WASHINGTON REPRESENTATIVES
1990

FOURTEENTH ANNUAL EDITION

Who Does What For Whom In The Nation's Capital

A compilation of Washington representatives of the major national associations, labor unions and U.S. companies, registered foreign agents, lobbyists, lawyers, law firms and special interest groups, together with their clients and areas of legislative and regulatory concern.

Arthur C. Close — Editor
Gregory L. Bologna — Editor
Curtis W. McCormick — Editor

COLUMBIA BOOKS INC., PUBLISHERS
1212 New York Ave., N.W.
Washington, D.C. 20005
(202) 898-0662

Fourteenth Edition — 1990

Copyright © by Columbia Books, Inc.

Library of Congress Catalog Card No. 76-21152

ISBN - 0910416-85-0

Price $55.00

TABLE OF CONTENTS

ORGANIZATION AND USE OF THIS DIRECTORY

This book is basically a list of people — the individuals in Washington who work in government affairs or public relations for American trade associations, professional societies, labor unions, corporations and a great variety of special interest and public interest groups. Some, but by no means all, are registered as lobbyists on Capitol Hill. Others represent foreign business or governmental interests and are registered at the Department of Justice as Foreign Agents. A third element consists of employees of the Executive Branch of the Federal Government who are charged with legislative affairs and Congressional liaison responsibilities and are, therefore a part of the lobbying community of Washington.

The information in this volume comes from one unique source — annual questionnaires sent to each Washington area office listed — and from many public sources, among which are:

- Lobby registrations filed with the Clerk of the House and Secretary of the Senate,
- Foreign Agent registrations at the Department of Justice,
- Files of the Federal Election Commission,
- Annual company reports to the various regulatory agencies, and
- Agency dockets and other open records too numerous to itemize.

All this material has been computer-processed into four sections:

- An alphabetical list of individuals showing for whom they work. *This list of Washington Representatives is the heart of the book.*

- An alphabetical list of companies and organizations showing who works for them. This can be used to lead a reader back to the appropriate representative.
- A listing of Federal Government departments and agencies and those responsible therein for legislative affairs.
- An index of companies and organizations by their industry group or the principal subject of their legislative concern.
- A country-by-country index of foreign governments and organizations with special representation in Washington.

The book thus provides a quick answer to such questions as:

- Who represents General Dynamics on Capitol Hill?
- What clients are represented in Washington by such prominent lobbying firms as Charls E. Walker Associates and Timmons and Company?
- What American law firms represent Japanese business interests in our Nation's Capital?
- What is Congress Watch and who speaks for it in dealings with the U.S. Government?

More than 12,500 individuals appear here, more than 600 law and public relations firms and more than 11,000 companies and interest groups in the U.S. and abroad which have retained Washington representation.

It is a unique guide to the people working to affect national decisions controlling the fate and futures of American business, labor, consumer and other interests.

WASHINGTON ADVOCACY:
A PROFILE OF THE PROFESSION

Washington is a city of representatives, a community of agents and advocates whose contending interests are a fascinating feature of American democracy.

Every other year each voting American sends someone to act for him in the House of Representatives. At different six year intervals he dispatches two senators to represent him on Capitol Hill. Every four years he tries to elect a President and Vice President who share his views on where this country should be headed and how it should be run. Yet this collection of 537 political representatives is dwarfed by the large and varied Washington community of *private* servants. Interacting with their political counterparts and the many *public* servants of the federal government, they also represent the interests and concerns of fellow Americans.

In much the same way, the foreign diplomatic corps in well over 100 embassies in Washington is reinforced by legions of private American representatives who lobby on behalf of foreign businesses and governments. Many are associated with Washington law firms which specialize in representing foreign clients in return for generous fees. Others represent particular foreign interests out of personal conviction — like the resilient Nationalist China lobby — or act as more general counselors and kibbitzers in the search for foreign and defense policies for a more dependent, less confident America. Some Americans who are especially conscious of their foreign roots have organized ethnic pressure groups which risk accusations of divided loyalty by consistently supporting the positions of their foreign homelands.

Some members of this fraternity are representatives in the strict sense: They man the Washington office outposts of, and are empowered to act for, the company, labor union, association or farmer organization that employs them. Some are independent consultants in government affairs who provide intelligence on their own government to confidential clients, or lobby for them on Capitol Hill and in the Executive Banch, or advise them how to win a larger share of governmental grants and subsidies. A few, veterans of years of Washington political infighting, are specialists in political organizations and activity. Many are lawyers whose services parallel those of the professional public affairs consultant but who also provide legal counsel in a wide variety of dealings or disputes with the government. Many are founders and leaders of activist groups focused sharply on specific concerns: the environment's pollution, the extravagance of energy consumption, the dangers of nuclear contamination — even the state of the nation's morals and its morale. Some claim to speak and act for "the consumer" and "the public" (whatever they are) without certification as to which of their rival organizations really represent those huge, heterogeneous constituencies.

Some representatives advertise their sponsors. Others invoke the confidentiality of client relationships to be much less forthcoming. Some are innocently mistaken for something they are not — like wildlife protectors who ultimately have hunting in mind. A very few deliberately hide the true nature of their interest behind some euphemistic organization name. Some work for several principals who pay them; some work for a few principles they believe in. Some educate and inform, some plead, some use pressure to persuade. All are advocates for some*one* or some*thing*. Together they have much to say about how this country is governed.

Washington representatives number in the thousands — the exact figure varying with the definition of "representative" used. By the criteria applied in compiling this directory — that is, persons working to influence government policies and actions to advance their own or their client's interest — the total approaches 12,500. The largest element (about 3,750) are officers of the 1,900 trade and professional associations and labor unions which keep a permanent presence in the Nation's Capital. Another 1,700 are representatives of individual corporations who, as distinguished from their marketing colleagues, are responsible for government and public relations. About 2,200 are advocates of special causes from ERA to environment, from handgun control to prison reform, from saving whales to saving unborn children. Lawyers who have registered as lobbyists or foreign agents or who have been identified as representing clients in regulatory matters and legal confrontations with the government currently number about 2,000. Public and government relations consultants and professional managers of client associations and interest groups also number about 2,000. Another 200 persons listed are officers of political parties or political action committees (PACs), and 100 others are active in policy think tanks which make their views known on a wide variety of domestic and foreign policy issues.

Over the past ten years the number of persons listed in this directory has grown steadily — in some measure we have found new sources of information, but in large part because there has actually been a continuing migration of association offices to Washington, an increase in the number of advocacy groups and a gradual expansion of the public affairs/government relations profession. It remains to be seen whether the trend will continue much longer in the face of the Republican Administration's efforts to eliminate excess federal regulation and to reduce the size, reach and generosity of the government. A large drop in numbers is unlikely, however; for most of the political and economic imperatives which prompted the need to have representation in company or association personnel has been balanced by a growth in independent consultants on whom these organizations are obliged to rely to present their views to government.

These special interest advocates, whose activities cut across geographic and party lines, have congregated in Washington over the past few decades for several reasons. First, they are here because of the extent of the federal government's involvement in, and control over, our daily lives. Regulation, whether of public utilities and interstate transportation or of the safety of mines and medicines and children's pajamas, has always been thought a burden by some and a blessing by others. It is not surprising, then, that those who want some new form of government aid or protection keep someone in Washington to assist at the birth of the appropriate law or regulation, that those who believe they will be adversely affected by some projected regulation hire lawyers to help them comment persuasively against the proposal, and that those whose fortunes have already been hurt by some measure enlist professional help to lobby for its repeal. Earlier conservatives have railed unsuccessfully against the pervasiveness of government and against the allegedly ambitious bureaucrat whose appetite for meddling is said to be the cause. This time things may turn out differently. But the strong suspicion remains that the blame for the size of intrusiveness of government has been misdirected: that we get more "government" because some among us ask for it; and that for every Washington representative who leaves town because some industry is deregulated or some reporting requirement rescinded at least another will appear to argue for new intervention to help or defend his client company, his consumer group or his version of the public interest.

Second, Washington is attractive as the principal dispensing station for financial assistance from the federal treasury. Price supports are vital to the farmer; protective tariffs, to the manufacturer threatened by cheap Korean labor; revenue sharing funds, to the survival of cities; and research grants, to the budgets of educational institutions. Virtually every state in the Union and every large city now has its own permanent Washington representative. So do major medical and charitable agencies, foundations and philanthropies. Many, together with universities and hospitals, are clients of the most influential law firms in town or of consultants who specialize in the art of begging for federal funds. Just as understandably, there are well staffed offices in Washington of all national farmer organizations and of trade associations of industries dependent on tariff protection or, like sugar producers, dependent on government decisions on quotas and allotments. Those who once decried the "strings" attached to government funding may well be among those who later employed several Washington representatives to argue the importance of federal help to "save the family farm" or rescue a bankrupt corporation. In the long run the Republican Administration's action to reduce federal funding of some "non-essential" programs or to shift responsibility for the administration of others to the state level may bring a decline in Washington representation. But for the present, the principal impact has been to increase competition for the scarcer funds and to reconfirm the value of having an effective advocate in Washington.

Finally, the phenomenon of private interest representation in the Nation's Capital is a manifestation of changing political dynamics in this country. People are not satisfied with the service they receive from their elected representatives. For better or for worse, this is a time of candor in admitting and facing up to personal problems and to society's problems and in the pursuit of what one wants or believes. It is also a time of growing concern about this country's future and the quality of life to be enjoyed by coming generations. It is thus, predictably, a time of impatience — impatience with indirect and evolutionary political processes, impatience with compromising, impatience with coalitions whose priorities may not be one's own and whose energies are necessarily diffused. "Instant gratification" has become perhaps as much a part of our political lifestyle as of our personal.

The most obvious result of this restlessness has been the decline of the traditional political party and the rise of activist, special interest or single issue organizations. Political parties are, after all, coalitions whose members differ widely on specific issues. How can one honestly submit to a party's discipline when its platform contains positions which one opposes or is so noncommittal as to say nothing? Why not join with people of exactly the same mind on some key issue — regardless of past party affiliation — and pursue that common objective with single-minded purpose? To many this reasoning has made sense. Groups focused as narrowly as preserving Alaska's environment, for example, reached a total of 40, and the overlapping membership of all environmentalist groups amounted to more than 2,000,000. They and other causes as diverse as SALT II and solar energy, nukes and nutrition, maintain

Washington representation in order to keep in daily touch with what the government is doing about their concerns and to push for government action as needed. Their number grows as new problems arise and someone invents a new approach to their solution.

The mood of the times has contributed in another way to the expansion of Washington's community of advocates. Impatient with political machinery which seems to ask for their opinions only at election time, Americans, through Washington lobbyists, increasingly volunteer their views directly to Congress. More and more they are striving to hold their elected representatives accountable on a current basis, rather than wait for a reckoning on election day. They are also dealing directly with key officials in the departments and agencies of the Executive Branch or taking initiatives in the courts if they despair of getting legislation responsive to their needs.

The same preference for clarity, directness and accountability in political activity has contributed to a new phenomenon, the Political Action Committee, which raises and dispenses campaign funds for candidates of its choice. With these committees, the sponsor of the fund-raising effort — a company, trade association, union or special issue group — is obvious to the contributor; the purpose of the donation is clear to the one who gives and the one who receives; and the return on the "investment" is relatively easy to monitor and measure, especially if the committee has a Washington representative who is in frequent touch with the successful candidate and can check closely on his subsequent voting record. Several hundred political action committees, including those of several prominent Washington law firms, now maintain an office in the Capital for these and related reasons.

Another important feature of the "new politics" has been the emergence of "public interest," "citizen" and "consumer" lobbies, most of which have made Washington their headquarters. Although they apparently sought broad, bi-partisan membership, the early public interest organizations became identified with middle class whites and with liberal political opinion. In reaction, groups with quite different, yet equally sincere, versions of what constitutes "the public interest" appeared. At about the same time the business community, which had held its own against organized labor's Washington lobby, responded to a new adversary, the vocal consumer advocate movements, by enlarging and revitalizing existing business lobby organizations and by creating new groups to defend "the free enterprise system."

On both sides of the political fence, public interest law firms also were established to provide "the little man" — the underpriviledged or the overlooked — with legal counsel in fighting for his rights or to undertake litigation in his interest. These groups also set up Washington offices whose staffs of politically aware and vocal lawyers further enlarged Washington's advocate community. In 1981, challenges to the concept of public funding of some legal services for the disadvantaged arose which brought deeper divisions among Washington's attorneys and new organizations to defend each side of the ensuing argument.

To the Capital also have come an assortment of over 30 religious lobbies — Seventh-day Adventists, Latter Day Saints, Catholics, Lutherans, Jews, Friends, Unitarians and more — all persuaded that they are acting in the true public interest in urging that moral, ethical and religious considerations be given greater weight in the domestic and foreign policy decisions of our government. Most controversial has been the religiously motivated, politically conservative Moral Majority, whose activities have prompted the formation of more than one rebutting organization with equally pretentious names.

* * * * * * * *

By task and tactic these Washington representatives divide into four general categories:

First, there are the information gatherers. These representatives collect, analyze and disseminate intelligence on national and international affairs either confidentially for the private use of clients or openly as a means of molding public opinion and the think-ing of decision-makers. A number of Washington firms specialize in this kind of activity; one even sought to organize a worldwide private intelligence service to rival the Central Intelligence Agency. The intelligence function is also cited as an important responsibility of corporate, union and association representatives in the city and their in-house legal staff. Phyllis McGrath of The Conference Board, a New York-based research group, was quoted in the *Wall Street Journal* as asserting that "the chief responsibility of the government affairs executive is monitoring, analyzing and communicating government related activity." A former Washington counsel for Westinghouse, commented to the *Legal Times of Washington* in January 1979 that corporate house counsel jobs in Washington "tend to get down to general information gathering." In the same category of information collection, research and dissemination are the activities of several Washington "think tanks" whose fellows often come from senior government positions and later return to them. Although the principle of scholarly objectivity is proclaimed, these institutions have not all shed their partisan colorations completely; and they provide prestigious Washington platforms from which the personal views (and biases) of their often transient scholars may influence government thinking.

Second, much Washington representation takes the form of legal counseling. Washington law firms specializing in communications, transportation or public utilities law help their client radio station, air line or gas company to comply with the routine licensing and reporting requirements of the regulatory agencies. They give legal counsel to corporate clients in regulatory commission hearings or in civil and criminal proceedings in a court of law. They provide legal expertise to clients commenting on proposed regulations or petitioning for special treatment under them. Increasingly, they are asked to undertake litigation against the government on their client's behalf. Several corporations have also included in-house legal staffs as part of their Washington representation. Some attorneys object to being called "representatives" and many disclaim any involvement in "lobbying." But as legal advisors to clients complying with or contesting some government regulation, they are surely representing the client's interest. And when they undertake a more activist role to prompt, revise or block some regulation or ruling, they are, in reality, lobbying, although not within the narrow definition of the existing statute.

A third element of the representative community is engaged in supporting political activity. The great majority are Washington contact points and managers of established political action committees of corporations, unions and associations. Others direct the activities of small, almost personal, political comittees established to give modest, sharply targeted assistance to candidates who agree with the sponsor's position on a particular issue. Some are specialized consultants in the arts of direct mail marketing of a candidate, issue definition and presentation, fund raising and campaign planning. Among the more recent — and more interesting — are the activists of highly partisan auxiliary committees of the established political parties. These aggressive groups, drawing up "hit lists" of opposition incumbents to defeat in coming elections and organizing fund raising and mail campaigning with similar focus, proved particularly effective for conservative Republicans in 1980. The last few years have seen the establishment of several Democratic groups committed to responding in kind against "most wanted" conservatives or to reviving and protecting, as appropriate, the political fortunes of prominent liberals.

By far the largest category of representational activity catalogued in this book is lobbying itself. Whether or not formally registered as lobbyists on Capitol Hill or as foreign agents with the Department of Justice, those Washington representatives whose principal objective is to stimulate government action favorable to (or block action unfavorable to) the interests of their employers, clients, or causes are lobbying. Their motives may be monetary or missionary or a mixture of both.

They lobby in both the Executive and Legislative Branches of government, dealing directly with legislators and policy makers in Washington's corridors and cocktail parties of power. To many their personal charm and persuasive powers are still major assets. More important to most is their ability to collect and present, factually and fairly, vital information for a member of Congress or the Cabinet trying to sort his way through the diversity and complexity of issues on which decisions must be made. One association executive summarized this aspect in *Association and Society Management* a few years ago:

"An effective lobbyist is well versed in the industry he represents, articulate, believable and known for his integrity. At some point an association may require someone who knows individual senators and who can shake a lot of hands, but congressmen and federal officials are mainly looking for someone who is informative and credible."

Significant also are the time and money which lobbyists spend at Washington fund raising functions for election candidates and the political action committee (PAC) contributions and generous speaking fees which their employers pay to influential political figures. One observer, quoted in the *Washington Post* in August 1983, noted that "fund raising from PACS winds up serving as a sort of business tax on lobbying." Another, commenting on the purpose of giving large speaking honoraria to public servants, used the words "It's more to get the body than the vote" to emphasize the value of winning favored personal access by such generosity. *(Wall Street Journal,* May 25, 1984).

A growing number of lobbyists now focuses on the media and the national public, recognizing the importance of public image to the cause they represent and the power of popular support from the "grass roots" in moving a reluctant legislator to action. In a day of instant and mass communications these are to a large extent public relations and media relations experts who can stir public concern about a given issue, prompt home district or national audience journals to print supportive editorials, or organize convincing phone-in or letter-writing campaigns which draw constituents and national trendsetters of opinion directly into the persuasion process. A successful Washington lobbyist, quoted in the *Washington Post* in July 1983, summarized this new broader form of lobbying as follows:

> "Politicians aren't loners; they don't want to be martyrs. They never do anything unless they feel there are formidable forces out there in the dark with them. You have to create a context of legitimacy for them to be with you."

The profession of lobbying in this country dates from its earliest days as a logical expression of the Constitutional right of citizens to "petition the government for a redress of grievances." Abuses in the intervening years gave lobbying a tarnished image, which has persisted to this day. Many lobbyists prefer to label their responsibilities as "government relations," "public affairs," "regulatory liaison," "legislative counseling" and "Washington activities." But attitudes are changing, witness the recent establishment of a professional association, The American League of Lobbyists, and the frequency with which legislators and others in government now acknowledge the contribution made by lobbyists in defining issues, amassing factual data on both sides of the question, preparing arguments, drafting legislation and helping to mobilize voting coalitions.

To say that there is greater understanding of the lobbyist's profession and increased (if sometimes grudging) acknowledgement of his contribution is not to ignore that fundamental concerns remain on Capitol Hill and in the country at large about the increase in lobbying for special interests and for differing interpretations of the public interest. Recently attention was given to two areas of concern — the need for an overall lobby law to replace the one that has existed since 1946 and the need to slow down the "revolving door" through which attorneys move back and forth from private practice on behalf of corporate clients to the government agencies responsible for regulating the very same corporations. New legislation in 1979 did impose greater restrictions on lawyers who leave government service to join a private law firm. The Ethics Reform Act of 1989 placed important new restrictions on influence-wielding by former members of Congress as well as former civil servants from the Executive Branch. It made more explicit the financial disclosure obligations of federal government appointees and placed limitations on the outside income earned by active members of the House and Senate.

* * * * * * * *

Despite all the words employed above and elsewhere, there is no easy way to describe the remarkable process by which interests, through private Washington representatives, help to shape America's future. The student of political affairs and the concerned citizen will have to probe more deeply on their own to understand the important interplay of influence that goes on in Washington and to judge its dangers. In such an effort, we believe this listing of the people and organizations involved can be of considerable value. Its scope was deliberately made broad in the belief that the forces at work are more diverse and extensive than those engaged in lobbying as such. It is intentionally a book about all advocates on the Washington political scene. It assumes no sinister conspiracy on their part to manipulate the body politic in secret. And, in turn, no secret sources, only exhaustive combing of public records and direct appeals for information from those it lists, have been used in its compilation. The result is, we trust, a comprehensive, informative, objective reference work which will help all who seek a fuller appreciation of if . . . and how . . . and why the American Democracy works.

WASHINGTON REPRESENTATIVES
1990

THE REPRESENTATIVES

Although some of this material has been provided by the individuals listed in this book, much of it has been compiled from public records. It is necessarily transitory. Washington representatives are sometimes retained for a specific purpose for a limited time. Once a point of view has been presented (and accepted or rejected) and a proposed measure passed (or voted down) the representative/client relationship may cease. This Directory shows the situation at the time the records were consulted. Every effort has been made to make it accurate. Columbia Books, however, accepts no responsibility for any errors.

AAGRE, Robert J.
Manager, Legislative Department, Chamber of Commerce of the U.S.A.
1615 H St., N.W., Washington, DC 20062
Telephone: (202) 463-5600
Registered as lobbyist at U.S. Congress.

AARON, Henry J.
Senior Fellow, Economic Studies Program, Brookings Institution
1775 Massachusetts Ave., N.W., Washington, DC 20036
Telephone: (202) 797-6000
Background: Assistant Secretary for Planning and Evaluation, Health, Education and Welfare (1977-78).

AARONSON, Robert J.
President, Air Transport Ass'n of America
1709 New York Ave., N.W., Washington, DC 20006-5206
Telephone: (202) 626-4000
Background: Associate Administrator for Airports, Federal Aviation Administration, 1978-81.

ABBEY, Richard H.
Mudge Rose Guthrie Alexander and Ferdon
2121 K St., N.W., Suite 700, Washington, DC 20037
Telephone: (202) 429-9355
Background: Assistant Chief Counsel, 1972-77; Deputy Chief Counsel, 1977-79; and Chief Counsel, 1979-85, U.S. Customs Service.
Clients:
Federal Express Corp.

Radix Group Internat'l Inc.
Rainbow Navigations, Inc.
Roanoke Companies, The
Societe Financiere d'Entreposage et de Commerce International de l'Alcool
Toshiba Corp.

ABBIN, Byrle M.
Mng. Dir., Office of Federal Tax Svcs., Andersen and Co., Arthur
1666 K St., N.W., Washington, DC 20006
Telephone: (202) 862-3368

ABBOTT, Ande M.
International Representative, Internat'l Brotherhood of Boilermakers, Iron Shipbuilders, Blacksmiths, Forgers and Helpers
400 First St., N.W., Suite 814, Washington, DC 20001
Telephone: (202) 638-5768
Registered as lobbyist at U.S. Congress.

ABBOTT, Keith F.
Senior Associate, Friedman Assoc. Inc., Cynthia
322 Massachusetts Ave., N.E., Washington, DC 20002
Telephone: (202) 546-4204
Background: Finance Director, Senator George Mitchell (D-ME), 1987. Finance Director, Democratic Senatorial Campaign Committee, 1984-86.
Organizations represented:
Committee for Nat'l Security
Simon for Senate '90

ABBOTT, Kelton
Lachelli, Waller and Associates
600 Maryland Ave., S.W., Suite 200A East Wing, Washington, DC 20024
Telephone: (202) 863-1472
Background: Special Assistant to Senator Alan Bible (D-TX), 1962-72. Legislative Assistant to Senator Howard Cannon (D-NV), 1972-83. Legislative Assistant to Senator Paul Laxalt (R-NV), 1983-87. Legislative Assistant to Senator Chic Hecht (R-NV), 1987.

ABDEL RAHMAN, Hasan
Director, Palestine Affairs Center
1730 K St., N.W., Suite 703, Washington, DC 20006
Telephone: (202) 785-8394
Registered as Foreign Agent: (#4133)

ABDNOR, Leanne J.
Director, Federal Government Affairs, Koch Industries
2000 Pennsylvania Ave., N.W. Suite 3580, Washington, DC 20006
Telephone: (202) 466-2789
Registered as lobbyist at U.S. Congress.

ABELES, Charles C.
Piper and Marbury
1200 19th St., N.W., Washington, DC 20036
Telephone: (202) 861-3900
Clients:
Nat'l Rural Electric Cooperative Ass'n

WASHINGTON REPRESENTATIVES

ABELL, Tyler
Bregman, Abell & Kay
1156 15th St., N.W., Suite 1212, Washington, DC 20005
Telephone: (202) 223-2900
Background: Associate Gen. Counsel, Post Office Dep't, 1963. Assistant Postmaster General, 1963-1967. Chief of Protocol of the United States, 1968-1969.

ABENANTE, Paul C.
President, American Bakers Ass'n
1111 14th St., N.W., Suite 300, Washington, DC 20005
Telephone: (202) 296-5800
Registered as lobbyist at U.S. Congress.
Background: Serves as Treasurer, BREAD Political Action Committee.

ABER, Robert E.
V. President, Deputy General Counsel, Nat'l Ass'n of Securities Dealers (NASDAQ)
1735 K St., N.W., Washington, DC 20006
Telephone: (202) 728-8000

ABERLY, Jessica R.
Field Organizer, Professionals' Coalition for Nuclear Arms Control
1616 P St., N.W., Suite 320, Washington, DC 20036
Telephone: (202) 332-4823
Registered as lobbyist at U.S. Congress.

ABERNATHY, Kathleen Q.
Director, Federal Affairs, Communications Satellite Corp. (COMSAT)
950 L'Enfant Plaza, S.W., Washington, DC 20024
Telephone: (202) 863-6000

ABINADER, J. R.
President, Nat'l U.S.-Arab Chamber of Commerce
1825 K St., N.W. Suite 1107, Washington, DC 20006
Telephone: (202) 331-8010
Registered as lobbyist at U.S. Congress.

ABLE, Edward H., Jr.
Exec. Director, American Ass'n of Museums
1225 Eye St., N.W., Washington, DC 20005
Telephone: (202) 289-1818
Background: Former staff aide to Senator Mike Mansfield (D-MT) and Senator Richard B. Russell (D-GA).

ABLER, Ronald F.
Exec. Director, Ass'n of American Geographers
1710 16th St., N.W., Washington, DC 20009
Telephone: (202) 234-1450

ABLONDI AND FOSTER, P.C.
2100 Pennsylvania Ave., N.W., Washington, DC 20006
Telephone: (202) 296-3355
Background: A law firm.
Members of firm representing listed organizations:
 Ablondi, Italo H.
  Background: Commissioner, U.S. Tariff Commission, 1972-74; U.S. Internat'l Trade Commission, 1975-78.
 Foster, F. David
  Background: Attorney Advisor, Office of the General Counsel, 1973-75 and Assistant to the Chairman, 1975-77, U.S. International Trade Commission. Trade Counsel, U.S. Senate Committee on Finance, 1977-81.
Clients:
 Ad Hoc Committee of Producers of Metal Castings *(Italo H. Ablondi)*
 China, Foreign Trade Board of the Republic of *(Italo H. Ablondi)*
 Far East Machinery Co. Ltd. *(Italo H. Ablondi, F. David Foster)*
 Guan Haur Industries Ltd. *(F. David Foster)*
 Taiwan Textile Federation *(Italo H. Ablondi)*
 United States Beet Sugar Ass'n *(F. David Foster)*

ABLONDI, Italo H.
Ablondi and Foster, P.C.
2100 Pennsylvania Ave., N.W., Washington, DC 20006
Telephone: (202) 296-3355
Registered as Foreign Agent: (#3235).
Background: Commissioner, U.S. Tariff Commission, 1972-74; U.S. Internat'l Trade Commission, 1975-78.
Clients:
 Ad Hoc Committee of Producers of Metal Castings
 China, Foreign Trade Board of the Republic of
 Far East Machinery Co. Ltd.
 Taiwan Textile Federation

ABOLT, Russ
Exec. V. President, Internat'l Sleep Products Ass'n
333 Commerce St., Alexandria, VA 22314
Telephone: (703) 683-8371

ABOUREZK, James G.
National Chairman, American-Arab Anti-Discrimination Committee
4201 Connecticut Ave., N.W. Suite 500, Washington, DC 20009
Telephone: (202) 244-2990
Background: Former U.S. Senator from South Dakota, 1973-79; Member, U.S. House of Representatives from South Dakota, 1971-73.

ABRAHAMSON, Jeffery A.
League Analyst, Citicorp
1275 Pennsylvania Ave., N.W., Suite 503, Washington, DC 20004
Telephone: (202) 879-6800
Registered as lobbyist at U.S. Congress.

ABRAMCZYK, Phyllis
Information Specialist, Nat'l Digestive Diseases Information Clearinghouse
P.O. Box NDDIC, Bethesda, MD 20892
Telephone: (301) 468-6344
Background: Serves also as Information Specialist, Nat'l Arthritis and Musculoskeletal and Skin Diseases Information Clearinghouse.

ABRAMOWITZ, George R.
Sutherland, Asbill and Brennan
1275 Pennsylvania, N.W., Washington, DC 20004-2404
Telephone: (202) 383-0100
Registered as lobbyist at U.S. Congress.

ABRAMOWITZ, Nancy S.
Arnold & Porter
1200 New Hampshire Ave., N.W., Washington, DC 20036
Telephone: (202) 872-6700
Registered as lobbyist at U.S. Congress.
Background: Law Clerk, U.S. Tax Court, 1975-77.

ABRAMS, Adele
Director, Government Affairs, Nat'l Stone Ass'n
1415 Elliot Place, N.W., Washington, DC 20007
Telephone: (202) 342-1100
Registered as lobbyist at U.S. Congress.

ABRAMS, Matthew J.
President, CANAMCO (The Canadian-American Company)
1220 19th St., N.W., Suite 202, Washington, DC 20036
Telephone: (202) 822-0707
Registered as lobbyist at U.S. Congress.
Registered as Foreign Agent: (#3884)
Background: Also represents the Canadian Shipowners Ass'n and the Aerospace Industries Ass'n of Canada.

ABRAMS, Robert G.
Howrey and Simon
1730 Pennsylvania Ave., N.W., Washington, DC 20006-4793
Telephone: (202) 783-0800
Clients:
 Exxon Co., U.S.A.

ABRAMSON ASSOCIATES
1275 K St., N.W., Washington, DC 20005
Telephone: (202) 289-6900
Members of firm representing listed organizations:
 Hartmann, Robert S., Sr. V. Pres. & Dir., Public Relations
 Webster, Wendy A., Account Supervisor and Dir., Media Rtns.

ABRAMSON, Mark A.
President, Council for Excellence in Government
1775 Pennsylvania Ave., N.W. Suite 750, Washington, DC 20006
Telephone: (202) 728-0418
Background: Served in the Office of the Assistant Secretary for Planning and Evaluation, U.S. Department of Health and Human Services, 1977-83.

ABSHIRE, David M.
President and CEO, Center for Strategic and Internat'l Studies
1800 K St., N.W., Washington, DC 20006
Telephone: (202) 887-0200
Background: Assistant Secretary of State for Congressional Relations, 1970-73. US ambassador to NATO, 1983-87. Special Counsellor to the President, 1987.

ABT ASSOCIATES INC.
4800 Montgomery Lane, Bethesda, MD 20814
Telephone: (301) 913-0500
Background: A Boston-based consulting firm specializing in policy and management research for business and government.
Members of firm representing listed organizations:
 Stein, (Dr.) Martin M.
  Background: Director, Transportation Research Department (Business Strategy Division), Abt Associates. Formerly, economist, U.S. Department of Transportation; and an officer in the U.S. Departments of Interior and Commerce.
 Wilson, (Dr.) Stephanie, V. Pres. & Magr., Internat'l Area
Clients:
 Wang Laboratories Inc.

ABU-JABER, Tariq
Exec. Director, United Palestinian Appeal
2100 M St., N.W., Suite 409, Washington, DC 20037
Telephone: (202) 659-5007

ABUKARI
Legislative Aide, Rainbow Lobby
1660 L St., N.W. Suite 204, Washington, DC 20036
Telephone: (202) 457-0700
Registered as lobbyist at U.S. Congress.

ACEVEDO, Elaine
Director, Government Affairs, Florists Transworld Delivery Ass'n
216 7th St., S.E., Washington, DC 20003
Telephone: (202) 546-1090
Registered as lobbyist at U.S. Congress.
Background: Treasurer, American League of Lobbyists, 1990.

ACKERMAN, Eric
Manager, Regulatory Policy, Edison Electric Institute
1111 19th St., N.W., Washington, DC 20036
Telephone: (202) 778-6400

ACKERMAN, Jerome
Covington and Burling
1201 Pennsylvania Ave., N.W., Box 7566, Washington, DC 20044
Telephone: (202) 662-6000

ACQUARD, Charles
Legislative Representative, American Public Power Ass'n
2301 M St., N.W., Washington, DC 20037
Telephone: (202) 775-8300
Registered as lobbyist at U.S. Congress.

ADAIR, Douglas E.
Exec. Director, Council on Hotel, Restaurant & Institutional Education
1200 17th St., N.W. 7th Floor, Washington, DC 20036
Telephone: (202) 331-5990

ADAM, Joe A.
Director, Dept. of Safety and Health, United Ass'n of Journeymen & Apprentices of the Plumbing & Pipe Fitting Industry of the US & Canada
901 Massachusetts Ave., N.W., Washington, DC 20001
Telephone: (202) 628-5823

ADAMS, A. John
President, Adams Associates, John
1825 K St., N.W. Suite 210, Washington, DC 20006
Telephone: (202) 466-8320
Registered as lobbyist at U.S. Congress.
Background: President, Grassroots Communications, Inc., a subsidiary of John Adams Associates. Serves as Chairman of the Executive Committee, Worldcom Group Inc., a PR Firm based in New York, NY with over 40 member firms located in the U.S., Canada, Europe, and the Far East.
Organizations represented:
 Solidarity

The listings in this directory are available as *Mailing Labels*. See last page.

ADAMS, ADAMS & ASSOC.
1213 Prince St., Alexandria, VA 22314
Telephone: (703) 548-4593
Members of firm representing listed organizations:
Adams, Ann Allen
  Background: Serves as Exec. Director, Professional Services Management Ass'n.
  Clients:
    A/E Pronet *(Ann Allen Adams)*
    Professional Services Management Ass'n *(Ann Allen Adams)*

ADAMS, Ann Allen
Adams, Adams & Assoc.
1213 Prince St., Alexandria, VA 22314
Telephone: (703) 548-4593
Background: Serves as Exec. Director, Professional Services Management Ass'n.
Clients:
  A/E Pronet
  Professional Services Management Ass'n

ADAMS ASSOCIATES, John
1825 K St., N.W. Suite 210, Washington, DC 20006
Telephone: (202) 466-8320
Members of firm representing listed organizations:
Adams, A. John, President
  Background: President, Grassroots Communications, Inc., a subsidiary of John Adams Associates. Serves as Chairman of the Executive Committee, Worldcom Group Inc., a PR Firm based in New York, NY with over 40 member firms located in the U.S., Canada, Europe, and the Far East.
Anderson, Carol Cofield, V. President
Green, Ann
Mater, Gene P., Senior Consultant
Schenk, Martha, Ass't ot the President & Corp. Sec'y
Organizations represented:
  American Pyrotechnics Ass'n
  Americares Foundation
  Environmental Industry Council
  Solidarity *(A. John Adams)*
  United Press Internat'l *(Gene P. Mater)*

ADAMS, Denvel D.
National Adjutant, Disabled American Veterans
807 Maine Ave., S.W., Washington, DC 20024
Telephone: (202) 554-3501

ADAMS, Gordon
Director, Defense Budget Project
236 Massachusetts Ave., N.E., Suite 401, Washington, DC 20002
Telephone: (202) 546-9737

ADAMS, Greg A.
V. President, November Group Inc.
1611 Connecticut Ave., N.W. 4th Floor, Washington, DC 20009
Telephone: (202) 265-2700

ADAMS, John
Director, Milk Safety and Animal Health, Nat'l Milk Producers Federation
1840 Wilson Blvd., Arlington, VA 22201
Telephone: (703) 243-6111

ADAMS, John J.
Hunton and Williams
2000 Pennsylvania Ave., N.W., Washington, DC 20006
Telephone: (202) 955-1500
Registered as lobbyist at U.S. Congress.
Registered as Foreign Agent: (#3650).

ADAMS, Kenneth L.
Dickstein, Shapiro and Morin
2101 L St., N.W., Washington, DC 20037
Telephone: (202) 785-9700
Background: Legislative Assistant to Congressman Abner Mikva, 1972.

ADAMS, Kenneth R.
Second V. President, Federal Relations, UNUM Life Insurance Co.
1919 Pennsylvania Ave., N.W. Suite 300, Washington, DC 20006
Telephone: (202) 775-9585

ADAMS, Lawrence
Internat'l Affairs & Economics Associate, Institute on Religion and Democracy
729 15th St., N.W., Suite 900, Washington, DC 20005
Telephone: (202) 393-3200
Background: Analyst, U.S. House of Representatives Committee on the Budget, 1987-89.

ADAMS, William T.
President, Radio Technical Commission for Maritime Services
655 15th St., N.W., Suite 300, Washington, DC 20005
Telephone: (202) 639-4006

ADAMSON, Stuart S.
Chairman, Todd Shipyards Corp. Political Action Committee
2341 Jefferson Davis Hwy., Arlington, VA 22202
Telephone: (703) 418-0133

ADDE, Elise
V. President, Industry Communications, Nat'l Cable Television Ass'n
1724 Massachusetts Ave., N.W., Washington, DC 20036
Telephone: (202) 775-3550

ADDLESTONE, David
Director, Vietnam Veterans Of America Legal Services Program
c/o Nat'l Veterans Legal Svc. 2001 S St., N.W., Suite 610, Washington, DC 20016
Telephone: (202) 265-8305

ADDUCI, D. M.
President and Director, Public Affairs, Adduci, Offices of V.J.
1140 Connecticut Ave., N.W., Suite 804, Washington, DC 20036
Telephone: (202) 452-6004

ADDUCI, Offices of V.J.
1140 Connecticut Ave., N.W., Suite 804, Washington, DC 20036
Telephone: (202) 452-6004
Background: An independent consultant in Washington representation, new products, investments and technology.
Members of firm representing listed organizations:
Adduci, D. M., President and Director, Public Affairs
Adduci, V. J.
  Background: Serves as Washington Representative, Mack Trucks, Inc.
Organizations represented:
  Innovation Technology, Inc.
  Invention Stores Internat'l
  Mack Trucks, Inc. *(V. J. Adduci)*
  Nat'l Commission Against Drunk Driving
  Novelty Manufacturing, Inc.

ADDUCI, V. J.
Adduci, Offices of V.J.
1140 Connecticut Ave., N.W., Suite 804, Washington, DC 20036
Telephone: (202) 452-6004
Background: Serves as Washington Representative, Mack Trucks, Inc.
Organizations represented:
  Mack Trucks, Inc.

ADELMAN, Roger M.
Partner, Kirkpatrick & Lockhart
1800 M St., N.W., Suite 900 South Lobby, Washington, DC 20036-5891
Telephone: (202) 778-9000
Background: Former prosecutor for the office of the U.S. Attorney.

ADERS, Robert O.
President, Food Marketing Institute
1750 K St., N.W., Washington, DC 20006
Telephone: (202) 452-8444
Registered as lobbyist at U.S. Congress.
Background: Formerly Special Ass't to the U.S. Attorney General and Undersecretary of Labor.

ADISE, Russell T.
Senior Associate, Armstrong, Byrd and Associates
1730 M St., N.W., Suite 808, Washington, DC 20036
Telephone: (202) 223-5880

Background: Former staff assistant to Rep. Don Young (R-AK) and Rep. Stephen Solarz (D-NY), 1977-79.
Clients:
  Kajima Corp.

ADKINSON, Austin
Exec. Director, Nat'l Ass'n of Life Underwriters Political Action Committee
1922 F St., N.W., Washington, DC 20006
Telephone: (202) 347-1444

ADLER, Allan Robert
Cohn and Marks
1333 New Hampshire Ave., N.W., Suite 600, Washington, DC 20036
Telephone: (202) 293-3860
Registered as lobbyist at U.S. Congress.
Registered as Foreign Agent: (#4303).
Clients:
  Maclean Hunter Cable TV

ADLER, Amy
Manager, Publications & Information, USO World
601 Indiana Ave., N.W., Washington, DC 20004
Telephone: (202) 783-8121

ADLER, Marsha Nye
Legislative Representative, People for the American Way
2000 M St., N.W., Suite 400, Washington, DC 20036
Telephone: (202) 467-4999
Registered as lobbyist at U.S. Congress.

ADLER, Prudence
Federal Relations Officer, Ass'n of Research Libraries
1527 New Hampshire Ave., N.W., Washington, DC 20036
Telephone: (202) 232-2466

ADLER, Robert
Senior Attorney, Natural Resources Defense Council
1350 New York Ave., N.W. Suite 300, Washington, DC 20005
Telephone: (202) 783-7800
Registered as lobbyist at U.S. Congress.

ADLER, W. F.
Exec. Dir., Federal Regulatory Matters, Pacific Telesis Group-Washington
1275 Pennsylvania Ave., N.W. Suite 400, Washington, DC 20004
Telephone: (202) 383-6400
Registered as lobbyist at U.S. Congress.

ADLHOCK, Terrance M.
Counsel, Southern California Edison Co.
1001 Pennsylvania Ave., N.W. Suite 450N, Washington, DC 20004
Telephone: (202) 393-3075
Registered as lobbyist at U.S. Congress.

ADOPACA, Jerry
President, Hispanic Ass'n on Corporate Responsibility
2000 L St., N.W. Suite 702, Washington, DC 20036
Telephone: (202) 835-9672
Background: Former Governor of New Mexico.

ADVOCACY SERVICES GROUP, INC.
1825 Eye St., N.W. Suite 400, Washington, DC 20006
Telephone: (202) 429-2096
Background: Government affairs representatives.
Members of firm representing listed organizations:
Anderson, Cheryl, Senior V. President
Ney, Richard T., President

ADVOCATES AT LAW CHARTERED
1899 L St., N.W., Suite 300, Washington, DC 20036
Telephone: (202) 466-7000
Members of firm representing listed organizations:
Morgan, Charles (Jr.)

AEA WASHINGTON, LTD.
905 16th St., N.W., Washington, DC 20006
Registered as Foreign Agent: (#4307)
Members of firm representing listed organizations:
Plunk, Daryl M., Director
Sheffer, Kenneth E. (Jr.), Director
Clients:
  Korean Overseas Information Service *(Daryl M. Plunk, Kenneth E. Sheffer, Jr.)*

AGNEW, Creigh H.
Government Affairs Manager, Weyerhaeuser Co.
2001 L St., N.W., Suite 304, Washington, DC 20036
Telephone: (202) 293-7222
Registered as lobbyist at U.S. Congress.

AGRI/WASHINGTON
1629 K St., N.W., Suite 1100, Washington, DC 20006
Telephone: (202) 785-6710
Members of firm representing listed organizations:
Weller, Paul S. (Jr.), President
Williams, Daren R., Public Relations Associate
Clients:
Agricultural Relations Council *(Paul S. Weller, Jr., Daren R. Williams)*
American Agricultural Editors Ass'n *(Paul S. Weller, Jr., Daren R. Williams)*
American Ass'n of Grain Inspection and Weighing Agencies *(Paul S. Weller, Jr., Daren R. Williams)*
Apple Processors Ass'n *(Paul S. Weller, Jr.)*

AHEARN, Vincent P., Jr.
President, Nat'l Ready Mixed Concrete Ass'n
900 Spring St., Silver Spring, MD 20910
Telephone: (301) 587-1400
Background: Also serves as Managing Director, Nat'l Industrial Sand Ass'n and President of the Nat'l Aggregates Ass'n.

AHERN, Catherine A.
V. President and Corporate Secretary, Internat'l Snowmobile Industry Ass'n
3975 University Drive Suite 310, Fairfax, VA 22030
Telephone: (703) 273-9606

AHLBERG, Brian
Communications Coordinator, Nat'l Family Farm Coalition
80 F St., N.W. Suite 714, Washington, DC 20001
Telephone: (202) 737-2215

AHO, David J.
Corp. V. Pres., Government Affairs, Baxter Internat'l Inc.
1667 K St., N.W., Suite 710, Washington, DC 20006
Telephone: (202) 223-4016
Registered as lobbyist at U.S. Congress.

AIKEN-O'NEILL, Patricia
President-CEO, Eye Bank Ass'n of America
1725 Eye St., N.W., Washington, DC 20006-2403
Telephone: (202) 775-4999

AIKEN, Robert S.
Manager of Federal Affairs, Pinnacle West Capital Corp.
1735 Eye St., N.W., Suite 916, Washington, DC 20006
Telephone: (202) 293-2655
Registered as lobbyist at U.S. Congress.

AILOR, David C.
Hauck and Associates
1255 23rd St., N.W., Washington, DC 20037
Telephone: (202) 452-8100
Background: Serves as Director, Regulatory Affairs, Nat'l Oilseed Processors Ass'n and American Coke and Coal Chemicals Institute.
Clients:
American Coke and Coal Chemicals Institute

AILSWORTH, Mike
V. President, Government Relations, Sandoz Corp.
1615 L St., N.W., Suite 320, Washington, DC 20036
Telephone: (202) 223-6262
Registered as lobbyist at U.S. Congress.

AIN, Ross D.
Van Ness, Feldman & Curtis
1050 Thomas Jefferson St., 7th Floor, Washington, DC 20007
Telephone: (202) 298-1800
Registered as lobbyist at U.S. Congress.
Background: Member, Office of the Legislative Counsel, U.S. House of Representatives 1971-76; Committee on Interstate and Foreign Commerce, U.S. House of Representatives, 1976-79. Federal Energy Regulatory Commission, 1979-80.
Clients:
LUZ Internat'l

AINSLIE ASSOCIATES
3812 N. Sixth Road, Arlington, VA 22203

Telephone: (703) 527-5404
Members of firm representing listed organizations:
Ainslie, Virginia, President

AINSLIE, Virginia
President, Ainslie Associates
3812 N. Sixth Road, Arlington, VA 22203
Telephone: (703) 527-5404

AIRES, Randolf H.
Vice President, Sears, Roebuck and Co.
633 Pennsylvania Ave., N.W., Washington, DC 20004
Telephone: (202) 737-4900
Registered as lobbyist at U.S. Congress.

AISENBERG, Michael A.
Manager, Federal Government Relations, Digital Equipment Corp.
1331 Pennsylvania Ave., N.W., Washington, DC 20004
Telephone: (202) 383-5630
Registered as lobbyist at U.S. Congress.

AISTARS, Sandra M.
Director of Public Relations, Joint Baltic American Nat'l Committee
Box 4578, Rockville, MD 20850
Telephone: (301) 340-1954

AITKEN, Bruce
Dorsey & Whitney
1330 Connecticut Ave., N.W., Suite 200, Washington, DC 20036
Telephone: (202) 857-0700
Registered as lobbyist at U.S. Congress.
Registered as Foreign Agent: (#4214).

AKER ASSOCIATES, INC.
1212 New York Ave., N.W., Suite 500, Washington, DC 20005
Telephone: (202) 789-2424
Background: A communications consulting firm.
Members of firm representing listed organizations:
Aker, G. Colburn, President
Background: Exec. Assistant to Senator John C. Culver (D-IA), 1973-77.
Clients:
Product Liability Coordinating Committee *(G. Colburn Aker)*

AKER, G. Colburn
President, Aker Associates, Inc.
1212 New York Ave., N.W., Suite 500, Washington, DC 20005
Telephone: (202) 789-2424
Registered as lobbyist at U.S. Congress.
Background: Exec. Assistant to Senator John C. Culver (D-IA), 1973-77.
Clients:
Product Liability Coordinating Committee

AKERS, James E.
Sullivan and Cromwell
1701 Pennsylvania Ave., N.W. Suite 800, Washington, DC 20006
Telephone: (202) 956-7500

AKIN, GUMP, STRAUSS, HAUER AND FELD
1333 New Hampshire Ave., N.W., Suite 400, Washington, DC 20036
Telephone: (202) 887-4000
Registered as Foreign Agent: (#3492).
Background: Washington office of a Dallas law firm.
Members of firm representing listed organizations:
Berg, Andrew G.
Connelly, Warren E.
Background: Attorney, Cost of Living Council, 1973-74.
Davis, Smith W.
Background: Counsel, House Judiciary Committee, Subcommittee on Crime, 1978-79.
Denvir, James P. (III)
Background: Trial Attorney, Antitrust Division, U.S. Departmemt of Justice, 1975-84. Chief Attorney Staff, Antitrust Division, 1982-84.
Donohoe, David A.
Eisenstat, David H.
Gallagher, John J.
Gardner, Michael R.

Background: Deputy Assistant Administrator, Energy Resource Development, 1975 and Director, Office of Planning and Evaluation, 1976, Federal Energy Administration. Council Member, Administrative Council of the U.S., 1981-.
Goldberg, Avrum M.
Background: Attorney, Division of Litigation, Office of the General Counsel, National Labor Relations Board, 1969-73.
Grealis, William J.
Hardee, David W.
Background: Former Minority Tax Counsel, U.S. Senate Finance Committee.
Hoffman, Lawrence J.
Background: Attorney, National Labor Relations Board, 1967-68.
Jankowsky, Joel
Background: Legislative Assistant to the Speaker, U.S. House of Representatives, 1972-76.
Johnson, Owen
Jordan, Vernon E. (Jr.)
Background: Member, Board of Directors, Corning Glass Works.
Knight, Edward S.
Background: Legislative Assistant to Senator Lloyd Bentsen of Texas, 1976-78.
Langdon, James C. (Jr.)
Lassman, Malcolm
Background: Serves as Treasurer, A.G.S.H.F. Civic Action Committee, the political action arm of the Akin, Gump, Strauss, Hauer and Feld firm.
Levien, Lawrence D.
Marcus, Michael S.
Markus, John F.
McLean, R. Bruce
Background: Attorney, Appellate Court Branch, Nat'l Labor Relations Board, 1971-73.
Mendelsohn, Bruce S.
Background: Attorney and Special Counsel, Division of Corporation Finance, Securities and Exchange Commission, 1977-80. Legal Assistant to Commissioner John R. Evans, SEC, 1980-82. Chief, Office of Regulatory Policy, Division of Investment, SEC, 1982-83.
O'Donnell, Kirk
Paolini, Angela J.
Rivers, Richard
Background: General Counsel of the Office of the Special Trade Representative for Trade Negotiations in the Executive Office of the President, 1977-79.
Rubinoff, Edward L.
Spiegel, Daniel
Background: Special Trade Representative of the U.S., 1977-79. Member, Board of Directors, PepsiCo, Inc. 1971-76. Special Assistant to Secretary of State Cyrus Vance, 1977-78. State Department Policy Planning Staff, 1978-79.
Strauss, Robert S.
Background: Special Trade Representative of the United States, 1977-79 and former Chairman, Democratic National Committee.
Teitz, Louise E.
Clients:
AB SKF, Inc.
Akin, Gump, Strauss, Hauer and Feld Civic Action Committee *(Malcolm Lassman)*
Amerada Hess Corp. *(Edward L. Rubinoff)*
American General Investment Corp.
AT&T
Bank of Nova Scotia *(Joel Jankowsky)*
Boone Co. *(Joel Jankowsky, Edward S. Knight)*
Buckeye Pipe Line Co. *(Joel Jankowsky)*
California Institute of Technology *(Joel Jankowsky)*
Cambridge Information Group *(Joel Jankowsky)*
Chilean Exporters Ass'n *(Lawrence D. Levien)*
Citizens and Southern Corp. *(Joel Jankowsky)*
Clarke/Bardes Organization, Inc.
Coca-Cola Co. *(Andrew G. Berg, Owen Johnson)*
Collagen Corp. *(John F. Markus, Kirk O'Donnell)*
Communications Satellite Corp. (COMSAT)
CRSS Constructors, Inc. *(Joel Jankowsky)*
Eastern Air Lines *(Joel Jankowsky)*
Enron Corp.
First City Bancorporation of Texas *(Joel Jankowsky)*
Fujitsu America, Inc. *(Warren E. Connelly, Joel Jankowsky)*
Fujitsu Ltd. *(Warren E. Connelly, Richard Rivers)*
Grand Met USA *(Smith W. Davis, Daniel Spiegel)*
Grand Metropolitan PLC

Guardian Savings and Loan Ass'n *(Joel Jankowsky)*
Harris County, Metropolitan Transit Authority of *(Joel Jankowsky)*
Houston Oilers *(Joel Jankowsky)*
Hoylake Investments Ltd. *(Joel Jankowsky)*
Industrial Indemnity Financial Corp. *(Joel Jankowsky)*
Kiewit Sons, Inc., Peter *(Joel Jankowsky)*
Levi Strauss and Co. *(Richard Rivers)*
Lone Star Steel Co. *(Warren E. Connelly, Angela J. Paolini)*
Long Island Lighting Co.
Loral/Fairchild Systems *(Joel Jankowsky)*
MacAndrews & Forbes Holdings, Inc.
Martin Marietta Corp. *(Joel Jankowsky)*
McDonnell Douglas Corp. *(Malcolm Lassman)*
Mesa Limited Partnership *(Joel Jankowsky)*
Miller Brewing Co. *(Kirk O'Donnell)*
Minnesota Power *(Joel Jankowsky)*
Morgan Stanley and Co. *(Joel Jankowsky)*
Motion Picture Ass'n of America *(James P. Denvir, III)*
Nat'l Football League *(Edward S. Knight)*
Nat'l Health Laboratories *(Joel Jankowsky)*
News America *(Joel Jankowsky)*
Oil, Chemical and Atomic Workers Internat'l Union *(Richard Rivers, Edward L. Rubinoff)*
PepsiCo, Inc.
Pillsbury Co. *(Joel Jankowsky)*
Plessey Co. PLC, The
Putnam's Sons, G. P. *(Andrew G. Berg, David A. Donohoe)*
R. Lacey, Inc. *(Joel Jankowsky)*
Revlon Group *(Andrew G. Berg, James P. Denvir, III, David A. Donohoe, Louise E. Teitz)*
RJR Nabisco Washington, Inc.
Sara Lee Corp. *(Joel Jankowsky)*
Southern California Edison Co. *(Joel Jankowsky)*
Staley Manufacturing Co., A. E. *(Joel Jankowsky)*
Texas Air Corp. *(John J. Gallagher)*
Texas Education Agency *(Joel Jankowsky)*
Texas Nat'l Research Laboratory Commission
UI Companies
Upjohn Co.
Warner-Lambert Co. *(Edward S. Knight)*
Wertheim Co.
Zink and Co., John *(Joel Jankowsky)*

AKINS, Julia L.
Counsel, Fed. Labor Rel. & Legis. Issues, Internat'l Federation of Professional and Technical Engineers
8701 Georgia Ave., Suite 701, Silver Spring, MD 20910
Telephone: (301) 565-9016
Registered as lobbyist at U.S. Congress.

AKMAN, Jerome P.
Arent, Fox, Kintner, Plotkin & Kahn
1050 Connecticut Ave., N.W., Washington, DC 20036-5339
Telephone: (202) 857-6000
Registered as Foreign Agent: (#2661).
Clients:
Outokumpu Oy

AL-GHARABLY, Marwan
Financial/Administrative Officer, Arab Information Center
1100 17th St., N.W., Suite 602, Washington, DC 20036
Telephone: (202) 265-3210

ALBERGER, Bill
Bishop, Cook, Purcell & Reynolds
1400 L St., N.W., Washington, DC 20005-3502
Telephone: (202) 371-5700
Registered as lobbyist at U.S. Congress.
Background: Special Assistant to Senator Bob Packwood (R-OR), 1969-71; Legislative and Administrative Assistant to Rep. Al Ullman (D-OR), 1972-77; Administrative Assistant, House Committee on Ways and Means, 1977; Commissioner (1977-82), Vice Chairman (1978-80), and Chairman (1980-82), U.S. International Trade Commission.
Clients:
Portland, Oregon, Port of

ALBERS AND CO.
1731 Connecticut Ave., N.W. Second Floor, Washington, DC 20009
Telephone: (202) 328-9333

Background: A public relations firm specializing in state legislative issues.
Members of firm representing listed organizations:
Albers, William E.
Blum, Jared O., V. President, Legislative Affairs
Forbes, Mari S., Senior V. President
Clients:
May Department Stores Co.

ALBERS, William E.
Albers and Co.
1731 Connecticut Ave., N.W. Second Floor, Washington, DC 20009
Telephone: (202) 328-9333
Registered as lobbyist at U.S. Congress.

ALBERSWERTH, David
Director, Public Lands and Energy Div., Nat'l Wildlife Federation
1412 16th St., N.W., Washington, DC 20036
Telephone: (202) 797-6859
Registered as lobbyist at U.S. Congress.

ALBERT, Ben
Director of Public Relations, AFL-CIO Committee on Political Education/Political Contributions Committee (COPE)
815 16th St., N.W., Washington, DC 20006
Telephone: (202) 637-5101

ALBIZO, Joel
Director, Public Relations, American Ass'n of Nurserymen
1250 Eye St., N.W., Suite 500, Washington, DC 20005
Telephone: (202) 789-2900

ALBRIGHT, David H.
Senior Scientist, Federation of American Scientists
307 Massachusetts Ave., N.E., Washington, DC 20002
Telephone: (202) 546-3300

ALBRIGHT, Madeleine K.
President, Center for Nat'l Policy
317 Massachusetts Ave., N.E. Suite 300, Washington, DC 20002
Telephone: (202) 546-9300

ALBUS, William N.
Senior Associate General Counsel, Nat'l Ass'n of Life Underwriters
1922 F St., N.W., Washington, DC 20006
Telephone: (202) 331-6000

ALCALDE, Hector
President, Alcalde & Rousselot
1901 North Fort Myer Dr., Suite 1204, Rosslyn, VA 22209
Telephone: (703) 841-0626
Registered as lobbyist at U.S. Congress.
Registered as Foreign Agent: (#3570).
Clients:
British Ass'n of Investment Trust Companies
Carnival Cruise Lines
China Airlines, Ltd.
Computer Sciences Corp.
Consolidated Freightways Corp.
Fountain Trading Co., Ltd.
Jacksonville, Florida, Port of
Las Vegas, Nevada, City of
Netherlands Antilles, Government of
Norwegian Caribbean Lines
Royal Caribbean Cruise Line

ALCALDE & ROUSSELOT
1901 North Fort Myer Dr., Suite 1204, Rosslyn, VA 22209
Telephone: (703) 841-0626
Background: A government and public affairs consulting firm.
Members of firm representing listed organizations:
Alcalde, Hector, President
Prowitt, Nancy Gibson
Clients:
Alliance for Clean Energy (ACE) *(Nancy Gibson Prowitt)*
British Ass'n of Investment Trust Companies *(Hector Alcalde)*
Carnival Cruise Lines *(Hector Alcalde)*
China Airlines, Ltd. *(Hector Alcalde)*
Computer Sciences Corp. *(Hector Alcalde)*
Consolidated Freightways Corp. *(Hector Alcalde)*
Fountain Trading Co., Ltd. *(Hector Alcalde)*
Hillsborough County Aviation Authority

Jacksonville, Florida, Port of *(Hector Alcalde)*
Las Vegas, Nevada, City of *(Hector Alcalde)*
Netherlands Antilles, Government of *(Hector Alcalde)*
Norwegian Caribbean Lines *(Hector Alcalde)*
Royal Caribbean Cruise Line *(Hector Alcalde)*
Tampa Electric Co.
Tampa Port Authority
Walter Corp., Jim

ALCORN, Daniel S.
Fensterwald & Alcorn, P.C.
2112 C Gallows Road, Vienna, VA 22180
Telephone: (703) 734-0500
Registered as lobbyist at U.S. Congress.

ALDEN, William F.
Cong and Public Affrs Office, DEPARTMENT OF JUSTICE - Drug Enforcement Administration
700 Army-Navy Drive, Arlington, VA 22202
Telephone: (703) 307-7363

ALDER, Thomas
President, Public Law Education Institute
1601 Connecticut Ave., N.W. Suite 450, Washington, DC 20009
Telephone: (202) 232-1400

ALDOCK, John D.
Shea and Gardner
1800 Massachusetts Ave., N.W., Washington, DC 20036
Telephone: (202) 828-2000
Registered as lobbyist at U.S. Congress.
Registered as Foreign Agent: (#3901).

ALDONAS, Grant D.
Member, Miller & Chevalier, Chartered
Metropolitan Square, 655 15th St., N.W., Washington, DC 20005
Telephone: (202) 626-5800
Registered as Foreign Agent: (#3626).
Background: Director, South American and Caribbean Affairs, Office of the U.S. Trade Representative, 1984-85. Special Assistant to the Under Secretary of State for Economic Affairs, 1983-84.

ALDRETE, Eddie
Director, Public Affairs, Nat'l Turkey Federation
11319 Sunset Hills Road, Reston, VA 22090
Telephone: (703) 435-7206
Registered as lobbyist at U.S. Congress.

ALDRIDGE, Bill G.
Exec. Director, Nat'l Science Teachers Ass'n
1742 Connecticut Ave., N.W., Washington, DC 20009
Telephone: (202) 328-5800

ALDRIDGE, Diana
Sr. V. Pres. and Unit Manager, Hill and Knowlton Public Affairs Worldwide
Washington Harbour, 901 31st St., N.W., Washington, DC 20007
Telephone: (202) 333-7400
Registered as Foreign Agent: (#3301).
Background: Former Legislative Assistant to Senator Haskell (D-CO) and Senator Edward Kennedy (D-MA).
Clients:
Larry Jones Ministries

ALEGI, August P.
V. Pres. and Legislative Counsel, GEICO Corp.
GEICO Plaza, Washington, DC 20076
Telephone: (301) 986-3000

ALESSI, Anthony
Mgr.-Federal Relations (Regulatory), Ameritech (American Information Technologies)
1050 Connecticut Ave., N.W., Suite 730, Washington, DC 20036
Telephone: (202) 955-3050

ALEXANDER, Claude D.
Director, Government Affairs, Ralston Purina Co.
2000 L St., N.W., Suite 801, Washington, DC 20036
Telephone: (202) 223-5302

ALEXANDER, Clifford J.
Kirkpatrick & Lockhart
1800 M St., N.W., Suite 900 South Lobby, Washington, DC 20036-5891
Telephone: (202) 778-9000
Background: Attorney/Analyst, Securities and Exchange Commission, 1967-70. Assistant Counsel, Securities Subcommittee of Senate Committee on Banking, Housing and Urban Affairs, 1975-77.

ALEXANDER, Donald C.
Cadwalader, Wickersham & Taft
1333 New Hampshire Ave., N.W. Suite 700, Washington, DC 20036
Telephone: (202) 862-2200
Registered as lobbyist at U.S. Congress.
Background: Commissioner of Internal Revenue, 1973-77. Commissioner, Commission on Federal Paperwork, 1975-77. Commissioner, Interior Department Coal Leasing Commission, 1983-84. Chairman, Internal Revenue Service Exempt Organization Advisory Group, 1987.
Clients:
Air Products and Chemicals, Inc.
Air Transport Ass'n of America
American Financial Corp.
Aon Corp.
Bechtel Group, Inc.
Bechtel Investments, Inc.
Family Life Insurance Co.
Harsco Corp.
Mortgage Guaranty Insurance Corp.
Nationwide Insurance Cos.
United Brands Co.

ALEXANDER, Fay
Exec. Director, Save Our Schools
655 15th St., N.W., Suite 310, Washington, DC 20005
Telephone: (202) 639-4419
Registered as lobbyist at U.S. Congress.

ALEXANDER, Koteles
Gartrell & Alexander
Lee Plaza, 8601 Georgia Ave. Suite 805, Silver Spring, MD 20910
Telephone: (301) 589-2222
Registered as lobbyist at U.S. Congress.
Clients:
Washington Metropolitan Area Transit Authority

ALEXANDER, Margaret
Finance Director, Republican Nat'l Committee
310 First St., S.E., Washington, DC 20003
Telephone: (202) 863-8500

ALEXANDER, Mary
Manager, Government Affairs, Matsushita Electric Corp. of America
1001 Pennsylvania Ave., N.W. Suite 1355 North, Washington, DC 20004
Telephone: (202) 347-7592
Registered as lobbyist at U.S. Congress.

ALEXANDER, Nancy L.
Legislative Secretary, Friends Committee on Nat'l Legislation
245 Second St., N.E., Washington, DC 20002
Telephone: (202) 547-6000
Registered as lobbyist at U.S. Congress.

ALEXANDER, Robin
Public Relations Director, Nat'l Ass'n of Black Women Attorneys
3711 Macomb St., N.W., Washington, DC 20016
Telephone: (202) 966-9693

ALFANO, Alphonse M.
Bassman, Mitchell & Alfano, Chartered
1750 K St., N.W., Suite 380, Washington, DC 20006
Telephone: (202) 466-6502

ALI, Richard F.
Director Goverment Affairs, Nat'l Spa and Pool Institute
2111 Eisenhower Ave., Alexandria, VA 22314
Telephone: (703) 838-0083

ALIRIZA, Dr. Bulent
Representative, Turkish Republic of Northern Cyprus
1667 K St., N.W., Suite 690, Washington, DC 20006
Telephone: (202) 887-6198

ALLAMANNO, Christine
General Counsel, Teamsters for a Democratic Union
2000 P St., N.W. Suite 612, Washington, DC 20036
Telephone: (202) 785-3707

ALLAN ASSOCIATES
900 17th St., N.W., Suite 520, Washington, DC 20006
Telephone: (202) 835-9685
Members of firm representing listed organizations:
Allan, Roger D., President
Clients:
American Council of Independent Laboratories
(*Roger D. Allan*)
Ass'n of Thrift Holding Companies (*Roger D. Allan*)
Institute of Electrical and Electronics Engineers, Inc. (*Roger D. Allan*)
Intermodal Marketing Ass'n (*Roger D. Allan*)
Nat'l Waterways Conference, Inc. (*Roger D. Allan*)

ALLAN, Richmond F.
Duncan, Weinberg, Miller & Pembroke, P.C.
1615 M St., N.W., Suite 800, Washington, DC 20036-3203
Telephone: (202) 467-6370
Background: Assistant U.S. Attorney, District of Montana, 1961-64. Trial Attorney, U.S. Department of Justice, 1965. Associate Solicitor, 1965-67, and Deputy Solicitor, 1968. Indian Affairs, Department of Interior.
Clients:
Basin Electric Power Cooperative
Beard Oil Co.
Derby Line, Vermont, Town of
Kenai Natives Ass'n, Inc.
Web Water Development Ass'n

ALLAN, Roger D.
President, Allan Associates
900 17th St., N.W., Suite 520, Washington, DC 20006
Telephone: (202) 835-9685
Clients:
American Council of Independent Laboratories
Ass'n of Thrift Holding Companies
Institute of Electrical and Electronics Engineers, Inc.
Intermodal Marketing Ass'n
Nat'l Waterways Conference, Inc.

ALLARD, Nicholas W.
Fox, Bennett and Turner
750 17th St., N.W., Suite 1100, Washington, DC 20006
Telephone: (202) 778-2300
Registered as lobbyist at U.S. Congress.
Background: Minority Counsel, U.S. Senate Committee on the Judiciary, 1984-86. Administrative Assistant to Senator Daniel P. Moynihan (D-NY), 1986-87.
Clients:
Wireless Cable Ass'n, Inc.

ALLEGRETTI, Thomas A.
V. President, Operations, American Waterways Operators
1600 Wilson Blvd. Suite 1000, Arlington, VA 22209
Telephone: (703) 841-9300

ALLEN, Alexis B.
Manager, Media Relations, Aerospace Industries Ass'n of America
1250 Eye St., N.W., Suite 1100, Washington, DC 20005
Telephone: (202) 371-8400

ALLEN, Anthony
Youth and Communications Director, World Federalist Ass'n
418 Seventh St., S.E., Washington, DC 20003
Telephone: (202) 546-3950

ALLEN, Barbara
Legislative Representative, Nat'l Committee to Preserve Social Security and Medicare
2000 K St., N.W. Suite 800, Washington, DC 20006
Telephone: (202) 822-9459
Registered as lobbyist at U.S. Congress.

ALLEN, Donald R.
Duncan, Allen and Talmage
1575 Eye St., N.W., Suite 300, Washington, DC 20005
Telephone: (202) 289-8400
Registered as lobbyist at U.S. Congress.
Registered as Foreign Agent: (#3505).

ALLEN, Edwin H.
Gen. Counsel & V. President, Health Industry Manufacturers Ass'n
1030 15th St., N.W. Suite 1100, Washington, DC 20005
Telephone: (202) 452-8240
Background: Former Associate Minority Counsel, House of Representatives Committee on Energy and Commerce.

ALLEN, Ernest
President, Nat'l Center for Missing and Exploited Children
2101 Wilson Blvd., Suite 550, Arlington, VA 22201
Telephone: (703) 235-3900

ALLEN-GIFFORD, Patrice
Exec. Assistant to the President, Air Transport Ass'n of America
1709 New York Ave., N.W., Washington, DC 20006-5206
Telephone: (202) 626-4000

ALLEN, Jeanne
Education Policy Analyst, Heritage Foundation
214 Massachusetts Ave., N.E., Washington, DC 20002
Telephone: (202) 546-4400
Background: Special Assistant, Department of Education, 1984-88.

ALLEN, Katherine E.
President, TADCO Enterprises
Box 65498, Washington, DC 20035-5498
Telephone: (202) 639-4787
Clients:
ADM Milling Co.
American River Transport Co.
Archer-Daniels-Midland Co.
Corn Sweeteners, Inc.

ALLEN, Kenneth B.
Senior V. President, Information Industry Ass'n
555 New Jersey Ave., N.W. Suite 800, Washington, DC 20001
Telephone: (202) 639-8262
Registered as lobbyist at U.S. Congress.

ALLEN, Marion H., III
Dow, Lohnes and Albertson
1255 23rd St., N.W., Suite 500, Washington, DC 20037
Telephone: (202) 857-2500
Clients:
Atlanta Falcons

ALLEN, Marjorie D.
Legislative Affairs Specialist, American Federation of State, County and Municipal Employees
1625 L St., N.W., Washington, DC 20036
Telephone: (202) 429-1000
Registered as lobbyist at U.S. Congress.
Background: Legislative Assistant to Rep. Chet Atkins (D-MA), 1987-88.

ALLEN, Pamela
Director, Legislative Services Division, Collier, Shannon & Scott
1055 Thomas Jefferson St., N.W., Suite 300, Washington, DC 20007
Telephone: (202) 342-8400
Registered as lobbyist at U.S. Congress.
Registered as Foreign Agent: (#3694).
Clients:
American Iron and Steel Institute
Footwear Industry Political Action Committee
Nat'l Ass'n of Mutual Insurance Companies
Zurich-American Insurance

ALLEN, Paul J.
Director of Communications, Natural Resources Defense Council
1350 New York Ave., N.W. Suite 300, Washington, DC 20005
Telephone: (202) 783-7800

ALLEN, Richard V.
Distinguished Fellow, Heritage Foundation
214 Massachusetts Ave., N.E., Washington, DC 20002
Telephone: (202) 546-4400
Background: Assistant to the President for National Security Affairs, 1981. Senior Staff Member, National Security Council and member of President's Commisssion on International Trade and Investment Policy under President Nixon.

ALLEN, Rita F.
Team Xerox PAC Administrator, Xerox Corp.
490 L'Enfant Plaza East, S.W., Suite 4200, Washington,
DC 20024
Telephone: (202) 646-8285

ALLEN, Ronald C.
Asst Chief Couns, Legis & General Law, DEPARTMENT
OF ARMY - Chief of Engineers
20 Massachusetts Ave., N.W., Washington, DC 20314
Telephone: (202) 272-0030

ALLEN, Susan Au
President, United States Pan Asian American Chamber of
Commerce
1625 K St., N.W., Suite 380, Washington, DC 20006
Telephone: (202) 638-1764

ALLEN, Susan S.
Chief Staff Executive, Vision Council of America
1800 North Kent St. Suite 1210, Arlington, VA 22209
Telephone: (703) 243-1508

ALLEN, William H.
Covington and Burling
1201 Pennsylvania Ave., N.W., Box 7566, Washington, DC
20044
Telephone: (202) 662-6000
Registered as lobbyist at U.S. Congress.
Clients:
Puerto Rico Ports Authority

ALLENDORF, Laura L.
Government Affairs Representative, American Soc. of Internal Medicine
1101 Vermont Ave., N.W. Suite 500, Washington, DC
20005
Telephone: (202) 289-1700
Registered as lobbyist at U.S. Congress.

ALLISON, Edward E.
Government Relations Consultant, McAuliffe, Kelly, Raffa-
elli & Siemens
1341 G St., N.W. Suite 200, Washington, DC 20005
Telephone: (202) 783-1800
Registered as lobbyist at U.S. Congress.
Registered as Foreign Agent: (#4332).
Background: Former Administrative Assistant to Senator
Paul Laxalt (R-NV). Active in Reagan and Bush Presi-
dential campaigns.
Clients:
American Nuclear Energy Council
Clark County, Nevada
Dalton Construction Co.
Environmental Research Center, University of
Nervada/Las Vegas
Massport/Commonwealth of Massachusetts
Nat'l Judicial College
Nat'l Medical Care, Inc.
University of Nevada/Reno

ALLISON, Richard G.
Exec. Officer, American Institute of Nutrition
9650 Rockville Pike, Bethesda, MD 20814
Telephone: (301) 530-7050

ALLISON, Col. Tom
Cong Inquiry, Legis Liaison, DEPARTMENT OF AIR
FORCE
The Pentagon, Washington, DC 20330
Telephone: (202) 697-8153

ALLMAN, Tina H.
President, Nat'l Composition and Prepress Ass'n
1730 North Lynn St., Arlington, VA 22209
Telephone: (703) 841-8165
Registered as lobbyist at U.S. Congress.

ALLNUTT, Robert F.
Exec. V. President, Pharmaceutical Manufacturers Ass'n
1100 15th St., N.W., Washington, DC 20005
Telephone: (202) 835-3430
Registered as lobbyist at U.S. Congress.

ALLPOINTS INTERNAT'L, LTD.
1250 Connecticut Ave., N.W., Suite 319, Washington, DC
20036
Telephone: (202) 371-6767

Members of firm representing listed organizations:
Denson, James L.
Clients:
Bophuthatswana, Government of *(James L. Denson)*

ALLRED, James E.
General V. Pres & Nat'l Legislative Rep., Brotherhood of
Railway Carmen of the U.S. and Canada
400 First St., N.W., Suite 804, Washington, DC 20001
Telephone: (202) 737-1541
Registered as lobbyist at U.S. Congress.

ALMQUIST, David D.
V. Pres, Membership/Organization Liaison, American Soc.
of Hospital Pharmacists
4630 Montgomery Ave., Bethesda, MD 20814
Telephone: (301) 657-3000

ALMSTEDT, Kermit W.
O'Melveny and Myers
555 13th St., N.W., Suite 500 West, Washington, DC
20004
Telephone: (202) 383-5300
Registered as lobbyist at U.S. Congress.
Clients:
Cargill, Inc.

ALPER AND MANN
400 First St., N.W. Suite 811, Washington, DC 20001
Telephone: (202) 298-9191
Clients:
Railway Labor Executives' Ass'n
United Transportation Union
Water Transport Ass'n

ALPERN, Robert Z.
Director, Washington Office, Unitarian Universalist Ass'n
of Congregations
100 Maryland Ave., N.E. Box #68, Washington, DC
20002
Telephone: (202) 547-0254

ALTER, Dr. Harvey
Manager, Resources Policy Department, Chamber of
Commerce of the U.S.A.
1615 H St., N.W., Washington, DC 20062
Telephone: (202) 463-5531
Registered as lobbyist at U.S. Congress.

ALTERMAN, Stephen A.
Meyers and Alterman
1710 Rhode Island Ave., N.W. Suite 200, Washington, DC
20036
Telephone: (202) 466-8270
Background: Attorney, Civil Aeronautics Board, 1968-73.
Chief, Legal Division, Civil Aeronautics Board, 1974-75.
Clients:
Air Freight Ass'n of America

ALTHEN, William I.
Smith, Heenan and Althen
1110 Vermont Ave., N.W., Suite 400, Washington, DC
20005
Telephone: (202) 887-0800
Background: Serves as General Counsel, American League
of Lobbyists, 1983.
Clients:
Internat'l Electronic Facsimile Users Ass'n
Nat'l Ass'n of Computer Stores

ALTIER, Michael J.
V. President & Legislative Counsel, Nat'l Retail Merchants
Ass'n
1000 Connecticut Ave., N.W., Washington, DC 20036
Telephone: (202) 223-8250
Registered as lobbyist at U.S. Congress.

ALTMAN, E. T.
President, Hardwood Plywood Manufacturers Ass'n
1825 Michael Faraday Dr., Reston, VA 22090
Telephone: (703) 435-2900

ALTMAN, Jeffrey P.
Chairman and Treasurer, Jewish Republican PAC
1575 I St., N.W. Suite 800, Washington, DC 20005
Telephone: (202) 789-7520

ALTMAN, John
Account Supervisor, Burson-Marsteller
1850 M St., N.W., Suite 900, Washington, DC 20036
Telephone: (202) 833-8550

ALTMAN, Richard H.
Exec. Director, Nat'l Political Action Committee, The
555 New Jersey Ave., N.W., Suite 718, Washington, DC
20000

ALTMAN, Robert A.
Clifford & Warnke
815 Connecticut Ave., N.W., Washington, DC 20006
Telephone: (202) 828-4200
Clients:
Nonprescription Drug Manfacturers Ass'n

ALTMAN, William A.
Legislative Counsel, American Psychological Ass'n
1200 17th St., N.W., Washington, DC 20036
Telephone: (202) 955-7600
Registered as lobbyist at U.S. Congress.

ALTMEYER, Thomas H.
Senior V. President, Gov't Affairs, Nat'l Coal Ass'n
1130 17th St., N.W., Washington, DC 20036
Telephone: (202) 463-2653
Registered as lobbyist at U.S. Congress.

ALVARADO GROUP, THE
655 15th St., N.W. Suite 300, Washington, DC 20005
Telephone: (202) 639-4019
Background: A lobbying firm.
Members of firm representing listed organizations:
Alvarado, Susan, President
Gerkin, David, Exec. V. President
Background: Former Legislative Assistant to former
Rep. Tony Coelho (D-CA).
Clients:
Chevron, U.S.A. *(Susan Alvarado)*
Clean Air Act Project *(Susan Alvarado)*
On the Potomac Productions, Inc. *(Susan Alvarado)*
UST Public Affairs, Inc. *(Susan Alvarado)*

ALVARADO, Susan
President, Alvarado Group, The
655 15th St., N.W. Suite 300, Washington, DC 20005
Telephone: (202) 639-4019
Clients:
Chevron, U.S.A.
Clean Air Act Project
On the Potomac Productions, Inc.
UST Public Affairs, Inc.

ALVAREZ, Margaret Ellen
Secretary-Treasurer, Cambridge Consulting Corp.
1893 Preston White Drive, Suite 110, Reston, VA 22091
Telephone: (703) 620-1911

ALVAREZ, Richard
Founder and CEO, Cambridge Consulting Corp.
1893 Preston White Drive, Suite 110, Reston, VA 22091
Telephone: (703) 620-1911

ALVAREZ, Robert L.
Nat'l Service Director, Military Order of the Purple Heart
of the U.S.A.
5413-B Backlick Rd., Springfield, VA 22151
Telephone: (703) 642-5360

ALVERSON, Cappie
Cong Liaison Specialist, DEPARTMENT OF COMMERCE
14th and Constitution Ave. S.W., Washington, DC 20230
Telephone: (202) 377-5485

ALVORD AND ALVORD
918 16th St., N.W. Suite 200, Washington, DC 20006
Telephone: (202) 393-2266
Clients:
Compania Peruana de Vapores
Internat'l Trade and Development, Inc.
Overseas Nat'l Airways

AMADOR, Rauol A.
Treasurer, Marine Engineers Beneficial Ass'n Retirees
Group Fund
444 North Capitol St. Suite 800, Washington, DC 20001
Telephone: (202) 347-8585

AMATETTI, John P.
Manager, Civil Aviation Affairs, Aerospace Industries Ass'n of America
1250 Eye St., N.W., Suite 1100, Washington, DC 20005
Telephone: (202) 371-8400

AMBACH, Gordon M.
Exec. Director, Council of Chief State School Officers
400 North Capitol St., N.W., Suite 379, Washington, DC 20001
Telephone: (202) 393-8161

AMBLER, John O.
Federal Government Affrs. Representative, Texaco U.S.A.
1050 17th St., N.W., Suite 500, Washington, DC 20036
Telephone: (202) 331-1427
Registered as lobbyist at U.S. Congress.

AMBRO ASSOCIATES, Jerome A.
4734 Timber Ridge Drive, Montclair, VA 22026
Telephone: (703) 690-4830
Background: A governmental and legislative consulting firm.
Members of firm representing listed organizations:
Ambro, Jerome A.
Organizations represented:
Associated Universities *(Jerome A. Ambro)*

AMBRO, Jerome A.
Ambro Associates, Jerome A.
4734 Timber Ridge Drive, Montclair, VA 22026
Telephone: (703) 690-4830
Registered as lobbyist at U.S. Congress.
Organizations represented:
Associated Universities

AMBROSE, John P.
Sr. Director, Advocacy, Nat'l Mental Health Ass'n
1021 Prince St., Alexandria, VA 22314
Telephone: (703) 684-7722

AMBUR, Owen
Legis Services Chief, DEPARTMENT OF INTERIOR - Fish and Wildlife Service
18th and C Sts., N.W., Washington, DC 20240
Telephone: (202) 343-2500

AMDUR, James A.
Corp Tax Counsel-Assoc General Counsel, Communications Satellite Corp. (COMSAT)
950 L'Enfant Plaza, S.W., Washington, DC 20024
Telephone: (202) 863-6000

AMERICAN SURVEYS INTERNAT'L
2000 N St., N.W., Washington, DC 20036
Telephone: (202) 331-1711
Members of firm representing listed organizations:
Rosenbloom, Morris Victor

AMERICAN TRADE ASS'N MANAGEMENT
9005 Congressional Court, Potomac, MD 20854
Telephone: (301) 365-4080
Members of firm representing listed organizations:
Mack, James E. (CAE)
Background: Serves as the Exec. Secretary and General Counsel, Nat'l Ass'n of Mirror Manufacturers and as Managing Director and General Counsel, Peanut Butter and Nut Processors Ass'n.
Clients:
Nat'l Ass'n of Mirror Manufacturers *(James E. Mack, CAE)*
Peanut Butter and Nut Processors Ass'n *(James E. Mack, CAE)*
Peanut Butter and Nut Processors Ass'n Political Action Committee *(James E. Mack, CAE)*

AMES, George F.
Exec. Director, Council of Infrastructure Financing Authorities
655 15th St., N.W., Suite 300, Washington, DC 20005
Telephone: (202) 347-6333
Background: Former Director, Water Policy, Environmental Protection Agency.

AMES, Joanne
Assistant Tax Counsel, American Bankers Ass'n
1120 Connecticut Ave., N.W., Washington, DC 20036
Telephone: (202) 663-5000
Registered as lobbyist at U.S. Congress.

AMES, Kristen
Junior Assoicate, Wexler, Reynolds, Fuller, Harrison and Schule, Inc.
1317 F St., N.W., Suite 600, Washington, DC 20004
Telephone: (202) 638-2121
Background: Staff Assistant, House Energy and Commerce Committee, 1985-88.
Clients:
Nat'l Ass'n of Social Workers

AMES, Robert G.
Venable, Baetjer, Howard and Civiletti
1201 New York Ave., N.W., Suite 1000, Washington, DC 20005
Telephone: (202) 962-4800

AMES-ZIERMAN, Susan
Exec. Director, Nat'l Ass'n of Developmental Disabilities Councils
1234 Massachusetts Ave., N.W. Suite 103, Washington, DC 20005
Telephone: (202) 347-1234

AMHAUS, Dean
Duncan and Associates
1213 29th St., N.W., Washington, DC 20007
Telephone: (202) 333-5841

AMICK, John
Campbell-Raupe, Inc.
1010 Pennsylvania Ave., S.E., Washington, DC 20003
Telephone: (202) 546-4991
Background: Former aide to Rep. Doug Bereuter (R-NE).

AMITAY, P.C., Morris J.
444 North Capitol St., N.W., Suite 712, Washington, DC 20001
Telephone: (202) 347-6613
Background: An attorney. Formerly served as Senior Legislative Aide to Senator Abraham Ribicoff of Connecticut, Foreign Service Officer, and Director of the American-Israel Public Affairs Committee.
Organizations represented:
Coalition for American Energy Security
Dietary Supplement Coalition
Elbit Inc./Inframetrics, Inc.
Howmet/Pechiney Corp.
LUZ, International
Northrop Corp.
Thompson Medical Co., Inc.
Washington Political Action Committee

AMITO, Eiji
Senior V. President, American Honda Motor Co.
955 L'Enfant Plaza Suite 5300, Washington, DC 20024
Telephone: (202) 554-1650
Registered as lobbyist at U.S. Congress.

AMS, John G.
V.P., Financial Affrs. & Administration, Interstate Natural Gas Ass'n of America
555 13th St., N.W. Suite 300 West, Washington, DC 20004
Telephone: (202) 626-3200
Registered as lobbyist at U.S. Congress.

AMUNDSON, Jan S.
V. President & General Counsel, Nat'l Ass'n of Manufacturers
1331 Pennsylvania Ave., N.W. Suite 1500 North, Washington, DC 20004-1703
Telephone: (202) 637-3000
Registered as lobbyist at U.S. Congress.

AN, Hong K.
Partner, Armstrong, Byrd and Associates
1730 M St., N.W., Suite 808, Washington, DC 20036
Telephone: (202) 223-5880
Registered as Foreign Agent: (#2734).
Background: Former Professional Staff Member, House Committee on Standards of Official Conduct, 1977-78.
Clients:
Korea Deep Sea Fisheries Ass'n

ANBENDER, Julie
Account Executive, Gallagher-Widmeyer Group Inc., The
1110 Vermont Ave., N.W., Suite 1020, Washington, DC 20005
Telephone: (202) 659-1606

Background: Former Press Secretary and Deputy Press Secretary, Democratic National Committee.

ANDERSON, Anthony A.
Eckert Seamans Cherin & Mellott
1818 N St., N.W., Suite 700, Washington, DC 20036
Telephone: (202) 452-1074
Registered as lobbyist at U.S. Congress.
Background: Attorney Advisor, Urban Mas Transportation Administration, 1980-84.
Clients:
New York Metropolitan Transportation Authority

ANDERSON, Becky
Admin Asst, Legis Affrs, EXECUTIVE OFFICE OF THE PRESIDENT - The White House
1600 Pennsylvania Ave., N.W., Washington, DC 20500
Telephone: (202) 456-2230

ANDERSON, BENJAMIN, READ & HANEY
1020 19th St., N.W., Suite 500, Washington, DC 20036
Telephone: (202) 659-5656
Background: A public affairs firm.
Members of firm representing listed organizations:
Consaul, Sheila A.
Knauer, Virginia H., Senior Consultant
Background: Former Director, U.S. Office of Consumer Affairs, Department of Health and Human Services, and former special advisor to President Reagan on consumer affairs.
Prendergast, Richard H.
Background: Former Special Assistant to the President for Legislative Affairs, House under President Reagan.

ANDERSON, Bette B.
Exec. V. President, KCI Inc.
1030 15th St., N.W., Washington, DC 20005
Telephone: (202) 371-2190
Registered as lobbyist at U.S. Congress.
Background: Undersecretary of the Treasury under President Jimmy Carter.
Clients:
SICPA Industries of America, Inc.
U.S. Banknote Corp.

ANDERSON, Bill
PAC Director, Nat'l Republican Congressional Committee
320 First St., S.E., Washington, DC 20003
Telephone: (202) 479-7000

ANDERSON, Carol Cofield
V. President, Adams Associates, John
1825 K St., N.W. Suite 210, Washington, DC 20006
Telephone: (202) 466-8320

ANDERSON, Charlene D.
Administrator, Toxicology Forum
1575 Eye St., N.W., Suite 800, Washington, DC 20005
Telephone: (202) 659-0030

ANDERSON, Cheryl
Senior V. President, Advocacy Services Group, Inc.
1825 Eye St., N.W. Suite 400, Washington, DC 20006
Telephone: (202) 429-2096

ANDERSON, Cynthia C.
Director, Federal Government Affairs, Enron Corp.
1020 16th St., N.W., Washington, DC 20036-5754
Telephone: (202) 828-3360
Registered as lobbyist at U.S. Congress.
Background: Former Legislative Assistant to Congressman Joe Barton (R-TX).

ANDERSON, Darryl
O'Donnell, Schwartz & Anderson
1300 L St., N.W., Suite 200, Washington, DC 20005-4178
Telephone: (202) 898-1707
Clients:
American Postal Workers Union

ANDERSON, David J.
Manager, Federal Relations, TRW Inc.
1000 Wilson Blvd., Arlington, VA 22209
Telephone: (703) 276-5000
Registered as lobbyist at U.S. Congress.

ANDERSON, Deborah E.
Assistant Director, Public Relations, American Textile
  Manufacturers Institute
1801 K St., N.W. Suite 900, Washington, DC 20006
Telephone: (202) 862-0500

ANDERSON, Desiree
Director, Gov'tl & Political Relations, Nat'l Ass'n of REAL-
  TORS
777 14th St., N.W., Washington, DC 20005
Telephone: (202) 383-1000
Registered as lobbyist at U.S. Congress.
Background: Serves also as Director, R-PAC.

ANDERSON, HIBEY, NAUHEIM AND BLAIR
1708 New Hampshire Ave., N.W., Washington, DC 20009
Telephone: (202) 483-1900
Members of firm representing listed organizations:
  Anderson, Stanton D.
    Background: Staff Assistant to the President of the
      United States, 1971-73. Deputy Assistant Secretary
      of State, 1973-75. Member, U.S. National Commis-
      sion for UNESCO, 1975-78. Member, President's
      Commission on Personnel Interchange, 1976-79.
      Serves also as Chairman of the Board, Global USA,
      Inc.
  Blair, Robert A.
  Nauheim, Stephen A.
    Background: Attorney-Advisor, 1967-70 and Assistant
      Chief, 1970-71, International Branch, Legislation and
      Regulations Division, IRS Chief Counsel's Office.
  Waldman, Byron, Principal
  Clients:
    Alamo Rent-a-Car *(Stanton D. Anderson, Robert A.
      Blair)*
    Bay Area Rapid Transit District *(Robert A. Blair)*
    Communication Industries Ass'n of Japan *(Stanton
      D. Anderson)*
    Curacao Internat'l Trust Co. *(Stephen A. Nauheim)*
    Eastern Air Lines *(Stanton D. Anderson)*
    ECO Corp. *(Robert A. Blair)*
    Electronic Industries Ass'n of Japan *(Stanton D.
      Anderson)*
    Institute of Financial and Fiscal Studies of Cura-
      cao *(Stanton D. Anderson, Stephen A. Nauheim)*
    Japan Machine Tool Builders Ass'n *(Stanton D. And-
      erson)*
    Japan Machinery Exporters Ass'n *(Stanton D. Ander-
      son)*
    Japan Metal Forming Machine Builders Ass'n
      (Stanton D. Anderson)
    NHK (Japanese Broadcasting Corp.) *(Stanton D.
      Anderson)*
    Project Orbis *(Robert A. Blair)*
    TECO Transport & Trade Corp. *(Robert A. Blair)*

ANDERSON, James A., Jr.
Senior Director, Government Relations, Nat'l Ass'n of
  Wholesaler-Distributors
1725 K St., N.W. Suite 710, Washington, DC 20006
Telephone: (202) 872-0885
Background: Serves as Exec. Director, The Product Liabili-
  ty Alliance.

ANDERSON, James E.
Loomis, Owen, Fellman and Howe
2020 K St., N.W. Suite 800, Washington, DC 20006
Telephone: (202) 296-5680
Background: Assistant United States Attorney for the Dis-
  trict of Maryland, 1970-76. Serves as General Counsel to
  the Greater Washington Soc. of Assocation Executives.
Clients:
  American Ass'n of State Highway and Trans-
    portation Officials
  Greater Washington Soc. of Ass'n Executives
  Hotel Sales and Marketing Ass'n Internat'l
  Industrial Diamond Ass'n of America
  Internat'l Business Forms Industries
  Optical Manufacturers Ass'n
  Washington Ass'n Research Foundation
  Wire Reinforcement Institute

ANDERSON, Jane M.
Director, Public Relations, American Soc. of Internal Medicine
1101 Vermont Ave., N.W. Suite 500, Washington, DC
  20005
Telephone: (202) 289-1700

ANDERSON, Jeannette
Internat'l Marketing Director, Nat'l Peanut Council
1500 King St., Suite 301, Alexandria, VA 22314-2730
Telephone: (703) 838-9500

ANDERSON, John A.
Exec. Director, Electricity Consumers Resource Council
1333 H St., N.W., West Tower - 8th Fl., Washington, DC
  20005
Telephone: (202) 466-4686

ANDERSON, John T.
Media Coordinator, Public Relats. Staff, General Motors
  Corp.
1660 L St., N.W., Washington, DC 20036
Telephone: (202) 775-5040

ANDERSON, Jon A.
Director, Federal Affairs, Eaton Corp.
1100 Connecticut Ave., N.W., Suite 410, Washington, DC
  20036
Telephone: (202) 955-6444
Registered as lobbyist at U.S. Congress.
Background: Former Legislative Assistant to the Secretary
  of Defense and Special Assistant to the Secretary of the
  Air Force.

ANDERSON, Kenneth C.
Squire, Sanders and Dempsey
1201 Pennsylvania Ave., N.W. P.O. Box 407, Washington,
  DC 20044
Telephone: (202) 626-6600
Background: Chief, Special Regulated Industries Section,
  Antitrust Division, Department of Justice, 1975-80.
Clients:
  Bessemer and Lake Erie Railroad Co.

ANDERSON, KILL, OLICK AND OSHINSKY
2000 Pennsylvania Ave., N.W., Suite 7500, Washington,
  DC 20006
Telephone: (202) 728-3100
Background: Washington office of a New York law firm.
Members of firm representing listed organizations:
  Oshinsky, Jerold
  Tydings, Joseph D.
    Background: Member, Maryland House of Delegates,
      1955-61. U.S. Attorney, District of Maryland, 1961-
      63. U.S. Senator from Maryland, 1965-71.
  Clients:
    Keene Corp. *(Jerold Oshinsky)*
    Population Crisis Committee *(Joseph D. Tydings)*

ANDERSON, Laurel
Associate, Meyers & Associates
412 First St., S.E., Suite 100, Washington, DC 20003
Telephone: (202) 484-2773

ANDERSON, Mark
Government Affairs Specialist, American Feed Industry
  Ass'n
1701 Fort Myer Dr. Suite 1200, Arlington, VA 22209
Telephone: (703) 524-0810
Registered as lobbyist at U.S. Congress.

ANDERSON, Marla
Exec. Director, Nat'l Ass'n of Neighborhoods
1651 Fuller St., N.W., Washington, DC 20009
Telephone: (202) 332-7766

ANDERSON & PARTNERS, P. W.
2070 Chain Bridge Road, Suite 500, Vienna, VA 22180
Telephone: (703) 442-0272
Registered as Foreign Agent: (#3806)
Background: An international consulting firm specializing
  in marketing, sales representation, study tours, and health
  services.
Members of firm representing listed organizations:
  Anderson, Philip W., President
  Organizations represented:
    Hannover, City of *(Philip W. Anderson)*

ANDERSON, Patricia
President, Public Office Corp.
911 Second St., N.E., Washington, DC 20002
Telephone: (202) 675-4900

ANDERSON AND PENDLETON, C.A.
1000 Connecticut Ave., N.W., Suite 1220, Washington, DC
  20036

Telephone: (202) 659-2334
Registered as Foreign Agent: (#2696)
Members of firm representing listed organizations:
  Johnson, Stephen S.
  McKenna, Francis G.
    Background: Attorney, Antitrust Division, Department
      of Justice, 1962-66. Hearing Division, Federal Com-
      munications Commission, 1966-68. Office of the
      General Counsel, Federal Home Loan Bank Board,
      1967-70.
  Pendleton, Edmund E.
  Whitehead, Donald
  Clients:
    Appalachian Regional Commission, States' Wash-
      ington Representative of *(Donald Whitehead)*
    Chile, Army Procurement Mission
    Emergent Technologies, Inc. *(Donald Whitehead)*
    Federation of Japan Tuna Fisheries Cooperative
      Ass'ns *(Francis G. McKenna)*
    Japan Tuna Fisheries Cooperative *(Francis G.
      McKenna)*
    West Virginia Railroad Maintenance Authority
      (Francis G. McKenna)

ANDERSON, Philip W.
President, Anderson & Partners, P. W.
2070 Chain Bridge Road, Suite 500, Vienna, VA 22180
Telephone: (703) 442-0272
Registered as Foreign Agent: (#3806).
Organizations represented:
  Hannover, City of

ANDERSON AND QUINN
12450 Fair Lakes Circle Suite 370, Fairfax, VA 22033-
  4900
Telephone: (703) 222-2200
Members of firm representing listed organizations:
  Corrie, Quentin R.
  Clients:
    American Automobile Ass'n *(Quentin R. Corrie)*

ANDERSON, Richard M.
Deputy General Manager, Hill and Knowlton Public Affairs
  Worldwide
Washington Harbour, 901 31st St., N.W., Washington, DC
  20007
Telephone: (202) 333-7400
Registered as Foreign Agent: (#4170).
Background: Formerly on the staff of the Liberal Party of
  Canada, 1974-77. Special Assistant to Canada's President
  of the Treasury Board and Minister of Science and Tech-
  nology, 1977-79. Policy Adviser to the Prime Minister of
  Canada, 1984.
Clients:
  Public Affairs Internat'l

ANDERSON, Stanton D.
Anderson, Hibey, Nauheim and Blair
1708 New Hampshire Ave., N.W., Washington, DC 20009
Telephone: (202) 483-1900
Registered as lobbyist at U.S. Congress.
Registered as Foreign Agent: (#3208).
Background: Staff Assistant to the President of the United
  States, 1971-73. Deputy Assistant Secretary of State,
  1973-75. Member, U.S. National Commission for UNES-
  CO, 1975-78. Member, President's Commission on Per-
  sonnel Interchange, 1976-79. Serves also as Chairman of
  the Board, Global USA, Inc.
Clients:
  Alamo Rent-a-Car
  Communication Industries Ass'n of Japan
  Eastern Air Lines
  Electronic Industries Ass'n of Japan
  Institute of Financial and Fiscal Studies of Cura-
    cao
  Japan Machine Tool Builders Ass'n
  Japan Machinery Exporters Ass'n
  Japan Metal Forming Machine Builders Ass'n
  NHK (Japanese Broadcasting Corp.)

ANDERSON, Steven C.
President, American Frozen Food Institute
1764 Old Meadow Lane Suite 350, McLean, VA 22102
Telephone: (703) 821-0770
Registered as lobbyist at U.S. Congress.
Background: Also serves as Executive Director, Frozen
  Potato Products Institute, Chairman of the Board, Ameri-
  can Frozen Food Institute Political Action Committee,
  and President, Nat'l Yogurt Ass'n. Former Special Assist-

ANDERSON, Steven C. (Cont'd)
ant to Rep. John B. Anderson (R-IL), 1975-79.

ANDERSON, Susan Stuebing
Manager, Government Affairs, Xerox Corp.
490 L'Enfant Plaza East, S.W., Suite 4200, Washington, DC 20024
Telephone: (202) 646-8285
Registered as lobbyist at U.S. Congress.

ANDERSON, Walter D.
Exec. Director, Contractors Pump Bureau
P.O. Box 5858, Rockville, MD 20855
Telephone: (301) 340-2094

ANDRAE, Charles N., III
V. President, RCF Group, The
1200 19th St., N.W. Suite 606, Washington, DC 20036
Telephone: (202) 659-8967
Background: Former Administrative Assistant to Senator Richard Lugar (R-IN).

ANDREAE, Chip
Exec. Director, Republican Majority Fund
503 Capitol Court, N.E., Suite 100, Washington, DC 20002
Telephone: (202) 547-6200

ANDRES, Gary J.
Spec Asst to Pres, Legis Affrs (House), EXECUTIVE OFFICE OF THE PRESIDENT - The White House
1600 Pennsylvania Ave., N.W. 112 East Wing, Washington, DC 20500
Telephone: (202) 456-7092

ANDREW, David C.
Partner, Baker, Worthington, Crossley, Stansberry & Woolf
1001 Pennsylvania Ave., N.W. Suite 1201, Washington, DC 20004
Telephone: (202) 347-4360

ANDREWS, A. Scott
V. President, Treasurer, WorldCorp
13873 Park Center Road Suite 490, Herndon, VA 22071
Telephone: (703) 834-9200

ANDREWS, Andrea
Sr. Manager/Washington Liaison, Price Waterhouse
1801 K St., N.W., Suite 700, Washington, DC 20006
Telephone: (202) 296-0800

ANDREWS' ASSOCIATES, INC.
2550 M St., N.W., Suite 695, Washington, DC 20037
Telephone: (202) 457-6512
Background: A governmental affairs consulting firm.
Members of firm representing listed organizations:
Andrews, Mark
Background: Member, U.S. House of Representatives (R-ND), 1963-81. Member, U.S. Senate (R-ND), 1981-87.
Balk-Tusa, Jacqueline, President
Background: Former Administrative Assistant to Senator Mark Andrews (R-ND).
Clients:
B.A.T. Industries, PLC *(Mark Andrews, Jacqueline Balk-Tusa)*
Denver, Colorado, City and County of *(Mark Andrews)*
Edison Electric Institute *(Mark Andrews, Jacqueline Balk-Tusa)*
Interstate Natural Gas Ass'n of America *(Mark Andrews, Jacqueline Balk-Tusa)*
M&M/Mars, Inc. *(Mark Andrews, Jacqueline Balk-Tusa)*
Safeguard America's Family Enterprises *(Mark Andrews, Jacqueline Balk-Tusa)*
Standard Federal Savings Bank *(Mark Andrews)*
Wayne County, Michigan *(Mark Andrews)*
Westinghouse Electric Corp. *(Mark Andrews, Jacqueline Balk-Tusa)*

ANDREWS, David
McCutchen, Doyle, Brown & Enersen
1455 Pennsylvania Ave., N.W., Suite 650, Washington, DC 20004
Telephone: (202) 628-4900
Registered as lobbyist at U.S. Congress.
Background: Legal Counsel and Special Assistant for Policy, Environmental Protection Agency, 1978-80. Deputy General Counsel, Department of Health and Human Services, 1980.

Clients:
DNA Plant Technology Corp.
Rohr Industries, Inc.

ANDREWS, Elaine
V. President, Federal Coordinator, Nat'l Ass'n of Life Companies
1455 Pennsylvania Ave., N.W., Suite 1250, Washington, DC 20004
Telephone: (202) 783-6252
Registered as lobbyist at U.S. Congress.

ANDREWS, Gregory B.
Smith Dawson & Andrews, Inc.
1000 Connecticut Ave., N.W., Suite 304, Washington, DC 20036
Telephone: (202) 835-0740
Registered as lobbyist at U.S. Congress.
Clients:
Clarke & Co.
Eugene, Oregon, City of
Power Packaging Inc.
S & F Warehouses, Inc.

ANDREWS, James H.
V. President, Government Affairs, Kellogg Co., M. W.
1317 F St., N.W., Suite 300, Washington, DC 20004-1105
Telephone: (202) 639-8870

ANDREWS AND KURTH
1701 Pennsylvania Ave., N.W., Suite 200, Washington, DC 20006
Telephone: (202) 662-2700
Background: Washington office of Houston law firm.
Members of firm representing listed organizations:
Butler, Michael F.
Background: Deputy General Counsel, United States Department of Commerce, 1969-1973. General Counsel, Federal Energy Administration, 1975-1977.
Green, Richard
Hardy, Robert G.
Moody, Rush (Jr.)
Background: Commissioner, Federal Power Commission, 1971-75.
Perdue, Robert
Steinwurtzel, Robert N.
Clients:
El Paso Natural Gas Co. *(Richard Green, Rush Moody, Jr.)*
Secondary Lead Smelters Ass'n *(Robert N. Steinwurtzel)*
Texas Gas Transmission Corp. *(Robert Perdue)*
Transco Energy Co. *(Robert G. Hardy)*

ANDREWS, Lewis D., Jr.
President, Glass Packaging Institute
1801 K St., N.W., Suite 1105L, Washington, DC 20006
Telephone: (202) 887-4850
Registered as lobbyist at U.S. Congress.

ANDREWS, Mark
Andrews' Associates, Inc.
2550 M St., N.W., Suite 695, Washington, DC 20037
Telephone: (202) 457-6512
Registered as lobbyist at U.S. Congress.
Registered as Foreign Agent: (#4062).
Background: Member, U.S. House of Representatives (R-ND), 1963-81. Member, U.S. Senate (R-ND), 1981-87.
Clients:
B.A.T. Industries, PLC
Denver, Colorado, City and County of
Edison Electric Institute
Interstate Natural Gas Ass'n of America
M&M/Mars, Inc.
Safeguard America's Family Enterprises
Standard Federal Savings Bank
Wayne County, Michigan
Westinghouse Electric Corp.

ANDREWS, Michael P.
Director, Salomon Brothers Inc.
1455 Pennsylvania Ave., N.W. Suite 350, Washington, DC 20005
Telephone: (202) 879-4100
Registered as lobbyist at U.S. Congress.
Background: Senior Legislative Assistant to Rep. Joseph P. Vigorito (D-PA), 1973-75. Executive Assistant and Counsel to the Chairman, Commodity Futures Trading Commission, 1981-83.

ANDREWS, Robert B.
Mgr., Gov't Relats., Trade Ass'n Liaison, Mobil Corp.
1100 Connecticut Ave., N.W., Suite 620, Washington, DC 20036
Telephone: (202) 862-1340
Registered as lobbyist at U.S. Congress.

ANDREWS, William Robert
Director, Congressional Relations, Rockwell Internat'l
1745 Jefferson Davis Hwy., Arlington, VA 22202
Telephone: (703) 553-6807
Registered as lobbyist at U.S. Congress.

ANDREWS, Wright H., Jr.
Sutherland, Asbill and Brennan
1275 Pennsylvania, N.W., Washington, DC 20004-2404
Telephone: (202) 383-0100
Registered as lobbyist at U.S. Congress.
Background: Chief Legislative Assistant to Senator Sam Nunn (D-GA), 1973-75.
Clients:
Acacia Mutual Life Insurance Co.
Bank of Baltimore
Equifax Inc.
First Financial Management Corp.
Nevada, State of
Philip Morris Cos., Inc.
Washington, State of

ANDRUKITIS, Barbara C.
President, Kendall and Associates
50 E St., S.E., Washington, DC 20003
Telephone: (202) 546-2600
Registered as lobbyist at U.S. Congress.

ANGELE, Al
Secretary-Treasurer, Internat'l Union of Police Ass'ns
1016 Duke St., Alexandria, VA 22314
Telephone: (703) 549-7473

ANGELL, Phillip S.
Consultant, Browning-Ferris Industries (D.C.), Inc.
1150 Connecticut Ave., N.W. Suite 500, Washington, DC 20036
Telephone: (202) 223-8151

ANGOFF, Jay
Counsel, Nat'l Insurance Consumer Organization
121 North Payne St., Alexandria, VA 22314
Telephone: (703) 549-8050

ANGUS, John, III
Duberstein Group, Inc., The
2100 Pennsylvania Ave., N.W. Suite 350, Washington, DC 20037
Telephone: (202) 728-1100
Clients:
Time Warner Inc.

ANIXT, Lawrence B.
Ordnance Div., Dir., Internat'l Mktg., Olin Corp.
1730 K St., N.W., Suite 1300, Washington, DC 20006
Telephone: (202) 331-7400

ANNIS, Sheldon
Senior Associate, Overseas Development Council
1717 Massachusetts Ave., N.W., Washington, DC 20036
Telephone: (202) 234-8701

ANSTROM, Decker
Exec. Vice President, Nat'l Cable Television Ass'n
1724 Massachusetts Ave., N.W., Washington, DC 20036
Telephone: (202) 775-3651
Registered as lobbyist at U.S. Congress.

ANTHONY, Betty
Federal Agencies, American Petroleum Institute
1220 L St., N.W., Washington, DC 20005
Telephone: (202) 682-8446

ANTHONY, Edwin
V. Pres., Corp. Affairs & Member Rtns., Edison Electric Institute
1111 19th St., N.W., Washington, DC 20036
Telephone: (202) 778-6657

ANTHONY, Tobias
Chairman, Federal Search, Inc.
6800 Fleetwood Road Suite 916, McLean, VA 22101
Telephone: (703) 821-8636

ANTHONY, Virginia Q.
Exec. Director, American Academy of Child and Adolescent Psychiatry
3615 Wisconsin Ave., N.W., Washington, DC 20016
Telephone: (202) 966-7300

ANTONE, Thomas M., IV
President, Nat'l Ass'n of Medical Equipment Suppliers
625 Slaters Lane, Suite 200, Alexandria, VA 22314
Telephone: (703) 836-6263
Registered as lobbyist at U.S. Congress.

ANTOS, Virginia
Assistant Director, Copyright, Ass'n of American Publishers
1718 Connecticut Ave., N.W. Suite 700, Washington, DC 20009-1148
Telephone: (202) 232-3335
Registered as lobbyist at U.S. Congress.

ANTRIM, Patrick S.
Senior Counsel, Bank of America NT & SA
1800 K St., N.W., Suite 900, Washington, DC 20006
Telephone: (202) 778-0532

ANZOATEGUI, Carlos
Exec. Director, Committee on Human Rights for the People of Nicaragua
11400 Falls Road, Potomac, MD 20854
Telephone: (301) 983-9333

APCO ASSOCIATES
1155 21st St., N.W., Suite 1000, Washington, DC 20036
Telephone: (202) 778-1000
Registered as Foreign Agent: (#3597)
Background: Formed as a consulting arm of the law firm Arnold & Porter.
Members of firm representing listed organizations:
Barbour, Nancy R., Senior Legislative Associate
Bonker, Don, Senior Trade Consultant
  Background: Former Member, House of Representatives (D-WA); Chairman, House Foreign Affairs Subcommittee on International Trade.
Bregman, Randy, Diretor, Soviet & Eastern European Svcs.
Bronk, Robin, Project Associate
Bushnell, David, Senior Associate
Cohen, Neal M., Director, Political Support Svcs.
D'Anastasio, Mark, Senior Associate
Eisner, Steve, Project Associate
Farr, Stephen, Project Associate
Grunberg, Carole, Senior Associate and Trade Consultant
  Background: Former Staff Director, House Foreign Affairs Subcommittee on Trade and Economic Policy.
Hartman, Arthur, Senior Consultant
  Background: Former U.S. Ambassador to the Soviet Union and to France.
Humpstone, Jane, Project Assistant
Judd, Terry W., Project Associate
Kraus, Margery, President and CEO
Lowenstein, James G., Senior Consultant
  Background: Former Ambassador to Luxembourg and Deputy Assistant Sec'y of State for European Affairs.
Navarrete, Andrew, Legislative Assistant
Nealer, Kevin G., Senior Associate
Sadoff, David, Legislative Ass't
Samors, Robert J., Legislative Associate
Schumacher, Barry J., Senior Associate
Sliz, Deborah R., Director, Energy Services
  Background: Former Counsel to the House Interior and Insular Affairs Subcommittee on Energy and Environment.
White, Jocelyn, V. President, Gov't Relations
Clients:
American Indian Trade Development Council *(Don Bonker)*
ASOCOLFLORES (Colombia Flower Growers Ass'n) *(Barry J. Schumacher)*
E Z America Ltd. *(Kevin G. Nealer)*
Excess Deferred Tax Coalition *(Deborah R. Sliz)*
Ferroalloys Ass'n *(Kevin G. Nealer)*
Heart of America Northwest *(Don Bonker)*
Honeywell, Inc. *(Margery Kraus)*
London Futures and Options Exchange
LymphoMed Inc. *(Neal M. Cohen)*
Niedermeyer-Martin Co. *(Don Bonker)*
Outboard Marine Corp. *(Jocelyn White)*

Philip Morris Management Corp. *(Neal M. Cohen, Margery Kraus)*
Profilo Holding A.S. *(Barry J. Schumacher)*
Recording Industry Ass'n of America *(Neal M. Cohen)*
Sacramento Municipal Utility District *(Deborah R. Sliz)*
Springfield, Missouri, City Utilities of *(Deborah R. Sliz)*
State Farm Insurance Cos. *(Barry J. Schumacher)*
Tennessee Valley Public Power Ass'n *(Deborah R. Sliz)*
Unilever United States, Inc. *(Margery Kraus)*
University of Michigan Medical Center *(Nancy R. Barbour)*

APICELLA, William
Treasurer, Greater Washington/Maryland Service Station and Automotive Repair Ass'n PAC
9420 Annapolis Road, Suite 307, Lanham, MD 20706
Telephone: (301) 577-2875

APPELBAUM, Judith C.
Reichler Appelbaum and Wippman
1701 K St., N.W. Suite 700, Washington, DC 20006
Telephone: (202) 429-0800
Registered as lobbyist at U.S. Congress.
Registered as Foreign Agent: (#3582).
Background: Attorney Advisor to the Chairman, Federal Trade Commission, 1978-81.
Clients:
Bazar San Jorge, S.A.
Nicaragua, Government of
United Coconut Ass'n of the Philippines

APPLEBAUM, Harvey M.
Covington and Burling
1201 Pennsylvania Ave., N.W., Box 7566, Washington, DC 20044
Telephone: (202) 662-6000
Clients:
AT&T
British Columbia, Canada, Government of
Chambre Syndicale des Producteurs d'Aciers Fins et Speciaux
Domtar, Inc.
Exxon Co., U.S.A.
Honda Motor Co.
Internat'l Minerals and Chemical Corp.
Motorola, Inc.
Quebec, Canada, Government of

APTAKER, Edward
Schmeltzer, Aptaker and Sheppard
The Watergate, 2600 Virginia Ave., N.W., Washington, DC 20037
Telephone: (202) 333-8800
Background: Counsel, Attorney, Interstate Commerce Commission, 1949-51. U.S. Maritime Administration, 1951-70.

APTER AND ASSOCIATES, David
1706 R St., N.W., Washington, DC 20009
Telephone: (202) 265-1212
Background: A public relations consulting firm.
Members of firm representing listed organizations:
Apter, Marc L.
Currie, Suzanne
Harrison, Summer, Exec. V. President
Stack, Richard, V. President
Organizations represented:
Airlines Reporting Corp. (ARC)
Best Western Internat'l, Inc.
Crest Hotels, Internat'l
Togo, Government of *(Marc L. Apter)*

APTER, Marc L.
Apter and Associates, David
1706 R St., N.W., Washington, DC 20009
Telephone: (202) 265-1212
Registered as lobbyist at U.S. Congress.
Registered as Foreign Agent: (#3133).
Organizations represented:
Togo, Government of

AQUAVIVA, Francis
Assoc. Exec. Dir., Member Services, American Occupational Therapy Ass'n
1383 Piccard Drive, Suite 300 P.O. Box 1725, Rockville, MD 20850
Telephone: (301) 948-9626

ARAMONY, William
President, United Way of America
701 N. Fairfax St., Alexandria, VA 22314-2045
Telephone: (703) 836-7100

ARANOW, Geoffrey
Arnold & Porter
1200 New Hampshire Ave., N.W., Washington, DC 20036
Telephone: (202) 872-6700
Clients:
American Institute of Certified Public Accountants

ARB CONSULTANTS
1309 Duke St., Alexandria, VA 22314
Telephone: (703) 836-0283
Members of firm representing listed organizations:
Battista, Anthony R.
Clients:
ITT Defense, Inc. *(Anthony R. Battista)*

ARBACK, Nina
Director of Communications, Nat'l Hospice Organization
1901 Moore St. Suite 901, Arlington, VA 22209
Telephone: (703) 243-5900

ARBUCKLE, J. Gordon
Patton, Boggs and Blow
2550 M St., N.W., Suite 800, Washington, DC 20037
Telephone: (202) 457-6000
Registered as lobbyist at U.S. Congress.
Registered as Foreign Agent: (#2165).
Clients:
Chemfix Technologies, Inc.
James Co., T. L.
LOOP, Inc.

ARCARI, Col. Paul W., USAF (Ret)
Director, Legislative Affairs, Retired Officers Ass'n, The (TROA)
201 N. Washington St., Alexandria, VA 22314
Telephone: (703) 549-2311
Registered as lobbyist at U.S. Congress.

ARCHER, John
Managing Director, Government Affairs, American Automobile Ass'n
500 E St. S.W., Suite 950, Washington, DC 20024
Telephone: (202) 554-6060
Registered as lobbyist at U.S. Congress.

ARCHEY, William T.
V. President, International Division, Chamber of Commerce of the U.S.A.
1615 H St., N.W., Washington, DC 20062
Telephone: (202) 659-6000
Background: Deputy Assistant Secretary for Trade Administration, U.S. Department of Commerce, 1982-86.

ARCHULETA, R. M. Julie
V. President, Government Affairs, Occidental Chemical Corporation
1747 Pennsylvania Ave., N.W., 3rd Floor, Washington, DC 20006
Telephone: (202) 857-3023
Registered as lobbyist at U.S. Congress.
Background: Served as President, Women in Government Relations, 1985.

ARENBERG, Cindy Joy
Klein & Saks, Inc.
1026 16th St., N.W., Suite 101, Washington, DC 20036
Telephone: (202) 783-0500
Background: Serves as Director, International Government Relations of the Gold Institute.
Clients:
Gold Institute

ARENBERG, Gerald S.
Exec. Director, American Federation of Police
1000 Connecticut Ave., N.W., Suite 9, Washington, DC 20036

ARENBERG, Gerald S. (Cont'd)
Telephone: (202) 293-9088

ARENT, FOX, KINTNER, PLOTKIN & KAHN
1050 Connecticut Ave., N.W., Washington, DC 20036-5339
Telephone: (202) 857-6000
Members of firm representing listed organizations:
Akman, Jerome P.
Aronofsky, David J.
Banoun, Raymond, Of Counsel
Bardin, David J.
  Background: Trial Attorney, 1958-65, Assistant General Counsel, 1965-67, and Deputy General Counsel 1967-69 in the Federal Power Commission. Commissioner, New Jersey Department of Environmental Protection, 1974-77. Deputy Administrator, Federal Energy Administration, 1977. Administrator of the Economic Regulatory Administration, Department of Energy, 1977-79.
Barnes, Michael D.
  Background: Member, U.S. House of Representatives (D-MD), 1979-86.
Berlack, Evan R.
  Background: Officer, U.S. Foreign Service, 1963-65; Attorney, Office of Legal Adviser, Department of State, 1965-68.
Christian, Claudette M.
Culver, John C.
  Background: Member, U.S. House of Representatives (D-IA), 1965-75. Member, U.S. Senate (D-IA), 1975-81.
Efron, Samuel
  Background: Securities and Exchange Commission 1939-40; Dep't of Labor 1940-1942; Office of Alien Property Custodian 1942-43; Dep't of Justice 1946-51; Assistant General Counsel, Internat'l Affairs, Dep't of Defense 1951-53.
Fleischaker, Marc L.
Gibson, Stephen L.
Goodrich, William W. (Jr.)
Henneberger, Lawrence F.
Hirsch, Robert B.
Hushon, John D.
Kurman, Michael J.
  Background: Attorney, Solicitor's Honors Program and Division of Surface Mining, and Special Assistant to the Solicitor, U.S. Department of Interior, 1977-81.
Leibowitz, Lewis E.
Malasky, Alan R.
Matelski, Wayne H.
Meigher, Eugene J.
  Background: Attorney, Antitrust Division, United States Dept of Justice, 1965-69.
Pendergast, William R.
Plotkin, Harry M.
  Background: Assistant General Counsel, Federal Communications Commission, 1943-51. Special Counsel to the Senate Committee on Interstate and Foreign Commerce, 1954-55. Member, Board of Directors, Viacom Internat'l, Inc.
Reichertz, Peter S.
Reider, Alan E.
  Background: Analyst, Department of Health, Education and Welfare, 1975-79. Chief, Review Policy Branch, Office of Special Standards Review Organization, Health Care Financing Administration, Department of Health and Human Services, 1979-80.
Roggensack, Margaret E.
Sandler, Joseph E.
Siegel, Allen G.
  Background: With National Labor Relations Board 1962-64.
Smith, Daniel C.
  Background: Attorney, Federal Trade Commission, 1966-1969.
Thurm, Gil, Of Counsel
Waters, Robert J.
Weiss, Arnold H.
  Background: Attorney, Office for International Finance and Congressional Liaison, U.S. Treasury Department, 1952-60.
Wides, Burton V.
  Background: Legislative Counsel, Sen. Philip A. Hart, 1970-76; Legislative Director and Administrative Assistant, Sen. Paul Sarbanes, 1976-77. Counsel, President's Intelligence Oversight Board, 1977-79. Legislative Counsel, 1979-80, and Counsel, 1981-84, U.S. Senate Committee on the Judiciary.

Clients:
  AIDA Engineering Ltd. *(Stephen L. Gibson)*
  American Ass'n of Bioanalysts *(Alan E. Reider)*
  American Medical Imaging Corp. *(Alan E. Reider)*
  Ass'n of Global Real Estate Executives (AGREE) *(Gil Thurm)*
  Ass'n of Professional Flight Attendants *(David J. Aronofsky, Michael D. Barnes, John C. Culver)*
  California Steel Industries Inc. *(Michael D. Barnes)*
  Clopay Corp. *(John D. Hushon)*
  Continental Grain Co. *(Samuel Efron, Lewis E. Leibowitz)*
  Elders Grain, Inc. *(Eugene J. Meigher)*
  Guardian Life Insurance Co. of America *(John D. Hushon)*
  Heckler & Koch *(Samuel Efron)*
  Ishikawajima-Harima Heavy Industries Co.
  Mercy Hospital of Des Moines, Iowa *(Alan E. Reider)*
  Mobile Diagnostic Systems *(Alan E. Reider)*
  Motor and Equipment Manufacturers Ass'n *(Marc L. Fleischaker)*
  Nat'l Ass'n of College Stores *(David J. Aronofsky, Michael D. Barnes, Marc L. Fleischaker, Burton V. Wides)*
  Nat'l Ass'n of Wheat Growers *(Samuel Efron, Stephen L. Gibson)*
  Nat'l Field Selling Ass'n *(Daniel C. Smith)*
  Nat'l Grain and Feed Ass'n *(Marc L. Fleischaker)*
  Nat'l Moving and Storage Ass'n *(Gil Thurm)*
  Nat'l Nutrition Coalition *(Burton V. Wides)*
  Nat'l Parking Ass'n *(Michael J. Kurman, Allen G. Siegel)*
  Nat'l Soft Drink Ass'n *(Evan R. Berlack)*
  Outokumpu Oy *(Jerome P. Akman, Stephen L. Gibson, Lewis E. Leibowitz)*
  Perrier Group
  Potash Corp. of Saskatchewan
  Prince George's County, Maryland
  Puerto Rico Federal Affairs Administration *(Michael D. Barnes, John C. Culver)*
  Puerto Rico, Popular Democratic Party of *(John C. Culver)*
  Salem Medical Laboratory *(Alan E. Reider)*
  San Diego, California, City of *(John C. Culver, Joseph E. Sandler, Burton V. Wides)*
  Sony Corp.
  STANT, Inc. *(Alan R. Malasky)*
  Toyota Motor Corp. *(John D. Hushon, Burton V. Wides)*
  Trailer Hitch Manufacturers Ass'n *(Lawrence F. Henneberger)*
  Video Software Dealers Ass'n *(Burton V. Wides)*

ARGYLE & ASSOCIATES
1117 G St., S.E., Washington, DC 20003
Members of firm representing listed organizations:
Deller, Susie
Steadley, Daniel M.
Clients:
  Nat'l Council of Savings Institutions *(Susie Deller, Daniel M. Steadley)*

ARIAS, Roger
Corp. Dir., Gov't Business Development, EG&G, Inc.
1850 K St., N.W., Suite 1190, Washington, DC 20006
Telephone: (202) 887-5570

ARIKAT, Said
Exec. Director, Palestinian Congress of North America
4401 East-West Highway Suite 301, Bethesda, MD 20814
Telephone: (301) 652-0052

ARKIN, William M.
Nuclear Information Director, Greenpeace, U.S.A.
1436 U St., N.W., Washington, DC 20009
Telephone: (202) 462-1177

ARKY, M. Elizabeth
Winthrop, Stimson, Putnam & Roberts
1133 Connecticut Ave., N.W. Suite 1000, Washington, DC 20036
Telephone: (202) 775-9800
Registered as lobbyist at U.S. Congress.
Registered as Foreign Agent: (#3873).
Background: Staff, House Telecommunications and Finance Subcommittee, 1986.
Clients:
  Navajo Nation, The

ARMENDARIS, Alex
Exec. Assistant to the Exec. Director, American Ass'n of Retired Persons
1909 K St., N.W., Washington, DC 20049
Telephone: (202) 872-4700
Background: Former head of the Office of Minority Business Enterprise under Presidents Nixon and Ford and Associate Director of White House Personnel under President Reagan.

ARMISTEAD, Lew
Director of Public Relations, Nat'l Ass'n of Secondary School Principals
1904 Association Drive, Reston, VA 22091
Telephone: (703) 860-0200

ARMSBY, Susan
Legislative Representative, People for the American Way
2000 M St., N.W., Suite 400, Washington, DC 20036
Telephone: (202) 467-4999
Registered as lobbyist at U.S. Congress.

ARMSTRONG, BYRD AND ASSOCIATES
1730 M St., N.W., Suite 808, Washington, DC 20036
Telephone: (202) 223-5880
Members of firm representing listed organizations:
Adise, Russell T., Senior Associate
  Background: Former staff assistant to Rep. Don Young (R-AK) and Rep. Stephen Solarz (D-NY), 1977-79.
An, Hong K., Partner
  Background: Former Professional Staff Member, House Committee on Standards of Official Conduct, 1977-78.
Armstrong, Rodney E., President
  Background: Former Foreign Service Officer, 1959-70. Director, Japan Society of New York 1970-73.
Clients:
  Kajima Corp. *(Russell T. Adise, Rodney E. Armstrong)*
  Korea Deep Sea Fisheries Ass'n *(Hong K. An, Rodney E. Armstrong)*

ARMSTRONG, Fred
Director, Government Services, Portland Cement Ass'n
1620 Eye St., N.W., Suite 520, Washington, DC 20006
Telephone: (202) 293-4260
Registered as lobbyist at U.S. Congress.

ARMSTRONG, Gayle
Manager, Communications, American Institute of Aeronautics and Astronautics
370 L'Enfant Promenade, Washington, DC 20024
Telephone: (202) 646-7432

ARMSTRONG, Jack
Staff Assistant, Dutko & Associates
412 First St., S.E. Suite 100, Washington, DC 20003
Telephone: (202) 484-4884
Registered as lobbyist at U.S. Congress.

ARMSTRONG, Jan M.
Newell-Payne Companies, Inc.
2011 Eye St., N.W., 5th Floor, Washington, DC 20006
Telephone: (202) 223-3217
Background: Serves as Exec. Director, American Car Rental Ass'n.
Clients:
  American Car Rental Ass'n

ARMSTRONG, Laura Q.
V. President, Media Relations, Ketchum Public Relations
1201 Connecticut Ave., N.W. Suite 300, Washington, DC 20036
Telephone: (202) 835-8800

ARMSTRONG, Phil
Sr. V.P., Grp. Dir., Grassroots Issues, Hill and Knowlton Public Affairs Worldwide
Washington Harbour, 901 31st St., N.W., Washington, DC 20007
Telephone: (202) 333-7400
Background: Former Deputy Assistant Secretary of Education for Public Affairs, Reagan Administration.
Clients:
  Seilbulite Internat'l, Inc.

ARMSTRONG, Rodney E.
President, Armstrong, Byrd and Associates
1730 M St., N.W., Suite 808, Washington, DC 20036
Telephone: (202) 223-5880

Registered as Foreign Agent: (#2724).
Background: Former Foreign Service Officer, 1959-70. Director, Japan Society of New York 1970-73.
Clients:
Kajima Corp.
Korea Deep Sea Fisheries Ass'n

ARMSTRONG, Tia
Assoc. Manager, Environmental Policy, Chamber of Commerce of the U.S.A.
1615 H St., N.W., Washington, DC 20062
Telephone: (202) 659-6000
Registered as lobbyist at U.S. Congress.

ARMSTRONG WHITING, Meredith
Director, Congressional Assistant Prgm., Conference Board
1755 Massachusetts Ave., N.W., Suite 312, Washington, DC 20036
Telephone: (202) 483-0580
Background: Serves also as Senior Fellow, Governmental Affairs. Public Affairs Aide, Office of the V. President, 1982-85; Director, Public Liaison, U.S. Dept. of Commerce, 1981-82.

ARNAIZ, Leo
Cong Hearings Coordinator, DEPARTMENT OF ENERGY
1000 Independence Ave. S.W., Washington, DC 20585
Telephone: (202) 586-5450

ARNDT, Randolph
Media Relations Director, Nat'l League of Cities
1301 Pennsylvania Ave., N.W., Washington, DC 20004
Telephone: (202) 626-3000

ARNESON, P.C., Paul
1555 Connecticut Ave., N.W. Suite 308, Washington, DC 20036
Telephone: (202) 462-4242
Members of firm representing listed organizations:
Arneson, Paul
   Background: Special Assistant to General Counsel, U.S. Department of Commerce, 1971-73.
Organizations represented:
Empire Blue Cross and Blue Shield *(Paul Arneson)*
High Speed Rail Ass'n *(Paul Arneson)*
Nat'l Ass'n of Water Companies *(Paul Arneson)*
Nat'l Ass'n of Water Companies Political Action Committee

ARNESON, Paul
Arneson, P.C., Paul
1555 Connecticut Ave., N.W. Suite 308, Washington, DC 20036
Telephone: (202) 462-4242
Registered as lobbyist at U.S. Congress.
Background: Special Assistant to General Counsel, U.S. Department of Commerce, 1971-73.
Organizations represented:
Empire Blue Cross and Blue Shield
High Speed Rail Ass'n
Nat'l Ass'n of Water Companies

ARNESS, John P.
Hogan and Hartson
555 13th St., N.W., Suite 1200, Washington, DC 20004-1109
Telephone: (202) 637-5600

ARNETT ASSOCIATES, Dixon
905 16th St., N.W. Suite 310, Washington, DC 20006
Telephone: (202) 393-1195
Members of firm representing listed organizations:
Arnett, Dixon, President
   Background: Former Leguslative Director to Senator Pete Wilson (R-CA). Former California State Assemblyman. Former Deputy Under Secretary, U.S. Department of Health and Human Services.
Organizations represented:
Foundation Health Corp. *(Dixon Arnett)*
Fresno Surgery and Recovery Care Center *(Dixon Arnett)*
Siemens Medical Systems, Inc. *(Dixon Arnett)*
Southern California Rapid Transit District *(Dixon Arnett)*
University of California Medical Centers *(Dixon Arnett)*

ARNETT, Dixon
President, Arnett Associates, Dixon
905 16th St., N.W. Suite 310, Washington, DC 20006
Telephone: (202) 393-1195
Registered as lobbyist at U.S. Congress.
Background: Former Legislative Director to Senator Pete Wilson (R-CA). Former California State Assemblyman. Former Deputy Under Secretary, U.S. Department of Health and Human Services.
Organizations represented:
Foundation Health Corp.
Fresno Surgery and Recovery Care Center
Siemens Medical Systems, Inc.
Southern California Rapid Transit District
University of California Medical Centers

ARNEY, Rex O.
Cong Liaison, NAT'L ENDOWMENT FOR THE HUMANITIES
1100 Pennsylvania Ave., N.W., Washington, DC 20506
Telephone: (202) 786-0328

ARNOLD, Carl F.
655 15th St., N.W., Suite 310, Washington, DC 20005
Telephone: (202) 659-3326
Registered as lobbyist at U.S. Congress.
Organizations represented:
Corporate Property Investors
Quintana Petroleum Corp.

ARNOLD, John E., Jay
Dir., Gov't Affrs - Defense Systems, Unisys Corp.
2001 L St., N.W., Suite 1000, Washington, DC 20036
Telephone: (202) 293-7720
Registered as lobbyist at U.S. Congress.

ARNOLD, Millard W.
Land, Lemle & Arnold
1701 K St., N.W., Washington, DC 20006
Telephone: (202) 785-1020
Registered as Foreign Agent: (#3824).
Background: Deputy Assistant Secretary of State, U.S. Department of State, 1980-81.
Clients:
Nigeria, Embassy of

ARNOLD & PORTER
1200 New Hampshire Ave., N.W., Washington, DC 20036
Telephone: (202) 872-6700
Background: The following information was obtained from public records and submitted to this firm for confirmation. It historically does not confirm or correct the listing.
Members of firm representing listed organizations:
Abramowitz, Nancy S.
   Background: Law Clerk, U.S. Tax Court, 1975-77.
Aranow, Geoffrey
Baer, William J.
   Background: Trial Attorney, Bureau of Consumer Protection, 1975-77. Attorney Advisor to the Chairman, 1977-78, and Assistant General Counsel, 1978-80, Federal Trade Commission. Serves as Coordinator, Lobbyists for Campaign Financing Reform.
Bennett, Alexander E.
Berger, Paul S.
Born, Brooksley E.
Burt, Jeffrey A.
Curzan, Myron P.
   Background: Legislative Assistant to Senator Robert F. Kennedy, 1965-66. Exec. Director, HUD Task Force on Improving the Operation of Federally Insured or Financed Housing Programs, 1972-73.
Dworkin, Douglas
Dwyer, Thomas R.
Ewing, Richard S.
Fitzpatrick, James F.
Garbow, Melvin C.
Garrett, Robert A.
   Background: Assistant to the General Counsel, Department of the Army, 1975-76.
Guttentag, Joseph H., Of Counsel
   Background: Special Assistant for International Tax Affairs, U.S. Department of Treasury, 1967-68.
Hawke, John D. (Jr.)
Hester, Stephen L.
Hubbard, Richard L.
Johnson, Janet Lee
Kim, Sukhan, Of Counsel
   Background: First Vice Chairman, U.S.-Asia Foreign Policy Council, 1983.

Krash, Abe
Letzler, Kenneth A.
Lyons, Dennis G.
   Background: Attorney, Office of the General Counsel, Department of the Air Force, 1955-58. Law Clerk to U.S. Supreme Court Justice, William Brennan, 1958-60.
Macrory, Patrick F. J.
Nowak, G. Philip
Quinn, John M.
   Background: Chief Legislative Assistant, Senator Floyd Haskell, 1974-75. Special Counsel, Senate Select Committee on Nutrition and Human Needs, 1976.
Reade, Claire
Rezneck, Daniel A.
Rockler, Walter J.
Rogers, William D.
   Background: Law Clerk to Justice Stanley Reed, U.S. Supreme Court, 1952-53. Special Counsel, U.S. Coordinator, Alliance for Progress, 1962-63. Deputy U.S. Coordinator, Alliance for Progress and Deputy Assistant Administrator, AID, 1963-65. Alternate U.S. Representative, Inter-American Economic and Social Council, 1964-65. Assistant Secretary of State for Inter-American Affairs, U.S. Coordinator, Alliance for Progress, 1974-76. Under Secretary of State for Economic Affairs, 1976.
Rosenbaum, Robert D.
Ross, Stanford G.
Sacks, Stephen M.
   Background: Assistant to the General Counsel, Department of the Army, 1967-1970.
Schneider, Lawrence A.
Seiden, Matthew J.
Sinel, Norman M.
Smith, Jeffrey H.
   Background: Member, Office of the Legal Adviser, U.S. Department of State, 1975-84. Staff, U.S. Senate Armed Services Committee, 1984-88.
Sohn, Michael N.
   Background: Attorney and Supervising Attorney, General Counsel's Office, National Labor Relations Board, 1964-69. General Counsel, Federal Trade Commission, 1977-80.
Vieth, G. Duane
   Background: Member of the Board of Directors of Mortgage Investors of Washington.
Vodra, William W.
   Background: Attorney, U.S. Department of Justice, Bureau of Narcotics and Dangerous Drugs/Drug Enforcement Administration, 1971-74. U.S. Department of Health, Education and Welfare, Office of General Counsel, Food and Drug Division, 1974-79.
Waldman, Daniel
Clients:
AFL-CIO - Building and Construction Trades Department
American Institute of Certified Public Accountants *(Geoffrey Aranow)*
Apex Ltd. *(Paul S. Berger)*
Arnold & Porter Political Action Committee *(John M. Quinn)*
Aruba, Government of *(Claire Reade)*
ASOCOLFLORES (Colombia Flower Growers Ass'n) *(Patrick F. J. Macrory, Claire Reade)*
Ass'n of Floral Importers of Florida
Banco Central do Brasil
Chile, Embassy of *(William D. Rogers)*
Continental Corp., The *(Thomas R. Dwyer)*
Earthquake Project, The *(John M. Quinn)*
Employee Benefit Research Institute
Fluor Corp.
General Mills
Golodetz Corp. *(Thomas R. Dwyer)*
Grain and Feed Trade Ass'n, The *(Brooksley E. Born, John M. Quinn, Daniel Waldman)*
Honeywell, Inc. *(Jeffrey H. Smith)*
Internat'l Commodities Clearing House, Ltd. *(Brooksley E. Born, John M. Quinn, Daniel Waldman)*
Internat'l Petroleum Exchange of London *(Brooksley E. Born)*
Israel, Embassy of *(Brooksley E. Born)*
Korea Foreign Trade Ass'n *(Claire Reade)*
Korea, Government of *(Sukhan Kim)*
League of Women Voters of the United States *(Brooksley E. Born)*
Lobbyists for Campaign Financing Reform

ARNOLD & PORTER (Cont'd)

London Commodity Exchange Co., Ltd. *(Brooksley E. Born, John M. Quinn, Daniel Waldman)*
London Internat'l Financial Futures Exchange
LymphoMed Inc.
Metal Market and Exchange Co. Ltd.
Miller Brewing Co.
Mutual of America *(Stanford G. Ross)*
Nat'l Coordinating Committee for Multiemployer Plans *(Paul S. Berger, Stephen L. Hester)*
New York City Board of Estimate *(Norman M. Sinel)*
Nissan Industrial Equipment Co. *(Patrick F. J. Macrory)*
Nissan Motor Co., Ltd. *(Patrick F. J. Macrory)*
Panama, Government of *(Douglas Dworkin, William D. Rogers)*
Pfizer, Inc. *(James F. Fitzpatrick)*
Philip Morris Cos., Inc.
Poland, Ministry of Finance of *(Jeffrey A. Burt)*
Profilo Holding A.S. *(Patrick F. J. Macrory)*
Recording Industry Ass'n of America *(James F. Fitzpatrick)*
Samsung Electronics Co., Ltd. *(Sukhan Kim)*
State Farm Insurance Cos. *(John M. Quinn)*
Survival Technology, Inc.
Washington Area Bankers Ass'n *(John D. Hawke, Jr.)*

ARNSTEIN, Sherry R.

Exec. Director, American Ass'n of Colleges of Osteopathic Medicine
1620 Eye St., N.W., Suite 220, Washington, DC 20006
Telephone: (202) 467-4131
Background: Staff Consultant, President's Committee on Juvenile Delinquency, 1963-65. Special Assistant to the Assistant Secretary of Health, Education and Welfare, 1965-67. Chief Citizen Participation Advisor, Department of Housing and Urban Development, 1967-68. Senior Research Fellow, Department of Health and Human Services, 1975-78. V. President for Government Relations, Nat'l Health Council, 1978-85.

ARNWINE, Barbara R.

Director, Lawyers' Committee for Civil Rights Under Law
1400 Eye St., N.W., Suite 400, Washington, DC 20005
Telephone: (202) 371-1212

ARON, Dr. Leon

Salvatori Fellow in Soviet Studies, Heritage Foundation
214 Massachusetts Ave., N.E., Washington, DC 20002
Telephone: (202) 546-4400

ARON, Nan

Exec. Director, Alliance for Justice
1601 Connecticut Ave., N.W. Suite 600, Washington, DC 20009
Telephone: (202) 332-3224
Registered as lobbyist at U.S. Congress.

ARONOFSKY, David J.

Arent, Fox, Kintner, Plotkin & Kahn
1050 Connecticut Ave., N.W., Washington, DC 20036-5339
Telephone: (202) 857-6000
Registered as lobbyist at U.S. Congress.
Clients:
Ass'n of Professional Flight Attendants
Nat'l Ass'n of College Stores

ARRASMITH, Thomas M.

Program Dir., Federal Government Rtns., Internat'l Business Machines Corp.
1801 K St., N.W., Suite 1200, Washington, DC 20006
Telephone: (202) 778-5000
Registered as lobbyist at U.S. Congress.

ARRINDELL, Deborah

Director of Public Policy, Wider Opportunities for Women
1325 G St., N.W. Lower Level, Washington, DC 20005
Telephone: (202) 638-3143

ARTER & HADDEN

1919 Pennsylvania Ave., N.W., Suite 400, Washington, DC 20006
Telephone: (202) 775-7100
Registered as Foreign Agent: (#3942)
Members of firm representing listed organizations:
Burke, Georgia H.
Dabaghi, William K.

Background: Director, Office of Congressional Affairs, Office of the Secretary, Department of Transportation, 1982-83.
Goodman, Bruce
Background: Former Mid-Atlantic Coordinator for Lawyers for Bush/Quayle.
Clients:
Amway Corp. *(Bruce Goodman)*
Central Union of Agricultural Cooperatives (ZENCHU) *(Georgia H. Burke, William K. Dabaghi)*
Coalition for Regional Banking and Economic Development *(William K. Dabaghi)*
Houston Clearing House Ass'n *(William K. Dabaghi)*
KREQ
KTXS-TV
WCVX
Westwood One, Inc. *(Bruce Goodman)*
WFMZ-TV
WGBA
WJPR
WJTC

ARTHURS, Jean

Legislative Liaison-President, Nat'l Ass'n of Military Widows
4023 25th Road North, Arlington, VA 22207
Telephone: (703) 527-4565
Registered as lobbyist at U.S. Congress.

ASBILL, JUNKIN, MYERS & BUFFONE

1615 New Hampshire Ave., N.W., Washington, DC 20009
Telephone: (202) 234-9000
Members of firm representing listed organizations:
Myers, Matthew L.
Background: Serves as Staff Director, Coalition on Smoking or Health.
Clients:
Coalition on Smoking or Health *(Matthew L. Myers)*

ASBILL, Mac, Jr.

Sutherland, Asbill and Brennan
1275 Pennsylvania, N.W., Washington, DC 20004-2404
Telephone: (202) 383-0100
Registered as lobbyist at U.S. Congress.
Background: Law Clerk to Justice Stanley Reed, U.S. Supreme Court, 1948-49.

ASH, Jon F.

Managing Director, Global Aviation Associates, Ltd.
1800 K St., N.W. Suite 1104, Washington, DC 20006
Telephone: (202) 457-0212
Registered as Foreign Agent: (#3943).
Clients:
Austrian Airlines
Memphis-Shelby County Airport Authority
Scandinavian Airlines System (SAS)

ASHBY AND ASSOCIATES

1140 Connecticut Ave., N.W., Suite 503, Washington, DC 20036
Telephone: (202) 296-3840
Background: Firm has provided consultant services to foreign and domestic industry, Nat'l Academy of Sciences, Nat'l Bureau of Standards, Dep't of Interior, Nat'l Wiretap Commission, and the Executive Office of the President of the United States. Specialists in marketing, international trade, electronic security, market research and technical assistance for industrial client interests in high technology applied to national needs.
Members of firm representing listed organizations:
Ashby, R. Barry, President
Kane, James L.
Montano, William B.
Stevens, John C.
Younts, George R.
Clients:
American Security Resources, Inc. *(William B. Montano)*
GT-Devices, Inc. *(R. Barry Ashby)*
Guernsey and Co., C. H. *(R. Barry Ashby)*
Industrial Heating Magazine *(R. Barry Ashby)*
Internat'l Microwave Systems Corp. (IMSCO) *(John C. Stevens)*
INTERSECT Corp. *(John C. Stevens)*
LAM Research Corp.
Oak Ridge Nat'l Laboratory
Phase Two Industries *(John C. Stevens)*
Physical Optics Corp. *(John C. Stevens)*

QuesTech, Inc. *(R. Barry Ashby)*
Refractory Composites, Inc. *(R. Barry Ashby)*
Security Systems Internat'l Corp., Geneva *(R. Barry Ashby)*
Zitel Corp. *(R. Barry Ashby)*

ASHBY, R. Barry

President, Ashby and Associates
1140 Connecticut Ave., N.W., Suite 503, Washington, DC 20036
Telephone: (202) 296-3840
Clients:
GT-Devices, Inc.
Guernsey and Co., C. H.
Industrial Heating Magazine
QuesTech, Inc.
Refractory Composites, Inc.
Security Systems Internat'l Corp., Geneva
Zitel Corp.

ASHCRAFT AND GEREL

2000 L St., N.W. Suite 700, Washington, DC 20036
Telephone: (202) 783-6400
Members of firm representing listed organizations:
Schaffer, Mark L.
Clients:
AFL-CIO (American Federation of Labor and Congress of Industrial Organizations) *(Mark L. Schaffer)*

ASHDOWN, C. Edward

President, Nat'l Peanut Council
1500 King St., Suite 301, Alexandria, VA 22314-2730
Telephone: (703) 838-9500

ASHEEKE, J. Wilson

Legislative Director, Washington Office on Africa
110 Maryland Ave., N.E. Suite 112, Washington, DC 20002
Telephone: (202) 546-7961
Registered as lobbyist at U.S. Congress.

ASHFORD, Deborah T.

Hogan and Hartson
555 13th St., N.W., Suite 1200, Washington, DC 20004-1109
Telephone: (202) 637-5600
Clients:
Alcide de Gasperi Foundation

ASHLEY, Thomas L.

President, Ass'n of Bank Holding Companies
730 15th St., N.W., Suite 820, Washington, DC 20005
Telephone: (202) 393-1158
Registered as lobbyist at U.S. Congress.
Background: Former Democratic Rep. from Ohio, 1955-81.

ASIS, Karen

Public Relations Director, American Ass'n of Zoological Parks and Aquariums
1110 Vermont Ave., N.W., Suite 1160, Washington, DC 20005
Telephone: (202) 429-0949

ASKINS, Mary Helen

Confidential Asst, Cong Rels, DEPARTMENT OF AGRICULTURE
14th and Independence Ave. S.W., Room 210-E, Washington, DC 20205
Telephone: (202) 447-7095

ASLANIAN, Kevin M.

Chairperson, Legislative Committee, Nat'l Welfare Rights and Reform Union
1000 Wisconsin Ave., N.W., Washington, DC 20007
Telephone: (202) 775-0925
Registered as lobbyist at U.S. Congress.

ASPEN HILL ENTERPRISES, LTD.

815 Connecticut Ave.,, N.W. Suite 800, Washington, DC 20006
Telephone: (202) 785-2525
Members of firm representing listed organizations:
Viets, Richard N.
Clients:
Jordan, Hashemite Kingdom of *(Richard N. Viets)*

ASPINWALL, Mark D.
Government Affairs Representative, United Shipowners of America
1627 K St., N.W., Suite 1200, Washington, DC 20006
Telephone: (202) 466-5388
Registered as lobbyist at U.S. Congress.

ASSAKO, Seichi
Chief Representative, Washington Office, Japan Tobacco, Inc.
1667 K St., N.W., Suite 330, Washington, DC 20006
Telephone: (202) 293-4289
Registered as Foreign Agent: (#3568)

ASS'N ADVOCATES
3312 Camden St., Silver Spring, MD 20902
Telephone: (301) 869-5800
Members of firm representing listed organizations:
  Oxley, Joanne
Clients:
  Alliance for Fair Competition *(Joanne Oxley)*
  Associated Specialty Contractors *(Joanne Oxley)*

ASS'N MANAGEMENT GROUP
3299 K St., N.W., 7th Floor, Washington, DC 20007
Telephone: (202) 965-7510
Members of firm representing listed organizations:
  Dolibois, Robert J., V. President
  Huey, Stewart M., Senior Account Executive
  Lederer, Robert F. (Jr.), V. President
  Rumbarger, Charles D., President
Clients:
  American Soc. of Home Inspectors *(Robert J. Dolibois)*
  Fiberglass Fabrication Ass'n *(Robert F. Lederer, Jr.)*
  Nat'l Ass'n of Independent Life Brokerage Agencies *(Charles D. Rumbarger)*
  Soc. of Nat'l Ass'n Publications *(Robert J. Dolibois)*

ASS'N MANAGEMENT SPECIALISTS
1717 Largo Rd., Upper Marboro, MD 20772
Telephone: (301) 659-1474
Members of firm representing listed organizations:
  Dunleavy, Liz

ASS'N RESOURCES MANAGEMENT, INC.
4222 King St., Alexandria, VA 22302
Telephone: (703) 549-4440
Members of firm representing listed organizations:
  Bomar, Ernest, Principal
  DeBolt, Don J. (CAE), Principal
  Fise, Thomas, Principal
Clients:
  American Ass'n of Gastroenterology *(Thomas Fise)*

ASS'N AND SOCIETY MANAGEMENT INTERNAT'L INC.
7297 Lee Highway, Unit N, Falls Church, VA 22042
Telephone: (703) 533-0251
Members of firm representing listed organizations:
  Buzzerd, Elizabeth A.
  Buzzerd, Harry W. (Jr.)
    Background: Serves as Exec. V. President, American Textile Machinery Ass'n; Exec. Director, Wire Industry Suppliers Ass'n; Exec. Director, Process Equipment Manufacturers Ass'n; and President, Meat Industry Suppliers Ass'n. Also serves as Acting Director, Nat'l Coordinating Council on Emergency Management.
  Tyeryar, Clay D.
Clients:
  American Textile Machinery Ass'n *(Harry W. Buzzerd, Jr.)*
  Meat Industry Suppliers Ass'n *(Harry W. Buzzerd, Jr., Clay D. Tyeryar)*
  Nat'l Coordinating Council on Emergency Management *(Elizabeth A. Buzzerd)*
  Process Equipment Manufacturers Ass'n *(Harry W. Buzzerd, Jr.)*
  Textile Machinery Good Government Committee *(Clay D. Tyeryar)*
  Wire Industry Suppliers Ass'n *(Clay D. Tyeryar)*

ASTE, George J.
V. Pres., Gov't and Internat'l Affairs, United Airlines
1707 L St., N.W., Suite 300, Washington, DC 20036
Telephone: (703) 892-7410
Registered as lobbyist at U.S. Congress.

ASTORGA, Lydia M.
Research Analyst, Gov't & Industry Afrs., Nat'l Ass'n of Professional Insurance Agents
400 North Washington St., Alexandria, VA 22314
Telephone: (703) 836-9340

ATHY, Andrew, Jr.
O'Neill and Athy, P.C.
1310 19th St., N.W., Washington, DC 20036
Telephone: (202) 466-6555
Registered as lobbyist at U.S. Congress.
Background: Counsel, Committee on Interstate and Foreign Commerce, U.S. House of Representatives, 1977-81.
Clients:
  American Bankers Ass'n
  Bank of New England
  Boston Bruins, Inc.
  Brandeis University
  Connecticut Bank and Trust Corp.
  Cruise America Line, Inc.
  Glass Packaging Institute
  Marathon Oil Co.
  Northeastern University
  Northwestern Mutual Life Insurance Co.
  Texas Utilities
  USX Corp.
  Viacom Internat'l, Inc.

ATKIN, James
Pillsbury, Madison and Sutro
1667 K St., N.W., Suite 1100, Washington, DC 20006
Telephone: (202) 887-0300

ATKINS, G. Lawrence
Director, Employee Benefit Policy, Winthrop, Stimson, Putnam & Roberts
1133 Connecticut Ave., N.W. Suite 1000, Washington, DC 20036
Telephone: (202) 775-9800
Registered as lobbyist at U.S. Congress.
Background: Minority Staff Director, Senate Special Committee on Aging, 1981-89.
Clients:
  Westinghouse Electric Corp.

ATKINSON, Diana
Secy, Legis Affairs, FEDERAL COMMUNICATIONS COMMISSION
1919 M St., N.W., Washington, DC 20554
Telephone: (202) 632-6405

ATKISSON, P.C., John McE.
1717 K St., N.W., Suite 610, Washington, DC 20036
Telephone: (202) 293-0104
Registered as lobbyist at U.S. Congress.
Background: An attorney. Former Chief Counsel, Subcommittee on Oversight and Investigations, House of Representatives Committee on Energy and Commerce.
Organizations represented:
  Daly City, California, City of
  Oxford Energy Co.
  Westinghouse Electric Corp.

ATTAWAY, Fritz E.
Sr. V. President, Government Relations, Motion Picture Ass'n of America
1600 Eye St., N.W., Washington, DC 20006
Telephone: (202) 293-1966
Registered as lobbyist at U.S. Congress.

ATWATER, Lee
Chairman, Republican Nat'l Committee
310 First St., S.E., Washington, DC 20003
Telephone: (202) 863-8500

ATWELL, Robert H.
President, American Council on Education
One Dupont Circle, N.W., Washington, DC 20036
Telephone: (202) 939-9300

ATWOOD, James R.
Covington and Burling
1201 Pennsylvania Ave., N.W., Box 7566, Washington, DC 20044
Telephone: (202) 662-6000
Registered as lobbyist at U.S. Congress.
Clients:
  BSA - Business Software Alliance

AUBIN, Leslie C.
Legislative Representative, Nat'l Federation of Independent Business
600 Maryland Ave., S.W., Suite 700, Washington, DC 20024
Telephone: (202) 554-9000
Registered as lobbyist at U.S. Congress.

AUD, Kenneth J.
Membership Administrator, Legis. Liaison, American Correctional Ass'n
8025 Laurel Lakes Court, Laurel, MD 20707
Telephone: (301) 206-5100

AUER, Kenneth E.
Acting President, Farm Credit Council
50 F St., N.W., Suite 900, Washington, DC 20001
Telephone: (202) 626-8710
Registered as lobbyist at U.S. Congress.

AUERBACH, James A.
V. President, Nat'l Planning Ass'n
1424 16th St., N.W. Suite 700, Washington, DC 20036
Telephone: (202) 265-7685

AUFHAUSER, David D.
Williams and Connolly
839 17th St., N.W. 1000 Hill Bldg., Washington, DC 20006
Telephone: (202) 331-5000
Clients:
  Loral/Fairchild Systems
  McKechnie Brothers (South Africa) Ltd.

AUGHTERON, Thomas G.
Technical Director, Industrial Safety Equipment Ass'n
1901 North Moore St., Suite 501, Arlington, VA 22209
Telephone: (703) 525-1695

AUGSBURGER, Myron S.
President, Christian College Coalition
327 8th St., N.E., Washington, DC 20002
Telephone: (202) 293-6177

AUKOFER, Mary
Editor, American Maritime Congress
444 N. Capitol St., N.W., Suite 801, Washington, DC 20001
Telephone: (202) 877-4477
Registered as lobbyist at U.S. Congress.

AULAKH, Dr. Gurmit Singh
President, Khalistan, Council of
2025 Eye St., N.W., Suite 901, Washington, DC 20007
Telephone: (202) 833-3262
Registered as Foreign Agent: (#4137)

AULD, Elaine, MPH
Director, Health Communications, Internat'l Food Information Council
1100 Connecticut Ave. N.W., Suite 430, Washington, DC 20036
Telephone: (202) 296-6540

AULICK, Dean D.
Shaw, Pittman, Potts and Trowbridge
2300 N St., N.W., Washington, DC 20037
Telephone: (202) 663-8000
Clients:
  Royal Air Maroc

AUSTIN & ASSOCIATES, Robb
600 New Hampshire Ave., N.W. Suite 1020, Washington, DC 20037
Telephone: (202) 333-5130
Registered as lobbyist at U.S. Congress.
Members of firm representing listed organizations:
  Austin, Robb

AUSTIN, Jeanie
Co-Chair, Republican Nat'l Committee
310 First St., S.E., Washington, DC 20003
Telephone: (202) 863-8500

AUSTIN, Jerry L.
President, Flight Engineers' Internat'l Ass'n
905 16th St., N.W. Suite 201, Washington, DC 20006
Telephone: (202) 347-4511

AUSTIN, Robb
Austin & Associates, Robb
600 New Hampshire Ave., N.W. Suite 1020, Washington, DC 20037
Telephone: (202) 333-5130
Registered as lobbyist at U.S. Congress.

AUSTIN, Ronald R.
Exec. Director and General Counsel, Overseas Education Ass'n
1201 16th St., N.W., Washington, DC 20036
Telephone: (202) 822-7850
Registered as lobbyist at U.S. Congress.

AUSTRIAN, Mark L.
Collier, Shannon & Scott
1055 Thomas Jefferson St., N.W., Suite 300, Washington, DC 20007
Telephone: (202) 342-8400
Registered as lobbyist at U.S. Congress.

AUTERY, C. Reuben
President, Gas Appliance Manufacturers Ass'n
1901 North Moore St., Arlington, VA 22209
Telephone: (703) 525-9565

AUTH, Catherine
Exec. Director, Nat'l Artists Equity Ass'n
P.O. Box 28068 Central Station, Washington, DC 20038
Telephone: (202) 628-9633
Background: Also represents the U.S. Committee of the Internat'l Ass'n of Art.

AUTHER, Sue
Staff Asst, Legis Affrs (Senate), EXECUTIVE OFFICE OF THE PRESIDENT - The White House
1600 Pennsylvania Ave., N.W. 107 East Wing, Washington, DC 20500
Telephone: (202) 456-6493

AUTRY, John S.
V. President, Government Relations, Unisys Corp.
2001 L St., N.W., Suite 1000, Washington, DC 20036
Telephone: (202) 293-7720
Registered as lobbyist at U.S. Congress.
Background: Also serves as Secretary-Treasurer, Unisys Political Action Committee.

AUXIER, Gary
Senior V. President, Burson-Marsteller
1850 M St., N.W., Suite 900, Washington, DC 20036
Telephone: (202) 833-8550
Background: Former Press Secretary to Senator Walter D. Huddleston (D-KY).

AVAKIAN, Michael
General Counsel, Center on Nat'l Labor Policy
5211 Port Royal Rd. Suite 400, Springfield, VA 22151
Telephone: (703) 321-9180

AVANT, Bob
Resident Tax Specialist, Independent Petroleum Ass'n of America
1101 16th St., N.W., Washington, DC 20036
Telephone: (202) 857-4734

AVARY, Robert P., Jr.
Wagner, Hines and Avary
1899 L St., N.W., Suite 500, Washington, DC 20036
Telephone: (202) 659-0930
Registered as lobbyist at U.S. Congress.
Registered as Foreign Agent: (#3845).
Clients:
American Heavy Lift Shipping Co.
H. E. Ventures, Inc.
Holmes & Narver, Inc.

AVERY, Dennis T.
Dir., Agricultural Technology Project, Hudson Institute
4401 Ford Ave. Suite 200, Alexandria, VA 22302
Telephone: (703) 824-2048

AVILA, Rebecca
Political Organizer, Common Cause
2030 M St., N.W., Washington, DC 20036
Telephone: (202) 833-1200
Registered as lobbyist at U.S. Congress.

AVRAAMIDES, Linda
Office Manager, American Hellenic Institute
1730 K St., N.W., Washington, DC 20006
Telephone: (202) 785-8430

AVRAKOTOS, Gus
Weiner, McCaffrey, Brodsky, Kaplan & Levin
1350 New York Ave., N.W., Suite 800, Washington, DC 20005-4797
Telephone: (202) 628-2000
Registered as lobbyist at U.S. Congress.

AWERBUCH, Leon
Manager, Business Development, Bechtel Group, Inc.
1620 Eye St., N.W., Suite 703, Washington, DC 20006
Telephone: (202) 393-4747

AXELRAD, Maurice
Newman & Holtzinger, P.C.
1615 L St., N.W., 10th Floor, Washington, DC 20005
Telephone: (202) 955-6600
Background: Attorney, Office of General Counsel, Atomic Energy Commission, 1958-61.

AYERS, Cindy
Confidential Asst, Cong Rels, DEPARTMENT OF AGRICULTURE
14th and Independence Ave. S.W., Room 239-E, Washington, DC 20205
Telephone: (202) 447-7095

AYLWARD, David K.
Nat'l Strategies Inc.
818 17th St., N.W., Washington, DC 20006
Telephone: (202) 429-8744
Background: Former Chief Counsel and Staff Director, House Subcommittee on Telecommunications, Consumer Protection and Finance. Serves as Exec. Director, Alliance for Capital Access.
Clients:
Alliance for Capital Access
Banner Industries

AYLWARD, Douglas
Director, Systems Development, Smith Industries
1225 Jefferson Davis Hwy., Suite 402, Arlington, VA 22202
Telephone: (703) 920-7640

AYLWARD & FINCHEM
888 17th St., N.W. 12th Floor, Washington, DC 20006
Telephone: (202) 429-2946
Background: Clients are represented by David K. Aylward of Nat'l Strategies Inc.
Clients:
Omak Wood Products Co.
Unimar Internat'l

AYOTTE, Christine
Director, Government Relations, Air Conditioning Contractors of America
1513 16th St., N.W., Washington, DC 20036
Telephone: (202) 483-9370

AYRES, Gretchen Y.
Staff Asst., Government Affairs, Sheet Metal and Air Conditioning Contractors' Nat'l Ass'n
8224 Old Courthouse Rd., Vienna, VA 22182
Telephone: (703) 790-9890

AYRES, Larry F.
Associate, Cassidy and Associates, Inc.
655 15th St., N.W., Suite 1100, Washington, DC 20005
Telephone: (202) 347-0773
Registered as lobbyist at U.S. Congress.
Background: Liaison to House of Representatives for the Office of the Secretary of Defense and Secretary of the Army, 1979-85.
Clients:
Medical University of South Carolina
Michigan Biotechnology Institute
Pennsylvania Turnpike Commission
University of Scranton

AYRES, Merribel S.
Exec. Director, Nat'l Independent Energy Producers
601 13th St., N.W. Suite 320S, Washington, DC 20004
Telephone: (202) 783-2244
Registered as lobbyist at U.S. Congress.
Background: Also serves as Treasurer, NIEPAC.

AYRES, Richard E.
Staff Attorney, Natural Resources Defense Council
1350 New York Ave., N.W. Suite 300, Washington, DC 20005
Telephone: (202) 783-7800
Registered as lobbyist at U.S. Congress.
Background: Also serves as Chairman, Nat'l Clean Air Coalition.

BAAB, Craig H.
Staff Director for Governmental Liaison, American Bar Ass'n
1800 M St., N.W., Washington, DC 20036
Telephone: (202) 331-2213
Registered as lobbyist at U.S. Congress.

BABB, John P.
Baker and Botts
555 13th St., N.W., Suite 500 East, Washington, DC 20004-1109
Telephone: (202) 639-7700
Clients:
Bundesverband der Deutschen Industrie

BABCO, Eleanor L.
Associate Director, Commission on Professionals in Science and Technology
1500 Massachusetts Ave., N.W. Suite 831, Washington, DC 20005
Telephone: (202) 223-6995
Background: Serves also as Exec. Secretary, Manpower Analysis and Planning Soc. of Washington.

BABCOCK, Anne H.
Director, Legislative Affairs, Council on Foundations
1828 L St., N.W. Suite 300, Washington, DC 20036
Telephone: (202) 466-6512
Background: Former Staff Member, Sen. Charles H. Percy.

BABCOCK, Hope M.
Counselor, Dir., Public Lands and Waters, Nat'l Audubon Soc.
801 Pennsylvania Ave., S.E., Washington, DC 20003
Telephone: (202) 547-9009
Registered as lobbyist at U.S. Congress.

BABER, Patti Jo
Exec. Director, American League of Lobbyists
P.O. Box 30005, Alexandria, VA 22310
Telephone: (703) 960-3011

BABINGTON, Maude A.
Associate Exec. Director, American Soc. of Consultant Pharmacists
2300 9th St., South, Arlington, VA 22204
Telephone: (703) 920-8492

BABIONE, Dale R.
Director, Government Business Relations, Boeing Co.
1700 North Moore St., Arlington, VA 22209
Telephone: (703) 558-9600
Registered as lobbyist at U.S. Congress.

BABYAK, Gregory R.
Royer, Mehle & Babyak
1747 Pennsylvania Ave., N.W. Suite 900, Washington, DC 20006
Telephone: (202) 296-0784
Registered as lobbyist at U.S. Congress.
Clients:
Contact Lens Institute
Municipal Finance Industry Ass'n
Nuveen & Co., Inc., John
Securities Industry Ass'n

BACH, Cristena
Director, Cong Afrs & State Liaison Div, DEPARTMENT OF ENERGY - Federal Energy Regulatory Commission
825 North Capitol St., Washington, DC 20426
Telephone: (202) 357-8004

BACHELLER, B. P.
Director, Public Relations, McDonnell Douglas Corp.
1735 Jefferson Davis Highway, Arlington, VA 22202
Telephone: (703) 553-3828

WASHINGTON REPRESENTATIVES

BACHENHEIMER, Cara C.
Director, Government Relations, Health Industry Distributors Ass'n
225 Reinekers Lane, Suite 650, Alexandria, VA 22314
Telephone: (703) 549-4432

BACHMAN, Gary
Van Ness, Feldman & Curtis
1050 Thomas Jefferson St., 7th Floor, Washington, DC 20007
Telephone: (202) 298-1800
Clients:
Committee of Hydroelectric Dam Owners

BACHMAN, Kenneth L., Jr.
Cleary, Gottlieb, Steen and Hamilton
1752 N St., N.W., Washington, DC 20036
Telephone: (202) 728-2700
Registered as lobbyist at U.S. Congress.
Clients:
Columbia Savings and Loan Ass'n

BACHMAN, Robert M.
Exec. Director, Nat'l Council on Patient Information and Education
666 11th St., N.W., Suite 810, Washington, DC 20001
Telephone: (202) 347-6711

BACHNER COMMUNICATIONS, INC.
8811 Colesville Rd., Suite G106, Silver Spring, MD 20910
Telephone: (301) 589-9121
Members of firm representing listed organizations:
Bachner, John P., President
Clients:
ASFE *(John P. Bachner)*
College of Property Management, The *(John P. Bachner)*
Consulting Engineers Council of Metropolitan Washington *(John P. Bachner)*
Institute of Professional Practice, The *(John P. Bachner)*
Mid-Atlantic Council of Shopping Center Managers *(John P. Bachner)*
Property Management Ass'n of America *(John P. Bachner)*
Property Management Ass'n of Metropolitan Washington *(John P. Bachner)*
Washington Area Council of Engineering Laboratories *(John P. Bachner)*

BACHNER, John P.
President, Bachner Communications, Inc.
8811 Colesville Rd., Suite G106, Silver Spring, MD 20910
Telephone: (301) 589-9121
Clients:
ASFE
College of Property Management, The
Consulting Engineers Council of Metropolitan Washington
Institute of Professional Practice, The
Mid-Atlantic Council of Shopping Center Managers
Property Management Ass'n of America
Property Management Ass'n of Metropolitan Washington
Washington Area Council of Engineering Laboratories

BACHRACH, Bronwyn R.
Hecht, Spencer & Associates
499 South Capitol St., S.W., Suite 507, Washington, DC 20003
Telephone: (202) 554-2881
Registered as lobbyist at U.S. Congress.
Background: Former Congressional Liaison officer, U.S. Department of State.
Clients:
BATUS, Inc.
Bixby Ranch
Boy Scouts of America
Brown and Williamson Tobacco Corp.
Marwais Steel Co.
Nat'l Ass'n for the Support of Long Term Care - NASL

BACHUS, Brig. Gen. Walter O., USA (Ret.)
Exec. Director, Soc. of American Military Engineers
P.O. Box 21289, Alexandria, VA 22320
Telephone: (703) 549-3800

BACK, Amy Bowling
Assistant, Gov't Affairs - Maryland, Potomac Electric Power Co.
1900 Pennsylvania Ave., N.W., Washington, DC 20068
Telephone: (202) 872-2000

BADER, Michael H.
Haley, Bader and Potts
2000 M St., N.W. Suite 600, Washington, DC 20036
Telephone: (202) 331-0606
Background: Member, Board of Directors, MCI Communications Corp.
Clients:
MCI Communications Corp.

BAER, Wendy J.
Exec. Vice President, Internat'l Hardwood Products Ass'n
Box 1308, Alexandria, VA 22313
Telephone: (703) 836-6696
Background: Responsibilities include the Ass'n INPAC.

BAER, William J.
Arnold & Porter
1200 New Hampshire Ave., N.W., Washington, DC 20036
Telephone: (202) 872-6700
Registered as lobbyist at U.S. Congress.
Background: Trial Attorney, Bureau of Consumer Protection, 1975-77. Attorney Advisor to the Chairman, 1977-78, and Assistant General Counsel, 1978-80, Federal Trade Commission. Serves as Coordinator, Lobbyists for Campaign Financing Reform.

BAFALIS, L. A., Skip
Evans Group, Ltd., The
1010 Wisconsin Ave., N.W. Suite 810, Washington, DC 20007
Telephone: (202) 333-8777
Registered as lobbyist at U.S. Congress.
Background: Former Member, U.S. House of Representatives (R-FL).
Clients:
Cain Hoy Plantation
Contraco, Inc.
Emergency Medical Services Associates
Matlack Systems, Inc.
Nigeria, Government of

BAGGETT, Joan N.
Dir., Congressional & Organizat'l Relats, Democratic Nat'l Committee
430 South Capitol St., S.E., Washington, DC 20003
Telephone: (202) 863-8000

BAGGETT, Madalene
Account Executive, Gallagher-Widmeyer Group Inc., The
1110 Vermont Ave., N.W., Suite 1020, Washington, DC 20005
Telephone: (202) 659-1606

BAGIN, Richard
Senior V. President, Madison Group/Earle Palmer Brown, The
2033 M St., N.W., 9th Floor, Washington, DC 20036
Telephone: (202) 223-0030
Clients:
Council for Solid Waste Solutions

BAGLEY, John F.
Director, External Relations, Battelle Memorial Institute
370 L'Enfant Promenade S.W. 901 D St., S.W., Suite 900, Washington, DC 20004-2115
Telephone: (202) 479-0500

BAHLER, Brent
Keene, Shirley & Associates, Inc.
919 Prince St., Alexandria, VA 22314
Telephone: (703) 684-0550
Registered as lobbyist at U.S. Congress.
Clients:
Boston Capital Partners, Inc.

BAHNER, Rita
Assistant Exec. Director, Ass'n of Official Analytical Chemists
2200 Wilson Blvd. Suite 400, Arlington, VA 22201-3301
Telephone: (703) 522-3032

BAHNSEN COMMUNICATIONS
1436 U St., N.W., Suite 204, Washington, DC 20009

Telephone: (202) 387-6556
Clients:
Independent Education Fund
Nat'l Ass'n of Independent Schools

BAHOUTH, Peter
Exec. Director, Greenpeace, U.S.A.
1436 U St., N.W., Washington, DC 20009
Telephone: (202) 462-1177

BAHR, Morton
President, Communications Workers of America
1925 K St., N.W., Washington, DC 20006
Telephone: (202) 728-2300

BAILAR, Barbara A.
Exec. Director, American Statistical Ass'n
1429 Duke St., Alexandria, VA 22314-3402
Telephone: (703) 684-1221

BAILEY, Arthur L.
Steptoe and Johnson
1330 Connecticut Ave., N.W., Washington, DC 20036
Telephone: (202) 429-3000
Clients:
New York Life Insurance Co.

BAILEY, Frank
Exec. Director, Volunteer-The Nat'l Center
1111 North 19th St. Suite 500, Arlington, VA 22209
Telephone: (703) 276-0542

BAILEY, Franklin E.
Asst Secy, Cong Rels, DEPARTMENT OF AGRICULTURE
14th and Independence Ave. S.W., Room 205-E, Washington, DC 20205
Telephone: (202) 447-7097

BAILEY, James H.
V. President, Federal Regulatory Affairs, Arkla, Inc.
1150 Connecticut Ave,m N.W. Suite 1125, Washington, DC 20036
Telephone: (202) 331-7175

BAILEY, James Michael
910 17th St., N.W. Suite 210, Washington, DC 20006
Telephone: (202) 296-7900
Registered as lobbyist at U.S. Congress.
Organizations represented:
Ass'n of U.S. Night Vision Manufacturers

BAILEY, Lois G.
Washington Rep., State & Commerce Depts., Loral/Fairchild Systems
1111 Jefferson Davis Hwy. Suite 811, Arlington, VA 22202
Telephone: (703) 685-5300

BAILEY, Myriam
Senior Analyst, American Ass'n of Retired Persons
1909 K St., N.W., Washington, DC 20049
Telephone: (202) 872-4700

BAILEY, Pamela G.
President, Nat'l Committee for Quality Health Care
1500 K St., N.W., Suite 360, Washington, DC 20005
Telephone: (202) 347-5731
Background: Director of Research, The White House (1973-74); Ass't Director, Domestic Council (1974-75); Ass't Secretary, Dept. of Health and Human Services (1981-83); Special Ass't to the President and Deputy Director, Office of Public Affairs (1983-84).

BAILEY, William A.
Legislative and Federal Affairs Officer, American Psychological Ass'n
1200 17th St., N.W., Washington, DC 20036
Telephone: (202) 955-7600
Registered as lobbyist at U.S. Congress.

BAILEY, William W.
Exec. V.P., Federal Government Affairs, Mutual of Omaha Insurance Companies
1700 Pennsylvania Ave., N.W. Suite 500, Washington, DC 20006
Telephone: (202) 393-6200
Registered as lobbyist at U.S. Congress.

BAIME, David
Director for Education Funding, Nat'l Ass'n of Independent Colleges and Universities
122 C St., N.W. Suite 750, Washington, DC 20001
Telephone: (202) 347-7512
Registered as lobbyist at U.S. Congress.

BAIN, Jackson
Sr. V.P., Grp. Dir., Elect. Media Svcs., Hill and Knowlton Public Affairs Worldwide
Washington Harbour, 901 31st St., N.W., Washington, DC 20007
Telephone: (202) 333-7400
Registered as Foreign Agent: (#3301).
Clients:
David Sarnoff Research Center
Nat'l Broadcasting Co.

BAINE, Kevin
Williams and Connolly
839 17th St., N.W. 1000 Hill Bldg., Washington, DC 20006
Telephone: (202) 331-5000
Clients:
Washington Post Co.

BAIR, James A.
Director, Government Relations, Millers' Nat'l Federation
600 Maryland Ave., S.W., Suite 305 West, Washington, DC 20024
Telephone: (202) 484-2200
Background: Former assistant to the Administrator, Federal Grain Inspection Service, U.S. Department of Agriculture.

BAIR, Jeanette
Exec. Director, American Occupational Therapy Ass'n
1383 Piccard Drive, Suite 300 P.O. Box 1725, Rockville, MD 20850
Telephone: (301) 948-9626

BAIRD, Jane C.
Dir, Cong Liaison, UNITED STATES INTERNAT'L TRADE COMMISSION
500 E St., S.W., Washington, DC 20436
Telephone: (202) 252-1151

BAIRD, Judith L.
Director, Federal Government Relations, ARCO
1333 New Hampshire Ave., N.W., Washington, DC 20036
Telephone: (202) 457-6256
Registered as lobbyist at U.S. Congress.

BAJER, Edward R.
Director of Energy, American Consulting Engineers Council
1015 15th St., N.W., Suite 802, Washington, DC 20005
Telephone: (202) 347-7474
Registered as lobbyist at U.S. Congress.

BAKER AND BOTTS
555 13th St., N.W., Suite 500 East, Washington, DC 20004-1109
Telephone: (202) 639-7700
Registered as Foreign Agent: (#4293)
Background: Washington office of a Houston law firm.
Members of firm representing listed organizations:
Babb, John P.
Baker, James A. (IV)
Berry, J. Patrick
   Background: Counsel, Committee on Energy and Natural Resources, U.S. Senate 1975-77.
Chapoton, O. Donaldson
   Background: Counsel. Former Deputy Assistant Secretary of the Treasury, 1986-87; Assistant Secretary of the Treasury, 1987-89.
Darling, Charles M. (IV)
Eastment, Thomas J.
Freedenberg, Paul
   Background: Consultant on international trade to the law firm of Baker and Botts. Former Under Secretary for Export Administration, U.S. Department of Commerce; Staff Director, Senate Banking Subcommittee on International Finance, 1981-85.
Hunsicker, Steven R.
Kiely, Bruce F.
Mathis, John P.
Picard, B. Donovan
Van Tine, Kirk K.
Veach, John B. (III)
Clients:

Ashland Exploration, Inc. *(Charles M. Darling, IV, John P. Mathis)*
Bundesverband der Deutschen Industrie *(John P. Babb, Paul Freedenberg, B. Donovan Picard, John B. Veach, III)*
Cabot Corp. *(James A. Baker, IV)*
Madison Gas and Electric Co. *(Bruce F. Kiely)*
NMTBA - The Ass'n for Manufacturing Technology *(B. Donovan Picard)*
Oryx Energy Co. *(Thomas J. Eastment)*
Pogo Producing Co. *(Thomas J. Eastment)*
Rhone-Poulenc Inc. *(B. Donovan Picard)*
Sonat Inc. *(James A. Baker, IV)*
US WEST, Inc. *(B. Donovan Picard)*
Wisconsin Distributor Group *(Bruce F. Kiely)*
Wisconsin Natural Gas Co.
Wisconsin Power and Light Co.

BAKER, Catherine A.
Director, Special Projects, Push Literacy Action Now (PLAN Inc.)
1332 G St., S.E., Washington, DC 20003
Telephone: (202) 547-8903

BAKER, Dr. Charles W.
V. President, Scientific Affairs, Sugar Ass'n, Inc.
1101 15th St., N.W., Suite 600, Washington, DC 20005
Telephone: (202) 785-1122

BAKER, David H.
Holland and Knight
888 17th St., N.W. Suite 900, Washington, DC 20006
Telephone: (202) 955-5550
Registered as Foreign Agent: (#3718).
Clients:
Bridgeport and Port Jefferson Steamboat Co.
Jamaica Nat'l Export Corp.
Lighter Ass'n, Inc.
Writing Instruments Manufacturers Ass'n

BAKER, Donald T.
1919 Pennsylvania Ave., N.W. Suite 800, Washington, DC 20006
Telephone: (202) 887-1457
Background: Formerly: Deputy Assistant Attorney General, U.S. Department of Justice, 1981-84; Deputy Assistant Secretary, U.S. Department of Commerce, 1984-85.

BAKER, Ellen Gay
Mgr., Regul. Affrs. (Enron/Interstate), Enron Corp.
1020 16th St., N.W., Washington, DC 20036-5754
Telephone: (202) 828-3360

BAKER, G. Tom
Staff V. President for Political Affairs, Nat'l Ass'n of Home Builders of the U.S.
15th and M Streets, N.W., Washington, DC 20005
Telephone: (202) 822-0470
Background: Also responsible for the Nat'l Ass'n of Home Builders Political Action Committee. Formerly aide to Senator Lloyd Bentsen (D-TX), 1975-78; Senate Democratic Policy Committee, 1978-79; Democratic Senate Campaign Committee, 1979-81.

BAKER, George D.
Williams and Jensen, P.C.
1101 Connecticut Ave., N.W., Suite 500, Washington, DC 20036
Telephone: (202) 659-8201
Registered as lobbyist at U.S. Congress.
Background: Former Attorney, Office of Hearings and Appeals, U.S. Department of Energy.
Clients:
Gamma Corp.
Lauder Inc., Estee
Mustang Fuel Corp.
Universal Foods Corp.

BAKER, Gerald E.
Senior Legislative Representative, Air Line Pilots Ass'n Internat'l
1625 Massachusetts Ave., N.W., Washington, DC 20036
Telephone: (202) 797-4039
Registered as lobbyist at U.S. Congress.

BAKER, Harold F.
Howrey and Simon
1730 Pennsylvania Ave., N.W., Washington, DC 20006-4793

Telephone: (202) 783-0800

BAKER AND HOSTETLER
1050 Connecticut Ave., N.W. Suite 1100, Washington, DC 20036
Telephone: (202) 861-1500
Background: Washington office of a Cleveland law firm.
Members of firm representing listed organizations:
Casey, Robert J.
   Background: Attorney, Office of Chief Counsel, Internal Revenue Service, 1950-52.
Graefe, Frederick H.
Hayes, Webb C. (III)
Jackson, Rebecca L.
Kies, Kenneth J.
Mattheis, Peter J.
Pinco, Robert G.
   Background: Attorney, Department of Justice, 1969-72. Assistant General Counsel, White House Special Action Office for Drug Abuse Prevention, 1972-74. Director, Over-the-Counter Drugs, Food and Drug Administration, 1974-77.
Pomeroy, Harlan
Reaves, John D.
Schweitzer, William H.
   Background: Assistant United States Attorney, Washington, DC 1970-73.
Skall, Gregg P.
Ward, Alan S.
   Background: Antitrust Division, Dep't of Justice 1956-61; Federal Trade Commission 1970-73.
Clients:
Aluminum Ass'n *(Alan S. Ward)*
American Protestant Health Ass'n
American Resort and Residential Development Ass'n Political Action Committee *(Kenneth J. Kies)*
Atchison, Topeka and Santa Fe Railway Co., The *(Robert J. Casey)*
Bell Canada *(Gregg P. Skall)*
BUILD-Political Action Committee
Chemed Corp. *(Kenneth J. Kies)*
Chubb Corp., The *(Kenneth J. Kies)*
CIGNA Corp.
Cleveland Clinic Foundation *(Frederick H. Graefe, Kenneth J. Kies)*
CNA Financial Corp. *(Kenneth J. Kies)*
Committee on Problems of Drug Dependence
Continental Insurance Investment Management *(Kenneth J. Kies)*
Elyria Memorial Hospital and Medical Center *(Frederick H. Graefe)*
Federal Deposit Insurance Corp. *(Kenneth J. Kies)*
Fireman's Fund Insurance Cos.
Greater New York Hospital Ass'n *(Frederick H. Graefe)*
Hermann Hospital *(Frederick H. Graefe)*
Homedco *(Frederick H. Graefe)*
Ivacare Corp. *(Frederick H. Graefe)*
Johnson & Johnson *(Robert G. Pinco)*
Lincoln Nat'l Life Insurance Co. *(Kenneth J. Kies)*
Lorain Community Hospital *(Frederick H. Graefe)*
Nat'l Ass'n of Professional Insurance Agents *(Kenneth J. Kies)*
Nat'l Congress of Parents and Teachers
PPG Industries *(Alan S. Ward)*
Renal Physicians of Texas *(Frederick H. Graefe)*
Rouse Company, The *(Kenneth J. Kies)*
Soc. of Cardiovascular and Interventional Radiology *(Frederick H. Graefe)*
Soc. of Vascular Technology *(Rebecca L. Jackson)*
St. Joseph Hospital and Health Center *(Frederick H. Graefe)*
St. Paul Fire and Marine Insurance Co. *(Kenneth J. Kies)*
Substance Abuse Management, Inc. *(Frederick H. Graefe)*
Travelers Insurance Co. *(Kenneth J. Kies)*
Uniden Corp. of America

BAKER, Howard H., Jr.
Senior Partner, Baker, Worthington, Crossley, Stansberry & Woolf
1001 Pennsylvania Ave., N.W. Suite 1201, Washington, DC 20004
Telephone: (202) 347-4360
Background: U.S. Senator (R-TN), 1966-85. Chief of Staff to President Ronald Reagan, The White House, 1987-88.

BAKER, James
PAC Contact, American Advertising Federation Political Action Committee
1400 K St., N.W., Suite 1000, Washington, DC 20005
Telephone: (202) 898-0089

BAKER, James A., IV
Baker and Botts
555 13th St., N.W., Suite 500 East, Washington, DC 20004-1109
Telephone: (202) 639-7700
Registered as lobbyist at U.S. Congress.
Clients:
Cabot Corp.
Sonat Inc.

BAKER, James Jay
Director, Federal Affairs Division, Nat'l Rifle Ass'n of America
1600 Rhode Island Ave., N.W., Washington, DC 20036
Telephone: (202) 828-6359
Registered as lobbyist at U.S. Congress.

BAKER, Jennifer A.
Assistant to the President, Bassin Assoc., Inc., Robert H.
499 South Capitol St., S.W. Suite 407, Washington, DC 20003
Telephone: (202) 863-2611

BAKER, Joe M., Jr.
Exec. V. President, Ass'n of the Wall and Ceiling Industries-Internat'l
1600 Cameron St., Alexandria, VA 22314
Telephone: (703) 684-2924
Background: Also serves as Treasurer, Wall and Ceiling Political Action Committee, and as Secretary, Foundation of the Wall and Ceiling Industry.

BAKER, John L.
President, Aircraft Owners and Pilots Ass'n
421 Aviation Way, Frederick, MD 21701
Telephone: (301) 695-2000

BAKER, Jules Evan
President, Nat'l Ass'n for Human Development
1424 16th St., N.W., Suite 102, Washington, DC 20036
Telephone: (202) 328-2191

BAKER AND MCKENZIE
815 Connecticut Ave., N.W. Suite 1100, Washington, DC 20006-4078
Telephone: (202) 452-7000
Background: Washington office of an international law firm.
Members of firm representing listed organizations:
Clubb, Bruce E.
Background: Attorney Advisor, Development Loan Fund and Agency for Internat'l Development, 1961-1962. Commissioner, U.S. Tariff Commission, 1967-1971.
Coward, Nicholas F.
Dyson, Edward E.
MacDonald, David R.
Background: Assistant Secretary of the Treasury, 1974-76. Under Secretary of the Navy, 1976-77. Deputy U.S. Trade Representative, 1981-83.
O'Brien, Kevin M.
O'Donnell, Thomas
Ondeck, Thomas P.
Outman, William D. (II)
Peele, B. Thomas (III)
Theroux, Eugene A.
Clients:
Acindar Industria Argentina de Aceros (Thomas P. Ondeck)
Amdahl Corp.
Camara Argentina de la Alumino y Metales Afines (Thomas P. Ondeck, B. Thomas Peele, III)
China, Government of the People's Republic of China Nat'l Chemical Import and Export Corp. (Eugene A. Theroux)
Clark Equipment Co. (Bruce E. Clubb)
Cold Spring Granite Co. (Bruce E. Clubb)
General Electric Co. (William D. Outman, II)
Melamine Chemicals (Thomas P. Ondeck)
Minnesota Mining and Manufacturing Co. (3M Co.) (Kevin M. O'Brien, Thomas P. Ondeck)
Mitsubishi Electric Corp. (Thomas P. Ondeck, William D. Outman, II)

Nat'l Club Ass'n (Thomas P. Ondeck)
Pizza Hut, Inc. (Eugene A. Theroux)
Samsonite Corp. (William D. Outman, II)
Stockton, California, Port of (Nicholas F. Coward)
Wang Laboratories Inc.

BAKER, Michael
Account Supervisor, Gallagher-Widmeyer Group Inc., The
1110 Vermont Ave., N.W., Suite 1020, Washington, DC 20005
Telephone: (202) 659-1606
Background: Former state press secretary to Vice President Walter Mondale in the 1984 presidential campaign.

BAKER, R. Garrity
Director, Internat'l Affairs, Chemical Manufacturers Ass'n
2501 M St., N.W., Washington, DC 20037
Telephone: (202) 887-1100
Registered as lobbyist at U.S. Congress.

BAKER-SMITH, Nancy
Exec. Director, Citizens for a Drug Free America
2230 George C. Marshall Drive, Falls Church, VA 22042
Telephone: (703) 207-9300
Registered as lobbyist at U.S. Congress.

BAKER, Stewart A.
Steptoe and Johnson
1330 Connecticut Ave., N.W., Washington, DC 20036
Telephone: (202) 429-3000
Registered as lobbyist at U.S. Congress.
Background: Law Clerk for Associate Justice John Paul Stevens, United States Supreme Court, 1977-78. Special Assistant to Secretary of Education, 1979-80. Deputy General Counsel, Department of Education, 1980-81.
Clients:
Outboard Marine Corp.

BAKER, Willie L., Jr.
Director, Public Affairs, United Food and Commercial Workers Internat'l Union
1775 K St., N.W., Washington, DC 20006
Telephone: (202) 223-3111
Registered as lobbyist at U.S. Congress.

BAKER, WORTHINGTON, CROSSLEY, STANSBERRY & WOOLF
1001 Pennsylvania Ave., N.W, Suite 1201, Washington, DC 20004
Telephone: (202) 347-4360
Members of firm representing listed organizations:
Andrew, David C., Partner
Baker, Howard H. (Jr.), Senior Partner
Background: U.S. Senator (R-TN), 1966-85. Chief of Staff to President Ronald Reagan, The White House, 1987-88.
Burgee, Michael B., Of Counsel.
Background: Deputy General Counsel, Federal Deposit Insurance Corp., 1984-87.
Hamberger, Edward R., Partner
Background: Staff Director, House Republican Policy Committee, 1979-81. Assistant Secretary for Governmental Affairs, U.S. Department of Transportation, 1988-89.
Montgomery, George Cranwell, Partner
Background: Counsel to the Majority Leader, U.S. Senate, 1981-85. U.S. Ambassador to Oman, 1985-89.
Murdock, (III) J. E., Partner
Background: FAA Chief Counsel, 1981-85. Acting FAA Deputy Administrator, 1984.
Rawls, W. Lee, Partner
Background: Legislative Director and Administrative Assistant to Senator Pete Domenici (R-NM), 1975-81, 1982-85.
Clients:
American Airlines (Edward R. Hamberger)
Austrian Airlines (III J. E. Murdock)
Bechtel Aviation Services (III J. E. Murdock)
Contel Corp. (Edward R. Hamberger)
Day & Zimmerman (Edward R. Hamberger)
DINAMO (Edward R. Hamberger)
DKT Memorial Fund (W. Lee Rawls)
Dunigan Companies (W. Lee Rawls)
Ebasco Services, Inc. (III J. E. Murdock)
Federal Express Corp. (W. Lee Rawls)
Guiness Peat Aviation (III J. E. Murdock)
Lawler/Wood, Inc. (Edward R. Hamberger)
Los Angeles County Transportation Commission (Edward R. Hamberger)

Nat'l Business Aircraft Ass'n (III J. E. Murdock)
Nat'l Label Co. (Edward R. Hamberger)
Nolisair (NationAir Canada) (III J. E. Murdock)
Occidental Petroleum Corp. (W. Lee Rawls)
Pennzoil Co. (W. Lee Rawls)
Philip Morris Management Corp. (W. Lee Rawls)
Pillsbury Co. (Edward R. Hamberger)
Public Service Co. of New Mexico (W. Lee Rawls)
Ryder System, Inc. (III J. E. Murdock)
Schering-Plough Corp. (W. Lee Rawls)
Southern California Edison Co. (W. Lee Rawls)
Warner-Lambert Co. (W. Lee Rawls)

BALDERSTON, Kris M.
Director, Office of Fed.-State Relations, Massachusetts, Commonwealth of
444 N. Capitol St., Suite 307, Washington, DC 20001
Telephone: (202) 628-1065
Background:

BALDI, Patricia A.
Director of Population Programs, Nat'l Audubon Soc.
801 Pennsylvania Ave., S.E., Washington, DC 20003
Telephone: (202) 547-9009
Registered as lobbyist at U.S. Congress.

BALDWIN, Anna J.
State Legislative Specialist, Automobile Importers of America
1725 Jefferson Davis Hwy., Suite 1002, Arlington, VA 22202
Telephone: (703) 979-5550

BALDWIN ASSOCIATES, Donald
1140 Connecticut Ave., N.W. Suite 804, Washington, DC 20036
Telephone: (202) 223-6850
Background: A Washington based government relations counsilting firm.
Members of firm representing listed organizations:
Baldwin, Donald, President
Background: Chairman, Nat'l Institute of Justice Advisory Board, 1986; member, 1981-86; White House Assistant; Administrative Assistant to Members of Congress. Serves as Exec. Director, Nat'l Law Enforcement Council.
Organizations represented:
Diagnostic Retrieval Systems, Inc. (Donald Baldwin)
Federal Criminal Investigators Ass'n (Donald Baldwin)
Mack Trucks, Inc. (Donald Baldwin)
Nat'l Commission Against Drunk Driving
Nat'l Law Enforcement Council (Donald Baldwin)

BALDWIN, Donald
President, Baldwin Associates, Donald
1140 Connecticut Ave., N.W. Suite 804, Washington, DC 20036
Telephone: (202) 223-6850
Registered as lobbyist at U.S. Congress.
Background: Chairman, Nat'l Institute of Justice Advisory Board, 1986; member, 1981-86; White House Assistant; Administrative Assistant to Members of Congress. Serves as Exec. Director, Nat'l Law Enforcement Council.
Organizations represented:
Diagnostic Retrieval Systems, Inc.
Federal Criminal Investigators Ass'n
Mack Trucks, Inc.
Nat'l Law Enforcement Council

BALDWIN, Elizabeth
Research Ethics Officer, American Psychological Ass'n
1200 17th St., N.W., Washington, DC 20036
Telephone: (202) 955-7600
Registered as lobbyist at U.S. Congress.

BALDWIN, Joan B.
United Internat'l Consultants
1800 Diagonal Rd., Alexandria, VA 22314
Telephone: (703) 684-4450
Registered as lobbyist at U.S. Congress.
Registered as Foreign Agent: (#3701).
Clients:
South Africa, Embassy of

WASHINGTON REPRESENTATIVES

BALEN, Samuel T.
Exec. Director, Nat'l Council of Architectural Registration Boards
1735 New York Ave., N.W. Suite 700, Washington, DC 20006
Telephone: (202) 783-6500

BALIS, Stanley W.
Miller, Balis and O'Neil
1101 14th St., N.W. Suite 1400, Washington, DC 20005
Telephone: (202) 789-1450
Background: Assistant Directror for Oil and Gas Pipeline and Producer Enforcement, Federal Energy Regulatory Commission, 1978-79.
Clients:
American Public Gas Ass'n

BALK-TUSA, Jacqueline
President, Andrews' Associates, Inc.
2550 M St., N.W., Suite 695, Washington, DC 20037
Telephone: (202) 457-6512
Registered as lobbyist at U.S. Congress.
Background: Former Administrative Assistant to Senator Mark Andrews (R-ND).

BALL, Helen M.
Director, Government Affairs, Brown Bridgman & Co Retiree Health Care Group
1016 16th St. N.W. Suite 100, Washington, DC 20036
Telephone: (202) 659-3507
Registered as lobbyist at U.S. Congress.

BALL, JANIK AND NOVACK
1101 Pennsylvania Ave., N.W. Suite 1035, Washington, DC 20004
Telephone: (202) 638-3307
Registered as Foreign Agent: (#4230)
Members of firm representing listed organizations:
Beall, James A., Partner
Background: Attorney-Advisor, U.S. Department of Interior, 1976-77. Legislative Director, Office of Rep. Al Ullman (D-OR), 1977-78; Staff Coordinator, House Committee on Ways and Means, 1978-81.
Cram, M. Victoria, Government Relations Consultant
Background: Staff Assistant to Rep. John Seiberling (D-OH), 1978-79. Legislative assistant, Democratic Study Group. 1979-81.
Giguere, Michelle E., Government Relations Consultant
Background: Former Legislative Director, office of Rep. Les AuCoin (D-OR).
Clients:
CH2M HILL
Clackamas County, Oregon *(James A. Beall, Michelle E. Giguere)*
Fresno, California, County of *(M. Victoria Cram)*
Fujitsu Microelectronics, Inc. *(James A. Beall)*
Greenbrier Leasing Corp. *(James A. Beall)*
Harsch Investment Corp. *(Michelle E. Giguere)*
Lower Columbia Regional Navy Task Force *(Michelle E. Giguere)*
Northwest Industrial Gas Users *(James A. Beall)*
Northwest Marine Iron Works *(James A. Beall, Michelle E. Giguere)*
Oregon Graduate Institute of Science and Technology *(Michelle E. Giguere)*
Portland, Oregon, City of *(M. Victoria Cram)*
Riedel Environmental Services *(James A. Beall)*
Section 8 Housing Group *(Michelle E. Giguere)*
Tillamook Bay, Oregon, Port of *(James A. Beall, Michelle E. Giguere)*

BALL, John
President, Nat'l Captioning Institute
5203 Leesburg Pike, Suite 1500, Falls Church, VA 22041
Telephone: (703) 998-2400

BALL, Thomas J.
Associate, Snyder Ball Kriser and Associates, Inc.
499 S. Capitol St., S.W., Suite 520, Washington, DC 20003
Telephone: (202) 488-4960
Registered as Foreign Agent: (#3655).

BALL, Whitney L.
Finance Director, Education and Research Institute
800 Maryland Ave., N.W., Washington, DC 20002
Telephone: (202) 546-1710

BALL, William L.
Director, Washington Office, General Motors Corp.
1660 L St., N.W., Washington, DC 20036
Telephone: (202) 775-5092
Registered as lobbyist at U.S. Congress.

BALL, William L., III
President, Nat'l Soft Drink Ass'n
1101 16th St., N.W., Washington, DC 20036
Telephone: (202) 463-6732
Registered as lobbyist at U.S. Congress.
Background: Former Secretary of the Navy.

BALLARD, B. Joseph
Associate Dir., Governmental Relations, Council for Exceptional Children
1920 Association Drive, Reston, VA 22091
Telephone: (703) 620-3660

BALLARD, D. Michael
President and General Manager, Barksdale Ballard & Co.
8027 Leesburg Pike Suite 200, Vienna, VA 22182
Telephone: (703) 827-8771
Background: Former Legislative Assistant and Press Secretary to Rep. Clement J. Zablocki (D-WI), 1968-70; Director of Communications, U.S. Postal Service, 1973-84.
Clients:
American Ass'n of State Highway and Transportation Officials
Public Broadcasting Service
TCOM Systems, Inc.
Virginia Wineries Ass'n

BALLARD, Frederic L., Jr.
Ballard, Spahr, Andrews and Ingersoll
555 13th St., N.W., Suite 900E, Washington, DC 20004
Telephone: (202) 383-8800
Clients:
AEG Aktiengesellschaft
Amexco
AVCO Financial Services
Beneficial Management Corp. of America
Citicorp Acceptance Corp.
Hallssen & Lyon
Haribo of America, Inc.

BALLARD, SPAHR, ANDREWS AND INGERSOLL
555 13th St., N.W., Suite 900E, Washington, DC 20004
Telephone: (202) 383-8800
Background: Washington office of a Philadelphia law firm.
Members of firm representing listed organizations:
Ballard, Frederic L. (Jr.)
Fanone, Joseph A.
Clients:
AEG Aktiengesellschaft *(Frederic L. Ballard, Jr.)*
Amexco *(Frederic L. Ballard, Jr.)*
AVCO Financial Services *(Frederic L. Ballard, Jr.)*
Beneficial Management Corp. of America *(Frederic L. Ballard, Jr.)*
Citicorp Acceptance Corp. *(Frederic L. Ballard, Jr.)*
Hallssen & Lyon *(Frederic L. Ballard, Jr.)*
Haribo of America, Inc. *(Frederic L. Ballard, Jr.)*

BALLEN, Debra T.
V. President, Policy Development/Rsrch., American Insurance Ass'n
1130 Connecticut Ave., N.W., Suite 1000, Washington, DC 20036
Telephone: (202) 828-7100
Registered as lobbyist at U.S. Congress.

BALLENGER, Sam
Lachelli, Waller and Associates
600 Maryland Ave., S.W., Suite 200A East Wing, Washington, DC 20024
Telephone: (202) 863-1472
Background: Legislative Assistant and Director of Legislation to Senator Paul Laxalt (R-NV), 1975-87.
Clients:
Imasco

BALLIN, Scott D.
V. President and Legislative Counsel, American Heart Ass'n
1250 Connecticut Ave., N.W., Suite 360, Washington, DC 20036
Telephone: (202) 822-9380

BALLOU, Col. DeForrest
Editor, National Defense, American Defense Preparedness Ass'n
2101 Wilson Blvd. Suite 400, Arlington, VA 22201-3061
Telephone: (703) 522-1820

BALMER, Thomas M.
Manager, Membership & Special Projects, Internat'l Ice Cream Ass'n
888 16th St., N.W., Washington, DC 20006
Telephone: (202) 296-4250
Registered as lobbyist at U.S. Congress.
Background: Also represents Milk Industry Foundation.

BALSAMO & ASSOCIATES, CHARTERED
1825 Eye St., N.W. Suite 400, Washington, DC 20006
Telephone: (202) 338-1260
Background: A law firm specializing in international tort claims, international insurance and commerciasl law, export finance, foreign investment and domestic civil litigation practice.
Members of firm representing listed organizations:
Balsamo, Richard W.
Background: Former Internat'l Taxation and Trade Law Attorney for the Internat'l Trade Administration, U.S. Dept. of Commerce.
Clients:
Global Medical Products, Inc. *(Richard W. Balsamo)*
Holzer, Inc., E. *(Richard W. Balsamo)*
Societe Chabert Duval, Ltd. *(Richard W. Balsamo)*

BALSAMO, Richard W.
Balsamo & Associates, Chartered
1825 Eye St., N.W. Suite 400, Washington, DC 20006
Telephone: (202) 338-1260
Background: Former Internat'l Taxation and Trade Law Attorney for the Internat'l Trade Administration, U.S. Dept. of Commerce.
Clients:
Global Medical Products, Inc.
Holzer, Inc., E.
Societe Chabert Duval, Ltd.

BALY, Michael, III
Exec. V. President and COO, American Gas Ass'n
1515 Wilson Blvd., Arlington, VA 22209
Telephone: (703) 841-8612
Registered as lobbyist at U.S. Congress.
Background: Former Special Assistant to Senator Jennings Randolph (D-WV).

BAMFORD, Gail
President, Nat'l Ass'n for Professional Saleswomen
712 West Broad St., Suite 5, Falls Church, VA 20046
Telephone: (703) 538-4390

BAND, Jonathan
Morrison & Foerster
2000 Pennsylvania Ave., N.W., Suite 5500, Washington, DC 20006
Telephone: (202) 887-1500
Registered as Foreign Agent: (#4282).
Clients:
Fujitsu Ltd.

BANDOW, Doug
Senior Fellow, Cato Institute
224 Second St., S.E., Washington, DC 20003
Telephone: (202) 546-0200
Background: Former Special Assistant to the President for Policy Development.

BANDY, Michael J.
Director, Communications, Internat'l Exhibitors Ass'n
5501 Backlick Road, Suite 200, Springfield, VA 22151
Telephone: (703) 941-3725

BANGERT, Philip A.
Director, Legislative Affairs, Century Public Affairs
1752 N St., N.W., Suite 800, Washington, DC 20036
Telephone: (202) 828-2375
Registered as lobbyist at U.S. Congress.
Clients:
New United Motor Manufacturing, Inc. (NUMMI)
Oakland, California, Port of
Transcontinental Development Corp.

BANK, Cindy
Congressional Liaison, Close Up Foundation
1235 Jefferson Davis Hwy., Arlington, VA 22202
Telephone: (703) 892-5400

BANK, Richard K.
Graham and James
2000 M St., N.W., Suite 700, Washington, DC 20036
Telephone: (202) 463-0800
Registered as Foreign Agent: (#3275).
Background: Director, Office of Maritime Affairs, U.S. Dept. of State.
Clients:
    Internat'l Ass'n of Independent Tanker Owners

BANKS, James T.
Director, Government Affairs, Waste Management, Inc.
1155 Connecticut Ave., N.W., Suite 800, Washington, DC 20036
Telephone: (202) 467-4480
Registered as lobbyist at U.S. Congress.

BANKS, Johnella
President, District of Columbia League for Nursing
5100 Wisconsin Ave., N.W. Suite 306, Washington, DC 20016
Telephone: (202) 244-0628

BANKS, MaryBeth
Director, Federal Regulatory Affairs, US Sprint Communications Co.
1850 M St., N.W., Suite 1100, Washington, DC 20036
Telephone: (202) 857-1030

BANKS, Terry M.
Federal Gov't Affrs V. Pres. & Attorney, AT&T
1120 20th St., N.W., Suite 1000, Washington, DC 20036
Telephone: (202) 457-3810

BANKSON, John P., Jr.
Hopkins and Sutter
888 16th St., N.W., Suite 700, Washington, DC 20006
Telephone: (202) 835-8000
Clients:
    KPVI
    KTTY
    WPXT

BANNAN, Kathryn E.
Federal Government Affairs Associate, Hoffmann-La Roche Inc.
1050 Connecticut Ave., N.W. Suite 401, Washington, DC 20036
Telephone: (202) 223-1975
Registered as lobbyist at U.S. Congress.

BANNER, Donald W.
President, Intellectual Property Owners, Inc.
1255 23rd St., N.W., Suite 850, Washington, DC 20037
Telephone: (202) 466-2396
Background: U.S. Commissioner of Patents and Trademarks, 1978-79.

BANNERMAN AND ASSOCIATES, INC.
888 16th St., N.W., Washington, DC 20006
Telephone: (202) 835-8188
Members of firm representing listed organizations:
    Bannerman, M. Graeme
        Background: Former Staff Director, Senate Foreign Relations Committee.
    Perugino, Roxanne
        Background: Former Staff Member, House Foreign Affairs Committee.
    Silvers, Curtis
        Background: Former staff member, Senate Foreign Relations Committee.
Clients:
    Bangladesh, People's Republic of *(M. Graeme Bannerman, Curtis Silvers)*
    Beirut University College *(M. Graeme Bannerman, Roxanne Perugino)*
    Egypt, Embassy of
    Egypt, Government of *(M. Graeme Bannerman)*
    Philippines, Government of the *(M. Graeme Bannerman, Curtis Silvers)*
    Tunisia, Embassy of *(M. Graeme Bannerman, Roxanne Perugino)*

BANNERMAN, M. Graeme
Bannerman and Associates, Inc.
888 16th St., N.W., Washington, DC 20006
Telephone: (202) 835-8188
Registered as lobbyist at U.S. Congress.
Registered as Foreign Agent: (#3964).
Background: Former Staff Director, Senate Foreign Relations Committee.
Clients:
    Bangladesh, People's Republic of
    Beirut University College
    Egypt, Government of
    Philippines, Government of the
    Tunisia, Embassy of

BANNISTER, Robert D
Sr. Staff V. Pres., Government Affairs, Nat'l Ass'n of Home Builders of the U.S.
15th and M Streets, N.W., Washington, DC 20005
Telephone: (202) 822-0470
Registered as lobbyist at U.S. Congress.
Background: Serves also as Secretary, BUILD-Political Action Committee.

BANOUN, Raymond
Of Counsel, Arent, Fox, Kintner, Plotkin & Kahn
1050 Connecticut Ave., N.W., Washington, DC 20036-5339
Telephone: (202) 857-6000

BANTLEON, David F.
Dow, Lohnes and Albertson
1255 23rd St., N.W., Suite 500, Washington, DC 20037
Telephone: (202) 857-2500
Clients:
    American Security Bank
    Avis Rent A Car Systems, Inc.
    Hertz Corp.
    Hilton Hotels Corp.
    Maryland Nat'l Bank
    Security Trust Co.
    U.S. Trust Co.

BANTON, Linda W.
Governemnt Relations Representative, Honeywell, Inc.
7900 Westpark Dr. Suite A-524, McLean, VA 22102
Telephone: (703) 827-3000
Registered as lobbyist at U.S. Congress.

BANVILLE, Anne
Public Affairs Representative, Alyeska Pipeline Service Co.
10009 Kensington Parkway, Kensington, MD 20895
Telephone: (301) 942-6121

BANZHAF, John F., III
Exec. Director and Chief Counsel, Action on Smoking and Health
2013 H St. N.W., Washington, DC 20006
Telephone: (202) 659-4310

BANZHAF, William H.
Exec. V. President, Soc. of American Foresters
5400 Grosvenor Lane, Bethesda, MD 20814
Telephone: (301) 897-8720

BAPTISTA, Samuel J.
President, Financial Services Council
1225 19th St., N.W., Suite 410, Washington, DC 20036
Telephone: (202) 785-1500
Registered as lobbyist at U.S. Congress.

BAPTISTE, J. Baron
Treasurer, QuesTech Inc. Political Action Committee
7600 A Leesburg Pike, Falls Church, VA 22043
Telephone: (703) 760-1000

BARAFF, KOERNER, OLENDER AND HOCHBERG
2033 M St., N.W., Suite 700, Washington, DC 20036
Telephone: (202) 452-8200
Members of firm representing listed organizations:
    Hochberg, Philip R.
        Background: Special Counsel, Communications Subcommittee, U.S. House of Representatives, 1977.
Clients:
    College Football Ass'n *(Philip R. Hochberg)*
    Nat'l Basketball Ass'n *(Philip R. Hochberg)*
    Nat'l Hockey League *(Philip R. Hochberg)*

BARAGAR, E. W.
Manager, Congressional Affairs, Boeing Co.
1700 North Moore St., Arlington, VA 22209
Telephone: (703) 558-9600
Registered as lobbyist at U.S. Congress.

BARALD, Patricia Anne
Covington and Burling
1201 Pennsylvania Ave., N.W., Box 7566, Washington, DC 20044
Telephone: (202) 662-6000
Clients:
    General Electric Co.

BARAN, Jan
Wiley, Rein & Fielding
1776 K St., N.W., Tenth Floor, Washington, DC 20006-2359
Telephone: (202) 429-7000
Background: Exec. Assistant to the Chairman, Federal Election Commission, 1977-79.
Clients:
    Nat'l Republican Congressional Committee
    Nat'l Republican Senatorial Committee

BARANIK, Diane
Child and Adolescent Mental Health, Nat'l Mental Health Ass'n
1021 Prince St., Alexandria, VA 22314
Telephone: (703) 684-7722
Background: Former Legislative Assistant to Senator John Kerry (D-MA).

BARAUTO, Juan N.
Resident Representative to the U.S., Northern Mariana Islands, Commonwealth of
2121 R St., N.W., Washington, DC 20008
Telephone: (202) 673-5869

BARBER, Daniel W.
President, NABADA - The Ass'n of Container Reconditioners
1030 15th St., N.W., Washington, DC 20005
Telephone: (202) 296-8028

BARBER, Douglas L.
Exec. V. President, Future Business Leaders of America
P.O. Box 17417-Dulles, Washington, DC 20041
Telephone: (703) 860-3334

BARBER, Randy
Director, Center for Economic Organizing
1522 K St., N.W., Suite 406, Washington, DC 20005
Telephone: (202) 775-9072

BARBERO, Albert
Regional Manager, Sundstrand Corp.
1000 Wilson Blvd., Suite 2400, Arlington, VA 22209
Telephone: (703) 276-1626

BARBIS, Patricia Q.
V. President, Hill and Knowlton Public Affairs Worldwide
Washington Harbour, 901 31st St., N.W., Washington, DC 20007
Telephone: (202) 333-7400
Registered as Foreign Agent: (#3301).
Background: Formerly served with the State Department's Office of Public Affairs and with USIA.

BARBOUR, Delta
V. President/Treasurer, Sugar Ass'n, Inc.
1101 15th St., N.W., Suite 600, Washington, DC 20005
Telephone: (202) 785-1122

BARBOUR, Nancy R.
Senior Legislative Associate, APCO Associates
1155 21st St., N.W., Suite 1000, Washington, DC 20036
Telephone: (202) 778-1000
Clients:
    University of Michigan Medical Center

BARBOUR, Rebecca T.
Government Affairs Representative, Shell Oil Co.
1025 Connecticut Ave., N.W., Suite 200, Washington, DC 20036
Telephone: (202) 466-1405
Registered as lobbyist at U.S. Congress.
Background: Former Special Assistant to the Minority, Senate Energy and Natural Resources Committee.

BARCLAY, Betsy
Director, Legislative Projects, Public Securities Ass'n
1000 Vermont Ave., N.W., Suite 800, Washington, DC 20005
Telephone: (202) 898-9390
Registered as lobbyist at U.S. Congress.
Background: Former aide to Senator Robert Taft, Jr. (R-OH) and to the Senate Commerce Committee.

BARCLAY, Charles
Exec. V. President, American Ass'n of Airport Executives
4212 King St., Alexandria, VA 22302
Telephone: (703) 824-0500
Background: Responsibilities include AAAE Good Government Committee. Former Chief Counsel, U.S. Senate Subcommittee on Aviation.

BARDIN, David J.
Arent, Fox, Kintner, Plotkin & Kahn
1050 Connecticut Ave., N.W., Washington, DC 20036-5339
Telephone: (202) 857-6000
Registered as lobbyist at U.S. Congress.
Background: Trial Attorney, 1958-65, Assistant General Counsel, 1965-67, and Deputy General Counsel 1967-69 in the Federal Power Commission. Commissioner, New Jersey Department of Environmental Protection, 1974-77. Deputy Administrator, Federal Energy Administration, 1977. Administrator of the Economic Regulatory Administration, Department of Energy, 1977-79.

BARER, Stanley H.
Garvey, Schubert & Barer
1000 Potomac St., N.W. Suite 500, Washington, DC 20007
Telephone: (202) 965-7880
Background: Counsel, U.S. Senate Committee on Commerce, 1966-69. Administrative Assistant to Senator Warren Magnuson (D-WA), 1969-74.
Clients:
China Ocean Shipping Co.

BARES, M. Camille
Director, Federal Relations, Southwestern Bell Corp.
1667 K St., N.W., Suite 1000, Washington, DC 20006
Telephone: (202) 293-8550
Registered as lobbyist at U.S. Congress.

BARHYTE, Leslie A.
Legislative Assistant, American Newspaper Publishers Ass'n
The Newspaper Center 11600 Sunrise Valley Drive, Reston, VA 22091
Telephone: (703) 648-1000
Registered as lobbyist at U.S. Congress.

BARIO ASSOCIATES, Patricia
512 11th St., S.E., Washington, DC 20003
Telephone: (202) 543-0923
Background: A public affairs/public relations representation firm.
Members of firm representing listed organizations:
Bario, Patricia, President
  Background: Served as Deputy White House Press Secretary under President Jimmy Carter.
Cohick, Chris
Franklin, Lesli
Jenkins, Pamela, Account Executive
Organizations represented:
Coalition Against Regressive Taxation *(Patricia Bario)*
Cox-Matthews *(Patricia Bario)*
History Factory, The *(Pamela Jenkins)*
Miller Brewing Co. *(Patricia Bario)*
Nat'l Ass'n of Retail Druggists *(Patricia Bario)*
Nat'l Institute for Automotive Service Excellence *(Patricia Bario)*

BARIO, Patricia
President, Bario Associates, Patricia
512 11th St., S.E., Washington, DC 20003
Telephone: (202) 543-0923
Background: Served as Deputy White House Press Secretary under President Jimmy Carter.
Organizations represented:
Coalition Against Regressive Taxation
Cox-Matthews
Miller Brewing Co.
Nat'l Ass'n of Retail Druggists

Nat'l Institute for Automotive Service Excellence

BARKER, Robert H.
V. Pres., Technical & Legislative Affrs., American Fiber Manufacturers Ass'n
1150 17th St., N.W., Suite 310, Washington, DC 20036
Telephone: (202) 296-6508
Registered as lobbyist at U.S. Congress.
Background: Former Administrative Assistant to Rep. Judd Gregg (R-NH).

BARKLEY, Liz
Administrator, Nat'l Certification Agency for Medical Laboratory Personnel
2021 L St., N.W. Suite 400, Washington, DC 20036
Telephone: (202) 857-1023

BARKSDALE BALLARD & CO.
8027 Leesburg Pike Suite 200, Vienna, VA 22182
Telephone: (703) 827-8771
Members of firm representing listed organizations:
Ballard, D. Michael, President and General Manager
  Background: Former Legislative Assistant and Press Secretary to Rep. Clement J. Zablocki (D-WI), 1968-70; Director of Communications, U.S. Postal Service, 1973-84.
Duka, Walter E., Exec. V. President
  Background: Information Director, President's Consumer Committee, 1965-67. Assistant Postmaster General for Communications, 1973-76 and 1978-82. Assistant Press Secretary to President Jimmy Carter, 1977. Assistant Postmaster General for International Affairs, 1982-88.
Clients:
American Ass'n of State Highway and Transportation Officials *(D. Michael Ballard, Walter E. Duka)*
Public Broadcasting Service *(D. Michael Ballard)*
TCOM Systems, Inc. *(D. Michael Ballard)*
Virginia Wineries Ass'n *(D. Michael Ballard)*

BARKSDALE, Thomas H., Jr.
McNair Law Firm, P.A.
1155 15th St., N.W. Suite 400, Washington, DC 20005
Telephone: (202) 659-3900
Registered as lobbyist at U.S. Congress.
Background: Counsel for U.S. Senate Committees on Judiciary and Commerce, 1966-70; Special Agent, Federal Bureau of Investigation, 1948-50.
Clients:
Gasoline Alliance to Preserve Competition

BARLOON, William J.
Manager, Federal Government Relations, United Telecommunications
1850 M St., N.W., Suite 1110, Washington, DC 20036
Telephone: (202) 857-1030

BARNARD, Geoffrey S.
V. President, International Program, Nature Conservancy, The
1815 N. Lynn St, Arlington, VA 22209
Telephone: (703) 841-5300

BARNARD, Robert C.
Counsel, Cleary, Gottlieb, Steen and Hamilton
1752 N St., N.W., Washington, DC 20036
Telephone: (202) 728-2700
Background: Attorney, Antitrust Division, U.S. Department of Justice, 1939-41. Attorney, 1941-47 and First Assistant, 1945-47, Office of the Assistant Solicitor General, U.S. Department of Justice.

BARNES, Ben
Evans Group, Ltd., The
1010 Wisconsin Ave., N.W. Suite 810, Washington, DC 20007
Telephone: (202) 333-8777
Registered as lobbyist at U.S. Congress.
Background: Former Lieutenant Governor of Texas and Speaker of the Texas House of Representatives. Serves as President, Nat'l Coalition for the Rehabilitation of Insured Institutions.

BARNES, Dennis N.
Morgan, Lewis and Bockius
1800 M St., N.W., Washington, DC 20036
Telephone: (202) 467-7000
Clients:

Atlantic Lines and Navigation Co., Ltd.
Puerto Rico Maritime Shipping Authority

BARNES, Donald J.
Director, Washington Office, Nat'l Anti-Vivisection Soc.
112 North Carolina Ave., S.E., Washington, DC 20003
Telephone: (202) 543-6601

BARNES, J. Craig
Hill Group, Inc.
1200 17th St., N.W., Suite 400, Washington, DC 20036
Telephone: (202) 296-9200
Clients:
Ceramic Tile Marketing Federation

BARNES, Col. James, USA (Ret.)
Director, Marketing & Membership Devlmnt, Retired Officers Ass'n, The (TROA)
201 N. Washington St., Alexandria, VA 22314
Telephone: (703) 549-2311

BARNES, Michael D.
Arent, Fox, Kintner, Plotkin & Kahn
1050 Connecticut Ave., N.W., Washington, DC 20036-5339
Telephone: (202) 857-6000
Registered as lobbyist at U.S. Congress.
Background: Member, U.S. House of Representatives (D-MD), 1979-86.
Clients:
Ass'n of Professional Flight Attendants
California Steel Industries Inc.
Nat'l Ass'n of College Stores
Puerto Rico Federal Affairs Administration

BARNES, Richard E., CAE
President, American Concrete Pipe Ass'n
8300 Boone Blvd., Suite 400, Vienna, VA 22182-2689
Telephone: (703) 821-1990
Background: Serves also as President, Concrete Pipe Ass'ns, Inc.

BARNES, Richard L.
Preston Gates Ellis & Rouvelas Meeds
1735 New York Ave., N.W., Suite 500, Washington, DC 20006-4759
Telephone: (202) 628-1700
Registered as lobbyist at U.S. Congress.
Background: Professional staff member, U.S. House of Representatives Government Operations Committee, 1977-79.
Clients:
Alaska Loggers Ass'n
American Forest Resource Alliance
American Plywood Ass'n
Nat'l Forest Products Ass'n
Nelbro Packing Co.
Simpson Investment Co.
Wickes Manufacturing Co.

BARNES, RICHARDSON AND COLBURN
1819 H St., N.W., Washington, DC 20006
Telephone: (202) 457-0300
Background: Washington office of a New York law firm.
Members of firm representing listed organizations:
Burke, Robert E.
  Background: Member, U.S. Foreign Service, 1967-68. Trial Attorney, Department of Justice, Customs Section, 1968-71.
Elliott, David O.
Honey, Edgar Thomas
Jarman, Rufus E. (Jr.)
Lehman, Leonard
  Background: Attorney Advisor, U.S. Tax Court, 1952-55. Assistant Chief Counsel, U.S. Customs Service, 1965-68. Deputy Chief Counsel, 1968-71 and Assistant Commissioner of Customs, 1971-79, U.S. Treasury Department.
Lundquist, James H.
McGrath, Matthew T.
O'Kelly, James S.
Sultan, Peter L.
Vance, Andrew P.
Von Conrad, Gunter
Clients:
Alfa Romeo, Inc. *(Rufus E. Jarman, Jr.)*
American Ass'n of Fastener Importers *(Matthew T. McGrath)*
Asahi Chemical Industry Co. *(James S. O'Kelly)*

Australian Wool Corp. (*Rufus E. Jarman, Jr.*)
Bowe Maschinenfabrik GmbH (*Rufus E. Jarman, Jr.*)
Budd Co. (*James H. Lundquist, Matthew T. McGrath*)
Case Co., J. I. (*Robert E. Burke, Matthew T. McGrath, Gunter Von Conrad*)
Consolidated Diesel Corp. (*Robert E. Burke, Matthew T. McGrath, Gunter Von Conrad*)
Florida Citrus Mutual (*James H. Lundquist, Matthew T. McGrath*)
Internat'l Tool Works Ltd. (*David O. Elliott*)
IPSCO Inc. (*Rufus E. Jarman, Jr.*)
Maple Leaf Fish Co. (*David O. Elliott, Matthew T. McGrath*)
Meat Importers Council of America (*Rufus E. Jarman, Jr., James H. Lundquist, Gunter Von Conrad*)
Medline Industries
Mercedes-Benz of North America, Inc. (*Edgar Thomas Honey*)
Miles, Inc. (*Matthew T. McGrath, Peter L. Sultan*)
Mitsubishi Corp. (*Edgar Thomas Honey*)
Mitsui and Co. (*James S. O'Kelly*)
Omstead Foods Ltd. (*David O. Elliott, Matthew T. McGrath*)
Orion Electric Co., Ltd.
Papeteries Bollore, S.A.
Sandoz Corp. (*James H. Lundquist*)
Sundstrand Corp. (*Matthew T. McGrath*)
West Bend Co.
West German Ceramic Exporters Ass'n
WMF of America

BARNES AND THORNBURG
1815 H St., N.W., Suite 800, Washington, DC 20006
Telephone: (202) 955-4500
Members of firm representing listed organizations:
Stayin, Randolph J.
Background: Administrative Assistant and Director of Legislation to Senator Robert Taft, Jr. (R-OH), 1973-76.
Stras, Marcela B.
Clients:
Headwear Institute of America (*Randolph J. Stayin, Marcela B. Stras*)
Indiana Gas Co.
Lilly and Co., Eli
Nat'l Candle Ass'n (*Randolph J. Stayin, Marcela B. Stras*)
Special Committee for Workplace Product Liability Reform (*Randolph J. Stayin*)

BARNES, William
Research Director, Nat'l League of Cities
1301 Pennsylvania Ave., N.W., Washington, DC 20004
Telephone: (202) 626-3000

BARNET, Richard J.
Senior Fellow, Institute for Policy Studies
1601 Connecticut Ave., N.W. 5th Floor, Washington, DC 20009
Telephone: (202) 234-9382

BARNETT, Frank R.
President, Nat'l Strategy Information Center
1730 Rhode Island Ave., N.W., Washington, DC 20036
Telephone: (202) 429-0129

BARNETT, Larry P.
V. President, Government Affairs, Air Transport Ass'n of America
1709 New York Ave., N.W., Washington, DC 20006-5206
Telephone: (202) 626-4186
Registered as lobbyist at U.S. Congress.

BARNETT, Robert B.
Williams and Connolly
839 17th St., N.W. 1000 Hill Bldg., Washington, DC 20006
Telephone: (202) 331-5000
Registered as lobbyist at U.S. Congress.
Background: Law clerk to U.S. Supreme Court Justice Byron R. White, 1972-73. Legislative Assistant to Senator Walter F. Mondale, 1973-75.

BARNEY, Daniel
Director, Litigation Center, American Trucking Ass'ns
2200 Mill Road, Alexandria, VA 22314
Telephone: (703) 838-1800

BARNSBACK, Richard E.
Chief Counsel, State Relations, American Council of Life Insurance
1001 Pennsylvania Ave., N.W., Washington, DC 20004-2599
Telephone: (202) 624-2190
Registered as lobbyist at U.S. Congress.

BARNUM, John W.
White & Case
1747 Pennsylvania Ave., N.W., Suite 500, Washington, DC 20006
Telephone: (202) 872-0013
Background: General Counsel, 1971-73; Under Secretary, 1973-74; Deputy Secretary, 1974-77; U.S. Department of Transportation.
Clients:
Federal Paper Board Co.
RIV-SKF Industrie S.p.A.

BAROODY, Michael E.
Sr. V. Pres, Policy and Communications, Nat'l Ass'n of Manufacturers
1331 Pennsylvania Ave., N.W. Suite 1500 North, Washington, DC 20004-1703
Telephone: (202) 637-3000
Registered as lobbyist at U.S. Congress.
Background: Former Assistant Secretary of Labor for Policy and former White House aide under President Reagan.

BARQUIN, Ramon C.
Exec. V. President and COO, Washington Consulting Group
1625 Eye St., N.W. Suite 214, Washington, DC 20006
Telephone: (202) 457-0233

BARR, Allison
Staff Assistant, Concerned Citizens Foundation
Capitol Hill Office Bldg. 412 First St., S.E., Suite 301, Washington, DC 20003
Telephone: (202) 479-9068

BARR, David S.
Barr, Peer & Cohen
1620 Eye St., N.W., Suite 603, Washington, DC 20006
Telephone: (202) 223-1900
Clients:
Newspaper Guild, The

BARR, James C.
Chief Exec. Officer, Nat'l Milk Producers Federation
1840 Wilson Blvd., Arlington, VA 22201
Telephone: (703) 243-6111
Registered as lobbyist at U.S. Congress.

BARR, James L.
Exec. Director, Nat'l Voluntary Health Agencies
1660 L St., N.W. Suite 601, Washington, DC 20036
Telephone: (202) 467-5913

BARR, PEER & COHEN
1620 Eye St., N.W., Suite 603, Washington, DC 20006
Telephone: (202) 223-1900
Members of firm representing listed organizations:
Barr, David S.
Clients:
Internat'l Brotherhood of Painters and Allied Trades
Internat'l Federation of Professional and Technical Engineers
Newspaper Guild, The (*David S. Barr*)

BARR, Roger W., Jr.
State Legislative Director-Kansas, Transportation, Communications Internat'l Union
815 16th St., N.W. Suite 511, Washington, DC 20036
Telephone: (202) 783-3660
Registered as lobbyist at U.S. Congress.

BARR, Terry N.
V. President, Agriculture & Trade Policy, Nat'l Council of Farmer Cooperatives
50 F St., N.W., Suite 900, Washington, DC 20001
Telephone: (202) 626-8700
Registered as lobbyist at U.S. Congress.

BARRACK, David W.
Internat'l Management Group, Inc.
1101 14th St., N.W. Suite 1100, Washington, DC 20005

Telephone: (202) 371-2200
Background: Serves as Exec. Director, Nat'l Ass'n of Public Insurance Adjusters; Exec. Director, Metal Construction Ass'n; Exec. Director, American Soc. of Electroplated Plastics; Exec. Director, American Cutlery Manufacturers Ass'n.
Clients:
American Cutlery Manufacturers Ass'n
American Soc. of Electroplated Plastics
Metal Construction Ass'n
Nat'l Ass'n of Public Insurance Adjusters

BARRENS, Ruth L.
Director of Education, Organization for the Protection and Advancement of Small Telephone Cos.
2000 K St., N.W., Suite 205, Washington, DC 20006
Telephone: (202) 659-5990

BARRETO, Julio, Jr.
Policy Analyst, Nat'l League of Cities
1301 Pennsylvania Ave., N.W., Washington, DC 20004
Telephone: (202) 626-3000

BARRETT, Bryan
V. President- Marconi Underwater Systems, Plessey Electronic Systems, Inc.
1215 Jefferson Davis Hwy., Suite 1203, Arlington, VA 22202
Telephone: (703) 920-7575

BARRETT, David C., Jr.
Director, Public Affairs, Nat'l Grain and Feed Ass'n
1201 New York Ave., N.W. Suite 830, Washington, DC 20005
Telephone: (202) 289-0873
Registered as lobbyist at U.S. Congress.

BARRETT, David M.
Barrett, Montgomery & Murphy
1055 Thomas Jefferson St., N.W., Suite 501, Washington, DC 20007
Telephone: (202) 293-3306
Background: Assistant U.S. Attorney for the District of Columbia, 1966-67. Member, President's Committee on Mental Retardation, 1976-79. Member and Vice President, Nat'l Center for Law and the Handicapped, 1979-. Special Counsel, U.S. House of Representative Committee on Standards of Official Conduct, 1979-.

BARRETT, Ford
Asst Dir (Regs), Legis & Regul Anal Div, DEPARTMENT OF TREASURY - Comptroller of the Currency
490 L'Enfant Plaza East, S.W., Washington, DC 20219
Telephone: (202) 447-1177

BARRETT, Michael
V. President, Jefferson Group, The
1341 G St., N.W., Suite 1100, Washington, DC 20005
Telephone: (202) 638-3535

BARRETT, MONTGOMERY & MURPHY
1055 Thomas Jefferson St., N.W., Suite 501, Washington, DC 20007
Telephone: (202) 293-3306
Members of firm representing listed organizations:
Barrett, David M.
Background: Assistant U.S. Attorney for the District of Columbia, 1966-67. Member, President's Committee on Mental Retardation, 1976-79. Member and Vice President, Nat'l Center for Law and the Handicapped, 1979-. Special Counsel, U.S. House of Representative Committee on Standards of Official Conduct, 1979-.
Montgomery, John H.
Murphy, Lynda M.
Background: Director, Office of State Agencies and Bond Financed Programs, 1980-82; Attorney Advisor to Assistant Secretary for Housing, FHA Commissioner, Department of Housing and Urban Development, 1979-80.
Clients:
Nat'l Rural Water Ass'n (*John H. Montgomery*)
Oklahoma City, Oklahoma, City of (*John H. Montgomery*)
San Diego, California, City of (*John H. Montgomery*)

BARRETT, Pat
Director, State & Local Gov't Relations, United Way of America
701 N. Fairfax St., Alexandria, VA 22314-2045
Telephone: (703) 836-7100

BARRETT, Thomas S.
Counsel, Public Resource Associates
1815 H St., N.W. Suite 600, Washington, DC 20006
Telephone: (202) 463-7456
Registered as lobbyist at U.S. Congress.

BARRIE, Robert W.
Mgr., Federal Legis. Relations, General Electric Co.
1331 Pennsylvania Ave., N.W., Washington, DC 20004
Telephone: (202) 637-4471
Registered as lobbyist at U.S. Congress.

BARRINGER, David
Director, Communications, Goodwill Industries of America, Inc.
9200 Wisconsin Ave., Bethesda, MD 20814-3896
Telephone: (301) 530-6500

BARRINGER, Steven G.
Holland and Hart
1001 Pennsylvania Suite 310, Washington, DC 20004
Telephone: (202) 638-5500
Registered as lobbyist at U.S. Congress.
Clients:
    Resource Conservation and Recovery Act Mine
        Waste Group

BARRINGER, William H.
Willkie Farr and Gallagher
1155 21st St., N.W., 6th Fl., Washington, DC 20036-3302
Telephone: (202) 328-8000
Registered as lobbyist at U.S. Congress.
Registered as Foreign Agent: (#3765).
Clients:
    ASEAN Federation of Textile Industries
    Associacao das Industrias de Calcados do Rio
        Grande do Sul
    Brazilian Iron and Steel Institute
    Fuji Heavy Industries Ltd.
    Instituto Brasileira de Siderugia
    Japan Iron and Steel Exporters Ass'n
    Japan Machinery Exporters Ass'n
    Nippon Kokan K.K.
    Siderbras
    Sucocitrico Cutrale
    Yamaha Corp. of America
    Yamaha Motor Corp. U.S.A.

BARRON, B. A.
Mgr., Fin. Anal. & Regulatory Opns., General Electric Co.
1331 Pennsylvania Ave., N.W. Suite 800S, Washington, DC 20004
Telephone: (202) 637-4000

BARRON, Kevin
Research and Demographic Analyst, Targeting Systems, Inc.
2111 Wilson Blvd., Suite 900, Arlington, VA 22201
Telephone: (703) 528-7555

BARRON, Thea Rossi
150 Little Falls St., Falls Church, VA 22046
Telephone: (703) 237-5959
Background: An attorney who provides legislative affairs counseling.

BARROW, Joe L., Jr.
Deputy Director, Communications, Democratic Nat'l Committee
430 South Capitol St., S.E., Washington, DC 20003
Telephone: (202) 863-8000

BARROW, Robert E.
National Master, Nat'l Grange
1616 H St., N.W., Washington, DC 20006
Telephone: (202) 628-3507
Registered as lobbyist at U.S. Congress.

BARRY, Capt. Kevin
Legislation Div., Office of Chief Counsel, DEPARTMENT OF TRANSPORTATION - United States Coast Guard
400 Seventh St., S.W., Washington, DC 20590
Telephone: (202) 366-4280

BARRY, Mark P.
Media Liaison, Internat'l Security Council
818 Connecticut Ave., N.W. Suite 600, Washington, DC 20006
Telephone: (202) 828-0802

BARRY, Peter F.
V. President - Washington Operations, Grumman Corp.
1000 Wilson Blvd., Suite 2800, Arlington, VA 22209
Telephone: (703) 875-8400

BARSH, Harry E., Jr.
Camp, Barsh, Bates and Tate
2550 M St., N.W., Suite 275, Washington, DC 20037
Telephone: (202) 887-5160
Registered as lobbyist at U.S. Congress.
Clients:
    ARCO Oil & Gas Co.
    Columbia Communications Corp.
    Columbia Gas System
    Exxon Corp.
    Mobil Corp.
    Natural Gas Supply Ass'n
    Pennzoil Co.
    Texaco U.S.A.
    Union Pacific Resources Co.

BARSHEFSKY, Charlene
Steptoe and Johnson
1330 Connecticut Ave., N.W., Washington, DC 20036
Telephone: (202) 429-3000
Clients:
    British Steel Corp.
    Coalition to Promote America's Trade
    Mitsui and Co.

BART, Dan
Legal, GTE Corp.
Suite 1200, 1850 M St., N.W., Washington, DC 20036
Telephone: (202) 463-5212

BARTH, Roger V.
Resident Counsel, Curtis, Mallet-Prevost, Colt & Mosle
1735 Eye St., N.W., Suite 715, Washington, DC 20006
Telephone: (202) 331-9797
Background: Assistant to the Commissioner, 1969-72, and Deputy Chief Counsel, 1972-73, Internal Revenue Service.

BARTHOLOMEW, Richard J.
Exec. Director, Washington Office, New York State Senate
444 North Capitol St., N.W. Suite 340, Washington, DC 20001
Telephone: (202) 624-5880

BARTLETT, David
President, Radio-Television News Directors Ass'n
1717 K St., N.W. Suite 615, Washington, DC 20006
Telephone: (202) 659-6510
Registered as lobbyist at U.S. Congress.

BARTLETT, Doyle C.
V. Pres & Director, Federal Legis. Srvcs, Conference of State Bank Supervisors
1015 18th St., N.W Suite 1100, Washington, DC 20036
Telephone: (202) 296-2840
Registered as lobbyist at U.S. Congress.
Background: Former Minority Counsel to the House of Representatives Committee on Banking, Finance and Urban Affairs.

BARTLETT, Linda Leigh
Director, Federal Government Affairs, Kraft General Foods, Inc.
1341 G St., N.W., 9th Floor, Washington, DC 20005
Telephone: (202) 637-1540
Registered as lobbyist at U.S. Congress.

BARTLETT, Robert G.
President, Nat'l Stone Ass'n
1415 Elliot Place, N.W., Washington, DC 20007
Telephone: (202) 342-1100
Registered as lobbyist at U.S. Congress.

BARTLEY, James E.
Exec. V. President, Nat'l Industrial Transportation League
1090 Vermont Ave., N.W. Suite 410, Washington, DC 20005-4905

Telephone: (202) 842-3870
Registered as lobbyist at U.S. Congress.

BARTON, Richard A.
Senior V. President, Government Affairs, Direct Marketing Ass'n
1101 17th St., N.W., Suite 900, Washington, DC 20036
Telephone: (202) 347-1222
Registered as lobbyist at U.S. Congress.
Background: Former Staff Director, Subcommittee on Postal Operations and Services, House Post Office and Civil Service Committee. Also serves as Treasurer of the Direct Marketing Political Action Committee.

BARTZ, Philip D.
Morrison & Foerster
2000 Pennsylvania Ave., N.W., Suite 5500, Washington, DC 20006
Telephone: (202) 887-1500
Registered as Foreign Agent: (#4282).
Clients:
    Coca-Cola Co.
    Fujitsu Ltd.

BARWICK, Debra
Research Assistant, Government Affairs, Nat'l Forest Products Ass'n
1250 Connecticut Ave., N.W. Suite 200, Washington, DC 20036
Telephone: (202) 463-2700

BASHIR, Mohammed
Washington Representative, People's Committee for Libyan Students
510 N. Washington St. Suite 400, Falls Church, VA 22045
Telephone: (703) 532-6262

BASILE, Jo-Anne R.
Director, Federal Relations, Cellular Telecommunications Industry Ass'n
1133 21St., N.W., Third Floor, Washington, DC 20036
Telephone: (202) 785-0081
Registered as lobbyist at U.S. Congress.

BASKIN, Maurice
Venable, Baetjer, Howard and Civiletti
1201 New York Ave., N.W., Suite 1000, Washington, DC 20005
Telephone: (202) 962-4800
Clients:
    Associated Builders and Contractors

BASKIN, Peter Jay
Sharretts, Paley, Carter and Blauvelt
1707 L St., N.W., Suite 725, Washington, DC 20036
Telephone: (202) 223-4433
Clients:
    Tandy Corp.

BASKIN, Zemphria R.
Director, Government Affairs, Air Transport Ass'n of America
1709 New York Ave., N.W., Washington, DC 20006
Telephone: (202) 626-4117

BASS, Dr. Gary D.
Exec. Director, OMB Watch
1731 Connecticut Ave., N.W., Washington, DC 20009-1146
Telephone: (202) 234-8494

BASS & HOWES
1601 Connecticut Ave., N.W. Suite 801, Washington, DC 20009
Telephone: (202) 328-2200
Background: A political consulting firm.
Members of firm representing listed organizations:
    Howes, Joanne
Clients:
    Women's Legal Defense Fund *(Joanne Howes)*

BASS, J. Mel
Manager, Government Affairs, Aluminum Co. of America
1615 M St., N.W., Suite 500, Washington, DC 20036
Telephone: (202) 956-5300

BASS, Kenneth C., III
Venable, Baetjer, Howard and Civiletti
1201 New York Ave., N.W., Suite 1000, Washington, DC 20005
Telephone: (202) 962-4800
Background: Former law clerk to Supreme Court Justice Black, 1969-70; legislative assistant to a Member of Congress; Counsel for Intelligence Policy, U.S. Department of Justice, 1979-81.

BASSECHES, Robert T.
Shea and Gardner
1800 Massachusetts Ave., N.W., Washington, DC 20036
Telephone: (202) 828-2000
Clients:
American President Companies

BASSETT, Judith F.
Dep Assoc Admin, Cong Affrs, GENERAL SERVICES ADMINISTRATION
18th and F Sts., N.W., Washington, DC 20405
Telephone: (202) 566-0563

BASSETT, Stephen R.
Sr. V. President, Gov't & Technical Afrs, Aircraft Owners and Pilots Ass'n
421 Aviation Way, Frederick, MD 21701
Telephone: (301) 695-2000
Registered as lobbyist at U.S. Congress.

BASSIN ASSOC., INC., Robert H.
499 South Capitol St., S.W. Suite 407, Washington, DC 20003
Telephone: (202) 863-2611
Background: A Democratic fundraising firm specializing in PAC solicitation, national finance strategies and telemarketing.
Members of firm representing listed organizations:
Baker, Jennifer A., Assistant to the President
Bassin, Robert H., President
Pederson, Steven R., Director, elemarketing

BASSIN, Robert H.
President, Bassin Assoc., Inc., Robert H.
499 South Capitol St., S.W. Suite 407, Washington, DC 20003
Telephone: (202) 863-2611

BASSMAN, MITCHELL & ALFANO, CHARTERED
1750 K St., N.W., Suite 380, Washington, DC 20006
Telephone: (202) 466-6502
Members of firm representing listed organizations:
Alfano, Alphonse M.
Bassman, Robert S.
Mitchell, Douglas B.
Clients:
Arkla, Inc.
British Petroleum Oil Marketers Ass'n
Chevron Petroleum Marketers Ass'n

BASSMAN, Robert S.
Bassman, Mitchell & Alfano, Chartered
1750 K St., N.W., Suite 380, Washington, DC 20006
Telephone: (202) 466-6502

BATCHELDER, Robert W.
Chief Cnsl/Dep Exec V. Pres, Govtal Affr, American Public Transit Ass'n
1201 New York Ave., N.W.,, Washington, DC 20005
Telephone: (202) 898-4000

BATEMAN, Diane
Assistant V. President, Gov't Relations, Fertilizer Institute
501 Second St., N.E., Washington, DC 20002
Telephone: (202) 675-8250
Registered as lobbyist at U.S. Congress.

BATES, Bradford L.
Transportation Counsel, Kimberly-Clark Corp.
1201 Pennsylvania Ave., N.W. Suite 730, Washington, DC 20004
Telephone: (202) 393-8280

BATES, Carl E.
Camp, Barsh, Bates and Tate
2550 M St., N.W., Suite 275, Washington, DC 20037
Telephone: (202) 887-5160
Registered as lobbyist at U.S. Congress.
Background: Legislation Attorney, Joint Committee on Taxation, U.S. Congress, 1975-80.

Clients:
PPG Industries

BATES, Christopher M.
Director, Policy Analysis, Motor and Equipment Manufacturers Ass'n
1325 Pennsylvania Ave., N.W. Suite 600, Washington, DC 20004
Telephone: (202) 393-6362
Registered as lobbyist at U.S. Congress.

BATES, Douglas P.
Director, Tax Analysis, American Council of Life Insurance
1001 Pennsylvania Ave., N.W., Washington, DC 20004-2599
Telephone: (202) 624-2107
Registered as lobbyist at U.S. Congress.

BATES, John C., Jr.
Reid & Priest
1111 19th St., N.W., Washington, DC 20036
Telephone: (202) 828-0100
Background: Special Assistant for Tax Policy, Treasury Department, 1973-76.

BATES, Michael J.
V. President, Timmons and Co., Inc.
1850 K St., N.W., Suite 850, Washington, DC 20006
Telephone: (202) 331-1760

BATES, Richard
Exec. Director, Democratic Congressional Campaign Committee
430 South Capitol St., S.E. 2nd Floor, Washington, DC 20003
Telephone: (202) 863-1500

BATES, Robert E., Jr.
Mgr., Gov't Relats., US Mktg. & Refg., Mobil Corp.
1100 Connecticut Ave., N.W., Suite 620, Washington, DC 20036
Telephone: (202) 862-1329
Registered as lobbyist at U.S. Congress.
Background: Legislative Assistant to Senator Edward M. Kennedy, 1969-1977.

BATES, Terri
Washington Representative, Nat'l Ass'n of State Foresters
444 North Capitol St., N.W., Washington, DC 20001
Telephone: (202) 624-5415

BATKY, Catharine R.
Director, Legislative Affairs, Burlington Northern Railroad
50 F St., N.W., Suite 1080, Washington, DC 20001
Telephone: (202) 383-4980
Registered as lobbyist at U.S. Congress.

BATLOUNI, Barbara Shahin
Exec. Director, American-Arab Anti-Discrimination Committee
4201 Connecticut Ave., N.W. Suite 500, Washington, DC 20009
Telephone: (202) 244-2990

BATSON, Arthur E., Jr.
President, Industrial Union of Marine and Shipbuilding Workers of America
5101 River Road, Suite 110, Bethesda, MD 20816
Telephone: (301) 951-4266

BATTAGLIA, Erica M.
Director, State Relations, Nat'l Ass'n for Home Care
519 C St., N.E., Washington, DC 20002
Telephone: (202) 547-7424
Registered as lobbyist at U.S. Congress.

BATTAGLIA, Richard D.
Associate Exec. Director, Special Libraries Ass'n
1700 18th St., N.W., Washington, DC 20009
Telephone: (202) 234-4700

BATTAGLIA, Thomas
Interlocke Associates
117 C St., S.E., Washington, DC 20003
Telephone: (202) 546-7973
Registered as Foreign Agent: (#3954).

BATTAGLINI, A. Robin
Dir., DOD and Congressional Liaison, ITT Defense, Inc.
1000 Wilson Blvd. Suite 3000, Arlington, VA 22209

Telephone: (703) 276-8300

BATTISTA, Anthony R.
ARB Consultants
1309 Duke St., Alexandria, VA 22314
Telephone: (703) 836-0283
Registered as lobbyist at U.S. Congress.
Clients:
ITT Defense, Inc.

BATTISTELLI, Ellen S.
Legislative Representative, Planned Parenthood Federation of America
2010 Massachusetts Ave., N.W. Fifth Floor, Washington, DC 20036
Telephone: (202) 785-3351
Registered as lobbyist at U.S. Congress.

BATTLE, Karen
Legis. Director, Community Development, Nat'l Ass'n of Counties
440 First St., N.W., Washington, DC 20001
Telephone: (202) 393-6226

BATTLE, Lucius D.
President, Middle East Institute
1761 N St., N.W., Washington, DC 20036
Telephone: (202) 785-1141
Background: Former U.S. Ambassador to Egypt and Assistant Secretary of State for Near Eastern and South Asian Affairs.

BATTLE, Mark
Exec. Director, Nat'l Ass'n of Social Workers
7981 Eastern Ave., Silver Spring, MD 20910
Telephone: (301) 565-0333

BATTS, Lana R.
Sr. V. President, Government Affairs, American Trucking Ass'ns
2200 Mill Road, Alexandria, VA 22314
Telephone: (703) 838-1787

BAUDHUIN, Michael D.
Corporate V. President, AT&T
Suite 1000, 1120 20th St., N.W., Washington, DC 20036
Telephone: (202) 457-3850

BAUER, Gary L.
President, Family Research Council, Inc.
601 Pennsylvania Ave., N.W., Suite 901, Washington, DC 20004
Telephone: (202) 393-2100
Registered as lobbyist at U.S. Congress.
Background: Former Assistant to the President, Policy Development, The White House, under President Reagan.

BAUER, John
Legis Officer, Cong & Intergovt'l Affrs, DEPARTMENT OF LABOR
200 Constitution Ave., N.W., Washington, DC 20210
Telephone: (202) 523-6141

BAUER, John L., Jr.
Manager, Legislative Affairs, Armco Inc.
1667 K St., N.W., Suite 650, Washington, DC 20006
Telephone: (202) 223-5370
Registered as lobbyist at U.S. Congress.

BAUER, Robert F.
Perkins Coie
1110 Vermont Ave., N.W., Suite 1200, Washington, DC 20005
Telephone: (202) 887-9030
Registered as Foreign Agent: (#3753).
Clients:
Democrats for the 90s

BAUGHMAN, Laura M.
C & M Internat'l L.P.
1001 Pennsylvania Ave., N.W., Washington, DC 20004-2505
Telephone: (202) 624-2895
Registered as Foreign Agent: (#3988).

BAUM, Mark W.
Senior V. President, Nat'l Food Brokers Ass'n
1010 Massachusetts Ave., N.W., Washington, DC 20001
Telephone: (202) 789-2844

BAUMAN, Barbara
Washington Representative, Detroit Edison Co.
1990 M St., N.W., Suite 480, Washington, DC 20036
Telephone: (202) 466-5495
Registered as lobbyist at U.S. Congress.

BAUMAN, Barry H.
Exec. Director, Lawyers for Civil Justice
1225 19th St., N.W. Suite 470, Washington, DC 20036
Telephone: (202) 479-0045
Registered as lobbyist at U.S. Congress.

BAUMANN, Henry L.
Exec. V. President and General Counsel, Nat'l Ass'n of
Broadcasters
1771 N St., N.W., Washington, DC 20036
Telephone: (202) 429-5300

BAUMBUSCH, Peter L.
Gibson, Dunn and Crutcher
1050 Connecticut Ave., N.W. Suite 900, Washington, DC
20036-5303
Telephone: (202) 955-8500
Registered as lobbyist at U.S. Congress.
Background: Serves as Treasurer, Fair Tax Foundation.
Clients:
    Dollar Drydock Savings Bank
    Teamwork America

BAUSER, Michael A.
Newman & Holtzinger, P.C.
1615 L St., N.W., 10th Floor, Washington, DC 20005
Telephone: (202) 955-6600
Clients:
    Utility Nuclear Waste Transportation Program

BAWDEN, Lee
Director, Human Resouces Policy Center, Urban Institute,
The
2100 M St., N.W., Washington, DC 20037
Telephone: (202) 833-7200

BAXTER, Allin P.
Elias, Matz, Tiernan and Herrick
734 15th St., N.W. 12th Fl., Washington, DC 20005
Telephone: (202) 347-0300
Background: Attorney, Securities and Exchange Commis-
sion, 1957-61.
Clients:
    Enterprise Bank

BAXTER, Thomas A.
Shaw, Pittman, Potts and Trowbridge
2300 N St., N.W., Washington, DC 20037
Telephone: (202) 663-8000
Background: Special Assistant for Litigation, Price Com-
mission and Cost of Living Council, 1972-73.
Clients:
    Carolina Power and Light Co.
    Union Electric Co.

BAYEA, Jan
Senior Staff Scientist, Nat'l Audubon Soc.
801 Pennsylvania Ave., S.E., Washington, DC 20003
Telephone: (202) 547-9009

BAYER, Patricia
Exec. Director, American School Food Service Ass'n
1600 Duke St., 7th Floor, Alexandria, VA 22314
Telephone: (703) 739-3900

BAYH, Birch, Jr.
Rivkin, Radler, Dunne and Bayh
1575 Eye St., N.W. Suite 1025, Washington, DC 20005
Telephone: (202) 289-8660
Background: Former Senator, (D-IN), 1963-81.
Clients:
    Nat'l Basketball Ass'n
    Nat'l Foreign Trade Council, Inc.
    Seagram & Sons, Inc., Joseph E.

BAYLESS & BOLAND, INC.
1072 Thomas Jefferson St., N.W., Washington, DC 20007
Telephone: (202) 342-0040
Members of firm representing listed organizations:
    Bayless, James L. (Jr.), President
        Background: Legislative Counsel to Senator John Tow-
        er (R-TX), 1978-81. Associate Director, White House
        Office of Presidential Personnel, 1981-82. Deputy
        Assistant Secretary for Congressional Affairs, Depart-

ment of Commerce, 1982-83.
    Boland, Michael J. P.
        Background: Chief Counsel and Floor Assistant to Rep.
        Trent Lott (R-MS), 1985-87. Senior Counsel, House
        Energy and Commerce Committee, 1978-84.
    Semerad, Samantha
Clients:
    Chevron, U.S.A. *(James L. Bayless, Jr., Michael J. P. Bo-*
        land)
    Pacific Toxicology Laboratories *(James L. Bayless, Jr.,*
        Michael J. P. Boland)
    Psychemedics Corp. *(James L. Bayless, Jr., Michael J. P.*
        Boland)
    Southwestern Bell Corp. *(James L. Bayless, Jr., Michael*
        J. P. Boland)
    Space Services Inc. *(James L. Bayless, Jr., Michael J. P.*
        Boland)

BAYLESS, James L., Jr.
President, Bayless & Boland, Inc.
1072 Thomas Jefferson St., N.W, Washington, DC 20007
Telephone: (202) 342-0040
Registered as lobbyist at U.S. Congress.
Background: Legislative Counsel to Senator John Tower
(R-TX), 1978-81. Associate Director, White House Office
of Presidential Personnel, 1981-82. Deputy Assistant
Secretary for Congressional Affairs, Department of Com-
merce, 1982-83.
Clients:
    Chevron, U.S.A.
    Pacific Toxicology Laboratories
    Psychemedics Corp.
    Southwestern Bell Corp.
    Space Services Inc.

BEA, Paul H., Jr.
Washington Representative, Director, Port Authority of
New York and New Jersey
1001 Connecticut Ave., N.W. Suite 610, Washington, DC
20036
Telephone: (202) 887-5240

BEACH, Bert B.
Director of Public Affairs, General Conference of Seventh-day Adventists
12501 Old Columbia Pike, Silver Spring, MD 20904
Telephone: (301) 680-6320

BEACH, Kristina M.
Manager, Congressional Relations, General Electric Co.
1331 Pennsylvania Ave., N.W., Washington, DC 20004
Telephone: (202) 637-4179
Registered as lobbyist at U.S. Congress.

BEACH, Richard
V. President, Governmental Affairs, Credit Union Nat'l
Ass'n
805 15th St., N.W. Suite 300, Washington, DC 20005
Telephone: (202) 682-4200
Registered as lobbyist at U.S. Congress.

BEAL, Dennis
Assistant to the President for Commo., AFL-CIO (American Federation of Labor and Congress of Industrial Organizations)
815 16th St., N.W., Washington, DC 20006
Telephone: (202) 637-5075

BEALL, James A.
Partner, Ball, Janik and Novack
1101 Pennsylvania Ave., N.W. Suite 1035, Washington,
DC 20004
Telephone: (202) 638-3307
Registered as lobbyist at U.S. Congress.
Background: Attorney-Advisor, U.S. Department of Interi-
or, 1976-77. Legislative Director, Office of Rep. Al Ull-
man (D-OR), 1977-78; Staff Coordinator, House Commit-
tee on Ways and Means, 1978-81.
Clients:
    Clackamas County, Oregon
    Fujitsu Microelectronics, Inc.
    Greenbrier Leasing Corp.
    Northwest Industrial Gas Users
    Northwest Marine Iron Works
    Riedel Environmental Services
    Tillamook Bay, Oregon, Port of

BEALL, Robert J.
Exec. V. President, Medical Affairs, Cystic Fibrosis Foundation
6931 Arlington Road Suite 200, Bethesda, MD 20814
Telephone: (301) 951-4422

BEAM, Bruce A.
V. President, Governmental Affairs, American Electric
Power Service Corp.
1667 K St., N.W. Suite 450, Washington, DC 20006
Telephone: (202) 659-0454
Registered as lobbyist at U.S. Congress.

BEAM, Kenneth
Deputy Exec. V. President, Soc. of American Foresters
5400 Grosvenor Lane, Bethesda, MD 20814
Telephone: (301) 897-8720

BEAM, Meg
Asst. Account Exec., Gov't Relations, Ketchum Public Relations
1201 Connecticut Ave., N.W. Suite 300, Washington, DC
20036
Telephone: (202) 835-8800

BEAN, Frank D.
Director, Population Studies Center, Urban Institute, The
2100 M St., N.W., Washington, DC 20037
Telephone: (202) 833-7200

BEAN, Michael
Director, Wildlife Program, Environmental Defense Fund
1616 P St., N.W., Suite 150, Washington, DC 20036
Telephone: (202) 387-3500

BEANG, Nancy
Exec. Director, Soc. for Neuroscience
11 Dupont Circle, N.W., Suite 500, Washington, DC 20036
Telephone: (202) 462-6688

BEARD, James E.
Dir., Nuclear Weapons Production Project, Friends of the
Earth
218 D St., S.E., Washington, DC 20003
Telephone: (202) 544-2600
Registered as lobbyist at U.S. Congress.

BEARD, Jeffrey L.
Manager, Regulatory Affairs, American Soc. of Civil Engineers
1015 15th St., N.W. Suite 600, Washington, DC 20005
Telephone: (202) 789-2200

BEARD, John G.
Legal Specialist, American Federation of Home Health
Agencies Political Action Committee
1320 Fenwick Lane, Suite 500, Silver Spring, MD 20910
Telephone: (301) 588-1454

BEARD, Jon
Cong Liaison Officer, UNITED STATES INFORMATION
AGENCY
301 4th St., S.W., Washington, DC 20547
Telephone: (202) 485-8828

BEARD, Michael K.
President & CEO, Nat'l Coalition to Ban Handguns
100 Maryland Ave., N.E., Washington, DC 20002
Telephone: (202) 544-7190
Registered as lobbyist at U.S. Congress.

BEARN, Gaston de
Assistant Director, Government Affairs, Hoffmann-La
Roche Inc.
1050 Connecticut Ave., N.W. Suite 401, Washington, DC
20036
Telephone: (202) 223-1975
Registered as lobbyist at U.S. Congress.

BEATTY, Hubert
Exec. V. President, Associated General Contractors of
America
1957 E St., N.W., Washington, DC 20006
Telephone: (202) 393-2040

BEAUCHAMP, Martha
Health & Environmental Affairs Director, American Petroleum Institute
1220 L St., N.W., Washington, DC 20005
Telephone: (202) 682-8470

BEAUCHEMIN, Tim
Legislative Director, American Legislative Exchange Council
214 Massachusetts Ave., N.W., Washington, DC 20002
Telephone: (202) 547-4646

BEAUMONT, Dina
Exec. Assistant to the President, Communications Workers of America
1925 K St., N.W., Washington, DC 20006
Telephone: (202) 728-2300

BEAUMONT, Enid
Director, Academy for State and Local Government
444 North Capitol St., N.W., Suite 349, Washington, DC 20001
Telephone: (202) 638-1445

BEAUMONT, Guy D.
Exec. Director, American College of Osteopathic Surgeons
123 North Henry St., Alexandria, VA 22314
Telephone: (703) 684-0416

BEAUREGARD, Gilles
Secretary-Treasurer, Office and Professional Employees Internat'l Union
815 16th St., N.W., Suite 606, Washington, DC 20006
Telephone: (202) 393-4464
Background: Also serves as Treasurer, Voice of the Electorate.

BEAUREGARD, Robert L.
V. President, Regulatory Affairs, Interstate Natural Gas Ass'n of America
555 13th St., N.W. Suite 300 West, Washington, DC 20004
Telephone: (202) 626-3200

BECHTEL AND COLE
2101 L St., N.W., Suite 502, Washington, DC 20037
Telephone: (202) 833-4190
Members of firm representing listed organizations:
  Cole, Harry F.
Clients:
  Shurberg Broadcasting of Hartford Inc. *(Harry F. Cole)*

BECHTOLD, Terry L.
Assistant Director, Ruff Political Action Committee
501 Capitol Court, N.E. Suite 100, Washington, DC 20002
Telephone: (202) 546-0023

BECK, Edward A., III
Washington Representative, American Petroleum Institute
1220 L St., N.W., Washington, DC 20005
Telephone: (202) 682-8418
Registered as lobbyist at U.S. Congress.

BECK, Robert
Director, Environmental Programs, Edison Electric Institute
1111 19th St., N.W., Washington, DC 20036
Telephone: (202) 778-6400

BECK, Robert E.
Director, Government Relations, Nat'l Ass'n of Plumbing-Heating-Cooling Contractors
180 South Washington St. Box 6808, Falls Church, VA 22046
Telephone: (703) 237-8100
Registered as lobbyist at U.S. Congress.

BECKEL, Robert G.
FMR Group Inc., The
1000 Potomac St., N.W. Suite 401, Washington, DC 20007
Telephone: (202) 333-2533
Registered as Foreign Agent: (#4213).

BECKER, Brenda Larsen
Director, CarePAC, The Blue Cross and Blue Shield Ass'n Political Action Committee
655 15th St., N.W. Suite 350, Washington, DC 20005
Telephone: (202) 626-4780

BECKER, Craig
Kirschner, Weinberg & Dempsey
1615 L St., N.W., Suite 1360, Washington, DC 20036
Telephone: (202) 775-5900
Clients:

American Federation of State, County and Municipal Employees

BECKER, Daniel F.
Wash. Dir., Global Warming & Energy Prog, Sierra Club
408 C St., N.E., Washington, DC 20002
Telephone: (202) 547-1141
Registered as lobbyist at U.S. Congress.

BECKER, Lee
Legislative Representative, American Bakers Ass'n
1111 14th St., N.W., Suite 300, Washington, DC 20005
Telephone: (202) 296-5800
Registered as lobbyist at U.S. Congress.

BECKER, Michael
Director, Research, Citizens for a Sound Economy
470 L'Enfant Plaza East, S.W. Suite 7112, Washington, DC 20024
Telephone: (202) 488-8200

BECKER, Robert H.
Kleinfeld, Kaplan and Becker
1140 19th St., N.W., Suite 700, Washington, DC 20036
Telephone: (202) 223-5120
Background: Trial Attorney, Food and Drug Division, Office of General Counsel, Department of Health, Education and Welfare, 1956-61.
Clients:
  Carter-Wallace, Inc.
  Cord Laboratories
  SmithKline Animal Health Products
  Squibb and Sons, Inc., E. R.

BECKER, S. William
Exec. Director, State and Territorial Air Pollution Program Administrators
444 North Capitol St., N.W. Suite 306, Washington, DC 20001
Telephone: (202) 624-7864
Background: Also represents the Ass'n of Local Air Pollution Control Officials.

BECKERMAN ASSOCIATES
1990 M St., N.W., Suite 400, Washington, DC 20036
Telephone: (202) 775-9022
Members of firm representing listed organizations:
  Beckerman, George
Clients:
  Donnelley & Sons, R. R. *(George Beckerman)*
  Dun & Bradstreet *(George Beckerman)*

BECKERMAN, George
Beckerman Associates
1990 M St., N.W., Suite 400, Washington, DC 20036
Telephone: (202) 775-9022
Clients:
  Donnelley & Sons, R. R.
  Dun & Bradstreet

BECKHARDT, Stacey
Government Liaison, Consortium of Social Science Ass'ns
1522 K St., N.W., Suite 836, Washington, DC 20005
Telephone: (202) 842-3525
Registered as lobbyist at U.S. Congress.

BECKINGTON, Jeffrey S.
Collier, Shannon & Scott
1055 Thomas Jefferson St., N.W., Suite 300, Washington, DC 20007
Telephone: (202) 342-8400
Clients:
  Chase Brass and Copper
  Hussey Copper Ltd.
  Miller Co.

BECKMAN, Steve
International Economist, United Automobile, Aerospace and Agricultural Implement Workers of America (UAW)
1757 N St., N.W., Washington, DC 20036
Telephone: (202) 828-8500
Registered as lobbyist at U.S. Congress.

BECKWITH ASSOCIATES, W. C.
205 Pennsylvania Ave., S.E. Suite 3, Washington, DC 20003
Telephone: (202) 671-4528
Background: A consulting firm with specialties in government affairs, marketing and management. Also provides general services of representation.

Members of firm representing listed organizations:
  Beckwith, Walter C. (IV)

BECKWITH, Elizabeth W.
Director, Gov't Relations, American Osteopathic Ass'n
300 5th St., N.E., Washington, DC 20002
Telephone: (202) 544-5060
Registered as lobbyist at U.S. Congress.

BECKWITH, Walter C., IV
Beckwith Associates, W. C.
205 Pennsylvania Ave., S.E. Suite 3, Washington, DC 20003
Telephone: (202) 671-4528

BECRAFT, Wayne E.
Exec. Director, American Ass'n of Collegiate Registrars and Admissions Officers
One Dupont Circle, N.W., Suite 330, Washington, DC 20036
Telephone: (202) 293-9161

BEDARD, Robert
Treasurer, Art PAC
707 8th St., S.E., Suite 200, Washington, DC 20003
Telephone: (202) 546-1821

BEDDOW, William W.
Governmental Affairs, Washington Manager, Caterpillar Inc.
1730 Pennsylvania Ave., N.W., Suite 750, Washington, DC 20006
Telephone: (202) 879-3050
Registered as lobbyist at U.S. Congress.

BEDLIN, Howard
Legislative Representative, American Ass'n of Retired Persons
1909 K St., N.W., Washington, DC 20049
Telephone: (202) 728-4612
Registered as lobbyist at U.S. Congress.

BEDNASH, Geraldine Polly
Exec. Director, American Ass'n of Colleges of Nursing
One Dupont Circle, N.W., Suite 530, Washington, DC 20036
Telephone: (202) 463-6930

BEEDON, Laurel
Senior Analyst, American Ass'n of Retired Persons
1909 K St., N.W., Washington, DC 20049
Telephone: (202) 872-4700

BEEMAN, Carole L.
Secretary and Director of Research, Ass'n of Oil Pipe Lines
1725 K St., N.W., Washington, DC 20006
Telephone: (202) 331-8228

BEEMAN, Josiah
15 Second St., N.E., Washington, DC 20002
Telephone: (202) 544-1285
Registered as lobbyist at U.S. Congress.
Organizations represented:
  California State Controller

BEEMAN, William J.
V. Pres. and Dir., Macroeconomic Studies, Committee for Economic Development
1700 K St., N.W., Suite 700, Washington, DC 20006
Telephone: (202) 296-5860
Background: Chief, National Income Section, Federal Reserve Board, 1975-78. Assistant Director, Fiscal Analysis, Congressional Budget Office, 1978-87.

BEERS, Robert M.
Congressional Liaison Officer, American Foreign Service Ass'n
2101 E St., N.W., Washington, DC 20037
Telephone: (202) 338-4045
Registered as lobbyist at U.S. Congress.

BEHAN, William
Director, Government Relations, Magnavox Government and Industrial Electronics Co.
1700 North Moore St. Suite 820, Arlington, VA 22209
Telephone: (703) 522-9610
Registered as lobbyist at U.S. Congress.

BEHRENS, Edwin L.
Assoc Dir, Tech Afrs & Nat'l Gov't Rtns, Procter and Gamble Mfg. Co.
Suite 400, 801 18th St., N.W., Washington, DC 20006
Telephone: (202) 833-9506
Registered as lobbyist at U.S. Congress.

BEIER, David
V. President, Government Affairs, Genentech, Inc.
1747 Pennsylvania Ave., N.W. Suite 1223, Washington, DC 20006
Telephone: (202) 296-7272
Registered as lobbyist at U.S. Congress.
Background: Former counsel to the House Judiciary Subcommittee on Courts, Civil Liberties and the Administration of Justice.

BEIGHTOL, David
Director, Washington Office, Wisconsin, State of
444 N. Capitol St., N.W. Suite 345, Washington, DC 20001
Telephone: (202) 624-5870

BEIRNE, Kenneth J.
Division V. Pres., Government Relations, Nat'l Ass'n of REALTORS
777 14th St., N.W., Washington, DC 20005
Telephone: (202) 383-1000
Registered as lobbyist at U.S. Congress.

BEIZER, James
Director of Communications, American Mining Congress
Suite 300, 1920 N St., N.W., Washington, DC 20036
Telephone: (202) 861-2891
Registered as lobbyist at U.S. Congress.

BELAIR, Robert R.
Kirkpatrick & Lockhart
1800 M St., N.W., Suite 900 South Lobby, Washington, DC 20036-5891
Telephone: (202) 778-9000
Registered as lobbyist at U.S. Congress.
Background: Attorney, Federal Trade Commission, 1973-75. Acting General Counsel, Committee on Privacy, Office of the President, 1975-76.
Clients:
Law Related Education
Nat'l Institute for Citizen Education in the Law Search Group, Inc.

BELAS, Richard S.
Partner, Dow, Lohnes and Albertson
1255 23rd St., N.W., Suite 500, Washington, DC 20037
Telephone: (202) 857-2500
Registered as lobbyist at U.S. Congress.
Clients:
American Integrity Insurance Co.
Fireman's Fund Insurance Cos.
First Boston Corp.
General Aviation Manufacturers Ass'n
Morgan Guaranty Trust Co.
Nat'l Business Aircraft Ass'n

BELDEN, Nancy
Belden and Russonello
1436 U St., N.W., Suite 204, Washington, DC 20009
Telephone: (202) 265-6887
Clients:
Independent Education Fund

BELDEN AND RUSSONELLO
1436 U St., N.W., Suite 204, Washington, DC 20009
Telephone: (202) 265-6887
Background: A survey research and communications consulting firm.
Members of firm representing listed organizations:
Belden, Nancy
Clients:
Independent Education Fund *(Nancy Belden)*

BELEW, Joe
President, Consumer Bankers Ass'n
1000 Wilson Blvd., 30th Floor, Arlington, VA 22209-3908
Telephone: (703) 276-1750
Registered as lobbyist at U.S. Congress.
Background: Former Executive Assistant to U.S. Rep. Doug Barnhard (D-GA).

BELL, BOYD & LLOYD
1615 L St., N.W. Suite 1200, Washington, DC 20036
Telephone: (202) 466-6300
Clients:
Deere & Co.

BELL, Denise
Legis. Director, Congressional Affairs, Nat'l Ass'n of REALTORS
777 14th St., N.W., Washington, DC 20005
Telephone: (202) 383-1000
Registered as lobbyist at U.S. Congress.

BELL, Howard Hughes
President, American Advertising Federation
1400 K St., N.W., Suite 1000, Washington, DC 20005
Telephone: (202) 898-0089
Registered as lobbyist at U.S. Congress.

BELL, Joseph C.
Hogan and Hartson
555 13th St., N.W., Suite 1200, Washington, DC 20004-1109
Telephone: (202) 637-5600
Registered as lobbyist at U.S. Congress.
Background: Assistant General Counsel, Federal Energy Administration, 1974-77.
Clients:
Poland, Ministry of Finance of

BELL, Peter
Exec. Director, Nat'l Housing Rehabilitation Ass'n
1726 18th St., N.W., Washington, DC 20009
Telephone: (202) 328-9171

BELL, R. Steve
President, Nat'l Air Traffic Controller Ass'n
444 N. Capitol St., Suite 845, Washington, DC 20001
Telephone: (202) 347-4572
Registered as lobbyist at U.S. Congress.
Background: Also represents the Nat'l Air Traffic Controllers Ass'n PAC.

BELL, Richard C.
V. President, Research Studies, Podesta Associates
424 C St., N.E., Washington, DC 20002
Telephone: (202) 544-6906

BELL, Sharon
Chairman, Nat'l Ass'n of Air Traffic Specialists
4740 Corridor Place, Suite c, Beltsville, MD 20705
Telephone: (301) 595-2012

BELL, Sharon Dworkin
Treasurer, Nat'l Housing Rehabilitation Ass'n Political Action Committee
1726 18th St., N.W., Washington, DC 20009
Telephone: (202) 328-9171

BELL, Stephen E.
Managing Director, Salomon Brothers Inc.
1455 Pennsylvania Ave., N.W. Suite 350, Washington, DC 20005
Telephone: (202) 879-4100
Registered as lobbyist at U.S. Congress.
Background: Former Staff Director, U.S. Senate Committee on the Budget.

BELL, Thomas D., Jr.
Vice Chairman, Burson-Marsteller
1850 M St., N.W., Suite 900, Washington, DC 20036
Telephone: (202) 833-8550

BELL, William C.
Research Associate, Mitsui and Co. (U.S.A.), Inc.
1701 Pennsylvania Ave., N.W., Suite 400, Washington, DC 20006
Telephone: (202) 861-0660

BELLER, Herbert N.
Bryan, Cave, McPheeters and McRoberts
1015 15th St., N.W., Suite 1000, Washington, DC 20005
Telephone: (202) 289-6100
Registered as lobbyist at U.S. Congress.

BELLISSIMO, Toni A.
Federal Government Relations Manager, Household Internat'l
1000 Connecticut Ave., N.W., Suite 507, Washington, DC 20036

Telephone: (202) 466-3561
Registered as lobbyist at U.S. Congress.

BELLO, Judith
Sidley and Austin
1722 Eye St., N.W. Sixth Floor, Washington, DC 20006
Telephone: (202) 429-4000
Background: Former General Counsel. Office of the U.S. Trade Representative.
Clients:
North West Timber Ass'n
Tootsie Roll Industries

BELMAN, Murray J.
Thompson and Mitchell
1120 Vermont Ave., N.W. Suite 1000, Washington, DC 20005
Telephone: (202) 857-0350
Registered as lobbyist at U.S. Congress.
Background: Deputy Legal Advisor, U.S. Department of State, 1967-69.
Clients:
Cold Finished Steel Bar Institute

BELMAR, Warren
Fulbright & Jaworski
1150 Connecticut Ave., N.W., Suite 400, Washington, DC 20036
Telephone: (202) 452-6800
Background: Law Clerk, U.S. Court of Appeals for District of Columbia Circuit, 1966-67. Attorney, Office of Legal Counsel, U.S. Department of Justice, 1967-69.
Clients:
Avis Rent A Car Systems, Inc.
Crysen Corp.
Federal Home Loan Bank of Dallas

BELOUS, Richard S.
V. President, Internat'l Affairs, Nat'l Planning Ass'n
1424 16th St., N.W. Suite 700, Washington, DC 20036
Telephone: (202) 265-7685

BELT, Terre H.
Exec. Dir., Hazardous Waste Act Coalit., American Consulting Engineers Council
1015 15th St., N.W., Suite 802, Washington, DC 20005
Telephone: (202) 347-7474
Registered as lobbyist at U.S. Congress.

BELTZ, William A.
President and Editor-in-Chief, Bureau of Nat'l Affairs, Inc., The
1231 25th St., N.W., Washington, DC 20037
Telephone: (202) 452-4200

BENCH, Robert R.
Principal, Financial Svcs. Indus. Pract., Price Waterhouse
1801 K St., N.W., Suite 700, Washington, DC 20006
Telephone: (202) 296-0800
Background: Formerly, Deputy Comptroller of the Currency.

BENCHMARKS, INC.
3248 Prospect St., N.W., Washington, DC 20007
Telephone: (202) 965-3983
Background: A consulting firm.
Members of firm representing listed organizations:
Scanlon, Thomas J.
Clients:
Chicago Ass'n of Commerce and Industry *(Thomas J. Scanlon)*

BENDER, David R.
Exec. Director, Special Libraries Ass'n
1700 18th St., N.W., Washington, DC 20009
Telephone: (202) 234-4700

BENDIXEN AND SCHROTH
1029 Vermont Ave., N.W., Suite 505, Washington, DC 20005
Telephone: (202) 628-4245
Background: A political consulting firm.
Members of firm representing listed organizations:
Bendixen, Sergio
Law, John
Schroth, Robert D., V. President

BENDIXEN, Sergio
Bendixen and Schroth
1029 Vermont Ave., N.W., Suite 505, Washington, DC 20005
Telephone: (202) 628-4245
Registered as lobbyist at U.S. Congress.

BENEDICK, Richard E.
Senior Fellow, Conservation Foundation
1250 24th St., N.W., Washington, DC 20037
Telephone: (202) 293-4800

BENEDICT, Mitchell P.
Neill and Co.
815 Connecticut Ave., N.W. Suite 800, Washington, DC 20006
Telephone: (202) 463-8877
Registered as lobbyist at U.S. Congress.
Registered as Foreign Agent: (#3320).
Background: U.S. Peace Corps, Belize, 1981-83. Recruiter, U.S. Peace Corps, New York, 1984-85. Intern, U.S. Embassy, Harare, Zimbabwe, 1987.

BENFIELD, James C.
Bracy Williams & Co.
1000 Connecticut Ave., N.W., Suite 304, Washington, DC 20036
Telephone: (202) 659-4805
Registered as lobbyist at U.S. Congress.
Clients:
Coin Coalition, The
Committee for Environmentally Effective Packaging
Rocky Co., The

BENJAMIN, Ben E.
O'Melveny and Myers
555 13th St., N.W., Suite 500 West, Washington, DC 20004
Telephone: (202) 383-5300
Registered as lobbyist at U.S. Congress.
Clients:
O'Melveny and Myers Political Action Committee

BENJAMIN, Ernst
General Secretary, American Ass'n of University Professors
1012 14th St., N.W., Suite 500, Washington, DC 20005
Telephone: (202) 737-5900

BENJAMIN, Maynard H.
Exec. V. President, Envelope Manufacturers Ass'n
1600 Duke St., Suite 440, Alexandria, VA 22314-3421
Telephone: (703) 739-2200

BENJAMIN, Michael L.
Legis. Rep., Human Services in Education, Nat'l Ass'n of Counties
440 First St., N.W., Washington, DC 20001
Telephone: (202) 393-6226

BENNA, Robert H.
Wright and Talisman
1050 17th St., N.W. Suite 600, Washington, DC 20036
Telephone: (202) 331-1194

BENNER, Mike
Special Ass't to the President, American Postal Workers Union
1300 L St., N.W., Washington, DC 20005
Telephone: (202) 842-4200
Registered as lobbyist at U.S. Congress.

BENNET, Daniel J.
Exec. V. President, Associated Builders and Contractors
729 15th St., N.W., Washington, DC 20005
Telephone: (202) 637-8800
Registered as lobbyist at U.S. Congress.

BENNET, Douglas J.
President, Nat'l Public Radio
2025 M St., N.W., Washington, DC 20036
Telephone: (202) 822-2010

BENNETT, Alan R.
Fox, Bennett and Turner
750 17th St., N.W., Suite 1100, Washington, DC 20006
Telephone: (202) 778-2300

Registered as lobbyist at U.S. Congress.
Background: Attorney, Office of the General Counsel, U.S. Food and Drug Administration, 1972-76. Special Counsel, U.S. Senate Committee on Governmental Affairs, 1877-81.
Clients:
Ares-Serono, Inc.
Johnson & Johnson
Serono Laboratories, Inc.

BENNETT, Alexander E.
Arnold & Porter
1200 New Hampshire Ave., N.W., Washington, DC 20036
Telephone: (202) 872-6700
Registered as lobbyist at U.S. Congress.

BENNETT, B. Timothy
SJS Advanced Strategies Inc.
1330 Connecticut Ave., N.W., Washington, DC 20036
Telephone: (202) 429-5500
Background: Former Exec. Director, U.S. Generalized System of Preferences, 1980-81. U.S. Trade Attache to the EEC, 1981-85. Deputy Assistant U.S. Trade Representative for Mexico, 1985-88.

BENNETT, Barbara
Cong Notifications, AGENCY FOR INTERNAT'L DEVELOPMENT
320 21st St., N.W., Washington, DC 20523
Telephone: (202) 647-8441

BENNETT, Catherine P.
Exec. Director, Government Relations, Pfizer, Inc.
1455 Pennsylvania Ave., N.W., Suite 925, Washington, DC 20004
Telephone: (202) 783-7070
Registered as lobbyist at U.S. Congress.

BENNETT, George E.
Public Relations Director, American Movers Conference
2200 Mill Road, Alexandria, VA 22314
Telephone: (703) 838-1930

BENNETT, Nancy
Asst. Dir., Political Action Program, Service Employees Internat'l Union
1313 L St., N.W., Washington, DC 20005
Telephone: (202) 898-3200

BENNETT, Peter H.
V. President, Telecommunications Industry Ass'n
1722 Eye St., N.W., Suite 440, Washington, DC 20006
Telephone: (202) 457-4912

BENNETT, Robert
Chief of Staff, American Legislative Exchange Council
214 Massachusetts Ave., N.W., Washington, DC 20002
Telephone: (202) 547-4646

BENNETT, William M.
Manager, Congressional Relations, Nat'l Soc. of Professional Engineers
1420 King St., Alexandria, VA 22314-2715
Telephone: (703) 684-2841
Registered as lobbyist at U.S. Congress.

BENNETT, William T.
General Secretary, Nat'l Vietnam Veterans Coalition
1000 Thomas Jefferson St., N.W., Suite 600, Washington, DC 20007
Telephone: (202) 338-6882
Background: Served in U.S. Army, 1967-71.

BENNISON, John Charles
V. President, Government Affairs, American Soc. of Travel Agents
1101 King St., Alexandria, VA 22314
Telephone: (703) 739-2782
Registered as lobbyist at U.S. Congress.

BENS, Jodean R.
Special Asst., Gov't Relations, United Fresh Fruit and Vegetable Ass'n
722 North Washington St., Alexandria, VA 22030
Telephone: (703) 836-3410

BENSIMON, Helen Frank
Director, Public Relations, American Soc. for Training and Development
1630 Duke St., Box 1443, Alexandria, VA 22313

Telephone: (703) 683-8100

BENSON, Daniel L.
Palatiello & Assoc., John M.
12020 Sunrise Valley Drive, Reston, VA 22091
Telephone: (703) 391-2739

BENSON, Frederick S., III
V. President, National Affairs, Weyerhaeuser Co.
2001 L St., N.W., Suite 304, Washington, DC 20036
Telephone: (202) 293-7222
Registered as lobbyist at U.S. Congress.

BENSON, Johan T.
Administrator, Public Policy, American Institute of Aeronautics and Astronautics
370 L'Enfant Promenade, Washington, DC 20024
Telephone: (202) 646-7430

BENSON, Mark
Ass't Staff VP, Political Field Operatns, Nat'l Ass'n of Home Builders of the U.S.
15th and M Streets, N.W., Washington, DC 20005
Telephone: (202) 822-0470
Background: Field Director for Senator Rudy Boschwitz (R-MN), 1984-85.

BENSON, Nancy C.
Dir., Agricultural Legislative Affairs, American Cyanamid Co.
1575 Eye St., N.W., Suite 200, Washington, DC 20005
Telephone: (202) 789-1222
Registered as lobbyist at U.S. Congress.

BENSON, Rory
Sr. V. Pres., Assistant to the President, Nat'l Ass'n of Broadcasters
1771 N St., N.W., Washington, DC 20036
Telephone: (202) 429-5300
Background: Also holds position of National Campaign Coordinator of the Association. Formerly served in the White House under President Jimmy Carter as Administrative Assistant to the Political Director.

BENTLEY, James D.
V. Pres., Division of Clinical Services, Ass'n of American Medical Colleges
One Dupont Circle, N.W., Suite 200, Washington, DC 20036
Telephone: (202) 828-0400

BENTLEY, Sheldon R.
Director, Government Affairs, Boeing Computer Services
7980 Boeing Court, CV-83, Vienna, VA 22182
Telephone: (703) 827-4390

BENTON, Hu A.
Associate, Thacher, Proffitt and Wood
1500 K St., N.W., Suite 200, Washington, DC 20005
Telephone: (202) 347-8400
Registered as lobbyist at U.S. Congress.
Clients:
Ranieri-Wilson

BENTSEN, Todd P.
Legislative Aide, Rainbow Lobby
1660 L St., N.W. Suite 204, Washington, DC 20036
Telephone: (202) 457-0700
Registered as lobbyist at U.S. Congress.

BENTZ, Joanne F.
Treasurer, Nat'l Ass'n of Air Traffic Specialists Political Action Fund
4780 Corridor Place, #B, Beltsville, MD 20705
Telephone: (301) 595-2012

BERARD, John
Sr. V. Pres. and Deputy General Manager, Hill and Knowlton Public Affairs Worldwide
Washington Harbour, 901 31st St., N.W., Washington, DC 20007
Telephone: (202) 333-7400

BERENSON, Adrienne
Treasurer, Armenian Assembly of America Political Action Committee
122 C St., N.W., Suite 350, Washington, DC 20001
Telephone: (202) 393-3434

BERG, Andrew G.
Akin, Gump, Strauss, Hauer and Feld
1333 New Hampshire Ave., N.W., Suite 400, Washington, DC 20036
Telephone: (202) 887-4000
Clients:
　Coca-Cola Co.
　Putnam's Sons, G. P.
　Revlon Group

BERG, George L., Jr.
Asst. Director, Nat'l Affairs Division, American Farm Bureau Federation
600 Maryland Ave., S.W. Suite 800, Washington, DC 20024
Telephone: (202) 484-1238
Registered as lobbyist at U.S. Congress.

BERG, Gracia M.
Steptoe and Johnson
1330 Connecticut Ave., N.W., Washington, DC 20036
Telephone: (202) 429-3000
Clients:
　Nashua Corp.

BERG, Joel
Policy Analyst, Ctr. for Civic Enterpr., Progressive Policy Institute
316 Pennsylvania Ave., S.E. Suite 516, Washington, DC 20003
Telephone: (202) 547-0001

BERG, Brother Joseph
Director for Special Programs, Catholic Charities USA
1319 F St., N.W., Suite 400, Washington, DC 20004
Telephone: (202) 639-8400

BERG, R. Christian
Cole, Corette & Abrutyn
1110 Vermont Ave., N.W., Suite 900, Washington, DC 20005
Telephone: (202) 872-1414
Registered as lobbyist at U.S. Congress.
Clients:
　Adidas U.S.A.

BERG, Rebecca Jane
Director, Federal Public Affairs, Sea-Land Service, Inc.
1331 Pennsylvania Ave., N.W. Suite 560 National Place, Washington, DC 20004
Telephone: (202) 783-1117
Registered as lobbyist at U.S. Congress.
Background: Also serves as Treasurer, Sea-Land Corp. Good Government Fund.

BERG, Richard Scott
V. President, Forest Policy & Research, American Forest Council
1250 Connecticut Ave., N.W. Suite 320, Washington, DC 20036
Telephone: (202) 463-2455
Registered as lobbyist at U.S. Congress.

BERGE, J. Hal
V. President, Telecommunications Industry Ass'n
1722 Eye St., N.W., Suite 440, Washington, DC 20006
Telephone: (202) 457-4912

BERGER, Douglas
Director, Public Affairs, Third Class Mail Ass'n
1333 F St., N.W., Suite 710, Washington, DC 20004-1108
Telephone: (202) 347-0055
Registered as lobbyist at U.S. Congress.

BERGER, Paul S.
Arnold & Porter
1200 New Hampshire Ave., N.W., Washington, DC 20036
Telephone: (202) 872-6700
Registered as lobbyist at U.S. Congress.
Clients:
　Apex Ltd.
　Nat'l Coordinating Committee for Multiemployer Plans

BERGER, Powell W.
Manager, Government Relations, Flexible Packaging Ass'n
1090 Vermont Ave., N.W Suite 500, Washington, DC 20005
Telephone: (202) 842-3880

BERGER, Renee A.
President, Teamworks
1117 North 19th St., Suite 900, Arlington, VA 22209
Telephone: (703) 528-7967

BERGER, Samuel R.
Hogan and Hartson
555 13th St., N.W., Suite 1200, Washington, DC 20004-1109
Telephone: (202) 637-5600
Registered as lobbyist at U.S. Congress.
Background: Legislative Assistant to Senator Harold E. Hughes, 1971-72. Deputy Director, Policy Planning Staff, U.S. Department of State, 1977-80.
Clients:
　Caterpillar Inc.
　May Department Stores Co.
　Poland, Ministry of Finance of
　Timex Corp.
　Toyota Motor Sales, U.S.A.

BERGHOFF, John C., Jr.
Mayer, Brown and Platt
2000 Pennsylvania Ave., N.W. Suite 6500, Washington, DC 20006
Telephone: (202) 463-2000
Registered as lobbyist at U.S. Congress.
Clients:
　Vulcan Materials Co.

BERGMAN, Allen I.
Deputy Director, Governmental Activities, United Cerebral Palsy Ass'ns
1522 K St., N.W., Suite 1112, Washington, DC 20005
Telephone: (202) 842-1266

BERGMAN ASSOCIATES, William S.
1001 Connecticut Ave., N.W., Suite 800, Washington, DC 20036
Telephone: (202) 452-1520
Background: An association management firm.
Members of firm representing listed organizations:
　Bergman, Valerie H.
　Bergman, William S. (CAE), President
　Devlin, Laura
　　Background: Serves as Director of Administration for the Food Industry Ass'n Executives and of Consumers for World Trade.
　Strickland, Suzette
　Weldon, Sara
　　Background: Serves as Director of Administration, Internat'l Ass'n of Cooking Professionals.
Organizations represented:
　Bank Card Servicers Ass'n *(Valerie H. Bergman)*
　Consumers for World Trade *(William S. Bergman, CAE, Laura Devlin)*
　Internat'l Ass'n of Cooking Professionals *(Sara Weldon)*
　Internat'l Biometric Ass'n *(William S. Bergman, CAE)*
　Nat'l Structured Settlements Political Action Committee *(Valerie H. Bergman)*
　Nat'l Structured Settlements Trade Ass'n *(William S. Bergman, CAE)*
　Outdoor Power Equipment Aftermarket Ass'n *(William S. Bergman, CAE)*
　TempNet *(Valerie H. Bergman)*

BERGMAN, Dr. Elihu
Exec. Director, Americans for Energy Independence
1629 K St., N.W., Washington, DC 20006
Telephone: (202) 466-2105

BERGMAN, Valerie H.
Bergman Associates, William S.
1001 Connecticut Ave., N.W., Suite 800, Washington, DC 20036
Telephone: (202) 452-1520
Organizations represented:
　Bank Card Servicers Ass'n
　Nat'l Structured Settlements Political Action Committee
　TempNet

BERGMAN, William S., CAE
President, Bergman Associates, William S.
1001 Connecticut Ave., N.W., Suite 800, Washington, DC 20036
Telephone: (202) 452-1520
Registered as lobbyist at U.S. Congress.
Organizations represented:

Consumers for World Trade
Internat'l Biometric Ass'n
Nat'l Structured Settlements Trade Ass'n
Outdoor Power Equipment Aftermarket Ass'n

BERGNER, BOYETTE & BOCKORNY, INC.
1016 16th St., N.W., Suite 700, Washington, DC 20036
Telephone: (202) 659-9111
Registered as Foreign Agent: (#3801)
Background: A government relations consulting firm.
Members of firm representing listed organizations:
　Bergner, Jeffrey T., Chairman and President
　Bockorny, David A., V. President
　　Background: Former Special Assistant to the President for Legislative Affairs, House under President Reagan.
　Boyette, Van R., Corp. Sec'y. & General Counsel
Clients:
　Avianca Airlines *(Van R. Boyette)*
　Bell Atlantic *(David A. Bockorny)*
　China External Trade Development Council *(Jeffrey T. Bergner)*
　First Boston Corp. *(David A. Bockorny)*
　Flo-Sun Land Corp. *(Van R. Boyette)*
　Forum Group, Inc. *(Van R. Boyette)*
　Fox Broadcasting Inc. *(David A. Bockorny)*
　Friendship in Freedom Ass'n *(Jeffrey T. Bergner)*
　Landmark Hotel Corp. *(David A. Bockorny, Van R. Boyette)*
　Lilly and Co., Eli *(Jeffrey T. Bergner, Van R. Boyette)*
　McDonnell Douglas Corp. *(Jeffrey T. Bergner)*
　Murry's, Inc. *(Van R. Boyette)*
　Nat'l Ass'n of Business and Educational Radio *(David A. Bockorny)*
　Nat'l Soft Drink Ass'n *(Jeffrey T. Bergner, David A. Bockorny, Van R. Boyette)*
　Nat'l-American Wholesale Grocers' Ass'n *(Van R. Boyette)*
　Natural Gas Supply Ass'n *(Jeffrey T. Bergner)*
　Okeelanta Corp. *(Van R. Boyette)*
　Orange & Rockland *(David A. Bockorny, Van R. Boyette)*

BERGNER, Jeffrey T.
Chairman and President, Bergner, Boyette & Bockorny, Inc.
1016 16th St., N.W., Suite 700, Washington, DC 20036
Telephone: (202) 659-9111
Registered as lobbyist at U.S. Congress.
Registered as Foreign Agent: (#3801).
Clients:
　China External Trade Development Council
　Friendship in Freedom Ass'n
　Lilly and Co., Eli
　McDonnell Douglas Corp.
　Nat'l Soft Drink Ass'n
　Natural Gas Supply Ass'n

BERGOFFEN, Gene S.
Exec. V. President, Nat'l Private Truck Council
1320 Braddock Place Suite 720, Alexandria, VA 22314
Telephone: (703) 683-1300
Registered as lobbyist at U.S. Congress.

BERGQUIST, Gloria
Sr. Acct. Exec, Grassroots & Issues Mgmt, Hill and Knowlton Public Affairs Worldwide
Washington Harbour, 901 31st St., N.W., Washington, DC 20007
Telephone: (202) 333-7400

BERGSTEN, C. Fred
Director, Institute for Internat'l Economics
11 Dupont Circle, N.W., Washington, DC 20036
Telephone: (202) 328-0583
Background: Former Assistant Secretary for International Affairs, Treasury Department, and Assistant for International Affairs, National Security Council.

BERGWIN, Jane W.
Federal Governmental Affairs Rep., Consumers Power Co.
1016 16th St., N.W. 5th Floor, Washington, DC 20036
Telephone: (202) 293-5794
Registered as lobbyist at U.S. Congress.

BERKE, Dayle
Director, Government Affairs, Nat'l Ass'n for Home Care
519 C St., N.E., Washington, DC 20002

Telephone: (202) 547-7424
Registered as lobbyist at U.S. Congress.

BERKERY, Peter M., Jr.
Dir., Congressional Relations/Tax Couns., Nat'l Soc. of Public Accountants
1010 N. Fairfax St., Alexandria, VA 22314
Telephone: (703) 549-6400
Registered as lobbyist at U.S. Congress.

BERKLEY, Nathan R.
Director, Government Traffic, American Movers Conference
2200 Mill Road, Alexandria, VA 22314
Telephone: (703) 838-1930
Registered as lobbyist at U.S. Congress.

BERKOFF, Barry I.
Legislative Representative, Reid & Priest
1111 19th St., N.W., Washington, DC 20036
Telephone: (202) 828-0100

BERKOWITZ, Deborah
Director, Safety and Health, United Food and Commercial Workers Internat'l Union
1775 K St., N.W., Washington, DC 20006
Telephone: (202) 223-3111

BERKOWITZ, Herbert
V. President, Public Relations, Heritage Foundation
214 Massachusetts Ave., N.E., Washington, DC 20002
Telephone: (202) 546-4400

BERKSHIRE, Linda K.
Exec. Director, Education Finance, Nat'l Ass'n of Independent Colleges and Universities
122 C St., N.W. Suite 750, Washington, DC 20001
Telephone: (202) 347-7512
Registered as lobbyist at U.S. Congress.

BERLACK, Evan R.
Arent, Fox, Kintner, Plotkin & Kahn
1050 Connecticut Ave., N.W., Washington, DC 20036-5339
Telephone: (202) 857-6000
Background: Officer, U.S. Foreign Service, 1963-65; Attorney, Office of Legal Adviser, Department of State, 1965-68.
Clients:
Nat'l Soft Drink Ass'n

BERLIN, Edward
Swidler & Berlin, Chartered
3000 K St., N.W., Suite 300, Washington, DC 20007
Telephone: (202) 944-4300
Background: Attorney, Department of Justice, 1961-66. Assistant General Counsel, Federal Power Commission, 1966-69.
Clients:
New England Power Co.

BERLIN, Kenneth
Winthrop, Stimson, Putnam & Roberts
1133 Connecticut Ave., N.W. Suite 1000, Washington, DC 20036
Telephone: (202) 775-9800

BERLINER AND MALONEY
1101 17th St., N.W., Suite 1004, Washington, DC 20036-4798
Telephone: (202) 293-1414
Members of firm representing listed organizations:
Kochinke, Clemens J.
Maloney, Barry C.
Rusch, Wayne H.

Clients:
Barbados, Government of (Bruce Zagaris)
Cayman Islands, Government of (Bruce Zagaris)
Elmont AG (Clemens J. Kochinke)

BERLINER, Roger A.
Brady and Berliner
1225 19th St., N.W. Suite 800, Washington, DC 20036
Telephone: (202) 955-6067
Registered as Foreign Agent: (#3656).
Clients:
Canadian Petroleum Ass'n
Independent Petroleum Ass'n of Canada

BERMAN, Bruce M.
Wilmer, Cutler and Pickering
2445 M St., N.W., Washington, DC 20037-1420
Telephone: (202) 663-6000
Clients:
Howard, Meedles, Tammen & Bergendoff

BERMAN AND CO.,INC., Richard B.
1025 Connecticut Ave., N.W. Suite 1010, Washington, DC 20036
Telephone: (202) 659-2800
Members of firm representing listed organizations:
Berman, Richard B.
Organizations represented:
Burger King (Richard B. Berman)
Chili's (Richard B. Berman)
Houston's (Richard B. Berman)
Minimum Wage Coalition to Save Jobs (Richard B. Berman)
Pillsbury Co. (Richard B. Berman)
S&A Restaurants Corp. (Richard B. Berman)
ShowBiz Pizza Time (Richard B. Berman)
TGI Friday's (Richard B. Berman)

BERMAN, Ellen
Exec. Director, Consumer Energy Council of America Research Foundation
2000 L St., N.W., Suite 802, Washington, DC 20036
Telephone: (202) 659-0404
Registered as lobbyist at U.S. Congress.

BERMAN, Jason S.
President, Recording Industry Ass'n of America
1020 19th St., N.W., Suite 200, Washington, DC 20036
Telephone: (202) 775-0101
Registered as lobbyist at U.S. Congress.

BERMAN, Jerry J.
Dir., Proj. Technology & Civil Liberties, American Civil Liberties Union
122 Maryland Ave., N.E., Washington, DC 20002
Telephone: (202) 544-1681
Registered as lobbyist at U.S. Congress.

BERMAN, Marshall F.
Dow, Lohnes and Albertson
1255 23rd St., N.W., Suite 500, Washington, DC 20037
Telephone: (202) 857-2500
Clients:
Harcourt Brace Jovanovich, Inc.

BERMAN, Michael
Duberstein Group, Inc., The
2100 Pennsylvania Ave., N.W. Suite 350, Washington, DC 20037
Telephone: (202) 728-1100

BERMAN, Richard B.
Berman and Co.,Inc., Richard B.
1025 Connecticut Ave., N.W. Suite 1010, Washington, DC 20036
Telephone: (202) 659-2800
Registered as lobbyist at U.S. Congress.
Organizations represented:
Burger King
Chili's
Houston's
Minimum Wage Coalition to Save Jobs
Pillsbury Co.
S&A Restaurants Corp.
ShowBiz Pizza Time
TGI Friday's

BERMAN, William R.
Director, Environment and Energy Dept., American Automobile Ass'n
500 E St. S.W., Suite 950, Washington, DC 20024
Telephone: (202) 554-6060
Registered as lobbyist at U.S. Congress.
Background: Serves as Chairman, Fuel Users for Equitable Levies.

BERNARD, Keith E.
V. Pres., Internat'l & Regulatory Affrs., Cable and Wireless North America
1919 Gallows Road, Vienna, VA 22182
Telephone: (703) 790-5300
Registered as Foreign Agent: (#4231)

BERNARD, William G.
President, Internat'l Ass'n of Heat and Frost Insulators and Asbestos Workers
1300 Connecticut Ave., N,W. Suite 505, Washington, DC 20036
Telephone: (202) 785-2388

BERNHARD, Berl
Verner, Liipfert, Bernhard, McPherson and Hand, Chartered
901 15th St., N.W., Suite 700, Washington, DC 20005
Telephone: (202) 371-6000
Registered as lobbyist at U.S. Congress.
Registered as Foreign Agent: (#3712)
Background: Supervisory General Attorney, U.S. Civil Rights Commission, 1959; Deputy Director, 1959-1960; Director, 1961-1963. General Counsel, Democratic Senatorial Campaign Committee, 1967-71. Special Counsel, Democratic Nat'l Committee, 1969-70. Senior advisor to the Secretary of State, 1980.
Clients:
Burlington Northern Railroad
Continental Airlines
Irving Ltd., J.D.
UNC Incorporated
Wings Holdings Inc.

BERNHARD, Mary E.
Manager, Environmental Policy, Chamber of Commerce of the U.S.A.
1615 H St., N.W., Washington, DC 20062
Telephone: (202) 463-5533
Registered as lobbyist at U.S. Congress.

BERNHARDT, Charles
Labor Relations Specialist, Nat'l Federation of Federal Employees
1016 16th St., N.W., Suite 400, Washington, DC 20036
Telephone: (202) 862-4400

BERNIER, J. Paul
President, Roxton, Inc.
2000 S. Eads St., Suite 1003, Arlington, VA 22202
Telephone: (703) 920-0564
Registered as lobbyist at U.S. Congress.

BERNSTEIN, Elizabeth
Rsrch. Asst., Campaign Finance Monitoring, Common Cause
2030 M St., N.W., Washington, DC 20036
Telephone: (202) 833-1200
Registered as lobbyist at U.S. Congress.

BERNSTEIN, George K.
Bernstein Law Off., George K.
1730 K St., N.W. Suite 313, Washington, DC 20006
Telephone: (202) 452-8010
Registered as Foreign Agent: (#4269)
Organizations represented:
Jauch & Hubener, O.H.G.
Nationwide Insurance Cos.

BERNSTEIN LAW OFF., George K.
1730 K St., N.W. Suite 313, Washington, DC 20006
Telephone: (202) 452-8010
Registered as lobbyist at U.S. Congress.
Registered as Foreign Agent: (#4269)
Members of firm representing listed organizations:
Bernstein, George K.
Shapiro, Robert B.
Organizations represented:
Jauch & Hubener, O.H.G. (George K. Bernstein, Robert B. Shapiro)
Nationwide Insurance Cos. (George K. Bernstein)

BERNSTEIN, Rachelle
Tax Manager, Andersen and Co., Arthur
1666 K St., N.W., Washington, DC 20006
Telephone: (202) 862-3100

BERNSTEIN, Roger D.
Director, State Government Affairs, Council for Solid Waste Solutions
1275 K St., N.W. Suite 400, Washington, DC 20005
Telephone: (202) 371-5319

BERNTHAL, Eric L.
Latham and Watkins
1001 Pennsylvania Ave., N.W., Suite 1300, Washington, DC 20004
Telephone: (202) 637-2200
Clients:
  T. A. Associates

BERRIEN, Glenn
President, Nat'l Postal Mail Handlers Union
One Thomas Circle, N.W. Suite 525, Washington, DC 20005
Telephone: (202) 833-9095

BERRIGAN, Thomas
Director of Communications, Travel Industry Ass'n of America
1133 21st St., N.W.,, Washington, DC 20036
Telephone: (202) 293-1433
Background: Former minority staff director, Subcommittee on Intergovernmental Relations, Senate Committee on Governmental Affairs.

BERRINGTON, Craig A.
General Counsel, American Insurance Ass'n
1130 Connecticut Ave., N.W., Suite 1000, Washington, DC 20036
Telephone: (202) 828-7100
Registered as lobbyist at U.S. Congress.

BERRY, C. Martin
Exec. V. President, Ass'n of Specialists in Cleaning and Restoration (ASCR Internat'l)
10830 Annapolis Junction Road, Suite 312, Annapolis Jct., MD 20701
Telephone: (301) 604-4411

BERRY, J. Patrick
Baker and Botts
555 13th St., N.W., Suite 500 East, Washington, DC 20004-1109
Telephone: (202) 639-7700
Registered as lobbyist at U.S. Congress.
Background: Counsel, Committee on Energy and Natural Resources, U.S. Senate 1975-77.

BERRY LAW OFFICES, Max N.
3213 O St., N.W., Washington, DC 20007
Telephone: (202) 298-6134
Members of firm representing listed organizations:
  Berry, Max N.
    Background: Attorney, Office of the Chief Counsel, Bureau of Customs, Department of the Treasury, 1963-1967. Member, Advisory Board, East-West Trade Council 1972.
  Echols, Marsha A.
    Background: Assistant to the Administrator, Foreign Agricultural Service, U.S. Dept. of Agriculture, 1977-80. Counsel to the Vice Chairman, U.S. International Trade Commission, 1980-82.
Organizations represented:
  American Importers Meat Products Group (*Max N. Berry*)
  Ass'n of Chocolate, Biscuit and Confectionery Industries of the EEC (*Max N. Berry*)
  Atalanta Corp. (*Max N. Berry*)
  BSN Groupe (*Max N. Berry*)
  Canada, Embassy of (*Max N. Berry*)
  Centre National Interprofessionel de L'Economie Laitiere (French Dairy Ass'n) (*Max N. Berry*)
  Committee to Assure the Availability of Casein (*Max N. Berry*)
  Federation of Wine and Spirits Exporters of France (*Max N. Berry*)
  Florida State Department of Citrus (*Max N. Berry*)
  Gallard-Schlesinger Chemical Manufacturing Corp. (*Max N. Berry*)
  Gilway Co., Ltd., The (*Marsha A. Echols*)
  Gist Brocades (*Max N. Berry*)
  Junex Enterprises (*Max N. Berry*)
  Nat'l Ass'n for the Specialty Food Trade (*Marsha A. Echols*)
  Nylo-Flex Manufacturing Co., Inc. (*Max N. Berry*)
  Prince des Bretagne (*Max N. Berry*)
  Valio Finnish Co-Operative Dairies Ass'n (*Max N. Berry*)

BERRY, Mark
Director, Media Relations, Washington Communications Group/Ruder Finn
1615 M St., N.W., Suite 220, Washington, DC 20036
Telephone: (202) 466-7800
Background: Former deputy press secretary for the presidential campaign of Rep. Jack Kemp (R-NY).

BERRY, Max N.
Berry Law Offices, Max N.
3213 O St., N.W., Washington, DC 20007
Telephone: (202) 298-6134
Registered as lobbyist at U.S. Congress.
Registered as Foreign Agent: (#2216).
Background: Attorney, Office of the Chief Counsel, Bureau of Customs, Department of the Treasury, 1963-1967. Member, Advisory Board, East-West Trade Council 1972.
Organizations represented:
  American Importers Meat Products Group
  Ass'n of Chocolate, Biscuit and Confectionery Industries of the EEC
  Atalanta Corp.
  BSN Groupe
  Canada, Embassy of
  Centre National Interprofessionel de L'Economie Laitiere (French Dairy Ass'n)
  Committee to Assure the Availability of Casein
  Federation of Wine and Spirits Exporters of France
  Florida State Department of Citrus
  Gallard-Schlesinger Chemical Manufacturing Corp.
  Gist Brocades
  Junex Enterprises
  Nylo-Flex Manufacturing Co., Inc.
  Prince des Bretagne
  Valio Finnish Co-Operative Dairies Ass'n

BERRY, Robert E.
Legislative Representative, American Gas Ass'n
1515 Wilson Blvd., Arlington, VA
Telephone: (703) 841-8654
Registered as lobbyist at U.S. Congress.
Background: Former Counsel, U.S. Senate Committee on Government Operations; and House Minority Reading Clerk.

BERRY, Steven K.
Dep Asst Secy, Legis Affairs, DEPARTMENT OF STATE
2201 C St., N.W., Washington, DC 20520
Telephone: (202) 647-4204

BERRY, Willard M.
V. President, Nat'l Foreign Trade Council, Inc.
1625 K St., N.W., Suite 1090, Washington, DC 20006
Telephone: (202) 887-0278
Registered as lobbyist at U.S. Congress.

BERSON, David W.
V. President and Chief Economist, Federal Nat'l Mortgage Ass'n
3900 Wisconsin Ave., N.W., Washington, DC 20016
Telephone: (202) 752-7000

BERTALAN, Imre
President, Hungarian Reformed Federation of America
2001 Massachusetts Ave., N.W., Washington, DC 20036
Telephone: (202) 328-2630

BERTELSEN, Michael J.
V. President, Counsel, Perkinson & Associates, Inc.
453 New Jersey Ave., S.E., Washington, DC 20003
Telephone: (202) 646-1260
Registered as lobbyist at U.S. Congress.
Background: Served in the federal government, 1985-89.
Clients:
  Alliance for America's Homeowners
  Beneficial Management Corp. of America
  Nat'l Coalition for Fair Bankruptcy Laws
  Nat'l Second Mortgage Ass'n

BERTERA, Bill
Managing Director, State Programs, Nat'l Solid Wastes Management Ass'n
1730 Rhode Island Ave., N.W., 10th Floor, Washington, DC 20036
Telephone: (202) 659-4613
Registered as lobbyist at U.S. Congress.

BERTRAM, Bruce M.
Technical Director, Salt Institute
700 North Fairfax St. Suite 600, Alexandria, VA 22314
Telephone: (703) 549-4648

BERY, R. N.
Vice President, Foster Wheeler Internat'l Corp.
1701 Pennsylvania Ave., N.W. Suite 460, Washington, DC 20006
Telephone: (202) 298-7750

BESCOND, Pierre
President, Spot Image Corp.
1897 Preston White Drive, Reston, VA 22091-4326
Telephone: (703) 620-2200

BESTEMAN, Karst
Exec. Director, Alcohol and Drug Problems Ass'n of North America
444 N. Capitol St., N.W., Washington, DC 20001
Telephone: (202) 737-4340

BESTER, Margot F.
Murphy and Demory, Ltd.
2300 N St., N.W. Suite 725, Washington, DC 20037
Telephone: (202) 785-3323
Registered as lobbyist at U.S. Congress.
Clients:
  United States Telephone Ass'n

BETAR, John F.
Legislative Counsel, Ass'n of Bank Holding Companies
730 15th St., N.W., Suite 820, Washington, DC 20005
Telephone: (202) 393-1158
Registered as lobbyist at U.S. Congress.

BETTAUER, Raija
Dir, Legis & Regul Analysis Div, DEPARTMENT OF TREASURY - Comptroller of the Currency
490 L'Enfant Plaza, S.W., Washington, DC 20219
Telephone: (202) 447-1632

BETTS, Richard K.
Defense Analyst, Brookings Institution
1775 Massachusetts Ave., N.W., Washington, DC 20036
Telephone: (202) 797-6000

BETZ ASSOCIATES, INC, Robert
1010 Vermont Ave., N.W., Suite 1116, Washington, DC 20005
Telephone: (202) 347-1990
Members of firm representing listed organizations:
  Betz, Robert B.
Organizations represented:
  Alabama Hospital Ass'n (*Robert B. Betz*)
  American Ass'n of Eye and Ear Hospitals (*Robert B. Betz*)

BETZ, Robert B.
Betz Associates, Inc, Robert
1010 Vermont Ave., N.W., Suite 1116, Washington, DC 20005
Telephone: (202) 347-1990
Registered as lobbyist at U.S. Congress.
Organizations represented:
  Alabama Hospital Ass'n
  American Ass'n of Eye and Ear Hospitals

BETZLER, Mary Roddy
Senior V. President, Kamber Group, The
1920 L St., N.W., Washington, DC 20036
Telephone: (202) 223-8700
Organizations represented:
  Amnesty Internat'l U.S.A.
  Internat'l Ass'n of Bridge, Structural and Ornamental Iron Workers
  Internat'l Brotherhood of Electrical Workers
  Nat'l Coordinating Committee for Multiemployer Plans

BEVELS, Terry D.
President, Wexler, Reynolds, Fuller, Harrison and Schule, Inc.
1317 F St., N.W., Suite 600, Washington, DC 20004
Telephone: (202) 638-2121
Registered as lobbyist at U.S. Congress.
Clients:
  American Public Transit Ass'n
  Consortium of State Maritime Schools

Massachusetts Maritime Academy
New England Aquarium
Oceanic Institute
Oregon, State of

BEVERIDGE, Albert J., III
Beveridge & Diamond, P.C.
1350 Eye St., N.W. Suite 700, Washington, DC 20005
Telephone: (202) 789-6000
Background: Attorney with Tax Division, U.S. Department
of Justice, 1965-1968.

BEVERIDGE & DIAMOND, P.C.
1350 Eye St., N.W. Suite 700, Washington, DC 20005
Telephone: (202) 789-6000
Registered as Foreign Agent: (#3772)
Members of firm representing listed organizations:
Beveridge, Albert J. (III)
Background: Attorney with Tax Division, U.S. Depart-
ment of Justice, 1965-1968.
Davis, Richard S.
Diamond, Henry L.
Background: Commissioner, New York State Dep't of
Conservation, 1970-1973; Chairman, President's Ad-
visory Commission on Environmental Quality, 1973-;
Executive Director, Commission on Critical Choices
for Americans, 1974. Member, Board of Directors,
Combustion Equipment Associates.
Hanson, John N.
Background: Trial Attorney, 1972-77 and Assistant Di-
rector, Civil Division, 1978-79, Department of Jus-
tice.
Himmelman, Harold
Background: U.S. Department of Justice, Civil Rights
Division, 1967-69.
Segall, Harold L.
Sierck, Alexander W.
Background: Director of Trade Policy, Antitrust Divi-
sion. U.S. Department of Justice, 1978-80.

Clients:
Airbus Industrie *(Alexander W. Sierck)*
Bluefield, West Virginia, City of *(Richard S. Davis,
Harold L. Segall)*
British Independent Steel Producers Ass'n *(Alexan-
der W. Sierck)*
Dana Corp. *(Alexander W. Sierck)*
FMC Corp.
Ingersoll Products Co. *(Alexander W. Sierck)*
Morgantown, West Virginia, City of *(Richard S. Dav-
is, Harold L. Segall)*
Northern Indiana Public Service Co.
People's Committee for Libyan Students

BEVEVINO, Christopher R.
President, Internat'l Business Forms Industries
2111 Wilson Blvd., Suite 350, Arlington, VA 22209
Telephone: (703) 841-9191

BEY, Barbara
Managing Director, External Affairs, American Council of
Life Insurance
1001 Pennsylvania Ave., N.W., Washington, DC 20004-
2599
Telephone: (202) 624-2440

BEYER, John C.
Nathan Associates Inc.
1301 Pennsylvania Ave., N.W., Washington, DC 20004
Telephone: (202) 393-2700

BEZOLD, Clement, Ph.D.
Exec. Director, Institute for Alternative Futures
108 North Alfred St., Alexandria, VA 22314
Telephone: (703) 684-5880

BHATIA, Joe
V. President, Governmental Affairs, Underwriters Laboratories Inc.
818 18th St., N.W., Washington, DC 20006
Telephone: (202) 296-7840

BIALOS, Jeffrey P.
Weil, Gotshal & Manges
1615 L St., N.W., Suite 700, Washington, DC 20036
Telephone: (202) 682-7000
Clients:
Matsushita Electronic Corp.
Mitsubishi Corp.

BIANCHI, Suzanne
Secretary/Treasurer, Population Ass'n of America
1429 Duke St., Alexandria, VA 22314-3402
Telephone: (703) 684-1221

BICKWIT, Leonard, Jr.
Member, Miller & Chevalier, Chartered
Metropolitan Square, 655 15th St., N.W., Washington, DC
20005
Telephone: (202) 626-5800
Registered as lobbyist at U.S. Congress.
Registered as Foreign Agent: (#3626).
Background: Counsel, Senate Subcommittee on the Envi-
ronment, 1969-74. Chief Legislative Assistant to Senator
John Glenn of Ohio, 1975-79. General Counsel, U.S. Nu-
clear Regulatory Commission, 1979-83.
Clients:
Ameribanc Investors Group
American Continental Corp.
American Nuclear Energy Council
Chevy Chase Savings Bank
Long Island Ass'n

BIDDLE, A. G. W.
President, Computer and Communications Industry Ass'n
666 Eleventh St., N.W., Sixth Floor, Washington, DC
20001
Telephone: (202) 783-0070

BIDDLE, Stephanie
Treasurer, Computer and Communications Industry Ass'n
Political Action Committee
666 Eleventh St., N.W., Sixth Floor, Washington, DC
20001
Telephone: (202) 783-0070

BIDDLE, Timothy M.
Crowell and Moring
1001 Pennsylvania Ave., N.W., Washington, DC 20004-
2505
Telephone: (202) 624-2500

BIDDLE, Walter H., CAE
Exec. Director, Internat'l Soc. for Hybrid Microelectronics
1861 Wiehle Ave., Suite 260, Box 2698, Reston, VA
22090
Telephone: (703) 471-0066

BIEBER, Sander M.
Dechert Price & Rhoads
1500 K St., N.W., Washington, DC 20005
Telephone: (202) 626-3300
Registered as lobbyist at U.S. Congress.
Clients:
Ryland Acceptance Advisers, Inc.

BIECHMAN, John C.
V. President, Safe Buildings Alliance
655 15th St., N.W., Suite 1200, Washington, DC 20005
Telephone: (202) 879-5120
Registered as lobbyist at U.S. Congress.

BIEGEL, Leonard
Sr. V. Pres./Dir., Media Relations, Burson-Marsteller
1850 M St., N.W., Suite 900, Washington, DC 20036
Telephone: (202) 833-8550
Clients:
Coalition Against Regressive Taxation

BIEGING, David A.
Dorsey & Whitney
1330 Connecticut Ave., N.W., Suite 200, Washington, DC
20036
Telephone: (202) 857-0700
Registered as lobbyist at U.S. Congress.
Background: Legislative Assistant to Senator Walter F.
Mondale (D-MN), 1975-76. Special Assistant to Vice
President Mondale, 1977-78. Administrative Assistant to
Rep. Martin O. Sabo (D-MN), 1979-87.

BIENS, AXELROD, OSBORNE & MOONEY, P.C.
2033 K St., N.W. Suite 300, Washington, DC 20006
Telephone: (202) 429-1900
Clients:
Nat'l Air Traffic Controller Ass'n

BIER, Joan T.
Corp. Staff V. President, Gov't Affairs, Internat'l Minerals
and Chemical Corp.
1726 M St., N.W., Suite 701, Washington, DC 20036
Telephone: (202) 659-1750
Registered as lobbyist at U.S. Congress.
Background: Serves also as contact for IMC-PAC, the political action committee of Internat'l Minerals and Chemical Corp.

BIERLY, Richard H.
V. Pres., Gov't Affrs & Internat'l Trade, Unisys Corp.
2001 L St., N.W., Suite 1000, Washington, DC 20036
Telephone: (202) 293-7720
Registered as lobbyist at U.S. Congress.
Background: Serves as Vice Chairman, Unisys Corp. Em-
ployee PAC.

BIERMAN, James N.
Foley & Lardner
1775 Pennsylvania Ave., N.W., Suite 1000, Washington,
DC 20006-4680
Telephone: (202) 862-5300
Registered as lobbyist at U.S. Congress.
Background: Member Civil Rights Reviewing Authority,
Department of Health, Education and Welfare, 1979.
Clients:
Duracell Inc.
Kohlberg Kravis Roberts & Co.
United Savings of America

BIERSTEIN, Karin, J.D., M.S.
Director, Socio-Economic Affairs, American Academy of
Otolaryngology-Head and Neck Surgery
One Prince St., Alexandria, VA 22314
Telephone: (703) 836-4444

BIGELOW, Claire
Exec. Director, Nat'l Ass'n of Commissions for Women
YWCA Bldg., Suite M-10, 624 Ninth St., N.W., Washing-
ton, DC 20001
Telephone: (202) 628-5030

BIGELOW, K K
V. President, Washington Operations, Martin Marietta
Corp.
6801 Rockledge Drive MP 335, Bethesda, MD 20817
Telephone: (301) 897-6164
Background: Also serves as Treasurer for the Martin Ma-
rietta Corp. Political Action Committee.

BIGELOW, Timothy
Asst. V. President, Conventions/Meetings, Nat'l Ass'n of
Life Underwriters
1922 F St., N.W., Washington, DC 20006
Telephone: (202) 331-6000

BIGGS, Heidi
Government Affairs Representative, American Forest Re-
source Alliance
1250 Connecticut Ave., N.W. Suite 200, Washington, DC
20036
Telephone: (202) 463-2747
Registered as lobbyist at U.S. Congress.
Background: Former Legislative Assistant to Senator Slade
Gorton (R-WA).

BIJLEFELD, Marjolijn
Associate Director, Nat'l Coalition to Ban Handguns
100 Maryland Ave., N.E., Washington, DC 20002
Telephone: (202) 544-7190

BILIK, Al
President, AFL-CIO - Public Employee Department
815 16th St., N.W., Suite 308, Washington, DC 20006
Telephone: (202) 393-2820

BILLER, Moe
President, American Postal Workers Union
1300 L St., N.W., Washington, DC 20005
Telephone: (202) 842-4246
Registered as lobbyist at U.S. Congress.

BILLINGS, Dick
Coordinator of Investigations, Christic Institute
1324 N. Capitol St., N.W., Washington, DC 20002
Telephone: (202) 797-8106

BILLINGS, INC., Leon G.
901 15th St., N.W. Suite 570, Washington, DC 20005
Telephone: (202) 371-0764
Members of firm representing listed organizations:
 Billings, Leon G., President
Organizations represented:
 Oxford Energy Co. *(Leon G. Billings)*
 Santa Barbara County Air Pollution Control District *(Leon G. Billings)*
 South Coast Air Quality Management District *(Leon G. Billings)*

BILLINGS, Leon G.
President, Billings, Inc., Leon G.
901 15th St., N.W. Suite 570, Washington, DC 20005
Telephone: (202) 371-0764
Registered as lobbyist at U.S. Congress.
Organizations represented:
 Oxford Energy Co.
 Santa Barbara County Air Pollution Control District
 South Coast Air Quality Management District

BILLINGS, Robert D.
Legislative Director, American Conservative Union
38 Ivy St., S.E., Washington, DC 20003
Telephone: (202) 546-6555
Registered as lobbyist at U.S. Congress.

BILLMAN, Paul
Director, Political Programs, Sheehan Associates, Inc.
727 15th St., N.W., Suite 1200, Washington, DC 20005
Telephone: (202) 347-0044
Clients:
 American Ass'n of Politically Active Citizens

BILLY, David B.
Political Action Assistant, Internat'l Ass'n of Fire Fighters
1750 New York Ave., N.W., Washington, DC 20006
Telephone: (202) 737-8484
Registered as lobbyist at U.S. Congress.

BILSON, Andrea
Manager, State Issues, Food Marketing Institute
1750 K St., N.W., Washington, DC 20006
Telephone: (202) 452-8444
Registered as lobbyist at U.S. Congress.

BINDEMAN, Deborah
Federal Affairs Representative, Insurance Services Office
1666 K St., N.W. Suite 915, Washington, DC 20006
Telephone: (202) 466-2800

BINDER, Elaine Kotell
Exec. Director, B'nai B'rith Women
1828 L St., N.W., Suite 250, Washington, DC 20036
Telephone: (202) 857-1310

BINGAMAN, Robert, Jr.
Nat'l Field Manager, Nat'l Abortion Rights Action League
1101 14th St., N.W., Suite 500, Washington, DC 20005
Telephone: (202) 371-0779
Registered as lobbyist at U.S. Congress.

BINNS, David M.
Exec. Director, Employee Stock Ownership Ass'n
1100 17th St., N.W. Suite 1207, Washington, DC 20036
Telephone: (202) 293-2971
Background: Also represents the Employee Stock Ownership Political Action Committee.

BINNS, Don
Chairman, Infomedia Corporation
7700 Leesburg Pike Centre Tower, Falls Church, VA 22042
Telephone: (703) 847-0077

BINSTOCK, Stuart
Associated General Contractors of America
1957 E St., N.W., Washington, DC 20006
Telephone: (202) 393-2040
Registered as lobbyist at U.S. Congress.

BINSWANGER, William B.
Treasurer, Nat'l Rifle Ass'n of America
1600 Rhode Island Ave., N.W., Washington, DC 20036
Telephone: (202) 828-6000

BINZEL, Peggy K.
Director, Government Affairs, Turner Broadcasting System, Inc.
111 Massachusetts Ave., N.W. Third Floor, Washington, DC 20001
Telephone: (202) 898-7670
Background: Former Legislative Assistant to Rp. Jack Fields (R-TX).

BIRCH, HORTON, BITTNER AND CHEROT
1155 Connecticut Ave., N.W., Suite 1200, Washington, DC 20036
Telephone: (202) 659-5800
Background: Washington office of an Alaskan law firm with offices in Anchorage, Juneau and Fairbanks. Specializes in natural resources issues.
Members of firm representing listed organizations:
 Birch, Ronald G.
  Background: Administrative Aide to Senator Ted Stevens of Alaska, 1968-71.
 Bumpers, William M.
 Carr, Geraldine
 Chomski, Joseph M.
 Eisen, Eric A.
 Horn, William P.
 Ross, Elisabeth
Clients:
 Alaska Pacific Refining, Inc. *(Joseph M. Chomski)*
 Alaska Teamster-Employer Pension Trust *(Joseph M. Chomski)*
 Chugach Alaska Corp. *(Joseph M. Chomski)*
 Cooney Enterprises, Gerry *(Joseph M. Chomski)*
 Entergy Corp. *(William M. Bumpers)*
 Grand Targhee Ski Resort *(Joseph M. Chomski)*
 Kodiak Island Borough *(Joseph M. Chomski)*
 Missouri Public Service Commission *(Eric A. Eisen)*
 North Slope Borough *(Ronald G. Birch)*
 Old Harbor Corp. *(Joseph M. Chomski)*
 Sealaska Corp. *(Joseph M. Chomski)*
 Security Pacific Bank of Alaska *(Joseph M. Chomski)*
 St. George, Alaska, City of *(Joseph M. Chomski)*
 St. George Tanaq Corp. *(Joseph M. Chomski)*
 Stebbins-Ambler Air Transport *(Joseph M. Chomski)*
 Tanadgusix Corp. *(Joseph M. Chomski)*
 U.S. Central, Inc. *(Joseph M. Chomski)*
 Wildlife Legislative Fund of America *(William P. Horn)*
 Yukon Pacific Inc. *(Ronald G. Birch, William P. Horn)*

BIRCH, Ronald G.
Birch, Horton, Bittner and Cherot
1155 Connecticut Ave., N.W., Suite 1200, Washington, DC 20036
Telephone: (202) 659-5800
Registered as lobbyist at U.S. Congress.
Background: Administrative Aide to Senator Ted Stevens of Alaska, 1968-71.
Clients:
 North Slope Borough
 Yukon Pacific Inc.

BIRCHER, John E., III
Neill and Co.
815 Connecticut Ave., N.W. Suite 800, Washington, DC 20006
Telephone: (202) 463-8877
Registered as lobbyist at U.S. Congress.
Registered as Foreign Agent: (# 3320).
Background: U.S. Army Security Agency Liaison Officer, Combined Arms Center, 1975-76. Defense and Army Attache to Lebanon, 1979-80. Middle East/Africa Director, Defense Attache System, DIA, 1980-82. Military Attache to Morocco, 1982-84. Director, Regional Affairs and Politico-Military Advisor to Assistant Secretary of State, Bureau of Near East/ South Asian Affairs, Department of State, 1984-88.
Clients:
 Contraves Italiana S.p.A.
 General Dynamics Corp.
 Morocco, Kingdom of
 Smith & Wesson

BIRD, Michael
Federal Affairs Counsel, Nat'l Conference of State Legislatures
444 North Capitol St., N.W. Suite 500, Washington, DC 20001
Telephone: (202) 624-5400

BIRD, Robert S.
Director, Washington Office, General Mills
555 13th St., N.W., Suite 490 West, Washington, DC 20004
Telephone: (202) 737-8200
Registered as lobbyist at U.S. Congress.

BIRD, Stephanie J.
President, Ass'n for Women in Science
1522 K St., N.W. Suite 820, Washington, DC 20005
Telephone: (202) 408-0742

BIRDSONG, James R.
Exec. Dir., Building Systems, Nat'l Ass'n of Home Builders of the U.S.
15th and M Streets, N.W., Washington, DC 20005
Telephone: (202) 822-0470

BIRDSONG, John G.
Associate, Templeton and Co.
1925 North Lynn St., Arlington, VA 22209
Telephone: (703) 525-3888
Clients:
 Beggs Associates, J. M.
 Bionetics Corp., The

BIRENBAUM, David E.
Fried, Frank, Harris, Shriver & Jacobson
1001 Pennsylvania Ave., N.W., Suite 800, Washington, DC 20004-2505
Telephone: (202) 639-7000
Registered as Foreign Agent: (# 3473).
Clients:
 California Pistachio Commission
 Handgun Control, Inc.

BIRKHOFER, William J.
V. President, Director of Gov't Affairs, Sverdrup Corp.
1500 Wilson Blvd., Arlington, VA 22209
Telephone: (703) 525-1600

BIRMINGHAM, Mary E.
Linton, Mields, Reisler and Cottone
1225 Eye St., N.W., Suite 300, Washington, DC 20005
Telephone: (202) 682-3901
Clients:
 Nat'l Ass'n of Activity Professionals

BIRNBAUM, Kenneth S.
General Cou, Bracy Williams & Co.
1000 Connecticut Ave., N.W., Suite 304, Washington, DC 20036
Telephone: (202) 659-4805
Registered as lobbyist at U.S. Congress.
Clients:
 American Home Satellite Ass'n
 American Southwest Financial Corp.
 Batman Corp.
 Daishowa America Co. Ltd.
 Fieldstone Co.
 Millicom Inc.
 Rocky Co., The

BIRNBAUM, S. Elizabeth
Counsel, Water Resources Division, Nat'l Wildlife Federation
1400 16th St., N.W., Washington, DC 20036-2266
Telephone: (202) 797-6800

BIRNEY, Jonelle
V. President, Fleishman-Hillard, Inc
1301 Connecticut Ave., N.W., Washington, DC 20036
Telephone: (202) 659-0330

BIRNEY, William
Chief, Legis Svcs Office, Real Estate, DEPARTMENT OF ARMY - Chief of Engineers
20 Massachusetts Ave., N.W., Washington, DC 20314
Telephone: (202) 272-0515

BIRNS, Laurence R.
Director, Council on Hemispheric Affairs
724 9th St., N.W., Washington, DC 20001
Telephone: (202) 393-3322

BISACQUINO, Thomas J.
Senior V. President, Nat'l Ass'n of Industrial and Office Parks
1215 Jefferson Davis Hwy., Suite 100, Arlington, VA 22202
Telephone: (703) 979-3400

BISCOE, Alvin B., Ph.D.
Exec. V. President, Mongoven, Biscoe & Duchin, Inc.
655 15th St., N.W., Suite 300, Washington, DC 20005
Telephone: (202) 639-4080

BISHOP, Charles O., Jr.
Director, Public Relations, American Public Transit Ass'n
1201 New York Ave., N.W., Washington, DC 20005
Telephone: (202) 898-4000

BISHOP, COOK, PURCELL & REYNOLDS
1400 L St., N.W., Washington, DC 20005-3502
Telephone: (202) 371-5700
Background: The following information was obtained from public records by the Editors. It is the policy of Bishop, Cook, Purcell & Reynolds neither to confirm nor to deny that an individual or an entity is a client of the firm unless the clients expressly directs, or the law requires, that such a disclosure be made.
Members of firm representing listed organizations:
Alberger, Bill
Background: Special Assistant to Senator Bob Packwood (R-OR), 1969-71; Legislative and Administrative Assistant to Rep. Al Ullman (D-OR), 1972-77; Administrative Assistant, House Committee on Ways and Means, 1977; Commissioner (1977-82), Vice Chairman (1978-80), and Chairman (1980-82), U.S. International Trade Commission.
Bor, Robert M.
Background: Supervising Attorney, Deputy Director and Division Director, Office of General Counsel, Department of Agriculture, 1954-75. Chief Counsel, House Committee on Agriculture, 1975-84.
Cook, Marlow W.
Background: Former U.S. Senator (R-KY), 1968-74.
Daniel, Royal (III), Partner
Background: Special Assistant for Tariff Policy Planning, General Counsel's Office, U.S. Treasury Department, 1978-79.
diGenova, Joseph E.
Background: Counsel, Senate Select Committee on Intelligence, 1975-76. Counsel, Subcommittee on the District of Columbia, Senate Committee on Governmental Affairs, 1976. Counsel, Senate Committee on the Judiciary, 1978. Administrative Assistant and Legislative Counsel to Senator Charles Mathias, 1979. Chief Counsel and Staff Director, Senate Committee on Rules and Administration, 1981. U.S. Attorney for the District of Columbia, 1983-88.
Fox, H. Lawrence
Background: Assistant Branch Chief, Legislation and Regulation Division, Chief Counsel's Office, Internal Revenue Service, 1965-69.
Head, C. J., Partner
Hiebert, Peter N., Partner
Hirschhorn, Eric L.
Background: Legislative Assistant to Representative Bella S. Abzug of New York, 1971-73. Chief Counsel, House of Representatives Subcommittee on Government Information and Individual Rights 1975-77. Deputy Associate Director, Office of Management and Budget (President's Reorganization Project), 1977-80. Deputy Assistant Secretary for Export Administration, U.S. Department of Commerce, 1980-81.
Jackson, James K.
Background: Attorney, Office of the Chief Counsel, Internal Revenue Service, 1966-70.
May, Randolph J., Partner
Background: Assistant General Counsel, Federal Communications Commission, 1978-80. Associate General Counsel, Federal Communications Commission, 1980-81.
McGarry, (III) J. Michael
O'Leary, Joseph E., Consultant
Background: Held several Congressional staff position, 1969-75.
Purcell, Graham B. (Jr.), Of Counsel
Background: Former Member, U.S. House of Representatives (D-TX), and former Chairman, House Committee on Agriculture.

Waits, John A.
Background: Administrative Assistant to Rep. David R. Bowen (D-MS), 1980-82, and Counsel to House Agriculture Subcommittee on Cotton, Rice and Sugar, 1979-80.
Clients:
Ad Hoc Committee for Western Utilities *(H. Lawrence Fox)*
Akhiok-Kaguyak, Inc. *(Marlow W. Cook)*
Brazil-U.S. Business Council
Cayman Airways Ltd.
Center of Industries of the State of San Paulo (CIESP) *(Royal Daniel, III)*
CNA Financial Corp. *(Marlow W. Cook)*
Colonial Sugar Refineries, Ltd. *(Graham B. Purcell, Jr.)*
CompuServe Inc. *(Randolph J. May)*
GPU Service Corp.
Houston Agricultural Credit Corp. *(Robert M. Bor)*
IBP, Inc. *(Robert M. Bor)*
Industry Coalition on Technology Transfer *(Eric L. Hirschhorn)*
Internat'l Llama Ass'n *(Marlow W. Cook)*
Kidder, Peabody & Co., Inc. *(H. Lawrence Fox)*
Milk Industry Foundation
Mississippi Department of Economic and Community Development *(John A. Waits)*
Nat'l Cotton Council of America *(Robert M. Bor)*
Oakland County Board of Supervisors *(H. Lawrence Fox)*
Portland, Oregon, Port of *(Bill Alberger)*
Puerto Rico, Commonwealth of *(Marlow W. Cook)*
Puerto Rico, Popular Democratic Party of *(Marlow W. Cook)*
Puget Sound Power and Light Co. *(H. Lawrence Fox)*
Rohm and Haas Co. *(James K. Jackson)*
Sierra Pacific Resources *(H. Lawrence Fox)*
Texaco U.S.A. *(Marlow W. Cook)*
Thousand Springs Generating Co.
Tobacco Institute
Tousand Spring Generating Co. *(H. Lawrence Fox)*
U.S. Rice Producers' Legislative Group *(Robert M. Bor)*
Virgin Islands, Government of the *(Peter N. Hiebert)*
Washington Public Power Supply System (WPPSS) *(Marlow W. Cook)*

BISHOP, Frank
Exec. Director, Nat'l Ass'n of State Energy Officials
122 C St., N.W., Suite 810, Washington, DC 20001
Telephone: (202) 639-8749

BISHOP, Karen
Exec. Secretary, Detachable Container Ass'n
1730 Rhode Island Ave., N.W., Suite 1000, Washington, DC 20036
Telephone: (202) 659-4613

BISHOP, McNair
Legislative Analyst, Ass'n of Nat'l Advertisers
1725 K St., N.W., Suite 601, Washington, DC 20006
Telephone: (202) 785-1525
Registered as lobbyist at U.S. Congress.

BISNOW, Mark C.
2717 Chesapeake St., N.W., Washington, DC 20008
Telephone: (202) 363-3788
Registered as Foreign Agent: (#4306)
Organizations represented:
Thailand, Embassy of

BISSELL, Mary Sue
Exec. Director, US-Asia Institute
232 East Capitol St., N.E., Washington, DC 20003
Telephone: (202) 544-3181

BITZER, J. Barry
Exec. Director, Conservative Alliance
1315 Duke St., Alexandria, VA 22314
Telephone: (703) 683-4329
Registered as lobbyist at U.S. Congress.

BJORK, Don
Associate Exec. Director, World Relief
220 Eye St., N.E. Suite 200, Washington, DC 20002
Telephone: (202) 544-4447

BJORNSON, Gerrie
Director, Government Relations, Goodrich Co., BF
1825 Eye St., N.W., Suite 400, Washington, DC 20006
Telephone: (202) 429-2060
Registered as lobbyist at U.S. Congress.

BLACK, Charles R.
Black, Manafort, Stone and Kelly Public Affairs Co.
211 N. Union St., Third Floor, Alexandria, VA 22314
Telephone: (703) 683-6612
Registered as lobbyist at U.S. Congress.
Registered as Foreign Agent: (#3600).
Clients:
Bethlehem Steel Corp.
Chicago Regional Transit Authority

BLACK, J. Thomas
Staff V. Pres. for Research & Education, Urban Land Institute
1090 Vermont Ave., N.W. Suite 300, Washington, DC 20005
Telephone: (202) 289-8500

BLACK, Judy A.
Staff V. President, Government Relations, Internat'l Council of Shopping Centers
1199 North Fairfax St. Suite 204, Alexandria, VA 22314
Telephone: (703) 549-7404
Registered as lobbyist at U.S. Congress.
Background: Former special assistant for inter-governmental affairs at the White House under President Reagan.

BLACK, MANAFORT, STONE AND KELLY PUBLIC AFFAIRS CO.
211 N. Union St., Third Floor, Alexandria, VA 22314
Telephone: (703) 683-6612
Registered as Foreign Agent: (#3600)
Background: A public affairs and government relations consulting firm.
Members of firm representing listed organizations:
Black, Charles R.
Dark, Linda Pinegar
Davis, Richard H., Senior V. President
Background: Former Associate Director, Office of Cabinet Affairs in the White House under President Reagan.
Donaldson, John
Fenig, David, V. President
Background: Former Legislative Director for Senator Spark Matsunaga (D-HI).
Freedman, Matthew
Gay, Lawrance W.
Healey, James H.
Kelly, Peter G.
Keyserling, Jonathan
Background: Serves as Senior V. President, Black, Manafort, Stone, and Kelly Public Affairs. Exec. Director, Congressional Tax Caucus (1981-83); Tax Council and Legislative Director to Sen. Robert T. Matsui (D-CA), (1983-86).
Levinson, Riva
Manafort, Paul J.
Panuzio, Nicholas A., Chairman of the Board
Pastrick, R. Scott, Senior V. President
Background: Former Special Ass't to the Ass't Secretary for Legislative Affairs (1978-80); Staff Director, Subcommittee on Census and Population (1983); Deputy Nat'l Financial Director for Democratic Presidential Nominee Walter F. Mondale (1984).
Roberts, Robin D.
Stone, Roger J.
Sweet, Stuart J.
Sweitzer, Donald R., V. President
Background: Former Finance Director, Democratic National Committee.
Clients:
Aetna Life & Casualty Co. *(Peter G. Kelly)*
Allied-Signal Inc.
Bethlehem Steel Corp. *(Charles R. Black)*
Casino Ass'n of New Jersey *(Nicholas A. Panuzio)*
Chicago Regional Transit Authority *(Charles R. Black)*
Edison Electric Institute *(Nicholas A. Panuzio)*
Financial Security Assurance, Inc. *(Paul J. Manafort)*
Johnson & Johnson *(James H. Healey)*
Kaman Corp. *(Paul J. Manafort)*
Kenya, Government of

BLACK, MANAFORT, STONE AND KELLY PUBLIC AFFAIRS CO. (Cont'd)
Large Public Power Council *(Nicholas A. Panuzio)*
Mortgage Insurance Companies of America
Nigeria, Government of
NOVA University *(Nicholas A. Panuzio)*
Puerto Rico Federal Affairs Administration *(Richard H. Davis, Paul J. Manafort)*
Revlon Group *(Nicholas A. Panuzio)*
Somalia, Government of *(Nicholas A. Panuzio)*
South Carolina Economic Development Board *(Nicholas A. Panuzio)*
Tobacco Institute
Trans World Airlines
Trump Organization, The *(Nicholas A. Panuzio)*
Uniao Nacional Para Independencia Total de Angola (UNITA) *(Paul J. Manafort)*
Zaire, Government of the Republic of

BLACK, Norman
Manager, News and Information, Ford Aerospace Corp.
1235 Jefferson Davis Hwy. Suite 1300, Arlington, VA 22202
Telephone: (703) 685-5500

BLACK, Phyllis S.
Secretary, Olin Corp. Good Government Fund
1730 K St., N.W., Suite 1300, Washington, DC 20006
Telephone: (202) 331-7400

BLACK, R. Randal
Collier, Shannon & Scott
1055 Thomas Jefferson St., N.W., Suite 300, Washington, DC 20007
Telephone: (202) 342-8400
Registered as lobbyist at U.S. Congress.
Background: Former Legislative Assistant to Senator Richard C. Shelby (D-AL).

BLACK, Rheada Michele
Associate Director, Nat'l Health Policy Forum
2011 Eye St., N.W. Suite 200, Washington, DC 20006
Telephone: (202) 872-1390

BLACK, Timothy N.
Wilmer, Cutler and Pickering
2445 M St., N.W., Washington, DC 20037-1420
Telephone: (202) 663-6000
Clients:
Columbia Gas Transmission Corp.

BLACK, Wayne V.
Keller and Heckman
1150 17th St., N.W. Suite 1000, Washington, DC 20036
Telephone: (202) 956-5600
Clients:
INDA, Ass'n of the Nonwoven Fabrics Industry

BLACK, Col. Wendell
House Liaison, Legis Liaison, DEPARTMENT OF ARMY
The Pentagon, Washington, DC 20310-0101
Telephone: (202) 697-6767

BLACKLOW, Roger
Legislative Analyst, Nat'l Ass'n of Letter Carriers of the United States of America
100 Indiana Ave., N.W., Washington, DC 20001
Telephone: (202) 393-4695
Registered as lobbyist at U.S. Congress.

BLACKWELDER, Brent
Dir., Water Resources/Internat'l & V. P., Friends of the Earth
218 D St., S.E., Washington, DC 20003
Telephone: (202) 544-2600
Registered as lobbyist at U.S. Congress.

BLACKWELL, Lisa
Legis. Analyst, Gov't Relations, Nat'l Ass'n of REALTORS
777 14th St., N.W., Washington, DC 20005
Telephone: (202) 383-1087
Registered as lobbyist at U.S. Congress.

BLACKWELL, Robert J.
Dir., Fed. Relats. & Mktg. -Mil & Space, Ebasco Services, Inc.
1025 Connecticut Ave., N.W. Suite 1014, Washington, DC 20036
Telephone: (202) 872-1352

Registered as lobbyist at U.S. Congress.

BLACKWOOD, Bev D.
Washington Representative, Exxon Corp.
Suite 1100, 1899 L St., N.W., Washington, DC 20036
Telephone: (202) 862-0220
Registered as lobbyist at U.S. Congress.

BLACKWOOD, Tanya
Assistant Director, Public Relations, Recording Industry Ass'n of America
1020 19th St., N.W., Suite 200, Washington, DC 20036
Telephone: (202) 775-0101

BLAHA, David R.
Associate, Perkinson & Associates, Inc.
453 New Jersey Ave., S.E., Washington, DC 20003
Telephone: (202) 646-1260
Registered as lobbyist at U.S. Congress.
Clients:
Alliance for America's Homeowners

BLAINE, Barbara S.
Bryan, Cave, McPheeters and McRoberts
1015 15th St., N.W., Suite 1000, Washington, DC 20005
Telephone: (202) 289-6100
Registered as lobbyist at U.S. Congress.

BLAINE, Jack H.
Executive V. President, Reinsurance Ass'n of America
1819 L St., N.W., Suite 700, Washington, DC 20036
Telephone: (202) 293-3335

BLAIR, Bruce G.
Brookings Institution
1775 Massachusetts Ave., N.W., Washington, DC 20036
Telephone: (202) 797-6000

BLAIR, Robert A.
Anderson, Hibey, Nauheim and Blair
1708 New Hampshire Ave., N.W., Washington, DC 20009
Telephone: (202) 483-1900
Registered as lobbyist at U.S. Congress.
Registered as Foreign Agent: (# 3208).
Clients:
Alamo Rent-a-Car
Bay Area Rapid Transit District
ECO Corp.
Project Orbis
TECO Transport & Trade Corp.

BLAIR, Stephen J.
President, Nat'l Ass'n of Trade and Technical Schools
2251 Wisconsin Ave., N.W. Suite 200, Washington, DC 20007
Telephone: (202) 333-1021
Registered as lobbyist at U.S. Congress.

BLAIR, Trudi
Exec. Director, Bell Atlantic
1710 Rhode Island Ave., N.W., Suite 1100, Washington, DC 20036
Telephone: (202) 392-6984

BLAKE, Ernest L., Jr.
Shaw, Pittman, Potts and Trowbridge
2300 N St., N.W., Washington, DC 20037
Telephone: (202) 663-8000
Clients:
GPU Service Corp.
Jersey Central Power and Light Co.
Louisiana Power and Light Co.

BLAKE, Francis S.
Swidler & Berlin, Chartered
3000 K St., N.W., Suite 300, Washington, DC 20007
Telephone: (202) 944-4300
Background: Deputy Counsel to the Vice President, 1981-83. General Counsel, Environmental Protection Agency, 1985-88.
Clients:
American Gas Ass'n
American Iron and Steel Institute

BLAKE, Jonathan D.
Covington and Burling
1201 Pennsylvania Ave., N.W., Box 7566, Washington, DC 20044
Telephone: (202) 662-6000

Registered as lobbyist at U.S. Congress.
Clients:
Ass'n of Maximum Service Telecasters, Inc.
Lin Broadcasting Corp.

BLAKE, Richard R., Jr.
Dir, Pol Commun Network, Pol Field Optns, Nat'l Ass'n of REALTORS
777 14th St., N.W., Washington, DC 20005
Telephone: (202) 383-1000
Registered as lobbyist at U.S. Congress.

BLAKEY, Allen
V. President, Harrison Co., E. Bruce
1440 New York Ave., N.W. Suite 300, Washington, DC 20005
Telephone: (202) 638-1200

BLAKEY, William A.
Clohan & Dean
1101 Vermont Ave., N.W. Suite 400, Washington, DC 20005
Telephone: (202) 289-3900
Background: Aide to Senator Paul Simon (D-IL), 1981-87. Staff Director, Senate Subcommittee on Employment and Productivity, 1987-89.
Clients:
Miles College
Nat'l Council of Educational Opportunity Ass'ns
United Negro College Fund

BLALOCK, Cecelia
Director, Public Relations, Young Astronaut Council
1211 Connecticut Ave., N.W. Suite 800, Washington, DC 20036
Telephone: (202) 682-1984

BLANCHARD, Larry
Director, Public Affairs, Credit Union Nat'l Ass'n
805 15th St., N.W. Suite 300, Washington, DC 20005
Telephone: (202) 682-4200

BLANCHE, John G., III
Exec. Director, Federal Bar Ass'n
1815 H St., N.W., Suite 408, Washington, DC 20006
Telephone: (202) 638-0252

BLANCHETTE, Robert W.
Special Counsel, Ass'n of American Railroads
50 F Street, N.W., Washington, DC 20001
Telephone: (202) 639-2100

BLANDIN, Don M.
Director, Business-Higher Education Forum
One Dupont Circle, N.W., Suite 800, Washington, DC 20036
Telephone: (202) 939-9345

BLANK, Helen K.
Director, Child Care, Children's Defense Fund
122 C St., N.W., Washington, DC 20001
Telephone: (202) 628-8787
Registered as lobbyist at U.S. Congress.

BLANK, Jonathan
Preston Gates Ellis & Rouvelas Meeds
1735 New York Ave., N.W., Suite 500, Washington, DC 20006-4759
Telephone: (202) 628-1700
Registered as lobbyist at U.S. Congress.
Clients:
OMI Corp.
Seatrain Tankers Corp.
Transportation Institute

BLANK, Linda
Account Executive, Gallagher-Widmeyer Group Inc., The
1110 Vermont Ave., N.W., Suite 1020, Washington, DC 20005
Telephone: (202) 659-1606

BLANKENSHIP, Julia
Legislative Affairs Representative, Edison Electric Institute
1111 19th St., N.W., Washington, DC 20036
Telephone: (202) 778-6400
Registered as lobbyist at U.S. Congress.
Background: Former Legislative Assistant to Rep. Michael Oxley (R-OH).

WASHINGTON REPRESENTATIVES

BLANKENSHIP, Norma
Legislative Representative, American Health Care Ass'n
1201 L St., N.W., Washington, DC 20005
Telephone: (202) 842-4444

BLANKS, Jack B.
Acting Exec. Director, Internat'l Eye Foundation/Soc. of
Eye Surgeons
7801 Norfolk Ave., Bethesda, MD 20814
Telephone: (301) 986-1830

BLANTON, Lt. Gen. Charles C., USAF (Ret)
President, Armed Forces Relief and Benefit Ass'n
909 N. Washington St., Alexandria, VA 22314
Telephone: (703) 659-5140

BLANTON, Thomas
Deputy Director, Nat'l Security Archive
1755 Massachusetts Ave., N.W. Suite 500, Washington,
DC 22036
Telephone: (202) 797-0882

BLASE, Kurt E.
Prather, Seeger, Doolittle and Farmer
1600 M St., N.W., Washington, DC 20036
Telephone: (202) 296-0500
Clients:
Cadmium Council
General Electric Co.
Greens Creek Mining Co.
Lead Industries Ass'n
QIT, Inc.
Ridgeway Mining Co.

BLATCHFORD, Joseph H.
O'Connor & Hannan
1919 Pennsylvania Ave., N.W., Suite 800, Washington, DC
20006
Telephone: (202) 887-1400
Registered as lobbyist at U.S. Congress.
Registered as Foreign Agent: (#2972).
Background: Director, Peace Corps, 1969-72. Director, Ac-
tion, 1971-72. Member, President's Cabinet Committee
on the Aging, 1972. Deputy Under Secretary of Com-
merce, 1976-77.
Clients:
Asociacion Nacional de la Empresa Privada de El
Salvador
El Salvador, Government of

BLAU, Robert
Director, Regulatory Policy Analysis, BellSouth Corp.
1133 21st St., N.W., Suite 900, Washington, DC 20036
Telephone: (202) 463-4100

BLAU, Thomas
President, InTecTran, Inc.
1129 20th St., N.W., Suite 500, Washington, DC 20036-
3403
Telephone: (202) 293-0154

BLECHMAN, Barry M.
Chairman of the Board, Henry L. Stimson Center
1350 Connecticut Ave., N.W. Suite 304, Washington, DC
20036
Telephone: (202) 223-5956

BLECKER, Robert
Research Economist, Economic Policy Institute
1424 16th St., N.W., Suite 501, Washington, DC 20036
Telephone: (202) 667-0400

BLEDSOE, Ralph C.
Director, Washington Public Affairs Ctr., University of
Southern California
512 10th St., N.W., Washington, DC 20004
Telephone: (202) 638-4949

BLEDSOE, Willie W.
Carmen Group, The
1667 K St., N.W., Suite 700, Washington, DC 20006
Telephone: (202) 785-0500
Registered as Foreign Agent: (#4233).
Clients:
Committee for Free Elections and Democracy in
Nicaragua

BLEE, David C.
V. President, Robinson, Lake, Lerer & Montgomery
1667 K St., N.W., Suite 900, Washington, DC 20006
Telephone: (202) 457-9270
Registered as lobbyist at U.S. Congress.
Background: Director of Public Affairs, 1983-87; Director,
External Affairs, 1987-88; and Deputy Assistant Secretary
for Congressional, Intergovernmental and Public Affairs,
1988-89, U.S. Department of Energy.
Clients:
Illinois Power Co.

BLEICHER, Beatrice
Counsel, Government Relations, Reed Smith Shaw &
McClay
1200 18th St., N.W., Washington, DC 20036
Telephone: (202) 457-6100
Registered as lobbyist at U.S. Congress.
Clients:
Owens-Illinios

BLESSINGTON, Christopher M.
Ass't. Director, Highway Division, Associated General
Contractors of America
1957 E St., N.W., Washington, DC 20006
Telephone: (202) 393-2040
Registered as lobbyist at U.S. Congress.

BLISS, Donald T., Jr.
O'Melveny and Myers
555 13th St., N.W., Suite 500 West, Washington, DC
20004
Telephone: (202) 383-5300
Registered as lobbyist at U.S. Congress.
Registered as Foreign Agent: (#3346).
Background: Assistant to the Secretary of HEW, 1969-73.
Special Assistant to the Administrator, EPA, 1973-74.
Deputy General Counsel, Department of Transporation,
1975-77. Acting General Counsel, Department of Trans-
portation, 1976-77.
Clients:
Ford Motor Co.

BLISS, John S.
Wunder, Ryan, Cannon & Thelen
1615 L St., N.W., Suite 650, Washington, DC 20036
Telephone: (202) 659-3005
Registered as lobbyist at U.S. Congress.
Background: Legislative Aide to Senator Arlen Specter
(R-PA), 1981-84.

BLISS, Julia Christine
Mudge Rose Guthrie Alexander and Ferdon
2121 K St., N.W., Suite 700, Washington, DC 20037
Telephone: (202) 429-9355
Registered as lobbyist at U.S. Congress.
Registered as Foreign Agent: (#3200).
Background: Attorney-Advisor, Office of the General
Counsel, U.S. International Trade Commission, 1979-81.
Legislative Assistant to Senator John Chafee (R-RI),
1981-82. Associate General Counsel, Office of the Gener-
al Counsel, U.S. Trade Representative, 1982-86.
Clients:
Japan Lumber Importers Ass'n
Ponds India
PROEXPO/INCOMEX
Sovcomflot
Toshiba Corp.

BLISS, Richard W.
1079 Papermill Court N.W., Washington, DC 20007
Telephone: (202) 337-6008
Registered as lobbyist at U.S. Congress.
Background: An attorney.
Organizations represented:
Amax Inc.
Figgie Internat'l
Fluor Corp.
Nat'l Paint and Coatings Ass'n
New Hampshire Ball Bearings, Inc.
Philip Morris Cos., Inc.
San Diego Gas and Electric Co.

BLISS-WALTERS, Rinelda
Special Assistant and Corp. Secretary, Center for Security Policy
1250 24th St., N.W., Washington, DC 20037
Telephone: (202) 466-0515

Background: Conference Ass't to Ass't Secretary, Dept. of
Energy, 1985; Delegate to Negotiations on Nuclear &
Space Arms in Geneva, State Dept., 1985-86; Conference
Ass't to Ass't Director, Strategic Programs, ACDA,
1985-86; Confidential Ass't to Ass't Secretary of Defense,
Internat'l Security Policy, 1987; Special Ass't to the
Secretary of Defense, 1988.

BLITZ, Mark N.
Director, Political and Social Studies, Hudson Institute
4401 Ford Ave. Suite 200, Alexandria, VA 22302
Telephone: (703) 824-2048
Background: Former Associate Director for Educational
and Cultural Affairs, United States Information Agency.

BLOBAUM, Roger
Dir., Americans for Safe Food Project, Center for Science
in the Public Interest
1501 16th St., N.W., Washington, DC 20036
Telephone: (202) 332-9110

BLOCH, Michele
Director, Women vs. Smoking
1730 Rhode Island Ave., N.W. Suite 600, Washington, DC
20036
Telephone: (202) 659-8475

BLOCH, Ronald A.
Counsel, McDermott, Will and Emery
1850 K St., N.W., Suite 500, Washington, DC 20006-2296
Telephone: (202) 887-8000
Background: Former Assistant Director for Litigation, Bu-
reau of Competition, Federal Trade Commission, 1978-85.
Clients:
Churfine-Central Corp.
Nat'l Grocers Ass'n

BLOCH, Stuart Marshall
Dow, Lohnes and Albertson
1255 23rd St., N.W., Suite 500, Washington, DC 20037
Telephone: (202) 857-2500
Clients:
American Real Estate Group
American Savings Bank, F.A.
Belin and Associates
Castine Partners
Crossland Savings Bank
Franklin Federal Bancorp
New West Savings and Loan Ass'n
Owens-Illinois Development Corp.

BLOCK, Edward L.
Exec. Director, Nat'l Ass'n of Community Action Agencies
1775 T St., N.W.,, Washington, DC 20009
Telephone: (202) 265-7546

BLOCK, John R.
President, Nat'l-American Wholesale Grocers' Ass'n
201 Park Washington Court, Falls Church, VA 22046
Telephone: (703) 532-9400
Registered as lobbyist at U.S. Congress.
Background: Former Secretary, U.S. Department of Agri-
culture in the Reagan Administration.

BLOCKLIN, Peter
Senior Legislative Representative-Senate, American Bank-
ers Ass'n
1120 Connecticut Ave., N.W., Washington, DC 20036
Telephone: (202) 663-5000
Registered as lobbyist at U.S. Congress.

BLODGETT, Virginia
Director, Communications, Senior Executives Ass'n
Box 7610, Ben Franklin Station, Washington, DC 20044
Telephone: (202) 535-4328

BLOM, Don
Assoc. Exec. Director, Program Services, Nat'l School
Boards Ass'n
1680 Duke St., Alexandria, VA 22314
Telephone: (703) 838-6722

BLOM, Stephen D.
Exec. Director, American College Health Ass'n
1300 Piccard Drive Suite 200, Rockville, MD 20850
Telephone: (301) 963-1100

WASHINGTON REPRESENTATIVES

BLOMMER, Michael W.
Exec. Director, American Intellectual Property Law Ass'n
2001 Jefferson Davis Hwy. Suite 203, Arlington, VA 22202
Telephone: (703) 521-1680
Background: Also serves as Treasurer, Intellectual Property
Political Action Committee.

BLOMQUIST, Jim
Washington Dir., Public Lands Program, Sierra Club
408 C St., N.E., Washington, DC 20002
Telephone: (202) 547-1141
Registered as lobbyist at U.S. Congress.

BLONG, Adele
Associate Director, Center on Social Welfare Policy and
Law
1029 Vermont Ave., N.W. Suite 850, Washington, DC
20005
Telephone: (202) 347-5615

BLOOD, Patricia A.
Legislative Affairs (Senate), Nat'l Ass'n of Broadcasters
1771 N St., N.W., Washington, DC 20036
Telephone: (202) 429-5300
Registered as lobbyist at U.S. Congress.

BLOOM, Anne W.
Staff Attorney, Congress Watch
215 Pennsylvania Ave., S.E., Washington, DC 20003
Telephone: (202) 546-4996
Registered as lobbyist at U.S. Congress.

BLOOM, Charleen, Ph.D.
Administrative Consultant, Nat'l Student Speech Language
Hearing Ass'n
10801 Rockville Pike, Rockville, MD 20852
Telephone: (301) 897-5700

BLOOM, David I.
Mayer, Brown and Platt
2000 Pennsylvania Ave., N.W. Suite 6500, Washington,
DC 20006
Telephone: (202) 463-2000

BLOOM, Jane
Senior Attorney, Natural Resources Defense Council
1350 New York Ave., N.W. Suite 300, Washington, DC
20005
Telephone: (202) 783-7800

BLOOM, John L.
Preston Gates Ellis & Rouvelas Meeds
1735 New York Ave., N.W., Suite 500, Washington, DC
20006-4759
Telephone: (202) 628-1700
Registered as lobbyist at U.S. Congress.
Clients:
Aurora Fisheries, Inc.
Bellingham Cold Storage
Golden Alaska Seafoods, Inc.
Marine Management, Inc.
SeaHarvest, Inc.
Sunmar Shipping, Inc.
United States Cruises, Inc.

BLOOM, Madeline
Legis and Strategic Plng Div., DEPARTMENT OF TRANS-
PORTATION - Federal Highway Administration
400 Seventh St., S.W., Washington, DC 20590
Telephone: (202) 366-9208

BLOOMBERG, Mary Beth
Senior V. President for Client Services, Reese Communi-
cations Companies
2111 Wilson Ave., Suite 900, Arlington, VA 22201
Telephone: (703) 528-4400
Background: Senior Special Assistant to the Secretary, U.S.
Department of Health and Human Services, 1983-86.

BLOOMCAMP, F. W.
Director-Air Force Programs, McDonnell Douglas Corp.
1735 Jefferson Davis Hwy., Arlington, VA 22202
Telephone: (703) 553-3825

BLOOMFIELD ASSOC., Douglas
13712 Wagon Way, Silver Spring, MD 20906
Telephone: (301) 460-3285
Background: A lobbying and consulting firm.

Members of firm representing listed organizations:
Bloomfield, Douglas M., President
Background: Held staff positions, U.S. Congress, 1971-
80.
Organizations represented:
Computerized Machine Tools, Inc. *(Douglas M.
Bloomfield)*
Security Pacific Trade Finance *(Douglas M. Bloom-
field)*

BLOOMFIELD, Douglas M.
President, Bloomfield Assoc., Douglas
13712 Wagon Way, Silver Spring, MD 20906
Telephone: (301) 460-3285
Registered as lobbyist at U.S. Congress.
Background: Held staff positions, U.S. Congress, 1971-80.
Organizations represented:
Computerized Machine Tools, Inc.
Security Pacific Trade Finance

BLOOMFIELD, Mark A.
President, American Council for Capital Formation
1850 K St., N.W. Suite 400, Washington, DC 20006
Telephone: (202) 293-5811
Registered as lobbyist at U.S. Congress.

BLOOMFIELD, Sara
Exec. Director, United States Holocaust Memorial Council
2000 L St., N.W., Suite 588, Washington, DC 20036
Telephone: (202) 653-9220

BLOOMFIELD, Shirley A.
Director, Government Affairs, Nat'l Telephone Cooperative
Ass'n
2626 Pennsylvania Ave., N.W., Washington, DC 20037
Telephone: (202) 298-2300
Registered as lobbyist at U.S. Congress.
Background: Responsibilities include the Nat'l Telephone
Cooperative Ass'n Education Committee Organization.

**BLOOSTON, MORDKOFSKY, JACKSON & DICK-
ENS**
2120 L St., N.W. Suite 300, Washington, DC 20037
Telephone: (202) 659-0830
Members of firm representing listed organizations:
Courtney, Jeremiah, Counsel
Background: Specializes in communications law other
than broadcasting law. Assistant General Counsel,
Federal Communications Commission, 1946.
Dickens, Benjamin
Clients:
Academy of Model Aeronautics *(Jeremiah Courtney)*
Central Station Electrical Protection Ass'n *(Benja-
min Dickens)*

BLOUNT, John B., Jr.
V. President, Congressional Affairs, Nat'l Ass'n of REAL-
TORS
777 14th St., N.W., Washington, DC 20005
Telephone: (202) 383-1120
Registered as lobbyist at U.S. Congress.

BLOW, George
Patton, Boggs and Blow
2550 M St., N.W., Suite 800, Washington, DC 20037
Telephone: (202) 457-6000
Clients:
American Internat'l Automobile Dealers Ass'n
Auto Dealers and Drivers for Free Trade PAC
Dealer Action Ass'n

BLUDWORTH, Robert S.
Government Affairs Coordinator, Nat'l Beer Wholesalers
Ass'n
5205 Leesburg Pike, Suite 1600, Falls Church, VA 22041
Telephone: (703) 578-4300
Registered as lobbyist at U.S. Congress.
Background: Former Legislative Liaison to the Senate,
Dept. of the Army.

BLUM, Charles H.
Director, Internat'l Advisory Services Group Ltd.
1400 L St., N.W., Suite 600, Washington, DC 20005
Telephone: (202) 342-1200
Registered as lobbyist at U.S. Congress.
Registered as Foreign Agent: (#4267).
Background: U.S. Foreign Service Officer, 1971-80. Assist-
ant U.S. Trade Representative, 1980-88.
Clients:

Siderbras
Steel Service Center Institute

BLUM, Jared O.
V. President, Legislative Affairs, Albers and Co.
1731 Connecticut Ave., N.W. Second Floor, Washington,
DC 20009
Telephone: (202) 328-9333

BLUM, Joanne S.
Assistant Director, Planned Parenthood Federation of
America
2010 Massachusetts Ave., N.W. Fifth Floor, Washington,
DC 20036
Telephone: (202) 785-3351
Registered as lobbyist at U.S. Congress.

BLUMENFELD, Sue D.
Willkie Farr and Gallagher
1155 21st St., N.W., 6th Fl., Washington, DC 20036-3302
Telephone: (202) 328-8000
Clients:
Cable and Wireless North America
Cellular Telecommunications Industry Ass'n
Dun & Bradstreet
Network Equipment Technologies
Prudential Insurance Co. of America
Time Warner Inc.

BLUMENSTOCK, Doni G.
Assistant Director, Nat'l Assembly of Nat'l Voluntary
Health and Social Welfare Organizations
1319 F St., N.W., Suite 601, Washington, DC 20004
Telephone: (202) 347-2080
Background: Serves as contact person for Nat'l Collabora-
tion for Youth, an affinity group of the Assembly.

BLUMER, Patti R.
Asst. Exec. Director for Gov't Affairs, American Dietetic
Ass'n
1667 K St., N.W., Suite 430, Washington, DC 20006
Telephone: (202) 296-3956
Registered as lobbyist at U.S. Congress.
Background: Also represents the American Dietetic Ass'n
Political Action Committee.

BOARDMAN, John A.
Director, Publc Affairs, AFL-CIO - Food and Allied Service
Trades Department
815 16th St., N.W., Suite 408, Washington, DC 20006
Telephone: (202) 737-7200
Registered as lobbyist at U.S. Congress.

BOARDMAN, William J.
Concord Associates, Inc.
1455 Pennsylvania Ave., N.W. Suite 560, Washington, DC
20004
Telephone: (202) 737-9300

BOAZ, David D.
Exec. V. President, Cato Institute
224 Second St., S.E., Washington, DC 20003
Telephone: (202) 546-0200

BOBBITT, Timothy
Associate, Suplizio Associates, Paul
5152 Woodmire Lane, Alexandria, VA 22311
Telephone: (703) 931-0103
Registered as lobbyist at U.S. Congress.
Organizations represented:
Targeted Jobs Tax Credit Coalition

BOBO, Donald A.
Treasurer, Responsible Citizen's Political League
3 Research Place, Rockville, MD 20850
Telephone: (301) 948-4910

BOBO, Jack E.
Exec. V. President, Nat'l Ass'n of Life Underwriters
1922 F St., N.W., Washington, DC 20006
Telephone: (202) 331-6000

BOCCHI, Gregory J.
Exec. Director, Powder Coating Institute
1800 Diagonal Road, Suite 370, Alexandria, VA 22314
Telephone: (703) 684-1770

BOCCHINO, Carmella A.
Director, Legislative Services Division, Nursing Economics
1511 K St., N.W., Washington, DC 20005

Mail one of these cards TODAY!

This Directory is available by subscription. It's easy to order. Just use one of the tear-out cards below.

Washington Representatives
1990

ISBN 0-910416-85-0

ORDER CARD

Please enter my order for *Washington Representatives*

☐ XIV Edition — 1990 .... $55.
☐ XV Edition — 1991 .... $60.
☐ Put me on Standing Order for future editions (at 10% reduction).
☐ Check enclosed.

NAME   TITLE

ORGANIZATION

ADDRESS

CITY   STATE   ZIP

DATE

SIGNATURE

REVISION FORM

Please   ☐ Add   ☐ Change

The following individual in future editions of this book.

NAME   TITLE

STREET   TEL.:

CITY   STATE   ZIP

ORGANIZATION REPRESENTED:

ADDRESS

CITY   STATE   ZIP

TELEPHONE:

ORDER CARD

Please enter my order for *Washington Representatives*

☐ XIV Edition — 1990 .... $55.0
☐ XV Edition — 1991 .... $60.0
☐ Put me on Standing Order for future editions (at 10% reduction).
☐ Check enclosed.

NAME   TITLE

ORGANIZATION

ADDRESS

CITY   STATE   ZIP

DATE

SIGNATURE

Mail one of these cards TODAY!

This Directory is available by subscription. It's easy to order. Just use one of these order cards.

Business Manager
COLUMBIA BOOKS, INC.
1212 New York Ave., N.W.
Washington, D.C. 20005

Business Manager
COLUMBIA BOOKS, INC.
1212 New York Ave., N.W.
Washington, D.C. 20005

Telephone: (202) 347-2187

BOCEK, Robert R.
Director - Space & Technology Programs, McDonnell Douglas Corp.
1735 Jefferson Davis Highway, Arlington, VA
Telephone: (703) 553-2192

BOCKORNY, David A.
V. President, Bergner, Boyette & Bockorny, Inc.
1016 16th St., N.W., Suite 700, Washington, DC 20036
Telephone: (202) 659-9111
Registered as lobbyist at U.S. Congress.
Registered as Foreign Agent: (#3801).
Background: Former Special Assistant to the President for Legislative Affairs, House under President Reagan.
Clients:
Bell Atlantic
First Boston Corp.
Fox Broadcasting Inc.
Landmark Hotel Corp.
Nat'l Ass'n of Business and Educational Radio
Nat'l Soft Drink Ass'n
Orange & Rockland

BODDIE, Judith Ann
Senior Legislative Representative, Edison Electric Institute
1111 19th St., N.W., Washington, DC 20036
Telephone: (202) 778-6400
Registered as lobbyist at U.S. Congress.

BODE AND ASSOCIATES, William
1150 Connecticut Ave., N.W. 9th Floor, Washington, DC 20036
Telephone: (202) 337-0400
Members of firm representing listed organizations:
Bode, William
Organizations represented:
Environmental Business Ass'n, The *(William Bode)*
Independent Terminal Operators Ass'n *(William Bode)*
Mount Airy Refining Co. *(William Bode)*
Peerless Petrochemicals, Inc. *(William Bode)*
Petrojam Ltd. *(William Bode)*
Shepherd Oil Co. *(William Bode)*

BODE, Denise A.
Gold and Liebengood, Inc.
1455 Pennsylvania Ave., N.W. Suite 950, Washington, DC 20004
Telephone: (202) 639-8899
Registered as lobbyist at U.S. Congress.
Background: Former Legal Counsel to Senator David Boren (D-OK).
Clients:
Equitable Life Assurance Soc. of the U.S.
Nat'l Cattlemen's Ass'n
Phillips Petroleum Co.
Public Securities Ass'n

BODE, John
Olsson, Frank and Weeda, P.C.
1400 16th St., N.W. Suite 400, Washington, DC 20036-2220
Telephone: (202) 789-1212
Registered as lobbyist at U.S. Congress.
Background: Former Assistant Secretary for Food and Consumer Services, U.S. Department of Agriculture.
Clients:
Duramed Pharmaceuticals, Inc.
Nat'l-American Wholesale Grocers' Ass'n
San Tomo Group
Schwan's Sales Enterprises
U.S. Surgical Corp.
VICAM
Western States Meat Ass'n

BODE, William
Bode and Associates, William
1150 Connecticut Ave., N.W. 9th Floor, Washington, DC 20036
Telephone: (202) 337-0400
Organizations represented:
Environmental Business Ass'n, The
Independent Terminal Operators Ass'n
Mount Airy Refining Co.
Peerless Petrochemicals, Inc.
Petrojam Ltd.
Shepherd Oil Co.

BODEN, Shirley
Chairman, Board of Trustees, Cooperative Housing Foundation
1010 Wayne Ave., Suite 240, Silver Spring, MD 20910
Telephone: (301) 587-4700

BODENHORN, Karen
Capitol Associates, Inc.
426 C St., N.E., Washington, DC 20002
Telephone: (202) 544-1880
Clients:
American Ass'n of Nurse Anesthetists
Citizens for the Treatment of High Blood Pressure
Nat'l Ass'n of Pediatric Nurse Associates and Practitioners
Nat'l Center for Health Education

BODLEY, Alice
Deputy Gerneral Counsel, Nat'l Federation of Federal Employees
1016 16th St., N.W., Suite 400, Washington, DC 20036
Telephone: (202) 862-4400
Registered as lobbyist at U.S. Congress.

BODNER, John, Jr.
Howrey and Simon
1730 Pennsylvania Ave., N.W., Washington, DC 20006-4793
Telephone: (202) 783-0800

BOEDE, Marvin J.
General President, United Ass'n of Journeymen & Apprentices of the Plumbing & Pipe Fitting Industry of the US & Canada
901 Massachusetts Ave., N.W., Washington, DC 20001
Telephone: (202) 628-5823

BOEGE, Robert S.
Consultant, Public Affairs Group, Inc.
1629 K St., N.W., Suite 1100, Washington, DC 20006
Telephone: (202) 785-6713
Background: Former Associate Director, White House Conference on Small Business.
Clients:
Braddock Communications
MTI Export Management, Inc.
STRATCO, Inc.
Strategic Leadership, Inc.

BOERNER, Robert J.
Exec. Director, Ass'n of Schools and Colleges of Optometry
6110 Executive Blvd., Suite 514, Rockville, MD 20852
Telephone: (301) 231-5944

BOERTLEIN, Paul L.
V. Chairman, Hannaford Co., Inc., The
655 15th St., N.W. Suite 200, Washington, DC 20005
Telephone: (202) 638-4600
Registered as lobbyist at U.S. Congress.
Registered as Foreign Agent: (#2850).

BOESCH, Doyce
Exec. Director, Nat'l Republican Senatorial Committee
425 Second St., N.E., Washington, DC 20002
Telephone: (202) 675-6000
Background: Former Admin. Ass't, Office of U.S. Senator Don Nickles (R-OK), 1981-88.

BOETTGE, William
President, Nat'l Shoe Retailers Ass'n
9861 Broken Land Pkwy., Columbia, MD 21046-1148
Telephone: (301) 381-8282

BOGAN, William
Exec. V. President, Nat'l Coalition of Hispanic Health and Human Services
1030 15th St., N.W. Suite 1053, Washington, DC 20005
Telephone: (202) 371-2100

BOGGS, Andrea
Philip Manuel Resource Group Ltd.
1747 Pennsylvania Ave., N.W. Suite 701, Washington, DC 20006
Telephone: (202) 861-0651
Clients:
Compania Peruana de Vapores

BOGGS, Roderic V. O.
Exec. Director, Washington Lawyers' Committee for Civil Rights Under Law
1400 Eye St., N.W., Suite 450, Washington, DC 20005
Telephone: (202) 682-5900

BOGGS, Thomas Hale, Jr.
Patton, Boggs and Blow
2550 M St., N.W., Suite 800, Washington, DC 20037
Telephone: (202) 457-6000
Registered as lobbyist at U.S. Congress.
Registered as Foreign Agent: (#2165).
Background: Special U.S. Representative to Internat'l Maritime Conference 1965. Serves as Special Counsel to the American Soc. of Ass'n Executives. Member, Board of Directors, Eastern Air Lines.
Clients:
Ass'n of Professional Flight Attendants
Ass'n of Trial Lawyers of America
BATUS, Inc.
Chicago Board Options Exchange
Doyon, Ltd.
Freedom to Advertise Coalition
Internat'l Thomson
Marathon Oil Co.
MCI Communications Corp.
Mocatta Metals Corp.
Nakajima All Co.
Nat'l Ass'n of Retail Druggists
New York Life Insurance Co.
Options Clearing Corp., The
Paine Webber Group
Retail Industry Trade Action Coalition
Retail Tax Committee
Smokeless Tobacco Council

BOGGS, Timothy A.
V. President, Public Affairs, Time Warner Inc.
1133 21st St., N.W., Suite 400, Washington, DC 20036
Telephone: (202) 223-8855
Registered as lobbyist at U.S. Congress.

BOGLE AND GATES
One Thomas Circle, N.W., Suite 900, Washington, DC 20005
Telephone: (202) 293-3600
Registered as Foreign Agent: (#3474).
Background: DC office of a Seattle, WA law firm.
Members of firm representing listed organizations:
Hayes, Robert G.
Leitzell, Terry L.
Background: Assistant Administrator of NOAA, U.S. Department of Commerce, 1977-81.
Ringwood, Irene
Clients:
American Dehydrated Onion and Garlic Ass'n *(Robert G. Hayes, Irene Ringwood)*
American Fishing Tackle Manufacturers Ass'n *(Robert G. Hayes, Irene Ringwood)*
Basic American Foods *(Robert G. Hayes, Irene Ringwood)*
Coastal Conservation Ass'n *(Robert G. Hayes)*
Cominco, Ltd.
Crystal Globe Ltd.
Exxon Corp.
Nat'l Apparel and Textile Ass'n
Northern Jaeger *(Terry L. Leitzell)*
Norwegian Fisheries Ass'n *(Terry L. Leitzell)*
Oceantrawl, Inc. *(Terry L. Leitzell)*
Puget Sound Cruiseship Alliance *(Terry L. Leitzell, Irene Ringwood)*
Sahlman Seafoods *(Terry L. Leitzell)*
United Sport Fishermen *(Robert G. Hayes)*
Washington Agriculture GATT Coalition *(Irene Ringwood)*
Wright Schuchart, Inc. *(Terry L. Leitzell)*

BOHAN, Robert Z.
Sr. V. President/General Counsel, Nat'l Soft Drink Ass'n
1101 16th St., N.W., Washington, DC 20036
Telephone: (202) 463-6740
Registered as lobbyist at U.S. Congress.

BOHI, Douglas R.
Dir., Energy & Natural Resources Div., Resources for the Future
1616 P St., N.W., Washington, DC 20036
Telephone: (202) 328-5000

WASHINGTON REPRESENTATIVES

BOHM, John
Exec. Director, Nat'l Assisted Housing Management Ass'n
1800 Diagonal Rd. Suite 600, Alexandria, VA 22314
Telephone: (703) 684-4476

BOHRNSTEDT, George W.
V. President and Director, American Institutes for Research
3333 K St., N.W., Suite 300, Washington, DC 20007
Telephone: (202) 342-5000

BOIDOCK, John K.
Mgr., Government Relations (Corporate), Texas Instruments
1455 Pennsylvania Ave., N.W., Suite 230, Washington, DC 20004
Telephone: (202) 628-3133

BOINSKI, Patricia M.
Director, Federal Government Relations, ARCO
1333 New Hampshire Ave., N.W., Suite 1001, Washington, DC 20036
Telephone: (202) 457-6220
Registered as lobbyist at U.S. Congress.

BOISTURE, Robert A.
Director, Washington Office, YMCA of the USA
1701 K St., N.W., Suite 903, Washington, DC 20006
Telephone: (202) 835-9043

BOK, Carol
Director, Gov't Relations, Exchange Aff., American Logistics Ass'n
1133 15th St., N.W. Suite 640, Washington, DC 20005
Telephone: (202) 466-2520
Registered as lobbyist at U.S. Congress.

BOKAT, Stephen
V. President and General Counsel, Chamber of Commerce of the U.S.A.
1615 H St., N.W., Washington, DC 20062
Telephone: (202) 463-5337
Background: Serves also as Vice President, Nat'l Chamber Litigation Center.

BOLAN, Robert S.
Executive V. President, American Diabetes Ass'n
Nat'l Service Center, 1660 Duke St., Alexandria, VA 22314
Telephone: (703) 549-1500

BOLAND, Christopher T.
Gallagher, Boland, Meiburger and Brosnan
1000 Vermont Ave., N.W. Suite 1100, Washington, DC 20005-4903
Telephone: (202) 289-7200
Background: Staff Director, U.S. Senate Committee on Atomic Energy; Counsel-Staff Director, Joint Congressional Committee on Atomic Energy, 1945-47.
Clients:
High Island Offshore Systems

BOLAND, Michael J. P.
Bayless & Boland, Inc.
1072 Thomas Jefferson St., N.W, Washington, DC 20007
Telephone: (202) 342-0040
Registered as lobbyist at U.S. Congress.
Background: Chief Counsel and Floor Assistant to Rep. Trent Lott (R-MS), 1985-87. Senior Counsel, House Energy and Commerce Committee, 1978-84.
Clients:
Chevron, U.S.A.
Pacific Toxicology Laboratories
Psychemedics Corp.
Southwestern Bell Corp.
Space Services Inc.

BOLCE, Don
Director, Information Services, Nat'l Head Start Ass'n
1220 King St., Suite 200, Alexandria, VA 22314
Telephone: (703) 739-0875

BOLDUC, Mark P.
Assistant Director, Mortgage Bankers Ass'n of America
1125 15th St., N.W., Suite 700, Washington, DC 20005
Telephone: (202) 861-6500
Background: Serves as contact for Mortgage Bankers Association Political Aciton Committee.

BOLEN, Michael
Assistant Director, Federal Legislation, Associated Builders and Contractors
729 15th St., N.W., Washington, DC 20005
Telephone: (202) 637-8800
Registered as lobbyist at U.S. Congress.

BOLGER, Richard O.
2007 N. 15th St., Suite 201, Arlington, VA 22201
Telephone: (703) 522-1781
Registered as lobbyist at U.S. Congress.
Organizations represented:
Professional Photographers of America, Inc.

BOLGER, Terry
Account Executive, Hill and Knowlton Public Affairs Worldwide
Washington Harbour, 901 31st St., N.W., Washington, DC 20007
Telephone: (202) 333-7400
Registered as Foreign Agent: (#4170).
Background: Legislative Correspondent for Rep. Michael Bilirakis (R-FL), 1985 and Rep. Rick Boucher (D-VA), 1984.

BOLGER, William A.
Exec. Director, Nat'l Resource Center for Consumers of Legal Services
1444 Eye St., N.W., Eighth Floor, Washington, DC 20005
Telephone: (202) 842-3503
Registered as lobbyist at U.S. Congress.

BOLICK, Clint
Director, Landmark Legal Foundation Center for Civil Rights
216 G St., N.E., Washington, DC 20002
Telephone: (202) 546-6045

BOLICK, Stephanie C.
Director, Public Affairs, BDM Internat'l, Inc.
7915 Jones Branch Drive, McLean, VA 22102
Telephone: (703) 821-5000

BOLLING, Andrea W.
Associate, Cassidy and Associates, Inc.
655 15th St., N.W., Suite 1100, Washington, DC 20005
Telephone: (202) 347-0773
Registered as lobbyist at U.S. Congress.
Background: Staff aide to Rep. Claude Pepper (D-FL), 1983-85.
Clients:
Cardinal Hill Hospital
Loyola University of Chicago
Massachusetts Corp. for Educational Telecommunications

BOLLON, Vincent J.
Secretary-Treasurer, Internat'l Ass'n of Fire Fighters
1750 New York Ave., N.W., Washington, DC 20006
Telephone: (202) 737-8484

BOLT, Katie M.
Exec. Director, Nat'l Council of Community Hospitals
1700 K St., N.W. Suite 906, Washington, DC 20006
Telephone: (202) 728-0830

BOLUSKY, Benjamin C.
Director, Government Affairs, American Ass'n of Nurserymen
1250 Eye St., N.W., Suite 500, Washington, DC 20005
Telephone: (202) 789-2900
Registered as lobbyist at U.S. Congress.

BOLZE, Ray S.
Howrey and Simon
1730 Pennsylvania Ave., N.W., Washington, DC 20006-4793
Telephone: (202) 783-0800
Clients:
Carolina Power and Light Co.

BOMAR, Ernest
Principal, Ass'n Resources Management, Inc.
4222 King St., Alexandria, VA 22302
Telephone: (703) 549-4440

BOMBELLES, Thomas
Government Relations Counselor, Internat'l Business-Government Counsellors, Inc.
818 Connecticut Ave., N.W. Suite 1200, Washington, DC 20006
Telephone: (202) 872-8181

BOMBERG, Neil
Research Associate for Employment & Tng, Nat'l Ass'n of Counties
440 First St., N.W., Washington, DC 20001
Telephone: (202) 393-6226

BOND, Dr. A. Dewey
Special Assistant to the President, American Meat Institute
Box 3556, Washington, DC 20007
Telephone: (703) 841-2424
Registered as lobbyist at U.S. Congress.
Background: Exec. Secy., Nat'l Meat Canners Ass'n; Exec. Secretary, Canned and Cooked Meat Importers Ass'n, and Washington Representative, Internat'l Natural Sausage Casing Ass'n.

BOND, Col. Arlan F., USA (Ret.)
Vice President, Nat'l Security Industrial Ass'n
1025 Connecticut Ave., N.W., Suite 300, Washington, DC 20036
Telephone: (202) 775-1440

BOND DONATELLI INC.
1414 Prince St., Suite 300, Alexandria, VA 22314
Telephone: (703) 684-5991
Registered as Foreign Agent: (#4215)
Members of firm representing listed organizations:
Bond, Richard
Background: Former Deputy Chief of Staff to Vice President George Bush and former Deputy Chairman, Republican National Committee.
Donatelli, Frank
Background: Former White House political director under President Ronald Reagan.
McInturff, Cecilia Cole, Exec. V. President
Clients:
American Financial Corp. *(Frank Donatelli)*
American Petroleum Institute *(Frank Donatelli)*
FMC Corp. *(Frank Donatelli)*
Grumman Corp. *(Frank Donatelli)*
Tuscaloosa Steel Corp. *(Frank Donatelli)*
US Sprint Communications Co.

BOND, Edward N.
V. President, Congressional Affairs, Boeing Co.
1700 North Moore St., Arlington, VA 22209
Telephone: (703) 558-9684
Registered as lobbyist at U.S. Congress.

BOND, Phillip J.
Exec Asst, Legis, Affrs, DEPARTMENT OF DEFENSE
The Pentagon, Washington, DC 20301
Telephone: (202) 697-6210

BOND, Rae Young
Director, Public Affairs, Nat'l Governors' Ass'n
Suite 250, 444 North Capitol St., N.W., Washington, DC 20001
Telephone: (202) 624-5330

BOND, Richard
Bond Donatelli Inc.
1414 Prince St., Suite 300, Alexandria, VA 22314
Telephone: (703) 684-5991
Background: Former Deputy Chief of Staff to Vice President George Bush and former Deputy Chairman, Republican National Committee.

BONDER, Joel F.
Treasurer, Nat'l Corporation For Housing Partnerships Political Action Committee
1225 Eye St., N.W. Suite700, Washington, DC 20005
Telephone: (202) 347-6247

BONDURANT, Amy L.
Verner, Liipfert, Bernhard, McPherson and Hand, Chartered
901 15th St., N.W., Suite 700, Washington, DC 20005
Telephone: (202) 371-6000
Registered as lobbyist at U.S. Congress.
Registered as Foreign Agent: (#3712).

The listings in this directory are available as *Mailing Labels*. See last page.

Background: Legislative Assistant to Senator Wendell Ford (D-KY), 1975-78; Consumer Counsel/Senior Counsel, U.S. Senate Committee on Commerce, Science and Transportation, 1978- 1987.
Clients:
General Aviation Manufacturers Ass'n
General Dynamics Corp.
McDonnell Douglas Corp.

BONEY DENISON, Mary
Graham and James
2000 M St., N.W., Suite 700, Washington, DC 20036
Telephone: (202) 463-0800

BONITATI, Robert F.
Senior V. President, Kamber Group, The
1920 L St., N.W., Washington, DC 20036
Telephone: (202) 223-8700
Organizations represented:
Internat'l Ass'n of Fire Fighters

BONITT, John E.
Legislative and Regulatory Affairs, Allied-Signal Inc.
1001 Pennsylvania Ave., N.W. Suite 700, Washington, DC 20004
Telephone: (202) 662-2650
Registered as lobbyist at U.S. Congress.

BONK, Kathy
Co-Director, Communications Consortium
1333 H St., N.W., 11th Floor, Washington, DC 20005
Telephone: (202) 682-1270

BONKER, Don
Senior Trade Consultant, APCO Associates
1155 21st St., N.W., Suite 1000, Washington, DC 20036
Telephone: (202) 778-1000
Background: Former Member, House of Representatives (D-WA); Chairman, House Foreign Affairs Subcommittee on International Trade.
Clients:
American Indian Trade Development Council
Heart of America Northwest
Niedermeyer-Martin Co.

BONNER & ASSOCIATES
1625 K St., N.W., Suite 300, Washington, DC 20006
Telephone: (202) 463-8880
Background: Firm specializes in organizing and conducting grassroots campaigns at the federal and state levels on legislative and regulatory issues.
Members of firm representing listed organizations:
Bonner, Jack, President
Background: Executive Assistant and Press Secretary, Sen. John Heinz (R-PA), 1979-82. Press Office, Republican Nat'l Committee, 1977-79. Public Relations Director, City of Tucson, AZ, 1972-77.
Bonner, Sandy Cohen, Director, Legislative Affairs
Background: Former Legislative Assistant to Senator John Heinz (R-PA), 1982-84; Attorney, Office of Special Counsel, U.S. Merit Systems Protection Board, 1979-80.
Collingwood, Marlin W., Senior Project Manager
Background: Former Press Assistant to Senator John Heinz (R-PA); Assistant to Senator Richard Lugar (R-IN) and Rep. William Clinger (R-PA); Press Assistant for the Jack Kemp President Exploratory Committee; and Co-Chairman, Nat'l Republican Collegiate Committee for Reagan/Bush campaign, 1984.
Feaster, Susan Smith, Manager, Corporate Affairs
Background: Special Assistant to Senator Paul Trible (R-VA), 1983-84. Legislative Assistant to Rep. Frank Wolf (R-VA), 1984-87.
Fletcher, Lynne, Manager, Corporate Affairs
Graham, Gretta, Project Manager
Background: Deputy Press Secretary, U.S. Senate Government Affairs Committee, 1982-87. Press Secretary to Gov. John Sununu of New Hampshire, 1988.
Hess, Vicki Totter, Manager, Corporate Affairs
Mannes, Gwynn Geiger, V. President
Mannes, Paul H., Manager, Information Systems
Murphy, Chris, Project Manager
Background: Legislative Assistant to Rep. James Scheuer (D-NY), 1985-85.
Murphy, Patrick, Director, Government Relations
Background: State Assemblyman, Nevada State Legislature, 1975-79. Intergovernmental Liaison, U.S. Department of Housing and Urban Development, 1980-

81. Manager, Government Affairs, Federal Home Loan Mortgage Corp., 1988-89.
Schuessler, Janet L., V. President
Background: Former Director of Legislation, Rep. Adam Benjamin, Jr. (D-IN), 1978-81.
Towle, Ray, Project Manager
Background: Staff member to Senator Carl Levin (D-MI), 1984. Aide to Rep. John Dingell (D-MI), 1984-88.
Clients:
Alliance of American Insurers
American Ref-Fuel Co.
Ameritech (American Information Technologies)
Amoco Corp.
Ass'n of Bank Holding Companies
Automobile Importers of America
BP America Inc.
Browning-Ferris Industries (D.C.), Inc.
Chase Manhattan Bank
Citicorp
Colorado Bankers Ass'n
Cosmetic, Toiletry and Fragrance Ass'n
Exxon Corp.
FMC Corp.
Ford Motor Co.
General Motors Corp.
Illinois Committee on Tort Reform
Insurance Ass'n of Connecticut
Internat'l Playtex, Inc.
Lederle Laboratories, American Cyanamid Co. Subsidiary
Michigan Bell Telephone Co.
Miller Brewing Co.
Mobil Corp.
Motor Vehicle Manufacturers Ass'n of the United States
Nat'l Solid Wastes Management Ass'n
Nationwide Insurance Cos.
New Jersey Federation of Advocates for Insurance Reform
New York Telephone Co.
NYNEX
Ohio Alliance for Civil Justice
Pacific Telesis Group-Washington
Pharmaceutical Manufacturers Ass'n
Philip Morris Cos., Inc.
Retail Industry Trade Action Coalition
Shell Oil Co.
Smokeless Tobacco Council
State Farm Insurance Cos.
Syntex Laboratories
Texas Civil Justice League
United Parcel Service

BONNER, Jack
President, Bonner & Associates
1625 K St., N.W., Suite 300, Washington, DC 20006
Telephone: (202) 463-8880
Background: Executive Assistant and Press Secretary, Sen. John Heinz (R-PA), 1979-82. Press Office, Republican Nat'l Committee, 1977-79. Public Relations Director, City of Tucson, AZ, 1972-77.

BONNER, Sandy Cohen
Director, Legislative Affairs, Bonner & Associates
1625 K St., N.W., Suite 300, Washington, DC 20006
Telephone: (202) 463-8880
Background: Former Legislative Assistant to Senator John Heinz (R-PA), 1982-84; Attorney, Office of Special Counsel, U.S. Merit Systems Protection Board, 1979-80.

BONNET, Brian C.
Associate Director, Government Relations, Nat'l Ass'n of Truck Stop Operators
1199 N. Fairfax St. Suite 801, Alexandria, VA 22314
Telephone: (703) 549-2100
Registered as lobbyist at U.S. Congress.
Background: Former staff member, U.S. Senate Committee on Veterans' Affairs.

BONOSARO, Carol A.
President, Senior Executives Ass'n
Box 7610, Ben Franklin Station, Washington, DC 20044
Telephone: (202) 535-4328
Background: Former senior executive, U.S. Commission on Civil Rights, 1966-86. Analyst, Office of Management and Budget, 1961-66.

BONSIB, INC.
P.O. Box 1807, Washington, DC 20013
Telephone: (202) 546-7000
Members of firm representing listed organizations:
Bonsib, L. W. "Bill", President
Clients:
Eliminate the Nat'l Debt (END) (L. W. "Bill" Bonsib)
Nat'l Conservative Congressional Committee (L. W. "Bill" Bonsib)

BONSIB, L. W. "Bill"
President, Bonsib, Inc.
P.O. Box 1807, Washington, DC 20013
Telephone: (202) 546-7000
Registered as lobbyist at U.S. Congress.
Clients:
Eliminate the Nat'l Debt (END)
Nat'l Conservative Congressional Committee

BONTEMPO, Lisa
Manager, Federal Affairs, Nat'l Propane Gas Ass'n
1235 Jefferson Davis Hwy., Suite 702, Arlington, VA 22202
Telephone: (703) 979-3560
Registered as lobbyist at U.S. Congress.

BOOE, James B.
Secretary-Treasurer, Communications Workers of America
1925 K St., N.W., Washington, DC 20006
Telephone: (202) 728-2344
Background: Also serves as Treasurer, CWA-COPE Political Contributions Committee.

BOOK, Edward R.
President, Travel Industry Ass'n of America
1133 21st St., N.W.,, Washington, DC 20036
Telephone: (202) 293-1433
Registered as lobbyist at U.S. Congress.
Background: Also represents the Travel Industry Ass'n PAC.

BOOKSHESTER, Steven A.
Assoc. Gen. Counsel & First Amend. Atty., Nat'l Ass'n of Broadcasters
1771 N St., N.W., Washington, DC 20036
Telephone: (202) 429-5300
Registered as lobbyist at U.S. Congress.

BOOTH, John K.
V. President and Chief Actuary, American Council of Life Insurance
1001 Pennsylvania Ave., N.W., Washington, DC 20004-2599
Telephone: (202) 624-2170
Registered as lobbyist at U.S. Congress.

BOOTH, Sidney
Newmyer Associates, Inc.
1220 L St., N.W., Washington, DC 20005
Telephone: (202) 289-6300
Clients:
Alexander & Alexander Inc.

BOOTHBY, Lee
General Counsel, Americans United for Separation of Church and State
8120 Fenton St., Silver Spring, MD 20910
Telephone: (301) 589-3707

BOOTHE, Jeffrey F.
Schwabe, Williamson and Wyatt
2000 Pennsylvania Ave., N.W., Suite 8335, Washington, DC 20006
Telephone: (202) 785-5960

BOOZER, Lindon
Manager, Government Relations, United States Telephone Ass'n
900 19th St., N.W., Suite 800, Washington, DC 20006-2102
Telephone: (202) 835-3100
Background: Serves as contact for the United States Telephone Ass'n PAC.

BOR, Robert M.
Bishop, Cook, Purcell & Reynolds
1400 L St., N.W., Washington, DC 20005-3502

WASHINGTON REPRESENTATIVES

BOR, Robert M. (Cont'd)
Telephone: (202) 371-5700
Registered as lobbyist at U.S. Congress.
Background: Supervising Attorney, Deputy Director and
Division Director, Office of General Counsel, Department
of Agriculture, 1954-75. Chief Counsel, House Committee
on Agriculture, 1975-84.
Clients:
Houston Agricultural Credit Corp.
IBP, Inc.
Nat'l Cotton Council of America
U.S. Rice Producers' Legislative Group

BORCK, Noel C.
Exec. V. President, Nat'l Erectors Ass'n
1501 Lee Hwy., Suite 202, Arlington, VA 22209
Telephone: (703) 524-3336

BOREK, Col. Ted, JAGC, USA
Dir, Legis and Legal Policy, DEPARTMENT OF DEFENSE
- Military Manpower and Personnel Policy, Office of Asst
Secy (Force Mgmt)
The Pentagon, Washington, DC 20301
Telephone: (202) 697-3387

BORGER, Henry A.
Exec. Secretary, Federal Construction Council
c/o Nat'l Academy of Sciences 2101 Constitution Ave.,
N.W., Washington, DC 20418
Telephone: (202) 334-3378

BORGHESANI, William H., Jr.
Keller and Heckman
1150 17th St., N.W. Suite 1000, Washington, DC 20036
Telephone: (202) 956-5600
Background: Serves as General Counsel, Private Carrier
Conference.
Clients:
Nat'l-American Wholesale Grocers' Ass'n

BORGHESE, Phyllis
Director, Government Relations, Nat'l Ass'n of Enrolled
Agents
6000 Executive Blvd., #205, Rockville, MD 20852
Telephone: (301) 984-6232

BORGSTROM, Karl F.
Exec. Director, Construction Management Ass'n of America
12355 Sunrise Valley Drive Suite 640, Reston, VA 22091
Telephone: (703) 391-1200

BORISH, Phillip
V. President and Treasurer, American Gas Ass'n
1515 Wilson Blvd., Arlington, VA 22209
Telephone: (703) 841-8400

BORISSOFF, Erast
Exec. Director, American Coal Ash Ass'n
1000 16th St., N.W., Suite 507, Washington, DC 20036
Telephone: (202) 659-2303

BORKOSKI, I. Regina
Administrative Secretary, Ass'n of Farmworker Opportunity Programs
408 7th St., S.E., Washington, DC 20003
Telephone: (202) 543-3443

BORLAND, Lydia A.
Research Assistant, Internat'l Advisers, Inc.
2300 M St., N.W., Suite 600, Washington, DC 20037
Telephone: (202) 293-1575
Registered as lobbyist at U.S. Congress.
Registered as Foreign Agent: (#4203).
Clients:
Turkey, Embassy of

BORMAN, William
V. Pres. & Dir., Internat'l Telecomms., Motorola, Inc.
1350 Eye St., N.W., Suite 400, Washington, DC 20005-3306
Telephone: (202) 371-6900

BORN, Brooksley E.
Arnold & Porter
1200 New Hampshire Ave., N.W., Washington, DC 20036
Telephone: (202) 872-6700
Registered as lobbyist at U.S. Congress.
Registered as Foreign Agent: (#1750).
Clients:

Grain and Feed Trade Ass'n, The
Internat'l Commodities Clearing House, Ltd.
Internat'l Petroleum Exchange of London
Israel, Embassy of
League of Women Voters of the United States
London Commodity Exchange Co., Ltd.

BORNEMANN, Richard H.
V. President, Gov'tl Afrs. & Corp. Comm., UI Companies
10 Fourth St., S.E., Washington, DC 20003
Telephone: (202) 544-4522
Registered as lobbyist at U.S. Congress.

BOROS AND GAROFALO
1255 23rd St., N.W., Suite 295, Washington, DC 20037
Telephone: (202) 857-2526
Members of firm representing listed organizations:
Garofalo, Gary B.
Background: Staff Attorney, Federal Aviation Administration, 1965-68.
Clients:
Air BVI *(Gary B. Garofalo)*
Lineas Aereas Paraguayes (LAP) *(Gary B. Garofalo)*
Rich Internat'l Airways *(Gary B. Garofalo)*
Spantax, S.A. *(Gary B. Garofalo)*

BOROWSKI, Patricia A., CPIW
V. President, Gov't and Industry Affairs, Nat'l Ass'n of
Professional Insurance Agents
400 North Washington St., Alexandria, VA 22314
Telephone: (703) 836-9340
Registered as lobbyist at U.S. Congress.

BOROWY, Carol
General Manager, Sverdrup Corp.
1500 Wilson Blvd., Arlington, VA 22209
Telephone: (703) 525-1600

BORTHWICK, Mark
Exec. Director, United States Nat'l Committee for Pacific
Economic Cooperation
1755 Massachusetts Ave., N.W., Suite 420, Washington,
DC 20036
Telephone: (202) 745-7444
Background: Consultant to Chairman, House of Representatives Sub-Committee on Asian and Pacific Affairs,
1979-80.

BORTON, Lynn
Deputy Director, Nat'l Alliance for the Mentally Ill
2101 Wilson Blvd., Suite 302, Arlington, VA 22201
Telephone: (703) 524-7600

BORUT, Donald J.
Exec. Director, Nat'l League of Cities
1301 Pennsylvania Ave., N.W., Washington, DC 20004
Telephone: (202) 626-3000

BORY, Laurence D.
Managing Director, Governmental Affairs, American Consulting Engineers Council
1015 15th St., N.W., Suite 802, Washington, DC 20005
Telephone: (202) 347-7474
Registered as lobbyist at U.S. Congress.

BOS, Laura
Director, Education, Employee Benefit Research Institute
2121 K St., N.W., Suite 600, Washington, DC 20037-2121
Telephone: (202) 659-0670

BOSCO, Cassandra
Manager, Public Affairs, Nat'l Business Aircraft Ass'n
1200 18th St., N.W. Suite 200, Washington, DC 20036
Telephone: (202) 783-9000

BOSLEY, John J.
General Counsel, Metropolitan Washington Council of
Governments
777 N. Capitol St., N.E. Suite 300, Washington, DC
20002-4201
Telephone: (202) 962-3200
Background: Also serves as Legal Counsel for Nat'l Ass'n
of Regional Counsels.

BOSS, Walter
Director, Federal Government Division, Dictaphone Corp.
8260 Greensboro Drive A-32, Mclean, VA 22102
Telephone: (703) 893-2390

BOSSART, Kent
Export License Supervisor, Mitsui and Co. (U.S.A.), Inc.
1701 Pennsylvania Ave., N.W., Suite 400, Washington, DC
20006
Telephone: (202) 861-0660
Background: Office of Export Licensing, Department of
Commerce, 1988-89.

BOSSONG, Ken
Director, Public Citizen's Critical Mass Energy Project
215 Pennsylvania Ave., S.E., Washington, DC 20003
Telephone: (202) 546-4996
Registered as lobbyist at U.S. Congress.
Background: Formerly Coordinator, Citizens' Energy Project.

BOSTROM CORP.
808 17th St., N.W., Suite 200, Washington, DC 20006
Telephone: (202) 223-9669
Background: Washington office of a Chicago association
management firm.
Members of firm representing listed organizations:
Donahue, John F.
Estrada, Ramon A.
Miller, Jerome A. (CAE)
Clients:
American Heartworm Soc. *(Ramon A. Estrada)*
Nat'l Ass'n of Boards of Examiners of Nursing
Home Administrators *(Jerome A. Miller, CAE)*
Nat'l Ass'n of School Psychologists *(John F. Donahue)*
Soc. for American Archaeology *(Jerome A. Miller,
CAE)*
USIR - The Internat'l Soc. of SIR Users *(Ramon A.
Estrada)*

BOSWELL, G. Stewart
President and Chief Operating Officer, American Apparel
Manufacturers Ass'n
2500 Wilson Blvd., Suite 301, Arlington, VA 22201
Telephone: (703) 524-1864
Registered as lobbyist at U.S. Congress.

BOSWELL, M. L.
Chairman, Italian Aerospace Industries (USA), Inc.
1235 Jefferson Davis Hwy. Suite 500, Arlington, VA 22202
Telephone: (703) 271-9000
Registered as Foreign Agent: (#3399)
Background: Represents Aeritalia S.A.I.p.A. and Finmeccanica.

BOTELER, Stephanie
Treasurer, Nat'l Federation of Federal Employees Public
Affairs Council
1016 16th St., N.W., Washington, DC 20036
Telephone: (202) 862-4400

BOTHWELL, Robert O.
Exec. Director, Nat'l Committee for Responsive Philanthropy
2001 S St., N.W., Suite 620, Washington, DC 20009
Telephone: (202) 387-9177

BOTKISS AND ASSOC., Dan
1001 Connecticut Ave., N.W. Suite 528, Washington, DC
20036
Telephone: (202) 296-2207
Members of firm representing listed organizations:
Botkiss, Daniel A., President
Organizations represented:
Dump Transport Industries Ass'n *(Daniel A. Botkiss)*
Nat'l Environmental Health Ass'n *(Daniel A. Botkiss)*

BOTKISS, Daniel A.
President, Botkiss and Assoc., Dan
1001 Connecticut Ave., N.W. Suite 528, Washington, DC
20036
Telephone: (202) 296-2207
Organizations represented:
Dump Transport Industries Ass'n
Nat'l Environmental Health Ass'n

BOTSFORD, Charles G.
Botsford Office, Charles G.
1730 M St., N.W. Suite 911, Washington, DC 20036
Telephone: (202) 466-2885
Registered as lobbyist at U.S. Congress.
Organizations represented:
Air-Log Ltd.

Ellerbe-Becket Architects, Inc.
Evergreen Internat'l Aviation

BOTSFORD OFFICE, Charles G.
1730 M St., N.W. Suite 911, Washington, DC 20036
Telephone: (202) 466-2885
Background: An independent government relations consultant office.
Members of firm representing listed organizations:
Botsford, Charles G.
Organizations represented:
Air-Log Ltd. *(Charles G. Botsford)*
Ellerbe-Becket Architects, Inc. *(Charles G. Botsford)*
Evergreen Internat'l Aviation *(Charles G. Botsford)*

BOUCHARD, Francis D.
Assistant Director, Public Affairs, Nat'l Ass'n of Life Underwriters
1922 F St., N.W., Washington, DC 20006
Telephone: (202) 331-6000

BOUCHEY, Amparo
Dep Asst Secy, Cong & Intergovt'l Affrs, DEPARTMENT OF LABOR
200 Constitution Ave., N.W., Washington, DC 20210
Telephone: (202) 523-6141

BOUCHEY, L. Francis
President, Council for Inter-American Security
122 C St., N.W., Suite 710, Washington, DC 20001
Telephone: (202) 393-6622

BOUDRIAS, Claude P.
Legislative Rep., Tax and Trade, Chemical Manufacturers Ass'n
2501 M St., N.W., Washington, DC 20037
Telephone: (202) 887-1100
Registered as lobbyist at U.S. Congress.

BOULDIN, Kenneth A.
President and COO, Computer Dealers and Lessors Ass'n
1212 Potomac St., N.W., Washington, DC 20007
Telephone: (202) 333-0102

BOUNDS, Lori A.
Washigton Representative, American Academy of Ophthalmology
1101 Vermont Ave., N.W., Suite 300, Washington, DC 20005
Telephone: (202) 737-6662
Registered as lobbyist at U.S. Congress.

BOURDETTE, Mary M.
Director of Governmental Affairs, Children's Defense Fund
122 C St., N.W., Washington, DC 20001
Telephone: (202) 628-8787
Registered as lobbyist at U.S. Congress.

BOURNE, Laura L.
Manager, Legislative Information, Food Marketing Institute
1750 K St., N.W., Washington, DC 20006
Telephone: (202) 452-8444
Registered as lobbyist at U.S. Congress.

BOURNE POTTER, Janet A.
Exec. V. President, Nat'l Ass'n of Medical Equipment Suppliers
625 Slaters Lane, Suite 200, Alexandria, VA 22314
Telephone: (703) 836-6263

BOURQUE, Daniel P.
Corporate Senior V. President, Voluntary Hospitals of America, Inc.
1150 Connecticut Ave., N.W. Suite 800, Washington, DC 20036
Telephone: (202) 822-9750
Background: Also represents the Voluntary Hospitals of America PAC.

BOUTWELL, Wayne A.
President, Nat'l Council of Farmer Cooperatives
50 F St., N.W., Suite 900, Washington, DC 20001
Telephone: (202) 626-8700
Registered as lobbyist at U.S. Congress.

BOVE, Edward J.
Staff Attorney, Banner Life Insurance Co.
1701 Research Blvd., Rockville, MD 20850
Telephone: (301) 279-4800

BOW, Joseph W., CAE
President, Foodservice & Packaging Institute, Inc.
1025 Connecticut Ave., N.W., Suite 513, Washington, DC 20036
Telephone: (202) 822-6420

BOWE, Richard W.
Miles and Stockbridge
1701 Pennsylvania Ave., N.W., Suite 500, Washington, DC 20006
Telephone: (202) 333-2350
Clients:
Black and Decker Corp., The
Inova Health Systems

BOWEN & ATKIN
11215 Empire Lane, Rockville, MD 20852
Telephone: (301) 881-8910
Members of firm representing listed organizations:
Bowen, Harry A.
Clients:
Aero B *(Harry A. Bowen)*
Air Haiti *(Harry A. Bowen)*
Florida West Indies Airlines *(Harry A. Bowen)*
Skywest Aviation, Inc.
Surinam Airways *(Harry A. Bowen)*
TACA Internat'l Airlines *(Harry A. Bowen)*
Trans Air Link, Inc. *(Harry A. Bowen)*

BOWEN, Harry A.
Bowen & Atkin
11215 Empire Lane, Rockville, MD 20852
Telephone: (301) 881-8910
Clients:
Aero B
Air Haiti
Florida West Indies Airlines
Surinam Airways
TACA Internat'l Airlines
Trans Air Link, Inc.

BOWEN, Loretta
Director of Political Affairs, Communications Workers of America
1925 K St., N.W., Washington, DC 20006
Telephone: (202) 728-2465
Background: Also serves as political contact, CWA-COPE Political Contributions Committee.

BOWENS-JONES, Jacqueline E.
Director, Gov't and Community Affairs, Children's Hospital Nat'l Medical Center
111 Michigan Ave., N.E., Washington, DC 20010
Telephone: (202) 745-5000

BOWER, Catherine D.
V.P., Communications & Public Relations, Soc. for Human Resources Management
606 N. Washington St., Alexandria, VA 22314
Telephone: (703) 548-3440

BOWER, Donna
Manager, State Affairs, Baxter Internat'l Inc.
1667 K St., N.W., Suite 710, Washington, DC 20006
Telephone: (202) 223-4016

BOWER, Dr. Leonard G.
Policy Analysis Director, American Petroleum Institute
1220 L St., N.W., Washington, DC 20005
Telephone: (202) 682-8530

BOWER, Stephen P.
Director of Marketing/Communications, Nat'l-American Wholesale Grocers' Ass'n
201 Park Washington Court, Falls Church, VA 22046
Telephone: (703) 532-9400

BOWERS, Albert D.
V. President, Government Affairs, Shell Oil Co.
1025 Connecticut Ave., N.W., Suite 200, Washington, DC 20036
Telephone: (202) 466-1405
Registered as lobbyist at U.S. Congress.

BOWERS, Caroline
Director, Legislative Affairs, American Ski Federation
207 Constitution Ave., N.E., Washington, DC 20002
Telephone: (202) 543-1595

BOWERS, John, Jr.
Legislative Director, Internat'l Longshoremen's Ass'n
815 16th St., N.W., Suite 104, Washington, DC 20006
Telephone: (202) 628-4546
Registered as lobbyist at U.S. Congress.

BOWERS, Josh
Staff Attorney, Nat'l Federation of Federal Employees
1016 16th St., N.W., Suite 400, Washington, DC 20036
Telephone: (202) 862-4400
Registered as lobbyist at U.S. Congress.

BOWERS, Michael
Assoc Exec Dir for Professional Practice, American Ass'n for Marriage and Family Therapy
1717 K St., N.W. Suite 407, Washington, DC 20006
Telephone: (202) 429-1825
Registered as lobbyist at U.S. Congress.

BOWLER, M. Kenneth
V. President, Washington Govt Affairs, Pfizer, Inc.
1455 Pennsylvania Ave., N.W., Suite 925, Washington, DC 20004
Telephone: (202) 783-7070
Registered as lobbyist at U.S. Congress.
Background: Former Staff Director, House Ways and Means Committee.

BOWLES, Larry G.
Director, Government Relations, Halliburton Co.
1150 Connecticut Ave., N.W. Suite 205, Washington, DC 20036
Telephone: (202) 223-0820
Registered as lobbyist at U.S. Congress.

BOWLEY, Ed
Legislative Consultant, Nat'l League of Postmasters of the U.S.
1023 North Royal St., Alexandria, VA 22314
Telephone: (703) 548-5922
Background: Serves as contact for the Nat'l League of Postmasters Political Action Committee.

BOWLIN, Christopher
Legis Officer, Cong & Intergovt'l Affrs, DEPARTMENT OF LABOR
200 Constitution Ave., N.W., Washington, DC 20210
Telephone: (202) 523-6141

BOWLING, Richard P.
President, Truck Trailer Manufacturers Ass'n
1020 Princess St., Alexandria, VA 22314
Telephone: (703) 549-3010
Registered as lobbyist at U.S. Congress.

BOWMAN, Peyton G., III
Reid & Priest
1111 19th St., N.W., Washington, DC 20036
Telephone: (202) 828-0100
Clients:
Great Plains Natural Gas Co.
Halecrest Co.
Philadelphia Electric Co.

BOWYER, Joan Costain
Asst. to the V. Pres., Gov't Relations, Phelps Dodge Corp.
1015 15th St., N.W., Suite 909, Washington, DC 20005
Telephone: (202) 789-1745
Registered as lobbyist at U.S. Congress.

BOWYTZ, Robert B.
Bowytz, Sherman and Mitchell
2828 Pennsylvania Ave., N.W., Suite 304, Washington, DC 20007-3719
Telephone: (202) 965-7150
Clients:
American Ass'n of Small Research Companies

BOWYTZ, SHERMAN AND MITCHELL
2828 Pennsylvania Ave., N.W., Suite 304, Washington, DC 20007-3719
Telephone: (202) 965-7150
Members of firm representing listed organizations:
Bowytz, Robert B.
Clients:
American Ass'n of Small Research Companies
(Robert B. Bowytz)

BOXER, Peter
Senior V. President, British Aerospace, Inc./Defense Programs Office
1101 Wilson Blvd. Suite 1200, Arlington, VA 22209
Telephone: (703) 243-3939

BOYADJIAN, Seto
Exec. Director, Armenian Nat'l Committee of America
1901 Pennsylvania Ave., N.W., Suite 206, Washington, DC 20006
Telephone: (202) 775-1918

BOYAJIAN, Pamela
Exec. Director, Nat'l Beverage Dispensing Equipment Ass'n
2011 Eye St., N.W., Fifth Floor, Washington, DC 20006
Telephone: (202) 775-4885
Background: Also represents the Committee to Eliminate Equipment Giveaways.

BOYCE, Katharine R.
Patton, Boggs and Blow
2550 M St., N.W., Suite 800, Washington, DC 20037
Telephone: (202) 457-6000
Registered as lobbyist at U.S. Congress.
Registered as Foreign Agent: (#2165).
Background: Legislative Aide to Rep. James G. O'Hara (D-MI), 1972-73. Legislative Assistant and Press Secretary to Rep. Brock Adams (D-WA), 1973-77.
Clients:
Cherokee Nation of Oklahoma
Fiart Cantieri Italiani S.p.A.
Waste Management, Inc.

BOYCE, Dr. Peter B.
Exec. Officer, American Astronomical Soc.
2000 Florida Ave., N.W., Suite 300, Washington, DC 20009
Telephone: (202) 328-2010

BOYD, Alan
Chairman, Airbus Industrie of North America
1825 Eye St., N.W., Suite 400, Washington, DC 20006
Telephone: (202) 429-2052

BOYD, Dennis W.
Exec. Director, Federal Physicians Ass'n
P.O. Box 45150, Washington, DC 20026
Telephone: (703) 455-5947

BOYD, John G.
Program Director, Public Affairs, Internat'l Business Machines Corp.
Suite 1200, 1801 K St., N.W., Washington, DC 20006
Telephone: (202) 778-5042
Registered as lobbyist at U.S. Congress.

BOYD, Robert
Managing Director, Secura Group, The
1155 21st St., N.W., Washington, DC 20036
Telephone: (202) 728-4920

BOYD, Robert K.
Special Assistant, Washington Gas Light Co.
1100 H St., N.W., Washington, DC 20080
Telephone: (202) 624-6091

BOYD, Rodger
Exec. Director, Navajo Nation, The
2033 M St., N.W., Suite 404, Washington, DC 20036
Telephone: (202) 775-0393

BOYD, Susan
Exec. Director, Concern, Inc.
1794 Columbia Road, N.W., Washington, DC 20009
Telephone: (202) 328-8160

BOYER, Carolyn A.
V. President & Associate Counsel, Equitable Life Assurance Soc. of the U.S.
1700 Pennsylvania Ave., N.W., Suite 525, Washington, DC 20006
Telephone: (202) 393-3210

BOYERS, Ellen
Development Director - Southeast Region, Conference Board
1755 Massachusetts Ave., N.W., Suite 312, Washington, DC 20036
Telephone: (202) 483-0580

BOYETTE, Van R.
Corp. Sec'y. & General Counsel, Bergner, Boyette & Bockorny, Inc.
1016 16th St., N.W., Suite 700, Washington, DC 20036
Telephone: (202) 659-9111
Registered as lobbyist at U.S. Congress.
Registered as Foreign Agent: (#3801).
Clients:
Avianca Airlines
Flo-Sun Land Corp.
Forum Group, Inc.
Landmark Hotel Corp.
Lilly and Co., Eli
Murry's, Inc.
Nat'l Soft Drink Ass'n
Nat'l-American Wholesale Grocers' Ass'n
Okeelanta Corp.
Orange & Rockland

BOYKIN, Hamilton
Colton and Boykin
1025 Thomas Jefferson St., N.W., Suite 500 East, Washington, DC 20007
Telephone: (202) 342-5400
Clients:
Nat'l Office Products Ass'n

BOYLE, J. Patrick
President and CEO, American Meat Institute
Box 3556, Washington, DC 20007
Telephone: (703) 841-2400
Background: Administrator, Agricultural Marketing Service, U.S. Department of Agriculture, 1986-89. Also was a former aide to Senator Pete Wilson (R-CA).

BOYLE, Jayne F.
Kirkland and Ellis
655 15th St., N.W. Suite 1200, Washington, DC 20005
Telephone: (202) 879-5000
Background: Former Tax Counsel, House Committee on Ways and Means.

BOYLE, Dr. Joseph F.
Exec. Vice President, American Soc. of Internal Medicine
1101 Vermont Ave., N.W. Suite 500, Washington, DC 20005
Telephone: (202) 289-1700

BOYLE, Paul J.
Government Affairs Representative, American Newspaper Publishers Ass'n
The Newspaper Center 11600 Sunrise Valley Drive, Reston, VA 22091
Telephone: (703) 648-1000
Registered as lobbyist at U.S. Congress.

BOYLE, Stephen T.
Cong and Public Affrs, DEPARTMENT OF JUSTICE - United States Marshals Service
600 Army-Navy Drive, Arlington, VA 22202
Telephone: (202) 307-9065

BRABHAM, Robert E., Ph.D.
Exec. Director, Nat'l Rehabilitation Ass'n
633 S. Washington St., Alexandria, VA 22314
Telephone: (703) 836-0850

BRACEWELL AND PATTERSON
2000 K St., N.W., Suite 500, Washington, DC 20006-1809
Telephone: (202) 828-5800
Background: Washington office of a law firm with other offices in Houston, Dallas, Austin and London.
Members of firm representing listed organizations:
Godley, Gene E.
Background: Serves also as Treasurer, Bracewell and Patterson Political Action Committee and the Conservative Democratic PAC. Administrative Assistant to Sen. Ralph Yarborough (D-TX), 1967-69. General Counsel, Senate Labor and Public Welfare Committee, 1969-70. General Counsel, Senate District Committee, 1970-71. Administrative Assistant to Sen. Thomas Eagleton (D-MO), 1971-76. Assistant Secretary of the Treasury for Legislative Affairs, 1976-80.
Pate, Michael L.
Background: Former Legislative Director for Senator Lloyd Bentsen (D-TX), 1980-86.
Segal, Scott H.
Clients:
American Council on Education

Bracewell and Patterson Political Action Committee *(Gene E. Godley)*
Centex Corp. *(Gene E. Godley)*
Chemical Manufacturers Ass'n *(Gene E. Godley)*
Computer Dealers and Lessors Ass'n *(Gene E. Godley)*
Conservative Democratic PAC *(Gene E. Godley)*
Enron Corp. *(Gene E. Godley)*
Genentech, Inc. *(Gene E. Godley)*
Higman Barge Lines *(Gene E. Godley)*
Louisiana Land and Exploration Co. *(Gene E. Godley)*
Massachusetts Mutual Life Insurance Co. *(Michael L. Pate)*
Southdown *(Gene E. Godley)*
Sterling Chemical Co. *(Gene E. Godley)*
Valero Energy Corp. *(Gene E. Godley)*

BRACK, William T.
Williams and Jensen, P.C.
1101 Connecticut Ave., N.W., Suite 500, Washington, DC 20036
Telephone: (202) 659-8201
Clients:
College Construction Loan Insurance Ass'n
Goldome FSB
GTE Corp.
Southwestern Bell Corp.
United States Telephone Ass'n

BRACKIN, Susan
Exec. Director, Eagle Forum
316 Pennsylvania Ave., S.E. Suite 203, Washington, DC 20003
Telephone: (202) 544-0353

BRACY, Terrence L.
CEO, Bracy Williams & Co.
1000 Connecticut Ave., N.W., Suite 304, Washington, DC 20036
Telephone: (202) 659-4805
Registered as lobbyist at U.S. Congress.
Background: Former Assistant Secretary for Congressional and Governmental Affairs, U.S. Department of Transportation.
Clients:
American Home Satellite Ass'n
American Southwest Financial Corp.
Batman Corp.
Daishowa America Co. Ltd.
Fieldstone Co.
Millicom Inc.
Pratt & Whitney
Rocky Co., The
Tucson, Arizona, City of

BRACY WILLIAMS & CO.
1000 Connecticut Ave., N.W., Suite 304, Washington, DC 20036
Telephone: (202) 659-4805
Background: A government affairs consulting firm.
Members of firm representing listed organizations:
Benfield, James C.
Birnbaum, Kenneth S., General Cou
Bracy, Terrence L., CEO
Background: Former Assistant Secretary for Congressional and Governmental Affairs, U.S. Department of Transportation.
Hennessey, Thomas J. (Jr.)
Kreizman, Janet
Stram, Kenneth M.
Williams, Susan J., President
Background: Former Assistant Secretary for Congressional and Governmental Affairs, U.S. Department of Transportation.
Clients:
American Home Satellite Ass'n *(Kenneth S. Birnbaum, Terrence L. Bracy, Thomas J. Hennessey, Jr., Susan J. Williams)*
American Southwest Financial Corp. *(Kenneth S. Birnbaum, Terrence L. Bracy, Susan J. Williams)*
Arkla, Inc.
Batman Corp. *(Kenneth S. Birnbaum, Terrence L. Bracy, Kenneth M. Stram, Susan J. Williams)*
Coin Coalition, The *(James C. Benfield)*
Committee for Environmentally Effective Packaging *(James C. Benfield)*

Daishowa America Co. Ltd. *(Kenneth S. Birnbaum, Terrence L. Bracy, Thomas J. Hennessey, Jr., Kenneth M. Stram, Susan J. Williams)*
Energy Absorption Systems, Inc. *(Susan J. Williams)*
Fieldstone Co. *(Kenneth S. Birnbaum, Terrence L. Bracy, Kenneth M. Stram, Susan J. Williams)*
Millicom Inc. *(Kenneth S. Birnbaum, Terrence L. Bracy, Thomas J. Hennessey, Jr., Susan J. Williams)*
Pratt & Whitney *(Terrence L. Bracy)*
Rocky Co., The *(James C. Benfield, Kenneth S. Birnbaum, Terrence L. Bracy, Thomas J. Hennessey, Jr., Kenneth M. Stram, Susan J. Williams)*
Tucson, Arizona, City of *(Terrence L. Bracy, Thomas J. Hennessey, Jr., Susan J. Williams)*

BRADBURNE, John
Director, Government Affairs, NUS Corp.
910 Clopper Road, Gaithersburg, MD 20877-0962
Telephone: (301) 258-6000

BRADBURY, Dorothy V.
Cong and Public Liaison, DEPARTMENT OF AGRICULTURE - Soil Conservation Service
12th and Independence Ave. S.W., Washington, DC 20250
Telephone: (202) 447-2771

BRADBURY, Col. James W., (Ret)
Treasurer, Nat'l Ass'n for Uniformed Services Political Action Committee
5535 Hempstead Way, Springfield, VA 22151
Telephone: (703) 750-1342

BRADEN, Susan G.
Wilner and Scheiner
1200 New Hampshire Ave., N.W., Suite 300, Washington, DC 20036
Telephone: (202) 861-7800
Registered as lobbyist at U.S. Congress.
Background: Senior Trial Attorney, Antitrust Division, Department of Justice, 1978-80. Senior Attorney Advisor to Commissioner and Acting Chairman, 1980-83 and Special Counsel to the Chairman, 1984-85, Federal Trade Commission.

BRADFIELD, Daniel Todd
Dir, Political Affrs/Sr Legislative Rep, Suburban Maryland Building Industry Ass'n
Executive Terrace 1400 Mercantile Lane, Landover, MD 20785
Telephone: (301) 925-9490
Registered as lobbyist at U.S. Congress.

BRADFORD, Marcia
Communications Director, Nat'l Small Business United
1155 15th St., N.W. 7th Floor, Washington, DC 20005
Telephone: (202) 293-8830

BRADFORD, Patricia
Admin. Assistant, Nat'l Homeowners Ass'n
1906 Sunderland Place, N.W., Washington, DC 20036
Telephone: (202) 223-1453

BRADFORD, William H., Jr.
Hopkins and Sutter
888 16th St., N.W., Suite 700, Washington, DC 20006
Telephone: (202) 835-8000
Registered as lobbyist at U.S. Congress.
Clients:
Amoco Corp.
Greenwich Capital Markets, Inc.

BRADLEY, David
Legislative Director, Nat'l Community Action Foundation
2100 M St., N.W. Suite 604, Washington, DC 20037
Telephone: (202) 775-0223
Registered as lobbyist at U.S. Congress.
Background: Repsonsibilities include the Nat'l Community Action Foundation PAC.

BRADLEY, Gene E.
Chairman and President, Internat'l Management and Development Institute
2600 Virginia Ave., N.W. Suite 905, Washington, DC 20037
Telephone: (202) 337-1022

BRADLEY, Harvey H.
V. President, Operations and Maintenance, Ass'n of American Railroads
50 F St., N.W., Suite 6102, Washington, DC 20001
Telephone: (202) 639-2200

BRADLEY, Mitchell
Exec. Director, American Ass'n of Engineering Societies
415 2nd St., N.E., Suite 200, Washington, DC 20002
Telephone: (202) 546-2237

BRADLEY, Richard H.
President, Internat'l Downtown Ass'n
915 15th St., N.W. Suite 900, Washington, DC 20005-2375
Telephone: (202) 783-4963

BRADLEY, William
Manager, Technical Division, American Gear Manufacturers Ass'n
1500 King St., Suite 201, Alexandria, VA 22314
Telephone: (703) 684-0211

BRADLEY WOODS & CO.
733 15th St., N.W. Suite 400, Washington, DC 20005
Telephone: (202) 628-0193
Background: A public policy research firm serving institutional investors.
Members of firm representing listed organizations:
Brush, C. E., Partner

BRADSHAW, Christina L.
Exec. Asst. to the President, Nat'l Center for Neighborhood Enterprise
1367 Connecticut Ave., N.W., 2nd Floor, Washington, DC 20036
Telephone: (202) 331-1103

BRADSHAW, Dennis
Director, Member Services, Sheet Metal and Air Conditioning Contractors' Nat'l Ass'n
8224 Old Courthouse Rd., Vienna, VA 22182
Telephone: (703) 790-9890
Registered as lobbyist at U.S. Congress.

BRADSHAW, Mary
Director, Industry Relations, North American Telecommunications Ass'n
2000 M Street, N.W., Suite 550, Washington, DC 20036
Telephone: (202) 296-9800
Background: Responsibilities include the North American Telecommunications Ass'n Political Action Committee.

BRADY AND BERLINER
1225 19th St., N.W. Suite 800, Washington, DC 20036
Telephone: (202) 955-6067
Members of firm representing listed organizations:
Berliner, Roger A.
Brady, Jerry M.
Clients:
Alberta Petroleum Marketing Commission
Canadian Petroleum Ass'n *(Roger A. Berliner, Jerry M. Brady)*
Independent Petroleum Ass'n of Canada *(Roger A. Berliner, Jerry M. Brady)*

BRADY, Frank B.
Exec. Director, Institute of Navigation
1026 16th St., N.W., Washington, DC 20036
Telephone: (202) 783-4121

BRADY, Hugh S.
Director, Legislative Affairs, BellSouth Corp.
1133 21st St., N.W., Suite 900, Washington, DC 20036
Telephone: (202) 463-4100

BRADY, J. Christopher
Legis Director, Cong Affrs, GENERAL SERVICES ADMINISTRATION
18th and F Sts., N.W., Washington, DC 20405
Telephone: (202) 566-0563

BRADY, Jerry M.
Brady and Berliner
1225 19th St., N.W. Suite 800, Washington, DC 20036
Telephone: (202) 955-6067
Registered as Foreign Agent: (#3656).
Clients:
Canadian Petroleum Ass'n

Independent Petroleum Ass'n of Canada

BRADY, John
President, Direct Impact Co., The
1414 Prince St. Suite 350, Alexandria, VA 22314
Telephone: (703) 684-1245
Clients:
American Petroleum Institute
Chemical Manufacturers Ass'n
Columbia Presbyterian Hospital
Dulles Area Rapid Transit, Inc.
Florida Commercial Developers Ass'n
FMC Corp.
Maglev Transit, Inc.
Rocky Mountain Oil and Gas Ass'n

BRADY, John F.
Exec. V. President, MEBA District II
490 L'Enfant Plaza East, S.W., Suite 3204, Washington, DC 20024
Telephone: (202) 479-1166

BRADY, Richard A.
Covington and Burling
1201 Pennsylvania Ave., N.W., Box 7566, Washington, DC 20044
Telephone: (202) 662-6000
Registered as lobbyist at U.S. Congress.

BRADY, Robert P.
Patton, Boggs and Blow
2550 M St., N.W., Suite 800, Washington, DC 20037
Telephone: (202) 457-6000
Background: Exec. Ass't to the Commissioner, Food and Drug Administration, 1981-83.

BRADY, Sarah
Chair, Handgun Control, Inc.
1225 Eye St., N.W., Suite 1100, Washington, DC 20005
Telephone: (202) 898-0792
Registered as lobbyist at U.S. Congress.
Background: Former Deputy Director for Law Enforcement, Bureau of Alcohol, Tobacco and Firearms, U.S. Department of the Treasury.

BRAGG, Raymond F., Jr.
President, Legislative Strategies Inc.
1275 Pennsylvania Ave., N.W. Suite 301, Washington, DC 20004
Telephone: (202) 626-6490
Registered as lobbyist at U.S. Congress.
Clients:
American Independent Refiners Ass'n
American Independent Refiners Ass'n PAC
Consolidated Natural Gas Co.
Environmental Power Corp.
Nat'l Hydropower Ass'n
Tosco Corp.

BRAHMS, Thomas W.
Exec. Director, Institute of Transportation Engineers
525 School St., S.W., Suite 410, Washington, DC 20024
Telephone: (202) 554-8050

BRAHS, Stuart J.
V. Pres., Federal Government Relations, Principal Financial Group, The
655 15th St., N.W., Suite 950, Washington, DC 20005
Telephone: (202) 737-5930
Registered as lobbyist at U.S. Congress.
Background: Former Special Assistant to Rep. Richard Ottinger (D-NY), 1965-71. Senior Legislative Assistant to Rep. Herman Badillo (D-NY), 1971-73 and Administrative Assistant to Rep Badillo, 1974. Senior Legislative Assistant to Rep. Stephen Solarz (D-NY), 1975-76. Senior Legislative Assistant to Rep. Ottinger, 1975-76. Legislative Assistant to Sen. Abraham Ribicoff (D-CT), 1976-79.

BRAIN, Sally M.
Director, Construction Economics, Associated General Contractors of America
1957 E St., N.W., Washington, DC 20006
Telephone: (202) 393-2040
Registered as lobbyist at U.S. Congress.

BRALLIAR, Lt. General Max B., USAF (Ret)
Exec. Director, Ass'n of Military Surgeons of the U.S.
9320 Old Georgetown Rd., Bethesda, MD 20814
Telephone: (301) 897-8800

BRALLIAR, Lt. General Max B., USAF (Ret) (Cont'd)
Background: Former surgeon general of the Air Force, 1982-85.

BRAMBLE, Barbara
Director, International Program, Nat'l Wildlife Federation
1400 16th St., N.W., Washington, DC 20036-2266
Telephone: (202) 797-6800
Registered as lobbyist at U.S. Congress.

BRAMER, Donald
Confidential Asst to the Asst Secy, DEPARTMENT OF COMMERCE
14th and Constitution Ave. S.W., Washington, DC 20230
Telephone: (202) 377-5485

BRANAND, David C.
Counsel, Director, Environmental Affairs, Nat'l Coal Ass'n
1130 17th St., N.W., Washington, DC 20036
Telephone: (202) 463-2637

BRAND, Herbert
Chairman of the Board, Transportation Institute
5201 Auth Way, Camp Springs, MD 20746
Telephone: (301) 423-3335

BRAND, Joseph L.
Patton, Boggs and Blow
2550 M St., N.W., Suite 800, Washington, DC 20037
Telephone: (202) 457-6000
Clients:
   Dole Fresh Fruit Co.

BRAND, Kelly
Assistant Director, Government Relations, American Optometric Ass'n
1505 Prince Street, Suite 300, Alexandria, VA 22314
Telephone: (703) 739-9200

BRAND AND LOWELL, P.C.
923 15th St., N.W., Washington, DC 20005
Telephone: (202) 662-9700
Members of firm representing listed organizations:
   Brand, Stanley M.
      Background: Legislative Assistant to House Majority Leader, Thomas P. O'Neill, Jr., 1971-74. Attorney/Advisor, U.S. Securities and Exchange Commission, Division of Investment Management, 1974-76. General Counsel to the Clerk of the House of Representatives, 1976-83.
   Lowell, Abbe David
   McLuckie, Sally F.
      Background: Administrator, Brand and Lowell. Also serves as Treasurer, Brand and Lowell Political Action Committee.
Clients:
   Brand and Lowell Political Action Committee
   Internat'l Brotherhood of Teamsters, Chauffeurs, Warehousemen and Helpers of America *(Stanley M. Brand)*
. Nat'l Ass'n for Home Care *(Stanley M. Brand)*
   Platte River Whooping Crane Trust *(Abbe David Lowell)*
   Schnitzer Investment Inc. *(Stanley M. Brand)*

BRAND, Stanley M.
Brand and Lowell, P.C.
923 15th St., N.W., Washington, DC 20005
Telephone: (202) 662-9700
Registered as lobbyist at U.S. Congress.
Background: Legislative Assistant to House Majority Leader, Thomas P. O'Neill, Jr., 1971-74. Attorney/Advisor, U.S. Securities and Exchange Commission, Division of Investment Management, 1974-76. General Counsel to the Clerk of the House of Representatives, 1976-83.
Clients:
   Internat'l Brotherhood of Teamsters, Chauffeurs, Warehousemen and Helpers of America
   Nat'l Ass'n for Home Care
   Schnitzer Investment Inc.

BRANDENBURG, Bert S.
Policy Analyst, Progressive Policy Institute
316 Pennsylvania Ave., S.E. Suite 516, Washington, DC 20003
Telephone: (202) 547-0001

BRANDENBURG, Dan S.
Sanders, Schnabel & Brandenburg, P.C.
1110 Vermont Ave., N.W., Suite 600, Washington, DC 20005
Telephone: (202) 638-2241
Registered as lobbyist at U.S. Congress.
Clients:
   American Soc. of Ass'n Executives

BRANDON, David L.
General Counsel, Nat'l Ass'n of Real Estate Investment Trusts
1129 20th St., N.W. Suite 705, Washington, DC 20036
Telephone: (202) 785-8717
Registered as lobbyist at U.S. Congress.
Background: Attorney, Advisor, Internal Revenue Service, 1983-89.

BRANDON, Mabel, Muffie
Dir. Corp. Programming & Cultural Affrs., Ford Motor Co.
1350 Eye St., N.W. Suite 1000, Washington, DC 20005
Telephone: (202) 962-5400
Background: Former social secretary, The White House, under President Ronald Reagan.

BRANDON, Robert M.
Exec. Director, Citizen/Labor Energy Coalition Project
1300 Connecticut Ave., N.W. Suite 401, Washington, DC 20036
Telephone: (202) 857-5153
Registered as lobbyist at U.S. Congress.
Background: Also serves as V. President, Political Director, Citizen Action.

BRANDT, David
Administrator, Spacecause
922 Pennsylvania Ave., S.E., Washington, DC 20003
Telephone: (202) 543-1900
Registered as lobbyist at U.S. Congress.

BRANDT, Irene M.
Government Affairs Associate, Lilly and Co., Eli
1901 L. St., N.W. Suite 705, Washington, DC 20036
Telephone: (202) 955-5350

BRANFMAN, Fred
Exec. Director, Rebuild America
201 Massachusetts Ave., N.E., Suite C-6, Washington, DC 20002
Telephone: (202) 547-1212
Background: A non-partisan group seeking a national policy commitment to foster greater productive economic investment.

BRANICK, Robert C.
Senior Program Analyst, Bechtel Group, Inc.
1620 Eye St., N.W., Suite 703, Washington, DC 20006
Telephone: (202) 393-4747

BRANSFORD, Louis A.
President, Public Service Satellite Consortium
600 Maryland Ave., S.W., Suite 220, Washington, DC 20024
Telephone: (202) 863-0890

BRANSFORD, William L.
Neill, Mullenholz and Shaw
815 Connecticut Ave., N.W. Suite 800, Washington, DC 20006
Telephone: (202) 463-8400
Background: Senior Attorney. General Legal Services Division, Office of Chief Counsel, Internal Revenue Service 1981-83. Specializes in Federal employee law, labor law and administrative law.

BRANSILVER, Edward
Shearman and Sterling
1001 30th St., N.W., Suite 400, Washington, DC 20007
Telephone: (202) 337-8200
Clients:
   Citicorp

BRANTLEY, Chris Julian
Administrator, Professional Programs, Institute of Electrical and Electronics Engineers, Inc.
1828 L St., N.W. Suite 1202, Washington, DC 20036-5104
Telephone: (202) 785-0017
Registered as lobbyist at U.S. Congress.

BRASHER, C. Donald, Jr.
Internat'l Development Systems
733 15th St., N.W., Suite 520, Washington, DC 20005
Telephone: (202) 783-0720
Registered as lobbyist at U.S. Congress.
Registered as Foreign Agent: (#4012).
Background: Former international trade specialist, Office of Textiles, U.S. Department of Commerce.
Clients:
   Bangladesh Garment Manufacturers and Exporters Ass'n

BRASWELL, Arnold W.
President, Air-Conditioning and Refrigeration Institute
1501 Wilson Blvd., Suite 600, Arlington, VA 22209
Telephone: (703) 524-8800
Background: Also represents the Air-Conditioning and Refrigeration Institute Political Action Committee.

BRASWELL, Glenn
President, Flexible Packaging Ass'n
1090 Vermont Ave., N.W Suite 500, Washington, DC 20005
Telephone: (202) 842-3880

BRATTON, Joseph K., Jr.
Sr. V. Pres., Manager, Washington Opns., Parsons Corp.
1133 15th St., N.W. Suite 800, Washington, DC 20005
Telephone: (202) 775-6010

BRAUN & COMPANY
1201 Connecticut Ave., N.W. Suite 300, Washington, DC 20036
Telephone: (202) 835-8880
Registered as Foreign Agent: (#3825)
Background: A public affairs firm, a unit of Kethcum Communications.
Members of firm representing listed organizations:
   Imus, Catherine L., V. President, Group Manager
      Background: With the U.S. House of Representatives Congressional Steel Caucus, 1982-84; and as an aide to Rep. Carroll Hubbard, Jr. (D-KY), 1984.
   Pulido, Anna
Clients:
   California Department of Commerce
   Chase Manhattan Bank
   Ecology & Environment, Inc.
   Great Western Financial Corp.
   Kaiser Steel Holdings
   Transamerica Occidental Life Insurance Co.
   Western States Petroleum Ass'n

BRAUNLICH, Christian N.
Exec. Director, Small Mfrs. Forum, Nat'l Ass'n of Manufacturers
1331 Pennsylvania Ave., N.W. Suite 1500 North, Washington, DC 20004-1703
Telephone: (202) 637-3000
Registered as lobbyist at U.S. Congress.

BRAUNSTEIN, Richard L.
Dow, Lohnes and Albertson
1255 23rd St., N.W., Suite 500, Washington, DC 20037
Telephone: (202) 857-2500
Clients:
   Cox Enterprises, Inc.

BRAUNSTEIN, Roy
Legislative Aide, American Postal Workers Union
1300 L St., N.W., Washington, DC 20005
Telephone: (202) 842-4200
Registered as lobbyist at U.S. Congress.

BRAUNSTEIN, Samuel A.
Treasurer, Nat'l Soc. of Public Accountants Political Action Committee
1010 N. Fairfax St., Alexandria, VA 22314
Telephone: (703) 549-6400

BRAVERMAN, Burt A.
Cole, Raywid, and Braverman
1919 Pennsylvania Ave., N.W. Suite 200, Washington, DC 20006
Telephone: (202) 659-9750

BRAZEAU, Christine
Coordinator, Govt'l Affairs, Geostar Corp.
1001 22nd St., N.W., Washington, DC 20037
Telephone: (202) 887-0870

BRAZEMAN, Cary A.
Assistant V. President, Public Relations, Nat'l Cooperative Bank
1630 Connecticut Ave., N.W., Washington, DC 20009-1004
Telephone: (202) 745-4610

BRAZIL, Harold E.
Mgr., DC and Federal Government Affairs, Potomac Electric Power Co.
1900 Pennsylvania Ave., N.W., Washington, DC 20068
Telephone: (202) 872-2000
Registered as lobbyist at U.S. Congress.

BRAZIL, Noel
Director, American Optometric Ass'n Political Action Committee
1505 Prince St. Suite 300, Alexandria, VA 22314
Telephone: (703) 739-9200

BREATHITT, Edward T.
Senior V. President, Public Affairs, Norfolk Southern Corp.
1500 K St., N.W., Suite 375, Washington, DC 20005
Telephone: (202) 383-4166
Registered as lobbyist at U.S. Congress.

BREATHITT, Linda
Fed. Liaison, Wash. Office of the Gov., Kentucky, Commonwealth of
400 N. Capitol St., N.W., Suite 330, Washington, DC 20001
Telephone: (202) 624-7741

BREAULT, Richard L.
Group V. President for Policy, Chamber of Commerce of the U.S.A.
1615 H St., N.W., Washington, DC 20062
Telephone: (202) 463-5417

BREDHOFF, Elliot
Bredhoff and Kaiser
1000 Connecticut Ave., N.W. Suite 1300, Washington, DC 20036
Telephone: (202) 833-9340
Background: Special Counsel, United Steelworkers of America, 1965 to present. Also serves as General Counsel of the Industrial Unions Department of the AFL-CIO, 1968 to present.
Clients:
AFL-CIO - Industrial Union Department
Pickands Mather and Co.
United Steelworkers of America

BREDHOFF AND KAISER
1000 Connecticut Ave., N.W. Suite 1300, Washington, DC 20036
Telephone: (202) 833-9340
Members of firm representing listed organizations:
Bredhoff, Elliot
  Background: Special Counsel, United Steelworkers of America, 1965 to present. Also serves as General Counsel of the Industrial Unions Department of the AFL-CIO, 1968 to present.
Clark, Julia Penny
Cohen, George H.
  Background: Attorney-Advisor, 1960-63 and Appellate Court Litigation Attorney, 1963-66, National Labor Relations Board.
Freund, Jeffrey R.
  Background: Trial Attorney (1972-76) and Training Director (1976-77), Public Defender Service of D.C.
Gibbs, Jeffrey L.
Gottesman, Michael H.
  Background: Trial Attorney, U.S. Department of Justice, 1959-61.
Clients:
AFL-CIO - Building and Construction Trades Department

AFL-CIO - Industrial Union Department *(Elliot Bredhoff, Jeffrey L. Gibbs)*
Bakery, Confectionery and Tobacco Workers Internat'l Union *(Julia Penny Clark, Jeffrey L. Gibbs)*
Pickands Mather and Co. *(Elliot Bredhoff)*
United Steelworkers of America *(Elliot Bredhoff, George H. Cohen, Michael H. Gottesman)*

BREECE, George W.
Exec. Director, American State of the Art Prosthetic Ass'n
403 1st St., S.E., Washington, DC 20003
Telephone: (202) 544-4441
Registered as lobbyist at U.S. Congress.

BREED, Nancy
Director, Administration, Food Processing Machinery and Supplies Ass'n
200 Daingerfield Road, Alexandria, VA 22314
Telephone: (703) 684-1080

BREED, Nathaniel P., Jr.
Shaw, Pittman, Potts and Trowbridge
2300 N St., N.W., Washington, DC 20037
Telephone: (202) 663-8000

BREEDEN, Claude S., Jr.
Exec. Director, Packaging Machinery Manufacturers Institute
1343 L St., N.W., Washington, DC 20005
Telephone: (202) 347-3838

BREEN, Barry
Director of Publications, Environmental Law Institute
1616 P St., N.W., Suite 200, Washington, DC 20036
Telephone: (202) 328-5150

BREGMAN, ABELL & KAY
1156 15th St., N.W., Suite 1212, Washington, DC 20005
Telephone: (202) 223-2900
Members of firm representing listed organizations:
Abell, Tyler
  Background: Associate Gen. Counsel, Post Office Dep't, 1963. Assistant Postmaster General, 1963-1967. Chief of Protocol of the United States, 1968-1969.
Bregman, Stanley I.
  Background: Assistant to Senator Hubert H. Humphrey, 1954-1956. Consultant to Postmaster General of the United States, 1965. Consultant to Deputy Administrator for Financial Assistance, Small Business Administration, 1965. Consultant, Agency for Internat'l Development, 1965.
Kay, Alan
  Background: Attorney, Office of Gen. Counsel, Dep't of Commerce, 1966-1967. Assistant U.S. Attorney, 1963-66.
Clients:
AFL-CIO (American Federation of Labor and Congress of Industrial Organizations) *(Stanley I. Bregman)*
Air Transport Ass'n Employees Political Action Committee *(Stanley I. Bregman)*
Air Transport Ass'n of America *(Stanley I. Bregman)*
American Federal Savings Bank *(Stanley I. Bregman)*
Car Rental Coalition *(Stanley I. Bregman)*
Committee to Eliminate Equipment Giveaways *(Stanley I. Bregman)*
Federal Home Loan Bank of San Francisco *(Stanley I. Bregman)*
Truck Renting and Leasing Ass'n *(Stanley I. Bregman)*

BREGMAN, Randy
Diretor, Soviet & Eastern European Svcs., APCO Associates
1155 21st St., N.W., Suite 1000, Washington, DC 20036
Telephone: (202) 778-1000

BREGMAN, Stanley I.
Bregman, Abell & Kay
1156 15th St., N.W., Suite 1212, Washington, DC 20005
Telephone: (202) 223-2900
Registered as lobbyist at U.S. Congress.
Background: Assistant to Senator Hubert H. Humphrey, 1954-1956. Consultant to Postmaster General of the United States, 1965. Consultant to Deputy Administrator for Financial Assistance, Small Business Administration, 1965. Consultant, Agency for Internat'l Development, 1965.
Clients:

AFL-CIO (American Federation of Labor and Congress of Industrial Organizations)
Air Transport Ass'n Employees Political Action Committee
American Federal Savings Bank
Car Rental Coalition
Committee to Eliminate Equipment Giveaways
Federal Home Loan Bank of San Francisco
Truck Renting and Leasing Ass'n

BREHM, Carolyn L.
Senior Washington Representative, General Motors Corp.
1660 L St., N.W., Washington, DC 20036
Telephone: (202) 775-5098
Registered as lobbyist at U.S. Congress.

BREITER, Jerome J.
President, Hides, Skins & Leather, American Meat Institute
Box 3556, Washington, DC 20007
Telephone: (703) 841-2400

BREMER, Frances W.
Exec. Director, Foreign Student Service Council
2337 18th St., N.W., Washington, DC 20009
Telephone: (202) 232-4979

BRENNAN, John V.
President, Brennan Research Internat'l, Inc.
2300 M St., N.W., Suite 800, Washington, DC 20037
Telephone: (202) 466-5544
Background: Former Ass't to Richard Nixon.

BRENNAN, Joseph P.
President, Bituminous Coal Operators Ass'n
918 16th St., N.W. Suite 303, Washington, DC 20006
Telephone: (202) 783-3195

BRENNAN, Michael J.
Legislative and Political Director, Internat'l Ass'n of Bridge, Structural and Ornamental Iron Workers
1750 New York Ave., N.W., Washington, DC 20006
Telephone: (202) 383-4880
Registered as lobbyist at U.S. Congress.
Background: Represents the Iron Workers Political Action League.

BRENT, J. Lytle
Administrative Assistant, French & Company
The Willard, 1455 Pennsylvania Ave., N.W., Suite 1260, Washington, DC 20004
Telephone: (202) 783-7272

BRESNAHAN, Mary
Director, Finance and Management, American Nuclear Energy Council
410 First St., S.E. Third Floor, Washington, DC 20003
Telephone: (202) 484-2670

BRESNAHAN, Thomas M., III
Manager, Federal Government Affairs, Chevron, U.S.A.
1700 K St., N.W., Suite 1200, Washington, DC 20006
Telephone: (202) 457-5800
Registered as lobbyist at U.S. Congress.

BRESNICK, William O.
Senior Federal Environmental Affairs Rep, Texaco U.S.A.
1050 17th St., N.W., Suite 500, Washington, DC 20036
Telephone: (202) 331-1427
Registered as lobbyist at U.S. Congress.

BREUER, James E.
Director of Communications, Ass'n for Information and Image Management
1100 Wayne Ave. Suite 1100, Silver Spring, MD 20910
Telephone: (301) 587-8202

BREUER, Paul J.
Associate National Legislative Director, Disabled American Veterans
807 Maine Ave., S.W., Washington, DC 20024
Telephone: (202) 554-3501
Registered as lobbyist at U.S. Congress.

BREVIK, Leonard C.
Director, State Government Affairs, Independent Insurance Agents of America
600 Pennsylvania Ave., S.E., Suite 200, Washington, DC 20003
Telephone: (202) 544-5833

BREWER, D. H.
Vice Chairman, Olin Corp. Good Government Fund
1730 K St., N.W., Suite 1300, Washington, DC 20006
Telephone: (202) 331-7400

BREWER, F. H., III
Director Legislative Affairs, Chemical Specialties Manufacturers Ass'n
1913 Eye St., N.W., Washington, DC 20006
Telephone: (202) 872-8110
Registered as lobbyist at U.S. Congress.
Background: Administrative Assistant to Rep. Peter Kostmayer (D-PA), 1984-89.

BREWER, Gene C.
President Emeritus, Nat'l Institute of Building Sciences
1201 L St., N.W., Suite 400, Washington, DC 20005
Telephone: (202) 289-7800

BREWER, Larry K.
Director, Legislative Affairs, Emerson Electric Co.
1235 Jefferson Davis Hwy., Suite 305, Arlington, VA 22202
Telephone: (703) 920-7600
Registered as lobbyist at U.S. Congress.

BREWER, Michael F.
V. President, Government Affairs, Dun & Bradstreet
600 Maryland Ave., S.W., Suite 240, Washington, DC 20024
Telephone: (202) 484-7381

BREWSTER, Christopher R.
Kaye, Scholer, Fierman, Hays and Handler
The McPherson Building 901 15th St., N.W., #1100, Washington, DC 20005
Telephone: (202) 682-3500
Registered as lobbyist at U.S. Congress.
Background: Assistant Attorney General, State of Missouri, 1975-77. Legislative Assistant to Senator John Danforth (R-MO), 1977-79. Chief Counsel, Subcommittee on Federal Expenditures, U.S. Senate Committee on Government Affairs, 1980-82.
Clients:
Benjamin Moore & Co.
Bosch Corporation, Robert
Brown Brothers Harriman & Co.
Carlon Co.
Eastern Air Lines
Educational Media
Industrial Fabrics Ass'n Internat'l
Londontown Corp.
Newport Beach, California, City of
Siemens Medical Systems, Inc.
Texaco U.S.A.
United States Industrial Fabrics Institute
Westwood One, Inc.

BREYFOGLE, Jon
Legis Officer, Cong & Intergovt'l Affrs, DEPARTMENT OF LABOR
200 Constitution Ave., N.W., Washington, DC 20210
Telephone: (202) 523-6141

BRICELAND-BETTS, Deborah
Deputy Director, Long Term Care Campaign
1334 G St., N.W., Suite 300, Washington, DC 20005
Telephone: (202) 628-3030

BRICKELL, Beatrice A.
Sharretts, Paley, Carter and Blauvelt
1707 L St., N.W., Suite 725, Washington, DC 20036
Telephone: (202) 223-4433
Clients:
An Mau Steel Ltd.
Argentina, Government of
Givaudan Corp.
Hamilton Copper and Steel Corp.
Sambo Copper Co., Ltd.
Thyssen Inc.

BRICKER, Kathryn
Exec. Director, U.S. English
818 Connecticut Ave., N.W. Suite 200, Washington, DC 20006
Telephone: (202) 833-0100

BRICKER, Ron
Sr. V. Pres.and Dir., Media Productions, Kamber Group, The
1920 L St., N.W., Washington, DC 20036
Telephone: (202) 223-8700

BRIDGEN, Pamela
Exec. Director, Ass'n of Biotechnology Companies
1120 Vermont Ave., N.W., Suite 601, Washington, DC 20005
Telephone: (202) 842-2229
Registered as lobbyist at U.S. Congress.

BRIER, M. William
V. President, Communications, Edison Electric Institute
1111 19th St., N.W., Washington, DC 20036
Telephone: (202) 778-6850

BRIERRE, William V., Jr.
Senior V. President, Lykes Bros. Steamship Co.
1001 Connecticut Ave., N.W., Suite 1010, Washington, DC 20036
Telephone: (202) 659-3737

BRIESE, Garry L.
Exec. Director, Internat'l Ass'n of Fire Chiefs
1329 18th St., N.W., Washington, DC 20036
Telephone: (202) 833-3420

BRIGGS, Ethel D.
Exec. Director (Acting), Nat'l Council on Disability
800 Independence Ave., S.W. Suite 814, Washington, DC 20591
Telephone: (202) 267-3846

BRIGGS, John DeQ., III
Howrey and Simon
1730 Pennsylvania Ave., N.W., Washington, DC 20006-4793
Telephone: (202) 783-0800
Clients:
Uniroyal Chemical Co., Inc.

BRIGGS, Richard E.
Exec. V. President, Ass'n of American Railroads
50 F Street, N.W., Washington, DC 20001
Telephone: (202) 639-2100

BRIGGUM, Sue M.
Director, Government Affairs, Waste Management, Inc.
1155 Connecticut Ave., N.W., Suite 800, Washington, DC 20036
Telephone: (202) 467-4480
Registered as lobbyist at U.S. Congress.

BRIGHAM, Karen A.
Assoc. Manager, Business & Gov't Policy, Chamber of Commerce of the U.S.A.
1615 H St., N.W., Washington, DC 20062
Telephone: (202) 659-6000
Registered as lobbyist at U.S. Congress.

BRIGHT, Marilee
Chief, Legis Affrs, DEPARTMENT OF COMMERCE - Nat'l Oceanic and Atmospheric Administration
14th and Constitution Ave. N.W., Washington, DC 20230
Telephone: (202) 377-4981

BRIGHTUP, Craig S.
Director of Government Relations, Nat'l Roofing Contractors Ass'n
206 E St., N.E., Washington, DC 20002
Telephone: (202) 546-7584
Background: Former Director of Congressional Relations, Federal Trade Commission.

BRILL, Bernard D.
Exec. V. President, Internat'l Ass'n of Wiping Cloth Manufacturers
7910 Woodmont Ave., Suite 1212, Bethesda, MD 20814
Telephone: (301) 656-1077

BRINK, Peter
V. President, Programs and Services, Nat'l Trust for Historic Preservation
1785 Massachusetts Ave., N.W., Washington, DC 20036
Telephone: (202) 673-4000

BRINKER, Andrew
President, Nat'l Labor Relations Board Professional Ass'n
1717 Pennsylvania Ave., N.W., Room 1148, Washington, DC 20570
Telephone: (202) 254-9372

BRINKLEY, Margot
Director, Washington Office, Foundation Center
1001 Connecticut Ave., N.W. Suite 938, Washington, DC 20036
Telephone: (202) 331-1400

BRINKMAN, C. B.
Manager, Washington Nuclear Operations, Asea Brown Boveri, Inc.
12300 Twinbrook Parkway Suite 330, Rockville, MD
Telephone: (301) 881-7040

BRINKMAN, Fred
Area Managing Partner, Andersen and Co., Arthur
1666 K St., N.W., Washington, DC 20006
Telephone: (202) 862-3100

BRINKMANN, Robert J.
General Counsel, Nat'l Newspaper Ass'n
1627 K St., N.W. Suite 400, Washington, DC 20006
Telephone: (202) 466-7200
Registered as lobbyist at U.S. Congress.

BRIOTTA, Patricia
Associate Director, Media Relations, Nat'l Ass'n of Life Underwriters
1922 F St., N.W., Washington, DC 20006
Telephone: (202) 331-6000

BRISSETT, Belva B.
Sr. V. President, Regulatory Affairs, Nat'l Ass'n of Broadcasters
1771 N St., N.W., Washington, DC 20036
Telephone: (202) 429-5304

BROADSTONE, James M.
Gallagher, Boland, Meiburger and Brosnan
1000 Vermont Ave., N.W. Suite 1100, Washington, DC 20005-4903
Telephone: (202) 289-7200
Background: Staff Attorney, Federal Power Commission, 1972-73.
Clients:
Gas Research Institute

BROADWELL, Bradly A.
Grassroots Manager, Chemical Manufacturers Ass'n
2501 M St., N.W., Washington, DC 20037
Telephone: (202) 887-1100
Registered as lobbyist at U.S. Congress.

BROBECK, Stephen
Exec. Director, Consumer Federation of America
1424 16th St., N.W. Suite 604, Washington, DC 20036
Telephone: (202) 387-6121
Registered as lobbyist at U.S. Congress.
Background: Also serves as Treasurer, Consumer Federation of America Political Action Fund.

BROCK, Cindy
Staff Assistant, Concerned Citizens Foundation
Capitol Hill Office Bldg. 412 First St., S.E., Suite 301, Washington, DC 20003
Telephone: (202) 479-9068

BROCK GROUP, THE
1130 Connecticut Ave., N.W. Suite 350, Washington, DC 20036
Telephone: (202) 296-1901
Registered as Foreign Agent: (#4310)
Background: A management advisory firm that provides long-term strategic planning as well as consultation and support on international trade and investment, labor-management relations, and human resource development.
Members of firm representing listed organizations:
Brock, William E., Senior Partner
Background: Member, U.S. House of Representatives (R-TN), 1962-70. Member, U.S. Senate (R-TN), 1970-76. Chairman, Republican National Committee, 1977-80. U.S. Trade Representative, 1980-84. U.S. Secretary of Labor, 1984-87.
Frierson, James W., Partner

Background: Special Assistant, Office of the U.S. Trade Representative, 1981-85. Chief of Staff, Office of the U.S. Trade Representative, 1985-89. Coordinator, U.S. Government's policy on the functioning of the GATT system in the Uruguay Round of Trade Negotiations, 1987-89.

McElheny, Richard L., Partner
Background: Assistant Secretary for Trade Development, Director General of the U.S. and Foreign Commercial Service U.S. Department of Commerce, 1981-84.

Reich, Otto J., Partner
Background: Assistant Administrator, U.S. Agency for International Development, 1981-83. Special Advisor to the Secretary of State, 1983-86. U.S. Ambassador to Venezuela, 1986-89.

Whitfield, Dennis E., Managing Partner
Background: Director of Political Affairs, Director of Education and Training, and Regional Political Director for the Southeast, Republican National Committee, 1977-80. Chief of Staff, Office of the U.S. Trade Representative, 1981-85. Deputy Secretary of Labor, 1985-89.

BROCK, William E.
Senior Partner, Brock Group, The
1130 Connecticut Ave., N.W. Suite 350, Washington, DC 20036
Telephone: (202) 296-1901
Registered as Foreign Agent: (#4310).
Background: Member, U.S. House of Representatives (R-TN), 1962-70. Member, U.S. Senate (R-TN), 1970-76. Chairman, Republican National Committee, 1977-80. U.S. Trade Representative, 1980-84. U.S. Secretary of Labor, 1984-87.

BROCKBANK & ASSOCIATES
918 16th St., N.W. Mezzanine Suite, Washington, DC 20006
Telephone: (202) 223-2803
Clients:
Puerto Rico, New Progressive Party Of

BROCKMAN, David M.
Director, Legislative Affairs, Nat'l Grain and Feed Ass'n
1201 New York Ave., N.W. Suite 830, Washington, DC 20005
Telephone: (202) 289-0873
Registered as lobbyist at U.S. Congress.
Background: Former Legislative Assistant to Rep. Charles Stenholm (D-TX).

BRODERICK, Kathryn P.
Preston Gates Ellis & Rouvelas Meeds
1735 New York Ave., N.W., Suite 500, Washington, DC 20006-4759
Telephone: (202) 628-1700
Registered as lobbyist at U.S. Congress.

BRODERICK, Mary
Director, Defender Division, Nat'l Legal Aid and Defender Ass'n
1625 K St., N.W., Washington, DC 20006
Telephone: (202) 452-0620
Registered as lobbyist at U.S. Congress.

BRODHEAD, William M.
Plunkett & Cooney , P.C.
2715 M St., N.W., Suite 300, Washington, DC 20007-3710
Telephone: (202) 333-8803
Registered as lobbyist at U.S. Congress.
Background: Member, U.S. House of Representatives from Michigan, 1974-82.
Clients:
Boysville of Michigan
Detroit Educational TV Foundation
Detroit, Michigan, City of
Michigan Humane Soc.

BRODSKY, James A.
Weiner, McCaffrey, Brodsky, Kaplan & Levin
1350 New York Ave., N.W., Suite 800, Washington, DC 20005-4797
Telephone: (202) 628-2000
Registered as lobbyist at U.S. Congress.
Background: Patent Examiner, U.S. Patent Office, 1968-72. Special Assistant to Commissioner Newman, U.S. Consumer Product Safety Commission, 1974-76. Deputy Assistant Secretary for Consumer Affairs, HUD, 1976-77.

BRODY, David A.
Attorney, American Fiber Manufacturers Ass'n
1150 17th St., N.W., Suite 310, Washington, DC 20036
Telephone: (202) 296-6508
Registered as lobbyist at U.S. Congress.

BRODY, Dr. Eugene B.
Secretary General, World Federation for Mental Health
1021 Prince St., Alexandria, VA 22314
Telephone: (703) 684-7722

BRODY, Marcia D.
Legislative Assistant, American Veterinary Medical Ass'n
1023 15th St., N.W., Suite 300, Washington, DC 20005
Telephone: (202) 659-2040
Registered as lobbyist at U.S. Congress.

BROE, Dwayne J.
Treasurer, Opticians Committee for Political Education
10341 Democracy Lane, Box 10110, Fairfax, VA 22030
Telephone: (703) 691-8355

BROGIOLA, Michael
Field Coordinator, Long Term Care Campaign
1334 G St., N.W., Suite 300, Washington, DC 20005
Telephone: (202) 628-3030

BROMBERG, Michael D.
Exec. Director, Federation of American Health Systems
1111 19th St., N.W. Suite 402, Washington, DC 20036
Telephone: (202) 833-3090
Registered as lobbyist at U.S. Congress.

BRONK, Robin
Project Associate, APCO Associates
1155 21st St., N.W., Suite 1000, Washington, DC 20036
Telephone: (202) 778-1000

BRONSTEIN, Alvin J.
Exec. Director, Nat'l Prison Project
1616 P St., N.W., Suite 340, Washington, DC 20036
Telephone: (202) 331-0500

BRONZ AND FARRELL
2021 K St., N.W., Washington, DC 20006
Telephone: (202) 298-5966
Members of firm representing listed organizations:
Farrell, Edward J.
Background: U.S. Court of Customs and Patent Appeals, 1971-82; U.S. Court of Appeals for the Federal Circuit, 1982.
Clients:
Canadian Cattlemen's Ass'n *(Edward J. Farrell)*

BROOKE, Edward W.
O'Connor & Hannan
1919 Pennsylvania Ave., N.W., Suite 800, Washington, DC 20006
Telephone: (202) 887-1400
Registered as lobbyist at U.S. Congress.
Registered as Foreign Agent: (#2972).
Background: Member, U.S. Senate (R-MA), 1967-79.

BROOKS, Barbara
Cong Liaison Div, ENVIRONMENTAL PROTECTION AGENCY
401 M St., S.W., Washington, DC 20460
Telephone: (202) 382-5200

BROOKS, Dale E.
Washington Representative, Chevron, U.S.A.
1700 K St., N.W., Suite 1200, Washington, DC 20006
Telephone: (202) 457-5800
Registered as lobbyist at U.S. Congress.

BROOKS, Mary E.
Senior Lobbyist, League of Women Voters of the United States
1730 M St., N.W., Tenth Floor, Washington, DC 20036
Telephone: (202) 429-1965
Registered as lobbyist at U.S. Congress.

BROOKS, Matthew
Political Director, Nat'l Jewish Coalition
415 Second St., N.E., Washington, DC 20002
Telephone: (202) 547-7701

BROOKS, Father Robert J.
Presiding Bishop's Staff Officer, Episcopal Church, Washington Office of the
110 Maryland Ave., N.E. Suite 309, Washington, DC 20002
Telephone: (202) 547-7300

BROOKS, Robert M.
Evergreen Associates, Ltd.
206 G St., N.E., Washington, DC 20002
Telephone: (202) 543-3383
Registered as lobbyist at U.S. Congress.
Clients:
Clover Park School District
DCL Industries
Military Impacted School Districts Ass'n
Nat'l Indian Impacted Schools
Suffolk County, New York
SuperComputers, Inc.
Washington State Democratic Party
Washington State Impact Aid Ass'n

BROOKS, Roger A.
Director, Asian Studies Center, Heritage Foundation
214 Massachusetts Ave., N.E., Washington, DC 20002
Telephone: (202) 546-4400
Background: Former Director, Policy Planning Staff, Bureau of International Organization Affairs, U.S. Department of State.

BROOKS, Ronald A.
Chief, Cong Liaison, OFFICE OF PERSONNEL MANAGEMENT
1900 E St., N.W., Washington, DC 20415
Telephone: (202) 632-6514

BROOME, David W.
V. President, Government Relations, Nat'l Marine Manufacturers Ass'n
1000 Thomas Jefferson St, N.W. Suite 525, Washington, DC 20007
Telephone: (202) 338-6662

BROSCH, Kevin J.
Steptoe and Johnson
1330 Connecticut Ave., N.W., Washington, DC 20036
Telephone: (202) 429-3000
Clients:
Nat'l Oilseed Processors Ass'n

BROSNAHAN, Timothy G.
Exec. V. President, Burson-Marsteller
1850 M St., N.W., Suite 900, Washington, DC 20036
Telephone: (202) 833-8550
Background: Former Legislative Assistant to Senator Lowell Weicker (R-CT).
Clients:
Bethlehem Steel Corp.

BROSNAN, Thomas F.
Gallagher, Boland, Meiburger and Brosnan
1000 Vermont Ave., N.W. Suite 1100, Washington, DC 20005-4903
Telephone: (202) 289-7200
Background: Attorney-Advisor, Tax Court of the U.S., 1953-55.
Clients:
Bay State Gas Co.
Florida Public Utilities Co.
Washington Natural Gas Co.

BROSSI, Mario
Counsel & V. President, Gov't Relations, Direct Selling Ass'n
1776 K St., N.W., Suite 600, Washington, DC 20006
Telephone: (202) 293-5760
Registered as lobbyist at U.S. Congress.
Background: Former Ass't to Sen. George Mitchell (D-ME). Serves as Counsel to the Democratic Nat'l Committee's Business Council.

BROTZMAN, Donald G.
.Hopkins and Sutter
888 16th St., N.W., Suite 700, Washington, DC 20006
Telephone: (202) 835-8000
Registered as lobbyist at U.S. Congress.
Clients:
COMDISCO, Inc.

BROUHA, Paul
Deputy Director, American Fisheries Soc.
5410 Grosvenor Lane, Bethesda, MD 20814
Telephone: (301) 897-8616

BROUSE ASSOCIATES, J. Robert
1299 Woodside Drive, McLean, VA 22102
Telephone: (703) 556-6114
Background: An association management and consulting firm.
Members of firm representing listed organizations:
  Brouse, J. Robert
    Background: Former Chairman, Association Executives for Reagan/Bush.
Organizations represented:
  Internat'l Teleconferencing Ass'n

BROUSE, J. Robert
Brouse Associates, J. Robert
1299 Woodside Drive, McLean, VA 22102
Telephone: (703) 556-6114
Background: Former Chairman, Association Executives for Reagan/Bush.

BROUSSE, Maria
Assistant Field Director, U.S. Public Interest Research Group
215 Pennsylvania Ave., S.E., Washington, DC 20003
Telephone: (202) 546-9707
Registered as lobbyist at U.S. Congress.

BROWDER, Joseph B.
Partner, Dunlap & Browder, Inc.
418 10th St., S.E., Washington, DC 20003
Telephone: (202) 546-3720
Registered as lobbyist at U.S. Congress.
Background: Former Special Assistant to the Assistant Secretary for Land and Water, Department of Interior, 1977-81. Cofounder and former President (1972-76), Environmental Policy Institute.

BROWN, A. Gilson
Executive Director, Ass'n for Childhood Education International
11141 Georgia Ave., Suite 200, Wheaton, MD 20902
Telephone: (301) 942-2443

BROWN, Alvin S.
Lobbyist, Robbins Associates, Liz
420 7th St., S.E., Washington, DC 20003
Telephone: (202) 544-6093
Background: Tax Attorney and Manager, Internal Revenue Service National Office, 1960-89.
Organizations represented:
  Babcock and Brown
  Standard Pacific Corp.
  Warburg Pincus & Co., E. M.

BROWN, Andrew
Special Counsel, Nat'l Telephone Cooperative Ass'n
2626 Pennsylvania Ave., N.W., Washington, DC 20037
Telephone: (202) 298-2300

BROWN & ASSOCIATES, T. G.
National Press Building Suite 995, Washington, DC 20045
Telephone: (202) 347-1440
Members of firm representing listed organizations:
  Brown, T. G., President
Organizations represented:
  Velsicol Chemical Corp.

BROWN, Benjamin L.
Exec. Director and Gen. Counsel, Nat'l Institute of Municipal Law Officers
1000 Connecticut Ave., N.W. Suite 902, Washington, DC 20036
Telephone: (202) 466-5424

BROWN, Carolyn
Exec. Director, American Astronautical Soc.
6352 Rolling Mill Place Suite 102, Springfield, VA 22152
Telephone: (703) 866-0020

BROWN, Clarence J.
Chairman, Brown & Co., Clarence J.
1101 Connecticut Ave., N.W. Suite 1000, Washington, DC 20036
Telephone: (202) 828-2300

Background: Former Member, U.S. House of Representatives (R-OH), 1965-83. Deputy Secretary of Commerce, 1983-88.

BROWN & CO., Clarence J.
1101 Connecticut Ave., N.W. Suite 1000, Washington, DC 20036
Telephone: (202) 828-2300
Members of firm representing listed organizations:
  Brown, Clarence J., Chairman
    Background: Former Member, U.S. House of Representatives (R-OH), 1965-83. Deputy Secretary of Commerce, 1983-88.
  Giese, Robert B., President
Organizations represented:
  BHC, Inc. *(Robert B. Giese)*
  Chris-Craft Industries Inc. *(Robert B. Giese)*
  Ohio Edison Co. *(Robert B. Giese)*
  United Television, Inc. *(Robert B. Giese)*

BROWN, COATES AND MCCARTHY
1825 K St., N.W., Suite 807, Washington, DC 20006
Telephone: (202) 293-4761
Registered as lobbyist at U.S. Congress.
Members of firm representing listed organizations:
  Coates, Vincent J. (Jr.)
Clients:
  Avco Research Lab, Inc. *(Vincent J. Coates, Jr.)*

BROWN, Cynthia A.
Manager, Washington Office, American College of Surgeons
1640 Wisconsin Ave., N.W., Washington, DC 20007
Telephone: (202) 337-2701

BROWN, Cynthia L.
V. President, Legislative Affairs, Shipbuilders Council of America
1110 Vermont Ave., N.W. Suite 1250, Washington, DC 20005
Telephone: (202) 775-9060
Registered as lobbyist at U.S. Congress.

BROWN, David S. J.
V. President, Government Affairs, Monsanto Co.
700 14th St., N.W., Suite 1100, Washington, DC 20005
Telephone: (202) 783-2460
Registered as lobbyist at U.S. Congress.
Background: Attorney Appellate Section, Antitrust Division, Dep't of Justice, 1966-1968. Administrative and Legislative Ass't to Rep. Paul McCloskey (R-Ca.), 1968-1973.

BROWN, Dennis
Director, State Advertising Coalition, American Advertising Federation
1400 K St., N.W., Suite 1000, Washington, DC 20005
Telephone: (202) 898-0089

BROWN, Doreen L.
President, Consumers for World Trade
1001 Connecticut Ave., N.W. Suite 800, Washington, DC 20036
Telephone: (202) 785-4835

BROWN, Ellen B.
Corp. Dir., Procure. & Acquisition Policy, General Dynamics Corp.
1745 Jefferson Davis Hwy., Suite 1000, Arlington, VA 22202
Telephone: (703) 553-1200

BROWN, Garry E.
Kirkpatrick & Lockhart
1800 M St., N.W., Suite 900 South Lobby, Washington, DC 20036-5891
Telephone: (202) 778-9000
Registered as lobbyist at U.S. Congress.
Background: Member, U.S. House of Representatives, 1967-79. Member, President's Commission on Housing, 1981-82.
Clients:
  Asociacion de Bancos de Ahorro Puerto Rico
  Federal Home Loan Bank of Boston
  Federal Home Loan Bank of Cincinnati
  First Federal Savings Bank
  Kirkpatrick & Lockhart Political Action Committee

BROWN, George L.
V. President - Washington Operations, Grumman Corp.
1000 Wilson Blvd., Suite 2800, Arlington, VA 22209
Telephone: (703) 875-8400
Registered as lobbyist at U.S. Congress.

BROWN, J. Michael
Federal Gov't Affrs V. Pres. & Attorney, AT&T
Suite 1000, 1120 20th St., N.W., Washington, DC 20036
Telephone: (202) 457-3831

BROWN, J. Noah
Director, Gov't Relations & Public Afrs, Nat'l University Continuing Education Ass'n
One Dupont Circle, N.W. Suite 615, Washington, DC 20036-1168
Telephone: (202) 659-3130

BROWN, Jack T.
Director of Marketing, Energy Research Corp.
1627 K St., N.W. Suite 403, Washington, DC 20006
Telephone: (202) 785-9321

BROWN, Jacqueline Knox
Asst Secy, Cong and Intergovt'l Affrs, DEPARTMENT OF ENERGY
1000 Independence Ave. S.W., Washington, DC 20585
Telephone: (202) 586-5450

BROWN, Jim
Director of Communications, Partnership for Improved Air Travel
1709 New York Ave., N.W. 5th Floor, Washington, DC 20006
Telephone: (202) 626-4200

BROWN, Judie
President, American Life League
P.O. Box 1350, Stafford, VA 22554
Telephone: (703) 659-4171

BROWN, Karen B.
Government Affairs Assistant, Potomac Electric Power Co.
1900 Pennsylvania Ave., N.W., Washington, DC 20068
Telephone: (202) 872-2000

BROWN, Karen H.
Vice President, Communications, Food Marketing Institute
1750 K St., N.W., Washington, DC 20006
Telephone: (202) 452-8444

BROWN, Ken
Campaigns Director, Clean Water Action Project
317 Pennsylvania Ave., S.E., Washington, DC 20003
Telephone: (202) 547-1196
Registered as lobbyist at U.S. Congress.

BROWN, Kim
Saunders and Company
1015 Duke St., Alexandria, VA 22314
Telephone: (703) 549-1555
Clients:
  Mitsubishi Internat'l Corp.
  Taiwan Textile Federation

BROWN, Laura L.
Director, Media Relations, Nat'l Ass'n of Manufacturers
1331 Pennsylvania Ave., N.W. Suite 1500 North, Washington, DC 20004-1703
Telephone: (202) 637-3000

BROWN, Lauren E.
Holland and Hart
1001 Pennsylvania Suite 310, Washington, DC 20004
Telephone: (202) 638-5500
Registered as lobbyist at U.S. Congress.
Background: Aide to Sen. Ted Stevens (R-AK), 1986-88.
Clients:
  Alyeska Pipeline Service Co.
  Council for Solid Waste Solutions
  Scott's Liquid Gold

BROWN, Lawrence C., Jr.
President, 70001 Training & Employment Institute
501 School St., S.W. Suite 600, Washington, DC 20024
Telephone: (202) 484-0103

BROWN, Leslie
V. President, Marketing & Communications, Can Manufacturers Institute
1625 Massachusetts Ave., N.W., Suite 500, Washington, DC 20036
Telephone: (201) 232-4677

BROWN, Lester R.
President, Worldwatch Institute
1776 Massachusetts Ave., N.W., Washington, DC 20036
Telephone: (202) 452-1999

BROWN, Melissa P.
Smith, Bucklin and Associates
1101 Connecticut Ave., N.W., Suite 700, Washington, DC 20036
Telephone: (202) 857-1100

BROWN, Michael G.
V. President, Jensen & Co.
2000 Pennsylvania Ave., N.W. Suite 3580, Washington, DC 20006
Telephone: (202) 833-3580
Clients:
Commission on Minority Business Development
Earth Corps
Maxima Corp.

BROWN, Michael J.
V. President, Klein & Saks, Inc.
1026 16th St., N.W., Suite 101, Washington, DC 20036
Telephone: (202) 783-0500
Background: Former Press Secretary, U.S. Mint. Serves as Director of Public Relations for the Gold Institute and the Silver Institute.
Clients:
Gold Institute
Silver Institute

BROWN, Michael W.
Director of Public Affairs, United States Conference of Mayors
1620 Eye St., N.W., Washington, DC 20006
Telephone: (202) 293-7330

BROWN, Omer F., II
Davis Wright Tremaine
1752 N St., N.W., Suite 800, Washington, DC 20036
Telephone: (202) 822-9775
Registered as lobbyist at U.S. Congress.
Clients:
Energy Contractors Price-Anderson Group

BROWN, Quincalee
Exec. Director, Water Pollution Control Federation
601 Wythe Street, Alexandria, VA 22314
Telephone: (703) 684-2400

BROWN, Reginald L., Jr.
Mgr, Policy/Gov't Afrs, Integ. Systm Org, Xerox Corp.
490 L'Enfant Plaza East, S.W., Suite 4200, Washington, DC 20024
Telephone: (202) 646-8285

BROWN, Richard A.
Senior V. President, Operations, Nat'l Grocers Ass'n
1825 Samuel Morse Drive, Reston, VA 22090
Telephone: (703) 437-5300

BROWN, Robert M.
Jones, Day, Reavis and Pogue
1450 G St., N.W., Suite 700, Washington, DC 20005-2088
Telephone: (202) 879-3939
Registered as Foreign Agent: (#3427).

BROWN, Ronald H.
Chairman, Democratic Nat'l Committee
430 South Capitol St., S.E., Washington, DC 20003
Telephone: (202) 863-8000
Background: Special Assistant to Senator Edward Kennedy (D-MA), 1969-77. Chief Counsel, U.S. Senate Committee on the Judiciary, 1980. General Counsel and Staff Director for Senator Edward Kennedy, 1981.

BROWN, S.M. Henry, Jr.
V. President, Governmental Affairs, Entergy Corp.
1776 Eye St., N.W., Suite 275, Washington, DC 20006
Telephone: (202) 785-8444

BROWN, Sharon
Senior Account Executive, Burson-Marsteller
1850 M St., N.W., Suite 900, Washington, DC 20036
Telephone: (202) 833-8550
Background: Former Deputy Press Secretary to Senator Joseph Biden (D-DE) and Press Secretary to Senator Gaylord Nelson (D-WI).

BROWN, Stephen H.
Associate, Vorys, Sater, Seymour and Pease
1828 L St., N.W., Suite 1111, Washington, DC 20036
Telephone: (202) 822-8200
Registered as lobbyist at U.S. Congress.
Clients:
Bell Communications Research, Inc.
Ohio Advanced Technology Center
Ohio Forestry Ass'n
Snow Aviation Internat'l

BROWN, Steven J.
V. Pres., Strategic Planning & Policy, Aircraft Owners and Pilots Ass'n
421 Aviation Way, Frederick, MD 21701
Telephone: (301) 695-2000

BROWN, Susan
Director, Public Affairs, Urban Institute, The
2100 M St., N.W., Washington, DC 20037
Telephone: (202) 833-7200

BROWN, T. G.
President, Brown & Associates, T. G.
National Press Building Suite 995, Washington, DC 20045
Telephone: (202) 347-1440
Registered as lobbyist at U.S. Congress.

BROWN, Tyrone
Steptoe and Johnson
1330 Connecticut Ave., N.W., Washington, DC 20036
Telephone: (202) 429-3000
Background: Law Clerk to Chief Justice Earl Warren, U.S. Supreme Court, 1967-68. Staff Director, Intergovernmental Relations Committee, U.S. Senate, 1970-71. Commissioner, Federal Communications Commission, 1977-81.

BROWN, Virginia W.
Thacher, Proffitt and Wood
1500 K St., N.W., Suite 200, Washington, DC 20005
Telephone: (202) 347-8400
Registered as lobbyist at U.S. Congress.
Clients:
Castine Partners
Citicorp Mortgage Finance, Inc.
Federal Home Loan Mortgage Corp.
General Electric Mortgage Insurance Co.
Standard Federal Savings Bank

BROWN, W. L. Lyons, Jr.
Chairman, American Business Conference
1730 K St., N.W. Suite 1200, Washington, DC 20006
Telephone: (202) 822-9300

BROWN, William E.
Senior Consultant, Mead Corp.
1667 K St., N.W., Suite 420, Washington, DC 20006
Telephone: (202) 833-9643
Registered as lobbyist at U.S. Congress.

BROWN, William R.
V. President, Nat'l Rural Letter Carriers' Ass'n
1448 Duke St., Alexandria, VA 22314
Telephone: (703) 684-5545

BROWN, William R.
President, Council of State Chambers of Commerce
122 C St., N.W. Suite 330, Washington, DC 20001
Telephone: (202) 484-8103
Registered as lobbyist at U.S. Congress.

BROWN, William Y.
Director, Government Affairs, Waste Management, Inc.
1155 Connecticut Ave., N.W., Suite 800, Washington, DC 20036
Telephone: (202) 467-4480
Registered as lobbyist at U.S. Congress.
Background: Former Executive Director, Endangered Species Scientific Authority, 1977-80, and of Internat'l Convention Advisory Commission, 1980-81.

BROWN, Winthrop N.
Shaw, Pittman, Potts and Trowbridge
2300 N St., N.W., Washington, DC 20037
Telephone: (202) 663-8000

BROWN & WOOD
815 Connecticut Ave., N.W. Suite 701, Washington, DC 20006
Telephone: (202) 223-0220
Members of firm representing listed organizations:
Eccard, Walter T.
Background: Deputy Ass't General Counsel (1984-85), Ass't General Counsel (1985-86), U.S. Dept. of Treasury.
Murray, James E.
Background: Senior V. President and General Counsel, Federal National Mortgage Association, 1971-81. President, Federal National Mortgage Association, 1981-83.
Clients:
Nat'l Ass'n of Small Business Investment Companies *(James E. Murray)*

BROWNELL, Arthur W.
Assoc. Director, Federal Corp. Affairs, Internat'l Paper Co.
1620 Eye St., N.W., Suite 700, Washington, DC 20006
Telephone: (202) 785-3666
Registered as lobbyist at U.S. Congress.
Background: Also represents the Voluntary Contributors for Better Government, a group supported by Internat'l Paper.

BROWNING, Carol
Hecht, Spencer & Associates
499 South Capitol St., S.W., Suite 507, Washington, DC 20003
Telephone: (202) 554-2881
Background: Former aide to former Senator Bill Brock (R-TN) in the Senate, the Office of U.S. Trade Representative and the U.S. Department of Labor.

BROWNING, Sally
Liaison Officer, Cong & Intergov'l Affrs, DEPARTMENT OF LABOR
200 Constitution Ave., N.W., Washington, DC 20210
Telephone: (202) 523-6141

BROWNING, Sue
Director, Fed. Regulatory Matters (FCC), NYNEX
1828 L St., N.W., Suite 1000, Washington, DC 20036
Telephone: (202) 416-0100

BROWNLEE, Don
Director, Public Affairs, Aerojet
1025 Connecticut Ave., N.W. Suite 1107, Washington, DC 20036
Telephone: (202) 828-6826

BROWNRIGG AND MULDOON
1730 M St., N.W. Suite 805, Washington, DC 20036
Telephone: (202) 466-8666
Members of firm representing listed organizations:
Muldoon, Charles P.
Background: Assistant General Counsel, U.S. Economic Cooperation Administration, 1947-49. Assistant to the Financial Consultant to the Secretary of State, 1950.
Clients:
Chile, Army Procurement Mission
Egypt, Embassy of
Yamaichi Internat'l
Yusen Air and Sea Service (USA) Inc. *(Charles P. Muldoon)*

BROWNSTEIN & ASSOC., C. M.
791 Woodmont Ave., Suite 1208, Bethessda, MD 20814-3015
Telephone: (301) 913-0010
Members of firm representing listed organizations:
Brownstein, Clifford M.
Shanley, Claire E., Account Executive
Organizations represented:
American Soc. of Access Professionals *(Claire E. Shanley)*
Ass'n of Practicing CPAs *(Clifford M. Brownstein)*
Continental Ass'n of Funeral and Memorial Societies *(Clifford M. Brownstein)*
Nat'l Business Owners Ass'n *(Clifford M. Brownstein)*

BROWNSTEIN, Clifford M.
Brownstein & Assoc., C. M.
791 Woodmont Ave., Suite 1208, Bethessda, MD 20814-3015
Telephone: (301) 913-0010
Organizations represented:
Ass'n of Practicing CPAs
Continental Ass'n of Funeral and Memorial Societies
Nat'l Business Owners Ass'n

BROWNSTEIN, Philip N.
Brownstein Zeidman and Schomer
1401 New York Ave., N.W., Suite 900, Washington, DC 20005
Telephone: (202) 879-5700
Registered as lobbyist at U.S. Congress.
Background: Director, Loan Guaranty Service, 1958-61 and Chief Benefits Director, 1961-63, Veterans Administration. Commissioner, Federal Housing Administration, 1963-69 and Assistant Secretary for Mortgage Credit, 1966-69, Department of Housing and Urban Development. Director, Federal Nat'l Mortgage Ass'n, 1963-68 and 1969-72. Member, President's Task Force on Low Income Housing, 1970.
Clients:
MGIC Investment Corp.

BROWNSTEIN ZEIDMAN AND SCHOMER
1401 New York Ave., N.W., Suite 900, Washington, DC 20005
Telephone: (202) 879-5700
Members of firm representing listed organizations:
Brownstein, Philip N.
Background: Director, Loan Guaranty Service, 1958-61 and Chief Benefits Director, 1961-63, Veterans Administration. Commissioner, Federal Housing Administration, 1963-69 and Assistant Secretary for Mortgage Credit, 1966-69, Department of Housing and Urban Development. Director, Federal Nat'l Mortgage Ass'n, 1963-68 and 1969-72. Member, President's Task Force on Low Income Housing, 1970.
Lore, Kenneth G.
Background: Office of General Counsel, U.S. Department of Housing and Urban Development, 1973-75. Counsel, Nat'l Housing and Rehabilitation Ass'n, 1980-present. Vice Chairman, Nat'l Housing Conference, 1985-present. Member, Federal Nat'l Mortgage Ass'n, 1989-present. Member, Low and Moderate Housing Task Force. Member, Federal Nat'l Mortgage Ass'n Office of Housing Policy Research.
Schreiberg, Sheldon L.
Background: Counsel, Committee on Banking, Finance and Urban Affairs, Subcommittee on Housing and Community Development, U.S. House of Representatives; Exec. Asst. to Asst. Secretary for Housing, Federal Housing Commission, 1977-78. Counsel, Nat'l Housing and Rehabilitation Ass'n, 1980-present.
Zeidman, Philip F.
Background: Federal Trade Commission, 1960-61. Staff Assistant, White House Committee on Small Business, 1961-63. General Counsel, Small Business Administration, 1964-68. Special Assistant to the Vice President of the U.S., 1968. General Counsel, Internat'l Franchise Ass'n. Washington Counsel, American Business Conference.
Clients:
Ass'n of Local Housing Finance Agencies
Industrias Resistol
MGIC Investment Corp. *(Philip N. Brownstein)*
New York City Housing Development Corp. *(Kenneth G. Lore)*
New York State Mortgage Loan Enforcement and Administrative Corp. *(Kenneth G. Lore)*
Schochet Associates *(Sheldon L. Schreiberg)*

BROYHILL, Jeanne
Regional Director, Federal Home Loan Mortgage Corp.
1759 Business Center Drive, Reston, VA 22090
Telephone: (703) 789-4700
Registered as lobbyist at U.S. Congress.

BRUCE, E. Edward
Covington and Burling
1201 Pennsylvania Ave., N.W., Box 7566, Washington, DC 20044

Telephone: (202) 662-6000

BRUCE, John F.
Howrey and Simon
1730 Pennsylvania Ave., N.W., Washington, DC 20006-4793
Telephone: (202) 783-0800
Clients:
American Cement Alliance
Tile Council of America
United States Beet Sugar Ass'n

BRUCE, Nancy
Dir, Cong Affrs Office, DEPARTMENT OF TRANSPORTATION
400 Seventh St., S.W., Washington, DC 20590
Telephone: (202) 366-4573

BRUCE, Robert R.
Partner, Debevoise and Plimpton
555 13th St., N.W. Eleventh Floor, Washington, DC 20004-1179
Telephone: (202) 383-8000
Registered as lobbyist at U.S. Congress.
Registered as Foreign Agent: (# 3527).
Background: General Counsel, Federal Communications Commission, 1977-81.
Clients:
Internat'l Telecom Japan
Sony Corp.

BRUCH, Herbert W.
Technical Director, Nat'l Petroleum Refiners Ass'n
1899 L St., N.W., Suite 1000, Washington, DC 20036
Telephone: (202) 457-0480

BRUDER, GENTILE & MARCOUX
1350 New York Ave., N.W., Suite 600, Washington, DC 20005
Telephone: (202) 783-1350
Members of firm representing listed organizations:
Bruder, George F.
Background: Trial Attorney, Federal Power Commission, 1964-1967.
Clients:
Boston Edison Co. *(George F. Bruder)*
Central Vermont Public Service Corp.
Florida Power Corp.
Montaup Electric Co. *(George F. Bruder)*
Northern States Power Co. *(George F. Bruder)*
Public Service Co. of Indiana *(George F. Bruder)*
Public Service Co. of New Hampshire *(George F. Bruder)*
Wisconsin Electric Power Co. *(George F. Bruder)*

BRUDER, George F.
Bruder, Gentile & Marcoux
1350 New York Ave., N.W., Suite 600, Washington, DC 20005
Telephone: (202) 783-1350
Background: Trial Attorney, Federal Power Commission, 1964-1967.
Clients:
Boston Edison Co.
Montaup Electric Co.
Northern States Power Co.
Public Service Co. of Indiana
Public Service Co. of New Hampshire
Wisconsin Electric Power Co.

BRUDERLE, Thomas P.
Director, Federal Legislative Affairs, American Soc. of Hospital Pharmacists
4630 Montgomery Ave., Bethesda, MD 20814
Telephone: (301) 657-3000
Registered as lobbyist at U.S. Congress.

BRUECKMANN, Dr. Wolf
Director, Internat'l Investment Policy, Chamber of Commerce of the U.S.A.
1615 H St., N.W., Washington, DC 20062
Telephone: (202) 659-6000
Registered as lobbyist at U.S. Congress.

BRUEGER, Maura
Political Director, Women's Campaign Fund
1601 Connecticut Ave., N.W. Suite 800, Washington, DC 20005
Telephone: (202) 234-3700

BRUGGER, David J.
President, Nat'l Ass'n of Public Television Stations
1350 Connecticut Ave., N.W. Suite 200, Washington, DC 20036
Telephone: (202) 887-1700

BRUGGER, Trina
Associate Director, American Council for Drug Education
204 Monroe St., Rockville, MD 20850
Telephone: (301) 294-0600

BRUNE, Louis J., III
Exec. Director, American Bankruptcy Institute
107 Second St., N.E., Washington, DC 20002
Telephone: (202) 543-1234

BRUNEEL, Larry
Senior Policy Analyst, Madison Group/Earle Palmer Brown, The
2033 M St., N.W., 9th Floor, Washington, DC 20036
Telephone: (202) 223-0030

BRUNELLI, Samuel A.
Exec. Director, American Legislative Exchange Council
214 Massachusetts Ave., N.W., Washington, DC 20002
Telephone: (202) 547-4646

BRUNER, Kathryne M.
Mgr., Energy Development Technologies, General Atomics
1100 17th St., N.W., Suite 1200, Washington, DC 20036
Telephone: (202) 659-3140
Registered as lobbyist at U.S. Congress.

BRUNER, Ronald G.
V. President, Communications, Soc. of the Plastics Industry
1275 K St., N.W., Suite 400, Washington, DC 20005
Telephone: (202) 371-5200

BRUNETTE, William Kent
Legislative Representative, American Ass'n of Retired Persons
1909 K St., N.W., Suite 600, Washington, DC 20049
Telephone: (202) 728-4734

BRUNKENHOEFER, James M.
Nat'l Legislative Director, United Transportation Union
400 First St., N.W., Suite 704, Washington, DC 20001
Telephone: (202) 783-3939
Registered as lobbyist at U.S. Congress.

BRUNNER, Michael E.
Exec. Vice President, Nat'l Telephone Cooperative Ass'n
2626 Pennsylvania Ave., N.W., Washington, DC 20037
Telephone: (202) 298-2300
Registered as lobbyist at U.S. Congress.

BRUNNER, Thomas W.
Wiley, Rein & Fielding
1776 K St., N.W., Tenth Floor, Washington, DC 20006-2359
Telephone: (202) 429-7000
Clients:
Nat'l Health Care Anti-Fraud Ass'n

BRUNO, Philippe M.
Dorsey & Whitney
1330 Connecticut Ave., N.W., Suite 200, Washington, DC 20036
Telephone: (202) 857-0700

BRUNSVOLD, Brian G.
Finnegan, Henderson, Farabow, Garrett and Dunner
1300 I St., N.W., Suite 600, Washington, DC 20005
Telephone: (202) 293-6850
Background: Law Clerk, U.S. Court of Claims, 1966-1967.
Clients:
Yamazaki Machinery Works, Ltd.

BRUSE, J. Charles
Asst. V. Pres. & Asst. General Counsel, Allstate Insurance Co.
633 Pennsylvania Ave., N.W., Suite 600, Washington, DC 20004
Telephone: (202) 737-4900
Registered as lobbyist at U.S. Congress.

BRUSER, Lawrence
Deputy General Manager, Mitsui and Co. (U.S.A.), Inc.
1701 Pennsylvania Ave., N.W., Suite 400, Washington, DC 20006
Telephone: (202) 861-0660

BRUSH, C. E.
Partner, Bradley Woods & Co.
733 15th St., N.W. Suite 400, Washington, DC 20005
Telephone: (202) 628-0193

BRYAN, CAVE, MCPHEETERS AND MCROBERTS
1015 15th St., N.W., Suite 1000, Washington, DC 20005
Telephone: (202) 289-6100
Background: Washington Office of a St. Louis law firm.
Members of firm representing listed organizations:
  Beller, Herbert N.
  Blaine, Barbara S.
  Cooper, J. Michael
    Background: Law Clerk, U.S. Court of Appeals, 1973-74.
  Ehrenhaft, Peter D.
    Background: Deputy Assistant Secretary and Special Counsel (Tariff Affairs) Department of the Treasury, 1977-79.
  Murphy, James J.
    Background: Trial Attorney, Civil Rights Division, Department of Justice, 1965-68. Counsel, U.S. Senate Subcommittee, 1969-76.
  O'Neill, Edward S.
  Schwartz, Daniel C.
    Background: Assistant to the Director, 1973-75; Assistant Director for Evaluation, 1975-77, and Deputy Director, 1977-79, Bureau of Competition, Federal Trade Commission.
  Clients:
    American Pediatric Soc. *(James J. Murphy)*
    Ben Franklin Savings Institution
    Czechoslovakia, Chamber of Commerce and Industry of *(J. Michael Cooper)*
    Farmland Industries
    Laclede Gas Co. *(James J. Murphy)*
    Lincoln Savings and Loan Ass'n

BRYANT, Dr. Anne L.
Exec. Director, American Ass'n of University Women
2401 Virginia Ave., N.W., Washington, DC 20037
Telephone: (202) 785-7700

BRYANT, Arthur
Exec. Director, Trial Lawyers for Public Justice
2000 P St., N.W., Suite 611, Washington, DC 20036
Telephone: (202) 463-8600

BRYANT, Barbara L.
Exec. Dir., Private Practice Section, American Physical Therapy Ass'n
1111 North Fairfax St., Alexandria, VA 22314
Telephone: (703) 684-2782

BRYANT, Bo
Staff Asst, Legis Affrs, EXECUTIVE OFFICE OF THE PRESIDENT - The White House
1600 Pennsylvania Ave., N.W., Washington, DC 20500
Telephone: (202) 456-2230

BRYANT, Kathy, J.D.
Associate Director, Government Relations, American College of Obstetricians and Gynecologists
409 12th St., S.W., Washington, DC 20024
Telephone: (202) 638-5577

BRYANT, Margaret H.
Director, Federal Affairs, Coastal Corp., The/ANR Pipeline Co.
2000 M St., N.W., Suite 500, Washington, DC 20036
Telephone: (202) 466-7430
Registered as lobbyist at U.S. Congress.

BRYANT, Nancy B.
Exec. V. President, Soc. of Industrial and Office Realtors
777 14th St., N.W. Suite 400, Washington, DC 20005-3271
Telephone: (202) 383-1150

BRYANT, Victor, Alex
Government Relations Associate, American Textile Manufacturers Institute
1801 K St., N.W. Suite 900, Washington, DC 20006

Telephone: (202) 862-0500
Registered as lobbyist at U.S. Congress.
Background: Former Legislative Assistant to Rep. Elton Gallegly (R-CA).

BRYDON, Dawn M.
Director, Industry Promotions, Internat'l Ice Cream Ass'n
888 16th St., N.W., Washington, DC 20006
Telephone: (202) 296-4250
Registered as lobbyist at U.S. Congress.
Background: Also represents Milk Industry Foundation.

BRYEN, Shoshana
Exec. Director, Jewish Institute for Nat'l Security Affairs
1100 17th St., N.W., Suite 330, Washington, DC 20036
Telephone: (202) 833-0020

BRYGGER, Mary Pat
Director, Nat'l Woman Abuse Prevention Project
2000 P St., N.W., 508, Washington, DC 20036
Telephone: (202) 857-0216

BUC, Nancy L.
Weil, Gotshal & Manges
1615 L St., N.W., Suite 700, Washington, DC 20036
Telephone: (202) 682-7000
Registered as lobbyist at U.S. Congress.
Background: Assistant General Counsel, Department of Health and Human Services, and Chief Counsel, Food and Drug Administration, 1980-81. Attorney, Federal Trade Commission, 1969-72.
Clients:
  Schering Internat'l

BUCHALTER, Alice
Legislative Assistant, New Jersey, State of
444 N. Capitol St., N.W. Suite 236, Washington, DC 20001
Telephone: (202) 638-0631

BUCHANAN, Don
Director, Railroad Workers, Sheet Metal Workers' Internat'l Ass'n
1750 New York Ave., N.W. Sixth Floor, Washington, DC 20006
Telephone: (202) 783-5880
Registered as lobbyist at U.S. Congress.

BUCHANAN, John
Chairman, People for the American Way
2000 M St., N.W., Suite 400, Washington, DC 20036
Telephone: (202) 467-4999
Registered as lobbyist at U.S. Congress.
Background: Also is Senior Associate for the Kettering Foundation.

BUCK, Kathleen A.
Kirkland and Ellis
655 15th St., N.W. Suite 1200, Washington, DC 20005
Telephone: (202) 879-5000
Background: Former General Counsel, Department of Defense and General Counsel, Department of the Air Force.

BUCK, Susan
V. President, Government Affairs, US Sprint Communications Co.
1850 M St., N.W., Suite 1100, Washington, DC 20036
Telephone: (202) 857-1030
Registered as lobbyist at U.S. Congress.

BUCKALEW, Judith A.
Manager, Government Affairs, Hoffmann-La Roche Inc.
1050 Connecticut Ave., N.W. Suite 401, Washington, DC 20036
Telephone: (202) 223-1975
Background: Former Legislative Assistant to former Senator Dan Quayle (R-IN) and former Special Assistant to President Reagan, Office of Public Liaison, The White House.

BUCKHOLD, Virginia M.
Legislative Coordinator, Sidley and Austin
1722 Eye St., N.W. Sixth Floor, Washington, DC 20006
Telephone: (202) 429-4000
Registered as lobbyist at U.S. Congress.
Clients:
  Commerce Clearing House

BUCKLES, Mary
Reed Smith Shaw & McClay
1200 18th St., N.W., Washington, DC 20036
Telephone: (202) 457-6100
Clients:
  Amgen, Inc.

BUCKLEY, David
Senior Account Executive, Reese Communications Companies
2111 Wilson Ave., Suite 900, Arlington, VA 22201
Telephone: (703) 528-4400

BUCKLEY, Jeremiah S.
Thacher, Proffitt and Wood
1500 K St., N.W., Suite 200, Washington, DC 20005
Telephone: (202) 347-8400
Registered as lobbyist at U.S. Congress.
Background: Assistant Counsel, Committee on Government Operations, U.S. House of Representatives, 1971-73. Minority Counsel, Subcommittee on Housing, Committee on Banking, Housing, and Urban Affairs, U.S. Senate, 1973-77. Minority Staff Director, Committee on Banking, Housing, and Urban Affairs, U.S. Senate, 1977-79.
Clients:
  Citicorp Mortgage Finance, Inc.
  Massachusetts Bankers Ass'n
  Mutual Savings Central Fund
  Savings Banks Ass'n of Massachusetts

BUCKLEY, John
V. President, Robinson, Lake, Lerer & Montgomery
1667 K St., N.W., Suite 900, Washington, DC 20006
Telephone: (202) 457-9270

BUCKLEY, Linda M.
Director, Public Relations, Organization for the Protection and Advancement of Small Telephone Cos.
2000 K St., N.W., Suite 205, Washington, DC 20006
Telephone: (202) 659-5990

BUCKMASTER, Thomas L.
Fleishman-Hillard, Inc
1301 Connecticut Ave., N.W., Washington, DC 20036
Telephone: (202) 659-0330
Registered as lobbyist at U.S. Congress.
Background: Serves as Exec. Director of Citizens for Sensible Control of Acid Rain.
Clients:
  Citizens for a Drug Free America

BUCKNER, Michael W.
Research Director, United Mine Workers of America
900 15th St., N.W., Washington, DC 20005
Telephone: (202) 842-7292

BUCKNER, Roy C.
Director, Congressional Relations, Textron Inc.
1090 Vermont Ave., N.W., Suite 1100, Washington, DC 20005
Telephone: (202) 289-5800
Registered as lobbyist at U.S. Congress.

BUDD, Mary H.
Manager, Government Affairs, Control Data Corp.
1201 Pennsylvania Ave., N.W. Suite 370, Washington, DC 20004
Telephone: (202) 789-6524

BUDDE, Bernadette A.
V. President, Political Education, Business-Industry Political Action Committee
1747 Pennsylvania Ave., N.W. Suite 250, Washington, DC 20006-4697
Telephone: (202) 833-1880

BUDEIRI, Priscilla
Staff Attorney, Trial Lawyers for Public Justice
2000 P St., N.W., Suite 611, Washington, DC 20036
Telephone: (202) 463-8600

BUDEITI, Maureen
Senior Government Relations Analyst, University of California
1523 New Hampshire Ave., N.W., Washington, DC 20036
Telephone: (202) 785-2666

The listings in this directory are available as *Mailing Labels.* See last page.

61

BUDWAY, Robert
General Counsel, Can Manufacturers Institute
1625 Massachusetts Ave., N.W., Suite 500, Washington,
DC 20036
Telephone: (201) 232-4677

BUDZIK, Philip M.
Director, Research and Analysis, Natural Gas Supply
Ass'n
1129 20th St., N.W. Suite 300, Washington, DC 20036
Telephone: (202) 331-8900

BUEHLER, Joanne M.
Director, Governmental Affairs, American Ecology Corp.
P.O. Box 3600, Gaithersburg, MD 20878
Telephone: (301) 590-9056

BUEK, Richard
Treasurer, Allied-Signal PAC, Allied-Signal Inc.
1001 Pennsylvania Ave., N.W. Suite 700, Washington, DC
20004
Telephone: (202) 662-2650

BUHL, Cindy M.
PAC Director, Pax Americas
122 Maryland Ave., N.E., Third Floor, Washington, DC
20002
Telephone: (202) 546-0116

BULCAO, Douglas W.
Deputy Exec. V. President, American Textile Manufactur-
ers Institute
1801 K St., N.W. Suite 900, Washington, DC 20006
Telephone: (202) 862-0500
Registered as lobbyist at U.S. Congress.
Background: Serves also as Director, Legislative Division.
Former Legislative Assistant to Rep. Joe D. Waggonner,
Jr. of Louisiana. Contact person for the political action
committee.

BULGER, Roger J.
President, Ass'n of Academic Health Centers
1400 16th St., N.W. Suite 410, Washington, DC 20036
Telephone: (202) 265-9600

BULGER, Thomas J.
Government Relations, Inc.
1620 Eye St., N.W. Suite 300, Washington, DC 20006
Telephone: (202) 775-0079
Registered as lobbyist at U.S. Congress.
Clients:
    Fairfax County, Virginia
    Metropolitan Transportation Commission of Oak-
        land
    Oakland County Board of Supervisors
    San Mateo, California, County of

BULL, Steve
PAC and Business Development Director, Nat'l Republican Senatorial Committee
425 Second St., N.E., Washington, DC 20002
Telephone: (202) 675-6000
Background: Special Assistant to President Richard Nixon,
1969-74.

BULLARD, Dr. John W.
Staff Asst. to the President, Soc. of Medical Consultants
to the Armed Forces
4301 Jones Bridge Road, Bethesda, MD 20814
Telephone: (301) 295-3106

BULLARD, Susan
Cong Liaison Div, ENVIRONMENTAL PROTECTION
AGENCY
401 M St., S.W., Washington, DC 20460
Telephone: (202) 382-5200

BULTHIUS, Jill
Dir, Public Relations & Membership Info., Nat'l Ass'n for
Foreign Student Affairs
1860 19th St., N.W., Washington, DC 20009
Telephone: (202) 462-4811

BUMBALO, Linda Knell
Associate Legislative Counsel, Mortgage Bankers Ass'n of
America
1125 15th St., N.W., Suite 700, Washington, DC 20005
Telephone: (202) 861-6500
Registered as lobbyist at U.S. Congress.

BUMGARNER, Fred
Legis Res Officer, Legis Liaison, DEPARTMENT OF AIR
FORCE
The Pentagon, Washington, DC 20330
Telephone: (202) 697-8153

BUMPERS, William M.
Birch, Horton, Bittner and Cherot
1155 Connecticut Ave., N.W., Suite 1200, Washington, DC
20036
Telephone: (202) 659-5800
Clients:
    Entergy Corp.

BUNN, David A.
Exec. V. President, Parcel Shippers Ass'n
1211 Connecticut Ave., N.W., Suite 406, Washington, DC
20036
Telephone: (202) 296-4618
Registered as lobbyist at U.S. Congress.
Background: Also represents the Parcel Shippers Ass'n Pol-
itical Action Committee.

BUNNELL, Robert A.
V. President, External Affairs, Airport Operators Council
Internat'l
1220 19th St., N.W. Suite 200, Washington, DC 20036
Telephone: (202) 293-8500

BUNTE, Arthur H., Jr.
President, Trucking Management, Inc.
2233 Wisconsin Ave., N.W. Suite 412, Washington, DC
20007
Telephone: (202) 965-7660

BUNTON, T. Scott
Senior Policy Advisor, Gov't Relations, MCI Communica-
tions Corp.
1133 19th St., N.W., Washington, DC 20036
Telephone: (202) 872-1600
Registered as lobbyist at U.S. Congress.
Background: Exec. Assistant to Senator Ralph Yarborough
(D-TX), 1973-74. Professional Staff Member, 1981-84;
Deputy Staff Director for Domestic Policy, 1984-85; and
Staff Director, 1985-87, Senate Democratic Policy Com-
mittee. Chief of Staff to Senator Timothy E Wirth (D-
CO), 1987-89.

BURBAGE, Tom
V. Pres., Wash. Off. (Aeronaut. Systems), Lockheed Corp.
1825 Eye St., N.W., Suite 1100, Washington, DC 20006
Telephone: (202) 955-3300

BURCH, Christine C.
Exec. V. President, Nat'l Ass'n of Public Hospitals
1212 New York Ave., N.W. Suite 800, Washington, DC
20004
Telephone: (202) 408-0223

BURCH, Dean
Director General, Internat'l Telecommunications Satellite
Organization (INTELSAT)
3400 International Drive, N.W., Washington, DC 20008-
3098
Telephone: (202) 944-6800
Background: Chairman, Republican National Committee,
1964-65. Chairman, Federal Communications Commission, 1969-74. Counselor to the President, 1974.

BURCH, J. Thomas, Jr.
Chairman, Nat'l Vietnam Veterans Coalition
1000 Thomas Jefferson St., N.W., Suite 600, Washington,
DC 20007
Telephone: (202) 338-6882
Background: Served in U.S. Army, 1966-74.

BURCH, Michael
V. President,Public Policy, Targeted Communications
Corp.
1807 Michael Faraday Court, Reston, VA 22090
Telephone: (703) 742-7888

BURCH, Norman D.
Ass't Dir., Dir., Congressional Rltns., College of American
Pathologists
1101 Vermont Ave., N.W., Washington, DC 20005
Telephone: (202) 371-6617
Registered as lobbyist at U.S. Congress.

BURCHAM, John B., Jr.
Exec. Director, Nat'l Liquor Stores Ass'n
5101 River Road Suite 108, Bethesda, MD 20816
Telephone: (301) 656-1494

BURCHETT, Barbara G.
National Affairs Manager, Hallmark Cards, Inc.
1615 L St., N.W., Suite 1220, Washington, DC 20036
Telephone: (202) 659-0946
Registered as lobbyist at U.S. Congress.

BURCHETTE & ASSOCIATES
Members of firm representing listed organizations:
    Burchette, William
    Lee, Kenneth
    Clients:
    AmBase Corp.
    New York University

BURCHETTE, William
Burchette & Associates
Registered as lobbyist at U.S. Congress.

BURCK, Gordon
Staff Assoc., Chem./Biological Warfare, Federation of
American Scientists
307 Massachusetts Ave., N.E., Washington, DC 20002
Telephone: (202) 546-3300

BURFORD, David P.
Legislative Affairs Coordinator, Southern Company Services, Inc.
1130 Connecticut Ave., N.W., Suite 830, Washington, DC
20036
Telephone: (202) 775-0944
Registered as lobbyist at U.S. Congress.

BURGEE, Michael B.
Of Counsel., Baker, Worthington, Crossley, Stansberry &
Woolf
1001 Pennsylvania Ave., N.W, Suite 1201, Washington,
DC 20004
Telephone: (202) 347-4360
Background: Deputy General Counsel, Federal Deposit In-
surance Corp., 1984-87.

BURGER, George B.
Lunde and Berger Inc.
1101 King St., Suite 601, Alexandria, VA 22314
Telephone: (703) 838-5511
Background: Former Political Director, Democratic Na-
tional Committee.

BURGER, Mary Louise
President, Ass'n for Childhood Education Internat'l
11141 Georgia Ave., Suite 200, Wheaton, MD 20902
Telephone: (301) 942-2443

BURGILLO, Luis, Jr.
Assoc Dir, Congressional & Federal Affrs, District of Co-
lumbia Office of Intergovernmental Relations
1350 Pennsylvania Ave., N.W., Room 416, Washington,
DC 20004
Telephone: (202) 727-6265

BURGUM & GRIMM, LTD.
106 North Carolina Ave., S.E., Washington, DC 20003
Telephone: (202) 546-3414
Registered as Foreign Agent: (#4301)
Members of firm representing listed organizations:
    Burgum, Thomas L., Exec. V. Pres., Sec'y &
        Treasurer
        Background: Formerly Deputy Under Secretary for Ru-
        ral Development, USDA.
    Grimm, Rodman D., President
        Background: Formerly Industry Program Officer, Office
        of Nuclear Energy, ERDA and Special Assistant, As-
        sistant Secretary for Economic Affairs, Department
        of Commerce. President of Burgum & Grimm Ltd.
    Lebrun-Yaffe, Cynthia, V. President
    Clients:
    Committee for Free Elections and Democracy in
        Nicaragua *(Thomas L. Burgum, Rodman D. Grimm,
        Cynthia Lebrun-Yaffe)*
    Illinois Department of Energy and Natural Re-
        sources *(Thomas L. Burgum)*
    JEFCO *(Thomas L. Burgum)*
    LBG Political Action Committee of Burgum &
        Grimm Ltd. *(Cynthia Lebrun-Yaffe)*

BURGUM, Thomas L.
Exec. V. Pres., Sec'y & Treasurer, Burgum & Grimm, Ltd.
106 North Carolina Ave., S.E., Washington, DC 20003
Telephone: (202) 546-3414
Registered as lobbyist at U.S. Congress.
Registered as Foreign Agent: (#3010).
Background: Formerly Deputy Under Secretary for Rural
Development, USDA.
Clients:
Committee for Free Elections and Democracy in
Nicaragua
Illinois Department of Energy and Natural Re-
sources
JEFCO

BURHOP, William J.
V. President, Federal Affairs, American Airlines
1101 17th St., N.W. Suite 600, Washington, DC 20036
Telephone: (202) 857-4221
Registered as lobbyist at U.S. Congress.

BURIAN, Lawrence L.
President, Nat'l Air Transportation Ass'n
4226 King St., Alexandria, VA 22302
Telephone: (703) 845-9000

BURK, Richard J., Jr.
President, Society and Association Services Corp.
8000 Westpark Drive Suite 130, McLean, VA 22102
Telephone: (703) 790-1745
Clients:
American Board of Health Physics
American Soc. for Photobiology
Health Physics Soc.
Soc. for Risk Analysis

BURKE, April
Sr. Acct. Exec., Corp./Political Issues, Hill and Knowlton
Public Affairs Worldwide
Washington Harbour, 901 31st St., N.W., Washington, DC
20007
Telephone: (202) 333-7400

BURKE, Diane B.
Legislative Affairs Specialist, American Federation of
State, County and Municipal Employees
1625 L St., N.W., Washington, DC 20036
Telephone: (202) 429-1000
Registered as lobbyist at U.S. Congress.

BURKE, Georgia H.
Arter & Hadden
1919 Pennsylvania Ave., N.W., Suite 400, Washington, DC
20006
Telephone: (202) 775-7100
Registered as Foreign Agent: (#3942).
Clients:
Central Union of Agricultural Cooperatives
(ZENCHU)

BURKE, John L., Jr.
Foley, Hoag and Eliot
1615 L St., N.W., Suite 950, Washington, DC 20036
Telephone: (202) 775-0600
Registered as lobbyist at U.S. Congress.
Clients:
Pittsburgh, Stadium Authority of

BURKE, Kelly H.
Stafford, Burke and Hecker
1006 Cameron St., Alexandria, VA 22314
Telephone: (703) 836-2696
Registered as Foreign Agent: (#3625).
Clients:
Construcciones Aeronauticas, S.A.
Sumitomo Corp.

BURKE, Kevin M.
Dir., Industrial & Regulatory Affairs, American Bakers
Ass'n
1111 14th St., N.W., Suite 300, Washington, DC 20005
Telephone: (202) 296-5800
Registered as lobbyist at U.S. Congress.

BURKE, Mary V.
Assistant Exec. Director, Secondary, Nat'l Catholic Educational Ass'n
1077 30th St., N.W. Suite 100, Washington, DC 20007
Telephone: (202) 337-6232

BURKE, Robert E.
Barnes, Richardson and Colburn
1819 H St., N.W., Washington, DC 20006
Telephone: (202) 457-0300
Registered as lobbyist at U.S. Congress.
Background: Member, U.S. Foreign Service, 1967-68. Trial
Attorney, Department of Justice, Customs Section, 1968-
71.
Clients:
Case Co., J. I.
Consolidated Diesel Corp.

BURKE, Robert L.
Senior V. President, American Newspaper Publishers
Ass'n
The Newspaper Center 11600 Sunrise Valley Drive, Res-
ton, VA 22091
Telephone: (703) 648-1000

BURKHALTER, Holly J.
Washington Director, Human Rights Watch
1522 K St., N.W., Suite 910, Washington, DC 20005
Telephone: (202) 371-6592

BURKHARDT, Francis X.
Special Asst. to the General President, Internat'l Brother-
hood of Painters and Allied Trades
1750 New York Ave., N.W., Washington, DC 20006
Telephone: (202) 637-0700
Registered as lobbyist at U.S. Congress.

BURNET, Lining
Programs Director, American Legislative Exchange Council
214 Massachusetts Ave., N.W., Washington, DC 20002
Telephone: (202) 547-4646

BURNETT, Phillip
Exec. V. President, Nat'l Cotton Council of America
1110 Vermont Ave., N.W. Suite 430, Washington, DC
20005
Telephone: (202) 833-2943

BURNETT, Stanton
Director of Studies, Center for Strategic and Internat'l
Studies
1800 K St., N.W., Washington, DC 20006
Telephone: (202) 887-0200
Background: Counselor, United States Information Agency,
1985-88. Counselor for Public Affairs, Rome, 1980-83;
U.S. Mission to NATO, 1983-84; Director of European
Affairs, 1984-85; Director of Research, 1978-80.

BURNETT, Susan
Attorney, Legislation Div, DEPARTMENT OF HEALTH
AND HUMAN SERVICES
200 Independence Ave., S.W., Washington, DC 20201
Telephone: (202) 245-7773

BURNETTE, Linda J.
Office Manager, Nat'l Insurance Consumer Organization
121 North Payne St., Alexandria, VA 22314
Telephone: (703) 549-8050

BURNETTE, Mahlon A., III
631 Walker Rd., Great Falls, VA 22066
Telephone: (703) 759-5984
Registered as lobbyist at U.S. Congress.
Organizations represented:
Nat'l Broiler Council

BURNEY, David
General Counsel/ Exec. Director, United States Tuna
Foundation
1101 17th St., N.W. Suite 609, Washington, DC 20036
Telephone: (202) 857-0610

BURNIM, Ira A.
Legal Director, Mental Health Law Project
2021 L St., N.W., Washington, DC 20036
Telephone: (202) 467-5730

BURNLEY, James H., IV
Shaw, Pittman, Potts and Trowbridge
2300 N St., N.W., Washington, DC 20037
Telephone: (202) 663-8000
Registered as lobbyist at U.S. Congress.
Clients:
Colebrand Ltd.

BURNS, Charles S.
Vice President, Government Relations, Phelps Dodge
Corp.
1015 15th St., N.W., Suite 909, Washington, DC 20005
Telephone: (202) 789-1745
Registered as lobbyist at U.S. Congress.

BURNS, Hugh P.
Dir., News and Information-Washington, Lockheed Corp.
1825 Eye St., N.W., Suite 1100, Washington, DC 20006
Telephone: (202) 955-3306

BURNS, Kevin R.
Counsel, American Mining Congress
1920 N St., N.W. Suite 300, Washington, DC 20036
Telephone: (202) 861-2800
Registered as lobbyist at U.S. Congress.

BURNS, Michael
Senior Fellow, Business Executives for Nat'l Security
601 Pennsylvania Ave., N.W. Suite 700, Washington, DC
20004
Telephone: (202) 737-1090
Registered as lobbyist at U.S. Congress.

BURNS, Nancy A.
Exec. Director, Color Marketing Group
4001 N. 9th St., Suite 102, Arlington, VA 22203
Telephone: (703) 528-7666

BURNS, Terry J.
V. President, Nat'l Ass'n of Tobacco Distributors
1199 North Fairfax St. Suite 701, Alexandria, VA 22314
Telephone: (703) 683-8336
Background: Serves as Treasurer, Nat'l Ass'n of Tobacco
Distributors Political Action Committee.

BURNS, Timothy F.
Director Federal Legislative Affairs, Chemical Manufactur-
ers Ass'n
2501 M St., N.W., Washington, DC 20037
Telephone: (202) 887-1100
Registered as lobbyist at U.S. Congress.

BURRIDGE ASSOCIATES
1612 K St., N.W. Suite 204, Washington, DC 20006
Telephone: (202) 955-0001
Members of firm representing listed organizations:
Burridge, James L.

BURRIDGE, James L.
Burridge Associates
1612 K St., N.W. Suite 204, Washington, DC 20006
Telephone: (202) 955-0001

BURROUGHS, James N.
V. Pres., Gov't Relations & Gen. Counsel, Nat'l Propane
Gas Ass'n
1235 Jefferson Davis Hwy., Suite 702, Arlington, VA
22202
Telephone: (703) 979-3560
Background: Former Legislative Assistant to Senator Paul
Trible (R-VA) and Rep. Frank Wolf (R-VA). Former At-
torney-Advisor to the Office of the Federal Register.

BURRUS, William
V. President, American Postal Workers Union
1300 L St., N.W., Washington, DC 20005
Telephone: (202) 842-4246
Registered as lobbyist at U.S. Congress.

BURSON-MARSTELLER
1850 M St., N.W., Suite 900, Washington, DC 20036
Telephone: (202) 833-8550
Background: Washington Office of a New York PR firm.
Members of firm representing listed organizations:
Altman, John, Account Supervisor
Auxier, Gary, Senior V. President
Background: Former Press Secretary to Senator Walter
D. Huddleston (D-KY).
Bell, Thomas D. (Jr.), Vice Chairman
Biegel, Leonard, Sr. V. Pres./Dir., Media Rela-
tions
Brosnahan, Timothy G., Exec. V. President
Background: Former Legislative Assistant to Senator
Lowell Weicker (R-CT).
Brown, Sharon, Senior Account Executive
Background: Former Deputy Press Secretary to Senator
Joseph Biden (D-DE) and Press Secretary to Senator
Gaylord Nelson (D-WI).

BURSON-MARSTELLER (Cont'd)

Caldwell, Ellen
Background: Former press aide to Senators Wyche Fowler, Jr. (D—GA) and Albert Gore (D-TN).
Callan, Jim, Constituency Relations Counselor
Cordia, Louis, V. President
Background: Special Assistant, Environmental Protection Agency, 1981-83.
DuPont, Daniel
Fitzsimmons, Richard, V. President, Government Relations
Ford, Patrick, V. President and Group Manager
Gilroy, Brent, Account Supervisor
Background: Former aide to Rep. George Darden (D-GA).
Halkias, Rebecca L., V. President
Hamrick, Peggy
Hartz, Michelle, Senior V.
Heilig, Paul T., V. President, Government Relations
Kehs, Michael, Account Supervisor
Leavell, Winston, Account Supervisor
Lengel, John B., V. President
Maloley, Nancy A., Sr. V. Pres. & Dir., Environment Policy
Background: Former Special Assistant to President Bush for Environmental, Energy and Natural Resources Policy, White House Office of Policy Development.
Moore, Richard, V. President, Director, Media Relations
Natanblut, Sharon, V. President
Newton, Charlotte, Constituency Relations Counselor
Pines, Wayne L., Exec. V. Pres. & Dir. of Medical Issues
Prothro, Pamela
Raviv, Sheila, Sr. V. Pres., Dir., Media Relations
Ray, Jerry, Senior Counsel, Media Relations
Background: Former press secretary to Senator Howell Heflin (D-AL).
Sklar, William E., V. President
Stephens, J. Gordon (Jr.)
Background: Senior V. President, Burson-Marsteller. Legislative Assistant to former Speaker of the House of Representatives Carl Albert (D-OK), 1973-77.
Tieger, Carolyn, Sr. V. President
Background: Former Communications and Special Projects Director, Office of Private Sector Initiatives, The White House.
Umansky, David J., Sr. V.P./Director, Grass Roots Mobiliztn
Wilson, Edie, V. President
Clients:
American Ass'n of Dental Schools *(Rebecca L. Halkias)*
American Handicapped Employers Ass'n *(Carolyn Tieger)*
American Paper Institute *(Wayne L. Pines)*
American Podiatric Medical Ass'n *(Sheila Raviv)*
American Soc. of Landscape Architects *(Michelle Hartz)*
Andersen and Co., Arthur
Asbestos Claims Facility *(Carolyn Tieger)*
Australia, Department of Industry, Technology and Resources of
Ball Corp.
Bethlehem Steel Corp. *(Timothy G. Brosnahan)*
Blue Cross of Pennsylvania *(Rebecca L. Halkias)*
Burson-Marsteller Political Action Committee
Carr Company, The Oliver *(Sharon Natanblut)*
Cigarette Export Ass'n
Coalition Against Regressive Taxation *(Leonard Biegel)*
du Pont de Nemours and Co., E. I. *(Carolyn Tieger)*
Emhart Corp. *(Paul T. Heilig, J. Gordon Stephens, Jr.)*
GPU Service Corp. *(Wayne L. Pines)*
Independent Blue Cross *(Rebecca L. Halkias)*
Lever Brothers Co. *(J. Gordon Stephens, Jr.)*
McNeil Consumer Products Co. *(Sheila Raviv)*
Nat'l Food Processors Ass'n
Nat'l Urban Coalition *(Sheila Raviv)*
Norway, Government of
NutraSweet Co. *(Sheila Raviv)*
Pennwalt Corp.
Pfizer, Inc. *(Wayne L. Pines)*
Philadelphia Industrial Development Corp.

Philadelphia, Pennsylvania, City of *(Rebecca L. Halkias)*
Philadelphia Port Corp. *(Rebecca L. Halkias)*
Philip Morris Cos., Inc.
Ridgeview Institute *(Carolyn Tieger)*
Safe Buildings Alliance *(Carolyn Tieger)*
Saudi Basic Industries Corp.
Saudi Refining, Inc.
Shell Chemical Co. *(Sheila Raviv)*
Temple University *(Rebecca L. Halkias)*
Thomson-CSF Inc.
Thomson Group

BURT, Jeffrey A.
Arnold & Porter
1200 New Hampshire Ave., N.W., Washington, DC 20036
Telephone: (202) 872-6700
Clients:
Poland, Ministry of Finance of

BURTLESS, Gary
Senior Fellow, Economic Studies Program, Brookings Institution
1775 Massachusetts Ave., N.W., Washington, DC 20036
Telephone: (202) 797-6000
Background: Economist, Department of Labor (1979-81); Economist, Health, Education and Welfare (1977-79).

BURTON, Daniel F., Jr.
Exec. V. President, Council on Competitiveness
1331 Pennsylvania Ave., N.W. Suite 900 North, Washington, DC 20004
Telephone: (202) 662-8760

BURTON, David
Manager, Tax Policy, Chamber of Commerce of the U.S-.A.
1615 H St., N.W., Washington, DC 20062
Telephone: (202) 659-6000
Registered as lobbyist at U.S. Congress.

BURTON, Ellen
Director, Federal Relations, US WEST, Inc.
1020 19th St., N.W., Suite 700, Washington, DC 20036
Telephone: (202) 429-3100

BURTON, Joel S.
Ginsburg, Feldman and Bress
1250 Connecticut Ave., N.W. Suite 800, Washington, DC 20036
Telephone: (202) 637-9000

BURTON, Julie
Exec. Director, Voters for Choice
2000 P St., N.W., Suite 515, Washington, DC 20036
Telephone: (202) 822-6640

BURTON, Kent
Resource Recovery Director, Nat'l Solid Wastes Management Ass'n
1730 Rhode Island Ave., N.W., 10th Floor, Washington, DC 20036
Telephone: (202) 659-4613
Registered as lobbyist at U.S. Congress.

BURTON, Larry D.
Ass't. Director, Federal Gov't. Affairs, BP America Inc.
1776 Eye St., N.W., Suite 1000, Washington, DC 20006
Telephone: (202) 785-4888
Registered as lobbyist at U.S. Congress.

BURTON, Shirley
Director of Communication, General Conference of Seventh-day Adventists
12501 Old Columbia Pike, Silver Spring, MD 20904
Telephone: (301) 680-6320

BURWELL, HANSEN, PETERS AND HOUSTON
1762 Church St., N.W., Washington, DC 20036
Telephone: (202) 745-0441
Members of firm representing listed organizations:
Hansen, Walter D.
Background: Special Counsel to the U.S. House of Representatives Judiciary Committee, 1966-67.
Clients:
Garuda Indonesian Airways *(Walter D. Hansen)*
Lyon Moving and Storage Co.
Transamerica Airlines *(Walter D. Hansen)*
Wardair Canada, Ltd. *(Walter D. Hansen)*

BURY, Craig E.
V. President, Chambers Associates Incorporated
1625 K St., N.W. Suite 200, Washington, DC 20006
Telephone: (202) 857-0670
Background: Former Professional Staff Member, Senate Appropriations Committee and Senate Budget Committee.
Clients:
American Ass'n of Retired Persons
American Postal Workers Union

BUSBY, David
Dorsey & Whitney
1330 Connecticut Ave., N.W., Suite 200, Washington, DC 20036
Telephone: (202) 857-0700
Registered as lobbyist at U.S. Congress.
Background: Counsel, Sub-Committee on Automobile Marketing Practices, U.S. Senate Interstate and Foreign Commerce Committee, 1955-1958. Counsel, Sub-Committee on Foreign Commerce, U.S. Senate Interstate and Foreign Commerce Committee, 1958.

BUSH, Barbara
Taxation Deputy Director, American Petroleum Institute
1220 L St., N.W., Washington, DC 20005
Telephone: (202) 682-8462

BUSH, Graeme
Caplin and Drysdale
One Thomas Circle, N.W. Suite 1100, Washington, DC 20005
Telephone: (202) 862-5000
Clients:
Mail Advertising Service Ass'n Internat'l

BUSH, James T.
Associate Director, Center for Defense Information
1500 Massachusetts Ave., N.W., Washington, DC 20005
Telephone: (202) 862-0700

BUSH, John S., Jr.
V. President, Governmental Affairs, USG Corporation
655 15th St., N.W., Suite 300, Washington, DC 20005
Telephone: (202) 639-4057

BUSH, Nicholas J.
President, Natural Gas Supply Ass'n
1129 20th St., N.W. Suite 300, Washington, DC 20036
Telephone: (202) 331-8900

BUSH, Robert D.
Exec. Director, Advisory Council on Historic Preservation
1100 Pennsylvania Ave., N.W. Suite 809, Washington, DC 20004
Telephone: (202) 786-0503

BUSHNELL, David
Senior Associate, APCO Associates
1155 21st St., N.W., Suite 1000, Washington, DC 20036
Telephone: (202) 778-1000

BUSHONG, David W.
Gold and Liebengood, Inc.
1455 Pennsylvania Ave., N.W. Suite 950, Washington, DC 20004
Telephone: (202) 639-8899
Registered as lobbyist at U.S. Congress.
Background: Former Counsel, Committee on Intelligence, and aide to Senator Nancy Kassebaum (R-KS).
Clients:
British Airports Authority (BAA plc)
Nat'l Business Aircraft Ass'n

BUSKER, William
Sr. V. President, Law and Finance, American Trucking Ass'ns
2200 Mill Road, Alexandria, VA 22314
Telephone: (703) 838-1858

BUTCHMAN, Alan A.
Garvey, Schubert & Barer
1000 Potomac St., N.W. Suite 500, Washington, DC 20007
Telephone: (202) 965-7880
Registered as lobbyist at U.S. Congress.
Background: Deputy Secretary, U.S. Department of Transportation, 1977-79. Administrative Assistant to Rep. Brock Adams, 1970-76.
Clients:

Aberdeen, Washington, City of
Bellingham, Port of
Early Winters Resort
Foss Maritime Co.
Garvey, Schubert & Barer Political Action Committee
Space Industries, Inc.
Totem Ocean Trailer Express, Inc.
Washington Citizens for World Trade

BUTERA, CHARTERED, James J.
4901 Quebec St., N.W., Washington, DC 20016
Telephone: (202) 362-8501
Background: A law and government relations firm.
Members of firm representing listed organizations:
Butera, James J., President
Organizations represented:
Bank of Baltimore
Dime Savings Bank of New York
Federal Home Loan Bank of Boston
Federal Home Loan Bank of New York
New Jersey Council of Savings Institutions
Peoples Bank
River Bank America
Rochester Community Savings Bank
Savings Bank of the Finger Lakes
Savings Banks Ass'n of New York
Wilmington Savings Fund Soc.

BUTERA, James J.
President, Butera, Chartered, James J.
4901 Quebec St., N.W., Washington, DC 20016
Telephone: (202) 362-8501
Registered as lobbyist at U.S. Congress.

BUTLER, Barbara
Exec. Director, Bell Atlantic
Suite 1200, 1710 Rhode Island Ave., N.W., Washington, DC 20036
Telephone: (202) 392-1384

BUTLER, Bill
Director, Government Relations, Beech Aircraft Corp.
1215 Jefferson Davis Hwy., 15th Floor, Arlington, VA 22202-4302
Telephone: (703) 521-2020

BUTLER, Carol Lynne
Director, Regulatory Affairs, Cable and Wireless North America
1919 Gallows Road, Vienna, VA 22182
Telephone: (703) 790-5300
Registered as Foreign Agent: (#4231)

BUTLER, Frances F.
President, EMJ Consultants
11481 Bingham Terrace, Reston, VA 22091
Telephone: (703) 860-9570
Clients:
American Ass'n for Internat'l Aging
Nat'l Ass'n of Foster Grandparent Program Directors
Nat'l Ass'n of Retired Senior Volunteer Program Directors
Nat'l Ass'n of Senior Companion Program Directors

BUTLER, Hedi
Acting Public Relations Director, Nat'l Center for Neighborhood Enterprise
1367 Connecticut Ave., N.W., 2nd Floor, Washington, DC 20036
Telephone: (202) 331-1103

BUTLER, Michael F.
Andrews and Kurth
1701 Pennsylvania Ave., N.W., Suite 200, Washington, DC 20006
Telephone: (202) 662-2700
Registered as lobbyist at U.S. Congress.
Background: Deputy General Counsel, United States Department of Commerce, 1969-1973. General Counsel, Federal Energy Administration, 1975-1977.

BUTLER, Nancy
V. President, Communications, Internat'l Sleep Products Ass'n
333 Commerce St., Alexandria, VA 22314
Telephone: (703) 683-8371

BUTLER, Patrick H.
V. President, Washington, Times Mirror Co.
1875 Eye St., N.W., Suite 1110, Washington, DC 20006
Telephone: (202) 293-3126
Registered as lobbyist at U.S. Congress.

BUTLER, Stuart M.
Director, Domestic Policy Studies, Heritage Foundation
214 Massachusetts Ave., N.E., Washington, DC 20002
Telephone: (202) 546-4400

BUTLER, Susan Lowell
Exec. V. President, Women in Communications
2101 Wilson Blvd., Suite 417, Arlington, VA 22201
Telephone: (703) 528-4200

BUTLER, Sydney J.
V. President, Conservation, Wilderness Soc.
1400 Eye St., N.W., 10th Floor, Washington, DC 20005
Telephone: (202) 842-3400
Registered as lobbyist at U.S. Congress.

BUTLER, William A.
Dickstein, Shapiro and Morin
2101 L St., N.W., Washington, DC 20037
Telephone: (202) 785-9700

BUTTERFIELD, Bruce
V. President, Public Affairs, Manufactured Housing Institute
1745 Jefferson Davis Hwy. Suite 511, Arlington, VA 22202
Telephone: (703) 979-6620
Registered as lobbyist at U.S. Congress.

BUTTERFIELD, Jane
V. President, Washington Communications Group/Ruder Finn
1615 M St., N.W., Suite 220, Washington, DC 20036
Telephone: (202) 466-7800

BUTTON, Christopher
Senior Policy Assoc., Gov'tl Activities, United Cerebral Palsy Ass'ns
1522 K St., N.W., Suite 1112, Washington, DC 20005
Telephone: (202) 842-1266

BUTTON, Kenneth R.
V. President, Economic Consulting Services Inc.
1225 19th St. N.W., Suite 210, Washington, DC 20036
Telephone: (202) 466-7720
Clients:
Non-Ferrous Metals Producers Committee

BUTTRAM CO., Jack E.
1629 K St., N.W. Suite 802, Washington, DC 20006
Telephone: (202) 296-5056
Members of firm representing listed organizations:
Buttram, Jack E.
Organizations represented:
Democratic Unionist Party of Northern Ireland
(Jack E. Buttram)
Friends of Free China

BUTTRAM, Jack E.
Buttram Co., Jack E.
1629 K St., N.W. Suite 802, Washington, DC 20006
Telephone: (202) 296-5056
Registered as Foreign Agent: (#3588).
Organizations represented:
Democratic Unionist Party of Northern Ireland

BUTYNSKI, Dr. William
Exec. Director, Nat'l Ass'n of State Alcohol and Drug Abuse Directors
444 North Capitol St., N.W. Suite 642, Washington, DC 20001
Telephone: (202) 783-6868

BUVINIC, Mayra
Director, Internat'l Center for Research on Women
1717 Massachusetts Ave., N.W., Suite 302, Washington, DC 20036
Telephone: (202) 797-0007

BUXTON, C. Michael
Vinson and Elkins
Willard Office Building, 1455 Pennsylvania Ave., N.W., Washington, DC 20004-1007
Telephone: (202) 639-6500

Background: Attorney-Advisor, Office of Legal Counsel, U.S. Department of Justice, 1971-73. Special Assistant U.S. Attorney, District of Columbia, 1972.

BUZBY, Barry
Exec. Director, State Ass'ns Group, Nat'l Industrial Council
1331 Pennsylvania Ave., N.W. N. Lobby Suite 1500, Washington, DC 20004-1703
Telephone: (202) 637-3053

BUZZELL, Charles H.
Exec. Director, American Vocational Ass'n
1410 King St., Alexandria, VA 22314
Telephone: (703) 683-3111
Background: Formerly with the Office of Vocational and Adult Education, U.S. Department of Education.

BUZZERD, Elizabeth A.
Ass'n and Society Management Internat'l Inc.
7297 Lee Highway, Unit N, Falls Church, VA 22042
Telephone: (703) 533-0251
Clients:
Nat'l Coordinating Council on Emergency Management

BUZZERD, Harry W., Jr.
Ass'n and Society Management Internat'l Inc.
7297 Lee Highway, Unit N, Falls Church, VA 22042
Telephone: (703) 533-0251
Background: Serves as Exec. V. President, American Textile Machinery Ass'n; Exec. Director, Wire Industry Suppliers Ass'n; Exec. Director, Process Equipment Manufacturers Ass'n; and President, Meat Industry Suppliers Ass'n. Also serves as Acting Director, Nat'l Coordinating Council on Emergency Management.
Clients:
American Textile Machinery Ass'n
Meat Industry Suppliers Ass'n
Process Equipment Manufacturers Ass'n

BYE, Dr. Raymond
Dir, Legis and Public Affrs, NAT'L SCIENCE FOUNDATION
1800 G St., N.W., Washington, DC 20550
Telephone: (202) 357-9838

BYER, David
Exec. Branch Advocate, Federal Relations, Nat'l School Boards Ass'n
1680 Duke St., Alexandria, VA 22314
Telephone: (703) 838-6722

BYERLEY LAW OFFICES, Walter E.
1625 K St., N.W. Suite 1190, Washington, DC 20006-1649
Telephone: (202) 628-5530
Members of firm representing listed organizations:
Byerley, Walter E.
Background: Trial Attorney, Food and Drug Administration, 1960-67.
Hill, Wayne K.
Background: General Counsel, National Bakery Suppliers Association.
Organizations represented:
Independent Cosmetic Manufacturers and Distributors, Inc. *(Walter E. Byerley)*
Internat'l Hydrolized Protein Council *(Walter E. Byerley)*
Nat'l Bakery Suppliers Ass'n *(Wayne K. Hill)*
Nat'l Kraut Packers Ass'n, Inc. *(Walter E. Byerley)*
Pickle Packers Internat'l, Inc. *(Walter E. Byerley)*

BYERLEY, Walter E.
Byerley Law Offices, Walter E.
1625 K St., N.W. Suite 1190, Washington, DC 20006-1649
Telephone: (202) 628-5530
Background: Trial Attorney, Food and Drug Administration, 1960-67.
Organizations represented:
Independent Cosmetic Manufacturers and Distributors, Inc.
Internat'l Hydrolized Protein Council
Nat'l Kraut Packers Ass'n, Inc.
Pickle Packers Internat'l, Inc.

BYINGTON, S. John
Pillsbury, Madison and Sutro
1667 K St., N.W., Suite 1100, Washington, DC 20006
Telephone: (202) 887-0300

BYINGTON, S. John (Cont'd)
Registered as lobbyist at U.S. Congress.

BYLER ASSOCIATES, William
1155 Connecticut Ave., N.W. Suite 300, Washington, DC 20036
Telephone: (202) 429-6633
Background: A consulting firm on legislative lobbying and government relations.
Members of firm representing listed organizations:
Byler, William, President
Organizations represented:
Havasupai Tribal Council *(William Byler)*
San Carlos Apache Tribe
Tohono O'odham Nation *(William Byler)*

BYLER, William
President, Byler Associates, William
1155 Connecticut Ave., N.W. Suite 300, Washington, DC 20036
Telephone: (202) 429-6633
Registered as lobbyist at U.S. Congress.
Organizations represented:
Havasupai Tribal Council
Tohono O'odham Nation

BYNUM, James L.
Dep Asst Secy, Cong Relations, DEPARTMENT OF HOUSING AND URBAN DEVELOPMENT
451 Seventh St., S.W., Washington, DC 20410
Telephone: (202) 755-7380

BYRLEY, Charles A.
Director, Washington Office, American Public Works Ass'n
1301 Pennsylvania Ave., N.W. Suite 501, Washington, DC 20004
Telephone: (202) 393-2792

BYRNE, John J.
Senior Legislative Counsel, American Bankers Ass'n
1120 Connecticut Ave., N.W., Washington, DC 20036
Telephone: (202) 663-5000
Registered as lobbyist at U.S. Congress.

BYRNE, Michael
Washington Rep/Administrative Officer, California, State of
444 North Capitol St., N.W., Suite 305, Washington, DC 20001
Telephone: (202) 347-6891

BYRNES, William J.
Haley, Bader and Potts
2000 M St., N.W. Suite 600, Washington, DC 20036
Telephone: (202) 331-0606
Clients:
MCI Communications Corp.

BYRON, James
Treasurer, Nat'l Committee for an Effective Congress
507 Capitol Court, N.E., Washington, DC 20002
Telephone: (202) 547-1151

BYWATER, William H.
President, Internat'l Union of Electronic, Electrical, Salaried, Machine, and Furniture Workers, AFL-CIO
1126 16th St., N.W., Washington, DC 20036
Telephone: (202) 296-1200

C & C CONSULTING GROUP, INC.
210 Cameron St., Alexandria, VA 22314
Telephone: (703) 548-1992
Members of firm representing listed organizations:
Clinkenbeard, Kirk L., Secretary-Treasurer
Cushing, Christopher T., President and CEO

C & M INTERNAT'L L.P.
1001 Pennsylvania Ave., N.W., Washington, DC 20004-2505
Telephone: (202) 624-2895
Registered as Foreign Agent: (#3988)
Background: An international trade consulting and lobbying firm associated with the law firm of Crowell and Moring.
Members of firm representing listed organizations:
Baughman, Laura M.
Cooper, Doral S.
Background: Former Assistant U.S. Trade Representative, Office of Bilateral Affairs, Reagan Administration.

Covell, Barbara J.
Keene, Thomas C.
Rickard, Claire A.
Clients:
China, Foreign Trade Board of the Republic of *(Doral S. Cooper)*
Korea Foreign Trade Ass'n *(Doral S. Cooper)*
Singapore Trade Development Board *(Doral S. Cooper)*
United Nations Conference on Trade and Development *(Doral S. Cooper)*

CABLE, William H.
V. President and General Counsel, Timmons and Co., Inc.
1850 K St., N.W., Suite 850, Washington, DC 20006
Telephone: (202) 331-1760
Background: Former Counsel to the House Committee on Education and Labor and Staff Director, House Administration Committee; Deputy Assistant (Legislative Affairs) to President Jimmy Carter, 1977-81.

CABRAL, Debra
Jefferson Group, The
1341 G St., N.W., Suite 1100, Washington, DC 20005
Telephone: (202) 638-3535
Background: Former aide to Rep. Thomes P. O'Neill, Jr. (D-MA).

CACCHIONE, Patrick J.
Director, Government Affairs, Nat'l Ass'n of Medical Equipment Suppliers
625 Slaters Lane, Suite 200, Alexandria, VA 22314
Telephone: (703) 836-6263
Registered as lobbyist at U.S. Congress.
Background: Also serves as contact for the Nat'l Ass'n of Medical Equipment Suppliers Political Action Committee.

CADWALADER, WICKERSHAM & TAFT
1333 New Hampshire Ave., N.W. Suite 700, Washington, DC 20036
Telephone: (202) 862-2200
Background: A law firm headquartered in New York City.
Members of firm representing listed organizations:
Alexander, Donald C.
Background: Commissioner of Internal Revenue, 1973-77. Commissioner, Commission on Federal Paperwork, 1975-77. Commissioner, Interior Department Coal Leasing Commission, 1983-84. Chairman, Internal Revenue Service Exempt Organization Advisory Group, 1987.
Carlisle, Linda E.
Background: Special Assistant to the Assistant Secretary for Tax Policy and Attorney Advisor, U.S. Treasury, 1984-87.
Eastman, Ronald D.
Background: Attorney, Office of the General Counsel, FPC, 1967-1969.
Granwell, Alan W.
Background: International Tax Counsel and Director, Office of International Tax Affairs, U.S. Dept. of the Treasury, 1981-4.
Mentz, J. Roger
Background: Assistant Secretary for Tax Policy, U.S. Treasury Department, 1985-87.
Clients:
Air Products and Chemicals, Inc. *(Donald C. Alexander)*
Air Transport Ass'n of America *(Donald C. Alexander)*
American Financial Corp. *(Donald C. Alexander)*
Aon Corp. *(Donald C. Alexander)*
Bechtel Group, Inc. *(Donald C. Alexander)*
Bechtel Investments, Inc. *(Donald C. Alexander)*
Clayton & Dubilier, Inc. *(Linda E. Carlisle, J. Roger Mentz)*
Coalition for Capital Import Neutrality *(J. Roger Mentz)*
Family Life Insurance Co. *(Donald C. Alexander)*
Harsco Corp. *(Donald C. Alexander)*
Kern River Gas Transmission Co.
Mercedes-Benz of North America, Inc. *(J. Roger Mentz)*
Michigan, State of *(Ronald D. Eastman)*
Mortgage Guaranty Insurance Corp. *(Donald C. Alexander)*
Nationwide Insurance Cos. *(Donald C. Alexander)*
Northwest Airlines, Inc. *(Ronald D. Eastman)*
PFIC Group *(J. Roger Mentz)*

United Brands Co. *(Donald C. Alexander)*

CADY, Elizabeth B.
Government Affairs Director, Steel Service Center Institute
1919 Pennsylvania Ave., N.W. Suite 400, Washington, DC 20006
Telephone: (202) 785-3642
Registered as lobbyist at U.S. Congress.

CADY, Fran
Staff V. President for Finance, Urban Land Institute
1090 Vermont Ave., N.W. Suite 300, Washington, DC 20005
Telephone: (202) 289-8500

CADY, John R.
President, Nat'l Food Processors Ass'n
1401 New York Ave., N.W. Suite 400, Washington, DC 20005
Telephone: (202) 639-5900
Registered as lobbyist at U.S. Congress.

CAFFIAUX, Jean A.
Senior V. President, Government Div., Electronic Industries Ass'n
2001 Pennsylvania Ave., N.W., Washington, DC 20006
Telephone: (202) 457-4940

CAFRUNY, Madalyn
Director of Public Information, American Public Power Ass'n
2301 M St., N.W., Washington, DC 20037
Telephone: (202) 775-8300

CAGGIANO, Paul J.
President, Coalition for Government Procurement
1990 M St., N.W., Suite 400, Washington, DC 20036
Telephone: (202) 331-0975

CAHILL, Catherine D.
Asst. V. Pres., Government Affairs, American Osteopathic Hospital Ass'n
1454 Duke St., Alexandria, VA 22314
Telephone: (703) 684-7700
Registered as lobbyist at U.S. Congress.
Background: Serves as contact for the Political Action Committee of the American Osteopathic Hospital Ass'n.

CAHILL, Jim
Confidential Asst, Cong Relations, DEPARTMENT OF AGRICULTURE
14th and Independence Ave. S.W., Room 211-E, Washington, DC 20205
Telephone: (202) 447-7095

CAHOON, Mark
V. President, Council of State Chambers of Commerce
122 C St., N.W. Suite 330, Washington, DC 20001
Telephone: (202) 484-8103
Registered as lobbyist at U.S. Congress.

CAIN, C. Marshall
Dep Gen Counsel, Litig, Legis & Reg Opns, ENVIRONMENTAL PROTECTION AGENCY
401 M St., S.W., Washington, DC 20460
Telephone: (202) 382-5200

CAIN, Morrison G.
Public Affairs Counsel, Internat'l Mass Retail Ass'n
1901 Pennsylvania Ave., N.W. Suite 200, Washington, DC 20006
Telephone: (202) 861-0774
Registered as lobbyist at U.S. Congress.

CAIN, Stephen Alexis
Senior Budget Analyst, Defense Budget Project
236 Massachusetts Ave., N.E., Suite 401, Washington, DC 20002
Telephone: (202) 546-9737

CAINE, Christopher G.
Program Dir., Federal Government Rtns., Internat'l Business Machines Corp.
1801 K St., N.W., Suite 1200, Washington, DC 20006
Telephone: (202) 778-5000
Registered as lobbyist at U.S. Congress.

CALABRESE, Michael R.
Morgan, Lewis and Bockius
1800 M St., N.W., Washington, DC 20036
Telephone: (202) 467-7000
Clients:
  PPG Industries

CALAIS, Mary Jane
Director, Public Policy & Mgmt. Programs, Nat'l Ass'n of
  College and University Business Officers
One Dupont Circle, N.W., Suite 500, Washington, DC
  20036-1178
Telephone: (202) 861-2500

CALAMARO, Raymond S.
Winthrop, Stimson, Putnam & Roberts
1133 Connecticut Ave., N.W. Suite 1000, Washington, DC
  20036
Telephone: (202) 775-9800
Registered as lobbyist at U.S. Congress.
Registered as Foreign Agent: (#3873).
Background: Legislative Director for Sen. Gaylord Nelson,
  1973-75. Deputy Assistant U.S. Attorney General, 1976-
  79.
Clients:
  Bowater, Inc.
  Connecticut Liquidity Investment Fund, Inc.
  IBJ Schroder Bank and Trust Co.
  Metallverken AB
  Swedish Steelproducers' Ass'n (Jernkontoret)

CALANDRO, Tony
Director, Governmental Relations, Nat'l Ass'n of Trade
  and Technical Schools
2251 Wisconsin Ave., N.W. Suite 200, Washington, DC
  20007
Telephone: (202) 333-1021
Registered as lobbyist at U.S. Congress.
Background: Serves as contact for the Ass'n Political Action Committee.

CALAWAY, James D.
Space Industries, Inc.
2011 Crystal Drive Suite 903, Arlington, VA
Registered as lobbyist at U.S. Congress.

CALDERWOOD, James A.
Grove, Jaskiewicz, Gilliam and Cobert
1730 M St., N.W. Suite 501, Washington, DC 20036
Telephone: (202) 296-2900
Background: Trial Attorney, Department of Justice, Anti-
  trust Division, 1970-73. Special Assistant U.S. Attorney
  for the District of Columbia, 1973. Trial Attorney and
  Senior Trial Attorney, Department of Justice, Antitrust
  Division, 1974-78.
Clients:
  Soc. of Glass and Ceramic Decorators
  United Van Lines, Inc.

CALDWELL, Alan C.
Director, Federal Government Affairs, RJR Nabisco Wash-
  ington, Inc.
1455 Pennsylvania Ave., N.W., Suite 525, Washington, DC
  20004
Telephone: (202) 626-7200
Registered as lobbyist at U.S. Congress.
Background: Represents Del Monte-USA and Nabisco
  Brands, Inc.

CALDWELL, Bonnie
Director, Government Relations, Public Securities Ass'n
1000 Vermont Ave., N.W., Suite 800, Washington, DC
  20005
Telephone: (202) 898-9390
Registered as lobbyist at U.S. Congress.
Background: Full title is V. President, Government Affairs
  for Housing Asset-Backed Finance.

CALDWELL, Ellen
Burson-Marsteller
1850 M St., N.W., Suite 900, Washington, DC 20036
Telephone: (202) 833-8550
Background: Former press aide to Senators Wyche Fowler,
  Jr. (D—GA) and Albert Gore (D-TN).

CALDWELL, Janice L.
Attorney/Government Relations, Direct Selling Ass'n
1776 K St., N.W., Suite 600, Washington, DC 20006
Telephone: (202) 293-5760

CALDWELL, Louise
Nat'l President, American War Mothers
2615 Woodley Place, N.W., Washington, DC 20008
Telephone: (202) 462-2791

CALENDER, John G.
Clifford & Warnke
815 Connecticut Ave., N.W., Washington, DC 20006
Telephone: (202) 828-4200

CALHOUN, Frank L.
Asst Chief Counsel, Legis and Regul, DEPARTMENT OF
  TRANSPORTATION - Federal Highway Administration
400 Seventh St., S.W., Washington, DC 20590
Telephone: (202) 366-0761

CALHOUN, John
Exec. Director, Nat'l Crime Prevention Council
1700 K St., N.W. 2nd Floor, Washington, DC 20005
Telephone: (202) 466-6272

CALHOUN, Robert L.
Sullivan and Worcester
1025 Connecticut Ave., N.W. Suite 806, Washington, DC
  20036
Telephone: (202) 775-8190
Background: Attorney-Advisor to Commissioner Charles
  A. Webb, 1963-67 and Legislative Counsel, 1967-69, In-
  terstate Commerce Commission. Deputy Director, Office
  of Policy Review, Department of Transportation, 1969-71.
Clients:
  Kansas City Southern Industries

CALIFA, Anthony J.
Legislative Counsel, American Civil Liberties Union
122 Maryland Ave., N.E., Washington, DC 20002
Telephone: (202) 544-1681
Registered as lobbyist at U.S. Congress.

CALIFANO, Joseph A., Jr.
Dewey, Ballantine, Bushby, Palmer and Wood
1775 Pennsylvania Ave., N.W. Suite 200, Washington, DC
  20006
Telephone: (202) 862-1000
Registered as lobbyist at U.S. Congress.
Background: Special Assistant to General Counsel, Depart-
  ment of Defense, 1961-62. Special Assistant to Secretary
  of the Army, 1962-63. General Counsel, Department of
  the Army, 1963-64. Special Assistant to the Secretary and
  Deputy Secretary of Defense, 1964-65. Special Assistant
  for Domestic Affairs to the President, 1965-69. Secretary
  of Health, Education and Welfare, 1977-79. Member,
  Board of Directors, Primerica Corp. and Chrysler Corp.
Clients:
  Chrysler Corp.
  Federal Nat'l Mortgage Ass'n
  Pfizer, Inc.
  Primerica Corp.

CALIFF, Lee H.
Manager, Government Relations, Reynolds Metals Co.
1620 Eye St., N.W., Washington, DC 20006
Telephone: (202) 833-3760
Registered as lobbyist at U.S. Congress.
Background: Legislative Assistant, Sen. John W. Warner
  (R-VA), 1979-1986.

CALIMAFDE, Paula A.
President, Small Business Council of America
4800 Hampden Lane, 7th Floor, Bethesda, MD 20814
Telephone: (301) 656-7603

CALIO, Nicholas E.
Dep Asst to Pres, Legis Affrs (House), EXECUTIVE OF-
  FICE OF THE PRESIDENT - The White House
1600 Pennsylvania Ave., N.W. 112 East Wing, Washing-
  ton, DC 20500
Telephone: (202) 456-6620

CALKINS, Barbara J.
Director of Legis. and Federal Affairs, American Psycho-
  logical Ass'n
1200 17th St., N.W., Washington, DC 20036
Telephone: (202) 955-7563
Registered as lobbyist at U.S. Congress.
Background: Former Legislative Director to Rep. John R.
  McKernan (R-ME).

CALKINS, Richard
Exec. Director, Council on Internat'l Non-Theatrical Events
1001 Connecticut Ave., N.W., Suite 1016, Washington, DC
  20036
Telephone: (202) 785-1136

CALL, Michael
Manager, Mitsubishi Internat'l Corp.
655 15th St., N.W., Suite 860, Washington, DC 20005
Telephone: (202) 638-1101

CALLAHAN, Patricia
Dir of Cong Affrs, DEPARTMENT OF COMMERCE - Pat-
  ent and Trademark Office
C/o Asst Secy and Commissioner of Patents and Trade-
  marks, Washington, DC 20231
Telephone: (703) 557-7578

CALLAN, Jim
Constituency Relations Counselor, Burson-Marsteller
1850 M St., N.W., Suite 900, Washington, DC 20036
Telephone: (202) 833-8550

CALLAWAY, Robbie
Director, Government Relations, Boys Clubs of America
611 Rockville Pike, Suite 230, Rockville, MD 20852
Telephone: (301) 251-6676

CALLAWAY, William H., Jr.
Zuckert, Scoutt and Rasenberger
888 17th St., N.W., Suite 600, Washington, DC 20006-
  3959
Telephone: (202) 298-8660
Clients:
  Air Afrique
  Challenge Air Cargo

CALLERY, T. Grant
V. President, Deputy General Counsel, Nat'l Ass'n of
  Securities Dealers (NASDAQ)
1735 K St., N.W., Washington, DC 20006
Telephone: (202) 728-8000

CALLICOTT, Robin F.
Washington Affairs Representative, American Home Products Corp.
1726 M St., N.W., Suite 1001, Washington, DC 20036
Telephone: (202) 659-8320

CALLOWAY, James R.
1101 Connecticut Ave., N.W., Suite 500, Washington, DC
Telephone: (202) 659-8163
Organizations represented:
  Pratt & Whitney

CALOMIRIS, William
Treasurer, Federal Commerce and Industry Political Action Committee
1129 20th St., N.W. Suite 200, Washington, DC 20036
Telephone: (202) 857-5934

CALVERT, E. Bruce
Director of Administration, Independent Liquid Terminals
  Ass'n
1133 15th St., N.W. Suite 204, Washington, DC 20005
Telephone: (202) 659-2301

CAMARA, Wayne J.
Testing and Assessment, American Psychological Ass'n
1200 17th St., N.W., Washington, DC 20036
Telephone: (202) 955-7600
Registered as lobbyist at U.S. Congress.

CAMBRIDGE CONSULTING CORP.
1893 Preston White Drive, Suite 110, Reston, VA 22091
Telephone: (703) 620-1911
Members of firm representing listed organizations:
  Alvarez, Margaret Ellen, Secretary-Treasurer
  Alvarez, Richard, Founder and CEO

CAMBRIDGE INTERNAT'L, INC.
1600 Wilson Blvd., Suite 713, Arlington, VA 22209
Telephone: (703) 524-1068
Members of firm representing listed organizations:
  White, Justus P., V. President
Clients:
  Eastern Technologies, Ltd. *(Justus P. White)*
  FMC Corp.
  General Dynamics Corp. *(Justus P. White)*

CAMBRIDGE INTERNAT'L, INC. (Cont'd)
General Dynamics Valley Systems Division *(Justus P. White)*
McDonnell Douglas Helicopter Co. *(Justus P. White)*
Optic-Electronic Corp. *(Justus P. White)*
Textron Inc. *(Justus P. White)*

CAMERON, Arthur E.
1111 14th St., N.W., Suite 1001, Washington, DC 20005
Telephone: (202) 289-8353
Registered as lobbyist at U.S. Congress.
Background: An attorney. Employee, U.S. House of Representatives, 1950-68. Associate Counsel, Select Congressional Committee on Crime, 1969-70.
Organizations represented:
Amerace Corp. (Stimsonite Division)
Highway Safety Corp.
Lukens Steel, Inc. (Flex-O-Lite Div.)
Minnesota Mining and Manufacturing Co. (Traffic Control Materials Division)
Nat'l Advertising Co.
Nat'l Greyhound Ass'n
Potters Industries, Inc.
Safetran Systems Corp.
Syro Steel Co.

CAMERON, Bruce P.
1725 17th St., Suite 109, Washington, DC 20009
Telephone: (202) 667-9563
Registered as lobbyist at U.S. Congress.
Registered as Foreign Agent: (#4043)
Organizations represented:
Guatemala, Government of
Mozambique, Government of

CAMERON, Don
Exec. Director, Nat'l Education Ass'n of the U.S.
1201 16th St., N.W., Washington, DC 20036
Telephone: (202) 822-7300
Background: Also represents the Nat'l Education Ass'n Political Action Committee.

CAMERON, Donald B., Jr.
Mudge Rose Guthrie Alexander and Ferdon
2121 K St., N.W., Suite 700, Washington, DC 20037
Telephone: (202) 429-9355
Registered as lobbyist at U.S. Congress.
Registered as Foreign Agent: (#3200).
Clients:
Climax Paper Converters Ltd.
Dong Sung Steel Industries Co., Ltd.
Futaba Corp.
Korea Consumer Goods Exporters Ass'n
Korea Foundry Forging Cooperative Ass'n
Korea Iron and Steel Ass'n
Mexinox, S.A. de C.V.

CAMERON, Duncan H.
Cameron and Hornbostel
818 Connecticut Ave., N.W. Suite 700, Washington, DC 20006
Telephone: (202) 293-4690
Registered as Foreign Agent: (#3164).
Background: Attorney, Office of the General Counsel, AID, 1963-1967.
Clients:
Papua New Guinea, Government of

CAMERON AND HORNBOSTEL
818 Connecticut Ave., N.W. Suite 700, Washington, DC 20006
Telephone: (202) 293-4690
Members of firm representing listed organizations:
Cameron, Duncan H.
Background: Attorney, Office of the General Counsel, AID, 1963-1967.
Ince, William K.
Clients:
British Columbia Raspberry Growers Ass'n *(William K. Ince)*
Canadian Pork Council *(William K. Ince)*
Papua New Guinea, Government of *(Duncan H. Cameron)*

CAMERON, Jared S.
V. President, Hannaford Co., Inc., The
655 15th St., N.W. Suite 200, Washington, DC 20005
Telephone: (202) 638-4600
Registered as lobbyist at U.S. Congress.

CAMERON, Mary Ann
Director of Communications, Music Educators Nat'l Conference
1902 Association Drive, Reston, VA 22091
Telephone: (703) 860-4000

CAMERON, William A.
V. Pres., Gov't Optns. - McDermott Int'l, McDermott Inc.
1850 K St., N.W. Suite 950, Washington, DC 20006
Telephone: (202) 296-0390

CAMM, Nancy
V. President and Washington Rep., Bank of America NT & SA
1800 K St., N.W., Suite 900, Washington, DC 20006
Telephone: (202) 778-0537
Registered as lobbyist at U.S. Congress.
Background: Serves also as Assistant Treasurer, BankAmerica Federal Election Fund.

CAMP, BARSH, BATES AND TATE
2550 M St., N.W., Suite 275, Washington, DC 20037
Telephone: (202) 887-5160
Background: Represents numerous corporate and institutional clients in legislative and administrative matters in areas as diverse as banking, telecommunications, taxation, trade, energy and transportation.
Members of firm representing listed organizations:
Barsh, Harry E. (Jr.)
Bates, Carl E.
Background: Legislation Attorney, Joint Committee on Taxation, U.S. Congress, 1975-80.
Camp, John C.
Collins, Meg
Migdail, Evan M.
Moss, Kate
Background: Special Assistant to Senator Charles McC. Mathias, Jr. (R-MD), 1970-71. Director for Congressional Liaison, Executive Office of the President, 1971-74.
Platt, Ronald L.
Background: Former aide to Senator Lloyd Bentsen (D-TX), Rep. Jack Brooks (D-TX), and Rep. Glenn English (D-OK).
Tate, Dan C.
Background: Legislative Assistant to Senator Herman (D-GA), 1969-76. Chief Legislative Representative (Senate) for President Jimmy Carter, 1977-80.
Clients:
Advance Petroleum, Inc. *(Ronald L. Platt)*
ARA Services *(Ronald L. Platt)*
ARCO Oil & Gas Co. *(Harry E. Barsh, Jr.)*
Associated Financial Corp. *(Ronald L. Platt)*
BellSouth Corp. *(John C. Camp)*
Blue Cross and Blue Shield of Missouri *(Ronald L. Platt)*
California Pipe Trades Council *(Dan C. Tate)*
Campbell Soup Co. *(Ronald L. Platt)*
CIC Enterprises, Inc. *(Ronald L. Platt)*
CITGO Petroleum Corp. *(Ronald L. Platt)*
Coalition for Equitable Compensation *(John C. Camp, Kate Moss)*
Columbia Communications Corp. *(Harry E. Barsh, Jr.)*
Columbia Gas System *(Harry E. Barsh, Jr.)*
Committee for Equitable Compensation *(John C. Camp, Kate Moss)*
Exxon Corp. *(Harry E. Barsh, Jr.)*
Goldbelt, Inc.
Home Intensive Care, Inc. *(Ronald L. Platt)*
Invacare Corp. *(Ronald L. Platt)*
K mart Corp. *(Ronald L. Platt)*
Mobil Corp. *(Harry E. Barsh, Jr., John C. Camp)*
NATCO *(Ronald L. Platt)*
Natural Gas Supply Ass'n *(Harry E. Barsh, Jr.)*
Pennzoil Co. *(Harry E. Barsh, Jr.)*
PGA Tour *(Dan C. Tate)*
PPG Industries *(Carl E. Bates)*
Russ Berrie Corp. *(Ronald L. Platt)*
Shell Oil Co. *(John C. Camp)*
Southland Corp., The *(Ronald L. Platt)*
Texaco U.S.A. *(Harry E. Barsh, Jr.)*
Union Pacific Resources Co. *(Harry E. Barsh, Jr.)*
World Airways *(Ronald L. Platt)*

CAMP, John C.
Camp, Barsh, Bates and Tate
2550 M St., N.W., Suite 275, Washington, DC 20037
Telephone: (202) 887-5160

Registered as lobbyist at U.S. Congress.
Clients:
BellSouth Corp.
Coalition for Equitable Compensation
Committee for Equitable Compensation
Mobil Corp.
Shell Oil Co.

CAMP, Sharon L.
Vice President, Population Crisis Committee
1120 19th St., N.W., Washington, DC 20036
Telephone: (202) 659-1833

CAMPAIGN CONSULTANTS INC.
211 N. Union St., Suite 200, Alexandria, VA 22314
Telephone: (703) 739-5260
Background: Affiliated with the public affairs and political consulting firm Black, Manafort, Stone and Kelly.

CAMPAIGN PERFORMANCE GROUP
507 Capital Court, N.E., Washington, DC 20002
Telephone: (202) 546-3170
Members of firm representing listed organizations:
Ward, Stephen D., V. President

CAMPAIGNE, Antony L.
Chairman, Council for Internat'l Development
1000 Potomac St., N.W. Plaza 100, Washington, DC 20007
Telephone: (703) 965-0900

CAMPAIGNE, Nancy
Director, Cong Affrs Div, DEPARTMENT OF COMMERCE - Minority Business Development Agency
14th and Constitution Ave. N.W., Washington, DC 20230
Telephone: (202) 377-5641

CAMPANELLA, Constance
President, Stateside Associates
Courthouse Plaza II, Suite 407 2300 Clarendon Blvd., Arlington, VA 22201
Telephone: (703) 525-7466
Clients:
Working Group Coalition, The

CAMPBELL, Alan J.
Exec. Director, Nat'l Ass'n of the Remodeling Industry
1901 North Moore St. Suite 808, Arlington, VA 22209
Telephone: (703) 276-7600

CAMPBELL, Angela J.
Associate Director, Citizens Communications Center
Georgetown Univ. Law Center, 600 New Jersey Ave., N.W., Washington, DC 20001
Telephone: (202) 662-9535
Background: Trial Attorney, U.S. Dept. of Justice, 1984-89.

CAMPBELL, Anne
Campbell, Falk & Selby
1101 30th St., N.W. Suite 500, Washington, DC 20007
Telephone: (202) 298-0427
Clients:
Puerto Rico, Commonwealth of
Puerto Rico Federal Affairs Administration

CAMPBELL, Argyll C.
Exec. Dir., Industrial Relations Group, Nat'l Industrial Council
1331 Pennsylvania Ave., N.W. N. Lobby Suite 1500, Washington, DC 20004-1703
Telephone: (202) 637-3053
Registered as lobbyist at U.S. Congress.

CAMPBELL & ASSOC., Thomas D.
113 South Alfred St., Alexandria, VA 22314
Telephone: (703) 683-0773
Members of firm representing listed organizations:
Campbell, Thomas D.
Organizations represented:
Cyprus Minerals Corp. *(Thomas D. Campbell)*

CAMPBELL, C. Russell, Jr.
Asst. Vice President - Legislative Affrs, GTE Corp.
Suite 1200, 1850 M St., N.W., Washington, DC 20036
Telephone: (202) 463-5220
Registered as lobbyist at U.S. Congress.

CAMPBELL, C. Thomas
Manager, Government Relations, Dow Chemical
1776 Eye St., N.W., Suite 575, Washington, DC 20006
Telephone: (202) 429-3400

CAMPBELL, Carl C.
Special Projects Representative, Nat'l Cotton Council of
America
1110 Vermont Ave., N.W. Suite 430, Washington, DC
20005
Telephone: (202) 833-2943
Registered as lobbyist at U.S. Congress.
Background: Also represents the Cotton Council Internat'l.

CAMPBELL, Charles O.
Director, Government Relations, Nat'l Soc. of Professional
Engineers
1420 King St., Alexandria, VA 22314-2715
Telephone: (703) 684-2841
Registered as lobbyist at U.S. Congress.
Background: Former Minority Counsel to House of Repre-
sentatives Government Operations Subcommittee.

CAMPBELL, Cindy
Field Organizer, Congress Watch
215 Pennsylvania Ave., S.E., Washington, DC 20003
Telephone: (202) 546-4996

CAMPBELL, David
Economist, Water Resources Division, Nat'l Wildlife Feder-
ation
1400 16th St., N.W., Washington, DC 20036-2266
Telephone: (202) 797-6800
Registered as lobbyist at U.S. Congress.

CAMPBELL, F. Hammer
Dir., Gov't. Affrs., Sr. Legis. Rep., Suburban Maryland
Building Industry Ass'n
Executive Terrace 1400 Mercantile Lane, Landover, MD
20785
Telephone: (301) 925-9490
Registered as lobbyist at U.S. Congress.

CAMPBELL, Dr. Faith Thompson
Senior Project Staff Officer, Natural Resources Defense
Council
1350 New York Ave., N.W. Suite 300, Washington, DC
20005
Telephone: (202) 783-7800
Registered as lobbyist at U.S. Congress.

CAMPBELL, FALK & SELBY
1101 30th St., N.W. Suite 500, Washington, DC 20007
Telephone: (202) 298-0427
Members of firm representing listed organizations:
Campbell, Anne
Falk, Jacqueline
Selby, Steven
Clients:
Puerto Rico, Commonwealth of *(Anne Campbell,*
Steven Selby)
Puerto Rico Federal Affairs Administration *(Anne*
Campbell, Steven Selby)

CAMPBELL, Geary
Manager, Public Relations, Internat'l Bottled Water Ass'n
113 North Henry St., Alexandria, VA 22314
Telephone: (703) 683-5213

CAMPBELL, INC., John G.
9300-D Old Keene Mill Road, Burke, VA 22015
Telephone: (703) 455-8885
Members of firm representing listed organizations:
Campbell, John G., President
Organizations represented:
ARCO *(John G. Campbell)*
BDM Internat'l, Inc. *(John G. Campbell)*
General Electric Co.
General Motors Corp.
ManTech Internat'l
Minnesota Mining and Manufacturing Co. (3M
Co.) *(John G. Campbell)*
Syracuse University *(John G. Campbell)*
Towerbank
West Virginia University

CAMPBELL, James I., Jr.
General Counsel, Professional Lobbying and Consulting
Center
1111 14th St., N.W., Suite 1001, Washington, DC 20005
Telephone: (202) 898-0084

CAMPBELL, James S.
Wilmer, Cutler and Pickering
2445 M St., N.W., Washington, DC 20037-1420
Telephone: (202) 663-6000
Registered as lobbyist at U.S. Congress.
Background: Special Assistant, Antitrust Division, Depart-
ment of Justice, 1967-68. General Counsel, Nat'l Com-
mission pn Causes and Prevention of Violence, 1968-69.
Counsel, Office of the Secretary, Department of Housing
and Urban Development, 1977-78.
Clients:
Handgun Control, Inc.
Lufthansa German Airlines

CAMPBELL, Jeanne M.
President, Campbell-Raupe, Inc.
1010 Pennsylvania Ave., S.E., Washington, DC 20003
Telephone: (202) 546-4991
Registered as lobbyist at U.S. Congress.
Background: Former Staff Assistant to Rep. Dan Rosten-
kowski of Illinois and Press Secretary to Rep. Margaret
Heckler of Massachusetts.
Clients:
Algonquin Gas Transmission Co.
American Airlines
American Ass'n of Advertising Agencies
Credit Union Nat'l Ass'n
Invest to Compete Alliance
Nat'l Ass'n of Auctioneers
Plantation Foods
Securities Industry Ass'n
Stone and Webster Engineering Corp.

CAMPBELL, John G.
President, Campbell, Inc., John G.
9300-D Old Keene Mill Road, Burke, VA 22015
Telephone: (703) 455-8885
Registered as lobbyist at U.S. Congress.
Organizations represented:
ARCO
BDM Internat'l, Inc.
Minnesota Mining and Manufacturing Co. (3M
Co.)
Syracuse University

CAMPBELL, Nancy Duff
Managing Attorney, Nat'l Women's Law Center
1616 P St., N.W., Washington, DC 20036
Telephone: (202) 328-5160

CAMPBELL-RAUPE, INC.
1010 Pennsylvania Ave., S.E., Washington, DC 20003
Telephone: (202) 546-4991
Members of firm representing listed organizations:
Amick, John
Background: Former aide to Rep. Doug Bereuter (R-
NE).
Campbell, Jeanne M., President
Background: Former Staff Assistant to Rep. Dan Ros-
tenkowski of Illinois and Press Secretary to Rep.
Margaret Heckler of Massachusetts.
Clients:
Algonquin Gas Transmission Co. *(Jeanne M. Camp-*
bell)
American Airlines *(Jeanne M. Campbell)*
American Ass'n of Advertising Agencies *(Jeanne*
M. Campbell)
Credit Union Nat'l Ass'n *(Jeanne M. Campbell)*
Invest to Compete Alliance *(Jeanne M. Campbell)*
Nat'l Ass'n of Auctioneers *(Jeanne M. Campbell)*
Plantation Foods *(Jeanne M. Campbell)*
Securities Industry Ass'n *(Jeanne M. Campbell)*
Stone and Webster Engineering Corp. *(Jeanne M.*
Campbell)

CAMPBELL, Scott L.
Washington Policy & Analysis
655 15th St., N.W., Ninth Floor, Washington, DC 20005-
5701
Telephone: (202) 626-5800
Registered as Foreign Agent: (#4211).
Clients:
Statoil North America, Inc.

Tohoku Electric Power Co.

CAMPBELL, Steve
Director, Safety Department, American Trucking Ass'ns
430 First St., S.E., Washington, DC 20003-1826
Telephone: (202) 544-6245

CAMPBELL, Thomas D.
Campbell & Assoc., Thomas D.
113 South Alfred St., Alexandria, VA 22314
Telephone: (703) 683-0773
Registered as lobbyist at U.S. Congress.
Organizations represented:
Cyprus Minerals Corp.

CAMPBELL, W. Douglas
V. President, Fleishman-Hillard, Inc
1301 Connecticut Ave., N.W., Washington, DC 20036
Telephone: (202) 659-0330
Registered as lobbyist at U.S. Congress.
Clients:
Apple & Eve
Citizens for a Drug Free America
Coalition for FDA Resources
Spectacor Management Group
United Network of Organ Sharing

CAMPO, Terry T.
Chairman, Young Republican Nat'l Federation
310 First St., S.E., Washington, DC 20003
Telephone: (202) 662-1340

CANAN, G. Patrick
Assistant Director, Gov't Liaison, United States Catholic
Conference
3200 4th St., N.E., Washington, DC 20017
Telephone: (202) 541-3000

CANAVAN, Robert
V. President, Public Affairs, United Way of America
701 N. Fairfax St., Alexandria, VA 22314-2045
Telephone: (703) 836-7100
Registered as lobbyist at U.S. Congress.

CANAVAN, Sharon M.
Staff V. Pres., Deputy Legis. Counsel, Mortgage Bankers
Ass'n of America
1125 15th St., N.W., Suite 700, Washington, DC 20005
Telephone: (202) 861-6500

CANCADE, Susan
Deputy Director, Committee for Nat'l Security
1601 Connecticut Ave., N.W. Suite 302, Washington, DC
20009
Telephone: (202) 745-2450

CANES, Dr. Michael E.
V. President, Fin. Analysis & Statistics, American Petroleum Institute
1220 L St., N.W., Washington, DC 20005
Telephone: (202) 682-8500

CANFIELD, Anne C.
Washington Rep., Government Relations, General Electric
Co.
1331 Pennsylvania Ave., N.W., Washington, DC 20004
Telephone: (202) 637-4308
Registered as lobbyist at U.S. Congress.

CANFIELD, Edward F.
Casey, Scott, Canfield & Heggestad
805 15th St., N.W., Suite 600, Washington, DC 20005
Telephone: (202) 682-4082
Registered as lobbyist at U.S. Congress.
Clients:
Liberty Homes, Inc.

CANFIELD, Stofford
Dep Dir, Senate Liaison, DEPARTMENT OF INTERIOR
18th and C Sts., N.W., Washington, DC 20240
Telephone: (202) 343-7693

CANFIELD, William B.
Legal Counsel, Nat'l Republican Senatorial Committee
425 Second St., N.E., Washington, DC 20002
Telephone: (202) 675-6000
Background: Republican Chief Counsel, Senate Rules Com-
mittee, 1979-87.

CANNER, Sharon F.
Assistant V. Pres., Industrial Relations, Nat'l Ass'n of Manufacturers
1331 Pennsylvania Ave., N.W. Suite 1500 North, Washington, DC 20004-1703
Telephone: (202) 637-3000
Registered as lobbyist at U.S. Congress.

CANNON AND ASSOC., Howard W.
1919 Pennsylvania Ave., N.W., Suite 800, Washington, DC 20006
Telephone: (202) 887-1417
Members of firm representing listed organizations:
Cannon, Howard W.
Background: Former U.S. Senator, (D-NV).

CANNON, Daniel W.
Director, Program Development, R & T, Nat'l Ass'n of Manufacturers
1331 Pennsylvania Ave., N.W. Suite 1500 North, Washington, DC 20004-1703
Telephone: (202) 637-3000

CANNON, Howard W.
Cannon and Assoc., Howard W.
1919 Pennsylvania Ave., N.W., Suite 800, Washington, DC 20006
Telephone: (202) 887-1417
Registered as lobbyist at U.S. Congress.
Background: Former U.S. Senator, (D-NV).

CANNON, Hugh C.
Assoc Commissioner, Legis Affrs, DEPARTMENT OF HEALTH AND HUMAN SERVICES - Food and Drug Administration
5600 Fishers Lane, Rockville, MD 20857
Telephone: (301) 443-3793

CANNON, James M.
Co-Exec. Director, American Agenda
Background: Former domestic policy advisor to President Gerald Ford.

CANNON, Kevin F.
Manager, Agricultural Affairs, Monsanto Co.
700 14th St., N.W., Suite 1100, Washington, DC 20005
Telephone: (202) 783-2460

CANNON, Richard J.
Jaenke & Associates, E. A.
777 14th St., Suite 666, Washington, DC 20005
Telephone: (202) 393-1793
Organizations represented:
Seaboard Corp.

CANNON, W. Stephen
Wunder, Ryan, Cannon & Thelen
1615 L St., N.W., Suite 650, Washington, DC 20036
Telephone: (202) 659-3005
Registered as lobbyist at U.S. Congress.
Registered as Foreign Agent: (#3971).
Background: Trial Attorney, Antitrust Division, Department of Justice, 1977-81; Chief Antitrust Counsel to the Senate Judiciary Committee, 1981-85; Deputy Assistant Attorney General, Antitrust Division, Department of Justice, 1985-86.
Clients:
Dresser Industries
Grocery Manufacturers of America
NEC Home Electronics (USA) Inc.
North American Philips Corp.
NYNEX
Rohm and Haas Co.
Section 8 Coalition
Trailer Train Co.

CANO, Paul G.
Director, Government Affairs, American Soc. of Consultant Pharmacists
2300 9th St., South, Arlington, VA 22204
Telephone: (703) 920-8492
Background: Represents the American Soc. of Consultants Political Action Committee.

CANOVA, Diane
Director of Public Policy, Nat'l Ass'n of State Alcohol and Drug Abuse Directors
444 North Capitol St., N.W. Suite 642, Washington, DC 20001

Telephone: (202) 783-6868

CANTLEY, Brent
Legislative Representative, Collier, Shannon & Scott
1055 Thomas Jefferson St., N.W., Suite 300, Washington, DC 20007
Telephone: (202) 342-8400
Registered as lobbyist at U.S. Congress.

CANTOR, Donna F.
Smith, Bucklin and Associates
1101 Connecticut Ave., N.W., Suite 700, Washington, DC 20036
Telephone: (202) 857-1100
Background: Exec. Director, Ass'n for Hospital Medical Education, Council on Continuing Education Unit, and Nat'l Certification Agency for Medical Personnel.
Clients:
Ass'n for Hospital Medical Education
Council on Continuing Education Unit

CANTREL, Francis J., Jr.
Communications Executive, MCI Communications Corp.
1133 19th St., N.W., Washington, DC 20036
Telephone: (202) 872-1600
Registered as lobbyist at U.S. Congress.

CANTRELL, Jean
Manager, Government Affairs, Dun & Bradstreet
600 Maryland Ave., S.W., Suite 240, Washington, DC 20024
Telephone: (202) 484-7381
Background: Serves as Administrator and Assistant Treasurer, Political Action Committee of Dun & Bradstreet Corporation.

CANTUS, H. Hollister
Group V. President (Missiles & Space), Lockheed Corp.
1825 Eye St., N.W., Suite 1100, Washington, DC 20006
Telephone: (202) 955-3375
Background: Associate Administrator, NASA, 1987-88; Director, Congressional Relations, ERDA, 1975-78; Deputy Assistant Secretary of Defense, 1974-75; Professional Staff Member, House Armed Services Committee, 1970-74.; Captain, USNR (Ret.).

CANTUS, Charles Hollister
Legislative Ass't, Union Pacific Corp.
555 13th St., N.W., Suite 450 West Columbia Square, Washington, DC 20004
Telephone: (202) 662-0100
Registered as lobbyist at U.S. Congress.

CAPELLE, Russell
Director of Research and Statistics, Regular Common Carrier Conference
2200 Mill Road Suite 350, Alexandria, VA 22314
Telephone: (703) 838-1967

CAPITAL COMMUNICATIONS GROUP
1317 F St., N.W., Suite 310, Washington, DC 20004
Telephone: (202) 347-5085
Background: A public relations consulting subsidiary of R. Duffy Wall Associates.
Clients:
Pittston Co., The

CAPITAL CONSULTANTS
643 Pennsylvania Ave., S.E., Suite 200, Washington, DC 20003
Telephone: (202) 546-2277
Background: A government relations and marketing consultant firm. Shares office space with The Jeanne Mahoney Group, a public relations firm.
Members of firm representing listed organizations:
Owens, (Dr.) Susan Weir
Owens, William H. (Jr.), President

CAPITAL LEGISLATIVE SERVICES
1440 New York Ave., N.W. Suite 320, Washington, DC 20005
Telephone: (202) 628-4229
Background: A lobbying firm subsidiary of the public relations firm E. Bruce Harrison Co.
Members of firm representing listed organizations:
Mullins, Mary A., Director, Government Relations
Clients:
Nat'l Environmental Development Ass'n

CAPITAL MARKETING ANALYTICS, INC.
2001 Jefferson Davis Hwy. Suite 1012, Arlington, VA 22202
Telephone: (703) 486-1030

CAPITAL SERVICES, INC.
1802 T St., N.W., Washington, DC 20009
Telephone: (202) 745-4900
Background:
Members of firm representing listed organizations:
Rendon, John W. (Jr.), President

CAPITOL ASSOCIATES, INC.
426 C St., N.E., Washington, DC 20002
Telephone: (202) 544-1880
Members of firm representing listed organizations:
Bodenhorn, Karen
Donoghue, Marguerite
Gampel, Gwen, V. President, Health Affairs
Guthrie, Anne
Hardy-Havens, Debra M., V. President and CEO
Jackson, Pamela Patrice
Kardell, Amy
Lierman, Terry, President
Background: Former Chief Clerk at Senate Appropriations for Sen. Warren G. Magnuson (D-WA).
MacDougall, Gordon P., V. President, Government Affairs
Background: Former Administrative Assistant to Rep. John Edward Porter (R-IL), 1984-86.
Ritley, Dominique
Trull, Frankie
Whooley, Barbara
Clients:
American Ass'n of Nurse Anesthetists *(Karen Bodenhorn, Debra M. Hardy-Havens)*
American Ass'n of Retired Persons *(Gwen Gampel)*
American Soc. of Nephrology *(Terry Lierman)*
American Soc. of Tropical Medicine and Hygiene *(Marguerite Donoghue)*
Child Welfare League of America *(Gwen Gampel)*
Citizens for the Treatment of High Blood Pressure *(Karen Bodenhorn, Terry Lierman)*
Cystic Fibrosis Foundation *(Debra M. Hardy-Havens, Terry Lierman)*
Endocrine Soc. *(Amy Kardell, Terry Lierman)*
FDA Council *(Marguerite Donoghue, Terry Lierman)*
Hutchinson Cancer Center *(Marguerite Donoghue, Terry Lierman)*
Illinois Collaboration on Youth *(Debra M. Hardy-Havens)*
Joint Council on Allergy and Immunology *(Debra M. Hardy-Havens, Terry Lierman)*
Museum of Science and Industry *(Gordon P. MacDougall)*
Nat'l Ass'n of Pediatric Nurse Associates and Practitioners *(Karen Bodenhorn, Debra M. Hardy-Havens)*
Nat'l Cancer Research Coalition *(Terry Lierman)*
Nat'l Center for Health Education *(Karen Bodenhorn, Terry Lierman)*
Nat'l Coalition for Cancer Research *(Marguerite Donoghue, Terry Lierman)*
Nat'l Coalition for Volunteer Protection *(Gordon P. MacDougall)*
Nat'l Crime Prevention Council *(Gordon P. MacDougall)*
Nat'l Multiple Sclerosis Soc. *(Debra M. Hardy-Havens, Terry Lierman)*
Nat'l Renal Administrators Ass'n *(Gwen Gampel)*
Ringling Brothers/Barnum & Bailey
TDS Healthcare Systems Corp. *(Debra M. Hardy-Havens, Terry Lierman, Gordon P. MacDougall)*
Wistar Institute, The *(Marguerite Donoghue, Terry Lierman)*

CAPITOL ECONOMICS
1730 Pennsylvania Ave., N.W., Washington, DC 20006
Telephone: (202) 783-0800
Background: Formed by the law firm of Howrey and Simon to provide economic consulting and research services to clients.
Members of firm representing listed organizations:
Kaplan, David P., President

CAPITOL GROUP
1001 Pennsylvania Ave., N.W., Suite 1385, Washington, DC 20004

Telephone: (202) 638-1400
Members of firm representing listed organizations:
Fuselier, Linda

CAPITOL NETWORK
c/o Kindness & Chatfield 1747 Pennsylvania Ave, NW, Washington, DC 20006
Telephone: (202) 429-6060
Background: A informal partnership of law and government relations consulting firms in the Washington area organized under the leadership of Thomas Kindness of Kindness Assopciates. Also included in the group is John Zagame Associates.

CAPITOL PESPECTIVES
1915 17th St., N.W., Washington, DC 20009
Telephone: (202) 265-5276
Members of firm representing listed organizations:
DeGonia, Mary Elise
Clients:
Alternative Schools Network *(Mary Elise DeGonia)*

CAPITOL STRATEGISTS GROUP
717 2nd St., N.E. Suite 303, Washington, DC 20002
Telephone: (202) 452-8060
Members of firm representing listed organizations:
Mahoney, Kieran
Background: Serves also as Political Director, Albanian American Civic League.
Clients:
Albanian American Civic League *(Kieran Mahoney)*

CAPLAN, Ruth
Exec. Director, Environmental Action
1525 New Hampshire Ave., N.W., Washington, DC 20036
Telephone: (202) 745-4870
Background: Also represents Environmental Action Foundation.

CAPLIN AND DRYSDALE
One Thomas Circle, N.W. Suite 1100, Washington, DC 20005
Telephone: (202) 862-5000
Registered as Foreign Agent: (#3821)
Members of firm representing listed organizations:
Bush, Graeme
Caplin, Mortimer M.
Background: Law Clerk, US 4th Circuit Court of Appeals; President's Task Force on Taxation 1960. US Commissioner of Internal Revenue 1961-64. Member of Board of Directors of Prentice-Hall, Inc. and Fairchild Industries. Member, Public Review Board, Arthur Andersen and Co.
Elliott, Robert H. (Jr.)
Background: Attorney, Office of Chief Counsel, Internal Revenue Service, 1961-62; Office of Tax Legislative Counsel, U.S. Treasury Department, 1962-64.
Klayman, Robert A.
Background: Attorney, Office of Chief Counsel, Internal Revenue Service, 1957-60. Office of Tax Legislative Counsel Treasury Department, 1960-64; Associate Tax Legislative Counsel. Treasury Department, 1964.
Rosenbaum, Daniel B.
Background: Attorney, U.S. Department of Justice, Tax Division, 1968-72.
Rosenbloom, H. David
Background: Special Assistant to U.S. Ambassador to United Nations, 1966-67; Law Clerk, U.S. Supreme Court, 1967-68; International Tax Counsel, U.S. Treasury Department, 1978-81.
Skillman, Richard W.
Background: Law Clerk to the Chief Justice of the U.S. Supreme Court, 1971-72.
Troyer, Thomas A.
Background: Tax Division, Department of Justice, 1962-64; Office of Assistant Secretary of the Treasury for Tax Policy, 1964-66; Associate Tax Legislative Counsel, 1966-67.
Clients:
Hoechst-Celanese Corp.
Independent Education Fund
Mail Advertising Service Ass'n Internat'l *(Graeme Bush)*
Nat'l Ass'n of Independent Schools
Nat'l Wildlife Federation

CAPLIN, Mortimer M.
Caplin and Drysdale
One Thomas Circle, N.W. Suite 1100, Washington, DC 20005
Telephone: (202) 862-5000
Background: Law Clerk, US 4th Circuit Court of Appeals; President's Task Force on Taxation 1960. US Commissioner of Internal Revenue 1961-64. Member of Board of Directors of Prentice-Hall, Inc. and Fairchild Industries. Member, Public Review Board, Arthur Andersen and Co.

CAPON, Ross
Exec. Director, Nat'l Ass'n of Railroad Passengers
236 Massachusetts Ave., N.E., Suite 603, Washington, DC 20002
Telephone: (202) 546-1550
Registered as lobbyist at U.S. Congress.
Background: Served as Special Assistant to the Massachusetts Secretary of Transportation, 1971-75.

CAPPS, Carol
Associate for Development Policy, Church World Service/Lutheran World Relief
110 Maryland Ave., N.E. Building Box #45, Washington, DC 20002-5694
Telephone: (202) 543-6336

CAPPS, Milton F.
Senior V. President, Corporate Affairs, United Press Internat'l
1400 Eye St., N.W., Washington, DC 20005
Telephone: (202) 898-8000

CARABILLO, Joseph
Counsel, Union Labor Life Insurance Co.
111 Massachusetts Ave., N.W., Washington, DC 20001
Telephone: (202) 682-0900

CARABISI, M. Joy
Assoc Dir, Govt Affrs, INTERSTATE COMMERCE COMMISSION
12th and Constitution Ave. N.W., Washington, DC 20423
Telephone: (202) 275-7231

CARAMANGO, Salvatore E.
Ross and Hardies
888 16th St., N.W., Washington, DC 20006
Telephone: (202) 296-8600
Clients:
Nat'l Hand Tool Corp.

CARBERRY, Michael G.
Chief Exec. Officer, Kaufman & Associates, Henry J.
2233 Wisconsin Ave., N.W., Washington, DC 20007
Telephone: (202) 333-0700
Organizations represented:
Brunei, Embassy of
Nat'l Dairy Promotion and Research Board

CARBONE, Leslie
Exec. Director, Accuracy in Academia
1275 K St., N.W., Suite 1150, Washington, DC 20005
Telephone: (202) 789-4076

CARD, Kathleene B.
Dir, External Affrs, DEPARTMENT OF ENERGY - Federal Energy Regulatory Commission
825 North Capitol St., Washington, DC 20426
Telephone: (202) 357-8004

CARDEL, James
Manager of Government Affairs, Legal Services Corp.
400 Virginia Ave., S.W., Washington, DC 20024
Telephone: (202) 863-1839

CARDENAS, Daniel
Assoc. Director, Policy Analysis, Nat'l Ass'n of Community Health Centers
1330 New Hampshire Ave., N.W. Suite 122, Washington, DC 20036
Telephone: (202) 659-8008

CARDMAN, Denise A.
Legislative Counsel, American Bar Ass'n
1800 M St., N.W., Washington, DC 20036
Telephone: (202) 331-2209
Registered as lobbyist at U.S. Congress.

CAREY, E. Niel
Exec. Director, Nat'l Career Development Ass'n
5999 Stevenson Ave., Alexandria, VA 22304
Telephone: (703) 823-9800

CAREY, Melissa C.
Legislative Representative, Harris Corp.
1201 East Abingdon Drive Suite 300, Alexandria, VA 22314
Telephone: (703) 548-9200

CAREY, Norval E.
Sr. V. President, Government Operations, General Atomics
1100 17th St., N.W., Suite 1200, Washington, DC 20036
Telephone: (202) 659-3140
Registered as lobbyist at U.S. Congress.

CAREY, Sarah
Steptoe and Johnson
1330 Connecticut Ave., N.W., Washington, DC 20036
Telephone: (202) 429-3000

CAREY, Stephen W., CAE
Exec. V. President, Greater Washington Soc. of Ass'n Executives
1426 21st St., N.W., Suite 200, Washington, DC 20036
Telephone: (202) 429-9370
Background: Also serves as Exec. Director, Washington Ass'n Research Foundation.

CARINO, Maurice E.
Manager, Government Programs, Bethlehem Steel Corp.
1667 K St., N.W., Suite 600, Washington, DC 20006
Telephone: (202) 775-6200
Registered as lobbyist at U.S. Congress.

CARLESON & ASSOC., Robert B.
Box 2205 Crystal City, Arlington, VA 22202
Telephone: (703) 521-4289
Members of firm representing listed organizations:
Carleson, Robert B.
Organizations represented:
Unisys Corp.

CARLESON, Robert B.
Carleson & Assoc., Robert B.
Box 2205 Crystal City, Arlington, VA 22202
Telephone: (703) 521-4289
Registered as lobbyist at U.S. Congress.

CARLILE, Jane
Asst. Director, Professional Relations, College of American Pathologists
1101 Vermont Ave., N.W., Washington, DC 20005
Telephone: (202) 371-6617

CARLINER, Michael S.
Staff V. Pres., Econ. and Housing Policy, Nat'l Ass'n of Home Builders of the U.S.
15th and M Streets, N.W., Washington, DC 20005
Telephone: (202) 822-0470

CARLISLE, L. Gerald
Secretary-Treasurer, Internat'l Union of Bricklayers and Allied Craftsmen Political Action Committee
815 15th St., N.W., 2nd Floor, Washington, DC 20005
Telephone: (202) 783-3788

CARLISLE, Linda E.
Cadwalader, Wickersham & Taft
1333 New Hampshire Ave., N.W. Suite 700, Washington, DC 20036
Telephone: (202) 862-2200
Registered as lobbyist at U.S. Congress.
Background: Special Assistant to the Assistant Secretary for Tax Policy and Attorney Advisor, U.S. Treasury, 1984-87.
Clients:
Clayton & Dubilier, Inc.

CARLISLE, Margo D. B.
V. President, Government Relations, Heritage Foundation
214 Massachusetts Ave., N.E., Washington, DC 20002
Telephone: (202) 546-4400
Background: Former Assistant Secretary of Defense.

CARLOUGH, Edward J.
General President, Sheet Metal Workers' Internat'l Ass'n
1750 New York Ave., N.W. Sixth Floor, Washington, DC 20006
Telephone: (202) 783-5880
Registered as lobbyist at U.S. Congress.

CARLSON, Anne E.
Manager, Federal Liaison Dept., Motor Vehicle Manufacturers Ass'n of the United States
1620 Eye St., N.W. Suite 1000, Washington, DC 20006
Telephone: (202) 775-2700
Registered as lobbyist at U.S. Congress.

CARLSON, Catharine A.
Legislative Representative, Nat'l Wildlife Federation
1400 16th St., N.W., Washington, DC 20036-2266
Telephone: (202) 797-6800
Registered as lobbyist at U.S. Congress.

CARLSON, V. Adm. Dudley L., USN, Ret.
Exec. Director, Navy League of the United States
2300 Wilson Blvd., Arlington, VA 22201
Telephone: (703) 528-1775
Background: Former Legislative Assistant to Senator Phil Gramm (R-TX) and Senator Pete Wilson (R-CA).

CARLSON, Eileen Shannon
Graham and James
2000 M St., N.W., Suite 700, Washington, DC 20036
Telephone: (202) 463-0800
Registered as lobbyist at U.S. Congress.
Background: Legislative Assistant, Rep. J.J. Pickle (D-TX), 1981-83; Attorney-Advisor, Office of Deputy Chief Counsel for Import Administration, Department of Commerce, 1984-86.
Clients:
Disney Productions, Walt
Federal Administrative Law Judges' Conference
Federal Judges Ass'n
Illinois Health Facilities Authority
Stock Information Group

CARLSON, George N.
Partner, Office of Federal Tax Services, Andersen and Co., Arthur
1666 K St., N.W., Washington, DC 20006
Telephone: (202) 862-3100
Background: Former Director, Office of Tax Analysis, Dept. of Treasury.

CARLSON, Ronald
Assoc Admin, Plng, Eval & Legislation, DEPARTMENT OF HEALTH AND HUMAN SERVICES - Health Resources and Services Administration
5600 Fishers Lane, Rockville, MD 20857
Telephone: (301) 443-2460

CARLSTROM, Robert, Jr.
Jefferson Group, The
1341 G St., N.W., Suite 1100, Washington, DC 20005
Telephone: (202) 638-3535
Registered as lobbyist at U.S. Congress.
Background: Formerly with Office of Management and Budget.
Clients:
Conundrum Joint Venture
Internat'l Lead Zinc Research Organization

CARLUCCI, Anne
Manager, Product Development, Student Loan Marketing Ass'n
1050 Thomas Jefferson St., N.W., Washington, DC 20007
Telephone: (202) 333-8000

CARMEN, David M.
Carmen Group, The
1667 K St., N.W., Suite 700, Washington, DC 20006
Telephone: (202) 785-0500
Registered as Foreign Agent: (#4066).
Background: Serves as Exec. Director, United Shareholders Ass'n.
Clients:
Committee for Free Elections and Democracy in Nicaragua

CARMEN, Gerald P.
Carmen Group, The
1667 K St., N.W., Suite 700, Washington, DC 20006

Telephone: (202) 785-0500
Background: Former Administrator, General Services Administration.

CARMEN GROUP, THE
1667 K St., N.W., Suite 700, Washington, DC 20006
Telephone: (202) 785-0500
Registered as Foreign Agent: (#4233)
Members of firm representing listed organizations:
  Bledsoe, Willie W.
  Carmen, David M.
    Background: Serves as Exec. Director, United Shareholders Ass'n.
  Carmen, Gerald P.
    Background: Former Administrator, General Services Administration.
  Hallett, Carol Boyd
  Lee, Page C.
  Merryman, Lori L., V. President, Communications
    Background: Former public affairs specialist, U.S. Department of Education.
  Whatley, George C.
  Clients:
  CareerCom Corp. *(Page C. Lee)*
  Committee for Free Elections and Democracy in Nicaragua *(Willie W. Bledsoe, David M. Carmen, Carol Boyd Hallett, George C. Whatley)*

CARNEAL, George U.
Hogan and Hartson
555 13th St., N.W., Suite 1200, Washington, DC 20004-1109
Telephone: (202) 637-5600
Registered as lobbyist at U.S. Congress.
Background: Special Assistant to the Secretary of Transportation, 1969-1970; General Counsel, Federal Aviation Administration, 1970-1972.

CARNEVALE, Anthony P.
Chief Economist and V.P., Nat'l Affrs., American Soc. for Training and Development
1630 Duke St., Box 1443, Alexandria, VA 22313
Telephone: (703) 683-8100

CARNEY, William
Government Affairs Consultant, Lipsen Whitten & Diamond
1725 DeSales St., N.W., Suite 800, Washington, DC 20036
Telephone: (202) 659-6540
Registered as lobbyist at U.S. Congress.
Background: Former U.S. Representative (R-NY), 1978-86. Former Member, House Merchant Marine and Fisheries Committee; House Armed Services Committee; House Science and Technology Committee.

CARNILLA, Phyllis D.
1700 17th St., N.W. Suite 301, Washington, DC 20009
Registered as lobbyist at U.S. Congress.
Organizations represented:
Arctic Sounder Enterprises, Inc.
Birting Fisheries
JOMM Limited Partnership

CAROL, Daniel S.
Director, Opposition Research, Democratic Nat'l Committee
430 South Capitol St., S.E., Washington, DC 20003
Telephone: (202) 863-8000

CAROL, David J.
Senior Director, Government Affairs, AMTRAK (Nat'l Rail Passenger Corp.)
60 Massachusetts Ave., N.E., Washington, DC 20002
Telephone: (202) 906-3942

CAROL, Ned
Dir., Washington Opns., Sierra Research, LTV Aircraft Products Group
1725 Jefferson Davis Hwy. Suite 900, Arlington, VA 22202
Telephone: (703) 521-6560

CAROZZA, Michael
Manager, Reimbursement Policy, Bristol-Myers Squibb Co.
655 15th St., N.W., Suite 410, Washington, DC 20005
Telephone: (202) 783-0900
Registered as lobbyist at U.S. Congress.
Background: Deputy Commissioner, Social Security Administration 1988-89; Senior Analyst, U.S. Senate Budget Committee 1982-87.

CARP, Bertram W.
V. President, Government Affairs, Turner Broadcasting System, Inc.
810 1st St., N.E., Washington, DC 20002
Telephone: (202) 898-7680
Registered as lobbyist at U.S. Congress.

CARPENTER, Ted Galen
Director, Foreign Policy Studies, Cato Institute
224 Second St., S.E., Washington, DC 20003
Telephone: (202) 546-0200

CARR, Donald A.
Of Counsel, Winthrop, Stimson, Putnam & Roberts
1133 Connecticut Ave., N.W. Suite 1000, Washington, DC 20036
Telephone: (202) 775-9800
Background: Acting Assistant Attorney General, Land and Natural Resources Division, U.S. Department of Justice, 1989.

CARR, Geraldine
Birch, Horton, Bittner and Cherot
1155 Connecticut Ave., N.W., Suite 1200, Washington, DC 20036
Telephone: (202) 659-5800

CARR, James H.
V. President, Housing Policy Research, Federal Nat'l Mortgage Ass'n
3900 Wisconsin Ave., N.W., Washington, DC 20016
Telephone: (202) 752-7000

CARR, Jeffrey W.
Director, Internat'l Advisory Services Group Ltd.
1400 L St., N.W., Suite 600, Washington, DC 20005
Telephone: (202) 342-1200
Registered as Foreign Agent: (#4267).
Clients:
Siderbras
Steel Service Center Institute

CARR, John
Sec'y, Social Development & World Peace, United States Catholic Conference
3200 4th St., N.E., Washington, DC 20017
Telephone: (202) 541-3000

CARR, John L., Jr.
Shaw, Pittman, Potts and Trowbridge
2300 N St., N.W., Washington, DC 20037
Telephone: (202) 663-8000
Registered as Foreign Agent: (#2580).

CARR, Lisa
Legislative Assistant, Catholic Charities USA
1319 F St., N.W., Suite 400, Washington, DC 20004
Telephone: (202) 639-8400

CARR, Ronald G.
Morrison & Foerster
2000 Pennsylvania Ave., N.W., Suite 5500, Washington, DC 20006
Telephone: (202) 887-1500
Registered as Foreign Agent: (#4282).
Clients:
Coca-Cola Co.
Fujitsu Ltd.

CARRO, Richard S.
Assoc Gen Counsel, Legis, Litig & Regul, DEPARTMENT OF TREASURY
15th and Pennsylvania Ave. N.W., Washington, DC 20220
Telephone: (202) 566-2558

CARROCCIO, A. Thomas
Santarelli, Smith, Kraut and Carroccio
1155 Connecticut Ave., N.W., Washington, DC 20036
Telephone: (202) 466-6800
Clients:
KJAZ-FM
Performing Arts Network of New Jersey

CARROLL, Bill
Staff Director, Government Relations, Nat'l Ass'n for Foreign Student Affairs
1860 19th St., N.W., Washington, DC 20009
Telephone: (202) 462-4811
Background: Serves also as Editor, Government Affairs Bulletin.

CARROLL, Charles T.
Assistant General Counsel, Nat'l Ass'n of Stevedores
2011 Eye St., N.W., Washington, DC 20006
Telephone: (202) 296-2810
Registered as lobbyist at U.S. Congress.

CARROLL, David W.
Director of Environmental Programs, Chemical Manufacturers Ass'n
2501 M St., N.W., Washington, DC 20037
Telephone: (202) 887-1164

CARROLL, Rear Admiral Eugene J., USN (Ret)
Deputy Director, Center for Defense Information
1500 Massachusetts Ave., N.W., Washington, DC 20005
Telephone: (202) 862-0700

CARROLL, Greg M.
Exec. Director, Computer Dealers and Lessors Ass'n
1212 Potomac St., N.W., Washington, DC 20007
Telephone: (202) 333-0102

CARROLL, Howard J.
Manager, Media Relations & Public Rtns., Nat'l Education Ass'n of the U.S.
1201 16th St., N.W., Washington, DC 20036
Telephone: (202) 822-7300

CARROLL, Lynn B.
Director for Development, Catholic Charities USA
1319 F St., N.W., Suite 400, Washington, DC 20004
Telephone: (202) 639-8400

CARROLL, Viveca M.
Government Relations Specialist, Coopers and Lybrand
1800 Pennsylvania Ave., N.W. Suite 400, Washington, DC 20036
Telephone: (202) 822-5517

CARSON, A. W.
Exec. Director, American Soc. of Appraisers
535 Herndon Parkway, Suite 150, Herndon, VA 22070
Telephone: (703) 478-2228

CARSON, John K.
Tax Specialist, Chamber of Commerce of the U.S.A.
1615 H St., N.W., Washington, DC 20062
Telephone: (202) 659-6000
Registered as lobbyist at U.S. Congress.

CARSON, John R.
Director of Governmental Affairs, American Podiatric Medical Ass'n
9312 Old Georgetown Road, Bethesda, MD 20814
Telephone: (301) 571-9200
Registered as lobbyist at U.S. Congress.
Background: Serves as liaison, Podiatry Political Action Committee.

CARSON, Marjorie V.
Assistant Treasurer, Tooling and Machining Industry Political Action Committee
Box 44162, Fort Washington, MD 20744
Telephone: (301) 248-6200

CARSON, Walter E.
Johns and Carson
12501 Old Columbia Pike, Silver Spring, MD 20904
Telephone: (301) 680-6320

CARTER, C. Carter
Exec. Director, Internat'l Mass Transit Ass'n
P.O. Box 40247, Washington, DC 20016-0247
Telephone: (202) 362-7960

CARTER, David C.
President, United States Beet Sugar Ass'n
1156 15th St., N.W., Washington, DC 20005
Telephone: (202) 296-4820
Registered as lobbyist at U.S. Congress.
Background: Serves also as Chairman, U.S. Sweetener Producers Group; Director, Sugar Information Bureau; Chairman, Beet Sugar PAC.

CARTER, David W.
Associate, Wexler, Reynolds, Fuller, Harrison and Schule, Inc.
1317 F St., N.W., Suite 600, Washington, DC 20004
Telephone: (202) 638-2121
Background: Former staff member, House Appropriations Committee.

CARTER, Gilmer T.
National Commander, Veterans of World War I of the U.S.-.A.
941 North Capitol St., N.E. Suite 1201-C, Washington, DC 20002
Telephone: (202) 275-1388

CARTER, Jean H.
Exec. Director, Business Council
888 17th St., N.W., Suite 506, Washington, DC 20006
Telephone: (202) 298-7650

CARTER, John R., Jr.
V. Pres., Space & Defense, Wash. Office, TRW Inc.
Suite 2600, 1000 Wilson Blvd., Arlington, VA 22209
Telephone: (703) 276-5120
Registered as lobbyist at U.S. Congress.

CARTER, Joseph L., Jr.
V. President - Legislative, Ass'n of American Railroads
50 F St., N.W., Suite 12900, Washington, DC 20001
Telephone: (202) 639-2536
Registered as lobbyist at U.S. Congress.

CARTER, Lisle C., Jr.
General Counsel, United Way of America
701 N. Fairfax St., Alexandria, VA 22314-2045
Telephone: (703) 836-7100

CARTER-MAGUIRE, Melanie
Director, Government Relations, Int'l, Northern Telecom Inc..
600 Maryland Ave., S.W. Suite 607, Washington, DC 20024
Telephone: (202) 554-1520

CARTER, Nick
Exec. Director, SANE/FREEZE
1819 H St., N.W., Suite 1000, Washington, DC 20006
Telephone: (202) 862-9740

CARTER, Rene
Manager, Public Affairs, American Insurance Ass'n
1130 Connecticut Ave., N.W., Suite 1000, Washington, DC 20036
Telephone: (202) 828-7100

CARTER, Rob
Cong Liaison Specialist, DEPARTMENT OF COMMERCE
14th and Constitution Ave. S.W., Washington, DC 20230
Telephone: (202) 377-5485

CARTER, Robert G.
V. President, Technical Analysis, Aircraft Owners and Pilots Ass'n
421 Aviation Way, Frederick, MD 21701
Telephone: (301) 695-2000

CARTER, Tom
Dep Asst Secy, Senate Affrs, Legis Affrs, DEPARTMENT OF DEFENSE
The Pentagon, Washington, DC 20301
Telephone: (202) 697-6210

CARTER, Tristan E.
Legislative Affairs (House), Nat'l Ass'n of Broadcasters
1771 N St., N.W., Washington, DC 20036
Telephone: (202) 429-5300
Registered as lobbyist at U.S. Congress.

CARTIER, Brian E.
Exec. Director, Foundation for Chiropractic Education and Research
1701 Clarendon Blvd., Arlington, VA 22209
Telephone: (703) 276-7445

CARTO, Willis A.
Treasurer, Liberty Lobby
300 Independence Ave., S.E., Washington, DC 20003
Telephone: (202) 546-5611

CARTWRIGHT, Julie
Media Director, Nat'l Center for Missing and Exploited Children
2101 Wilson Blvd., Suite 550, Arlington, VA 22201
Telephone: (703) 235-3900

CARTWRIGHT, Suzanne
Director of Legislative Affairs, Verner, Liipfert, Bernhard, McPherson and Hand, Chartered
901 15th St., N.W., Suite 700, Washington, DC 20005
Telephone: (202) 371-6000
Registered as Foreign Agent: (#3712).
Background: Legislative Assistant to Rep. Jim Moody (D-WI), 1983-85.

CARTY, James P.
V. Pres., Gov't Relations & Competition, Nat'l Ass'n of Manufacturers
1331 Pennsylvania Ave., N.W. Suite 1500 North, Washington, DC 20004-1703
Telephone: (202) 637-3000
Registered as lobbyist at U.S. Congress.

CARTY, Lee
Administrator, Mental Health Law Project
2021 L St., N.W., Washington, DC 20036
Telephone: (202) 467-5730

CARVER, Caroline
Director, Legis. and Gov't Activities, American Traffic Safety Services Ass'n
ATSSA Building 5440 Jefferson Davis Highway, Fredericksburg, VA 22401
Telephone: (703) 898-5400

CARVER, Susan B.
Director, Legislative Affairs, Nat'l Coal Ass'n
1130 17th St., N.W., Washington, DC 20036
Telephone: (202) 463-2650
Registered as lobbyist at U.S. Congress.

CASALI, Richard A.
Vice President, Columbia Gas System Service Corp.
1250 Eye St., N.W., Suite 703, Washington, DC 20005
Telephone: (202) 842-7403
Background: Also represents the following subsidiaries of Columbia Gas System: Columbia Gas Development Corp., Columbia Gas Transmission Corp., Columbia Gulf Transmission Corp. and Columbia LNG Corp.

CASE, Dr. Larry D.
National Adviser, Future Farmers of America
Box 15160, Alexandria, VA 22309-0160
Telephone: (703) 360-3600

CASEY, Carol F.
Associate & Exec. Asst. to the Chairman, Cassidy and Associates, Inc.
655 15th St., N.W., Suite 1100, Washington, DC 20005
Telephone: (202) 347-0773
Registered as lobbyist at U.S. Congress.
Background: Head of Political Institutions and Processes Section, Government Division, Congressional Research Service, Library of Congress, 1974-79.
Clients:
Ocean Spray Cranberries
The Univeristy Hospital
Tufts University
University of Pennsylvania
University of the Arts
University of Vermont

CASEY, Daniel L.
Exec. Director, American Conservative Union
38 Ivy St., S.E., Washington, DC 20003
Telephone: (202) 546-6555
Registered as lobbyist at U.S. Congress.
Background: Serves also as contact for American Conservative Union Political Action Committee.

CASEY, Donald J.
Director, Regulatory Programs, Fertilizer Institute
501 Second St., N.E., Washington, DC 20002
Telephone: (202) 675-8250

CASEY, James L.
Assistant General Counsel, Air Transport Ass'n of America
1709 New York Ave., N.W., Washington, DC 20006-5206
Telephone: (202) 626-4000

CASEY, Joanne
Exec. Director, Intermodal Council, American Trucking Ass'ns
430 First St., S.E., Washington, DC 20003-1826

The listings in this directory are available as *Mailing Labels*. See last page.

73

CASEY, Joanne (Cont'd)
Telephone: (202) 544-6245

CASEY, Martha L.
O'Neill and Athy, P.C.
1310 19th St., N.W., Washington, DC 20036
Telephone: (202) 466-6555
Registered as lobbyist at U.S. Congress.
Background: Legislative Assistant to Rep. Joseph Early (D-MA), 1977-79. Counsel to Rep. Brian Donnelly (D-MA), 1982-87.
Clients:
Allegheny County, Pennsylvania
Beth Israel Hospital
Coalition of Boston Teaching Hospitals
Compu Chem Corp.
Massachusetts General Hospital
Massachusetts Hospital Ass'n
New England Deaconess Hospital
New England Medical Center

CASEY, Robert J.
Baker and Hostetler
1050 Connecticut Ave., N.W. Suite 1100, Washington, DC 20036
Telephone: (202) 861-1500
Background: Attorney, Office of Chief Counsel, Internal Revenue Service, 1950-52.
Clients:
Atchison, Topeka and Santa Fe Railway Co., The

CASEY, SCOTT, CANFIELD & HEGGESTAD
805 15th St., N.W., Suite 600, Washington, DC 20005
Telephone: (202) 682-4082
Members of firm representing listed organizations:
Canfield, Edward F.
Heggestad, Robert E.
Clients:
Liberty Homes, Inc. *(Edward F. Canfield)*

CASEY, Thomas J.
Mintz, Levin, Cohn, Ferris, Glovsky and Popeo, P.C.
1825 Eye St., N.W. 12th Floor, Washington, DC 20006
Telephone: (202) 293-0500
Background: Special Assistant to Chief, Cable TV Bureau, Federal Communications Commission, 1978. Special Assistant to Chairman, 1978-79 and Deputy Chief Common Carrier Bureau, Federal Communications Commission, 1979-81.

CASHDOLLAR-JONES & CO.
1000 16th St., N.W. Suite 702, Washington, DC 20036
Telephone: (202) 728-4058
Members of firm representing listed organizations:
Cashdollar, Robert, President
Background: Former staff director, House Agriculture Subcommittee on Conservation, Credit and Rural Development.
Jones, Ed
Background: Former Member, U.S. House of Representatives (D-TN).
Clients:
Council for Educational Development and Research *(Robert Cashdollar)*
Triad Development Corp. *(Robert Cashdollar)*
Tyson Foods, Inc. *(Robert Cashdollar)*
United Foods, Inc. *(Robert Cashdollar, Ed Jones)*

CASHDOLLAR, Robert
President, Cashdollar-Jones & Co.
1000 16th St., N.W. Suite 702, Washington, DC 20036
Telephone: (202) 728-4058
Background: Former staff director, House Agriculture Subcommittee on Conservation, Credit and Rural Development.
Clients:
Council for Educational Development and Research
Triad Development Corp.
Tyson Foods, Inc.
United Foods, Inc.

CASHDOLLAR, Winthrop
Legislative Representative, American Health Care Ass'n
1201 L St., N.W., Washington, DC 20005
Telephone: (202) 842-4444

CASHEN, Henry C., II
Dickstein, Shapiro and Morin
2101 L St., N.W., Washington, DC 20037
Telephone: (202) 785-9700
Registered as Foreign Agent: (#3028).
Background: Deputy Counsel to the President of the United States, 1969-70. Deputy Assistant to the President of the United States, 1971-73.
Clients:
ABD Securities Corp.
Alitalia Airlines
American Greyhound Track Operators Ass'n
Paulucci Enterprises

CASKEY, Paul S.
Wash. Rep. (Taxation & Natural Gas), Chevron, U.S.A.
1700 K St., N.W., Suite 1200, Washington, DC 20006
Telephone: (202) 457-5800
Registered as lobbyist at U.S. Congress.

CASKIE, Allen R.
Senior Counsel, American Council of Life Insurance
1001 Pennsylvania Ave., N.W., Washington, DC 20004-2599
Telephone: (202) 624-2111
Registered as lobbyist at U.S. Congress.

CASNER, Bruce M.
President, Morgan Casner Associates, Inc.
1332 Independence Ave., S.E., Washington, DC 20003
Telephone: (202) 543-4600
Background: Former Congressional Staff member. Specializes in legislative and political matters.

CASS, Richard W.
Wilmer, Cutler and Pickering
2445 M St., N.W., Washington, DC 20037-1420
Telephone: (202) 663-6000
Registered as Foreign Agent: (#3355).
Clients:
Polaroid Corp.

CASSEDY, Brian
President, Internat'l Management Group, Inc.
1101 14th St., N.W. Suite 1100, Washington, DC 20005
Telephone: (202) 371-2200
Background: Also serves as Exec. Director, Nat'l Soc. for Cardiovascular and Pulmonary Technology.
Clients:
Internat'l Soc. of Transport Aircraft Traders
Nat'l Soc. for Cardiovascular and Pulmonary Technology

CASSEDY, Joan Walsh
Chairman, Internat'l Management Group, Inc.
1101 14th St., N.W. Suite 1100, Washington, DC 20005
Telephone: (202) 371-2200
Background: Also serves as Exec. Director, Soc. for Toxicology and Exec. Director, Specialty Coffee Ass'n of America.
Clients:
Internat'l Ass'n of Energy Economists
Soc. of Toxicology
Specialty Coffee Ass'n of America

CASSELL, Mary
Director of Outreach, Christic Institute
1324 N. Capitol St., N.W., Washington, DC 20002
Telephone: (202) 797-8106

CASSELMAN, William E., II
Popham, Haik, Schnobrich & Kaufman, Ltd.
1800 M St., N.W. Suite 300 South, Washington, DC 20036
Telephone: (202) 828-5300
Registered as lobbyist at U.S. Congress.
Registered as Foreign Agent: (#4247).
Background: Legislative Assistant to Rep. Robert McClory (R-IL), 1965-69. Deputy Special Assistant to the President (Congressional Relations), 1969-71. General Counsel, General Services Administration, 1971-73. Legal Counsel to the Vice President of the U.S. and Deputy Assistant for Executive Branch Liaison, 1973-74. Counsel to the President of the U.S., 1974-75.
Clients:
Japan Steel Works, Ltd.
Ova Noss Family Partnership

CASSERLY, James L.
Squire, Sanders and Dempsey
1201 Pennsylvania Ave., N.W. P.O. Box 407, Washington, DC 20044
Telephone: (202) 626-6600
Clients:
Independent Data Communications Manufacturers Ass'n

CASSERLY, Michael
Senior Associate, Legislative, Council of Great City Schools
1413 K St., N.W. Suite 400, Washington, DC 20005
Telephone: (202) 371-0163
Registered as lobbyist at U.S. Congress.

CASSIDY AND ASSOCIATES, INC.
655 15th St., N.W., Suite 1100, Washington, DC 20005
Telephone: (202) 347-0773
Registered as Foreign Agent: (#4259)
Background: A public affairs consulting firm. Also maintains offices in Philadelphia and Boston.
Members of firm representing listed organizations:
Ayres, Larry F., Associate
Background: Liaison to House of Representatives for the Office of the Secretary of Defense and Secretary of the Army, 1979-85.
Bolling, Andrea W., Associate
Background: Staff aide to Rep. Claude Pepper (D-FL), 1983-85.
Casey, Carol F., Associate & Exec. Asst. to the Chairman
Background: Head of Political Institutions and Processes Section, Government Division, Congressional Research Service, Library of Congress, 1974-79.
Cassidy, Gerald S. J., Chairman of the Board and CEO
Background: Inc., 1975- . General Counsel, U.S. Senate Select Committee on Nutrition and Human Needs, 1969-73 and 1974-75. General Counsel to the Commission on Delegate Selection and Party Structure, Democratic National Committee, 1973.
Cloherty, William M., Senior Associate
Background: Office of U.S. Trade Representative, 1979.
Collins, James P., Associate
Background: Member of the Massachusetts State Legislature, 1977-78.
Cox, Willard F., Associate
Background: Special Assistant to Rep. Don Fuqua (D-FL), 1979-83.
Dawson, Robert K., V. President, Management
Background: Deputy Assistant Secretary of the Army for Civil Works, 1981-84. Assistant Secretary of the Army for Civil Works, 1984-87. Associate Director, Office of Management and Budget, 1987-88.
Dolan, Charles H. (Jr.), Senior V. President
Background: Former Exec. Director, Democratic Governors' Ass'n.
Dougherty, Charles F., Resident Associate (Philadelphia)
Background: Member of the U.S. House of Representatives, 1979-83. Member of the Pennsylvania Senate, 1972-78.
Fabiani, James P., President and COO
Background: Senior Minority Staff Member, U.S. House Labor, Health and Human Services, and Education Subcommittee of the House Appropriations Committee.
Farmer, Robert A., Senior V. President
Background: Treasurer, Democratic Governors' Ass'n, 1986- . Treasurer, Democratic Nat'l Committee, 1989- . Treasurer, Dukakis for President Campaign.
Fiedler, Elliott M., Associate
Background: Legislative and Staff Director to Rep. David Obey (D-WI), 1976-87.
Gannon, Thomas M., General Counsel
Glavas, Pete W., Associate
Background: Former Chief of Staff and Special Assistant to Senator David L. Boren (D-OK).
Godfrey, C. Frank (Jr.), Sr. Associate & Dir. of Administration
Background: Exec. Assistant to the Speaker, U.S. House of Representatives, 1979-83.
Hogness, John R. (M.D.), Senior Consultant
Kelley, (General) Paul X. (USMC-Ret.), V. President, Corporate Marketing
Background: Commander, President's Rapid Deployment Task Force, 1980. Commandant of the U.S. Marine Corps, 1983-87.

McNamara, Daniel J., Account Executive

Meyers, Roy C.
Background: Director of Communications, Cassidy and Associates, Inc, 1987- . Press Secretary to Senator Howard Metzenbaum (D-OH), 1977-85.

Murphy, Peter
Background: Formerly in the Office of the U.S. Trade Representative.

Ramonas, George A., Associate
Background: Legislative Director to Sen. Pete V. Domenici (R-NM), 1977-85.

Rose, (Dr.) Frank A., Senior Consultant

Singletary, (Dr.) Otis A. (Jr.), Sr. Consultant

Smith, Donald P., Sr. Assoc. & Director of Legis. Affairs
Background: Staff Ass't to the House Committee on Appropriations, 1975-87. Budget Examiner, Office of Management and Budget, 1972-75.

Stahr, (Dr.) Elvis J. (Jr.), Senior Consultant
Background: Former Secretary of the Army.

Tate, Sheila B., V. Chairman, Communications
Background: White House Press Secretary to Nancy Reagan, 1981-85. Campaugn and Transition Press Secretary to President Bush, 1988.

Versage, Vincent M., Associate
Background: Legislative Director to Rep. Timothy Wirth (D-CO), 1984-85. Senior Legislative Assistant to Senator Spark Matsunaga (D-HI), 1976-84.

Clients:
Acorn Data Systems, Inc. *(Thomas M. Gannon)*
Action for Boston Community Development *(James P. Collins)*
Alexander Graham Bell Ass'n for the Deaf *(James P. Fabiani)*
American Dredging Co. *(Robert K. Dawson, Thomas M. Gannon)*
American Hospital in Shanghai Foundation *(Gerald S. J. Cassidy, William M. Cloherty, Elliott M. Fiedler)*
American Science & Engineering Inc. *(Thomas M. Gannon, Pete W. Glavas)*
Arizona State University *(George A. Ramonas)*
Ass'n for the Safe Handling of Medical Waste *(Thomas M. Gannon)*
Atlantic Financial *(Gerald S. J. Cassidy, Pete W. Glavas, George A. Ramonas)*
Barry University *(Gerald S. J. Cassidy, C. Frank Godfrey, Jr.)*
Biopure Corp. *(Thomas M. Gannon)*
Bolt, Beranek and Newman *(C. Frank Godfrey, Jr.)*
Boston Carmen's Union, Local 589 *(James P. Collins, Thomas M. Gannon)*
Boston College *(James P. Fabiani, C. Frank Godfrey, Jr.)*
Boston University *(Gerald S. J. Cassidy, James P. Collins, C. Frank Godfrey, Jr., Donald P. Smith)*
Cardinal Hill Hospital *(Andrea W. Bolling, C. Frank Godfrey, Jr., Dr. Frank A. Rose)*
Catholic University of America *(Gerald S. J. Cassidy, Donald P. Smith)*
Challenger Center for Space Science Education *(Dr. Frank A. Rose, Donald P. Smith)*
Children's Hospital and Health Center
Children's Hospital Nat'l Medical Center *(James P. Fabiani, Thomas M. Gannon, Donald P. Smith)*
Children's Hospital of Michigan *(Gerald S. J. Cassidy, John R. Hogness, M.D., Donald P. Smith)*
Children's Hospital (Pittsburgh) *(James P. Fabiani)*
Clark Atlanta University *(James P. Fabiani, Vincent M. Versage)*
Columbia University *(Gerald S. J. Cassidy, Thomas M. Gannon, C. Frank Godfrey, Jr.)*
Critical Languages Consortium *(William M. Cloherty, Elliott M. Fiedler)*
DataCom Systems Corp. *(James P. Collins, Thomas M. Gannon)*
Delaware State Department of Transportation *(Thomas M. Gannon)*
Donaldson, Lufkin & Jenrette *(Gerald S. J. Cassidy)*
Drexel University *(Gerald S. J. Cassidy, Charles F. Dougherty, C. Frank Godfrey, Jr.)*
Enid Joint Industrial Foundation *(Pete W. Glavas)*
Experiment in Internat'l Living *(Elliott M. Fiedler)*
Fudan Foundation *(Gerald S. J. Cassidy, William M. Cloherty, Elliott M. Fiedler)*
Gonzaga University *(C. Frank Godfrey, Jr.)*
Great Lakes Dredge and Dock Co. *(Robert K. Dawson, Thomas M. Gannon)*

Hawaii State Department of Business and Economic Development *(Thomas M. Gannon, Vincent M. Versage)*
Hawaii, University of *(Vincent M. Versage)*
Hexagon Technical Co. Inc. *(Gerald S. J. Cassidy, Thomas M. Gannon)*
Indiana Department of Commerce *(Thomas M. Gannon)*
Infirmary Health System, Inc. *(Robert K. Dawson, James P. Fabiani, Dr. Frank A. Rose)*
Internat'l Data Corp. *(Gerald S. J. Cassidy, Thomas M. Gannon, General Paul X. Kelley, USMC-Ret., Sheila B. Tate)*
ITT Gilfillan *(Thomas M. Gannon)*
James Co., T. L. *(Robert K. Dawson, Thomas M. Gannon)*
Kerr-McGee Corp. *(Thomas M. Gannon)*
Lee Company, Thomas H. *(Thomas M. Gannon)*
Lehigh University *(Robert K. Dawson, Vincent M. Versage)*
LiTel Telecommunications Corp. *(C. Frank Godfrey, Jr.)*
Loma Linda University *(Donald P. Smith)*
Louisiana Public Facilities Authority *(Gerald S. J. Cassidy, Dr. Frank A. Rose, Donald P. Smith)*
Loyola College *(James P. Fabiani, Vincent M. Versage)*
Loyola Marymount University *(Thomas M. Gannon, C. Frank Godfrey, Jr.)*
Loyola University of Chicago *(Andrea W. Bolling, C. Frank Godfrey, Jr.)*
Massachusetts Ass'n of Community Health Agencies *(James P. Collins)*
Massachusetts Corp. for Educational Telecommunications *(Andrea W. Bolling, Vincent M. Versage)*
Massachusetts League of Community Banks *(James P. Collins)*
Medical College of Wisconsin *(Thomas M. Gannon)*
Medical University of South Carolina *(Larry F. Ayres, C. Frank Godfrey, Jr.)*
Michigan Biotechnology Institute *(Larry F. Ayres, Donald P. Smith)*
Michigan Technological University *(Thomas M. Gannon, Donald P. Smith, Vincent M. Versage)*
Monterey Institute of Internat'l Studies *(C. Frank Godfrey, Jr.)*
Mount Sinai Medical Center *(Gerald S. J. Cassidy, Vincent M. Versage)*
Mount Sinai Medical Center of Greater Miami *(Thomas M. Gannon, Donald P. Smith)*
Mutual Interest Transactions *(Thomas M. Gannon)*
Nat'l Jewish Center for Immunology and Respiratory Medicine *(Gerald S. J. Cassidy, Elliott M. Fiedler, Vincent M. Versage)*
NeoRx, Inc. *(Gerald S. J. Cassidy, George A. Ramonas)*
Ocean Spray Cranberries *(Carol F. Casey, Gerald S. J. Cassidy, James P. Collins, C. Frank Godfrey, Jr.)*
O'Connell Management Co. *(Gerald S. J. Cassidy, James P. Fabiani)*
Pennsylvania Turnpike Commission *(Larry F. Ayres, Charles F. Dougherty, Donald P. Smith)*
Pirelli Cable Corp. *(James P. Fabiani, Thomas M. Gannon, Vincent M. Versage)*
Polytechnic University of New York *(James P. Fabiani, Vincent M. Versage)*
Presbyterian Hospital/University of Pittsburgh *(Gerald S. J. Cassidy, C. Frank Godfrey, Jr.)*
Puerto Rico Federal Affairs Administration *(Gerald S. J. Cassidy, Robert A. Farmer)*
Rochester Institute of Technology *(James P. Fabiani, Vincent M. Versage)*
Schutz American School *(William M. Cloherty, Elliott M. Fiedler)*
Seragen Inc. *(Gerald S. J. Cassidy)*
Societa Cavi Pirelli S.p.A. *(James P. Fabiani, C. Frank Godfrey, Jr., Vincent M. Versage)*
Spring Garden College *(Thomas M. Gannon)*
St. Joseph's University *(Charles F. Dougherty, Vincent M. Versage)*
St. Norberts College *(Elliott M. Fiedler)*
The University Hospital *(Carol F. Casey)*
Thomas Jefferson University *(C. Frank Godfrey, Jr.)*
Tougaloo College *(Gerald S. J. Cassidy, Robert A. Farmer)*
Tread Corp. *(William M. Cloherty)*
Tufts University *(Carol F. Casey, Gerald S. J. Cassidy, C. Frank Godfrey, Jr.)*
Twentieth Century Fox *(Thomas M. Gannon)*
U.S. Healthcare, Inc. *(C. Frank Godfrey, Jr.)*

Universal Medical Center *(Gerald S. J. Cassidy, C. Frank Godfrey, Jr., Dr. Otis A. Singletary, Jr.)*
University Hospital of Cleveland *(Roy C. Meyers, George A. Ramonas)*
University of Bridgeport *(George A. Ramonas)*
University of Kentucky Foundation *(C. Frank Godfrey, Jr., George A. Ramonas)*
University of Nebraska *(James P. Fabiani, Donald P. Smith)*
University of Nebraska Foundation *(James P. Fabiani, Donald P. Smith)*
University of Pennsylvania *(Carol F. Casey, Gerald S. J. Cassidy, C. Frank Godfrey, Jr.)*
University of Scranton *(Larry F. Ayres, James P. Fabiani)*
University of Southern Mississippi *(C. Frank Godfrey, Jr.)*
University of the Arts *(Carol F. Casey, Charles F. Dougherty, Thomas M. Gannon, C. Frank Godfrey, Jr.)*
University of Utah *(George A. Ramonas)*
University of Vermont *(Carol F. Casey, Gerald S. J. Cassidy)*
Utah, State of
Valley Children's Hospital *(C. Frank Godfrey, Jr.)*
West Virginia University *(Donald P. Smith, Dr. Elvis J. Stahr, Jr.)*
Western Townships Utilities Authority *(Robert K. Dawson, Donald P. Smith)*
World Trade Center Boston *(William M. Cloherty)*
20th Century Fox *(Gerald S. J. Cassidy, Pete W. Glavas)*

CASSIDY, Esther C.
Director, Cong & Legis Affrs, DEPARTMENT OF COMMERCE - Nat'l Institute of Standards and Technology
A-1111 Adm. Bldg., Gaithersburg, MD 20899
Telephone: (301) 975-3080

CASSIDY, Gerald S. J.
Chairman of the Board and CEO, Cassidy and Associates, Inc.
655 15th St., N.W., Suite 1100, Washington, DC 20005
Telephone: (202) 347-0773
Registered as lobbyist at U.S. Congress.
Background: Inc., 1975- . General Counsel, U.S. Senate Select Committee on Nutrition and Human Needs, 1969-73 and 1974-75. General Counsel to the Commission on Delegate Selection and Party Structure, Democratic National Committee, 1973.
Clients:
American Hospital in Shanghai Foundation
Atlantic Financial
Barry University
Boston University
Catholic University of America
Children's Hospital of Michigan
Columbia University
Donaldson, Lufkin & Jenrette
Drexel University
Fudan Foundation
Hexagon Technical Co. Inc.
Internat'l Data Corp.
Louisiana Public Facilities Authority
Mount Sinai Medical Center
Nat'l Jewish Center for Immunology and Respiratory Medicine
NeoRx, Inc.
Ocean Spray Cranberries
O'Connell Management Co.
Presbyterian Hospital/University of Pittsburgh
Puerto Rico Federal Affairs Administration
Seragen Inc.
Tougaloo College
Tufts University
Universal Medical Center
University of Pennsylvania
University of Vermont
20th Century Fox

CASSIDY, J. Warren
Exec. V. President, Nat'l Rifle Ass'n of America
1600 Rhode Island Ave., N.W., Washington, DC 20036
Telephone: (202) 828-6000
Registered as lobbyist at U.S. Congress.

CASSIDY, Lawrence J.
General Secretary-Treasurer, Sheet Metal Workers' Inter-nat'l Ass'n
1750 New York Ave., N.W. Sixth Floor, Washington, DC 20006
Telephone: (202) 783-5880

CASSIDY, Robert C., Jr.
Wilmer, Cutler and Pickering
2445 M St., N.W., Washington, DC 20037-1420
Telephone: (202) 663-6000
Registered as lobbyist at U.S. Congress.
Registered as Foreign Agent: (#3355).
Background: International Trade Counsel, Senate Finance Committee, 1975-79. General Counsel, Office of the U.S. Trade Representative, Exec. Office of the President, 1979-81.
Clients:
Ford Motor Co.
Lufthansa German Airlines
Yamaha Motor Corp. U.S.A.

CASSO, Mark Anthony
Gen. Counsel & Mng. Dir., Administration, American Consulting Engineers Council
1015 15th St., N.W., Suite 802, Washington, DC 20005
Telephone: (202) 347-7474
Registered as lobbyist at U.S. Congress.

CASSON, HARKINS & LAPALLO
1233 20th St., N.W. Suite 800, Washington, DC 20036-2396
Telephone: (202) 778-1100
Clients:
Foundation for Eye Research
Healthcare Recoveries Inc.

CASTELLANI, John J.
V. President, Government Relations, TRW Inc.
Suite 2700, 1000 Wilson Blvd., Arlington, VA 22209
Telephone: (703) 276-5030
Registered as lobbyist at U.S. Congress.

CASTELLON, Margarita T.
Director of Government Relations, Republic Group, The
5801 Lee Hwy., Arlington, VA 22207
Telephone: (703) 533-8555
Background: Former Special Assistant to Senator Lawton Chiles (D-FL).

CASTOR, C. R.
Nat'l Exec. Secretary, United States Coast Guard Chief Petty Officers Ass'n
5520 G Hempstead Way, Springfield, VA 22151
Telephone: (703) 941-0395

CATE CORP., THE
11480 Sunset Hills Road Suite 100E, Reston, VA 22090
Telephone: (703) 435-6708
Members of firm representing listed organizations:
Cate, George M.
Clients:
American Soc. for Extra-Corporeal Technology
(George M. Cate)

CATE, George M.
Cate Corp., The
11480 Sunset Hills Road Suite 100E, Reston, VA 22090
Telephone: (703) 435-6708
Clients:
American Soc. for Extra-Corporeal Technology

CATH, Stan
Exec. Director, Agricultural Research Institute
9650 Rockville Pike, Bethesda, MD 20814
Telephone: (301) 530-7122

CATO, Phillip C.
Senior V. President, Pagan Internat'l Inc.
1925 N. Lynn St. Suite 903, Washington, DC 22209
Telephone: (703) 528-4177

CATOR, G. Thomas
President, Neece, Cator and Associates
1050 17th St., N.W. Suite 810, Washington, DC 20036
Telephone: (202) 887-5599
Registered as lobbyist at U.S. Congress.
Clients:
Nat'l Small Business United

Southeastern Lumber Manufacturers Ass'n

CATUCCI, W. V.
Corporate V. President, AT&T
Suite 1000, 1120 20th St., N.W., Washington, DC 20036
Telephone: (202) 457-3890

CAUDELL-FEAGAN, Michael
Exec. Director, Nat'l Ass'n for Public Interest Law
1666 Connecticut Ave., N.W., Suite 424, Washington, DC 20009
Telephone: (202) 462-0120

CAVANAGH, Mary
Director, Washington Office, Mercury Stainless Corp.
305 3rd St., S.E., Washington, DC 20003
Telephone: (202) 546-3538
Registered as lobbyist at U.S. Congress.

CAVANAGH, Michael F.
Exec. Director, Electronic Mail Ass'n
1555 Wilson Blvd., Suite 555, Arlington, VA 22209
Telephone: (703) 522-7111

CAVANAUGH, Gordon
Reno, Cavanaugh & Hornig
122 C St., N.W., Suite 875, Washington, DC 20001
Telephone: (202) 783-5120
Registered as lobbyist at U.S. Congress.
Background: Administrator, Farmers Home Administration, Department of Agriculture, 1977-81.
Clients:
Council of Large Public Housing Authorities

CAVANAUGH, J. Michael
Graham and James
2000 M St., N.W., Suite 700, Washington, DC 20036
Telephone: (202) 463-0800
Background: Attorney-Advisor, Office of the General Counsel, Maritime Administration, Department of Commerce, 1974-77.
Clients:
American Hawaii Cruises

CAVAROCCHI, Nicholas G.
CR Associates
317 Massachusetts Ave., N.E., Suite 100, Washington, DC 20002
Telephone: (202) 546-4732
Registered as lobbyist at U.S. Congress.
Clients:
Alzheimer's Ass'n
American Academy of Orthopaedic Surgeons
American Ass'n for Dental Research

CAVE, Robert B.
Hogan and Hartson
555 13th St., N.W., Suite 1200, Washington, DC 20004-1109
Telephone: (202) 637-5600
Registered as lobbyist at U.S. Congress.

CAVE, Robert S.
Exec. Director, American Public Gas Ass'n
Box 1426, Vienna, VA 22183
Telephone: (703) 281-2910

CAWELTI, Dr. Gordon
Exec. Director, Ass'n for Supervision and Curriculum Development
1250 North Pitt Street, Alexandria, VA 22314
Telephone: (703) 549-9110

CEBULA, Andrew V.
Director, Government Affairs, Nat'l Air Transportation Ass'n
4226 King St., Alexandria, VA 22302
Telephone: (703) 845-9000

CECELSKI, Dorothy D.
Director, State Communications, Common Cause
2030 M St., N.W., Washington, DC 20036
Telephone: (202) 833-1200
Background: Serves also as Secretary to the National Governing Board.

CECERE, Jacob
Associate, Gilberg & Kurent
1250 I St., N.W. Suite 600, Washington, DC 20005
Telephone: (202) 842-3222

CEDERBERG AND ASSOCIATES
7100 Sussex Place, Alexandria, VA 22307
Telephone: (703) 768-9130
Members of firm representing listed organizations:
Cederberg, Elford A.
Background: Also serves as Treasurer, Americans for Constitutional Action.
Clients:
Americans for Constitutional Action *(Elford A. Cederberg)*
Grumman Aerospace Corp. *(Elford A. Cederberg)*

CEDERBERG, Elford A.
Cederberg and Associates
7100 Sussex Place, Alexandria, VA 22307
Telephone: (703) 768-9130
Background: Also serves as Treasurer, Americans for Constitutional Action.
Clients:
Americans for Constitutional Action
Grumman Aerospace Corp.

CEHP, INC.
1333 Connecticut Ave., N.W. Suite 400, Washington, DC 20036
Telephone: (202) 293-1774
Members of firm representing listed organizations:
McCann, Theodore, V. President
Neumann, Loretta, President
Reinburg, Kathleen, V. President

CELLA, Glenn R.
Exec. Director, American Institute for Shippers' Ass'ns
Box 33457, Washington, DC 20033
Telephone: (202) 628-0933
Background: U.S. Dept. of State. 1960-89.

CENTURY PUBLIC AFFAIRS
1752 N St., N.W., Suite 800, Washington, DC 20036
Telephone: (202) 828-2375
Background: A lobbying firm in limited partnership with the law firm of Davis Wright & Jones.
Members of firm representing listed organizations:
Bangert, Philip A., Director, Legislative Affairs
Sinnott, Richard L., President
Clients:
Dallas-Ft. Worth Internat'l Airport
Intermec Corp.
New United Motor Manufacturing, Inc. (NUM-MI) *(Philip A. Bangert)*
Oakland, California, Port of *(Philip A. Bangert, Richard L. Sinnott)*
Transcontinental Development Corp. *(Philip A. Bangert, Richard L. Sinnott)*

CEOL, Ed
PAC Director, Free Congress Political Action Committee
717 2nd St., N.E., Washington, DC 20002
Telephone: (202) 546-3000

CERAR, Jeffrey O.
Squire, Sanders and Dempsey
1201 Pennsylvania Ave., N.W. P.O. Box 407, Washington, DC 20044
Telephone: (202) 626-6600
Background: Deputy Associate General Counsel, U.S. Environmental Protection Agency, 1978-79.
Clients:
Ferro Corp.
Northeast Ohio Regional Sewer District
White Consolidated Industries

CERGOL, Jack
Director, Communications, Nat'l Spa and Pool Institute
2111 Eisenhower Ave., Alexandria, VA 22314
Telephone: (703) 838-0083

CERIN, Elmer
5432 Connecticut Ave., N.W. Suite 705, Washington, DC 20015
Telephone: (202) 362-0923
Background: Voluntary lobbyist on health issues, bio-medical research, and the environment.

CERNY, Louis T.
Exec. Director, American Railway Engineering Ass'n
50 F St., N.W., Suite 7702, Washington, DC 20001
Telephone: (202) 639-2190

CEROTZKE, David
Manager, Regulatory Affairs, American Gas Ass'n
1515 Wilson Blvd., Arlington, VA 22209
Telephone: (703) 841-8656

CERTAIN, Bettie-Julia
Senate Liaison, DEPARTMENT OF DEFENSE - Defense
Security Assistance Agency
The Pentagon, Washington, DC 20301-2800
Telephone: (202) 697-9201

CERTNER, Cathy Ellen
Director, Public Policy, Washington Business Group on
Health
229 1/2 Pennsylvania Ave., S.E., Washington, DC 20003
Telephone: (202) 547-6644

CERTNER, David
Legislative Representative, American Ass'n of Retired
Persons
1909 K St., N.W., Washington, DC 20049
Telephone: (202) 728-4738
Registered as lobbyist at U.S. Congress.

CESTON, Dr. T. Stephan
Exec V Pres., Internat'l/ Govt'l Affairs, Geostar Corp.
1001 22nd St., N.W., Washington, DC 20037
Telephone: (202) 887-0870

CHADBOURNE AND PARKE
1101 Vermont Ave., N.W. Suite 900, Washington, DC
20005
Telephone: (202) 289-3000
Background: Washington office of a New York law firm.
Members of firm representing listed organizations:
D'Amico, William
Golden, Cornelius (Jr.)
Martin, Keith
Background: Legislative Assistant, Sen. Henry M. Jackson, 1974-77. Legislative Counsel, Sen. Daniel Patrick Moynihan, 1979-1982.
Muskie, Edmund S.
Background: Former U.S. Senator (D-ME), 1959-80 and Secretary of State, 1980-81.
Clients:
AES Corporation, The
Amalgamated Metal Corp. PLC *(Cornelius Golden, Jr.)*
American Paper Institute
Burnett & Hallamshire Holdings, PLC
Inter-Power of New York
Napp Chemicals
Ormat Energy Systems
Oxbow Power Cprp.
Purdue Frederick Co., The
Ruan Leasing Co.

CHADWICK, Lynn
President and CEO, Nat'l Federation of Community
Broadcasters
666 11th St., N.W. Suite 805, Washington, DC 20001
Telephone: (202) 393-2355

CHAFER, Charles M.
V. President for Government Affairs, Space Services Inc.
600 Water St., S.W., Suite 207, Washington, DC 20024
Telephone: (202) 646-1025

CHAFETZ, Dr. Morris E.
President, Health Education Foundation
600 New Hampshire Ave., N.W., Suite 452, Washington,
DC 20037
Telephone: (202) 338-3501

CHAKARUN, Michael J.
Tax Analyst, American Mining Congress
1920 N St., N.W. Suite 300, Washington, DC 20036
Telephone: (202) 861-2800
Registered as lobbyist at U.S. Congress.
Background: Former Legislative Assistant to Senator Malcolm Wallop (R-WY).

CHALEF, Ira
President, Congressional Management Foundation
513 Capitol Court, N.E. Suite 100, Washington, DC 20002
Telephone: (202) 546-0100
Background: Also serves as President of the Congress of
American Homeowners.

CHALFIE, Deborah M.
Legislative Director, HALT-An Organization of Americans
for Legal Reform
1319 F St., N.W., Suite 300, Washington, DC 20004
Telephone: (202) 347-9600
Registered as lobbyist at U.S. Congress.

CHALLENGE AMERICA, INC.
1700 K St., N.W., Suite 1100, Washington, DC 20006
Telephone: (202) 429-9400
Background: A political consulting firm.
Members of firm representing listed organizations:
Sloan, Richard S., President
Clients:
American Federation of Teachers *(Richard S. Sloan)*
Internat'l Ass'n of Machinists and Aerospace
Workers *(Richard S. Sloan)*
Service Employees Internat'l Union *(Richard S. Sloan)*

CHALMERS, Walton M.
President, Hilton/Chalmers, Hilton/Chalmers Inc.
923 15th St., N.W., Washington, DC 20005
Telephone: (202) 638-1535
Background: Former Exec. Director, Democratic Nat'l
Committee.

CHALPIN, Mark G.
V. Pres., Gov't & Internat'l Affrs., Nat'l Constructors Ass'n
1730 M St., N.W., Suite 900, Washington, DC 20036-4571
Telephone: (202) 466-8880
Registered as lobbyist at U.S. Congress.
Background: Formerly in Office of General Counsel, General Accounting Office. Also represents the Nat'l Constructors Ass'n Political Action Committee.

CHAMBERLAIN, Charles E.
Webster, Chamberlain and Bean
1747 Pennsylvania Ave., N.W., Suite 1000, Washington,
DC 20006
Telephone: (202) 785-9500
Background: Member, U.S. House of Representatives from
Michigan, 1957-74.
Clients:
Committee for Production Sharing

CHAMBERLAIN, Henry
V. President, Communications, Building Owners and
Managers Ass'n Internat'l
1201 New York Ave., N.W. Suite 300, Washington, DC
20005
Telephone: (202) 289-7000

CHAMBERLAIN, Terry M.
Director, Internat'l Construction, Associated General Contractors of America
1957 E St., N.W., Washington, DC 20006
Telephone: (202) 393-2040
Registered as lobbyist at U.S. Congress.

CHAMBERLIN, Holly
Manager, State Tax Government Relations, Price Waterhouse
1801 K St., N.W., Suite 700, Washington, DC 20006
Telephone: (202) 296-0800

CHAMBERLIN, R. Webster
Director, Public/Media Relations, Chesapeake and Potomac Telephone Co.
2055 L St., N.W., Washington, DC 20036
Telephone: (202) 392-5108

CHAMBERLIN, W. George
Manager, Washington Operations, Lockheed, Sanders Inc.
1735 Jefferson Davis Hwy., Suite 700, Arlington, VA
22202
Telephone: (703) 920-5204

CHAMBERS ASSOCIATES INCORPORATED
1625 K St., N.W. Suite 200, Washington, DC 20006
Telephone: (202) 857-0670
Background: Public policy consultants.
Members of firm representing listed organizations:
Bury, Craig E., V. President
Background: Former Professional Staff Member, Senate
Appropriations Committee and Senate Budget Committee.
Chambers, Letitia, President
Background: Former Staff Director, Senate Committee
on Labor and Human Resources; Minortiy Staff Director, Senate Special Committee on Aging; Senior
Budget and Policy Analyst, Senate Budget Committee.
Lyman, Mary S., Project Manager, Tax Counsel
Background: Former Tax Counsel to Congressman Jim
Shannon, House Ways and Means Committee.
Merisotis, Jamie P.
Smith, James N., V. President
Background: Former Ass't Administrator, EPA; Deputy
Director, National Commission on Water Quality.
Stringer, William L., V. President
Background: Formerly Deputy Treasurer, State of New
Jersey; Chief Economist, Senate Budget Committee;
and Assistant to the Chairman, Federal Home Loan
Bank Board.
Summerton, Allison B., Project Manager
Clients:
AFL-CIO (American Federation of Labor and
Congress of Industrial Organizations) *(Letitia
Chambers)*
American Ass'n of Retired Persons *(Craig E. Bury)*
American Postal Workers Union *(Craig E. Bury)*
Belk Stores Services, Inc. *(Mary S. Lyman)*
Ben Franklin Advanced Technology Center *(William L. Stringer)*
Coalition of Publicly Traded Partnerships *(Letitia
Chambers, Mary S. Lyman)*
Coalition of Publicly Traded Partnerships Political Action Committee *(Letitia Chambers)*
Committee for Equitable Compensation *(Letitia
Chambers)*
Eagle-Picher Industries *(Letitia Chambers)*
Infrastructure Bond Coalition *(James N. Smith)*
Manville Corp. *(James N. Smilh)*
Nat'l Ass'n of Home Builders of the U.S. *(William
L. Stringer)*
Newhall Land and Farming Co. *(William L. Stringer)*
North Jersey District Water Supply Commission
(William L. Stringer)
Southwest Realty, Inc. *(Mary S. Lyman, James N.
Smith)*
State Higher Education Executive Officers *(Letitia
Chambers, Jamie P. Merisotis)*
Utah League of Cities and Towns *(William L. Stringer)*

CHAMBERS, Caroline M.
Director, Congressional Relations, Nat'l Ass'n of Regulatory Utility Commissioners
Box 684, I.C.C. Bldg., Washington, DC 20044-0684
Telephone: (202) 898-2200

CHAMBERS, Dr. Charles M.
Exec. Director, American Institute of Biological Sciences
730 11th St., N.W., Washington, DC 20001-4521
Telephone: (202) 628-1500

CHAMBERS, Jerry L.
Assistant Director, Government Relations, American
Cyanamid Co.
1575 Eye St., N.W., Suite 200, Washington, DC 20005
Telephone: (202) 789-1222
Background: Serves as Chairman, American Cyanamid
Employee Political Action Committee.

CHAMBERS, Letitia
President, Chambers Associates Incorporated
1625 K St., N.W. Suite 200, Washington, DC 20006
Telephone: (202) 857-0670
Registered as lobbyist at U.S. Congress.
Background: Former Staff Director, Senate Committee on
Labor and Human Resources; Minortiy Staff Director,
Senate Special Committee on Aging; Senior Budget and
Policy Analyst, Senate Budget Committee.
Clients:
AFL-CIO (American Federation of Labor and
Congress of Industrial Organizations)
Coalition of Publicly Traded Partnerships
Coalition of Publicly Traded Partnerships Political Action Committee
Committee for Equitable Compensation
Eagle-Picher Industries
State Higher Education Executive Officers

CHAMBERS, Mary
Senior Associate, Robinson, Lake, Lerer & Montgomery
1667 K St., N.W., Suite 900, Washington, DC 20006
Telephone: (202) 457-9270
Background: Former Chief of Staff to Rep. Robert Matsui
(D-CA).

CHAMBERS, Ray B.
Chairman, RBC Associates, Inc.
324 Fourth St., N.E., Washington, DC 20002
Telephone: (202) 543-0038
Registered as lobbyist at U.S. Congress.
Background: Administrative Assistant to Rep. Phil Ruppe
(R-MI), 1967-71. Deputy Assistant Secretary for Field
Administration, U.S. Department of Health, Education
and Welfare, 1971-73. Director, Congressional Relations,
Department of Transportation, 1973-75.
Clients:
Bangor and Aroostook Railroad
Chicago and Northwestern Transportation Co.
Delaware Otsego System
Genesee and Wyoming Corp.
Long Island Rail Road Co.

CHAMBERS, Reid Peyton
Sonosky, Chambers and Sachse
1250 Eye St., N.W., Suite 1000, Washington, DC 20005
Telephone: (202) 682-0240
Registered as lobbyist at U.S. Congress.

CHAMEIDES, Steven B.
Foley & Lardner
1775 Pennsylvania Ave., N.W., Suite 1000, Washington,
DC 20006-4680
Telephone: (202) 862-5300

CHAMP, Lorraine
Controller, American Bakers Ass'n
1111 14th St., N.W., Suite 300, Washington, DC 20005
Telephone: (202) 296-5800
Registered as lobbyist at U.S. Congress.

CHAMP-WILSON, Ann
Exec. Director, Deafpride
1350 Potomac Ave., S.E., Washington, DC 20003
Telephone: (202) 675-6700

CHAMPION, Maxine C.
V. President, Government Relations, LTV Corp.
1025 Thomas Jefferson St., N.W., Suite 511 West, Wash-
ington, DC 20007
Telephone: (202) 944-5700
Registered as lobbyist at U.S. Congress.
Background: Former Tax Counsel, Committee on Ways
and Means, U.S. House of Representative.

CHANCLER, Robert T.
V. President, Smith, Bucklin and Associates
1101 Connecticut Ave., N.W., Suite 700, Washington, DC
20036
Telephone: (202) 857-1100
Background: Serves as Exec. Director of Commercial Re-
frigerator Manufacturers Ass'n, American Wire Producers
Ass'n, Internat'l Ass'n of Airport Duty Free Shops and of
the Nat'l Ass'n of Corporate Treasurers.
Clients:
American Wire Producers Ass'n
Commercial Refrigerator Manufacturers Ass'n
Internat'l Ass'n of Airport Duty Free Stores
Nat'l Ass'n of Corporate Treasurers

CHANDLER ASSOCIATES, W. J.
Suite 1100, 1511 K St., N.W., Washington, DC 20005
Telephone: (202) 783-7762
Background: A natural resource policy and government re-
lations consulting firm.
Members of firm representing listed organizations:
Chandler, William J.

CHANDLER, Ed
Legislative Representative, NMTBA - The Ass'n for Manu-
facturing Technology
7901 Westpark Dr., McLean, VA 22102
Telephone: (703) 893-2900
Registered as lobbyist at U.S. Congress.

CHANDLER, J. W.
V. President (MM&G Division), York Internat'l Corp.
8301-B Patuxent Range, Jessup, MD 20794-9620

Telephone: (301) 953-0520

CHANDLER, Dr. John W.
President, Ass'n of American Colleges
1818 R St., N.W., Washington, DC 20009
Telephone: (202) 387-3760

CHANDLER, William J.
Chandler Associates, W. J.
Suite 1100, 1511 K St., N.W., Washington, DC 20005
Telephone: (202) 783-7762
Registered as lobbyist at U.S. Congress.

CHANEY, Carolyn
Nat'l Center for Municipal Development
1620 Eye St., N.W., Suite 300, Washington, DC 20006
Telephone: (202) 429-0160
Clients:
Beaumont, Texas, City of
Lincoln, Nebraska, City of
Pasadena, California, City of
Springfield, Illinois, City of

CHANIN, Michael H.
Powell, Goldstein, Frazer and Murphy
1001 Pennsylvania, N.W., Sixth Fl., Washington, DC
20004
Telephone: (202) 347-0066
Registered as lobbyist at U.S. Congress.
Background: Special Assistant, Office of the Secretary of
Commerce, 1977-78. Deputy Assistant to the President of
the U.S., 1978-81.
Clients:
Palau, Government of

CHANIN, Robert H.
General Counsel, Nat'l Education Ass'n of the U.S.
1201 16th St., N.W., Washington, DC 20036
Telephone: (202) 822-7300

CHAPIN, Isolde
Exec. Director, Washington Independent Writers
220 Woodward Building 733 15th St., N.W., Washington,
DC 20005
Telephone: (202) 347-4973
Registered as lobbyist at U.S. Congress.

CHAPIN, Roger
President & Founder, Citizens for a Drug Free America
2230 George C. Marshall Drive, Falls Church, VA 22042
Telephone: (703) 207-9300

CHAPMAN, Amy
Field Director, Service Employees Internat'l Union
1313 L St., N.W., Washington, DC 20005
Telephone: (202) 898-3200

CHAPMAN, Kelly G.
Legislative Representative, Flanagan Group, Inc.
11 Canal Center Plaza Suite 250, Alexandria, VA 22314
Telephone: (703) 739-8822

CHAPMAN, Linda
Director, Government Affairs, Biscuit and Cracker Manu-
facturers Ass'n
1400 L St., N.W. Suite 400, Washington, DC 20005
Telephone: (202) 898-1636
Registered as lobbyist at U.S. Congress.

CHAPMAN, Michael D.
Legis. Director, Congressional Affairs, Nat'l Ass'n of
REALTORS
777 14th St., N.W., Washington, DC 20005
Telephone: (202) 383-1000
Registered as lobbyist at U.S. Congress.

CHAPMAN, Tom
V. Pres., Legislative Affairs & Counsel, Aircraft Owners
and Pilots Ass'n
421 Aviation Way, Frederick, MD 21701
Telephone: (301) 695-2000
Registered as lobbyist at U.S. Congress.

CHAPOTON, John E.
Vinson and Elkins
Willard Office Building, 1455 Pennsylvania Ave., N.W.,
Washington, DC 20004-1007
Telephone: (202) 639-6500
Registered as lobbyist at U.S. Congress.
Registered as Foreign Agent: (#4277).

Background: Tax Legislative Counsel, U.S. Treasury De-
partment, 1970-72. Assistant Secretary of the Treasury
for Tax Policy, 1981-84.
Clients:
ENSERCH Corp.
Goldman, Sachs and Co.
Merrill Lynch and Co., Inc.
Vitro, S.A.

CHAPOTON, O. Donaldson
Baker and Botts
555 13th St., N.W., Suite 500 East, Washington, DC
20004-1109
Telephone: (202) 639-7700
Registered as lobbyist at U.S. Congress.
Background: Counsel. Former Deputy Assistant Secretary
of the Treasury, 1986-87; Assistant Secretary of the
Treasury, 1987-89.

CHAPPIE, Gene
Government Affairs Consultant, Fleishman-Hillard, Inc
1301 Connecticut Ave., N.W., Washington, DC 20036
Telephone: (202) 659-0330
Background: Member, U.S. House of Representatives (R-
CA), 1981-86.

CHARMATZ, Marc
Counsel, Nat'l Ass'n of the Deaf
800 Florida Ave., N.E., Washington, DC 20002
Telephone: (202) 651-5373

CHARNOFF, Gerald
Shaw, Pittman, Potts and Trowbridge
2300 N St., N.W., Washington, DC 20037
Telephone: (202) 663-8000
Registered as lobbyist at U.S. Congress.
Background: Atomic Energy Commission, 1957-60.
Clients:
Duquesne Light Co.
Indiana and Michigan Electric Co.
Indiana Michigan Power Co.
Northern States Power Co.
Public Service Co. of New Hampshire
Toledo Edison Co.
Union Electric Co.
Wisconsin Electric Power Co.

CHARRIER, J. William
President, American Automar, Inc.
1025 Thomas Jefferson St., N.W., Suite 308, Washington,
DC 20007
Telephone: (202) 342-2410

CHASEN, Nancy
Director, Public Affairs, Fusion Systems Corp.
7600 Standish Place, Rockville, MD 20855
Telephone: (301) 251-0300

CHASEY ORGANIZATION, The William
1015 33rd St., N.W., Suite 509, Washington, DC 20007
Telephone: (202) 333-1968
Registered as Foreign Agent: (#4221)
Background: A professional lobbying firm based in La Jol-
la, California.
Members of firm representing listed organizations:
Chasey, Virginia
Chasey, William C. (Ph.D.)
Williams, Paul A.
Organizations represented:
CASA (Church Alliance of South Africa) *(Virginia
Chasey)*
City University *(Virginia Chasey)*
Coalition for the Promotion of Costa Rica
Abroad *(William C. Chasey, Ph.D.)*
Financial Northeastern Corp. *(Virginia Chasey)*
Indo-U.S. Political Action Committee *(William C.
Chasey, Ph.D.)*
Palomar/Pomerado Hospital District *(William C.
Chasey, Ph.D.)*
Preuss Foundation, The Peter *(William C. Chasey,
Ph.D.)*
Research and Development Laboratories *(William
C. Chasey, Ph.D.)*
Response Dynamics Inc. *(Virginia Chasey)*
ST Systems Corp. (STX) *(William C. Chasey, Ph.D.)*
Sunshine Makers, Inc. *(Virginia Chasey)*
Third World Prosthetic Foundation *(William C.
Chasey, Ph.D.)*
Trident Trading Corp. *(Virginia Chasey)*

CHASEY, Virginia
Chasey Organization, The William
1015 33rd St., N.W., Suite 509, Washington, DC 20007
Telephone: (202) 333-1968
Registered as lobbyist at U.S. Congress.
Organizations represented:
 CASA (Church Alliance of South Africa)
 City University
 Financial Northeastern Corp.
 Response Dynamics Inc.
 Sunshine Makers, Inc.
 Trident Trading Corp.

CHASEY, William C., Ph.D.
Chasey Organization, The William
1015 33rd St., N.W., Suite 509, Washington, DC 20007
Telephone: (202) 333-1968
Registered as lobbyist at U.S. Congress.
Registered as Foreign Agent: (#4221).
Organizations represented:
 Coalition for the Promotion of Costa Rica
  Abroad
 Indo-U.S. Political Action Committee
 Palomar/Pomerado Hospital District
 Preuss Foundation, The Peter
 Research and Development Laboratories
 ST Systems Corp. (STX)
 Third World Prosthetic Foundation

CHASNOW, Robert M.
Dow, Lohnes and Albertson
1255 23rd St., N.W., Suite 500, Washington, DC 20037
Telephone: (202) 857-2500
Clients:
 Acton Corp.
 Erie Islands Resort and Marina
 Nat'l American Corp.
 Westinghouse Community Development Group

CHATAK, Elmer
Secretary-Treasurer, AFL-CIO - Industrial Union Department
815 16th St., N.W., Washington, DC 20006
Telephone: (202) 842-7848

CHATFIELD, William A.
Kindness & Chatfield Associates
1747 Pennsylvania Ave., N.W., Suite 1100, Washington, DC 20006
Telephone: (202) 429-6060
Background: U.S. House of Representatives Floor Staff, 1978-79. Staff of the Deputy Undersecretary for Policy, Department of Defense, 1981-82. Regional Director, Civil Aeronautics Board, 1982-84. Special Assistant to Director, Office of Personnel Management; Assistant to Chairman, Consumer Products Safety Commission; Special Assistant for Congressional Liaison, Department of Interior; Staff Advisor to Commissioner, Interstate Commerce Commission, 1985-87.

CHAVKIN, David F.
Senior Prog. Assoc., Public Pol & Educa., Nat'l Center for Clinical Infant Programs
733 15th St., N.W., Suite 912, Washington, DC 20005
Telephone: (202) 347-0308
Registered as lobbyist at U.S. Congress.

CHEATHAM, John H., III
Sr. V. Pres., Gen. Counsel and Secretary, Interstate Natural Gas Ass'n of America
555 13th St., N.W. Suite 300 West, Washington, DC 20004
Telephone: (202) 626-3200

CHEEK, Leslie, III
Senior V. President, Federal Affairs, Crum and Forster Corp.
1025 Connecticut Ave., N.W. Suite 414, Washington, DC 20036
Telephone: (202) 296-5850
Registered as lobbyist at U.S. Congress.

CHEEK, Leslye
Communications Associate, Nat'l Urban League
1114 14th St., N.W., 6th Floor, Washington, DC 20005
Telephone: (202) 898-1604

CHEEK, Marilyn
Manager, Public Affairs, American Insurance Ass'n
1130 Connecticut Ave., N.W., Suite 1000, Washington, DC 20036
Telephone: (202) 828-7100

CHEEK, Warren L.
Secretary, Nat'l Rifle Ass'n of America
1600 Rhode Island Ave., N.W., Washington, DC 20036
Telephone: (202) 828-6000

CHENEY, Carolyn
V. President, Robinson, Lake, Lerer & Montgomery
1667 K St., N.W., Suite 900, Washington, DC 20006
Telephone: (202) 457-9270
Clients:
 Staley Manufacturing Co., A. E.

CHERKASKY, William B.
President, Internat'l Franchise Ass'n
1350 New York Ave., N.W. Suite 900, Washington, DC 20005
Telephone: (202) 628-8000
Registered as lobbyist at U.S. Congress.
Background: Former Exec. Director of the U.S. Senate Select Committee on Small Business.

CHERNIKOFF AND CO.
1826 Jefferson Place, N.W., Suite 101, Washington, DC 20036
Telephone: (202) 223-9280
Members of firm representing listed organizations:
 Chernikoff, Larry
Clients:
 American Museum of Natural History *(Larry Chernikoff)*
 Corcoran Gallery of Art, The *(Larry Chernikoff)*
 Directors Guild of America *(Larry Chernikoff)*
 Field Museum of Natural History, The *(Larry Chernikoff)*
 Fine Arts Museums of San Francisco *(Larry Chernikoff)*
 Ford's Theater *(Larry Chernikoff)*
 Los Angeles County Museum of Art *(Larry Chernikoff)*
 Los Angeles County Museum of Natural History *(Larry Chernikoff)*
 Meridian House Internat'l *(Larry Chernikoff)*
 Nat'l Learning Center, The *(Larry Chernikoff)*
 Nat'l Museum of Women in the Arts *(Larry Chernikoff)*
 Nat'l Symphony Orchestra, The *(Larry Chernikoff)*
 Phillips Collection, The *(Larry Chernikoff)*
 Shakespeare Theater at the Folger, The *(Larry Chernikoff)*
 Textile Museum *(Larry Chernikoff)*
 The University Museum (University of Pennsylvania) *(Larry Chernikoff)*
 Washington Ballet, The *(Larry Chernikoff)*
 Washington Opera, The *(Larry Chernikoff)*
 Washington Performing Arts Soc., The *(Larry Chernikoff)*

CHERNIKOFF, Larry
Chernikoff and Co.
1826 Jefferson Place, N.W., Suite 101, Washington, DC 20036
Telephone: (202) 223-9280
Clients:
 American Museum of Natural History
 Corcoran Gallery of Art, The
 Directors Guild of America
 Field Museum of Natural History, The
 Fine Arts Museums of San Francisco
 Ford's Theater
 Los Angeles County Museum of Art
 Los Angeles County Museum of Natural History
 Meridian House Internat'l
 Nat'l Learning Center, The
 Nat'l Museum of Women in the Arts
 Nat'l Symphony Orchestra, The
 Phillips Collection, The
 Shakespeare Theater at the Folger, The
 Textile Museum
 The University Museum (University of Pennsylvania)
 Washington Ballet, The
 Washington Opera, The

Washington Performing Arts Soc., The

CHERRY, Barbara F.
Legis Affrs Specialist, NAT'L AERONAUTICS AND SPACE ADMINISTRATION
400 Maryland Ave., S.W., Washington, DC 20546
Telephone: (202) 453-1055

CHERRY, Dicken
Nat'l Center for Municipal Development
1620 Eye St., N.W., Suite 300, Washington, DC 20006
Telephone: (202) 429-0160
Clients:
 Jefferson Parish, Louisiana
 New Orleans, Louisiana, City of

CHERTOFF, Stephen E.
Government Affairs Representative, Electronic Data Systems Corp.
1331 Pennsylvania Ave., N.W., Suite 1300 North, Washington, DC 20004
Telephone: (202) 637-6700

CHESSER, Judy L.
Director, New York City (Washington Office)
555 New Jersey Ave., N.W. Suite 700, Washington, DC 20001
Telephone: (202) 393-3903

CHETTLE, John H.
Freedman, Levy, Kroll and Simonds
1050 Connecticut Ave., N.W., Suite 825, Washington, DC 20036
Telephone: (202) 457-5100
Clients:
 Investors Internat'l
 South Africa, Chamber of Mines of
 Universal Frutrading Cooperative Ltd.

CHIDESTER, Becky
V. President for Client Services, Reese Communications Companies
2111 Wilson Ave., Suite 900, Arlington, VA 22201
Telephone: (703) 528-4400

CHILCOTE, Samuel D., Jr.
President, Tobacco Institute
1875 Eye St., N.W., Suite 800, Washington, DC 20006
Telephone: (202) 457-4810
Registered as lobbyist at U.S. Congress.

CHILCOTT, Thomas E.
Federal Gov't Affairs V. President, AT&T
Suite 1000, 1120 20th St., N.W., Washington, DC 20036
Telephone: (202) 457-0839
Registered as lobbyist at U.S. Congress.
Background: Serves as Administrator, AT&T PAC.

CHIMES, Marc
V. President, Nordlinger Associates
1620 Eye St., N.W. 7th Floor, Washington, DC 20006
Telephone: (202) 785-0440

CHIODO, Ronald A.
Director, Legislative Liaison, United Technologies Corp.
1825 Eye St., N.W. Suite 700, Washington, DC 20006
Telephone: (202) 785-7400

CHIPLEY, Ann
Director of Program and Policy, American Ass'n of University Women
2401 Virginia Ave., N.W., Washington, DC 20037
Telephone: (202) 785-7700

CHIRCOP, Jeanne N.
Mgr., Communications, Consumer Group, Electronic Industries Ass'n
2001 Pennsylvania Ave., N.W., Washington, DC 20006
Telephone: (202) 457-4900

CHIRON, Stuart
Senior Attorney, Sprint International
12490 Sunrise Valley Drive, Reston, VA 22096
Telephone: (703) 689-7103

CHISHOLM, Phillip R.
Exec. V. President, Petroleum Marketers Ass'n of America
1120 Vermont Ave., N.W., Suite 1130, Washington, DC 20005
Telephone: (202) 331-1198

The listings in this directory are available as *Mailing Labels*. See last page.

79

CHISHOLM, Phillip R. (Cont'd)
Registered as lobbyist at U.S. Congress.
Background: Responsibilities include Petroleum Marketers
Ass'n of America Small Businessmen's Committee.

CHO, Don Young
Director, Korea Trade Center
1129 20th St. N.W. 4th Floor, Washington, DC 20036
Telephone: (202) 857-7919

CHO, Nam Hong
President, Korea Foreign Trade Ass'n
1800 K St., N.W.,, Washington, DC 20006
Telephone: (202) 408-0100
Registered as Foreign Agent: (#3636)

CHOAT, Darrel
Keene, Shirley & Associates, Inc.
919 Prince St., Alexandria, VA 22314
Telephone: (703) 684-0550
Registered as lobbyist at U.S. Congress.
Clients:
  Australian Barley Board
  The Limited, Inc.

CHOATE, Pat
V. President, Policy Analysis, TRW Inc.
Suite 2700, 1000 Wilson Blvd., Arlington, VA 22209
Telephone: (703) 276-5060
Background: Serves as Chairman, Congressional Economic
Leadership Institute.

CHOMSKI, Joseph M.
Birch, Horton, Bittner and Cherot
1155 Connecticut Ave., N.W., Suite 1200, Washington, DC
20036
Telephone: (202) 659-5800
Registered as lobbyist at U.S. Congress.
Clients:
  Alaska Pacific Refining, Inc.
  Alaska Teamster-Employer Pension Trust
  Chugach Alaska Corp.
  Cooney Enterprises, Gerry
  Grand Targhee Ski Resort
  Kodiak Island Borough
  Old Harbor Corp.
  Sealaska Corp.
  Security Pacific Bank of Alaska
  St. George, Alaska, City of
  St. George Tanaq Corp.
  Stebbins-Ambler Air Transport
  Tanadgusix Corp.
  U.S. Central, Inc.

CHOPKO, Mark E.
General Counsel, United States Catholic Conference
3200 4th St., N.E., Washington, DC 20017
Telephone: (202) 541-3000
Background: Also represents the Nat'l Conference of Cath-
olic Bishops.

CHOPPIN, Purnell W.
President, Howard Hughes Medical Institute
6701 Rockledge Drive, Bethesda, MD 20817
Telephone: (301) 571-0305

CHRISS, Richard
Dir., Cong. Rels., PACs & Fiscal Affrs., Associated Gener-
al Contractors of America
1957 E St., N.W., Washington, DC 20006
Telephone: (202) 393-2040
Registered as lobbyist at U.S. Congress.

CHRIST-ERWIN, Mary
V. President, Edelman, Inc., Daniel J.
1420 K St., N.W., Washington, DC 20005
Telephone: (202) 371-0200

CHRISTENSEN, Karen
Assistant General Counsel, Nat'l Public Radio
2025 M St., N.W., Washington, DC 20036
Telephone: (202) 822-2000

CHRISTENSEN, Ronald R.
Exec. Director, Ass'n of Official Analytical Chemists
2200 Wilson Blvd. Suite 400, Arlington, VA 22201-3301
Telephone: (703) 522-3032

CHRISTENSON, Linda E.
Counsel, Kilpatrick & Cody
2501 M St., N.W., Suite 500, Washington, DC 20037
Telephone: (202) 463-2500
Registered as lobbyist at U.S. Congress.
Clients:
  Coors Brewing Company

CHRISTIAN, Betty Jo
Steptoe and Johnson
1330 Connecticut Ave., N.W., Washington, DC 20036
Telephone: (202) 429-3000
Background: Attorney, Interstate Commerce Commission,
1961-68. Associate General Counsel, Interstate Com-
merce Commission, 1971-76. Commissioner, 1976-79 and
Vice Chairman, 1976-78.
Clients:
  Burlington Northern Railroad

CHRISTIAN, Claudette M.
Arent, Fox, Kintner, Plotkin & Kahn
1050 Connecticut Ave., N.W., Washington, DC 20036-
5339
Telephone: (202) 857-6000
Registered as Foreign Agent: (#2661). ·

CHRISTIAN, Cliff
Nat'l Field Director, Nat'l Tax Limitation Committee
201 Massachusetts Ave., N.E., Suite C-7, Washington,
DC 20002
Telephone: (202) 547-4196

CHRISTIAN, Ernest S., Jr.
Patton, Boggs and Blow
2550 M St., N.W., Suite 800, Washington, DC 20037
Telephone: (202) 457-6000
Registered as lobbyist at U.S. Congress.
Registered as Foreign Agent: (#2165).
Background: Tax Legislative Counsel, U.S. Treasury De-
partment, 1973-74. Deputy Assistant Secretary of Treas-
ury for Tax Policy, 1974-75.
Clients:
  Air Products and Chemicals, Inc.
  American Ass'n of Equipment Lessors
  Cherokee Nation Industries, Inc.
  Nat'l Intergroup, Inc.

CHRISTIAN, James B., Jr.
Patton, Boggs and Blow
2550 M St., N.W., Suite 800, Washington, DC 20037
Telephone: (202) 457-6000
Registered as lobbyist at U.S. Congress.
Registered as Foreign Agent: (#2165).
Background: Legislative Counsel and Professional Staff
Member, Senate Appropriations Committee, 1975-77.
Clients:
  Alaska Crab Coalition
  Bethlehem Steel Corp.
  College Savings Bank
  Flexi-Van Leasing
  Fundacion Pro-Imagen de Colombia en el Exteri-
    or
  Gana-A' Yoo, Ltd.
  Itel Containers Internat'l Corp.
  Magnuson Act Coalition
  Nat'l Marine Manufacturers Ass'n
  NCNB Texas Nat'l Bank
  Olympic Fibers
  Royal Trustco Ltd.
  Save Chanute Committee
  Smokeless Tobacco Council
  Speciality Seafoods
  Standard Federal Savings Bank
  Trans Ocean Ltd.
  Transamerica Leasing, Inc.
  Triton Container Co.
  Wayne County, Michigan
  XTRA Corp.

CHRISTIAN, James M., Sr.
Laxalt, Washington, Perito & Dubuc
1120 Connecticut Ave., N.W., Suite 1000, Washington, DC
20036
Telephone: (202) 857-4000
Registered as lobbyist at U.S. Congress.
Background: Deputy Minority Counsel, House Committee
on the District of Columbia, 1973-75. Chief Counsel, Urban Mass Transportation Administration, U.S. Department of Transportation.
Clients:

Inglewood, California, City of
Oakland, California, City of
Tobacco Institute
Washington, DC, City of

CHRISTIAN, James W.
Sr. V. President & Chief Economist, United States League
of Savings Institutions
1709 New York Ave., N.W., Suite 801, Washington, DC
20006
Telephone: (202) 637-8900

CHRISTIE, Michael R.
Director for North America, South Africa Foundation
1225 19th St., N.W. Suite 700, Washington, DC 20036
Telephone: (202) 223-5486

CHRISTINE, Samuel W., III
Manager, Legislative Bureau, Greater Washington Board
of Trade
1129 20th St., N.W., Washington, DC 20036
Telephone: (202) 857-5910
Registered as lobbyist at U.S. Congress.

CHRISTOPHER, Warren
O'Melveny and Myers
555 13th St., N.W., Suite 500 West, Washington, DC
20004
Telephone: (202) 383-5300
Background: Law Clerk to Mr. Justice Douglas, U.S. Su-
preme Court, 1949-50. Deputy Attorney General of the
U.S., 1967-69. Deputy Secretary of State, 1977-81.
Clients:
  Southern California Edison Co.

CHRISTY, Betty
Asst. Staff V. President, Public Affairs, Nat'l Ass'n of
Home Builders of the U.S.
15th and M Streets, N.W., Washington, DC 20005
Telephone: (202) 822-0470

CHRISTY, James T.
Director, Federal Government Relations, Air Products and
Chemicals, Inc.
805 15th St., N.W. Southern Bldg., Washington, DC 20006
Telephone: (202) 289-4110
Registered as lobbyist at U.S. Congress.
Background: Administrative Ass't to Rep. Thomas Kind-
ness (R-OH) (1975-76); Minority Counsel, Subcommittee
on Oversight and Investigations, Committee on Energy
and Commerce, U.S. House of Representatives (1981-84);
Legislative Counsel, U.S. Dept. of the Interior (1984-85).

CHUNG, Sung K
Manager, Korea Foreign Trade Ass'n
1800 K St., N.W.,, Washington, DC 20006
Telephone: (202) 408-0100
Registered as Foreign Agent: (#3636)

CHURBA, Dr. Joseph
President, Internat'l Security Council
818 Connecticut Ave., N.W. Suite 600, Washington, DC
20006
Telephone: (202) 828-0802

CHURCH, Elaine K.
Principal, Employee Benefits Svcs., Price Waterhouse
1801 K St., N.W., Suite 700, Washington, DC 20006
Telephone: (202) 296-0800
Registered as lobbyist at U.S. Congress.

CHVOTKIN, Alan L.
Senior Corporate Attorney, Sundstrand Corp.
1000 Wilson Blvd., Suite 2400, Arlington, VA 22209
Telephone: (703) 276-1626
Registered as lobbyist at U.S. Congress.

CHWAT, John S.
Chwat/Weigend Associates
400 First St., N.W. Suite 100, Washington, DC 20001
Telephone: (202) 638-6400
Registered as lobbyist at U.S. Congress.
Registered as Foreign Agent: (#4320).
Background: Former Legislative Assistant to Rep. Sy Halpern of New York, 1971-73. Member, Senate Labor and
Public Welfare Committee Staff, 1973. U.S. Department
of Agriculture, Congressional Relations, 1973-74. Congressional Research Service, Library of Congress, 1974-
76. Administrative Assistant to Rep. John Breckenridge
of Kentucky, 1976-78. Administrative Assistant to Rep.

Bill Boner of Tennessee, 1978-80.
Clients:
American Home Sewing Ass'n
American Radio Relay League
Associated Locksmiths of America
Cheese Importers Ass'n of America
Lockwood Trade Journal
Nat'l Exchange Carriers Ass'n
Nat'l Licensed Beverage Ass'n
Nat'l Weather Service Employees Organization

CHWAT/WEIGEND ASSOCIATES
400 First St., N.W. Suite 100, Washington, DC 20001
Telephone: (202) 638-6400
Registered as Foreign Agent: (#4320)
Background: A lobbying firm founded in 1981 specializing in government and public relations services in Washington, D.C. for corporations, trade associations, professional organizations, industries, small businesses and individuals.
Members of firm representing listed organizations:
Chwat, John S.
Background: Former Legislative Assistant to Rep. Sy Halpern of New York, 1971-73. Member, Senate Labor and Public Welfare Committee Staff, 1973. U.S. Department of Agriculture, Congressional Relations, 1973-74. Congressional Research Service, Library of Congress, 1974-76. Administrative Assistant to Rep. John Breckenridge of Kentucky, 1976-78. Administrative Assistant to Rep. Bill Boner of Tennessee, 1978-80.
Weigend, Robert E.
Clients:
American Home Sewing Ass'n *(John S. Chwat, Robert E. Weigend)*
American Radio Relay League *(John S. Chwat, Robert E. Weigend)*
Associated Locksmiths of America *(John S. Chwat, Robert E. Weigend)*
Cheese Importers Ass'n of America *(John S. Chwat)*
Lockwood Trade Journal *(John S. Chwat, Robert E. Weigend)*
Nat'l Exchange Carriers Ass'n *(John S. Chwat, Robert E. Weigend)*
Nat'l Licensed Beverage Ass'n *(John S. Chwat, Robert E. Weigend)*
Nat'l Weather Service Employees Organization *(John S. Chwat, Robert E. Weigend)*
Nat'l Weather Service Employees Organization Political Action Committee *(Robert E. Weigend)*

CIARAVELLA, Jo Ann
McAuliffe, Kelly, Raffaelli & Siemens
1341 G St., N.W. Suite 200, Washington, DC 20005
Telephone: (202) 783-1800
Background: Former Staff Director, House Commission on Congressional Mailing Standards.

CICALA, Jane H.
Director, Boeing Commercial Airplane Co., Boeing Co.
1700 North Moore St., Arlington, VA 22209
Telephone: (703) 558-9650

CICCO, Dr. Robert
Legislative Chairperson, Nat'l Perinatal Ass'n
101 1/2 South Union St., Alexandria, VA 22314-3323
Telephone: (703) 549-5523
Background: Serves also as President, Alliance for Perinatal Research and Services.

CIOCCI, Linda Church
Legislative Representative, American Public Power Ass'n
2301 M St., N.W., Washington, DC 20037
Telephone: (202) 775-8300
Registered as lobbyist at U.S. Congress.

CIORLETTI, Julia
Keyman Coordinator, College of American Pathologists
1101 Vermont Ave., N.W., Washington, DC 20005
Telephone: (202) 371-6617

CISZEK, Dr. Raymond
Exec. Director, Ass'n for Research, Administration, Professional Councils and Societies
1900 Association Drive, Reston, VA 22091
Telephone: (703) 476-3430
Background: Serves also as Staff Liaison for The Safety Society.

CIVIC SERVICE, INC.
1050 Connecticut Ave., N.W., Suite 870, Washington, DC 20036
Telephone: (202) 785-2070
Registered as Foreign Agent: (#3385)
Members of firm representing listed organizations:
Pfautch, Roy, President
Clients:
Internat'l Public Relations Co. *(Roy Pfautch)*
Mitsubishi Trust and Banking Corp. *(Roy Pfautch)*
Nippon Telephone and Telegraph Corp. *(Roy Pfautch)*
PR Service Co., Ltd. *(Roy Pfautch)*
Sanwa Bank Ltd.

CIVILETTI, Benjamin R.
Venable, Baetjer, Howard and Civiletti
1201 New York Ave., N.W., Suite 1000, Washington, DC 20005
Telephone: (202) 962-4800
Registered as lobbyist at U.S. Congress.
Background: Deputy Attorney General and Attorney General in the Administration of President Jimmy Carter.
Clients:
Associated Builders and Contractors

CIZIK, Richard C.
Policy Analyst, Nat'l Ass'n of Evangelicals
1023 15th St., N.W., Suite 500, Washington, DC 20005
Telephone: (202) 789-1011

CLADOUHOS, Harry W.
Pettit & Martin
1800 Massachusetts Ave., N.W., Washington, DC 20036
Telephone: (202) 785-5153
Registered as lobbyist at U.S. Congress.
Registered as Foreign Agent: (#3815).
Background: Legal Assistant, Office of Commissioner, Federal Communications Commission, 1954-55. Foreign Service Officer, Secretary in the Diplomatic Service and Vice Consul, Department of State, 1955-57. Senior Trial Attorney, Trial Section, Antitrust Division, Department of Justice, 1957-69.
Clients:
Suzuki Motors Co., Ltd.
United States Suzuki Motor Corp.

CLAGETT, Brice M.
Covington and Burling
1201 Pennsylvania Ave., N.W., Box 7566, Washington, DC 20044
Telephone: (202) 662-6000

CLAPP, Archie J.
Exec. V. President, Wholesale Florists and Florist Suppliers of America
5313 Lee Highway, Arlington, VA 22207
Telephone: (703) 241-1100

CLAPP, Philip E.
Nat'l Strategies Inc.
818 17th St., N.W., Washington, DC 20006
Telephone: (202) 429-8744
Background: Former Legislative Director to Congressman Timothy Wirth and Associate Staff Member, House Committee on the Budget.

CLARK & ASSOCIATES, Vern
1730 M St., N.W. Suite 911, Washington, DC 20036
Telephone: (202) 737-1123
Members of firm representing listed organizations:
Clark, Vernon, President
Thompson, Michael A., Legislative Assistant
Organizations represented:
Metromedia Co. *(Vernon Clark)*
RJR Nabisco Washington, Inc. *(Vernon Clark)*
Vern Clark & Associates, Inc. PAC *(Michael A. Thompson)*

CLARK, Bob
Director, Federal Affairs, Ryder System, Inc.
400 Madison St., Suite 1908, Alexandria, VA 22314
Telephone: (703) 549-4416
Registered as lobbyist at U.S. Congress.

CLARK, Dana
Legis Officer, Cong & Intergovt'l Affrs, DEPARTMENT OF LABOR
200 Constitution Ave., N.W., Washington, DC 20210

Telephone: (202) 523-6141

CLARK, Donald J.
Exec. Director, American Academy of Otolaryngic Allergy
8455 Colesville Road Suite 745, Silver Spring, MD 20910-9998
Telephone: (301) 588-1800

CLARK, Fred D., Jr.
Legislative Representative - Agriculture, Nat'l Rural Electric Cooperative Ass'n
1800 Massachusetts Ave., N.W., Washington, DC
Telephone: (202) 857-4880
Registered as lobbyist at U.S. Congress.

CLARK, Gilbert M.
Exec. Director, American Ass'n of Blood Banks
1117 North 19th St. Suite 600, Arlington, VA 22209
Telephone: (703) 528-8200
Registered as lobbyist at U.S. Congress.
Background: Legal Assistant to Senator Robert P. Griffin (Michigan), 1975-1977.

CLARK, Howard
Director, Nat'l Insurance Consumer Organization
121 North Payne St., Alexandria, VA 22314
Telephone: (703) 549-8050

CLARK, Julia Penny
Bredhoff and Kaiser
1000 Connecticut Ave., N.W. Suite 1300, Washington, DC 20036
Telephone: (202) 833-9340
Clients:
Bakery, Confectionery and Tobacco Workers Internat'l Union

CLARK, Julie
Director, Government Relations, Nat'l Legal Aid and Defender Ass'n
1625 K St., N.W., Washington, DC 20006
Telephone: (202) 452-0620
Registered as lobbyist at U.S. Congress.

CLARK, Kathleen B.
Legislative Representative, Collier, Shannon & Scott
1055 Thomas Jefferson St., N.W., Suite 300, Washington, DC 20007
Telephone: (202) 342-8400
Registered as lobbyist at U.S. Congress.
Registered as Foreign Agent: (#3694).

CLARK, Linda
Public Relations Manager, Washington Times Corp., The
3600 New York Ave., N.E., Washington, DC 20002
Telephone: (202) 636-4858

CLARK, Louis
Exec. Director, Government Accountability Project (GAP)
25 E St., N.W. Suite 700, Washington, DC 20001
Telephone: (202) 347-0460

CLARK, Lynn C.
Deputy Director, District of Columbia Chamber of Commerce
1411 K St., N.W., Suite 500, Washington, DC 20005
Telephone: (202) 347-7202
Registered as lobbyist at U.S. Congress.

CLARK, Michael S.
President, Friends of the Earth
218 D St., S.E., Washington, DC 20003
Telephone: (202) 544-2600
Registered as lobbyist at U.S. Congress.

CLARK, Penelope
Account Executive, Edelman, Inc., Daniel J.
1420 K St., N.W., Washington, DC 20005
Telephone: (202) 371-0200

CLARK, Rudy I.
Director, Military & Gov't Relations, Air Force Sergeants Ass'n
P.O. Box 50, Temple Hills, MD 20748
Telephone: (301) 899-3500
Registered as lobbyist at U.S. Congress.

CLARK, Vernon
President, Clark & Associates, Vern
1730 M St., N.W. Suite 911, Washington, DC 20036

CLARK, Vernon (Cont'd)
Telephone: (202) 737-1123
Registered as lobbyist at U.S. Congress.
Organizations represented:
Metromedia Co.
RJR Nabisco Washington, Inc.

CLARKE, Denise
Dep Dir, Info & Legis Affrs Staff, DEPARTMENT OF AG-
RICULTURE - Food Safety and Inspection.Service
14th and Independence Ave. S.W., Washington, DC 20250
Telephone: (202) 447-7943

CLARKE, Gail
Acting Chief Exec. Officer, Nat'l Soc. of Fund Raising Executives
1101 King St., Suite 3000, Alexandria, VA 22314
Telephone: (703) 684-0410

CLARKE, Jan
Legislative Analyst, American Maritime Congress
444 N. Capitol St., N.W., Suite 801, Washington, DC
20001
Telephone: (202) 877-4477
Registered as lobbyist at U.S. Congress.

CLARKE, John, Jr.
Highsaw, Mahoney & Clarke
Suite 210, 1050 17th St., N.W., Washington, DC 20036
Telephone: (202) 296-8500

CLARKE, Capt. Sandy
Weapons Syst & Current Opns, Legis Affrs, DEPART-
MENT OF DEFENSE
The Pentagon, Washington, DC 20301
Telephone: (202) 697-6210

CLARKSON, John J.
Exec. Director, American Ass'n for Dental Research
1111 14th St., N.W. Suite 1000, Washington, DC 20005
Telephone: (202) 898-1050
Background: Becomes Exec. Director June 1, 1990.

CLARY, Sara
Senior Washington Representative, Alliance of American
Insurers
1629 K St., N.W. Suite 1010, Washington, DC 20006
Telephone: (202) 822-8811
Registered as lobbyist at U.S. Congress.

CLAWSON, James B.
Executive V. President, Internat'l Business-Government
Counsellors, Inc.
818 Connecticut Ave., N.W. Suite 1200, Washington, DC
20006
Telephone: (202) 872-8181
Clients:
Uniroyal Chemical Co., Inc.

CLAWSON, Cdr. Steve
Public Affrs, Legis Affairs, DEPARTMENT OF NAVY
The Pentagon, Washington, DC 20350-1300
Telephone: (202) 697-7146

CLAXTON, David F.
Director, Political Affairs, United Food and Commercial
Workers Internat'l Union
1775 K St., N.W., Washington, DC 20006
Telephone: (202) 223-3111

CLAYBROOK, Joan B.
President, Public Citizen
2000 P St., N.W., Suite 610, Washington, DC 20036
Telephone: (202) 293-9142
Registered as lobbyist at U.S. Congress.

CLAYTON, Gary
Senior Analyst, American Ass'n of Retired Persons
1909 K St., N.W., Washington, DC 20049
Telephone: (202) 872-4700

CLAYTON, Warren
Exec. Director, Foundation, Future Homemakers of America
1910 Association Drive, Reston, VA 22091
Telephone: (703) 476-4900

CLEARY, GOTTLIEB, STEEN AND HAMILTON
1752 N St., N.W., Washington, DC 20036
Telephone: (202) 728-2700

Registered as Foreign Agent: (#0508)
Background: Washington office of a multi-city law firm.
Members of firm representing listed organizations:
Bachman, Kenneth L. (Jr.)
Barnard, Robert C., Counsel
Background: Attorney, Antitrust Division, U.S. Depart-
ment of Justice, 1939-41. Attorney, 1941-47 and
First Assistant, 1945-47, Office of the Assistant So-
licitor General, U.S. Department of Justice.
Duncan, R. Michael
Background: Trial Attorney, Tax Division, Department
of Justice, 1958-62.
Hinds, Richard deC.
Kliever, Douglas E.
Marans, J. Eugene
Morgan, Donald L.
Plog, Henry J. (Jr.)
Schotland, Sara D.
Silver, Daniel B.
Background: General Counsel, National Security Agen-
cy, 1978-79; Central Intelligence Agency, 1979-81.
Clients:
American Cyanamid Co. *(Donald L. Morgan)*
Colonial Sugar Refineries, Ltd.
Columbia Savings and Loan Ass'n *(Kenneth L. Bach-
man, Jr.)*
Day-Glo Color Corp. *(Richard deC. Hinds)*
Electricity Consumers Resource Council *(Sara D.
Schotland)*
Guggenheim Foundation, The Harry Frank *(J. Eu-
gene Marans)*
La Metalli Industriale S.p.A. *(Richard deC. Hinds,
Daniel B. Silver)*
Mexico, Ministry of Finance and Public Credit
(Douglas E. Kliever)
Petroleos de Venezuela, S.A.
Security Pacific Nat'l Bank *(J. Eugene Marans)*
UNOCAL Corp. *(Henry J. Plog, Jr.)*

CLEARY, John M.
Donelan, Cleary, Wood and Maser, P.C.
1275 K St., N.W., Suite 850, Washington, DC 20005
Telephone: (202) 371-9500
Clients:
Southwestern Electric Power Co.

CLEMENT, John R.B.
Chairman Government Activities, American Federation of
Information Processing Societies
1899 Preston White Drive, Reston, VA 22091-4366
Telephone: (703) 620-8900
Background: Also represents: American Soc. for Informa-
tion Science, American Statistical Ass'n, Ass'n for Com-
putational Linguistics, Ass'n for Computing Machinery,
Data Processing Management Ass'n, Institute of Electri-
cal & Electronics Engineers Computer Soc., Instrument
Soc. of America, Soc. for Computer Simulation, Soc. for
Industrial Applied Mathematics and Soc. for Information
Display, and Internat'l Ass'n for Computing in Education.

CLEMENTS, Jack
President, Mutual Broadcasting System
1755 South Jefferson Davis Hwy., Suite 1200, Arlington,
VA 22202
Telephone: (703) 685-2000

CLIFFORD, Clark M.
Clifford & Warnke
815 Connecticut Ave., N.W., Washington, DC 20006
Telephone: (202) 828-4200
Registered as Foreign Agent: (#2564).
Background: Special Counsel to the President of the Unit-
ed States, 1946-1950. Secretary of Defense, 1968-1969.
Member, Board of Directors, Knight-Ridder Newspapers.

CLIFFORD & WARNKE
815 Connecticut Ave., N.W., Washington, DC 20006
Telephone: (202) 828-4200
Members of firm representing listed organizations:
Altman, Robert A.
Calender, John G.
Clifford, Clark M.
Background: Special Counsel to the President of the
United States, 1946-1950. Secretary of Defense,
1968-1969. Member, Board of Directors, Knight-Rid-
der Newspapers.
Granger, David I.
Background: Attorney, Tax Division, U.S. Department
of Justice, 1961-1965.

Hecht, Philip H.
Kovin, John F.
Lesher, J. Griffin
Murry, Harold D. (Jr.)
Background: Attorney, U.S. Department of Justice,
1971-74. Special Assistant U.S. Attorney, 1972.
Reznick, Robert P.
Warnke, Paul C.
Background: General Counsel, Department of Defense,
1966-67. Assistant Secretary of Defense, Interna-
tional Security Affairs, 1967-69. Director, Arms Con-
trol and Disarmament Agency and Chief U.S. Strate-
gic Arms Negotiator, 1977-78.
Yolles, Bryan Jay
Background: Trial Attorney, Civil Aeronautics Board,
1977-79.
Clients:
Australian Meat and Livestock Corp.
Keene Corp.
Knight-Ridder Newspapers
Nonprescription Drug Manfacturers Ass'n *(Robert
A. Altman)*

CLINE, William R.
Senior Fellow, Institute for Internat'l Economics
11 Dupont Circle, N.W., Washington, DC 20036
Telephone: (202) 328-0583

CLINKENBEARD, Kirk L.
Secretary-Treasurer, C & C Consulting Group, Inc.
210 Cameron St., Alexandria, VA 22314
Telephone: (703) 548-1992

CLODIUS, Robert L.
President, Nat'l Ass'n of State Universities and Land-
Grant Colleges
One Dupont Circle, N.W., Suite 710, Washington, DC
20036-1191
Telephone: (202) 778-0818

CLOHAN & DEAN
1101 Vermont Ave., N.W. Suite 400, Washington, DC
20005
Telephone: (202) 289-3900
Members of firm representing listed organizations:
Blakey, William A.
Background: Aide to Senator Paul Simon (D-IL),
1981-87. Staff Director, Senate Subcommittee on
Employment and Productivity, 1987-89.
Clohan, William C. (Jr.)
Background: Former Undersecretary, U.S. Department
of Education. Former Republican Education Counsel,
Education and Labor Committee, U.S. House of Rep-
resentatives. Serves as General Counsel, Ass'n of In-
dependent Colleges and Schools.
Dean, John E.
Background: Assistant Counsel, House Committee on
Education and Labor, 1983-85.
Clients:
Ass'n of Independent Colleges and Schools *(Wil-
liam C. Clohan, Jr.)*
Ass'n of Independent Colleges and Schools Poli-
tical Action Committee
Coalition of Higher Education Assistance Organi-
zations *(John E. Dean)*
Miles College *(William A. Blakey)*
Nat'l Council of Educational Opportunity Ass'ns
(William A. Blakey)
Student Loan Funding Corp. of Ohio *(John E. Dean)*
United Negro College Fund *(William A. Blakey)*

CLOHAN, William C., Jr.
Clohan & Dean
1101 Vermont Ave., N.W. Suite 400, Washington, DC
20005
Telephone: (202) 289-3900
Background: Former Undersecretary, U.S. Department of
Education. Former Republican Education Counsel, Edu-
cation and Labor Committee, U.S. House of Representa-
tives. Serves as General Counsel, Ass'n of Independent
Colleges and Schools.
Clients:
Ass'n of Independent Colleges and Schools

CLOHERTY, William M.
Senior Associate, Cassidy and Associates, Inc.
655 15th St., N.W., Suite 1100, Washington, DC 20005
Telephone: (202) 347-0773
Registered as lobbyist at U.S. Congress.
Background: Office of U.S. Trade Representative, 1979.

WASHINGTON REPRESENTATIVES

Clients:
American Hospital in Shanghai Foundation
Critical Languages Consortium
Fudan Foundation
Schutz American School
Tread Corp.
World Trade Center Boston

CLONEY, Gordon J.
President, Internat'l Insurance Council
1212 New York Ave., N.W. Suite 205, Washington, DC 20005
Telephone: (202) 682-2345

CLOUD, Deborah A.
Manager of Public Relations, American Ass'n of Homes for the Aging
1129 20th St., N.W., Suite 400, Washington, DC 20036
Telephone: (202) 296-5960

CLOUD, Pilar M.
Director of Operations, BSA - Business Software Alliance
1201 Pennsylvania Ave., N.W. Suite 250, Washington, DC 20004
Telephone: (202) 737-7060
Registered as lobbyist at U.S. Congress.

CLOUD, Stephen J.
Legislative Research Manager, American Petroleum Institute
1220 L St., N.W., Washington, DC 20005
Telephone: (202) 682-8413
Registered as lobbyist at U.S. Congress.

CLOUGH, Guy
Director, Federal Legislation, Air Transport Ass'n of America
1709 New York Ave., N.W., Washington, DC 20006-5206
Telephone: (202) 626-4000
Registered as lobbyist at U.S. Congress.
Background: Former Legislative Ass't to Sen. Nancy Kassebaum (R-KN).

CLOW, Byron B.
Exec. V. President, Internat'l Magnesium Ass'n
2010 Corporate Ridge Suite 700, McLean, VA 22102
Telephone: (703) 442-8888

CLOWER, W. Dewey
President, Nat'l Ass'n of Truck Stop Operators
1199 N. Fairfax St. Suite 801, Alexandria, VA 22314
Telephone: (703) 549-2100
Registered as lobbyist at U.S. Congress.

CLUBB, Bruce E.
Baker and McKenzie
815 Connecticut Ave., N.W. Suite 1100, Washington, DC 20006-4078
Telephone: (202) 452-7000
Background: Attorney Advisor, Development Loan Fund and Agency for Internat'l Development, 1961-1962. Commissioner, U.S. Tariff Commission, 1967-1971.
Clients:
Clark Equipment Co.
Cold Spring Granite Co.

CLUFF, Dr. Anthony
Exec. Director, Ass'n of Reserve City Bankers
1710 Rhode Island Ave., N.W. Suite 500, Washington, DC 20036
Telephone: (202) 296-5709

CLYBURN, Gay
Director of Public Affairs, American Ass'n of State Colleges and Universities
One Dupont Circle, N.W. Suite 700, Washington, DC 20036
Telephone: (202) 293-7070

CM SERVICES, INC.
1655 North Ft. Myer Drive Suite 700, Arlington, VA 22209
Telephone: (703) 522-2176
Members of firm representing listed organizations:
Martin, David F., Director of Government Affairs
Background: Serves as Director, Government Affairs, Plumbing Manufacturers Institute.
Clients:
Plumbing Manufacturers Institute *(David F. Martin)*

CMF&Z PUBLIC RELATIONS
655 15th St., N.W., Suite 300, Washington, DC 20005
Telephone: (202) 639-4059
Members of firm representing listed organizations:
Hoffer, Audrey S., Senior Account Executive
Neely, Susan K., V. President and General Manager
Background: Former Press Secretary to Rep. Jim Leach (R-IA).

COALITIONS, INC.
505 2nd St., N.E., Washington, DC 20002
Telephone: (202) 675-4050
Members of firm representing listed organizations:
Jones, Roy, President
Clients:
Washington Times Corp., The *(Roy Jones)*

COAN, Carl A. S., Jr.
Coan & Lyons
1625 Eye St., N.W., Suite 1015, Washington, DC 20006
Telephone: (202) 728-1070
Registered as lobbyist at U.S. Congress.
Clients:
Nat'l Assisted Housing Management Ass'n
Trafalgar Capital Associates, Inc.

COAN & LYONS
1625 Eye St., N.W., Suite 1015, Washington, DC 20006
Telephone: (202) 728-1070
Members of firm representing listed organizations:
Coan, Carl A. S. (Jr.)
Murphy, Andrew P. (Jr.), Of Counsel
Clients:
Nat'l Assisted Housing Management Ass'n *(Carl A. S. Coan, Jr.)*
Trafalgar Capital Associates, Inc. *(Carl A. S. Coan, Jr.)*

COATES, Vincent J., Jr.
Brown, Coates and McCarthy
1825 K St., N.W., Suite 807, Washington, DC 20006
Telephone: (202) 293-4761
Registered as lobbyist at U.S. Congress.
Clients:
Avco Research Lab, Inc.

COATS, Dr. Betty A.
Presiding Bishop's Staff Officer, Episcopal Church, Washington Office of the
110 Maryland Ave., N.E. Suite 309, Washington, DC 20002
Telephone: (202) 547-7300

COATS, Judith D.
Director, Rural Coalition
2001 S St., N.W., Suite 500, Washington, DC 20009
Telephone: (202) 483-1500

COBB, Alan J.
V. Pres., Legislative & Political Affrs., Petroleum Marketers Ass'n of America
1120 Vermont Ave., N.W., Suite 1130, Washington, DC 20005
Telephone: (202) 331-1198
Registered as lobbyist at U.S. Congress.

COBB, Calvin H., Jr.
Nat'l President, Navy League of the United States
2300 Wilson Blvd., Arlington, VA 22201
Telephone: (703) 528-1775

COBB, William B., Jr.
Exec. Director, Diplomatic and Consular Officers, Retired (Dacor)
1801 F St., N.W., Washington, DC 20006
Telephone: (202) 682-0500

COBERT, Ronald N.
Grove, Jaskiewicz, Gilliam and Cobert
1730 M St., N.W. Suite 501, Washington, DC 20036
Telephone: (202) 296-2900
Background: General Counsel, American Institute for Shippers' Ass'ns.
Clients:
American Institute for Shippers' Ass'ns

COBLE, Karen
Director of Washington Communications, Nat'l Pork Producers Council
501 School St., N.W. Suite 400, Washington, DC 20024
Telephone: (202) 552-3600

COBURN, Lucy
Director, Legislative Communications, Nat'l Ass'n of Life Underwriters
1922 F St., N.W., Washington, DC 20006
Telephone: (202) 331-6000

COCCHI, Raymond
V. Pres., Congressional & State Liaison, Nat'l Ass'n of Securities Dealers (NASDAQ)
1735 K St., N.W., Washington, DC 20006
Telephone: (202) 728-8000

COCHRAN, J. Thomas
Exec. Director, United States Conference of Mayors
1620 Eye St., N.W., Washington, DC 20006
Telephone: (202) 293-7330

COCHRAN, Thomas B.
Senior Scientist, Natural Resources Defense Council
1350 New York Ave., N.W. Suite 300, Washington, DC 20005
Telephone: (202) 783-7800

CODDING, Fred H.
Exec. Director and General Counsel, Nat'l Ass'n of Reinforcing Steel Contractors
10382 Main St., Suite 200 Box 280, Fairfax, VA 22030
Telephone: (703) 591-1870
Background: Also represents the Nat'l Ass'n of Miscellaneous, Ornamental and Architectural Products Contractors.

COE, JoAnne
President & Exec. Director, Campaign America
511 Capitol Court N. E. Suite 100, Washington, DC 20002
Telephone: (202) 543-5016
Background: Senior Advisor to Sen. Robert Dole (R-KS).

COERPER, Milo C.
Coudert Brothers
1627 Eye St., N.W. 12th Floor, Washington, DC 20006
Telephone: (202) 775-5100
Clients:
Centrale Marketinggesellschaft der Deutschen Agrarwirtschaft
Edelstahlwerke Buderus AG
German Flatware Manufacturers Ass'n
German Specialty Steel Ass'n
Krupp Internat'l
Nippon Electric Co., Ltd.
West German Iron and Steel Federation

COFFEY, Matthew B.
President and Chief Operating Officer, Nat'l Tooling and Machining Ass'n
9300 Livingston Rd., Fort Washington, MD 20744
Telephone: (301) 248-6200

COFFEY, MCGOVERN AND NOEL, LTD.
2445 M St., N.W., Suite 260, Washington, DC 20037
Telephone: (202) 872-8123
Members of firm representing listed organizations:
Falk, James H.
Clients:
Designers & Planners, Inc. *(James H. Falk)*
Support Systems Associates, Inc. *(James H. Falk)*

COFFIELD UNGARETTI HARRIS & SLAVIN
1747 Pennsylvania Ave., N.W. Suite 900, Washington, DC 20006
Telephone: (202) 872-4310
Members of firm representing listed organizations:
Kramer, Andrea S.
Macari, Robert
Menell, Howard
Clients:
COMDISCO, Inc. *(Andrea S. Kramer, Robert Macari, Howard Menell)*

COFFIN, William Sloane
President, SANE/FREEZE
1819 H St., N.W., Suite 1000, Washington, DC 20006
Telephone: (202) 862-9740

The listings in this directory are available as *Mailing Labels.* See last page.

83

WASHINGTON REPRESENTATIVES

COGEN, Ruth P.
Exec. Director, Washington Area Lawyers for the Arts
2025 Eye St., N.W. Suite 1114, Washington, DC 20006
Telephone: (202) 861-0055

COHEN AND ASSOCIATES, Scott
1625 Massachusetts Ave., N.W. Suite 402, Washington, DC 20036
Telephone: (202) 232-6872
Background: A government relations and international public affairs consulting firm. Clients include the InterAction Council of Former Heads of Government and various corporations, scientific groups and international refugee organizations.
Members of firm representing listed organizations:
Cohen, Scott
Background: Former foreign affairs advisor to Senator Charles H. Percy (R-IL) and former Staff Director, Senate Foreign Relations Committee. Supervises and coordinates the work of nine associates who are specialized in such areas as trade, financing, marketing, economics, privatization, technology transfer and maritime affairs.

COHEN, Bob
Director, Communications, ADAPSO, the Computer Software & Services Industry Ass'n
1300 North 17th St. Suite 300, Arlington, VA 22209
Telephone: (703) 522-5055

COHEN, Calman J.
Vice President, Emergency Committee for American Trade
1211 Connecticut Ave., N.W. Suite 801, Washington, DC 20036
Telephone: (202) 659-5147
Background: Former Director of Congressional Affairs, Office of the U.S. Trade Representative.

COHEN, Dan
Legislative Liaison, American Israel Public Affairs Committee
440 First St., N.W. Suite 600, Washington, DC 20001
Telephone: (202) 639-5200
Registered as lobbyist at U.S. Congress.

COHEN, Daniel L.
Director, National Affairs, Ass'n of Trial Lawyers of America
1050 31st St., N.W., Washington, DC 20007
Telephone: (202) 965-3500
Registered as lobbyist at U.S. Congress.

COHEN, David
Co-director, Advocacy Institute, The
1730 Rhode Island Ave., N.W. Suite 600, Washington, DC 20036
Telephone: (202) 659-8475
Registered as lobbyist at U.S. Congress.
Background: President of Professionals' Coalition for Nuclear Arms Control. Former President, Common Cause.

COHEN, David B.
Dir., Small Company and REA Affairs, United States Telephone Ass'n
900 19th St., N.W., Suite 800, Washington, DC 20006-2102
Telephone: (202) 835-3100
Background: Former Chief, Loans Management Branch, Telecommunications Division, Rural Electrification Administration and Acting Chief, Revenue Requirements and Valuations Branch, REA.

COHEN, David S.
Cohen and White
1055 Thomas Jefferson St., Suite 504, Washington, DC 20007
Telephone: (202) 342-2550
Registered as lobbyist at U.S. Congress.
Clients:
Computer and Communications Industry Ass'n

COHEN, Don
President, Volunteers in Overseas Cooperative Assistance
50 F St., N.W., Suite 1075, Washington, DC 20001
Telephone: (202) 626-8750

COHEN, Edward B.
Davis Wright Tremaine
1752 N St., N.W., Suite 800, Washington, DC 20036
Telephone: (202) 822-9775
Registered as lobbyist at U.S. Congress.
Background: Deputy Special Assistant to the President of the U.S., 1979-81. General Counsel, U.S. Office of Consumer Affairs, 1977-79. Staff Counsel, Senate Committee on Commerce, Science and Transportation, 1974-77.
Clients:
American Honda Motor Co.
Davis Wright Political Action Committee
McCaw Cellular Communications Cos.

COHEN, Edwin S.
Covington and Burling
1201 Pennsylvania Ave., N.W., Box 7566, Washington, DC 20044
Telephone: (202) 662-6000
Registered as lobbyist at U.S. Congress.
Background: Assistant Secretary of the Treasury, 1969-1972; Under Secretary of the Treasury, 1972-1973.

COHEN, George H.
Bredhoff and Kaiser
1000 Connecticut Ave., N.W. Suite 1300, Washington, DC 20036
Telephone: (202) 833-9340
Background: Attorney-Advisor, 1960-63 and Appellate Court Litigation Attorney, 1963-66, National Labor Relations Board.
Clients:
United Steelworkers of America

COHEN, Herbert
Chairman of the Board, Wigman and Cohen
1735 Jefferson Davis Hwy. Crystal Sq. 3, Suite 200, Arlington, VA 22202
Telephone: (703) 892-4300

COHEN, Irwin
Fulbright & Jaworski
1150 Connecticut Ave., N.W., Suite 400, Washington, DC 20036
Telephone: (202) 452-6800
Clients:
Soc. of Cardiovascular and Interventional Radiology

COHEN, Jacqueline A.
Director, Government Relations, Nat'l Ass'n of Tobacco Distributors
1199 North Fairfax St. Suite 701, Alexandria, VA 22314
Telephone: (703) 683-8336
Registered as lobbyist at U.S. Congress.
Background: Legislative Assistant to Sen. Jacob Javits (D-NY), 1969-80; Sen. Arlen Specter (R-PA).

COHEN, John
Assoc. Dir., Energy & Natural Resources, Nat'l Ass'n of Manufacturers
1331 Pennsylvania Ave., N.W. Suite 1500 North, Washington, DC 20004-1703
Telephone: (202) 637-3000
Registered as lobbyist at U.S. Congress.

COHEN, Karen
Exec. Director, Nat'l Gaucher Foundation
1424 K St., N.W., 4th Floor, Washington, DC 20005
Telephone: (202) 393-2777

COHEN, Laurence J.
Sherman, Dunn, Cohen, Leifer and Counts
1125 15th St., N.W. Suite 801, Washington, DC 20005
Telephone: (202) 785-9300
Background: Legal Assistant and Supervising Attorney, 1964-67, Nat'l Labor Relations Board. Alternate Member, Chairman's Task force on the NLRB, 1976-77.
Clients:
Internat'l Brotherhood of Electrical Workers

COHEN, Maura S.
Marketing and Sales Manager, Targeting Systems, Inc.
2111 Wilson Blvd., Suite 900, Arlington, VA 22201
Telephone: (703) 528-7555

COHEN, N. Jerold
Sutherland, Asbill and Brennan
1275 Pennsylvania, N.W., Washington, DC 20004-2404
Telephone: (202) 383-0100
Registered as lobbyist at U.S. Congress.
Background: Chief Counsel, Internal Revenue Service, 1979-81.

COHEN, Neal M.
Director, Political Support Svcs., APCO Associates
1155 21st St., N.W., Suite 1000, Washington, DC 20036
Telephone: (202) 778-1000
Clients:
LymphoMed Inc.
Philip Morris Management Corp.
Recording Industry Ass'n of America

COHEN, Roger
Ass't. to the V. Pres. Gov't Affairs, Air Transport Ass'n of America
1709 New York Ave., N.W., Washington, DC 20006-5206
Telephone: (202) 626-4000

COHEN, Scott
Cohen and Associates, Scott
1625 Massachusetts Ave., N.W. Suite 402, Washington, DC 20036
Telephone: (202) 232-6872
Background: Former foreign affairs advisor to Senator Charles H. Percy (R-IL) and former Staff Director, Senate Foreign Relations Committee. Supervises and coordinates the work of nine associates who are specialized in such areas as trade, financing, marketing, economics, privatization, technology transfer and maritime affairs.

COHEN, Sharon L.
Director, Health Policy, Alliance for Aging Research
2021 K St., N.W. Suite 305, Washington, DC 20006
Telephone: (202) 293-2856

COHEN, Sheldon S.
Morgan, Lewis and Bockius
1800 M St., N.W., Washington, DC 20036
Telephone: (202) 467-7000
Registered as lobbyist at U.S. Congress.
Background: Chief Counsel, Internal Revenue Service, 1964. Commissioner of Internal Revenue, 1965-69.
Clients:
WEI Enterprises Corp.

COHEN, Stanley B.
Cohn and Marks
1333 New Hampshire Ave., N.W., Suite 600, Washington, DC 20036
Telephone: (202) 293-3860
Registered as lobbyist at U.S. Congress.
Clients:
General Electric Co.

COHEN, Susan
Account Supervisor, Health Care, Hill and Knowlton Public Affairs Worldwide
Washington Harbour, 901 31st St., N.W., Washington, DC 20007
Telephone: (202) 333-7400
Clients:
Allergan
Intermedics, Inc.

COHEN, Vincent H.
Hogan and Hartson
555 13th St., N.W., Suite 1200, Washington, DC 20004-1109
Telephone: (202) 637-5600
Registered as lobbyist at U.S. Congress.
Background: Trail Attorney, U.S. Department of Justice, 1962-67.

COHEN AND WHITE
1055 Thomas Jefferson St., Suite 504, Washington, DC 20007
Telephone: (202) 342-2550
Members of firm representing listed organizations:
Cohen, David S.
Clients:
Computer and Communications Industry Ass'n
(David S. Cohen)

COHICK, Chris
Bario Associates, Patricia
512 11th St., S.E., Washington, DC 20003
Telephone: (202) 543-0923

The listings in this directory are available as *Mailing Labels*. See last page.

COHN AND MARKS
1333 New Hampshire Ave., N.W., Suite 600, Washington, DC 20036
Telephone: (202) 293-3860
Registered as Foreign Agent: (#4303)
Background: Law firm specializing in communications matters.
Members of firm representing listed organizations:
Adler, Allan Robert
Cohen, Stanley B.
Schmidt, Richard M. (Jr.)
  Background: Counsel, Special Investigating Subcommittee, U.S. Senate, 1959-60. General Counsel, U.S.A., 1965-68.
Siegel, Ronald A.
Volner, Ian D.
  Background: Serves as General Counsel, Third Class Mail Ass'n. Staff Attorney, Federal Communications Commission Review Board, 1968-70.
Clients:
American Soc. of Newspaper Editors *(Richard M. Schmidt, Jr.)*
Ass'n of American Publishers
Direct Marketing Ass'n *(Ian D. Volner)*
General Electric Co. *(Stanley B. Cohen)*
KBMT
KCFW-TV
KCOS-TV
KCTZ-TV
KDOC-TV
KECI-TV
KEDT-TV
KETA-TV
KFDX-TV
KIEM-TV
KIII
KJAC-TV
KLNO-TV
KMSG
KNOE-TV
KOCV-TV
KOED-TV
KOET-TV
KRBK-TV
KRGV-TV
KSMQ-TV
KSNF-TV
KTKA
KTNW
KTVM
KTVN
KUAC-TV
KUSK
KVCT-TV
KWET-TV
KWHY-TV
KWSU-TV
KXRM-TV
Maclean Hunter Cable TV *(Allan Robert Adler, Ronald A. Siegel, Ian D. Volner)*
Nat'l Ass'n of Trade and Technical Schools *(Richard M. Schmidt, Jr., Ian D. Volner)*
Nat'l Electric Sign Ass'n *(Richard M. Schmidt, Jr.)*
Third Class Mail Ass'n *(Ian D. Volner)*
WAPT-TV
WBBH-TV
WBRA-TV
WBRZ
WCBD-TV
WCET-TV
WCIU-TV
WEIU-TV
WGBU-TV
WGVC-TV
WGVK-TV
WHA-TV
WJKS-TV
WJSU-TV
WMDT
WMSY-TV
WOI-TV
WOST-TV
WOUB-TV
WOUC-TV
WPEC
WQTV-TV
WRCB-TV
WSBN-TV
WSEE-TV
WSFP-TV
WSIU-TV
WSNS-TV
WUCM-TV
WUCX-TV
WUSF-TV
WVIR-TV
WVSB-TV
WXFL
WZZM-TV

COHN, Robert E.
Shaw, Pittman, Potts and Trowbridge
2300 N St., N.W., Washington, DC 20037
Telephone: (202) 663-8000

COIA, Arthur A.
General Secretary - Treasurer, Laborers' Internat'l Union of North America
905 16th St., N.W., Washington, DC 20006
Telephone: (202) 737-8320

COLAIANNI, Peter L.
Exec. Director, Nat'l Business Forms Ass'n
433 East Monroe Ave., Alexandria, VA 22301
Telephone: (703) 836-6225

COLANERI, Joseph L.
Washington Representative, UNOCAL Corp.
1050 Connecticut Ave., N.W., Suite 760, Washington, DC 20036
Telephone: (202) 659-7600
Registered as lobbyist at U.S. Congress.

COLBORN, Carol
Reed Smith Shaw & McClay
1200 18th St., N.W., Washington, DC 20036
Telephone: (202) 457-6100
Clients:
Amgen, Inc.

COLBURN, Cordis
Programs Div, Legis Liaison, DEPARTMENT OF ARMY
The Pentagon, Washington, DC 20310-0101
Telephone: (202) 697-6767

COLBY, William E.
Donovan Leisure Rogovin Huge & Schiller
1250 24th St., N.W., Washington, DC 20037
Telephone: (202) 467-8300
Clients:
Nissho-Iwai American Corp.
Usinor-Sacilor, S.A.

COLE, Albert M.
McKenna, Conner and Cuneo
1575 Eye St., N.W. Suite 800, Washington, DC 20005
Telephone: (202) 789-7500
Background: Former Member, U.S. House of Representatives (R-KN).

COLE, Basil
Of Counsel, Hopkins and Sutter
888 16th St., N.W., Suite 700, Washington, DC 20006
Telephone: (202) 835-8000

COLE, CORETTE & ABRUTYN
1110 Vermont Ave., N.W., Suite 900, Washington, DC 20005
Telephone: (202) 872-1414
Members of firm representing listed organizations:
Berg, R. Christian
Cole, Robert T.
  Background: International Tax Counsel, U.S. Treasury Department, 1971-1973.
Corette, John E. (III)
  Background: General Counsel, Export-Import Bank of the United States, 1969-75.
Lieberman, Edward H.
  Background: Tax Law Specialist, 1977-80, Reviewer, 1980-81, Internal Revenue Service.
Musher, Steven A.
  Background: An international taxation specialist.
Clients:
Adidas U.S.A. *(R. Christian Berg)*
Internat'l Electronics Manufacturers and Consumers of America *(Robert T. Cole)*

Louisiana Land and Exploration Co. *(Edward H. Lieberman)*
Matsushita Electric Corp. of America *(Robert T. Cole)*
Netherlands Antilles, Government of *(Robert T. Cole, Steven A. Musher)*

COLE, Douglas
Manager, Government Sales/Service, American President Companies
1101 17th St., N.W. Suite 400, Washington, DC 20036
Telephone: (202) 331-1424
Registered as lobbyist at U.S. Congress.

COLE, Harry F.
Bechtel and Cole
2101 L St., N.W., Suite 502, Washington, DC 20037
Telephone: (202) 833-4190
Clients:
Shurberg Broadcasting of Hartford Inc.

COLE, Dr. Henry S.
Research and Science Director, Clean Water Action Project
317 Pennsylvania Ave., S.E., Washington, DC 20003
Telephone: (202) 547-1196

COLE, Kenneth W.
Corp. V. Pres., Government Relations, Allied-Signal Inc.
1001 Pennsylvania Ave., N.W. Suite 700, Washington, DC 20004
Telephone: (202) 662-2650
Registered as lobbyist at U.S. Congress.

COLE, Michael F.
Laxalt, Washington, Perito & Dubuc
1120 Connecticut Ave., N.W., Suite 1000, Washington, DC 20036
Telephone: (202) 857-4000
Registered as lobbyist at U.S. Congress.
Clients:
American College of Neuropsychopharmacology
Committee on Problems of Drug Dependence
Group Hospital and Medical Services, Inc.
Nordisk USA
Pharmakinetics Laboratories, Inc.

COLE, Philip J.
Director of Nat'l Activities, Nat'l Security Industrial Ass'n
1025 Connecticut Ave., N.W., Suite 300, Washington, DC 20036
Telephone: (202) 775-1440

COLE, Randall I.
Director, Legislative Affairs, Burlington Resources, Inc.
50 F St., N.W., Suite 1080, Washington, DC 20001
Telephone: (202) 383-4960
Registered as lobbyist at U.S. Congress.

COLE, RAYWID, AND BRAVERMAN
1919 Pennsylvania Ave., N.W. Suite 200, Washington, DC 20006
Telephone: (202) 659-9750
Members of firm representing listed organizations:
Braverman, Burt A.
James, Robert L.
Raywid, Alan
  Background: Trial Attorney, Admiralty and Shipping Section, U.S. Department of Justice, 1957-63; 1965. Special Assistant to the Assistant Attorney General of the U.S., Civil Division, 1963-66.
Clients:
United Video Inc. *(Robert L. James)*

COLE, Robert E.
Vice President, Kaiser Aluminum and Chemical Corp.
900 17th St., N.W. Suite 706, Washington, DC 20006
Telephone: (202) 296-5474
Registered as lobbyist at U.S. Congress.

COLE, Robert T.
Cole, Corette & Abrutyn
1110 Vermont Ave., N.W., Suite 900, Washington, DC 20005
Telephone: (202) 872-1414
Registered as lobbyist at U.S. Congress.
Background: International Tax Counsel, U.S. Treasury Department, 1971-1973.
Clients:

COLE, Robert T. (Cont'd)
Internat'l Electronics Manufacturers and Consumers of America
Matsushita Electric Corp. of America
Netherlands Antilles, Government of

COLE, Steven J.
V. President and Senior Counsel, Council of Better Business Bureaus
4200 Wilson Blvd. Suite 800, Arlington, VA 22203
Telephone: (703) 276-0100

COLE, Thomas E.
President, Rubber Manufacturers Ass'n
1400 K St., N.W., Washington, DC 20005
Telephone: (202) 682-4800
Background: Also serves as President, Natural Rubber Shippers Ass'n and Chairman, Rubber Manufacturers Ass'n Political Action Committee.

COLE, Timothy R.
Sparkman and Cole, Inc.
1925 North Lynn St. Suite 308, Arlington, VA 22209
Telephone: (703) 522-7555
Registered as lobbyist at U.S. Congress.
Clients:
Air Transport Ass'n of America
Delta Air Lines
Nat'l Business Aircraft Ass'n
Regional Airport Authority of Louisville

COLEMAN, Colette
Director, State Relations, Nat'l Restaurant Ass'n
1200 17th St., N.W., Washington, DC 20036-3097
Telephone: (202) 331-5900
Registered as lobbyist at U.S. Congress.

COLEMAN, Cynthia
Legislative Representative, AFL-CIO - Food and Allied Service Trades Department
815 16th St., N.W., Suite 408, Washington, DC 20006
Telephone: (202) 737-7200

COLEMAN, Lynn R.
Skadden, Arps, Slate, Meagher and Flom
1440 New York Ave., N.W., Washington, DC 20005
Telephone: (202) 371-7000
Registered as lobbyist at U.S. Congress.
Background: Serves also as Treasurer, Skadden Arps Political Action Committee. General Counsel, U.S. Department of Energy, 1978-80. Deputy Secretary, U.S. Department of Energy, 1980-81.
Clients:
Enron Corp.
Natural Gas Alliance for Generative Electricity
Natural Gas Supply Ass'n

COLEMAN, Michael D.
V. President, International Operations, DeLeuw, Cather and Co.
1133 15th St., N.W. Suite 800, Washington, DC 20005
Telephone: (202) 775-3300

COLEMAN, Paul D.
Hoppel, Mayer and Coleman
1000 Connecticut Ave., N.W. Suite 410, Washington, DC 20036
Telephone: (202) 296-5460
Registered as Foreign Agent: (# 3470).
Clients:
Crown Central Petroleum Corp.
Tropical Shipping and Construction Co.

COLEMAN, Ronald D.
Chairman & CEO, Internat'l Televent Inc.
2000 Corporate Ridge Suite 815, McLean, VA 22102
Telephone: (703) 556-7778

COLEMAN, Walter S.
V. President, Operations, Air Transport Ass'n of America
1709 New York Ave., N.W., Washington, DC 20006-5206
Telephone: (202) 626-4000

COLEMAN, William T., Jr.
O'Melveny and Myers
555 13th St., N.W., Suite 500 West, Washington, DC 20004
Telephone: (202) 383-5300
Registered as Foreign Agent: (# 3346).

Background: Chief Legislative Assistant to U.S. Senator Howard H. Baker of Tennessee, 1973-76. Member, Board of Directors, CIGNA Corp.
Clients:
Alaska Airlines
Ford Motor Co.
Pan American World Airways
Security Pacific Nat'l Bank

COLING, George
Great Lakes Washington Specialist, Sierra Club
408 C St., N.E., Washington, DC 20002
Telephone: (202) 547-1141

COLLADO, Emilio G., III
Exec. Director, American Watch Ass'n
1201 Pennsylvania Ave., N.W. P.O. Box 464, Washington, DC 20044
Telephone: (703) 759-3377
Registered as lobbyist at U.S. Congress.

COLLATZ, Mark L.
Manager, Public Relations, Nat'l Air Transportation Ass'n
4226 King St., Alexandria, VA 22302
Telephone: (703) 845-9000

COLLENDER, Stanley E.
Dir, Fed Budget Plcy, Wash Nat'l Tax Svc, Price Waterhouse
1801 K St., N.W., Suite 700, Washington, DC 20006
Telephone: (202) 296-0800

COLLETTE, Will
Organizing Director, Citizens Clearinghouse for Hazardous Wastes
P.O. Box 926, Arlington, VA 22216
Telephone: (703) 276-7070

COLLIE, H. Cris
Exec. V. President, Employee Relocation Council
1720 N St., N.W., Washington, DC 20036
Telephone: (202) 857-0857
Registered as lobbyist at U.S. Congress.

COLLIER, Jr. Earl
Hogan and Hartson
555 13th St., N.W., Suite 1200, Washington, DC 20004-1109
Telephone: (202) 637-5600
Registered as lobbyist at U.S. Congress.

COLLIER, SHANNON & SCOTT
1055 Thomas Jefferson St., N.W., Suite 300, Washington, DC 20007
Telephone: (202) 342-8400
Members of firm representing listed organizations:
Allen, Pamela, Director, Legislative Services Division
Austrian, Mark L.
Beckington, Jeffrey S.
Black, R. Randal
Background: Former Legislative Assistant to Senator Richard C. Shelby (D-AL).
Cantley, Brent, Legislative Representative
Clark, Kathleen B., Legislative Representative
Columbus, R. Timothy
Cullen, Paul D.
Fazzone, Patrick B.
Gilbert, Robin H.
Hartquist, David A.
Background: Legislative Assistant to Senator Richard S. Schweiker, 1970-1973. Assistant to the President, Overseas Private Investment Corp., 1973-1974. Gen. Counsel, White House Council on Internat'l Economic Policy, 1974-1976.
Howard, Lauren R.
Kershow, Michael R.
Lasoff, Laurence J.
Background: Special Assistant to the Assistant Secretary of Commerce for Internat'l Trade, 1977-79.
Leiter, Jeffrey L.
Logan, Mark
Background: Former Counsel to the Senate Budget Committee. Specializes in legislative and environmental issues.
McDermott, Kathleen
O'Connell, K. Michael
Background: Senior Policy Analyst, Assistant Secretary for Trade Development, International Trade Administration, U.S. Dept. of Commerce, 1983-4.

Oldham, Judy
Porter, Robert W., Legislative Representative
Rosenthal, Paul C.
Background: Counsel, U.S. Senate Committee on Governmental Affairs, 1975-81.
Schneeberger, Dana L., Legislative Representative
Scott, William W.
Shannon, Thomas F.
Background: Legislative Counsel to Senator Styles Bridges, 1955-1957. Chief Minority Counsel, Committee on Appropriations, U. S. Senate, 1957-1958.
Sherman, Michael D.
Staley, Mary T.
Sullivan, Anne, Legislative Representative
Williams, John B.
Clients:
Alliance for Capital Access *(R. Timothy Columbus)*
American Car Rental Ass'n *(R. Timothy Columbus)*
American Couplings Coalition *(David A. Hartquist, Paul C. Rosenthal, Thomas F. Shannon)*
American Flint Glass Workers Union *(Paul D. Cullen, David A. Hartquist, Thomas F. Shannon)*
American Iron and Steel Institute *(Pamela Allen, Thomas F. Shannon)*
American Textile Machinery Ass'n *(William W. Scott)*
Armco Inc. *(David A. Hartquist, Thomas F. Shannon)*
Bethlehem Steel Corp. *(David A. Hartquist)*
Bicycle Manufacturers Ass'n of America *(Lauren R. Howard, Thomas F. Shannon)*
Carpenter Technology Corp. *(David A. Hartquist)*
Chase Brass and Copper *(Jeffrey S. Beckington, David A. Hartquist, Mary T. Staley)*
Coalition for Equitable Compensation
Coalition for Safe Ceramicware *(David A. Hartquist)*
Committee of American Ammunition Manufacturers *(Lauren R. Howard, Thomas F. Shannon)*
Copper and Brass Fabricators Council *(David A. Hartquist)*
Crop Insurance Research Bureau *(David A. Hartquist)*
Ferrous Scrap Consumers Coalition *(Paul C. Rosenthal)*
Food Marketing Institute
Footwear Industries of America *(Lauren R. Howard, Thomas F. Shannon)*
Footwear Industry Political Action Committee *(Pamela Allen, Lauren R. Howard, Thomas F. Shannon)*
Gerico *(Michael R. Kershow)*
Hussey Copper Ltd. *(Jeffrey S. Beckington, David A. Hartquist, Mary T. Staley)*
Hyster Co.
Independent Lubricant Manufacturers Ass'n *(William W. Scott)*
Independent Lubricant Manufacturers Ass'n Political Action Committee
Inland Steel Co.
Internat'l Ass'n of Machinists and Aerospace Workers *(Paul D. Cullen, Laurence J. Lasoff)*
Leather Industries of America *(Thomas F. Shannon)*
Lykes Brothers, Inc. *(Paul C. Rosenthal)*
Magnavox Consumer Electronics Co. *(Paul D. Cullen, David A. Hartquist, Thomas F. Shannon)*
Miller Co. *(Jeffrey S. Beckington, David A. Hartquist, Mary T. Staley)*
Municipal Castings Fair Trade Council *(Paul C. Rosenthal)*
Nat'l Ass'n of Convenience Stores *(R. Timothy Columbus)*
Nat'l Ass'n of Convenience Stores Political Action Committee
Nat'l Ass'n of Mutual Insurance Companies *(Pamela Allen, David A. Hartquist)*
Nat'l Broiler Council
Nat'l Cosmetology Ass'n
Nat'l Juice Products Ass'n *(Robin H. Gilbert, Paul C. Rosenthal)*
Nat'l Pasta Ass'n
Outdoor Power Equipment Institute *(Thomas F. Shannon)*
Owner-Operator Independent Drivers Ass'n Political Action Committee *(K. Michael O'Connell)*
Petrojam Ltd. *(R. Timothy Columbus)*
Petroleos de Venezuela, S.A. *(Paul D. Cullen, William W. Scott, Thomas F. Shannon)*
Pittsburgh Corning Corp. *(David A. Hartquist)*
Reynolds Tobacco Co., R. J. *(Judy Oldham)*
Shipbuilders Council of America

Siemens Corp. (Paul D. Cullen, Michael D. Sherman)
Soc. of Independent Gasoline Marketers of
America (R. Timothy Columbus, Jeffrey L. Leiter, William
W. Scott)
Soc. of Independent Gasoline Marketers Political
Action Committee (R. Timothy Columbus)
Specialty Steel Industry of the United States (David A. Hartquist, Thomas F. Shannon)
Stanley Bostitch Inc. (David A. Hartquist, Thomas F.
Shannon)
Steel Manufacturers Ass'n
Tropicana Products Inc. (Robin H. Gilbert, Paul C. Rosenthal)
United Steelworkers of America (David A. Hartquist,
Laurence J. Lasoff)
Valve Manufacturers Ass'n of America (David A.
Hartquist)
Western Union Corp.
Wyman-Gordon Co. (Robin H. Gilbert, David A. Hartquist, Michael R. Kershow)
Zurich-American Insurance (Pamela Allen)

COLLIER, Thomas C., Jr.
Steptoe and Johnson
1330 Connecticut Ave., N.W., Washington, DC 20036
Telephone: (202) 429-3000
Background: Special Assistant to the General Counsel. Department of Housing and Urban Development (HUD),
1979-80. Deputy Assistant Secretary for Regulatory
Functions and Interstate Land Sales Administrator, HUD,
1980-81.

COLLING, Terese
Exec. V. President, Davidson Colling Group, Inc., The
1211 Connecticut Ave., N.W., Suite 610, Washington, DC
20036
Telephone: (202) 293-2180
Registered as lobbyist at U.S. Congress.
Clients:
Garden State Paper Co.
Media General, Inc.

COLLINGWOOD, Marlin W.
Senior Project Manager, Bonner & Associates
1625 K St., N.W., Suite 300, Washington, DC 20006
Telephone: (202) 463-8880
Background: Former Press Assistant to Senator John Heinz
(R-PA); Assistant to Senator Richard Lugar (R-IN) and
Rep. William Clinger (R-PA); Press Assistant for the Jack
Kemp President Exploratory Committee; and Co-Chairman, Nat'l Republican Collegiate Committee for Reagan/
Bush campaign, 1984.

COLLINS, Aase J.
Assistant Exec. Director, Nat'l Ass'n of Private Residential
Resources
4200 Evergreen Lane, Suite 315, Annandale, VA 22003
Telephone: (703) 642-6614

COLLINS & ASSOCIATES
6269 Franconia Road, Alexandria, VA 22310
Telephone: (703) 971-1700
Members of firm representing listed organizations:
Taylor, Sunny, V. President, Government Affairs
Background: Legislative Assistant and Chief Legislative
Director to Rep. Dan Mica (D-FL), 1982-87.
Clients:
First Page (Sunny Taylor)
New Era Communications (Sunny Taylor)
Pompano Beach, Florida, City of (Sunny Taylor)
USA Telecommunications (Sunny Taylor)

COLLINS, Bryan P.
Johnson & Gibbs, P.C.
1001 Pennsylvania Ave., N.W. Suite 745, Washington, DC
20004
Telephone: (202) 682-4500
Registered as lobbyist at U.S. Congress.
Clients:
Permanente Medical Group, Inc., The

COLLINS, Carrie
V. President, Washington Communications Group/Ruder
Finn
1615 M St., N.W., Suite 220, Washington, DC 20036
Telephone: (202) 466-7800

COLLINS, Chantee
Staff Assistant, Concerned Citizens Foundation
Capitol Hill Office Bldg. 412 First St., S.E., Suite 301,
Washington, DC 20003
Telephone: (202) 479-9068

COLLINS, Eileen M.
Sr. Assoc, Director, Div. of Legislation, American Hospital
Ass'n
50 F St., N.W., Suite 1100, Washington, DC 20001
Telephone: (202) 638-1100
Registered as lobbyist at U.S. Congress.

COLLINS, Gail
Legislative Director, General Federation of Women's
Clubs
1734 N St., N.W., Washington, DC 20036
Telephone: (202) 347-3168

COLLINS, Harold M.
Exec. Director, Nat'l Agricultural Aviation Ass'n
1005 E St., S.E, Washington, DC 20003
Telephone: (202) 546-5722
Registered as lobbyist at U.S. Congress.

COLLINS, James E.
President, Steel Manufacturers Ass'n
815 Connecticut Ave., N.W. Suite 304, Washington, DC
20006
Telephone: (202) 331-7027

COLLINS, James P.
Associate, Cassidy and Associates, Inc.
655 15th St., N.W., Suite 1100, Washington, DC 20005
Telephone: (202) 347-0773
Registered as lobbyist at U.S. Congress.
Background: Member of the Massachusetts State Legislature, 1977-78.
Clients:
Action for Boston Community Development
Boston Carmen's Union, Local 589
Boston University
DataCom Systems Corp.
Massachusetts Ass'n of Community Health Agencies
Massachusetts League of Community Banks
Ocean Spray Cranberries

COLLINS, Jeremiah C.
Williams and Connolly
839 17th St., N.W. 1000 Hill Bldg., Washington, DC 20006
Telephone: (202) 331-5000

COLLINS, John
V. President, American Trucking Ass'ns
2200 Mill Road, Alexandria, VA 22314
Telephone: (703) 838-1800
Background: Former Assistant General Counsel for Legislation, U.S. Department of Transportation.

COLLINS, John T.
Steptoe and Johnson
1330 Connecticut Ave., N.W., Washington, DC 20036
Telephone: (202) 429-3000
Registered as lobbyist at U.S. Congress.
Background: General Counsel, U.S. Senate Committee on
Banking, Housing and Urban Affairs, 1982-85.
Clients:
Citizens Savings Financial Corp.
Coast Savings and Loan Ass'n
Commercial Federal Savings and Loan Ass'n
Cooperative Central Bank
CSO Co.
Glendale Federal Savings and Loan Ass'n
MeraBank
Pioneer Financial
Western Financial Savings Bank

COLLINS, Kathleen W.
Dow, Lohnes and Albertson
1255 23rd St., N.W., Suite 500, Washington, DC 20037
Telephone: (202) 857-2500
Clients:
Washington Bancorporation

COLLINS, LaVerne
Nat'l President, Nat'l Federation of Business and Professional Women's Clubs
2012 Massachusetts Ave., N.W., Washington, DC 20036

Telephone: (202) 293-1100

COLLINS, Mary Jean
Director, Public Affairs, Catholics for a Free Choice
1436 U St., N. W. Suite 301, Washington, DC 20009
Telephone: (202) 638-1706
Registered as lobbyist at U.S. Congress.

COLLINS, Meg
Camp, Barsh, Bates and Tate
2550 M St., N.W., Suite 275, Washington, DC 20037
Telephone: (202) 887-5160
Registered as lobbyist at U.S. Congress.

COLLINS, Michael A.
Legislative Representative, United Ass'n of Journeymen &
Apprentices of the Plumbing & Pipe Fitting Industry of
the US & Canada
901 Massachusetts Ave., N.W., Washington, DC 20001
Telephone: (202) 628-5823
Registered as lobbyist at U.S. Congress.
Background: Serves as Treasurer, Plumbers Local Union
#5 Political Action Fund.

COLLINS, Paula J.
Director, Government Affairs, American Express Co.
1020 19th St., N.W. Suite 600, Washington, DC 20036
Telephone: (202) 822-6680
Registered as lobbyist at U.S. Congress.

COLLINS, R. J.
Government Affairs Representative, Amdahl Corp.
1667 K St., N.W., Suite 300, Washington, DC 20006
Telephone: (202) 835-2220
Registered as lobbyist at U.S. Congress.

COLLINS, Stephen J.
Director, Econ. & International Affairs, Motor Vehicle
Manufacturers Ass'n of the United States
1620 Eye St., N.W. Suite 1000, Washington, DC 20006
Telephone: (202) 775-2700
Registered as lobbyist at U.S. Congress.

COLLINS, William P.
Farragut Group, The
1825 K St., N.W., Suite 807, Washington, DC 20006
Telephone: (202) 331-9669
Registered as lobbyist at U.S. Congress.

COLLISHAW, Karen
Director, Government Relations, American College of Cardiology
9111 Old Georgetown Road, Bethesda, MD 20814
Telephone: (301) 897-5400

COLLISHAW, William C.
Squire, Sanders and Dempsey
1201 Pennsylvania Ave., N.W. P.O. Box 407, Washington,
DC 20044
Telephone: (202) 626-6600
Clients:
Population Crisis Committee

COLLOVA, Camilla L.
Deputy Director, Government Relations, Armstrong World
Industries, Inc.
1025 Connecticut Ave., N.W., Suite 1007, Washington, DC
20036
Telephone: (202) 296-2830
Registered as lobbyist at U.S. Congress.

COLMAN, Richard T.
Howrey and Simon
1730 Pennsylvania Ave., N.W., Washington, DC 20006-
4793
Telephone: (202) 783-0800
Background: Trial Attorney, Antitrust Division, Department of Justice, 1962-66.
Clients:
Caterpillar Inc.
PepsiCo, Inc.

COLON, Dominique
Public Affairs Associate, Medtronic, Inc.
2000 L St., N.W., Suite 200, Washington, DC 20036
Telephone: (202) 293-7035
Registered as lobbyist at U.S. Congress.

COLOPY, Michael
Legislative Coordinator, O'Connor & Hannan
1919 Pennsylvania Ave., N.W., Suite 800, Washington, DC 20006
Telephone: (202) 887-1400
Registered as lobbyist at U.S. Congress.
Clients:
China External Trade Development Council
Healthcare Financing Study Group

COLOSI, Thomas R.
Vice President, National Affairs, American Arbitration Ass'n
Suite 909, 1730 Rhode Island Ave., N.W, Washington, DC 20036
Telephone: (202) 331-7073

COLOSIMO, E. Thomas
Exec. Director, ARROW (Americans for Restitution, Righting Old Wrongs)
1000 Connecticut Ave., N.W. Suite 401, Washington, DC 20036
Telephone: (202) 296-0685
Background: Also represents the Nat'l American Indian Court Clerks Ass'n.

COLSON, Charles W.
Chairman of the Board, Prison Fellowship Ministries
P.O. Box 17500, Washington, DC 20041-0500
Telephone: (703) 478-0100
Background: Former Special Counsel to President Richard Nixon.

COLTON AND BOYKIN
1025 Thomas Jefferson St., N.W., Suite 500 East, Washington, DC 20007
Telephone: (202) 342-5400
Members of firm representing listed organizations:
Boykin, Hamilton
Colton, Herbert S.
Background: Former Chief Counsel, Rental Housing Division, Federal Housing Administration, 1936-46.
Segal, Peter W.
Background: Serves as General Counsel, Nat'l Ass'n of Home Builders of the U.S.
Winn, Allan R.
Clients:
Countrywide Credit Industries *(Peter W. Segal)*
Home Owners Warranty Corp.
Nat'l Ass'n of Home Builders of the U.S. *(Peter W. Segal)*
Nat'l Office Products Ass'n *(Hamilton Boykin)*

COLTON & COMPANY
600 New Hampshire Ave., N.W., Suite 1020, Washington, DC 20037-2403
Telephone: (202) 333-1555
Members of firm representing listed organizations:
Colton, T. J. V., President
Hillman, J. F., V. President

COLTON, Herbert S.
Colton and Boykin
1025 Thomas Jefferson St., N.W., Suite 500 East, Washington, DC 20007
Telephone: (202) 342-5400
Background: Former Chief Counsel, Rental Housing Division, Federal Housing Administration, 1936-46.

COLTON, Kent W.
Exec. V. President and CEO, Nat'l Ass'n of Home Builders of the U.S.
15th and M Streets, N.W., Washington, DC 20005
Telephone: (202) 822-0470
Registered as lobbyist at U.S. Congress.

COLTON, Sterling D.
Senior V. President and General Counsel, Marriott Corp.
One Marriott Drive, Washington, DC 20058
Telephone: (301) 380-9000

COLTON, T. J. V.
President, Colton & Company
600 New Hampshire Ave., N.W., Suite 1020, Washington, DC 20037-2403
Telephone: (202) 333-1555

COLUMBUS, R. Timothy
Collier, Shannon & Scott
1055 Thomas Jefferson St., N.W., Suite 300, Washington, DC 20007
Telephone: (202) 342-8400
Registered as lobbyist at U.S. Congress.
Registered as Foreign Agent: (#3694).
Clients:
Alliance for Capital Access
American Car Rental Ass'n
Nat'l Ass'n of Convenience Stores
Petrojam Ltd.
Soc. of Independent Gasoline Marketers of America
Soc. of Independent Gasoline Marketers Political Action Committee

COLVILLE, Mary M.
Director of Government Relations, Nat'l Broiler Council
1155 15th St., N.W. Suite 614, Washington, DC 20005
Telephone: (202) 296-2622
Registered as lobbyist at U.S. Congress.
Background: Responsibilities include Nat'l Broiler Council PAC.

COLZA, Carol A.
Schagrin Associates
1112 16th St., N.W. Suite 1000, Washington, DC 20036
Telephone: (202) 223-1700
Registered as lobbyist at U.S. Congress.
Background: Former Legislative Director for Rep. Adam Benjamin, Jr., 1978-82.
Clients:
Copperweld Corp.
Cyclops Industries
Grinnell Corp.
LTV Tubular
Maverick Tube Corp.
Quanex Corp.
Wheatland Tube Co.

COMEAU, Lori A.
Washington Representative, C F Industries, Inc.
805 15th St., N.W., Washington, DC 20005
Telephone: (202) 371-9279
Registered as lobbyist at U.S. Congress.

COMER, Meryl
V. President, Communications Development, Chamber of Commerce of the U.S.A.
1615 H St., N.W., Washington, DC 20062
Telephone: (202) 659-6000

COMER, Suzanne
Senior Account Executive, Powell, Adams & Rinehart
1901 L St., N.W., 3rd Floor, Washington, DC 20036
Telephone: (202) 466-7590

COMLISH, Donald C.
V. President, Internat'l Affairs, Air Transport Ass'n of America
1709 New York Ave., N.W., Washington, DC 20006-5206
Telephone: (202) 626-4000

COMMERCE CONSULTANTS INTERNAT'L LTD.
1025 Thomas Jefferson St, N.W. Suite 105, Washington, DC 20007
Telephone: (202) 342-9610
Registered as Foreign Agent: (#4248)
Members of firm representing listed organizations:
Hatcher, David M.
Richards, Richard, President
Clients:
Hughes Aircraft Co. *(David M. Hatcher, Richard Richards)*
Thailand, Office of the Prime Minister *(David M. Hatcher, Richard Richards)*

COMMITTEE MANAGEMENT ASSOCIATES
Box 470, Arlington, VA 22210
Telephone: (703) 241-1741
Background: A management consulting firm specializing in management of Political Action Committees.
Members of firm representing listed organizations:
de Blois, Michael

COMMONWEALTH CONSULTING CORP.
9507 Beach Mill Road, Great Falls, VA 22066
Telephone: (703) 759-7120

Registered as Foreign Agent: (#4261)
Background: A consulting firm providing government relations, public affairs and international marketing expertise.
Members of firm representing listed organizations:
Lehman, Christopher M., President
Background: Associate Staff member, Senate Armed Services Committee, 1976-81. Director, Office of Strategic Nuclear Policy, Department of State, 1981-83. Special Assistant to the President, The White House, 1983-85.
Clients:
Foundation for Democracy in Namibia *(Christopher M. Lehman)*

COMMUNICATIONS MANAGEMENT ASSOCIATES
1724 N. Wakefield St., Arlington, VA 22207
Telephone: (202) 525-7062
Members of firm representing listed organizations:
Martin, David K.
Clients:
Friends of the Earth *(David K. Martin)*
Intellectual Property Owners, Inc. *(David K. Martin)*

COMPA, Lance
Washington Counsel, United Electrical, Radio and Machine Workers of America
1411 K St., N.W., Suite 1005, Washington, DC 20005
Telephone: (202) 737-3072
Registered as lobbyist at U.S. Congress.

CONAWAY, Ellen
Deputy Exec. Director, Nat'l Republican Senatorial Committee
425 Second St., N.E., Washington, DC 20002
Telephone: (202) 675-6000

CONAWAY, Harry J.
Mercer, Inc., William M.
1001 22nd St., N.W. Suite 400, Washington, DC 20037
Telephone: (202) 293-9422
Registered as lobbyist at U.S. Congress.

CONBOY, Brian
V. President, Government Affairs, Time Warner Inc.
1050 Connecticut Ave., N.W. Suite 850, Washington, DC 20036
Telephone: (202) 861-4000

CONBOY, Kenneth
Deputy Director, Asian Studies Center, Heritage Foundation
214 Massachusetts Ave., N.E., Washington, DC 20002
Telephone: (202) 546-4400

CONCKLIN, Bert M.
V. President, Government Relations, Planning Research Corp.
1500 Planning Research Drive, McLean, VA 22102
Telephone: (703) 556-1500
Registered as lobbyist at U.S. Congress.
Background: Also serves as Treasurer, Planning Research Corp. Political Action Committee.

CONCORD ASSOCIATES, INC.
1455 Pennsylvania Ave., N.W. Suite 560, Washington, DC 20004
Telephone: (202) 737-9300
Members of firm representing listed organizations:
Boardman, William J.
Rock, James W.
Background: Former House Ways and Means Committee Assistant to Rep. Ed Jenkins (D-GA), 1984-88, and to Rep. Kent Hance (D-TX), 1980-84.
Thevenot, E. Wayne
Background: Former Executive Assistant to Senator Russell B. Long (D-LA), 1963-75.
Clients:
American Resort and Residential Development Ass'n
Broad, Inc.
Cogentrix, Inc.
Fort Howard Corp.
General Chemical Corp.
Henley Group, Inc., The
J & B Management Co.
Maglev USA
Mutual Life Insurance Legislative Committee
Wheelabrator Technologies‡ Inc.

CONDEELIS, Mary
Exec. Director, Bankers' Ass'n for Foreign Trade
1600 M St., N.W., Washington, DC 20036
Telephone: (202) 452-0952

CONDON AND FORSYTH
1100 15th St., N.W., Suite 300, Washington, DC 20005
Telephone: (202) 289-0500
Background: Washington office of a New York-based law firm.
Members of firm representing listed organizations:
Whalen, Thomas J.
Clients:
Air Pacific Ltd. *(Thomas J. Whalen)*
British Airtours Ltd. *(Thomas J. Whalen)*
Qantas Airways *(Thomas J. Whalen)*

CONDRELL, William K.
Steptoe and Johnson
1330 Connecticut Ave., N.W., Washington, DC 20036
Telephone: (202) 429-3000

CONES, Carole K.
DCM Group
1355 Beverly Rd., Suite 200, McLean, VA 22101
Telephone: (703) 883-1355
Registered as lobbyist at U.S. Congress.

CONLEY, Jeffrey B.
Exec. V. President, Harrison Co., E. Bruce
1440 New York Ave., N.W. Suite 300, Washington, DC 20005
Telephone: (202) 638-1200
Registered as lobbyist at U.S. Congress.
Organizations represented:
Clean Air Act Project

CONLEY, John
V. President, Nat'l Tank Truck Carriers
2200 Mill Road, Suite 601, Alexandria, VA 22314
Telephone: (703) 838-1960
Registered as lobbyist at U.S. Congress.
Background: Serves also as Treasurer, Nat'l Tank Truck Carriers Political Action Committee.

CONLON, FRANTZ, PHELAN & KNAPP
1818 N St., N.W., Suite 200, Washington, DC 20036
Telephone: (202) 331-7050
Members of firm representing listed organizations:
Conlon, Michael J.
Clients:
Automotive Parts Rebuilders Ass'n *(Michael J. Conlon)*
Automotive Refrigeration Products Institute *(Michael J. Conlon)*

CONLON, Michael J.
Conlon, Frantz, Phelan & Knapp
1818 N St., N.W., Suite 200, Washington, DC 20036
Telephone: (202) 331-7050
Registered as lobbyist at U.S. Congress.
Clients:
Automotive Parts Rebuilders Ass'n
Automotive Refrigeration Products Institute

CONN, Joseph L.
Mng. Edit., Church and State Magazine, Americans United for Separation of Church and State
8120 Fenton St., Silver Spring, MD 20910
Telephone: (301) 589-3707

CONNARN, John J.
V. President-Federal Relations, Ameritech (American Information Technologies)
1050 Connecticut Ave., N.W., Suite 730, Washington, DC 20036
Telephone: (202) 955-3050

CONNAUGHTON, Thomas A.
Rivkin, Radler, Dunne and Bayh
1575 Eye St., N.W. Suite 1025, Washington, DC 20005
Telephone: (202) 289-8660
Registered as lobbyist at U.S. Congress.
Background: Former Administrative Assistant to Senator Birch Bayh of Indiana.
Clients:
ALC Communications Corp.
Chemical Bank
Cook Group

Nat'l Basketball Ass'n
Nat'l Soft Drink Ass'n
RRD & B Good Government Committee

CONNELL, Lawrence
Prather, Seeger, Doolittle and Farmer
1600 M St., N.W., Washington, DC 20036
Telephone: (202) 296-0500
Registered as lobbyist at U.S. Congress.
Background: Chairman, Nat'l Credit Union Administration, 1977-81.

CONNELL, Peter J.
Vice President and Washington Counsel, Aetna Life & Casualty Co.
1667 K St., N.W., Suite 400, Washington, DC 20006
Telephone: (202) 223-2821

CONNELLY, Jeanne K.
V. President, Government Affairs, Champion Internat'l Corp.
1875 Eye St., N.W., Suite 540, Washington, DC 20006
Telephone: (202) 785-9888
Registered as lobbyist at U.S. Congress.

CONNELLY, Warren E.
Akin, Gump, Strauss, Hauer and Feld
1333 New Hampshire Ave., N.W., Suite 400, Washington, DC 20036
Telephone: (202) 887-4000
Background: Attorney, Cost of Living Council, 1973-74.
Clients:
Fujitsu America, Inc.
Fujitsu Ltd.
Lone Star Steel Co.

CONNER, Colleen
Exec. Secretary, Ass'n of Physical Plant Administrators of Universities and Colleges
1446 Duke St., Alexandria, VA 22314
Telephone: (703) 684-1446

CONNER, James J.
Exec. V. President, Motor and Equipment Manufacturers Ass'n
1325 Pennsylvania Ave., N.W. Suite 600, Washington, DC 20004
Telephone: (202) 393-6362

CONNER, Robert J.
Director, Federal Relations, Chrysler Corp.
1100 Connecticut Ave., N.W., Washington, DC 20036
Telephone: (202) 862-5411
Registered as lobbyist at U.S. Congress.
Background: Serves also as V. President, Government Affairs, Chrysler Technologies.

CONNER, Roger L.
Exec. Director, American Alliance for Rights and Responsibilities
1819 H St., N.W., Suite 500, Washington, DC 20006
Telephone: (202) 785-7844

CONNER, Troy B., Jr.
Conner and Wetterhahn, P.C.
1747 Pennsylvania Ave., N.W. Suite 1050, Washington, DC 20006
Telephone: (202) 833-3500
Clients:
Cincinnati Gas and Electric Co.
Gulf States Utilities Co.
Niagara Mohawk Power Corp.
Philadelphia Electric Co.
Public Service Electric and Gas Co.

CONNER AND WETTERHAHN, P.C.
1747 Pennsylvania Ave., N.W. Suite 1050, Washington, DC 20006
Telephone: (202) 833-3500
Members of firm representing listed organizations:
Conner, Troy B. (Jr.)
Rader, Robert M.
Background: Trial Attorney, Civil Division, U.S. Department of Justice, 1973-78.
Wetterhahn, Mark J.
Clients:
Cincinnati Gas and Electric Co. *(Troy B. Conner, Jr., Mark J. Wetterhahn)*
Columbus and Southern Ohio Electric Co.

Dayton Power and Light Co.
Gulf States Utilities Co. *(Troy B. Conner, Jr., Mark J. Wetterhahn)*
Niagara Mohawk Power Corp. *(Troy B. Conner, Jr., Mark J. Wetterhahn)*
Philadelphia Electric Co. *(Troy B. Conner, Jr.)*
Public Service Electric and Gas Co. *(Troy B. Conner, Jr., Mark J. Wetterhahn)*
U.S. Ecology *(Robert M. Rader, Mark J. Wetterhahn)*

CONNERS, Francis J.
Exec. V. President, Nat'l Ass'n of Letter Carriers of the United States of America
100 Indiana Ave., N.W., Washington, DC 20001
Telephone: (202) 393-4695
Registered as lobbyist at U.S. Congress.

CONNERTON, Peggy
Director, Public Policy, Service Employees Internat'l Union
1313 L St., N.W., Washington, DC 20005
Telephone: (202) 898-3200

CONNERTON, RAY AND SIMON
1920 L St., N.W., Washington, DC 20036-5004
Telephone: (202) 466-6790
Members of firm representing listed organizations:
Connerton, Robert J.
Background: Serves as General Counsel for the Laborers' Internat'l Union of North America.
Mallino, David L., Chief Lobbyist
Ray, James S.
Clients:
Laborers' Internat'l Union of North America *(Robert J. Connerton)*

CONNERTON, Robert J.
Connerton, Ray and Simon
1920 L St., N.W., Washington, DC 20036-5004
Telephone: (202) 466-6790
Background: Serves as General Counsel for the Laborers' Internat'l Union of North America.
Clients:
Laborers' Internat'l Union of North America

CONNOLLY, Stephen J.
Jellinek, Schwartz, Connolly & Freshman, Inc.
1015 15th St., N.W. Suite 500, Washington, DC 20005
Telephone: (202) 789-8181

CONNOR, Brian L.
Government Relations Director, Nat'l Utility Contractors Ass'n
1235 Jefferson Davis Hwy. Suite 606, Arlington, VA 22202
Telephone: (703) 486-2100
Registered as lobbyist at U.S. Congress.
Background: Responsibilities include Nat'l Utility Contractors Ass'n Legislative and Action Committee.

CONNOR, Catherine
Manager, Government Relations, Parsons Brinkerhoff Quade & Douglas Inc.
555 13th St., N.W. Suite 460 West Tower, Washington, DC 20004
Telephone: (202) 637-8150
Registered as lobbyist at U.S. Congress.

CONNOR, John T.
Managing Partner, Deloitte & Touche Washington Services Group
1001 Pennsylvania Ave., N.W. Suite 350N, Washington, DC 20004
Telephone: (202) 879-5600

CONNOR, Martin F.
President, American Tort Reform Ass'n
1212 New York Ave., N.W. Suite 515, Washington, DC 20005
Telephone: (202) 682-1163
Background: Also serves as Chairman of the Board of Stateside Associates.

CONNOR, Richard J., Jr.
Director, Federal Affairs, Seagram & Sons, Inc., Joseph E.
1455 Pennsylvania Ave., N.W., Suite 600, Washington, DC 20004
Telephone: (202) 638-3090
Registered as lobbyist at U.S. Congress.

CONNORS, Jerry C.
President, Manufactured Housing Institute
1745 Jefferson Davis Hwy. Suite 511, Arlington, VA 22202
Telephone: (703) 979-6620
Registered as lobbyist at U.S. Congress.

CONOVER, David W.
Federal Liaison, Nat'l Rifle Ass'n of America
1600 Rhode Island Ave., N.W., Washington, DC
Telephone: (202) 828-6364
Registered as lobbyist at U.S. Congress.

CONRAD, David R.
Water Resource Specialist, Nat'l Wildlife Federation
1400 16th St., N.W., Washington, DC 20036-2266
Telephone: (202) 797-6800
Registered as lobbyist at U.S. Congress.

CONRAD, James
Assoc Asst Secy, Intergovt'l Affrs, DEPARTMENT OF LA-
BOR
200 Constitution Ave., N.W., Washington, DC 20210
Telephone: (202) 523-6141

CONRAD, Robin S.
Dir. of Litigat., Nat'l Chamb. Lit. Ctr., Chamber of Commerce of the U.S.A.
1615 H St., N.W., Washington, DC 20062
Telephone: (202) 659-6000

CONROY, Amy S.
Senior Account Executive, Washington Resources and
Strategy, Inc.
536 7th St., S.E., Washington, DC 20003
Telephone: (202) 544-1988

CONSAUL, Sheila A.
Anderson, Benjamin, Read & Haney
1020 19th St., N.W., Suite 500, Washington, DC 20036
Telephone: (202) 659-5656

CONTEE, Christine
Director of Public Affairs/Fellow, Overseas Development
Council
1717 Massachusetts Ave., N.W., Washington, DC 20036
Telephone: (202) 234-8701

CONTI, William J.
Shea and Gould
1775 Pennsylvania Ave., N.W., Suite 700, Washington, DC
20006
Telephone: (202) 833-9850

CONTRATTO, Dana C.
Crowell and Moring
1001 Pennsylvania Ave., N.W., Washington, DC 20004-
2505
Telephone: (202) 624-2500
Registered as lobbyist at U.S. Congress.
Clients:
Associated Gas Distributors
Brooklyn Union Gas Co.
Central Nebraska Public Power and Irrigation
District
Lehn & Fink Products Group
Nebraska Public Power District

CONWAY AND COMPANY
1120 Connecticut Ave., N.W. Suite 469, Washington, DC
20036
Telephone: (202) 289-0800
Registered as lobbyist at U.S. Congress.
Members of firm representing listed organizations:
Hayden, Robert T.

CONWAY, Daniel J.
Sr. V. President, General Counsel, Reinsurance Ass'n of
America
1819 L St., N.W., Suite 700, Washington, DC 20036
Telephone: (202) 293-3335
Registered as lobbyist at U.S. Congress.

CONWAY, Edward F., Jr.
Assistant General Counsel, Recreation Vehicle Industry
Ass'n
1896 Preston White Drive P.O. Box 2999, Reston, VA
22090
Telephone: (703) 620-6003
Background: Formerly Assistant Chief Counsel, Federal
Railroad Administration for 16 years.

CONWAY, James F., Jr.
Manager, Government Affairs, Siemens Capital Corp.
1455 Pennsylvania Ave., N.W. Suite 300, Washington, DC
20004
Telephone: (202) 347-0444

CONWAY, John A.
Political Specialist, Nat'l Education Ass'n of the U.S.
1201 16th St., N.W., Washington, DC 20036
Telephone: (202) 822-7300
Registered as lobbyist at U.S. Congress.

CONWAY, Margaret
Director, State and Local Projects, Catholics for a Free
Choice
1436 U St., N. W. Suite 301, Washington, DC 20009
Telephone: (202) 638-1706

COOGAN, John J.
Director, Health Affairs, Eastman Kodak Co.
1776 Eye St., N.W. Suite 1050, Washington, DC 20006
Telephone: (202) 857-3461
Registered as lobbyist at U.S. Congress.

COOK, Alexandra
Government Affairs Representative, Electronic Data Sys-
tems Corp.
1331 Pennsylvania Ave., N.W., Suite 1300 North, Wash-
ington, DC 20004
Telephone: (202) 637-6700
Registered as lobbyist at U.S. Congress.
Background: Serves as President, Women in Government
Relations.

COOK AND ASSOCIATES
2000 P St., N.W., Suite 505, Washington, DC 20036
Telephone: (202) 223-9786
Members of firm representing listed organizations:
Cook, Howard L. (Jr.)
Clients:
Metcor Inc. *(Howard L. Cook, Jr.)*

COOK, Bette
Senate For Relats Cttee, Off For Disast, AGENCY FOR
INTERNAT'L DEVELOPMENT
320 21st St., N.W., Washington, DC 20523
Telephone: (202) 647-8440

COOK, Charles E., Jr.
V. President, Hill and Knowlton Public Affairs Worldwide
Washington Harbour, 901 31st St., N.W., Washington, DC
20007
Telephone: (202) 333-7400
Registered as Foreign Agent: (#4170).
Background: Research Director, Democratic Senatorial
Campaign Committee, 1977-79. Staff Member, Senate
Democratic Policy Committee, 1982-84.

COOK, Cheryl
Legislative Assistant, Nat'l Farmers Union
600 Maryland Ave., S.W., Suite 202W, Washington, DC
20024
Telephone: (202) 554-1600
Registered as lobbyist at U.S. Congress.

COOK, David B.
Shea and Gardner
1800 Massachusetts Ave., N.W., Washington, DC 20036
Telephone: (202) 828-2000
Clients:
American President Companies

COOK, Gayla
Director, International Division, Nat'l Council of Negro Women
1211 Connecticut Ave. N.W. Suite 702, Washington, DC
20036
Telephone: (202) 659-0006

COOK, Harry N.
President, Nat'l Waterways Conference, Inc.
1130 17th St., N.W., Washington, DC 20036
Telephone: (202) 296-4415
Registered as lobbyist at U.S. Congress.

COOK, Howard L., Jr.
Cook and Associates
2000 P St., N.W., Suite 505, Washington, DC 20036
Telephone: (202) 223-9786

Registered as lobbyist at U.S. Congress.
Clients:
Metcor Inc.

COOK, Jonathan
Exec. Director, Support Center
1410 Q St., N.W., Washington, DC 20009
Telephone: (202) 462-2000

COOK, Joseph A.
Account Executive, Hill Group, Inc.
1200 17th St., N.W., Suite 400, Washington, DC 20036
Telephone: (202) 296-9200
Background: Serves as Exec. V. President, Nat'l Ass'n of
Chemical Distributors.
Clients:
Nat'l Ass'n of Chemical Distributors
Work Glove Manufacturers Ass'n

COOK, Judith Wise
Taggart and Associates, Inc.
1155 15th St., N.W., Suite 1108, Washington, DC 20005
Telephone: (202) 429-1940

COOK, Judy
Research Assistant, Public Housing, Public Housing Authorities Directors Ass'n
511 Capitol Court, N.E., Washington, DC 20002-4937
Telephone: (202) 546-5445

COOK, K. Richard
Wash. Representative, Gov't Relations, General Electric
Co.
1331 Pennsylvania Ave., N.W., Washington, DC 20004
Telephone: (202) 637-4307
Registered as lobbyist at U.S. Congress.

COOK, Lauren A.
Coordinator, State Scanning Network, Council of State
Policy and Planning Agencies
400 North Capitol St., N.W. Suite 285, Washington, DC
20001
Telephone: (202) 624-5386

COOK, Lauren M.
Director, Public Affairs and Development, George Mason
University Law School
3401 N. Fairfax Drive, Arlington, VA 22201-4498
Telephone: (703) 841-7114

COOK, Liz
Ozone Campaign Director, Friends of the Earth
218 D St., S.E., Washington, DC 20003
Telephone: (202) 544-2600

COOK, Marlow W.
Bishop, Cook, Purcell & Reynolds
1400 L St., N.W., Washington, DC 20005-3502
Telephone: (202) 371-5700
Registered as lobbyist at U.S. Congress.
Registered as Foreign Agent: (# 3050).
Background: Former U.S. Senator (R-KY), 1968-74.
Clients:
Akhiok-Kaguyak, Inc.
CNA Financial Corp.
Internat'l Llama Ass'n
Puerto Rico, Commonwealth of
Puerto Rico, Popular Democratic Party of
Texaco U.S.A.
Washington Public Power Supply System
(WPPSS)

COOK, Richard K.
Vice President, Lockheed Corp.
1825 Eye St., N.W., Suite 1100, Washington, DC 20006
Telephone: (202) 955-3350
Background: Admin. Assistant, Congressman Edwin B.
Dooley, 1960-1963. Legislative Assistant, Congressman
Oliver P. Bolton, 1963-1965. Professional staff member,
House Banking and Currency Committee, 1965-1969.
Deputy Assistant to the President for Legislative Affairs,
1969-1973.

COOK, Stephen K.
Exec. V. President/General Manager, Edelman, Inc., Dan-
iel J.
1420 K St., N.W., Washington, DC 20005
Telephone: (202) 371-0200
Registered as Foreign Agent: (# 3634).

Background: Press Secretary to Rep. Teno Roncalio (D-WY), 1973-75. Press Secretary to Rep. Berkley Bedell (D-IA), 1975-79.
Organizations represented:
CDM/Federal Programs Corp.
Hughes Aircraft Co.
Japan Tobacco, Inc.
Nat'l Gypsum Co.

COOK, Suzanne N.
Regulatory Assistant, Columbia Gas System Service Corp.
1250 Eye St., N.W., Suite 703, Washington, DC 20005
Telephone: (202) 842-7414

COOK, Thomas M.
Director, Industry Affairs, Nat'l Cattlemen's Ass'n
1301 Pennsylvania Ave., N.W., Suite 300, Washington, DC 20004
Telephone: (202) 347-0228
Registered as lobbyist at U.S. Congress.

COOKE, Charles E.
Washington Representative, Southern California Edison Co.
1001 Pennsylvania Ave., N.W. Suite 450N, Washington, DC 20004
Telephone: (202) 393-3075
Registered as lobbyist at U.S. Congress.

COOKE, Eileen D.
Director, Washington Office, American Library Ass'n
110 Maryland Ave., N.E., Suite 101, Washington, DC 20002
Telephone: (202) 547-4440
Registered as lobbyist at U.S. Congress.

COOKE, Terence S.
Counsel, Home Owners Warranty Corp.
2000 L St., N.W. Suite 400, Washington, DC 20036
Telephone: (202) 463-4770

COOKE, Willie E., Jr.
Exec. Director, Neighborhood Legal Services Program
701 4th St., N.W., Washington, DC 20001
Telephone: (202) 682-2700

COOKS, Shirley
Director, South/North Development Group, Ltd.
610 Fourth Place, S.W., Washington, DC 20024
Telephone: (202) 554-7032
Registered as lobbyist at U.S. Congress.
Registered as Foreign Agent: (#4219).

COOKS, Stoney
President, South/North Development Group, Ltd.
610 Fourth Place, S.W., Washington, DC 20024
Telephone: (202) 554-7032
Registered as lobbyist at U.S. Congress.
Registered as Foreign Agent: (#4219).
Background: Administrative Assistant, U.S. Congress, 5th District, Georgia, 1973-77. Exec. Assistant to U.S. Ambassador to the United Nations, 1977-79.
Clients:
Minorco Societe Anonyme

COOKSEY, Janie
Cong Liaison, DEPARTMENT OF COMMERCE - Patent and Trademark Office
C/o Asst Secy and Commissioner Patents and Trademarks, Washington, DC 20231
Telephone: (703) 557-1310

COOKSIN, Matthew
Legislative Specialist, Connecticut, State of
444 North Capitol St., N.W. Suite 317, Washington, DC 20001
Telephone: (202) 347-4535
Background: Former Legislative Assistant to Rep. Stan Lundine (D-NY).

COONEY, Bente E.
Policy Analyst, Nat'l Committee to Preserve Social Security and Medicare
2000 K St., N.W. Suite 800, Washington, DC 20006
Telephone: (202) 822-9459
Registered as lobbyist at U.S. Congress.

COONEY, Caroline
Public Relations Associate, Heritage Foundation
214 Massachusetts Ave., N.E., Washington, DC 20002
Telephone: (202) 546-4400

COONEY, David M.
President, Goodwill Industries of America, Inc.
9200 Wisconsin Ave., Bethesda, MD 20814-3896
Telephone: (301) 530-6500

COONEY, Edward
Deputy Director, Food Research and Action Center
1319 F St., N.W. Suite 500, Washington, DC 20004
Telephone: (202) 393-5060
Registered as lobbyist at U.S. Congress.
Background: Also represents the Child Nutrition Forum.

COONEY, Joanne M.
Administrative Director, OPERA America
777 14th St., N.W. Suite 520, Washington, DC 20005
Telephone: (202) 347-9262

COONEY, Nelson J.
President, Brick Institute of America
11490 Commerce Park Drive, Reston, VA 22091
Telephone: (703) 620-0010
Background: Also serves as Treasurer, Brick Political Action Committee.

COONEY, Paul E.
Foley & Lardner
1775 Pennsylvania Ave., N.W., Suite 1000, Washington, DC 20006-4680
Telephone: (202) 862-5300
Registered as lobbyist at U.S. Congress.
Clients:
American Red Cross
Aurora Health Care, Inc.
Central Bank of Tampa

COONEY, Stephen
Director, Internat'l Investment, Nat'l Ass'n of Manufacturers
1331 Pennsylvania Ave., N.W. Suite 1500 North, Washington, DC 20004-1703
Telephone: (202) 637-3000

COONS, Barbara
V. President & Director, Research Svcs., Hill and Knowlton Public Affairs Worldwide
Washington Harbour, 901 31st St., N.W., Washington, DC 20007
Telephone: (202) 333-7400
Registered as Foreign Agent: (#3301).
Background: Former Education Liaison Specialist, Library of Congress.

COOPER, Aileen
Director, Program & Public Affairs, B'nai B'rith Women
1828 L St., N.W., Suite 250, Washington, DC 20036
Telephone: (202) 857-1310

COOPER, B. Jay
Director of Communications, Republican Nat'l Committee
310 First St., S.E., Washington, DC 20003
Telephone: (202) 863-8500
Background: Former Deputy Press Secretary, The White House.

COOPER, Benjamin Y.
Sr. V. President of Government Affairs, Printing Industries of America
1730 North Lynn St., Arlington, VA 22209
Telephone: (703) 841-8115
Registered as lobbyist at U.S. Congress.
Background: Serves as Treasurer, Printing Industries of America Political Action Committee and also represents the Graphic Arts Legislative Council, Nat'l Ass'n of Printers and Lithographers, and the Graphic Arts Technical Foundation.

COOPER, Col. Charles D., USAF (Ret)
Director, Communications, Retired Officers Ass'n, The (TROA)
201 N. Washington St., Alexandria, VA 22314
Telephone: (703) 549-2311

COOPER, Doral S.
C & M Internat'l L.P.
1001 Pennsylvania Ave., N.W., Washington, DC 20004-2505
Telephone: (202) 624-2895
Registered as lobbyist at U.S. Congress.
Registered as Foreign Agent: (#3988).
Background: Former Assistant U.S. Trade Representative, Office of Bilateral Affairs, Reagan Administration.
Clients:
China, Foreign Trade Board of the Republic of
Korea Foreign Trade Ass'n
Singapore Trade Development Board
United Nations Conference on Trade and Development

COOPER, J. Michael
Bryan, Cave, McPheeters and McRoberts
1015 15th St., N.W., Suite 1000, Washington, DC 20005
Telephone: (202) 289-6100
Registered as lobbyist at U.S. Congress.
Background: Law Clerk, U.S. Court of Appeals, 1973-74.
Clients:
Czechoslovakia, Chamber of Commerce and Industry of

COOPER, John Sherman
Covington and Burling
1201 Pennsylvania Ave., N.W., Box 7566, Washington, DC 20044
Telephone: (202) 662-6000
Background: Former U.S. Senator (R-KY).

COOPER, Josephine S.
Senior V. President, Hill and Knowlton Public Affairs Worldwide
Washington Harbour, 901 31st St., N.W., Washington, DC 20007
Telephone: (202) 333-7400
Background: Air Quality Planning and Standards Program, Environmental Protection Agency, 1969-79. Environmental Legislative Staff Aide to Senator Howard Baker (R-TN), 1979-83. Assistant Administrator, EPA, 1983-85.
Clients:
Chlorine Institute
Distilled Spirits Council of the United States
FMC Corp.
Hastings, Nebraska, City of

COOPER, Mario M.
Laxalt, Washington, Perito & Dubuc
1120 Connecticut Ave., N.W., Suite 1000, Washington, DC 20036
Telephone: (202) 857-4000
Background: Staff Assistant to the President, Executive Office of the President, 1979-81.

COOPER, Mark N.
Research Director, Consumer Federation of America
1424 16th St., N.W. Suite 604, Washington, DC 20036
Telephone: (202) 387-6121
Registered as lobbyist at U.S. Congress.

COOPER, Mary Anderson
Acting Director, Nat'l Council of the Churches of Christ in the USA
110 Maryland Ave., N.E., Washington, DC 20002
Telephone: (202) 544-2350

COOPER, Milton
V. President, Program Development, Computer Sciences Corp. (Systems Group)
3160 Fairview Park Drive, Falls Church, VA 22042
Telephone: (703) 876-1000

COOPER, Sara
Director of Public Information, Nat'l Consumers League
815 15th St., N.W., Suite 516, Washington, DC 20005
Telephone: (202) 639-8140

COOPER, Stephanie
Coordinator, Member and Student Services, American Council of the Blind
1010 Vermont Ave., N.W. Suite 1100, Washington, DC 20005
Telephone: (202) 393-3666
Background: Also represents: American Blind Lawyers Ass'n, American Council of Blind Federal Employees, American Council of Blind Parents, American Council of Blind Radio Amateurs, Braille Revival League, Council of

COOPER, Stephanie (Cont'd)
Citizens with Low Vision, Council of Rehabilitation Specialists, Guide Dog Users, Inc., Independent Visually Impaired Enterprisers, Nat'l Alliance of Blind Students, Nat'l Ass'n of Blind Teachers, Randolph-Sheppard Vendors of America, Visually Impaired Data Processors Internat'l, Visually Impaired Secretarial/Transcribers Ass'n, Visually Impaired Veterans of America, American Council of Blind Lions, Library Users of America, Visually Impaired Piano Tuners Internat'l.

COOPERMAN, Richard M.
Chairman of the Board, Counselors For Management, Inc.
1000 16th St., N.W., Suite 603, Washington, DC 20006
Telephone: (202) 785-0550
Registered as Foreign Agent: (#3431).
Clients:
Cominco, Ltd.
Independent Zinc Alloyers Ass'n, Inc.

COORS, J. Bradford
Asst, Cong Rels, Legis & Cong Rels, DEPARTMENT OF HOUSING AND URBAN DEVELOPMENT
451 Seventh St., S.W., Washington, DC 20410
Telephone: (202) 755-7380

COOVER, Darrell
Sr. V. President, Government Relations, Nat'l Ass'n of Independent Insurers
499 South Capitol St., S.W. Suite 401, Washington, DC 20003
Telephone: (202) 484-2350
Registered as lobbyist at U.S. Congress.

COPAKEN, Richard D.
Covington and Burling
1201 Pennsylvania Ave., N.W., Box 7566, Washington, DC 20044
Telephone: (202) 662-6000
Registered as lobbyist at U.S. Congress.
Clients:
Puerto Rico Federal Affairs Administration
Puerto Rico, Popular Democratic Party of

COPE, Beulah M.
Adjutant General, United Spanish War Veterans
Box 1915, Washington, DC 20013
Telephone: (202) 347-1898

COPE, Bill
Manager, Federal Financial Relations, American Gas Ass'n
1515 Wilson Blvd., Arlington, VA 22209
Telephone: (703) 841-8651

COPE, James D.
President, Nonprescription Drug Manfacturers Ass'n
1150 Connecticut Ave., N.W.,, Washington, DC 20036
Telephone: (202) 429-9260

COPELAND, Jack L.
Consultant, Fidelity Pacific Group
1250 24th St., N.W., Suite 600, Washington, DC 20037
Telephone: (202) 466-0576
Registered as Foreign Agent: (#4300).
Clients:
Philippines, Government of the

COPELAND, James M., Jr.
Government Relations Consultant, McAuliffe, Kelly, Raffaelli & Siemens
1341 G St., N.W. Suite 200, Washington, DC 20005
Telephone: (202) 783-1800
Registered as lobbyist at U.S. Congress.
Registered as Foreign Agent: (#4332).
Background: Administrative Assistant to Rep. Pete Stark (D-CA), 1973-77. Director, Congressional Relations, Federal Home Loan Bank Board, 1977. Deputy Assistant to the President for Congressional Relations, 1978-80.
Clients:
Alameda County, California
Bay Area Rapid Transit District
Chicago Mercantile Exchange
Nat'l Telephone Services, Inc.
Pacific Mutual Life Insurance Co.
Sweetener Users Ass'n
Transamerica Corp.

COPELAND, John B.
Director of Export Administration, Motorola, Inc.
1350 Eye St., N.W., Suite 400, Washington, DC 20005-3306
Telephone: (202) 371-6900

COPLE, William J., III
King and Spalding
1730 Pennsylvania Ave., N.W. Suite 1200, Washington, DC 20006-4706
Telephone: (202) 737-0500
Background: Office of the Secretary of Defense, Office of General Counsel, 1980-83.

COPPELMAN, Peter
V. President, Wilderness Soc.
1400 Eye St., N.W., 10th Floor, Washington, DC 20005
Telephone: (202) 842-3400

COPPERTHITE, Michael C.
President, Washington Special Events
329 F St., N.E., Washington, DC 20002
Telephone: (202) 544-4286
Background: Former Deputy Political Director, Gephardt for President Committee.

COPPOLA, Felicia B.
Legislative Assistant, BP America Inc.
1776 Eye St., N.W., Suite 1000, Washington, DC 20006
Telephone: (202) 785-4888

COPPS, Michael J.
Sr. V. Pres., Public & Congress'l Affrs., American Meat Institute
Box 3556, Washington, DC 20007
Telephone: (703) 841-2400
Registered as lobbyist at U.S. Congress.
Background: Former Administrative Assistant to Senator Ernest Hollings (D-SC).

CORAZZINI, Robert F.
Pepper and Corazzini
1776 K St., N.W., Suite 700, Washington, DC 20006
Telephone: (202) 296-0600
Registered as lobbyist at U.S. Congress.
Clients:
Satellite Syndicated Systems, Inc.

CORBER, Robert J.
Steptoe and Johnson
1330 Connecticut Ave., N.W., Washington, DC 20036
Telephone: (202) 429-3000
Registered as lobbyist at U.S. Congress.
Background: Commissioner, Interstate Commerce Commission, 1975-76.

CORBETT, John J., Jr.
Spiegel and McDiarmid
1350 New York Ave., N.W., Suite 1100, Washington, DC 20005
Telephone: (202) 879-4000
Registered as lobbyist at U.S. Congress.
Clients:
Airline Passengers of America
Colorado Aviation Department (City and County of Denver)
Florida High Speed Rail Commission

CORBIN, Dr. Carlyle
Washington Representative, Virgin Islands, Office of the Governor
900 17th St., N.W., Suite 500, Washington, DC 20006
Telephone: (202) 293-3707

CORCORAN, James T.
V. President, Government Affairs, Greyhound Corp., The
2000 K St., N.W., Suite 203, Washington, DC 20006
Telephone: (202) 223-8630

CORCORAN, John F.
Assistant V. President, Public Affairs, Norfolk Southern Corp.
1500 K St., N.W. Suite 375, Washington, DC 20005
Telephone: (202) 383-4551
Registered as lobbyist at U.S. Congress.

CORCORAN, Patrick H.
Exec. Director, Ass'n of Oil Pipe Lines
1725 K St., N.W., Washington, DC 20006

Telephone: (202) 331-8228
Registered as lobbyist at U.S. Congress.

CORCORAN, Thomas G., Jr.
Corcoran, Youngman and Rowe
1511 K St., N.W. Suite 1100, Washington, DC 20005
Telephone: (202) 783-7900
Clients:
Coordination Council for North American Affairs

CORCORAN, YOUNGMAN AND ROWE
1511 K St., N.W. Suite 1100, Washington, DC 20005
Telephone: (202) 783-7900
Members of firm representing listed organizations:
Corcoran, Thomas G. (Jr.)
Cronin, Donald J., Counsel
Background: Former Administrative Assistant to Sen. Lister Hill of Alabama, 1953-69.
Clients:
Coordination Council for North American Affairs
(Thomas G. Corcoran, Jr.)

CORDARO, J. B.
President, Council for Responsible Nutrition
1300 19th St., N.W. Suite 310, Washington, DC 20036
Telephone: (202) 872-1488

CORDIA, Louis
V. President, Burson-Marsteller
1850 M St., N.W., Suite 900, Washington, DC 20036
Telephone: (202) 833-8550
Background: Special Assistant, Environmental Protection Agency, 1981-83.

CORDON, Alfred C.
Cordon and Kelly
1920 N St., N.W., Suite 200, Washington, DC 20036
Telephone: (202) 293-2300
Registered as lobbyist at U.S. Congress.

CORDON AND KELLY
1920 N St., N.W., Suite 200, Washington, DC 20036
Telephone: (202) 293-2300
Members of firm representing listed organizations:
Cordon, Alfred C.
Clients:
KBTX-TV
KFNB
KFNE
KFNR
KLFY-TV
KROC-TV
KWTX-TV
KXII
WENY-TV
WEVU
WIVB-TV
WKPT-TV
WMGM-TV

CORDONE, Maria C.
Legislative Representative, Internat'l Ass'n of Machinists and Aerospace Workers
1300 Connecticut Ave., N.W. Suite 404, Washington, DC 20036
Telephone: (202) 857-5200
Registered as lobbyist at U.S. Congress.

CORDTZ, Richard W.
Secretary-Treasurer, Service Employees Internat'l Union
1313 L St., N.W., Washington, DC 20005
Telephone: (202) 898-3200

CORETTE, John E., III
Cole, Corette & Abrutyn
1110 Vermont Ave., N.W., Suite 900, Washington, DC 20005
Telephone: (202) 872-1414
Registered as lobbyist at U.S. Congress.
Background: General Counsel, Export-Import Bank of the United States, 1969-75.

CORMAN, James C.
Silverstein and Mullens
1776 K St., N.W., Suite 800, Washington, DC 20006
Telephone: (202) 452-7900
Registered as lobbyist at U.S. Congress.
Background: Member, U.S. House of Representatives (D-CA), 1961-81. Member, House Committee on Ways and Means, 1968-81. Chairman, House Democratic Campaign

Committee, 1976-81.
Clients:
Majestic Realty Co.
MCA Inc.
Nat'l Structured Settlements Trade Ass'n
United States League of Savings Institutions

CORN, Robert S.
V. President, Landmark Strategies, Inc.
101 South Whiting St. Suite 319, Alexandria, VA 22304
Telephone: (703) 370-8500
Background: Former Western Regional Political Director,
Democratic National Party.

CORNELL, William A., Jr.
Lipsen Whitten & Diamond
1725 DeSales St., N.W., Suite 800, Washington, DC
20036
Telephone: (202) 659-6540
Registered as lobbyist at U.S. Congress.
Background: Administrative Assistant to Congressman Bill
Goodling, 1976-79; Executive Assistant to U.S. Senator
John Heinz, 1980-82.

CORNISH, Edward S.
President, World Future Soc.
4916 St. Elmo Ave., Bethesda, MD 20814
Telephone: (301) 656-8274

CORNISH, Jill
Publisher, Association Trends
4948 St. Elmo Ave., Suite 306, Bethesda, MD 20814
Telephone: (301) 652-8666

CORNISH, Norman G.
10209 Lloyd Road, Potomac, MD 20854
Telephone: (301) 762-6239
Background: A consultant to industry and government in
various fields, including the Defense Production Act, industrial modernization, economic development and energy. Serves as consultant to the Subcommittee on Economic Stabilization of the House Committee on Banking, Finance and Urban Affairs. Former President, Nat'l Council
to Preserve the U.S. Defense Industrial Base. Former senior Congressional staff member.
Organizations represented:
Nat'l Defense Contractors Expo
New Directions Group, Inc.

CORNISH, Paul L.
Exec. Director, Nat'l Ass'n of Public Insurance Adjusters
1101 14th St., N.W., Suite 1100, Washington, DC 20005
Telephone: (292) 371-1258

CORNMAN, John M.
Exec. Director, Gerontological Soc. of America
1275 K St., N.W., Suite 350, Washington, DC 20005
Telephone: (202) 842-1275

CORPORATE CONSULTING INTERNAT'L LTD.
1700 North Moore St., Suite 1610, Arlington, VA 22209
Telephone: (703) 524-8957
Background: A consulting firm specializing in advice and
project management to foreign firms investing in the U.S.,
foreign firm product liability assessment, trade networks,
U.S. firms investing abroad, identification of major project
opportunities and the registration/protection of patents,
trademarks and copyrights for U.S. and foreign firms.
Members of firm representing listed organizations:
McClure, William D.
Wallop, French C., President

CORPORATE CPR
2601 Babcock Rd., Vienna, VA 22180
Telephone: (703) 281-2734
Background: A consulting firm specializing in crisis public
relations (CPR).
Clients:
Fur Institute of Canada

CORRADO, Ernest J.
President, American Institute of Merchant Shipping
1000 16th St., N.W., Suite 511, Washington, DC 20036-
5705
Telephone: (202) 775-4399
Registered as lobbyist at U.S. Congress.

CORRIE, Quentin R.
Anderson and Quinn
12450 Fair Lakes Circle Suite 370, Fairfax, VA 22033-
4900
Telephone: (703) 222-2200
Clients:
American Automobile Ass'n

CORRIGAN, Mary Marcotte
Dir., Research and Information, ILA, Nat'l Rifle Ass'n of
America
1600 Rhode Island Ave., N.W., Washington, DC 20036
Telephone: (202) 828-6360
Registered as lobbyist at U.S. Congress.

CORRIGAN, Richard L.
Vice President, Government Affairs, CH2M HILL
Metropolitan Square, 655 15th St., N.W., Suite 444, Wash-
ington, DC 20005
Telephone: (202) 393-2426
Registered as lobbyist at U.S. Congress.

CORRIGAN, Robert F.
Washington Representative, United Brands Co.
1331 Pennsylvania Ave., N.W. Suite 1100, Washington,
DC 20004
Telephone: (202) 879-2410

CORRIGAN, Susan
Exec. V. President & CEO, Gifts in Kind, Inc.
700 North Fairfax St., Suite 300, Alexandria, VA 22314
Telephone: (703) 836-2121

CORRY, Martin C.
Director, Federal Affairs, American Ass'n of Retired Per-
sons
1909 K St., N.W., Washington, DC 20049
Telephone: (202) 728-4730
Registered as lobbyist at U.S. Congress.

CORS, Al, Jr.
Legislative and Political Director, Nat'l Tax Limitation
Committee
201 Massachusettes Ave., N.E., Suite C-7, Washington,
DC 20002
Telephone: (202) 547-4196

CORS, Allan D.
Sr. V. Pres. and Dir. of Gov't Affairs, Corning
1455 Pennsylvania Ave., N.W. Suite 500, Washington, DC
·20004
Telephone: (202) 347-2270
Registered as lobbyist at U.S. Congress.
Background: Counsel to the Minority, House Judiciary
Committee, 1962-1966. Serves also as Chairman, CORE-
PAC.

CORSO, Anthony R.
General Mgr., Corp. Government Relations, Mobil Corp.
1100 Connecticut Ave., N.W., Suite 620, Washington, DC
20036
Telephone: (202) 862-1300
Registered as lobbyist at U.S. Congress.

CORTESE, Alfred W.
Kirkland and Ellis
655 15th St., N.W. Suite 1200, Washington, DC 20005
Telephone: (202) 879-5000
Background: Former Assistant Exec. Director, Federal
Trade Commission.
Clients:
General Motors Corp.

CORWIN, Philip S.
Dir., Office of Optns. & Retail Banking, American Bankers
Ass'n
1120 Connecticut Ave., N.W., Washington, DC 20036
Telephone: (202) 663-5000
Registered as lobbyist at U.S. Congress.

COSMAN, Catherine
Washington Representative-Helsinki Watch, Human Rights
Watch
1522 K St., N.W., Suite 910, Washington, DC 20005
Telephone: (202) 371-6592

COSSON, David
V. President, Legal and Industry, Nat'l Telephone Cooper-
ative Ass'n
2626 Pennsylvania Ave., N.W., Washington, DC 20037
Telephone: (202) 298-2300
Background: General attorney, Federal Communications
Commission 1971-73; Public utilities specialist, FCC,
1967-71.

COSTA, Gregory J.
Manager, Political Affairs, Public Securities Ass'n
1000 Vermont Ave., N.W., Suite 800, Washington, DC
20005
Telephone: (202) 898-9390
Registered as lobbyist at U.S. Congress.
Background: Responsibilities include the political action
committee.

COSTELLO, Ann
Williams and Jensen, P.C.
1101 Connecticut Ave., N.W., Suite 500, Washington, DC
20036
Telephone: (202) 659-8201
Clients:
USAA

COSTELLO, Rev. Charles P., S.J.
President, Jesuit Secondary Education Ass'n
1424 16th St., N.W. Suite 300, Washington, DC 20036
Telephone: (202) 667-3888

COSTELLO, Daniel
Director of House Liaison, Chamber of Commerce of the
U.S.A.
1615 H St., N.W., Washington, DC 20062
Telephone: (202) 463-5600
Registered as lobbyist at U.S. Congress.

COSTELLO, Frank J.
Zuckert, Scoutt and Rasenberger
888 17th St., N.W., Suite 600, Washington, DC 20006-
3959
Telephone: (202) 298-8660
Clients:
Air Aruba
Air-Sea Forwarders, Inc.
Martinair Holland

COSTELLO, John H.
President, Citizens Network for Foreign Affairs
1616 H St., N.W., Washington, DC 20006
Telephone: (202) 639-8889

COSTELLO, Lisa M.
Administrator, Independent Insurance Agents of America,
Inc. Political Action Committee
600 Pennsylvania Ave., S.E. Suite 200, Washington, DC
20003
Telephone: (202) 675-6485

COSTELLO, Michael E.
Director, Government Affairs, Panhandle Eastern Corp.
1025 Connecticut Ave., N.W., Suite 404, Washington, DC
20036
Telephone: (202) 331-8090
Registered as lobbyist at U.S. Congress.

COSTELLO, Paul
V. President, Powell, Adams & Rinehart
1901 L St., N.W., 3rd Floor, Washington, DC 20036
Telephone: (202) 466-7590

COSTLOW, Donna J.
Assoc. Director, Risk Management, Nat'l Ass'n of Manufacturers
1331 Pennsylvania Ave., N.W. Suite 1500 North, Washington, DC 20004-1703
Telephone: (202) 637-3000
Registered as lobbyist at U.S. Congress.

COTTEN, DAY AND SELFON
1899 L St., N.W., 12th Floor, Washington, DC 20036
Telephone: (202) 659-9505
Members of firm representing listed organizations:
Day, James M.
Background: Director, Office of Hearings and Appeals,
Department of Interior, 1970-73. Administrator, U.S.
Mining Enforcement and Safety Administration,
1973-75.
Clients:

COTTEN, DAY AND SELFON (Cont'd)
American Samoa, Government of

COTTER, Francis P.
Advisor, Lipsen Whitten & Diamond
1725 DeSales St., N.W., Suite 800, Washington, DC 20036
Telephone: (202) 659-6540
Background: Staff Joint Congressional Committee on Atomic Energy, 1952-54.

COTTONE, Mello
Linton, Mields, Reisler and Cottone
1225 Eye St., N.W., Suite 300, Washington, DC 20005
Telephone: (202) 682-3901
Clients:
Linton, Mields Reisler and Cottone Political Action Committee

COUDERT BROTHERS
1627 Eye St., N.W. 12th Floor, Washington, DC 20006
Telephone: (202) 775-5100
Background: Washington office of a New York law firm.
Members of firm representing listed organizations:
Coerper, Milo C.
Herlach, Mark D.
Katz, Sherman E.
Linowitz, Sol M.
Background: U.S. Ambassador to the Organization of American States, 1966-69. Co-negotiator of the Panama Canal Treaty, 1977. Member of the Board of Directors, Pan American World Airways.
Lipstein, Robert A.
Wachtmeister, (Count) Wilhelm, Senior International Advisor
Background: Former Swedish Ambassador to the United States.
Clients:
AB Bofors
Australia, Commonwealth of *(Sherman E. Katz)*
Bundesvereinigung der Deutschen Ernahrangsindustrie *(Robert A. Lipstein)*
Canada, Government of
Centrale Marketinggesellschaft der Deutschen Agrarwirtschaft *(Milo C. Coerper, Robert A. Lipstein)*
China, Government of the People's Republic of
Colombia, Embassy of
Edelstahlwerke Buderus AG *(Milo C. Coerper)*
German Flatware Manufacturers Ass'n *(Milo C. Coerper)*
German Specialty Steel Ass'n *(Milo C. Coerper)*
Krupp Internat'l *(Milo C. Coerper)*
L'Air Liquide *(Robert A. Lipstein)*
Marshall Islands, Government of
Nat'l Ass'n of Sugar Cane Growers
NEC Corp. *(Mark D. Herlach)*
Nippon Electric Co., Ltd. *(Milo C. Coerper)*
West German Iron and Steel Federation *(Milo C. Coerper)*

COUGHLAN, William D.
Exec. V. President and CEO, American Physical Therapy Ass'n
1111 North Fairfax St., Alexandria, VA 22314
Telephone: (703) 684-2782

COUGHLIN, Edward T.
Director, Regulatory Affairs, Nat'l Milk Producers Federation
1840 Wilson Blvd., Arlington, VA 22201
Telephone: (703) 243-6111
Registered as lobbyist at U.S. Congress.
Background: Former Director, Regulatory Affairs Marketing Service, USDA.

COUILLARD, Walter E.
Director of Retired Members, Nat'l Ass'n of Letter Carriers of the United States of America
100 Indiana Ave., N.W., Washington, DC 20001
Telephone: (202) 393-4695
Registered as lobbyist at U.S. Congress.

COULSON, E. Bret
Dir, Legis Affrs, EXECUTIVE OFFICE OF THE PRESIDENT - Nat'l Security Council
1600 Pennsylvania Ave., N.W., Washington, DC 20500
Telephone: (202) 395-3055

COULTER, William
V. President, Policy and Affairs, COMSAT General Corp.
950 L'Enfant Plaza, S.W., Washington, DC 20024
Telephone: (202) 863-6000

COUNSELORS FOR MANAGEMENT, INC.
1000 16th St., N.W., Suite 603, Washington, DC 20006
Telephone: (202) 785-0550
Registered as Foreign Agent: (#3431)
Members of firm representing listed organizations:
Cooperman, Richard M., Chairman of the Board
Lipsen, Janice C., President
Background: Serves as Director, Washington Office of the Governor, State of Hawaii and as Deputy Exec. Director, Aluminum Recycling Ass'n and Independent Zinc Alloyers Ass'n. Was an assistant to House Speaker Carl Albert, 1970-75.
Clients:
Cominco, Ltd. *(Richard M. Cooperman)*
Hawaii, Washington Office of *(Janice C. Lipsen)*
Independent Zinc Alloyers Ass'n, Inc. *(Richard M. Cooperman, Janice C. Lipsen)*

COUNTERTERRORISM CONSULTANTS L.P.
1800 Diagonal Road, Suite 230, Alexandria, VA 22314
Telephone: (703) 683-6988
Registered as Foreign Agent: (#4294)
Members of firm representing listed organizations:
McCormick, L. Carter (Jr.)
Walker, Gerald S.
Clients:
Jamaica, Government of *(L. Carter McCormick, Jr., Gerald S. Walker)*

COUNTS, Alex
Legislative Director, RESULTS
236 Massachusetts Ave., N.E. Suite 110, Washington, DC 20002
Telephone: (202) 543-9340

COURTNEY, Jeremiah
Counsel, Blooston, Mordkofsky, Jackson & Dickens
2120 L St., N.W. Suite 300, Washington, DC 20037
Telephone: (202) 659-0830
Background: Specializes in communications law other than broadcasting law. Assistant General Counsel, Federal Communications Commission, 1946.
Clients:
Academy of Model Aeronautics

COURTNEY, MCCAMANT AND TURNEY
1725 K St., N.W., Washington, DC 20006
Telephone: (202) 331-9825
Background: Represents clients on Capitol Hill and with federal agencies.
Members of firm representing listed organizations:
Turney, Richard F.
Background: Washington Representative, Automotive Service Industry Ass'n.
Clients:
Automotive Service Industry Ass'n *(Richard F. Turney)*
Interstate Taxation Coalition *(Richard F. Turney)*
Nat'l Ass'n of Chain Manufacturers *(Richard F. Turney)*

COURTNEY, Roger C.
Director of Government Relations, American Ass'n of Colleges of Osteopathic Medicine
1620 Eye St., N.W., Suite 220, Washington, DC 20006
Telephone: (202) 467-4131
Background: Special Expert, Nat'l Heart, Lung, and Blood Institute, NIH, 1983-84; Research Analyst (1984-85) and Special Consultant (1985-86), Prospective Payment Commission, NIH.

COURTOT, Marilyn
Director, Standard & Technology, Ass'n for Information and Image Management
1100 Wayne Ave. Suite 1100, Silver Spring, MD 20910
Telephone: (301) 587-8202
Background: Former Ass't Secretary, U.S. Senate.

COUSINS, James H.
Sr. V. President, Legislative Affairs, United States League of Savings Institutions
1709 New York Ave., N.W., Suite 801, Washington, DC 20006
Telephone: (202) 637-8900

Registered as lobbyist at U.S. Congress.

COUSINS, Susan M.
Associate Manager, Legislation, Chamber of Commerce of the U.S.A.
1615 H St., N.W., Washington, DC 20062
Telephone: (202) 659-6000
Registered as lobbyist at U.S. Congress.

COUTTEE, Douglas
Internat'l V. President, Civil Rights, United Food and Commercial Workers Internat'l Union
1775 K St., N.W., Washington, DC 20006
Telephone: (202) 223-3111

COUTURE, Kym
Legis Officer, Legis & Cong Rels, DEPARTMENT OF HOUSING AND URBAN DEVELOPMENT
451 Seventh St., S.W., Washington, DC 20410
Telephone: (202) 755-5005

COVALL, Mark
Director, Congressional Affairs, Nat'l Ass'n of Private Psychiatric Hospitals
1319 F St., N.W., Suite 1000, Washington, DC 20004
Telephone: (202) 393-6700
Registered as lobbyist at U.S. Congress.

COVE ASSOCIATES
918 16th St., N.W. Suite 702, Washington, DC 20006
Telephone: (202) 638-3707
Background: A consulting firm.
Members of firm representing listed organizations:
Cove, John F.
Background: Serves as Exec. V. President, Ass'n of U.S. Night Vision Manufacturers.
Clients:
Ass'n of U.S. Night Vision Manufacturers *(John F. Cove)*
Grumman Corp. *(John F. Cove)*

COVE, John F.
Cove Associates
918 16th St., N.W. Suite 702, Washington, DC 20006
Telephone: (202) 638-3707
Registered as lobbyist at U.S. Congress.
Background: Serves as Exec. V. President, Ass'n of U.S. Night Vision Manufacturers.
Clients:
Ass'n of U.S. Night Vision Manufacturers
Grumman Corp.

COVE, Maurice
Treasurer, Syscon Corp. Political Action Committee
1000 Thomas Jefferson St., N.W., Washington, DC 20007
Telephone: (202) 342-4000

COVELL, Andrea M.
Asst. V. Pres. & Asst. Legislat. Counsel, GEICO Corp.
GEICO Plaza, Washington, DC 20076
Telephone: (301) 986-3000

COVELL, Barbara J.
C & M Internat'l L.P.
1001 Pennsylvania Ave., N.W., Washington, DC 20004-2505
Telephone: (202) 624-2895
Registered as Foreign Agent: (#3988).

COVER, Michael W.
Dir., Cong. Relations/Asst. to Pres., Recording Industry Ass'n of America
1020 19th St., N.W., Suite 200, Washington, DC 20036
Telephone: (202) 775-0101
Registered as lobbyist at U.S. Congress.

COVERT, John
Director, Communications, Nat'l Ass'n of Chain Drug Stores
Box 1417-D49, Alexandria, VA 22313
Telephone: (703) 549-3001

COVINGTON AND BURLING
1201 Pennsylvania Ave., N.W., Box 7566, Washington, DC 20044
Telephone: (202) 662-6000
Members of firm representing listed organizations:
Ackerman, Jerome
Allen, William H.

Applebaum, Harvey M.
Atwood, James R.
Barald, Patricia Anne
Blake, Jonathan D.
Brady, Richard A.
Bruce, E. Edward
Clagett, Brice M.
Cohen, Edwin S.
  Background: Assistant Secretary of the Treasury, 1969-1972; Under Secretary of the Treasury, 1972-1973.
Cooper, John Sherman
  Background: Former U.S. Senator (R-KY).
Copaken, Richard D.
DeArment, Roderick A.
  Background: Former Chief Counsel, Senate Finance Committee.
Douglas, John W.
  Background: Ass't Attorney General, Civil Division, U.S. Dep't of Justice, 1963-66.
Dunnan, Weaver W.
Dym, Herbert
Ellicott, John
Ely, Clausen (Jr.)
Fels, Nicholas W.
Garrett, Theodore L.
Gilbert, Scott D.
Grace, David R.
Gribbon, Daniel M.
Horne, Michael S.
Horsky, Charles A., Counsel
  Background: Solicitor General's Office, 1935-37, Adviser to the President for National Capital Affairs, 1962-67. Director, Attorney General's Committee on Bankruptcy, 1935-40. Office of Chief Counsel for War Crimes, 1945-47; assistant prosecutor at Nuremberg, 1948.
Hutt, Peter Barton
  Background: Former General Counsel, Food and Drug Administration, 1971-1975.
Iverson, William D.
Johnson, (Jr.) O. Thomas
Jones, John B. (Jr.), Partner
Lambert, Eugene I.
Leverich, Bingham B.
Levy, Gregg H.
Levy, Michael R.
Livingston, S. William (Jr.)
Ludwig, Eugene A.
McGiffert, David E.
  Background: Under Secretary of the Army, 1966-69. Assistant Secretary of Defense, Internat'l Security Affairs, 1977-81.
Michaelson, Michael G.
Miller, Charles A.
Nickles, Peter J.
Owen, Roberts B.
  Background: Legal Advisor, U.S. Department of State, 1979-81.
Paul, William M.
Roach, Arvid E. (II)
Ruff, Charles
Sailer, Henry P.
Sayler, Robert N.
Smith, John T. (II)
Spear, Sandra L.
Stock, Stuart C.
Teel, Keith A.
Temko, Stanley L.
Topol, Allan J.
Trooboff, Peter D.
Vine, John M.
Watkin, Virginia G.
Weiss, Mark A.
Williamson, Thomas S. (Jr.), Partner
Winner, Sonya D.
Clients:
Air Products and Chemicals, Inc. *(Nicholas W. Fels)*
American Cyanamid Co.
American Watch Ass'n
Amoco Corp. *(John M. Vine)*
Animal Health Institute *(Eugene I. Lambert)*
Armstrong World Industries, Inc. *(Robert N. Sayler)*
Asphalt Institute *(Peter Barton Hutt)*
Ass'n of Maximum Service Telecasters, Inc. *(Jonathan D. Blake)*
AT&T *(Harvey M. Applebaum, Jr. O. Thomas Johnson)*
Bristol-Myers Squibb Co.

British Columbia, Canada, Government of *(Harvey M. Applebaum)*
BSA - Business Software Alliance *(James R. Atwood)*
Business Men's Assurance Co. of America
Campbell Soup Co. *(Sandra L. Spear)*
Chambre Syndicale des Producteurs d'Aciers Fins et Speciaux *(Harvey M. Applebaum)*
Coalition to Preserve the Integrity of American Trademarks *(Scott D. Gilbert, Eugene A. Ludwig)*
Copper and Brass Fabricators Council
Cranston, Rhode Island, Department of Human Services *(Thomas S. Williamson, Jr.)*
Direct Marketing Ass'n
Domtar, Inc. *(Harvey M. Applebaum)*
du Pont de Nemours and Co., E. I. *(Daniel M. Gribbon)*
ERISA Industry Committee (ERIC), The *(John M. Vine)*
Exxon Co., U.S.A. *(Harvey M. Applebaum)*
First Federal Savings Bank of Western Maryland
General Electric Co. *(Patricia Anne Barald, Allan J. Topol)*
General Telephone Co. of California
Honda Motor Co. *(Harvey M. Applebaum)*
Internat'l Ice Cream Ass'n
Internat'l Minerals and Chemical Corp. *(Harvey M. Applebaum, Jr. O. Thomas Johnson, Sonya D. Winner)*
Internat'l Swap Dealers Ass'n *(Eugene A. Ludwig)*
Investment Company Institute
Lansing, Michigan, Department of Social Services *(Thomas S. Williamson, Jr.)*
Lin Broadcasting Corp. *(Jonathan D. Blake)*
Maui Land and Pineapple Co., Inc. *(William M. Paul)*
Mental Health Law Project *(Peter J. Nickles)*
Merck and Co. *(Herbert Dym, Stanley L. Temko)*
Milk Industry Foundation
Monarch Capital Corp.
Montana Power Co.
Motorola, Inc. *(Harvey M. Applebaum)*
Nat'l Ass'n for Biomedical Research
Oklahoma Department of Human Services *(Charles A. Miller)*
Puerto Rico, Commonwealth of *(Michael G. Michaelson)*
Puerto Rico Federal Affairs Administration *(Richard D. Copaken)*
Puerto Rico, Popular Democratic Party of *(Richard D. Copaken)*
Puerto Rico Ports Authority *(William H. Allen)*
Quebec, Canada, Government of *(Harvey M. Applebaum)*
Silver Group, Inc. *(Eugene I. Lambert)*
SmithKline Beecham *(Stanley L. Temko)*
Sun Life Assurance Co. of Canada (U.S. Division) *(Michael R. Levy, Eugene A. Ludwig)*
Tobacco Institute
Upjohn Co. *(Herbert Dym, Eugene I. Lambert, Stanley L. Temko)*
Uranium Producers of America
Washington Area Bankers Ass'n *(Stuart C. Stock)*

COWAN, Glenn A.
FMR Group Inc., The
1000 Potomac St., N.W. Suite 401, Washington, DC 20007
Telephone: (202) 333-2533

COWAN, James W.
Dir., Fed. Rtns. - Agr./Natural Resouces, Nat'l Ass'n of State Universities and Land-Grant Colleges
One Dupont Circle, N.W., Suite 710, Washington, DC 20036-1191
Telephone: (202) 778-0818

COWAN, Mark D.
Chief Executive Officer, Jefferson Group, The
1341 G St., N.W., Suite 1100, Washington, DC 20005
Telephone: (202) 638-3535
Background: Former Assistant Legislative Counsel, Central Intelligence Agency and former chief of staff to ex-Secretary of Labor, Raymond Donovan.
Clients:
Boonestroo, Rosene, Anderlik & Associates
Gerson and Co., L. M.
Industrial Safety Equipment Ass'n
Minnesota Mining and Manufacturing Co. (3M Co.)

Pittston Co., The

COWAN, Sharon R.
Federal Government Relations Manager, American Soc. of Mechanical Engineers
1825 K St., N.W., Suite 218, Washington, DC 20006
Telephone: (202) 785-3756
Registered as lobbyist at U.S. Congress.

COWARD, Nicholas F.
Baker and McKenzie
815 Connecticut Ave., N.W. Suite 1100, Washington, DC 20006-4078
Telephone: (202) 452-7000
Clients:
Stockton, California, Port of

COWDEN, Dick
Exec. Director, American Ass'n of Enterprise Zones
1730 K St., N.W., Suite 915, Washington, DC 20006
Telephone: (202) 466-2687

COWLES, C. Deming, IV
1050 Thomas Jefferson St., N.W., Washington, DC 20007
Telephone: (202) 333-1617
Registered as lobbyist at U.S. Congress.
Background: An attorney.
Organizations represented:
  Alaska Crab Coalition
  Bering Sea Fishermen's Ass'n
  Cordova District Fishermen United
  Fairbanks/North Star Borough
  Florida Crushed Orange, Inc.
  Institute of Resource Management
  Kodiak Longline Vessel Owners Ass'n
  Pacific States Marine Fisheries Commission
  Southeast Alaska Seiners Ass'n
  United Fishermen of Alaska

COX, Archibald
Chairman, Common Cause
2030 M St., N.W., Washington, DC 20036
Telephone: (202) 833-1200
Registered as lobbyist at U.S. Congress.

COX, Carol G.
President, Committee for a Responsible Federal Budget
220 1/2 E St., N.E., Washington, DC 20002
Telephone: (202) 547-4484

COX, Eric
Exec. Director, Campaign for United Nations Reform
418 7th St., S.E., Washington, DC 20003
Telephone: (202) 546-3956
Registered as lobbyist at U.S. Congress.

COX, Ms. Garylee
Regional V. President, American Arbitration Ass'n
1730 Rhode Island Ave., N.W., Suite 509, Washington, DC 20036
Telephone: (202) 296-8510

COX, Dr. Geraldine V.
Vice President, Technical Director, Chemical Manufacturers Ass'n
2501 M St., N.W., Washington, DC 20037
Telephone: (202) 887-1260
Background: Also serves as National President, Federation of Organizations for Professional Women.

COX, Dr. James E.
Director of Government Affairs, American Soc. of Heating, Refrigerating and Air Conditioning Engineers
1825 K St., N.W., Suite 215, Washington, DC 20006-1202
Telephone: (202) 833-1830

COX, Jerry W.
Murphy and Demory, Ltd.
2300 N St., N.W. Suite 725, Washington, DC 20037
Telephone: (202) 785-3323
Registered as lobbyist at U.S. Congress.
Background: Former Legislative Counsel to Senator John Danforth (R-MO).
Clients:
Anglo-American Auto Auctions Inc.

COX, John A., Jr.
Manager, Government Affairs, Nat'l Tooling and Machining Ass'n
9300 Livingston Rd., Fort Washington, MD 20744
Telephone: (301) 248-6200
Background: Serves as Staff Executive, Tooling and Machining Industry Political Action Committee.

COX, John B.
Director of Communications, Nat'l Ass'n of College and University Business Officers
One Dupont Circle, N.W., Suite 500, Washington, DC 20036-1178
Telephone: (202) 861-2500

COX, Joseph J.
V. President, American Institute of Merchant Shipping
1000 16th St., N.W., Suite 511, Washington, DC 20036-5705
Telephone: (202) 775-4399

COX, Kenneth A.
Of Counsel, Haley, Bader and Potts
2000 M St., N.W. Suite 600, Washington, DC 20036
Telephone: (202) 331-0606
Background: Special Counsel, Senate Commerce Committee, 1956-1957. Chief, Broadcast Bureau, Federal Communications Commission, 1961-1963. Member, Federal Communications Commission, 1963-1970. Serves as Senior Vice President and Counsel, MCI Telecommunications Corp. and member of its Board of Directors.
Clients:
MCI Communications Corp.

COX, Patricia
Cong Correspondent, EXECUTIVE OFFICE OF THE PRESIDENT - The White House
1600 Pennsylvania Ave., N.W. 102 East Wing, Washington, DC 20500
Telephone: (202) 456-7500

COX, Col. Philip, USAF (Ret)
Military Analyst, American Security Council Foundation
733 15th St., N.W. Suite 700, Washington, DC 20005
Telephone: (202) 484-1676

COX, Tamara
V. President, Hill and Knowlton Public Affairs Worldwide
Washington Harbour, 901 31st St., N.W., Washington, DC 20007
Telephone: (202) 333-7400
Registered as lobbyist at U.S. Congress.
Background: Former aide to Rep. John Napier (R-SC).
Clients:
American Mining Congress
Brewster Heights Packing Co.
Larry Jones Ministries
Tobacco Institute

COX, Thomas
Policy Analyst, Latin America, Heritage Foundation
214 Massachusetts Ave., N.E., Washington, DC 20002
Telephone: (202) 546-4400

COX, Willard F.
Associate, Cassidy and Associates, Inc.
655 15th St., N.W., Suite 1100, Washington, DC 20005
Telephone: (202) 347-0773
Registered as lobbyist at U.S. Congress.
Background: Special Assistant to Rep. Don Fuqua (D-FL), 1979-83.

COX, William J.
V. President, Div. of Gov't Services, Catholic Health Ass'n of the United States
1776 K St., N.W. Suite 204, Washington, DC 20006
Telephone: (202) 296-3993

COXSON, Harold P.
Thompson, Mann and Hutson
3000 K St., N.W. Suite 600, Washington, DC 20007
Telephone: (202) 783-1900
Registered as lobbyist at U.S. Congress.
Clients:
Bechtel Civil & Minerals, Inc.
Construction Industry Labor Law Coalition
Fluor-Daniel Corp.
Milliken and Co.

COY, John
Senior V. President, Jefferson Group, The
1341 G St., N.W., Suite 1100, Washington, DC 20005
Telephone: (202) 638-3535
Clients:
Children's Survival Plan
du Pont de Nemours and Co., E. I.
St. Ambrose University

COYLE, Kevin J.
President, American Rivers
801 Pennsylvania Ave., S.E. Suite 303, Washington, DC 20003-2155
Telephone: (202) 547-6900
Registered as lobbyist at U.S. Congress.

COYLE, Timothy L.
Asst Secy, Legislation & Cong Relations, DEPARTMENT OF HOUSING AND URBAN DEVELOPMENT
451 Seventh St., S.W., Washington, DC 20410
Telephone: (202) 755-5005

CR ASSOCIATES
317 Massachusetts Ave., N.E., Suite 100, Washington, DC 20002
Telephone: (202) 546-4732
Background: A government and public relations firm.
Members of firm representing listed organizations:
Cavarocchi, Nicholas G.
Forster, Theresa
Background: Former Legislative Aide to Senator David Pryor (D-AR).
Lacoste, Rene, Senior Associate
Background: Former Staff, Federal Reserve System's Board of Governors.
Ruscio, Domenic R.
Background: Former Staff Member, U. S. Senate Committee on Appropriations and Deputy Assistant Secretary of Management and Budget, U.S. Department of Health, Education and Welfare.
Clients:
Alzheimer's Ass'n *(Nicholas G. Cavarocchi, Domenic R. Ruscio)*
American Academy of Orthopaedic Surgeons *(Nicholas G. Cavarocchi)*
American Ass'n for Dental Research *(Nicholas G. Cavarocchi)*
American Ass'n of Colleges of Podiatric Medicine *(Domenic R. Ruscio)*
Ass'n of University Programs in Health Administration *(Domenic R. Ruscio)*
Conjoint Committee on Diagnostic Radiology *(Domenic R. Ruscio)*
Delta Dental Plans Ass'n
Seton Hall School of Law *(Domenic R. Ruscio)*

CRACO, Louis A.
Willkie Farr and Gallagher
1155 21st St., N.W., 6th Fl., Washington, DC 20036-3302
Telephone: (202) 328-8000
Clients:
American Institute of Certified Public Accountants

CRAFT BAKER, Nancy
V. President, Communications, Institute for Research on the Economics of Taxation (IRET)
1331 Pennsylvania Ave., N.W. Suite 515, Washington, DC 20004
Telephone: (202) 347-9570

CRAFT, Gretchen
Cong Liaison Asst, DEPARTMENT OF COMMERCE
14th and Constitution Ave. S.W., Washington, DC 20230
Telephone: (202) 377-5485

CRAFT AND LOESCH
1050 Thomas Jefferson St, N.W. 6th Floor, Washington, DC 20007
Telephone: (202) 965-6290
Members of firm representing listed organizations:
Swanson, David L.

CRAFT, Robert H., Jr.
Sullivan and Cromwell
1701 Pennsylvania Ave., N.W. Suite 800, Washington, DC 20006
Telephone: (202) 956-7500
Registered as lobbyist at U.S. Congress.

Background: Special Assistant to Under Secretary of State, 1974-76. Exec. Assistant to Chairman, Securities and Exchange Commission, 1976.

CRAIG ASSOCIATES
1701 K St., N.W., Suite 200, Washington, DC 20006
Telephone: (202) 466-0001
Background: A firm specializing in legislative representation, grants consultation and federal agency liaison.
Members of firm representing listed organizations:
Craig, (Patricia) Johnson, President
Rothaar, Jessica
Clients:
County Welfare Directors of California *(Patricia Johnson Craig)*
Dakota County, Minnesota *(Patricia Johnson Craig)*
Ramsey County, Minnesota *(Patricia Johnson Craig)*
San Bernardino County, California *(Patricia Johnson Craig)*

CRAIG, Bruce
Coordinator, Cultural Resources, Nat'l Parks and Conservation Ass'n
1015 31st St., N.W., Washington, DC 20007
Telephone: (202) 944-8530
Registered as lobbyist at U.S. Congress.

CRAIG, Daniel
Director, Legislative Policy, Nat'l Cable Television Ass'n
1724 Massachusetts Ave., N.W., Washington, DC 20036
Telephone: (202) 775-3550
Registered as lobbyist at U.S. Congress.
Background: Former aide to Senator Daniel Inouye (D-HI).

CRAIG, Gregory
Williams and Connolly
839 17th St., N.W. 1000 Hill Bldg., Washington, DC 20006
Telephone: (202) 331-5000

CRAIG, Jim C.
Public Relations Director, American Petroleum Institute
1220 L St., N.W., Washington, DC 20005
Telephone: (202) 682-8120

CRAIG, Patricia Johnson
President, Craig Associates
1701 K St., N.W., Suite 200, Washington, DC 20006
Telephone: (202) 466-0001
Clients:
County Welfare Directors of California
Dakota County, Minnesota
Ramsey County, Minnesota
San Bernardino County, California

CRAIG, William D.
Manager, Energy Programs, Bechtel Group, Inc.
1620 Eye St., N.W., Suite 703, Washington, DC 20006
Telephone: (202) 393-4747

CRAIGUE, Alan
Regional Manager, Kollmorgen Corp.
Box 2306, Falls Church, VA 22042
Telephone: (703) 573-7050

CRAIN, Douglas
Dir., Wash. Office, Aircraft Prod. Grp., LTV Aircraft Products Group
1725 Jefferson Davis Hwy. Suite 900, Arlington, VA 22202
Telephone: (703) 521-6560

CRAM, M. Victoria
Government Relations Consultant, Ball, Janik and Novack
1101 Pennsylvania Ave., N.W. Suite 1035, Washington, DC 20004
Telephone: (202) 638-3307
Background: Staff Assistant to Rep. John Seiberling (D-OH), 1978-79. Legislative assistant, Democratic Study Group. 1979-81.
Clients:
Fresno, California, County of
Portland, Oregon, City of

CRAMER AND HABER
1029 Vermont Ave., N.W. 4th Floor, Washington, DC 20005
Telephone: (202) 872-8103
Members of firm representing listed organizations:
 Cramer, Mark C.
 Cramer, William C.
  Background: Member of U.S. House of Reps. (R-FL), 1954-70. Republican National Committeeman from Florida 1964-72. Chairman Rules Committee, Republican National Convention 1972.
 Williams, Eliazer A.
Clients:
 Canaveral Port Authority
 China, Administration of Shantou Special Economic Zone of *(William C. Cramer, Eliazer A. Williams)*
 Dade County Internat'l Airport *(William C. Cramer)*

CRAMER, James P.
Exec V. President/Chief Exec. Officer, American Institute of Architects, The
1735 New York Ave., N.W., Washington, DC 20006
Telephone: (202) 626-7300
Registered as lobbyist at U.S. Congress.

CRAMER, Mark C.
Cramer and Haber
1029 Vermont Ave., N.W. 4th Floor, Washington, DC 20005
Telephone: (202) 872-8103
Registered as Foreign Agent: (#3688).

CRAMER, William C.
Cramer and Haber
1029 Vermont Ave., N.W. 4th Floor, Washington, DC 20005
Telephone: (202) 872-8103
Registered as lobbyist at U.S. Congress.
Registered as Foreign Agent: (#3688).
Background: Member of U.S. House of Reps. (R-FL), 1954-70. Republican National Committeeman from Florida 1964-72. Chairman Rules Committee, Republican National Convention 1972.
Clients:
 China, Administration of Shantou Special Economic Zone of
 Dade County Internat'l Airport

CRANDALL, Derrick A.
President, American Recreation Coalition
1331 Pennsylvania Ave., N.W., Suite 726, Washington, DC 20004
Telephone: (202) 662-7420
Background: Served as Chairman, Government Affairs Committee, American Soc. of Ass'n Executives, 1985-86.

CRANE, David C.
V. Pres, Issues Development and Research, People for the American Way
2000 M St., N.W., Suite 400, Washington, DC 20036
Telephone: (202) 467-4999

CRANE, Donald A.
Assoc. Director, Government Relations, Grace and Co., W. R.
919 18th St., N.W., Suite 400, Washington, DC 20006
Telephone: (202) 452-6700
Registered as lobbyist at U.S. Congress.
Background: Staff Member, Interior and Insular Affairs Committee, U.S. House of Representatives, 1965-72.

CRANE, Edward H.
President, Cato Institute
224 Second St., S.E., Washington, DC 20003
Telephone: (202) 546-0200

CRANE, Mary
Legislative Representative, American Heart Ass'n
1250 Connecticut Ave., N.W., Suite 360, Washington, DC 20036
Telephone: (202) 822-9380

CRANE, Rhonda
District Manager, Federal Gov't Affairs, AT&T
Suite 1000, 1120 20th St., N.W., Washington, DC 20036
Telephone: (202) 457-2402

CRANE, Stacey L.
Exec. Director, Municipal Treasurers Ass'n of the United States and Canada
1420 16th St., N.W., Suite 302, Washington, DC 20036
Telephone: (202) 797-7347

CRANER, Lorne W.
Dep Asst Secy, Legis Affrs, DEPARTMENT OF STATE
2201 C St., N.W., Washington, DC 20520
Telephone: (202) 647-4204

CRANWELL, George E.
Cranwell & O'Connell
4113 Lee Highway, Arlington, VA 22207
Telephone: (703) 522-2255
Clients:
 American Soc. for Photogrammetry and Remote Sensing
 Internat'l Soc. for Photogrammetry and Remote Sensing

CRANWELL & O'CONNELL
4113 Lee Highway, Arlington, VA 22207
Telephone: (703) 522-2255
Members of firm representing listed organizations:
 Cranwell, George E.
Clients:
 American Soc. for Photogrammetry and Remote Sensing *(George E. Cranwell)*
 Internat'l Soc. for Photogrammetry and Remote Sensing *(George E. Cranwell)*

CRATER, Tim
Special Representative, Nat'l Ass'n of Evangelicals
1023 15th St., N.W., Suite 500, Washington, DC 20005
Telephone: (202) 789-1011

CRAUN-HARPER, Diane
Director, Congressional Relations, Grumman Corp.
1000 Wilson Blvd., Suite 2800, Arlington, VA 22209
Telephone: (703) 875-8400
Registered as lobbyist at U.S. Congress.

CRAVEN, Donald B.
Member, Miller & Chevalier, Chartered
Metropolitan Square, 655 15th St., N.W., Washington, DC 20005
Telephone: (202) 626-5800
Background: Trial Attorney, Tax Division, U.S. Department of Justice, 1968-73. Associate Assistant Administrator and Acting Assistant Administrator, Federal Energy Administration, 1974-75.
Clients:
 American Petroleum Institute

CRAVEN, Kelly
Polit. Director, Political Field Optns., Nat'l Ass'n of REALTORS
777 14th St., N.W., Washington, DC 20005
Telephone: (202) 383-1000
Registered as lobbyist at U.S. Congress.

CRAVER, MATHEWS, SMITH AND CO.
300 North Washington St., Falls Church, VA 22046
Telephone: (703) 237-0600
Background: A direct-mail fund-raising and consulting firm for non- profit, progressive organizations.
Members of firm representing listed organizations:
 Craver, Roger M., President
Clients:
 Nat'l Abortion Rights Action League *(Roger M. Craver)*

CRAVER, Roger M.
President, Craver, Mathews, Smith and Co.
300 North Washington St., Falls Church, VA 22046
Telephone: (703) 237-0600
Clients:
 Nat'l Abortion Rights Action League

CRAWFORD, Diane
Government Affairs Representative, Dresser Industries
1100 Connecticut Ave., N.W. Suite 310, Washington, DC 20036
Telephone: (202) 296-3070

CRAWFORD, Donald J.
Sr. V. Pres. and Dir. of Gov't Rel., Securities Industry Ass'n
1850 M St., N.W., Suite 550, Washington, DC 20036
Telephone: (202) 296-9410
Registered as lobbyist at U.S. Congress.
Background: Responsible for Securities Industry Ass'n Political Action Committee.

CRAWFORD, Franklin J.
Director, Government and Public Affairs, Nissan Motor Corp. in U.S.A.
750 17th St., N.W. Suite 901, Washington, DC 20006
Telephone: (202) 862-5523
Registered as lobbyist at U.S. Congress.

CRAWFORD, John M., Jr.
President, Screen Printing Ass'n Internat'l
10015 Main St., Fairfax, VA 22031-3489
Telephone: (703) 385-1335

CRAWFORD, Kelly A.
Foley & Co.
206 G St. N.E. Suite 201, Washington, DC 20002
Telephone: (202) 543-8601
Registered as lobbyist at U.S. Congress.
Clients:
 PolyPhaser Corp.

CRAWFORD, Marjorie O.
Manager, Government Relations, Pfizer, Inc.
1455 Pennsylvania Ave., N.W., Suite 925, Washington, DC 20004
Telephone: (202) 783-7070

CRAWFORD, Milly
Member Legislative Services, Van Ness, Feldman & Curtis
1050 Thomas Jefferson St., 7th Floor, Washington, DC 20007
Telephone: (202) 298-1800
Clients:
 Geothermal Resources Ass'n

CRAWFORD, Richard C.
Director, Government Relations, Nat'l Grocers Ass'n
1825 Samuel Morse Drive, Reston, VA 22090
Telephone: (703) 437-5300
Registered as lobbyist at U.S. Congress.
Background: Serves also as Treasurer, Nat'l Grocers Ass'n PAC.

CRAWFORD, Richard L.
Director, Government Affairs, Lipsen Whitten & Diamond
1725 DeSales St., N.W., Suite 800, Washington, DC 20036
Telephone: (202) 659-6540
Registered as lobbyist at U.S. Congress.
Background: Administrative Assistant/Legislative Director to Rep. Bill Boner (D-TN), 1979-82. Associate Staff, House Committee on Apprpriations, 1982-85.

CRAWFORD, Ronald
F/P Research Associates
1700 K St., N.W., Suite 404, Washington, DC 20006
Telephone: (202) 296-5505
Registered as lobbyist at U.S. Congress.

CRAYCRAFT, Charlene Baker
Chairman of the Board, Americans for Constitutional Action
955 L'Enfant Plaza North, S.W. Suite 1000, Washington, DC 20024
Telephone: (202) 484-5525

CREAL, Richard C.
Exec. Director, College and University Personnel Ass'n
1233 20th St., N.W., Suite 503, Washington, DC 20036
Telephone: (202) 429-0311

CREEDON, Michael
Director, Corporate Programs, Nat'l Council on the Aging
600 Maryland Ave., S.W. West Wing 100, Washington, DC 20024
Telephone: (202) 479-1200

CREGAN, John P.
V. President, United States Business and Industrial Council
220 Nat'l Press Building, Washington, DC 20045

WASHINGTON REPRESENTATIVES

CREGAN, John P. (Cont'd)
Telephone: (202) 662-8744
Registered as lobbyist at U.S. Congress.
Background: Researcher, House Education and Labor Committee, 1981-82. Assistant to Rep. John M. Ashbrook (R-OH), 1982.

CREIGHTON, Richard C.
President, American Cement Alliance
1331 Pennsylvania Ave., N.W. Suite 910, Washington, DC 20004
Telephone: (202) 662-7416
Registered as lobbyist at U.S. Congress.
Background: Also responsible for the American Cement Trade Alliance Political Action Committee.

CREMIN, Mary M.
Exec. Secretary, Institute of Gas Technology
1825 K St., N.W. Suite 503, Washington, DC 20006
Telephone: (202) 785-3511

CRERAR, Ken A.
V. President, Government Affairs, Nat'l Ass'n of Casualty and Surety Agents
600 Pennsylvania Ave., S.E., Suite 211, Washington, DC 20003
Telephone: (202) 547-6616
Registered as lobbyist at U.S. Congress.

CREW, Douglas P.
Washington Representative, Caterpillar Inc.
1730 Pennsylvania Ave., N.W., Suite 750, Washington, DC 20006
Telephone: (202) 879-3050
Registered as lobbyist at U.S. Congress.

CREYKE, Cynthia Shearin
Program Manager, Nat'l Council on the Aging
600 Maryland Ave., S.W. West Wing 100, Washington, DC 20024
Telephone: (202) 479-1200
Background: Represents the Nat'l Institute of Senior Citizens and the Nat'l Center on Rural Aging.

CRIBB, Dicksie J.
Cong Liaison Specialist, FEDERAL COMMUNICATIONS COMMISSION
1919 M St., N.W., Washington, DC 20554
Telephone: (202) 632-6405

CRIBBEN, Joseph
Research and Legislation, United Ass'n of Journeymen & Apprentices of the Plumbing & Pipe Fitting Industry of the US & Canada
901 Massachusetts Ave., N.W., Washington, DC 20001
Telephone: (202) 628-5823

CRIGLER, Winfield P.
Williams and Jensen, P.C.
1101 Connecticut Ave., N.W., Suite 500, Washington, DC 20036
Telephone: (202) 659-8201
Clients:
Higher Education Assistance Foundation
Student Loan Marketing Ass'n

CRIPPEN, Dan
Duberstein Group, Inc., The
2100 Pennsylvania Ave., N.W. Suite 350, Washington, DC 20037
Telephone: (202) 728-1100

CRISCUOLI, Ernest J., Jr.
Exec. Vice President, American Soc. for Industrial Security
1655 N. Ft. Myer Drive Suite 1200, Arlington, VA 22209
Telephone: (703) 522-5800

CRISP, Mary Dent
Senior Political Advisor, Business Executives for Nat'l Security
601 Pennsylvania Ave., N.W. Suite 700, Washington, DC 20004
Telephone: (202) 737-1090
Registered as lobbyist at U.S. Congress.
Background: Former Co-Chairperson, Republican National Committee

CRISPEN, Elaine D.
Senior V. President, Hill and Knowlton Public Affairs Worldwide
Washington Harbour, 901 31st St., N.W., Washington, DC 20007
Telephone: (202) 333-7400
Background: Former Press Secretary to First Lady Nancy Reagan.
Clients:
Tobacco Institute

CRISTOL, Richard E.
Kellen Co., Robert H.
1101 15th St., N.W., Washington, DC 20005
Telephone: (202) 785-3232
Registered as lobbyist at U.S. Congress.
Background: Serves as Exec. Director, Nat'l Ass'n of Margarine Manufacturers.
Organizations represented:
Nat'l Ass'n of Margarine Manufacturers

CROCKETT, Judy C.
Legislative Representative, American Civil Liberties Union
122 Maryland Ave., N.E., Washington, DC 20002
Telephone: (202) 544-1681

CROKER, Mrs. Kay A.
Exec. Officer, American Soc. for Pharmacology and Experimental Therapeutics
9650 Rockville Pike, Bethesda, MD 20814
Telephone: (301) 530-7060

CROLIUS, Robert W.
V. President, Washington Affairs, Portland Cement Ass'n
1620 Eye St., N.W., Suite 520, Washington, DC 20006
Telephone: (202) 293-4260
Registered as lobbyist at U.S. Congress.
Background: Serves also as Treasurer, Portland Cement Ass'n Political Action Committee.

CROMARTIE, Robert W.
Legislative Representative, Nat'l Rural Electric Cooperative Ass'n
1800 Massachusetts Ave., N.W., Washington, DC 20036
Telephone: (202) 857-9721
Registered as lobbyist at U.S. Congress.

CROMER, Harry C.
Neill and Co.
815 Connecticut Ave., N.W. Suite 800, Washington, DC 20006
Telephone: (202) 463-8877
Registered as lobbyist at U.S. Congress.
Registered as Foreign Agent: (#3320).
Background: U.S. General Accounting Office, 1952-59. Staff Member, Committee on Foreign Affairs, House of Representatives, 1959-74. Auditor General, Agency for International Development, 1974-77.

CROMWELL, Charles H.
Cromwell Inc., Charles H.
2009 N. 14th St., Suite 101, Arlington, VA 22201
Telephone: (703) 528-3373
Registered as lobbyist at U.S. Congress.
Background: Former Professional Staff Member, U.S. Senate Armed Services Committee.
Organizations represented:
EDO Corp.
McDonnell Douglas Helicopter Co.

CROMWELL INC., Charles H.
2009 N. 14th St., Suite 101, Arlington, VA 22201
Telephone: (703) 528-3373
Background: A public affairs and management consulting firm.
Members of firm representing listed organizations:
Cromwell, Charles H.
Background: Former Professional Staff Member, U.S. Senate Armed Services Committee.
Organizations represented:
EDO Corp. *(Charles H. Cromwell)*
McDonnell Douglas Helicopter Co. *(Charles H. Cromwell)*

CROMWELL, James
Research Advocate, Nat'l Alliance for the Mentally Ill
2101 Wilson Blvd., Suite 302, Arlington, VA 22201
Telephone: (703) 524-7600

CRONIN, Anne
Secretary of Board of Policy, Liberty Lobby
300 Independence Ave., S.E., Washington, DC 20003
Telephone: (202) 546-5611

CRONIN, Carol A.
V. President, Washington Business Group on Health
229 1/2 Pennsylvania Ave., S.E., Washington, DC 20003
Telephone: (202) 547-6644

CRONIN, Donald J.
Counsel, Corcoran, Youngman and Rowe
1511 K St., N.W. Suite 1100, Washington, DC 20005
Telephone: (202) 783-7900
Registered as lobbyist at U.S. Congress.
Background: Former Administrative Assistant to Sen. Lister Hill of Alabama, 1953-69.

CRONIN, Earl
President, Police Ass'n of the District of Columbia
1441 Pennsylvania Ave., S.E., Washington, DC 20003
Telephone: (202) 543-9557

CRONIN, Kevin T.
Washington Counsel, Nat'l Ass'n of Insurance Commissioners
444 N. Capitol St., Suite 316, Washington, DC 20001
Telephone: (202) 624-7790

CRONMILLER, Rae E.
Environmental Counsel, Nat'l Rural Electric Cooperative Ass'n
1800 Massachusetts Ave., N.W., Washington, DC 20036
Telephone: (202) 857-9593
Registered as lobbyist at U.S. Congress.

CROPP, Dwight S.
Director, District of Columbia Office of Intergovernmental Relations
1350 Pennsylvania Ave., N.W., Room 416, Washington, DC 20004
Telephone: (202) 727-6265

CROSBY, Dana
Exec. Assistant, Progressive Policy Institute
316 Pennsylvania Ave., S.E. Suite 516, Washington, DC 20003
Telephone: (202) 547-0001

CROSBY, Harriett
President, Institute for Soviet-American Relations
1608 New Hampshire Ave., N.W., Washington, DC 20009
Telephone: (202) 387-3034

CROSBY, Kenneth G., Ed.D.
Exec. Director, Internat'l Ass'n of Boards of Examiners in Optometry
5530 Wisconsin Ave. Suite 711, Chevy Chase, MD 20815
Telephone: (301) 951-6330

CROSBY, Mark E.
President and Managing Director, Special Industrial Radio Service Ass'n
1110 North Glebe Road Suite 500, Arlington, VA 22201
Telephone: (703) 528-5115
Registered as lobbyist at U.S. Congress.

CROSBY, Mary
Assistant Director for Gov't Affairs, American Academy of Child and Adolescent Psychiatry
3615 Wisconsin Ave., N.W., Washington, DC 20016
Telephone: (202) 966-7300

CROSBY, Ralph D., Jr.
V. P. & Manager, Washington Office, Northrop Corp.
1000 Wilson Blvd., Suite 2300, Arlington, VA 22209
Telephone: (703) 525-6767

CROSER, M. Doreen
Exec. Director, American Ass'n on Mental Retardation
1719 Kalorama Road, N.W., Washington, DC 20009
Telephone: (202) 387-1968

CROSLAND, Page Dahl
V. President, Director, Media Relations, Kamber Group, The
1920 L St., N.W., Washington, DC 20036
Telephone: (202) 223-8700

CROSS, S. Lorraine
Director, Executive Branch Relations, American Gas Ass'n
1515 Wilson Blvd., Arlington, VA 22209
Telephone: (703) 841-8474

CROSS, William A.
President, Southern Technical Services
Suite 610 Three Metro Center, Bethesda, MD 20814
Telephone: (301) 652-2500

CROSS, William L.
Treasurer, ULLILPAC - Ullilco Inc. Political Action Committee
111 Massachusetts Ave., N.W., Washington, DC 20001
Telephone: (202) 682-6689

CROW, David T.
V. President, Legislative Affairs, Jefferson Group, The
1341 G St., N.W., Suite 1100, Washington, DC 20005
Telephone: (202) 638-3535
Registered as lobbyist at U.S. Congress.
Clients:
Lockheed Corp.
Scott and Sons, O. M.

CROW, Douglas L.
V. President, Ass'n of Publicly Traded Companies
1707 L St., N.W., Suite 950, Washington, DC 20036
Telephone: (202) 785-9200

CROWELL AND MORING
1001 Pennsylvania Ave., N.W., Washington, DC 20004-2505
Telephone: (202) 624-2500
Members of firm representing listed organizations:
Biddle, Timothy M.
Contratto, Dana C.
Davison, Calvin
Eberhardt, Michael
Background: Assistant Inspector General, Department of Defense, 1982-87.
Elmer, Brian C.
Ferrall, Victor E. (Jr.)
Fleming, Philip A.
Flexner, Donald L.
Background: Deputy Assistant Attorney General, Antitrust Division Department of Justice, 1978-80.
Hall, Ridgway M. (Jr.)
Background: Associate General Counsel, Environmental Protection Agency, 1976-77.
Hathaway, C. Michael
Background: Former Senior Deputy General Counsel, Office of the United States Trade Representative.
Heltzer, Harold J.
Background: Attorney, Civil and Tax Divisions, Department of Justice, 1966-72. Attorney-Advisor, Office of Tax Legislative Counsel, Department of Treasury, 1972-74.
Johnson, W. Stanfield
Keiner, R. Bruce (Jr.)
Moring, Frederick
Mullen, Michael J., Of Counsel
Background: Deputy Counsel, Subcommittee on Judicial Improvements, Senate Committee on the Judiciary, 1971-74. Staff Counsel to Sen. Philip A. Hart (D-MI), 1975-76. Counsel, Consumer Subcommittee, Senate Committee on Commerce, Science and Transportation, 1977-83.
Quarles, Steven P.
Background: Deputy Under Secretary, Department of the Interior, 1979-81.
Regan, James J., Of Counsel
Background: Chief Counsel and Hearing Examiner, General Services Administration Board of Contract Appeals, 1982-86.
Ryan, Jerry W.
Schwartz, Victor E., Of Counsel
Background: Chairman, Federal Interagency Task Force on Product Liability, 1976-80. Exec. Director, Federal Interagency Council on Insurance, 1978-80.
Souk, Fred S.
Williams, Karen Hastie, Of Counsel
Background: Administrator, Office of Federal Procurement Policy, Office of Management and Budget, 1980-81.
Work, Peter B.
Clients:
Aer Lingus *(Jerry W. Ryan)*

American Forest Resource Alliance *(Steven P. Quarles)*
Associated Gas Distributors *(Dana C. Contratto)*
Avon Products, Inc. *(Harold J. Heltzer)*
Brooklyn Union Gas Co. *(Dana C. Contratto)*
Burlington Resources, Inc. *(Steven P. Quarles)*
Central Nebraska Public Power and Irrigation District *(Dana C. Contratto)*
Communications Satellite Corp. (COMSAT) *(Harold J. Heltzer)*
Cook Inlet Region Inc. *(Steven P. Quarles)*
Crowell and Moring PAC *(Karen Hastie Williams)*
Design Professionals Coalition *(Karen Hastie Williams)*
Eagle-Picher Industries *(Victor E. Schwartz)*
Emery Worldwide *(R. Bruce Keiner, Jr.)*
KAIT-TV
KDLH-TV
KLRT
KTNV-TV
Lawyers Alliance for Nuclear Arms Control *(Philip A. Fleming)*
Lehn & Fink Products Group *(Dana C. Contratto)*
Minnesota Mining and Manufacturing Co. (3M Co.) *(Victor E. Schwartz)*
Nashua Corp. *(Brian C. Elmer)*
Nat'l Ass'n of Wholesaler-Distributors *(Michael J. Mullen, Victor E. Schwartz)*
Nebraska Public Power District *(Dana C. Contratto)*
North Miami, City of *(Steven P. Quarles)*
Pan American World Airways *(Jerry W. Ryan)*
Product Liability Alliance, The *(Victor E. Schwartz)*
Product Liability Coordinating Committee *(Victor E. Schwartz)*
Product Liability Information Bureau *(Victor E. Schwartz)*
Tiffany & Co. *(Harold J. Heltzer)*
United Cities Gas Co. *(Harold J. Heltzer)*
United Technologies Corp. *(Brian C. Elmer, W. Stanfield Johnson)*
United Telecommunications *(James J. Regan)*
WBKO
WBNS-TV
WCLQ-TV
WTHR

CROWLEY, Paul
Tax Representative, Shell Oil Co.
1025 Connecticut Ave., N.W. Suite 200, Washington, DC 20036
Telephone: (202) 466-1444
Registered as lobbyist at U.S. Congress.

CROWLEY, Thomas P.
Director, Internat'l Business Support, Asea Brown Boveri, Inc.
1101 15th St., N.W. Suite 500, Washington, DC 20005
Telephone: (202) 429-9180

CROZE, Gilbert
President & CEO, Matra Aerospace, Inc.
1213 Jefferson Davis Hwy. Crystal City IV, Suite 1102, Arlington, VA 22202
Telephone: (703) 979-3600

CRUDEN, Col. John C.
Investigations & Legislation, Legis Lias, DEPARTMENT OF ARMY
The Pentagon, Washington, DC 20310-0101
Telephone: (202) 697-6767

CRUIT, Charles W.
Senior Procurement Policy Representative, Rockwell Internat'l
1745 Jefferson Davis Hwy. Suite 1200, Arlington, VA 22202
Telephone: (703) 553-6600

CRUM, John Kistler
Exec. Director, American Chemical Soc.
1155 16th St., N.W., Washington, DC 20036
Telephone: (202) 872-4534

CRUMP, John
Exec. Director, Nat'l Bar Ass'n
1225 11th St., N.W., Washington, DC 20001
Telephone: (202) 842-3900

CRUTCHFIELD, Sam S.
Exec. Director, Internat'l Legal Fraternity-Phi Delta Phi
1750 N St., N.W., Washington, DC 20036
Telephone: (202) 628-0148
Background: General Counsel, U.S. Postal Rate Commission, 1973-1974.

CRYOR, Michael
Regional V. President, Davis Companies, The Susan
1146 19th St., N.W., Washington, DC 20036
Telephone: (202) 775-8881
Background: Former Special Assistant to Rep. Parren Mitchell (D-MD). Former Consultant to Senate Judiciary Committee. Former Deputy Director, Democratic Platform Committee. Former aide to Rep. Mike Barnes (D-MD).
Organizations represented:
Career Communications

CSONTOS, Stephen J.
Sr Legis Couns, Office of Legis & Policy, DEPARTMENT OF JUSTICE - Tax Division
555 4th St., N.W., Washington, DC 20001
Telephone: (202) 724-6419

CUADERES, John D.
Manager, Legislative Projects, Emerson Electric Co.
1235 Jefferson Davis Hwy., Suite 305, Arlington, VA 22202
Telephone: (703) 920-7600
Registered as lobbyist at U.S. Congress.
Background: Former Legislative Assistant to Rep. Dave McCurdy (D-OK).

CULHANE, Brien F.
Assistant Director, Nat'l Parks Program, Wilderness Soc.
1400 Eye St., N.W., 10th Floor, Washington, DC 20005
Telephone: (202) 842-3400
Registered as lobbyist at U.S. Congress.

CULKIN, Douglas S.
Sr. V. President, Nat'l Ass'n of Professional Insurance Agents
400 North Washington St., Alexandria, VA 22314
Telephone: (703) 836-9340

CULLEN, Barry M.
President, Nat'l Forest Products Ass'n
1250 Connecticut Ave., N.W. Suite 200, Washington, DC 20036
Telephone: (202) 463-2700
Background: Former Legislative Assistant to Senator Warren Magnuson (D-WA).

CULLEN, David
V. President of Public Affairs, Nat'l Federation of Independent Business
600 Maryland Ave., S.W., Suite 700, Washington, DC 20024
Telephone: (202) 554-9000

CULLEN AND DYKMAN
1225 19th St., N.W. Suite 320, Washington, DC 20036
Telephone: (202) 223-8890
Background: Washington office of a Brooklyn, NY, law firm.
Members of firm representing listed organizations:
Hall, Michael W.
Clients:
Brooklyn Union Gas Co. *(Michael W. Hall)*

CULLEN, Paul D.
Collier, Shannon & Scott
1055 Thomas Jefferson St., N.W., Suite 300, Washington, DC 20007
Telephone: (202) 342-8400
Registered as lobbyist at U.S. Congress.
Registered as Foreign Agent: (#3694).
Clients:
American Flint Glass Workers Union
Internat'l Ass'n of Machinists and Aerospace Workers
Magnavox Consumer Electronics Co.
Petroleos de Venezuela, S.A.
Siemens Corp.

WASHINGTON REPRESENTATIVES

CULLINAN, Christine M.
Associate for Public Policy, Nat'l Recreation and Park Ass'n
3101 Park Center Drive, Alexandria, VA 22302
Telephone: (703) 820-4940
Background: Former Staff Assistant to Rep. Bill McCollum (R-FL).

CULLINANE, Maurice
Exec. V. President, Washington Area Bankers Ass'n
1750 New York Ave., N.W., Suite 240, Washington, DC 20006
Telephone: (202) 783-4555
Background: Chief, D.C. Police Department, 1974-78. Represents the Washington Area Bankers Ass'n Bankpac as well as the Association itself.

CULVER, John C.
Arent, Fox, Kintner, Plotkin & Kahn
1050 Connecticut Ave., N.W., Washington, DC 20036-5339
Telephone: (202) 857-6000
Registered as lobbyist at U.S. Congress.
Background: Member, U.S. House of Representatives (D-IA), 1965-75. Member, U.S. Senate (D-IA), 1975-81.
Clients:
  Ass'n of Professional Flight Attendants
  Puerto Rico Federal Affairs Administration
  Puerto Rico, Popular Democratic Party of
  San Diego, California, City of

CUMBERLAND, William E.
Staff V. President & General Counsel, Mortgage Bankers Ass'n of America
1125 15th St., N.W., Suite 700, Washington, DC 20005
Telephone: (202) 861-6500

CUMMER, Sara
Federal Compliance Counsel, Credit Union Nat'l Ass'n
805 15th St., N.W. Suite 300, Washington, DC 20005
Telephone: (202) 682-4200

CUMMINGS, Daniel
Dir, Legis Affrs & Public Information, DEPARTMENT OF AGRICULTURE - Rural Electrification Administration
14th and Independence Ave. S.W., Washington, DC 20250
Telephone: (202) 382-1255

CUMMINGS, Norman B.
Director of Political Division, Republican Nat'l Committee
310 First St., S.E., Washington, DC 20003
Telephone: (202) 863-8500

CUMMINGS, Philip T.
McCutchen, Doyle, Brown & Enersen
1455 Pennsylvania Ave., N.W., Suite 650, Washington, DC 20004
Telephone: (202) 628-4900
Registered as lobbyist at U.S. Congress.
Background: Chief Counsel, U.S. Senate Committee on Environment andf Public Works, 1970-88.
Clients:
  Browning-Ferris Industries (D.C.), Inc.
  DNA Plant Technology Corp.
  Nat'l Ass'n of Regional Councils
  Rohr Industries, Inc.
  Southern California Ass'n of Governments

CUMMINS, Cheryl
Staff V. President, Programs, Urban Land Institute
1090 Vermont Ave., N.W. Suite 300, Washington, DC 20005
Telephone: (202) 289-8500

CUNARD, Jeffrey P.
Partner, Debevoise and Plimpton
555 13th St., N.W. Eleventh Floor, Washington, DC 20004-1179
Telephone: (202) 383-8000
Registered as lobbyist at U.S. Congress.
Registered as Foreign Agent: (#3527).
Clients:
  Internat'l Telecom Japan
  Sony Corp.

CUNEO, Jonathan W.
Principal, Cuneo Law Offices, Jonathan W.
1300 Eye St., N.W. Suite 480 East Tower, Washington, DC 20005

Telephone: (202) 962-3860
Registered as lobbyist at U.S. Congress.
Background: Also of counsel to Opperman, Heins and Pasquin.
Organizations represented:
  Committee to Support the Antitrust Laws
  Nat'l Ass'n of Securities and Commercial Law Attorneys
  Nat'l Coalition of Petroleum Retailers

CUNEO LAW OFFICES, Jonathan W.
1300 Eye St., N.W. Suite 480 East Tower, Washington, DC 20005
Telephone: (202) 962-3860
Members of firm representing listed organizations:
  Cuneo, Jonathan W., Principal
    Background: Also of counsel to Opperman, Heins and Pasquin.
  Schweitzer, James J.
Organizations represented:
  Committee to Support the Antitrust Laws *(Jonathan W. Cuneo)*
  Nat'l Ass'n of Securities and Commercial Law Attorneys *(Jonathan W. Cuneo)*
  Nat'l Coalition of Petroleum Retailers *(Jonathan W. Cuneo)*
  Songwriters Guild, The *(James J. Schweitzer)*

CUNNIFF, Mark A.
Exec. Director, Nat'l Ass'n of Criminal Justice Planners
1511 K St., N.W., Suite 445, Washington, DC 20005
Telephone: (202) 347-0501

CUNNIFF, Michael M.
State Legislative Director-Missouri, Transportation, Communications Internat'l Union
815 16th St., N.W. Suite 511, Washington, DC 20036
Telephone: (202) 783-3660
Registered as lobbyist at U.S. Congress.

CUNNINGHAM, Charles H.
State Liaison, Inst. for Legis. Action, Nat'l Rifle Ass'n of America
1600 Rhode Island Ave., N.W., Washington, DC 20036
Telephone: (202) 828-6377

CUNNINGHAM, Drusilla
Program Assistant, Food Processors Institute, The
1401 New York Ave., N.W., Washington, DC 20005
Telephone: (202) 393-0890

CUNNINGHAM, Richard O.
Steptoe and Johnson
1330 Connecticut Ave., N.W., Washington, DC 20036
Telephone: (202) 429-3000
Clients:
  British Steel Corp.
  Cargill, Inc.
  Harley-Davidson, Inc.
  Mitsui and Co.

CUNNINGHAM, Robert
Senior Counsel, Nat'l Paint and Coatings Ass'n
1500 Rhode Island Ave., N.W., Washington, DC 20005
Telephone: (202) 462-6272

CUNNINGHAM, Robert E., Jr.
Legislative Analyst, Korea Trade Center
1129 20th St. N.W. 4th Floor, Washington, DC 20036
Telephone: (202) 857-7919

CUNNINGHAM, William J., Jr.
Legislative Representative, AFL-CIO (American Federation of Labor and Congress of Industrial Organizations)
815 16th St., N.W., Washington, DC 20006
Telephone: (202) 637-5088
Registered as lobbyist at U.S. Congress.

CURLIN, Peggy
President and CEO, Centre for Development and Population Activity
1717 Massachusetts Ave., N.W., Washington, DC 20036
Telephone: (202) 667-1142

CURRAN, Jack
Legislative Director, Laborers' Internat'l Union of North America
905 16th St., N.W., Washington, DC 20006
Telephone: (202) 737-8320

Registered as lobbyist at U.S. Congress.

CURRAN, Jean E.
Neill and Co.
815 Connecticut Ave., N.W. Suite 800, Washington, DC 20006
Telephone: (202) 463-8877
Registered as lobbyist at U.S. Congress.
Registered as Foreign Agent: (#3320).
Background: International Affairs Specialist, U.S. Department of Agriculture, 1987-88. Program Coordinator, U.S. Department of Agriculture, 1988-89.

CURRIE, Suzanne
Apter and Associates, David
1706 R St., N.W., Washington, DC 20009
Telephone: (202) 265-1212

CURRIER, Jerry
Director, Graphics Services, Hill and Knowlton Public Affairs Worldwide
Washington Harbour, 901 31st St., N.W., Washington, DC 20007
Telephone: (202) 333-7400

CURRIO, James R.
Director, VFW-Political Action Committee, Inc.
200 Maryland Ave., N.E. Suite 506, Washington, DC 20002
Telephone: (202) 544-5868
Registered as lobbyist at U.S. Congress.

CURRY, Anne McGhee
Sr. Government Relations Representative, Food Marketing Institute
1750 K St., N.W., Washington, DC 20006
Telephone: (202) 452-8444
Registered as lobbyist at U.S. Congress.

CURRY AND ASSOCIATES, Richard
P.O. Box 66, McLean, VA 22101
Telephone: (703) 821-1404
Background: A governmental affairs consulting firm.
Members of firm representing listed organizations:
  Curry, Richard C.
    Background: Former Special Assistant to the Secretary, and Special Assistant to Assistant Secretary for Fish, Wildlife and Parks, Department of the Interior. Also former Director of Legislation, Nat'l Park Service.
  Stoddard, Gerard
Organizations represented:
  Barrier Beach Preservation Ass'n *(Richard C. Curry)*
  Coastal Reports, Inc. *(Richard C. Curry, Gerard Stoddard)*
  Fire Island Ass'n, Inc. *(Richard C. Curry)*
  Grand Canyon Chamber Music Festival Inc. *(Richard C. Curry)*
  Long Island Coastal Alliance *(Richard C. Curry, Gerard Stoddard)*
  Seaview Property Owners Ass'n, Inc. *(Richard C. Curry)*
  Stamats Film and Video *(Richard C. Curry)*

CURRY, Brenda
Asst Dir (Legis), Legis & Regul Anal Div, DEPARTMENT OF TREASURY - Comptroller of the Currency
490 L'Enfant Plaza, S.W., Washington, DC 20219
Telephone: (202) 447-1632

CURRY, John J.
Exec. Director, American College of Radiology
1891 Preston White Drive, Reston, VA 22091
Telephone: (703) 648-8900

CURRY, Richard C.
Curry and Associates, Richard
P.O. Box 66, McLean, VA 22101
Telephone: (703) 821-1404
Registered as lobbyist at U.S. Congress.
Background: Former Special Assistant to the Secretary, and Special Assistant to Assistant Secretary for Fish, Wildlife and Parks, Department of the Interior. Also former Director of Legislation, Nat'l Park Service.
Organizations represented:
  Barrier Beach Preservation Ass'n
  Coastal Reports, Inc.
  Fire Island Ass'n, Inc.
  Grand Canyon Chamber Music Festival Inc.
  Long Island Coastal Alliance

Seaview Property Owners Ass'n, Inc.
Stamats Film and Video

CURRY SANTORA, Kathleen
Exec. Dir. for Operations, Nat'l Ass'n of Independent Colleges and Universities
122 C St., N.W. Suite 750, Washington, DC 20001
Telephone: (202) 347-7512
Registered as lobbyist at U.S. Congress.

CURTIN, Wayne T.
Assistant Director, Wealth Management Corp.
Washington Harbour 3000 K St., N.W., P.H. 3-A, Washington, DC 20007
Telephone: (202) 944-4920
Registered as lobbyist at U.S. Congress.
Clients:
Motorcycle Riders Foundation

CURTIS, Charles B.
Van Ness, Feldman & Curtis
1050 Thomas Jefferson St., 7th Floor, Washington, DC 20007
Telephone: (202) 298-1800
Registered as lobbyist at U.S. Congress.
Background: Supervisory Attorney, Comptroller of the Currency, Department of the Treasury, 1965-67. Special Counsel, Chief Branch of Market Regulation, and Inspection, Securities and Exchange Commission, 1967-71. Counsel, House Committee on Interstate and Foreign Commerce, 1971-76. Chairman, Federal Power Commission, 1977. Federal Energy Regulatory Commission, 1977-81.
Clients:
American Institute of Certified Public Accountants

CURTIS, Kevin S.
Nat'l Strategies Inc.
818 17th St., N.W., Washington, DC 20006
Telephone: (202) 429-8744
Background: Senate Liaison, Department of Energy, 1978-80. Legislative Assistant to Rep. Timothy E. Wirth (D-CO), 1980-83.

CURTIS, MALLET-PREVOST, COLT & MOSLE
1735 Eye St., N.W., Suite 715, Washington, DC 20006
Telephone: (202) 331-9797
Members of firm representing listed organizations:
Barth, Roger V., Resident Counsel
Background: Assistant to the Commissioner, 1969-72, and Deputy Chief Counsel, 1972-73, Internal Revenue Service.
Clients:
Ass'n of Government Accountants

CURTIS, Richard E.
Dir., Policy, Development and Research, Health Insurance Ass'n of America
1025 Connecticut Ave., N.W. Suite 1200, Washington, DC 20036
Telephone: (202) 223-7780

CURTIS, Tom
Dir., Natural Resources Group, Nat'l Governors' Ass'n
444 North Capitol St., N.W., Suite 250, Washington, DC 20001
Telephone: (202) 624-5300

CURTIS, Vincent J., Jr.
Fletcher, Heald and Hildreth
1225 Connecticut Ave. N.W. Suite 400, Washington, DC 20036
Telephone: (202) 828-5700
Registered as lobbyist at U.S. Congress.

CURTISS, Catherine
Miller & Chevalier, Chartered
Metropolitan Square, 655 15th St., N.W., Washington, DC 20005
Telephone: (202) 626-5800
Clients:
Saudi Basic Industries Corp.

CURZAN, Myron P.
Arnold & Porter
1200 New Hampshire Ave., N.W., Washington, DC 20036
Telephone: (202) 872-6700
Registered as Foreign Agent: (#1750).

Background: Legislative Assistant to Senator Robert F. Kennedy, 1965-66. Exec. Director, HUD Task Force on Improving the Operation of Federally Insured or Financed Housing Programs, 1972-73.

CUSHENBERRY, Kent T.
Prog. Dir., Federal Government Relations, Internat'l Business Machines Corp.
Suite 1200, 1801 K St., N.W., Washington, DC 20006
Telephone: (202) 778-5003

CUSHING, Christopher T.
President and CEO, C & C Consulting Group, Inc.
210 Cameron St., Alexandria, VA 22314
Telephone: (703) 548-1992

CUSIC, Rebecca
Deputy Director, AYUDA, Inc.
1736 Columbia Road, N.W., Washington, DC 20009
Telephone: (202) 387-4848

CUSKADEN, Eileen
Director, Program Operations, Very Special Arts
1331 Pennsylvania Ave., N.W. Suite 1205, Washington, DC 20004
Telephone: (202) 662-8899

CUTCHINS, Kimberly
Director of Industry Services, Nat'l Peanut Council
1500 King St., Suite 301, Alexandria, VA 22314-2730
Telephone: (703) 838-9500

CUTHBERTSON, Betsy A.
Dir. of Gov't Affairs & Public Relats., American Soc. of Landscape Architects
4401 Connecticut Ave., N.W., Washington, DC 20008
Telephone: (202) 686-2752

CUTLER, Dr. Herschel
Exec. Director, Institute of Scrap Recycling Industries, Inc.
1627 K St., N.W. Suite 700, Washington, DC 20006
Telephone: (202) 466-4050
Background: Responsibilities include Institute of Scrap Iron and Steel Political Action Committee.

CUTLER, Jay B.
Dir. of Gov't Relations & Special Couns., American Psychiatric Ass'n
1400 K St., N.W., Washington, DC 20005
Telephone: (202) 682-6060
Registered as lobbyist at U.S. Congress.

CUTLER, Lloyd N.
Wilmer, Cutler and Pickering
2445 M St., N.W., Washington, DC 20037-1420
Telephone: (202) 663-6000
Registered as Foreign Agent: (#3355).
Background: Counsel to the President under President Jimmy Carter.
Clients:
Ford Motor Co.
Long Island Savings Bank

CUTLER, Lynn
V. Chairwoman, Democratic Nat'l Committee
430 South Capitol St., S.E., Washington, DC 20003
Telephone: (202) 863-8000

CUTLER, M. Rupert
President, Defenders of Wildlife
1244 19th St., N.W., Washington, DC 20036
Telephone: (202) 659-9510
Registered as lobbyist at U.S. Congress.

CUTLER AND STANFIELD
1850 M St., N.W. Suite 1000, Washington, DC 20036
Telephone: (202) 822-6400
Members of firm representing listed organizations:
Reffe, Paige E., Of Counsel
Background: Special Assistant, Office of Management and Budget, 1977. Special Assistant to the Administrator, General Services Administration, 1978. Trial Attorney, Tax Division, Department of Justice, 1979-83. Chief of Staff to Rep/Senator Timothy Wirth (D-CO), 1985-87.
Stanfield, Jeffrey L.
Background: Assistant to the Secretary, 1977-79 and Associate Under Secretary, 1979-80, U.S. Department of Energy. Assistant to the General Counsel, Federal Administration, 1977.

Clients:
General Atomics *(Jeffrey L. Stanfield)*
University of Colorado, Office of the President *(Jeffrey L. Stanfield)*

CUTLER, Walter L.
President, Meridian House Internat'l
1630 Crescent Place, N.W., Washington, DC 20009
Telephone: (202) 667-6800
Background: U.S. Ambassador to Zaire, 1975-79; Dep. Ass't Sec. of State Congressional Relations, 1979-81; U.S. Ambassador to Tunisia, 1982-84; U.S. Ambassador to Saudi Arabia, 1984-87, 1988-89.

CUTRONA, Joseph F. H.
Exec. Director, Nat'l Small Shipments Traffic Conference - NASSTRAC
1750 Pennsylvania Ave., N.W., Suite 1111, Washington, DC 20006
Telephone: (202) 393-5505

CUTRONE, Roseann
Skadden, Arps, Slate, Meagher and Flom
1440 New York Ave., N.W., Washington, DC 20005
Telephone: (202) 371-7000
Clients:
American Electronics Ass'n

CYLKE, Owen
President, Ass'n of Big Eight Universities
Box 9513, Arlington, VA 22209
Telephone: (202) 479-0651

CZECH, Grover E.
V. President, State Affairs, American Insurance Ass'n
1130 Connecticut Ave., N.W., Suite 1000, Washington, DC 20036
Telephone: (202) 828-7100

CZEKANSKI, Peter C.
Director, Government Relations, NYNEX
1828 L St., N.W., Suite 1000, Washington, DC 20036
Telephone: (202) 416-0100

CZEPLUCH, Ralf W.K.
Manager, Federal Legislative Affairs, Gulf Power Co.
1130 Connecticut Ave., N.W. Suite 830, Washington, DC 20036
Telephone: (202) 775-0944
Registered as lobbyist at U.S. Congress.

DABAGHI, William K.
Arter & Hadden
1919 Pennsylvania Ave., N.W., Suite 400, Washington, DC 20006
Telephone: (202) 775-7100
Registered as lobbyist at U.S. Congress.
Registered as Foreign Agent: (#3686).
Background: Director, Office of Congressional Affairs, Office of the Secretary, Department of Transportation, 1982-83.
Clients:
Central Union of Agricultural Cooperatives (ZENCHU)
Coalition for Regional Banking and Economic Development
Houston Clearing House Ass'n

DACEK, Raymond F.
Reid & Priest
1111 19th St., N.W., Washington, DC 20036
Telephone: (202) 828-0100
Registered as lobbyist at U.S. Congress.
Clients:
CIAC Group, The
Edison Electric Institute
Florida Progress Corp.
Gulf States Utilities Co.
Utility Decommissioning Tax Group

DACH, Leslie
Senior V. Pres., Director, Public Affrs., Edelman, Inc., Daniel J.
1420 K St., N.W., Washington, DC 20005
Telephone: (202) 371-0200
Registered as lobbyist at U.S. Congress.
Background: Formerly Communications Director of the Dukakis Presidential Campaign, 1988.
Organizations represented:

DACH, Leslie (Cont'd)
Advo-Systems, Inc.
Collagen Corp.
Fuji Photo Film U.S.A.
Fujitsu America, Inc.
Hughes Aircraft Co.
United Parcel Service

D'AGOSTINO, Bruce
Public Relations Director, Dairy and Food Industries Supply Ass'n
6245 Executive Blvd., Rockville, MD 20852
Telephone: (301) 984-1444

DAHLMAN, George
Manager, Press Office, British Aerospace, Inc.
13873 Park Center Road, Herndon, VA 22071
Telephone: (703) 478-9420
Background: Former Press Secretary to Senator Alan Dixon (D-IL).

DAHLQUIST, Susan
Legislative Rep./Asst. PAC Director, Nat'l Committee to Preserve Social Security and Medicare
2000 K St., N.W. Suite 800, Washington, DC 20006
Telephone: (202) 822-9459
Registered as lobbyist at U.S. Congress.

DAIGLER, Stephen
Director, Information Services, Soc. of American Florists
1601 Duke St., Alexandria, VA 22314
Telephone: (703) 836-8700
Registered as lobbyist at U.S. Congress.

DAILEY, Ann Armstrong
Founding Director, Children's Hospice Internat'l
1101 King St., Suite 131, Alexandria, VA 22314
Telephone: (703) 684-0330

DAINES, William Kay
Exec. V. President and General Counsel, American Retail Federation
1616 H St., N.W. 6th Floor, Washington, DC 20006
Telephone: (202) 783-7971
Registered as lobbyist at U.S. Congress.
Background: Active in the Pro-Trade Group.

DALE, Charles
President, Newspaper Guild, The
8611 2nd Ave., Silver Spring, MD 20910
Telephone: (301) 585-2990

DALEY, Donna
Director, Federal Advocacy, American Psychological Ass'n
1200 17th St., N.W., Washington, DC 20036
Telephone: (202) 955-7600
Registered as lobbyist at U.S. Congress.

DALLEY, George A.
Neill and Co.
815 Connecticut Ave., N.W. Suite 800, Washington, DC 20006
Telephone: (202) 463-8877
Registered as lobbyist at U.S. Congress.
Background: Staff Attorney, Office of EEO, U.S. Department of State, 1966-67. Counsel, House of Representatives Committee on the Judiciary, 1971-72. Administrative Assistant to Rep. Charles Rangel (D-NY), 1972-77. Deputy Assistant Secretary of State, Bureau of International Affairs, Department of State, 1977-80. Member, Civil Aeronautics Board, 1985-89. Counsel and Staff Director to Rep Charles Rangel (D-NY).
Clients:
American Methanol Institute
Ivory Coast, Government of
Jamaica, Government of
Puerto Rico Economic Development Administration

DALLOS, Lisa
Director, Public Relations, Turner Broadcasting System, Inc.
111 Massachusetts Ave., N.W. Third Floor, Washington, DC 20001
Telephone: (202) 898-7670

DALRYMPLE, Dack
Director, Medical Government Affairs, American Cyanamid Co.
1575 Eye St., N.W., Suite 200, Washington, DC 20005
Telephone: (202) 789-1222
Registered as lobbyist at U.S. Congress.
Background: Also represents the subsidiary Lederle Laboratories. Former Counsel, Subcommittee on Health and the Environment, Committee on Energy and Commerce, U.S. House of Representatives, 1974-79; Legislative Assistant to Rep. Paul Rogers (D-FL), 1970, 1973-74.

DALRYMPLE, Marcia Bresee
Manager, Government Affairs, Aluminum Co. of America
1615 M St., N.W., Suite 500, Washington, DC 20036
Telephone: (202) 956-5300

DALTON, Anne
Dir. of Commun. Research & Policy Group, Ass'n of Junior Leagues, Internat'l
1319 F St., N.W., Suite 604, Washington, DC 20004
Telephone: (202) 393-3364

DALTON, Helen
Director, Public Relations, Federal Home Loan Mortgage Corp.
1759 Business Center Drive, Reston, VA 22090
Telephone: (703) 789-4700

DALTON, James G.
Deputy Exec. Director, Programs, Nat'l Soc. of Professional Engineers
1420 King St., Alexandria, VA 22314-2715
Telephone: (703) 684-2841

DALY ASSOCIATES, INC.
702 World Center Bldg., 918 16th St., N.W., Washington, DC 20006-2993
Telephone: (202) 659-2925
Members of firm representing listed organizations:
Daly, John Jay, President
Background: Former Director, American League of Lobbyists and former President, National Capital Chapter of the Public Relations Society of America (1973);
Montgomery, Nellie
Clients:
Bell and Howell (Business Equipment Division)
(John Jay Daly)
Direct Marketing Guaranty Trust *(John Jay Daly)*
Group 1 Software *(John Jay Daly)*

DALY, John Jay
President, Daly Associates, Inc.
702 World Center Bldg., 918 16th St., N.W., Washington, DC 20006-2993
Telephone: (202) 659-2925
Background: Former Director, American League of Lobbyists and former President, National Capital Chapter of the Public Relations Society of America (1973),
Clients:
Bell and Howell (Business Equipment Division)
Direct Marketing Guaranty Trust
Group 1 Software

DALY, Thomas A.
Of Counsel, Nat'l Soft Drink Ass'n
1101 16th St., N.W., Washington, DC 20036
Telephone: (202) 463-6732

DALY, Thomas R.
Legal Counsel, American Chiropractic Ass'n
1701 Clarendon Blvd., Arlington, VA 22209
Telephone: (703) 276-8800

DALY, William J.
Senior Legislative Representative, Shearman and Sterling
1001 30th St., N.W., Suite 400, Washington, DC 20007
Telephone: (202) 337-8200

DAMERON, Del S.
McKenna, Conner and Cuneo
1575 Eye St., N.W. Suite 800, Washington, DC 20005
Telephone: (202) 789-7500
Clients:
Oshkosh Truck Corp.

DAMGARD, John M.
President, Futures Industry Ass'n
1825 Eye St., N.W. Suite 1040, Washington, DC 20006
Telephone: (202) 466-5460
Registered as lobbyist at U.S. Congress.

D'AMICO, William
Chadbourne and Parke
1101 Vermont Ave., N.W. Suite 900, Washington, DC 20005
Telephone: (202) 289-3000

DANAS, Andrew M.
Grove, Jaskiewicz, Gilliam and Cobert
1730 M St., N.W. Suite 501, Washington, DC 20036
Telephone: (202) 296-2900

D'ANASTASIO, Mark
Senior Associate, APCO Associates
1155 21st St., N.W., Suite 1000, Washington, DC 20036
Telephone: (202) 778-1000

DANCY, Carla M.
International Affairs Representative, Electronic Data Systems Corp.
1331 Pennsylvania Ave., N.W., Suite 1300 North, Washington, DC 20004
Telephone: (202) 637-6700

DANE, John
Manager, State Government Relations, Nat'l Marine Manufacturers Ass'n
1000 Thomas Jefferson St, N.W. Suite 525, Washington, DC 20007
Telephone: (202) 338-6662

DANFORTH, John
Managing Director, Secura Group, The
1155 21st St., N.W., Washington, DC 20036
Telephone: (202) 728-4920

DANIEL, Aubrey M., III
Williams and Connolly
839 17th St., N.W. 1000 Hill Bldg., Washington, DC 20006
Telephone: (202) 331-5000
Clients:
General Motors Corp.
Navistar Internat'l Corp.

DANIEL, John E.
Corp. V. President, Government Affairs, Internat'l Technology Corp.
1233 20th St., N.W. 7th Floor, Washington, DC 20036
Telephone: (202) 778-8760
Registered as lobbyist at U.S. Congress.
Background: Chief of Staf, U.S. Environmental Protection Agency, 1981-83.

DANIEL, Royal, III
Partner, Bishop, Cook, Purcell & Reynolds
1400 L St., N.W., Washington, DC 20005-3502
Telephone: (202) 371-5700
Registered as lobbyist at U.S. Congress.
Background: Special Assistant for Tariff Policy Planning, General Counsel's Office, U.S. Treasury Department, 1978-79.
Clients:
Center of Industries of the State of San Paulo (CIESP)

DANIELIAN, Ronald L.
President, Internat'l Economic Policy Ass'n
12605 Native Daneer Place, Gaithersburg, MD 20878
Telephone: (301) 990-1255

DANIELS, Michael P.
Mudge Rose Guthrie Alexander and Ferdon
2121 K St., N.W., Suite 700, Washington, DC 20037
Telephone: (202) 429-9355
Registered as lobbyist at U.S. Congress.
Registered as Foreign Agent: (#3200).
Clients:
Asociacion Nacional de Industriales (ANDI)
China Nat'l Textiles Import and Export Corp.
Footwear Distributors and Retailers of America
Hong Kong Trade, Industry and Customs Department
PROEXPO/INCOMEX

DANIELS, Molly
Field Coordinator, Long Term Care Campaign
1334 G St., N.W., Suite 300, Washington, DC 20005
Telephone: (202) 628-3030

DANIELS, Ronda
Associate Regulatory Counsel, Nat'l Ass'n of Home Builders of the U.S.
15th and M Streets, N.W., Washington, DC 20005
Telephone: (202) 822-0470

DANIELSON, David S.
Assistant Director, Gov't Relations, American Optometric Ass'n
1505 Prince Street, Suite 300, Alexandria, VA 22314
Telephone: (703) 739-9200
Registered as lobbyist at U.S. Congress.

DANIELSON, Nancy
Legislative Assistant, Nat'l Farmers Union
600 Maryland Ave., S.W., Suite 202W, Washington, DC 20024
Telephone: (202) 554-1600
Registered as lobbyist at U.S. Congress.

DANNENFELDT, Paula
Legislative & Public Affairs Director, Ass'n of Metropolitan Sewerage Agencies
1000 Connecticut Ave., N.W. Suite 1006, Washington, DC 20036
Telephone: (202) 833-2672

DANNER, Pamela
Ross and Hardies
888 16th St., N.W., Washington, DC 20006
Telephone: (202) 296-8600

DANOVITCH, David
Regulatory Counsel, Nat'l Council of Savings Institutions
1101 15th St., N.W. Suite 400, Washington, DC 20005
Telephone: (202) 857-3100
Registered as lobbyist at U.S. Congress.

DANOWITZ, Jane
Exec. Director, Women's Campaign Fund
1601 Connecticut Ave., N.W. Suite 800, Washington, DC 20005
Telephone: (202) 234-3700

D'ANTONIO, Dr. William V.
Exec. Officer, American Sociological Ass'n
1722 N St., N.W., Washington, DC 20036
Telephone: (202) 833-3410

DANZIG, Amy
Director of Communications, American Diabetes Ass'n
Nat'l Service Center, 1660 Duke St., Alexandria, VA 22314
Telephone: (703) 549-1500

DANZIG, Richard J.
Latham and Watkins
1001 Pennsylvania Ave., N.W., Suite 1300, Washington, DC 20004
Telephone: (202) 637-2200
Background: Law Clerk to Justice Byron R. White, U.S. Supreme Court, 1971-2. Deputy Assistant Secretary of Defense, 1977-81.
Clients:
Daewoo Internat'l

DAPPER, Nancy
Dir, Legislation & Policy Office (Act), DEPARTMENT OF HEALTH AND HUMAN SERVICES - Health Care Financing Administration
200 Independence Ave., S.W., Washington, DC 20201
Telephone: (202) 426-3960

DARBY, Douglas W.
Dir., Spec. Projects, Legislative Anal., Nat'l Ass'n of Manufacturers
1331 Pennsylvania Ave., N.W. Suite 1500 North, Washington, DC 20004-1703
Telephone: (202) 637-3000

DARBY, Paul B.
Director of Information, Farm Credit Council
50 F St., N.W., Suite 900, Washington, DC 20001
Telephone: (202) 626-8710

Background: Previously employed by former Governor, Farm Credit Administration as researcher and writer, 1985.

DARCY, Jo Ellen
Legislative Affairs Associate, Investment Company Institute
1600 M St., N.W. Suite 600, Washington, DC 20036
Telephone: (202) 293-7700
Registered as lobbyist at U.S. Congress.
Background: Former staff member, House Banking Committee.

DARK, Linda Pinegar
Black, Manafort, Stone and Kelly Public Affairs Co.
211 N. Union St., Third Floor, Alexandria, VA 22314
Telephone: (703) 683-6612
Registered as lobbyist at U.S. Congress.
Registered as Foreign Agent: (#3600).

DARLING, Charles M., IV
Baker and Botts
555 13th St., N.W., Suite 500 East, Washington, DC 20004-1109
Telephone: (202) 639-7700
Clients:
Ashland Exploration, Inc.

DARLING, Richard C.
Manager, Federal Gov't Relations, Penney Co., J. C.
Suite 1015, 1156 15th St., N.W., Washington, DC 20005
Telephone: (202) 862-4811
Registered as lobbyist at U.S. Congress.

D'ARMIENTO, Paul R.
V. President, McKevitt Group, The
1101 16th St., N.W., Suite 333, Washington, DC 20036
Telephone: (202) 822-0604
Background: Consultant in public relations and communications.

DARNEILLE, Diane D.
Staff V. President, Legislative Affairs, Schering-Plough Corp.
1850 K St., N.W. Suite 1195, Washington, DC 20006
Telephone: (202) 463-7372
Registered as lobbyist at U.S. Congress.

DARNEILLE, Hopewell H., III
Verner, Liipfert, Bernhard, McPherson and Hand, Chartered
901 15th St., N.W., Suite 700, Washington, DC 20005
Telephone: (202) 371-6000
Clients:
Indiana Port Commission

DARR, Anne
DeHart and Darr Associates, Inc.
1360 Beverly Road, Suite 201, McLean, VA 22101
Telephone: (703) 448-1000
Clients:
University of New Mexico

DARRELL, Mark C.
Miller, Balis and O'Neil
1101 14th St., N.W. Suite 1400, Washington, DC 20005
Telephone: (202) 789-1450
Registered as lobbyist at U.S. Congress.
Clients:
American Public Gas Ass'n

D'ARRIGO, Diane
Regulatory Oversight Coordinator, Nuclear Information and Resource Service
1424 16th St., N.W. Suite 601, Washington, DC 20036
Telephone: (202) 328-0002

DARROW, Alan
V. President, Administration, Nat'l Business Aircraft Ass'n
1200 18th St., N.W. Suite 200, Washington, DC 20036
Telephone: (202) 783-9000

DARROW, Carl E.
President, American Wood Council
1250 Connecticut Ave., N.W., Suite 230, Washington, DC 20036
Telephone: (202) 833-1595

DASCHLE, Linda
V. President, Federal Affairs, American Ass'n of Airport Executives
4212 King St., Alexandria, VA 22302
Telephone: (703) 824-0500
Registered as lobbyist at U.S. Congress.

DASKAL, Jim
Counsel, Service Station Dealers of America
499 S. Capitol St., S.E. Suite 407, Washington, DC 20003
Telephone: (202) 479-0196

DATT, John C.
Executive & Director, Washington Office, American Farm Bureau Federation
600 Maryland Ave., S.W., Washington, DC 20024
Telephone: (202) 484-3600
Registered as lobbyist at U.S. Congress.

DAUB, Hal
Director, Government Affairs, Deloitte & Touche Washington Services Group
1001 Pennsylvania Ave., N.W. Suite 350N, Washington, DC 20004
Telephone: (202) 879-5600
Background: Member, U.S. House of Representatives (R-NE), 1981-88.

DAUBON, Ramon
V. President, Nat'l Puerto Rican Coalition
1700 K St., N.W., Suite 500, Washington, DC 20006
Telephone: (703) 223-3915

DAVENPORT, Becky L.
Exec. Asst., Mmbrship & Public Affrs., Internat'l Ice Cream Ass'n
888 16th St., N.W., Washington, DC 20006
Telephone: (202) 296-4250
Registered as lobbyist at U.S. Congress.
Background: Also represents Milk Industry Foundation.

DAVENPORT, James
Tanaka, Ritger and Middleton
1919 Pennsylvania Ave., N.W., Suite 303, Washington, DC 20006
Telephone: (202) 223-1670
Registered as lobbyist at U.S. Congress.
Registered as Foreign Agent: (#0948).
Clients:
Japan Automobile Tire Manufacturers Ass'n
Japan Bearing Industrial Ass'n
Japan Export Metal Flatware Industry Ass'n
Japan General Merchandise Exporters Ass'n
Japan Trade Center

DAVENPORT, Linda G.
COO, Affordable Housing & Exec. V. Pres., Nat'l Corp. for Housing Partnerships
1225 Eye St., N.W. Suite 700, Washington, DC 20005
Telephone: (202) 347-6247

DAVENPORT, Rory
Political Director, Politics Inc.
1920 L St., N.W., Suite 700, Washington, DC 20036
Telephone: (202) 331-7654

DAVID, Earl F.
Federal Relations Representative, Phillips Petroleum Co.
1776 Eye St., N.W. Suite 700, Washington, DC 20006
Telephone: (202) 833-0900
Registered as lobbyist at U.S. Congress.

DAVID, John C.
V.P., Broadcaster-Congressional Relats., Nat'l Ass'n of Broadcasters
1771 N St., N.W., Washington, DC 20036
Telephone: (202) 429-5300
Registered as lobbyist at U.S. Congress.

DAVIDSON COLLING GROUP, INC., THE
1211 Connecticut Ave., N.W., Suite 610, Washington, DC 20036
Telephone: (202) 293-2180
Members of firm representing listed organizations:
Colling, Terese, Exec. V. President
Davidson, James H., President
Background: Chief Counsel and Staff Director, U.S. Senate Judiciary Subcommittee on Administrative Practice and Procedure, 1979-81. Chief Counsel, U.S. Senate Governmental Affairs Subcommittee on Inter-

DAVIDSON COLLING GROUP, INC., THE (Cont'd)
governmental Relations, 1974-79. Special Assistant to Senator Stuart Symington (D-MO), 1971-74.
Clients:
American Advertising Federation *(James H. David-son)*
American Ass'n of Advertising Agencies *(James H. Davidson)*
American Newspaper Publishers Ass'n *(James H. Davidson)*
Ass'n of Nat'l Advertisers *(James H. Davidson)*
Direct Marketing Ass'n
Garden State Paper Co. *(Terese Colling)*
Magazine Publishers of America *(James H. Davidson)*
Media General, Inc. *(Terese Colling)*
Nat'l Ass'n of Broadcasters *(James H. Davidson)*
Nat'l Ass'n of Industrial and Office Parks *(James H. Davidson)*
Rouse Company, The *(James H. Davidson)*
Yellow Pages Publishers Ass'n *(James H. Davidson)*

DAVIDSON, Daniel I.
Spiegel and McDiarmid
1350 New York Ave., N.W., Suite 1100, Washington, DC 20005
Telephone: (202) 879-4000
Registered as lobbyist at U.S. Congress.
Background: Law Clerk, U.S. Court of Appeals, Second Circuit, 1959-60. U.S. Department of State, 1965-68. Delegate to Paris Peace Talks on Viet Nam, 1968. Senior Staff, Nat'l Security Council, 1969.

DAVIDSON, Glenn K.
Director, Virginia Liaison Office, Virginia, Governor of
444 N. Capitol St., N.W. Suite 246, Washington, DC 20001
Telephone: (202) 783-1769

DAVIDSON, Howard
Director, Center on Children and the Law
1800 M St., N.W., Washington, DC 20036
Telephone: (202) 331-2250

DAVIDSON, James H.
President, Davidson Colling Group, Inc., The
1211 Connecticut Ave., N.W., Suite 610, Washington, DC 20036
Telephone: (202) 293-2180
Registered as lobbyist at U.S. Congress.
Background: Chief Counsel and Staff Director, U.S. Senate Judiciary Subcommittee on Administrative Practice and Procedure, 1979-81. Chief Counsel, U.S. Senate Governmental Affairs Subcommittee on Intergovernmental Relations, 1974-79. Special Assistant to Senator Stuart Symington (D-MO), 1971-74.
Clients:
American Advertising Federation
American Ass'n of Advertising Agencies
American Newspaper Publishers Ass'n
Ass'n of Nat'l Advertisers
Direct Marketing Ass'n
Magazine Publishers of America
Nat'l Ass'n of Broadcasters
Nat'l Ass'n of Industrial and Office Parks
Rouse Company, The
Yellow Pages Publishers Ass'n

DAVIDSON, Richard H.
Wright and Talisman
1050 17th St., N.W. Suite 600, Washington, DC 20036
Telephone: (202) 331-1194
Background: Attorney, Federal Energy Regulatory Commission, 1985-86.

DAVIE, Bruce F.
Manager, Federal Tax Services, Andersen and Co., Arthur
1666 K St., N.W., Washington, DC 20006
Telephone: (202) 862-3100
Background: For Chief Tax Economist, House Ways and Means Committee.

DAVIES, Dionne
American Bankers Ass'n
1120 Connecticut Ave., N.W., Washington, DC 20036
Telephone: (202) 663-5000
Registered as lobbyist at U.S. Congress.

D'AVINO, Richard
King and Spalding
1730 Pennsylvania Ave., N.W. Suite 1200, Washington, DC 20006-4706
Telephone: (202) 737-0500
Clients:
Alliance for Capital Access

DAVIS, Alan C.
V. President for Public Affairs, American Cancer Soc. (Public Affairs Office)
316 Pennsylvania Ave., S.E. Suite 200, Washington, DC 20003
Telephone: (202) 546-4011

DAVIS, Anna Holmquist
Dir, Legis Affrs, DEPARTMENT OF TREASURY
15th and Pennsylvania Ave. N.W., Washington, DC 20220
Telephone: (202) 566-2037

DAVIS, Carl
East Coast Counsel, NIKE, Inc.
507 Second St., N.E., Washington, DC 20002
Telephone: (202) 543-8500

DAVIS, Christopher L.
President, Investment Partnership Ass'n
1100 Connecticut Ave., N.W., Suite 500, Washington, DC 20036-5303
Telephone: (202) 775-9750
Background: Also represents InvestAmerica, the association's political action committee.

DAVIS COMPANIES, The Susan
1146 19th St., N.W., Washington, DC 20036
Telephone: (202) 775-8881
Members of firm representing listed organizations:
Cryor, Michael, Regional V. President
Background: Former Special Assistant to Rep. Parren Mitchell (D-MD). Former Consultant to Senate Judiciary Committee. Former Deputy Director, Democratic Platform Committee. Former aide to Rep. Mike Barnes (D-MD).
Davis, Susan A., Chairman
Gay, Timothy, Director of Communications
Background: Former Press Secretary to Senator John D. Rockefeller, IV (D-WV); Senator John Heinz (R-PA); Rep. Thomas Carper (D-DE); Rep. James Coyne (D-PA); and Rep. William Clinger (R-PA).
Rhatican, William F., Senior V. President
Background: Special Assistant to President Nixon, 1970-73; Special Assistant/Director of Communications - Treasury, Commerce and Interior, 1974-75; Special Assistant to President Ford, 1976.
Whittlesey, Judy
Background: Exec. V. President, The Susan Davis Communications Group. Former Chief of Staff, Press Secretary to Joan Mondale. Former Chief of Staff to B.A. Bentsen, Dukakis-Bentsen Campaign, 1988.
Winnick, Jeanne M.
Background: Director, Los Angeles Office, The Susan Davis Companies. Former Staff Assistant, Press Secretay's Office, The White House, under President Ronald Reagan.
Organizations represented:
American Institute of Architects, The *(Susan A. Davis)*
Career Communications *(Michael Cryor)*
Children's Hospice Internat'l
Computer and Business Equipment Manufacturers Ass'n *(Timothy Gay)*
Eastman Kodak Co.
MayCenters, Inc. *(Judy Whittlesey)*
McDonald's Corp.
Nat'l Ass'n of Home Builders of the U.S. *(William F. Rhatican)*
Nat'l Cattlemen's Ass'n
Philip Morris Cos., Inc.

DAVIS, Debra
Market Opinion Research, Inc.
1400 L St., N.W., Suite 650, Washington, DC 20005
Telephone: (202) 289-0420

DAVIS, Drew M.
Director, Congressional Affairs, Nat'l Soft Drink Ass'n
1101 16th St., N.W., Washington, DC 20036
Telephone: (202) 463-6732
Registered as lobbyist at U.S. Congress.

DAVIS, Edward M.
President, American Nuclear Energy Council
410 First St., S.E. Third Floor, Washington, DC 20003
Telephone: (202) 484-2670
Registered as lobbyist at U.S. Congress.

DAVIS, Edwin H.
Associate Director, Issues Development, Common Cause
2030 M St., N.W., Washington, DC 20036
Telephone: (202) 833-1200
Registered as lobbyist at U.S. Congress.

DAVIS, Fred G.
Director, Legislative Affairs (Nuclear), Edison Electric Institute
1111 19th St., N.W., Washington, DC 20036
Telephone: (202) 778-6477
Registered as lobbyist at U.S. Congress.
Background: Serves as contact for Power PAC.

DAVIS, Garry
World Coordinator, World Service Authority
1012 14th St., N.W. Suite 1101, Washington, DC 20005
Telephone: (202) 638-2662
Background: Also serves as World Coordinator, World Government of World Citizens.

DAVIS, GRAHAM AND STUBBS
1200 19th St., N.W., Suite 500, Washington, DC 20036
Telephone: (202) 822-8660
Members of firm representing listed organizations:
Hosenball, S. Neil
Background: Assistant General Counsel for Procurement, 1965-67, Deputy General Counsel, 1967-75 and General Counsel, 1975-85, National Aeronautics and Space Administration.
Clients:
American Wire Producers Ass'n

DAVIS & HARMAN
1455 Pennsylvania Ave., N.W. Suite 1200, Washington, DC 20004
Telephone: (202) 347-2230
Members of firm representing listed organizations:
Davis, Thomas A.
Background: Office of the Chief Counsel, Internal Revenue Service, 1966-70.
Harman, William B. (Jr.)
Mattox, Barbara G., Partner
Wilkins, Gail B.
Clients:
Alcoma Packing Co. *(Thomas A. Davis)*
American General Corp.
American Horse Council *(Thomas A. Davis)*
Armco Inc. *(Thomas A. Davis)*
Associated Electric and Gas Insurance Services, Ltd. *(Thomas A. Davis, Gail B. Wilkins)*
Bethlehem Steel Corp. *(Thomas A. Davis)*
Chicago Board of Trade *(Thomas A. Davis)*
CIGNA Corp.
Committee of Annuity Insurers
Dresser Industries *(Gail B. Wilkins)*
Florida Power and Light Co.
Lincoln Nat'l Life Insurance Co.
Lloyds of London, Underwriters at *(Thomas A. Davis, Gail B. Wilkins)*
Nat'l Ass'n of Life Companies
Nat'l Cattlemen's Ass'n
Stock Information Group *(William B. Harman, Jr.)*

DAVIS, James W.
Federal Gov't Affairs Director, AT&T
Suite 1000, 1120 20th St., N.W., Washington, DC 20036
Telephone: (202) 457-3855

DAVIS, Jana
Jefferson Group, The
1341 G St., N.W., Suite 1100, Washington, DC 20005
Telephone: (202) 638-3535

DAVIS, Jerry
Senior V. President, Nat'l Office Products Ass'n
301 North Fairfax St., Alexandria, VA 22314
Telephone: (703) 549-9040

DAVIS, John W.
Manager, Congressional Relations, General Electric Co.
1331 Pennsylvania Ave., N.W., Washington, DC
Telephone: (202) 637-4407

Registered as lobbyist at U.S. Congress.

DAVIS, Julius A.
V. President, United States Student Ass'n
1012 14th St., N.W., Suite 207, Washington, DC 20005
Telephone: (202) 347-8772

DAVIS, Kenneth E.
Director, Government Relations, Rohm and Haas Co.
1667 K St., N.W., Suite 210, Washington, DC 20006
Telephone: (202) 872-0660
Registered as lobbyist at U.S. Congress.
Background: Legislative Assistant (1967-73) and Administrative Assistant (1974-76) for U.S. Senator Hugh Scott.

DAVIS, Lanny J.
Patton, Boggs and Blow
2550 M St., N.W., Suite 800, Washington, DC 20037
Telephone: (202) 457-6000
Registered as lobbyist at U.S. Congress.
Clients:
ALTA Technology
Hobby Industries Ass'n

DAVIS, Dr. Lynda
Director, Washington Office, Florida Washington Office, State of
444 N. Capitol St., Suite 287, Washington, DC 20001
Telephone: (202) 624-5885

DAVIS, Martin
President, November Group Inc.
1611 Connecticut Ave., N.W. 4th Floor, Washington, DC 20009
Telephone: (202) 265-2700

DAVIS, Rebecca McPherson
Wallace & Edwards
1150 Connecticut Ave., N.W., Suite 507, Washington, DC 20036
Telephone: (202) 331-4331
Registered as lobbyist at U.S. Congress.
Background: Serves as Treasurer, Cotton Warehouse Government Relations Committee.

DAVIS, Michele M.
Exec. Director, Republican Governors Ass'n
310 First St., S.E., Washington, DC 20003
Telephone: (202) 863-8587

DAVIS POLK & WARDWELL
1300 Eye St., N.W. 11th Fl. East, Washington, DC 20005
Telephone: (202) 962-7000
Background: Washington office of a New York law firm.
Members of firm representing listed organizations:
Doremus, Theodore A. (Jr.), Of Counsel
Background: Senior Branch Attorney, Securities and Exchange Commission, 1970-75. General Counsel, Minority Staff, House Committee on Banking, Finance and Urban Affairs, 1975-79.
Moe, Richard
Background: Administrative Assistant to Senator Walter F. Mondale (D-MN), 1972-77. Chief of Staff to the Vice President of the United States, 1977-81.
Rollyson, Mikel M.
Clients:
American Institute of Certified Public Accountants *(Richard Moe)*
Kohlberg Kravis Roberts & Co. *(Mikel M. Rollyson)*
Manville Corp. *(Richard Moe)*
Morgan Guaranty Trust Co. *(Theodore A. Doremus, Jr., Richard Moe)*
Morgan Stanley and Co. *(Mikel M. Rollyson)*
Norwest Corp. *(Theodore A. Doremus, Jr.)*

DAVIS, Randall E.
Jones, Day, Reavis and Pogue
1450 G St., N.W., Suite 700, Washington, DC 20005-2088
Telephone: (202) 879-3939
Registered as lobbyist at U.S. Congress.
Background: Former Associate Director, Natural Resources, Energy and Science, Office of Management and Budget.
Clients:
Castle-Harlan, Inc.
Centex Corp.
Chevy Chase Savings Bank
Consumers for Competitive Fuels
Day Kimball Hospital

Fairfield Communities, Inc.
Kentucky Utilities Co.
Preussag AG
Royal Trustco Ltd.
Windham Community Memorial Hospital

DAVIS/REPLOGLE & ASSOCIATES, INC.
335 Commerce St., Alexandria, VA 22314
Telephone: (703) 548-5016
Members of firm representing listed organizations:
Sullivan, Brandi
Clients:
City & Regional Magazine Ass'n *(Brandi Sullivan)*

DAVIS, Richard H.
Senior V. President, Black, Manafort, Stone and Kelly Public Affairs Co.
211 N. Union St., Third Floor, Alexandria, VA 22314
Telephone: (703) 683-6612
Registered as lobbyist at U.S. Congress.
Registered as Foreign Agent: (#3600).
Background: Former Associate Director, Office of Cabinet Affairs in the White House under President Reagan.
Clients:
Puerto Rico Federal Affairs Administration

DAVIS, Richard S.
Beveridge & Diamond, P.C.
1350 Eye St., N.W. Suite 700, Washington, DC 20005
Telephone: (202) 789-6000
Registered as lobbyist at U.S. Congress.
Clients:
Bluefield, West Virginia, City of
Morgantown, West Virginia, City of

DAVIS, Robert W.
Aerospace Progam Development, Ford Aerospace Corp.
1235 Jefferson Davis Hwy. Suite 1300, Arlington, VA 22202
Telephone: (703) 685-5500
Registered as lobbyist at U.S. Congress.

DAVIS, Ron H.
Director, Research and Chief Economist, Printing Industries of America
1730 North Lynn St., Arlington, VA 22209
Telephone: (703) 841-8100

DAVIS, Smith W.
Akin, Gump, Strauss, Hauer and Feld
1333 New Hampshire Ave., N.W., Suite 400, Washington, DC 20036
Telephone: (202) 887-4000
Background: Counsel, House Judiciary Committee, Subcommittee on Crime, 1978-79.
Clients:
Grand Met USA

DAVIS, Steve G.
Exec. Director, Nat'l Newspaper Publishers Ass'n
948 National Press Building, Washington, DC 20045
Telephone: (202) 662-7324

DAVIS, Susan
Account Executive, Jefferson Group, The
1341 G St., N.W., Suite 1100, Washington, DC 20005
Telephone: (202) 638-3535
Background: Former Chief Counsel, House Committee on Agriculture.

DAVIS, Susan A.
Chairman, Davis Companies, The Susan
1146 19th St., N.W., Washington, DC 20036
Telephone: (202) 775-8881
Registered as lobbyist at U.S. Congress.
Registered as Foreign Agent: (#3444).
Organizations represented:
American Institute of Architects, The

DAVIS, Thomas A.
Davis & Harman
1455 Pennsylvania Ave., N.W. Suite 1200, Washington, DC 20004
Telephone: (202) 347-2230
Registered as lobbyist at U.S. Congress.
Registered as Foreign Agent: (#4018).
Background: Office of the Chief Counsel, Internal Revenue Service, 1966-70.
Clients:

Alcoma Packing Co.
American Horse Council
Armco Inc.
Associated Electric and Gas Insurance Services, Ltd.
Bethlehem Steel Corp.
Chicago Board of Trade
Lloyds of London, Underwriters at

DAVIS, William
Director, Policy Analysis & Development, Nat'l League of Cities
1301 Pennsylvania Ave., N.W., Washington, DC 20004
Telephone: (202) 626-3000

DAVIS WRIGHT TREMAINE
1752 N St., N.W., Suite 800, Washington, DC 20036
Telephone: (202) 822-9775
Background: Washington office of a Seattle law firm.
Members of firm representing listed organizations:
Brown, Omer F. (II)
Cohen, Edward B.
Background: Deputy Special Assistant to the President of the U.S., 1979-81. General Counsel, U.S. Office of Consumer Affairs, 1977-79. Staff Counsel, Senate Committee on Commerce, Science and Transportation, 1974-77.
Evans, Walter H. (III)
Waggoner, Daniel
Walsh, James P., Of Counsel
Background: Staff Counsel, Senate Committee on Commerce, 1972-77. General Counsel, Senate Committee on Commerce, Science and Transportation, 1977-78. Deputy Administrator, National Oceanic and Atmospheric Administration, 1978-81.
Clients:
American Honda Motor Co. *(Edward B. Cohen)*
American Tunaboat Ass'n *(James P. Walsh)*
Davis Wright Political Action Committee *(Edward B. Cohen)*
Energy Contractors Price-Anderson Group *(Omer F. Brown, II)*
F/V American Empire *(James P. Walsh)*
Japan, Embassy of *(Walter H. Evans, III)*
Klukwan Forest Products, Inc. *(James P. Walsh)*
Knappton Corp. *(Walter H. Evans, III)*
McCaw Cellular Communications Cos. *(Edward B. Cohen, Daniel Waggoner)*
Nike, Inc. *(Walter H. Evans, III)*
Oregon Economic Development Dept., Ports Division *(Walter H. Evans, III)*
Oregon, State of, Department of Economic Development, Ports Division *(Walter H. Evans, III)*
Qatar, Embassy of *(Walter H. Evans, III)*

DAVISON, Calvin
Crowell and Moring
1001 Pennsylvania Ave., N.W., Washington, DC 20004-2505
Telephone: (202) 624-2500
Registered as lobbyist at U.S. Congress.

DAW, Richard
Director, Dept. of Communications, United States Catholic Conference
3200 4th St., N.E., Washington, DC 20017
Telephone: (202) 541-3000

DAWSON AND ASSOCIATES, MATHIS
1900 L St., N.W., Suite 300, Washington, DC 20036
Telephone: (202) 872-1699
Registered as Foreign Agent: (#4278)
Members of firm representing listed organizations:
Mathis, Dawson
Background: Former Member, U.S. House of Representatives (D-GA).
Clients:
American Electronics Laboratories *(Dawson Mathis)*
B.A.T. Industries, PLC *(Dawson Mathis)*
Crowley Maritime Corp. *(Dawson Mathis)*
Long Lake Energy Corp. *(Dawson Mathis)*
Massachusetts Mutual Life Insurance Co. *(Dawson Mathis)*

DAWSON, Mimi Weyforth
Lobbyist, Wiley, Rein & Fielding
1776 K St., N.W., Tenth Floor, Washington, DC 20006-2359
Telephone: (202) 429-7000

DAWSON, Mimi Weyforth (Cont'd)
Registered as lobbyist at U.S. Congress.
Background: Former Deputy Secretary of Transportation.
Clients:
BMW of North America
General Electric Information Services

DAWSON, Rhett B.
Sr. V. Pres., Law and Public Policy, Potomac Electric
Power Co.
1900 Pennsylvania Ave., N.W., Washington, DC 20068
Telephone: (202) 872-2000
Registered as lobbyist at U.S. Congress.
Background: Former assistant to President Reagan for operations.

DAWSON, Robert K.
V. President, Management, Cassidy and Associates, Inc.
655 15th St., N.W., Suite 1100, Washington, DC 20005
Telephone: (202) 347-0773
Registered as lobbyist at U.S. Congress.
Background: Deputy Assistant Secretary of the Army for
Civil Works, 1981-84. Assistant Secretary of the Army
for Civil Works, 1984-87. Associate Director, Office of
Management and Budget, 1987-88.
Clients:
American Dredging Co.
Great Lakes Dredge and Dock Co.
Infirmary Health System, Inc.
James Co., T. L.
Lehigh University
Western Townships Utilities Authority

DAWSON, Robert M.
Manager, Legis. Research and Information, Nat'l Rural
Electric Cooperative Ass'n
1800 Massachusetts Ave., N.W., Washington, DC 20036
Telephone: (202) 857-9570
Registered as lobbyist at U.S. Congress.

DAWSON, Thomas C.
Smith Dawson & Andrews, Inc.
1000 Connecticut Ave., N.W., Suite 304, Washington, DC
20036
Telephone: (202) 835-0740
Registered as lobbyist at U.S. Congress.
Clients:
Bank St. College
Eugene, Oregon, City of
New York Metropolitan Transportation Authority
San Francisco, California, City of
San Francisco Public Utilities Commission

DAY, Brenda T.
Director, Environmental Affairs, Chrysler Corp.
1100 Connecticut Ave., N.W., Washington, DC 20036
Telephone: (202) 862-5414
Registered as lobbyist at U.S. Congress.

DAY, Charles W.
Manager, Washington Public Affairs, Ford Motor Co.
1350 Eye St., N.W. Suite 1000, Washington, DC 20005
Telephone: (202) 962-5400

DAY, Harry F.
Regulatory Counsel, New York Stock Exchange
1800 K St., N.W., Suite 1100, Washington, DC 20006
Telephone: (202) 293-5740
Registered as lobbyist at U.S. Congress.

DAY, James M.
Cotten, Day and Selfon
1899 L St., N.W., 12th Floor, Washington, DC 20036
Telephone: (202) 659-9505
Background: Director, Office of Hearings and Appeals, Department of Interior, 1970-73. Administrator, U.S. Mining
Enforcement and Safety Administration, 1973-75.

DAY, Robert D.
Exec. Director, Renewable Natural Resources Foundation
5430 Grosvenor Lane, Bethesda, MD 20814
Telephone: (301) 493-9101

DC INTERNAT'L, INC.
8401 Colesville Road Suite 361-A, Silver Spring, MD
20910-3312
Telephone: (301) 589-0226
Registered as Foreign Agent: (#4210)

Members of firm representing listed organizations:
Hernandez, Andres R.
Clients:
Christian Democrat Internat'l *(Andres R. Hernandez)*
Christian Democrat Organization of the Americas
(Andres R. Hernandez)
European Union of Christian Democrats/Europe-
an People'sParty *(Andres R. Hernandez)*
Guatemala, Government of *(Andres R. Hernandez)*

DCM GROUP
1355 Beverly Rd., Suite 200, McLean, VA 22101
Telephone: (703) 883-1355
Background: A public relations and communications consulting firm.
Members of firm representing listed organizations:
Cones, Carole K.
DeBolt, Edward S., President

DEAKIN, Philip C.
Director, Defense Programs, Internat'l Technology Corp.
1233 20th St., N.W. 7th Floor, Washington, DC 20036
Telephone: (202) 778-8760

DEAL, William F., CAE
Exec. Vice President, Internat'l Bottled Water Ass'n
113 North Henry St., Alexandria, VA 22314
Telephone: (703) 683-5213

DEAMICIS, Don S.
Ropes and Gray
1001 Pennsylvania Ave., N.W., Washington, DC 20004
Telephone: (202) 626-3900
Registered as lobbyist at U.S. Congress.

DEAN, Carol A.
Exec. V. President, Building Service Contractors Ass'n, Internat'l
10201 Lee Hwy. Suite 225, Fairfax, VA 22030
Telephone: (703) 359-7090

DEAN, John E.
Clohan & Dean
1101 Vermont Ave., N.W. Suite 400, Washington, DC
20005
Telephone: (202) 289-3900
Registered as lobbyist at U.S. Congress.
Background: Assistant Counsel, House Committee on Education and Labor, 1983-85.
Clients:
Coalition of Higher Education Assistance Organizations
Student Loan Funding Corp. of Ohio

DEAN, Maggie
Ass't Director, Government Affairs, Georgia-Pacific Corp.
1875 Eye St., N.W. Suite 775, Washington, DC 20006
Telephone: (202) 659-3600
Registered as lobbyist at U.S. Congress.

DEAN, Norman L., Jr.
Director, Environmental Quality Division, Nat'l Wildlife Federation
1400 16th St., N.W., Washington, DC 20036-2266
Telephone: (202) 797-6800

DEAN, Robert W.
Senior V. Pres., Washington Operations, Ball Corp.
2200 Clarendon Blvd. Suite 1006, Arlington, VA 22201
Telephone: (703) 284-5400

DEAN, S. Bobo
Hobbs, Straus, Dean and Wilder
1819 H St., N.W., Suite 800, Washington, DC 20006
Telephone: (202) 783-5100
Registered as lobbyist at U.S. Congress.
Clients:
Ass'n of Navajo Community Controlled School
Boards
Bristol Bay Health Corp.
Maniilaq Ass'n
Metlakatla Indian Community
Miccosukee Tribe of Indians of Florida
Oglala Sioux Tribe

DEAN, Virginia
Director, Gov't and Membership Relations, American
Bankers Ass'n
1120 Connecticut Ave., N.W., Washington, DC 20036

Telephone: (202) 663-5000

DEANE, Curtis C.
Managing Director, American Soc. of Civil Engineers
1015 15th St., N.W. Suite 600, Washington, DC 20005
Telephone: (202) 789-2200

DEANE, James G.
Co-Chairman, Canada-United States Environmental Council
1244 19th St., N.W., Washington, DC 20036
Telephone: (202) 659-9510

DEANE, John Russell, II
Trainum, Snowdon, Holland, Hyland & Deane
888 17th St., N.W., Suite 500, Washington, DC 20006
Telephone: (202) 835-0900
Background: Staff Assistant to the President of the U.S.,
1971-72 Deputy Assistant General Counsel, Federal Energy Administration, 1974-75. Serves as Counsel for the
Specialty Equipment Market Ass'n, Performance Warehouse Ass'n, Nat'l Hot Rod Ass'n, and Coalition of Automotive Ass'ns.

DEANER, Milton
President, American Iron and Steel Institute
1133 15th St., N.W. Suite 300, Washington, DC 20005-
2701
Telephone: (202) 452-7146

DEARDORFF, Howard
Director, Membership Services, Pet Industry Joint Advisory Council
1710 Rhode Island Ave., N.W. Suite 200, Washington, DC
20036
Telephone: (202) 452-1525

DEARMENT, Roderick A.
Covington and Burling
1201 Pennsylvania Ave., N.W., Box 7566, Washington, DC
20044
Telephone: (202) 662-6000
Registered as lobbyist at U.S. Congress.
Background: Former Chief Counsel, Senate Finance Committee.

DEBEVOISE AND PLIMPTON
555 13th St., N.W. Eleventh Floor, Washington, DC
20004-1179
Telephone: (202) 383-8000
Members of firm representing listed organizations:
Bruce, Robert R., Partner
Background: General Counsel, Federal Communications Commission, 1977-81.
Cunard, Jeffrey P., Partner
Clients:
Internat'l Telecom Japan *(Robert R. Bruce, Jeffrey P. Cunard)*
Sony Corp. *(Robert R. Bruce, Jeffrey P. Cunard)*

DE BLOIS, Michael
Committee Management Associates
Box 470, Arlington, VA 22210
Telephone: (703) 241-1741

DEBOER, Jeffrey
Chief Legislative Counsel, Nat'l Ass'n of Industrial and Office Parks
1215 Jefferson Davis Hwy., Suite 100, Arlington, VA
22202
Telephone: (703) 979-3400
Registered as lobbyist at U.S. Congress.
Background: Also serves as Treasurer, Nat'l Ass'n of Industrial and Office Parks American Development PAC.

DEBOISSIERE, Alex J.
Washington Representative, Tenneco Inc.
490 L'Enfant Plaza East, S.W. Suite 2202, S.W., Washington, DC 20024
Telephone: (202) 554-2850
Registered as lobbyist at U.S. Congress.
Background: Former Staff Attorney, Federal Energy Regulatory Commission.

DEBOLT, Don J., CAE
Principal, Ass'n Resources Management, Inc.
4222 King St., Alexandria, VA 22302
Telephone: (703) 549-4440

DEBOLT, Edward S.
President, DCM Group
1355 Beverly Rd., Suite 200, McLean, VA 22101
Telephone: (703) 883-1355
Registered as lobbyist at U.S. Congress.

DEBOR, Marydale
Attorney, MacAndrews & Forbes Holdings, Inc.
1001 Pennsylvania Ave., N.W. Suite 715 South Concourse, Washington, DC 20004
Telephone: (202) 628-2600
Registered as lobbyist at U.S. Congress.

DEBRUYCKER, Thomas E.
Director, Governmental Affairs, Morrison-Knudsen Corp.
555 13th St., N.W. Suite 410 West Tower, Washington, DC 20004-1109
Telephone: (202) 638-6355

DEBUSK, F. Amanda
O'Melveny and Myers
555 13th St., N.W., Suite 500 West, Washington, DC 20004
Telephone: (202) 383-5300
Clients:
Nippon Zeon

DECHERT PRICE & RHOADS
1500 K St., N.W., Washington, DC 20005
Telephone: (202) 626-3300
Background: Washington office of a Philadelphia-based law firm.
Members of firm representing listed organizations:
Bieber, Sander M.
Mostoff, Allan S.
Background: Staff Member, Securities and Exchange Commission, 1962-1976. Associate Director, 1968-1972 and Director, 1972-1976, Division of Investment Management Regulation, Director of Policy Studies, 1976.
Clients:
Export-Import Bank of Japan *(Allan S. Mostoff)*
Japan, Embassy of *(Allan S. Mostoff)*
Ryland Acceptance Advisers, Inc. *(Sander M. Bieber)*

DECKER, Mark O.
Exec. V. President, Nat'l Ass'n of Real Estate Investment Trusts
1129 20th St., N.W. Suite 705, Washington, DC 20036
Telephone: (202) 785-8717
Registered as lobbyist at U.S. Congress.

DECONCINI, John
President, Bakery, Confectionery and Tobacco Workers Internat'l Union
10401 Connecticut Ave., Kensington, MD 20895
Telephone: (301) 933-8600

DECONCINI, Matt
Legislative Representative, Engineers' Political and Education Committee
1125 17th St., N.W., Washington, DC 20036
Telephone: (202) 429-9100
Registered as lobbyist at U.S. Congress.

DEDEKIAN, Elaine P.
Government Affairs Liaison, Siemens Capital Corp.
1455 Pennsylvania Ave., N.W. Suite 300, Washington, DC 20004
Telephone: (202) 347-0444

DEEGAN, Margaret
Director of Publications, Food and Drug Law Institute
1000 Vermont Ave., N.W., Suite 1200, Washington, DC 20005
Telephone: (202) 371-1420

DEEGAN, Michael W.
Director, Government Relations, Teledyne Industries Inc.
1501 Wilson Blvd., Suite 900, Arlington, VA 22209
Telephone: (703) 522-2550

DEEGANS, William E.
Surface Mining Project Coordinator, Nat'l Wildlife Federation
1400 16th St., N.W., Washington, DC 20036-2266
Telephone: (202) 797-6800
Registered as lobbyist at U.S. Congress.

DEEM, Richard A.
Asst. Director, Dept. of Federal Affairs, American Medical Ass'n
1101 Vermont Ave., N.W., Washington, DC 20005
Telephone: (202) 789-7400
Registered as lobbyist at U.S. Congress.

DE EMILIO, Michael
Assistant to the President, Brotherhood of Maintenance of Way Employees
400 First St., N.W., Room 801, Washington, DC 20001
Telephone: (202) 638-2135
Registered as lobbyist at U.S. Congress.

DEEN, Thomas B.
Exec. Director, Transportation Research Board (of Nat'l Research Council)
2101 Constitution Ave., N.W., Washington, DC 20418
Telephone: (202) 334-2933

DEERE, William R.
Director, Congressional Affairs, Aircraft Owners and Pilots Ass'n
500 E St., S.W. Suite 920, Washington, DC 20024
Telephone: (202) 479-4050
Registered as lobbyist at U.S. Congress.

DEERY, Brian
Director, Municipal Utilities Division, Associated General Contractors of America
1957 E St., N.W., Washington, DC 20006
Telephone: (202) 393-2040
Registered as lobbyist at U.S. Congress.

DEESE, C. Michael
Fehrenbacher, Sale, Quinn, and Deese
910 16th St., N.W., 5th Floor, Washington, DC 20006
Telephone: (202) 833-4170
Clients:
American Correctional Ass'n
Better Working Environments, Inc.
Decorative Window Coverings Ass'n
Industrial Fabrics Ass'n Internat'l
Nat'l Decorating Products Ass'n
Nat'l Waterbed Retailers Ass'n
Trophy Dealers and Manufacturers Ass'n
United States Industrial Fabrics Institute
Waterbed Manufacturers Ass'n

DEESE, Pamela M.
Robins, Kaplan, Miller & Ciresi
1627 Eye St., N.W., Suite 610, Washington, DC 20006
Telephone: (202) 861-6800
Clients:
Ad Hoc Granite Trade Group
Cold Spring Granite Co.
Ecolab

DEETS, Horace B.
Exec. Director, American Ass'n of Retired Persons
1909 K St., N.W., Washington, DC 20049
Telephone: (202) 872-4700

DEFRANCIS, James U.
V. President, Corporate Relations, Ebasco Services, Inc.
1025 Connecticut Ave., N.W. Suite 1014, Washington, DC 20036
Telephone: (202) 872-1352
Registered as lobbyist at U.S. Congress.

DEFRANCIS, Joseph A.
Latham and Watkins
1001 Pennsylvania Ave., N.W., Suite 1300, Washington, DC 20004
Telephone: (202) 637-2200
Clients:
Supermarket Development Corp.
Vons Co.

DE FRIES, C. E.
President, Marine Engineers Beneficial Ass'n
444 North Capitol St., N.W. Suite 800, Washington, DC 20001
Telephone: (202) 347-8585

DEFUSCO, Lisa M.
Legislative Assistant, Soc. of Real Estate Appraisers
600 New Hampshire Ave., N.W. Suite 1111, Washington, DC 20037

Telephone: (202) 298-8497
Registered as lobbyist at U.S. Congress.

DEGASPERIS, Siro
V. President, United Parcel Service
316 Pennsylvania Ave., S.E. Suite 304, Washington, DC 20003
Telephone: (202) 675-4220

DEGNON ASSOCIATES, INC.
6728 Old McLean Village Drive, McLean, VA 22101
Telephone: (703) 556-9222
Members of firm representing listed organizations:
Degnon, George K., President
Background: Serves as Executive Director of the Ass'n of State and Territorial Health Officials, the Soc. for Health and Human Values, the Ass'n for the Behavioral Sciences and Medical Education and the American Psychosomatic Soc.
Degnon, Marge
Background: Serves as Exec. Secretary, Ambulatory Pediatric Ass'n and Women in Government Relations.
Kiner, Carol Ann
Mantell, Maxine, Associate Director
White, Valerie
Clients:
Ambulatory Pediatric Ass'n *(Marge Degnon)*
American Psychosomatic Soc. *(George K. Degnon, Carol Ann Kiner)*
Ass'n for the Behavioral Sciences and Medical Education *(George K. Degnon, Carol Ann Kiner)*
Ass'n of State and Territorial Health Officials *(George K. Degnon, Valerie White)*
Soc. for Health and Human Values *(George K. Degnon, Carol Ann Kiner)*
Women in Government Relations *(Marge Degnon)*

DEGNON, George K.
President, Degnon Associates, Inc.
6728 Old McLean Village Drive, McLean, VA 22101
Telephone: (703) 556-9222
Registered as lobbyist at U.S. Congress.
Background: Serves as Executive Director of the Ass'n of State and Territorial Health Officials, the Soc. for Health and Human Values, the Ass'n for the Behavioral Sciences and Medical Education and the American Psychosomatic Soc.
Clients:
American Psychosomatic Soc.
Ass'n for the Behavioral Sciences and Medical Education
Ass'n of State and Territorial Health Officials
Soc. for Health and Human Values

DEGNON, Marge
Degnon Associates, Inc.
6728 Old McLean Village Drive, McLean, VA 22101
Telephone: (703) 556-9222
Background: Serves as Exec. Secretary, Ambulatory Pediatric Ass'n and Women in Government Relations.
Clients:
Ambulatory Pediatric Ass'n
Women in Government Relations

DEGONIA, Mary Elise
Capitol Pespectives
1915 17th St., N.W., Washington, DC 20009
Telephone: (202) 265-5276
Registered as lobbyist at U.S. Congress.
Clients:
Alternative Schools Network

DEHART AND DARR ASSOCIATES, INC.
1360 Beverly Road, Suite 201, McLean, VA 22101
Telephone: (703) 448-1000
Members of firm representing listed organizations:
Darr, Anne
DeHart, Edward H.
Newburg, Janice
Clients:
University of New Mexico *(Anne Darr, Edward H. DeHart)*

DEHART, Edward H.
DeHart and Darr Associates, Inc.
1360 Beverly Road, Suite 201, McLean, VA 22101
Telephone: (703) 448-1000
Clients:

DEHART, Edward H. (Cont'd)
University of New Mexico

DEIGH, Robb
Director of Corporate Information, Public Broadcasting Service
1320 Braddock Place, Alexandria, VA 22314
Telephone: (703) 739-5000

DEITZ, William T.
V. Pres., Legislat. & Regul. Affairs, Palumbo & Cerrell, Inc.
1629 K St., N.W., Suite 1100, Washington, DC 20006
Telephone: (202) 785-6705
Background: Former Administrative Assistant to Rep. Frank Thompson, Jr. (D-NJ) and Special Counsel to the House of Representatives Public Works and Transportation Committee.

DEKIEFFER, Donald E.
Pillsbury, Madison and Sutro
1667 K St., N.W., Suite 1100, Washington, DC 20006
Telephone: (202) 887-0300
Registered as lobbyist at U.S. Congress.
Clients:
Internat'l Anti-Counterfeiting Coalition
Nat'l Semiconductor Corp.
Titanium Metals Corp. (TIMET)

DE LA CRUZ, Arcadio R.
Exec. Director, Policy and Programs, American Public Transit Ass'n
1201 New York Ave., N.W.,, Washington, DC 20005
Telephone: (202) 898-4000
Registered as lobbyist at U.S. Congress.

DELACY, Catharine M.
Director, Federal Government Affairs, Council for Solid Waste Solutions
1275 K St., N.W. Suite 400, Washington, DC 20005
Telephone: (202) 371-5319

DELAHANTY, Kathryn A.
Legislative Assistant, Foley & Co.
206 G St. N.E. Suite 201, Washington, DC 20002
Telephone: (202) 543-8601
Registered as lobbyist at U.S. Congress.
Clients:
PolyPhaser Corp.

DELANEY AND ASSOCIATES, EDWARD N.
1629 K St., N.W., Suite 1000, Washington, DC 20006
Telephone: (202) 955-5600
Members of firm representing listed organizations:
Delaney, Edward N.
Background: Trial Attorney, Office of the Regional Counsel, New York Region, Internal Revenue Service, 1955-60. Member, Business Advisory Committee, Securities and Exchange Commission Inter-Agency Tax Force On Off Shore Funds.
Clients:
Ass'n of Outplacement Consulting Firms *(Edward N. Delaney)*
Harcourt Brace Jovanovich, Inc. *(Edward N. Delaney)*
Nat'l Ass'n of Independent Insurers *(Edward N. Delaney)*

DELANEY, Edward N.
Delaney and Associates, Edward N.
1629 K St., N.W., Suite 1000, Washington, DC 20006
Telephone: (202) 955-5600
Registered as lobbyist at U.S. Congress.
Background: Trial Attorney, Office of the Regional Counsel, New York Region, Internal Revenue Service, 1955-60. Member, Business Advisory Committee, Securities and Exchange Commission Inter-Agency Tax Force On Off Shore Funds.
Clients:
Ass'n of Outplacement Consulting Firms
Harcourt Brace Jovanovich, Inc.
Nat'l Ass'n of Independent Insurers

DELANEY, Edward N., II
President, NTEA/Bankers Committee, The
1629 K St., N.W., Suite 1000, Washington, DC 20036
Telephone: (202) 466-8308
Registered as lobbyist at U.S. Congress.

DELANEY LAW OFFICES, Paul H.
1826 Jefferson Place, N.W. Suite 201, Washington, DC 20036
Telephone: (202) 785-1766
Members of firm representing listed organizations:
DeLaney, Paul H. (Jr.)
Background: Deputy Chief Counsel and Acting Chief Counsel, Office of Foreign Direct Investments, U.S. Department of Commerce, 1971-72. Consultant to Council on International Economic Policy and Office of the Special Representative for Trade Negotiaions, Exec. Office of the President, 1972-73.
Organizations represented:
Continental Grain Co.
Groth Air Services, Inc. *(Paul H. DeLaney, Jr.)*
Japan, Embassy of *(Paul H. DeLaney, Jr.)*
South Africa, Chamber of Mines of *(Paul H. DeLaney, Jr.)*
Universal Frutrading Cooperative Ltd. *(Paul H. DeLaney, Jr.)*

DELANEY, Paul H., Jr.
DeLaney Law Offices, Paul H.
1826 Jefferson Place, N.W. Suite 201, Washington, DC 20036
Telephone: (202) 785-1766
Registered as lobbyist at U.S. Congress.
Registered as Foreign Agent: (#4127).
Background: Deputy Chief Counsel and Acting Chief Counsel, Office of Foreign Direct Investments, U.S. Department of Commerce, 1971-72. Consultant to Council on International Economic Policy and Office of the Special Representative for Trade Negotiaions, Exec. Office of the President, 1972-73.
Organizations represented:
Groth Air Services, Inc.
Japan, Embassy of
South Africa, Chamber of Mines of
Universal Frutrading Cooperative Ltd.

DELANEY, Susan F.
Exec. Asst., American Internat'l Group
1455 Pennsylvania Ave., N.W. Suite 900, Washington, DC 20004
Telephone: (202) 783-5690

DELANEY, Thomas J.
Exec. Director, Ass'n of Labor-Management Administrators and Consultants on Alcoholism
4601 N. Fairfax Drive Suite 1001, Arlington, VA 22203
Telephone: (703) 522-6272

DELEE, Debra
Director, Government Relations, Nat'l Education Ass'n of the U.S.
1201 16th St., N.W., Washington, DC 20036
Telephone: (202) 822-7300
Registered as lobbyist at U.S. Congress.
Background: Also represents the Nat'l Education Ass'n Political Action Committee.

DE LELLIS, John
V. Pres., Communications & Member Svcs., American Chamber of Commerce Executives
4232 King St., Alexandria, VA 22302
Telephone: (703) 998-0072

DELEON, Dona
Dir, Cong Liaison Div (Act), ENVIRONMENTAL PROTECTION AGENCY
401 M St., S.W., Washington, DC 20460
Telephone: (202) 382-5200

DELGADO, Jane L., Ph.D.
President, Nat'l Coalition of Hispanic Health and Human Services
1030 15th St., N.W. Suite 1053, Washington, DC 20005
Telephone: (202) 371-2100
Background: Senior Health Policy Advisor, Office of the Secretary, 1983-85; Program Analyst, Office of Community Services, 1981-83; Social Science Analyst, Office of Human Development Services, 1979-81, Department of Health and Human Services.

DEL GANDIO, Frank S.
Secretary, Internat'l Soc. of Air Safety Investigators
Technology Trading Park, 5 Export Drive, Sterling, VA 22170-4421
Telephone: (703) 430-9668

DELGAUDIO, Columbia Eugene
Director, Public Advocate
6001 Leesburg Pike, #3, Falls Church, VA 22041
Telephone: (202) 546-3224

DELLER, Susie
Argyle & Associates
1117 G St., S.E., Washington, DC 20003
Registered as lobbyist at U.S. Congress.
Clients:
Nat'l Council of Savings Institutions

DELLON, Leslie K.
Lepon, McCarthy, Jutkowitz & Holzworth
1146 19th St., N.W. Third Fl., Washington, DC 20036
Telephone: (202) 857-0242
Registered as Foreign Agent: (#4302).
Background: Trial Attorney, Civil Division, Department of Justice, 1983-86.

DELMONTAGNE, Regis J.
President, Nat'l Printing Equipment and Supply Ass'n
1899 Preston White Drive, Reston, VA 22091
Telephone: (703) 264-7200
Registered as lobbyist at U.S. Congress.

DELOACH, Roy
Legis. Analyst, Gov't Relations, Nat'l Ass'n of REALTORS
777 14th St., N.W., Washington, DC 20005
Telephone: (202) 383-1171
Registered as lobbyist at U.S. Congress.

DELOGU, Nancy N.
Associate Director, Institute for a Drug-Free Workplace
P.O. Box 65708, Washington, DC 20035-5708
Telephone: (202) 463-5530

DELOOSE, Michael J.
Assoc Admin, Cong Affrs, GENERAL SERVICES ADMINISTRATION
18th and F Sts., N.W., Washington, DC 20405
Telephone: (202) 566-0563

DELPOLITO, Carolyn M., Ph.D.
Smith, Bucklin and Associates
1101 Connecticut Ave., N.W., Suite 700, Washington, DC 20036
Telephone: (202) 857-1100
Background: Exec. Director, American Soc. of Allied Health Professions.
Clients:
American Soc. of Allied Health Professions

DEL POLITO, Gene A.
Exec. Director, Third Class Mail Ass'n
1333 F St., N.W., Suite 710, Washington, DC 20004-1108
Telephone: (202) 347-0055
Registered as lobbyist at U.S. Congress.

DELPONTE, Paul
Director, Communications, Alliance for Aging Research
2021 K St., N.W. Suite 305, Washington, DC 20006
Telephone: (202) 293-2856

DELUCA, Fred R.
CFO, Group Executive, American Institute of Architects, The
1735 New York Ave., N.W., Washington, DC 20006
Telephone: (202) 626-7300
Registered as lobbyist at U.S. Congress.

DELUCIA, Robert
V. President and Treasurer, Airline Industrial Relations Conference
1920 N St., N.W., Suite 250, Washington, DC 20036
Telephone: (202) 861-7550

DEMARCO, Nancy
Exec. Director, Independent Lubricant Manufacturers Ass'n
651 S. Washington, Alexandria, VA 22314
Telephone: (703) 684-5574
Registered as lobbyist at U.S. Congress.

DEMAREST, William F., Jr.
Holland and Hart
1001 Pennsylvania Suite 310, Washington, DC 20004
Telephone: (202) 638-5500
Registered as lobbyist at U.S. Congress.

Background: Counsel, House Subcommittee on Energy and Power, 1975-79; Counsel, House Committee on Small Business, 1973-75.
Clients:
Council for Solid Waste Solutions
Grocery Manufacturers of America
Southland Corp., The

DE MARINES, Jane M.
Staff V. Pres., Public Affairs/Marketing, Mortgage Bankers Ass'n of America
1125 15th St., N.W., Washington, DC 20005
Telephone: (202) 861-6554

DEMARTINO, Gaelyn
Washington Counsel, American Hospital Ass'n
50 F St., N.W., Suite 1100, Washington, DC 20001
Telephone: (202) 638-1100
Registered as lobbyist at U.S. Congress.

DEMATO, Elizabeth C.
Legislative Representative, Seafarers Internat'l Union of North America
5201 Auth Way, Camp Springs, MD 20746
Telephone: (301) 899-0675
Registered as lobbyist at U.S. Congress.
Background: Former Staff Member, House of Representatives Subcommittee on Merchant Marine.

DEMATTEIS, Mary Jo
Senior V. President, Malatesta & Co., J. Thomas
600 New Hampshire Ave., N.W., Suite 300, Washington, DC 20037
Telephone: (202) 457-0393

DEMCHUK, Tania
Public Affairs Specialist, Nat'l Ass'n of Independent Insurers
499 South Capitol St., S.W. Suite 401, Washington, DC 20003
Telephone: (202) 484-2350
Registered as lobbyist at U.S. Congress.

DE MESONES, Dr. Pedro
President, Foundation for the Advancement of Hispanic Americans
P.O. Box 66012, Washington, DC 20035
Telephone: (703) 866-1578

DEMINO, Leonard J.
V. Pres., Pharmacy & Professional Affrs., Nat'l Ass'n of Chain Drug Stores
Box 1417-D49, Alexandria, VA 22313
Telephone: (703) 549-3001

DEMOCKER, Wendy M.
Communications Director, Nat'l Republican Senatorial Committee
425 Second St., N.E., Washington, DC 20002
Telephone: (202) 675-6000
Background: Former Assistant Secretary for Public Affairs, U.S. Department of Transportation.

DEMORY, Willard L.
President, Murphy and Demory, Ltd.
2300 N St., N.W. Suite 725, Washington, DC 20037
Telephone: (202) 785-3323
Registered as lobbyist at U.S. Congress.
Clients:
California Energy Co.
United States Telephone Ass'n

DEMOUGEOT, George
1825 I St., N.W., Suite 400, Washington, DC 20006
Telephone: (202) 429-2087
Registered as lobbyist at U.S. Congress.
Registered as Foreign Agent: (#3874)
Background: A public relations consultant.
Organizations represented:
Kellwood Co.

DEMPSEY, Donna S.
Government Affairs Exec. Administrator, Oracle Corp.
1627 Eye St., N.W., Suite 880, Washington, DC 20006
Telephone: (202) 657-7860
Registered as lobbyist at U.S. Congress.

DEMPSEY, John C.
Kirschner, Weinberg & Dempsey
1615 L St., N.W., Suite 1360, Washington, DC 20036
Telephone: (202) 775-5900

DEMPSEY, William H.
President and Chief Exec. Officer, Ass'n of American Railroads
50 F St., N.W., Suite 12503, Washington, DC 20001
Telephone: (202) 639-2402

DEMUTH, Christopher C.
President, American Enterprise Institute for Public Policy Research
1150 17th St., N.W., Washington, DC 20036
Telephone: (202) 862-5800
Background: Former Regulatory Chief, Office of Management and Budget, 1981-84.

DENBY, Stephen
Exec. Director, Vocational Industrial Clubs of America
Box 3000, Leesburg, VA 22075
Telephone: (703) 777-8810

DENHOLM, David Y.
President, Public Service Research Council
1761 Business Center Drive Suite 230, Reston, VA 22090
Telephone: (703) 438-3966

DENHOLM, Nancy
Spec Asst, Legis Affrs, ACTION
1100 Vermont Ave., N.W., Washington, DC 20525
Telephone: (202) 634-9772

DENISON, George H.
4801 Massachusetts Ave., N.W. Suite 400, Washington, DC 20016
Telephone: (202) 244-3125
Registered as lobbyist at U.S. Congress.
Background: An attorney at law. Formerly an aide to Senator Barry Goldwater, (R-AZ); Minority Counsel, Senate Labor Committee, 1962-65; Legislative Assistant to Rep. Robert Griffin, 1965; speechwriter for President Gerald Ford, 1976-77.
Organizations represented:
Edison Electric Institute
USX Corp.
Westinghouse Electric Corp.

DENMAN, Robert A.
Legislative Assistant, Nat'l Farmers Union
600 Maryland Ave., S.W., Suite 202W, Washington, DC 20024
Telephone: (202) 554-1600
Registered as lobbyist at U.S. Congress.

DENMAN, Scott
Director, Safe Energy Communication Council
1717 Massachusetts Ave., N.W. Suite LL215, Washington, DC 20036
Telephone: (202) 483-8491

DENNE, Eileen E.
Director, Public Relations, Nat'l Ass'n of Small Business Investment Companies
1156 15th St., N.W. Suite 1101, Washington, DC 20005
Telephone: (202) 833-8230

DENNETT, Paul W.
Wash. Rep./Legislative Policy Analyst, Blue Cross and Blue Shield Ass'n
655 15th St., N.W., Suite 350, Washington, DC 20005
Telephone: (202) 626-4780
Registered as lobbyist at U.S. Congress.
Background: Former legislative aide to Sen. Max Baucus (D-LA).

DENNING, D. B.
V. President, Government Services, General Electric Co.
1331 Pennsylvania Ave., N.W. Suite 800S, Washington, DC 20004
Telephone: (202) 637-4000
Registered as lobbyist at U.S. Congress.

DENNING AND WOHLSTETTER
1700 K St., N.W., Washington, DC 20006
Telephone: (202) 833-8884
Members of firm representing listed organizations:
    Mullins, Joseph F. (Jr.)

Wohlstetter, Alan F.
Background: Trial Attorney for Federal Maritime Board and Maritime Administration 1951-52.
Clients:
Central Freight Forwarding (Alan F. Wohlstetter)
Compagnie d'Affretement et de Transport USA (Joseph F. Mullins, Jr.)
Express Forwarding and Storage, Inc.
Gulf Atlantic Transport Corp. (Joseph F. Mullins, Jr.)
Household Goods Forwarders Ass'n of America (Alan F. Wohlstetter)
Karlander Kangaroo Lines (Alan F. Wohlstetter)
Marine Transport Overseas Services (Joseph F. Mullins, Jr.)
Mobley Inc., E. L. (Alan F. Wohlstetter)
Northland Marine Lines
Pacific Inland Navigation
Richmond Transfer and Storage Co. (Alan F. Wohlstetter)
Transconex, Inc.
United Kingdom Express (Joseph F. Mullins, Jr.)
West India Line (Joseph F. Mullins, Jr.)

DENNIS, C. W.
Spec Asst for Legis Affrs, DEPARTMENT OF DEFENSE - Comptroller's Office
The Pentagon, Washington, DC 20301
Telephone: (202) 697-1101

DENNIS, Debra H.
Exec. Director, Associated Landscape Contractors of America
405 North Washington St. Suite 104, Falls Church, VA 22046
Telephone: (703) 241-4004

DENNIS, Gary
Director, Federal Regulatory Affairs, BellSouth Corp.
1133 21st St., N.W., Suite 900, Washington, DC 20036
Telephone: (202) 463-4100

DENNIS, Thomas J.
V. President, Washington Region, Southern California Edison Co.
Suite 303, 1111 19th St., N.W., Washington, DC 20036
Telephone: (202) 872-1900
Registered as lobbyist at U.S. Congress.

DENNY, David L.
Director, Research, U.S.-China Business Council
1818 N St., N.W., Suite 500, Washington, DC 20036
Telephone: (202) 429-0340

DENNY, Jeff
Research Associate, Common Cause
2030 M St., N.W., Washington, DC 20036
Telephone: (202) 833-1200
Registered as lobbyist at U.S. Congress.
Background: Former Press Secretary to Rep. Nancy Johnson (R-CT).

DENNY, John, Jr.
Mahe Company, The Eddie
900 Second St., N.E. Suite 200, Washington, DC 20002
Telephone: (202) 842-4100

DENSON, James L.
Allpoints Internat'l, Ltd.
1250 Connecticut Ave., N.W., Suite 319, Washington, DC 20036
Telephone: (202) 371-6767
Registered as Foreign Agent: (#4157).
Clients:
Bophuthatswana, Government of

DENT, Edward A.
Director, Americans for the Nat'l Voter Initiative Amendment
3115 N St., N.W., Washington, DC 20007
Telephone: (202) 333-4846
Registered as lobbyist at U.S. Congress.

DENTON, Harold
Dir, Govt'l and Public Affairs Office, NUCLEAR REGULATORY COMMISSION
11555 Rockville Pike, Rockville, MD 20852
Telephone: (301) 492-1780

DENTON, Janet Ann
Director, Federal Relations, Pacific Telesis Group-Washington
1275 Pennsylvania Ave., N.W. Suite 400, Washington, DC 20004
Telephone: (202) 383-6400
Registered as lobbyist at U.S. Congress.

DENTON, Robert Neal
Assistant Director, Alliance of Nonprofit Mailers
2001 S St., N.W., Suite 301, Washington, DC 20009
Telephone: (202) 462-5132
Registered as lobbyist at U.S. Congress.

DENTON, Susan T.
Consultant, Rowland & Sellery
1023 15th St., N.W. 7th Fl., Washington, DC 20005
Telephone: (202) 289-1780
Clients:
    Product Liability Coordinating Committee

DENVIR, James P., III
Akin, Gump, Strauss, Hauer and Feld
1333 New Hampshire Ave., N.W., Suite 400, Washington, DC 20036
Telephone: (202) 887-4000
Background: Trial Attorney, Antitrust Division, U.S. Departmemt of Justice, 1975-84. Chief Attorney Staff, Antitrust Division, 1982-84.
Clients:
    Motion Picture Ass'n of America
    Revlon Group

DENYES, Wells
Director, Federal Gov't Rtns & V. Pres., Eastman Kodak Co.
1776 Eye St., N.W., Suite 1050, Washington, DC 20006
Telephone: (202) 857-3400
Registered as lobbyist at U.S. Congress.

DENYSYK, Dr. Bohdan
Senior V. President, Global USA, Inc.
2121 K St., N.W., Suite 650, Washington, DC 20037
Telephone: (202) 296-2400
Registered as Foreign Agent: (#3489).
Background: Former Deputy Assistant Secretary of Commerce.
Clients:
    Fanuc, Ltd.
    Japan Federation of Construction Contractors
    Japanese Aero Engines Corp.
    Japanese Aircraft Development Corp.
    Mazak Corp.
    Murata Machinery, Ltd.

DEPEW, Marilyn
Cong Liaison Officer, DEPARTMENT OF COMMERCE - Inspector General
15th and Constitution Ave. N.W., Washington, DC 20230
Telephone: (202) 377-4661

DEPONT, Robert A.
Fletcher, Heald and Hildreth
1225 Connecticut Ave., N.W. Suite 400, Washington, DC 20036
Telephone: (202) 828-5700

DEPOY, Martin L.
Legis. Director, Congressional Affairs, Nat'l Ass'n of REALTORS
777 14th St., N.W., Washington, DC 20005
Telephone: (202) 383-1000
Registered as lobbyist at U.S. Congress.

DEPRIEST, Gregory L.
V. President, Ass'n of Maximum Service Telecasters, Inc.
1400 16th St., N.W. Suite 610, Washington, DC 20036
Telephone: (202) 462-4351
Registered as lobbyist at U.S. Congress.

DEQUATRO, Maria
Senior Associate, Kamber Group, The
1920 L St., N.W., Washington, DC 20036
Telephone: (202) 223-8700

DE RAVEL, Pierre F.
Donovan Leisure Rogovin Huge & Schiller
1250 24th St., N.W., Washington, DC 20037
Telephone: (202) 467-8300

DEREUTER, William R.
Government Relations Representative, Merrill Lynch and Co., Inc.
1828 L St., N.W., Suite 906, Washington, DC 20036
Telephone: (202) 822-3600
Registered as lobbyist at U.S. Congress.

DERR, Derl I.
President, Internat'l Apple Institute
Box 1137, McLean, VA 22101
Telephone: (703) 442-8850

DERRICK, John M., Jr.
Exec. V. President & C.O.O., Potomac Electric Power Co.
1900 Pennsylvania Ave., N.W., Washington, DC 20068
Telephone: (202) 872-2000

DERRICKSON, Lloyd J.
Legal Counsel, Ass'n of Publicly Traded Companies
1707 L St., N.W., Suite 950, Washington, DC 20036
Telephone: (202) 785-9200

DERWINSKI, Bonnie
Director, Cong and Public Affairs, DEPARTMENT OF JUSTICE - Immigration and Naturalization Service
425 I St., N.W., Washington, DC 20536
Telephone: (202) 633-5231

DE SANCTIS, Dona
Ass't Dir., Communications & Public Rel., American Hospital Ass'n
50 F St., N.W., Suite 1100, Washington, DC 20001
Telephone: (202) 638-1100

DESANTO, Pamela
Dir. of Communications, Public Relations, Nat'l Burglar and Fire Alarm Ass'n
7101 Wisconsin Ave. Suite 1390, Bethesda, MD 20814-1100
Telephone: (301) 907-3202

DESAVAGE, Janet M.
Government Affairs, Nat'l Electrical Manufacturers Ass'n
2101 L St., N.W., Washington, DC 20037
Telephone: (202) 457-8400

DESISTI & ASSOCIATES
901 15th St., N.W. Suite 700, Washington, DC 20005
Telephone: (202) 371-6172
Members of firm representing listed organizations:
    DeSisti, Judith A.
        Background: Former Exec. Director, Democratic House and Senate Council; Exec. Assistant to Rep. J. Edward Roush (D-IN).

DESISTI, Judith A.
DeSisti & Associates
901 15th St., N.W. Suite 700, Washington, DC 20005
Telephone: (202) 371-6172
Background: Former Exec. Director, Democratic House and Senate Council; Exec. Assistant to Rep. J. Edward Roush (D-IN).

DESOTO, Patricia
General Manager, Woman's Nat'l Democratic Club
1526 New Hampshire Ave., N.W., Washington, DC 20036
Telephone: (202) 232-7363

DESROSIERS, Eva, FASI
Secretary, American Soc. of Interpreters
P.O. Box 9603, Washington, DC 20016
Telephone: (703) 998-8636

DETTER, Brian R.
Director, Federal Relations, Internat'l Council of Shopping Centers
1199 North Fairfax St. Suite 204, Alexandria, VA 22314
Telephone: (703) 549-7404
Registered as lobbyist at U.S. Congress.
Background: Former Press Secretary to Senator Jay Rockefeller (D-WV).

DEUSCHL, Vivian A.
V. President, Harrison Co., E. Bruce
1440 New York Ave., N.W. Suite 300, Washington, DC 20005
Telephone: (202) 638-1200
Background: Former Special Assistant to Undersecretary of Commerce for Travel and Tourism.

DEUTSCH, Jo Ellen
Manager, Government Affairs, Ass'n of Flight Attendants
1625 Massachusetts Ave., N.W. 3rd Floor, Washington, DC 20036
Telephone: (202) 328-5400
Registered as lobbyist at U.S. Congress.
Background: Serves as contact for the Ass'n of Flight Attendants PAC.

DEVALL, James L.
Zuckert, Scoutt and Rasenberger
888 17th St., N.W., Suite 600, Washington, DC 20006-3959
Telephone: (202) 298-8660
Clients:
    All Nippon Airways Co.
    Empresa Consolidada Cubana de Aviacion
    Korean Air Lines
    Nippon Cargo Airlines
    Pakistan Internat'l Airlines

DE VEGH, Diana
Director, Institute for Policy Studies
1601 Connecticut Ave., N.W. 5th Floor, Washington, DC 20009
Telephone: (202) 234-9382

DEVIERNO, John A.
Preston Gates Ellis & Rouvelas Meeds
1735 New York Ave., N.W., Suite 500, Washington, DC 20006-4759
Telephone: (202) 628-1700
Registered as lobbyist at U.S. Congress.
Background: Office of General Counsel, U.S. Department of Transportation, 1977-81.
Clients:
    Nat'l Private Truck Council
    South Dakota Department of Transportation

DEVINE, Donald J.
Consultant, Citizens for America
214 Massachusetts Ave., N.E. Suite 480, Washington, DC 20002
Telephone: (202) 544-7888

DEVINE, Thomas
Government Accountability Project (GAP)
25 E St., N.W. Suite 700, Washington, DC 20001
Telephone: (202) 347-0460

DE VISSER, John T.
Director, Corporate Affairs, Martin Marietta Corp.
6801 Rockledge Drive MP 220, Bethesda, MD 20817
Telephone: (301) 897-6862

DEVLIN, Joseph A.
V. President, Government Affairs, Harnischfeger Corp.
2828 Pennsylvania Ave., N.W. Suite 500, Washington, DC 20007
Telephone: (202) 342-0150

DEVLIN, Laura
Bergman Associates, William S.
1001 Connecticut Ave., N.W., Suite 800, Washington, DC 20036
Telephone: (202) 452-1520
Background: Serves as Director of Administration for the Food Industry Ass'n Executives and of Consumers for World Trade.
Organizations represented:
    Consumers for World Trade

DEVLIN, R. Daniel
Director, Legislative Affairs, Trans World Airlines
808 17th St., N.W., Suite 520, Washington, DC 20006
Telephone: (202) 457-4752

DEVRIES, Christine
Ass't Dir., Congressional & Agency Rtns., American Nurses' Ass'n
1101 14th St., N.W., Suite 200, Washington, DC 20005
Telephone: (202) 789-1800
Registered as lobbyist at U.S. Congress.

DEWEY, BALLANTINE, BUSHBY, PALMER AND WOOD
1775 Pennsylvania Ave., N.W. Suite 200, Washington, DC 20006
Telephone: (202) 862-1000

Background: New York law firm with an office in Washington.

Members of firm representing listed organizations:

Califano, Joseph A. (Jr.)
Background: Special Assistant to General Counsel, Department of Defense, 1961-62. Special Assistant to Secretary of the Army, 1962-63. General Counsel, Department of the Army, 1963-64. Special Assistant to the Secretary and Deputy Secretary of Defense, 1964-65. Special Assistant for Domestic Affairs to the President, 1965-69. Secretary of Health, Education and Welfare, 1977-79. Member, Board of Directors, Primerica Corp. and Chrysler Corp.

Dowley, Joseph K.
Background: Administraive Assistant to Rep. Dan Rostenkowski (D-IL), 1977-80. Assistant Counsel, 1980-84 and Chief Counsel, House Committee on Ways and Means, 1985-87.

Gadbaw, R. Michael
Background: Former Deputy General Counsel, Office of the Special Representative for Trade Negotiations.

Howell, Thomas R.

McFadden, Clark

O'Brien, Lawrence F. (III)
Background: Deputy for Tax Legislation to the Assistant Secretary of Treasury for Legislative Affairs, 1977-79.

Salmon, John J.
Background: Former Chief Counsel, House of Representatives Ways and Means Committee.

Stein, Michael H.
Background: Former General Counsel, U.S. International Trade Commission.

Wolff, Alan W.
Background: Attorney, Office of General Counsel, Internat'l Affairs Section, U.S. Treasury Department, 1968-73. Deputy General Counsel, 1973-74. General Counsel, 1974-76, and Deputy Special Representative for Trade Negotiations , 1977-79, Office of Special Representative for Trade Negotiations.

Clients:
American Iron and Steel Institute *(Joseph K. Dowley)*
Armco Inc.
Bankers Trust Co. *(Lawrence F. O'Brien, III)*
Beneficial Corp. *(Lawrence F. O'Brien, III)*
Bethlehem Steel Corp.
Bristol-Myers Squibb Co. *(Joseph K. Dowley)*
Chrysler Corp. *(Joseph A. Califano, Jr.)*
Coalition for Fair Lumber Imports *(Michael H. Stein, Alan W. Wolff)*
Digital Equipment Corp. *(R. Michael Gadbaw)*
Disney Productions, Walt *(Lawrence F. O'Brien, III)*
Edgcomb Corp. *(John J. Salmon)*
Federal Nat'l Mortgage Ass'n *(Joseph A. Califano, Jr., Lawrence F. O'Brien, III)*
Federation of American Health Systems *(John J. Salmon)*
General Electric Pension Trust
General Reinsurance *(Lawrence F. O'Brien, III)*
Hanschell Iniss Ltd. *(John J. Salmon)*
Health Insurance Ass'n of America *(Lawrence F. O'Brien, III)*
Hospital Corp. of America *(John J. Salmon)*
Household Internat'l *(John J. Salmon)*
Household Internat'l Political Action Committee *(John J. Salmon)*
Inland Steel Co. *(Michael H. Stein)*
Integrated Resources, Inc. *(John J. Salmon)*
Intel Corporation *(R. Michael Gadbaw, Alan W. Wolff)*
Labor-Industry Coalition for Internat'l Trade *(Alan W. Wolff)*
McCown De Leeuw & Co. *(Joseph K. Dowley)*
Morgan Stanley and Co. *(Joseph K. Dowley, Lawrence F. O'Brien, III)*
Nat'l Ass'n of Wholesaler-Distributors *(Lawrence F. O'Brien, III)*
Nat'l Forest Products Ass'n *(Michael H. Stein, Alan W. Wolff)*
NYNEX *(Lawrence F. O'Brien, III)*
Pfizer, Inc. *(Joseph A. Califano, Jr.)*
Premark Internat'l *(Joseph K. Dowley)*
Primerica Corp. *(Joseph A. Califano, Jr., Lawrence F. O'Brien, III)*
Prudential Insurance Co. of America *(Joseph K. Dowley)*
Seagram & Sons, Inc., Joseph E. *(John J. Salmon)*
SEMATECH *(Clark McFadden)*

Semiconductor Industry Ass'n *(R. Michael Gadbaw, Thomas R. Howell, John J. Salmon, Michael H. Stein, Alan W. Wolff)*
Teachers Insurance and Annuity Ass'n *(Lawrence F. O'Brien, III)*
Tribune Broadcasting Co. *(John J. Salmon)*
West Indies Rum and Spirits Producers' Ass'n *(John J. Salmon)*
Wickes Companies, Inc. *(John J. Salmon)*
Xerox Corp. *(John J. Salmon)*

DEWHIRST, Mary
Dir, Cong Relations, DEPARTMENT OF COMMERCE - Economic Development Administration
14th and Constitution Ave. N.W., Washington, DC 20230
Telephone: (202) 377-5314

DEWTON, Doris J.
Assoc. Director, Federal Gov't Relations, Ashland Oil, Inc.
1025 Connecticut Ave., N.W., Suite 507, Washington, DC 20036
Telephone: (202) 223-8290
Registered as lobbyist at U.S. Congress.
Background: Former Assistant Administrator for Petroleum Operations, Economic Regulatory Administration, Department of Energy.

DEYULIA, Thomas R.
V. President, Program & Support Services, CNA Insurance Cos.
7361 Calhoun Place, Rockville, MD 20855
Telephone: (301) 738-1216
Registered as lobbyist at U.S. Congress.
Background: Former Staff Director, Committee on the Post Office and Civil Service, U.S. House of Representatives.

DGA INTERNAT'L
1133 Connecticut Ave., N.W. Suite 700, Washington, DC 20036
Telephone: (202) 223-4001
Members of firm representing listed organizations:
Mahan, David L.
Meredith, Sandra K.
Mitchell, Gerald C.
Preslar, Lloyd T., V. President
Warner, Ernest R. (Jr.)
Clients:
Delegation General pour l' Armement (DRI) *(Sandra K. Meredith)*
Societe Nationale des Poudres et Explosifs
Societe Nationale d'Etude et Construction de Moteurs d'Aviation (SNECMA) *(Sandra K. Meredith)*
Sofreavia *(Sandra K. Meredith)*
Teledyne Brown Engineering *(David L. Mahan)*

DGM INTERNAT'L INC.
9271 Old Keene Mill Road, Springfield, VA 22152
Telephone: (703) 644-4587
Members of firm representing listed organizations:
Ellison, Donald E., Managing Partner
Jones, Gordon S.
Background: Former Exec. Director, House Republican Policy Committee.
Clients:
Aero Consultants *(Donald E. Ellison)*
Louisiana Tanners *(Donald E. Ellison)*
Multiprogres *(Gordon S. Jones)*
Questar Corp. *(Gordon S. Jones)*
Texstor *(Donald E. Ellison)*

DIAMOND, Henry L.
Beveridge & Diamond, P.C.
1350 Eye St., N.W. Suite 700, Washington, DC 20005
Telephone: (202) 789-6000
Background: Commissioner, New York State Dep't of Conservation, 1970-1973; Chairman, President's Advisory Commission on Environmental Quality, 1973-; Executive Director, Commission on Critical Choices for Americans, 1974. Member, Board of Directors, Combustion Equipment Associates.

DIAMOND, Robert M.
Lipsen Whitten & Diamond
1725 DeSales St., N.W., Suite 800, Washington, DC 20036
Telephone: (202) 659-6540
Registered as lobbyist at U.S. Congress.

DIBONA, Charles J.
President, American Petroleum Institute
1220 L St., N.W., Washington, DC 20005
Telephone: (202) 682-8100
Registered as lobbyist at U.S. Congress.

DICKENS, Benjamin
Blooston, Mordkofsky, Jackson & Dickens
2120 L St., N.W. Suite 300, Washington, DC 20037
Telephone: (202) 659-0830
Clients:
Central Station Electrical Protection Ass'n

DICKENS, Col. Samuel T., USAF (Ret)
Director, Inter-American Affairs, American Security Council Foundation
733 15th St., N.W. Suite 700, Washington, DC 20005
Telephone: (202) 484-1676

DICKENSON, Jim
Van Dyk Associates, Inc.
1250 24th St., N.W., Suite 600, Washington, DC 20037
Telephone: (202) 223-4880
Clients:
Browning-Ferris Industries (D.C.), Inc.
Insurance Information Institute
Star Tribune Co,

DICKERSON, Chester T., Jr.
Director, Agricultural Affairs, Monsanto Co.
700 14th St., N.W., Suite 1100, Washington, DC 20005
Telephone: (202) 783-2460
Registered as lobbyist at U.S. Congress.

DICKERSON, J. Spencer
Senior V. President, American Ass'n of Airport Executives
4212 King St., Alexandria, VA 22302
Telephone: (703) 824-0500

DICKEY, Ann Sanders
Senior Manager, State & Federal Affairs, Federal Express Corp.
300 Maryland Ave., N.E., Washington, DC 20002
Telephone: (202) 546-1631
Registered as lobbyist at U.S. Congress.

DICKINSON, Elaine
Associate Editor, Public Affairs, Boat Owners Ass'n of The United States (BOAT/U.S.)
880 South Pickett St., Alexandria, VA 22304
Telephone: (703) 823-9550
Registered as lobbyist at U.S. Congress.

DICKINSON, John
Director, Statistical Services, Aluminum Ass'n
900 19th St., N.W., Suite 300, Washington, DC 20006
Telephone: (202) 862-5100

DICKINSON, Dr. Torry D.
Exec. Director, Ass'n for Women in Science
1522 K St., N.W. Suite 820, Washington, DC 20005
Telephone: (202) 408-0742

DICKINSON, WRIGHT, MOON, VAN DUSEN AND FREEMAN
1901 L St., N.W. Suite 800, Washington, DC 20036
Telephone: (202) 457-0160
Background: Washington office of Michigan-based law firm.
Members of firm representing listed organizations:
Nedzi, Lucien N., Of Counsel
Background: Member, U.S. House of Representatives (D-MI), 1961-81.
Petrash, Jeffrey M.
Clients:
United Technologies Corp. *(Lucien N. Nedzi)*

DICKMAN, Dr. Donna McCord
Exec. Director, Alexander Graham Bell Ass'n for the Deaf
3417 Volta Place, N.W., Washington, DC 20007
Telephone: (202) 337-5220

DICKSON, R. Bruce
Paul, Hastings, Janofsky and Walker
1050 Connecticut Ave., N.W. Suite 1200, Washington, DC 20036-5331
Telephone: (202) 223-9000
Clients:
Aspirin Foundation of America, Inc.

DICKSON, Timothy E.
Exec. Director, Project 500
6 E St., S.E., Washington, DC 20003
Telephone: (202) 543-9200

DICKSTEIN, SHAPIRO AND MORIN
2101 L St., N.W., Washington, DC 20037
Telephone: (202) 785-9700
Registered as lobbyist at U.S. Congress.
Members of firm representing listed organizations:
Adams, Kenneth L.
Background: Legislative Assistant to Congressman Abner Mikva, 1972.
Butler, William A.
Cashen, Henry C. (II)
Background: Deputy Counsel to the President of the United States, 1969-70. Deputy Assistant to the President of the United States, 1971-73.
Dickstein, Sidney
Dill, John C.
Background: Legislative Director to Rep. James R. Jones (D-OK), 1977-81; Counsel to the Chairman, House Budget Committee, U.S. House of Representatives, 1981-85.
Garment, Leonard
Background: Special Consultant to the President of the United States, 1973-74. Assistant to the President, 1974. Vice Chairman, Administrative Conference of the United States 1973-74. U.S. Representative to the Commission on Human Rights of the United Nations Economic and Social Council, 1975-77. Counselor to U.S. Delegation to the UN, 1975-77. Chairman, Commission on Federal Judiciary of Sen. Daniel P. Moynihan, 1976-. Member, Committee on the Judiciary, Judicial Conference of the U.S., 1981-.
Jones, James R.
Background: Special Assistant to President Lyndon B. Johnson, 1964-68. Member, U.S. House of Representatives (D-OK), 1972-86. Member, House Ways and Means Committee, 1974-86; Member, House Subcommittee on Trade. Chairman, House Committee on the Budget, 1981-85. Chairman, House Social Security Subcommittee, 1985-86.
Kadzik, Peter J.
Background: Campaign advisor to the national campaigns of Senator Edward Kennedy (1980), Rep. Geraldine Ferraro (1984) and Michael Dukakis (1988). Member, Technical and Legal Advisory Committee, Compliance Review Commissiom (1984) and Task Force on Voting Rights and Voter Participation (1987), Democratic Nat'l Committee.
Kaufmann, George
Kolick, Joseph (Jr.)
Libby, I. Lewis
Background: Director of Special Projects, Bureau of East Asian and Pacific Affairs, Department of State, 1982-85.
Lowther, Frederick M.
Background: Special Assistant to General Counsel, U.S. Maritime Administration, 1971-72. Director, Office of Energy Policy, U.S. Department of Commerce, 1972-73.
Miller, Andrew P.
Background: Attorney General, Commonwealth of Virginia, 1970-77.
Minetti, G. Joseph
Background: Special Assistant to the Attorney General of the United States, 1940-43. Member, Federal Maritime Board, 1954-56. Member Civil Aeronautics Board, 1956-78. Vice Chairman, Civil Aeronautics Board, 1978.
Morin, Charles H.
Nash, Bernard
Background: Counsel, U.S. Senate Committee on Judiciary Subcommittee on Antitrust and Monopolies, 1971-77.
Robertson, Linda
Walvick, Walter J.
Welsh, Peggy, Government Relations Rep.
Yost, Nicholas C.

Background: General Counsel, Council on Environmental Quality, Executive Office of the President, 1977-81.
Clients:
ABD Securities Corp. *(Henry C. Cashen, II)*
Advance Publications, Inc. *(Leonard Garment)*
Alitalia Airlines *(Henry C. Cashen, II)*
American Greyhound Track Operators Ass'n *(Henry C. Cashen, II, John C. Dill)*
Arkansas, State of *(Andrew P. Miller, Bernard Nash)*
Avondale Industries, Inc. *(John C. Dill, James R. Jones)*
Bank of Oklahoma *(James R. Jones)*
Batman Corp. *(John C. Dill)*
Bear, Stearns and Co. *(Charles H. Morin)*
Boundary Gas *(Frederick M. Lowther)*
Car Audio Specialists Ass'n *(Sidney Dickstein)*
Coalition for Competitive Capital *(John C. Dill)*
Cordova District Fishermen United *(John C. Dill)*
Delaware, State of *(Andrew P. Miller, Bernard Nash)*
Dickstein, Shapiro and Morin Political Action Committee *(John C. Dill)*
Falconbridge Ltd. *(I. Lewis Libby)*
Federal Nat'l Mortgage Ass'n *(John C. Dill)*
Federated Cash Management Systems *(Charles H. Morin)*
First Annapolis Savings Bank F.S.B. *(John C. Dill)*
Guess, Inc. *(John C. Dill, James R. Jones)*
Harbour Group Ltd. *(Sidney Dickstein, John C. Dill)*
Home Box Office *(Bernard Nash)*
Illinois Department of Children and Family Services *(John C. Dill)*
Iowa, State of *(Andrew P. Miller, Bernard Nash)*
IPP Working Group *(John C. Dill)*
Iroquois Gas, Inc. *(Linda Robertson)*
Kuwait Airways *(G. Joseph Minetti, Walter J. Walvick)*
Louisiana, State of *(Andrew P. Miller, Bernard Nash)*
Malaysia, Government of
Marine Engineers Beneficial Ass'n *(John C. Dill, Charles H. Morin)*
Medtronic, Inc. *(John C. Dill, Peter J. Kadzik, George Kaufmann, Joseph Kolick, Jr., Andrew P. Miller, Bernard Nash)*
Middle East Airlines *(G. Joseph Minetti, Walter J. Walvick)*
Morgan & Co., J. P. *(John C. Dill, James R. Jones)*
Nat'l Bank of Washington, The
Nat'l Federation of Societies for Clinical Social Work *(John C. Dill)*
Newport Group *(John C. Dill)*
North Carolina Department of Natural Resources *(Bernard Nash)*
North Dakota, State of *(Andrew P. Miller, Bernard Nash)*
Ocean State Power *(John C. Dill)*
Paulucci Enterprises *(Henry C. Cashen, II)*
Rhode Island, State of *(Andrew P. Miller, Bernard Nash)*
Sea Hawk Seafoods, Inc. *(John C. Dill)*
Security Life Insurance Co. of Denver *(James R. Jones)*
Toshiba Corp. *(Leonard Garment, James R. Jones, G. Joseph Minetti)*
Utah, State of *(Andrew P. Miller, Bernard Nash)*
West Virginia, State of *(Andrew P. Miller, Bernard Nash)*

DICKSTEIN, Sidney
Dickstein, Shapiro and Morin
2101 L St., N.W., Washington, DC 20037
Telephone: (202) 785-9700
Clients:
Car Audio Specialists Ass'n
Harbour Group Ltd.

DIEBOLD, Larry A.
Special Assistant, State Relations, Nat'l Council of State Education Ass'ns
1201 16th St., N.W., Washington, DC 20036
Telephone: (202) 822-7745

DIEDRICH, William S.
President, Transatlantic Security Council
2323 Virginia Ave., N.W., Washington, DC 20037
Telephone: (202) 338-2539
Background: Foreign Service Officer, U.S. Department of State, 1963-82.

DIEGEL, Rick
Political Director, Internat'l Brotherhood of Electrical Workers
1125 15th St., N.W., Washington, DC 20005
Telephone: (202) 833-7000
Registered as lobbyist at U.S. Congress.

DIENER, Patricia L.
Director of Communications, YMCA of Metropolitan Washington
1625 Massachusetts Ave., N.W., Suite 700, Washington, DC 20036
Telephone: (202) 797-4497

DIERCKS, Walter E.
Rubin, Winston and Diercks
1730 M St., N.W., Suite 412, Washington, DC 20036
Telephone: (202) 861-0870
Registered as lobbyist at U.S. Congress.
Background: Staff Attorney (1972-76) and Deputy Assistant Director (1976-77), Bureau of Consumer Protection, Federal Trade Commission.
Clients:
Outdoor Advertising Ass'n of America

DIETZ, Paula
External Liaison Associate, American Petroleum Institute
1220 L St., N.W., Washington, DC 20005
Telephone: (202) 682-8286

DIGENOVA, Joseph E.
Bishop, Cook, Purcell & Reynolds
1400 L St., N.W., Washington, DC 20005-3502
Telephone: (202) 371-5700
Registered as lobbyist at U.S. Congress.
Background: Counsel, Senate Select Committee on Intelligence, 1975-76. Counsel, Subcommittee on the District of Columbia, Senate Committee on Governmental Affairs, 1976. Counsel, Senate Committee on the Judiciary, 1978. Administrative Assistant and Legislative Counsel to Senator Charles Mathias, 1979. Chief Counsel and Staff Director, Senate Committee on Rules and Administration, 1981. U.S. Attorney for the District of Columbia, 1983-88.

DIGGES, Robert, Jr.
Law Department, American Trucking Ass'ns
2200 Mill Road, Alexandria, VA 22314
Telephone: (703) 838-1857

DILDINE, Larry L.
Partner, Wasington Nat'l Tax Svc, Price Waterhouse
1801 K St., N.W., Suite 700, Washington, DC 20006
Telephone: (202) 296-0800
Registered as lobbyist at U.S. Congress.
Background: Former economist, U.S. Treasury Department.

DILL, John C.
Dickstein, Shapiro and Morin
2101 L St., N.W., Washington, DC 20037
Telephone: (202) 785-9700
Registered as lobbyist at U.S. Congress.
Background: Legislative Director to Rep. James R. Jones (D-OK), 1977-81; Counsel to the Chairman, House Budget Committee, U.S. House of Representatives, 1981-85.
Clients:
American Greyhound Track Operators Ass'n
Avondale Industries, Inc.
Batman Corp.
Coalition for Competitive Capital
Cordova District Fishermen United
Dickstein, Shapiro and Morin Political Action Committee
Federal Nat'l Mortgage Ass'n
First Annapolis Savings Bank F.S.B.
Guess, Inc.
Harbour Group Ltd.
Illinois Department of Children and Family Services
IPP Working Group
Marine Engineers Beneficial Ass'n
Medtronic, Inc.
Morgan & Co., J. P.
Nat'l Federation of Societies for Clinical Social Work
Newport Group
Ocean State Power
Sea Hawk Seafoods, Inc.

DILLER, Janelle
Legal Director, Internat'l Human Rights Law Group
1601 Connecticut Ave., N.W. Suite 700, Washington, DC 20009
Telephone: (202) 232-8500

DILLINGHAM, P. W., Jr.
V. President, Government Operations, Cray Research, Inc.
1331 Pennsylvania Ave., N.W., Suite 1331 North, Washington, DC 20004
Telephone: (202) 638-6000

DILLMAN, Rusty
Legis Analyst, SECURITIES AND EXCHANGE COMMISSION
450 5th St., N.W., Washington, DC 20549
Telephone: (202) 272-2500

DILLON, Elizabeth
Health and Medicine Counsel of Washington
511 Capitol Court, N.E., Suite 300, Washington, DC 20002
Telephone: (202) 544-7499

DIMARZIO, Rev. Msgr. Nicholas
Exec. Dir., Migration & Refugee Svcs., United States Catholic Conference
3200 4th St., N.E., Washington, DC 20017
Telephone: (202) 541-3000

DIMAS, James T.
Exec. Director, Public Health Foundation
1220 L St., N.W., Suite 350, Washington, DC 20005
Telephone: (202) 898-5600

DIMICHAEL, Nicholas J.
Donelan, Cleary, Wood and Maser, P.C.
1275 K St., N.W., Suite 850, Washington, DC 20005
Telephone: (202) 371-9500
Registered as lobbyist at U.S. Congress.
Clients:
Nat'l Industrial Transportation League

DIMOFF, Steven A.
Director, Washington Office, United Nations Ass'n of the U.S.A.
1010 Vermont Ave., N.W., Suite 904, Washington, DC 20005
Telephone: (202) 347-5004

DINAPOLI, Rose
Dir, Cong Liaison, NAT'L ENDOWMENT FOR THE ARTS
1100 Pennsylvania Ave., N.W. Room 524, Washington, DC 20506
Telephone: (202) 682-5434

DINE, Thomas A.
Exec. Director, American Israel Public Affairs Committee
440 First St., N.W. Suite 600, Washington, DC 20001
Telephone: (202) 639-5200
Registered as lobbyist at U.S. Congress.
Background: Formerly deputy foreign policy advisor to Senator Edward Kennedy.

DINEEN, Alison C.
Director of Fellowship Program, Women's Research and Education Institute
1700 18th St., N.W., Suite 400, Washington, DC 20009
Telephone: (202) 328-7070

DINEEN, Michael F.
Director of Federal Relations, Kemper Group
600 Pennsylvania Ave., S.E., Suite 206, Washington, DC 20003
Telephone: (202) 547-0120
Registered as lobbyist at U.S. Congress.
Background: Administrative Assistant to Rep. Dan Kuykendall (R-TN) (1970-1974) and Rep. Matthew J. Rinaldo (R-NJ) (1974-1975).

DINEGAR, James C.
V. President, Gov't & Industry Affairs, Building Owners and Managers Ass'n Internat'l
1201 New York Ave., N.W. Suite 300, Washington, DC 20005
Telephone: (202) 289-7000
Registered as lobbyist at U.S. Congress.

DINGES, Casey
Legislative Affairs Manager, American Soc. of Civil Engineers
1015 15th St., N.W. Suite 600, Washington, DC 20005
Telephone: (202) 789-2200

DINNERSTEIN, Michael
Staff Attorney, United Mine Workers of America
900 15th St., N.W., Washington, DC 20005
Telephone: (202) 842-7280
Registered as lobbyist at U.S. Congress.

DINSMORE, Alan M.
Legislative Network Coordinator, American Foundation for the Blind (Government Relations Department)
1615 M St., N.W., Suite 250, Washington, DC 20036
Telephone: (202) 457-1487

DIRECT IMPACT CO., THE
1414 Prince St. Suite 350, Alexandria, VA 22314
Telephone: (703) 684-1245
Background: A grassroots lobbying firm.
Members of firm representing listed organizations:
Brady, John, President
Dittus, Gloria
Herrity, Tom, V. President
Clients:
American Nuclear Energy Council
American Petroleum Institute *(John Brady, Tom Herrity)*
Chemical Manufacturers Ass'n *(John Brady, Tom Herrity)*
Columbia Presbyterian Hospital *(John Brady, Tom Herrity)*
Dulles Area Rapid Transit, Inc. *(John Brady, Tom Herrity)*
Florida Commercial Developers Ass'n *(John Brady, Gloria Dittus, Tom Herrity)*
FMC Corp. *(John Brady, Gloria Dittus, Tom Herrity)*
Maglev Transit, Inc. *(John Brady, Gloria Dittus, Tom Herrity)*
Nat'l Dairy Promotion and Research Board
President's Drug Advisory Counsel
Rocky Mountain Oil and Gas Ass'n *(John Brady, Tom Herrity)*

DIRENFELD, Barry
Swidler & Berlin, Chartered
3000 K St., N.W., Suite 300, Washington, DC 20007
Telephone: (202) 944-4300
Clients:
American Bakers Ass'n
Business Coalition for RICO Reform
Laidlaw, Inc.
Merrill Lynch and Co., Inc.

DIRKS, Dale P.
President, Health and Medicine Counsel of Washington
511 Capitol Court, N.E., Suite 300, Washington, DC 20002
Telephone: (202) 544-7499
Clients:
American Academy of Family Physicians
American Ass'n of Gastroenterology
American Lung Ass'n/American Thoracic Soc.
American Narcolepsy Ass'n
Ass'n of Minority Health Professions Schools
Digestive Disease Nat'l Coalition
Environmental Sciences Ass'n
Nat'l Sudden Infant Death Syndrome Foundation
St. George's University School of Medicine

DIRKSEN, Cathy
Manager, Special Activities, Defenders of Wildlife
1244 19th St., N.W., Washington, DC 20036
Telephone: (202) 659-9510

DISNEY, Peggy L.
Divisional V. Pres., Public Relations, Hecht's
685 N. Glebe Road, Arlington, VA 22203
Telephone: (703) 558-1414

DITLOW, Clarence M.
Exec. Director, Center for Auto Safety
2001 S St., N.W., Room 410, Washington, DC 20009
Telephone: (202) 328-7700

DITTUS, Gloria
Direct Impact Co., The
1414 Prince St. Suite 350, Alexandria, VA 22314

Telephone: (703) 684-1245
Clients:
Florida Commercial Developers Ass'n
FMC Corp.
Maglev Transit, Inc.

DIUGUID AND EPSTEIN
1000 Connecticut Ave., N.W. Suite 1107, Washington, DC 20036
Telephone: (202) 872-0700
Members of firm representing listed organizations:
Diuguid, John
Background: Served in Organized Crime and Racketeering Section, U.S. Department of Justice, 1960-65; and with Judge Advocate's office of the U.S. Air Force as a reservist, 1954-84.
Epstein, Howard
Background: Served with Federal Trade Commission, 1961-68; Anti-Trust Division, U.S. Department of Justice, 1969-75.
Clients:
American Logistics Ass'n

DIUGUID, John
Diuguid and Epstein
1000 Connecticut Ave., N.W. Suite 1107, Washington, DC 20036
Telephone: (202) 872-0700
Background: Served in Organized Crime and Racketeering Section, U.S. Department of Justice, 1960-65; and with Judge Advocate's office of the U.S. Air Force as a reservist, 1954-84.

DIVILA, Walter
President, Greater Washington Ibero-American Chamber of Commerce
733 15th St., N.W., Suite 315, Washington, DC 20005
Telephone: (202) 737-2676

DIX, Dennis C.
Exec. Director & Chief Operating Officer, Outdoor Power Equipment Institute
341 S. Patrick St., Alexandria, VA 22314
Telephone: (703) 549-7600

DIX, Patsy B.
Legislative Specialist, Nat'l Education Ass'n of the U.S.
1201 16th St., N.W., Washington, DC 20036
Telephone: (202) 822-7300
Registered as lobbyist at U.S. Congress.

DIXON, Barbara A.
V. President, Motion Picture Ass'n of America
1600 Eye St., N.W., Washington, DC 20006
Telephone: (202) 293-1966
Registered as lobbyist at U.S. Congress.

DOAK, David M.
Partner, Doak, Shrum & Associates
1200 Eaton Court, Washington, DC 20007
Telephone: (202) 333-7901

DOAK, SHRUM & ASSOCIATES
1200 Eaton Court, Washington, DC 20007
Telephone: (202) 333-7901
Background: A political consulting firm.
Members of firm representing listed organizations:
Doak, David M., Partner
Shrum, Robert M.

DOANE, Hollye
Nat'l Superconducting Super Collider Coalition
1725 DeSales St., N.W. Suite 800, Washington, DC 20036
Telephone: (202) 659-6568
Registered as lobbyist at U.S. Congress.
Background: Federal Energy Regulatory Commission, Legal Advisor to Commissioner Charles Stalon (3 yrs.).

DOBBINS, Cheryl
Consulting Director, American Ass'n of Blacks in Energy
1220 L St., N.W., Suite 605, Washington, DC 20005
Telephone: (202) 898-0828

DOBBINS, Thomas B.
Director, Legislative Services, American Consulting Engineers Council
1015 15th St., N.W., Suite 802, Washington, DC 20005
Telephone: (202) 347-7474
Registered as lobbyist at U.S. Congress.

DOBBINS, Thomas B. (Cont'd)
Background: Also serves as contact for the American Consulting Engineers Council PAC (ACE/PAC).

DOCKSAI, Ronald F.
V. President, Government Relations, Marion Merrell Dow, Inc.
1776 Eye St., N.W. Suite 575, Washington, DC 20006
Telephone: (202) 429-3400
Background: Formerly served as Staff Director, U.S. Senate Committee on Labor and Human Resources, and as Assistant Secretary for Legislation, U.S. Department of Health and Human Services.

DODSON, Diane
Deputy Director, Family Programs, Women's Legal Defense Fund
2000 P St., N.W., Suite 400, Washington, DC 20036
Telephone: (202) 887-0364
Registered as lobbyist at U.S. Congress.

DODSON, Katherine
Director, Public Relations, American Health Assistance Foundation
15825 Shady Grove Road, Rockville, MD 20850
Telephone: (301) 948-3244
Background: Served as a Congressional press secretary for six years.

DOERFLINGER, Richard
Asst. Dir., Office for Pro-Life Activ., Nat'l Conference of Catholic Bishops
3211 4th St., N.E., Washington, DC 20017
Telephone: (202) 541-3000

DOERR, Karl
V. President, Federal Government Mktg., Nat'l Computer Systems
4601 N. Fairfax Drive, Arlington, VA 22203
Telephone: (703) 516-4306

DOERRER, John
State Legislative Director-Illinois, Transportation, Communications Internat'l Union
815 16th St., N.W. Suite 511, Washington, DC 20036
Telephone: (202) 783-3660
Registered as lobbyist at U.S. Congress.

DOERSAM, Harold A.
Federal Government Relations Manager, Household Internat'l
1000 Connecticut Ave., N.W., Suite 507, Washington, DC 20036
Telephone: (202) 466-3561
Registered as lobbyist at U.S. Congress.
Background: Represents also these subsidiaries of Household Internat'l: Alexander Hamilton Life Insurance Co. of America, HFC Leasing, Inc., Household Bank, F.S.B., Household Finance Corp., Household Bank, N.A.

DOGOLOFF, Lee I.
Exec. Director, American Council for Drug Education
204 Monroe St., Rockville, MD 20850
Telephone: (301) 294-0600
Background: Director, Government Assistant Division, Special Action Office for Drug Abuse Prevention, The White House, 1972-73. Director, Division of Community Assistant, Nat'l Institute on Drug Abuse, 1974-75. Deputy, Federal Drug Management, Office of Management and Budget, 1975-76. White House Advisor on Drug Policy, 1977-81.

DOHENY, David A.
Vice President, General Counsel, Nat'l Trust for Historic Preservation
1785 Massachusetts Ave., N.W., Washington, DC 20036
Telephone: (202) 673-4000

DOHERTY, Daniel P.
Exec. Director, Alliance of Nonprofit Mailers
2001 S St., N.W., Suite 301, Washington, DC 20009
Telephone: (202) 462-5132
Registered as lobbyist at U.S. Congress.

DOHERTY, James F.
President, Group Health Ass'n of America
1129 20th St., N.W. Suite 600, Washington, DC 20036
Telephone: (202) 778-3200

DOHERTY, John
Senior Consultant, Government Relations, Hill and Knowlton Public Affairs Worldwide
Washington Harbour, 901 31st St., N.W., Washington, DC 20007
Telephone: (202) 333-7400
Clients:
Chase Manhattan Bank
Marine Midland Banks, Inc.

DOHERTY, Robert B.
V. Pres., Gov't Affrs. & Public Policy, American Soc. of Internal Medicine
1101 Vermont Ave., N.W. Suite 500, Washington, DC 20005
Telephone: (202) 289-1700

DOHERTY, RUMBLE, AND BUTLER
1625 M St., N.W., Washington, DC 20036
Telephone: (202) 293-0555
Members of firm representing listed organizations:
Glaser, Peter S.
Clients:
Western Fuels Ass'n *(Peter S. Glaser)*

DOHERTY, William C., Jr.
Exec. Director, American Institute for Free Labor Development
1015 20th St., N.W., Washington, DC 20036
Telephone: (202) 659-6300

DOI, David
Director, Law Enforcement Relations, Handgun Control, Inc.
1225 Eye St., N.W., Suite 1100, Washington, DC 20005
Telephone: (202) 898-0792

DOLAN, Brian M.
Director, Federal Government Relations, Brooklyn Union Gas Co.
1225 19th St., N.W., Suite 320, Washington, DC 20036
Telephone: (202) 659-4716

DOLAN, Charles H., Jr.
Senior V. President, Cassidy and Associates, Inc.
655 15th St., N.W., Suite 1100, Washington, DC 20005
Telephone: (202) 347-0773
Background: Former Exec. Director, Democratic Governors' Ass'n.

DOLAN, Christine
Kostmayer Communications, Inc.
2300 M St., N.W., Suite 920, Washington, DC 20037
Telephone: (202) 223-6655
Clients:
Keep America Beautiful

DOLAN, Julie A.
V. President, Communications, American Advertising Federation
1400 K St., N.W., Suite 1000, Washington, DC 20005
Telephone: (202) 898-0089

DOLAN, Michael W.
Winthrop, Stimson, Putnam & Roberts
1133 Connecticut Ave., N.W. Suite 1000, Washington, DC 20036
Telephone: (202) 775-9800
Registered as lobbyist at U.S. Congress.
Registered as Foreign Agent: (#3873).
Background: Deputy Ass't Attorney General, Office of Legislative Affairs, U.S. Dept. of Justice 1979-85.
Clients:
Bowater, Inc.
Connecticut Liquidity Investment Fund, Inc.
Nat'l Vehicle Leasing Ass'n
Snappy Car Rental
Thrifty Rent-A-Car System, Inc.

DOLE, Gregory S.
Director, Commercial Programs, McDonnell Douglas Corp.
1735 Jefferson Davis Highway, Arlington, VA 22202
Telephone: (703) 553-3809

DOLE, Robin
Director of Government Relations, Century 21 Real Estate Corp.
1101 Connecticut Ave., N.W., Suite 500, Washington, DC 20036

Telephone: (202) 463-8850

DOLIBOIS, Robert J.
V. President, Ass'n Management Group
3299 K St., N.W., 7th Floor, Washington, DC 20007
Telephone: (202) 965-7510
Clients:
American Soc. of Home Inspectors
Soc. of Nat'l Ass'n Publications

DOLLASE, Ellen K.
Assistant Director, State Gov't Affairs, Independent Insurance Agents of America
600 Pennsylvania Ave., S.E., Suite 200, Washington, DC 20003
Telephone: (202) 544-5833

DOMENECH, Douglas
Director, Forestry Programs, American Pulpwood Ass'n
1025 Vermont Ave., N.W., Suite 1020, Washington, DC 20005
Telephone: (202) 347-2900
Registered as lobbyist at U.S. Congress.

DOMENICK, Julie
V. President, Legislative Affairs, Investment Company Institute
1600 M St., N.W. Suite 600, Washington, DC 20036
Telephone: (202) 293-7700
Registered as lobbyist at U.S. Congress.

DOMINY, Maj. Gen. Charles E.
Chief, Legis Liaison, DEPARTMENT OF ARMY
The Pentagon, Washington, DC 20310-0101
Telephone: (202) 697-6767

DONADIO, Brian
Executive Director, American College of Osteopathic Internists
300 5th St., N.E., Washington, DC 20002
Telephone: (202) 546-0095

DONAHUE, Alice C.
Internat'l President, General Federation of Women's Clubs
1734 N St., N.W., Washington, DC 20036
Telephone: (202) 347-3168

DONAHUE, Dr. D. Joseph
Sr. V. Pres., Tech. & Business Devel'pt., Thomson Consumer Electronics, Inc.
1200 19th St., N.W., Suite 601, Washington, DC 20036
Telephone: (202) 872-0670

DONAHUE, John F.
Bostrom Corp.
808 17th St., N.W., Suite 200, Washington, DC 20006
Telephone: (202) 223-9669
Clients:
Nat'l Ass'n of School Psychologists

DONAHUE, Karen L.
Neill and Co.
815 Connecticut Ave., N.W. Suite 800, Washington, DC 20006
Telephone: (202) 463-8877
Registered as lobbyist at U.S. Congress.
Registered as Foreign Agent: (#3320).

DONAHUE, Thomas R.
Secretary/ Treasurer, AFL-CIO Committee on Political Education/Political Contributions Committee (COPE)
815 16th St., N.W., Washington, DC 20006
Telephone: (202) 637-5101

DONALDSON, Gerald A.
Highway Safety Project Director, Center for Auto Safety
2001 S St., N.W., Room 410, Washington, DC 20009
Telephone: (202) 328-7700

DONALDSON, John
Black, Manafort, Stone and Kelly Public Affairs Co.
211 N. Union St., Third Floor, Alexandria, VA 22314
Telephone: (703) 683-6612
Registered as lobbyist at U.S. Congress.
Registered as Foreign Agent: (#3600).

DONALDSON, John C. L.
JCLD Consultancy
1000 Potomac St., N.W., Suite 102-A, Washington, DC 20007

Telephone: (202) 965-6685
Background: Editor, EuroMarket Digest.
Clients:
Eurofer

DONALDSON, Nancy A.
Assistant Director, Legislation, Service Employees Inter-nat'l Union
1313 L St., N.W., Washington, DC 20005
Telephone: (202) 898-3200
Registered as lobbyist at U.S. Congress.

DONATELLI, Frank
Bond Donatelli Inc.
1414 Prince St., Suite 300, Alexandria, VA 22314
Telephone: (703) 684-5991
Registered as lobbyist at U.S. Congress.
Background: Former White House political director under President Ronald Reagan.
Clients:
American Financial Corp.
American Petroleum Institute
FMC Corp.
Grumman Corp.
Tuscaloosa Steel Corp.

DONEGAN, Thomas J., Jr.
V. President and General Counsel, Cosmetic, Toiletry and Fragrance Ass'n
1110 Vermont Ave., N.W. Suite 800, Washington, DC 20005
Telephone: (202) 331-1770

DONELAN, CLEARY, WOOD AND MASER, P.C.
1275 K St., N.W., Suite 850, Washington, DC 20005
Telephone: (202) 371-9500
Background: Represents listed clients in transportation and distribution related regulatory matters.
Members of firm representing listed organizations:
Cleary, John M.
DiMichael, Nicholas J.
Donelan, John F.
Gerarden, Ted P.
Wood, Frederic L.
Clients:
American Frozen Food Institute *(John F. Donelan, Frederic L. Wood)*
American Paper Institute *(John F. Donelan)*
Carolina Power and Light Co. *(John F. Donelan)*
Cascade Natural Gas Co. *(Ted P. Gerarden)*
Duke Power Co. *(John F. Donelan)*
Iowa-Illinois Gas and Electric Co.
Iowa Public Service Co.
Iowa Southern Utilities Co.
Minnesota Power *(John F. Donelan, Frederic L. Wood)*
Nat'l Industrial Transportation League *(Nicholas J. DiMichael)*
Public Service Co. of Oklahoma
South Carolina Electric and Gas Co.
Southwestern Electric Power Co. *(John M. Cleary)*
Tampa Electric Co.

DONELAN, John F.
Donelan, Cleary, Wood and Maser, P.C.
1275 K St., N.W., Suite 850, Washington, DC 20005
Telephone: (202) 371-9500
Registered as lobbyist at U.S. Congress.
Clients:
American Frozen Food Institute
American Paper Institute
Carolina Power and Light Co.
Duke Power Co.
Minnesota Power

DONELSON, Andrew J.
Manager, Regulatory Affairs, Minnesota Mining and Manu-facturing Co. (3M Co.)
1101 15th St., N.W., Washington, DC 20005
Telephone: (202) 331-6948
Registered as lobbyist at U.S. Congress.

DONIGER, David D.
Senior Staff Attorney, Natural Resources Defense Council
1350 New York Ave., N.W. Suite 300, Washington, DC 20005
Telephone: (202) 783-7800

DONNELLAN, Kevin J.
Legislative Counsel, American Ass'n of Retired Persons
1909 K St., N.W., Washington, DC 20049
Telephone: (202) 872-4700
Registered as lobbyist at U.S. Congress.

DONNELLY, Mary Adele
Director, Sea Turtle Rescue Fund
1725 DeSales St., N.W. Suite 500, Washington, DC 20036
Telephone: (202) 429-5609

DONNELLY, Mary Beth
V. President, Government Relations, Newmont Mining Corp.
1233 20th St., N.W., Suite 200, Washington, DC 20036
Telephone: (202) 659-2080
Registered as lobbyist at U.S. Congress.

DONNELLY, Thomas F.
Exec. V. President, Nat'l Water Resources Ass'n
3800 North Fairfax Dr. Suite 4, Arlington, VA 22203
Telephone: (703) 524-1544
Registered as lobbyist at U.S. Congress.

DONNELLY, Thomas R., Jr.
Pagonis and Donnelly Group
1620 Eye St., N.W., Suite 603, Washington, DC 20006
Telephone: (202) 452-8811
Registered as lobbyist at U.S. Congress.
Background: Former Special Assistant to the President, The White House.
Clients:
Air Products and Chemicals, Inc.
Asea Brown Boveri, Inc.
Ass'n of High Medicare Hospitals
Burroughs Wellcome Co.
Dow Chemical
Harrah's
Holiday Corp.
Nord Resources Corp.
Transkei, Government of

DONNER, Sally S.
Manager, Federal Government Relations, Kraft General Foods, Inc.
1341 G St., N.W., 9th Floor, Washington, DC 20005
Telephone: (202) 637-1540
Registered as lobbyist at U.S. Congress.

D'ONOFRIO, Stephen J.
Dep. General Counsel/Anti-Piracy Opertns, Recording In-dustry Ass'n of America
1020 19th St., N.W., Suite 200, Washington, DC 20036
Telephone: (202) 775-0101

DONOGHUE, Daniel J.
Manager, Stone and Webster Engineering Corp.
1201 Connecticut Ave., N.W. Suite 850, Washington, DC 20036-2605
Telephone: (202) 466-7415

DONOGHUE, Marguerite
Capitol Associates, Inc.
426 C St., N.E., Washington, DC 20002
Telephone: (202) 544-1880
Registered as lobbyist at U.S. Congress.
Clients:
American Soc. of Tropical Medicine and Hygiene
FDA Council
Hutchinson Cancer Center
Nat'l Coalition for Cancer Research
Wistar Institute, The

DONOHOE, David A.
Akin, Gump, Strauss, Hauer and Feld
1333 New Hampshire Ave., N.W., Suite 400, Washington, DC 20036
Telephone: (202) 887-4000
Clients:
Putnam's Sons, G. P.
Revlon Group

DONOHUE, Thomas J.
President and CEO, American Trucking Ass'ns
2200 Mill Road, Alexandria, VA 22314
Telephone: (703) 838-1800
Registered as lobbyist at U.S. Congress.
Background: Serves also as President, American Trucking Ass'ns Foundation and the Trucking Research Institute.

DONOVAN, Charles
Family Research Council, Inc.
601 Pennsylvania Ave., N.W., Suite 901, Washington, DC 20004
Telephone: (202) 393-2100
Registered as lobbyist at U.S. Congress.

DONOVAN, David L.
V. President, Legal & Legislat. Affairs, Ass'n of Indepen-dent Television Stations
1200 18th St., N.W. Suite 502, Washington, DC 20036
Telephone: (202) 887-1970

DONOVAN, George J.
V.P., Dir., Wash. Opns. (Def Syst & EI), Texas Instruments
1745 Jefferson Davis Hwy. Suite 605, Artlington, VA 22202
Telephone: (703) 892-9333

DONOVAN LEISURE ROGOVIN HUGE & SCHIL-LER
1250 24th St., N.W., Washington, DC 20037
Telephone: (202) 467-8300
Background: The law firms of Donovan Leisure Newton & Irvine and Rogovin, Huge & Schiller were in the process of merging to form Donovan Leisure Rogovin Huge & Schiller as this edition of WASHINGTON REPRESEN-TATIVES went to press.
Members of firm representing listed organizations:
Colby, William E.
de Ravel, Pierre F.
Clients:
Nissho-Iwai American Corp. *(William E. Colby)*
Usinor-Sacilor, S.A. *(William E. Colby)*

DONOVAN, Paul M.
LaRoe, Winn, Moerman & Donovan
1120 G St., N.W., Suite 800, Washington, DC 20005
Telephone: (202) 628-2788
Registered as lobbyist at U.S. Congress.
Clients:
Jones Chemicals Political Action Committee
Western Transportation Co.

DONOVAN, William J.
V. President, Government Affrs. Counsel, Nat'l Ass'n of Federal Credit Unions
3138 N. 10th St., Arlington, VA 22201
Telephone: (703) 522-4770
Registered as lobbyist at U.S. Congress.
Background: Also serves as Treasurer, Nat'l Ass'n of Fed-eral Credit Unions Political Action Committee.

DOOLEY, Betty
Exec. Director, Women's Research and Education Institute
1700 18th St., N.W., Suite 400, Washington, DC 20009
Telephone: (202) 328-7070

DOOLITTLE, J. William
Prather, Seeger, Doolittle and Farmer
1600 M St., N.W., Washington, DC 20036
Telephone: (202) 296-0500
Background: Clerk to Justice Felix Frankfurter, U.S. Su-preme Court, 1957-58. Assistant to Solicitor General of the U.S., 1961-63. First Assistant, Civil Division, Depart-ment of Justice, 1963-66. General Counsel, 1966-68 and Assistant Secretary, 1968-69, Department of the Air Force.
Clients:
Elsevier U.S. Holdings, Inc.
Greenwood Press

DOON, Melanie K.
Manager, Business-Government Policy, Professional Ser-vices Council
918 16th St., N.W., Suite 406, Washington, DC 20006
Telephone: (202) 296-2030

DORANZ, Jeffrey D.
General Counsel, Palumbo & Cerrell, Inc.
1629 K St., N.W., Suite 1100, Washington, DC 20006
Telephone: (202) 785-6705
Background: Special Counsel, Senate Committee on Labor and Public Welfare, 1973-75. Counsel, Office of the Solic-itor, U.S. Department of Labor, 1976-86.
Clients:
American Insurance Ass'n
ARCO Chemical Co.
Order of Sons of Italy in America

DORANZ, Jeffrey D. (Cont'd)
Palmer Associates, G. H.

DORCY, Jim
Sr. Government Relations Associate, Federation for American Immigration Reform (FAIR)
1666 Connecticut Ave., N.W., Suite 400, Washington, DC 20009
Telephone: (202) 328-7004
Registered as lobbyist at U.S. Congress.

DOREMUS, Theodore A., Jr.
Of Counsel, Davis Polk & Wardwell
1300 Eye St., N.W. 11th Fl. East, Washington, DC 20005
Telephone: (202) 962-7000
Registered as lobbyist at U.S. Congress.
Background: Senior Branch Attorney, Securities and Exchange Commission, 1970-75. General Counsel, Minority Staff, House Committee on Banking, Finance and Urban Affairs, 1975-79.
Clients:
Morgan Guaranty Trust Co.
Norwest Corp.

DORFMAN, Ira H.
V. President, Government Affairs, American Bakers Ass'n
1111 14th St., N.W., Suite 300, Washington, DC 20005
Telephone: (202) 296-5800
Registered as lobbyist at U.S. Congress.

DORIAN, Linda Colvard
Exec. Director, Nat'l Federation of Business and Professional Women's Clubs
2012 Massachusetts Ave., N.W., Washington, DC 20036
Telephone: (202) 293-1100
Registered as lobbyist at U.S. Congress.
Background: Formerly had government service with the Equal Employment Opportunity Commission and as Deputy Director for Consumer Protection, Federal Trade Commission.

DORMAN, Richard F.
Exec. Director, American Congress on Surveying and Mapping
5410 Grosvenor Lane, Suite 100, Bethesda, MD 20814-2122
Telephone: (301) 493-0200

DORN, James A.
V. President, Academic Affairs, Cato Institute
224 Second St., S.E., Washington, DC 20003
Telephone: (202) 546-0200

DORN, Joseph W.
Kilpatrick & Cody
2501 M St., N.W., Suite 500, Washington, DC 20037
Telephone: (202) 463-2500
Registered as lobbyist at U.S. Congress.
Registered as Foreign Agent: (#3610).
Clients:
Atlantic-Southeast Airlines
Bromon Aircraft Corp.
Cookware Manufacturers Ass'n
Farberware
General Housewares Corp.
Hand Tools Institute
Oregon Caneberry Commission
Revere Copper and Brass Co.
Southdown
Washington Raspberry Commission

DORNSIFE, N. Cinnamon
Washington Representative, Asia Foundation, The
2301 E St., N.W., Suite 713, Washington, DC 20037
Telephone: (202) 223-5268

DORSCH, James A.
Washington Counsel, Health Insurance Ass'n of America
1025 Connecticut Ave., N.W. Suite 1200, Washington, DC 20036
Telephone: (202) 223-7780
Registered as lobbyist at U.S. Congress.

DORSEY, Frederick D.
People's Counsel, District of Columbia Office of the People's Counsel
1101 14th St., N.W., Suite 900, Washington, DC 20005
Telephone: (202) 727-3071

DORSEY & WHITNEY
1330 Connecticut Ave., N.W., Suite 200, Washington, DC 20036
Telephone: (202) 857-0700
Members of firm representing listed organizations:
Aitken, Bruce
Bieging, David A.
Background: Legislative Assistant to Senator Walter F. Mondale (D-MN), 1975-76. Special Assistant to Vice President Mondale, 1977-78. Administrative Assistant to Rep. Martin O. Sabo (D-MN), 1979-87.
Bruno, Philippe M.
Busby, David
Background: Counsel, Sub-Committee on Automobile Marketing Practices, U.S. Senate Interstate and Foreign Commerce Committee, 1955-1958. Counsel, Sub-Committee on Foreign Commerce, U.S. Senate Interstate and Foreign Commerce Committee, 1958.
Glazier, Jonathan H.
Hall, Munford Page (II)
Israel, Barry J.
Leonard, Will E.
Background: Legislative Assistant to Senator Russell B. Long of Louisiana, 1960-66. Professional Staff Member, U.S. Senate Committee on Finance, 1966-68. Commissioner, 1966-77 and Chairman, 1975-76, U.S. International Trade Commission.
Mullaney, L. Daniel
Rehm, John B.
Background: Office of the Legal Advisor, Department of State, 1953-1963. General Counsel, Office of the Special Representative for Trade Negotiations, 1963-1969.
Reppert, Linda P.
Sam Bai, Sanyung
Taylor, (Jr.) James
Tuttle, Jon F.
Clients:
American Suzuki Motor Corp.
Black and Decker Corp., The
BMW of North America
Canai Inc.
Chilean Nitrate Sales Corp.
Colgate-Palmolive Co.
Computer and Business Equipment Manufacturers Ass'n
Florists Transworld Delivery Ass'n
Genetics Institute Inc. *(Will E. Leonard)*
Guam Commission on Self-Determination
Guam, Office of the Attorney General of
Guam, Port Authority of
Hyundai Motor America
Hyundai Motor Co.
Internat'l Electronics Manufacturers and Consumers of America
Leaf Tobacco Exporters Ass'n
Nissan Motor Corp. in U.S.A.
Nissho-Iwai American Corp.
Pechiney Corp.
Philipp Brothers, Inc.
Ricoh Corp.
Societe Nationale des Poudres et Explosifs
Texas Ass'n of Steel Importers
Thailand, Embassy of
Tokyo Juki Industrial Co., Ltd.
Toyota Motor Corp.

DORT, Dean R., II
Washington Counsel, Deere & Co.
1667 K St., N.W., Suite 1230, Washington, DC 20006
Telephone: (202) 223-4817
Registered as lobbyist at U.S. Congress.

DORT, Terrie
Legislative Director, Rowland & Sellery
1023 15th St., N.W. 7th Fl., Washington, DC 20005
Telephone: (202) 289-1780
Registered as lobbyist at U.S. Congress.
Clients:
Borg-Warner Automotive, Inc.
Coalition for Uniform Product Liability Law
Drugfree Workplace Coalition
Fire Equipment Manufacturers and Services Ass'n
Job Opportunities Business Symposium

DOSWELL, W. Carter
V. President, Goldman, Sachs and Co.
1101 Pennsylvania Ave., N.W. Suite 900, Washington, DC 20004
Telephone: (202) 637-3700
Registered as lobbyist at U.S. Congress.

DOTCHIN, Robert J.
V. President, Industry & Federal Relats., Smokeless Tobacco Council
2550 M St., N.W., Suite 300, Washington, DC 20037
Telephone: (202) 452-1252
Registered as lobbyist at U.S. Congress.
Background: Former Minority Staff Director, Senate Small Business Committee.

DOTSON, Betsy
Legislative Rep., Federal Liaison Center, Government Finance Officers Ass'n
1750 K St., N.W. Suite 200, Washington, DC 20006
Telephone: (202) 429-2750

DOUBRAVA, Richard J.
Manager, Government Affairs, Delta Air Lines
1629 K St., N.W., Suite 501, Washington, DC 20006
Telephone: (202) 296-6464
Registered as lobbyist at U.S. Congress.

DOUDS, H. James
Senior V. President and General Counsel, Nat'l Ass'n of Life Underwriters
1922 F St., N.W., Washington, DC 20006
Telephone: (202) 331-6020

DOUGHERTY, Charles F.
Resident Associate (Philadelphia), Cassidy and Associates, Inc.
655 15th St., N.W., Suite 1100, Washington, DC 20005
Telephone: (202) 347-0773
Registered as lobbyist at U.S. Congress.
Background: Member of the U.S. House of Representatives, 1979-83. Member of the Pennsylvania Senate, 1972-78.
Clients:
Drexel University
Pennsylvania Turnpike Commission
St. Joseph's University
University of the Arts

DOUGHERTY, Thomas J., Jr.
Fletcher, Heald and Hildreth
1225 Connecticut Ave., N.W. Suite 400, Washington, DC 20036
Telephone: (202) 828-5700

DOUGHTY, Roger
President, Gay and Lesbian Activists Alliance
1517 U St., N.W., Suite 1A, Washington, DC 20009
Telephone: (202) 667-5139

DOUGLAS, Jacalyn
Research Assistant, Mitsui and Co. (U.S.A.), Inc.
1701 Pennsylvania Ave., N.W., Suite 400, Washington, DC 20006
Telephone: (202) 861-0660

DOUGLAS, John W.
Covington and Burling
1201 Pennsylvania Ave., N.W., Box 7566, Washington, DC 20044
Telephone: (202) 662-6000
Background: Ass't Attorney General, Civil Division, U.S. Dep't of Justice, 1963-66.

DOUGLAS, Roberta
Director of Development, American Council of the Blind
1010 Vermont Ave., N.W. Suite 1100, Washington, DC 20005
Telephone: (202) 393-3666

DOUGLAS, Sally L.
Asst. Dir., Fed. Gov't Afrs./Res. & Pol., Nat'l Federation of Independent Business
600 Maryland Ave., S.W., Suite 700, Washington, DC 20024
Telephone: (202) 554-9000
Registered as lobbyist at U.S. Congress.

WASHINGTON REPRESENTATIVES

DOUGLAS, Suzanne G.
Director, Information and Research, Public Service Satellite Consortium
600 Maryland Ave., S.W., Suite 220, Washington, DC 20024
Telephone: (202) 863-0890

DOVE, Tim
Federal Affairs Issues Manager, Insurance Information Institute
1101 17th St, N.W., Suite 408, Washington, DC 20036
Telephone: (202) 833-1580

DOVER, G. Jack
Principal, Griffin, Johnson & Associates
1211 Connecticut Ave., N.W., Suite 700, Washington, DC 20036
Telephone: (202) 775-8116
Registered as lobbyist at U.S. Congress.
Background: Former aide to Rep. Dennis Eckert (D-OH) and Senator John Glenn (D-OH) and a former member of President Jimmy Carter's Domestic Policy Staff.

DOW, LOHNES AND ALBERTSON
1255 23rd St., N.W. Suite 500, Washington, DC 20037
Telephone: (202) 857-2500
Members of firm representing listed organizations:
  Allen, Marion H. (III)
  Bantleon, David F.
  Belas, Richard S., Partner
  Berman, Marshall F.
  Bloch, Stuart Marshall
  Braunstein, Richard L.
  Chasnow, Robert M.
  Collins, Kathleen W.
  Hardy, Ralph W. (Jr.)
   Background: Serves as Vice President and Secretary of First Media Corp., a company owned by members of the Marriott Family.
  Hildebrandt, David A.
  Hill, Jonathan B.
  Ingersoll, William B.
  Kelly, Joseph F. (Jr.)
  Kurzweil, Jeffrey
   Background: Special Assistant to the General Counsel, U.S. Department of Commerce, 1977-79.
  Long, Bernard J. (Jr.)
  Lutzker, Arnold P.
  Robertson, Reuben B.
  Salomon, Kenneth D., Partner
  Sheldon, Stuart A.
  Sher, Stanley O.
  Silverman, Arthur H.
  Silverman, William
  Stern, Jeffrey B.
  Thompson, Philip C.
Clients:
  Acton Corp. *(Robert M. Chasnow)*
  Advance Publications, Inc. *(Bernard J. Long, Jr.)*
  Agricultural Satellite Corp. *(Kenneth D. Salomon)*
  Algoma Steel Corp., Ltd. *(William Silverman)*
  American Integrity Insurance Co. *(Richard S. Belas)*
  American Psychological Ass'n *(William B. Ingersoll)*
  American Real Estate Group *(Stuart Marshall Bloch)*
  American Resort and Residential Development Ass'n *(William B. Ingersoll)*
  American Savings Bank, F.A. *(Stuart Marshall Bloch)*
  American Security Bank *(David F. Bantleon)*
  Atlanta Falcons *(Marion H. Allen, III)*
  Avis Rent A Car Systems, Inc. *(David F. Bantleon)*
  Belin and Associates *(Stuart Marshall Bloch)*
  Blue Cross and Blue Shield of Maryland *(Arnold P. Lutzker)*
  Branigar Organization *(William B. Ingersoll)*
  California Wine Commission *(Arthur H. Silverman)*
  Campolonghi Italia S.p.A. *(William Silverman)*
  Carlyle Group, The *(Jeffrey Kurzweil)*
  Castine Partners *(Stuart Marshall Bloch)*
  Century Property Fund *(Jeffrey B. Stern)*
  Chamber of Commerce of the U.S.A. *(Arthur H. Silverman)*
  Citibank, N.A. *(Ralph W. Hardy, Jr.)*
  Colonial Village, Inc. *(Reuben B. Robertson)*
  Compania Trasatlantica Espanola, S.A. *(Stanley O. Sher)*
  Cox Enterprises, Inc. *(Richard L. Braunstein)*
  Crossland Savings Bank *(Stuart Marshall Bloch)*
  Directors Guild of America *(Arnold P. Lutzker)*
  Dofasco, Inc. *(William Silverman)*
  Envases de Plastico, S.A. de C.V. *(William Silverman)*
  Erie Islands Resort and Marina *(Robert M. Chasnow)*
  Euromarble, S.p.A. *(William Silverman)*
  Fireman's Fund Insurance Cos. *(Richard S. Belas)*
  First Boston Corp. *(Richard S. Belas, Jeffrey Kurzweil)*
  First Media Corp. *(Ralph W. Hardy, Jr.)*
  First Nat'l Bank of Chicago *(Bernard J. Long, Jr.)*
  Flyer Industries Ltd. *(William Silverman)*
  Franklin Federal Bancorp *(Stuart Marshall Bloch)*
  Gannett Co., Inc. *(Arnold P. Lutzker)*
  General Aviation Manufacturers Ass'n *(Richard S. Belas)*
  GoldStar Co., Ltd. *(William Silverman)*
  Governors Club Development Corp. *(William B. Ingersoll)*
  Hapag-Lloyd AG *(Stanley O. Sher)*
  Harcourt Brace Jovanovich, Inc. *(Marshall F. Berman)*
  Hawaiian Airlines *(Jonathan B. Hill)*
  Henraux S.p.A. *(William Silverman)*
  Hercules, Inc. *(Arthur H. Silverman)*
  Hertz Corp. *(David F. Bantleon, Stanley O. Sher)*
  Hilton Hotels Corp. *(David F. Bantleon)*
  Johnson-Simmons Co., The *(Jeffrey Kurzweil)*
  Lazard Freres *(Bernard J. Long, Jr.)*
  Life Card, Inc. *(Arnold P. Lutzker)*
  Lifecare Services Co. *(Jeffrey Kurzweil)*
  Marriott Corp. *(Jeffrey Kurzweil)*
  Maryland Nat'l Bank *(David F. Bantleon)*
  Masstock Internat'l Limited *(Philip C. Thompson)*
  Mobil Land Development Co. *(William B. Ingersoll)*
  Morgan Guaranty Trust Co. *(Richard S. Belas, Jeffrey Kurzweil)*
  Morgan Stanley and Co. *(Bernard J. Long, Jr.)*
  Nat'l American Corp. *(Robert M. Chasnow)*
  Nat'l Business Aircraft Ass'n *(Richard S. Belas)*
  Nat'l Technological University *(Kenneth D. Salomon)*
  New West Savings and Loan Ass'n *(Stuart Marshall Bloch)*
  NTS Corp. *(William B. Ingersoll)*
  OEL/Norfin S.p.A. *(William Silverman)*
  Owens-Illinois Development Corp. *(Stuart Marshall Bloch)*
  Patten Corp. *(William B. Ingersoll)*
  PLIVA Pharmaceutical and Chemical Works *(William Silverman)*
  Procter and Gamble Mfg. Co. *(David A. Hildebrandt)*
  Product Liability Coordinating Committee *(Arthur H. Silverman)*
  Profit Sharing Council of America *(David A. Hildebrandt)*
  Salomon Brothers Inc. *(Stuart A. Sheldon)*
  Savema S.p.A. *(William Silverman)*
  Security Trust Co. *(David F. Bantleon)*
  Sefri Construction Internat'l *(Philip C. Thompson)*
  SOFICIA *(Arthur H. Silverman)*
  Sporicidin Co., The *(Arthur H. Silverman)*
  ST Systems Corp. (STX) *(Ralph W. Hardy, Jr.)*
  Stelco, Inc. *(William Silverman)*
  Tak Communications, Inc. *(Ralph W. Hardy, Jr.)*
  Trapp Family Lodge *(William B. Ingersoll)*
  U.S. Home Corp. *(William B. Ingersoll)*
  U.S. Trust Co. *(David F. Bantleon, Joseph F. Kelly, Jr.)*
  Virginia Beach Federal Savings Bank *(Reuben B. Robertson)*
  Washington Bancorporation *(Kathleen W. Collins)*
  Westinghouse Community Development Group *(Robert M. Chasnow)*
  Wilmington Savings Fund Soc. *(Jeffrey B. Stern)*

DOWD, John P.
State Legislative Director-Massachusetts, Transportation, Communications Internat'l Union
815 16th St., N.W. Suite 511, Washington, DC 20036
Telephone: (202) 783-3660
Registered as lobbyist at U.S. Congress.

DOWD, Michael G.
Porter, Wright, Morris and Arthur
1233 20th St., N.W., Suite 400, Washington, DC 20005
Telephone: (202) 778-3000
Clients:
  Coalition for Environmental-Energy Balance

DOWDEN, C. James
Exec. V. President, Community Ass'ns Institute
1423 Powhatan St., Suite 7, Alexandria, VA 22314
Telephone: (703) 548-8600

DOWER, Roger
Dir, Climate Energy & Pollution Program, World Resources Institute
1709 New York Ave., N.W., Washington, DC 20006
Telephone: (202) 638-6300
Background: Economic Consultant, Exec. Office of the President, 1980-81; Chief, Energy and Environmental Unit, Congressional Budget Office, 1986-89.

DOWHOWER, Kay S., H.H.D.
Director, Lutheran Office for Governmental Affairs/Evangelical Lutheran Church in America
122 C St., N.W. Suite 300, Washington, DC 20001
Telephone: (202) 783-7508

DOWLEY, Joseph K.
Dewey, Ballantine, Bushby, Palmer and Wood
1775 Pennsylvania Ave., N.W. Suite 200, Washington, DC 20006
Telephone: (202) 862-1000
Background: Administraive Assistant to Rep. Dan Rostenkowski (D-IL), 1977-80. Assistant Counsel, 1980-84 and Chief Counsel, House Committee on Ways and Means, 1985-87.
Clients:
  American Iron and Steel Institute
  Bristol-Myers Squibb Co.
  McCown De Leeuw & Co.
  Morgan Stanley and Co.
  Premark Internat'l
  Prudential Insurance Co. of America

DOWLING, Paul Bruce
Exec. Director, America the Beautiful Fund
219 Shoreham Bldg., Washington, DC 20005
Telephone: (202) 638-1649

DOWN, A. Graham
Exec. Director, Council for Basic Education
725 15th St., N.W., Suite 801, Washington, DC 20005
Telephone: (202) 347-4171

DOWNEN, Robert L.
V. President, Neill and Co.
815 Connecticut Ave., N.W. Suite 800, Washington, DC 20006
Telephone: (202) 463-8877
Registered as lobbyist at U.S. Congress.
Registered as Foreign Agent: (#3320).
Background: Legislative Assistant to Senator Robert Dole (R-KS), 1973-79. Director of Special Projects and Policy Adviser, Bureau of East Asian and Pacific Affairs, U.S. Department of State, 1984-88.
Clients:
  China External Trade Development Council

DOWNER, Charles P.
Industrial Preparedness Representative, NMTBA - The Ass'n for Manufacturing Technology
7901 Westpark Dr., McLean, VA 22102
Telephone: (703) 893-2900
Registered as lobbyist at U.S. Congress.

DOWNES, Rose R.
Exec. Administrator, Ass'n of Small Research, Engineering and Technical Services Companies
450 Maple Ave., East Suite 204, Vienna, VA 22180
Telephone: (703) 255-5011

DOWNEY, Jane L.
General Counsel, American Movers Conference
2200 Mill Road, Alexandria, VA 22314
Telephone: (703) 838-1930

DOWNEY, Rita E.
Government Affairs Specialist, Hewlett-Packard Co.
900 17th St., N.W. Suite 1100, Washington, DC 20006
Telephone: (202) 785-7943

DOWNING, Mary Louise
V. President, Powell, Adams & Rinehart
1901 L St., N.W., 3rd Floor, Washington, DC 20036
Telephone: (202) 466-7590

DOWNS, Jill
Manager, Corp. Affairs, Potomac Electric Power Co.
1900 Pennsylvania Ave., N.W., Washington, DC 20068
Telephone: (202) 872-2000

DOWNS, Mary E.
Asst. General Counsel and Secretary, Air Transport Ass'n of America
1709 New York Ave., N.W., Washington, DC 20006-5206
Telephone: (202) 626-4161

DOYLE, J. Andrew
Exec. Director, Nat'l Paint and Coatings Ass'n
1500 Rhode Island Ave., N.W., Washington, DC 20005
Telephone: (202) 462-6272

DOYLE, Jack
Agricultural & Biotechnology Director, Friends of the Earth
218 D St., S.E., Washington, DC 20003
Telephone: (202) 544-2600
Registered as lobbyist at U.S. Congress.

DOYLE, John A.
Exec. Director, Nat'l Ass'n of Rehabilitation Facilities
Box 17675, Washington, DC 20041-0675
Telephone: (703) 648-9300

DOYLE, Kenneth A.
Exec. V. President, Soc. of Independent Gasoline Marketers of America
1730 K St., N.W., Suite 907, Washington, DC 20006
Telephone: (202) 429-9333
Background: Responsibilities include Soc. of Independent Gasoline Marketers Political Action Committee.

DOYLE, Rev. Kenneth J.
Director, Office of Media Affairs, United States Catholic Conference
3211 4th St., N.E., Washington, DC 20017
Telephone: (202) 541-3100
Background: Responsibilities also include the Nat'l Conference of Catholic Bishops.

DOYLE, M. Theresa
Senior Legislative Representative, Mutual of Omaha Insurance Companies
1700 Pennsylvania Ave., N.W. Suite 500, Washington, DC 20006
Telephone: (202) 393-6200
Registered as lobbyist at U.S. Congress.

DOYLE, Stephen P.
Wilmer, Cutler and Pickering
2445 M St., N.W., Washington, DC 20037-1420
Telephone: (202) 663-6000
Clients:
American Petroleum Institute

DOYNE, Karen
V. President, Fleishman-Hillard, Inc
1301 Connecticut Ave., N.W., Washington, DC 20036
Telephone: (202) 659-0330

DOZSA, George
V. President, Hungarian Reformed Federation of America
2001 Massachusetts Ave., N.W., Washington, DC 20036
Telephone: (202) 328-2630

DRAGNICH, David W.
Director, Program Development, Battelle Memorial Institute
370 L'Enfant Promenade S.W. 901 D St., S.W., Suite 900, Washington, DC 20004-2115
Telephone: (202) 479-0500

DRAGOTTA, George V.
Exec. V. President, Nat'l Parking Ass'n
1112 16th St., N.W., Suite 300, Washington, DC 20036
Telephone: (202) 296-4336

DRAGOUMIS, Paul
Exec. V. President, Potomac Electric Power Co.
1900 Pennsylvania Ave., N.W., Washington, DC 20068
Telephone: (202) 872-2000

DRAKE, David P., Jr.
Manager, Federal Government Relations, CIBA-GEIGY Corp.
1747 Pennsylvania Ave., N.W., Suite 700, Washington, DC 20006
Telephone: (202) 293-3019
Registered as lobbyist at U.S. Congress.

DRAKE, James E.
Ass't Dir., Dept. of Congress'l Affairs, American Medical Ass'n
1101 Vermont Ave., N.W., Washington, DC 20005
Telephone: (202) 789-7400
Registered as lobbyist at U.S. Congress.

DRASNER, Fred
Counsel, Shaw, Pittman, Potts and Trowbridge
2300 N St., N.W., Washington, DC 20037
Telephone: (202) 663-8000

DRATH, Viola
Chairman of the Board, Transatlantic Security Council
2323 Virginia Ave., N.W., Washington, DC 20037
Telephone: (202) 338-2539

DRAVO, Andrea N.
Vice President, American Nuclear Energy Council
410 First St., S.E. Third Floor, Washington, DC 20003
Telephone: (202) 484-2670
Registered as lobbyist at U.S. Congress.

DRAY, Marie E.
Director, Regulatory Agency Relations, Merck and Co.
1615 L St., N.W., Suite 1320, Washington, DC 20036
Telephone: (202) 833-8205

DRAZEK, Paul A.
Asst. Director, Nat'l Affairs Division, American Farm Bureau Federation
600 Maryland Ave., S.W., Washington, DC 20024
Telephone: (202) 484-3600
Registered as lobbyist at U.S. Congress.

DREA, Stephanie
Communications Director, League of Women Voters of the United States
1730 M St., N.W., Tenth Floor, Washington, DC 20036
Telephone: (202) 429-1965

DREHER, Robert
Staff Attorney & Co-Director, Sierra Club Legal Defense Fund
1531 P St., N.W. Suite 200, Washington, DC 20005
Telephone: (202) 667-4500

DRESDEN, Anthony V.
Director, Public Affairs, Nat'l Air Traffic Controller Ass'n
444 N. Capitol St., Suite 845, Washington, DC 20001
Telephone: (202) 347-4572
Registered as lobbyist at U.S. Congress.

DRESING, Robert K.
President, Cystic Fibrosis Foundation
6931 Arlington Road Suite 200, Bethesda, MD 20814
Telephone: (301) 951-4422

DRESSENDORFER, John H.
Dressendorfer-Laird, Inc.
1730 Rhode Island Ave., N.W., Suite 210, Washington, DC 20036
Telephone: (202) 887-5073
Clients:
General Dynamics Corp.

DRESSENDORFER-LAIRD, INC.
1730 Rhode Island Ave., N.W., Suite 210, Washington, DC 20036
Telephone: (202) 887-5073
Background: A governmental relations consulting firm.
Members of firm representing listed organizations:
Dressendorfer, John H.
Laird, David M., V. President
Clients:
General Dynamics Corp. *(John H. Dressendorfer)*
Metropolitan Insurance Cos. *(David M. Laird)*
Science Applications, Inc. *(David M. Laird)*

DREUX, Joan Albert
VP, Fed. Legislative & Regulatory Affrs., Mutual of Omaha Insurance Companies
1700 Pennsylvania Ave., N.W. Suite 500, Washington, DC 20006
Telephone: (202) 393-6200
Registered as lobbyist at U.S. Congress.

DREW, Jerry
V. Pres. & Director, Washington Office, African American Institute
1625 Massachusetts Ave., N.W. Suite 210, Washington, DC 20036
Telephone: (202) 667-5636

DREW, Robert T.
Health & Environmental Sciences Director, American Petroleum Institute
1220 L St., N.W., Washington, DC 20005
Telephone: (202) 682-8308

DREYFUS, Daniel A.
V. Pres., Strat. Analysis & Energy Fcstn, Gas Research Institute
1331 Pennsylvania Ave., N.W., Suite 730 North, Washington, DC 20004
Telephone: (202) 662-8989

DRIESLER, Stephen D.
Sr. V. Pres, Gov't Affairs & Polit. Rtns, Nat'l Ass'n of REALTORS
777 14th St., N.W., Washington, DC 20005
Telephone: (202) 383-1026
Registered as lobbyist at U.S. Congress.
Background: Serves as the chief lobbyist of the Nat'l Ass'n of Realtors. Also represents Nat'l Ass'n of Realtors Political Action Committee. Former Administrative Assistant to Rep. Larry J. Hopkins (R-KY).

DRIESSEN, J. Kenneth
V. Pres. & Gen. Mgr., Gov't Systems, MRJ, Inc.
10455 White Granite Dr. Suite 305, Oakton, VA 22124
Telephone: (703) 385-0703

DRIGGERS, William B.
Legislative Liaison (Def. Syst. & Elec.), Texas Instruments
1745 Jefferson Davis Hwy. Suite 605, Arlington, VA 22202
Telephone: (703) 892-9333
Registered as lobbyist at U.S. Congress.

DRISCOLL, Daniel J.
V. President, Corporate Communications, Federal Home Loan Mortgage Corp.
1759 Business Center Drive, Reston, VA 22090
Telephone: (703) 789-4700

DRISCOLL, Edward J.
Chairman of the Board, President & CEO, Nat'l Air Carrier Ass'n
1730 M St., N.W. Suite 806, Washington, DC 20036
Telephone: (202) 833-8200
Background: Also represents the Aviation Bilateral Conference.

DRISCOLL, Kevin J.
Staff Director for Bar Liaison, American Bar Ass'n
1800 M St., N.W., Washington, DC 20036
Telephone: (202) 331-2211
Registered as lobbyist at U.S. Congress.

DRISCOLL, Lorraine
Legislative Director, Citizen Action
1300 Connecticut Ave., N.W. Suite 401, Washington, DC 20036
Telephone: (202) 857-5153
Registered as lobbyist at U.S. Congress.

DRISKELL AND ASSOCIATES. PAUL
1819 H St., N.W. Suite 1175, Washington, DC 20006
Telephone: (202) 898-0734
Clients:
Rouse Company, The

DROGULA, Fred W.
Verner, Liipfert, Bernhard, McPherson and Hand, Chartered
901 15th St., N.W., Suite 700, Washington, DC 20005
Telephone: (202) 371-6000
Registered as lobbyist at U.S. Congress.
Background: Law Clerk to the Chief Judge of the U.S. Court of Appeals, District of Columbia, 1961-63; Trial Attorney with the U.S. Dept. of Justice, 1963-67; Special Ass't to the Deputy Attorney General of the U.S., 1967-69.

DROHAN MANAGEMENT GROUP
1600 Wilson Blvd., Suite 905, Arlington, VA 22209

Telephone: (703) 525-2722
Background: An association management and government relations firm.
Members of firm representing listed organizations:
Drohan, William M., President
Background: Serves as Exec. Director, Soc. of Automotive Analysts.
Guggolz, Richard A.
Background: Serves as Exec. Director, Nat'l Ass'n of Rehabilitation Agencies and Exec. Director, American Ass'n of Surgeon's Assistants.
Clients:
American Ass'n of Surgeons Assistants (Richard A. Guggolz)
American Blood Commission (William M. Drohan)
Nat'l Ass'n of Rehabilitation Agencies (Richard A. Guggolz)

DROHAN, William M.
President, Drohan Management Group
1600 Wilson Blvd., Suite 905, Arlington, VA 22209
Telephone: (703) 525-2722
Background: Serves as Exec. Director, Soc. of Automotive Analysts.
Clients:
American Blood Commission

DROSS AND LEVENSTEIN
3016 St. Clair Dr., Temple Hills, MD 20748
Telephone: (301) 899-3330
Members of firm representing listed organizations:
Levenstein, William
Clients:
Borden Internat'l (William Levenstein)
Carborundum Co. (William Levenstein)
Commercial Solvents Corp. (William Levenstein)

DRUCKENMILLER, Robert
Porter/Novelli
1001 30th St., N.W., Washington, DC 20007
Telephone: (202) 342-7000

DRUMMOND, Anita
Legislative Assistant, Nat'l Tire Dealers and Retreaders Ass'n
1250 I St., N.W. Suite 400, Washington, DC 20005
Telephone: (202) 789-2300

DSP INTERNAT'L CONSULTANTS
777 14th St., N.W., Suite 700, Washington, DC 20005
Telephone: (202) 638-1789
Background: Provides consulting services to U.S. and European corporations, especially regarding doing business with the People's Republic of China and France.
Members of firm representing listed organizations:
Dubost, Jean Claude, President
Rahal, Pierre, Director of Communications
Clients:
Ass'n for Research on Cancer (Jean Claude Dubost, Pierre Rahal)

DUBECK, John B.
Keller and Heckman
1150 17th St., N.W. Suite 1000, Washington, DC 20036
Telephone: (202) 956-5600
Clients:
Vestal Laboratories

DUBERSTEIN GROUP, INC., THE
2100 Pennsylvania Ave., N.W. Suite 350, Washington, DC 20037
Telephone: (202) 728-1100
Background: A government relations and lobbying firm.
Members of firm representing listed organizations:
Angus, John (III)
Berman, Michael
Crippen, Dan
Duberstein, Kenneth M.
Background: Research Assistant to Senator Jacob Javits (R-NY), 1965-67. Director, Congressional and Intergovernmental Affairs, General Services Administration, 1972-76. Deputy Under Secretary of Labor, 1976-77. Deputy Assistant, 1981, and Assistant to the President for Legislative Affairs, 1981-83. Deputy Chief and Chief of Staff, The White House, 1987-89.
Kuhn, James
Clients:
Aetna Life & Casualty Co.
Consolidated Rail Corp. (CONRAIL)

General Motors Corp.
Goldman, Sachs and Co.
McCaw Cellular Communications Cos.
Monsanto Co.
Time Warner Inc. (John Angus, III)

DUBERSTEIN, Kenneth M.
Duberstein Group, Inc., The
2100 Pennsylvania Ave., N.W. Suite 350, Washington, DC 20037
Telephone: (202) 728-1100
Background: Research Assistant to Senator Jacob Javits (R-NY), 1965-67. Director, Congressional and Intergovernmental Affairs, General Services Administration, 1972-76. Deputy Under Secretary of Labor, 1976-77. Deputy Assistant, 1981, and Assistant to the President for Legislative Affairs, 1981-83. Deputy Chief and Chief of Staff, The White House, 1987-89.

DUBESTER, Ernest
Legislative Representative, AFL-CIO (American Federation of Labor and Congress of Industrial Organizations)
815 16th St., N.W., Washington, DC 20006
Telephone: (202) 637-5078
Registered as lobbyist at U.S. Congress.

DUBIN, Lawrence M.
Hopkins and Sutter
888 16th St., N.W., Suite 700, Washington, DC 20006
Telephone: (202) 835-8000
Clients:
Peoples Energy Corp.

DUBINA, Cpt. Victor
Director, Public Relations, Nat'l Guard Ass'n of the U.S.
One Massachusetts Ave., N.W., Washington, DC 20001
Telephone: (202) 789-0031

DUBOIS, Marcel
Legis Officer, Cong & Intergov't'l Affrs, DEPARTMENT OF LABOR
200 Constitution Ave., N.W., Washington, DC 20210
Telephone: (202) 523-6141

DUBOSE, William P., IV
Government Affairs Representative, Nat'l Ocean Industries Ass'n
1050 17th St., N.W. Suite 700, Washington, DC 20036
Telephone: (202) 785-5116
Registered as lobbyist at U.S. Congress.

DUBOST, Jean Claude
President, DSP Internat'l Consultants
777 14th St., N.W., Suite 700, Washington, DC 20005
Telephone: (202) 638-1789
Clients:
Ass'n for Research on Cancer

DUBOW, Sy
Legal Director, Nat'l Center for Law and the Deaf
Gallaudet University 800 Florida Ave., N.E., Washington, DC 20002
Telephone: (202) 651-5373

DUBROW, Evelyn
V. President and Legislative Director, Internat'l Ladies Garment Workers Union
815 16th St., N.W. Suite 103, Washington, DC 20006
Telephone: (202) 347-7417
Registered as lobbyist at U.S. Congress.

DUBROW, Morgan D.
Chief Engineer, Nat'l Rural Electric Cooperative Ass'n
1800 Massachusetts Ave., N.W., Washington, DC 20036
Telephone: (202) 857-9592
Registered as lobbyist at U.S. Congress.
Background: Manager, Bonneville Power Administration DC office, 1951-1957. Department of the Interior, 1957-1970. Chief, Civilian Power Applications Branch, Division of Reactor Development, AEC, 1970-1972.

DUBUC, Carroll E.
Laxalt, Washington, Perito & Dubuc
1120 Connecticut Ave., N.W., Suite 1000, Washington, DC 20036
Telephone: (202) 857-4000
Registered as Foreign Agent: (#4107).
Clients:
Air China Internat'l Corp., Ltd.

Institut de la Vie

DUCHIN, Ronald A.
Senior V. President, Mongoven, Biscoe & Duchin, Inc.
655 15th St., N.W., Suite 300, Washington, DC 20005
Telephone: (202) 639-4080
Background: Former Director of Media Relations, U.S. Department of Defense, 1979-84.

DUCKENFIELD, Thomas A.
President, Nat'l Bar Ass'n
1225 11th St., N.W., Washington, DC 20001
Telephone: (202) 842-3900

DUCKWILDER, LaVern
Secretary/Treasurer, Nat'l Center for Religious Involvement
1115 P. St., N.W., Washington, DC 20005
Telephone: (202) 667-2338

DUCKWORTH, Frank A.
President, Food and Drug Law Institute
1000 Vermont Ave., N.W., Suite 1200, Washington, DC 20005
Telephone: (202) 371-1420

DUDEN, Dana D.
Legislative Assistant, Reinsurance Ass'n of America
1819 L St., N.W., Suite 700, Washington, DC 20036
Telephone: (202) 293-3335
Registered as lobbyist at U.S. Congress.

DUDGEON, Tim
Asst. Director, Federal Gov't Relations, Distilled Spirits Council of the United States
1250 Eye St., N.W., Suite 900, Washington, DC 20005
Telephone: (202) 628-3544
Registered as lobbyist at U.S. Congress.

DUDINSKY, John, Jr.
Mica, Dudinsky & Associates
201 Massachusetts Ave., N.E., Suite C-9, Washington, DC 20002
Telephone: (202) 543-2143
Registered as lobbyist at U.S. Congress.
Background: Legislative Assistant to Rep. John H. Dent (D-PA), 1972-76. Legislative Assistant to the House Education and Labor Committee, 1978-80. Legislative Assistant to Senator Paula Hawkins (R-FL), 1980-82. Staff Director and Chief Counsel, Senate Subcommittee on Children, Family, Drugs and Alcohol and the 48-member Senate Drug Caucus, 1982-86.
Clients:
American Specialty Chemical Corp.
Antimony Products of America
Broward County, Office of the Sheriff
Champon Flavors & Fragrances
Champon Pet Products
Coopers and Lybrand
Darome, Inc.
Genix Corp.
Greater Orlando Aviation Authority
Harris Government Systems
Hvide Shipping, Inc.
IAMUS/Internat'l Unlimited

DUDLEY, Deana Francis
Schmeltzer, Aptaker and Sheppard
The Watergate, 2600 Virginia Ave., N.W., Washington, DC 20037
Telephone: (202) 333-8800
Clients:
Maritima Transligra

DUENSING, Hollis G.
General Solicitor, Ass'n of American Railroads
50 F St., N.W., Suite 12302, Washington, DC 20001
Telephone: (202) 639-2506
Registered as lobbyist at U.S. Congress.

DUFEK, Paul C.
Exec. V. President and Treasurer, Nat'l Alcoholic Beverage Control Ass'n
4216 King St. West, Alexandria, VA 22302-1507
Telephone: (703) 578-4200

DUFF, Daniel
Asst Chief Counsel, Off of Chief Counsel, DEPARTMENT OF TRANSPORTATION - Urban Mass Transportation Administration
400 Seventh St., S.W., Washington, DC 20590
Telephone: (202) 366-4011

DUFF, Michael J.
V. President, Public Affairs, SAMA Group of Ass'ns
225 Reinekers Lane Suite 625, Washington, DC 22314
Telephone: (703) 836-1360
Registered as lobbyist at U.S. Congress.
Background: Staff Member, Subcommittee on Investigations, House Interstate and Foreign Commerce Committee, 1971. Serves also as Director, Analytical Instruments Ass'n.

DUFFY, Daniel A.
Government Relations Associate, Rubber Manufacturers Ass'n
1400 K St., N.W., Washington, DC 20005
Telephone: (202) 682-4800
Registered as lobbyist at U.S. Congress.

DUFFY, Dennis M.
Director, Cong Relations, DEPARTMENT OF VETERANS AFFAIRS
810 Vermont Ave., N.W., Washington, DC 20420
Telephone: (202) 233-2831

DUFFY, Henry A.
President, Air Line Pilots Ass'n Internat'l
1625 Massachusetts Ave., N.W., Washington, DC 20036
Telephone: (202) 797-4003
Background: Also represenets the Air Line Pilots Political Action Committee.

DUFFY, Jennifer E.
Account Executive, Hill and Knowlton Public Affairs Worldwide
Washington Harbour, 901 31st St., N.W., Washington, DC 20007
Telephone: (202) 333-7400
Registered as Foreign Agent: (#4170).
Background: Office of Public Liaison, USIA/Voice of America, 1983-85. Spokesperson/Regional Communications Assistant, 1985-87 and Deputy Director for Press Relations, 1987-88, Republican Senatorial Committee.

DUFFY, Richard E.
Rep. for Fed. Assistance, Dept. of Educ., United States Catholic Conference
3211 4th St., N.E., Washington, DC 20017
Telephone: (202) 541-3148
Background: Also represents the Nat'l Conference of Catholic Bishops.

DUFFY, Richard M.
Occupatonal Safety and Health Director, Internat'l Ass'n of Fire Fighters
1750 New York Ave., N.W., Washington, DC 20006
Telephone: (202) 737-8484

DUFFY, Stephen C.
Asst. Dir., Dept. of Congress'l Affairs, American Medical Ass'n
1101 Vermont Ave., N.W., Washington, DC 20005
Telephone: (202) 789-7400
Registered as lobbyist at U.S. Congress.

DUFFY, Thomas N.
Nat'l Center for Municipal Development
1620 Eye St., N.W., Suite 300, Washington, DC 20006
Telephone: (202) 429-0160
Clients:
Fort Worth, Texas, City of
Nat'l Organization to Insure a Sound-Controlled Environment-N.O.I.S.E.
Sparks, Nevada, City of

DUGAN, Robert P., Jr.
Director, Office of Public Affairs, Nat'l Ass'n of Evangelicals
1023 15th St., N.W., Suite 500, Washington, DC 20005
Telephone: (202) 789-1011

DUGGAN, C. Ray
Regional Legislative Director, Transportation, Communications Internat'l Union
815 16th St., N.W. Suite 511, Washington, DC 20036
Telephone: (202) 783-3660
Registered as lobbyist at U.S. Congress.

DUGGER, Robert H.
Chief Economist. Dir., Policy Develop't, American Bankers Ass'n
1120 Connecticut Ave., N.W., Washington, DC 20036
Telephone: (202) 663-5000
Registered as lobbyist at U.S. Congress.
Background: Former Chief Economist, U.S. Senate Committee on Banking, Housing and Urban Affairs.

DUGGIN, Thelma
Director, Political Outreach, Republican Nat'l Committee
310 First St., S.E., Washington, DC 20003
Telephone: (202) 863-8500

DUKA, Walter E.
Exec. V. President, Barksdale Ballard & Co.
8027 Leesburg Pike Suite 200, Vienna, VA 22182
Telephone: (703) 827-8771
Background: Information Director, President's Consumer Committee, 1965-67. Assistant Press Secretary for Communications, 1973-76 and 1978-82. Assistant Press Secretary to President Jimmy Carter, 1977. Assistant Postmaster General for International Affairs, 1982-88.
Clients:
American Ass'n of State Highway and Transportation Officials

DUKE, Debbie
Co-Director, American Labor Education Center
1730 Connecticut Ave., N.W., Washington, DC 20009
Telephone: (202) 387-6780

DULA, Brig. Gen. Brett M.
Dep Dir, Legis Liaison, DEPARTMENT OF AIR FORCE
The Pentagon, Washington, DC 20330
Telephone: (202) 697-8153

DUMELLE, Fran
Director of Government Relations, American Lung Ass'n/American Thoracic Soc.
1726 M St., N.W. Suite 902, Washington, DC 20005
Telephone: (202) 785-3355
Registered as lobbyist at U.S. Congress.

DUNAWAY & CROSS
1146 19th St., N.W. Suite 400, Washington, DC 20036
Telephone: (202) 862-9700
Members of firm representing listed organizations:
Dunaway, Mac S.
Clients:
Aerospace Industries Ass'n of America *(Mac S. Dunaway)*
American Electric Power Service Corp. *(Mac S. Dunaway)*
American Mining Congress *(Mac S. Dunaway)*
Avianca Airlines *(Mac S. Dunaway)*
Crown Controls Corp. *(Mac S. Dunaway)*
Edgell Communications *(Mac S. Dunaway)*
Florida Power and Light Co. *(Mac S. Dunaway)*
Industrial Truck Ass'n *(Mac S. Dunaway)*
Lord Corp. *(Mac S. Dunaway)*
Portable Power Equipment Manufacturers Ass'n *(Mac S. Dunaway)*
Southern Company Services, Inc. *(Mac S. Dunaway)*
Walbro Corp. *(Mac S. Dunaway)*

DUNAWAY, Mac S.
Dunaway & Cross
1146 19th St., N.W. Suite 400, Washington, DC 20036
Telephone: (202) 862-9700
Registered as lobbyist at U.S. Congress.
Clients:
Aerospace Industries Ass'n of America
American Electric Power Service Corp.
American Mining Congress
Avianca Airlines
Crown Controls Corp.
Edgell Communications
Florida Power and Light Co.
Industrial Truck Ass'n
Lord Corp.
Portable Power Equipment Manufacturers Ass'n

Southern Company Services, Inc.
Walbro Corp.

DUNBAR, Amy K.
Director, Governmental Affairs, Nat'l Ass'n of Bond Lawyers
2000 Pennsylvania Ave., N.W., Suite 9000, Washington, DC 20006
Telephone: (202) 778-2244
Registered as lobbyist at U.S. Congress.
Background: Legislative Correspondent/Analysts to Senator Paul Tsongas (D-MA), 1979-81. Social Science Analyst, U.S. Department of Transportation, 1981-83.

DUNBAR, James R.
Director, Washington Operations, Learjet Corp.
1825 Eye St., Suite 400, Washington, DC 20006
Telephone: (202) 331-1610

DUNCAN, ALLEN AND TALMAGE
1575 Eye St., N.W., Suite 300, Washington, DC 20005
Telephone: (202) 289-8400
Members of firm representing listed organizations:
Allen, Donald R.
Duncan, C. Emerson (II)

DUNCAN AND ASSOCIATES
1213 29th St., N.W., Washington, DC 20007
Telephone: (202) 333-5841
Members of firm representing listed organizations:
Amhaus, Dean
Duncan, Jack G.
Background: An attorney specializing in public interest law. Counsel and Staff Director, House Subcommittee on Select Education, 1969-79; Legislative Assistant, Social and Rehabilitative Service, HEW, 1968-69; Chief Legislative Officer, Rehabilitation Services Administration, HEW, 1967-68; Attorney, Foreign Claims Settlement Commission, Department of State, 1964-67.
Clients:
American Council for the Arts
Conference of Educational Administrators Serving the Deaf
Federation of State Humanities Councils
Nat'l Ass'n of Private Residential Resources
Nat'l Council on Rehabilitation Education
Nat'l Head Injury Foundation
Nat'l Rehabilitation Ass'n
Nat'l Rehabilitation Political Action Committee
Self Help for Hard of Hearing People

DUNCAN, Bonnie
Director, Communications, Nat'l Electrical Contractors Ass'n
13th floor, 7315 Wisconsin Ave., Bethesda, MD 20814
Telephone: (301) 657-3110

DUNCAN, C. Emerson, II
Duncan, Allen and Talmage
1575 Eye St., N.W., Suite 300, Washington, DC 20005
Telephone: (202) 289-8400
Registered as Foreign Agent: (#3505).

DUNCAN, Charles T.
Counsel, Reid & Priest
1111 19th St., N.W., Washington, DC 20036
Telephone: (202) 828-0100
Background: General Counsel, U.S. Equal Employment Opportunity Commission, 1965-66. Corporation Counsel, District of Columbia, 1966-70.
Clients:
Broadcast Music Inc.

DUNCAN, Don R.
Dir., Federal Tax & Nat. Resource Issues, Phillips Petroleum Co.
1776 Eye St., N.W. Suite 700, Washington, DC 20006
Telephone: (202) 833-0900
Registered as lobbyist at U.S. Congress.

DUNCAN, Harley T.
Exec. Director, Federation of Tax Administrators
444 North Capitol St., N.W., Suite 334, Washington, DC 20001
Telephone: (202) 624-5890

DUNCAN, Jack G.
Duncan and Associates
1213 29th St., N.W., Washington, DC 20007
Telephone: (202) 333-5841
Background: An attorney specializing in public interest law. Counsel and Staff Director, House Subcommittee on Select Education, 1969-79; Legislative Assistant, Social and Rehabilitative Service, HEW, 1968-69; Chief Legislative Officer, Rehabilitation Services Administration, HEW, 1967-68; Attorney, Foreign Claims Settlement Commission, Department of State, 1964-67.

DUNCAN, John
Dir, Legis & Public Affrs, DEPARTMENT OF AGRICULTURE - Animal and Plant Health Inspection Service
14th and Independence Ave. S.W., Room 1147 South Bldg., Washington, DC 20250
Telephone: (202) 447-2511

DUNCAN, Mallory B.
Attorney, Penney Co., J. C.
Suite 1015, 1156 15th St., N.W., Washington, DC 20005
Telephone: (202) 862-4833

DUNCAN, R. Michael
Cleary, Gottlieb, Steen and Hamilton
1752 N St., N.W., Washington, DC 20036
Telephone: (202) 728-2700
Registered as lobbyist at U.S. Congress.
Background: Trial Attorney, Tax Division, Department of Justice, 1958-62.

DUNCAN, Wallace L.
Duncan, Weinberg, Miller & Pembroke, P.C.
1615 M St., N.W., Suite 800, Washington, DC 20036-3203
Telephone: (202) 467-6370
Registered as Foreign Agent: (#2763).
Background: Special Assistant to the Solicitor, Department of the Interior, 1962-1965.
Clients:
Arkansas Public Service Commission
Delaware Municipal Electric Corp. (DEMEC)
Endicott, New York, Municipality of
Freeport, New York, Village of
Jamestown, New York, City of
Lubbock, Brownfield, Floyada and Tulia, Texas, Municipalities of
Lubbock Power and Light
Massena, New York, Town of
Modesto Irrigation District
MSR Public Power Agency
Municipal Electric Utilities Ass'n of New York State
Newark, Seaford, Smyrna, Middletown, Dover, Lewes, Clayton, New Castle & Milford, Delaware, Municipalities of
Penn Yan, New York, Municipality of
Plattsburgh, New York, Municipality of
Santa Clara, California, City of
Transmission Agency of Northern California
Tupper Lake, New York, Municipality of
Watkins Glen, New York, Municipality of

DUNCAN, WEINBERG, MILLER & PEMBROKE, P.C.
1615 M St., N.W., Suite 800, Washington, DC 20036-3203
Telephone: (202) 467-6370
Members of firm representing listed organizations:
Allan, Richmond F.
  Background: Assistant U.S. Attorney, District of Montana, 1961-64. Trial Attorney, U.S. Department of Justice, 1965. Associate Solicitor, 1965-67, and Deputy Solicitor, 1968. Indian Affairs, Department of Interior.
Duncan, Wallace L.
  Background: Special Assistant to the Solicitor, Department of the Interior, 1962-1965.
Genzer, Jeffrey C.
  Background: Staff Counsel, Nat'l Governors' Ass'n, Energy and Environment Committee, 1983-85.
Lower, Janice L.
Miller, Frederick L. (Jr.)
  Background: Trial Attorney Land and Natural Resources Division Department of Justice, 1970-74.
Pembroke, James D.
Weinberg, Edward
  Background: Dep't of the Interior, Attorney, 1944-1951 and Assistant Chief Counsel, 1951-54 Bureau of Reclamation; Assistant Solicitor, Branch of Power, 1955-

1961; Associate Solicitor, Water and Power, 1961-1963; Deputy Solicitor, 1963-1968; Solicitor, 1968-1969. Principal Consultant, The Nat'l Water Commission, 1969-1973.
Weinberg, Robert
Clients:
Allegheny Electric Cooperative, Inc. (*Robert Weinberg*)
Arkansas Public Service Commission (*Wallace L. Duncan, Janice L. Lower, James D. Pembroke*)
Auburn, Avilla, Bluffton, Columbia City and Other Indiana Municipalities (*Janice L. Lower, James D. Pembroke*)
Basin Electric Power Cooperative (*Richmond F. Allan, Edward Weinberg*)
Beard Oil Co. (*Richmond F. Allan, Edward Weinberg*)
Bentonville, Arkansas, City of (*Robert Weinberg*)
Cajun Rural Electric Power Cooperative, Inc. (*James D. Pembroke, Robert Weinberg*)
Central Montana Electric Power Cooperative, Inc. (*Janice L. Lower, James D. Pembroke*)
Central Virginia Electric Cooperative, Inc. (*Robert Weinberg*)
Colorado River Commission of Nevada (*Frederick L. Miller, Jr., Edward Weinberg*)
Craig-Botetourt Electric Cooperative (*Robert Weinberg*)
Delaware Municipal Electric Corp. (DEMEC) (*Wallace L. Duncan, Janice L. Lower*)
Derby Line, Vermont, Town of (*Richmond F. Allan*)
Endicott, New York, Municipality of (*Wallace L. Duncan, Jeffrey C. Genzer*)
Freeport, New York, Village of (*Wallace L. Duncan, Jeffrey C. Genzer*)
Illinois Department of Energy and Natural Resources (*Jeffrey C. Genzer*)
Indiana and Michigan Municipal Distributors Ass'n (*Janice L. Lower, James D. Pembroke*)
Jamestown, New York, City of (*Wallace L. Duncan, Jeffrey C. Genzer, Frederick L. Miller, Jr.*)
Kenai Natives Ass'n, Inc. (*Richmond F. Allan, Edward Weinberg*)
Lake Andes-Wagner Water Systems, Inc. (*Frederick L. Miller, Jr., Edward Weinberg*)
Lubbock, Brownfield, Floyada and Tulia, Texas, Municipalities of (*Wallace L. Duncan, Robert Weinberg*)
Lubbock Power and Light (*Wallace L. Duncan, Janice L. Lower, Robert Weinberg*)
Massena, New York, Town of (*Wallace L. Duncan, Jeffrey C. Genzer*)
Mid-West Electric Consumers Ass'n (*Frederick L. Miller, Jr., Edward Weinberg*)
Modesto Irrigation District (*Wallace L. Duncan, James D. Pembroke*)
Montana Electric Power Cooperatives Ass'n (*Janice L. Lower, James D. Pembroke*)
MSR Public Power Agency (*Wallace L. Duncan, Frederick L. Miller, Jr.*)
Municipal Electric Utilities Ass'n of New York State (*Wallace L. Duncan, Jeffrey C. Genzer*)
Nat'l Ass'n of State Energy Officials (*Jeffrey C. Genzer*)
Newark, Delaware, City of (*Janice L. Lower, Frederick L. Miller, Jr.*)
Newark, Seaford, Smyrna, Middletown, Dover, Lewes, Clayton, New Castle & Milford, Delaware, Municipalities of (*Wallace L. Duncan, Janice L. Lower*)
Niles, Michigan, Utilities Department of (*Janice L. Lower, James D. Pembroke*)
Penn Yan, New York, Municipality of (*Wallace L. Duncan, Jeffrey C. Genzer*)
Plattsburgh, New York, Municipality of (*Wallace L. Duncan, Jeffrey C. Genzer*)
Santa Clara, California, City of (*Wallace L. Duncan, James D. Pembroke*)
Seaford, Delaware, City of (*Janice L. Lower, Frederick L. Miller, Jr.*)
Southern Maryland Electric Cooperative, Inc. (*Jeffrey C. Genzer, Robert Weinberg*)
Sturgis, Michigan, Municipality of (*Janice L. Lower, James D. Pembroke*)
Transmission Agency of Northern California (*Wallace L. Duncan, James D. Pembroke, Edward Weinberg*)
Tupper Lake, New York, Municipality of (*Wallace L. Duncan, Jeffrey C. Genzer*)

Watkins Glen, New York, Municipality of (*Wallace L. Duncan, Jeffrey C. Genzer*)
Web Water Development Ass'n (*Richmond F. Allan, Edward Weinberg*)
Western Fuels Ass'n (*Frederick L. Miller, Jr., Edward Weinberg*)

DUNCAN, William C.
Deputy General Director, Japan Automobile Manufacturers Ass'n
1050 17th St., N.W. Suite 410, Washington, DC 20036
Telephone: (202) 296-8537
Registered as lobbyist at U.S. Congress.
Registered as Foreign Agent: (#3101)

DUNGAN, Arthur E.
V. Pres., Safety, Health & Environment, Chlorine Institute
2001 L St., N.W., Suite 506, Washington, DC 20036
Telephone: (202) 775-2790

DUNGAN, Diane R.
Director, Government Relations, Chlorine Institute
2001 L St., N.W., Suite 506, Washington, DC 20036
Telephone: (202) 775-2790
Registered as lobbyist at U.S. Congress.

DUNLAP & BROWDER, INC.
418 10th St., S.E., Washington, DC 20003
Telephone: (202) 546-3720
Background: Natural resources, energy and environmental consulting and legislative and regulatory strategies. Clients include aerospace, chemical, utility, mining, oil and gas companies; industry and public interest associations.
Members of firm representing listed organizations:
Browder, Joseph B., Partner
  Background: Former Special Assistant to the Assistant Secretary for Land and Water, Department of Interior, 1977-81. Cofounder and former President (1972-76), Environmental Policy Institute.
Dunlap, Louise C., Partner
  Background: Cofounder and former President (1976-85), Environmental Policy Institute.
Clients:
Acurex Corp.

DUNLAP, Louise C.
Partner, Dunlap & Browder, Inc.
418 10th St., S.E., Washington, DC 20003
Telephone: (202) 546-3720
Registered as lobbyist at U.S. Congress.
Background: Cofounder and former President (1976-85), Environmental Policy Institute.

DUNLEAVY, Liz
Ass'n Management Specialists
1717 Largo Rd., Upper Marboro, MD 20772
Telephone: (301) 659-1474

DUNLOP, Becky Norton
Sr. Fellow, Envir. & Natural Res. Policy, Citizens for a Sound Economy
470 L'Enfant Plaza East, S.W. Suite 7112, Washington, DC 20024
Telephone: (202) 488-8200
Background: Former Asssistant Secretary of Interior for Fish and Wildlife and Parks.

DUNN, Anita B.
Communications Director, Democratic Senatorial Campaign Committee
430 South Capitol St., S.E., Washington, DC 20003
Telephone: (202) 224-2447

DUNN, Christopher A.
Willkie Farr and Gallagher
1155 21st St., N.W., 6th Fl., Washington, DC 20036-3302
Telephone: (202) 328-8000
Registered as Foreign Agent: (#3765).
Clients:
AOC Internat'l, Inc.
Frutropic, S.A.
Kobe Steel Co.
Louis Dreyfus Corp.
Sampo Corp.
Silver Reed America
Standard Commerical Tobacco Co.
Stelco, Inc.
Sucocitrico Cutrale
Sun Moon Star Group

DUNN, Christopher A. (Cont'd)
Tatung Co.

DUNN, David E., III
Patton, Boggs and Blow
2550 M St., N.W., Suite 800, Washington, DC 20037
Telephone: (202) 457-6000
Registered as lobbyist at U.S. Congress.
Registered as Foreign Agent: (#2165).
Background: Assistant Attorney General, State of Alabama, 1975-76. Assistant to President, Overseas Private Investment Corp., 1977.
Clients:
Fiart Cantieri Italiani S.p.A.
Fundacion Pro-Imagen de Colombia en el Exterior
Oman, Embassy of the Sultanate of
Spain, Government of

DUNN, H. Stewart, Jr.
Ivins, Phillips and Barker
1700 Pennsylvania Ave., N.W., Suite 600, Washington, DC 20006
Telephone: (202) 393-7600
Registered as lobbyist at U.S. Congress.
Clients:
Rochester Tax Council

DUNN, J. Michael
President, Can Manufacturers Institute
1625 Massachusetts Ave., N.W., Suite 500, Washington, DC 20036
Telephone: (201) 232-4677

DUNN, James M.
Exec. Director, Baptist Joint Committee on Public Affairs
200 Maryland Ave., N.E. Suite 303, Washington, DC 20002
Telephone: (202) 544-4226

DUNN, Jean B.
V. President, Development & Admin., Nat'l Democratic Institute for Internat'l Affairs
1717 Massachusetts Ave., N.W. Suite 605, Washington, DC 20036
Telephone: (202) 328-3136

DUNN, Jeffrey A.
Venable, Baetjer, Howard and Civiletti
1201 New York Ave., N.W., Suite 1000, Washington, DC 20005
Telephone: (202) 962-4800

DUNN, Mari Lee
Vice President, American Council for Capital Formation
1850 K St., N.W. Suite 400, Washington, DC 20006
Telephone: (202) 293-5811
Registered as lobbyist at U.S. Congress.

DUNN, Mary Mitchell
Federal Regulatory Counsel, Credit Union Nat'l Ass'n
805 15th St., N.W. Suite 300, Washington, DC 20005
Telephone: (202) 682-4200

DUNN, Michael V
V. President, Legislative Services, Nat'l Farmers Union
600 Maryland Ave., S.W., Suite 202W, Washington, DC 20024
Telephone: (202) 554-1600
Registered as lobbyist at U.S. Congress.

DUNNAN, Weaver W.
Covington and Burling
1201 Pennsylvania Ave., N.W., Box 7566, Washington, DC 20044
Telephone: (202) 662-6000

DUNNE, John H.
Secy.-Treas., Internat'l Federation of Professional and Technical Engineers
8701 Georgia Ave., Suite 701, Silver Spring, MD 20910
Telephone: (301) 565-9016
Registered as lobbyist at U.S. Congress.
Background: Responsible for Internat'l Federation of Professional and Technical Engineers LEAP-PAC.

DUNNIGAN, John H.
Cong Affrs Officer, DEPARTMENT OF COMMERCE - Nat'l Marine Fisheries Service
1335 East-West Hwy., Silver Spring, MD 20917
Telephone: (301) 427-2263

DUPONT, Daniel
Burson-Marsteller
1850 M St., N.W., Suite 900, Washington, DC 20036
Telephone: (202) 833-8550

DUPREE, James A.
Director, National Affairs Office, Ford Motor Co.
1350 Eye St., N.W. Suite 1000, Washington, DC 20005
Telephone: (202) 962-5400
Registered as lobbyist at U.S. Congress.

DUPREE, Robert F., Jr.
Government Relations Associate, American Textile Manufacturers Institute
1801 K St., N.W. Suite 900, Washington, DC 20006
Telephone: (202) 862-0500
Registered as lobbyist at U.S. Congress.
Background: Former Legislative Director for Rep. Bill Chappell, Jr. (D-FL).

DURANT, Andrew G.
V. President, Hill and Knowlton Public Affairs Worldwide
Washington Harbour, 901 31st St., N.W., Washington, DC 20007
Telephone: (202) 333-7400
Background: Legislative Assistant to Rep. Clive Benedict (R-WV), 1980-81. Press and Legislative Assistant to Rep. E. Thomas Coleman (R-MO), 1982-84.
Clients:
Hitachi Research Institute
Japan Trade Center
Toyota Motor Corp.

DURANT, Gail D.
Exec. Director, Federated Ambulatory Surgery Ass'n
700 N. Fairfax St., Suite 520, Alexandria, VA 22314
Telephone: (703) 836-8808

DURANT, Jean
Cong Liaison Div, ENVIRONMENTAL PROTECTION AGENCY
401 M St., S.W., Washington, DC 20460
Telephone: (202) 382-5200

DURANTE ASSOCIATES
1129 20th St., N.W. Suite 500, Washington, DC 20036
Telephone: (202) 822-1713
Members of firm representing listed organizations:
Durante, Douglas A.
Background: Nat'l Transportation Policy Study Commission, 1977-79; Director of Public Affairs, Nat'l Alcohol Fuels Commission, 1979-81; U.S. Department of Energy, 1981-82. Also a partner in the Denver, Colorado consulting firm of Stratton, Reiter, Dupree & Durante.
Durante, Raymond W.
Background: Former Special Projects Manager, US Department of Interior.
Clients:
AECL Research Co.
American Nuclear Soc.
Atomic Energy of Canada Ltd.
Avac Systems, Inc.
Carlucci Construction Co.
Clean Fuels Development Coalition

DURANTE, Douglas A.
Durante Associates
1129 20th St., N.W. Suite 500, Washington, DC 20036
Telephone: (202) 822-1713
Registered as lobbyist at U.S. Congress.
Background: Nat'l Transportation Policy Study Commission, 1977-79; Director of Public Affairs, Nat'l Alcohol Fuels Commission, 1979-81; U.S. Department of Energy, 1981-82. Also a partner in the Denver, Colorado consulting firm of Stratton, Reiter, Dupree & Durante.

DURANTE, Raymond W.
Durante Associates
1129 20th St., N.W. Suite 500, Washington, DC 20036
Telephone: (202) 822-1713
Background: Former Special Projects Manager, US Department of Interior.

DURBOROW, Margaret C.
President, Chief Operating Officer, Cable Television Administration and Marketing Soc.
635 Slaters Lane, Suite 250, Alexandria, VA 22314
Telephone: (703) 549-4200

DURDEN, Lou
Prog. Dir., Community & Ext'l Programs, Internat'l Business Machines Corp.
1801 K St., N.W., Suite 1200, Washington, DC 20006
Telephone: (202) 778-5000

DURHAM, R. V.
Director, Safety and Health Department, Internat'l Brotherhood of Teamsters, Chauffeurs, Warehousemen and Helpers of America
25 Louisiana Ave., N.W., Washington, DC 20001
Telephone: (202) 624-6800

DURKIN, Ed
Coordinator of Special Projects, United Brotherhood of Carpenters and Joiners of America
101 Constitution Ave., N.W., Washington, DC 20001
Telephone: (202) 546-6206
Registered as lobbyist at U.S. Congress.

DUROCHER, Cort
Exec. Director, American Institute of Aeronautics and Astronautics
370 L'Enfant Promenade, Washington, DC 20004
Telephone: (202) 646-7400

DURSO, Emily F.
Exec. V. President, Hotel Ass'n of Washington
1201 New York Ave., N.W. Suite 601, Washington, DC 20005
Telephone: (202) 289-3141

DURST, Joseph L.
Dir., Occupational Safety and Health, United Brotherhood of Carpenters and Joiners of America
101 Constitution Ave., N.W., Washington, DC 20001
Telephone: (202) 546-6206

DUTILH, Katherine D.
Lobbyist, Milliken and Co.
1100 Connecticut Ave., N.W. 13th Floor, Washington, DC 20036
Telephone: (202) 543-9374
Registered as lobbyist at U.S. Congress.

DUTKO & ASSOCIATES
412 First St., S.E. Suite 100, Washington, DC 20003
Telephone: (202) 484-4884
Members of firm representing listed organizations:
Armstrong, Jack, Staff Assistant
Dutko, Daniel A., Managing Partner, President
Background: Former Administrative Assistant to Sen. Donald Stewart of Alabama, 1978-80. Former Administrative Assistant to Rep. Robert Krueger of Texas, 1975-78.
Goodman, Susan, Associate
Hankla, L. L. Hank, Partner, V. President, General Counsel
Background: Former Enforcement Attorney, Environmental Protection Agency. Formerly on the staffs of Sen. Mike Monroney and Sen. Fred R. Harris, both of Oklahoma.
McKenney, William R., Senior Associate
Background: Former Press Secretary to Rep. Clarence Brown (R-OH), 1982; Legislative/Communications Director to Rep. Tom Kindness (R-OH), 1983-84; Legislative Director to Rep. Rod Chandler (R-WA), 1985-90.
Perry, Steve, Partner, V. President
Background: Former Legis. Ass't to Senator John Heinz (R-PA), 1980-83.
Raffensperger, Juliette, Associate
Background: Former Professional Staff member, Senate Commerce Committee, 1984-87.
Seely, Richard L., V. President
Background: Former Coordinator of Plans and Programs, World Tourism Organization, 1980-83; Consultant to U.S. Travel and Tourism Administration, 1984; Assistant Secretary of Commerce, 1985-88.
Young, Emily, Senior Associate
Background: Former Special Assistant to U.S. Senate Energy and Natural Resources Committee, 1984-85; Legislative Assistant to Rep. Billy Tauzin (D-LA),

1985-89.

Clients:
American Iron and Steel Institute *(Emily Young)*
American Nuclear Energy Council *(Daniel A. Dutko)*
Anchor Industries, Inc. *(L. L. Hank Hankla)*
Ass'n of Oil Pipe Lines *(Emily Young)*
Ass'n of Progressive Rental Organizations
Bedford Group *(L. L. Hank Hankla)*
Building Industry Ass'n of Southern California *(L. L. Hank Hankla)*
CITGO Petroleum Corp. *(Daniel A. Dutko)*
Communications Satellite Corp. (COMSAT) *(Steve Perry)*
Council for Solid Waste Solutions *(Emily Young)*
Council of Great Lakes Governors *(Richard L. Seely)*
Creditors Alliance to Preserve Freight Undercharge Assets *(Emily Young)*
DSC Communications Corp. *(Steve Perry)*
Grenada, Government of *(L. L. Hank Hankla)*
H.C. Internat'l Trade, Inc. *(Daniel A. Dutko)*
Internat'l Craniofacial Foundations *(Daniel A. Dutko)*
Internat'l Telecharge, Inc. *(Steve Perry)*
Jewish Nat'l Fund *(Daniel A. Dutko, Susan Goodman, Richard L. Seely)*
Lusk Company, The *(L. L. Hank Hankla)*
McDonald's Corp. *(Emily Young)*
Nat'l Cellular Resellers Ass'n *(Steve Perry)*
Pacificare Health Systems, Inc. *(Emily Young)*
Phoenix Mutual Life Insurance Co. *(Daniel A. Dutko, William R. McKenney)*
Puerto Rico, Senate of *(Richard L. Seely)*
Rmax, Inc. *(L. L. Hank Hankla)*
Satellite Broadcasting and Communications Ass'n *(Emily Young)*
Waste Conversion Systems, Inc. *(L. L. Hank Hankla)*
Yavapai Telephone Exchange *(Daniel A. Dutko, Steve Perry)*

DUTKO, Daniel A.
Managing Partner, President, Dutko & Associates
412 First St., S.E. Suite 100, Washington, DC 20003
Telephone: (202) 484-4884
Registered as lobbyist at U.S. Congress.
Background: Former Administrative Assistant to Sen. Donald Stewart of Alabama, 1978-80. Former Administrative Assistant to Rep. Robert Krueger of Texas, 1975-78.
Clients:
American Nuclear Energy Council
CITGO Petroleum Corp.
H.C. Internat'l Trade, Inc.
Internat'l Craniofacial Foundations
Jewish Nat'l Fund
Phoenix Mutual Life Insurance Co.
Yavapai Telephone Exchange

DUTTON AND DUTTON, P.C.
1507 Tilden St., N.W., Washington, DC 20016
Telephone: (202) 686-3500
Members of firm representing listed organizations:
Dutton, Frederick G.
   Background: Special Assistant to the President, 1961-1962. Assistant Secretary of State for Congressional Relations, 1962-1964.
Clients:
PETROMIN *(Frederick G. Dutton)*
Saudi Basic Industries Corp. *(Frederick G. Dutton)*

DUTTON, Frederick G.
Dutton and Dutton, P.C.
1507 Tilden St., N.W., Washington, DC 20016
Telephone: (202) 686-3500
Registered as Foreign Agent: (#2591).
Background: Special Assistant to the President, 1961-1962. Assistant Secretary of State for Congressional Relations, 1962-1964.
Clients:
PETROMIN
Saudi Basic Industries Corp.

DUVAL, William A.
President, Internat'l Brotherhood of Painters and Allied Trades
1750 New York Ave., N.W., Washington, DC 20006
Telephone: (202) 637-0700

DUVALL, Donald
President, Inter-American Bar Ass'n
1889 F St., N.W. Suite LL2, Washington, DC 20006

Telephone: (202) 789-2747
Background: Serves also as member of the Council of the Inter-American Bar Ass'n. Former Chief Administrative Law Judge, U.S. International Trade Commission.

DUXBURY, Lloyd L.
Legislative Representative, Nat'l Committee to Preserve Social Security and Medicare
2000 K St., N.W. Suite 800, Washington, DC 20006
Telephone: (202) 822-9459
Registered as lobbyist at U.S. Congress.

DWORKIN, Douglas
Arnold & Porter
1200 New Hampshire Ave., N.W., Washington, DC 20036
Telephone: (202) 872-6700
Registered as lobbyist at U.S. Congress.
Registered as Foreign Agent: (#1750).
Clients:
Panama, Government of

DWOSKIN, Gary
President, Nat'l Assistance Management Ass'n
Box 57051, Washington, DC 20037
Telephone: (202) 223-1448

DWYER, Denis J.
Chief Operating Officer, McNair Group Inc.
1155 15th St., N.W., Washington, DC 20005
Telephone: (202) 659-8866
Registered as lobbyist at U.S. Congress.
Clients:
Gateway Freight Services Inc.
Harmon Industries, Inc.
Hawaii Department of Transportation
Paine Webber Group
Puerto Rico Ports Authority
Railstar Control Technology, Inc.
World Airways

DWYER, Roderick T.
Assistant V. President, American Mining Congress
1920 N St., N.W. Suite 300, Washington, DC 20036
Telephone: (202) 861-2800
Registered as lobbyist at U.S. Congress.

DWYER, Shawn F.
Director of Public Relations, Regular Common Carrier Conference
2200 Mill Road Suite 350, Alexandria, VA 22314
Telephone: (703) 838-1967

DWYER, Thomas J.
State Legislative Director-Minnesota, Transportation, Communications Internat'l Union
815 16th St., N.W. Suite 511, Washington, DC 20036
Telephone: (202) 783-3660

DWYER, Thomas R.
Arnold & Porter
1200 New Hampshire Ave., N.W., Washington, DC 20036
Telephone: (202) 872-6700
Registered as lobbyist at U.S. Congress.
Clients:
Continental Corp., The
Golodetz Corp.

DYE, Alan P.
Webster, Chamberlain and Bean
1747 Pennsylvania Ave., N.W., Suite 1000, Washington, DC 20006
Telephone: (202) 785-9500
Clients:
Nat'l Tooling and Machining Ass'n

DYE, Stuart S.
Graham and James
2000 M St., N.W., Suite 700, Washington, DC 20036
Telephone: (202) 463-0800
Background: Secretary, Navy Staff, Deep Submergence Systems Review Group, Office of Legislative Affairs, 1963-64. Special Assistant for Law of the Sea Matters, International Law Division, Office of the Judge Advocate General, 1965-66.
Clients:
Internat'l Ass'n of Independent Tanker Owners

DYER, ELLIS, JOSEPH & MILLS
600 New Hampshire Ave., N.W., Suite 1000, Washington, DC 20037
Telephone: (202) 944-3040
Registered as Foreign Agent: (#4121)
Background: A law firm specializing in international trade and finance.
Members of firm representing listed organizations:
Dyer, Thomas M.
Ellis, James B. (II)
Joseph, Michael
   Background: Attorney, Office of the General Counsel, Securities and Exchange Commission, 1961-66.
Mills, Thomas L.
Vine, Howard A.
Clients:
Ace Frosty Shipping Co., Ltd. *(Thomas M. Dyer, James B. Ellis, II, Michael Joseph, Thomas L. Mills, Howard A. Vine)*
Alliance for Corporate Growth *(Howard A. Vine)*
Apex Marine Co. *(Thomas L. Mills)*
Atlantic Richfield Company (ARCO) Marine Co. *(Thomas L. Mills)*
Bay Area Renal Stone Center *(Thomas L. Mills)*
Bender Shipbuilding & Repair Co., Inc. *(Thomas L. Mills)*
Bobbie Brooks *(Howard A. Vine)*
Bristol Bay Native Corp. *(Thomas L. Mills)*
Competitive Health Care Coalition *(Thomas L. Mills, Howard A. Vine)*
Crowley Maritime Corp. *(Thomas L. Mills)*
Internat'l Ass'n of Independent Tanker Owners
Liberty Shipping Group
Medical Care Internat'l *(Thomas L. Mills)*
PubCo Corp. *(Howard A. Vine)*
Renal Physican Ass'n *(Thomas L. Mills)*
Smith Corona Corp. *(Howard A. Vine)*
Torrington Co. *(Howard A. Vine)*
Trunkline LNG Co.
T2 Medical
Viktor Lenac Shipyard

DYER, James W.
Director, Washington Relations, Philip Morris Management Corp.
1341 G St., N.W., Suite 900, Washington, DC 20005
Telephone: (202) 637-1500
Registered as lobbyist at U.S. Congress.

DYER, Thomas M.
Dyer, Ellis, Joseph & Mills
600 New Hampshire Ave., N.W., Suite 1000, Washington, DC 20037
Telephone: (202) 944-3040
Registered as Foreign Agent: (#4121).
Clients:
Ace Frosty Shipping Co., Ltd.

DYER, Timothy J.
Exec. Director, Nat'l Ass'n of Secondary School Principals
1904 Association Drive, Reston, VA 22091
Telephone: (703) 860-0200

DYESS, Mary A.
Ass't Exec. Director, Nat'l Ass'n of Stevedores
2011 Eye St., N.W., Washington, DC 20006
Telephone: (202) 296-2810
Registered as lobbyist at U.S. Congress.

DYKEMA GOSSETT
1752 N St., N.W., 6th Floor, Washington, DC 20036
Telephone: (202) 466-7185
Background: Washington office of a law firm based in Michigan.
Members of firm representing listed organizations:
Jenkins, Judy P.
O'Leary, Howard E. (Jr.)
   Background: Chief Counsel and Staff Director, U.S. Senate Committee on The Judiciary, Subcommittee on Antitrust and Monopoly, 1969-77.
Sullivan, Timothy
Clients:
Military Boot Manufacturers Ass'n *(Judy P. Jenkins)*
Total Petroleum, Inc. *(Howard E. O'Leary, Jr.)*

DYM, Herbert
Covington and Burling
1201 Pennsylvania Ave., N.W., Box 7566, Washington, DC 20044

DYM, Herbert (Cont'd)
Telephone: (202) 662-6000
Clients:
Merck and Co.
Upjohn Co.

DYSON, Edward E.
Baker and McKenzie
815 Connecticut Ave., N.W. Suite 1100, Washington, DC
20006-4078
Telephone: (202) 452-7000

DZIUBAN, Robert L.
Director, Convention Services, Nat'l Petroleum Refiners
Ass'n
1899 L St., N.W., Suite 1000, Washington, DC 20036
Telephone: (202) 457-0480

EADER, Michael
Associate Exec. Director, Nat'l School Boards Ass'n
1680 Duke St., Alexandria, VA 22314
Telephone: (703) 838-6722

EAGLES, Warren, Sr.
National Commander, American Veterans of World War II,
Korea and Vietnam (AMVETS)
4647 Forbes Blvd., Lanham, MD 20706
Telephone: (301) 459-9600

EAKIN, Robert N.
Mgr., Government Accounts, New Products, Ingersoll-
Rand Co.
1627 K St., N.W., Suite 900, Washington, DC 20006
Telephone: (202) 955-1450

EARLE, Ralph, II
National Policy Director, Lawyers Alliance for Nuclear
Arms Control
1001 Pennsylvania Ave., N.W.,, Washington, DC 20004
Telephone: (202) 624-2755

EARLES, Lucius, M.D.
Chairman, Nat'l Medical Ass'n Political Action Committee
Box 56241 Brightwood Station, Washington, DC 20011
Telephone: (202) 347-1895

EARLEY, Penelope
Director, Governmental Relations, American Ass'n of Col-
leges for Teacher Education
One Dupont Circle, N.W., Suite 610, Washington, DC
20036
Telephone: (202) 293-2450

EARLY, A. Blakeman
Wash. Dir., Pollution & Toxics Program, Sierra Club
408 C St., N.E., Washington, DC 20002
Telephone: (202) 547-1141
Registered as lobbyist at U.S. Congress.

EASTERLING, Barbara J.
Exec. V. President, Communications Workers of America
1925 K St., N.W., Washington, DC 20006
Telephone: (202) 728-2344
Background: Heads up all legislative and political activities.

EASTLAND, Terry H.
Resident Scholar, Nat'l Legal Center for the Public Interest
1000 16th St., N.W., Suite 301, Washington, DC 20036
Telephone: (202) 296-1683
Background: Former public affairs director, U.S. Department of Justice.

EASTMAN, Ronald D.
Cadwalader, Wickersham & Taft
1333 New Hampshire Ave., N.W. Suite 700, Washington,
DC 20036
Telephone: (202) 862-2200
Background: Attorney, Office of the General Counsel,
FPC, 1967-1969.
Clients:
Michigan, State of
Northwest Airlines, Inc.

EASTMENT, Thomas J.
Baker and Botts
555 13th St., N.W., Suite 500 East, Washington, DC
20004-1109
Telephone: (202) 639-7700
Clients:

Oryx Energy Co.
Pogo Producing Co.

EASTWOOD, Mary
President, Nat'l Woman's Party
144 Constitution Ave., N.E., Washington, DC 20002
Telephone: (202) 546-1210

EATMAN, George H.
Executive Consultant, Coal & Slurry Technology Ass'n
1156 15th St., N.W., Suite 525, Washington, DC 20005
Telephone: (202) 296-1133
Registered as lobbyist at U.S. Congress.

EATON ASSOCIATES
1725 K St., N.W., Suite 1111, Washington, DC 20006
Telephone: (202) 296-9166
Background: A consulting firm in space, energy and de-
fense-related matters.
Members of firm representing listed organizations:
Eaton, (Maj. Gen.) Robert E. L. (USAF (Ret))

EATON, Charles H. S.
Manager, Washington Operations, Acurex Corp.
1725 K St., N.W., Suite 1111, Washington, DC 20006
Telephone: (202) 296-8498

EATON, Pam
Refuge Program Assistant, Wilderness Soc.
1400 Eye St., N.W., 10th Floor, Washington, DC 20005
Telephone: (202) 842-3400
Registered as lobbyist at U.S. Congress.

EATON, Maj. Gen. Robert E. L., USAF (Ret)
Eaton Associates
1725 K St., N.W., Suite 1111, Washington, DC 20006
Telephone: (202) 296-9166

EBEL, Robert E.
V. President International Affairs, ENSERCH Corp.
1025 Connecticut Ave., N.W., Suite 1014, Washington, DC
20036
Telephone: (202) 872-1352
Registered as lobbyist at U.S. Congress.

EBELL, Myron
Washington Representative, Nat'l Inholders Ass'n
4 Library Court, S.E., Washington, DC 20003
Telephone: (202) 544-6156
Registered as lobbyist at U.S. Congress.
Background: Also represents the Multiple-Use Land Al-
liance.

EBERHARDT, Michael
Crowell and Moring
1001 Pennsylvania Ave., N.W., Washington, DC 20004-
2505
Telephone: (202) 624-2500
Background: Assistant Inspector General, Department of
Defense, 1982-87.

EBERLE & ASSOC., Bruce W.
8330 Old Court House Road Suite 700, Vienna, VA 22180
Telephone: (703) 821-1550
Members of firm representing listed organizations:
Eberle, Bruce W., President

EBERLE, Bruce W.
President, Eberle & Assoc., Bruce W.
8330 Old Court House Road Suite 700, Vienna, VA 22180
Telephone: (703) 821-1550

EBERLY, Donald J.
Exec. Director, Nat'l Service Secretariat
5140 Sherrier Place, N.W., Washington, DC 20016
Telephone: (202) 244-5828
Background: Formerly with ACTION, 1971-80, and the
Selective Service, 1980-84.

EBERT, Andrew
Kellen Co., Robert H.
1101 15th St., N.W., Washington, DC 20005
Telephone: (202) 785-3232
Background: Serves as Exec. Director, The Cranberry In-
stitute.
Organizations represented:
Cranberry Institute, The

EBY, C. C.
V. President, DeLeuw, Cather and Co.
1133 15th St., N.W. Suite 800, Washington, DC 20005
Telephone: (202) 775-3300

EBY, Charles J.
Senior Consultant, Biotechnology Div., Hill and Knowlton
Public Affairs Worldwide
Washington Harbour, 901 31st St., N.W., Washington, DC
20007
Telephone: (202) 333-7400
Registered as lobbyist at U.S. Congress.

EBZERY, Joan
Director, Public Affairs, Clean Sites, Inc.
1199 North Fairfax St., Alexandria, VA 22314
Telephone: (703) 739-1275
Background: Former Assistant Attorney General for Administration, Justice Management Division, U.S. Department of Justice.

ECCARD, Walter T.
Brown & Wood
815 Connecticut Ave., N.W. Suite 701, Washington, DC
20006
Telephone: (202) 223-0220
Registered as lobbyist at U.S. Congress.
Background: Deputy Ass't General Counsel (1984-85),
Ass't General Counsel (1985-86), U.S. Dept. of Treasury.

ECHEVERRIA, John D.
Gen. Cous./Dir, Nat'l Hydro-Pwr Plcy Ctr, American Rivers
801 Pennsylvania Ave., S.E. Suite 303, Washington, DC
20003-2155
Telephone: (202) 547-6900
Registered as lobbyist at U.S. Congress.

ECHOLS, Marsha A.
Berry Law Offices, Max N.
3213 O St., N.W., Washington, DC 20007
Telephone: (202) 298-6134
Registered as lobbyist at U.S. Congress.
Background: Assistant to the Administrator, Foreign Agri-
cultural Service, U.S. Dept. of Agriculture, 1977-80.
Counsel to the Vice Chairman, U.S. International Trade
Commission, 1980-82.
Organizations represented:
Gilway Co., Ltd., The
Nat'l Ass'n for the Specialty Food Trade

ECHOLS, William D.
Federal and Legislative Affairs Officer, American Psycho-
logical Ass'n
1200 17th St., N.W., Washington, DC 20036
Telephone: (202) 955-7600
Registered as lobbyist at U.S. Congress.

ECKER, N. Boyd
Mgr., Gov't Relats, Expl. & Producing, Mobil Corp.
1100 Connecticut Ave., N.W., Suite 620, Washington, DC
20036
Telephone: (202) 862-1331
Registered as lobbyist at U.S. Congress.

ECKERLY, Susan
Legis Officer, Cong & Intergovt'l Affrs, DEPARTMENT OF
LABOR
200 Constitution Ave., N.W., Washington, DC 20210
Telephone: (202) 523-6141

ECKERT SEAMANS CHERIN & MELLOTT
1818 N St., N.W., Suite 700, Washington, DC 20036
Telephone: (202) 452-1074
Background: A full service law firm.
Members of firm representing listed organizations:
Anderson, Anthony A.
Background: Attorney Advisor, Urban Mas Transporta-
tion Administration, 1980-84.
Quealy, Patricia A., Special Counsel
Background: Counsel, 1980-81; Deputy Chief Counsel,
1982-85; and Chief Counsel, 1986-89, U.S. House of
Representatives Committee on the Budget.
Starke, Jane Sutter
Background: Minority Counsel, Committee on Energy
and Commerce, U.S. House of Representatives,
1981-87.
Woodman, G. Kent

Background: Formerly served in the Office of the Legislative Counsel, U.S. House of Representatives, 1974-81; and in the Urban Mass Transportation Administration, 1981-84.
Clients:
  Blockbuster Entertainment Corp. *(Patricia A. Quealy, Jane Sutter Starke)*
  Blue Cross and Blue Shield Ass'n *(Patricia A. Quealy)*
  Continental Medical Systems, Inc. *(Patricia A. Quealy)*
  New York Metropolitan Transportation Authority *(Anthony A. Anderson, Jane Sutter Starke, G. Kent Woodman)*

ECKL, Christopher
Assistant Washington Representative, Tennessee Valley Authority
412 First St., S.E., Suite 300, Washington, DC 20444
Telephone: (202) 479-4412

ECKLAND, William S.
Morrison & Foerster
2000 Pennsylvania Ave., N.W., Suite 5500, Washington, DC 20006
Telephone: (202) 887-1500
Registered as lobbyist at U.S. Congress.
Clients:
  Federal Home Loan Bank of Seattle
  First Nationwide Bank
  Ford Motor Co.

ECONOMIC CONSULTING SERVICES INC.
1225 19th St. N.W., Suite 210, Washington, DC 20036
Telephone: (202) 466-7720
Members of firm representing listed organizations:
  Button, Kenneth R., V. President
  Love, Mark W., V. President
  Malashevich, Bruce P., President
  Swartz, Deborah, Director, Government Relations
Clients:
  Amalgamated Clothing and Textile Workers Union *(Mark W. Love, Deborah Swartz)*
  Cordage Institute *(Mark W. Love)*
  Footwear Industries of America *(Deborah Swartz)*
  Goody Products, Inc. *(Mark W. Love, Deborah Swartz)*
  Internat'l Leather Goods, Plastics and Novelty Workers Union, AFL-CIO *(Deborah Swartz)*
  Luggage and Leather Goods Manufacturers of America *(Mark W. Love, Deborah Swartz)*
  Neckwear Ass'n of America *(Deborah Swartz)*
  Non-Ferrous Metals Producers Committee *(Kenneth R. Button)*
  Outboard Marine Corp. *(Bruce P. Malashevich, Deborah Swartz)*
  Work Glove Manufacturers Ass'n *(Deborah Swartz)*

EDELEN, Stephen R.
Exec. V. President, Council for Inter-American Security
122 C St., N.W., Suite 710, Washington, DC 20001
Telephone: (202) 393-6622

EDELIN, Ramona H., Ph.D.
President and CEO, Nat'l Urban Coalition
8601 Georgia Ave., Suite 500. Silver Spring, MD 20910
Telephone: (301) 495-4999

EDELMAN, Daniel B.
Yablonski, Both & Edelman
1140 Connecticut Ave., N.W. Suite 800, Washington, DC 20036
Telephone: (202) 833-9060
Background: Law Clerk to Justice Harry A. Blackmun, U.S. Supreme Court, 1970-71.
Clients:
  United Mine Workers of America

EDELMAN, INC., Daniel J.
1420 K St., N.W., Washington, DC 20005
Telephone: (202) 371-0200
Registered as Foreign Agent: (#3634)
Background: International public relations firm with offices in eight U.S. and eleven foreign cities.
Members of firm representing listed organizations:
  Christ-Erwin, Mary, V. President
  Clark, Penelope, Account Executive
  Cook, Stephen K., Exec. V. President/General Manager

Background: Press Secretary to Rep. Teno Roncalio (D-WY), 1973-75. Press Secretary to Rep. Berkley Bedell (D-IA), 1975-79.
  Dach, Leslie, Senior V. Pres., Director, Public Affrs.
  Background: Formerly Communications Director of the Dukakis Presidential Campaign, 1988.
  Feichgraeber, Michelle
  Fillip, Christine, V. President
  Gidez, Christopher, V. President
  Background: Former Press Secretary to Rep. Harold Hollenbeck (R-NJ).
  Hanes, Joanna, Senior V. President
  Kelley, Elizabeth, Account Supervisor
  Lyons, Charles (Jr.), Account Executive
  Background: Former press aide to Rep. Frank Wolf (R-VA).
  Nerney, Christopher, Senior Account Executive
  Rainey, Jean, Senior V. President
  Yui, Ellen Moulton, Account Supervisor
Organizations represented:
  Advo-Systems, Inc. *(Leslie Dach, Michelle Feichgraeber)*
  American Academy of Actuaries *(Elizabeth Kelley)*
  CDM/Federal Programs Corp. *(Stephen K. Cook, Christine Fillip)*
  Collagen Corp. *(Leslie Dach, Christopher Gidez)*
  du Pont de Nemours and Co., E. I. *(Joanna Hanes)*
  Ernst & Young *(Christopher Gidez)*
  Friendswood Development Corp. *(Christopher Gidez)*
  Fuji Photo Film U.S.A. *(Leslie Dach)*
  Fujitsu America, Inc. *(Leslie Dach)*
  General Foods Foundation *(Elizabeth Kelley)*
  Hall-Kimbrell *(Jean Rainey)*
  Hughes Aircraft Co. *(Stephen K. Cook, Leslie Dach)*
  Japan Tobacco, Inc. *(Stephen K. Cook)*
  Korea Foreign Trade Ass'n
  Nat'l Coffee Ass'n *(Jean Rainey)*
  Nat'l Dairy Promotion and Research Board *(Mary Christ-Erwin, Jean Rainey)*
  Nat'l Fish and Seafood Promotion Council *(Mary Christ-Erwin, Jean Rainey)*
  Nat'l Gypsum Co. *(Stephen K. Cook)*
  Sugar Ass'n, Inc. *(Mary Christ-Erwin, Jean Rainey)*
  United Parcel Service *(Leslie Dach)*

EDELMAN, Marian Wright
President, Children's Defense Fund
122 C St., N.W., Washington, DC 20001
Telephone: (202) 628-8787

EDELSON, Neal
Associate General Counsel, Recording Industry Ass'n of America
1020 19th St., N.W., Suite 200, Washington, DC 20036
Telephone: (202) 775-0101

EDELSTON, Bruce S.
Director, Public Policy, Edison Electric Institute
. 1111 19th St., N., Washington, DC 20036
Telephone: (202) 778-6523

EDES, R. Hartley
Exec. Director, Insulation Contractors Ass'n of America
15819 Crabbs Branch Way, Rockville, MD 20855
Telephone: (301) 590-0030

EDGAR, G.
Newman & Holtzinger, P.C.
1615 L St., N.W., 10th Floor, Washington, DC 20005
Telephone: (202) 955-6600
Clients:
  Texas Utilities

EDGAR, Robert
Director, Committee for Nat'l Security
1601 Connecticut Ave., N.W. Suite 302, Washington, DC 20009
Telephone: (202) 745-2450
Background: Former staff member, U.S. Arms Control and Disarmament Agency and Department of Defense.

EDGE, Helen H.
V. President, Government Affairs, Railway Progress Institute
700 North Fairfax St., Alexandria, VA 22314
Telephone: (703) 836-2332
Registered as lobbyist at U.S. Congress.
Background: Former aide to Rep. Paul Rogers of Florida.

EDGERTON, Russell
President, American Ass'n for Higher Education
One Dupont Circle, N.W. Suite 600, Washington, DC 20036
Telephone: (202) 293-6440

EDIE, John
General Counsel, Council on Foundations
1828 L St., N.W. Suite 300, Washington, DC 20036
Telephone: (202) 466-6512

EDINGTON, William H.
Ginn, Edington, Moore and Wade
803 Prince St., Alexandria, VA 22314
Telephone: (703) 836-3328
Registered as lobbyist at U.S. Congress.
Registered as Foreign Agent: (#4134).

EDLUND, Anne
Vice President, Public Affairs, Motor Vehicle Manufacturers Ass'n of the United States
1620 Eye St., N.W. Suite 1000, Washington, DC 20006
Telephone: (202) 775-2700
Registered as lobbyist at U.S. Congress.

EDMONDSON, Eric
Saunders and Company
1015 Duke St., Alexandria, VA 22314
Telephone: (703) 549-1555
Clients:
  Internat'l Public Relations Co.
  Japan, Embassy of
  Mitsubishi Electric Corp.
  Ohbayashi Corp.

EDMONDSON, June E.
Williams and Jensen, P.C.
1101 Connecticut Ave., N.W., Suite 500, Washington, DC 20036
Telephone: (202) 659-8201
Clients:
  Nat'l Realty Political Action Committee (REALPAC)

EDSON, Charles L.
Kelley, Drye and Warren
2300 M St., N.W., Washington, DC 20037
Telephone: (202) 463-8333
Registered as lobbyist at U.S. Congress.
Background: General Counsel, President's Commission on Postal Organizations, 1967-68. Chief, Public Housing Section, Office of General Counsel, Department of Housing and Urban Development, 1968-70.
Clients:
  Coalition to Preserve the Low Income Housing Tax Credit
  Council for Rural Housing and Development
  Nat'l Leased Housing Ass'n

EDWARDS, Christine A.
Sr. V. President/Director, Gov'tl Affrs., Dean Witter Financial Services Group
633 Pennsylvania Ave., N.W., Washington, DC 20004
Telephone: (202) 737-4900
Registered as lobbyist at U.S. Congress.
Background: Also represents Sears Savings Bank.

EDWARDS, Gary
Exec. Director, Ethics Resource Center Inc.
600 New Hampshire Ave., N.W. Suite 400, Washington, DC 20037
Telephone: (202) 333-3419

EDWARDS, Jack
Hand, Arendall, Bedsole, Greaves & Johnston
1667 K St., N.W. Suite 310, Washington, DC 20006
Telephone: (202) 785-8893
Registered as lobbyist at U.S. Congress.
Background: Member, U.S. House of Representatives (R-AL), 1965-84.
Clients:
  Northrop Corp.

EDWARDS, John David
Exec. Director, Joint Nat'l Committee for Languages
300 I St., N.E., Suite 211, Washington, DC 20002
Telephone: (202) 546-7855

EDWARDS, Macon T.
President, Wallace & Edwards
1150 Connecticut Ave., N.W., Suite 507, Washington, DC 20036
Telephone: (202) 331-4331
Registered as lobbyist at U.S. Congress.
Clients:
  American Soc. of Farm Managers and Rural Appraisers
  Fiber, Fabric and Apparel Coalition for Trade
  Flue-Cured Tobacco Cooperative Stabilization Corp.

EDWARDS, Mencer D.
Exec. Director, Nat'l Minority AIDS Council
Telephone: (202) 544-1076

EDWARDS, Michael D.
Manager, Congressional Relations, Nat'l Education Ass'n of the U.S.
1201 16th St., N.W., Washington, DC 20036
Telephone: (202) 822-7300
Registered as lobbyist at U.S. Congress.

EDWARDS, Sharon
Robbins Associates, Liz
420 7th St., S.E., Washington, DC 20003
Telephone: (202) 544-6093
Organizations represented:
  Deleuw/Greeley/Hyman
  Gaymar Industries, Inc.
  New York Medical Care Facilities Finance Agency
  New York Public Library
  New York State Housing Finance Agency
  Spectrascan Imaging Services
  Vail Valley Associates

EDWARDS, Tony M.
Morrison & Foerster
2000 Pennsylvania Ave., N.W., Suite 5500, Washington, DC 20006
Telephone: (202) 887-1500
Registered as lobbyist at U.S. Congress.
Background: Internal Revenue Service, 1975-79.
Clients:
  RREEF Funds, The

EFFROS, P.C., Stephen R.
P.O. Box 1005, 3977 Chain Bridge Road, Fairfax, VA 22030-1005
Telephone: (703) 691-8875
Members of firm representing listed organizations:
  Effros, Stephen R.
  Ewalt, James H.
Organizations represented:
  Community Antenna Television Ass'n *(Stephen R. Effros)*

EFFROS, Stephen R.
Effros, P.C., Stephen R.
P.O. Box 1005, 3977 Chain Bridge Road, Fairfax, VA 22030-1005
Telephone: (703) 691-8875
Registered as lobbyist at U.S. Congress.
Organizations represented:
  Community Antenna Television Ass'n

EFRON, Samuel
Arent, Fox, Kintner, Plotkin & Kahn
1050 Connecticut Ave., N.W., Washington, DC 20036-5339
Telephone: (202) 857-6000
Background: Securities and Exchange Commission 1939-40; Dep't of Labor 1940-1942; Office of Alien Property Custodian 1942-43; Dep't of Justice 1946-51; Assistant General Counsel, Internat'l Affairs, Dep't of Defense 1951-53.
Clients:
  Continental Grain Co.
  Heckler & Koch
  Nat'l Ass'n of Wheat Growers

EGAN, Leonard
Fort and Schlefer
1401 New York Ave., N.W. Twelfth Floor, Washington, DC 20005
Telephone: (202) 467-5900
Clients:

Grand Metropolitan PLC
Wendell Investments Ltd.

EGAN, Paul S.
Director of Legislative Affairs, Vietnam Veterans of America, Inc.
2001 S St., N.W., Washington, DC 20009
Telephone: (202) 332-2700
Registered as lobbyist at U.S. Congress.

EGGE, George V., Jr.
1825 Eye St., N.W. Suite 400, Washington, DC 20006
Telephone: (202) 833-2420
Background: An attorney. Served as an Internat'l Economist with the Department of Commerce, 1960-61.
Organizations represented:
  Aceitunas de Mesa, S.A.
  Acerinox, S.A.
  Asturiana de Zinc, S.A.
  Espanola del Zinc, S.A.
  Union de Empresas y Entidades Siderugicas

EGGER, Roscoe L., Jr.
Partner, Washington Nat'l Tax Svc, Price Waterhouse
1801 K St., N.W., Suite 700, Washington, DC 20006
Telephone: (202) 296-0800
Background: Former Commissioner, Internal Revenue Service.

EGGERS, Bruce J.
Dir.-Federal Relations (Congressional), Ameritech (American Information Technologies)
1050 Connecticut Ave., N.W., Suite 730, Washington, DC 20036
Telephone: (202) 955-3050
Background: Attorney, Office of the Solicitor, U.S. Department of the Interior, 1975-77. Chief Legislative Counsel to former U.S. Senator Howard W. Cannon (D-NV), 1977-83.

EHRENHAFT, Peter D.
Bryan, Cave, McPheeters and McRoberts
1015 15th St., N.W., Suite 1000, Washington, DC 20005
Telephone: (202) 289-6100
Registered as Foreign Agent: (# 3599).
Background: Deputy Assistant Secretary and Special Counsel (Tariff Affairs) Department of the Treasury, 1977-79.

EHRHARDT, Robert F.
V. President, Nat'l Ass'n of Environmental Professionals
Box 15210, Alexandria, VA 22309-0210
Telephone: (703) 660-2364

EHRLICH, Bernard H.
2000 L St., N.W., Suite 504, Washington, DC 20036
Telephone: (202) 296-5848
Background: An attorney.
Organizations represented:
  American Forestry Ass'n
  Commission of Accredited Truck Driving Schools (CATDS)
  KEX Nat'l Ass'n

EHRLICH-MANES AND ASSOCIATES
4901 Fairmont Ave., Bethesda, MD 20814
Telephone: (301) 657-1800
Background: Advertising, marketing and public relations firm.
Members of firm representing listed organizations:
  Manes, Nella
  Stein, Sherwin B.
Clients:
  Fokker B.V. *(Sherwin B. Stein)*

EICHENLAUB, Alfred J.
Ginsburg, Feldman and Bress
1250 Connecticut Ave., N.W. Suite 800, Washington, DC 20036
Telephone: (202) 637-9000
Clients:
  Ball Brothers, Inc.

EICHER, Jill A.
Manager, State Affairs, Health Industry Manufacturers Ass'n
1030 15th St., N.W. Suite 1100, Washington, DC 20005
Telephone: (202) 452-8240

EICK, Gretchen C.
Nat'l Director, IMPACT
100 Maryland Ave., N.E. Suite 502, Washington, DC 20002
Telephone: (202) 544-8636

EISCHEID, Linda G.
Dir, Policy, Plng and Legislation, DEPARTMENT OF HEALTH AND HUMAN SERVICES - Human Development Services
200 Independence Ave. S.W., Washington, DC 20201
Telephone: (202) 245-7027

EISEN, Eric A.
Birch, Horton, Bittner and Cherot
1155 Connecticut Ave., N.W., Suite 1200, Washington, DC 20036
Telephone: (202) 659-5800
Clients:
  Missouri Public Service Commission

EISEN, Phyllis
Director, Risk Management, Nat'l Ass'n of Manufacturers
1331 Pennsylvania Ave., N.W. Suite 1500 North, Washington, DC 20004-1703
Telephone: (202) 637-3000

EISENBERG, Albert C.
Senior Director, Federal Liaison, American Institute of Architects, The
1735 New York Ave., N.W., Washington, DC 20006
Telephone: (202) 626-7300
Registered as lobbyist at U.S. Congress.
Background: Former Minority Staff Director, U.S. Senate Housing and Urban Affairs Subcommittee.

EISENBERG, Diane U.
Exec. Director, Council for the Advancement of Citizenship
1724 Massachusetts Ave., N.W., Suite 300, Washington, DC 20036
Telephone: (202) 857-0578

EISENBERG, Pablo
President, Center for Community Change
1000 Wisconsin Ave., N.W., Washington, DC 20007
Telephone: (202) 342-0519
Background: Former Deputy Director of Research and Demonstration Programs, Office of Economic Opportunity.

EISENBERG, Ron
Senior V. President, Public Relations, Jefferson Group, The
1341 G St., N.W., Suite 1100, Washington, DC 20005
Telephone: (202) 638-3535
Clients:
  B E & K Daycare
  Cleartel Communication
  Lipman Hearne

EISENBERG, Warren W.
Director, B'nai B'rith Internat'l
1640 Rhode Island Ave., N.W., Washington, DC 20036
Telephone: (202) 857-6600

EISENBUD, Robert
Managing Director, Environmental Policy, Nat'l Solid Wastes Management Ass'n
1730 Rhode Island Ave., N.W., 10th Floor, Washington, DC 20036
Telephone: (202) 659-4613
Registered as lobbyist at U.S. Congress.
Background: Counsel, Senate Commerce, Science and Transportation Committee, 1985-89.

EISENHART, Earl B.
V. President, Government Affairs, Nat'l Private Truck Council
1320 Braddock Place Suite 720, Alexandria, VA 22314
Telephone: (703) 683-1300
Registered as lobbyist at U.S. Congress.

EISENSTAT, David H.
Akin, Gump, Strauss, Hauer and Feld
1333 New Hampshire Ave., N.W., Suite 400, Washington, DC 20036
Telephone: (202) 887-4000

WASHINGTON REPRESENTATIVES

EISNER, David
Public Affairs Manager, Legal Services Corp.
400 Virginia Ave., S.W., Washington, DC 20024
Telephone: (202) 863-1839

EISNER, Steve
Project Associate, APCO Associates
1155 21st St., N.W., Suite 1000, Washington, DC 20036
Telephone: (202) 778-1000

EITELBERG, Cathie G.
Ass't Director, Federal Liaison Center, Government Finance Officers Ass'n
1750 K St., N.W. Suite 200, Washington, DC 20006
Telephone: (202) 429-2750

EIZENSTAT, Stuart E.
Powell, Goldstein, Frazer and Murphy
1001 Pennsylvania, N.W., Sixth Fl., Washington, DC 20004
Telephone: (202) 347-0066
Registered as lobbyist at U.S. Congress.
Registered as Foreign Agent: (#3274).
Background: Formerly Assistant to the President for Domestic Affairs and Policy under President Jimmy Carter. Member, Board of Directors, Hercules, Inc., Public Service Co. of Indiana and Israel Discount Bank of New York. Serves as Adjunct Lecturer, JFK School of Government, Harvard University.
Clients:
Committee for Equitable Compensation
Council on Research and Technology (CORE-TECH)
Flood Control Advisory Committee
Fluor Corp.
Hadson Corp.
Hercules, Inc.
Hewlett-Packard Co.
Hitachi Ltd.
Hitachi Sales Corp. of America
Internat'l Telecommunications Satellite Organization (INTELSAT)
Stride Rite Corp., The
Union of Councils for Soviet Jews
Weizman Institute of Science

EKEDAHL, Duane H.
Smith, Bucklin and Associates
1101 Connecticut Ave., N.W., Suite 700, Washington, DC 20036
Telephone: (202) 857-1100
Background: Serves as Exec. Manager, Regional Airline Ass'n and Exec. Director, Pet Food Institute.
Clients:
Pet Food Institute
Regional Airline Ass'n
Regional Airlines Ass'n Political Action Committee

EKFELT, Richard H.
V. President, Hauck and Associates
1255 23rd St., N.W., Washington, DC 20037
Telephone: (202) 452-8100
Background: Serves as Exec. Director, Electromagnetic Energy Policy Alliance and Exec. Director, Nat'l Health Care Anti-Fraud Ass'n.
Clients:
Electromagnetic Energy Policy Alliance
Nat'l Health Care Anti-Fraud Ass'n

EL-ASHRY, Mohamed T.
V. Pres., Research and Policy Affairs, World Resources Institute
1709 New York Ave., N.W., Washington, DC 20006
Telephone: (202) 638-6300

ELASS, Majed
Vice President, U.S. Office, Arabian American Oil Co.
1667 K St., N.W., Suite 1200, Washington, DC 20006
Telephone: (202) 223-7750

ELBERT, Stephen A.
Director, Federal Relations, Amoco Corp.
1615 M St., N.W., Suite 200, Washington, DC 20036
Telephone: (202) 857-5304
Registered as lobbyist at U.S. Congress.

ELDRED, John S.
Keller and Heckman
1150 17th St., N.W. Suite 1000, Washington, DC 20036
Telephone: (202) 956-5600
Background: Trial Attorney, Food and Drug Administration, 1970-75.
Clients:
K-Line Pharmaceuticals, Ltd.

ELIADES, George K., CAE
President and Chief Exec. Officer, Soc. of American Wood Preservers, Inc.
7297 Lee Hwy., Unit P, Falls Church, VA 22042
Telephone: (703) 237-0900
Registered as lobbyist at U.S. Congress.
Background: Also serves as Treasurer, Wood Preservers Political Action Committee and Exec. Director, Fire Retardant Trated Wood Chemical Manufacturers Council.

ELIAS, Jack I.
Elias, Matz, Tiernan and Herrick
734 15th St., N.W. 12th Fl., Washington, DC 20005
Telephone: (202) 347-0300
Background: Member of Staff, Securities Exchange Commission, 1938-58. Director, Holding Company Section of Federal Home Loan Bank Board, 1968-72.

ELIAS, MATZ, TIERNAN AND HERRICK
734 15th St., N.W. 12th Fl., Washington, DC 20005
Telephone: (202) 347-0300
Members of firm representing listed organizations:
Baxter, Allin P.
Background: Attorney, Securities and Exchange Commission, 1957-61.
Elias, Jack I.
Background: Member of Staff, Securities Exchange Commission, 1938-58. Director, Holding Company Section of Federal Home Loan Bank Board, 1968-72.
Matz, Timothy B.
Background: Associate General Counsel, Federal Home Loan Mortgage Corp., 1971-72.
Clients:
Baldwin Co., D. H.
Bayamon Federal Savings and Loan Ass'n
Beneficial Corp.
Coast Federal Savings and Loan Ass'n
Enterprise Bank *(Allin P. Baxter)*
Entex, Inc.
Financial Corp. of America
First Federal Savings and Loan Ass'n of Raleigh
Haven Federal Savings and Loan Ass'n
Homestead Financial Corp.
North American Securities Administrators Ass'n
Richardson Savings and Loan Ass'n

ELICKER, Paul H.
Exec. Director, Center for Privatization
2000 Pennsylvania Ave., N.W. Suite 2500, Washington, DC 20006
Telephone: (202) 872-9250

ELLER, J. Burton, Jr.
Sr. V. President, Government Affairs, Nat'l Cattlemen's Ass'n
1301 Pennsylvania Ave., N.W., Suite 300, Washington, DC 20004
Telephone: (202) 347-0228
Registered as lobbyist at U.S. Congress.

ELLICOTT, John
Covington and Burling
1201 Pennsylvania Ave., N.W., Box 7566, Washington, DC 20044
Telephone: (202) 662-6000

ELLIE, Palmateer
Research Analyst, Panhandle Eastern Corp.
1025 Connecticut Ave., N.W., Suite 404, Washington, DC 20036
Telephone: (202) 331-8090

ELLINGSWORTH, William D.
Sr. Staff V. President, Public Affairs, Nat'l Ass'n of Home Builders of the U.S.
15th and M Streets, N.W., Washington, DC 20005
Telephone: (202) 822-0470

ELLIOTT ASSOCIATES
308 Constitution Ave., N.E., Washington, DC 20002

Telephone: (202) 546-1808
Members of firm representing listed organizations:
Elliott, M. Diane
Clients:
American Ass'n of Private Railroad Car Owners, Inc. *(M. Diane Elliott)*
Kansas City Southern Industries *(M. Diane Elliott)*

ELLIOTT, David O.
Barnes, Richardson and Colburn
1819 H St., N.W., Washington, DC 20006
Telephone: (202) 457-0300
Clients:
Internat'l Tool Works Ltd.
Maple Leaf Fish Co.
Omstead Foods Ltd.

ELLIOTT, H. John
10172 Main St., Box 366, Fairfax, VA 22030
Telephone: (703) 273-1788
Background: An engineering consultant.
Organizations represented:
Belmont Development
Kennedy Engine Service Co.
Power Technology Inc.
Site Evaluators & Consultants

ELLIOTT, M. Diane
Elliott Associates
308 Constitution Ave., N.E., Washington, DC 20002
Telephone: (202) 546-1808
Clients:
American Ass'n of Private Railroad Car Owners, Inc.
Kansas City Southern Industries

ELLIOTT, R. Lance
Exec. Director, Nat'l Bowling Council
1919 Pennsylvania Ave., N.W., Washington, DC 20006
Telephone: (202) 659-9070

ELLIOTT, Robert H., Jr.
Caplin and Drysdale
One Thomas Circle, N.W. Suite 1100, Washington, DC 20005
Telephone: (202) 862-5000
Registered as Foreign Agent: (#3821).
Background: Attorney, Office of Chief Counsel, Internal Revenue Service, 1961-62; Office of Tax Legislative Counsel, U.S. Treasury Department, 1962-64.

ELLIOTT, Dr. T. Michael
Exec. Director, Computer Society, The
1730 Massachusetts Ave., N.W., Washington, DC 20036
Telephone: (202) 371-0101

ELLIOTT, Warren G.
Nossaman, Guthner, Knox and Elliott
1227 25th St., N.W., Suite 700, Washington, DC 20037
Telephone: (202) 223-9100
Registered as lobbyist at U.S. Congress.
Background: Legislative Counsel to Senator Gordon Allott of Colorado, 1955-61.
Clients:
Aetna Life & Casualty Co.
Northwestern Nat'l Life Insurance Co.
PKR Foundation

ELLIS, Emory N., Jr.
Fulbright & Jaworski
1150 Connecticut Ave., N.W., Suite 400, Washington, DC 20036
Telephone: (202) 452-6800
Background: Attorney, Civil Aeronautics Board, 1961-70.

ELLIS, James B., II
Dyer, Ellis, Joseph & Mills
600 New Hampshire Ave., N.W., Suite 1000, Washington, DC 20037
Telephone: (202) 944-3040
Registered as Foreign Agent: (#4121).
Clients:
Ace Frosty Shipping Co., Ltd.

ELLIS, Margaret
Exec. Assistant, Arms Control and Foreign Policy Caucus
House Annex 2 Room 501, Washington, DC 20515
Telephone: (202) 226-3440

ELLIS, Mark G.
Counsel, American Mining Congress
1920 N St., N.W. Suite 300, Washington, DC 20036
Telephone: (202) 861-2800
Registered as lobbyist at U.S. Congress.

ELLISAGE, Chet
Nat'l Commander, Catholic War Veterans of the U.S.A.
419 N. Lee St., Alexandria, VA 22314
Telephone: (703) 549-3622

ELLISON, Donald E.
Managing Partner, DGM Internat'l Inc.
9271 Old Keene Mill Road, Springfield, VA 22152
Telephone: (703) 644-4587
Clients:
    Aero Consultants
    Louisiana Tanners
    Texstor

ELLISON, Mark C.
V. Pres., Gov't Affairs & Gen. Counsel, Satellite Broadcasting and Communications Ass'n
300 N. Washington St. Suite 600, Alexandria, VA 22314
Telephone: (703) 549-6990
Registered as lobbyist at U.S. Congress.

ELLISON, Mark M.
Senior V. President, French & Company
The Willard, 1455 Pennsylvania Ave., N.W., Suite 1260, Washington, DC 20004
Telephone: (202) 783-7272
Registered as lobbyist at U.S. Congress.
Registered as Foreign Agent: (#3666).
Clients:
    BATUS, Inc.
    Internat'l Electronics Manufacturers and Consumers of America
    Montgomery Ward & Co., Inc.
    Wheels, Inc.

ELLSWORTH, Cheryl N.
Partner, Harris & Ellsworth
1101 30th St., N.W. Suite 103, Washington, DC 20007
Telephone: (202) 337-8338

ELLSWORTH, Dorothy
Assistant Director, Legislative Affairs, Internat'l Ass'n of Machinists and Aerospace Workers
1300 Connecticut Ave., N.W. Suite 404, Washington, DC 20036
Telephone: (202) 857-5200
Registered as lobbyist at U.S. Congress.

ELMENDORF, Edward
V. President, Governmental Relations, American Ass'n of State Colleges and Universities
One Dupont Circle, N.W. Suite 700, Washington, DC 20036
Telephone: (202) 293-7070
Background: Former Assistant Secretary for Postsecondary Education, U.S. Department of Education.

ELMENDORF, Fritz M.
V. President - Communications, Consumer Bankers Ass'n
1000 Wilson Blvd., 30th Floor, Arlington, VA 22209-3908
Telephone: (703) 276-1750

ELMER, Brian C.
Crowell and Moring
1001 Pennsylvania Ave., N.W., Washington, DC 20004-2505
Telephone: (202) 624-2500
Clients:
    Nashua Corp.
    United Technologies Corp.

ELMER, Ivan C.
Director, Small Business Programs, Chamber of Commerce of the U.S.A.
1615 H St., N.W., Washington, DC 20062
Telephone: (202) 463-5580

ELWELL, Robert G.
V. President-Special Advisor, Internat'l Business-Government Counsellors, Inc.
818 Connecticut Ave., N.W. Suite 1200, Washington, DC 20006
Telephone: (202) 872-8181

ELWOOD, Nancy
Senior Legislative Representative, Nat'l Ass'n of Home Builders of the U.S.
15th and M Streets, N.W., Washington, DC 20005
Telephone: (202) 822-0470
Registered as lobbyist at U.S. Congress.

ELY, Clausen, Jr.
Covington and Burling
1201 Pennsylvania Ave., N.W., Box 7566, Washington, DC 20044
Telephone: (202) 662-6000

ELY, Jeffrey R.
President, Landmark Strategies, Inc.
101 South Whiting St. Suite 319, Alexandria, VA 22304
Telephone: (703) 370-8500
Background: Former Political Director, Democratic National Committee.

EMANUEL, Alyson A.
Manager, Government Relations, BASF Corp.
2100 Pennsylvania Ave., N.W. Suite 755, Washington, DC 20037
Telephone: (202) 296-4894
Registered as lobbyist at U.S. Congress.

EMERLING, Stanley J.
Exec. V. President, Nat'l Ass'n of Meat Purveyors
8365-B Greensboro Drive, McLean, VA 22102-3585
Telephone: (703) 827-5754

EMERSON, Peter
V. Pres., Rsrch, Planning & Economics, Wilderness Soc.
1400 Eye St., N.W., 10th Floor, Washington, DC 20005
Telephone: (202) 842-3400

EMERY, Jack M.
Assistant Director, Federal Affairs, American Medical Ass'n
1101 Vermont Ave., N.W., Washington, DC 20005
Telephone: (202) 789-7400
Registered as lobbyist at U.S. Congress.

EMERY, N. Beth
Paul, Hastings, Janofsky and Walker
1050 Connecticut Ave., N.W. Suite 1200, Washington, DC 20036-5331
Telephone: (202) 223-9000
Background: Attorney, Electric and Telephone Division, Office of the General Counsel, Department of Agriculture, 1977-79. Legal Advisor to Commissioner Matthew Holden, Jr., Federal Energy Regulatory Commission, 1979-81.

EMERY, William F.
Exec. Director, Military Chaplains Ass'n of the U.S.
Box 645, Riverdale, MD 20737-0645
Telephone: (301) 674-3306

EMIG, Michael J.
Legislative Director, Internat'l Brotherhood of Electrical Workers
Telephone: (202) 728-6060
Registered as lobbyist at U.S. Congress.

EMJ CONSULTANTS
11481 Bingham Terrace, Reston, VA 22091
Telephone: (703) 860-9570
Background: A consulting firm specializing in Washington representation and consulting services for public service organizations, particularly those dealing with the aging.
Members of firm representing listed organizations:
    Butler, Frances F., President
Clients:
    American Ass'n for Internat'l Aging *(Frances F. Butler)*
    Nat'l Ass'n of Foster Grandparent Program Directors *(Frances F. Butler)*
    Nat'l Ass'n of Retired Senior Volunteer Program Directors *(Frances F. Butler)*
    Nat'l Ass'n of Senior Companion Program Directors *(Frances F. Butler)*

EMRICH, Rick
Director of Communications, Christic Institute
1324 N. Capitol St., N.W., Washington, DC 20002
Telephone: (202) 797-8106

EMSELLEM, Irene R.
Staff Director for Member Liaison, American Bar Ass'n
1800 M St., N.W., Washington, DC 20036
Telephone: (202) 331-2210
Registered as lobbyist at U.S. Congress.

EMURA, Takashi
General Manager, Sumitomo Corp. of America
1747 Pennsylvania Ave., N.W. Suite 703, Washington, DC 20006
Telephone: (202) 785-9210

ENCE, Ronald K.
Dir., Agricultural and Rural Affairs, Independent Bankers Ass'n of America
One Thomas Circle, N.W., Suite 950, Washington, DC 20005
Telephone: (202) 659-8111
Registered as lobbyist at U.S. Congress.
Background: Legal Aide to U.S. Rep. Bud Shuster (R-PA), 1972-75; Aide to U.S. Rep. Tom Hagedorn (R-MN), 1980-83.

ENDEAN, Howard John
V. President, Policy, American Business Conference
1730 K St., N.W. Suite 1200, Washington, DC 20006
Telephone: (202) 822-9300
Registered as lobbyist at U.S. Congress.

ENDERS, John H.
President, Flight Safety Foundation
2200 Wilson Blvd., Suite 500, Arlington, VA 22201
Telephone: (703) 522-8300

ENDERS, Michael A.
V. President, Internat'l Ass'n for Continuing Education and Training
P.O. Box 27043, Washington, DC 20038
Telephone: (301) 384-1059

ENERGY RESOURCES INTERNAT'L
1015 18th St., N.W. Suite 500, Washington, DC 20036
Telephone: (202) 785-8833
Members of firm representing listed organizations:
    Schwartz, Michael H.
Clients:
    Utility Nuclear Waste Transportation Program
        (Michael H. Schwartz)

ENG, Jacqueline
Director of Public Affairs, American Ass'n of Colleges of Pharmacy
1426 Prince St., Alexandria, VA 22314
Telephone: (703) 739-2330

ENGEBRETSON, Gary D.
President, Contract Services Ass'n of America
1350 New York Ave., N.W., Suite 200, Washington, DC 20005
Telephone: (202) 347-0600
Registered as lobbyist at U.S. Congress.
Background: Responsibilities include the Contract Services Ass'n Political Action Committee.

ENGEL, Ralph
President, Chemical Specialties Manufacturers Ass'n
1913 Eye St., N.W., Washington, DC 20006
Telephone: (202) 872-8110
Registered as lobbyist at U.S. Congress.

ENGEL, Rob
Fenn & King Communications
1043 Cecil Place, N.W., Washington, DC 20007
Telephone: (202) 337-6995

ENGELEN, John T.
Ass't Dir., Agricultural Legis. Affairs, American Cyanamid Co.
1575 Eye St., N.W., Suite 200, Washington, DC 20005
Telephone: (202) 789-1222
Registered as lobbyist at U.S. Congress.

ENGELKEN, Albert
Deputy Exec. Director, American Public Transit Ass'n
1201 New York Ave., N.W.,, Washington, DC 20005
Telephone: (202) 898-4000

The listings in this directory are available as *Mailing Labels*. See last page.

ENGEN, Donald D.
President, Air Safety Foundation, Aircraft Owners and Pilots Ass'n
421 Aviation Way, Frederick, MD 21701
Telephone: (301) 695-2000

ENGLAND, Catherine
Director, Regulatory Studies, Cato Institute
224 Second St., S.E., Washington, DC 20003
Telephone: (202) 546-0200

ENGLAND, Leslie
Conservation Assistant, Sierra Club
408 C St., N.E., Washington, DC 20002
Telephone: (202) 547-1141
Registered as lobbyist at U.S. Congress.

ENGLE, Mark T.
V. President, Hauck and Associates
1255 23rd St., N.W., Washington, DC 20037
Telephone: (202) 452-8100
Background: Serves as President, American Coke and Coal Chemicals Institute; Exec. Director Nat'l Ass'n of Video Distributors; and Exec. Director, Nat'l Ass'n of Telecommunications Dealers.
Clients:
American Coke and Coal Chemicals Institute
Nat'l Ass'n of Telecommunications Dealers
Nat'l Ass'n of Video Distributors

ENGLE, Paul H., Jr.
Exec. Director, American Pipe Fittings Ass'n
6203 Old Keene Mill Court, Springfield, VA 22152
Telephone: (703) 644-0001

ENGLERT, Roy T.
Walker Associates, Charls E.
1730 Pennsylvania Ave., N.W. Suite 200, Washington, DC 20006
Telephone: (202) 393-4760

ENGLISH, Mary J. Pepper
Director, Congressional Relations, BellSouth Corp.
1133 21st St., N.W., Suite 900, Washington, DC 20036
Telephone: (202) 463-4100

ENGLISH, Phillip
V. President, Communications Services, American Ass'n of Community and Junior Colleges
One Dupont Circle, N.W. Suite 410, Washington, DC 20036
Telephone: (202) 293-7050

ENGLISH, Raymond
Senior Vice President, Ethics and Public Policy Center
1030 15th St., N.W. Suite 300, Washington, DC 20005
Telephone: (202) 682-1200

ENGLUND, Jon
Manager, Government Affairs, American Electronics Ass'n
1225 Eye St., N.W., Suite 950, Washington, DC 20005
Telephone: (202) 682-9110
Registered as lobbyist at U.S. Congress.

ENGMAN, Patricia H.
Deputy Exec. Director, Business Roundtable
1615 L St., N.W., Suite 1350, Washington, DC 20036
Telephone: (202) 872-1260
Registered as lobbyist at U.S. Congress.

ENGQUIST, Christopher
Director, Manpower Training Division, Associated General Contractors of America
1957 E St., N.W., Washington, DC 20006
Telephone: (202) 393-2040
Registered as lobbyist at U.S. Congress.

ENGSTROM, Eric
Exec. Director, Nat'l AIDS Network
2033 M St., N.W., Suite 800, Washington, DC 20036
Telephone: (202) 293-2437

ENNIS, James G.
Fletcher, Heald and Hildreth
1225 Connecticut Ave., N.W. Suite 400, Washington, DC 20036
Telephone: (202) 828-5700

ENRIGHT, Nancy
Head, Public Communication, American Chemical Soc.
1155 16th St., N.W., Washington, DC 20036
Telephone: (202) 872-4440

ENS RESOURCES, INC.
1333 H St., N.W., Suite 400, Washington, DC 20005
Telephone: (202) 789-1226
Members of firm representing listed organizations:
Sapirstein, Eric
Clients:
California Ass'n of Sanitation Agencies
In-Situ, Inc. *(Eric Sapirstein)*
Orange County Sanitation Districts *(Eric Sapirstein)*

ENVIRON CORP.
4350 North Fairfax Drive Suite 300, Arlington, VA 22203
Telephone: (703) 516-2300
Members of firm representing listed organizations:
Wrenn, Grover, President

EPPARD, Lynn
Legislative Director, Federally Employed Women, Inc.
1400 Eye St., N.W. Suite 425, Washington, DC 20005
Telephone: (202) 898-0994

EPPLER, David
Staff Attorney, Congress Watch
215 Pennsylvania Ave., S.E., Washington, DC 20003
Telephone: (202) 546-4996
Registered as lobbyist at U.S. Congress.

EPPS, Cheryl Anthony
Legislative Analyst, Internat'l Ass'n of Chiefs of Police
1110 N. Glebe Road Suite 200, Arlington, VA 22201
Telephone: (703) 243-6500
Registered as lobbyist at U.S. Congress.

EPSTEIN, Anita
Legislative Director, Shearman and Sterling
1001 30th St., N.W., Suite 400, Washington, DC 20007
Telephone: (202) 337-8200
Registered as lobbyist at U.S. Congress.
Registered as Foreign Agent: (#4208).
Background: Legislative Director, Shearman and Sterling.
Clients:
Claro y Cia

EPSTEIN BECKER AND GREEN
1227 25th St., N.W., Suite 700, Washington, DC 20037
Telephone: (202) 861-0900
Background: Washington office of a New York law firm.
Members of firm representing listed organizations:
Kerman, Leslie
Kopit, William G.
Main, David S.
Background: Professional Staff Member, Minority Policy Committee 1974-76, Legislative Ass't to Sen. Richard S. Schweiker (R-PA) 1976-77, Minority Counsel, Subcommittee on Health and Scientific Research, U.S. Senate 1977-79.
Snyder, Lynn S.
Steelman, Deborah
Background: Legislative Director to Sen. John Heinz (R-PA) 1982-83; Director, State Relations, Environmental Protection Agency 1983-84; Deputy Ass't to the President for Intergovernmental Affairs 1985; Assoc. Director for Human Resources Veterans and Labor, Office of Management and Budget, 1986-87.
Clients:
American Academy of Dermatology *(Deborah Steelman)*
American Managed Care and Review Ass'n *(Lynn S. Snyder)*
American Managed Care and Review Ass'n Political Action Committee (AMCRA PAC)
Bank of Tokyo Trust Co.
Blue Cross and Blue Shield of Missouri *(Deborah Steelman)*
Central Virginia Health Systems Agency *(William G. Kopit)*
Doctors Nat'l Homecare Corp. *(Deborah Steelman)*
Epstein Becker and Green Political Committee
Independent Action *(Leslie Kerman)*
Morgan Stanley and Co.
Pfizer, Inc. *(Deborah Steelman)*
Pharmaceutical Manufacturers Ass'n *(Deborah Steelman)*

Professional Ass'n for Quality Home Respiratory Care *(Deborah Steelman)*
Social Democratic and Labor Party of Northern Ireland (SDLP) *(William G. Kopit)*
Voluntary Hospitals of America, Inc.

EPSTEIN, David
Government Affairs Specialist, Service Station Dealers of America
499 S. Capitol St., S.E. Suite 407, Washington, DC 20003
Telephone: (202) 479-0196

EPSTEIN, Gary M.
Latham and Watkins
1001 Pennsylvania Ave., N.W., Suite 1300, Washington, DC 20004
Telephone: (202) 637-2200
Background: Chief, Common Carrier Bureau, Federal Communications Commission, 1981-83.

EPSTEIN, Gordon
Manager, Mitsubishi Internat'l Corp.
655 15th St., N.W., Suite 860, Washington, DC 20005
Telephone: (202) 638-1101

EPSTEIN, Howard
Diuguid and Epstein
1000 Connecticut Ave., N.W. Suite 1107, Washington, DC 20036
Telephone: (202) 872-0700
Background: Served with Federal Trade Commission, 1961-68; Anti-Trust Division, U.S. Department of Justice, 1969-75.

EPSTEIN, Mark A.
Internat'l Advisers, Inc.
2300 M St., N.W., Suite 600, Washington, DC 20037
Telephone: (202) 293-1575
Registered as lobbyist at U.S. Congress.
Registered as Foreign Agent: (#4203).
Background: Issues Director, Hollings for President and U.S. Senate Staff, 1983-84. Visiting Scholar, Foreign Service Institute, U.S. Department of State, 1984. Professional Staff, House Government Operations Committee, 1987. Professional Staff, European Economics Division, West German Foreign Ministry, Bonn, 1988-89.

EPSTEIN, Samuel S., M.D.
Chairperson, Commission for the Advancement of Public Interest Organizations
P.O. Box 53424, Washington, DC 20009
Telephone: (202) 462-0505

EPSTEIN, Seymour G.
Tech. Dir.-Env. Res'ch, Health & Safety, Aluminum Ass'n
900 19th St., N.W. Suite 300, Washington, DC 20006
Telephone: (202) 862-5135

EQUALE, Paul A.
V. President, Government Affairs, Independent Insurance Agents of America
600 Pennsylvania Ave., S.E., Suite 200, Washington, DC 20003
Telephone: (202) 544-5833
Registered as lobbyist at U.S. Congress.
Background: Responsibilities include the Independent Insurance Agents of America, Inc. Political Action Committee.

ERBEN, Randall H.
Deputy Director, Texas, State of, Office of State-Federal Relations
600 Maryland Ave., S.W., Suite 255, Washington, DC 20024
Telephone: (202) 488-3927

ERCOLANO, Alfred S.
Director, Washington Office, College of American Pathologists
1101 Vermont Ave., N.W., Washington, DC 20005
Telephone: (202) 371-6617

ERENBAUM, Allen
Preston Gates Ellis & Rouvelas Meeds
1735 New York Ave., N.W., Suite 500, Washington, DC 20006-4759
Telephone: (202) 628-1700
Registered as lobbyist at U.S. Congress.
Clients:

ERENBAUM, Allen (Cont'd)
Albion, Michigan, City of
Clyde Hill, Washington, Town of
Grand Haven, Michigan, City of
Loudoun County, Virginia
Orange, Texas, City of
Sacramento, California, City of
Somerville, Massachusetts, City of
Spokane, Washington, City of

ERICKSEN, Jack
Director of Federal Relations, Aetna Life & Casualty Co.
1667 K St., N.W., Suite 400, Washington, DC 20006
Telephone: (202) 223-2821

ERICKSON, Ronald H., Jr.
Cong and Public Affrs Officer, FARM CREDIT ADMINIS-
TRATION
1501 Farm Credit Drive, McLean, VA 22102
Telephone: (703) 883-4056

ERLENBORN, John N.
Seyfarth, Shaw, Fairweather and Geraldson
815 Connecticut Ave., N.W., Washington, DC 20006-4004
Telephone: (202) 463-2400
Background: U.S. Representative (R-IL), 1965-1985. Serves
as government affairs consultant to the American Soc. of
Pension Actuaries.
Clients:
American Soc. of Pension Actuaries
Employers Council on Flexible Compensation

ERNEST, Pamela K.
Director, Federal Affairs, Honeywell, Inc.
1100 Connecticut Ave., N.W., Suite 710, Washington, DC
20036
Telephone: (202) 872-0495
Registered as lobbyist at U.S. Congress.

ERNST, Jerome B.
Exec. Director, Nat'l Catholic Conference for Interracial
Justice
3033 Fourth St., N.E., Washington, DC 20017
Telephone: (202) 529-6480

ERNST, John
Director, Office of Legislative Affairs, Nat'l Wildlife Feder-
ation
1400 16th St., N.W., Washington, DC 20036-2266
Telephone: (202) 797-6800
Registered as lobbyist at U.S. Congress.

ERVIN, James L.
President, Ervin Technical Associates, Inc. (ETA)
1667 K St., N.W., Suite 310, Washington, DC 20006
Telephone: (202) 863-0001
Registered as lobbyist at U.S. Congress.
Registered as Foreign Agent: (#4296)
Background: Served in the U.S. Air Force, 1967-87.
Clients:
Baldt, Inc.
Kaman Corp.
Martin Marietta Corp.
MIP Instandsetzungsbetriebe GmbH
SKF USA, Inc.

ERVIN TECHNICAL ASSOCIATES, INC. (ETA)
1667 K St., N.W., Suite 310, Washington, DC 20006
Telephone: (202) 863-0001
Registered as Foreign Agent: (#4296)
Members of firm representing listed organizations:
Ervin, James L., President
Background: Served in the U.S. Air Force, 1967-87.
Clients:
Baldt, Inc. *(James L. Ervin)*
Kaman Corp. *(James L. Ervin)*
Martin Marietta Corp. *(James L. Ervin)*
MIP Instandsetzungsbetriebe GmbH *(James L. Er-
vin)*
SKF USA, Inc. *(James L. Ervin)*

ESCH, Michael D.
Patton, Boggs and Blow
2550 M St., N.W., Suite 800, Washington, DC 20037
Telephone: (202) 457-6000

ESCUDERO, Mario F.
Morgan, Lewis and Bockius
1800 M St., N.W., Washington, DC 20036
Telephone: (202) 467-7000
Clients:
Puerto Rico Maritime Shipping Authority

ESDERS, Ingolf G.
Assistant to the Director, Internat'l Longshoremen's Ass'n
815 16th St., N.W., Suite 104, Washington, DC 20006
Telephone: (202) 628-4546
Registered as lobbyist at U.S. Congress.

ESHER, Cynthia
President, SAMA Group of Ass'ns
225 Reinekers Lane Suite 625, Washington, DC 22314
Telephone: (703) 836-1360

ESHERICK, George T.
Vice President, Government Relations, American Iron and
Steel Institute
1133 15th St., N.W. Suite 300, Washington, DC 20005-
2701
Telephone: (202) 452-7230
Registered as lobbyist at U.S. Congress.

ESHERICK, Mark Richard
Manager, Legislative Affairs, Cable and Wireless North
America
1919 Gallows Road, Vienna, VA 22182
Telephone: (703) 790-5300
Registered as lobbyist at U.S. Congress.
Registered as Foreign Agent: (#4231)

ESHMAN, Dennis
Counsel, Legislat. & Regulatory Affairs, American Gas
Ass'n
1515 Wilson Blvd., Arlington, VA 22209
Telephone: (703) 841-8481

ESKIN, Andrew D.
Verner, Liipfert, Bernhard, McPherson and Hand, Chart-
ered
901 15th St., N.W., Suite 700, Washington, DC 20005
Telephone: (202) 371-6000
Registered as lobbyist at U.S. Congress.
Background: Legislative Aide to Rep. James Santini (D-
NV), 1977-78. Attorney, Federal Trade Commission,
1985-86. Legislative Director to Senator Richard Bryan
(D-NV), 1989-90.

ESLEECK, Samuel H.
Mgr. Wash. Liaison, Contract Resrch Div., Babcock and
Wilcox Co.
c/o McDermott Internat'l Inc. 1850 K St., N.W., Suite 950,
Washington, DC 20006
Telephone: (202) 296-0390

ESSAYE, Anthony F.
Rogers and Wells
1737 H St., N.W., Washington, DC 20006
Telephone: (202) 331-7760
Registered as lobbyist at U.S. Congress.
Registered as Foreign Agent: (#3428).
Background: Office of the General Counsel, 1963-65;
Deputy General Counsel, 1965-66, Peace Corps.
Clients:
Compagnie Financiere de Paris et des Pays Bas

ESSERMAN, Susan G.
Steptoe and Johnson
1330 Connecticut Ave., N.W., Washington, DC 20036
Telephone: (202) 429-3000
Registered as Foreign Agent: (#3975).
Clients:
Aluminum Co. of America
Canadian Sugar Institute
Cargill, Inc.
Mitsui and Co.

ESSLINGER, J. Thomas
Schmeltzer, Aptaker and Sheppard
The Watergate, 2600 Virginia Ave., N.W., Washington, DC
20037
Telephone: (202) 333-8800
Clients:
South Carolina State Port Authority

ESTERLY, Jane B.
Funke and Associates, Karl A.
729 2nd St., N.E., Washington, DC 20002
Telephone: (202) 544-4166
Registered as lobbyist at U.S. Congress.
Organizations represented:
Chitimacha Tribe of Louisiana

ESTRADA, Ramon A.
Bostrom Corp.
808 17th St., N.W., Suite 200, Washington, DC 20006
Telephone: (202) 223-9669
Clients:
American Heartworm Soc.
USIR - The Internat'l Soc. of SIR Users

ETCHISON, Glenda Leggitt
Senior Staff Executive, American Ass'n of Advertising
Agencies
1899 L St., N.W., Suite 700, Washington, DC 20036
Telephone: (202) 331-7345
Background: Former aide to Representative Margaret
Heckler of Massachusetts.

ETKIN, Nancy U.
Legislative Affairs Specialist, Arkla, Inc.
1150 Connecticut Ave,m N.W. Suite 1125, Washington,
DC 20036
Telephone: (202) 331-7175

ETTLESON, Sherry E.
Staff Attorney, Congress Watch
215 Pennsylvania Ave., S.E., Washington, DC 20003
Telephone: (202) 546-4996
Registered as lobbyist at U.S. Congress.

ETTLINGER, Michael P.
State Tax Policy Director, Citizens for Tax Justice
1311 L St., N.W. 4th Floor, Washington, DC 20005
Telephone: (202) 626-3780

EURE, Stephen E.
Director, Government Relations, Snack Food Ass'n
1711 King St., Suite One, Alexandria, VA 22314
Telephone: (703) 836-4500
Registered as lobbyist at U.S. Congress.

EVANS, Andreas 'Red'
Dir. of Publications & Public Relations, Nat'l Federation of
Federal Employees
1016 16th St., N.W., Suite 400, Washington, DC 20036
Telephone: (202) 862-4400
Registered as lobbyist at U.S. Congress.

EVANS & ASSOC. INC., B. L.
1301 Connecticut Ave., N.W., Washington, DC 20036
Telephone: (202) 659-0330
Members of firm representing listed organizations:
Evans, Billy Lee, President
Background: Member, U.S. House of Representatives
(D-GA), 1977-83.
Organizations represented:
BATUS, Inc. *(Billy Lee Evans)*
Brown and Williamson Tobacco Corp. *(Billy Lee
Evans)*
Great Western Financial Corp. *(Billy Lee Evans)*

EVANS ASSOCIATES, Dave
406 3rd St., S.E., Washington, DC 20003
Background: A government relations and political consult-
ing firm.
Members of firm representing listed organizations:
Evans, David W.
Background: Member, U.S. House of Representatives
(D-IN), 1975-83.
Organizations represented:
Harmon-Motive
Mortgage Insurance Companies of America *(David
W. Evans)*
United California Savings Bank *(David W. Evans)*

EVANS & ASSOCIATES, P.C.
655 15th St., N.W., Suite 310, Washington, DC 20005
Telephone: (202) 978-3333
Members of firm representing listed organizations:
Evans, Donald C. (Jr.)
Background: A lawyer/lobbyist.
Clients:
American Family Corp.
Stepan Chemical Co.

EVANS, Billy Lee
President, Evans & Assoc. Inc., B. L.
1301 Connecticut Ave., N.W., Washington, DC 20036
Telephone: (202) 659-0330
Registered as lobbyist at U.S. Congress.
Background: Member, U.S. House of Representatives (D-GA), 1977-83.
Organizations represented:
BATUS, Inc.
Brown and Williamson Tobacco Corp.
Great Western Financial Corp.

EVANS, Brock
V. President for Nat'l Issues, Nat'l Audubon Soc.
801 Pennsylvania Ave., S.E., Washington, DC 20003
Telephone: (202) 547-9009
Registered as lobbyist at U.S. Congress.

EVANS, C. Lawrence, Jr.
V. President, Government Relations, Acacia Mutual Life Insurance Co.
51 Louisiana Ave., N.W., Washington, DC 20001
Telephone: (202) 628-4506
Registered as lobbyist at U.S. Congress.

EVANS, Cindy
Environmental Counsel, Nat'l Forest Products Ass'n
1250 Connecticut Ave., N.W. Suite 200, Washington, DC 20036
Telephone: (202) 463-2700
Registered as lobbyist at U.S. Congress.

EVANS, David C.
Reed Smith Shaw & McClay
1200 18th St., N.W., Washington, DC 20036
Telephone: (202) 457-6100
Registered as lobbyist at U.S. Congress.
Clients:
Brick Institute of America
Building Owners and Managers Ass'n Internat'l

EVANS, David W.
Evans Associates, Dave
406 3rd St., S.E., Washington, DC 20003
Registered as lobbyist at U.S. Congress.
Background: Member, U.S. House of Representatives (D-IN), 1975-83.
Organizations represented:
Mortgage Insurance Companies of America
United California Savings Bank

EVANS, Donald C., Jr.
Evans & Associates, P.C.
655 15th St., N.W., Suite 310, Washington, DC 20005
Telephone: (202) 978-3333
Registered as lobbyist at U.S. Congress.
Background: A lawyer/lobbyist.

EVANS, Donald D.
Deputy General Counsel, Chemical Manufacturers Ass'n
2501 M St., N.W., Washington, DC 20037
Telephone: (202) 887-1100

EVANS, Elaine
Exec. Director, Nat'l Hydropower Ass'n
555 13th St., N.W. Suite 900 East, Washington, DC 20004
Telephone: (202) 637-8115
Registered as lobbyist at U.S. Congress.
Background: Also represents the Nat'l Hydropower Ass'n Political Action Committee.

EVANS, Gordon R.
Exec. Dir, Fed, Regulatory Matters (FCC), NYNEX
1828 L St., N.W., Suite 1000, Washington, DC 20036
Telephone: (202) 416-0100

EVANS GROUP, LTD., THE
1010 Wisconsin Ave., N.W. Suite 810, Washington, DC 20007
Telephone: (202) 333-8777
Registered as Foreign Agent: (#4222)
Members of firm representing listed organizations:
Bafalis, L. A. (Skip)
Background: Former Member, U.S. House of Representatives (R-FL).
Barnes, Ben
Background: Former Lieutenant Governor of Texas and Speaker of the Texas House of Representatives. Serves as President, Nat'l Coalition for the Rehabilitation of Insured Institutions.

Evans, Thomas B. (Jr.), President
Background: Former Member, U.S. House of Representatives (R-DE).
Meltsner, James R.
Riley, Susan
Taylor, Mary Ellen
Clients:
Cain Hoy Plantation (*L. A., Skip Bafalis, Thomas B. Evans, Jr.*)
Contraco, Inc. (*L. A., Skip Bafalis, Thomas B. Evans, Jr.*)
Cyprus, Embassy of the Republic of (*Thomas B. Evans, Jr., James R. Meltsner*)
Cyprus, Government of the Republic of
Emergency Medical Services Associates (*L. A., Skip Bafalis, Thomas B. Evans, Jr.*)
Federal Home Loan Bank of Pittsburgh (*Thomas B. Evans, Jr., Mary Ellen Taylor*)
Matlack Systems, Inc. (*L. A., Skip Bafalis, Thomas B. Evans, Jr., James R. Meltsner*)
Matteson Investment Corp. (*Thomas B. Evans, Jr., Susan Riley*)
Mortgage Bankers Ass'n of America (*Thomas B. Evans, Jr., Susan Riley, Mary Ellen Taylor*)
Nat'l Multi Housing Council (*Thomas B. Evans, Jr., Susan Riley*)
New York State Mortgage Loan Enforcement and Administrative Corp. (*Susan Riley*)
Nigeria, Government of (*L. A., Skip Bafalis, Thomas B. Evans, Jr.*)
Remodelers Nat'l Funding Corp. (*Thomas B. Evans, Jr.*)
Rollins Environmental Services, Inc. (*Thomas B. Evans, Jr.*)
Towers Financial Corp. (*Thomas B. Evans, Jr.*)

EVANS, Jennifer
Assistant to the President, American Waterways Operators
1600 Wilson Blvd. Suite 1000, Arlington, VA 22209
Telephone: (703) 841-9300

EVANS, John K.
Consultant, Pacific Resources, Inc.
1700 K St., N.W., Suite 502, Washington, DC 20006
Telephone: (202) 223-4623

EVANS, Julie
Office Manager/Administrative Asst., Salt River Project
214 Massachusetts Ave., N.E. Suite 310, Washington, DC 20002
Telephone: (202) 546-8940

EVANS, Lawrence H.
Director, Domestic Marine Affairs, Transportation Institute
5201 Auth Way, Camp Springs, MD 20746
Telephone: (301) 423-3335

EVANS, M. Stanton
Chairman, Education and Research Institute
800 Maryland Ave., N.W., Washington, DC 20002
Telephone: (202) 546-1710

EVANS, Rae Forker
Staff V. President, Nat'l Affairs, Hallmark Cards, Inc.
1615 L St., N.W., Suite 1220, Washington, DC 20036
Telephone: (202) 659-0946
Registered as lobbyist at U.S. Congress.

EVANS, Robert B.
President, American Financial Services Ass'n
1101 14th St., N.W., Washington, DC 20005
Telephone: (202) 289-0400

EVANS, Robert D.
Director, ABA Washington Office, American Bar Ass'n
1800 M St., N.W., Washington, DC 20036
Telephone: (202) 331-2214
Registered as lobbyist at U.S. Congress.

EVANS, Thomas B., Jr.
President, Evans Group, Ltd., The
1010 Wisconsin Ave., N.W. Suite 810, Washington, DC 20007
Telephone: (202) 333-8777
Registered as lobbyist at U.S. Congress.
Background: Former Member, U.S. House of Representatives (R-DE).
Clients:
Cain Hoy Plantation

Contraco, Inc.
Cyprus, Embassy of the Republic of
Emergency Medical Services Associates
Federal Home Loan Bank of Pittsburgh
Matlack Systems, Inc.
Matteson Investment Corp.
Mortgage Bankers Ass'n of America
Nat'l Multi Housing Council
Nigeria, Government of
Remodelers Nat'l Funding Corp.
Rollins Environmental Services, Inc.
Towers Financial Corp.

EVANS, Walter H., III
Davis Wright Tremaine
1752 N St., N.W., Suite 800, Washington, DC 20036
Telephone: (202) 822-9775
Registered as lobbyist at U.S. Congress.
Registered as Foreign Agent: (#3021).
Clients:
Japan, Embassy of
Knappton Corp.
Nike, Inc.
Oregon Economic Development Dept., Ports Division
Oregon, State of, Department of Economic Development, Ports Division
Qatar, Embassy of

EVANS, William J.
Systems Director, Government Affairs, Pan American World Airways
1200 17th St., N.W., Suite 500, Washington, DC 20036
Telephone: (202) 659-7805
Registered as lobbyist at U.S. Congress.
Background: Serves as assistant treasurer for the Pan Am PAC.

EVENSON, Fawn K.
President, Footwear Industries of America
1420 K St., N.W., Suite 600, Washington, DC 20005
Telephone: (202) 789-1420
Registered as lobbyist at U.S. Congress.
Background: Office of Congressional Affairs, Office of Economic Opportunity, 1968-1971. Office of Congressional Affairs, Price Commission/Cost of Living Council, 1971-1974. Also represents the Footwear Industries of America Political Action Committee.

EVER-JONES, Beverly
Exec. Director, Nat'l Ass'n of Black Accountants
900 2nd St., N.E., Suite 205, Washington, DC 20002
Telephone: (202) 682-0222

EVERETT, Ralph B.
Paul, Hastings, Janofsky and Walker
1050 Connecticut Ave., N.W. Suite 1200, Washington, DC 20036-5331
Telephone: (202) 223-9000
Background: Special Assistant to Senator Ernest Hollings (D-SC), 1977-78. Legislative Assistant to Senator Hollings, 1979-82. Minority Chief Counsel and Staff Director, Senate Commerce, Science and Transportation Committee, 1983-86; Chief Counsel and Staff Director, same Committee, 1987-89.
Clients:
American Trucking Ass'ns
Ameritech (American Information Technologies)
Bell Atlantic
BellSouth Corp.
Government Affairs Policy Council of the Regional Bell Operating Companies
NYNEX
Pacific Telesis Group-Washington
Paul, Hastings, Janofsky and Walker Political Action Committee
Southwestern Bell Corp.
US WEST, Inc.

EVERGREEN ASSOCIATES, LTD.
206 G St., N.E., Washington, DC 20002
Telephone: (202) 543-3383
Members of firm representing listed organizations:
Brooks, Robert M.
Frank, Robert
Kauffman, Jo Ann
Pate, Leigh
Weaver, Gerald
Clients:

EVERGREEN ASSOCIATES, LTD. (Cont'd)
American Indian Healthcare Ass'n *(Jo Ann Kauffman)*
Clover Park School District *(Robert M. Brooks)*
DCL Industries *(Robert M. Brooks)*
Gundle Lining Systems, Inc. *(Gerald Weaver)*
Military Impacted School Districts Ass'n *(Robert M. Brooks)*
Nat'l Indian Impacted Schools *(Robert M. Brooks)*
Nez Perce Tribe *(Jo Ann Kauffman)*
Suffolk County, New York *(Robert M. Brooks, Robert Frank, Leigh Pate)*
SuperComputers, Inc. *(Robert M. Brooks)*
United Video Inc. *(Gerald Weaver)*
Washington State Democratic Party *(Robert M. Brooks)*
Washington State Impact Aid Ass'n *(Robert M. Brooks)*
Zambelli Internationale *(Gerald Weaver)*

EVERS, Kathleen
Chief of Staff to the Co-Chair, Republican Nat'l Committee
310 First St., S.E., Washington, DC 20003
Telephone: (202) 863-8500

EVERSOL, Paige
Ketchum Public Relations
1201 Connecticut Ave., N.W. Suite 300, Washington, DC 20036
Telephone: (202) 835-8800
Clients:
Road Information Program, The (TRIP)

EWALT, James H.
Effros, P.C., Stephen R.
P.O. Box 1005, 3977 Chain Bridge Road, Fairfax, VA 22030-1005
Telephone: (703) 691-8875
Registered as lobbyist at U.S. Congress.

EWING, Ky P., Jr.
Vinson and Elkins
Willard Office Building, 1455 Pennsylvania Ave., N.W., Washington, DC 20004-1007
Telephone: (202) 639-6500
Registered as lobbyist at U.S. Congress.
Background: Deputy Assistant Attorney General, Antitrust Division, U.S. Department of Justice, 1978-80.
Clients:
Travelers, The

EWING, Richard S.
Arnold & Porter
1200 New Hampshire Ave., N.W., Washington, DC 20036
Telephone: (202) 872-6700

EXECUTIVES CONSULTANTS, INC.
13542 Union Village Circle, Clifton, VA 22024
Telephone: (703) 830-5369
Background: An association management firm.
Members of firm representing listed organizations:
LaGasse, Robert C. (CAE)
Clients:
Internat'l Microwave Power Institute *(Robert C. LaGasse, CAE)*
Nat'l Bark Producers Ass'n *(Robert C. LaGasse, CAE)*

EXLEY, Robbie G., CAE
Labor Relations Specialist, Nat'l Federation of Federal Employees
1016 16th St., N.W., Suite 400, Washington, DC 20036
Telephone: (202) 862-4400
Registered as lobbyist at U.S. Congress.

EYER, Paul
Assoc. Director,, American Osteopathic Ass'n
300 5th St., N.E., Washington, DC 20002
Telephone: (202) 544-5060
Registered as lobbyist at U.S. Congress.

EYOB, Daniel
Treasurer, Atlantic Research Corp. Political Action Committee
5390 Cherokee Ave., Alexandria, VA 22314
Telephone: (703) 642-4000

EZZELL, Susan
Cong Afrs Specialist, DEPARTMENT OF DEFENSE - Joint Chiefs of Staff
The Pentagon, Washington, DC 20301
Telephone: (202) 697-1137

F/P RESEARCH ASSOCIATES
1700 K St., N.W., Suite 404, Washington, DC 20006
Telephone: (202) 296-5505
Members of firm representing listed organizations:
Crawford, Ronald

FABER, Michael W.
Reid & Priest
1111 19th St., N.W., Washington, DC 20036
Telephone: (202) 828-0100
Registered as lobbyist at U.S. Congress.
Background: Attorney Advisor to Commissioner, Federal Communications Commission, 1971.
Clients:
Committee of Corporate Telecommunications Users

FABERMAN, Edward
Associate General Counsel, American Airlines
1101 17th St., N.W. Suite 600, Washington, DC 20036
Telephone: (202) 857-4221

FABIANI, James P.
President and COO, Cassidy and Associates, Inc.
655 15th St., N.W., Suite 1100, Washington, DC 20005
Telephone: (202) 347-0773
Registered as lobbyist at U.S. Congress.
Registered as Foreign Agent: (#4259).
Background: Senior Minority Staff Member, U.S. House Labor, Health and Human Services, and Education Subcommittee of the House Appropriations Committee.
Clients:
Alexander Graham Bell Ass'n for the Deaf
Boston College
Children's Hospital Nat'l Medical Center
Children's Hospital (Pittsburgh)
Clark Atlanta University
Infirmary Health System, Inc.
Loyola College
O'Connell Management Co.
Pirelli Cable Corp.
Polytechnic University of New York
Rochester Institute of Technology
Societa Cavi Pirelli S.p.A.
University of Nebraska
University of Nebraska Foundation
University of Scranton

FAGA, Betsy
President, American Corn Millers Federation
6707 Old Dominion Drive Suite 240, McLean, VA 22101
Telephone: (703) 821-3025

FAGER, Dan L.
Washington Representative, Chevron, U.S.A.
1700 K St., N.W., Suite 1200, Washington, DC 20006
Telephone: (202) 457-5800
Registered as lobbyist at U.S. Congress.

FAHERTY, Robert L.
Program Director, Publications Program, Brookings Institution
1775 Massachusetts Ave., N.W., Washington, DC 20036
Telephone: (202) 797-6000

FAHEY, J. Noel
V. President & Assoc. Dir. of Research, United States League of Savings Institutions
1709 New York Ave., N.W., Suite 801, Washington, DC 20006
Telephone: (202) 637-8900

FAHEY, Mary L.
Assistant Tax Counsel, Tax Executives Institute
1001 Pennsylvania Ave., N.W., Suite 320, Washington, DC 20004-2505
Telephone: (202) 638-5601

FAHS, Robert R.
V. President & Washington Representative, Cargill, Inc.
1101 15th St., N.W., Suite 205, Washington, DC 20005
Telephone: (202) 785-3060
Registered as lobbyist at U.S. Congress.

FAIN, Leslie
Legislative Director, Committee for Humane Legislation
1506 19th St., N.W. Suite 3, Washington, DC 20036
Telephone: (202) 483-8998
Registered as lobbyist at U.S. Congress.

FAIR, Rita
Managing Director, Secura Group, The
1155 21st St., N.W., Washington, DC 20036
Telephone: (202) 728-4920

FAIRBANKS, Richard M., III
Paul, Hastings, Janofsky and Walker
1050 Connecticut Ave., N.W. Suite 1200, Washington, DC 20036-5331
Telephone: (202) 223-9000
Registered as lobbyist at U.S. Congress.
Registered as Foreign Agent: (#3763).
Background: Associate Director, White House Domestic Council, 1972-74. Assistant Secretary of State, 1981-82; Special Negotiator, Middle East Peace Process, 1982-83; Ambassador at Large, 1984-85.
Clients:
Iraq, Embassy of
Koito Manufacturing Co.

FAKE, Barent L.
Miles and Stockbridge
1701 Pennsylvania Ave., N.W., Suite 500, Washington, DC 20006
Telephone: (202) 333-2350
Clients:
Inova Health Systems

FALASCA, Robert J.
Assistant to the Exec. V. President, American Seed Trade Ass'n
1030 15th St., N.W. Suite 964, Washington, DC 20005
Telephone: (202) 223-4080
Background: Also serves as Secretary of the Nat'l Council of Commercial Plant Breeders and of the American Seed Research Foundation.

FALEY, Gary M.
State Legislative Director-Michigan, Transportation, Communications Internat'l Union
815 16th St., N.W. Suite 511, Washington, DC 20036
Telephone: (202) 783-3660

FALEY, Kevin O.
Rivkin, Radler, Dunne and Bayh
1575 Eye St., N.W. Suite 1025, Washington, DC 20005
Telephone: (202) 289-8660
Registered as lobbyist at U.S. Congress.
Background: Counsel, U.S. Senate Subcommittee on Juvenile Delinquency, 1974-77. General Counsel, Senate Subcommittee on the Constitution, 1977-78. Chief Counsel and Exec. Director, Senate Subcommittee on the Constitution, 1978-80.
Clients:
Nat'l Basketball Ass'n
Nat'l Foreign Trade Council, Inc.

FALEY, Roland, TOR
Exec. Director, Conference of Major Superiors of Men of the U.S.A.
8808 Cameron St., Silver Spring, MD 20910
Telephone: (301) 588-4030

FALIG, Alejandro M.
Federal Programs Coordinator, Northern Mariana Islands, Commonwealth of
2121 R St., N.W., Washington, DC 20008
Telephone: (202) 673-5869

FALK, Bernard H.
President, Nat'l Electrical Manufacturers Ass'n
2101 L St., N.W., Washington, DC 20037
Telephone: (202) 457-8400

FALK, Jacqueline
Campbell, Falk & Selby
1101 30th St., N.W. Suite 500, Washington, DC 20007
Telephone: (202) 298-0427

FALK, James H.
Coffey, McGovern and Noel, Ltd.
2445 M St., N.W., Suite 260, Washington, DC 20037
Telephone: (202) 872-8123
Clients:

WASHINGTON REPRESENTATIVES

Designers & Planners, Inc.
Support Systems Associates, Inc.

FALLE, J. Gary
Director, Washington Office, Ohio, State of
444 N. Capitol St., N.W., Suite 528, Washington, DC 20001
Telephone: (202) 624-5844

FALLON, John B.
Sr. V. President, Internat'l, Rockwell Internat'l
1745 Jefferson Davis Hwy. Suite 1200, Arlington, VA 22202
Telephone: (703) 553-6600

FALLON, Joseph B.
President, Nat'l Organization Against Invisible Disease Spread
Telephone: (202) 462-8640
Registered as lobbyist at U.S. Congress.

FALLTRICK, George
State Legislative Director-California, Transportation, Communications Internat'l Union
815 16th St., N.W. Suite 511, Washington, DC 20036
Telephone: (202) 783-3660
Registered as lobbyist at U.S. Congress.

FANELLI, Joseph J.
President, Business-Industry Political Action Committee
1747 Pennsylvania Ave., N.W. Suite 250, Washington, DC 20006-4697
Telephone: (202) 833-1880

FANG, Paul
Director, Public Relations, Boeing Co.
1700 North Moore St., Arlington, VA 22209
Telephone: (703) 558-9600

FANNING, Leo C.
Staff Director, Professional Activities, Institute of Electrical and Electronics Engineers, Inc.
1828 L St., N.W. Suite 1202, Washington, DC 20036-5104
Telephone: (202) 785-0017

FANNING, William M.
Manager, Technical Services, Nat'l Business Aircraft Ass'n
1200 18th St., N.W. Suite 200, Washington, DC 20036
Telephone: (202) 783-9000

FANONE, Joseph A.
Ballard, Spahr, Andrews and Ingersoll
555 13th St., N.W., Suite 900E, Washington, DC 20004
Telephone: (202) 383-8800

FANT, Lester C., III
Sidley and Austin
1722 Eye St., N.W. Sixth Floor, Washington, DC 20006
Telephone: (202) 429-4000
Registered as lobbyist at U.S. Congress.
Registered as Foreign Agent: (#3731).
Clients:
Cayman Islands, Government of

FARAH, Robert
Exec. Director, Lebanese Information and Research Center
1730 M St., N.W., Suite 807, Washington, DC 20036
Telephone: (202) 785-6666
Registered as Foreign Agent: (#2935)

FARBER, Ted B.
Exec. V. President, United Jewish Appeal Federation of Greater Washington
6101 Montrose Rd., Rockville, MD 20852
Telephone: (301) 230-7200

FARBMAN, Andrea H.
Exec. Director, Nat'l Ass'n for Music Therapy
505 11th St., S.E., Washington, DC 20003
Telephone: (202) 543-6864

FARFONE, Frank J.
Manager, Government Affairs, Dow Chemical
1776 Eye St., N.W. Suite 575, Washington, DC 20006
Telephone: (202) 429-3400
Registered as lobbyist at U.S. Congress.

FARHA, Cheri L.
Director, Media and Public Relations, Aircraft Owners and Pilots Ass'n
500 E St., S.W. Suite 920, Washington, DC 20024
Telephone: (202) 479-4050
Registered as lobbyist at U.S. Congress.
Background: Former aide to Rep. Dan Glickman (D-KS).

FARLEY, Charles
Marketing Director, Brick Institute of America
11490 Commerce Park Drive, Reston, VA 22091
Telephone: (703) 620-0010

FARLEY, Thomas B., II
Washington Representative, American Petroleum Institute
1220 L St., N.W., Washington, DC 20005
Telephone: (202) 682-8416
Registered as lobbyist at U.S. Congress.

FARMER, David M.
V. President, Federal Affairs, Alliance of American Insurers
1629 K St., N.W. Suite 1010, Washington, DC 20006
Telephone: (202) 822-8811
Registered as lobbyist at U.S. Congress.

FARMER, Greg
Director, Government Relations, Northern Telecom Inc..
600 Maryland Ave., S.W. Suite 607, Washington, DC 20024
Telephone: (202) 554-1520
Registered as lobbyist at U.S. Congress.

FARMER, Martha P.
National Exec. Director, Foundation for Women's Resources
700 North Fairfax St., Suite 302, Alexandria, VA 22314
Telephone: (703) 549-1102
Background: Also represents Leadership America.

FARMER, Robert A.
Senior V. President, Cassidy and Associates, Inc.
655 15th St., N.W., Suite 1100, Washington, DC 20005
Telephone: (202) 347-0773
Background: Treasurer, Democratic Governors' Ass'n, 1986- . Treasurer, Democratic Nat'l Committee, 1989- . Treasurer, Dukakis for President Campaign.
Clients:
Puerto Rico Federal Affairs Administration
Tougaloo College

FARMER, Thomas L.
Prather, Seeger, Doolittle and Farmer
1600 M St., N.W., Washington, DC 20036
Telephone: (202) 296-0500
Registered as lobbyist at U.S. Congress.
Registered as Foreign Agent: (#1815).
Background: Chairman, Advisory Board, National Capital Transportation Agency, 1961-1964. Gen. Counsel, Agency for Internat'l Development, 1964-1968. Director and Gen. Counsel, Overseas Development Council, 1968- . Chairman, President's Intelligence Oversight Board, 1977-81.
Clients:
Bankers' Ass'n for Foreign Trade
Bremer Lagerhaus-Gesellschaft
John Hancock Mutual Life Insurance Co.
Nigeria, Government of
North Rhine Westphalia, Government of
Royal Bank of Canada
Salzgitter AG

FARNHAM, Peter
Public Affairs Officer, American Soc. for Biochemistry and Molecular Biology
9650 Rockville Pike, B-22, Bethesda, MD 20814
Telephone: (301) 530-7145

FARNSWORTH, Marianne
Administrator, Union Pacific Fund for Effective Government
555 13th St., N.W. Suite 450 West Columbia Square, Washington, DC 20004
Telephone: (202) 662-0100

FARR, Dagmar T.
V. President, Consumer Affairs, Food Marketing Institute
1750 K St., N.W., Washington, DC 20006
Telephone: (202) 452-8444

Registered as lobbyist at U.S. Congress.

FARR, J. Dent
Director, Government Relations, North American Telecommunications Ass'n
2000 M Street, N.W., Suite 550, Washington, DC 20036
Telephone: (202) 296-9800
Registered as lobbyist at U.S. Congress.

FARR, Stephen
Project Associate, APCO Associates
1155 21st St., N.W., Suite 1000, Washington, DC 20036
Telephone: (202) 778-1000

FARRAGUT GROUP, THE
1825 K St., N.W., Suite 807, Washington, DC 20006
Telephone: (202) 331-9669
Members of firm representing listed organizations:
Collins, William P.

FARRAND, Christopher G.
V. President for Government Relations, Peabody Holding Co.
122 C St., N.W., Suite 240, Washington, DC 20001
Telephone: (202) 393-4366
Registered as lobbyist at U.S. Congress.

FARRAR, Eleanor
V. President, Joint Center for Political Studies
1301 Pennsylvania Ave., N.W., Washington, DC 20004
Telephone: (202) 626-3500

FARRAR, Michael C.
V. Pres., Environmental & Health Affairs, American Paper Institute
1250 Connecticut Ave., N.W. Suite 210, Washington, DC 20036
Telephone: (202) 463-2420
Registered as lobbyist at U.S. Congress.

FARRELL, Brian P.
Program Manager, Utility Nuclear Waste Transportation Program
1111 19th St., N.W., Suite 600, Washington, DC 20036
Telephone: (202) 778-6511

FARRELL, Dianne
V. President, Government Affairs, Recreation Vehicle Industry Ass'n
1896 Preston White Drive P.O. Box 2999, Reston, VA 22090
Telephone: (703) 620-6003

FARRELL, Edward J.
Bronz and Farrell
2021 K St., N.W., Washington, DC 20006
Telephone: (202) 298-5966
Background: U.S. Court of Customs and Patent Appeals, 1971-82; U.S. Court of Appeals for the Federal Circuit, 1982.
Clients:
Canadian Cattlemen's Ass'n

FARRELL, J. Michael
Manatt, Phelps, Rothenberg & Phillips
1200 New Hampshire Ave., N.W., Suite 200, Washington, DC 20036
Telephone: (202) 463-4300
Registered as lobbyist at U.S. Congress.
Background: General Counsel, U.S. Department of Energy, 1985-87.
Clients:
NEC Corp.

FARRELL, Joseph A., III
President, American Waterways Operators
1600 Wilson Blvd. Suite 1000, Arlington, VA 22209
Telephone: (703) 841-9300
Registered as lobbyist at U.S. Congress.

FARRELL, Richard
V. President, Government Affairs, Syntex (USA) Inc.
1133 15th St., N.W., Suite 210, Washington, DC 20005
Telephone: (202) 429-2225
Registered as lobbyist at U.S. Congress.
Background: Former Chief of Staff to Senator Lawton Chiles (D-FL).

The listings in this directory are available as *Mailing Labels*. See last page.

133

FARRELL, Timothy
Keene, Shirley & Associates, Inc.
919 Prince St., Alexandria, VA 22314
Telephone: (703) 684-0550
Registered as lobbyist at U.S. Congress.
Registered as Foreign Agent: (# 3997).

FARRIS, Robert E.
V. President, Policy, American Trucking Ass'ns
430 First St., S.E., Washington, DC 20003-1826
Telephone: (202) 544-6245
Background: Former Director, Federal Highway Administration.

FARTHING, Penelope S.
Patton, Boggs and Blow
2550 M St., N.W., Suite 800, Washington, DC 20037
Telephone: (202) 457-6000
Registered as lobbyist at U.S. Congress.
Background: Staff Attorney, Federal Communications Commission, 1970-72. Congressional Liaison, Federal Trade Commission, 1974-77. Special Assistant to the Administrator, USDA Food Safety and Quality Service, 1977-78.
Clients:
 Incorporated Research Institutions for Seismology

FASIG, Bill
Manager, Government Affairs, Apple Computer, Inc.
1550 M St., N.W. Suite 1000, Washington, DC 20005
Telephone: (202) 872-6260
Registered as lobbyist at U.S. Congress.

FASSETT, Thom White Wolf
General Secretary, United Methodist Church Board of Church and Society
100 Maryland Ave., N.E. Suite 300, Washington, DC 20002
Telephone: (202) 488-5600

FAUGHT, Thomas F., Jr.
Exec. Director, Nat'l Center for Advanced Technologies
1250 Eye St., N.W., Suite 1100, Washington, DC 20005
Telephone: (202) 371-8544
Background: Assistant Secretary of the Navy (1987-89)

FAULKNER, Barbara J.
V. Pres. for Policy and Legal Affairs, Petroleum Marketers Ass'n of America
1120 Vermont Ave., N.W., Suite 1130, Washington, DC 20005
Telephone: (202) 331-1198

FAUST, Marcus G.
322 Constitution Ave., N.E., Washington, DC 20002
Telephone: (202) 547-4276
Registered as lobbyist at U.S. Congress.
Organizations represented:
 Clark County, Nevada
 Desert Research Institute
 Geneva Steel Co.
 Nevada Power Co.
 Public Service Co. of New Mexico
 Sierra Pacific Resources

FAUX, Jeff
President, Economic Policy Institute
1424 16th St., N.W., Suite 501, Washington, DC 20036
Telephone: (202) 667-0400

FAWCETT-HOOVER, Jane
Assoc. Dir., Nat'l Government Relations, Procter and Gamble Mfg. Co.
Suite 400, 801 18 St., N.W., Washington, DC 20006
Telephone: (202) 833-9555
Registered as lobbyist at U.S. Congress.

FAY, Kevin J.
Exec. Director, Alliance for Responsible CFC Policy
2011 Eye St., N.W. Suite 500, Washington, DC 20006
Telephone: (202) 429-1614
Registered as lobbyist at U.S. Congress.

FAY, Robert C.
Exec. V. President, American Amusement Machine Ass'n
12731 Directors Loop, Woodbridge, VA 22192
Telephone: (703) 548-8044
Registered as lobbyist at U.S. Congress.

FAY, William D.
V. President, Congressional Affairs, Nat'l Coal Ass'n
1130 17th St., N.W., Washington, DC 20036
Telephone: (202) 463-2649
Registered as lobbyist at U.S. Congress.
Background: Former legislative aide to Sen. Steve Symms (R-ID). Serves as Administrator, Clean Air Working Group.

FAYAD, Elizabeth
Park Threats Coordinator, Nat'l Parks and Conservation Ass'n
1015 31st St., N.W., Washington, DC 20007
Telephone: (202) 944-8530
Registered as lobbyist at U.S. Congress.
Background: Also represents the American Hiking Society.

FAZZONE, Patrick B.
Collier, Shannon & Scott
1055 Thomas Jefferson St., N.W., Suite 300, Washington, DC 20007
Telephone: (202) 342-8400

FEAGLES, Prentiss E.
Hogan and Hartson
555 13th St., N.W., Suite 1200, Washington, DC 20004-1109
Telephone: (202) 637-5600
Registered as lobbyist at U.S. Congress.

FEASTER, Susan Smith
Manager, Corporate Affairs, Bonner & Associates
1625 K St., N.W., Suite 300, Washington, DC 20006
Telephone: (202) 463-8880
Background: Special Assistant to Senator Paul Trible (R-VA), 1983-84. Legislative Assistant to Rep. Frank Wolf (R-VA), 1984-87.

FEDCHOCK, Bonnie
Assistant Manager, Governmental Affairs, Club Managers Ass'n of America
1733 King St., Alexandria, VA 22314
Telephone: (703) 739-9500

FEDDIS, Nessa
Fed. Couns., Gov't Rels./Retail Banking, American Bankers Ass'n
1120 Connecticut Ave., N.W., Washington, DC 20036
Telephone: (202) 663-5000

FEDELI, Frederick
Assistant Director, Government Relations, American Psychiatric Ass'n
1400 K St., N.W., Washington, DC 20005
Telephone: (202) 682-6039
Registered as lobbyist at U.S. Congress.

FEDER, Laurence M.
Ass't Director, Program Development, Institute of Gas Technology
1825 K St., N.W. Suite 503, Washington, DC 20006
Telephone: (202) 785-3511

FEDERAL SEARCH, INC.
6800 Fleetwood Road Suite 916, McLean, VA 22101
Telephone: (703) 821-8636
Members of firm representing listed organizations:
 Anthony, Tobias, Chairman

FEDIAY, Elizabeth I.
Exec. Director, Nat'l Security Political Action Committee
Washington Harbor West 3050 K St., N.W., Suite 310, Washington, DC 20007
Telephone: (202) 363-9472

FEDOURK, Nick
Policy Director, Energy Conservation Coalition
1525 New Hampshire Ave., N.W., Washington, DC 20036
Telephone: (202) 745-4870

FEGE, Arnold F.
Director of Governmental Relations, Nat'l Congress of Parents and Teachers
1201 16th St., N.W. Room 621, Washington, DC 20036
Telephone: (202) 822-7878

FEGLEY, Karen
Director, Wheat Export Trade Education Committee
415 2nd St., N.E., Suite 300, Washington, DC 20002
Telephone: (202) 547-2004

FEHRENBACHER, SALE, QUINN, AND DEESE
910 16th St., N.W., 5th Floor, Washington, DC 20006
Telephone: (202) 833-4170
Members of firm representing listed organizations:
 Deese, C. Michael
 Sale, Stephen
Clients:
 American Correctional Ass'n (*C. Michael Deese*)
 Better Working Environments, Inc. (*C. Michael Deese*)
 CSC Credit Services, Inc. (*Stephen Sale*)
 Decorative Window Coverings Ass'n (*C. Michael Deese*)
 Industrial Fabrics Ass'n Internat'l (*C. Michael Deese*)
 Nat'l Decorating Products Ass'n (*C. Michael Deese*)
 Nat'l Waterbed Retailers Ass'n (*C. Michael Deese*)
 Trophy Dealers and Manufacturers Ass'n (*C. Michael Deese*)
 United States Industrial Fabrics Institute (*C. Michael Deese*)
 Waterbed Manufacturers Ass'n (*C. Michael Deese*)

FEICHGRAEBER, Michelle
Edelman, Inc., Daniel J.
1420 K St., N.W., Washington, DC 20005
Telephone: (202) 371-0200
Organizations represented:
 Advo-Systems, Inc.

FEIERABEND, J. Scott
Director, Fisheries and Wildlife Div., Nat'l Wildlife Federation
1400 16th St., N.W., Washington, DC 20036-2266
Telephone: (202) 797-6800
Registered as lobbyist at U.S. Congress.

FEINBERG, Kenneth R.
Kaye, Scholer, Fierman, Hays and Handler
The McPherson Building 901 15th St., N.W., #1100, Washington, DC 20005
Telephone: (202) 682-3500
Registered as lobbyist at U.S. Congress.
Background: Administrative Assistant to Sen. Edward M. Kennedy, 1976-79. Special Counsel, U.S. Senate Judiciary Committee, 1979.
Clients:
 Goldman, Sachs and Co.

FEINBERG, Richard E.
V. President, Overseas Development Council
1717 Massachusetts Ave., N.W., Washington, DC 20036
Telephone: (202) 234-8701

FEINBERG, Robert S.
President, Washington Financial Information Services, Inc.
406 3rd St., S.E., Washington, DC 20003
Registered as lobbyist at U.S. Congress.
Clients:
 Downey Savings and Loan

FEINSTEIN, Lee A.
Senior Research Analyst, Arms Control Ass'n
11 Dupont Circle, N.W., Washington, DC 20036
Telephone: (202) 797-6450

FEITH, Douglas J.
Internat'l Advisers, Inc.
2300 M St., N.W., Suite 600, Washington, DC 20037
Telephone: (202) 293-1575
Registered as lobbyist at U.S. Congress.
Registered as Foreign Agent: (#4203).
Background: Member, National Security Council Staff, 1981-82. Special Counsel to the Assistant Secretary of Defense for International Security Policy, 1982-84. Deputy Assistant Secretary of Defense for Negotiations Policy, 1984-86.
Clients:
 Turkey, Embassy of

FEKETE, Paul J.
Account Executive, Hill and Knowlton Public Affairs Worldwide
Washington Harbour, 901 31st St., N.W., Washington, DC 20007
Telephone: (202) 333-7400
Registered as Foreign Agent: (#4170).
Clients:
 Public Affairs Internat'l

FELDBLUM, Chai R.
Legislative Counsel, American Civil Liberties Union
122 Maryland Ave., N.E., Washington, DC 20002
Telephone: (202) 544-1681
Registered as lobbyist at U.S. Congress.

FELDMAN, Howard G.
Seamon, Wasko and Ozment
1015 18th St., N.W. Suite 800, Washington, DC 20036
Telephone: (202) 331-0770
Background: Attorney, Senior Attorney and Assistant
Chief, Legal Division, Bureau of Operating Rights, Civil
Aeronautics Board, 1958-67. Chief, Agreements Division,
Civil Aeronautics Board, 1967-69.
Clients:
Northeastern Airlines

FELDMAN, Howard J.
Van Ness, Feldman & Curtis
1050 Thomas Jefferson St., 7th Floor, Washington, DC
20007
Telephone: (202) 298-1800
Registered as lobbyist at U.S. Congress.
Background: Attorney, Tax Division, U.S. Department of
Justice, 1964-1968. Chief Counsel, U.S. Senate Permanent
Committee on Investigations, 1973-1977.
Clients:
Bumble Bee Seafoods, Inc.
McKesson Corp.
Wagner and Brown

FELDMAN, Jay
National Coordinator, Nat'l Coalition Against the Misuse of
Pesticides
530 7th St., S.E., Washington, DC 20003
Telephone: (202) 543-5450

FELDMAN, Lloyd
Dir., Planning, Policy and Legislation, DEPARTMENT OF
LABOR - Employment and Training Administration
200 Constitution Ave., N.W., Washington, DC 20210
Telephone: (202) 535-0664

FELDMAN, Mark B.
Internat'l Advisers, Inc.
2300 M St., N.W., Suite 600, Washington, DC 20037
Telephone: (202) 293-1575
Registered as lobbyist at U.S. Congress.
Registered as Foreign Agent: (#4203).
Background: Assistant Legal Adviser, 1968-74, Deputy Le-
gal Adviser, 1974-80, Acting Legal Adviser, 1981, U.S.
Department of State.

FELDMAN, Myer
Ginsburg, Feldman and Bress
1250 Connecticut Ave., N.W. Suite 800, Washington, DC
20036
Telephone: (202) 637-9000
Background: Special Counsel to the Securities and Exchange Commission, 1946-55; Counsel, Senate Banking
and Currency Committee, 1955-57; Legislative Assistant
to Senator J. F. Kennedy, 1958-61; Deputy Special Counsel to the President, 1961-64 and Counsel, 1964-65.

FELDMAN, Timothy
Manager, Legislative Affairs, Oracle Corp.
1627 Eye St., N.W. Suite 880, Washington, DC 20006
Telephone: (202) 907-2753
Registered as lobbyist at U.S. Congress.

FELLER, Mimi A.
V. Pres., Public Affrs. & Gov't Relats., Gannett Co., Inc.
1100 Wilson Blvd., Arlington, VA 22234
Telephone: (703) 284-6046
Registered as lobbyist at U.S. Congress.
Background: Chief of Staff to Senator John Chafee (R-RI),
1981-83. Deputy Assistant Secretary/Legislative Affairs,
U.S. Treasury Department, 1983-85.

FELLER, Peter Buck
McKenna, Conner and Cuneo
1575 Eye St., N.W. Suite 800, Washington, DC 20005
Telephone: (202) 789-7500
Clients:
American Pipe Fittings Ass'n
Cast Iron Pipefittings Committee
Cigar Ass'n of America

FELLMAN, Steven John
Loomis, Owen, Fellman and Howe
2020 K St., N.W. Suite 800, Washington, DC 20006
Telephone: (202) 296-5680
Background: Federal Trade Commission 1962-64.
Clients:
Nat'l Ass'n of Theatre Owners
Nat'l Erectors Ass'n
Textile Rental Services Ass'n of America

FELS, Nicholas W.
Covington and Burling
1201 Pennsylvania Ave., N.W., Box 7566, Washington, DC
20044
Telephone: (202) 662-6000
Clients:
Air Products and Chemicals, Inc.

FELTMAN, Kenneth E.
Director, Employers Council on Flexible Compensation
927 15th St., N.W., Suite 1000, Washington, DC 20005
Telephone: (202) 659-4300
Registered as lobbyist at U.S. Congress.

FENIG, David
V. President, Black, Manafort, Stone and Kelly Public Af-
fairs Co.
211 N. Union St., Third Floor, Alexandria, VA 22314
Telephone: (703) 683-6612
Background: Former Legislative Director for Senator Spark
Matsunaga (D-HI).

FENN & KING COMMUNICATIONS
1043 Cecil Place, N.W., Washington, DC 20007
Telephone: (202) 337-6995
Background: A multi-service campaign consulting firm spe-
cializing in media production, direct mail and general
strategy.
Members of firm representing listed organizations:
Engel, Rob
Fenn, Peter H.
Background: Senate Intelligence Committee, 1975-76;
Chief of Staff to Senator Frank Church, 1977-80;
Exec. Director, Democrats for the 80's, 1981-82.
Goodman, Lisa, Media Director
King, Thomas J. (Jr.)
Background: Political Director, Democratic Congres-
sional Campaign Committee, 1985-86.
Murphy, Steve
Putnam, Mark C., Creative Director

FENN, Peter H.
Fenn & King Communications
1043 Cecil Place, N.W., Washington, DC 20007
Telephone: (202) 337-6995
Background: Senate Intelligence Committee, 1975-76;
Chief of Staff to Senator Frank Church, 1977-80; Exec.
Director, Democrats for the 80's, 1981-82.

FENNELL, Karen S.
Government Relations Coordinator, American College of
Nurse-Midwives
1522 K St., N.W., Suite 1000, Washington, DC 20005
Telephone: (202) 289-0171
Registered as lobbyist at U.S. Congress.

FENNINGER, Randolph B.
MARC Associates, Inc.
1030 15th St., N.W. Suite 468, Washington, DC 20005
Telephone: (202) 371-8090
Registered as lobbyist at U.S. Congress.
Clients:
American Ass'n of Clinical Urologists
American Ass'n of Colleges of Osteopathic Medi-
cine
American College of Nuclear Physicians
American Soc. for Gastrointestinal Endoscopy
American Soc. of Clinical Pathologists
American Urological Ass'n
Nat'l Hemophilia Foundation

FENSTER, Larry
Senior Analyst, American Ass'n of Retired Persons
1909 K St., N.W., Washington, DC 20049
Telephone: (202) 872-4700

FENSTERWALD & ALCORN, P.C.
2112 C Gallows Road, Vienna, VA 22180
Telephone: (703) 734-0500

Members of firm representing listed organizations:
Alcorn, Daniel S.
Fensterwald, Bernard (III)
Clients:
Assassination Archive and Research Center *(Ber-
nard Fensterwald, Jr.)*
Concerned Federal Railroad Administration Em-
ployees *(Bernard Fensterwald, III)*
Open Government Institute *(Bernard Fensterwald, III)*

FENSTERWALD, Bernard, III
Fensterwald & Alcorn, P.C.
2112 C Gallows Road, Vienna, VA 22180
Telephone: (703) 734-0500
Registered as lobbyist at U.S. Congress.
Clients:
Concerned Federal Railroad Administration Em-
ployees
Open Government Institute

FENTON COMMUNICATIONS, INC.
1755 S St., N.W., Second Floor, Washington, DC 20009
Telephone: (202) 745-0707
Registered as Foreign Agent: (#3857)
Members of firm representing listed organizations:
Fenton, David, President
McDowell-Head, Leila, Senior Account Execu-
tive
Clients:
Angola, Government of the People's Republic of
(David Fenton)
Jamaica, Government of *(David Fenton, Leila McDo-
well-Head)*

FENTON, David
President, Fenton Communications, Inc.
1755 S St., N.W., Second Floor, Washington, DC 20009
Telephone: (202) 745-0707
Registered as Foreign Agent: (#3857).
Clients:
Angola, Government of the People's Republic of
Jamaica, Government of

FENTON, Frank
Senior V. President, Public Policy, American Iron and
Steel Institute
1133 15th St., N.W. Suite 300, Washington, DC 20005
Telephone: (202) 452-7130

FENTON, George F., Jr.
V. President - Government Affairs, American Mining Con-
gress
1920 N St., N.W. Suite 300, Washington, DC 20036
Telephone: (202) 861-2800
Registered as lobbyist at U.S. Congress.
Background: Staff Member (Transportation), Senate Envi-
ronment & Public Works Committee; 1973-1985.

FERGUSON, Allen R.
President, AFE, Inc.
4440 Sedgwick St., N.W., Washington, DC 20016
Telephone: (202) 244-0987

FERGUSON ASSOCIATES, Jack
203 Maryland Ave., N.E., Washington, DC 20002
Telephone: (202) 544-6655
Members of firm representing listed organizations:
Ferguson, Jack, President
Background: Was Legislative Aide to Congressman
Floyd Hicks (D-WA) 1970-73; Administrative Aide
to Congressman Don Young (R-AK) 1973-76; Ad-
ministrative Aide to Senate Assistant Minority Lead-
er, Senator Ted Stevens (R-AK) 1976-78. Established
Jack Ferguson Associates in 1978.
Knieriemen, Theresa
Background: Former Legislative Analyst to the House
Republican Party Conference under Chairmanship of
Reps. Dick Cheney (R-WY) and Jack Kemp (R-NY).
Organizations represented:
Alaskan Loggers Ass'n *(Jack Ferguson)*
Art Dealers Ass'n of America *(Jack Ferguson)*
Christie's Internat'l *(Jack Ferguson)*
Conoco, Inc.
Crystal Cruises, Inc. *(Jack Ferguson)*
Dillingham Construction N.A., Inc.
Dillingham Construction Pacific, Ltd.
Global Marine, Inc.
Haida Corp.
Klukwan, Inc. *(Jack Ferguson)*

FERGUSON ASSOCIATES, Jack (Cont'd)
Northern Air Cargo *(Jack Ferguson)*
Sotheby's Holdings, Inc. *(Jack Ferguson)*
Tacoma Boatbuilding Co.
United States Borax and Chemical Corp.
Western Forest Industries Ass'n *(Jack Ferguson)*
Williams Companies, The

FERGUSON CO., The
1730 Rhode Island Ave., N.W., Suite 400, Washington, DC 20036
Telephone: (202) 331-8500
Members of firm representing listed organizations:
Ferguson, William (Jr.)
Jordan, Patricia
Young, Thane
Organizations represented:
Alhambra, California, City of *(William Ferguson, Jr., Patricia Jordan, Thane Young)*
Berg-Revoir Corp. *(William Ferguson, Jr., Patricia Jordan, Thane Young)*
Imperial Irrigation District *(William Ferguson, Jr., Patricia Jordan, Thane Young)*
Inglewood, California, City of *(William Ferguson, Jr., Patricia Jordan, Thane Young)*
Irvine Co., The *(William Ferguson, Jr., Patricia Jordan, Thane Young)*
Long Beach Transit *(William Ferguson, Jr., Patricia Jordan, Thane Young)*
Oceanside, California, City of *(William Ferguson, Jr., Patricia Jordan, Thane Young)*
Oceanside Redevelopment Agency *(William Ferguson, Jr., Patricia Jordan, Thane Young)*
Provo, Utah, City of *(William Ferguson, Jr., Patricia Jordan, Thane Young)*
Redondo Beach, California, City of *(William Ferguson, Jr., Patricia Jordan, Thane Young)*
Santa Ana, California, City of *(William Ferguson, Jr., Patricia Jordan, Thane Young)*
Santa Cruz Properties, Inc. *(William Ferguson, Jr., Patricia Jordan, Thane Young)*
South Salt Lake, Utah, City of *(William Ferguson, Jr., Patricia Jordan, Thane Young)*

FERGUSON, Denise G.
V. President, Government Affairs, American Express Co.
1020 19th St., N.W., Suite 600, Washington, DC 20036
Telephone: (202) 822-6680
Registered as lobbyist at U.S. Congress.

FERGUSON, Edward E.
Deputy Exec. Director, Nat'l Ass'n of Counties
440 First St., N.W., Washington, DC 20001
Telephone: (202) 393-6226
Background: Serves as principal contact for the Nat'l Ass'n of Elected County Officials, the Nat'l Ass'n of County Administrators, the Nat'l Ass'n of County Association Executives, and the Nat'l Ass'n of County Park and Recreation Officials.

FERGUSON, Jack
President, Ferguson Associates, Jack
203 Maryland Ave., N.E., Washington, DC 20002
Telephone: (202) 544-6655
Registered as lobbyist at U.S. Congress.
Background: Was Legislative Aide to Congressman Floyd Hicks (D-WA) 1970-73; Administrative Aide to Congressman Don Young (R-AK) 1973-76; Administrative Aide to Senate Assistant Minority Leader, Senator Ted Stevens (R-AK) 1976-78. Established Jack Ferguson Associates in 1978.
Organizations represented:
Alaskan Loggers Ass'n
Art Dealers Ass'n of America
Christie's Internat'l
Crystal Cruises, Inc.
Klukwan, Inc.
Northern Air Cargo
Sotheby's Holdings, Inc.
Western Forest Industries Ass'n

FERGUSON, James H.
Senior Legislative Specialist, Institute of Electrical and Electronics Engineers, Inc.
1828 L St., N.W. Suite 1202, Washington, DC 20036-5104
Telephone: (202) 785-0017
Registered as lobbyist at U.S. Congress.

FERGUSON, Karen W.
Director, Pension Rights Center
918 16th St., N.W., Suite 704, Washington, DC 20006
Telephone: (202) 296-3776
Registered as lobbyist at U.S. Congress.

FERGUSON, Robert
President, Nat'l Ass'n of Chiefs of Police
1000 Connecticut Ave., N.W. Suite 9, Washington, DC 20036
Telephone: (202) 293-9088

FERGUSON, Shannon
Technical Coordinator, OMB Watch
1731 Connecticut Ave., N.W., Washington, DC 20009-1146
Telephone: (202) 234-8494

FERGUSON, W. Scott
General Counsel, Nat'l Agricultural Chemicals Ass'n
Madison Bldg., 1155 15th St., Suite 900, Washington, DC 20005
Telephone: (202) 296-1585

FERGUSON, William, Jr.
Ferguson Co., The
1730 Rhode Island Ave., N.W., Suite 400, Washington, DC 20036
Telephone: (202) 331-8500
Registered as lobbyist at U.S. Congress.
Organizations represented:
Alhambra, California, City of
Berg-Revoir Corp.
Imperial Irrigation District
Inglewood, California, City of
Irvine Co., The
Long Beach Transit
Oceanside, California, City of
Oceanside Redevelopment Agency
Provo, Utah, City of
Redondo Beach, California, City of
Santa Ana, California, City of
Santa Cruz Properties, Inc.
South Salt Lake, Utah, City of

FERLIN, Douglas E.
International Marketing, Gulfstream Aerospace Corp.
1000 Wilson Blvd., Suite 2701, Arlington, VA 22209
Telephone: (703) 276-9500
Background: Serves as Chairman, Gulf Aerospace Corp. Political Action Committee.

FERRALL, Victor E., Jr.
Crowell and Moring
1001 Pennsylvania Ave., N.W., Washington, DC 20004-2505
Telephone: (202) 624-2500
Registered as lobbyist at U.S. Congress.

FERRARA, Peter
Senior Fellow, Cato Institute
224 Second St., S.E., Washington, DC 20003
Telephone: (202) 546-0200

FERRARA, Peter J.
Shaw, Pittman, Potts and Trowbridge
2300 N St., N.W., Washington, DC 20037
Telephone: (202) 663-8000

FERREIRA, Rick A.
Policy Associate, American Public Welfare Ass'n
810 First St., N.E., Suite 300, Washington, DC 20002
Telephone: (202) 682-0100

FERRELL, Michael J.
Sr. Staff V.P. & Legislative Counsel, Mortgage Bankers Ass'n of America
1125 15th St., N.W., Suite 700, Washington, DC 20005
Telephone: (202) 861-6500
Registered as lobbyist at U.S. Congress.
Background: Former Staff Director, House Post Office and Civil Service Subcommittee on Postal Operations and Services.

FERRI, Robert J., Jr.
Manager, Press Relations, Nat'l Ass'n of Securities Dealers (NASDAQ)
1735 K St., N.W., Washington, DC 20006
Telephone: (202) 728-8000

Background: Former Exec. Assistant for Communications to Senator John Heinz (R-PA).

FERRIS, Charles D.
Mintz, Levin, Cohn, Ferris, Glovsky and Popeo, P.C.
1825 Eye St., N.W. 12th Floor, Washington, DC 20006
Telephone: (202) 293-0500
Registered as lobbyist at U.S. Congress.
Registered as Foreign Agent: (#3933).
Background: General Counsel to U.S. Senate Majority, 1963-76, to the Speaker of the House of Representatives, 1976-77. Chairman, Federal Communications Commission, 1977-81.
Clients:
Coalition for High Definition Television 1125/60 Production
Communication Industries Ass'n of Japan
Home Recording Rights Coalition

FERRIS, Frank
Director of Negotiations, Nat'l Treasury Employees Union
1730 K St., N.W., Suite 1100, Washington, DC 20006
Telephone: (202) 785-4411

FERRY ASSOCIATES, J. D.
P.O. Box 849, Stevensville, MD 21666
Telephone: (301) 643-4161
Background: A multiple association management firm.
Members of firm representing listed organizations:
Ferry, John D., President
Organizations represented:
American Wood Preservers Ass'n *(John D. Ferry)*
Fourdrinier Wire Council *(John D. Ferry)*
Wire Rope Technical Board *(John D. Ferry)*

FERRY, John D.
President, Ferry Associates, J. D.
P.O. Box 849, Stevensville, MD 21666
Telephone: (301) 643-4161
Organizations represented:
American Wood Preservers Ass'n
Fourdrinier Wire Council
Wire Rope Technical Board

FERSH, Robert J.
Exec. Director, Food Research and Action Center
1319 F St., N.W. Suite 500, Washington, DC 20004
Telephone: (202) 393-5060
Registered as lobbyist at U.S. Congress.
Background: Senior Analyst, U.S. Senate Committee on the Budget, 1978-79. Assistant to the Administrator, Food and Nutrition Service, Department of Agriculture, 1979-81. Assistant Minority Counsel, Senate Committee on Agriculture, Nutrition and Forestry, 1981-83. Staff Director, House of Representatives Subcommittee on Marketing, Consumer Relations and Nutrition, 1983-86.

FESTA, John L.
Director, Chemical Control Programs, American Paper Institute
1250 Connecticut Ave., N.W. Suite 210, Washington, DC 20036
Telephone: (202) 463-2420
Registered as lobbyist at U.S. Congress.

FEULNER, Edwin J., Jr.
President, Heritage Foundation
214 Massachusetts Ave., N.E., Washington, DC 20002
Telephone: (202) 546-4400
Background: Special Assistant, Office of the Secretary of Defense, 1969-1970; Administrative Assistant to Rep. Philip M. Crane, 1970-1974; Exec. Director, Republican Study Committee, U.S. House of Representatives, 1974-1977. Chairman, U.S. Advisory Commission on Public Diplomacy.

FEW, Richard L.
Senior V. President, Federation Relats., American Trucking Ass'ns
430 First St., S.E., Washington, DC 20003-1826
Telephone: (202) 544-6245

FICHTER, Edwin P.
Coordinating Director, Holy Childhood Ass'n
1720 Massachusetts Ave., N.W., Washington, DC 20036
Telephone: (202) 775-8637

FIDELITY PACIFIC GROUP
1250 24th St., N.W., Suite 600, Washington, DC 20037

Telephone: (202) 466-0576
Registered as Foreign Agent: (#4300)
Members of firm representing listed organizations:
Copeland, Jack L., Consultant
Clients:
Philippines, Government of the *(Jack L. Copeland)*

FIDUCCIA, Paul C.
Winston and Strawn
2550 M St., N.W., Suite 500, Washington, DC 20037
Telephone: (202) 828-8400
Registered as lobbyist at U.S. Congress.
Registered as Foreign Agent: (#3689).
Clients:
Nat'l Council of Health Facilities Finance Authorities

FIEDLER, Donald B.
National Director, Nat'l Organization for the Reform of Marijuana Laws
2001 S St., N.W., Suite 640, Washington, DC 20009
Telephone: (202) 483-5500

FIEDLER, Elliott M.
Associate, Cassidy and Associates, Inc.
655 15th St., N.W., Suite 1100, Washington, DC 20005
Telephone: (202) 347-0773
Registered as lobbyist at U.S. Congress.
Background: Legislative and Staff Director to Rep. David Obey (D-WI), 1976-87.
Clients:
American Hospital in Shanghai Foundation
Critical Languages Consortium
Experiment in Internat'l Living
Fudan Foundation
Nat'l Jewish Center for Immunology and Respiratory Medicine
Schutz American School
St. Norberts College

FIEDLER, Jeff
Director, Corporate Affairs, AFL-CIO - Food and Allied Service Trades Department
815 16th St., N.W., Suite 408, Washington, DC 20006
Telephone: (202) 737-7200

FIEGEL, John L.
V. President, Internat'l Management Group, Inc.
1101 14th St., N.W. Suite 1100, Washington, DC 20005
Telephone: (202) 371-2200
Background: Serves as Exec. Director, Ass'n of Unmanned Vehicle Systems
Clients:
Ass'n for Unmanned Vehicle Systems

FIELD, Charles G.
Staff V. Pres. Regulatory & Tech. Svcs., Nat'l Ass'n of Home Builders of the U.S.
15th and M Streets, N.W., Washington, DC 20005
Telephone: (202) 822-0470

FIELD, Thomas F.
Exec. Director, Tax Analysts
6830 North Fairfax Drive, Arlington, VA 22213
Telephone: (703) 532-1850

FIELDS, Gary W.
Director, State Ass'n Division, American Bankers Ass'n
1120 Connecticut Ave., N.W., Washington, DC 20036
Telephone: (202) 663-5000

FIELDS, Mrs. Rubye S.
President, Blacks in Government
1424 K St., N.W. Suite 604, Washington, DC 20005
Telephone: (202) 638-7767

FIER, Steven I.
Dir., Gov't Relations & Legis. Counsel, Associated Credit Bureaus, Inc.
1090 Vermont Ave., N.W., Suite 501, Washington, DC 20005
Telephone: (202) 371-0910
Registered as lobbyist at U.S. Congress.

FIERCE AND ASSOCIATES
Watergate Bldg., 600 New Hampshire Ave., NW, Suite 1010, Washington, DC 20037
Telephone: (202) 333-8667
Background: A consultant.

Members of firm representing listed organizations:
Fierce, Donald L.
Clients:
AB Hagglund & Soner *(Donald L. Fierce)*
Apex Marine Co.
Bollinger Machine Shop and Shipyard, Inc. *(Donald L. Fierce)*
Coca-Cola Foods *(Donald L. Fierce)*
General Electric Co. *(Donald L. Fierce)*
Liberty Shipping Group *(Donald L. Fierce)*
Nat'l Steel and Shipbuilding Co. *(Donald L. Fierce)*
Pinnacle Data Corp. *(Donald L. Fierce)*
Spar Industries
Superior Farms
Williams & Co., A. L. *(Donald L. Fierce)*

FIERCE, Donald L.
Fierce and Associates
Watergate Bldg., 600 New Hampshire Ave., NW, Suite 1010, Washington, DC 20037
Telephone: (202) 333-8667
Registered as lobbyist at U.S. Congress.
Clients:
AB Hagglund & Soner
Bollinger Machine Shop and Shipyard, Inc.
Coca-Cola Foods
General Electric Co.
Liberty Shipping Group
Nat'l Steel and Shipbuilding Co.
Pinnacle Data Corp.
Williams & Co., A. L.

FIERS, Alan D.
Corp V. Pres. & Dir., Gov't Relations, Grace and Co., W. R.
919 18th St., N.W., Suite 400, Washington, DC 20006
Telephone: (202) 452-6700
Registered as lobbyist at U.S. Congress.
Background: U.S. Diplomatic Service, 1968-88.

FIKE, Harold L.
President, Sulphur Institute
1725 K St., N.W., Washington, DC 20006
Telephone: (202) 331-9660

FIKES, Jay
Legislative Secretary, Friends Committee on Nat'l Legislation
245 Second St., N.E., Washington, DC 20002
Telephone: (202) 547-6000
Registered as lobbyist at U.S. Congress.

FILERMAN, Gary L.
President, Ass'n of University Programs in Health Administration
1911 N. Fort Myer Dr. Suite 503, Arlington, VA 22209
Telephone: (703) 524-5500

FILIPPINI, John C.
Chief, Legis Unit, Legal Policy Sect, DEPARTMENT OF JUSTICE - Antitrust Division
10th and Constitution Ave. N.W., Washington, DC 20530
Telephone: (202) 633-2497

FILLER, Eileen
Associate, Friedman Assoc. Inc., Cynthia
322 Massachusetts Ave., N.E., Washington, DC 20002
Telephone: (202) 546-4204
Background: Former Washington Finance Director, Peter Hoagland for Congress, 1987-88.
Organizations represented:
Simon for Senate '90

FILLER, P.C., Marshall S.
1330 Connecticut Ave., N.W. Suite 250, Washington, DC 20036
Telephone: (202) 457-7760
Organizations represented:
Continental Airlines
Eastern Air Lines
Texas Air Corp.

FILLIP, Christine
V. President, Edelman, Inc., Daniel J.
1420 K St., N.W., Washington, DC 20005
Telephone: (202) 371-0200
Organizations represented:
CDM/Federal Programs Corp.

FIMIANI, Betty Hall
Manager, Information, Battelle Memorial Institute
370 L'Enfant Promenade S.W. 901 D St., S.W., Suite 900, Washington, DC 20004-2115
Telephone: (202) 479-0500

FINAN, William F.
Quick, Finan and Associates
1133 21st. N.W. Suite 200, Washington, DC 20036
Telephone: (202) 223-4044
Background: Former Special Assistant to the Undersecretary of Commerce for International Trade.

FINCKE & WHITE
1900 L St., N.W., Suite 500, Washington, DC 20036
Telephone: (202) 331-8414
Members of firm representing listed organizations:
White, Stephanie A.
Background: Attorney Advisor to Assistant Secretary for Civil Rights, U.S. Department of Education. Minority Counsel, House Committee on the District of Columbia, 1986-87.
Clients:
Magnetic Technologies Corp. *(Stephanie A. White)*
Pitney-Bowes, Inc. *(Stephanie A. White)*

FINE, David
Exec. Director, Federal Relations, Southwestern Bell Corp.
1667 K St., N.W., Suite 1000, Washington, DC 20006
Telephone: (202) 293-8550
Registered as lobbyist at U.S. Congress.

FINE, Hyman
President, Hyman Fine & Associates Ltd.
1725 Jefferson Davis Hwy Suite 213, Arlington, VA 22202
Telephone: (703) 892-2232

FINERAN, Lawrence A.
Director, Regulation and Competition, Nat'l Ass'n of Manufacturers
1331 Pennsylvania Ave., N.W. Suite 1500 North, Washington, DC 20004-1703
Telephone: (202) 637-3000
Registered as lobbyist at U.S. Congress.

FINERFROCK, William A.
Director of Federal Affairs, American Academy of Physician Assistants
950 North Washington St., Alexandria, VA 22314
Telephone: (703) 836-2272
Registered as lobbyist at U.S. Congress.

FINGER, Harold B.
President and Chief Exec. Officer, U.S. Council for Energy Awareness
1776 Eye St., N. W. Suite 400, Washington, DC 20006
Telephone: (202) 293-0770

FINGERHUT, Michael
General Regional Attorney-Federal, US Sprint Communications Co.
1850 M St., N.W., Suite 1100, Washington, DC 20036
Telephone: (202) 857-1030

FINK, Matthew P.
Senior V. President and General Counsel, Investment Company Institute
1600 M St., N.W., Suite 600, Washington, DC 20036
Telephone: (202) 293-7700
Registered as lobbyist at U.S. Congress.

FINK, Nelson L.
Legislative Assistant, Gov't & Mil. Rel., Air Force Sergeants Ass'n
P.O. Box 50, Temple Hills, MD 20748
Telephone: (301) 899-3500
Registered as lobbyist at U.S. Congress.

FINK, Patricia M.
Staff Administrator, Mechanical Contractors Ass'n of America/PAC
1385 Piccard Drive, Rockville, MD 20850
Telephone: (301) 869-5800
Registered as lobbyist at U.S. Congress.

FINKEL, E. Jay
Of Counsel, Porter, Wright, Morris and Arthur
1233 20th St., N.W., Suite 400, Washington, DC 20005

FINKEL, E. Jay (Cont'd)
Telephone: (202) 778-3000
Registered as lobbyist at U.S. Congress.
Background: U.S. Member, Board of Directors, Inter-American Development Bank, 1977-80; Asst. Secretary, Development Committee, World Bank and International Monetary Fund, 1975-77; U.S. Treasury, International Finance, 1952-1974.
Clients:
Harza Engineering Co.
Huntington Nat'l Bank
Maryland People's Counsel

FINKEL, Karen E.
Exec. Director, Nat'l School Transportation Ass'n
Box 2639, Springfield, VA 22152
Telephone: (703) 644-0700
Background: Also serves as Treasurer, Non-Partisan Transportation Action Committee

FINKELSTEIN, Ben
Spiegel and McDiarmid
1350 New York Ave., N.W., Suite 1100, Washington, DC 20005
Telephone: (202) 879-4000
Registered as lobbyist at U.S. Congress.
Clients:
South Hadley, Massachusetts, Town of

FINKELSTEIN, Jim B.
V. President, Communications, Nat'l Soft Drink Ass'n
1101 16th St., N.W., Washington, DC 20036
Telephone: (202) 463-6732

FINKLE, Jeffrey A.
Exec. Director, Nat'l Council for Urban Economic Development
1730 K St., N.W., Suite 915, Washington, DC 20006
Telephone: (202) 223-4735

FINLEY, James K.
Director of Government Relations, Nat'l Council of Community Mental Health Centers
12300 Twinbrook Parkway Suite 320, Rockville, MD 20852
Telephone: (301) 984-6200
Registered as lobbyist at U.S. Congress.

FINLEY, William T., Jr.
Pierson, Semmes, and Finley
1054 31st St., N.W. Suite 300, Washington, DC 20007
Telephone: (202) 333-4000
Registered as lobbyist at U.S. Congress.
Background: Law Clerk to Mr. Justice Brennan, 1964; Chief Counsel, Subcommittee on Improvements in Judicial Machinery, Committee on the Judiciary, U.S. Senate, 1965-1967; Associate Deputy Attorney General, Department of Justice, 1968-1969.
Clients:
Six Flags, Inc.

FINN, Gene L.
V. President and Chief Economist, Nat'l Ass'n of Securities Dealers (NASDAQ)
1735 K St., N.W., Washington, DC 20006
Telephone: (202) 728-8000

FINN, Susan Kudla
Smith, Bucklin and Associates
1101 Connecticut Ave., N.W., Suite 700, Washington, DC 20036
Telephone: (202) 857-1100
Background: Serves as Director of Legislative Affairs, Pet Food Institute and Exec. Director, American Women in Radio and Television
Clients:
American Women in Radio and Television
Pet Food Institute

FINNEGAN, HENDERSON, FARABOW, GARRETT AND DUNNER
1300 I St., N.W., Suite 600, Washington, DC 20005
Telephone: (202) 293-6850
Members of firm representing listed organizations:
Brunsvold, Brian G.
Background: Law Clerk, U.S. Court of Claims, 1966-1967.
Payne, Kenneth E.
Background: Assistant General Counsel, U.S. Department of Commerce, 1971-73.

Clients:
Reserve Bank of Australia *(Kenneth E. Payne)*
Yamazaki Machinery Works, Ltd. *(Brian G. Brunsvold)*

FINNERTY, Peter J.
V. President, Public Affairs, Sea-Land Service, Inc.
1331 Pennsylvania Ave., N.W. Suite 560 National Place, Washington, DC 20004
Telephone: (202) 783-1117
Registered as lobbyist at U.S. Congress.

FINNIGAN, Thomas D.
Assistant Director of Federal Affairs, Union Carbide Corp.
1100 15th St., N.W., Suite 1200, Washington, DC 20005
Telephone: (202) 872-8555
Registered as lobbyist at U.S. Congress.

FINUCAN, Karen
Director, Public Information, American Planning Ass'n
1776 Massachusetts Ave., N.W., Washington, DC 20036
Telephone: (202) 872-0611

FINUCANE, Matthew H.
Director, Air Safety, Ass'n of Flight Attendants
1625 Massachusetts Ave., N.W. 3rd Floor, Washington, DC 20036
Telephone: (202) 328-5400

FIOCCO, M. J.
Director of Legislative Communications, Nat'l Industrial Transportation League
1090 Vermont Ave., N.W. Suite 410, Washington, DC 20005-4905
Telephone: (202) 842-3870
Registered as lobbyist at U.S. Congress.

FIRILAS, Michael
Treasurer, American Hellenic Educational Progressive Ass'n Political Action Committee
1707 L St., N.W., Suite 200, Washington, DC 20036
Telephone: (202) 785-9284

FIRST ASSOCIATES INC.
4320 Lorcom Lane, Arlington, VA 22207
Telephone: (703) 276-0091
Registered as Foreign Agent: (#3941)
Members of firm representing listed organizations:
Roberson, Floyd I.
Clients:
Toa Nenryo Kogyo Kabushiki Kaisha *(Floyd I. Roberson)*

FISCHER, Ken
Administrative Coordinator, Soc. of American Travel Writers
1155 Connecticut Ave., N.W. Suite 500, Washington, DC 20036
Telephone: (202) 429-6639

FISCHER, L. Richard
Morrison & Foerster
2000 Pennsylvania Ave., N.W., Suite 5500, Washington, DC 20006
Telephone: (202) 887-1500
Registered as lobbyist at U.S. Congress.
Clients:
California Bankers Clearinghouse Ass'n
Federal Home Loan Bank of Des Moines
Federal Home Loan Bank of Topeka
MasterCard Internat'l. Inc.
VISA U.S.A., Inc.

FISCHER, Richard L.
V. Pres., Gov't Affairs, Washington, Amoco Corp.
1615 M St., N.W., Suite 200, Washington, DC 20036
Telephone: (202) 857-5310
Registered as lobbyist at U.S. Congress.

FISCHIONE, Deborah A.
Director, Government Relations, Chicago Mercantile Exchange
2000 Pennsylvania Ave., N.W. Suite 6200, Washington, DC 20006
Telephone: (202) 223-6965
Registered as lobbyist at U.S. Congress.
Background: Legislative aide to Rep. Sid Morrison (R-WA), 1981-85.

FISE, Mary Ellen
Product Safety Director, Consumer Federation of America
1424 16th St., N.W. Suite 604, Washington, DC 20036
Telephone: (202) 387-6121
Registered as lobbyist at U.S. Congress.

FISE, Thomas
Principal, Ass'n Resources Management, Inc.
4222 King St., Alexandria, VA 22302
Telephone: (703) 549-4440
Clients:
American Ass'n of Gastroenterology

FISH, Howard
V. President, International, LTV Aircraft Products Group
1725 Jefferson Davis Hwy. Suite 900, Arlington, VA 22202
Telephone: (703) 521-6560

FISHBEIN, Allen
Dir., Neighborhood Revitalization Proj., Center for Community Change
1000 Wisconsin Ave., N.W., Washington, DC 20007
Telephone: (202) 342-0519

FISHEL, Madeline
Ass't Director of Federal Projects, Trust for Public Land
312 Massachusetts Ave., N.E., Washington, DC 20002
Telephone: (202) 543-7552
Registered as lobbyist at U.S. Congress.

FISHER, Bart S.
Patton, Boggs and Blow
2550 M St., N.W., Suite 800, Washington, DC 20037
Telephone: (202) 457-6000
Registered as lobbyist at U.S. Congress.
Registered as Foreign Agent: (#2165).
Clients:
Agri-Energy Roundtable
Rice Millers' Ass'n

FISHER, Bruce L.
Research Director, Citizens for Tax Justice
1311 L St., N.W. 4th Floor, Washington, DC 20005
Telephone: (202) 626-3780

FISHER, Colleen
V. President, Government Relations, Nat'l Apartment Ass'n
1111 14th St., N.W., 9th Floor, Washington, DC 20005
Telephone: (202) 842-4050
Registered as lobbyist at U.S. Congress.
Background: Former Legislative Aide to Senator Richard S. Schweiker of Pennsylvania and staff member, Senate Subcommittee on Housing and Urban Development. Serves also as Treasurer, Apartment Political Committee of the Nat'l Apartment Ass'n

FISHER, Dick
V. President, Administration, Cosmetic, Toiletry and Fragrance Ass'n
1110 Vermont Ave., N.W. Suite 800, Washington, DC 20005
Telephone: (202) 331-1770

FISHER, Dr. Donald W., CAE
Exec. Vice President, American Group Practice Ass'n
1422 Duke St., Alexandria, VA 22314
Telephone: (703) 838-0033
Registered as lobbyist at U.S. Congress.
Background: Serves also as Treasurer, Group Practice Political Action Committee.

FISHER, Gary K.
Washington Representative (Marketing), Chevron, U.S.A.
1700 K St., N.W., Suite 1200, Washington, DC 20006
Telephone: (202) 457-5800
Registered as lobbyist at U.S. Congress.

FISHER, J. Paris
Director, Gov't Relations - Defense, Westinghouse Electric Corp.
1801 K St., N.W., Washington, DC 20006
Telephone: (202) 835-2331
Registered as lobbyist at U.S. Congress.

FISHER, Janet S.
Director, Federal Government Relations, ARCO
1333 New Hampshire Ave., N.W., Suite 1001, Washington, DC 20036

Telephone: (202) 457-6223
Registered as lobbyist at U.S. Congress.

FISHER, John M.
Chairman, American Security Council
499 South Capitol St., S.W., Washington, DC 20003
Telephone: (202) 484-1677
Background: Also represents the Coalition for Peace Through Strength.

FISHER, Quinn R.
Legislative Analyst, USX Corp.
818 Connecticut Ave., N.W., Washington, DC 20006
Telephone: (202) 331-1340

FISHER, Richard
Policy Analyst, Asian Studies, Heritage Foundation
214 Massachusetts Ave., N.E., Washington, DC 20002
Telephone: (202) 546-4400

FISHER, Richard L.
Dir., Federal Regulations & Gas Planning, Washington Gas Light Co.
6801 Industrial Road, Springfield, VA 22151
Telephone: (703) 750-4440

FISHER, WAYLAND, COOPER AND LEADER
1255 23rd St., N.W., Suite 800, Washington, DC 20037-1125
Telephone: (202) 659-3494
Members of firm representing listed organizations:
Moir, Brian R.
Clients:
Internat'l Communications Ass'n *(Brian R. Moir)*
KATU
KCEN-TV
KCIK
KCWT
KDRV
KDUH-TV
KENI-TV
KFAR-TV
KGMC
KHSD-TV
KIHS-TV
KMOS-TV
KMSO-TV
KOMO-TV
KOMU-TV
KOTA-TV
KSGW-TV
KTUU
KTVB
KXMA-TV
KXMB
KXMC-TV
KXMD-TV
KXTX-TV
WANX-TV
WBBS-TV
WBFF
WCCT-TV
WCFC-TV
WFCB-TV
WFMJ-TV
WGGS-TV
WHAE-TV
WPTT-TV
WTLW
WTTE
WXNE-TV
WYAH

FISHER, William P.
Exec. V. President, Nat'l Restaurant Ass'n
1200 17th St., N.W., Washington, DC 20036-3097
Telephone: (202) 331-5900
Registered as lobbyist at U.S. Congress.

FISHKIN, Jane G.
Dir., Social Science Computation Center, Brookings Institution
1775 Massachusetts Ave., N.W., Washington, DC 20036
Telephone: (202) 797-6000

FISHMAN, Ann
Treasurer, ASDC Democratic Victory Fund
430 South Capitol St., S.E., Washington, DC 20003
Telephone: (202) 863-8000

FISHMAN, Charles Louis
Fishman, P.C., Charles Louis
1129 20th St., N.W., Suite 500, Washington, DC 20036
Telephone: (202) 293-0150
Registered as Foreign Agent: (#4054).
Organizations represented:
Nissan Aerospace Division
Nissan Motor Co., Ltd.

FISHMAN, Ira
Patton, Boggs and Blow
2550 M St., N.W., Suite 800, Washington, DC 20037
Telephone: (202) 457-6000
Registered as lobbyist at U.S. Congress.
Registered as Foreign Agent: (#2165).

FISHMAN, P.C., Charles Louis
1129 20th St., N.W., Suite 500, Washington, DC 20036
Telephone: (202) 293-0150
Registered as Foreign Agent: (#4054)
Members of firm representing listed organizations:
Fishman, Charles Louis
Organizations represented:
Nissan Aerospace Division *(Charles Louis Fishman)*
Nissan Motor Co., Ltd. *(Charles Louis Fishman)*

FISHMAN, William L.
Sullivan and Worcester
1025 Connecticut Ave., N.W. Suite 806, Washington, DC 20036
Telephone: (202) 775-8190
Background: Deputy Associate Administrator for Policy, 1974-77, and Senior Policy Advisor, 1979-80, National Telecommunications and Information Administration, U.S. Department of Commerce.

FITCH, John H., Jr.
Exec. Director, American Automotive Leasing Ass'n
1001 Connecticut Ave., N.W., Suite 1201, Washington, DC 20036
Telephone: (202) 223-2600
Registered as lobbyist at U.S. Congress.

FITCHEARD, Linda G.
Manager of Policy and Development, Nat'l Ass'n of REAL-TORS
777 14th St., N.W., Washington, DC 20005
Telephone: (202) 383-1000
Registered as lobbyist at U.S. Congress.

FITHIAN, John F.
Patton, Boggs and Blow
2550 M St., N.W., Suite 800, Washington, DC 20037
Telephone: (202) 457-6000
Registered as lobbyist at U.S. Congress.

FITHIAN, Lisa
Coordinator, Washington Peace Center
2111 Florida Ave., N.W., Washington, DC 20008
Telephone: (202) 234-2000

FITZ-PEGADO, Lauri J.
Sr. V. President and Unit Manager, Hill and Knowlton Public Affairs Worldwide
Washington Harbour, 901 31st St., N.W., Washington, DC 20007
Telephone: (202) 333-7400
Registered as lobbyist at U.S. Congress.
Registered as Foreign Agent: (#3301).
Background: Formerly with U.S. Information Agency.

FITZGERALD, Eileen
Consultant, Kent & O'Connor, Incorp.
1825 K St., N.W., Suite 305, Washington, DC 20006
Telephone: (202) 223-6222
Background: Served in the federal government, 1975-88.

FITZGERALD, John M., Esq.
Counsel for Wildlife Policy, Defenders of Wildlife
1244 19th St., N.W., Washington, DC 20036
Telephone: (202) 659-9510
Registered as lobbyist at U.S. Congress.

FITZGERALD, Mary Clare
Senior V. President, Secura Group, The
1155 21st St., N.W., Washington, DC 20036
Telephone: (202) 728-4920
Registered as lobbyist at U.S. Congress.
Background: V. President, Chase Manhattan Bank. Serves also as Treasurer, SecuraPAC.

Clients:
Chase Manhattan Bank
SecuraPAC

FITZGERALD, Thomas E.
Federal Government Relations Manager, Household Internat'l
1000 Connecticut Ave., N.W., Suite 507, Washington, DC 20036
Telephone: (202) 466-3561
Registered as lobbyist at U.S. Congress.

FITZPATRICK, James F.
Arnold & Porter
1200 New Hampshire Ave., N.W., Washington, DC 20036
Telephone: (202) 872-6700
Registered as lobbyist at U.S. Congress.
Clients:
Pfizer, Inc.
Recording Industry Ass'n of America

FITZPATRICK, John J.
Director of Public Affairs, Internat'l Center for Development Policy
731 Eighth St., S.E., Washington, DC 20003
Telephone: (202) 547-3800

FITZPATRICK, Joyce
Partner, Peabody Fitzpatrick Communications
1400 K St., N.W., Suite 1212, Washington, DC 20005
Telephone: (202) 842-5000
Clients:
Nature Conservancy, The
Pew Health Professions Commission
University of North Carolina

FITZPATRICK, Robert B.
Fitzpatrick & Verstegen
4801 Massachusetts Ave., N.W. Suite 400, Washington, DC 20016-2087
Telephone: (202) 364-8710
Registered as lobbyist at U.S. Congress.

FITZPATRICK & VERSTEGEN
4801 Massachusetts Ave., N.W. Suite 400, Washington, DC 20016-2087
Telephone: (202) 364-8710
Members of firm representing listed organizations:
Fitzpatrick, Robert B.

FITZSIMMONS, Richard
V. President, Government Relations, Burson-Marsteller
1850 M St., N.W., Suite 900, Washington, DC 20036
Telephone: (202) 833-8550
Registered as lobbyist at U.S. Congress.

FLACK INC.
1320 19th St., N.W. Suite 400, Washington, DC 20036
Telephone: (202) 659-2608
Members of firm representing listed organizations:
Flack, Susan Garber
Clients:
Dayton Hudson Corp. *(Susan Garber Flack)*
Nat'l Ass'n of Chain Drug Stores *(Susan Garber Flack)*
Spiegel Inc. *(Susan Garber Flack)*

FLACK, Susan Garber
Flack Inc.
1320 19th St., N.W. Suite 400, Washington, DC 20036
Telephone: (202) 659-2608
Registered as lobbyist at U.S. Congress.
Clients:
Dayton Hudson Corp.
Nat'l Ass'n of Chain Drug Stores
Spiegel Inc.

FLAGG, Robert B.
Legis Rep, Hazardous Waste & Groundwater, Chemical Manufacturers Ass'n
2501 M St., N.W., Washington, DC 20037
Telephone: (202) 887-1100
Registered as lobbyist at U.S. Congress.

FLAGG, Ronald S.
Sidley and Austin
1722 Eye St., N.W. Sixth Floor, Washington, DC 20006
Telephone: (202) 429-4000

FLAHERTY, James E.
Program Manager, Utility Nuclear Waste Transportation Program
1111 19th St., N.W., Suite 600, Washington, DC 20036
Telephone: (202) 778-6511

FLAHERTY, Linda D.
Sr. Legislative Representative, Soc. of American Florists
1601 Duke St., Alexandria, VA 22314
Telephone: (703) 836-8700
Registered as lobbyist at U.S. Congress.

FLAJSER, Steven H.
Director, Government Relations, Fairchild Space & Defense Corp.
20301 Century Blvd, G-17, Germantown, MD 20874
Telephone: (301) 428-6325

FLAMM, Barry
Chief Forester, Wilderness Soc.
1400 Eye St., N.W., 10th Floor, Washington, DC 20005
Telephone: (202) 842-3400
Registered as lobbyist at U.S. Congress.

FLANAGAN, Daniel V., Jr.
Flanagan Group, Inc.
11 Canal Center Plaza Suite 250, Alexandria, VA 22314
Telephone: (703) 739-8822
Registered as lobbyist at U.S. Congress.
Clients:
Dominion Resources, Inc.
Fritz Companies, The
North Carolina Power Co.
San Francisco, California, Port of
Virginia Power Co.

FLANAGAN GROUP, INC.
11 Canal Center Plaza Suite 250, Alexandria, VA 22314
Telephone: (703) 739-8822
Members of firm representing listed organizations:
Chapman, Kelly G., Legislative Representative
Flanagan, Daniel V. (Jr.)
Fontecilla, Herbert M., V. President, Regulatory Affairs
Garrish, Theodore J.
  Background: General Counsel, Dept. of Energy, 1983-85; Ass't Secretary for Intergov't and Public Affairs, 1985-87; Ass't Secretary for Nuclear Energy, 1987-89.
Clients:
American Nuclear Energy Council *(Theodore J. Garrish)*
California Desert Coalition *(Theodore J. Garrish)*
Dominion Resources, Inc. *(Daniel V. Flanagan, Jr.)*
Fritz Companies, The *(Daniel V. Flanagan, Jr.)*
North Carolina Power Co. *(Daniel V. Flanagan, Jr.)*
San Francisco, California, Port of *(Daniel V. Flanagan, Jr.)*
Virginia Power Co. *(Daniel V. Flanagan, Jr.)*

FLANAGAN, James J.
V. President, Yankee Atomic Electric Co.
905 Sixth St., S.W., Washington, DC 20024
Telephone: (202) 488-3789
Registered as lobbyist at U.S. Congress.

FLANAGAN, Kevin
Nat'l Center for Municipal Development
1620 Eye St., N.W., Suite 300, Washington, DC 20006
Telephone: (202) 429-0160
Background: A tenant in the National Center offices, representing the City of Boston.
Clients:
Boston, Massachusetts, City of

FLANAGAN, Richard
National Public Relations Director, American Veterans of World War II, Korea and Vietnam (AMVETS)
4647 Forbes Blvd., Lanham, MD 20706
Telephone: (301) 459-9600

FLANAGAN, Rear Adm. William J.
Chief, Legis Affrs, DEPARTMENT OF NAVY
The Pentagon, Washington, DC 20350-1300
Telephone: (202) 697-7146

FLASK, Jon T.
Grossman and Flask
1101 14th St., N.W. Suite 800, Washington, DC 20005

Telephone: (202) 842-4840
Background: Trial Attorney, Office of Chief Counsel, Internal Revenue Service, 1971-75.

FLAVIN, Christopher
V. President, Worldwatch Institute
1776 Massachusetts Ave., N.W., Washington, DC 20036
Telephone: (202) 452-1999

FLAX, Shira A.
Toxics Specialist, Sierra Club
408 C St., N.E., Washington, DC 20002
Telephone: (202) 547-1141
Registered as lobbyist at U.S. Congress.

FLEISCHAKER, Marc L.
Arent, Fox, Kintner, Plotkin & Kahn
1050 Connecticut Ave., N.W., Washington, DC 20036-5339
Telephone: (202) 857-6000
Registered as lobbyist at U.S. Congress.
Clients:
Motor and Equipment Manufacturers Ass'n
Nat'l Ass'n of College Stores
Nat'l Grain and Feed Ass'n

FLEISCHMAN AND WALSH, P.C.
1400 16th St., N.W. Suite 600, Washington, DC 20036
Telephone: (202) 939-7900
Members of firm representing listed organizations:
Walsh, Charles S.
  Background: Serves as Treasurer, Nat'l Cable Television Political Action Committee.
Clients:
KFBB-TV

FLEISHMAN-HILLARD, INC
1301 Connecticut Ave., N.W., Washington, DC 20036
Telephone: (202) 659-0330
Registered as Foreign Agent: (#3775)
Members of firm representing listed organizations:
Birney, Jonelle, V. President
Buckmaster, Thomas L.
  Background: Serves as Exec. Director of Citizens for Sensible Control of Acid Rain.
Campbell, W. Douglas, V. President
Chappie, Gene, Government Affairs Consultant
  Background: Member, U.S. House of Representatives (R-CA), 1981-86.
Doyne, Karen, V. President
Gregory, Jack
Johnson, Paul
Kochenderfer, Karil L., Account Supervisor
Laitin, Joseph, Public Affairs Consultant
McLean, Elizabeth C., Account Supervisor
Miller, Martha L., Account Supervisor
Nolan, Kathleen D., V. President
Overstreet, John
Redicker, Jane
Royer, Bill
  Background: Former Member, U.S. House of Representatives (R-CA).
Sonnenfeldt, Marjorie
Sullivan, Richard, Exec. V.P. & Sr. Partner
Turner, Caren
Wickenden, David, V. President
Clients:
American Ambulance Ass'n *(Paul Johnson, Caren Turner)*
Apple & Eve *(W. Douglas Campbell, Paul Johnson)*
Automotive Refrigeration Products Institute *(Paul Johnson, Elizabeth C. McLean)*
Chilean Exporters Ass'n
Citizens for a Drug Free America *(Thomas L. Buckmaster, W. Douglas Campbell, Paul Johnson, John Overstreet)*
Citizens for Sensible Control of Acid Rain *(Martha L. Miller)*
Coalition for FDA Resources *(W. Douglas Campbell)*
Coastal Barrier Relief Fund *(Paul Johnson, John Overstreet)*
Eveready *(Jack Gregory, John Overstreet)*
Mexico, Ministry of Commerce
Nat'l Pasta Ass'n
Pathology Practice Ass'n *(Paul Johnson, Caren Turner)*
Processed Apples Institute *(Paul Johnson, Elizabeth C. McLean)*
Ricoh Electronics, Inc.

Spectacor Management Group *(W. Douglas Campbell, Paul Johnson, John Overstreet)*
Syva Co. *(Paul Johnson)*
United Network of Organ Sharing *(W. Douglas Campbell, Paul Johnson, Elizabeth C. McLean)*
United States Navy Memorial Foundation
Wheelabrator Corp., The

FLEISHMAN, Robert W.
Steptoe and Johnson
1330 Connecticut Ave., N.W., Washington, DC 20036
Telephone: (202) 429-3000
Registered as lobbyist at U.S. Congress.

FLEMING, Bartlett S.
President, Ass'n of High Medicare Hospitals
1015 18th St., N.W., Suite 900, Washington, DC 20026
Telephone: (202) 785-9670

FLEMING, Harold C.
Pres. Emeritus & Senior Consultant, Potomac Institute
1400 20th St., N.W. Suite 5, Washington, DC 20036
Telephone: (202) 331-0087

FLEMING, Helen
Chief Deputy Director, Project Vote!
1424 16th St., N.W., Suite 101, Washington, DC 20005
Telephone: (202) 328-1500

FLEMING, J. Roger
Sr. V. President, Tech. Services, Air Transport Ass'n of America
1709 New York Ave., N.W., Washington, DC 20006-5206
Telephone: (202) 626-4021

FLEMING, Jonathan W.
Director, Government Liaison, United Technologies Corp.
1825 Eye St., N.W. Suite 700, Washington, DC 20006
Telephone: (202) 785-7400
Background: Attorney, Office of the General Counsel, 1964-69 and Special Assistant to the Staff Director, 1969-73, U.S. Commission on Civil Rights. Legislative Assistant to Senator Alan Cranston (D-CA), 1973-87.

FLEMING, Michael J.
President, American Ass'n of Equipment Lessors
1300 North 17th St. Suite 1010, Arlington, VA 22209
Telephone: (703) 527-8655
Registered as lobbyist at U.S. Congress.
Background: Also represents the American Ass'n of Equipment Lessors Capital Investment Political Action Committee.

FLEMING, Philip A.
Crowell and Moring
1001 Pennsylvania Ave., N.W., Washington, DC 20004-2505
Telephone: (202) 624-2500
Clients:
Lawyers Alliance for Nuclear Arms Control

FLEMMING, Arthur S.
Co-Chair, Save Our Security
1201 16th St., N.W., Suite 222, Washington, DC 20036
Telephone: (202) 822-7848
Registered as lobbyist at U.S. Congress.

FLESSATE, Gerald C.
Cong Affrs, DEPARTMENT OF DEFENSE - Defense Logistics Agency
Cameron Station, Alexandria, VA 22314-6100
Telephone: (202) 274-6133

FLETCHER, HEALD AND HILDRETH
1225 Connecticut Ave., N.W. Suite 400, Washington, DC 20036
Telephone: (202) 828-5700
Members of firm representing listed organizations:
Curtis, Vincent J. (Jr.)
DePont, Robert A.
Dougherty, Thomas J. (Jr.)
Ennis, James G.
Hildreth, Richard
Hummers, Edward W. (Jr.)
Jazzo, Frank R.
Mahoney, Patricia A.
Petrutsas, George
Raish, Leonard R.
Riley, James P.

Rosenberg, Marvin
Ross, Stephen R.
Clients:
KADN
KAKE-TV
KARK
KBCP
KCMY
KCSO
KCWC-TV
KEVU
KFTL
KFTY
KGW-TV
KHNL-TV
KING-TV
KISU-TV
KITN
KJCT-TV
KJNP
KMPH
KOB-TV
KOBF
KOGG
KPOM-TV
KRDO-TV
KREM-TV
KREN-TV
KRON-TV
KSCH-TV
KSMS-TV
KSTP-TV
KTBS-TV
KTEN
KTVB
KUPK-TV
KUSI
KWTV
K17BA
K21AG
K45AC
San Francisco Chronicle
WAPA-TV
WATE-TV
WBAY-TV
WBEN-TV
WCCL
WDHN
WDHN-TV
WFFT
WFME
WIEC
WJBF
WJZY
WLEX-TV
WLOX-TV
WOAY-TV
WOWT
WRAL-TV
WRWR-TV
WSKP-TV
WTOG
WTRA
WVGA
WVUT-TV
WXEX-TV
810409XO

FLETCHER, Lynne
Manager, Corporate Affairs, Bonner & Associates
1625 K St., N.W., Suite 300, Washington, DC 20006
Telephone: (202) 463-8880

FLETCHER, Michael
Conference Manager, American Legislative Exchange
Council
214 Massachusetts Ave., N.W., Washington, DC 20002
Telephone: (202) 547-4646

FLEXNER, Donald L.
Crowell and Moring
1001 Pennsylvania Ave., N.W., Washington, DC 20004-2505
Telephone: (202) 624-2500
Background: Deputy Assistant Attorney General, Antitrust
Division Department of Justice, 1978-80.

FLOBERG, Gregory V.
National Membership Director, American Veterans of
World War II, Korea and Vietnam (AMVETS)
4647 Forbes Blvd., Lanham, MD 20706
Telephone: (301) 459-9600

FLOOD AND ASSOCIATES, Randolph G.
422 First St., S.E., Suite 210, Washington, DC 20003
Telephone: (202) 544-6675
Background: A government affairs consulting firm.
Members of firm representing listed organizations:
Flood, Randolph G., President and CEO
Background: Legislative Assistant to Former Senator
Harry F. Byrd, Jr. Professional Staff, U.S. Senate
Committee on Environment and Public Works,
1972-82.
Organizations represented:
Jaycees Internat'l
Norfolk Shipbuilding & Drydock Corp.
Puerto Rico Marine Management, Inc.
Virginia Independent Network Political Action
Committee *(Randolph G. Flood)*
Virginia Letter on Public Business *(Randolph G.
Flood)*

FLOOD, Randolph G.
President and CEO, Flood and Associates, Randolph G.
422 First St., S.E., Suite 210, Washington, DC 20003
Telephone: (202) 544-6675
Background: Legislative Assistant to Former Senator Harry
F. Byrd, Jr. Professional Staff, U.S. Senate Committee on
Environment and Public Works, 1972-82.
Organizations represented:
Virginia Independent Network Political Action
Committee
Virginia Letter on Public Business

FLOOD, William F.
Exec. V. President, Nat'l Ass'n of Health Underwriters
1000 Connecticut Ave., N.W., Suite 1111, Washington, DC
20036
Telephone: (202) 223-5533

FLORES, Apolonio
President, Nat'l Ass'n of Housing and Redevelopment Officials
1320 18th St., N.W., Washington, DC 20036
Telephone: (202) 429-2960

FLORES, Dan
Patton, Boggs and Blow
2550 M St., N.W., Suite 800, Washington, DC 20037
Telephone: (202) 457-6000
Registered as lobbyist at U.S. Congress.

FLORINI, Karen
Senior Staff Attorney, Toxics Program, Environmental De-
fense Fund
1616 P St., N.W., Suite 150, Washington, DC 20036
Telephone: (202) 387-3500
Background: Trial Attorney for the U.S. Department of
Justice Land and Natural Resources Division, 1984-87.

FLORIO, Dale J.
Partner, Princeton Public Affairs Group
3333 K St., N.W., Suite 110, Washington, DC 20007
Telephone: (202) 785-2203

FLOWER, Ludlow
Managing Director, Council of the Americas
1625 K St., N.W., Suite 1200, Washington, DC 20006
Telephone: (202) 659-1547

FLOWER, Ruth
Legislative Secretary, Friends Committee on Nat'l Legisla-
tion
245 Second St., N.E., Washington, DC 20002
Telephone: (202) 547-6000
Registered as lobbyist at U.S. Congress.

FLOWERS, R. Allen
Deputy Exec. Secretary, Industry Coalition on Technology
Transfer
c/o Bishop, Cook, Purcell & Reynolds, 1400 L St., N.W.,
Washington, DC 20005
Telephone: (202) 371-5994

FLOYD, Jeremiah
Assoc. Exec. Director, Public Relations, Nat'l School
Boards Ass'n
1680 Duke St., Alexandria, VA 22314
Telephone: (703) 838-6722

FLOYD, Selma
Legis Reference Unit, DEPARTMENT OF HEALTH AND
HUMAN SERVICES
200 Independence Ave., S.W., Washington, DC 20201
Telephone: (202) 245-7750

FLUG, James F.
Lobel, Novins, Lamont and Flug
1275 K St., N.W., Suite 770, Washington, DC 20005
Telephone: (202) 371-6626
Registered as lobbyist at U.S. Congress.
Background: Legal Assistant to the Assistant Attorney
General, Tax Division, 1964-65. Confidential Assistant to
the Attorney General of the U.S. 1965-67. Legislative As-
sistant to Sen. Edward M. Kennedy of Massachusetts,
1967-69. Chief Counsel, Subcommittee on Administrative
Practice and Procedure, Senate Committee on the Judici-
ary, 1969-73.
Clients:
Consumers Union of the United States
Generic Pharmaceutical Industry Ass'n
Phone Medium

FLYE, Richard A.
McKenna, Conner and Cuneo
1575 Eye St., N.W. Suite 800, Washington, DC 20005
Telephone: (202) 789-7500
Registered as lobbyist at U.S. Congress.
Background: Chief, Water Enforcement Branch, Environ-
mental Protection Agency, 1972-78.
Clients:
Fertilizer Institute

FLYNN, Barbara S.
Director, Public Affairs, Nat'l Hydropower Ass'n
555 13th St., N.W. Suite 900 East, Washington, DC 20004
Telephone: (202) 637-8115

FLYNN, Janet
Director, Public Affairs, Distilled Spirits Council of the United States
1250 Eye St., N.W., Suite 900, Washington, DC 20005
Telephone: (202) 628-3544

FLYNN, John J.
Director of Legislation and Politics, Internat'l Union of Op-
erating Engineers
1125 17th St., N.W., Washington, DC 20036
Telephone: (202) 429-9100
Registered as lobbyist at U.S. Congress.

FLYNN, Laurie
Exec. Director, Nat'l Alliance for the Mentally Ill
2101 Wilson Blvd., Suite 302, Arlington, VA 22201
Telephone: (703) 524-7600

FLYNN, Paul M.
Wright and Talisman
1050 17th St., N.W. Suite 600, Washington, DC 20036
Telephone: (202) 331-1194

FLYNN, Pauline
Exec. Director, Nat'l Ass'n of Consumer Agency Administrators
1010 Vermont Ave., N.W., Suite 514, Washington, DC
20005
Telephone: (202) 347-7395

FLYNN, Richard J.
Sidley and Austin
1722 Eye St., N.W. Sixth Floor, Washington, DC 20006
Telephone: (202) 429-4000
Registered as Foreign Agent: (#2658).

FLYNN, Thomas R.
V. President, Brunswick Corp. Defense Division
1745 Jefferson Davis Hwy. Suite 410, Arlington, VA 22202
Telephone: (703) 521-5650

FMR GROUP INC., THE
1000 Potomac St., N.W. Suite 401, Washington, DC
20007
Telephone: (202) 333-2533
Background: A public affairs consulting firm.

WASHINGTON REPRESENTATIVES

FMR GROUP INC., THE (Cont'd)

Members of firm representing listed organizations:
Beckel, Robert G.
Cowan, Glenn A.
Francis, Leslie C.
  Background: Deputy Chief of Staff and Deputy Assistant to the President of the United States, 1977-79. Administrative Assistant to Rep. Norman Y. Mineta, 1975-77.
McGinnis, Patricia G.
  Background: Deputy Associate Director, Office of Management and Budget, 1977-81. Staff Member, U.S. Senate Budget Committee, 1976-77. Policy Analyst, U.S. Department of Health and Human Services and U.S. Department of Commerce, 1973-76.
Rees, Joseph M.
Clients:
California Department of Education *(Patricia G. McGinnis)*
Chrysler Corp.
Ford Motor Co.
General Motors Corp.
Nat'l Coalition of Burn Center Hospitals *(Joseph M. Rees)*
United Hospital Fund of New York *(Joseph M. Rees)*
Waste Management, Inc.

FOELAK, Florence
Special Asst. for Public Information, American College of Obstetricians and Gynecologists
409 12th St., S.W., Washington, DC 20024
Telephone: (202) 638-5577

FOER, Esther
Schmertz Co., The
555 13th St. N.W. Suite 1220 East, Washington, DC 20004
Telephone: (202) 637-6680

FOERSTER, Lloyd C.
Director, Lutheran Resources Commission
5 Thomas Circle, N.W., Washington, DC 20005
Telephone: (202) 667-9844

FOERSTER, Mary C.
Senior V. President, Hill and Knowlton Public Affairs Worldwide
Washington Harbour, 901 31st St., N.W., Washington, DC 20007
Telephone: (202) 333-7400
Registered as Foreign Agent: (#3301).
Background: Former Deputy Director of Commerce, City of Philadelphia.
Clients:
Baden-Wuerttemberg, State of, Development Corp.
Bank of Hungary
Electronic Industries Ass'n of Japan
German Nat'l Tourist Office
Royal Danish Embassy

FOGEL, Cathleen A.
Associate Washington Representative, Sierra Club
408 C St., N.E., Washington, DC 20002
Telephone: (202) 547-1141
Registered as lobbyist at U.S. Congress.

FOGEL, Robert
Legis. Rep., Transp. & Intergovt'l Afrs., Nat'l Ass'n of Counties
440 First St., N.W., Washington, DC 20001
Telephone: (202) 393-6226
Background: Serves as contact for the Nat'l Ass'n of County Engineers and the Nat'l Ass'n of Counties Council of Intergovernmental Coordinators.

FOLCARELLI, Cynthia
Coordinator, Public Policy Information, Nat'l Council of Community Mental Health Centers
12300 Twinbrook Parkway Suite 320, Rockville, MD 20852
Telephone: (301) 984-6200
Registered as lobbyist at U.S. Congress.

FOLEY & CO.
206 G St. N.E. Suite 201, Washington, DC 20002
Telephone: (202) 543-8601

Background: A legislative, public affairs and market research firm. Specializes in electronics, health care services and systems, international trade relations, light industrial manufacturing, Congressional political issue generation and Federal sector contract identification and procurement.
Members of firm representing listed organizations:
Crawford, Kelly A.
Delahanty, Kathryn A., Legislative Assistant
Foley, Joseph P., President
  Background: Formerly Floor Assistant to Rep. Bill Chappell (D-FL), 1974-80. Director of Congressional Affairs, Selective Service System, 1980-82. Legislative Affairs Officer, Federal Emergency Management Agency, 1982-85.
Horst, Toni A., Market Research Assistant
Lavery, Paul C.
Clients:
American Security Fence Corp. *(Joseph P. Foley)*
PolyPhaser Corp. *(Kelly A. Crawford, Kathryn A. Delahanty, Joseph P. Foley, Paul C. Lavery)*

FOLEY, HOAG AND ELIOT
1615 L St., N.W., Suite 950, Washington, DC 20036
Telephone: (202) 775-0600
Members of firm representing listed organizations:
Burke, John L. (Jr.)
Gross, Richard A.
  Background: Exec. Director, U.S. Consumer Protection Safety Commission, 1979-81.
Kanin, Dennis
Tsongas, Paul
Clients:
Humane Soc. of the United States *(Dennis Kanin, Paul Tsongas)*
Pittsburgh, Stadium Authority of *(John L. Burke, Jr.)*

FOLEY, Joseph P.
President, Foley & Co.
206 G St. N.E. Suite 201, Washington, DC 20002
Telephone: (202) 543-8601
Registered as lobbyist at U.S. Congress.
Background: Formerly Floor Assistant to Rep. Bill Chappell (D-FL), 1974-80. Director of Congressional Affairs, Selective Service System, 1980-82. Legislative Affairs Officer, Federal Emergency Management Agency, 1982-85.
Clients:
American Security Fence Corp.
PolyPhaser Corp.

FOLEY & LARDNER
1775 Pennsylvania Ave., N.W., Suite 1000, Washington, DC 20006-4680
Telephone: (202) 862-5300
Background: Washington office of a Milwaukee-based law firm.
Members of firm representing listed organizations:
Bierman, James N.
  Background: Member Civil Rights Reviewing Authority, Department of Health, Education and Welfare, 1979.
Chameides, Steven B.
Cooney, Paul E.
Kamm, Linda Heller, Of Counsel
  Background: General Counsel, Committee on the Budget, U.S. House of Representatives, 1975-77. General Counsel, U.S. Department of Transportation, 1977-80.
Varon, Jay N.
Clients:
American Red Cross *(Paul E. Cooney)*
Aurora Health Care, Inc. *(Paul E. Cooney)*
Central Bank of Tampa *(Paul E. Cooney)*
Coldwell Banker *(Jay N. Varon)*
Duracell Inc. *(James N. Bierman)*
Kohlberg Kravis Roberts & Co. *(James N. Bierman)*
United Savings of America *(James N. Bierman)*

FOLEY, M. Todd
Cong Liaison Div, ENVIRONMENTAL PROTECTION AGENCY
401 M St., S.W., Washington, DC 20460
Telephone: (202) 382-5200

FOLEY, Martin
Exec. Director, Nat'l Motor Freight Traffic Ass'n
2200 Mill Road, Alexandria, VA 22314
Telephone: (703) 838-1818

Background: Former career executive with the Interstate Commerce Commission, 1961-85; served as Managing Director, 1983-85.

FOLEY, Michael
Director, Financial Analysis, Nat'l Ass'n of Regulatory Utility Commissioners
Box 684, I.C.C. Bldg., Washington, DC 20044-0684
Telephone: (202) 898-2200

FOLSOM, R. D.
Wall and Associates, R. Duffy
1317 F St., N.W., Suite 400, Washington, DC 20004
Telephone: (202) 737-0100
Registered as lobbyist at U.S. Congress.
Organizations represented:
Footwear Distributors and Retailers of America
Glaxo, Inc.
Hong Kong Trade Development Council
Pharmaceutical Manufacturers Ass'n

FONTAINE, Monita W.
Exec. Director, Licensed Beverage Information Council
1225 Eye St., N.W. Suite 500, Washington, DC 20005
Telephone: (202) 682-4775

FONTECILLA, Herbert M.
V. President, Regulatory Affairs, Flanagan Group, Inc.
11 Canal Center Plaza Suite 250, Alexandria, VA 22314
Telephone: (703) 739-8822

FORAN, Dr. James
V. President, Educational Affairs, Ass'n of Independent Colleges and Schools
One Dupont Circle, N.W., Suite 350, Washington, DC 20036
Telephone: (202) 659-2460

FORBES, Mari S.
Senior V. President, Albers and Co.
1731 Connecticut Ave., N.W. Second Floor, Washington, DC 20009
Telephone: (202) 328-9333

FORBES, Michael P.
Asst Admin, Cong and Legis Affrs, SMALL BUSINESS ADMINISTRATION
1441 L St., N.W. Room 1028, Washington, DC 20416
Telephone: (202) 653-7581

FORBES, Phyllis R.
V. President, Nat'l Ass'n of College and University Business Officers
One Dupont Circle, N.W., Suite 500, Washington, DC 20036-1178
Telephone: (202) 861-2500

FORD, David
V. President, Public Timber, Nat'l Forest Products Ass'n
1250 Connecticut Ave., N.W. Suite 200, Washington, DC 20036
Telephone: (202) 463-2700
Registered as lobbyist at U.S. Congress.

FORD, James E.
Director, Federal Government Relations, ARCO
1333 New Hampshire Ave., N.W., Suite 1001, Washington, DC 20036
Telephone: (202) 457-6221
Registered as lobbyist at U.S. Congress.

FORD, John
Director, Government Relations, Kellogg Co.
2000 L St., N.W., Suite 200, Washington, DC 20036
Telephone: (202) 833-2443

FORD, John J.
President, Jeford-McManus Internat'l, Inc.
513 Capitol Court, N.E., Suite 300, Washington, DC 20002
Telephone: (202) 546-0073
Registered as lobbyist at U.S. Congress.

FORD, Martha
Assistant Director, Government Affairs, Ass'n for Retarded Citizens of the U.S.
1522 K St., N.W. Suite 516, Washington, DC 20005
Telephone: (202) 785-3388

FORD, Patrick
V. President and Group Manager, Burson-Marsteller
1850 M St., N.W., Suite 900, Washington, DC 20036
Telephone: (202) 833-8550

FORD-ROEGNER, Pat, R.N.
Director, American Nurses' Ass'n Political Action Committee (ANA-PAC)
1101 14th St., N.W. Suite 200, Washington, DC 20005
Telephone: (202) 789-1800

FOREMAN, Carol Tucker
Partner, Foreman & Heidepriem
1112 16th St., N.W. Suite 750, Washington, DC 20036
Telephone: (202) 822-8060
Registered as lobbyist at U.S. Congress.
Background: Former Asst. Secretary of Agriculture for Food and Consumer Service, 1977-81. Director, Nat'l Consumer Cooperative Bank, 1979-81 and Exec Director, Consumer Federation of America, 1973-77.
Clients:
Aetna Life & Casualty Co.
American Insurance Ass'n
Coalition to Preserve the Integrity of American Trademarks
Columbia Hospital for Women Medical Center
Procter and Gamble Mfg. Co.
Rockefeller Foundation
United Food and Commercial Workers Internat'l Union

FOREMAN, E. David
Director, Government Affairs, Todd Shipyards Corp. Political Action Committee
2341 Jefferson Davis Hwy., Arlington, VA 22202
Telephone: (703) 418-0133

FOREMAN & HEIDEPRIEM
1112 16th St., N.W. Suite 750, Washington, DC 20036
Telephone: (202) 822-8060
Background: A public policy consulting firm.
Members of firm representing listed organizations:
Foreman, Carol Tucker, Partner
Background: Former Asst. Secretary of Agriculture for Food and Consumer Service, 1977-81. Director, Nat'l Consumer Cooperative Bank, 1979-81 and Exec Director, Consumer Federation of America, 1973-77.
Heidepriem, Nikki, Partner
Background: Former Special Assistant to HEW Secretary Joseph Califano, Jr., 1978-79.
Clients:
Aetna Life & Casualty Co. *(Carol Tucker Foreman, Nikki Heidepriem)*
American Insurance Ass'n *(Carol Tucker Foreman, Nikki Heidepriem)*
Coalition to Preserve the Integrity of American Trademarks *(Carol Tucker Foreman, Nikki Heidepriem)*
Columbia Hospital for Women Medical Center *(Carol Tucker Foreman, Nikki Heidepriem)*
Nat'l Abortion Rights Action League *(Nikki Heidepriem)*
Procter and Gamble Mfg. Co. *(Carol Tucker Foreman, Nikki Heidepriem)*
Rockefeller Foundation *(Carol Tucker Foreman, Nikki Heidepriem)*
United Food and Commercial Workers Internat'l Union *(Carol Tucker Foreman)*

FORESIGHT SCIENCE & TECHNOLOGY, INC.
2000 P St., N.W. Suite 305, Washington, DC 20036
Telephone: (202) 833-2322
Background: A science and technology consulting firm.
Members of firm representing listed organizations:
Speser, (Dr.) Philip, Chairman

FORGASH, Michael
Info and Govt'l Affrs Div., DEPARTMENT OF AGRICULTURE - Federal Crop Insurance Corp.
14th and Independence Ave. S.W., Washington, DC 20250
Telephone: (202) 447-3287

FORGOTSON, Edward H.
1350 Eye St., N.W., Suite 700, Washington, DC 20005
Telephone: (202) 789-6027
Registered as lobbyist at U.S. Congress.
Background: An attorney at law.
Organizations represented:
ENSERCH Corp.
GNB, Inc.

Northern Indiana Public Service Co.
Superior Nat'l Insurance Group

FORKAN, Patricia
Senior V. President, Humane Soc. of the United States
2100 L St., N.W., Washington, DC 20037
Telephone: (202) 452-1100

FORKENBROCK, John
Exec. Director, Nat'l Ass'n of Federally Impacted Schools
444 North Capitol St., N.W., Suite 405, Washington, DC 20001
Telephone: (202) 624-5455

FORMAN, Sallie H.
V. President, Government Relations, Nat'l Broadcasting Co.
1331 Pennsylvania Ave., N.W. Suite 700S, Washington, DC 20004
Telephone: (202) 637-4522
Registered as lobbyist at U.S. Congress.

FORNACIARI, John R.
Steele & Fornaciari
2020 K St., N.W. Suite 850, Washington, DC 20006-1857
Telephone: (202) 887-1779
Registered as lobbyist at U.S. Congress.
Clients:
K mart Corp.

FORNOS, Werner
President, Population Institute
110 Maryland Ave., N.E. Suite 207, Washington, DC 20002
Telephone: (202) 544-3300

FORREST, James E.
Exec. Director, Naval Reserve Ass'n
1619 King St., Alexandria, VA 22314-2793
Telephone: (703) 548-5800

FORSCEY, Michael A.
Wunder, Ryan, Cannon & Thelen
1615 L St., N.W., Suite 650, Washington, DC 20036
Telephone: (202) 659-3005
Registered as lobbyist at U.S. Congress.
Background: Counsel, U.S. Senate Subcommittee on Labor, 1977-80. Special Assistant to the Majority Whip of the U.S. House of Representatives, 1980-81. Chief Minority Counsel, U.S. Senate Committee on Labor and Human Resources, 1981-85.
Clients:
American Iron and Steel Institute
Kelly Services, Inc.
KRC Research and Consulting
Manville Corp.
Metropolitan Insurance Cos.
Mylan Laboratories, Inc.
Nat'l Ass'n of Temporary Services
Tobacco Industry Labor Management Committee

FORSEE, Joseph B.
Exec. Director, Internat'l Circulation Managers Ass'n
Newspaper Center, 11600 Sunrise Valley Dr., Reston, VA 22091
Telephone: (703) 620-9555

FORSTER & ASSOCIATES
827 25th St. South, Arlington, VA 22202
Telephone: (703) 548-1360
Members of firm representing listed organizations:
Forster, Johann R., President
Background: Chief U.S. Navy Foreign Liaison (3yrs); Head USN Foreign Military Sales, PACOM (2yrs).
Clients:
Bruker Meerestechnik GmbH *(Johann R. Forster)*
LITEF GmbH *(Johann R. Forster)*
Trinity Marine Group *(Johann R. Forster)*

FORSTER, Johann R.
President, Forster & Associates
827 25th St. South, Arlington, VA 22202
Telephone: (703) 548-1360
Background: Chief U.S. Navy Foreign Liaison (3yrs); Head USN Foreign Military Sales, PACOM (2yrs).
Clients:
Bruker Meerestechnik GmbH
LITEF GmbH
Trinity Marine Group

FORSTER, Theresa
CR Associates
317 Massachusetts Ave., N.E., Suite 100, Washington, DC 20002
Telephone: (202) 546-4732
Background: Former Legislative Aide to Senator David Pryor (D-AR).

FORSYTH, Robert N.
Exec. Director, Marine Corps League
8626 Lee Highway Suite 201, Fairfax, VA 22031
Telephone: (703) 207-9588

FORT AND SCHLEFER
1401 New York Ave., N.W. Twelfth Floor, Washington, DC 20005
Telephone: (202) 467-5900
Members of firm representing listed organizations:
Egan, Leonard
Fort, William H.
Schlefer, Mark P.
Clients:
Australia-New Zealand Direct Line *(William H. Fort)*
Avia Footwear, Inc.
Bollinger Machine Shop and Shipyard, Inc.
Crowley Maritime Corp. *(Mark P. Schlefer)*
Grand Metropolitan PLC *(Leonard Egan)*
Wendell Investments Ltd. *(Leonard Egan)*

FORT, William H.
Fort and Schlefer
1401 New York Ave., N.W. Twelfth Floor, Washington, DC 20005
Telephone: (202) 467-5900
Clients:
Australia-New Zealand Direct Line

FORTE, Lori
Director, Public Affairs, Business Software Ass'n
1201 Pennsylvania Ave., N.W. Suite 250, Washington, DC 20044
Telephone: (202) 737-7060

FORTE, Patrick A.
President, Ass'n of Thrift Holding Companies
888 17th St., N.W., Suite 312, Washington, DC 20006
Telephone: (202) 223-6575
Registered as lobbyist at U.S. Congress.
Background: Also represents the Ass'n of Thrift Holding Companies Political Action Committee.

FORTIER, Alison B.
Manager, Legislative Programs, Rockwell Internat'l
1745 Jefferson Davis Hwy. Suite 1200, Arlington, VA 22202
Telephone: (703) 553-6600
Registered as lobbyist at U.S. Congress.
Background: Former Senior Director, Legislative Affairs, Nat'l Security Council.

FORTUNA, Richard C.
Executive Director, Hazardous Waste Treatment Council
1440 New York Ave., N.W., Suite 310, Washington, DC 20005
Telephone: (202) 783-0870
Background: Also represents the Hazardous Waste Treatment Council Political Action Committee.

FORTUNE, Terence J.
Paul, Weiss, Rifkind, Wharton and Garrison
1615 L St., N.W., Suite 1300, Washington, DC 20036
Telephone: (202) 223-7300
Registered as Foreign Agent: (#3647).
Background: Assistant Legal Adviser, Department of State, 1977-83.
Clients:
NEC America
NEC Corp.

FOSCARINIS, Maria
Director, Nat'l Law Center on Homelessness and Poverty
1575 Eye St., N.W., Suite 1135, Washington, DC 20005
Telephone: (202) 289-1680
Registered as lobbyist at U.S. Congress.

FOSCO, Angelo
General President, Laborers' Internat'l Union of North America
905 16th St., N.W., Washington, DC 20006

The listings in this directory are available as *Mailing Labels*. See last page.

FOSCO, Angelo (Cont'd)
Telephone: (202) 737-8320
Background: Responsibilities include Laborers' Political
League.

FOSLER, R. Scott
V. Pres., & Director, Government Studies, Committee for
Economic Development
1700 K St., N.W., Suite 700, Washington, DC 20006
Telephone: (202) 296-5860
Background: Serves also as President, Washington Council
of Governments.

FOSS, Brian
V. President, Assistant to the President, Independent Sector
1828 L St., N.W., Washington, DC 20036
Telephone: (202) 223-8100

FOSS, Joe
President, Nat'l Rifle Ass'n of America
1600 Rhode Island Ave., N.W., Washington, DC 20036
Telephone: (202) 828-6000

FOSTER, Andrea
President, Nat'l Dental Hygienists' Ass'n
5506 Connecticut Ave., N.W., Suite 24-25, Washington,
DC 20015
Telephone: (202) 699-3710

FOSTER, Bruce
V. President, Washington Affairs, New England Electric
System
2100 Pennsylvania Ave. N.W., Suite 695, Washington, DC
20037
Telephone: (202) 488-3789

FOSTER, F. David
Ablondi and Foster, P.C.
2100 Pennsylvania Ave., N.W., Washington, DC 20006
Telephone: (202) 296-3355
Background: Attorney Advisor, Office of the General
Counsel, 1973-75 and Assistant to the Chairman, 1975-
77, U.S. International Trade Commission. Trade Counsel,
U.S. Senate Committee on Finance, 1977-81.
Clients:
Far East Machinery Co. Ltd.
Guan Haur Industries Ltd.
United States Beet Sugar Ass'n

FOSTER, Hope S.
O'Connor & Hannan
1919 Pennsylvania Ave., N.W., Suite 800, Washington, DC
20006
Telephone: (202) 887-1400
Clients:
American Clinical Laboratory Ass'n
American Clinical Laboratory Ass'n Political Ac-
tion Committee
Nat'l Ass'n of Portable X-Ray Providers

FOSTER, Jean
V. President, Corporate Development, Nat'l Council of
Savings Institutions
1101 15th St., N.W. Suite 400, Washington, DC 20005
Telephone: (202) 857-3100

FOSTER, Nancy E.
Staff V. Pres., Public Affairs Dept., American Soybean
Ass'n
1300 L St., N.W., Suite 950, Washington, DC 20005-4107
Telephone: (202) 371-5511
Registered as lobbyist at U.S. Congress.
Background: Deputy Director, Office of Public Liaison,
U.S. Department of Agriculture, 1985-86.

FOSTER, William C.
Patton, Boggs and Blow
2550 M St., N.W., Suite 800, Washington, DC 20037
Telephone: (202) 457-6000
Registered as lobbyist at U.S. Congress.
Registered as Foreign Agent: (#2165).
Background: Deputy Director, Alaska Legislative Council
and Legislative Counsel to Senator E. L. Bartlett, 1961-
64. Counsel, U.S. Senate Commerce Committee, 1964-66.

FOWLER, Becky
Staff Assistant, State Gov't Rels., American Petroleum Institute
1220 L St., N.W., Washington, DC 20005
Telephone: (202) 682-8213

FOWLER, C. Grayson
Secretary, Internat'l Public Strategies, Inc.
1030 15th St., N.W., Suite 408, Washington, DC 20005
Telephone: (202) 371-5604
Registered as lobbyist at U.S. Congress.
Registered as Foreign Agent: (#4200).
Background: Former foreign relations aide to the late Sena-
tor Edward Zorinski (D-NE).
Clients:
Aruba, Government of

FOWLER, R. Mark
Manager, Legislative Programs, Rockwell Internat'l
1745 Jefferson Davis Hwy. Suite 1200, Arlington, VA
22202
Telephone: (703) 553-6600
Registered as lobbyist at U.S. Congress.

FOWLER, William A.
Exec. Director, Nat'l Home Study Council
1601 18th St., N.W., Washington, DC 20009
Telephone: (202) 234-5100

FOX, Albert A.
V. President, Riley and Fox
1101 17th St., N.W., Suite 606, Washington, DC 20036
Telephone: (202) 223-9800

FOX, Alissa
Senior Washington Representative, Blue Cross and Blue
Shield Ass'n
655 15th St., N.W., Suite 350, Washington, DC 20005
Telephone: (202) 626-4780
Registered as lobbyist at U.S. Congress.

FOX, Allan M.
Fox, Bennett and Turner
750 17th St., N.W., Suite 1100, Washington, DC 20006
Telephone: (202) 778-2300
Registered as lobbyist at U.S. Congress.
Background: General Counsel, Health and Scientific Re-
search Subcommittee, Committee on Labor and Public
Welfare, U.S. Senate, 1975-77. Legislative Assistant to
Senator Jacob K. Javits (D-NY), 1977-79.
Clients:
American Social Health Ass'n
Ares-Serono, Inc.
Johnson & Johnson
Lederle Laboratories, American Cyanamid Co.
Subsidiary
Nat'l Coalition for Cancer Research

FOX, Arthur L., II
Staff Attorney, Public Citizen Litigation Group
2000 P St., N.W., Suite 700, Washington, DC 20036
Telephone: (202) 785-3704

FOX, Barbara
Manager, Government Affairs, Federal Home Loan Mort-
gage Corp.
1759 Business Center Drive, Reston, VA 22090
Telephone: (703) 789-4700
Registered as lobbyist at U.S. Congress.

➡ **FOX, BENNETT AND TURNER**
750 17th St., N.W., Suite 1100, Washington, DC 20006
Telephone: (202) 778-2300
Members of firm representing listed organizations:
Allard, Nicholas W.
Background: Minority Counsel, U.S. Senate Committee
on the Judiciary, 1984-86. Administrative Assistant
to Senator Daniel P. Moynihan (D-NY), 1986-87.
Bennett, Alan R.
Background: Attorney, Office of the General Counsel,
U.S. Food and Drug Administration, 1972-76. Special
Counsel, U.S. Senate Committee on Governmental
Affairs, 1877-81.
Fox, Allan M.
Background: General Counsel, Health and Scientific
Research Subcommittee, Committee on Labor and
Public Welfare, U.S. Senate, 1975-77. Legislative As-
sistant to Senator Jacob K. Javits (D-NY), 1977-79.
Kiser, John Daniel

Background: Assistant Regional Attorney, 1976-80;
Senior Attorney/ Litigation, Public Health Division,
1980-83; Special Assistant to the Deputy General
Counsel, 1983-85, U.S. Department of Health and
Human Services.
Turner, Samuel D.
Background: Deputy General Counsel, U.S. Depart-
ment of Health and Human Services, 1981-84.
Clients:
American Social Health Ass'n *(Allan M. Fox)*
Ares-Serono, Inc. *(Alan R. Bennett, Allan M. Fox)*
Johnson & Johnson *(Alan R. Bennett, Allan M. Fox)*
Lederle Laboratories, American Cyanamid Co.
Subsidiary *(Allan M. Fox, Samuel D. Turner)*
Nat'l Coalition for Cancer Research *(Allan M. Fox)*
New MediCo Associates, Inc. *(Samuel D. Turner)*
Serono Laboratories, Inc. *(Alan R. Bennett)*
Wireless Cable Ass'n, Inc. *(Nicholas W. Allard)*

FOX, Chuck
Director of Legislative Affairs, Friends of the Earth
218 D St., S.E., Washington, DC 20003
Telephone: (202) 544-2600
Registered as lobbyist at U.S. Congress.

FOX, David E.
1325 18th St., N.W. Suite 103, Washington, DC 20036
Telephone: (202) 887-0725
Organizations represented:
Institutional and Municipal Parking Congress

FOX, Eric R.
Ivins, Phillips and Barker
1700 Pennsylvania Ave., N.W., Suite 600, Washington, DC
20006
Telephone: (202) 393-7600
Registered as lobbyist at U.S. Congress.

FOX, H. Lawrence
Bishop, Cook, Purcell & Reynolds
1400 L St., N.W., Washington, DC 20005-3502
Telephone: (202) 371-5700
Registered as lobbyist at U.S. Congress.
Background: Assistant Branch Chief, Legislation and Regu-
lation Division, Chief Counsel's Office, Internal Revenue
Service, 1965-69.
Clients:
Ad Hoc Committee for Western Utilities
Kidder, Peabody & Co., Inc.
Oakland County Board of Supervisors
Puget Sound Power and Light Co.
Sierra Pacific Resources
Tousand Spring Generating Co.

FOX, Howard I.
Staff Attorney & Co-Director, Sierra Club Legal Defense
Fund
1531 P St., N.W. Suite 200, Washington, DC 20005
Telephone: (202) 667-4500

FOX, J. Edward
Mintz, Levin, Cohn, Ferris, Glovsky and Popeo, P.C.
1825 Eye St., N.W. 12th Floor, Washington, DC 20006
Telephone: (202) 293-0500
Background: A government relations consultant to the
firm. Former Assistant Secretary of State for Legislative
Affairs.

FOX, Richard K.
Senior V. President, Meridian House Internat'l
1630 Crescent Place, N.W., Washington, DC 20009
Telephone: (202) 667-6800
Background: U.S. Ambassador to Trinidad & Tobago,
1977-80; Deputy Inspector General, U.S. Dept. of State
and Foreign Service, 1981-83.

FOX, Thomas H.
Director, Center for Internat'l Development and Environment
1709 New York Ave., N.W. 7th Floor, Washington, DC
20006
Telephone: (202) 638-6300

FRAAS, Phillip L.
Partner, McLeod & Pires
2501 M St., N.W., Suite 400, Washington, DC 20037
Telephone: (202) 861-1234
Registered as lobbyist at U.S. Congress.

FRADO, Dennis
Assistant Director for Foreign Affairs, Lutheran Office for Governmental Affairs/Evangelical Lutheran Church in America
122 C St., N.W. Suite 300, Washington, DC 20001
Telephone: (202) 783-7508

FRAHM, John R.
Manager, Gov't Activities-Internat'l, Minnesota Mining and Manufacturing Co. (3M Co.)
Suite 1100, 1101 15th St., N.W., Washington, DC 20005
Telephone: (202) 331-6950
Registered as lobbyist at U.S. Congress.

FRAIOLI/JOST
122 C St., N.W., Suite 500-A, Washington, DC 20001
Telephone: (202) 347-3042
Members of firm representing listed organizations:
 Fraioli, Michael J.
 Jost, Steven J.
  Background: Former Administrative Assistant to Rep. Richard H. Lehman (D-CA) and former Deputy Director for Finance, Democratic Congressional Campaign Committee.

FRAIOLI, Michael J.
Fraioli/Jost
122 C St., N.W., Suite 500-A, Washington, DC 20001
Telephone: (202) 347-3042

FRAMPTON, George T., Jr.
President, Wilderness Soc.
1400 Eye St., N.W., 10th Floor, Washington, DC 20005
Telephone: (202) 842-3400

FRANASIAK, David
Senior Manager, Government Relations, Ernst & Young
1200 19th St., N.W., Suite 400, Washington, DC 20036
Telephone: (202) 862-9300

FRANCALANGRIA, James L.
FTS2000 Program Manager, Boeing Computer Services
7980 Boeing Court, CV-83, Vienna, VA 22182
Telephone: (703) 827-4390

FRANCIOSI, Pat
Nat'l President, Nat'l Mental Health Ass'n
1021 Prince St., Alexandria, VA 22314
Telephone: (703) 684-7722

FRANCIS, Charles
V. President and Unit Manager, Hill and Knowlton Public Affairs Worldwide
Washington Harbour, 901 31st St., N.W., Washington, DC 20007
Telephone: (202) 333-7400
Registered as Foreign Agent: (#3301).
Clients:
 Carlyle Group, The
 Federal Express Corp.
 Versar, Inc.
 WorldCorp

FRANCIS, Frances E.
Spiegel and McDiarmid
1350 New York Ave., N.W., Suite 1100, Washington, DC 20005
Telephone: (202) 879-4000
Registered as lobbyist at U.S. Congress.
Background: Assistant to Federal Power Commission Commissioner, 1965-68. Attorney, Federal Power Commissioner, 1965-68.
Clients:
 Connecticut Municipal Electric Energy Cooperative
 Richmond Power and Light Co.
 Sacramento Municipal Utility District

FRANCIS, Harry
Technical Manager, Nat'l Lime Ass'n
3601 North Fairfax Drive, Arlington, VA 22201
Telephone: (703) 243-5463

FRANCIS, Leslie C.
FMR Group Inc., The
1000 Potomac St., N.W. Suite 401, Washington, DC 20007
Telephone: (202) 333-2533
Registered as lobbyist at U.S. Congress.

Background: Deputy Chief of Staff and Deputy Assistant to the President of the United States, 1977-79. Administrative Assistant to Rep. Norman Y. Mineta, 1975-77.

FRANCIS, Michael A.
Counsel, National Forest Issues, Wilderness Soc.
1400 Eye St., N.W., 10th Floor, Washington, DC 20005
Telephone: (202) 842-3400
Registered as lobbyist at U.S. Congress.
Background: Former aide to Senator Robert Stafford (R-VT).

FRANCISCO, Douglas L.
V. President, Independent Petroleum Ass'n of America
1101 16th St., N.W., Washington, DC 20036
Telephone: (202) 857-4742
Registered as lobbyist at U.S. Congress.

FRANCOIS, Francis B.
Exec. Director, American Ass'n of State Highway and Transportation Officials
444 N. Capitol St., N.W., Suite 225, Washington, DC 20001
Telephone: (202) 624-5800

FRANK, Barbara
Associate Director, Nat'l Citizens Coalition for Nursing Home Reform
1424 16th St., N.W., Suite L2, Washington, DC 20036
Telephone: (202) 797-0657

FRANK, BERNSTEIN, CONAWAY & GOLDMAN
4300 Wisconsin Ave., N.W., Washington, DC 20016
Telephone: (202) 833-1914
Clients:
 Coalition for Equitable Compensation

FRANK, Dr. Martin
Exec. Director, American Physiological Soc.
9650 Rockville Pike, Bethesda, MD 20814
Telephone: (301) 530-7164

FRANK, Pamela D.
Legislative Representative, Federal Managers Ass'n
1000 16th St., N.W., Suite 701, Washington, DC 20006
Telephone: (202) 778-1500

FRANK, Peter M.
Manager, Washington Office, Kerr-McGee Corp.
1667 K St., N.W., Suite 250, Washington, DC 20006
Telephone: (202) 728-9600
Registered as lobbyist at U.S. Congress.

FRANK, RICHARD A., LAW OFFICES OF
1120 19th St., N.W. Suite 600, Washington, DC 20036
Telephone: (202) 785-0235
Clients:
 Japan Fisheries Ass'n

FRANK, Richard L.
Olsson, Frank and Weeda, P.C.
1400 16th St., N.W. Suite 400, Washington, DC 20036-2220
Telephone: (202) 789-1212
Registered as lobbyist at U.S. Congress.
Clients:
 Nat'l-American Wholesale Grocers' Ass'n
 Pillsbury Co.

FRANK, Robert
Evergreen Associates, Ltd.
206 G St., N.E., Washington, DC 20002
Telephone: (202) 543-3383
Registered as lobbyist at U.S. Congress.
Clients:
 Suffolk County, New York

FRANK, Susan M.
Sonnenschein Nath & Rosenthal
1201 Pennsylvania Ave., N.W. Suite 700, Washington, DC 20004
Telephone: (202) 637-2000
Registered as lobbyist at U.S. Congress.
Clients:
 Geneva Steel Co.

FRANKFORT, Faye B.
Ass't Director, Government Affairs, American Podiatric Medical Ass'n
9312 Old Georgetown Road, Bethesda, MD 20814

Telephone: (301) 571-9200
Registered as lobbyist at U.S. Congress.
Background: Serves as liaison, Podiatry Political Action Committee.

FRANKHAUSER, Mahlon
Partner, Lord Day & Lord, Barrett Smith
1201 Pennsylvania Ave., N.W., Suite 821, Washington, DC 20004
Telephone: (202) 393-5024
Clients:
 Coffee, Sugar and Cocoa Exchange
 Merrill Lynch Futures Inc.
 Prudential-Bache Securities, Inc.
 Shearson Lehman Hutton

FRANKIL, David
Director, Federal Government Affairs, Champion Internat'l Corp.
1875 Eye St., N.W., Suite 540, Washington, DC 20006
Telephone: (202) 785-9888
Registered as lobbyist at U.S. Congress.

FRANKLAND, Walter L., Jr.
Exec. Vice President, Silver Users Ass'n
1730 M St., N.W., Suite 911, Washington, DC 20036
Telephone: (202) 785-3050
Registered as lobbyist at U.S. Congress.
Background: Represents also Compass Internat'l Inc.

FRANKLIN, Gen. Charles D., USA (Ret)
President, Franklin Group
10826 Henderson Road, Fairfax Station, VA 22038
Telephone: (703) 764-0100

FRANKLIN, Ellis B.
Internat'l Exec. V. President, Amalgamated Transit Union
5025 Wisconsin Ave., N.W., Washington, DC 20016
Telephone: (202) 537-1645

FRANKLIN GROUP
10826 Henderson Road, Fairfax Station, VA 22038
Telephone: (703) 764-0100
Members of firm representing listed organizations:
 Franklin, (Gen.) Charles D. (USA (Ret)), President
Clients:
 McDonnell Douglas Helicopter Co. (Gen. Charles D. Franklin, USA *(Ret)*)

FRANKLIN, Lesli
Bario Associates, Patricia
512 11th St., S.E., Washington, DC 20003
Telephone: (202) 543-0923

FRANKLIN, Ruth W.
Admin. Officer, Council of Defense and Space Industry Ass'ns
1722 Eye St., N.W., Suite 300, Washington, DC 20006
Telephone: (202) 457-8713

FRANKOVICH, Kevin
Director of Government Relations, Contract Services Ass'n of America
1350 New York Ave., N.W., Suite 200, Washington, DC 20005
Telephone: (202) 347-0600
Registered as lobbyist at U.S. Congress.

FRANKS, Martin D.
V. President, Washington, CBS, Inc.
1800 M St., N.W. Suite 300 North, Washington, DC 20036
Telephone: (202) 457-4501
Background: Former Exec. Director, Democratic Congressional Campaign Committee.

FRANKS, Thomas C.
V. President for Government Relations, American Resort and Residential Development Ass'n
1220 L St., N.W. Suite 510, Washington, DC 20005
Telephone: (202) 371-6700
Registered as lobbyist at U.S. Congress.
Background: Responsibilites include American Resort and Residential Development Ass'n Political Action Committee.

FRANTZ, Diann
Cong Liaison Div, ENVIRONMENTAL PROTECTION
AGENCY
401 M St., S.W., Washington, DC 20460
Telephone: (202) 382-5200

FRANZ, Delton
Director, Washington Office, Mennonite Central Committee, Peace Section
110 Maryland Ave., N.E. Suite 502, Washington, DC
20002
Telephone: (202) 544-6564

FRANZ, Jerry
Porter/Novelli
1001 30th St., N.W., Washington, DC 20007
Telephone: (202) 342-7000
Clients:
Internat'l Apple Institute

FRANZ, Marian C.
Exec. Director, Nat'l Campaign for a Peace Tax Fund
2121 Decatur Place, N.W., Washington, DC 20008
Telephone: (202) 483-3751
Registered as lobbyist at U.S. Congress.

FRASER, Edie
President and CEO, Public Affairs Group, Inc.
1629 K St., N.W., Suite 1100, Washington, DC 20006
Telephone: (202) 785-6713
Background: Government service, 1965-73.
Clients:
Ass'n of the Wall and Ceiling Industries-Internat'l
Braddock Communications
Center for the Study of the Presidency
Community Foundation of Greater Washington
MTI Export Management, Inc.
Novophalt America, Inc.
STRATCO, Inc.
Strategic Leadership, Inc.
Youth in Philanthropy

FRATRIK, Mark
V. President/Economist, Nat'l Ass'n of Broadcasters
1771 N St., N.W., Washington, DC 20036
Telephone: (202) 429-5300

FRAZIER, Charles L.
Director, Washington Office, Nat'l Farmers Organization
475 L'Enfant Plaza, S.W., Washington, DC 20024
Telephone: (202) 484-7075
Registered as lobbyist at U.S. Congress.
Background: Also serves as Treasurer of Grass Roots in
Politics (GRIP).

FRAZIER, Frances B.
Director, Government/Corporate Relations, American
Business Conference
1730 K St., N.W. Suite 1200, Washington, DC 20006
Telephone: (202) 822-9300
Registered as lobbyist at U.S. Congress.
Background: Former Staff Assistant, White House Office
of Legislative Affairs, Reagan Administration.

FRAZIER, Harry
Kostmayer Communications, Inc.
2300 M St., N.W., Suite 920, Washington, DC 20037
Telephone: (202) 223-6655
Clients:
Competitive Health Care Coalition
Mothers Against Drunk Driving (MADD)
Nat'l Law Enforcement Officers' Memorial Fund

FRAZIER, Mark
Chairman, Services Group, The
1815 N. Lynn St. Suite 200, Arlington, VA 22209
Telephone: (702) 528-7486

FRAZIER, Russell F.
Exec. V. President, American Soc. of Agricultural Consul-
tants
8301 Greensboro Drive Suite 260, McLean, VA 22102
Telephone: (703) 356-2455
Background: Serves as principal contact for the American
Soc. of Agricultural Consultants Internat'l Political Action
Committee.

FREAD, Joan P.
Mayer, Brown and Platt
2000 Pennsylvania Ave., N.W. Suite 6500, Washington,
DC 20006
Telephone: (202) 463-2000
Registered as lobbyist at U.S. Congress.
Registered as Foreign Agent: (#3076).
Clients:
Dome Petroleum Ltd.

FREDERICK, Robert M.
Legislative Director, Nat'l Grange
1616 H St., N.W., Washington, DC 20006
Telephone: (202) 628-3507
Registered as lobbyist at U.S. Congress.

FREDERICKS, Joe
Bur for Africa, Food for Peace, AGENCY FOR INTER-
NAT'L DEVELOPMENT
320 21st St., N.W., Washington, DC 20523
Telephone: (202) 647-8190

FREDERICKSEN, John S.
Smith, Bucklin and Associates
1101 Connecticut Ave., N.W., Suite 700, Washington, DC
20036
Telephone: (202) 857-1100
Registered as lobbyist at U.S. Congress.
Background: Serves as President, Regional Airline Ass'n.

FREDRIKSSON, John
Asst. Dir. for Immig. and Refugee Affrs., Lutheran Office
for Governmental Affairs/Evangelical Lutheran Church in
America
122 C St., N.W. Suite 300, Washington, DC 20001
Telephone: (202) 783-7508

FREE, James C.
Walker Associates, Charls E.
1730 Pennsylvania Ave., N.W. Suite 200, Washington, DC
20006
Telephone: (202) 393-4760
Registered as lobbyist at U.S. Congress.
Registered as Foreign Agent: (#4180).
Background: Former Congressional Liaison, The White
House, under President Jimmy Carter.
Organizations represented:
Broadcast Music Inc.
CBS Records Group
CSX Corp.

FREEDENBERG, Paul
Baker and Botts
555 13th St., N.W., Suite 500 East, Washington, DC
20004-1109
Telephone: (202) 639-7700
Registered as lobbyist at U.S. Congress.
Registered as Foreign Agent: (#4293).
Background: Consultant on international trade to the law
firm of Baker and Botts. Former Under Secretary for Ex-
port Administration, U.S. Department of Commerce; Staff
Director, Senate Banking Subcommittee on International
Finance, 1981-85.
Clients:
Bundesverband der Deutschen Industrie

FREEDMAN, Anthony S.
Powell, Goldstein, Frazer and Murphy
1001 Pennsylvania, N.W., Sixth Fl., Washington, DC
20004
Telephone: (202) 347-0066
Registered as lobbyist at U.S. Congress.
Background: Deputy Director, Legislation, U.S. Environ-
mental Protection Agency, 1977-78. Deputy Assistant
Secretary, Housing Policy and Budget, U.S. Department
of Housing and Urban Development, 1979-81.
Clients:
Massachusetts Housing Finance Agency

FREEDMAN, Joel
V. President & Federal Affairs Counsel, Hartford Insurance Group
1600 M St., N.W., Washington, DC 20036
Telephone: (202) 775-7361

FREEDMAN, LEVY, KROLL AND SIMONDS
1050 Connecticut Ave., N.W., Suite 825, Washington, DC
20036
Telephone: (202) 457-5100

Members of firm representing listed organizations:
Chettle, John H.
Hughes, Phyllis Eileen, Legal Assistant
Clients:
Investors Internat'l *(John H. Chettle)*
South Africa, Chamber of Mines of *(John H. Chettle)*
Universal Frutrading Cooperative Ltd. *(John H.
Chettle)*

FREEDMAN, Marc
Director, Federal Regulation, Associated Builders and
Contractors
729 15th St., N.W., Washington, DC 20005
Telephone: (202) 637-8800
Registered as lobbyist at U.S. Congress.

FREEDMAN, Matthew
Black, Manafort, Stone and Kelly Public Affairs Co.
211 N. Union St., Third Floor, Alexandria, VA 22314
Telephone: (703) 683-6612
Registered as lobbyist at U.S. Congress.
Registered as Foreign Agent: (#3600).

FREEDMAN, Robert
Exec. Assistant, Nat'l Waterways Conference, Inc.
1130 17th St., N.W., Washington, DC 20036
Telephone: (202) 296-4415

FREEDMAN, Robert L.
Silver, Freedman & Taff
1735 Eye St., N.W., Washington, DC 20006
Telephone: (202) 429-6100
Registered as lobbyist at U.S. Congress.
Clients:
Hiawatha Savings and Loan Ass'n

FREEMAN, James T.
Legislative Staff Assistant, Mortgage Bankers Ass'n of
America
1125 15th St., N.W., Suite 700, Washington, DC 20005
Telephone: (202) 861-6500
Registered as lobbyist at U.S. Congress.

FREEMAN, Lewis R., Jr.
V. President, Government Affairs, Soc. of the Plastics In-
dustry
1275 K St., N.W., Suite 400, Washington, DC 20005
Telephone: (202) 371-5200
Registered as lobbyist at U.S. Congress.

FREEMAN, Mary Ann
Mgr., Congressional & Industry Relations, General Electric
Co.
1331 Pennsylvania Ave., N.W., Washington, DC 20004
Telephone: (202) 637-4368
Registered as lobbyist at U.S. Congress.

FREEMAN, Raymond L.
Government Affairs Consultant, American Soc. of Landscape Architects
4401 Connecticut Ave., N.W., Washington, DC 20008
Telephone: (202) 686-2752

FREEMAN, Terri
Director, Community Communications, Federal Home
Loan Mortgage Corp.
1759 Business Center Drive, Reston, VA 22090
Telephone: (703) 789-4700

FREER, David W.
Manager, Federal Governmental Affairs, Southern California Gas Co.
1150 Connecticut Ave., N.W., Suite 717, Washington, DC
20036
Telephone: (202) 822-3700
Registered as lobbyist at U.S. Congress.

FREER, Paula D.
Manager, Governmental Affairs, USX Corp.
818 Connecticut Ave., N.W., Washington, DC 20006
Telephone: (202) 331-1340
Registered as lobbyist at U.S. Congress.

FREIBERG, Ronna A.
Director, Legislative Affairs, Winthrop, Stimson, Putnam &
Roberts
1133 Connecticut Ave., N.W. Suite 1000, Washington, DC
20036
Telephone: (202) 775-9800

Registered as lobbyist at U.S. Congress.
Background: Admin. Ass't to U.S. Rep. Peter Rodino, Jr., 1975-76; Congressional Liaison, The White House, 1976-80.
Clients:
America West Airlines
BASF Corp.
Connecticut Liquidity Investment Fund, Inc.
Macrovision
Nat'l Vehicle Leasing Ass'n
Queen City Home Health Care Co.
Snappy Car Rental
Thrifty Rent-A-Car System, Inc.

FREIBERT, David
Mahe Company, The Eddie
900 Second St., N.E. Suite 200, Washington, DC 20002
Telephone: (202) 842-4100

FRENCH, Catherine
Exec. Vice President and CEO, American Symphony Orchestra League
777 14th St., N.W., Suite 500, Washington, DC 20005
Telephone: (202) 628-0099

FRENCH & COMPANY
The Willard, 1455 Pennsylvania Ave., N.W., Suite 1260, Washington, DC 20004
Telephone: (202) 783-7272
Background: A governmental affairs consulting firm.
Members of firm representing listed organizations:
Brent, J. Lytle, Administrative Assistant
Ellison, Mark M., Senior V. President
French, Verrick O., President
Iskenderian, Sally D., Legislative Assistant
Kurtz, Ruth M., Senior V. President
Clients:
BATUS, Inc. (Mark M. Ellison, Verrick O. French)
Internat'l Electronics Manufacturers and Consumers of America (Mark M. Ellison, Verrick O. French, Sally D. Iskenderian)
Montgomery Ward & Co., Inc. (Mark M. Ellison, Verrick O. French)
Wheels, Inc. (Mark M. Ellison, Verrick O. French)

FRENCH, Mark D.
Sr. V. President, Development, American Trucking Ass'ns
2200 Mill Road, Alexandria, VA 22314
Telephone: (703) 838-1955

FRENCH, Verrick O.
President, French & Company
The Willard, 1455 Pennsylvania Ave., N.W., Suite 1260, Washington, DC 20004
Telephone: (202) 783-7272
Registered as lobbyist at U.S. Congress.
Registered as Foreign Agent: (#3666).
Clients:
BATUS, Inc.
Internat'l Electronics Manufacturers and Consumers of America
Montgomery Ward & Co., Inc.
Wheels, Inc.

FRENCH, Walter C., Col.
Director, Nat'l Public Affairs, Salvation Army
1025 Vermont Ave., N.W., Washington, DC 20005
Telephone: (202) 639-8414
Background: Full title is Director, Nat'l Public Affairs; Nat'l Consultant, World Service.

FRESHMAN, John D.
Jellinek, Schwartz, Connolly & Freshman, Inc.
1015 15th St., N.W. Suite 500, Washington, DC 20005
Telephone: (202) 789-8181
Registered as lobbyist at U.S. Congress.
Clients:
Coors Brewing Company
Los Angeles County Sanitation District

FRESON, Raymond D.
Director, Public Relations & Advertising, Blue Cross and Blue Shield of the National Capital Area
550 12th St., S.W., Washington, DC 20065
Telephone: (202) 479-8000

FRETZ, Burton D.
Exec. Director, Nat'l Senior Citizens Law Center
2025 M St., N.W. Suite 400, Washington, DC 20036

Telephone: (202) 887-5280

FREUND, Jeffrey R.
Bredhoff and Kaiser
1000 Connecticut Ave., N.W. Suite 1300, Washington, DC 20036
Telephone: (202) 833-9340
Background: Trial Attorney (1972-76) and Training Director (1976-77), Public Defender Service of D.C.

FREY, Andrew
Mayer, Brown and Platt
2000 Pennsylvania Ave., N.W. Suite 6500, Washington, DC 20006
Telephone: (202) 463-2000

FREYMILLER, Donald
Treasurer, Interstate Truckload Carriers Conference Political Action Committee
2200 Mill Road, Alexandria, VA 22314
Telephone: (703) 838-1950

FRI, Robert W.
President, Resources for the Future
1616 P St., N.W., Washington, DC 20036
Telephone: (202) 328-5000
Background: Deputy Administrator, Environmental Protection Agency, 1971-73. Deputy Administrator, Energy Research and Development Administration, 1975-77.

FRIBOURG, Annette P.
V. President for Congressional Relations, Federal Nat'l Mortgage Ass'n
3900 Wisconsin Ave., N.W., Washington, DC 20016
Telephone: (202) 752-6675
Registered as lobbyist at U.S. Congress.

FRICK, G. William
V. President, General Counsel & Sec'y, American Petroleum Institute
1220 L St., N.W., Washington, DC 20005
Telephone: (202) 682-8240
Background: Former General Counsel, Environmental Protection Agency.

FRIDAY, Lisa A.
Dir, Polit Reforms & Indep. Expenditures, Nat'l Ass'n of REALTORS
777 14th St., N.W., Washington, DC 20005
Telephone: (202) 383-1000

FRIED, FRANK, HARRIS, SHRIVER & JACOBSON
1001 Pennsylvania Ave., N.W., Suite 800, Washington, DC 20004-2505
Telephone: (202) 639-7000
Registered as Foreign Agent: (#3473)
Background: Washington office of a New York law firm.
Members of firm representing listed organizations:
Birenbaum, David E.
Hubschman, Henry A.
Background: Executive Assistant to the Secretary of Housing and Urban Development, 1977-79. Director, Federal Nat'l Mortgage Ass'n, 1979-81.
Kashdan, Alan G.
Kraemer, Jay R.
Kramer, Kenneth S.
Lazarus, Arthur (Jr.)
Miles, David Michael
Pitt, Harvey L.
Background: Special Counsel, Office of the General Counsel, 1971-72; Chief Counsel, Division of Market Regulation, 1972-73; Exec. Assistant to the Chairman, 1973-75; and General Counsel, 1975-78, Securities Exchange Commission.
Rishe, Melvin
Background: Deputy General Counsel, Claims and Litigation, Office of the General Counsel, Dept. of the Navy, 1967-74. Counsel, Navy Contract Adjustment Board, 1967-74.
Rowden, Marcus A.
Sauber, Richard
Shriver, Sargent
Background: Director, Peace Corps, 1961-1966; Director, Office of Economic Opportunity, 1964-1968; United States Ambassador to France, 1968-1970.
Stanislawski, Howard J.
Zahler, Eric J.
Zax, Leonard A., Partner
Clients:

California Pistachio Commission (David E. Birenbaum)
Canadair Challenger, Inc. Advanced Unmanned Systems Directorate
Forstmann, Little & Co. (Leonard A. Zax)
General Electric Co. (Marcus A. Rowden)
Grumman Corp.
Handgun Control, Inc. (David E. Birenbaum)
Israel, Embassy of (Melvin Rishe)
Israel, Government of (Alan G. Kashdan, Melvin Rishe)
Israel Military Industries
Israel, Ministry of Defense
Lonza Inc. (Henry A. Hubschman)
Virgin Island Rum Industries (Jay R. Kraemer)

FRIED, Ronald A.
Senior Consultant, Government Relations, Holland and Knight
888 17th St., N.W. Suite 900, Washington, DC 20006
Telephone: (202) 955-5550
Registered as lobbyist at U.S. Congress.
Background: Former Legislative Assistant to Rep. Claude Pepper (D-FL).
Clients:
Hialeah Hospital

FRIEDHEIM, Jerry W.
President, American Newspaper Publishers Ass'n
The Newspaper Center 11600 Sunrise Valley Drive, Reston, VA 22091
Telephone: (703) 648-1000
Registered as lobbyist at U.S. Congress.

FRIEDLANDER, James S.
Mitchell, Friedlander & Gittleman
1201 Connecticut Ave., N.W. Suite 720, Washington, DC 20036
Telephone: (202) 835-0720
Registered as Foreign Agent: (#4295).
Clients:
Liberia, Nat'l Bank of

FRIEDLANDER, Philip P., Jr.
Exec. V. President, Nat'l Tire Dealers and Retreaders Ass'n
1250 I St., N.W. Suite 400, Washington, DC 20005
Telephone: (202) 789-2300
Registered as lobbyist at U.S. Congress.

FRIEDMAN ASSOC. INC., Cynthia
322 Massachusetts Ave., N.E., Washington, DC 20002
Telephone: (202) 546-4204
Members of firm representing listed organizations:
Abbott, Keith F., Senior Associate
Background: Finance Director, Senator George Mitchell (D-ME), 1987. Finance Director, Democratic Senatorial Campaign Committee, 1984-86.
Filler, Eileen, Associate
Background: Former Washington Finance Director, Peter Hoagland for Congress, 1987-88.
Friedman, Cynthia, President
Background: Deputy Finance Director, Democratic Senatorial Campaign Committee, 1984-86.
McCabe, Ellen, Associate
Organizations represented:
Ann Richards for Governor Committee '90 (Cynthia Friedman, Ellen McCabe)
Committee for Nat'l Security (Keith F. Abbott)
Nat'l Organization for Women (Cynthia Friedman)
Simon for President '86 (Cynthia Friedman)
Simon for Senate '90 (Keith F. Abbott, Eileen Filler)

FRIEDMAN, Cynthia
President, Friedman Assoc. Inc., Cynthia
322 Massachusetts Ave., N.E., Washington, DC 20002
Telephone: (202) 546-4204
Background: Deputy Finance Director, Democratic Senatorial Campaign Committee, 1984-86.
Organizations represented:
Ann Richards for Governor Committee '90
Nat'l Organization for Women
Simon for President '86

FRIEDMAN, David N.
Manager, Environmental Affairs, Interstate Natural Gas Ass'n of America
555 13th St., N.W. Suite 300 West, Washington, DC 20004
Telephone: (202) 626-3200

FRIEDMAN, Deborah H.
V. President, Kamber Group, The
1920 L St., N.W., Washington, DC 20036
Telephone: (202) 223-8700

FRIEDMAN, John
Public Affairs Administrator, American Academy of Physician Assistants
950 North Washington St., Alexandria, VA 22314
Telephone: (703) 836-2272

FRIEDMAN, Karen D.
Congressional Liaison, Human Rights Campaign Fund
1012 14th St., N.W. Suite 607, Washington, DC 20005
Telephone: (202) 628-4160
Registered as lobbyist at U.S. Congress.

FRIEDMAN, Margery Sinder
Morgan, Lewis and Bockius
1800 M St., N.W., Washington, DC 20036
Telephone: (202) 467-7000

FRIEDMAN, Miles
Exec. Director, Nat'l Ass'n of State Development Agencies
444 North Capitol St., N.W. Suite 611, Washington, DC 20001
Telephone: (202) 624-5411

FRIEDMAN, Paul A.
Political Director, Environmental Action's Political Action Committee (ENACT/PAC)
1525 New Hampshire Ave., N.W., Washington, DC 20036
Telephone: (202) 745-4870
Background: Former staff associate for Small Business Subcommittee on Regulation and Business Opportunities under Cong. Ron Wyder (D-OR).

FRIEDMAN, Robert
General Counsel, Internat'l Union of Electronic, Electrical, Salaried, Machine, and Furniture Workers, AFL-CIO
1126 16th St., N.W., Washington, DC 20036
Telephone: (202) 296-1200

FRIEDMAN, Robert E.
President, Corporation for Enterprise Development
1725 K St., N.W. Suite 1401, Washington, DC 20006
Telephone: (202) 293-7963

FRIEDMANN, Gay H.
Director, Federal Government Affairs, Northern States Power Co.
655 15th St., N.W., Suite 300, Washington, DC 20005
Telephone: (202) 639-4051
Registered as lobbyist at U.S. Congress.

FRIEDMANN, Peter
Lindsay, Hart, Neil & Weigler
1225 19th St., N.W. Suite 200, Washington, DC 20036
Telephone: (202) 393-4460
Registered as lobbyist at U.S. Congress.
Background: Legislative Counsel, Senator Bob Packwood, 1979. Chief Counsel, Subcommittee on Merchant Marine, Committee on Commerce, Science and Transportation, Senate, 1980-85.
Clients:
Agriculture Ocean Transportation Coalition
Avia Footwear, Inc.
Crowley Maritime Corp.
Oregon Economic Development Dept., Ports Division
Pacific Coast Council of Freight Forwarders
Portland, Oregon, Port of
Redwood City, California, Port of
Reebok Internat'l Ltd.

FRIEDRICH, Albert H.
V. President, Washington Operations, Kollsman
2001 Jefferson Davis Hwy. Suite 807, Arlington, VA 22202
Telephone: (703) 979-1200

FRIEL, Tom
Group V. President, Consumer Group, Electronic Industries Ass'n
2001 Pennsylvania Ave., N.W., Washington, DC 20006
Telephone: (202) 457-4900

FRIEND, Gary
Director, Corporate Government Services, Dun & Bradstreet
600 Maryland Ave., S.W., Suite 240, Washington, DC 20024
Telephone: (202) 484-7381

FRIENDS, Nathaniel L.
Regulatory Affrs. V. Pres. & Attorney, AT&T
Suite 1000, 1120 20th St., N.W., Washington, DC 20036
Telephone: (202) 457-3895

FRIERSON, James W.
Partner, Brock Group, The
1130 Connecticut Ave., N.W. Suite 350, Washington, DC 20036
Telephone: (202) 296-1901
Registered as Foreign Agent: (#4310).
Background: Special Assistant, Office of the U.S. Trade Representative, 1981-85. Chief of Staff, Office of the U.S. Trade Representative, 1985-89. Coordinator, U.S. Government's policy on the functioning of the GATT system in the Uruguay Round of Trade Negotiations, 1987-89.

FRIES, R. Roger
Director, Federal and Technical Affairs, Glass Packaging Institute
1801 K St., N.W., Suite 1105L, Washington, DC 20006
Telephone: (202) 887-4850
Registered as lobbyist at U.S. Congress.

FRINGS, Carole L.
Federal Relations Representative, American Dental Ass'n
1111 14th St., N.W. Suite 1200, Washington, DC 20005
Telephone: (202) 898-2400

FRISCHKORN, Allen R., Jr.
President, Telecommunications Industry Ass'n
1722 Eye St., N.W., Suite 440, Washington, DC 20006
Telephone: (202) 457-4912

FRITSCHLE, Elizabeth
Government Affairs Specialist, Transco Energy Co.
555 13th St., N.W., Suite 430 West, Washington, DC 20004
Telephone: (202) 628-3060

FRITTS, Charles
Director, Government Affairs, Federal Home Loan Mortgage Corp.
1759 Business Center Drive, Reston, VA 22090
Telephone: (703) 789-4700
Registered as lobbyist at U.S. Congress.

FRITTS, Edward O.
President, Nat'l Ass'n of Broadcasters
1771 N St., N.W., Washington, DC 20036
Telephone: (202) 429-5300
Registered as lobbyist at U.S. Congress.

FRITTS, William D., Jr.
Asst Secy, Legis & Intergovt'l Affrs, DEPARTMENT OF COMMERCE
14th and Constitution Ave. S.W., Washington, DC 20230
Telephone: (202) 377-5485

FRITZ, Joni
Exec. Director, Nat'l Ass'n of Private Residential Resources
4200 Evergreen Lane, Suite 315, Annandale, VA 22003
Telephone: (703) 642-6614

FRITZ, Thomas
Exec. Editor, Tax, Prentice Hall Information Services
1819 L St., N.W. Suite 400, Washington, DC 20036
Telephone: (202) 293-0707

FRITZ, Thomas V.
V. Chairman, Government Relations, Ernst & Young
1200 19th St., N.W., Suite 400, Washington, DC 20036
Telephone: (202) 862-9300

FRITZEL, Charles H.
Asst. V. President, Government Relations, Nat'l Ass'n of Independent Insurers
499 South Capitol St., S.W. Suite 401, Washington, DC 20003
Telephone: (202) 484-2350
Registered as lobbyist at U.S. Congress.

FRITZLEN, Jeffrey A.
Director of Washington Affairs-Resources, Union Pacific Corp.
555 13th St., N.W., Suite 450 West Columbia Square, Washington, DC 20004
Telephone: (202) 662-0100
Registered as lobbyist at U.S. Congress.
Background: Also represents Union Pacific Resources Co., a subsidiary of Union Pacific Corp.

FROH, Richard
V. President, Government Relations, Kaiser Foundation Health Plan, Inc.
1700 K St., N.W. Suite 601, Washington, DC 20006
Telephone: (202) 296-1314

FROHLICHER, Jean S.
Exec. Director, Nat'l Council of Higher Education Loan Programs
804 E St., S.E., Washington, DC 20003
Telephone: (202) 547-1571

FROM, Alvin
President & Exec. Director, Democratic Leadership Council
316 Pennsylvania Ave., S.E., Suite 500, Washington, DC 20003
Telephone: (202) 546-0007

FROMYER, Mary O.
Government Relations Counsellor, Internat'l Business-Government Counsellors, Inc.
818 Connecticut Ave., N.W. Suite 1200, Washington, DC 20006
Telephone: (202) 872-8181

FROSH, Marcy
Senior Research Associate, Common Cause
2030 M St., N.W., Washington, DC 20036
Telephone: (202) 833-1200
Registered as lobbyist at U.S. Congress.

FROST, Douglas
Dir., Wash. Office of the Governor, Michigan, State of
444 N. Capitol St., N.W. Suite 390, Washington, DC 20001
Telephone: (202) 624-5840

FROST, Ellen L.
Director, International Affairs, United Technologies Corp.
1825 Eye St., N.W. Suite 700, Washington, DC 20006
Telephone: (202) 785-7400

FROST, Susan
Exec. Director, Committee For Education Funding
505 Capitol Court, N.E. Suite 200, Washington, DC 20002
Telephone: (202) 543-6300

FRUMIN, Eric
Health and Safety Director, Amalgamated Clothing and Textile Workers Union
815 16th St., N.W., Suite 507, Washington, DC 20006
Telephone: (202) 628-0214

FRUMKIN, Peter
V. President, Institute for Educational Affairs
1112 16th St., N.W. Suite 520, Washington, DC 20036
Telephone: (202) 833-1801

FRUSCELLO, Mary
Divisional V. Pres., Real Estate Finance, Nat'l Ass'n of REALTORS
777 14th St., N.W., Washington, DC 20005
Telephone: (202) 383-1000

FRY, Gordon H.
Manager, State-Local Gov't Relations, Edison Electric Institute
1111 19th St., N.W., Washington, DC
Telephone: (202) 778-6461
Registered as lobbyist at U.S. Congress.

FRY, Kevin
Senior Director, Public Affairs, American Institute of Architects, The
1735 New York Ave., N.W., Washington, DC 20006
Telephone: (202) 626-7300

FRY, Paul
Deputy Exec. Director, American Public Power Ass'n
2301 M St., N.W., Washington, DC 20037
Telephone: (202) 775-8300

FRY, William R.
President, Nat'l Public Law Training Center
1441 E. Capitol St., S.E., Washington, DC 20003
Telephone: (202) 544-0180

FRYE, Alton
V. President and Washington Director, Council on Foreign Relations
2400 N St., N.W., Washington, DC 20037
Telephone: (202) 862-7780

FRYXELL, Joseph O.
Wright and Talisman
1050 17th St., N.W. Suite 600, Washington, DC 20036
Telephone: (202) 331-1194

FUJIMURA, Shun-Ichi
Chief Representative, Nippon Cargo Airlines
888 17th St., N.W., Suite 600, Washington, DC 20006
Telephone: (202) 298-8660

FUJIWARA, Donna A.
Exec. Director, Eye Care
1319 F St., N.W., Suite 905, Washington, DC 20004
Telephone: (202) 628-3816

FULBRIGHT, J. William
Of Counsel, Hogan and Hartson
555 13th St., N.W., Suite 1200, Washington, DC 20004-1109
Telephone: (202) 637-5600
Background: U.S. Senator from Arkansas 1945-75. Dep't of Justice 1934-35. President of the University of Arkansas 1939-41. U.S. House of Representatives 1943-45.

FULBRIGHT & JAWORSKI
1150 Connecticut Ave., N.W., Suite 400, Washington, DC 20036
Telephone: (202) 452-6800
Background: Washington office of a Houston law firm. The following information was obtained from public records and submitted to this firm for confirmation and correction. The firm did not respond.
Members of firm representing listed organizations:
  Belmar, Warren
    Background: Law Clerk, U.S. Court of Appeals for District of Columbia Circuit, 1966-67. Attorney, Office of Legal Counsel, U.S. Department of Justice, 1967-69.
  Cohen, Irwin
  Ellis, Emory N. (Jr.)
    Background: Attorney, Civil Aeronautics Board, 1961-70.
  Harrington, John F.
  Keeley, Patrick J.
  Schoonover, Martha J.
  Vogt, Carl W.
  Wellen, Robert H.
Clients:
  Avis Rent A Car Systems, Inc. *(Warren Belmar)*
  Crysen Corp. *(Warren Belmar)*
  Federal Home Loan Bank of Dallas *(Warren Belmar)*
  Maxus Energy
  Memorial Hospital System *(Robert H. Wellen)*
  Merichem Co. *(Martha J. Schoonover)*
  Nat'l Cottonseed Products Ass'n *(Carl W. Vogt)*
  Soc. of Cardiovascular and Interventional Radiology *(Irwin Cohen)*
  Texas Gas Transmission Corp. *(John F. Harrington)*
  Textile Fibers and By-Products Ass'n (TFBA) *(Carl W. Vogt)*

FULBRIGHT, Lu
Manager, Communications Projects, American Ass'n of School Administrators
1801 North Moore St., Arlington, VA 22209
Telephone: (703) 528-0700

FULCO, Nancy Reed
Human Resource Attorney, Chamber of Commerce of the U.S.A.
1615 H St., N.W., Washington, DC 20062
Telephone: (202) 463-5503
Registered as lobbyist at U.S. Congress.

Background: Former Minority Counsel, House of Representatives Sub-Committee on General Oversight and the Economy, Committee on Small Business.

FULLARTON, David C.
President, Information Industry Ass'n
555 New Jersey Ave., N.W. Suite 800, Washington, DC 20001
Telephone: (202) 639-8262

FULLER, Craig L.
President, Wexler, Reynolds, Fuller, Harrison and Schule, Inc.
1317 F St., N.W., Suite 600, Washington, DC 20004
Telephone: (202) 638-2121
Background: Former Chief of Staff to Vice President George Bush.

FULLER, Kathryn S.
President, World Wildlife Fund/The Conservation Foundation
1250 24th St., N.W., Washington, DC 20037
Telephone: (202) 293-4800

FULLER, Lee O.
Walker Associates, Charls E.
1730 Pennsylvania Ave., N.W. Suite 200, Washington, DC 20006
Telephone: (202) 393-4760
Background: Former Minority Staff Director and Majority Staff Director, Senate Committee on Environment and Public Works.
Organizations represented:
  Atchison, Topeka and Santa Fe Railway Co., The

FULLER, Mary
Exec. Dir., Ass'n of Graphic Arts Cons., Printing Industries of America
1730 North Lynn St., Arlington, VA 22209
Telephone: (703) 841-8100
Background: Also directs other affiliate organizations of the Printing Industries of America: Internat'l Thermographers Ass'n, Magazine Printers Section and Printing Industry Financial Executives.

FULTON, C. Michael
Sr. Ass't Gov't Relations Specialist, Ryan-McGinn
1110 Vermont Ave., N.W. Suite 820, Washington, DC 20005
Telephone: (202) 775-4370
Clients:
  Concord College
  Independent Oil and Gas Ass'n of West Virginia
  Wheeling Jesuit College

FULTON, Donna
Regulatory Specialist (Enron/Interstate), Enron Corp.
1020 16th St., N.W., Washington, DC 20036-5754
Telephone: (202) 828-3360

FULTON, Richard A.
White, Fine, and Verville
1156 15th St., N.W. Suite 1100, Washington, DC 20005
Telephone: (202) 659-2900
Background: Assistant to Senator Allen J. Ellender of Louisiana, 1960-62.
Clients:
  American Chiropractic Registry of Radiologic Technologists
  Ass'n of Theological Schools in the United States and Canada, The
  Illinois Ass'n of Colleges and Schools
  Marketing Education Ass'n
  Nat'l Ass'n of Health Career Schools

FULTON, William J.
Lipsen Whitten & Diamond
1725 DeSales St., N.W., Suite 800, Washington, DC 20036
Telephone: (202) 659-6540
Registered as lobbyist at U.S. Congress.

FUNK, Karen J.
Hobbs, Straus, Dean and Wilder
1819 H St., N.W., Suite 800, Washington, DC 20006
Telephone: (202) 783-5100
Clients:
  Nat'l Indian Education Ass'n

FUNK, Kristen
Grassroots Coordinator, Nat'l Committee to Preserve Social Security and Medicare
2000 K St., N.W. Suite 800, Washington, DC 20006
Telephone: (202) 822-9459
Registered as lobbyist at U.S. Congress.

FUNKE AND ASSOCIATES, Karl A.
729 2nd St., N.E., Washington, DC 20002
Telephone: (202) 544-4166
Members of firm representing listed organizations:
  Esterly, Jane B.
  Funke, Karl A.
  Spotted Elk, Clara
Organizations represented:
  Cheyenne River Sioux Tribe *(Clara Spotted Elk)*
  Chitimacha Tribe of Louisiana *(Jane B. Esterly)*
  Council of Energy Resource Tribes *(Karl A. Funke)*
  Eastern Band of Cherokee Indians *(Karl A. Funke)*
  Lac du Flambeau Chippewa Tribe *(Karl A. Funke)*
  Lac Vieux Desert Tribe *(Karl A. Funke)*
  Miccosukee Tribe of Indians of Florida *(Karl A. Funke)*
  Native American Fish and Wildlife Society *(Karl A. Funke)*
  Nisqually Indian Tribal Business Committee *(Karl A. Funke)*
  Saginaw Chippewa Tribe of Michigan *(Karl A. Funke)*
  United South and Eastern Tribes *(Karl A. Funke)*

FUNKE, Karl A.
Funke and Associates, Karl A.
729 2nd St., N.E., Washington, DC 20002
Telephone: (202) 544-4166
Registered as lobbyist at U.S. Congress.
Organizations represented:
  Council of Energy Resource Tribes
  Eastern Band of Cherokee Indians
  Lac du Flambeau Chippewa Tribe
  Lac Vieux Desert Tribe
  Miccosukee Tribe of Indians of Florida
  Native American Fish and Wildlife Society
  Nisqually Indian Tribal Business Committee
  Saginaw Chippewa Tribe of Michigan
  United South and Eastern Tribes

FUQUA, Don
President, Aerospace Industries Ass'n of America
1250 Eye St., N.W., Suite 1100, Washington, DC 20005
Telephone: (202) 371-8400
Registered as lobbyist at U.S. Congress.
Background: Member, U.S. House of Representatives from Florida, 1963-87. Chairman of the House Science and Technology Committee, 1979-87.

FUQUAY, Claudia
Director, Congressional Relations, United Fresh Fruit and Vegetable Ass'n
722 North Washington St., Alexandria, VA 22030
Telephone: (703) 836-3410
Registered as lobbyist at U.S. Congress.

FURHWIRTH, Dennis
Treasurer, COMSATPAC
950 L'Enfant Plaza, S.W., Washington, DC 20024
Telephone: (202) 863-6000

FURMAN, Harold W., II
Partner, McLeod & Pires
2501 M St., N.W., Suite 400, Washington, DC 20037
Telephone: (202) 861-1234
Background: Former Deputy Assistant Secretary for Water and Science, U.S. Department of the Interior.
Clients:
  Florida Lime & Avocado Commission, Trustees of
  South Dade Land Corp.

FURR, Coleman
Chairman of the Board, Ass'n of Independent Colleges and Schools
One Dupont Circle, N.W., Suite 350, Washington, DC 20036
Telephone: (202) 659-2460

WASHINGTON REPRESENTATIVES

FURTEK, Ed
Asst. Dir., Fed. Governmental Relations, University of California
1523 New Hampshire Ave., N.W., Washington, DC 20036
Telephone: (202) 785-2666

FUSELIER, Linda
Capitol Group
1001 Pennsylvania Ave., N.W., Suite 1385, Washington, DC 20004
Telephone: (202) 638-1400

FUTRELL, J. William
President, Environmental Law Institute
1616 P St., N.W., Suite 200, Washington, DC 20036
Telephone: (202) 328-5150

FUTTERMAN, Marlene W.
Exec. Director, Direct Selling Education Foundation
1776 K St., N.W., Washington, DC 20006
Telephone: (202) 293-5760

GABAUER, Peter A., Jr.
Deputy General Counsel, Nat'l Coal Ass'n
1130 17th St., N.W., Washington, DC 20036
Telephone: (202) 463-2643

GABBERT & ASSOC., J. Stephen
2000 M St., N.W., Suite 200, Washington, DC 20036
Telephone: (202) 452-1846

GABERLAVAGE, George
Senior Analyst, American Ass'n of Retired Persons
1909 K St., N.W., Washington, DC 20049
Telephone: (202) 872-4700

GABLE, Wayne E.
President, Citizens for a Sound Economy
470 L'Enfant Plaza East, S.W. Suite 7112, Washington, DC 20024
Telephone: (202) 488-8200
Background: Also serves as President, Tax Foundation, Inc.

GABOR, Marc P.
Nat'l Legislative Representative, United Mine Workers of America
900 15th St., N.W., Washington, DC 20005
Telephone: (202) 842-7334
Registered as lobbyist at U.S. Congress.

GABOURY, Col. Laurence., USMC (Ret)
Exec. Director, Marine Corps Reserve Officers Ass'n
201 North Washington St. Suite 206, Alexandria, VA 22314
Telephone: (703) 548-7607

GABRIEL, Edward M.
Madison Group/Earle Palmer Brown, The
2033 M St., N.W., 9th Floor, Washington, DC 20036
Telephone: (202) 223-0030
Registered as lobbyist at U.S. Congress.
Clients:
General Electric Co.
Keystone Center, The

GABUSI, John
Senior V. President, Marketing, Professional Lobbying and Consulting Center
1111 14th St., N.W., Suite 1001, Washington, DC 20005
Telephone: (202) 898-0084

GADBAW, R. Michael
Dewey, Ballantine, Bushby, Palmer and Wood
1775 Pennsylvania Ave., N.W. Suite 200, Washington, DC 20006
Telephone: (202) 862-1000
Background: Former Deputy General Counsel, Office of the Special Representative for Trade Negotiations.
Clients:
Digital Equipment Corp.
Intel Corporation
Semiconductor Industry Ass'n

GADDY, Steven
Dep Asst Secy, Govt'l Affrs, DEPARTMENT OF TRANSPORTATION
400 Seventh St., S.W., Washington, DC 20590
Telephone: (202) 366-4573

GAFFIN, Barbara
Congressional Liaison, Nat'l Conference on Soviet Jewry
1522 K St., N.W., Suite 1100, Washington, DC 20005
Telephone: (202) 898-2500

GAFFNEY, Frank J., Jr.
President and Director, Center for Security Policy
1250 24th St., N.W., Washington, DC 20037
Telephone: (202) 466-0515
Background: Staff, Senate Armed Services Committee, 1981-83; Deputy Ass't Secretary of Defense for Nuclear Arms Control Policy, 1983-87; Ass't Secretary of Defense for Internat'l Security Policy, 1987.

GAFNEY, Lorraine
Director, Wine Institute
1575 Eye St., N.W., Suite 325, Washington, DC 20005
Telephone: (202) 408-0870

GAGE, Franklin
Director, Task Force Against Nuclear Pollution
Box 1817, Washington, DC 20013
Telephone: (301) 474-8311

GAGE, Kit
Washington Representative, Nat'l Committee Against Repressive Legislation
236 Massachusetts Ave., N.E., Suite 406, Washington, DC 20002
Telephone: (202) 543-7659
Registered as lobbyist at U.S. Congress.

GAGE, Larry S.
Powell, Goldstein, Frazer and Murphy
1001 Pennsylvania, N.W., Sixth Fl., Washington, DC 20004
Telephone: (202) 347-0066
Background: Legal Counsel to Commissioner Nicholas Johnson, Federal Communications Commission, 1972-73. Counsel, U.S. Senate Subcommittee on Employment, Poverty and Migratory Labor, 1973-75. Staff Director, U.S. Senate Subcommittee on Alcoholism and Drug Abuse, 1975-77. Special Assistant and Deputy Assistant Secretary, Health Legislation, Department of Health and Human Services, 1977-81. Serves as President and General Counsel of the Nat'l Ass'n of Public Hospitals.
Clients:
Nat'l Ass'n of Public Hospitals

GAGER, William C.
Exec. V. President, Automotive Parts Rebuilders Ass'n
6849 Old Dominion Drive, Suite 352, McLean, VA 22101
Telephone: (703) 790-1050
Registered as lobbyist at U.S. Congress.

GAGNON, Kathy
Asst. to the Sr. V.P., Gov't Relations, Chicago Mercantile Exchange
2000 Pennsylvania Ave., N.W. Suite 6200, Washington, DC 20006
Telephone: (202) 223-6965

GAIBLER, Floyd D.
Exec. Director, Nat'l Cheese Institute
888 16th St., N.W., Washington, DC 20006
Telephone: (202) 659-1454
Registered as lobbyist at U.S. Congress.
Background: Also serves as Exec. Director of the American Butter Institute.

GAINER, R. I.
V. President for Finance, Adventist Development and Relief Agency Internat'l
12501 Old Columbia Pike, Silver Spring, MD 20904
Telephone: (301) 680-6380

GAINES, Beverly E.
Cong Svcs Coordinator, DEPARTMENT OF ENERGY
1000 Independence Ave. S.W., Washington, DC 20585
Telephone: (202) 586-5450

GAINES, Frank W., Jr.
Olwine, Connelly, Chase, O'Donnell and Weyher
1701 Pennsylvania Ave., N.W. Suite 1000, Washington, DC 20006
Telephone: (202) 835-0500

GALANTY, Walter E., Jr.
President, Nat'l Ass'n of Brick Distributors
212 South Henry St., Alexandria, VA 22314
Telephone: (703) 549-2555

GALAVIZ, Fernando
V. President, Government Liaison, United States Pan Asian American Chamber of Commerce
1625 K St., N.W., Suite 380, Washington, DC 20006
Telephone: (202) 638-1764

GALBRAITH, J. Alan
Williams and Connolly
839 17th St., N.W. 1000 Hill Bldg., Washington, DC 20006
Telephone: (202) 331-5000
Clients:
Navistar Internat'l Corp.

GALE, Michael
Dep Dir, Legis Affrs, DEPARTMENT OF COMMERCE
14th and Constitution Ave. S.W., Washington, DC 20230
Telephone: (202) 377-5485

GALE, Robert A.
President, American Machine Tool Distributors Ass'n
1335 Rockville Pike Suite 300, Rockville, MD 20852
Telephone: (301) 738-1200

GALE, Robert L.
President, Ass'n of Governing Boards of Universities and Colleges
One Dupont Circle, N.W. Suite 400, Washington, DC 20036
Telephone: (202) 296-8400

GALINSKY, Ellen
President, Nat'l Ass'n for the Education of Young Children
1834 Connecticut Ave., N.W., Washington, DC 20009
Telephone: (202) 232-8777

GALL, John
Treasurer, Advanced Technology Inc. Political Action Committee
12005 Sunrise Valley Drive, Reston, VA 22091
Telephone: (703) 620-8000

GALLAGHER & ASSOC., Linda Parke
1225 Eye St. N.W., Suite 600, Washington, DC 20005
Telephone: (202) 326-8402
Background: A public and government relations firm, focusing on issues surrounding finance, housing, conservation and economic development.
Members of firm representing listed organizations:
Gallagher, Linda Parke, President
Background: Formerly Senior V. President, Federal Nat'l Mortgage Ass'n.
Organizations represented:
Affordable Housing Preservation Center *(Linda Parke Gallagher)*
Nat'l Housing Partnership *(Linda Parke Gallagher)*
Urban Land Institute *(Linda Parke Gallagher)*

GALLAGHER, BOLAND, MEIBURGER AND BROSNAN
1000 Vermont Ave., N.W. Suite 1100, Washington, DC 20005-4903
Telephone: (202) 289-7200
Members of firm representing listed organizations:
Boland, Christopher T.
Background: Staff Director, U.S. Senate Committee on Atomic Energy; Counsel-Staff Director, Joint Congressional Committee on Atomic Energy, 1945-47.
Broadstone, James M.
Background: Staff Attorney, Federal Power Commission, 1972-73.
Brosnan, Thomas F.
Background: Attorney-Advisor, Tax Court of the U.S., 1953-55.
Kelly, Frank X.
Lesch, Peter C.
Background: Staff Attorney, Federal Power Commission, 1973-77; Legal Advisor to Commissioner, Federal Energy Regulatory Commission, 1978-79.
Meiburger, George J.
Clients:
Bay State Gas Co. *(Thomas F. Brosnan)*
Enron Corp. *(Frank X. Kelly, George J. Meiburger)*
Florida Public Utilities Co. *(Thomas F. Brosnan)*
Gas Research Institute *(James M. Broadstone)*

High Island Offshore Systems *(Christopher T. Boland)*
Tampa Electric Co. *(Peter C. Lesch)*
U-T Offshore System
Washington Natural Gas Co. *(Thomas F. Brosnan)*

GALLAGHER, John J.

Akin, Gump, Strauss, Hauer and Feld
1333 New Hampshire Ave., N.W., Suite 400, Washington,
DC 20036
Telephone: (202) 887-4000
Clients:
Texas Air Corp.

GALLAGHER, Linda Parke

President, Gallagher & Assoc., Linda Parke
1225 Eye St. N.W., Suite 600, Washington, DC 20005
Telephone: (202) 326-8402
Registered as lobbyist at U.S. Congress.
Background: Formerly Senior V. President, Federal Nat'l
Mortgage Ass'n.
Organizations represented:
Affordable Housing Preservation Center
Nat'l Housing Partnership
Urban Land Institute

GALLAGHER, Mark

Assistant Director, Gov't Liaison, United States Catholic
Conference
3200 4th St., N.E., Washington, DC 20017
Telephone: (202) 541-3000

GALLAGHER, Mary Jane

Gallagher-Widmeyer Group Inc., The
1110 Vermont Ave., N.W., Suite 1020, Washington, DC
20005
Telephone: (202) 659-1606
Background: Former Press Secretary to John D. Rockefel-
ler, IV, now U.S. Senator (D-WV). Also formerly directed
public affairs for the Nat'l Conference of State Legisla-
tures.
Clients:
Ass'n of Flight Attendants
Minnesota AFL-CIO
Nat'l Commission to Prevent Infant Mortality
Nat'l Forum on the Future of Children and Their
Families
Project 500
Renew America Project
Southern Governors Ass'n
TransAfrica

GALLAGHER-WIDMEYER GROUP INC., THE

1110 Vermont Ave., N.W., Suite 1020, Washington, DC
20005
Telephone: (202) 659-1606
Background: A public relations and public affairs consult-
ing firm.
Members of firm representing listed organizations:
Anbender, Julie, Account Executive
Background: Former Press Secretary and Deputy Press
Secretary, Democratic National Committee.
Baggett, Madalene, Account Executive
Baker, Michael, Account Supervisor
Background: Former state press secretary to Vice Presi-
dent Walter Mondale in the 1984 presidential cam-
paign.
Blank, Linda, Account Executive
Gallagher, Mary Jane
Background: Former Press Secretary to John D. Rock-
efeller, IV, now U.S. Senator (D-WV). Also formerly
directed public affairs for the Nat'l Conference of
State Legislatures.
Griggs, Henry, Account Supervisor
Hoff, Tina, Assistant Account Executive
Kogan, Joanne, Account Executive
Krell, Paul, Director, Creative-Strategic Services
Background: Former political director of the political
action committee of Rep. Richard Gephardt (D-MO)
during the 1985-86 political cycle. Served as Senior
National Scheduler for the Carter-Mondale presiden-
tial campaign 1979-80 and on the national campaign
staff of Senator John Glenn (D-OH), 1983-84.
Ranbom, Shepard, Director, Education Projects
Background: Formerly served on the Congressional Ad-
visory Committee on Student Financial Aid.
Roberts, Anne Marie, Assistant Account Executive
St. Denis, Cathy, Account Executive

Background: Formerly served as Deputy Communica-
tions Director, Democratic Senatorial Committee and
as Deputy Press Secretary to Senator Tom Daschle
(D-SD).
Widmeyer, Scott D.
Background: Deputy Press Secretary in the 1980 Presi-
dential campaign of Jimmy Carter and also served in
press aide roles in the 1984 campaigns of Walter
Mondale and Geraldine Ferraro.
Clients:
American Ass'n for the Advancement of Science
(Scott D. Widmeyer)
American Federation of Teachers *(Scott D. Widmey-
er)*
Ass'n of Flight Attendants *(Mary Jane Gallagher)*
Carnegie Council on Adolescent Development
(Scott D. Widmeyer)
Education Commission of the States *(Scott D. Wid-
meyer)*
Education Week *(Scott D. Widmeyer)*
Edunetics *(Scott D. Widmeyer)*
Grant Foundation, W. T. *(Scott D. Widmeyer)*
Institute for Educational Leadership *(Scott D. Wid-
meyer)*
Minnesota AFL-CIO *(Mary Jane Gallagher)*
Nat'l Alliance of Business *(Scott D. Widmeyer)*
Nat'l Ass'n of Trade and Technical Schools *(Scott
D. Widmeyer)*
Nat'l Board of Professional Teaching Standards
(Scott D. Widmeyer)
Nat'l Center on Education and the Economy
(Scott D. Widmeyer)
Nat'l Commission to Prevent Infant Mortality
(Mary Jane Gallagher)
Nat'l Forum on the Future of Children and Their
Families *(Mary Jane Gallagher)*
Pelavin Associates *(Scott D. Widmeyer)*
Project 500 *(Mary Jane Gallagher)*
Renew America Project *(Mary Jane Gallagher)*
RJR Nabisco Washington, Inc. *(Scott D. Widmeyer)*
Southern Governors Ass'n *(Mary Jane Gallagher)*
TransAfrica *(Mary Jane Gallagher)*
United Automobile, Aerospace and Agricultural
Implement Workers of America (UAW) *(Scott D.
Widmeyer)*
Whittle Communications *(Scott D. Widmeyer)*

GALLAND, KHARASCH, MORSE AND GARFIN-KLE

Canal Square, 1054 31st St., N.W., Washington, DC
20007
Telephone: (202) 342-5200
Registered as Foreign Agent: (#4006)
Members of firm representing listed organizations:
Garfinkle, Morris R.
Ginsberg, Marc C., Partner
Greenberg, Edward D.
Background: Regional Counsel, Interstate Commerce
Commission, 1973-76. Special Counsel for Pipelines,
Interstate Commerce Commission, 1977. Director
and Chief Counsel, Trans Alaska Pipeline System
Project, Federal Energy Regulatory Commission,
1978.
Jollie, Susan B.
Background: Associate General Counsel for Antitrust
and Litigation, Civil Aeronautics Board, 1980-84. Ex-
ecutive Assistant to the Vice Chairman, Civil
Aeronautics Board, 1982-83.
Kahan, Mark S.
Background: Associate Director, Legal Economic and
Regulatory Affairs, Civil Aeronautics Board, 1981-82.
Deputy Solicitor for Administrative Enforcement and
Litigation, Office of Special Counsel. Department of
Energy, 1977-78.
Kharasch, Robert N.
Background: Consultant to U.S. Department of Trans-
portation, 1967-68.
Morse, Robert H.
Background: Trial Attorney and Senior Trial Attorney,
Patent Section, Antitrust Division, Department of
Justice, 1971-75. Senior Trial Attorney, Trial Section,
Antitrust Division, Department of Justice, 1975-78.
Clients:
Air Jamaica *(Morris R. Garfinkle, Susan B. Jollie, Mark S.
Kahan)*
Alamo Rent-a-Car *(Susan B. Jollie)*
California Shipping Line, Inc.
Freight-Savers Shipping Co. Ltd.

Hong Kong Aircraft Engineering Co., Ltd. *(Morris
R. Garfinkle, Susan B. Jollie)*
Israel Aircraft Industries *(Morris R. Garfinkle, Susan B.
Jollie)*
Orient Airlines Ass'n *(Morris R. Garfinkle, Susan B. Jol-
lie)*
South African Sugar Ass'n *(Marc C. Ginsberg)*
Surface Freight Corp. *(Edward D. Greenberg)*

GALLANT, Karl

V.P. & Director, Federal Legislation, Nat'l Right to Work
Committee
8001 Braddock Road, Springfield, VA 22160
Telephone: (703) 321-9820
Registered as lobbyist at U.S. Congress.

GALLANT, Mark

Nat'l Lumber and Building Material Dealers Ass'n
40 Ivy St., S.E., Washington, DC 20003
Telephone: (202) 547-2230
Registered as lobbyist at U.S. Congress.

GALLEGOS, Kathy E.

Director, Conmgressional Affairs, McNair Group Inc.
1155 15th St., N.W., Washington, DC 20005
Telephone: (202) 659-8866
Background: Former Legislative Director to Rep. James
Hansen (R-UT).
Clients:
Defense Group, Inc.
GTE Corp.
Texas Instruments, Industrial Automation
Westinghouse Environmental Services

GALLEN, Kevin P.

Newman & Holtzinger, P.C.
1615 L St., N.W., 10th Floor, Washington, DC 20005
Telephone: (202) 955-6600
Clients:
Dairyland Power Cooperative

GALLES, John Paul

Exec. V. President and COO, Nat'l Small Business United
1155 15th St., N.W. 7th Floor, Washington, DC 20005
Telephone: (202) 293-8830
Registered as lobbyist at U.S. Congress.
Background: Also represents the Nat'l Small Business
United PAC.

GALLINA, Emil

V. President, Kamber Group, The
1920 L St., N.W., Washington, DC 20036
Telephone: (202) 223-8700

GALTNEY, Liz

Director, Project on Government Procurement
613 Pennsylvania Ave., S.E. 2nd Floor, Washington, DC
20003
Telephone: (202) 543-0883

GALVIN, STANLEY & HAZARD

111 Massachusetts Ave., N.W., Washington, DC 20001
Telephone: (202) 289-4854
Members of firm representing listed organizations:
Hazard, Holly Eliz.
Clients:
Animal Legal Defense Fund
Doris Day Animal League *(Holly Eliz. Hazard)*

GAMBER, Glenn

Legislative Representative, Nat'l Food Processors Ass'n
1401 New York Ave., N.W. Suite 400, Washington, DC
20005
Telephone: (202) 639-5900
Background: Serves as contact for the Nat'l Food Processors Ass'n Political Action Committee.

GAMBILL, John

Sr. Res. Assoc, Dir. of Publications, Federation of Tax Administrators
444 North Capitol St., N.W., Suite 334, Washington, DC
20001
Telephone: (202) 624-5890

GAMBLE, Bruce

V. President, External Affairs, Nat'l Bankers Ass'n
122 C St., N.W. Suite 580, Washington, DC 20001
Telephone: (202) 783-3200
Registered as lobbyist at U.S. Congress.

GAMMON AND GRANGE
1925 K St., N.W., Suite 300, Washington, DC 20006
Telephone: (202) 862-2000
Clients:
Institute on Religion and Democracy
KARK-TV
KFCB
WCLF
WEJC
WLIG-TV
WLYJ
WNFT
WPCB-TV
WTGI-TV

GAMMON, Samuel R.
Exec. Director, American Historical Ass'n
400 A St., S.E., Washington, DC 20003
Telephone: (202) 544-2422

GAMPEL, Gwen
V. President, Health Affairs, Capitol Associates, Inc.
426 C St., N.E., Washington, DC 20002
Telephone: (202) 544-1880
Clients:
American Ass'n of Retired Persons
Child Welfare League of America
Nat'l Renal Administrators Ass'n

GANGLOFF, Deborah
V. President for Program Services, American Forestry
Ass'n
P.O. Box 2000, Washington, DC 20013
Telephone: (202) 667-3300

GANNON, Cheryl
Legislative Representative, Nat'l Committee to Preserve
Social Security and Medicare
2000 K St., N.W. Suite 800, Washington, DC 20006
Telephone: (202) 822-9459
Registered as lobbyist at U.S. Congress.

GANNON, John A.
Legislative Liaison, Internat'l Union of Police Ass'ns
1016 Duke St., Alexandria, VA 22314
Telephone: (703) 549-7473
Registered as lobbyist at U.S. Congress.

GANNON, Thomas M.
General Counsel, Cassidy and Associates, Inc.
655 15th St., N.W., Suite 1100, Washington, DC 20005
Telephone: (202) 347-0773
Registered as lobbyist at U.S. Congress.
Clients:
Acorn Data Systems, Inc.
American Dredging Co.
American Science & Engineering Inc.
Ass'n for the Safe Handling of Medical Waste
Biopure Corp.
Boston Carmen's Union, Local 589
Children's Hospital Nat'l Medical Center
Columbia University
DataCom Systems Corp.
Delaware State Department of Transportation
Great Lakes Dredge and Dock Co.
Hawaii State Department of Business and Eco-
nomic Development
Hexagon Technical Co. Inc.
Indiana Department of Commerce
Internat'l Data Corp.
ITT Gilfillan
James Co., T. L.
Kerr-McGee Corp.
Lee Company, Thomas H.
Loyola Marymount University
Medical College of Wisconsin
Michigan Technological University
Mount Sinai Medical Center of Greater Miami
Mutual Interest Transactions
Pirelli Cable Corp.
Spring Garden College
Twentieth Century Fox
University of the Arts

GANS, Curtis B.
Exec. Director, Committee for the Study of the American
Electorate
421 New Jersey, Ave., S.E., Washington, DC 20003
Telephone: (202) 546-3221

Registered as lobbyist at U.S. Congress.

GANS, John A.
Exec. V. President and CEO, American Pharmaceutical
Ass'n
2215 Constitution Ave., N.W., Washington, DC 20037
Telephone: (202) 628-4410

GANTS, Robert M.
Vice President, Government Relations, Ass'n of Home Ap-
pliance Manufacturers
200 Dangerfield Road, Alexandria, VA 22314
Telephone: (703) 683-8822
Background: Also represents the Ass'n of Home Appliance
Manufacturers PAC.

GANTT, John B.
1025 Thomas Jefferson St, N.W. Suite 500-East, Wash-
ington, DC 20007
Telephone: (202) 944-3212
Registered as Foreign Agent: (#4120)
Organizations represented:
European Space Agency

GANTZ, David A.
Oppenheimer Wolff and Donnelly
1020 19th St., N.W., Suite 400, Washington, DC 20036
Telephone: (202) 293-5096
Registered as lobbyist at U.S. Congress.
Registered as Foreign Agent: (#3485).
Background: Attorney, Office of the Legal Adviser, De-
partment of State, 1970-73. Assistant Legal Adviser: In-
ter-American Affairs, 1974-76; European Affairs, 1976-
77, Department of State.
Clients:
Daewoo Electronics Co.
Korea Footwear Exporters Ass'n
Nishika Corp.

GARA, Nicole
Director, Gov't and Professional Affairs, American Acade-
my of Physician Assistants
950 North Washington St., Alexandria, VA 22314
Telephone: (703) 836-2272
Registered as lobbyist at U.S. Congress.

GARBER, Felicia
Communications Director, Internat'l Magnesium Ass'n
2010 Corporate Ridge Suite 700, McLean, VA 22102
Telephone: (703) 442-8888

GARBOW, Melvin C.
Arnold & Porter
1200 New Hampshire Ave., N.W., Washington, DC 20036
Telephone: (202) 872-6700
Registered as Foreign Agent: (#1750).

GARCIA, Ernest E.
V. President, Eastern Operations, Source One Management, Inc.
1155 15th St., N.W., Suite 1108, Washington, DC 20005
Telephone: (202) 429-1944

GARCIA, Isabelle
Legislative Specialist, Nat'l Education Ass'n of the U.S.
1201 16th St., N.W., Washington, DC 20036
Telephone: (202) 822-7300
Registered as lobbyist at U.S. Congress.

GARCIA, Lou
Exec. Director, Soc. of Consumer Affairs Professionals in
Business
4900 Leesburg Pike Suite 400, Alexandria, VA 22302
Telephone: (703) 998-7371

GARCIA, Mildred R.
Director of Adminstration, Hispanic Policy Development
Project
1001 Connecticut Ave., N.W. Suite 310, Washington, DC
20036
Telephone: (202) 822-8414

GARCIA, Raymond
Director, Legislative Affairs, Rockwell Internat'l
1745 Jefferson Davis Hwy., Arlington, VA 22202
Telephone: (703) 553-6638
Registered as lobbyist at U.S. Congress.

GARDINER, Arthur Z., Jr.
Wilmer, Cutler and Pickering
2445 M St., N.W., Washington, DC 20037-1420
Telephone: (202) 663-6000
Registered as Foreign Agent: (#3355).

GARDINER, David McLane
Legislative Director, Sierra Club
408 C St., N.E., Washington, DC 20002
Telephone: (202) 547-1141
Registered as lobbyist at U.S. Congress.

GARDINER, Donald K., CAE
Exec. V. President, Nat'l Ass'n of Professional Insurance
Agents
400 North Washington St., Alexandria, VA 22314
Telephone: (703) 836-9340

GARDINER, Elizabeth
EPA/Environment Project Manager, Organization for
American-Soviet ExchangeS (OASES-DC)
1302 R St., N.W., Washington, DC 20009
Telephone: (202) 332-1145

GARDINER, Richard
Director, State & Local Affairs Division, Nat'l Rifle Ass'n of
America
1600 Rhode Island Ave., N.W., Washington, DC 20036
Telephone: (202) 828-6000

GARDNER, CARTON AND DOUGLAS
1001 Pennsylvania Ave., N.W., Suite 750, Washington, DC
20004
Telephone: (202) 347-9200
Background: Washington office of a Chicago law firm.
Members of firm representing listed organizations:
Griner, G. Christopher
Johnson, M. Scott
Moffat, J. Curtis
Background: Legal Assistant to the Chairman, Federal
Energy Regulatory Commission, 1977-79.
Clients:
Alamo Rent-a-Car *(J. Curtis Moffat)*
American Community TV Ass'n *(M. Scott Johnson)*
Andrew Corporation *(J. Curtis Moffat)*
Ansell Inc. *(J. Curtis Moffat)*
Minnesota Mining and Manufacturing Co. (3M
Co.) *(J. Curtis Moffat)*
Pharmaceutical Aerosol CFC Coalition *(J. Curtis
Moffat)*

GARDNER, Jack H.
Dir., Regul. Affrs. & Asst. Gen. Counsel, ITT Corp.
1600 M St., N.W., Washington, DC 20036
Telephone: (202) 775-7355

GARDNER, Marsha W.
V. President, International Affairs, Cosmetic, Toiletry and
Fragrance Ass'n
1110 Vermont Ave., N.W. Suite 800, Washington, DC
20005
Telephone: (202) 331-1770

GARDNER, Michael R.
Akin, Gump, Strauss, Hauer and Feld
1333 New Hampshire Ave., N.W., Suite 400, Washington,
DC 20036
Telephone: (202) 887-4000
Registered as Foreign Agent: (#3492).
Background: Deputy Assistant Administrator, Energy Re-
source Development, 1975 and Director, Office of Plan-
ning and Evaluation, 1976, Federal Energy Administra-
tion. Council Member, Administrative Council of the
U.S., 1981-.

GARDNER, Sherwin
Vice President, Science and Technology, Grocery Manufacturers of America
1010 Wisconsin Ave., N.W., Suite 800, Washington, DC
20007
Telephone: (202) 337-9400
Registered as lobbyist at U.S. Congress.

GARFINKEL, Steve
Account Executive, Powell, Adams & Rinehart
1901 L St., N.W., 3rd Floor, Washington, DC 20036
Telephone: (202) 466-7590

GARFINKLE, Morris R.
Galland, Kharasch, Morse and Garfinkle
Canal Square, 1054 31st St., N.W., Washington, DC 20007
Telephone: (202) 342-5200
Registered as Foreign Agent: (#3513).
Clients:
Air Jamaica
Hong Kong Aircraft Engineering Co., Ltd.
Israel Aircraft Industries
Orient Airlines Ass'n

GARIN, Geoffrey
President, Garin-Hart Strategic Research, Inc.
1724 Connecticut Ave., N.W., Washington, DC 20009
Telephone: (202) 234-5570

GARIN-HART STRATEGIC RESEARCH, INC.
1724 Connecticut Ave., N.W., Washington, DC 20009
Telephone: (202) 234-5570
Background: A Democratic political polling firm.
Members of firm representing listed organizations:
Garin, Geoffrey, President

GARLAND ASSOCIATES
137 13th St., N.E., Washington, DC 20002
Telephone: (202) 546-8486
Background: A legislative affairs consultant firm.
Members of firm representing listed organizations:
Garland, Sara G.
Background: Former aide to Rep. Margaret Heckler (R-MA) and Senator Quentin Burdick (D-ND).
Clients:
Nat'l Ass'n of Public Television Stations *(Sara G. Garland)*
Patlex Corp. *(Sara G. Garland)*
University of North Dakota *(Sara G. Garland)*

GARLAND, Kristine
Exec. V. President and CEO, Composite Can and Tube Institute
1818 N St., N.W. Suite T-10, Washington, DC 20036
Telephone: (202) 223-4840

GARLAND, Nancy
Government Relations Counsel, American Optometric Ass'n
1505 Prince Street, Suite 300, Alexandria, VA 22314
Telephone: (703) 739-9200
Registered as lobbyist at U.S. Congress.

GARLAND, Sara G.
Garland Associates
137 13th St., N.E., Washington, DC 20002
Telephone: (202) 546-8486
Registered as lobbyist at U.S. Congress.
Background: Former aide to Rep. Margaret Heckler (R-MA) and Senator Quentin Burdick (D-ND).
Clients:
Nat'l Ass'n of Public Television Stations
Patlex Corp.
University of North Dakota

GARMENT, Leonard
Dickstein, Shapiro and Morin
2101 L St., N.W., Washington, DC 20037
Telephone: (202) 785-9700
Registered as lobbyist at U.S. Congress.
Background: Special Consultant to the President of the United States, 1973-74. Assistant to the President, 1974. Vice Chairman, Administrative Conference of the United States 1973-74. U.S. Representative to the Commission on Human Rights of the United Nations Economic and Social Council, 1975-77. Counselor to U.S. Delegation to the UN, 1975-77. Chairman, Commission on Federal Judiciary of Sen. Daniel P. Moynihan, 1976-. Member, Committee on the Judiciary, Judicial Conference of the U.S., 1981-.
Clients:
Advance Publications, Inc.
Toshiba Corp.

GARNER, Carol
Director, Election Center, Academy for State and Local Government
444 North Capitol St., N.W., Suite 349, Washington, DC 20001
Telephone: (202) 638-1445
Background: Responsibilities include the Election Center.

GAROFALO, Gary B.
Boros and Garofalo
1255 23rd St., N.W., Suite 295, Washington, DC 20037
Telephone: (202) 857-2526
Background: Staff Attorney, Federal Aviation Administration, 1965-68.
Clients:
Air BVI
Lineas Aereas Paraguayes (LAP)
Rich Internat'l Airways
Spantax, S.A.

GARRETSON, Merv
Interim Exec. Director, Nat'l Ass'n of the Deaf
814 Thayer Ave., Silver Spring, MD 20910
Telephone: (301) 587-1788

GARRETT AND COMPANY
1630 Connecticut Ave., N.W. Suite 202, Washington, DC 20009
Telephone: (202) 332-0200
Registered as Foreign Agent: (#4279)
Members of firm representing listed organizations:
Garrett, Thaddeus A. (Jr.)
Clients:
Congo, Office of the President of the *(Thaddeus A. Garrett, Jr.)*

GARRETT, E. Norbert
Dir, Cong Affrs, EXECUTIVE OFFICE OF THE PRESIDENT - Central Intelligence Agency
Washington, DC 20505
Telephone: (703) 482-6121

GARRETT, Harley
Manager, Northeast Region, SCI Technology, Inc.
1215 Jefferson Davis Hwy. Suite 307, Arlington, VA 22202
Telephone: (703) 486-0011

GARRETT, James H., Jr.
V.P., Electronics Gov't Affairs & Mktg, Rockwell Internat'l
1745 Jefferson Davis Hwy. Suite 1200, Arlington, VA 22202
Telephone: (703) 553-6600

GARRETT, Robert A.
Arnold & Porter
1200 New Hampshire Ave., N.W., Washington, DC 20036
Telephone: (202) 872-6700
Background: Assistant to the General Counsel, Department of the Army, 1975-76.

GARRETT, Robert M.
Exec. Director, American Traffic Safety Services Ass'n
ATSSA Building 5440 Jefferson Davis Highway, Fredericksburg, VA 22401
Telephone: (703) 898-5400

GARRETT, Thaddeus A., Jr.
Garrett and Company
1630 Connecticut Ave., N.W. Suite 202, Washington, DC 20009
Telephone: (202) 332-0200
Registered as lobbyist at U.S. Congress.
Registered as Foreign Agent: (#4279).
Clients:
Congo, Office of the President of the

GARRETT, Theodore L.
Covington and Burling
1201 Pennsylvania Ave., N.W., Box 7566, Washington, DC 20044
Telephone: (202) 662-6000

GARRETT, William C.
Exec. V. President, Nat'l Medical Ass'n
1012 10th St., N.W., Washington, DC 20001
Telephone: (202) 347-1895
Background: Also represents the Nat'l Medical Ass'n Political Action Committee.

GARRISH, Theodore J.
Flanagan Group, Inc.
11 Canal Center Plaza Suite 250, Alexandria, VA 22314
Telephone: (703) 739-8822
Registered as lobbyist at U.S. Congress.
Background: General Counsel, Dept. of Energy, 1983-85; Ass't Secretary for Intergovt'l and Public Affairs, 1985-87; Ass't Secretary for Nuclear Energy, 1987-89.
Clients:

American Nuclear Energy Council
California Desert Coalition

GARRISON, Preston J.
Nat'l Exec. Director, Nat'l Mental Health Ass'n
1021 Prince St., Alexandria, VA 22314
Telephone: (703) 684-7722

GARRITY, Gary L.
Vice President, Public Affairs, American Land Title Ass'n
1828 L St., N.W., Suite 705, Washington, DC 20036
Telephone: (202) 296-3671

GARSIDE, Grenville
Van Ness, Feldman & Curtis
1050 Thomas Jefferson St., 7th Floor, Washington, DC 20007
Telephone: (202) 298-1800
Registered as lobbyist at U.S. Congress.
Background: Special Assistant to the Secretary of Interior, 1967-68. Staff Director and Counsel, Senate Committee on Energy and Natural Resources, 1975-78.
Clients:
Consumers United for Rail Equity
Uranium Producers of America

GARTHOFF, Raymond L.
Senior Fellow, Foreign Studies Program, Brookings Institution
1775 Massachusetts Ave., N.W., Washington, DC 20036
Telephone: (202) 797-6000
Background: Ambassador to Bulgaria 91977-79); Deputy Director, Politico-Military Affairs, State Department (1970-73); Member of SALT I and ABM treaty delegation (1969-73).

GARTLAND, John C.
Director, Washington Office, Amway Corp.
214 Massachusetts Ave., N.E., Suite 210, Washington, DC 20002
Telephone: (202) 547-5005
Registered as lobbyist at U.S. Congress.

GARTRELL & ALEXANDER
Lee Plaza, 8601 Georgia Ave. Suite 805, Silver Spring, MD 20910
Telephone: (301) 589-2222
Members of firm representing listed organizations:
Alexander, Koteles
Clients:
Washington Metropolitan Area Transit Authority *(Koteles Alexander)*

GARVELINK, Linda A.
Operations Liaison, Independent Bankers Ass'n of America
One Thomas Circle, N.W., Suite 950, Washington, DC 20005
Telephone: (202) 659-8111

GARVER, Ann L.
Director of Legislative Affairs, Nat'l Ass'n of Casualty and Surety Agents
600 Pennsylvania Ave., S.E., Suite 211, Washington, DC 20003
Telephone: (202) 547-6616
Registered as lobbyist at U.S. Congress.

GARVEY, SCHUBERT & BARER
1000 Potomac St., N.W. Suite 500, Washington, DC 20007
Telephone: (202) 965-7880
Background: Washington office of a Seattle law firm.
Members of firm representing listed organizations:
Barer, Stanley H.
Background: Counsel, U.S. Senate Committee on Commerce, 1966-69. Administrative Assistant to Senator Warren Magnuson (D-WA), 1969-74.
Butchman, Alan A.
Background: Deputy Secretary, U.S. Department of Transportation, 1977-79. Administrative Assistant to Rep. Brock Adams, 1970-76.
Hoff, Paul S.
Background: Associate Chief Counsel, Senate Governmental Affairs Committee, 1975-81.
Wegman, Richard A.
Background: Appellate Attorney, Antitrust Division, U.S. Department of Justice, 1965-68. Staff Director, Senate Subcommittee on Executive Reorganization, and Legislative Counsel to Senator William Proxmire

GARVEY, SCHUBERT & BARER (Cont'd)
(D-WI), 1968-74. Exec. Director, President's Commission on a National Agenda for the 80's, 1979-81. Chief Counsel and Staff Director, Senate Committee on Government Affairs, 1975-81.
Clients:
Aberdeen, Washington, City of *(Alan A. Butchman)*
American Iron and Steel Institute *(Richard A. Wegman)*
Bellingham, Port of *(Alan A. Butchman)*
Canada, Embassy of *(Richard A. Wegman)*
Canada, Government of *(Richard A. Wegman)*
China Ocean Shipping Co. *(Stanley H. Barer)*
Dade County Aviation Department *(Richard A. Wegman)*
Early Winters Resort *(Alan A. Butchman)*
Foss Maritime Co. *(Alan A. Butchman)*
Garvey, Schubert & Barer Political Action Committee *(Alan A. Butchman)*
J & B Management Co. *(Paul S. Hoff)*
Japan Fisheries Ass'n
Manitoba, Province of *(Richard A. Wegman)*
Miami Internat'l Airport *(Richard A. Wegman)*
Ontario, Province of *(Richard A. Wegman)*
Space Industries, Inc. *(Alan A. Butchman)*
Totem Ocean Trailer Express, Inc. *(Alan A. Butchman)*
Washington Citizens for World Trade *(Alan A. Butchman)*

GARVIE, Pamela J.
Preston Gates Ellis & Rouvelas Meeds
1735 New York Ave., N.W., Suite 500, Washington, DC 20006-4759
Telephone: (202) 628-1700
Registered as lobbyist at U.S. Congress.
Background: Former Chief Counsel to the Subcommittees on Aviation, Surface Transportation and Business, Trade and Tourism of the Senate Commerce Committee, 1986. Counsel to the Subcommittee on Surface Transportation, 1981-86. Assistant Legislative Counsel, Interstate Commerce Commission, 1978-80, Counsel to Rep. Robert Duncan (D-OR), 1976-78.
Clients:
Burlington Northern Railroad
Nat'l Business Aircraft Ass'n

GARVIN, E. June
Director, State Government Relations, American Petroleum Institute
1220 L St., N.W., Washington, DC 20005
Telephone: (202) 682-8203

GARY, W. Bradford
V. President, Government Relations, Warner-Lambert Co.
1667 K St., N.W., Suite 1270, Washington, DC 20006
Telephone: (202) 862-3840
Registered as lobbyist at U.S. Congress.
Background: Staff Assistant, U.S. Senate, 1970-72, Committee on Labor and Human Resources, 1970-72. Legislative Assistant to U.S. Representative Les Aspin, 1973-75.

GARZA, Jose
Nat'l Director, Political Access Program, Mexican-American Legal Defense and Educational Fund
1430 K St., N.W., Suite 700, Washington, DC 20005
Telephone: (202) 628-4074

GASCOIGNE, Joseph A.
Exec. Director, Construction Specifications Institute
601 Madison St., Alexandria, VA 22314-1791
Telephone: (703) 684-0300

GASKILL, Stephen
Associate, Wexler, Reynolds, Fuller, Harrison and Schule, Inc.
1317 F St., N.W., Suite 600, Washington, DC 20004
Telephone: (202) 638-2121

GASKIN, Lillian B.
Legislative Counsel, American Bar Ass'n
1800 M St., N.W., Washington, DC 20036
Telephone: (202) 331-2209
Registered as lobbyist at U.S. Congress.

GASKINS, Pat
Cong Liaison Div, ENVIRONMENTAL PROTECTION AGENCY
401 M St., S.W., Washington, DC 20460

Telephone: (202) 382-5200

GASPAR, Russell J.
Hanna, Gaspar and Osborne
2550 M St., N.W. Suite 375, Washington, DC 20037
Telephone: (202) 296-7666

GASPEROW, Robert
Exec. Director, Construction Labor Research Council
1730 M St., N.W., Suite 900B, Washington, DC 20036
Telephone: (202) 223-8045

GASS, Ronald S.
Senior Counsel, American Insurance Ass'n
1130 Connecticut Ave., N.W., Suite 1000, Washington, DC 20036
Telephone: (202) 828-7100

GASSAMA, Ibrahim
Legislative Assistant, TransAfrica
545 Eighth St., S.E. Suite 200, Washington, DC 20003
Telephone: (202) 547-2550

GASTEYER, Philip
Exec. V. Pres./General Counsel, United States League of Savings Institutions
1709 New York Ave., N.W., Suite 801, Washington, DC 20006
Telephone: (202) 637-8900
Registered as lobbyist at U.S. Congress.

GATES, Bruce A.
V. President, Government Relations, Nat'l-American Wholesale Grocers' Ass'n
201 Park Washington Court, Falls Church, VA 22046
Telephone: (703) 532-9400
Registered as lobbyist at U.S. Congress.
Background: Former Legislative Assistant to Rep. Carroll A. Campbell, Jr. (R-SC). Also represents the Nat'l-American Wholesale Grocers' Ass'n Political Action Committee.

GATES, Jacquelyn
Nat'l President, Nat'l Ass'n of Negro Business & Professional Women's Clubs, Inc.
1806 New Hampshire Ave., N.W., Washington, DC 20009
Telephone: (202) 483-4206

GATES, James D.
Exec. Director, Nat'l Council of Teachers of Mathematics
1906 Association Dr., Reston, VA 22091
Telephone: (703) 620-9840

GATEWOOD, Lottie
Public Relations & Marketing Director, Soc. of Industrial and Office Realtors
777 14th St., N.W. Suite 400, Washington, DC 20005-3271
Telephone: (202) 383-1150

GAUDINO, Dr. James L.
Exec. Director, Speech Communication Ass'n
Bldg. E., 5105 Backlick Road, Annandale, VA 22003
Telephone: (703) 750-0533

GAVAGHAN, Paul F.
V. President, Research and Education, Distilled Spirits Council of the United States
1250 Eye St., N.W., Suite 900, Washington, DC 20005
Telephone: (202) 628-3544
Background: Serves also as contact for the Alliance for Traffic Safety.

GAVETT, Kathy J.
Manager, State Government Affairs, Nat'l Ass'n of Chain Drug Stores
Box 1417-D49, Alexandria, VA 22313
Telephone: (703) 549-3001

GAVIN, Joseph G., III
Associate Washington Representative, United States Council for Internat'l Business
1015 15th St., N.W. Suite 1200, Washington, DC 20005
Telephone: (202) 371-1316

GAWELL, Karl
Director, Government Relations, Zero Population Growth, Inc.
1400 16th St., N.W., Suite 320, Washington, DC 20036
Telephone: (202) 332-2200

Registered as lobbyist at U.S. Congress.

GAY, Lawrance W.
Black, Manafort, Stone and Kelly Public Affairs Co.
211 N. Union St., Third Floor, Alexandria, VA 22314
Telephone: (703) 683-6612
Registered as lobbyist at U.S. Congress.
Registered as Foreign Agent: (# 3600).

GAY, Timothy
Director of Communications, Davis Companies, The Susan
1146 19th St., N.W., Washington, DC 20036
Telephone: (202) 775-8881
Registered as lobbyist at U.S. Congress.
Background: Former Press Secretary to Senator John D. Rockefeller, IV (D-WV); Senator John Heinz (R-PA); Rep. Thomas Carper (D-DE); Rep. James Coyne (D-PA); and Rep. William Clinger (R-PA).
Organizations represented:
Computer and Business Equipment Manufacturers Ass'n

GAYLE, Catherine Ludwig
9901 Phoenix Lane, Great Falls, VA 22066
Telephone: (703) 759-6952
Background: A public relations consultant.
Organizations represented:
Nat'l Center for Neighborhood Enterprise

GAYNER, Jeffrey
Counselor for International Relations, Heritage Foundation
214 Massachusetts Ave., N.E., Washington, DC 20002
Telephone: (202) 546-4400
Background: Also holds position of Director, International Resource Bank. Former foreign policy advisor in the 1980 election campaign of Ronald Reagan.

GAYNER, Lewis F.
Director, Regulatory & Legis. Affairs, Dow Chemical
1776 Eye St., N.W., Suite 575, Washington, DC 20006
Telephone: (202) 429-3400

GAYNOR, Margaret C.
Director, Office of Cong. Liaison, Smithsonian Institution
1000 Jefferson Drive, S.W., Washington, DC 20560
Telephone: (202) 357-2962

GAYNOR, Richard D.
Exec. V. President, Nat'l Aggregates Ass'n
900 Spring St., Silver Spring, MD 20910
Telephone: (301) 587-1400
Background: Also represents the Nat'l Ready Mixed Concrete Ass'n.

GEARAN, Mark D.
Exec. Director, Democratic Governors Ass'n
430 South Capitol St., S.E., Washington, DC 20003
Telephone: (202) 863-8096

GEATZ, Ronald J.
Manager, Media Relations, Nature Conservancy, The
1815 N. Lynn St, Arlington, VA 22209
Telephone: (703) 841-5300

GEBLER, Fred, III
Government Affairs Representative, Electronic Data Systems Corp.
1331 Pennsylvania Ave., N.W., Suite 1300 North, Washington, DC 20004
Telephone: (202) 637-6700
Registered as lobbyist at U.S. Congress.

GECHAS, Olga
Development Director, World Federalist Ass'n
418 Seventh St., S.E., Washington, DC 20003
Telephone: (202) 546-3950

GEDDES, Betsy
V. President, Kamber Group, The
1920 L St., N.W., Washington, DC 20036
Telephone: (202) 223-8700

GEDNEY, David S.
President, DeLeuw, Cather and Co.
1133 15th St., N.W. Suite 800, Washington, DC 20005
Telephone: (202) 775-3300

GEER, Shirley K.
Press Relations, World Resources Institute
1709 New York Ave., N.W., Washington, DC 20006

Telephone: (202) 638-6300

GEERS, Karen
Congressional Liaison, Concerned Women for America
370 L'Enfant Promenade, S.W., Suite 800, Washington,
DC 20024
Telephone: (202) 488-7000
Registered as lobbyist at U.S. Congress.

GEFFERT, Garry
Counsel, Farmworker Justice Fund
2001 S St., N.W., Suite 210, Washington, DC 20009
Telephone: (202) 462-8192
Registered as lobbyist at U.S. Congress.

GEGG, Joseph C.
Senior V. President, Wine and Spirits Wholesalers of
America
1023 15th St., N.W., 4th Floor, Washington, DC 20005
Telephone: (202) 371-9792

GEHRING, Craig J.
Preston Gates Ellis & Rouvelas Meeds
1735 New York Ave., N.W., Suite 500, Washington, DC
20006-4759
Telephone: (202) 628-1700
Registered as lobbyist at U.S. Congress.
Registered as Foreign Agent: (#3567).
Background: Counsel, Committee on Government Operations, Subcommittee on Legislation and National Security, 1976-79.
Clients:
Albion, Michigan, City of
Birmingham, Alabama, City of
Clyde Hill, Washington, Town of
Grand Haven, Michigan, City of
Internat'l Telecommunications Satellite Organization (INTELSAT)
Loudoun County, Virginia
Ludington, Michigan, City of
Orange, Texas, City of
Sacramento, California, City of
Somerville, Massachusetts, City of
Southfield, Michigan, City of
Spokane, Washington, City of
Wickes Manufacturing Co.

GEHRKE, Craig
Director, Intermountain Region, Wilderness Soc.
1400 Eye St., N.W., 10th Floor, Washington, DC 20005
Telephone: (202) 842-3400
Registered as lobbyist at U.S. Congress.

GEIB, Ruthann
Administrative Assistant, American Sugar Beet Growers
Ass'n
1156 15th St., N.W. Suite 1020, Washington, DC 20005
Telephone: (202) 833-2398
Registered as lobbyist at U.S. Congress.
Background: Responsibilities include the American Sugar Beet Growers Ass'n Political Action Committee.

GEIER, Bernard A.
Exec. Director, Nat'l Ass'n of Flight Instructors
5021 Powell Road, Fairfax, VA 22032
Telephone: (703) 323-8763

GEIGER, Susan B.
Preston Gates Ellis & Rouvelas Meeds
1735 New York Ave., N.W., Suite 500, Washington, DC
20006-4759
Telephone: (202) 628-1700
Registered as lobbyist at U.S. Congress.
Registered as Foreign Agent: (#3567).
Background: Senior staff, Office of Management and Budget, 1970-80.
Clients:
Calista Corp.
Interlake Holding Corp.
Maryland, Aviation Administration of the State of
Mormac Marine Group, Inc.
Nat'l Council on Compensation Insurance
OMI Corp.
Southeast Alaska Regional Health Corp. (SEARHC)
University of Washington

GEISLER, Raymond H.
Exec. Director, American College of Healthcare Marketing
4200 Wisconsin Ave., N.W. Suite 106, Box 340, Washington, DC 20016
Telephone: (202) 331-1223

GEKAS, Constantine W.
Exec. Director, American Hellenic Educational Progressive
Ass'n (AHEPA)
1707 L St., N.W., Suite 200, Washington, DC 20036
Telephone: (202) 785-9284

GELACEK, Michael S.
McNair Law Firm, P.A.
1155 15th St., N.W. Suite 400, Washington, DC 20005
Telephone: (202) 659-3900
Registered as lobbyist at U.S. Congress.
Background: Minority Staff Director, Senate Judiciary Committee; Staff Director, Senate Subcommittee on Criminal Law; and Chief Counsel, Senate Subcommittee on Penitentiaries, 1977-85. Legislative Director to Senator Joseph R. Biden, Jr. (D-DE), 1983-85.
Clients:
Ass'n of Independent Television Stations
Seagram & Sons, Inc., Joseph E.

GELBAND, Stephen L.
Hewes, Morella, Gelband and Lamberton, P.C.
1000 Potomac St., N.W. Suite 300, Washington, DC
20007
Telephone: (202) 337-6200
Background: Trial Attorney, Bureau of Economic Regulation, Civil Aeronautics Board, 1968-71.
Clients:
Orion Air
Tower Air, Inc.
Washington Airports Task Force

GELLER, Henry
Director, Washington Center for Public Policy Research
1776 K St., N.W., Suite 900, Washington, DC 20006
Telephone: (202) 429-7360

GELLER, Howard S.
Associate Director, American Council for an Energy-Efficient Economy
1001 Connecticut Ave., N.W., Suite 535, Washington, DC
20036
Telephone: (202) 429-8873

GELLER, Kenneth
Mayer, Brown and Platt
2000 Pennsylvania Ave., N.W. Suite 6500, Washington,
DC 20006
Telephone: (202) 463-2000
Clients:
Medtronic, Inc.

GELMAN, Sherril B.
Exec. Director, Accrediting Commission on Education for
Health Services Administration
1911 North Fort Myer Drive Suite 503, Arlington, VA
22209
Telephone: (703) 524-0511

GELTMAN, Edward A.
Squire, Sanders and Dempsey
1201 Pennsylvania Ave., N.W. P.O. Box 407, Washington,
DC 20044
Telephone: (202) 626-6600
Background: Trial Attorney, Federal Trade Commission,
1971-73.
Clients:
United Technologies Carrier

GELTMAN, Richard B.
V. President, Inter-Governmental Relats., Public Securities
Ass'n
1000 Vermont Ave., N.W., Suite 800, Washington, DC
20005
Telephone: (202) 898-9390
Registered as lobbyist at U.S. Congress.

GEMEINHARDT, Elise A.
Public Policy Associate, Washington Business Group on
Health
229 1/2 Pennsylvania Ave., S.E., Washington, DC 20003
Telephone: (202) 547-6644

GEMMA, Peter B., Jr.
President, Associated Direct Marketing Services
P.O. Box 3296, Falls Church, VA 22043
Telephone: (703) 284-3651

GEMMELL, Michael
Exec. Director, Ass'n of Schools of Public Health
Suite 404, 1015 15th St., N.W., Washington, DC 20005
Telephone: (202) 842-4668
Background: Serves also as Treasurer of Educators for Public Health, Inc., a political action committee.

GENCARELLI, David F.
General Counsel & Secretary, Nat'l Ass'n of Beverage
Importers
1025 Vermont Ave., N.W. Suite 1205, Washington, DC
20005
Telephone: (202) 638-1617

GENDERSON, Bruce R.
Williams and Connolly
839 17th St., N.W. 1000 Hill Bldg., Washington, DC 20006
Telephone: (202) 331-5000
Clients:
McKechnie Brothers (South Africa) Ltd.

GENDRON, Nancy E.
Humane Soc. of the United States
2100 L St., N.W., Washington, DC 20037
Telephone: (202) 452-1100
Registered as lobbyist at U.S. Congress.

GENEROUS, Diane
Assoc. Director, Employee Relations, Nat'l Ass'n of Manufacturers
1331 Pennsylvania Ave., N.W. Suite 1500 North, Washington, DC 20004-1703
Telephone: (202) 637-3000
Registered as lobbyist at U.S. Congress.
Background: Former aide to Rep. Arlan Stangeland (R-MN).

GENEVIE, Cheryl K.
Senior Legislative Associate, LaRoe, Winn, Moerman &
Donovan
1120 G St., N.W., Suite 800, Washington, DC 20005
Telephone: (202) 628-2788
Registered as lobbyist at U.S. Congress.

GENOVESE, Samuel A.
Director, State Affairs, Health Industry Manufacturers
Ass'n
1030 15th St., N.W. Suite 1100, Washington, DC 20005
Telephone: (202) 452-8240
Registered as lobbyist at U.S. Congress.
Background: Also represents the Health Industry Manufacturers Ass'n Political Action Committee.

GENTILLE, John R.
Exec. Director, Market Services, Associated General Contractors of America
1957 E St., N.W., Washington, DC 20006
Telephone: (202) 393-2040
Registered as lobbyist at U.S. Congress.
Background: Serves as a Washington Contact for the Associated General Contractors of America Political Committee.

GENTRY, Jan
District Manager, Public Affairs, AT&T
Suite 1000, 1120 20th St., N.W., Washington, DC
Telephone: (202) 457-3919

GENZER, Jeffrey C.
Duncan, Weinberg, Miller & Pembroke, P.C.
1615 M St., N.W., Suite 800, Washington, DC 20036-3203
Telephone: (202) 467-6370
Registered as lobbyist at U.S. Congress.
Background: Staff Counsel, Nat'l Governors' Ass'n, Energy
and Environment Committee, 1983-85.
Clients:
Endicott, New York, Municipality of
Freeport, New York, Village of
Illinois Department of Energy and Natural Resources
Jamestown, New York, City of
Massena, New York, Town of
Municipal Electric Utilities Ass'n of New York State

GENZER, Jeffrey C. (Cont'd)
Nat'l Ass'n of State Energy Officials
Penn Yan, New York, Municipality of
Plattsburgh, New York, Municipality of
Southern Maryland Electric Cooperative, Inc.
Tupper Lake, New York, Municipality of
Watkins Glen, New York, Municipality of

GEOGHEGAN, William A.
Reed Smith Shaw & McClay
1200 18th St., N.W., Washington, DC 20036
Telephone: (202) 457-6100
Registered as lobbyist at U.S. Congress.
Background: Assistant Deputy Attorney General, Department of Justice, 1961-65.
Clients:
Dun & Bradstreet
Securities Industry Ass'n

GEORG, John
Manager, Public Relations, Litton Industries
490 L'Enfant Plaza East, S.W., Washington, DC 20024
Telephone: (202) 554-2570

GEORGE & ASSOCIATES, Nancy Whorton, P.C.
555 13th St., N.W. Suite 1010 East, Washington, DC 20004-1109
Telephone: (202) 863-2226
Members of firm representing listed organizations:
George, Nancy Whorton
Organizations represented:
Enron Corp. *(Nancy Whorton George)*
Natural Gas Alliance for Generative Electricity *(Nancy Whorton George)*
Transco Energy Co. *(Nancy Whorton George)*

GEORGE, Elizabeth
Dir, Public Infor. & Public Relations, Washington Airports Task Force
P.O. Box 17349, Washington Dulles Internat'l Airport, Washington, DC 20041
Telephone: (703) 661-8040

GEORGE, Howard
Exec. Director, Airport Operators Council Internat'l
1220 19th St., N.W. Suite 200, Washington, DC 20036
Telephone: (202) 293-8500

GEORGE, Jawad F.
Exec. Director, Nat'l Ass'n of Arab Americans
2033 M St., N.W., Suite 300, Washington, DC 20036
Telephone: (202) 467-4800
Registered as lobbyist at U.S. Congress.
Background: Serves as contact for the Nat'l Ass'n Arab Americans PAC.

GEORGE, John David
President, American Mental Health Fund
2735 Hartland Road, Suite 302, Falls Church, VA 22043
Telephone: (703) 573-2200
Background: Former legislative aide to Senator Jeremiah Denton (R-AL), 1981-83.

GEORGE, Katherine
Communications Manager, American Ass'n of Equipment Lessors
1300 North 17th St. Suite 1010, Arlington, VA 22209
Telephone: (703) 527-8655

GEORGE, Nancy Whorton
George & Associates, Nancy Whorton, P.C.
555 13th St., N.W. Suite 1010 East, Washington, DC 20004-1109
Telephone: (202) 863-2226
Registered as lobbyist at U.S. Congress.
Organizations represented:
Enron Corp.
Natural Gas Alliance for Generative Electricity
Transco Energy Co.

GEORGETOWN ECONOMIC SERVICES
1055 Jefferson St., N.W., Washington, DC 20007
Telephone: (202) 342-8610
Background: An economic research and consulting firm associated with the law firm of Collier, Shannon, Rill and Scott.
Members of firm representing listed organizations:
Magrath, Patrick, Managing Director

GEORGINE, Robert A.
President, AFL-CIO - Building and Construction Trades Department
815 16th St., N.W., Suite 603, Washington, DC 20006
Telephone: (202) 347-1461
Registered as lobbyist at U.S. Congress.
Background: Also serves as Chairman, Nat'l Coordinating Committee for Multiemployer Plans, and President, Center to Protect Workers' Rights.

GERARD & ASSOCIATES, Forrest
1155 Connecticut Ave., N.W. Suite 400, Washington, DC 20036
Telephone: (202) 429-6677
Members of firm representing listed organizations:
Gerard, Forrest J.
Organizations represented:
Commissioned Officers Ass'n of the U.S. Public Health Service *(Forrest J. Gerard)*
Leech Lake Reservation Business Committee *(Forrest J. Gerard)*
Santa Clara Indian Pueblo *(Forrest J. Gerard)*
Sault Ste. Marie Tribe of Chippewa Indians *(Forrest J. Gerard)*
Siletz Tribal Council *(Forrest J. Gerard)*
Tulalip Tribes *(Forrest J. Gerard)*
White Earth Tribal Council *(Forrest J. Gerard)*

GERARD, Forrest J.
Gerard & Associates, Forrest
1155 Connecticut Ave., N.W. Suite 400, Washington, DC 20036
Telephone: (202) 429-6677
Registered as lobbyist at U.S. Congress.
Organizations represented:
Commissioned Officers Ass'n of the U.S. Public Health Service
Leech Lake Reservation Business Committee
Santa Clara Indian Pueblo
Sault Ste. Marie Tribe of Chippewa Indians
Siletz Tribal Council
Tulalip Tribes
White Earth Tribal Council

GERARD, John C.
Washington Representative, Nat'l Fire Protection Ass'n
1110 North Glebe Road, Suite 560, Arlington, VA 22201
Telephone: (703) 524-3505

GERARD, Joseph G.
Vice President, Government Affairs, American Furniture Manufacturers Ass'n
918 16th St., N.W., Suite 402, Washington, DC 20006
Telephone: (202) 466-7362
Registered as lobbyist at U.S. Congress.

GERARDEN, Ted P.
Donelan, Cleary, Wood and Maser, P.C.
1275 K St., N.W., Suite 850, Washington, DC 20005
Telephone: (202) 371-9500
Clients:
Cascade Natural Gas Corp.

GERBER, Louis M.
Legislative Representative, Communications Workers of America
1925 K St., N.W., Washington, DC 20006
Telephone: (202) 728-2468
Registered as lobbyist at U.S. Congress.
Background: Legislative Assistant to Senator Stephen M. Young (Ohio), 1970. Professional Staff Consultant, Joint Committee on Congressional Operations, 1971. Legislative Assistant to Representative Bertram L. Podell (New York), 1971-1972.

GERBER, Robin
Assoc. Dir., Political & Legis. Affairs, United Brotherhood of Carpenters and Joiners of America
101 Constitution Ave., N.W., Washington, DC 20001
Telephone: (202) 546-6206
Registered as lobbyist at U.S. Congress.

GERCHICK, Mark L.
Paul, Hastings, Janofsky and Walker
1050 Connecticut Ave., N.W. Suite 1200, Washington, DC 20036-5331
Telephone: (202) 223-9000
Registered as lobbyist at U.S. Congress.
Clients:

Kawasaki Motors Corp., USA

GERDES, Ronald W.
Sandler, Travis & Rosenberg. P.A.
1120 19th St., N.W. Suite 420, Washington, DC 20036
Telephone: (202) 457-0078
Background: U.S. Customs Service: Assistant Chief Counsel, Administration and Legislation, 1980-85; Senior Attorney, Office of Regulation and Rulings, 1973-1980.
Clients:
American Ass'n of Exporters and Importers
Florida Customs Brokers and Forwarders
Florida District Export Council
Florida Exporters and Importers Ass'n

GEREAU, Gerald R.
Senior V. President, Hoffmann & Assoc., F. Nordy
400 North Capitol St., N.W. Suite 327, Washington, DC 20001
Telephone: (202) 393-4848
Registered as lobbyist at U.S. Congress.
Background: Professional Staff Member, Senate Interior Committee, 1972-74. Legislative Director for Senator Howard Metzenbaum (D-OH), 1974-75. Chief Investigator, Senate Rules Committee, 1977-88. Also served on personal or committee staffs of Senators Henry Jackson (D-WA), Lee Metcalf (D-MT) and John Warner (R-VA); and Reps. Frank Thompson (D-NJ), Jack Brooks (D-TX) and Augustus Hawkins (D-CA).
Organizations represented:
Nat'l Education Ass'n of the U.S.

GEREBEN, Istvan B.
Exec. Secretary, Coordinating Committee of the Hungarian Organizations of North America
4101 Blackpool Road, Rockville, MD 20853
Telephone: (301) 871-7018

GERKE, Scott A.
Government Relations Assistant, Honda North America, Inc.
955 L'Enfant Plaza S.W., Suite 5300, Washington, DC 20024
Telephone: (202) 554-1650
Registered as lobbyist at U.S. Congress.

GERKIN, Daniel R.
Sr. V. Pres., Public & Constituent Rels., Nat'l Coal Ass'n
1130 17th St., N.W., Washington, DC 20036
Telephone: (202) 463-2659

GERKIN, David
Exec. V. President, Alvarado Group, The
655 15th St., N.W. Suite 300, Washington, DC 20005
Telephone: (202) 639-4019
Background: Former Legislative Assistant to former Rep. Tony Coelho (D-CA).

GERMAN, Michael I.
Senior V. President, American Gas Ass'n
1515 Wilson Blvd., Arlington, VA 22209
Telephone: (703) 841-8400

GERSH, Mark H.
Director, Washington Office, Nat'l Committee for an Effective Congress
507 Capitol Court, N.E., Washington, DC 20002
Telephone: (202) 547-1151

GERSHMAN, Carl
President, Nat'l Endowment for Democracy
1101 15th St., N.W. Suite 203, Washiongton, DC 20005
Telephone: (202) 293-9072

GERSON, David B.
Exec. V. President, American Enterprise Institute for Public Policy Research
1150 17th St., N.W., Washington, DC 20036
Telephone: (202) 862-5800
Background: Former Executive Assistant to the Director, Office of Management and Budget, David A. Stockman.

GERSON, Matthew T.
Asst. V. Pres., Congressional Affairs, Motion Picture Ass'n of America
1600 Eye St., N.W., Washington, DC 20006
Telephone: (202) 293-1966
Registered as lobbyist at U.S. Congress.

Background: Former Counsel, Legal Staff, Federal Election Commission; former Counsel, U.S. Senate Subcommittee on Patents, Copyrights and Trademarks.

GERSTEL, Deborah
Lipsen Whitten & Diamond
1725 DeSales St., N.W., Suite 800, Washington, DC 20036
Telephone: (202) 659-6540
Background: Served with the Congressional Research Service, 1988.

GERSUK, John J.
Congressional Affairs Manager, Bechtel Group, Inc.
1620 Eye St., N.W., Suite 703, Washington, DC 20006
Telephone: (202) 393-4747
Registered as lobbyist at U.S. Congress.

GERTZ, G. D.
Ass't Counsel, GEICO Corp.
GEICO Plaza, Washington, DC 20076
Telephone: (301) 986-3000

GESKE, Alvin J.
Sills & Brodsky, P.C.
1016 16th St., N.W., Sixth Floor, Washington, DC 20036
Telephone: (202) 955-1000
Registered as lobbyist at U.S. Congress.
Registered as Foreign Agent: (#4178).
Background: Attorney, Legislation and Regulation Division, Office of Chief Counsel, Internal Revenue Service, 1970-72, and Assistant Branch Chief, 1972-74. Legislation Attorney, Joint Committee on Taxation, U.S. Congress, 1975-77, and Assistant Legislation Counsel, 1978-81.
Clients:
Grupo Industrial Alfa, S.A.
Renewable Fuels Ass'n

GETTINGS, Robert M.
Exec. Director, Nat'l Ass'n of State Mental Retardation Program Directors
113 Oronoco St., Alexandria, VA 22314
Telephone: (703) 683-4202

GEVINSON, Dorothy F.
Assoc. Dir., Nat'l Government Relations, Procter and Gamble Mfg. Co.
Suite 400, 801 18th St., N.W., Washington, DC 20006
Telephone: (202) 833-4015
Registered as lobbyist at U.S. Congress.

GEZEN, Asil
President, Turkish-American Political Action Committee
7921 Woodruff Court, Suite 200, Springfield, VA 22151
Telephone: (703) 321-6175

GHEBREHIWEP, Hagos
Exec. Director, Eritrean People's Liberation Front
1418 15th St., N.W., Suite 1, Washington, DC 20005
Telephone: (202) 234-9282

GHORBANI, Daniel D.
President, Ass'n for Regulatory Reform
1331 Pennsylvania Ave., N.W., Suite 508, Washington, DC 20004
Telephone: (202) 783-4087
Registered as lobbyist at U.S. Congress.

GHYLIN, Clair
V. President, Chevron, U.S.A.
1700 K St., N.W., Suite 1200, Washington, DC 20006
Telephone: (202) 457-5800
Registered as lobbyist at U.S. Congress.
Background: Also represents Chevron Corp., the parent company.

GIAIMO, Christopher J.
Deputy Director, Legislative Affairs, Retired Officers Ass'n, The (TROA)
201 N. Washington St., Alexandria, VA 22314
Telephone: (703) 549-2311
Registered as lobbyist at U.S. Congress.

GIAIMO, Robert N.
Nossaman, Guthner, Knox and Elliott
1227 25th St., N.W., Suite 700, Washington, DC 20037
Telephone: (202) 223-9100
Background: Member, U.S. House of Representatives (D-CT), 1959-80.
Clients:
Committee for a Responsible Federal Budget

GIARAMITA, Phillip S.
Exec. Director, Public Relations, Martin Marietta Corp.
6801 Rockledge Drive MP 221, Bethesda, MD 20817
Telephone: (301) 897-6121

GIBB, William T.
Chief Counsel, Federal Taxes & Pensions, American Council of Life Insurance
1001 Pennsylvania Ave., N.W., Washington, DC 20004-2599
Telephone: (202) 624-2110
Registered as lobbyist at U.S. Congress.

GIBBENS, Wayne
President, Mid-Continent Oil and Gas Ass'n
1919 Pennsylvania Ave., N.W. Suite 503, Washington, DC 20006
Telephone: (202) 785-3515
Registered as lobbyist at U.S. Congress.

GIBBONS, Anne Marie
Legislative Representative, American Public Power Ass'n
2301 M St., N.W., Washington, DC 20037
Telephone: (202) 775-8300
Registered as lobbyist at U.S. Congress.

GIBBONS, Clifford S.
Legislative Consultant, Hogan and Hartson
555 13th St., N.W., Suite 1200, Washington, DC 20004-1109
Telephone: (202) 637-5600
Registered as lobbyist at U.S. Congress.
Registered as Foreign Agent: (#2440).
Background: Special Assistant to the U.S. Special Trade Representative, Executive Office of the President, 1979-81.
Clients:
Aermacchi, S.p.A.
American Medical Internat'l
Cryo-Chem Internat'l, Inc.
Lloyds of London, Underwriters at
May Department Stores Co.
Mercedes-Benz of North America, Inc.
Mutual Life Insurance Co. of New York
Ontario, Province of
Toyota Motor Sales, U.S.A.
Whitman Distributing Co.

GIBBONS, Sheila J.
Director, Public Affairs, Gannett Co., Inc.
1100 Wilson Blvd., Arlington, VA 22234
Telephone: (703) 284-6048

GIBBS, Jeffrey L.
Bredhoff and Kaiser
1000 Connecticut Ave., N.W. Suite 1300, Washington, DC 20036
Telephone: (202) 833-9340
Clients:
AFL-CIO - Industrial Union Department
Bakery, Confectionery and Tobacco Workers Internat'l Union

GIBBS, Lawrence B.
Johnson & Gibbs, P.C.
1001 Pennsylvania Ave., N.W. Suite 745, Washington, DC 20004
Telephone: (202) 682-4500
Registered as lobbyist at U.S. Congress.
Clients:
Permanente Medical Group, Inc., The

GIBBS, Leon B.
Dir, Gov't Afrs (Lat Amer & Carib Basin), Johnson & Johnson
1667 K St., N.W., Suite 410, Washington, DC 20006
Telephone: (202) 293-2620

GIBBS, Lois Marie
Exec. Director, Citizens Clearinghouse for Hazardous Wastes
P.O. Box 926, Arlington, VA 22216
Telephone: (703) 276-7070

GIBLIN, Joan E.
Manager, Communications, Nat'l Spa and Pool Institute
2111 Eisenhower Ave., Alexandria, VA 22314
Telephone: (703) 838-0083

GIBSON, DUNN AND CRUTCHER
1050 Connecticut Ave., N.W. Suite 900, Washington, DC 20036-5303
Telephone: (202) 955-8500
Background: Washington office of a Los Angeles law firm.
Members of firm representing listed organizations:
Baumbusch, Peter L.
Background: Serves as Treasurer, Fair Tax Foundation.
Herfort, John A.
Kilberg, William J.
Background: White House Fellow, Special Assistant to the Secretary of Labor, 1969-70. General Counsel, Federal Mediation and Conciliation Service, 1970-71. Associate Solicitor, Department of Labor, 1971-73. Solicitor, Department of Labor, 1973-77.
Lebow, Cynthia C., Of Counsel
McConnell, Robert A.
Background: Of Counsel. Assistant Attorney General, U.S. Department of Justice, 1981-84.
Muckenfuss, C. F. (III)
Background: Special Assistant to the Director, 1974-77 and Counsel to the Chairman, 1977-78, Federal Deposit Insurance Corporation. Member, Administrative Conference of the U.S., 1977-78. Senior Deputy Comptroller for Policy, Office of the Comptroller of the Currency, 1978-81.
Olson, John F.
Parsky, Gerald L.
Background: Assistant Secretary of the Treasury for International Affairs, 1974-77.
Price, Joseph H.
Background: Law Clerk to Supreme Court Justice Hugo L. Black, 1967-68. Vice President for Insurance, Overseas Private Investment Corp., 1971-73.
Rosenauer, David B.
Turza, Peter
Clients:
Alyeska Pipeline Service Co. *(Cynthia C. Lebow, Robert A. McConnell)*
Dollar Drydock Savings Bank *(Peter L. Baumbusch)*
First Republic Bank Corp. *(Cynthia C. Lebow)*
Internat'l Electronics Manufacturers and Consumers of America *(Robert A. McConnell)*
Prudential Insurance Co. of America *(Cynthia C. Lebow)*
Smith Barney, Harris Upham and Co.
Teamwork America *(Peter L. Baumbusch)*
UNOCAL Corp.
Volvo North America
Washington Mutual Savings Bank *(C. F. Muckenfuss, III)*
Wespar Financial Services *(Robert A. McConnell)*
Wheeling-Pittsburgh Steel Co.

GIBSON, Joseph
Wunder, Ryan, Cannon & Thelen
1615 L St., N.W., Suite 650, Washington, DC 20036
Telephone: (202) 659-3005
Registered as Foreign Agent: (#3971).
Background: Research Assistant, Senate Judiciary Committee, 1983-84. Law Clerk to the Hon. R. Lanier Anderson, III, 1987-88.

GIBSON, Robert E.
V. Pres., Gen. Mgr., Alt. Dispute Resol., Council of Better Business Bureaus
4200 Wilson Blvd. Suite 800, Arlington, VA 22203
Telephone: (703) 276-0100

GIBSON, Stephen L.
Arent, Fox, Kintner, Plotkin & Kahn
1050 Connecticut Ave., N.W., Washington, DC 20036-5339
Telephone: (202) 857-6000
Registered as Foreign Agent: (#2661).
Clients:
AIDA Engineering Ltd.
Nat'l Ass'n of Wheat Growers
Outokumpu Oy

GIBSON, Thomas
V. President, Government Affairs, Porter/Novelli
1001 30th St., N.W., Washington, DC 20007
Telephone: (202) 342-7000
Background: Former Special Assistant and Director of Public Affairs, The White House in the Reagan Administration.

WASHINGTON REPRESENTATIVES

GIDEZ, Christopher
V. President, Edelman, Inc., Daniel J.
1420 K St., N.W., Washington, DC 20005
Telephone: (202) 371-0200
Background: Former Press Secretary to Rep. Harold Hollenbeck (R-NJ).
Organizations represented:
Collagen Corp.
Ernst & Young
Friendswood Development Corp.

GIDLEY, Barry F.
Cong & Public Affrs (Int'l Org Affrs), DEPARTMENT OF STATE
2201 C St., N.W., Washington, DC 20520
Telephone: (202) 647-4001

GIEL, Ken
Dep. Dir., Anti-Piracy Investigative Opn, Recording Industry Ass'n of America
1020 19th St., N.W., Suite 200, Washington, DC 20036
Telephone: (202) 775-0101

GIESE, Robert B.
President, Brown & Co., Clarence J.
1101 Connecticut Ave., N.W. Suite 1000, Washington, DC 20036
Telephone: (202) 828-2300
Registered as lobbyist at U.S. Congress.
Organizations represented:
BHC, Inc.
Chris-Craft Industries Inc.
Ohio Edison Co.
United Television, Inc.

GIESE, Robert B.
3811 Garfield St., N.W., Washington, DC 20007
Telephone: (202) 342-6660
Background: An attorney-at-law.

GIFFORD, Dawn
Swidler & Berlin, Chartered
3000 K St., N.W., Suite 300, Washington, DC 20007
Telephone: (202) 944-4300
Registered as lobbyist at U.S. Congress.
Registered as Foreign Agent: (#4079).
Background: Former Administrative Assistant to Senator Robert Kasten (R-WI).
Clients:
China External Trade Development Council
External Tanks Corp.
Internat'l Environmental Policy Coalition
Product Liability Alliance, The

GIFFORD, Laurence S.
Manager, Regulatory Operations, GE Nuclear Energy
12300 Twinbrook Pkwy., Rockville, MD 20852
Telephone: (301) 770-9650
Background: Represents Nuclear Energy Business Operation (licensing and consulting services) in regulatory matters regarding licensing of power reactors and associated products.

GIGLIO, William P.
Reg. V.P., Wash. & V.P., Wash. Affairs, McGraw-Hill, Inc.
1750 K St., N.W., Suite 1170, Washington, DC 20006
Telephone: (202) 955-3830

GIGUERE, Michelle E.
Government Relations Consultant, Ball, Janik and Novack
1101 Pennsylvania Ave., N.W. Suite 1035, Washington, DC 20004
Telephone: (202) 638-3307
Background: Former Legislative Director, office of Rep. Les AuCoin (D-OR).
Clients:
Clackamas County, Oregon
Harsch Investment Corp.
Lower Columbia Regional Navy Task Force
Northwest Marine Iron Works
Oregon Graduate Institute of Science and Technology
Section 8 Housing Group
Tillamook Bay, Oregon, Port of

GILARDI, Robert C.
Staff Manager, Compressed Gas Ass'n
1235 Jefferson Davis Hwy., Arlington, VA 22202
Telephone: (703) 979-0900

Registered as lobbyist at U.S. Congress.

GILBERG, David J.
Rogers and Wells
1737 H St., N.W., Washington, DC 20006
Telephone: (202) 331-7760
Clients:
Futures Industry Ass'n

GILBERG, Donald M.
Gilberg & Kurent
1250 I St., N.W. Suite 600, Washington, DC 20005
Telephone: (202) 842-3222

GILBERG & KURENT
1250 I St., N.W. Suite 600, Washington, DC 20005
Telephone: (202) 842-3222
Members of firm representing listed organizations:
Cecere, Jacob, Associate
Gilberg, Donald M.
Knutson, Martha, Associate
Kurent, Edward A.
Read, Todd, Associate
Stockel, Mary, Associate
Westerfield, Mark G., Associate

GILBERT, Gary G.
Director, Banking Agency Liaison, United States League of Savings Institutions
1709 New York Ave., N.W., Suite 801, Washington, DC 20006
Telephone: (202) 637-8900

GILBERT, Gerald E.
Hogan and Hartson
555 13th St., N.W., Suite 1200, Washington, DC 20004-1109
Telephone: (202) 637-5600
Registered as lobbyist at U.S. Congress.
Background: U.S. Dep't of Commerce 1965-66.
Clients:
Toyota Motor Sales, U.S.A.

GILBERT, Gregory A.
Treasurer, American Soc. of Appraisers PAC
535 Herndon Pkwy., Herndon, VA 22070
Telephone: (703) 478-2228

GILBERT, Pamela
Legislative Director, Congress Watch, Congress Watch
215 Pennsylvania Ave., S.E., Washington, DC 20003
Telephone: (202) 546-4996
Registered as lobbyist at U.S. Congress.

GILBERT, Richard
Dir., State & Local Affrs., Gov't Relat., American Public Health Ass'n
1015 15th St., N.W. Third Floor, Washington, DC 20005
Telephone: (202) 789-5600
Registered as lobbyist at U.S. Congress.

GILBERT, Robin H.
Collier, Shannon & Scott
1055 Thomas Jefferson St., N.W., Suite 300, Washington, DC 20007
Telephone: (202) 342-8400
Clients:
Nat'l Juice Products Ass'n
Tropicana Products Inc.
Wyman-Gordon Co.

GILBERT, Scott D.
Covington and Burling
1201 Pennsylvania Ave., N.W., Box 7566, Washington, DC 20044
Telephone: (202) 662-6000
Clients:
Coalition to Preserve the Integrity of American Trademarks

GILBERTSON, Gene
Exec. V. President, Banner Life Insurance Co.
1701 Research Blvd., Rockville, MD 20850
Telephone: (301) 279-4800

GILBERTSON, Peter A.
Weiner, McCaffrey, Brodsky, Kaplan & Levin
1350 New York Ave., N.W., Suite 800, Washington, DC 20005-4797

Telephone: (202) 628-2000
Registered as lobbyist at U.S. Congress.

GILCHRIST, James E.
V. President - Environmental Affairs, American Mining Congress
1920 N St., N.W. Suite 300, Washington, DC 20036
Telephone: (202) 861-2800
Registered as lobbyist at U.S. Congress.

GILDEA, Michael W.
Assistant to the Director, Legislation, AFL-CIO (American Federation of Labor and Congress of Industrial Organizations)
Room 309, 815 16th St., N.W., Washington, DC 20006
Telephone: (202) 637-5246
Registered as lobbyist at U.S. Congress.

GILL, Brian W.
President, Master Printers of America
1730 North Lynn St., Suite 805, Arlington, VA 22209
Telephone: (703) 841-8130

GILL, John J.
General Counsel, American Bankers Ass'n
1120 Connecticut Ave., N.W., Washington, DC 20036
Telephone: (202) 663-5000

GILL, Samuel H.
Exec. Director, Nat'l Accounting and Finance Council
2200 Mill Road, Second Floor, Alexandria, VA 22314
Telephone: (703) 838-1915

GILL, William
Exec. Director, Catholic War Veterans of the U.S.A.
419 N. Lee St., Alexandria, VA 22314
Telephone: (703) 549-3622

GILLAN, Jacqueline
Assistant Director, Ohio, State of
444 N. Capitol St., N.W., Suite 528, Washington, DC 20001
Telephone: (202) 624-5844

GILLEN, Neal P.
General Counsel, American Cotton Shippers Ass'n
1725 K St., N.W. Suite 1210, Washington, DC 20006
Telephone: (202) 296-7116
Registered as lobbyist at U.S. Congress.
Background: Serves as Treasurer, Committee Organized for the Trading of Cotton (COTCO). Serves also as Secretary-Treasurer of The Washington Discussion Group.

GILLESPIE, Annelise B.
Congressional Representative, Nat'l Forest Products Ass'n
1250 Connecticut Ave., N.W. Suite 200, Washington, DC 20036
Telephone: (202) 463-2700
Registered as lobbyist at U.S. Congress.
Background: Contact for the Forest Industries Political Action Committee.

GILLESPIE, T. J., Jr.
Asst. V. Pres., Gov't & Public Affairs, AMTRAK (Nat'l Rail Passenger Corp.)
60 Massachusetts Ave., N.E., Washington, DC 20002
Telephone: (202) 906-3939

GILLICK, John E.
Of Counsel, Winthrop, Stimson, Putnam & Roberts
1133 Connecticut Ave., N.W. Suite 1000, Washington, DC 20036
Telephone: (202) 775-9800
Registered as lobbyist at U.S. Congress.
Clients:
America West Airlines
Nat'l Vehicle Leasing Ass'n
Saab-Scania of America

GILLIGAN, Daniel
President, Nat'l Manufactured Housing Federation
1701 K St., N.W., Suite 400, Washington, DC 20006
Telephone: (202) 822-6470
Registered as lobbyist at U.S. Congress.
Background: Serves also as Assistant Treasurer and contact for the Nat'l Manufactured Housing Federation Political Action Committee.

The listings in this directory are available as *Mailing Labels.* See last page.

GILLMAN, Dorothy M.
Legislative Representative, Independent Bankers Ass'n of America
One Thomas Circle, N.W., Suite 950, Washington, DC 20005
Telephone: (202) 659-8111
Registered as lobbyist at U.S. Congress.
Background: Writer/Researcher, Democratic Policy Committee, US Senate, 1983-86. Legislative Assistant, Rep. Barbara A. Mikulski (D-MD), 1980-81.

GILMAN, Brad
Robertson, Monagle and Eastaugh
1050 Thomas Jefferson St., NW Sixth Floor, Washington, DC 20007
Telephone: (202) 333-4400
Registered as lobbyist at U.S. Congress.
Clients:
Anchorage School District
Coastal Coalition
Reeve Aleutian Airways

GILMAN, Maureen
Assistant Director of Legislation, Nat'l Treasury Employees Union
1730 K St., N.W., Suite 1100, Washington, DC 20006
Telephone: (202) 785-4411
Registered as lobbyist at U.S. Congress.

GILMAN, OLSON & PANGIA
1815 H St., N.W. Suite 600, Washington, DC 20005
Telephone: (202) 466-5100
Members of firm representing listed organizations:
Olson, William J.
Clients:
Industry Council for Tangible Assets *(William J. Olson)*

GILMORE, Yvonne
Associate Director, Regulatory Affairs, Nat'l Ass'n of Federal Credit Unions
3138 N. 10th St., Arlington, VA 22201
Telephone: (703) 522-4770

GILROY, Brent
Account Supervisor, Burson-Marsteller
1850 M St., N.W., Suite 900, Washington, DC 20036
Telephone: (202) 833-8550
Background: Former aide to Rep. George Darden (D-GA).

GILSTRAP, Jack R.
Exec. V. President, American Public Transit Ass'n
1201 New York Ave., N.W.,, Washington, DC 20005
Telephone: (202) 898-4000

GIMBEL, Tod I.
Federal Affairs Representative, Miller Brewing Co.
1341 G St., N.W., Suite 900, Washington, DC 20005
Telephone: (202) 637-1520
Registered as lobbyist at U.S. Congress.

GINGRICH, Claud L.
V. President, Motley and Co., L. A.
1800 K St., N.W., Suite 1000, Washington, DC 20006
Telephone: (202) 223-8222
Registered as lobbyist at U.S. Congress.
Registered as Foreign Agent: (#3723).
Organizations represented:
Associacao das Industrias de Calcados do Rio Grande do Sul
Associacao Nacional das Industrias de Citricos

GINN, EDINGTON, MOORE AND WADE
803 Prince St., Alexandria, VA 22314
Telephone: (703) 836-3328
Background: Other office located at 1133 Connecticut Ave., N.W. Washington, DC 20036. (202) 457-6558.
Members of firm representing listed organizations:
Edington, William H.
Ginn, Ronald B. "Bo'
Background: Member, U.S. House of Representatives (D-GA), 1973-83.
Moore, Powell A.
Background: Assistant Secretary of State, 1982-83; Deputy Assistant to the President for Legislative Affairs (Senate), 1981.
Wade, T. Rogers
Clients:
AB Bofors

Agusta Group, The
Allied-Signal Inc.
American League for Exports and Security Assistance (ALESA)
Chrysler Corp.
Equifax Inc.
Lockheed Corp.
Oglethorpe Power Corp.
Outdoor Advertising Ass'n of America
Regan Group Insurance Marketing, The
Turner Broadcasting System, Inc.
United States Cane Sugar Refiners' Ass'n
Watkins Associated Industries, Inc.

GINN, Ronald B. "Bo'
Ginn, Edington, Moore and Wade
803 Prince St., Alexandria, VA 22314
Telephone: (703) 836-3328
Registered as lobbyist at U.S. Congress.
Registered as Foreign Agent: (#4134).
Background: Member, U.S. House of Representatives (D-GA), 1973-83.

GINSBERG, Benjamin L.
General Counsel, Republican Nat'l Committee
310 First St., S.E., Washington, DC 20003
Telephone: (202) 863-8500

GINSBERG, Marc C.
Partner, Galland, Kharasch, Morse and Garfinkle
Canal Square, 1054 31st St., N.W., Washington, DC 20007
Telephone: (202) 342-5200
Registered as Foreign Agent: (#4006).
Clients:
South African Sugar Ass'n

GINSBERG, Mark R., Ph.D.
Executive Director, American Ass'n for Marriage and Family Therapy
1717 K St., N.W. Suite 407, Washington, DC 20006
Telephone: (202) 429-1825
Registered as lobbyist at U.S. Congress.

GINSBERG, Susan Woolum
Ass't Manager, Regulatory Affairs, Hadson Gas Systems
1001 30th St., N.W. Suite 340, Washington, DC 20007
Telephone: (202) 337-5430

GINSBURG, David
Ginsburg, Feldman and Bress
1250 Connecticut Ave., N.W. Suite 800, Washington, DC 20036
Telephone: (202) 637-9000
Registered as Foreign Agent: (#3106).
Background: With Securities and Exchange Commission, 1935-39. Law Secretary to U.S. Supreme Court Justice William O. Douglas, 1939. Gen. Counsel, Office of Price Administration, 1940-1943. Admin. Assistant to Senator M. M. Neely (W. Va.), 1950. Member, Presidential Emergency Board 166, 1966. Chairman, Presidential Emergency Board 169, 1967. Member, Commission on Postal Organization, 1967. Member, Board of Directors, Fifth Dimension, Inc. and Ranco, Inc.
Clients:
Airship Industries, Ltd.
Japan Fisheries Ass'n
Morocco, Kingdom of
Ranco, Inc.

GINSBURG, FELDMAN AND BRESS
1250 Connecticut Ave., N.W. Suite 800, Washington, DC 20036
Telephone: (202) 637-9000
Members of firm representing listed organizations:
Burton, Joel S.
Eichenlaub, Alfred J.
Feldman, Myer
Background: Special Counsel to the Securities and Exchange Commission, 1946-55; Counsel, Senate Banking and Currency Committee, 1955-57; Legislative Assistant to Senator J. F. Kennedy, 1958-61; Deputy Special Counsel to the President, 1961-64 and Counsel, 1964-65.
Ginsburg, David
Background: With Securities and Exchange Commission, 1935-39. Law Secretary to U.S. Supreme Court Justice William O. Douglas, 1939. Gen. Counsel, Office of Price Administration, 1940-1943. Admin. Assistant to Senator M. M. Neely (W. Va.), 1950.

Member, Presidential Emergency Board 166, 1966.
Chairman, Presidential Emergency Board 169, 1967.
Member, Commission on Postal Organization, 1967.
Member, Board of Directors, Fifth Dimension, Inc. and Ranco, Inc.
Hawkins, Robert W.
Henry, E. William
Background: Chairman, Federal Communications Commission, 1963-66.
Joyce, Rodney, Partner
Kirby, Peter M.
Marks, Lee R.
Background: Attorney, Office of the Legal Adviser, Department of State, 1961-63. Special Assistant to the Legal Advisor, Deparment of State, 1964. Senior Deputy Legal Advisor, Department of State, 1977-79.
Rabinovitz, Bruce H.
Background: Attorney-Advisor, Procurement Division, General Services Administration, 1971-72. Rates and Agreements Division, Office of General Counsel, Civil Aeronautics Board, 1972-76.
Rosenthal, Jacob W.
Background: Counsel to Bureau of Safety Regulation, 1947-49; Assistant Chief, Opinion Writing Division, 1950-56; Chief, Special Authorities Division, 1957-61; Chief, Routes and Agreements Division, 1961-65; and Director, Bureau of Operating Rights, 1966-67, all of the Civil Aeronautics Board. Member, Board of Directors, Systems Automation Corp.
Sears, Mary Helen
Clients:
Airship Industries, Ltd. *(David Ginsburg, Robert W. Hawkins)*
Ball Brothers, Inc. *(Alfred J. Eichenlaub)*
Executive Air Fleet Corp. *(Jacob W. Rosenthal)*
Genetics Institute Inc. *(Peter M. Kirby, Mary Helen Sears)*
Japan Fisheries Ass'n *(David Ginsburg)*
Konishoruku Photo Industry U.S.A.
Michigan Channel 38 *(E. William Henry)*
Midway Airlines *(Jacob W. Rosenthal)*
Morocco, Kingdom of *(David Ginsburg, Lee R. Marks)*
Northern Pacific Transport, Inc. *(Jacob W. Rosenthal)*
Ranco, Inc. *(David Ginsburg)*
United States Telephone Ass'n *(Rodney Joyce)*
Upjohn Co. *(E. William Henry, Peter M. Kirby)*

GIORDINO, Tino
Staff Assistant, Concerned Citizens Foundation
Capitol Hill Office Bldg. 412 First St., S.E., Suite 301, Washington, DC 20003
Telephone: (202) 479-9068

GIOVANIELLO, Gerard
Staff V. Pres., Congressional Affairs, Nat'l Ass'n of REALTORS
777 14th St., N.W., Washington, DC 20005
Telephone: (202) 383-1000
Registered as lobbyist at U.S. Congress.

GIROUX, Terrence J.
Exec. Director, Horatio Alger Ass'n of Distinguished Americans
11 Canal Center Plaza Suite 210, Alexandria, VA 22314
Telephone: (703) 684-9444

GIRTON, Brenda
Legislative Counsel, Sears, Roebuck and Co.
633 Pennsylvania Ave., N.W., Washington, DC 20004
Telephone: (202) 737-4900

GIST, John
Senior Analyst, American Ass'n of Retired Persons
1909 K St., N.W., Washington, DC 20049
Telephone: (202) 872-4700

GITENSTEIN, Mark H.
Exec. Director, Foundation for Change
310 Pennsylvania Ave., S.E., Washington, DC 20003
Telephone: (202) 546-8410

GITTINGS, Thomas Morton, Jr.
Shoreham Bldg. Suite 425, Washington, DC 20005
Telephone: (202) 628-2878
Background: An attorney. Serves as legal counsel to Fleet Reserve Ass'n.
Organizations represented:
Fleet Reserve Ass'n

WASHINGTON REPRESENTATIVES

GIUFFRIDA ASSOCIATES, INC.
204 E St., N.E., Washington, DC 20002
Telephone: (202) 547-6340
Members of firm representing listed organizations:
Giuffrida, Mike, President
Purcell, John R., V. President
Clients:
Nat'l Frozen Food Ass'n *(Mike Giuffrida, John R. Purcell)*

GIUFFRIDA, Mike
President, Giuffrida Associates, Inc.
204 E St., N.E., Washington, DC 20002
Telephone: (202) 547-6340
Registered as lobbyist at U.S. Congress.
Clients:
Nat'l Frozen Food Ass'n

GLADSTONE, David J.
President, Ass'n of Government Guaranteed Lenders Political Action Committee
1666 K St., N.W., Suite 901, Washington, DC 20006
Telephone: (202) 331-1112

GLAKAS, Nicholas J.
Director, Government Affairs, ITT Corp.
1600 M St., N.W., Washington, DC 20036
Telephone: (202) 775-7419
Registered as lobbyist at U.S. Congress.
Background: Former General Counsel, U.S. Senate Appropriations Committee and former Assistant Director for Enforcement, Commodity Futures Trading Commission.

GLANZMAN, Wanda
Regulatory Manager, Sprint International
12490 Sunrise Valley Drive, Reston, VA 22096
Telephone: (703) 689-5302

GLASER, Peter S.
Doherty, Rumble, and Butler
1625 M St., N.W., Washington, DC 20036
Telephone: (202) 293-0555
Clients:
Western Fuels Ass'n

GLASMANN, Jay W.
Ivins, Phillips and Barker
1700 Pennsylvania Ave., N.W., Suite 600, Washington, DC 20006
Telephone: (202) 393-7600
Registered as lobbyist at U.S. Congress.
Background: Ass't General Counsel, Treasury Dep't, 1959. Ass't to Secretary of the Treasury, 1959-61.
Clients:
American Textile Manufacturers Institute
Digital Equipment Corp.
Employee Relocation Council

GLASSER, Melvin
Director, Health Security Action Council
1757 N St., N.W., Washington, DC 20036
Telephone: (202) 223-9685

GLASSMAN, Lynne
Director, Network Operations, Nat'l School Boards Ass'n
1680 Duke St., Alexandria, VA 22314
Telephone: (703) 838-6722

GLAVAS, Pete W.
Associate, Cassidy and Associates, Inc.
655 15th St., N.W., Suite 1100, Washington, DC 20005
Telephone: (202) 347-0773
Registered as lobbyist at U.S. Congress.
Background: Former Chief of Staff and Special Assistant to Senator David L. Boren (D-OK).
Clients:
American Science & Engineering Inc.
Atlantic Financial
Enid Joint Industrial Foundation
20th Century Fox

GLAVES, Dennis
Director, Legislative Affairs, GTE Corp.
Suite 1200, 1850 M St., N.W., Washington, DC 20036
Telephone: (202) 463-5222

GLAZIER, Jonathan H.
Dorsey & Whitney
1330 Connecticut Ave., N.W., Suite 200, Washington, DC 20036
Telephone: (202) 857-0700

GLEASON, Barbara
Assistant Director, Public Affairs, Nonprescription Drug Manfacturers Ass'n
1150 Connecticut Ave., N.W.,, Washington, DC 20036
Telephone: (202) 429-9260

GLEASON, Donna Siss
Director, Government Affairs, Unisys Corp.
2001 L St., N.W., Suite 1000, Washington, DC 20036
Telephone: (202) 293-7720
Registered as lobbyist at U.S. Congress.

GLEASON, John P.
President, Portland Cement Ass'n
1620 Eye St., N.W., Suite 520, Washington, DC 20006
Telephone: (202) 293-4260

GLEASON, Joseph B., APR
Managing Director, Manning, Selvage & Lee/Washington
1250 Eye St., N.W., Suite 300, Washington, DC 20005
Telephone: (202) 682-1660

GLEASON, Patricia A.
Director of Communication, Industrial Safety Equipment Ass'n
1901 North Moore St., Suite 501, Arlington, VA 22209
Telephone: (703) 525-1695

GLEASON, Robert E.
Assistant Legislative Director, Internat'l Longshoremen's Ass'n
815 16th St., N.W., Suite 104, Washington, DC 20006
Telephone: (202) 628-4546

GLEIBER, John
Exec. Secretary, Soc. for Animal Protective Legislation
Box 3719, Georgetown Station, Washington, DC 20007
Telephone: (202) 337-2334

GLENN, Donald R.
V. President, Energy Research Corp.
1627 K St., N.W. Suite 403, Washington, DC 20006
Telephone: (202) 785-9321
Registered as lobbyist at U.S. Congress.
Background: Also serves as Contact, Energy Research Corp. PAC.

GLENN, Martha Cole
Director, Federal Affairs, Humane Soc. of the United States
2100 L St., N.W., Washington, DC 20037
Telephone: (202) 452-1100
Registered as lobbyist at U.S. Congress.

GLENN, Sara B.
Government Relations Advisor, Mobil Corp.
1100 Connecticut Ave., N.W., Suite 620, Washington, DC 20036
Telephone: (202) 862-1354
Registered as lobbyist at U.S. Congress.
Background: Full title is Government Relations Advisor, Environmental Affairs, Employee Relations, Research and Exploration.

GLENNON, Robert E., Jr.
Williams and Jensen, P.C.
1101 Connecticut Ave., N.W., Suite 500, Washington, DC 20036
Telephone: (202) 659-8201
Clients:
Ass'n of Family Farmers
Bass Group, Robert M.
CIGNA Corp.
Keystone Provident Life Insurance Co.

GLESKE, Elmer G.
V. President, Governmental Affairs, FlightSafety Internat'l
655 15th St., N.W., Suite 300, Washington, DC 20005-5701
Telephone: (202) 639-4066
Registered as lobbyist at U.S. Congress.

GLICKMAN, David G.
Managing Director, Washington Office, Johnson & Gibbs, P.C.
1001 Pennsylvania Ave., N.W. Suite 745, Washington, DC 20004
Telephone: (202) 682-4500
Registered as lobbyist at U.S. Congress.
Background: With Chief Counsel's Office, Internal Revenue Service, 1964-68. Deputy Assistant Secretary of the Treasury, Tax Policy, 1981-83.
Clients:
Centex Corp.
Church Alliance
Compaq Computer
EPIC Healthcare Group, Inc.
Oryx Energy Co.
Permanente Medical Group, Inc., The
Republic Health Corp.

GLISSON, JoAnne
Legislative Representative, Kaiser Foundation Health Plan, Inc.
1700 K St., N.W. Suite 601, Washington, DC 20006
Telephone: (202) 296-1314
Registered as lobbyist at U.S. Congress.

GLITZENSTEIN, Eric
Harmon, Curran and Tousley
2001 S St., N.W., Suite 430, Washington, DC 20009
Telephone: (202) 328-3500
Clients:
Natural Resources Defense Council

GLOBAL AVIATION ASSOCIATES, LTD.
1800 K St., N.W. Suite 1104, Washington, DC 20006
Telephone: (202) 457-0212
Registered as Foreign Agent: (#3943)
Members of firm representing listed organizations:
Ash, Jon F., Managing Director
Trent, Judith M.
Clients:
Austrian Airlines *(Jon F. Ash)*
Huntsville-Madison County Airport *(Judith M. Trent)*
Memphis-Shelby County Airport Authority *(Jon F. Ash)*
Phoenix Sky Harbour Internat'l Airport *(Judith M. Trent)*
Scandinavian Airlines System (SAS) *(Jon F. Ash)*

GLOBAL USA, INC.
2121 K St., N.W., Suite 650, Washington, DC 20037
Telephone: (202) 296-2400
Background: An international consulting and government relations firm. Stanton D. Anderson, senior partner in the law firm of Anderson, Hibey, Nauheim, and Blair, serves as Chairman of the Board, Global USA.
Members of firm representing listed organizations:
Denysyk, (Dr.) Bohdan, Senior V. President
Background: Former Deputy Assistant Secretary of Commerce.
Kopp, George S., V. President and General Counsel
Background: Former Staff Dir. and Chief Counsel, House Subcommittee on Natural Resources.
Morris, William H. (Jr.), President and CEO
Background: Former Assistant Secretary of Commerce for Trade, 1981-83. Former Assistant to Senator Bill Brock, (R-TN) and member of the President's Commission on Industrial Competitiveness.
Nugent, John M. (Jr.), V. President
Background: Former Ass't for Congressional Affairs to the Administrator, Energy Administration.
Clients:
All Nippon Airways Co. *(John M. Nugent, Jr.)*
Earth Observation Satellite Co. *(George S. Kopp)*
Fanuc, Ltd. *(Dr. Bohdan Denysyk)*
Hitachi Ltd. *(John M. Nugent, Jr.)*
Hyundai Motor America *(William H. Morris, Jr.)*
Japan Federation of Construction Contractors *(Dr. Bohdan Denysyk)*
Japanese Aero Engines Corp. *(Dr. Bohdan Denysyk)*
Japanese Aircraft Development Corp. *(Dr. Bohdan Denysyk)*
Komatsu Ltd. *(William H. Morris, Jr.)*
Kyocera Corp. *(William H. Morris, Jr.)*
Mazak Corp. *(Dr. Bohdan Denysyk)*
Murata Machinery, Ltd. *(Dr. Bohdan Denysyk)*

South Louisiana Port Commission *(William H. Morris, Jr.)*

TECO Transport & Trade Corp. *(William H. Morris, Jr.)*

GLODDECK, Alfred
Manager, Regulatory Affairs, Subaru of America
1700 K St., N.W., Suite 1007, Washington, DC 20006
Telephone: (202) 296-4994

GLOSSON, Brig. Gen. Buster C.
Dep Asst Secy, Plans & Opns, Legis Affrs, DEPARTMENT OF DEFENSE
The Pentagon, Washington, DC 20301
Telephone: (202) 697-6210

GLOVER, Eugene
President, Nat'l Council of Senior Citizens
925 15th St., N.W., Washington, DC 20005
Telephone: (202) 347-8800

GLOVER, Jere W.
1725 K St., N.W., Suite 308, Washington, DC 20006
Telephone: (202) 775-0628
Registered as lobbyist at U.S. Congress.
Organizations represented:
  Associated Enterprises, Inc.
  Nat'l Ass'n for the Self-Employed

GNESS, Melanie P.
Assistant Director, Government Relations, Flexible Packaging Ass'n
1090 Vermont Ave., N.W Suite 500, Washington, DC 20005
Telephone: (202) 842-3880

GNESSIN, Alan M.
Gnessin Law Offices, Alan M.
1220 19th St., N.W., Suite 400, Washington, DC 20036
Telephone: (202) 833-1547
Registered as lobbyist at U.S. Congress.
Organizations represented:
  CHP
  Family Health Plan, Inc.

GNESSIN LAW OFFICES, Alan M.
1220 19th St., N.W., Suite 400, Washington, DC 20036
Telephone: (202) 833-1547
Members of firm representing listed organizations:
  Gnessin, Alan M.
Organizations represented:
  CHP *(Alan M. Gnessin)*
  Family Health Plan, Inc. *(Alan M. Gnessin)*

GODDARD, Pamela
Conservation Assistant, Sierra Club
408 C St., N.E., Washington, DC 20002
Telephone: (202) 547-1141

GODFREY, C. Frank, Jr.
Sr. Associate & Dir. of Administration, Cassidy and Associates, Inc.
655 15th St., N.W., Suite 1100, Washington, DC 20005
Telephone: (202) 347-0773
Registered as lobbyist at U.S. Congress.
Registered as Foreign Agent: (#4259).
Background: Exec. Assistant to the Speaker, U.S. House of Representatives, 1979-83.
Clients:
  Barry University
  Bolt, Beranek and Newman
  Boston College
  Boston University
  Cardinal Hill Hospital
  Columbia University
  Drexel University
  Gonzaga University
  LiTel Telecommunications Corp.
  Loyola Marymount University
  Loyola University of Chicago
  Medical University of South Carolina
  Monterey Institute of Internat'l Studies
  Ocean Spray Cranberries
  Presbyterian Hospital/University of Pittsburgh
  Societa Cavi Pirelli S.p.A.
  Thomas Jefferson University
  Tufts University
  U.S. Healthcare, Inc.
  Universal Medical Center

University of Kentucky Foundation
University of Pennsylvania
University of Southern Mississippi
University of the Arts
Valley Children's Hospital

GODLEY, Gene E.
Bracewell and Patterson
2000 K St., N.W., Suite 500, Washington, DC 20006-1809
Telephone: (202) 828-5800
Registered as lobbyist at U.S. Congress.
Background: Serves also as Treasurer, Bracewell and Patterson Political Action Committee and the Conservative Democratic PAC. Administrative Assistant to Sen. Ralph Yarborough (D-TX), 1967-69. General Counsel, Senate Labor and Public Welfare Committee, 1969-70. General Counsel, Senate District Committee, 1970-71. Administrative Assistant to Sen. Thomas Eagleton (D-MO), 1971-76. Assistant Secretary of the Treasury for Legislative Affairs, 1976-80.
Clients:
  Bracewell and Patterson Political Action Committee
  Centex Corp.
  Chemical Manufacturers Ass'n
  Computer Dealers and Lessors Ass'n
  Conservative Democratic PAC
  Enron Corp.
  Genentech, Inc.
  Higman Barge Lines
  Louisiana Land and Exploration Co.
  Southdown
  Sterling Chemical Co.
  Valero Energy Corp.

GODLEY, Stephanie
Director, Legislative Services, American Apparel Manufacturers Ass'n
2500 Wilson Blvd., Suite 301, Arlington, VA 22201
Telephone: (703) 524-1864
Registered as lobbyist at U.S. Congress.

GODLOVE, James W.
Federal Relations Representative, Phillips Petroleum Co.
1776 Eye St., N.W. Suite 700, Washington, DC 20006
Telephone: (202) 833-0900
Registered as lobbyist at U.S. Congress.

GODOWN, Richard D.
President, Industrial Biotechnology Ass'n
1625 K St., N.W., Suite 1100, Washington, DC 20006
Telephone: (202) 857-0244

GODSON, Dr. Roy
Director, Washington Office, Nat'l Strategy Information Center
1730 Rhode Island Ave., N.W., Washington, DC 20036
Telephone: (202) 429-0129

GOELLER, David
Media Coordinator, Environmental Action
1525 New Hampshire Ave., N.W., Washington, DC 20036
Telephone: (202) 745-4870

GOELZER, KayLynn
Government Relations Associate, American Waterways Operators
1600 Wilson Blvd. Suite 1000, Arlington, VA 22209
Telephone: (703) 841-9300
Registered as lobbyist at U.S. Congress.

GOETZL, Alberto
V. Pres., Economics & Info. Services, Nat'l Forest Products Ass'n
1250 Connecticut Ave., N.W., Washington, DC 20036
Telephone: (202) 463-2713

GOEWEY, Sarah M.
Account Coordinator, Kaufman & Associates, Henry J.
2233 Wisconsin Ave., N.W., Washington, DC 20007
Telephone: (202) 333-0700
Registered as Foreign Agent: (#4093).
Organizations represented:
  Brunei, Embassy of

GOEWEY, Susan E,
Director, Public Relations, Information Industry Ass'n
555 New Jersey Ave., N.W. Suite 800, Washington, DC 20001

Telephone: (202) 639-8262
Background: Former aide to Rep. Mike Andrews (D-TX).

GOFF, Karen
Exec Asst, Legis Affrs, EXECUTIVE OFFICE OF THE PRESIDENT - The White House
1600 Pennsylvania Ave., N.W., Washington, DC 20500
Telephone: (202) 456-2230

GOGGINS, James
Exec. Director, Nat'l Contract Management Ass'n
1912 Woodford Road, Vienna, VA 22182
Telephone: (703) 448-9231

GOGOL, David U.
President, Sagamore Associates, Inc.
1701 K St., N.W., Suite 400, Washington, DC 20006
Telephone: (202) 223-0964
Registered as lobbyist at U.S. Congress.
Background: Legislative Assistant to Senator Richard Lugar (R-IN), 1978-81. Assistant to the Chairman, Senate Subcommittee on Housing and Urban Affairs, 1981-83. Legislative Director to Senator Lugar, 1983-85.
Clients:
  Columbus, Indiana, City of
  Comprehensive Marketing Systems, Inc.
  Indiana State University
  Indianapolis Center for Advanced Research
  Indianapolis, Indiana, City of
  Manufacturers Hanover Trust Co.
  Nobelsville, Indiana, City of
  North Las Vegas, Nevada, City of
  Seattle Organizing Committee, 1990 Goodwill Games
  South Bend, Indiana, City of
  1993 World University Games

GOHLA, Richard C.
Exec. V. President, Retail Bakers of America
Presidential Bldg. 6525 Belcrest Rd., Suite 250, Hyattsville, MD 20782
Telephone: (301) 277-0990
Registered as lobbyist at U.S. Congress.

GOINS, Jace
Saunders and Company
1015 Duke St., Alexandria, VA 22314
Telephone: (703) 549-1555

GOLAB, Thom
Director Development, Capitol Research Center
1612 K St., N.W., Suite 704, Washington, DC 20006
Telephone: (202) 822-8666

GOLATO, Al James
Corporate Director of Public Affairs, Block, H. & R.
1641 Rt. 3 North, Suite 101, Crofton, MD 21114
Telephone: (301) 858-1210
Registered as lobbyist at U.S. Congress.
Background: Former Assistant to the Commissioner of Internal Revenue for six years.

GOLD, Harvey S.
Exec. V. President, Nat'l Pest Control Ass'n
8100 Oak St., Dunn Loring, VA 22027
Telephone: (703) 573-8330
Registered as lobbyist at U.S. Congress.

GOLD, Laurence
General Counsel, AFL-CIO (American Federation of Labor and Congress of Industrial Organizations)
815 16th St., N.W., Washington, DC 20006
Telephone: (202) 637-5075

GOLD AND LIEBENGOOD, INC.
1455 Pennsylvania Ave., N.W. Suite 950, Washington, DC 20004
Telephone: (202) 639-8899
Registered as Foreign Agent: (#3700)
Background: Government relations consultants. Acquired by Burson-Marsteller in late 1989.
Members of firm representing listed organizations:
  Bode, Denise A.
    Background: Former Legal Counsel to Senator David Boren (D-OK).
  Bushong, David W.
    Background: Former Counsel, Committee on Intelligence, and aide to Senator Nancy Kassebaum (R-KS).

GOLD AND LIEBENGOOD, INC. (Cont'd)

Gold, Martin B.
Background: Former Counsel to U.S. Senate Majority Leader Howard Baker (R-TN).

Griffith, Melanie
Background: Former Aide to U.S. Senate Committee on Finance.

Hildenbrand, William F.
Background: Former Secretary of the U.S. Senate.

Jarvis, Patricia J.
Background: Former Special Assistant, Office of Legislation, U.S. Department of Health and Human Services.

Liebengood, Howard S.
Background: Former Sergeant-at-Arms of the U.S. Senate.

McCormick, Mary Lou
Background: Former Press Secretary to Senator Bob Packwood (R-OR).

Merin, Charles L.

Morin, Mary Kay
Background: Former Aide to U.S. Senate Majority Leader Howard Baker (R-TN).

Powers Grisso, Cindy J.
Background: Former Aide to U.S. Representative Michael A. Andrews and Congressman Lloyd Benton (both D-TX).

Ratchford, William R.
Background: Former U.S. Representative (D-CT).

Scruggs, John F.
Background: Former Assistant Secretary for Legislation, U.S. Department of Health and Human Services.

Slaton, Sally

Slone, Peter B.
Background: Former U.S. House Appropriations Committee Associate Staff.

Clients:
Alaska Loggers Ass'n *(Martin B. Gold)*
American Academy of Ophthalmology *(John F. Scruggs)*
American Medical Ass'n *(Martin B. Gold)*
Bausch & Lomb, Inc. *(Martin B. Gold)*
Beretta U.S.A. Corp. *(Howard S. Liebengood)*
British Airports Authority (BAA plc) *(David W. Bushong, Howard S. Liebengood, John F. Scruggs)*
College of American Pathologists *(Martin B. Gold)*
Electronic Data Systems Corp. *(John F. Scruggs)*
Energy Research Corp. *(William R. Ratchford)*
Equitable Life Assurance Soc. of the U.S. *(Denise A. Bode)*
Eye Bank Ass'n of America *(John F. Scruggs)*
Federated Investors, Inc. *(William F. Hildenbrand)*
Fiat Washington *(Howard S. Liebengood)*
Ford Motor Co.
Hopi Tribe *(Howard S. Liebengood)*
Internat'l Committee of Passenger Lines *(Martin B. Gold)*
Investment Company Institute *(Howard S. Liebengood)*
MCI Communications Corp. *(Martin B. Gold, Charles L. Merin)*
Nat'l Business Aircraft Ass'n *(David W. Bushong, Howard S. Liebengood)*
Nat'l Cattlemen's Ass'n *(Denise A. Bode)*
Nat'l Football League *(Martin B. Gold)*
Nat'l Restaurant Ass'n *(Charles L. Merin)*
Nat'l School Transportation Ass'n *(Charles L. Merin, Peter B. Slone)*
Pacific Enterprises *(Martin B. Gold)*
Pennzoil Co. *(Martin B. Gold, Howard S. Liebengood)*
Philip Morris Management Corp. *(Martin B. Gold, Howard S. Liebengood)*
Phillips Petroleum Co. *(Denise A. Bode)*
Public Securities Ass'n *(Denise A. Bode)*
Salomon Brothers Inc. *(Martin B. Gold)*
Thomson-CSF Inc. *(Howard S. Liebengood)*
Times Mirror Co. *(Martin B. Gold)*
Washington Metropolitan Area Transit Authority *(Charles L. Merin)*

GOLD, Martin B.
Gold and Liebengood, Inc.
1455 Pennsylvania Ave., N.W. Suite 950, Washington, DC 20004
Telephone: (202) 639-8899
Registered as lobbyist at U.S. Congress.
Background: Former Counsel to U.S. Senate Majority Leader Howard Baker (R-TN).

Clients:
Alaska Loggers Ass'n
American Medical Ass'n
Bausch & Lomb, Inc.
College of American Pathologists
Internat'l Committee of Passenger Lines
MCI Communications Corp.
Nat'l Football League
Pacific Enterprises
Pennzoil Co.
Philip Morris Management Corp.
Salomon Brothers Inc.
Times Mirror Co.

GOLD, Peter F.
Winthrop, Stimson, Putnam & Roberts
1133 Connecticut Ave., N.W. Suite 1000, Washington, DC 20036
Telephone: (202) 775-9800
Registered as lobbyist at U.S. Congress.
Registered as Foreign Agent: (# 3873).
Background: Legislative Director, U.S. Senator Gary Hart (D-CO), 1975-81.
Clients:
Amoco Performance Products, Inc.
BASF Corp.
BASF Structural Materials, Inc.
Brown and Bain
Fiberite Corp.
Hercules Aerospace Co. (Aerospace Products Group)
Navajo Nation, The
Snappy Car Rental
Thrifty Rent-A-Car System, Inc.

GOLD, Stephen
Director of Public Policy, Citizens for a Sound Economy
470 L'Enfant Plaza East, S.W. Suite 7112, Washington, DC 20024
Telephone: (202) 488-8200

GOLDBECK, Willis B.
President, Washington Business Group on Health
229 1/2 Pennsylvania Ave., S.E., Washington, DC 20003
Telephone: (202) 547-6644

GOLDBERG, Allen
Sr. Associate, Gov't & Media Relations, Grocery Manufacturers of America
1010 Wisconsin Ave., N.W., Suite 800, Washington, DC 20007
Telephone: (202) 337-9400
Registered as lobbyist at U.S. Congress.

GOLDBERG, Avrum M.
Akin, Gump, Strauss, Hauer and Feld
1333 New Hampshire Ave., N.W., Suite 400, Washington, DC 20036
Telephone: (202) 887-4000
Background: Attorney, Division of Litigation, Office of the General Counsel, National Labor Relations Board, 1969-73.

GOLDBERG, David M.
Director of Communications, Nat'l Ass'n of Plumbing-Heating-Cooling Contractors
180 South Washington St. Box 6808, Falls Church, VA 22046
Telephone: (703) 237-8100

GOLDBERG, FIELDMAN AND LETHAM
1100 15th St., N.W. Suite 200, Washington, DC 20005
Telephone: (202) 463-8300
Members of firm representing listed organizations:
Goldberg, Reuben
Clients:
Community Public Service Co.
North Penn Gas Co.
Sierra Pacific Resources

GOLDBERG, Henry
Goldberg & Spector
1229 19th St., N.W., Washington, DC 20036
Telephone: (202) 429-4900

GOLDBERG, James M.
Tendler, Goldberg & Biggins, Chtd.
1090 Vermont Ave., N.W., Suite 1200, Washington, DC 20005-4905

Telephone: (202) 682-9000
Clients:
American Soc. for Biotechnology
Michigan Retailers Ass'n
Nat'l Alcoholic Beverage Control Ass'n
Nat'l Ass'n of Meat Purveyors
Nat'l Ass'n of Music Merchants
Nat'l Ass'n of Retail Dealers of America
Nat'l Ass'n of School Music Dealers
Nat'l Peanut Council
Nat'l Shoe Retailers Ass'n
Nat'l Wine Distributors Ass'n
Prescription Footwear Ass'n
TDCC: The Electronic Data Interchange Ass'n

GOLDBERG, Michael I.
Exec. Director, American Soc. for Microbiology
1325 Massachusetts Ave., N.W., Washington, DC 20005
Telephone: (202) 737-3600

GOLDBERG, Milton
Exec. Director, Council on Governmental Relations
1 Dupont Circle, N.W. Suite 670, Washington, DC 20036
Telephone: (202) 861-2595

GOLDBERG, Neal M.
Hopkins and Sutter
888 16th St., N.W., Suite 700, Washington, DC 20006
Telephone: (202) 835-8000
Clients:
WTKR-TV

GOLDBERG, Peter B.
Senior Associate, Institute for Educational Leadership
1001 Connecticut Ave., N.W. Suite 310, Washington, DC 20036
Telephone: (202) 822-8405

GOLDBERG, Reuben
Goldberg, Fieldman and Letham
1100 15th St., N.W. Suite 200, Washington, DC 20005
Telephone: (202) 463-8300

GOLDBERG, Sandra
Law Associate, Sierra Club Legal Defense Fund
1531 P St., N.W. Suite 200, Washington, DC 20005
Telephone: (202) 667-4500

GOLDBERG, Sheldon L.
President, American Ass'n of Homes for the Aging
1129 20th St., N.W., Suite 400, Washington, DC 20036
Telephone: (202) 296-5960

GOLDBERG, Sherwood D.
Director, Worldwide Associates, Inc
1155 15th St., N.W. Suite 800, Washington, DC 20005
Telephone: (202) 429-9788

GOLDBERG & SPECTOR
1229 19th St., N.W., Washington, DC 20036
Telephone: (202) 429-4900
Members of firm representing listed organizations:
Goldberg, Henry
Spector, Phillip L.
Clients:
Pan American Satellite Corp.
Turner Broadcasting System, Inc.

GOLDBLOOM, Irwin
Latham and Watkins
1001 Pennsylvania Ave., N.W., Suite 1300, Washington, DC 20004
Telephone: (202) 637-2200
Background: Trial Attorney, 1958-71, Special Litigation Counsel, 1971-74 and Deputy Assistant Attorney General, 1974-78, Civil Division, Department of Justice.
Clients:
PPG Industries

GOLDEN, Cornelius, Jr.
Chadbourne and Parke
1101 Vermont Ave., N.W., Suite 900, Washington, DC 20005
Telephone: (202) 289-3000
Registered as lobbyist at U.S. Congress.
Clients:
Amalgamated Metal Corp. PLC

GOLDEN, FREDA AND SCHRAUB, P.C.
1400 16th St., N.W. Suite 700, Washington, DC 20036
Telephone: (202) 939-6000
Members of firm representing listed organizations:
Irwin, David A.
Background: Special Counsel to Chief, Common Carrier Bureau/Chief Program Evaluation Staff, Federal Communications Commission, 1975-79.

GOLDEN, Jim
Director of Research, Nat'l Ass'n of Counties
440 First St., N.W., Washington, DC 20001
Telephone: (202) 393-6226

GOLDEN, Mark J.
V. President, Ass'n of Telemessaging Services Internat'l
1150 South Washington St. Suite 150, Alexandria, VA 22314
Telephone: (703) 684-0016

GOLDEN, Martha A.
V. President, Support Programs, Citicorp
1275 Pennsylvania Ave., N.W., Suite 503, Washington, DC 20004
Telephone: (202) 879-6800
Background: Serves as Treasurer, Citicorp Voluntary Political Fund - Federal.

GOLDEN, Patrick G.
Attorney, Law Department, Pacific Gas and Electric Co.
1726 M St., N.W., Suite 1100, Washington, DC 20036-4502
Telephone: (202) 466-7980

GOLDFARB, Kathryn
Sr. Acct. Superv., Grassroots/issues Mgt, Hill and Knowlton Public Affairs Worldwide
Washington Harbour, 901 31st St., N.W., Washington, DC 20007
Telephone: (202) 333-7400

GOLDFARB, KAUFMAN & O'TOOLE
918 16th St., N.W., Suite 503, Washington, DC 20006
Telephone: (202) 466-3030
Members of firm representing listed organizations:
Goldfarb, Ronald L.
Clients:
Washington Independent Writers (Ronald L. Goldfarb)

GOLDFARB, Ronald L.
Goldfarb, Kaufman & O'Toole
918 16th St., N.W., Suite 503, Washington, DC 20006
Telephone: (202) 466-3030
Registered as lobbyist at U.S. Congress.
Clients:
Washington Independent Writers

GOLDFIELD, H. P.
Strategic Resources Corp.
3000 K St., N.W., Suite 300, Washington, DC 20007
Telephone: (202) 944-4772
Registered as lobbyist at U.S. Congress.
Clients:
Bermuda, Government of
China External Trade Development Council
Hyundai Motor Co.

GOLDHAMMER, Alan R.
Director, Technical Affairs, Industrial Biotechnology Ass'n
1625 K St., N.W., Suite 1100, Washington, DC 20006
Telephone: (202) 857-0244

GOLDMAN, Andrew
Spec Asst, Foreign Affrs, Legis Affrs, DEPARTMENT OF DEFENSE
The Pentagon, Washington, DC 20301
Telephone: (202) 697-6210

GOLDMAN-CARTER, Janice
Counsel, Nat'l Wildlife Federation
1400 16th St., N.W., Washington, DC 20036-2266
Telephone: (202) 797-6800
Registered as lobbyist at U.S. Congress.

GOLDMAN, Charles
1010 Vermont Ave., N.W., Suite 1100, Washington, DC 20005
Telephone: (202) 347-7550
Organizations represented:
Disability Focus, Inc.

GOLDMAN, Jack H.
Manager, Technical Services, Aluminum Ass'n
900 19th St., N.W., Suite 300, Washington, DC 20006
Telephone: (202) 862-5100

GOLDMAN, Janlori
Legislative Counsel, American Civil Liberties Union
122 Maryland Ave., N.E., Washington, DC 20002
Telephone: (202) 544-1681
Registered as lobbyist at U.S. Congress.

GOLDMAN, Max
Sr. Federal Gov't Affairs Representative, Texaco U.S.A.
1050 17th St., N.W., Suite 500, Washington, DC 20036
Telephone: (202) 331-1427
Registered as lobbyist at U.S. Congress.

GOLDMAN, Patricia
Sr. V. Pres., Corporate Communications, USAir Group Inc.
Crystal Park 4 2345 Crystal Dr., Arlington, VA 22227
Telephone: (703) 418-5111

GOLDMAN, Patricia R.
Sr. Assoc. Director, Div. of Legislation, American Hospital Ass'n
50 F St., N.W., Suite 1100, Washington, DC 20001
Telephone: (202) 638-1100
Registered as lobbyist at U.S. Congress.

GOLDMAN, Patti
Staff Attorney, Public Citizen Litigation Group
2000 P St., N.W., Suite 700, Washington, DC 20036
Telephone: (202) 785-3704

GOLDRICH, Anna
Assistant to the Director, League of Conservation Voters
1150 Connecticut Ave., N.W. Suite 501, Washington, DC 20036
Telephone: (202) 785-8683

GOLDSBOROUGH, Robert H.
Legislative Director, Americans for Immigration Control
721 2nd St., N.E., Suite 307, Washington, DC 20002
Telephone: (202) 543-3719

GOLDSTEIN, Alan
Director, Communications, Nat'l Food Brokers Ass'n
1010 Massachusetts Ave., N.W., Washington, DC 20001
Telephone: (202) 789-2844

GOLDSTEIN, Carl A.
V. President, Public and Media Relations, U.S. Council for Energy Awareness
1776 Eye St., N. W. Suite 400, Washington, DC 20006
Telephone: (202) 293-0770

GOLDSTEIN, Ellen
Director, Health & Public Affairs, Ass'n of Private Pension and Welfare Plans
1212 New York Ave., N.W. 12th Floor, Washington, DC 20005
Telephone: (202) 737-6666

GOLDSTEIN, Jeffery M.
Skadden, Arps, Slate, Meagher and Flom
1440 New York Ave., N.W., Washington, DC 20005
Telephone: (202) 371-7000
Clients:
MacMillan Publishing Co.

GOLDSTEIN, Jordan
Staff Consultant, Arms Control and Foreign Policy Caucus
House Annex 2 Room 501, Washington, DC 20515
Telephone: (202) 226-3440

GOLDSTEIN, Leonard J.
Chairman, Beer Institute
1225 Eye St., N.W., Suite 825, Washington, DC 20005
Telephone: (202) 737-2337

GOLEMBE, Carter
Chairman of the Board/Managing Director, Secura Group, The
1155 21st St., N.W., Washington, DC 20036
Telephone: (202) 728-4920

GOLLATTSCHECK, Dr. James F.
Exec. V. President, American Ass'n of Community and Junior Colleges
One Dupont Circle, N.W. Suite 410, Washington, DC 20036
Telephone: (202) 293-7050

GOLLICK, Donna M.
Interim Exec. Director, Nat'l Council for Accreditation of Teacher Education
2029 K St.,, N.W. Suite 500, Washington, DC 20006
Telephone: (202) 466-7496

GOLODNER, Linda F.
Exec. Director, Nat'l Consumers League
815 15th St., N.W., Suite 516, Washington, DC 20005
Telephone: (202) 639-8140
Registered as lobbyist at U.S. Congress.

GOLUB, Alvin
Executive Director, Washington Psychiatric Soc.
1400 K St., N.W. Suite 202, Washington, DC 20005
Telephone: (202) 682-6270

GOLUB, Judy
Associate Washington Representative, American Jewish Committee
2027 Massachusetts Ave., N.W., Washington, DC 20036
Telephone: (202) 265-2000

GOMPERTS, John S.
Legislative Counsel, People for the American Way
2000 M St., N.W., Suite 400, Washington, DC 20036
Telephone: (202) 467-4999
Registered as lobbyist at U.S. Congress.

GON, Sylvia
Assistant Director, South Africa Foundation
1225 19th St., N.W. Suite 700, Washington, DC 20036
Telephone: (202) 223-5486

GONCZ, Paul
Director, Wash. Operations, AM General, LTV Aircraft Products Group
1725 Jefferson Davis Hwy. Suite 900, Arlington, VA 22202
Telephone: (703) 521-6560
Registered as lobbyist at U.S. Congress.

GONNELLY, William
Internat'l Representative, Sheet Metal Workers' Internat'l Ass'n
1750 New York Ave., N.W. Sixth Floor, Washington, DC 20006
Telephone: (202) 783-5880
Registered as lobbyist at U.S. Congress.

GONYEA, Dr. Meredith A.
President, Center for Studies in Health Policy
1155 Connecticut Ave., N.W. Suite 500, Washington, DC 20036
Telephone: (202) 659-3270

GONZALES, Michael A.
V. President, Nat'l Ass'n of Trade and Technical Schools
2251 Wisconsin Ave., N.W. Suite 200, Washington, DC 20007
Telephone: (202) 333-1021

GONZALES, Tomasa
Community Liaison, Nat'l Hispanic Council on Aging
2713 Ontario Road, N.W. Suite 200, Washington, DC 20009
Telephone: (202) 265-1288

GONZALEZ, Cecilia
Howrey and Simon
1730 Pennsylvania Ave., N.W., Washington, DC 20006-4793
Telephone: (202) 783-0800
Clients:
Amgen, Inc.

GONZALEZ, Helen
Attorney/Legislative Specialist, Nat'l Consumer Law Center
236 Massachusetts Ave., N.E. Suite 504, Washington, DC 20002
Telephone: (202) 543-6060

GONZALEZ, John A.
Manager, Legislative Programs, Rockwell Internat'l
1745 Jefferson Davis Hwy. Suite 1200, Arlington, VA
22202
Telephone: (703) 553-6600
Registered as lobbyist at U.S. Congress.

GONZALEZ, Dr. Jose
Director, International Affairs, Internat'l Hospital Federation
50 F St., N.W., Suite 1100, Washington, DC 20001
Telephone: (202) 638-1100

GONZE, Ruth
Policy Analyst, American Public Power Ass'n
2301 M St., N.W., Washington, DC 20037
Telephone: (202) 775-8300
Registered as lobbyist at U.S. Congress.

GOOCH, R. Gordon
Travis & Gooch
1100 15th St., N.W. Suite 1200, Washington, DC 20005
Telephone: (202) 457-9100
Registered as lobbyist at U.S. Congress.
Background: General Counsel, Federal Power Commission,
1969-72.
Clients:
Anadarko Petroleum Corp.
Coalition to Oppose Energy Taxes

GOOD, Larry I.
Senior V. President, Hill and Knowlton Public Affairs
Worldwide
Washington Harbour, 901 31st St., N.W., Washington, DC
20007
Telephone: (202) 333-7400
Registered as Foreign Agent: (#4170).
Clients:
American General Corp.
Internat'l Business Machines Corp.
UNUM Corp.

GOODFADER, Alan
Murphy and Demory, Ltd.
2300 N St., N.W. Suite 725, Washington, DC 20037
Telephone: (202) 785-3323
Registered as lobbyist at U.S. Congress.

GOODFELLOW, William C.
Director, Center for Internat'l Policy
1755 Massachusetts Ave., N.W., Suite 500, Washington,
DC 20036
Telephone: (202) 232-3317
Background: Research Director of Indochina Resource
Center, 1973-75.

GOODMAN, Bruce
Arter & Hadden
1919 Pennsylvania Ave., N.W., Suite 400, Washington, DC
20006
Telephone: (202) 775-7100
Background: Former Mid-Atlantic Coordinator for Law-
yers for Bush/Quayle.
Clients:
Amway Corp.
Westwood One, Inc.

GOODMAN, G. Thomas
Director, Public Affairs, Nat'l Ass'n of Counties
440 First St., N.W., Washington, DC 20001
Telephone: (202) 393-6226

GOODMAN, Leslie
Press Secretary, Republican Nat'l Committee
310 First St., S.E., Washington, DC 20003
Telephone: (202) 863-8500

GOODMAN, Lisa
Media Director, Fenn & King Communications
1043 Cecil Place, N.W., Washington, DC 20007
Telephone: (202) 337-6995

GOODMAN, Mark
Exec. Director, Student Press Law Center
1735 Eye St., N.W. Suite 504, Washington, DC 20006
Telephone: (202) 466-5242

GOODMAN, Nancy
Director of Development, Internat'l Human Rights Law
Group
1601 Connecticut Ave., N.W. Suite 700, Washington, DC
20009
Telephone: (202) 232-8500

GOODMAN, Richard
V. President, Government Affairs, Continental Grain Co.
818 Connecticut Ave., N.W., 8th Floor, Washington, DC
20006
Telephone: (202) 331-1922

GOODMAN, Susan
Associate, Dutko & Associates
412 First St., S.E. Suite 100, Washington, DC 20003
Telephone: (202) 484-4884
Registered as lobbyist at U.S. Congress.
Clients:
Jewish Nat'l Fund

GOODRICH, Bernard A.
Director, Public Communications, MCI Communications
Corp.
1133 19th St., N.W., Washington, DC 20036
Telephone: (202) 872-1600

GOODRICH, William W., Jr.
Arent, Fox, Kintner, Plotkin & Kahn
1050 Connecticut Ave., N.W., Washington, DC 20036-
5339
Telephone: (202) 857-6000
Registered as lobbyist at U.S. Congress.

GOODSTEIN, Richard F.
Div. V. Pres, Nat'l Government Affairs, Browning-Ferris Industries (D.C.), Inc.
1150 Connecticut Ave., N.W., Suite 500, Washington, DC
20036
Telephone: (202) 223-8153
Registered as lobbyist at U.S. Congress.

GOODWEATHER, Melvin G.
Director, Government Relations, Pratt & Whitney
1825 Eye St., N.W., Suite 700, Washington, DC 20006
Telephone: (202) 785-7430

GOODWIN, Robert F.
Staff V.P., Dir. of Governmental Affairs, Meredith Corp.
1850 K St., N.W., Suite 275, Washington, DC 20006
Telephone: (202) 223-2406
Registered as lobbyist at U.S. Congress.

GOOLD, Linda
Dir., Fed. Tax Programs, Gov't Relations, Nat'l Ass'n of
REALTORS
777 14th St., N.W., Washington, DC 20005
Telephone: (202) 383-1000
Registered as lobbyist at U.S. Congress.

GORDON, Bezalel
Director, Press Relations, B'nai B'rith Internat'l
1640 Rhode Island Ave., N.W., Washington, DC 20036
Telephone: (202) 857-6600

GORDON, David F.
Director, Public Affairs, American Trucking Ass'ns
2200 Mill Road, Alexandria, VA 22314
Telephone: (703) 838-1875

GORDON, Deborah
Energy Analyst, Union of Concerned Scientists
1616 P St., N.W., Suite 310, Washington, DC 20036
Telephone: (202) 332-0900
Registered as lobbyist at U.S. Congress.

GORDON, H. Stephan
General Counsel, Nat'l Federation of Federal Employees
1016 16th St., N.W., Suite 400, Washington, DC 20036
Telephone: (202) 862-4400
Registered as lobbyist at U.S. Congress.
Background: Former General Counsel, Federal Labor Rela-
tions Authority.

GORDON, Harold
Exec. Director, Internat'l Healthcare Safety Professional
Certification Board
5010-A Nicholson Lane, Rockville, MD 20852
Telephone: (301) 984-8969

GORDON, Mary S.
Manager, Government Relations, Northern Telecom Inc..
600 Maryland Ave., S.W. Suite 607, Washington, DC
20024
Telephone: (202) 554-1520
Registered as lobbyist at U.S. Congress.

GORDON, Randall C.
V.P., Communications and Gov't Relations, Nat'l Grain
and Feed Ass'n
1201 New York Ave., N.W. Suite 830, Washington, DC
20005
Telephone: (202) 289-0873
Registered as lobbyist at U.S. Congress.

GORDON, Robert E.
Nat'l Center for Municipal Development
1620 Eye St., N.W., Suite 300, Washington, DC 20006
Telephone: (202) 429-0160
Clients:
Spokane, Washington, City of

GORDON, Ronald
Director, American Hispanic PAC
c/o ZGS, 2300 Clarendon Blvd., Arlington, VA 22201
Telephone: (703) 351-5656

GORE, Brenda J.
Manager, Congressional Relations, TRW Inc.
Suite 2600, 1000 Wilson Blvd., Arlington, VA 22209
Telephone: (703) 276-5124
Registered as lobbyist at U.S. Congress.

GORE, John C.
V. President, Internat'l Affairs, BP America Inc.
1776 Eye St., N.W., Suite 1000, Washington, DC 20006
Telephone: (202) 785-4888
Registered as lobbyist at U.S. Congress.

GORELICK, Jamie S.
Miller, Cassidy, Larroca and Lewin
2555 M St., N.W. Suite 500, Washington, DC 20037
Telephone: (202) 293-6400
Registered as lobbyist at U.S. Congress.
Background: Assistant to Secretary and Counsellor to the
Deputy Secretary, Department of Energy, 1979-80. Vice
Chairman, Task Force on Evaluation of Audit, Investiga-
tive and Inspection Components of the Department of
Defense, 1979-80.
Clients:
Nat'l Ass'n of Life Underwriters
Nat'l Ass'n of Professional Insurance Agents
47th Street Photo

GORHAM, Millicent
Assistant Director, Gov't Relations, American Optometric
Ass'n
1505 Prince Street, Suite 300, Alexandria, VA 22314
Telephone: (703) 739-9200
Registered as lobbyist at U.S. Congress.

GORHAM, William
President, Urban Institute, The
2100 M St., N.W., Washington, DC 20037
Telephone: (202) 833-7200

GORIN, David
Exec. V. President, Nat'l Campground Owners Ass'n
11307 Sunset Hills Rd. Suite B-7, Reston, VA 22090
Telephone: (703) 471-0143

GORIN, Joe
Coordinator, Network in Solidarity with the People of
Guatemala
1314 14th St., N.W., 3rd Floor, Washington, DC 20005
Telephone: (202) 483-0050

GORMAN, Eleanor
EPA Project Assistant, Organization for American-Soviet
ExchangeS (OASES-DC)
1302 R St., N.W., Washington, DC 20009
Telephone: (202) 332-1145

GORMAN, Faye A.
Government Relations Representative, Dow Corning Corp.
1800 M St., N.W., Suite 325·South, Washington, DC
20036
Telephone: (202) 785-0585

GORMAN, Mark S.
Senior Director, Government Affairs, Nat'l Restaurant Ass'n
1200 17th St., N.W., Washington, DC 20036-3097
Telephone: (202) 331-5900
Registered as lobbyist at U.S. Congress.

GORMLEY, James D.
President, General Aviation Manufacturers Ass'n
1400 K St., Suite 801, Washington, DC 20005
Telephone: (202) 393-1500
Registered as lobbyist at U.S. Congress.
Background: Also serves as Secy.-Treas., General Aviation Manufacturers Ass'n Political Action Committee.

GORSKI, Thomas A.
Director, Public Relations & Market Res., American Soc. of Ass'n Executives
1575 Eye St., N.W., Washington, DC 20005-1168
Telephone: (202) 626-2723

GOSIER, Ann M.
V. President, Manufacturers Services, American Mining Congress
Suite 300, 1920 N St., N.W., Washington, DC 20036
Telephone: (202) 861-2862
Registered as lobbyist at U.S. Congress.

GOSLIN, Dr. David A.
President and Chief Exec. Officer, American Institutes for Research
3333 K St., N.W., Suite 300, Washington, DC 20007
Telephone: (202) 342-5000

GOSS, Frederick D.
Exec. Director, Newsletter Ass'n, The
1401 Wilson Blvd, Suite 403, Arlington, VA 22209
Telephone: (703) 527-2333

GOSS, Kenneth A.
Director, National Defense Issues, Air Force Ass'n
1501 Lee Hwy., Arlington, VA 22209-1198
Telephone: (703) 247-5800

GOSS, Leslie
Cong Liaison Div, ENVIRONMENTAL PROTECTION AGENCY
401 M St., S.W., Washington, DC 20460
Telephone: (202) 382-5200

GOSSENS, Peter J.
Corporate Manager, Legislative Affairs, General Dynamics Corp.
1745 Jefferson Davis Hwy., Suite 1000, Arlington, VA 22202
Telephone: (703) 553-1200
Registered as lobbyist at U.S. Congress.

GOTTEHRER, Barry H.
Senior V. President, Public Affairs, Massachusetts Mutual Life Insurance Co.
600 Pennsylvania Ave., N.W., Suite 601, Washington, DC 20004
Telephone: (202) 737-0440
Registered as lobbyist at U.S. Congress.

GOTTESMAN, Michael H.
Bredhoff and Kaiser
1000 Connecticut Ave., N.W. Suite 1300, Washington, DC 20036
Telephone: (202) 833-9340
Background: Trial Attorney, U.S. Department of Justice, 1959-61.
Clients:
United Steelworkers of America

GOTTFRIED, Pamela
Manager, Government Affairs, Columbia Gas System Service Corp.
1250 Eye St., N.W., Suite 703, Washington, DC 20005
Telephone: (202) 842-7400

GOTTLIEB, Margaret
Director, State Government Affairs, Direct Marketing Ass'n
1101 17th St., N.W., Suite 900, Washington, DC 20036
Telephone: (202) 347-1222
Registered as lobbyist at U.S. Congress.

GOTTSCHALK, Thomas A.
Kirkland and Ellis
655 15th St., N.W. Suite 1200, Washington, DC 20005
Telephone: (202) 879-5000

GOUABAULT, Veronica
Eastern Regional Manager, U.S. Hispanic Chamber of Commerce
111 Massachusetts Ave., N.W., Suite 200, Washington, DC 20001
Telephone: (202) 789-2717

GOULD, George B.
Legis. and Polit. Ass't to the President, Nat'l Ass'n of Letter Carriers of the United States of America
100 Indiana Ave., N.W., Washington, DC 20001
Telephone: (202) 393-4695
Registered as lobbyist at U.S. Congress.
Background: Also represents the Committee on Letter Carriers' Political Education, the association's political action committee.

GOULD, J. D.
V. President, Washington Operations, Ferranti Defense and Space Group
1111 Jefferson Davis Hwy, Suite 800, Arlington, VA 22202
Telephone: (703) 979-0005

GOULD, James C.
Vinson and Elkins
Willard Office Building, 1455 Pennsylvania Ave., N.W., Washington, DC 20004-1007
Telephone: (202) 639-6500
Registered as lobbyist at U.S. Congress.
Registered as Foreign Agent: (#4277).
Background: Legislative Assistant to Senator Lloyd Bentsen (D-TX), 1984-86. Chief Tax Counsel, 1987, and Staff Director and Chief Counsel, 1988, Senate Finance Committee.
Clients:
Modar, Inc.
Nat'l Refrigerants, Inc.
Pennsylvania Engineering Co.
Sterling Group, Inc., The
Trammell Crow, Inc.

GOULD, Noel
Exec. Director, Democratic Senatorial Campaign Committee
430 South Capitol St., S.E., Washington, DC 20003
Telephone: (202) 224-2447

GOULD, Rebecca M.J.
Verner, Liipfert, Bernhard, McPherson and Hand, Chartered
901 15th St., N.W., Suite 700, Washington, DC 20005
Telephone: (202) 371-6000
Registered as lobbyist at U.S. Congress.

GOULDEN, Joseph C.
Director of Media Analysis, Accuracy in Media
1275 K St., N.W., Suite 1150, Washington, DC 20005
Telephone: (202) 371-6710

GOULDING, Miriam B.
Gen. Counsel & Dir. of Gov'tl Affairs, Goodwill Industries of America, Inc.
9200 Wisconsin Ave., Bethesda, MD 20814-3896
Telephone: (301) 530-6500

GOULDRICK, Rev. John W., C.M.
Exec. Director, Committee for Pro-Life Activities
3211 4th St., N.E., Washington, DC 20017
Telephone: (202) 541-3070

GOVERNMENT RELATIONS, INC.
1620 Eye St., N.W. Suite 300, Washington, DC 20006
Telephone: (202) 775-0079
Members of firm representing listed organizations:
Bulger, Thomas J.
Clients:
Fairfax County, Virginia *(Thomas J. Bulger)*
Metropolitan Transportation Commission of Oakland *(Thomas J. Bulger)*
Oakland County Board of Supervisors *(Thomas J. Bulger)*
San Mateo, California, County of *(Thomas J. Bulger)*

GOWDY, Richard
Legislative Director, American Legislative Exchange Council
214 Massachusetts Ave., N.W., Washington, DC 20002
Telephone: (202) 547-4646

GOZONSKY, Moses
Program Associate, Nat'l Council on the Aging
600 Maryland Ave., S.W. West Wing 100, Washington, DC 20024
Telephone: (202) 479-1200
Background: Represents the Nat'l Institute of Senior Housing.

GRABER, Edmund C.
Dir., Cong. Rel./Public Works/Internat'l, Associated General Contractors of America
1957 E St., N.W., Washington, DC 20006
Telephone: (202) 393-2040
Registered as lobbyist at U.S. Congress.

GRABOWSKI, Gene
Director, Media Relations, American Council of Life Insurance
1001 Pennsylvania Ave. N.W., Washington, DC 20004-2599
Telephone: (202) 624-2000

GRACE, David R.
Covington and Burling
1201 Pennsylvania Ave., N.W., Box 7566, Washington, DC 20044
Telephone: (202) 662-6000

GRADY, Gregory
Wright and Talisman
1050 17th St., N.W. Suite 600, Washington, DC 20036
Telephone: (202) 331-1194
Background: Attorney, Federal Power Commission, 1973-74.

GRAEFE, Frederick H.
Baker and Hostetler
1050 Connecticut Ave., N.W. Suite 1100, Washington, DC 20036
Telephone: (202) 861-1500
Registered as lobbyist at U.S. Congress.
Clients:
Cleveland Clinic Foundation
Elyria Memorial Hospital and Medical Center
Greater New York Hospital Ass'n
Hermann Hospital
Homedco
Ivacare Corp.
Lorain Community Hospital
Renal Physicians of Texas
Soc. of Cardiovascular and Interventional Radiology
St. Joseph Hospital and Health Center
Substance Abuse Management, Inc.

GRAF, James E., II
V. President, Governmental Relations, Contel Corp.
555 13th St. Suite 480 West, Washington, DC 20004
Telephone: (202) 383-3700
Registered as lobbyist at U.S. Congress.
Background: Serves as Chairman, Contel Corporation Political Action Committee. Formerly Communications Counsel to the U.S. Senate Committee on Commerce, 1976-77, and Legal Assistant to FCC Commissioner, 1977-83.

GRAFF, John R.
Exec. Dir., Counsel and Dir., Govt. Rels., Internat'l Ass'n of Amusement Parks and Attractions
4230 King St., Alexandria, VA 22302
Telephone: (703) 671-5800
Registered as lobbyist at U.S. Congress.
Background: Also serves as Chairman, Internat'l Ass'n of Amusement Parks and Attractions Political Action Committee.

GRAHAM, Amy
Heating Fuels Counsel, Petroleum Marketers Ass'n of America
1120 Vermont Ave., N.W., Suite 1130, Washington, DC 20005
Telephone: (202) 331-1198

GRAHAM, Daniel O., Jr.
Exec. Director, Americans for the High Frontier
2800 Shirlington Road Suite 405 A, Arlington, VA 22206
Telephone: (703) 671-4111

GRAHAM, Lt. Gen. Daniel, USA (Ret.)
Chairman, Americans for the High Frontier
2800 Shirlington Road Suite 405 A, Arlington, VA 22206
Telephone: (703) 671-4111
Background: Serves also as Chairman, American Space
Frontier Committee Political Action Committee.

GRAHAM, David W.
Environmental Issues Manager, Dow Chemical
1776 Eye St., N.W., Suite 575, Washington, DC 20006
Telephone: (202) 429-3400
Registered as lobbyist at U.S. Congress.

GRAHAM, Deborah J.
Commo and Legis Affrs, EQUAL EMPLOYMENT OPPOR-
TUNITY COMMISSION
1801 L St., N.W., Washington, DC 20507
Telephone: (202) 663-4900

GRAHAM, Elaine
Director, Federal Relations, Nat'l Restaurant Ass'n
1200 17th St., N.W., Washington, DC 20036-3097
Telephone: (202) 331-5900
Registered as lobbyist at U.S. Congress.

GRAHAM, Gretta
Project Manager, Bonner & Associates
1625 K St., N.W., Suite 300, Washington, DC 20006
Telephone: (202) 463-8880
Background: Deputy Press Secretary, U.S. Senate Govern-
ment Affairs Committee, 1982-87. Press Secretary to
Gov. John Sununu of New Hampshire, 1988.

GRAHAM AND JAMES
2000 M St., N.W., Suite 700, Washington, DC 20036
Telephone: (202) 463-0800
Background: Washington office of a San Francisco law
firm.
Members of firm representing listed organizations:
Bank, Richard K.
Background: Director, Office of Maritime Affairs, U.S.
Dept. of State.
Boney Denison, Mary
Carlson, Eileen Shannon
Background: Legislative Assistant, Rep. J.J. Pickle (D-
TX), 1981-83; Attorney-Advisor, Office of Deputy
Chief Counsel for Import Administration, Depart-
ment of Commerce, 1984-86.
Cavanaugh, J. Michael
Background: Attorney-Advisor, Office of the General
Counsel, Maritime Administration, Department of
Commerce, 1974-77.
Dye, Stuart S.
Background: Secretary, Navy Staff, Deep Submergence
Systems Review Group, Office of Legislative Affairs,
1963-64. Special Assistant for Law of the Sea Mat-
ters, International Law Division, Office of the Judge
Advocate General, 1965-66.
Halperin, Eliot J.
Manelli, Daniel J.
McGill, Brian E.
Railsback, Thomas F.
Background: Member, U.S. House of Representatives
(R-IL), 1967-82.
Saito, Yoshihiro
Snyder, Jeffrey L.
Walders, Lawrence R.
Zhang, Samuel X.
Clients:
A/S Ivarans Rederi
American Hawaii Cruises *(J. Michael Cavanaugh,
Thomas F. Railsback)*
Cape Verde, Embassy of the Republic of
China Nat'l Machinery and Equipment Import
and Export Corp.
Contact Lens Manufacturers Ass'n *(Daniel J. Manel-
li)*
Contact Lens Manufacturers Ass'n Political Ac-
tion Committee *(Daniel J. Manelli)*
Disney Productions, Walt *(Eileen Shannon Carlson,
Thomas F. Railsback)*
Federal Administrative Law Judges' Conference
(Eileen Shannon Carlson, Thomas F. Railsback)

Federal Judges Ass'n *(Eileen Shannon Carlson, Thomas
F. Railsback)*
Frontier Express Inc. *(Eliot J. Halperin)*
Hitachi Zosen Corp. *(Brian E. McGill, Yoshihiro Saito)*
Holland America Line Westours Inc. *(Thomas F.
Railsback)*
ICI Americas Inc. *(Jeffrey L. Snyder)*
Illinois Health Facilities Authority *(Eileen Shannon
Carlson, Thomas F. Railsback)*
Internat'l Ass'n of Independent Tanker Owners
(Richard K. Bank, Stuart S. Dye)
Japan Electronic Industry Development Ass'n
Komatsu Ltd. *(Lawrence R. Walders)*
Mutual of Omaha Insurance Companies *(Thomas F.
Railsback)*
Nat'l Council of U.S. Magistrates *(Thomas F. Rails-
back)*
Neptune Orient Lines
Nippon Benkan Kogyo Co., Ltd. *(Yoshihiro Saito)*
Nippon Mining Co. *(Brian E. McGill, Yoshihiro Saito)*
Ohbayashi Corp.
Overseas Shipping Co. *(Eliot J. Halperin)*
Pacific Coast European Conference
Sierra Pacific Resources *(Thomas F. Railsback)*
Stock Information Group *(Eileen Shannon Carlson,
Thomas F. Railsback)*
TDK U.S.A. Corp. *(Jeffrey L. Snyder)*

GRAHAM, Lawrence T.
Exec. Director, Institute of Industrial Launderers
1730 M St., N.W. Suite 610, Washington, DC 20036
Telephone: (202) 296-6744

GRAHAM, Michael N.
Exec. V. President and COO, Reese Communications
Companies
2111 Wilson Ave., Suite 900, Arlington, VA 22201
Telephone: (703) 528-4400

GRAHAM, Nancy A.
Senior Associate, Institute for Soviet-American Relations
1608 New Hampshire Ave., N.W., Washington, DC 20009
Telephone: (202) 387-3034

GRAHAM, Thomas R.
Skadden, Arps, Slate, Meagher and Flom
1440 New York Ave., N.W., Washington, DC 20005
Telephone: (202) 371-7000
Background: Deputy General Counsel, Office of the United
States Trade Representative, Executive Office of the
President, 1974-79.
Clients:
Fuji Photo Film U.S.A.

GRAMLEY, Lyle E.
Sr. Staff V. President & Chief Economist, Mortgage Bank-
ers Ass'n of America
1125 15th St., N.W., Suite 700, Washington, DC 20005
Telephone: (202) 861-6500
Background: Former Governor, Federal Reserve Bank.

GRANAHAN, Frances M. Turk
Manager, Government Affairs, Panhandle Eastern Corp.
1025 Connecticut Ave., N.W., Suite 404, Washington, DC
20036
Telephone: (202) 331-8090
Registered as lobbyist at U.S. Congress.

GRANDISON, W. George
Steptoe and Johnson
1330 Connecticut Ave., N.W., Washington, DC 20036
Telephone: (202) 429-3000
Clients:
Nippon Steel Corp.

GRANESE, Nancy L.
Government Relations Advisor, Kutak Rock & Campbell
1101 Connecticut Ave., N.W. Suite 1000, Washington, DC
20036
Telephone: (202) 828-2400
Registered as lobbyist at U.S. Congress.
Background: Exec. V. President, KRC Resources Inc.
Clients:
Capital Markets Assurance Corp.
Financial Security Assurance, Inc.
Kutak Rock & Campbell Political Action Com-
mittee
Municipal Bond Insurance Ass'n
Summit, Ltd.

GRANGENOIS, Mireille
Director, Minority Affairs, American Soc. of Newspaper
Editors
11600 Sunrise Valley Drive, Reston, VA 22091
Telephone: (703) 684-1144

GRANGER, David I.
Clifford & Warnke
815 Connecticut Ave., N.W., Washington, DC 20006
Telephone: (202) 828-4200
Background: Attorney, Tax Division, U.S. Department of
Justice, 1961-1965.

GRANT, Andrea
Verner, Liipfert, Bernhard, McPherson and Hand, Chart-
ered
901 15th St., N.W., Suite 700, Washington, DC 20005
Telephone: (202) 371-6000
Registered as lobbyist at U.S. Congress.
Background: Attorney on the Oil Import Appeals Board,
1974-76.

GRANT, Dr. Carl
Group V. President, Communications, Chamber of Commerce of the U.S.A.
1615 H St., N.W., Washington, DC 20062
Telephone: (202) 463-5425

GRANT, James B.
Exec. Secretary, Nat'l Ass'n of State Departments of Agriculture
1616 H St., N.W., Washington, DC 20006
Telephone: (202) 628-1566

GRANT, Jeff
Federal Contracts Manager, Memorex Corp.
8609 Westwood Center Drive Suite 500, Vienna, VA
22182
Telephone: (703) 761-5600

GRANT, Kevin
Manager, State Affairs, American Newspaper Publishers
Ass'n
The Newspaper Center 11600 Sunrise Valley Drive, Res-
ton, VA 22091
Telephone: (703) 648-1000

GRANT, Robert
Dep Dir, Regul/Legis Analysis, DEPARTMENT OF COM-
MERCE - Office of Policy Analysis
14th and Constitution Ave. N.W., Room 4876, Washington,
DC 20230
Telephone: (202) 377-1985

GRANUM, James L.
Assistant V. President, Public Affairs, Norfolk Southern
Corp.
1500 K St., N.W., Suite 375, Washington, DC 20005
Telephone: (202) 383-4550
Registered as lobbyist at U.S. Congress.

GRANWELL, Alan W.
Cadwalader, Wickersham & Taft
1333 New Hampshire Ave., N.W. Suite 700, Washington,
DC 20036
Telephone: (202) 862-2200
Registered as Foreign Agent: (#3665).
Background: International Tax Counsel and Director, Of-
fice of International Tax Affairs, U.S. Dept. of the Treas-
ury, 1981-4.

GRASSER, John L. C.
Director, Media Relations, Nat'l Coal Ass'n
1130 17th St., N.W., Washington, DC 20036
Telephone: (202) 463-2651

GRASSI, Wendy Sears
Director, Communications, Citizens Network for Foreign
Affairs
1616 H St., N.W., Washington, DC 20006
Telephone: (202) 639-8889

GRASSO, Michele
Government Relations Manager, United States Trademark
Ass'n
6 East 45th St., New York, NY 10017
Telephone: (212) 986-5880

GRAU, John
Exec. V. President, Nat'l Electrical Contractors Ass'n
13th floor, 7315 Wisconsin Ave., Bethesda, MD 20814
Telephone: (301) 657-3110

GRAVELINK, Linda A.
Director of Regulation, Independent Bankers Ass'n of America
One Thomas Circle, N.W., Suite 950, Washington, DC 20005
Telephone: (202) 659-8111

GRAVES, David R.
President, Rice Millers' Ass'n
1235 Jefferson Davis Hwy. Suite 302, Arlington, VA 22202-3270
Telephone: (703) 920-1281

GRAVES, Ellen
Exec. Director, Nat'l Ass'n of Negro Business & Professional Women's Clubs, Inc.
1806 New Hampshire Ave., N.W., Washington, DC 20009
Telephone: (202) 483-4206

GRAVES RENEAU, Julia D.
Manager, Communications, Air Line Pilots Ass'n Internat'l
1625 Massachusetts Ave., N.W., Washington, DC 20036
Telephone: (202) 797-4003

GRAVES, Ruth P.
President, Reading is Fundamental, Inc.
600 Maryland Ave., S.W. Suite 500, Washington, DC 20560
Telephone: (202) 287-3220
Registered as lobbyist at U.S. Congress.

GRAVES, Thomas J.
Director Federal Affairs, Nat'l Paint and Coatings Ass'n
1500 Rhode Island Ave., N.W., Washington, DC 20005
Telephone: (202) 462-6272
Background: Former Counsel, U.S. Senate; Formerly with Office of General Counsel, Pension Benefit Guarantee Corp.

GRAVES, William J.
Assoc. Exec. Dir., Finan., Bus. Adm., American Occupational Therapy Ass'n
1383 Piccard Drive, Suite 300 P.O. Box 1725, Rockville, MD 20850
Telephone: (301) 948-9626
Background: Also serves as Treasurer, American Occupational Therapy Political Action Committee.

GRAY, Alan G.
President, Lonington, Inc.
218 N. Lee St., Alexandria, VA 22314
Telephone: (703) 548-6647
Clients:
AB Electronics Group Ltd.
Trackpower Transmissions, Ltd.

GRAY AND ASSOCIATES, DAVID C.
3728 Kanawha St., N.W., Washington, DC 20015
Telephone: (202) 966-0202
Background: Legislative consultants.
Members of firm representing listed organizations:
  Gray, David C.
Clients:
Portsmouth-Kittery Armed Services Committee, Inc. *(David C. Gray)*

GRAY, Carol J.
Federal Legislative Representative, American Council of Life Insurance
1001 Pennsylvania Ave., N.W., Washington, DC
Telephone: (202) 624-2158
Registered as lobbyist at U.S. Congress.

GRAY, Charles D.
Assistant General Counsel, Nat'l Ass'n of Regulatory Utility Commissioners
Box 684, I.C.C. Bldg., Washington, DC 20044-0684
Telephone: (202) 898-2200

GRAY, David C.
Gray and Associates, David C.
3728 Kanawha St., N.W., Washington, DC 20015
Telephone: (202) 966-0202
Registered as lobbyist at U.S. Congress.
Clients:

Portsmouth-Kittery Armed Services Committee, Inc.

GRAY, Gerald
Director of Resource Policy, American Forestry Ass'n
P.O. Box 2000, Washington, DC 20013
Telephone: (202) 667-3300

GRAY, General John O., (Ret.)
Exec. Director, Air Force Ass'n
1501 Lee Hwy., Arlington, VA 22209-1198
Telephone: (703) 247-5800

GRAY, John W., Jr.
Corp. V. Pres., Federal Gov't Affairs, AT&T
Suite 1000, 1120 20th St., N.W., Washington, DC 20036
Telephone: (202) 457-3843

GRAY, Larry
Legislative Coordinator, Nat'l Family Farm Coalition
80 F St., N.W. Suite 714, Washington, DC 20001
Telephone: (202) 737-2215

GRAY, Neil A.
Director, Government Relations, Highway Users Federation for Safety and Mobility
1776 Massachusetts Ave., N.W., Washington, DC
Telephone: (202) 857-1217
Registered as lobbyist at U.S. Congress.

GRAY, Peter
V. President, Domestic Government Rltns., Citicorp
1275 Pennsylvania Ave., N.W., Suite 503, Washington, DC 20004
Telephone: (202) 879-6800
Registered as lobbyist at U.S. Congress.

GRAY, Peter
Economist and Policy Analyst, Environmental Law Institute
1616 P St., N.W., Suite 200, Washington, DC 20036
Telephone: (202) 328-5150

GRAY, Robert Keith
Chairman, Hill and Knowlton Public Affairs Worldwide
Washington Harbour, 901 31st St., N.W., Washington, DC 20007
Telephone: (202) 333-7400
Registered as lobbyist at U.S. Congress.
Registered as Foreign Agent: (# 3301).
Background: Former Secretary of the Cabinet, Eisenhower Administration.
Clients:
American Airlines
AMR Corp.
Shaklee Corp.
Turkey, Government of

GRAY, Robert Reed
Of Counsel, Winthrop, Stimson, Putnam & Roberts
1133 Connecticut Ave., N.W. Suite 1000, Washington, DC 20036
Telephone: (202) 775-9800
Background: Staff of General Counsel, Civil Aeronautics Board, 1951-52 and Assistant Chief, International and Rules Division, CAB, 1953-55. Legal Advisor, DCNO (Air), 1952-53.
Clients:
CP Air
El Al Israel Airlines, Ltd.
Israel Aircraft Industries
Nigeria Airways
Polskie Linie Lotnicze
Quebecair
Saab-Scania of America
Scandinavian Airlines System (SAS)
Transportes Aereos Mercantiles Panamericanos
Varig Brazilian Airlines

GRAY, Robin B., Jr.
V. President, Admin. & Mbr. Svcs., American Soc. of Travel Agents
1101 King St., Alexandria, VA 22314
Telephone: (703) 739-2782

GRAY, Robin C.
Director of Public Affairs, Internat'l Life Sciences Institute Nutrition Foundation
1126 16th St., N.W., Suite 300, Washington, DC 20036
Telephone: (202) 659-0074

Background: Exec. Asst. to the Secretary, Dept. of Energy, 1985-89; Ass't Press Secretary to the President, The White House, 1981-85.

GRAY, Sandra Trice
V. President, Give Five Program, Independent Sector
1828 L St., N.W., Washington, DC 20036
Telephone: (202) 223-8100

GRAYBILL, Ginny L.
Assistant to the Exec. Director, American Pharmaceutical Institute
2215 Constitution Ave., N.W., Washington, DC 20037
Telephone: (202) 429-7514
Background: Former district office manager and legislative assistant to Rep. Terry L. Bruce (D-IL).

GREALIS, William J.
Akin, Gump, Strauss, Hauer and Feld
1333 New Hampshire Ave., N.W., Suite 400, Washington, DC 20036
Telephone: (202) 887-4000

GREALY COHEN, Catherine
Director, Washington Office, American Soc. of Clinical Pathologists
1101 Vermont Ave., N.W. 6th Floor, Washington, DC 20005
Telephone: (202) 371-0515

GREALY, Mary R.
Deputy Director and Executive Counsel, Federation of American Health Systems
1111 19th St., N.W. Suite 402, Washington, DC 20036
Telephone: (202) 833-3090
Registered as lobbyist at U.S. Congress.

GREELEGS, Ed
Director, Government Relations, Federal Nat'l Mortgage Ass'n
3900 Wisconsin Ave., N.W., Washington, DC 20016
Telephone: (202) 752-7000
Registered as lobbyist at U.S. Congress.

GREELEY, Donald R.
V. President, Government Relations, Hoechst-Celanese Corp.
919 18th St., N.W., Suite 700, Washington, DC 20006
Telephone: (202) 296-2890
Registered as lobbyist at U.S. Congress.
Background: Admin. Assistant to Representative Ralph J. Rivers (Alaska), 1959-1966. Exec. Assistant to Senator Ernest Gruening (Alaska), 1966-1968.

GREELEY, Paul J., Jr., CAE
President, American Chamber of Commerce Executives
4232 King St., Alexandria, VA 22302
Telephone: (703) 998-0072

GREEN, Ann
Adams Associates, John
1825 K St., N.W. Suite 210, Washington, DC 20006
Telephone: (202) 466-8320

GREEN, Barton C.
Sr. V. Pres., Gen. Counsel & Secy-Treas., American Iron and Steel Institute
1133 15th St., N.W., Suite 300, Washington, DC 20005-2701
Telephone: (202) 452-7143

GREEN, Bobby
Board Chairman, Nat'l Coalition of Title I/Chapter I Parents
Edmond School Bldg., 9th & D Sts., N.E., Rm. 201, Washington, DC 20002
Telephone: (202) 547-9286

GREEN, Brian
Director, Legislative Research, Air Force Ass'n
1501 Lee Hwy., Arlington, VA 22209-1198
Telephone: (703) 247-5800

GREEN, Carl J.
Milbank, Tweed, Hadley & McCloy
1825 Eye St., N.W. Suite 900, Washington, DC 20006
Telephone: (202) 835-7500
Background: Attorney/Advisor, U.S. Department of Transportation, 1968-69.

WASHINGTON REPRESENTATIVES

GREEN, Carol
Associate Director, American Cast Metals Ass'n
918 16th St., N.W., Suite 403, Washington, DC 20006
Telephone: (202) 833-1316

GREEN, Deborah
Administrative Director, Rainbow Lobby
1660 L St., N.W. Suite 204, Washington, DC 20036
Telephone: (202) 457-0700

GREEN, Edward M.
Chief Counsel, American Mining Congress
1920 N St., N.W. Suite 300, Washington, DC 20036
Telephone: (202) 861-2800
Registered as lobbyist at U.S. Congress.
Background: Formerly an attorney with the Department of Interior.

GREEN, Col. Fred K.
Legal & Legis Counsel to Chairman, JCS, DEPARTMENT OF DEFENSE - Joint Chiefs of Staff
The Pentagon, Washington, DC 20301
Telephone: (202) 697-1137

GREEN, Gary
Director, Legal Department, Air Line Pilots Ass'n Internat'l
1625 Massachusetts Ave., N.W., Washington, DC 20036
Telephone: (202) 797-4003

GREEN, George R.
V. President and Asst. General Counsel, Food Marketing Institute
1750 K St., N.W., Washington, DC 20006
Telephone: (202) 452-8444
Registered as lobbyist at U.S. Congress.

GREEN, Gretchen
Government Relations Analyst, Japan Economic Institute of America
1000 Connecticut Ave., N.W. Suite 211, Washington, DC 20036
Telephone: (202) 296-5633
Registered as lobbyist at U.S. Congress.
Registered as Foreign Agent (#0929)

GREEN, James E.
Manager, Government Relations, Mobil Corp.
1100 Connecticut Ave., N.W., Suite 620, Washington, DC 20036
Telephone: (202) 862-1300
Registered as lobbyist at U.S. Congress.

GREEN, Kaylene H.
Director, Washington Operations, Bath Iron Works Corp.
2341 Jefferson Davis Highway Suite 1100, Arlington, VA 22202
Telephone: (703) 979-2030
Registered as lobbyist at U.S. Congress.
Background: Serves also as contact for Bath Iron Works Corp. Political Action Committee.

GREEN, Lynn S.
Manager, Governmental Services, Institute of Makers of Explosives
1120 19th St., N.W., Suite 310, Washington, DC 20036-3605
Telephone: (202) 429-9280
Registered as lobbyist at U.S. Congress.

GREEN, Martin S.
Program Manager, Nat'l Ass'n of College and University Business Officers
One Dupont Circle, N.W., Suite 500, Washington, DC 20036-1178
Telephone: (202) 861-2500

GREEN, Micah S.
Sr. V. President, Legislative Affairs, Public Securities Ass'n
1000 Vermont Ave., N.W., Suite 800, Washington, DC 20005
Telephone: (202) 898-9390
Registered as lobbyist at U.S. Congress.

GREEN, Oliver W.
Internat'l Secretary-Treasurer, Amalgamated Transit Union
5025 Wisconsin Ave., N.W., Washington, DC 20016
Telephone: (202) 537-1645
Registered as lobbyist at U.S. Congress.

GREEN, Richard
Andrews and Kurth
1701 Pennsylvania Ave., N.W., Suite 200, Washington, DC 20006
Telephone: (202) 662-2700
Clients:
El Paso Natural Gas Co.

GREEN, Robert H.
Staff V. Pres, Fed. Taxation, Gov't Rtns, Nat'l Ass'n of REALTORS
777 14th St., N.W., Washington, DC 20005
Telephone: (202) 383-1124
Registered as lobbyist at U.S. Congress.

GREEN, Stanley J.
V. President-General Counsel, General Aviation Manufacturers Ass'n
1400 K St., Suite 801, Washington, DC 20005
Telephone: (202) 393-1500

GREEN, William J.
V. President, Government Relations, MacAndrews & Forbes Holdings, Inc.
1001 Pennsylvania Ave., N.W. Suite 715 South Concourse, Washington, DC 20004
Telephone: (202) 628-2600
Registered as lobbyist at U.S. Congress.

GREENAN, Linda
Director of Public Policy, Child Welfare League of America
440 First St., N.W., Suite 310, Washington, DC 20001
Telephone: (202) 638-2952

GREENBAUM, Dr. Leon J.
Exec. Director, Undersea and Hyperbaric Medical Soc.
9650 Rockville Pike, Bethesda, MD 20814
Telephone: (301) 571-1818

GREENBERG, David I.
Staff V. President, Washington Relations, Philip Morris Management Corp.
1341 G St., N.W., Suite 900, Washington, DC 20005
Telephone: (202) 637-1500
Registered as lobbyist at U.S. Congress.

GREENBERG, Edward D.
Galland, Kharasch, Morse and Garfinkle
Canal Square, 1054 31st St., N.W., Washington, DC 20007
Telephone: (202) 342-5200
Background: Regional Counsel, Interstate Commerce Commission, 1973-76. Special Counsel for Pipelines, Interstate Commerce Commission, 1977. Director and Chief Counsel, Trans Alaska Pipeline System Project, Federal Energy Regulatory Commission, 1978.
Clients:
Surface Freight Corp.

GREENBERG, Jon
Manager, Environmental Policy, Browning-Ferris Industries (D.C.), Inc.
1150 Connecticut Ave., N.W. Suite 500, Washington, DC 20036
Telephone: (202) 223-8151

GREENBERG, Judith M.
Miller & Steuart
1825 I St., N.W. Suite 400, Washington, DC 20006
Telephone: (202) 429-2017
Registered as lobbyist at U.S. Congress.
Clients:
Coastal Corp., The/ANR Pipeline Co.
Squibb and Sons, Inc., E. R.

GREENBERG, Mark
Senior Staff Attorney, Center for Law and Social Policy
1616 P St., N.W., Suite 350, Washington, DC 20036
Telephone: (202) 328-5140

GREENBERG, Robert
Vice President and General Counsel, American Soc. of Hospital Pharmacists
4630 Montgomery Ave., Bethesda, MD 20814
Telephone: (301) 657-3000

GREENBERGER, Marcia D.
Managing Attorney, Nat'l Women's Law Center
1616 P St., N.W., Washington, DC 20036
Telephone: (202) 328-5160

GREENBERGER, Phyllis
Ass't Dir., Political Ed. Coord., American Psychiatric Ass'n
1400 K St., N.W., Washington, DC 20005
Telephone: (202) 682-6046
Registered as lobbyist at U.S. Congress.

GREENBURG, David J.
Exec. Director, Nat'l Health Lawyers Ass'n
1620 Eye St., N.W. Suite 900, Washington, DC 20006
Telephone: (202) 833-1100
Background: Department of Labor, 1959-66.

GREENE, Col. Fred W., (Ret.)
V. President, Miller Associates, Denny
400 N. Capitol St., N.W. Suite 325, Washington, DC 20001
Telephone: (202) 783-0280
Registered as lobbyist at U.S. Congress.
Background: Former Chief of Staff, U.S. Army Armor Center, Fort Knox, Kentucky.

GREENE, H. Thomas
Exec. Director of Legislative Affairs, Nat'l Automobile Dealers Ass'n
412 First St., S.E., Washington, DC 20003
Telephone: (202) 547-5500
Registered as lobbyist at U.S. Congress.

GREENE, Ronald J.
Wilmer, Cutler and Pickering
2445 M St., N.W., Washington, DC 20037-1420
Telephone: (202) 663-6000
Registered as lobbyist at U.S. Congress.
Clients:
American Honda Motor Co.
Lederle Laboratories, American Cyanamid Co. Subsidiary
Trans Ocean Leasing Corp.

GREENER, Charles V.
V. President and Senior Associate, Mahe Company, The Eddie
900 Second St., N.E. Suite 200, Washington, DC 20002
Telephone: (202) 842-4100
Registered as lobbyist at U.S. Congress.
Background: Former Special Assistant, Legislative Affairs Office, The White House, under President Reagan.

GREENFIELD, Anne
Polit. Director, Political Field Optns., Nat'l Ass'n of REALTORS
777 14th St., N.W., Washington, DC 20005
Telephone: (202) 383-1000
Registered as lobbyist at U.S. Congress.

GREENFIELD, Suzanne
Political Organizer, Common Cause
2030 M St., N.W., Washington, DC 20036
Telephone: (202) 833-1200
Registered as lobbyist at U.S. Congress.

GREENLY, Ray
V. President, Public Relations, American Soc. of Travel Agents
1101 King St., Alexandria, VA 22314
Telephone: (703) 739-2782

GREENSTEIN, Robert
Exec. Director, Center on Budget and Policy Priorities
236 Massachusetts Ave., N.E., Suite 305, Washington, DC 20002
Telephone: (202) 544-0591
Registered as lobbyist at U.S. Congress.
Background: Special Assistant to the Secretary of Agriculture, 1977-78. Administrator, Food and Nutrition Service, Department of Agriculture, 1978-80.

GREENWALD, John D.
Wilmer, Cutler and Pickering
2445 M St., N.W., Washington, DC 20037-1420
Telephone: (202) 663-6000
Clients:
du Pont de Nemours and Co., E. I.

GREENWALT, Lynn A.
V. President, Internat'l Affairs, Nat'l Wildlife Federation
1412 16th St., N.W., Washington, DC 20036
Telephone: (202) 797-6669
Registered as lobbyist at U.S. Congress.

GREENWOOD, Richard
Assistant to the President, Internat'l Ass'n of Machinists and Aerospace Workers
1300 Connecticut Ave., N.W. Suite 404, Washington, DC 20036
Telephone: (202) 857-5200

GREER, Frank
Greer, Margolis, Mitchell & Associates
2626 Pennsylvania Ave., N.W. Suite 301, Washington, DC 20037
Telephone: (202) 338-8700
Clients:
Nat'l Abortion Rights Action League

GREER, John M.
Chairman, Graphic Communications Internat'l Union Political Contributions Committee
1900 L St., N.W., Washington, DC 20036
Telephone: (202) 462-1400

GREER, MARGOLIS, MITCHELL & ASSOCIATES
2626 Pennsylvania Ave., N.W. Suite 301, Washington, DC 20037
Telephone: (202) 338-8700
Background: A media consultant firm.
Members of firm representing listed organizations:
Greer, Frank
Clients:
Nat'l Abortion Rights Action League *(Frank Greer)*
Nat'l ORT Project

GREFE, Richard
V. President, Nat'l Ass'n of Public Television Stations
1350 Connecticut Ave., N.W. Suite 200, Washington, DC 20036
Telephone: (202) 887-1700

GREGG, Arthur J.
7736 Rockledge Court, Springfield, VA 22152
Telephone: (703) 978-7063
Registered as lobbyist at U.S. Congress.
Organizations represented:
Cable Television Ass'n of Maryland, Delaware and the District of Columbia

GREGG, R. T.
Director, Government Relations, United States Telephone Ass'n
900 19th St., N.W., Suite 800, Washington, DC 20006-2102
Telephone: (202) 835-3100
Registered as lobbyist at U.S. Congress.

GREGG, Sarah Massengal
Manager, Health Affairs, Baxter Internat'l Inc.
1667 K St., N.W., Suite 710, Washington, DC 20006
Telephone: (202) 223-4016
Registered as lobbyist at U.S. Congress.

GREGORY CO., THE
2300 N St., N.W., Suite 600, Washington, DC 20037
Telephone: (202) 663-9053
Background: A public and government relations firm.
Members of firm representing listed organizations:
Gregory, Neal, President
Background: U.S. House of Representatives, Committee on House Administration, 1976-81.
Clients:
Australia, Commonwealth of *(Neal Gregory)*
Australia, Embassy of *(Neal Gregory)*
Benevolent and Protective Order of Elks (BPOE) *(Neal Gregory)*
Ramirez & Co., T. *(Neal Gregory)*

GREGORY, Dolores
Consultant, Browning-Ferris Industries (D.C.), Inc.
1150 Connecticut Ave., N.W. Suite 500, Washington, DC 20036
Telephone: (202) 223-8151

GREGORY, Francis M., Jr.
Sutherland, Asbill and Brennan
1275 Pennsylvania, N.W., Washington, DC 20004-2404
Telephone: (202) 383-0100
Background: Law Clerk to U.S. Supreme Court Justice William J. Brennan, 1967-68.
Clients:
Equifax Inc.

GREGORY, Gwendolyn H.
Deputy General Counsel, Nat'l School Boards Ass'n
1680 Duke St., Alexandria, VA 22314
Telephone: (703) 838-6722

GREGORY, Jack
Fleishman-Hillard, Inc
1301 Connecticut Ave., N.W., Washington, DC 20036
Telephone: (202) 659-0330
Registered as lobbyist at U.S. Congress.
Clients:
Eveready

GREGORY, Janice M.
Legislative Director, ERISA Industry Committee (ERIC), The
1726 M St., N.W., Suite 1101, Washington, DC 20036
Telephone: (202) 833-2800
Registered as lobbyist at U.S. Congress.

GREGORY, Neal
President, Gregory Co., The
2300 N St., N.W., Suite 600, Washington, DC 20037
Telephone: (202) 663-9053
Registered as lobbyist at U.S. Congress.
Registered as Foreign Agent: (#156).
Background: U.S. House of Representatives, Committee on House Administration, 1976-81.
Clients:
Australia, Commonwealth of
Australia, Embassy of
Benevolent and Protective Order of Elks (BPOE)
Ramirez & Co., T.

GREINER, Linda W.
Manager, Government Relations, White Consolidated Industries
1317 F St., N.W. Suite 510, Washington, DC 20004
Telephone: (202) 638-7878
Registered as lobbyist at U.S. Congress.

GREISSING, Edward F., Jr.
V. President, Government Affairs, Upjohn Co.
1455 F St., N.W., Suite 450, Washington, DC 20005
Telephone: (202) 393-6040
Registered as lobbyist at U.S. Congress.

GREMEL, Lori
Legis Officer, Cong & Intergovt'l Affrs, DEPARTMENT OF LABOR
200 Constitution Ave., N.W., Washington, DC 20210
Telephone: (202) 523-6141

GRENIER, Edward J., Jr.
Sutherland, Asbill and Brennan
1275 Pennsylvania, N.W., Washington, DC 20004-2404
Telephone: (202) 383-0100
Clients:
American Industrial Clay Co.
Armco Inc.
Georgia Kaolin Co.
Process Gas Consumers Group

GREVE, Michael
Exec. Director, Center for Individual Rights
2300 N St., N.W. Suite 600, Washington, DC 20037
Telephone: (202) 663-9041

GRIBBIN, David
Asst Secy, Legis Affrs, DEPARTMENT OF DEFENSE
The Pentagon, Washington, DC 20301
Telephone: (202) 697-6210

GRIBBIN, David J., IV
Legislative Representative, Nat'l Federation of Independent Business
600 Maryland Ave., S.W., Suite 700, Washington, DC 20024
Telephone: (202) 554-9000
Registered as lobbyist at U.S. Congress.

GRIBBIN, Lori
Legis Affrs Office, DEPARTMENT OF COMMERCE - Nat'l Oceanic and Atmospheric Administration
14th and Constitution Ave. N.W., Washington, DC 20230
Telephone: (202) 377-4981

GRIBBON, Daniel M.
Covington and Burling
1201 Pennsylvania Ave., N.W., Box 7566, Washington, DC 20044
Telephone: (202) 662-6000
Clients:
du Pont de Nemours and Co., E. I.

GRIECO, Jeffrey J.
Murphy and Demory, Ltd.
2300 N St., N.W. Suite 725, Washington, DC 20037
Telephone: (202) 785-3323
Registered as lobbyist at U.S. Congress.
Clients:
California Energy Co.
Haiti, Government of
Korea Tacoma Marine Industries Inc.

GRIER, Phillip M.
Exec. Director, Nat'l Ass'n of College and University Attorneys
One Dupont Circle, N.W. Suite 620, Washington, DC 20036
Telephone: (202) 833-8390

GRIESINGER, Kathryn Joy
Mica, Dudinsky & Associates
201 Massachusetts Ave., N.E., Suite C-9, Washington, DC 20002
Telephone: (202) 543-2143
Background: Staff aide to Rep. Dick Schulze (R-PA), 1984-85. Minority Staff Member, House Committee on Science, Space and Technology, 1985-87.

GRIESSBACH, Dr. Lothar
President and CEO, Representative for German Industry and Trade
One Farragut Square South 1634 Eye St., N.W., Washington, DC 20006
Telephone: (202) 347-0247
Registered as Foreign Agent: (#4274).
Clients:
Bundesverband der Deutschen Industrie
Deutscher Industrie und Handelstag

GRIFFEE, Ellen
Government Relations Director, Ass'n of Science-Technology Centers
1413 K St., N.W. 10th Floor, Washington, DC 20005
Telephone: (202) 371-1171
Registered as lobbyist at U.S. Congress.

GRIFFIN COMMUNICATIONS
713 Park St., S.E., Vienna, VA 22180
Telephone: (703) 255-2211
Registered as Foreign Agent: (#3913)
Background: A public relations consulting firm.
Members of firm representing listed organizations:
Griffin, Frances, President
Clients:
Eagle Forum *(Frances Griffin)*
Free Angola Information Service *(Frances Griffin)*

GRIFFIN, Frances
President, Griffin Communications
713 Park St., S.E., Vienna, VA 22180
Telephone: (703) 255-2211
Registered as Foreign Agent: (#3913).
Clients:
Eagle Forum
Free Angola Information Service

GRIFFIN, JOHNSON & ASSOCIATES
1211 Connecticut Ave., N.W., Suite 700, Washington, DC 20036
Telephone: (202) 775-8116
Members of firm representing listed organizations:
Dover, G. Jack, Principal
Background: Former aide to Rep. Dennis Eckert (D-OH) and Senator John Glenn (D-OH) and a former member of President Jimmy Carter's Domestic Policy Staff.
Griffin, Patrick J.

The listings in this directory are available as *Mailing Labels*. See last page.

169

GRIFFIN, JOHNSON & ASSOCIATES (Cont'd)

Background: Former Secretary to the Minority, 1982-85, U.S. Senate; Professional staff, Democratic Policy Committee, Senate Budget Committee and Department of Health and Human Services.

Johnson, David E.
Background: Former Executive Director, Democratic Senatorial Campaign Committee, 1985-86; Administrative Assistant to Senator George Mitchell (D-ME); Deputy Assistant Secretary, Department of Health and Human Services; Counsel, U.S. Governmental Affairs Committee, U.S. Senate.

Johnston, N. Hunter
Background: Former law clerk, U.S. District Court, Eastern District of Louisiana.

Kitzmiller, W. Michael, Principal
Background: Former Staff Director, House Energy and Commerce Committee.

Smith, Larry E.
Background: Former Minority Staff Director, Senate Committee on Rules and Administration. Deputy Sergeant at Arms, U.S. Senate, 1981-83. Sergeant at Arms, U.S. Senate, 1983-85.

Clients:
Air Transport Ass'n of America
American Coal Ash Ass'n
American Nuclear Energy Council
American Psychological Ass'n
Andersen and Co., Arthur
Blue Cross and Blue Shield Ass'n *(David E. Johnson)*
CBS, Inc.
Communications Satellite Corp. (COMSAT)
Grumman Corp. *(David E. Johnson)*
Martin Marietta Corp.
McCaw Cellular Communications Cos.
Merck and Co.
Nat'l Music Publishers' Ass'n
NUS Corp.
Outdoor Advertising Ass'n of America *(Patrick J. Griffin, David E. Johnson)*
Pharmaceutical Manufacturers Ass'n
Puyallup Tribe of Indians
Tobacco Institute
United Cable Television

GRIFFIN, Melanie
Associate Washington Representative, Sierra Club
408 C St., N.E., Washington, DC 20002
Telephone: (202) 547-1141
Registered as lobbyist at U.S. Congress.

GRIFFIN, Patrick J.
Griffin, Johnson & Associates
1211 Connecticut Ave., N.W., Suite 700, Washington, DC 20036
Telephone: (202) 775-8116
Registered as lobbyist at U.S. Congress.
Background: Former Secretary to the Minority, 1982-85, U.S. Senate; Professional staff, Democratic Policy Committee, Senate Budget Committee and Department of Health and Human Services.
Clients:
Outdoor Advertising Ass'n of America

GRIFFIN, Richard
Director, Government Relations, General Signal Corp.
1735 Eye St., N.W., Suite 917, Washington, DC 20006
Telephone: (202) 785-3076

GRIFFIN, Robert T.
Staff Executive, Washington Office, Chrysler Corp.
1100 Connecticut Ave., N.W., Washington, DC 20036
Telephone: (202) 862-5422
Registered as lobbyist at U.S. Congress.

GRIFFITH, Melanie
Gold and Liebengood, Inc.
1455 Pennsylvania Ave., N.W. Suite 950, Washington, DC 20004
Telephone: (202) 639-8899
Background: Former Aide to U.S. Senate Committee on Finance.

GRIFFITHS, Ann Mills
Exec. Director, Nat'l League of Families of American Prisoners and Missing in Southeast Asia
1001 Connecticut Ave., N.W. Suite 219, Washington, DC 20036
Telephone: (202) 223-6846

GRIFFITHS, Mark N.
Smith, Bucklin and Associates
1101 Connecticut Ave., N.W., Suite 700, Washington, DC 20036
Telephone: (202) 857-1100
Background: Director of Government Relations, Nat'l Ass'n of Metal Finishers and Adhesive Manufacturers Ass'n.
Clients:
Adhesives Manufacturers Ass'n
Nat'l Ass'n of Metal Finishers

GRIGGS, Henry
Account Supervisor, Gallagher-Widmeyer Group Inc., The
1110 Vermont Ave., N.W., Suite 1020, Washington, DC 20005
Telephone: (202) 659-1606

GRIGSBY, McGee
Latham and Watkins
1001 Pennsylvania Ave., N.W., Suite 1300, Washington, DC 20004
Telephone: (202) 637-2200

GRILL, Phillip M.
V. President, Government Relations, Matson Navigation Co.
444 North Capitol St., Suite 514, Washington, DC 20001
Telephone: (202) 833-3555

GRIM, Rebecca W.
Exec. Secretary, Nat'l Ass'n of Educational Office Personnel
7223 Lee Highway, #301, Falls Church, VA 22046
Telephone: (703) 533-0810

GRIMALDI, Alan M.
Howrey and Simon
1730 Pennsylvania Ave., N.W., Washington, DC 20006-4793
Telephone: (202) 783-0800
Clients:
Shell Oil Co.

GRIMES, A. Jack
Director of Government Affairs, Nat'l Pest Control Ass'n
8100 Oak St., Dunn Loring, VA 22027
Telephone: (703) 573-8330
Registered as lobbyist at U.S. Congress.
Background: Also serves as contact for the Nat'l Pest Control Ass'n Political Action Committee.

GRIMES, Kathy J.
Exec. Director, Nat'l Ass'n of Development Companies
1730 Rhode Island Ave., N.W., Suite 209, Washington, DC 20036
Telephone: (202) 785-8484
Registered as lobbyist at U.S. Congress.

GRIMM, Craig N.
Asst. Dir., Manpower & Training Svcs., Associated General Contractors of America
1957 E St., N.W., Washington, DC 20006
Telephone: (202) 393-2040
Registered as lobbyist at U.S. Congress.

GRIMM, Rodman D.
President, Burgum & Grimm, Ltd.
106 North Carolina Ave., S.E., Washington, DC 20003
Telephone: (202) 546-3414
Registered as Foreign Agent: (#4301).
Background: Formerly Industry Program Officer, Office of Nuclear Energy, ERDA and Special Assistant, Assistant Secretary for Economic Affairs, Department of Commerce. President of Burgum & Grimm Ltd.
Clients:
Committee for Free Elections and Democracy in Nicaragua

GRINER, G. Christopher
Gardner, Carton and Douglas
1001 Pennsylvania Ave., N.W., Suite 750, Washington, DC 20004
Telephone: (202) 347-9200
Registered as lobbyist at U.S. Congress.

GRISKIVICH, Peter
V. President, Motor Truck Mfrs. Division, Motor Vehicle Manufacturers Ass'n of the United States
1620 Eye St., N.W. Suite 1000, Washington, DC 20006
Telephone: (202) 775-2700

GRISSO, Michael E.
Director, Legislative Affairs, Pagonis and Donnelly Group
1620 Eye St., N.W., Suite 603, Washington, DC 20006
Telephone: (202) 452-8811
Registered as lobbyist at U.S. Congress.
Background: Former legislative assistant to House Speaker Jim Wright (D-TX).
Clients:
Burroughs Wellcome Co.
Dow Chemical
Harrah's
Holiday Corp.

GRKAVAC, Olga
Sr. V. President, Government Relations, ADAPSO, the Computer Software & Services Industry Ass'n
1300 North 17th St. Suite 300, Arlington, VA 22209
Telephone: (703) 522-5055
Registered as lobbyist at U.S. Congress.
Background: Also responsible for the ADAPSO PAC.

GROAH, William J.
Technical Director, Hardwood Plywood Manufacturers Ass'n
1825 Michael Faraday Dr., Reston, VA 22090
Telephone: (703) 435-2900

GROFF, James B.
Exec. Director, Nat'l Ass'n of Water Companies
1725 K St., N.W. Suite 1212, Washington, DC 20006
Telephone: (202) 833-8383
Background: Served for over 24 years in the Civil Engineer Corps, U.S. Navy, retiring as a Captain.

GROHL, James
Sr. VP, Spec Ass't to the Pres, Commun., United States League of Savings Institutions
1709 New York Ave., N.W., Suite 801, Washington, DC 20006
Telephone: (202) 637-8900

GROHL, Renie Yoshida
Sr. V. Pres., Group Exec. Regul. Affairs, United States League of Savings Institutions
1709 New York Ave., N.W., Suite 801, Washington, DC 20006
Telephone: (202) 637-8900

GRONER, N. Isaac
1615 L St., N.W., Suite 970, Washington, DC 20036-5602
Telephone: (202) 331-8888
Members of firm representing listed organizations:
Groner, Isaac N.
Background: Law Clerk to Chief Justice Vinson 1948-50; Dep't of Justice 1950-51; Chief Counsel, Wage Stabilization Board 1951-53.
Organizations represented:
Nat'l Ass'n of Postmasters of the U.S. *(Isaac N. Groner)*

GRONER, Isaac N.
Groner, N. Isaac
1615 L St., N.W., Suite 970, Washington, DC 20036-5602
Telephone: (202) 331-8888
Background: Law Clerk to Chief Justice Vinson 1948-50; Dep't of Justice 1950-51; Chief Counsel, Wage Stabilization Board 1951-53.
Organizations represented:
Nat'l Ass'n of Postmasters of the U.S.

GRONINGER, James N.
Federal Gov't Affairs Representative, Texaco U.S.A.
1050 17th St., N.W., Suite 500, Washington, DC 20036
Telephone: (202) 331-1427
Registered as lobbyist at U.S. Congress.

GROOM, Beverly L.
Federal Legislative Representative, American Council of Life Insurance
1001 Pennsylvania Ave., N.W., Washington, DC 20004-2599
Telephone: (202) 624-2159
Registered as lobbyist at U.S. Congress.

GROOM AND NORDBERG
1701 Pennsylvania Ave., N.W., Suite 1200, Washington, DC 20006
Telephone: (202) 857-0620
Members of firm representing listed organizations:
Groom, Theodore R.
Harding, Robert B.
  Background: Assistant to Rep. Charles A. Halleck, Office of Minority Leader, House of Representatives, 1963-67. Attorney, Securities and Exchange Commission, 1967-68. Special Assistant to the Secretary for Congressional Affairs, HEW, 1970-71.
Holmes, Peter E., Legislative Affairs Consultant
Howell, Elizabeth C , Legislative Affairs Consultant
Nordberg, Carl A. (Jr.)
Rabinowitz, Julie M.
Schiffbauer, William G.
Clients:
  Ad Hoc MGA Group *(Theodore R. Groom)*
  American Petroleum Institute *(Carl A. Nordberg, Jr.)*
  Chevron Corp. *(Robert B. Harding, Carl A. Nordberg, Jr.)*
  Lilly and Co., Eli *(Robert B. Harding, Carl A. Nordberg, Jr.)*
  Murphy Oil U.S.A. *(Carl A. Nordberg, Jr.)*
  Nebraska Public Power District *(William G. Schiffbauer)*
  Phillips Petroleum Co. *(Robert B. Harding, Carl A. Nordberg, Jr.)*
  Physicians Mutual Insurance Co. *(Theodore R. Groom, Robert B. Harding)*
  Principal Financial Group, The *(Theodore R. Groom, Robert B. Harding)*
  Prudential-Bache Securities, Inc. *(Robert B. Harding)*
  Prudential Insurance Co. of America *(Theodore R. Groom, Robert B. Harding)*
  Puerto Rico, U.S.A. Foundation *(Peter E. Holmes, Carl A. Nordberg, Jr.)*
  Reading and Bates Corp. *(Carl A. Nordberg, Jr.)*
  Southern California Edison Co. *(Robert B. Harding)*
  Sunflower Electric Cooperative, Inc. *(Robert B. Harding, William G. Schiffbauer)*
  True Oil Co. *(Julie M. Rabinowitz)*
  Union Texas Petroleum *(Robert B. Harding, Carl A. Nordberg, Jr.)*
  Westinghouse Electric Corp. *(Robert B. Harding, Carl A. Nordberg, Jr.)*

GROOM, Theodore R.
Groom and Nordberg
1701 Pennsylvania Ave., N.W., Suite 1200, Washington, DC 20006
Telephone: (202) 857-0620
Registered as lobbyist at U.S. Congress.
Clients:
  Ad Hoc MGA Group
  Physicians Mutual Insurance Co.
  Principal Financial Group, The
  Prudential Insurance Co. of America

GROSS, Anne
Program Manager, Nat'l Ass'n of College and University Business Officers
One Dupont Circle, N.W., Suite 500, Washington, DC 20036-1178
Telephone: (202) 861-2500

GROSS, Beth
Senior Account Executive, Powell, Adams & Rinehart
1901 L St., N.W., 3rd Floor, Washington, DC 20036
Telephone: (202) 466-7590

GROSS, George
Exec. V. President, Government Affairs, Magazine Publishers of America
1211 Connecticut Ave., N.W. Suite 406, Washington, DC 20036
Telephone: (202) 296-7277
Registered as lobbyist at U.S. Congress.
Background: Also serves as Treasurer, Magazine Publishers of America Political Action Committee.

GROSS, Kenneth A.
Skadden, Arps, Slate, Meagher and Flom
1440 New York Ave., N.W., Washington, DC 20005
Telephone: (202) 371-7000
Background: Former Associate General Counsel, Federal Election Commission.

GROSS, Malvern J.
President, Nat'l Aeronautic Ass'n of the U.S.A.
1763 R St., N.W., Washington, DC 20009
Telephone: (202) 265-8720

GROSS, Nina
Dir, Legis Affrs, SECURITIES AND EXCHANGE COMMISSION
450 5th St., N.W., Washington, DC 20549
Telephone: (202) 272-2500

GROSS, Richard
Chairperson, Nat'l Consortium for Child Mental Health Services
3615 Wisconsin Ave., N.W., Washington, DC 20016
Telephone: (202) 966-7300

GROSS, Richard A.
Foley, Hoag and Eliot
1615 L St., N.W., Suite 950, Washington, DC 20036
Telephone: (202) 775-0600
Registered as lobbyist at U.S. Congress.
Background: Exec. Director, U.S. Consumer Protection Safety Commission, 1979-81.

GROSSI, Ralph E.
President, American Farmland Trust
1920 N St., N.W., Suite 400, Washington, DC 20036
Telephone: (202) 659-5170

GROSSMAN AND FLASK
1101 14th St., N.W. Suite 800, Washington, DC 20005
Telephone: (202) 842-4840
Members of firm representing listed organizations:
Flask, Jon T.
  Background: Trial Attorney, Office of Chief Counsel, Internal Revenue Service, 1971-75.
Grossman, Robert D. (Jr.)
  Background: Senior Trial Attorney, Office of Chief Counsel, Internal Revenue Service, 1971-75.

GROSSMAN, Jerome, Jr.
Treasurer, PEACE PAC
100 Maryland Ave., N.E., Washington, DC 20002
Telephone: (202) 543-4100
Registered as lobbyist at U.S. Congress.

GROSSMAN, Robert D., Jr.
Grossman and Flask
1101 14th St., N.W. Suite 800, Washington, DC 20005
Telephone: (202) 842-4840
Background: Senior Trial Attorney, Office of Chief Counsel, Internal Revenue Service, 1971-75.

GROSSMAN, Steven A.
V. President, Corporate & Polit. Affairs, Hill and Knowlton Public Affairs Worldwide
Washington Harbour, 901 31st St., N.W., Washington, DC 20007
Telephone: (202) 333-7400
Background: Former Deputy Assistant Secretary for Health, U.S. Department of Health and Human Services.
Clients:
  Mary Kay Cosmetics

GROSVENOR, Gilbert M.
President & Chairman of the Board, Nat'l Geographic Soc.
1145 17th St., N.W., Washington, DC 20036
Telephone: (202) 857-7000

GROVE, JASKIEWICZ, GILLIAM AND COBERT
1730 M St., N.W. Suite 501, Washington, DC 20036
Telephone: (202) 296-2900
Members of firm representing listed organizations:
Calderwood, James A.
  Background: Trial Attorney, Department of Justice, Antitrust Division, 1970-73. Special Assistant U.S. Attorney for the District of Columbia, 1973. Trial Attorney and Senior Trial Attorney, Department of Justice, Antitrust Division, 1974-78.
Cobert, Ronald N.
  Background: General Counsel, American Institute for Shippers' Ass'ns.
Danas, Andrew M.
Jaskiewicz, Leonard A.
Clients:
  American Institute for Shippers' Ass'ns *(Ronald N. Cobert)*
  Bulk Carrier Conference, Inc. *(Leonard A. Jaskiewicz)*

Intermodal Marketing Ass'n
Intermodal Transportation Ass'n *(Leonard A. Jaskiewicz)*
Soc. of Glass and Ceramic Decorators *(James A. Calderwood)*
United Van Lines, Inc. *(James A. Calderwood)*

GROVE, Jon P., CAE
Exec. Vice President, American Soc. of Ass'n Executives
1575 Eye St., N.W., Washington, DC 20005-1168
Telephone: (202) 626-2723

GROVE, V. P.
V. President, Government Affairs, Oshkosh Truck Corp.
4660 Kenmore Ave. Suite 1018, Alexandria, VA 22304
Telephone: (703) 823-9778

GROVE, William A., Jr.
Exec. Director - Congressional Relations, Chesapeake and Potomac Telephone Co.
1710 H St., N.W., Washington, DC 20006
Telephone: (202) 392-1905
Background: Serves as Vice Chairman and Administrator, Chesapeake and Potomac Telephone Co. Federal Political Action Committee.

GRUBB, Leslae
Agriculture Council of America
1250 I St., N.W., Suite 601, Washington, DC 20005
Telephone: (202) 682-9200

GRUENBURG, Drew
V. President, Government Relations, Soc. of American Florists
1601 Duke St., Alexandria, VA 22314
Telephone: (703) 836-8700

GRUENINGER, Antoinette
Manager, Public Relations, Center for Media and Public Affairs
2101 L St., N.W., Suite 505, Washington, DC 20037
Telephone: (202) 223-2942

GRUMBLY, Thomas P.
President, Clean Sites, Inc.
1199 North Fairfax St., Alexandria, VA 22314
Telephone: (703) 739-1275

GRUNBERG, Carole
Senior Associate and Trade Consultant, APCO Associates
1155 21st St., N.W., Suite 1000, Washington, DC 20036
Telephone: (202) 778-1000
Background: Former Staff Director, House Foreign Affairs Subcommittee on Trade and Economic Policy.

GRUNDMAN, Stacey
Podesta Associates
424 C St., N.E., Washington, DC 20002
Telephone: (202) 544-6906

GRUPENHOFF, Dr. John T.
6410 Rockledge Drive, Bethesda, MD 20817
Telephone: (301) 571-9790
Background: A government relations consultant.
Organizations represented:
  American Academy of Dermatology
  American Academy of Otolaryngology-Head and Neck Surgery
  American Soc. of Clinical Oncology
  Cooley's Anemia Foundation

GUBSER, Peter A.
President, American Near East Refugee Aid
1522 K St., N.W. Suite 202, Washington, DC 20005
Telephone: (202) 347-2558

GUENTHER, Kenneth A.
Exec. V. President, Independent Bankers Ass'n of America
One Thomas Circle, N.W., Suite 950, Washington, DC 20005
Telephone: (202) 659-8111
Registered as lobbyist at U.S. Congress.
Background: Former Assistant to the Board of Governors of the Federal Reserve System, Presidential appointee in the Treaury Department, economic assistant to Sen. Jacob Javits (D-NY) and Foreign Service Officer, Department of State.

WASHINGTON REPRESENTATIVES

GUERRA-MONDRAGON, Gabriel
V. President, Keefe Co., The
444 North Capitol St., N.W., Suite 711, Washington, DC
20001
Telephone: (202) 638-7030
Registered as lobbyist at U.S. Congress.
Background: President, TKC Internat'l.

GUERRERO, Gene
Field Coordinator & Legislative Rep., American Civil Liberties Union
122 Maryland Ave., N.E., Washington, DC 20002
Telephone: (202) 544-1681
Registered as lobbyist at U.S. Congress.

GUEST, Mary Scott
Legislative Consultant, O'Connor & Hannan
1919 Pennsylvania Ave., N.W., Suite 800, Washington, DC
20006
Telephone: (202) 887-1400
Registered as lobbyist at U.S. Congress.
Clients:
Naegle Outdoor Advertising
Paine Webber Group
Western Electrochemical Co.

GUGGOLZ, Richard A.
Drohan Management Group
1600 Wilson Blvd., Suite 905, Arlington, VA 22209
Telephone: (703) 525-2722
Background: Serves as Exec. Director, Nat'l Ass'n of
Rehabilitation Agencies and Exec. Director, American
Ass'n of Surgeon's Assistants.
Clients:
American Ass'n of Surgeons Assistants
Nat'l Ass'n of Rehabilitation Agencies

GUINEY, Shannon P.
Washington Representative, Sun Co.
555 13th St., N.W., Suite 1010 East, Washington, DC
20004
Telephone: (202) 628-1010
Registered as lobbyist at U.S. Congress.

GUINIVEN, John E.
Director, Washington Public Relations, Chrysler Corp.
1100 Connecticut Ave., N.W., Washington, DC 20036
Telephone: (202) 862-5409
Registered as lobbyist at U.S. Congress.

GUION, John F.
President, Ass'n of Publicly Traded Companies
1707 L St., N.W., Suite 950, Washington, DC 20036
Telephone: (202) 785-9200

GUIRARD, James E., Jr.
1730 Rhode Island Ave., N.W. Suite 419, Washington, DC
20036
Telephone: (202) 293-3411
Background: An attorney and government relations consultant. Served as Nat'l Affairs Director, American Security
Council Foundation, 1981. Formerly Administrative Assistant to Senator Russell Long of Louisiana, 1972-80; to
Senator Allen Ellender of Louisiana, 1968-72; and to
Rep. Edwin E. Willis of Lousiana, 1964-68.
Organizations represented:
BASF Corp.
KMS Industries, Inc.
Walk-Haydel & Associates Inc.

GULICK, Lewis
President, American Great Lakes Ports
1911 North Fort Meyer Drive, Arlington, VA 22209
Telephone: (703) 276-9093
Registered as lobbyist at U.S. Congress.

GULINO, Denny
V. President, Media Relations, Nat'l Ass'n of Manufacturers
1331 Pennsylvania Ave., N.W. Suite 1500 North, Washington, DC 20004-1703
Telephone: (202) 637-3000

GULLETT, John
Exec. Director, American Council on the Environment
1301 20th St., N.W. Suite 113, Washington, DC 20036
Telephone: (202) 659-1900

GUM, Deborah H.
Office Supervisor, Government Relations, Capital Cities/
ABC Inc.
2445 M St., N.W., Suite 480, Washington, DC 20037-1420
Telephone: (202) 887-7777
Registered as lobbyist at U.S. Congress.

GUNDERSON, Christine
Confidental Asst, Cong Rels, DEPARTMENT OF AGRICULTURE
14th and Independence Ave. S.W., Room 234-E, Washington, DC 20205
Telephone: (202) 447-7095

GUNDLING, Lisa
Public Information Specialist, American Running and Fitness Ass'n
9310 Old Georgetown Rd., Bethesda, MD 20814
Telephone: (301) 897-0197

GURECK, William
V. President, Field Operations, Lockheed, Sanders Inc.
1735 Jefferson Davis Hwy., Suite 700, Arlington, VA
22202
Telephone: (703) 920-5204

GURVITCH, Gerry
Executive Director, Genetics Soc. of America
9650 Rockville Pike, Bethesda, MD 20814
Telephone: (301) 571-1825

GUSLER, Dorothy J.
Sr. Federal Affairs Representative, Amax Inc.
1819 L St., N.W., Suite 300, Washington, DC 20036-3895
Telephone: (202) 466-6966

GUTHRIE, Anne
Capitol Associates, Inc.
426 C St., N.E., Washington, DC 20002
Telephone: (202) 544-1880
Registered as lobbyist at U.S. Congress.

GUTHRIE, Robert F.
Asst. Dir., Dept. for Prof. Employees, AFL-CIO (American
Federation of Labor and Congress of Industrial Organizations)
Room 608, 815 16th St., N.W., Washington, DC 20006
Telephone: (202) 638-0320
Registered as lobbyist at U.S. Congress.

GUTSCHICK, Kenneth A.
Technical Director, Nat'l Lime Ass'n
3601 North Fairfax Drive, Arlington, VA 22201
Telephone: (703) 243-5463

GUTTENBERG & COMPANY
700 S. Washington St. Suite 218, Alexandria, VA 22314
Telephone: (703) 836-6100
Background: A public relations/public affairs counseling
firm.
Members of firm representing listed organizations:
Guttenberg, John P. (Jr.), President
Clients:
Council on Competitiveness *(John P. Guttenberg, Jr.)*
Federal Data Corp. *(John P. Guttenberg, Jr.)*
Health Industry Manufacturers Ass'n *(John P. Guttenberg, Jr.)*

GUTTENBERG, John P., Jr.
President, Guttenberg & Company
700 S. Washington St. Suite 218, Alexandria, VA 22314
Telephone: (703) 836-6100
Clients:
Council on Competitiveness
Federal Data Corp.
Health Industry Manufacturers Ass'n

GUTTENTAG, Joseph H.
Of Counsel, Arnold & Porter
1200 New Hampshire Ave., N.W., Washington, DC 20036
Telephone: (202) 872-6700
Background: Special Assistant for International Tax Affairs, U.S. Department of Treasury, 1967-68.

GUTTING, Richard
V. President, Government Relations, Nat'l Fisheries Institute
1525 Wilson Blvd., Suite 500, Arlington, VA 22209
Telephone: (703) 524-8880

Registered as lobbyist at U.S. Congress.

GUTTMAN, Alvin M.
1924 N St., N.W., Washington, DC 20036
Telephone: (202) 293-2525
Background: An attorney. Serves as Legislative Counsel to
the Towing and Recovery Ass'n of America.
Organizations represented:
Towing and Recovery Ass'n of America

GUTTMAN, Daniel
Special Counsel, Spiegel and McDiarmid
1350 New York Ave., N.W., Suite 1100, Washington, DC
20005
Telephone: (202) 879-4000
Registered as lobbyist at U.S. Congress.
Background: Subcommittee on Civil Service and General
Services, U.S. Senate Committee on Governmental Affairs, 1980.

GUTTMAN, Robert M.
Consultant, Interstate Conference of Employment Security
Agencies
444 North Capitol St., N.W. Suite 126, Washington, DC
20001-1571
Telephone: (202) 628-5588
Background: Formerly Minority Counsel, Senate Labor and
Human Resouces Subcommittee on Labor; Counsel to
then Senator Dan Quayle (R-IN); and Chief of Staff to
Vice President Quayle.

GUY, John H., IV
Deputy Exec. Director, Nat'l Petroleum Council
1625 K St., N.W., Suite 600, Washington, DC 20006
Telephone: (202) 393-6100

GUYER, Susanne
Director, Fed., Regulatory Matters (FCC), NYNEX
1828 L St., N.W., Suite 1000, Washington, DC 20036
Telephone: (202) 416-0100

GUZICK, William J.
Skadden, Arps, Slate, Meagher and Flom
1440 New York Ave., N.W., Washington, DC 20005
Telephone: (202) 371-7000
Clients:
Chain Pharmacy Ass'n of New York State

GWIRTZMAN, Milton
Van Dyk Associates, Inc.
1250 24th St., N.W., Suite 600, Washington, DC 20037
Telephone: (202) 223-4880
Registered as lobbyist at U.S. Congress.
Clients:
Boston Co., The
Browning-Ferris Industries (D.C.), Inc.

HAAKE, Jane Scherer
Senior Washington Representative, Mead Corp.
1667 K St., N.W., Suite 420, Washington, DC 20006
Telephone: (202) 833-9643
Registered as lobbyist at U.S. Congress.

HAAKE, Timothy M.
O'Connor & Hannan
1919 Pennsylvania Ave., N.W., Suite 800, Washington, DC
20006
Telephone: (202) 887-1400
Registered as lobbyist at U.S. Congress.
Registered as Foreign Agent: (#2972).
Background: Tax Counsel to Congressman Cecil Heftel,
1980-82, and to Senator H. John Heinz, 1979-80. Legislative Director to Congressman Richard T. Schulze, 1977-79. Attorney, Internal Revenue Service, 1973-77.
Clients:
American Bus Ass'n
American Health Care Ass'n
American Orthotic and Prosthetic Ass'n
American Soc. of Ass'n Executives
British Consortium, The
Connaught Laboratories, Inc.
Electronic Data Processing Auditors Ass'n
Internat'l Ass'n of Convention and Visitor Bureaus
Nat'l Funeral Directors Ass'n
Nat'l Retail Hardware Ass'n
SmithKline Beecham
Warner-Lambert Co.

HAAN, L. Russell
Treasurer, Internat'l Hardwood Products Ass'n INPAC
Box 1308, Alexandria, VA 22313
Telephone: (703) 836-6696

HAAS, Barbara
Director, Corporate Conservation Council, Nat'l Wildlife
Federation
1400 16th St., N.W., Washington, DC 20036-2266
Telephone: (202) 797-6800

HAAS, Dana W.
1800 K St., N.W., Suite 1018, Washington, DC 20006
Telephone: (202) 887-0497
Background: A federal affairs representative. Legislative
Assistant to Rep. Robert Whittaker (R-KS), 1978-82; and
to Rep. James Slattery (D-KS), 1983.
Organizations represented:
Empire District Electric Co.
Kansas City Power & Light Co.
Kansas Gas & Electric Co.

HAAS, Ellen
Exec. Director, Public Voice for Food and Health Policy
1001 Connecticut Ave., N.W., Suite 522, Washington, DC
20036
Telephone: (202) 659-5930

HAAS, Richard T.
V. President, Public Affairs, Associated Builders and Contractors
729 15th St., N.W., Washington, DC 20005
Telephone: (202) 637-8800

HABEEB, Wm. Mark
Neill and Co.
815 Connecticut Ave., N.W. Suite 800, Washington, DC
20006
Telephone: (202) 463-8877
Registered as lobbyist at U.S. Congress.
Registered as Foreign Agent: (# 3320).

HABER, Sherry J.
Director, Government & Public Affairs, Nat'l Wholesale
Druggists' Ass'n
105 Oronoco St., Alexandria, VA 22314
Telephone: (202) 684-6400

HABIG, Charles J.
Secretary-Treasurer, United Ass'n of Journeymen & Ap-
prentices of the Plumbing & Pipe Fitting Industry of the
US & Canada
901 Massachusetts Ave., N.W., Washington, DC 20001
Telephone: (202) 628-5823

HACALA, Joseph R., S. J.
Director, Jesuit Social Ministries
1424 16th St., N.W., Suite 300, Washington, DC 20036
Telephone: (202) 462-7008

HACK, Capt. Ted
Navy Program, Legis Affrs, DEPARTMENT OF NAVY
The Pentagon, Washington, DC 20350-1300
Telephone: (202) 697-7146

HACKER, Kenneth F.
Manager, Public Affairs, American Insurance Ass'n
1130 Connecticut Ave., N.W., Suite 1000, Washington, DC
20036
Telephone: (202) 828-7100

HACKETT, Robert D.
Director, Contract Policies, Aerospace Industries Ass'n of
America
1250 Eye St., N.W., Suite 1100, Washington, DC 20005
Telephone: (202) 371-8400

HACKLER, W. Craig
President, Independent Consultants
1616 H St., N.W. Suite 600, Washington, DC 20006
Telephone: (202) 347-7555
Registered as lobbyist at U.S. Congress.

HACKNEY, Charles W.
Senior Congressional Liaison, Nat'l Ass'n of Home Build-
ers of the U.S.
15th and M Streets, N.W., Washington, DC 20005
Telephone: (202) 822-0470
Registered as lobbyist at U.S. Congress.

HADDELAND, William G.
Director, Federal Gov't Relations, Ashland Oil, Inc.
1025 Connecticut Ave., N.W., Suite 507, Washington, DC
20036
Telephone: (202) 223-8290
Registered as lobbyist at U.S. Congress.

HADELY, Jack
Co-director, Center for Health Policy Studies
c/o Georgetown University, 2233 Wisconsin Ave., N.W.,
Washington, DC 20007
Telephone: (202) 342-0107

HADEN & BISKER, P.C.
450 Maple Ave. East, Suites 202 & 203, Vienna, VA
22180
Telephone: (703) 255-7200
Members of firm representing listed organizations:
Haden, Fred M., President
Background: Serves as General Counsel for numerous
credit unions throughout the United States. Former
General Counsel, Nat'l Credit Union Administration.
Clients:
Nat'l Ass'n of Federal Credit Unions

HADEN, Fred M.
President, Haden & Bisker, P.C.
450 Maple Ave. East, Suites 202 & 203, Vienna, VA
22180
Telephone: (703) 255-7200
Background: Serves as General Counsel for numerous cred-
it unions throughout the United States. Former General
Counsel, Nat'l Credit Union Administration.

HADEN, Mabel Dole
President, Nat'l Ass'n of Black Women Attorneys
3711 Macomb St., N.W., Washington, DC 20016
Telephone: (202) 966-9693

HADLEY, Joseph E., Jr.
Hadley and McKenna
1815 H St., N.W., Suite 1000, Washington, DC 20006-
3604
Telephone: (202) 296-6300
Clients:
Acrylonitrile Group, Inc., The

HADLEY, Lawrence M.
Director of Marine Affairs, American Institute of Merchant
Shipping
1000 16th St., N.W., Suite 511, Washington, DC 20036-
5705
Telephone: (202) 775-4399

HADLEY AND MCKENNA
1815 H St., N.W., Suite 1000, Washington, DC 20006-
3604
Telephone: (202) 296-6300
Members of firm representing listed organizations:
Hadley, Joseph E. (Jr.)
Clients:
Acrylonitrile Group, Inc., The *(Joseph E. Hadley, Jr.)*

HAGAN, William J. M., II
Chief Lobbyist, Congressional Relations, Nat'l Conference
of State Legislatures
444 North Capitol St., N.W. Suite 500, Washington, DC
20001
Telephone: (202) 624-5400

HAGEE, Charles G., CAE
Exec. Director, Nat'l Shorthand Reporters Ass'n
118 Park St., S.E., Vienna, VA 22180
Telephone: (703) 281-4677
Background: Serves as Treasurer, Nat'l Shorthand Reporters Ass'n Political Action Committee and also represents
the Nat'l Shorthand Reporters Ass'n Heritage Foundation.

HAGEL, Charles T.
President, USO World
601 Indiana Ave., N.W., Washington, DC 20004
Telephone: (202) 783-8121

HAGEN, Katherine Ann
Federal Gov't Affairs Director, AT&T
Suite 1000, 1120 20th St., N.W., Washington, DC 20036
Telephone: (202) 457-3838

HAGER, Barry M.
Keefe Co., The
444 North Capitol St., N.W., Suite 711, Washington, DC
20001
Telephone: (202) 638-7030
Registered as lobbyist at U.S. Congress.

HAGER, S. Dilworth
Washington Representative, Nat'l Ass'n of Dredging Contractors
1625 Eye St., N.W. Suite 321, Washington, DC 20006
Telephone: (202) 223-4820

HAGER SHARP INC.
1101 17th St., N.W., Suite 1001, Washington, DC 20036
Telephone: (202) 466-5430
Members of firm representing listed organizations:
Hager, Susan, President
Hofman, Steven I., V. President
Background: Former Director, House Republican Re-
search Committee.
Jordan, Ruth, V. President
Sharp, Marcia, Chairman
Clients:
Nat'l Ass'n of Small Business Investment Compa-
nies *(Susan Hager)*
Women's College Coalition *(Marcia Sharp)*

HAGER, Susan
President, Hager Sharp Inc.
1101 17th St., N.W., Suite 1001, Washington, DC 20036
Telephone: (202) 466-5430
Clients:
Nat'l Ass'n of Small Business Investment Compa-
nies

HAGERTY, Kenneth C. O.
Public Affairs Services, Inc.
1155 15th St., N.W., Suite 710, Washington, DC 20005
Telephone: (202) 659-9101
Clients:
Nat'l Venture Capital Ass'n

HAGGART, Roni
V. President, Internat'l Trade, Motorola, Inc.
1350 Eye St., N.W., Suite 400, Washington, DC 20005-
3306
Telephone: (202) 371-6900

HAGGERT, Veronica A.
V. Pres. & Dir., Internat'l Trade Rels., Motorola, Inc.
1350 Eye St., N.W., Suite 400, Washington, DC 20005-
3306
Telephone: (202) 371-6900
Background: Commissioner, International Trade Commission, 1982-84.

HAHN-BAKER, David K.
Environmental Quality Coordinator, Nat'l Wildlife Federation
1400 16th St., N.W., Washington, DC 20036-2266
Telephone: (202) 797-6800

HAHN, Bruce N.
V. President, Public Affairs, Nat'l Ass'n of Manufacturers
1331 Pennsylvania Ave., N.W. Suite 1500 North, Washing-
ton, DC 20004-1703
Telephone: (202) 637-3000
Registered as lobbyist at U.S. Congress.

HAHN, Lorna
Exec. Director, Ass'n on Third World Affairs
1629 K St., N.W., Suite 802, Washington, DC 20006
Telephone: (202) 331-8455

HAHN, Nancy
Treasurer, Nat'l Ass'n of Business and Educational Radio
Political Action Committee
1501 Duke St., Suite 200, Alexandria, VA 22314
Telephone: (703) 739-0300

HAHN, Patricia A.
Assoc General Counsel, Legislation, INTERSTATE COM-
MERCE COMMISSION
12th and Constitution Ave. N.W., Washington, DC 20423
Telephone: (202) 275-7104

HAHN, Peter H.
Legislative Representative, Chromalloy Gas Turbine Corp.
1155 Connecticut Ave., N.W. Suite 500, Washington, DC
20036
Telephone: (202) 659-4280
Registered as lobbyist at U.S. Congress.

HAIFLEY, John F.
Director of Federal Relations, American Automobile Ass'n
8111 Gatehouse Rd., Fairfax, VA 22047
Telephone: (703) 222-6199
Registered as lobbyist at U.S. Congress.

HAIG, Alexander M., Jr.
President, Worldwide Associates, Inc
1155 15th St., N.W. Suite 800, Washington, DC 20005
Telephone: (202) 429-9788

HAILES, Dr. Edward A.
Exec. Director, District of Columbia, Opportunities Industrialization Centers
3224 16th St., N.W., Washington, DC 20010
Telephone: (202) 265-2626

HAILPERN, Nancy
Legislative Assistant, American Cancer Soc. (Public Affairs Office)
316 Pennsylvania Ave., S.E. Suite 200, Washington, DC
20003
Telephone: (202) 546-4011
Registered as lobbyist at U.S. Congress.
Background: Former staff member, House of Representatives Subcommittee on Health and the Environment.

HAIR, Jay D., Ph.D.
President, Nat'l Wildlife Federation
1412 16th St., N.W., Washington, DC 20036
Telephone: (202) 797-6842
Registered as lobbyist at U.S. Congress.

HAIRSTON, Thomas F.
V. President, Washington Office, UNOCAL Corp.
1050 Connecticut Ave., N.W., Suite 760, Washington, DC
20036
Telephone: (202) 659-7600
Registered as lobbyist at U.S. Congress.

HAISLMAIER, Edmund
Policy Analyst, Health Care, Heritage Foundation
214 Massachusetts Ave., N.E., Washington, DC 20002
Telephone: (202) 546-4400

HAKIM, Peter
Staff Director, Inter-American Dialogue
1333 New Hampshire Ave., N.W., Washington, DC 20036
Telephone: (202) 466-6410

HAKOLA, Edith
V. President and General Counsel, Nat'l Right to Work Legal Defense Foundation
8001 Braddock Road, Springfield, VA 22160
Telephone: (703) 321-9820

HALAMANDARIS, Val J.
President, Nat'l Ass'n for Home Care
519 C St., N.E., Washington, DC 20002
Telephone: (202) 547-7424

HALE, Alma P.
Legislative and Regulatory Analyst, American Mining Congress
1920 N St., N.W. Suite 300, Washington, DC 20036
Telephone: (202) 861-2800
Registered as lobbyist at U.S. Congress.
Background: Former staff member, House Interior and Insular Affairs Subcommittee on Mining and Natural Resources.

HALE AND DORR
1455 Pennsylvania Ave., N.W. Suite 1000, Washington,
DC 20004
Telephone: (202) 393-0800
Members of firm representing listed organizations:
Quarles, James L., Senior Partner
Urwitz, Jay P., Senior Partner
Background: Legislative Assistant to Senator Edward
Kennedy (D-MA), 1977-81.
Clients:
Boston Museum of Science *(Jay P. Urwitz)*

Dakota Wesleyan University *(Jay P. Urwitz)*
Gay Head Taxpayers' Ass'n *(Jay P. Urwitz)*
Genetics Institute Inc. *(Jay P. Urwitz)*
Mashpee, Massachusetts, Town of *(James L. Quarles)*
Metalor USA Refining Corp. *(Jay P. Urwitz)*
Northeastern University *(Jay P. Urwitz)*
Prime Computer, Inc. *(Jay P. Urwitz)*
USS Constitution Museum *(Jay P. Urwitz)*

HALE, Randolph M.
V. President, Industrial Relations, Nat'l Ass'n of Manufacturers
1331 Pennsylvania Ave., N.W. Suite 1500 North, Washington, DC 20004-1703
Telephone: (202) 637-3000
Registered as lobbyist at U.S. Congress.

HALES, Shirley I.
Manager, Constituent Relations, TRW Inc.
Suite 2700. 1000 Wilson Blvd., Arlington, VA 22209
Telephone: (703) 276-5043

HALEY, BADER AND POTTS
2000 M St., N.W. Suite 600, Washington, DC 20036
Telephone: (202) 331-0606
Background: The information below was obtained from
public sources and submitted to the firm for confirmation.
The firm declined to confirm or correct the information
and asked to be omitted from the book.
Members of firm representing listed organizations:
Bader, Michael H.
Background: Member, Board of Directors, MCI Com-
munications Corp.
Byrnes, William J.
Cox, Kenneth A., Of Counsel
Background: Special Counsel, Senate Commerce Com-
mittee, 1956-1957. Chief, Broadcast Bureau, Federal
Communications Commission, 1961-1963. Member,
Federal Communications Commission, 1963-1970.
Serves as Senior Vice President and Counsel, MCI
Telecommunications Corp. and member of its Board
of Directors.
Pelkey, John M.
Clients:
American Electronics Ass'n *(John M. Pelkey)*
MCI Communications Corp. *(Michael H. Bader, Wil-
liam J. Byrnes, Kenneth A. Cox)*

HALEY, Frances
Exec. Director, Nat'l Council for the Social Studies
3501 Newark St., N.W., Washington, DC 20016
Telephone: (202) 966-7840

HALEY, Timothy F.
Seyfarth, Shaw, Fairweather and Geraldson
815 Connecticut Ave., N.W., Washington, DC 20006-4004
Telephone: (202) 463-2400

HALIK, Heide
Conservation Assistant, Sierra Club
408 C St., N.E., Washington, DC 20002
Telephone: (202) 547-1141
Registered as lobbyist at U.S. Congress.

HALKIAS, Rebecca L.
V. President, Burson-Marsteller
1850 M St., N.W., Suite 900, Washington, DC 20036
Telephone: (202) 833-8550
Registered as lobbyist at U.S. Congress.
Registered as Foreign Agent: (#2469).
Clients:
American Ass'n of Dental Schools
Blue Cross of Pennsylvania
Independent Blue Cross
Philadelphia, Pennsylvania, City of
Philadelphia Port Corp.
Temple University

HALL, Angelynn
Director, Federal Legislation, Air Transport Ass'n of
America
1709 New York Ave., N.W., Washington, DC 20006
Telephone: (202) 626-4119

HALL-CRAWFORD, Mel
Manager, Federal Governmental Affairs, San Diego Gas
and Electric Co.
316 Pennsylvania Ave., S.E., Suite 301, Washington, DC
20003

Telephone: (202) 546-7676
Registered as lobbyist at U.S. Congress.

HALL, Dorian
Dep Dir, Cong Relations (Act), FEDERAL TRADE COM-
MISSION
6th and Pennsylvania Ave. N.W., Washington, DC 20580
Telephone: (202) 326-2195

HALL, Edwin K.
V. President, Government Relations, MCI Communications
Corp.
1133 19th St., N.W., Washington, DC 20036
Telephone: (202) 872-1600
Registered as lobbyist at U.S. Congress.
Background: Former General Counsel, U.S. Senate Com-
mittee on Commerce, Science and Transportation. Re-
sponsible for MCI Telecommunications Political Action
Committee.

HALL, Elliott S.
V. President, Washington Affairs, Ford Motor Co.
1350 Eye St., N.W. Suite 1000, Washington, DC 20005
Telephone: (202) 962-5400
Registered as lobbyist at U.S. Congress.

**HALL, ESTILL, HARDWICK, GABLE, GOLDEN &
NELSON**
1120 20th St., N.W., Suite 750 - South Bldg., Washington,
DC 20036
Telephone: (202) 822-9100
Members of firm representing listed organizations:
Rudolph, John
Clients:
Arkla, Inc. *(John Rudolph)*

HALL, Janet
Director, International Affairs, Westinghouse Electric Corp.
1801 K St., N.W., Washington, DC 20006
Telephone: (202) 835-2368

HALL, John F.
President, American Wood Preservers Institute
1945 Old Gallows Road Suite 550, Vienna, VA 22182
Telephone: (703) 893-4005
Registered as lobbyist at U.S. Congress.
Background: Serves as Treasurer, American Wood Preserv-
ers Institute Political Action Committee.

➤HALL, John P., Jr.
V. President, Federal Relations, Johnson & Johnson
1667 K St., N.W., Suite 410, Washington, DC 20006
Telephone: (202) 293-2620
Registered as lobbyist at U.S. Congress.

HALL, Joseph
Manager, Congressional Relations, Harris Corp.
1201 East Abingdon Drive Suite 300, Alexandria, VA
22314
Telephone: (703) 548-9200

HALL, Judy A.
Associate Director, Program Division, Nat'l Ass'n of Social
Workers
7981 Eastern Ave., Silver Spring, MD 20910
Telephone: (301) 565-0333

HALL, Julius L.
Legislative Counsel, Nat'l Federation of Federal Em-
ployees
1016 16th St., N.W., Suite 400, Washington, DC 20036
Telephone: (202) 862-4400
Registered as lobbyist at U.S. Congress.
Background: Former Legislative Counsel to Rep. Lindsay
Thomas (D-GA).

HALL, Michael W.
Cullen and Dykman
1225 19th St., N.W. Suite 320, Washington, DC 20036
Telephone: (202) 223-8890
Clients:
Brooklyn Union Gas Co.

HALL, Munford Page, II
Dorsey & Whitney
1330 Connecticut Ave., N.W., Suite 200, Washington, DC
20036
Telephone: (202) 857-0700

HALL, Reggie
Exec. Director, Internat'l Newspaper Advertising and Marketing Executives
Box 17210, Washington, DC 20041
Telephone: (703) 648-1168

HALL, Richard
Sive, Paget & Riesel
1055 Thomas Jefferson St, N.W. Suite 501, Washington, DC 20007
Telephone: (202) 965-1500
Background: Former Assistant Director, Surface Mining Reclamation and Enforcement, U.S. Department of Interior.

HALL, Richard F.
V. President, Government Affairs, Pacific Resources, Inc.
1700 K St., N.W., Suite 502, Washington, DC 20006
Telephone: (202) 223-4623
Registered as lobbyist at U.S. Congress.

HALL, Ridgway M., Jr.
Crowell and Moring
1001 Pennsylvania Ave., N.W., Washington, DC 20004-2505
Telephone: (202) 624-2500
Registered as lobbyist at U.S. Congress.
Background: Associate General Counsel, Environmental Protection Agency, 1976-77.

HALL, Roger
First V. President, Air Line Pilots Ass'n Internat'l
1625 Massachusetts Ave., N.W., Washington, DC 20036
Telephone: (202) 797-4003
Background: Also represents the Air Line Pilots Ass'n Political Action Committee.

HALLADAY, J. R.
Counselor to the President, American Trucking Ass'ns
2200 Mill Road, Alexandria, VA 22314
Telephone: (703) 838-1803

HALLADAY, Roberta L.
Morgan, Lewis and Bockius
1800 M St., N.W., Washington, DC 20036
Telephone: (202) 467-7000

HALLAHAN, Michael J.
Director, ACV Marketing, Textron Marine Systems
1090 Vermont Ave., N.W., Suite 1100, Washington, DC 20005
Telephone: (202) 289-5800

HALLER, Keith
President, Potomac Survey Research
7940 Norfolk Ave., Bethesda, MD 20814
Telephone: (301) 656-7900

HALLER, Tracy
Manager, Legislative Affairs, Sandoz Corp.
1615 L St., N.W., Suite 320, Washington, DC 20036
Telephone: (202) 223-6262

HALLETT, Carol Boyd
Carmen Group, The
1667 K St., N.W., Suite 700, Washington, DC 20006
Telephone: (202) 785-0500
Registered as Foreign Agent: (#4233).
Clients:
  Committee for Free Elections and Democracy in Nicaragua

HALLETT, Frederick H.
V. Pres., Industry & Gov't Relations, White Consolidated Industries
1317 F St., N.W. Suite 510, Washington, DC 20004
Telephone: (202) 638-7878

HALLIDAY, Toby
Director, Government Affairs, American Symphony Orchestra League
777 14th St., N.W., Suite 500, Washington, DC 20005
Telephone: (202) 628-0099
Background: Former Aide to U.S. Rep. Alan Wheat (D-MO), 1987-89.

HALLISAY, Paul
Director, Legislative Affairs, Air Line Pilots Ass'n Internat'l
1625 Massachusetts Ave., N.W., Washington, DC 20036
Telephone: (202) 797-4003

Registered as lobbyist at U.S. Congress.

HALLMAN, Paul W.
MultiState Associates
515 King St., Suite 310, Alexandria, VA 22314
Telephone: (703) 684-1110

HALLORAN, Deidre
Associate General Counsel, United States Catholic Conference
3200 4th St., N.E., Washington, DC 20017
Telephone: (202) 541-3000

HALPERIN, Eliot J.
Graham and James
2000 M St., N.W., Suite 700, Washington, DC 20036
Telephone: (202) 463-0800
Clients:
  Frontier Express Inc.
  Overseas Shipping Co.

HALPERIN, Jerome
Exec. Director, United States Pharmacopeial Convention
12601 Twinbrook Parkway, Rockville, MD 20852
Telephone: (301) 881-0666

HALPERIN, Morton H.
Director, Washington Office, American Civil Liberties Union
122 Maryland Ave., N.E., Washington, DC 20002
Telephone: (202) 544-1681
Registered as lobbyist at U.S. Congress.
Background: Serves also as Director, Center for National Security Studies. Former staff member, National Security Council, and former Deputy Ass't Secretary of Defense.

HALSEY, Steven C.
McAuliffe, Kelly, Raffaelli & Siemens
1341 G St., N.W. Suite 200, Washington, DC 20005
Telephone: (202) 783-1800
Registered as lobbyist at U.S. Congress.
Registered as Foreign Agent: (#4332).
Clients:
  Dallas/Fort Worth RAILTRAN
  Nat'l Telephone Services, Inc.

HALUZA, Paul T.
Dir., Gov'tal Relations & Public Affairs, Motor and Equipment Manufacturers Ass'n
1325 Pennsylvania Ave., N.W. Suite 600, Washington, DC 20004
Telephone: (202) 393-6362
Registered as lobbyist at U.S. Congress.

HALVERSON, Rhonda Lee
V. President, Administration, American Business Conference
1730 K St., N.W. Suite 1200, Washington, DC 20006
Telephone: (202) 822-9300
Registered as lobbyist at U.S. Congress.

HALVORSEN, Jerald V.
President, Interstate Natural Gas Ass'n of America
555 13th St., N.W. Suite 300 West, Washington, DC 20004
Telephone: (202) 626-3200

HAMBERGER, Edward R.
Partner, Baker, Worthington, Crossley, Stansberry & Woolf
1001 Pennsylvania Ave., N.W., Suite 1201, Washington, DC 20004
Telephone: (202) 347-4360
Registered as lobbyist at U.S. Congress.
Background: Staff Director, House Republican Policy Committee, 1979-81. Assistant Secretary for Governmental Affairs, U.S. Department of Transportation, 1988-89.
Clients:
  American Airlines
  Contel Corp.
  Day & Zimmerman
  DINAMO
  Lawler/Wood, Inc.
  Los Angeles County Transportation Commission
  Nat'l Label Co.
  Pillsbury Co.

HAMBERGER, Martin G.
Counsel, Corp. Devel. & Public Affairs, Chambers Development Co., Inc.
1150 17th St., N.W., Suite 307, Washington, DC 20036
Telephone: (202) 463-0306

HAMBLEY, Win
Cong Liaison, FEDERAL RESERVE SYSTEM
20th and C Sts., N.W., Washington, DC 20551
Telephone: (202) 452-3456

HAMBY, Martha R.
Director, Federal Affairs, American Insurance Ass'n
1130 Connecticut Ave., N.W., Suite 1000, Washington, DC 20036
Telephone: (202) 828-7100
Registered as lobbyist at U.S. Congress.
Background: Assistant Press Secretary to Senator Russell Long (D-LA), 1979-80. Press Secretary to Rep. Beryl Anthony (D-AR), 1980-81.

HAMDEN, Dr. Raymond H.
Chairman of the Board, Foundation for Internat'l Human Relations
P.O. Box 18206, Washington, DC 20036
Telephone: (202) 659-5552
Background: Also serves as President, Human Relations Institute.

HAMILL, Bruce
General Counsel, Nat'l Paint and Coatings Ass'n
1500 Rhode Island Ave. N.W., Washington, DC 20005
Telephone: (202) 462-6272

HAMILTON, David
Field Director, U.S. Public Interest Research Group
215 Pennsylvania Ave., S.E., Washington, DC 20003
Telephone: (202) 546-9707
Registered as lobbyist at U.S. Congress.

HAMILTON, James A.
General Secretary, Nat'l Council of the Churches of Christ in the USA
110 Maryland Ave., N.E., Washington, DC 20002
Telephone: (202) 544-2350

HAMILTON, Joyce
Director, Government Relations, Nat'l-American Wholesale Grocers' Ass'n
201 Park Washington Court, Falls Church, VA 22046
Telephone: (703) 532-9400
Registered as lobbyist at U.S. Congress.

HAMILTON, Larry
Director, Public Affairs -Wash. Office, Grumman Corp.
1000 Wilson Blvd., Suite 2800, Arlington, VA 22209
Telephone: (703) 875-8400

HAMILTON, Lee
Sr. V. Pres., Membership & Public Affrs., Nat'l Ass'n of Manufacturers
1331 Pennsylvania Ave., N.W. Suite 1500 North, Washington, DC 20004-1703
Telephone: (202) 637-3000
Registered as lobbyist at U.S. Congress.

HAMILTON, Patricia
Director, Communications, American Wood Preservers Institute
1945 Old Gallows Road Suite 550, Vienna, VA 22182
Telephone: (703) 893-4005

HAMILTON, Philip W.
Managing Director, Public Affairs, American Soc. of Mechanical Engineers
1825 K St., N.W., Suite 218, Washington, DC 20006
Telephone: (202) 785-3756
Registered as lobbyist at U.S. Congress.

HAMILTON, Rae M.
Director of Communications, Police Foundation
1001 22nd St., N.W., Suite 200, Washington, DC 20037
Telephone: (202) 833-1460

HAMILTON & STAFF
1019 19th St., N.W., Suite 1300, Washington, DC 20036
Telephone: (202) 857-1980
Background: A political and public affairs consulting firm.
Members of firm representing listed organizations:
  Hamilton, William, President

HAMILTON & STAFF (Cont'd)
Patterson, Sally, Senior V. President
Background: Also serves as President, Women in Government Relations.

HAMILTON, William
President, Hamilton & Staff
1019 19th St., N.W., Suite 1300, Washington, DC 20036
Telephone: (202) 857-1980

HAMILTON, William W., Jr.
Director, Washington Office, Planned Parenthood Federation of America
2010 Massachusetts Ave., N.W. Fifth Floor, Washington, DC 20036
Telephone: (202) 785-3351
Registered as lobbyist at U.S. Congress.
Background: Former Senate staff member.

HAMLIN, Joyce V.
Exec. Secretary for Public Policy, United Methodist Church Board of Global Ministries, Women's Div.
100 Maryland Ave., N.E., Room 501, Washington, DC 20002
Telephone: (202) 488-5660

HAMM, Michael
Smith, Bucklin and Associates
1101 Connecticut Ave., N.W., Suite 700, Washington, DC 20036
Telephone: (202) 857-1100
Background: Serves as Exec. Director, American Ass'n for Medical Systems and Informatics and Exec. Director, Nat'l Organization for Competency Assurance.
Clients:
American Ass'n for Medical Systems and Informatics (AAMSI)
Nat'l Commission Certifying Agencies
Nat'l Organization for Competency Assurance

HAMM, Ronald P.
Manager, Federal Liaison Dept., Motor Vehicle Manufacturers Ass'n of the United States
1620 Eye St., N.W. Suite 1000, Washington, DC 20006
Telephone: (202) 775-2700
Registered as lobbyist at U.S. Congress.

HAMMER, Amy R.
Washington Representative, Exxon Corp.
Suite 1100, 1899 L St., N.W., Washington, DC 20036
Telephone: (202) 862-0216
Registered as lobbyist at U.S. Congress.

HAMMER, Michael H.
Dir., Communications Policy Development, Time Warner Inc.
1050 Connecticut Ave., N.W. Suite 850, Washington, DC 20036
Telephone: (202) 861-4000

HAMMER, Thomas A.
President, Sweetener Users Ass'n
2100 Pennsylvania Ave., N.W. Suite 695, Washington, DC 20037
Telephone: (202) 872-8676
Registered as lobbyist at U.S. Congress.

HAMMICK, Patricia A.
V. President, Natural Gas Supply Ass'n
1129 20th St., N.W. Suite 300, Washington, DC 20036
Telephone: (202) 331-8900

HAMMOND, Mark N.
Treasurer, Soft Drink Political Action Committee
1101 16th St., N.W., Washington, DC 20036
Telephone: (202) 463-6732

HAMOVIT, Jerry M.
Melrod, Redman and Gartlan, A Professional Corporation
1801 K St., N.W. Suite 1100, Washington, DC 20006
Telephone: (202) 822-5300
Background: Trial Attorney, Tax Division, U.S. Department of Justice, 1959-1962; Attorney, Office of the Tax Legislative Counsel, U.S. Treasury Department, 1965-1967.

HAMPTON, Ronald E.
Exec. Director, Nat'l Black Police Ass'n
1100 17th St., N.W., Suite 1000, Washington, DC 20036

Telephone: (202) 457-0563

HAMRICK, Peggy
Burson-Marsteller
1850 M St., N.W., Suite 900, Washington, DC 20036
Telephone: (202) 833-8550

HAMRIN, Robert
Van Dyk Associates, Inc.
1250 24th St., N.W., Suite 600, Washington, DC 20037
Telephone: (202) 223-4880
Clients:
Council on United States Internat'l Trade Policy

HANAGAN, Mary Dreape
Director, Government Affairs, Ass'n for Advanced Life Underwriting
1922 F St., N.W., Washington, DC 20006
Telephone: (202) 331-6081
Background: Former Special Assistant to Senate Majority Leader Howard Baker (R-TN).

HANAN, Timothy A.
Manager, Federal Government Relations, Mobil Corp.
1100 Connecticut Ave., N.W., Suite 620, Washington, DC 20036
Telephone: (202) 862-1319
Registered as lobbyist at U.S. Congress.

HANAVER, Jill
PAC Manager, Nat'l Abortion Rights Action League Political Action Committee
1101 14th St., N.W., Suite 500, Washington, DC 20005
Telephone: (202) 371-0779

HANC, Dr. George
Exec. V. Pres., Finance & Administration, Nat'l Council of Savings Institutions
1101 15th St., N.W. Suite 400, Washington, DC 20005
Telephone: (202) 857-3100

HANCHER, Renee S.
Manager, International Trade, Air-Conditioning and Refrigeration Institute
1501 Wilson Blvd., Suite 600, Arlington, VA 22209
Telephone: (703) 524-8800

HANCOCK, Charles C.
Exec. Officer, American Soc. for Biochemistry and Molecular Biology
9650 Rockville Pike, B-22, Bethesda, MD 20814
Telephone: (301) 530-7145

HANCOCK, Michael
Exec. Director, Farmworker Justice Fund
2001 S St., N.W., Suite 210, Washington, DC 20009
Telephone: (202) 462-8192
Registered as lobbyist at U.S. Congress.

HANCOCK, Nolan W.
Citizenship-Legislative Director, Oil, Chemical and Atomic Workers Internat'l Union
1126 16th St., N.W., Suite 411, Washington, DC 20036
Telephone: (202) 223-5770
Registered as lobbyist at U.S. Congress.
Background: Also represents the Political Action Committee.

HANCOCK, William E., Jr.
Chairman, Dealers Election Action Committee of the Nat'l Automobile Dealers Ass'n (DEAC)
8400 Westpark Drive, McLean, VA 22102
Telephone: (703) 821-7110

HAND, ARENDALL, BEDSOLE, GREAVES & JOHNSTON
1667 K St., N.W. Suite 310, Washington, DC 20006
Telephone: (202) 785-8893
Members of firm representing listed organizations:
Edwards, Jack
Background: Member, U.S. House of Representatives (R-AL), 1965-84.
Clients:
Northrop Corp. *(Jack Edwards)*

HAND, Lloyd N.
Verner, Liipfert, Bernhard, McPherson and Hand, Chartered
901 15th St., N.W., Suite 700, Washington, DC 20005
Telephone: (202) 371-6000

Registered as lobbyist at U.S. Congress.
Registered as Foreign Agent: (# 3712).
Background: Assistant to Senate Majority Leader and Vice President Lyndon B. Johnson, 1957-61. U.S. Chief of Protocol, 1965-66.
Clients:
Alcatel
Bell Atlantic
GenCorp
Irving Ltd., J.D.
Nat'l Wildlife Federation
TRW Inc.

HANDELMAN, Rubin
President, Nat'l Ass'n of Postal Supervisors
490 L'Enfant Plaza., S.W., Suite 3200, Washington, DC 20024
Telephone: (202) 484-6070

HANDFIELD, William G.
Assistant V. President, Ass'n of American Railroads
50 F St., N.W., Suite 12800, Washington, DC 20001
Telephone: (202) 639-2530
Registered as lobbyist at U.S. Congress.

HANDRAHAN, Kay
Sr. V. Pres. & Washington Business Mgr., Hill and Knowlton Public Affairs Worldwide
Washington Harbour, 901 31st St., N.W., Washington, DC 20007
Telephone: (202) 333-7400

HANES, Donald K.
Vice President, Communications, Nat'l Council of Farmer Cooperatives
50 F St., N.W., Suite 900, Washington, DC 20001
Telephone: (202) 626-8700
Registered as lobbyist at U.S. Congress.

HANES, Joanna
Senior V. President, Edelman, Inc., Daniel J.
1420 K St., N.W., Washington, DC 20005
Telephone: (202) 371-0200
Organizations represented:
du Pont de Nemours and Co., E. I.

HANES, Rose M.
Exec. Director, Population - Environment Balance
1325 G St., N.W., Suite 1003, Washington, DC 20005-3104
Telephone: (202) 879-3000
Registered as lobbyist at U.S. Congress.

HANKINS, Rita
Exec. Director, Bell Atlantic
Suite 1200, 1710 Rhode Island Ave., N.W., Washington, DC 20036
Telephone: (202) 392-6987

HANKLA, L. L. Hank
Partner, V. President, General Counsel, Dutko & Associates
412 First St., S.E. Suite 100, Washington, DC 20003
Telephone: (202) 484-4884
Registered as lobbyist at U.S. Congress.
Background: Former Enforcement Attorney, Environmental Protection Agency. Formerly on the staffs of Sen. Mike Monroney and Sen. Fred R. Harris, both of Oklahoma.
Clients:
Anchor Industries, Inc.
Bedford Group
Building Industry Ass'n of Southern California
Grenada, Government of
Lusk Company, The
Rmax, Inc.
Waste Conversion Systems, Inc.

HANLEY, Edward T.
President, Hotel Employees and Restaurant Employees Internat'l Union
1219 28th St., N.W., Washington, DC 20007
Telephone: (202) 393-4373

HANLEY, Mary
V. President, Public Affairs, Wilderness Soc.
1400 Eye St., N.W., 10th Floor, Washington, DC 20005
Telephone: (202) 842-3400

HANLIN, Elisabeth
Dir., Gov't Affairs - State and Federal, Unisys Corp.
2001 L St., N.W., Suite 1000, Washington, DC 20036
Telephone: (202) 293-7720
Registered as lobbyist at U.S. Congress.

HANLON, R. Timothy
Shaw, Pittman, Potts and Trowbridge
2300 N St., N.W., Washington, DC 20037
Telephone: (202) 663-8000
Registered as Foreign Agent: (#2580).
Background: Honors Program, Office of the General Counsel, Department of the Air Force, 1961-64.
Clients:
Taiwan Power Co.

HANNA, GASPAR AND OSBORNE
2550 M St., N.W. Suite 375, Washington, DC 20037
Telephone: (202) 296-7666
Members of firm representing listed organizations:
Gaspar, Russell J.

HANNA, Thomas H.
President/Chief Exec. Officer, Motor Vehicle Manufacturers Ass'n of the United States
1620 Eye St., N.W. Suite 1000, Washington, DC 20006
Telephone: (202) 775-2700

HANNAFORD CO., INC., The
655 15th St., N.W. Suite 200, Washington, DC 20005
Telephone: (202) 638-4600
Registered as Foreign Agent: (#2850)
Background: A public relations/public affairs consulting firm.
Members of firm representing listed organizations:
Boertlein, Paul L., V. Chairman
Cameron, Jared S., V. President
Hannaford, Donald R., V. President
Hannaford, Peter D., Chairman of the Board
Leggett, Carroll H., Exec. V. President, Public Affairs
Norton, Joe M., Senior V. President
Williamson, John L., V. President
Organizations represented:
China, Government Information Office of the Republic of
Congo, People's Republic of the
Coordination Council for North American Affairs
Minnesota Mining and Manufacturing Co. (3M Co.)
Saudi Arabia, Royal Embassy of

HANNAFORD, Donald R.
V. President, Hannaford Co., Inc., The
655 15th St., N.W. Suite 200, Washington, DC 20005
Telephone: (202) 638-4600

HANNAFORD, Peter D.
Chairman of the Board, Hannaford Co., Inc., The
655 15th St., N.W. Suite 200, Washington, DC 20005
Telephone: (202) 638-4600
Registered as lobbyist at U.S. Congress.
Registered as Foreign Agent: (#2850).

HANNAH, John
Deputy Director of Research, Washington Institute for Near East Policy
50 F St., N.W., Suite 8800, Washington, DC 20001
Telephone: (202) 783-0226

HANNAS, Polly S.
Manager, Legislative Affairs, Grace and Co., W. R.
919 18th St., N.W., Suite 400, Washington, DC 20006
Telephone: (202) 452-6700
Registered as lobbyist at U.S. Congress.

HANNEMAN, Richard L.
President, Salt Institute
700 North Fairfax St. Suite 600, Alexandria, VA 22314
Telephone: (703) 549-4648
Registered as lobbyist at U.S. Congress.

HANNETT, Frederick J.
Jefferson Group, The
1341 G St., N.W., Suite 1100, Washington, DC 20005
Telephone: (202) 638-3535
Registered as lobbyist at U.S. Congress.
Clients:
American Health Care Advisory Ass'n

Bell Atlantic
Children's Health System, Inc.
Gibraltar, P.R., Inc.
Independent Health Plan
Maxicare HealthPlans, Inc.
Peat Marwick
Preferred Health
Tidewater Health Care

HANRAHAN, Dolly A.
Manager, Government Affairs, Health Industry Manufacturers Ass'n
1030 15th St., N.W. Suite 1100, Washington, DC 20005
Telephone: (202) 452-8240
Registered as lobbyist at U.S. Congress.

HANRAHAN, Robert P.
President, RPH & Associates
7268 Evans Mill Road, McLean, VA 22101
Telephone: (703) 448-0931
Background: Former Superintendent of Schools, Cook County, Illinois, 1967-71. Member of U.S. House of Representatives (R-IL), 1973-75. Deputy Assistant Secretary of Education, 1975-77. Lake County, Illinois, Commissioner, 1980-82.
Clients:
Diversified Realty Corp. and Financial Group

HANRAHAN, William F.
Sr. Dir., Standards/Technology Program, Computer and Business Equipment Manufacturers Ass'n
311 First St., N.W. Suite 500, Washington, DC 20001
Telephone: (202) 737-8888

HANSELL, Herbert J.
Jones, Day, Reavis and Pogue
1450 G St., N.W., Suite 700, Washington, DC 20005-2088
Telephone: (202) 879-3939
Registered as lobbyist at U.S. Congress.
Registered as Foreign Agent: (#3427).
Background: Legal Advisor, Department of State, 1977-79.

HANSELL, William H., Jr.
Exec. Director, Internat'l City Management Ass'n
777 North Capitol St., N.E., Suite 500, Washington, DC 20002
Telephone: (202) 289-4262

HANSEN, Bill
Dep Asst Secy, Legislation, DEPARTMENT OF EDUCATION
400 Maryland Ave., S.W., Washington, DC 20202
Telephone: (202) 732-5020

HANSEN, Christopher W.
Deputy Director, Congressional Affairs, Boeing Co.
1700 North Moore St., Arlington, VA 22209
Telephone: (703) 558-9600
Registered as lobbyist at U.S. Congress.

HANSEN, Erling
General Counsel, Group Health Ass'n of America
1129 20th St., N.W. Suite 600, Washington, DC 20036
Telephone: (202) 778-3200
Registered as lobbyist at U.S. Congress.

HANSEN, Orval
President, Columbia Institute
8 E St., S.E., Washington, DC 20003
Telephone: (202) 547-2470
Background: U.S. Representative (R), State of Idaho, 1969-74.

HANSEN, W. Darryl
Exec. Director, Entomological Soc. of America
9301 Annapolis Rd., Lanham, MD 20706-3115
Telephone: (301) 731-4535

HANSEN, Walter D.
Burwell, Hansen, Peters and Houston
1762 Church St., N.W., Washington, DC 20036
Telephone: (202) 745-0441
Background: Special Counsel to the U.S. House of Representatives Judiciary Committee, 1966-67.
Clients:
Garuda Indonesian Airways
Transamerica Airlines
Wardair Canada, Ltd.

HANSMANN, Jack
Exec. Secretary, Nat'l Certified Pipe Welding Bureau
1385 Piccard Drive, Rockville, MD 20850
Telephone: (301) 897-0770

HANSON, Brian T.
Government Affairs Representative, Deere & Co.
1667 K St., N.W., Suite 1230, Washington, DC 20006
Telephone: (202) 223-4817
Registered as lobbyist at U.S. Congress.
Background: Former Legislative Assistant to Senator Alan Dixon (D-IL).

HANSON, Eric R.
Chairman, CEO and President, U.S. Strategies Corp.
1321 Duke St., Suite 200, Alexandria, VA 22314-3563
Telephone: (703) 739-7999
Registered as lobbyist at U.S. Congress.

HANSON, Heidi A.
V. President, Public Affairs, U.S. Strategies Corp.
1321 Duke St., Suite 200, Alexandria, VA 22314-3563
Telephone: (703) 739-7999
Background: Ass't to U.S. Rep. John Buchanan, 1976; Special Ass't, U.S. Dept. of State, 1977-79; Special Ass't to the Secretary, Dept. of Health and Human Services, 1979-80.
Clients:
Cities in Schools, Inc.

HANSON, John N.
Beveridge & Diamond, P.C.
1350 Eye St., N.W. Suite 700, Washington, DC 20005
Telephone: (202) 789-6000
Background: Trial Attorney, 1972-77 and Assistant Director, Civil Division, 1978-79, Department of Justice.

HANSON, Mary
Director, Landscape Architecture Foundation
4401 Connecticut Ave., N.W. Suite 500, Washington, DC 20009
Telephone: (202) 686-0068

HARADA, Daisaku
Director, U.S. Office, Japan Productivity Center
1729 King St., Suite 100, Alexandria, VA 22314
Telephone: (703) 838-0414

HARADA, Mitsuhiko
Representative, Hitachi Ltd.
1850 K St., N.W., Suite 475, Washington, DC 20006
Telephone: (202) 828-9272
Registered as Foreign Agent: (#3855)

HARAF, William S.
V. President, Policy Analysis, Citicorp
1275 Pennsylvania Ave., N.W., Suite 503, Washington, DC 20004
Telephone: (202) 879-6800
Background: Former Senior Economist, Council of Economic Advisers.

HARAHAN, Samuel
Exec. Director, Council for Court Excellence
1025 Vermont Ave., N.W., Suite 510, Washington, DC 20005
Telephone: (202) 783-7736

HARBRANT, Robert F.
President, AFL-CIO - Food and Allied Service Trades Department
815 16th St., N.W., Suite 408, Washington, DC 20006
Telephone: (202) 737-7200

HARDEE, David W.
Akin, Gump, Strauss, Hauer and Feld
1333 New Hampshire Ave., N.W., Suite 400, Washington, DC 20036
Telephone: (202) 887-4000
Background: Former Minority Tax Counsel, U.S. Senate Finance Committee.

HARDIMAN, Joseph R.
President & CEO, Nat'l Ass'n of Securities Dealers (NASDAQ)
1735 K St., N.W., Washington, DC 20006
Telephone: (202) 728-8000

HARDING, Robert B.
Groom and Nordberg
1701 Pennsylvania Ave., N.W., Suite 1200, Washington, DC 20006
Telephone: (202) 857-0620
Registered as lobbyist at U.S. Congress.
Background: Assistant to Rep. Charles A. Halleck, Office of Minority Leader, House of Representatives, 1963-67. Attorney, Securities and Exchange Commission, 1967-68. Special Assistant to the Secretary for Congressional Affairs, HEW, 1970-71.
Clients:
  Chevron Corp.
  Lilly and Co., Eli
  Phillips Petroleum Co.
  Physicians Mutual Insurance Co.
  Principal Financial Group, The
  Prudential-Bache Securities, Inc.
  Prudential Insurance Co. of America
  Southern California Edison Co.
  Sunflower Electric Cooperative, Inc.
  Union Texas Petroleum
  Westinghouse Electric Corp.

HARDING, Sandra K.
Staff Associate for Legislation, Nat'l Ass'n of Social Workers
7981 Eastern Ave., Silver Spring, MD 20910
Telephone: (301) 565-0333
Registered as lobbyist at U.S. Congress.

HARDY-HAVENS, Debra M.
V. President and CEO, Capitol Associates, Inc.
426 C St., N.E., Washington, DC 20002
Telephone: (202) 544-1880
Registered as lobbyist at U.S. Congress.

HARDY, Ralph W., Jr.
Dow, Lohnes and Albertson
1255 23rd St., N.W., Suite 500, Washington, DC 20037
Telephone: (202) 857-2500
Background: Serves as Vice President and Secretary of First Media Corp., a company owned by members of the Marriott Family.
Clients:
  Citibank, N.A.
  First Media Corp.
  ST Systems Corp. (STX)
  Tak Communications, Inc.

HARDY, Robert G.
Andrews and Kurth
1701 Pennsylvania Ave., N.W., Suite 200, Washington, DC 20006
Telephone: (202) 662-2700
Clients:
  Transco Energy Co.

HARDY, Dr. Stuart B.
Manager, Food and Agriculture Policy, Chamber of Commerce of the U.S.A.
1615 H St., N.W., Washington, DC 20062
Telephone: (202) 463-5533
Registered as lobbyist at U.S. Congress.

HARDY, Timothy S.
Kirkland and Ellis
655 15th St., N.W. Suite 1200, Washington, DC 20005
Telephone: (202) 879-5000
Background: Member, Office of Counsel to the President, 1975-76.

HARE, Philip J.
927 15th St., N.W. Suite 1100, Washington, DC 20005
Telephone: (202) 898-0800
Registered as Foreign Agent: (#3974)
Organizations represented:
  South Africa, Embassy of

HARFF, James W.
Senior V. President, Washington Communications Group/ Ruder Finn
1615 M St., N.W., Suite 220, Washington, DC 20036
Telephone: (202) 466-7800
Registered as Foreign Agent: (#4315).
Clients:
  Axa Midi Assurances

HARGETT, W. Jack
Manager, Governmental Affairs, Parsons Corp.
1133 15th St., N.W. Suite 800, Washington, DC 20005
Telephone: (202) 775-6010

HARGROVE, John Lawrence
Exec. Director, American Soc. of Internat'l Law
2223 Massachusetts Ave., N.W., Washington, DC 20008
Telephone: (202) 265-4313

HARKAWAY, William I.
McCarthy, Sweeney and Harkaway, P.C.
1750 Pennsylvania Ave. N.W. Suite 1105, Washington, DC 20006
Telephone: (202) 393-5710
Background: Senior Staff Attorney, Federal Power Commission 1958-67.
Clients:
  Consolidated Edison Co. of New York

HARKER, R. Charles
Director, Government Affairs, American Physical Therapy Ass'n
1111 North Fairfax St., Alexandria, VA 22314
Telephone: (703) 684-2782
Background: Responsible for American Physical Therapy Ass'n Congressional Action Committee.

HARKEY, Charles 'Andy'
Federal Legislative Representative, American Financial Services Ass'n
1101 14th St., N.W., Washington, DC 20005
Telephone: (202) 289-0400
Background: Former staff member, House Appropriations Committee.

HARKINS, Francis J.
Chairman, 70001 Training & Employment Institute
501 School St., S.W. Suite 600, Washington, DC 20024
Telephone: (202) 484-0103

HARKINS, James C.
Exec. Director, Regular Common Carrier Conference
2200 Mill Road Suite 350, Alexandria, VA 22314
Telephone: (703) 838-1967

HARKNESS, Kim
Treasurer, American Federation of Teachers Staff Union Committee on Political Education
555 New Jersey Ave., N.W., Washington, DC 20001
Telephone: (202) 879-4471

HARLEY, William G.
Exec. Director, Nat'l Utility Contractors Ass'n
1235 Jefferson Davis Hwy. Suite 606, Arlington, VA 22202
Telephone: (703) 486-2100
Registered as lobbyist at U.S. Congress.
Background: Responsibilities include Nat'l Utility Contractors Ass'n Legislative and Action Committee.

HARLOE, D. Lynn
Government Relations Representative, Ass'n of Independent Colleges and Schools
One Dupont Circle, N.W., Suite 350, Washington, DC 20036
Telephone: (202) 659-2460

HARLOW, Bryce L.
Asst Secy, Legis Affrs, DEPARTMENT OF TREASURY
15th and Pennsylvania Ave. N.W., Washington, DC 20220
Telephone: (202) 566-2037

HARMAN, Charles R.
Director, Public Relations, Nat'l Alliance for the Mentally Ill
2101 Wilson Blvd., Suite 302, Arlington, VA 22201
Telephone: (703) 524-7600

HARMAN, Donna Akers
Director, Government Affairs, Champion Internat'l Corp.
1875 Eye St., N.W., Suite 540, Washington, DC 20006
Telephone: (202) 785-9888
Registered as lobbyist at U.S. Congress.

HARMAN, John R.
Wall and Associates, R. Duffy
1317 F St., N.W., Suite 400, Washington, DC 20004
Telephone: (202) 737-0100
Registered as lobbyist at U.S. Congress.

HARMAN, Robert E.
Director, Public Affairs, American Federation of State, County and Municipal Employees
1625 L St., N.W., Washington, DC 20036
Telephone: (202) 429-1000

HARMAN, William B., Jr.
Davis & Harman
1455 Pennsylvania Ave., N.W. Suite 1200, Washington, DC 20004
Telephone: (202) 347-2230
Clients:
  Stock Information Group

HARMENING, Patricia L.
Governmental Affairs Representative, San Diego Gas and Electric Co.
316 Pennsylvania Ave., S.E., Suite 301, Washington, DC 20003
Telephone: (202) 546-7676
Registered as lobbyist at U.S. Congress.

HARMON, CURRAN AND TOUSLEY
2001 S St., N.W., Suite 430, Washington, DC 20009
Telephone: (202) 328-3500
Members of firm representing listed organizations:
  Glitzenstein, Eric
  Harmon, Gail
Clients:
  Independent Sector *(Gail Harmon)*
  Nat'l Abortion Rights Action League
  Natural Resources Defense Council *(Eric Glitzenstein)*

HARMON, Gail
Harmon, Curran and Tousley
2001 S St., N.W., Suite 430, Washington, DC 20009
Telephone: (202) 328-3500
Clients:
  Independent Sector

HARMON AND WILMOT
1010 Vermont Ave., N.W., Suite 310, Washington, DC 20005
Telephone: (202) 783-9100
Background: An attorney.
Members of firm representing listed organizations:
  Wilmot, David W.
Clients:
  Anheuser-Busch Cos., Inc. *(David W. Wilmot)*
  Hotel Ass'n of Washington *(David W. Wilmot)*

HARPER-DIGGS, Brenda
Chairwoman, Nat'l Center for Religious Involvement
1115 P. St., N.W., Washington, DC 20005
Telephone: (202) 667-2338

HARPER-FAHEY, Christine
Legislative Representative, Nat'l Low Income Housing Coalition
1012 14th St., N.W. Suite 1500, Washington, DC 20005
Telephone: (202) 662-1530
Registered as lobbyist at U.S. Congress.

HARPER, Rosemary
V. President, Ass'n Services, American Chamber of Commerce Executives
4232 King St., Alexandria, VA 22302
Telephone: (703) 998-0072
Background: Serves as contact for American Chamber of Commerce Executives Communications Council.

HARPRING, Mary Gabriel
Staff Asst, Legis Affrs (House), EXECUTIVE OFFICE OF THE PRESIDENT - The White House
1600 Pennsylvania Ave., N.W. 112 East Wing, Washington, DC 20500
Telephone: (202) 456-7766

HARRELL, Wiley C., Jr.
Director, National Affairs, Anheuser-Busch Cos., Inc.
1776 I St., Suite 200, Washington, DC 20006
Telephone: (202) 293-9494
Registered as lobbyist at U.S. Congress.

HARRIGAN, Anthony
President, United States Business and Industrial Council
220 Nat'l Press Building, Washington, DC 20045
Telephone: (202) 662-8744

HARRILL, Edward D.
Dir, Office of Cong Relations, CONSUMER PRODUCT SAFETY COMMISSION
5401 Westbard Ave., Bethesda, MD 20816
Telephone: (301) 492-5515

HARRIMAN, Pamela
Chairperson, Democrats for the 90s
Box 3797 3038 N St., N.W., Washington, DC 20007
Telephone: (202) 338-9092

HARRINGTON, Anthony
Hogan and Hartson
555 13th St., N.W., Suite 1200, Washington, DC 20004-1109
Telephone: (202) 637-5600
Registered as lobbyist at U.S. Congress.
Clients:
  Center for Democracy
  Nat'l Telecommunications Network

HARRINGTON, John F.
Fulbright & Jaworski
1150 Connecticut Ave., N.W., Suite 400, Washington, DC 20036
Telephone: (202) 452-6800
Clients:
  Texas Gas Transmission Corp.

HARRINGTON, Kathleen
Asst Secy, Cong & Intergov'l Affrs, DEPARTMENT OF LABOR
200 Constitution Ave., N.W., Washington, DC 20210
Telephone: (202) 523-6141

HARRINGTON, Larry
Political Director, Democratic Senatorial Campaign Committee
430 South Capitol St., S.E., Washington, DC 20003
Telephone: (202) 224-2447

HARRINGTON, Toni
Manager, Government and Industry Rtns., Honda North America, Inc.
955 L'Enfant Plaza S.W., Suite 5300, Washington, DC 20024
Telephone: (202) 554-1650
Registered as lobbyist at U.S. Congress.

HARRINGTON, W. Brendan
Public Affairs Counselor, Cargill, Inc.
1101 15th St., N.W., Suite 205, Washington, DC 20005
Telephone: (202) 785-3060
Registered as lobbyist at U.S. Congress.

HARRIS, A. J., II
V. President, Federal Affairs, CIGNA Corp.
1825 Eye St., N.W., Suite 750, Washington, DC 20006
Telephone: (202) 296-7174
Registered as lobbyist at U.S. Congress.

HARRIS, Bill
Senior V. President, U.S. Council for Energy Awareness
1776 Eye St., N. W. Suite 400, Washington, DC 20006
Telephone: (202) 293-0770

HARRIS, C. Coleman
Exec. Secretary, Future Farmers of America
Box 15160, Alexandria, VA 22309-0160
Telephone: (703) 360-3600

HARRIS, Caspa L., Jr.
President, Nat'l Ass'n of College and University Business Officers
One Dupont Circle, N.W., Suite 500, Washington, DC 20036-1178
Telephone: (202) 861-2500

HARRIS, David A.
Washington Representative, American Jewish Committee
2027 Massachusetts Ave., N.W., Washington, DC 20036
Telephone: (202) 265-2000

HARRIS, David A., A.I.A.
President, Nat'l Institute of Building Sciences
1201 L St., N.W., Suite 400, Washington, DC 20005
Telephone: (202) 289-7800

HARRIS & ELLSWORTH
1101 30th St., N.W. Suite 103, Washington, DC 20007
Telephone: (202) 337-8338
Background: A law firm.
Members of firm representing listed organizations:
  Ellsworth, Cheryl N., Partner
  Harris, Herbert E. (II)
    Background: Member, U.S. House of Representatives (D-VA), 1975-81.
Clients:
  American Railway Car Institute *(Herbert E. Harris, II)*
  Ass'n of Food Industries, Inc. *(Herbert E. Harris, II)*
  Cheese Importers Ass'n of America *(Herbert E. Harris, II)*
  Committee of American Axle Producers *(Herbert E. Harris, II)*
  Committee of Domestic Steel Wire Rope and Specialty Cable Manufacturers *(Herbert E. Harris, II)*
  Tuna Canners Ass'n of the Philippines

HARRIS, Herbert E., II
Harris & Ellsworth
1101 30th St., N.W. Suite 103, Washington, DC 20007
Telephone: (202) 337-8338
Background: Member, U.S. House of Representatives (D-VA), 1975-81.
Clients:
  American Railway Car Institute
  Ass'n of Food Industries, Inc.
  Cheese Importers Ass'n of America
  Committee of American Axle Producers
  Committee of Domestic Steel Wire Rope and Specialty Cable Manufacturers

HARRIS, Kevin
Project Director, Nat'l Student Educational Fund
1012 14th St. N.W., Suite 403, Washington, DC 20005
Telephone: (202) 347-4769

HARRIS, LaDonna
President/ Exec. Director, Americans for Indian Opportunity
3508 Garfield St., N.W., Washington, DC 20007
Telephone: (202) 338-8809

HARRIS, Leslie
Chief Legislative Counsel, American Civil Liberties Union
122 Maryland Ave., N.E., Washington, DC 20002
Telephone: (202) 544-1681
Registered as lobbyist at U.S. Congress.

HARRIS, Lois
Admin Ofcr, Policy, Plng & Legislation, DEPARTMENT OF HEALTH AND HUMAN SERVICES - Human Development Services
200 Independence Ave. S.W., Washington, DC 20201
Telephone: (202) 245-7027

HARRIS, Marilyn A.
Gen Mgr-Govt'l Afrs, Steel & Diversified, USX Corp.
818 Connecticut Ave., N.W., Washington, DC 20006
Telephone: (202) 331-1340
Registered as lobbyist at U.S. Congress.
Background: Former Administrative Assistant to Rep. Mary Rose Oakar (D-OH) and Exec. Administrator, U.S. Senate Committee on Governmental Affairs. Responsibilities include the USX Corp. PAC.

HARRIS, Marra
Director, Political Affairs, Associated Builders and Contractors
729 15th St., N.W., Washington, DC 20005
Telephone: (202) 637-8800
Registered as lobbyist at U.S. Congress.
Background: Also serves as Director of the ABC-PAC.

HARRIS, Richard M.
Exec. V. President, American Road and Transportation Builders Ass'n
501 School St., S.W. Suite 800, Washington, DC 20024
Telephone: (202) 488-2722
Registered as lobbyist at U.S. Congress.
Background: Serves as contact for the American Road and Transportation Builders Ass'n PAC.

HARRIS, Robert L.
V. President, Legislative Affairs, Jefferson Group, The
1341 G St., N.W., Suite 1100, Washington, DC 20005
Telephone: (202) 638-3535
Registered as lobbyist at U.S. Congress.
Clients:
  Alumax, Inc.
  Doe Run Co.
  Horsehead Resource Development Co.
  Lockheed Corp.

HARRIS, Sam
Exec. Director, RESULTS
236 Massachusetts Ave., N.E. Suite 110, Washington, DC 20002
Telephone: (202) 543-9340

HARRIS, Sheldon J.
Rivkin, Radler, Dunne and Bayh
1575 Eye St., N.W. Suite 1025, Washington, DC 20005
Telephone: (202) 289-8660
Clients:
  Chemical Bank

HARRIS, Stuart H.
Howrey and Simon
1730 Pennsylvania Ave., N.W., Washington, DC 20006-4793
Telephone: (202) 783-0800
Clients:
  Timex Corp.

HARRIS, Sunny
Staff Associate for Legislation, Nat'l Ass'n of Social Workers
7981 Eastern Ave., Silver Spring, MD 20910
Telephone: (301) 565-0333
Registered as lobbyist at U.S. Congress.

HARRIS, Teena M.
Goverment Relations Legislative Ass't, Nat'l Newspaper Ass'n
1627 K St., N.W. Suite 400, Washington, DC 20006
Telephone: (202) 466-7200
Registered as lobbyist at U.S. Congress.

HARRISON, Alisa
Manager, Washington Information, Nat'l Cattlemen's Ass'n
1301 Pennsylvania Ave., N.W., Suite 300, Washington, DC 20004
Telephone: (202) 347-0228

HARRISON-CLARK, Anne
V. President for Public Affairs, March of Dimes Birth Defects Foundation
1725 K St., N.W., Suite 814, Washington, DC 20006
Telephone: (202) 659-1800
Registered as lobbyist at U.S. Congress.

HARRISON CO., E. Bruce
1440 New York Ave., N.W. Suite 300, Washington, DC 20005
Telephone: (202) 638-1200
Background: A public relations firm. Acquired Ernest Wittenberg Associates in 1986.
Members of firm representing listed organizations:
  Blakey, Allen, V. President
  Conley, Jeffrey B., Exec. V. President
  Deuschl, Vivian A., V. President
    Background: Former Special Assistant to Undersecretary of Commerce for Travel and Tourism.
  Harrison, E. Bruce, Chairman
  Harrison, Patricia S., Senior V. President and Partner
    Background: Serves as President, Nat'l Women's Economic Alliance.
  Hellem, Steven B., Senior V. President
  Klose, Christopher, V. President
  Soll, Joy A., V. President, Travel and Tourism Group
  Wittenberg, Ernest, V. Chairma
Organizations represented:
  Alternative Materials Institute
  Clean Air Act Project *(Jeffrey B. Conley, Steven B. Hellem)*
  Electricity Consumers Resource Council *(Steven B. Hellem)*
  Nat'l Environmental Development Ass'n *(Steven B. Hellem)*
  Nat'l Women's Economic Alliance *(Patricia S. Harrison)*
  Natural Gas Consumers Information Center
  Process Gas Consumers Group *(Steven B. Hellem)*
  Sorptive Minerals Institute *(Steven B. Hellem)*

HARRISON, E. Bruce
Harrison, Harrison Co., E. Bruce
1440 New York Ave., N.W. Suite 300, Washington, DC 20005
Telephone: (202) 638-1200

HARRISON, Gail
Senior V. President, Wexler, Reynolds, Fuller, Harrison and Schule, Inc.
1317 F St., N.W., Suite 600, Washington, DC 20004
Telephone: (202) 638-2121
Registered as lobbyist at U.S. Congress.
Registered as Foreign Agent: (#3306).
Clients:
Columbia Hospital for Women Medical Center
Foothills Pipe Lines (Yukon), Ltd.

HARRISON, Jim
President, Ass'n of Urban Universities
501 I St., S.W., Washington, DC 20024
Telephone: (202) 863-2027
Registered as lobbyist at U.S. Congress.

HARRISON, Joseph M.
President, Household Goods Carrier's Bureau
1611 Duke St., Alexandria, VA 22314
Telephone: (703) 683-7410

HARRISON, Mark
Lobbyist, SANE/FREEZE
1819 H St., N.W., Suite 1000, Washington, DC 20006
Telephone: (202) 862-9740
Registered as lobbyist at U.S. Congress.

HARRISON, Nancy F.
Admin Officer, Cong and Legis Affrs, DEPARTMENT OF INTERIOR
18th and C Sts., N.W., Washington, DC 20240
Telephone: (202) 343-7693

HARRISON, Patricia S.
Senior V. President and Partner, Harrison Co., E. Bruce
1440 New York Ave., N.W. Suite 300, Washington, DC 20005
Telephone: (202) 638-1200
Background: Serves as President, Nat'l Women's Economic Alliance.
Organizations represented:
Nat'l Women's Economic Alliance

HARRISON, Robert W.
Director, Washington Operations, CAE-LINK Corp.
1213 Jefferson Davis Hwy. Suite 1400, Gateway 4, Arlington, VA 22202
Telephone: (703) 553-0084
Registered as lobbyist at U.S. Congress.

HARRISON, Summer
Exec. V. President, Apter and Associates, David
1706 R St., N.W., Washington, DC 20009
Telephone: (202) 265-1212

HARSANYI, Dr. Fruzsina M.
V. President, Gov't & Internat'l Affairs, Asea Brown Boveri, Inc.
1101 15th St., N.W. Suite 500, Washington, DC 20005
Telephone: (202) 429-9180

HARSCH, J. William W.
Harsh, W. J. William
1722 Eye St., N.W., 6th Floor, Washington, DC 20006
Telephone: (202) 466-5770
Registered as lobbyist at U.S. Congress.
Organizations represented:
ANG Coal Gasification Co.
Aspen Technology, Inc.
Cranston, Rhode Island, City of
Fleet Nat'l Bank
Medical Care Development
Pyropower Corp.

HARSH, W. J. William
1722 Eye St., N.W., 6th Floor, Washington, DC 20006
Telephone: (202) 466-5770
Members of firm representing listed organizations:
Harsch, J. William W.
Organizations represented:
ANG Coal Gasification Co. *(J. William W. Harsch)*
Aspen Technology, Inc. *(J. William W. Harsch)*

Cranston, Rhode Island, City of *(J. William W. Harsch)*
Fleet Nat'l Bank *(J. William W. Harsch)*
Medical Care Development *(J. William W. Harsch)*
Pyropower Corp. *(J. William W. Harsch)*

HARSHA, Barbara
Exec. Director, Nat'l Ass'n of Governors' Highway Safety Representatives
444 North Capitol St., N.W. Suite 530, Washington, DC 20001
Telephone: (202) 624-5877

HARSHAW, John W.
President, American League of Financial Institutions
1709 New York Ave., N.W. Suite 801, Washington, DC 20006
Telephone: (202) 628-5624

HART, Betty K.
Public Information Officer, Investment Company Institute
1600 M St., N.W. Suite 600, Washington, DC 20036
Telephone: (202) 293-7700

HART, Col. Herbert M., USMC (Ret)
Director, Public Affairs, Reserve Officers Ass'n of the U.S.
1 Constitution Ave., N.E., Washington, DC 20002
Telephone: (202) 479-2200
Background: Serves also as volunteer National Secretary, Council on America's Military Past, a non-profit educational military history association, and Editor, ROA National Security Report, a bi-monthly publication with a circulation of 130,000.

HART, Hilary
Conservation Associate, Grand Canyon Trust
1400 16th St. N.W., Suite 300, Washington, DC 20036
Telephone: (202) 797-5429

HART, J. Steven
President, Williams and Jensen, P.C.
1101 Connecticut Ave., N.W. Suite 500, Washington, DC 20036
Telephone: (202) 659-8201
Background: Former Ass't to the Chair, President's Task Force on ERISA Reorganization, Office of Management and Budget, 1978-79. Special Assistant to the Assistant Attorney General for Legal Policy, Department of Justice, 1981-82.
Clients:
Nat'l Board for Professional Training Standards
Pittston Co., The
Recording Industry Ass'n of America
Texas Air Corp.
Turner Broadcasting System, Inc.

HART, Jayne A.
Ass't Dir., Dept. of Congress'l Affairs, American Medical Ass'n
1101 Vermont Ave., N.W., Washington, DC 20005
Telephone: (202) 789-7400
Registered as lobbyist at U.S. Congress.

HART, Lynn S.
Director, Federal Legislation, Federation of American Health Systems
1111 19th St., N.W. Suite 402, Washington, DC 20036
Telephone: (202) 833-3090
Registered as lobbyist at U.S. Congress.
Background: Serves as contact for the Federation of American Health Systems Political Action Committee.

HART, Tanya
Program Manager, Nat'l Council on the Aging
600 Maryland Ave., S.W. West Wing 100, Washington, DC 20024
Telephone: (202) 479-1200
Background: Represents the Nat'l Institute on Adult Daycare and Nat'l Institute on Community-Based Long-Term Care.

HART, Thomas D.
Dir., Legislative and Regulatory Affairs, Allied-Signal Inc.
1001 Pennsylvania Ave., N.W. Suite 700, Washington, DC 20004
Telephone: (202) 662-2650
Registered as lobbyist at U.S. Congress.

HART, William R.
Deputy Director, Legislative Affairs, Retired Officers Ass'n, The (TROA)
201 N. Washington St., Alexandria, VA 22314
Telephone: (703) 549-2311
Registered as lobbyist at U.S. Congress.

HARTL, Gabriel A.
President, Air Traffic Control Ass'n
2020 North 14th St., Arlington, VA 22201
Telephone: (703) 522-5717
Registered as lobbyist at U.S. Congress.

HARTLEY, H. Benjamin
Piper and Marbury
1200 19th St., N.W., Washington, DC 20036
Telephone: (202) 861-3900
Registered as lobbyist at U.S. Congress.
Clients:
Nat'l Ass'n of Independent Colleges and Universities

HARTLEY, Kathleen L.
Exec. Assistant, Voluntary Hospitals of America, Inc.
1150 Connecticut Ave., N.W. Suite 800, Washington, DC 20036
Telephone: (202) 822-9750

HARTMAN, Arthur
Senior Consultant, APCO Associates
1155 21st St., N.W., Suite 1000, Washington, DC 20036
Telephone: (202) 778-1000
Background: Former U.S. Ambassador to the Soviet Union and to France.

HARTMAN, Charles H.
Exec. V. President, American Alliance for Health, Physical Education, Recreation and Dance
1900 Association Drive, Reston, VA 22091
Telephone: (703) 476-3400

HARTMAN, Richard C.
Exec. Director, Nat'l Ass'n of Regional Councils
1700 K St., N.W., Suite 1300, Washington, DC 20006-0011
Telephone: (202) 457-0710

HARTMANN, Arthur W.
Government Policy Specialist, Nat'l Rural Electric Cooperative Ass'n
1800 Massachusetts Ave., N.W., Washington, DC 20036
Telephone: (202) 857-9571
Registered as lobbyist at U.S. Congress.

HARTMANN, Dr. C. David
President, Fellowship Square Foundation
11718 Bowman Green Drive, Reston, VA 22090
Telephone: (703) 471-5370

HARTMANN, Carolyn
Staff Attorney, U.S. Public Interest Research Group
215 Pennsylvania Ave., S.E., Washington, DC 20003
Telephone: (202) 546-9707
Registered as lobbyist at U.S. Congress.

HARTMANN, Robert S.
Sr. V. Pres. & Dir., Public Relations, Abramson Associates
1275 K St., N.W., Washington, DC 20005
Telephone: (202) 289-6900

HARTNETT & ASSOCIATES
4590 MacArthur Blvd., N.W., Suite 200, Washington, DC 20007
Telephone: (202) 337-1502
Members of firm representing listed organizations:
Hartnett, Catherine B., President
Hartnett, Douglas
Kunz, Cynthia
Clients:
Baking Industry and Teamster Labor Conference *(Cynthia Kunz)*
Environmental and Energy Study Institute *(Douglas Hartnett)*
Spina Bifida Ass'n of America *(Catherine B. Hartnett)*

HARTNETT, Catherine B.
President, Hartnett & Associates
4590 MacArthur Blvd., N.W., Suite 200, Washington, DC 20007

Telephone: (202) 337-1502
Clients:
Spina Bifida Ass'n of America

HARTNETT, Douglas
Hartnett & Associates
4590 MacArthur Blvd., N.W., Suite 200, Washington, DC 20007
Telephone: (202) 337-1502
Clients:
Environmental and Energy Study Institute

HARTNETT, Janet S.
Dep Dir, Polcy, Plng and Legislation, DEPARTMENT OF HEALTH AND HUMAN SERVICES - Human Development Services
200 Independence Ave. S.W., Washington, DC 20201
Telephone: (202) 245-7027

HARTNETT, Kathleen
Assoc. Dir., Private Lands & Envir Mgmt, Nat'l Cattlemen's Ass'n
1301 Pennsylvania Ave., N.W., Suite 300, Washington, DC 20004
Telephone: (202) 347-0228
Registered as lobbyist at U.S. Congress.

HARTQUIST, David A.
Collier, Shannon & Scott
1055 Thomas Jefferson St., N.W., Suite 300, Washington, DC 20007
Telephone: (202) 342-8400
Registered as lobbyist at U.S. Congress.
Registered as Foreign Agent: (#2937).
Background: Legislative Assistant to Senator Richard S. Schweiker, 1970-1973. Assistant to the President, Overseas Private Investment Corp., 1973-1974. Gen. Counsel, White House Council on Internat'l Economic Policy, 1974-1976.
Clients:
American Couplings Coalition
American Flint Glass Workers Union
Armco Inc.
Bethlehem Steel Corp.
Carpenter Technology Corp.
Chase Brass and Copper
Coalition for Safe Ceramicware
Copper and Brass Fabricators Council
Crop Insurance Research Bureau
Hussey Copper Ltd.
Magnavox Consumer Electronics Co.
Miller Co.
Nat'l Ass'n of Mutual Insurance Companies
Pittsburgh Corning Corp.
Specialty Steel Industry of the United States
Stanley Bostitch Inc.
United Steelworkers of America
Valve Manufacturers Ass'n of America
Wyman-Gordon Co.

HARTWELL, Keith O.
President, RBC Associates, Inc.
324 Fourth St., N.E., Washington, DC 20002
Telephone: (202) 543-0038
Background: Former Administrative Assistant to Rep. Marvin Esch (R-MI), 1971-76. Director, State Senate Legislative Staff, 1978-80.
Clients:
Dakota, Minnesota & Eastern
Pinsly Railroad Co.
Regional Railroads of America
Turbomeca Engine Corp.

HARTY, Christopher E.
Winkelmann & Associates, Inc.
1250 Connecticut Ave. NW Suite 620, Washington, DC 20036
Telephone: (202) 466-7263
Registered as lobbyist at U.S. Congress.

HARTZ, Jim
Hartz/Meek Internat'l
806 15th St., N.W. Suite 210, Washington, DC 20006
Telephone: (202) 737-7370
Clients:
Arizona, State of

HARTZ/MEEK INTERNAT'L
806 15th St., N.W. Suite 210, Washington, DC 20006

Telephone: (202) 737-7370
Background: A public relations firm.
Members of firm representing listed organizations:
Hartz, Jim
Meek, John
Clients:
Arizona, State of *(Jim Hartz, John Meek)*
GEICO Corp.

HARTZ, Michelle
Senior V., Burson-Marsteller
1850 M St., N.W., Suite 900, Washington, DC 20036
Telephone: (202) 833-8550
Clients:
American Soc. of Landscape Architects

HARVEY, Lt. Col. Thomas
SDI, Legis Affrs, DEPARTMENT OF DEFENSE
The Pentagon, Washington, DC 20301
Telephone: (202) 697-6210

HARVEY, Rev. Thomas J.
Exec. Director, Catholic Charities USA
1319 F St., N.W., Suite 400, Washington, DC 20004
Telephone: (202) 639-8400

HARVISON, Clifford J.
President, Nat'l Tank Truck Carriers
2200 Mill Road, Suite 601, Alexandria, VA 22314
Telephone: (703) 838-1960
Registered as lobbyist at U.S. Congress.

HASFURTHER, Donald J.
Director, East-West Internat'l Division, Chamber of Commerce of the U.S.A.
1615 H St., N.W., Washington, DC 20062
Telephone: (202) 659-6000

HASH, Michael M.
Health Policy Alternatives
122 C St., N.W., Suite 820, Washington, DC 20001
Telephone: (202) 737-3390
Background: Serves as Washington consultant for the American Nurses' Ass'n.

HASKELL, Elizabeth R.
Exec. Director, American Council of Young Political Leaders
1000 Connecticut Ave., N.W. Suite 208, Washington, DC 20036
Telephone: (202) 857-0999

HASLEBACHER, Fanny L.
Washington Legislative Counsel, American Medical Ass'n
1101 Vermont Ave., N.W., Washington, DC 20005
Telephone: (202) 789-7400
Registered as lobbyist at U.S. Congress.

HASPEL, Donald P.
Exec. V. President, Nat'l Office Products Ass'n
301 North Fairfax St., Alexandria, VA 22314
Telephone: (703) 549-9040
Background: Serves as contact for the Nat'l Office Products Ass'n PAC.

HASSETT, Holly
Manager, Washington Office, Hershey Foods Corp.
1730 Rhode Island Ave., N.W., Suite 206, Washington, DC 20036
Telephone: (202) 223-9070
Registered as lobbyist at U.S. Congress.

HASSETT, James C., Jace
Government Relations Representative, Grocery Manufacturers of America
1010 Wisconsin Ave., N.W., Suite 800, Washington, DC 20007
Telephone: (202) 337-9400
Registered as lobbyist at U.S. Congress.

HASTIE, Rod
Confidential Asst, Cong Rels, DEPARTMENT OF AGRICULTURE
14th and Independence Ave. S.W., Room 210-E, Washington, DC 20205
Telephone: (202) 447-7095

HATCH, F. Whitney
Asst. V. President - Regulatory Affairs, GTE Corp.
Suite 1200, 1850 M St., N.W., Washington, DC 20036

Telephone: (202) 463-5292

HATCHER, David M.
Commerce Consultants Internat'l Ltd.
1025 Thomas Jefferson St, N.W. Suite 105, Washington, DC 20007
Telephone: (202) 342-9610
Registered as Foreign Agent: (#4248).
Clients:
Hughes Aircraft Co.
Thailand, Office of the Prime Minister

HATCHER, Edgar
Senior Manager, Tax Policy, American Electronics Ass'n
1225 Eye St., N.W., Suite 950, Washington, DC 20005
Telephone: (202) 682-9110
Registered as lobbyist at U.S. Congress.
Background: Former Administrative Assistant to Rep. Robert Matsui (D-CA).

HATFIELD, Frederick W.
Government Relations Consultant, McAuliffe, Kelly, Raffaelli & Siemens
1341 G St., N.W. Suite 200, Washington, DC 20005
Telephone: (202) 783-1800
Registered as lobbyist at U.S. Congress.
Registered as Foreign Agent: (#4332).
Background: Former Chief of Staff to Rep. Tony Coelho (D-CA).
Clients:
American Tunaboat Ass'n
Coalition for Affordable Home Financing
Monarch Wines
Valley Children's Hospital
Wine Institute

HATFIELD, Dr. Thomas A.
Exec. Director, Nat'l Art Education Ass'n
1916 Association Dr., Reston, VA 22091
Telephone: (703) 860-8000

HATHAWAY, C. Michael
Crowell and Moring
1001 Pennsylvania Ave., N.W., Washington, DC 20004-2505
Telephone: (202) 624-2500
Background: Former Senior Deputy General Counsel, Ofice of the United States Trade Representative.

HATHAWAY, Janet S.
Senior Project Attorney, Natural Resources Defense Council
1350 New York Ave., N.W., Suite 300, Washington, DC 20005
Telephone: (202) 783-7800
Registered as lobbyist at U.S. Congress.

HATHAWAY, Spencer K.
State Government Affairs Manager, Syntex (USA) Inc.
1133 15th St., N.W., Suite 210, Washington, DC 20005
Telephone: (202) 429-2225

HATHAWAY, William D.
Patton, Boggs and Blow
2550 M St., N.W., Suite 800, Washington, DC 20037
Telephone: (202) 457-6000
Registered as lobbyist at U.S. Congress.
Registered as Foreign Agent: (#2165).
Background: Member U.S. House of Representatives (D-ME), 1965-72. Member U.S. Senate (D-ME), 1973-78.
Clients:
Fidelity Investors

HAUB, Carl
Director, Demographic Analysis, Population Reference Bureau
777 14th St., N.W. Suite 800, Washington, DC 20005
Telephone: (202) 639-8040

HAUCK AND ASSOCIATES
1255 23rd St., N.W., Washington, DC 20037
Telephone: (202) 452-8100
Background: A professional association management firm.
Members of firm representing listed organizations:
Ailor, David C.
Background: Serves as Director, Regulatory Affairs, Nat'l Oilseed Processors Ass'n and American Coke and Coal Chemicals Institute.
Ekfelt, Richard H., V. President

WASHINGTON REPRESENTATIVES

HAUCK AND ASSOCIATES (Cont'd)
Background: Serves as Exec. Director, Electromagnetic Energy Policy Alliance and Exec. Director, Nat'l Health Care Anti-Fraud Ass'n.
Engle, Mark T., V. President
Background: Serves as President, American Coke and Coal Chemicals Institute; Exec. Director Nat'l Ass'n of Video Distributors; and Exec. Director, Nat'l Ass'n of Telecommunications Dealers.
Hauck, Sheldon J., President
Background: Serves as President, Nat'l Oilseed Processors Ass'n and Exec. V. President, Soy Protein Council.
McElfresh, Dinah D.
Background: Serves as Director, Regulatory Affairs Committee, Soy Protein Council; Director of Gov't Relations, Hearing Industries Ass'n; and Director of Administration, State Governmental Affairs Council.
McVey, Brose A.
Background: Serves as Exec. V. President, Nat'l Oilseed Processors Ass'n.
Rogin, Carole M., Exec. V. President
Background: Serves as Exec. Director, Hearing Industries Ass'n and Exec. Director, State Governmental Affairs Council.
Clients:
American Coke and Coal Chemicals Institute *(David C. Ailor, Mark T. Engle)*
Electromagnetic Energy Policy Alliance *(Richard H. Ekfelt)*
Hearing Industries Ass'n *(Carole M. Rogin)*
Nat'l Ass'n of Telecommunications Dealers *(Mark T. Engle)*
Nat'l Ass'n of Video Distributors *(Mark T. Engle)*
Nat'l Health Care Anti-Fraud Ass'n *(Richard H. Ekfelt)*
Nat'l Oilseed Processors Ass'n *(Sheldon J. Hauck, Brose A. McVey)*
Soy Protein Council *(Sheldon J. Hauck, Dinah D. McElfresh)*
State Governmental Affairs Council *(Dinah D. McElfresh, Carole M. Rogin)*

HAUCK, Sheldon J.
President, Hauck and Associates
1255 23rd St., N.W., Washington, DC 20037
Telephone: (202) 452-8100
Background: Serves as President, Nat'l Oilseed Processors Ass'n and Exec. V. President, Soy Protein Council.
Clients:
Nat'l Oilseed Processors Ass'n
Soy Protein Council

HAUERCAMP, Dawn
Director of Federation Relations, American Soc. of Internal Medicine
1101 Vermont Ave., N.W. Suite 500, Washington, DC 20005
Telephone: (202) 289-1700

HAUGEN, Barbara
Director, Federal Affairs, Nat'l Ass'n of Insurance Brokers
1401 New York Ave., N.W., Suite 720, Washington, DC 20005
Telephone: (202) 628-6700
Registered as lobbyist at U.S. Congress.
Background: Former Director of Information Services, The White House.

HAUGEN, Marilyn Beth
Mgr., Groundwater/Drinking Water Prgrms, American Paper Institute
1250 Connecticut Ave., N.W. Suite 210, Washington, DC 20036
Telephone: (202) 463-2420
Registered as lobbyist at U.S. Congress.

HAUGH, Barbara J.
Manager, Federal Affairs, UNOCAL Corp.
1050 Connecticut Ave., N.W. Suite 760, Washington, DC 20036
Telephone: (202) 659-7600
Registered as lobbyist at U.S. Congress.

HAUGH, Leroy J.
V. President, Procurement and Finance, Aerospace Industries Ass'n of America
1250 Eye St., N.W., Suite 1100, Washington, DC 20005
Telephone: (202) 371-8400

HAUGHT, Mary W.
Consultant, Sun Co.
555 13th St., N.W., Suite 1010 East, Washington, DC 20004
Telephone: (202) 628-1010

HAUGHTON-DENNISTON, Pamela
Director, Legislative Program, Religious Coalition for Abortion Rights
100 Maryland Ave., N.E., Washington, DC 20002
Telephone: (202) 543-7032
Registered as lobbyist at U.S. Congress.

HAUPT, E. H.
Manager, Airport & Environmental Svcs., Nat'l Business Aircraft Ass'n
1200 18th St., N.W. Suite 200, Washington, DC 20036
Telephone: (202) 783-9000

HAUSER, Kathryn F.
Exec. Director, Bell Atlantic
1710 Rhode Island Ave., N.W., Suite 1100, Washington, DC 20036
Telephone: (202) 392-0929

HAUSMAN, Shawn
Director, External Affairs, American Council of Life Insurance
1001 Pennsylvania Ave., N.W., Washington, DC 20004-2599
Telephone: (202) 624-2438

HAVEL, James
Director, Government Relations, Nat'l Alliance for the Mentally Ill
2101 Wilson Blvd., Suite 302, Arlington, VA 22201
Telephone: (703) 524-7600

HAVEL, Roberta
Director, Save Our Security
1201 16th St., N.W., Suite 222, Washington, DC 20036
Telephone: (202) 822-7848
Registered as lobbyist at U.S. Congress.
Background: Former congressional legislative assistant.

HAVENS, Arnold I.
White, Fine, and Verville
1156 15th St., N.W. Suite 1100, Washington, DC 20005
Telephone: (202) 659-2900
Registered as lobbyist at U.S. Congress.
Clients:
Armstrong World Industries, Inc.
Ass'n of American Railroads
Burlington Northern Railroad
CSX Corp.
MetPath Inc.

HAVENS, Charles W., III
LeBoeuf, Lamb, Leiby, and MacRae
1333 New Hampshire Ave., N.W. Suite 1100, Washington, DC 20036
Telephone: (202) 457-7500
Registered as lobbyist at U.S. Congress.
Registered as Foreign Agent: (#2868).
Clients:
Lloyds of London, Underwriters at

HAWES, Kathryn JoAnn
Assistant to the President, Internat'l Federation of Professional and Technical Engineers
8701 Georgia Ave., Suite 701, Silver Spring, MD 20910
Telephone: (301) 565-9016
Registered as lobbyist at U.S. Congress.

HAWK, Robert M.
Dir., Public Relations & Advertising, Fokker Aircraft U.S.A., Inc.
1199 North Fairfax St. Suite 500, Alexandria, VA 22314
Telephone: (703) 838-0100

HAWKE, John D., Jr.
Arnold & Porter
1200 New Hampshire Ave., N.W., Washington, DC 20036
Telephone: (202) 872-6700
Clients:
Washington Area Bankers Ass'n

HAWKES, Sidney G.
Vice President, Washington Affairs, Mead Corp.
1667 K St., N.W., Suite 420, Washington, DC 20006
Telephone: (202) 833-9643
Registered as lobbyist at U.S. Congress.

HAWKINS, Charles E., III
V. President, Government Affairs, Associated Builders and Contractors
729 15th St., N.W., Washington, DC 20005
Telephone: (202) 637-8800
Registered as lobbyist at U.S. Congress.
Background: Responsible also for ABC-PAC.

HAWKINS, David G.
Attorney, Natural Resources Defense Council
1350 New York Ave., N.W. Suite 300, Washington, DC 20005
Telephone: (202) 783-7800

HAWKINS, Edward J.
Squire, Sanders and Dempsey
1201 Pennsylvania Ave., N.W. P.O. Box 407, Washington, DC 20044
Telephone: (202) 626-6600
Registered as lobbyist at U.S. Congress.
Background: Chief Tax Counsel, Senate Finance Committee, 1979-80. Minority Tax Counsel, Senate Finance Committee, 1981.
Clients:
White Consolidated Industries

HAWKINS, James W., III
Director, Government Affairs, Health Industry Manufacturers Ass'n
1030 15th St., N.W. Suite 1100, Washington, DC 20005
Telephone: (202) 452-8240
Registered as lobbyist at U.S. Congress.
Background: Responsibilities include the Health industry Manufacturers Ass'n PAC.

HAWKINS, Kit
Director, Government Relations, United States Telephone Ass'n
900 19th St., N.W., Suite 800, Washington, DC 20006-2102
Telephone: (202) 835-3100
Registered as lobbyist at U.S. Congress.

HAWKINS, Robert W.
Ginsburg, Feldman and Bress
1250 Connecticut Ave., N.W. Suite 800, Washington, DC 20036
Telephone: (202) 637-9000
Registered as Foreign Agent: (#3106).
Clients:
Airship Industries, Ltd.

HAWKS, Jack
Director, Public Information, American Gas Ass'n
1515 Wilson Blvd., Arlington, VA 22209
Telephone: (703) 841-8661

HAWLEY, Dale
Exec. Director, Nat'l Honor Soc.
1904 Association Drive, Reston, VA 22091
Telephone: (703) 860-0200

HAWLEY, F. William, III
V. President, Internat'l Gov't Relations, Citicorp
1275 Pennsylvania Ave., N.W., Suite 503, Washington, DC 20004
Telephone: (202) 879-6800

HAWLEY, Kip
V. President, External Relations, Union Pacific Corp.
555 13th St., N.W., Suite 450 West Columbia Square, Washington, DC 20004
Telephone: (202) 662-0100
Registered as lobbyist at U.S. Congress.
Background: Serves as head of Washington, DC office.

HAY, John F.
Assoc. Dir., Gov't Relations - Defense, Westinghouse Electric Corp.
1801 K St., N.W., Washington, DC
Telephone: (202) 835-2409
Registered as lobbyist at U.S. Congress.

The listings in this directory are available as *Mailing Labels.* See last page.

WASHINGTON REPRESENTATIVES

HAYCOCK, Kati
V. President, Children's Defense Fund
122 C St., N.W., Washington, DC 20001
Telephone: (202) 628-8787

HAYDEN, Robert T.
Conway and Company
1120 Connecticut Ave., N.W. Suite 469, Washington, DC 20036
Telephone: (202) 289-0800
Registered as lobbyist at U.S. Congress.

HAYDEN, Samuel
Senior Counsel, International, Public Affairs Group, Inc.
1629 K St., N.W., Suite 1100, Washington, DC 20006
Telephone: (202) 785-6713

HAYES, Carnie
Director, Federal-State Relations, Council of Chief State School Officers
400 North Capitol St., N.W., Suite 379, Washington, DC 20001
Telephone: (202) 393-8161

HAYES, Peter M.
Manager, Federal Affairs, Salt River Project
214 Massachusetts Ave., N.E. Suite 310, Washington, DC 20002
Telephone: (202) 546-8940
Registered as lobbyist at U.S. Congress.

HAYES, Robert G.
Bogle and Gates
One Thomas Circle, N.W., Suite 900, Washington, DC 20005
Telephone: (202) 293-3600
Registered as lobbyist at U.S. Congress.
Clients:
American Dehydrated Onion and Garlic Ass'n
American Fishing Tackle Manufacturers Ass'n
Basic American Foods
Coastal Conservation Ass'n
United Sport Fishermen

HAYES, Stephen D.
V. President, Public Information, Air Transport Ass'n of America
1709 New York Ave., N.W., Washington, DC 20006-5206
Telephone: (202) 626-4000
Background: FAA Public Affairs Assistant Administrator, 1985-87.

HAYES, Webb C., III
Baker and Hostetler
1050 Connecticut Ave., N.W. Suite 1100, Washington, DC 20036
Telephone: (202) 861-1500

HAYNES, Caroline
Dep Asst Secy, Legis Affrs (Senate), DEPARTMENT OF TREASURY
15th and Pennsylvania Ave. N.W., Washington, DC 20220
Telephone: (202) 566-2037

HAYNES, Dr. Charles C.
Project Director, Americans United Research Foundation
900 Silver Spring Ave., Silver Spring, MD 20910
Telephone: (301) 588-2282

HAYNES, Fred
V.P., Plng. & Anal., Miss. & Elect. Grp., LTV Aircraft Products Group
1725 Jefferson Davis Hwy. Suite 900, Arlington, VA 22202
Telephone: (703) 521-6560

HAZARD, Holly Eliz.
Galvin, Stanley & Hazard
111 Massachusetts Ave., N.W., Washington, DC 20001
Telephone: (202) 289-4854
Clients:
Doris Day Animal League

HAZARD, John W., Jr.
Webster, Chamberlain and Bean
1747 Pennsylvania Ave., N.W., Suite 1000, Washington, DC 20006
Telephone: (202) 785-9500
Registered as lobbyist at U.S. Congress.
Clients:

American Academy of Optometry

HAZEN, Paul
V. President, Government Relations, Nat'l Cooperative Business Ass'n
1401 New York Ave., N.W. Suite 1100, Washington, DC 20005
Telephone: (202) 638-6222
Registered as lobbyist at U.S. Congress.

HEAD, C. J.
Partner, Bishop, Cook, Purcell & Reynolds
1400 L St., N.W., Washington, DC 20005-3502
Telephone: (202) 371-5700

HEALEY, James H.
Black, Manafort, Stone and Kelly Public Affairs Co.
211 N. Union St., Third Floor, Alexandria, VA 22314
Telephone: (703) 683-6612
Registered as lobbyist at U.S. Congress.
Registered as Foreign Agent: (#3600).
Clients:
Johnson & Johnson

HEALEY, Maureen
Ass't Director, Federal Gov't Affairs, Soc. of the Plastics Industry
1275 K St., N.W., Suite 400, Washington, DC 20005
Telephone: (202) 371-5200

HEALTH AND MEDICINE COUNSEL OF WASHINGTON
511 Capitol Court, N.E., Suite 300, Washington, DC 20002
Telephone: (202) 544-7499
Members of firm representing listed organizations:
Dillon, Elizabeth
Dirks, Dale P., President
Clients:
American Academy of Family Physicians *(Dale P. Dirks)*
American Ass'n of Gastroenterology *(Dale P. Dirks)*
American Lung Ass'n/American Thoracic Soc. *(Dale P. Dirks)*
American Narcolepsy Ass'n *(Dale P. Dirks)*
American Sleep Disorders Ass'n
Ass'n of Minority Health Professions Schools *(Dale P. Dirks)*
Digestive Disease Nat'l Coalition *(Dale P. Dirks)*
Environmental Sciences Ass'n *(Dale P. Dirks)*
Nat'l Sudden Infant Death Syndrome Foundation *(Dale P. Dirks)*
St. George's University School of Medicine *(Dale P. Dirks)*

HEALTH POLICY ALTERNATIVES
122 C St., N.W., Suite 820, Washington, DC 20001
Telephone: (202) 737-3390
Members of firm representing listed organizations:
Hash, Michael M.
Background: Serves as Washington consultant for the American Nurses' Ass'n.
Clients:
American Nurses' Ass'n

HEALY, Gigi A.
Director of Public Affairs, Suppliers of Advanced Composite Materials Ass'n (SACMA)
1600 Wilson Blvd., Suite 1008, Arlington, VA 22209
Telephone: (703) 841-1556

HEALY, John J.
Exec. V. President and CEO, Nat'l Wooden Pallet and Container Ass'n
1625 Massachusetts Ave., N.W., Washington, DC 20036
Telephone: (202) 667-3670

HEALY, Monica M.
Director, Maryland Washington Office, State of
444 N. Capitol St., N.W. Suite 315, Washington, DC 20001
Telephone: (202) 638-2215

HEALY, Patricia M.
Reid & Priest
1111 19th St., N.W., Washington, DC 20036
Telephone: (202) 828-0100
Clients:
Utility Decommissioning Tax Group

HEALY, Dr. Robert
Washington Representative, ARCO
1333 New Hampshire Ave., N.W., Suite 1001, Washington, DC 20036
Telephone: (202) 457-6253
Registered as lobbyist at U.S. Congress.

HEALY, Robert L., Jr.
Government Affairs Director, American Public Transit Ass'n
1201 New York Ave., N.W.,, Washington, DC 20005
Telephone: (202) 898-4000
Registered as lobbyist at U.S. Congress.

HEANUE, Anne A.
Associate Director, American Library Ass'n
110 Maryland Ave., N.E., Suite 101, Washington, DC 20002
Telephone: (202) 547-4440
Registered as lobbyist at U.S. Congress.

HEARD, B. Keith
Exec. V. President, Nat'l Corn Growers Ass'n
201 Massachusetts Ave., N.E., Suite C4, Washington, DC 20002
Telephone: (202) 546-7611
Registered as lobbyist at U.S. Congress.

HEARNE, Paul G.
President, Dole Foundation for Employment of People with Disabilities, The
1819 H St., N.W., Suite 850, Washington, DC 20006
Telephone: (202) 457-0318
Background: Deputy Postmaster General of the U.S., 1985-86. Serves also as Exec. Director, Nat'l Council on Disabilities and Just One Break, Inc.

HEATHERLY, Charles L.
V. President, Academic Relations, Heritage Foundation
214 Massachusetts Ave., N.E., Washington, DC 20002
Telephone: (202) 546-4400

HEATON, Suzanne M.
Staff Dir., Gov't Affairs, Consumer Grp., Electronic Industries Ass'n
2001 Pennsylvania Ave., N.W., Washington, DC 20006
Telephone: (202) 457-4900

HEBDA, Robert E.
Steele & Fornaciari
2020 K St., N.W. Suite 850, Washington, DC 20006-1857
Telephone: (202) 887-1779
Registered as lobbyist at U.S. Congress.
Clients:
K mart Corp.

HEBERT, David E.
Government Affairs Counsel, Nat'l Ass'n of Life Underwriters
1922 F St., N.W., Washington, DC 20006
Telephone: (202) 331-6000
Registered as lobbyist at U.S. Congress.
Background: Former Legislative Director to Rep. Jack Buechner (R-MO).

HEBERT, Richard
Communications Director, HALT-An Organization of Americans for Legal Reform
1319 F St., N.W., Suite 300, Washington, DC 20004
Telephone: (202) 347-9600

HECHT, Philip H.
Clifford & Warnke
815 Connecticut Ave., N.W., Washington, DC 20006
Telephone: (202) 828-4200

HECHT, SPENCER & ASSOCIATES
499 South Capitol St., S.W., Suite 507, Washington, DC 20003
Telephone: (202) 554-2881
Background: A government relations consulting firm.
Members of firm representing listed organizations:
Bachrach, Bronwyn R.
Background: Former Congressional Liaison officer, U.S. Department of State.
Browning, Carol
Background: Former aide to former Senator Bill Brock (R-TN) in the Senate, the Office of U.S. Trade Representative and the U.S. Department of Labor.

HECHT, SPENCER & ASSOCIATES (Cont'd)

Hecht, William H.

Huddleston, Walter D., Exec. V. President
Background: Former U.S. Senator (D-KY), 1973-85.

Locke, W. Timothy
Background: Former White House assistant, U.S. Interior Departmen official and aide to Senator Howard Baker (R-TN).

Spencer, Stuart K.
Background: Chairman of the Board, Hecht, Spencer & Associates.

Wiles, Lanny F.

Clients:
AIRTRAX *(William H. Hecht, Walter D. Huddleston, W. Timothy Locke)*
BATUS, Inc. *(Bronwyn R. Bachrach, William H. Hecht, Walter D. Huddleston, W. Timothy Locke)*
Bixby Ranch *(Bronwyn R. Bachrach, William H. Hecht)*
Boy Scouts of America *(Bronwyn R. Bachrach, William H. Hecht, W. Timothy Locke)*
Brown and Williamson Tobacco Corp. *(Bronwyn R. Bachrach, William H. Hecht, Walter D. Huddleston, W. Timothy Locke)*
Jacksonville, Florida, City of *(Lanny F. Wiles)*
Los Angeles Raiders *(William H. Hecht)*
Marwais Steel Co. *(Bronwyn R. Bachrach, William H. Hecht, W. Timothy Locke)*
Nat'l Ass'n for the Support of Long Term Care - NASL *(Bronwyn R. Bachrach, William H. Hecht, W. Timothy Locke)*
Texas Clinical Laboratories *(William H. Hecht)*
Traditional Industries *(William H. Hecht)*

HECHT, William H.

Hecht, Spencer & Associates
499 South Capitol St., S.W., Suite 507, Washington, DC 20003
Telephone: (202) 554-2881
Registered as lobbyist at U.S. Congress.
Registered as Foreign Agent: (#3740).
Clients:
AIRTRAX
BATUS, Inc.
Bixby Ranch
Boy Scouts of America
Brown and Williamson Tobacco Corp.
Los Angeles Raiders
Marwais Steel Co.
Nat'l Ass'n for the Support of Long Term Care - NASL
Texas Clinical Laboratories
Traditional Industries

HECKER, Guy L.

Stafford, Burke and Hecker
1006 Cameron St., Alexandria, VA 22314
Telephone: (703) 836-2696
Registered as Foreign Agent: (#3625).
Clients:
Construcciones Aeronauticas, S.A.
Sumitomo Corp.

HEDDEN, Herbert A.

Assistant Director, Government Relations, Internat'l Franchise Ass'n
1350 New York Ave., N.W. Suite 900, Washington, DC 20005
Telephone: (202) 628-8000
Registered as lobbyist at U.S. Congress.

HEDLUND, Elizabeth

Director, Government Relations, Public Voice for Food and Health Policy
1001 Connecticut Ave., N.W., Suite 522, Washington, DC 20036
Telephone: (202) 659-5930
Registered as lobbyist at U.S. Congress.

HEDLUND, James B.

President, Ass'n of Independent Television Stations
1200 18th St., N.W. Suite 502, Washington, DC 20036
Telephone: (202) 887-1970
Registered as lobbyist at U.S. Congress.
Background: Responsible for the Ass'n of Independent Television Stations Political Action Committee. Former Deputy Director, Council on Wage and Price Stability, 1975-76, and Minority Staff Director, House Budget Committee, 1977-81.

HEDLUND, Jay

Director, Grassroots Lobbying, Common Cause
2030 M St., N.W., Washington, DC 20036
Telephone: (202) 833-1200
Registered as lobbyist at U.S. Congress.

HEDRICK, Susan

Asst, Cong Rels, Legis & Cong Rels, DEPARTMENT OF HOUSING AND URBAN DEVELOPMENT
451 Seventh St., S.W., Washington, DC 20410
Telephone: (202) 755-7380

HEENAN, Michael T.

Smith, Heenan and Althen
1110 Vermont Ave., N.W., Suite 400, Washington, DC 20005
Telephone: (202) 887-0800
Background: Trial Attorney, Division of Mine Health and Safety, Office of the Solicitor, U.S. Department of Interior, 1973-74.
Clients:
Barnes and Tucker Co.
General Portland Inc.
Hulcher Quarry, Inc.
Lone Star Florida, Inc.
Lone Star Industries
Nemacolin Mines Corp.
Peter White Coal Mining Co.
Youngstown Mines Corp.

HEFFERNAN, Edward D.

1019 19th St., N.W., Penthouse One, Washington, DC 20036
Telephone: (202) 331-7444
Registered as lobbyist at U.S. Congress.
Background: An attorney-at-law.
Organizations represented:
American Cast Iron Pipe Co.
Chicago Board Options Exchange
CSX Corp.
Harza Engineering Co.
Renewable Fuels Ass'n
Sealaska Corp.

HEFFERNAN, James P.

Exec. Director, American Horse Racing Federation
1700 K St., N.W., Suite 300, Washington, DC 20006
Telephone: (202) 296-4031

HEFFERON DAVIS, Lizanne

Manager, Regulatory Affairs, FMC Corp.
1627 K St., N.W., Suite 500, Washington, DC 20006
Telephone: (202) 956-5200

HEFFNER, John

Assoc. Dir., Manpower & Training Div., Associated General Contractors of America
1957 E St., N.W., Washington, DC 20006
Telephone: (202) 393-2040
Registered as lobbyist at U.S. Congress.

HEFFRON, Howard A.

1850 K St., N.W., Suite 500, Washington, DC 20006
Telephone: (202) 778-8045
Background: An attorney.
Organizations represented:
Center for Auto Safety

HEFTI, M. L.

V.P. & Chief, Cong. Rtns., Aerosp. Prgms, Allied-Signal Inc.
1001 Pennsylvania Ave., N.W. Suite 700, Washington, DC 20004
Telephone: (202) 662-2650
Registered as lobbyist at U.S. Congress.

HEGELIN, Rebecca

Communications Coordinator, Concerned Women for America
370 L'Enfant Promenade, S.W., Suite 800, Washington, DC 20024
Telephone: (202) 488-7000

HEGGESTAD, Robert E.

Casey, Scott, Canfield & Heggestad
805 15th St., N.W., Suite 600, Washington, DC 20005
Telephone: (202) 682-4082
Registered as lobbyist at U.S. Congress.

HEHIR, Rev. J. Bryan

Consultant, United States Catholic Conference
3211 4th St., N.E., Washington, DC 20017
Telephone: (202) 541-3198
Background: Also represents the Nat'l Conference of Catholic Bishops.

HEIDEPRIEM, Nikki

Partner, Foreman & Heidepriem
1112 16th St., N.W. Suite 750, Washington, DC 20036
Telephone: (202) 822-8060
Registered as lobbyist at U.S. Congress.
Background: Former Special Assistant to HEW Secretary Joseph Califano, Jr., 1978-79.
Clients:
Aetna Life & Casualty Co.
American Insurance Ass'n
Coalition to Preserve the Integrity of American Trademarks
Columbia Hospital for Women Medical Center
Nat'l Abortion Rights Action League
Procter and Gamble Mfg. Co.
Rockefeller Foundation

HEIGHT, Dr. Dorothy I.

Nat'l President, Nat'l Council of Negro Women
1211 Connecticut Ave. N.W. Suite 702, Washington, DC 20036
Telephone: (202) 659-0006

HEILIG, Paul T.

V. President, Government Relations, Burson-Marsteller
1850 M St., N.W., Suite 900, Washington, DC 20036
Telephone: (202) 833-8550
Registered as lobbyist at U.S. Congress.
Registered as Foreign Agent: (#4690).
Clients:
Emhart Corp.

HEILMAN, John F.

National Legislative Director, Disabled American Veterans
807 Maine Ave., S.W., Washington, DC 20024
Telephone: (202) 554-3501
Registered as lobbyist at U.S. Congress.

HEIMAN, Bruce J.

Preston Gates Ellis & Rouvelas Meeds
1735 New York Ave., N.W., Suite 500, Washington, DC 20006-4759
Telephone: (202) 628-1700
Registered as lobbyist at U.S. Congress.
Registered as Foreign Agent: (#3567).
Background: Legislative Director and Trade Counsel to Senator Daniel P. Moynihan, 1984-87.
Clients:
American Plywood Ass'n
American President Companies
Go-Video
Instituto Latinoamericano del Fierro y el Acero (ILAFA)
Internat'l Telecommunications Satellite Organization (INTELSAT)
TeleCommunications, Inc.

HEIMERS, Patricia A.

V. President, Public Relations, Recording Industry Ass'n of America
1020 19th St., N.W., Suite 200, Washington, DC 20036
Telephone: (202) 775-0101

HEIN, Werner J.

Wilkinson, Barker, Knauer and Quinn
1735 New York Ave., N.W., Suite 600, Washington, DC 20006
Telephone: (202) 783-4141
Registered as Foreign Agent: (#4075).

HEINE, Kristine

Leighton and Regnery
1667 K St., N.W., Suite 801, Washington, DC 20006
Telephone: (202) 955-3900

HEINE, Robert

Sr. Washington Representative, du Pont de Nemours and Co., E. I.
1701 Pennsylvania Ave., N.W., Suite 900, Washington, DC 20006
Telephone: (202) 728-3600
Registered as lobbyist at U.S. Congress.

HEINEMEIER, Dan C.
Exec. Director, Government Relations, Electronic Industries Ass'n
2001 Pennsylvania Ave., N.W., Washington, DC 20006
Telephone: (202) 457-4900
Registered as lobbyist at U.S. Congress.

HEININGER, Marvin W.
Dir. of Communications & Public Relats., Air-Conditioning and Refrigeration Institute
1501 Wilson Blvd., Suite 600, Arlington, VA 22209
Telephone: (703) 524-8800

HEINTZE, Juliette
V. President, Investor Relations, USAir Group Inc.
Crystal Park 4 2345 Crystal Dr., Arlington, VA 22227
Telephone: (703) 418-5111

HELFER, Michael S.
Wilmer, Cutler and Pickering
2445 M St., N.W., Washington, DC 20037-1420
Telephone: (202) 663-6000
Registered as lobbyist at U.S. Congress.
Clients:
Bank Capital Markets Ass'n
Long Island Savings Bank
Peoples Heritage Savings Bank
Southeast Banking Corp.

HELLEM, Steven B.
Senior V. President, Harrison Co., E. Bruce
1440 New York Ave., N.W. Suite 300, Washington, DC 20005
Telephone: (202) 638-1200
Registered as lobbyist at U.S. Congress.
Organizations represented:
Clean Air Act Project
Electricity Consumers Resource Council
Nat'l Environmental Development Ass'n
Process Gas Consumers Group
Sorptive Minerals Institute

HELLER, J. Roderick, III
Chairman, President and CEO, Nat'l Corp. for Housing Partnerships
1225 Eye St., N.W. Suite 700, Washington, DC 20005
Telephone: (202) 347-6247

HELLINGER, Douglas
Managing Director, Development Group for Alternative Policies
1400 Eye St., N.W., Suite 520 Suite 520, Washington, DC 20005
Telephone: (202) 898-1566

HELLINGER, Stephen
Exec. Director, Development Group for Alternative Policies
1400 Eye St., N.W., Suite 520 Suite 520, Washington, DC 20005
Telephone: (202) 898-1566

HELLMANN, Donald
Associate Counselor, Wilderness Soc.
1400 Eye St., N.W., 10th Floor, Washington, DC 20005
Telephone: (202) 842-3400
Registered as lobbyist at U.S. Congress.

HELLWEGE, Richard L.
Director, Business Development, Smith Industries
1225 Jefferson Davis Hwy., Suite 402, Arlington, VA 22202
Telephone: (703) 920-7640
Registered as lobbyist at U.S. Congress.

HELM, DeWitt F., Jr.
President, Ass'n of Nat'l Advertisers
1725 K St., N.W., Suite 601, Washington, DC 20006
Telephone: (202) 785-1525
Registered as lobbyist at U.S. Congress.

HELM, Robert W.
V. President, Legislative Affairs, Northrop Corp.
1000 Wilson Blvd., Suite 2300, Arlington, VA 22209
Telephone: (703) 525-6767
Registered as lobbyist at U.S. Congress.

HELME, Edward A. 'Ned'
Director, Alliance for Acid Rain Control
444 North Capitol St., N.W., Suite 526, Washington, DC 20001
Telephone: (202) 624-5475
Registered as lobbyist at U.S. Congress.

HELMES, Dr. C. Tucker
Exec. Director, Ecological and Toxicological Ass'n of the Dyestuffs Manufacturing Industry
1330 Connecticut Ave., N.W., Washington, DC 20036-1702
Telephone: (202) 659-0060

HELMKE, Mark
Robinson, Lake, Lerer & Montgomery
1667 K St., N.W., Suite 900, Washington, DC 20006
Telephone: (202) 457-9270
Registered as lobbyist at U.S. Congress.
Background: Press Secretary to Senator Richard G. Lugar (R-IN), 1981-86.
Clients:
Atari Games Corp.
Guam Commission on Self-Determination
Nat'l Venture Capital Ass'n

HELMS, Robert B.
Exec. Director, American Pharmaceutical Institute
2215 Constitution Ave., N.W., Washington, DC 20037
Telephone: (202) 429-7514
Background: Former Assistant Secretary for Planning and Evaluation, Dept. of Health and Human Services.

HELSCHER, Thomas M.
Director, Congressional Affairs, Monsanto Co.
700 14th St., N.W., Suite 1100, Washington, DC 20005
Telephone: (202) 783-2460
Registered as lobbyist at U.S. Congress.

HELTZER, Harold J.
Crowell and Moring
1001 Pennsylvania Ave., N.W., Washington, DC 20004-2505
Telephone: (202) 624-2500
Registered as lobbyist at U.S. Congress.
Background: Attorney, Civil and Tax Divisions, Department of Justice, 1966-72. Attorney-Advisor, Office of Tax Legislative Counsel, Department of Treasury, 1972-74.
Clients:
Avon Products, Inc.
Communications Satellite Corp. (COMSAT)
Tiffany & Co.
United Cities Gas Co.

HEMENWAY, Russell D.
National Director, Nat'l Committee for an Effective Congress
507 Capitol Court, N.E., Washington, DC 20002
Telephone: (202) 547-1151

HEMLEY, Ginette
Director, TRAFFIC, World Wildlife Fund
1250 24th St., N.W., Washington, DC 20037
Telephone: (202) 293-4800

HEMMINGS, Madeline B.
Exec. Director, Nat'l Ass'n of State Directors of Vocational Technical Education Consortium
1420 16th St., N.W., Washington, DC 20036
Telephone: (202) 328-0216

HEMPLING, Scott
Legislative Representative, Environmental Action
1525 New Hampshire Ave., N.W., Washington, DC 20036
Telephone: (202) 745-4870
Registered as lobbyist at U.S. Congress.

HENBERGER, Linda
Director, Operations, Convention II, Inc.
Box 1987, Washington, DC 20013-1987
Telephone: (202) 544-1789

HENDERSON, Bruce D.
V. President, State & Local Resources, State & Local Resources
901 Sixth St., S.W., Suite 503A, Washington, DC 20024
Telephone: (202) 488-1460
Background: Formerly with Environmental Protection Agency, 1982-83.
Clients:

G. W. Electronics
Mid-American Network
Nat'l Academy of Engineering
Nevada Development Authority
Nevada, State of
T. M. Community College

HENDERSON, Carol C.
Deputy Director, Washington Office, American Library Ass'n
110 Maryland Ave., N.E., Suite 101, Washington, DC 20002
Telephone: (202) 547-4440
Registered as lobbyist at U.S. Congress.

HENDERSON, David
Pagonis and Donnelly Group
1620 Eye St., N.W., Suite 603, Washington, DC 20006
Telephone: (202) 452-8811
Clients:
Americans for Nat'l Dividend Act

HENDERSON, Leonard N.
Senior Washington Representative, Metropolitan Insurance Cos.
1615 L St., N.W., Suite 1210, Washington, DC 20036
Telephone: (202) 659-3575
Registered as lobbyist at U.S. Congress.

HENDERSON, Robert E.
V. President, Nat'l Republican Institute for Internat'l Affairs
601 Indiana Ave., N.W., Washington, DC 20004
Telephone: (202) 783-2280

HENDERSON, Thomas H.
Exec. Director, Ass'n of Trial Lawyers of America
1050 31st St., N.W., Washington, DC 20007
Telephone: (202) 965-3500

HENDERSON, Wade J.
Associate Director, American Civil Liberties Union
122 Maryland Ave., N.E., Washington, DC 20002
Telephone: (202) 544-1681
Registered as lobbyist at U.S. Congress.

HENDRICKS, Diane
Westermann and Hendricks, Inc.
1225 Jefferson Davis Hwy., Suite 600, Arlington, VA 22202
Telephone: (703) 486-5659
Registered as lobbyist at U.S. Congress.
Background: Second Vice President, American League of Lobbyists, 1990.
Clients:
Partnerships in Education
Young Astronaut Council

HENDRICKS, Gary
Director of Gov't Info & Chief Economist, American Academy of Actuaries
1720 Eye St., N.W., 7th Floor, Washington, DC 20006
Telephone: (202) 223-8196

HENDRICKS, Karen M.
Director of Government Affairs, Ass'n of Junior Leagues, Internat'l
1319 F St., N.W., Suite 604, Washington, DC 20004
Telephone: (202) 393-3364
Registered as lobbyist at U.S. Congress.

HENDRICKSON, Ron
Exec. Director, Internat'l Chiropractors Ass'n
1110 N. Glebe Rd. Suite 1000, Arlington, VA 22201
Telephone: (703) 528-5000
Background: Responsibilities include the Internat'l Chiropractors Ass'n Political Action Committee.

HENINGER, Lynn W.
Asst Admin, Cong Relations (Act), NAT'L AERONAUTICS AND SPACE ADMINISTRATION
400 Maryland Ave., S.W., Washington, DC 20546
Telephone: (202) 453-1055

HENINGTON, C. Dayle
Sr. V. President, Government Relations, Chicago Mercantile Exchange
2000 Pennsylvania Ave., N.W. Suite 6200, Washington, DC 20006
Telephone: (202) 223-6965

HENINGTON, C. Dayle (Cont'd)
Registered as lobbyist at U.S. Congress.

HENKEL, Christopher J.
Program Manager, Utility Nuclear Waste Transportation Program
1111 19th St., N.W., Suite 600, Washington, DC 20036
Telephone: (202) 778-6511

HENKEL, Dr. Don
Staff Liaison, Soc. of Park and Recreation Educators
3101 Park Center Drive, Alexandria, VA 22302
Telephone: (703) 820-4940

HENLEY, Susan A.
Exec. Director, American Hiking Soc.
1015 31st St., N.W., Washington, DC 20007
Telephone: (202) 385-3252

HENNEBERGER, Lawrence F.
Arent, Fox, Kintner, Plotkin & Kahn
1050 Connecticut Ave., N.W., Washington, DC 20036-5339
Telephone: (202) 857-6000
Registered as lobbyist at U.S. Congress.
Clients:
Trailer Hitch Manufacturers Ass'n

HENNEBERRY, Edward P.
Howrey and Simon
1730 Pennsylvania Ave., N.W., Washington, DC 20006-4793
Telephone: (202) 783-0800
Background: Trial Attorney, Honors Program Department of Justice, Antitrust Division, 1970-75.

HENNEBERRY, Margaretha M.
Exec. V. President, World Peace Through Law Center
1000 Connecticut Ave., N.W. Suite 800, Washington, DC 20036
Telephone: (202) 466-5428

HENNESSEY, Stacy L.
Assistant Counsel, American Insurance Ass'n
1130 Connecticut Ave., N.W., Suite 1000, Washington, DC 20036
Telephone: (202) 828-7100

HENNESSEY, Thomas J., Jr.
Bracy Williams & Co.
1000 Connecticut Ave., N.W., Suite 304, Washington, DC 20036
Telephone: (202) 659-4805
Registered as lobbyist at U.S. Congress.
Clients:
American Home Satellite Ass'n
Daishowa America Co. Ltd.
Millicom Inc.
Rocky Co., The
Tucson, Arizona, City of

HENNESSY, Ellen A.
Willkie Farr and Gallagher
1155 21st St., N.W., 6th Fl., Washington, DC 20036-3302
Telephone: (202) 328-8000
Clients:
New York State Employees Retirement System
Sharon Steel Co.

HENNING, C. Randall
Research Fellow, Institute for Internat'l Economics
11 Dupont Circle, N.W., Washington, DC 20036
Telephone: (202) 328-0583

HENRICH, Carolyn
Government Relations Specialist, Nat'l Congress of Parents and Teachers
1201 16th St., N.W. Room 621, Washington, DC 20036
Telephone: (202) 822-7878

HENRY, Bruce B.
President/Exec. Director, Nat'l Ass'n of Air Traffic Specialists
4740 Corridor Place, Suite c, Beltsville, MD 20705
Telephone: (301) 595-2012

HENRY, E. William
Ginsburg, Feldman and Bress
1250 Connecticut Ave., N.W. Suite 800, Washington, DC 20036

Telephone: (202) 637-9000
Background: Chairman, Federal Communications Commission, 1963-66.
Clients:
Michigan Channel 38
Upjohn Co.

HENRY, George H.
Senior Counsel, American Insurance Ass'n
1130 Connecticut Ave., N.W., Suite 1000, Washington, DC 20036
Telephone: (202) 828-7100
Registered as lobbyist at U.S. Congress.
Background: Former Tax Counsel to Rep. Robert Matsui (D-CA).

HENRY, James L.
President, Transportation Institute
5201 Auth Way, Camp Springs, MD 20746
Telephone: (301) 423-3335
Registered as lobbyist at U.S. Congress.

HENRY, John H.
Manager, Federal Legislative Affairs, McDermott Inc.
1850 K St., N.W. Suite 950, Washington, DC 20006
Telephone: (202) 296-0390
Registered as lobbyist at U.S. Congress.
Background: Also represents McDermott Internat'l and Babcock and Wilcox Co.

HENSCHE, LeAnn R.
Sr. Assoc., Federal Government Relations, RJR Nabisco Washington, Inc.
1455 Pennsylvania Ave., N.W., Suite 525, Washington, DC 20004
Telephone: (202) 626-7200
Registered as lobbyist at U.S. Congress.

HENSLER, David J.
Hogan and Hartson
555 13th St., N.W., Suite 1200, Washington, DC 20004-1109
Telephone: (202) 637-5600
Registered as lobbyist at U.S. Congress.
Background: Attorney, General Counsel's Office, Securities and Exchange Commission, 1967-68.

HENSLEY, Jan
Director, Professional Insurance Agents' Political Action Committee
400 N. Washington St., Alexandria, VA 22314
Telephone: (703) 836-9340
Background: Former Political Fundraiser for Sen. Jeff Bingaman (D-NM).

HENSTRUDGE, Paula
Legis Specialist, DEPARTMENT OF AGRICULTURE - Animal and Plant Health Inspection Service
14th and Independence Ave. S.W., Room 1147 South Bldg., Washington, DC 20250
Telephone: (202) 447-2511

HENTELEFF, Thomas O.
Kleinfeld, Kaplan and Becker
1140 19th St., N.W., Suite 700, Washington, DC 20036
Telephone: (202) 223-5120

HENWOOD, Roy M.
President, Millers' Nat'l Federation
600 Maryland Ave., S.W., Suite 305 West, Washington, DC 20024
Telephone: (202) 484-2200

HENZKE, Leonard J., Jr.
Lehrfeld Cantor & Henzke, P.C.
1101 Connecticut Ave., N.W., Suite 403, Washington, DC 20036
Telephone: (202) 659-4772
Background: Trial Attorney, Antitrust Division, Justice Department, 1965-69. Special Assistant to Assistant Attorney General, Tax Division, Justice Department, 1979-81.
Clients:
Nat'l Club Ass'n

HEPPES, Jerry
Assistant to the Exec. V. President, Door and Hardware Institute
7711 Old Springhouse Road, McLean, VA 22102-3474

Telephone: (703) 556-3990

HERBER, Catharine
Legislative Counsel, Nat'l School Boards Ass'n
1680 Duke St., Alexandria, VA 22314
Telephone: (703) 838-6703

HERBERT, Jule R., Jr.
Dir, Govt and Public Affrs Office (Act), INTERSTATE COMMERCE COMMISSION
12th and Constitution Ave. N.W., Washington, DC 20423
Telephone: (202) 275-7231

HERBOLSHEIMER, Robert T.
Manatt, Phelps, Rothenberg & Phillips
1200 New Hampshire Ave., N.W., Suite 200, Washington, DC 20036
Telephone: (202) 463-4300
Registered as lobbyist at U.S. Congress.
Clients:
Akhiok-Kaguyak, Inc.
Bowling Proprietors' Ass'n of America
Centre Point Associates
EDU-DYNE Systems, Inc.
Fairfield Communities, Inc.
Melrose Co., The
Missouri Ass'n of Private Career Schools
North Beach Property Owner's Ass'n
Vero Beach Oceanfront Investors Limited Partnership

HERBST, Peter R.
Assistant Exec. Director, Soc. for Technical Communication
901 North Stuart St., Arlington, VA 22203
Telephone: (703) 522-4114

HERBST, Robert L.
Exec. Director, Trout Unlimited
501 Church St., N.E., Vienna, VA 22180
Telephone: (703) 281-1100
Background: Former Assistant Secretary of Interior for Fish, Wildlife and Parks and Acting Secretary of Interior.

HERCENBERG, Jerrold J.
McDermott, Will and Emery
1850 K St., N.W., Suite 500, Washington, DC 20006-2296
Telephone: (202) 887-8000
Background: Former Senior Legal Advisor, Office of Pre-paid Health Care, Health Care Financing Administration, U.S. Department of Health and Human Services.

HERDT, Mary Lyn
Associate Director, Fed. Gov't. Affairs, BP America Inc.
1776 Eye St., N.W., Suite 1000, Washington, DC 20006
Telephone: (202) 785-4888
Registered as lobbyist at U.S. Congress.

HERFORT, John A.
Gibson, Dunn and Crutcher
1050 Connecticut Ave., N.W. Suite 900, Washington, DC 20036-5303
Telephone: (202) 955-8500

HERGE, J. Curtis
Secretary, Stone and Associates, Ann E. W.
1315 Duke St., Alexandria, VA 22314
Telephone: (703) 836-7717
Registered as Foreign Agent: (#3914).

HERLACH, Mark D.
Coudert Brothers
1627 Eye St., N.W. 12th Floor, Washington, DC 20006
Telephone: (202) 775-5100
Clients:
NEC Corp.

HERLIHY-GEARAN, Mary H.
Associate, Wexler, Reynolds, Fuller, Harrison and Schule, Inc.
1317 F St., N.W., Suite 600, Washington, DC 20004
Telephone: (202) 638-2121

HERLIHY, Thomas
Asst Gen Counsel, Legislation, DEPARTMENT OF TRANSPORTATION
400 Seventh St., S.W., Washington, DC 20590
Telephone: (202) 366-4687

HERMAN, Alexis M.
Chief of Staff, Democratic Nat'l Committee
430 South Capitol St., S.E., Washington, DC 20003
Telephone: (202) 863-8000

HERMAN, Betsy M.
Exec. Director, American Podiatric Medical Students Ass'n
9312 Old Georgetown Road, Bethesda, MD 20814
Telephone: (301) 493-9667

HERMAN, Ruth C.
Exec. Director, Women in Community Service
1900 North Beauregard St., Suite 14, Alexandria, VA 22311
Telephone: (703) 671-0500

HERMAN, Stephen A.
Kirkland and Ellis
655 15th St., N.W. Suite 1200, Washington, DC 20005
Telephone: (202) 879-5000

HERMELIN, William M.
Director, Government Affairs, American Pharmaceutical Ass'n
2215 Constitution Ave., N.W., Washington, DC 20037
Telephone: (202) 628-4410
Registered as lobbyist at U.S. Congress.
Background: Former staff member, White House Policy Staff to Pres. Gerald R. Ford, former Admin Asst. to Rep. Tom Railsback (R-IL), former legal advisor, Dept. of Health, Education, and Welfare. Serves as contact for the Ass'n Political Action Committee.

HERNANDEZ, Andres R.
DC Internat'l, Inc.
8401 Colesville Road Suite 361-A, Silver Spring, MD 20910-3312
Telephone: (301) 589-0226
Registered as Foreign Agent: (#4210).
Clients:
Christian Democrat Internat'l
Christian Democrat Organization of the Americas
European Union of Christian Democrats/European People's Party
Guatemala, Government of

HERNANDEZ, Peter A.
V. President, Employee Relations, American Iron and Steel Institute
1133 15th St., N.W., Suite 300, Washington, DC 20005-2701
Telephone: (202) 452-7212

HEROLD, Arthur L.
Webster, Chamberlain and Bean
1747 Pennsylvania Ave., N.W., Suite 1000, Washington, DC 20006
Telephone: (202) 785-9500
Background: Trial Attorney, Federal Trade Commission 1967-70.
Clients:
Amana Refrigeration, Inc.
American Financial Services Ass'n
American Financial Services Ass'n Political Action Committee
Internat'l Taxicab Ass'n
Nat'l Ass'n of Temporary Services
Power Tool Institute
Vocational Industrial Clubs of America

HERR, Wendy W.
Director, Regulatory Issues, Healthcare Financial Management Ass'n
1050 17th St., N.W., Suite 510, Washington, DC 20036
Telephone: (202) 296-2920

HERRENBRUCK, Susan
Manager, Public & Economic Affairs, American Gear Manufacturers Ass'n
1500 King St., Suite 201, Alexandria, VA 22314
Telephone: (703) 684-0211

HERRETT, Richard A.
Government Relations Scientific Liaison, ICI Americas Inc.
1600 M St., N.W., Suite 702, Washington, DC 20036
Telephone: (202) 775-9722
Registered as lobbyist at U.S. Congress.

HERRICK, Jo-Ann
Washington Representative, Tesoro Petroleum Corp.
1800 K St., N.W. Suite 530, Washington, DC 20006
Telephone: (202) 775-8840

HERRITY, Tom
V. President, Direct Impact Co., The
1414 Prince St. Suite 350, Alexandria, VA 22314
Telephone: (703) 684-1245
Clients:
American Petroleum Institute
Chemical Manufacturers Ass'n
Columbia Presbyterian Hospital
Dulles Area Rapid Transit, Inc.
Florida Commercial Developers Ass'n
FMC Corp.
Maglev Transit, Inc.
Rocky Mountain Oil and Gas Ass'n

HERSH, Alice S.
Exec. Director, Ass'n for Health Services Research
2100 M St., N.W., Suite 402, Washington, DC 20037
Telephone: (202) 223-2477

HERSHAFT, Alex
President, Farm Animal Reform Movement
P.O. Box 30654, Bethesda, MD 20824
Telephone: (301) 530-1737

HERTFELDER, Eric
Exec. Director, Nat'l Conference of State Historic Preservation Officers
444 N. Capitol St., N.W. Suite 332, Washington, DC 20001
Telephone: (202) 624-5465

HERTZBERG, Michael A.
Howrey and Simon
1730 Pennsylvania Ave., N.W., Washington, DC 20006-4793
Telephone: (202) 783-0800
Clients:
ICI Americas Inc.

HERZSTEIN, Marsha
Government Liaison, American Logistics Ass'n
1133 15th St., N.W. Suite 640, Washington, DC 20005
Telephone: (202) 466-2520
Registered as lobbyist at U.S. Congress.

HERZSTEIN, Robert
Shearman and Sterling
1001 30th St., N.W., Suite 400, Washington, DC 20007
Telephone: (202) 337-8200
Registered as Foreign Agent: (#4208).
Clients:
Claro y Cia
Komatsu Ltd.

HESCOCK, George C.
Exec. V. President, Direct Selling Ass'n
1776 K St., N.W., Suite 600, Washington, DC 20006
Telephone: (202) 293-5760
Background: Also serves as Treasurer, Direct Selling Ass'n Political Action Committee.

HESLIP, John A.
President, Nat'l Concrete Masonry Ass'n
P.O. Box 781, Herndon, VA 22070
Telephone: (703) 435-4900
Registered as lobbyist at U.S. Congress.
Background: Responsibilities include Nat'l Concrete Masonry Ass'n Political Action Committee.

HESS, Don
Exec. V. President, United States Army Warrant Officers Ass'n
Box 2040, Reston, VA 22090
Telephone: (703) 620-3986

HESS, Stephen
Sr. Fellow, Governmental Studies Program, Brookings Institution
1775 Massachusetts Ave., N.W., Washington, DC 20036
Telephone: (202) 797-6000
Background: U.S. Rep to the UN General Assembly (1976); U.S. Rep to the UNESCO General Conference (1974); Nat'l Chair for White House Conference on Children and Youth (1969-71); Deputy Asst. to President for Urban Affairs (1969).

HESS, Vicki Totter
Manager, Corporate Affairs, Bonner & Associates
1625 K St., N.W., Suite 300, Washington, DC 20006
Telephone: (202) 463-8880

HESSBERG, Rufus R., M.D.
Exec. V. President, Aerospace Medical Ass'n
320 South Henry St., Alexandria, VA 22314
Telephone: (703) 739-2240

HESSE, Richard J.
Manager, Washington Office, Harza Engineering Co.
1060 Leighmill Road, Great Falls, VA 22066
Telephone: (703) 759-6746

HESTER, Stephen L.
Arnold & Porter
1200 New Hampshire Ave., N.W., Washington, DC 20036
Telephone: (202) 872-6700
Registered as lobbyist at U.S. Congress.
Clients:
Nat'l Coordinating Committee for Multiemployer Plans

HESTER, Theodore M.
King and Spalding
1730 Pennsylvania Ave., N.W. Suite 1200, Washington, DC 20006-4706
Telephone: (202) 737-0500
Registered as lobbyist at U.S. Congress.
Registered as Foreign Agent: (#3812).
Background: Legislative Assistant to United States Senator David H. Gambrell, 1971-72.
Clients:
Georgia Internat'l Investment Coalition
GPIA Animal Drug Alliance

HETRICK, Greg
Director of Government Affairs, Menswear Retailers of America
2011 Eye St., N.W. Suite 600, Washington, DC 20006
Telephone: (202) 347-1932
Background: Also represents the Menswear Retailers of America Political Action Committee.

HETTINGER, William S.
Director, Business Programs, Grumman Corp.
1000 Wilson Blvd., Suite 2800, Arlington, VA 22209
Telephone: (703) 875-8400
Registered as lobbyist at U.S. Congress.

HETU, Herbert E.
V. President, Communications, Aerospace Industries Ass'n of America
1250 Eye St., N.W., Suite 1100, Washington, DC 20005
Telephone: (202) 371-8400
Background: Former Director of Public Affairs, Central Intelligence Agency and spokesman for a number of Presidential commissions.

HEWES, Mary D.
Director of Projects, Nat'l Park Foundation
P.O. Box 57473, Washington, DC 20037
Telephone: (202) 785-4500

HEWES, MORELLA, GELBAND AND LAMBERTON, P.C.
1000 Potomac St., N.W. Suite 300, Washington, DC 20007
Telephone: (202) 337-6200
Members of firm representing listed organizations:
Gelband, Stephen L.
Background: Trial Attorney, Bureau of Economic Regulation, Civil Aeronautics Board, 1968-71.
Clients:
Conquest Tours Ltd.
Orion Air *(Stephen L. Gelband)*
Tower Air, Inc. *(Stephen L. Gelband)*

The listings in this directory are available as *Mailing Labels*. See last page.

187

HEWES, MORELLA, GELBAND AND LAMBERTON, P.C. (Cont'd)
Washington Airports Task Force *(Stephen L. Gelband)*

HEWETT, Edward A.
Senior Fellow, Brookings Institution
1775 Massachusetts Ave., N.W., Washington, DC 20036
Telephone: (202) 797-6000

HEWITT, Charles C.
President, Satellite Broadcasting and Communications Ass'n
300 N. Washington St. Suite 600, Alexandria, VA 22314
Telephone: (703) 549-6990

HEWITT, Mary E.
V. President, Morgan Casner Associates, Inc.
1332 Independence Ave., S.E., Washington, DC 20003
Telephone: (202) 543-4600
Background: Specializes in matters pertaining to the media.

HEYDINGER, Ted A.
V. President, Domestic Issues, Computer and Business Equipment Manufacturers Ass'n
311 First St., N.W. Suite 500, Washington, DC 20001
Telephone: (202) 737-8888
Registered as lobbyist at U.S. Congress.

HEYDLAUFF, Dale E.
Director, Federal Agency Affairs, American Electric Power Service Corp.
1667 K St., N.W. Suite 450, Washington, DC 20006
Telephone: (202) 659-0454
Registered as lobbyist at U.S. Congress.

HEYER, Albert W., III
President, Construction Management Ass'n of America
12355 Sunrise Valley Drive Suite 640, Reston, VA 22091
Telephone: (703) 391-1200

HEYL, John L.
V. President, Resources Development, Nat'l Trust for Historic Preservation
1785 Massachusetts Ave., N.W., Washington, DC 20036
Telephone: (202) 673-4000

HEYLIN, G. Brockwell
Director, Government Affairs, American Ass'n of Colleges of Nursing
One Dupont Circle, N.W., Suite 530, Washington, DC 20036
Telephone: (202) 463-6930

HHL FINANCIAL SERVICES, INC.
2000 L St., N.W. Suite 200, Washington, DC 20036
Telephone: (202) 785-2735
Members of firm representing listed organizations:
Reffkin, Alan D.

HIBBS, Gwenn
V. President, Legislative Analysis, Federal Nat'l Mortgage Ass'n
3900 Wisconsin Ave., N.W., Washington, DC 20016
Telephone: (202) 752-7127

HICKERSON, David B.
Washington Rep., Human Resource Affairs, Eastman Kodak Co.
1776 Eye St., N.W., Suite 1050, Washington, DC 20006
Telephone: (202) 857-3400
Registered as lobbyist at U.S. Congress.

HICKEY, Barbara C.
Exec. Director, Nat'l Soc. of Accountants for Cooperatives
6320 Augusta Drive, #800C, Springfield, VA 22150
Telephone: (703) 569-3088

HICKEY, Caroline
Washington Liaison, Education Commission of the States
444 North Capitol St., N.W. Suite 248, Washington, DC 20001
Telephone: (202) 624-5838

HICKEY, James J., Jr.
Counsel & Director, Government Relations, American Horse Council
1700 K St., N.W. Suite 300, Washington, DC 20006
Telephone: (202) 296-4031

HICKEY, Michael
Director, Gov't Relations (Agencies), NYNEX
1828 L St., N.W., Suite 1000, Washington, DC 20036
Telephone: (202) 416-0100

HICKEY, Roger
V. President, Public Affairs, Economic Policy Institute
1424 16th St., N.W., Suite 501, Washington, DC 20036
Telephone: (202) 667-0400

HICKMAN, Harrison
Hickman-Maslin Research
1827 Jefferson Place, N.W., Washington, DC 20036
Telephone: (202) 659-4000
Clients:
Nat'l Abortion Rights Action League

HICKMAN-MASLIN RESEARCH
1827 Jefferson Place, N.W., Washington, DC 20036
Telephone: (202) 659-4000
Members of firm representing listed organizations:
Hickman, Harrison
Clients:
Nat'l Abortion Rights Action League *(Harrison Hickman)*

HICKMAN, Tom
Exec. Assistant to the President, Internat'l Brotherhood of Electrical Workers
1125 15th St., N.W., Washington, DC 20005
Telephone: (202) 833-7000

HICKS, Deborah Davis
Communications Director, EMILY'S List
2000 P St., N.W., Suite 412, Washington, DC 20036
Telephone: (202) 887-1957

HICKS, Diane
Cong Liaison Div, ENVIRONMENTAL PROTECTION AGENCY
401 M St., S.W., Washington, DC 20460
Telephone: (202) 382-5200

HICKS, Doin, Ed.D.
Exec. Director, Council on Education of the Deaf
c/o Gallaudet, EMG Room 206 800 Florida Ave., N.E., Washington, DC 20002
Telephone: (202) 651-5020

HICKS, Donita
Deputy Director, Americans for Democratic Action
1511 K St., N.W. Suite 941, Washington, DC 20005
Telephone: (202) 638-6447
Registered as lobbyist at U.S. Congress.

HICKS, Marshall M.
Secretary-Treasurer, Utility Workers Union of America
815 16th St., N.W. Suite 605, Washington, DC 20006
Telephone: (202) 347-8105
Background: Also represents Utility Workers of America Political Contributions Committee.

HICKS, Scottie B.
Secretary-Treasurer, Nat'l Rural Letter Carriers' Ass'n
1448 Duke St., Alexandria, VA 22314
Telephone: (703) 684-5545

HICKS, Thomas E.
Senior Consultant, Southern Technical Services
Suite 610 Three Metro Center, Bethesda, MD 20814
Telephone: (301) 652-2500

HIDALGO, Edward
1828 L St., N.W., Suite 1111, Washington, DC 20036
Telephone: (202) 822-8200
Background: An attorney. Special Assistant to the Director, 1972 and General Counsel and Congressional Liaison, 1973-76. U.S. Information Agency. Special Assistant to the Secretary of the Navy, 1945-46, 1965-66. Assistant Secretary of the Navy, 1977-79. Secretary of the Navy, 1979-81.

HIDEN, Barbara L.
Legislative Analyst, Nat'l Soft Drink Ass'n
1101 16th St., N.W., Washington, DC 20036
Telephone: (202) 463-6732
Registered as lobbyist at U.S. Congress.

HIDUSKEY, Roddy L.
Director, Public Relations, Nat'l Apartment Ass'n
1111 14th St., N.W., 9th Floor, Washington, DC 20005
Telephone: (202) 842-4050
Background: Former Press Aide to Secretary of Housing and Urban Development Samuel R. Pierce, Jr.

HIEBERT, Peter N.
Partner, Bishop, Cook, Purcell & Reynolds
1400 L St., N.W., Washington, DC 20005-3502
Telephone: (202) 371-5700
Registered as lobbyist at U.S. Congress.
Clients:
Virgin Islands, Government of the

HIEMSTRA, Hal
Policy Director, Scenic America
216 7th St., S.E., Washington, DC 20003
Telephone: (202) 546-1100
Registered as lobbyist at U.S. Congress.

HIGGINBOTHAM, J. Thomas
V. President, Legislative Affairs, American Institute of Certified Public Accountants
1455 Pennsylvania Ave., N.W. Suite 400, Washington, DC 20004
Telephone: (202) 737-6600
Registered as lobbyist at U.S. Congress.

HIGGINS, Billy K.
Congressional Liaison, American Ass'n of State Highway and Transportation Officials
444 N. Capitol St., N.W., Suite 225, Washington, DC 20001
Telephone: (202) 624-5800

HIGGINS, C. B., Jr.
Chief Marketing Officer, Ferranti Defense and Space Group
1111 Jefferson Davis Hwy, Suite 800, Arlington, VA 22202
Telephone: (703) 979-0005

HIGGINS, Carol Ann
Legislative Affairs Representative, Investment Company Institute
1600 M St., N.W. Suite 600, Washington, DC 20036
Telephone: (202) 293-7700
Registered as lobbyist at U.S. Congress.

HIGGINS, Duane
Director of House Relations, Heritage Foundation
214 Massachusetts Ave., N.E., Washington, DC 20002
Telephone: (202) 546-4400
Background: Former Legislative Assistant to Rep. Mark Siljander (R-MI).

HIGGINS, Lawrence P.
Wunder, Ryan, Cannon & Thelen
1615 L St., N.W., Suite 650, Washington, DC 20036
Telephone: (202) 659-3005
Registered as lobbyist at U.S. Congress.
Background: Chief Counsel, Federal Taxes and Pension, American Council of Life Insurance, 1982-84.
Clients:
Metropolitan Insurance Cos.
Mutual Life Insurance Co. Tax Committee
Northwestern Mutual Life Insurance Co.

HIGGINS, Richard
Exec. Director, Immigration Reform Law Institute
1666 Connecticut Ave., N.W. Suite 402, Washington, DC 20009
Telephone: (202) 462-1969

HIGGINS, Terrence S.
Assistant Technical Director, Nat'l Petroleum Refiners Ass'n
1899 L St., N.W., Suite 1000, Washington, DC 20036
Telephone: (202) 457-0480

HIGHLEY & ASSOCIATES
One Colonial Place, Suite 531 2111 Wilson Blvd., Arlington, VA 22201-3008
Telephone: (202) 522-0557
Background: A government relations consulting firm specializing in agriculture.
Members of firm representing listed organizations:
Highley, Vern F., Chairman

Background: Formerly held several executive level positions in the U.S. Department of Agriculture including Special Assistant to the Secretary and Administrator, Agricultural Marketing Service.

Clients:
American Cotton Growers *(Vern F. Highley)*
Cotton Cooperatives *(Vern F. Highley)*
Cottongrowers Warehouse Ass'n *(Vern F. Highley)*
Marlin Group, The *(Vern F. Highley)*
Nat'l Honey Board *(Vern F. Highley)*
Nat'l Watermelon Ass'n *(Vern F. Highley)*
Processed Cherries *(Vern F. Highley)*
Red Tart Cherries *(Vern F. Highley)*
Signal Produce Co. *(Vern F. Highley)*

HIGHLEY, Vern F.
Chairman, Highley & Associates
One Colonial Place, Suite 531 2111 Wilson Blvd., Arlington, VA 22201-3008
Telephone: (202) 522-0557
Registered as lobbyist at U.S. Congress.
Background: Formerly held several executive level positions in the U.S. Department of Agriculture including Special Assistant to the Secretary and Administrator, Agricultural Marketing Service.
Clients:
American Cotton Growers
Cotton Cooperatives
Cottongrowers Warehouse Ass'n
Marlin Group, The
Nat'l Honey Board
Nat'l Watermelon Ass'n
Processed Cherries
Red Tart Cherries
Signal Produce Co.

HIGHSAW, MAHONEY & CLARKE
Suite 210, 1050 17th St., N.W., Washington, DC 20036
Telephone: (202) 296-8500
Members of firm representing listed organizations:
Clarke, John (Jr.)
Mahoney, William G.
Clients:
Railway Labor Executives' Ass'n *(William G. Mahoney)*

HIGHT, Evelyn
Treasurer, American Ass'n for Marriage and Family Therapy PAC
1717 K St., N.W., Suite 407, Washington, DC 20006
Telephone: (202) 429-1825

HIGHT, Martin
Staff Assistant, Public Affairs, American Soc. for Microbiology
1325 Massachusetts Ave., N.W., Washington, DC 20005
Telephone: (202) 737-3600

HIGHTOWER, Vivian A.
Senior Research Associate, Nat'l Ass'n of Broadcasters
1771 N St., N.W., Washington, DC 20036
Telephone: (202) 429-5300
Registered as lobbyist at U.S. Congress.

HILDEBRANDT, David A.
Dow, Lohnes and Albertson
1255 23rd St., N.W., Suite 500, Washington, DC 20037
Telephone: (202) 857-2500
Clients:
Procter and Gamble Mfg. Co.
Profit Sharing Council of America

HILDENBRAND, William F.
Gold and Liebengood, Inc.
1455 Pennsylvania Ave., N.W. Suite 950, Washington, DC 20004
Telephone: (202) 639-8899
Registered as lobbyist at U.S. Congress.
Background: Former Secretary of the U.S. Senate.
Clients:
Federated Investors, Inc.

HILDERLEY, Clifton T., Jr.
Assoc. Director, Federal Gov't Relations, Ashland Oil, Inc.
Suite 507, 1025 Connecticut Ave., N.W., Washington, DC 20036
Telephone: (202) 223-8297
Registered as lobbyist at U.S. Congress.

HILDRETH, Richard
Fletcher, Heald and Hildreth
1225 Connecticut Ave., N.W. Suite 400, Washington, DC 20036
Telephone: (202) 828-5700

HILL, Anne R.
Executive Director, Kids Project
1101 Connecticut Ave., N.W. Suite 500, Washington, DC 20036
Telephone: (202) 429-7470
Registered as lobbyist at U.S. Congress.

HILL, BETTS AND NASH
1818 N St., N.W., Suite 700, Washington, DC 20036
Telephone: (202) 452-0586
Background: Washington office of a New York law firm.
Members of firm representing listed organizations:
Kehoe, Brien E.
Background: General Counsel, Federal Maritime Commission, 1979-81. Marine Legal Counsel, Department of Transportation, 1981-82. Exec. Assistant to Maritime Administrator, Department of Transportation, 1982-83.
Clients:
Internat'l Ass'n of Independent Tanker Owners
Resources Trucking Inc. *(Brien E. Kehoe)*
Waterman Steamship Co. *(Brien E. Kehoe)*

HILL, Rear Adm. C. A., USN (Ret.)
V. President for Government Affairs, Ass'n of Naval Aviation
5205 Leesburg Pike, Suite 200, Falls Church, VA 22041
Telephone: (703) 998-7733

HILL, Carolyn C.
Washington Counsel, United Telecommunications
1875 Eye St., N.W., Suite 1250, Washington, DC 20006
Telephone: (202) 659-4600

HILL, Charles E.
Managing Attorney, Nat'l Consumer Law Center
236 Massachusetts Ave., N.E. Suite 504, Washington, DC 20002
Telephone: (202) 543-6060

HILL, Cynthia A.
Research Specialist, Nat'l Ass'n of REALTORS
777 14th St., N.W., Washington, DC 20005
Telephone: (202) 383-1000
Registered as lobbyist at U.S. Congress.

HILL, Damian P.
Assistant Director, Highway Division, Associated General Contractors of America
1957 E St., N.W., Washington, DC 20006
Telephone: (202) 393-2040
Registered as lobbyist at U.S. Congress.

HILL, Dumond Peck
Kirkpatrick & Lockhart
1800 M St., N.W., Suite 900 South Lobby, Washington, DC 20036-5891
Telephone: (202) 778-9000
Registered as Foreign Agent: (#2840).
Background: Member of Staff, U.S. Atomic Energy Commission, 1950-1951. Assistant Counsel, Internat'l Security Affairs, Office of Secretary of Defense, 1950-1953. Associate Counsel, Dep't of the Army, 1953-1954. Trial Attorney, Dep't of Justice, 1954-1956. Staff Consultant, Committee on Foreign Affairs, House of Representatives, 1956-1959.

HILL GROUP, INC.
1200 17th St., N.W., Suite 400, Washington, DC 20036
Telephone: (202) 296-9200
Background: A multiple association management firm.
Members of firm representing listed organizations:
Barnes, J. Craig
Cook, Joseph A., Account Executive
Background: Serves as Exec. V. President, Nat'l Ass'n of Chemical Distributors.
Hill, Sanford J., President
Smith, Jay H.
Background: Serves as Exec. V. President, Nat'l Ass'n of Hose and Accessories Distributors.
Clients:
Ceramic Tile Marketing Federation *(J. Craig Barnes)*

Medical-Dental Hospital Services Bureaus of America *(Sanford J. Hill)*
Nat'l Ass'n of Chemical Distributors *(Joseph A. Cook)*
Nat'l Ass'n of Hose and Accessories Distributors *(Jay H. Smith)*
Nat'l Ass'n of NIDSPORT Users *(Sanford J. Hill)*
Work Glove Manufacturers Ass'n *(Joseph A. Cook)*

HILL, J. Eldred, Jr.
President, UBA, Inc.
Suite 603, 600 Maryland Ave., S.W., Washington, DC 20024
Telephone: (202) 484-3344
Registered as lobbyist at U.S. Congress.
Background: Assistant Attorney General of Virginia 1954-58; Counsel, Legislative Committee, Interstate Conference of Employment Security Agencies 1957-59. Commissioner, Virginia Employment Commission 1959-66. Exec. Assistant to Governor of Virginia and State Director of Industrial Development 1966-67.

HILL, Jonathan B.
Dow, Lohnes and Albertson
1255 23rd St., N.W., Suite 500, Washington, DC 20037
Telephone: (202) 857-2500
Clients:
Hawaiian Airlines

HILL, Kent R.
Exec. Director, Institute on Religion and Democracy
729 15th St., N.W., Suite 900, Washington, DC 20005
Telephone: (202) 393-3200

HILL AND KNOWLTON PUBLIC AFFAIRS WORLDWIDE
Washington Harbour, 901 31st St., N.W., Washington, DC 20007
Telephone: (202) 333-7400
Registered as lobbyist at U.S. Congress.
Registered as Foreign Agent: (#3301)
Members of firm representing listed organizations:
Aldridge, Diana, Sr. V. Pres. and Unit Manager
Background: Former Legislative Assistant to Senator Haskell (D-CO) and Senator Edward Kennedy (D-MA).
Anderson, Richard M., Deputy General Manager
Background: Formerly on the staff of the Liberal Party of Canada, 1974-77. Special Assistant to Canada's President of the Treasury Board and Minister of Science and Technology, 1977-79. Policy Adviser to the Prime Minister of Canada, 1984.
Armstrong, Phil, Sr. V.P., Grp. Dir., Grassroots Issues
Background: Former Deputy Assistant Secretary of Education for Public Affairs, Reagan Administration.
Bain, Jackson, Sr. V.P., Grp. Dir., Elect. Media Svcs.
Barbis, Patricia Q., V. President
Background: Formerly served with the State Department's Office of Public Affairs and with USIA.
Berard, John, Sr. V. Pres. and Deputy General Manager
Bergquist, Gloria, Sr. Acct. Exec, Grassroots & Issues Mgmt
Bolger, Terry, Account Executive
Background: Legislative Correspondent for Rep. Michael Bilirakis (R-FL), 1985 and Rep. Rick Boucher (D-VA), 1984.
Burke, April, Sr. Acct. Exec., Corp./Political Issues
Cohen, Susan, Account Supervisor, Health Care
Cook, Charles E. (Jr.), V. President
Background: Research Director, Democratic Senatorial Campaign Committee, 1977-79. Staff Member, Senate Democratic Policy Committee, 1982-84.
Coons, Barbara, V. President & Director, Research Svcs.
Background: Former Education Liaison Specialist, Library of Congress.
Cooper, Josephine S., Senior V. President
Background: Air Quality Planning and Standards Program, Environmental Protection Agency, 1969-79. Environmental Legislative Staff Aide to Senator Howard Baker (R-TN), 1979-83. Assistant Administrator, EPA, 1983-85.
Cox, Tamara, V. President
Background: Former aide to Rep. John Napier (R-SC).

WASHINGTON REPRESENTATIVES

HILL AND KNOWLTON PUBLIC AFFAIRS WORLDWIDE (Cont'd)

Crispen, Elaine D., Senior V. President
Background: Former Press Secretary to First Lady Nancy Reagan.

Currier, Jerry, Director, Graphics Services

Doherty, John, Senior Consultant, Government Relations

Duffy, Jennifer E., Account Executive
Background: Office of Public Liaison, USIA/Voice of America, 1983-85. Spokesperson/Regional Communications Assistant, 1985-87 and Deputy Director for Press Relations, 1987-88, Republican Senatorial Committee.

Durant, Andrew G., V. President
Background: Legislative Assistant to Rep. Clive Benedict (R-WV), 1980-81. Press and Legislative Assistant to Rep. E. Thomas Coleman (R-MO), 1982-84.

Eby, Charles J., Senior Consultant, Biotechnology Div.

Fekete, Paul J., Account Executive

Fitz-Pegado, Lauri J., Sr. V. President and Unit Manager
Background: Formerly with U.S. Information Agency.

Foerster, Mary C., Senior V. President
Background: Former Deputy Director of Commerce, City of Philadelphia.

Francis, Charles, V. President and Unit Manager

Goldfarb, Kathryn, Sr. Acct. Superv., Grassroots/issues Mgt

Good, Larry I., Senior V. President

Gray, Robert Keith, Chairman
Background: Former Secretary of the Cabinet, Eisenhower Administration.

Grossman, Steven A., V. President, Corporate & Polit. Affairs
Background: Former Deputy Assistant Secretary for Health, U.S. Department of Health and Human Services.

Handrahan, Kay, Sr. V. Pres. & Washington Business Mgr.

Hoog, Tom, Sr. V.P. & Pract. Dir., St. & Local Govt
Background: Former Chief of Staff to Senator Gary Hart (D-CO).

Hoting, Hilarie, V. President, Health Care

Hubbard, Henry W. (Sr.), Sr. V. Pres. & Group Dir., Biotechnology

Hyde, Barbara, Sr. Acct. Exec., Biotechnology Group

Hymel, Gary, Chief Lobbyist and Vice Chairman
Background: Former Administrative Assistant to former Speaker of the House Thomas P. O'Neill, U.S. House of Representatives.

Janata, Gloria, V. President, Health Care

Jennings, James C., General Manager

Kaminow, (Dr.) Ira P., V. President
Background: V. President and Ecopnomic Adviser, Federal Reserve Bank of Philadelphia, 1969-79.

Kauffman, Frank, V.P., Grassroots & Issues Management

Kaufman, Steve, Deputy Dir., Electronic Media Svcs.

Kaulius, Ghana, Sr. Consultant, State & Local Govt Svcs.

Lathem, Ellen, V.P., Grassroots & Issues Management

Lawson, Dale, V. President
Background: Community Organizer, Office of Economic Opportunity, U.S. Department of Labor, 1967-69. Director, Educational Involvement Program, Department of Labor, 1969. Advisor to Senator Walter Huddleston (D-KY), 1979.

Lindberg, Roger, V. President, Government Relations
Background: Former Administrative Assistant to Rep. Robert T. Matsui (D-CA).

Mankiewicz, Frank, Vice Chairman
Background: Former President, National Public Radio and Press Secretary to Sen. Robert F. Kennedy (D-NY).

Manning, Mary Jo, Senior V. President
Background: Counsel, House Armed Services Committee, 1968-70; Attorney/Advisor, Dept. of Justice, 1970-71; Chief Legislative Ass't, Sen. Ernest F. Hollings (D-SC), 1971-76; Chief Counsel, Communications Subcommittee, Senate Commerce, Science, and Transporation Committee, 1976-81.

Marshall, Cathy, V. Pres., Environment/Energy Group

Massey, Donald F., Sr. V. Pres. & Group Dir., Gov't Relats.

McElroy, James R., V. President
Background: Automotive Trade Analyst, U.S. International Trade Commission, 1977-86.

McGarity, Neal, Acct. Supervisor, Corp/Int'l Counseling

Meeter, Stephen H., V. President
Background: Assistant to House Minority Leader Gerald Ford (R-MI), 1973.

Mefford, T. Fleetwood, V. President, International Trade

Miller, David, Senior Consultant, Government Relations

Miller, Melanie, Sr. Acct. Exec., Biotechnolgy Group

Phipps, John G., Account Executive

Pucie, Charles R. (Jr.), Sr. V.P., Grp. Dir., Corp & Int'l Couns.

Qualls, John, V. President, GRC Economics Group

Rabin, Ken, Sr. V.P. & Nat'l Pract. Dir, Health Care

Reece, Beverly, Senior Account Supervisor

Robertson, Mark, V. President
Background: Former Staff Assistant to Senator David Pryor (D-AR).

Rubin, Jason, V. President, Biotechnology Group

Samuels, (Ambassador) Michael A., Sr. V.P. & Nat'l Pract. Dir, Int'l Trade
Background: Former Deputy U.S. Trade Representative.

Schneider, Robert V., V. President

Schuker, Jill, Senior V. President
Background: Former Press and Public Affairs Counselor, U.S. Mission, United Nations.

Seman, Jep, V.P., Public Affrs., State & Local Govt

Sills, Hilary, V. President
Background: Staff Representative to Rep. William Whitehurst (R-VA), 1970-71.

Silverman, Harold, Sr. V. President, Health Care

Small, Karna, Senior Consultant
Background: Former Special Assistant to the President and Senior Director of Public Affairs, Nat'l Security Council in the Reagan Administration.

Trammell, Jeffrey B., V.P., Gov't Rels./State & Local Affairs

Urbanchuk, John, V. President
Background: Desk Officer, Soviet Union/Eastern Europe, Politico-Military Division, Strategic Plans and Policy Directorate, Office of the Deputy Chief of Staff for Operations and Plans, Department of the Army, 1982-86.

Williams, Marci, Senior V. President and Unit Manager

Witeck, Robert, Sr. V. Pres and Creative Director
Background: Former Communications Director to Senator Bob Packwood (R-OR).

Wolf, Kenneth L., Account Executive, Gov't Relations

Worden, George M., Senior Consultant

Worden, Joan, V. President

Clients:
Abbott Laboratories *(Dale Lawson)*
ADIG-Investment GmbH *(Dr. Ira P. Kaminow)*
Alexander Laing & Cruickshank *(Dr. Ira P. Kaminow)*
Allergan *(Susan Cohen)*
American Airlines *(Robert Keith Gray)*
American General Corp. *(Larry I. Good)*
American Meat Institute *(Harold Silverman)*
American Mining Congress *(Tamara Cox)*
Amerijet Internat'l Inc.
AMR Corp. *(Robert Keith Gray, Gary Hymel)*
Apple Computer, Inc. *(Marci Williams)*
Applied Recovery Technologies, Inc.
ARCO *(Hilary Sills)*
ASARCO Incorporated *(Tom Hoog)*
Baden-Wuerttemberg, State of, Development Corp. *(Mary C. Foerster)*
Bank of Hungary *(Mary C. Foerster, Frank Mankiewicz)*
Blue Cross and Blue Shield Ass'n *(Jeffrey B. Trammell)*
Boeing Co.
Boots Co. *(Ken Rabin)*

Brewster Heights Packing Co. *(Tamara Cox)*
Browning-Ferris Industries (D.C.), Inc.
Bureau National Interprofessionel du Cognac *(Charles R. Pucie, Jr.)*
Caisse des Depots et Consignations *(Dr. Ira P. Kaminow)*
Carlyle Group, The *(Charles Francis)*
Casino *(Dr. Ira P. Kaminow)*
Central Bureau for Fruit and Vegetable Auctions in Holland
Cetus Corp.
Chase Enterprises *(Jill Schuker)*
Chase Manhattan Bank *(John Doherty, David Miller)*
Chemical Waste Management, Inc. *(Tom Hoog)*
Chlorine Institute *(Josephine S. Cooper)*
Chugai Pharmaceutical Co., Ltd. *(Ken Rabin)*
Citicorp Acceptance Corp. *(John Qualls)*
Colorado State University *(Tom Hoog)*
Corcoran Gallery of Art, The *(Frank Mankiewicz, Lauri J. Fitz-Pegado)*
David Sarnoff Research Center *(Jackson Bain, Marci Williams)*
Distilled Spirits Council of the United States *(Josephine S. Cooper)*
Dow Corning Corp. *(Dale Lawson)*
Dresdnerbank *(Dr. Ira P. Kaminow)*
Electronic Industries Ass'n of Japan *(Mary C. Foerster)*
Electronic Industries Ass'n of Korea *(Stephen H. Meeter)*
European Investment Bank *(Dr. Ira P. Kaminow)*
Exxon Co., U.S.A. *(Hilary Sills)*
F&C Management Ltd. *(Dr. Ira P. Kaminow)*
Farmland Industries
Federal Express Corp. *(Charles Francis)*
FMC Corp. *(Josephine S. Cooper)*
Food and Drug Law Institute
Friends' Provident Life Office *(Dr. Ira P. Kaminow)*
Frontec Logistics Corp. *(Robert V. Schneider)*
General Development Corp.
General Electric Co. *(Dale Lawson)*
Gerber Products Corp. *(Donald F. Massey)*
German Nat'l Tourist Office *(Mary C. Foerster)*
Hastings, Nebraska, City of *(Josephine S. Cooper)*
Hecht's *(Mark Robertson)*
Hertz Corp. *(Jeffrey B. Trammell, Kenneth L. Wolf)*
Hill and Knowlton Inc. Political Action Committee *(Gary Hymel)*
Hitachi Ltd. *(Stephen H. Meeter)*
Hitachi Research Institute *(Andrew G. Durant)*
Indonesia, Government of *(Gary Hymel)*
Indonesia, Nat'l Development Information Office *(Donald F. Massey)*
Intermedics, Inc. *(Susan Cohen, Ken Rabin)*
Internat'l Business Machines Corp. *(Larry I. Good)*
ITT Corp. *(James C. Jennings)*
Japan Trade Center *(Andrew G. Durant)*
Johnson Controls, Inc. *(Roger Lindberg)*
Larry Jones Ministries *(Diana Aldridge, Tamara Cox)*
Lederle Laboratories, American Cyanamid Co. Subsidiary *(Jason Rubin)*
MacAndrews & Forbes Holdings, Inc. *(Tom Hoog)*
Marine Midland Banks, Inc. *(John Doherty, David Miller)*
Marubeni America Inc.
Mary Kay Cosmetics *(Steven A. Grossman)*
Merck and Co. *(Ken Rabin)*
Monsanto Co. *(John Urbanchuk)*
Nat'l Broadcasting Co. *(Jackson Bain)*
Nat'l Cancer Institute *(Ken Rabin, Jill Schuker)*
Nat'l Cattlemen's Ass'n *(Barbara Hyde)*
Nat'l Institute on Mental Health *(Ken Rabin)*
Nat'l Realty Committee *(Dr. Ira P. Kaminow)*
New Hampshire Ball Bearings, Inc.
Nintendo *(Roger Lindberg, Donald F. Massey)*
Occidental Petroleum Corp. *(Dale Lawson)*
Peat Marwick *(Joan Worden)*
Petroleos de Venezuela, S.A. *(Lauri J. Fitz-Pegado)*
Phillips & Drew *(Dr. Ira P. Kaminow)*
Procter and Gamble Mfg. Co. *(Barbara Hyde)*
Promodes *(Dr. Ira P. Kaminow)*
Prudential-Bache Securities, Inc. *(Tom Hoog)*
Public Affairs Internat'l *(Richard M. Anderson, Paul J. Fekete, Hilary Sills)*
Rohm and Haas Co. *(John Urbanchuk)*
Royal Danish Embassy *(Mary C. Foerster)*
Ryder System, Inc. *(Gary Hymel)*
Sanwa Bank Ltd. *(Gary Hymel)*

Scottish Equitable Life Assurance Society (*Dr. Ira P. Kaminow*)

Seilbulite Internat'l, Inc. (*Phil Armstrong*)

Shaklee Corp. (*Robert Keith Gray, Gary Hymel, Roger Lindberg, Frank Mankiewicz*)

SmithKline Animal Health Products (*Barbara Hyde*)

SNA Canada Inc. (*Robert V. Schneider*)

Syntex (USA) Inc.

Television Operators Caucus, Inc. (*Mary Jo Manning*)

Telocator (*Mary Jo Manning*)

Thomson Consumer Electronics, Inc. (*Mary Jo Manning, Marci Williams*)

Tobacco Institute (*Tamara Cox, Elaine D. Crispen*)

Toyota Motor Corp. (*Andrew G. Durant*)

Turkey, Embassy of (*Gary Hymel, Donald F. Massey, Charles R. Pucie, Jr.*)

Turkey, Government of (*Robert Keith Gray, Gary Hymel, Frank Mankiewicz, Donald F. Massey, Charles R. Pucie, Jr.*)

UNUM Corp. (*Larry I. Good*)

Upjohn Co. (*Dale Lawson*)

USF&G (*John Urbanchuk*)

Versar, Inc. (*Charles Francis*)

Wistar Institute, The (*Henry W. Hubbard, Sr.*)

WorldCorp (*Charles Francis*)

Wyeth-Ayerst Internat'l, Inc. (*Ken Rabin*)

Yemen Arab Republic, Government of (*Charles R. Pucie, Jr.*)

HILL, Michael
Assistant Director, Gov't Liaison, United States Catholic Conference
3200 4th St., N.E., Washington, DC 20017
Telephone: (202) 541-3000

HILL, Patricia K.
Dir., Water Quality & Waste Disposal Pgm, American Paper Institute
1250 Connecticut Ave., N.W. Suite 210, Washington, DC 20036
Telephone: (202) 463-2420
Registered as lobbyist at U.S. Congress.

HILL, Penny
Ketchum Public Relations
1201 Connecticut Ave., N.W. Suite 300, Washington, DC 20036
Telephone: (202) 835-8800
Clients:
Road Information Program, The (TRIP)

HILL, Richard B.
Exec. Director, American Soc. for Information Science
1424 16th St., N.W. Suite 404, Washington, DC 20036
Telephone: (202) 462-1000

HILL, Robert B.
Legislative Tax Representative, Chemical Manufacturers Ass'n
2501 M St., N.W., Washington, DC 20037
Telephone: (202) 887-1100
Registered as lobbyist at U.S. Congress.

HILL, Robert L.
V. Pres., Consumer and Community Affairs, American Gas Ass'n
1515 Wilson Blvd., Arlington, VA 22209
Telephone: (703) 841-8529

HILL, Sanford J.
President, Hill Group, Inc.
1200 17th St., N.W., Suite 400, Washington, DC 20036
Telephone: (202) 296-9200
Clients:
Medical-Dental Hospital Services Bureaus of America
Nat'l Ass'n of NIDSPORT Users

HILL, Terry
Manager, Nat'l Media Relations, Nat'l Federation of Independent Business
600 Maryland Ave., S.W., Suite 700, Washington, DC 20024
Telephone: (202) 554-9000

HILL, Thomas M.
Director, Federal Legislative Relations, Pacific Gas and Electric Co.
1726 M St., N.W., Suite 1100, Washington, DC 20036-4502
Telephone: (202) 466-7980
Registered as lobbyist at U.S. Congress.
Background: Formerly with the Department of Interior.

HILL, Wayne K.
Byerley Law Offices, Walter E.
1625 K St., N.W. Suite 1190, Washington, DC 20006-1649
Telephone: (202) 628-5530
Background: General Counsel, National Bakery Suppliers Association.
Organizations represented:
Nat'l Bakery Suppliers Ass'n

HILLA, Elizabeth
Exec. Director, Educational Foundation, Health Industry Distributors Ass'n
225 Reinekers Lane, Suite 650, Alexandria, VA 22314
Telephone: (703) 549-4432

HILLEN, Cheryl E.
V. President, Valis Associates
1747 Pennsylvania Ave., N.W., Suite 1201, Washington, DC 20006
Telephone: (202) 833-5055
Clients:
Transportation Reform Alliance

HILLENBRAND, Karen K.
Washington Representative, Pennzoil Co.
1155 15th St., N.W., Suite 600, Washington, DC 20005
Telephone: (202) 331-0212
Registered as lobbyist at U.S. Congress.
Background: Former Legislative Director to Rep. Mary Rose Oakar (D-OH).

HILLIARD, Andrea Riddle
Dir., Leg. & Reg. Affrs. & AGC, American Gas Ass'n
1515 Wilson Blvd., Arlington, VA 22209
Telephone: (703) 841-8469

HILLINGS, Edward J.
V. President, Fed. Gov't Affairs, Enron Corp.
1020 16th St., N.W., Washington, DC 20036-5754
Telephone: (202) 828-3360
Registered as lobbyist at U.S. Congress.

HILLMAN, J. F.
V. President, Colton & Company
600 New Hampshire Ave., N.W., Suite 1020, Washington, DC 20037-2403
Telephone: (202) 333-1555

HILLS, John L.
Corp. Director, Congressional Relations, Sundstrand Corp.
1000 Wilson Blvd., Suite 2400, Arlington, VA 22209
Telephone: (703) 276-1626
Registered as lobbyist at U.S. Congress.

HILLS, John M.
V. President, External Affairs, Brookings Institution
1775 Massachusetts Ave., N.W., Washington, DC 20036
Telephone: (202) 797-6000

HILLS, Laura H.
Patton, Boggs and Blow
2550 M St., N.W., Suite 800, Washington, DC 20037
Telephone: (202) 457-6000
Registered as lobbyist at U.S. Congress.

HILT, Richard H.
Ass't Dir., Energy Analysis & Forcasting, Gas Research Institute
1331 Pennsylvania Ave., N.W., Suite 730 North, Washington, DC 20004
Telephone: (202) 662-8989

HILTON/CHALMERS INC.
923 15th St., N.W., Washington, DC 20005
Telephone: (202) 638-1535
Members of firm representing listed organizations:
Chalmers, Walton M., President, Hilton/Chalmers
Background: Former Exec. Director, Democratic Nat'l Committee.

HILTON, Gregg
Exec. Director, American Security Council
733 15th St., N.W. Suite 700, Washington, DC 20005
Telephone: (202) 484-1676

HIMMELBERG, John M.
Holland and Knight
888 17th St., N.W. Suite 900, Washington, DC 20006
Telephone: (202) 955-5550
Clients:
Florida Celery Exchange
Florida Fruit and Vegetable Ass'n
Florida Tomato Exchange
Indian River Citrus League

HIMMELMAN, Harold
Beveridge & Diamond, P.C.
1350 Eye St., N.W. Suite 700, Washington, DC 20005
Telephone: (202) 789-6000
Background: U.S. Department of Justice, Civil Rights Division, 1967-69.

HINCHMAN, Grace L.
Manager, Public Affairs, Digital Equipment Corp.
1331 Pennsylvania Ave., N.W. Suite 600, Washington, DC 20004
Telephone: (202) 383-5600
Registered as lobbyist at U.S. Congress.

HIND, Richard
Environmental Program Director, U.S. Public Interest Research Group
215 Pennsylvania Ave., S.E., Washington, DC 20003
Telephone: (202) 546-9707
Registered as lobbyist at U.S. Congress.

HINDS, Richard deC.
Cleary, Gottlieb, Steen and Hamilton
1752 N St., N.W., Washington, DC 20036
Telephone: (202) 728-2700
Registered as lobbyist at U.S. Congress.
Registered as Foreign Agent: (#0508).
Clients:
Day-Glo Color Corp.
La Metalli Industriale S.p.A.

HINE, Kenneth F.
Exec. V. President and CEO, American Hotel and Motel Ass'n
1201 New York Ave., N.W. Suite 600, Washington, DC 20005
Telephone: (202) 289-3100

HINES, Eugene E.
Exec. Director, American Soc. of Notaries
918 16th St., N.W., Washington, DC 20006
Telephone: (202) 955-6162
Background: Trial Attorney, Office of the Chief Counsel, Internal Revenue Service, 1954-1958.

HINES, Virginia K.
Deputy Director, American Youth Work Center, The
1751 N St., N.W., Suite 302, Washington, DC 20036
Telephone: (202) 785-0764

HINES, William J.
Wagner, Hines and Avary
1899 L St., N.W., Suite 500, Washington, DC 20036
Telephone: (202) 659-0930
Registered as lobbyist at U.S. Congress.
Registered as Foreign Agent: (#3845).
Clients:
American Heavy Lift Shipping Co.
H. E. Ventures, Inc.
Holmes & Narver, Inc.

HINKLE, Maureen K.
Director of Agriculture Policy, Nat'l Audubon Soc.
801 Pennsylvania Ave., S.E., Washington, DC 20003
Telephone: (202) 547-9009
Registered as lobbyist at U.S. Congress.

HINSON, J. Philip
Dir, West Europe & Near East/US C of C, European Council of American Chambers of Commerce in Europe
1615 H St., N.W., Washington, DC 20062
Telephone: (202) 463-5487

HIOTT, Yvonne
Manager, Public Relations, Recreation Vehicle Industry Ass'n
1896 Preston White Drive P.O. Box 2999, Reston, VA 22090
Telephone: (703) 620-6003

HIPPLE, Thomas
Political Affairs Director, Nat'l Ass'n of Home Builders of the U.S.
15th and M Streets, N.W., Washington, DC 20005
Telephone: (202) 822-0470
Background: Served on the staff of Senator Vance Hartke (D-IN), 1969-71; as an aide to Rep. Andrew Jacobs (D-IN), 1975-78; and in the Office of the Secretary of Health and Human Services, 1978-80.

HIPPLER, Melissa
Secretary, Environmental Federation of America
3007 Tilden St., N.W. Suite 4L, Washington, DC 20008
Telephone: (202) 537-7100

HIRD, David B.
Weil, Gotshal & Manges
1615 L St., N.W., Suite 700, Washington, DC 20036
Telephone: (202) 682-7000
Clients:
Schering Internat'l

HIRN, Richard J.
General Counsel, Nat'l Weather Service Employees Organization
400 North Capitol St., N.W. Suite 326, Washington, DC 20001
Telephone: (202) 783-3131

HIRSCH, Robert A.
General Counsel/Dir. of Regulatory Afrs., Nat'l Private Truck Council
1320 Braddock Place Suite 720, Alexandria, VA 22314
Telephone: (703) 683-1300
Registered as lobbyist at U.S. Congress.

HIRSCH, Robert B.
Arent, Fox, Kintner, Plotkin & Kahn
1050 Connecticut Ave., N.W., Washington, DC 20036-5339
Telephone: (202) 857-6000

HIRSCHFELD, Tamara
Manager, Gov't Relations, American Stock Exchange
888 17th St., N.W., Suite 308, Washington, DC 20006
Telephone: (202) 887-6880

HIRSCHHORN, Eric L.
Bishop, Cook, Purcell & Reynolds
1400 L St., N.W., Washington, DC 20005-3502
Telephone: (202) 371-5700
Background: Legislative Assistant to Representative Bella S. Abzug of New York, 1971-73. Chief Counsel, House of Representatives Subcommittee on Government Information and Individual Rights 1975-77. Deputy Associate Director, Office of Management and Budget (President's Reorganization Project), 1977-80. Deputy Assistant Secretary for Export Administration, U.S. Department of Commerce, 1980-81.
Clients:
Industry Coalition on Technology Transfer

HIRSCHMANN, David
Director, Research and Liaison, Council for Inter-American Security
122 C St., N.W., Suite 710, Washington, DC 20001
Telephone: (202) 393-6622

HIRSHBERG, Jennefer
Rogers & Cowan, Inc.
2233 Wisconsin Ave., N.W. Suite 500, Washington, DC 20007
Telephone: (202) 338-1900
Background: As Asst. V. President, Kaufman Public Relations, handles public relations for Rogers & Cowan, Inc. Both firms are units of Shandwick PLC.

HISER, Wray C.
Senior Counsel, Government Relations, Thomson Consumer Electronics, Inc.
1200 19th St., N.W., Suite 601, Washington, DC 20036
Telephone: (202) 872-0670

HITCHCOCK, Cornish F.
Staff Attorney, Public Citizen Litigation Group
2000 P St., N.W., Suite 700, Washington, DC 20036
Telephone: (202) 785-3704
Registered as lobbyist at U.S. Congress.
Background: Also serves as Legal Director, Aviation Consumer Action Project.

HITCHCOCK, Jamie
Exec. Assistant, American Educational Research Ass'n
1230 17th St., N.W., Washington, DC 20036
Telephone: (202) 223-9485

HITCHINGS, Ward
Washington Representative, Nat'l Wood Window and Door Ass'n
1250 Connecticut Ave., N.W. Suite 300, Washington, DC 20036
Telephone: (202) 463-2799

HITCHNER, Stephen B., Jr.
Senior V. President, Urban Institute, The
2100 M St., N.W., Washington, DC 20037
Telephone: (202) 833-7200

HITT, Dan L.
V. President, Federal Gov't Affairs, Minnesota Mining and Manufacturing Co. (3M Co.)
1101 15th St., N.W., Washington, DC 20005
Telephone: (202) 331-6900

HITZ, Frederick P.
Schwabe, Williamson and Wyatt
2000 Pennsylvania Ave., N.W., Suite 8335, Washington, DC 20006
Telephone: (202) 785-5960
Registered as lobbyist at U.S. Congress.
Background: Deputy Assistant Secretary of Defense for Legislative Affairs, 1975-77. Member, Energy Policy and Planning Staff, Exec Office of the President, 1977. Director of Congressional Affairs, U.S. Department of Energy, 1977-78. Legislative Counsel to the Director of Central Intelligence, 1978-81.
Clients:
Eugene Water and Electric Board
Grant County P.U.D.
Multnomah County, Oregon
Oregon METRO
Oregon, State of
Oregon Steel Mills, Inc.
Physicians Medical Laboratories
Portland Metropolitan Service District
Portland, Oregon, City of
Public Generating Pool
Tri-County Metropolitan Transportation District of Oregon

HIXSON, Sheila E.
V. President, Stateside Associates
Courthouse Plaza II, Suite 407 2300 Clarendon Blvd., Arlington, VA 22201
Telephone: (703) 525-7466
Registered as lobbyist at U.S. Congress.

HOADLEY, John F.
Senior Research Associate, Nat'l Health Policy Forum
2011 Eye St., N.W. Suite 200, Washington, DC 20006
Telephone: (202) 872-1390
Background: Former Legislative Aide to Rep. Barbara B. Kennelly (D-CT).

HOAGLAND, K. Elaine
Exec. Director, Ass'n of Systematics Collections
730 11th St., N.W., 2nd Floor, Washington, DC 20001
Telephone: (202) 347-2850

HOAGLAND, Ken
Spec. Asst. to the Exec. Director, Nat'l Council of Senior Citizens
925 15th St., N.W., Washington, DC 20005
Telephone: (202) 347-8800

HOBART, Karen
Field Organizer, Congress Watch
215 Pennsylvania Ave., S.E., Washington, DC 20003
Telephone: (202) 546-4996

HOBART, Lawrence S.
Exec. Director, American Public Power Ass'n
2301 M St., N.W., Washington, DC 20037
Telephone: (202) 775-8300
Registered as lobbyist at U.S. Congress.

HOBBS, Caswell O., III
Morgan, Lewis and Bockius
1800 M St., N.W., Washington, DC 20036
Telephone: (202) 467-7000
Clients:
Bird and Son
Nat'l Spa and Pool Institute

HOBBS, Charles A.
Hobbs, Straus, Dean and Wilder
1819 H St., N.W., Suite 800, Washington, DC 20006
Telephone: (202) 783-5100
Registered as lobbyist at U.S. Congress.
Clients:
Quinault Indian Nation
Three Afiliated Tribes of Fort Berthold Reservation

HOBBS, STRAUS, DEAN AND WILDER
1819 H St., N.W., Suite 800, Washington, DC 20006
Telephone: (202) 783-5100
Members of firm representing listed organizations:
Dean, S. Bobo
Funk, Karen J.
Hobbs, Charles A.
Straus, Jerry C.
  Background: Attorney, Civil Division, Appellate Section, U.S. Department of Justice, 1961-63. Member, Washington D.C. Regional Selection Panel, President's Commission on White House Fellows, 1973.
Clients:
Aroostook Bank of Micmacs *(Jerry C. Straus)*
Ass'n of Navajo Community Controlled School Boards *(S. Bobo Dean)*
Bristol Bay Health Corp. *(S. Bobo Dean)*
Maniilaq Ass'n *(S. Bobo Dean)*
Menominee Indian Tribe *(Jerry C. Straus)*
Metlakatla Indian Community *(S. Bobo Dean)*
Miccosukee Tribe of Indians of Florida *(S. Bobo Dean)*
Nat'l Indian Education Ass'n *(Karen J. Funk)*
Oglala Sioux Tribe *(S. Bobo Dean)*
Quinault Indian Nation *(Charles A. Hobbs)*
Seminole Tribe of Florida *(Jerry C. Straus)*
Three Afiliated Tribes of Fort Berthold Reservation *(Charles A. Hobbs)*

HOBSON, David
Smith, Bucklin and Associates
1101 Connecticut Ave., N.W., Suite 700, Washington, DC 20036
Telephone: (202) 857-1100
Background: Administrative Director, Internat'l District Heating and Cooling Ass'n and Exec. Director, Ass'n for Governmental Leasing and Financing.
Clients:
Ass'n for Governmental Leasing and Financing
Internat'l District Heating and Cooling Ass'n

HOBSON, James R.
Legal, GTE Corp.
Suite 1200, 1850 M St., N.W., Washington, DC 20036
Telephone: (202) 463-5210

HOBSON, Tina C.
Exec. Director, Renew America Project
1400 16th St., N.W. Suite 710, Washington, DC 20036
Telephone: (202) 232-2252

HOCHBERG, Philip R.
Baraff, Koerner, Olender and Hochberg
2033 M St., N.W., Suite 700, Washington, DC 20036
Telephone: (202) 452-8200
Registered as lobbyist at U.S. Congress.
Background: Special Counsel, Communications Subcommittee, U.S. House of Representatives, 1977.
Clients:
College Football Ass'n
Nat'l Basketball Ass'n
Nat'l Hockey League

HOCKER, Stephen A.
Exec. Director, District of Columbia Special Olympics
220 Eye St., N.E., Suite 280, Washington, DC 20002
Telephone: (202) 544-7770

HOCKETT, Ruth Ann
Dep Dir, Legis Affrs & Public Info, DEPARTMENT OF AG-
RICULTURE - Rural Electrification Administration
14th and Independence Ave. S.W., Washington, DC 20250
Telephone: (202) 382-1255

HODGE, Charles
President, American Council of the Blind Federal Employees
1010 Vermont Ave., N.W. Suite 1100, Washington, DC
20005
Telephone: (202) 393-3666

HODGE, Deanna
Manager, Congressional Affairs, Soc. for Human Re-
sources Management
606 N. Washington St., Alexandria, VA 22314
Telephone: (703) 548-3440
Registered as lobbyist at U.S. Congress.
Background: Former Staff Assistant, House Committee on
Education and Labor. Legislative Liaison, Department of
Labor, 1986-88.

HODGES, Ann C.
Director, Congressional Affairs, Aircraft Owners and Pilots
Ass'n
500 E St., S.W. Suite 920, Washington, DC 20024
Telephone: (202) 479-4050
Registered as lobbyist at U.S. Congress.
Background: Former Legislative Assistant to Rep. T. Cass
Ballenger (R-NC).

HODGES, John A.
Wiley, Rein & Fielding
1776 K St., N.W., Tenth Floor, Washington, DC 20006-
2359
Telephone: (202) 429-7000
Registered as lobbyist at U.S. Congress.
Registered as Foreign Agent: (#4154).
Clients:
  Marine Mammal Coalition

HODGKINSON, Harold L.
Director, Center for Demographic Policy, Institute for Educational Leadership
1001 Connecticut Ave., N.W. Suite 310, Washington, DC
20036
Telephone: (202) 822-8405

HODGKINSON, Virginia Ann
V. President, Research, Independent Sector
1828 L St., N.W., Washington, DC 20036
Telephone: (202) 223-8100

HOECHSTETTER, Susan
Director, Legislation, Nat'l Ass'n of Social Workers
7981 Eastern Ave., Silver Spring, MD 20910
Telephone: (301) 565-0333
Registered as lobbyist at U.S. Congress.

HOEGLE, Robert L.
Olwine, Connelly, Chase, O'Donnell and Weyher
1701 Pennsylvania Ave., N.W. Suite 1000, Washington,
DC 20006
Telephone: (202) 835-0500
Clients:
  Companhia de Navagacao Maritima NETUMAR
  Liberty Mutual Insurance Co.

HOEHN, Elmer L.
5914 Woodley Road, McLean, VA 22101
Telephone: (703) 532-3320
Background: Director, Oil and Gas, State of Indiana,
1949-53. Chairman, Interstate Oil Compabt Commission,
1962. Administrator, U.S. Oil Import Administration,
1965-69.
Organizations represented:
  Liaison Committee of Cooperating Oil and Gas
  Ass'ns

HOELTER, Herbert
Director, Nat'l Center on Institutions and Alternatives
635 Slaters Lane Suite G-100, Alexandria, VA 22314
Telephone: (703) 684-0373

HOEWING, Raymond L.
President, Public Affairs Council
1019 19th St., N.W., Suite 200, Washington, DC 20036
Telephone: (202) 872-1790

HOFER, Lydia
Dir, House Liaison, DEPARTMENT OF INTERIOR
18th and C Sts., N.W., Washington, DC 20240
Telephone: (202) 343-7693

HOFF, John S.
Swidler & Berlin, Chartered
3000 K St., N.W., Suite 300, Washington, DC 20007
Telephone: (202) 944-4300
Registered as lobbyist at U.S. Congress.
Clients:
  Nat'l Council of Community Hospitals

HOFF, Paul S.
Garvey, Schubert & Barer
1000 Potomac St., N.W. Suite 500, Washington, DC
20007
Telephone: (202) 965-7880
Registered as lobbyist at U.S. Congress.
Background: Associate Chief Counsel, Senate Govern-
mental Affairs Committee, 1975-81.
Clients:
  J & B Management Co.

HOFF, Tina
Assistant Account Executive, Gallagher-Widmeyer Group
Inc., The
1110 Vermont Ave., N.W., Suite 1020, Washington, DC
20005
Telephone: (202) 659-1606

HOFFER, Audrey S.
Senior Account Executive, CMF&Z Public Relations
655 15th St., N.W., Suite 300, Washington, DC 20005
Telephone: (202) 639-4059

HOFFMAN, Adonis E.
Hopkins and Sutter
888 16th St., N.W., Suite 700, Washington, DC 20006
Telephone: (202) 835-8000
Registered as lobbyist at U.S. Congress.
Background: Legislative Assistant to Rep. Mervyn M. Dy-
mally (D-CA), 1981-84.

HOFFMAN, Cheryl W.
Director of Communications, Interstate Natural Gas Ass'n
of America
555 13th St., N.W. Suite 300 West, Washington, DC
20004
Telephone: (202) 626-3200

HOFFMAN, Gail H.
Legislative Director, Handgun Control, Inc.
1225 Eye St., N.W., Suite 1100, Washington, DC 20005
Telephone: (202) 898-0792
Registered as lobbyist at U.S. Congress.
Background: Contact for Handgun Control, Inc. Political
Action Committee.

HOFFMAN, Joel E.
Sutherland, Asbill and Brennan
1275 Pennsylvania, N.W., Washington, DC 20004-2404
Telephone: (202) 383-0100
Background: Trial Attorney, Appellate Section, Antitrust
Division, U.S. Department of Justice, 1960-63.
Clients:
  Lederle Laboratories, American Cyanamid Co.
  Subsidiary

HOFFMAN, Katherine, APR
Associate Director, Nat'l Ass'n of Professional Insurance
Agents
400 North Washington St., Alexandria, VA 22314
Telephone: (703) 836-9340

HOFFMAN, Kathy
Washington Rep, Transportation, California, State of
444 North Capitol St., N.W., Suite 305, Washington, DC
20001
Telephone: (202) 347-6891

HOFFMAN, Lawrence J.
Akin, Gump, Strauss, Hauer and Feld
1333 New Hampshire Ave., N.W., Suite 400, Washington,
DC 20036
Telephone: (202) 887-4000
Background: Attorney, National Labor Relations Board,
1967-68.

HOFFMAN, Linda J.
V. President, Gov't Affairs and Trade, Automotive Parts
and Accessories Ass'n
5100 Forbes Blvd., Lanham, MD 20706
Telephone: (301) 459-9110
Registered as lobbyist at U.S. Congress.

HOFFMAN, Melane Kinney
V. President, Porter/Novelli
1001 30th St., N.W., Washington, DC 20007
Telephone: (202) 342-7000

HOFFMAN, Steven A.
Deputy Dir., Couns., Off. of Fed. Affrs., New York, State
of
444 N. Capitol St., N.W. Suite 301, Washington, DC
20001
Telephone: (202) 638-1311

HOFFMAN, William L.
516 First St., S.E., Washington, DC 20003
Telephone: (202) 546-5639
Registered as lobbyist at U.S. Congress.
Registered as Foreign Agent: (#3847)
Background: A consultant. Former Chief of Staff and
Legislative Director to U.S. Senator Mike Gravel.
Organizations represented:
  American University of Beirut
  Richardson Lawrie Associates

HOFFMANN & ASSOC., F. Nordy
400 North Capitol St., N.W. Suite 327, Washington, DC
20001
Telephone: (202) 393-4848
Members of firm representing listed organizations:
  Gereau, Gerald R., Senior V. President
    Background: Professional Staff Member, Senate Interior
    Committee, 1972-74. Legislative Director for Senator
    Howard Metzenbaum (D-OH), 1974-75. Chief Inves-
    tigator, Senate Rules Committee, 1977-88. Also
    served on personal or committee staffs of Senators
    Henry Jackson (D-WA), Lee Metcalf (D-MT) and
    John Warner (R-VA); and Reps. Frank Thompson
    (D-NJ), Jack Brooks (D-TX) and Augustus Hawkins
    (D-CA).
  Hoffmann, F. Nordy, President
    Background: Former Exec. Director, Democratic
    Senatorial Campaign Committee. Former Sergeant at
    Arms, U.S. Senate.
Organizations represented:
  Archer-Daniels-Midland Co. *(F. Nordy Hoffmann)*
  Coca-Cola Co. *(F. Nordy Hoffmann)*
  Marine Engineers Beneficial Ass'n *(F. Nordy Hoff-
  mann)*
  Nat'l Education Ass'n of the U.S. *(Gerald R. Gereau,
  F. Nordy Hoffmann)*
  Wilmorite, Inc. *(F. Nordy Hoffmann)*

HOFFMANN, F. Nordy
President, Hoffmann & Assoc., F. Nordy
400 North Capitol St., N.W. Suite 327, Washington, DC
20001
Telephone: (202) 393-4848
Registered as lobbyist at U.S. Congress.
Background: Former Exec. Director, Democratic Senatorial
Campaign Committee. Former Sergeant at Arms, U.S.
Senate.
Organizations represented:
  Archer-Daniels-Midland Co.
  Coca-Cola Co.
  Marine Engineers Beneficial Ass'n
  Nat'l Education Ass'n of the U.S.
  Wilmorite, Inc.

HOFFMANN, Walter F.
Exec. Director, World Federalist Ass'n
418 Seventh St., S.E., Washington, DC 20003
Telephone: (202) 546-3950
Background: Formerly Staff Attorney for Congressional
Investigations Committee and Trial Attorney, National
Labor Relations Board.

HOFMAN, Steven I.
V. President, Hager Sharp Inc.
1101 17th St., N.W., Suite 1001, Washington, DC 20036
Telephone: (202) 466-5430
Background: Former Director, House Republican Research Committee.

HOGAN, Elizabeth A.
Manager, Congressional Relations, MCI Communications Corp.
1133 19th St., N.W., Washington, DC 20036
Telephone: (202) 872-1600
Registered as lobbyist at U.S. Congress.

HOGAN, Gerald F.
V. President, Government Relations, Corporation for Public Broadcasting
901 E St., N.W. Suite 2209, Washington, DC 20004-2006
Telephone: (202) 879-9712
Background: Former Deputy Legislative Council, U.S. Merit Systems Protection Board.

HOGAN AND HARTSON
555 13th St., N.W., Suite 1200, Washington, DC 20004-1109
Telephone: (202) 637-5600
Background: The information below was obtained from public records and submitted for confirmation to this firm, which declined to confirm or correct the information and asked to be omitted from the book.
Members of firm representing listed organizations:
  Arness, John P.
  Ashford, Deborah T.
  Bell, Joseph C.
    Background: Assistant General Counsel, Federal Energy Administration, 1974-77.
  Berger, Samuel R.
    Background: Legislative Assistant to Senator Harold E. Hughes, 1971-72. Deputy Director, Policy Planning Staff, U.S. Department of State, 1977-80.
  Carneal, George U.
    Background: Special Assistant to the Secretary of Transportation, 1969-1970; General Counsel, Federal Aviation Administration, 1970-1972.
  Cave, Robert B.
  Cohen, Vincent H.
    Background: Trail Attorney, U.S. Department of Justice, 1962-67.
  Collier, (Jr.) Earl
  Feagles, Prentiss E.
  Fulbright, J. William, Of Counsel
    Background: U.S. Senator from Arkansas 1945-75. Dep't of Justice 1934-35. President of the University of Arkansas 1939-41. U.S. House of Representatives 1943-45.
  Gibbons, Clifford S., Legislative Consultant
    Background: Special Assistant to the U.S. Special Trade Representative, Executive Office of the President, 1979-81.
  Gilbert, Gerald E.
    Background: U.S. Dep't of Commerce 1965-66.
  Harrington, Anthony
  Hensler, David J.
    Background: Attorney, General Counsel's Office, Securities and Exchange Commission, 1967-68.
  Johnson, Arnold C.
    Background: Attorney, Legal Advisory Staff, U.S. Treasury Department, 1954-56. Attorney, staff of the Joint Committee on Internal Revenue Taxation, 1956-59.
  Kilcarr, Andrew J.
    Background: Trial Attorney, Antitrust Division, U.S. Department of Justice, 1959-64.
  Korwek, Edward L.
  Kushner, Gary J.
  Leary, Thomas B.
  Lloyd, Timothy A.
  Mayo, George W. (Jr.)
  McConnell, Mark S.
  Mernick, George (III)
  Michel, Laurie
  Miller, George T.
  Miller, H. Todd
  Miller, Randy E.
  O'Bryon, Maureen E.
  Odle, Bob Glen
  Prettyman, E. Barrett (Jr.)

Background: Law Clerk to U.S. Supreme Court Justices Robert Jackson (1953-54), Felix Frankfurter (1954-55) and John Harlan (1955). Special Assistant to the Attorney General of the U.S.(1963) and to the White House (1963-64). Special Counsel to the House of Representatives Committee on Standards of Official Conduct, 1980-82.
  Rogers, Paul G.
    Background: Member of Congress (D-FL) 1955-1979. Chairman, Subcommittee on Health and the Environment, U.S. House of Representatives, 1971-79. Member, Board of Directors, Merck and Co. and of Mutual Life Insurance Co. of New York.
  Rothkopf, Arthur J.
    Background: Attorney, Securities and Exchange Commission, 1960-63. Associate Tax Legislative Counsel (International), U.S. Treasury Department, 1963-66.
  Rousselot, Peter F.
  Sonosky, Jerome N.
    Background: Special Assistant to the Assistant Secretary for Legislation, Department of Health, Education and Welfare, 1961-63. Legislative Assistant to Senator Abraham Ribicoff of Connecticut 1963-65. Staff Director and General Counsel, Senate Subcommittee on Executive Reorganization, 1965-67.
  Stanton, John S.
    Background: Member, Professional Staff, House Banking Committee, U.S. Congress, 1974-77.
  Taylor, (Jr.) Chester
  Trilling, Helen R.
  Vickery, Ann Morgan
  Von Salzen, Eric A.
  Winnik, Joel S.
Clients:
  Aermacchi, S.p.A. *(Clifford S. Gibbons)*
  Air Transport Ass'n of America
  Alcide de Gasperi Foundation *(Deborah T. Ashford)*
  American Council of Young Political Leaders
  American Frozen Food Institute *(Gary J. Kushner)*
  American Medical Internat'l *(Clifford S. Gibbons, John S. Stanton)*
  American Physical Therapy Ass'n *(Helen R. Trilling, Ann Morgan Vickery)*
  American Soybean Ass'n *(Gary J. Kushner)*
  Amgen, Inc. *(Ann Morgan Vickery)*
  Bahamas, Government of the
  Caremark/Home Health Care of America *(Bob Glen Odle, Ann Morgan Vickery)*
  Caterpillar Inc. *(Samuel R. Berger)*
  Center for Democracy *(Anthony Harrington)*
  Champon Flavors & Fragrances *(Edward L. Korwek)*
  Cryo-Chem Internat'l, Inc. *(Clifford S. Gibbons, Laurie Michel)*
  Daimler-Berry A.G.
  Denver and Rio Grande Western Railroad Co. *(Thomas B. Leary, George W. Mayo, Jr., E. Barrett Prettyman, Jr., Peter F. Rousselot, Eric A. Von Salzen)*
  Dianon Systems *(Helen R. Trilling)*
  Farmworker Justice Fund *(George Mernick, III)*
  Fox Broadcasting Inc.
  Freightliner Corp.
  Internat'l Committee of Passenger Lines
  Japan, Embassy of
  Korean Soybean Processors Ass'n
  Lloyds of London, Underwriters at *(Clifford S. Gibbons, Arthur J. Rothkopf, John S. Stanton)*
  Manufacturers Hanover Trust Co. *(Arthur J. Rothkopf, John S. Stanton)*
  May Department Stores Co. *(Samuel R. Berger, Clifford S. Gibbons, Bob Glen Odle)*
  Mercedes-Benz of North America, Inc. *(Clifford S. Gibbons)*
  Mutual Life Insurance Co. of New York *(Clifford S. Gibbons)*
  Nat'l Broiler Council
  Nat'l Hospice Organization
  Nat'l Pasta Ass'n *(Gary J. Kushner)*
  Nat'l Telecommunications Network *(Anthony Harrington)*
  Ontario, Province of *(Clifford S. Gibbons, Mark S. McConnell, Bob Glen Odle)*
  Poland, Ministry of Finance of *(Joseph C. Bell, Samuel R. Berger)*
  SouthernNet, Inc. *(John S. Stanton)*
  Timex Corp. *(Samuel R. Berger)*
  Toyota Motor Sales, U.S.A. *(Samuel R. Berger, Clifford S. Gibbons, Gerald E. Gilbert)*
  Washington Post Co.

Whitman Distributing Co. *(Clifford S. Gibbons, George T. Miller, Jr. Chester Taylor)*

HOGAN, Ilona M.
Venable, Baetjer, Howard and Civiletti
1201 New York Ave., N.W., Suite 1000, Washington, DC 20005
Telephone: (202) 962-4800
Clients:
Alliance of Metalworking Industries

HOGAN, Joseph Michael, Jr.
Asst. Director, Governmental Relations, American Chiropractic Ass'n
1701 Clarendon Blvd., Arlington, VA 22209
Telephone: (703) 276-8800
Registered as lobbyist at U.S. Congress.
Background: Serves as PAC director for the American Chiropractic Ass'n Political Action Committee.

HOGAN, Sandra
Legis Liaison Office, DEPARTMENT OF AGRICULTURE - Agricultural Marketing Staff
14th and Independence Ave. S.W., Room 3510 South Bldg., Washington, DC 20250
Telephone: (202) 447-3203

HOGNESS, John R., M.D.
Senior Consultant, Cassidy and Associates, Inc.
655 15th St., N.W., Suite 1100, Washington, DC 20005
Telephone: (202) 347-0773
Registered as lobbyist at U.S. Congress.
Clients:
Children's Hospital of Michigan

HOGUE, Phillip A.
Internat'l Technical Expertise, Ltd.
150 South Washington St., Suite 403, Falls Church, VA 22046
Telephone: (703) 536-4500
Registered as lobbyist at U.S. Congress.

HOHBACH, Barbara
Coordinator, Media Relations, Heritage Foundation
214 Massachusetts Ave., N.E., Washington, DC 20002
Telephone: (202) 546-4400

HOHMANN, Kathryn
Associate Washington Representative, Sierra Club
408 C St., N.E., Washington, DC 20002
Telephone: (202) 547-1141
Registered as lobbyist at U.S. Congress.

HOLAHAN, John
Director, Health Policy Center, Urban Institute, The
2100 M St., N.W., Washington, DC 20037
Telephone: (202) 833-7200

HOLAYTER, William J.
Dir., Legislation & Political Action, Internat'l Ass'n of Machinists and Aerospace Workers
1300 Connecticut Ave., N.W. Suite 404, Washington, DC 20036
Telephone: (202) 857-5295
Registered as lobbyist at U.S. Congress.
Background: Responsibilities include the Machinists Non-Partisan Political League.

HOLBERT, Martha A.
Legislative Assistant, Health Insurance Plan of Greater New York
1150 17th St., N.W., Suite 600, Washington, DC 20036
Telephone: (202) 659-9460
Registered as lobbyist at U.S. Congress.

HOLBROOK, Douglas C.
Secretary-Treasurer, American Postal Workers Union
1300 L St., N.W., Washington, DC 20005
Telephone: (202) 842-4215

HOLCOMB, Howard E.
Government Affairs Counsel, Council of Independent Colleges
One Dupont Circle, N.W. Suite 320, Washington, DC 20036
Telephone: (202) 466-7230

HOLCOMB, Terry
Senior Associate, Mahe Company, The Eddie
900 Second St., N.E. Suite 200, Washington, DC 20002

Telephone: (202) 842-4100
Background: Former Chief of Staff to Rep. James Imhofe (R-OK).

HOLDEN, Gwen A.
Exec. V. President, Nat'l Criminal Justice Ass'n
444 N. Capitol St., N.W. Suite 608, Washington, DC 20001
Telephone: (202) 347-4900

HOLDEN, James P.
Steptoe and Johnson
1330 Connecticut Ave., N.W., Washington, DC 20036
Telephone: (202) 429-3000
Background: Member, Advisory Group to Commissioner of Internal Revenue, 1979-80.

HOLDER, Elma
Exec. Director, Nat'l Citizens Coalition for Nursing Home Reform
1424 16th St., N.W., Suite L2, Washington, DC 20036
Telephone: (202) 797-0657

HOLDGREIWE, Daniel C.
Exec. Director, Coalition for Religious Freedom
515 Wyhte St., Suite 201, Alexandria, VA 22314
Telephone: (703) 684-9010

HOLDSWORTH, Thomas W.
Director, Communications & Public Affrs., Vocational Industrial Clubs of America
Box 3000, Leesburg, VA 22075
Telephone: (703) 777-8810

HOLIK, Susan Z.
Legislative Representative, American Foreign Service Ass'n
2101 E St., N.W., Washington, DC 20037
Telephone: (202) 338-4045
Registered as lobbyist at U.S. Congress.

HOLLADAY, Philip C., Jr.
Washington Rep., House and Senate, Shell Oil Co.
Suite 200, 1025 Connecticut Ave., N.W., Washington, DC 20036
Telephone: (202) 466-1415
Registered as lobbyist at U.S. Congress.

HOLLAND AND HART
1001 Pennsylvania Suite 310, Washington, DC 20004
Telephone: (202) 638-5500
Registered as lobbyist at U.S. Congress.
Background: The Washington, DC office of a Rocky Mountain, CO based law firm.
Members of firm representing listed organizations:
 Barringer, Steven G.
 Brown, Lauren E.
  Background: Aide to Sen. Ted Stevens (R-AK), 1986-88.
 Demarest, William F. (Jr.)
  Background: Counsel, House Subcommitte on Energy and Power, 1975-79; Counsel, House Committee on Small Business, 1973-75.
 Luedtke, J. Peter
 Maddox, Adelia
  Background: Administrative Ass't (1983-85) and Legislative Ass't (1979-83) to Rep. Richard Shelby (D-AL).
 O'Connell, Quinn
Clients:
 Alyeska Pipeline Service Co. *(Lauren E. Brown, Quinn O'Connell)*
 Council for Solid Waste Solutions *(Lauren E. Brown, William F. Demarest, Jr.)*
 Grocery Manufacturers of America *(William F. Demarest, Jr.)*
 Resource Conservation and Recovery Act Mine Waste Group *(Steven G. Barringer)*
 Scott's Liquid Gold *(Lauren E. Brown, J. Peter Luedtke)*
 Southland Corp., The *(William F. Demarest, Jr.)*

HOLLAND, Howard
Program Manager, External Affairs, American Occupational Therapy Ass'n
1383 Piccard Drive, Suite 300 P.O. Box 1725, Rockville, MD 20850
Telephone: (301) 948-9626

HOLLAND, James R.
Director, Office of Communications, American Ass'n of Retired Persons
1909 K St., N.W., Washington, DC 20049
Telephone: (202) 728-4300
Background: Former Deputy Assistant Secretary for Public Affairs, U.S. Department of Health, Education and Welfare. Served also as Deputy Director of Communications for Presidents Richard Nixon and Gerald Ford.

HOLLAND AND KNIGHT
888 17th St., N.W. Suite 900, Washington, DC 20006
Telephone: (202) 955-5550
Background: Washington office of a Florida law firm.
Members of firm representing listed organizations:
 Baker, David H.
 Fried, Ronald A., Senior Consultant, Government Relations
  Background: Former Legislative Assistant to Rep. Claude Pepper (D-FL).
 Himmelberg, John M.
 Kimbrell, Eddie, Senior Consultant, Gov't Relations
  Background: Former Deputy Administrator, Agricultural Marketing Service, U.S. Department of Agriculture.
 Loos, Dickson R.
 Matz, Marshall L.
  Background: Counsel and General Counsel, U.S. Senate Select Committee on Nutrition and Human Needs, 1973-77. Special Counsel, Senate Committee on Agriculture, Nutrition and Forestry, 1978-80.
 Studley, Janet R.
  Background: Former Chief Counsel, Senate Subcommittee on Federal Spending Practices / Senator Lawton Chiles (D-FL).
Clients:
 Abbott Laboratories *(Marshall L. Matz)*
 Avianca Airlines
 Bridgeport and Port Jefferson Steamboat Co. *(David H. Baker)*
 Carnival Cruise Lines *(Marshall L. Matz)*
 Florida Celery Exchange *(John M. Himmelberg)*
 Florida Fruit and Vegetable Ass'n *(John M. Himmelberg)*
 Florida Tomato Exchange *(John M. Himmelberg)*
 General Development Corp. *(Janet R. Studley)*
 Hialeah Hospital *(Ronald A. Fried)*
 Holland and Knight Committee for Effective Government *(Janet R. Studley)*
 Hospice Care, Inc.
 Indian River Citrus League *(John M. Himmelberg)*
 Jamaica, Government of
 Jamaica Nat'l Export Corp. *(David H. Baker)*
 Lighter Ass'n, Inc. *(David H. Baker)*
 Millers' Nat'l Federation
 Orlando, Florida, City of
 Pan American Satellite Corp. *(Janet R. Studley)*
 United Fresh Fruit and Vegetable Ass'n *(Dickson R. Loos)*
 Varig Brazilian Airlines
 Writing Instruments Manufacturers Ass'n *(David H. Baker)*

HOLLAND, Nancy R.
Exec. Director, American Council on Transplantation
700 North Fairfax St., Suite 505, Alexandria, VA 22314
Telephone: (703) 836-4301

HOLLAND, Robert A.
Director, Federal Affairs, SmithKline Beecham
1020 19th St., N.W., Suite 420, Washington, DC 20036
Telephone: (202) 452-8490
Registered as lobbyist at U.S. Congress.

HOLLAND, Dr. Robert C.
President, Committee for Economic Development
1700 K St., N.W., Suite 700, Washington, DC 20006
Telephone: (202) 296-5860
Background: Member, Federal Reserve Board, 1973-76.

HOLLAND, Robert J.
Dep Dir, Cong Relations, DEPARTMENT OF TREASURY - Thrift Supervision Office
1700 G St., N.W., Washington, DC 20552
Telephone: (202) 906-6804

HOLLANDER, Kenneth N.
V. President, Marketing, Ford Aerospace Corp.
1235 Jefferson Davis Hwy. Suite 1300, Arlington, VA 22202
Telephone: (703) 685-5500

HOLLANS, Irby N., Jr.
Exec. Director, Optical Laboratories Ass'n
Box 2000, Merrifield, VA 22116-2000
Telephone: (703) 849-8550

HOLLAR, Larry
Department Director, Issues, Bread for the World
802 Rhode Island Ave., N.E., Washington, DC 20018
Telephone: (202) 269-0200

HOLLESTELLE, Kay
Exec. Director, Children's Foundation
725 15th St., N.W., Washington, DC 20005
Telephone: (202) 347-3300

HOLLINGSWORTH, E. Boyd, Jr.
Dep Asst to Pres, Legis Affrs (Senate), EXECUTIVE OFFICE OF THE PRESIDENT - The White House
1600 Pennsylvania Ave., N.W. 107 East Wing, Washington, DC 20500
Telephone: (202) 456-7054

HOLLINGSWORTH, Joe G.
Spriggs & Hollingsworth
1350 Eye St., N.W. 9th Floor, Washington, DC 20005-3304
Telephone: (202) 898-5800
Clients:
 Armstrong World Industries, Inc.

HOLLINS, Cheryl J.
Exec. V. President, Car Audio Specialists Ass'n
2101 L St., N.W., Suite 800, Washington, DC 20037
Telephone: (202) 828-2270

HOLLIS, Nicholas E.
Exec. Director, Agri-Energy Roundtable
2550 M St., N.W., Suite 300, Washington, DC 20037
Telephone: (202) 887-0528
Background: Serves also as President and Chief Executive, The Agribusiness Council.

HOLLOWAY, Wendell M.
Corp. & Financial Legis. Mgr, Wash. Afrs, Ford Motor Co.
1350 Eye St., N.W. Suite 1000, Washington, DC 20005
Telephone: (202) 962-5400
Registered as lobbyist at U.S. Congress.

HOLMAN COMMUNICATIONS
1667 K St., N.W., Suite 390, Washington, DC 20006
Telephone: (202) 822-6804
Background: A communications consulting firm.
Members of firm representing listed organizations:
 Holman, Diana L., General Partner
Clients:
 Design Cuisine
 WETA *(Diana L. Holman)*
 Women's Sports Foundation *(Diana L. Holman)*

HOLMAN, Diana L.
General Partner, Holman Communications
1667 K St., N.W., Suite 390, Washington, DC 20006
Telephone: (202) 822-6804
Clients:
 WETA
 Women's Sports Foundation

HOLMAN, Francis W., Jr.
V. President and Secretary, Manufacturers' Alliance for Productivity and Innovation (MAPI)
1200 18th St., N.W. Suite 400, Washington, DC 20036
Telephone: (202) 331-8430

HOLMES, Constance D.
Senior V. President, Policy Analysis, Nat'l Coal Ass'n
1130 17th St., N.W., Washington, DC 20036
Telephone: (202) 463-2654

HOLMES, Diane S.
Director, Special Programs, American Nuclear Energy Council
410 First St., S.E. Third Floor, Washington, DC 20003
Telephone: (202) 484-2670
Registered as lobbyist at U.S. Congress.

HOLMES, Kim R.
Dir., Foreign Policy & Defense Studies, Heritage Foundation
214 Massachusetts Ave., N.E., Washington, DC 20002
Telephone: (202) 546-4400

HOLMES, Lee B.
Exec. V. President, Corporate Relations, Federal Home Loan Mortgage Corp.
1759 Business Center Drive, Reston, VA 22090
Telephone: (703) 789-4700

HOLMES, Lynn R.
Director, Legislative Affairs, BellSouth Corp.
1133 21st St., N.W., Suite 900, Washington, DC 20036
Telephone: (202) 463-4100

HOLMES, Moses D., Jr.
Legislative Specialist, Nat'l Education Ass'n of the U.S.
1201 16th St., N.W., Washington, DC 20036
Telephone: (202) 822-7300
Registered as lobbyist at U.S. Congress.

HOLMES, Peter E.
Legislative Affairs Consultant, Groom and Nordberg
1701 Pennsylvania Ave., N.W., Suite 1200, Washington, DC 20006
Telephone: (202) 857-0620
Registered as lobbyist at U.S. Congress.
Clients:
Puerto Rico, U.S.A. Foundation

HOLMGRAIN, Floyd H., Jr., Ed.D.
Exec. Director, Nat'l Academy of Opticianry
10111 Martin Luther King, Jr. Hwy., Suite 112, Bowie, MD 20720
Telephone: (301) 577-4828

HOLMSTROM, Engin
Internat'l Advisers, Inc.
2300 M St., N.W., Suite 600, Washington, DC 20037
Telephone: (202) 293-1575
Registered as lobbyist at U.S. Congress.
Registered as Foreign Agent: (#4203).
Clients:
Turkey, Embassy of

HOLSEY, Rosita Stevens
National Office Director, Nat'l Dental Ass'n
5506 Connecticut Ave., N.W. Suite 25, Washington, DC 20015
Telephone: (202) 244-7555

HOLSTEIN, Elgie
Director, Bankcard Holders of America
560 Herndon Parkway Suite 120, Herndon, VA 22070
Telephone: (703) 481-1110

HOLT, E. Y., Jr.
V. President, Finance and Administration, Nat'l Ass'n of Federal Credit Unions
3138 N. 10th St., Arlington, VA 22201
Telephone: (703) 522-4770
Registered as lobbyist at U.S. Congress.

HOLT, Fred H.
President, Animal Health Institute
119 Oronoco St., Box 1417-D50, Alexandria, VA 22313-1480
Telephone: (703) 684-0011
Registered as lobbyist at U.S. Congress.

HOLT, James
Potomac Partners
1250 24th St., N.W. Suite 875, Washington, DC 20037
Telephone: (202) 466-0560

HOLT, John W.
Senior Counsel, American Council of Life Insurance
1001 Pennsylvania Ave., N.W., Washington, DC 20004-2599
Telephone: (202) 624-2108
Registered as lobbyist at U.S. Congress.

HOLT, MILLER & ASSOCIATES
2111 Wilson Blvd., Suite 531, Arlington, VA 22201-3008
Telephone: (703) 276-8009
Members of firm representing listed organizations:
Kirby, Michael G.
Miller, Harris N., Managing Partner

Background: Formerly served on the staff of the House Judiciary Committee and as Legislative Director to Senator John Durkin (D-NH). Former Director, Congressional Affairs, Office of Personnel Management.
Sullivan, Ann M., V. President
Background: Former aide to Senators George Mitchell (D-ME) and Carl Levin (D-MI) and to Rep. Philip Sharp (D-IN).
Clients:
Ada Software Alliance (ASA) *(Harris N. Miller)*
Agricultural Producers, Inc. *(Harris N. Miller)*
AmBase Corp. *(Harris N. Miller)*
American Council on Internat'l Personnel *(Harris N. Miller)*
Interstate Natural Gas Ass'n of America *(Ann M. Sullivan)*
Irish Immigration Reform Movement *(Michael G. Kirby, Harris N. Miller)*
McDonald's Corp. *(Harris N. Miller)*
Mountain Plains Agricultural Service *(Michael G. Kirby, Harris N. Miller)*
Nat'l Agricultural Coalition *(Harris N. Miller)*
Natural Gas Vehicle Coalition *(Ann M. Sullivan)*
Snake River Farmers Ass'n *(Harris N. Miller)*
Texas Ranchers Labor Ass'n *(Harris N. Miller)*
U.S. English *(Harris N. Miller)*
Western Range Ass'n *(Harris N. Miller)*

HOLT, Robert
V. President, CRSS Constructors, Inc.
1201 New York Ave., N.W., Suite 1250, Washington, DC 20005
Telephone: (202) 898-1110

HOLT, Timothy
Exec. V. President, Nat'l School Supply and Equipment Ass'n
2020 North 14th St., Arlington, VA 22201
Telephone: (703) 524-8819

HOLTHUS, C. G.
President, American Bankers Ass'n
1120 Connecticut Ave., N.W., Washington, DC 20036
Telephone: (202) 663-5000

HOLTON, Robert J.
General President, Operative Plasterers' and Cement Masons' Internat'l Ass'n of the U.S. and Canada
1125 17th St., N.W. 6th Floor, Washington, DC 20036
Telephone: (202) 393-6569
Background: Serves also as Chairman, Plasterers' and Cement Masons' Action Committee.

HOLTZINGER, John E.
Newman & Holtzinger, P.C.
1615 L St., N.W., 10th Floor, Washington, DC 20005
Telephone: (202) 955-6600

HOLTZMAN, Jon C.
Vice President, Communications, Chemical Manufacturers Ass'n
2501 M St., N.W., Washington, DC 20037
Telephone: (202) 887-1100

HOLUM, John D.
O'Melveny and Myers
555 13th St., N.W., Suite 500 West, Washington, DC 20004
Telephone: (202) 383-5300
Registered as lobbyist at U.S. Congress.

HOLWERDA-HOYT, Lois
Assistant Director, American Academy of Family Physicians
600 Maryland Ave., S.W., Suite 770, Washington, DC 20024
Telephone: (202) 488-7448
Registered as lobbyist at U.S. Congress.

HOLZWORTH, David A.
Lepon, McCarthy, Jutkowitz & Holzworth
1146 19th St., N.W. Third Fl., Washington, DC 20036
Telephone: (202) 857-0242
Registered as lobbyist at U.S. Congress.
Registered as Foreign Agent: (#4302).
Clients:
Chilean Exporters Ass'n

HOMBS, Mary Ellen
Director, Nat'l Coalition for the Homeless
1621 Connecticut Ave., N.W. 4th Fl., Washington, DC 20007
Telephone: (202) 265-2371

HONBERG, Ron
Legislative Associate, Nat'l Alliance for the Mentally Ill
2101 Wilson Blvd., Suite 302, Arlington, VA 22201
Telephone: (703) 524-7600

HONBERGER, Roger F.
Washington Representative, San Diego, California, County of
440 First St., N.W. Suite 501, Washington, DC 20001
Telephone: (202) 737-7523
Background: Also represents the counties of Riverside and Ventura, California, as well as the San Diego and North San Diego Metropolitan Transit Development Board.

HONEY, Edgar Thomas
Barnes, Richardson and Colburn
1819 H St., N.W., Washington, DC 20006
Telephone: (202) 457-0300
Clients:
Mercedes-Benz of North America, Inc.
Mitsubishi Corp.

HONOR, Lt. Gen. Edward, USA (Ret)
President, Nat'l Defense Transportation Ass'n
50 S. Pickett St., Suite 220, Alexandria, VA 22304
Telephone: (703) 751-5011

HOOD, Elouise
Cong Correspondence, AGENCY FOR INTERNAT'L DEVELOPMENT
320 21st St., N.W., Washington, DC 20523
Telephone: (202) 647-8440

HOOG, Tom
Sr. V.P. & Pract. Dir, St. & Local Govt, Hill and Knowlton Public Affairs Worldwide
Washington Harbour, 901 31st St., N.W., Washington, DC 20007
Telephone: (202) 333-7400
Background: Former Chief of Staff to Senator Gary Hart (D-CO).
Clients:
ASARCO Incorporated
Chemical Waste Management, Inc.
Colorado State University
MacAndrews & Forbes Holdings, Inc.
Prudential-Bache Securities, Inc.

HOOLEY, James L.
Senior V. President for Marketing, Reese Communications Companies
2111 Wilson Ave., Suite 900, Arlington, VA 22201
Telephone: (703) 528-4400
Background: Assistant to the President, The White House, 1981-89.

HOOPER, Dr. Billy E.
Exec. Director, Ass'n of American Veterinary Medical Colleges
1023 15th St., N.W., 3rd Floor, Washington, DC 20005
Telephone: (202) 371-9195
Registered as lobbyist at U.S. Congress.

HOOPER, Helen D.
Congressional Liaison, Nat'l Trust for Historic Preservation
1785 Massachusetts Ave., N.W., Washington, DC 20036
Telephone: (202) 673-4000
Registered as lobbyist at U.S. Congress.

HOOPER, Joyce
Legislative Assistant, American Academy of Orthopaedic Surgeons
317 Massachusetts Ave., N.E., Suite 100, Washington, DC 20002
Telephone: (202) 546-4430

HOOPER, Katherine
Exec. Director, Committee for Dulles
P.O. Box 17053-Washington/ Dulles Airport, Washington, DC 20041
Telephone: (703) 481-4278
Background: Also serves as Exec. Director, Dulles Area Transportation Ass'n.

HOOPER, Linsay D.
Winburn, VanScoyoc, and Hooper
453 New Jersey Ave., S.E., Washington, DC 20003
Telephone: (202) 488-3581
Registered as lobbyist at U.S. Congress.
Clients:
Hallmark Cards, Inc.
Jackson Nat'l Life Insurance Co.
Kansas City Southern Industries

HOOVER, Karen A.
Asst. Legislative Director, American Maritime Officers Service
490 L'Enfant Plaza East, S.W., Suite 490, Washington, DC 20024
Telephone: (202) 479-1133
Registered as lobbyist at U.S. Congress.

HOOVER, Stephanie
Associate Exec. Director, American Occupational Therapy Ass'n
1383 Piccard Drive, Suite 300 P.O. Box 1725, Rockville, MD 20850
Telephone: (301) 948-9626

HOOVER, William W.
Exec. V. Pres., Operations and Safety, Air Transport Ass'n of America
1709 New York Ave., N.W., Washington, DC 20006-5206
Telephone: (202) 626-4000

HOPE, Judith Richards
Paul, Hastings, Janofsky and Walker
1050 Connecticut Ave., N.W. Suite 1200, Washington, DC 20036-5331
Telephone: (202) 223-9000
Registered as lobbyist at U.S. Congress.
Background: Associate Director, The Domestic Council, The White House, 1975-77. Member, Nat'l Highway Traffic Safety Commission, 1977-78. Member, President's Commission on Organized Crime, 1985-86.
Clients:
CalMat Co.
Government Affairs Policy Council of the Regional Bell Operating Companies
Security Life Insurance Co. of Denver

HOPE, Samuel
Exec. Director, Nat'l Ass'n of Schools of Music
11250 Roger Bacon Drive, #21, Reston, VA 22090
Telephone: (703) 437-0700
Background: Also serves as Exec. Director of the Nat'l Ass'n of Schools of Art and Design, Exec. Director of the Nat'l Ass'n of Schools of Dance and Exec. Director of the Nat'l Ass'n of Schools of Theatre.

HOPKINS, Bruce R.
Steptoe and Johnson
1330 Connecticut Ave., N.W., Washington, DC 20036
Telephone: (202) 429-3000
Clients:
American Ass'n of Colleges for Teacher Education

HOPKINS, Charles I., Jr.
Chairman, Nat'l Railway Labor Conference
1901 L St., N.W. Suite 500, Washington, DC 20036
Telephone: (202) 862-7200

HOPKINS, Deborah M.
Manager, Consumer Affairs, Automotive Consumer Action Program
8400 Westpark Drive, McLean, VA 22102
Telephone: (202) 821-7144

HOPKINS, Frank Snowden
V. President, World Future Soc.
4916 St. Elmo Ave., Bethesda, MD 20814
Telephone: (301) 656-8274

HOPKINS, Grover Prevatte
Secretary General, Inter-American Bar Ass'n
1889 F St., N.W. Suite LL2, Washington, DC 20006
Telephone: (202) 789-2747

HOPKINS, Marian E.
Director of Senate Liaison, Chamber of Commerce of the U.S.A.
1615 H St., N.W., Washington, DC 20062

Telephone: (202) 463-5600
Registered as lobbyist at U.S. Congress.
Background: Former Legislative Assistant to Sen. S. I. Hayakawa (R-CA).

HOPKINS, Mark
Director of Corporate Relations, Alliance to Save Energy
1725 K St., N.W., Suite 914, Washington, DC 20006
Telephone: (202) 857-0666
Registered as lobbyist at U.S. Congress.

HOPKINS, Stephen A.
V. President, Domestic Government Rltns., Citicorp
1275 Pennsyylvania Ave., N.W. Suite 503, Washington, DC 20004
Telephone: (202) 879-6837
Registered as lobbyist at U.S. Congress.

HOPKINS AND SUTTER
888 16th St., N.W., Suite 700, Washington, DC 20006
Telephone: (202) 835-8000
Members of firm representing listed organizations:
Bankson, John P. (Jr.)
Bradford, William H. (Jr.)
Brotzman, Donald G.
Cole, Basil, Of Counsel
Dubin, Lawrence M.
Goldberg, Neal M.
Hoffman, Adonis E.
Background: Legislative Assistant to Rep. Mervyn M. Dymally (D-CA), 1981-84.
Hou, William
Lambert, Steven C.
Marquez, Joaquin A.
Background: Former Director, Puerto Rico Federal Affairs Administration in Washington.
McDermott, Francis O.
McPhee, Henry Roemer
Background: Special Assistant, The White House, 1954-57. Assistant Special Counsel to the President of the United States, 1957-1961.
Oyler, Gregory K.
Background: Law Clerk, U.S. Tax Court, 1978-80.
Pettit, John W.
Background: General Counsel, Federal Communications Commission, 1972-74.
Petty, Charles W. (Jr.)
Pfunder, Malcolm R.
Background: Associate Director, 1977-78, and Assistant Director, 1978-81, Bureau of Competition, Federal Trade Commission.
Phillips, William D.
Background: Chief of Staff to Senator Ted Stevens (R-AK), 1983-86; Legislative Director and Legislative Assistant, 1981-83.
vom Eigen, Robert P.
Worthy, K. Martin
Background: Chief Counsel, Internal Revenue Service, 1969-72. Member, Board of Directors, Beneficial Corp.
Clients:
Alaska Joint Venture Seafoods, Inc. *(William D. Phillips)*
Allstate Insurance Co. *(Francis O. McDermott)*
Amoco Corp. *(William H. Bradford, Jr.)*
Ass'n Management Corp. *(Francis O. McDermott)*
Chicago Mercantile Exchange *(Francis O. McDermott)*
COMDISCO, Inc. *(Donald G. Brotzman)*
First Chicago Corp. *(Francis O. McDermott)*
First Federal Savings Bank *(Joaquin A. Marquez)*
Grand Trunk Corp. *(Robert P. vom Eigen)*
Greenwich Capital Markets, Inc. *(William H. Bradford, Jr.)*
Infinite Research, Inc. *(William D. Phillips)*
Inland Steel Co. *(Francis O. McDermott)*
Korean Air Lines *(William D. Phillips)*
KPVI *(John P. Bankson, Jr.)*
KTTY *(John P. Bankson, Jr.)*
Louisiana Pacific Corp. *(Steven C. Lambert)*
Martel Laboratory Services, Inc. *(William D. Phillips)*
Organization of Chinese Americans *(William Hou)*
Peoples Energy Corp. *(Lawrence M. Dubin)*
Puerto Rico Manufacturers Ass'n *(Joaquin A. Marquez)*
Rubber Manufacturers Ass'n *(John W. Pettit)*
Tandy Corp. *(John W. Pettit, Malcolm R. Pfunder)*
United Video Inc. *(William D. Phillips)*
WPXT *(John P. Bankson, Jr.)*

WTKR-TV *(Neal M. Goldberg)*

HOPKINS, Virginia E.
Taft, Stettinius and Hollister
1620 Eye St., N.W., Suite 800, Washington, DC 20006
Telephone: (202) 785-1620
Registered as lobbyist at U.S. Congress.
Clients:
Great American Broadcasting Co.
Kings Entertainment Co.
Telephone and Data Systems, Inc.
Wald Manufacturing Co.

HOPPEL, MAYER AND COLEMAN
1000 Connecticut Ave., N.W. Suite 410, Washington, DC 20036
Telephone: (202) 296-5460
Registered as Foreign Agent: (#3470)
Members of firm representing listed organizations:
Coleman, Paul D.
Mayer, Neal M.
Clients:
Brazil, Secretariat of Waterborne Transportation (STA) *(Neal M. Mayer)*
Companhia de Navagacao Maritima NETUMAR *(Neal M. Mayer)*
Companhia de Navegacao Lloyd Brasileiro *(Neal M. Mayer)*
Crown Central Petroleum Corp. *(Paul D. Coleman)*
Japan Tobacco, Inc. *(Neal M. Mayer)*
P & O (TFL) Ltd./Trans Freight Lines *(Neal M. Mayer)*
Showa Line, Ltd. *(Neal M. Mayer)*
Tropical Shipping and Construction Co. *(Paul D. Coleman, Neal M. Mayer)*

HOPWOOD, Frank
Dir., Federal Regulatory Relations, Pacific Telesis Group-Washington
1275 Pennsylvania Ave., N.W. Suite 400, Washington, DC 20004
Telephone: (202) 383-6400

HORAN, Deborah L.
Director, Congressional Relations, Close Up Foundation
1235 Jefferson Davis Hwy., Arlington, VA 22202
Telephone: (703) 892-5400

HORANBERG, Richard C.
Dir, Legis Affrs, OVERSEAS PRIVATE INVESTMENT CORP.
1615 M St., N.W., Washington, DC 20527
Telephone: (202) 457-7072

HORDES, Jess N.
Director, Washington Office, Anti-Defamation League of B'nai B'rith
1100 Connecticut Ave., N.W., Washington, DC 20036
Telephone: (202) 452-8320

HOREN, Dr. Ian R.
Exec. Director, Orthotic and Prosthetic Nat'l Office
717 Pendleton St., Alexandria, VA 22314
Telephone: (703) 836-7114
Background: Also serves as Treasurer, American Orthotic and Prosthetic Ass'n Political Action Committee.

HORIO, Darnell K.
Legislative Assistant, GPU Service Corp.
600 Maryland Ave., S.W., Suite 520, Washington, DC 20024
Telephone: (202) 554-7616
Registered as lobbyist at U.S. Congress.

HORLICK, Gary N.
O'Melveny and Myers
555 13th St., N.W., Suite 500 West, Washington, DC 20004
Telephone: (202) 383-5300
Registered as Foreign Agent: (#3346).
Clients:
Emergency Committee for American Trade
Ford Motor Co.

HORN, Bernard P.
Director, State Legislation, Handgun Control, Inc.
1225 Eye St., N.W., Suite 1100, Washington, DC 20005
Telephone: (202) 898-0792
Registered as lobbyist at U.S. Congress.

HORN, Robert J.
Asst. V. Pres. and Mgr., Federal Affairs, Detroit Edison Co.
1990 M St., N.W., Suite 480, Washington, DC 20036
Telephone: (202) 466-5495
Registered as lobbyist at U.S. Congress.

HORN, William P.
Birch, Horton, Bittner and Cherot
1155 Connecticut Ave., N.W., Suite 1200, Washington, DC 20036
Telephone: (202) 659-5800
Registered as lobbyist at U.S. Congress.
Clients:
Wildlife Legislative Fund of America
Yukon Pacific Inc.

HORNADAY, Richard M., CAE
Exec. V. President, Door and Hardware Institute
7711 Old Springhouse Road, McLean, VA 22102-3474
Telephone: (703) 556-3990
Background: Responsibilities include Door and Hardware Institute Political Action Committee.

HORNE, Michael S.
Covington and Burling
1201 Pennsylvania Ave., N.W., Box 7566, Washington, DC 20044
Telephone: (202) 662-6000

HORNER, Patricia I.
Smith, Bucklin and Associates
1101 Connecticut Ave., N.W., Suite 700, Washington, DC 20036
Telephone: (202) 857-1100
Background: Serves as Exec. Director of Alliance for Engineering in Medicine and Biology, Rehabilitation Engineering Society of North America, Society of Non-Invasive Vascular Technology and Ass'n for the Advancement of Rehabilitative Technology.
Clients:
RESNA
Soc. of Vascular Technology

HORNING, Mark F.
Steptoe and Johnson
1330 Connecticut Ave., N.W., Washington, DC 20036
Telephone: (202) 429-3000
Clients:
Independent Insurance Agents of America

HOROWITT, Sanford
Political Consultant, Nat'l Coalition to Ban Handguns Political Action Committee
100 Maryland Ave., N.E., Washington, DC 20002
Telephone: (202) 544-7213

HOROWITZ, Rachelle
Political Director, American Federation of Teachers
555 New Jersey Ave., N.W., Washington, DC 20001
Telephone: (202) 879-4436
Background: Contact for the Ass'n Political Action Committee.

HORSKY, Charles A.
Counsel, Covington and Burling
1201 Pennsylvania Ave., N.W., Box 7566, Washington, DC 20044
Telephone: (202) 662-6000
Registered as lobbyist at U.S. Congress.
Background: Solicitor General's Office, 1935-37, Adviser to the President for National Capital Affairs, 1962-67. Director, Attorney General's Committee on Bankruptcy, 1935-40. Office of Chief Counsel for War Crimes, 1945-47; assistant prosecutor at Nuremberg, 1948.

HORST, R. Kyle
Director, Refugee Affairs, Armenian Assembly of America
122 C St., N.W., Suite 350, Washington, DC 20001
Telephone: (202) 393-3434
Registered as lobbyist at U.S. Congress.

HORST, Toni A.
Market Research Assistant, Foley & Co.
206 G St. N.E. Suite 201, Washington, DC 20002
Telephone: (202) 543-8601
Registered as lobbyist at U.S. Congress.

HORSTMAN, Douglass C.
Gov't Affairs Counsel and PAC Manager, Maytag Corp.
McLean Office Square 1319 Vincent Place, McLean, VA 22101
Telephone: (703) 790-1611
Registered as lobbyist at U.S. Congress.
Background: Serves as contact for Maytag Corp. Good Government Committee

HORTUM, Leslie Wheeler
V. President, Communications, American Trucking Ass'ns
2200 Mill Road, Alexandria, VA 22314
Telephone: (703) 838-1866

HORTY, John F.
President, Nat'l Council of Community Hospitals
1700 K St., N.W. Suite 906, Washington, DC 20006
Telephone: (202) 728-0830
Registered as lobbyist at U.S. Congress.

HORVATH, Jan
Policy Associate, State Medicaid Directors Ass'n
810 First St., N.E., Suite 500, Washington, DC 20002
Telephone: (202) 682-0100

HORVATH, R. Skip
V. Pres., Rate and Policy Analysis, Interstate Natural Gas Ass'n of America
555 13th St., N.W. Suite 300 West, Washington, DC 20004
Telephone: (202) 626-3200

HORWITZ, Jamie
Assistant Director, Public Relations, American Federation of Teachers
555 New Jersey Ave., N.W., Washington, DC 20001
Telephone: (202) 879-4400

HORWITZ, Joshua M.
Legal Director, Educational Fund to End Handgun Violence
100 Maryland Ave., N.E., Washington, DC 20002
Telephone: (202) 544-7227

HOSENBALL, S. Neil
Davis, Graham and Stubbs
1200 19th St., N.W., Suite 500, Washington, DC 20036
Telephone: (202) 822-8660
Background: Assistant General Counsel for Procurement, 1965-67, Deputy General Counsel, 1967-75 and General Counsel, 1975-85, National Aeronautics and Space Administration.

HOSKING, James H.
Strother and Hosking Associates
6301 Stevenson Ave., Suite 1, Alexandria, VA 22304
Telephone: (703) 823-1732
Registered as lobbyist at U.S. Congress.

HOSPODOR, Sarah
Dir, Energy, Envir. & Dvmn't, Gov't Rtns, Nat'l Ass'n of REALTORS
777 14th St., N.W., Washington, DC 20005
Telephone: (202) 383-1000
Registered as lobbyist at U.S. Congress.

HOSTETLER, James S.
Kirkland and Ellis
655 15th St., N.W. Suite 1200, Washington, DC 20005
Telephone: (202) 879-5000
Background: Former Legislative Counsel to Department of Health, Education and Welfare; Special Assistant to the Administrator, Economic Development Administration, U.S. Department of Commerce.
Clients:
American Ass'n for Laboratory Accreditation

HOTES, William J.
President, Telocator
2000 M St., N.W., Suite 230, Washington, DC 20036
Telephone: (202) 467-4770

HOTING, Hilarie
V. President, Health Care, Hill and Knowlton Public Affairs Worldwide
Washington Harbour, 901 31st St., N.W., Washington, DC 20007
Telephone: (202) 333-7400

HOTVEDT, Richard C.
Morgan, Lewis and Bockius
1800 M St., N.W., Washington, DC 20036
Telephone: (202) 467-7000

HOU, William
Hopkins and Sutter
888 16th St., N.W., Suite 700, Washington, DC 20006
Telephone: (202) 835-8000
Clients:
Organization of Chinese Americans

HOUDESHELDT, Bruce
Assoc. Dir., Gov't. Affrs., Suburban Maryland Building Industry Ass'n
Executive Terrace 1400 Mercantile Lane, Landover, MD 20785
Telephone: (301) 925-9490
Registered as lobbyist at U.S. Congress.

HOULIHAN, David P.
Mudge Rose Guthrie Alexander and Ferdon
2121 K St., N.W., Suite 700, Washington, DC 20037
Telephone: (202) 429-9355
Registered as lobbyist at U.S. Congress.
Registered as Foreign Agent: (#3200).
Clients:
C.V.G. Siderurgica del Orinoco Ca. (SIDOR)
Camara de la Industria Curtidora Argentina
Dalmine Siderica
Flachglas A.G.
Futaba Corp.
Japan Lumber Importers Ass'n
Propulsora Siderurgica S.A.I.C.
Sovcomflot
TENAX Corp.
Toshiba Corp.

HOUSE, Thomas B., CAE
President Emeritus, American Frozen Food Institute
1764 Old Meadow Lane Suite 350, McLean, VA 22102
Telephone: (703) 821-0770
Background: Director General, Internat'l Frozen Food Ass'n.

HOUSE, William Mike
Shaw, Pittman, Potts and Trowbridge
2300 N St., N.W., Washington, DC 20037
Telephone: (202) 663-8000
Registered as lobbyist at U.S. Congress.
Registered as Foreign Agent: (#2580).
Background: Former Administrative Assistant to Senator Howell Heflin (D-AL).
Clients:
ADDSCO Industries
Alabama Power Co.
American Coke and Coal Chemicals Institute
American Hellenic Institute
American Savings and Loan of Florida
Auburn University
Drummond Co., Inc.
Energy Efficient Insulation Manufacturers
Florida Citrus Mutual
Georgia Power Co.
INCO U.S.
Intergraph Corp.
Michelin Tire Co.
Munitions Carrier Conference
Nat'l Industries, Inc.
Rust Engineering
South Central Bell
Southern Company Services, Inc.
Vulcan Materials Co.
Walter Corp., Jim

HOUSEMAN, Alan W.
Director, Center for Law and Social Policy
1616 P St., N.W., Suite 350, Washington, DC 20036
Telephone: (202) 328-5140

HOUSER, Kathy G.
Manager, KPMG Peat Marwick
2001 M St., N.W., Washington, DC 20036
Telephone: (202) 467-3846

HOUSTON ASSOCIATES, INC.
1901 North Moore St., Arlington, VA 22209
Telephone: (703) 525-2514

Members of firm representing listed organizations:
Houston, James J., President
Background: Exec. V. President, Industrial Heating
Equipment Ass'n.
Clients:
Industrial Heating Equipment Ass'n *(James J. Houston)*
Industrial Heating Equipment Ass'n Political Action Committee *(James J. Houston)*

HOUSTON, Betsy
Exec. V. President, Siegel, Houston and Associates
1707 L St., N.W., Suite 333, Washington, DC 20036
Telephone: (202) 296-2606
Clients:
Federation of Materials Societies
Nat'l Ass'n of Career Development Consultants

HOUSTON, James J.
President, Houston Associates, Inc.
1901 North Moore St., Arlington, VA 22209
Telephone: (703) 525-2514
Background: Exec. V. President, Industrial Heating Equipment Ass'n.
Clients:
Industrial Heating Equipment Ass'n
Industrial Heating Equipment Ass'n Political Action Committee

HOVERMALE, David
Dir, Legis Affrs, DEPARTMENT OF AGRICULTURE - Foreign Agricultural Service
14th and Independence Ave. S.W., Washington, DC 20250
Telephone: (202) 447-6829

HOVEY, Denise S.
Managing Editor, State Policy Research, Inc.
7706 Lookout Court, Alexandria, VA 22306
Telephone: (703) 765-8389

HOVEY, Harold A.
President, State Policy Research, Inc.
7706 Lookout Court, Alexandria, VA 22306
Telephone: (703) 765-8389

HOVING GROUP, The
910 17th St., N.W. Suite 318, Washington, DC 20006
Telephone: (202) 429-0120
Members of firm representing listed organizations:
Hoving, John H. F., President
Sherman, Norman, V. President
Organizations represented:
American Film Marketing Ass'n *(John H. F. Hoving)*
Barnes and Tucker Co.
Coalition for Equitable Compensation
Eagle-Picher Industries *(John H. F. Hoving)*
Western Southern *(John H. F. Hoving)*

HOVING, John H. F.
President, Hoving Group, The
910 17th St., N.W. Suite 318, Washington, DC 20006
Telephone: (202) 429-0120
Registered as lobbyist at U.S. Congress.
Registered as Foreign Agent: (#3720).
Organizations represented:
American Film Marketing Ass'n
Eagle-Picher Industries
Western Southern

HOWARD, Ann B.
Exec. Director, American Federation of Home Health Agencies
1320 Fenwick Lane, Suite 100, Silver Spring, MD 20910
Telephone: (301) 588-1454

HOWARD, Gerald Michael
Tax Counsel, Nat'l Ass'n of Home Builders of the U.S.
15th and M Streets, N.W., Washington, DC 20005
Telephone: (202) 822-0470
Registered as lobbyist at U.S. Congress.

HOWARD, Glen S.
Sutherland, Asbill and Brennan
1275 Pennsylvania, N.W., Washington, DC 20004-2404
Telephone: (202) 383-0100
Clients:
Process Gas Consumers Group

HOWARD, Jack
Spec Asst to Pres, Legis Affrs (House), EXECUTIVE OFFICE OF THE PRESIDENT - The White House
1600 Pennsylvania Ave., N.W. 112 East Wing, Washington, DC 20500
Telephone: (202) 456-7766

HOWARD, Janet A.
Director, Democrats for the 90s
Box 3797 3038 N St., N.W., Washington, DC 20007
Telephone: (202) 338-9092

HOWARD, John
Director, Internat'l Finance, Chamber of Commerce of the U.S.A.
1615 H St., N.W., Washington, DC 20062
Telephone: (202) 463-5464
Registered as lobbyist at U.S. Congress.

HOWARD, Karen E.
Assistant Director, Government Relations, American Psychiatric Ass'n
1400 K St., N.W., Washington, DC 20005
Telephone: (202) 682-6000
Registered as lobbyist at U.S. Congress.
Background: Former Staff Assistant, House of Representatives Post Office and Civil Service Committee.

HOWARD, Lauren R.
Collier, Shannon & Scott
1055 Thomas Jefferson St., N.W., Suite 300, Washington, DC 20007
Telephone: (202) 342-8400
Registered as lobbyist at U.S. Congress.
Clients:
Bicycle Manufacturers Ass'n of America
Committee of American Ammunition Manufacturers
Footwear Industries of America
Footwear Industry Political Action Committee

HOWARD, Patricia
Cong and Public Affairs Director, DEPARTMENT OF JUSTICE - Office of Justice Programs
633 Indiana Ave., N.W., Washington, DC 20531
Telephone: (202) 724-7694

HOWARD, Patricia Digh
Manager, International Relations, Soc. for Human Resources Management
606 N. Washington St., Alexandria, VA 22314
Telephone: (703) 548-3440

HOWARD, Rachel
Exec. Director, American Design Drafting Ass'n
5522 Noreck Road, Suite 391, Rockville, MD 20853
Telephone: (301) 460-6875

HOWARD, Robert M.
Legs. Mgr., Washington Afrs (Automotive), Ford Motor Co.
1350 Eye St., N.W. Suite 1000, Washington, DC 20005
Telephone: (202) 962-5400
Registered as lobbyist at U.S. Congress.

HOWARD, William W., Jr.
Exec. V. President, Nat'l Wildlife Federation
1400 16th St., N.W., Washington, DC 20036-2266
Telephone: (202) 797-6800

HOWARTH, Thomas J.
Peyser Associates, Inc.
1000 Vermont Ave., N.W. Suite 400, Washington, DC 20005
Telephone: (202) 842-4545
Registered as lobbyist at U.S. Congress.
Background: Former Legis. Ass't to Senator Frank Lautenberg (D-NJ); Former Washington Representative, City of New York.
Clients:
Mothers Against Drunk Driving (MADD)

HOWE, Allynn
Legislative Representative, United Brotherhood of Carpenters and Joiners of America
101 Constitution Ave., N.W., Washington, DC 20001
Telephone: (202) 546-6206
Registered as lobbyist at U.S. Congress.

HOWE, Chris W.
Washington Representative, Chevron, U.S.A.
1700 K St., N.W., Suite 1200, Washington, DC 20006
Telephone: (202) 457-5800
Registered as lobbyist at U.S. Congress.

HOWE, Jonathan
President, Nat'l Business Aircraft Ass'n
1200 18th St., N.W. Suite 200, Washington, DC 20036
Telephone: (202) 783-9000
Registered as lobbyist at U.S. Congress.

HOWE, Patty
Dep Asst Secy, House Affrs, Legis Affrs, DEPARTMENT OF DEFENSE
The Pentagon, Washington, DC 20301
Telephone: (202) 697-6210

HOWE, Susan E.
Asst. to the Dir., Federal Legislation, Associated Builders and Contractors
729 15th St., N.W., Washington, DC 20005
Telephone: (202) 637-8800
Registered as lobbyist at U.S. Congress.

HOWE, William H.
Loomis, Owen, Fellman and Howe
2020 K St., N.W. Suite 800, Washington, DC 20006
Telephone: (202) 296-5680
Registered as lobbyist at U.S. Congress.
Background: Secretary and General Counsel, Association of Bituminous Contractors.
Clients:
Ass'n of Bituminous Contractors

HOWELL, Elizabeth C.
Legislative Affairs Consultant, Groom and Nordberg
1701 Pennsylvania Ave., N.W., Suite 1200, Washington, DC 20006
Telephone: (202) 857-0620
Registered as lobbyist at U.S. Congress.

HOWELL, Gary
V.P., Cong. Liais. (Def. Sys. & Elect.), Texas Instruments
1745 Jefferson Davis Hwy. Suite 605, Arlington, VA 22202
Telephone: (703) 892-9333
Registered as lobbyist at U.S. Congress.

HOWELL, J. William
IBM Director, Government Relations, Internat'l Business Machines Corp.
1801 K St., N.W., Suite 1200, Washington, DC 20006
Telephone: (202) 778-5000
Registered as lobbyist at U.S. Congress.

HOWELL, James P.
Director, Legislative Affairs, Nat'l Council of Farmer Cooperatives
50 F St., N.W., Suite 900, Washington, DC 20001
Telephone: (202) 626-8700
Registered as lobbyist at U.S. Congress.

HOWELL, John C.
Ross and Hardies
888 16th St., N.W., Washington, DC 20006
Telephone: (202) 296-8600

HOWELL, Marcela
PAC Chair, Nat'l Abortion Rights Action League Political Action Committee
1101 14th St., N.W., Suite 500, Washington, DC 20005
Telephone: (202) 371-0779

HOWELL, Mary L.
V. President, Government Affairs, Textron Inc.
1090 Vermont Ave., N.W., Suite 1100, Washington, DC 20005
Telephone: (202) 289-5800
Registered as lobbyist at U.S. Congress.

HOWELL, Thomas R.
Dewey, Ballantine, Bushby, Palmer and Wood
1775 Pennsylvania Ave., N.W. Suite 200, Washington, DC 20006
Telephone: (202) 862-1000
Clients:
Semiconductor Industry Ass'n

HOWES, Dwight A.
Legislative Counsel, Consolidated Natural Gas Co.
1819 L St., N.W. Suite 900, Washington, DC 20036
Telephone: (202) 833-3900
Registered as lobbyist at U.S. Congress.
Background: Former Legislative Assistant to Senator John Heinz (R-PA) and former Associate Counsel, Senate Select Committee on Intelligence.

HOWES, Hal W.
V. President, Washington Operations, Aerojet
1025 Connecticut Ave., N.W. Suite 1107, Washington, DC 20036
Telephone: (202) 828-6826

HOWES, Joanne
Bass & Howes
1601 Connecticut Ave., N.W. Suite 801, Washington, DC 20009
Telephone: (202) 328-2200
Clients:
Women's Legal Defense Fund

HOWES, John A.
Director of Federal Governmental Affairs, Consumers Power Co.
1016 16th St., N.W. 5th Floor, Washington, DC 20036
Telephone: (202) 293-5794
Registered as lobbyist at U.S. Congress.

HOWLETT, C. T. "Kip", Jr.
V. President, Government Affairs, Georgia-Pacific Corp.
1875 Eye St., N.W. Suite 775, Washington, DC 20006
Telephone: (202) 659-3600
Registered as lobbyist at U.S. Congress.

HOWREY AND SIMON
1730 Pennsylvania Ave., N.W., Washington, DC 20006-4793
Telephone: (202) 783-0800
Background: Specialists in commercial and antitrust litigation, international, intellectual property, government contracts and white collar crime.
Members of firm representing listed organizations:
Abrams, Robert G.
Baker, Harold F.
Bodner, John (Jr.)
Bolze, Ray S.
Briggs, John DeQ. (III)
Bruce, John F.
Colman, Richard T.
   Background: Trial Attorney, Antitrust Division, Department of Justice, 1962-66.
Gonzalez, Cecilia
Grimaldi, Alan M.
Harris, Stuart H.
Henneberry, Edward P.
   Background: Trial Attorney, Honors Program Department of Justice, Antitrust Division, 1970-75.
Hertzberg, Michael A.
Jacobsen, Raymond A. (Jr.)
   Background: Special Assistant to Senator William Roth, Jr., 1971-74.
Kaufman, Joel D.
Kingdon, John S.
   Background: Trial Attorney, Tax Division, Department of Justice, 1967-70.
Murchison, David C.
   Background: Legal Assistant to Under Secretary of the Army 1949-51; Associate General Counsel, Small Defense Plants Administration 1952-53. Federal Trade Commission 1953-55. U.S. Delegation to UNESCO 1955.
Nields, John W. (Jr.)
   Background: Chief Counsel, Committee on Standards of Official Conduct, Korea Influence Investigation, U.S. House of Representatives, 1977-78. Special Counsel, Department of Justice, 1979-80. Chief Counsel, House Select Committee to Investigate Covert Arms Transactions with Iran, 1987.
O'Brien, William R.
Plaia, Paul (Jr.)
Pugh, Keith E. (Jr.)
Roberts, William A. (III)
Savarese, Ralph J.
Sheehy, Terrence C.
Shelley, Herbert C.

Background: Attorney-Advisor, U.S. Internat'l Trade Commission, 1973-74; Ass't Director, office of Tariff Affairs, U.S. Dept. of Treasury, 1974-76; Member, U.S. Delegation to the Multilateral Trade Negotiations, 1976-79.
Sherzer, Harvey G.
Whitaker, A. Duncan
   Background: Trial Attorney, Antitrust Division, Department of Justice, 1957-59.
Wiseman, Alan M.
Clients:
American Cement Alliance *(John F. Bruce)*
Amgen, Inc. *(Cecilia Gonzalez, Paul Plaia, Jr.)*
Anheuser-Busch Cos., Inc. *(Terrence C. Sheehy)*
Carolina Power and Light Co. *(Ray S. Bolze)*
Caterpillar Inc. *(Richard T. Colman, David C. Murchison)*
Exxon Co., U.S.A. *(Robert G. Abrams)*
General Mills *(Ralph J. Savarese)*
Heinz Co., H. J. *(Keith E. Pugh, Jr.)*
Hershey Foods Corp. *(Keith E. Pugh, Jr.)*
Heublein, Inc. *(Ralph J. Savarese)*
ICI Americas Inc. *(Michael A. Hertzberg)*
Johnson & Johnson *(John W. Nields, Jr.)*
MCI Communications Corp. *(William A. Roberts, III)*
Mead Corp. *(Alan M. Wiseman)*
Mobil Corp. *(A. Duncan Whitaker)*
PepsiCo, Inc. *(Richard T. Colman, Raymond A. Jacobsen, Jr.)*
Quaker Oats Co. *(John S. Kingdon)*
Royal Dutch Shell Group *(Keith E. Pugh, Jr.)*
Shell Oil Co. *(Alan M. Grimaldi)*
Siemens Corp.
SKF USA, Inc. *(Paul Plaia, Jr.)*
Sun Pipe Line Co. *(A. Duncan Whitaker)*
Sun Refining and Marketing Co. *(Keith E. Pugh, Jr.)*
Taiwan Transportation Vehicle Manufacturing Ass'n *(Herbert C. Shelley)*
Teledyne Industries Inc. *(Harvey G. Sherzer)*
Tile Council of America *(John F. Bruce)*
Timex Corp. *(Stuart H. Harris, Ralph J. Savarese)*
Uniroyal Chemical Co., Inc. *(John DeQ. Briggs, III)*
United States Beet Sugar Ass'n *(John F. Bruce)*
VSI Corp. *(Terrence C. Sheehy)*
Wallcovering Manufacturers Ass'n *(David C. Murchison)*

HOYLE, Leonard H.
Exec. V. President, Hotel Sales and Marketing Ass'n Internat'l
1300 L St., N.W., Suite 800, Washington, DC 20005
Telephone: (202) 789-0089

HOYT, John A.
President, Humane Soc. of the United States
2100 L St., N.W., Washington, DC 20037
Telephone: (202) 452-1100

HOYT, Mary Finch
Director, Public Relations, Nat'l Trust for Historic Preservation
1785 Massachusetts Ave., N.W., Washington, DC 20036
Telephone: (202) 673-4000

HUARD, Paul R.
V. Pres., Taxation and Fiscal Policy, Nat'l Ass'n of Manufacturers
1331 Pennsylvania Ave., N.W. Suite 1500 North, Washington, DC 20004-1703
Telephone: (202) 637-3000
Registered as lobbyist at U.S. Congress.

HUBBARD, David S.
Legislative Director, American Cement Alliance
1331 Pennsylvania Ave., N.W. Suite 910, Washington, DC 20004
Telephone: (202) 662-7416
Registered as lobbyist at U.S. Congress.

HUBBARD, Henry W., Sr.
Sr. V. Pres. & Group Dir., Biotechnology, Hill and Knowlton Public Affairs Worldwide
Washington Harbour, 901 31st St., N.W., Washington, DC 20007
Telephone: (202) 333-7400
Registered as lobbyist at U.S. Congress.
Registered as Foreign Agent: (# 3301).
Clients:
Wistar Institute, The

HUBBARD, Pat Hill
V. President, Education & Science Policy, American Electronics Ass'n
1225 Eye St., N.W., Suite 950, Washington, DC 20005
Telephone: (202) 682-9110

HUBBARD, Richard L.
Arnold & Porter
1200 New Hampshire Ave., N.W., Washington, DC 20036
Telephone: (202) 872-6700
Registered as lobbyist at U.S. Congress.

HUBER, J. Martin
Exec. V. President, Nat'l Ass'n of Surety Bond Producers
6931 Arlington Road, Suite 308, Bethesda, MD 20814
Telephone: (301) 986-4166
Registered as lobbyist at U.S. Congress.
Background: Also serves as Exec. Director of the Nat'l Ass'n of Casulty and Surety Agents.

HUBER, John J.
Staff Attorney, Interstate Truckload Carriers Conference
2200 Mill Road Suite 600, Alexandria, VA 22314
Telephone: (703) 838-1950
Registered as lobbyist at U.S. Congress.

HUBER, R. James
Treasurer, Nat'l Ass'n of Chain Drug Stores Political Action Committee
Box 1417-D49, Alexandria, VA 22313
Telephone: (703) 549-3001

HUBERTY, Robert
Director, Resource Bank, Heritage Foundation
214 Massachusetts Ave., N.E., Washington, DC 20002
Telephone: (202) 546-4400

HUBLITZ, Lisa Shuger
Director, Government Relations, Nat'l Family Planning and Reproductive Health Ass'n
122 C St., N.W., Suite 380, Washington, DC 20001-2109
Telephone: (202) 628-3535
Registered as lobbyist at U.S. Congress.

HUBSCHMAN, Henry A.
Fried, Frank, Harris, Shriver & Jacobson
1001 Pennsylvania Ave., N.W., Suite 800, Washington, DC 20004-2505
Telephone: (202) 639-7000
Registered as lobbyist at U.S. Congress.
Background: Executive Assistant to the Secretary of Housing and Urban Development, 1977-79. Director, Federal Nat'l Mortgage Ass'n, 1979-81.
Clients:
Lonza Inc.

HUDAK, Martha
Ketchum Public Relations
1201 Connecticut Ave., N.W. Suite 300, Washington, DC 20036
Telephone: (202) 835-8800
Clients:
Road Information Program, The (TRIP)

HUDDLESTON, Walter D.
Exec. V. President, Hecht, Spencer & Associates
499 South Capitol St., S.W., Suite 507, Washington, DC 20003
Telephone: (202) 554-2881
Registered as lobbyist at U.S. Congress.
Registered as Foreign Agent: (# 3740).
Background: Former U.S. Senator (D-KY), 1973-85.
Clients:
AIRTRAX
BATUS, Inc.
Brown and Williamson Tobacco Corp.

HUDGINS, Edward L.
Dir., Center for Internat'l Econ. Growth, Heritage Foundation
214 Massachusetts Ave., N.E., Washington, DC 20002
Telephone: (202) 546-4400

HUDSON, Betty L.
V. President, Government Relations, Fluor Corp.
1627 K St., N.W., Washington, DC 20006
Telephone: (202) 955-9313
Registered as lobbyist at U.S. Congress.

HUDSON, CREYKE, KOEHLER AND TACKE
1101 King St., Suite 601, Alexandria, VA 22314
Telephone: (703) 838-9230
Clients:
 Bata Shoe Co.
 Dillingham Corp.
 Dorr-Oliver, Inc.
 Fischbach and Moore
 General Railway Signal Co.
 Keuffel and Esser Co.
 Omaha Public Power District
 Springs Industries, Inc.

HUDSON, J. William
President, Internat'l Ass'n of Refrigerated Warehouses
7315 Wisconsin Ave., Suite 1200N, Bethesda, MD 20814
Telephone: (301) 652-5674

HUDSON, Margaret Renken
Legislative Representative, Nat'l Federation of Independent Business
600 Maryland Ave., S.W., Suite 700, Washington, DC 20024
Telephone: (202) 544-9000
Registered as lobbyist at U.S. Congress.

HUDSON, Stewart
Legis. Rep., Internat'l Program, Nat'l Wildlife Federation
1400 16th St., N.W., Washington, DC 20036-2266
Telephone: (202) 797-6800
Registered as lobbyist at U.S. Congress.

HUETER, Ernest B.
President, Nat'l Legal Center for the Public Interest
1000 16th St., N.W., Suite 301, Washington, DC 20036
Telephone: (202) 296-1683

HUEY, Robert H.
Squire, Sanders and Dempsey
1201 Pennsylvania Ave., N.W. P.O. Box 407, Washington, DC 20044
Telephone: (202) 626-6600
Registered as lobbyist at U.S. Congress.
Clients:
 California Steel Industries Inc.

HUEY, Stewart M.
Senior Account Executive, Ass'n Management Group
3299 K St., N.W., 7th Floor, Washington, DC 20007
Telephone: (202) 965-7510

HUFFMAN, Robert
Member, Miller & Chevalier, Chartered
Metropolitan Square, 655 15th St., N.W., Washington, DC 20005
Telephone: (202) 626-5800

HUGE, Harry
Kamber Group, The
1920 L St., N.W., Washington, DC 20036
Telephone: (202) 223-8700
Organizations represented:
 Sheet Metal Workers' Internat'l Ass'n

HUGEL, Charles E.
Chairman and CEO, Nat'l Foreign Trade Council, Inc.
1625 K St., N.W., Suite 1090, Washington, DC 20006
Telephone: (202) 887-0278

HUGGINS, Esther
Member Services Manager, Nonprofit Mailers Federation
4351 Garden City Drive Suite 655, Landover, MD 20785
Telephone: (301) 577-6388

HUGGINS, M. Wayne
Director, Nat'l Institute of Corrections
320 First St., N.W. Room 200, Washington, DC 20534
Telephone: (202) 724-3106

HUGHES, Cindy
Technical Director, Independent Liquid Terminals Ass'n
1133 15th St., N.W. Suite 204, Washington, DC 20005
Telephone: (202) 659-2301

HUGHES, Della
Exec. Director, Nat'l Network of Runaway and Youth Services
1400 Eye St., N.W., Suite 330, Washington, DC 20005
Telephone: (202) 682-4114

HUGHES, Gary E.
Chief Counsel, Securities, American Council of Life Insurance
1001 Pennsylvania Ave., N.W., Washington, DC 20004-2599
Telephone: (202) 624-2120
Registered as lobbyist at U.S. Congress.

HUGHES HUBBARD AND REED
901 15th St., N.W., Washington, DC 20005-2301
Telephone: (202) 371-6240
Background: Washington office of a New York law firm.
Clients:
 Coopers and Lybrand
 Merck and Co.
 Northwest Airlines, Inc.
 United States Catholic Conference

HUGHES, J. Vance
Kilpatrick & Cody
2501 M St., N.W., Suite 500, Washington, DC 20037
Telephone: (202) 463-2500
Registered as lobbyist at U.S. Congress.
Background: Formerly with the U.S. Environmental Protection Agency and the U.S. Department of Justice.
Clients:
 Greenpeace, U.S.A.
 Kootznoowoo, Inc.

HUGHES, James J.
V. Pres., Communications & Admin. Svcs., American Iron and Steel Institute
1133 15th St., N.W., Suite 300, Washington, DC 20005-2701
Telephone: (202) 452-7122

HUGHES, John
Technical Affairs Director, Electricity Consumers Resource Council
1333 H St., N.W., West Tower - 8th Fl., Washington, DC 20005
Telephone: (202) 466-4686

HUGHES, Julia K.
Director of Government Relations, Associated Merchandising Corp.
1615 L St., N.W. Suite 700, Washington, DC 20036
Telephone: (202) 682-7098

HUGHES, Kathleen
Director, Media Relations, BellSouth Corp.
1133 21st St., N.W., Suite 900, Washington, DC 20036
Telephone: (202) 463-4100

HUGHES, Kent H.
President, Council on Competitiveness
1331 Pennsylvania Ave., N.W. Suite 900 North, Washington, DC 20004
Telephone: (202) 662-8760

HUGHES LANE, Scott
Legislative Representative, Nat'l Automobile Dealers Ass'n
412 First St., S.E., Washington, DC 20003
Telephone: (202) 547-5500
Registered as lobbyist at U.S. Congress.

HUGHES, Michael
Manager, Advanced Unmanned Systems, Canadair Challenger, Inc. Advanced Unmanned Systems Directorate
1215 Jefferson Davis Highway Suite 901, Arlington, VA 22202
Telephone: (703) 486-5850

HUGHES, Peg
Exec. Secretary, Federal Gov't Relations, Air Products and Chemicals, Inc.
805 15th St., N.W. Southern Bldg., Washington, DC 20006
Telephone: (202) 289-4110

HUGHES, Phyllis Eileen
Legal Assistant, Freedman, Levy, Kroll and Simonds
1050 Connecticut Ave., N.W., Suite 825, Washington, DC 20036
Telephone: (202) 457-5100

HUGHES, Ruth A.
Exec. Director, Internat'l Ass'n of Psychosocial Rehabilitation Services
5550 Sterrett Place, Suite 214, Columbia, MD 21044
Telephone: (301) 730-7190

HUGHES, Sharon M.
Exec. V. President, Nat'l Council of Agricultural Employers
1735 Eye St., N.W. Suite 704, Washington, DC 20003
Telephone: (202) 728-0300
Registered as lobbyist at U.S. Congress.

HUGHES, William G.
General Counsel, Nat'l Ass'n of Federal Veterinarians
1023 15th St., N.W. Suite 300, Washington, DC 20005
Telephone: (202) 289-6334
Registered as lobbyist at U.S. Congress.

HUGO & ASSOCIATES, Michael
3414 North Emerson St., Arlington, VA 22207
Telephone: (703) 237-6950
Background: A lobbying and information systems firm.
Members of firm representing listed organizations:
 Hugo, F. Michael, President
 Background: Former Minority Counsel and Staff Director, House Appropriations Committee.
Organizations represented:
 Geo-Centers, Inc. *(F. Michael Hugo)*
 Professional Services Council *(F. Michael Hugo)*
 Warner-Lambert Co. *(F. Michael Hugo)*

HUGO, F. Michael
President, Hugo & Associates, Michael
3414 North Emerson St., Arlington, VA 22207
Telephone: (703) 237-6950
Registered as lobbyist at U.S. Congress.
Background: Former Minority Counsel and Staff Director, House Appropriations Committee.
Organizations represented:
 Geo-Centers, Inc.
 Professional Services Council
 Warner-Lambert Co.

HUHN, S. Peter
Director, Legislative Education, Navy League of the United States
2300 Wilson Blvd., Arlington, VA 22201
Telephone: (703) 528-1775

HUIZENGA, Walter E.
Exec. V. President, American Internat'l Automobile Dealers Ass'n
1128 16th St., N.W., Washington, DC 20036
Telephone: (202) 659-2561

HULL, B. Jeanine
Manager, Hadson Corp.
1001 30th St., N.W. Suite 340, Washington, DC 20007
Telephone: (202) 337-5430
Registered as lobbyist at U.S. Congress.

HULL, William J.
V. President and Counsel, Nat'l Waterways Conference, Inc.
1130 17th St., N.W., Washington, DC 20036
Telephone: (202) 296-4415

HULTMAN, Dwight Eric
Van Ness, Feldman & Curtis
1050 Thomas Jefferson St., 7th Floor, Washington, DC 20007
Telephone: (202) 298-1800
Registered as lobbyist at U.S. Congress.
Clients:
 America First Companies

HULTMAN, Maj. Gen. Evan, AUS (Ret)
Exec. Director, Reserve Officers Ass'n of the U.S.
1 Constitution Ave., N.E., Washington, DC 20002
Telephone: (202) 479-2200
Registered as lobbyist at U.S. Congress.

HUMM, Marilyn J.
Director, Scientific and Public Affairs, American Statistical Ass'n
1429 Duke St., Alexandria, VA 22314-3402
Telephone: (703) 684-1221

The listings in this directory are available as *Mailing Labels*. See last page.

201

HUMMEL, Harlan
Exec. V. President, Nat'l Lumber and Building Material
Dealers Ass'n
40 Ivy St., S.E., Washington, DC 20003
Telephone: (202) 547-2230

HUMMERS, Edward W., Jr.
Fletcher, Heald and Hildreth
1225 Connecticut Ave., N.W. Suite 400, Washington, DC
20036
Telephone: (202) 828-5700
Registered as lobbyist at U.S. Congress.

HUMPHREY, Bruce G.
Assistant to the President, Strat. Plng., Edison Electric Institute
1111 19th St., N.W., Washington, DC 20036
Telephone: (202) 778-6400

HUMPHREY, Gregory A.
Legislative Director, American Federation of Teachers
555 New Jersey Ave., N.W., Washington, DC 20001
Telephone: (202) 879-4450
Registered as lobbyist at U.S. Congress.

HUMPHREY, Margot Smiley
Koteen and Naftalin
1150 Connecticut Ave., N.W. Suite 1000, Washington, DC
20036
Telephone: (202) 467-5700
Registered as lobbyist at U.S. Congress.
Clients:
Alascom, Inc.
Telephone and Data Systems, Inc.

HUMPHREYS, Allison
Wallace & Edwards
1150 Connecticut Ave., N.W., Suite 507, Washington, DC
20036
Telephone: (202) 331-4331
Registered as lobbyist at U.S. Congress.
Clients:
Cotton Warehouse Government Relations Com-
mittee

HUMPHREYS, David J.
President and CEO, Recreation Vehicle Industry Ass'n
1896 Preston White Drive P.O. Box 2999, Reston, VA
22090
Telephone: (703) 620-6003

HUMPHREYS, Frances
Director, Washington Office, Gray Panthers Nat'l Office in
Washington
1424 16th St., N.W., Washington, DC 20036
Telephone: (202) 387-3111

HUMPHREYS, Robert R.
MARC Associates, Inc.
1030 15th St., N.W. Suite 468, Washington, DC 20005
Telephone: (202) 371-8090
Registered as lobbyist at U.S. Congress.
Clients:
Affiliated Leadership League of and for the Blind
of America
Boys Town Nat'l Research Hospital
Helen Keller Nat'l Center for Deaf-Blind Youths
and Adults
Nat'l Coalition on Immune System Disorders
Recording for the Blind, Inc.

HUMPSTONE, Jane
Project Assistant, APCO Associates
1155 21st St., N.W., Suite 1000, Washington, DC 20036
Telephone: (202) 778-1000

HUNGATE, Bob
Government Affairs, Health Care Manager, Hewlett-Packard Co.
900 17th St., N.W. Suite 1100, Washington, DC 20006
Telephone: (202) 785-7943

HUNKELER, Dr. John
Treasurer, American Soc. of Cataract and Refractive
Surgery Political Action Committee
3702 Pender Drive, Suite 250, Fairfax, VA 22033
Telephone: (703) 591-2220

HUNNICUTT, Charles A.
Robins, Kaplan, Miller & Ciresi
1627 Eye St., N.W., Suite 610, Washington, DC 20006
Telephone: (202) 861-6800
Registered as lobbyist at U.S. Congress.

HUNNICUTT, John E.
Partner, KPMG Peat Marwick
2001 M St., N.W., Washington, DC 20036
Telephone: (202) 467-3846

HUNNINGS, Adrian
Exec. Director, Cotton Council Internat'l
Suite 430, 1110 Vermont Ave., N.W., Washington, DC
20005
Telephone: (202) 833-2943
Background: Also represents Nat'l Cotton Council of
America.

HUNSICKER, Steven R.
Baker and Botts
555 13th St., N.W., Suite 500 East, Washington, DC
20004-1109
Telephone: (202) 639-7700

HUNT, F. Milton
Gov't Relats. Mgr., Agricultural Product, Dow Chemical
1776 Eye St., N.W., Suite 575, Washington, DC 20006
Telephone: (202) 429-3400

HUNT, Frances A.
Resource Specialist, Forestry, Nat'l Wildlife Federation
1400 16th St., N.W., Washington, DC 20036-2266
Telephone: (202) 797-6800
Registered as lobbyist at U.S. Congress.

HUNT, Frederick D., Jr.
President, Hunt Management Systems
2033 M St., N.W., Suite 605, Washington, DC 20036
Telephone: (202) 223-6413
Background: Also serves as President, Society of Profes-
sional Benefit Administrators.
Clients:
Soc. of Professional Benefit Administrators

HUNT, James H.
Director, Nat'l Insurance Consumer Organization
121 North Payne St., Alexandria, VA 22314
Telephone: (703) 549-8050
Registered as lobbyist at U.S. Congress.

HUNT, Jayne E.
Treasurer, Consumer Bankers Ass'n Political Action Committee
1300 North 17th St., Arlington, VA 22209
Telephone: (703) 276-1750

HUNT MANAGEMENT SYSTEMS
2033 M St., N.W., Suite 605, Washington, DC 20036
Telephone: (202) 223-6413
Members of firm representing listed organizations:
Hunt, Frederick D. (Jr.), President
Background: Also serves as President, Society of
Professional Benefit Administrators.
Lennan, Anne C.
Background: Serves as Director of Federal Affairs, Soc.
of Professional Benefit Administrators.
Ysla, Elizabeth
Background: Serves as Director of Government Rela-
tions, Soc. of Professional Benefit Administrators.
Clients:
Soc. of Professional Benefit Administrators (Frede-
rick D. Hunt, Jr., Anne C. Lennan, Elizabeth Ysla)

HUNT, Meg
Director of Senate Relations, Heritage Foundation
214 Massachusetts Ave., N.E., Washington, DC 20002
Telephone: (202) 546-4400
Background: Legislative Assistant to Rep. Dan Marriott
(R-UT), 1982. Legislative Assistant to Senator Jeremiah
Denton (R-AL), 1982-86.

HUNT, Olive
Public Relations Director, Nat'l Committee on Public Employee Pension Systems
1221 Connecticut Ave., N.W., 4th Floor, Washington, DC
20036
Telephone: (202) 293-3960

Background: Legislative Assistant to former Congressman
and Senator William Brock (R-TN), 1962-72; Press Secretary to Rep. C. L. Baker (R-TN), 1972-74.

HUNT, Scott
Exec. Director, Endocrine Soc.
9650 Rockville Pike, Bethesda, MD 20814
Telephone: (301) 571-1802

HUNTER, Angela M.
Assistant Legislative Representative, Internat'l Brother-
hood of Teamsters, Chauffeurs, Warehousemen and
Helpers of America
25 Louisiana Ave., N.W., Washington, DC 20001
Telephone: (202) 624-6800
Registered as lobbyist at U.S. Congress.

HUNTER, Bruce
Assoc. Exec. Director, Gov't Relations, American Ass'n of
School Administrators
1801 North Moore St., Arlington, VA 22209
Telephone: (703) 528-0700

HUNTER, Daniel J.
Sr. Government Relations Representative, Nat'l Cotton
Council of America
1110 Vermont Ave., N.W. Suite 430, Washington, DC
20005
Telephone: (202) 833-2943
Registered as lobbyist at U.S. Congress.

HUNTER, J. Robert
President, Nat'l Insurance Consumer Organization
121 North Payne St., Alexandria, VA 22314
Telephone: (703) 549-8050
Registered as lobbyist at U.S. Congress.

HUNTER, Janet
V. President, Internat'l Business-Government Counsellors,
Inc.
818 Connecticut Ave., N.W. Suite 1200, Washington, DC
20006
Telephone: (202) 872-8181
Registered as lobbyist at U.S. Congress.
Clients:
Xerox Corp.

HUNTER, John W.
McNair Law Firm, P.A.
1155 15th St., N.W. Suite 400, Washington, DC 20005
Telephone: (202) 659-3900
Registered as lobbyist at U.S. Congress.
Background: Staff Attorney, Federal Communications
Commission, 1972-80; Legislative Assistant to Rep. Guy
Vander Jagt (R-MI), 1969-72.
Clients:
GTE Government Systems

HUNTER, Larry
Deputy Chief Economist, Chamber of Commerce of the
U.S.A.
1615 H St., N.W., Washington, DC 20062
Telephone: (202) 659-6000

HUNTER, Michael M.
Director, Corporate Affairs, ITT Corp.
1600 M St., N.W., Washington, DC 20036
Telephone: (202) 775-7366

HUNTER, Richard C.
Deputy Secretary General, World Federation for Mental
Health
1021 Prince St., Alexandria, VA 22314
Telephone: (703) 684-7722

HUNTER, Robert E.
V. Pres., Regional Programs, Center for Strategic and In-
ternat'l Studies
1800 K St., N.W., Washington, DC 20006
Telephone: (202) 887-0200
Background: Nat'l Security Council: Director of Middle
East Affairs, 1979-81 and West European Affairs, 1977-
79.

HUNTER, Robert W.
Director of Corporate Communications, Communications
Satellite Corp. (COMSAT)
950 L'Enfant Plaza, S.W., Washington, DC 20024
Telephone: (202) 863-6000

HUNTER, William
Acting Director, American Ass'n for Counseling and Development
5999 Stevenson Ave., Alexandria, VA 22304
Telephone: (703) 823-9800

HUNTINGTON, Charlie
Legislative Representative, American Academy of Family Physicians
600 Maryland Ave., S.W., Suite 770, Washington, DC 20024
Telephone: (202) 488-7448
Registered as lobbyist at U.S. Congress.

HUNTINGTON, Judith A.
Director, Washington Office, American Nurses' Ass'n
1101 14th St., N.W., Suite 200, Washington, DC 20005
Telephone: (202) 789-1800

HUNTON AND WILLIAMS
2000 Pennsylvania Ave., N.W., Washington, DC 20006
Telephone: (202) 955-1500
Background: Washington office of a 400-lawyer law firm whose main office is in Richmond, Virginia.
Members of firm representing listed organizations:
  Adams, John J.
  Nickel, Henry V.
  Ossola, Charles D.
  Rhodes, John J., Of Counsel
    Background: Member, U.S. House of Representatives (R-AZ). House Minority Leader, 1973-81.
Clients:
  American Soc. of Magazine Photographers *(Charles D. Ossola)*
  Arkansas Power and Light Co.
  Committee for a Responsible Federal Budget *(John J. Rhodes)*
  Copyright Justice Coalition *(Charles D. Ossola)*
  Crestar
  Delmarva Power and Light Co.
  Ethyl Corp.
  Long Island Lighting Co.
  Northeast Utilities Service Co.
  Oklahoma Gas and Electric Co.
  Pennsylvania Power and Light Co.
  Southern California Edison Co.
  Tampa Electric Co.
  Utility Air Regulatory Group *(Henry V. Nickel)*
  Virginia Power Co.
  Western Carolina Telephone Co.
  Westvaco Corp.

HURAY, Frank T.
Ass't. Exec. Director, Nat'l Svc. Fdn., American Veterans of World War II, Korea and Vietnam (AMVETS)
4647 Forbes Blvd., Lanham, MD 20706
Telephone: (301) 459-9600

HURKEY, Chuck
V. President, Communications, Insurance Institute for Highway Safety
1005 North Glebe Rd. Suite 800, Arlington, VA 22201
Telephone: (703) 247-1500

HURLBURT, Carol J.
Director of Communications, Nat'l Printing Equipment and Supply Ass'n
1899 Preston White Drive, Reston, VA 22091
Telephone: (703) 264-7200

HURLEY, Gerard F., CAE
Exec. V. President, Nat'l Club Ass'n
1625 Eye St., N.W., Suite 609, Washington, DC 20006
Telephone: (202) 466-8424
Registered as lobbyist at U.S. Congress.

HURLEY, Karen
Asst. Director, Legislat. Communications, Nat'l Ass'n of Life Underwriters
1922 F St., N.W., Washington, DC 20006
Telephone: (202) 331-6000

HURLEY, Paul E.
President, Malaysian Rubber Bureau
1925 K St., N.W. Suite 204, Washington, DC 20006
Telephone: (202) 452-0544

HURST, Michael E.
President and Chairman of the Board, Nat'l Restaurant Ass'n
1200 17th St., N.W., Washington, DC 20036-3097
Telephone: (202) 331-5900

HURST, Ronald A.
Exec. V. President, American Managed Care and Review Ass'n Political Action Committee (AMCRA PAC)
1227 25th St., N.W. Suite 610, Washington, DC 20037
Telephone: (202) 728-0506
Registered as lobbyist at U.S. Congress.

HURTT, Melissa
District Director, Muscular Dystrophy Ass'n
5350 Shawnee Rd., Suite 330, Alexandria, VA 22312
Telephone: (703) 941-5001

HURWIT, Cathy
Director, Federal Health Policy, Nat'l Health Care Campaign
1334 G St., N.W. LL, Washington, DC 20005
Telephone: (202) 639-8833
Registered as lobbyist at U.S. Congress.

HURWITZ, Geoffrey B.
Director, State Government Relations, Rohm and Haas Co.
1667 K St., N.W., Suite 210, Washington, DC 20006
Telephone: (202) 872-0660
Registered as lobbyist at U.S. Congress.

HURWITZ, Mark W.
Exec. V. President, Building Owners and Managers Ass'n Internat'l
1201 New York Ave., N.W. Suite 300, Washington, DC 20005
Telephone: (202) 289-7000
Registered as lobbyist at U.S. Congress.
Background: Also serves as contact for the Building Owners and Managers Ass'n Political Action Committee.

HUSHBECK, Judy
Senior Analyst, American Ass'n of Retired Persons
1909 K St., N.W., Washington, DC 20049
Telephone: (202) 872-4700

HUSHEN, John W.
V. President, Government Relations, Eaton Corp.
1100 Connecticut Ave., N.W., Suite 410, Washington, DC 20036
Telephone: (202) 955-6444

HUSHON, John D.
Arent, Fox, Kintner, Plotkin & Kahn
1050 Connecticut Ave., N.W., Washington, DC 20036-5339
Telephone: (202) 857-6000
Registered as lobbyist at U.S. Congress.
Registered as Foreign Agent: (#2661).
Clients:
  Clopay Corp.
  Guardian Life Insurance Co. of America
  Toyota Motor Corp.

HUSK, Samuel B.
Exec. Director, Council of the Great City Schools
1413 K St., N.W. 4th Floor, Washington, DC 20006
Telephone: (202) 371-0163

HUSSEY, John F.
V. President, Corporate Affairs, Nestle Enterprises, Inc.
1511 K St., N.W., Suite 1100, Washington, DC 20005
Telephone: (202) 639-8894

HUSSEY, Michael F.
Legis. Director, Congressional Affairs, Nat'l Ass'n of REALTORS
777 14th St., N.W., Washington, DC 20005
Telephone: (202) 383-1000
Registered as lobbyist at U.S. Congress.

HUTCHINS, Lawrence G.
Vice President, Nat'l Ass'n of Letter Carriers of the United States of America
100 Indiana Ave., N.W., Washington, DC 20001
Telephone: (202) 393-4695

HUTCHINSON, Dan
Director, Federal Systems, McDonnell Douglas Systems Integration
2070 Chain Bridge Rd. Suite 200, Vienna, VA 22182
Telephone: (703) 734-0088

HUTCHINSON, Philip A., Jr.
V.P., Public Aff., Gen. Counsel & Sec'y, Volkswagen of America, Inc.
490 L'Enfant Plaza, S.W., Suite 7204, Washington, DC 20024
Telephone: (202) 484-6096
Registered as lobbyist at U.S. Congress.

HUTCHINSON, Suzanne C.
Exec. V. President, Mortgage Insurance Companies of America
805 15th St., N.W., Suite 1110, Washington, DC 20005
Telephone: (202) 371-2899
Registered as lobbyist at U.S. Congress.

HUTCHISON AND CO., F. H.
901 King St., Suite 101, Alexandria, VA 22314
Telephone: (703) 684-8885
Background: A government and public affairs consulting firm specializing in Western U.S. policy issues.
Members of firm representing listed organizations:
  Hutchison, Fred H., President and Owner
    Background: Is also president, Hutchison Software Corp. Former Legislative Assistant to Senator Frank Church (D-ID), 1975-81.
Organizations represented:
  Bennett Lumber Products, Inc. *(Fred H. Hutchison)*
  Boise, Idaho, City of *(Fred H. Hutchison)*
  Coalition of ARBA Licensees *(Fred H. Hutchison)*
  Evergreen Forest Products, Inc. *(Fred H. Hutchison)*
  Fibreboard Corp. *(Fred H. Hutchison)*
  Fine Hardwood Veneer Ass'n *(Fred H. Hutchison)*
  GeoProducts Corp. *(Fred H. Hutchison)*
  Hydrocel Corp. *(Fred H. Hutchison)*
  Idapine Mills/Clearwater Forest Industries *(Fred H. Hutchison)*
  Inter-Industry Log Export Action Committee *(Fred H. Hutchison)*
  Sequoia Forest Industries *(Fred H. Hutchison)*

HUTCHISON, Fred H.
President and Owner, Hutchison and Co., F. H.
901 King St., Suite 101, Alexandria, VA 22314
Telephone: (703) 684-8885
Registered as lobbyist at U.S. Congress.
Background: Is also president, Hutchison Software Corp. Former Legislative Assistant to Senator Frank Church (D-ID), 1975-81.
Organizations represented:
  Bennett Lumber Products, Inc.
  Boise, Idaho, City of
  Coalition of ARBA Licensees
  Evergreen Forest Products, Inc.
  Fibreboard Corp.
  Fine Hardwood Veneer Ass'n
  GeoProducts Corp.
  Hydrocel Corp.
  Idapine Mills/Clearwater Forest Industries
  Inter-Industry Log Export Action Committee
  Sequoia Forest Industries

HUTT, Peter Barton
Covington and Burling
1201 Pennsylvania Ave., N.W., Box 7566, Washington, DC 20044
Telephone: (202) 662-6000
Background: Former General Counsel, Food and Drug Administration, 1971-1975.
Clients:
  Asphalt Institute

HUTTER, Jean
Director of Legislation, Nat'l Housing Conference
1126 16th St., N.W., Suite 211, Washington, DC 20036
Telephone: (202) 223-4844

HUWA, Randy
V. President, Membership & Media Commun., Common Cause
2030 M St., N.W., Washington, DC 20036
Telephone: (202) 833-1200

HYDE, Barbara
Sr. Acct. Exec., Biotechnology Group, Hill and Knowlton
Public Affairs Worldwide
Washington Harbour, 901 31st St., N.W., Washington, DC
20007
Telephone: (202) 333-7400
Clients:
Nat'l Cattlemen's Ass'n
Procter and Gamble Mfg. Co.
SmithKline Animal Health Products

HYDE, David E.
President, Nat'l Ass'n of Postmasters of the U.S.
8 Herbert St., Alexandria, VA 22305-2600
Telephone: (703) 683-9027

HYDE, Floyd H.
Consultant, Simon & Co., Inc.
1001 Connecticut Ave., N.W. Suite 435, Washington, DC
20005
Telephone: (202) 659-2229
Registered as lobbyist at U.S. Congress.
Background: Former Ass't Sec'y, Community Develop-
ment, U.S. Department of Housing and Urban Dvlmt.
(HUD) 1971-73, Under Secretary HUD, 1973-74.

HYDE, Isabel E.
Director, Federal & Legislative Affairs, Goodyear Tire and
Rubber Co.
901 15th St., N.W. Suite 350, Washington, DC 20005
Telephone: (202) 682-9250
Registered as lobbyist at U.S. Congress.

HYMAN FINE & ASSOCIATES LTD.
1725 Jefferson Davis Hwy Suite 213, Arlington, VA 22202
Telephone: (703) 892-2232
Members of firm representing listed organizations:
Fine, Hyman, President
Clients:
British Aerospace, Inc.
Lockheed Missiles and Space Co.
Magnavox Government and Industrial Elec-
tronics Co.
Rolls-Royce, Inc.
United Technologies Corp.

HYMAN, Lester S.
Swidler & Berlin, Chartered
3000 K St., N.W., Suite 300, Washington, DC 20007
Telephone: (202) 944-4300
Registered as lobbyist at U.S. Congress.
Registered as Foreign Agent: (#4079).
Background: Attorney, Securities and Exchange Commis-
sion, 1955-56.
Clients:
Bermuda, Government of
Hyundai Motor Co.

HYMAN, PHELPS AND MCNAMERA
1120 G St., N.W., Suite 1040, Washington, DC 20005
Telephone: (202) 737-5600
Members of firm representing listed organizations:
Theis, Roger
Clients:
Lederle Laboratories, American Cyanamid Co.
Subsidiary *(Roger Theis)*

HYMEL, Gary
Chief Lobbyist and Vice Chairman, Hill and Knowlton Pub-
lic Affairs Worldwide
Washington Harbour, 901 31st St., N.W., Washington, DC
20007
Telephone: (202) 333-7400
Registered as lobbyist at U.S. Congress.
Registered as Foreign Agent: (#3301).
Background: Former Administrative Assistant to former
Speaker of the House Thomas P. O'Neill, U.S. House of
Representatives.
Clients:
AMR Corp.
Hill and Knowlton Inc. Political Action Commit-
tee
Indonesia, Government of
Ryder System, Inc.
Sanwa Bank Ltd.
Shaklee Corp.
Turkey, Embassy of
Turkey, Government of

HYNAN, William E.
Sr. V. President, Law Dept., Nat'l Coal Ass'n
1130 17th St., N.W., Washington, DC 20036
Telephone: (202) 463-2652

HYNES, Robert D., Jr.
V. President, Washington, Nat'l Broadcasting Co.
1331 Pennsylvania Ave., N.W. Suite 700S, Washington,
DC 20004
Telephone: (202) 637-4531
Registered as lobbyist at U.S. Congress.

HYPS, Brian M.
Government Affairs Assistant, American Pharmaceutical
Ass'n
2215 Constitution Ave., N.W., Washington, DC 20037
Telephone: (202) 628-4410
Registered as lobbyist at U.S. Congress.

I AND J ASSOCIATES
648 Anderson Hall 4400 Massachusetts Ave., N.W.,
Washington, DC 20016-8101
Telephone: (202) 885-7953
Members of firm representing listed organizations:
Jersey, Ira F. (Jr.)
Regan, John J.
Clients:
Mixmor, Inc. *(Ira F. Jersey, Jr., John J. Regan)*
Public Image Printing *(Ira F. Jersey, Jr., John J. Regan)*
Public Images *(Ira F. Jersey, Jr., John J. Regan)*
T and J Electronics *(Ira F. Jersey, Jr., John J. Regan)*

ICG INC.
2550 M St., N.W. Suite 460, Washington, DC 20037
Telephone: (202) 789-1188
Members of firm representing listed organizations:
Knapp, John, Senior Consultant
Background: Senior Consultant, ICG Inc. Former Gen-
eral Counsel, Former Gen. Counsel, Department of
Housing and Urban Development.

ICHORD, J. William
Director, Federal Affairs, UNOCAL Corp.
1050 Connecticut Ave., N.W., Suite 760, Washington, DC
20036
Telephone: (202) 659-7600
Registered as lobbyist at U.S. Congress.

ICHORD, Richard H.
Washington Industrial Team, Inc.
499 South Capitol St., S.W. Suite 520, Washington, DC
20003
Telephone: (202) 347-0633
Registered as lobbyist at U.S. Congress.
Background: Member, U.S. House of Representatives from
Missouri, 1961-81. Serves as Co-Chairman, American
Freedom Coalition.

IGASAKI, Paul M.
Washington Representative, Japanese American Citizens
League
1730 Rhode Island Ave., N.W., Suite 204, Washington, DC
20036
Telephone: (202) 223-1240

IGLI, Kevin J.
Regulatory Affairs Manager, Waste Management, Inc.
1155 Connecticut Ave., N.W., Suite 800, Washington, DC
20036
Telephone: (202) 467-4480
Registered as lobbyist at U.S. Congress.

IGNAGNI, Karen
Dir., Occ. Safety & Health Issues, AFL-CIO (American
Federation of Labor and Congress of Industrial Organi-
zations)
815 16th St., N.W., Washington, DC 20006
Telephone: (202) 637-5075

IIZUKA, Shogo
Senior V. President, Honda North America, Inc.
955 L'Enfant Plaza S.W., Suite 5300, Washington, DC
20024
Telephone: (202) 554-1650

IKARD, Frank N.
Laxalt, Washington, Perito & Dubuc
1120 Connecticut Ave., N.W., Suite 1000, Washington, DC
20036

Telephone: (202) 857-4000
Background: Former Member, U.S. House of Representatives (D-TX).

IKEJIRI, Kris H.
General Counsel, Interstate Truckload Carriers Confer-
ence
2200 Mill Road Suite 600, Alexandria, VA 22314
Telephone: (703) 838-1950
Registered as lobbyist at U.S. Congress.
Background: Trial Attorney, U.S. Dept. of Agriculture
1980-86.

IKENSON, Frederick L.
Ikenson, P.C., Frederick L.
1621 New Hampshire Ave., N.W., Washington, DC 20009
Telephone: (202) 483-8900
Background: Trial Attorney, Customs Section, Civil Divi-
sion, U.S. Department of Justice, 1968-71. Assistant
Chief, Customs Section, Civil Division, Department of
Justice, 1971-73.
Organizations represented:
General Electric Co.
Hand Tools Institute
Zenith Electronics Corp.

IKENSON, P.C., Frederick L.
1621 New Hampshire Ave., N.W., Washington, DC 20009
Telephone: (202) 483-8900
Members of firm representing listed organizations:
Ikenson, Frederick L.
Background: Trial Attorney, Customs Section, Civil
Division, U.S. Department of Justice, 1968-71. As-
sistant Chief, Customs Section, Civil Division, De-
partment of Justice, 1971-73.
Organizations represented:
General Electric Co. *(Frederick L. Ikenson)*
Hand Tools Institute *(Frederick L. Ikenson)*
Zenith Electronics Corp. *(Frederick L. Ikenson)*

IMIG, David G.
Exec. Director, American Ass'n of Colleges for Teacher
Education
One Dupont Circle, N.W., Suite 610, Washington, DC
20036
Telephone: (202) 293-2450

IMUS, Catherine L.
V. President, Group Manager, Braun & Company
1201 Connecticut Ave., N.W. Suite 300, Washington, DC
20036
Telephone: (202) 835-8880
Registered as lobbyist at U.S. Congress.
Background: With the U.S. House of Representatives Con-
gressional Steel Caucus, 1982-84; and as an aide to Rep.
Carroll Hubbard, Jr. (D-KY), 1984.

INCE, William K.
Cameron and Hornbostel
818 Connecticut Ave., N.W. Suite 700, Washington, DC
20006
Telephone: (202) 293-4690
Registered as Foreign Agent: (#3887).
Clients:
British Columbia Raspberry Growers Ass'n
Canadian Pork Council

INDEPENDENT CONSULTANTS
1616 H St., N.W. Suite 600, Washington, DC 20006
Telephone: (202) 347-7555
Members of firm representing listed organizations:
Hackler, W. Craig, President

INDYK, Martin
Exec. Director, Washington Institute for Near East Policy
50 F St., N.W., Suite 8800, Washington, DC 20001
Telephone: (202) 783-0226

ING, Charles E.
Legislative Affairs Manager, Toyota Motor Sales, U.S.A.
1850 M St., N.W., Suite 600, Washington, DC 20036
Telephone: (202) 775-1700
Registered as lobbyist at U.S. Congress.

ING, Edwin T. C.
2000 Pennsylvania Ave., N.W., Suite 7400, Washington,
DC 20006
Telephone: (202) 457-6630
Registered as lobbyist at U.S. Congress.

Background: Tax Law Specialist, Internal Revenue Service, 1975-77. Legislative Counsel to Senator Spark Matsunaga (D-HI), 1977-83.
Organizations represented:
First Hawaiian Bank
Hawaiian Sugar Planters' Ass'n
Kamehameha Schools
San Diego Gas and Electric Co.
United States Windpower, Inc.

INGEMIE, David
President, United Ski Industries Ass'n
8377-B Greensboro Drive, McLean, VA 22102
Telephone: (703) 556-9020

INGERSOLL, William B.
Dow, Lohnes and Albertson
1255 23rd St., N.W., Suite 500, Washington, DC 20037
Telephone: (202) 857-2500
Clients:
American Psychological Ass'n
American Resort and Residential Development Ass'n
Branigar Organization
Governors Club Development Corp.
Mobil Land Development Co.
NTS Corp.
Patten Corp.
Trapp Family Lodge
U.S. Home Corp.

INGHAM, Mark W.
Exec. Dir., Newspaper Pers. Relat. Ass'n, American Newspaper Publishers Ass'n
The Newspaper Center 11600 Sunrise Valley Drive, Reston, VA 22091
Telephone: (703) 648-1000

INGLE, R. Edward
Associate, Wexler, Reynolds, Fuller, Harrison and Schule, Inc.
1317 F St., N.W., Suite 600, Washington, DC 20004
Telephone: (202) 638-2121
Background: Former Senior Budget Examiner, Office of Management and Budget.

INGRAHAM, Ronwyn
Director, Washington Office, CARE
2025 I St., N.W., Suite 1003, Washington, DC 20006
Telephone: (202) 296-5696

INGRAM, Mark A.
Treasurer, Independent Action
1511 K St., N.W. Suite 619, Washington, DC 20005
Telephone: (202) 628-4321

INGRAO, Jean F.
Exec. Secretary-Treasurer, AFL-CIO - Martime Trades Department
815 16th St., N.W., Suite 510, Washington, DC 20006
Telephone: (202) 628-6300

INKLEY, Doug
Wildlife Resource Specialist, Nat'l Wildlife Federation
1400 16th St., N.W., Washington, DC 20036-2266
Telephone: (202) 797-6800
Registered as lobbyist at U.S. Congress.

INLOW, Allen
Treasurer, Nat'l Ass'n of Plumbing-Heating-Cooling Contractors Political Action Committee
180 South Washington St. Box 6808, Falls Church, VA 22046
Telephone: (703) 237-8100

INMAN, Harry A.
Patton, Boggs and Blow
2550 M St., N.W., Suite 800, Washington, DC 20037
Telephone: (202) 457-6000
Registered as Foreign Agent: (#165).

INNES, Andrea L.
Director, Political Affairs, Nat'l Coal Ass'n
1130 17th St., N.W., Washington, DC 20036
Telephone: (202) 463-2645

INSTITUTIONAL DEVELOPMENT ASSOCIATES
7799 Leesburg Pike, Suite 900, Falls Church, VA 22043
Telephone: (703) 827-5932

Registered as Foreign Agent: (#3828)
Background: A management consulting and support services firm specializing in weapons and technology transfer.
Members of firm representing listed organizations:
Lucas, John A. (Jr.)
Clients:
Saudi Arabia, Royal Embassy of *(John A. Lucas, Jr.)*

INTERLOCKE ASSOCIATES
117 C St., S.E., Washington, DC 20003
Telephone: (202) 546-7973
Registered as lobbyist at U.S. Congress.
Registered as Foreign Agent: (#3954)
Members of firm representing listed organizations:
Battaglia, Thomas
Vitali, Andrew
Clients:
Bolova System and Instrument Division
Eberhard Manufacturing
GKN Defense, Plc.

INTERNAT'L ADVISERS, INC.
2300 M St., N.W., Suite 600, Washington, DC 20037
Telephone: (202) 293-1575
Registered as Foreign Agent: (#4203)
Background: An international government affairs consulting subsidiary of the law firm of Feith & Zell.
Members of firm representing listed organizations:
Borland, Lydia A., Research Assistant
Epstein, Mark A.
Background: Issues Director, Hollings for President and U.S. Senate Staff, 1983-84. Visiting Scholar, Foreign Service Institute, U.S. Department of State, 1984. Professional Staff, House Government Operations Committee, 1987. Professional Staff, European Economics Division, West German Foreign Ministry, Bonn, 1988-89.
Feith, Douglas J.
Background: Member, National Security Council Staff, 1981-82. Special Counsel to the Assistant Secretary of Defense for International Security Policy, 1982-84. Deputy Assistant Secretary of Defense for Negotiations Policy, 1984-86.
Feldman, Mark B.
Background: Assistant Legal Adviser, 1968-74, Deputy Legal Adviser, 1974-80, Acting Legal Adviser, 1981, U.S. Department of State.
Holmstrom, Engin
McNamara, Michael J., V. Pres., Director, Defense Affairs
Background: Graduate of British Royal College of Defence Studies, London, 1978. Senior Staff Officer, Allied Forces Central Europe, Netherlands, 1979-83. Graduate of NATO Defense College, Rome, 1983. Country Director for Turkey, the U.K., Ireland and Yugoslavia, Office of the Secretary of Defense, International Security Policy, 1984-88. Retired as Colonel, U.S. Army, 1989.
Clients:
Turkey, Embassy of *(Lydia A. Borland, Douglas J. Feith, Engin Holmstrom, Michael J. McNamara)*

INTERNAT'L ADVISORY SERVICES GROUP LTD.
1400 L St., N.W., Suite 600, Washington, DC 20005
Telephone: (202) 342-1200
Registered as Foreign Agent: (#4267)
Background: A trade policy consulting firm.
Members of firm representing listed organizations:
Blum, Charles H., Director
Background: U.S. Foreign Service Officer, 1971-80. Assistant U.S. Trade Representative, 1980-88.
Carr, Jeffrey W., Director
Clients:
Siderbras *(Charles H. Blum, Jeffrey W. Carr)*
Steel Service Center Institute *(Charles H. Blum, Jeffrey W. Carr)*

INTERNAT'L BUSINESS AND ECONOMIC RESEARCH CORP.
2121 K St, N.W., Suite 700, Washington, DC 20037
Telephone: (202) 955-6155
Members of firm representing listed organizations:
Lenahan, Wally
Background: Former Deputy Assistant Secretary of Commerce for Textiles and Apparel, Department of Commerce.
Clients:

Asociacion Nacional de Industriales (ANDI) *(Wally Lenahan)*
Hong Kong Trade, Industry and Customs Department
Indonesia, Government of
Indonesian Ass'n of Textile Industries
Japan Chemical Fibers Ass'n
Japan Lumber Importers Ass'n
Japan Woolen and Linen Textiles Exporters Ass'n
Korea Federation of Footwear Industries
Korea Iron and Steel Ass'n
Korea Leather and Fur Exporters Ass'n
Korea Plastic Goods Exporters Ass'n
Retail Industry Trade Action Coalition

INTERNAT'L BUSINESS-GOVERNMENT COUNSELLORS, INC.
818 Connecticut Ave., N.W. Suite 1200, Washington, DC 20006
Telephone: (202) 872-8181
Members of firm representing listed organizations:
Bombelles, Thomas, Government Relations Counselor
Clawson, James B., Executive V. President
Elwell, Robert G., V. President-Special Advisor
Fromyer, Mary O., Government Relations Counsellor
Hunter, Janet, V. President
McDermid, John F.
Background: President and General Counsel, Internat'l Business-Government Counsellors, Inc.
Spielmann, Solveig B., Chairman and CEO
Vaughn, Philip, Government Relations Counselor
Clients:
Allen-Bradley Corp. *(Solveig B. Spielmann)*
ANSAC *(John F. McDermid)*
Uniroyal Chemical Co., Inc. *(James B. Clawson)*
Xerox Corp. *(Janet Hunter)*

INTERNAT'L DEVELOPMENT SYSTEMS
733 15th St., N.W., Suite 520, Washington, DC 20005
Telephone: (202) 783-0720
Background: Provides quota analyses on textile and apparel trade and other information and advice on the U.S. textile program to firms operating in the international marketplace and to foreign countries trading with the United States.
Members of firm representing listed organizations:
Brasher, C. Donald (Jr.)
Background: Former international trade specialist, Office of Textiles, U.S. Department of Commerce.
Stack, Clinton J.
Background: Former Deputy Director, Implementation Division, Office of Textiles, U.S. Department of Commerce.
Clients:
Bangladesh Garment Manufacturers and Exporters Ass'n *(C. Donald Brasher, Jr.)*
Costa Rica Shirt Manufacturers
Guatemala, Government of

INTERNAT'L MANAGEMENT GROUP, INC.
1101 14th St., N.W. Suite 1100, Washington, DC 20005
Telephone: (202) 371-2200
Background: A multiple association management firm.
Members of firm representing listed organizations:
Barrack, David W.
Background: Serves as Exec. Director, Nat'l Ass'n of Public Insurance Adjusters; Exec. Director, Metal Construction Ass'n; Exec. Director, American Soc. of Electroplated Plastics; Exec. Director, American Cutlery Manufacturers Ass'n.
Cassedy, Brian, President
Background: Also serves as Exec. Director, Nat'l Soc. for Cardiovascular and Pulmonary Technology.
Cassedy, Joan Walsh, Chairman
Background: Also serves as Exec. Director, Soc. for Toxicology and Exec. Director, Specialty Coffee Ass'n of America.
Fiegel, John L., V. President
Background: Serves as Exec. Director, Ass'n of Unmanned Vehicle Systems.
McElgunn, Peggy, V. President
Background: Serves as Exec. Director, Soc. of Environmental Toxicology and Chemistry and Associate Director, Nat'l Soc. for Cardiovascular Technologists/ Nat'l Soc. for Pulmonary Technologists.

WASHINGTON REPRESENTATIVES

INTERNAT'L MANAGEMENT GROUP, INC.
(Cont'd)
Sanasack, David, Exec. V. President
Background: Serves also as Exec. V. President, Institute of Ass'n Management Companies; Exec. Director, Soc. of Environmental Toxicology and Chemistry; and Exec. Director, Internat'l Soc. of Transport Aircraft Traders.
Steinkuller, William P.
Background: V. President, Internat'l Management Group. Also serves as Exec. Director, Automotive Dismantlers and Recyclers Ass'n.
Clients:
American Cutlery Manufacturers Ass'n *(David W. Barrack)*
American Soc. of Electroplated Plastics *(David W. Barrack)*
Ass'n for Unmanned Vehicle Systems *(John L. Fiegel)*
Auto Dismantlers & Recyclers Ass'n *(William P. Steinkuller)*
Automotive Dismantlers and Recyclers Ass'n *(William P. Steinkuller)*
Internat'l Ass'n of Energy Economists *(Joan Walsh Cassedy)*
Internat'l Soc. of Transport Aircraft Traders *(Brian Cassedy)*
Metal Construction Ass'n *(David W. Barrack)*
Nat'l Ass'n of Public Insurance Adjusters *(David W. Barrack)*
Nat'l Soc. for Cardiovascular and Pulmonary Technology *(Brian Cassedy, Peggy McElgunn)*
Soc. of Toxicology *(Joan Walsh Cassedy)*
Specialty Coffee Ass'n of America *(Joan Walsh Cassedy)*

INTERNAT'L PUBLIC STRATEGIES, INC.
1030 15th St., N.W., Suite 408, Washington, DC 20005
Telephone: (202) 371-5604
Registered as Foreign Agent: (#4200)
Background: A government relations consulting firm specializing in aiding foreign clients. The firm is headed by Mark A. Siegel, whose related company, Mark A. Siegel & Associates, represents domestic clients.
Members of firm representing listed organizations:
Fowler, C. Grayson, Secretary
Background: Former foreign relations aide to the late Senator Edward Zorinski (D-NE).
Posada, Ricardo, Account Representative
Wilder, Timothy E., Account Representative
Clients:
Aruba, Government of *(C. Grayson Fowler)*
Pakistan, Government of

INTERNAT'L TECHNICAL EXPERTISE, LTD.
150 South Washington St., Suite 403, Falls Church, VA 22046
Telephone: (703) 536-4500
Background: A consulting firm.
Members of firm representing listed organizations:
Hogue, Phillip A.
Petersen, Dennis L.
Rohrkemper, Stephen F.

INTERNAT'L TRADE AND DEVELOPMENT AGENCY
1911 North Fort Meyer Dr. Suite 703, Arlington, VA 22209
Telephone: (703) 243-1456
Registered as Foreign Agent: (#3690)
Clients:
China External Trade Development Council
Korea, Embassy of
Thailand, Embassy of

IOVINO, Peter
Manager, Corporate Programs, Ford Aerospace Corp.
1235 Jefferson Davis Hwy. Suite 1300, Arlington, VA 22202
Telephone: (703) 685-5500
Registered as lobbyist at U.S. Congress.

IPPOLITO, Frank
Govt'l Affrs Staff, DEPARTMENT OF AGRICULTURE - Food and Nutrition Service
3101 Park Center Drive, Alexandria, VA 22302
Telephone: (703) 756-3039

IRBY, Richard, III
V. President, Government Relations, American Gas Ass'n
1515 Wilson Blvd., Arlington, VA 22209
Telephone: (703) 841-8621

IRIONS, Charles C.
President, American Movers Conference
2200 Mill Road, Alexandria, VA 22314
Telephone: (703) 838-1930
Registered as lobbyist at U.S. Congress.

IRONFIELD, Susan
Liaison Officer, Cong & Intergov'l Affrs, DEPARTMENT OF LABOR
200 Constitution Ave., N.W., Washington, DC 20210
Telephone: (202) 523-6141

IRVIN, William Robert
Counsel, Fisheries & Wildlife Div., Nat'l Wildlife Federation
1400 16th St., N.W., Washington, DC 20036-2266
Telephone: (202) 797-6800
Registered as lobbyist at U.S. Congress.

IRVINE, Edrie
Sr. Econ. Analyst, Econ. & Int'l Affrs., Motor Vehicle Manufacturers Ass'n of the United States
1620 Eye St., N.W. Suite 1000, Washington, DC 20006
Telephone: (202) 775-2700
Registered as lobbyist at U.S. Congress.

IRVINE, Reed J.
Chairman of the Board, Accuracy in Media
1275 K St., N.W., Suite 1150, Washington, DC 20005
Telephone: (202) 371-6710

IRWIN, David A.
Golden, Freda and Schraub, P.C.
1400 16th St., N.W. Suite 700, Washington, DC 20036
Telephone: (202) 939-6000
Registered as lobbyist at U.S. Congress.
Background: Special Counsel to Chief, Common Carrier Bureau/Chief Program Evaluation Staff, Federal Communications Commission, 1975-79.

IRWIN, Edward L.
Manager, Federal Regulatory Affairs, Southern California Gas Co.
Suite 717, 1150 Connecticut Ave., N.W., Washington, DC 20036
Telephone: (202) 822-3716

IRWIN, Paul
Executive V. President, Humane Soc. of the United States
2100 L St., N.W., Washington, DC 20037
Telephone: (202) 452-1100

IRWIN, William
Director of Operations, American Logistics Ass'n
1133 15th St., N.W. Suite 640, Washington, DC 20005
Telephone: (202) 466-2520

ISAAC, William M.
Managing Director and COO, Secura Group, The
1155 21st St., N.W., Washington, DC 20036
Telephone: (202) 728-4920
Background: Also a partner in the law firm of Arnold and Porter. Chairman, Federal Deposit Insurance Corp., 1981-85.
Clients:
Chase Manhattan Bank

ISAACS, Amy
National Director, Americans for Democratic Action
1511 K St., N.W. Suite 941, Washington, DC 20005
Telephone: (202) 638-6447
Registered as lobbyist at U.S. Congress.

ISAACS, John D.
Legislative Director, Council for a Livable World
100 Maryland Ave., N.E. Suite 211, Washington, DC 20002
Telephone: (202) 543-4100
Registered as lobbyist at U.S. Congress.

ISAACS, Joseph C.
V. President for Government Relations, Nat'l Health Council
1700 K St., N.W. Suite 1005, Washington, DC 20006
Telephone: (202) 785-3913

ISAACSON, Sandra
Jefferson Group, The
1341 G St., N.W., Suite 1100, Washington, DC 20005
Telephone: (202) 638-3535
Registered as lobbyist at U.S. Congress.
Background: Former staff member, Senate Committee on Veterans' Affairs.

ISACCO, Caroline
Cong Liaison Officer, UNITED STATES INFORMATION AGENCY
301 4th St., S.W., Washington, DC 20547
Telephone: (202) 485-8828

ISHAK, Magenta
Director, Independent Insurance Agents of America, Inc. Political Action Committee
600 Pennsylvania Ave., S.E. Suite 200, Washington, DC 20003
Telephone: (202) 675-6485

ISKENDERIAN, Sally D.
Legislative Assistant, French & Company
The Willard, 1455 Pennsylvania Ave., N.W., Suite 1260, Washington, DC 20004
Telephone: (202) 783-7272
Clients:
Internat'l Electronics Manufacturers and Consumers of America

ISOKAIT, William A.
Ass't. Director, Open Shop, Associated General Contractors of America
1957 E St., N.W., Washington, DC 20006
Telephone: (202) 393-2040
Registered as lobbyist at U.S. Congress.

ISPAHANI, Mahnaz
Research Director, Nat'l Democratic Institute for Internat'l Affairs
1717 Massachusetts Ave., N.W. Suite 605, Washington, DC 20036
Telephone: (202) 328-3136

ISRAEL, Barry J.
Dorsey & Whitney
1330 Connecticut Ave., N.W., Suite 200, Washington, DC 20036
Telephone: (202) 857-0700

ISRAEL, Lesley
Kamber Group, The
1920 L St., N.W., Washington, DC 20036
Telephone: (202) 223-8700
Organizations represented:
AFL-CIO - Industrial Union Department

ISRAEL, Mark S.
Nat'l Center for Municipal Development
1620 Eye St., N.W., Suite 300, Washington, DC 20006
Telephone: (202) 429-0160
Clients:
Miami, Florida, City of
Riverside, California, City of
Waukegan, Illinois, City of

ISRAEL, Paul
Director, Washington Office, Buyers Up
P.O. Box 33757, Washington, DC 20009
Telephone: (202) 328-3800

ISSUE DYNAMICS INC.
901 15th St., N.W. Suite 230, Washington, DC 20005
Telephone: (202) 408-1400
Background: Public affairs consulting firm.
Members of firm representing listed organizations:
Klass, Kathie, Exec. Director
Simon, Samuel A., President

IUDICELLO, Suzanne
Assoc. Dir., Fisheries & the Environ., Alaska, State of
444 N. Capitol St., N.W. Suite 518, Washington, DC 20001
Telephone: (202) 624-5858

IVERSON, George D.
Director - Army Programs, McDonnell Douglas Corp.
1735 Jefferson Davis Highway, Arlington, VA 22202
Telephone: (703) 553-2193

The listings in this directory are available as *Mailing Labels*. See last page.

IVERSON, J. R.
President and CEO, American Electronics Ass'n
1225 Eye St., N.W., Suite 950, Washington, DC 20005
Telephone: (202) 682-9110

IVERSON, William D.
Covington and Burling
1201 Pennsylvania Ave., N.W., Box 7566, Washington, DC 20044
Telephone: (202) 662-6000

IVES, Suzanne L., APR
Senior V. President, Manning, Selvage & Lee/Washington
1250 Eye St., N.W., Suite 300, Washington, DC 20005
Telephone: (202) 682-1660

IVEY, David L.
Exec. V. President, Institutional and Municipal Parking Congress
P.O. Box 7167, Fredericksburg, VA 22404
Telephone: (703) 371-7535
Background: Staff Assistant, Congressman David Pryor, 1967. Staff Assistant, Senator J. W. Fulbright, 1968-1969. Assistant to Senate Superintendent of Documents, 1972-1973.

IVEY, Glenn F.
Preston Gates Ellis & Rouvelas Meeds
1735 New York Ave., N.W., Suite 500, Washington, DC 20006-4759
Telephone: (202) 628-1700
Registered as lobbyist at U.S. Congress.
Background: Former Legislative Assistant to Rep, John Conyers, Jr. (D-MI).

IVEY, Hilma Lou
Associate Executive, Nat'l Counsel Associates
421 New Jersey Ave., S.E., Washington, DC 20003
Telephone: (202) 547-5000
Registered as lobbyist at U.S. Congress.
Clients:
Tosco Corp.

IVINS, PHILLIPS AND BARKER
1700 Pennsylvania Ave., N.W., Suite 600, Washington, DC 20006
Telephone: (202) 393-7600
Background: A law firm specializing in tax matters.
Members of firm representing listed organizations:
Dunn, H. Stewart (Jr.)
Fox, Eric R.
Glasmann, Jay W.
Background: Ass't General Counsel, Treasury Dep't, 1959. Ass't to Secretary of the Treasury, 1959-61.
Keenan, Laurie E.
Morrison, Philip D.
Background: Counsel, Senate Finance Committee, 1981-83.
O'Brien, Kevin P.
Rumph, Alan D.
Savage, Carroll J.
Sollee, William
Solomon, Michael F.
Clients:
American Textile Manufacturers Institute *(Jay W. Glasmann, Philip D. Morrison)*
Digital Equipment Corp. *(Jay W. Glasmann, Philip D. Morrison)*
Employee Relocation Council *(Jay W. Glasmann, Alan D. Rumph)*
Family Holding Co. Advocacy Group *(Philip D. Morrison)*
Oberlin College *(Philip D. Morrison)*
Rochester Tax Council *(H. Stewart Dunn, Jr., Philip D. Morrison)*
The Limited, Inc. *(Michael F. Solomon)*

IVORY, Elenora Gidding
Director, Washington Office, Presbyterian Church (U.S.A.)
110 Maryland Ave., N.E., Washington, DC 20002
Telephone: (202) 543-1126

IWANCIW, Eugene M.
Director, Washington Office, Ukrainian Nat'l Ass'n
400 First St., N.W. Suite 710, Washington, DC 20001
Telephone: (202) 347-8629
Background: Special Assistant: Social Security Administration (1986-88), Office of Personnel Management (1986), Housing and Urban Development (1986); Professional Staff, Senate Select Committee on Intelligence (1981-85);

Legislative Assistant, Sen. Harrison Schmitt (R-NM); Staff Asst., Sen. James Buckley (C-NY), (1971-72 & 75-77).

J T & A, INC.
1000 Connecticut Ave., N.W., Suite 300, Washington, DC 20036
Telephone: (202) 833-3380
Members of firm representing listed organizations:
Taggart, Judith F., President
Clients:
North American Lake Management Soc. *(Judith F. Taggart)*

JABARA, Abdeen
President, American-Arab Anti-Discrimination Committee
4201 Connecticut Ave., N.W. Suite 500, Washington, DC 20009
Telephone: (202) 244-2990
Background: Serves also as President, Middle East Women's and Children's Fund.

JABLON, Robert A.
Spiegel and McDiarmid
1350 New York Ave., N.W., Suite 1100, Washington, DC 20005
Telephone: (202) 879-4000
Registered as lobbyist at U.S. Congress.

JACKMAN, Dennis
Director, Legislative Affairs, Schering-Plough Corp.
1850 K St., N.W. Suite 1195, Washington, DC 20006
Telephone: (202) 463-7372
Registered as lobbyist at U.S. Congress.
Background: Former Legislative Assistant to Senator Arlen Specter (R-PA).

JACKMAN, William E.
Asst. V. President, Public Information, Air Transport Ass'n of America
1709 New York Ave., N.W., Washington, DC 20006-5206
Telephone: (202) 626-4000

JACKS, Maston T.
V. President, Legal & External Affairs, Inova Health Systems
8001 Braddock Road, Springfield, VA 22151
Telephone: (703) 321-4213

JACKSON, Alice M.
Assoc. Director, Policy Analysis, Nat'l Ass'n of Community Health Centers
1330 New Hampshire Ave., N.W. Suite 122, Washington, DC 20036
Telephone: (202) 659-8008

JACKSON, Benjamin R.
TechLaw
14500 Avion Pkwy. Suite 300, Chantilly, VA 22021
Telephone: (703) 263-7327
Registered as lobbyist at U.S. Congress.
Background: Formerly Deputy Assistant Administrator, U.S. Environmental Protection Agency.

JACKSON, Betty Ruth
Treasurer, Seaboard System Railroad Political Action Committee
1331 Pennsylvania Ave., N.W. Suite 560, Washington, DC 20004
Telephone: (202) 783-8124

JACKSON, Bobby J.
V. President, Human Resources, American Mining Congress
1920 N St., N.W. Suite 300, Washington, DC 20036
Telephone: (202) 861-2800
Registered as lobbyist at U.S. Congress.

JACKSON, C. R.
V. President for Gov't Affairs, Non Commissioned Officers Ass'n of the U.S.A.
225 North Washington St., Alexandria, VA 22314
Telephone: (703) 549-0311
Registered as lobbyist at U.S. Congress.

JACKSON, Carlton
External Liaison Director, American Petroleum Institute
1220 L St., N.W., Washington, DC 20005
Telephone: (202) 682-8280

JACKSON, Glenn F.
Asst. V. Pres., Legislative Affairs, Interstate Natural Gas Ass'n of America
555 13th St., N.W. Suite 300 West, Washington, DC 20004
Telephone: (202) 626-3200
Registered as lobbyist at U.S. Congress.

JACKSON, Jacquelyn L.
Director, Times Mirror Co.
1875 Eye St., N.W., Suite 1110, Washington, DC 20006
Telephone: (202) 293-3126
Registered as lobbyist at U.S. Congress.

JACKSON, James K.
Bishop, Cook, Purcell & Reynolds
1400 L St., N.W., Washington, DC 20005-3502
Telephone: (202) 371-5700
Registered as lobbyist at U.S. Congress.
Background: Attorney, Office of the Chief Counsel, Internal Revenue Service, 1966-70.
Clients:
Rohm and Haas Co.

JACKSON AND JESSUP, P.C.
3426 North Washington Blvd., Box 1240, Arlington, VA 22210
Telephone: (703) 525-4050
Members of firm representing listed organizations:
Jackson, William P. (Jr.), President and Senior Attorney
Background: Serves as Exec. Director, Southern Transportation League.
Clients:
Southern Transportation League, Inc. *(William P. Jackson, Jr.)*

JACKSON, Joseph C.
Exec. Director, Suppliers of Advanced Composite Materials Ass'n (SACMA)
1600 Wilson Blvd., Suite 1008, Arlington, VA 22209
Telephone: (703) 841-1556
Registered as lobbyist at U.S. Congress.

JACKSON, Julia
Government Affairs Representative, Nat'l Telephone Cooperative Ass'n
2626 Pennsylvania Ave., N.W., Washington, DC 20037
Telephone: (202) 298-2300
Registered as lobbyist at U.S. Congress.
Background: Former Chief Counsel to Senator John Breaux (D-LA).

JACKSON, Pamela Patrice
Capitol Associates, Inc.
426 C St., N.E., Washington, DC 20002
Telephone: (202) 544-1880

JACKSON, Rebecca L.
Baker and Hostetler
1050 Connecticut Ave., N.W. Suite 1100, Washington, DC 20036
Telephone: (202) 861-1500
Clients:
Soc. of Vascular Technology

JACKSON, Sheri
Manager, Federal Affairs, US WEST, Inc.
1020 19th St., N.W., Suite 700, Washington, DC 20036
Telephone: (202) 429-3100

JACKSON, Thad M., Ph.D.
Special Issues Director, Nestle Enterprises, Inc.
1511 K St., N.W., Suite 1100, Washington, DC 20005
Telephone: (202) 639-8894

JACKSON, William P., Jr.
President and Senior Attorney, Jackson and Jessup, P.C.
3426 North Washington Blvd., Box 1240, Arlington, VA 22210
Telephone: (703) 525-4050
Background: Serves as Exec. Director, Southern Transportation League.
Clients:
Southern Transportation League, Inc.

JACOB, Chuck
Manager, Government Affairs, Apple Computer, Inc.
1550 M St., N.W. Suite 1000, Washington, DC 20005

JACOB, Chuck (Cont'd)
Telephone: (202) 872-6260
Registered as lobbyist at U.S. Congress.

JACOBE, Dennis J.
Sr. V. Pres. & Director, Research Econ., United States
League of Savings Institutions
1709 New York Ave., N.W., Suite 801, Washington, DC
20006
Telephone: (202) 637-8900

JACOBS, Maj. Gen. Bruce
Asst. Exec. Director, Nat'l Guard Ass'n of the U.S.
One Massachusetts Ave., N.W., Washington, DC 20001
Telephone: (202) 789-0031

JACOBS, Jeffrey P.
Congressional Liaison, American Public Health Ass'n
1015 15th St., N.W. Third Floor, Washington, DC 20005
Telephone: (202) 789-5600
Registered as lobbyist at U.S. Congress.

JACOBS, Jerald A.
Jenner and Block
21 Dupont Circle, N.W., Washington, DC 20036
Telephone: (202) 223-4400
Registered as lobbyist at U.S. Congress.
Clients:
  Adhesive and Sealant Council
  American Film Marketing Ass'n
  American Soc. of Cataract and Refractive Surg-
  ery

JACOBS, Lois G.
Silver, Freedman & Taff
1735 Eye St., N.W., Washington, DC 20006
Telephone: (202) 429-6100
Registered as lobbyist at U.S. Congress.
Clients:
  Hiawatha Savings and Loan Ass'n

JACOBS, Lynn S.
Assistant V. President, Federal Affairs, CIGNA Corp.
1825 Eye St., N.W., Suite 750, Washington, DC 20006
Telephone: (202) 296-7174

JACOBS, Stephen I.
V. President, Congressional Liaison, Nat'l Ass'n of Broad-
casters
1771 N St., N.W., Washington, DC 20036
Telephone: (202) 429-5300
Registered as lobbyist at U.S. Congress.

JACOBSEN, John L.
Director, Government and Public Affairs, AMTRAK (Nat'l
Rail Passenger Corp.)
60 Massachusetts Ave., N.E., Washington, DC 20002
Telephone: (202) 906-3860

JACOBSEN, Mary Jeanne
Manager, Broadcast Media Relations, Nat'l Geographic
Soc.
1145 17th St., N.W., Washington, DC 20036
Telephone: (202) 857-7000

JACOBSEN, Raymond A., Jr.
Howrey and Simon
1730 Pennsylvania Ave., N.W., Washington, DC 20006-
4793
Telephone: (202) 783-0800
Background: Special Assistant to Senator William Roth,
Jr., 1971-74.
Clients:
  PepsiCo, Inc.

JACOBSON, Caroline
Contact, Bakery, Confectionery and Tobacco Workers Internat'l Union Political Action Committee
10401 Connecticut Ave., Kensington, MD 20895
Telephone: (301) 933-8600

JACOBSON, David E.
Reid & Priest
1111 19th St., N.W., Washington, DC 20036
Telephone: (202) 828-0100

JACOBSON, Kenneth
Public Affairs Manager, du Pont de Nemours and Co., E. I.
1701 Pennsylvania Ave., N.W., Suite 900, Washington, DC
20006

Telephone: (202) 728-3600

JACOBSON, Dr. Michael F.
Exec. Director, Center for Science in the Public Interest
1501 16th St., N.W., Washington, DC 20036
Telephone: (202) 332-9110

JACOBUS, Cheri
Director, Press and Media, Nat'l-American Wholesale Grocers' Ass'n
201 Park Washington Court, Falls Church, VA 22046
Telephone: (703) 532-9400
Background: Former Press Secretary and Legislative Assistant to Rep. Helen Bentley (R-MD).

JACOBY, Irene
V. President, Administration, Nat'l Legal Center for the
Public Interest
1000 16th St., N.W., Suite 301, Washington, DC 20036
Telephone: (202) 296-1683

JACOBY, Paul B.
Provorny, Jacoby & Robinson
1350 Connecticut Ave., Suite 502, Washington, DC 20036
Telephone: (202) 223-4200
Background: Staff Counsel, Office of the Chairman, Occu-
pational Safety and Health Review Commission, 1972-76.
Clients:
  Mycogen Corp.

JACQUEZ, Albert S.
President, Latin American Manufacturers Ass'n
419 New Jersey Ave., S.E., Washington, DC 20003
Telephone: (202) 546-3803

JACQUEZ, Lynnette R.
McAuliffe, Kelly, Raffaelli & Siemens
1341 G St., N.W. Suite 200, Washington, DC 20005
Telephone: (202) 783-1800
Registered as lobbyist at U.S. Congress.
Background: Former Staff Director, House Judiciary Immi-
gration Subcommittee.
Clients:
  China West
  Epoc Water, Inc.
  Latin American Management Ass'n
  Nat'l Jai Alai Ass'n
  Native American Industrial Trade Ass'n
  White Mountain Apache Tribe
  World Airways

JAENKE & ASSOCIATES, E. A.
777 14th St., Suite 666, Washington, DC 20005
Telephone: (202) 393-1793
Background: A consulting firm specializing in agricultural
and international matters.
Members of firm representing listed organizations:
  Cannon, Richard J.
  Jaenke, E. A., President
  Lowerre, Robert T.
Organizations represented:
  Nat'l Bank for Cooperatives *(Robert T. Lowerre)*
  Nat'l Cooperative Bank *(E. A. Jaenke)*
  Seaboard Corp. *(Richard J. Cannon)*

JAENKE, E. A.
President, Jaenke & Associates, E. A.
777 14th St., Suite 666, Washington, DC 20005
Telephone: (202) 393-1793
Registered as lobbyist at U.S. Congress.
Organizations represented:
  Nat'l Cooperative Bank

JAFFE, Daniel L.
Exec. V. President, Ass'n of Nat'l Advertisers
1725 K St., N.W., Suite 601, Washington, DC 20006
Telephone: (202) 785-1525
Registered as lobbyist at U.S. Congress.
Background: Formerly Counsel, U.S. Senate Commerce
Committee.

JAFFEE, Edward L.
Washington Rep. & Mgr., Wash. Office, PPG Industries
1730 Rhode Island Ave., N.W., Suite 715, Washington, DC
20036
Telephone: (202) 659-9894
Registered as lobbyist at U.S. Congress.

JAHN, Laurence R.
President, Wildlife Management Institute
1101 14th St., N.W., Suite 725, Washington, DC 20005
Telephone: (202) 371-1808

JAHSHAN, Khalil E.
Associate Exec. Director, Public Affairs, Nat'l Ass'n of
Arab Americans
2033 M St., N.W., Suite 300, Washington, DC 20036
Telephone: (202) 467-4800
Registered as lobbyist at U.S. Congress.

JALOSKY, Lynn A.
Treasurer, Ice Cream and Milk PAC
888 16th St., N.W. 2nd Floor, Washington, DC 20006
Telephone: (202) 296-4250

JAMES, C. L., III
Keefe Co., The
444 North Capitol St., N.W., Suite 711, Washington, DC
20001
Telephone: (202) 638-7030
Clients:
  Executive Leadership Council

JAMES, Clarence L., Jr.
President, Keefe Co., The
444 North Capitol St., N.W., Suite 711, Washington, DC
20001
Telephone: (202) 638-7030
Registered as lobbyist at U.S. Congress.
Clients:
  Ameri-Cable Internat'l, Inc.
  Aruba, Government of
  Bechtel Civil & Minerals, Inc.
  Broward County Governmental Center
  Hillsborough Area Regional Transit Authority
  Homewood Corp.
  Tampa, Florida, City of
  Westinghouse Transportation Division

JAMES, Claudia M.
V. President/Legal & Governmental Afrs., American
Newspaper Publishers Ass'n
The Newspaper Center 11600 Sunrise Valley Drive, Res-
ton, VA 22091
Telephone: (703) 648-1000
Registered as lobbyist at U.S. Congress.

JAMES, Dennis, Jr.
Kaplan, Russin and Vecchi
1215 17th St., N.W., Washington, DC 20036
Telephone: (202) 887-0353

JAMES, Luanne
Exec. Director, ADAPSO, the Computer Software & Ser-
vices Industry Ass'n
1300 North 17th St. Suite 300, Arlington, VA 22209
Telephone: (703) 522-5055
Background: Serves as contact for ADAPSO-PAC.

JAMES, Philip J.
Group Vice President & CEO, Nat'l Glass Ass'n
8200 Greensboro Drive Suite 302, McLean, VA 22102
Telephone: (703) 442-4890
Background: Serves also as contact for Nat'l Glass Ass'n
Political Action Committee.

JAMES, Robert L.
Cole, Raywid, and Braverman
1919 Pennsylvania Ave., N.W. Suite 200, Washington, DC
20006
Telephone: (202) 659-9750
Clients:
  United Video Inc.

JAMESON, Paul
Schagrin Associates
1112 16th St., N.W. Suite 1000, Washington, DC 20036
Telephone: (202) 223-1700

JAMIESON, Ballard J., Jr.
Laxalt Group, The Paul
1455 Pennsylvania Ave., N.W., Suite 975, Washington, DC
20004
Telephone: (202) 624-0640

JANATA, Gloria
V. President, Health Care, Hill and Knowlton Public Affairs Worldwide
Washington Harbour, 901 31st St., N.W., Washington, DC 20007
Telephone: (202) 333-7400

JANDROWITZ, Frank J.
V. President, Field Operations, American Petroleum Institute
1220 L St., N.W., Washington, DC 20005
Telephone: (202) 682-8200

JANGER, Stephen A.
President, Close Up Foundation
1235 Jefferson Davis Hwy., Arlington, VA 22202
Telephone: (703) 892-5400

JANKA, Leslie A.
Neill and Co.
815 Connecticut Ave., N.W. Suite 800, Washington, DC 20006
Telephone: (202) 463-8877
Registered as lobbyist at U.S. Congress.
Registered as Foreign Agent: (#3320).
Background: Special Assistant, National Security Council, 1971-75. Assistant Secretary, U.S. Department of Defense, 1976-78.
Clients:
Guinea, Government of
Jordan, Hashemite Kingdom of

JANKOWSKY, Joel
Akin, Gump, Strauss, Hauer and Feld
1333 New Hampshire Ave., N.W., Suite 400, Washington, DC 20036
Telephone: (202) 887-4000
Registered as lobbyist at U.S. Congress.
Background: Legislative Assistant to the Speaker, U.S. House of Representatives, 1972-76.
Clients:
Bank of Nova Scotia
Boone Co.
Buckeye Pipe Line Co.
California Institue of Technology
Cambridge Information Group
Citizens and Southern Corp.
CRSS Constructors, Inc.
Eastern Air Lines
First City Bancorporation of Texas
Fujitsu America, Inc.
Guardian Savings and Loan Ass'n
Harris County, Metropolitan Transit Authority of
Houston Oilers
Hoylake Investments Ltd.
Industrial Indemnity Financial Corp.
Kiewit Sons, Inc., Peter
Loral/Fairchild Systems
Martin Marietta Corp.
Mesa Limited Partnership
Minnesota Power
Morgan Stanley and Co.
Nat'l Health Laboratories
News America
Pillsbury Co.
R. Lacey, Inc.
Sara Lee Corp.
Southern California Edison Co.
Staley Manufacturing Co., A. E.
Texas Education Agency
Zink and Co., John

JANOPANL, Mona M.
Attorney, Consumers Power Co.
Telephone: (202) 293-5795

JANSSON, Erik T.
Coordinator, Nat'l Network to Prevent Birth Defects
Box 15309 Southeast Station, Washington, DC 20003
Telephone: (202) 543-5450

JAQUAY, Joseph N.
Research Director, Amalgamated Transit Union
5025 Wisconsin Ave., N.W., Washington, DC 20016
Telephone: (202) 537-1645

JAR-MON CONSULTANTS, INC.
214 Massachusetts Ave., N.E. Suite 300, Washington, DC 20002

Telephone: (202) 547-7150
Members of firm representing listed organizations:
Jarmin, Gary L., President
Background: Serves also as Chairman, American Council for Free Asia.
Jarmin, Gina, Senior V. President
Smyth, Matthew D., V. President
Clients:
American Council for Free Asia *(Matthew D. Smyth)*

JARDOT, Leo C.
Sr. Director and Counsel, Fed. Relations, American Home Products Corp.
1726 M St., N.W., Suite 1001, Washington, DC 20036
Telephone: (202) 659-8320

JARMAN, Rufus E., Jr.
Barnes, Richardson and Colburn
1819 H St., N.W., Washington, DC 20006
Telephone: (202) 457-0300
Registered as lobbyist at U.S. Congress.
Clients:
Alfa Romeo, Inc.
Australian Wool Corp.
Bowe Maschinenfabrik GmbH
IPSCO Inc.
Meat Importers Council of America

JARMIN, Gary L.
President, Jar-Mon Consultants, Inc.
214 Massachusetts Ave., N.E. Suite 300, Washington, DC 20002
Telephone: (202) 547-7150
Registered as lobbyist at U.S. Congress.
Background: Serves also as Chairman, American Council for Free Asia.

JARMIN, Gina
Senior V. President, Jar-Mon Consultants, Inc.
214 Massachusetts Ave., N.E. Suite 300, Washington, DC 20002
Telephone: (202) 547-7150
Registered as lobbyist at U.S. Congress.

JARTMAN, Marc R.
V. Pres., Gov't Affairs and Marketing, UNC Incorporated
175 Admiral Cochrane Drive, Annapolis, MD 21401-7333
Telephone: (301) 266-7333
Registered as lobbyist at U.S. Congress.

JARVIS, Patricia J.
Gold and Liebengood, Inc.
1455 Pennsylvania Ave., N.W. Suite 950, Washington, DC 20004
Telephone: (202) 639-8899
Registered as lobbyist at U.S. Congress.
Background: Former Special Assistant, Office of Legislation, U.S. Department of Health and Human Services.

JARVIS, Sonia R., Esq.
Exec. Director, Nat'l Coalition on Black Voter Participation, Inc.
1101 14th St., N.W., Suite 925, Washington, DC 20005
Telephone: (202) 898-2220

JASEN, Edward
7826 Eastern Ave., N.W. Suite 304, Washington, DC 20012
Telephone: (202) 723-1900
Background: An attorney.
Organizations represented:
Internat'l Ass'n of Independent Producers

JASINOWSKI, Jerry J.
President, Nat'l Ass'n of Manufacturers
1331 Pennsylvania Ave., N.W. Suite 1500 North, Washington, DC 20004-1703
Telephone: (202) 637-3000
Registered as lobbyist at U.S. Congress.
Background: Former Assistant Secretary of Commerce for Policy.

JASINSKI, Robert J.
Public Relations Manager, NYNEX
1828 L St., N.W., Suite 1000, Washington, DC 20036
Telephone: (202) 416-0100

JASKIEWICZ, Leonard A.
Grove, Jaskiewicz, Gilliam and Cobert
1730 M St., N.W. Suite 501, Washington, DC 20036
Telephone: (202) 296-2900
Clients:
Bulk Carrier Conference, Inc.
Intermodal Transportation Ass'n

JAUSSI, Judy
Washington Rep, Health & Welfare, California, State of
444 North Capitol St., N.W., Suite 305, Washington, DC 20001
Telephone: (202) 347-6891

JAWER, Michael A.
Legislative Director, Building Owners and Managers Ass'n Internat'l
1201 New York Ave., N.W. Suite 300, Washington, DC 20005
Telephone: (202) 289-7000
Registered as lobbyist at U.S. Congress.
Background: Former aide to Sen. Donald Riegle (D-MI).

JAY, Dennis
Asst. V. President, Communications, Nat'l Ass'n of Professional Insurance Agents
400 North Washington St., Alexandria, VA 22314
Telephone: (703) 836-9340

JAZZO, Frank R.
Fletcher, Heald and Hildreth
1225 Connecticut Ave., N.W. Suite 400, Washington, DC 20036
Telephone: (202) 828-5700

JCLD CONSULTANCY
1000 Potomac St., N.W., Suite 102-A, Washington, DC 20007
Telephone: (202) 965-6685
Members of firm representing listed organizations:
Donaldson, John C. L.
Background: Editor, EuroMarket Digest.
Clients:
Eurofer *(John C. L. Donaldson)*

JEFFERS, Gene
V. Pres., Public Affrs. & Communications, Nat'l Ass'n of Broadcasters
1771 N St., N.W., Washington, DC 20036
Telephone: (202) 429-5300

JEFFERS, Margaret O.
Exec. Director, Apartment and Office Building Ass'n of Metropolitan Washington
Suite 600, 1413 K St., N.W., Washington, DC 20005
Telephone: (202) 289-1717
Registered as lobbyist at U.S. Congress.

JEFFERSON GROUP, THE
1341 G St., N.W., Suite 1100, Washington, DC 20005
Telephone: (202) 638-3535
Background: A public affairs, lobbying, regulatory affairs and marketing consultant firm.
Members of firm representing listed organizations:
Barrett, Michael, V. President
Cabral, Debra
Background: Former aide to Rep. Thomes P. O'Neill, Jr. (D-MA).
Carlstrom, Robert (Jr.)
Background: Formerly with Office of Management and Budget.
Cowan, Mark D., Chief Executive Officer
Background: Former Assistant Legislative Counsel, Central Intelligence Agency and former chief of staff to ex-Secretary of Labor, Raymond Donovan.
Coy, John, Senior V. President
Crow, David T., V. President, Legislative Affairs
Davis, Jana
Davis, Susan, Account Executive
Background: Former Chief Counsel, House Committee on Agriculture.
Eisenberg, Ron, Senior V. President, Public Relations
Hannett, Frederick J.
Harris, Robert L., V. President, Legislative Affairs
Isaacson, Sandra
Background: Former staff member, Senate Committee on Veterans' Affairs.

JEFFERSON GROUP, THE (Cont'd)

Johnson, Stephen M., Senior V. President
McLaughlin, Carolyn
Nutter, Jack O., Sr. V. President, Dir Legis. Affairs
  Background: Minority Tax Counsel, Senate Finance Committee, 1977-80.
Ortiz-Daliot, Jose, V. President, Inter-American Affairs
  Background: Former Director, Puerto Rico Federal Affairs Administration.
Schumacher, Randal, V. Pres., Occ. Safety, Health & Environ.
Serwer, David
Susman, Julie, V. President
Upston, John
Wheeler, Porter, V. President
Wolf, James W., V. President
  Background: Legislative Director to then-Senator Dan Quayle (R-IN), 1981-83.
  Clients:
  Alumax, Inc. *(Robert L. Harris)*
  American Health Care Advisory Ass'n *(Frederick J. Hannett)*
  B E & K Daycare *(Ron Eisenberg)*
  Bell Atlantic *(Frederick J. Hannett)*
  Boonestroo, Rosene, Anderlik & Associates *(Mark D. Cowan, Julie Susman)*
  Bridgeway Plan for Health *(David Serwer)*
  Carolina, Puerto Rico, City of *(Jose Ortiz-Daliot)*
  Children's Health System, Inc. *(Frederick J. Hannett)*
  Children's Survival Plan *(John Coy)*
  Cleartel Communication *(Ron Eisenberg)*
  Conundrum Joint Venture *(Robert Carlstrom, Jr.)*
  Direct Health, Inc. *(David Serwer)*
  Doe Run Co. *(Robert L. Harris)*
  du Pont de Nemours and Co., E. I. *(John Coy)*
  Georgia-Pacific Corp. *(Randal Schumacher)*
  Gerson and Co., L. M. *(Mark D. Cowan)*
  Gibraltar, P.R., Inc. *(Frederick J. Hannett)*
  Gurabo, Puerto Rico, City of *(Jose Ortiz-Daliot)*
  H.S.I. *(Julie Susman)*
  Health Management Strategies, Internat'l *(David Serwer)*
  HIP Network of Florida *(David Serwer)*
  Horsehead Resource Development Co. *(Robert L. Harris)*
  Independent Health Plan *(Frederick J. Hannett)*
  Industrial Safety Equipment Ass'n *(Mark D. Cowan)*
  Inter-American University *(Jose Ortiz-Daliot)*
  Internat'l Lead Zinc Research Organization *(Robert Carlstrom, Jr.)*
  Investment Partnership Ass'n *(Porter Wheeler)*
  Lipman Hearne *(Ron Eisenberg)*
  Lockheed Corp. *(David T. Crow, Robert L. Harris, Jack O. Nutter)*
  Maxicare HealthPlans, Inc. *(Frederick J. Hannett)*
  Minnesota Mining and Manufacturing Co. (3M Co.) *(Mark D. Cowan, Randal Schumacher)*
  Peat Marwick *(Frederick J. Hannett)*
  Pittston Co., The *(Mark D. Cowan, Jack O. Nutter)*
  Planning Research Corp. *(Julie Susman)*
  Preferred Health *(Frederick J. Hannett)*
  Puerto Rico Department of Justice *(Jose Ortiz-Daliot)*
  San Juan, Puerto Rico, City of *(Jose Ortiz-Daliot)*
  Scott and Sons, O. M. *(David T. Crow, Jack O. Nutter)*
  Si.A.C./Italy *(Jose Ortiz-Daliot, John Upston)*
  Simpson Paper Co. *(Randal Schumacher)*
  St. Ambrose University *(John Coy)*
  Tidewater Health Care *(Frederick J. Hannett, David Serwer)*
  Total Health Plan *(David Serwer)*
  Trujillo Alto, Puerto Rico, City of *(Jose Ortiz-Daliot)*
  Zinc Corp. of America

JEFFREY, David

Public Affairs Director, Airline Passengers of America
4212 King St., Alexandria, VA 22302
Telephone: (703) 824-0505

JEFFREY, Dennis

President, Designers & Planners, Inc.
2611 Jefferson Davis Highway, Suite 3000, Arlington, VA 22202
Telephone: (703) 418-3800

JEFFREY, Joseph A.

Vice President, Taxation, American Mining Congress
1920 N St., N.W. Suite 300, Washington, DC 20036
Telephone: (202) 861-2800
Registered as lobbyist at U.S. Congress.

JEFFREYS, Steven Kent

Energy and Environmental Policy Analyst, Heritage Foundation
214 Massachusetts Ave., N.E., Washington, DC 20002
Telephone: (202) 546-4400

JEFFRIES, Craig S.

Exec Dir & Gen Couns, Home Care Mkt Grp, Health Industry Distributors Ass'n
225 Reinekers Lane, Suite 650, Alexandria, VA 22314
Telephone: (703) 549-4432

JEFORD-McMANUS INTERNAT'L, INC.

513 Capitol Court, N.E., Suite 300, Washington, DC 20002
Telephone: (202) 546-0073
Background: A government affairs consulting firm.
Members of firm representing listed organizations:
  Ford, John J., President
  McManus, Paul E., Exec. V. President

JEHLE, Philip F.

Washington Office Director, Pennsylvania, Commonwealth of
444 N. Capitol St., N.W., Suite 700, Washington, DC 20001
Telephone: (202) 624-7828

JELLINEK, SCHWARTZ, CONNOLLY & FRESHMAN, INC.

1015 15th St., N.W. Suite 500, Washington, DC 20005
Telephone: (202) 789-8181
Background: A consulting firm on environmental, health and energy issues.
Members of firm representing listed organizations:
  Connolly, Stephen J.
  Freshman, John D.
  Jellinek, Steven D., Principal
    Background: Former Assistant Administrator of Pesticides and Toxic Substances, Environmental Protection Agency and Former Staff Director, Council on Environmental Quality.
  Schwartz, Jeffrey H.
  Clients:
  ASARCO Incorporated *(Jeffrey H. Schwartz)*
  Coors Brewing Company *(John D. Freshman)*
  Los Angeles County Sanitation District *(John D. Freshman)*
  Nat'l Ass'n of Wheat Growers *(Steven D. Jellinek)*
  Nat'l Independent Energy Producers *(Jeffrey H. Schwartz)*
  Rhone-Poulenc Ag Co. *(Steven D. Jellinek)*

JELLINEK, Steven D.

Principal, Jellinek, Schwartz, Connolly & Freshman, Inc.
1015 15th St., N.W. Suite 500, Washington, DC 20005
Telephone: (202) 789-8181
Background: Former Assistant Administrator of Pesticides and Toxic Substances, Environmental Protection Agency and Former Staff Director, Council on Environmental Quality.
  Clients:
  Nat'l Ass'n of Wheat Growers
  Rhone-Poulenc Ag Co.

JENCKES, Joseph S.

Vice President, Washington, Abbott Laboratories
1710 Rhode Island Ave., N.W. Suite 300, Washington, DC 20036
Telephone: (202) 659-8524
Registered as lobbyist at U.S. Congress.
Background: Assistant U.S. Attorney, Dep't of Justice, 1969-1973. Admin. Assistant to Senator Paul Fannin (Arizona), 1973-1975. Special Assistant to President Ford, Legislative Affairs (Senate), 1976.

JENCKES, Linda

Vice President, Federal Affairs, Health Insurance Ass'n of America
1025 Connecticut Ave., N.W. Suite 1200, Washington, DC 20036
Telephone: (202) 223-7780
Registered as lobbyist at U.S. Congress.

JENKINS, Barry L.

Director of Communications, Nat'l Ass'n of Wheat Growers
415 Second St., N.E. Suite 300, Washington, DC 20002
Telephone: (202) 547-7800

JENKINS, David M.

V. President, Federal Gov't Affairs, SmithKline Beecham
1020 19th St., N.W., Suite 420, Washington, DC 20036
Telephone: (202) 452-8490
Registered as lobbyist at U.S. Congress.

JENKINS, James F.

Advisory Board Chairperson, Nat'l Soc. of Black Engineers
344 Commerce St., Alexandria, VA 22314
Telephone: (703) 549-2207

JENKINS, Judy P.

Dykema Gossett
1752 N St., N.W., 6th Floor, Washington, DC 20036
Telephone: (202) 466-7185
  Clients:
  Military Boot Manufacturers Ass'n

JENKINS, Pamela

Account Executive, Bario Associates, Patricia
512 11th St., S.E., Washington, DC 20003
Telephone: (202) 543-0923
Organizations represented:
  History Factory, The

JENNER AND BLOCK

21 Dupont Circle, N.W., Washington, DC 20036
Telephone: (202) 223-4400
Background: Washington office of a Chicago law firm.
Members of firm representing listed organizations:
  Jacobs, Jerald A.
  Nadler, Carl
  Clients:
  Adhesive and Sealant Council *(Jerald A. Jacobs)*
  American Ass'n of Electromyography and Electrodiagnosis
  American Dental Trade Ass'n
  American Diabetes Ass'n
  American Film Marketing Ass'n *(Jerald A. Jacobs)*
  American Soc. of Cataract and Refractive Surgery *(Jerald A. Jacobs)*
  Dental Gold Institute
  Internat'l Soc. for Hybrid Microelectronics
  Nat'l Glass Ass'n

JENNINGS, Carole P., Ph.D.

American Academy of Nurse Practitioners
8904 1st Ave., Silver Spring, MD 20910
Telephone: (301) 726-3794
Registered as lobbyist at U.S. Congress.

JENNINGS, Horace, III

Staff Consultant, Neill and Co.
815 Connecticut Ave., N.W. Suite 800, Washington, DC 20006
Telephone: (202) 463-8877
Registered as lobbyist at U.S. Congress.
Registered as Foreign Agent: (# 3320).
Background: Legislative Assistant to Senator Lloyd Bentsen (D-TX), 1983-85. Attorney Advisor, Board of Veterans Appeals, Veterans Administration, 1985-87.

JENNINGS, James C.

General Manager, Hill and Knowlton Public Affairs Worldwide
Washington Harbour, 901 31st St., N.W., Washington, DC 20007
Telephone: (202) 333-7400
  Clients:
  ITT Corp.

JENNINGS, Mary L.

Legis Counsel, MERIT SYSTEMS PROTECTION BOARD
1120 Vermont Ave., N.W., Washington, DC 20419
Telephone: (202) 653-7162

JENSEN & CO.

2000 Pennsylvania Ave., N.W. Suite 3580, Washington, DC 20006
Telephone: (202) 833-3580
Background: A public relations/political consulting firm.

Members of firm representing listed organizations:
Brown, Michael G., V. President
Jensen, Ronald R., Chairman
Background: Formerly associated with the George Bush presidential campaign, The Fund for America's Future and the Reagan-Bush '84 re-election campaign.
Clients:
Commission on Minority Business Development
(*Michael G. Brown, Ronald R. Jensen*)
Earth Corps (*Michael G. Brown, Ronald R. Jensen*)
Maxima Corp. (*Michael G. Brown, Ronald R. Jensen*)

JENSEN, Frank L., Jr.
President, Helicopter Ass'n Internat'l
1619 Duke St., Alexandria, VA 22314-3406
Telephone: (703) 683-4646

JENSEN, Robert E.
Williams and Jensen, P.C.
1101 Connecticut Ave., N.W., Suite 500, Washington, DC 20036
Telephone: (202) 659-8201

JENSEN, Ronald R.
Chairman, Jensen & Co.
2000 Pennsylvania Ave., N.W. Suite 3580, Washington, DC 20006
Telephone: (202) 833-3580
Background: Formerly associated with the George Bush presidential campaign, The Fund for America's Future and the Reagan-Bush '84 re-election campaign.
Clients:
Commission on Minority Business Development
Earth Corps
Maxima Corp.

JERSEY, Ira F., Jr.
I and J Associates
648 Anderson Hall 4400 Massachusetts Ave., N.W., Washington, DC 20016-8101
Telephone: (202) 885-7953
Registered as lobbyist at U.S. Congress.
Clients:
Mixmor, Inc.
Public Image Printing
Public Images
T and J Electronics

JESSAMY, Howard T.
President, District of Columbia Hospital Ass'n
1250 Eye St., N.W., Suite 700, Washington, DC 20005-3922
Telephone: (202) 682-1581

JESSICK, Nancy H.
Director of Government Affairs, Hiram Walker and Sons, Inc.
1331 Pennsylvania Ave., N.W., Suite 720, Washington, DC 20004
Telephone: (202) 628-5877
Registered as lobbyist at U.S. Congress.

JETTON, C. Loring, Jr.
Wilmer, Cutler and Pickering
2445 M St., N.W., Washington, DC 20037-1420
Telephone: (202) 663-6000
Registered as Foreign Agent: (#3355).

JEWELL & ASSOCIATES, David A.
1615 M St., N.W. Suite 730, Washington, DC 20036
Telephone: (202) 659-6506
Members of firm representing listed organizations:
Jewell, David A., President
Organizations represented:
Earthquake Project, The (*David A. Jewell*)

JEWELL, David A.
President, Jewell & Associates, David A.
1615 M St., N.W. Suite 730, Washington, DC 20036
Telephone: (202) 659-6506
Organizations represented:
Earthquake Project, The

JEWELL-KELLY, Starla
Exec. Director, Nat'l Community Education Ass'n
801 N. Fairfax St. Suite 209, Alexandria, VA 22314

JIGGETTS, Chuck
Government Affairs Representative, Electronic Data Systems Corp.
1331 Pennsylvania Ave., N.W., Suite 1300 North, Washington; DC 20004
Telephone: (202) 637-6700
Registered as lobbyist at U.S. Congress.

JIMERSON, Melva
Legislative Associate, Church of the Brethren
110 Maryland Ave., N.E., Washington, DC 20002
Telephone: (202) 546-3202

JOE, Tom
Director, Washington Office, Center for the Study of Social Policy
1250 Eye St., N.W., Suite 503, Washington, DC 20005
Telephone: (202) 371-1565

JOFFE, Bruce
Director of Communications, Screen Printing Ass'n Internat'l
10015 Main St., Fairfax, VA 22031-3489
Telephone: (703) 385-1335

JOHANNSSEN, Howard E.
President, Professional Airways Systems Specialists
444 North Capitol St., N.W., Suite 840, Washington, DC 20001
Telephone: (202) 347-6065

JOHANSEN, Eivind H.
President, Nat'l Industries for the Severely Handicapped
2235 Cedar Lane, Vienna, VA 22182
Telephone: (703) 560-6800

JOHNS AND CARSON
12501 Old Columbia Pike, Silver Spring, MD 20904
Telephone: (301) 680-6320
Members of firm representing listed organizations:
Carson, Walter E.
Johns, Warren L.
Nixon, Robert W.
Wetmore, Thomas E.
Clients:
Adventist Development and Relief Agency Internat'l
Adventist Health System/United States
General Conference of Seventh-day Adventists
Internat'l Religious Liberty Ass'n
Loma Linda Foods
Loma Linda University
Pacific Press Publishing Ass'n
Review and Herald Publishing Co.

JOHNS, Michael
Policy Analyst, Third World & Africa, Heritage Foundation
214 Massachusetts Ave., N.E., Washington, DC 20002
Telephone: (202) 546-4400

JOHNS, Warren L.
Johns and Carson
12501 Old Columbia Pike, Silver Spring, MD 20904
Telephone: (301) 680-6320

JOHNSEN, Dawn
Legal Research Director, Nat'l Abortion Rights Action League
1101 14th St., N.W., Suite 500, Washington, DC 20005
Telephone: (202) 371-0779

JOHNSEN, Ronald P.
Legislative Representative, Columbia Gas System Service Corp.
1250 Eye St., N.W., Suite 703, Washington, DC 20005
Telephone: (202) 842-7407
Registered as lobbyist at U.S. Congress.

JOHNSON, A. Sidney, III
Exec. Director, American Public Welfare Ass'n
810 First St., N.E., Suite 300, Washington, DC 20002
Telephone: (202) 682-0100

JOHNSON, Arnold C.
Hogan and Hartson
555 13th St., N.W., Suite 1200, Washington, DC 20004-1109
Telephone: (202) 637-5600

Background: Attorney, Legal Advisory Staff, U.S. Treasury Department, 1954-56. Attorney, staff of the Joint Committee on Internal Revenue Taxation, 1956-59.

JOHNSON & ASSOCIATES, INC.
3240 North Albemarle St., Arlington, VA 22207
Telephone: (703) 241-0727
Members of firm representing listed organizations:
Johnson, James H.
Background: Also associated with Cassidy and Associates, Inc. Special Assistant to Secretary, USDA, 1981-82; Deputy Undersecretary, USDA, 1982-1984.
Clients:
Commodity Storage, Ltd. (*James H. Johnson*)

JOHNSON, Betsy
Exec. Director, Washington Council of Agencies
1001 Connecticut Ave., N.W. Sute 925, Washington, DC 20036
Telephone: (202) 457-0540

JOHNSON, Beverley
Exec. Director, Ass'n for the Care of Children's Health
3615 Wisconsin Ave., N.W., Washington, DC 20016
Telephone: (202) 244-1801

JOHNSON, Brad C.
Director, Office of Federal Affairs, New York, State of
444 N. Capitol St., N.W. Suite 301, Washington, DC 20001
Telephone: (202) 638-1311

JOHNSON, Bradley
Exec. Director, Public Risk and Insurance Management Ass'n
1117 19th St. North Suite 900, Arlington, VA 22209
Telephone: (703) 528-7701

JOHNSON, Calvin P.
Legislative Representative, AFL-CIO (American Federation of Labor and Congress of Industrial Organizations)
815 16th St., N.W., Washington, DC 20006
Telephone: (202) 637-5075
Registered as lobbyist at U.S. Congress.

JOHNSON, Carl T.
President, Compressed Gas Ass'n
1235 Jefferson Davis Hwy., Arlington, VA 22202
Telephone: (703) 979-0900
Registered as lobbyist at U.S. Congress.
Background: Former Special Assistant to Rep. Amory Houghton, Jr. (R-NY). Serves also as Chairman of the Helium Advisory Council of the Compressed Gas Ass'n.

JOHNSON, Carolyn I.
Legis Aide, INTERSTATE COMMERCE COMMISSION
12th and Constitution Ave. N.W., Washington, DC 20423
Telephone: (202) 275-7231

JOHNSON, Cliff
Director, Family Support, Children's Defense Fund
122 C St., N.W., Washington, DC 20001
Telephone: (202) 628-8787

JOHNSON, Cynthia
Washington Government Affairs Manager, Hewlett-Packard Co.
900 17th St., N.W. Suite 1100, Washington, DC 20006
Telephone: (202) 785-7943

JOHNSON, Dallas
President, Health and Education Resources
4733 Bethesda Ave., Suite 735, Bethesda, MD 20814
Telephone: (301) 656-3178

JOHNSON, Darwin G.
Policy Economics Group of KPMG Peat Marwick
2001 M St., N.W., Washington, DC 20036
Telephone: (202) 467-3818
Background: Former Chief, Fiscal Analysis Branch, Office of Management and Budget.

JOHNSON, David E.
Griffin, Johnson & Associates
1211 Connecticut Ave., N.W., Suite 700, Washington, DC 20036
Telephone: (202) 775-8116
Registered as lobbyist at U.S. Congress.
Background: Former Executive Director, Democratic Senatorial Campaign Committee, 1985-86; Administrative Assistant to Senator George Mitchell (D-ME); Deputy

JOHNSON, David E. (Cont'd)
Assistant Secretary, Department of Health and Human Services; Counsel, U.S. Governmental Affairs Committee, U.S. Senate.
Clients:
Blue Cross and Blue Shield Ass'n
Grumman Corp.
Outdoor Advertising Ass'n of America

JOHNSON, Dr. David H.
Exec. Director, Federation of Behavioral, Psychological and Cognitive Sciences
1200 17th St., N.W., Room 517, Washington, DC 20036
Telephone: (202) 955-7758
Registered as lobbyist at U.S. Congress.

JOHNSON, David T.
Research Director, Center for Defense Information
1500 Massachusetts Ave., N.W., Washington, DC 20005
Telephone: (202) 862-0700

JOHNSON, Douglas
Legislative Director, Nat'l Right to Life Committee
419 7th St., N.W. Suite 500, Washington, DC 20004
Telephone: (202) 626-8820
Registered as lobbyist at U.S. Congress.

JOHNSON & GIBBS, P.C.
1001 Pennsylvania Ave., N.W. Suite 745, Washington, DC 20004
Telephone: (202) 682-4500
Members of firm representing listed organizations:
Collins, Bryan P.
Gibbs, Lawrence B.
Glickman, David G., Managing Director, Washington Office
Background: With Chief Counsel's Office, Internal Revenue Service, 1964-68. Deputy Assistant Secretary of the Treasury, Tax Policy, 1981-83.
Miller, Evan
Sacher, Steven J.
Background: Associate Solicitor of Labor, ERISA, 1974-77. Special Counsel for ERISA, 1977-80 and General Counsel, 1980-81 U.S. Senate Committee on Labor and Human Resources.
Stark, Richard C.
Tour, Jeffrey H.
Clients:
Centex Corp. *(David G. Glickman)*
Church Alliance *(David G. Glickman)*
Compaq Computer *(David G. Glickman)*
EPIC Healthcare Group, Inc. *(David G. Glickman)*
Oryx Energy Co. *(David G. Glickman)*
Permanente Medical Group, Inc., The *(Bryan P. Collins, Lawrence B. Gibbs, David G. Glickman, Richard C. Stark)*
Redmond Industries *(Evan Miller, Steven J. Sacher)*
Republic Health Corp. *(David G. Glickman)*

JOHNSON, Gregory N.
Legislative Counsel, NTEA/Bankers Committee, The
1629 K St., N.W., Suite 1000, Washington, DC 20036
Telephone: (202) 466-8308
Registered as lobbyist at U.S. Congress.

JOHNSON, Jacquelyn M.
Manager, Environmental Affairs, Grace and Co., W. R.
919 18th St., N.W., Suite 400, Washington, DC 20006
Telephone: (202) 452-6700

JOHNSON, James A. R.
Director of Government Affairs, Apple Computer, Inc.
1550 M St., N.W. Suite 1000, Washington, DC 20005
Telephone: (202) 872-6260
Registered as lobbyist at U.S. Congress.

JOHNSON, James H.
Johnson & Associates, Inc.
3240 North Albemarle St., Arlington, VA 22207
Telephone: (703) 241-0727
Registered as lobbyist at U.S. Congress.
Background: Also associated with Cassidy and Associates, Inc. Special Assistant to Secretary, USDA, 1981-82; Deputy Undesecretary, USDA, 1982-1984.
Clients:
Commodity Storage, Ltd.

JOHNSON, James R.
Acting Manager, Washington Office, Electric Power Research Institute
1019 19th St., N.W., Washington, DC 20036
Telephone: (202) 872-9222

JOHNSON, James W., Jr.
Director, Public Affairs, United States Beet Sugar Ass'n
1156 15th St., N.W., Washington, DC 20005
Telephone: (202) 296-4820
Registered as lobbyist at U.S. Congress.

JOHNSON, Janet Lee
Arnold & Porter
1200 New Hampshire Ave., N.W., Washington, DC 20036
Telephone: (202) 872-6700

JOHNSON, Jed, Jr.
Exec. Director, Ass'n of Former Members of Congress
1755 Massachusetts Ave., N.W., Suite 412, Washington, DC 20036
Telephone: (202) 332-3532

JOHNSON, Jerry
Director of Research, Powell, Adams & Rinehart
1901 L St., N.W., 3rd Floor, Washington, DC 20036
Telephone: (202) 466-7590

JOHNSON, Dr. Jimmy D.
President, Ass'n of Physical Fitness Centers
600 Jefferson St., Suite 202, Rockville, MD 20852
Telephone: (301) 424-7744

JOHNSON, Joel L.
V. President, International, Aerospace Industries Ass'n of America
1250 Eye St., N.W., Suite 1100, Washington, DC 20005
Telephone: (202) 371-8400

JOHNSON, John D., M.D.
Physicians' Representative, Kaiser Foundation Health Plan, Inc.
1700 K St., N.W. Suite 601, Washington, DC 20006
Telephone: (202) 296-1314
Registered as lobbyist at U.S. Congress.

JOHNSON, John Paul
Director of Industry Relations, Natural Gas Supply Ass'n
1129 20th St., N.W. Suite 300, Washington, DC 20036
Telephone: (202) 331-8900

JOHNSON, Karen
Director of Communications, Nat'l Federation of Republican Women
310 First St., S.E., Washington, DC 20003
Telephone: (202) 547-9341

JOHNSON, Kay
Director, Child Health, Children's Defense Fund
122 C St., N.W., Washington, DC 20001
Telephone: (202) 628-8787
Registered as lobbyist at U.S. Congress.

JOHNSON, L. Oakley
V. President, Corporate Affairs, American Internat'l Group
1455 Pennsylvania Ave., N.W. Suite 900, Washington, DC 20004
Telephone: (202) 783-5690
Registered as lobbyist at U.S. Congress.
Background: Former Manager of Internat'l Programs, U.S. Chamber of Commerce.

JOHNSON, Linda Meyer
Program Manager, Governmental Programs, Internat'l Business Machines Corp.
1801 K St., N.W., Suite 1200, Washington, DC 20006
Telephone: (202) 778-5000

JOHNSON, M. Scott
Gardner, Carton and Douglas
1001 Pennsylvania Ave., N.W., Suite 750, Washington, DC 20004
Telephone: (202) 347-9200
Clients:
American Community TV Ass'n

JOHNSON, Mark R.
General Mgr.-Governmental Affairs, Maersk Inc.
1667 K St., N.W., Suite 350, Washington, DC 20006
Telephone: (202) 887-6770

Registered as lobbyist at U.S. Congress.

JOHNSON, Marlene
Public Affairs Specialist, District of Columbia Office of the People's Counsel
1101 14th St., N.W., Suite 900, Washington, DC 20005
Telephone: (202) 727-3071

JOHNSON, May
Treasurer, American Security Council Political Action Committee
499 South Capitol St., S.W., Washington, DC 20003
Telephone: (202) 484-1677

JOHNSON, Michael J.
V. President, International Affairs, FMC Corp.
1627 K St., N.W., Suite 500, Washington, DC 20006
Telephone: (202) 956-5214

JOHNSON, Michael S.
Loeffler Group, The
555 13th St., N.W., Suite 300, Washington, DC 20004
Telephone: (202) 637-6850
Background: Former Press Secretary and Chief of Staff to House Minority Leader Robert H. Michel (R-IL).

JOHNSON, Mildred
Exec. Director, Nat'l Technical Ass'n
206 N. Washington St., Suite 202, Alexandria, VA 22314
Telephone: (202) 829-6100

JOHNSON, Nancie
Manager, Internat'l Trade & Investment, du Pont de Nemours and Co., E. I.
1701 Pennsylvania Ave., N.W., Suite 900, Washington, DC 20006
Telephone: (202) 728-3600
Registered as lobbyist at U.S. Congress.

JOHNSON, Nancy
Director, Public Affairs and Research, Professional Services Council
918 16th St., N.W, Suite 406, Washington, DC 20006
Telephone: (202) 296-2030

JOHNSON, Jr. O. Thomas
Covington and Burling
1201 Pennsylvania Ave., N.W., Box 7566, Washington, DC 20044
Telephone: (202) 662-6000
Clients:
AT&T
Internat'l Minerals and Chemical Corp.

JOHNSON, Owen
Akin, Gump, Strauss, Hauer and Feld
1333 New Hampshire Ave., N.W., Suite 400, Washington, DC 20036
Telephone: (202) 887-4000
Clients:
Coca-Cola Co.

JOHNSON, Patricia L.
Administrative Assistant, Concerned Citizens Foundation
Capitol Hill Office Bldg. 412 First St., S.E., Suite 301, Washington, DC 20003
Telephone: (202) 479-9068
Registered as lobbyist at U.S. Congress.
Background: Former aide to Rep. Tom DeLay (R-TX), 1988.

JOHNSON, Paul
Fleishman-Hillard, Inc
1301 Connecticut Ave., N.W., Washington, DC 20036
Telephone: (202) 659-0330
Registered as lobbyist at U.S. Congress.
Clients:
American Ambulance Ass'n
Apple & Eve
Automotive Refrigeration Products Institute
Citizens for a Drug Free America
Coastal Barrier Relief Fund
Pathology Practice Ass'n
Processed Apples Institute
Spectacor Management Group
Syva Co.
United Network of Organ Sharing

JOHNSON, Peter B.
Exec. Director, Caribbean/Central American Action
1211 Connecticut Ave., N.W. Suite 510, Washington, DC 20036
Telephone: (202) 466-7464

JOHNSON, Richard
Assistant Exec. Director, United States Conference of Mayors
1620 Eye St., N.W., Washington, DC 20006
Telephone: (202) 293-7330

JOHNSON, Richard C.
General Counsel, Nat'l Restaurant Ass'n
1200 17th St., N.W., Washington, DC 20036-3097
Telephone: (202) 331-5900

JOHNSON, Richard C.
Nat'l Center for Municipal Development
1620 Eye St., N.W., Suite 300, Washington, DC 20006
Telephone: (202) 429-0160
Clients:
Duluth, Minnesota, City of
Providence, Rhode Island, City of
Trenton, New Jersey, City of

JOHNSON, Richard C.
Seyfarth, Shaw, Fairweather and Geraldson
815 Connecticut Ave., N.W., Washington, DC 20006-4004
Telephone: (202) 463-2400
Registered as Foreign Agent: (#3122).
Background: Member, Office of the General Counsel, Department of the Air Force, 1962-66. Assistant Executive Director, Federal Power Commission, 1966-68.

JOHNSON, Richard D.
Deputy Exec. Director, United States Conference of Local Health Officers
1620 Eye St., N.W., Washington, DC 20006
Telephone: (202) 293-7330

JOHNSON, Richard W., Jr.
Director of Legislation, Non Commissioned Officers Ass'n of the U.S.A.
225 North Washington St., Alexandria, VA 22314
Telephone: (703) 549-0311
Registered as lobbyist at U.S. Congress.

JOHNSON, Robert W., II
McClure and Trotter
1100 Connecticut Ave., N.W., Suite 600, Washington, DC 20036
Telephone: (202) 659-3400
Registered as lobbyist at U.S. Congress.
Background: Attorney, Office of the General Counsel, U.S. Department of Agriculture, 1976-1977. Senior Staff Assistant to Chairman George Mahon, Committee on Appropriations, House of Representatives, 1977-1979.

JOHNSON, Roger
Public Information Officer, Federation of American Societies for Experimental Biology
9650 Rockville Pike, Bethesda, MD 20814
Telephone: (301) 530-7000

JOHNSON-SCHULKE, Collette
V. President, State and Municipal, Nat'l Ass'n of REALTORS
777 14th St., N.W., Washington, DC 20005
Telephone: (202) 383-1094
Registered as lobbyist at U.S. Congress.

JOHNSON, Spencer A.
V. President, Paperboard Packaging Council
1101 Vermont Ave., N.W. Suite 411, Washington, DC 20005
Telephone: (202) 289-4100
Registered as lobbyist at U.S. Congress.

JOHNSON, Stephen M.
Senior V. President, Jefferson Group, The
1341 G St., N.W., Suite 1100, Washington, DC 20005
Telephone: (202) 638-3535

JOHNSON, Stephen S.
Anderson and Pendleton, C.A.
1000 Connecticut Ave., N.W., Suite 1220, Washington, DC 20036
Telephone: (202) 659-2334

Registered as Foreign Agent: (#2696).

JOHNSON, Steven
Field Organizer, Congress Watch
215 Pennsylvania Ave., S.E., Washington, DC 20003
Telephone: (202) 546-4996

JOHNSON, W. Stanfield
Crowell and Moring
1001 Pennsylvania Ave., N.W., Washington, DC 20004-2505
Telephone: (202) 624-2500
Clients:
United Technologies Corp.

JOHNSON, Wallace
Exec. Director, Public Housing Authorities Directors Ass'n
511 Capitol Court, N.E., Washington, DC 20002-4937
Telephone: (202) 546-5445

JOHNSON, Willa Ann
Chairman, Capitol Research Center
1612 K St., N.W., Suite 704, Washington, DC 20006
Telephone: (202) 822-8666

JOHNSTON, Barbara W.
Washington Representative, BHP-Utah Internat'l Inc.
1700 K St., N.W., Suite 502, Washington, DC 20006
Telephone: (202) 775-1389
Registered as lobbyist at U.S. Congress.

JOHNSTON, Douglas M., Jr.
Exec. V. President and COO, Center for Strategic and Internat'l Studies
1800 K St., N.W., Washington, DC 20006
Telephone: (202) 887-0200
Background: Deputy Assistant Secretary of the Navy (Manpower), 1975-77. Director, Policy Planning and Management, Manpower and Reserve Affairs, Office of Secretary of Defense, 1974-75. Deputy Administrator, Office of Wage Stabilization, 1972-73.

JOHNSTON, George Allen
Dir., Grassroots & Member Relations, Nat'l Committee to Preserve Social Security and Medicare
2000 K St., N.W. Suite 800, Washington, DC 20006
Telephone: (202) 822-9459
Registered as lobbyist at U.S. Congress.
Background: Former Majority Staff Director, House of Representatives Subcommittee on Retirement Income and Employment, Select Committee on Aging.

JOHNSTON, James D.
V. Pres., Industry & Gov't Relations, General Motors Corp.
1660 L St., N.W., Washington, DC 20036
Telephone: (202) 775-5090
Registered as lobbyist at U.S. Congress.

JOHNSTON, Martha
Dir, Office of Cong Liaison, UNITED STATES INFORMATION AGENCY
301 4th St., S.W., Washington, DC 20547
Telephone: (202) 485-8828

JOHNSTON, Michael
Director of Safety & Training, United States Parachute Ass'n
1440 Duke St., Alexandria, VA 22314
Telephone: (703) 836-3495

JOHNSTON, N. Hunter
Griffin, Johnson & Associates
1211 Connecticut Ave., N.W., Suite 700, Washington, DC 20036
Telephone: (202) 775-8116
Registered as lobbyist at U.S. Congress.
Background: Former law clerk, U.S. District Court, Eastern District of Louisiana.

JOLLEY, Michael
V. President, Public Affairs, British Aerospace, Inc.
13873 Park Center Road, Herndon, VA 22071
Telephone: (703) 478-9420

JOLLIE, Susan B.
Galland, Kharasch, Morse and Garfinkle
Canal Square, 1054 31st St., N.W., Washington, DC 20007
Telephone: (202) 342-5200
Registered as Foreign Agent: (#4006).

Background: Associate General Counsel for Antitrust and Litigation, Civil Aeronautics Board, 1980-84. Executive Assistant to the Vice Chairman, Civil Aeronautics Board, 1982-83.
Clients:
Air Jamaica
Alamo Rent-a-Car
Hong Kong Aircraft Engineering Co., Ltd.
Israel Aircraft Industries
Orient Airlines Ass'n

JOLLY, Mary K.
Federal Liaison, Nat'l Rifle Ass'n of America
1600 Rhode Island Ave., N.W., Washington, DC 20036
Telephone: (202) 828-6357
Registered as lobbyist at U.S. Congress.

JOLLY, Thomas R.
O'Connor & Hannan
1919 Pennsylvania Ave., N.W., Suite 800, Washington, DC 20006
Telephone: (202) 887-1400
Registered as lobbyist at U.S. Congress.
Background: Legislative Assistant, 1970-73 and Legislative Counsel, 1973-78 to Rep. William D. Ford (D-MI). Counsel and Staff Director, Subcommittee on Agricultural Labor, 1973-77 and Subcommittee on Postsecondary Education, 1977-78, House of Representatives Committee on Education and Labor.
Clients:
American Family Corp.
CareerCom Corp.
CNA Financial Corp.
CNA Insurance Cos.
Distilled Spirits Council of the United States
Eastern Michigan University
Seagram & Sons, Inc., Joseph E.

JONAS, John
Patton, Boggs and Blow
2550 M St., N.W., Suite 800, Washington, DC 20037
Telephone: (202) 457-6000
Registered as lobbyist at U.S. Congress.
Registered as Foreign Agent: (#2165).
Background: Tax Counsel, Committee on Ways and Means, U.S. House of Representatives, 1981-86.
Clients:
Council of Graduate Schools
Massachusetts Mutual Life Insurance Co.
Metropolitan Insurance Cos.
Mutual Benefit Life Insurance Co.
Mutual Life Insurance Co. Tax Committee
Mutual Life Insurance Legislative Committee
Nat'l Ass'n of Life Underwriters
Northwestern Mutual Life Insurance Co.
Reinsurance Ass'n of America

JONES, Allan R.
Manager, Legislative Affairs, American Trucking Ass'ns
430 First St., S.E., Washington, DC 20003
Telephone: (202) 544-6245
Registered as lobbyist at U.S. Congress.

JONES, Anne P.
Sutherland, Asbill and Brennan
1275 Pennsylvania, N.W., Washington, DC 20004-2404
Telephone: (202) 383-0100
Background: Attorney, 1968-77 and Director, Division of Investment Management, 1976-77, Securities and Exchange Commission. General Counsel, Federal Home Loan Bank Board, 1978-79. Commissioner, Federal Communications Commission, 1979-83.
Clients:
Argo Communications Corp.
Columbia Federal Savings and Loan
New England Digital Distribution Corp.
Pacific Telesis Group-Washington

JONES, Annette
Liaison, Nat'l Federation of Democratic Women
5422 2nd St., N.W., Washington, DC 20011
Telephone: (202) 723-8182

JONES, Anthony L.
President, Tonya, Inc.
1620 Eye St., N.W., Suite 515, Washington, DC 20006
Telephone: (202) 835-3300
Registered as lobbyist at U.S. Congress.
Clients:

JONES, Anthony L. (Cont'd)
Birmingham, Alabama, City of

JONES & ASSOCIATES, C. Darrell
1101 King St. Suite 601, Alexandria, VA 22314
Telephone: (703) 838-9203
Members of firm representing listed organizations:
  Jones, C. Darrell, President, Managing Director
    Background: Professional Staff member, Senate Committee on Governmental Affairs, 1977-79. Congressional Affairs Officer, General Services Administration, 1979-80. Legislative Analyst, U.S. Department of Labor, 1980-87. Legislative Assistant to Rep. Julian C. Dixon (D-CA), 1988.

JONES, Barbara
Legislative Representative, Dresser Industries
1100 Connecticut Ave., N.W. Suite 310, Washington, DC 20036
Telephone: (202) 296-3070

JONES, Belva W.
Kellen Co., Robert H.
1101 15th St., N.W., Washington, DC 20005
Telephone: (202) 785-3232
Registered as lobbyist at U.S. Congress.
Background: Serves as Associate Director, Nat'l Ass'n of Margarine Manufacturers.
Organizations represented:
  Nat'l Ass'n of Margarine Manufacturers

JONES, Ben
Director, Washington Office, Council of State Governments
444 North Capitol St., N.W., Washington, DC 20001
Telephone: (202) 624-5450

JONES, Bertrand F.
Special Assistant to the President, Sonicraft, Inc.
6303 Little River Turnpike Suite 320, Alexandria, VA 22312
Telephone: (703) 642-0371

JONES, Beverly E.
V. President, Government Affairs, Consolidated Natural Gas Co.
1819 L St., N.W. Suite 900, Washington, DC 20036
Telephone: (202) 833-3900

JONES, C. Darrell
President, Managing Director, Jones & Associates, C. Darrell
1101 King St. Suite 601, Alexandria, VA 22314
Telephone: (703) 838-9203
Registered as lobbyist at U.S. Congress.
Background: Professional Staff member, Senate Committee on Governmental Affairs, 1977-79. Congressional Affairs Officer, General Services Administration, 1979-80. Legislative Analyst, U.S. Department of Labor, 1980-87. Legislative Assistant to Rep. Julian C. Dixon (D-CA), 1988.

JONES, Carleton S.
Shaw, Pittman, Potts and Trowbridge
2300 N St., N.W., Washington, DC 20037
Telephone: (202) 663-8000
Registered as lobbyist at U.S. Congress.
Clients:
  Nat'l Air Transportation Ass'n

JONES, Clayton M.
V. Pres., Aerospace Gov't Affairs & Mktg, Rockwell Inter-nat'l
1745 Jefferson Davis Hwy. Suite 1200, Arlington, VA 22202
Telephone: (703) 553-6600

JONES, David R.
President, NFIB Foundation, Nat'l Federation of Independent Business
600 Maryland Ave., S.W., Suite 700, Washington, DC 20024
Telephone: (202) 554-9000

JONES, DAY, REAVIS AND POGUE
1450 G St., N.W., Suite 700, Washington, DC 20005-2088
Telephone: (202) 879-3939
Background: Washington office of a Cleveland-based law firm; merged with Surrey & Morse in 1986.

Members of firm representing listed organizations:
  Brown, Robert M.
  Davis, Randall E.
    Background: Former Associate Director, Natural Resources, Energy and Science, Office of Management and Budget.
  Hansell, Herbert J.
    Background: Legal Advisor, Department of State, 1977-79.
  Lataif, Lawrence P.
  Long, C. Thomas
    Background: Deputy General Counsel, Federal Home Loan Bank Board, 1984-85.
  Lowe, Randall B.
  Mathias, Charles McC.
    Background: Member, U.S. House of Representatives from Maryland, 1961-69. Member, U.S. Senate from Maryland, 1969-87.
  McDermott, Robert F.
    Background: Staff Ass't to the President 1971-72; Staff Ass't to the Deputy Attorney General 1974-75; Assoc. Deputy Attorney General 1975; U.S. Dept. of Justice, Ass't U.S. Attorney for the Eastern District of Virginia 1976-79.
  O'Hara, James T.
    Background: Section Chief, Reorganization Branch, Internal Revenue Service, 1967-69.
  Rose, Jonathan C.
    Background: White House Staff Assistant, 1969-71. Special Assistant to the President, 1971-72. General Counsel, Council on International Economic Policy, 1972-74. Associate Deputy Attorney General, 1974-75. Director, Office of Justice Policy and Planning, 1974-75. Deputy Assistant Attorney General, Anti-trust Division, Department of Justice, 1975-77. Assistant Attorney General, Office of Legal Policy, 1981-84.
  Scanlon, Melissa
  Sims, Joe
  Sudow, William E.
    Background: Assistant to Staff Director, U.S. Commission on Civil Rights, 1970-71. Special Assistant and Counsel to Rep. John Brademas of Indiana, 1972-75.
  Szabat, Mary Eleanor
  Von Keszycki, Alexine I.
  Wallison, Frieda K.
    Background: Special Counsel, Securities and Exchange Commission, 1975. Executive Director and General Counsel, Municipal Securities Rulemaking Board, 1975-78.
  Wiacek, Raymond J.
  Wilderotter, James A.
    Background: Special Assistant to the Under Secretary, Department of Commerce, 1971-73. Exec. Assistant to the Secretary, Department of Housing and Urban Development, 1973-74. Associate Deputy Attorney General, Department of Justice, 1974-75. Associate Counsel to the President, 1975-76. General Counsel, Energy Research and Development Administration, 1976-77.
Clients:
  AmeriTrust Co. N.A. *(C. Thomas Long)*
  Arkla, Inc.
  Castle-Harlan, Inc. *(Randall E. Davis)*
  Centex Corp. *(Randall E. Davis)*
  Chevy Chase Savings Bank *(Randall E. Davis)*
  China, Embassy of the People's Republic of
  China, Government of the People's Republic of
  Consumers for Competitive Fuels *(Randall E. Davis)*
  Day Kimball Hospital *(Randall E. Davis)*
  Fairfield Communities, Inc. *(Randall E. Davis)*
  First Church of Christ-Scientist *(Lawrence P. Lataif)*
  Health Policy Coalition
  Heron Internat'l, Ltd. *(C. Thomas Long)*
  Internat'l Telecharge, Inc. *(Randall B. Lowe)*
  Jones, Day, Reavis and Pogue Good Government Fund
  Kentucky Utilities Co. *(Randall E. Davis)*
  Laurel Industries *(James A. Wilderotter)*
  Los Angeles County, California *(Frieda K. Wallison)*
  Lubrizol Corp.
  Morgan Grenfell and Co., Ltd. *(James A. Wilderotter)*
  Nat'l Ass'n of State Auditors, Comptrollers and Treasurers *(Frieda K. Wallison)*
  Nat'l Beer Wholesalers Ass'n
  Pfizer, Inc. *(Raymond J. Wiacek)*
  Preussag AG *(Randall E. Davis, Charles McC. Mathias)*

RJR Nabisco Washington, Inc. *(Robert F. McDermott)*
Royal Trustco Ltd. *(Randall E. Davis)*
State Ass'n of County Retirement Systems *(Frieda K. Wallison)*
TeleCommunications, Inc.
USAA Federal Savings Bank *(C. Thomas Long)*
Windham Community Memorial Hospital *(Randall E. Davis)*

JONES, Donald
Director of State Programs, Nat'l League of Cities
1301 Pennsylvania Ave., N.W., Washington, DC 20004
Telephone: (202) 626-3000

JONES, E. Dale
Exec. Director, Ass'n of Transportation Practitioners
1725 K St., N.W. Suite 301, Washington, DC 20006
Telephone: (202) 466-2080

JONES, Ed
Cashdollar-Jones & Co.
1000 16th St., N.W. Suite 702, Washington, DC 20036
Telephone: (202) 728-4058
Background: Former Member, U.S. House of Representatives (D-TN).
Clients:
  United Foods, Inc.

JONES, Dr. Effie
Assoc. Exec. Director, Minority Affairs, American Ass'n of School Administrators
1801 North Moore St., Arlington, VA 22209
Telephone: (703) 528-0700

JONES, Elaine R.
Director, Deputy/Counsel, NAACP Legal Defense and Educational Fund, Inc.
1275 K St., N.W. Suite 301, Washington, DC 20005
Telephone: (202) 682-1300

JONES, Ernest W.
Dir., Construction Education Services, Associated General Contractors of America
1957 E St., N.W., Washington, DC 20006
Telephone: (202) 393-2040
Registered as lobbyist at U.S. Congress.

JONES, Frank P., Jr.
V. President, Government Affairs, Aluminum Co. of America
1615 M St., N.W., Suite 500, Washington, DC 20036
Telephone: (202) 956-5300

JONES, Gordon S.
DGM Internat'l Inc.
9271 Old Keene Mill Road, Springfield, VA 22152
Telephone: (703) 644-4587
Background: Former Exec. Director, House Republican Policy Committee.
Clients:
  Multiprogres
  Questar Corp.

JONES, Huda
President, Nat'l Federation of Republican Women
310 First St., S.E., Washington, DC 20003
Telephone: (202) 547-9341

JONES, James D. E.
Washington Representative, Port Authority of New York and New Jersey
1001 Connecticut Ave., N.W. Suite 610, Washington, DC 20036
Telephone: (202) 887-5240

JONES, James R.
Dickstein, Shapiro and Morin
2101 L St., N.W., Washington, DC 20037
Telephone: (202) 785-9700
Background: Special Assistant to President Lyndon B. Johnson, 1964-68. Member, U.S. House of Representatives (D-OK), 1972-86. Member, House Ways and Means Committee, 1974-86; Member, House Subcommittee on Trade. Chairman, House Committee on the Budget, 1981-85. Chairman, House Social Security Subcommittee, 1985-86.
Clients:
  Avondale Industries, Inc.

Bank of Oklahoma
Guess, Inc.
Morgan & Co., J. P.
Security Life Insurance Co. of Denver
Toshiba Corp.

JONES, Jennifer
Assistant Development Director, Defenders of Wildlife
1244 19th St., N.W., Washington, DC 20036
Telephone: (202) 659-9510

JONES, John B., Jr.
Partner, Covington and Burling
1201 Pennsylvania Ave., N.W., Box 7566, Washington, DC 20044
Telephone: (202) 662-6000
Registered as lobbyist at U.S. Congress.

JONES, Judith Miller
Director, Nat'l Health Policy Forum
2011 Eye St., N.W. Suite 200, Washington, DC 20006
Telephone: (202) 872-1390

JONES, Larry
Legis. Rep., Employment/Labor Relations, Nat'l Ass'n of Counties
440 First St., N.W., Washington, DC 20001
Telephone: (202) 393-6226
Background: Also serves as Coordinator of the Caucus of Black County Officials, Nat'l Ass'n of Counties.

JONES, Lora Lynn
V. President, Stone and Associates, Ann E. W.
1315 Duke St., Alexandria, VA 22314
Telephone: (703) 836-7717
Registered as Foreign Agent: (#3914).
Organizations represented:
Conservative Alliance

JONES, Phillip J.
Southern Regional Political Director, Democratic Nat'l Committee
430 South Capitol St., S.E., Washington, DC 20003
Telephone: (202) 863-8000

JONES, Randall T.
Sr. V. Pres., Gov't & Public Affairs, Nat'l Council of Farmer Cooperatives
50 F St., N.W., Suite 900, Washington, DC 20001
Telephone: (202) 626-8700
Registered as lobbyist at U.S. Congress.
Background: Responsibilities include Nat'l Council of Farmer Cooperatives Political Action Committee (Co-op/PAC).

JONES, Robert L.
National Exec. Director, American Veterans of World War II, Korea and Vietnam (AMVETS)
4647 Forbes Blvd., Lanham, MD 20706
Telephone: (301) 459-9600
Registered as lobbyist at U.S. Congress.

JONES, Ronald W.
PAI Management Corp.
5530 Wisconsin Ave., N.W., Suite 1149, Washington, DC 20815
Telephone: (301) 656-4224
Clients:
Ophthalmic Research Institute

JONES, Roy
President, Coalitions, Inc.
505 2nd St., N.E., Washington, DC 20002
Telephone: (202) 675-4050
Clients:
Washington Times Corp., The

JONES, Stephen R.
V. President, Law and Policy, Council of Better Business Bureaus
4200 Wilson Blvd. Suite 800, Arlington, VA 22203
Telephone: (703) 276-0100

JONES, Theodore L.
412 First St., S.E., Suite 60, Washington, DC 20003
Telephone: (202) 393-0711
Organizations represented:
Mall Properties, Inc.
Maxicare HealthPlans, Inc.

United Companies Life Insurance Co.
Zapata Corp.
Zapata Gulf Marine Service Corp.

JONES, W. Patrick
V. President, Government Relations, American Ass'n of Port Authorities
1010 Duke St., Alexandria, VA 22314
Telephone: (703) 684-5700
Registered as lobbyist at U.S. Congress.

JONES, Wiley N.
V. President, Governmental Relations, Southern Pacific Transportation Co.
816 Connecticut Ave., N.W. Suite 800, Washington, DC 20006
Telephone: (202) 393-0100
Registered as lobbyist at U.S. Congress.
Background: Legislative Assistant to Rep. Gillis Long (D-LA), 1973-74. Legislative Assistant to Sen. Russell B. Long (D-LA), 1974-82.

JONES, William
Exec. Director, American Ass'n of University Affiliated Programs
8630 Fenton St., Suite 410, Silver Spring, MD 20910
Telephone: (301) 588-8252

JORDAN, Alexander H.
Asst. V. Pres., Governmental Affairs, Southern Pacific Transportation Co.
816 Connecticut Ave., N.W. Suite 800, Washington, DC 20006
Telephone: (202) 393-0100
Registered as lobbyist at U.S. Congress.

JORDAN, Cleveland
Washington Liaison, Nat'l Ass'n of State Directors of Veterans Affairs
941 North Capitol St., N.E., Suite 1211-F, Washington, DC 20421
Telephone: (202) 737-5050

JORDAN, G. Harris
Director, Government Affairs, American Soc. of Ass'n Executives
1575 Eye St., N.W., Washington, DC 20005-1168
Telephone: (202) 626-2703
Registered as lobbyist at U.S. Congress.
Background: Former Legislative Director for Rep. Philip Crane (R-IL).

JORDAN, Mary Lu
Attorney, United Mine Workers of America
900 15th St., N.W., Washington, DC 20005
Telephone: (202) 842-7338

JORDAN, Patricia
Ferguson Co., The
1730 Rhode Island Ave., N.W., Suite 400, Washington, DC 20036
Telephone: (202) 331-8500
Registered as lobbyist at U.S. Congress.
Organizations represented:
Alhambra, California, City of
Berg-Revoir Corp.
Imperial Irrigation District
Inglewood, California, City of
Irvine Co., The
Long Beach Transit
Oceanside, California, City of
Oceanside Redevelopment Agency
Provo, Utah, City of
Redondo Beach, California, City of
Santa Ana, California, City of
Santa Cruz Properties, Inc.
South Salt Lake, Utah, City of

JORDAN, Robert E., III
Steptoe and Johnson
1330 Connecticut Ave., N.W., Washington, DC 20036
Telephone: (202) 429-3000
Background: Special Assistant for Civil Rights, Office of the Secretary of Defense, 1963-64. Assistant U.S. Attorney for the District of Columbia, 1964-65. Executive Assistant for Law Enforcement, Office of the Secretary of the Treasury, 1965-67. General Counsel of the Army and Special Assistant to the Secretary of the Army for Civil Functions, 1967-71.

JORDAN, Ruth
V. President, Hager Sharp Inc.
1101 17th St., N.W., Suite 1001, Washington, DC 20036
Telephone: (202) 466-5430

JORDAN, Vernon E., Jr.
Akin, Gump, Strauss, Hauer and Feld
1333 New Hampshire Ave., N.W., Suite 400, Washington, DC 20036
Telephone: (202) 887-4000
Background: Member, Board of Directors, Corning Glass Works.

JORDAN, Whit
Director, Federal Regulatory Affairs, BellSouth Corp.
1133 21st St., N.W., Suite 900, Washington, DC 20036
Telephone: (202) 463-4100

JORDIN, John N.
V.P. & Dir., Human Resources/Gov't Affrs, Armstrong World Industries, Inc.
1025 Connecticut Ave., N.W., Suite 1007, Washington, DC 20036
Telephone: (202) 296-2830

JORPELAND, M. S.
Communications Director, Nat'l Shorthand Reporters Ass'n
118 Park St., S.E., Vienna, VA 22180
Telephone: (703) 281-4677

JORY, David C.
V. President, Government Relations, Citicorp
1275 Pennsylvania Ave., N.W., Suite 503, Washington, DC 20004
Telephone: (202) 879-6800

JOSEPH, GAJARSA, McDERMOTT AND REINER, P.C.
1300 19th St., N.W. Suite 400, Washington, DC 20036
Telephone: (202) 331-1955
Members of firm representing listed organizations:
McDermott, Mark T.
Background: Trial Attorney, Federal Aviation Administration, 1974-78.
Clients:
Civil Pilots for Regulatory Reform *(Mark T. McDermott)*

JOSEPH, James A.
President, Council on Foundations
1828 L St., N.W. Suite 300, Washington, DC 20036
Telephone: (202) 466-6512
Background: Under Secretary of Interior in the Carter administration.

JOSEPH, Jeffrey H.
V. President, Domestic Policy, Chamber of Commerce of the U.S.A.
1615 H St., N.W., Washington, DC 20062
Telephone: (202) 463-5493

JOSEPH, Mary Lou
Director, National Affairs, Nat'l Public Radio
2025 M St., N.W., Washington, DC 20036
Telephone: (202) 822-2342
Registered as lobbyist at U.S. Congress.

JOSEPH, Michael
Dyer, Ellis, Joseph & Mills
600 New Hampshire Ave., N.W., Suite 1000, Washington, DC 20037
Telephone: (202) 944-3040
Registered as Foreign Agent: (#4121).
Background: Attorney, Office of the General Counsel, Securities and Exchange Commission, 1961-66.
Clients:
Ace Frosty Shipping Co., Ltd.

JOSEPH, Thomas L., III
Legislative Representative, Health, Nat'l Ass'n of Counties
440 First St., N.W., Washington, DC 20001
Telephone: (202) 393-6226
Background: Serves as contact for the Nat'l Ass'n of County Human Services Administrators, the Nat'l Ass'n of County Aging Programs, and the Nat'l Ass'n of County Health Facility Administrators.

JOSEPHS, Melvin
Exec. Director, American Soc. of Plant Physiologists
15501 Monona Drive, Rockville, MD 20855
Telephone: (301) 251-0560

JOSEPHSON, Marvin
Treasurer, Nat'l Political Action Committee, The
555 New Jersey Ave., N.W., Suite 718, Washington, DC 20000

JOST, Diana
Exec. Dir., Private Market Programs, Blue Cross and Blue Shield Ass'n
655 15th St., N.W., Suite 350, Washington, DC 20005
Telephone: (202) 626-4780
Registered as lobbyist at U.S. Congress.

JOST, Steven J.
Fraioli/Jost
122 C St., N.W., Suite 500-A, Washington, DC 20001
Telephone: (202) 347-3042
Background: Former Administrative Assistant to Rep. Richard H. Lehman (D-CA) and former Deputy Director for Finance, Democratic Congressional Campaign Committee.

JOURNEY, Drexel D.
Schiff Hardin & Waite
1101 Connecticut Ave., N.W. Suite 600, Washington, DC 20036
Telephone: (202) 857-0600
Background: Member, 1952-77, and General Counsel, 1974-77, Federal Power Commission.

JOY, James, Jr.
President, Utility Workers Union of America
815 16th St., N.W. Suite 605, Washington, DC 20006
Telephone: (202) 347-8105

JOYCE, Carleen
Director, Information Clearinghouse, Nat'l Citizens Coalition for Nursing Home Reform
1424 16th St., N.W., Suite L2, Washington, DC 20036
Telephone: (202) 797-0657

JOYCE, John J.
Director, Nat'l Housing Program, Internat'l Brotherhood of Teamsters, Chauffeurs, Warehousemen and Helpers of America
25 Louisiana Ave., N.W., Washington, DC 20001
Telephone: (202) 624-6800
Registered as lobbyist at U.S. Congress.

JOYCE, John T.
President, Internat'l Union of Bricklayers and Allied Craftsmen
815 15th St., N.W., 2nd Floor, Washington, DC 20005
Telephone: (202) 783-3788
Registered as lobbyist at U.S. Congress.

JOYCE, Mary Ellen
Federal Agencies, American Petroleum Institute
1220 L St., N.W., Washington, DC 20005
Telephone: (202) 682-8450

JOYCE, Rodney
Partner, Ginsburg, Feldman and Bress
1250 Connecticut Ave., N.W. Suite 800, Washington, DC 20036
Telephone: (202) 637-9000
Registered as lobbyist at U.S. Congress.
Clients:
United States Telephone Ass'n

JOYNER, John R.
Deputy Exec. Director, Nat'l League of Cities
1301 Pennsylvania Ave., N.W., Washington, DC 20004
Telephone: (202) 626-3000

JOYNER, Nelson T.
Chairman, Federation of Internat'l Trade Ass'ns
1851 Alexander Bell Drive, Reston, VA 22091
Telephone: (703) 391-6106

JUARBE, Frederico, Jr.
Director, Nat'l Veterans Service, Veterans of Foreign Wars of the U.S.
200 Maryland Ave., N.E., Washington, DC 20002
Telephone: (202) 543-2239

JUDAH, Jeffrey N.
Government Affairs, Thacher, Proffitt and Wood
1500 K St., N.W., Suite 200, Washington, DC 20005
Telephone: (202) 347-8400
Registered as lobbyist at U.S. Congress.
Clients:
Citicorp

JUDD, Ardon B., Jr.
Staff V. President, Washington Counsel, Dresser Industries
1100 Connecticut Ave., N.W. Suite 310, Washington, DC 20036
Telephone: (202) 296-3070
Registered as lobbyist at U.S. Congress.

JUDD, Katherine L.
Area Representative (Chevron Chem), Chevron, U.S.A.
1700 K St., N.W., Suite 1200, Washington, DC 20006
Telephone: (202) 457-5800
Registered as lobbyist at U.S. Congress.

JUDD, Terry W.
Project Associate, APCO Associates
1155 21st St., N.W., Suite 1000, Washington, DC 20036
Telephone: (202) 778-1000

JUDKINS, H. Keith
Exec. V. President, Architectural Woodwork Institute
2310 South Walter Reed Dr., Arlington, VA 22206
Telephone: (703) 671-9100

JUDSON, Margaret
Meyers & Associates
412 First St., S.E., Suite 100, Washington, DC 20003
Telephone: (202) 484-2773
Clients:
Nat'l Institute of Oilseed Products

JUDY, Amy
Political Organizer, Common Cause
2030 M St., N.W., Washington, DC 20036
Telephone: (202) 833-1200
Registered as lobbyist at U.S. Congress.

JUKES, James J.
Chief, Econ Sci & Gen Govt Br, Legis Ref, EXECUTIVE OFFICE OF THE PRESIDENT - Office of Management and Budget
Old Executive Office Bldg., Washington, DC 20500
Telephone: (202) 395-4790

JULIANA, James N.
Wagner, Hines and Avary
1899 L St., N.W., Suite 500, Washington, DC 20036
Telephone: (202) 659-0930
Registered as Foreign Agent: (# 3845).
Clients:
H. E. Ventures, Inc.

JULIANO ASSOCIATES, Robert E.
2555 M St., N.W., Suite 303, Washington, DC 20037
Telephone: (202) 223-4175
Members of firm representing listed organizations:
Juliano, Robert E.
Organizations represented:
AFL-CIO - Food and Allied Service Trades Department
Hotel Employees and Restaurant Employees Internat'l Union *(Robert E. Juliano)*
Internat'l Speedway Corp. *(Robert E. Juliano)*
Stock Information Group

JULIANO, Robert E.
Juliano Associates, Robert E.
2555 M St., N.W., Suite 303, Washington, DC 20037
Telephone: (202) 223-4175
Registered as lobbyist at U.S. Congress.
Organizations represented:
Hotel Employees and Restaurant Employees Internat'l Union
Internat'l Speedway Corp.

JULYAN, David S.
Exec. V. President, Spot Image Corp.
1897 Preston White Drive, Reston, VA 22091-4326
Telephone: (703) 620-2200
Background: Legislative Director for Senator Patrick J. Leahy (D-VT), 1976-80.

JUNN, S. Chull
Reid & Priest
1111 19th St., N.W., Washington, DC 20036
Telephone: (202) 828-0100
Clients:
Korea, Embassy of
Korea Foreign Trade Ass'n

JURGELA, Elena
Exec. Director, Nat'l Republican Heritage Groups Council
310 First St., S.E., Washington, DC 20003
Telephone: (202) 662-1345

JURKOVICH, Celesta S.
V. President, Government Relations, Chicago Board of Trade
1455 Pennsylvania Ave., N.W. Suite 1225, Washington, DC 20004
Telephone: (202) 783-1190

JUSTIS, Doris
Exec. Secretary, Interfaith Forum on Religion, Art and Architecture
1777 Church St., N.W., Washington, DC 20036
Telephone: (202) 387-8333

JYRON, Kathleen
Manager, Business Information Center, U.S.-China Business Council
1818 N St., N.W., Suite 500, Washington, DC 20036
Telephone: (202) 429-0340

KABEL, Robert J.
Manatt, Phelps, Rothenberg & Phillips
1200 New Hampshire Ave., N.W., Suite 200, Washington, DC 20036
Telephone: (202) 463-4300
Registered as lobbyist at U.S. Congress.
Background: Former Legislative Director for Senator Richard Lugar (R-IN) and Special Assistant to President Reagan for Legislative Affairs.
Clients:
American Institute of Real Estate Appraisers
California Bankers Ass'n
Federal Express Corp.
Manufacturers Hanover Trust Co.
Money Store, The
Occidental Petroleum Corp.
Philip Morris Management Corp.
Security First Group
Sterling & Associates, Donald T.
United Airlines
Western Bank

KACHURIK, Catherine A.
Director, Internat'l & Gov't Relations, Electronic Data Interchange Ass'n
225 Reinekers Lane Suite 550, Alexandria, VA 22314
Telephone: (703) 838-8042

KADIS, Phillip M.
Education Director, Newspaper Guild, The
8611 2nd Ave., Silver Spring, MD 20910
Telephone: (301) 585-2990
Background: Former Director of Policy Development, Asst to the Chairperson, Nat'l Endowment for the Arts.

KADRICH, Lee
Managing Dir., Gov't Affairs & Trade, Automotive Parts and Accessories Ass'n
5100 Forbes Blvd., Lanham, MD 20706
Telephone: (301) 459-9110

KADZIK, Peter J.
Dickstein, Shapiro and Morin
2101 L St., N.W., Washington, DC 20037
Telephone: (202) 785-9700
Background: Campaign advisor to the national campaigns of Senator Edward Kennedy (1980), Rep. Geraldine Ferraro (1984) and Michael Dukakis (1988). Member, Technical and Legal Advisory Committee, Compliance Review Commissiom (1984) and Task Force on Voting Rights and Voter Particiapation (1987), Democratic Nat'l Committee.
Clients:
Medtronic, Inc.

KAGAN, Cheryl C.
Exec. Director, Independent Action
1511 K St., N.W. Suite 619, Washington, DC 20005
Telephone: (202) 628-4321

KAGANOWICH, Gar
Director, Office of Public Affairs, Federation of American
Societies for Experimental Biology
9650 Rockville Pike, Bethesda, MD 20814
Telephone: (301) 530-7000

KAGIWADA, JoAnne
Acting Exec. Dir., Legis. Educ. Comm., Japanese American Citizens League
1730 Rhode Island Ave., N.W., Suite 204, Washington, DC
20036
Telephone: (202) 223-1240

KAHAN, Mark S.
Galland, Kharasch, Morse and Garfinkle
Canal Square, 1054 31st St., N.W., Washington, DC
20007
Telephone: (202) 342-5200
Background: Associate Director, Legal Economic and Reg-
ulatory Affairs, Civil Aeronautics Board, 1981-82. Deputy
Solicitor for Administrative Enforcement and Litigation,
Office of Special Counsel. Department of Energy, 1977-
78.
Clients:
Air Jamaica

KAHN, B. Franklin
President, Washington Real Estate Investment Trust
4936 Fairmont Ave., Bethesda, MD 20814
Telephone: (301) 652-4300

KAIMAN, Sherry F.
Rapoza Associates, Robert A.
122 C St., N.W., Suite 875, Washington, DC 20001
Telephone: (202) 393-5225
Registered as lobbyist at U.S. Congress.
Clients:
Nat'l Rural Health Ass'n

KAISER, Harry
Senior Account Executive, Powell, Adams & Rinehart
1901 L St., N.W., 3rd Floor, Washington, DC 20036
Telephone: (202) 466-7590
Background: Former Press Secretary and Special Assistant
to Rep. Marcy Kaptur (D-OH).

KAITZ, James A.
Director - Government Relations, Financial Executives In-
stitute
1100 17th St., N.W., Suite 1203, Washington, DC 20036
Telephone: (202) 659-3700
Registered as lobbyist at U.S. Congress.

KAL/PR
911 Duke St., Alexandria, VA 22314
Telephone: (703) 683-0357
Members of firm representing listed organizations:
Lubieniecki, Karen A.
Clients:
Nat'l Council on Patient Information and Educa-
tion *(Karen A. Lubieniecki)*

KALDENBACH, Isabel
Director, Public & Governmental Affairs, Farmworker Jus-
tice Fund
2001 S St., N.W., Suite 210, Washington, DC 20009
Telephone: (202) 462-8192
Registered as lobbyist at U.S. Congress.

KALDY, Joanne
Director of Communications, American Soc. of Consultant
Pharmacists
2300 9th St., South, Arlington, VA 22204
Telephone: (703) 920-8492

KALIAN, S. J.
V. President, American Soc. of Internal Medicine
1101 Vermont Ave., N.W. Suite 500, Washington, DC
20005
Telephone: (202) 289-1700

KALISH, Susan
Exec. Director, American Running and Fitness Ass'n
9310 Old Georgetown Rd., Bethesda, MD 20814
Telephone: (301) 897-0197

KALLSEN, Patricia G.
Senior V. President, American Ass'n of Homes for the Aging
1129 20th St., N.W., Suite 400, Washington, DC 20036
Telephone: (202) 296-5960

KAMASAKI, Charles K.
V. Pres, Office of Resrch, Advoc & Legis, Nat'l Council of
La Raza
810 1st St., N.E., Suite 300, Washington, DC 20002
Telephone: (202) 289-1380

KAMBER GROUP, The
1920 L St., N.W., Washington, DC 20036
Telephone: (202) 223-8700
Members of firm representing listed organizations:
Betzler, Mary Roddy, Senior V. President
Bonitati, Robert F., Senior V. President
Bricker, Ron, Sr. V. Pres.and Dir., Media Pro-
ductions
Crosland, Page Dahl, V. President, Director,
Media Relations
DeQuatro, Maria, Senior Associate
Friedman, Deborah H., V. President
Gallina, Emil, V. President
Geddes, Betsy, V. President
Huge, Harry
Israel, Lesley
Kamber, Victor S., President, CEO, and Chair-
man of Board
Kinsella, Katherine, Senior V. President, Direc-
tor, Marketing
Leslie, John W., Exec. V. President
Lowe, Florence S., Senior Consultant
McClure, Donovan, Senior V. President
Sandman, Jeffrey M., V. President and General
Counsel
Sonnenberg, Martin J., V. President and Produc-
er
Spellane, C. James, V. President
Staton, Cliff, V. Pres. & Director, West Coast
Office
Walston, Dennis, Sr. V. Pres., and Director, Art
Dept.
Weiss, Richard A., Senior V. President
Organizations represented:
AFL-CIO - Building and Construction Trades
Department *(Victor S. Kamber)*
AFL-CIO - Industrial Union Department *(Lesley
Israel)*
American Federation of Musicians *(Richard A.
Weiss)*
American University, The *(Dennis Walston)*
Amnesty Internat'l U.S.A. *(Mary Roddy Betzler)*
Coalition of Labor Union Women *(John W. Leslie)*
Internat'l Ass'n of Bridge, Structural and Orna-
mental Iron Workers *(Mary Roddy Betzler)*
Internat'l Ass'n of Fire Fighters *(Robert F. Bonitati)*
Internat'l Brotherhood of Boilermakers, Iron
Shipbuilders, Blacksmiths, Forgers and Helpers
Internat'l Brotherhood of Electrical Workers *(Mary
Roddy Betzler)*
Kamber Group Political Action Fund (TKG
PAC) *(Victor S. Kamber, Jeffrey M. Sandman)*
Kelly Press, Inc.
Nat'l Ass'n of Social Workers *(Dennis Walston)*
Nat'l Coordinating Committee for Multiemployer
Plans *(Mary Roddy Betzler)*
Nat'l Education Ass'n of the U.S. *(Katherine Kinsel-
la)*
Plasterers' and Cement Masons' Action Commit-
tee *(Donovan McClure)*
Police Foundation *(Dennis Walston)*
Retail, Wholesale and Department Store Workers
Union *(Richard A. Weiss)*
Sheet Metal Workers' Internat'l Ass'n *(Harry Huge)*
Transportation, Communications Internat'l Union
(Donovan McClure)
United Food and Commercial Workers Internat'l
Union *(Jeffrey M. Sandman)*
Washington Court Hotel *(Katherine Kinsella)*
Wyatt Communications *(Dennis Walston)*

KAMBER, Victor S.
President, CEO, and Chairman of Board, Kamber Group,
The
1920 L St., N.W., Washington, DC 20036
Telephone: (202) 223-8700
Organizations represented:
AFL-CIO - Building and Construction Trades
Department
Kamber Group Political Action Fund (TKG
PAC)

KAMELA, Bill
Public Policy Director, Nat'l SAFE KIDS Campaign, Children's Hospital Nat'l Medical Center, The
111 Michigan Ave., N.W., Washington, DC 20010
Telephone: (202) 939-4993

KAMEN, Laurel
V. President, Government Affairs, American Express Co.
1020 19th St., N.W., Suite 600, Washington, DC 20036
Telephone: (202) 822-6680
Registered as lobbyist at U.S. Congress.

KAMENAR, Paul D.
Exec. Legal Director, Washington Legal Foundation
1705 N St., N.W., Washington, DC 20036
Telephone: (202) 857-0240

KAMERMAN, Dan
Community and Econ. Devel't Specialist, Nat'l Rural Electric Cooperative Ass'n
1800 Massachusetts Ave., N.W., Washington, DC 20036
Telephone: (202) 857-9562

KAMINOW, Dr. Ira P.
V. President, Hill and Knowlton Public Affairs Worldwide
Washington Harbour, 901 31st St., N.W., Washington, DC
20007
Telephone: (202) 333-7400
Background: V. President and Ecopnomic Adviser, Federal
Reserve Bank of Philadelphia, 1969-79.
Clients:
ADIG-Investment GmbH
Alexander Laing & Cruickshank
Caisse des Depots et Consignations
Casino
Dresdnerbank
European Investment Bank
F&C Management Ltd.
Friends' Provident Life Office
Nat'l Realty Committee
Phillips & Drew
Promodes
Scottish Equitable Life Assurance Society

KAMM, Linda Heller
Of Counsel, Foley & Lardner
1775 Pennsylvania Ave., N.W., Suite 1000, Washington,
DC 20006-4680
Telephone: (202) 862-5300
Registered as lobbyist at U.S. Congress.
Registered as Foreign Agent: (#4010).
Background: General Counsel, Committee on the Budget,
U.S. House of Representatives, 1975-77. General Counsel,
U.S. Department of Transportation, 1977-80.

KAMP, John F.
V. President, American Ass'n of Advertising Agencies
1899 L St., N.W., Suite 700, Washington, DC 20036
Telephone: (202) 331-7345

KANE, James L.
Ashby and Associates
1140 Connecticut Ave., N.W., Suite 503, Washington, DC
20036
Telephone: (202) 296-3840

KANE, John E.
Director, Federal Relations, American Council of Life Insurance
1001 Pennsylvania Ave., N.W., Washington, DC 20004-
2599
Telephone: (202) 624-2115
Registered as lobbyist at U.S. Congress.

KANE, Mary
PAC Representative, Nat'l Committee to Preserve Social
Security and Medicare Political Action Committee
2000 K St., N.W., Suite 800, Washington, DC 20006

KANE, Mary (Cont'd)
Telephone: (202) 822-9459
Registered as lobbyist at U.S. Congress.

KANIEWSKI, Donald
Assistant to the Legislat. Director, Laborers' Internat'l Union of North America
905 16th St., N.W., Washington, DC 20006
Telephone: (202) 737-8320
Registered as lobbyist at U.S. Congress.

KANIN, Dennis
Foley, Hoag and Eliot
1615 L St., N.W., Suite 950, Washington, DC 20036
Telephone: (202) 775-0600
Clients:
Humane Soc. of the United States

KANITZ, Bud
Exec. Director, Nat'l Neighborhood Coalition
810 First St., N.E. 3rd Floor, Washington, DC 20002
Telephone: (202) 289-1551

KANNER, Martin B.
Director of Government Relations, American Public Power Ass'n
2301 M St., N.W., Washington, DC 20037
Telephone: (202) 775-8300
Registered as lobbyist at U.S. Congress.

KANOUSE, James W.
Manager, Congressional Affairs, Boeing Co.
1700 North Moore St., Arlington, VA 22209
Telephone: (703) 558-9600
Registered as lobbyist at U.S. Congress.

KANTOR, L. Eric
V. President, Public Information, Investment Company Institute
1600 M St., N.W. Suite 600, Washington, DC 20036
Telephone: (202) 293-7700

KANTOR, Mickey
Manatt, Phelps, Rothenberg & Phillips
1200 New Hampshire Ave. N.W., Suite 200, Washington, DC 20036
Telephone: (202) 463-4300

KANY, Katherine
Professional Issues Coordinator, Federation of Nurses and Health Professionals/AFT
555 New Jersey Ave., N.W., Washington, DC 20001
Telephone: (202) 879-4491

KAPELSOHN, Emanuel
Exec. Director, American Shooting Sports Coalition

KAPLAN, Alan H.
Kleinfeld, Kaplan and Becker
1140 19th St., N.W., Suite 700, Washington, DC 20036
Telephone: (202) 223-5120
Background: Trial Attorney, Food and Drug Division, Office of General Counsel, Department of Health, Education and Welfare, 1957-60.
Clients:
Adria Laboratories, Inc.
Carter-Wallace, Inc.
Cord Laboratories
Mead Johnson and Co.
Par Pharmaceutical Inc.
Quad Pharmaceutical Inc.
Vitarine Pharmaceuticals Inc.

KAPLAN, Allen H.
Secretary-Treasurer, American Federation of Government Employees
80 F St., N.W., Washington, DC 20001
Telephone: (202) 737-8700

KAPLAN, David P.
President, Capitol Economics
1730 Pennsylvania Ave., N.W., Washington, DC 20006
Telephone: (202) 783-0800

KAPLAN, Elaine
Deputy Director, Litigation, Nat'l Treasury Employees Union
1730 K St., N.W., Suite 1100, Washington, DC 20006
Telephone: (202) 785-4411

KAPLAN, Julius
Kaplan, Russin and Vecchi
1215 17th St., N.W., Washington, DC 20036
Telephone: (202) 887-0353
Registered as lobbyist at U.S. Congress.
Registered as Foreign Agent: (#4092).
Clients:
Israel Electric Corp., Ltd.

KAPLAN, Dr. Karen Orloff
Director, Nat'l Center for Social Policy and Practice
7981 Eastern Ave., Silver Spring, MD 20910
Telephone: (301) 565-0333

KAPLAN, Linda
Exec. Director, Nat'l Women's Political Caucus
1275 K St., N.W., Suite 750, Washington, DC 20005
Telephone: (202) 898-1100
Background: Responsibilites also include the Nat'l Women's Political Caucus Campaign Support Committee. Serves as Coordinator for the Coalition for Women's Appointments.

KAPLAN, Nancey
PAC Director, American Health Care Ass'n Political Action Committee
1201 L St., N.W., Washington, DC 20005
Telephone: (202) 842-4444

KAPLAN, RUSSIN AND VECCHI
1215 17th St., N.W., Washington, DC 20036
Telephone: (202) 887-0353
Registered as Foreign Agent: (#4092)
Members of firm representing listed organizations:
James, Dennis (Jr.)
Kaplan, Julius
Patterson, Kathleen F.
Russin, Jonathan
Background: With Office of the Gen. Counsel, Agency for Internat'l Development, Dep't of State, 1964-1969 (Regional Legal Adviser, Dominican Republic, 1967-1969).
Schroeder, James W.
White, William R.
Background: Administrative Assistant to Senator John Glenn (D-OH), 1975-84.
Wiss, Marcia A.
Clients:
Canned and Cooked Meat Importers Ass'n *(Marcia A. Wiss)*
Caribbean Trade and Apparel Coalition (C-TAC) *(Jonathan Russin, William R. White)*
Israel Electric Corp., Ltd. *(Julius Kaplan)*
Sea-Land Service, Inc.
Venezuela, Government of

KAPLAR, Richard T.
V. President, Media Institute
3017 M St., N.W., Washington, DC 20007
Telephone: (202) 298-7512

KARAS, William
Steptoe and Johnson
1330 Connecticut Ave., N.W., Washington, DC 20036
Telephone: (202) 429-3000
Registered as Foreign Agent: (#4207).
Clients:
Atlantic Container Line
Gulf Container Line
Swissair

KARBER, Phillip A.
Sr. V. Pres., Nat'l Security Programs, BDM Internat'l, Inc.
7915 Jones Branch Drive, McLean, VA 22102
Telephone: (703) 821-5000

KARCHER, David A.
Exec. Director, American Soc. of Cataract and Refractive Surgery
3702 Pender Drive, Suite 250, Fairfax, VA 22030
Telephone: (703) 591-2220
Registered as lobbyist at U.S. Congress.

KARDELL, Amy
Capitol Associates, Inc.
426 C St., N.E., Washington, DC 20002
Telephone: (202) 544-1880
Registered as lobbyist at U.S. Congress.
Clients:

Endocrine Soc.

KARDY, Walter M.
President, Specialty Contractors Management, Inc.
P.O. Box 42558, Northwest Station, Washington, DC 20015-0458
Telephone: (301) 933-7430
Background: Serves as Exec. Director, Instrument Constructing and Engineering Ass'n, Inc.; Exec. Director, Quality Control Council of America; Exec. Director, Internat'l Council of Employers of Bricklayers and Allied Craftsmen; Director, Special Events, Foundation of Internat'l Meetings.
Clients:
Instrument Constructing and Engineering Ass'n, Inc.
Instrument Technicians Labor-Management Cooperation Fund
Quality Control Council of America, Inc.

KARI, Judith
Director of Programs, American Kidney Fund
6110 Executive Blvd., Rockville, MD 20852
Telephone: (301) 881-3052

KARINCH, Maryann
Director, Communications, Computer and Business Equipment Manufacturers Ass'n
311 First St., N.W. Suite 500, Washington, DC 20001
Telephone: (202) 737-8888

KARL, Malcolm S.
Director of Finance, American Soc. of Ass'n Executives
1575 Eye St., N.W., Washington, DC 20005-1168
Telephone: (202) 626-2723
Background: Serves also as Treasurer, A-PAC.

KARMAN, Alexander F.
Assistant V. President, Pacific Telecom, Inc.
1726 M St., N.W. Suite 801, Washington, DC 20036
Telephone: (202) 223-5200
Background: Also represents Alascom, Inc.

KARPINSKI, Gene
Exec. Director, U.S. Public Interest Research Group
215 Pennsylvania Ave., S.E., Washington, DC 20003
Telephone: (202) 546-9707
Registered as lobbyist at U.S. Congress.

KARPINSKI, Joseph
Princ Dep Asst Secy, Cong & Intergovt'l, DEPARTMENT OF ENERGY
1000 Independence Ave. S.W., Washington, DC 20585
Telephone: (202) 586-5450

KARSON, Stanley G.
Director, Center for Corporate Public Involvement
1001 Pennsylvania Ave., N.W., Washington, DC 20004
Telephone: (202) 624-2425

KARWOWSKI, Marlene
Editor, Nat'l Head Start Ass'n
1220 King St., Suite 200, Alexandria, VA 22314
Telephone: (703) 739-0875

KASEMAN, A. Carl, III
Piper and Marbury
1200 19th St., N.W., Washington, DC 20036
Telephone: (202) 861-3900
Registered as lobbyist at U.S. Congress.

KASHDAN, Alan G.
Fried, Frank, Harris, Shriver & Jacobson
1001 Pennsylvania Ave., N.W., Suite 800, Washington, DC 20004-2505
Telephone: (202) 639-7000
Clients:
Israel, Government of

KASINITZ, Barry
Legislative Assistant, Internat'l Ass'n of Fire Fighters
1750 New York Ave., N.W., Washington, DC 20006
Telephone: (202) 737-8484
Registered as lobbyist at U.S. Congress.

KASSINGER, Theodore W.
Vinson and Elkins
Willard Office Building, 1455 Pennsylvania Ave., N.W., Washington, DC 20004-1007
Telephone: (202) 639-6500

Background: Attorney, Office of the Legal Adviser, Department of State, 1980-81. International Trade Counsel, Senate Committee on Finance, 1981-85.
Clients:
Vitro, S.A.

KASSOUF, George
Director, Judicial Selection Project, Alliance for Justice
1601 Connecticut Ave., N.W. Suite 600, Washington, DC 20009
Telephone: (202) 332-3224
Registered as lobbyist at U.S. Congress.

KASTNER, Michael E.
Director of Government Relations, Nat'l Truck Equipment Ass'n
1350 New York Ave., N.W. Suite 800, Washington, DC 20005
Telephone: (202) 628-2010
Registered as lobbyist at U.S. Congress.
Background: Also represents the Nat'l Truck Equipment Ass'n PAC.

KASWELL, Stuart
Winthrop, Stimson, Putnam & Roberts
1133 Connecticut Ave., N.W. Suite 1000, Washington, DC 20036
Telephone: (202) 775-9800
Registered as lobbyist at U.S. Congress.
Background: Served with Securities and Exchange Commission, 1979-86, including as Special Counsel, 1983-84, and Branch Chief, OTC Regulation, 1984-86. Minority Counsel, House Energy and Commerce Committee, 1986-90.

KATOR, Michael J.
Kator, Scott and Heller
1275 K St., N.W. Suite 950, Washington, DC 20005
Telephone: (202) 898-4800
Clients:
Nat'l Ass'n of Retired Federal Employees

KATOR, SCOTT AND HELLER
1275 K St., N.W. Suite 950, Washington, DC 20005
Telephone: (202) 898-4800
Members of firm representing listed organizations:
Kator, Michael J.
Clients:
Nat'l Ass'n of Retired Federal Employees *(Michael J. Kator)*

KATSENES, Andrea
Director of Communications, American Soc. of Cataract and Refractive Surgery
3702 Pender Drive, Suite 250, Fairfax, VA 22030
Telephone: (703) 591-2220

KATTEN, MUCHIN, ZAVIS & DOMBROFF
1275 Pennsylvania Ave., N.W. Suite 301, Washington, DC 20004
Telephone: (202) 626-6400
Members of firm representing listed organizations:
Sperling, Gilbert
Clients:
Cogeneration and Independent Power Coalition of America *(Gilbert Sperling)*

KATZ, Barbara J.
Legislative Counsel, Consumer Federation of America
1424 16th St., N.W. Suite 604, Washington, DC 20036
Telephone: (202) 387-6121
Registered as lobbyist at U.S. Congress.

KATZ, John W.
Director of State/Federal Relations, Alaska, State of
444 N. Capitol St., N.W. Suite 518, Washington, DC 20001
Telephone: (202) 624-5858
Background: Also holds title of Special Counsel to the Governor of Alaska.

KATZ, Jonathan
Exec. Director, Nat'l Assembly of State Arts Agencies
1010 Vermont Ave., N.W., Suite 920, Washington, DC 20005
Telephone: (202) 347-6352

KATZ, Philip C.
V. President, Research Services, Beer Institute
1225 Eye St., N.W., Suite 825, Washington, DC 20005
Telephone: (202) 737-2337

KATZ, Sherman E.
Coudert Brothers
1627 Eye St., N.W. 12th Floor, Washington, DC 20006
Telephone: (202) 775-5100
Registered as Foreign Agent: (#3743).
Clients:
Australia, Commonwealth of

KATZEN, Sally
Wilmer, Cutler and Pickering
2445 M St., N.W., Washington, DC 20037-1420
Telephone: (202) 663-6000
Registered as lobbyist at U.S. Congress.
Background: General Counsel, Council on Wage and Price Stability, Exec. Office of the President, 1979-81.
Clients:
Amerada Hess Corp.
Communications Satellite Corp. (COMSAT)
Federal Home Loan Bank of San Francisco
Trans-Alaska Pipeline Liability Fund

KAUFFMAN, Frank
V.P., Grassroots & Issues Management, Hill and Knowlton Public Affairs Worldwide
Washington Harbour, 901 31st St., N.W., Washington, DC 20007
Telephone: (202) 333-7400

KAUFFMAN, Jo Ann
Evergreen Associates, Ltd.
206 G St., N.E., Washington, DC 20002
Telephone: (202) 543-3383
Registered as lobbyist at U.S. Congress.
Clients:
American Indian Healthcare Ass'n
Nez Perce Tribe

KAUFFMAN, Marvin E.
Exec. Director, American Geological Institute
4220 King St., Alexandria, VA 22302
Telephone: (703) 379-2480

KAUFMAN & ASSOCIATES, Henry J.
2233 Wisconsin Ave., N.W., Washington, DC 20007
Telephone: (202) 333-0700
Background: Public relations, government affairs and product promotion services for national and international clients.
Members of firm representing listed organizations:
Carberry, Michael G., Chief Exec. Officer
Goewey, Sarah M., Account Coordinator
Seng, John, V. President
Sullivan, Helen
Yerrick, Mary, Senior V. President
Organizations represented:
Brunei, Embassy of *(Michael G. Carberry, Sarah M. Goewey)*
Financial Services Council *(John Seng)*
Generic Pharmaceutical Industry Ass'n *(John Seng)*
Healthcare Compliance Packaging Council *(John Seng)*
Internat'l Sleep Products Ass'n *(Helen Sullivan)*
Nat'l Dairy Promotion and Research Board *(Michael G. Carberry, John Seng)*

KAUFMAN, Joel D.
Howrey and Simon
1730 Pennsylvania Ave., N.W., Washington, DC 20006-4793
Telephone: (202) 783-0800

KAUFMAN, Steve
Deputy Dir., Electronic Media Svcs., Hill and Knowlton Public Affairs Worldwide
Washington Harbour, 901 31st St., N.W., Washington, DC 20007
Telephone: (202) 333-7400

KAUFMANN, George
Dickstein, Shapiro and Morin
2101 L St., N.W., Washington, DC 20037
Telephone: (202) 785-9700
Clients:
Medtronic, Inc.

KAUFMANN, Robert C.
Director, Air Quality Program, American Paper Institute
1250 Connecticut Ave., N.W. Suite 210, Washington, DC 20036
Telephone: (202) 463-2420
Registered as lobbyist at U.S. Congress.

KAULIUS, Ghana
Sr. Consultant, State & Local Govt Svcs., Hill and Knowlton Public Affairs Worldwide
Washington Harbour, 901 31st St., N.W., Washington, DC 20007
Telephone: (202) 333-7400

KAUTT, Philip C.
V. President, EG&G, Inc.
1850 K St., N.W., Suite 1190, Washington, DC 20006
Telephone: (202) 887-5570

KAVANAGH, Anthony P.
Government Affairs Representative, Consolidated Edison Co. of New York
2100 Pennsylvania Ave., N.W., Suite 695, Washington, DC 20037
Telephone: (202) 331-2020
Registered as lobbyist at U.S. Congress.

KAVANAUGH, E. Edward
President, Cosmetic, Toiletry and Fragrance Ass'n
1110 Vermont Ave., N.W. Suite 800, Washington, DC 20005
Telephone: (202) 331-1770
Registered as lobbyist at U.S. Congress.

KAVITS, Philip
Director, Radio-TV, Nat'l Wildlife Federation
1400 16th St., N.W., Washington, DC 20036-2266
Telephone: (202) 797-6800

KAVJIAN, Edward M.
Washington Representative, General Motors Corp.
1660 L St., N.W., 4th Floor, Washington, DC 20036
Telephone: (202) 775-5027
Registered as lobbyist at U.S. Congress.

KAY, Alan
Bregman, Abell & Kay
1156 15th St., N.W., Suite 1212, Washington, DC 20005
Telephone: (202) 223-2900
Background: Attorney, Office of Gen. Counsel, Dep't of Commerce, 1966-1967. Assistant U.S. Attorney, 1963-66.

KAY, Kenneth R.
Preston Gates Ellis & Rouvelas Meeds
1735 New York Ave., N.W., Suite 500, Washington, DC 20006-4759
Telephone: (202) 628-1700
Registered as lobbyist at U.S. Congress.
Background: Legislative Director to Sen. Max Baucus, 1982-84. Counsel, Senate Judiciary Committee, 1979-82. Legislative Assistant, Cong. Ed Koch, 1976-77. Serves as Exec. Director, Council on Research and Technology.
Clients:
Council on Research and Technology (CORE-TECH)
Data General Corp.
Hewlett-Packard Co.
Nat'l Council on Compensation Insurance

KAYE, Bronwen A.
Assistant Director, Medical Gov't Affrs., American Cyanamid Co.
1575 Eye St., N.W., Suite 200, Washington, DC 20005
Telephone: (202) 789-1222
Registered as lobbyist at U.S. Congress.

KAYE, SCHOLER, FIERMAN, HAYS AND HANDLER
The McPherson Building 901 15th St., N.W., #1100, Washington, DC 20005
Telephone: (202) 682-3500
Background: Washington office of a New York law firm.
Members of firm representing listed organizations:
Brewster, Christopher R.
Background: Assistant Attorney General, State of Missouri, 1975-77. Legislative Assistant to Senator John Danforth (R-MO), 1977-79. Chief Counsel, Subcommittee on Federal Expenditures, U.S. Senate Committee on Government Affairs, 1980-82.

KAYE, SCHOLER, FIERMAN, HAYS AND HANDLER (Cont'd)

Feinberg, Kenneth R.
Background: Administrative Assistant to Sen. Edward M. Kennedy, 1976-79. Special Counsel, U.S. Senate Judiciary Committee, 1979.
Ribicoff, Abraham A.
Background: U.S. Senator from Connecticut, 1963-81. Secretary of Health, Education and Welfare, 1961-63.
Shrinsky, Jason
Weitzman, James M.
Zevnik, Paul A.
Clients:
Adams Communications Corp. *(Jason Shrinsky)*
Barnstable Broadcasting *(Jason Shrinsky)*
Benjamin Moore & Co. *(Christopher R. Brewster)*
Bosch Corporation, Robert *(Christopher R. Brewster)*
Brown Brothers Harriman & Co. *(Christopher R. Brewster)*
Carlon Co. *(Christopher R. Brewster)*
Eastern Air Lines *(Christopher R. Brewster)*
Educational Media *(Christopher R. Brewster)*
GAF Corp. *(Paul A. Zevnik)*
Golden West Broadcasters *(Jason Shrinsky)*
Goldman, Sachs and Co. *(Kenneth R. Feinberg)*
H & D Communications Group *(Jason Shrinsky)*
Holt Communications Corp. *(Jason Shrinsky)*
Industrial Fabrics Ass'n Internat'l *(Christopher R. Brewster)*
Katz Communications, Inc. *(Jason Shrinsky)*
Keymarket Communications, Inc. *(Jason Shrinsky)*
Lincoln Group, The *(Jason Shrinsky)*
Londontown Corp. *(Christopher R. Brewster)*
Malrite Communications Group, Inc. *(Jason Shrinsky)*
Metroplex Communications, Inc. *(Jason Shrinsky)*
NewCity Communications, Inc. *(Jason Shrinsky)*
Newport Beach, California, City of *(Christopher R. Brewster)*
Pennsylvania Power and Light Co.
Saga Communications, Inc. *(Jason Shrinsky)*
Sage Communications Corp. *(Jason Shrinsky)*
Siemens Medical Systems, Inc. *(Christopher R. Brewster)*
Spanish Broadcasting System, Inc. *(Jason Shrinsky)*
Texaco U.S.A. *(Christopher R. Brewster)*
United States Industrial Fabrics Institute *(Christopher R. Brewster)*
Westwood One, Inc. *(Christopher R. Brewster, Jason Shrinsky)*

KAYSON, Sarah
Public Policy Associate, Nat'l Council on Alcoholism and Drug Dependence
1511 K St., N.W., Suite 926, Washington, DC 20005
Telephone: (202) 737-8122

KAZMAN, Sam
Dir., Free Market Legal Prog. & GC, Competitive Enterprise Institute
233 Pennsylvania Ave., S.E., Suite 200, Washington, DC 20003
Telephone: (202) 547-1010

KCI INC.
1030 15th St., N.W., Washington, DC 20005
Telephone: (202) 371-2190
Members of firm representing listed organizations:
Anderson, Bette B., Exec. V. President
Background: Undersecretary of the Treasury under President Jimmy Carter.
Clients:
SICPA Industries of America, Inc. *(Bette B. Anderson)*
U.S. Banknote Corp. *(Bette B. Anderson)*

KEALY, Edward
Director, Federal Programs, Nat'l School Boards Ass'n
1680 Duke St., Alexandria, VA 22314
Telephone: (703) 838-6722

KEANE, Vincent A.
Special Ass't, Resource Development, Nat'l Ass'n of Community Health Centers
1330 New Hampshire Ave., N.W. Suite 122, Washington, DC 20036
Telephone: (202) 659-8008
Background: Serves as contact for Soc. for the Advancement of Ambulatory Care Political Action Committee.

KEARNS, Kevin L.
Fellow, Economic Strategy Institute
1100 Connecticut Ave., N.W. Suite 330, Washington, DC 20036
Telephone: (202) 728-0993
Background: Former Director, Office of Defense Trade Policy, Politico-Military Affairs Bureau, U.S. Department of State.

KEATING, David L.
Exec. V. President, Nat'l Taxpayers Union
713 Maryland Ave., N.E., Washington, DC 20002
Telephone: (202) 543-1300
Registered as lobbyist at U.S. Congress.

KEATING, Richard F.
V. President, Nat'l Affairs, Anheuser-Busch Cos., Inc.
1776 I St., Suite 200, Washington, DC 20006
Telephone: (202) 293-9494
Registered as lobbyist at U.S. Congress.

KECK, MAHIN AND CATE
1201 New York Ave., N.W., Penthouse Suite, Washington, DC 20005
Telephone: (202) 347-7006
Background: Washington office of a Chicago law firm.
Members of firm representing listed organizations:
Landry, Brock R.
Raclin, Victoria R.
Schaffer, Rebecca
Clients:
American Ass'n for Marriage and Family Therapy
American Petroleum Institute *(Rebecca Schaffer)*
Arkla Exploration Co. *(Rebecca Schaffer)*
Arkla, Inc.
General Instrument Corp.
Nat'l Particleboard Ass'n *(Brock R. Landry)*
Nat'l Tire Dealers and Retreaders Ass'n *(Brock R. Landry)*
Water Quality Ass'n
Williams Companies, The *(Rebecca Schaffer)*

KEEFE CO., THE
444 North Capitol St., N.W., Suite 711, Washington, DC 20001
Telephone: (202) 638-7030
Registered as Foreign Agent: (#4228)
Background: A management consultant firm. Foreign business conducted under the name of TKC International, Inc., at the same address.
Members of firm representing listed organizations:
Guerra-Mondragon, Gabriel, V. President
Background: President, TKC Internat'l.
Hager, Barry M.
James, C. L. (III)
James, Clarence L. (Jr.), President
Keefe, Robert J., Chairman of the Board
Background: Chairman of the Board of Directors of the Keefe Co. and TKC Internat'l.
McGhee, Camilla A.
O'Connell, Terry M., Exec. V. President
Roberts, William A., Senior V. President
Signer, William A.
Slade, Jonathon A.
Clients:
Adler Group *(Jonathon A. Slade)*
Ameri-Cable Internat'l, Inc. *(Clarence L. James, Jr., Robert J. Keefe, Terry M. O'Connell)*
Aruba, Government of *(Clarence L. James, Jr., Robert J. Keefe, Terry M. O'Connell)*
Bechtel Civil & Minerals, Inc. *(Clarence L. James, Jr., Robert J. Keefe, Terry M. O'Connell)*
Broward County Governmental Center *(Clarence L. James, Jr., William A. Roberts)*
Capital Hill Group, Inc., The *(Robert J. Keefe, Terry M. O'Connell)*
Cuban American Foundation *(Jonathon A. Slade)*
Dallas Area Rapid Transit Authority *(William A. Roberts)*
Executive Leadership Council *(C. L. James, III)*
Fairfax County, Virginia *(William A. Roberts)*
Federal Express Corp. *(Robert J. Keefe, Terry M. O'Connell)*
Foodservice and Lodging Institute *(Camilla A. McGhee, William A. Signer)*
Glick & Glick *(Camilla A. McGhee, William A. Signer)*
Greater New York Hospital Ass'n *(Camilla A. McGhee, William A. Signer)*
Hillsborough Area Regional Transit Authority *(Clarence L. James, Jr., William A. Roberts)*
Homewood Corp. *(Clarence L. James, Jr., Terry M. O'Connell)*
Internat'l Public Relations Co. *(Robert J. Keefe, Terry M. O'Connell)*
Nat'l Burglar and Fire Alarm Ass'n *(William A. Signer)*
NATJ and NATE *(Camilla A. McGhee, William A. Signer)*
New York Hospital *(Camilla A. McGhee, William A. Signer)*
Polysar Limited *(Robert J. Keefe, Terry M. O'Connell)*
RJR Nabisco Washington, Inc. *(William A. Signer)*
Security, Inc. *(Robert J. Keefe)*
Seminole Tribe of Florida *(William A. Roberts, Jonathon A. Slade)*
Spillis Candela & Partners, Inc. *(William A. Roberts)*
Tampa, Florida, City of *(Clarence L. James, Jr., William A. Roberts)*
University of Miami *(William A. Roberts)*
Westinghouse Transportation Division *(Clarence L. James, Jr., William A. Roberts)*

KEEFE, Patrick
Director of Communications, Nat'l Ass'n of Federal Credit Unions
3138 N. 10th St., Arlington, VA 22201
Telephone: (703) 522-4770

KEEFE, Robert J.
Chairman of the Board, Keefe Co., The
444 North Capitol St., N.W., Suite 711, Washington, DC 20001
Telephone: (202) 638-7030
Registered as lobbyist at U.S. Congress.
Registered as Foreign Agent: (#3333).
Background: Chairman of the Board of Directors of the Keefe Co. and TKC Internat'l.
Clients:
Ameri-Cable Internat'l, Inc.
Aruba, Government of
Bechtel Civil & Minerals, Inc.
Capital Hill Group, Inc., The
Federal Express Corp.
Internat'l Public Relations Co.
Polysar Limited
Security, Inc.

KEEGAN-AYER, M. C.
Ass't Director, Federal Affairs, Independent Insurance Agents of America
600 Pennsylvania Ave., S.E., Suite 200, Washington, DC 20003
Telephone: (202) 544-5833
Registered as lobbyist at U.S. Congress.

KEELEY, Patrick J.
Fulbright & Jaworski
1150 Connecticut Ave., N.W., Suite 400, Washington, DC 20036
Telephone: (202) 452-6800

KEELING, J. Michael
Zuckert, Scoutt and Rasenberger
888 17th St., N.W., Suite 600, Washington, DC 20006-3959
Telephone: (202) 298-8660
Clients:
Employee Stock Ownership Ass'n
Nat'l Ass'n of Royalty Owners
Small Business Council of America

KEELING, John R.
Ass't Director, Nat'l Affairs Division, American Farm Bureau Federation
600 Maryland Ave., S.W., Washington, DC 20024
Telephone: (202) 484-3600
Registered as lobbyist at U.S. Congress.

KEENAN, Laurie E.
Ivins, Phillips and Barker
1700 Pennsylvania Ave., N.W., Suite 600, Washington, DC 20006
Telephone: (202) 393-7600

KEENE, David A.
Keene, Shirley & Associates, Inc.
919 Prince St., Alexandria, VA 22314
Telephone: (703) 684-0550
Registered as lobbyist at U.S. Congress.
Registered as Foreign Agent: (#3997).
Clients:
Australian Barley Board
Conservative Political Action Conference
Legal Services Reform Coalition
Marine Engineers Beneficial Ass'n
Nat'l Farmers' Federation of Australia
The Limited, Inc.
World Freedom Foundation

KEENE, Murray
Mng. Dir., Communications & Member Svcs., American
Consulting Engineers Council
1015 15th St., N.W., Suite 802, Washington, DC 20005
Telephone: (202) 347-7474

KEENE, Russell T.
Assistant the Exec. V.P. and COO, American Gas Ass'n
1515 Wilson Blvd., Arlington, VA 22209
Telephone: (703) 841-8595
Background: Also serves as Manager, Gas Employees Political Action Committee.

KEENE, SHIRLEY & ASSOCIATES, INC.
919 Prince St., Alexandria, VA 22314
Telephone: (703) 684-0550
Members of firm representing listed organizations:
Bahler, Brent
Choat, Darrel
Farrell, Timothy
Keene, David A.
Mueller, Gregory R.
Newton, Lisa
Olson, Lisa M., V. President
Shirley, Craigan P.
Clients:
American Maritime Congress
Australian Barley Board *(Darrel Choat, David A. Keene, Craigan P. Shirley)*
AXS *(Lisa M. Olson)*
Boston Capital Partners, Inc. *(Brent Bahler, Craigan P. Shirley)*
Conservative Political Action Conference *(David A. Keene)*
Conservative Victory Committee *(Gregory R. Mueller)*
Kendall and Associates, John *(Lisa M. Olson)*
Legal Services Reform Coalition *(David A. Keene)*
Marine Engineers Beneficial Ass'n *(David A. Keene, Craigan P. Shirley)*
Nat'l Farmers' Federation of Australia *(David A. Keene, Craigan P. Shirley)*
The Limited, Inc. *(Darrel Choat, David A. Keene, Craigan P. Shirley)*
World Freedom Foundation *(David A. Keene, Craigan P. Shirley)*

KEENE, Thomas C.
C & M Internat'l L.P.
1001 Pennsylvania Ave., N.W., Washington, DC 20004-2505
Telephone: (202) 624-2895
Registered as Foreign Agent: (#3988).

KEENEY, Eugene Adams
Exec. V. President, Optical Manufacturers Ass'n
6055A Arlington Blvd., Falls Church, VA 22044
Telephone: (703) 237-8433

KEENEY, Robin E.
Director, Government Relations, American Land Title Ass'n
1828 L St., N.W., Suite 705, Washington, DC 20036
Telephone: (202) 296-3671
Registered as lobbyist at U.S. Congress.
Background: Serves as contact for Title Industry Political Action Committee.

KEENY, Spurgeon M., Jr.
President and Exec. Director, Arms Control Ass'n
11 Dupont Circle, N.W., Washington, DC 20036
Telephone: (202) 797-6450
Background: Former Deputy and Assistant Director, U.S. Arms Control and Disarmament Agency; Senior staff member, Nat'l Security Council.

KEHOE, Brien E.
Hill, Betts and Nash
1818 N St., N.W., Suite 700, Washington, DC 20036
Telephone: (202) 452-0586
Registered as lobbyist at U.S. Congress.
Background: General Counsel, Federal Maritime Commission, 1979-81. Marine Legal Counsel, Department of Transportation, 1981-82. Exec. Assistant to Maritime Administrator, Department of Transportation, 1982-83.
Clients:
Resources Trucking Inc.
Waterman Steamship Co.

KEHOE, Danea M.
Associate General Counsel, Nat'l Ass'n of Life Underwriters
1922 F St., N.W., Washington, DC 20006
Telephone: (202) 331-6000
Registered as lobbyist at U.S. Congress.

KEHOE, Keiki
Dir., Nuclear Accoun./Global Warming, Friends of the Earth
218 D St., S.E., Washington, DC 20003
Telephone: (202) 544-2600
Registered as lobbyist at U.S. Congress.

KEHS, Michael
Account Supervisor, Burson-Marsteller
1850 M St., N.W., Suite 900, Washington, DC 20036
Telephone: (202) 833-8550

KEIFFER, Sebert H.
General Counsel, Hardwood Plywood Manufacturers Ass'n
7111 Allentown Rd. Suite 108, Camp Springs,, MD 20744
Telephone: (301) 248-7400

KEIMOWITZ, Hazel
Acting Exec. Director, American College of Preventive Medicine
Suite 403, 1015 15th St., N.W., Washington, DC 20005
Telephone: (202) 789-0003

KEINER, R. Bruce, Jr.
Crowell and Moring
1001 Pennsylvania Ave., N.W., Washington, DC 20004-2505
Telephone: (202) 624-2500
Clients:
Emery Worldwide

KEIR, Rick
Director, Communications, Recreation Vehicle Industry Ass'n
1896 Preston White Drive P.O. Box 2999, Reston, VA 22090
Telephone: (703) 620-6003

KEISER, Joan F.
Legislative Representative, Nat'l Rural Electric Cooperative Ass'n
1800 Massachusetts Ave., N.W., Washington, DC 20036
Telephone: (202) 857-9500
Registered as lobbyist at U.S. Congress.

KEISTER, Rick
Legis. Rep., Public Lands, Nat'l Ass'n of Counties
440 First St., N.W., Washington, DC 20001
Telephone: (202) 393-6226

KEITH, Hastings
Co-Chairman, Nat'l Committee on Public Employee Pension Systems
1221 Connecticut Ave., N.W., 4th Floor, Washington, DC 20036
Telephone: (202) 293-3960
Background: Former Member, U.S. House of Representatives, 1959-72.

KEITH, Jefferson D.
Exec. Director, American Driver and Traffic Safety Education Ass'n
239 Florida Ave., Salisbury, MD 21801
Telephone: (301) 860-0075
Background: Also represents the Alliance for Traffic Safety.

KEITH, Kendell W.
Exec. V. President, Nat'l Grain and Feed Ass'n
1201 New York Ave., N.W. Suite 830, Washington, DC 20005
Telephone: (202) 289-0873
Registered as lobbyist at U.S. Congress.

KEITHLEY, Carter E.
V. President, Smith, Bucklin and Associates
1101 Connecticut Ave., N.W., Suite 700, Washington, DC 20036
Telephone: (202) 857-1100
Background: Serves as Exec. Director, Wood Heating Alliance, and Exec. Director, Regulatory Affairs Professionals Soc.
Clients:
Regulatory Affairs Professionals Soc.
Wood Heating Alliance

KEITHLEY, Jay C.
V. President, Law & External Affairs, United Telecommunications
1875 Eye St., N.W., Suite 1250, Washington, DC 20006
Telephone: (202) 659-4600
Registered as lobbyist at U.S. Congress.

KELER, Marianne M.
V. President and Assoc. General Counsel, Student Loan Marketing Ass'n
1050 Thomas Jefferson St., N.W., Washington, DC 20007
Telephone: (202) 333-8000

KELL, Bonnie
Account Executive, Powell, Adams & Rinehart
1901 L St., N.W., 3rd Floor, Washington, DC 20036
Telephone: (202) 466-7590

KELLEHER, William D.
Manager, Community Development, Chamber of Commerce of the U.S.A.
1615 H St., N.W., Washington, DC 20062
Telephone: (202) 463-5533
Registered as lobbyist at U.S. Congress.

KELLEN CO., Robert H.
1101 15th St., N.W., Washington, DC 20005
Telephone: (202) 785-3232
Background: The Washington office of an Atlanta-based association management firm.
Members of firm representing listed organizations:
Cristol, Richard E.
Background: Serves as Exec. Director, Nat'l Ass'n of Margarine Manufacturers.
Ebert, Andrew
Background: Serves as Exec. Director, The Cranberry Institute.
Jones, Belva W.
Background: Serves as Associate Director, Nat'l Ass'n of Margarine Manufacturers.
Kellen, Robert H., President
Organizations represented:
Cranberry Institute, The *(Andrew Ebert, Robert H. Kellen)*
Nat'l Ass'n of Margarine Manufacturers *(Richard E. Cristol, Belva W. Jones)*

KELLEN, Robert H.
President, Kellen Co., Robert H.
1101 15th St., N.W., Washington, DC 20005
Telephone: (202) 785-3232
Organizations represented:
Cranberry Institute, The

KELLER, Charles L.
Director, Bureau of Explosives, Ass'n of American Railroads
50 F St., N.W., Suite 6501, Washington, DC 20001
Telephone: (202) 639-2133

KELLER, Elizabeth
Deputy Director, Internat'l City Management Ass'n
777 North Capitol St., N.E., Suite 500, Washington, DC 20002
Telephone: (202) 289-4262

KELLER AND HECKMAN
1150 17th St., N.W. Suite 1000, Washington, DC 20036
Telephone: (202) 956-5600

The listings in this directory are available as *Mailing Labels.* See last page.

221

KELLER AND HECKMAN (Cont'd)

Members of firm representing listed organizations:

Black, Wayne V.

Borghesani, William H. (Jr.)

Background: Serves as General Counsel, Private Carrier Conference.

Dubeck, John B.

Eldred, John S.

Background: Trial Attorney, Food and Drug Administration, 1970-75.

Keller, Joseph E.

MacArthur, Malcolm D.

Background: Trial Attorney, Antitrust Division, U.S. Department of Justice, 1959-63.

Mayberry, Peter G.

McNamara, Mary Martha

Susser, Peter A.

Clients:

Art Supply Labeling Coalition *(Mary Martha McNamara)*

Contractors Pump Bureau *(Malcolm D. MacArthur)*

Dayton Power and Light Co.

Dean Witter Financial Services Group *(Mary Martha McNamara)*

Georgia Power Co.

Gulf States Utilities Co.

Healthcare Compliance Packaging Council

INDA, Ass'n of the Nonwoven Fabrics Industry *(Wayne V. Black, Peter G. Mayberry)*

Internat'l Ass'n of Fire Chiefs

Iowa Power and Light Co.

K-Line Pharmaceuticals, Ltd. *(John S. Eldred, Joseph E. Keller)*

Monongahela Power Co.

Montana Power Co.

Nat'l-American Wholesale Grocers' Ass'n *(William H. Borghesani, Jr., Peter A. Susser)*

New Mexico Electric Service Co.

Northern States Power Co.

Soc. of the Plastics Industry

Special Industrial Radio Service Ass'n

Specialty Advertising Ass'n, Internat'l

Texas Gas Transmission Corp.

Vestal Laboratories *(John B. Dubeck)*

Wisconsin Electric Power Co.

KELLER, Joseph E.

Keller and Heckman

1150 17th St., N.W. Suite 1000, Washington, DC 20036

Telephone: (202) 956-5600

Clients:

K-Line Pharmaceuticals, Ltd.

KELLER, Lisa

Communications Specialist, Nat'l Milk Producers Federation

1840 Wilson Blvd., Arlington, VA 22201

Telephone: (703) 243-6111

KELLER-REIS, Lee

Director, Communications, Nat'l Wildlife Federation

1400 16th St., N.W., Washington, DC 20036-2266

Telephone: (202) 797-6800

KELLER, Thomas J.

Verner, Liipfert, Bernhard, McPherson and Hand, Chartered

901 15th St., N.W., Suite 700, Washington, DC 20005

Telephone: (202) 371-6000

Registered as lobbyist at U.S. Congress.

Registered as Foreign Agent: (#3712).

KELLERS, Peggy

Exec. Director, Nat'l Ass'n for Girls and Women in Sport

1900 Association Drive, Reston, VA 22091

Telephone: (703) 476-3450

KELLEY, Dr. Daniel

Director, Regulatory Policy & Analysis, MCI Communications Corp.

1133 19th St., N.W., Washington, DC 20036

Telephone: (202) 872-1600

KELLEY, DRYE AND WARREN

2300 M St., N.W., Washington, DC 20037

Telephone: (202) 463-8333

Members of firm representing listed organizations:

Edson, Charles L.

Background: General Counsel, President's Commission on Postal Organizations, 1967-68. Chief, Public Housing Section, Office of General Counsel, Department of Housing and Urban Development, 1968-70.

Lebow, Edward M.

Lemov, Michael R., Of Counsel

Lorber, Lawrence Z.

Marinaccio, Charles L.

Clients:

Baltimore, Maryland, City of *(Michael R. Lemov)*

Coalition to Preserve the Low Income Housing Tax Credit *(Charles L. Edson)*

Council for Rural Housing and Development *(Charles L. Edson)*

Cushman & Wakefield, Inc.

Great Western Financial Corp. *(Michael R. Lemov)*

Guinness PLC

Morgan & Co., J. P.

Nat'l Glass Ass'n *(Michael R. Lemov)*

Nat'l Independent Automobile Dealers Ass'n *(Michael R. Lemov)*

Nat'l Leased Housing Ass'n *(Charles L. Edson)*

New York Hospital *(Charles L. Marinaccio)*

Pyropower Corp. *(Michael R. Lemov)*

Soc. for Human Resources Management *(Lawrence Z. Lorber)*

Tokyo Electric Co., Ltd. *(Edward M. Lebow)*

KELLEY, Elizabeth

Account Supervisor, Edelman, Inc., Daniel J.

1420 K St., N.W., Washington, DC 20005

Telephone: (202) 371-0200

Organizations represented:

American Academy of Actuaries

General Foods Foundation

KELLEY, J. Tyrone

Government Relations Representative, Food Marketing Institute

1750 K St., N.W., Washington, DC 20006

Telephone: (202) 452-8444

Registered as lobbyist at U.S. Congress.

KELLEY, Joseph B.

Manager, State and Outreach Affairs, Grace and Co., W. R.

919 18th St., N.W., Suite 400, Washington, DC 20006

Telephone: (202) 452-6700

KELLEY, Keith

Staff Director for Public Relations, Federal Bar Ass'n

1815 H St., N.W., Suite 408, Washington, DC 20006

Telephone: (202) 638-0252

KELLEY, Kevin J.

V. President, Cellular Telecommunications Industry Ass'n

1133 21St., N.W., Third Floor, Washington, DC 20036

Telephone: (202) 785-0081

KELLEY, Margaret

External Liaison Representative, American Petroleum Institute

1220 L St., N.W., Washington, DC 20005

Telephone: (202) 682-8284

KELLEY, Michelle Spivak

Nat'l Program Director, Jewish War Veterans of the U.S.-A.

1811 R St., N.W., Washington, DC 20009

Telephone: (202) 265-6280

KELLEY, General Paul X., USMC-Ret.

V. President, Corporate Marketing, Cassidy and Associates, Inc.

655 15th St., N.W., Suite 1100, Washington, DC 20005

Telephone: (202) 347-0773

Background: Commander, President's Rapid Deployment Task Force, 1980. Commandant of the U.S. Marine Corps, 1983-87.

Clients:

Internat'l Data Corp.

KELLEY, Robert

Sears Law Offices, John P.

2021 K St., N.W., Suite 750, Washington, DC 20006

Telephone: (202) 331-3300

Registered as lobbyist at U.S. Congress.

Registered as Foreign Agent: (#3584).

Background: Former deputy legal counsel, U.S. Senate.

Organizations represented:

South Africa, Embassy of

KELLEY, Robert H., Jr.

Treasurer, Fairchild Political Action Committee

300 West Service Road Dulles Internat'l Airport, Chantilly, VA 22021-9998

Telephone: (703) 478-5800

KELLIHER, Joseph T.

Legislative Programs Director, American Nuclear Energy Council

410 First St., S.E. Third Floor, Washington, DC 20003

Telephone: (202) 484-2670

Registered as lobbyist at U.S. Congress.

KELLNER, Stephen S.

Vice President, Legal Affairs, Chemical Specialties Manufacturers Ass'n

1913 Eye St., N.W., Washington, DC 20006

Telephone: (202) 872-8110

Registered as lobbyist at U.S. Congress.

Background: Also repoonsible for Chemical Specialties Manufacturers Ass'n Political Action Committee.

KELLOGG, Paulette

Regulatory Representative, American College of Emergency Physicians

900 17th St., N.W., Suite 1250, Washington, DC 20006

Telephone: (202) 728-0610

KELLY AND ASSOCIATES, INC.

1025 Thomas Jefferson St., N.W., Suite 105, Washington, DC 20007

Telephone: (202) 342-9610

Background: A government/public affairs firm.

Members of firm representing listed organizations:

Kelly, John A., President

Background: Dep. Exec. Director, 1989 Presidential Inaugural Committee Lead Advance, Vice President Dan Quayle, 1988 Bush/Quayle Committee; Director, Office of Presidential Liaison and Special Assistant for Political Affairs, Republican National Committee, 1981-82; Member, Presidential Transition Team, 1980; Legislative Assistant to Rep. Charles B. Rangel (D-NY), 1974-78.

Clients:

Globe Securities System Inc. *(John A. Kelly)*

Internat'l Narcotic Enforcement Officers Ass'n *(John A. Kelly)*

Merit Protection System, Inc. *(John A. Kelly)*

Perdue Farms Inc. *(John A. Kelly)*

Sahlen and Associates, Inc. *(John A. Kelly)*

Universidad Autonoma de Guadalajara *(John A. Kelly)*

KELLY, Biruta P.

Scribner, Hall and Thompson

1850 K St., N.W. Suite 1100, Washington, DC 20006-2201

Telephone: (202) 331-8585

Registered as Foreign Agent: (#4253).

Background: Attorney, Interpretative Division, Chief Counsel's Office, Internal Revenue Service, 1982-83.

KELLY, Carol A.

V. President, Metropolitan Insurance Cos.

1615 L St., N.W., Suite 1210, Washington, DC 20036

Telephone: (202) 659-3575

Registered as lobbyist at U.S. Congress.

KELLY, Cynthia K.

Manager, Government and Legal Affairs, American Ass'n of Blood Banks

1117 North 19th St. Suite 600, Arlington, VA 22209

Telephone: (703) 528-8200

Registered as lobbyist at U.S. Congress.

KELLY, Donald E.

VP & Director of Washington Operations, Soc. of Real Estate Appraisers

600 New Hampshire Ave., N.W. Suite 1111, Washington, DC 20037

Telephone: (202) 298-8497

Registered as lobbyist at U.S. Congress.

Background: Counsel, Committee of Standards of Official Conduct, U.S. House of Representatives, 1980-82. Chief Counsel, Subcommittee on Oversight and Investigations, House Banking, Finance and Urban Affairs Committee, 1982-85.

KELLY, Doug
Policy Analyst, Citizens for Tax Justice
1311 L St., N.W. 4th Floor, Washington, DC 20005
Telephone: (202) 626-3780

KELLY, Earl
Director, Governmental Affairs, American Wind Energy
Ass'n
1730 N. Lynn St., Suite 610, Arlington, VA 22209
Telephone: (703) 276-8334
Registered as lobbyist at U.S. Congress.

KELLY, Edward
Director, Regulatory Affairs, Nat'l Ass'n of Private Psy-
chiatric Hospitals
1319 F St., N.W., Suite 1000, Washington, DC 20004
Telephone: (202) 393-6700
Registered as lobbyist at U.S. Congress.
Background: Formerly with the Department of Health and
Human Services.

KELLY, Ellen I.
Manager, Member Relations, Aerospace Industries Ass'n
of America
1250 Eye St., N.W., Suite 1100, Washington, DC 20005
Telephone: (202) 371-8400

KELLY, Ernest B., III
Director, Government Relations, Communications Satellite
Corp. (COMSAT)
950 L'Enfant Plaza, S.W., Washington, DC 20024
Telephone: (202) 863-6000
Registered as lobbyist at U.S. Congress.

KELLY, Frank X.
Gallagher, Boland, Meiburger and Brosnan
1000 Vermont Ave., N.W. Suite 1100, Washington, DC
20005-4903
Telephone: (202) 289-7200
Clients:
Enron Corp.

KELLY, John A.
President, Kelly and Associates, Inc.
1025 Thomas Jefferson St., N.W., Suite 105, Washington,
DC 20007
Telephone: (202) 342-9610
Registered as lobbyist at U.S. Congress.
Background: Dep. Exec. Director, 1989 Presidential
Inaugural Committee Lead Advance, Vice President Dan
Quayle, 1988 Bush/Quayle Committee; Director, Office
of Presidential Liaison and Special Assistant for Political
Affairs, Republican National Committee, 1981-82; Mem-
ber, Presidential Transition Team, 1980; Legislative As-
sistant to Rep. Charles B. Rangel (D-NY), 1974-78.
Clients:
Globe Securities System Inc.
Internat'l Narcotic Enforcement Officers Ass'n
Merit Protection System, Inc.
Perdue Farms Inc.
Sahlen and Associates, Inc.
Universidad Autonoma de Guadalajara

KELLY, John F.
Government Relations Representative, Merrill Lynch and
Co., Inc.
1828 L St., N.W., Suite 906, Washington, DC 20036
Telephone: (202) 822-3600
Registered as lobbyist at U.S. Congress.

KELLY, John P., Jr.
President, Nat'l Bankers Ass'n
122 C St., N.W. Suite 580, Washington, DC 20001
Telephone: (202) 783-3200
Background: Responsibilities include Nat'l Bankers Ass'n
Political Action Committee.

KELLY, Jon F.
Thompson, Hine and Flory
1920 N St., N.W., Washington, DC 20036
Telephone: (202) 331-8800

KELLY, Joseph F., Jr.
Dow, Lohnes and Albertson
1255 23rd St., N.W., Suite 500, Washington, DC 20037
Telephone: (202) 857-2500
Clients:
U.S. Trust Co.

KELLY, Michael S.
Morgan, Lewis and Bockius
1800 M St., N.W., Washington, DC 20036
Telephone: (202) 467-7000
Registered as Foreign Agent: (#3794).
Clients:
Scotch Whiskey Ass'n
United Kingdom of Great Britain and Northern
Ireland, Government of the

KELLY, Paul A., Jr.
Plant Safety and Energy Manager, Ford Motor Co.
1350 Eye St., N.W. Suite 1000, Washington, DC 20005
Telephone: (202) 962-5400
Registered as lobbyist at U.S. Congress.

KELLY, Paul T.
Director of Governmental Relations, American Chiroprac-
tic Ass'n
1701 Clarendon Blvd., Arlington, VA 22209
Telephone: (703) 276-8800
Registered as lobbyist at U.S. Congress.

KELLY, Peter G.
Black, Manafort, Stone and Kelly Public Affairs Co.
211 N. Union St., Third Floor, Alexandria, VA 22314
Telephone: (703) 683-6612
Registered as Foreign Agent: (#3600).
Clients:
Aetna Life & Casualty Co.

KELLY, Susan N.
Miller, Balis and O'Neil
1101 14th St., N.W. Suite 1400, Washington, DC 20005
Telephone: (202) 789-1450
Registered as lobbyist at U.S. Congress.
Clients:
American Public Gas Ass'n

KELLY, William C., Jr.
Latham and Watkins
1001 Pennsylvania Ave., N.W., Suite 1300, Washington,
DC 20004
Telephone: (202) 637-2200
Registered as lobbyist at U.S. Congress.
Background: Law Clerk to Supreme Court Justice Lewis F.
Powell, Jr., 1972-73. Assistant to Special Counsel, Office
of Secretary of the Navy, 1973-75. Exec. Assistant to
Secretary of Housing and Urban Development, 1975-77.
Clients:
Los Angeles Community Redevelopment Agency

KELMAR, Steven
Asst Secy, Legislation (Act), DEPARTMENT OF HEALTH
AND HUMAN SERVICES
200 Independence Ave. S.W., Washington, DC 20201
Telephone: (202) 245-7627

KELSCH, E. Taylor
Senior Planning and Programs Analyst, Arabian American
Oil Co.
1667 K St., N.W., Suite 1200, Washington, DC 20006
Telephone: (202) 223-7750

KELSEY, Peter B.
V. President, Law & Coprorate Secretary, Edison Electric
Institute
1111 19th St., N.W., Washington, DC 20036
Telephone: (202) 778-6620
Registered as lobbyist at U.S. Congress.

KEMBLE, Penn
Chairman, Executive Committee, Coalition for a Democratic Majority
1001 Connecticut Ave., N.W., Suite 707, Washington, DC
20036
Telephone: (202) 466-4702

KEMMER, Mark L.
Senior Washington Representative, General Motors Corp.
1660 L St., N.W., Washington, DC 20036
Telephone: (202) 775-5066
Registered as lobbyist at U.S. Congress.

KEMPER, Coletta I.
Director, Public Affairs, Nat'l Ass'n of Insurance Brokers
1401 New York Ave., N.W., Suite 720, Washington, DC
20005
Telephone: (202) 628-6700

Registered as lobbyist at U.S. Congress.

KEMPER, Jackson, Jr.
V. President, Washington Operations, Diagnostic Retrieval
Systems, Inc.
1215 South Jefferson Davis Hwy., Suite 1004, Arlington,
VA 22202
Telephone: (703) 521-8000
Registered as lobbyist at U.S. Congress.

KEMPNER, Jonathan L.
President, Nat'l Multi Housing Council
1250 Connecticut Ave., N.W., Suite 620, Washington, DC
20036
Telephone: (202) 659-3381
Registered as lobbyist at U.S. Congress.
Background: Serves as contact for the Nat'l Multi Housing
Council PAC.

KENARY, Patrick
Spec Asst, Legis Affrs, EXECUTIVE OFFICE OF THE
PRESIDENT - Office of Management and Budget
Old Executive Office Bldg., Washington, DC 20500
Telephone: (202) 395-4790

KENDALL AND ASSOCIATES
50 E St., S.E., Washington, DC 20003
Telephone: (202) 546-2600
Members of firm representing listed organizations:
Andrukitis, Barbara C., President
Kendall, William T., Chairman
Clients:
ALC Communications Corp. *(William T. Kendall)*
Manville Corp. *(William T. Kendall)*
Toyota Motor Sales, U.S.A. *(William T. Kendall)*

KENDALL, Beverly C.
Secretary and Tresurer, Shipbuilders Council of America
1110 Vermont Ave., N.W. Suite 1250, Washington, DC
20005
Telephone: (202) 775-9060

KENDALL, David E.
Williams and Connolly
839 17th St., N.W. 1000 Hill Bldg., Washington, DC 20006
Telephone: (202) 331-5000
Background: Law Clerk to U.S. Supreme Court Justice By-
ron R. White, 1971-72.
Clients:
MCA Inc.
Washington Post Co.

KENDALL, William T.
Chairman, Kendall and Associates
50 E St., S.E., Washington, DC 20003
Telephone: (202) 546-2600
Registered as lobbyist at U.S. Congress.
Clients:
ALC Communications Corp.
Manville Corp.
Toyota Motor Sales, U.S.A.

KENDRICK, John
Director, Congressional Relations, Grumman Corp.
1000 Wilson Blvd., Suite 2800, Arlington, VA 22209
Telephone: (703) 875-8400
Registered as lobbyist at U.S. Congress.

KENDRICK, Martha M.
Patton, Boggs and Blow
2550 M St., N.W., Suite 800, Washington, DC 20037
Telephone: (202) 457-6000
Registered as lobbyist at U.S. Congress.

KENKEL, Mary
Public Information Representative, Edison Electric Institute
1111 19th St., N.W., Washington, DC 20036
Telephone: (202) 778-6662

KENNAN, Stephanie A.
Legislative Representative, American College of Emergen-
cy Physicians
900 17th St., N.W., Suite 1250, Washington, DC 20006
Telephone: (202) 728-0610
Registered as lobbyist at U.S. Congress.

KENNEBECK, Joseph W.
Government Affairs Manager, Volkswagen of America, Inc.
490 L'Enfant Plaza, S.W., Suite 7204, Washington, DC 20024
Telephone: (202) 484-6096
Registered as lobbyist at U.S. Congress.

KENNEDY, David
Assoc. Dir, State Legislative Afairs, Aircraft Owners and Pilots Ass'n
421 Aviation Way, Frederick, MD 21701
Telephone: (301) 695-2000
Registered as lobbyist at U.S. Congress.

KENNEDY, James J.
Exec. Secretary-Treasurer, Railway Labor Executives' Ass'n
400 First St., N.W. Suite 804, Washington, DC 20001
Telephone: (202) 737-1541
Registered as lobbyist at U.S. Congress.
Background: Registered as lobbyist at U.S. Congress.

KENNEDY, Joseph B.
Consulting Attorney, Government Accountability Project (GAP)
25 E St., N.W. Suite 700, Washington, DC 20001
Telephone: (202) 347-0460
Background: Former Administrative Law Judge, Mine Safety and Health Review Commission.

KENNEDY, Judith A.
V. President, Government Affairs, Federal Home Loan Mortgage Corp.
1759 Business Center Drive, Reston, VA 22090
Telephone: (703) 789-4700
Registered as lobbyist at U.S. Congress.

KENNEDY, Mary A.
Managing Director, Government Affairs, American Airlines
1101 17th St., N.W. Suite 600, Washington, DC 20036
Telephone: (202) 857-4221

KENNEDY, Michael E.
Director, Equal Employment Opportunity, Associated General Contractors of America
1957 E St., N.W., Washington, DC 20006
Telephone: (202) 393-2040

KENNEDY, Nancy Mohr
Asst Secy, Legislation, DEPARTMENT OF EDUCATION
400 Maryland Ave., S.W., Washington, DC 20202
Telephone: (202) 732-5020

KENNEDY, Sean W.
President and CEO, Electronic Funds Transfer Ass'n
1421 Prince St., Suite 310, Alexandria, VA 22314
Telephone: (703) 549-9800
Registered as lobbyist at U.S. Congress.

KENNEDY, Thomas
Exec. Director, Ass'n of State and Territorial Solid Waste Management Officials
444 North Capitol St., N.W., Suite 388, Washington, DC 20001
Telephone: (202) 624-5828

KENNER, Mary Ellen
Director, Marketing and Communications, Printing Industries of America
1730 North Lynn St., Arlington, VA 22209
Telephone: (703) 841-8100

KENNERDELL, Peter B.
Exec. Director of Programs, Public Affairs Council
1019 19th St., N.W., Suite 200, Washington, DC 20036
Telephone: (202) 872-1790

KENNEY, Jeremiah J., Jr.
Director of Federal Affairs, Union Carbide Corp.
1100 15th St., N.W., Suite 1200, Washington, DC 20005
Telephone: (202) 872-8555
Registered as lobbyist at U.S. Congress.

KENNEY, Sarah
Manager, Public Relations and Marketing, Soc. of Industrial and Office Realtors
777 14th St., N.W. Suite 400, Washington, DC 20005-3271
Telephone: (202) 383-1150

KENNY, Brendan M.
Legislative Representative, Air Line Pilots Ass'n Internat'l
1625 Massachusetts Ave., N.W., Washington, DC 20036
Telephone: (202) 797-4003
Registered as lobbyist at U.S. Congress.
Background: Former Congressional Relations Officer for U.S. Department of Transportation.

KENNY, Henry J.
V. President, American League for Exports and Security Assistance (ALESA)
122 C St., N.W., Suite 740, Washington, DC 20001
Telephone: (202) 783-0051
Registered as lobbyist at U.S. Congress.

KENOPENSKY, Andrew
Automotive Coordinator, Internat'l Ass'n of Machinists and Aerospace Workers
1300 Connecticut Ave., N.W. Suite 404, Washington, DC 20036
Telephone: (202) 857-5200

KENT, J. H.
Chairman, Kent & O'Connor, Incorp.
1825 K St., N.W., Suite 305, Washington, DC 20006
Telephone: (202) 223-6222
Registered as lobbyist at U.S. Congress.
Clients:
American Soc. of Plastic and Reconstructive Surgeons
American Supply Ass'n
Internat'l Ass'n of Airport Duty Free Stores
Nat'l Ass'n of Steel Pipe Distributors
Nat'l Customs Brokers and Forwarders Ass'n of America
Vista Chemical Co.

KENT & O'CONNOR, INCORP.
1825 K St., N.W., Suite 305, Washington, DC 20006
Telephone: (202) 223-6222
Background: A corporate government affairs consulting firm.
Members of firm representing listed organizations:
Fitzgerald, Eileen, Consultant
Background: Served in the federal government, 1975-88.
Kent, J. H., Chairman
O'Connor, Patrick C., President
Thomas, Cindy, Attorney
Background: Served in the federal government, 1973-77.
Clients:
American College of Occupational Medicine *(Patrick C. O'Connor)*
American Soc. of Plastic and Reconstructive Surgeons *(J. H. Kent)*
American Supply Ass'n *(J. H. Kent, Patrick C. O'Connor)*
American Warehousemen's Ass'n *(Patrick C. O'Connor)*
Internat'l Ass'n of Airport Duty Free Stores *(J. H. Kent)*
Nat'l Ass'n of Fleet Administrators *(Patrick C. O'Connor)*
Nat'l Ass'n of Steel Pipe Distributors *(J. H. Kent)*
Nat'l Customs Brokers and Forwarders Ass'n of America *(J. H. Kent)*
Steel Tank Institute *(Patrick C. O'Connor)*
Transportation Lawyers Ass'n *(Patrick C. O'Connor)*
Vista Chemical Co. *(J. H. Kent)*

KENWORTHY, James L., Esq.
905 Sixth St., S.W. Suite 708-B, Washington, DC 20024
Telephone: (202) 863-0426
Background: A consultant in government affairs and international trade. Held U.S. Senate Staff position with two Senators from Missouri, 1959-62 and 1964-66. Served with the Foreign Claims Settlement Commission, 1966-67, and in the U.S. Department of Commerce in the Office of Foreign Direct Investments (1969-70) and the Office of the General Counsel (1974-81).
Organizations represented:
Coalition to End the Permanent Congress
Nat'l Economists Club

KENYON, Capt. Chris
Exec Officer, Legis Liaison, DEPARTMENT OF AIR FORCE
The Pentagon, Washington, DC 20330

Telephone: (202) 697-8153

KENYON, Tom
Exec. Director, Nat'l Alliance to End Homelessness
1518 K St., N.W., Suite 206, Washington, DC 20005
Telephone: (202) 638-1526
Background: Public Welfare Analyst, Legislative Reference Service, Library of Congress, 1963-65. Public Welfare Analyst, Office of Assistant Secretary for Planning and Evaluation, Department of Health, Education and Welfare, 1967-70.

KEPHART, Kelly
Treasurer, Independent Lubricant Manufacturers Ass'n Political Action Committee
651 S. Washington St., Alexandria, VA 22314
Telephone: (703) 684-5574

KEPLEY, Elizabeth Y.
Director, Government Relations, Family Research Council, Inc.
601 Pennsylvania Ave., N.W., Suite 901, Washington, DC 20004
Telephone: (202) 393-2100
Registered as lobbyist at U.S. Congress.

KERAMIDAS, Sherry
Assoc. Exec. V. President, American Physical Therapy Ass'n
1111 North Fairfax St., Alexandria, VA 22314
Telephone: (703) 684-2782

KERCHERVAL SHORT, Mary
Secretary for Women's Concerns, United Methodist Church Board of Global Ministries, Women's Div.
100 Maryland Ave., N.E., Room 501, Washington, DC 20002
Telephone: (202) 488-5660

KEREKES, Steven C.
Director, Public Relations, Nat'l Right to Work Committee
8001 Braddock Road, Springfield, VA 22160
Telephone: (703) 321-9820

KERESTER, Thomas P.
Exec. Director, Tax Executives Institute
1001 Pennsylvania Ave., N.W., Suite 320, Washington, DC 20004-2505
Telephone: (202) 638-5601

KERIN, Kenneth J.
Senior V. President, Nat'l Ass'n of REALTORS
777 14th St., N.W., Washington, DC 20005
Telephone: (202) 383-1000

KERLEY, Michael L.
V. President, Government Affairs, Nat'l Ass'n of Life Underwriters
1922 F St., N.W., Washington, DC 20006
Telephone: (202) 331-6022
Registered as lobbyist at U.S. Congress.

KERMAN, Leslie
Epstein Becker and Green
1227 25th St., N.W., Suite 700, Washington, DC 20037
Telephone: (202) 861-0900
Clients:
Independent Action

KERN, Robert G.
Wright and Talisman
1050 17th St., N.W. Suite 600, Washington, DC 20036
Telephone: (202) 331-1194
Registered as lobbyist at U.S. Congress.

KERN, Sheila
Manager, International Programs, Motorola, Inc.
1350 Eye St., N.W., Suite 400, Washington, DC 20005-3306
Telephone: (202) 371-6900

KERNAN, Timothy C.
Director, Congressional Relations, Fluor Corp.
1627 K St., N.W., Suite 300, Washington, DC 20006
Telephone: (202) 955-9300
Registered as lobbyist at U.S. Congress.

KERNUS, Susan A.
Manager , Government Affairs, Synthetic Organic Chemical Manufacturers Ass'n
1330 Connecticut Ave., N.W. Suite 300, Washington, DC 20036
Telephone: (202) 659-0060
Registered as lobbyist at U.S. Congress.

KERR, Stuart
Exec. Director, Internat'l Law Institute
1615 New Hampshire Ave., N.W., Washington, DC 20009
Telephone: (202) 483-3036
Background: A non-profit organization which conducts training programs in DC and abroad for gov't officials in developing countries.

KERR, Suzanne S.
Legislative Director, Women's Action for Nuclear Disarmament
305 7th St., S.E., Suite 204, Washington, DC 20003
Telephone: (202) 543-8505
Registered as lobbyist at U.S. Congress.

KERR, T. Michael
Assistant Director of Legislation, American Federation of State, County and Municipal Employees
1625 L St., N.W., Washington, DC 20036
Telephone: (202) 429-1000
Registered as lobbyist at U.S. Congress.

KERRIGAN, Michael J.
President, Smokeless Tobacco Council
2550 M St., N.W., Suite 300, Washington, DC 20037
Telephone: (202) 452-1252
Registered as lobbyist at U.S. Congress.
Background: Also directs the Smokeless Tobacco Council Political Action Committee.

KERSCHNER, Helen K., Ph.D.
Exec. Director, American Ass'n for Internat'l Aging
1511 K St., N.W., Suite 443, Washington, DC 20005
Telephone: (202) 638-6815

KERSCHNER, Paul
Senior V. President, Nat'l Council on the Aging
600 Maryland Ave., S.W. West Wing 100, Washington, DC 20024
Telephone: (202) 479-1200

KERSHOW, Michael R.
Collier, Shannon & Scott
1055 Thomas Jefferson St., N.W., Suite 300, Washington, DC 20007
Telephone: (202) 342-8400
Registered as lobbyist at U.S. Congress.
Clients:
Gerico
Wyman-Gordon Co.

KERWIN, Mary D.
Dir, Cong Liaison, NAT'L AERONAUTICS AND SPACE ADMINISTRATION
400 Maryland Ave., S.W., Washington, DC 20546
Telephone: (202) 453-1055

KERWOOD, Lewis O.
Exec. V. President, Nat'l Soc. for Real Estate Finance
2300 M St., N.W., Suite 800, Washington, DC 20037
Telephone: (202) 466-6015

KESSLER AND ASSOCIATES
126 Kentucky Ave., S.E., Washington, DC 20003
Telephone: (202) 547-6808
Members of firm representing listed organizations:
Kessler, Richard S., President
Luhn, Kathy, Director, Government Relations
Clients:
American Ass'n of Fastener Importers
Jimmie Heuga Center
Ripon Soc.
Sandoz Corp.
Seagram & Sons, Inc., Joseph E. *(Richard S. Kessler)*
Upjohn Co.

KESSLER, Judd L.
Of Counsel, Porter, Wright, Morris and Arthur
1233 20th St., N.W., Suite 400, Washington, DC 20005
Telephone: (202) 778-3000
Registered as lobbyist at U.S. Congress.

Background: Asst. General Counsel, U.S. Agency for Internat'l Development; Chief Counsel for Middle East Programs, 1980-82; Chief Counsel for Latin America and the Caribbean, 1976-80.

KESSLER, Lee
Deputy Director, American Arts Alliance
1319 F St., N.W., Suite 307, Washington, DC 20004-1182
Telephone: (202) 737-1727

KESSLER, Lorence L.
McGuiness and Williams
1015 15th St., N.W., Suite 1200, Washington, DC 20005
Telephone: (202) 789-8600
Clients:
Equal Employment Advisory Council

KESSLER, Richard S.
President, Kessler and Associates
126 Kentucky Ave., S.E., Washington, DC 20003
Telephone: (202) 547-6808
Registered as lobbyist at U.S. Congress.
Clients:
Seagram & Sons, Inc., Joseph E.

KEST, Steven
Exec. Director, ACORN (Ass'n of Community Organizations for Reform Now)
522 8th St., S.E., Washington, DC 20003
Telephone: (202) 547-9292

KESTENBAUM, Leon M.
V. President, Regulatory Affairs, US Sprint Communications Co.
1850 M St., N.W., Suite 1100, Washington, DC 20036
Telephone: (202) 857-1030

KESTER, John
Williams and Connolly
839 17th St., N.W. 1000 Hill Bldg., Washington, DC 20006
Telephone: (202) 331-5000
Clients:
Loral/Fairchild Systems

KESTON, Joan
Exec. Director, Public Employees Roundtable
Box 6184, Ben Franklin Station, Washington, DC 20044
Telephone: (202) 535-4324

KETCHAM, John T.
Wright and Talisman
1050 17th St., N.W. Suite 600, Washington, DC 20036
Telephone: (202) 331-1194

KETCHUM PUBLIC RELATIONS
1201 Connecticut Ave., N.W. Suite 300, Washington, DC 20036
Telephone: (202) 835-8800
Registered as Foreign Agent: (#4254)
Background: Headquartered in Pittsburgh, PA.
Members of firm representing listed organizations:
Armstrong, Laura Q., V. President, Media Relations
Beam, Meg, Asst. Account Exec., Gov't Relations
Eversol, Paige
Hill, Penny
Hudak, Martha
McCahill, Julie P., V. President, Government Relations
Mueller, Ronald R., Washington Director
Olszewski, Gerald B., V. President
Shaw, Gregory M., Account Executive
Thelian, Lorraine, Sr. V. Pres., Assoc. Director
Clients:
American Council on Science and Health
American Industrial Health Council *(Lorraine Thelian)*
Aspirin Foundation of America, Inc. *(Lorraine Thelian)*
Chemical Specialties Manufacturers Ass'n
Dow Chemical *(Gerald B. Olszewski)*
Road Information Program, The (TRIP) *(Paige Eversol, Penny Hill, Martha Hudak, Ronald R. Mueller, Gregory M. Shaw)*

KETLER, Lt. Col. Richard, USMC
Dep Dir, Legis and Legal Policy, DEPARTMENT OF DEFENSE - Military Manpower and Personnel Policy, Office of Asst Secy (Force Mgmt)
The Pentagon, Washington, DC 20301
Telephone: (202) 697-3387

KEVILLE, Dorothy A.
Regional Government Affairs Manager, Burroughs Wellcome Co.
1500 K St., N.W., Suite 625, Washington, DC 20005
Telephone: (202) 393-1420
Registered as lobbyist at U.S. Congress.

KEYES, Allan
President, Citizens Against Government Waste
1301 Connecticut Ave., N.W. Suite 400, Washington, DC 20036
Telephone: (202) 467-5300

KEYES, Evelyn V.
Government Affairs Director, Farley Industries
1455 Pennsylvania Ave., N.W. Suite 1170, Washington, DC 20004
Telephone: (202) 737-1930
Registered as lobbyist at U.S. Congress.

KEYES, Joseph A., Jr.
General Counsel, Ass'n of American Medical Colleges
One Dupont Circle, N.W., Suite 200, Washington, DC 20036
Telephone: (202) 828-0400

KEYS, Arthur
Executive Director, Interfaith Action for Economic Justice
110 Maryland Ave., N.E. Suite 509, Washington, DC 20002
Telephone: (202) 543-2800

KEYS, G. Chandler, III
Director, Congressional Relations, Nat'l Cattlemen's Ass'n
1301 Pennsylvania Ave., N.W., Suite 300, Washington, DC 20004
Telephone: (202) 347-0228
Registered as lobbyist at U.S. Congress.

KEYSER, Earline A.
Domestic Issues Manager, Bechtel Group, Inc.
1620 Eye St., N.W., Suite 703, Washington, DC 20006
Telephone: (202) 393-4747

KEYSERLING, Jonathan
Black, Manafort, Stone and Kelly Public Affairs Co.
211 N. Union St., Third Floor, Alexandria, VA 22314
Telephone: (703) 683-6612
Registered as lobbyist at U.S. Congress.
Registered as Foreign Agent: (#3600).
Background: Serves as Senior V. President, Black, Manafort, Stone, and Kelly Public Affairs. Exec. Director, Congressional Tax Caucus (1981-83); Tax Council and Legislative Director to Sen. Robert T. Matsui (D-CA), (1983-86).

KEYSERLING, Judy
Kostmayer Communications, Inc.
2300 M St., N.W., Suite 920, Washington, DC 20037
Telephone: (202) 223-6655
Registered as lobbyist at U.S. Congress.
Clients:
Police Executive Research Forum

KHARASCH, Robert N.
Galland, Kharasch, Morse and Garfinkle
Canal Square, 1054 31st St., N.W., Washington, DC 20007
Telephone: (202) 342-5200
Background: Consultant to U.S. Department of Transportation, 1967-68.

KIBBE, Arthur H.
Dir., Scientific Affairs, Policy Div., American Pharmaceutical Ass'n
2215 Constitution Ave., N.W., Washington, DC 20037
Telephone: (202) 628-4410

KIDD AND CO.
6609 E. Wakefield Drive #A2, Alexandria, VA 22307
Telephone: (703) 768-7738

KIDD AND CO. (Cont'd)

Members of firm representing listed organizations:
Kidd, Yvonne, President
Clients:
Ass'n for Information and Image Management
Prison Industries Reform Council *(Yvonne Kidd)*

KIDD, Yvonne

President, Kidd and Co.
6609 E. Wakefield Drive # A2, Alexandria, VA 22307
Telephone: (703) 768-7738
Clients:
Prison Industries Reform Council

KIEDROWSKI, Katherine

Health Services Specialist, Nat'l Ass'n of Community
Health Centers
1330 New Hampshire Ave., N.W. Suite 122, Washington,
DC 20036
Telephone: (202) 659-8008

KIEFFER, Charles

Spec Asst, Legis Affrs, EXECUTIVE OFFICE OF THE
PRESIDENT - Office of Management and Budget
Old Executive Office Bldg., Washington, DC 20500
Telephone: (202) 395-4790

KIEFFER, Dr. Jarold A.

Secretary/Treasurer, Advanced Transit Ass'n
9019 Hamilton Drive, Fairfax, VA 22031
Telephone: (703) 591-8328

KIEHL, Kristina

President, Voters for Choice
2000 P St., N.W., Suite 515, Washington, DC 20036
Telephone: (202) 822-6640

KIELY, Bruce F.

Baker and Botts
555 13th St., N.W., Suite 500 East, Washington, DC
20004-1109
Telephone: (202) 639-7700
Clients:
Madison Gas and Electric Co.
Wisconsin Distributor Group

KIERNAN, Peter

Legis Counsel, SECURITIES AND EXCHANGE COMMIS-
SION
450 5th St., N.W., Washington, DC 20549
Telephone: (202) 272-2500

KIES, Kenneth J.

Baker and Hostetler
1050 Connecticut Ave., N.W. Suite 1100, Washington, DC
20036
Telephone: (202) 861-1500
Registered as lobbyist at U.S. Congress.
Clients:
American Resort and Residential Development
Ass'n Political Action Committee
Chemed Corp.
Chubb Corp., The
Cleveland Clinic Foundation
CNA Financial Corp.
Continental Insurance Investment Management
Federal Deposit Insurance Corp.
Lincoln Nat'l Life Insurance Co.
Nat'l Ass'n of Professional Insurance Agents
Rouse Company, The
St. Paul Fire and Marine Insurance Co.
Travelers Insurance Co.

KIES, William S., Jr.

Sr V. Pres, Marketing & Field Services, Food Marketing
Institute
1750 K St., N.W., Washington, DC 20006
Telephone: (202) 452-8444
Registered as lobbyist at U.S. Congress.

KIGGINS, Katherine D.

Director, Public Affairs, Professional Services Council
918 16th St., N.W. Suite 406, Washington, DC 20006
Telephone: (202) 296-2030

KIGHT, Leila

President, Washington Researchers
2612 P St., N.W., Washington, DC 20007
Telephone: (202) 333-3499

KIGIN, Joseph P.

Director, Government/Public Affairs, Westinghouse Electric Corp.
1801 K St., N.W., Washington, DC 20006
Telephone: (202) 835-2336

KILAND, Ingolf N., Jr.

Senior Washington Representative, General Motors Corp.
1660 L St., N.W., Washington, DC 20036
Telephone: (202) 775-5028
Registered as lobbyist at U.S. Congress.

KILBERG, William J.

Gibson, Dunn and Crutcher
1050 Connecticut Ave., N.W. Suite 900, Washington, DC
20036-5303
Telephone: (202) 955-8500
Background: White House Fellow, Special Assistant to the
Secretary of Labor, 1969-70. General Counsel, Federal
Mediation and Conciliation Service, 1970-71. Associate
Solicitor, Department of Labor, 1971-73. Solicitor, De-
partment of Labor, 1973-77.

KILBRY, Brian

State Legis. Director-Washington State, Transportation,
Communications Internat'l Union
815 16th St., N.W. Suite 511, Washington, DC 20036
Telephone: (202) 783-3660
Registered as lobbyist at U.S. Congress.

KILCARR, Andrew J.

Hogan and Hartson
555 13th St., N.W., Suite 1200, Washington, DC 20004-
1109
Telephone: (202) 637-5600
Background: Trial Attorney, Antitrust Division, U.S. Department of Justice, 1959-64.

KILCLINE, V. Admiral Thomas J., USN (Ret.)

President, Retired Officers Ass'n, The (TROA)
201 N. Washington St., Alexandria, VA 22314
Telephone: (703) 549-2311
Registered as lobbyist at U.S. Congress.
Background: Former Commander Naval Air Force, Atlan-
tic Fleet, Chief of Legislative Affairs.

KILDUFF, Maryann

Director of Government Relations, Telocator
2000 M St., N.W., Suite 230, Washington, DC 20036
Telephone: (202) 467-4770
Registered as lobbyist at U.S. Congress.
Background: Also represents the Telocator Political Action
Commmittee.

KILLEEN, John J.

Director, Legislative Affairs, Textron Inc.
1090 Vermont Ave., N.W., Suite 1100, Washington, DC
20005
Telephone: (202) 289-5800
Registered as lobbyist at U.S. Congress.

KILLMER, William

Legis Officer, Cong & Intergovt'l Affrs, DEPARTMENT OF
LABOR
200 Constitution Ave., N.W., Washington, DC 20210
Telephone: (202) 523-6141

KILPATRICK & CODY

2501 M St., N.W., Suite 500, Washington, DC 20037
Telephone: (202) 463-2500
Background: Washington office of an Atlanta law firm.
Members of firm representing listed organizations:
Christenson, Linda E., Counsel
Dorn, Joseph W.
Hughes, J. Vance
Background: Formerly with the U.S. Environmental
Protection Agency and the U.S. Department of Jus-
tice.
Levitas, Elliott H.
Background: Former Member, U.S. House of Represen-
tatives (D-GA).
Nuckolls, C. Randall
Background: Legislative Counsel to Senator Herman
Talmadge (D-GA), 1977-80. Chief Counsel and
Legislative Director to Senator Sam Nunn (D-GA),
1980-86.
Rice, Robert
Background: Former Special Counsel for Litigation,
General Services Administration.

von Unwerth, Frederick H., Counsel
Background: Staff Director and Legislative Counsel to
Rep. Wyche Fowler, Jr., U.S. House of Representa-
tives, 1981-84.
Wincek, Mark D.
Background: Member of Staff, U.S. House of Represen-
tatives Committee on Ways and Means, Subcommit-
tee on Oversight, 1976-81; Senior Subcommittee
Counsel, 1980-81.
Clients:
Atlantic-Southeast Airlines *(Joseph W. Dorn, C. Ran-
dall Nuckolls)*
Bank South *(Mark D. Wincek)*
Bromon Aircraft Corp. *(Joseph W. Dorn, C. Randall
Nuckolls)*
Cookware Manufacturers Ass'n *(Joseph W. Dorn)*
Coors Brewing Company *(Linda E. Christenson)*
Eye Bank Ass'n of America *(Frederick H. von Un-
werth)*
Farberware *(Joseph W. Dorn)*
Federal Express Corp. *(Elliott H. Levitas, C. Randall
Nuckolls)*
First Carolina Communications *(Frederick H. von Un-
werth)*
Forest Farmers Ass'n *(C. Randall Nuckolls)*
Frito-Lay, Inc. *(C. Randall Nuckolls, Frederick H. von Un-
werth, Mark D. Wincek)*
Furniture Rental Ass'n of America *(Frederick H. von
Unwerth)*
General Housewares Corp. *(Joseph W. Dorn)*
Georgia Tech Research Corp. *(C. Randall Nuckolls)*
Granite Industrial Development *(C. Randall Nuckolls)*
Greenpeace, U.S.A. *(J. Vance Hughes)*
Hand Tools Institute *(Joseph W. Dorn)*
Kootznoowoo, Inc. *(J. Vance Hughes, C. Randall Nuck-
olls)*
Oregon Caneberry Commission *(Joseph W. Dorn)*
PepsiCo, Inc. *(C. Randall Nuckolls, Mark D. Wincek)*
Revere Copper and Brass Co. *(Joseph W. Dorn)*
Scientific-Atlanta, Inc. *(C. Randall Nuckolls, Frederick
H. von Unwerth)*
Siemens Energy and Automation, Inc. *(C. Randall
Nuckolls)*
Southdown *(Joseph W. Dorn, C. Randall Nuckolls)*
Spalding-Evenflo *(C. Randall Nuckolls)*
United Airlines *(Elliott H. Levitas, C. Randall Nuckolls)*
University of Georgia *(C. Randall Nuckolls)*
US Sprint Communications Co. *(C. Randall Nuckolls)*
Washington Raspberry Commission *(Joseph W.
Dorn)*
Zayre Corp. *(Mark D. Wincek)*

KILROY, Richard I.

Internat'l President, Transportation, Communications Internat'l Union
815 16th St., N.W. Suite 511, Washington, DC 20036
Telephone: (202) 783-3660
Registered as lobbyist at U.S. Congress.
Background: Serves also as Chairman, Railway Labor Executives' Ass'n.

KIM, Dae Kyum

Senior Trade Analyst, Korea Foreign Trade Ass'n
1800 K St., N.W.,, Washington, DC 20006
Telephone: (202) 408-0100
Registered as Foreign Agent: (# 3636)

KIM, Jae Ho

Managing Director, Daewoo Internat'l (America) Corp.
1120 19th St., N.W., Suite 500, Washington, DC 20036
Telephone: (202) 293-8030

KIM, K. H.

General Manager, Pohang Iron & Steel Co., Ltd.
1730 Rhode Island Ave., N.W. Suite 1215, Washington,
DC 20036
Telephone: (202) 785-5643

KIM, Sukhan

Of Counsel, Arnold & Porter
1200 New Hampshire Ave., N.W., Washington, DC 20036
Telephone: (202) 872-6700
Registered as Foreign Agent: (# 1750).
Background: First Vice Chairman, U.S.-Asia Foreign Policy
Council, 1983.
Clients:
Korea, Government of
Samsung Electronics Co., Ltd.

KIMBALL, Amy B.
Government Affairs Representative, Rowland & Sellery
1023 15th St., N.W. 7th Fl., Washington, DC 20005
Telephone: (202) 289-1780
Clients:
Libbey-Owens-Ford Co.

KIMBALL, Lee A.
Exec. Director, Council on Ocean Law
1709 New York Ave., N.W. Suite 700, Washington, DC 20006
Telephone: (202) 347-3766

KIMBALL, Philips H.
Director of Communications, Nat'l Confectioners Ass'n
7900 Westpark Drive Suite A-320, McLean, VA 22102
Telephone: (703) 790-5750
Background: Former press and legislative aide to U.S. Rep. Kenneth Robinson of Virginia.

KIMBALL, Phillips T., Jr.
Director, Labor Relations Designate, Sheet Metal and Air Conditioning Contractors' Nat'l Ass'n
8224 Old Courthouse Rd., Vienna, VA 22182
Telephone: (703) 790-9890
Registered as lobbyist at U.S. Congress.

KIMBERLY, Richard H.
Director, Federal Government Relations, Kimberly-Clark Corp.
1201 Pennsylvania Ave., N.W. Suite 730, Washington, DC 20004
Telephone: (202) 393-8280
Registered as lobbyist at U.S. Congress.
Background: First Vice President, American League of Lobbyists, 1990.

KIMBLE, James L.
Senior Counsel, American Insurance Ass'n
1130 Connecticut Ave., N.W., Suite 1000, Washington, DC 20036
Telephone: (202) 828-7100
Registered as lobbyist at U.S. Congress.

KIMBRELL, Andrew
Policy Director, Foundation on Economic Trends
1130 17th St., N.W. Suite 630, Washington, DC 20026
Telephone: (202) 466-2823

KIMBRELL, Eddie
Senior Consultant, Gov't Relations, Holland and Knight
888 17th St., N.W. Suite 900, Washington, DC 20006
Telephone: (202) 955-5550
Background: Former Deputy Administrator, Agricultural Marketing Service, U.S. Department of Agriculture.

KIMMELMAN, Gene
Legislative Director, Consumer Federation of America
1424 16th St., N.W. Suite 604, Washington, DC 20036
Telephone: (202) 387-6121
Registered as lobbyist at U.S. Congress.

KIMMITT, J. S. 'Stan'
Assistant to the Pres., Gov't Affairs, McDonnell Douglas Helicopter Co.
1735 Jefferson Davis Hwy. Suite 1200, Arlington, VA 22202
Telephone: (703) 553-3885
Background: Former Secretary of the U.S. Senate.

KINARD, Lisa P.
Associate, Wexler, Reynolds, Fuller, Harrison and Schule, Inc.
1317 F St., N.W., Suite 600, Washington, DC 20004
Telephone: (202) 638-2121
Background: Former Legislative Assistant to Rep. Augustus F. Hawkins (D-CA).

KINAS, John
Staff Director, Political Affairs, Nat'l Ass'n of Home Builders of the U.S.
15th and M Streets, N.W., Washington, DC 20005
Telephone: (202) 822-0470
Background: Legislative Director to Rep. Floyd Fithian (D-IN), 1975-80. Exec. Assistant to Rep. Fithian, 1980-82. Exec. Assistant to Rep. Bill Patman (D-TX), 1983.

KINDNESS & CHATFIELD ASSOCIATES
1747 Pennsylvania Ave., N.W., Suite 1100, Washington, DC 20006
Telephone: (202) 429-6060
Background: A governmental affairs consulting service.
Members of firm representing listed organizations:
Chatfield, William A.
Background: U.S. House of Representatives Floor Staff, 1978-79. Staff of the Deputy Undersecretary for Policy, Department of Defense, 1981-82. Regional Director, Civil Aeronautics Board, 1982-84. Special Assistant to Director, Office of Personnel Management; Assistant to Chairman, Consumer Products Safety Commission; Special Assistant for Congressional Liaison, Department of Interior; Staff Advisor to Commissioner, Interstate Commerce Commission, 1985-87.
Kindness, Thomas N.
Background: Member, U.S. House of Representatives (R-OH), 1975-86. Member, Ohio State Legislature, 1971-74.

KINDNESS, Thomas N.
Kindness & Chatfield Associates
1747 Pennsylvania Ave., N.W., Suite 1100, Washington, DC 20006
Telephone: (202) 429-6060
Registered as lobbyist at U.S. Congress.
Background: Member, U.S. House of Representatives (R-OH), 1975-86. Member, Ohio State Legislature, 1971-74.

KINER, Carol Ann
Degnon Associates, Inc.
6728 Old McLean Village Drive, McLean, VA 22101
Telephone: (703) 556-9222
Clients:
American Psychosomatic Soc.
Ass'n for the Behavioral Sciences and Medical Education
Soc. for Health and Human Values

KING, Ann Ottoson
Leighton and Regnery
1667 K St., N.W., Suite 801, Washington, DC 20006
Telephone: (202) 955-3900
Clients:
American Cordage and Netting Manufacturers

KING, Aubrey C.
Exec. Director, Travel and Tourism Government Affairs Council
Two Lafayette Center 1133 21st St., N.W., Washington, DC 20036
Telephone: (202) 293-5407
Registered as lobbyist at U.S. Congress.

KING, Barrett T.
Director, Media Relations, Chamber of Commerce of the U.S.A.
1615 H St., N.W., Washington, DC 20062
Telephone: (202) 659-6000

KING, Charles M., Jr.
Exec. V. Pres., Res. & Educ. Foundation, American Soc. of Hospital Pharmacists
4630 Montgomery Ave., Bethesda, MD 20814
Telephone: (301) 657-3000

KING, Doug
President, Challenger Center for Space Science Education
1101 King St. Suite 190, Alexandria, VA 22314
Telephone: (703) 683-9740

KING, George
Director, Public Relations, Nat'l Treasury Employees Union
1730 K St., N.W., Suite 1100, Washington, DC 20006
Telephone: (202) 785-4411

KING, Gregory
Communications Director, Human Rights Campaign Fund
1012 14th St., N.W. Suite 607, Washington, DC 20005
Telephone: (202) 628-4160

KING, Jack
Exec. V. President, Occidental Internat'l Corp.
1747 Pennsylvania Ave., N.W., Suite 375, Washington, DC 20006

Telephone: (202) 857-3000

KING, John A.
Director, Laidlaw, Inc.
1155 Connecticut Ave., N.W., Suite 300, Washington, DC 20036
Telephone: (202) 429-6533

KING, Kim
Communications Coordinator, Consumer Grp, Electronic Industries Ass'n
2001 Pennsylvania Ave., N.W., Washington, DC 20006
Telephone: (202) 457-4900

KING, Neil J.
Wilmer, Cutler and Pickering
2445 M St., N.W., Washington, DC 20037-1420
Telephone: (202) 663-6000
Registered as lobbyist at U.S. Congress.
Clients:
Ford Motor Co.
Internat'l Metals Reclamation Co.

KING AND NORDLINGER
1000 Connecticut Ave., N.W. Suite 311, Washington, DC 20036
Telephone: (202) 833-9310
Clients:
Apartment and Office Building Ass'n of Metropolitan Washington

KING, Dr. Ruth E.G.
Nat'l Office Administrator, Ass'n of Black Psychologists
Box 55999, Washington, DC 20040
Telephone: (202) 722-0808

KING AND SPALDING
1730 Pennsylvania Ave., N.W. Suite 1200, Washington, DC 20006-4706
Telephone: (202) 737-0500
Registered as Foreign Agent: (#3812)
Background: Washington office of an Atlanta law firm.
Members of firm representing listed organizations:
Cople, William J. (III)
Background: Office of the Secretary of Defense, Office of General Counsel, 1980-83.
D'Avino, Richard
Hester, Theodore M.
Background: Legislative Assistant to United States Senator David H. Gambrell, 1971-72.
Lipsky, Abbott B. (Jr.)
Background: Deputy Assistant Attorney General, Antitrust Division, U.S. Department of Justice, 1981-83. Special Assistant to the Chairman, Council on Wage and Price Stability, 1981.
McKee, William S.
Background: Tax Legislative Counsel, Department of the Treasury, 1981-83.
Pfeifer, Eugene M.
Background: Trial Attorney, 1968-73 and Associate Chief Counsel for Enforcement, 1975-79, Office of General Counsel, Food and Drug Administration. Attorney, Office of General Counsel, Federal Trade Commission, 1974.
Stribling, Jess H.
Talmadge, William C.
Background: Legislative Assistant to U.S. Senator Herman Talmadge. Administrative Assistant to Congressman Richard Ray.
Clients:
Alliance for Capital Access *(Richard D'Avino)*
Chater Medical Corp.
Generic Pharmaceutical Industry Ass'n
Georgia Internat'l Investment Coalition *(Theodore M. Hester)*
GPIA Animal Drug Alliance *(Theodore M. Hester, Jess H. Stribling)*
Nat'l Pharmaceutical Alliance *(Eugene M. Pfeifer)*
Nat'l Pharmaceutical Alliance Political Action Committee
Superpharm Corp. *(Eugene M. Pfeifer)*
Trammell Crow, Inc. *(William S. McKee)*
West Point Pepperell *(Abbott B. Lipsky, Jr.)*

KING, Terry
Director, Congressional Relations, Aerojet
1025 Connecticut Ave., N.W. Suite 1107, Washington, DC 20036
Telephone: (202) 828-6826

WASHINGTON REPRESENTATIVES

KING, Thomas J., Jr.
Fenn & King Communications
1043 Cecil Place, N.W., Washington, DC 20007
Telephone: (202) 337-6995
Background: Political Director, Democratic Congressional
Campaign Committee, 1985-86.

KING, W. Russell
President, Freeport-McMoRan D.C., Freeport-McMoRan
Inc.
50 F St., N.W., Suite 1050, Washington, DC 20001
Telephone: (202) 737-1400
Registered as lobbyist at U.S. Congress.
Background: Responsibilities include Freeport-McMoRan
Inc. Citizenship Committee.

KING, William B.
Director, Government Relations, Armstrong World Industries, Inc.
1025 Connecticut Ave., N.W., Suite 1007, Washington, DC
20036
Telephone: (202) 296-2830

KING, William K.
Reg. Mgr, Auto Sfty, Emissns & Fuel Econ, Ford Motor
Co.
1350 Eye St., N.W. Suite 1000, Washington, DC 20005
Telephone: (202) 962-5400
Background: Responsible for regulatory matters in automo-
tive safety, emissions and fuel economy.

KINGDON, John S.
Howrey and Simon
1730 Pennsylvania Ave., N.W., Washington, DC 20006-
4793
Telephone: (202) 783-0800
Background: Trial Attorney, Tax Division, Department of
Justice, 1967-70.
Clients:
Quaker Oats Co.

KINGHORN & ASSOC., Edward J., Jr.
900 2nd St., N.E., Washington, DC 20002
Telephone: (208) 420-0219
Organizations represented:
Ferroalloys Ass'n

KINGMAN, A. Gay
Exec. Director (Interim), Nat'l Congress of American Indians
900 Pennsylvania Ave., S.E., Washington, DC 20003
Telephone: (202) 546-9404

KINGSCOTT, Kathleen N.
Program Dir., Federal Government Relats., Internat'l Busi-
ness Machines Corp.
1801 K St., N.W., Suite 1200, Washington, DC 20006
Telephone: (202) 778-5000
Registered as lobbyist at U.S. Congress.

KINGSLEY, Daniel T.
Exec. Director, Nat'l Venture Capital Ass'n
1655 N. Fort Myer Drive Suite 700, Arlington, VA 22209
Telephone: (703) 528-4370
Registered as lobbyist at U.S. Congress.

KINGSLEY, Robert
Political Director, United Electrical, Radio and Machine
Workers of America
1411 K St., N.W., Suite 1005, Washington, DC 20005
Telephone: (202) 737-3072
Registered as lobbyist at U.S. Congress.

KINGSLEY, Dr. Roger P.
Director, Congressional Relations Div., American Speech-
Language-Hearing Ass'n
10801 Rockville Pike, Rockville, MD 20852
Telephone: (301) 897-5700
Registered as lobbyist at U.S. Congress.

KINGSLEY, Thomas
Dir., Public Finance & Housing Center, Urban Institute,
The
2100 M St., N.W., Washington, DC 20037
Telephone: (202) 833-7200

KINGSLEY, William E.
Exec. V. President, Public Affairs, American Council of
Life Insurance
1001 Pennsylvania Ave., N.W., Washington, DC 20004-
2599
Telephone: (202) 624-2400

KINN, John M.
Staff V. Pres., Engineering Department, Electronic Industries Ass'n
2001 Pennsylvania Ave., N.W., Washington, DC 20006
Telephone: (202) 457-4961
Background: Also represents Joint Electronic Device Engineering Council.

KINNAIRD, Jula J.
V. President, Communications, Nat'l Pasta Ass'n
2101 Wilson Blvd. Suite 920, Arlington, VA 22201
Telephone: (703) 841-0818

KINNE, Theodore L.
V. Pres., Safety Environment & Operatns., Interstate Natural Gas Ass'n of America
555 13th St., N.W. Suite 300 West, Washington, DC
20004
Telephone: (202) 626-3200

KINNEY, Jan
Director, Washington Operations, Sporting Goods Manu-
facturers Ass'n
1625 K St., N.W., Suite 900, Washington, DC 20006
Telephone: (202) 775-1762
Registered as lobbyist at U.S. Congress.
Background: Also represents: Archery Manufacturers Or-
ganization, Bowling and Billiard Institute of America,
Diving Equipment Manufacturers Ass'n, Non-Powder
Gun Ass'n, Tennis Manufacturers Ass'n and Water Ski
Industry Ass'n.

KINNEY, Janie A.
Counsel, Congressional Relations, Merck and Co.
1615 L St., N.W., Suite 1320, Washington, DC 20036
Telephone: (202) 833-8205
Registered as lobbyist at U.S. Congress.

KINNEY, Joyce
Office Manager, Bank of America NT & SA
1800 K St., N.W., Suite 900, Washington, DC 20006
Telephone: (202) 778-0535

KINSELLA, Brian
Manager, Government Affairs, American Hotel and Motel
Ass'n
1201 New York Ave., N.W. Suite 600, Washington, DC
20005
Telephone: (202) 289-3100
Registered as lobbyist at U.S. Congress.
Background: Special Assistant to the Secretary of Labor,
1954-61. Alternate Representative, President's Pay Board,
1971-73. Member, Federal Service Impasses Panel, 1972-
78. Contact for the American Hotel Motel Political Action Committee.

KINSELLA, Katherine
Senior V. President, Director, Marketing, Kamber Group,
The
1920 L St., N.W., Washington, DC 20036
Telephone: (202) 223-8700
Organizations represented:
Nat'l Education Ass'n of the U.S.
Washington Court Hotel

KINSMAN, David B.
Manager, Program Support and Development, Public Affairs Council
1019 19th St., N.W., Suite 200, Washington, DC 20036
Telephone: (202) 872-1790

KINTER, Marci
Director, Government Affairs, Screen Printing Ass'n Internat'l
10015 Main St., Fairfax, VA 22031-3489
Telephone: (703) 385-1335

KIPKE, Ronald
Secretary-Treasurer, Nat'l Federation of Federal Employees
1016 16th St., N.W., Suite 400, Washington, DC 20036
Telephone: (202) 862-4400

Registered as lobbyist at U.S. Congress.

KIPLINGER, Walter M., Jr.
V. President, Government Affairs, American Cast Metals
Ass'n
918 16th St., N.W., Suite 403, Washington, DC 20006
Telephone: (202) 833-1316

KIRBY, Michael G.
Holt, Miller & Associates
2111 Wilson Blvd., Suite 531, Arlington, VA 22201-3008
Telephone: (703) 276-8009
Registered as lobbyist at U.S. Congress.
Clients:
Irish Immigration Reform Movement
Mountain Plains Agricultural Service

KIRBY, Peter M.
Ginsburg, Feldman and Bress
1250 Connecticut Ave., N.W. Suite 800, Washington, DC
20036
Telephone: (202) 637-9000
Registered as lobbyist at U.S. Congress.
Clients:
Genetics Institute Inc.
Upjohn Co.

KIRCHHOFF, Richard W.
Director, State Relations, Smokeless Tobacco Council
2550 M St., N.W., Suite 300, Washington, DC 20037
Telephone: (202) 452-1252
Background: Former Minority Consultant, House Commit-
tee on Agriculture, Subcommittee on Tobacco & Peanuts.

KIRCHNER, Kevin
Legislative Assistant, New Jersey, State of
444 N. Capitol St., N.W. Suite 236, Washington, DC
20001
Telephone: (202) 638-0631

KIRCHNER, Paul G.
Kurrus and Kirchner
1055 Thomas Jefferson St., NW Suite 418, Washington,
DC 20007
Telephone: (202) 342-0204
Registered as lobbyist at U.S. Congress.
Clients:
American Pilots Ass'n
St. Lawrence Seaway Pilots Ass'n

KIRK, Ken
Exec. Director, Ass'n of Metropolitan Sewerage Agencies
1000 Connecticut Ave., N.W. Suite 1006, Washington, DC
20036
Telephone: (202) 833-2672
Background: Legal Advisor, Office of Legislation, Environmental Protection Agency, 1973-75.

KIRK, Michael K.
Asst Commissioner for External Affairs, DEPARTMENT
OF COMMERCE - Patent and Trademark Office
c/o Asst Secy and Commissioner of Patents and Trade-
marks, Washington, DC 20231
Telephone: (703) 557-3065

KIRK, William A., Jr.
Silverstein and Mullens
1776 K St., N.W., Suite 800, Washington, DC 20006
Telephone: (202) 452-7900
Registered as lobbyist at U.S. Congress.
Background: Professional staff, U.S. House of Representa-
tives Committee on Ways and Means, 1980-84. Staff Di-
rector, House Subcommittee on Oversight, 1982-84.
Legislative aide, Capitol Hill, 1975-80.
Clients:
American Newspaper Publishers Ass'n
Kelso & Co.
Republic Nat'l Bank of New York
Tropicana Energy Co.

KIRKLAND AND ELLIS
655 15th St., N.W. Suite 1200, Washington, DC 20005
Telephone: (202) 879-5000
Members of firm representing listed organizations:
Boyle, Jayne F.
Background: Former Tax Counsel, House Committee
on Ways and Means.
Buck, Kathleen A.

Background: Former General Counsel, Department of Defense and General Counsel, Department of the Air Force.

Cortese, Alfred W.
Background: Former Assistant Exec. Director, Federal Trade Commission.

Gottschalk, Thomas A.

Hardy, Timothy S.
Background: Member, Office of Counsel to the President, 1975-76.

Herman, Stephen A.

Hostetler, James S.
Background: Former Legislative Counsel to Department of Health, Education and Welfare; Special Assistant to the Administrator, Economic Development Administration, U.S. Department of Commerce.

Metzger, David P.
Background: Former Staff Director of the Energy, Environment, Safety and Research Subcommittee, House Small Business Committee. Former Director, Innovation and Procurement Policy Office, U.S. Small Business Administration.

Miskovsky, Milan C.
Background: Former Assistant General Counsel, Department of Treasury. Former General Counsel, Federal Home Loan Bank Board.

Norrell, David G.
Background: Law Clerk to U.S. Supreme Court Justice Thurgood Marshall, 1978-79.

Sampson, Arthur F.

Singer, William S.
Background: Former Member, Chicago City Council.

Warren, Edward W.

Wine, L. Mark
Background: Member, Land and Natural Resources Division, U.S. Department of Justice, 1972-78.

Yannucci, Thomas D.
Background: Former Law Clerk to Hon. John A Danaher, U.S. Court of Appeals for the District of Columbia.

Young, Mark D.
Background: Former Assistant General Counsel, Commodity Futures Trading Commission.

Clients:
American Ass'n for Laboratory Accreditation *(James S. Hostetler)*
American Council of Independent Laboratories
American Petroleum Institute
Amoco Corp.
Asbestos Information Ass'n/North America
C F Industries, Inc.
Chicago Board of Trade
General Motors Corp. *(Alfred W. Cortese)*
Safe Buildings Alliance *(L. Mark Wine)*
Service Master, Limited Partnership
Valhi, Inc.

KIRKMAN, Natalie
Director, National Office, Nat'l Council of University Research Administrators
One Dupont Circle, N.W. Suite 420, Washington, DC 20036
Telephone: (202) 466-3894

KIRKPATRICK, Jeane J.
Counselor, Foreign Policy Studies, American Enterprise Institute for Public Policy Research
1150 17th St., N.W., Washington, DC 20036
Telephone: (202) 862-5800
Background: Former U.S. Ambassador to the United Nations, 1981-85.

KIRKPATRICK & LOCKHART
1800 M St., N.W., Suite 900 South Lobby, Washington, DC 20036-5891
Telephone: (202) 778-9000
Background: Washington law firm with offices in Pittsburgh, Harrisburg, Boston and Miami.
Members of firm representing listed organizations:
Adelman, Roger M., Partner
Background: Former prosecutor for the office of the U.S. Attorney.
Alexander, Clifford J.
Background: Attorney/Analyst, Securities and Exchange Commission, 1967-70. Assistant Counsel, Securities Subcommittee of Senate Committee on Banking, Housing and Urban Affairs, 1975-77.
Belair, Robert R.

Background: Attorney, Federal Trade Commission, 1973-75. Acting General Counsel, Committee on Privacy, Office of the President, 1975-76.

Brown, Garry E.
Background: Member, U.S. House of Representatives, 1967-79. Member, President's Commission on Housing, 1981-82.

Hill, Dumond Peck
Background: Member of Staff, U.S. Atomic Energy Commission, 1950-1951. Assistant Counsel, Internat'l Security Affairs, Office of Secretary of Defense, 1950-1953. Associate Counsel, Dep't of the Army, 1953-1954. Trial Attorney, Dep't of Justice, 1954-1956. Staff Consultant, Committee on Foreign Affairs, House of Representatives, 1956-1959.

Phillips, Richard M.
Background: Securities and Exchange Commission, 1960-68: Legal Asst. to Commissioner, 1962-1964; Special Counsel, 1964-1966; Assistant General Counsel, 1966-1968; Staff Director, Disclosure Study, 1968.

Reichardt, Glenn R.

Udall, Stewart L., Of Counsel
Background: Member, U.S. House of Representatives (D-AZ), 1955-61. Secretary of the Interior, 1961-69.

Clients:
Ahmanson & Co., H. F.
American Chipper Knife Coalition *(Glenn R. Reichardt)*
Asociacion de Bancos de Ahorro Puerto Rico *(Garry E. Brown)*
Federal Home Loan Bank of Boston *(Garry E. Brown)*
Federal Home Loan Bank of Cincinnati *(Garry E. Brown)*
Federal Home Loan Bank of New York
First Federal Savings Bank *(Garry E. Brown)*
Grocery Manufacturers of America
Kirkpatrick & Lockhart Political Action Committee *(Garry E. Brown)*
Law Related Education *(Robert R. Belair)*
Nat'l Institute for Citizen Education in the Law *(Robert R. Belair)*
Nat'l U.S.-Arab Chamber of Commerce
Search Group, Inc. *(Robert R. Belair)*

KIRLIN, CAMPBELL AND KEATING
One Farragut Square South 2nd Floor, Washington, DC 20006
Telephone: (202) 639-8000
Background: Washington office of a New York law firm, one of the oldest in the country, established in 1865, specializing in transportation law.
Members of firm representing listed organizations:
Pewett, James W.
Weil, Russell T.
Clients:
Council of European and Japanese Nat'l Shipowners' Ass'ns *(Russell T. Weil)*

KIRSCHNER, Richard
Kirschner, Weinberg & Dempsey
1615 L St., N.W., Suite 1360, Washington, DC 20036
Telephone: (202) 775-5900
Clients:
American Federation of State, County and Municipal Employees

KIRSCHNER, WEINBERG & DEMPSEY
1615 L St., N.W., Suite 1360, Washington, DC 20036
Telephone: (202) 775-5900
Background: A law firm with offices in Washington, D.C., Fairfax, VA, and Philadelphia, PA. The firm serves as General Counsel to the American Federation of State, County and Municipal Employees and as Counsel to a large number and variety of local unions affiliated with other international unions.
Members of firm representing listed organizations:
Becker, Craig
Dempsey, John C.
Kirschner, Richard
Weinberg, Larry P.
Clients:
American Federation of State, County and Municipal Employees *(Craig Becker, Richard Kirschner, Larry P. Weinberg)*

KIRSHNER, Robert A.
Environmental Counsel, Nat'l Forest Products Ass'n
1250 Connecticut Ave., N.W. Suite 200, Washington, DC 20036
Telephone: (202) 463-2700
Registered as lobbyist at U.S. Congress.

KIRTLEY, Jane E.
Exec. Director, Reporters Committee for Freedom of the Press
1735 I St., N.W., Suite 504, Washington, DC 20006
Telephone: (202) 466-6312

KISER, David M.
Manager Environmental Affairs, Eastman Kodak Co.
1776 Eye St., N.W., Suite 1050, Washington, DC 20006
Telephone: (202) 857-3400
Registered as lobbyist at U.S. Congress.

KISER, John Daniel
Fox, Bennett and Turner
750 17th St., N.W., Suite 1100, Washington, DC 20006
Telephone: (202) 778-2300
Background: Assistant Regional Attorney, 1976-80; Senior Attorney/Litigation, Public Health Division, 1980-83; Special Assistant to the Deputy General Counsel, 1983-85, U.S. Department of Health and Human Services.

KISSICK, Ralph L.
Zuckert, Scoutt and Rasenberger
888 17th St., N.W., Suite 600, Washington, DC 20006-3959
Telephone: (202) 298-8660

KISSLING, Frances
President, Catholics for a Free Choice
1436 U St., N. W. Suite 301, Washington, DC 20009
Telephone: (202) 638-1706

KISTNER, William
Staff Writer, Center for Investigative Reporting
309 Pennsylvania Ave., S.E. 3rd Floor, Washington, DC 20003
Telephone: (202) 546-1880

KITCHEN, Emmett B., Jr.
President and General Manager, Nat'l Ass'n of Business and Educational Radio
1501 Duke St., Suite 200, Alexandria, VA 22314
Telephone: (703) 739-0300
Registered as lobbyist at U.S. Congress.
Background: Responsible for Nat'l Ass'n of Business and Educational Radio Political Action Committee.

KITTLE, Ralph W.
McNair Law Firm, P.A.
1155 15th St., N.W. Suite 400, Washington, DC 20005
Telephone: (202) 659-3900
Registered as lobbyist at U.S. Congress.
Background: Counsel to Senator Robert Taft (R-OH) and the Senate Labor Committee, 1953. President's Advisory Committee on Pollution Control, 1967-70.

KITTREDGE, Frank D.
President, Nat'l Foreign Trade Council, Inc.
1625 K St., N.W., Suite 1090, Washington, DC 20006
Telephone: (202) 887-0278

KITZMILLER, W. Michael
Principal, Griffin, Johnson & Associates
1211 Connecticut Ave., N.W., Suite 700, Washington, DC 20036
Telephone: (202) 775-8116
Registered as lobbyist at U.S. Congress.
Background: Former Staff Director, House Energy and Commerce Committee.

KJAER, Lisa K.
Exec. Director, Government Relations, Electronic Industries Ass'n
2001 Pennsylvania Ave., N.W., Washington, DC 20006
Telephone: (202) 457-4900
Registered as lobbyist at U.S. Congress.

KJELLBERG, Sandra D.
Government Relations, Maritime Institute for Research and Industrial Development
1133 15th St., N.W. Suite 600, Washington, DC 20005
Telephone: (202) 463-6505

WASHINGTON REPRESENTATIVES

KJELLBERG, Sandra D. (Cont'd)
Registered as lobbyist at U.S. Congress.

KLASS, Kathie
Exec. Director, Issue Dynamics Inc.
901 15th St., N.W. Suite 230, Washington, DC 20005
Telephone: (202) 408-1400

KLAUS, Vincent J.
Treasurer, Pharmaceutical Manufacturers Ass'n Better Government Committee
1100 15th St., N.W. Suite 900, Washington, DC 20005
Telephone: (202) 835-3400

KLAYMAN, Robert A.
Caplin and Drysdale
One Thomas Circle, N.W. Suite 1100, Washington, DC 20005
Telephone: (202) 862-5000
Registered as lobbyist at U.S. Congress.
Background: Attorney, Office of Chief Counsel, Internal Revenue Service, 1957-60. Office of Tax Legislative Counsel Treasury Department, 1960-64; Associate Tax Legislative Counsel. Treasury Department, 1964.

KLECKLEY, Alicia G.
Nat'l Affairs Representative, American Soc. for Training and Development
1630 Duke St., Box 1443, Alexandria, VA 22313
Telephone: (703) 683-8100

KLEIN, Andrew M.
Schiff Hardin & Waite
1101 Connecticut Ave., N.W. Suite 600, Washington, DC 20036
Telephone: (202) 857-0600
Background: Director, Division of Market Regulation, Securities and Exchange Commission, 1977-79. Special Counsel, Assistant Director, and Associate Director of Division of Market Regulation, 1973-77.
Clients:
Chicago Board Options Exchange

KLEIN, Gary
Verner, Liipfert, Bernhard, McPherson and Hand, Chartered
901 15th St., N.W., Suite 700, Washington, DC 20005
Telephone: (202) 371-6000
Registered as lobbyist at U.S. Congress.
Background: Legislative ass't to Sen. Jacob Javits (R-NY), 1973-75; Minority Counsel to the Energy Subcommittee of the Senate Government Affairs Committee, 1975-77.

KLEIN, James A.
Deputy Exec. Director, Ass'n of Private Pension and Welfare Plans
1212 New York Ave., N.W. 12th Floor, Washington, DC 20005
Telephone: (202) 737-6666
Registered as lobbyist at U.S. Congress.

KLEIN, Joel I.
Onek, Klein & Farr
2550 M St., N.W., Suite 350, Washington, DC 20037
Telephone: (202) 775-0184
Background: Law Clerk to Justice Lewis F. Powell, U.S. Supreme Court, 1974-75.
Clients:
American Psychiatric Ass'n

KLEIN, Kenneth H.
Counsel, Government Affairs, Xerox Corp.
490 L'Enfant Plaza East, S.W., Suite 4200, Washington, DC 20024
Telephone: (202) 646-8285

KLEIN & SAKS, INC.
1026 16th St., N.W., Suite 101, Washington, DC 20036
Telephone: (202) 783-0500
Members of firm representing listed organizations:
Arenberg, Cindy Joy
Background: Serves as Director, International Government Relations of the Gold Institute.
Brown, Michael J., V. President
Background: Former Press Secretary, U.S. Mint. Serves as Director of Public Relations for the Gold Institute and the Silver Institute.
Lutley, John H., President
Background: Serves as Managing Director of the Gold Institute and Exec. Director of the Silver Institute.

Clients:
Ball Corp.
Gold Institute *(Cindy Joy Arenberg, Michael J. Brown, John H. Lutley)*
Silver Institute *(Michael J. Brown, John H. Lutley)*

KLEINFELD, Eric F.
Manatt, Phelps, Rothenberg & Phillips
1200 New Hampshire Ave., N.W., Suite 200, Washington, DC 20036
Telephone: (202) 463-4300
Registered as lobbyist at U.S. Congress.

KLEINFELD, KAPLAN AND BECKER
1140 19th St., N.W., Suite 700, Washington, DC 20036
Telephone: (202) 223-5120
Members of firm representing listed organizations:
Becker, Robert H.
Background: Trial Attorney, Food and Drug Division, Office of General Counsel, Department of Health, Education and Welfare, 1956-61.
Henteleff, Thomas O.
Kaplan, Alan H.
Background: Trial Attorney, Food and Drug Division, Office of General Counsel, Department of Health, Education and Welfare, 1957-60.
Mathers, Peter R.
Morey, Richard S.
Reagan, Kinsey S.
Background: Attorney, U.S. Department of Health and Human Services, 1975-80.
Safir, Peter O.
Clients:
Adria Laboratories, Inc. *(Alan H. Kaplan)*
Carter-Wallace, Inc. *(Robert H. Becker, Alan H. Kaplan, Peter O. Safir)*
Cord Laboratories *(Robert H. Becker, Alan H. Kaplan, Richard S. Morey)*
Inwood Laboratories, Inc. *(Peter R. Mathers)*
Jones Medical Industries, Inc. *(Peter R. Mathers)*
Kleinfeld, Kaplan and Becker Political Action Committee
Mead Johnson and Co. *(Alan H. Kaplan, Richard S. Morey)*
Par Pharmaceutical Inc. *(Alan H. Kaplan)*
Quad Pharmaceutical Inc. *(Alan H. Kaplan)*
SmithKline Animal Health Products *(Robert H. Becker, Kinsey S. Reagan)*
Squibb and Sons, Inc., E. R. *(Robert H. Becker, Kinsey S. Reagan, Peter O. Safir)*
Vitarine Pharmaceuticals Inc. *(Alan H. Kaplan)*

KLEMOW, Marvin G.
1700 North Moore St. Suite 830, Arlington, VA 22209
Telephone: (703) 243-2223
Organizations represented:
Israel Aircraft Industries

KLEPNER, Jerry D.
Director of Legislation, American Federation of State, County and Municipal Employees
1625 L St., N.W., Washington, DC 20036
Telephone: (202) 429-1000
Registered as lobbyist at U.S. Congress.
Background: Former Staff Director, Subcommittee on Compensation and Employee Benefits, House Post Office and Civil Service Committee.

KLIESMET, Robert B.
President, Internat'l Union of Police Ass'ns
1016 Duke St., Alexandria, VA 22314
Telephone: (703) 549-7473

KLIEVER, Douglas E.
Cleary, Gottlieb, Steen and Hamilton
1752 N St., N.W., Washington, DC 20036
Telephone: (202) 728-2700
Registered as lobbyist at U.S. Congress.
Clients:
Mexico, Ministry of Finance and Public Credit

KLINE, Lawrence Y., M.D.
Treasurer, Washington Psychiatric Soc. Political Action Committee
1400 K St., N.W. Suite 202, Washington, DC 20005
Telephone: (202) 682-6270

KLINE, Ray
President, Nat'l Academy of Public Administration
1120 G St., N.W. Suite 540, Washington, DC 20005
Telephone: (202) 347-3190

KLINEFELTER, Bill
Sr. Legislative Representative, Nat'l Wildlife Federation
1400 16th St., N.W., Washington, DC 20036-2266
Telephone: (202) 797-6800
Registered as lobbyist at U.S. Congress.

KLING, Joanne Marie
Coalition Coordinator, Chamber of Commerce of the U.S.-A.
1615 H St., N.W., Washington, DC 20062
Telephone: (202) 659-6000
Registered as lobbyist at U.S. Congress.
Background: Full title is Coalition Coordinator & Research Analyst/ Health Care & Employment.

KLING, Thomas
Treasurer, American Gear Political Action Committee
1500 King St., Suite 201, Alexandria, VA 22209
Telephone: (703) 684-0211

KLINGER, Jeffrey L.
Eastern Regional Counsel, Peabody Holding Co.
122 C St., N.W., Suite 240, Washington, DC 20001
Telephone: (202) 393-4366
Registered as lobbyist at U.S. Congress.

KLIPPER, Michael R.
Leventhal, Senter & Lerman
2000 K St., N.W., Suite 600, Washington, DC 20006
Telephone: (202) 429-8970
Registered as lobbyist at U.S. Congress.
Clients:
Committee for America's Copyright Community
Copyright Remedies Coalition

KLITZMAN, Stephen
Assoc Dir, Legis Affrs, FEDERAL COMMUNICATIONS COMMISSION
1919 M St., N.W., Washington, DC 20554
Telephone: (202) 632-6405

KLOCKE, Mary Jane
Government Affairs Representative, Shell Oil Co.
1025 Connecticut Ave., N.W., Suite 200, Washington, DC 20036
Telephone: (202) 466-1405
Registered as lobbyist at U.S. Congress.

KLOSE, Christopher
V. President, Harrison Co., E. Bruce
1440 New York Ave., N.W. Suite 300, Washington, DC 20005
Telephone: (202) 638-1200

KLOSE, Eliza K.
Exec. Director, Institute for Soviet-American Relations
1608 New Hampshire Ave., N.W., Washington, DC 20009
Telephone: (202) 387-3034

KLOTZBAUGH, George R.
Senior Counsel, American Insurance Ass'n
1130 Connecticut Ave., N.W., Suite 1000, Washington, DC 20036
Telephone: (202) 828-7100

KLV ASSOCIATES
1110 Vermont Ave., N.W., Suite 1160, Washington, DC 20005
Telephone: (202) 429-0949
Members of firm representing listed organizations:
Vehrs, Kristin L.
Clients:
American Ass'n of Zoological Parks and Aquariums *(Kristin L. Vehrs)*
Texas Shrimp Ass'n *(Kristin L. Vehrs)*

KMETZ, Martin J.
Manager, Gov't Affairs - Maryland, Potomac Electric Power Co.
1900 Pennsylvania Ave., N.W., Washington, DC 20068
Telephone: (202) 872-2000
Background: Serves as Chairman, PEPCO Political Action Committee.

KNAPP, Gail
V. President, Corporate Communications, MCI Communications Corp.
1133 19th St., N.W., Washington, DC 20036
Telephone: (202) 872-1600
Background: Serves as Treasurer, Motion Picture Ass'n PAC.

KNAPP, John
Senior Consultant, ICG Inc.
2550 M St., N.W. Suite 460, Washington, DC 20037
Telephone: (202) 789-1188
Background: Senior Consultant, ICG Inc. Former General Counsel, Former Gen. Counsel, Department of Housing and Urban Development.

KNAPP, Mary
Exec. Secretary to S.V.P., Gov't Relats., Motion Picture Ass'n of America
1600 Eye St., N.W., Washington, DC 20006
Telephone: (202) 293-1966

KNAPP, Dr. Richard M.
Senior V. President, Ass'n of American Medical Colleges
One Dupont Circle, N.W., Suite 200, Washington, DC 20036
Telephone: (202) 828-0400

KNAPPEN, Theodore C.
Senior V. President/Gov't Affairs, Greyhound Lines, Inc.
1101 14th St., Suite 1201, Washington, DC 20005
Telephone: (202) 347-3827

KNAUER, Leon T.
Wilkinson, Barker, Knauer and Quinn
1735 New York Ave., N.W., Suite 600, Washington, DC 20006
Telephone: (202) 783-4141
Registered as Foreign Agent: (#4075).

KNAUER, Virginia H.
Senior Consultant, Anderson, Benjamin, Read & Haney
1020 19th St., N.W., Suite 500, Washington, DC 20036
Telephone: (202) 659-5656
Background: Former Director, U.S. Office of Consumer Affairs, Department of Health and Human Services, and former special advisor to President Reagan on consumer affairs.

KNAUFT, Edwin B.
Exec. V. President, Independent Sector
1828 L St., N.W., Washington, DC 20036
Telephone: (202) 223-8100

KNEALE, James E.
Manager, Legislative Affairs, Lockheed Corp.
1825 Eye St., N.W., Suite 1100, Washington, DC 20006
Telephone: (202) 955-3311
Registered as lobbyist at U.S. Congress.

KNEBEL, John A.
President, American Mining Congress
1920 N St., N.W. Suite 300, Washington, DC 20036
Telephone: (202) 861-2800
Registered as lobbyist at U.S. Congress.
Background: Assistant Counsel, House Committee on Agriculture, 1969-71. General Counsel, Small Business Administration, 1971-73. General Counsel, 1973-75; Under Secretary, 1975-76; Deputy Secretary, 1976 and Secretary, 1976-77, U.S. Department of Agriculture.

KNEISLEY, Robert W.
Wilner and Scheiner
1200 New Hampshire Ave., N.W., Suite 300, Washington, DC 20036
Telephone: (202) 861-7800
Background: Attorney/Advisor, Office of General Counsel, Civil Aeronautics Board, 1976-78. Trial Attorney, Bureau of Internat'l Aviation and Bureau of Consumer Protection, Antitrust Division, Civil Aeronautics Board, 1978-80.

KNEISS, John
Exec. Director, Aspirin Foundation of America, Inc.
1330 Connecticut Ave., N.W., Suite 300, Washington, DC 20036
Telephone: (202) 659-0060

KNIERIEMEN, Theresa
Ferguson Associates, Jack
203 Maryland Ave., N.E., Washington, DC 20002
Telephone: (202) 544-6655
Background: Former Legislative Analyst to the House Republican Party Conference under Chairmanship of Reps. Dick Cheney (R-WY) and Jack Kemp (R-NY).

KNIGHT, Bruce I.
Dir., Gov't Affairs & Mktg. Svcs., Nat'l Ass'n of Wheat Growers
415 Second St., N.E. Suite 300, Washington, DC 20002
Telephone: (202) 547-7800
Registered as lobbyist at U.S. Congress.
Background: Former Legislative Assistant to Rep. Fred Grandy (R-IA).

KNIGHT, Edward S.
Akin, Gump, Strauss, Hauer and Feld
1333 New Hampshire Ave., N.W., Suite 400, Washington, DC 20036
Telephone: (202) 887-4000
Background: Legislative Assistant to Senator Lloyd Bentsen of Texas, 1976-78.
Clients:
Boone Co.
Nat'l Football League
Warner-Lambert Co.

KNIGHT, Gary D.
Dep Asst Secy, House Liaison, DEPARTMENT OF ENERGY
1000 Independence Ave. S.W., Washington, DC 20585
Telephone: (202) 586-5450

KNIGHT, Guyon D.
V. President, Communications, Washington Post Co.
1150 15th St., N.W., Washington, DC 20071
Telephone: (202) 334-6642

KNIGHT, Patricia
Dep Asst Secy, Legis & Intergovt'l Affrs, DEPARTMENT OF COMMERCE
14th and Constitution Ave. S.W., Washington, DC 20230
Telephone: (202) 377-5485

KNIGHT, Peter E.
V. President and Dir., Mortgage Finance, Nat'l Council of Savings Institutions
1101 15th St., N.W. Suite 400, Washington, DC 20005
Telephone: (202) 857-3100
Registered as lobbyist at U.S. Congress.

KNIGHT, Robert
President, Nat'l Ass'n of Private Industry Councils
1201 New York Ave., N.W. Suite 800, Washington, DC 20005
Telephone: (202) 289-2950

KNIPMEYER, Mary C., Ph.D.
Dir, Div of Legis & Policy Implementat'n, DEPARTMENT OF HEALTH AND HUMAN SERVICES - Alcohol Drug Abuse and Mental Health Administration
5600 Fishers Lane Room 12C-26, Rockville, MD 20857
Telephone: (301) 443-4640

KNIPPERS, Diane L.
Deputy Director, Institute on Religion and Democracy
729 15th St., N.W., Suite 900, Washington, DC 20005
Telephone: (202) 393-3200

KNOBLOCH, Karen Theibert
Government Relations Representative, Food Marketing Institute
1750 K St., N.W., Washington, DC 20006
Telephone: (202) 452-8444
Registered as lobbyist at U.S. Congress.

KNOBLOCH, Kevin T.
Legis. Dir., Arms Control & Nat'l Secur., Union of Concerned Scientists
1616 P St., N.W., Suite 310, Washington, DC 20036
Telephone: (202) 332-0900
Registered as lobbyist at U.S. Congress.
Background: Press Secretary/Legislative Assistant to Rep. Ted Weiss (D-NY), 1983-85. Legislative Director to Senator Timothy Wirth (D-CO), 1985-89.

KNOBLOCK, Keith R.
V.P., Minerals Avail'ty & Public Lands, American Mining Congress
Suite 300, 1920 N St., N.W., Washington, DC 20036
Telephone: (202) 861-2851
Registered as lobbyist at U.S. Congress.

KNOFF, Patti
Director, Government Affairs, Nat'l Ass'n of the Remodeling Industry
1901 North Moore St. Suite 808, Arlington, VA 22209
Telephone: (703) 276-7600

KNOLL, Albert B.
Washington Representative, Sun Co.
555 13th St., N.W., Suite 1010 East, Washington, DC 20004
Telephone: (202) 628-1010
Registered as lobbyist at U.S. Congress.

KNOPP, Gregory V.
DEAC Director, Dealers Election Action Committee of the Nat'l Automobile Dealers Ass'n (DEAC)
8400 Westpark Drive, McLean, VA 22102
Telephone: (703) 821-7111

KNOUSE, Mark S.
Dir., Washington Affairs - Environment, Union Pacific Corp.
555 13th St., N.W., Suite 450 West Columbia Square, Washington, DC 20004
Telephone: (202) 662-0100
Registered as lobbyist at U.S. Congress.
Background: Represents USPCI, a subidiary of Union Pacific Corp.

KNOWLES, Gearold L.
Schiff Hardin & Waite
1101 Connecticut Ave., N.W. Suite 600, Washington, DC 20036
Telephone: (202) 857-0600
Registered as Foreign Agent: (#3387).
Background: Attorney, Division of Corporate Regulation, Securities and Exchange Commission, 1973-76. Senior Attorney, Office of the General Counsel, U.S. Railway Ass'n, 1976-77.
Clients:
China, Directorate General of Telecommunications, Ministry of Communications of Republic of

KNOWLES, Louis J.
Director, Planning & Internat'l Affairs, Council on Foundations
1828 L St., N.W. Suite 300, Washington, DC 20036
Telephone: (202) 466-6512

KNOWLES, Mark R.
President, Nat'l Pharmaceutical Council
1894 Preston White Drive, Reston, VA 22091
Telephone: (703) 620-6390

KNUTSON, Martha
Associate, Gilberg & Kurent
1250 I St., N.W. Suite 600, Washington, DC 20005
Telephone: (202) 842-3222

KOACH, Joseph L.
Exec. Director, Service Station Dealers of America
499 S. Capitol St., S.E. Suite 407, Washington, DC 20003
Telephone: (202) 479-0196
Background: Serves as contact for the Service Station Dealers of America PAC.

KOBOR, Patricia
Legislative & Federal Affairs Officer, American Psychological Ass'n
1200 17th St., N.W., Washington, DC 20036
Telephone: (202) 955-7600
Registered as lobbyist at U.S. Congress.

KOCH, Bradley R.
Dir., Energy and Environmental Policy, Nat'l Rural Electric Cooperative Ass'n
1800 Massachusetts Ave., N.W., Washington, DC 20036
Telephone: (202) 857-9569
Registered as lobbyist at U.S. Congress.

KOCH, F. James
Director - Government Affairs, GTE Corp.
Suite 1200, 1850 M St., N.W., Washington, DC 20036
Telephone: (202) 463-5271
Background: Serves also as Treasurer, GTE Good Government Club.

KOCH, Patrick C.
Wunder, Ryan, Cannon & Thelen
1615 L St., N.W., Suite 650, Washington, DC 20036
Telephone: (202) 659-3005
Registered as lobbyist at U.S. Congress.
Clients:
    Grocery Manufacturers of America
    United States Telephone Ass'n

KOCHAN, Richard S.
President, PPED, Inc.
1620 Eye St., N.W., Suite 509, Washington, DC 20006
Telephone: (202) 659-2187
Clients:
    Benton Harbor, Michigan, City of
    Richmond, California, City of
    San Lorenzo Guaynabo, Puerto Rico, City of

KOCHEISEN, Carol
Legislative Counsel, Nat'l League of Cities
1301 Pennsylvania Ave., N.W., Washington, DC 20004
Telephone: (202) 626-3000

KOCHENDERFER, Karil L.
Account Supervisor, Fleishman-Hillard, Inc
1301 Connecticut Ave., N.W., Washington, DC 20036
Telephone: (202) 659-0330

KOCHERSPERGER, Jane
Information and Research Coordinator, Nat'l Coalition Against the Misuse of Pesticides
530 7th St., S.E., Washington, DC 20003
Telephone: (202) 543-5450

KOCHINKE, Clemens J.
Berliner and Maloney
1101 17th St., N.W., Suite 1004, Washington, DC 20036-4798
Telephone: (202) 293-1414
Registered as lobbyist at U.S. Congress.
Registered as Foreign Agent: (#3512).
Clients:
    Elmont AG

KOEHLER, Robert H.
Patton, Boggs and Blow
2550 M St., N.W., Suite 800, Washington, DC 20037
Telephone: (202) 457-6000
Registered as lobbyist at U.S. Congress.
Background: Legal Advisor, U.S. Army Procurement Agency, Vietnam, 1970-71. Trial Attorney, Contract Appeals Division, Office of the Judge Advocate General, 1971-73.
Clients:
·   Bristol-Myers Squibb Co.

KOELEMAY, J. Douglas
Senior Associate, Peabody Fitzpatrick Communications
1400 K St., N.W., Suite 1212, Washington, DC 20005
Telephone: (202) 842-5000
Background: Legislative Assistant to Rep. Robert Mollohan (D-WV), 1980-82. Legislative Assistant to Senator Frank Lautenberg (D-NJ), 1983-84.
Clients:
    American Ass'n of Retired Persons
    Nature Conservancy, The
    Pennsylvania State System of Higher Education
    Pew Health Professions Commission

KOENIG, David G.
Tax Attorney, Texaco U.S.A.
1050 17th St., N.W., Suite 500, Washington, DC 20036
Telephone: (202) 331-1427
Registered as lobbyist at U.S. Congress.

KOEPPEN, Cathy
Senior Staff Specialist/Communications, American Nurses' Ass'n
1101 14th St., N.W., Suite 200, Washington, DC 20005
Telephone: (202) 789-1800

KOEZE, R. Todd
Cong Liaison Div, ENVIRONMENTAL PROTECTION AGENCY
401 M St., S.W., Washington, DC 20460
Telephone: (202) 382-5200

KOFFLER, Warren W.
1730 K St., N.W., Suite 304, Washington, DC 20006
Telephone: (202) 463-0662
Background: Trial attorney, Federal Aviation Agency, 1963. Hearing Officer, Federal Home Loan Bank Board, 1964-1966.
Organizations represented:
    All American Nat'l Bank
    Asian American Nat'l Bank
    Banco Cooperativo
    Banco Nacional, N.A.
    Brenton Banks
    First Federal Savings and Loan Ass'n (Inverness)
    First Nat'l Bank of Douglasville
    First Nat'l Bank of Hollywood
    Florida Bankshares
    Hollywood Federal Savings and Loan Ass'n
    Jefferson Bancorp
    Tourist Cablevision Corp.
    VIP Hotel Representatives, Inc.
    Virgin Island Nat'l Bank

KOGAN, Joanne
Account Executive, Gallagher-Widmeyer Group Inc., The
1110 Vermont Ave., N.W., Suite 1020, Washington, DC 20005
Telephone: (202) 659-1606

KOGEL, Ross
Treasurer, Nat'l Tire Dealers and Retreaders Ass'n Political Action Committee
1250 Eye St., N.W., Suite 400, Washington, DC 20005
Telephone: (202) 789-2300

KOGOVSEK & ASSOCIATES, INC.
1455 Pennsylvania Ave., N.W., Suite 950, Washington, DC 20004
Telephone: (202) 639-8899
Background: A lobbying firm based in Colorado with offices in Denver and Pueblo as well as Washington, DC.
Members of firm representing listed organizations:
Kogovsek, Ray, President
    Background: Former, U.S. House of Representatives (D-CO).
Mulick, Christine Ann, V. President
    Background: Former aide to former Rep. Ray Kogovsek (D-CO), 1979-84.
Wiessner, Andy, V. President
    Background: Former Counsel, U.S. House of Representatives Interior Subcommittee on Public Lands.
Clients:
    American Public Land Exchange Co.
    Animas-La Plata Water Conservancy District
    Blue Cross and Blue Shield of Colorado
    Blue Cross and Blue Shield of Nevada
    Blue Cross and Blue Shield of New Mexico
    Bonneville Pacific Corp.
    FLEX Land Exchange, Inc.
    Greater Denver Corporation
    Longview Fibre Co.
    Page Land and Cattle Co.
    Public Employees' Retirement Ass'n of Colorado
    Pueblo, Colorado, City of
    Regional Transportation District
    Rio Grande Water Conservation District
    Southern Ute Indian Tribe
    Southwestern Water Conservation District
    Union Pacific Resources Co.
    United States Olympic Committee
    Upper Yampa Water Conservancy District
    Ute Mountain Ute Indian Tribe
    Walker Field Airport Authority
    Western Land Exchange Co.

KOGOVSEK, Ray
President, Kogovsek & Associates, Inc.
1455 Pennsylvania Ave., N.W., Suite 950, Washington, DC 20004
Telephone: (202) 639-8899
Registered as lobbyist at U.S. Congress.
Background: Former, U.S. House of Representatives (D-CO).

KOHL, Karen K.
Congressional Liaison, Concerned Women for America
370 L'Enfant Promenade, S.W., Suite 800, Washington, DC 20024
Telephone: (202) 488-7000
Registered as lobbyist at U.S. Congress.
Background: Responsibilities include the Concerned Women for America Legislative Action Committee.

KOHL, Kay J.
Exec. Director, Nat'l University Continuing Education Ass'n
One Dupont Circle, N.W. Suite 615, Washington, DC 20036-1168
Telephone: (202) 659-3130

KOHLMEYER, Robert W.
Public Affairs Counselor, Cargill, Inc.
1101 15th St., N.W., Suite 205, Washington, DC 20005
Telephone: (202) 785-3060

KOHN, Gary J.
Legislative Counsel, Independent Bankers Ass'n of America
One Thomas Circle, N.W., Suite 950, Washington, DC 20005
Telephone: (202) 659-8111
Registered as lobbyist at U.S. Congress.
Background: Research Assistant to U.S. Rep. Donald Mitchell, 1973-74; Research Librarian, Library of Congress, 1974-85.

KOLAR, Joseph M.
Thacher, Proffitt and Wood
1500 K St., N.W., Suite 200, Washington, DC 20005
Telephone: (202) 347-8400
Clients:
    Ranieri-Wilson

KOLAR, Mary Jane, CAE
Exec. Director, Ass'n of Government Accountants
601 Wythe St., Suite 204, Alexandria, VA 22314
Telephone: (703) 684-6931
Registered as lobbyist at U.S. Congress.

KOLBE, Stanley E., Jr.
Director of Governmental Affairs, Sheet Metal and Air Conditioning Contractors' Nat'l Ass'n
305 4th St., N.E., Washington, DC 20002
Telephone: (202) 547-8202
Registered as lobbyist at U.S. Congress.
Background: Responsibilities include Sheet Metal and Air Conditioning Contractors' Nat'l Ass'n Political Action Committee (SMACPAC).

KOLBERG, William H.
President and CEO, Nat'l Alliance of Business
1201 New York Ave., N.W., Suite 700, Washington, DC 20005
Telephone: (202) 289-2888

KOLICK, Joseph, Jr.
Dickstein, Shapiro and Morin
2101 L St., N.W., Washington, DC 20037
Telephone: (202) 785-9700
Clients:
    Medtronic, Inc.

KOLKER, Ann
Public Policy Director, Nat'l Women's Law Center
1616 P St., N.W., Washington, DC 20036
Telephone: (202) 328-5160
Registered as lobbyist at U.S. Congress.

KOLLER, Diane J.
Managing Director, Gov't Affairs, American Airlines
1101 17th St., N.W. Suite 600, Washington, DC 20036
Telephone: (202) 857-4221
Registered as lobbyist at U.S. Congress.
Background: Serves also as Treasurer, American Airlines Political Action Committee.

KOLODZIEJ, Richard R.
Senior V. President, American Gas Ass'n
1515 Wilson Blvd., Arlington, VA 22209
Telephone: (703) 841-8620

KOLOSKI, Judith Ann
Exec. Director, American Ass'n for Adult and Continuing Education
1112 16th St., N.W., Suite 420, Washington, DC 20036
Telephone: (202) 463-6333

KOMINUS, Nicholas
President, United States Cane Sugar Refiners' Ass'n
1001 Connecticut Ave., N.W., Suite 735, Washington, DC 20036
Telephone: (202) 331-1458
Registered as lobbyist at U.S. Congress.

KONDO, Takeshi
Senior V. President, Itoh (America), Inc., C.
1155 21st St., N.W. Suite 710, Washington, DC 20036
Telephone: (202) 822-9082
Registered as lobbyist at U.S. Congress.

KONNOR, Delbert D.
Exec. V. President, American Managed Care Pharmacy Ass'n
2300 9th St. South, Suite 210, Arlington, VA 22204
Telephone: (703) 920-8480

KONOPKO, Bernard L.
P.O. Box 4571, Rockville, MD 20850
Telephone: (301) 340-6076

KONOSHIMA, Joji
President and Trustee, US-Asia Institute
232 East Capitol St., N.E., Washington, DC 20003
Telephone: (202) 544-3181

KONOSHIMA, Mari
Assoc. Director, International Trade, Nat'l Ass'n of Manufacturers
1331 Pennsylvania Ave., N.W. Suite 1500 North, Washington, DC 20004-1703
Telephone: (202) 637-3000

KONTNIK, Ginnie
Director, Harriman Communun. Center, Democratic Congressional Campaign Committee
430 South Capitol St., S.E. 2nd Floor, Washington, DC 20003
Telephone: (202) 863-1500

KOONCE, Norman L.
President, AIA Foundation, American Institute of Architects, The
1735 New York Ave., N.W., Washington, DC 20006
Telephone: (202) 626-7300

KOOPERSMITH, Jeffrey M.
Treasurer, Radon Industry PAC
1 D St. S.E., Washington, DC 20002
Telephone: (202) 543-3859

KOPECKY, George M.
President, Nat'l Electric Sign Ass'n
801 North Fairfax St. Suite 205, Alexandria, VA 22314
Telephone: (703) 836-4012
Background: Also responsible for the Nat'l Electric Sign Ass'n Political Action Committee.

KOPIT, Neil R.
V. President of Client Services, Reese Communications Companies
2111 Wilson Ave., Suite 900, Arlington, VA 22201
Telephone: (703) 528-4400

KOPIT, William G.
Epstein Becker and Green
1227 25th St., N.W., Suite 700, Washington, DC 20037
Telephone: (202) 861-0900
Registered as lobbyist at U.S. Congress.
Clients:
Central Virginia Health Systems Agency
Social Democratic and Labor Party of Northern Ireland (SDLP)

KOPLAN, Stephen
V. President, Governmental Affairs, Seagram & Sons, Inc., Joseph E.
1455 Pennsylvania Ave., N.W., Suite 600, Washington, DC 20004
Telephone: (202) 638-3090
Registered as lobbyist at U.S. Congress.

Background: Trial Attorney, Tax Division (1962-67), Civil Rights Division (1971-74), and Chief of the Federal Programs Section, Civil Rights Division (1975-79), Department of Justice, General Counsel for U.S. Senate Committee for Post Office and Civil Service (1974-75). Staff Attorney for Senator Lee Metcalf (D-MT), 1967-70.

KOPP, George S.
V. President and General Counsel, Global USA, Inc.
2121 K St., N.W., Suite 650, Washington, DC 20037
Telephone: (202) 296-2400
Registered as lobbyist at U.S. Congress.
Registered as Foreign Agent: (#3489).
Background: Former Staff Dir. and Chief Counsel, House Subcommittee on Natural Resources.
Clients:
Earth Observation Satellite Co.

KOPP, Harry
V. President, Motley and Co., L. A.
1800 K St., N.W., Suite 1000, Washington, DC 20006
Telephone: (202) 223-8222
Registered as lobbyist at U.S. Congress.
Registered as Foreign Agent: (#3723).
Organizations represented:
Associacao das Industrias de Calcados do Rio Grande do Sul
Associacao Nacional das Industrias de Citricos

KOPP, Raymond J.
Dir., Quality of the Environment Div., Resources for the Future
1616 P St., N.W., Washington, DC 20036
Telephone: (202) 328-5000

KOPPELMAN, Jane
Research Associate, Nat'l Health Policy Forum
2011 Eye St., N.W. Suite 200, Washington, DC 20006
Telephone: (202) 872-1390

KOPPERUD, Steven
V. President, Legislation, American Feed Industry Ass'n
1701 Fort Myer Dr. Suite 1200, Arlington, VA 22209
Telephone: (703) 524-0810
Registered as lobbyist at U.S. Congress.
Background: Also represents Feed Industry Political Action Committee and the Animal Industry Foundation.

KORAB, Henry E.
Exec. Director, Soc. of Soft Drink Technologists
P.O. Box 259, Brentwood, MD 20722
Telephone: (301) 277-0018

KORB, Lawrence J.
Dir., Center for Public Policy Education, Brookings Institution
1775 Massachusetts Ave., N.W., Washington, DC 20036
Telephone: (202) 797-6000
Background: Asst. Secretary of Defense for Manpower, Reserve Affairs, Installations and Logistics (1981-85).

KORB, Thomas
Coordinator, Legislative Issues, Ass'n for Advanced Life Underwriting
1922 F St., N.W., Washington, DC 20006
Telephone: (202) 331-6081

KOREN, Edward
Staff Attorney, Nat'l Prison Project
1616 P St., N.W. Suite 340, Washington, DC 20036
Telephone: (202) 331-0500

KORNS, John H.
Pettit & Martin
1800 Massachusetts Ave., N.W., Washington, DC 20036
Telephone: (202) 785-5153
Registered as lobbyist at U.S. Congress.
Background: Law Clerk to Chief Justice Warren E. Burger, U.S. Supreme Court, 1971-72. Assistant U.S. Attorney for District of Columbia, 1976-80.

KORODY, Paul A.
V. President, Government Affairs, ConAgra, Inc.
888 17th St., N.W., Suite 300, Washington, DC 20006
Telephone: (202) 223-5115
Registered as lobbyist at U.S. Congress.
Background: Former Chief Legislative Assistant to Senator Stephen Young of Ohio and Senator Robert C. Byrd of West Virginia. Legislative Assistant to three members of the House of Representatives.

KOROLOGOS, Tom C.
President, Timmons and Co., Inc.
1850 K St., N.W., Suite 850, Washington, DC 20006
Telephone: (202) 331-1760
Background: Dep. Ass't, Legis. to Presidents Nixon and Ford, 1970-74. Former Assistant to Sen. Wallace F. Bennett.

KORTH, Fred
Korth and Korth
1700 K St., N.W. Suite 501, Washington, DC 20006
Telephone: (202) 223-3630
Background: Assistant Secretary of the Army, 1952-53. Secretary of the Navy, 1962-63.
Clients:
Bernard Johnson, Inc.
First Financial Corp.

KORTH, Fritz-Alan
Korth and Korth
1700 K St., N.W. Suite 501, Washington, DC 20006
Telephone: (202) 223-3630
Clients:
Del Norte Technology
OKC Limited Partnership

KORTH AND KORTH
1700 K St., N.W. Suite 501, Washington, DC 20006
Telephone: (202) 223-3630
Members of firm representing listed organizations:
Korth, Fred
Background: Assistant Secretary of the Army, 1952-53. Secretary of the Navy, 1962-63.
Korth, Fritz-Alan
Clients:
Bernard Johnson, Inc. *(Fred Korth)*
Del Norte Technology *(Fritz-Alan Korth)*
First Financial Corp. *(Fred Korth)*
First Savings and Loan
OKC Limited Partnership *(Fritz-Alan Korth)*

KORWEK, Edward L.
Hogan and Hartson
555 13th St., N.W., Suite 1200, Washington, DC 20004-1109
Telephone: (202) 637-5600
Registered as lobbyist at U.S. Congress.
Clients:
Champon Flavors & Fragrances

KOSCIUSZKO, Patricia L.
Manager, Public Relations, Building Owners and Managers Ass'n Internat'l
1201 New York Ave., N.W. Suite 300, Washington, DC 20005
Telephone: (202) 289-7000

KOSH, Ronald W.
General Manager, AAA Potomac, American Automobile Ass'n
12600 Fair Lakes Circle, Fairfax, VA 22030
Telephone: (703) 222-6000
Registered as lobbyist at U.S. Congress.

KOSMINSKY, Jay
Deputy Director, Defense Policy Studies, Heritage Foundation
214 Massachusetts Ave., N.E., Washington, DC 20002
Telephone: (202) 546-4400

KOSS, Marilyn S.
Wash. Representative, Ass't V. President, New York Life Insurance Co.
600 New Hampshire Ave., N.W., Suite 200, Washington, DC 20037
Telephone: (202) 331-8733
Registered as lobbyist at U.S. Congress.

KOSTERS, Marvin H.
Director, Economic Policy Studies, American Enterprise Institute for Public Policy Research
1150 17th St., N.W., Washington, DC 20036
Telephone: (202) 862-5800

KOSTIW, Michael V.
Sr. Federal Gov't Affairs Representative, Texaco U.S.A.
1050 17th St., N.W., Suite 500, Washington, DC 20036
Telephone: (202) 331-1427

WASHINGTON REPRESENTATIVES

KOSTMAYER COMMUNICATIONS, INC.
2300 M St., N.W., Suite 920, Washington, DC 20037
Telephone: (202) 223-6655
Members of firm representing listed organizations:
 Dolan, Christine
 Frazier, Harry
 Keyserling, Judy
 Kostmayer, Pamela, President
Clients:
 Competitive Health Care Coalition *(Harry Frazier)*
 Keep America Beautiful *(Christine Dolan)*
 Mothers Against Drunk Driving (MADD) *(Harry Frazier)*
 Nat'l Law Enforcement Officers' Memorial Fund *(Harry Frazier)*
 Police Executive Research Forum *(Judy Keyserling)*

KOSTMAYER, Pamela
President, Kostmayer Communications, Inc.
2300 M St., N.W., Suite 920, Washington, DC 20037
Telephone: (202) 223-6655

KOSTUK, Barbara M.
Manager, Government Relations, LTV Corp.
1025 Thomas Jefferson St., N.W., Suite 511 West, Washington, DC 20007
Telephone: (202) 944-5700
Registered as lobbyist at U.S. Congress.
Background: Former Special Assistant, Legislative Affairs, Office of Management and Budget.

KOTEEN, Bernard
Koteen and Naftalin
1150 Connecticut Ave., N.W. Suite 1000, Washington, DC 20036
Telephone: (202) 467-5700
Registered as lobbyist at U.S. Congress.
Background: Chief, Review Section, Federal Communications Commission, 1946-48.

KOTEEN AND NAFTALIN
1150 Connecticut Ave., N.W., Suite 1000, Washington, DC 20036
Telephone: (202) 467-5700
Background: The information below was obtained from public sources and submitted to this firm for confirmation or correction. The firm declined to confirm or correct the listing.
Members of firm representing listed organizations:
 Humphrey, Margot Smiley
 Koteen, Bernard
  Background: Chief, Review Section, Federal Communications Commission, 1946-48.
 Naftalin, Alan Y.
  Background: Attorney, Federal Communications Commission, 1952-53.
Clients:
 Alascom, Inc. *(Margot Smiley Humphrey, Alan Y. Naftalin)*
 KCNA-TV
 KCPQ
 KCRA-TV
 KERO-TV
 KFSM-TV
 KGTV
 KIVA-TV
 KLBK-TV
 KMGH-TV
 KMIR-TV
 KMOM-TV
 KPLR-TV
 KTSP-TV
 KTVV
 KTXA
 KTXH
 KWAB-TV
 KXAS-TV
 Telephone and Data Systems, Inc. *(Margot Smiley Humphrey, Alan Y. Naftalin)*
 WAGM-TV
 WBRC
 WCKT
 WDAF-TV
 WFRV-TV
 WGHP-TV
 WGR-TV
 WGTQ
 WGTU
 WHNT-TV
 WILX-TV
 WJMN-TV
 WKRC-TV
 WNEP-TV
 WQAD-TV
 WREG-TV
 WRTV
 WSVN
 WTAF-TV
 WTSP-TV
 WTVN-TV

KOTLER, Milton
V. President, CRG Marketing Group
1000 16th St., N.W. Suite 500, Washington, DC 20036
Telephone: (202) 223-2400

KOUAKOU, Amour
Manager, Public Information, Cogema, Inc.
7401 Wisconsin Ave., Bethesda, MD 20814
Telephone: (301) 986-8585
Registered as Foreign Agent: (#3587)

KOUBA, Dennis
Director, Communications, American Public Transit Ass'n
1201 New York Ave., N.W.,, Washington, DC 20005
Telephone: (202) 898-4000

KOURPIAS, George
President, Internat'l Ass'n of Machinists and Aerospace Workers
1300 Connecticut Ave., N.W. Suite 404, Washington, DC 20036
Telephone: (202) 857-5200

KOUTSOUMPAS, J. Thomas
Lash Group, The
555 13th St., N.W., Washington, DC 20004
Telephone: (202) 637-5600
Registered as lobbyist at U.S. Congress.

KOVACH, Gerald J.
Senior V. President, External Affairs, MCI Communications Corp.
1133 19th St., N.W., Washington, DC 20036
Telephone: (202) 872-1600
Registered as lobbyist at U.S. Congress.
Background: Former Chief Counsel, U.S. Senate Science, Commerce and Transportation Committee.

KOVACK, Kenneth S.
Assistant Director, Legislative Dept., United Steelworkers of America
815 16th St., N.W. Suite 706, Washington, DC 20006
Telephone: (202) 638-6929
Registered as lobbyist at U.S. Congress.

KOVALIC, Joan M.
Manager, Government Relations, BASF Corp.
2100 Pennsylvania Ave., N.W. Suite 755, Washington, DC 20037
Telephone: (202) 296-4894
Registered as lobbyist at U.S. Congress.

KOVENER, R. R.
Vice President, Healthcare Financial Management Ass'n
1050 17th St., N.W., Suite 510, Washington, DC 20036
Telephone: (202) 296-2920

KOVIN, John F.
Clifford & Warnke
815 Connecticut Ave., N.W., Washington, DC 20006
Telephone: (202) 828-4200

KOWOLSKI, Jeanne
Assoc Dir, Govt Affrs, INTERSTATE COMMERCE COMMISSION
12th and Constitution Ave. N.W., Washington, DC 20423
Telephone: (202) 275-7231

KOYANAGI, Chris
Sr. Director, Government Affairs, Nat'l Mental Health Ass'n
1021 Prince St., Alexandria, VA 22314
Telephone: (703) 684-7722

KOZAK, Jerome J.
V. President, Internat'l Ice Cream Ass'n
888 16th St., N.W., Washington, DC 20006

Telephone: (202) 296-4250
Registered as lobbyist at U.S. Congress.

KOZICHAROW, Eugene
Director, Public Affairs (Washington), Textron Inc.
1090 Vermont Ave., N.W., Suite 1100, Washington, DC 20005
Telephone: (202) 289-5800

KRACH, Gary
Director, Internat'l Affairs, GTE Corp.
Suite 1200, 1850 M St., N.W., Washington, DC 20036
Telephone: (202) 463-5232

KRAEMER, Jay R.
Fried, Frank, Harris, Shriver & Jacobson
1001 Pennsylvania Ave., N.W., Suite 800, Washington, DC 20004-2505
Telephone: (202) 639-7000
Clients:
 Virgin Island Rum Industries

KRAEMER, Sven F.
Deputy Director, Center for Security Policy
1250 24th St., N.W., Washington, DC 20037
Telephone: (202) 466-0515
Background: Staff, Nat'l Security Council, 1967-76; U.S. Senate Republican Policy Committee Senior Staff, 1979-80; GOP Platform Committee, 1980; Nat'l Security Council Director of Arms Control, 1981-87; Ass't for Defense & Foreign Policy to Cong. Jack Kemp (R-NY), 1987-88.

KRAFT, Betsy
Exec. Director, Coal Exporters Ass'n of the U.S.
1130 17th St., N.W. 9th Floor, Washington, DC 20036
Telephone: (202) 463-2654
Background: Also serves as Director, Internat'l Affairs, Nat'l Coal Ass'n.'

KRAFT, Michael B.
Exec. V. President, Sagamore Associates, Inc.
1701 K St., N.W., Suite 400, Washington, DC 20006
Telephone: (202) 223-0964
Registered as lobbyist at U.S. Congress.
Background: Press Secretary to Senator Vance Hartke (D-IN), 1963-65. Director, Nat'l Advisory Council on Small Business, 1979-81. Administrative Assistant to Rep. Phil Sharp (D-IN), 1981-89.
Clients:
 Indiana Electric Ass'n
 Nat'l Institute for Fitness and Sport
 1993 World University Games

KRAFT, Steven P.
Director, Utility Nuclear Waste Transportation Program
1111 19th St., N.W., Suite 600, Washington, DC 20036
Telephone: (202) 778-6511

KRAJA, Mylio S.
Exec. Director, Washington Office, American Legion
1608 K St., N.W., Washington, DC 20006
Telephone: (202) 861-2700

KRAJEC, Richard A.
Treasurer, Gulfstream Aerospace Corp. Political Action Committee
1000 Wilson Blvd., Suite 2701, Arlington, VA 22209
Telephone: (703) 276-9500

KRAKOVEC, Laura L.
Weil, Gotshal & Manges
1615 L St., N.W., Suite 700, Washington, DC 20036
Telephone: (202) 682-7000
Clients:
 Schering Internat'l

KRAMER, Andrea S.
Coffield Ungaretti Harris & Slavin
1747 Pennsylvania Ave., N.W. Suite 900, Washington, DC 20006
Telephone: (202) 872-4310
Clients:
 COMDISCO, Inc.

KRAMER, Franklin D.
Shea and Gardner
1800 Massachusetts Ave., N.W., Washington, DC 20036
Telephone: (202) 828-2000
Registered as lobbyist at U.S. Congress.

Registered as Foreign Agent: (#3901).
Background: Special Assistant to the Assistant Secretary of Defense for International Security Affairs, 1977-79. Principal Deputy Assistant Secretary of Defense for International Security Affairs, 1979-81. Undersecretary of Defense for Policy, 1981.

KRAMER, Kenneth S.
Fried, Frank, Harris, Shriver & Jacobson
1001 Pennsylvania Ave., N.W., Suite 800, Washington, DC 20004-2505
Telephone: (202) 639-7000

KRAMER, William D.
Squire, Sanders and Dempsey
1201 Pennsylvania Ave., N.W. P.O. Box 407, Washington, DC 20044
Telephone: (202) 626-6600
Registered as lobbyist at U.S. Congress.
Clients:
Nat'l Collegiate Athletic Ass'n

KRAMERICH, Leslie
Verner, Liipfert, Bernhard, McPherson and Hand, Chartered
901 15th St., N.W., Suite 700, Washington, DC 20005
Telephone: (202) 371-6000
Registered as lobbyist at U.S. Congress.
Background: Professional Staff Member, Senate Committee on Aging, 1984-86. Aide to Senator Dave Durenberger (R-MN), 1986-87. Staff Member, House Appropriations Committee, 1987-89.

KRANOWITZ, Alan M.
Senior V. President, Gov't Relations, Nat'l Ass'n of Wholesaler-Distributors
1725 K St., N.W. Suite 710, Washington, DC 20006
Telephone: (202) 872-0885
Registered as lobbyist at U.S. Congress.
Background: Former Assistant for Legislative Affairs to President Ronald Reagan and former floor assistant to House Minority Whip Dick Cheney (R-WY), 1989. Serves also Exec. Director, Wholesaler-Distributor PAC.

KRANZ, Sally
Director, Public Relations, General Federation of Women's Clubs
1734 N St., N.W., Washington, DC 20036
Telephone: (202) 347-3168

KRASH, Abe
Arnold & Porter
1200 New Hampshire Ave., N.W., Washington, DC 20036
Telephone: (202) 872-6700

KRASNER, Wendy L.
McDermott, Will and Emery
1850 K St., N.W., Suite 500, Washington, DC 20006-2296
Telephone: (202) 887-8000
Background: Office of General Counsel, U.S. Department of Health and Human Services, 1978-80.

KRATZ, Donald F.
Senior Counsel, Amax Inc.
1819 L St., N.W., Suite 300, Washington, DC 20036-3895
Telephone: (202) 466-6966

KRAUS, Bonnie D.
Legislative Ass't, Committee For Education Funding
505 Capitol Court, N.E. Suite 200, Washington, DC 20002
Telephone: (202) 543-6300

KRAUS, Margery
President and CEO, APCO Associates
1155 21st St., N.W., Suite 1000, Washington, DC 20036
Telephone: (202) 778-1000
Registered as lobbyist at U.S. Congress.
Clients:
Honeywell, Inc.
Philip Morris Management Corp.
Unilever United States, Inc.

KRAUS, Stephen W.
Senior Counsel - Pensions, American Council of Life Insurance
1001 Pennsylvania Ave., N.W., Washington, DC 20004-2599
Telephone: (202) 624-2109
Registered as lobbyist at U.S. Congress.

KRAUS, Susan
V. President, Media Relations, Nat'l Ass'n of Broadcasters
1771 N St., N.W., Washington, DC 20036
Telephone: (202) 429-5300

KRAUTHAMER, Judith
Manager, State Government Relations, American Soc. of Mechanical Engineers
1825 K St., N.W., Suite 218, Washington, DC 20006
Telephone: (202) 785-3756

KRAWIEC, Elaine M.
Director of Government Relations, Nat'l Ass'n of Water Companies
1725 K St., N.W. Suite 1212, Washington, DC 20006
Telephone: (202) 833-8383
Background: Former Aide to Rep. Nancy L. Johnson (D-CT).

KREAMER, Capt. Thomas J.
V. President, Internat'l Soc. of Air Safety Investigators
Technology Trading Park, 5 Export Drive, Sterling, VA 22170-4421
Telephone: (703) 430-9668

KREBS, Frederick L.
Manager, Business-Government Policy, Chamber of Commerce of the U.S.A.
1615 H St., N.W., Washington, DC 20062
Telephone: (202) 659-6000

KREBS, Robert S.
Dir., Public & Gov't Affrs., AAA Potomac, American Automobile Ass'n
12600 Fair Oaks Circle, Fairfax, VA 22033
Telephone: (703) 222-6000
Registered as lobbyist at U.S. Congress.

KREHER, Earl R.
Sr. Econ. Analyst, Econ. & Int'l Afrs., Motor Vehicle Manufacturers Ass'n of the United States
1620 Eye St., N.W. Suite 1000, Washington, DC 20006
Telephone: (202) 775-2700
Registered as lobbyist at U.S. Congress.

KREIZMAN, Janet
Bracy Williams & Co.
1000 Connecticut Ave., N.W., Suite 304, Washington, DC 20036
Telephone: (202) 659-4805
Registered as lobbyist at U.S. Congress.

KRELL, Kate
Public Relations Director, American Federation of Teachers
555 New Jersey Ave., N.W., Washington, DC 20001
Telephone: (202) 879-4400

KRELL, Paul
Director, Creative-Strategic Services, Gallagher-Widmeyer Group Inc., The
1110 Vermont Ave., N.W., Suite 1020, Washington, DC 20005
Telephone: (202) 659-1606
Background: Former political director of the political action committee of Rep. Richard Gephardt (D-MO) during the 1985-86 political cycle. Served as Senior National Scheduler for the Carter-Mondale presidential campaign 1979-80 and on the national campaign staff of Senator John Glenn (D-OH), 1983-84.

KREPON, Michael
President, Henry L. Stimson Center
1350 Connecticut Ave., N.W. Suite 304, Washington, DC 20036
Telephone: (202) 223-5956

KRESS, Martin P.
Asst Admin, Legis Affrs, NAT'L AERONAUTICS AND SPACE ADMINISTRATION
400 Maryland Ave, S.W., Washington, DC 20546
Telephone: (202) 453-1055

KRETZER, Gilbert L.
V. Pres. & Exec. Dir., IFDA, Nat'l-American Wholesale Grocers' Ass'n
201 Park Washington Court, Falls Church, VA 22046
Telephone: (703) 532-9400

KRIEGEL, Henry
Executive Director, Committee for a Free Afghanistan
214 Massachusetts Ave., N.E. Suite 480, Washington, DC 20002
Telephone: (202) 546-7577

KRIEGER, Kathy L.
General Counsel, United Brotherhood of Carpenters and Joiners of America
101 Constitution Ave., N.W., Washington, DC 20001
Telephone: (202) 546-6206

KRIESBERG, Simeon M.
Mayer, Brown and Platt
2000 Pennsylvania Ave., N.W. Suite 6500, Washington, DC 20006
Telephone: (202) 463-2000
Clients:
American Farm Bureau Federation

KRIKORIAN, Van Z.
Government and Legal Affairs Director, Armenian Assembly of America
122 C St., N.W., Suite 350, Washington, DC 20001
Telephone: (202) 393-3434
Registered as lobbyist at U.S. Congress.

KRIMSKY, George A.
V. President and Exec. Director, Center for Foreign Journalists
11690-A Sunrise Valley Drive, Reston, VA 22091
Telephone: (703) 620-5984

KRINSKY, Adam
Legislative Analyst, Nat'l Ass'n of Development Organizations
400 North Capitol St., N.W. Suite 372, Washington, DC 20001
Telephone: (202) 624-7806

KRISER, Lou
President, Snyder Ball Kriser and Associates, Inc.
499 S. Capitol St., S.W., Suite 520, Washington, DC 20003
Telephone: (202) 488-4960
Registered as lobbyist at U.S. Congress.
Registered as Foreign Agent: (#3655).
Clients:
Alloy Surfaces, Inc.
General Motors (Allison Gas Turbines Division)
Service Engineering Co.

KRISSOFF & ASSOCIATES, INC.
3 Church Circle, Suite 250, Annapolis, MD 21401
Telephone: (301) 267-0023
Members of firm representing listed organizations:
Krissoff, Michael, President
Background: Serves as Exec. Director, Asphalt Emulsion Manufacturers Ass'n and Exec. Director, Asphalt Recycling and Reclaiming Ass'n.
Clients:
Asphalt Emulsion Manufacturers Ass'n
Asphalt Recycling and Reclaiming Ass'n *(Michael Krissoff)*

KRISSOFF, Michael
President, Krissoff & Associates, Inc.
3 Church Circle, Suite 250, Annapolis, MD 21401
Telephone: (301) 267-0023
Background: Serves as Exec. Director, Asphalt Emulsion Manufacturers Ass'n and Exec. Director, Asphalt Recycling and Reclaiming Ass'n.
Clients:
Asphalt Recycling and Reclaiming Ass'n

KRIST, William K.
V. President, Internat'l Affairs, American Electronics Ass'n
1225 Eye St., N.W., Suite 950, Washington, DC 20005
Telephone: (202) 682-9110

KRISTOF, Dawn C.
President, Water and Wastewater Equipment Manufacturers Ass'n
Box 17402 Dulles Internat'l Airport, Washington, DC 20041
Telephone: (703) 661-8011
Registered as lobbyist at U.S. Congress.

KRISTY, Jack
Asst Gen Counsel, Legis Counsel, DEPARTMENT OF EDUCATION
400 Maryland Ave., S.W., Washington, DC 20202
Telephone: (202) 732-2670

KRIVIT, Daniel H.
Krivit and Krivit
50 E St., S.E., Washington, DC 20003
Telephone: (202) 544-1112
Clients:
Bayonne Board of Education
Bayonne, New Jersey, City of
Clifton, New Jersey, City of
Gloucester County, New Jersey
Hoboken, New Jersey, City of
Hudson County, New Jersey
Irvington, New Jersey, Town of
Jersey City Office of Grants Management
Kearny, New Jersey, Town of
Lake County Job Training Corp.
Ponce, Puerto Rico, City of

KRIVIT AND KRIVIT
50 E St., S.E., Washington, DC 20003
Telephone: (202) 544-1112
Members of firm representing listed organizations:
Krivit, Daniel H.
Clients:
Bayonne Board of Education *(Daniel H. Krivit)*
Bayonne, New Jersey, City of *(Daniel H. Krivit)*
Clifton, New Jersey, City of *(Daniel H. Krivit)*
Gloucester County, New Jersey *(Daniel H. Krivit)*
Hoboken, New Jersey, City of *(Daniel H. Krivit)*
Hudson County, New Jersey *(Daniel H. Krivit)*
Irvington, New Jersey, Town of *(Daniel H. Krivit)*
Jersey City Office of Grants Management *(Daniel H. Krivit)*
Kearny, New Jersey, Town of *(Daniel H. Krivit)*
Lake County Job Training Corp. *(Daniel H. Krivit)*
Ponce, Puerto Rico, City of *(Daniel H. Krivit)*

KROES, Donald J.
V.P., Federation Develop't & Field Opns., Chamber of Commerce of the U.S.A.
1615 H St., N.W., Washington, DC 20062
Telephone: (202) 463-5406

KROLL, Steven
Assoc. Director, Political Affairs, American Hospital Ass'n
50 F St., N.W., Washington, DC 20001
Telephone: (202) 638-1100
Registered as lobbyist at U.S. Congress.

KROLOFF, George M.
Kroloff Marshall and Associates
1350 Connecticut Ave., N.W. Suite 900, Washington, DC 20036
Telephone: (202) 429-8877
Registered as Foreign Agent: (#3947).
Clients:
European Communities, Commission of the

KROLOFF MARSHALL AND ASSOCIATES
1350 Connecticut Ave., N.W. Suite 900, Washington, DC 20036
Telephone: (202) 429-8877
Members of firm representing listed organizations:
Kroloff, George M.
Clients:
European Communities, Commission of the
(George M. Kroloff)

KROMKOWSKI, John A.
President, Nat'l Center for Urban Ethnic Affairs
20 Cardinal Station, Washington, DC 20064
Telephone: (202) 232-3600

KRONMILLER, Theodore G.
Patton, Boggs and Blow
2550 M St., N.W., Suite 800, Washington, DC 20037
Telephone: (202) 457-6000
Registered as lobbyist at U.S. Congress.
Registered as Foreign Agent: (#2165).
Background: Counsel, Subcommittee on Oceanography, U.S. House of Representatives, 1978-79. Counsel, House Subcommittee on Fisheries and Wildlife Conservation and the Environment, 1979-81. Deputy Assistant Secretary of State for Ocean and Fisheries Affairs, 1982-83.
Clients:
Fishing Vessel Owners Ass'n
Iceland, Government of
Marshall Islands, Government of

KROOTH & ALTMAN
2101 L St., N.W., Suite 210, Washington, DC 20037
Telephone: (202) 293-8200
Members of firm representing listed organizations:
Mazer, Michael E.
Clients:
Housing Study Group *(Michael E. Mazer)*

KROPF, Robin L.
Assistant Director, Federal Affairs, American Medical Ass'n
1101 Vermont Ave., N.W., Washington, DC 20005
Telephone: (202) 789-7400
Registered as lobbyist at U.S. Congress.

KROPP, Arthur
President, People for the American Way
2000 M St., N.W., Suite 400, Washington, DC 20036
Telephone: (202) 467-4999

KRUG, Larry L.
Director of Public Affairs, Nat'l 4-H Council
7100 Connecticut Ave., Chevy Chase, MD 20815
Telephone: (301) 961-2800

KRUGER, Ann
Seminar Director, American Security Council Foundation
733 15th St., N.W. Suite 700, Washington, DC 20005
Telephone: (202) 484-1676

KRUKE, Kevin H.
V. President, Public & Int'l Affairs, American Trucking Ass'ns
430 First St., S.E., Washington, DC 20003-1826
Telephone: (202) 544-6245

KRULISCH, Lee
Exec. Director, Scientists Center for Animal Welfare
4805 St. Elmo Ave., Bethesda, MD 20814
Telephone: (301) 654-6390

KRUMBOLTZ, Ann
Director, Earth Day Program, Nat'l Wildlife Federation
1400 16th St., N.W., Washington, DC 20036-2266
Telephone: (202) 797-6800

KRUMHOLTZ, Jack
Verner, Liipfert, Bernhard, McPherson and Hand, Chartered
901 15th St., N.W., Suite 700, Washington, DC 20005
Telephone: (202) 371-6000
Registered as lobbyist at U.S. Congress.

KRUPIN, Jay P.
Reid & Priest
1111 19th St., N.W., Washington, DC 20036
Telephone: (202) 828-0100

KRUSE, Earl J.
Internat'l President, United Union of Roofers, Waterproofers and Allied Workers
1125 17th St., N.W., Washington, DC 20036
Telephone: (202) 638-3228

KRUSE, Paul R.
Senior Washington Representative, Pennzoil Co.
1155 15th St., N.W., Suite 600, Washington, DC 20005
Telephone: (202) 331-0212
Registered as lobbyist at U.S. Congress.

KRUSE, Richard A.
Assistant Director, Government Relations, Nat'l Ass'n of Secondary School Principals
1904 Association Drive, Reston, VA 22091
Telephone: (703) 860-0200

KRZYMINSKI, James S.
Sr. V. Pres., Corp. Svcs. & Gen. Couns., Nat'l Council of Farmer Cooperatives
50 F St., N.W., Suite 900, Washington, DC 20001
Telephone: (202) 626-8700
Registered as lobbyist at U.S. Congress.

KUCHLER, Joseph A.
Director, Federal Issues, Healthcare Financial Management Ass'n
1050 17th St., N.W., Suite 510, Washington, DC 20036
Telephone: (202) 296-2920

KUCHNICKI, Richard P.
President, Council of American Building Officials
5203 Leesburg Pike, Falls Church, VA 22041
Telephone: (703) 931-4533

KUGLER, Eileen
Director of Communications, Public Voice for Food and Health Policy
1001 Connecticut Ave., N.W., Suite 522, Washington, DC 20036
Telephone: (202) 659-5930
Registered as lobbyist at U.S. Congress.

KUHN, Herb B.
Sr Assoc. Director, Div. of Leg. Affairs, American Hospital Ass'n
50 F St., N.W., Suite 1100, Washington, DC 20001
Telephone: (202) 638-1100
Registered as lobbyist at U.S. Congress.

KUHN, James
Duberstein Group, Inc., The
2100 Pennsylvania Ave., N.W. Suite 350, Washington, DC 20037
Telephone: (202) 728-1100

KUHN, Thomas R.
President, Edison Electric Institute
1111 19th St., N.W., Washington, DC 20036
Telephone: (202) 778-6555
Registered as lobbyist at U.S. Congress.

KULESBER, Kate
Legislative Analyst, Nat'l Wholesale Druggists' Ass'n
105 Oronoco St., Alexandria, VA 22314
Telephone: (202) 684-6400

KUN, John A.
Assistant Director, Washington Office, Ukrainian Nat'l Ass'n
400 First St., N.W. Suite 710, Washington, DC 20001
Telephone: (202) 347-8629

KUNDU, Jai
Exec. Dir., Safety Management Council, American Trucking Ass'ns
430 First St., S.E., Washington, DC 20003-1826
Telephone: (202) 544-6245

KUNZ, Cynthia
Hartnett & Associates
4590 MacArthur Blvd., N.W., Suite 200, Washington, DC 20007
Telephone: (202) 337-1502
Clients:
Baking Industry and Teamster Labor Conference

KUNZ, Lt. Col. Eric
Legis Asst to the Chairman, JCS, DEPARTMENT OF DEFENSE - Joint Chiefs of Staff
The Pentagon, Washington, DC 20301
Telephone: (202) 697-1137

KUPPER, Rebecca L.
Ass't Director, Government Relations, American College of Radiology
1891 Preston White Drive, Reston, VA 22091
Telephone: (703) 648-8900

KUPPERMAN, Charles M.
Dir.-Quality Processes & Strat. Planning, McDonnell Douglas Corp.
1735 Jefferson Davis Highway, Arlington, VA 22202
Telephone: (703) 553-4117

KURIANSKY, Joan A.
Exec. Director, Older Women's League
730 11th St., N.W. Suite 300, Washington, DC 20001
Telephone: (202) 783-6686

KURKUL, Doug
Director, Legislative Analysis, Nat'l Ass'n of Manufacturers
1331 Pennsylvania Ave., N.W. Suite 1500 North, Washington, DC 20004-1703

Telephone: (202) 637-3000

KURMAN, Michael J.
Arent, Fox, Kintner, Plotkin & Kahn
1050 Connecticut Ave., N.W., Washington, DC 20036-5339
Telephone: (202) 857-6000
Registered as lobbyist at U.S. Congress.
Background: Attorney, Solicitor's Honors Program and Division of Surface Mining, and Special Assistant to the Solicitor, U.S. Department of Interior, 1977-81.
Clients:
Nat'l Parking Ass'n

KURRELMEYER, Louis H.
Winthrop, Stimson, Putnam & Roberts
1133 Connecticut Ave., N.W. Suite 1000, Washington, DC 20036
Telephone: (202) 775-9800
Registered as Foreign Agent: (#3873).
Clients:
Swedish Steelproducers' Ass'n (Jernkontoret)

KURRENT, Edward A.
Gilberg & Kurent
1250 I St., N.W. Suite 600, Washington, DC 20005
Telephone: (202) 842-3222

KURRUS AND KIRCHNER
1055 Thomas Jefferson St., NW Suite 418, Washington, DC 20007
Telephone: (202) 342-0204
Members of firm representing listed organizations:
Kirchner, Paul G.
Kurrus, Richard W.
Background: Special Assistant to Federal Maritime Board, 1951-53. Chief Counsel, House Select Committee on Crime, 1969.
Clients:
American Pilots Ass'n (Paul G. Kirchner)
St. Lawrence Seaway Pilots Ass'n (Paul G. Kirchner)

KURRUS, Richard W.
Kurrus and Kirchner
1055 Thomas Jefferson St., NW Suite 418, Washington, DC 20007
Telephone: (202) 342-0204
Registered as lobbyist at U.S. Congress.
Background: Special Assistant to Federal Maritime Board, 1951-53. Chief Counsel, House Select Committee on Crime, 1969.

KURTZ, Angela Y.
Government Relations Represenative, Hershey Foods Corp.
1730 Rhode Island Ave., N.W., Suite 206, Washington DC 20036
Telephone: (202) 223-9070

KURTZ, Ruth M.
Senior V. President, French & Company
The Willard, 1455 Pennsylvania Ave., N.W., Suite 1260, Washington, DC 20004
Telephone: (202) 783-7272

KURUCZA, Robert M.
Morrison & Foerster
2000 Pennsylvania Ave., N.W., Suite 5500, Washington, DC 20006
Telephone: (202) 887-1500
Registered as lobbyist at U.S. Congress.
Background: Securities and Exchange Commission, 1978-80. Office of the Comptroller of the Currency, 1980-82.
Clients:
California Bankers Clearinghouse Ass'n
MasterCard Internat'l. Inc.
VISA U.S.A., Inc.

KURZ, Ester
Legislative Director, American Israel Public Affairs Committee
440 First St., N.W. Suite 600, Washington, DC 20001
Telephone: (202) 639-5200
Registered as lobbyist at U.S. Congress.

KURZ, Norman J.
Kurz & Volk
733 15th St., N.W., Suite 700, Washington, DC 20005
Telephone: (202) 783-5233

KURZ & VOLK
733 15th St., N.W., Suite 700, Washington, DC 20005
Telephone: (202) 783-5233
Background: A consulting firm specializing in campaign strategy, political fundraising and public affairs.
Members of firm representing listed organizations:
Kurz, Norman J.
Volk, Mary Jane

KURZMAN, Stephen
Nixon, Hargrave, Devans and Doyle
One Thomas Circle, N.W., Eighth Floor, Washington, DC 20005
Telephone: (202) 223-7200
Registered as lobbyist at U.S. Congress.
Background: Legislative Assistant and Counsel to Sen. Jacob K. Javits of New York, 1961-65. Minority Counsel, U.S. Senate Committee on Labor and Public Welfare, 1965-66. Assistant Secretary for Legislation, Department of Health, Education and Welfare, 1971-76.
Clients:
American Free Trade Ass'n
Bausch & Lomb, Inc.
Coalition for Competitive Imports
Eastman Savings & Loan Ass'n
Lawyers Co-operative Publishing Co.
Thompson Medical Co., Inc.

KURZWEIL, Jeffrey
Dow, Lohnes and Albertson
1255 23rd St., N.W., Suite 500, Washington, DC 20037
Telephone: (202) 857-2500
Registered as lobbyist at U.S. Congress.
Background: Special Assistant to the General Counsel, U.S. Department of Commerce, 1977-79.
Clients:
Carlyle Group, The
First Boston Corp.
Johnson-Simmons Co., The
Lifecare Services Co.
Marriott Corp.
Morgan Guaranty Trust Co.

KUSAK, Laurie
Communication, Nat'l Recreation and Park Ass'n
3101 Park Center Drive, Alexandria, VA 22302
Telephone: (703) 820-4940

KUSH, Daniel M.
BizNet Congressional Correspondent, Chamber of Commerce of the U.S.A.
1615 H St., N.W., Washington, DC 20062
Telephone: (202) 463-5928

KUSHNER, Gary J.
Hogan and Hartson
555 13th St., N.W., Suite 1200, Washington, DC 20004-1109
Telephone: (202) 637-5600
Clients:
American Frozen Food Institute
American Soybean Ass'n
Nat'l Pasta Ass'n

KUSHNICK, Michael G.
Rose, Schmidt, Hasley & DiSalle
1701 Pennsylvania Ave., N.W., Suite 1040, Washington, DC 20006
Telephone: (202) 293-8600
Registered as lobbyist at U.S. Congress.
Registered as Foreign Agent: (#2275).
Background: Army Judge Advocate, 1958-61. Trial Attorney, Federal Trade Commission, 1961-64. Principal Legal Assistant to Federal Trade Commissioner Mary Gardiner Jones, 1964-66.
Clients:
Equimark Corp.
Federation of the Swiss Watch Industry
Joy Technologies Inc.
Social Security Protection Bureau

KUTAK ROCK & CAMPBELL
1101 Connecticut Ave., N.W. Suite 1000, Washington, DC 20036
Telephone: (202) 828-2400
Members of firm representing listed organizations:
Granese, Nancy L., Government Relations Advisor
Background: Exec. V. President, KRC Resources Inc.
Clients:

Capital Markets Assurance Corp. (Nancy L. Granese)
Financial Security Assurance, Inc. (Nancy L. Granese)
Kutak Rock & Campbell Political Action Committee (Nancy L. Granese)
Municipal Bond Insurance Ass'n (Nancy L. Granese)
Summit, Ltd. (Nancy L. Granese)

KUTSKA, Melanie A.
Administrative Secretary, Federal Express Corp.
300 Maryland Ave., N.E., Washington, DC 20002
Telephone: (202) 546-1631

KUTZNER, Patricia L.
Exec. Director, World Hunger Education Service
3018 Fourth St., N.E., Washington, DC 20017
Telephone: (202) 269-1075

KUYKENDALL CO.
517 3rd St., S.E., Washington, DC 20003
Telephone: (202) 546-2196
Members of firm representing listed organizations:
Kuykendall, Dan H., President
Background: Former Member, U.S. House of Representatives (R-TN), 1967-75.
Clients:
Alpha Environmental, Inc. (Dan H. Kuykendall)
Alpha 21 Corp. (Dan H. Kuykendall)
First Construction Fund (Dan H. Kuykendall)
Shoup Corp., R. F. (Dan H. Kuykendall)

KUYKENDALL, Dan H.
President, Kuykendall Co.
517 3rd St., S.E., Washington, DC 20003
Telephone: (202) 546-2196
Registered as lobbyist at U.S. Congress.
Background: Former Member, U.S. House of Representatives (R-TN), 1967-75.
Clients:
Alpha Environmental, Inc.
Alpha 21 Corp.
First Construction Fund
Shoup Corp., R. F.

KUYKENDALL, Dawn E.
Office Manager, Mortgage Insurance Companies of America
805 15th St., N.W., Suite 1110, Washington, DC 20005
Telephone: (202) 371-2899

KWAPISZ, John D.
Exec. Director, Center for Peace and Freedom
214 Massachusetts Ave., N.E., Suite 360, Washington, DC 20002
Telephone: (202) 547-5607
Background: Serves also as Exec. Secretary, Science and Engineering Committee for a Secure World.

KYLE, John E.
Dir., Children & Families in Cities, Nat'l League of Cities
1301 Pennsylvania Ave., N.W., Washington, DC 20004
Telephone: (202) 626-3000

KYNOCH, Kimberly R.
PAC Director, Equitable Life Assurance Soc. of the U.S.
1700 Pennsylvania Ave., N.W., Suite 525, Washington, DC 20006
Telephone: (202) 393-3210
Background: Staff Assistant to U.S. Senator Sam Nunn, 1983-85.

KYROS AND ASSOCIATES
1055 Thomas Jefferson St., N.W., Suite 418, Washington, DC 20007
Telephone: (202) 342-0204
Members of firm representing listed organizations:
Kyros, Peter N., Founding Partner
Background: Former Member, U.S. House of Representatives (D-ME), 1967-75.

KYROS, Peter N.
Founding Partner, Kyros and Associates
1055 Thomas Jefferson St., N.W., Suite 418, Washington, DC 20007
Telephone: (202) 342-0204
Registered as lobbyist at U.S. Congress.
Background: Former Member, U.S. House of Representatives (D-ME), 1967-75.

KYTE, John
Sr. Legislative Representative, Yankee Atomic Electric Co.
905 Sixth St., S.W., Washington, DC 20024
Telephone: (202) 488-3789
Registered as lobbyist at U.S. Congress.

LABELLA, Gary M.
V. President, Public Relations, Recreation Vehicle Industry
Ass'n
1896 Preston White Drive P.O. Box 2999, Reston, VA
22090
Telephone: (703) 620-6003

LABELLE, Ernest W.
Director, State & Constituent Relations, TRW Inc.
Suite 2700, 1000 Wilson Blvd., Arlington, VA 22209
Telephone: (703) 276-5020

LABOR BUREAU, INC., The
1101 15th St., N.W., Suite 1010, Washington, DC 20005
Telephone: (202) 296-7420
Background: A labor relations consulting firm.
Members of firm representing listed organizations:
Rosen, Mark A., V. President
Roth, Thomas R., President

LACH, Joseph L.
Manager, Government Marketing, Manville Corp.
1625 K St., N.W., Suite 750, Washington, DC 20006
Telephone: (202) 785-4940
Registered as lobbyist at U.S. Congress.

LACHANCE, Janice R.
Director, Commun. & Political Action, American Federation
of Government Employees
80 F St., N.W., Washington, DC 20001
Telephone: (202) 737-8700
Registered as lobbyist at U.S. Congress.

LACHELLI, Kim M., Lam
Lachelli, Waller and Associates
600 Maryland Ave., S.W., Suite 200A East Wing, Wash-
ington, DC 20024
Telephone: (202) 863-1472
Clients:
Hong Kong Press Publishers

LACHELLI, Vincent P.
Lachelli, Waller and Associates
600 Maryland Ave., S.W., Suite 200A East Wing, Wash-
ington, DC 20024
Telephone: (202) 863-1472
Registered as lobbyist at U.S. Congress.
Clients:
Interspace Inns Internat'l
Las Vegas Paiute Indian Tribe
Nationwide Auction Co.
Reno Sparks Indian Colony
Shenzhen Municipality Industrial Development
Corp.

LACHELLI, WALLER AND ASSOCIATES
600 Maryland Ave., S.W., Suite 200A East Wing, Wash-
ington, DC 20024
Telephone: (202) 863-1472
Background: A government relations consulting firm.
Members of firm representing listed organizations:
Abbott, Kelton
Background: Special Assistant to Senator Alan Bible
(D-TX), 1962-72. Legislative Assistant to Senator
Howard Cannon (D-NV), 1972-83. Legislative Assist-
ant to Senator Paul Laxalt (R-NV), 1983-87. Legisla-
tive Assistant to Senator Chic Hecht (R-NV), 1987.
Ballenger, Sam
Background: Legislative Assistant and Director of
Legislation to Senator Paul Laxalt (R-NV), 1975-87.
Lachelli, Kim M. (Lam)
Lachelli, Vincent P.
Waller, John D.
Whitaker, L. Paige
Clients:
Advanced Management & Technologies *(John D.
Waller)*
Applied Expertise
Aurora University *(John D. Waller)*
Caribbean Investment Group
Charming Shops
Hong Kong Press Publishers *(Kim M., Lam Lachelli)*
Imasco *(Sam Ballenger)*

Inter Tribal Council of Nevada *(John D. Waller)*
Interspace Inns Internat'l *(Vincent P. Lachelli)*
Ka Pono Hawaii Nei Inc.
Kaempen Internat'l
Las Vegas Paiute Indian Tribe *(Vincent P. Lachelli)*
Nationwide Auction Co. *(Vincent P. Lachelli)*
Reno Sparks Indian Colony *(Vincent P. Lachelli)*
Shenzhen Municipality Industrial Development
Corp. *(Vincent P. Lachelli)*
Sierra Press *(John D. Waller)*
Silent Partner *(John D. Waller)*
Undersea Tours Inc.

LACHTER, Stephen
Of Counsel, Patton, Boggs and Blow
2550 M St., N.W., Suite 800, Washington, DC 20037
Telephone: (202) 457-6000
Background: Trial Attorney, Civil Aeronautics Board,
1969-1975. Supervisory Trial Attorney, Antitrust Divi-
sion, U.S. Department of Justice, 1975-1978. Executive
Assistant to CAB Member, 1978-1982. Deputy Director
and Associate Director, Legal Affairs, Bureau of Domes-
tic Aviation, CAB, 1982-1985 . Special Aviation Counsel,
U.S. Department of Transportation, 1985.
Clients:
USAir Group Inc.

LACKEY, Mary Lou
Manager, State Government Relations, Motorola, Inc.
1350 Eye St., N.W., Suite 400, Washington, DC 20005-
3306
Telephone: (202) 371-6900
Registered as lobbyist at U.S. Congress.

LACKEY, Phillip Ray
Exec. V. President, Internat'l Masonry Institute
Suite 1001, 823 15th St., N.W., Washington, DC 20005
Telephone: (202) 783-3908
Registered as lobbyist at U.S. Congress.

LACKRITZ, Marc E.
Exec. V. President, Securities Industry Ass'n
1850 M St., N.W., Suite 550, Washington, DC 20036
Telephone: (202) 296-9410

LACOPO, John D.
V. Pres., Office of Government Affairs, Electronic Data
Systems Corp.
1331 Pennsylvania Ave., N.W., Suite 1300 North, Wash-
ington, DC 20004
Telephone: (202) 637-6700
Registered as lobbyist at U.S. Congress.

LACOSTE, Rene
Senior Associate, CR Associates
317 Massachusetts Ave., N.E., Suite 100, Washington, DC
20002
Telephone: (202) 546-4732
Background: Former Staff, Federal Reserve System's Board
of Governors.

LADD, Bruce C., Jr.
V. President of Legislative Affairs, Motorola, Inc.
1350 Eye St., N.W., Suite 400, Washington, DC 20005-
3306
Telephone: (202) 371-6900
Registered as lobbyist at U.S. Congress.
Background: Serves as PAC Administrator for the Motoro-
la Employees' Good Government Committee.

LADD, Katherine D.
Director, Federal Health Policy, Glaxo, Inc.
1500 K St., N.W., Suite 650, Washington, DC 20005
Telephone: (202) 783-1277
Registered as lobbyist at U.S. Congress.

LADD, Richard B.
V. President, Robison Internat'l, Inc.
2300 N St., N.W., Suite 600, Washington, DC 20037
Telephone: (202) 663-9048
Registered as lobbyist at U.S. Congress.
Registered as Foreign Agent: (#3950).
Clients:
McDonnell Douglas Helicopter Co.

LADD, William D.
V. President, Government Affairs, Marriott Corp.
One Marriott Drive Dept. 904, Washington, DC 20058
Telephone: (301) 380-1073

Background: Responsibilities include Marriott Political Action Committee.

LADOMIRAK, Deborah
Smith, Bucklin and Associates
1101 Connecticut Ave., N.W., Suite 700, Washington, DC
20036
Telephone: (202) 857-1100
Background: Serves as V. President, Director of Public Af-
fairs, Regional Airline Ass'n.
Clients:
Regional Airline Ass'n

LAFEVRE, Sandra L.
Assistant V. President, Reinsurance Ass'n of America
1819 L St., N.W., Suite 700, Washington, DC 20036
Telephone: (202) 293-3335
Registered as lobbyist at U.S. Congress.

LAFIELD, William L., Jr.
Manager, State Government Relations-East, Shell Oil Co.
Suite 200, 1025 Connecticut Ave., N.W., Washington, DC
20036
Telephone: (202) 466-1450

LAFRANCE, Ann J.
Squire, Sanders and Dempsey
1201 Pennsylvania Ave., N.W. P.O. Box 407, Washington,
DC 20044
Telephone: (202) 626-6600
Clients:
McGraw-Hill, Inc.

LAGASSE, Alfred B., III
Exec. V. President, Internat'l Taxicab Ass'n
3849 Farragut Ave., Kensington, MD 20898
Telephone: (301) 946-5701
Background: Also serves as Treasurer, Internat'l Taxicab
Ass'n Political Action Committee.

LAGASSE, Robert C., CAE
Executives Consultants, Inc.
13542 Union Village Circle, Clifton, VA 22024
Telephone: (703) 830-5369
Clients:
Internat'l Microwave Power Institute
Nat'l Bark Producers Ass'n

LAHAYE, Beverly
President, Concerned Women for America
370 L'Enfant Promenade, S.W., Suite 800, Washington,
DC 20024
Telephone: (202) 488-7000

LAHR, Donald
Administrator, Nat'l Energy Management Institute
601 North Fairfax St., Alexandria, VA 22314
Telephone: (703) 739-7100

LAHUE, Sally Ann
Associate Director, Congressional Afrs., Nat'l Council of
Savings Institutions
1101 15th St., N.W. Suite 400, Washington, DC 20005
Telephone: (202) 857-3100
Registered as lobbyist at U.S. Congress.

LAIBLE, Myron F.
V. President, Outdoor Advertising Ass'n of America
1212 New York Ave., N.W., Suite 1210, Washington, DC
20005
Telephone: (202) 371-5566
Registered as lobbyist at U.S. Congress.

LAIRD, David M.
V. President, Dressendorfer-Laird, Inc.
1730 Rhode Island Ave., N.W., Suite 210, Washington, DC
20036
Telephone: (202) 887-5073
Registered as lobbyist at U.S. Congress.
Clients:
Metropolitan Insurance Cos.
Science Applications, Inc.

LAITIN, Joseph
Public Affairs Consultant, Fleishman-Hillard, Inc
1301 Connecticut Ave., N.W., Washington, DC 20036
Telephone: (202) 659-0330

LAKE, F. David, Jr.
Wilmer, Cutler and Pickering
2445 M St., N.W., Washington, DC 20037-1420
Telephone: (202) 663-6000

LAKE, James H.
Chairman, Robinson, Lake, Lerer & Montgomery
1667 K St., N.W., Suite 900, Washington, DC 20006
Telephone: (202) 457-9270
Registered as lobbyist at U.S. Congress.
Registered as Foreign Agent: (#3911).
Clients:
Atari Games Corp.
California Prune Board
California Walnut Commission
Connell Rice and Sugar Co.
Japan Auto Parts Industry Ass'n
Mitsubishi Electric Corp.
Napa Flood Control and Water Conservation
District
Rice Growers Ass'n of California
Sun Diamond Growers of California
Tri-Valley Growers of California

LAKE, Kerry L.
Exec. V. President, Adhesive and Sealant Council
1627 K St., N.W., Washington, DC 20006
Telephone: (202) 452-1500

LAKE, William T.
Wilmer, Cutler and Pickering
2445 M St., N.W., Washington, DC 20037-1420
Telephone: (202) 663-6000
Registered as Foreign Agent: (#3555).
Background: Deputy Legal Adviser, Department of State,
1980-81. Counsel, Council on Environmental Quality,
1970-73.
Clients:
Tibet, Government of (in Exile)

LAKIN, Steven
V. President, Institute for Research on the Economics of
Taxation (IRET)
1331 Pennsylvania Ave., N.W. Suite 515, Washington, DC
20004
Telephone: (202) 347-9570

LALLY, Richard F.
V. President, Security, Air Transport Ass'n of America
1709 New York Ave., N.W., Washington, DC 20006-5206
Telephone: (202) 626-4000

LAMAR, Harry
President, Monticello Associates
818 Connecticut Ave., N.W., 12th Floor, Washington, DC
20006
Telephone: (202) 466-5490
Background: Former Trade Advisor, House Ways and
Means Committee, 1967-80.
Clients:
Joint Industry Group

LAMAR, Brig. Gen. Kirby, USA (Ret.)
V. President & Treasurer, Armed Forces Communications
and Electronics Ass'n Headquarters
4400 Fair Lakes Court, Fairfax, VA 22033
Telephone: (703) 631-6100

LAMB, A. Gretchen
Account Executive, Madison Group/Earle Palmer Brown,
The
2033 M St., N.W., 9th Floor, Washington, DC 20036
Telephone: (202) 223-0030
Registered as lobbyist at U.S. Congress.

LAMB, Ellen C.
Ass't Dir., Federal Legislative Services, Conference of
State Bank Supervisors
1015 18th St., N.W Suite 1100, Washington, DC 20036
Telephone: (202) 296-2840
Registered as lobbyist at U.S. Congress.

LAMB, Eugene
Programs Analyst, Nat'l Ass'n of Conservation Districts
509 Capitol Court, N.E., Washington, DC 20002
Telephone: (202) 547-6223

LAMB, Gerard F.
Director, Government Affairs, Bath Iron Works Corp.
2341 Jefferson Davis Highway Suite 1100, Arlington, VA
22202
Telephone: (703) 979-2030
Registered as lobbyist at U.S. Congress.

LAMB, James Michael
Dep Asst Dir and Chief, Office of Legis, DEPARTMENT
OF INTERIOR - Nat'l Park Service
18th and C Sts., N.W., Washington, DC 20240
Telephone: (202) 343-5883

LAMB, Robert H.
McGuire, Woods, Battle and Boothe
1627 Eye St., N.W. Suite 1000, Washington, DC 20006
Telephone: (202) 857-1700
Registered as lobbyist at U.S. Congress.
Clients:
Armstrong World Industries, Inc.
Doe Run Co.
James River Corp.
Nat'l Paint and Coatings Ass'n
Sun Co.

LAMBERT, Blanche
Pagonis and Donnelly Group
1620 Eye St., N.W., Suite 603, Washington, DC 20006
Telephone: (202) 452-8811

LAMBERT, Constance A.
Asst. to the Pres., Administration, Internat'l Union of Brick-
layers and Allied Craftsmen
815 15th St., N.W., 2nd Floor, Washington, DC 20005
Telephone: (202) 783-3788
Background: Former Exec. Assisant to Senator Edward
Kennedy (D-MA).

LAMBERT, David P.
Sr. V. President, Public Affairs, New York Stock Exchange
1800 K St., N.W., Suite 1100, Washington, DC 20006
Telephone: (202) 293-5740
Registered as lobbyist at U.S. Congress.

LAMBERT, David R.
Director of Government Affairs, American Seed Trade
Ass'n
1030 15th St., N.W. Suite 964, Washington, DC 20005
Telephone: (202) 223-4080
Registered as lobbyist at U.S. Congress.
Background: Serves as principal contact for American Seed
Trade Ass'n Political Action Committee.

LAMBERT, Eugene I.
Covington and Burling
1201 Pennsylvania Ave., N.W., Box 7566, Washington, DC
20044
Telephone: (202) 662-6000
Clients:
Animal Health Institute
Silver Group, Inc.
Upjohn Co.

LAMBERT, Steven C.
Hopkins and Sutter
888 16th St., N.W., Suite 700, Washington, DC 20006
Telephone: (202) 835-8000
Clients:
Louisiana Pacific Corp.

LAMBRAKOPOULOS, Stavroula
Deputy Director, Washington Office, New Jersey, State of
444 N. Capitol St., N.W. Suite 236, Washington, DC
20001
Telephone: (202) 638-0631

LAMM, Carolyn B.
White & Case
1747 Pennsylvania Ave., N.W., Suite 500, Washington, DC
20006
Telephone: (202) 872-0013
Clients:
George Washington Corp.
Parker Drilling Co.
Turkey, Government of

LAMM, Lester P.
President, Highway Users Federation for Safety and Mobility
1776 Massachusette Ave., N.W., Washington, DC 20036
Telephone: (202) 857-1200
Background: Former Deputy Administrator, Federal Highway Administration.

LAMONT, William J.
Lobel, Novins, Lamont and Flug
1275 K St., N.W., Suite 770, Washington, DC 20005
Telephone: (202) 371-6626
Background: Attorney, Office of Alien Property Custodian,
1942-46. Department of Justice, 1946-72.

LAMPLEY, Virginia A.
Spec Asst to Pres & Sr Dir, Legis Affrs, EXECUTIVE OF-
FICE OF THE PRESIDENT - Nat'l Security Council
1600 Pennsylvania Ave., N.W., Washington, DC 20500
Telephone: (202) 395-3055

LANCASTER, Ray H.
V. Pres., Federal Governmental Affairs, Texas Gas Transmission Corp.
555 13th St., N.W. Suite 430 West, Washington, DC
20004
Telephone: (202) 393-8577
Registered as lobbyist at U.S. Congress.

LANCELOT, Jill
Director of Congressional Affairs, Nat'l Taxpayers Union
713 Maryland Ave., N.E., Washington, DC 20002
Telephone: (202) 543-1300
Registered as lobbyist at U.S. Congress.

LAND, LEMLE & ARNOLD
1701 K St., N.W., Washington, DC 20006
Telephone: (202) 785-1020
Registered as Foreign Agent: (#3824)
Members of firm representing listed organizations:
Arnold, Millard W.
Background: Deputy Assistant Secretary of State, U.S.
Department of State, 1980-81.
Lemle, J. Stuart
Background: Assistant Director, Domestic Policy Staff,
The White House, 1977-78.
Clients:
Nigeria, Embassy of *(Millard W. Arnold, J. Stuart Lemle)*

LANDE, Stephen L.
Manchester Trade, Inc.
1155 15th St., N.W., Suite 314, Washington, DC 20005
Telephone: (202) 331-9464
Registered as Foreign Agent: (#4149).
Clients:
HYLSA
Korea Foreign Trade Ass'n
Sidermex Internat'l, Inc.
Tubos de Acero de Mexico, S.A.

LANDEAU, Deborah
Chair, Voters for Choice
2000 P St., N.W., Suite 515, Washington, DC 20036
Telephone: (202) 822-6640

LANDERS, Jay
Director, Government Affairs, Recreation Vehicle Dealers
Ass'n of North America
3251 Old Lee Hwy. Suite 500, Fairfax, VA 22030
Telephone: (703) 591-7130

LANDGREBE, Carl
Special Assistant to the President, Marine Engineers
Beneficial Ass'n
444 North Capitol St., N.W. Suite 800, Washington, DC
20001
Telephone: (202) 347-8585

LANDIS, Robert D.
Politcal Dir, Political Field Operations, Nat'l Ass'n of
REALTORS
777 14th St., N.W., Washington, DC 20005
Telephone: (202) 383-1000
Registered as lobbyist at U.S. Congress.

LANDMARK STRATEGIES, INC.
101 South Whiting St. Suite 319, Alexandria, VA 22304
Telephone: (703) 370-8500

The listings in this directory are available as *Mailing Labels*. See last page.

LANDMARK STRATEGIES, INC. (Cont'd)
Members of firm representing listed organizations:
Corn, Robert S., V. President
   Background: Former Western Regional Political Director, Democratic National Party.
Ely, Jeffrey R., President
   Background: Former Political Director, Democratic National Committee.

LANDOLFO, Maria
Director, Legislation & Political Action, Internat'l Union of Electronic, Electrical, Salaried, Machine, and Furniture Workers, AFL-CIO
1126 16th St., N.W., Washington, DC 20036
Telephone: (202) 296-1213
Registered as lobbyist at U.S. Congress.
Background: Also serves as contact for the IUE Committee on Political Education.

LANDRY, Brock R.
Keck, Mahin and Cate
1201 New York Ave., N.W., Penthouse Suite, Washington, DC 20005
Telephone: (202) 347-7006
Clients:
   Nat'l Particleboard Ass'n
   Nat'l Tire Dealers and Retreaders Ass'n

LANDRY, James E.
Sr. V. President and General Counsel, Air Transport Ass'n of America
Suite 500, 1709 New York Ave., N.W., Washington, DC 20006-5206
Telephone: (202) 626-4156

LANDSIDLE, David W.
Director, Washington Affairs, Abbott Laboratories
1710 Rhode Island Ave., N.W. Suite 300, Washington, DC 20036
Telephone: (202) 659-8524
Registered as lobbyist at U.S. Congress.

LANE, Dennis
Wilner and Scheiner
1200 New Hampshire Ave., N.W., Suite 300, Washington, DC 20036
Telephone: (202) 861-7800
Background: Trial Attorney, Rate Section, Federal Power Commission, 1975-77.

LANE, John D.
Wilkes, Artis, Hedrick and Lane, Chartered
1666 K St., N.W., Suite 1100, Washington, DC 20006
Telephone: (202) 457-7800
Clients:
   Westinghouse Broadcasting Co., Inc.

LANE, L. Lee
Exec. Dir., Intermodal Policy Division, Ass'n of American Railroads
50 F St., N.W., Suite 4900, Washington, DC 20001
Telephone: (202) 639-2163

LANE, Marcia S.
Dir., Communications & Public Relations, American Ass'n of Blood Banks
1117 North 19th St. Suite 600, Arlington, VA 22209
Telephone: (703) 528-8200

LANE, Mark
Associate Editor, New American View
132 Third St., S.E., Washington, DC 20003
Telephone: (202) 547-1036

LANE AND MITTENDORF
919 18th St., N.W., Suite 800, Washington, DC 20006
Telephone: (202) 785-4949
Background: Washington office of a New York law firm.
Members of firm representing listed organizations:
Woody, Robert J.
   Background: Legislative Assistant to Sen. James B. Pearson, 1969-71. Counsel, Senate Committee on Commerce, 1971-73.
Clients:
   University of South Carolina

LANG, Adrienne
Director of Governmental Affairs, American Soc. of Anesthesiologists
1111 14th St., N.W., Suite 501, Washington, DC 20005
Telephone: (202) 289-2222
Registered as lobbyist at U.S. Congress.

LANG, Jeffrey M.
Of Counsel, Winthrop, Stimson, Putnam & Roberts
1133 Connecticut Ave., N.W. Suite 1000, Washington, DC 20036
Telephone: (202) 775-9800
Background: Deputy General Counsel, International Trade Commission, 1976-79. Senate Finance Committee Staff, 1979-90, including Chief, International Trade Counsel, 1987-90.

LANG, Ronald A.
President, Synthetic Organic Chemical Manufacturers Ass'n
1330 Connecticut Ave., N.W. Suite 300, Washington, DC 20036
Telephone: (202) 659-0060
Background: Also represents the American Industrial Health Council.

LANGDON, James C., Jr.
Akin, Gump, Strauss, Hauer and Feld
1333 New Hampshire Ave., N.W., Suite 400, Washington, DC 20036
Telephone: (202) 887-4000

LANGE, Dieter G. F.
Wilmer, Cutler and Pickering
2445 M St., N.W., Washington, DC 20037-1420
Telephone: (202) 663-6000
Clients:
   Lufthansa German Airlines

LANGE, Robert
Manager, Congressional Affairs, Boeing Co.
1700 North Moore St., Arlington, VA 22209
Telephone: (703) 558-9600
Registered as lobbyist at U.S. Congress.

LANGE, William M.
Assistant General Counsel, Consumers Power Co.
Telephone: (202) 293-5795

LANGFORD SANFORD, Suzanne
Schmeltzer, Aptaker and Sheppard
The Watergate, 2600 Virginia Ave., N.W., Washington, DC 20037
Telephone: (202) 333-8800

LANGLEY, Patricia
Director, Washington Office, Family Service America
1319 F St., N.W., Suite 606, Washington, DC 20004
Telephone: (202) 347-1124

LANGSDORF, Roger W.
Dir., Antitrust Compliance & Sr. Counsel, ITT Corp.
1600 M St., N.W., Washington, DC 20036
Telephone: (202) 775-7360
Registered as lobbyist at U.S. Congress.

LANGWORTHY, Col. Everett W., USAF (Ret)
Exec. V. President, Nat'l Aeronautic Ass'n of the U.S.A.
1763 R St., N.W., Washington, DC 20009
Telephone: (202) 265-8720
Background: Also represents: Academy of Model Aeronautics, Balloon Federation of America, Soaring Soc. of America, United States Hang Gliding Ass'n, United States Parachute Ass'n, Experimental Aircraft Ass'n, the Internat'l Aerobatic Ass'n and the United States Ultralight Ass'n.

LANIER, Robin
Sr. Legislative Representative, Internat'l Mass Retail Ass'n
1901 Pennsylvania Ave., N.W. Suite 200, Washington, DC 20006

Telephone: (202) 861-0774
Registered as lobbyist at U.S. Congress.

LANOFF, Sheri
Political Specialist, Nat'l Education Ass'n of the U.S.
1201 16th St., N.W., Washington, DC 20036
Telephone: (202) 822-7300

LANSING, Kathleen
Communication Director, Nat'l Peace Institute Foundation
110 Maryland Ave., N.E., Suite 409, Washington, DC 20002
Telephone: (202) 546-9500

LAPIDUS, Fern M.
Washington Representative, New York City Board of Education
555 New Jersey Ave., N.W. Suite 702, Washington, DC 20001
Telephone: (202) 783-6262

LAPIDUS, Dr. Jules B.
President, Council of Graduate Schools
One Dupont Circle, N.W. Suite 430, Washington, DC 20036
Telephone: (202) 223-3791

LAPIERRE, Wayne R., Jr.
Exec. Dir., Inst. For Legis. Action, Nat'l Rifle Ass'n of America
1600 Rhode Island Ave. N.W., Washington, DC 20036
Telephone: (202) 828-6000
Registered as lobbyist at U.S. Congress.
Background: Serves as Political Director for the Nat'l Rifle Ass'n Political Victory Fund.

LAPLANTE, Clifford C.
Mgr., Cong. & Exec. Aircraft Engineering, General Electric Co.
1331 Pennsylvania Ave., N.W., Washington, DC 20004
Telephone: (202) 637-4158
Registered as lobbyist at U.S. Congress.

LAPOINTE, George D.
Legislative Counsel, Internat'l Ass'n of Fish and Wildlife Agencies
444 North Capitol St., N.W. Suite 534, Washington, DC 20001
Telephone: (202) 624-7890
Registered as lobbyist at U.S. Congress.

LAQUEUR, Maria
Exec. Director, Ass'n of Part-Time Professionals
7700 Leesburg Pike, Suite 216, Falls Church, VA 22043-2615
Telephone: (703) 734-7975

LARCHER, Constance C.
Exec. Director, Washington Legal Foundation
1705 N St., N.W., Washington, DC 20036
Telephone: (202) 857-0240

LARGER, Christine
Program Manager, Nat'l Ass'n of College and University Business Officers
One Dupont Circle, N.W., Suite 500, Washington, DC 20036-1178
Telephone: (202) 861-2500

LARIGAKIS, Nicholas
Special Projects Coordinator, American Hellenic Institute Public Affairs Committee
1730 K St., N.W. Suite 1005, Washington, DC 20006
Telephone: (202) 659-4608
Registered as lobbyist at U.S. Congress.

LARKIN, Mary Ann
Director, Major Donor Relations, Africare
440 R St., N.W., Washington, DC 20001
Telephone: (202) 462-3614

LARKIN, Peter J.
Director, State Government Relations, Food Marketing Institute
1750 K St., N.W., Washington, DC 20006
Telephone: (202) 452-8444
Registered as lobbyist at U.S. Congress.

LAROCHELLE, Richard
Legislative Representative, Nat'l Rural Electric Cooperative Ass'n
1800 Massachusetts Ave., N.W., Washington, DC 20036
Telephone: (202) 857-9528
Registered as lobbyist at U.S. Congress.

LA ROCQUE, Rear Admiral Gene R., USN (Ret)
Founder and Director, Center for Defense Information
1500 Massachusetts Ave., N.W., Washington, DC 20005
Telephone: (202) 862-0700

LAROE, WINN, MOERMAN & DONOVAN
1120 G St., N.W., Suite 800, Washington, DC 20005
Telephone: (202) 628-2788
Members of firm representing listed organizations:
Donovan, Paul M.
Genevie, Cheryl K., Senior Legislative Associate
Moerman, Samuel H., Of Counsel
Richman, Gerald L.
Clients:
Jones Chemicals Political Action Committee *(Paul M. Donovan)*
North Atlantic Ports Ass'n
Pennwalt Corp. *(Gerald L. Richman)*
Western Transportation Co. *(Paul M. Donovan, Gerald L. Richman)*

LARSEN, William L.
Ass't V. Pres. and Dir., Reg. Relations, Securities Industry Ass'n
1850 M St., N.W., Suite 550, Washington, DC 20036
Telephone: (202) 296-9410

LARSON, Mary Ellen
Manager, Congressional Relations, Nat'l Soc. of Professional Engineers
1420 King St., Alexandria, VA 22314-2715
Telephone: (703) 684-2841
Registered as lobbyist at U.S. Congress.

LARSON, Reed E.
President, Nat'l Right to Work Committee
8001 Braddock Road, Springfield, VA 22160
Telephone: (703) 321-9820
Registered as lobbyist at U.S. Congress.
Background: Also serves as President, Nat'l Right to Work Legal Defense Foundation. Also reponsible for the Right to Work Political Action Committee.

LASAGNA, Dr. Louis
Chairman, Medicine in the Public Interest
600 New Hampshire Ave., N.W., Suite 720, Washington, DC 20037
Telephone: (202) 338-8255
Background: Located at group's headquarters in Boston, MA.

LASEAU, Joseph N.
Exec. V. President, Ass'n of Telemessaging Services Internat'l
1150 South Washington St. Suite 150, Alexandria, VA 22314
Telephone: (703) 684-0016
Background: Also serves as Treasurer, Ass'n of Telemessaging Services Internat'l Political Action Committee.

LASH GROUP, THE
555 13th St., N.W., Washington, DC 20004
Telephone: (202) 637-5600
Background: A health-care consulting group associated with the law firm of Hogan and Hartson.
Members of firm representing listed organizations:
Koutsoumpas, J. Thomas
Lash, Myles

LASH, Myles
Lash Group, The
555 13th St., N.W., Washington, DC 20004
Telephone: (202) 637-5600

LASKO, Warren
Exec. V. President, Mortgage Bankers Ass'n of America
1125 15th St., N.W., Suite 700, Washington, DC 20005
Telephone: (202) 861-6500
Registered as lobbyist at U.S. Congress.

LASOFF, Laurence J.
Collier, Shannon & Scott
1055 Thomas Jefferson St., N.W., Suite 300, Washington, DC 20007
Telephone: (202) 342-8400
Registered as lobbyist at U.S. Congress.
Registered as Foreign Agent: (#3694).
Background: Special Assistant to the Assistant Secretary of Commerce for Internat'l Trade, 1977-79.
Clients:
Internat'l Ass'n of Machinists and Aerospace Workers
United Steelworkers of America

LASPADA, Carmella
Chairman of the Board, No Greater Love
1750 New York Ave., N.W., Washington, DC 20006
Telephone: (202) 783-4665

LASSMAN, Malcolm
Akin, Gump, Strauss, Hauer and Feld
1333 New Hampshire Ave., N.W., Suite 400, Washington, DC 20036
Telephone: (202) 887-4000
Registered as lobbyist at U.S. Congress.
Background: Serves as Treasurer, A.G.S.H.F. Civic Action Committee, the political action arm of the Akin, Gump, Strauss, Hauer and Feld firm.
Clients:
Akin, Gump, Strauss, Hauer and Feld Civic Action Committee
McDonnell Douglas Corp.

LATAIF, Lawrence P.
Jones, Day, Reavis and Pogue
1450 G St., N.W., Suite 700, Washington, DC 20005-2088
Telephone: (202) 879-3939
Clients:
First Church of Christ-Scientist

LATAPPI, Francis
Director, External Relations, Internat'l Telecommunications Satellite Organization (INTELSAT)
3400 International Drive, N.W., Washington, DC 20008-3098
Telephone: (202) 944-6800

LATHAM, Donald C.
President, Lockheed C31 Systems Division, Lockheed Corp.
12015 Lee-Jackson Hwy., Fairfax, VA 22033
Telephone: (703) 924-5200
Background: Former Assistant Secretary of Defense for Command, Control, Communications and Intelligence.

LATHAM AND WATKINS
1001 Pennsylvania Ave., N.W., Suite 1300, Washington, DC 20004
Telephone: (202) 637-2200
Background: Washington office of a Los Angeles law firm.
Members of firm representing listed organizations:
Bernthal, Eric L.
Danzig, Richard J.
Background: Law Clerk to Justice Byron R. White, U.S. Supreme Court, 1971-2. Deputy Assistant Secretary of Defense, 1977-81.
DeFrancis, Joseph A.
Epstein, Gary M.
Background: Chief, Common Carrier Bureau, Federal Communications Commission, 1981-83.
Goldbloom, Irwin
Background: Trial Attorney, 1958-71, Special Litigation Counsel, 1971-74 and Deputy Assistant Attorney General, 1974-78, Civil Division, Department of Justice.
Grigsby, McGee
Kelly, William C. (Jr.)
Background: Law Clerk to Supreme Court Justice Lewis F. Powell, Jr., 1972-73. Assistant to Special Counsel, Office of Secretary of the Navy, 1973-75. Exec. Assistant to Secretary of Housing and Urban Development, 1975-77.
Salem, Irving
Background: Attorney, Office of Chief Counsel, Internal Revenue Service, 1960-62. Office of Tax Legislative Counsel, Treasury Department, 1962-64. Technical Assistant to Chief Counsel, Internal Revenue Service, 1964-65.
Sussman, Robert M.

Winik, Peter L.
Clients:
Daewoo Internat'l *(Richard J. Danzig)*
Los Angeles Community Redevelopment Agency *(William C. Kelly, Jr.)*
PPG Industries *(Irwin Goldbloom)*
Supermarket Development Corp. *(Joseph A. DeFrancis)*
T. A. Associates *(Eric L. Bernthal)*
Vons Co. *(Joseph A. DeFrancis)*

LATHEM, Ellen
V.P., Grassroots & Issues Management, Hill and Knowlton Public Affairs Worldwide
Washington Harbour, 901 31st St., N.W., Washington, DC 20007
Telephone: (202) 333-7400

LATTA, Kate
Bur for Sci & Tech, Bur for Priv Enter, AGENCY FOR INTERNAT'L DEVELOPMENT
320 21st St., N.W., Washington, DC 20523
Telephone: (202) 647-8190

LAU, K. P.
V. President, Technical, American Nuclear Energy Council
410 First St., S.E. Third Floor, Washington, DC 20003
Telephone: (202) 484-2670
Registered as lobbyist at U.S. Congress.

LAUDERDALE, Larry
Sr. Mktg. Speclst, Contract Research Div, Babcock and Wilcox Co.
c/o McDermott Internat'l Inc. 1850 K St., N.W., Suite 950, Washington, DC 20006
Telephone: (202) 296-0390

LAUDICINA, Paul A.
V. President, SRI International
1611 North Kent St., Arlington, VA 22209
Telephone: (703) 524-2053

LAUENSTEIN, Karl F.
Corp. Dir., Legis. Affairs - Internat'l, General Dynamics Corp.
1745 Jefferson Davis Hwy., Suite 1000, Arlington, VA 22202
Telephone: (703) 553-1240
Registered as lobbyist at U.S. Congress.

LAUGHARN, Elizabeth
Dep Dir, Legis Affrs, DEPARTMENT OF AGRICULTURE - Food Safety and Inspection Service
14th and Independence Ave. S.W., Washington, DC 20250
Telephone: (202) 447-7943

LAUTERBACK, Tom
Staff V. Pres., Commo., Consumer Group, Electronic Industries Ass'n
2001 Pennsylvania Ave., N.W., Washington, DC 20006
Telephone: (202) 457-4900

LAUTIERI, Joseph K.
Ass't Manager, Bell Communications Research, Inc.
2101 L St., N.W. Suite 600, Washington, DC 20037
Telephone: (202) 955-4600

LAUTZENHEISER AND ASSOCIATES
1900 L St., N.W. Suite 500, Washington, DC 20036
Telephone: (202) 452-0532
Members of firm representing listed organizations:
Lautzenheiser, Barbara J.
Clients:
Phoenix Mutual Life Insurance Co. *(Barbara J. Lautzenheiser)*
Transamerica Occidental Life Insurance Co. *(Barbara J. Lautzenheiser)*

LAUTZENHEISER, Barbara J.
Lautzenheiser and Associates
1900 L St., N.W. Suite 500, Washington, DC 20036
Telephone: (202) 452-0532
Clients:
Phoenix Mutual Life Insurance Co.
Transamerica Occidental Life Insurance Co.

The listings in this directory are available as *Mailing Labels*. See last page.

LAUWERS, Daniel
Legislative Representative, Nat'l Milk Producers Federation
1840 Wilson Blvd., Arlington, VA 22201
Telephone: (703) 243-6111
Registered as lobbyist at U.S. Congress.
Background: Former legislative assistant to Rep. Bill Schuette (R-MI).

LAV, Iris J.
Assistant Director for Economic Policy, American Federation of State, County and Municipal Employees
1625 L St., N.W., Washington, DC 20036
Telephone: (202) 429-1000

LAVALLEE, Dennis, CAE
Director, Member & Government Relations, Nat'l Candy Wholesalers Ass'n
1120 Vermont Ave., N.W., Suite 1120, Washington, DC 20005
Telephone: (202) 463-2124
Registered as lobbyist at U.S. Congress.

LAVANTY, Don
Rutherford & Assoc., J. T.
1301 North Courthouse Road Room 1802, Arlington, VA 22201
Telephone: (703) 525-5424
Registered as lobbyist at U.S. Congress.
Organizations represented:
American College of Radiology
American Optometric Ass'n

LAVERDY, Marina
Deputy Director, Congressional Hispanic Caucus Institute
504 C St., N.E., Washington, DC 20002
Telephone: (202) 543-1771

LAVERY, Paul C.
Foley & Co.
206 G St. N.E. Suite 201, Washington, DC 20002
Telephone: (202) 543-8601
Registered as lobbyist at U.S. Congress.
Clients:
PolyPhaser Corp.

LAVET, Lorraine
Dir., Procurement Policy, Bus-Gov't Pol., Chamber of Commerce of the U.S.A.
1615 H St., N.W., Washington, DC 20062
Telephone: (202) 463-5500
Registered as lobbyist at U.S. Congress.

LAVIE, Ann Ferrill
Director, Federal Affairs, Insurance Services Office
1666 K St., N.W. Suite 915, Washington, DC 20006
Telephone: (202) 466-2800

LAVIN, Charles B., Jr.
Exec. Director, Nat'l Burglar and Fire Alarm Ass'n
7101 Wisconsin Ave. Suite 1390, Bethesda, MD 20814-1100
Telephone: (301) 907-3202
Registered as lobbyist at U.S. Congress.
Background: Serves also as Exec. Director, Central Alarm Ass'n.

LAVIN, Franklin L.
Smick Medley Internat'l Inc.
1050 Connecticut Ave., N.W., Washington, DC 20036
Telephone: (202) 861-0770

LAVINE, Eileen M.
Information Counsel, Intersociety Committee on Pathology Information
4733 Bethesda Ave., Suite 735, Bethesda, MD 20814
Telephone: (301) 656-2944

LAVOR, Joan H.
Director, Cong'l Relations/PAC Manager, Associated General Contractors of America
1957 E St., N.W., Washington, DC 20006
Telephone: (202) 393-2040
Registered as lobbyist at U.S. Congress.
Background: Also represents the Associated General Contractors Political Action Committee.

LAVRIHA, Kathryn M.
Manager, State Government Affairs, Nat'l Ass'n of Chain Drug Stores
Box 1417-D49, Alexandria, VA 22313
Telephone: (703) 549-3001
Registered as lobbyist at U.S. Congress.

LAW, John
Bendixen and Schroth
1029 Vermont Ave., N.W., Suite 505, Washington, DC 20005
Telephone: (202) 628-4245
Registered as lobbyist at U.S. Congress.

LAWNICZAK, Johnathon
Senior Legislative Assistant, Nat'l Council of Senior Citizens
925 15th St., N.W., Washington, DC 20005
Telephone: (202) 347-8800
Registered as lobbyist at U.S. Congress.

LAWRENCE & ASSOC., Bob
803 Prince St., Alexandria, VA 22314
Telephone: (703) 836-3654
Members of firm representing listed organizations:
Lawrence, Bob
Organizations represented:
Mechanical Technology Inc. *(Bob Lawrence)*
Radian Corp. *(Bob Lawrence)*
University City Science Center *(Bob Lawrence)*
Valmont Industries, Inc. *(Bob Lawrence)*

LAWRENCE, Bob
Lawrence & Assoc., Bob
803 Prince St., Alexandria, VA 22314
Telephone: (703) 836-3654
Registered as lobbyist at U.S. Congress.
Organizations represented:
Mechanical Technology Inc.
Radian Corp.
University City Science Center
Valmont Industries, Inc.

LAWRENCE, George H.
President, American Gas Ass'n
1515 Wilson Blvd., Arlington, VA 22209
Telephone: (703) 841-8400
Registered as lobbyist at U.S. Congress.

LAWRENCE, John D.
Neill and Co.
815 Connecticut Ave., N.W. Suite 800, Washington, DC 20006
Telephone: (202) 463-8877
Registered as lobbyist at U.S. Congress.
Registered as Foreign Agent: (#3320).

LAWRENCE, Lynne
Director, Government Relations, American Fertility Soc.
409 12th St., S.W. Suite 110, Washington, DC 20024
Telephone: (202) 863-2576

LAWRENCE, Michael
Legis Officer, Cong & Intergov't Affrs, DEPARTMENT OF LABOR
200 Constitution Ave., N.W., Washington, DC 20210
Telephone: (202) 523-6141

LAWRENCE, Sharon
Director, Federal Affairs, Nat'l Ass'n of Towns and Townships
1522 K St., N.W. Suite 730, Washington, DC 20005
Telephone: (202) 737-5200

LAWRENCE, William
Office of Cong Affrs, DEPARTMENT OF TREASURY - United States Customs Service
1301 Constitution Ave., N.W., Washington, DC 20229
Telephone: (202) 566-5644

LAWS, Elliott P.
Patton, Boggs and Blow
2550 M St., N.W., Suite 800, Washington, DC 20037
Telephone: (202) 457-6000
Registered as lobbyist at U.S. Congress.
Background: Attorney, U.S. Dept. of Justice, head of Natural Resources Division, 1985-87; Attorney, Environmental Protection Agency, Office of Enforcement and Compliance Monitoring, 1984-85.

LAWS, Patricia
Legislative Assistant, MidCon Corp.
1747 Pennsylvania Ave., N.W. Suite 300, Washington, DC 20006
Telephone: (202) 857-3075

LAWSON, Dale
V. President, Hill and Knowlton Public Affairs Worldwide
Washington Harbour, 901 31st St., N.W., Washington, DC 20007
Telephone: (202) 333-7400
Registered as Foreign Agent: (#4170).
Background: Community Organizer, Office of Economic Opportunity, U.S. Department of Labor, 1967-69. Director, Educational Involvement Program, Department of Labor, 1969. Advisor to Senator Walter Huddleston (D-KY), 1979.
Clients:
Abbott Laboratories
Dow Corning Corp.
General Electric Co.
Occidental Petroleum Corp.
Upjohn Co.

LAWSON, Elizabeth
Senior Lobbyist, League of Women Voters of the United States
1730 M St., N.W., Tenth Floor, Washington, DC 20036
Telephone: (202) 429-1965
Registered as lobbyist at U.S. Congress.

LAWSON, John M.
Director, National Affairs, Nat'l Ass'n of Public Television Stations
1350 Connecticut Ave., N.W. Suite 200, Washington, DC 20036
Telephone: (202) 887-1700
Registered as lobbyist at U.S. Congress.

LAWSON, Madeline
Deputy Director, Martin Luther King, Jr. Federal Holiday Commission
451 Seventh St, S.W. Suite 5182, Washington, DC 20410
Telephone: (202) 755-1005

LAWSON, Marcia G.
Manager, Communications, American Industrial Health Council
1330 Connecticut Ave., N.W. Suite 300, Washington, DC 20036-1702
Telephone: (202) 659-0060

LAWSON, Richard L.
President, Nat'l Coal Ass'n
1130 17th St., N.W., Washington, DC 20036
Telephone: (202) 463-2647
Registered as lobbyist at U.S. Congress.

LAWTON, Stephan E.
Reed Smith Shaw & McClay
1200 18th St., N.W., Washington, DC 20036
Telephone: (202) 457-6100
Registered as lobbyist at U.S. Congress.
Background: Chief Counsel, Subcommittee on Health and the Environment, U.S. House of Representatives, 1971-78.
Clients:
American Academy of Pediatrics
American College of Osteopathic Surgeons
Amgen, Inc.
Ass'n of Schools of Public Health
Infectious Disease Soc. of America
Soc. of Critical Care Medicine

LAXALT, CONSULTANT, John M.
1515 Jefferson Davis Hwy. PH-12, Arlington, VA 22202
Telephone: (703) 979-7609

LAXALT CORP., The
1455 Pennsylvania Ave., N.W., Suite 985, Washington, DC 20004
Telephone: (202) 393-0688
Background: A government and legislative public relations firm.
Members of firm representing listed organizations:
Laxalt, Michelle D.
Organizations represented:
Boone Co. *(Michelle D. Laxalt)*
Mesa Limited Partnership *(Michelle D. Laxalt)*

Milliken and Co. *(Michelle D. Laxalt)*
Motion Picture Ass'n of America *(Michelle D. Laxalt)*
United Shareholders Ass'n *(Michelle D. Laxalt)*

LAXALT GROUP, The Paul
1455 Pennsylvania Ave., N.W., Suite 975, Washington, DC 20004
Telephone: (202) 624-0640
Members of firm representing listed organizations:
Jamieson, Ballard J. (Jr.)
Laxalt, Paul, President
Background: Member, U.S. Senate (R-NV), 1974-87. Retains position as Senior Counsel of the law firm of Laxalt, Washington, Perito & Dubuc.
Laxalt, Peter
Loranger, Tom
Organizations represented:
Martin Marietta Corp. *(Paul Laxalt)*

LAXALT, Michelle D.
Laxalt Corp., The
1455 Pennsylvania Ave., N.W., Suite 985, Washington, DC 20004
Telephone: (202) 393-0688
Registered as lobbyist at U.S. Congress.
Organizations represented:
Boone Co.
Mesa Limited Partnership
Milliken and Co.
Motion Picture Ass'n of America
United Shareholders Ass'n

LAXALT, Paul
President, Laxalt Group, The Paul
1455 Pennsylvania Ave., N.W., Suite 975, Washington, DC 20004
Telephone: (202) 624-0640
Background: Member, U.S. Senate (R-NV), 1974-87. Retains position as Senior Counsel of the law firm of Laxalt, Washington, Perito & Dubuc.
Organizations represented:
Martin Marietta Corp.

LAXALT, Peter
Laxalt Group, The Paul
1455 Pennsylvania Ave., N.W., Suite 975, Washington, DC 20004
Telephone: (202) 624-0640

LAXALT, WASHINGTON, PERITO & DUBUC
1120 Connecticut Ave., N.W., Suite 1000, Washington, DC 20036
Telephone: (202) 857-4000
Background: A Washington, D.C. firm with offices in New York City and Baltimore.
Members of firm representing listed organizations:
Christian, James M. (Sr.)
Background: Deputy Minority Counsel, House Committee on the District of Columbia, 1973-75. Chief Counsel, Urban Mass Transportation Administration, U.S. Department of Transportation.
Cole, Michael F.
Cooper, Mario M.
Background: Staff Assistant to the President, Executive Office of the President, 1979-81.
Dubuc, Carroll E.
Ikard, Frank N.
Background: Former Member, U.S. House of Representatives (D-TX).
Perito, Paul L.
Background: Assistant U.S. Attorney, Department of Justice, 1966-70. Chief Counsel and Staff Director, House Select Committee on Crime, 1970-71. General Counsel and Deputy Director, Special Action Office for Drug Abuse Prevention, Executive Office of the President, 1971-73.
Pruitt, Steven, Legislative Consultant
Background: Special Assistant to Senator Howard Metzenbaum, (D-OH), 1977-79. Staff Director, Census and Population Subcommittee, House Committeee on Post Office and Civil Service, 1984. Exec. Director, House Committee on the Budget, 1985-88.
Scheineson, Marc J.
Background: Tax Counsel and Legislative Assistant to Rep. Willis D. Gradison, Jr. (R-OH), 1980-82.
Trible, Paul S.

Background: Member, U.S. House of Representatives (R-VA), 1977-83. Member, U.S. Senate (R-VA), 1983-89. Member, U.S. Delegation to the United Nations, 1989.
Valdez, Abelardo L.
Background: Attorney-Advisor, U.S. Overseas Private Investment Corp., 1971-73. General Counsel, Inter-American Foundation, 1973-75. Assistant Administrator for Latin America and the Caribbean, U.S. Agency for International Dvelopment, 1977-79. Ambassador, Chief of Protocol, U.S. Department of State, 1979-81.
Washington, Robert B. (Jr.)
Background: Counsel, Committee on the District of Columbia, U.S. Senate, 1971-1972. Chief Counsel and Staff Director, Committee on the District of Columbia, U.S. House of Representatives, 1973-1975.
Clients:
Air China Internat'l Corp., Ltd. *(Carroll E. Dubuc)*
American College of Neuropsychopharmacology *(Michael F. Cole)*
Angola, Government of the People's Republic of *(Robert B. Washington, Jr.)*
Antigua and Barbuda, Government of *(Robert B. Washington, Jr.)*
Appraisal Foundation *(Marc J. Scheineson)*
Arizona, State of
Asociacion de Empresas RENFE/Patentes TALGO, S.A. *(Abelardo L. Valdez)*
AVW Electronics Systems, Inc. *(Marc J. Scheineson)*
BTS Development Corp. *(Marc J. Scheineson)*
Burlington Resources, Inc.
Cohen Flax Investments *(Marc J. Scheineson)*
Committee on Problems of Drug Dependence *(Michael F. Cole)*
District of Columbia Armory Board
Greenbaum & Rose Associates *(Marc J. Scheineson)*
Group Hospital and Medical Services, Inc. *(Michael F. Cole)*
Home Group, The *(Robert B. Washington, Jr.)*
Inglewood, California, City of *(James M. Christian, Sr.)*
Institut de la Vie *(Carroll E. Dubuc)*
Laxalt Washington Perito and Dubuc PAC *(Robert B. Washington, Jr.)*
LTV Corp.
Martin Marietta Corp.
Nordisk USA *(Michael F. Cole)*
Oakland, California, City of *(James M. Christian, Sr.)*
Operaciones Turisticas, S.A.
OPTUR - La Sociedad Mercantil Operaciones Turisticas *(Marc J. Scheineson)*
Pharmakinetics Laboratories, Inc. *(Michael F. Cole)*
Puerto Rico Department of Health *(Paul L. Perito)*
Sea-Land Service, Inc.
Soc. of Real Estate Appraisers *(Marc J. Scheineson)*
Southwest Gas Corp. *(Marc J. Scheineson)*
Standard Federal Savings Bank
Tobacco Institute *(James M. Christian, Sr.)*
Washington, DC, City of *(James M. Christian, Sr.)*
Western States Steel Producers Coalition
Yukon Pacific Inc.

LAYMAN-HEITMAN, Jennifer
Coord. & Res. Assoc., State Issues Dev., Common Cause
2030 M St., N.W., Washington, DC 20036
Telephone: (202) 833-1200
Registered as lobbyist at U.S. Congress.

LAYTON, Amy Jill
Manager, Public Affairs, American Insurance Ass'n
1130 Connecticut Ave., N.W., Suite 1000, Washington, DC 20036
Telephone: (202) 828-7100

LAZARUS, Arthur, Jr.
Fried, Frank, Harris, Shriver & Jacobson
1001 Pennsylvania Ave., N.W., Suite 800, Washington, DC 20004-2505
Telephone: (202) 639-7000

LAZARUS, Edward H.
Partner, Mellman & Lazarus Inc.
1054 31st St., N.W. Suite 530, Washington, DC 20007
Telephone: (202) 625-0370

LAZARUS, Simon, III
Powell, Goldstein, Frazer and Murphy
1001 Pennsylvania, N.W., Sixth Fl., Washington, DC 20004
Telephone: (202) 347-0066
Registered as lobbyist at U.S. Congress.
Background: Legal Assistant to Federal Communications Commissioner Nicholas Johnson, 1967-68. Associate Director, White House Domestic Policy Staff, 1977-81.
Clients:
Computer and Business Equipment Manufacturers Ass'n
Hayes Microcomputer Products, Inc.

LEACH, Barbara
Polit. Director, Political Field Optns., Nat'l Ass'n of REALTORS
777 14th St., N.W., Washington, DC 20005
Telephone: (202) 383-1000
Registered as lobbyist at U.S. Congress.

LEACH, Daniel E.
Leach, McGreevy, Eliassen & Leach
1619 New Hampshire Ave., N.W., Washington, DC 20009
Telephone: (202) 265-3700
Registered as lobbyist at U.S. Congress.
Registered as Foreign Agent: (#3550).
Clients:
Manufacturers Life Insurance Co.
Washington Psychiatric Soc.

LEACH, MCGREEVY, ELIASSEN & LEACH
1619 New Hampshire Ave., N.W., Washington, DC 20009
Telephone: (202) 265-3700
Members of firm representing listed organizations:
Leach, Daniel E.
Clients:
Manufacturers Life Insurance Co. *(Daniel E. Leach)*
Washington Psychiatric Soc. *(Daniel E. Leach)*

LEADER, Shelah
Policy Analyst, American Ass'n of Retired Persons
1909 K St., N.W., Washington, DC 20049
Telephone: (202) 728-4859

LEAHY, Edward R.
Thacher, Proffitt and Wood
1500 K St., N.W., Suite 200, Washington, DC 20005
Telephone: (202) 347-8400
Registered as lobbyist at U.S. Congress.
Clients:
Chicago Board Options Exchange
Citicorp

LEAMOND, Nancy
President and Exec. Director, Congressional Economic Leadership Institute
1000 Wilson Blvd., Suite 2700, Arlington, VA 22209
Telephone: (703) 276-5007
Background: Formerly Administrative Asst to Rep. Mary Rose Oakar, (D-OH); 9 years in Executive Branch at OMB, Commerce, HEW, Education.

LEAPE, Gerald B.
Legislative Director, Wildlife, Greenpeace, U.S.A.
1436 U St., N.W., Washington, DC 20009
Telephone: (202) 462-1177
Registered as lobbyist at U.S. Congress.

LEARNER, Alisa J.
Issue Analyst/Policy Develmnt. Director, Chrysler Corp.
1100 Connecticut Ave., N.W., Washington, DC 20036
Telephone: (202) 862-5432
Registered as lobbyist at U.S. Congress.
Background: Former legislative assistant to Senator Donald Riegle, Jr. (D-MI).

LEARY, Richard J.
Exec. Director, Internat'l Service Agencies
6000 Executive Blvd, Suite 608, Rockville, MD 20852
Telephone: (301) 881-2468

LEARY, Thomas B.
Hogan and Hartson
555 13th St., N.W., Suite 1200, Washington, DC 20004-1109
Telephone: (202) 637-5600
Registered as lobbyist at U.S. Congress.
Clients:

LEARY, Thomas B. (Cont'd)
Denver and Rio Grande Western Railroad Co.

LEASURE, Mark
Deputy Exec. V. President, American Soc. of Internal Medicine
1101 Vermont Ave., N.W. Suite 500, Washington, DC 20005
Telephone: (202) 289-1700

LEAVELL, Winston
Account Supervisor, Burson-Marsteller
1850 M St., N.W., Suite 900, Washington, DC 20036
Telephone: (202) 833-8550

LEAVITT, Herman
Treasurer, Hotel Employees and Restaurant Employees International TIP Union To Insure Progress
1219 28th St., N.W., Washington, DC 20006
Telephone: (202) 393-4373

LEBOEUF, Kerley
President, Nat'l Ass'n of Convenience Stores
1605 King St., Alexandria, VA 22314
Telephone: (703) 684-3600

LEBOEUF, LAMB, LEIBY, AND MACRAE
1333 New Hampshire Ave., N.W. Suite 1100, Washington, DC 20036
Telephone: (202) 457-7500
Background: Washington office of a New York law firm.
Members of firm representing listed organizations:
Havens, Charles W. (III)
Meagher, John K.
Background: Former Assistant Secretary for Legislative Affairs, U.S. Treasury Department.
Olney, Austin P.
Background: Counsel, U.S. House of Representatives Committee on Merchant Marine and Fisheries, 1975-77.
Clients:
Basic Industry Coalition *(John K. Meagher)*
Golden Nugget, Inc. *(John K. Meagher)*
Lloyds of London, Underwriters at *(Charles W. Havens, III)*
Maritrans Operating Partners, L.P. *(Austin P. Olney)*
Physician Insurers Ass'n of America *(John K. Meagher)*
STS Corp. *(John K. Meagher)*

LEBOW, Cynthia C.
Of Counsel, Gibson, Dunn and Crutcher
1050 Connecticut Ave., N.W. Suite 900, Washington, DC 20036-5303
Telephone: (202) 955-8500
Registered as lobbyist at U.S. Congress.
Clients:
Alyeska Pipeline Service Co.
First Republic Bank Corp.
Prudential Insurance Co. of America

LEBOW, Edward M.
Kelley, Drye and Warren
2300 M St., N.W., Washington, DC 20037
Telephone: (202) 463-8333
Registered as lobbyist at U.S. Congress.
Registered as Foreign Agent: (#3681).
Clients:
Tokyo Electric Co., Ltd.

LEBOW, Morton A.
Assoc. Director of Public Information, American College of Obstetricians and Gynecologists
409 12th St., S.W., Washington, DC 20024
Telephone: (202) 638-5577

LEBRUN-YAFFE, Cynthia
V. President, Burgum & Grimm, Ltd.
106 North Carolina Ave., S.E., Washington, DC 20003
Telephone: (202) 546-3414
Registered as Foreign Agent: (#4301).

LECHNER, Wendy
Legislative Representative, Nat'l Federation of Independent Business
600 Maryland Ave., S.W., Suite 700, Washington, DC 20024
Telephone: (202) 554-9000
Registered as lobbyist at U.S. Congress.

LEDBETTER, Marc
Senior Associate, American Council for an Energy-Efficient Economy
1001 Connecticut Ave., N.W., Suite 535, Washington, DC 20036
Telephone: (202) 429-8873

LEDERER, Gerard L.
Exec. Director, Government Relations, United States Telephone Ass'n
900 19th St., N.W., Suite 800, Washington, DC 20006-2102
Telephone: (202) 835-3100
Registered as lobbyist at U.S. Congress.
Registered as Foreign Agent: (#000₂)

LEDERER, Robert F., Jr.
V. President, Ass'n Management Group
3299 K St., N.W., 7th Floor, Washington, DC 20007
Telephone: (202) 965-7510
Clients:
Fiberglass Fabrication Ass'n

LEDERMAN, Dr. Harvey
Treasurer, Podiatry Political Action Committee
9312 Old Georgetown Road, Bethesda, MD 20814
Telephone: (301) 571-9200

LEDLEY, Robert S.
Exec. Director, Pattern Recognition Soc.
Georgetown Medical Ctr. Pre-Clinical Sci. Bldg. LR3, Washington, DC 20007
Telephone: (202) 687-2121
Background: Also represents the Computerized Radiology Soc.

LEE, Anthony
President, Coastal Soc.
3202 Tower Oaks Blvd., Rockville, MD 20852
Telephone: (301) 231-5250

LEE, Bernard Z.
Deputy Chairman, Federal Affairs, American Institute of Certified Public Accountants
1455 Pennsylvania Ave., N.W. Suite 400, Washington, DC 20004
Telephone: (202) 737-6600

LEE, Carol F.
Partner, Wilmer, Cutler and Pickering
2445 M St., N.W., Washington, DC 20037-1420
Telephone: (202) 663-6000
Registered as lobbyist at U.S. Congress.
Clients:
Lufthansa German Airlines

LEE, Cora
Treasurer, Nat'l Ass'n of Postmasters of the U.S. PAC for Postmasters
8 Herbert St., Alexandria, VA 22305
Telephone: (703) 683-9027

LEE, Douglas O.
Chairman, Americans for Nuclear Energy
2525 Wilson Blvd., Arlington, VA 22201
Telephone: (703) 528-4430
Registered as lobbyist at U.S. Congress.

LEE, Eric
Federal Gov't Affrs Director & Attorney, AT&T
Suite 1000, 1120 20th St., N.W., Washington, DC 20036
Telephone: (202) 457-2951

LEE, F. Gordon
O'Connor & Hannan
1919 Pennsylvania Ave., N.W., Suite 800, Washington, DC 20006
Telephone: (202) 887-1400
Registered as Foreign Agent: (#2972).

LEE, Franklin M.
Exec. V. Pres. and Chief Counsel, Minority Business Enterprise Legal Defense and Education Fund
300 Eye St., N.E., Suite 200, Washington, DC 20002
Telephone: (202) 543-0040
Registered as lobbyist at U.S. Congress.
Background: Former antitrust attorney, Federal Trade Commission.

LEE, Gary A.
Corporate V. President, Gov't Affairs, Whitman Corp.
1667 K St., N.W., Suite 605, Washington, DC 20006
Telephone: (202) 293-6410
Background: Member, U.S. House of Representatives from New York, 1979-83.

LEE, Kathryn
Smith, Heenan and Althen
1110 Vermont Ave., N.W., Suite 400, Washington, DC 20005
Telephone: (202) 887-0800
Registered as lobbyist at U.S. Congress.
Clients:
American League of Lobbyists

LEE, Kenneth
Burchette & Associates
Registered as lobbyist at U.S. Congress.

LEE, L. Courtland
Public Resource Associates
1815 H St., N.W. Suite 600, Washington, DC 20006
Telephone: (202) 463-7456
Registered as lobbyist at U.S. Congress.
Background: Staff of House of Representatives Subcommittee on Mining, 1979-80.

LEE, Ladonna Y.
President, Mahe Company, The Eddie
900 Second St., N.E. Suite 200, Washington, DC 20002
Telephone: (202) 842-4100

LEE, Lansing B.
Patton, Boggs and Blow
2550 M St., N.W., Suite 800, Washington, DC 20037
Telephone: (202) 457-6000
Registered as lobbyist at U.S. Congress.
Background: Administrative Ass't to Gov. Jimmy Carter (D-GA), 1970-72, Exec. Director, Democratic Party of Georgia, 1983-85.
Clients:
CIGNA Corp.

LEE, Page C.
Carmen Group, The
1667 K St., N.W., Suite 700, Washington, DC 20006
Telephone: (202) 785-0500
Registered as lobbyist at U.S. Congress.
Clients:
CareerCom Corp.

LEE, Rex E.
Sidley and Austin
1722 Eye St., N.W. Sixth Floor, Washington, DC 20006
Telephone: (202) 429-4000
Background: Assistant Attorney General of the U.S., 1975-77. Solicitor General of the U.S., 1981-85.

LEE, Robert A.
Director, Government Liaison, Varian Associates Inc.
2101 Wilson Blvd., Suite 832, Arlington, VA 22201
Telephone: (703) 522-8002

LEE, Steve
Director, Aerospace Education Foundation
1501 Lee Hwy., Arlington, VA 22209
Telephone: (703) 247-5839

LEE, TOOMEY & KENT
1200 18th St., N.W., 8th Floor, Washington, DC 20036
Telephone: (202) 457-8500
Clients:
Abbott Laboratories
American Home Products Corp.
ASARCO Incorporated
Avon Products, Inc.
Bell Atlantic
Beneficial Corp.
Boise Cascade Corp.
Carter-Wallace, Inc.
CBS, Inc.
Colgate-Palmolive Co.
Cummins Engine Co., Inc.
Deere & Co.
Fireman's Fund Insurance Cos.
General Development Corp.
General Mills
Georgia-Pacific Corp.

Great Northern Nekoosa Corp.
Hertz Corp.
Hewlett-Packard Co.
Household Internat'l
ICI Americas Inc.
James River Corp.
Johnson & Johnson
MGM/UA Communications Co.
Minnesota Mining and Manufacturing Co. (3M
Co.)
Morton Internat'l, Inc.
NCR Corporation
Pfizer, Inc.
Premark Internat'l
RJR Nabisco, Inc.
Schering-Plough Corp.
Signet Banking Corp.
Texaco, Inc.
Texaco U.S.A.
Towers, Perrin, Forster & Crosby
United Airlines - EXOCT
Upjohn Co.
Viacom Internat'l, Inc.
Wachovia Corp.
Westvaco Corp.

LEEDS, Morton
Program Associate, Nat'l Council on the Aging
600 Maryland Ave., S.W. West Wing 100, Washington, DC
20024
Telephone: (202) 479-1200
Background: Represents the Nat'l Institute of Senior Housing.

LEET, Rebecca
Potomac Partners
1250 24th St., N.W. Suite 875, Washington, DC 20037
Telephone: (202) 466-0560

LEFEVE, David A.
V. Pres., State & Local Gov't Relations, Merrill Lynch and
Co., Inc.
1828 L St., N.W., Suite 906, Washington, DC 20036
Telephone: (202) 822-3600

LEFKIN, Peter A.
Asst. V. Pres. & Dir., Fed. Relations, Fireman's Fund Insurance Cos.
1730 Rhode Island Ave., N.W. Suite 1117, Washington,
DC 20036
Telephone: (202) 785-3575
Registered as lobbyist at U.S. Congress.
Background: Former Legislative Counsel to Rep. Matthew
J. Rinaldo (R-NJ).

LEFKOVITS, Marsha
Sr. Associate Federal Gov't Affairs, RJR Nabisco Washington, Inc.
1455 Pennsylvania Ave., N.W., Suite 525, Washington, DC
20004
Telephone: (202) 626-7200
Registered as lobbyist at U.S. Congress.
Background: Former Executive Assistant to Rep. Richard
Shelby (D-AL).

LEGATO, Carmen D.
Swidler & Berlin, Chartered
3000 K St., N.W., Suite 300, Washington, DC 20007
Telephone: (202) 944-4300
Registered as lobbyist at U.S. Congress.
Background: Law Clerk to Justice William J. Brennan, U.S.
Supreme Court, 1977-78.
Clients:
Intercontinental Energy Corp.

LEGATSKI, Mary James
Manager, Government Affairs, Synthetic Organic Chemical
Manufacturers Ass'n
1330 Connecticut Ave., N.W. Suite 300, Washington, DC
20036
Telephone: (202) 659-0060
Registered as lobbyist at U.S. Congress.

LEGGETT, C. Hoke
Director, Agricultural Relations, Tobacco Institute
1875 Eye St., N.W., Suite 800, Washington, DC 20006
Telephone: (202) 457-4800
Registered as lobbyist at U.S. Congress.

LEGGETT, Carroll H.
Exec. V. President, Public Affairs, Hannaford Co., Inc.,
The
655 15th St., N.W. Suite 200, Washington, DC 20005
Telephone: (202) 638-4600
Registered as lobbyist at U.S. Congress.
Registered as Foreign Agent: (#2850).

LEGISLATIVE STRATEGIES INC.
1275 Pennsylvania Ave., N.W. Suite 301, Washington, DC
20004
Telephone: (202) 626-6490
Background: A political and governmental affairs consulting subsidiary of the law firm of Katten Muchin Zavis &
Dombroff.
Members of firm representing listed organizations:
Bragg, Raymond F. (Jr.), President
Clients:
American Independent Refiners Ass'n *(Raymond F.
Bragg, Jr.)*
American Independent Refiners Ass'n PAC *(Raymond F. Bragg, Jr.)*
Consolidated Natural Gas Co. *(Raymond F. Bragg, Jr.)*
Environmental Power Corp. *(Raymond F. Bragg, Jr.)*
Nat'l Hydropower Ass'n *(Raymond F. Bragg, Jr.)*
Tosco Corp. *(Raymond F. Bragg, Jr.)*

LEGNINI, Meric L.
V. Pres, Government & Industry Relations, Scheduled Airlines Traffic Offices, Inc. (SatoTravel)
1005 North Glebe Road,, Arlington, VA 22210
Telephone: (703) 358-1450

LEHMAN, Bruce A.
Swidler & Berlin, Chartered
3000 K St., N.W., Suite 300, Washington, DC 20007
Telephone: (202) 944-4300
Registered as lobbyist at U.S. Congress.
Background: Counsel, Committee on the Judiciary,
1974-83 and Chief Counsel, Subcommittee on Courts,
Civil Liberties and the Administration of Justice, 1977-83,
U.S. House of Representatives.
Clients:
Aldus
Ashton-Tate
Autodesk, Inc.
BSA - Business Software Alliance
Design Protection Coalition
Lotus Development Corp.
Microsoft
Software Publishers Ass'n
United States Trademark Ass'n
WordPerfect

LEHMAN, Christopher M.
President, Commonwealth Consulting Corp.
9507 Beach Mill Road, Great Falls, VA 22066
Telephone: (703) 759-7120
Registered as Foreign Agent: (#4261).
Background: Associate Staff member, Senate Armed Services Committee, 1976-81. Director, Office of Strategic
Nuclear Policy, Department of State, 1981-83. Special
Assistant to the President, The White House, 1983-85.
Clients:
Foundation for Democracy in Namibia

LEHMAN, Leonard
Barnes, Richardson and Colburn
1819 H St., N.W., Washington, DC 20006
Telephone: (202) 457-0300
Registered as lobbyist at U.S. Congress.
Background: Attorney Advisor, U.S. Tax Court, 1952-55.
Assistant Chief Counsel, U.S. Customs Service, 1965-68.
Deputy Chief Counsel, 1968-71 and Assistant Commissioner of Customs, 1971-79, U.S. Treasury Department.

LEHMAN, Thomas
Associate Director, Minnesota, State of
400 North Capitol St., N.W. Suite 322, Washington, DC
20001
Telephone: (202) 624-5308

LEHNHARD, Mary Nell
V. President, Office of Gov't Relations, Blue Cross and
Blue Shield Ass'n
655 15th St., N.W., Suite 350, Washington, DC 20005
Telephone: (202) 626-4780
Registered as lobbyist at U.S. Congress.
Background: Former staff assistant to the House Ways and
Means Subcommittee on Health.

LEHRFELD, Betsy
Potomac Partners
1250 24th St., N.W. Suite 875, Washington, DC 20037
Telephone: (202) 466-0560

LEHRFELD CANTOR & HENZKE, P.C.
1101 Connecticut Ave., N.W., Suite 403, Washington, DC
20036
Telephone: (202) 659-4772
Background: The following information was obtained from
public records and submitted to this firm for confirmation. It did not confirm or correct the information and
asked to be omitted from the book.
Members of firm representing listed organizations:
Henzke, Leonard J. (Jr.)
Background: Trial Attorney, Antitrust Division, Justice
Department, 1965-69. Special Assistant to Assistant
Attorney General, Tax Division, Justice Department,
1979-81.
Lehrfeld, William J.
Background: Tax Law Specialist, Exempt Organizations
and Pension Trust Division, Internal Revenue Service, 1960-65.
Clients:
Nat'l Club Ass'n *(Leonard J. Henzke, Jr., William J. Lehrfeld)*

LEHRFELD, William J.
Lehrfeld Cantor & Henzke, P.C.
1101 Connecticut Ave., N.W., Suite 403, Washington, DC
20036
Telephone: (202) 659-4772
Registered as lobbyist at U.S. Congress.
Background: Tax Law Specialist, Exempt Organizations
and Pension Trust Division, Internal Revenue Service,
1960-65.
Clients:
Nat'l Club Ass'n

LEIBACH, Dale
Powell, Adams & Rinehart
1901 L St., N.W., 3rd Floor, Washington, DC 20036
Telephone: (202) 466-7590
Registered as lobbyist at U.S. Congress.
Background: Former aide to Senator Tom Harkin (D-IA)
and Assistant Press Secretary to President Jimmy Carter.
Clients:
American Iron and Steel Institute

LEIBIG, Michael
Zwerdling, Paul, Leibig & Thompson
1025 Connecticut Ave., N.W. Suite 307, Washington, DC
20036
Telephone: (202) 857-5000
Clients:
Internat'l Union of Police Ass'ns

LEIBOWITZ, David
Sr. V. President and General Counsel, Recording Industry
Ass'n of America
1020 19th St., N.W., Suite 200, Washington, DC 20036
Telephone: (202) 775-0101

LEIBOWITZ, Lewis E.
Arent, Fox, Kintner, Plotkin & Kahn
1050 Connecticut Ave., N.W., Washington, DC 20036-
5339
Telephone: (202) 857-6000
Registered as lobbyist at U.S. Congress.
Registered as Foreign Agent: (#2661).
Clients:
Continental Grain Co.
Outokumpu Oy

LEIDEN, Warren R.
Exec. Director, American Immigration Lawyers Ass'n
1000 16th St., N.W. Suite 604, Washington, DC 20036
Telephone: (202) 331-0046
Registered as lobbyist at U.S. Congress.

LEIDL, Richard J.
Reid & Priest
1111 19th St., N.W., Washington, DC 20036
Telephone: (202) 828-0100
Clients:
Pride Refining, Inc.

WASHINGTON REPRESENTATIVES

LEIFER, Elihu I.
Sherman, Dunn, Cohen, Leifer and Counts
1125 15th St., N.W. Suite 801, Washington, DC 20005
Telephone: (202) 785-9300
Background: Attorney, Civil Rights Division, U.S. Department of Justice, 1964-67.

LEIGH, Ann
Manager, Federal Liaison Office, American Soc. for Engineering Education
11 Dupont Circle, N.W., Suite 200, Washington, DC 20036
Telephone: (202) 293-7080
Background: Legislative Assistant, U.S. Congress, 1980-84.

LEIGH, Monroe
Steptoe and Johnson
1330 Connecticut Ave., N.W., Washington, DC 20036
Telephone: (202) 429-3000
Registered as lobbyist at U.S. Congress.
Registered as Foreign Agent: (#2792).
Background: Assistant Gen. Counsel for Internat'l Affairs, Office of Secretary of Defense, 1955-1959. Legal Adviser, Dep't of State, 1975-1977. Member on the part of the U.S. of the Permanent Court on Arbitration, 1975-80.
Clients:
Chile, Embassy of

LEIGH, Robert J.
Senior V. President, Nat'l Telephone Cooperative Ass'n
2626 Pennsylvania Ave., N.W., Washington, DC 20037
Telephone: (202) 298-2300
Registered as lobbyist at U.S. Congress.
Background: Attorney, Federal Communications Commission, 1961-1965.

LEIGHTON, G. Timothy
President, Internat'l Ass'n for Continuing Education and Training
P.O. Box 27043, Washington, DC 20038
Telephone: (301) 384-1059
Registered as lobbyist at U.S. Congress.
Background: Serves also as President, Convention II, Inc.

LEIGHTON AND REGNERY
1667 K St., N.W., Suite 801, Washington, DC 20006
Telephone: (202) 955-3900
Members of firm representing listed organizations:
Heine, Kristine
King, Ann Ottoson
Leighton, Richard J.
   Background: Council on Administrative Law, Chamber of Commerce of the United States, 1983-87. Consultant, Subcommittee on Regulatory Reform, Senate Judiciary Committee, U.S. Senate, 1980. Chairman, Adjudication Conference of the United States, 1984-87. Committee, U.S. Visiting Nurses Ass'n.
Mann, Richard F.
Regnery, Alfred S.
Clients:
Alpo Pet Foods, Inc. *(Richard J. Leighton)*
American Cordage and Netting Manufacturers *(Ann Ottoson King)*
American Dairy Products Institute *(Richard J. Leighton)*
Clorox Co., The *(Richard J. Leighton)*
Express Foods Co., Inc. *(Richard J. Leighton)*
GTE Products Corp. *(Richard J. Leighton)*
Land O'Lakes, Inc.
Leprino Foods, Inc. *(Richard J. Leighton)*
Rexnord, Inc.
Visiting Nurses Ass'n of America *(Alfred S. Regnery)*

LEIGHTON, Richard J.
Leighton and Regnery
1667 K St., N.W., Suite 801, Washington, DC 20006
Telephone: (202) 955-3900
Registered as lobbyist at U.S. Congress.
Background: Council on Administrative Law, Chamber of Commerce of the United States, 1983-87. Consultant, Subcommittee on Regulatory Reform, Senate Judiciary Committee, U.S. Senate, 1980. Chairman, Adjudication Conference of the United States, 1984-87. Committee, U.S. Visiting Nurses Ass'n.
Clients:
Alpo Pet Foods, Inc.
American Dairy Products Institute
Clorox Co., The
Express Foods Co., Inc.
GTE Products Corp.

Leprino Foods, Inc.

LEIGHTON AND SHERLINE
1010 Massachusetts Ave., N.W., Suite 101, Washington, DC 20001-5402
Telephone: (202) 898-1122
Members of firm representing listed organizations:
Sherline, Lee S.
Clients:
Idaho Power Co. *(Lee S. Sherline)*
PacifiCorp *(Lee S. Sherline)*
Utah Power and Light Co. *(Lee S. Sherline)*
Washington Water Power Co. *(Lee S. Sherline)*

LEINBACH, Linda A.
V. President, Vote America Foundation
1200 19th St., N.W., Suite 6030, Washington, DC 20036
Telephone: (202) 659-4595

LEISHER, Catherine A.
Exec. Director, Home Economics Education Ass'n
1201 16th St., N.W., Washington, DC 20036
Telephone: (202) 822-7844

LEITER, Jeffrey L.
Collier, Shannon & Scott
1055 Thomas Jefferson St., N.W., Suite 300, Washington, DC 20007
Telephone: (202) 342-8400
Registered as lobbyist at U.S. Congress.
Clients:
Soc. of Independent Gasoline Marketers of America

LEITZELL, Terry L.
Bogle and Gates
One Thomas Circle, N.W., Suite 900, Washington, DC 20005
Telephone: (202) 293-3600
Registered as lobbyist at U.S. Congress.
Registered as Foreign Agent: (#3474).
Background: Assistant Administrator of NOAA, U.S. Department of Commerce, 1977-81.
Clients:
Northern Jaeger
Norwegian Fisheries Ass'n
Oceantrawl, Inc.
Puget Sound Cruiseship Alliance
Sahlman Seafoods
Wright Schuchart, Inc.

LE, Khoa X.
President, Indochina Resource Action Center
1628 16th St., N.W. 3rd Floor, Washington, DC 20037
Telephone: (202) 667-4690

LEMA, Joseph E.
V. President, Transportation, Nat'l Coal Ass'n
1130 17th St., N.W., Washington, DC 20036
Telephone: (202) 463-2629

LEMASTER, Roger J.
Dep. Dir., Fed. Relations & Sr. Counsel, American Council of Life Insurance
1001 Pennsylvania Ave., N.W, Washington, DC 20004-2599
Telephone: (202) 624-2114
Registered as lobbyist at U.S. Congress.

LEMBESIS, Steve
Dir. of Advocacy & Public Affairs, Nat'l Urban Coalition
8601 Georgia Ave., Suite 500, Silver Spring, MD 20910
Telephone: (301) 495-4999

LEMBO, Bob
Director, State Relations, Ass'n of Trial Lawyers of America
1050 31st St., N.W., Washington, DC 20007
Telephone: (202) 965-3500

LEMLE, J. Stuart
Land, Lemle & Arnold
1701 K St., N.W., Washington, DC 20006
Telephone: (202) 785-1020
Registered as Foreign Agent: (#3824).
Background: Assistant Director, Domestic Policy Staff, The White House, 1977-78.
Clients:
Nigeria, Embassy of

LEMOAL, Danielle
Director, Administrative Services, American Mental Health Counselors Ass'n
5999 Stevenson Ave., Alexandria, VA 22304
Telephone: (703) 823-9800

LEMON, T. I.
V. President, General Manager, Natural Rubber Shippers Ass'n
1400 K St., N.W. 9th Floor, Washington, DC 20005
Telephone: (202) 682-1325

LEMOV, Michael R.
Of Counsel, Kelley, Drye and Warren
2300 M St., N.W., Washington, DC 20037
Telephone: (202) 463-8333
Registered as lobbyist at U.S. Congress.
Clients:
Baltimore, Maryland, City of
Great Western Financial Corp.
Nat'l Glass Ass'n
Nat'l Independent Automobile Dealers Ass'n
Pyropower Corp.

LENABURG, Dave
CEO and President, Banner Life Insurance Co.
1701 Research Blvd., Rockville, MD 20850
Telephone: (301) 279-4800

LENAHAN, Wally
Internat'l Business and Economic Research Corp.
2121 K St, N.W., Suite 700, Washington, DC 20037
Telephone: (202) 955-6155
Registered as Foreign Agent: (#2944).
Background: Former Deputy Assistant Secretary of Commerce for Textiles and Apparel, Department of Commerce.
Clients:
Asociacion Nacional de Industriales (ANDI)

LENARD, Lynette
Director of Federal Relations, Browning-Ferris Industries (D.C.), Inc.
1150 Connecticut Ave., N.W. Suite 500, Washington, DC 20036
Telephone: (202) 223-8151
Registered as lobbyist at U.S. Congress.

LENARD, Myra
Exec. Director, Polish-American Congress
1625 Eye St., N.W., Suite 326, Washington, DC 20006
Telephone: (202) 296-6955

LENGEL, John B.
V. President, Burson-Marsteller
1850 M St., N.W., Suite 900, Washington, DC 20036
Telephone: (202) 833-8550

LENHART, Cynthia R.
Wildlife Specialist, Nat'l Audubon Soc.
801 Pennsylvania Ave., S.E., Washington, DC 20003
Telephone: (202) 547-9009
Registered as lobbyist at U.S. Congress.

LENHOFF, Donna R.
Director, Legal Policy and Programs, Women's Legal Defense Fund
2000 P St., N.W., Suite 400, Washington, DC 20036
Telephone: (202) 887-0364
Registered as lobbyist at U.S. Congress.

LENIHAN, Patricia
Washington Bureau Chief, Prentice Hall Information Services
1819 L St., N.W. Suite 400, Washington, DC 20036
Telephone: (202) 293-0707

LENKOWSKY, Dr. Leslie
President, Institute for Educational Affairs
1112 16th St., N.W. Suite 520, Washington, DC 20036
Telephone: (202) 833-1801
Background: Ass't and Deputy Director, U.S. Information Agency, 1983-84;

LENNAN, Anne C.
Hunt Management Systems
2033 M St., N.W., Suite 605, Washington, DC 20036
Telephone: (202) 223-6413
Background: Serves as Director of Federal Affairs, Soc. of Professional Benefit Administrators.

The listings in this directory are available as *Mailing Labels*. See last page.

Clients:
Soc. of Professional Benefit Administrators

LENZ, Allen J.
Director, Trade and Economics, Chemical Manufacturers Ass'n
2501 M St., N.W., Washington, DC 20037
Telephone: (202) 887-1100

LENZ, Edward A.
Sr. V. President and General Counsel, Nat'l Ass'n of Temporary Services
119 South St. Asaph St., Alexandria, VA 22314
Telephone: (703) 549-6287

LENZ, Msgr. Paul A.
Exec. Director, Catholic Indian Missions, Bureau of
2021 H St., N.W., Washington, DC 20006
Telephone: (202) 331-8542

LEON, Denele
Area Development Director, United Negro College Fund
1025 Vermont Ave., N.W. Suite 810, Washington, DC 20005
Telephone: (202) 785-8623

LEONARD, Burleigh C. W.
V. President, Federal Gov't Affrs., RJR Nabisco Washington, Inc.
1455 Pennsylvania Ave., N.W., Suite 525, Washington, DC 20004
Telephone: (202) 626-7200
Registered as lobbyist at U.S. Congress.
Background: Legislative Assistant to Senator John Danforth (R-MO), 1977-79. Staff Member U.S. Senate Committee on Agriculture, Nutrition and Forestry 1979-81. Special Assistant to the President for Policy Development and Exec. Secretary of the Cabinet Council on Food and Agriculture, 1981-84.

LEONARD, Lloyd J.
Legislative Director, League of Women Voters of the United States
1730 M St., N.W., Tenth Floor, Washington, DC 20036
Telephone: (202) 429-1965
Registered as lobbyist at U.S. Congress.

LEONARD, Ned
Manager Communications/Gov't Affairs, Western Fuels Ass'n
1625 M St., N.W. Magruder Bldg., Washington, DC 20036-3264
Telephone: (202) 463-6580

LEONARD, Patrick
President, World Mercy Fund
121 S. Saint Asaph St., Alexandria, VA 22314
Telephone: (703) 548-4646

LEONARD, Paul A.
Budget/Housing Analyst, Center on Budget and Policy Priorities
236 Massachusetts Ave., N.E., Suite 305, Washington, DC 20002
Telephone: (202) 544-0591

LEONARD, Raymond G.
President, Water Resources Congress
3800 N. Fairfax Drive Suite 7, Arlington, VA 22203
Telephone: (703) 525-4881

LEONARD, Rodney E.
Exec. Director, Community Nutrition Institute
2001 S St., N.W. Suite 530, Washington, DC 20009
Telephone: (202) 462-4700
Background: Former Deputy Director, Officer of Consumer Affairs, The White House. Serves also as Exec. Director, American Ass'n for World Health.

LEONARD, Roger W.
Legis Affrs Staff, DEPARTMENT OF AGRICULTURE - Forest Service
12 and Independence Ave. S.W., Washington, DC 20250
Telephone: (202) 447-7531

LEONARD, Scott
Assistant Director, Nat'l Ass'n of Railroad Passengers
236 Massachusetts Ave., N.E., Suite 603, Washington, DC 20002
Telephone: (202) 546-1550

Registered as lobbyist at U.S. Congress.

LEONARD, Will E.
Dorsey & Whitney
1330 Connecticut Ave., N.W., Suite 200, Washington, DC 20036
Telephone: (202) 857-0700
Background: Legislative Assistant to Senator Russell B. Long of Louisiana, 1960-66. Professional Staff Member, U.S. Senate Committee on Finance, 1966-68. Commissioner, 1966-77 and Chairman, 1975-76, U.S. International Trade Commission.
Clients:
Genetics Institute Inc.

LEPON, Jeffrey M.
Lepon, McCarthy, Jutkowitz & Holzworth
1146 19th St., N.W. Third Fl., Washington, DC 20036
Telephone: (202) 857-0242
Registered as Foreign Agent: (#4302).
Clients:
Chilean Exporters Ass'n

LEPON, MCCARTHY, JUTKOWITZ & HOLZWORTH
1146 19th St., N.W. Third Fl., Washington, DC 20036
Telephone: (202) 857-0242
Registered as Foreign Agent: (#4302)
Members of firm representing listed organizations:
Dellon, Leslie K.
Background: Trial Attorney, Civil Division, Department of Justice, 1983-86.
Holzworth, David A.
Lepon, Jeffrey M.
Clients:
Chilean Exporters Ass'n *(David A. Holzworth, Jeffrey M. Lepon)*

LEPOVITZ, Teri
Senior V. President, Nat'l Ass'n of Broadcasters
1771 N St., N.W., Washington, DC 20036
Telephone: (202) 429-5300

LEPPERT, Charles, Jr.
Director, Fed. Affairs, Nat'l Gov't Rtns, Procter and Gamble Mfg. Co.
Suite 400, 801 18th St., N.W., Washington, DC 20006
Telephone: (202) 833-9502
Registered as lobbyist at U.S. Congress.
Background: Minority Counsel, Committee on Interior and Insular Affairs, U.S. House of Representatives, 1965-74; Assistant to the President, Legislative Affairs, 1975-76; Counsel and Director, Republican Policy Relations Committe, U.S. House of Representatives, 1977-79.

LERCH AND CO., INC.
1030 15th St., N.W., Washington, DC 20005
Telephone: (202) 466-2804
Background: A public relations/government affairs consulting firm.
Members of firm representing listed organizations:
Lerch, Donald G. (Jr.), President
Clients:
Japan Economic Institute of America *(Donald G. Lerch, Jr.)*
Japan, Government of *(Donald G. Lerch, Jr.)*

LERCH, Donald G., Jr.
President, Lerch and Co., Inc.
1030 15th St., N.W., Washington, DC 20005
Telephone: (202) 466-2804
Registered as Foreign Agent: (#0929).
Clients:
Japan Economic Institute of America
Japan, Government of

LERMAN, Arnold M.
Wilmer, Cutler and Pickering
2445 M St., N.W., Washington, DC 20037-1420
Telephone: (202) 663-6000
Clients:
Citicorp

LERNER ASSOCIATES, Charles S.
7201 Marbury Rd., Bethesda, MD 20817
Telephone: (301) 320-2938
Members of firm representing listed organizations:
Lerner, Charles S.
Organizations represented:

Nat'l Council on Patient Information and Education *(Charles S. Lerner)*

LERNER, Charles S.
Lerner Associates, Charles S.
7201 Marbury Rd., Bethesda, MD 20817
Telephone: (301) 320-2938
Organizations represented:
Nat'l Council on Patient Information and Education

LEROY, Wayne E.
Associate V. President, Ass'n of Physical Plant Administrators of Universities and Colleges
1446 Duke St., Alexandria, VA 22314
Telephone: (703) 684-1446

LESCH, Peter C.
Gallagher, Boland, Meiburger and Brosnan
1000 Vermont Ave., N.W. Suite 1100, Washington, DC 20005-4903
Telephone: (202) 289-7200
Background: Staff Attorney, Federal Power Commission, 1973-77; Legal Advisor to Commissioner, Federal Energy Regulatory Commission, 1978-79.
Clients:
Tampa Electric Co.

LESH, Donald R.
President, Global Tomorrow Coalition
1325 G St., N.W., Suite 915, Washington, DC 20005-3104
Telephone: (202) 628-4016

LESHER, J. Griffin
Clifford & Warnke
815 Connecticut Ave., N.W., Washington, DC 20006
Telephone: (202) 828-4200

LESHER, Dr. Richard L.
President, Chamber of Commerce of the U.S.A.
1615 H St., N.W., Washington, DC 20062
Telephone: (202) 463-5300
Registered as lobbyist at U.S. Congress.

LESHER & RUSSELL, INC.
517 C St., N.E., Washington, DC 20002
Telephone: (202) 546-6501
Members of firm representing listed organizations:
Lesher, William
Moos, Eugene, V. President
Russell, Randy M.
Clients:
Agricultural Policy Working Group *(William Lesher, Randy M. Russell)*

LESHER, William
Lesher & Russell, Inc.
517 C St., N.E., Washington, DC 20002
Telephone: (202) 546-6501
Registered as lobbyist at U.S. Congress.
Clients:
Agricultural Policy Working Group

LESLIE, John W.
Exec. V. President, Kamber Group, The
1920 L St., N.W., Washington, DC 20036
Telephone: (202) 223-8700
Organizations represented:
Coalition of Labor Union Women

LESSARD, William J., Jr.
Director of Policy and Research, Nat'l Committee to Preserve Social Security and Medicare
2000 K St., N.W. Suite 800, Washington, DC 20006
Telephone: (202) 822-9459
Registered as lobbyist at U.S. Congress.

LESSEN, Frank J.
Director, Legislative Affairs & Press, Ass'n of Biotechnology Companies
1120 Vermont Ave., N.W., Suite 601, Washington, DC 20005
Telephone: (202) 842-2229
Registered as lobbyist at U.S. Congress.

LESSENCO, Gilbert B.
Wilner and Scheiner
1200 New Hampshire Ave., N.W., Suite 300, Washington, DC 20036

LESSENCO, Gilbert B. (Cont'd)
Telephone: (202) 861-7800
Registered as lobbyist at U.S. Congress.
Clients:
   General Mills
   Graco, Inc.

LESSER, Craig S.
Manager, Legislative Affairs - Federal, Georgia Power Co.
1130 Connecticut Ave., N.W. Suite 830, Washington, DC 20036
Telephone: (202) 775-0944

LESTER, Joseph S., Jr.
Assistant General Counsel, Control Data Corp.
Suite 370, 1201 Pennsylvania Ave., N.W., Washington, DC
Telephone: (202) 789-6462
Registered as lobbyist at U.S. Congress.

LESTER, Robert M.
Asst Gen Counsel, Legis & Policy, OGC, AGENCY FOR INTERNAT'L DEVELOPMENT
320 21st St., N.W., Washington, DC 20523
Telephone: (202) 647-8371

LESTINA, Dale
Assistant Director, Special Projects, Nat'l Education Ass'n of the U.S.
1201 16th St., N.W., Washington, DC 20036
Telephone: (202) 822-7300
Registered as lobbyist at U.S. Congress.

LESTRADE, Swinburne A.S.
Exec. Director, Eastern Caribbean Investment Promotion Service
1730 M St., N.W., Suite 901, Washington, DC 20036
Telephone: (202) 659-8689
Registered as Foreign Agent: (#4080)

LETZLER, Kenneth A.
Arnold & Porter
1200 New Hampshire Ave., N.W., Washington, DC 20036
Telephone: (202) 872-6700

LEUCHTENBURG, Thomas T.
Dir, Gov't Rels. & Public Communications, Gas Research Institute
1331 Pennsylvania Ave., N.W., Suite 730 North, Washington, DC 20004
Telephone: (202) 662-8989

LEUGS, Brian
Manager, State & Local Affairs, Nat'l Soft Drink Ass'n
1101 16th St., N.W., Washington, DC 20036
Telephone: (202) 463-6732

LEVA, HAWES, MASON AND MARTIN
1220 19th St., N.W. Suite 700, Washington, DC 20036
Telephone: (202) 775-0725
Registered as Foreign Agent: (#3881)
Members of firm representing listed organizations:
   Leva, Marx
      Background: Law Clerk to U.S. Supreme Court Justice Hugo Black, 1940-41. General Counsel, Department of Defense, 1947-49. Assistant Secretary of Defense for Legal and Legislative Affairs, 1949-51.
   Martin, Robert
   Mason, Arthur K.
   Mesirow, Harold E.
   Sack, James M.
   Sherbill, Raymond J.
   Turnbull, Lowell D.
Clients:
   American Waterways Operators *(Harold E. Mesirow)*
   Ass'n of the United States Army *(Arthur K. Mason, Raymond J. Sherbill)*
   British Embassy *(Lowell D. Turnbull)*
   Electro- & Electronik Appartebau Gesellschaft mbH *(Lowell D. Turnbull)*
   Foss Maritime Co. *(Harold E. Mesirow)*
   Global Marine, Inc. *(Harold E. Mesirow)*
   United Kingdom Defence Export Services Organization *(Marx Leva, Robert Martin)*

LEVA, Marx
Leva, Hawes, Mason and Martin
1220 19th St., N.W., Suite 700, Washington, DC 20036
Telephone: (202) 775-0725
Registered as Foreign Agent: (#3881).

Background: Law Clerk to U.S. Supreme Court Justice Hugo Black, 1940-41. General Counsel, Department of Defense, 1947-49. Assistant Secretary of Defense for Legal and Legislative Affairs, 1949-51.
Clients:
   United Kingdom Defence Export Services Organization

LEVANDOSKI, Carrie
Public Awareness Officer, Nat'l Academy of Engineering
2101 Constitution Ave., N.W., Washington, DC 20037
Telephone: (202) 334-2195

LEVENSTEIN, William
Dross and Levenstein
3016 St. Clair Dr., Temple Hills, MD 20748
Telephone: (301) 899-3330
Clients:
   Borden Internat'l
   Carborundum Co.
   Commercial Solvents Corp.

LEVENTHAL, Paul
President, Nuclear Control Institute
1000 Connecticut Ave., N.W. Suite 704, Washington, DC 20036
Telephone: (202) 822-8444

LEVENTHAL, Robert B.
Counsel, AFL-CIO Maritime Committee
444 North Capitol St., N.W., Suite 820, Washington, DC 20001
Telephone: (202) 347-5980
Registered as lobbyist at U.S. Congress.

LEVENTHAL, SENTER & LERMAN
2000 K St., N.W., Suite 600, Washington, DC 20006
Telephone: (202) 429-8970
Members of firm representing listed organizations:
   Klipper, Michael R.
   Rodriguez, Raul R.
Clients:
   Aeronautical Radio, Inc. *(Raul R. Rodriguez)*
   Committee for America's Copyright Community *(Michael R. Klipper)*
   Copyright Remedies Coalition *(Michael R. Klipper)*

LEVENTHAL, Sharon
Exec. Director, Nuclear Control Institute
1000 Connecticut Ave., N.W. Suite 704, Washington, DC 20036
Telephone: (202) 822-8444

LEVERE, Andrea
Director, Nat'l Development Council
1025 Connecticut Ave., N.W., Suite 317, Washington, DC 20036
Telephone: (202) 466-3906

LEVERICH, Bingham B.
Covington and Burling
1201 Pennsylvania Ave., N.W., Box 7566, Washington, DC 20044
Telephone: (202) 662-6000

LEVERING, Robert J.
V.P., Gov't Affrs. & Legislative Couns., Direct Marketing Ass'n
1101 17th St., N.W., Suite 900, Washington, DC 20036
Telephone: (202) 347-1222
Registered as lobbyist at U.S. Congress.

LEVIEN, Lawrence D.
Akin, Gump, Strauss, Hauer and Feld
1333 New Hampshire Ave., N.W., Suite 400, Washington, DC 20036
Telephone: (202) 887-4000
Registered as Foreign Agent: (#3492).
Clients:
   Chilean Exporters Ass'n

LEVIN, Betsy
Exec. Director, Ass'n of American Law Schools
1201 Connecticut Ave., N.W. Suite 800, Washington, DC 20036
Telephone: (202) 296-8851
Registered as lobbyist at U.S. Congress.
Background: General Counsel, Dept. of Education, 1980-81.

LEVIN-EPSTEIN, Jodie
State Policy Advocate, Center for Law and Social Policy
1616 P St., N.W., Suite 350, Washington, DC 20036
Telephone: (202) 328-5140

LEVIN-JARDOT, Debra
Deputy Exec. Director, Democratic Congressional Campaign Committee
430 South Capitol St., S.E. 2nd Floor, Washington, DC 20003
Telephone: (202) 863-1500

LEVIN, Mark
Exec. V. President, Chain Link Fence Manufacturers Ass'n
1776 Massachusetts Ave., N.W. Suite 521, Washington, DC 20036
Telephone: (202) 659-3536

LEVIN, Mark B.
Assoc. Exec. Director, Washington Office, Nat'l Conference on Soviet Jewry
1522 K St., N.W., Suite 1100, Washington, DC 20005
Telephone: (202) 898-2500

LEVIN, Mark M.
Weiner, McCaffrey, Brodsky, Kaplan & Levin
1350 New York Ave., N.W., Suite 800, Washington, DC 20005-4797
Telephone: (202) 628-2000
Background: Trial Attorney, Public Counsel Section, Antitrust Division, U.S. Department of Justice, 1973-77.

LEVINE, Barbara W.
Dir., Federal Affairs, Gov't Relations, American Public Health Ass'n
1015 15th St., N.W. Third Floor, Washington, DC 20005
Telephone: (202) 789-5600
Registered as lobbyist at U.S. Congress.
Background: Former Legislative Assistant to Rep. Matthew J. Rinaldo of New Jersey.

LEVINE, Kenneth S.
Wunder, Ryan, Cannon & Thelen
1615 L St., N.W., Suite 650, Washington, DC 20036
Telephone: (202) 659-3005
Registered as lobbyist at U.S. Congress.
Registered as Foreign Agent: (#3971).
Background: Director, Office of Congressional Consumer and Public Affairs, Federal Energy Regulatory Commission, 1979-81. Deputy Assistant Secretary for Legislation, U.S. Department of Health, Education and Welfare, 1977-79. Administrative Assistant to Rep. Bob Eckhardt (D-TX), 1975-76.
Clients:
   American Internat'l Group
   Bermuda, Government of
   Environmental Air Control Inc.
   Falcon Safety Products
   Gesamtverband der Deutschen Versicherungswirtschaft e.V.
   Hook-SupeRx, Inc.
   Kohlberg Kravis Roberts & Co.
   Pfizer, Inc.
   Philip Morris Management Corp.

LEVINE, Leonard B.
Director, U.S. Government Affairs, TransCanada PipeLines
1701 Pennsylvania Ave., N.W. Suite 1110, Washington, DC 20006
Telephone: (202) 785-5270

LEVINE, Leslie
Director, Communications, Nat'l Ass'n of the Remodeling Industry
1901 North Moore St. Suite 808, Arlington, VA 22209
Telephone: (703) 276-7600

LEVINE, Peter J.
TransNational, Inc.
1511 K St., N.W., Suite 1100, Washington, DC 20005
Telephone: (202) 393-7690
Registered as Foreign Agent: (#3779).
Clients:
   Associacao das Industrias de Calcados do Rio Grande do Sul
   Companhia Siderurgica de Tubarao

LEVINE, Phyllis
Counsel, Legis. & Regulatory Affairs, American Gas Ass'n
1515 Wilson Blvd., Arlington, VA 22209
Telephone: (703) 841-8400

LEVINSON, Ellen S.
Partner, Lord Day & Lord, Barrett Smith
1201 Pennsylvania Ave., N.W., Suite 821, Washington, DC
20004
Telephone: (202) 393-5024
Clients:
Coffee, Sugar and Cocoa Exchange

LEVINSON, Lawrence E.
Sr. V. President, Government Relations, Paramount Communications, Inc.
1875 Eye St., N.W., Suite 1225, Washington, DC 20006
Telephone: (202) 429-9690
Registered as lobbyist at U.S. Congress.

LEVINSON, Riva
Black, Manafort, Stone and Kelly Public Affairs Co.
211 N. Union St., Third Floor, Alexandria, VA 22314
Telephone: (703) 683-6612
Registered as lobbyist at U.S. Congress.
Registered as Foreign Agent: (#3600).

LEVITAN, Sar
Chairman, Steering Committee, Nat'l Council on Employment Policy
1730 K St., N.W., Suite 701, Washington, DC 20006
Telephone: (202) 833-2532

LEVITAS, Elliott H.
Kilpatrick & Cody
2501 M St., N.W., Suite 500, Washington, DC 20037
Telephone: (202) 463-2500
Registered as lobbyist at U.S. Congress.
Background: Former Member, U.S. House of Representatives (D-GA).
Clients:
Federal Express Corp.
United Airlines

LEVRIO, Jay
Director, Council on Podiatric Medical Education
9312 Old Georgetown Road, Bethesda, MD 20015
Telephone: (301) 571-9200

LEVY, Charles S.
Mayer, Brown and Platt
2000 Pennsylvania Ave., N.W. Suite 6500, Washington,
DC 20006
Telephone: (202) 463-2000
Registered as lobbyist at U.S. Congress.
Background: Legislative Assistant to Cong. John Culver,
1971. Legislative Assistant to Sen. Adlai Stevenson,
1973-75. Legal Advisor to the Commissioner, U.S. International Trade Commission, 1979-80. Member, Investment Policy Advisory Committee, Office of the U.S.
Trade Representative.
Clients:
American Farm Bureau Federation
Continental Illinois Nat'l Bank and Trust Co.
Dome Petroleum Ltd.
Hewlett-Packard Co.
SAMA Group of Ass'ns

LEVY, David
Sidley and Austin
1722 Eye St., N.W. Sixth Floor, Washington, DC 20006
Telephone: (202) 429-4000
Clients:
Alliance of Nonprofit Mailers

LEVY, David L.
President, Nat'l Council for Children's Rights
721 2nd St., N.E. Suite 103, Washington, DC 20002
Telephone: (202) 223-6227

LEVY, Edward, Jr.
President, American Israel Public Affairs Committee
440 First St., N.W. Suite 600, Washington, DC 20001
Telephone: (202) 639-5200

LEVY, Gregg H.
Covington and Burling
1201 Pennsylvania Ave., N.W., Box 7566, Washington, DC
20044

Telephone: (202) 662-6000

LEVY, Herbert J.
Exec. Director, Nat'l Ass'n of Housing Cooperatives
1614 King St., Alexandria, VA 22314
Telephone: (703) 549-5201
Registered as lobbyist at U.S. Congress.

LEVY, Michael R.
Covington and Burling
1201 Pennsylvania Ave., N.W., Box 7566, Washington, DC
20044
Telephone: (202) 662-6000
Registered as lobbyist at U.S. Congress.
Clients:
Sun Life Assurance Co. of Canada (U.S. Division)

LEVY, Paul Alan
Staff Attorney, Public Citizen Litigation Group
2000 P St., N.W., Suite 700, Washington, DC 20036
Telephone: (202) 785-3704

LEVY-REINER, Dr. Sherry
Director, Public Info & Publications, Ass'n of American
Colleges
1818 R St., N.W., Washington, DC 20009
Telephone: (202) 387-3760

LEVY, Roger N.
V. President, Federal Gov't Affairs, Travelers, The
901 15th St., N.W. Suite 520, Washington, DC 20005
Telephone: (202) 789-1380
Registered as lobbyist at U.S. Congress.

LEW, Jacob J.
Van Ness, Feldman & Curtis
1050 Thomas Jefferson St., 7th Floor, Washington, DC
20007
Telephone: (202) 298-1800
Clients:
LUZ Internat'l

LEWIN, Martin J.
Mudge Rose Guthrie Alexander and Ferdon
2121 K St., N.W., Suite 700, Washington, DC 20037
Telephone: (202) 429-9355
Registered as lobbyist at U.S. Congress.
Registered as Foreign Agent: (#3200).
Background: Staff Attorney, Special Project Counsel to Interstate Commerce Commission, 1973-74. Attorney/Advisor, Office of the General Counsel, General Accounting
Office, 1974-77. Staff Member, House Committee on International Relations, 1977-78, Legal Advisor to Commissioner Stern, U.S. International Trade Commission, 1978-
79.
Clients:
American Import Shippers Ass'n
China Nat'l Textiles Import and Export Corp.
Hong Kong Trade, Industry and Customs Department
United States Ass'n of Importers of Textile and
Apparel (USITA)

LEWIN, Nathan
Miller, Cassidy, Larroca and Lewin
2555 M St., N.W. Suite 500, Washington, DC 20037
Telephone: (202) 293-6400
Background: Law Clerk to U.S. Supreme Court Justice
John M. Harlan, 1961-62. Special Assistant to the Assistant Attorney General, Criminal Division, Department of
Justice, 1962-63. Assistant to Solicitor General 1963-67.
Deputy Administrator, Bureau of Security and Consular
Affairs Department of State, 1967-68. Deputy Assistant
Attorney General, Civil Rights Division, 1968-69.
Clients:
47th Street Photo

LEWIS, Caroline
Schmertz Co., The
555 13th St. N.W. Suite 1220 East, Washington, DC
20004
Telephone: (202) 637-6680

LEWIS, Cathy A.
Vinson and Elkins
Willard Office Building, 1455 Pennsylvania Ave., N.W.,
Washington, DC 20004-1007
Telephone: (202) 639-6500

Registered as lobbyist at U.S. Congress.
Background: Assistant to Counsel to Chairman, 1974-78
and Attorney, 1978-79, Board of Governors of the Federal Reserve System.
Clients:
United Savings of Texas, FSB

LEWIS, Charles
Exec. Director, Center for Public Integrity
P.O. Box 18134, Washington, DC 20036
Telephone: (202) 223-0299

LEWIS, Daniel N.
Dir, Cong & Legis Affrs Staff, DEPARTMENT OF INTERIOR - Indian Affairs
18th and C Sts., N.W. Room 4641, Washington, DC
20240
Telephone: (202) 343-5706

LEWIS, David A.
PAI Management Corp.
5530 Wisconsin Ave., N.W., Suite 1149, Washington, DC
20815
Telephone: (301) 656-4224
Background: Serves as Executive Director, American
Academy of Optometry, American Soc. for Adolescent
Psychiatry and American College of Internat'l Physicians.
Clients:
American Academy of Optometry
American Soc. for Adolescent Psychiatry
Physicians for Social Responsibility

LEWIS, Edward
Director, Tire Industry Safety Council
National Press Bldg. Suite 844, Washington, DC 20045
Telephone: (202) 783-1022

LEWIS, Frank J.
Sr. V. P. & Spec. Ass't to the CEO, Harris Corp.
1201 East Abingdon Drive Suite 300, Alexandria, VA
22314
Telephone: (703) 548-9200

LEWIS, Gail W.
V. President, Regional Affairs, Aircraft Owners and Pilots
Ass'n
421 Aviation Way, Frederick, MD 21701
Telephone: (301) 695-2000

LEWIS, Howard K., III
V. President, Internat'l Economic Affrs., Nat'l Ass'n of
Manufacturers
1331 Pennsylvania Ave., N.W. Suite 1500 North, Washington, DC 20004-1703
Telephone: (202) 637-3000
Registered as lobbyist at U.S. Congress.

LEWIS, Jack W.
V. President, Government Affairs, Nat'l Beer Wholesalers
Ass'n
5205 Leesburg Pike, Suite 1600, Falls Church, VA 22041
Telephone: (703) 578-4300
Registered as lobbyist at U.S. Congress.
Background: Former staff aide to Senators Harry Byrd and
William B. Spong (D-VA) and Senator Thomas F. Eagleton (D-MO).

LEWIS & LEWIS
4601 N. Fairfax Drive Suite 720, Arlington, VA 22203
Telephone: (703) 243-2333
Members of firm representing listed organizations:
Lewis, Staffanie J.

LEWIS, Linda R.
Corporate V. President, Nat'l Cooperative Bank
1630 Connecticut Ave., N.W., Washington, DC 20009-
1004
Telephone: (202) 745-4610

LEWIS, Mark
Director of Communications, Nat'l Organization on Disability
910 16th St., N.W., Suite 600, Washington, DC 20006
Telephone: (202) 293-5960

LEWIS, Marx
Chairman, Council for the Defense of Freedom
1275 K St., N.W., Suite 1150, Washington, DC 20005
Telephone: (202) 789-4294

LEWIS, Michael R.
Washington Representative, Internat'l Longshoremen's and Warehousemen's Union
1133 15th St., N.W. Suite 600, Washington, DC 20005
Telephone: (202) 463-6265
Registered as lobbyist at U.S. Congress.

LEWIS, Mike
Director, Communications, American Institute of Aeronautics and Astronautics
370 L'Enfant Promenade, Washington, DC 20024
Telephone: (202) 646-7405

LEWIS, Richard
President, American Pulpwood Ass'n
1025 Vermont Ave., N.W., Suite 1020, Washington, DC 20005
Telephone: (202) 347-2900
Registered as lobbyist at U.S. Congress.
Background: Also represents the Forest Products Trucking Council.

LEWIS, Richard W.
Washington Representative, Chevron, U.S.A.
1700 K St., N.W., Suite 1200, Washington, DC 20006
Telephone: (202) 457-5800
Registered as lobbyist at U.S. Congress.

LEWIS, Rita
Verner, Liipfert, Bernhard, McPherson and Hand, Chartered
901 15th St., N.W., Suite 700, Washington, DC 20005
Telephone: (202) 371-6000
Registered as lobbyist at U.S. Congress.

LEWIS, Robert J.
Senior V. President, Federal Relations, Tobacco Institute
1875 Eye St., N.W., Suite 800, Washington, DC 20006
Telephone: (202) 457-4899
Registered as lobbyist at U.S. Congress.

LEWIS, Samuel W.
President, United States Institute for Peace
1550 M St., N.W. Suite 700, Washington, DC 20005-1708
Telephone: (202) 457-1700
Background: Deputy Director, Policy Planning Staff, U.S. State Dept., 1974-75; Ass't Secretary of State for Internat'l Organization Affairs, 1975-77; U.S. Ambassador to Israel, 1977-85.

LEWIS, Staffanie J.
Lewis & Lewis
4601 N. Fairfax Drive Suite 720, Arlington, VA 22203
Telephone: (703) 243-2333
Registered as lobbyist at U.S. Congress.

LEYDEN, John F.
Secretary-Treasurer, AFL-CIO - Public Employee Department
815 16th St., N.W., Suite 308, Washington, DC 20006
Telephone: (202) 393-2820
Registered as lobbyist at U.S. Congress.

LEYH, J. Robert
Sr. V. President, Government Relations, Waterman Steamship Co.
1000 16th St., N.W. Suite 802, Washington, DC 20036
Telephone: (202) 659-3804

LEYTON, Peter S.
White, Fine, and Verville
1156 15th St., N.W., Suite 1100, Washington, DC 20005
Telephone: (202) 659-2900

LIANG, Fern Z.
Director, Gov't Affairs Division, American Soc. of Hospital Pharmacists
4630 Montgomery Ave., Bethesda, MD 20814
Telephone: (301) 657-3000
Registered as lobbyist at U.S. Congress.

LIBBY, I. Lewis
Dickstein, Shapiro and Morin
2101 L St., N.W., Washington, DC 20037
Telephone: (202) 785-9700
Registered as Foreign Agent: (#3028).
Background: Director of Special Projects, Bureau of East Asian and Pacific Affairs, Department of State, 1982-85.
Clients:

Falconbridge Ltd.

LIBERATORE, Robert G.
Exec Dir, Public Policy/Legisltv. Affrs, Chrysler Corp.
1100 Connecticut Ave., N.W., Washington, DC 20036
Telephone: (202) 862-5447
Registered as lobbyist at U.S. Congress.

LIBIN, Jerome B.
Sutherland, Asbill and Brennan
1275 Pennsylvania, N.W., Washington, DC 20004-2404
Telephone: (202) 383-0100
Registered as lobbyist at U.S. Congress.
Registered as Foreign Agent: (#3307).
Background: Law Clerk to Justice Charles E. Whittaker, U.S. Supreme Court, 1959-60.

LICHENSTEIN, Charles M.
Distinguished Scholar, Heritage Foundation
214 Massachusetts Ave., N.E., Washington, DC 20002
Telephone: (202) 546-4400
Background: Alternate U.S. Representative to the United Nations, 1981-84.

LICHT, Eric
President, Coalitions for America
717 2nd St., N.E., Washington, DC 20002
Telephone: (202) 546-3003
Background: Also holds the position of Chairman, Nat'l Pro-Family Coalition at the same address.

LICHTENBERG, Joseph M.
President, Nat'l Pasta Ass'n
2101 Wilson Blvd. Suite 920, Arlington, VA 22201
Telephone: (703) 841-0818

LICHTENSTEIN, Sarah
Treasurer, Nat'l Women's Political Caucus Victory Fund
1275 K St., N.W. Suite 750, Washington, DC 20005
Telephone: (202) 898-1100

LICHTER, Linda S.
Co-Director, Center for Media and Public Affairs
2101 L St., N.W., Suite 505, Washington, DC 20037
Telephone: (202) 223-2942

LICHTER, S. Robert
Co-Director, Center for Media and Public Affairs
2101 L St., N.W., Suite 505, Washington, DC 20037
Telephone: (202) 223-2942

LICHTMAN, Judith L.
President, Women's Legal Defense Fund
2000 P St., N.W., Suite 400, Washington, DC 20036
Telephone: (202) 887-0364
Registered as lobbyist at U.S. Congress.
Background: Serves also as Secretary, Leadership Conference on Civil Rights. Formerly an attorney with the U.S. Commission on Civil Rights and HEW.

LICHTMAN, Pamela
Legislative Assistant, Zero Population Growth, Inc.
1400 16th St., N.W., Suite 320, Washington, DC 20036
Telephone: (202) 332-2200
Registered as lobbyist at U.S. Congress.

LIDER, Robert Y.
V. President, Tax Dept., Citicorp
1275 Pennsylvania Ave., N.W., Suite 503, Washington, DC 20004
Telephone: (202) 879-6800

LIDINSKY, Richard A., Jr.
V. President, Governmental Affairs, Sea Containers America Inc.
1440 New York Ave., N.W., Suite 430, Washington, DC 20005
Telephone: (202) 638-4140
Registered as lobbyist at U.S. Congress.

LIEBENGOOD, Howard S.
Gold and Liebengood, Inc.
1455 Pennsylvania Ave., N.W. Suite 950, Washington, DC 20004
Telephone: (202) 639-8899
Registered as lobbyist at U.S. Congress.
Background: Former Sergeant-at-Arms of the U.S. Senate.
Clients:
Beretta U.S.A. Corp.
British Airports Authority (BAA plc)

Fiat Washington
Hopi Tribe
Investment Company Institute
Nat'l Business Aircraft Ass'n
Pennzoil Co.
Philip Morris Management Corp.
Thomson-CSF Inc.

LIEBENOW, Robert C.
President, Corn Refiners Ass'n
1100 Connecticut Ave., N.W. Suite 1120, Washington, DC 20036
Telephone: (202) 331-1634
Registered as lobbyist at U.S. Congress.

LIEBERMAN, Edward H.
Cole, Corette & Abrutyn
1110 Vermont Ave., N.W., Suite 900, Washington, DC 20005
Telephone: (202) 872-1414
Registered as Foreign Agent: (#2968).
Background: Tax Law Specialist, 1977-80, Reviewer, 1980-81, Internal Revenue Service.
Clients:
Louisiana Land and Exploration Co.

LIEBERMAN, Janet
Legislative Director, United States Student Ass'n
1012 14th St., N.W., Suite 207, Washington, DC 20005
Telephone: (202) 347-8772
Registered as lobbyist at U.S. Congress.

LIEBERMAN, Michael
Washington Counsel/Associate Director, Anti-Defamation League of B'nai B'rith
1100 Connecticut Ave., N.W., Washington, DC 20036
Telephone: (202) 452-8320

LIEBMAN, Diane S.
V. Pres., Legislative & Media Relations, CSX Corp.
1331 Pennsylvania Ave., N.W., Suite 560, Washington, DC 20004
Telephone: (202) 783-8124
Registered as lobbyist at U.S. Congress.

LIEBMAN, Ronald S.
Patton, Boggs and Blow
2550 M St., N.W., Suite 800, Washington, DC 20037
Telephone: (202) 457-6000
Registered as lobbyist at U.S. Congress.
Registered as Foreign Agent: (#2165).
Background: Assistant U.S. Attorney, District of Maryland, 1972-78.
Clients:
Cryolife Inc.

LIEBSCHUTZ, David S.
Manager, External Affairs, Public Securities Ass'n
1000 Vermont Ave., N.W., Suite 800, Washington, DC 20005
Telephone: (202) 898-9390
Background: Public Affairs Officer for the Bureau of Debt, U.S. Treasury Dept., 1986-89.

LIEDERMAN, David S.
Exec. Director, Child Welfare League of America
440 First St., N.W., Suite 310, Washington, DC 20001
Telephone: (202) 638-2952

LIEG, Robert
V. Pres., Admin. & Contracts, Atlantic Research Corp.
5390 Cherokee Ave., Alexandria, VA 22312-2302
Telephone: (703) 642-4000

LIENESCH, William C.
Director, Federal Activities, Nat'l Parks and Conservation Ass'n
1015 31st St., N.W., Washington, DC 20007
Telephone: (202) 944-8530
Registered as lobbyist at U.S. Congress.

LIERMAN, Terry
President, Capitol Associates, Inc.
426 C St., N.E., Washington, DC 20002
Telephone: (202) 544-1880
Registered as lobbyist at U.S. Congress.
Background: Former Chief Clerk at Senate Appropriations for Sen. Warren G. Magnuson (D-WA).
Clients:

American Soc. of Nephrology
Citizens for the Treatment of High Blood Pressure
Cystic Fibrosis Foundation
Endocrine Soc.
FDA Council
Hutchinson Cancer Center
Joint Council on Allergy and Immunology
Nat'l Cancer Research Coalition
Nat'l Center for Health Education
Nat'l Coalition for Cancer Research
Nat'l Multiple Sclerosis Soc.
TDS Healthcare Systems Corp.
Wistar Institute, The

LIESEMER, Ronald N., Ph.D.
V. President, Technology, Council for Solid Waste Solutions
1275 K St., N.W. Suite 400, Washington, DC 20005
Telephone: (202) 371-5319

LIGGETT, Martha
Asst. Exec. Dir., Government Affairs, American Ass'n of Dental Schools
1625 Massachusetts Ave., N.W., Washington, DC 20036
Telephone: (202) 667-9433

LIGGITT, Richard K.
Deputy Director, Bank Capital Markets Ass'n
Nat'l Press Building Second Floor, Washington, DC 20045
Telephone: (202) 347-5510
Registered as lobbyist at U.S. Congress.
Background: Also serves as Treasurer for the Ass'ns Political Action Committee.

LIGHTFOOT, Susan A.
Government Relations Representative, American College of Obstetricians and Gynecologists
409 12th St., S.W., Washington, DC 20024
Telephone: (202) 638-5577

LIGHTHIZER, Robert E.
Skadden, Arps, Slate, Meagher and Flom
1440 New York Ave., N.W., Washington, DC 20005
Telephone: (202) 371-7000
Registered as lobbyist at U.S. Congress.
Background: Chief Minority Counsel, Senate Committee on Finance, 1978-81. Chief Counsel and Staff Director, Senate Committee on Finance, 1981-83. Deputy United States Trade Representative, Ambassador, 1983-85.
Clients:
Akzo America, Inc.
Anheuser-Busch Cos., Inc.
Bethlehem Steel Corp.
General Development Corp.
General Mills
Hoylake Investments Ltd.
Merrill Lynch and Co., Inc.
Mesa Limited Partnership
Questar Corp.
Sara Lee Corp.

LIKES, Peter
Chairman, Alliance for Responsible CFC Policy
2011 Eye St., N.W. Suite 500, Washington, DC 20006
Telephone: (202) 429-1614

LILLEY, William, III
President, Policy Communications Inc.
1615 L St., N.W., Suite 650, Washington, DC 20036
Telephone: (202) 659-1023
Background: Dep. Ass't Sec'y, Housing and Urban Development, 1973-75. Director, Council on Wage and Price Stability, 1975-77. Minority Staff Director, House Budget Committee, 1977-78.

LILLIE, Rev. John
Assistant Director, Lutheran Office for Governmental Affairs/Evangelical Lutheran Church in America
122 C St. N.W. Suite 300, Washington, DC 20001
Telephone: (202) 783-7508

LILLQUIST, Richard A., CAE
President, Nat'l Center for Ass'n Resources
1511 K St., N.W. Suite 715, Washington, DC 20005
Telephone: (202) 628-7144

LILLYWHITE, Jack W.
Manager, Federal Programs, Bechtel Group, Inc.
1620 Eye St., N.W., Suite 703, Washington, DC 20006
Telephone: (202) 393-4747

LILYGREN, Sara
Director of Public Relations, American Meat Institute
Box 3556, Washington, DC 20007
Telephone: (703) 841-2400

LIMBACH, Bonnie
External Communications Manager, Soc. of the Plastics Industry
1275 K St., N.W., Suite 400, Washington, DC 20005
Telephone: (202) 371-5200

LINCK, Peter G.
Exec. Director, Nat'l Alliance for Animal Legislation
P.O. Box 75116, Washington, DC 20013-5116
Telephone: (703) 684-0654
Registered as lobbyist at U.S. Congress.

LINCOLN, Peter M.
Director-Corporate Communications, Ameritech (American Information Technologies)
1050 Connecticut Ave., N.W., Suite 730, Washington, DC 20036
Telephone: (202) 955-3050
Background: Former press aide to Sen. Dan Quayle (R-IN).

LIND, Michael
Visiting Fellow, Heritage Foundation
214 Massachusetts Ave., N.E., Washington, DC 20002
Telephone: (202) 546-4400

LINDAUR, Martha
Director, Communications, Associated Landscape Contractors of America
405 North Washington St. Suite 104, Falls Church, VA 22046
Telephone: (703) 241-4004

LINDBERG, Roger
V. President, Government Relations, Hill and Knowlton Public Affairs Worldwide
Washington Harbour, 901 31st St., N.W., Washington, DC 20007
Telephone: (202) 333-7400
Registered as lobbyist at U.S. Congress.
Background: Former Administrative Assistant to Rep. Robert T. Matsui (D-CA).
Clients:
Johnson Controls, Inc.
Nintendo
Shaklee Corp.

LINDEN, Nancy
Legislative Representative, Nat'l Marine Manufacturers Ass'n
1000 Thomas Jefferson St, N.W. Suite 525, Washington, DC 20007
Telephone: (202) 338-6662

LINDENHEIM, Victor E.
V. President, Regulatory Affairs, American Wood Preservers Institute
1945 Old Gallows Road Suite 550, Vienna, VA 22182
Telephone: (703) 893-4005
Registered as lobbyist at U.S. Congress.

LINDON, Timothy
President, Washington Council of Lawyers
1200 New Hampshire Ave., N.W. Suite 700, Washington, DC 20036
Telephone: (202) 659-5964

LINDREW, Jerry
Asst Dir of Policy & Legis Analysis, DEPARTMENT OF LABOR - Pension and Welfare Benefits Administration
200 Constitution Ave., N.W., Washington, DC 20210
Telephone: (202) 523-7933

LINDSAY, HART, NEIL & WEIGLER
1225 19th St., N.W. Suite 200, Washington, DC 20036
Telephone: (202) 393-4460
Members of firm representing listed organizations:
Friedmann, Peter

Background: Legislative Counsel, Senator Bob Packwood, 1979. Chief Counsel, Subcommittee on Merchant Marine, Committee on Commerce, Science and Transportation, Senate, 1980-85.
Clients:
Agriculture Ocean Transportation Coalition *(Peter Friedmann)*
Avia Footwear, Inc. *(Peter Friedmann)*
Crowley Maritime Corp. *(Peter Friedmann)*
Oregon Economic Development Dept., Ports Division *(Peter Friedmann)*
Pacific Coast Council of Freight Forwarders *(Peter Friedmann)*
Portland, Oregon, Port of *(Peter Friedmann)*
Redwood City, California, Port of *(Peter Friedmann)*
Reebok Internat'l Ltd. *(Peter Friedmann)*

LINDSEY, Dawn
Associate Director, Internal Relations, Nat'l Ass'n of Life Underwriters
1922 F St., N.W., Washington, DC 20006
Telephone: (202) 331-6000

LINDSEY, Donald
V. Pres. and Nat'l Legislative Rep., Brotherhood of Locomotive Engineers
400 First St., N.W., Suite 819, Washington, DC 20001
Telephone: (202) 347-7936
Registered as lobbyist at U.S. Congress.

LINDSLEY, Thomas A.
V. President, Congressional Affairs, Nat'l Alliance of Business
1201 New York Ave., N.W., Suite 700, Washington, DC 20005
Telephone: (202) 289-2888

LINEHAN, Kathleen M.
Senior Director, Washington Relations, Philip Morris Management Corp.
1341 G St., N.W., Suite 900, Washington, DC 20005
Telephone: (202) 637-1500
Registered as lobbyist at U.S. Congress.

LINER, David
Bur for Latin America & the Caribbean, AGENCY FOR INTERNAT'L DEVELOPMENT
320 21st St., N.W., Washington, DC 20523
Telephone: (202) 647-8190

LINER, E. Blaine
Director, State Policy Center, Urban Institute, The
2100 M St., N.W., Washington, DC 20037
Telephone: (202) 833-7200

LINETT, Howard
Staff Counsel, Nat'l Postal Mail Handlers Union
One Thomas Circle, N.W. Suite 525, Washington, DC 20005
Telephone: (202) 833-9095

LINFIELD, Jon
Government'l Services Liaison Officer, Housing Assistance Council
1025 Vermont Ave., N.W. Suite 606, Washington, DC 20005
Telephone: (202) 842-8600

LINKOUS, Jonathan D.
Exec. Director, Nat'l Ass'n of Area Agencies on Aging
600 Maryland Ave., S.W. Suite 208 West Wing, Washington, DC 20024
Telephone: (202) 484-7520

LINOWITZ, Sol M.
Coudert Brothers
1627 Eye St., N.W. 12th Floor, Washington, DC 20006
Telephone: (202) 775-5100
Background: U.S. Ambassador to the Organization of American States, 1966-69. Co-negotiator of the Panama Canal Treaty, 1977. Member of the Board of Directors, Pan American World Airways.

LINTNER, Rev. Jay
Director, United Church of Christ Office for Church in Society
110 Maryland Ave., N.E. Suite 504, Washington, DC 20002
Telephone: (202) 543-1517

LINTON, MIELDS, REISLER AND COTTONE
1225 Eye St., N.W., Suite 300, Washington, DC 20005
Telephone: (202) 682-3901
Background: Intergovernmental relations and legislative affairs consultants.
Members of firm representing listed organizations:
Birmingham, Mary E.
Cottone, Mello
Linton, Ron M.
  Background: Executive Director, Nat'l Ass'n of Flood and Stormwater Management Agencies, Instrumentation Testing Service, Inc.
Masri, Bashar
McCarty, Kevin
Mields, Hugh
  Background: Washington Representative, City of Norfolk, VA.
Price, Charles F.
Reisler, Irwin
Clients:
Council of Industrial Development Bond Issuers
  (Kevin McCarty)
Instrumentation Testing Ass'n *(Bashar Masri)*
Linton, Mields Reisler and Cottone Political Action Committee *(Mello Cottone)*
Nat'l Ass'n of Activity Professionals *(Mary E. Birmingham, Charles F. Price)*
Nat'l Ass'n of Flood and Stormwater Management Agencies *(Kevin McCarty)*
Nat'l Water Alliance *(Ron M. Linton)*

LINTON, Otha W.
Associate Exec. Director, American College of Radiology
1891 Preston White Drive, Reston, VA 22091
Telephone: (703) 648-8900
Background: Also represents the American Soc. of Therapeutic Radiologists and the Ass'n of University Radiologists.

LINTON, Ron M.
Linton, Mields, Reisler and Cottone
1225 Eye St., N.W., Suite 300, Washington, DC 20005
Telephone: (202) 682-3901
Registered as lobbyist at U.S. Congress.
Background: Executive Director, Nat'l Ass'n of Flood and Stormwater Management Agencies, Instrumentation Testing Service, Inc.
Clients:
Nat'l Water Alliance

LIPMAN, Deborah Swartz
Director, Government Relations, Washington Metropolitan Area Transit Authority
600 5th St., N.W., Washington, DC 20001
Telephone: (202) 962-1003

LIPSCOMB, Bently
Deputy Director, Operations, Nat'l Ass'n of Partners in Education
601 Wythe St., Suite 200, Alexandria, VA 22314
Telephone: (703) 836-4880

LIPSCOMB, Gregory Owen
National Coordinator, OPT IN AMERICA
1020 19th St., N.W. Suite 500, Washington, DC 20036
Telephone: (202) 659-5212
Registered as lobbyist at U.S. Congress.

LIPSCOMB, Sharron
Asst, Cong Rels, Legis & Cong Rels, DEPARTMENT OF HOUSING AND URBAN DEVELOPMENT
451 Seventh St., S.W., Washington, DC 20410
Telephone: (202) 755-7380

LIPSEN, Janice C.
President, Counselors For Management, Inc.
1000 16th St., N.W., Suite 603, Washington, DC 20006
Telephone: (202) 785-0550
Registered as lobbyist at U.S. Congress.
Registered as Foreign Agent: (#3431).
Background: Serves as Director, Washington Office of the Governor, State of Hawaii and as Deputy Exec. Director, Aluminum Recycling Ass'n and Independent Zinc Alloyers Ass'n. Was an assistant to House Speaker Carl Albert, 1970-75.
Clients:
Hawaii, Washington Office of
Independent Zinc Alloyers Ass'n, Inc.

LIPSEN, Linda A.
Legislative/Regulatory Counsel, Consumers Union of the United States
2001 S St., N.W., Suite 520, Washington, DC 20009
Telephone: (202) 462-6262
Registered as lobbyist at U.S. Congress.

LIPSEN WHITTEN & DIAMOND
1725 DeSales St., N.W., Suite 800, Washington, DC 20036
Telephone: (202) 659-6540
Members of firm representing listed organizations:
Carney, William, Government Affairs Consultant
  Background: Former U.S. Representative (R-NY), 1978-86. Former Member, House Merchant Marine and Fisheries Committee; House Armed Services Committee; House Science and Technology Committee.
Cornell, William A. (Jr.)
  Background: Administrative Assistant to Congressman Bill Goodling, 1976-79; Executive Assistant to U.S. Senator John Heinz, 1980-82.
Cotter, Francis P., Advisor
  Background: Staff Joint Congressional Committee on Atomic Energy, 1952-54.
Crawford, Richard L., Director, Government Affairs
  Background: Administrative Assistant/Legislative Director to Rep. Bill Boner (D-TN), 1979-82. Associate Staff, House Committee on Apprpriations, 1982-85.
Diamond, Robert M.
  Background: Administrative Assistant and Tax Counsel to U.S. Representatives Ray Lederer, 1977-80, and Don Bailey, 1980-82. House Liaison, Mondale for President, 1984. Counsel, Democratic Party Platform Drafting Committee, 1988.
Fulton, William J.
Gerstel, Deborah
  Background: Served with the Congressional Research Service, 1988.
Lipsen, Zel E.
  Background: Staff Assistant to U.S. Senator Clair Engle, 1959-63. Member, Select Committee on Government Research, U.S. House of Representatives, 1963. Legal Assistant, House Select Committee on Government Research, 1964-65. Held several positions with Democratic National Committee.
Mellon, Regina M., Government Affairs Representative
Simpson, Charles W., Sr. Director, Government Affairs
  Background: Former Adm. Assistant to Senator Lloyd Bentsen (1984-87), and Charles Wilson (1973-84).
Singley, Elizabeth, Govt'l Affairs Specialist
  Background: Ass't for Legislative Affairs, The White House, 1981-84; Administrative Officer, National Commission on Air Quality, 1979-81.
Whitten, Jamie L.
  Background: Trial Attorney, Office of U.S. Attorney, Miami, 1966-70. Trial Attorney, U.S. Department of Justice, 1970-73.
Clients:
Amarillo/Pantex
Americans for the Supercollider
ANR Pipeline, Inc.
Century Internat'l
Colebrand Ltd.
Dallas County Utility and Reclamation District
Engineers and Architects Ass'n
ENSERCH Corp.
Federal Record Service Corp.
Fleisher-Smythe Co.
John Gray Institute
McKesson Corp.
Nat'l Rural Letter Carriers' Ass'n
Olivetti, USA
OMI Corp.
Pennsylvania Ass'n of Nurse Anesthetists
Perot Group, The
Perot Systems Inc.
Pioneer Hi-Bred Seed Internat'l
RJR Nabisco Washington, Inc.
Rolls-Royce, Inc.
United Kingdom, Ministry of Defence of the
Vickers Shipbuilding and Engineering, Ltd.
Westinghouse Electric Corp.

LIPSEN, Zel E.
Lipsen Whitten & Diamond
1725 DeSales St., N.W., Suite 800, Washington, DC 20036
Telephone: (202) 659-6540
Registered as lobbyist at U.S. Congress.
Registered as Foreign Agent: (#3586).
Background: Staff Assistant to U.S. Senator Clair Engle, 1959-63. Member, Select Committee on Government Research, U.S. House of Representatives, 1963. Legal Assistant, House Select Committee on Government Research, 1964-65. Held several positions with Democratic National Committee.

LIPSKY, Abbott B., Jr.
King and Spalding
1730 Pennsylvania Ave., N.W. Suite 1200, Washington, DC 20006-4706
Telephone: (202) 737-0500
Background: Deputy Assistant Attorney General, Antitrust Division, U.S. Department of Justice, 1981-83. Special Assistant to the Chairman, Council on Wage and Price Stability, 1981.
Clients:
West Point Pepperell

LIPSON, Debra J.
Assistant Dir., Program & Policy, Children's Defense Fund
122 C St., N.W., Washington, DC 20001
Telephone: (202) 628-8787
Registered as lobbyist at U.S. Congress.

LIPSTEIN, Robert A.
Coudert Brothers
1627 Eye St., N.W. 12th Floor, Washington, DC 20006
Telephone: (202) 775-5100
Clients:
Bundesvereinigung der Deutschen Ernahrangsindustrie
Centrale Marketinggesellschaft der Deutschen Agrarwirtschaft
L'Air Liquide

LISACK, John, Jr.
Exec. V. President, Nat'l Ass'n of Personnel Consultants
3133 Mt. Vernon Ave., Alexandria, VA 22305
Telephone: (703) 684-0180

LISANSKY, Judith
Director, Programs, American Anthropological Ass'n
1703 New Hampshire Ave., N.W., Washington, DC 20009
Telephone: (202) 232-8800

LISBOA ASSOCIATES, INC.
1317 F St., N.W., Suite 202, Washington, DC 20004
Telephone: (202) 737-2622
Members of firm representing listed organizations:
Lisboa-Farrow, Elizabeth, President
Michaels, Eileen F.
O'Keefe, Eileen
  Background: Associate, Lisboa Associates, Inc.
Clients:
Virgin Islands, University of the *(Elizabeth Lisboa-Farrow, Eileen F. Michaels, Eileen O'Keefe)*

LISBOA-FARROW, Elizabeth
President, Lisboa Associates, Inc.
1317 F St., N.W., Suite 202, Washington, DC 20004
Telephone: (202) 737-2622
Registered as lobbyist at U.S. Congress.

LISCHER, James F.
Asst Gen Counsel, Legislation, DEPARTMENT OF HOUSING AND URBAN DEVELOPMENT
451 Seventh St., S.W., Washington, DC 20410
Telephone: (202) 755-7093

LISMEZ, Daniel
Legislative Representative, Nat'l Rural Electric Cooperative Ass'n
1800 Massachusetts Ave., N.W., Washington, DC 20036
Telephone: (202) 857-9500
Registered as lobbyist at U.S. Congress.

LITAN, Robert E.
Dir., Ctr. For Econ. Progress & Employ., Brookings Institution
1775 Massachusetts Ave., N.W., Washington, DC 20036
Telephone: (202) 797-6000

Background: Staff Member, Council of Economic Advisers (1977-79).

LITCH, Scott
Legislative Counsel, American Ass'n of Dental Schools
1625 Massachusetts Ave., N.W., Washington, DC 20036
Telephone: (202) 667-9433

LITJEN, Tom
Associate Director, Illinois, State of
444 N. Capitol St., N.W. Suite 210, Washington, DC 20001
Telephone: (202) 624-7760

LITMAN, Irwin
Exec. Dir., Legislative Tax Matters, NYNEX
1828 L St., N.W., Suite 1000, Washington, DC 20036
Telephone: (202) 416-0100

LITTELL, Barbara
Assoc. Dir., Ctr. for Public Pol. Educ., Brookings Institution
1775 Massachusetts Ave., N.W., Washington, DC 20036
Telephone: (202) 797-6000

LITTLE, Barbara A.
Sr. Government Relations Representative, Ethyl Corp.
1155 15th St., N.W., Suite 611, Washington, DC 20005
Telephone: (202) 223-4411
Registered as lobbyist at U.S. Congress.

LITTLE, Charles B.
Exec. Assistant, UBA, Inc.
Suite 603, 600 Maryland Ave., S.W., Washington, DC 20024
Telephone: (202) 484-3344
Registered as lobbyist at U.S. Congress.

LITTLE, INC., Arthur D.
500 E St., S.W. Suite 940, Washington, DC 20024
Telephone: (202) 488-5850
Registered as Foreign Agent: (#3804)
Background: The Washington office of an industrial research and management consulting firm based in Boston.
Organizations represented:
Thailand, Board of Investment of the Government of

LITTLE, Jeanne Marie
Government Affairs Representative, Nat'l Tooling and Machining Ass'n
9300 Livingston Rd., Fort Washington, MD 20744
Telephone: (301) 248-6200

LITTLE, William F.
Legislative Assoc., Washington Affrs., Ford Motor Co.
1350 Eye St., N.W. Suite 1000, Washington, DC 20005
Telephone: (202) 962-5400
Registered as lobbyist at U.S. Congress.

LITTLEFIELD, Amy
Director, Government Affairs, Service Station Dealers of America
499 S. Capitol St., S.E. Suite 407, Washington, DC 20003
Telephone: (202) 479-0196

LITTLEFIELD, Robert G.
Manager, Government Sales, Ingersoll-Rand Co.
1627 K St., N.W., Suite 900, Washington, DC 20006
Telephone: (202) 955-1450

LITTLEFIELD, Roy E.
Exec. Director, Greater Washington/Maryland Service Station and Automotive Repair Ass'n
9420 Annapolis Road, Suite 307, Lanham, MD 20706
Telephone: (301) 577-2875
Registered as lobbyist at U.S. Congress.

LITTLEHALE, E. Geoffrey
V. President, Government Relations, Glaxo, Inc.
1500 K St., N.W., Suite 650, Washington, DC 20005
Telephone: (202) 783-1277
Registered as lobbyist at U.S. Congress.

LITZ, Joyce
CarePac Coordinator, CarePAC, The Blue Cross and Blue Shield Ass'n Political Action Committee
655 15th St., N.W. Suite 350, Washington, DC 20005
Telephone: (202) 626-4780

LIVAUDAIS, E. F., Jr.
Manager, Federal Government Relations, ARCO
1333 New Hampshire Ave., N.W., Suite 1001, Washington, DC 20036
Telephone: (202) 457-6242
Registered as lobbyist at U.S. Congress.

LIVELY, Carol A.
Smith, Bucklin and Associates
1101 Connecticut Ave., N.W., Suite 700, Washington, DC 20036
Telephone: (202) 857-1100
Background: V. President, Smith, Bucklin and Associates. Serves as Exec. Director, Nat'l Ass'n of Hospital Admitting Managers; Exec. Director, Forum for Health Care Planning; and Exec. Director, American College of Nuclear Physicians.
Clients:
American College of Nuclear Physicians
Forum for Health Care Planning
Nat'l Ass'n of Hospital Admitting Managers

LIVELY, Robert W.
Legislative Representative, Nat'l Rural Electric Cooperative Ass'n
1800 Massachusetts Ave., N.W., Washington, DC 20036
Telephone: (202) 857-9633
Registered as lobbyist at U.S. Congress.

LIVINGSTON, S. William, Jr.
Covington and Burling
1201 Pennsylvania Ave., N.W., Box 7566, Washington, DC 20044
Telephone: (202) 662-6000

LIVINGSTON, Scott D.
Morrison & Foerster
2000 Pennsylvania Ave., N.W., Suite 5500, Washington, DC 20006
Telephone: (202) 887-1500
Clients:
Coca-Cola Co.

LLOYD AND ASSOCIATES, INC.
932 Hungerford Drive, Suite 36, Rockville, MD 20850
Telephone: (301) 738-2448
Background: An association management firm.
Members of firm representing listed organizations:
Lloyd, Raymond J.
Background: Serves as Exec. Secretary, American Chain Ass'n, Exec. Director, Scale Manufacturers Ass'n and Exec. V. President, Conveyor Equipment Manufacturers Ass'n.
Reinfried, Robert A.
Background: Serves as Exec. Director, Mechanical Power Transmission Ass'n.
Clients:
American Chain Ass'n *(Raymond J. Lloyd)*
Conveyor Equipment Manufacturers Ass'n *(Raymond J. Lloyd)*
Mechanical Power Transmission Ass'n *(Robert A. Reinfried)*
Scale Manufacturers Ass'n *(Raymond J. Lloyd)*

LLOYD, David
Director, State Affairs, Nat'l Paint and Coatings Ass'n
1500 Rhode Island Ave., N.W., Washington, DC 20005
Telephone: (202) 462-6272
Registered as lobbyist at U.S. Congress.
Background: Responsibilities include state and federal legislative affairs.

LLOYD, Raymond J.
Lloyd and Associates, Inc.
932 Hungerford Drive, Suite 36, Rockville, MD 20850
Telephone: (301) 738-2448
Background: Serves as Exec. Secretary, American Chain Ass'n, Exec. Director, Scale Manufacturers Ass'n and Exec. V. President, Conveyor Equipment Manufacturers Ass'n.
Clients:
American Chain Ass'n
Conveyor Equipment Manufacturers Ass'n
Scale Manufacturers Ass'n

LLOYD, Timothy A.
Hogan and Hartson
555 13th St., N.W., Suite 1200, Washington, DC 20004-1109

Telephone: (202) 637-5600
Registered as lobbyist at U.S. Congress.

LLOYD, Wingate
Director, International Relations, ITT Corp.
1600 M St, N.W., Washington, DC 20036
Telephone: (202) 775-7378

LOBEL, NOVINS, LAMONT AND FLUG
1275 K St., N.W., Suite 770, Washington, DC 20005
Telephone: (202) 371-6626
Members of firm representing listed organizations:
Flug, James F.
Background: Legal Assistant to the Assistant Attorney General, Tax Division, 1964-65. Confidential Assistant to the Attorney General of the U.S. 1965-67. Legislative Assistant to Sen. Edward M. Kennedy of Massachusetts, 1967-69. Chief Counsel, Subcommittee on Administrative Practice and Procedure, Senate Committee on the Judiciary, 1969-73.
Lamont, William J.
Background: Attorney, Office of Alien Property Custodian, 1942-46. Department of Justice, 1946-72.
Clients:
Consumers Union of the United States *(James F. Flug)*
Generic Pharmaceutical Industry Ass'n *(James F. Flug)*
Phone Medium *(James F. Flug)*

LOBLE, Leslie
Legislative Representative, Communications Workers of America
1925 K St., N.W., Washington, DC 20006
Telephone: (202) 728-2471
Registered as lobbyist at U.S. Congress.

LOCATELLI, Mario
President, Fiat Washington
1776 Eye St., N.W. Suite 775, Washington, DC 20006
Telephone: (202) 862-1610

LOCKARD, Susan A.
Research & Admin Dir., Legis Affrs, DEPARTMENT OF DEFENSE
The Pentagon, Washington, DC 20301
Telephone: (202) 697-6210

LOCKE, John W.
President, American Ass'n for Laboratory Accreditation
656 Quince Orchard Road, Suite 704, Gaithersburg, MD 20878
Telephone: (301) 670-1377

LOCKE, Judy
Manager, Regulatory Relations, Transco Energy Co.
555 13th St., N.W., Suite 430 West, Washington, DC 20004
Telephone: (202) 628-3060

LOCKE, W. Timothy
Hecht, Spencer & Associates
499 South Capitol St., S.W., Suite 507, Washington, DC 20003
Telephone: (202) 554-2881
Registered as lobbyist at U.S. Congress.
Background: Former White House assistant, U.S. Interior Departmen official and aide to Senator Howard Baker (R-TN).
Clients:
AIRTRAX
BATUS, Inc.
Boy Scouts of America
Brown and Williamson Tobacco Corp.
Marwais Steel Co.
Nat'l Ass'n for the Support of Long Term Care - NASL

LOCKHART, Robert F., Jr.
Government Affairs Representative, Amdahl Corp.
1667 K St., N.W., Suite 300, Washington, DC 20006
Telephone: (202) 835-2220
Registered as lobbyist at U.S. Congress.

LOCKWOOD, Charles H.
V. President and General Counsel, Automobile Importers of America
1725 Jefferson Davis Hwy., Suite 1002, Arlington, VA 22202

LOCKWOOD, Charles H. (Cont'd)
Telephone: (703) 979-5550

LOCKWOOD, James
Legal Counsel, DeLeuw, Cather and Co.
1133 15th St., N.W. Suite 800, Washington, DC 20005
Telephone: (202) 775-3300

LOCONTE, Joe
Director, Communications, Council for Inter-American Security
122 C St., N.W., Suite 710, Washington, DC 20001
Telephone: (202) 393-6622

LODGE, James E.
Exec. Dir., Communications, American Bankers Ass'n
1120 Connecticut Ave., N.W., Washington, DC 20036
Telephone: (202) 663-5000
Background: Serves also as Exec. Director, Corporation for American Banking.

LODGE, Stephen
Director, Legislative Affairs, Nat'l Confectioners Ass'n
7900 Westpark Drive Suite A-320, McLean, VA 22102
Telephone: (703) 790-5750
Registered as lobbyist at U.S. Congress.

LODICK, George
Exec. Director, Young Americans for Freedom
380 Maple Ave. West Suite 303, Vienna, VA 22180
Telephone: (703) 938-3305

LOEB, G. Hamilton
Paul, Hastings, Janofsky and Walker
1050 Connecticut Ave., N.W. Suite 1200, Washington, DC 20036-5331
Telephone: (202) 223-9000
Registered as lobbyist at U.S. Congress.
Registered as Foreign Agent: (#3763).
Clients:
Amdahl Corp.
Koito Manufacturing Co.
Telequest, Inc.
Tubos de Acero de Mexico, S.A.

LOEB, Laura
Public Policy Director, Older Women's League
730 11th St., N.W. Suite 300, Washington, DC 20001
Telephone: (202) 783-6686
Registered as lobbyist at U.S. Congress.

LOEFFLER GROUP, THE
555 13th St., N.W., Suite 300, Washington, DC 20004
Telephone: (202) 637-6850
Background: The lobbying arm of the law firm of McCamish, Brown, Martin & Loeffler.
Members of firm representing listed organizations:
Johnson, Michael S.
Background: Former Press Secretary and Chief of Staff to House Minority Leader Robert H. Michel (R-IL).
Clients:
Citicorp
SEMATECH

LOEFFLER, Tom
McCamish, Martin, Brown & Loeffler
555 13th St., N.W. Suite 300 East, Washington, DC 20004
Telephone: (202) 637-6850
Registered as lobbyist at U.S. Congress.
Background: Former Member, U.S. House of Representatives (R-TX).
Clients:
Central and South West Services, Inc.
SEMATECH

LOFTUS, C. Michael
Slover and Loftus
1224 17th St., N.W., Washington, DC 20036
Telephone: (202) 347-7170
Registered as lobbyist at U.S. Congress.
Clients:
Western Coal Traffic League

LOFTUS, Jerome
General Counsel, Recreation Vehicle Industry Ass'n
1896 Preston White Drive P.O. Box 2999, Reston, VA 22090
Telephone: (703) 620-6003

LOFTUS, Robert
Public and Cong Affrs, NAT'L CREDIT UNION ADMINISTRATION
1776 G St., N.W., Washington, DC 20456
Telephone: (202) 682-9650

LOFTUS, William E.
President, American Short Line Railroad Ass'n
2000 Massachusetts Ave., N.W., Washington, DC 20036
Telephone: (202) 785-2250
Registered as lobbyist at U.S. Congress.

LOGAN, Mark
Collier, Shannon & Scott
1055 Thomas Jefferson St., N.W., Suite 300, Washington, DC 20007
Telephone: (202) 342-8400
Registered as lobbyist at U.S. Congress.
Background: Former Counsel to the Senate Budget Committee. Specializes in legislative and environmental issues.

LOHNES, Robin C.
Exec. Director, American Horse Protection Ass'n
1000 29th St., N.W., Suite T-100, Washington, DC 20007
Telephone: (202) 965-0500

LOICHLE, Janice
Treasurer, Allnet Communications Services Inc. Good Government Fund
1990 M St., N.W., Suite 500, Washington, DC 20036
Telephone: (202) 293-0593

LONDON ASSOC., INC., Paul A.
1250 Connecticut Ave., N.W., Suite 800, Washington, DC 20036
Telephone: (202) 637-9126
Registered as Foreign Agent: (#3935).
Members of firm representing listed organizations:
London, Paul A.
Organizations represented:
Hydro-Quebec (Paul A. London)
Japan Soc. of Industrial Machinery Manufacturers (Paul A. London)

LONDON, Paul A.
London Assoc., Inc., Paul A.
1250 Connecticut Ave., N.W., Suite 800, Washington, DC 20036
Telephone: (202) 637-9126
Registered as Foreign Agent: (#3935).
Organizations represented:
Hydro-Quebec
Japan Soc. of Industrial Machinery Manufacturers

LONDON AND SATAGAJ, ATTORNEYS-AT-LAW
1025 Vermont Ave., N.W. Suite 1201, Washington, DC 20005
Telephone: (202) 639-8888
Members of firm representing listed organizations:
London, Sheldon I.
Satagaj, John S.
Background: Also serves as President of the Small Business Legislative Council.
Clients:
American Floorcovering Ass'n (Sheldon I. London, John S. Satagaj)
American Hardware Manufacturers Ass'n (Sheldon I. London, John S. Satagaj)
American Supply and Machinery Manufacturers' Ass'n (Sheldon I. London, John S. Satagaj)
Hand Tools Institute (Sheldon I. London, John S. Satagaj)
Jewelers of America (Sheldon I. London, John S. Satagaj)
Nat'l Ass'n of Exposition Managers (Sheldon I. London, John S. Satagaj)
Nat'l Home Furnishings Ass'n (Sheldon I. London, John S. Satagaj)
Photo Marketing Ass'n-Internat'l (Sheldon I. London, John S. Satagaj)
Small Business Legislative Council (John S. Satagaj)
Wood Machinery Manufacturers of America (Sheldon I. London, John S. Satagaj)

LONDON, Sheldon I.
London and Satagaj, Attorneys-at-Law
1025 Vermont Ave., N.W. Suite 1201, Washington, DC 20005
Telephone: (202) 639-8888

Registered as lobbyist at U.S. Congress.
Clients:
American Floorcovering Ass'n
American Hardware Manufacturers Ass'n
American Supply and Machinery Manufacturers' Ass'n
Hand Tools Institute
Jewelers of America
Nat'l Ass'n of Exposition Managers
Nat'l Home Furnishings Ass'n
Photo Marketing Ass'n-Internat'l
Wood Machinery Manufacturers of America

LONDONER, Laurie E.
Ass't V.P./ Dir., Gov't & Industry Affrs, Alexander & Alexander Inc.
555 13th St., N.W. Suite 1180E, Washington, DC 20004-1109
Telephone: (202) 783-2550

LONERGAN, Vincent P.
Director, State Relations, Smokeless Tobacco Council
2550 M St., N.W., Suite 300, Washington, DC 20037
Telephone: (202) 452-1252

LONG, Bernard J., Jr.
Dow, Lohnes and Albertson
1255 23rd St., N.W., Suite 500, Washington, DC 20037
Telephone: (202) 857-2500
Clients:
Advance Publications, Inc.
First Nat'l Bank of Chicago
Lazard Freres
Morgan Stanley and Co.

LONG, C. Thomas
Jones, Day, Reavis and Pogue
1450 G St., N.W., Suite 700, Washington, DC 20005-2088
Telephone: (202) 879-3939
Registered as lobbyist at U.S. Congress.
Registered as Foreign Agent: (#3427).
Background: Deputy General Counsel, Federal Home Loan Bank Board, 1984-85.
Clients:
AmeriTrust Co. N.A.
Heron Internat'l, Ltd.
USAA Federal Savings Bank

LONG, Carole
Public Affairs Director, Armenian Assembly of America
122 C St., N.W., Suite 350, Washington, DC 20001
Telephone: (202) 393-3434

LONG, Charles E.
Exec. V. President and Secretary, Citicorp
1275 Pennsylvania Ave., N.W., Suite 503, Washington, DC 20004
Telephone: (202) 879-6868

LONG, Cheryl
V. President, Corporate Development, Institute for Research on the Economics of Taxation (IRET)
1331 Pennsylvania Ave., N.W. Suite 515, Washington, DC 20004
Telephone: (202) 347-9570

LONG, John J.
Director, Legislative Task Force, Republican Nat'l Committee
310 First St., S.E., Washington, DC 20003
Telephone: (202) 863-8500

LONG, Linda
Associate, Montgomery, McCracken, Walker & Rhoads
1156 15th St., N.W. Suite 550, Washington, DC 20005
Telephone: (202) 828-6901
Registered as lobbyist at U.S. Congress.
Clients:
Carpenter Labs
Nat'l Ass'n of Private Schools for Exceptional Children
Nat'l Check Cashers Coalition

LONG, P. Richard
External Liaison Representative, American Petroleum Institute
1220 L St., N.W., Washington, DC 20005
Telephone: (202) 682-8283

LONG, Richard
Government Relations Specialist, Nat'l Council of Teachers of Mathematics
444 North Capitol St., N.W., Suite 321, Washington, DC 20001
Telephone: (202) 347-3992

LONG, Robert
Director, Congressional Affairs, Nat'l Coal Ass'n
1130 17th St., N.W., Washington, DC 20036
Telephone: (202) 463-2663
Registered as lobbyist at U.S. Congress.

LONGBERRY, Joan
Chairman, ASMT-PAC, American Soc. for Medical Technology Political Action Committee
2021 L St., N.W., Washington, DC 20036
Telephone: (202) 785-3311

LONGORIA, Jose
Exec. Director, League of United Latin American Citizens
777 N. Capitol St., N.E. Suite 305, Washington, DC 20002
Telephone: (202) 408-0060

LONGSTRETH, John L.
Preston Gates Ellis & Rouvelas Meeds
1735 New York Ave., N.W., Suite 500, Washington, DC 20006-4759
Telephone: (202) 628-1700
Registered as lobbyist at U.S. Congress.
Background: Clerk for U.S. District Court for the Eastern District of Pennsylvania.
Clients:
Data General Corp.

LONGSTRETH, Thomas
Assoc. Dir., Strategic Weapons Policy, Federation of American Scientists
307 Massachusetts Ave., N.E., Washington, DC 20002
Telephone: (202) 546-3300
Background: Former Military Legislative Assistant to Sen. Edward Kennedy (D-MA).

LONGSWORTH, Nellie
President, Preservation Action
1350 Connecticut Ave., N.W. Suite 401, Washington, DC 20036
Telephone: (202) 659-0915
Registered as lobbyist at U.S. Congress.

LONINGTON, INC.
218 N. Lee St., Alexandria, VA 22314
Telephone: (703) 548-6647
Background: A Washington representation and consultancy firm.
Members of firm representing listed organizations:
Gray, Alan G., President
Clients:
AB Electronics Group Ltd. *(Alan G. Gray)*
Trackpower Transmissions, Ltd. *(Alan G. Gray)*

LOOMIS, OWEN, FELLMAN AND HOWE
2020 K St., N.W. Suite 800, Washington, DC 20006
Telephone: (202) 296-5680
Members of firm representing listed organizations:
Anderson, James E.
Background: Assistant United States Attorney for the District of Maryland, 1970-76. Serves as General Counsel to the Greater Washington Soc. of Assocation Executives.
Fellman, Steven John
Background: Federal Trade Commission 1962-64.
Howe, William H.
Background: Secretary and General Counsel, Association of Bituminous Contractors.
Owen, Stephen F. (Jr.)
Background: Attorney, Division of Corporate Finance, Securities Exchange Commission, 1962-64. Serves as General Counsel, Classroom Publishers Ass'n.
Clients:
American Ass'n of State Highway and Transportation Officials *(James E. Anderson)*
Ass'n of Bituminous Contractors *(William H. Howe)*
Classroom Publishers Ass'n *(Stephen F. Owen, Jr.)*
First Co.
Greater Washington Soc. of Ass'n Executives *(James E. Anderson)*
Hotel Sales and Marketing Ass'n Internat'l *(James E. Anderson)*

Industrial Diamond Ass'n of America *(James E. Anderson)*
Internat'l Business Forms Industries *(James E. Anderson)*
Nat'l Ass'n of Theatre Owners *(Steven John Fellman)*
Nat'l Erectors Ass'n *(Steven John Fellman)*
Optical Manufacturers Ass'n *(James E. Anderson)*
Textile Rental Services Ass'n of America *(Steven John Fellman)*
Washington Ass'n Research Foundation *(James E. Anderson)*
Wire Reinforcement Institute *(James E. Anderson)*

LOOMIS, Susan J.
Exec. Director, Congressional Relations, Associated General Contractors of America
1957 E St., N.W., Washington, DC 20006
Telephone: (202) 393-2040
Registered as lobbyist at U.S. Congress.
Background: Also responsible for the Associated General Contractors Political Action Committee.

LOOMIS, Wilhelmina T.
Exec. Director, Nat'l Ass'n of Decorative Architectural Finishes
112 North Alfred St., Alexandria, VA 22314
Telephone: (703) 836-6504
Background: Also serves as Exec. Director, Tile Contractors Ass'n of America.

LOON, Jenifer
Washington Representative, Associated Builders and Contractors
729 15th St., N.W., Washington, DC 20005
Telephone: (202) 637-8800
Registered as lobbyist at U.S. Congress.

LOOPER, Ann
Ass't Dir., Gov't Afrs./Federal Liaison, American Institute of Architects, The
1735 New York Ave., N.W., Washington, DC 20006
Telephone: (202) 626-7300
Registered as lobbyist at U.S. Congress.

LOOPER, Lisa
Associate Exec. V. President, American Medical Peer Review Ass'n
810 First St., N.E., Suite 410, Washington, DC 20002
Telephone: (202) 371-5610

LOOS, Dickson R.
Holland and Knight
888 17th St., N.W. Suite 900, Washington, DC 20006
Telephone: (202) 955-5550
Registered as Foreign Agent: (#3718).
Clients:
United Fresh Fruit and Vegetable Ass'n

LOPER, Lt. Col. William B.
Exec Officer, Legis Liaison (Act), DEPARTMENT OF ARMY
The Pentagon, Washington, DC 20310-0101
Telephone: (202) 697-6767

LOPEZ, Dr. Gonzalo
Washington Director, InterAmerican College of Physicians and Surgeons
1101 15th St., N.W. Suite 602, Washington, DC 20005
Telephone: (202) 467-4756

LOPEZ, Sherri
Administrator, Internat'l Life Sciences Institute
1126 16th St., N.W. Suite 300, Washington, DC 20036
Telephone: (202) 659-0074
Background: Also serves as Administrator of the Internat'l Life Sciences Institute Nutrition Foundation.

LOPEZ, Virginia C.
Exec Director, Aerospace Research Center, Aerospace Industries Ass'n of America
1250 Eye St., N.W., Suite 1100, Washington, DC 20005
Telephone: (202) 371-8400
Registered as lobbyist at U.S. Congress.

LOPINA, Brian
Director of Government Relations, Citizens for a Sound Economy
470 L'Enfant Plaza East, S.W. Suite 7112, Washington, DC 20024

Telephone: (202) 488-8200
Registered as lobbyist at U.S. Congress.

LORANGER, Tom
Laxalt Group, The Paul
1455 Pennsylvania Ave., N.W., Suite 975, Washington, DC 20004
Telephone: (202) 624-0640

LORBER, Lawrence Z.
Kelley, Drye and Warren
2300 M St., N.W., Washington, DC 20037
Telephone: (202) 463-8333
Registered as lobbyist at U.S. Congress.
Clients:
Soc. for Human Resources Management

LORD, Albert L.
Exec. V. President and Chief Fin. Off., Student Loan Marketing Ass'n
1050 Thomas Jefferson St., N.W., Washington, DC 20007
Telephone: (202) 333-8000

LORD, Christopher
Legis Officer, Legis & Cong Rels, DEPARTMENT OF HOUSING AND URBAN DEVELOPMENT
451 Seventh St., S.W., Washington, DC 20410
Telephone: (202) 755-5000

LORD DAY & LORD, BARRETT SMITH
1201 Pennsylvania Ave., N.W., Suite 821, Washington, DC 20004
Telephone: (202) 393-5024
Background: Washington office of a New York law firm.
Members of firm representing listed organizations:
Frankhauser, Mahlon, Partner
Levinson, Ellen S., Partner
Viehe-Naess, Brenda, Partner
Young, Joanne W., Partner
Clients:
Aeromexico *(Joanne W. Young)*
Aeroservicios Ecuatorianos, C.A. *(Joanne W. Young)*
American Trans Air *(Joanne W. Young)*
Ass'n of British Insurers *(Brenda Viehe-Naess)*
Bangor Internat'l Airport *(Joanne W. Young)*
Coffee, Sugar and Cocoa Exchange *(Mahlon Frankhauser, Ellen S. Levinson)*
Iceland Air *(Joanne W. Young)*
Iceland Steamship Co. *(Joanne W. Young)*
Lineas Aereas del Caribe *(Joanne W. Young)*
Merrill Lynch Futures Inc. *(Mahlon Frankhauser)*
Miami Internat'l Airport *(Joanne W. Young)*
Prudential-Bache Securities, Inc. *(Mahlon Frankhauser)*
Shearson Lehman Hutton *(Mahlon Frankhauser)*
Tradewinds Airways Ltd. *(Joanne W. Young)*
Transbrasil *(Joanne W. Young)*
Worldways Canada, Ltd. *(Joanne W. Young)*

LORE, Gerald D.
Asst. V. Pres. & Dir., Gov't Affrs., Hoffmann-La Roche Inc.
1050 Connecticut Ave., N.W. Suite 401, Washington, DC 20036
Telephone: (202) 223-1975
Registered as lobbyist at U.S. Congress.

LORE, Kenneth G.
Brownstein Zeidman and Schomer
1401 New York Ave., N.W., Suite 900, Washington, DC 20005
Telephone: (202) 879-5700
Registered as lobbyist at U.S. Congress.
Background: Office of General Counsel, U.S. Department of Housing and Urban Development, 1973-75. Counsel, Nat'l Housing and Rehabilitation Ass'n, 1980-present. Vice Chairman, Nat'l Housing Conference, 1985-present. Member, Federal Nat'l Mortgage Ass'n, 1989-present. Member, Low and Moderate Housing Task Force. Member, Federal Nat'l Mortgage Ass'n Office of Housing Policy Research.
Clients:
New York City Housing Development Corp.
New York State Mortgage Loan Enforcement and Administrative Corp.

LORENZ, Jack
Exec. Director, Izaak Walton League of America
1401 Wilson Blvd., Level B, Arlington, VA 22209
Telephone: (703) 528-1818

LORETZ, John W.
Director, Communications, Physicians for Social Responsibility
1000 16th St., N.W., Suite 810, Washington, DC 20036
Telephone: (202) 785-3777

LORSUNG, Thomas N.
Director and Editor-in-Chief, Nat'l Catholic News Service
1312 Massachusetts Ave., N.W., Washington, DC 20005
Telephone: (202) 541-3250

LOTRIDGE, Calva
Exec. Director, Soc. for Imaging Science and Technology
7003 Kilworth Lane, Springfield, VA 22151
Telephone: (703) 642-9090

LOTTER, Lisa E.
Director, Regulatory Affairs, Nat'l Ass'n of Federal Credit Unions
3138 N. 10th St., Arlington, VA 22201
Telephone: (703) 522-4770
Background: Responsibilities include Nat'l Ass'n of Federal Credit Unions Political Action Committee.

LOTZ, Denton
General Secretary-Treasurer, Baptist World Alliance
6733 Curran St., McLean, VA 22101-6005
Telephone: (703) 790-8980

LOUGHREY, Bill
Director of Government Affairs, Scientific-Atlanta, Inc.
2011 Crystal Drive, Suite 308, Arlington, VA 22202
Telephone: (703) 486-0701

LOUIS, Claudia
Legislative Representative, American Heart Ass'n
1250 Connecticut Ave., N.W., Suite 360, Washington, DC 20036
Telephone: (202) 822-9380

LOUIS, Francois
Director, Governmental Affairs, Renault USA, Inc.
1111 19th St., N.W. Suite 1000, Washington, DC 20036
Telephone: (202) 331-9345

LOVAIN, Timothy
V. President and General Counsel, Miller Associates, Denny
400 N. Capitol St., N.W. Suite 325, Washington, DC 20001
Telephone: (202) 783-0280
Registered as lobbyist at U.S. Congress.
Background: Former Legislative Assistant to Senator Slade Gorton and Legislative Director to Rep. Helen Meyner.

LOVE, Mark W.
V. President, Economic Consulting Services Inc.
1225 19th St. N.W., Suite 210, Washington, DC 20036
Telephone: (202) 466-7720
Clients:
Amalgamated Clothing and Textile Workers Union
Cordage Institute
Goody Products, Inc.
Luggage and Leather Goods Manufacturers of America

LOVELESS, Charles M.
Associate Director, Legislation, American Federation of State, County and Municipal Employees
1625 L St., N.W., Washington, DC 20036
Telephone: (202) 429-1000
Registered as lobbyist at U.S. Congress.

LOVELL, Celia C.
Washington Representative, Norfolk Southern Corp.
1500 K St., N.W., Suite 375, Washington, DC 20005
Telephone: (202) 383-4166
Registered as lobbyist at U.S. Congress.

LOVELL, James
Chairman, Business Coalition for Fair Competition
1725 K St., N.W. Suite 412, Washington, DC 20006
Telephone: (202) 887-5872

LOVELL, Rose Ann
Director, Business Development, McNair Group Inc.
1155 15th St., N.W., Washington, DC 20005
Telephone: (202) 659-8866
Background: Former aide to Rep. Jerry Lewis (R-CA).

LOVENDUSKY, Michael
Counsel, American Insurance Ass'n
1130 Connecticut Ave., N.W., Suite 1000, Washington, DC 20036
Telephone: (202) 828-7100

LOVETT, Steve
V. President, Internat'l Trade Council, Nat'l Forest Products Ass'n
1250 Connecticut Ave., N.W. Suite 200, Washington, DC 20036
Telephone: (202) 463-2700

LOW, James P.
Exec. V. President and CEO, Ass'n of Foreign Investors in U.S. Real Estate
2300 M St., N.W., Washington, DC 20037
Telephone: (202) 887-0937
Background: Also serves as Chairman, Dynamics, a consulting and training company; Vice Chairman, Foundation for International Meetings; and Director, Association Consulting of Lawrence-Leiter and Co.

LOWE, Eugene
Assistant Exec. Director, United States Conference of Mayors
1620 Eye St., N.W., Washington, DC 20006
Telephone: (202) 293-7330

LOWE, Florence S.
Senior Consultant, Kamber Group, The
1920 L St., N.W., Washington, DC 20036
Telephone: (202) 223-8700

LOWE, Randall B.
Jones, Day, Reavis and Pogue
1450 G St., N.W., Suite 700, Washington, DC 20005-2088
Telephone: (202) 879-3939
Registered as lobbyist at U.S. Congress.
Clients:
Internat'l Telecharge, Inc.

LOWELL, Abbe David
Brand and Lowell, P.C.
923 15th St., N.W., Washington, DC 20005
Telephone: (202) 662-9700
Registered as lobbyist at U.S. Congress.
Clients:
Platte River Whooping Crane Trust

LOWENSTEIN, Douglas
Nat'l Strategies Inc.
818 17th St., N.W., Washington, DC 20006
Telephone: (202) 429-8744
Registered as lobbyist at U.S. Congress.
Background: Former Legislative Director to Sen. Howard Metzenbaum. Serves also as V. President, Alliance for Capital Access.
Clients:
Alliance for Capital Access

LOWENSTEIN, Helen P.
V. President, United States Cane Sugar Refiners' Ass'n
1001 Connecticut Ave., N.W., Suite 735, Washington, DC 20036
Telephone: (202) 331-1458

LOWENSTEIN, James G.
Senior Consultant, APCO Associates
1155 21st St., N.W., Suite 1000, Washington, DC 20036
Telephone: (202) 778-1000
Background: Former Ambassador to Luxembourg and Deputy Assistant Sec'y of State for European Affairs.

LOWER, Janice L.
Duncan, Weinberg, Miller & Pembroke, P.C.
1615 M St., N.W., Suite 800, Washington, DC 20036-3203
Telephone: (202) 467-6370
Clients:
Arkansas Public Service Commission
Auburn, Avilla, Bluffton, Columbia City and Other Indiana Municipalities
Central Montana Electric Power Cooperative, Inc.
Delaware Municipal Electric Corp. (DEMEC)
Indiana and Michigan Municipal Distributors Ass'n
Lubbock Power and Light
Montana Electric Power Cooperatives Ass'n

Newark, Delaware, City of
Newark, Seaford, Smyrna, Middletown, Dover, Lewes, Clayton, New Castle & Milford, Delaware, Municipalities of
Niles, Michigan, Utilities Department of
Seaford, Delaware, City of
Sturgis, Michigan, Municipality of

LOWERRE, Robert T.
Jaenke & Associates, E. A.
777 14th St., Suite 666, Washington, DC 20005
Telephone: (202) 393-1793
Organizations represented:
Nat'l Bank for Cooperatives

LOWERY, Leon
Legislative Representative, Environmental Action
1525 New Hampshire Ave., N.W., Washington, DC 20036
Telephone: (202) 745-4870
Registered as lobbyist at U.S. Congress.

LOWMAN, Rodney W.
V. President, Government Affairs, Council for Solid Waste Solutions
1275 K St., N.W. Suite 400, Washington, DC 20005
Telephone: (202) 371-5319

LOWREY, Carmen G.
Parry and Romani Associates Inc.
233 Constitution Ave., N.E., Washington, DC 20002
Telephone: (202) 547-4000
Registered as Foreign Agent: (#3814).

LOWRIE, Diane G.
V. President, Global Tomorrow Coalition
1325 G St., N.W., Suite 915, Washington, DC 20005-3104
Telephone: (202) 628-4016

LOWRIE, Gerald M.
Sr. V. President, Federal Gov't Affairs, AT&T
Suite 1000, 1120 20th St., N.W., Washington, DC 20036
Telephone: (202) 457-2233

LOWRY, Suellen
Preston Gates Ellis & Rouvelas Meeds
1735 New York Ave., N.W., Suite 500, Washington, DC 20006-4759
Telephone: (202) 628-1700
Registered as lobbyist at U.S. Congress.
Clients:
Council on Research and Technology (CORE-TECH)

LOWTHER, Frederick M.
Dickstein, Shapiro and Morin
2101 L St., N.W., Washington, DC 20037
Telephone: (202) 785-9700
Background: Special Assistant to General Counsel, U.S. Maritime Administration, 1971-72. Director, Office of Energy Policy, U.S. Department of Commerce, 1972-73.
Clients:
Boundary Gas

LOY, Frank E.
President, German Marshall Fund of the United States
11 Dupont Circle, N.W., Suite 750, Washington, DC 20036
Telephone: (202) 745-3950

LOYLESS, Betsy
Assistant Political Director, Sierra Club
408 C St., N.E., Washington, DC 20002
Telephone: (202) 547-1141
Registered as lobbyist at U.S. Congress.

LOZA, Moises
Exec. Director, Housing Assistance Council
1025 Vermont Ave., N.W. Suite 606, Washington, DC 20005
Telephone: (202) 842-8600

LUBAR, Jeff
V. President, Public Affairs, Nat'l Ass'n of REALTORS
777 14th St., N.W., Washington, DC 20005
Telephone: (202) 383-1000

LUBERDA, R. Alan
Schagrin Associates
1112 16th St., N.W. Suite 1000, Washington, DC 20036
Telephone: (202) 223-1700
Clients:

NEPTCO

LUBIENIECKI, Karen A.
KAL/PR
911 Duke St., Alexandria, VA 22314
Telephone: (703) 683-0357
Clients:
Nat'l Council on Patient Information and Education

LUBINSKI, Christine B.
Director for Public Policy, Nat'l Council on Alcoholism and Drug Dependence
1511 K St., N.W., Suite 926, Washington, DC 20005
Telephone: (202) 737-8122

LUBY, Arthur M.
O'Donnell, Schwartz & Anderson
1300 L St., N.W., Suite 200, Washington, DC 20005-4178
Telephone: (202) 898-1707
Registered as lobbyist at U.S. Congress.
Clients:
Transport Workers Union of America, AFL-CIO

LUCAK, Paula D.
Legislative Coordinator, AFL-CIO - Public Employee Department
815 16th St., N.W., Suite 308, Washington, DC 20006
Telephone: (202) 393-2820
Registered as lobbyist at U.S. Congress.

LUCAS, C. Payne
Exec. Director, Africare
440 R St., N.W., Washington, DC 20001
Telephone: (202) 462-3614

LUCAS, Freddie H.
Senior Washington Representative, General Motors Corp.
1660 L St., N.W., Washington, DC 20036
Telephone: (202) 775-5080
Registered as lobbyist at U.S. Congress.

LUCAS, John A., Jr.
Institutional Development Associates
7799 Leesburg Pike, Suite 900, Falls Church, VA 22043
Telephone: (703) 827-5932
Registered as Foreign Agent: (#3828).
Clients:
Saudi Arabia, Royal Embassy of

LUCAS, Michael J.
Lobbyist, Robbins Associates, Liz
420 7th St., S.E., Washington, DC 20003
Telephone: (202) 544-6093
Organizations represented:
Authors Guild, The
Carlan Homes
Coalition of Religious Press Ass'ns
Dramatists Guild
Songwriters Guild, The
Southern Baptist Press Ass'n
Spectrascan Imaging Services

LUCAS, Steven M.
Shaw, Pittman, Potts and Trowbridge
2300 N St., N.W., Washington, DC 20037
Telephone: (202) 663-8000
Registered as lobbyist at U.S. Congress.
Background: Attorney, Office of the Judge Advocate General, Dept. of the Army, 1974-5. Legal Adviser, Panama Canal Negotiations Working Group, Dept. of Defense, 1975-77.
Clients:
Institute of Internat'l Bankers

LUCASSEN, Sigurd
General President, United Brotherhood of Carpenters and Joiners of America
101 Constitution Ave., N.W., Washington, DC 20001
Telephone: (202) 546-6206

LUCCA, William J., Jr.
Exec. Director, Commissioned Officers Ass'n of the U.S. Public Health Service
1400 Eye St., N.W., Suite 725, Washington, DC 20005
Telephone: (202) 289-6400

LUCCHINO, Lawrence
Williams and Connolly
839 17th St., N.W. 1000 Hill Bldg., Washington, DC 20006
Telephone: (202) 331-5000
Background: Counsel, Impeachment Inquiry, U.S. House of Representatives Committee on the Judiciary.
Clients:
Baltimore Orioles

LUCY, William
Secretary-Treasurer, American Federation of State, County and Municipal Employees
1625 L St., N.W., Washington, DC 20036
Telephone: (202) 429-1200
Background: Responsible for AFSCME Nat'l Public Employees Organized to Promote Legislative Equality (PEOPLE). Serves as President, Coalition of Black Trade Unionists.

LUDKE, Mary R.
Washington Representative, Chevron, U.S.A.
1700 K St., N.W., Suite 1200, Washington, DC 20006
Telephone: (202) 457-5800
Registered as lobbyist at U.S. Congress.

LUDWICK, Leslie C.
Ass't Director, Congressional Affairs, American Medical Ass'n
1101 Vermont Ave., N.W., Washington, DC 20005
Telephone: (202) 789-7400
Registered as lobbyist at U.S. Congress.

LUDWIG, Eugene A.
Covington and Burling
1201 Pennsylvania Ave., N.W., Box 7566, Washington, DC 20044
Telephone: (202) 662-6000
Registered as lobbyist at U.S. Congress.
Clients:
Coalition to Preserve the Integrity of American Trademarks
Internat'l Swap Dealers Ass'n
Sun Life Assurance Co. of Canada (U.S. Division)

LUEDTKE, J. Peter
Holland and Hart
1001 Pennsylvania Suite 310, Washington, DC 20004
Telephone: (202) 638-5500
Registered as lobbyist at U.S. Congress.
Clients:
Scott's Liquid Gold

LUGBILL, Carolyn
Manager, Government & Industry Affairs, Nat'l Glass Ass'n
8200 Greensboro Drive Suite 302, McLean, VA 22102
Telephone: (703) 442-4890
Background: Serves as contact for the Nat'l Glass Ass'n Political Action Committee.

LUGBILL, Tim
Legislative Analyst, Nat'l Ass'n of Manufacturers
1331 Pennsylvania Ave., N.W. Suite 1500 North, Washington, DC 20004-1703
Telephone: (202) 637-3000

LUHN, Kathy
Director, Government Relations, Kessler and Associates
126 Kentucky Ave., S.E., Washington, DC 20003
Telephone: (202) 547-6808
Registered as lobbyist at U.S. Congress.

LUKENS, David R.
Director, Highway Division, Associated General Contractors of America
1957 E St., N.W., Washington, DC 20006
Telephone: (202) 393-2040
Registered as lobbyist at U.S. Congress.

LUKENS, Walter P.
V. President, Litton Industries
490 L'Enfant Plaza East, S.W., Washington, DC 20024
Telephone: (202) 554-2570

LUMAN AND ASSOC., J. C.
1030 15th St., N.W., Suite 816, Washington, DC 20005
Telephone: (202) 682-9191

Background: A firm representing various clients with interests in employment, engineering, education, federal consulting and other federal activities.
Members of firm representing listed organizations:
Luman, Joseph C.
Background: Formerly Staff Director, U.S. House of Representatives Subcommittee on Manpower and Housing.
Organizations represented:
Nat'l Ass'n of Personnel Consultants *(Joseph C. Luman)*
Nat'l Home Study Council *(Joseph C. Luman)*
Nat'l Industries for the Severely Handicapped *(Joseph C. Luman)*

LUMAN, Joseph C.
Luman and Assoc., J. C.
1030 15th St., N.W., Suite 816, Washington, DC 20005
Telephone: (202) 682-9191
Registered as lobbyist at U.S. Congress.
Background: Formerly Staff Director, U.S. House of Representatives Subcommittee on Manpower and Housing.
Organizations represented:
Nat'l Ass'n of Personnel Consultants
Nat'l Home Study Council
Nat'l Industries for the Severely Handicapped

LUMB, Randolph C.
Federal Gov't Affairs V. President, AT&T
Suite 1000, 1120 20th St., N.W., Washington, DC 20036
Telephone: (202) 457-2398

LUND, Elisa M.
Director, Washington Programs, New England Council, Inc., The
1455 Pennsylvania Ave., N.W. Suite 1000, Washington, DC 20004
Telephone: (202) 639-8955

LUND AND O'BRIEN
1625 Eye St., N.W., Suite 406, Washington, DC 20006
Telephone: (202) 331-1377
Members of firm representing listed organizations:
Lund, Wendell
Background: War Production Broad, 1943. War Manpower Commission, 1942.
O'Brien, James D.
Background: Attorney for Power Matters, U.S. Department of the Interior, 1963-1964.
Clients:
Montana Power Co.
Pennsylvania Mines Corp.
Pennsylvania Power and Light Co. *(James D. O'Brien)*

LUND, Wendell
Lund and O'Brien
1625 Eye St., N.W., Suite 406, Washington, DC 20006
Telephone: (202) 331-1377
Registered as lobbyist at U.S. Congress.
Background: War Production Broad, 1943. War Manpower Commission, 1942.

LUNDE AND BERGER INC.
1101 King St., Suite 601, Alexandria, VA 22314
Telephone: (703) 838-5511
Background: A political consulting firm.
Members of firm representing listed organizations:
Burger, George B.
Background: Former Political Director, Democratic National Committee.
Lunde, Brian R.
Background: Formerly managed the 1988 Presidential campaign of Senator Paul Simon (D-IL) and also a former Exec. Director, Democratic National Committee.

LUNDE, Brian R.
Lunde and Berger Inc.
1101 King St., Suite 601, Alexandria, VA 22314
Telephone: (703) 838-5511
Background: Formerly managed the 1988 Presidential campaign of Senator Paul Simon (D-IL) and also a former Exec. Director, Democratic National Committee.

LUNDQUIST, James H.
Barnes, Richardson and Colburn
1819 H St., N.W., Washington, DC 20006
Telephone: (202) 457-0300

LUNDQUIST, James H. (Cont'd)
Registered as lobbyist at U.S. Congress.
Clients:
Budd Co.
Florida Citrus Mutual
Meat Importers Council of America
Sandoz Corp.

LUNETTA, Carla
Assoc. Dir., Div. of Legislative Affairs, American Hospital Ass'n
50 F St., N.W., Suite 1100, Washington, DC 20001
Telephone: (202) 638-1100
Registered as lobbyist at U.S. Congress.

LUNN, Deborah
Exec. V. President, Airport Operators Council Internat'l
1220 19th St., N.W. Suite 200, Washington, DC 20036
Telephone: (202) 293-8500

LUNNIE, Francis M., Jr.
Director, Employee Relations, Nat'l Ass'n of Manufacturers
1331 Pennsylvania Ave., N.W. Suite 1500 North, Washington, DC 20004-1703
Telephone: (202) 637-3000
Registered as lobbyist at U.S. Congress.

LUSKEY, Charlene
Sr Cong Relations Officer, OFFICE OF PERSONNEL MANAGEMENT
1900 E St., N.W., Washington, DC 20415
Telephone: (202) 632-6514

LUTHER, Laura
Legislative Assistant, Equitable Life Assurance Soc. of the U.S.
1700 Pennsylvania Ave., N.W., Suite 525, Washington, DC 20006
Telephone: (202) 393-3210
Background: Legislative Ass't to Sen. Jim Exon (D-NE), 1983-86.

LUTLEY, John H.
President, Klein & Saks, Inc.
1026 16th St., N.W., Suite 101, Washington, DC 20036
Telephone: (202) 783-0500
Background: Serves as Managing Director of the Gold Institute and Exec. Director of the Silver Institute.
Clients:
Gold Institute
Silver Institute

LUTZKER, Arnold P.
Dow, Lohnes and Albertson
1255 23rd St., N.W., Suite 500, Washington, DC 20037
Telephone: (202) 857-2500
Clients:
Blue Cross and Blue Shield of Maryland
Directors Guild of America
Gannett Co., Inc.
Life Card, Inc.

LYCETTE, Margaret
Deputy Director, Internat'l Center for Research on Women
1717 Massachusetts Ave., N.W., Suite 302, Washington, DC 20036
Telephone: (202) 797-0007

LYDEN, Michael E.
V. Pres., Storage and Transportation, Chlorine Institute
2001 L St., N.W., Suite 506, Washington, DC 20036
Telephone: (202) 775-2790

LYLE-DURHAM, Beth
Grassroots Coordinator, Nat'l Committee to Preserve Social Security and Medicare
2000 K St., N.W. Suite 800, Washington, DC 20006
Telephone: (202) 822-9459
Registered as lobbyist at U.S. Congress.

LYLES, Tammy J.
President, Ruff Political Action Committee
501 Capitol Court, N.E. Suite 100, Washington, DC 20002
Telephone: (202) 546-0023

LYMAN, Howard T.
Legislative Assistant, Nat'l Farmers Union
600 Maryland Ave., S.W., Suite 202W, Washington, DC 20024
Telephone: (202) 554-1600
Registered as lobbyist at U.S. Congress.

LYMAN, Mary S.
Project Manager, Tax Counsel, Chambers Associates Incorporated
1625 K St., N.W. Suite 200, Washington, DC 20006
Telephone: (202) 857-0670
Background: Former Tax Counsel to Congressman Jim Shannon, House Ways and Means Committee.
Clients:
Belk Stores Services, Inc.
Coalition of Publicly Traded Partnerships
Southwest Realty, Inc.

LYNCH, Constance E.
Director, State Liaison, American Speech-Language-Hearing Ass'n
10801 Rockville Pike, Rockville, MD 20852
Telephone: (301) 897-5700
Registered as lobbyist at U.S. Congress.

LYNCH, David H.
Polit. Director, Political Field Optns., Nat'l Ass'n of REALTORS
777 14th St., N.W., Washington, DC 20005
Telephone: (202) 383-1000
Registered as lobbyist at U.S. Congress.

LYNCH, Deborah Ball
Director, Regulatory Affairs, Williams Companies, The
1120 20th St., N.W. Suite S 700, Washington, DC 20036
Telephone: (202) 833-8994

LYNCH, Jennifer C.
Associate, Valis Associates
1747 Pennsylvania Ave., N.W., Suite 1201, Washington, DC 20006
Telephone: (202) 833-5055

LYNCH, Julia E.
Legislative Assistant, Nat'l Ass'n of Insurance Commissioners
444 N. Capitol St., Suite 316, Washington, DC 20001
Telephone: (202) 624-7790

LYNCH, Mary Ellen
Manager, Environmental Planning, Browning-Ferris Industries (D.C.), Inc.
1150 Connecticut Ave., N.W. Suite 500, Washington, DC 20036
Telephone: (202) 223-8151
Registered as lobbyist at U.S. Congress.

LYNCH, Michael P.
Director of Administration, Nat'l Center for Missing and Exploited Children
2101 Wilson Blvd., Suite 550, Arlington, VA 22201
Telephone: (703) 235-3900

LYNCH, Robert
President/CEO, Nat'l Assembly of Local Arts Agencies
1420 K St., N.W., Suite 204, Washington, DC 20005
Telephone: (202) 371-2830

LYNCH, Rev. Robert N.
General Secretary, United States Catholic Conference
3211 4th St., N.E., Washington, DC 20017
Telephone: (202) 541-3200
Background: Also represents the Nat'l Conference of Catholic Bishops.

LYNCH, Timothy P.
V. President, Government Affairs, Roadway Express, Inc.
1901 North Ft. Myer Drive, Suite 204, Arlington, VA 22209
Telephone: (703) 528-0233
Registered as lobbyist at U.S. Congress.

LYNN, Barry W.
Legislative Counsel, American Civil Liberties Union
122 Maryland Ave., N.E., Washington, DC 20002
Telephone: (202) 544-1681
Registered as lobbyist at U.S. Congress.

LYNN, John
Government Affairs Representative, Electronic Data Systems Corp.
1331 Pennsylvania Ave., N.W., Suite 1300 North, Washington, DC 20004
Telephone: (202) 637-6700

LYNN, John E.
Sr. Director, Congressional Relations, American Trucking Ass'ns
430 First St., S.E., Washington, DC 20003-1826
Telephone: (202) 544-6245
Registered as lobbyist at U.S. Congress.
Background: Former Special Assistant to the Chairman, House Budget Committee and Exec. Director, House Democratic Research Organization.

LYNN, Sarah
Legislative Counsel, American Psychological Ass'n
1200 17th St., N.W., Washington, DC 20036
Telephone: (202) 955-7600
Registered as lobbyist at U.S. Congress.

LYONS, Charles, Jr.
Account Executive, Edelman, Inc., Daniel J.
1420 K St., N.W., Washington, DC 20005
Telephone: (202) 371-0200
Background: Former press aide to Rep. Frank Wolf (R-VA).

LYONS, Clinton
Exec. Director, Nat'l Legal Aid and Defender Ass'n
1625 K St., N.W., Washington, DC 20006
Telephone: (202) 452-0620

LYONS, Dennis G.
Arnold & Porter
1200 New Hampshire Ave., N.W., Washington, DC 20036
Telephone: (202) 872-6700
Background: Attorney, Office of the General Counsel, Department of the Air Force, 1955-58. Law Clerk to U.S. Supreme Court Justice, William Brennan, 1958-60.

LYONS, Ellis
Volpe, Boskey and Lyons
918 16th St., N.W., Washington, DC 20006
Telephone: (202) 737-6580
Clients:
American Ass'n of Equipment Lessors Capital Investment Political Action Committee

LYONS, James J.
Exec. Director, Nat'l Ass'n for Bilingual Education
810 First St., N.E. 3rd Floor, Washington, DC 20002-4205
Telephone: (202) 898-1829

LYONS, Kenneth T.
President, Nat'l Ass'n of Government Employees
1313 L St., N.W., 2nd Floor, Washington, DC 20005
Telephone: (202) 371-6644

LYONS, Maggie
Publications Director, Nat'l Coffee Service Ass'n
4000 Williamsburg Square, Fairfax, VA 22032
Telephone: (703) 273-9008

LYONS, Marge
Manager, Washington Office, CIBA-GEIGY Corp.
1747 Pennsylvania Ave., N.W., Suite 700, Washington, DC 20006
Telephone: (202) 293-3019
Registered as lobbyist at U.S. Congress.

LYONS, William T.
Director, Federal Government Relations, CIBA-GEIGY Corp.
1747 Pennsylvania Ave., N.W., Suite 700, Washington, DC 20006
Telephone: (202) 293-3019
Registered as lobbyist at U.S. Congress.

MABRY, Samuel A.
Director, Federal Affairs, Hercules, Inc.
1800 K St., N.W., Suite 710, Washington, DC 20006
Telephone: (202) 223-8590
Registered as lobbyist at U.S. Congress.

MACAN, Nancy
Member, Legislative Services Group, Van Ness, Feldman & Curtis
1050 Thomas Jefferson St., 7th Floor, Washington, DC 20007
Telephone: (202) 298-1800
Clients:
Consumers United for Rail Equity

MACARI, Robert
Coffield Ungaretti Harris & Slavin
1747 Pennsylvania Ave., N.W. Suite 900, Washington, DC 20006
Telephone: (202) 872-4310
Clients:
COMDISCO, Inc.

MACARTHUR, Malcolm D.
Keller and Heckman
1150 17th St., N.W. Suite 1000, Washington, DC 20036
Telephone: (202) 956-5600
Background: Trial Attorney, Antitrust Division, U.S. Department of Justice, 1959-63.
Clients:
Contractors Pump Bureau

MACARTHUR, Stephen M.
Washington Representative, Nestle Enterprises, Inc.
1511 K St., N.W., Suite 1100, Washington, DC 20005
Telephone: (202) 639-8894
Background: Serves as contact for Carnation Corp.

MACAULAY, Joseph H.
5981 Searl Terrace, Bethesda, MD 20816
Telephone: (301) 320-4387

MACBETH, Angus
Sidley and Austin
1722 Eye St., N.W. Sixth Floor, Washington, DC 20006
Telephone: (202) 429-4000
Background: Chief Pollution Control Section, 1977-79 and Deputy Assistant Attorney General, 1979-81, Land and Natural Resources Division, Department of Justice.

MACCABEE, Julie W.
Corporate Manager, Congressional Affairs, Hughes Aircraft Co.
1100 Wilson Blvd. 20th Floor, Arlington, VA 22209
Telephone: (703) 525-1550

MACCARTHY, Mark M.
V. President, Government Affairs, Capital Cities/ABC Inc.
2445 M St., N.W., Suite 480, Washington, DC 20037-1420
Telephone: (202) 887-7777
Registered as lobbyist at U.S. Congress.
Background: Former aide to Rep. John Dingell (D-MI), Chairman of the House Energy and Commerce Committee.

MACCARTHY, Timothy C.
Director of Federal Liaison, Motor Vehicle Manufacturers Ass'n of the United States
1620 Eye St., N.W. Suite 1000, Washington, DC 20006
Telephone: (202) 775-2700
Registered as lobbyist at U.S. Congress.

MACCOULL, Dr. Leslie S.B.
U.S. Rep. and Sr. Research Scholar, Soc. for Coptic Archaeology
2800 Wisconsin Ave., N.W. Suite 702, Washington, DC 20007
Telephone: (202) 363-3480

MACDONALD, David R.
Baker and McKenzie
815 Connecticut Ave., N.W. Suite 1100, Washington, DC 20006-4078
Telephone: (202) 452-7000
Background: Assistant Secretary of the Treasury, 1974-76. Under Secretary of the Navy, 1976-77. Deputy U.S. Trade Representative, 1981-83.

MACDONALD, Jack A.
V. President, Beverly Enterprises
1901 N. Fort Myer Drive Suite 302, Arlington, VA 22209
Telephone: (703) 276-0808
Registered as lobbyist at U.S. Congress.

MACDONALD, Paige
Exec. V. President, World Wildlife Fund/The Conservation Foundation
1250 24th St., N.W., Washington, DC 20037
Telephone: (202) 293-4800

MACDONALD, Sheila
Director, Government Relations, Nat'l Taxpayers Union
713 Maryland Ave., N.E., Washington, DC 20002
Telephone: (202) 543-1300
Registered as lobbyist at U.S. Congress.

MACDOUGALL, Gordon P.
V. President, Government Affairs, Capitol Associates, Inc.
426 C St., N.E., Washington, DC 20002
Telephone: (202) 544-1880
Registered as lobbyist at U.S. Congress.
Background: Former Administrative Assistant to Rep. John Edward Porter (R-IL), 1984-86.
Clients:
Museum of Science and Industry
Nat'l Coalition for Volunteer Protection
Nat'l Crime Prevention Council
TDS Healthcare Systems Corp.

MACH, Leta
Director of Communications, Cooperative League of the USA Political Action Committee (Nat'l Coop Business PAC)
1401 New York Ave., N.W., Suite 1100, Washington, DC 20005
Telephone: (202) 638-6222

MACHINIST, Ben
V. President, American Internat'l Automobile Dealers Ass'n
1128 16th St., N.W., Washington, DC 20036
Telephone: (202) 659-2561

MACHUSIC, Karen
Director, Education & Info. Services, Nat'l Ass'n of Rehabilitation Facilities
Box 17675, Washington, DC 20041-0675
Telephone: (703) 648-9300

MACK, James E., CAE
American Trade Ass'n Management
9005 Congressional Court, Potomac, MD 20854
Telephone: (301) 365-4080
Registered as lobbyist at U.S. Congress.
Background: Serves as the Exec. Secretary and General Counsel, Nat'l Ass'n of Mirror Manufacturers and as Managing Director and General Counsel, Peanut Butter and Nut Processors Ass'n.
Clients:
Nat'l Ass'n of Mirror Manufacturers
Peanut Butter and Nut Processors Ass'n
Peanut Butter and Nut Processors Ass'n Political Action Committee

MACK, James H.
V. President, Government Relations, NMTBA - The Ass'n for Manufacturing Technology
7901 Westpark Dr., McLean, VA 22102
Telephone: (703) 893-2900
Registered as lobbyist at U.S. Congress.
Background: Also serves as Treasurer, Machine Tool Political Action Committee.

MACK, Thomas L.
Manager and V. President, Bechtel Group, Inc.
1620 Eye St., N.W., Suite 703, Washington, DC 20006
Telephone: (202) 393-4747
Registered as lobbyist at U.S. Congress.

MACKAY, William
Legis Mgr - Enforcement, DEPARTMENT OF TREASURY
15th and Pennsylvania Ave. N.W., Washington, DC 20220
Telephone: (202) 566-2037

MACKENZIE, I. R.
MacKenzie McCheyne, Inc.
2475 Virginia Ave., N.W. Suite 812, Washington, DC 20037
Telephone: (202) 338-9431
Registered as Foreign Agent: (#2721).
Clients:
Buenaventura Industrial Free Zone
El Salvador Freedom Foundation

Guatemala Freedom Foundation
Latin American Management Ass'n

MACKENZIE MCCHEYNE, INC.
2475 Virginia Ave., N.W. Suite 812, Washington, DC 20037
Telephone: (202) 338-9431
Members of firm representing listed organizations:
MacKenzie, I. R.
O'Brien, Ana Colomar, V. President
Clients:
Buenaventura Industrial Free Zone *(I. R. MacKenzie)*
Cuban Patriotic Council *(Ana Colomar O'Brien)*
El Salvador Freedom Foundation *(I. R. MacKenzie, Ana Colomar O'Brien)*
Guatemala Freedom Foundation *(I. R. MacKenzie, Ana Colomar O'Brien)*
Latin American Management Ass'n *(I. R. MacKenzie)*

MACKIN, Olivia C.
Federal Relations Analyst, Phillips Petroleum Co.
1776 Eye St., N.W. Suite 700, Washington, DC 20006
Telephone: (202) 833-0900
Registered as lobbyist at U.S. Congress.

MACKLER AND GIBBS
1120 Vermont Ave., N.W. Suite 600, Washington, DC 20005
Telephone: (202) 842-1690
Clients:
Ass'n of Biotechnology Companies

MACKLIN, Laura
Associate Director, Institute for Public Representation
600 New Jersey Ave., N.W., Washington, DC 20001
Telephone: (202) 662-9535

MACLAURIN, William A.
Manager, Washington Public Relations, Westinghouse Electric Corp.
1801 K St., N.W., Washington, DC 20006
Telephone: (202) 835-2364

MACLAURY, Bruce K.
President, Brookings Institution
1775 Massachusetts Ave., N.W., Washington, DC 20036
Telephone: (202) 797-6000
Background: Deputy Undersecretary for Monetary Affairs, Treasury Department (1969-71).

MACLEOD, Sarah
Obadal and O'Leary
1612 K St., N.W. Suite 1400, Washington, DC 20006
Telephone: (202) 457-0260
Clients:
Aeronautical Repair Station Ass'n

MACMEEKIN, Daniel H.
MacMeekin & Woodworth
1776 Massachusetts Ave., N.W. Suite 604, Washington, DC 20036
Telephone: (202) 223-1717
Background: Executive Director, Northern Mariana Islands Commission on Federal Laws, 1980-85.

MACMEEKIN & WOODWORTH
1776 Massachusetts Ave., N.W. Suite 604, Washington, DC 20036
Telephone: (202) 223-1717
Members of firm representing listed organizations:
MacMeekin, Daniel H.
Background: Executive Director, Northern Mariana Islands Commission on Federal Laws, 1980-85.
Woodworth, Donald C.
Background: Former General Counsel to the Resident Representative for the Northern Mariana Islands.

MACMILLAN, Douglas
Treasurer, Ensco Fund for Safer Waste Treatment
211 North Union St., Suite 100, Alexandria, VA 22314
Telephone: (703) 549-5528

MACMURDY, Paul
Legislative Programs Director, American Nuclear Energy Council
410 First St., S.E. Third Floor, Washington, DC 20003
Telephone: (202) 484-2670
Registered as lobbyist at U.S. Congress.

WASHINGTON REPRESENTATIVES

MACNABB, Richard R.
Senior V. President and Chief Economist, Manufacturers' Alliance for Productivity and Innovation (MAPI)
1200 18th St., N.W. Suite 400, Washington, DC 20036
Telephone: (202) 331-8430

MACRORY, Patrick F. J.
Arnold & Porter
1200 New Hampshire Ave., N.W., Washington, DC 20036
Telephone: (202) 872-6700
Registered as lobbyist at U.S. Congress.
Registered as Foreign Agent: (#1750).
Clients:
ASOCOLFLORES (Colombia Flower Growers Ass'n)
Nissan Industrial Equipment Co.
Nissan Motor Co., Ltd.
Profilo Holding A.S.

MADAN, Rafael A.
Thompson, Hine and Flory
1920 N St., N.W., Washington, DC 20036
Telephone: (202) 331-8800
Background: Foreign language specialist with firm.
Clients:
Yale Materials Handling Corp.

MADDA, Anthony V.
Ass't Director, Field Services Division, Nat'l Rifle Ass'n of America
1600 Rhode Island Ave., N.W., Washington, DC 20036
Telephone: (202) 828-6110

MADDEN, Murdaugh Stuart
2100 L St., N.W., Washington, DC 20037
Telephone: (202) 833-3360
Organizations represented:
World Federation for the Protection of Animals

MADDEN, Thomas J.
Venable, Baetjer, Howard and Civiletti
1201 New York Ave., N.W., Suite 1000, Washington, DC 20005
Telephone: (202) 962-4800
Background: Deputy General Counsel, Department of Justice, Law Enforcement Assistance Administration, 1970-71. General Counsel, Law Enforcement Assistance Administration, 1972-79. Office of Justice Assistance, Research and Statistics, Department of Justice, 1980. Director, National Advisory Commission on Criminal Justice Standards and Goals, 1971-73.

MADDOX, Adelia
Holland and Hart
1001 Pennsylvania Suite 310, Washington, DC 20004
Telephone: (202) 638-5500
Registered as lobbyist at U.S. Congress.
Background: Administrative Ass't (1983-85) and Legislative Ass't (1979-83) to Rep. Richard Shelby (D-AL).

MADDOX, John G.
Campaign Director, Nat'l Republican Congressional Committee
320 First St., S.E., Washington, DC 20003
Telephone: (202) 479-7000

MADDOX, Rev. Robert L.
Exec. Director, Americans United for Separation of Church and State
8120 Fenton St., Silver Spring, MD 20910
Telephone: (301) 589-3707
Background: Served as a speechwriter and religious liaison aide to President Jimmy Carter. Also represents Americans United Research Foundation.

MADDY, James D.
Exec. Director, League of Conservation Voters
1150 Connecticut Ave., N.W. Suite 501, Washington, DC 20036
Telephone: (202) 785-8683

MADIGAN, John H., Jr.
Asst. V. President for Public Affairs, American Cancer Soc. (Public Affairs Office)
316 Pennsylvania Ave., S.E. Suite 200, Washington, DC 20003
Telephone: (202) 546-4011
Registered as lobbyist at U.S. Congress.

Background: Assistant to Senator Birch Bayh (D-IN), 1977-80. Assistant Director of Public Affairs, U.S. National Alcohol Fuels Commission, 1980-81.

MADIGAN, Peter
Sr Dep Asst Secy, Legis Affrs, DEPARTMENT OF STATE
2201 C St., N.W., Washington, DC 20520
Telephone: (202) 647-4204

MADISON, Alan
Powell, Adams & Rinehart
1901 L St., N.W., 3rd Floor, Washington, DC 20036
Telephone: (202) 466-7590
Background: Senior Account Executive, Ogilvy & Mather Public Affairs, Inc.

MADISON GROUP/EARLE PALMER BROWN, THE
2033 M St., N.W., 9th Floor, Washington, DC 20036
Telephone: (202) 223-0030
Members of firm representing listed organizations:
Bagin, Richard, Senior V. President
Bruneel, Larry, Senior Policy Analyst
Gabriel, Edward M.
Lamb, A. Gretchen, Account Executive
Martin, Peggy L., Senior V. President
Roberts, Laura, Deputy Director, Coalition Development
Rosenzweig, Richard, Partner
Segal, Ed, V. President
Clients:
American Federation for Clinical Research *(Ed Segal)*
Council for Solid Waste Solutions *(Richard Bagin)*
DO IT Coalition *(Ed Segal)*
General Electric Co. *(Edward M. Gabriel)*
Keystone Center, The *(Edward M. Gabriel, Richard Rosenzweig)*
Nat'l Ass'n of Discount Theatres *(Peggy L. Martin)*
Northern States Power Co. *(Richard Rosenzweig)*
Philip Morris Cos., Inc.
Polystyrene Packaging Council *(Peggy L. Martin)*
STRATCO, Inc. *(Richard Rosenzweig)*
Tobacco Institute *(Peggy L. Martin)*

MADISON, John J.
Legis Affrs Specialist, NAT'L AERONAUTICS AND SPACE ADMINISTRATION
400 Maryland Ave, S.W., Washington, DC 20546
Telephone: (202) 453-1055

MADISON, Juliette B.
Exec. Director, Nat'l Housing Conference
1126 16th St., N.W., Suite 211, Washington, DC 20036
Telephone: (202) 223-4844

MADSEN, Stephany A.
V. President, State Government Relations, Vacation Ownership Council of ARRDA
1220 L St., N.W., Fifth Floor, Washington, DC 20005
Telephone: (202) 371-6700

MADSON, Gary K.
Dep Asst Secy, Cong Rels, DEPARTMENT OF AGRICULTURE
14th and Independence Ave. S.W., Room 205-E, Washington, DC 20205
Telephone: (202) 447-7095

MAEDER, Edward C.
Winston and Strawn
2550 M St., N.W., Suite 500, Washington, DC 20037
Telephone: (202) 828-8400
Background: Legislative Assistant to Sen. William B. Spong, 1967-70. Counsel, Senate Committee on the District of Columbia, 1970-71.
Clients:
Internat'l Council of Shopping Centers

MAENZA, Terry
Mahe Company, The Eddie
900 Second St., N.E. Suite 200, Washington, DC 20002
Telephone: (202) 842-4100

MAGALLAN, Rafael
Exec. Director, Hispanic Higher Education Coalition
20 F St., N.W., Suite 108, Washington, DC 20001
Telephone: (202) 638-7339

MAGAVERN, Bill
Staff Attorney, U.S. Public Interest Research Group
215 Pennsylvania Ave., S.E., Washington, DC 20003
Telephone: (202) 546-9707
Registered as lobbyist at U.S. Congress.

MAGAZINE, Alan H.
President, Health Industry Manufacturers Ass'n
1030 15th St., N.W. Suite 1100, Washington, DC 20005
Telephone: (202) 452-8240

MAGER, Mimi
Grass Roots Coordinator, Leadership Conference on Civil Rights
2027 Massachusetts Ave., N.W., Washington, DC 20036
Telephone: (202) 667-1780
Registered as lobbyist at U.S. Congress.
Background: Legislative Assistant to Senator James Abourezk (D-SD), 1976-78. Special Assistant to VISTA Director, 1979-80. Director, Friends of VISTA, 1981-86.

MAGGIO AND KATTAR, P.C.
11 Dupont Circle, N.W. Suite 775, Washington, DC 20009
Telephone: (202) 483-0052
Members of firm representing listed organizations:
Maggio, Michael
Clients:
Center for Constitutional Rights *(Michael Maggio)*

MAGGIO, Michael
Maggio and Kattar, P.C.
11 Dupont Circle, N.W. Suite 775, Washington, DC 20009
Telephone: (202) 483-0052
Clients:
Center for Constitutional Rights

MAGILL, James N.
Director, Nat'l Legislative Service, Veterans of Foreign Wars of the U.S.
200 Maryland Ave., N.E., Washington, DC 20002
Telephone: (202) 543-2239
Registered as lobbyist at U.S. Congress.

MAGNER & ASSOC. INC., James J.
314 Massachusetts Ave., N.E., Washington, DC 20002
Telephone: (202) 543-3171
Members of firm representing listed organizations:
Magner, James J., President
Organizations represented:
ASARCO Incorporated *(James J. Magner)*
Kaibab Industries *(James J. Magner)*
Kalber Forest Products Co. *(James J. Magner)*
Superconducting Core Technologies *(James J. Magner)*

MAGNER, James J.
President, Magner & Assoc. Inc., James J.
314 Massachusetts Ave., N.E., Washington, DC 20002
Telephone: (202) 543-3171
Registered as lobbyist at U.S. Congress.
Organizations represented:
ASARCO Incorporated
Kaibab Industries

Superconducting Core Technologies

MAGNO, Linda
Director, Regulatory Affairs, American Hospital Ass'n
50 F St., N.W., Suite 1100, Washington, DC 20001
Telephone: (202) 638-1100

MAGNOTTI ENTERPRISES, INC.
1029 Vermont Ave., N.W., Suite 800, Washington, DC 20005
Telephone: (202) 737-2696
Members of firm representing listed organizations:
Magnotti, (Dr.) John F. (Jr.)
Background: Serves as Exec. V. President, Nat'l Candle Ass'n, American Surety Ass'n, and Nat'l Council of Small Federal Contractors.
Clients:
American Surety Ass'n *(Dr. John F. Magnotti, Jr.)*
Nat'l Council of Small Federal Contractors *(Dr. John F. Magnotti, Jr.)*

MAGNOTTI, Dr. John F., Jr.
Magnotti Enterprises, Inc.
1029 Vermont Ave., N.W., Suite 800, Washington, DC 20005

Telephone: (202) 737-2696
Background: Serves as Exec. V. President, Nat'l Candle Ass'n, American Surety Ass'n, and Nat'l Council of Small Federal Contractors.
Clients:
American Surety Ass'n
Nat'l Council of Small Federal Contractors

MAGNUSON, Mark G.
Assistant General Counsel-Washington, Consolidated Natural Gas Co.
1819 L St., N.W. Suite 900, Washington, DC 20036
Telephone: (202) 833-3900

MAGNUSON, R. Gary
Director, Coastal States Organization
444 North Capitol St., N.W. Suite 312, Washington, DC 20001
Telephone: (202) 628-9636

MAGRATH, Patrick
Managing Director, Georgetown Economic Services
1055 Jefferson St., N.W., Washington, DC 20007
Telephone: (202) 342-8610

MAGUIRE, A. John
V. President, Washington Operations, Nat'l Cotton Council of America
1110 Vermont Ave., N.W. Suite 430, Washington, DC 20005
Telephone: (202) 833-2943
Registered as lobbyist at U.S. Congress.
Background: Serves as Washington Representative, Committee for the Advancement of Cotton.

MAGUIRE, Frank
Sr Dep Compt, Legis and Public Affrs, DEPARTMENT OF TREASURY - Comptroller of the Currency
490 L'Enfant Plaza East, S.W., Washington, DC 20219
Telephone: (202) 447-1820

MAGUIRE, Col. Joseph
Acquisions Policy, Legis Affrs, DEPARTMENT OF DEFENSE
The Pentagon, Washington, DC 20301
Telephone: (202) 697-6210

MAGUIRE, Margaret
Managing Director, Secura Group, The
1155 21st St., N.W., Washington, DC 20036
Telephone: (202) 728-4920
Background: Also a partner in the law firm of Arnold and Porter.

MAGUIRE, Mary F.
Director, External Communications, Corporation for Public Broadcasting
901 E St., N.W. Suite 2209, Washington, DC 20004-2006
Telephone: (202) 879-9712

MAGUIRE, Michael A.
Legislation Dir, NAT'L AERONAUTICS AND SPACE ADMINISTRATION
400 Maryland Ave., S.W., Washington, DC 20546
Telephone: (202) 453-1055

MAGUIRE, W. Terry
Senior V. President, American Newspaper Publishers Ass'n
The Newspaper Center 11600 Sunrise Valley Drive, Reston, VA 22091
Telephone: (703) 648-1000
Registered as lobbyist at U.S. Congress.

MAHAN, Connie
Grassroots Coordinator, Nat'l Audubon Soc.
801 Pennsylvania Ave., S.E., Washington, DC 20003
Telephone: (202) 547-9009
Registered as lobbyist at U.S. Congress.

MAHAN, David L.
DGA Internat'l
1133 Connecticut Ave., N.W. Suite 700, Washington, DC 20036
Telephone: (202) 223-4001
Clients:
Teledyne Brown Engineering

MAHE COMPANY, The Eddie
900 Second St., N.E. Suite 200, Washington, DC 20002
Telephone: (202) 842-4100
Members of firm representing listed organizations:
Denny, John (Jr.)
Freibert, David
Greener, Charles V., V. President and Senior Associate
Background: Former Special Assistant, Legislative Affairs Office, The White House, under President Reagan.
Holcomb, Terry, Senior Associate
Background: Former Chief of Staff to Rep. James Imhofe (R-OK).
Lee, Ladonna Y., President
Maenza, Terry
Mahe, Eddie (Jr.)
Sparks, David, V. President & Sr. Associate
Weber, James D., Senior Associate
Background: Managed the Virginia gubernatorial primary campaign of Rep. Stan Parris (R-VA), 1989.
Organizations represented:
Communications Satellite Corp. (COMSAT)
Hanford-Tridec
Island Development Corp.
Japan, Ministry of Foreign Affairs of
Preston Trucking Co.
Public Service Co. of New Mexico
Thompson Development Co., Kathryn G.
Utah Power and Light Co.

MAHE, Eddie, Jr.
Mahe Company, The Eddie
900 Second St., N.E. Suite 200, Washington, DC 20002
Telephone: (202) 842-4100

MAHER, James R.
Exec. V. President, American Land Title Ass'n
1828 L St., N.W., Suite 705, Washington, DC 20036
Telephone: (202) 296-3671
Background: Former Attorney, U.S. Department of Housing and Urban Development.

MAHER, Robert W.
President, Cellular Telecommunications Industry Ass'n
1133 21St., N.W., Third Floor, Washington, DC 20036
Telephone: (202) 785-0081
Registered as lobbyist at U.S. Congress.

MAHER, Walter B.
Dir., Fed. Rtns./Human Resources Office, Chrysler Corp.
1100 Connecticut Ave., N.W., Washington, DC 20036
Telephone: (202) 862-5431
Registered as lobbyist at U.S. Congress.

MAHLMANN, John J.
Exec. Director, Music Educators Nat'l Conference
1902 Association Drive, Reston, VA 22091
Telephone: (703) 860-4000

MAHONEY, John J.
President, Nat'l Hospice Organization
1901 Moore St. Suite 901, Arlington, VA 22209
Telephone: (703) 243-5900

MAHONEY, Kieran
Capitol Strategists Group
717 2nd St., N.E. Suite 303, Washington, DC 20002
Telephone: (202) 452-8060
Registered as lobbyist at U.S. Congress.
Background: Serves also as Political Director, Albanian American Civic League.
Clients:
Albanian American Civic League

MAHONEY, Patricia A.
Fletcher, Heald and Hildreth
1225 Connecticut Ave., N.W. Suite 400, Washington, DC 20036
Telephone: (202) 828-5700

MAHONEY, William G.
Highsaw, Mahoney & Clarke
Suite 210, 1050 17th St., N.W., Washington, DC 20036
Telephone: (202) 296-8500
Registered as lobbyist at U.S. Congress.
Clients:
Railway Labor Executives' Ass'n

MAHONY, Terence P.
V. President, Government Relations, Nat'l Broadcasting Co.
1331 Pennsylvania Ave., N.W. Suite 700S, Washington, DC 20004
Telephone: (202) 637-4533
Registered as lobbyist at U.S. Congress.

MAIBACH, Michael C.
Government Affairs Director, Intel Corporation
1825 Eye St., N.W., Suite 400, Washington, DC 20006
Telephone: (202) 429-2054
Registered as lobbyist at U.S. Congress.

MAILLARD, Eugene
Chief Executive Officer, Very Special Arts
1331 Pennsylvania Ave., N.W. Suite 1205, Washington, DC 20004
Telephone: (202) 662-8899

MAIN, David S.
Epstein Becker and Green
1227 25th St., N.W., Suite 700, Washington, DC 20037
Telephone: (202) 861-0900
Registered as lobbyist at U.S. Congress.
Background: Professional Staff Member, Minority Policy Committee 1974 -76, Legislative Ass't to Sen. Richard S. Schweiker (R-PA) 1976-77, Minority Counsel, Subcommittee on Health and Scientific Research, U.S. Senate 1977-79.

MAINES, Patrick D.
President, Media Institute
3017 M St., N.W., Washington, DC 20007
Telephone: (202) 298-7512

MAISONPIERRE, Andre
President, Reinsurance Ass'n of America
1819 L St., N.W., Suite 700, Washington, DC 20036
Telephone: (202) 293-3335
Registered as lobbyist at U.S. Congress.

MAJAK, Roger
Manager, Federal Government Affairs, Tektronix, Inc.
1700 N. Moore St., Suite 1620, Arlington, VA 22209
Telephone: (703) 522-4500
Registered as lobbyist at U.S. Congress.
Background: Staff Director, House Subcommittee on Internat'l Economic Policy, 1975-1985; Chairman, Industry Committee on Technology Transfer (ICOTT).

MAJOROS, Michael
V. President, Snavely, King and Associates
1220 L St., N.W., Suite 410, Washington, DC 20005
Telephone: (202) 371-1111

MAK, William
Executive Director, Nat'l Chinese Welfare Council
803 H St., N.W., Washington, DC 20001
Telephone: (202) 638-1041

MAKARECHIAN, David A.
Project Director, Tax and Budget, Citizens for a Sound Economy
470 L'Enfant Plaza East, S.W. Suite 7112, Washington, DC 20024
Telephone: (202) 488-8200
Registered as lobbyist at U.S. Congress.

MAKOSKY, Vivian
Assistant Exec. Director and Counsel, Institute of Scrap Recycling Industries, Inc.
1627 K St., N.W. Suite 700, Washington, DC 20006
Telephone: (202) 466-4050

MALASHEVICH, Bruce P.
President, Economic Consulting Services Inc.
1225 19th St. N.W., Suite 210, Washington, DC 20036
Telephone: (202) 466-7720
Clients:
Outboard Marine Corp.

MALASKY, Alan R.
Arent, Fox, Kintner, Plotkin & Kahn
1050 Connecticut Ave., N.W., Washington, DC 20036-5339
Telephone: (202) 857-6000
Registered as lobbyist at U.S. Congress.
Clients:

MALASKY, Alan R. (Cont'd)
STANT, Inc.

MALATESTA & CO., J. Thomas
600 New Hampshire Ave., N.W., Suite 300, Washington, DC 20037
Telephone: (202) 457-0393
Background: A marketing, events, public relations and public affairs firm; engages in international business.
Members of firm representing listed organizations:
DeMatteis, Mary Jo, Senior V. President
Malatesta, J. Thomas, President
Organizations represented:
Nat'l Commission Against Drunk Driving

MALATESTA, J. Thomas
President, Malatesta & Co., J. Thomas
600 New Hampshire Ave., N.W., Suite 300, Washington, DC 20037
Telephone: (202) 457-0393

MALBIN, Irene L.
V. President, Public Affairs, Cosmetic, Toiletry and Fragrance Ass'n
1110 Vermont Ave., N.W. Suite 800, Washington, DC 20005
Telephone: (202) 331-1770

MALBON, K. Wayne
Associate Director, Nat'l Tire Dealers and Retreaders Ass'n
1250 I St., N.W. Suite 400, Washington, DC 20005
Telephone: (202) 789-2300
Registered as lobbyist at U.S. Congress.
Background: Responsibilities include TIDE-PAC, the political action committee of the Nat'l Tire Dealers and Retreaders Ass'n.

MALCOLM, Ellen R.
President, EMILY'S List
2000 P St., N.W., Suite 412, Washington, DC 20036
Telephone: (202) 887-1957

MALDONADO, Daniel C.
MARC Associates, Inc.
1030 15th St., N.W. Suite 468, Washington, DC 20005
Telephone: (202) 371-8090
Registered as lobbyist at U.S. Congress.
Clients:
American Soc. for Bone and Mineral Research
American Soc. of Anesthesiologists
Merck Sharp and Dohme
Nat'l Hemophilia Foundation
NI Industries
Research Soc. on Alcoholism

MALDONADO, Irma
President, Mexican American Women's Nat'l Ass'n
1201 16th St., N.W., Suite 230, Washington, DC 20036
Telephone: (202) 822-7888

MALLECK, Andrew T.
Nat'l Legislative Representative, Brotherhood of Maintenance of Way Employees
400 First St., N.W., Room 801, Washington, DC 20001
Telephone: (202) 638-2135
Registered as lobbyist at U.S. Congress.

MALLICK, Earl W.
V. President, Public Affairs, USX Corp.
818 Connecticut Ave., N.W., Washington, DC 20006
Telephone: (202) 331-1340
Background: Serves as chairman for the Clean Air Working Group.

MALLINO, David L.
Chief Lobbyist, Connerton, Ray and Simon
1920 L St., N.W., Washington, DC 20036-5004
Telephone: (202) 466-6790
Registered as lobbyist at U.S. Congress.

MALLON, Francis J.
Assoc. Exec. V. Pres., Prof. Rel. Dept., American Physical Therapy Ass'n
1111 North Fairfax St., Alexandria, VA 22314
Telephone: (703) 684-2782

MALLOY, Alice
Exec. Ass't to Group V.P., Ext. Affairs, American Institute of Architects, The
1735 New York Ave., N.W., Washington, DC 20006
Telephone: (202) 626-7300

MALLOY, Cyril I.
Vice President, Government Relations, American Concrete Pipe Ass'n
8300 Boone Blvd., Suite 400, Vienna, VA 22182-2689
Telephone: (703) 821-1990

MALLOY, Jerry G.
Treasurer, BUILD-Political Action Committee
15th and M Sts., N.W., Washington, DC 20005
Telephone: (202) 822-0470

MALMGREN, Kurt
Senior V. President, State Activities, Tobacco Institute
1875 Eye St., N.W., Suite 800, Washington, DC 20006
Telephone: (202) 457-4857

MALOLEY, Nancy A.
Sr. V. Pres. & Dir., Environment Policy, Burson-Marsteller
1850 M St., N.W., Suite 900, Washington, DC 20036
Telephone: (202) 833-8550
Background: Former Special Assistant to President Bush for Environmental, Energy and Natural Resources Policy, White House Office of Policy Development.

MALONE, William R.
Murphy and Malone
1901 L St., N.W., Suite 200, Washington, DC 20036-3506
Telephone: (202) 223-5062
Clients:
Micronesian Telecommunications Corp.

MALONEY, Barry C.
Berliner and Maloney
1101 17th St., N.W., Suite 1004, Washington, DC 20036-4798
Telephone: (202) 293-1414
Registered as Foreign Agent: (#3512).

MALONEY, Gary W.
Director, Legislative Services, Sheehan Associates, Inc.
727 15th St., N.W., Suite 1200, Washington, DC 20005
Telephone: (202) 347-0044
Background: Former aide to Rep. Elton Gallegly (R-CA), 1987-88, and to Rep. Jim McCrery (R-LA), 1988.
Clients:
Searle Co., G. D.

MALONEY, Joseph F.
Secretary-Treasurer, AFL-CIO - Building and Construction Trades Department
815 16th St., N.W., Suite 603, Washington, DC 20006
Telephone: (202) 347-1461
Background: Responsibilities include the Political Education Fund of the Building and Construction Trades Department.

MALONEY, Robert
Director, Government Relations, Federal Nat'l Mortgage Ass'n
3900 Wisconsin Ave., N.W., Washington, DC 20016
Telephone: (202) 752-7000
Registered as lobbyist at U.S. Congress.

MALONI, William R.
Sr. V. Pres., Policy & Public Affrs., Federal Nat'l Mortgage Ass'n
3900 Wisconsin Ave., N.W., Washington, DC 20016
Telephone: (202) 752-7120
Registered as lobbyist at U.S. Congress.

MALOUFF, Frank J.
Exec. Director, American Podiatric Medical Ass'n
9312 Old Georgetown Road, Bethesda, MD
Telephone: (301) 571-9200

MALSON, Robert A.
Exec. V. President and COO, Close Up Foundation
1235 Jefferson Davis Hwy., Arlington, VA 22202
Telephone: (703) 892-5400

MALTER, Barry L.
Swidler & Berlin, Chartered
3000 K St., N.W., Suite 300, Washington, DC 20007
Telephone: (202) 944-4300

Registered as lobbyist at U.S. Congress.
Background: Attorney, Federal Trade Commission, 1973-76. Acting Deputy Associate General Counsel, Environmental Protection Agency, 1976-80.
Clients:
Internat'l Environmental Policy Coalition
Laidlaw, Inc.

MANAFORT, Paul J.
Black, Manafort, Stone and Kelly Public Affairs Co.
211 N. Union St., Third Floor, Alexandria, VA 22314
Telephone: (703) 683-6612
Registered as lobbyist at U.S. Congress.
Registered as Foreign Agent: (#3600).
Clients:
Financial Security Assurance, Inc.
Kaman Corp.
Puerto Rico Federal Affairs Administration
Uniao Nacional Para Independencia Total de Angola (UNITA)

MANATOS, Andrew E.
Manatos & Manatos, Inc.
1750 New York Ave., N.W. Suite 210, Washington, DC 20006
Telephone: (202) 393-7790
Registered as lobbyist at U.S. Congress.
Clients:
American Hellenic Alliance, Inc.
Committee for Citizen Awareness
Greece, Embassy of
Hellenic American Council of Southern California
MetPath Inc.
Pancyprian Ass'n of America
San Francisco, California, City of
Specialty Vehicle Institute of America
United Hellenic American Congress
United Refining Co.

MANATOS & MANATOS, INC.
1750 New York Ave., N.W. Suite 210, Washington, DC 20006
Telephone: (202) 393-7790
Members of firm representing listed organizations:
Manatos, Andrew E.
Matthews, Kimberly A.
Van Koevering, Dyck
Clients:
American Hellenic Alliance, Inc. *(Andrew E. Manatos, Dyck Van Koevering)*
Committee for Citizen Awareness *(Andrew E. Manatos, Kimberley A. Matthews)*
Greece, Embassy of *(Andrew E. Manatos)*
Hellenic American Council of Southern California *(Andrew E. Manatos, Dyck Van Koevering)*
MetPath Inc. *(Andrew E. Manatos, Kimberley A. Matthews)*
Pancyprian Ass'n of America *(Andrew E. Manatos, Dyck Van Koevering)*
San Francisco, California, City of *(Andrew E. Manatos, Kimberley A. Matthews)*
Specialty Vehicle Institute of America *(Andrew E. Manatos)*
United Hellenic American Congress *(Andrew E. Manatos, Kimberley A. Matthews)*
United Refining Co. *(Andrew E. Manatos, Kimberley A. Matthews)*

MANATT, Charles T.
Manatt, Phelps, Rothenberg & Phillips
1200 New Hampshire Ave., N.W., Suite 200, Washington, DC 20036
Telephone: (202) 463-4300
Registered as lobbyist at U.S. Congress.
Registered as Foreign Agent: (#3736).
Background: Former Chairman of the Democratic Nat'l Committee.
Clients:
California Bankers Ass'n
NEC Corp.
Northrop Corp.
Philip Morris Management Corp.
Sterling & Associates, Donald T.

MANATT, PHELPS, ROTHENBERG & PHILLIPS
1200 New Hampshire Ave., N.W., Suite 200, Washington, DC 20036

WASHINGTON REPRESENTATIVES

Telephone: (202) 463-4300
Background: Washington office of a Los Angeles law firm.
Members of firm representing listed organizations:
Farrell, J. Michael
  Background: General Counsel, U.S. Department of Energy, 1985-87.
Herbolsheimer, Robert T.
Kabel, Robert J.
  Background: Former Legislative Director for Senator Richard Lugar (R-IN) and Special Assistant to President Reagan for Legislative Affairs.
Kantor, Mickey
Kleinfeld, Eric F.
Manatt, Charles T.
  Background: Former Chairman of the Democratic Nat'l Committee.
Oldaker, William C.
  Background: Special Assistant, Equal Employment Opportunity Commission, 1969-73. Assistant General Counsel for Litigation and Enforcement, Federal Election Commission, 1975-76. General Counsel, Federal Election Commission, 1976-79.
Utrecht, Lyn
Wager, Robert J.
  Background: General Counsel and Staff Director, House Subcommittee on Reorganization, Research and International Operations, 1970-74.
Walton, June L.
Clients:
  Akhiok-Kaguyak, Inc. (Robert T. Herbolsheimer)
  AMBASE (William C. Oldaker)
  American Ass'n of Nurse Anesthetists (William C. Oldaker, June L. Walton)
  American Institute of Real Estate Appraisers (Robert J. Kabel, Robert J. Wager, June L. Walton)
  Bowling Proprietors' Ass'n of America (Robert T. Herbolsheimer)
  California Bankers Ass'n (Robert J. Kabel, Charles T. Manatt)
  Centre Point Associates (Robert T. Herbolsheimer)
  Citizen Action (William C. Oldaker)
  Edison Electric Institute (June L. Walton)
  EDU-DYNE Systems, Inc. (Robert T. Herbolsheimer)
  Fairfield Communities, Inc. (Robert T. Herbolsheimer)
  Federal Express Corp. (Robert J. Kabel, William C. Oldaker)
  Manufacturers Hanover Trust Co. (Robert J. Kabel)
  Melrose Co., The (Robert T. Herbolsheimer)
  Missouri Ass'n of Private Career Schools (Robert T. Herbolsheimer)
  Money Store, The (Robert J. Kabel)
  Nat'l Cable Television Ass'n Political Action Committee (William C. Oldaker)
  NEC Corp. (J. Michael Farrell, Charles T. Manatt)
  North Beach Property Owner's Ass'n (Robert T. Herbolsheimer)
  Northrop Corp. (Charles T. Manatt, Robert J. Wager)
  Occidental Petroleum Corp. (Robert J. Kabel)
  Philip Morris Management Corp. (Robert J. Kabel, Charles T. Manatt, William C. Oldaker)
  Security First Group (Robert J. Kabel)
  Sterling & Associates, Donald T. (Robert J. Kabel, Charles T. Manatt)
  United Airlines (Robert J. Kabel)
  Vero Beach Oceanfront Investors Limited Partnership (Robert T. Herbolsheimer)
  Western Bank (Robert J. Kabel)

MANCE, Katherine T.
Vice President, American Retail Federation
1616 H St., N.W. 6th Floor, Washington, DC 20006
Telephone: (202) 783-7971
Registered as lobbyist at U.S. Congress.

MANCHESTER ASSOCIATES, LTD.
1707 L St., N.W. Suite 725, Washington, DC 20036
Telephone: (202) 872-9333
Members of firm representing listed organizations:
  Moller, John V., V. President
Clients:
  Ampco-Pittsburgh Co. (John V. Moller)
  Nissan Motor Co., Ltd. (John V. Moller)
  Nissan Motor Manufacturing Corp. U.S.A. (John V. Moller)

MANCHESTER TRADE, INC.
1155 15th St., N.W., Suite 314, Washington, DC 20005
Telephone: (202) 331-9464

Registered as Foreign Agent: (#4149)
Members of firm representing listed organizations:
  Lande, Stephen L.
Clients:
  HYLSA (Stephen L. Lande)
  Korea Foreign Trade Ass'n (Stephen L. Lande)
  Sidermex Internat'l, Inc. (Stephen L. Lande)
  Tubos de Acero de Mexico, S.A. (Stephen L. Lande)

MANCINI, John
V. President, Domestic Public Affairs, American Electronics Ass'n
1225 Eye St., N.W., Suite 950, Washington, DC 20005
Telephone: (202) 682-9110
Registered as lobbyist at U.S. Congress.

MANCUSI, Michael
Managing Director, Secura Group, The
1155 21st St., N.W., Washington, DC 20036
Telephone: (202) 728-4920
Background: Former Senior Deputy Comptroller of the Currency.

MANCUSO, Dawn M.
Exec. Director, Nat'l Campground Owners Ass'n
11307 Sunset Hills Rd. Suite B-7, Reston, VA 22090
Telephone: (703) 471-0143

MANDEL, Robert L.
Director of Taxation, Air Transport Ass'n of America
1709 New York Ave., N.W., Washington, DC 20006-5206
Telephone: (202) 626-4000

MANELLI, Daniel J.
Graham and James
2000 M St., N.W., Suite 700, Washington, DC 20036
Telephone: (202) 463-0800
Clients:
  Contact Lens Manufacturers Ass'n
  Contact Lens Manufacturers Ass'n Political Action Committee

MANES, Joseph
Senior Policy Analyst, Mental Health Law Project
2021 L St., N.W., Washington, DC 20036
Telephone: (202) 467-5730

MANES, Nella
Ehrlich-Manes and Associates
4901 Fairmont Ave., Bethesda, MD 20814
Telephone: (301) 657-1800

MANES, Susan
V. President, Issue Development, Common Cause
2030 M St., N.W., Washington, DC 20036
Telephone: (202) 833-1200
Registered as lobbyist at U.S. Congress.

MANESS, Ted
Director of Political Affairs, Chamber of Commerce of the U.S.A.
1615 H St., N.W., Washington, DC 20062
Telephone: (202) 463-5606

MANGELLI, Peter J.
Vice President, Internat'l Exhibitors Ass'n
5501 Backlick Road, Suite 200, Springfield, VA 22151
Telephone: (703) 941-3725

MANGIONE, Peter T.
President, Footwear Distributors and Retailers of America
1319 F St., N.W. Suite 700, Washington, DC 20004
Telephone: (202) 737-5660
Registered as lobbyist at U.S. Congress.

MANKIEWICZ, Frank
Vice Chairman, Hill and Knowlton Public Affairs Worldwide
Washington Harbour, 901 31st St., N.W., Washington, DC 20007
Telephone: (202) 333-7400
Registered as lobbyist at U.S. Congress.
Registered as Foreign Agent: (#3301).
Background: Former President, National Public Radio and Press Secretary to Sen. Robert F. Kennedy (D-NY).
Clients:
  Bank of Hungary
  Corcoran Gallery of Art, The
  Shaklee Corp.
  Turkey, Government of

MANN, Lawrence O.
Exec. Director, American Soc. of Military Comptrollers
Box 338, Burgess, VA 22432-0338
Telephone: (703) 462-5637

MANN, Mary
Legislative Representative, Nat'l Marine Manufacturers Ass'n
1000 Thomas Jefferson St, N.W. Suite 525, Washington, DC 20007
Telephone: (202) 338-6662

MANN, Phillip L.
Member, Miller & Chevalier, Chartered
Metropolitan Square, 655 15th St., N.W., Washington, DC 20005
Telephone: (202) 626-5800
Background: Deputy Tax Legislative Counsel, 1973-74, and Tax Legislative Counsel, 1974-75, Department of the Treasury.
Clients:
  Rouse Company, The

MANN, Richard F.
Leighton and Regnery
1667 K St., N.W., Suite 801, Washington, DC 20006
Telephone: (202) 955-3900
Registered as lobbyist at U.S. Congress.

MANN, Robert W.
Senior Associate, Reese Communications Companies
2111 Wilson Ave., Suite 900, Arlington, VA 22201
Telephone: (703) 528-4400
Background: Former Administrative Assistant to Rep. Robert C. Smith (R-NH).

MANN, Thomas E.
Director, Governmental Studies Program, Brookings Institution
1775 Massachusetts Ave., N.W., Washington, DC 20036
Telephone: (202) 797-6000

MANNEN, Ted R.
Sr V. President, Policy & Communications, Health Industry Manufacturers Ass'n
1030 15th St., N.W. Suite 1100, Washington, DC 20005
Telephone: (202) 452-8240

MANNES, Gwynn Geiger
V. President, Bonner & Associates
1625 K St., N.W., Suite 300, Washington, DC 20006
Telephone: (202) 463-8880

MANNES, Paul H.
Manager, Information Systems, Bonner & Associates
1625 K St., N.W., Suite 300, Washington, DC 20006
Telephone: (202) 463-8880

MANNINA, George J., Jr.
O'Connor & Hannan
1919 Pennsylvania Ave., N.W., Suite 800, Washington, DC 20006
Telephone: (202) 887-1400
Registered as lobbyist at U.S. Congress.
Registered as Foreign Agent: (#2972).
Background: Administrative Aide to Rep. Gilbert Gude (R-MD), 1971-73. Legislative Assistant to Rep. Edwin B. Forsythe (R-NJ), 1973-75. Counsel House Subcommittee on Fisheries, Wildlife, Conservation and the Environment, 1975-81. Chief Minority Counsel, House Merchant Marine and Fisheries Committee, 1982-85.
Clients:
  Alaska, State of
  American Maritime Transport, Inc.
  Center for Marine Conservation
  Ecomarine
  Hutchinson Island Limited, Inc.
  Israel, Government of
  Kawasaki Kisen Kaisha, Ltd.
  Summer Island, Inc.
  United States Tuna Foundation

MANNING, Mary Jo
Senior V. President, Hill and Knowlton Public Affairs Worldwide
Washington Harbour, 901 31st St., N.W., Washington, DC 20007
Telephone: (202) 333-7400

MANNING, Mary Jo (Cont'd)
Background: Counsel, House Armed Services Committee, 1968-70; Attorney/Advisor, Dept. of Justice, 1970-71; Chief Legislative Ass't, Sen. Ernest F. Hollings (D-SC), 1971- 76; Chief Counsel, Communications Subcommittee, Senate Commerce, Science, and Transporation Committee, 1976-81.
Clients:
Television Operators Caucus, Inc.
Telocator
Thomson Consumer Electronics, Inc.

MANNING, Nora
Asst Dir, Legis Affrs (Act), ACTION
1100 Vermont Ave., N.W., Washington, DC 20525
Telephone: (202) 634-9772

MANNING, SELVAGE & LEE/WASHINGTON
1250 Eye St., N.W., Suite 300, Washington, DC 20005
Telephone: (202) 682-1660
Background: An international public relations agency, headquartered in New York City.
Members of firm representing listed organizations:
Gleason, Joseph B. (APR), Managing Director
Ives, Suzanne L. (APR), Senior V. President
Warner, Harland (apr), Exec. V. President & Deputy Mng. Dir.
Clients:
Honeywell, Inc.
Nat'l Ass'n of Business and Educational Radio
Nat'l School Boards Ass'n
Pennsylvania Builders Ass'n
Upjohn Co.
YMCA of Metropolitan Washington

MANNING, Thurston E.
President, Council on Postsecondary Accreditation
One Dupont Circle, N.W., Suite 305, Washington, DC 20036
Telephone: (202) 452-1433

MANSFIELD, Barbara I.
Ass't Manager, Washington Public Affairs, Ford Motor Co.
1350 Eye St., N.W. Suite 1000, Washington, DC 20005
Telephone: (202) 962-5400

MANSFIELD, Cynthia
Director, Government Affairs, GPU Service Corp.
600 Maryland Ave., S.W., Suite 520, Washington, DC 20024
Telephone: (202) 554-7616
Registered as lobbyist at U.S. Congress.

MANSFIELD, Linda K. C.
Assoc. Exec. Director, Communication, Paralyzed Veterans of America
801 18th St., N.W., Washington, DC 20006
Telephone: (202) 872-1300

MANTEL, Robert
Sr Adv., Cong & Public Affrs (Polit-Mil), DEPARTMENT OF STATE
2201 C St., N.W., Washington, DC 20520
Telephone: (202) 647-1256

MANTELL, Maxine
Associate Director, Degnon Associates, Inc.
6728 Old McLean Village Drive, McLean, VA 22101
Telephone: (703) 556-9222

MANTELL, Michael A.
General Counsel, Conservation Foundation
1250 24th St., N.W., Washington, DC 20037
Telephone: (202) 293-4800

MANUEL, Anne
Research Director, Americas Watch, Human Rights Watch
1522 K St., N.W., Suite 910, Washington, DC 20005
Telephone: (202) 371-6592

MANUEL, Philip R.
Philip Manuel Resource Group Ltd.
1747 Pennsylvania Ave., N.W. Suite 701, Washington, DC 20006
Telephone: (202) 861-0651
Clients:
Compania Peruana de Vapores

MANVILLE, Albert M, II, Ph.D.
Senior Staff Wildlife Biologist, Defenders of Wildlife
1244 19th St., N.W., Washington, DC 20036
Telephone: (202) 659-9510
Registered as lobbyist at U.S. Congress.

MANZANARES, Anthony, Jr.
Senior Counsel, American Council of Life Insurance
1001 Pennsylvania Ave., N.W., Washington, DC 20004-2599
Telephone: (202) 624-2106
Registered as lobbyist at U.S. Congress.

MAPLES, Robert Y.
Washington Representative, Philip Morris Management Corp.
1341 G St., N.W., Suite 900, Washington, DC 20005
Telephone: (202) 637-1500
Registered as lobbyist at U.S. Congress.

MARA, Wayne
Oversight & Investig Staff, Legis Affrs, DEPARTMENT OF HEALTH AND HUMAN SERVICES - Food and Drug Administration
5600 Fishers Lane, Rockville, MD 20857
Telephone: (301) 443-3793

MARANEY, John V.
Exec. Director, Nat'l Star Route Mail Contractors Ass'n
324 East Capitol St., S.E., Washington, DC 20003
Telephone: (202) 543-1661
Registered as lobbyist at U.S. Congress.
Background: Serves as contact for the Nat'l Star Route Mail Contractors Ass'n PAC.

MARANO, Cynthia E.
Exec. Director, Wider Opportunities for Women
1325 G St., N.W. Lower Level, Washington, DC 20005
Telephone: (202) 638-3143

MARANS, J. Eugene
Cleary, Gottlieb, Steen and Hamilton
1752 N St., N.W., Washington, DC 20036
Telephone: (202) 728-2700
Registered as lobbyist at U.S. Congress.
Clients:
Guggenheim Foundation, The Harry Frank
Security Pacific Nat'l Bank

MARC ASSOCIATES, INC.
1030 15th St., N.W. Suite 468, Washington, DC 20005
Telephone: (202) 371-8090
Background: A medical organization representational firm.
Members of firm representing listed organizations:
Fenninger, Randolph B.
Humphreys, Robert R.
Maldonado, Daniel C.
Riker, Ellen
Clients:
Affiliated Leadership League of and for the Blind of America *(Robert R. Humphreys)*
American Ass'n of Clinical Urologists *(Randolph B. Fenninger)*
American Ass'n of Colleges of Osteopathic Medicine *(Randolph B. Fenninger)*
American College of Nuclear Physicians *(Randolph B. Fenninger)*
American Soc. for Bone and Mineral Research *(Daniel C. Maldonado)*
American Soc. for Gastrointestinal Endoscopy *(Randolph B. Fenninger)*
American Soc. of Anesthesiologists *(Daniel C. Maldonado, Ellen Riker)*
American Soc. of Clinical Pathologists *(Randolph B. Fenninger, Ellen Riker)*
American Urological Ass'n *(Randolph B. Fenninger)*
Boys Town Nat'l Research Hospital *(Robert R. Humphreys)*
Helen Keller Nat'l Center for Deaf-Blind Youths and Adults *(Robert R. Humphreys)*
Merck Sharp and Dohme *(Daniel C. Maldonado, Ellen Riker)*
Nat'l Ass'n of Epilepsy Centers *(Ellen Riker)*
Nat'l Coalition on Immune System Disorders *(Robert R. Humphreys)*
Nat'l Hemophilia Foundation *(Randolph B. Fenninger, Daniel C. Maldonado)*
NI Industries *(Daniel C. Maldonado)*
Recording for the Blind, Inc. *(Robert R. Humphreys)*

Research Soc. on Alcoholism *(Daniel C. Maldonado)*

MARCHAND, Paul
Director of Governmental Affairs, Ass'n for Retarded Citizens of the U.S.
1522 K St., N.W. Suite 516, Washington, DC 20005
Telephone: (202) 785-3388

MARCHANT, Major General T. Eston
President, Adjutants General Ass'n of the United States
One Massachusetts Ave., N.W., Washington, DC 20001
Telephone: (202) 789-0031
Background: Has offices in South Carolina and Washington.

MARCHETTI, Victor
Editor, New American View
132 Third St., S.E., Washington, DC 20003
Telephone: (202) 547-1036

MARCK, Charles T.
V. President & Director, Gov't Relations, Dow Chemical
1776 Eye St., N.W., Suite 575, Washington, DC 20006
Telephone: (202) 429-3400
Registered as lobbyist at U.S. Congress.

MARCOE, Jeffery D.
Editor/Spec. Ass't Cong. Relations Div., Chamber of Commerce of the U.S.A.
1615 H St., N.W., Washington, DC 20062
Telephone: (202) 463-5604

MARCOU, George
Deputy Exec. Director, American Planning Ass'n
1776 Massachusetts Ave., N.W., Washington, DC 20036
Telephone: (202) 872-0611

MARCUS, Daniel
Wilmer, Cutler and Pickering
2445 M St., N.W., Washington, DC 20037-1420
Telephone: (202) 663-6000
Registered as lobbyist at U.S. Congress.
Registered as Foreign Agent: (#3355).
Background: Deputy General Counsel, Department of Health, Education and Welfare, 1977-79. General Counsel, Department of Agriculture, 1979-80.
Clients:
du Pont de Nemours and Co., E. I.
Superpharm Corp.

MARCUS, Michael S.
Akin, Gump, Strauss, Hauer and Feld
1333 New Hampshire Ave., N.W., Suite 400, Washington, DC 20036
Telephone: (202) 887-4000

MARCUS, Richard
Senior V. President, Powell, Adams & Rinehart
1901 L St., N.W., 3rd Floor, Washington, DC 20036
Telephone: (202) 466-7590

MARCUSS, Stanley J.
Milbank, Tweed, Hadley & McCloy
1825 Eye St., N.W. Suite 900, Washington, DC 20006
Telephone: (202) 835-7500
Registered as lobbyist at U.S. Congress.
Background: Counsel, International Finance Subcommittee, U.S. Senate, 1973-77. Senior Deputy Assistant Secretary for Industry and Trade, Department of Commerce, 1977-79; Acting Assistant Secretary for Industry and Trade, Department of Commerce, 1979-80.

MARDEN, Judith C.
Director of Communications, American Academy of Facial Plastic and Reconstructive Surgery
1101 Vermont Ave., N.W. Suite 404, Washington, DC 20005
Telephone: (202) 842-4500

MARESCA, Charles A., Jr.
Staff Attorney, Nat'l Interreligious Service Board for Conscientious Objectors
1601 Connecticut Ave., N.W. Suite 750, Washington, DC 20009
Telephone: (202) 293-5962

MARGARITIS, William G.
Manager, State Government Affairs, Occidental Chemical Corporation
1747 Pennsylvania Ave., N.W., Suite 375, Washington, DC 20006
Telephone: (202) 857-3000
Registered as lobbyist at U.S. Congress.

MARIANI, Robert
Regional Legislative Director, Transportation, Communications Internat'l Union
815 16th St., N.W. Suite 511, Washington, DC 20036
Telephone: (202) 783-3660
Registered as lobbyist at U.S. Congress.

MARIANO, Joseph N.
Associate Counsel & Mgr., Gov't Affairs, Direct Selling Ass'n
1776 K St., N.W., Suite 600, Washington, DC 20006
Telephone: (202) 293-5760
Registered as lobbyist at U.S. Congress.

MARIASCHIN, Daniel S.
Director, Public Affairs, B'nai B'rith Internat'l
1640 Rhode Island Ave., N.W., Washington, DC 20036
Telephone: (202) 857-6600

MARINACCIO, Charles L.
Kelley, Drye and Warren
2300 M St., N.W., Washington, DC 20037
Telephone: (202) 463-8333
Registered as lobbyist at U.S. Congress.
Clients:
New York Hospital

MARIOTTE, Michael
Exec. Director, Nuclear Information and Resource Service
1424 16th St., N.W. Suite 601, Washington, DC 20036
Telephone: (202) 328-0002

MARK, Richard F.
Director, Research and Communications, 20/20 Vision Nat'l Project
1000 16th St., N.W., Washington, DC 20036
Telephone: (202) 728-1157

MARKER, Dennis
Co-director, Witness for Peace
P.O. Box 33273, Washington, DC 20033
Telephone: (202) 797-1169

MARKET OPINION RESEARCH, INC.
1400 L St., N.W., Suite 650, Washington, DC 20005
Telephone: (202) 289-0420
Registered as Foreign Agent: (#3795)
Background: A national public opinion research firm.
Members of firm representing listed organizations:
Davis, Debra
Murphy, Maureen
Van Lohuiven, Jan
Venkateswaran, Indira

MARKEY, David J.
V. Pres., Federal Regulatory Affairs, BellSouth Corp.
1133 21st St., N.W., Suite 900, Washington, DC 20036
Telephone: (202) 463-4100
Background: Formerly Assistant Secretary of Commerce; special advisor to the Chairman, Federal Communications Commission; Chief of Staff for Senators Frank Murkowski (R-AK) and Glen Beall, Jr. (R-MD); V. President, Congressional Relations, Nat'l Ass'n of Broadcasters, 1974-81.

MARKHAM, Allan W.
2733 36th St., N.W., Washington, DC 20007
Telephone: (202) 364-8886
Background: An attorney. Serves as General Counsel, Coastal Airlines, Inc. and Railways Systems Design and Director, Suncoast Airlines, Inc. Special Assistant to the Administrator, Federal Aviation Administration, 1970-71. Chief Legislative Counsel, Federal Aviation Administration, 1971-73.
Organizations represented:
Arrow Air
Coastal Airlines, Inc.
First Co-operative Airlines
Railway Systems Design
SunCoast Airlines, Inc.
U.S. Express, Inc.

MARKOSKI, Joseph P.
Squire, Sanders and Dempsey
1201 Pennsylvania Ave., N.W. P.O. Box 407, Washington, DC 20044
Telephone: (202) 626-6600
Clients:
ADAPSO, the Computer Software & Services Industry Ass'n

MARKS, Herbert E.
Squire, Sanders and Dempsey
1201 Pennsylvania Ave., N.W. P.O. Box 407, Washington, DC 20044
Telephone: (202) 626-6600
Clients:
ADAPSO, the Computer Software & Services Industry Ass'n
Independent Data Communications Manufacturers Ass'n

MARKS, John
V. President, Regional Office, Loral/Fairchild Systems
1111 Jefferson Davis Hwy. Suite 811, Arlington, VA 22202
Telephone: (703) 685-5300

MARKS, John
Exec. Director, Search for Common Ground
2005 Massachusetts Ave., N.W., Lower Level, Washington, DC 20036
Telephone: (202) 265-4300

MARKS, Lee R.
Ginsburg, Feldman and Bress
1250 Connecticut Ave., N.W. Suite 800, Washington, DC 20036
Telephone: (202) 637-9000
Registered as Foreign Agent: (#3106).
Background: Attorney, Office of the Legal Adviser, Department of State, 1961-63. Special Assistant to the Legal Advisor, Deparment of State, 1964. Senior Deputy Legal Advisor, Department of State, 1977-79.
Clients:
Morocco, Kingdom of

MARKS, Matthew J.
Marks Murase and White
2001 L St., N.W., Suite 750, Washington, DC 20036
Telephone: (202) 955-4900
Registered as Foreign Agent: (#4141).
Background: Deputy to Assistant Secretary of the Treasury, 1967-1973; Deputy Assistant Secretary of the Treasury for Tariff and Trade Affairs, 1973-1974.
Clients:
Japan Steel Works, Ltd.
Mitsui and Co.

MARKS MURASE AND WHITE
2001 L St., N.W., Suite 750, Washington, DC 20036
Telephone: (202) 955-4900
Background: Washington office of a New York law firm.
Members of firm representing listed organizations:
Marks, Matthew J.
Background: Deputy to Assistant Secretary of the Treasury, 1967-1973; Deputy Assistant Secretary of the Treasury for Tariff and Trade Affairs, 1973-1974.
Rose, Frederic B.
Clients:
Bibby-Ste. Croix Foundries, Inc.
Japan Steel Works, Ltd. *(Matthew J. Marks, Frederic B. Rose)*
Mitsui and Co. *(Matthew J. Marks)*

MARKS, Richard P.
Exec. Secretary, Pan American Health and Education Foundation
525 23rd St., N.W., Washington, DC 20037
Telephone: (202) 861-3416

MARKS, Robert H.
Director, Publications, American Chemical Soc.
1155 16th St., N.W., Washington, DC
Telephone: (202) 872-6215

MARKUS, John F.
Akin, Gump, Strauss, Hauer and Feld
1333 New Hampshire Ave., N.W., Suite 400, Washington, DC 20036
Telephone: (202) 887-4000
Registered as lobbyist at U.S. Congress.
Clients:

Collagen Corp.

MARKWART, Luther
Exec. Vice President, American Sugar Beet Growers Ass'n
1156 15th St., N.W. Suite 1020, Washington, DC 20005
Telephone: (202) 833-2398
Registered as lobbyist at U.S. Congress.
Background: Responsibilities include American Sugar Beet Growers Ass'n Political Action Committee.

MARLER, Joseph S.
Asst Dir, External Affrs, DEPARTMENT OF INTERIOR - Fish and Wildlife Service
18th and C Sts., N.W., Washington, DC 20240
Telephone: (202) 343-2500

MARLETTE, C. Alan
Exec. Director, Automotive Trade Ass'n Executives
8400 Westpark Dr., McLean, VA 22102
Telephone: (703) 821-7072

MARLEY, Julianne
President, United States Student Ass'n
1012 14th St., N.W., Suite 207, Washington, DC 20005
Telephone: (202) 347-8772

MARLOW, E. Robert
V. President, Region IV, Internat'l Chemical Workers Union
1126 16th St., N.W., Suite 200, Washington, DC 20036
Telephone: (202) 659-3747
Registered as lobbyist at U.S. Congress.

MARLOWE AND CO.
1667 K St., N.W., Suite 480, Washington, DC 20006
Telephone: (202) 775-1796
Background: A public affairs consulting firm.
Members of firm representing listed organizations:
Marlowe, Howard, President
Background: President, American League of Lobbyists, 1988-89.
Nix, Michael
Background: Former aide to Rep. Les Aspin (D-WI).
Williams, Timothy, Legislative Representative
Clients:
AFL-CIO (American Federation of Labor and Congress of Industrial Organizations)
Amalgamated Clothing and Textile Workers Union
Amalgamated Transit Union
American Chiropractic Ass'n
Ass'n of Flight Attendants
Carlon Electrical Sciences, Inc.
Coalition to Keep Alaska Oil *(Howard Marlowe)*
Commercial Metals Co.
Connecticut Ass'n of REALTORS
Edison Electric Institute
End Notch Discrimination, Inc.
Independent Sector
Lazare Kaplan International, Inc.
Memphis-Shelby County Airport Authority *(Howard Marlowe)*
U.S. Trademark Ass'n
Venice, Florida, City of *(Howard Marlowe)*

MARLOWE, Howard
President, Marlowe and Co.
1667 K St., N.W., Suite 480, Washington, DC 20006
Telephone: (202) 775-1796
Registered as lobbyist at U.S. Congress.
Background: President, American League of Lobbyists, 1988-89.
Clients:
Coalition to Keep Alaska Oil
Memphis-Shelby County Airport Authority
Venice, Florida, City of

MARLOWE, Robert S.
Exec. Director, Citizens for Educational Freedom
927 S. Walter Reed Drive, Suite 1, Arlington, VA 22204
Telephone: (703) 486-8311
Background: Also serves as Exec. Director, Clearinghouse on Educational Choice.

MARMET AND MCCOMBS, P.C.
1822 Jefferson Place, N.W., Washington, DC 20036-2549
Telephone: (202) 331-7300
Background: Law firm specializing in work with the regulatory agencies, the FCC in particular.

The listings in this directory are available as *Mailing Labels.* See last page.

265

MARMET AND MCCOMBS, P.C. (Cont'd)
Clients:
KABY-TV
KATC
KBMY
KHAW-TV
KHON-TV
KMLY
KPRY-TV
KSFY-TV
KTMA-TV
KWCH
WDAY-TV
WDAZ-TV
WDRB-TV
WEAL-TV
WGAL-TV
WLKY-TV
WLNE-TV
WSJU
WSVI-TV
WTEV
WWL-TV

MAROON, Rosanne
Treasurer, Preston Gates Ellis & Rouvelas Meeds Political Action Committee
1735 New York Ave., N.W., Suite 500, Washington, DC 20006
Telephone: (202) 628-1700

MAROULIS-CRONMILLER, Alexandra
Administrator, Independent Bankers Political Action Committee
One Thomas Circle, N.W., Suite 950, Washington, DC 20005
Telephone: (202) 659-8111
Background: Serves also as State Liaison, Independent Bankers Ass'n of America.

MARQUEZ, Joaquin A.
Hopkins and Sutter
888 16th St., N.W., Suite 700, Washington, DC 20006
Telephone: (202) 835-8000
Registered as lobbyist at U.S. Congress.
Background: Former Director, Puerto Rico Federal Affairs Administration in Washington.
Clients:
First Federal Savings Bank
Puerto Rico Manufacturers Ass'n

MARQUIS, Chalmers
Congressional Affairs, Nat'l Ass'n of Public Television Stations
1350 Connecticut Ave., N.W. Suite 200, Washington, DC 20036
Telephone: (202) 887-1700

MARRINAN, James T.
Director, Federal Agency Affairs, American Hospital Ass'n
50 F St., N.W., Suite 1100, Washington, DC 20001
Telephone: (202) 638-1100

MARRIOTT, Frank S.
Director, Public Programs, Westinghouse Electric Corp.
1801 K St., N.W., Washington, DC 20006
Telephone: (202) 835-2329

MARRONE, Nick
Director, Dept. of Cong. and Gov't Rtns., Seafarers International Union of North America
5201 Auth Way, Camp Springs, MD 20746
Telephone: (301) 899-0675
Background: Serves as Contact for the Seafarers Political Activity Donation (SPAD).

MARSHALL, Brian
Director, U.S. Membership & Publishing, United States-Mexico Chamber of Commerce
1900 L St., N.W., Suite 612, Washington, DC 20036
Telephone: (202) 296-5198

MARSHALL, C. Travis
Sr. V. Pres., Director, Gov't Relations, Motorola, Inc.
1350 Eye St., N.W., Suite 400, Washington, DC 20005-3306
Telephone: (202) 371-6900
Registered as lobbyist at U.S. Congress.
Background: Also serves as Treasurer, Motorola Employees' Good Government Committee.

MARSHALL, Carmen
Exec. Director, Nat'l Black Media Coalition
38 New York Ave., N.E., Washington, DC 20002
Telephone: (202) 387-8155

MARSHALL, Cathy
V. Pres., Environment/Energy Group, Hill and Knowlton Public Affairs Worldwide
Washington Harbour, 901 31st St., N.W., Washington, DC 20007
Telephone: (202) 333-7400

MARSHALL, James J.
President, Education Funding Research Council
1611 North Kent St. Suite 508, Arlington, VA 22209
Telephone: (703) 528-1082

MARSHALL, Pluria W.
Chairman, Nat'l Black Media Coalition
38 New York Ave., N.E., Washington, DC 20002
Telephone: (202) 387-8155

MARSHALL, Robert
Chairman, Nat'l Rural Housing Coalition
122 C St., N.W., Washington, DC 20001
Telephone: (202) 393-5229

MARSHALL, Robert G.
Director of Research, American Life League
P.O. Box 1350, Stafford, VA 22554
Telephone: (703) 659-4171

MARSHALL, Scott
Director, Governmental Relations Dept., American Foundation for the Blind (Government Relations Department)
1615 M St., N.W., Suite 250, Washington, DC 20036
Telephone: (202) 457-1487

MARSHALL, Sylvan M.
Marshall, Tenzer, Greenblatt, Fallon and Kaplan
4545 42nd St., N.W., Suite 214, Washington, DC 20016
Telephone: (202) 362-6300
Background: Office of Price Stabilization 1951-53.
Clients:
Brunei, Embassy of
Bulgaria, Embassy of
China, Embassy of the People's Republic of
Finland, Embassy of
German Democratic Republic, Embassy of the
Mongolia People's Republic, Embassy of
Nepal, Embassy of
Singapore, Embassy of
Thailand, Embassy of
Tunisia, Embassy of

MARSHALL, TENZER, GREENBLATT, FALLON AND KAPLAN
4545 42nd St., N.W., Suite 214, Washington, DC 20016
Telephone: (202) 362-6300
Background: Washington office of New York law firm.
Members of firm representing listed organizations:
Marshall, Sylvan M.
Background: Office of Price Stabilization 1951-53.
Clients:
Brunei, Embassy of (Sylvan M. Marshall)
Bulgaria, Embassy of (Sylvan M. Marshall)
China, Embassy of the People's Republic of (Sylvan M. Marshall)
Finland, Embassy of (Sylvan M. Marshall)
German Democratic Republic, Embassy of the (Sylvan M. Marshall)
Mongolia People's Republic, Embassy of (Sylvan M. Marshall)
Nepal, Embassy of (Sylvan M. Marshall)
Singapore, Embassy of (Sylvan M. Marshall)
Thailand, Embassy of (Sylvan M. Marshall)
Tunisia, Embassy of (Sylvan M. Marshall)

MARSHALL, Will
President, Progressive Policy Institute
316 Pennsylvania Ave., S.E. Suite 516, Washington, DC 20003
Telephone: (202) 547-0001
Background: Former Policy Director, Democratic Leadership Council.

MARTENSTEIN, Lynn
Director, Media Coordination, American Red Cross
430 17th St., N.W., Washington, DC 20006

Telephone: (202) 639-3200
Background: Director, Media Coordination, of the American Red Cross National Office.

MARTIN, Dr. A. Dallas, Jr.
President, Nat'l Ass'n of Student Financial Aid Administrators
1920 L St., N.W., Suite 200, Washington, DC 20036
Telephone: (202) 785-0453

MARTIN, Allan L.
Asst Chief Couns., Tariff, Trade & Legis, DEPARTMENT OF TREASURY
15th and Pennsylvania Ave. N.W., Washington, DC 20220
Telephone: (202) 566-2482

MARTIN, Caroline
Peyser Associates, Inc.
1000 Vermont Ave., N.W. Suite 400, Washington, DC 20005
Telephone: (202) 842-4545
Registered as lobbyist at U.S. Congress.
Background: Former Legislative Aide to Rep. Byron Dorgan (D-ND).
Clients:
Mothers Against Drunk Driving (MADD)

MARTIN, Cornel
Director, Shipyard Operations, American Waterways Operators
1600 Wilson Blvd. Suite 1000, Arlington, VA 22209
Telephone: (703) 841-9300
Registered as lobbyist at U.S. Congress.

MARTIN, Cynthia L.
Director, Government Relations, Diagnostic Retrieval Systems, Inc.
1215 South Jefferson Davis Hwy., Suite 1004, Arlington, VA 22202
Telephone: (703) 521-8000
Registered as lobbyist at U.S. Congress.

MARTIN, David F.
Director of Government Affairs, CM Services, Inc.
1655 North Ft. Myer Drive Suite 700, Arlington, VA 22209
Telephone: (703) 522-2176
Registered as lobbyist at U.S. Congress.
Background: Serves as Director, Government Affairs, Plumbing Manufacturers Institute.
Clients:
Plumbing Manufacturers Institute

MARTIN, David H.
Porter, Wright, Morris and Arthur
1233 20th St., N.W., Suite 400, Washington, DC 20005
Telephone: (202) 778-3000
Background: Former Chief Counsel, U.S. Secret Service, 1974-77. Former Director, U.S. Office of Government Ethics, 1983-87.

MARTIN, David K.
Communications Management Associates
1724 N. Wakefield St., Arlington, VA 22207
Telephone: (202) 525-7062
Clients:
Friends of the Earth
Intellectual Property Owners, Inc.

MARTIN, Elizabeth M.
V. President, Communications, Ass'n of American Medical Colleges
One Dupont Circle, N.W., Suite 200, Washington, DC 20036
Telephone: (202) 828-0400

MARTIN, Fred
Perkins Coie
1110 Vermont Ave., N.W., Suite 1200, Washington, DC 20005
Telephone: (202) 887-9030
Registered as lobbyist at U.S. Congress.
Background: President, The Bancroft Group, the lobbying affiliate of Perkins Coie.

MARTIN, Fred J., Jr.
Sr. V. Pres. & Director, Gov't Relations, Bank of America NT & SA
1800 K St., N.W., Suite 900, Washington, DC 20006
Telephone: (202) 778-0533

Registered as lobbyist at U.S. Congress.
Background: Serves also as Treasurer, BankAmerica Federal Election Fund.

MARTIN, Gilbert A.
V. President, Regulatory Affairs, Columbia Gas System Service Corp.
1250 Eye St., N.W., Suite 703, Washington, DC 20005
Telephone: (202) 842-7404

MARTIN, Guy R.
Perkins Coie
1110 Vermont Ave., N.W., Suite 1200, Washington, DC 20005
Telephone: (202) 887-9030
Registered as lobbyist at U.S. Congress.
Background: Assistant Secretary of the Interior for Land and Water Resources, 1977-81.
Clients:
  Arctic Alaska Fishing Corp.
  Boeing Co.
  Burlington Resources, Inc.
  Geothermal Resources Ass'n
  James River Corp.
  Kootznoowoo, Inc.
  Ormat Energy Systems
  Perkins Coie Political Action Committee
  Wood Heating Alliance

MARTIN, Jack
Senior Adviser, Democratic Nat'l Committee
430 South Capitol St., S.E., Washington, DC 20003
Telephone: (202) 863-8000

MARTIN, James L.
Legislative Counsel, Nat'l Governors' Ass'n
Suite 250, 444 North Capitol St., N.W., Washington, DC 20001
Telephone: (202) 624-5315

MARTIN, Joan
Director of Communication, American Congress on Surveying and Mapping
5410 Grosvenor Lane, Suite 100, Bethesda, MD 20814-2122
Telephone: (301) 493-0200

MARTIN, John M.
Exec. V. President, Dairy and Food Industries Supply Ass'n
6245 Executive Blvd., Rockville, MD 20852
Telephone: (301) 984-1444
Background: Also represents the Dairy Industry Committee.

MARTIN, John M., Jr.
6909 Fort Hunt Road, Alexandria, VA 22307
Telephone: (703) 768-3606
Background: A legislative affairs consultant and tax counsel. Former Chief Counsel and Staff Director, House of Representatives Ways and Means Committee.
Organizations represented:
  Food Marketing Institute

MARTIN, John R.
President, Nat'l Ass'n of Railroad Passengers
236 Massachusetts Ave., N.E., Suite 603, Washington, DC 20002
Telephone: (202) 546-1550

MARTIN, Kate
Director, Nat'l Security Litigation Proj, Center for Nat'l Security Studies
122 Maryland Ave., N.E., Washington, DC 20002
Telephone: (202) 544-1681

MARTIN, Katherine E.
Asst. to V. President, Legislative Dept., Ass'n of American Railroads
50 F St., N.W., Suite 12904, Washington, DC 20001
Telephone: (202) 639-2540
Registered as lobbyist at U.S. Congress.

MARTIN, Keith
Chadbourne and Parke
1101 Vermont Ave., N.W. Suite 900, Washington, DC 20005
Telephone: (202) 289-3000
Registered as lobbyist at U.S. Congress.

Registered as Foreign Agent: (#3490).
Background: Legislative Assistant, Sen. Henry M. Jackson, 1974-77. Legislative Counsel, Sen. Daniel Patrick Moynihan, 1979-1982.

MARTIN, Larry K.
Director, Government Relations, American Apparel Manufacturers Ass'n
2500 Wilson Blvd., Suite 301, Arlington, VA 22201
Telephone: (703) 524-1864
Registered as lobbyist at U.S. Congress.
Background: Serves as Treasurer, American Apparel Manufacturers Political Action Committee.

MARTIN, Lewe B.
Thompson, Hine and Flory
1920 N St., N.W., Washington, DC 20036
Telephone: (202) 331-8800
Clients:
  American Cutlery Manufacturers Ass'n
  Bicycle Wholesale Distributors Ass'n
  Interface Group, Inc., The
  Manufacturing Jewelers and Silversmiths of America, Inc.

MARTIN, Peggy L.
Senior V. President, Madison Group/Earle Palmer Brown, The
2033 M St., N.W., 9th Floor, Washington, DC 20036
Telephone: (202) 223-0030
Clients:
  Nat'l Ass'n of Discount Theatres
  Polystyrene Packaging Council
  Tobacco Institute

MARTIN, R. Eden
Sidley and Austin
1722 Eye St., N.W. Sixth Floor, Washington, DC 20006
Telephone: (202) 429-4000

MARTIN, Renee M.
Attorney, Ameritech (American Information Technologies)
1050 Connecticut Ave., N.W., Suite 730, Washington, DC 20036
Telephone: (202) 955-3050

MARTIN, Robert
Leva, Hawes, Mason and Martin
1220 19th St., N.W. Suite 700, Washington, DC 20036
Telephone: (202) 775-0725
Registered as Foreign Agent: (#3881).
Clients:
  United Kingdom Defence Export Services Organization

MARTIN, Robert L.
Dir., Employee Relations Policy Center, Chamber of Commerce of the U.S.A.
1615 H. St., N.W., Washington, DC 20062
Telephone: (202) 463-5533
Registered as lobbyist at U.S. Congress.

MARTIN, Sue
Senior Director, Public Affairs, AMTRAK (Nat'l Rail Passenger Corp.)
60 Massachusetts Ave., N.E., Washington, DC 20002
Telephone: (202) 906-2513

MARTIN, William F.
Washington Policy & Analysis
655 15th St., N.W., Ninth Floor, Washington, DC 20005-5701
Telephone: (202) 626-5800
Registered as Foreign Agent: (#4211).
Clients:
  Statoil North America, Inc.
  Tohoku Electric Power Co.

MARTIN YOCHIM, Mrs. Eldred
President General, Daughters of the American Revolution
1776 D St., N.W., Washington, DC 20006-5392
Telephone: (202) 628-1776

MARTINEAU, Frank, CAE
Chairman, Association Trends
4948 St. Elmo Ave., Suite 306, Bethesda, MD 20814
Telephone: (301) 652-8666

MARTINEZ, Alice Conde
Exec. Director, American College of Psychiatrists, The
Box 365, Greenbelt, MD 20768
Telephone: (301) 345-3534
Background: Also represents the American Academy of Psychiatrists in Alcoholism and Addictions and the American Ass'n for Geriatric Psychiatry.

MARTINEZ, Jose Roberto
Director, Puerto Rico Federal Affairs Administration
1100 17th St., N.W. Suite 800, Washington, DC 20036
Telephone: (202) 778-0710

MARTINEZ, Robert J.
Of Counsel, Williams and Jensen, P.C.
1101 Connecticut Ave., N.W., Suite 500, Washington, DC 20036
Telephone: (202) 659-8201

MARTSON, Philip M.
V. President, Hadson Gas Systems
1001 30th St., N.W. Suite 340, Washington, DC 20007
Telephone: (202) 337-5430

MARTYAK, Joseph J.
Director, Corporate Affairs, Rhone-Poulenc Inc.
Metropolitan Square, Suite 225 655 15th St., N.W., Washington, DC 20005
Telephone: (202) 628-0500
Registered as lobbyist at U.S. Congress.
Registered as Foreign Agent: (#4188)

MARUMOTO, William 'Mo'
Exec. V. President, United States Pan Asian American Chamber of Commerce
1625 K St., N.W., Suite 380, Washington, DC 20006
Telephone: (202) 638-1764
Background: Assistant to the President of the United States, 1970-73.

MARVIN, Michael L.
Legislative Director, White, Fine, and Verville
1156 15th St., N.W. Suite 1100, Washington, DC 20005
Telephone: (202) 659-2900
Registered as lobbyist at U.S. Congress.
Background: Legislative Director/Press Secretary to Rep. Frank Horton (R-NY), 1985-88. Administrative Assistant to Rep. Silvio Conte (R-MA), 1988-89.
Clients:
  CSX Corp.

MARX, Gary
Associate Exec. Director, Communications, American Ass'n of School Administrators
1801 North Moore St., Arlington, VA 22209
Telephone: (703) 528-0700

MARX, William B.
President, Council of Industrial Boiler Owners
6035 Burke Centre Pkwy. Suite 360, Burke, VA 22015
Telephone: (703) 250-9042
Registered as lobbyist at U.S. Congress.

MARY, Ponder
Deputy Director, Nat'l Consumers League
815 15th St., N.W., Suite 516, Washington, DC 20005
Telephone: (202) 639-8140

MARZULLA, Roger J.
Powell, Goldstein, Frazer and Murphy
1001 Pennsylvania, N.W., Sixth Fl., Washington, DC 20004
Telephone: (202) 347-0066
Registered as lobbyist at U.S. Congress.
Background: Served in the U.S. Department of Justice, 1983-89. Held positions of Special Litigation Counsel, 1982-83, Deputy Assistant Attorney General, 1984-87, and Assistant Attorney General, 1987-89, in the Land and Natural Resources Division.
Clients:
  Public Service Co. of Indiana

MASAOKA ASSOCIATES, Mike
900 17th St., N.W., Suite 520, Washington, DC 20006
Telephone: (202) 296-4484
Registered as Foreign Agent: (#2521)
Members of firm representing listed organizations:
  Masaoka, Mike M., Chairman
  Smith, Jennifer

MASAOKA ASSOCIATES, Mike (Cont'd)
Tilson, Patti A.
Yamada, T. Albert, President
Organizations represented:
Japan, Embassy of
Japan External Trade Organization (JETRO)
Toyota Motor Sales, U.S.A. *(Mike M. Masaoka, Patti A. Tilson, T. Albert Yamada)*
West Mexico Vegetable Distributors Ass'n *(T. Albert Yamada)*

MASAOKA, Mike M.
Chairman, Masaoka Associates, Mike
900 17th St., N.W., Suite 520, Washington, DC 20006
Telephone: (202) 296-4484
Registered as lobbyist at U.S. Congress.
Registered as Foreign Agent: (#2521).
Organizations represented:
Toyota Motor Sales, U.S.A.

MASCARO, Albert J.
Exec. Director, Intermodal Transportation Ass'n
6410 Kenilworth Ave. Suit 108, Riverdale, MD 20737
Telephone: (301) 864-2661

MASIN, Michael T.
O'Melveny and Myers
555 13th St., N.W., Suite 500 West, Washington, DC 20004
Telephone: (202) 383-5300
Registered as lobbyist at U.S. Congress.

MASLYN, Mark A.
Asst. Director, Nat'l Affairs Division, American Farm Bureau Federation
600 Maryland Ave., S.W., Washington, DC 20024
Telephone: (202) 484-3600
Registered as lobbyist at U.S. Congress.

MASON, Arthur K.
Leva, Hawes, Mason and Martin
1220 19th St., N.W. Suite 700, Washington, DC 20036
Telephone: (202) 775-0725
Registered as lobbyist at U.S. Congress.
Clients:
Ass'n of the United States Army

MASON, David
Director, Executive Branch Liaison, Heritage Foundation
214 Massachusetts Ave., N.E., Washington, DC 20002
Telephone: (202) 546-4400
Background: Formerly a Deputy Assistant Secretary of Defense and Staff Director of the House Minority Whip's Office.

MASON, Karen A.
Media Relations Manager, Recreation Vehicle Industry Ass'n
1896 Preston White Drive P.O. Box 2999, Reston, VA 22090
Telephone: (703) 620-6003

MASON, Michael J.
Washington Representative, American Petroleum Institute
1220 L St., N.W., Washington, DC 20005
Telephone: (202) 682-8420
Registered as lobbyist at U.S. Congress.

MASON, Nancy H.
Dir., Cong Affrs and Public Programs, DEPARTMENT OF COMMERCE - Nat'l Telecommunications and Information Administration
14th and Constitution Ave. N.W., Washington, DC 20230
Telephone: (202) 377-1551

MASRI, Bashar
Linton, Mields, Reisler and Cottone
1225 Eye St., N.W., Suite 300, Washington, DC 20005
Telephone: (202) 682-3901
Clients:
Instrumentation Testing Ass'n

MASSA, Cliff, III
Patton, Boggs and Blow
2550 M St., N.W., Suite 800, Washington, DC 20037
Telephone: (202) 457-6000
Registered as lobbyist at U.S. Congress.
Registered as Foreign Agent: (#2165).
Clients:

May Department Stores Co.
Nat'l Ass'n of Wholesaler-Distributors

MASSA, Paul P.
President, Elsevier U.S. Holdings, Inc.
4520 East-West Highway Suite 800, Bethesda, MD 20814
Telephone: (301) 654-1550

MASSABNY, Judith T.
Public Relations Director, Nat'l Grange
1616 H St., N.W., Washington, DC 20006
Telephone: (202) 628-3507

MASSEY, Donald F.
Sr. V. Pres. & Group Dir., Gov't Relats., Hill and Knowlton Public Affairs Worldwide
Washington Harbour, 901 31st St., N.W., Washington, DC 20007
Telephone: (202) 333-7400
Registered as lobbyist at U.S. Congress.
Registered as Foreign Agent: (#3301).
Clients:
Gerber Products Corp.
Indonesia, Nat'l Development Information Office
Nintendo
Turkey, Embassy of
Turkey, Government of

MASSEY, William L.
Mayer, Brown and Platt
2000 Pennsylvania Ave., N.W. Suite 6500, Washington, DC 20006
Telephone: (202) 463-2000
Registered as lobbyist at U.S. Congress.
Clients:
Arkansas Electric Cooperative Corp.
Brambles USA, Inc.
Entergy Corp.

MASSIE, James
Wall and Associates, R. Duffy
1317 F St., N.W., Suite 400, Washington, DC 20004
Telephone: (202) 737-0100
Registered as lobbyist at U.S. Congress.

MASTERS, Edward E.
President, Nat'l Planning Ass'n
1424 16th St., N.W. Suite 700, Washington, DC 20036
Telephone: (202) 265-7685

MASUR, Sandra
Director, Public Policy Analysis, Eastman Kodak Co.
1776 Eye St., N.W. Suite 1050, Washington, DC 20006
Telephone: (202) 857-3463

MATALIN, Mary
Chief of Staff, Republican Nat'l Committee
310 First St., S.E., Washington, DC 20003
Telephone: (202) 863-8500

MATELSKI, Wayne H.
Arent, Fox, Kintner, Plotkin & Kahn
1050 Connecticut Ave., N.W., Washington, DC 20036-5339
Telephone: (202) 857-6000

MATER, Gene P.
Senior Consultant, Adams Associates, John
1825 K St., N.W. Suite 210, Washington, DC 20006
Telephone: (202) 466-8320
Organizations represented:
United Press Internat'l

MATHEIS, Cheryl
Legislative Representative, American Ass'n of Retired Persons
1909 K St., N.W., Washington, DC 20049
Telephone: (202) 728-4640
Registered as lobbyist at U.S. Congress.

MATHERLEE, Karen
Deputy Director, Nat'l Health Policy Forum
2011 Eye St., N.W. Suite 200, Washington, DC 20006
Telephone: (202) 872-1390

MATHERS, Peter R.
Kleinfeld, Kaplan and Becker
1140 19th St., N.W., Suite 700, Washington, DC 20036
Telephone: (202) 223-5120
Clients:

Inwood Laboratories, Inc.
Jones Medical Industries, Inc.

MATHES, Elizabeth M.
V. President, Marketing & Communications, Health Industry Distributors Ass'n
225 Reinekers Lane, Suite 650, Alexandria, VA 22314
Telephone: (703) 549-4432

MATHEWS, Colin D.
Vinson and Elkins
Willard Office Building, 1455 Pennsylvania Ave., N.W., Washington, DC 20004-1007
Telephone: (202) 639-6500
Registered as lobbyist at U.S. Congress.

MATHEWS, Jessica Tuchman
V. President, World Resources Institute
1709 New York Ave., N.W., Washington, DC 20006
Telephone: (202) 638-6300

MATHEWS, Patricia N.
Sr. V. President, Public Affairs, Nat'l Bank of Washington, The
4340 Connecticut Ave., N.W., Washington, DC 20006
Telephone: (202) 364-6938
Background: Serves as Treasurer, Washington Bancorporation Political Action Committee.

MATHIAS, Barbara
Assistant Director, Public Affairs, Brookings Institution
1775 Massachusetts Ave., N.W., Washington, DC 20036
Telephone: (202) 797-6000

MATHIAS, Charles McC.
Jones, Day, Reavis and Pogue
1450 G St., N.W., Suite 700, Washington, DC 20005-2088
Telephone: (202) 879-3939
Background: Member, U.S. House of Representatives from Maryland, 1961-69. Member, U.S. Senate from Maryland, 1969-87.
Clients:
Preussag AG

MATHIAS, Richard D.
Senior V. President, Government Affairs, Pan American World Airways
1200 17th St., N.W., Suite 500, Washington, DC 20036
Telephone: (202) 659-7805
Registered as lobbyist at U.S. Congress.

MATHIS, Dawson
Dawson and Associates, Mathis
1900 L St., N.W., Suite 300, Washington, DC 20036
Telephone: (202) 872-1699
Registered as lobbyist at U.S. Congress.
Registered as Foreign Agent: (#2780).
Background: Former Member, U.S. House of Representatives (D-GA).
Clients:
American Electronics Laboratories
B.A.T. Industries, PLC
Crowley Maritime Corp.
Long Lake Energy Corp.
Massachusetts Mutual Life Insurance Co.

MATHIS, John P.
Baker and Botts
555 13th St., N.W., Suite 500 East, Washington, DC 20004-1109
Telephone: (202) 639-7700
Registered as lobbyist at U.S. Congress.
Clients:
Ashland Exploration, Inc.

MATHIS, Weldon L.
Secretary-Treasurer, Internat'l Brotherhood of Teamsters, Chauffeurs, Warehousemen and Helpers of America
25 Louisiana Ave., N.W., Washington, DC 20001
Telephone: (202) 624-6800

MATLACK, Jim
Exec. Director, Nat'l Head Start Ass'n
1220 King St., Suite 200, Alexandria, VA 22314
Telephone: (703) 739-0875

MATLACK, Jim
Director, Washington Office, American Friends Service Committee
1822 R St., N.W., Washington, DC 20009
Telephone: (202) 483-3341
Background: An organization of the Society of Friends (Quakers) which seeks to bring together persons holding key positions in government and others influential in the formulation of US policies and public opinion to explore points of view on domestic and international issues and to share AFSC's field experience in humanitarian aid, development, peace and social justice programs.

MATLICK, Susan J., CAE
Suburban Maryland Building Industry Ass'n
Executive Terrace 1400 Mercantile Lane, Landover, MD 20785
Telephone: (301) 925-9490

MATT, Peter K.
Spiegel and McDiarmid
1350 New York Ave., N.W., Suite 1100, Washington, DC 20005
Telephone: (202) 879-4000
Registered as lobbyist at U.S. Congress.
Clients:
  Sacramento Municipal Utility District

MATTAR, Deborah
Government Affairs & Public Rtns. Ass't., American Soc. of Landscape Architects
4401 Connecticut Ave., N.W., Washington, DC 20008
Telephone: (202) 686-2752

MATTHEIS, Ann H.
Manager, Government Relations, American Paper Institute
1250 Connecticut Ave., N.W. Suite 210, Washington, DC 20036
Telephone: (202) 463-2420
Registered as lobbyist at U.S. Congress.

MATTHEIS, Peter J.
Baker and Hostetler
1050 Connecticut Ave., N.W. Suite 1100, Washington, DC 20036
Telephone: (202) 861-1500
Registered as lobbyist at U.S. Congress.

MATTHEWS, Charles D.
President, Nat'l Ocean Industries Ass'n
1050 17th St., N.W. Suite 700, Washington, DC 20036
Telephone: (202) 785-5116
Registered as lobbyist at U.S. Congress.
Background: Also serves as Chairman, Nat'l Ocean Industries Ass'n Political Action Committee.

MATTHEWS, K. Michael
V. President, Government Relations, U.S. Strategies Corp.
1321 Duke St., Suite 200, Alexandria, VA 22314-3563
Telephone: (703) 739-7999
Registered as lobbyist at U.S. Congress.
Clients:
  BioMed Services, Inc.
  Envirotech Operating Services, Inc.
  HealthSouth Rehabilitation Corp.
  O'Brien Energy Systems, Inc.
  Service Employees Internat'l Union
  Ultrasystems Development Corp.
  USSI, Inc.

MATTHEWS, Kimberley A.
Manatos & Manatos, Inc.
1750 New York Ave., N.W. Suite 210, Washington, DC 20006
Telephone: (202) 393-7790
Registered as lobbyist at U.S. Congress.
Clients:
  Committee for Citizen Awareness
  MetPath Inc.
  San Francisco, California, City of
  United Hellenic American Congress
  United Refining Co.

MATTHEWS, Robert A.
President, Railway Progress Institute
700 North Fairfax St., Alexandria, VA 22314
Telephone: (703) 836-2332
Registered as lobbyist at U.S. Congress.
Background: Secretary, American League of Lobbyists, 1990.

MATTHEWS, Stuart
President & Chief Exec. Officer, Fokker Aircraft U.S.A., Inc.
1199 North Fairfax St. Suite 500, Alexandria, VA 22314
Telephone: (703) 838-0100

MATTHEWS, Suzette
2020 North 14th St., Suite 410, Arlington, VA 22201
Telephone: (703) 522-5717
Background: Attorney with an independent practice.
Organizations represented:
  Air Traffic Control Ass'n

MATTINGLY, Joseph M.
Director, Gov't Affrs & General Counsel, Gas Appliance Manufacturers Ass'n
1901 North Moore St., Arlington, VA 22209
Telephone: (703) 525-9565
Registered as lobbyist at U.S. Congress.

MATTISON, Lindsay
Exec. Director, Internat'l Center for Development Policy
731 Eighth St., S.E., Washington, DC 20003
Telephone: (202) 547-3800

MATTISON, William E.
President, Nat'l Slag Ass'n
300 South Washington St., Alexandria, VA 22314
Telephone: (703) 549-3111

MATTOON, Daniel J.
Director, Congressional Affairs, BellSouth Corp.
1133 21st St., N.W., Suite 900, Washington, DC 20036
Telephone: (202) 463-4100
Registered as lobbyist at U.S. Congress.

MATTOX, Barbara G.
Partner, Davis & Harman
1455 Pennsylvania Ave., N.W. Suite 1200, Washington, DC 20004
Telephone: (202) 347-2230
Registered as lobbyist at U.S. Congress.

MATTOX, William C.
V. President and Dir., Federal Relations, Equitable Life Assurance Soc. of the U.S.
1700 Pennsylvania Ave., N.W., Suite 525, Washington, DC 20006
Telephone: (202) 393-3210
Registered as lobbyist at U.S. Congress.

MATZ, Marshall L.
Holland and Knight
888 17th St., N.W. Suite 900, Washington, DC 20006
Telephone: (202) 955-5550
Registered as lobbyist at U.S. Congress.
Background: Counsel and General Counsel, U.S. Senate Select Committee on Nutrition and Human Needs, 1973-77. Special Counsel, Senate Committee on Agriculture, Nutrition and Forestry, 1978-80.
Clients:
  Abbott Laboratories
  Carnival Cruise Lines

MATZ, Michael
Washington Dir., Public Lands Program, Sierra Club
408 C St., N.E., Washington, DC 20002
Telephone: (202) 547-1141
Registered as lobbyist at U.S. Congress.

MATZ, Timothy B.
Elias, Matz, Tiernan and Herrick
734 15th St., N.W. 12th Fl., Washington, DC 20005
Telephone: (202) 347-0300
Background: Associate General Counsel, Federal Home Loan Mortgage Corp., 1971-72.

MAUDLIN, C. V. & R. V.
1511 K St., N.W., Suite 535, Washington, DC 20005
Telephone: (202) 628-8777
Members of firm representing listed organizations:
  Maudlin, Robert V., Owner
    Background: Sec'y, Nat'l Ass'n of Scissors and Shears Manufacturers. Consultant to Alabama Power Co., Gulf Power Co., Southern Company Services, Inc.
Organizations represented:
  Alabama Power Co. *(Robert V. Maudlin)*
  Gulf Power Co. *(Robert V. Maudlin)*

Nat'l Ass'n of Scissors and Shears Manufacturers *(Robert V. Maudlin)*
Southern Company Services, Inc. *(Robert V. Maudlin)*

MAUDLIN, Robert V.
Owner, Maudlin, C. V. & R. V.
1511 K St., N.W., Suite 535, Washington, DC 20005
Telephone: (202) 628-8777
Registered as lobbyist at U.S. Congress.
Background: Sec'y, Nat'l Ass'n of Scissors and Shears Manufacturers. Consultant to Alabama Power Co., Gulf Power Co., Southern Company Services, Inc.
Organizations represented:
  Alabama Power Co.
  Gulf Power Co.
  Nat'l Ass'n of Scissors and Shears Manufacturers
  Southern Company Services, Inc.

MAUER, Marc
Assistant Director, Sentencing Project, The
918 F St., N.W. Suite 501, Washington, DC 20004
Telephone: (202) 628-0871

MAUPIN TAYLOR ELLIS & ADAMS, P.C.
1130 Connecticut Ave., N.W. Suite 750, Washington, DC 20036
Telephone: (202) 429-8910
Registered as Foreign Agent: (#4242)
Members of firm representing listed organizations:
  Wilson, Scott A.
    Background: Chief Legislative Assistant for Domestic Policy to Senator Jesse Helms (R-NC), 1979-85.
Clients:
  Glaxo Australia Pty. Ltd. *(Scott A. Wilson)*

MAURER, William W.
Corporate Director, Legislative Affairs, General Dynamics Corp.
1745 Jefferson Davis Hwy., Suite 1000, Arlington, VA 22202
Telephone: (703) 553-1286
Registered as lobbyist at U.S. Congress.

MAURY, Samuel L.
Exec. Director, Business Roundtable
1615 L St., N.W., Suite 1350, Washington, DC 20036
Telephone: (202) 872-1260
Registered as lobbyist at U.S. Congress.

MAWBY, Michael
Lobbyist, Common Cause
2030 M St., N.W., Washington, DC 20036
Telephone: (202) 833-1200
Registered as lobbyist at U.S. Congress.

MAXFIELD, Elizabeth F.
V. President, Cellular Telecommunications Industry Ass'n
1133 21 St., N.W., Third Floor, Washington, DC 20036
Telephone: (202) 785-0081

MAXIM, Susan
Staff Assistant, Equitable Life Assurance Soc. of the U.S.
1700 Pennsylvania Ave., N.W., Suite 525, Washington, DC 20006
Telephone: (202) 393-3210

MAXSON, F. Gordon
Director - Regulatory Matters, GTE Corp.
Suite 1200, 1850 M St., N.W., Washington, DC 20036
Telephone: (202) 463-5291

MAXSON, John S.
Director, Governmental Affairs, Commonwealth Edison Co.
1722 Eye St., N.W., Suite 600, Washington, DC 20006
Telephone: (202) 452-6278
Registered as lobbyist at U.S. Congress.

MAXWELL, Robert J.
President, Nat'l Ass'n of Beverage Importers
1025 Vermont Ave., N.W. Suite 1205, Washington, DC 20005
Telephone: (202) 638-1617
Background: Serves also as Treasurer, Nat'l Ass'n of Beverage Importers Political Action Committee.

MAXWELL, William A.
V. President, International Issues, Computer and Business Equipment Manufacturers Ass'n
311 First St., N.W. Suite 500, Washington, DC 20001
Telephone: (202) 737-8888
Registered as lobbyist at U.S. Congress.
Background: Former Legislative Analyst and Budget Examiner, Office of Management and Budget.

MAY, Albert E.
Exec. Vice President, United Shipowners of America
1627 K St., N.W., Suite 1200, Washington, DC 20006
Telephone: (202) 466-5388
Registered as lobbyist at U.S. Congress.

MAY, F. Lynn
Exec. V. President, American Academy of Physician Assistants
950 North Washington St., Alexandria, VA 22314
Telephone: (703) 836-2272
Background: Former Deputy Assistant Secretary for Public Affairs, U.S. Department of Health and Human Services.

MAY, James C.
Exec. V. President, Government Relations, Nat'l Ass'n of Broadcasters
1771 N St., N.W., Washington, DC 20036
Telephone: (202) 429-5300
Registered as lobbyist at U.S. Congress.

MAY, Mr. Lynn
Exec. Director, Ass'n of Physician Assistant Programs
950 N. Washington St., Alexandria, VA 22314
Telephone: (703) 836-2272

MAY, Randolph J.
Partner, Bishop, Cook, Purcell & Reynolds
1400 L St., N.W., Washington, DC 20005-3502
Telephone: (202) 371-5700
Registered as lobbyist at U.S. Congress.
Background: Assistant General Counsel, Federal Communications Commission, 1978-80. Associate General Counsel, Federal Communications Commission, 1980-81.
Clients:
CompuServe Inc.

MAY, Richard E.
Federal Affairs Counsel, Nat'l Conference of State Legislatures
444 North Capitol St., N.W. Suite 500, Washington, DC 20001
Telephone: (202) 624-5400
Background: Former Legislative Director for Rep. John Kasich (R-OH).

MAY, Timothy J.
Patton, Boggs and Blow
2550 M St., N.W., Suite 800, Washington, DC 20037
Telephone: (202) 457-6000
Registered as Foreign Agent: (#2165).
Background: Law Clerk, U.S. Court of Appeals, D.C. Circuit 1957-58. Consultant, Executive Office of the President 1961-62. Acting Chief Counsel, U.S. Senate National Stockpile Investigating Committee 1962-63. Managing Director Federal Maritime Commission 1963-66. U.S. Representative to International Maritime Conferences 1964-66.
Clients:
Avon Products, Inc.
Beckett Packaging, Ltd.
Cargolux Airlines Internat'l
Coalition on State Use Taxes
Nat'l Ass'n of Postal Supervisors
Nat'l Ass'n of Postal Supervisors Political Action Committee
New Process Co.
Parcel Shippers Ass'n Political Action Committee

MAYBERRY & ASSOC., Richard
888 16th St., N.W., Washington, DC 20006
Telephone: (202) 785-6677
Members of firm representing listed organizations:
Mayberry, Richard, President

MAYBERRY, Peter G.
Keller and Heckman
1150 17th St., N.W. Suite 1000, Washington, DC 20036
Telephone: (202) 956-5600
Registered as lobbyist at U.S. Congress.
Clients:
INDA, Ass'n of the Nonwoven Fabrics Industry

MAYBERRY, Richard
President, Mayberry & Assoc., Richard
888 16th St., N.W., Washington, DC 20006
Telephone: (202) 785-6677

MAYER, BROWN AND PLATT
2000 Pennsylvania Ave., N.W. Suite 6500, Washington, DC 20006
Telephone: (202) 463-2000
Background: Washington office of a Chicago based law firm.
Members of firm representing listed organizations:
Berghoff, John C. (Jr.)
Bloom, David I.
Fread, Joan P.
Frey, Andrew
Geller, Kenneth
Kriesberg, Simeon M.
Levy, Charles S.
  Background: Legislative Assistant to Cong. John Culver, 1971. Legislative Assistant to Sen. Adlai Stevenson, 1973-75. Legal Advisor to the Commissioner, U.S. International Trade Commission, 1979-80. Member, Investment Policy Advisory Committee, Office of the U.S. Trade Representative.
Massey, William L.
Nathan, Amy L.
Oppenheimer, Jerry L.
  Background: Treasury Department, Associate Tax Legislative Counsel, 1970-71; Deputy Tax Legislative Counsel, 1972; Acting Tax Legislative Counsel, 1973.
Smith, Richard M.
  Background: Special Counsel, Federal Power Commission, 1977. Member, White House Energy, Policy and Planning Staff, 1978. Director, Office of Policy Coordination, Department of Energy, 1978-79.
Williamson, Joel V.
Clients:
Accountant's Liability Assurance Co., Ltd. *(Jerry L. Oppenheimer)*
American Farm Bureau Federation *(Simeon M. Kriesberg, Charles S. Levy)*
Arkansas Electric Cooperative Corp. *(William L. Massey)*
Attorneys' Liability Assurance Soc. *(Jerry L. Oppenheimer)*
Brambles USA, Inc. *(William L. Massey)*
Business Roundtable
Cabot, Cabot & Forbes Realty Advisors *(Jerry L. Oppenheimer)*
COMDISCO, Inc. *(Jerry L. Oppenheimer)*
Continental Illinois Nat'l Bank and Trust Co. *(Charles S. Levy, Jerry L. Oppenheimer)*
Dome Petroleum Ltd. *(Joan P. Fread, Charles S. Levy, Jerry L. Oppenheimer)*
Entergy Corp. *(William L. Massey)*
First Chicago Corp. *(Jerry L. Oppenheimer)*
FMC Corp. *(Jerry L. Oppenheimer)*
Hewlett-Packard Co. *(Charles S. Levy)*
Honeywell, Inc.
Household Commercial Financial Services, Inc. *(Jerry L. Oppenheimer)*
Inland Steel Co.
LaSalle Partners Inc. *(Jerry L. Oppenheimer)*
Lehndorff & Babson Real Estate Counsel *(Jerry L. Oppenheimer)*
London Metal Exchange, Ltd.
Medtronic, Inc. *(Kenneth Geller)*
Nalco Chemical Co. *(Jerry L. Oppenheimer)*
Nestle, S.A. *(Joel V. Williamson)*
Quaker Oats Co.
SAMA Group of Ass'ns *(Charles S. Levy)*
Sara Lee Corp. *(Jerry L. Oppenheimer)*
Shearson Lehman Hutton *(Jerry L. Oppenheimer)*
Smith Barney, Harris Upham and Co. *(Jerry L. Oppenheimer)*
Solid Waste Agency of Northern Cook County
TeleCommunications, Inc. *(Jerry L. Oppenheimer)*
Vulcan Materials Co. *(John C. Berghoff, Jr.)*

MAYER, Joseph L.
President, Copper and Brass Fabricators Council
1050 17th St., N.W. Suite 440, Washington, DC 20036
Telephone: (202) 833-8575

MAYER, Joseph T.
Manager, Legislative Programs, Rockwell Internat'l
1745 Jefferson Davis Hwy. Suite 1200, Arlington, VA
Telephone: (703) 553-6851
Registered as lobbyist at U.S. Congress.

MAYER, Marion R.
Legislative Representative, American Ass'n of Retired Persons
1909 K St., N.W., Washington, DC 20049
Telephone: (202) 872-4700
Registered as lobbyist at U.S. Congress.

MAYER, Mike
Editor, Nat'l Alliance to End Homelessness
1518 K St., N.W., Suite 206, Washington, DC 20005
Telephone: (202) 638-1526

MAYER, Neal M.
Hoppel, Mayer and Coleman
1000 Connecticut Ave., N.W. Suite 410, Washington, DC 20036
Telephone: (202) 296-5460
Registered as Foreign Agent: (#3470).
Clients:
Brazil, Secretariat of Waterborne Transportation (STA)
Companhia de Navagacao Maritima NETUMAR
Companhia de Navegacao Lloyd Brasileiro
Japan Tobacco, Inc.
P & O (TFL) Ltd./Trans Freight Lines
Showa Line, Ltd.
Tropical Shipping and Construction Co.

MAYER, Robert C.
821 15th St., N.W. Suite 925, Washington, DC 20005
Telephone: (202) 737-1717

MAYER, Ruth
Program Manager, Nat'l Council on the Aging
600 Maryland Ave., S.W. West Wing 100, Washington, DC 20024
Telephone: (202) 479-1200
Background: Serves as contact for the Health Promotion Institute.

MAYERS, Daniel K.
Wilmer, Cutler and Pickering
2445 M St., N.W., Washington, DC 20037-1420
Telephone: (202) 663-6000
Registered as Foreign Agent: (#3355).

MAYFIELD, Martin
Legislative Assistant, Nat'l Right to Work Committee
8001 Braddock Road, Springfield, VA 22160
Telephone: (703) 321-9820
Registered as lobbyist at U.S. Congress.

MAYO, George W., Jr.
Hogan and Hartson
555 13th St., N.W., Suite 1200, Washington, DC 20004-1109
Telephone: (202) 637-5600
Clients:
Denver and Rio Grande Western Railroad Co.

MAYS, Jeffrey G.
Director, Government Relations, American Optometric Ass'n
1505 Prince Street, Suite 300, Alexandria, VA 22314
Telephone: (703) 739-9200
Registered as lobbyist at U.S. Congress.

MAZER, Ellen
Grassroots Lobbying Specialist, League of Women Voters of the United States
1730 M St., N.W., Tenth Floor, Washington, DC 20036
Telephone: (202) 429-1965
Registered as lobbyist at U.S. Congress.

MAZER, Michael E.
Krooth & Altman
2101 L St., N.W., Suite 210, Washington, DC 20037
Telephone: (202) 293-8200
Registered as lobbyist at U.S. Congress.
Clients:
Housing Study Group

MAZOR, John
Communications Specialist, Air Line Pilots Ass'n Internat'l
1625 Massachusetts Ave., N.W., Washington, DC 20036
Telephone: (202) 797-4003

MAZZAGLIA, Enzo
U.S. Representative, Selenia Industria Elettronica, S.p.A.
1101 15th St., N.W., Suite 610, Washington, DC 20005
Telephone: (202) 223-5504

MAZZASCHI, Anthony J.
Public Affairs Officer, American Soc. for Pharmacology
and Experimental Therapeutics
9650 Rockville Pike, Bethesda, MD 20814
Telephone: (301) 530-7060

MCADAMS, Michael J.
Ass't Director, Federal Gov't Affairs, BP America Inc.
1776 Eye St., N.W., Suite 1000, Washington, DC 20006
Telephone: (202) 785-4888
Registered as lobbyist at U.S. Congress.

MCADEN ASSOCIATES, LTD.
1155 15th St., N.W., Suite 504, Washington, DC 20005
Telephone: (202) 452-1003
Members of firm representing listed organizations:
  McAden, H. Wesley
Clients:
  Supima Ass'n of America *(H. Wesley McAden)*

MCADEN, H. Wesley
McAden Associates, Ltd.
1155 15th St., N.W., Suite 504, Washington, DC 20005
Telephone: (202) 452-1003
Registered as lobbyist at U.S. Congress.
Clients:
  Supima Ass'n of America

MCADOO, Jennifer M.
Dir., Community Involvement/GroundWater, Friends of the
Earth
218 D St., S.E., Washington, DC 20003
Telephone: (202) 544-2600
Registered as lobbyist at U.S. Congress.

MCAFEE, Skip
Exec. Director, American Soc. for Horticultural Science
113 South West St., Alexandria, VA 22314-2824
Telephone: (703) 836-4606

MCALEXANDER, Kirk
Exec. V. President, United States Business and Industrial
Council
220 Nat'l Press Building, Washington, DC 20045
Telephone: (202) 662-8744

MCALLISTER, Douglas B.
Director, Communications, Computer Dealers and Lessors
Ass'n
1212 Potomac St., N.W., Washington, DC 20007
Telephone: (202) 333-0102

MCALLISTER, M.
Government Affairs Coordinator, Matsushita Electric Corp.
of America
1001 Pennsylvania Ave., N.W. Suite 1355 North, Washington, DC 20004
Telephone: (202) 347-7592

MCALLISTER, Dr. Ray
Director, Regulatory Affairs, Nat'l Agricultural Chemicals
Ass'n
Madison Bldg., 1155 15th St., Suite 900, Washington, DC
20005
Telephone: (202) 296-1585

MCALPIN, James J.
Exec. Director, Commission of Accredited Truck Driving
Schools (CATDS)
1899 L St., N.W. Suite 500, Washington, DC 20036
Telephone: (202) 331-8866

MCALPINE, Robert
Director, Policy & Gov't Relations, Nat'l Urban League
1114 14th St., N.W., 6th Floor, Washington, DC 20005
Telephone: (202) 898-1604

MCANDREW, Paul
Confidential Asst, Cong Rels, DEPARTMENT OF AGRI-
CULTURE
14th adn Independence Ave. S.W., Room 239-E, Washington, DC 20205
Telephone: (202) 447-7095

MCATEER, J. Davitt
Director, Occupational Safety and Health Law Center
1536 16th St., N.W., Washington, DC 20036
Telephone: (202) 328-8300

MCAULIFFE, KELLY, RAFFAELLI & SIEMENS
1341 G St., N.W. Suite 200, Washington, DC 20005
Telephone: (202) 783-1800
Registered as lobbyist at U.S. Congress.
Background: A law firm with general business and govern-
ment relations practice, emphasizing corporate, banking,
tax, trade, real estate, venture capital and administrative
law.
Members of firm representing listed organizations:
  Allison, Edward E., Government Relations
    Consultant
    Background: Former Administrative Assistant to Sena-
    tor Paul Laxalt (R-NV). Active in Reagan and Bush
    Presidential campaigns.
  Ciaravella, Jo Ann
    Background: Former Staff Director, House Commission
    on Congressional Mailing Standards.
  Copeland, James M. (Jr.), Government Relations
    Consultant
    Background: Administrative Assistant to Rep. Pete
    Stark (D-CA), 1973-77. Director, Congressional Re-
    lations, Federal Home Loan Bank Board, 1977.
    Deputy Assistant to the President for Congressional
    Relations, 1978-80.
  Halsey, Steven C.
  Hatfield, Frederick W., Government Relations
    Consultant
    Background: Former Chief of Staff to Rep. Tony Coel-
    ho (D-CA).
  Jacquez, Lynnette R.
    Background: Former Staff Director, House Judiciary
    Immigration Subcommittee.
  Raffaelli, John D.
    Background: Tax and Trade Counsel to Senator Lloyd
    Bentsen (D-TX), 1980-84.
Clients:
  Alameda County, California *(James M. Copeland, Jr.)*
  American Nuclear Energy Council *(Edward E. Alli-
    son)*
  American Tunaboat Ass'n *(Frederick W. Hatfield)*
  Bay Area Rapid Transit District *(James M. Copeland,
    Jr.)*
  Browning-Ferris Industries (D.C.), Inc. *(John D.
    Raffaelli)*
  Chicago Mercantile Exchange *(James M. Copeland,
    Jr.)*
  China West *(Lynnette R. Jacquez)*
  Clark County, Nevada *(Edward E. Allison)*
  Coalition for Affordable Home Financing *(Frederick
    W. Hatfield)*
  Council of South Texas Economic Progress *(John
    D. Raffaelli)*
  Dallas/Fort Worth RAILTRAN *(Steven C. Halsey,
    John D. Raffaelli)*
  Dalton Construction Co. *(Edward E. Allison)*
  Dean Witter Realty *(John D. Raffaelli)*
  Environmental Research Center, University of
    Nervada/Las Vegas *(Edward E. Allison)*
  Epoc Water, Inc. *(Lynnette R. Jacquez)*
  Latin American Management Ass'n *(Lynnette R.
    Jacquez)*
  Lloyd's U.S. *(John D. Raffaelli)*
  Massport/Commonwealth of Massachusetts *(Ed-
    ward E. Allison)*
  Monarch Wines *(Frederick W. Hatfield)*
  Nat'l Jai Alai Ass'n *(Lynnette R. Jacquez)*
  Nat'l Judicial College *(Edward E. Allison)*
  Nat'l Medical Care, Inc. *(Edward E. Allison)*
  Nat'l Telephone Services, Inc. *(James M. Copeland,
    Jr., Steven C. Halsey, John D. Raffaelli)*
  Native American Industrial Trade Ass'n *(Lynnette
    R. Jacquez)*
  Pacific Mutual Life Insurance Co. *(James M. Cope-
    land, Jr.)*
  Philip Morris Cos., Inc. *(John D. Raffaelli)*
  Philip Morris Management Corp. *(John D. Raffaelli)*

  Sweetener Users Ass'n *(James M. Copeland, Jr.)*
  Transamerica Corp. *(James M. Copeland, Jr.)*
  Turkey, Government of *(John D. Raffaelli)*
  University of Nevada/Reno *(Edward E. Allison)*
  Valley Children's Hospital *(Frederick W. Hatfield)*
  White Mountain Apache Tribe *(Lynnette R. Jacquez)*
  Wine Institute *(Frederick W. Hatfield)*
  World Airways *(Lynnette R. Jacquez)*

MCAULIFFE, Mary E.
Dir., Wash. Affairs - Transportat. & Tax, Union Pacific
Corp.
555 13th St., N.W., Suite 450 West Columbia Square,
Washington, DC 20004
Telephone: (202) 662-0100
Registered as lobbyist at U.S. Congress.
Background: Represents the Union Pacific Railroad Co.
and Overnight Trucking subsidiaries of Union Pacific
Corp.

MCAULIFFE, Rebecca
Legislative Assistant, Public Securities Ass'n
1000 Vermont Ave., N.W., Suite 800, Washington, DC
20005
Telephone: (202) 898-9390
Registered as lobbyist at U.S. Congress.
Background: Former Staff Member, Senate Finance Com-
mittee.

MCAVOY, James
Exec. Director, Nat'l Coal Council
Box 17370, Arlington, VA 22216
Telephone: (703) 527-1191

MCAVOY, John J.
White & Case
1747 Pennsylvania Ave., N.W., Suite 500, Washington, DC
20006
Telephone: (202) 872-0013
Clients:
  Turkey, Government of

MCBEATH, Dr. William H.
Exec. Director, American Public Health Ass'n
1015 15th St., N.W. Third Floor, Washington, DC 20005
Telephone: (202) 789-5600

MCBRIDE, Ann
Senior V. President, Common Cause
2030 M St., N.W., Washington, DC 20036
Telephone: (202) 833-1200
Registered as lobbyist at U.S. Congress.

MCBRIDE ASSOC, INC., Charlie
1101 Connecticut Ave., N.W., Suite 906, Washington, DC
20036
Telephone: (202) 466-4210
Members of firm representing listed organizations:
  McBride, Charlie, President
  Womack, Stephanie
Organizations represented:
  American Electric Power Co. *(Charlie McBride)*
  American Nuclear Energy Council *(Charlie McBride)*
  Carolina Power and Light Co. *(Charlie McBride)*
  Commonwealth Edison Co. *(Charlie McBride)*
  Consolidated Edison Co. of New York *(Charlie
    McBride)*
  General Atomics *(Charlie McBride)*
  Louisiana Energy Services *(Charlie McBride, Stephanie
    Womack)*
  Oxford Energy Co. *(Charlie McBride)*
  Sealaska Corp. *(Charlie McBride)*
  Southern California Edison Co. *(Charlie McBride)*
  Tri-City Industrial Development Council *(Charlie
    McBride)*
  UI Companies *(Charlie McBride)*
  University of Alaska - Fairbanks *(Charlie McBride)*
  University of Nevada - Las Vegas *(Charlie McBride)*
  Westinghouse Electric Corp. *(Charlie McBride)*
  Yukon Pacific Inc. *(Charlie McBride)*

MCBRIDE, Charlie
President, McBride Assoc, Inc., Charlie
1101 Connecticut Ave., N.W., Suite 906, Washington, DC
20036
Telephone: (202) 466-4210
Registered as lobbyist at U.S. Congress.
Organizations represented:
  American Electric Power Co.

WASHINGTON REPRESENTATIVES

MCBRIDE, Charlie (Cont'd)
American Nuclear Energy Council
Carolina Power and Light Co.
Commonwealth Edison Co.
Consolidated Edison Co. of New York
General Atomics
Louisiana Energy Services
Oxford Energy Co.
Sealaska Corp.
Southern California Edison Co.
Tri-City Industrial Development Council
UI Companies
University of Alaska - Fairbanks
University of Nevada - Las Vegas
Westinghouse Electric Corp.
Yukon Pacific Inc.

MCBRIDE, Maurice H.
Attorney, Nat'l Petroleum Refiners Ass'n
1899 L St., N.W., Suite 1000, Washington, DC 20036
Telephone: (202) 457-0480

MCCABE, Ann
Associate Director, Illinois, State of
444 N. Capitol St., N.W. Suite 210, Washington, DC 20001
Telephone: (202) 624-7760

MCCABE, Ellen
Associate, Friedman Assoc. Inc., Cynthia
322 Massachusetts Ave., N.E., Washington, DC 20002
Telephone: (202) 546-4204
Organizations represented:
Ann Richards for Governor Committee '90

MCCABE, Michael K.
General Counsel, Nat'l Rifle Ass'n of America
1600 Rhode Island Ave., N.W., Washington, DC 20036
Telephone: (202) 828-6335
Background: Serves as Director of Legal Affairs of the Institute for Legislative Action of the Nat'l Rifle Ass'n.

MCCABE, Nancy R.
Assistant Manager, Government Relations, Centel Corp.
1350 Eye St., N.W., Suite 500, Washington, DC 20005
Telephone: (202) 778-8700

MCCAFFREY, R. Lawrence
Weiner, McCaffrey, Brodsky, Kaplan & Levin
1350 New York Ave., N.W., Suite 800, Washington, DC 20005-4797
Telephone: (202) 628-2000
Registered as lobbyist at U.S. Congress.
Background: Attorney Advisor, Office of General Counsel, U.S. Department of Housing and Urban Development, 1971-74. Special Assistant to the General Counsel, U.S. Department of Transportation, 1974-75. Chief Counsel, Federal Railroad Administration, 1975-77.

MCCAFFREY, Susan
State Analyst, Nat'l Solid Wastes Management Ass'n
1730 Rhode Island Ave., N.W., 10th Floor, Washington, DC 20036
Telephone: (202) 659-4613
Registered as lobbyist at U.S. Congress.

MCCAHEY, Hugh
Manager, Association Department, Chamber of Commerce of the U.S.A.
1615 H St., N.W., Washington, DC 20062
Telephone: (202) 463-5560

MCCAHILL, Julie P.
V. President, Government Relations, Ketchum Public Relations
1201 Connecticut Ave., N.W. Suite 300, Washington, DC 20036
Telephone: (202) 835-8800

MCCALEB, Brent
Ryan-McGinn
1110 Vermont Ave., N.W. Suite 820, Washington, DC 20005
Telephone: (202) 775-4370
Clients:
St. Vincent Hospital and Medical Center

MCCALL, Barbara T.
Nat'l Center for Municipal Development
1620 Eye St., N.W., Suite 300, Washington, DC 20006
Telephone: (202) 429-0160
Clients:
Columbia, South Carolina, City of
Henderson, Nevada, City of
Newburgh, New York, City of
Orange, Texas, City of
Texas Cities Legislative Coalition (TCLC)

MCCALLUM, John D.
Assistant Comptroller, Potomac Electric Power Co.
1900 Pennsylvania Ave., N.W., Washington, DC 20068
Telephone: (202) 872-2000
Registered as lobbyist at U.S. Congress.

MCCAMISH, MARTIN, BROWN & LOEFFLER
555 13th St., N.W. Suite 300 East, Washington, DC 20004
Telephone: (202) 637-6850
Background: Washington, D.C. office of a San Antonio, Texas law firm.
Members of firm representing listed organizations:
Loeffler, Tom
Background: Former Member, U.S. House of Representatives (R-TX).
Clients:
Central and South West Services, Inc. *(Tom Loeffler)*
SEMATECH *(Tom Loeffler)*

MCCANN, Theodore
V. President, CEHP, Inc.
1333 Connecticut Ave., N.W. Suite 400, Washington, DC 20036
Telephone: (202) 293-1774

MCCARL, Kathryn A.
Mgr. Gov't Affairs, Consumer Group, Electronic Industries Ass'n
2001 Pennsylvania Ave., N.W., Washington, DC 20006
Telephone: (202) 457-4900

MCCARTER, Katherine
Assoc. Exec. Director, Gov't Relations, American Public Health Ass'n
1015 15th St., N.W. Third Floor, Washington, DC 20005
Telephone: (202) 789-5600
Registered as lobbyist at U.S. Congress.

MCCARTHY AND ASSOC., Bettie
733 15th St., N.W., Suite 700, Washington, DC 20005
Telephone: (202) 393-0020
Members of firm representing listed organizations:
McCarthy, Bettie S., President
Organizations represented:
Productive Employment Foundation *(Bettie S. McCarthy)*
Proprietary Industries Ass'n *(Bettie S. McCarthy)*
Trinova Corp. *(Bettie S. McCarthy)*

MCCARTHY, Bettie S.
President, McCarthy and Assoc., Bettie
733 15th St., N.W., Suite 700, Washington, DC 20005
Telephone: (202) 393-0020
Organizations represented:
Productive Employment Foundation
Proprietary Industries Ass'n
Trinova Corp.

MCCARTHY, Carolyn Kim
Legis. Couns. & Dir., Fed. Gov't Affairs, Corning
1455 Pennsylvania Ave., N.W. Suite 500, Washington, DC 20004
Telephone: (202) 347-2270
Registered as lobbyist at U.S. Congress.

MCCARTHY, Edward J.
V. President, Industrial Products, Rubber Manufacturers Ass'n
1400 K St., N.W., Washington, DC 20005
Telephone: (202) 682-4800

MCCARTHY, Frank E.
Exec. V. President, Nat'l Automobile Dealers Ass'n
8400 Westpark Dr., McLean, VA 22102
Telephone: (703) 821-7000
Registered as lobbyist at U.S. Congress.

MCCARTHY, James R.
Director, Wash. Energy Tax Practice, Price Waterhouse
1801 K St., N.W., Suite 700, Washington, DC 20006
Telephone: (202) 296-0800
Registered as lobbyist at U.S. Congress.

MCCARTHY, John B.
Senior Program Specialist, American Veterinary Medical Ass'n
1023 15th St., N.W., Suite 300, Washington, DC 20005
Telephone: (202) 659-2040
Registered as lobbyist at U.S. Congress.

MCCARTHY, Dr. John F.
V. Pres., Dir., Scient. & Regul. Affairs, Nat'l Agricultural Chemicals Ass'n
Madison Bldg., 1155 15th St., Suite 900, Washington, DC 20005
Telephone: (202) 296-1585

MCCARTHY, Kevin
Dir., Communications/Entertainment/Mktg., USO World
601 Indiana Ave., N.W., Washington, DC 20004
Telephone: (202) 783-8121

MCCARTHY, Margaret
Public Information Officer, California, State of
444 North Capitol St., N.W. Suite 305, Washington, DC 20001
Telephone: (202) 347-6891

MCCARTHY, Matthew H.
Stroock & Stroock & Lavan
1150 17th St., N.W. Sixth Floor, Washington, DC 20036
Telephone: (202) 452-9250

MCCARTHY, Robert
Railroad Coordinator, Internat'l Ass'n of Machinists and Aerospace Workers
1300 Connecticut Ave., N.W. Suite 404, Washington, DC 20036
Telephone: (202) 857-5200

MCCARTHY, SWEENEY AND HARKAWAY, P.C.
1750 Pennsylvania Ave. N.W. Suite 1105, Washington, DC 20006
Telephone: (202) 393-5710
Members of firm representing listed organizations:
Harkaway, William I.
Background: Senior Staff Attorney, Federal Power Commission 1958-67.
Reiter, Harvey L.
Background: Trial Attorney, Federal Power Commission, 1975-78. Special Assistant to the Deputy General Counsel for Litigation, Federal Energy Regulatory Commission, 1979-84.
Sweeney, Daniel J.
Clients:
Consolidated Edison Co. of New York *(William I. Harkaway)*
Green Bay and Western Railroad Co.
Missouri Public Service Co.
Montana Power Co.
Nat'l Small Shipments Traffic Conference - NAS-STRAC *(Daniel J. Sweeney)*
Pennsylvania Power and Light Co.
Union Electric Co.
Vermont Department of Public Service *(Harvey L. Reiter)*
Virginia Power Co.
Wisconsin Electric Power Co.
Wisconsin Power and Light Co.
Wisconsin Public Service Corp.

MCCARTHY, Timothy S.
Director, Communications, American Forest Council
1250 Connecticut Ave., N.W. Suite 320, Washington, DC 20036
Telephone: (202) 463-2455

MCCARTHY, William J.
Chairman, Democratic-Republican-Independent Voter Education (DRIVE) Committee
25 Louisiana Ave., N.W., Washington, DC 20001
Telephone: (202) 624-8741

MCCARTY, Donald J.
President, Nat'l Ass'n of Stevedores
2011 Eye St., N.W., Washington, DC 20006

Telephone: (202) 296-2810

MCCARTY, J. Laurence
V. President, Government Relations, Prudential Insurance
Co. of America
1140 Connecticut Ave., N.W. Suite 510, Washington, DC
20036
Telephone: (202) 293-2777

MCCARTY, Kevin
Linton, Mields, Reisler and Cottone
1225 Eye St., N.W., Suite 300, Washington, DC 20005
Telephone: (202) 682-3901
Clients:
Council of Industrial Development Bond Issuers
Nat'l Ass'n of Flood and Stormwater Manage-
ment Agencies

MCCASTLIAN, Hugh
Manager, Energy Technology Development, American
Gas Ass'n
1515 Wilson Blvd., Arlington, VA 22209
Telephone: (703) 841-8653

MCCAUL, James R.
President, Internat'l Maritime Associates
2600 Virginia Ave., N.W., Washington, DC 20037
Telephone: (202) 333-8501
Registered as lobbyist at U.S. Congress.

MCCAULEY, Alfred R.
Sharretts, Paley, Carter and Blauvelt
1707 L St., N.W., Suite 725, Washington, DC 20036
Telephone: (202) 223-4433
Clients:
AM&S/BHAS
SAE Electric
Thyssen Inc.

MCCAULEY, Michael
Field Organizer, Congress Watch
215 Pennsylvania Ave., S.E., Washington, DC 20003
Telephone: (202) 546-4996

MCCLAIN, W. R.
V. President, Gov't and Int'l Operations, E-Systems, Inc.
1901 North Moore St. Suite 609, Arlington, VA 22209
Telephone: (703) 524-2310

MCCLELLAN, Dr. James
President, Center for Judicial Studies
Box 15499, Washington, DC 20003
Telephone: (202) 544-1776

MCCLELLAND, Pamela
Resource Director, Trout Unlimited
501 Church St., N.E., Vienna, VA 22180
Telephone: (703) 281-1100

MCCLESKEY, James S.
Legislative Director, Simon & Co., Inc.
1001 Connecticut Ave., N.W. Suite 435, Washington, DC
20005
Telephone: (202) 659-2229
Background: Staff Assistant to Senator Daniel P. Moynihan (D-NY), 1986-87.

MCCLOSKEY, Michael
Chairman, Sierra Club
408 C St., N.E., Washington, DC 20002
Telephone: (202) 547-1141
Registered as lobbyist at U.S. Congress.

MCCLOSKEY, Peter F.
President, Electronic Industries Ass'n
2001 Pennsylvania Ave., N.W., Washington, DC 20006
Telephone: (202) 457-4900

MCCLOSKEY, William
Manager, Media Relations, BellSouth Corp.
1133 21st St., N.W., Suite 900, Washington, DC 20036
Telephone: (202) 463-4100

MCCLUNG, John M.
V. President, Government Relations, United Fresh Fruit
and Vegetable Ass'n
722 North Washington St., Alexandria, VA 22030
Telephone: (703) 836-3410
Registered as lobbyist at U.S. Congress.

Background: Former Director of Information, U.S. Dept. of
Agriculture. Serves also as contact for the United Fresh
Fruit and Vegetable Ass'n PAC (UNIPAC).

MCCLURE, Donovan
Senior V. President, Kamber Group, The
1920 L St., N.W., Washington, DC 20036
Telephone: (202) 223-8700
Organizations represented:
Plasterers' and Cement Masons' Action Commit-
tee
Transportation, Communications Internat'l Union

MCCLURE, Frederick D.
Asst to the President for Legis Affrs, EXECUTIVE OFFICE
OF THE PRESIDENT - The White House
1600 Pennsylvania Ave., N.W., Washington, DC 20500
Telephone: (202) 456-2230

MCCLURE, Phyllis
Div. of Policy and Information, NAACP Legal Defense and
Educational Fund, Inc.
1275 K St., N.W. Suite 301, Washington, DC 20005
Telephone: (202) 682-1300

MCCLURE AND TROTTER
1100 Connecticut Ave., N.W., Suite 600, Washington, DC
20036
Telephone: (202) 659-3400
Members of firm representing listed organizations:
Johnson, Robert W. (II)
Background: Attorney, Office of the General Counsel,
U.S. Department of Agriculture, 1976-1977. Senior
Staff Assistant to Chairman George Mahon, Commit-
tee on Appropriations, House of Representatives,
1977-1979.
McClure, William P.
Clients:
Ass'n of American Publishers
Coca-Cola Enterprises Inc.
Dominican Republic Internat'l Sugar Policy
Coordinating Commission
Dominican Sugar Institute
Met-Fuel Inc.
Motion Picture Ass'n of America (William P.
McClure)
TeknaMed Corp.

MCCLURE, William D.
Corporate Consulting Internat'l Ltd.
1700 North Moore St., Suite 1610, Arlington, VA 22209
Telephone: (703) 524-8957

MCCLURE, William P.
McClure and Trotter
1100 Connecticut Ave., N.W., Suite 600, Washington, DC
20036
Telephone: (202) 659-3400
Registered as lobbyist at U.S. Congress.
Clients:
Motion Picture Ass'n of America

MCCLUSKEY, Sandra H.
Director of Public Affairs, Cato Institute
224 Second St., S.E., Washington, DC 20003
Telephone: (202) 546-0200

MCCOMAS, Harry G., Skip
Smith, Bucklin and Associates
1101 Connecticut Ave., N.W., Suite 700, Washington, DC
20036
Telephone: (202) 857-1100
Background: Account Executive for Chain Link Fence
Manufacturers Institute, Independent Electrical Contrac-
tors and Internat'l Slurry Seal Ass'n.
Clients:
Internat'l Slurry Seal Ass'n
Southern Cemetery Ass'n

MCCOMMONS, Richard E.
Exec. Director, Ass'n of Collegiate Schools of Architecture
1735 New York Ave., N.W. Seventh Floor, Washington,
DC 20006
Telephone: (202) 785-2324

MCCONAGHY, Mark
Principal, Washington Nat'l Tax Svc, Price Waterhouse
1801 K St., N.W., Suite 700, Washington, DC 20006
Telephone: (202) 296-0800

Background: Former staff chief, Congressional Joint Committee on Taxation.

MCCONNAUGHEY, Robert S.
Senior Counsel, American Council of Life Insurance
1001 Pennsylvania Ave., N.W., Washington, DC 20004-
2599
Telephone: (202) 624-2119
Registered as lobbyist at U.S. Congress.

MCCONNELL, Cynthia W.
Field Director, Federation for American Immigration Reform (FAIR)
1666 Connecticut Ave., N.W., Suite 400, Washington, DC
20009
Telephone: (202) 328-7004
Registered as lobbyist at U.S. Congress.

MCCONNELL, James F.
1730 Rhode Island Ave., N.W. Suite 400, Washington, DC
20036
Telephone: (202) 223-2451
Registered as lobbyist at U.S. Congress.
Organizations represented:
Orange, California, County of
Orange County Transit District
Orange County Transportation Commission
Orange County Water District
Santa Ana River Flood Protection Agency
Transportation Corridor Agencies

MCCONNELL, Janet
Cong Inquiries, AGENCY FOR INTERNAT'L DEVELOP-
MENT
320 21st St., N.W., Washington, DC 20523
Telephone: (202) 647-8190

MCCONNELL, Mark S.
Hogan and Hartson
555 13th St., N.W., Suite 1200, Washington, DC 20004-
1109
Telephone: (202) 637-5600
Registered as lobbyist at U.S. Congress.
Registered as Foreign Agent: (#2244).
Clients:
Ontario, Province of

MCCONNELL, Nancy Fifield
Director, Washington Office, Population Resource Center
1725 K St., N.W., Suite 1102, Washington, DC 20006
Telephone: (202) 467-5030

MCCONNELL, Robert A.
Gibson, Dunn and Crutcher
1050 Connecticut Ave., N.W. Suite 900, Washington, DC
20036-5303
Telephone: (202) 955-8500
Registered as lobbyist at U.S. Congress.
Background: Of Counsel. Assistant Attorney General, U.S.
Department of Justice, 1981-84.
Clients:
Alyeska Pipeline Service Co.
Internat'l Electronics Manufacturers and Con-
sumers of America
Wespar Financial Services

MCCONNELL, Stephen R.
Director, Washington Office, Alzheimer's Ass'n
1334 G St., N.W. Suite 500, Washington, DC 20005
Telephone: (202) 393-7737
Registered as lobbyist at U.S. Congress.
Background: Staff aide to the House Select Committee on
Aging, 1980-84 and Staff Director to Senate Special Ag-
ing Committee, 1984-87.

MCCORD, Rob
Exec. Director, Congressional Institute for the Future
412 First St., S.E., Washington, DC 20003
Telephone: (202) 544-7994

MCCORMACK, Nellie
Chief of Staff, Nat'l Federation of Republican Women
310 First St., S.E., Washington, DC 20003
Telephone: (202) 547-9341

WASHINGTON REPRESENTATIVES

MCCORMACK, Susan
Cong Correspondent, EXECUTIVE OFFICE OF THE
PRESIDENT - The White House
1600 Pennsylvania Ave., N.W. 102 East Wing, Washington, DC 20500
Telephone: (202) 456-7500

MCCORMALLY, Timothy J.
Tax Counsel, Tax Executives Institute
1001 Pennsylvania Ave., N.W., Suite 320, Washington, DC 20004-2505
Telephone: (202) 638-5601

MCCORMICK, Diann
Assistant to the Dir., Federal Relations, Kemper Group
600 Pennsylvania Ave., S.E., Suite 206, Washington, DC 20003
Telephone: (202) 547-0120
Background: Assistant to Rep. Ken Hechler (D-WV), 1965-77.

MCCORMICK, Judith A.
Assistant Federal Counsel, American Bankers Ass'n
1120 Connecticut Ave., N.W., Washington, DC 20036
Telephone: (202) 663-5479
Registered as lobbyist at U.S. Congress.

MCCORMICK, L. Carter, Jr.
CounterTerrorism Consultants L.P.
1800 Diagonal Road, Suite 230, Alexandria, VA 22314
Telephone: (703) 683-6988
Registered as Foreign Agent: (#4294).
Clients:
Jamaica, Government of

MCCORMICK, Mary Lou
Gold and Liebengood, Inc.
1455 Pennsylvania Ave., N.W. Suite 950, Washington, DC 20004
Telephone: (202) 639-8899
Background: Former Press Secretary to Senator Bob Packwood (R-OR).

MCCORMICK, Robert P.
President, Nat'l Constructors Ass'n
1730 M St., N.W., Suite 900, Washington, DC 20036-4571
Telephone: (202) 466-8880

MCCOY, Garland
Director of Development, American Legislative Exchange Council
214 Massachusetts Ave., N.W., Washington, DC 20002
Telephone: (202) 547-4646

MCCOY, Meredith
Staff Counsel, Nat'l Rural Electric Cooperative Ass'n
1800 Massachusetts Ave., N.W., Washington, DC 20036
Telephone: (202) 857-9500
Registered as lobbyist at U.S. Congress.

MCCOY, Steven A.
President, North American Export Grain Ass'n
1030 15th St., N.W. Suite 1020, Washington, DC 20005
Telephone: (202) 682-4030
Registered as lobbyist at U.S. Congress.

MCCOY, Victor
Assoc. Exec. Director, Veterans Benefits, Paralyzed Veterans of America
801 18th St., N.W., Washington, DC 20006
Telephone: (202) 872-1300

MCCOY, Virginia
Legislative Analyst, State & Local Afrs., Nat'l Soft Drink Ass'n
1101 16th St., N.W., Washington, DC 20036
Telephone: (202) 463-6732

MCCRACKEN, Todd
Legislative Director, Nat'l Small Business United
1155 15th St., N.W. 7th Floor, Washington, DC 20005
Telephone: (202) 293-8830
Registered as lobbyist at U.S. Congress.

MCCRAY, Joyce G.
Exec. Director, Council for American Private Education
1726 M St., N.W. Suite 1102, Washington, DC 20036
Telephone: (202) 659-0016

MCCREDIE, William H.
Exec. V. President, Nat'l Particleboard Ass'n
18928 Premiere Court, Gaithersburg, MD 20879
Telephone: (301) 670-0604

MCCREEDY, Cliff
Cong Liaison Div, ENVIRONMENTAL PROTECTION AGENCY
401 M St., S.W., Washington, DC 20460
Telephone: (202) 382-5200

MCCUE, Martin T.
V. President & General Counsel, United States Telephone Ass'n
900 19th St., N.W., Suite 800, Washington, DC 20006-2102
Telephone: (202) 835-3100

MCCULLOCH, Donna A.
Legislative Representative, Nat'l Apartment Ass'n
1111 14th St., N.W., 9th Floor, Washington, DC 20005
Telephone: (202) 842-4050
Registered as lobbyist at U.S. Congress.

MCCULLOCH, Edgar 'Ned' H., III
Legislative Representative, Service Employees Internat'l Union
1313 L St., N.W., Washington, DC 20005
Telephone: (202) 898-3200
Registered as lobbyist at U.S. Congress.

MCCULLOUGH, Kim
Media Consultant, State & Local Resources
901 Sixth St., S.W., Suite 503A, Washington, DC 20024
Telephone: (202) 488-1460

MCCURDY, Dr. Harry W.
Exec. V. President, American Academy of Otolaryngology-Head and Neck Surgery

MCCURDY, Patrick
Director of Communications, American Chemical Soc.
1155 16th St., N.W., Washington, DC 20036
Telephone: (202) 872-6280

MCCURRY, Michael D.
Communications Director, Democratic Nat'l Committee
430 South Capitol St., S.E., Washington, DC 20003
Telephone: (202) 863-8000

MCCUTCHEN, DOYLE, BROWN & ENERSEN
1455 Pennsylvania Ave., N.W., Suite 650, Washington, DC 20004
Telephone: (202) 628-4900
Members of firm representing listed organizations:
Andrews, David
  Background: Legal Counsel and Special Assistant for Policy, Environmental Protection Agency, 1978-80. Deputy General Counsel, Department of Health and Human Services, 1980.
Cummings, Philip T.
  Background: Chief Counsel, U.S. Senate Committee on Environment andf Public Works, 1970-88.
Clients:
Browning-Ferris Industries (D.C.), Inc. *(Philip T. Cummings)*
DNA Plant Technology Corp. *(David Andrews, Philip T. Cummings)*
General Electric Co.
Nat'l Ass'n of Regional Councils *(Philip T. Cummings)*
Rohr Industries, Inc. *(David Andrews, Philip T. Cummings)*
Southern California Ass'n of Governments *(Philip T. Cummings)*

MCCUTCHEON, Aubrey, III
Exec. Director, Washington Office on Africa
110 Maryland Ave., N.E. Suite 112, Washington, DC 20002
Telephone: (202) 546-7961
Registered as lobbyist at U.S. Congress.
Background: Legislative Assistant to Rep. George W. Crockett, Jr. (D-MI), 1982-83. Staff Director to Rep. John Conyers (D-MI), 1983-86.

MCDANIEL, Capt. Eugene B.
President/Founder, American Defense Foundation
214 Massachusetts Ave., N.E. Suite 200, Washington, DC 20002
Telephone: (202) 544-4704
Background: Former Navy/Marine Corps. Liaison to the U.S. House of Representatives, 1979-81.

MCDAVITT, Jack
Director, Publications, Nat'l Committee to Preserve Social Security and Medicare
2000 K St., N.W. Suite 800, Washington, DC 20006
Telephone: (202) 822-9459
Registered as lobbyist at U.S. Congress.
Background: Staff positions with U.S. House of Representatives, 1973-84. Special Assistant for Public Affairs to the Assistant Secretary of Labor for OSHA, 1984-86.

MCDERMID, John F.
Internat'l Business-Government Counsellors, Inc.
818 Connecticut Ave., N.W. Suite 1200, Washington, DC 20006
Telephone: (202) 872-8181
Background: President and General Counsel, Internat'l Business-Government Counsellors, Inc.
Clients:
ANSAC

MCDERMOTT, Ann
Director, Government Relations, Manor Care
10750 Columbia Pike, Silver Spring, MD 20901
Telephone: (301) 593-9600

MCDERMOTT, Charles
Government Affairs Director, Waste Management, Inc.
1155 Connecticut Ave., N.W., Suite 800, Washington, DC 20036
Telephone: (202) 467-4480
Registered as lobbyist at U.S. Congress.

MCDERMOTT, Daniel J.
Legislative Counsel, Financial Services Council
1225 19th St., N.W., Suite 410, Washington, DC 20036
Telephone: (202) 785-1500
Registered as lobbyist at U.S. Congress.

MCDERMOTT, Francis O.
Hopkins and Sutter
888 16th St., N.W., Suite 700, Washington, DC 20006
Telephone: (202) 835-8000
Registered as lobbyist at U.S. Congress.
Clients:
Allstate Insurance Co.
Ass'n Management Corp.
Chicago Mercantile Exchange
First Chicago Corp.
Inland Steel Co.

MCDERMOTT, Kathleen
Collier, Shannon & Scott
1055 Thomas Jefferson St., N.W., Suite 300, Washington, DC 20007
Telephone: (202) 342-8400

MCDERMOTT, Marianne
Resources for Group Management, Inc.
1350 New York Ave., N.W. Suite 615, Washington, DC 20005
Telephone: (202) 393-1780
Registered as lobbyist at U.S. Congress.
Background: Serves as Exec. V. President, Greeting Card Ass'n and Nat'l Candle Ass'n and as Treasurer, Committee Assisting Republicans and Democrats (CARD-PAC).
Clients:
Committee Assisting Republicans and Democrats (CARD-PAC)
Greeting Card Ass'n
Nat'l Ass'n of Legal Search Consultants
Nat'l Candle Ass'n
Purchasing Management Ass'n of Washington

MCDERMOTT, Mark T.
Joseph, Gajarsa, McDermott and Reiner, P.C.
1300 19th St., N.W. Suite 400, Washington, DC 20036
Telephone: (202) 331-1955
Registered as lobbyist at U.S. Congress.
Background: Trial Attorney, Federal Aviation Administration, 1974-78.
Clients:

WASHINGTON REPRESENTATIVES

Civil Pilots for Regulatory Reform

MCDERMOTT, Robert F.
Jones, Day, Reavis and Pogue
1450 G St., N.W., Suite 700, Washington, DC 20005-2088
Telephone: (202) 879-3939
Registered as lobbyist at U.S. Congress.
Background: Staff Ass't to the President 1971-72; Staff Ass't to the Deputy Attorney General 1974-75; Assoc. Deputy Attorney General 1975; U.S. Dept. of Justice, Ass't U.S. Attorney for the Eastern District of Virginia 1976-79.
Clients:
RJR Nabisco Washington, Inc.

MCDERMOTT, WILL AND EMERY
1850 K St., N.W., Suite 500, Washington, DC 20006-2296
Telephone: (202) 887-8000
Background: Washington office of a national law firm.
Members of firm representing listed organizations:
  Bloch, Ronald A., Counsel
    Background: Former Assistant Director for Litigation, Bureau of Competition, Federal Trade Commission, 1978-85.
  Hercenberg, Jerrold J.
    Background: Former Senior Legal Advisor, Office of Prepaid Health Care, Health Care Financing Administration, U.S. Department of Health and Human Services.
  Krasner, Wendy L.
    Background: Office of General Counsel, U.S. Department of Health and Human Services, 1978-80.
  Nicholas, Robert B.
  Romansky, Michael A.
  Ruckert, Edward
  Schwartz, Robert S.
    Background: Trial Attorney, Antitrust Division, Intellectual Property Section, U.S. Department of Justice, 1975-79.
  Schwarz, Carl W.
    Background: Trial Attorney, U.S. Department of Justice, 1961-69.
  Sneed, James
  Warden, Robert A.
    Background: Assistant Legislation Counsel, 1975-79; Legislation Counsel, 1977 and Assistant Chief of Staff, 1978, Joint Committee on Taxation, U.S. Congress.
Clients:
Accreditation Ass'n for Ambulatory Healthcare, Inc.
American Dental Hygienists' Ass'n
American Imaging Ass'n *(Michael A. Romansky)*
American Soc. for Medical Technology Political Action Committee
American Soc. of Outpatient Surgeons
Animal Health Institute *(Robert B. Nicholas)*
Ass'n of Freestanding Radiation Oncology Centers
California Table Grape Commission *(Edward Ruckert)*
Churfine-Central Corp. *(Ronald A. Bloch)*
Electronic Industries Ass'n of Japan *(Robert S. Schwartz)*
Globe Corp. *(Robert A. Warden)*
Hitachi America Ltd. *(Robert S. Schwartz, Carl W. Schwarz)*
Hitachi Ltd. *(Robert S. Schwartz, Carl W. Schwarz)*
Illinois Cereal Mills *(James Sneed)*
Internat'l Apple Institute *(Edward Ruckert)*
Juvenile Diabetes Foundation
Nat'l Foundation for the Handicapped
Nat'l Grocers Ass'n *(Ronald A. Bloch)*
Nat'l Potato Council *(Edward Ruckert)*
Public Employees' Retirement Ass'n of Colorado *(Robert A. Warden)*
Western Ass'n of Children's Hospitals

MCDIARMID, Robert C.
Spiegel and McDiarmid
1350 New York Ave., N.W., Suite 1100, Washington, DC 20005
Telephone: (202) 879-4000
Registered as lobbyist at U.S. Congress.
Background: Attorney, Civil Division, Appellate Section, Department of Justice 1964-68. Assistant to the General Counsel, Federal Power Commission, 1968-70.
Clients:

Northern California Power Agency

MCDIVITT, James A.
Sr. V. President, Government Operations, Rockwell Internat'l
1745 Jefferson Davis Hwy., Suite 1200, Arlington, VA 22202
Telephone: (703) 553-6625

MCDONALD, Charles S.
Assistant to the Secretary-Treasurer, AFL-CIO (American Federation of Labor and Congress of Industrial Organizations)
815 16th St., N.W., Washington, DC 20006
Telephone: (202) 637-5075

MCDONALD CO., Jack
1001 Pennsylvania Ave., N.W., Suite 625 South, Washington, DC 20004
Telephone: (202) 624-7269
Members of firm representing listed organizations:
  McDonald, Jack
    Background: Former Member, U.S. House of Representatives (R-MI).
  Sandifer, Myron G. (III)
    Background: Former Staff Assistant to Senator Walter D. Huddleston (D-KY).
Organizations represented:
  Ameritech (American Information Technologies) *(Jack McDonald)*
  Dow Corning Corp. *(Jack McDonald, Myron G. Sandifer, III)*
  Hitachi America Ltd. *(Jack McDonald, Myron G. Sandifer, III)*
  Hitachi Sales Corp. of America *(Jack McDonald, Myron G. Sandifer, III)*
  Outboard Marine Corp. *(Jack McDonald)*
  Planeta North America, Inc. *(Jack McDonald, Myron G. Sandifer, III)*
  Tuteur Associates, Inc. *(Jack McDonald, Myron G. Sandifer, III)*
  WMW Machinery, Inc. *(Jack McDonald, Myron G. Sandifer, III)*

MCDONALD, Craig
Director, Clean Up Congress Campaign, Congress Watch
215 Pennsylvania Ave., S.E., Washington, DC 20003
Telephone: (202) 546-4996

MCDONALD, Edward
Regional Legislative Director, Transportation, Communications Internat'l Union
815 16th St., N.W. Suite 511, Washington, DC 20036
Telephone: (202) 783-3660
Registered as lobbyist at U.S. Congress.

MCDONALD, Gail C.
Manager, Regulatory Affairs, Gas Research Institute
1331 Pennsylvania Ave., N.W., Suite 730 North, Washington, DC 20004
Telephone: (202) 662-8989

MCDONALD, Greg
Exec. Director, Nat'l Ass'n for Search and Rescue
Box 3709, Fairfax, VA 22038
Telephone: (703) 352-1349

MCDONALD, Jack
McDonald Co., Jack
1001 Pennsylvania Ave., N.W., Suite 625 South, Washington, DC 20004
Telephone: (202) 624-7269
Registered as lobbyist at U.S. Congress.
Registered as Foreign Agent: (#3956).
Background: Former Member, U.S. House of Representatives (R-MI).
Organizations represented:
  Ameritech (American Information Technologies)
  Dow Corning Corp.
  Hitachi America Ltd.
  Hitachi Sales Corp. of America
  Outboard Marine Corp.
  Planeta North America, Inc.
  Tuteur Associates, Inc.
  WMW Machinery, Inc.

MCDONALD, Mary
Washington Rep, Natural Resources, California, State of
444 North Capitol St., N.W., Suite 305, Washington, DC 20001
Telephone: (202) 347-6891

MCDONALD, Patricia A.
Director, Public Lands, Nat'l Cattlemen's Ass'n
1301 Pennsylvania Ave., N.W., Suite 300, Washington, DC 20004
Telephone: (202) 347-0228
Registered as lobbyist at U.S. Congress.
Background: Serves also as Exec. Director, Public Lands Council.

MCDONALD, Robert A.
V. President, Nat'l Ass'n of Environmental Professionals
Box 15210, Alexandria, VA 22309-0210
Telephone: (703) 660-2364

MCDONNELL, James A.
Director, Military Relations, Air Force Ass'n
1501 Lee Hwy., Arlington, VA 22209-1198
Telephone: (703) 247-5800

MCDONOUGH, Peter
Partner, Princeton Public Affairs Group
3333 K St., N.W., Suite 110, Washington, DC 20007
Telephone: (202) 785-2203

MCDONOUGH, Sandra K.
Federal Affairs Manager, Pacific Power & Light
1350 New York Ave., N.W. Suite 600, Washington, DC 20005-4702
Telephone: (202) 347-5242

MCDOUGALL, Gay
Director, Southern Africa Project, Lawyers' Committee for Civil Rights Under Law
1400 Eye St., N.W., Suite 400, Washington, DC 20005
Telephone: (202) 371-1212

MCDOWELL, Douglas S.
McGuiness and Williams
1015 15th St., N.W., Suite 1200, Washington, DC 20005
Telephone: (202) 789-8600
Clients:
Equal Employment Advisory Council

MCDOWELL-HEAD, Leila
Senior Account Executive, Fenton Communications, Inc.
1755 S St., N.W., Second Floor, Washington, DC 20009
Telephone: (202) 745-0707
Registered as Foreign Agent: (#3857).

MCDOWELL, Joyce
Director of Public Affairs, Nat'l Moving and Storage Ass'n
1500 North Beauregard St. Suite 320, Alexandria, VA 22311
Telephone: (703) 671-8813

MCDOWELL, Marian E.
Director, Federal Relations, Pacific Telesis Group-Washington
1275 Pennsylvania Ave., N.W. Suite 400, Washington, DC 20004
Telephone: (202) 383-6400
Registered as lobbyist at U.S. Congress.

MCDOWELL, Suzanne Ross
Ropes and Gray
1001 Pennsylvania Ave., N.W., Washington, DC 20004
Telephone: (202) 626-3900
Registered as lobbyist at U.S. Congress.
Background: Attorney-Advisor, 1983-85, Associate Tax Legislative Counsel, 1985-87, U.S. Department of the Treasury.
Clients:
Butler Capital Corp.

MCELFRESH, Dinah D.
Hauck and Associates
1255 23rd St., N.W., Washington, DC 20037
Telephone: (202) 452-8100
Registered as lobbyist at U.S. Congress.
Background: Serves as Director, Regulatory Affairs Committee, Soy Protein Council; Director of Gov't Relations, Hearing Industries Ass'n; and Director of Administration, State Governmental Affairs Council.
Clients:

MCELFRESH, Dinah D. (Cont'd)
Soy Protein Council
State Governmental Affairs Council

MCELGUNN, Peggy
V. President, Internat'l Management Group, Inc.
1101 14th St., N.W. Suite 1100, Washington, DC 20005
Telephone: (202) 371-2200
Background: Serves as Exec. Director, Soc. of Environmental Toxicology and Chemistry and Associate Director, Nat'l Soc. for Cardiovascular Technologists/Nat'l Soc. for Pulmonary Technologists.
Clients:
Nat'l Soc. for Cardiovascular and Pulmonary Technology

MCELHENY, Richard L.
Partner, Brock Group, The
1130 Connecticut Ave., N.W. Suite 350, Washington, DC 20036
Telephone: (202) 296-1901
Background: Assistant Secretary for Trade Development, Director General of the U.S. and Foreign Commercial Service U.S. Department of Commerce, 1981-84.

MCELIGOT, Patrick
Rea, Cross & Auchincloss
1920 N St., N.W., Suite 420, Washington, DC 20036
Telephone: (202) 785-3700
Clients:
New England Motor Rate Bureau

MCELROY, James R.
V. President, Hill and Knowlton Public Affairs Worldwide
Washington Harbour, 901 31st St., N.W., Washington, DC 20007
Telephone: (202) 333-7400
Background: Automotive Trade Analyst, U.S. International Trade Commission, 1977-86.

MCELROY, Michelle
Manager, Public Information, Gas Research Institute
1331 Pennsylvania Ave., N.W., Suite 730 North, Washington, DC 20004
Telephone: (202) 662-8989

MCELROY, Roland
President, Outdoor Advertising Ass'n of America
1212 New York Ave., N.W., Suite 1210, Washington, DC 20005
Telephone: (202) 371-5566
Registered as lobbyist at U.S. Congress.
Background: Former Press Secretary and Chief of Staff to Senator Sam Nunn (D-GA).

MCENTEE, Christine W.
Director, Div. of Membership Relations, American Hospital Ass'n
50 F St., N.W., Suite 1100, Washington, DC 20001
Telephone: (202) 638-1100
Registered as lobbyist at U.S. Congress.

MCENTEE, Elliott C.
President, Nat'l Automated Clearing House Ass'n
607 Herndon Parkway Suite 200, Herndon, VA 22070
Telephone: (703) 742-9190

MCENTEE, Gerald W.
President, American Federation of State, County and Municipal Employees
1625 L St., N.W., Washington, DC 20036
Telephone: (202) 429-1100

MCEVOY, John T.
Exec. V. Director, Nat'l Council of State Housing Agencies
444 N. Capitol St., N.W., Suite 118, Washington, DC 20001
Telephone: (202) 624-7710
Background: Former Staff Director, Senate Budget Committee.

MCEWEN, Darryl D.
Exec. V. President, Machinery Dealers Nat'l Ass'n
1110 Spring St., Silver Spring, MD 20910
Telephone: (301) 585-9494
Registered as lobbyist at U.S. Congress.
Background: Also serves as Treasurer of the Machinery Dealers Nat'l Ass'n PAC.

MCEWEN, Dr. Gerald N., Jr.
V. President, Science, Cosmetic, Toiletry and Fragrance Ass'n
1110 Vermont Ave., N.W. Suite 800, Washington, DC 20005
Telephone: (202) 331-1770

MCFADDEN, Clark
Dewey, Ballantine, Bushby, Palmer and Wood
1775 Pennsylvania Ave., N.W. Suite 200, Washington, DC 20006
Telephone: (202) 862-1000
Clients:
SEMATECH

MCFADDEN, Robert
Director, Washington Information Bureau, Ad Hoc Committee in Defense of Life
1187 Nat'l Press Bldg., Washington, DC 20045
Telephone: (202) 347-8686
Registered as lobbyist at U.S. Congress.

MCFADDEN, Robert H.
Senior Analyst, Fed. Liaison Dept., Motor Vehicle Manufacturers Ass'n of the United States
1620 Eye St., N.W. Suite 1000, Washington, DC 20006
Telephone: (202) 775-2700
Registered as lobbyist at U.S. Congress.

MCFARLAND, Leslie
Deputy Director, Nat'l Coalition on Black Voter Participation, Inc.
1101 14th St., N.W., Suite 925, Washington, DC 20005
Telephone: (202) 898-2220

MCFARLANE, Carolyn
Cong Liaison, DEPARTMENT OF TREASURY - Comptroller of the Currency
490 L'Enfant Plaza East, S.W., Washington, DC 20219
Telephone: (202) 447-9704

MCFARLANE, Randall H.
Sr VP & Dep Gen Counsel, Leg & Reg Afrs., United States League of Savings Institutions
1709 New York Ave., N.W., Suite 801, Washington, DC 20006
Telephone: (202) 637-8900

MCFEELEY, Tim
Exec. Director, Human Rights Campaign Fund
1012 14th St., N.W. Suite 607, Washington, DC 20005
Telephone: (202) 628-4160

MCFILLEN, Teresa L.
Deputy PAC Director, Nat'l Republican Congressional Committee
320 First St., S.E., Washington, DC 20003
Telephone: (202) 479-7000

MCGANN, Albert J.
Federal Gov't Affairs V. President, AT&T
Suite 1000, 1120 20th St., N.W., Washington, DC 20036
Telephone: (202) 457-3852

MCGARITY, Neal
Acct. Supervisor, Corp/Int'l Counseling, Hill and Knowlton Public Affairs Worldwide
Washington Harbour, 901 31st St., N.W., Washington, DC 20007
Telephone: (202) 333-7400

MCGARRY, III J. Michael
Bishop, Cook, Purcell & Reynolds
1400 L St., N.W., Washington, DC 20005-3502
Telephone: (202) 371-5700

MCGEE, Becky
Senior Attorney, Oryx Energy Co.
1212 New York Ave., N.W. Suite 1200, Washington, DC 20005-3987
Telephone: (202) 682-1212
Registered as lobbyist at U.S. Congress.

MCGEE, Dana
V. President - Congressional Liaison, Grumman Corp.
1000 Wilson Blvd., Suite 2800, Arlington, VA 22209
Telephone: (703) 875-8400
Registered as lobbyist at U.S. Congress.

MCGEE, Donna Lee
Director, Government Relations, Burlington Industries Inc.
1001 Connecticut Ave., N.W. Suite 701, Washington, DC 20036
Telephone: (202) 223-3167
Registered as lobbyist at U.S. Congress.

MCGEE, James
President, Nat'l Alliance of Postal and Federal Employees
1628 11th St., N.W., Washington, DC 20001
Telephone: (202) 939-6325
Background: Also represents the Nat'l Alliance for Political Action.

MCGEE, Karen
Federal Legislative Representative, Credit Union Nat'l Ass'n
805 15th St., N.W. Suite 300, Washington, DC 20005
Telephone: (202) 682-4200
Registered as lobbyist at U.S. Congress.

MCGEE, Kate
Manager, Government Affairs, Oracle Corp.
1627 Eye St., N.W., Suite 880, Washington, DC 20006
Telephone: (202) 907-2264
Registered as lobbyist at U.S. Congress.

MCGEE, Myricks E.
Manager, Bell Atlantic
1710 Rhode Island Ave., N.W., Suite 1200, Washington, DC 20036
Telephone: (202) 392-6983

MCGEHEE, Meredith
Lobbyist, Common Cause
2030 M St., N.W., Washington, DC 20036
Telephone: (202) 833-1200
Registered as lobbyist at U.S. Congress.

MCGHEE, Camilla A.
Keefe Co., The
444 North Capitol St., N.W., Suite 711, Washington, DC 20001
Telephone: (202) 638-7030
Clients:
Foodservice and Lodging Institute
Glick & Glick
Greater New York Hospital Ass'n
NATJ and NATE
New York Hospital

MCGIFFERT, David E.
Covington and Burling
1201 Pennsylvania Ave., N.W., Box 7566, Washington, DC 20044
Telephone: (202) 662-6000
Background: Under Secretary of the Army, 1966-69. Assistant Secretary of Defense, Internat'l Security Affairs, 1977-81.

MCGILL, Brian E.
Graham and James
2000 M St., N.W., Suite 700, Washington, DC 20036
Telephone: (202) 463-0800
Clients:
Hitachi Zosen Corp.
Nippon Mining Co.

MCGILL, John R.
Executive Assistant to the President, American Ass'n of Community and Junior Colleges
One Dupont Circle, N.W. Suite 410, Washington, DC 20036
Telephone: (202) 293-7050

MCGILL, Patricia
Ass't Dir., Congress'l & Agency Relat'ns, American Nurses' Ass'n
1101 14th St., N.W., Suite 200, Washington, DC 20005
Telephone: (202) 789-1800
Registered as lobbyist at U.S. Congress.

MCGILLICUDDY, Hugh J.
Government Marketing Representative, Grace and Co., W. R.
919 18th St., N.W., Suite 400, Washington, DC 20006
Telephone: (202) 452-6700

MCGINLY, Dr. William C.
President, Nat'l Ass'n for Hospital Development
112-B East Broad St., Falls Church, VA 22046
Telephone: (703) 532-6243

MCGINN, Daniel
V. President, Ryan-McGinn
1110 Vermont Ave., N.W. Suite 820, Washington, DC 20005
Telephone: (202) 775-4370
Registered as lobbyist at U.S. Congress.
Clients:
 Ashland Coal
 Batman Corp.
 Cabot Oil & Gas
 Health Industry Manufacturers Ass'n
 Humana, Inc.
 Independent Oil and Gas Ass'n of West Virginia
 Massey Coal Services
 Midwest Corp.
 Oregon Ass'n of Hospitals
 Texas A & M College of Medicine
 West Virginia Bankers Ass'n
 West Virginia Hospital Ass'n
 Wheeling Hospital

MCGINNIS, Patricia G.
FMR Group Inc., The
1000 Potomac St., N.W. Suite 401, Washington, DC 20007
Telephone: (202) 333-2533
Background: Deputy Associate Director, Office of Management and Budget, 1977-81. Staff Member, U.S. Senate Budget Committee, 1976-77. Policy Analyst, U.S. Department of Health and Human Services and U.S. Department of Commerce, 1973-76.
Clients:
 California Department of Education

MCGLOTTEN, Robert M.
Director, Dept. of Legislation, AFL-CIO (American Federation of Labor and Congress of Industrial Organizations)
815 16th St., N.W., Washington, DC 20006
Telephone: (202) 637-5075
Registered as lobbyist at U.S. Congress.
Background: Served as President, American League of Lobbyists in 1985.

MCGOVERN, John J., Jr.
Wunder, Ryan, Cannon & Thelen
1615 L St., N.W., Suite 650, Washington, DC 20036
Telephone: (202) 659-3005
Registered as lobbyist at U.S. Congress.
Registered as Foreign Agent: (#3971).
Background: Legislative Assistant to Senator Richard Lugar (R-IN), 1977-83. Legislative Assistant to Chairman John S. R. Shad, Securities and Exchange Commission, 1983-85.
Clients:
 Aermacchi, S.p.A.
 Airship Industries, Ltd.
 Bond Internat'l Gold
 FFA Fluzeugwerke
 Finanziaria Mirabella SpA
 Intermarine S.p.A.
 Mirabella
 Westinghouse Airship
 Westinghouse Electric Corp.

MCGOVERN, Nancy
District Director, Muscular Dystrophy Ass'n
5350 Shawnee Rd., Suite 330, Alexandria, VA 22312
Telephone: (703) 941-5001

MCGOVERN, Phyllis M.
Treasurer, Tobacco Institute Political Action Committee
1875 Eye St., N.W. Suite 800, Washington, DC 20006
Telephone: (202) 457-4800
Registered as lobbyist at U.S. Congress.

MCGOWAN, Gail
Corporate Secretary, American Bankers Ass'n
1120 Connecticut Ave., N.W., Washington, DC 20036
Telephone: (202) 663-5000

MCGRATH, Matthew T.
Barnes, Richardson and Colburn
1819 H St., N.W., Washington, DC 20006
Telephone: (202) 457-0300

Registered as lobbyist at U.S. Congress.
Registered as Foreign Agent: (#2751).
Clients:
 American Ass'n of Fastener Importers
 Budd Co.
 Case Co., J. I.
 Consolidated Diesel Corp.
 Florida Citrus Mutual
 Maple Leaf Fish Co.
 Miles, Inc.
 Omstead Foods Ltd.
 Sundstrand Corp.

MCGRAW, Marvin A.
Legislative Counsel, Nat'l League of Cities
1301 Pennsylvania Ave., N.W., Washington, DC 20004
Telephone: (202) 626-3000

MCGRAW, Richard L.
V. President, Corporate Affairs, Communications Satellite Corp. (COMSAT)
950 L'Enfant Plaza, S.W., Washington, DC 20024
Telephone: (202) 863-6000
Registered as lobbyist at U.S. Congress.

MCGREEVY, Martha
Admin Officer, Cong Liaison Asst, DEPARTMENT OF COMMERCE
14th and Constitution Ave. S.W., Washington, DC 20230
Telephone: (202) 377-5485

MCGUIGAN, Patrick B.
Sr. Scholar, Ctr for Law and Democracy, Coalitions for America
717 2nd St., N.E., Washington, DC 20002
Telephone: (202) 546-3003

MCGUINESS, Ann
Development Director, Nat'l Abortion Rights Action League
1101 14th St., N.W., Suite 500, Washington, DC 20005
Telephone: (202) 371-0779

MCGUINESS, Jeffrey C.
McGuiness and Williams
1015 15th St., N.W., Suite 1200, Washington, DC 20005
Telephone: (202) 789-8600
Registered as lobbyist at U.S. Congress.
Background: Chairman, Civil Rights Reviewing Authority, Department of Health and Human Services, 1981-83. Serves as President, Labor Policy Ass'n.
Clients:
 Labor Policy Ass'n
 Pony Express Courier Corp.
 Wells Fargo Armored Service Corp.

MCGUINESS AND WILLIAMS
1015 15th St., N.W., Suite 1200, Washington, DC 20005
Telephone: (202) 789-8600
Members of firm representing listed organizations:
 Kessler, Lorence L.
 McDowell, Douglas S.
 McGuiness, Jeffrey C.
  Background: Chairman, Civil Rights Reviewing Authority, Department of Health and Human Services, 1981-83. Serves as President, Labor Policy Ass'n.
 Norris, Jeffrey A.
 Tysse, G. John
  Background: Director of Labor Law, U.S. Chamber of Commerce, 1980-84.
 Yohay, Stephen C.
  Background: Attorney, Enforcement Division, National Labor Relations Board, 1971-74. Supervisory Attorney, OSHA Division, U.S. Department of Labor, 1974-75.
Clients:
 Equal Employment Advisory Council *(Lorence L. Kessler, Douglas S. McDowell, Jeffrey A. Norris)*
 Internat'l Theatrical Agencies Ass'n *(G. John Tysse)*
 Labor Policy Ass'n *(Jeffrey C. McGuiness)*
 Nat'l Ass'n of Orchestra Leaders *(G. John Tysse)*
 Nat'l Club Ass'n *(G. John Tysse)*
 Pony Express Courier Corp. *(Jeffrey C. McGuiness)*
 Wells Fargo Armored Service Corp. *(Jeffrey C. McGuiness)*

MCGUIRE, Jean F.
Exec. Director, AIDS Action Council
2033 M St., N.W., Suite 801, Washington, DC 20036

Telephone: (202) 293-2886
Registered as lobbyist at U.S. Congress.

MCGUIRE, Joseph M.
Sr. V. President, Policy & Gov't Affairs, Air-Conditioning and Refrigeration Institute
1501 Wilson Blvd., Suite 600, Arlington, VA 22209
Telephone: (703) 524-8800
Registered as lobbyist at U.S. Congress.

MCGUIRE, Monica M.
Director, Fiscal and Monetary Policy, Nat'l Ass'n of Manufacturers
1331 Pennsylvania Ave., N.W. Suite 1500 North, Washington, DC 20004-1703
Telephone: (202) 637-3000
Registered as lobbyist at U.S. Congress.

MCGUIRE, Raymond L.
Exec. V. President, Governmental Affairs, BellSouth Corp.
1133 21st St., N.W., Suite 900, Washington, DC 20036
Telephone: (202) 463-4100

MCGUIRE, WOODS, BATTLE AND BOOTHE
1627 Eye St., N.W. Suite 1000, Washington, DC 20006
Telephone: (202) 857-1700
Members of firm representing listed organizations:
 Lamb, Robert H.
 Sharp, Larry D.
Clients:
 Armstrong World Industries, Inc. *(Robert H. Lamb)*
 Doe Run Co. *(Robert H. Lamb)*
 James River Corp. *(Robert H. Lamb)*
 Nat'l Paint and Coatings Ass'n *(Robert H. Lamb)*
 Richmond, Fredericksburg and Potomac Railroad
 Signet Banking Corp.
 Sun Co. *(Robert H. Lamb)*
 Viobin Corp. *(Larry D. Sharp)*
 Vulcan Materials Co.

MCHALE, James M.
Seyfarth, Shaw, Fairweather and Geraldson
815 Connecticut Ave., N.W., Washington, DC 20006-4004
Telephone: (202) 463-2400
Registered as Foreign Agent: (#3122).

MCHALE, Sharon
Public Affairs Officer, American Medical Student Ass'n
1890 Preston White Drive, Reston, VA 22091
Telephone: (703) 620-6600

MCHENRY, George W., Jr.
McHenry and Staffier, P.C.
1300 19th St., N.W. Suite 408, Washington, DC 20036
Telephone: (202) 467-5880
Registered as lobbyist at U.S. Congress.
Background: Trial Attorney, Federal Trade Commission, 1969-70. Federal Power Commission, 1970-73. Solicitor, Federal Power Commission, 1973-75.
Clients:
 Foothills Pipe Lines (Yukon), Ltd.
 NOVA, An Alberta Corp.
 Pan-Alberta Gas, Ltd.

MCHENRY AND STAFFIER, P.C.
1300 19th St., N.W. Suite 408, Washington, DC 20036
Telephone: (202) 467-5880
Members of firm representing listed organizations:
 McHenry, George W. (Jr.)
  Background: Trial Attorney, Federal Trade Commission, 1969-70. Federal Power Commission, 1970-73. Solicitor, Federal Power Commission, 1973-75.
 Staffier, John R.
  Background: Staff Attorney, Federal Power Commission, Office of the Solicitor, 1972-75.
Clients:
 Foothills Pipe Lines (Yukon), Ltd. *(George W. McHenry, Jr., John R. Staffier)*
 NOVA, An Alberta Corp. *(George W. McHenry, Jr., John R. Staffier)*
 Pan-Alberta Gas, Ltd. *(George W. McHenry, Jr.)*
 Westcoast Transmission Co. *(John R. Staffier)*

MCHENRY, William P.
Manager, Government Relations, Coopers and Lybrand
1800 M St., N.W., Washington, DC 20036
Telephone: (202) 822-4226

MCILHENNY, James H.
President, Council of Better Business Bureaus
4200 Wilson Blvd. Suite 800, Arlington, VA 22203
Telephone: (703) 276-0100

MCINERNEY, James E., Jr.
Exec. V. President, American League for Exports and
Security Assistance (ALESA)
122 C St., N.W., Suite 740, Washington, DC 20001
Telephone: (202) 783-0051
Registered as lobbyist at U.S. Congress.

MCINTURFF, Cecilia Cole
Exec. V. President, Bond Donatelli Inc.
1414 Prince St., Suite 300, Alexandria, VA 22314
Telephone: (703) 684-5991

MCINTYRE, James, Jr.
McNair Law Firm, P.A.
1155 15th St., N.W. Suite 400, Washington, DC 20005
Telephone: (202) 659-3900
Registered as lobbyist at U.S. Congress.
Background: Former Director of Office of Management
and Budget under President Jimmy Carter.
Clients:
Adwell Corp.
Edison Electric Institute
Insurance/Financial Affiliates of America
Internat'l Ass'n for Financial Planning

MCINTYRE, John A.
Exec. V. President, Can Manufacturers Institute
1625 Massachusetts Ave., N.W., Suite 500, Washington,
DC 20036
Telephone: (201) 232-4677

MCINTYRE, Marla
Director of Information, Nat'l Conference of States on
Building Codes and Standards
481 Carlisle Drive, Herndon, VA 22070
Telephone: (703) 437-0100
Background: Serves as Secretariat, Ass'n of Major City
Building Officials.

MCINTYRE, Michelle P.
Confidential Asst, Legis Affrs, DEPARTMENT OF DE-
FENSE
The Pentagon, Washington, DC 20301
Telephone: (202) 697-6210

MCINTYRE, Robert S.
Director, Citizens for Tax Justice
1311 L St., N.W. 4th Floor, Washington, DC 20005
Telephone: (202) 626-3780
Registered as lobbyist at U.S. Congress.

MCKAIG, J. Carter
Wilkes, Artis, Hedrick and Lane, Chartered
1666 K St., N.W., Suite 1100, Washington, DC 20006
Telephone: (202) 457-7800

MCKASY-DONLIN, Maureen
Director, Center for Historic Houses
1785 Massachusetts Ave., N.W., Washington, DC 20036
Telephone: (202) 673-4025

MCKAY, Bernard F.
Federal Procurement Policy Manager, Hewlett-Packard
Co.
900 17th St., N.W. Suite 1100, Washington, DC 20006
Telephone: (202) 785-7943

MCKAY, Robert E.
Exec. Director, Council of Large Public Housing Authorities
122 C St., S.E. Suite 865, Washington, DC 20001
Telephone: (202) 638-1300

MCKECHNIE, John J., III
Director, Political Action, Credit Union Nat'l Ass'n
805 15th St., N.W. Suite 300, Washington, DC 20005
Telephone: (202) 682-4200
Registered as lobbyist at U.S. Congress.

MCKEE, William S.
King and Spalding
1730 Pennsylvania Ave., N.W. Suite 1200, Washington,
DC 20006-4706
Telephone: (202) 737-0500
Registered as lobbyist at U.S. Congress.

Background: Tax Legislative Counsel, Department of the
Treasury, 1981-83.
Clients:
Trammell Crow, Inc.

MCKEEVER, Ira E.
Slover and Loftus
1224 17th St., N.W., Washington, DC 20036
Telephone: (202) 347-7170
Registered as lobbyist at U.S. Congress.
Clients:
Western Coal Traffic League

MCKENNA, CONNER AND CUNEO
1575 Eye St., N.W. Suite 800, Washington, DC 20005
Telephone: (202) 789-7500
Background: Washington office of a Los Angeles law firm.
The following information was obtained from public rec-
ords and submitted to this firm for confirmation or cor-
rection. The firm did not confirm the information and
asked to be omitted from the book.
Members of firm representing listed organizations:
Cole, Albert M.
Background: Former Member, U.S. House of Represen-
tatives (R-KN).
Dameron, Del S.
Feller, Peter Buck
Flye, Richard A.
Background: Chief, Water Enforcement Branch, Envi-
ronmental Protection Agency, 1972-78.
McVey, Lane L.
Tomenga, Michael K.
Clients:
American Pipe Fittings Ass'n *(Peter Buck Feller)*
Cast Iron Pipefittings Committee *(Peter Buck Feller)*
Chemical Specialties Manufacturers Ass'n
Cigar Ass'n of America *(Peter Buck Feller)*
Fertilizer Institute *(Richard A. Flye)*
Oshkosh Truck Corp. *(Del S. Dameron, Lane L. McVey)*
Savings and Loan League of Colorado
Southwire Co. *(Michael K. Tomenga)*
Toxicology Forum

MCKENNA, Francis G.
Anderson and Pendleton, C.A.
1000 Connecticut Ave., N.W., Suite 1220, Washington, DC
20036
Telephone: (202) 659-2334
Background: Attorney, Antitrust Division, Department of
Justice, 1962-66. Hearing Division, Federal Communica-
tions Commission, 1966-68. Office of the General Coun-
sel, Federal Home Loan Bank Board, 1967-70.
Clients:
Federation of Japan Tuna Fisheries Cooperative
Ass'ns
Japan Tuna Fisheries Cooperative
West Virginia Railroad Maintenance Authority

MCKENNA, Jim
Special Asst to the Asst Secy, DEPARTMENT OF COM-
MERCE
14th and Constitution Ave. S.W., Washington, DC 20230
Telephone: (202) 377-5485

MCKENNEY, James
Ass't V. President, Federal Relations, American Ass'n of
Community and Junior Colleges
One Dupont Circle, N.W. Suite 410, Washington, DC
20036
Telephone: (202) 293-7050

MCKENNEY, William R.
Senior Associate, Dutko & Associates
412 First St., S.E. Suite 100, Washington, DC 20003
Telephone: (202) 484-4884
Registered as lobbyist at U.S. Congress.
Background: Former Press Secretary to Rep. Clarence
Brown (R-OH), 1982; Legislative/Communications Direc-
tor to Rep. Tom Kindness (R-OH), 1983-84; Legislative
Director to Rep. Rod Chandler (R-WA), 1985-90.
Clients:
Phoenix Mutual Life Insurance Co.

MCKENZIE, James J.
Senior Associate, World Resources Institute
1709 New York Ave., N.W., Washington, DC 20006
Telephone: (202) 638-6300

MCKENZIE, Lisa
Staff Manager, Congressional Relations, BellSouth Corp.
1133 21st St., N.W., Suite 900, Washington, DC 20036
Telephone: (202) 463-4100

MCKENZIE SHAIN, Victoria
Director, Federal Health Policy, Abbott Laboratories
1710 Rhode Island Ave., N.W. Suite 300, Washington, DC
20036
Telephone: (202) 659-8524
Registered as lobbyist at U.S. Congress.

MCKENZIE, William P.
Exec. Director, Ripon Soc.
6 Library Court, S.E., Washington, DC 20003
Telephone: (202) 546-1292
Background: Serves also as Editor, Ripon Forum.

MCKERNAN, Robert T.
V. President, Policy Planning & Commun., American Paper
Institute
1250 Connecticut Ave., N.W. Suite 210, Washington, DC
20036
Telephone: (202) 463-2420
Registered as lobbyist at U.S. Congress.

MCKEVITT GROUP, THE
1101 16th St., N.W., Suite 333, Washington, DC 20036
Telephone: (202) 822-0604
Members of firm representing listed organizations:
D'Armiento, Paul R., V. President
Background: Consultant in public relations and com-
munications.
McKevitt, James D. 'Mike', President
Background: Attorney-at-Law. Former District Attor-
ney, City and County of Denver, Colorado, 1967-71.
Member, U.S. House of Representatives from Colora-
do, 1971-72. Assistant Attorney General for Legisla-
tive Affairs, U.S. Department of Justice, 1973. Coun-
sel, Energy Policy Office, The White House, 1973-
74. Member, President's Korean War Veterans
Memorial Advisory Board; President, Arlington Na-
tional Cemetery Historical Society.
Schneier, Abraham L., V. President
Background: Legislative Representative and Tax Coun-
sel for the Nat'l Federation of Independent Business.
Advisor to the Securities and Exchange Commission.
Past member of the American Legislative Exchange
Council and of its Editorial Board on the Impact of
Tax Reform on States.
Clients:
Bureau of Wholesale Sales Representatives
Kelly Services, Inc.
Lab Support, Inc.
Nat'l Ass'n of Wholesaler-Distributors
Nat'l Federation of Independent Business
Private Sector Council
70001 Training & Employment Institute

MCKEVITT, James D. 'Mike'
President, McKevitt Group, The
1101 16th St., N.W., Suite 333, Washington, DC 20036
Telephone: (202) 822-0604
Registered as lobbyist at U.S. Congress.
Background: Attorney-at-Law. Former District Attorney,
City and County of Denver, Colorado, 1967-71. Member,
U.S. House of Representatives from Colorado, 1971-72.
Assistant Attorney General for Legislative Affairs, U.S.
Department of Justice, 1973. Counsel, Energy Policy Of-
fice, The White House, 1973-74. Member, President's Ko-
rean War Veterans Memorial Advisory Board; President,
Arlington National Cemetery Historical Society.

MCKEW, Robert
Assoc. Counsel, Ass't Dir., Regul. Affrs, American Finan-
cial Services Ass'n
1101 14th St., N.W., Washington, DC 20005
Telephone: (202) 289-0400
Registered as lobbyist at U.S. Congress.

MCKIERNAN, Gerald J.
V. President, Legislative Affairs, American Trucking Ass'ns
430 First St., S.E., Washington, DC 20003-1826
Telephone: (202) 544-6245
Registered as lobbyist at U.S. Congress.
Background: Former Special Assistant, Legislative Affairs,
to President Reagan. Serves as contact for the American
Trucking Ass'ns Truck PAC.

WASHINGTON REPRESENTATIVES

MCKINNEY, C. A.
Legislative Counsel, Non Commissioned Officers Ass'n of the U.S.A.
225 North Washington St., Alexandria, VA 22314
Telephone: (703) 549-0311
Registered as lobbyist at U.S. Congress.

MCKINNEY, John P.
Representative, Federal Government Affrs, UST Public Affairs, Inc.
1825 Eye St., N.W., Suite 400, Washington, DC 20006
Telephone: (202) 429-2010
Registered as lobbyist at U.S. Congress.

MCKINNEY, Dr. Joseph C.
Treasurer, African Methodist Episcopal Church
1134 11th St., N.W., Washington, DC 20001
Telephone: (202) 371-8700

MCKINNEY, Robert L.
Director, State & Local Affairs, Nat'l Soft Drink Ass'n
1101 16th St., N.W., Washington, DC 20036
Telephone: (202) 463-6740

MCKINNEY, Rufus W.
V. President, National Public Affairs, Southern California Gas Co.
1150 Connecticut Ave., N.W., Washington, DC 20036
Telephone: (202) 822-3707

MCKINNON, Monette
Grassroots Coordinator, Nat'l Committee to Preserve Social Security and Medicare
2000 K St., N.W. Suite 800, Washington, DC 20006
Telephone: (202) 822-9459
Registered as lobbyist at U.S. Congress.

MCKINNON, Russell F., CAE
Exec. Director, Nat'l Child Support Enforcement Ass'n
444 North Capitol St., N.W., Suite 613, Washington, DC 20001
Telephone: (202) 624-8180

MCKITTRICK, Charles E., Jr.
IBM V. President, Governmental Programs, Internat'l Business Machines Corp.
1801 K St., N.W., Suite 1200, Washington, DC 20006
Telephone: (202) 778-5000

MCLAIN, Patrick M.
Rowan & Blewitt, Inc.
1000 Vermont Ave., N.W. Suite 1000, Washington, DC 20005
Telephone: (202) 842-1010
Registered as lobbyist at U.S. Congress.
Clients:
Cosmetic, Toiletry and Fragrance Ass'n

MCLAUGHLIN, Carolyn
Jefferson Group, The
1341 G St., N.W., Suite 1100, Washington, DC 20005
Telephone: (202) 638-3535

MCLAUGHLIN, Edmumd
Past President, Nat'l Ass'n of Rehabilitation Facilities
Box 17675, Washington, DC 20041-0675
Telephone: (703) 648-9300

MCLAUGHLIN, Francis X.
Director, Nat'l Treasury Employees Union Political Action Committee
1730 K St., N.W. Suite 1101, Washington, DC 20006
Telephone: (202) 785-4411
Background: Legislative Assistant to the former Speaker of the U.S. House of Representatives, Thomas P. O'Neill, Jr. (D-MA), 1981-86.

MCLAUGHLIN, James D.
Dir., Agency Relations, Trust/Securities, American Bankers Ass'n
1120 Connecticut Ave., N.W., Washington, DC 20036
Telephone: (202) 663-5000
Registered as lobbyist at U.S. Congress.

MCLAUGHLIN, John P.
V. President, General Counsel, Genentech, Inc.
1747 Pennsylvania Ave., N.W. Suite 1223, Washington, DC 20006
Telephone: (202) 296-7272
Registered as lobbyist at U.S. Congress.

MCLAURIN, John R.
Director, Federal Affairs, American President Companies
1101 17th St., N.W. Suite 400, Washington, DC 20036
Telephone: (202) 331-1424
Registered as lobbyist at U.S. Congress.

MCLEAN, Elizabeth C.
Account Supervisor, Fleishman-Hillard, Inc
1301 Connecticut Ave., N.W., Washington, DC 20036
Telephone: (202) 659-0330
Clients:
Automotive Refrigeration Products Institute
Processed Apples Institute
United Network of Organ Sharing

MCLEAN, R. Bruce
Akin, Gump, Strauss, Hauer and Feld
1333 New Hampshire Ave., N.W., Suite 400, Washington, DC 20036
Telephone: (202) 887-4000
Background: Attorney, Appellate Court Branch, Nat'l Labor Relations Board, 1971-73.

MCLEAN, Robert E.
Legislative Counsel, Nat'l Ass'n of Postal Supervisors
490 L'Enfant Plaza., S.W., Suite 3200, Washington, DC 20024
Telephone: (202) 484-6070
Registered as lobbyist at U.S. Congress.
Background: Responsibilities include the Supervisors Political Action Committee. Editor of 'The Postal Supervisor' magazine and the NAPSletter.

MCLELLAN, Bruce
Director of Government Relations, Nat'l Office Products Ass'n
301 North Fairfax St., Alexandria, VA 22314
Telephone: (703) 549-9040
Background: Serves as a Director, Coalition for Common Sense in Government Procurement and is also responsible for the Nat'l Office Products Ass'n Political Action Committee. Former Legislative Assistant to Rep. Robert Roe, 1971-73.

MCLENNAN, Kenneth
President, Manufacturers' Alliance for Productivity and Innovation (MAPI)
1200 18th St., N.W. Suite 400, Washington, DC 20036
Telephone: (202) 331-8430

MCLEOD, Brooke W.
Media Relations Specialist, Nat'l Right to Work Committee
8001 Braddock Road, Springfield, VA 22160
Telephone: (703) 321-9820

MCLEOD, Michael R.
Partner, McLeod & Pires
2501 M St., N.W., Suite 400, Washington, DC 20037
Telephone: (202) 861-1234
Registered as lobbyist at U.S. Congress.
Background: Legislative Assistant to Sen. Herman E. Talmadge of Georgia, 1967-71. Counsel to Senate Committee on Agriculture and Forestry, 1971-74. General Counsel and Staff Director, Senate Committee on Agriculture and Forestry, 1974-78.
Clients:
American Ass'n of Crop Insurers
American Ass'n of Crop Insurers Political Action Committee
American Soybean Ass'n
Chicago Board of Trade
Florida State Department of Citrus
Mushroom Council
United Egg Ass'n
United Egg Producers

MCLEOD & PIRES
2501 M St., N.W., Suite 400, Washington, DC 20037
Telephone: (202) 861-1234
Members of firm representing listed organizations:
Fraas, Phillip L., Partner
Furman, Harold W. (II), Partner
Background: Former Deputy Assistant Secretary for Water and Science, U.S. Department of the Interior.
McLeod, Michael R., Partner
Background: Legislative Assistant to Sen. Herman E. Talmadge of Georgia, 1967-71. Counsel to Senate Committee on Agriculture and Forestry, 1971-74. General Counsel and Staff Director, Senate Committee on Agriculture and Forestry, 1974-78.

Murray, Margaret R., Government Relations Consultant
Nelson, Christine, Government Relations Consultant
Phelps, Laura, Government Relations Consultant
Watkinson, Wayne R., Partner
Westwater, Joseph, Government Relations Consultant
Clients:
American Ass'n of Crop Insurers *(Michael R. McLeod, Margaret R. Murray, Laura Phelps)*
American Ass'n of Crop Insurers Political Action Committee *(Michael R. McLeod)*
American Soybean Ass'n *(Michael R. McLeod, Wayne R. Watkinson)*
Cattlemen's Beef Promotion and Research Board *(Wayne R. Watkinson)*
Chicago Board of Trade *(Michael R. McLeod)*
Florida Lime & Avocado Commission, Trustees of *(Harold W. Furman, II)*
Florida State Department of Citrus *(Michael R. McLeod)*
Mushroom Council *(Michael R. McLeod, Laura Phelps)*
Nat'l Dairy Promotion and Research Board *(Wayne R. Watkinson)*
South Dade Land Corp. *(Harold W. Furman, II)*
United Egg Ass'n *(Michael R. McLeod, Christine Nelson)*
United Egg Producers *(Michael R. McLeod, Christine Nelson)*

MCLIN, William M.
Exec. V. President, Epilepsy Foundation of America
4351 Garden City Drive, Landover, MD 20785
Telephone: (301) 459-3700

MCLUCKIE, Sally F.
Brand and Lowell, P.C.
923 15th St., N.W., Washington, DC 20005
Telephone: (202) 662-9700
Background: Administrator, Brand and Lowell. Also serves as Treasurer, Brand and Lowell Political Action Committee.

MCMACKIN, John J., Jr.
Williams and Jensen, P.C.
1101 Connecticut Ave., N.W., Suite 500, Washington, DC 20036
Telephone: (202) 659-8201
Clients:
American Home Products Corp.
Nippon Cargo Airlines
Southern Pacific Transportation Co.
Southwest Airlines
Trailer Train Co.

MCMAHON AND ASSOCIATES
1331 Pennsylvania Ave., N.W., Suite 909, Washington, DC 20004
Telephone: (202) 662-7400
Background: A public affairs consulting firm.
Members of firm representing listed organizations:
McMahon, Joseph E.
Background: Former Executive Assistant to Lt. Governor Francis W. Sargent of Massachusetts; Assistant to Attorney General and Senator Edward W. Brooke (MA).
Schlicker, Sandra A.
Background: Formerly with the U.S. Dept. of Agriculture, Food and Nutrition Service.
Clients:
Bedford Stuyvesant Restoration Corp.
Covenant House
Procter and Gamble Mfg. Co.
Rodale Press, Inc. *(Joseph E. McMahon, Sandra A. Schlicker)*
Stone and Webster Engineering Corp.
Westinghouse Electric Corp.

MCMAHON, Edward T.
Exec. Director, Scenic America
216 7th St., S.E., Washington, DC 20003
Telephone: (202) 546-1100
Registered as lobbyist at U.S. Congress.

MCMAHON, John J., Jr.
Exec. Director, Institute of the Ironworking Industry
1750 New York Ave., N.W. Suite 400, Washington, DC 20006
Telephone: (202) 783-3998

MCMAHON, Joseph E.
McMahon and Associates
1331 Pennsylvania Ave., N.W., Suite 909, Washington, DC 20004
Telephone: (202) 662-7400
Registered as lobbyist at U.S. Congress.
Background: Former Executive Assistant to Lt. Governor Francis W. Sargent of Massachusetts; Assistant to Attorney General and Senator Edward W. Brooke (MA).
Clients:
Rodale Press, Inc.

MCMAHON, Patrick J.
Sedam and Shearer
1700 Pennsylvania Ave., N.W. Suite 620, Washington, DC 20006
Telephone: (703) 691-2010
Clients:
Nat'l Soc. of Fund Raising Executives
Tomen Corp.

MCMAHON, Tara L.
Assistant Washington Counsel, Health Insurance Ass'n of America
1025 Connecticut Ave., N.W. Suite 1200, Washington, DC 20036
Telephone: (202) 223-7780
Registered as lobbyist at U.S. Congress.
Background: Former Majority Counsel, Senate Subcommittee on Patents, Copyrights and Trademarks.

MCMAHON, Thomas
Eastern Manager and Counsel, Nat'l Automatic Merchandising Ass'n
11718 Bowman Green Drive, Reston, VA 22090
Telephone: (703) 435-1210

MCMANUS, Allegra P.
Associate Legislative Representative, AFL-CIO - Industrial Union Department
815 16th St., N.W., Washington, DC 20006
Telephone: (202) 842-7800
Background: Also represents the AFL-CIO Industrial Union Department Voluntary Fund.

MCMANUS, Frank M., Jr.
Exec. Director, American Paper Machinery Ass'n
5313 38th St., N.W., Washington, DC 20015
Telephone: (202) 362-6034

MCMANUS, James T.
Wright and Talisman
1050 17th St., N.W. Suite 600, Washington, DC 20036
Telephone: (202) 331-1194
Background: Attorney, Federal Power Commission, 1975-77.

MCMANUS, John J.
Exec. V. President, Professional Insurance Mass-Marketing Ass'n
4733 Bethesda Ave., Suite 33, Bethesda, MD 20814
Telephone: (301) 951-1260

MCMANUS, Paul E.
Exec. V. President, Jeford-McManus Internat'l, Inc.
513 Capitol Court, N.E., Suite 300, Washington, DC 20002
Telephone: (202) 546-0073
Registered as lobbyist at U.S. Congress.

MCMANUS, Roger E.
President, Center for Marine Conservation
1725 DeSales St., N.W. Suite 500, Washington, DC 20036
Telephone: (202) 429-5609

MCMANUS, Fr. Sean
Nat'l Director, Irish Nat'l Caucus
413 E. Capitol St., S.E., Washington, DC 20003
Telephone: (202) 544-0568

MCMANUS, William F.
Washington Rep., Gov't Relations, General Electric Co.
1331 Pennsylvania Ave., N.W., Washington, DC 20004
Telephone: (202) 637-4421
Registered as lobbyist at U.S. Congress.

MCMILLAN, C. W.
President, McMillan and Farrell Associates
2021 K St., N.W., Washington, DC 20006
Telephone: (202) 429-0676

Registered as lobbyist at U.S. Congress.
Background: Former Ass't Sec'y for Marketing and Inspection Service, U.S. Department of Agriculture.
Clients:
American Cyanamid Co. (Agricultural Division)
Campbell Soup Co.
Elanco Products Co.
Federal Agricultural Mortgage Corp.
IMC/Pittman Moore
Protatek Internat'l, Inc.
SmithKline Animal Health Products
Texas Cattle Feeders Ass'n

MCMILLAN AND FARRELL ASSOCIATES
2021 K St., N.W., Washington, DC 20006
Telephone: (202) 429-0676
Background: An agribusiness consulting firm.
Members of firm representing listed organizations:
McMillan, C. W., President
Background: Former Ass't Sec'y for Marketing and Inspection Service, U.S. Department of Agriculture.
Clients:
American Cyanamid Co. (Agricultural Division) (*C. W. McMillan*)
Campbell Soup Co. (*C. W. McMillan*)
Elanco Products Co. (*C. W. McMillan*)
Federal Agricultural Mortgage Corp. (*C. W. McMillan*)
IMC/Pittman Moore (*C. W. McMillan*)
Protatek Internat'l, Inc. (*C. W. McMillan*)
SmithKline Animal Health Products (*C. W. McMillan*)
Texas Cattle Feeders Ass'n (*C. W. McMillan*)

MCMILLAN, James D.
Washington Representative, Exxon Corp.
Suite 1100, 1899 L St., N.W., Washington, DC 20036
Telephone: (202) 862-0225
Registered as lobbyist at U.S. Congress.

MCMILLAN, Michael M.
V. President, Internat'l Operations, E-Systems, Inc.
1901 North Moore St. Suite 609, Arlington, VA 22209
Telephone: (703) 524-2310

MCMULLAN, Sandra H.
Exec. Dir. for Tax Policy & Gen Counsel, Nat'l Ass'n of Independent Colleges and Universities
122 C St., N.W. Suite 750, Washington, DC 20001
Telephone: (202) 347-7512
Registered as lobbyist at U.S. Congress.

MCMULLEN, Janet Oppenheim
Exec. Dir., Asbestos Abatement Council, Ass'n of the Wall and Ceiling Industries-Internat'l
1600 Cameron St., Alexandria, VA 22314
Telephone: (703) 684-2924

MCMURPHY, Michael A.
President and CEO, Cogema, Inc.
7401 Wisconsin Ave., Bethesda, MD 20814
Telephone: (301) 986-8585
Registered as Foreign Agent: (#3587)

MCMURRAY, Gerald R.
V. President, Housing Initiatives, Federal Nat'l Mortgage Ass'n
3900 Wisconsin Ave., N.W., Washington, DC 20016
Telephone: (202) 752-7000
Background: Former Staff Director, House Subcommittee on Housing and Community Development.

MCMURRAY, Jose
Exec. Director, Nat'l Ass'n of Hispanic Journalists
National Press Building Room 634, Washington, DC 20045
Telephone: (202) 783-6228

MCNAIR GROUP INC.
1155 15th St., N.W., Washington, DC 20005
Telephone: (202) 659-8866
Background: A government affairs consulting firm.
Members of firm representing listed organizations:
Dwyer, Denis J., Chief Operating Officer
Gallegos, Kathy E., Director, Conmgressional Affairs
Background: Former Legislative Director to Rep. James Hansen (R-UT).
Lovell, Rose Ann, Director, Business Development
Background: Former aide to Rep. Jerry Lewis (R-CA).

Rankin, Dennis R., Assistant V. President
Taylor, Elizabeth L., Director, Government Affairs
Clients:
Clemson University (*Elizabeth L. Taylor*)
Defense Group, Inc. (*Kathy E. Gallegos, Dennis R. Rankin*)
Gateway Freight Services Inc. (*Denis J. Dwyer*)
GTE Corp. (*Kathy E. Gallegos*)
Harmon Industries, Inc. (*Denis J. Dwyer*)
Hawaii Department of Transportation (*Denis J. Dwyer*)
Nat'l Composites Consortium, Inc. (*Elizabeth L. Taylor*)
Paine Webber Group (*Denis J. Dwyer*)
Puerto Rico Ports Authority (*Denis J. Dwyer*)
Railstar Control Technology, Inc. (*Denis J. Dwyer*)
Sotheby's Holdings, Inc. (*Elizabeth L. Taylor*)
South Carolina State College (*Elizabeth L. Taylor*)
Texas Instruments, Industrial Automation (*Kathy E. Gallegos, Dennis R. Rankin*)
University of Delaware
Virginia Polytechnic Institute and State University (*Elizabeth L. Taylor*)
Westinghouse Environmental Services (*Kathy E. Gallegos, Dennis R. Rankin*)
World Airways (*Denis J. Dwyer*)

MCNAIR LAW FIRM, P.A.
1155 15th St., N.W. Suite 400, Washington, DC 20005
Telephone: (202) 659-3900
Members of firm representing listed organizations:
Barksdale, Thomas H. (Jr.)
Background: Counsel for U.S. Senate Committees on Judiciary and Commerce, 1966-70; Special Agent, Federal Bureau of Investigation, 1948-50.
Gelacek, Michael S.
Background: Minority Staff Director, Senate Judiciary Committee; Staff Director, Senate Subcommittee on Criminal Law; and Chief Counsel, Senate Subcommittee on Penitentiaries, 1977-85. Legislative Director to Senator Joseph R. Biden, Jr. (D-DE), 1983-85.
Hunter, John W.
Background: Staff Attorney, Federal Communications Commission, 1972-80; Legislative Assistant to Rep. Guy Vander Jagt (R-MI), 1969-72.
Kittle, Ralph W.
Background: Counsel to Senator Robert Taft (R-OH) and the Senate Labor Committee, 1953. President's Advisory Committee on Pollution Control, 1967-70.
McIntyre, James (Jr.)
Background: Former Director of Office of Management and Budget under President Jimmy Carter.
McNair, Robert E.
Background: Member, South Carolina House of Representatives, 1951-62. Lieutenant Governor of South Carolina, 1962-65. Governor of South Carolina, 1965-71. Vice Chairman, Democratic National Committee, 1969-70.
Napier, John L.
Scocozza, Matthew
Background: Senior Counsel, U.S. Senate Committee on Commerce, Science and Transportation, 1977-82. Deputy Assistant Secretary for Transportation and Telecommunications, U.S. Department of State, 1982-83. Assistant Secretary for Policy and and International Affairs, U.S. Department of Transportation, 1984-88.
Taylor, Warren P.
Background: Command Judge Advocate, Delta Regional Assistance Command, Republic of Vietnam, 1972-73. Legislative Counsel, Office of the Secretary of the Army, 1976. Staff Judge Advocate, 2nd Infantry Division, 1981. Team Chief and Senior Trial Attorney, U.S. Army, 1982-83. Legislative Assistant to the Secretary of Defense, 1983-87.
Clients:
Adwell Corp. (*James McIntyre, Jr.*)
Allied-Signal Inc.
Ass'n of Independent Television Stations (*Michael S. Gelacek*)
Edison Electric Institute (*James McIntyre, Jr.*)
Gasoline Alliance to Preserve Competition (*Thomas H. Barksdale, Jr.*)
Gateway Freight Services Inc. (*Matthew Scocozza*)
Georgia-Pacific Corp.
GTE Government Systems (*John W. Hunter*)

Hawaii Department of Transportation *(Matthew Scocozza)*
Insurance/Financial Affiliates of America *(James McIntyre, Jr.)*
Internat'l Ass'n for Financial Planning *(James McIntyre, Jr.)*
Michelin Tire Co.
New York State Bankers Ass'n
Phillips Petroleum Co. *(John L. Napier)*
Seagram & Sons, Inc., Joseph E. *(Michael S. Gelacek)*
South Carolina Research Authority *(John L. Napier)*

MCNAIR, Robert E.
McNair Law Firm, P.A.
1155 15th St., N.W. Suite 400, Washington, DC 20005
Telephone: (202) 659-3900
Registered as lobbyist at U.S. Congress.
Background: Member, South Carolina House of Representatives, 1951-62. Lieutenant Governor of South Carolina, 1962-65. Governor of South Carolina, 1965-71. Vice Chairman, Democratic National Committee, 1969-70.

MCNALLY, Susan
Manager, Alternate Site & Reimbursement, Baxter Internat'l Inc.
1667 K St., N.W., Suite 710, Washington, DC 20006
Telephone: (202) 223-4016
Registered as lobbyist at U.S. Congress.

MCNAMARA, Daniel J.
Account Executive, Cassidy and Associates, Inc.
655 15th St., N.W., Suite 1100, Washington, DC 20005
Telephone: (202) 347-0773

MCNAMARA, Kathryn 'Kelly'
Manager, Federal Government Affairs, Dean Witter Financial Services Group
633 Pennsylvania Ave., N.W., Washington, DC 20004
Telephone: (202) 737-4900
Registered as lobbyist at U.S. Congress.

MCNAMARA, Laramie F.
Director, Federal Relations, TRW Inc.
Suite 2700, 1000 Wilson Blvd., Arlington, VA 22209
Telephone: (703) 276-5037
Registered as lobbyist at U.S. Congress.

MCNAMARA, Mary Martha
Keller and Heckman
1150 17th St., N.W. Suite 1000, Washington, DC 20036
Telephone: (202) 956-5600
Registered as lobbyist at U.S. Congress.
Clients:
Art Supply Labeling Coalition
Dean Witter Financial Services Group

MCNAMARA, Michael J.
V. Pres., Director, Defense Affairs, Internat'l Advisers, Inc.
2300 M St., N.W., Suite 600, Washington, DC 20037
Telephone: (202) 293-1575
Registered as lobbyist at U.S. Congress.
Registered as Foreign Agent: (#4203).
Background: Graduate of British Royal College of Defence Studies, London, 1978. Senior Staff Officer, Allied Forces Central Europe, Netherlands, 1979-83. Graduate of NATO Defense College, Rome, 1983. Country Director for Turkey, the U.K., Ireland and Yugoslavia, Office of the Secretary of Defense, International Security Policy, 1984-88. Retired as Colonel, U.S. Army, 1989.
Clients:
Turkey, Embassy of

MCNAMEE, Catherine T., CSJ
President, Nat'l Catholic Educational Ass'n
1077 30th St., N.W. Suite 100, Washington, DC 20007
Telephone: (202) 337-6232

MCNAMEE, Nikki
Dir., Washington Office of the Governor, South Carolina, State of
444 N. Capitol St., N.W. Suite 234, Washington, DC 20001
Telephone: (202) 624-7784

MCNEIL, Jerald
Sr Proj. Dir., Employment & Training, Nat'l Ass'n of Counties
440 First St., N.W., Washington, DC 20001
Telephone: (202) 393-6226

Background: Serves as contact for the Nat'l Ass'n of County Training and Employment Professionals.

MCNEILL, Robert L.
Exec. Vice Chairman, Emergency Committee for American Trade
1211 Connecticut Ave., N.W. Suite 801, Washington, DC 20036
Telephone: (202) 659-5147
Background: Former White House aide to President Kennedy and a U.S. negotiator in the "Kennedy Round" of trade talks.

MCNEISH, Peter F.
President, Nat'l Ass'n of Small Business Investment Companies
1156 15th St., N.W. Suite 1101, Washington, DC 20005
Telephone: (202) 833-8230
Registered as lobbyist at U.S. Congress.

MCNELIS, Marcie
V. President, MultiState Associates
515 King St., Suite 310, Alexandria, VA 22314
Telephone: (703) 684-1110

MCNERNEY, John C.
Dir., Wash. Off., Missiles Division, LTV Aircraft Products Group
1725 Jefferson Davis Hwy. Suite 900, Arlington, VA 22202
Telephone: (703) 521-6560

MCNETT, Cheri
Legislative Assistant, American Soc. of Clinical Pathologists
1101 Vermont Ave., N.W. 6th Floor, Washington, DC 20005
Telephone: (202) 371-0515

MCNEVIN, Anthony
President, American Ass'n of Colleges of Podiatric Medicine
6110 Executive Blvd. Suite 204, Rockville, MD 20852
Telephone: (301) 984-9350

MCNICHOLAS, John P.
Dir, Gov't Affairs, Gov't Systems Divsn, Unisys Corp.
2001 L St., N.W., Suite 1000, Washingn, DC 20036
Telephone: (202) 293-7720
Registered as lobbyist at U.S. Congress.

MCNICKLE, Larry
Director, Housing and Tax Policy, American Ass'n of Homes for the Aging
1129 20th St., N.W., Suite 400, Washington, DC 20036
Telephone: (202) 296-5960
Registered as lobbyist at U.S. Congress.

MCNULTY, Col. John
Cong Inquiry, Legis Liaison, DEPARTMENT OF ARMY
The Pentagon, Washington, DC 20310-0101
Telephone: (202) 697-6767

MCNULTY, Molly
Senior Health Specialist, Children's Defense Fund
122 C St., N.W., Washington, DC 20001
Telephone: (202) 628-8787
Registered as lobbyist at U.S. Congress.

MCNULTY, Robert H.
President, Partners for Livable Places
1429 21st St., N.W., Washington, DC 20036
Telephone: (202) 887-5990

MCPHEE, Henry Roemer
Hopkins and Sutter
888 16th St., N.W., Suite 700, Washington, DC 20006
Telephone: (202) 835-8000
Registered as lobbyist at U.S. Congress.
Background: Special Assistant, The White House, 1954-57. Assistant Special Counsel to the President of the United States, 1957-1961.

MCPHERSON, Harry C.
Verner, Liipfert, Bernhard, McPherson and Hand, Chartered
901 15th St., N.W., Suite 700, Washington, DC 20005
Telephone: (202) 371-6000
Registered as lobbyist at U.S. Congress.
Registered as Foreign Agent: (#3712).

Background: General Counsel, Senate Democratic Policy Committee, 1956-63. Deputy Undersecretary of the Army, 1963-64. Assistant Secretary of State for Educational and Cultural Affairs, 1964-65. Special Counsel to the President, 1965-69. General Counsel for the John F. Kennedy Center.
Clients:
ARCO
Boston Mass Transit Authority
Consolidated Grain and Barge Co.
Irving Ltd., J.D.
Puerto Rico, New Progressive Party 0f
Rayburn County Electric Cooperative

MCQUAID, John A.
Exec. Director, Intermodal Marketing Ass'n
2111 Wilson Blvd., Suite 700, Arlington, VA 22201
Telephone: (703) 875-8665

MCQUIRE, Phillip
Law Enforcement Advisor, Handgun Control, Inc.
1225 Eye St., N.W., Suite 1100, Washington, DC 20005
Telephone: (202) 898-0792
Registered as lobbyist at U.S. Congress.

MCRAE, Karen A.
Interim Adminstrator, Congressional Black Caucus Foundation
1004 Pennsylvania Ave., S.E., Washington, DC 20003
Telephone: (202) 675-6730

MCSHANE, Michael
Manager, Government Relations, Nat'l Computer Systems
4601 N. Fairfax Drive, Arlington, VA 22203
Telephone: (703) 516-4306

MCSHERRY, Michael
Asst, Cong Rels, Legis & Cong Rels, DEPARTMENT OF HOUSING AND URBAN DEVELOPMENT
451 Seventh St., S.W., Washington, DC 20410
Telephone: (202) 755-7380

MCSORLEY, Mary T.
Associate Director, Government Relations, American Osteopathic Ass'n
300 5th St., N.E., Washington, DC 20002
Telephone: (202) 544-5060
Registered as lobbyist at U.S. Congress.

MCSTEEN, Martha A.
President, Nat'l Committee to Preserve Social Security and Medicare
2000 K St., N.W. Suite 800, Washington, DC 20006
Telephone: (202) 822-9459
Registered as lobbyist at U.S. Congress.

MCSWEENEY, Tim
Director of Technical Services, Screen Printing Ass'n Internat'l
10015 Main St., Fairfax, VA 22031-3489
Telephone: (703) 385-1335

MCVEY, Brose A.
Hauck and Associates
1255 23rd St., N.W., Washington, DC 20037
Telephone: (202) 452-8100
Registered as lobbyist at U.S. Congress.
Background: Serves as Exec. V. President, Nat'l Oilseed Processors Ass'n.
Clients:
Nat'l Oilseed Processors Ass'n

MCVEY, Lane L.
McKenna, Conner and Cuneo
1575 Eye St., N.W. Suite 800, Washington, DC 20005
Telephone: (202) 789-7500
Clients:
Oshkosh Truck Corp.

MCWETHY, Patricia J.
Exec. Director, Nat'l Ass'n of Biology Teachers
11250 Roger Bacon Dr. Suite 19, Reston, VA 22090
Telephone: (703) 471-1134

MCWHORTER, Celane
Director of Government Relations, Ass'n for Persons with Severe Handicaps
1511 King St., Alexandria, VA 22314
Telephone: (703) 683-5586

MCWHORTER, Celane (Cont'd)
Background: Legislative Director for Rep. G.V. 'Sonny' Montgomery, (D-MS); 1978-85.

MEAD, Leslie S.
Associate General Counsel, Nat'l Council of Farmer Cooperatives
50 F St., N.W. Suite 900, Washington, DC 20001
Telephone: (202) 626-8700
Registered as lobbyist at U.S. Congress.

MEADER, Glenn S.'Steve', Jr.
Asst. V. Pres., Governmental Relations, Contel Corp.
555 13th St. Suite 480 West, Washington, DC 20004
Telephone: (202) 383-3700
Background: Also serves as V. Chairman, Contel Corporation Political Action Committee.

MEADOWS, Johnette L.
Director, Minority Affairs, American Physical Therapy Ass'n
1111 North Fairfax St., Alexandria, VA 22314
Telephone: (703) 684-2782

MEAGHER, John K.
LeBoeuf, Lamb, Leiby, and MacRae
1333 New Hampshire Ave., N.W. Suite 1100, Washington, DC 20036
Telephone: (202) 457-7500
Background: Former Assistant Secretary for Legislative Affairs, U.S. Treasury Department.
Clients:
   Basic Industry Coalition
   Golden Nugget, Inc.
   Physician Insurers Ass'n of America
   STS Corp.

MEANEY, Francis X.
Mintz, Levin, Cohn, Ferris, Glovsky and Popeo, P.C.
1825 Eye St., N.W. 12th Floor, Washington, DC 20006
Telephone: (202) 293-0500
Registered as lobbyist at U.S. Congress.
Clients:
   Goldman, Sachs and Co.
   Securities Industry Ass'n

MEANS, Betty J.
Field Coordinator, Planned Parenthood Federation of America
2010 Massachusetts Ave., N.W. Fifth Floor, Washington, DC 20036
Telephone: (202) 785-3351

MEANY, Mary-Liz
Manager, Public Relations, American Bankers Ass'n
1120 Connecticut Ave., N.W., Washington, DC 20036
Telephone: (202) 663-5000

MEAUX, William A.
Government Relations Specialist, ICI Americas Inc.
1600 M St., N.W., Suite 702, Washington, DC 20036
Telephone: (202) 775-9722
Registered as lobbyist at U.S. Congress.

MEDER, Joseph J.
Washington Representative, Interlake Corp.
1730 M St., N.W., Suite 911, Washington, DC 20036
Telephone: (202) 659-1601
Registered as lobbyist at U.S. Congress.

MEDIA ENTERPRISES CORP.
1650 30th St., N.W., Washington, DC 20007
Telephone: (202) 337-9122
Clients:
   Nat'l Ass'n of Public Television Stations

MEDIN, Mark
Ass't Director, Anti-Defamation League of B'nai B'rith
1100 Connecticut Ave., N.W., Washington, DC 20036
Telephone: (202) 452-8320

MEDLEY, Richard
Smick Medley Internat'l Inc.
1050 Connecticut Ave., N.W., Washington, DC 20036
Telephone: (202) 861-0770

MEDLIN, Paul L.
Sr. V. President, Nat'l Foundation for the Handicapped
1850 K St., N.W., Suite 500, Washington, DC 20006
Telephone: (202) 778-8117

Background: Seeks to influence national policy via targeted initiatives such as the Self-Sufficiency Trust, Anna Emery Hanson Canter for the Arts, PBS film series, Imagine This World, highlighting the contributions of people with disabilities.

MEDVED, Beverly
President, Nat'l Council of Catholic Women
1275 K St., N.W. Suite 975, Washington, DC 20005
Telephone: (202) 682-0334

MEDWAY, Lawrence E.
Dir, Cong Inquiries, NAT'L AERONAUTICS AND SPACE ADMINISTRATION
400 Maryland Ave., S.W., Washington, DC 20546
Telephone: (202) 453-1055

MEEDS, Lloyd
Preston Gates Ellis & Rouvelas Meeds
1735 New York Ave., N.W., Suite 500, Washington, DC 20006-4759
Telephone: (202) 628-1700
Registered as lobbyist at U.S. Congress.
Registered as Foreign Agent: (#3567).
Background: Member, U.S. House of Representatives from Washington State's 2nd District, 1965-79.
Clients:
   Alaska Loggers Ass'n
   American Nuclear Insurers
   Boeing Co.
   Calista Corp.
   Earthquake Project, The
   Fluke Manufacturing Co., John
   Internat'l Telecommunications Satellite Organization (INTELSAT)
   Mutual Atomic Energy Liability Underwriters
   Pitney-Bowes, Inc.
   Seattle Organizing Committee, 1990 Goodwill Games
   Southeast Alaska Regional Health Corp. (SEARHC)
   TeleCommunications, Inc.
   University of Washington

MEEHAN, John J.
V. President, Corporate Relations, Chamber of Commerce of the U.S.A.
1615 H St., N.W., Washington, DC 20062
Telephone: (202) 463-5409

MEEK, John
Hartz/Meek Internat'l
806 15th St., N.W. Suite 210, Washington, DC 20006
Telephone: (202) 737-7370
Clients:
   Arizona, State of

MEEK, Katherine A.
Exec. Director, IMPAC 2000
122 C St., N.W., Suite 500A, Washington, DC 20001
Telephone: (202) 628-0617

MEESE, Edwin, III
Distinguished Fellow, Heritage Foundation
214 Massachusetts Ave., N.E., Washington, DC 20002
Telephone: (202) 546-4400
Background: Counselor to the President, 1981-85. Attorney General of the U.S., 1985-88.

MEETER, Stephen H.
V. President, Hill and Knowlton Public Affairs Worldwide
Washington Harbour, 901 31st St., N.W., Washington, DC 20007
Telephone: (202) 333-7400
Background: Assistant to House Minority Leader Gerald Ford (R-MI), 1973.
Clients:
   Electronic Industries Ass'n of Korea
   Hitachi Ltd.

MEFFORD, T. Fleetwood
V. President, International Trade, Hill and Knowlton Public Affairs Worldwide
Washington Harbour, 901 31st St., N.W., Washington, DC 20007
Telephone: (202) 333-7400

MEGIVERN, Kathleen
Exec. Director, Ass'n for Education & Rehabilitation of the Blind & Visually Impaired
206 North Washington St., Suite 320, Alexandria, VA 22314
Telephone: (703) 548-1884

MEHL, Ted
Parry and Romani Associates Inc.
233 Constitution Ave., N.E., Washington, DC 20002
Telephone: (202) 547-4000
Clients:
   Cessna Aircraft Co.

MEHLMAN, Ira
Public Relations Director, Federation for American Immigration Reform (FAIR)
1666 Connecticut Ave., N.W., Suite 400, Washington, DC 20009
Telephone: (202) 328-7004

MEIBURGER, George J.
Gallagher, Boland, Meiburger and Brosnan
1000 Vermont Ave., N.W. Suite 1100, Washington, DC 20005-4903
Telephone: (202) 289-7200
Clients:
   Enron Corp.

MEIER, Michelle
Counsel for Governmental Affairs, Consumers Union of the United States
2001 S St., N.W., Suite 520, Washington, DC 20009
Telephone: (202) 462-6262
Registered as lobbyist at U.S. Congress.

MEIER, Vernon H.
President, Nat'l Rural Letter Carriers' Ass'n
1448 Duke St., Alexandria, VA 22314
Telephone: (703) 684-5545
Registered as lobbyist at U.S. Congress.

MEIGHER, Eugene J.
Arent, Fox, Kintner, Plotkin & Kahn
1050 Connecticut Ave., N.W., Washington, DC 20036-5339
Telephone: (202) 857-6000
Background: Attorney, Antitrust Division, United States Dept of Justice, 1965-69.
Clients:
   Elders Grain, Inc.

MEIJER, John
Legislative/Joint State Liaison, Internat'l Fabricare Institute
12251 Tech Road, Silver Spring, MD 20904
Telephone: (301) 622-1900

MEISER, P.C., Robert N.
1825 I St., N.W., Suite 400, Washington, DC 20006
Telephone: (202) 296-6660
Background: An attorney in independent practice.
Organizations represented:
   "K" Line Air Service (U.S.A.), Inc.
   Kintetsu World Express (U.S.A.) Inc.
   Kuehne and Nagel, Inc.
   Royal Jordanian Airline, The
   Sumitomo Corp. of America
   Sumitronics Inc.

MEISINGER, J. Reese
Manager, Government Relations, American Soc. of Ass'n Executives
1575 Eye St., N.W., Washington, DC 20005-1168
Telephone: (202) 626-2723
Registered as lobbyist at U.S. Congress.
Background: Former aide to Rep. Roy Dyson (D-MD).

MEISINGER, Susan R.
V. President, Government Affairs, Soc. for Human Resources Management
606 N. Washington St., Alexandria, VA 22314
Telephone: (703) 548-3440
Registered as lobbyist at U.S. Congress.
Background: Exec. Assistant, 1981-87; Acting Director, OFCCP, 1986-87. Deputy Under Secretary of Labor for Employment Standards, 1984-87.

MEISSNER, Lt. Cdr. Robert
Intel & Spec Opns, Legis Affrs, DEPARTMENT OF DE-
FENSE
The Pentagon, Washington, DC 20301
Telephone: (202) 697-6210

MEISTER, Brenda
Congressional & Intergovt'l Relations, NAT'L TRANS-
PORTATION SAFETY BOARD
800 Independence Ave., S.W., Washington, DC 20594
Telephone: (202) 382-6757

MEISTER, F. A.
President and CEO, Distilled Spirits Council of the United
States
1250 Eye St., N.W., Suite 900, Washington, DC 20005
Telephone: (202) 628-3544

MELIA, Thomas O.
Program Director, Nat'l Democratic Institute for Internat'l
Affairs
1717 Massachusetts Ave., N.W. Suite 605, Washington,
DC 20036
Telephone: (202) 328-3136

MELINCOFF, David R.
O'Connor & Hannan
1919 Pennsylvania Ave., N.W., Suite 800, Washington, DC
20006
Telephone: (202) 887-1400
Registered as Foreign Agent: (#2972).
Background: Member, Trial Section, Antitrust Division,
Department of Justice, 1961-69.

MELLEY, Kenneth F.
Exec. Manager, Advocacy Programs, Nat'l Education
Ass'n of the U.S.
1201 16th St., N.W., Washington, DC 20036
Telephone: (202) 822-7300
Background: Also representes the Nat'l Education Ass'n
Political Action Committee.

MELLMAN & LAZARUS INC.
1054 31st St., N.W. Suite 530, Washington, DC 20007
Telephone: (202) 625-0370
Members of firm representing listed organizations:
Lazarus, Edward H., Partner

MELLON, Margaret G.
Director, Nat'l Biotechnology Policy Ctr, Nat'l Wildlife Fed-
eration
1400 16th St., N.W., Washington, DC 20036-2266
Telephone: (202) 797-6800
Registered as lobbyist at U.S. Congress.

MELLON, Regina M.
Government Affairs Representative, Lipsen Whitten & Diamond
1725 DeSales St., N.W., Suite 800, Washington, DC
20036
Telephone: (202) 659-6540
Registered as lobbyist at U.S. Congress.

MELLOR, John W.
Director, Internat'l Food Policy Research Institute
1776 Massachusetts Ave., N.W. Suite 800, Washington,
DC 20036
Telephone: (202) 862-5600
Background: Former economist with the U.S. Agency for
International Development (AID).

MELNYKOVICH, George O.
President and CEO, Food Processing Machinery and Supplies Ass'n
200 Daingerfield Road, Alexandria, VA 22314
Telephone: (703) 684-1080

**MELROD, REDMAN AND GARTLAN, A PROFES-
SIONAL CORPORATION**
1801 K St., N.W. Suite 1100, Washington, DC 20006
Telephone: (202) 822-5300
Members of firm representing listed organizations:
Hamovit, Jerry M.
Background: Trial Attorney, Tax Division, U.S. Depart-
ment of Justice, 1959-1962; Attorney, Office of the
Tax Legislative Counsel, U.S. Treasury Department,
1965-1967.
Clients:
American Speech-Language-Hearing Ass'n

Greyhound Leasing and Financial Corp.

MELTON, Carol A.
Washington Counsel, Time Warner Inc.
1133 21st St., N.W., Suite 400, Washington, DC 20036
Telephone: (202) 223-8855
Registered as lobbyist at U.S. Congress.

MELTON, George E.
Deputy Exec. Director, Nat'l Ass'n of Secondary School
Principals
1904 Association Drive, Reston, VA 22091
Telephone: (703) 860-0200

MELTON, Raymond
Assoc. Exec. Dir. and Dir, NASE, American Ass'n of
School Administrators
1801 North Moore St., Arlington, VA 22209
Telephone: (703) 528-0700

MELTSNER, James R.
Evans Group, Ltd., The
1010 Wisconsin Ave., N.W. Suite 810, Washington, DC
20007
Telephone: (202) 333-8777
Registered as lobbyist at U.S. Congress.
Clients:
Cyprus, Embassy of the Republic of
Matlack Systems, Inc.

MELTZER, Richard
Winston and Strawn
2550 M St., N.W., Suite 500, Washington, DC 20037
Telephone: (202) 828-8400
Registered as lobbyist at U.S. Congress.
Clients:
American Ass'n of Museums
CNA Financial Corp.
Tucson, Arizona, City of

MENA, Armando L.
Exec. Director, Republican Nat'l Hispanic Assembly of the
U.S.
440 First St., N.W. Suite 400, Washington, DC 20001
Telephone: (202) 662-1355

MENAKER, Howard N.
General Counsel, Nat'l Ass'n of Truck Stop Operators
1199 N. Fairfax St. Suite 801, Alexandria, VA 22314
Telephone: (703) 549-2100
Registered as lobbyist at U.S. Congress.
Background: Serves as Contact, Nat'l Ass'n of Truck Stop
Operators Political Action Committee.

MENAPACE, Jerry
Secretary-Treasurer, Active Ballot Club
1775 K St., N.W., c/o UFCW, Washington, DC 20006
Telephone: (202) 223-3111

MENDELSOHN, Bruce S.
Akin, Gump, Strauss, Hauer and Feld
1333 New Hampshire Ave., N.W., Suite 400, Washington,
DC 20036
Telephone: (202) 887-4000
Background: Attorney and Special Counsel, Division of
Corporation Finance, Securities and Exchange Commis-
sion, 1977-80. Legal Assistant to Commissioner John R.
Evans, SEC, 1980-82. Chief, Office of Regulatory Policy,
Division of Investment, SEC, 1982-83.

MENDELSOHN, Jack
Deputy Director, Arms Control Ass'n
11 Dupont Circle, N.W., Washington, DC 20036
Telephone: (202) 797-6450

MENDELSOHN, Martin
Treasurer, Fund for Freedom
1001 Pennsylvania Ave., N.W. Suite 275N, Washington,
DC 20503
Telephone: (202) 624-5914

MENDELSON, Keith J.
Pillsbury, Madison and Sutro
1667 K St., N.W., Suite 1100, Washington, DC 20006
Telephone: (202) 887-0300
Registered as Foreign Agent: (#4212).
Clients:
Korea Foreign Trade Ass'n

MENDEZ, Juan E.
Washington Exec Director, Americas Watch, Human
Rights Watch
1522 K St., N.W., Suite 910, Washington, DC 20005
Telephone: (202) 371-6592

MENDOZA, Julie C.
Mudge Rose Guthrie Alexander and Ferdon
2121 K St., N.W., Suite 700, Washington, DC 20037
Telephone: (202) 429-9355
Registered as Foreign Agent: (#3200).
Clients:
Camara de la Industria Curtidora Argentina
Dalmine Siderica
Dong Sung Steel Industries Co., Ltd.
Korea Iron and Steel Ass'n
Mexinox, S.A. de C.V.
Propulsora Siderurgica S.A.I.C.

MENDS-COLE, Joyce
Washington Representative - Africa Watch, Human Rights
Watch
1522 K St., N.W., Suite 910, Washington, DC 20005
Telephone: (202) 371-6592

MENELL, Howard
Coffield Ungaretti Harris & Slavin
1747 Pennsylvania Ave., N.W. Suite 900, Washington, DC
20006
Telephone: (202) 872-4310
Registered as lobbyist at U.S. Congress.
Clients:
COMDISCO, Inc.

MENGEBIER, David
Legislative Counsel, Handgun Control, Inc.
1225 Eye St., N.W., Suite 1100, Washington, DC 20005
Telephone: (202) 898-0792
Registered as lobbyist at U.S. Congress.
Background: Former Legislative Director to Rep. Carl D.
Pursell (R-MI).

MENGEBIER, William P.
Assistant Director, Government Relations, Rhone-Poulenc
Inc.
Metropolitan Square, Suite 225 655 15th St., N.W., Wash-
ington, DC 20005
Telephone: (202) 628-0500
Registered as lobbyist at U.S. Congress.
Registered as Foreign Agent: (#4188).

MENNING, Edward L.
Exec. V. President, Nat'l Ass'n of Federal Veterinarians
1023 15th St., N.W. Suite 300, Washington, DC 20005
Telephone: (202) 289-6334
Registered as lobbyist at U.S. Congress.
Background: Serves also as Treasurer of the Nat'l Ass'n of
Federal Veterinarians Political Action Committee.

MENSCH, Donald H.
Executive Director, Household Goods Forwarders Ass'n of
America
2111 Eisenhower Ave. Suite 404, Alexandria, VA 22314
Telephone: (703) 684-3780

MENSEL, Frank
V. President for Federal Relations, American Ass'n of
Community and Junior Colleges
One Dupont Circle, N.W. Suite 410, Washington, DC
20036
Telephone: (202) 293-7050

MENSH, Stephanie C.
Washington Representative, American Academy of Ophthalmology
1101 Vermont Ave., N.W., Suite 300, Washington, DC
20005
Telephone: (202) 737-6662
Registered as lobbyist at U.S. Congress.

MENTZ, J. Roger
Cadwalader, Wickersham & Taft
1333 New Hampshire Ave., N.W. Suite 700, Washington,
DC 20036
Telephone: (202) 862-2200
Registered as lobbyist at U.S. Congress.
Background: Assistant Secretary for Tax Policy, U.S.
Treasury Department, 1985-87.
Clients:

The listings in this directory are available as *Mailing Labels.* See last page.

283

MENTZ, J. Roger (Cont'd)
Clayton & Dubilier, Inc.
Coalition for Capital Import Neutrality
Mercedes-Benz of North America, Inc.
PFIC Group

MENTZER, Kenneth D.
Exec. V. President, Mineral Insulation Manufacturers Ass'n
1420 King St., 4th Floor, Alexandria, VA 22314
Telephone: (703) 684-0084

MENTZINGER, Jane
Spokeswoman, Common Cause
2030 M St., N.W., Washington, DC 20036
Telephone: (202) 833-1200

MERCADO-LLORENS, Segundo
Director, Government Affairs, United Food and Commercial Workers Internat'l Union
1775 K St., N.W., Washington, DC 20006
Telephone: (202) 223-3111

MERCER, INC., William M.
1001 22nd St., N.W. Suite 400, Washington, DC 20037
Telephone: (202) 293-9422
Members of firm representing listed organizations:
   Conaway, Harry J.
   Turner, Audrey S.

MERCER, Robert G.
Manager, Public Relations, Goodyear Tire and Rubber Co.
901 15th St., N.W. Suite 350, Washington, DC 20005
Telephone: (202) 682-9250

MEREDITH, Bruce
Van Fleet, Metzner & Meredith
499 South Capitol St., S.W. Suite 520, Washington, DC 20003
Telephone: (202) 488-1749

MEREDITH, James M.
President, American Nat'l Metric Council
1620 I St., N.W., Suite 220, Washington, DC 20006
Telephone: (202) 628-5757

MEREDITH, Julia
Legis Affrs Specialist, NAT'L AERONAUTICS AND SPACE ADMINISTRATION
400 Maryland Ave., S.W., Washington, DC 20546
Telephone: (202) 453-1055

MEREDITH, Dr. Leslie H.
Group Director, American Geophysical Union
2000 Florida Ave., N.W., Washington, DC 20009
Telephone: (202) 462-6900

MEREDITH, Sandra K.
DGA Internat'l
1133 Connecticut Ave., N.W. Suite 700, Washington, DC 20036
Telephone: (202) 223-4001
Registered as lobbyist at U.S. Congress.
Clients:
   Delegation General pour l' Armement (DRI)
   Societe Nationale d'Etude et Construction de Moteurs d'Aviation (SNECMA)
   Sofreavia

MERELMAN, Jack W.
Washington Representative, County Supervisors Ass'n of California
440 First St., N.W., Suite 503, Washington, DC 20001
Telephone: (202) 783-7575

MERENDA, Dan W.
Exec. Director, Nat'l Ass'n of Partners in Education
601 Wythe St., Suite 200, Alexandria, VA 22314
Telephone: (703) 836-4880

MERIN, Charles L.
Gold and Liebengood, Inc.
1455 Pennsylvania Ave., N.W. Suite 950, Washington, DC 20004
Telephone: (202) 639-8899
Registered as lobbyist at U.S. Congress.
Clients:
   MCI Communications Corp.
   Nat'l Restaurant Ass'n
   Nat'l School Transportation Ass'n
   Washington Metropolitan Area Transit Authority

MERISOTIS, Jamie P.
Chambers Associates Incorporated
1625 K St., N.W. Suite 200, Washington, DC 20006
Telephone: (202) 857-0670
Clients:
   State Higher Education Executive Officers

MERKIN, Jane P.
Exec. Director, National Capital Region, American Jewish Congress
2027 Massachusetts Ave., N.W., Washington, DC 20036
Telephone: (202) 332-4001

MERKIN, William S.
Senior V. President, International, Strategic Policy, Inc.
1615 L St., N.W., Suite 650, Washington, DC 20036
Telephone: (202) 659-0878
Registered as Foreign Agent: (#4206).
Clients:
   Grey, Clark, Shih and Associates, Ltd.
   Labatt Limited, John

MERKOWITZ, David R.
Director, Public Affairs, American Council on Education
One Dupont Circle, N.W., Washington, DC 20036
Telephone: (202) 939-9300

MERLIS, Edward
V. President, Policy and Planning, Air Transport Ass'n of America
1709 New York Ave., N.W., Washington, DC 20006-5206
Telephone: (202) 626-4000
Background: Formerly on staffs of Senate Commerce, Judiciary and Appropriations Committees.

MERNICK, George, III
Hogan and Hartson
555 13th St., N.W., Suite 1200, Washington, DC 20004-1109
Telephone: (202) 637-5600
Clients:
   Farmworker Justice Fund

MERRICK, Mrs. Libby
Secretary to the President, United States Defense Committee
3238 Wynford Drive, Fairfax, VA 22031
Telephone: (703) 914-2010

MERRICK, Thomas W.
President, Population Reference Bureau
777 14th St., N.W. Suite 800, Washington, DC 20005
Telephone: (202) 639-8040

MERRIFIELD, D. Bruce
Consultant, American Electronics Ass'n
1225 Eye St., N.W., Suite 950, Washington, DC 20005
Telephone: (202) 682-9110
Background: Former Assistant Secretary for Productivity, Technology and Innovation, U.S. Department of Commerce.

MERRIGAN, John A.
Verner, Liipfert, Bernhard, McPherson and Hand, Chartered
901 15th St., N.W., Suite 700, Washington, DC 20005
Telephone: (202) 371-6000
Registered as lobbyist at U.S. Congress.
Registered as Foreign Agent: (#3712).
Background: Staff of Sen. Russell Long (D-LA), 1971.
Clients:
   Central Gulf Lines
   Consolidated Grain and Barge Co.
   Coopers and Lybrand
   Investment Company Institute
   Irving Ltd., J.D.
   Puerto Rico, New Progressive Party Of
   Travelers, The
   UNC Incorporated
   Verner, Liipfert, Bernhard, McPherson and Hand Political Action Committee

MERRILL, Jo
Deputy Director - State Public Affairs, March of Dimes Birth Defects Foundation
1725 K St., N.W., Suite 814, Washington, DC 20006
Telephone: (202) 659-1800
Registered as lobbyist at U.S. Congress.

MERRIMAN, Richard M.
Reid & Priest
1111 19th St., N.W., Washington, DC 20036
Telephone: (202) 828-0100
Clients:
   Entergy Corp.
   Green Mountain Power Corp.

MERRITT, Gordon L.
Asst. Director, Congressional Affairs, Hughes Aircraft Co.
1100 Wilson Blvd. 20th Floor, Arlington, VA 22209
Telephone: (703) 525-1550

MERRITT, General Jack N., USA (Ret)
Exec. V. President, Ass'n of the United States Army
2425 Wilson Blvd., Arlington, VA 22201
Telephone: (703) 841-4300

MERRITT, Richard
Director, Intergovernmental Health Policy Project
2011 Eye St., N.W. Suite 200, Washington, DC 20006
Telephone: (202) 872-1445

MERRITT, William D.
V. President, Government Operations, Hughes Aircraft Co.
1100 Wilson Blvd. 20th Floor, Arlington, VA 22209
Telephone: (703) 525-1550

MERRY, Susan P.
Assoc. Exec. Director & Controller, Nat'l School Boards Ass'n
1680 Duke St., Alexandria, VA 22314
Telephone: (703) 838-6722

MERRYMAN, Lori L.
V. President, Communications, Carmen Group, The
1667 K St., N.W., Suite 700, Washington, DC 20006
Telephone: (202) 785-0500
Background: Former public affairs specialist, U.S. Department of Education.

MERRYMAN, Walker
V. President, Tobacco Institute
1875 Eye St., N.W., Suite 800, Washington, DC 20006
Telephone: (202) 457-4800

MERSKI, Paul G.
Director of Fiscal Affairs, Tax Foundation, Inc.
470 L'Enfant Plaza S.W., East Bldg., Suite 7112, Washington, DC 20024
Telephone: (202) 863-5454

MERSKI, Richard P.
Director, Government Affairs, American Internat'l Group
1455 Pennsylvania Ave., N.W. Suite 900, Washington, DC 20004
Telephone: (202) 783-5690
Registered as lobbyist at U.S. Congress.

MESIROW, Harold E.
Leva, Hawes, Mason and Martin
1220 19th St., N.W. Suite 700, Washington, DC 20036
Telephone: (202) 775-0725
Registered as lobbyist at U.S. Congress.
Clients:
   American Waterways Operators
   Foss Maritime Co.
   Global Marine, Inc.

MESSICK, Neil T.
Washington Rep., Government Relations, General Electric Co.
1331 Pennsylvania Ave., N.W., Washington, DC 20004
Telephone: (202) 637-4222
Registered as lobbyist at U.S. Congress.

MESSICK, Richard
Patton, Boggs and Blow
2550 M St., N.W., Suite 800, Washington, DC 20037
Telephone: (202) 457-6000
Registered as lobbyist at U.S. Congress.
Background: Chief Counsel, U.S. Senate Foreign Relations Committee, 1985-86.

MESSINA, Raymond A.
Attorney, Penney Co., J. C.
Suite 1015, 1156 15th St., N.W., Washington, DC 20005
Telephone: (202) 862-4827

MESSING, F. Andy, Jr.
Exec. Director, Nat'l Defense Council Foundation
228 S. Washington St., Suite 230, Alexandria, VA 22314-3626
Telephone: (703) 836-3443

MESSMORE, Ann
Director, Administration, American Chemical Soc.
1155 16th St., N.W., Washington, DC
Telephone: (202) 872-4091

MESSNER, Howard M.
Exec. V. Pres., Chief Operating Officer, American Consulting Engineers Council
1015 15th St., N.W., Suite 802, Washington, DC 20005
Telephone: (202) 347-7474
Registered as lobbyist at U.S. Congress.

MESTRES, Jean L.
Manager, Federal Relations, OXY USA Inc.
1747 Pennsylvania Ave., N.W. Suite 300, Washington, DC 20006
Telephone: (202) 857-3082
Registered as lobbyist at U.S. Congress.

MESTRICH, Keith
Director, Health and Safety, AFL-CIO - Food and Allied Service Trades Department
815 16th St., N.W., Suite 408, Washington, DC 20006
Telephone: (202) 737-7200

METALITZ, Stephen J.
V. President and Counsel, Information Industry Ass'n
555 New Jersey Ave., N.W. Suite 800, Washington, DC 20001
Telephone: (202) 639-8262
Registered as lobbyist at U.S. Congress.
Background: Formerly Special Counsel-Chief Nominations Counsel, Senate Judiciary Committee.

METHENY, Earl L.
Silver, Freedman & Taff
1735 Eye St., N.W., Washington, DC 20006
Telephone: (202) 429-6100
Clients:
Nat'l Homeowners Ass'n

METZ, Douglas W.
Exec. V. President, Wine and Spirits Wholesalers of America
1023 15th St., N.W., 4th Floor, Washington, DC 20005
Telephone: (202) 371-9792
Background: Responsibilities include Wine and Spirits Wholesalers of America Political Action Committee.

METZGER, David P.
Kirkland and Ellis
655 15th St., N.W. Suite 1200, Washington, DC 20005
Telephone: (202) 879-5000
Background: Former Staff Director of the Energy, Environment, Safety and Research Subcommittee, House Small Business Committee. Former Director, Innovation and Procurement Policy Office, U.S. Small Business Administration.

METZLER, Cynthia
Exec. Director, Overseas Education Fund Internat'l
1815 H St., N.W., 11th Floor, Washington, DC 20006
Telephone: (202) 466-3430

MEUSER, Kenneth G.
Walker Associates, Charls E.
1730 Pennsylvania Ave., N.W. Suite 200, Washington, DC 20006
Telephone: (202) 393-4760
Organizations represented:
Atchison, Topeka and Santa Fe Railway Co., The

MEUSER, Robert L.
Thompson and Co.
1001 G St., N.W. 7th Floor, Washington, DC 20001
Telephone: (202) 383-5590
Clients:
CareerCom Corp.

MEYER, Alden
Director, Climate Change & Energy Prgm., Union of Concerned Scientists
1616 P St., N.W., Suite 310, Washington, DC 20036
Telephone: (202) 332-0900
Registered as lobbyist at U.S. Congress.

MEYER, Brian M.
Director, American Bankers Ass'n BankPac
1120 Connecticut Ave., N.W., Washington, DC 20036
Telephone: (202) 663-5076

MEYER, Douglas
Director, Research & Internat'l Affairs, Internat'l Union of Electronic, Electrical, Salaried, Machine, and Furniture Workers, AFL-CIO
1126 16th St., N.W., Washington, DC 20036
Telephone: (202) 296-1200

MEYER, Eugene B.
Exec. Director, Federalist Soc. for Law
1700 K St., N.W. Suite 901, Washington, DC 20006
Telephone: (202) 822-8138

MEYER, FALLER, WEISMAN AND GREENBURG
4400 Jennifer St., N.W., Suite 380, Washington, DC 20015
Telephone: (202) 362-1100
Members of firm representing listed organizations:
Weisman, David E.
Clients:
Nat'l Ass'n of Business and Educational Radio *(David E. Weisman)*
Nat'l Ass'n of Business and Educational Radio Political Action Committee

MEYER, Jack A.
President, New Directions for Policy
1101 Vermont Ave., N.W. Suite 400, Washington, DC 20005
Telephone: (202) 289-3907

MEYER, Lindsay
Venable, Baetjer, Howard and Civiletti
1201 New York Ave., N.W., Suite 1000, Washington, DC 20005
Telephone: (202) 962-4800

MEYER, M. Barry
V.P., Gov't Rel. & Assoc. Gen'l Counsel, Aluminum Ass'n
900 19th St., N.W. Suite 300, Washington, DC 20006
Telephone: (202) 862-5177
Registered as lobbyist at U.S. Congress.
Background: Legislative Attorney, Bureau of Public Roads, Dep't of Commerce, 1956-1959. Senate Public Works Committee: Chief Counsel, 1967-1976; Staff Director, 1972-1976. Serves also as contact person for the Aluminum Ass'n PAC.

MEYER, Sean
Coordinator, Arms Cntrl & Nat'l Security, Union of Concerned Scientists
1616 P St., N.W., Suite 310, Washington, DC 20036
Telephone: (202) 332-0900
Registered as lobbyist at U.S. Congress.

MEYER, Steven R.
Director, Governmental Affairs, Nat'l Ass'n of Conservation Districts
509 Capitol Court, N.E., Washington, DC 20002
Telephone: (202) 547-6223

MEYERS AND ALTERMAN
1710 Rhode Island Ave., N.W. Suite 200, Washington, DC 20036
Telephone: (202) 466-8270
Members of firm representing listed organizations:
Alterman, Stephen A.
Background: Attorney, Civil Aeronautics Board, 1968-73. Chief, Legal Division, Civil Aeronautics Board, 1974-75.
Meyers, N. Marshall
Clients:
Air Freight Ass'n of America *(Stephen A. Alterman)*
Pet Industry Joint Advisory Council *(N. Marshall Meyers)*

MEYERS & ASSOCIATES
412 First St., S.E., Suite 100, Washington, DC 20003
Telephone: (202) 484-2773
Background: A lobbying firm. Affiliated with White Associates.
Members of firm representing listed organizations:
Anderson, Laurel, Associate

Judson, Margaret
Meyers, Larry D., President
Background: Legis. Dir. to Sen. Lloyd Bentsen (D-TX), 1972-76. Dir., Congressional Affairs, U.S. Department of Agriculture, 1976-80.
Meyers, Rick, V. President
Shirley, Kimberly
White, Keith
Wilson, Shelley
Clients:
Alnor Oil Co. *(Rick Meyers)*
American Beekeeping Federation *(Keith White)*
American Sheep Industry Ass'n *(Rick Meyers)*
American Sheep Industry Ass'n RAMSPAC *(Larry D. Meyers)*
Anodyne, Inc. *(Rick Meyers)*
Centergas, Inc. *(Larry D. Meyers)*
Internat'l Ass'n of Refrigerated Warehouses *(Rick Meyers)*
Nat'l Agricultural Chemicals Ass'n *(Larry D. Meyers)*
Nat'l Institute of Oilseed Products *(Margaret Judson, Rick Meyers)*
Nat'l Peanut Growers Group *(Larry D. Meyers)*
Ricebelt Warehouses *(Larry D. Meyers)*
Southwest Virginia and Carolinas Peanut Growers *(Larry D. Meyers)*
Texas A & M University Research Foundation *(Larry D. Meyers, Shelley Wilson)*
Texas Cotton Marketing *(Larry D. Meyers)*
Texas Internat'l Education Consortium *(Rick Meyers)*

MEYERS, Bradley
Confidential Asst, Cong Rels, DEPARTMENT OF AGRICULTURE
14th and Independence Ave. S.W., Room 208-E, Washington, DC 20205
Telephone: (202) 447-7095

MEYERS, Edward R.
Program Director, Citizens for Tax Justice
1311 L St., N.W. 4th Floor, Washington, DC 20005
Telephone: (202) 626-3780

MEYERS, Erik J.
General Counsel, Environmental Law Institute
1616 P St., N.W., Suite 200, Washington, DC 20036
Telephone: (202) 328-5150

MEYERS, Larry D.
President, Meyers & Associates
412 First St., S.E., Suite 100, Washington, DC 20003
Telephone: (202) 484-2773
Registered as lobbyist at U.S. Congress.
Background: Legis. Dir. to Sen. Lloyd Bentsen (D-TX), 1972-76. Dir., Congressional Affairs, U.S. Department of Agriculture, 1976-80.
Clients:
American Sheep Industry Ass'n RAMSPAC
Centergas, Inc.
Nat'l Agricultural Chemicals Ass'n
Nat'l Peanut Growers Group
Ricebelt Warehouses
Southwest Virginia and Carolinas Peanut Growers
Texas A & M University Research Foundation
Texas Cotton Marketing

MEYERS, Marshall
General Counsel, Pet Industry Joint Advisory Council
1710 Rhode Island Ave., N.W. Suite 200, Washington, DC 20036
Telephone: (202) 452-1525

MEYERS, N. Marshall
Meyers and Alterman
1710 Rhode Island Ave., N.W. Suite 200, Washington, DC 20036
Telephone: (202) 466-8270
Clients:
Pet Industry Joint Advisory Council

MEYERS, Rick
V. President, Meyers & Associates
412 First St., S.E., Suite 100, Washington, DC 20003
Telephone: (202) 484-2773
Registered as lobbyist at U.S. Congress.
Clients:
Alnor Oil Co.
American Sheep Industry Ass'n

MEYERS, Rick (Cont'd)
Anodyne, Inc.
Internat'l Ass'n of Refrigerated Warehouses
Nat'l Institute of Oilseed Products
Texas Internat'l Education Consortium

MEYERS, Roy C.
Cassidy and Associates, Inc.
655 15th St., N.W., Suite 1100, Washington, DC 20005
Telephone: (202) 347-0773
Registered as lobbyist at U.S. Congress.
Background: Director of Communications, Cassidy and Associates, Inc, 1987- . Press Secretary to Senator Howard Metzenbaum (D-OH), 1977-85.
Clients:
University Hospital of Cleveland

MEYERS, Tedson J.
Reid & Priest
1111 19th St., N.W., Washington, DC 20036
Telephone: (202) 828-0100
Background: Assistant to Chairman, Federal Communications Commission, 1961-62.

MICA, Daniel A.
Exec. V. President, Federal Affairs, American Council of Life Insurance
1001 Pennsylvania Ave., N.W., Washington, DC 20004-2599
Telephone: (202) 624-2121
Registered as lobbyist at U.S. Congress.
Background: Former Member, U.S. House of Representatives (D-FL).

MICA, DUDINSKY & ASSOCIATES
201 Massachusetts Ave., N.E., Suite C-9, Washington, DC 20002
Telephone: (202) 543-2143
Members of firm representing listed organizations:
Dudinsky, John (Jr.)
Background: Legislative Assistant to Rep. John H. Dent (D-PA), 1972-76. Legislative Assistant to the House Education and Labor Committee, 1978-80. Legislative Assistant to Senator Paula Hawkins (R-FL), 1980-82. Staff Director and Chief Counsel, Senate Subcommittee on Children, Family, Drugs and Alcohol and the 48-member Senate Drug Caucus, 1982-86.
Griesinger, Kathryn Joy
Background: Staff aide to Rep. Dick Schulze (R-PA), 1984-85. Minority Staff Member, House Committee on Science, Space and Technology, 1985-87.
Mica, John L.
Background: Member, Florida House of Representatives, 1976-80. Administrative Assistant to Senator Paula Hawkins (R-FL), 1980-85.
Clients:
American Specialty Chemical Corp. *(John Dudinsky, Jr., John L. Mica)*
Antimony Products of America *(John Dudinsky, Jr., John L. Mica)*
Broward County, Office of the Sheriff *(John Dudinsky, Jr., John L. Mica)*
Champon Flavors & Fragrances *(John Dudinsky, Jr., John L. Mica)*
Champon Pet Products *(John Dudinsky, Jr., John L. Mica)*
Coopers and Lybrand *(John Dudinsky, Jr., John L. Mica)*
Darome, Inc. *(John Dudinsky, Jr., John L. Mica)*
Genix Corp. *(John Dudinsky, Jr., John L. Mica)*
Greater Orlando Aviation Authority *(John Dudinsky, Jr., John L. Mica)*
Harris Government Systems *(John Dudinsky, Jr., John L. Mica)*
Harris RF Communications *(John L. Mica)*
Hvide Shipping, Inc. *(John Dudinsky, Jr., John L. Mica)*
IAMUS/Internat'l Unlimited *(John Dudinsky, Jr., John L. Mica)*

MICA, John L.
Mica, Dudinsky & Associates
201 Massachusetts Ave., N.E., Suite C-9, Washington, DC 20002
Telephone: (202) 543-2143
Registered as lobbyist at U.S. Congress.
Background: Member, Florida House of Representatives, 1976-80. Administrative Assistant to Senator Paula Hawkins (R-FL), 1980-85.
Clients:

American Specialty Chemical Corp.
Antimony Products of America
Broward County, Office of the Sheriff
Champon Flavors & Fragrances
Champon Pet Products
Coopers and Lybrand
Darome, Inc.
Genix Corp.
Greater Orlando Aviation Authority
Harris Government Systems
Harris RF Communications
Hvide Shipping, Inc.
IAMUS/Internat'l Unlimited

MICALI, Mark Allan
Manager, Government Affairs, Nat'l Business Aircraft Ass'n
1200 18th St., N.W. Suite 200, Washington, DC 20036
Telephone: (202) 783-9000
Registered as lobbyist at U.S. Congress.
Background: Formerly Legislative Assistant to Rep. Dan Rostenkowski (D-IL).

MICCICHE, Laurie J.
Manager, Federal Government Affairs, Occidental Chemical Corporation
1747 Pennsylvania Ave., N.W., Suite 375, Washington, DC 20006
Telephone: (202) 857-3000
Registered as lobbyist at U.S. Congress.

MICELI, Keith L.
Exec. V. President, Ass'n of American Chambers of Commerce in Latin America
1615 H St., N.W., Washington, DC 20062
Telephone: (202) 463-5485

MICHAD, Jay E.
Chicago Washington Office, City of
499 South Capitol St., S.E., Washington, DC 20003
Telephone: (202) 554-7900

MICHAELS, Eileen F.
Lisboa Associates, Inc.
1317 F St., N.W., Suite 202, Washington, DC 20004
Telephone: (202) 737-2622
Registered as lobbyist at U.S. Congress.
Clients:
Virgin Islands, University of the

MICHAELS, Joel L.
Michaels and Wishner, P.C.
1726 M St., N.W., Suite 500, Washington, DC 20036
Telephone: (202) 223-9212
Background: Serves as Washington Representative, Nat'l Ass'n for Ambulatory Care.
Clients:
Nat'l Ass'n for Ambulatory Care

MICHAELS AND WISHNER, P.C.
1726 M St., N.W., Suite 500, Washington, DC 20036
Telephone: (202) 223-9212
Members of firm representing listed organizations:
Michaels, Joel L.
Background: Serves as Washington Representative, Nat'l Ass'n for Ambulatory Care.
Clients:
Nat'l Ass'n for Ambulatory Care *(Joel L. Michaels)*

MICHAELSON, Leslie
Manager, Ass'n Research & Economics, Shriner-Midland Co.
6432 Quincy Place, Falls Church, VA 22042
Telephone: (703) 795-4356

MICHAELSON, Michael G.
Covington and Burling
1201 Pennsylvania Ave., N.W., Box 7566, Washington, DC 20044
Telephone: (202) 662-6000
Registered as lobbyist at U.S. Congress.
Clients:
Puerto Rico, Commonwealth of

MICHEL, Laurie
Hogan and Hartson
555 13th St., N.W., Suite 1200, Washington, DC 20004-1109
Telephone: (202) 637-5600
Clients:

Cryo-Chem Internat'l, Inc.

MICHELMAN, Kate
Exec. Director, Nat'l Abortion Rights Action League
1101 14th St., N.W., Suite 500, Washington, DC 20005
Telephone: (202) 371-0779

MICHELS, Kathleen
Ass't Dir., Congress'l & Agency Relat'ns, American Nurses' Ass'n
1101 14th St., N.W., Suite 200, Washington, DC 20005
Telephone: (202) 789-1800
Registered as lobbyist at U.S. Congress.

MICHIEL, Richard
Dir., Income & Benefits Policy Center, Urban Institute, The
2100 M St., N.W., Washington, DC 20037
Telephone: (202) 833-7200

MICHNICH, Dr. Marie E.
Assoc. Exec. V. Pres. for Health Policy, American College of Cardiology
9111 Old Georgetown Road, Bethesda, MD 20814
Telephone: (301) 897-5400
Background: Assistant to Senate Majority Leader Robert Dole (R-KS), 1984-87.

MIDDLEBROOK, William C.
International Secretary, American Soc. of Appraisers
535 Herndon Parkway, Suite 150, Herndon, VA 22070
Telephone: (703) 478-2228

MIDDLETON, B. Jenkins
Tanaka, Ritger and Middleton
1919 Pennsylvania Ave., N.W., Suite 303, Washington, DC 20006
Telephone: (202) 223-1670
Registered as lobbyist at U.S. Congress.
Registered as Foreign Agent: (#0948).
Clients:
Electronic Industries Ass'n of Japan
Japan Automobile Tire Manufacturers Ass'n
Japan Trade Center

MIDDLETON, E. Alan
Congressional Relations, Grumman Corp.
1000 Wilson Blvd., Suite 2800, Arlington, VA 22209
Telephone: (703) 875-8400
Registered as lobbyist at U.S. Congress.

MIDDLETON, Roger E.
Antitrust and Corporate Policy Attorney, Chamber of Commerce of the U.S.A.
1615 H St., N.W., Washington, DC 20062
Telephone: (202) 463-5500
Registered as lobbyist at U.S. Congress.

MIELDS, Hugh
Linton, Mields, Reisler and Cottone
1225 Eye St., N.W., Suite 300, Washington, DC 20005
Telephone: (202) 682-3901
Background: Washington Representative, City of Norfolk, VA.

MIERZWINSKI, Edmund
Consumer Lobbyist, U.S. Public Interest Research Group
215 Pennsylvania Ave., S.E., Washington, DC 20003
Telephone: (202) 546-9707
Registered as lobbyist at U.S. Congress.

MIETUS, Andrea
Administrative Director, Democratic Leadership Council
316 Pennsylvania Ave., S.E., Suite 500, Washington, DC 20003
Telephone: (202) 546-0007

MIGDAIL, Evan M.
Camp, Barsh, Bates and Tate
2550 M St., N.W., Suite 275, Washington, DC 20037
Telephone: (202) 887-5160
Registered as lobbyist at U.S. Congress.

MIGNINI, Paul J., Jr.
President, Nat'l Ass'n of Credit Management
8815 Centre Park Drive Suite 200, Columbia, MD 21045-2117
Telephone: (301) 740-5560

MIKESELL, Libby
Manager, Editorial Services, Internat'l Food Information Council
1100 Connecticut Ave. N.W., Suite 430, Washington, DC 20036
Telephone: (202) 296-6540

MIKO, Jason
Exec. Director, College Republican Nat'l Committee
310 First St., S.E., Washington, DC 20003
Telephone: (202) 662-1330

MILAM, Rene P.
Counsel, American Newspaper Publishers Ass'n
The Newspaper Center 11600 Sunrise Valley Drive, Reston, VA 22091
Telephone: (703) 648-1000
Registered as lobbyist at U.S. Congress.

MILANESE, Sylvia
Cong and Legis Affrs (Act), DEPARTMENT OF LABOR - Mine Safety and Health Administration
4015 Wilson Blvd., Arlington, VA 22203
Telephone: (703) 235-1392

MILAZZO, Janice I.
Washington Representative, BP America Inc.
1776 Eye St., N.W., Suite 1000, Washington, DC 20006
Telephone: (202) 785-4888
Registered as lobbyist at U.S. Congress.

MILBANK, TWEED, HADLEY & MCCLOY
1825 Eye St., N.W. Suite 900, Washington, DC 20006
Telephone: (202) 835-7500
Registered as Foreign Agent: (#1839)
Background: Washington office of a New York law firm.
Members of firm representing listed organizations:
  Green, Carl J.
    Background: Attorney/Advisor, U.S. Department of Transportation, 1968-69.
  Marcuss, Stanley J.
    Background: Counsel, International Finance Subcommittee, U.S. Senate, 1973-77. Senior Deputy Assistant Secretary for Industry and Trade, Department of Commerce, 1977-79; Acting Assistant Secretary for Industry and Trade, Department of Commerce, 1979-80.
  Richardson, Elliot L.
    Background: Assistant Secretary for Legislation, Dept. of Health, Education and Welfare, 1957-59. United States Attorney, Massachusetts, 1959-61. Special Assistant to the Attorney General of the U.S., 1961. Lieutenant Governor, 1965-67 and Attorney General, 1967-69, Commonwealth of Massachusetts. Under Secretary, U.S. Department of State, 1969-70. Secretary of Health, Education and Welfare, 1970-73. Secretary of Defense, 1973. Attorney General of the U.S., 1973. Ambassador to the Court of St. James, 1975-76. Secretary of Commerce, 1976-77. Ambassador at Large for the Law of the Sea, 1977-80.
  Tuttle, Baldwin B.
    Background: Assistant General Counsel, 1973-76 and Deputy General Counsel, 1976-77, Board of Governors of the Federal Reserve System.
  Clients:
  Ass'n for Internat'l Investment *(Elliot L. Richardson)*
  Japan, Embassy of
  Kuwait, Government of
  Mexico, Government of
  Midland Bank plc *(Elliot L. Richardson)*

MILBURN, Richard A.
V. President, Washington Operations, Grumman Corp.
1000 Wilson Blvd., Suite 2800, Arlington, VA 22209
Telephone: (703) 875-8400

MILCO, George
Staff Attorney, HALT-An Organization of Americans for Legal Reform
1319 F St., N.W., Suite 300, Washington, DC 20004
Telephone: (202) 347-9600

MILDER, Nelson L.
Assistant Director, Government Relations, American Soc. of Mechanical Engineers
1825 K St., N.W., Suite 218, Washington, DC 20006
Telephone: (202) 785-3756
Registered as lobbyist at U.S. Congress.

MILES, David Michael
Fried, Frank, Harris, Shriver & Jacobson
1001 Pennsylvania Ave., N.W., Suite 800, Washington, DC 20004-2505
Telephone: (202) 639-7000

MILES AND STOCKBRIDGE
1701 Pennsylvania Ave., N.W., Suite 500, Washington, DC 20006
Telephone: (202) 333-2350
Background: Washington office of a Baltimore law firm.
Members of firm representing listed organizations:
  Bowe, Richard W.
  Fake, Barent L.
  Clients:
  Black and Decker Corp., The *(Richard W. Bowe)*
  Inova Health Systems *(Richard W. Bowe, Barent L. Fake)*

MILES, W. Leanna
Managing Director, Associated Publishers, Inc.
1407 14th St., N.W., Washington, DC 20005-3704
Telephone: (202) 265-1441

MILHOLLAND, John
General Counsel, DEPARTMENT OF COMMERCE - Nat'l Weather Service
1325 East-West Hwy., Silver Spring, MD 20910
Telephone: (301) 427-7448

MILKMAN, Beverly Lyford
Exec. Director, Committee for Purchase from the Blind and Other Severely Handicapped
1755 Jeff Davis Hwy., Crystal Square 5, Rm. 1107, Arlington, VA 22202-3509
Telephone: (703) 557-1145

MILLAR, Fred
Wash Rep., Nuclear & Hazardous Waste, Friends of the Earth
218 D St., S.E., Washington, DC 20003
Telephone: (202) 544-2600
Registered as lobbyist at U.S. Congress.

MILLARD, Gaylen
Director, Science and Health Policy, American Industrial Health Council
1330 Connecticut Ave., N.W. Suite 300, Washington, DC 20036-1702
Telephone: (202) 659-0060

MILLENSON, Roy H.
1156 15th St., N.W., Suite 1100, Washington, DC 20005
Telephone: (202) 659-2900
Background: A government relations consultant. Retired U.S. Senate Staff member.

MILLER, Allen
Government Affairs Representative, Electronic Data Systems Corp.
1331 Pennsylvania Ave., N.W., Suite 1300 North, Washington, DC 20004
Telephone: (202) 637-6700

MILLER, Andrew P.
Dickstein, Shapiro and Morin
2101 L St., N.W., Washington, DC 20037
Telephone: (202) 785-9700
Background: Attorney General, Commonwealth of Virginia, 1970-77.
Clients:
  Arkansas, State of
  Delaware, State of
  Iowa, State of
  Louisiana, State of
  Medtronic, Inc.
  North Dakota, State of
  Rhode Island, State of
  Utah, State of
  West Virginia, State of

MILLER ASSOCIATES, Denny
400 N. Capitol St., N.W. Suite 325, Washington, DC 20001
Telephone: (202) 783-0280
Background: A public affairs and management consulting firm.
Members of firm representing listed organizations:
  Greene, (Col.) Fred W. ((Ret.)), V. President

  Background: Former Chief of Staff, U.S. Army Armor Center, Fort Knox, Kentucky.
  Lovain, Timothy, V. President and General Counsel
    Background: Former Legislative Assistant to Senator Slade Gorton and Legislative Director to Rep. Helen Meyner.
  Miller, Denny, President
    Background: Former Admin. Assistant to Senator Henry Jackson (D-WA), 1968-83.
  Miller, Sandra B., Exec. V. President
  Organizations represented:
  Alloy Surfaces, Inc.
  American Cyanamid Co.
  Boeing Co.
  Coeur d'Alene Mines
  Educational Clinics Inc.
  Keydata Systems, Inc.
  Makah Tribal Council
  Marine Engineers Beneficial Ass'n
  McCann Construction Co., Inc.
  Momentum '88
  Olin Corp.
  Olin Corp. (Aerospace, Brass, Ordnance and Winchester Divisions) *(Denny Miller)*
  Pacific Nuclear Systems
  Sabey Corp.
  Spokane Region Economic Development (Momentum 90)
  Sunshine Mining Co.
  Tacoma, Port of
  Tri-City Industrial Development Council
  University of Washington
  Washington Public Gaming Ass'n *(Denny Miller)*
  Washington, State of, Department of Transportation

MILLER, BALIS AND O'NEIL
1101 14th St., N.W. Suite 1400, Washington, DC 20005
Telephone: (202) 789-1450
Members of firm representing listed organizations:
  Balis, Stanley W.
    Background: Assistant Directror for Oil and Gas Pipeline and Producer Enforcement, Federal Energy Regulatory Commission, 1978-79.
  Darrell, Mark C.
  Kelly, Susan N.
  Miller, William T.
  Clients:
  American Public Gas Ass'n *(Stanley W. Balis, Mark C. Darrell, Susan N. Kelly, William T. Miller)*
  Citizen/Labor Energy Coalition Project
  New Jersey, Public Advocate of
  Northern States Power Co.

MILLER, Brent
Director, Government Relations, American Group Practice Ass'n
1422 Duke St., Alexandria, VA 22314
Telephone: (703) 838-0033
Registered as lobbyist at U.S. Congress.
Background: Former Administrative Assistant to Rep. Michael Andrews (D-TX).

MILLER, Carolyn C.
Exec. Secretary, Committee for Production Sharing
1629 K St., N.W., Suite 802, Washington, DC 20006
Telephone: (202) 223-6270

MILLER, Carolynn E.
Legislative Representative, Nat'l Federation of Independent Business
600 Maryland Ave., S.W., Suite 700, Washington, DC 20024
Telephone: (202) 554-9000
Registered as lobbyist at U.S. Congress.

MILLER, CASSIDY, LARROCA AND LEWIN
2555 M St., N.W. Suite 500, Washington, DC 20037
Telephone: (202) 293-6400
Members of firm representing listed organizations:
  Gorelick, Jamie S.
    Background: Assistant to Secretary and Counsellor to the Deputy Secretary, Department of Energy, 1979-80. Vice Chairman, Task Force on Evaluation of Audit, Investigative and Inspection Components of the Department of Defense, 1979-80.
  Lewin, Nathan

MILLER, CASSIDY, LARROCA AND LEWIN (Cont'd)

Background: Law Clerk to U.S. Supreme Court Justice John M. Harlan, 1961-62. Special Assistant to the Assistant Attorney General, Criminal Division, Department of Justice, 1962-63. Assistant to Solicitor General 1963-67. Deputy Administrator, Bureau of Security and Consular Affairs Department of State, 1967-68. Deputy Assistant Attorney General, Civil Rights Division, 1968-69.

Sallet, Jonathan

Clients:
Independent Insurance Agents of America *(Jonathan Sallet)*
Nat'l Ass'n of Casualty and Surety Agents *(Jonathan Sallet)*
Nat'l Ass'n of Life Underwriters *(Jamie S. Gorelick)*
Nat'l Ass'n of Professional Insurance Agents *(Jamie S. Gorelick)*
47th Street Photo *(Jamie S. Gorelick, Nathan Lewin)*

MILLER, Charles A.

Covington and Burling
1201 Pennsylvania Ave., N.W., Box 7566, Washington, DC 20044
Telephone: (202) 662-6000
Clients:
Oklahoma Department of Human Services

MILLER, Charles H.

Federal Gov't Affairs V. President, AT&T
Suite 1000, 1120 20th St., N.W., Washington, DC 20036
Telephone: (202) 457-3824

MILLER, Charles R.

Director, Media Relations, Nat'l Wildlife Federation
1412 16th St., N.W., Washington, DC 20036-2266
Telephone: (202) 797-6853

MILLER, Chaz

Recycling Director, Glass Packaging Institute
1801 K St., N.W., Suite 1105L, Washington, DC 20006
Telephone: (202) 887-4850
Registered as lobbyist at U.S. Congress.

MILLER & CHEVALIER, CHARTERED

Metropolitan Square, 655 15th St., N.W., Washington, DC 20005
Telephone: (202) 626-5800
Members of firm representing listed organizations:

Aldonas, Grant D., Member
Background: Director, South American and Caribbean Affairs, Office of the U.S. Trade Representative, 1984-85. Special Assistant to the Under Secretary of State for Economic Affairs, 1983-84.

Bickwit, Leonard (Jr.), Member
Background: Counsel, Senate Subcommittee on the Environment, 1969-74. Chief Legislative Assistant to Senator John Glenn of Ohio, 1975-79. General Counsel, U.S. Nuclear Regulatory Commission, 1979-83.

Craven, Donald B., Member
Background: Trial Attorney, Tax Division, U.S. Department of Justice, 1968-73. Associate Assistant Administrator and Acting Assistant Administrator, Federal Energy Administration, 1974-75.

Curtiss, Catherine

Huffman, Robert, Member

Mann, Phillip L., Member
Background: Deputy Tax Legislative Counsel, 1973-74, and Tax Legislative Counsel, 1974-75, Department of the Treasury.

Moran, Anne E., Member
Background: Tax Counsel, Senate Committee on Finance, 1983-86.

Neal, Philip S., Member

Nolan, John S., Member
Background: Deputy Assistant Secretary of the Treasury for Tax Policy, 1969-1972.

Oliphant, C. Frederick (III), Member

Porter, Catherine T., Member
Background: Tax Counsel, House Committee on Small Business, 1979-80. Assistant Counsel, Oversight Subcommittee, House Committee on Ways and Means, 1981-82. Tax and Trade Legislative Aide to Senator John Chafee (R-RI), 1983-88.

Yuspeh, Alan R., Member

Background: Legislative Assistant and Administrative Assistant to Senator J. Bennett Johnston (D-LA), 1974-78. General Counsel, Committee on the Armed Services, U.S. Senate, 1982-85.

Zakupowsky, Alexander (Jr.), Member
Background: Advisor on Tax Accounting Matters, Office of Tax Policy, Department of Treasury, 1976-78.

Clients:
Aerospace Industries Ass'n of America *(Alexander Zakupowsky, Jr.)*
Ameribanc Investors Group *(Leonard Bickwit, Jr.)*
American Continental Corp. *(Leonard Bickwit, Jr.)*
American Mining Congress
American Nuclear Energy Council *(Leonard Bickwit, Jr.)*
American Petroleum Institute *(Donald B. Craven)*
Boeing Co. *(Alan R. Yuspeh)*
Business-Industry Political Action Committee
Canada, Government of
Chevy Chase Savings Bank *(Leonard Bickwit, Jr.)*
Electronic Industries Ass'n *(Anne E. Moran)*
Export Source Rule Coalition *(Catherine T. Porter)*
Great Northern Insured Annuity Corporation *(Anne E. Moran)*
Hewlett-Packard Co. *(Catherine T. Porter)*
Long Island Ass'n *(Leonard Bickwit, Jr.)*
McDonnell Douglas Corp. *(Alan R. Yuspeh)*
Metropolitan Life Insurance Co. *(John S. Nolan)*
Nat'l Ass'n of Temporary Services *(C. Frederick Oliphant, III)*
Office of Fair Treatment of Internat'l Investment *(Catherine T. Porter)*
Organization for Fair Treatment of Internat'l Investment *(Catherine T. Porter)*
Pacific Medical Center *(Alan R. Yuspeh)*
Professional Services Council *(Alan R. Yuspeh)*
Rouse Company, The *(Phillip L. Mann, John S. Nolan)*
Saudi Basic Industries Corp. *(Catherine Curtiss)*
Section 482 Study Group *(John S. Nolan)*
Texas Instruments *(John S. Nolan)*
Toyota Motor Sales, U.S.A. *(John S. Nolan)*
USF&G *(Anne E. Moran)*
Varian Associates Inc. *(Alan R. Yuspeh)*
Yamaha Motor Corp. U.S.A. *(John S. Nolan)*

MILLER, Dale

4000 Reno Road, N.W., Washington, DC 20008
Telephone: (202) 362-5667
Organizations represented:
Corpus Christi, Nueces County, Port Authority of
Texasgulf Inc.

MILLER, David

Senior Consultant, Government Relations, Hill and Knowlton Public Affairs Worldwide
Washington Harbour, 901 31st St., N.W., Washington, DC 20007
Telephone: (202) 333-7400
Clients:
Chase Manhattan Bank
Marine Midland Banks, Inc.

MILLER, Deborah Imle

Staff VP, Congressional Affairs & Admin., Nat'l Ass'n of Home Builders of the U.S.
15th and M Streets, N.W., Washington, DC 20005
Telephone: (202) 822-0470
Registered as lobbyist at U.S. Congress.

MILLER, Denny

President, Miller Associates, Denny
400 N. Capitol St., N.W. Suite 325, Washington, DC 20001
Telephone: (202) 783-0280
Registered as lobbyist at U.S. Congress.
Background: Former Admin. Assistant to Senator Henry Jackson (D-WA), 1968-83.
Organizations represented:
Olin Corp. (Aerospace, Brass, Ordnance and Winchester Divisions)
Washington Public Gaming Ass'n

MILLER, Dr. Edward D.

Chief Exec. Officer, Future Business Leaders of America
P.O. Box 17417-Dulles, Washington, DC 20041
Telephone: (703) 860-3334

MILLER, Ellen S.

Director, Center for Responsive Politics
1320 19th St., N.W., Washington, DC 20036
Telephone: (202) 857-0044

MILLER, Evan

Johnson & Gibbs, P.C.
1001 Pennsylvania Ave., N.W. Suite 745, Washington, DC 20004
Telephone: (202) 682-4500
Registered as lobbyist at U.S. Congress.
Clients:
Redmond Industries

MILLER AND FIELDS

1990 M St., N.W., Suite 760, Washington, DC 20036-3404
Telephone: (202) 785-2720
Clients:
KAIL
KRLR
WTJC

MILLER, Francine

Legislative Assistant, Rainbow Lobby
1660 L St., N.W. Suite 204, Washington, DC 20036
Telephone: (202) 457-0700
Registered as lobbyist at U.S. Congress.

MILLER, Fred

Treasurer, American Internat'l Automobile Dealers Ass'n Political Action Committee
1128 16th St., N.W., Washington, DC 20036
Telephone: (202) 659-2561

MILLER, Frederick L., Jr.

Duncan, Weinberg, Miller & Pembroke, P.C.
1615 M St., N.W., Suite 800, Washington, DC 20036-3203
Telephone: (202) 467-6370
Registered as lobbyist at U.S. Congress.
Background: Trial Attorney Land and Natural Resources Division Department of Justice, 1970-74.
Clients:
Colorado River Commission of Nevada
Jamestown, New York, City of
Lake Andes-Wagner Water Systems, Inc.
Mid-West Electric Consumers Ass'n
MSR Public Power Agency
Newark, Delaware, City of
Seaford, Delaware, City of
Western Fuels Ass'n

MILLER, George T.

Hogan and Hartson
555 13th St., N.W., Suite 1200, Washington, DC 20004-1109
Telephone: (202) 637-5600
Registered as lobbyist at U.S. Congress.
Clients:
Whitman Distributing Co.

MILLER, Dr. Gerald H.

Exec. Director, Nat'l Ass'n of State Budget Officers
400 North Capitol St., N.W. Suite 295, Washington, DC 20001
Telephone: (202) 624-5382

MILLER, Grant

Director, Legislative Affairs, LTV Aircraft Products Group
1725 Jefferson Davis Hwy. Suite 900, Arlington, VA 22202
Telephone: (703) 521-6560
Registered as lobbyist at U.S. Congress.

MILLER, H. Todd

Hogan and Hartson
555 13th St., N.W., Suite 1200, Washington, DC 20004-1109
Telephone: (202) 637-5600
Registered as lobbyist at U.S. Congress.

MILLER, Harris N.

Managing Partner, Holt, Miller & Associates
2111 Wilson Blvd., Suite 531, Arlington, VA 22201-3008
Telephone: (703) 276-8009
Registered as lobbyist at U.S. Congress.
Background: Formerly served on the staff of the House Judiciary Committee and as Legislative Director to Senator John Durkin (D-NH). Former Director, Congressional Affairs, Office of Personnel Management.
Clients:

Ada Software Alliance (ASA)
Agricultural Producers, Inc.
AmBase Corp.
American Council on Internat'l Personnel
Irish Immigration Reform Movement
McDonald's Corp.
Mountain Plains Agricultural Service
Nat'l Agricultural Coalition
Snake River Farmers Ass'n
Texas Ranchers Labor Ass'n
U.S. English
Western Range Ass'n

MILLER AND HOLBROOKE
1225 19th St., N.W. Suite 400, Washington, DC 20036
Telephone: (202) 785-0600
Clients:
Laredo, Texas, City of
St. Louis, Missouri, City of

MILLER, Hydi
Senior Legislative Associate, U.S. English
818 Connecticut Ave., N.W. Suite 200, Washington, DC
20006
Telephone: (202) 833-0100
Registered as lobbyist at U.S. Congress.

MILLER, James C., III
Distinguished Fellow, Chairman, Citizens for a Sound
Economy
470 L'Enfant Plaza East, S.W. Suite 7112, Washington,
DC 20024
Telephone: (202) 488-8200
Background: Director, Office of Management and Budget,
1985-88.

MILLER, Jeanne
Associate, Suplizio Associates, Paul
5152 Woodmire Lane, Alexandria, VA 22311
Telephone: (703) 931-0103
Registered as lobbyist at U.S. Congress.
Organizations represented:
Internat'l Reciprocal Trade Ass'n
Targeted Jobs Tax Credit Coalition

MILLER, Jerome A., CAE
Bostrom Corp.
808 17th St., N.W., Suite 200, Washington, DC 20006
Telephone: (202) 223-9669
Clients:
Nat'l Ass'n of Boards of Examiners of Nursing
Home Administrators
Soc. for American Archaeology

MILLER, Jerome G.
President, Nat'l Center on Institutions and Alternatives
635 Slaters Lane Suite G-100, Alexandria, VA 22314
Telephone: (703) 684-0373

MILLER, Joseph S.
19 Third St., N.E., Washington, DC 20002
Telephone: (202) 546-6660
Organizations represented:
Ass'n of American Railroads
Marine Engineers Beneficial Ass'n
O and C Counties Ass'n
Portland, Oregon, Port of
Western Forest Industries Ass'n

MILLER, K. Michael
Assistant V. President, Federal Affairs, CIGNA Corp.
1825 Eye St., N.W., Suite 750, Washington, DC 20006
Telephone: (202) 296-7174

MILLER, Lane F.
Principal, Internat'l Inv./Venture Cap'l, Transnational Development Consortium
2745 29th St., N.W., Suite 216, Washington, DC 20008
Telephone: (202) 462-8314
Background: Former Executive Director, Office of Internat'l Business for the government of the District of Columbia. Member of the Economic Policy Council of the
United Nations Ass'n/USA. Senior Advisor; Internat'l
Economics/ Investment Policy/Pacific Rim, George Bush
for President campaign; 1987-88. Co-chairman, Foreign
Affairs Advisory Group, Fund for America's Future;
1985-87.

MILLER, Brig. Gen. Leonard D.
Dep Chief, Legis Liaison, DEPARTMENT OF ARMY
The Pentagon, Washington, DC 20310-0101
Telephone: (202) 697-6767

MILLER, Linda B.
President, Volunteer Trustees of Not-for-Profit Hospitals
1625 Eye St., N.W., Suite 810, Washington, DC 20006
Telephone: (202) 659-0338
Registered as lobbyist at U.S. Congress.

MILLER, Loye W.
Director, Public Information, Northrop Corp.
1000 Wilson Blvd., Suite 2300, Arlington, VA 22209
Telephone: (703) 525-6767

MILLER, Mark L.
Finance Director, Campaign America
511 Capitol Court N. E. Suite 100, Washington, DC 20002
Telephone: (202) 543-5016

MILLER, Mark W.
Mgr., Int'l Gov't Afrs - McDermott Int'l, McDermott Inc.
1850 K St., N.W. Suite 950, Washington, DC 20006
Telephone: (202) 296-0390
Background: Also holds the position of Manager, State
Government Affairs, McDermott, Inc. Also represents
Babcock and Wilcox Co.

MILLER, Marshall V.
Miller & Steuart
1825 I St., N.W. Suite 400, Washington, DC 20006
Telephone: (202) 429-2017
Registered as lobbyist at U.S. Congress.
Clients:
Coastal Corp., The/ANR Pipeline Co.
Squibb and Sons, Inc., E. R.

MILLER, Martha L.
Account Supervisor, Fleishman-Hillard, Inc
1301 Connecticut Ave., N.W., Washington, DC 20036
Telephone: (202) 659-0330
Registered as lobbyist at U.S. Congress.
Clients:
Citizens for Sensible Control of Acid Rain

MILLER, Martin
President, State and Federal Associates
1101 King St., Suite 600, Alexandria, VA 22314
Telephone: (703) 739-0200
Registered as lobbyist at U.S. Congress.

MILLER, Marye T.
1200 East Capitol St., N.E., Washington, DC 20002
Telephone: (202) 544-2613
Registered as lobbyist at U.S. Congress.
Registered as Foreign Agent: (#4246)
Organizations represented:
Cristal Services, Inc.

MILLER, Matthew
Administrator, Coal Miners Political Action Committee
900 15th St., N.W., Washington, DC 20005
Telephone: (202) 842-7280
Registered as lobbyist at U.S. Congress.

MILLER, Melanie
Sr. Acct. Exec., Biotechnolgy Group, Hill and Knowlton
Public Affairs Worldwide
Washington Harbour, 901 31st St., N.W., Washington, DC
20007
Telephone: (202) 333-7400

MILLER, Meredith
Employee Benefit Specialist, AFL-CIO (American Federation of Labor and Congress of Industrial Organizations)
815 16th St., N.W., Washington, DC 20006
Telephone: (202) 637-5075

MILLER, Michael J.
Exec. Director, Ass'n for the Advancement of Medical Instrumentation
3330 Washington Blvd. Suite 400, Arlington, VA 22201
Telephone: (703) 525-4890

MILLER, Michael V.
Wagner, Hines and Avary
1899 L St., N.W., Suite 500, Washington, DC 20036
Telephone: (202) 659-0930

MILLER, Oral O.
Director, American Council of the Blind
1010 Vermont Ave., N.W. Suite 1100, Washington, DC
20005
Telephone: (202) 393-3666

MILLER, Peggy
Legislative Representative, Consumer Federation of
America
1424 16th St., N.W. Suite 604, Washington, DC 20036
Telephone: (202) 387-6121
Registered as lobbyist at U.S. Congress.

MILLER, Randy E.
Hogan and Hartson
555 13th St., N.W., Suite 1200, Washington, DC 20004-
1109
Telephone: (202) 637-5600
Registered as lobbyist at U.S. Congress.

MILLER, Richard
Legislative Representative, American Health Care Ass'n
1201 L St., N.W., Washington, DC 20005
Telephone: (202) 842-4444

MILLER, Dr. Richard
Executive Director, Nat'l Ass'n of Federal Education Program Administrators
1801 N. Moore St., Arlington, VA 22209
Telephone: (703) 528-0700

MILLER, Richard D.
Exec. Director, American Ass'n of School Administrators
1801 North Moore St., Arlington, VA 22209
Telephone: (703) 528-0700

MILLER, Robert H.
V. President, Tenneco Inc.
490 L'Enfant Plaza East, S.W. Suite 2202, S.W., Washing-
ton, DC 20024
Telephone: (202) 554-2850
Registered as lobbyist at U.S. Congress.

MILLER, Robin
Legis Officer, Cong & Intergovt'l Affrs, DEPARTMENT OF
LABOR
200 Constitution Ave., N.W., Washington, DC 20210
Telephone: (202) 523-6141

MILLER, Ronald L., Ph.D.
Exec. Director, Blinded Veterans Ass'n
477 H St., N.W., Washington, DC 20001
Telephone: (202) 371-8880

MILLER, Sandra B.
Exec. V. President, Miller Associates, Denny
400 N. Capitol St., N.W. Suite 325, Washington, DC
20001
Telephone: (202) 783-0280
Registered as lobbyist at U.S. Congress.

MILLER, Sarah
Senior Government Relations Counsel, American Bankers
Ass'n
1120 Connecticut Ave., N.W., Washington, DC 20036
Telephone: (202) 663-5000
Registered as lobbyist at U.S. Congress.

MILLER & STEUART
1825 I St., N.W. Suite 400, Washington, DC 20006
Telephone: (202) 429-2017
Members of firm representing listed organizations:
Greenberg, Judith M.
Miller, Marshall V.
Steuart, George C.
Clients:
Coastal Corp., The/ANR Pipeline Co. *(Judith M.
Greenberg, Marshall V. Miller, George C. Steuart)*
Squibb and Sons, Inc., E. R. *(Judith M. Greenberg,
Marshall V. Miller, George C. Steuart)*

MILLER, Susan
Director, Communications, Nat'l Agricultural Chemicals
Ass'n
Madison Bldg., 1155 15th St., Suite 900, Washington, DC
20005
Telephone: (202) 296-1585

WASHINGTON REPRESENTATIVES

MILLER, Thomas H.
Dir., Gov't'l & Community Relations, Blinded Veterans Ass'n
477 H St., N.W., Washington, DC 20001
Telephone: (202) 371-8880

MILLER, Tom
Policy Analyst, Cong. Ratings/Antitrust, Competitive Enterprise Institute
233 Pennsylvania Ave., S.E., Suite 200, Washington, DC 20003
Telephone: (202) 547-1010

MILLER, William Green
President, American Committee on U.S.-Soviet Relations
109 11th St., S.E., Washington, DC 20003
Telephone: (202) 546-1700

MILLER, William T.
Miller, Balis and O'Neil
1101 14th St., N.W. Suite 1400, Washington, DC 20005
Telephone: (202) 789-1450
Registered as lobbyist at U.S. Congress.
Clients:
  American Public Gas Ass'n

MILLERT, Gregory T.
Federal Gov't Affrs. V. Pres. & Attorney, AT&T
Suite 1000, 1120 20th St., N.W., Washington, DC 20036
Telephone: (202) 457-2716

MILLIAN, Kenneth Y.
Corp. V. Pres. & Dir., Envirmnt'l Afrs., Grace and Co., W. R.
919 18th St., N.W., Suite 400, Washington, DC 20006
Telephone: (202) 452-6700
Registered as lobbyist at U.S. Congress.

MILLIKEN, Christine T.
Exec. Director and General Counsel, Nat'l Ass'n of Attorneys General
444 North Capitol St., N.W., Suite 403, Washington, DC 20001
Telephone: (202) 628-0435

MILLIKEN, John G.
Winston and Strawn
2550 M St., N.W., Suite 500, Washington, DC 20037
Telephone: (202) 828-8400
Registered as lobbyist at U.S. Congress.
Background: Exec. Assistant, Congressman Joseph L. Fisher of Virginia, 1975-78.
Clients:
  American Appraisal Associates, Inc.
  Gillett Group Management, Inc.

MILLMAN, Amy J.
Washington Representative, Philip Morris Management Corp.
1341 G St., N.W., Suite 900, Washington, DC 20005
Telephone: (202) 637-1500
Registered as lobbyist at U.S. Congress.

MILLS, Carol Ward
Admin. Asst. to the Pres. & Office Mgr., Nat'l Federation of Independent Business
600 Maryland Ave., S.W., Suite 700, Washington, DC 20024
Telephone: (202) 554-9000

MILLS, Loring E.
V. President, Nuclear Activities, Edison Electric Institute
1111 19th St., N.W., Washington, DC 20036
Telephone: (202) 778-6450

MILLS, Thomas L.
Dyer, Ellis, Joseph & Mills
600 New Hampshire Ave., N.W., Suite 1000, Washington, DC 20037
Telephone: (202) 944-3040
Registered as lobbyist at U.S. Congress.
Registered as Foreign Agent: (#4121).
Clients:
  Ace Frosty Shipping Co., Ltd.
  Apex Marine Co.
  Atlantic Richfield Company (ARCO) Marine Co.
  Bay Area Renal Stone Center
  Bender Shipbuilding & Repair Co., Inc.
  Bristol Bay Native Corp.

Competitive Health Care Coalition
Crowley Maritime Corp.
Medical Care Internat'l
Renal Physican Ass'n

MILLS, Wilbur D.
Shea and Gould
1775 Pennsylvania Ave., N.W., Suite 700, Washington, DC 20006
Telephone: (202) 833-9850
Background: Former Member, House of Representatives (D-AR).

MILSTEIN, Bonnie
Senior Staff Attorney, Mental Health Law Project
2021 L St., N.W., Washington, DC 20036
Telephone: (202) 467-5730

MILTENBERGER, Joseph H.
Director, Government Relations, U.S. Strategies Corp.
1321 Duke St., Suite 200, Alexandria, VA 22314-3563
Telephone: (703) 739-7999
Registered as lobbyist at U.S. Congress.
Clients:
  American Medical EEG Ass'n
  Economy Fastners, Inc.
  HealthSouth Rehabilitation Corp.
  Nat'l Alliance of Outpatient Cancer Therapy Centers
  Oncology Services, Inc.

MIN, Kyoung Sun
Ass't Manager, Korea Foreign Trade Ass'n
1800 K St., N.W.,, Washington, DC 20006
Telephone: (202) 408-0100
Registered as Foreign Agent: (#3636)

MINAYA, Anna
Legislative Assistant, Helicopter Ass'n Internat'l
1619 Duke St., Alexandria, VA 22314-3406
Telephone: (703) 683-4646

MINCBERG, Elliot M.
Director, Legal Department, People for the American Way
2000 M St., N.W., Suite 400, Washington, DC 20036
Telephone: (202) 467-4999
Registered as lobbyist at U.S. Congress.

MINCK, Richard V.
Exec. V. President, American Council of Life Insurance
1001 Pennsylvania Ave., N.W., Washington, DC 20004-2599
Telephone: (202) 624-2100
Registered as lobbyist at U.S. Congress.

MINEAR, Larry
Representative for Development Policy, Church World Service/Lutheran World Relief
110 Maryland Ave., N.E. Building Box #45, Washington, DC 20002-5694
Telephone: (202) 543-6336

MINER, Thomas H.
Chairman, Mid-America Committee
1201 Connecticut Ave., N.W. Suite 300, Washington, DC 20036
Telephone: (202) 835-8813

MINETTI, G. Joseph
Dickstein, Shapiro and Morin
2101 L St., N.W., Washington, DC 20037
Telephone: (202) 785-9700
Registered as Foreign Agent: (#3028).
Background: Special Assistant to the Attorney General of the United States, 1940-43. Member, Federal Maritime Board, 1954-56. Member Civil Aeronautics Board, 1956-78. Vice Chairman, Civil Aeronautics Board, 1978.
Clients:
  Kuwait Airways
  Middle East Airlines
  Toshiba Corp.

MINIKES, Stephan M.
Reid & Priest
1111 19th St., N.W., Washington, DC 20036
Telephone: (202) 828-0100
Registered as lobbyist at U.S. Congress.
Background: Senior V. President, Export-Import Bank, 1974-77. Counsel to the Special Consultant to the President of the United States for Energy, 1973. Counsel and

Special Assistant to the Chief of Naval Operations, 1972-74.
Clients:
  Derecktor of Rhode Island, Robert E.
  Philadelphia Industrial Development Corp.
  Philadelphia, Pennsylvania, City of
  SPD Technologies

MINK, Phillip S.
Gen. Couns., Legal & Reg. Reform Project, Citizens for a Sound Economy
470 L'Enfant Plaza East, S.W. Suite 7112, Washington, DC 20024
Telephone: (202) 488-8200

MINSHEW, George R.
Northern Sector V. President, Tobacco Institute
1875 Eye St., N.W., Suite 800, Washington, DC 20006
Telephone: (202) 457-4889

MINTER, J. Robert
Coordinator, Governmental Affairs, Southern Company Services, Inc.
1130 Connecticut Ave., N.W., Suite 830, Washington, DC 20036
Telephone: (202) 775-0944
Registered as lobbyist at U.S. Congress.

MINTON, David
Contact, NAATS Political Action Fund
4740 Corridor Place, Suite C, Beltsville, MD 20705-1165
Telephone: (301) 595-2012

MINTON, David
1211 Connecticut Ave., N.W., Washington, DC 20036
Telephone: (202) 861-0420
Background: An attorney.
Organizations represented:
  Magazine Publishers of America

MINTZ, Alan L.
Van Ness, Feldman & Curtis
1050 Thomas Jefferson St., 7th Floor, Washington, DC 20007
Telephone: (202) 298-1800
Registered as lobbyist at U.S. Congress.
Background: Senior Attorney, Office of Exceptions and Appeals, Federal Energy Administration, 1974-77.
Clients:
  Arctic Slope Regional Corp.
  Collier County, Florida
  Energy Fuels Nuclear, Inc.

MINTZ, LEVIN, COHN, FERRIS, GLOVSKY AND POPEO, P.C.
1825 Eye St., N.W. 12th Floor, Washington, DC 20006
Telephone: (202) 293-0500
Background: Washington office of a Boston law firm.
Members of firm representing listed organizations:
  Casey, Thomas J.
    Background: Special Assistant to Chief, Cable TV Bureau, Federal Communications Commission, 1978. Special Assistant to Chairman, 1978-79 and Deputy Chief Common Carrier Bureau, Federal Communications Commission, 1979-81.
  Ferris, Charles D.
    Background: General Counsel to U.S. Senate Majority, 1963-76, to the Speaker of the House of Representatives, 1976-77. Chairman, Federal Communications Commission, 1977-81.
  Fox, J. Edward
    Background: A government relations consultant to the firm. Former Assistant Secretary of State for Legislative Affairs.
  Meaney, Francis X.
  Schuyler, James H.
  Sokler, Bruce D.
  Wergeles, Amy S.
Clients:
  Cablevision System Development Co.
  Chain Pharmacy Ass'n of New York State (*Bruce D. Sokler, Amy S. Wergeles*)
  Coalition for High Definition Television 1125/60 Production (*Charles D. Ferris*)
  Communication Industries Ass'n of Japan (*Charles D. Ferris*)
  Goldman, Sachs and Co. (*Francis X. Meaney*)
  GTE Corp.
  Home Recording Rights Coalition (*Charles D. Ferris*)

The listings in this directory are available as *Mailing Labels*. See last page.

Houghton Mifflin Co.
Mortgage Insurance Companies of America *(James H. Schuyler)*
Securities Industry Ass'n *(Francis X. Meaney)*
Siemens Capital Corp.
Turner Broadcasting System, Inc.

MIRABELLI, Mario V.
Shea and Gould
1775 Pennsylvania Ave., N.W., Suite 700, Washington, DC 20006
Telephone: (202) 833-9850
Background: Trial Attorney, Bureau of Deceptive Practices, Federal Trade Commission, 1967-69; Division of Corporation Finance, Branch of Administrative Proceedings, Securities and Exchange Commission, 1969-73.

MIRON, George
Wyman, Bautzer, Christensen, Kuchel and Silbert
1919 Pennsylvania Ave., N.W., Suite 800, Washington, DC 20006
Telephone: (202) 887-5236
Registered as lobbyist at U.S. Congress.
Background: Assistant Chief, General Litigation Section and Trial Attorney, Anti-trust Division, Dep't of Justice, 1959-1965. Special Assistant to the Solicitor and Associate Solicitor for Reclamation and Power, Dep't of the Interior, 1965-1968.
Clients:
American Boiler Manufacturers Ass'n

MISHEL, Lawrence R.
Research Director, Economic Policy Institute
1424 16th St., N.W., Suite 501, Washington, DC 20036
Telephone: (202) 667-0400

MISHKIN, David G.
Staff V. Pres., Regul. & Internat'l Aff., Texas Air Corp.
901 15th St., N.W. Suite 500, Washington, DC 20005
Telephone: (202) 289-6060

MISKOVSKY, Milan C.
Kirkland and Ellis
655 15th St., N.W. Suite 1200, Washington, DC 20005
Telephone: (202) 879-5000
Background: Former Assistant General Counsel, Department of Treasury. Former General Counsel, Federal Home Loan Bank Board.

MITCHELL, Anthony
Legis Officer, Legis & Cong Rels, DEPARTMENT OF HOUSING AND URBAN DEVELOPMENT
451 Seventh St., S.W., Washington, DC 20410
Telephone: (202) 755-5005

MITCHELL, Billy P.
Mgr., Office of Chamber of Commerce Rtns, Chamber of Commerce of the U.S.A.
1615 H St., N.W., Washington, DC 20062
Telephone: (202) 463-5580

MITCHELL, Cary A.
Chairperson, Science Priorities Cmte., American Soc. for Horticultural Science
113 South West St., Alexandria, VA 22314-2824
Telephone: (703) 836-4606

MITCHELL, Charles P.
Staff Attorney, Center for Science in the Public Interest
1501 16th St., N.W., Washington, DC 20036
Telephone: (202) 332-9110
Registered as lobbyist at U.S. Congress.

MITCHELL, Daniel J.
Senior Fellow, Political Economy, Heritage Foundation
214 Massachusetts Ave., N.E., Washington, DC 20002
Telephone: (202) 546-4400
Background: Former advisor to Senator Bob Packwood (R-OR).

MITCHELL, Douglas B.
Bassman, Mitchell & Alfano, Chartered
1750 K St., N.W., Suite 380, Washington, DC 20006
Telephone: (202) 466-6502

MITCHELL, FRIEDLANDER & GITTLEMAN
1201 Connecticut Ave., N.W. Suite 720, Washington, DC 20036
Telephone: (202) 835-0720

Registered as Foreign Agent: (#4295)
Members of firm representing listed organizations:
Friedlander, James S.
Mitchell, Patrick H.
Background: Special Assistant to Minority Counsel, Interior and Insular Affairs Committee, U.S. Senate, 1969-70.
Clients:
Liberia, Nat'l Bank of *(James S. Friedlander, Patrick H. Mitchell)*

MITCHELL, Gerald C.
DGA Internat'l
1133 Connecticut Ave., N.W. Suite 700, Washington, DC 20036
Telephone: (202) 223-4001
Registered as lobbyist at U.S. Congress.

MITCHELL, Gina Shea
Senior Technical Associate, Financial Executives Institute
1100 17th St., N.W., Suite 1203, Washington, DC 20036
Telephone: (202) 659-3700
Registered as lobbyist at U.S. Congress.

MITCHELL, John
Manager, Federal Marketing Relations, American Gas Ass'n
1515 Wilson Blvd., Arlington, VA 22209
Telephone: (703) 841-8651

MITCHELL, Katherine
Senior Account Executive, Reese Communications Companies
2111 Wilson Ave., Suite 900, Arlington, VA 22201
Telephone: (703) 528-4400

MITCHELL, Lawrence W.
Director, Federal & State Relations, American Agriculture Movement, Inc.
100 Maryland Ave., N.E. Suite 500A, Washington, DC 20002
Telephone: (202) 544-5750
Registered as lobbyist at U.S. Congress.

MITCHELL, Michael
State and Federal Associates
1101 King St., Suite 600, Alexandria, VA 22314
Telephone: (703) 739-0200

MITCHELL, Michael C.
Legislative Affairs, Lockheed Corp.
1825 Eye St., N.W., Suite 1100, Washington, DC 20006
Telephone: (202) 955-3300
Registered as lobbyist at U.S. Congress.
Background: Former Deputy Minority Staff Director, Senate Governmental Affairs Committee.

MITCHELL, Parren
Founder and Chairman, Minority Business Enterprise Legal Defense and Education Fund
300 Eye St., N.E., Suite 200, Washington, DC 20002
Telephone: (202) 543-0040

MITCHELL, Patrick H.
Mitchell, Friedlander & Gittleman
1201 Connecticut Ave., N.W. Suite 720, Washington, DC 20036
Telephone: (202) 835-0720
Registered as Foreign Agent: (#4295).
Background: Special Assistant to Minority Counsel, Interior and Insular Affairs Committee, U.S. Senate, 1969-70.
Clients:
Liberia, Nat'l Bank of

MITCHELL, Samuel
Director, Research and Federal Relations, Federation of American Health Systems
1111 19th St., N.W. Suite 402, Washington, DC 20036
Telephone: (202) 833-3090

MITCHELL, Willard
V. President, Teledyne Industries Inc.
1501 Wilson Blvd., Suite 900, Arlington, VA 22209
Telephone: (703) 522-2550

MITCHLER, Al
Finance Director, Nat'l Republican Senatorial Committee
425 Second St., N.E., Washington, DC 20002
Telephone: (202) 675-6000

MITTELSTAT, Pamela
Ass't Dir., Congress'l & Agency Relat'ns, American Nurses' Ass'n
1101 14th St., N.W., Suite 200, Washington, DC 20005
Telephone: (202) 789-1800

MITTERMEIER, Russell A.
President, Conservation Internat'l Foundation
1015 18th St., N.W. Suite 1000, Washington, DC 20036
Telephone: (202) 429-5660

MIYASAKA, Tadahisa
Chief Representative, Electric Power Development Co., Ltd.
1825 K St., N.W., Suite 1205, Washington, DC 20006
Telephone: (202) 429-0670

MIYOSHI, Akihiko
General Director, Washington Office, Japan Automobile Manufacturers Ass'n
1050 17th St., N.W. Suite 410, Washington, DC 20036
Telephone: (202) 296-8537

MOAG, John, Jr.
Patton, Boggs and Blow
2550 M St., N.W., Suite 800, Washington, DC 20037
Telephone: (202) 457-6000
Clients:
University of Arizona

MOATES, G. Paul
Sidley and Austin
1722 Eye St., N.W. Sixth Floor, Washington, DC 20006
Telephone: (202) 429-4000

MOBLEY, Daniel E.
Exec. V. President, Washington Convention and Visitors Ass'n
1212 New York Ave., N.W., Sixth Floor, Washington, DC 20005
Telephone: (202) 789-7000

MOBLEY, Stacey J.
V. President, Federal Affairs, du Pont de Nemours and Co., E. I.
1701 Pennsylvania Ave., N.W., Suite 900, Washington, DC 20006
Telephone: (202) 728-3600
Registered as lobbyist at U.S. Congress.

MOCK, Richard C.
V. President, Public Information, Volunteer-The Nat'l Center
1111 North 19th St. Suite 500, Arlington, VA 22209
Telephone: (703) 276-0542

MODE, Paul J., Jr.
Wilmer, Cutler and Pickering
2445 M St., N.W., Washington, DC 20037-1420
Telephone: (202) 663-6000
Clients:
UNOCAL Corp.

MODI, Dave
Director, Federal Government Affairs, Georgia-Pacific Corp.
1875 Eye St., N.W. Suite 775, Washington, DC 20006
Telephone: (202) 659-3600

MODZELEWSKI, Kenneth S.
V. President, Promotional Activities, Nat'l Wildlife Federation
1400 16th St., N.W., Washington, DC 20036-2266
Telephone: (202) 797-6800

MOE, Richard
Davis Polk & Wardwell
1300 Eye St., N.W. 11th Fl. East, Washington, DC 20005
Telephone: (202) 962-7000
Registered as lobbyist at U.S. Congress.
Background: Administrative Assistant to Senator Walter F. Mondale (D-MN), 1972-77. Chief of Staff to the Vice President of the United States, 1977-81.
Clients:
American Institute of Certified Public Accountants
Manville Corp.
Morgan Guaranty Trust Co.

WASHINGTON REPRESENTATIVES

MOEHLMANN, Jennie L.
Special Assistant for Policy Development, American Institute of Biological Sciences
730 11th St., N.W., Washington, DC 20001-4521
Telephone: (202) 628-1500

MOEHRING, John
Director of Tax Policy, American Movers Conference
2200 Mill Road, Alexandria, VA 22314
Telephone: (703) 838-1930
Registered as lobbyist at U.S. Congress.

MOEHRING, Mary Runkel
Director of State Laws, American Trucking Ass'ns
2200 Mill Road, Alexandria, VA 22314
Telephone: (703) 838-1797

MOELLER, James
Account Executive, Powell, Adams & Rinehart
1901 L St., N.W., 3rd Floor, Washington, DC 20036
Telephone: (202) 466-7590
Registered as lobbyist at U.S. Congress.

MOELTNER, Joan
Associate for Membership Liaison, Nat'l Federation of Independent Business
600 Maryland Ave., S.W., Suite 700, Washington, DC 20024
Telephone: (202) 554-9000

MOERMAN, Samuel H.
Of Counsel, LaRoe, Winn, Moerman & Donovan
1120 G St., N.W., Suite 800, Washington, DC 20005
Telephone: (202) 628-2788

MOFFAT, J. Curtis
Gardner, Carton and Douglas
1001 Pennsylvania Ave., N.W., Suite 750, Washington, DC 20004
Telephone: (202) 347-9200
Background: Legal Assistant to the Chairman, Federal Energy Regulatory Commission, 1977-79.
Clients:
Alamo Rent-a-Car
Andrew Corporation
Ansell Inc.
Minnesota Mining and Manufacturing Co. (3M Co.)
Pharmaceutical Aerosol CFC Coalition

MOFFAT, Pamela
Washington Representative, Nat'l Council of Women of the U.S.
4341 Forest Lane, N.W., Washington, DC 20007
Telephone: (202) 363-2192
Background: Also a member of Executive Committee.

MOFFET, Barbara S.
Manager, Print Media Relations, Nat'l Geographic Soc.
1145 17th St., N.W., Washington, DC 20036
Telephone: (202) 857-7000

MOGGE, Harriet M.
Director of Meetings and Conventions, Music Educators Nat'l Conference
1902 Association Drive, Reston, VA 22091
Telephone: (703) 860-4000

MOHLER, Martha
Policy & Research Representative, Nat'l Committee to Preserve Social Security and Medicare
2000 K St., N.W. Suite 800, Washington, DC 20006
Telephone: (202) 822-9459
Registered as lobbyist at U.S. Congress.

MOHUNLALL, Roop
Legislative Director, American Legislative Exchange Council
214 Massachusetts Ave., N.W., Washington, DC 20002
Telephone: (202) 547-4646

MOIR, Brian R.
Fisher, Wayland, Cooper and Leader
1255 23rd St., N.W., Suite 800, Washington, DC 20037-1125
Telephone: (202) 659-3494
Registered as lobbyist at U.S. Congress.
Clients:
Internat'l Communications Ass'n

MOLCHON, Diane J.
Exec. Assistant, Chemical Producers and Distributors Ass'n
1220 19th St., N.W., Suite 202, Washington, DC 20036
Telephone: (202) 785-2732

MOLINARO, Peter
Washington Representative, Union Carbide Corp.
1100 15th St., N.W., Suite 1200, Washington, DC 20005
Telephone: (202) 872-8555
Registered as lobbyist at U.S. Congress.

MOLITER, Robert M.
Manager, Gov't Prog. Op'tns, Medical Sy., General Electric Co.
1331 Pennsylvania Ave., N.W., Washington, DC 20004
Telephone: (202) 637-4137
Registered as lobbyist at U.S. Congress.

MOLITOR, Graham T. T.
V. President and Secretary, World Future Soc.
4916 St. Elmo Ave., Bethesda, MD 20814
Telephone: (301) 656-8274

MOLLER, John V.
V. President, Manchester Associates, Ltd.
1707 L St., N.W. Suite 725, Washington, DC 20036
Telephone: (202) 872-9333
Registered as lobbyist at U.S. Congress.
Registered as Foreign Agent: (#3046).
Clients:
Ampco-Pittsburgh Co.
Nissan Motor Co., Ltd.
Nissan Motor Manufacturing Corp. U.S.A.

MOLLER, W. C.
Manager, Legislative Affairs, Lockheed Corp.
1825 Eye St., N.W., Suite 1100, Washington, DC 20006
Telephone: (202) 955-3315
Registered as lobbyist at U.S. Congress.

MOLLISON, Char
V. President, Membership, Independent Sector
1828 L St., N.W., Washington, DC 20036
Telephone: (202) 223-8100

MOLOFSKY, Robert A.
Legislative Director, Amalgamated Transit Union
5025 Wisconsin Ave., N.W., Washington, DC 20016
Telephone: (202) 537-1645
Background: Served in U.S. Department of Labor, 1972-77; and for Nat'l Labor Relations Board, 1977-81.

MOLONEY, John M.
Manager, Internat'l Government Relations, Trans World Airlines
808 17th St., N.W., Suite 520, Washington, DC 20006
Telephone: (202) 457-4764

MOLPUS, C. Manly
President and Chief Executive Officer, Grocery Manufacturers of America
1010 Wisconsin Ave., N.W., Suite 800, Washington, DC 20007
Telephone: (202) 337-9400
Registered as lobbyist at U.S. Congress.

MOMBERGER, William G., CAE
Exec. Director, Tissue Culture Ass'n
19110 Montgomery Village Ave., Suite 300, Gaithersburg, MD 20879
Telephone: (301) 869-2900

MONACO, Anthony J.
President, Hospital Council of the Nat'l Capital Area
1250 Eye St., N.W., Suite 700, Washington, DC 20005
Telephone: (202) 789-1500

MONAGHAN, James P.
Vice President, Government Affairs, Alcan Aluminum Corp.
918 16th St., N.W. Suite 304, Washington, DC 20006
Telephone: (202) 785-3018

MONAHAN, Frank
Director of Government Liaison, United States Catholic Conference
3211 4th St., N.E., Washington, DC 20017
Telephone: (202) 541-3140
Background: Also represents the Nat'l Conference of Catholic Bishops.

MONBORNE, Mark A.
Winthrop, Stimson, Putnam & Roberts
1133 Connecticut Ave., N.W. Suite 1000, Washington, DC 20036
Telephone: (202) 775-9800
Registered as Foreign Agent: (#3873).

MONCRIEF, Dr. William H.
President, American Medical Peer Review Ass'n
810 First St., N.E., Suite 410, Washington, DC 20002
Telephone: (202) 371-5610

MONDERER, Howard
Consultant, Law, Nat'l Broadcasting Co.
1331 Pennsylvania Ave., N.W. Suite 700S, Washington, DC 20004
Telephone: (202) 637-4536

MONEK, Christopher S.
Director, Building Division, Associated General Contractors of America
1957 E St., N.W., Washington, DC 20006
Telephone: (202) 393-2040
Registered as lobbyist at U.S. Congress.

MONGOVEN, BISCOE & DUCHIN, INC.
655 15th St., N.W., Suite 300, Washington, DC 20005
Telephone: (202) 639-4080
Background: A public affairs/public policy development firm.
Members of firm representing listed organizations:
Biscoe, Alvin B. (Ph.D.), Exec. V. President
Duchin, Ronald A., Senior V. President
Background: Former Director of Media Relations, U.S. Department of Defense, 1979-84.
Mongoven, John O., President
Background: Former Assistant Secretary, U.S. Treasury Department.

MONGOVEN, John O.
President, Mongoven, Biscoe & Duchin, Inc.
655 15th St., N.W., Suite 300, Washington, DC 20005
Telephone: (202) 639-4080
Background: Former Assistant Secretary, U.S. Treasury Department.

MONK, Carl C.
Deputy Director, Ass'n of American Law Schools
1201 Connecticut Ave., N.W. Suite 800, Washington, DC 20036
Telephone: (202) 296-8851
Registered as lobbyist at U.S. Congress.

MONROE ASSOCIATES, Wilbur F.
2101 Connecticut Ave., N.W., Washington, DC 20008
Telephone: (202) 332-8395
Members of firm representing listed organizations:
Monroe, Wilbur F., President
Organizations represented:
Industrial Bank of Japan, Ltd. *(Wilbur F. Monroe)*
Japan, Government of *(Wilbur F. Monroe)*
Nomura Research Institute (America), Inc. *(Wilbur F. Monroe)*

MONROE, J. P.
Director-USN/USMC Aircraft Programs, McDonnell Douglas Corp.
1735 Jefferson Davis Hwy., Arlington, VA 22202
Telephone: (703) 553-3845

MONROE, Wilbur F.
President, Monroe Associates, Wilbur F.
2101 Connecticut Ave., N.W., Washington, DC 20008
Telephone: (202) 332-8395
Registered as Foreign Agent: (#2888).
Organizations represented:
Industrial Bank of Japan, Ltd.
Japan, Government of
Nomura Research Institute (America), Inc.

MONRONEY, Michael
Senior Advisor, Citizens for a Sound Economy
470 L'Enfant Plaza East, S.W. Suite 7112, Washington, DC 20024
Telephone: (202) 488-8200
Registered as lobbyist at U.S. Congress.

The listings in this directory are available as *Mailing Labels*. See last page.

MONTAGNA, Donald
Senior Leader, Washington Ethical Soc.
7750 16th St., N.W., Washington, DC 20012
Telephone: (202) 882-6650

MONTANINO, Debra
Director, Institutional Relations, Resources for the Future
1616 P St., N.W., Washington, DC 20036
Telephone: (202) 328-5000

MONTANO, William B.
Ashby and Associates
1140 Connecticut Ave., N.W., Suite 503, Washington, DC 20036
Telephone: (202) 296-3840
Clients:
    American Security Resources, Inc.

MONTENEGRO, Mario A., FASI
President, American Soc. of Interpreters
P.O. Box 9603, Washington, DC 20016
Telephone: (703) 998-8636

MONTGOMERY, Forest D.
Counsel, Nat'l Ass'n of Evangelicals
1023 15th St., N.W., Suite 500, Washington, DC 20005
Telephone: (202) 789-1011

MONTGOMERY, George Cranwell
Partner, Baker, Worthington, Crossley, Stansberry & Woolf
1001 Pennsylvania Ave., N.W, Suite 1201, Washington, DC 20004
Telephone: (202) 347-4360
Background: Counsel to the Majority Leader, U.S. Senate, 1981-85. U.S. Ambassador to Oman, 1985-89.

MONTGOMERY, John H.
Barrett, Montgomery & Murphy
1055 Thomas Jefferson St., N.W., Suite 501, Washington, DC 20007
Telephone: (202) 293-3306
Clients:
    Nat'l Rural Water Ass'n
    Oklahoma City, Oklahoma, City of
    San Diego, California, City of

MONTGOMERY, John Nixon
Deputy Director, South Africa Foundation
1225 19th St., N.W. Suite 700, Washington, DC 20036
Telephone: (202) 523-5486

MONTGOMERY, MCCRACKEN, WALKER & RHOADS
1156 15th St., N.W. Suite 550, Washington, DC 20005
Telephone: (202) 828-6901
Members of firm representing listed organizations:
    Long, Linda, Associate
    Norcross, David F.
Clients:
    Ass'n of Schools and Agencies for the Handicapped *(David F. Norcross)*
    Carpenter Labs *(Linda Long, David F. Norcross)*
    Center for Democracy *(David F. Norcross)*
    Delaware River and Bay Pilots Ass'n *(David F. Norcross)*
    Nat'l Ass'n of Private Schools for Exceptional Children *(Linda Long, David F. Norcross)*
    Nat'l Check Cashers Coalition *(Linda Long)*
    Nat'l Republican Institute for Internat'l Affairs *(David F. Norcross)*
    Ports of Philadelphia Maritime Exchange *(David F. Norcross)*
    RailPort *(David F. Norcross)*

MONTGOMERY, Nellie
Daly Associates, Inc.
702 World Center Bldg., 918 16th St., N.W., Washington, DC 20006-2993
Telephone: (202) 659-2925

MONTGOMERY, Robert E., Jr.
Paul, Weiss, Rifkind, Wharton and Garrison
1615 L St., N.W., Suite 1300, Washington, DC 20036
Telephone: (202) 223-7300
Registered as lobbyist at U.S. Congress.
Registered as Foreign Agent: (#3647).
Background: Assistant to General Counsel, Department of the Army, 1969-1971; General Counsel, Office of Consumer Affairs, Exec. Office of the President, 1971-1972;

Ass't General Counsel, Federal Trade Commission, 1973; General Counsel, Federal Energy Administration, 1974-1975.
Clients:
    McDonnell Douglas Corp.
    NEC America
    NEC Corp.

MONTICELLO ASSOCIATES
818 Connecticut Ave., N.W., 12th Floor, Washington, DC 20006
Telephone: (202) 466-5490
Background: An international trade consulting firm.
Members of firm representing listed organizations:
    Lamar, Harry, President
        Background: Former Trade Advisor, House Ways and Means Committee, 1967-80.
Clients:
    Joint Industry Group *(Harry Lamar)*

MONTOYA, Alfredo C.
Exec. Director, Labor Council for Latin American Advancement
815 16th St., N.W. Suite 707, Washington, DC 20006
Telephone: (202) 347-4223
Registered as lobbyist at U.S. Congress.

MONTWIELER, William J.
Exec. Director, Industrial Truck Ass'n
1750 K St., N.W. Suite 210, Washington, DC 20006
Telephone: (202) 296-9880
Registered as lobbyist at U.S. Congress.

MOODY, Joan
Communications Director, Scenic America
216 7th St., S.E., Washington, DC 20003
Telephone: (202) 546-1100

MOODY, Kathleen
Cong Liaison (African Affrs), DEPARTMENT OF STATE
2201 C St., N.W., Washington, DC 20520
Telephone: (202) 647-6480

MOODY, Rush, Jr.
Andrews and Kurth
1701 Pennsylvania Ave., N.W., Suite 200, Washington, DC 20006
Telephone: (202) 662-2700
Background: Commissioner, Federal Power Commission, 1971-75.
Clients:
    El Paso Natural Gas Co.

MOONEY, James P.
President and CEO, Nat'l Cable Television Ass'n
1724 Massachusetts Ave., N.W., Washington, DC 20036
Telephone: (202) 775-3651
Registered as lobbyist at U.S. Congress.

MOORE, Alan J.
Representative of the President, Atchison, Topeka and Santa Fe Railway Co., The
1001 Pennsylvania Ave., N.W., Suite 675 North, Washington, DC 20004
Telephone: (202) 637-1250
Registered as lobbyist at U.S. Congress.

MOORE, Albert W.
President, NMTBA - The Ass'n for Manufacturing Technology
7901 Westpark Dr., McLean, VA 22102
Telephone: (703) 893-2900
Registered as lobbyist at U.S. Congress.

MOORE, Allen
President, Nat'l Solid Wastes Management Ass'n
1730 Rhode Island Ave., N.W., 10th Floor, Washington, DC 20036
Telephone: (202) 659-4613
Registered as lobbyist at U.S. Congress.
Background: Former Under Secretary of Commerce for International Trade.

MOORE, Maj. Gen. Burton R.
Dir, Legis Liaison, DEPARTMENT OF AIR FORCE
The Pentagon, Washington, DC 20330
Telephone: (202) 697-8153

MOORE, Carlos
Exec. V. President, American Textile Manufacturers Institute
1801 K St., N.W. Suite 900, Washington, DC 20006
Telephone: (202) 862-0500
Registered as lobbyist at U.S. Congress.
Background: International Economist, Office of Fuels and Energy, U.S. Department of State, 1978-80. Deputy Chief Economist, U.S. Delegation to Multilateral Trade Negotiations, 1974-78.

MOORE, Carolyn
PAC Contact, Nat'l Licensed Beverage Ass'n Beverage Alcohol Retailer PAC
4214 King St., Alexandria, VA 22302-1507
Telephone: (703) 671-7575

MOORE AND CO., Timothy X.
2900 M St., N.W., Suite 300, Washington, DC 20007
Telephone: (202) 333-4318
Background: A government relations consulting firm with special interest in telecommunications, commerce and judicial matters.
Members of firm representing listed organizations:
    Moore, Timothy X.
        Background: Former Legislative Assistant to Senator Richard Stone (D-FL), 1975-76; and Exec. Assistant to then Rep. Timothy Wirth (D-CO), 1976-80.
Organizations represented:
    Design Protection Coalition *(Timothy X. Moore)*
    Internat'l Environmental Policy Coalition *(Timothy X. Moore)*
    Software Rental Coalition *(Timothy X. Moore)*
    Typeface Design Coalition *(Timothy X. Moore)*

MOORE, Colleen M.
Legislative Specialist, Consolidated Natural Gas Co.
1819 L St., N.W. Suite 900, Washington, DC 20036
Telephone: (202) 833-3900

MOORE, Evelyn K.
Exec. Director, Nat'l Black Child Development Institute
1463 Rhode Island Ave., N.W., Washington, DC 20005
Telephone: (202) 387-1281

MOORE, Jack F.
Internat'l Secretary, Internat'l Brotherhood of Electrical Workers
1125 15th St., N.W., Washington, DC 20005
Telephone: (202) 833-7000
Background: Responsible for Internat'l Brotherhood of Electrical Workers Committee on Political Education.

MOORE, Joan Hartman
Director, Public Relations, Ass'n of American Medical Colleges
One Dupont Circle, N.W., Suite 200, Washington, DC 20036
Telephone: (202) 828-0400

MOORE, John Norton
Chairman of the Board of Directors, United States Institute for Peace
1550 M St., N.W. Suite 700, Washington, DC 20005-1708
Telephone: (202) 457-1700
Background: Counselor on Internatonal Law, U.S. State Dept., 1972-73; Chairman, Nat'l Security Council Task Force on Law of the Sea, Ambassador, Law of the Sea Conference, 1973-76.

MOORE, Jonathon R.
Windels, Marx, Davies and Ives
1701 Pennsylvania Ave., N.W. Suite 940, Washington, DC 20006
Telephone: (202) 775-5980
Registered as lobbyist at U.S. Congress.
Clients:
    Crown Controls Corp.

MOORE, Julia A.
V. President, Communications, World Wildlife Fund/The Conservation Foundation
1250 24th St., N.W., Washington, DC 20037
Telephone: (202) 293-4800

MOORE, Linda
Director of Field Operations, Democratic Leadership Council
316 Pennsylvania Ave., S.E., Suite 500, Washington, DC 20003
Telephone: (202) 546-0007

MOORE, Lisa
Director, Government Division, United Jewish Appeal Federation of Greater Washington
6101 Montrose Rd., Rockville, MD 20852
Telephone: (301) 230-7200

MOORE, M. Eddie
Assistant General President, United Ass'n of Journeymen & Apprentices of the Plumbing & Pipe Fitting Industry of the US & Canada
901 Massachusetts Ave., N.W., Washington, DC 20001
Telephone: (202) 628-5823

MOORE, M. Melissa
Director, Communications & Public Affrs., American Ass'n of Engineering Societies
415 2nd St., N.E., Suite 200, Washington, DC 20002
Telephone: (202) 546-2237
Background: Legislative Ass't, Sen. Hayakawa (R-CA).

MOORE, Mark P.
Manager, Policy Analysis, Public Securities Ass'n
1000 Vermont Ave., N.W., Suite 800, Washington, DC 20005
Telephone: (202) 898-9390

MOORE, Michael D.
Director, Federal Agency Relations, Burlington Resources, Inc.
50 F St., N.W., Suite 1080, Washington, DC 20001
Telephone: (202) 383-4960

MOORE, Obie L.
Senior Federal Legislative Manager, Penney Co., J. C.
Suite 1015 1156 15th St., N.W., Washington, DC
Telephone: (202) 862-4817
Registered as lobbyist at U.S. Congress.

MOORE, Powell A.
Ginn, Edington, Moore and Wade
803 Prince St., Alexandria, VA 22314
Telephone: (703) 836-3328
Registered as lobbyist at U.S. Congress.
Registered as Foreign Agent: (#4134).
Background: Assistant Secretary of State, 1982-83; Deputy Assistant to the President for Legislative Affairs (Senate), 1981.

MOORE, Richard
V. President, Director, Media Relations, Burson-Marsteller
1850 M St., N.W., Suite 900, Washington, DC 20036
Telephone: (202) 833-8550

MOORE, Robert
Director, California, State of
444 North Capitol St., N.W., Suite 305, Washington, DC 20001
Telephone: (202) 347-6891

MOORE, Robert H.
Senior V. President, Corp. Relations, Alexander & Alexander Inc.
555 13th St., N.W. Suite 1180E, Washington, DC 20004-1109
Telephone: (202) 783-2550

MOORE, Robert M.
President, Internat'l Banana Ass'n
1101 Vermont Ave., N.W. Suite 306, Washington, DC 20005
Telephone: (202) 371-1620

MOORE, Stephen J.
Exec. Director, American Immigration Institute
4401 Ford Ave., Suite 200, Alexandria, VA 22302
Telephone: (703) 824-2048

MOORE, Susan
Staff Asst, Legis Affrs (Senate), EXECUTIVE OFFICE OF THE PRESIDENT - The White House
1600 Pennsylvania Ave., N.W. 107 East Wing, Washington, DC 20500
Telephone: (202) 456-7557

MOORE, Timothy X.
Moore and Co., Timothy X.
2900 M St., N.W., Suite 300, Washington, DC 20007
Telephone: (202) 333-4318
Registered as lobbyist at U.S. Congress.
Background: Former Legislative Assistant to Senator Richard Stone (D-FL), 1975-76; and Exec. Assistant to then Rep. Timothy Wirth (D-CO), 1976-80.
Organizations represented:
Design Protection Coalition
Internat'l Environmental Policy Coalition
Software Rental Coalition
Typeface Design Coalition

MOORE, Walter K.
Director, Congressional Relations, Pfizer, Inc.
1455 Pennsylvania Ave., N.W., Suite 925, Washington, DC 20004
Telephone: (202) 783-7070

MOOREHEAD, Donald V.
Patton, Boggs and Blow
2550 M St., N.W., Suite 800, Washington, DC 20037
Telephone: (202) 457-6000
Registered as lobbyist at U.S. Congress.
Registered as Foreign Agent: (#2165).
Background: Chief Minority Counsel, Committee on Finance, U.S. Senate, 1975-76.
Clients:
Kaiser Aluminum and Chemical Corp.

MOOREHEAD, Laura W.
Legislative Affairs Manager, NCR Corporation
1156 15th St., N.W. Suite 1201, Washington, DC 20005
Telephone: (202) 872-0717

MOOREHEAD, Randall B.
Director, Government Affairs, North American Philips Corp.
1300 Eye St., N.W., Washington, DC 20005
Telephone: (202) 962-8550
Registered as lobbyist at U.S. Congress.
Background: Former Deputy Director for Legislative Affairs, Nat'l Oceanic and Atmospheric Administration, U.S. Department of Commerce.

MOOS, Eugene
V. President, Lesher & Russell, Inc.
517 C St., N.E., Washington, DC 20002
Telephone: (202) 546-6501

MOOSE, Richard M.
Sr. V. President, Government Affairs, American Express Co.
1020 19th St., N.W., Suite 600, Washington, DC 20036
Telephone: (202) 822-6680
Registered as lobbyist at U.S. Congress.
Background: Assistant Secretary of State for African Affairs in the Carter Administration. Responsibilities include the American Express Committee for Responsible Government.

MORAGLIO, Joseph
V. President, Federal Government, American Institute of Certified Public Accountants
1455 Pennsylvania Ave., N.W. Suite 400, Washington, DC 20004
Telephone: (202) 737-6600

MORAI, Edward C.
Director, Plns, Policy, and Evaluation, Nat'l Guard Ass'n of the U.S.
One Massachusetts Ave., N.W., Washington, DC 20001
Telephone: (202) 789-0031

MORALES, Martha R.
Assoc. Exec. Director, American Intellectual Property Law Ass'n
2001 Jefferson Davis Hwy. Suite 203, Arlington, VA 22202
Telephone: (703) 521-1680

MORAN, Anne E.
Member, Miller & Chevalier, Chartered
Metropolitan Square, 655 15th St., N.W., Washington, DC 20005
Telephone: (202) 626-5800
Registered as lobbyist at U.S. Congress.
Background: Tax Counsel, Senate Committee on Finance, 1983-86.
Clients:

Electronic Industries Ass'n
Great Northern Insured Annuity Corporation
USF&G

MORAN, Brennan D.
Director, Media Relations, Tobacco Institute
1875 Eye St., N.W., Suite 800, Washington, DC 20006
Telephone: (202) 457-4800

MORAN, Lori A.
Governmental Affairs Representative, American Consulting Engineers Council
1015 15th St., N.W., Suite 802, Washington, DC 20005
Telephone: (202) 347-7474
Registered as lobbyist at U.S. Congress.

MORAN, Margaret A.
Spec. Ass't, Arctic Nat'l Wildlife Ref., Alaska, State of
444 N. Capitol St., N.W. Suite 518, Washington, DC 20001
Telephone: (202) 624-5858

MORAN, Mark A.
Steptoe and Johnson
1330 Connecticut Ave., N.W., Washington, DC 20036
Telephone: (202) 429-3000
Clients:
Aluminum Co. of America

MORAN, Mark E.
1129 20th St., N.W., Suite 500, Washington, DC 20036
Telephone: (202) 775-0742
Registered as Foreign Agent: (#3945)
Organizations represented:
Mexico, Government of

MORAN, Peter
Sr. V. President, Consumer Relations, Soc. of American Florists
1601 Duke St., Alexandria, VA 22314
Telephone: (703) 836-8700

MORANDI, Larry
Program Manager, Natural Resources, Nat'l Conference of State Legislatures
444 North Capitol St., N.W. Suite 500, Washington, DC 20001
Telephone: (202) 624-5400

MORDINI, Kathleen
V. President, Public Affairs, American Internat'l Automobile Dealers Ass'n
1128 16th St., N.W., Washington, DC 20036
Telephone: (202) 659-2561

MORE, Tim E.
Associated General Contractors of America
1957 E St., N.W., Washington, DC 20006
Telephone: (202) 393-2040
Registered as lobbyist at U.S. Congress.

MOREHEAD, David L.
V. President, Communications, Petroleum Marketers Ass'n of America
1120 Vermont Ave., N.W., Suite 1130, Washington, DC 20005
Telephone: (202) 331-1198

MOREHEAD, Florida
Exec. Director, Nat'l Soc. of Black Engineers
344 Commerce St., Alexandria, VA 22314
Telephone: (703) 549-2207

MOREHOUSE, Judith
Manager, Government Business Relations, Boeing Co.
1700 North Moore St., Arlington, VA 22209
Telephone: (703) 558-9600
Registered as lobbyist at U.S. Congress.

MORELAND, Terri
Associate Director, Illinois, State of
444 N. Capitol St., N.W. Suite 210, Washington, DC 20001
Telephone: (202) 624-7760

MORELLI, Genevieve
General Counsel, Competitive Telecommunications Ass'n (COMPTEL)
120 Maryland Ave., N.E., Washington, DC 20002
Telephone: (202) 546-9022

MORENO, G. Mario
Regional Counsel, Mexican-American Legal Defense and Educational Fund
1430 K St., N.W., Suite 700, Washington, DC 20005
Telephone: (202) 628-4074

MOREY, Richard S.
Kleinfeld, Kaplan and Becker
1140 19th St., N.W., Suite 700, Washington, DC 20036
Telephone: (202) 223-5120
Clients:
Cord Laboratories
Mead Johnson and Co.

MORGAN, Anne
Staff Attorney, Nat'l Federation of Federal Employees
1016 16th St., N.W., Suite 400, Washington, DC 20036
Telephone: (202) 862-4400
Registered as lobbyist at U.S. Congress.

MORGAN CASNER ASSOCIATES, INC.
1332 Independence Ave., S.E., Washington, DC 20003
Telephone: (202) 543-4600
Background: A political and public affairs consulting firm that specializes in Washington representation and Federal Government liaison. Also sets up and operates political action committees for clients. Established 1973.
Members of firm representing listed organizations:
Casner, Bruce M., President
Background: Former Congressional Staff member. Specializes in legislative and political matters.
Hewitt, Mary E., V. President
Background: Specializes in matters pertaining to the media.
Walls, Richard A., Senior Associate

MORGAN, Charles, Jr.
Advocates at Law Chartered
1899 L St., N.W., Suite 300, Washington, DC 20036
Telephone: (202) 466-7000

MORGAN, Donald L.
Cleary, Gottlieb, Steen and Hamilton
1752 N St., N.W., Washington, DC 20036
Telephone: (202) 728-2700
Clients:
American Cyanamid Co.

MORGAN, E. Joyce
Managing Editor, American Mining Congress
1920 N St., N.W. Suite 300, Washington, DC 20036
Telephone: (202) 861-2800
Registered as lobbyist at U.S. Congress.

MORGAN, Gerald D., Jr.
Winthrop, Stimson, Putnam & Roberts
1133 Connecticut Ave., N.W. Suite 1000, Washington, DC 20036
Telephone: (202) 775-9800
Background: Attorney, 1971-74, Deputy Vice President for Insurance, 1974-75, Vice President and General Counsel, 1975-76, Overseas Private Investment Corp. General Counsel, Agency for International Development, 1976-77.

MORGAN, J. Ray
Exec. V. President, American Chiropractic Ass'n
1701 Clarendon Blvd., Arlington, VA 22209
Telephone: (703) 276-8800

MORGAN, Jay Railton
Legislative Rep., Automotive Group, Ford Motor Co.
1350 Eye St., N.W. Suite 1000, Washington, DC 20005
Telephone: (202) 962-5400
Registered as lobbyist at U.S. Congress.

MORGAN, John
Asst. to Exec. V.P., Legis./Gov't Affrs., Communications Workers of America
1925 K St., N.W., Washington, DC 20006
Telephone: (202) 728-2465
Registered as lobbyist at U.S. Congress.

MORGAN, Juanita Kennedy
Exec. Secretary/Org. Director, Nat'l Black Women's Political Leadership Caucus
3005 Bladensburg Road, N.E. Suite 217, Washington, DC 20018
Telephone: (202) 529-2806

MORGAN, Lance I.
V. President, Robinson, Lake, Lerer & Montgomery
1667 K St., N.W., Suite 900, Washington, DC 20006
Telephone: (202) 457-9270
Registered as lobbyist at U.S. Congress.
Background: Former Press Sec'y to Senate Select Committee on Secret Military Assistance for Iran and the Nicaraguan Opposition and former Press Secretary to Sen. Daniel Patrick Moynihan (D-NY).
Clients:
Atari Games Corp.

MORGAN, Larry
Dir, Legis and Public Affrs, DEPARTMENT OF INTERIOR - Territorial and Internat'l Affairs
18th and C Sts., N.W., Washington, DC 20240
Telephone: (202) 343-3003

MORGAN, LEWIS AND BOCKIUS
1800 M St., N.W., Washington, DC 20036
Telephone: (202) 467-7000
Registered as Foreign Agent: (#3794)
Background: Washington office of a Philadelphia law firm. The following information was obtained from public records and submitted to this firm for confirmation. The firm declined to confirm or correct information on client listings as a matter of policy.
Members of firm representing listed organizations:
Barnes, Dennis N.
Calabrese, Michael R.
Cohen, Sheldon S.
Background: Chief Counsel, Internal Revenue Service, 1964. Commissioner of Internal Revenue, 1965-69.
Escudero, Mario F.
Friedman, Margery Sinder
Halladay, Roberta L.
Hobbs, Caswell O. (III)
Hotvedt, Richard C.
Kelly, Michael S.
Quarles, John R. (Jr.)
Ritts, Leslie Sue
Schaeffer, Eric V.
Sender, Stanton P.
Background: Heads the firm's government relations practice.
Sheehan, Arline M., Associate
Sommer, A. A. (Jr.)
Background: Commissioner, Securities and Exchange Commission, 1973-76. Member, Board of Directors, Consolidated Natural Gas Co.
Topelius, Kathleen E.
Background: Attorney, Office of General Counsel, Federal Home Loan Bank Board, 1978-80.
Uehlein, E. Carl (Jr.)
Wotring, Thomas K.
Clients:
Ass'n of American Railroads
Atlantic Lines and Navigation Co., Ltd. *(Dennis N. Barnes)*
Baldwin United Corp.
Banco de Santander, S.A.d.c. *(Kathleen E. Topelius)*
Bird and Son *(Caswell O. Hobbs, III)*
Communications Satellite Corp. (COMSAT)
Consolidated Natural Gas Co. *(A. A. Sommer, Jr.)*
Council of Mutual Savings Institutions
Disabled American Veterans
Eastern Shore Natural Gas Co.
Florida Power Corp.
Florida Public Utilities Co. *(Thomas K. Wotring)*
Harsco Corp. *(Thomas K. Wotring)*
Lloyds of London, Underwriters at
Mexico, Government of
MIP Instandsetzungsbetriebe GmbH
Nat'l Environmental Development Ass'n *(John R. Quarles, Jr., Leslie Sue Ritts)*
Nat'l Lime Ass'n *(Eric V. Schaeffer)*
Nat'l Spa and Pool Institute *(Caswell O. Hobbs, III)*
Pan American World Airways
PPG Industries *(Michael R. Calabrese)*
Public Service Co. of New Mexico
Puerto Rico Maritime Shipping Authority *(Dennis N. Barnes, Mario F. Escudero)*
Ralston Purina Co. *(John R. Quarles, Jr.)*
Reading Railway System
Safeguard Industries
Safety-Kleen Corp. *(Eric V. Schaeffer, Arline M. Sheehan)*

Scotch Whiskey Ass'n *(Michael S. Kelly, E. Carl Uehlein, Jr.)*
Sears, Roebuck and Co. *(Stanton P. Sender)*
Sierra Pacific Resources
Skyline Corp.
Union Mechling Corp.
United Kingdom of Great Britain and Northern Ireland, Government of the *(Michael S. Kelly)*
USG Corporation *(Eric V. Schaeffer)*
Washington Post Co.
WEI Enterprises Corp. *(Sheldon S. Cohen)*

MORGAN, Peter Denis
Dir, Housing & Commun. Devmt, Gov't Rtns, Nat'l Ass'n of REALTORS
777 14th St., N.W., Washington, DC 20005
Telephone: (202) 383-1102
Registered as lobbyist at U.S. Congress.
Background: Former Senior Legislative Specialist, U.S. Department of Housing and Urban Development.

MORGAN, Dr. Russell E.
President, Nat'l Council for Internat'l Health
1701 K St., N.W. Suite 600, Washington, DC 20006
Telephone: (202) 833-5900

MORGAN, Stephen L.
Exec. V. President, American Cemetery Ass'n
Three Skyline Place 5201 Leesburg Pike, Suite 1111, Falls Church, VA 22041
Telephone: (703) 379-5838
Registered as lobbyist at U.S. Congress.

MORIAK, Susan
Asst. Director, Government Affairs, Recreation Vehicle Industry Ass'n
1896 Preston White Drive P.O. Box 2999, Reston, VA 22090
Telephone: (703) 620-6003

MORIN, Charles H.
Dickstein, Shapiro and Morin
2101 L St., N.W., Washington, DC 20037
Telephone: (202) 785-9700
Clients:
Bear, Stearns and Co.
Federated Cash Management Systems
Marine Engineers Beneficial Ass'n

MORIN, Gayle
Asst to the Commissioner (Legis Liaison), DEPARTMENT OF TREASURY - Internal Revenue Service
1111 Constitution Ave., N.W., Washington, DC 20224
Telephone: (202) 566-4071

MORIN, Mary Kay
Gold and Liebengood, Inc.
1455 Pennsylvania Ave., N.W. Suite 950, Washington, DC 20004
Telephone: (202) 639-8899
Background: Former Aide to U.S. Senate Majority Leader Howard Baker (R-TN).

MORIN, William G.
Dir., High Tech. Couns. & Defense Forum, Nat'l Ass'n of Manufacturers
1331 Pennsylvania Ave., N.W. Suite 1500 North, Washington, DC 20004-1703
Telephone: (202) 637-3000
Registered as lobbyist at U.S. Congress.

MORING, Frederick
Crowell and Moring
1001 Pennsylvania Ave., N.W., Washington, DC 20004-2505
Telephone: (202) 624-2500

MORITZ, Amy
President, Nat'l Center for Public Policy Research
300 Eye St., N.E., Suite 3, Washington, DC 20002
Telephone: (202) 543-1286
Background: Also serves as director of several foreign affairs-oriented committees; as Editor of the newsletter The Liberty Letter; on the board of directors of The Nat'l Center for Public Policy Research, The Liberty Institute (Chairman), American Freedom Institute, and others.

MORITZ, Donald I.
Chairman, Gov't Relations Committee, American Gas Ass'n
1515 Wilson Blvd., Arlington, VA 22209
Telephone: (703) 841-8400

MORRILL, James A.
Staff V. Pres., Federal Gov't Affairs, Scott Paper Co.
1726 M St., N.W., Suite 901, Washington, DC 20036
Telephone: (202) 331-0730
Registered as lobbyist at U.S. Congress.
Background: Former Staff Assistant, House Appropriations Committee, 1977-79; Legislative Assistant to the Assistant Secretary for Legislative Affairs, Department of Housing and Urban Development.

MORRIS, Barbara A.
Exec. Director, Government Relations, NYNEX
1828 L St., N.W., Suite 1000, Washington, DC 20036
Telephone: (202) 416-0100

MORRIS, Gerald
Deputy Director, American Federation of Teachers
555 New Jersey Ave., N.W., Washington, DC 20001
Telephone: (202) 879-4453
Registered as lobbyist at U.S. Congress.

MORRIS, Jack
President, Nat'l Military Intelligence Ass'n
Pentagon Station, Box 46583, Washington, DC 20050-6583
Telephone: (301) 840-6642

MORRIS, Jay H.
Associate Director, Public Affairs, Nat'l Ass'n of Life Underwriters
1922 F St., N.W., Washington, DC 20006
Telephone: (202) 331-6000

MORRIS, Julian C.
President, Automotive Parts and Accessories Ass'n
5100 Forbes Blvd., Lanham, MD 20706
Telephone: (301) 459-9110

MORRIS, Marion
Director of Legislative Services, Nat'l Ass'n of Housing and Redevelopment Officials
1320 18th St., N.W., Washington, DC 20036
Telephone: (202) 429-2960
Background: Former legislative assistant to Senator Charles McC. Mathias, Jr. (R-MD).

MORRIS, Michael
Director, Governmental Activities Office, United Cerebral Palsy Ass'ns
1522 K St., N.W., Suite 1112, Washington, DC 20005
Telephone: (202) 842-1266

MORRIS, Milton D.
Director of Research, Joint Center for Political Studies
1301 Pennsylvania Ave., N.W., Washington, DC 20004
Telephone: (202) 626-3500

MORRIS, R. K.
Director, International Trade, Nat'l Ass'n of Manufacturers
1331 Pennsylvania Ave., N.W. Suite 1500 North, Washington, DC 20004-1703
Telephone: (202) 637-3000

MORRIS, Rebecca
Assoc Asst Secy, Cong Affrs, DEPARTMENT OF LABOR
200 Constitution Ave., N.W., Washington, DC 20210
Telephone: (202) 523-6141

MORRIS, Richard A.
V. Pres., Gov't Relations & Public Affs., Nat'l Aggregates Ass'n
900 Spring St., Silver Spring, MD 20910
Telephone: (301) 587-1400
Background: Also represents the Nat'l Ready Mixed Concrete Ass'n as V. President, Government Relations and Public Affairs and the Nat'l Industrial Sand Ass'n as Director of Government Relations and Public Affairs.

MORRIS, Robert J.
Senior V. President, Washington, United States Council for Internat'l Business
1015 15th St., N.W. Suite 1200, Washington, DC 20005
Telephone: (202) 371-1316

Background: Former U.S. Foreign Service Officer, most recently Deputy to the Under Secretary of State for Economic Affairs.

MORRIS, Tom C.
Manager, Federal Relations, Phillips Petroleum Co.
1776 Eye St., N.W. Suite 700, Washington, DC 20006
Telephone: (202) 833-0900
Registered as lobbyist at U.S. Congress.

MORRIS, W. Patrick
V. President and General Counsel, Shipbuilders Council of America
1110 Vermont Ave., N.W. Suite 1250, Washington, DC 20005
Telephone: (202) 775-9060
Registered as lobbyist at U.S. Congress.

MORRIS, William
Rogers and Wells
1737 H St., N.W., Washington, DC 20006
Telephone: (202) 331-7760
Registered as lobbyist at U.S. Congress.
Background: General Counsel to Committee on Finance, U.S. Senate, 1972-80.
Clients:
American Express Co.
Dreyfus Corp.
Investment Partnership Ass'n
Merrill Lynch and Co., Inc.
Nat'l Ass'n of Beverage Importers
Rutgers, The State University of New Jersey
Shearson Lehman Hutton
Turner Corp., The
Wine and Spirits Wholesalers of America

MORRIS, William H., Jr.
President and CEO, Global USA, Inc.
2121 K St., N.W., Suite 650, Washington, DC 20037
Telephone: (202) 296-2400
Registered as lobbyist at U.S. Congress.
Registered as Foreign Agent: (# 3489).
Background: Former Assistant Secretary of Commerce for Trade, 1981-83. Former Assistant to Senator Bill Brock, (R-TN) and member of the President's Commission on Industrial Competitiveness.
Clients:
Hyundai Motor America
Komatsu Ltd.
Kyocera Corp.
South Louisiana Port Commission
TECO Transport & Trade Corp.

MORRIS WILLIAMS, Loretta
Legislative Analyst, March of Dimes Birth Defects Foundation
1725 K St., N.W., Suite 814, Washington, DC 20006
Telephone: (202) 659-1800
Registered as lobbyist at U.S. Congress.

MORRISON, Alan B.
Director, Public Citizen Litigation Group
2000 P St., N.W., Suite 700, Washington, DC 20036
Telephone: (202) 785-3704
Registered as lobbyist at U.S. Congress.

MORRISON ASSOCIATES
815 Connecticut Ave., N.W. Suite 800, Washington, DC 20006
Telephone: (202) 872-8996
Background: A government relations firm specializing in representing the federal legislative and regulatory interests of major companies in the services sector of the nation's economy.
Members of firm representing listed organizations:
Morrison, James W. (Jr.), President
Background: Formerly served on professional staff of Department of Defense agencies and NASA, 1959-74. Senior Management Associate, Office of Management and Budget, 1974-79. Director of Congressional Affairs, Office of Personnel Management, 1979-81. Associate Director, Office of Personnel Management, 1981-87.
Clients:
American Express Travel Related Services Co., Inc. *(James W. Morrison, Jr.)*
ARA Services *(James W. Morrison, Jr.)*
Blue Cross and Blue Shield Ass'n *(James W. Morrison, Jr.)*

Blue Cross and Blue Shield of Chicago *(James W. Morrison, Jr.)*
Children's World Learning Centers *(James W. Morrison, Jr.)*
Spectrum Emergency Care *(James W. Morrison, Jr.)*

MORRISON, Christine E.
Director, Public Relations, Recreation Vehicle Industry Ass'n
1896 Preston White Drive P.O. Box 2999, Reston, VA 22090
Telephone: (703) 620-6003

MORRISON & FOERSTER
2000 Pennsylvania Ave., N.W., Suite 5500, Washington, DC 20006
Telephone: (202) 887-1500
Registered as Foreign Agent: (# 4282)
Background: Washington office of a San Francisco law firm.
Members of firm representing listed organizations:
Band, Jonathan
Bartz, Philip D.
Carr, Ronald G.
Eckland, William S.
Edwards, Tony M.
Background: Internal Revenue Service, 1975-79.
Fischer, L. Richard
Kurucza, Robert M.
Background: Securities and Exchange Commission, 1978-80. Office of the Comptroller of the Currency, 1980-82.
Livingston, Scott D.
Rosenthal, Steven S.
Roster, Michael
Schwartz, Tamar R.
Squadron, William F.
Clients:
Bethlehem Steel Corp.
California Bankers Clearinghouse Ass'n *(L. Richard Fischer, Robert M. Kurucza)*
Coca-Cola Co. *(Philip D. Bartz, Ronald G. Carr, Scott D. Livingston, William F. Squadron)*
Federal Home Loan Bank of Des Moines *(L. Richard Fischer)*
Federal Home Loan Bank of Seattle *(William S. Eckland, Michael Roster)*
Federal Home Loan Bank of Topeka *(L. Richard Fischer)*
First Nationwide Bank *(William S. Eckland, Michael Roster)*
Ford Motor Co. *(William S. Eckland, Michael Roster)*
Fujitsu Ltd. *(Jonathan Band, Philip D. Bartz, Ronald G. Carr, Tamar R. Schwartz)*
MasterCard Internat'l. Inc. *(L. Richard Fischer, Robert M. Kurucza)*
Micron Technology, Inc.
Nat'l Electrical Manufacturers Ass'n *(Steven S. Rosenthal)*
RREEF Funds, The *(Tony M. Edwards)*
VISA U.S.A., Inc. *(L. Richard Fischer, Robert M. Kurucza)*

MORRISON, James W.
V. President for Policy, Business Executives for Nat'l Security
601 Pennsylvania Ave., N.W. Suite 700, Washington, DC 20004
Telephone: (202) 737-1090
Registered as lobbyist at U.S. Congress.

MORRISON, James W., Jr.
President, Morrison Associates
815 Connecticut Ave., N.W. Suite 800, Washington, DC 20006
Telephone: (202) 872-8996
Registered as lobbyist at U.S. Congress.
Background: Formerly served on professional staff of Department of Defense agencies and NASA, 1959-74. Senior Management Associate, Office of Management and Budget, 1974-79. Director of Congressional Affairs, Office of Personnel Management, 1979-81. Associate Director, Office of Personnel Management, 1981-87.
Clients:
American Express Travel Related Services Co., Inc.
ARA Services
Blue Cross and Blue Shield Ass'n

Blue Cross and Blue Shield of Chicago
Children's World Learning Centers
Spectrum Emergency Care

MORRISON, John W.
Legislative Counsel, Nat'l Ass'n for Uniformed Services
5535 Hempstead Way, Springfield, VA 22151
Telephone: (703) 750-1342
Registered as lobbyist at U.S. Congress.

MORRISON, Philip D.
Ivins, Phillips and Barker
1700 Pennsylvania Ave., N.W., Suite 600, Washington, DC 20006
Telephone: (202) 393-7600
Registered as lobbyist at U.S. Congress.
Background: Counsel, Senate Finance Committee, 1981-83.
Clients:
American Textile Manufacturers Institute
Digital Equipment Corp.
Family Holding Co. Advocacy Group
Oberlin College
Rochester Tax Council

MORRISON, William C.
Exec. Director, Meat Importers Council of America
1901 North Ft. Myer Dr. Suite 1110, Arlington, VA 22209
Telephone: (703) 522-1910
Registered as lobbyist at U.S. Congress.

MORRISSETTE, Peggy
Director of Public and Gov't Affairs, Manufacturers' Alliance for Productivity and Innovation (MAPI)
1200 18th St., N.W. Suite 400, Washington, DC 20036
Telephone: (202) 331-8430

MORRISSEY, H. T. Steve
President, Nat'l Ass'n of Retired Federal Employees
1533 New Hampshire Ave., N.W., Washington, DC 20036
Telephone: (202) 234-0832
Registered as lobbyist at U.S. Congress.

MORRISSEY, James A.
Director, Communications, American Textile Manufacturers Institute
1801 K St., N.W. Suite 900, Washington, DC
Telephone: (202) 862-0552

MORROW, Robert R.
Sutherland, Asbill and Brennan
1275 Pennsylvania, N.W., Washington, DC 20004-2404
Telephone: (202) 383-0100
Clients:
Process Gas Consumers Group

MORROW, Ward
National Chair, Youths for Democratic Action
1511 K St., N.W., Suite 941, Washington, DC 20005
Telephone: (202) 638-6447

MORSE, Anne R.
Pillsbury, Madison and Sutro
1667 K St., N.W., Suite 1100, Washington, DC 20006
Telephone: (202) 887-0300
Registered as Foreign Agent: (#4212).
Clients:
Korea Foreign Trade Ass'n

MORSE, Marie
Political Director, Nat'l Women's Political Caucus
1275 K St., N.W., Suite 750, Washington, DC 20005
Telephone: (202) 898-1100

MORSE, Robert H.
Galland, Kharasch, Morse and Garfinkle
Canal Square, 1054 31st St., N.W., Washington, DC 20007
Telephone: (202) 342-5200
Background: Trial Attorney and Senior Trial Attorney, Patent Section, Antitrust Division, Department of Justice, 1971-75. Senior Trial Attorney, Trial Section, Antitrust Division, Department of Justice, 1975-78.

MORSE, Valerie T.
V. President, Government Affairs, American Express Co.
1020 19th St., N.W., Suite 600, Washington, DC 20036
Telephone: (202) 822-6680
Registered as lobbyist at U.S. Congress.

MORTENSON, Lee E.
Exec. Director, Ass'n of Community Cancer Centers
11600 Nebel St., Suite 201, Rockville, MD 20852
Telephone: (301) 984-9496

MORTON, Evelyn
Legislative Representative, American Ass'n of Retired Persons
1909 K St., N.W., Washington, DC 20049
Telephone: (202) 872-4700
Registered as lobbyist at U.S. Congress.

MORTON, Michael L.
V. President, Florida Sugar Cane League
910 16th St., N.W., Suite 402, Washington, DC 20006
Telephone: (202) 785-4070
Registered as lobbyist at U.S. Congress.

MORTON, Sandy I.
Director, Gov't Relations, Special Libraries Ass'n
1700 18th St., N.W., Washington, DC 20009
Telephone: (202) 234-4700
Background: Legislative Assistant for Senator Charles Mathias, (R-MD), 1975-86.

MOSEDALE, Roberta
Exec. Secretary, Nat'l Soc. for Histotechnology
5900 Princess Garden Pkwy. Suite 805, Lanham, MD 20706
Telephone: (301) 577-4907

MOSELEY, Stephen F.
President, Academy for Educational Development
1255 23rd St., N.W., Washington, DC 20037
Telephone: (202) 862-1900

MOSER, Anna M.
Exec. Director, Council for Rural Housing and Development
2300 M St., N.W., Suite 260, Washington, DC 20037
Telephone: (202) 955-9715

MOSES, Nancy
Manager, Media Relations, Potomac Electric Power Co.
1900 Pennsylvania Ave., N.W., Washington, DC 20068
Telephone: (202) 872-2000

MOSHAVI, Dan
Director, Communications, Environmental Law Institute
1616 P St., N.W., Suite 200, Washington, DC 20036
Telephone: (202) 328-5150

MOSHENBERG, Sammie S.
Director of Washington Operations, Nat'l Council of Jewish Women
1101 15th St., N.W., Suite 1012, Washington, DC 20005
Telephone: (202) 296-2588

MOSHER, Russell N.
Exec. Director, American Boiler Manufacturers Ass'n
950 North Glebe Road, Suite 160, Arlington, VA 22203
Telephone: (703) 522-7350
Registered as lobbyist at U.S. Congress.

MOSHER, Sol
Sr. Advisor and Fed. Afrs. & Int'l Trade, Preston Gates Ellis & Rouvelas Meeds
1735 New York Ave., N.W., Suite 500, Washington, DC 20006-4759
Telephone: (202) 628-1700
Background: Former Assistant U.S. Trade Representative.

MOSKOWITZ, Jack
V. President, Government Relations, United Way of America
701 N. Fairfax St., Alexandria, VA 22314-2045
Telephone: (703) 836-7100
Registered as lobbyist at U.S. Congress.

MOSKOWITZ, Dr. Jay
Assoc Dir for Science Policy & Legislat, DEPARTMENT OF HEALTH AND HUMAN SERVICES - Nat'l Institutes of Health
Bldg. 1, 9000 Rockville Pike, Bethesda, MD 20892
Telephone: (301) 496-3152

MOSS, Dorothy J.
Director, Dept. of Federal Affairs, American Medical Ass'n
1101 Vermont Ave., N.W., Washington, DC 20005
Telephone: (202) 789-7400

Registered as lobbyist at U.S. Congress.

MOSS, Kate
Camp, Barsh, Bates and Tate
2550 M St., N.W., Suite 275, Washington, DC 20037
Telephone: (202) 887-5160
Registered as lobbyist at U.S. Congress.
Background: Special Assistant to Senator Charles McC. Mathias, Jr. (R-MD), 1970-71. Director for Congressional Liaison, Executive Office of the President, 1971-74.
Clients:
Coalition for Equitable Compensation
Committee for Equitable Compensation

MOSS, Robert E.
V. President, Federal Affairs, Coastal Corp., The/ANR Pipeline Co.
2000 M St., N.W., Suite 500, Washington, DC 20036
Telephone: (202) 466-7430
Registered as lobbyist at U.S. Congress.

MOSSINGHOFF, Gerald J.
President, Pharmaceutical Manufacturers Ass'n
1100 15th St., N.W., Washington, DC 20005
Telephone: (202) 835-3420
Registered as lobbyist at U.S. Congress.

MOSTOFF, Allan S.
Dechert Price & Rhoads
1500 K St., N.W., Washington, DC 20005
Telephone: (202) 626-3300
Registered as Foreign Agent: (#2777).
Background: Staff Member, Securities and Exchange Commission, 1962-1976. Associate Director, 1968-1972 and Director, 1972-1976, Division of Investment Management Regulation, Director of Policy Studies, 1976.
Clients:
Export-Import Bank of Japan
Japan, Embassy of

MOSTOFI, F. K.
Secretary Treasurer, Internat'l Council of Societies of Pathology
7001 Georgia St., Chevy Chase, MD 20815
Telephone: (301) 654-0095

MOTEN, Beth
Legislative Representative, American Federation of Government Employees
80 F St., N.W., Washington, DC 20001
Telephone: (202) 737-8700
Registered as lobbyist at U.S. Congress.

MOTLEY AND CO., L. A.
1800 K St., N.W., Suite 1000, Washington, DC 20006
Telephone: (202) 223-8222
Registered as Foreign Agent: (#3723).
Members of firm representing listed organizations:
Gingrich, Claud L., V. President
Kopp, Harry, V. President
Motley, Langhorne A., President
Organizations represented:
Associacao Brasileira dos Exportadores de Citricos (Langhorne A. Motley)
Associacao das Industrias de Calcados do Rio Grande do Sul (Claud L. Gingrich, Harry Kopp, Langhorne A. Motley)
Associacao Nacional das Industrias de Citricos (Claud L. Gingrich, Harry Kopp, Langhorne A. Motley)
Associacao Nacional dos Fabricantes de Papel e Celulose (Langhorne A. Motley)
Companhia de Navagacao Maritima NETUMAR (Langhorne A. Motley)
Eluma S/A Industria e Comercio
Lees Co, J B & S (Langhorne A. Motley)
Sharp S.A. Equipamentos Eletronicos (Langhorne A. Motley)

MOTLEY, John J.
V. Pres., Federal Governmental Affairs, Nat'l Federation of Independent Business
600 Maryland Ave., S.W., Suite 700, Washington, DC 20024
Telephone: (202) 554-9000
Registered as lobbyist at U.S. Congress.

MOTLEY, Langhorne A.
President, Motley and Co., L. A.
1800 K St., N.W., Suite 1000, Washington, DC 20006

MOTLEY, Langhorne A. (Cont'd)
Telephone: (202) 223-8222
Registered as lobbyist at U.S. Congress.
Registered as Foreign Agent: (#3723).
Organizations represented:
  Associacao Brasileira dos Exportadores de Citricos
  Associacao das Industrias de Calcados do Rio Grande do Sul
  Associacao Nacional das Industrias de Citricos
  Associacao Nacional dos Fabricantes de Papel e Celulose
  Companhia de Navagacao Maritima NETUMAR
  Lees Co, J B & S
  Sharp S.A. Equipamentos Eletronicos

MOULTON, Thomas O., Jr.
V. President, Federal Relations, Pacific Telesis Group-Washington
1275 Pennsylvania Ave., N.W. Suite 400, Washington, DC 20004
Telephone: (202) 383-6400
Registered as lobbyist at U.S. Congress.

MOUNTCASTLE, Katharine
Director, Campaign Finance Monitoring, Common Cause
2030 M St., N.W., Washington, DC 20036
Telephone: (202) 833-1200
Registered as lobbyist at U.S. Congress.

MOUSSEAU, Paul W.
Director, Wealth Management Corp.
Washington Harbour 3000 K St., N.W., P.H. 3-A, Washington, DC 20007
Telephone: (202) 944-4920
Registered as lobbyist at U.S. Congress.
Clients:
  Finryan Internat'l Ltd.

MOWE, Jeanne C.
Exec. Director, American Ass'n of Tissue Banks
1350 Beverly Road, Suite 220A, McLean, VA 22101
Telephone: (703) 827-9582

MOYA, Susan
Mgr., Energy & Natural Resources Policy, Chamber of Commerce of the U.S.A.
1615 H St., N.W., Washington, DC 20062
Telephone: (202) 463-5533
Registered as lobbyist at U.S. Congress.

MOYER, Bruce
Legislative Counsel, Federal Managers Ass'n
1000 16th St., N.W., Suite 701, Washington, DC 20006
Telephone: (202) 778-1500
Registered as lobbyist at U.S. Congress.
Background: Contact for the Federal Manager's Ass'n PAC.

MOYER, Steven
Legislative Representative, Fisheries, Nat'l Wildlife Federation
1400 16th St., N.W., Washington, DC 20036-2266
Telephone: (202) 797-6800
Registered as lobbyist at U.S. Congress.

MUCHNICK, Jeffrey Y.
Political Affairs Director, Nat'l Coalition to Ban Handguns
100 Maryland Ave., N.E., Washington, DC 20002
Telephone: (202) 544-7190
Registered as lobbyist at U.S. Congress.

MUCHOW, David J.
Gen. Counsel/Corporate Secretary, American Gas Ass'n
1515 Wilson Blvd., Arlington, VA 22209
Telephone: (703) 841-8608
Background: Aide to Congressman James A. Haley (Florida), 1962-1966. Budget Bureau, 1968-1970. Nat'l Security Council, 1970-1971. Special Asst. to Asst. Atty. Gen., Criminal Div., of U.S. Dept. of Justice, 1973-1976.

MUCKENFUSS, C. F., III
Gibson, Dunn and Crutcher
1050 Connecticut Ave., N.W. Suite 900, Washington, DC 20036-5303
Telephone: (202) 955-8500
Registered as lobbyist at U.S. Congress.
Background: Special Assistant to the Director, 1974-77 and Counsel to the Chairman, 1977-78, Federal Deposit Insurance Corporation. Member, Administrative Conference of the U.S., 1977-78. Senior Deputy Comptroller for Policy, Office of the Comptroller of the Currency, 1978-81.
Clients:
  Washington Mutual Savings Bank

MUDGE ROSE GUTHRIE ALEXANDER AND FERDON
2121 K St., N.W., Suite 700, Washington, DC 20037
Telephone: (202) 429-9355
Registered as Foreign Agent: (#3200)
Background: Washington office of a New York law firm.
Members of firm representing listed organizations:
Abbey, Richard H.
  Background: Assistant Chief Counsel, 1972-77; Deputy Chief Counsel, 1977-79; and Chief Counsel, 1979-85, U.S. Customs Service.
Bliss, Julia Christine
  Background: Attorney-Advisor, Office of the General Counsel, U.S. International Trade Commission, 1979-81. Legislative Assistant to Senator John Chafee (R-RI), 1981-82. Associate General Counsel, Office of the General Counsel, U.S. Trade Representative, 1982-86.
Cameron, Donald B. (Jr.)
Daniels, Michael P.
Houlihan, David P.
Lewin, Martin J.
  Background: Staff Attorney, Special Project Counsel to Interstate Commerce Commission, 1973-74. Attorney/Advisor, Office of the General Counsel, General Accounting Office, 1974-77. Staff Member, House Committee on International Relations, 1977-78, Legal Advisor to Commissioner Stern, U.S. International Trade Commission, 1978-79.
Mendoza, Julie C.
Neeley, Jeffrey S.
  Background: Attorney, Office of the General Counsel, U.S. International Trade Commission, 1979-83.
Palmeter, N. David
  Background: Trial Attorney, Civil Division, U.S. Department of Justice, 1966-68.
Vaughan, David A.
  Background: Assistant General Counsel, Federal Energy Administration, 1974-76.
Walker, William N.
  Background: General Counsel, Cost of Living Council, 1972-74. Federal Energy Office, 1974. Deputy U.S. Special Trade Representative, serving as Ambassador and Head of U.S. Delegation to Multilateral Trade Negotiations in Geneva, Switzerland, 1975-77.
Clients:
  Altos Hornos de Mexico, S.A. *(N. David Palmeter)*
  American Import Shippers Ass'n *(Martin J. Lewin)*
  Asociacion Nacional de Industriales (ANDI) *(Michael P. Daniels)*
  C.V.G. Siderurgica del Orinoco Ca. (SIDOR) *(David P. Houlihan, William N. Walker)*
  Camara de la Industria Curtidora Argentina *(David P. Houlihan, Julie C. Mendoza)*
  Camara de la Industria Aceitara de la Republica
  China Nat'l Chemical Import and Export Corp.
  China Nat'l Metals and Minerals Import and Export Corp. *(N. David Palmeter)*
  China Nat'l Textiles Import and Export Corp. *(Michael P. Daniels, Martin J. Lewin)*
  Cho Heung Chemical Ind. Co., Ltd. *(N. David Palmeter)*
  Climax Paper Converters Ltd. *(Donald B. Cameron, Jr.)*
  Creusot Loire Steel Products Co.
  Dai Lim Trading Co., Ltd. *(N. David Palmeter)*
  Daicel Chemical Industries, Ltd. *(N. David Palmeter)*
  Dalmine Siderica *(David P. Houlihan, Julie C. Mendoza)*
  Dong Sung Steel Industries Co., Ltd. *(Donald B. Cameron, Jr., Julie C. Mendoza)*
  Electronic Industries Ass'n of Japan *(William N. Walker)*
  Erie Lackawanna Railway Co.
  Federal Express Corp. *(Richard H. Abbey)*
  Federation of European Bearing Manufacturers Ass'ns *(N. David Palmeter)*
  Flachglas A.G. *(David P. Houlihan)*
  Footwear Distributors and Retailers of America *(Michael P. Daniels)*
  Futaba Corp. *(Donald B. Cameron, Jr., David P. Houlihan)*
  Grip-Rite, Ltd. *(N. David Palmeter)*
  Hong Kong Trade, Industry and Customs Department *(Michael P. Daniels, Martin J. Lewin)*
  Israel, Government of
  Japan Aluminum Federation *(William N. Walker)*
  Japan Lumber Importers Ass'n *(Julia Christine Bliss, David P. Houlihan)*
  Korea Consumer Goods Exporters Ass'n *(Donald B. Cameron, Jr.)*
  Korea Foundry Forging Cooperative Ass'n *(Donald B. Cameron, Jr.)*
  Korea Iron and Steel Ass'n *(Donald B. Cameron, Jr., Julie C. Mendoza)*
  Korea Iron and Steel Works, Ltd. *(N. David Palmeter)*
  Korea Leather and Fur Exporters Ass'n *(N. David Palmeter)*
  Korea Metal Flatware Exporters Ass'n *(N. David Palmeter)*
  Korea Metal Industry Cooperative *(N. David Palmeter)*
  Mercedes-Benz of North America, Inc. *(David A. Vaughan)*
  Mexinox, S.A. de C.V. *(Donald B. Cameron, Jr., Julie C. Mendoza)*
  Miwon Trading and Shipping Co., Ltd. *(N. David Palmeter)*
  Nippon Synthetic Chemical Industry Co. *(N. David Palmeter)*
  Norseland Foods *(N. David Palmeter)*
  Norske Fiskeoppdretternes Salgslag (FO) *(Jeffrey S. Neeley, N. David Palmeter)*
  Norwegian Dairies Ass'n *(N. David Palmeter)*
  Occidental Coating Co. *(N. David Palmeter)*
  Philipp Brothers, Inc. *(Jeffrey S. Neeley)*
  Ponds India *(Julia Christine Bliss)*
  PROEXPO/INCOMEX *(Julia Christine Bliss, Michael P. Daniels)*
  Propulsora Siderurgica S.A.I.C. *(David P. Houlihan, Julie C. Mendoza)*
  Radix Group Internat'l Inc. *(Richard H. Abbey)*
  Rainbow Navigations, Inc. *(Richard H. Abbey)*
  Roanoke Companies, The *(Richard H. Abbey)*
  Sidermex Internat'l, Inc. *(N. David Palmeter)*
  Siderurgica Lazaro Cardenas, S.A. *(N. David Palmeter)*
  Societe Financiere d'Entreposage et de Commerce International de l'Alcool *(Richard H. Abbey)*
  Sovcomflot *(Julia Christine Bliss, David P. Houlihan)*
  TENAX Corp. *(David P. Houlihan, Jeffrey S. Neeley)*
  Toshiba America, Inc. *(Jeffrey S. Neeley, N. David Palmeter)*
  Toshiba Corp. *(Richard H. Abbey, Julia Christine Bliss, David P. Houlihan, Jeffrey S. Neeley, David A. Vaughan)*
  United States Ass'n of Importers of Textile and Apparel(USITA) *(Martin J. Lewin)*
  Western Union Corp. *(David A. Vaughan)*

MUDRYK, Laura M.
Legislative Ass't, Government Affairs, Sterling Drug Inc.
1776 Eye St., N.W. Suite 1060, Washington, DC 20006
Telephone: (202) 857-3450

MUELLER, Athena
General Counsel, Action on Smoking and Health
2013 H St. N.W., Washington, DC 20006
Telephone: (202) 659-4310

MUELLER, Gregory R.
Keene, Shirley & Associates, Inc.
919 Prince St., Alexandria, VA 22314
Telephone: (703) 684-0550
Registered as lobbyist at U.S. Congress.
Registered as Foreign Agent: (#3997).
Clients:
  Conservative Victory Committee

MUELLER, Richard
Dep Asst Secy, Legis Affrs, DEPARTMENT OF STATE
2201 C St., N.W., Washington, DC 20520
Telephone: (202) 647-4204

MUELLER, Ronald R.
Washington Director, Ketchum Public Relations
1201 Connecticut Ave., N.W. Suite 300, Washington, DC 20036
Telephone: (202) 835-8800
Clients:
  Road Information Program, The (TRIP)

MUHA, Denise
Staff Director, Nat'l Leased Housing Ass'n
2300 M St., N.W., Suite 260, Washington, DC 20037
Telephone: (202) 785-8888

MULDOON, Charles P.
Brownrigg and Muldoon
1730 M St., N.W. Suite 805, Washington, DC 20036
Telephone: (202) 466-8666
Background: Assistant General Counsel, U.S. Economic
Cooperation Administration, 1947-49. Assistant to the Financial Consultant to the Secretary of State, 1950.
Clients:
Yusen Air and Sea Service (USA) Inc.

MULDOON, James
Director, Metropolitan Education and Training Corp.
2000 P St., N.W., Suite 505, Washington, DC 20036
Telephone: (202) 833-9624

MULHERN, Dr. Frank
Consultant, Scientific and Gov't Affairs, Nat'l Pork Producers Council
501 School St., N.W. Suite 400, Washington, DC 20024
Telephone: (202) 552-3600
Background: Director, Animal Disease Eradication, 1962-67, Deputy of Regulatory Programs, 1967-70, Administrator of APHIS, 1972- 80; United States Dept. of Agriculture.

MULHERN, James
Director of Legislation, Nat'l Milk Producers Federation
1840 Wilson Blvd., Arlington, VA 22201
Telephone: (703) 243-6111
Registered as lobbyist at U.S. Congress.

MULICK, Christine Ann
V. President, Kogovsek & Associates, Inc.
1455 Pennsylvania Ave., N.W., Suite 950, Washington, DC 20004
Telephone: (202) 639-8899
Registered as lobbyist at U.S. Congress.
Background: Former aide to former Rep. Ray Kogovsek (D-CO), 1979-84.

MULL, Lynda D.
Exec. Director, Ass'n of Farmworker Opportunity Programs
408 7th St., S.E., Washington, DC 20003
Telephone: (202) 543-3443

MULLAN, Rita
Exec. Director, Irish Nat'l Caucus
413 E. Capitol St., S.E., Washington, DC 20003
Telephone: (202) 544-0568

MULLANEY, L. Daniel
Dorsey & Whitney
1330 Connecticut Ave., N.W., Suite 200, Washington, DC 20036
Telephone: (202) 857-0700

MULLEN, Michael J.
Of Counsel, Crowell and Moring
1001 Pennsylvania Ave., N.W., Washington, DC 20004-2505
Telephone: (202) 624-2500
Registered as lobbyist at U.S. Congress.
Background: Deputy Counsel, Subcommittee on Judicial Improvements, Senate Committee on the Judiciary, 1971-74. Staff Counsel to Sen. Philip A. Hart (D-MI), 1975-76. Counsel, Consumer Subcommittee, Senate Committee on Commerce, Science and Transportation, 1977-83.
Clients:
Nat'l Ass'n of Wholesaler-Distributors

MULLENHOLZ, John J.
Neill, Mullenholz and Shaw
815 Connecticut Ave., N.W. Suite 800, Washington, DC 20006
Telephone: (202) 463-8400
Registered as lobbyist at U.S. Congress.
Registered as Foreign Agent: (#3320).
Background: Trial Attorney, General Litigation Section, Tax Division, U.S. Department of Justice, 1968-73. See also Neill and Co.
Clients:
Florida East Coast Railway Co.

Nat'l Farm and Power Equipment Dealers Ass'n
Soo Line Railroad, Inc.

MULLER, Richard J.
Public Affairs Consultant, Chrysler Corp.
1100 Connecticut Ave., N.W., Washington, DC 20036
Telephone: (202) 862-5407

MULLETT, John A.
Director, Legislative Affairs, FMC Corp.
1627 K St., N.W., Suite 500, Washington, DC 20006
Telephone: (202) 956-5200
Registered as lobbyist at U.S. Congress.

MULLIGAN, Robert
Senior Washington Representative, Blue Cross and Blue Shield Ass'n
655 15th St., N.W., Suite 350, Washington, DC 20005
Telephone: (202) 626-4780
Registered as lobbyist at U.S. Congress.

MULLIKEN, Charles W.
Exec. Director, Typographers Internat'l Ass'n
2262 Hall Place, N.W. Suite 101, Washington, DC 20007
Telephone: (202) 965-3400

MULLIN, RHYNE, EMMONS AND TOPEL, P.C.
1000 Connecticut Ave., N.W., Suite 500, Washington, DC 20036
Telephone: (202) 659-4700
Clients:
Fidelity Television, Inc.
KADN-TV
KXLN-TV
WDBB
WVII-TV

MULLIN, Tracy
Exec. V. President, Governmental Affair, Nat'l Retail Merchants Ass'n
1000 Connecticut Ave., N.W., Washington, DC 20036
Telephone: (202) 223-8250
Registered as lobbyist at U.S. Congress.
Background: Also represents the Nat'l Retail Merchants Ass'n Political Action Committee.

MULLIN, William F.
V. President, Metropolitan Insurance Cos.
1615 L St., N.W., Suite 1210, Washington, DC 20036
Telephone: (202) 659-3575
Registered as lobbyist at U.S. Congress.

MULLINS, Edgar
Director, Gov't Relations (Sikorsky Div), United Technologies Corp.
1825 Eye St., N.W. Suite 700, Washington, DC 20006
Telephone: (202) 785-7400

MULLINS, Janet G.
Asst Secy, Legis Affrs, DEPARTMENT OF STATE
2201 C St., N.W., Washington, DC 20520
Telephone: (202) 647-4204

MULLINS, Joseph F., Jr.
Denning and Wohlstetter
1700 K St., N.W., Washington, DC 20006
Telephone: (202) 833-8884
Clients:
Compagnie d'Affretement et de Transport USA
Gulf Atlantic Transport Corp.
Marine Transport Overseas Services
United Kingdom Express
West India Line

MULLINS, Mary A.
Director, Government Relations, Capital Legislative Services
1440 New York Ave., N.W. Suite 320, Washington, DC 20005
Telephone: (202) 628-4229

MULLINS, Morton L.
Director, Regulatory Affairs, Monsanto Co.
700 14th St., N.W., Suite 1100, Washington, DC 20005
Telephone: (202) 783-2460

MULLINS, W. H. L.
Corp. V. President, Government Relations, General Dynamics Corp.
1745 Jefferson Davis Hwy, Suite 1000, Arlington, VA 22202
Telephone: (703) 553-1290
Registered as lobbyist at U.S. Congress.
Background: Also serves as Chairman, General Dynamics Voluntary Political Contribution Plan.

MULTINATIONAL BUSINESS SERVICES, INC.
11 Dupont Circle, N.W. Suite 700, Washington, DC 20003
Telephone: (202) 293-5886
Background: A consulting firm which represents clients before Federal regulatory agencies.
Members of firm representing listed organizations:
Tozzi, James J., Director
Background: Former Dep. Administrator, Office of Management and Budget
Clients:
General Motors Corp. *(James J. Tozzi)*
Goodyear Tire and Rubber Co. *(James J. Tozzi)*

MULTISTATE ASSOCIATES
515 King St., Suite 310, Alexandria, VA 22314
Telephone: (703) 684-1110
Background: Through a 50-state network of over 1,500 professional lobbyists, provides customized state and local government relations services to corporations and associations to meet their information and lobbying needs on legislative and regulatory matters.
Members of firm representing listed organizations:
Hallman, Paul W.
McNelis, Marcie, V. President

MULVANEY, Susan
Info Officer, Cong Liaison Div, ENVIRONMENTAL PROTECTION AGENCY
401 M St., S.W., Washington, DC 20460
Telephone: (202) 382-5200

MUMMA, Richard D., Jr.
Exec. Director, American Ass'n of Dental Schools
1625 Massachusetts Ave., N.W., Washington, DC 20036
Telephone: (202) 667-9433

MUNDELL, George H.
Exec. Director, Film, Air and Package Carriers Conference
2200 Mill Road, Alexandria, VA 22314
Telephone: (703) 838-1887

MUNIS, Betty J.
Staff Assistant, Public Lands Council
1301 Pennsylvania Ave., N.W. Suite 300, Washington, DC 20004
Telephone: (202) 347-5355
Registered as lobbyist at U.S. Congress.

MUNLEY, Evelyn Fieman
Health Policy Analyst, American Ass'n of Homes for the Aging
1129 20th St., N.W., Suite 400, Washington, DC 20036
Telephone: (202) 296-5960
Registered as lobbyist at U.S. Congress.

MUNOZ, Cecelia
Senior Immigration Policy Analyst, Nat'l Council of La Raza
810 1st St., N.E., Suite 300, Washington, DC 20002
Telephone: (202) 289-1380

MUNOZ, Patricia
Director, Donor & Foundation Relations, American Rivers
801 Pennsylvania Ave., S.E. Suite 303, Washington, DC 20003-2155
Telephone: (202) 547-6900

MUNSON, Barbara L.
V. Pres./Manager, Congressional Affairs, Consumer Bankers Ass'n
1000 Wilson Blvd., 30th Floor, Arlington, VA 22209-3908
Telephone: (703) 276-1750
Registered as lobbyist at U.S. Congress.
Background: Former Legislative Assistant to Rep. Stan Lundine (D-NY).

MUNSON, Dick
Exec. Director, Northeast-Midwest Institute
218 D St., S.E., Washington, DC 20003
Telephone: (202) 544-5200

MURCH, Roger A.
Newell-Payne Companies, Inc.
2011 Eye St., N.W., 5th Floor, Washington, DC 20006
Telephone: (202) 223-3217
Background: Serves as Exec. V. President for American
Car Rental Ass'n, Nat'l Beverage Dispensing Equipment
Ass'n, Nat'l Truck Renting and Leasing Ass'n and Nat'l
Corrugated Steel Pipe Ass'n.

MURCHISON, David C.
Howrey and Simon
1730 Pennsylvania Ave., N.W., Washington, DC 20006-
4793
Telephone: (202) 783-0800
Background: Legal Assistant to Under Secretary of the
Army 1949-51; Associate General Counsel, Small De-
fense Plants Administration 1952-53. Federal Trade Com-
mission 1953-55. U.S. Delegation to UNESCO 1955.
Clients:
Caterpillar Inc.
Wallcovering Manufacturers Ass'n

MURDOCK, III J. E.
Partner, Baker, Worthington, Crossley, Stansberry &
Woolf
1001 Pennsylvania Ave., N.W, Suite 1201, Washington,
DC 20004
Telephone: (202) 347-4360
Background: FAA Chief Counsel, 1981-85. Acting FAA
Deputy Administrator, 1984.
Clients:
Austrian Airlines
Bechtel Aviation Services
Ebasco Services, Inc.
Guiness Peat Aviation
Nat'l Business Aircraft Ass'n
Nolisair (NationAir Canada)
Ryder System, Inc.

MURDOCK, Patricia C.
Legislative Affairs Specialist, American Federation of
State, County and Municipal Employees
1625 L St., N.W., Washington, DC 20036
Telephone: (202) 429-1000
Registered as lobbyist at U.S. Congress.

MUROYAMA & ASSOC., Paul
1511 K St., N.W., Suite 732, Washington, DC 20005
Telephone: (202) 393-3308
Background: Specializes in U.S.-Japan political and busi-
ness consultation.
Members of firm representing listed organizations:
Muroyama, Paul, President & CEO
Organizations represented:
NTT America *(Paul Muroyama)*

MUROYAMA, Paul
President & CEO, Muroyama & Assoc., Paul
1511 K St., N.W., Suite 732, Washington, DC 20005
Telephone: (202) 393-3308
Organizations represented:
NTT America

MURPHINE GROUP, The
1010 Wisconsin Ave., N.W. Suite 215, Washington, DC
20007
Telephone: (202) 298-7272
Background: A political consultant firm.
Members of firm representing listed organizations:
Murphine, Ralph D.

MURPHINE, Ralph D.
Murphine Group, The
1010 Wisconsin Ave., N.W. Suite 215, Washington, DC
20007
Telephone: (202) 298-7272

MURPHY, Andrew P., Jr.
Of Counsel, Coan & Lyons
1625 Eye St., N.W., Suite 1015, Washington, DC 20006
Telephone: (202) 728-1070

MURPHY, Anne G.
Exec. Director, American Arts Alliance
1319 F St., N.W., Suite 307, Washington, DC 20004-1182
Telephone: (202) 737-1727
Registered as lobbyist at U.S. Congress.

MURPHY AND ASSOCIATES
1250 24th St., N.W., Suite 600, Washington, DC 20037
Telephone: (202) 466-0550
Members of firm representing listed organizations:
Murphy, William T. (Jr.), President
Background: Served with Department of State, 1963-
64, and on the staff of the House of Representatives
Administration Committee, 1975.
Clients:
American Cement Alliance *(William T. Murphy, Jr.)*
Amoco Corp. *(William T. Murphy, Jr.)*
ARCO *(William T. Murphy, Jr.)*
Coalition for Environmental-Energy Balance *(Wil-
liam T. Murphy, Jr.)*
Darome, Inc. *(William T. Murphy, Jr.)*
Natural Gas Supply Ass'n *(William T. Murphy, Jr.)*
O'Connor and Associates *(William T. Murphy, Jr.)*
Options Policy Ass'n, The *(William T. Murphy, Jr.)*

MURPHY, Chris
Project Manager, Bonner & Associates
1625 K St., N.W., Suite 300, Washington, DC 20006
Telephone: (202) 463-8880
Background: Legislative Assistant to Rep. James Scheuer
(D-NY), 1985-85.

MURPHY, Admiral Daniel J., USN (Ret.)
Chairman, Murphy and Demory, Ltd.
2300 N St., N.W. Suite 725, Washington, DC 20037
Telephone: (202) 785-3323

MURPHY AND DEMORY, LTD.
2300 N St., N.W. Suite 725, Washington, DC 20037
Telephone: (202) 785-3323
Registered as Foreign Agent: (#4095)
Members of firm representing listed organizations:
Bester, Margot F.
Cox, Jerry W.
Background: Former Legislative Counsel to Senator
John Danforth (R-MO).
Demory, Willard L., President
Goodfader, Alan
Grieco, Jeffrey J.
Murphy, (Admiral) Daniel J. (USN (Ret.)),
Chairman
Clients:
Anglo-American Auto Auctions Inc. *(Jerry W. Cox)*
California Energy Co. (Admiral Daniel J. Mur-
phy, USN *(Ret.), Willard L. Demory, Jeffrey J. Grieco)*
Haiti, Government of (Admiral Daniel J. Mur-
phy, USN *(Ret.), Jeffrey J. Grieco)*
Korea Tacoma Marine Industries Inc. (Admiral
Daniel J. Murphy, USN *(Ret.), Jeffrey J. Grieco)*
PACO Enterprises (Admiral Daniel J. Murphy,
USN *(Ret.))*
PCI, Inc. (Admiral Daniel J. Murphy, USN *(Ret.))*
Samsung Electronics Co., Ltd.
TRIDEC/Westinghouse (Admiral Daniel J. Mur-
phy, USN *(Ret.))*
United States Telephone Ass'n *(Margot F. Bester, Wil-
lard L. Demory)*

MURPHY, Edward
Legis and Regul Office, General Counsel, DEPARTMENT
OF HOUSING AND URBAN DEVELOPMENT
451 Seventh St., S.W., Washington, DC 20410
Telephone: (202) 755-7093

MURPHY, Edward L.
Legislative Counsel, Nat'l Ass'n of Government Em-
ployees
1313 L St., N.W., 2nd Floor, Washington, DC 20005
Telephone: (202) 371-6644
Registered as lobbyist at U.S. Congress.
Background: Also represents the Internat'l Brotherhood of
Police Officers.

MURPHY, Elizabeth A.
Manager, State Government Affairs, Roadway Express,
Inc.
1901 North Ft. Myer Drive, Suite 204, Arlington, VA 22209
Telephone: (703) 528-0233
Registered as lobbyist at U.S. Congress.

MURPHY, Gerald E.
Exec. Director, Nat'l Licensed Beverage Ass'n
4214 King St. West, Alexandria, VA 22302
Telephone: (703) 671-7575
Background: Also represents the Nat'l Licensed Beverage
Ass'n Beverage Alcohol Retailer PAC.

MURPHY, Gerard P., MD
Senior V. President, Medical Affairs, American Cancer
Soc. (Public Affairs Office)
316 Pennsylvania Ave., S.E. Suite 200, Washington, DC
20003
Telephone: (202) 546-4011

MURPHY, James J.
Bryan, Cave, McPheeters and McRoberts
1015 15th St., N.W., Suite 1000, Washington, DC 20005
Telephone: (202) 289-6100
Background: Trial Attorney, Civil Rights Division, Depart-
ment of Justice, 1965-68. Counsel, U.S. Senate Subcom-
mittee, 1969-76.
Clients:
American Pediatric Soc.
Laclede Gas Co.

MURPHY, James J.
Exec. V. President, American Academy of Actuaries
1720 Eye St., N.W., 7th Floor, Washington, DC 20006
Telephone: (202) 223-8196
Registered as lobbyist at U.S. Congress.

MURPHY, Dr. James P.
Exec. Director, Nat'l Ass'n of Accredited Cosmetology
Schools
5201 Leesburg Pike, Suite 205, Falls Church, VA 22041
Telephone: (703) 845-1333
Background: Serves also as Treasurer of the Nat'l Ass'n of
Accredited Cosmetology Schools Political Action Com-
mittee.

MURPHY, Jeanne Marie
V. President, Congressional Affairs, Credit Union Nat'l
Ass'n
805 15th St., N.W. Suite 300, Washington, DC 20005
Telephone: (202) 682-4200
Registered as lobbyist at U.S. Congress.

MURPHY, Jeremiah L.
V. Pres., Public Policy & Gov't Affairs, Siemens Capital
Corp.
1455 Pennsylvania Ave., N.W. Suite 300, Washington, DC
20004
Telephone: (202) 347-0444

MURPHY, John C.
Smith, Bucklin and Associates
1101 Connecticut Ave., N.W., Suite 700, Washington, DC
20036
Telephone: (202) 857-1100
Background: Serves as Exec. Director, Ass'n of Local
Housing Finance Agencies and Privatization Council.
Clients:
Ass'n of Local Housing Finance Agencies
Privatization Council

MURPHY, Ken
Exec. Director, Environmental and Energy Study Institute
122 C St., N.W., Suite 700, Washington, DC 20001
Telephone: (202) 628-1400

MURPHY, Lynda M.
Barrett, Montgomery & Murphy
1055 Thomas Jefferson St., N.W., Suite 501, Washington,
DC 20007
Telephone: (202) 293-3306
Background: Director, Office of State Agencies and Bond
Financed Programs, 1980-82; Attorney Advisor to Assist-
ant Secretary for Housing, FHA Commissioner, Depart-
ment of Housing and Urban Development, 1979-80.

MURPHY, Lynne
Director, Communication, Nature Conservancy, The
1815 N. Lynn St, Arlington, VA 22209
Telephone: (703) 841-5300

MURPHY AND MALONE
1901 L St., N.W., Suite 200, Washington, DC 20036-3506
Telephone: (202) 223-5062

Members of firm representing listed organizations:
Malone, William R.
Murphy, Terence R.
Clients:
British Telecom plc *(Terence R. Murphy)*
Micronesian Telecommunications Corp. *(William R. Malone)*

MURPHY, Maureen
Market Opinion Research, Inc.
1400 L St., N.W., Suite 650, Washington, DC 20005
Telephone: (202) 289-0420

MURPHY, Michael M.
V. President, Government Affairs, American President Companies
1101 17th St., N.W. Suite 400, Washington, DC 20036
Telephone: (202) 331-1424
Registered as lobbyist at U.S. Congress.

MURPHY, Patrick
Director, Government Relations, Bonner & Associates
1625 K St., N.W., Suite 300, Washington, DC 20006
Telephone: (202) 463-8880
Background: State Assemblyman, Nevada State Legislature, 1975-79. Intergovernmental Liaison, U.S. Department of Housing and Urban Development, 1980-81. Manager, Government Affairs, Federal Home Loan Mortgage Corp., 1988-89.

MURPHY, Patrick M.
President, State & Local Resources
901 Sixth St., S.W., Suite 503A, Washington, DC 20024
Telephone: (202) 488-1460
Background: Democractic Nat'l Committee, 1974-80. U.S. Dept. of Housing and Urban Development, 1980-81. Former Director, State and Local Government Relations, U.S. Synthetic Fuels Corp.
Clients:
G. W. Electronics
Mid-American Network
Nat'l Academy of Engineering
Nevada Development Authority
Nevada, State of
T. M. Community College

MURPHY, Peter
Cassidy and Associates, Inc.
655 15th St., N.W., Suite 1100, Washington, DC 20005
Telephone: (202) 347-0773
Background: Formerly in the Office of the U.S. Trade Representative.

MURPHY, Richard J.
Dir., Legis. Affrs. - Public Sector Syst, Unisys Corp.
2001 L St., N.W., Suite 1000, Washington, DC 20036
Telephone: (202) 293-7720

MURPHY, Richard W.
Nat'l Coordinator, Combined Fed Campaign, Internat'l Service Agencies
6000 Executive Blvd, Suite 608, Rockville, MD 20852
Telephone: (301) 881-2468

MURPHY, Robin
V. President, Porter/Novelli
1001 30th St., N.W., Washington, DC 20007
Telephone: (202) 342-7000

MURPHY, Stephen P.
Sr. V. President and Secretary, Yellow Freight System
908 King St., Suite 300, Alexandria, VA 22314
Telephone: (703) 836-9406
Registered as lobbyist at U.S. Congress.

MURPHY, Steve
Fenn & King Communications
1043 Cecil Place, N.W., Washington, DC 20007
Telephone: (202) 337-6995

MURPHY, Terence R.
Murphy and Malone
1901 L St., N.W., Suite 200, Washington, DC 20036-3506
Telephone: (202) 223-5062
Clients:
British Telecom plc

MURPHY, William T., Jr.
President, Murphy and Associates
1250 24th St., N.W., Suite 600, Washington, DC 20037
Telephone: (202) 466-0550
Background: Served with Department of State, 1963-64, and on the staff of the House of Representatives Administration Committee, 1975.
Clients:
American Cement Alliance
Amoco Corp.
ARCO
Coalition for Environmental-Energy Balance
Darome, Inc.
Natural Gas Supply Ass'n
O'Connor and Associates
Options Policy Ass'n, The

MURR, James C.
Asst Dir, Legis Reference, EXECUTIVE OFFICE OF THE PRESIDENT - Office of Management and Budget
Old Executive Office Bldg., Washington, DC 20500
Telephone: (202) 395-4790

MURRAY, D. Michael
Murray, Scheer & Montgomery
2715 M St., N.W., Suite 300, Washington, DC 20037
Telephone: (202) 333-8830
Registered as lobbyist at U.S. Congress.
Registered as Foreign Agent: (#2927).
Clients:
Bear, Stearns and Co.
Cleveland-Cliffs Iron Co.
Connecticut Mutual Life Insurance Co.
Home Life Insurance Co.
Industry Council for Tangible Assets
Iron Ore Lessors Ass'n, Inc.
Nat'l Council of Coal Lessors, Inc.
New England, The
Pacific Mutual Life Insurance Co.
Penn Mutual Life Insurance Co.
Provident Mutual Life Insurance
Shubert Organization Inc.
Swaziland Sugar Ass'n

MURRAY, Daniel H.
Director, Congressional Affairs, BellSouth Corp.
1133 21st St., N.W., Suite 900, Washington, DC 20036
Telephone: (202) 463-4100
Registered as lobbyist at U.S. Congress.

MURRAY, Donald
Legis. Rep., Justice/Public Safety, Nat'l Ass'n of Counties
440 First St., N.W., Washington, DC 20001
Telephone: (202) 393-6226
Background: Serves as contact for the Nat'l Ass'n of County Civil Attorneys.

MURRAY, Isobel
Legislative Counsel, Nat'l Food Brokers Ass'n
1010 Massachusetts Ave., N.W., Washington, DC 20001
Telephone: (202) 789-2844
Registered as lobbyist at U.S. Congress.

MURRAY, James E.
Brown & Wood
815 Connecticut Ave., N.W. Suite 701, Washington, DC 20006
Telephone: (202) 223-0220
Registered as lobbyist at U.S. Congress.
Background: Senior V. President and General Counsel, Federal National Mortgage Association, 1971-81. President, Federal National Mortgage Association, 1981-83.
Clients:
Nat'l Ass'n of Small Business Investment Companies

MURRAY, Jim
Regional Manager, Smith Industries
1225 Jefferson Davis Hwy., Suite 402, Arlington, VA 22202
Telephone: (703) 920-7640

MURRAY, John F.
Exec. Director, Formaldehyde Institute
1330 Connecticut Ave., N.W. Suite 300, Washington, DC 20036
Telephone: (202) 659-0060
Background: Also serves as Director, Project Management Dept., Synthetic Organic Chemical Manufacturers Ass'n.

MURRAY, Margaret R.
Government Relations Consultant, McLeod & Pires
2501 M St., N.W., Suite 400, Washington, DC 20037
Telephone: (202) 861-1234
Registered as lobbyist at U.S. Congress.
Clients:
American Ass'n of Crop Insurers

MURRAY, Peggy Roth
V. President, Communications, American Business Conference
1730 K St., N.W. Suite 1200, Washington, DC 20006
Telephone: (202) 822-9300
Registered as lobbyist at U.S. Congress.

MURRAY, Samuel H.
Tax Counsel, Nat'l Forest Products Ass'n
1250 Connecticut Ave., N.W. Suite 200, Washington, DC 20036
Telephone: (202) 463-2700
Background: Serves also as V. President, Government Affairs, Profit- Sharing Council of America.

MURRAY, SCHEER & MONTGOMERY
2715 M St., N.W., Suite 300, Washington, DC 20037
Telephone: (202) 333-8830
Background: A government relations/public affairs consulting firm.
Members of firm representing listed organizations:
Murray, D. Michael
Prager, Rollinde
Clients:
Bear, Stearns and Co. *(D. Michael Murray)*
Cleveland-Cliffs Iron Co. *(D. Michael Murray)*
Connecticut Mutual Life Insurance Co. *(D. Michael Murray)*
Home Life Insurance Co. *(D. Michael Murray)*
Industry Council for Tangible Assets *(D. Michael Murray)*
Iron Ore Lessors Ass'n, Inc. *(D. Michael Murray)*
Nat'l Council of Coal Lessors, Inc. *(D. Michael Murray)*
Nat'l Federation of Coffee Growers of Colombia *(Rollinde Prager)*
New England, The *(D. Michael Murray)*
Pacific Mutual Life Insurance Co. *(D. Michael Murray)*
Penn Mutual Life Insurance Co. *(D. Michael Murray)*
Provident Mutual Life Insurance *(D. Michael Murray)*
Shubert Organization Inc. *(D. Michael Murray)*
Swaziland Sugar Ass'n *(D. Michael Murray)*

MURRAY, William R.
Natural Resources Counsel, American Forest Resource Alliance
1250 Connecticut Ave., N.W. Suite 200, Washington, DC 20036
Telephone: (202) 463-2747
Background: Former Assistant Solicitor, Onshore Minerals, Department of the Interior.

MURRELL, Wanda
Admin Officer, Legis & Cong Rels, DEPARTMENT OF HOUSING AND URBAN DEVELOPMENT
451 Seventh St., S.W., Washington, DC 20410
Telephone: (202) 755-7380

MURRY, Harold D., Jr.
Clifford & Warnke
815 Connecticut Ave., N.W., Washington, DC 20006
Telephone: (202) 828-4200
Background: Attorney, U.S. Department of Justice, 1971-74. Special Assistant U.S. Attorney, 1972.

MUSHER, Steven A.
Cole, Corette & Abrutyn
1110 Vermont Ave., N.W., Suite 900, Washington, DC 20005
Telephone: (202) 872-1414
Registered as Foreign Agent: (#2968).
Background: An international taxation specialist.
Clients:
Netherlands Antilles, Government of

MUSIC, Kimberley A.
Legislative Assistant, BP America Inc.
1776 Eye St., N.W., Suite 1000, Washington, DC 20006
Telephone: (202) 785-4888

MUSICA, Frank
Staff Director, Professional Engineers in Private Practice
1420 King St., Alexandria, VA 22314
Telephone: (703) 684-2862

MUSIL, Robert
Exec. Director, Professionals' Coalition for Nuclear Arms Control
1616 P St., N.W., Suite 320, Washington, DC 20036
Telephone: (202) 332-4823
Registered as lobbyist at U.S. Congress.

MUSKIE, Edmund S.
Chadbourne and Parke
1101 Vermont Ave., N.W. Suite 900, Washington, DC 20005
Telephone: (202) 289-3000
Registered as lobbyist at U.S. Congress.
Registered as Foreign Agent: (#3490).
Background: Former U.S. Senator (D-ME), 1959-80 and Secretary of State, 1980-81.

MUTH, Jean
Regulatory Affairs, ConAgra, Inc.
888 17th St., N.W., Suite 300, Washington, DC 20006
Telephone: (202) 223-5115

MUTH, Roy W.
President and Chief Exec. Officer, Internat'l Snowmobile Industry Ass'n
3975 University Drive Suite 310, Fairfax, VA 22030
Telephone: (703) 273-9606

MYER, Paul J.
V. President, Government Relations, Northern Telecom Inc..
600 Maryland Ave., S.W. Suite 607, Washington, DC 20024
Telephone: (202) 554-1520
Registered as lobbyist at U.S. Congress.

MYERS, Bradley
Legislative Ass't, Staley Manufacturing Co., A. E. Decatur, IL
Background: Responsibilities include the Staley PAC.

MYERS, Charles
President, Leather Industries of America
1000 Thomas Jefferson St. N.W., Suite 515, Washington, DC 20007
Telephone: (202) 342-8086

MYERS, Gary D.
President, Fertilizer Institute
501 Second St., N.E., Washington, DC 20002
Telephone: (202) 675-8250
Registered as lobbyist at U.S. Congress.

MYERS, Karen Magee
Government Affairs Representative, Electronic Data Systems Corp.
1331 Pennsylvania Ave., N.W., Suite 1300 North, Washington, DC 20004
Telephone: (202) 637-6700
Registered as lobbyist at U.S. Congress.

MYERS, Matthew L.
Asbill, Junkin, Myers & Buffone
1615 New Hampshire Ave., N.W., Washington, DC 20009
Telephone: (202) 234-9000
Registered as lobbyist at U.S. Congress.
Background: Serves as Staff Director, Coalition on Smoking or Health.
Clients:
Coalition on Smoking or Health

MYERS, Robert H.
Thompson and Mitchell
1120 Vermont Ave., N.W. Suite 1000, Washington, DC 20005
Telephone: (202) 857-0350

MYERS, Dr. Samuel L.
President, Nat'l Ass'n for Equal Opportunity in Higher Education
400 12th St., N.E. 2nd Floor, Washington, DC 20002
Telephone: (202) 543-9111

MYERS, Susan L.
Executive Secretary, Mineralogical Soc. of America
1625 Eye St., N.W., Suite 414, Washington, DC 20006
Telephone: (202) 775-4344

MYERS, William C.
Director, Free Congress Center for State Policy
721 2nd St., N.E., Washington, DC 20002
Telephone: (202) 546-3004
Background: Staff at U.S. Senate Republican Policy Committee, 1978-79.

MYERSON, Priscilla N.
Associate Director, Government Marketing, Grace and Co., W. R.
919 18th St., N.W., Suite 400, Washington, DC 20006
Telephone: (202) 452-6700

MYHRE, William N.
Preston Gates Ellis & Rouvelas Meeds
1735 New York Ave., N.W., Suite 500, Washington, DC 20006-4759
Telephone: (202) 628-1700
Registered as lobbyist at U.S. Congress.
Registered as Foreign Agent: (#3567).
Clients:
Arctic Sounder Enterprises, Inc.
Aurora Fisheries, Inc.
Bellingham Cold Storage
Coastal Transportation, Inc.
Golden Alaska Seafoods, Inc.
Marine Management, Inc.
Nelbro Packing Co.
Northwest Marine Terminal Ass'n
SeaHarvest, Inc.
Sunmar Shipping, Inc.
United States Cruises, Inc.

MYRICK, Christopher A.
Nat'l AgriChemical Retailers Ass'n
Box 65493, Washington, DC 20035-5493
Telephone: (202) 467-0825
Registered as lobbyist at U.S. Congress.
Background: Former Legislative Assistant to Rep. Hank Brown (R-CO).

NADASH, Daniel
Polit. Director, Political Field Optns., Nat'l Ass'n of REALTORS
777 14th St., N.W., Washington, DC 20005
Telephone: (202) 383-1000
Registered as lobbyist at U.S. Congress.
Background: Former aide to Rep. Tom McMillan (D-MD).

NADEL, Steve
Senior Associate, American Council for an Energy-Efficient Economy
1001 Connecticut Ave., N.W., Suite 535, Washington, DC 20036
Telephone: (202) 429-8873

NADER, Ralph
Managing Trustee, Center for Study of Responsive Law
Box 19367, Washington, DC 20036
Telephone: (202) 387-8030
Background: Also a contact for Public Citizen and the Telecommunications Research and Action Center.

NADLER, Carl
Jenner and Block
21 Dupont Circle, N.W., Washington, DC 20036
Telephone: (202) 223-4400

NAEGELE AND ASSOC., Timothy D.
1250 24th St., N.W., Suite 600, Washington, DC 20037
Telephone: (202) 466-7500
Background: A law firm.
Members of firm representing listed organizations:
Naegele, Timothy D.
Background: Assistant Counsel, U.S. Senate Committee on Banking, Housing and Urban Affairs, 1969-71; Administrative Assistant to Senator Edward W. Brooke, 1971-72.
Organizations represented:
Home Federal Savings and Loan Ass'n *(Timothy D. Naegele)*

NAEGELE, Timothy D.
Naegele and Assoc., Timothy D.
1250 24th St., N.W., Suite 600, Washington, DC 20037
Telephone: (202) 466-7500
Registered as lobbyist at U.S. Congress.
Background: Assistant Counsel, U.S. Senate Committee on Banking, Housing and Urban Affairs, 1969-71; Administrative Assistant to Senator Edward W. Brooke, 1971-72.
Organizations represented:
Home Federal Savings and Loan Ass'n

NAEVE, Mike
Skadden, Arps, Slate, Meagher and Flom
1440 New York Ave., N.W., Washington, DC 20005
Telephone: (202) 371-7000
Registered as lobbyist at U.S. Congress.
Background: Legislative Director for Senator Lloyd Bentsen (D-TX), 1978-80. Commissioner, Federal Energy Regulatory Commission, 1985-88.
Clients:
Amoco Corp.
Anadarko Petroleum Corp.
ATMOS Energy Corp.
Enron Corp.
Mesa Limited Partnership
Natural Gas Alliance for Generative Electricity
Natural Gas Supply Ass'n
Oryx Energy Co.
Public Service Co. of Indiana
Sonat Inc.

NAFTALIN, Alan Y.
Koteen and Naftalin
1150 Connecticut Ave., N.W. Suite 1000, Washington, DC 20036
Telephone: (202) 467-5700
Registered as lobbyist at U.S. Congress.
Background: Attorney, Federal Communications Commission, 1952-53.
Clients:
Alascom, Inc.
Telephone and Data Systems, Inc.

NAGASE, Masato
Manager, Mitsubishi Internat'l Corp.
655 15th St., N.W., Suite 860, Washington, DC 20005
Telephone: (202) 638-1101

NAGY, Gerald P.
V. President, Internat'l Sleep Products Ass'n
333 Commerce St., Alexandria, VA 22314
Telephone: (703) 683-8371

NAHAS, Rebecca
Director, Media Relations, Nat'l Ass'n of Arab Americans
2033 M St., N.W., Suite 300, Washington, DC 20036
Telephone: (202) 467-4800

NAIFEH, George A.
President, American-Arab Affairs Council
1730 M St., N.W. Suite 512, Washington, DC 20036
Telephone: (202) 296-6767
Background: U.S. Foreign Service, 1951-82. U.S. Information Agency, Washington, 1972-73.

NAKAMURA, John
Washington Representative, Agriculture, California, State of
444 North Capitol St., N.W., Suite 305, Washington, DC 20001
Telephone: (202) 347-6891

NAKAO, Masayuki
Senior Representative, Matsushita Electric Corp. of America
1001 Pennsylvania Ave., N.W. Suite 1355 North, Washington, DC 20004
Telephone: (202) 347-7592
Registered as Foreign Agent: (#4275)

NALLY, Terri L.
Manager, Office of College Chemistry, American Chemical Soc.
1155 16th St., N.W., Washington, DC 20036
Telephone: (202) 872-4587

NANCE, David Scott
Stewart and Stewart
808 17th St., N.W. Suite 301, Washington, DC 20006

Telephone: (202) 785-4185
Clients:
  PPG Industries

NAPIER, John L.
McNair Law Firm, P.A.
1155 15th St., N.W. Suite 400, Washington, DC 20005
Telephone: (202) 659-3900
Registered as lobbyist at U.S. Congress.
Clients:
  Phillips Petroleum Co.
  South Carolina Research Authority

NAPPI, Ralph J.
Director, Communication and Education, American Machine Tool Distributors Ass'n
1335 Rockville Pike Suite 300, Rockville, MD 20852
Telephone: (301) 738-1200
Background: Serves as the contact person for the associations government affairs activities.

NASH, Bernard
Dickstein, Shapiro and Morin
2101 L St., N.W., Washington, DC 20037
Telephone: (202) 785-9700
Background: Counsel, U.S. Senate Committee on Judiciary Subcommittee on Antitrust and Monopolies. 1971-77.
Clients:
  Arkansas, State of
  Delaware, State of
  Home Box Office
  Iowa, State of
  Louisiana, State of
  Medtronic, Inc.
  North Carolina Department of Natural Resources
  North Dakota, State of
  Rhode Island, State of
  Utah, State of
  West Virginia, State of

NASH, Cdr., Don
House Liaison, Legis Affrs, DEPARTMENT OF NAVY
The Pentagon, Washington, DC 20350-1300
Telephone: (202) 697-7146

NASH, James A.
Exec. Director, Churches' Center for Theology and Public Policy
4500 Massachusetts Ave., N.W., Washington, DC 20016
Telephone: (202) 885-9100

NASH, John F., Jr.
Washington Counsel, Milliken and Co.
1100 Connecticut Ave., N.W. 13th Floor, Washington, DC 20036
Telephone: (202) 543-9374
Registered as lobbyist at U.S. Congress.

NASH, John M.
President, Nat'l Ass'n of Corporate Directors
1707 L St., N.W., Suite 560, Washington, DC 20036
Telephone: (202) 775-0509

NASH, Pamela A.
Director, Government Affairs, American Ass'n for Clinical Chemistry
2029 K St., N.W., 7th Floor, Washington, DC 20006
Telephone: (202) 857-0717

NASON, Charles T.
Chairman of the Board, Acacia Mutual Life Insurance Co.
51 Louisiana Ave., N.W., Washington, DC 20001
Telephone: (202) 628-4506

NASRALLAH, Karen
Thompson and Co.
1001 G St., N.W. 7th Floor, Washington, DC 20001
Telephone: (202) 383-5590
Registered as lobbyist at U.S. Congress.
Clients:
  CareerCom Corp.

NASU, Akiyosha
Chief Representative, Mitsubishi Research Institute
655 15th St., N.W. Suite 880, Washington, DC 20005
Telephone: (202) 393-2424

NATANBLUT, Sharon
V. President, Burson-Marsteller
1850 M St., N.W., Suite 900, Washington, DC 20036
Telephone: (202) 833-8550
Clients:
  Carr Company, The Oliver

NATEMAN, Gary M.
V. President and General Counsel, Beer Institute
1225 Eye St., N.W., Suite 825, Washington, DC 20005
Telephone: (202) 737-2337
Registered as lobbyist at U.S. Congress.

NATHAN, Amy L.
Mayer, Brown and Platt
2000 Pennsylvania Ave., N.W. Suite 6500, Washington, DC 20006
Telephone: (202) 463-2000
Registered as lobbyist at U.S. Congress.

NATHAN ASSOCIATES INC.
1301 Pennsylvania Ave., N.W., Washington, DC 20004
Telephone: (202) 393-2700
Background: An internationally-renowned firm of consulting economists whose clients include a wide variety of major U.S. and foreign corporations, banks, governmental agencies and law firms.
Members of firm representing listed organizations:
  Beyer, John C.
  Nathan, Robert R., Chairman and Founder
Clients:
  Motion Picture Ass'n of America *(Robert R. Nathan)*

NATHAN, Hardy L.
Director, Government Relations, Food Marketing Institute
1750 K St., N.W., Washington, DC 20006
Telephone: (202) 452-8444
Registered as lobbyist at U.S. Congress.

NATHAN, Robert R.
Chairman and Founder, Nathan Associates Inc.
1301 Pennsylvania Ave., N.W., Washington, DC 20004
Telephone: (202) 393-2700
Clients:
  Motion Picture Ass'n of America

NATHANSON, Kenneth L.
Representative, Citizens for Safe Drivers Against Drunk Drivers and Chronic Offenders (CSD)
7401 MacKenzie Court, Bethesda, MD 20817
Telephone: (301) 469-6282

NATHANSON, Neal W.
President and Chief Executive Officer, Nat'l Rural Development and Finance Corp.
1818 N St., N.W., Suite 410, Washington, DC 20036
Telephone: (202) 429-9017
Registered as lobbyist at U.S. Congress.

NAT'L CENTER FOR MUNICIPAL DEVELOPMENT
1620 Eye St., N.W., Suite 300, Washington, DC 20006
Telephone: (202) 429-0160
Background: Founded in 1966 as the Man in Washington program, the National Center for Municipal Development became a non-profit corporation in 1974 affiliated with the National League of Cities and the United States Conference of Mayors. It exists to assist individual municipalities in matters which affect their interests at the federal level.
Members of firm representing listed organizations:
  Chaney, Carolyn
  Cherry, Dicken
  Duffy, Thomas N.
  Flanagan, Kevin
    Background: A tenant in the National Center offices, representing the City of Boston.
  Gordon, Robert E.
  Israel, Mark S.
  Johnson, Richard C.
  McCall, Barbara T.
  O'Donnell, John R.
  Seeley, James F.
Clients:
  Albuquerque, New Mexico, City of *(John R. O'Donnell)*
  Beaumont, Texas, City of *(Carolyn Chaney)*
  Boston, Massachusetts, City of *(Kevin Flanagan)*
  Columbia, South Carolina, City of *(Barbara T. McCall)*
  Duluth, Minnesota, City of *(Richard C. Johnson)*
  Fort Worth, Texas, City of *(Thomas N. Duffy)*
  Henderson, Nevada, City of *(Barbara T. McCall)*
  Jefferson Parish, Louisiana *(Dicken Cherry)*
  Lincoln, Nebraska, City of *(Carolyn Chaney)*
  Los Angeles, California, City of *(James F. Seeley)*
  Miami, Florida, City of *(Mark S. Israel)*
  Nat'l Organization to Insure a Sound-Controlled Environment-N.O.I.S.E. *(Thomas N. Duffy)*
  New Orleans, Louisiana, City of *(Dicken Cherry)*
  Newburgh, New York, City of *(Barbara T. McCall)*
  Orange, Texas, City of *(Barbara T. McCall)*
  Pasadena, California, City of *(Carolyn Chaney)*
  Phoenix, Arizona, City of *(John R. O'Donnell)*
  Providence, Rhode Island, City of *(Richard C. Johnson)*
  Riverside, California, City of *(Mark S. Israel)*
  Sparks, Nevada, City of *(Thomas N. Duffy)*
  Spokane, Washington, City of *(Robert E. Gordon)*
  Springfield, Illinois, City of *(Carolyn Chaney)*
  Texas Cities Legislative Coalition (TCLC) *(Barbara T. McCall)*
  Trenton, New Jersey, City of *(Richard C. Johnson)*
  Waukegan, Illinois, City of *(Mark S. Israel)*

NAT'L COUNSEL ASSOCIATES
421 New Jersey Ave., S.E., Washington, DC 20003
Telephone: (202) 547-5000
Background: A governmental relations lobbying company.
Members of firm representing listed organizations:
  Ivey, Hilma Lou, Associate Executive
  Rosenblatt, Maurice, President
Clients:
  Tosco Corp. *(Hilma Lou Ivey)*

NAT'L ECONOMIC RESEARCH ASSOCIATES INC.
1800 M St., N.W. Suite 600 South, Washington, DC 20006
Telephone: (202) 466-3510
Members of firm representing listed organizations:
  Netschert, Bruce C., Special Consultant

NAT'L MEDIA INC.
211 N. Union St., 2nd Floor, Alexandria, VA 22314
Telephone: (703) 683-4877
Background: A media relations and political consulting firm which spun off from Black, Manafort, Stone & Kelly Public Affairs.

NAT'L STRATEGIES INC.
818 17th St., N.W., Washington, DC 20006
Telephone: (202) 429-8744
Background: A government relations consulting firm.
Members of firm representing listed organizations:
  Aylward, David K.
    Background: Former Chief Counsel and Staff Director, House Subcommittee on Telecommunications, Consumer Protection and Finance. Serves as Exec. Director, Alliance for Capital Access.
  Clapp, Philip E.
    Background: Former Legislative Director to Congressman Timothy Wirth and Associate Staff Member, House Committee on the Budget.
  Curtis, Kevin S.
    Background: Senate Liaison, Department of Energy, 1978-80. Legislative Assistant to Rep. Timothy E. Wirth (D-CO), 1980-83.
  Lowenstein, Douglas
    Background: Former Legislative Director to Sen. Howard Metzenbaum. Serves also as V. President, Alliance for Capital Access.
  Scott, Gregory
  Skardon, Steve
    Background: Exec. Floor Assistant, Office of the Chief Deputy Majority Whip, U.S. House of Representatives, 1983-87.
  Tropp, Richard A.
    Background: Special Assistant to the Administrator, U.S. Agency for International Development, 1982-88. Earlier served in four Executive Branch agencies, the White House and as Legislative Assistant to a U.S. Senator from New York.
Clients:
  Alliance for Capital Access *(David K. Aylward, Douglas Lowenstein, Gregory Scott)*
  Banner Industries *(David K. Aylward)*
  Manor Care
  Manor Healthcare Federal Political Action Committee

NAT'L STRATEGIES INC. (Cont'd)
Triangle Industries

NAUGHTON, Mary A.
Office Mgr/TV Conf. Coordinator, ARCO
1333 New Hampshire Ave., N.W., Suite 1001, Washington,
DC 20036
Telephone: (202) 457-6226

NAUHEIM, Stephen A.
Anderson, Hibey, Nauheim and Blair
1708 New Hampshire Ave., N.W., Washington, DC 20009
Telephone: (202) 483-1900
Registered as lobbyist at U.S. Congress.
Registered as Foreign Agent: (#3208).
Background: Attorney-Advisor, 1967-70 and Assistant
Chief, 1970-71, International Branch, Legislation and
Regulations Division, IRS Chief Counsel's Office.
Clients:
Curacao Internat'l Trust Co.
Institute of Financial and Fiscal Studies of Cura-
cao

NAVARRETE, Andrew
Legislative Assistant, APCO Associates
1155 21st St., N.W., Suite 1000, Washington, DC 20036
Telephone: (202) 778-1000

NAVARRETE, Isabel M.
Public Information Director, Nat'l Council of La Raza
810 1st St., N.E., Suite 300, Washington, DC 20002
Telephone: (202) 289-1380
Registered as lobbyist at U.S. Congress.

NAVARRO, Bruce C.
Acting Asst Attorney General, DEPARTMENT OF JUS-
TICE
10th and Constitution Ave., Washington, DC 20530
Telephone: (202) 633-3752

NAYLOR, Michael W.
Dir., Legislative and Regulatory Affairs, Allied-Signal Inc.
1001 Pennsylvania Ave., N.W. Suite 700, Washington, DC
20004
Telephone: (202) 662-2650
Registered as lobbyist at U.S. Congress.

NAYLOR, Sarah
Assistant Director for Advocacy, Lutheran Office for Governmental Affairs/Evangelical Lutheran Church in America
122 C St., N.W. Suite 300, Washington, DC 20001
Telephone: (202) 783-7508

NEAL, Anne D.
Deputy General Counsel, Recording Industry Ass'n of
America
1020 19th St., N.W., Suite 200, Washington, DC 20036
Telephone: (202) 775-0101

NEAL, John
Mgr. of Energy Research and Development, Nat'l Rural
Electric Cooperative Ass'n
1800 Massachusetts Ave., N.W., Washington, DC 20036
Telephone: (202) 857-9598
Registered as lobbyist at U.S. Congress.

NEAL, Landis
Exec. Director, American Tax Reduction Movement
2113 National Press Building, Washington, DC 20045
Telephone: (202) 232-7443
Registered as lobbyist at U.S. Congress.

NEAL, Philip S.
Member, Miller & Chevalier, Chartered
Metropolitan Square, 655 15th St., N.W., Washington, DC
20005
Telephone: (202) 626-5800

NEALE, Erica
Legislative Assistant, Alzheimer's Ass'n
1334 G St., N.W. Suite 500, Washington, DC 20005
Telephone: (202) 393-7737

NEALE, Karen J.
Legislative Manager/Environment, Chemical Manufactur-
ers Ass'n
2501 M St., N.W., Washington, DC 20037
Telephone: (202) 887-1100
Registered as lobbyist at U.S. Congress.

NEALE, Tim
Director of Public Information, Air Transport Ass'n of
America
1709 New York Ave., N.W., Washington, DC 20006-5206
Telephone: (202) 626-4000

NEALER, Kevin G.
Senior Associate, APCO Associates
1155 21st St., N.W., Suite 1000, Washington, DC 20036
Telephone: (202) 778-1000
Clients:
E Z America Ltd.
Ferroalloys Ass'n

NEAS, Ralph Graham
Exec. Director, Leadership Conference on Civil Rights
2027 Massachusetts Ave., N.W., Washington, DC 20036
Telephone: (202) 667-1780
Registered as lobbyist at U.S. Congress.
Background: Former Chief Legislative Counsel to Senator
David F. Durenberger of Minnesota (1979-80) and to
Senator Edward W. Brooke of Massachusetts (1973-79).

NEDELMAN, Jeffrey
V. President, Public Affairs, Grocery Manufacturers of
America
1010 Wisconsin Ave., N.W., Suite 800, Washington, DC
20007
Telephone: (202) 337-9400
Registered as lobbyist at U.S. Congress.

NEDZI, Lucien N.
Of Counsel, Dickinson, Wright, Moon, Van Dusen and
Freeman
1901 L St., N.W. Suite 800, Washington, DC 20036
Telephone: (202) 457-0160
Registered as lobbyist at U.S. Congress.
Background: Member, U.S. House of Representatives (D-
MI), 1961-81.
Clients:
United Technologies Corp.

NEECE, Allen, Jr.
Chairman, Neece, Cator and Associates
1050 17th St., N.W. Suite 810, Washington, DC 20036
Telephone: (202) 887-5599
Registered as lobbyist at U.S. Congress.
Background: Also serves as Treasurer, Nat'l Venture Capi-
tal Ass'n PAC and Legislative Counsel, Nat'l Venture
Capital Ass'n
Clients:
Ass'n of Small Business Development Centers
Nat'l Small Business United
Nat'l Venture Capital Ass'n
Nat'l Venture Capital Ass'n Political Action
Committee

NEECE, CATOR AND ASSOCIATES
1050 17th St., N.W. Suite 810, Washington, DC 20036
Telephone: (202) 887-5599
Background: A government relations consulting firm.
Members of firm representing listed organizations:
Cator, G. Thomas, President
Neece, Allen (Jr.), Chairman
Background: Also serves as Treasurer, Nat'l Venture
Capital Ass'n PAC and Legislative Counsel, Nat'l
Venture Capital Ass'n
Clients:
Ass'n of Small Business Development Centers *(Al-
len Neece, Jr.)*
Design Professionals Coalition
Nat'l Small Business United *(G. Thomas Cator, Allen
Neece, Jr.)*
Nat'l Venture Capital Ass'n *(Allen Neece, Jr.)*
Nat'l Venture Capital Ass'n Political Action
Committee *(Allen Neece, Jr.)*
Southeastern Lumber Manufacturers Ass'n *(G.
Thomas Cator)*

NEEDHAM, Pamela Davis
President, Open Challenge Candidate Fund
403 First St., S.E., Wasgindton, DC 20003
Telephone: (202) 547-4935

NEELEY, Jeffrey S.
Mudge Rose Guthrie Alexander and Ferdon
2121 K St., N.W., Suite 700, Washington, DC 20037
Telephone: (202) 429-9355
Background: Attorney, Office of the General Counsel, U.S.
International Trade Commission, 1979-83.

Clients:
Norske Fiskeoppdretternes Salgslag (FO)
Philipp Brothers, Inc.
TENAX Corp.
Toshiba America, Inc.
Toshiba Corp.

NEELY, Capt. Pat
President, American Pilots Ass'n
1055 Thomas Jefferson St, N.W. Suite 404, Washington,
DC 20007
Telephone: (202) 333-9377
Background: Serves as Treasurer, American Pilots Ass'n
Political Action Committee.

NEELY, Susan K.
V. President and General Manager, CMF&Z Public Rela-
tions
655 15th St., N.W., Suite 300, Washington, DC 20005
Telephone: (202) 639-4059
Background: Former Press Secretary to Rep. Jim Leach
(R-IA).

NEIDLE, Dr. Enid
Director, Scientific Affairs, American Dental Ass'n
1111 14th St., N.W. Suite 1200, Washington, DC 20005
Telephone: (202) 898-2400

NEIGH, Janet
Exec. Director, Hospice Ass'n of America
519 C St., N.E., Washington, DC 20002
Telephone: (202) 546-4759

NEILL AND CO.
815 Connecticut Ave., N.W. Suite 800, Washington, DC
20006
Telephone: (202) 463-8877
Registered as Foreign Agent: (#3320)
Background: A government relations firm run by Denis M.
Neill, a partner in the law firm of Neill, Mullenholz and
Shaw at the same address.
Members of firm representing listed organizations:
Benedict, Mitchell P.
Background: U.S. Peace Corps, Belize, 1981-83. Re-
cruiter, U.S. Peace Corps, New York, 1984-85. In-
tern, U.S. Embassy, Harare, Zimbabwe, 1987.
Bircher, John E. (III)
Background: U.S. Army Security Agency Liaison Offi-
cer, Combined Arms Center, 1975-76. Defense and
Army Attache to Lebanon, 1979-80. Middle East/
Africa Director, Defense Attache System, DIA,
1980-82. Military Attache to Morocco, 1982-84. Di-
rector, Regional Affairs and Politico-Military Advisor
to Assistant Secretary of State, Bureau of Near East/
South Asian Affairs, Department of State, 1984-88.
Cromer, Harry C.
Background: U.S. General Accounting Office, 1952-59.
Staff Member, Committee on Foreign Affairs, House
of Representatives, 1959-74. Auditor General, Agen-
cy for International Development, 1974-77.
Curran, Jean E.
Background: International Affairs Specialist, U.S. De-
partment of Agriculture, 1987-88. Program Coordina-
tor, U.S. Department of Agriculture, 1988-89.
Dalley, George A.
Background: Staff Attorney, Office of EEO, U.S. De-
partment of State, 1966-67. Counsel, House of Rep-
resentatives Committee on the Judiciary, 1971-72.
Administrative Assistant to Rep. Charles Rangel (D-
NY), 1972-77. Deputy Assistant Secretary of State,
Bureau of International Affairs, Department of State,
1977-80. Member, Civil Aeronautics Board, 1985-89.
Counsel and Staff Director to Rep Charles Rangel
(D-NY).
Donahue, Karen L.
Downen, Robert L., V. President
Background: Legislative Assistant to Senator Robert
Dole (R-KS), 1973-79. Director of Special Projects
and Policy Adviser, Bureau of East Asian and Pacific
Affairs, U.S. Department of State, 1984-88.
Habeeb, Wm. Mark
Janka, Leslie A.
Background: Special Assistant, National Security Coun-
cil, 1971-75. Assistant Secretary, U.S. Department of
Defense, 1976-78.
Jennings, Horace (III), Staff Consultant
Background: Legislative Assistant to Senator Lloyd
Bentsen (D-TX), 1983-85. Attorney Advisor, Board
of Veterans Appeals, Veterans Administration, 1985-

87.

Lawrence, John D.

Neill, Denis M.

Background: General Attorney, Office of Chief Counsel, Internal Revenue Service, 1967-68. Attorney-Advisor, 1972-73 Assistant General Counsel, 1973-75 and Assistant Administrator, 1975-77, Agency for International Development. See also Neill, Mullenholz and Shaw.

Notkin, Jennifer

Perry, William

Background: Professional Staff Member, Senate Foreign Relations Committee, 1985-86. Director, Latin American Affairs, Nat'l Security Council, 1986-87.

Printz, Albert C. (Jr.)

Background: U.S. Department of Health, Education and Welfare, 1961-69. Chief, Federal Activities, Department of Interior, 1969-70. Director, Permit Program, Environmental Protection Agency, 1970-76. Environmental Coordinator, A.I.D., 1976-86.

Rosendahl, Jennifer E.

Background: Office of Congressman Don Bonker, 1981. Member, U.S. House of Representatives Export Task Force, 1982-83.

Shea, James T.

Background: U.S. Embassy, Nouakchott, Mauretania, 1981-82.

Clients:

Adobe Forms *(Denis M. Neill, Albert C. Printz, Jr.)*

American Methanol Institute *(George A. Dalley, Denis M. Neill)*

AT&T Technologies, Inc. *(Denis M. Neill, Albert C. Printz, Jr.)*

China External Trade Development Council *(Robert L. Downen, Denis M. Neill)*

Contraves Italiana S.p.A. *(John E. Bircher, III, Denis M. Neill)*

General Dynamics Corp. *(John E. Bircher, III, Denis M. Neill)*

General Electric Co. *(Denis M. Neill)*

Guinea, Government of *(Leslie A. Janka, Denis M. Neill)*

Ivory Coast, Government of *(George A. Dalley, Denis M. Neill)*

Jamaica, Government of *(George A. Dalley, Denis M. Neill)*

Jordan, Hashemite Kingdom of *(Leslie A. Janka, Denis M. Neill)*

Kenya, Government of *(Denis M. Neill)*

Morocco, Kingdom of *(John E. Bircher, III, Denis M. Neill)*

Puerto Rico Economic Development Administration *(George A. Dalley)*

Rhone-Poulenc Ag Co. *(Denis M. Neill, Albert C. Printz, Jr.)*

Smith & Wesson *(John E. Bircher, III, Denis M. Neill)*

NEILL, Denis M.

Neill and Co.

815 Connecticut Ave., N.W. Suite 800, Washington, DC 20006

Telephone: (202) 463-8877

Registered as lobbyist at U.S. Congress.

Registered as Foreign Agent: (#3320).

Background: General Attorney, Office of Chief Counsel, Internal Revenue Service, 1967-68. Attorney-Advisor, 1972-73 Assistant General Counsel, 1973-75 and Assistant Administrator, 1975-77, Agency for International Development. See also Neill, Mullenholz and Shaw.

Clients:

Adobe Forms

American Methanol Institute

AT&T Technologies, Inc.

China External Trade Development Council

Contraves Italiana S.p.A.

General Dynamics Corp.

General Electric Co.

Guinea, Government of

Ivory Coast, Government of

Jamaica, Government of

Jordan, Hashemite Kingdom of

Kenya, Government of

Morocco, Kingdom of

Rhone-Poulenc Ag Co.

Smith & Wesson

NEILL, MULLENHOLZ AND SHAW

815 Connecticut Ave., N.W. Suite 800, Washington, DC 20006

Telephone: (202) 463-8400

Members of firm representing listed organizations:

Bransford, William L.

Background: Senior Attorney. General Legal Services Division, Office of Chief Counsel, Internal Revenue Service 1981-83. Specializes in Federal employee law, labor law and administrative law.

Mullenholz, John J.

Background: Trial Attorney, General Litigation Section, Tax Division, U.S. Department of Justice, 1968-73. See also Neill and Co.

O'Rourke, Thomas J.

Background: Office of Chief Counsel, Internal Revenue Service 1974-83. Specializes in tax law.

Shaw, G. Jerry (Jr.)

Background: Director, General Legal Services Division, Office of the Chief Counsel, Internal Revenue Service, 1975-81. President, Senior Executive Ass'n, 1980-82. General Counsel, Senior Executive Ass'n, 1982-present. Chairman, Public Employees Roundtable, 1982-present.

Clients:

Florida East Coast Railway Co. *(John J. Mullenholz)*

Nat'l Ass'n of Chapter Thirteen Bankruptcy Trustees *(G. Jerry Shaw, Jr.)*

Nat'l Council of Social Security Management Ass'ns *(G. Jerry Shaw, Jr.)*

Nat'l Farm and Power Equipment Dealers Ass'n *(John J. Mullenholz)*

PHH-Homequity *(G. Jerry Shaw, Jr.)*

Public Employees Roundtable *(G. Jerry Shaw, Jr.)*

Senior Executives Ass'n *(G. Jerry Shaw, Jr.)*

Soo Line Railroad, Inc. *(John J. Mullenholz)*

TACA Internat'l Airlines

NEILL, Thomas

Director, Industrial Relations, American Postal Workers Union

1300 L St., N.W., Washington, DC 20005

Telephone: (202) 842-4200

NEIMAN, Joshua

Legislative Director, Nat'l Federation of Federal Employees

1016 16th St., N.W., Suite 400, Washington, DC 20036

Telephone: (202) 862-4400

Registered as lobbyist at U.S. Congress.

NEIPRIS, Deborah

Patton, Boggs and Blow

2550 M St., N.W., Suite 800, Washington, DC 20037

Telephone: (202) 457-6000

Registered as lobbyist at U.S. Congress.

Registered as Foreign Agent: (#2165).

Clients:

Cryolife Inc.

NEJELSKI, Marilyn

Exec. Director, Women Judges Fund for Justice

1900 L St., N.W., 300, Washington, DC 20036

Telephone: (202) 331-7343

NELLIGAN, William D., CAE

Exec. V. President, American College of Cardiology

9111 Old Georgetown Road, Bethesda, MD 20814

Telephone: (301) 897-5400

NELLIS, Joseph L.

Of Counsel, Spriggs & Hollingsworth

1350 Eye St., N.W. 9th Floor, Washington, DC 20005-3304

Telephone: (202) 898-5800

Registered as lobbyist at U.S. Congress.

Background: Chief Counsel. Senate Committee to Investigate Crime in Interstate Commerce, 1949-51. Special Counsel, Senate Antitrust Subcommittee, 1963-64. Chief Counsel, Investigations Subcommittee, House Select Business Committee, 1967-68. Special Counsel, House Crime Committee, 1969-70. Chief Counsel, House Narcotics Committee and General Counsel House Judiciary Committee, 1976-81.

NELSEN, Dr. Peter T.

President, Internat'l Trade Council

3114 Circle Hill Road, Alexandria, VA 22305

Telephone: (703) 548-1234

Registered as lobbyist at U.S. Congress.

NELSEN, Sandy

Director, Internat'l Trade Council

3114 Circle Hill Road, Alexandria, VA 22305

Telephone: (703) 548-1234

NELSON, Alan C.

Consultant, Federation for American Immigration Reform (FAIR)

1666 Connecticut Ave., N.W., Suite 400, Washington, DC 20009

Telephone: (202) 328-7004

Registered as lobbyist at U.S. Congress.

NELSON, Carl B., Jr.

Prather, Seeger, Doolittle and Farmer

1600 M St., N.W., Washington, DC 20036

Telephone: (202) 296-0500

Clients:

American Airlines

Bremer Lagerhaus-Gesellschaft

NELSON, Charles A.

V. President & Washington Representative, Bunge Corp.

1101 15th St., N.W., Suite 503, Washington, DC 20005

Telephone: (202) 785-3885

NELSON, Christine

Government Relations Consultant, McLeod & Pires

2501 M St., N.W., Suite 400, Washington, DC 20037

Telephone: (202) 861-1234

Clients:

United Egg Ass'n

United Egg Producers

NELSON, Clark A.

Director, Corp. Communications, Spot Image Corp.

1897 Preston White Drive, Reston, VA 22091-4326

Telephone: (703) 620-2200

NELSON, Dale

Director, Support Operations, Air Force Sergeants Ass'n

P.O. Box 50, Temple Hills, MD 20748

Telephone: (301) 899-3500

NELSON, Donald M., Jr.

Director, Internat'l Trade Relations, Philip Morris Management Corp.

1341 G St., N.W., Suite 900, Washington, DC 20005

Telephone: (202) 637-1500

NELSON, E. Colette

V. President of Government Relations, American Subcontractors Ass'n

1004 Duke St., Alexandria, VA 22314

Telephone: (703) 684-3450

Registered as lobbyist at U.S. Congress.

Background: Serves also as Treasurer, American Subcontractors Ass'n, Inc. Political Action Committee.

NELSON, Elizabeth S.

Public Relations/Communications Manager, Nat'l Spa and Pool Institute

2111 Eisenhower Ave., Alexandria, VA 22314

Telephone: (703) 838-0083

NELSON, Eric

Director, Market Research, North American Telecommunications Ass'n

2000 M Street, N.W., Suite 550, Washington, DC 20036

Telephone: (202) 296-9800

NELSON, Gaylord

Counselor, Wilderness Soc.

1400 Eye St., N.W., 10th Floor, Washington, DC 20005

Telephone: (202) 842-3400

Registered as lobbyist at U.S. Congress.

Background: U.S. Senator from Wisconsin, 1963-81.

NELSON, J. Thomas, III

V. Pres., Federal Government Relations, Household Internat'l

1000 Connecticut Ave., N.W., Suite 507, Washington, DC 20036

Telephone: (202) 466-3561

Registered as lobbyist at U.S. Congress.

WASHINGTON REPRESENTATIVES

NELSON, Joan M.
Senior Associate, Overseas Development Council
1717 Massachusetts Ave., N.W., Washington, DC 20036
Telephone: (202) 234-8701

NELSON, Mark
Director, Government Relations, SEMATECH
1825 Eye St., N.W. Suite 400, Washington, DC 20006
Telephone: (202) 429-2021

NELSON, Mark D.
Washington Counsel, du Pont de Nemours and Co., E. I.
1701 Pennsylvania Ave., N.W., Washington, DC 20006
Telephone: (202) 728-3661
Registered as lobbyist at U.S. Congress.
Background: Also serves as Director, Legislative Affairs for Consolidation Coal Co.

NELSON, Ralph F.
V. President and Ass't to the President, Flight Safety Foundation
2200 Wilson Blvd., Suite 500, Arlington, VA 22201
Telephone: (703) 522-8300

NELSON, Rebecca
Princial Staff Asst, Legis Affrs (House), EXECUTIVE OFFICE OF THE PRESIDENT - The White House
1600 Pennsylvania Ave., N.W. 112 East Wing, Washington, DC 20500
Telephone: (202) 456-6620

NELSON, Richard C.
Secretary/Treasurer, American Hotel and Motel Ass'n
1201 New York Ave., N.W. Suite 600, Washington, DC 20005
Telephone: (202) 289-3100

NELSON, Richard Y., Jr.
Exec. Director, Nat'l Ass'n of Housing and Redevelopment Officials
1320 18th St., N.W., Washington, DC 20036
Telephone: (202) 429-2960

NELSON, Robert L.
General Counsel, Paralyzed Veterans of America
801 18th St., N.W., Washington, DC 20006
Telephone: (202) 872-1300

NELSON, Robert W.
Director, Public & Ass'n Affairs Dept., Nat'l Rural Electric Cooperative Ass'n
1800 Massachusetts Ave., N.W., Washington, DC 20036
Telephone: (202) 857-9500

NELSON, Sara
Exec. Director, Christic Institute
1324 N. Capitol St., N.W., Washington, DC 20002
Telephone: (202) 797-8106

NELSON, William
Senior Director, Nat'l Automated Clearing House Ass'n
607 Herndon Parkway Suite 200, Herndon, VA 22070
Telephone: (703) 742-9190

NEME, Chris
Senior Policy Analyst, Center for Clean Air Policy
444 N. Capitol St., Suite 526, Washington, DC 20001
Telephone: (202) 624-7709
Background: Program Analyst for U.S. Environmental Angency (less than one year).

NEMEROFF, Michael A.
Sidley and Austin
1722 Eye St., N.W. Sixth Floor, Washington, DC 20006
Telephone: (202) 429-4000

NERNEY, Christopher
Senior Account Executive, Edelman, Inc., Daniel J.
1420 K St., N.W., Washington, DC 20005
Telephone: (202) 371-0200

NERNEY, Thomas
Director, Autism Soc. of America
1234 Massachusetts Ave., N.W., Suite C-1017, Washington, DC 20005
Telephone: (202) 783-0125

NERO, Janis A.
Ass't Director, Div. of Regulatory Afrs., American Hospital Ass'n
50 F St., N.W., Suite 1100, Washington, DC 20001
Telephone: (202) 638-1100
Registered as lobbyist at U.S. Congress.

NERSESIAN, Lynda L.
Deputy V. Pres., Government Relations, Pharmaceutical Manufacturers Ass'n
1100 15th St., N.W., Washington, DC 20005
Telephone: (202) 835-3480
Registered as lobbyist at U.S. Congress.

NESBITT, Frederick H.
Legislative and Political Director, Internat'l Ass'n of Fire Fighters
1750 New York Ave., N.W., Washington, DC 20006
Telephone: (202) 737-8484
Registered as lobbyist at U.S. Congress.

NESLUND, Thomas R.
Exec. Director, Internat'l Commission for the Prevention of Alcoholism and Drug Dependency
12501 Old Columbia Pike, Silver Spring, MD 20904-1600
Telephone: (301) 680-6719

NESMITH, E. Archie, Jr.
V.P., Congressonal Afrs, Aerosp. Prgrams, Allied-Signal Inc.
1001 Pennsylvania Ave., N.W. Suite 700, Washington, DC 20004
Telephone: (202) 662-2650
Registered as lobbyist at U.S. Congress.

NESS, Debra
Associate Director, Programs, Nat'l Abortion Rights Action League
1101 14th St., N.W., Suite 500, Washington, DC 20005
Telephone: (202) 371-0779

NESTLEN, Mark
Director, Congressional Relations, American Soybean Ass'n
1300 L St., N.W., Suite 950, Washington, DC 20005-4107
Telephone: (202) 371-5511
Registered as lobbyist at U.S. Congress.

NETSCHERT, Bruce C.
Special Consultant, Nat'l Economic Research Associates Inc.
1800 M St., N.W. Suite 600 South, Washington, DC 20006
Telephone: (202) 466-3510

NEUBERGER, Neal I.
Assoc. Director, Div. of Legislation, American Hospital Ass'n
50 F St., N.W., Suite 1100, Washington, DC 20001
Telephone: (202) 638-1100
Registered as lobbyist at U.S. Congress.
Background: Former Legislative Assistant to Rep. David R. Obey (D-WI).

NEUMAN, A. Mark
Dir, Office of Cong Affrs, DEPARTMENT OF COMMERCE - Bureau of the Census
Federal Center, Suitland, MD 20233
Telephone: (301) 763-2446

NEUMAN, Connie
Director, Communications, Chemical Specialties Manufacturers Ass'n
1913 Eye St., N.W., Washington, DC 20006
Telephone: (202) 872-8110
Background: Former staff assistant to Senator Alan Cranston (D-CA).

NEUMAN, Mike
Washington Representative, Seafarers Internat'l Union of North America
5201 Auth Way, Camp Springs, MD 20746
Telephone: (301) 899-0675
Background: Serves as contact for Seafarers Political Activity Donation.

NEUMAN, Nancy M.
President, League of Women Voters of the United States
1730 M St., N.W., Tenth Floor, Washington, DC 20036
Telephone: (202) 429-1965

NEUMAN, Robert A.
V. President, Powell, Adams & Rinehart
1901 L St., N.W., 3rd Floor, Washington, DC 20036
Telephone: (202) 466-7590
Background: Former Chief of Staff to Rep. Morris Udall (D-AZ).
Clients:
Amgen, Inc.

NEUMANN, E. John
Director, Governmental Affairs, Southern Company, The
1130 Connecticut Ave., N.W., Suite 830, Washington, DC 20036
Telephone: (202) 775-0944
Registered as lobbyist at U.S. Congress.

NEUMANN, Loretta
President, CEHP, Inc.
1333 Connecticut Ave., N.W. Suite 400, Washington, DC 20036
Telephone: (202) 293-1774
Registered as lobbyist at U.S. Congress.

NEVARES, Lorie J.
Manager, State and Local Affairs, Nat'l Soft Drink Ass'n
1101 16th St., N.W., Washington, DC 20036
Telephone: (202) 463-6732

NEVINS, Louis H.
Partner, Thacher, Proffitt and Wood
1500 K St., N.W., Suite 200, Washington, DC 20005
Telephone: (202) 347-8400
Registered as lobbyist at U.S. Congress.
Background: Attorney, Federal Housing Administration, 1963-67.
Clients:
Apple Bank for Savings
Binghampton Savings Bank
Boston Five Cents Savings Bank, FSB
Dollar Bank
Federal Home Loan Mortgage Corp.
General Electric Mortgage Insurance Co.
Great Western Financial Corp.
New Hampshire Savings Bank
Peoples Westchester Savings Bank
Ranieri-Wilson
River Bank America
Rochester Community Savings Bank
Standard Federal Savings Bank

NEW, Barry J.
V. President, Government Programs, Rolls-Royce, Inc.
1001 Pennsylvania Ave., N.W., Suite 490, Washington, DC 20004
Telephone: (202) 737-1010

NEWBOLD & ASSOC., Bill
1355 Beverly Rd., Suite 200, McLean, VA 22101
Telephone: (703) 243-3100
Members of firm representing listed organizations:
Newbold, Bill, President
Reeves, Robert, General Counsel
Organizations represented:
Partners of the Americas *(Bill Newbold)*
Presbyterian Health Center *(Bill Newbold)*
Rogers and Rogers Investments *(Bill Newbold)*
Southwest Center for Study of Hospital and Health Care Systems *(Bill Newbold)*

NEWBOLD, Bill
President, Newbold & Assoc., Bill
1355 Beverly Rd., Suite 200, McLean, VA 22101
Telephone: (703) 243-3100
Registered as lobbyist at U.S. Congress.
Organizations represented:
Partners of the Americas
Presbyterian Health Center
Rogers and Rogers Investments
Southwest Center for Study of Hospital and Health Care Systems

NEWBOULD, E. Jack
Counsel, Nat'l Clay Pipe Institute
206 Vassar Place, Alexandria, VA 22314
Telephone: (703) 370-5750

NEWBURG, Janice
DeHart and Darr Associates, Inc.
1360 Beverly Road, Suite 201, McLean, VA 22101

Telephone: (703) 448-1000
Registered as lobbyist at U.S. Congress.

NEWBY, Lilian Ann
Legislative Representative, American Public Power Ass'n
2301 M St., N.W., Washington, DC 20037
Telephone: (202) 775-8300
Registered as lobbyist at U.S. Congress.

NEWELL, Hal H.
1629 K St., N.W., Suite 802, Washington, DC 20006
Telephone: (202) 628-0222

NEWELL, Lisa
Newman and Newell
1920 N St., N.W., Suite 430 Suite 400, Washington, DC 20036
Telephone: (202) 857-5650

NEWELL-PAYNE COMPANIES, INC.
2011 Eye St., N.W., 5th Floor, Washington, DC 20006
Telephone: (202) 223-3217
Members of firm representing listed organizations:
   Armstrong, Jan M.
      Background: Serves as Exec. Director, American Car Rental Ass'n.
   Murch, Roger A.
      Background: Serves as Exec. V. President for American Car Rental Ass'n, Nat'l Beverage Dispensing Equipment Ass'n, Nat'l Truck Renting and Leasing Ass'n and Nat'l Corrugated Steel Pipe Ass'n.
   Preston, Leigh Anne
      Background: Serves as Acting Exec. Director, Truck Renting and Leasing Ass'n.
   Wolfsohn, Venlo J.
      Background: Serves as Exec. Director, Nat'l Corrugated Steel Pipe Ass'n.
Clients:
   American Car Rental Ass'n (Jan M. Armstrong)
   Nat'l Corrugated Steel Pipe Ass'n (Venlo J. Wolfsohn)
   Truck Renting and Leasing Ass'n (Leigh Anne Preston)

NEWKIRK, Caroline
Staff Attorney, Nat'l Women's Law Center
1616 P St., N.W., Washington, DC 20036
Telephone: (202) 328-5160

NEWKIRK, Ingrid
National Director, People for the Ethical Treatment of Animals (PETA)
4980 Wyaconda Road, Rockville, MD 20852
Telephone: (301) 770-7444

NEWMAN, George S.
V. President, Gov't and Public Affairs, BDM Internat'l, Inc.
7915 Jones Branch Drive, McLean, VA 22102
Telephone: (703) 821-5000
Registered as lobbyist at U.S. Congress.

NEWMAN & HOLTZINGER, P.C.
1615 L St., N.W., 10th Floor, Washington, DC 20005
Telephone: (202) 955-6600
Background: The information below was obtained from public records and submitted for confirmation to this firm. It replied that the listing contained errors but declined to correct them and asked to be omitted from the book.
Members of firm representing listed organizations:
   Axelrad, Maurice
      Background: Attorney, Office of General Counsel, Atomic Energy Commission, 1958-61.
   Bauser, Michael A.
   Edgar, G.
   Gallen, Kevin P.
   Holtzinger, John E.
   Newman, Jack R.
      Background: Atomic Energy Commission 1959-64. Joint Congressional Committee on Atomic Energy.
   Reis, Harold F.
      Background: Chief, Legal Branch, Office of Alien Property (1949-52), First Assistant, Office of Legal Counsel (1960-64), and Executive Assistant to the Attorney General (1964-67), U.S. Department of Justice.
   Shea, Kathleen H.
      Background: Attorney, Office of the General Counsel, Atomic Energy Commission, 1957-69, 1972-73. Legal Advisor, U.S. Mission to the European Atomic Energy Community, 1964-68.

Clients:
   CNG Transmission Corp.
   Dairyland Power Cooperative (Kevin P. Gallen)
   Florida Power and Light Co. (Harold F. Reis)
   Houston Lighting & Power Co. (Jack R. Newman)
   Houston Power and Lighting Co. (Jack R. Newman)
   Iowa Electric Light and Power Co. (Jack R. Newman, Kathleen H. Shea)
   Iowa Power and Light Co. (Jack R. Newman, Kathleen H. Shea)
   Mississippi River Transmission Corp.
   Texas Utilities (G. Edgar)
   Utility Nuclear Waste Transportation Program (Michael A. Bauser)

NEWMAN, Jack R.
Newman & Holtzinger, P.C.
1615 L St., N.W., 10th Floor, Washington, DC 20005
Telephone: (202) 955-6600
Background: Atomic Energy Commission 1959-64. Joint Congressional Committee on Atomic Energy.
Clients:
   Houston Lighting & Power Co.
   Houston Power and Lighting Co.
   Iowa Electric Light and Power Co.
   Iowa Power and Light Co.

NEWMAN AND NEWELL
1920 N St., N.W., Suite 430 Suite 400, Washington, DC 20036
Telephone: (202) 857-5650
Background: Represents labor unions, public interest organizations and individual clients.
Members of firm representing listed organizations:
   Newell, Lisa
   Newman, Winn I.
   Owens, Christine

NEWMAN, Sanford A.
Exec. Director, Project Vote!
1424 16th St., N.W., Suite 101, Washington, DC 20005
Telephone: (202) 328-1500

NEWMAN, William A.
Chief Legal Counsel, Nat'l Automobile Dealers Ass'n
8400 Westpark Dr., McLean, VA 22102
Telephone: (703) 821-7000

NEWMAN, William B., Jr.
Vice President and Washington Counsel, Consolidated Rail Corp. (CONRAIL)
990 L'Enfant Plaza, S.W., Washington, DC 20024
Telephone: (202) 789-5885
Registered as lobbyist at U.S. Congress.
Background: Former Professional Staff Member to the House of Representatives Committee on Interstate and Foreign Commerce.

NEWMAN, Winn I.
Newman and Newell
1920 N St., N.W., Suite 430 Suite 400, Washington, DC 20036
Telephone: (202) 857-5650

NEWMAN, Yale
Director, Public Affairs, U.S. English
818 Connecticut Ave., N.W. Suite 200, Washington, DC 20006
Telephone: (202) 833-0100

NEWMYER, A. G., III
President, Newmyer Associates, Inc.
1220 L St., N.W., Washington, DC 20005
Telephone: (202) 289-6300
Clients:
   Alexander & Alexander Inc.

NEWMYER ASSOCIATES, INC.
1220 L St., N.W., Washington, DC 20005
Telephone: (202) 289-6300
Members of firm representing listed organizations:
   Booth, Sidney
   Newmyer, A. G. (III), President
Clients:
   Alexander & Alexander Inc. (Sidney Booth, A. G. Newmyer, III)
   Capital Group
   Citicorp
   Dana Corp.

   Federal Nat'l Mortgage Ass'n
   Gillette Co.
   INCO U.S.
   Internat'l Business Machines Corp.
   KPMG Peat Marwick
   Westinghouse Electric Corp.

NEWPORT, Janet G.
Manager, Federal Affairs, FHP, Inc.
1225 19th St., N.W., Washington, DC 20036
Telephone: (202) 223-5718
Registered as lobbyist at U.S. Congress.

NEWSOM, Graham H.
Assistant Director, Government Liaison, American Academy of Pediatrics
1331 Pennsylvania Ave., N.W., Suite 721 North, Washington, DC 20004-1703
Telephone: (202) 662-7460

NEWSOM, Jean
Editor, Middle East Journal, Middle East Institute
1761 N St., N.W., Washington, DC 20036
Telephone: (202) 785-1141

NEWSOME, Sharon L.
V. President, Resources Conservation, Nat'l Wildlife Federation
1412 16th St., N.W., Washington, DC 20036
Telephone: (202) 797-6827
Registered as lobbyist at U.S. Congress.

NEWTON & ASSOC., E. G.
P.O. Box 65335, Washington, DC 20035
Telephone: (202) 827-9597
Background: Provides government relations consulting services with emphasis on science and engineering.
Members of firm representing listed organizations:
   Newton, Elisabeth G., President
Organizations represented:
   American Institute of Professional Geologists (Elisabeth G. Newton)
   Ass'n of Engineering Geologists (Elisabeth G. Newton)
   Stevenson & Associates (Elisabeth G. Newton)

NEWTON & ASSOC., Hugh C.
618 South Lee St., Alexandria, VA 22314
Telephone: (703) 549-5825
Background: The Washington media contact of the Coordination Council for North American Affairs, an information arm of the Republic of China (Taiwan).
Members of firm representing listed organizations:
   Newton, Hugh C., President
Organizations represented:
   Coordination Council for North American Affairs (Hugh C. Newton)
   Heritage Foundation (Hugh C. Newton)

NEWTON, Charlotte
Constituency Relations Counselor, Burson-Marsteller
1850 M St., N.W., Suite 900, Washington, DC 20036
Telephone: (202) 833-8550

NEWTON, Elisabeth G.
President, Newton & Assoc., E. G.
P.O. Box 65335, Washington, DC 20035
Telephone: (202) 827-9597
Organizations represented:
   American Institute of Professional Geologists
   Ass'n of Engineering Geologists
   Stevenson & Associates

NEWTON, Hugh C.
President, Newton & Assoc., Hugh C.
618 South Lee St., Alexandria, VA 22314
Telephone: (703) 549-5825
Organizations represented:
   Coordination Council for North American Affairs
   Heritage Foundation

NEWTON, Lisa
Keene, Shirley & Associates, Inc.
919 Prince St., Alexandria, VA 22314
Telephone: (703) 684-0550
Registered as Foreign Agent: (#3997).

NEY, Richard T.
President, Advocacy Services Group, Inc.
1825 Eye St., N.W. Suite 400, Washington, DC 20006
Telephone: (202) 429-2096

NEY, W. Roger
Exec. Director, Nat'l Council on Radiation Protection and Measurement
7910 Woodmont Ave. Suite 800, Bethesda, MD 20814
Telephone: (301) 657-2652

NICHOLAS, Robert B.
McDermott, Will and Emery
1850 K St., N.W., Suite 500, Washington, DC 20006-2296
Telephone: (202) 887-8000
Clients:
Animal Health Institute

NICHOLS, David A.
Legislative Director, Internat'l Ass'n for Continuing Education and Training
P.O. Box 27043, Washington, DC 20038
Telephone: (301) 384-1059

NICHOLS, Marshall W.
Exec. Director, Nat'l Petroleum Council
1625 K St., N.W., Suite 600, Washington, DC 20006
Telephone: (202) 393-6100

NICHOLS, Nexus
Policy Associate, Nat'l Network of Runaway and Youth Services
1400 Eye St., N.W., Suite 330, Washington, DC 20005
Telephone: (202) 682-4114

NICHOLS, Willard R.
V. President and General Counsel, Communications Satellite Corp. (COMSAT)
950 L'Enfant Plaza, S.W., Washington, DC 20024
Telephone: (202) 863-6130
Background: Former Chief of Staff to Federal Communications Commission Member Mark S. Fowler.

NICHOLSON, Bruce
Legislative Counsel, American Bar Ass'n
1800 M St., N.W., Washington, DC 20036
Telephone: (202) 331-2212
Registered as lobbyist at U.S. Congress.

NICHOLSON, Fred
Exec. Director, Nat'l Lighting Bureau
2101 L St., N.W., Suite 300, Washington, DC 20037
Telephone: (202) 457-8437

NICHOLSON, Marlene
Director, Government Relations, Barclays Bank PLC
1722 Eye St., N.W., 5th Floor, Washington, DC 20006
Telephone: (202) 429-4298
Registered as lobbyist at U.S. Congress.

NICHOLSON, Richard S.
Exec. Officer, American Ass'n for the Advancement of Science
1333 H St., N.W., Washington, DC 20005
Telephone: (202) 326-6400

NICKEL, Henry V.
Hunton and Williams
2000 Pennsylvania Ave., N.W., Washington, DC 20006
Telephone: (202) 955-1500
Clients:
Utility Air Regulatory Group

NICKELS, Thomas P.
Director, Government Affairs, American College of Emergency Physicians
900 17th St., N.W., Suite 1250, Washington, DC 20006
Telephone: (202) 728-0610
Registered as lobbyist at U.S. Congress.

NICKELSON, Daniel E.
Director, Government Affairs, Cleveland Clinic Foundation
2000 L St., N.W., Suite 200, Washington, DC 20036
Telephone: (202) 861-0955
Registered as lobbyist at U.S. Congress.
Background: U.S. Health Care Financing Administration (1979-83).

NICKELSON, Marian
Assistant Director for Advocacy, Lutheran Office for Governmental Affairs/Evangelical Lutheran Church in America
122 C St., N.W. Suite 300, Washington, DC 20001
Telephone: (202) 783-7508

NICKERSON, Christine E.
Director, Standards Program, American Academy of Actuaries
1720 Eye St., N.W., 7th Floor, Washington, DC 20006
Telephone: (202) 223-8196

NICKLAS, Bob
Deputy Director, Partnership for Democracy
2335 18th St., N.W., Washington, DC 20009
Telephone: (202) 483-0030

NICKLES, Peter J.
Covington and Burling
1201 Pennsylvania Ave., N.W., Box 7566, Washington, DC 20044
Telephone: (202) 662-6000
Registered as lobbyist at U.S. Congress.
Clients:
Mental Health Law Project

NICOLL, Anne
Assoc. Director, Division of Legislation, American Hospital Ass'n
50 F St., N.W., Suite 1100, Washington, DC 20001
Telephone: (202) 638-1100
Registered as lobbyist at U.S. Congress.
Background: Former legislative aide to Rep. Byron Dorgan (D-ND).

NIELD, George C.
President, Automobile Importers of America
1725 Jefferson Davis Hwy., Suite 1002, Arlington, VA 22202
Telephone: (703) 979-5550

NIELDS, John W., Jr.
Howrey and Simon
1730 Pennsylvania Ave., N.W., Washington, DC 20006-4793
Telephone: (202) 783-0800
Background: Chief Counsel, Committee on Standards of Official Conduct, Korea Influence Investigation, U.S. House of Representatives, 1977-78. Special Counsel, Department of Justice, 1979-80. Chief Counsel, House Select Committee to Investigate Covert Arms Transactions with Iran, 1987.
Clients:
Johnson & Johnson

NIELSEN, Louisa A.
Exec. Director, Broadcast Education Ass'n
1771 N St., N.W., Washington, DC 20036
Telephone: (202) 429-5355

NIEMANN, Doyle
Director, Union Labor Life Insurance Co.
111 Massachusetts Ave., N.W., Washington, DC 20001
Telephone: (202) 682-0900

NILAN, Patrick J.
Director of Legislation, American Postal Workers Union
1300 L St., N.W., Washington, DC 20005
Telephone: (202) 842-4210
Registered as lobbyist at U.S. Congress.
Background: Also serves as Secretary-Treasurer, Committee on Political Action of the American Postal Workers Union.

NILES, O'Jay
Director, Product Services Division, American Textile Manufacturers Institute
1801 K St., N.W. Suite 900, Washington, DC 20006
Telephone: (202) 862-0500

NISHIBORI, Satoshi
V. President, Nissan Research & Development
750 17th St., N.W., Suite 901, Washington, DC 20006
Telephone: (202) 466-5284

NISHIMURA, Glenn
Exec. Director, HALT-An Organization of Americans for Legal Reform
1319 F St., N.W., Suite 300, Washington, DC 20004
Telephone: (202) 347-9600

NISKANEN, William A., Jr.
Chairman, Cato Institute
224 Second St., S.E., Washington, DC 20003
Telephone: (202) 546-0200
Background: Former senior member, President's Council of Economic Advisers.

NISSENBAUM, Ellen
Legislative Director, Center on Budget and Policy Priorities
236 Massachusetts Ave., N.E., Suite 305, Washington, DC 20002
Telephone: (202) 544-0591
Registered as lobbyist at U.S. Congress.

NITZSCHE, Ronald E.
Chief Operating Officer, American College of Nurse-Midwives
1522 K St., N.W., Suite 1000, Washington, DC 20005
Telephone: (202) 289-0171

NIX, Michael
Marlowe and Co.
1667 K St., N.W., Suite 480, Washington, DC 20006
Telephone: (202) 775-1796
Registered as lobbyist at U.S. Congress.
Background: Former aide to Rep. Les Aspin (D-WI).

NIXON, HARGRAVE, DEVANS AND DOYLE
One Thomas Circle, N.W., Eighth Floor, Washington, DC 20005
Telephone: (202) 223-7200
Background: Washington office of a law firm based in Rochester, New York.
Members of firm representing listed organizations:
Kurzman, Stephen
Background: Legislative Assistant and Counsel to Sen. Jacob K. Javits of New York, 1961-65. Minority Counsel, U.S. Senate Committee on Labor and Public Welfare, 1965-66. Assistant Secretary for Legislation, Department of Health, Education and Welfare, 1971-76.
Clients:
American Free Trade Ass'n *(Stephen Kurzman)*
Bausch & Lomb, Inc. *(Stephen Kurzman)*
Coalition for Competitive Imports *(Stephen Kurzman)*
Eastman Savings & Loan Ass'n *(Stephen Kurzman)*
Lawyers Co-operative Publishing Co. *(Stephen Kurzman)*
Ogden Martin Systems
Tetrapak Inc.
Thompson Medical Co., Inc. *(Stephen Kurzman)*

NIXON, Nan F.
Washington Representative, Harvard University
499 South Capitol St., S.W., Washington, DC 20003
Telephone: (292) 863-1292

NIXON, Robert W.
Johns and Carson
12501 Old Columbia Pike, Silver Spring, MD 20904
Telephone: (301) 680-6320

NOACK, William H.
Director, Public Relations - Washington, General Motors Corp.
1660 L St., N.W., Washington, DC 20036
Telephone: (202) 775-5008

NOAH, Jeffrey P.
Director, Government Relations, Associated Builders and Contractors
729 15th St., N.W., Washington, DC 20005
Telephone: (202) 637-8800
Registered as lobbyist at U.S. Congress.

NOBLE, James R.
Exec. V. President, Mechanical Contractors Ass'n of America
1385 Piccard Drive, Rockville, MD 20850
Telephone: (301) 869-5800
Background: Serves also as Exec. Secretary, Nat'l Mechanical Equipment Service and Maintenance Bureau.

NOCERA, Barbara
Asst. Manager, Government Relations, Honda North America, Inc.
955 L'Enfant Plaza S.W., Suite 5300, Washington, DC 20024
Telephone: (202) 554-1650
Registered as lobbyist at U.S. Congress.

NOE, A. Allan
Director, Washington Affairs, Unilever United States, Inc.
816 Connecticut Ave., N.W. 7th Floor, Washington, DC 20006
Telephone: (202) 393-2839
Registered as lobbyist at U.S. Congress.

NOEL, Elizabeth A.
Deputy People's Counsel, District of Columbia Office of the People's Counsel
1101 14th St., N.W., Suite 900, Washington, DC 20005
Telephone: (202) 727-3071

NOEL, Lisa
Government Relations Specialist, Nat'l Manufactured Housing Finance Ass'n
1350 New York Ave., N.W., Suite 800, Washington, DC 20005
Telephone: (202) 628-2009

NOFZIGER COMMUNICATIONS
919 18th St., N.W. Suite 800, Washington, DC 20006
Telephone: (202) 785-6956
Members of firm representing listed organizations:
Nofziger, Franklyn 'Lyn'
   Background: Assistant to the President for Political Affairs, 1981-82.

NOFZIGER, Franklyn 'Lyn'
Nofziger Communications
919 18th St., N.W. Suite 800, Washington, DC 20006
Telephone: (202) 785-6956
Background: Assistant to the President for Political Affairs, 1981-82.

NOLAN, James P.
Internat'l President, Nat'l Ass'n of Broadcast Employees and Technicians
7101 Wisconsin Ave. Suite 800, Bethesda, MD 20814
Telephone: (301) 657-8420

NOLAN, John E., Jr.
Steptoe and Johnson
1330 Connecticut Ave., N.W., Washington, DC 20036
Telephone: (202) 429-3000
Registered as lobbyist at U.S. Congress.
Background: Law Clerk to Mr. Justice Clark, U.S. Supreme Court, 1955-56. Administrative Assistant to U.S. Attorney General Robert F. Kennedy, 1963-64.

NOLAN, John S.
Member, Miller & Chevalier, Chartered
Metropolitan Square, 655 15th St., N.W., Washington, DC 20005
Telephone: (202) 626-5800
Registered as lobbyist at U.S. Congress.
Background: Deputy Assistant Secretary of the Treasury for Tax Policy, 1969-1972.
Clients:
Metropolitan Life Insurance Co.
Rouse Company, The
Section 482 Study Group
Texas Instruments
Toyota Motor Sales, U.S.A.
Yamaha Motor Corp. U.S.A.

NOLAN, Kathleen D.
V. President, Fleishman-Hillard, Inc
1301 Connecticut Ave., N.W., Washington, DC 20036
Telephone: (202) 659-0330

NOLAN, Michael J.
Siegel & Associates, Mark A.
1030 15th St., N.W., Suite 408, Washington, DC 20005
Telephone: (202) 371-5600
Background: Also serves with Internat'l Public Strategies, Inc., the international arm of Mark A. Siegel & Associates.

NOLAN, Walker F.
Sr. V. President, Government Affairs, Edison Electric Institute
1111 19th St., N.W., Washington, DC 20036
Telephone: (202) 778-6510
Registered as lobbyist at U.S. Congress.

NOLAND, April L.
V. President, Operations, Foundation for Internat'l Meetings
4200 Wilson Blvd. Suite 1100, Arlington, VA 22203
Telephone: (703) 243-3288

NOLAND, Royce P.
President/ CEO, Institute for Professional Health Services Administrators
1101 King St., Suite 601, Alexandria, VA 22314
Telephone: (703) 684-0288

NOLIN, Christine L.
Exec. Director, Cogeneration and Independent Power Coalition of America
1133 21st St., N.W. Suite 420, Washington, DC 20036
Telephone: (202) 785-8776
Registered as lobbyist at U.S. Congress.

NOLIN, Raymond K.
V. President, Federal Relations, BellSouth Corp.
1133 21st St., N.W., Suite 900, Washington, DC 20036
Telephone: (202) 463-4100

NOON, Susan M.
Director, Legislative Activities, Profit Sharing Council of America
Chicago, IL

NOONAN, David J.
Deputy Exec. Vice President, American Academy of Ophthalmology
1101 Vermont Ave., N.W., Suite 300, Washington, DC 20005
Telephone: (202) 737-6662

NOOTER, Robert I.
Asst. Director, Nat'l Affairs Division, American Farm Bureau Federation
600 Maryland Ave., S.W., Washington, DC 20024
Telephone: (202) 484-3600
Registered as lobbyist at U.S. Congress.

NORBERG, Robert L.
Assistant to the V. President, Arabian American Oil Co.
1667 K St., N.W., Suite 1200, Washington, DC 20006
Telephone: (202) 223-7750

NORCROSS, David F.
Montgomery, McCracken, Walker & Rhoads
1156 15th St., N.W. Suite 550, Washington, DC 20005
Telephone: (202) 828-6901
Registered as lobbyist at U.S. Congress.
Clients:
Ass'n of Schools and Agencies for the Handicapped
Carpenter Labs
Center for Democracy
Delaware River and Bay Pilots Ass'n
Nat'l Ass'n of Private Schools for Exceptional Children
Nat'l Republican Institute for Internat'l Affairs
Ports of Philadelphia Maritime Exchange
RailPort

NORD, Nancy Ann
Exec. Director, American Corporate Counsel Ass'n
1225 Connecticut Ave., N.W., Suite 302, Washington, DC 20036
Telephone: (202) 296-4523

NORDBERG, Carl A., Jr.
Groom and Nordberg
1701 Pennsylvania Ave., N.W., Suite 1200, Washington, DC 20006
Telephone: (202) 857-0620
Registered as lobbyist at U.S. Congress.
Clients:
American Petroleum Institute
Chevron Corp.
Lilly and Co., Eli
Murphy Oil U.S.A.

Phillips Petroleum Co.
Puerto Rico, U.S.A. Foundation
Reading and Bates Corp.
Union Texas Petroleum
Westinghouse Electric Corp.

NORDHAUS, Robert R.
Van Ness, Feldman & Curtis
1050 Thomas Jefferson St., 7th Floor, Washington, DC 20007
Telephone: (202) 298-1800
Registered as lobbyist at U.S. Congress.
Clients:
Lower Colorado River Authority

NORDLINGER ASSOCIATES
1620 Eye St., N.W. 7th Floor, Washington, DC 20006
Telephone: (202) 785-0440
Background: A communications, public relations and grassroots firm specializing in politics and public affairs.
Members of firm representing listed organizations:
Chimes, Marc, V. President
Nordlinger, Gary, President
Shapiro, Lauren, Account Supervisor
Clients:
AFL-CIO (American Federation of Labor and Congress of Industrial Organizations)
AFL-CIO - Labor Heritage Foundation
American Psychological Ass'n
Gallatin Institute
Internat'l Council of Shopping Centers
Nat'l Ass'n of Homes for Children
Nat'l Ass'n of Letter Carriers of the United States of America
Nat'l Center for Policy Alternatives
Nat'l Education Ass'n of the U.S.
United Steelworkers of America

NORDLINGER, Gary
President, Nordlinger Associates
1620 Eye St., N.W. 7th Floor, Washington, DC 20006
Telephone: (202) 785-0440

NORE, Stephanie D.
Administrative Secretary, Cold Finished Steel Bar Institute
1120 Vermont Ave., N.W. Suite 1000, Washington, DC 20005
Telephone: (202) 857-0059

NOREN, Leif E.
Chairman, Conservative Victory Committee
111 South Columbus St., Alexandria, VA 22316
Telephone: (703) 684-6603

NORLAND, Donald R.
Program Director, Center for Internat'l Private Enterprise
1615 H St., N.W., Washington, DC 20062
Telephone: (202) 463-5901

NORMAN, Mark
Director, Policy Development, Highway Users Federation for Safety and Mobility
1776 Massachusette Ave., N.W., Washington, DC 20036
Telephone: (202) 857-1200

NORMAN-QUATTRONE, Teddi
National Affairs Coordinator, Hallmark Cards, Inc.
1615 L St., N.W., Suite 1220, Washington, DC 20036
Telephone: (202) 659-0946

NORMENT, Richard B.
Exec. Director, American Gear Manufacturers Ass'n
1500 King St., Suite 201, Alexandria, VA 22314
Telephone: (703) 684-0211
Background: Also represents the American Gear Political Action Committee.

NORRELL, David G.
Kirkland and Ellis
655 15th St., N.W. Suite 1200, Washington, DC 20005
Telephone: (202) 879-5000
Background: Law Clerk to U.S. Supreme Court Justice Thurgood Marshall, 1978-79.

NORRIS, Frances M.
Spec Asst to Pres, Legis Affrs (House), EXECUTIVE OFFICE OF THE PRESIDENT - The White House
1600 Pennsylvania Ave., N.W. 112 East Wing, Washington, DC 20500

NORRIS, Frances M. (Cont'd)
Telephone: (202) 456-7030

NORRIS, Grady
Asst Gen Counsel, Regulations, DEPARTMENT OF HOUSING AND URBAN DEVELOPMENT
451 Seventh St., S.W., Washington, DC 20410
Telephone: (202) 755-7055

NORRIS, James P.
Exec. Vice President, Air Conditioning Contractors of America
1513 16th St., N.W., Washington, DC 20036
Telephone: (202) 483-9370
Background: Also serves as Treasurer for the Air Conditioning Contractors of America Political Action Committee.

NORRIS, Jeffrey A.
McGuiness and Williams
1015 15th St., N.W., Suite 1200, Washington, DC 20005
Telephone: (202) 789-8600
Clients:
Equal Employment Advisory Council

NORRIS, Robert
Research Director, Democratic Congressional Campaign Committee
430 South Capitol St., S.E. 2nd Floor, Washington, DC 20003
Telephone: (202) 863-1500
Background: Former Legislative Assistant to Rep. Barney Frank (D-MA).

NORRIS, Robert S.
Senior Research Analyst, Natural Resources Defense Council
1350 New York Ave., N.W. Suite 300, Washington, DC 20005
Telephone: (202) 783-7800

NORRIS, T. H.
Corporate V. President, AT&T
Suite 1000, 1120 20th St., N.W., Washington, DC 20036
Telephone: (202) 457-3892

NORTH-RUDIN, Patrice
Ass't Exec. Director, Travel and Tourism Government Affairs Council
Two Lafayette Center 1133 21st St., N.W., Washington, DC 20036
Telephone: (202) 293-5407
Registered as lobbyist at U.S. Congress.

NORTH, William D.
Exec. V. President, Nat'l Ass'n of REALTORS
777 14th St., N.W., Washington, DC 20005
Telephone: (202) 383-1000

NORTHCOTT, Hall
Director, Government and Public Affairs, Matsushita Electric Corp. of America
1001 Pennsylvania Ave., N.W. Suite 1355 North, Washington, DC 20004
Telephone: (202) 347-7592
Registered as lobbyist at U.S. Congress.

NORTHCUTT, Allan
Exec. Director, Corporate Communications, Southwestern Bell Telephone Co.
1667 K St., N.W., Suite 1000, Washington, DC 20006
Telephone: (202) 293-8553

NORTHUP, Clifford
V. President, Walker Associates, Charls E.
1730 Pennsylvania Ave., N.W. Suite 200, Washington, DC 20006
Telephone: (202) 393-4760
Background: Former Legislative Ass't to Sen. Wm. Armstrong (R-CO).

NORTON, Edward M., Jr.
President, Grand Canyon Trust
1400 16th St. N.W., Suite 300, Washington, DC 20036
Telephone: (202) 797-5429
Registered as lobbyist at U.S. Congress.
Background: Ass't U.S. Attorney for the District of Maryland, 1978-81.

NORTON, Floyd L.
Reid & Priest
1111 19th St., N.W., Washington, DC 20036
Telephone: (202) 828-0100

NORTON, James J.
President, Graphic Communications Internat'l Union
1900 L St., N.W., Washington, DC 20036
Telephone: (202) 462-1400

NORTON, Joe M.
Senior V. President, Hannaford Co., Inc., The
655 15th St., N.W. Suite 200, Washington, DC 20005
Telephone: (202) 638-4600
Registered as lobbyist at U.S. Congress.
Registered as Foreign Agent: (#2850).

NORTON, John B.
General Attorney, Ass'n of American Railroads
50 F St., N.W., Suite 12300, Washington, DC 20001
Telephone: (202) 639-2504

NORTON, Marlee
Public Relations Director, Nat'l Telephone Cooperative Ass'n
2626 Pennsylvania Ave., N.W., Washington, DC 20037
Telephone: (202) 298-2300

NOSSAMAN, GUTHNER, KNOX AND ELLIOTT
1227 25th St., N.W., Suite 700, Washington, DC 20037
Telephone: (202) 223-9100
Registered as lobbyist at U.S. Congress.
Background: Washington office of a Los Angeles law firm.
Members of firm representing listed organizations:
Elliott, Warren G.
Background: Legislative Counsel to Senator Gordon Allott of Colorado, 1955-61.
Giaimo, Robert N.
Background: Member, U.S. House of Representatives (D-CT), 1959-80.
Zweben, Murray
Background: Assistant Parliamentarian (1963-75), Parliamentarian (1975-81), Parliamentarian Emeritus, 1986-present, U.S. Senate.
Clients:
Advo-Systems, Inc. *(Murray Zweben)*
Aetna Life & Casualty Co. *(Warren G. Elliott)*
Anheuser-Busch Cos., Inc. *(Murray Zweben)*
California Co-Compost Systems *(Murray Zweben)*
Committee for a Responsible Federal Budget *(Robert N. Giaimo)*
Edison Electric Institute *(Murray Zweben)*
General Cellular Corp. *(Murray Zweben)*
Nat'l Shorthand Reporters Ass'n *(Murray Zweben)*
Northwestern Nat'l Life Insurance Co. *(Warren G. Elliott)*
PKR Foundation *(Warren G. Elliott)*
Southern California Edison Co. *(Murray Zweben)*
Sun Microsystems *(Murray Zweben)*

NOTAR, Russell C.
Senior V. Pres., Domestic Operations, Nat'l Cooperative Business Ass'n
1401 New York Ave., N.W. Suite 1100, Washington, DC 20005
Telephone: (202) 638-6222
Registered as lobbyist at U.S. Congress.

NOTERMAN, Peter A.
Noterman and Ward
1616 H St., N.W. Suite 902, Washington, DC 20006-4995
Telephone: (202) 347-1820
Clients:
Nat'l AIDS Network

NOTERMAN AND WARD
1616 H St., N.W. Suite 902, Washington, DC 20006-4995
Telephone: (202) 347-1820
Members of firm representing listed organizations:
Noterman, Peter A.
Clients:
Nat'l AIDS Network *(Peter A. Noterman)*

NOTKIN, Jennifer
Neill and Co.
815 Connecticut Ave., N.W. Suite 800, Washington, DC 20006
Telephone: (202) 463-8877
Registered as lobbyist at U.S. Congress.

Registered as Foreign Agent: (#3320).

NOVAK, Mary Ann
Program Director - Energy, Parsons Brinkerhoff Quade & Douglas Inc.
555 13th St., N.W. Suite 460 West Tower, Washington, DC 20004
Telephone: (202) 637-8150

NOVAK, Michael
Dir., Social & Political Studies, American Enterprise Institute for Public Policy Research
1150 17th St., N.W., Washington, DC 20036
Telephone: (202) 862-5800

NOVEMBER GROUP INC.
1611 Connecticut Ave., N.W. 4th Floor, Washington, DC 20009
Telephone: (202) 265-2700
Background: A consulting firm specializing in voter contact and lobbying.
Members of firm representing listed organizations:
Adams, Greg A., V. President
Davis, Martin, President

NOWAK, G. Philip
Arnold & Porter
1200 New Hampshire Ave., N.W., Washington, DC 20036
Telephone: (202) 872-6700
Registered as lobbyist at U.S. Congress.

NOWERS, Philip P.
Exec. Director, Ass'n of Reproduction Materials Manufacturers
901 North Washington St., Alexandria, VA 22314
Telephone: (703) 548-7500

NOYES, Elizabeth J.
Director, Government Liaison, American Academy of Pediatrics
1331 Pennsylvania Ave., N.W., Suite 721 North, Washington, DC 20004-1703
Telephone: (202) 662-7460
Background: Also serves as Treasurer of Pediatricians for Children Inc.

NOZOE, Kuniaki
General Manager, Fujitsu Ltd.
1776 Eye St., N.W., Suite 880, Washington, DC 20006
Telephone: (202) 331-8750
Registered as Foreign Agent: (#4288).

NUCCIO, Richard A.
Senior Associate, Inter-American Dialogue
1333 New Hampshire Ave., N.W., Washington, DC 20036
Telephone: (202) 466-6410

NUCKOLLS, C. Randall
Kilpatrick & Cody
2501 M St., N.W., Suite 500, Washington, DC 20037
Telephone: (202) 463-2500
Registered as lobbyist at U.S. Congress.
Background: Legislative Counsel to Senator Herman Talmadge (D-GA), 1977-80. Chief Counsel and Legislative Director to Senator Sam Nunn (D-GA), 1980-86.
Clients:
Atlantic-Southeast Airlines
Bromon Aircraft Corp.
Federal Express Corp.
Forest Farmers Ass'n
Frito-Lay, Inc.
Georgia Tech Research Corp.
Granite Industrial Development
Kootznoowoo, Inc.
PepsiCo, Inc.
Scientific-Atlanta, Inc.
Siemens Energy and Automation, Inc.
Southdown
Spalding-Evenflo
United Airlines
University of Georgia
US Sprint Communications Co.

NUGENT, John M., Jr.
V. President, Global USA, Inc.
2121 K St., N.W., Suite 650, Washington, DC 20037
Telephone: (202) 296-2400
Registered as lobbyist at U.S. Congress.
Registered as Foreign Agent: (#3489).

Background: Former Ass't for Congressional Affairs to the Administrator, Energy Administration.
Clients:
All Nippon Airways Co.
Hitachi Ltd.

NUGENT, Patrick J.
Director of Finance Taxes, MCI Communications Corp.
1133 19th St., N.W., Washington, DC 20036
Telephone: (202) 872-1600
Registered as lobbyist at U.S. Congress.

NUGENT, Richard
Director of Government Liaison, Epilepsy Foundation of America
4351 Garden City Drive, Landover, MD 20785
Telephone: (301) 459-3700

NUNEZ, Louis
President, Nat'l Puerto Rican Coalition
1700 K St., N.W., Suite 500, Washington, DC 20006
Telephone: (703) 223-3915

NUNN, Silas O.
V. President, Programs, Shipbuilders Council of America
1110 Vermont Ave., N.W. Suite 1250, Washington, DC 20005
Telephone: (202) 775-9060
Registered as lobbyist at U.S. Congress.

NUSLOCH, George H.
Chairman, Olin Corp. Good Government Fund
1730 K St., N.W., Suite 1300, Washington, DC 20006
Telephone: (202) 331-7400

NUSS, Dr. Elizabeth
Executive Director, Nat'l Ass'n of Student Personnel Administrators
1700 18th Street, N.W. Suite 301, Washington, DC 20009
Telephone: (202) 265-7500

NUSSDORF, Melanie Franco
Steptoe and Johnson
1330 Connecticut Ave., N.W., Washington, DC 20036
Telephone: (202) 429-3000
Clients:
Ass'n of Private Pension and Welfare Plans

NUTTER, Jack O.
Sr. V. President, Dir Legis. Affairs, Jefferson Group, The
1341 G St., N.W., Suite 1100, Washington, DC 20005
Telephone: (202) 638-3535
Registered as lobbyist at U.S. Congress.
Background: Minority Tax Counsel, Senate Finance Committee, 1977-80.
Clients:
Lockheed Corp.
Pittston Co., The
Scott and Sons, O. M.

NUTTLE, R. Marc
Exec. Director, Nat'l Republican Congressional Committee
320 First St., S.E., Washington, DC 20003
Telephone: (202) 479-7000

NUZZACO, Mark J.
Director of Government Affairs, Nat'l Printing Equipment and Supply Ass'n
1899 Preston White Drive, Reston, VA 22091
Telephone: (703) 264-7200

NYBERG, Lars T.
V. President, Maersk Inc.
1667 K St., N.W., Suite 350, Washington, DC 20006
Telephone: (202) 887-6770

NYE, Zhi Marie
President, Real Trends
9200 Centerway Road, Gaithersburg, MD 20879
Telephone: (301) 840-6642
Clients:
Nat'l Military Intelligence Ass'n

NYERGES, Yolanda
Exec. Director, Council on Legal Education Opportunity
1800 M St., N.W. Suite 290, N. Lobby, Washington, DC 20036
Telephone: (202) 785-4840

NYHOUS, Lt. Col. Terry
House Affrs Dir, Legis Affrs, DEPARTMENT OF DEFENSE
The Pentagon, Washington, DC 20301
Telephone: (202) 697-6210

NYKWEST, Beverly C.
Assoc Dir, Communications/Public./PR, Nat'l Ass'n of Towns and Townships
1522 K St., N.W. Suite 730, Washington, DC 20005
Telephone: (202) 737-5200

OAKES, Maribeth
Policy Analyst/Editor, Nat'l Congress of Parents and Teachers
1201 16th St., N.W. Room 621, Washington, DC 20036
Telephone: (202) 822-7878

OAKLEY, Jana R.
Director, Federal Governmental Affairs, Entergy Corp.
1776 Eye St., N.W., Suite 275, Washington, DC 20006
Telephone: (202) 785-8444

OAKLEY, Janet
Associate for Government Affairs, Nat'l Ass'n of Regional Councils
1700 K St., N.W., Suite 1300, Washington, DC 20006-0011
Telephone: (202) 457-0710

OAKLEY, Paul C.
Exec. Director, State Rail Programs, Ass'n of American Railroads
50 F St., N.W., Suite 6904, Washington, DC 20001
Telephone: (202) 639-2206
Registered as lobbyist at U.S. Congress.

OBADAL, Anthony J.
Obadal and O'Leary
1612 K St., N.W. Suite 1400, Washington, DC 20006
Telephone: (202) 457-0260
Registered as lobbyist at U.S. Congress.
Clients:
Associated Equipment Distributors
Concrete Pipe Ass'ns, Inc.

OBADAL AND O'LEARY
1612 K St., N.W. Suite 1400, Washington, DC 20006
Telephone: (202) 457-0260
Members of firm representing listed organizations:
MacLeod, Sarah
Obadal, Anthony J.
O'Leary, John T.
Clients:
Aeronautical Repair Station Ass'n *(Sarah MacLeod)*
Associated Equipment Distributors *(Anthony J. Obadal, John T. O'Leary)*
Associated Equipment Distributors Political Action Committee *(John T. O'Leary)*
Concrete Pipe Ass'ns, Inc. *(Anthony J. Obadal)*

O'BANNON & CO.
2550 M St., N.W. Suite 250, Washington, DC 20037
Telephone: (202) 833-1914
Members of firm representing listed organizations:
O'Bannon, Dona
Clients:
Committee for Equitable Compensation *(Dona O'Bannon)*
Nat'l Ass'n of Women Business Owners *(Dona O'Bannon)*
PIMA (A Trade Association) *(Dona O'Bannon)*
Playtex, Inc. *(Dona O'Bannon)*

O'BANNON, Dona
O'Bannon & Co.
2550 M St., N.W. Suite 250, Washington, DC 20037
Telephone: (202) 833-1914
Registered as lobbyist at U.S. Congress.
Clients:
Committee for Equitable Compensation
Nat'l Ass'n of Women Business Owners
PIMA (A Trade Association)
Playtex, Inc.

O'BANNON, Hubert K., Jr.
Assistant V. President - Legislation, Ass'n of American Railroads
50 F Street, N.W., Washington, DC 20001

Telephone: (202) 639-2100
Registered as lobbyist at U.S. Congress.

O'BEA, George, Jr.
Vice President, United Paperworkers Internat'l Union
815 16th St., N.W. Suite 701, Washington, DC 20006
Telephone: (202) 783-5238
Registered as lobbyist at U.S. Congress.
Background: Also responsible for the United Paperworkers Internat'l Union Political Education Program.

O'BEIRNE, Elizabeth
Director, Public Affairs, Sprint International
12490 Sunrise Valley Drive, Reston, VA 22096
Telephone: (703) 689-7722

O'BEIRNE, Kate Walsh
Deputy Dir. for Domestic Policy Studies, Heritage Foundation
214 Massachusetts Ave., N.E., Washington, DC 20002
Telephone: (202) 546-4400
Background: Former Deputy Assistant Secretary of Health and Human Services for Human Service Legislation.

OBERDORFER, John L.
Patton, Boggs and Blow
2550 M St., N.W., Suite 800, Washington, DC 20037
Telephone: (202) 457-6000
Registered as lobbyist at U.S. Congress.
Registered as Foreign Agent: (#2165).
Background: Attorney, Office of the General Counsel, U.S. Department of Transportation, 1971-74.
Clients:
Institute of Scrap Recycling Industries, Inc.

O'BERRY, Dinah Kay
Legislative Representative, Nat'l Committee to Preserve Social Security and Medicare
2000 K St., N.W. Suite 800, Washington, DC 20006
Telephone: (202) 822-9459
Registered as lobbyist at U.S. Congress.
Background: Former Legislative Assistant to Rep. Fernand St. Germain.

OBOZ, Kim M.
Assistant V. Pres., Federal Relations, US WEST, Inc.
1020 19th St., N.W., Suite 700, Washington, DC 20036
Telephone: (202) 429-3100
Registered as lobbyist at U.S. Congress.

OBOZ, M. Kenneth
V. President, Government Relations, Prudential Insurance Co. of America
1140 Connecticut Ave., N.W., Suite 510, Washington, DC 20036
Telephone: (202) 463-0060

O'BRIEN, Ana Colomar
V. President, MacKenzie McCheyne, Inc.
2475 Virginia Ave., N.W. Suite 812, Washington, DC 20037
Telephone: (202) 338-9431
Registered as Foreign Agent: (#2721).
Clients:
Cuban Patriotic Council
El Salvador Freedom Foundation
Guatemala Freedom Foundation

O'BRIEN AND ASSOCIATES, DAVID
600 New Hampshire Ave., N.W., Suite 1010, Washington, DC 20037
Telephone: (202) 338-6650
Members of firm representing listed organizations:
O'Brien, David D.
Clients:
AB Hagglund & Soner *(David D. O'Brien)*
Competitive Health Care Coalition *(David D. O'Brien)*
Harley-Davidson, Inc. *(David D. O'Brien)*
Williams & Co., A. L. *(David D. O'Brien)*

O'BRIEN, BIRNEY AND BUTLER
888 17th St., N.W., Suite 1000, Washington, DC 20006
Telephone: (202) 298-6161
Members of firm representing listed organizations:
O'Brien, Paul L.
Clients:
American Pharmaceutical Ass'n *(Paul L. O'Brien)*
American Soc. of Appraisers *(Paul L. O'Brien)*

O'BRIEN, BIRNEY AND BUTLER (Cont'd)
Nat'l Institute for Automotive Service Excellence

O'BRIEN, Coleman C.
Sr. V. President, Legislative Counsel, United States
League of Savings Institutions
1709 New York Ave., N.W., Suite 801, Washington, DC
20006
Telephone: (202) 637-8900
Registered as lobbyist at U.S. Congress.

O'BRIEN, David D.
O'Brien and Associates, David
600 New Hampshire Ave., N.W., Suite 1010, Washington,
DC 20037
Telephone: (202) 338-6650
Registered as lobbyist at U.S. Congress.
Registered as Foreign Agent: (#4165).
Clients:
AB Hagglund & Soner
Competitive Health Care Coalition
Harley-Davidson, Inc.
Williams & Co., A. L.

O'BRIEN, Edward I.
President, Securities Industry Ass'n
1850 M St., N.W., Suite 550, Washington, DC 20036
Telephone: (202) 296-9410

O'BRIEN, Edward L.
Co-Director, Nat'l Institute for Citizen Education in the Law
711 G St., S.E., Washington, DC 20003
Telephone: (202) 662-9620

O'BRIEN, James D.
Lund and O'Brien
1625 Eye St., N.W., Suite 406, Washington, DC 20006
Telephone: (202) 331-1377
Registered as lobbyist at U.S. Congress.
Background: Attorney for Power Matters, U.S. Department
of the Interior, 1963-1964.
Clients:
Pennsylvania Power and Light Co.

O'BRIEN, John E.
Director, Engineering and Air Safety, Air Line Pilots Ass'n
Internat'l
1625 Massachusetts Ave., N.W., Washington, DC 20036
Telephone: (202) 797-4003

O'BRIEN, Kevin M.
Baker and McKenzie
815 Connecticut Ave., N.W. Suite 1100, Washington, DC
20006-4078
Telephone: (202) 452-7000
Clients:
Minnesota Mining and Manufacturing Co. (3M
Co.)

O'BRIEN, Kevin P.
Ivins, Phillips and Barker
1700 Pennsylvania Ave., N.W., Suite 600, Washington, DC
20006
Telephone: (202) 393-7600
Registered as lobbyist at U.S. Congress.

O'BRIEN, Lawrence F., III
Dewey, Ballantine, Bushby, Palmer and Wood
1775 Pennsylvania Ave., N.W. Suite 200, Washington, DC
20006
Telephone: (202) 862-1000
Registered as lobbyist at U.S. Congress.
Background: Deputy for Tax Legislation to the Assistant
Secretary of Treasury for Legislative Affairs, 1977-79.
Clients:
Bankers Trust Co.
Beneficial Corp.
Disney Productions, Walt
Federal Nat'l Mortgage Ass'n
General Reinsurance
Health Insurance Ass'n of America
Morgan Stanley and Co.
Nat'l Ass'n of Wholesaler-Distributors
NYNEX
Primerica Corp.
Teachers Insurance and Annuity Ass'n

O'BRIEN, Michael
Direcor, State and Local Affairs, Nat'l Ass'n of Home
Builders of the U.S.
15th and M Streets, N.W., Washington, DC 20005
Telephone: (202) 822-0470

O'BRIEN, Nancy
Associate Dir, Governmental Relations, Nat'l Ass'n of
Trade and Technical Schools
2251 Wisconsin Ave., N.W. Suite 200, Washington, DC
20007
Telephone: (202) 333-1021
Registered as lobbyist at U.S. Congress.

O'BRIEN, Patrick
Exec. Director, Police Ass'n of the District of Columbia
1441 Pennsylvania Ave., S.E., Washington, DC 20003
Telephone: (202) 543-9557
Background: Serves as contact for the Police Ass'n of the
District of Columbia PAC.

O'BRIEN, Paul L.
O'Brien, Birney and Butler
888 17th St., N.W., Suite 1000, Washington, DC 20006
Telephone: (202) 298-6161
Clients:
American Pharmaceutical Ass'n
American Soc. of Appraisers

O'BRIEN, Raymond V.
Director, Public Affairs, ITT Corp.
1600 M St., N.W., Washington, DC 20036
Telephone: (202) 775-7364
Registered as lobbyist at U.S. Congress.

O'BRIEN, Rindy
Director, Governmental Affairs, Wilderness Soc.
1400 Eye St., N.W., 10th Floor, Washington, DC 20005
Telephone: (202) 842-3400
Registered as lobbyist at U.S. Congress.

O'BRIEN, Robert
Director, Washington Public Relations, McDonnell Douglas
Corp.
1735 Jefferson Davis Highway, Arlington, VA 22202
Telephone: (703) 553-2117

O'BRIEN, Rosemary L.
V. President, Public Affairs, C F Industries, Inc.
805 15th St., N.W., Washington, DC 20005
Telephone: (202) 371-9279
Registered as lobbyist at U.S. Congress.

O'BRIEN, William R.
Howrey and Simon
1730 Pennsylvania Ave., N.W., Washington, DC 20006-
4793
Telephone: (202) 783-0800

O'BRYON, Maureen E.
Hogan and Hartson
555 13th St., N.W., Suite 1200, Washington, DC 20004-
1109
Telephone: (202) 637-5600

OCHOA, Mario
Exec. V. President, Adventist Development and Relief
Agency Internat'l
12501 Old Columbia Pike, Silver Spring, MD 20904
Telephone: (301) 680-6380

OCHS, Thomas
V. President, Squier & Eskew Communications, Inc.
511 2nd St., N.E., Washington, DC 20002
Telephone: (202) 547-4970
Registered as Foreign Agent: (#4237).
Clients:
Venezuela, Government of

O'COIN, Thomas A.
Deputy Dir. of Development, Corp. Affrs., Meridian House
Internat'l
1630 Crescent Place, N.W., Washington, DC 20009
Telephone: (202) 667-6800

O'CONNELL, Brian
President, Independent Sector
1828 L St., N.W., Washington, DC 20036
Telephone: (202) 223-8100

O'CONNELL, Brian F.
Peace, Freedom and Security Studies Prgm, Nat'l Ass'n
of Evangelicals
1023 15th St., N.W., Suite 500, Washington, DC 20005
Telephone: (202) 789-1011

O'CONNELL, James J.
Director, Int'l Trade Services, Control Data Corp.
Suite 370, 1201 Pennsylvania Ave., N.W., Washington, DC
20004
Telephone: (202) 789-6525
Registered as lobbyist at U.S. Congress.

O'CONNELL, K. Michael
Collier, Shannon & Scott
1055 Thomas Jefferson St., N.W., Suite 300, Washington,
DC 20007
Telephone: (202) 342-8400
Registered as lobbyist at U.S. Congress.
Registered as Foreign Agent: (#3694).
Background: Senior Policy Analyst, Assistant Secretary for
Trade Development, International Trade Administration,
U.S. Dept. of Commerce, 1983-4.
Clients:
Owner-Operator Independent Drivers Ass'n Poli-
tical Action Committee

O'CONNELL, Quinn
Holland and Hart
1001 Pennsylvania Suite 310, Washington, DC 20004
Telephone: (202) 638-5500
Registered as lobbyist at U.S. Congress.
Clients:
Alyeska Pipeline Service Co.

O'CONNELL, Richard T., CAE
President, Chocolate Manufacturers Ass'n of the U.S.A.
7900 Westpark Drive Suite A320, McLean, VA 22101
Telephone: (703) 790-5011
Background: Serves also as President, American Cocoa Research Institute, and as Exec. Director, Nat'l Confectioners Ass'n. Serves as Treasurer, Nat'l Confectioners Ass'n
of the U.S. Political Action Committee.

O'CONNELL, Terry M.
Exec. V. President, Keefe Co., The
444 North Capitol St., N.W., Suite 711, Washington, DC
20001
Telephone: (202) 638-7030
Registered as lobbyist at U.S. Congress.
Clients:
Ameri-Cable Internat'l, Inc.
Aruba, Government of
Bechtel Civil & Minerals, Inc.
Capital Hill Group, Inc., The
Federal Express Corp.
Homewood Corp.
Internat'l Public Relations Co.
Polysar Limited

O'CONNOR, Cindy
Manager, Regulatory Affairs, Chemical Producers and
Distributors Ass'n
1220 19th St., N.W., Suite 202, Washington, DC 20036
Telephone: (202) 785-2732
Registered as lobbyist at U.S. Congress.
Background: Also serves as Manager, Government Affairs,
Synthetic Organic Chemical Manufacturers Ass'n.

O'CONNOR, David M.
Regional Director, United States, Internat'l Air Transport
Ass'n
1001 Pennsylvania Ave., N.W. Suite 285, Washington, DC
20004
Telephone: (202) 624-2977

O'CONNOR, Emily
Dir, Land Use/Prop Rights, State & Munic, Nat'l Ass'n of
REALTORS
777 14th St., N.W., Washington, DC 20005
Telephone: (202) 383-1000
Registered as lobbyist at U.S. Congress.

O'CONNOR & HANNAN
1919 Pennsylvania Ave., N.W., Suite 800, Washington, DC
20006
Telephone: (202) 887-1400
Background: Washington office of a Minneapolis law firm.

WASHINGTON REPRESENTATIVES

Members of firm representing listed organizations:

Blatchford, Joseph H.
Background: Director, Peace Corps, 1969-72. Director, Action, 1971-72. Member, President's Cabinet Committee on the Aging, 1972. Deputy Under Secretary of Commerce, 1976-77.

Brooke, Edward W.
Background: Member, U.S. Senate (R-MA), 1967-79.

Colopy, Michael, Legislative Coordinator

Foster, Hope S.

Guest, Mary Scott, Legislative Consultant

Haake, Timothy M.
Background: Tax Counsel to Congressman Cecil Heftel, 1980-82, and to Senator H. John Heinz, 1979-80. Legislative Director to Congressman Richard T. Schulze, 1977-79. Attorney, Internal Revenue Service, 1973-77.

Jolly, Thomas R.
Background: Legislative Assistant, 1970-73 and Legislative Counsel, 1973-78 to Rep. William D. Ford (D-MI). Counsel and Staff Director, Subcommittee on Agricultural Labor, 1973-77 and Subcommittee on Postsecondary Education, 1977-78, House of Representatives Committee on Education and Labor.

Lee, F. Gordon

Mannina, George J. (Jr.)
Background: Administrative Aide to Rep. Gilbert Gude (R-MD), 1971-73. Legislative Assistant to Rep. Edwin B. Forsythe (R-NJ), 1973-75. Counsel House Subcommittee on Fisheries, Wildlife, Conservation and the Environment, 1975-81. Chief Minority Counsel, House Merchant Marine and Fisheries Committee, 1981-85.

Melincoff, David R.
Background: Member, Trial Section, Antitrust Division, Department of Justice, 1961-69.

O'Connor, Patrick J.
Background: Treasurer, Democratic National Committee, 1969-1970.

O'Donnell, Patrick E.
Background: Assistant Corporate Counsel, District of Columbia, 1962-70. Deputy Assistant Attorney General, Department of Justice, 1972-73. Special Assistant to the President for Legislative Affairs, The White House, 1970-72, 1974-76. Board member, Radio Marti, 1982-84.

Quinn, Thomas H.
Background: Attorney, Office of the Controller of the Currency, U.S. Treasury Department, 1963-1967. Member, U.S. Government Board for Internat'l Broadcasting, 1974-80.

Symington, James W.
Background: United States Chief of Protocol, 1966; United States Congressman (D-MO), 1969-77.

Wice, Jeffrey M.

Clients:
Alaska, State of *(George J. Mannina, Jr.)*
American Bus Ass'n *(Timothy M. Haake)*
American Clinical Laboratory Ass'n *(Hope S. Foster)*
American Clinical Laboratory Ass'n Political Action Committee *(Hope S. Foster)*
American Family Corp. *(Thomas R. Jolly)*
American Health Care Ass'n *(Timothy M. Haake)*
American Institute of Certified Public Accountants *(Thomas H. Quinn)*
American Maritime Transport, Inc. *(George J. Mannina, Jr.)*
American Orthotic and Prosthetic Ass'n *(Timothy M. Haake)*
American Soc. of Ass'n Executives *(Timothy M. Haake)*
American Soc. of Cataract and Refractive Surgery *(Thomas H. Quinn)*
Andersen and Co., Arthur
Asociacion Nacional de la Empresa Privada de El Salvador *(Joseph H. Blatchford, Patrick E. O'Donnell)*
Bionox, Inc.
British Consortium, The *(Timothy M. Haake)*
CareerCom Corp. *(Thomas R. Jolly)*
Center for Marine Conservation *(George J. Mannina, Jr.)*
China External Trade Development Council *(Michael Colopy, Thomas H. Quinn)*
CNA Financial Corp. *(Thomas R. Jolly)*
CNA Insurance Cos. *(Thomas R. Jolly)*
Coalition for Affordable Home Financing
Coca-Cola Co. *(Patrick E. O'Donnell)*
Connaught Laboratories, Inc. *(Timothy M. Haake)*

Democratic State Legislative Leaders Ass'n *(Jeffrey M. Wice)*
Distilled Spirits Council of the United States *(Thomas R. Jolly, Patrick E. O'Donnell)*
Eastern Michigan University *(Thomas R. Jolly)*
Ecomarine, Inc. *(George J. Mannina, Jr.)*
El Salvador, Government of *(Joseph H. Blatchford)*
Electronic Data Processing Auditors Ass'n *(Timothy M. Haake)*
Electronic Data Systems Corp.
Federal Home Loan Bank of Des Moines
Federal Home Loan Bank of Seattle
Federal Home Loan Bank of Topeka
Forstmann, Little & Co. *(Thomas H. Quinn)*
Grand Metropolitan PLC
Healthcare Financing Study Group *(Michael Colopy, Thomas H. Quinn)*
Hennepin County, Minnesota
Hutchinson Island Limited, Inc. *(George J. Mannina, Jr.)*
Internat'l Ass'n of Convention and Visitor Bureaus *(Timothy M. Haake)*
Investment Company Institute
Israel, Government of *(George J. Mannina, Jr.)*
Kawasaki Kisen Kaisha, Ltd. *(George J. Mannina, Jr.)*
MasterCard Internat'l. Inc.
Mercedes-Benz of North America, Inc. *(Patrick E. O'Donnell)*
Minnesota Mutual Life Insurance Co. *(Patrick J. O'Connor)*
Morgan Grenfell and Co., Ltd. *(Thomas H. Quinn)*
Naegele Outdoor Advertising *(Mary Scott Guest)*
Nat'l Apartment Ass'n *(Thomas H. Quinn)*
Nat'l Ass'n of Portable X-Ray Providers *(Hope S. Foster)*
Nat'l Club Ass'n *(Patrick E. O'Donnell, Thomas H. Quinn)*
Nat'l Funeral Directors Ass'n *(Timothy M. Haake)*
Nat'l Retail Hardware Ass'n *(Timothy M. Haake)*
New York State Assembly *(Jeffrey M. Wice)*
Outdoor Advertising Ass'n of America
Pacific Telesis Group-Washington *(Thomas H. Quinn)*
Paine Webber Group *(Mary Scott Guest)*
Penney Co., J. C. *(Patrick E. O'Donnell)*
Perpetual Savings Bank *(Thomas H. Quinn)*
Prudential Insurance Co. of America *(Thomas H. Quinn)*
Seagram & Sons, Inc., Joseph E. *(Thomas R. Jolly, Patrick E. O'Donnell)*
Securities Industry Ass'n *(Thomas H. Quinn)*
SmithKline Beecham *(Timothy M. Haake)*
Summer Island, Inc. *(George J. Mannina, Jr.)*
United States Tuna Foundation *(George J. Mannina, Jr.)*
VISA U.S.A., Inc.
Warner-Lambert Co. *(Timothy M. Haake, Patrick E. O'Donnell)*
Western Electrochemical Co. *(Mary Scott Guest)*
Westinghouse Electric Corp.

O'CONNOR, James E.
V. President and Dir., Tax Legislation, Nat'l Council of Savings Institutions
1101 15th St., N.W. Suite 400, Washington, DC 20005
Telephone: (202) 857-3100
Registered as lobbyist at U.S. Congress.

O'CONNOR, K. James
Associate Director, Internat'l Trade, Chemical Manufacturers Ass'n
2501 M St., N.W., Washington, DC 20037
Telephone: (202) 887-1100
Registered as lobbyist at U.S. Congress.

O'CONNOR, Michael J.
Director, Government Relations, Adhesive and Sealant Council
1627 K St., N.W., Washington, DC 20006
Telephone: (202) 452-1500
Registered as lobbyist at U.S. Congress.
Background: Staff Director, House Small Business Subcommittee on General Oversight and the Economy, 1985-87.

O'CONNOR, Patrick C.
President, Kent & O'Connor, Incorp.
1825 K St., N.W., Suite 305, Washington, DC 20006
Telephone: (202) 223-6222
Registered as lobbyist at U.S. Congress.
Clients:

American College of Occupational Medicine
American Supply Ass'n
American Warehousemen's Ass'n
Nat'l Ass'n of Fleet Administrators
Steel Tank Institute
Transportation Lawyers Ass'n

O'CONNOR, Patrick J.
O'Connor & Hannan
1919 Pennsylvania Ave., N.W., Suite 800, Washington, DC 20006
Telephone: (202) 887-1400
Registered as lobbyist at U.S. Congress.
Registered as Foreign Agent: (#2972).
Background: Treasurer, Democratic National Committee, 1969-1970.
Clients:
Minnesota Mutual Life Insurance Co.

O'CONNOR, Tom
V. President, Snavely, King and Associates
1220 L St., N.W., Suite 410, Washington, DC 20005
Telephone: (202) 371-1111
Background: Economist, Interstate Commerce Commission, 1973-75. Manager, Local Rail Planning, United States Railroad Administration, 1975-77.

O'CONOR, Kelley
Governmental Affairs Representative, Florists Transworld Delivery Ass'n
216 7th St., S.E., Washington, DC 20003
Telephone: (202) 546-1090
Registered as lobbyist at U.S. Congress.

O'DAY, Paul T.
President, American Fiber Manufacturers Ass'n
1150 17th St., N.W., Suite 310, Washington, DC 20036
Telephone: (202) 296-6508
Registered as lobbyist at U.S. Congress.
Background: Formerly a Deputy Assistant Secretary in the U.S. Department of Commerce.

O'DAY, Thomas A.
Associate V. President, Alliance of American Insurers
1629 K St., N.W. Suite 1010, Washington, DC 20006
Telephone: (202) 822-8811
Registered as lobbyist at U.S. Congress.

ODDIS, Joseph A.
Exec. Vice President, American Soc. of Hospital Pharmacists
4630 Montgomery Ave., Bethesda, MD 20814
Telephone: (301) 657-3000

O'DEA, James
Director, Washington Office, Amnesty Internat'l U.S.A.
304 Pennsylvania Ave., S.E., Washington, DC 20003
Telephone: (202) 544-0200

ODEN, Thomas J.
1503 North Fillmore St., Arlington, VA 22201
Telephone: (703) 528-3838
Organizations represented:
Nat'l Milk Producers Federation

ODLE, Bob Glen
Hogan and Hartson
555 13th St., N.W., Suite 1200, Washington, DC 20004-1109
Telephone: (202) 637-5600
Registered as lobbyist at U.S. Congress.
Clients:
Caremark/Home Health Care of America
May Department Stores Co.
Ontario, Province of

ODLE, Robert C., Jr.
Weil, Gotshal & Manges
1615 L St., N.W., Suite 700, Washington, DC 20036
Telephone: (202) 682-7000
Registered as lobbyist at U.S. Congress.
Background: Staff Assistant to the President of the U.S., 1969-71. Deputy Assistant Secretary, Department of Housing and Urban Development, 1973-76. Assistant Secretary, Department of Energy, 1981-85.
Clients:
Marine Shale Processors, Inc.
Noranda, Inc.

ODOM, Sheralyn J.
Exec. Director, Nat'l Ass'n of State Credit Union Supervisors
1901 North Ft. Myer Dr. Suite 201, Arlington, VA 22209
Telephone: (703) 528-8351

ODOM, Lt. Gen. William E., USA (Ret)
Director, Nat'l Security Studies, Hudson Institute
4401 Ford Ave. Suite 200, Alexandria, VA 22302
Telephone: (703) 824-2048

O'DONNELL, Denise
Sr. Government Affairs Representative, Georgia-Pacific Corp.
1875 Eye St., N.W. Suite 775, Washington, DC 20006
Telephone: (202) 659-3600
Background: Serves as Treasurer, G-P Employees Fund of Georgia-Pacific.

O'DONNELL, Earle H.
Sutherland, Asbill and Brennan
1275 Pennsylvania, N.W., Washington, DC 20004-2404
Telephone: (202) 383-0100
Clients:
Ad Hoc Committee for a Competitive Electric Supply System (ACCESS)
Armco Inc.

O'DONNELL, John F.
Dir., Legislation and Legislative Policy, American Dental Ass'n
1111 14th St., N.W. Suite 1200, Washington, DC 20005
Telephone: (202) 898-2400
Registered as lobbyist at U.S. Congress.

O'DONNELL, John R.
Nat'l Center for Municipal Development
1620 Eye St., N.W., Suite 300, Washington, DC 20006
Telephone: (202) 429-0160
Clients:
Albuquerque, New Mexico, City of
Phoenix, Arizona, City of

O'DONNELL, Karen
Director, Taxation & Fiscal Affairs, Associated General Contractors of America
1957 E St., N.W., Washington, DC 20006
Telephone: (202) 393-2040
Registered as lobbyist at U.S. Congress.

O'DONNELL, Kirk
Akin, Gump, Strauss, Hauer and Feld
1333 New Hampshire Ave., N.W., Suite 400, Washington, DC 20036
Telephone: (202) 887-4000
Registered as lobbyist at U.S. Congress.
Clients:
Collagen Corp.
Miller Brewing Co.

O'DONNELL, Patrick E.
O'Connor & Hannan
1919 Pennsylvania Ave., N.W., Suite 800, Washington, DC 20006
Telephone: (202) 887-1400
Registered as lobbyist at U.S. Congress.
Registered as Foreign Agent: (#2972).
Background: Assistant Corporate Counsel, District of Columbia, 1962-70. Deputy Assistant Attorney General, Department of Justice, 1972-73. Special Assistant to the President for Legislative Affairs, The White House, 1970-72, 1974-76. Board member, Radio Marti, 1982-84.
Clients:
Asociacion Nacional de la Empresa Privada de El Salvador
Coca-Cola Co.
Distilled Spirits Council of the United States
Mercedes-Benz of North America, Inc.
Nat'l Club Ass'n
Penney Co., J. C.
Seagram & Sons, Inc., Joseph E.
Warner-Lambert Co.

O'DONNELL, SCHWARTZ & ANDERSON
1300 L St., N.W., Suite 200, Washington, DC 20005-4178
Telephone: (202) 898-1707
Registered as lobbyist at U.S. Congress.
Members of firm representing listed organizations:
Anderson, Darryl

Luby, Arthur M.
Clients:
American Postal Workers Union *(Darryl Anderson)*
Transport Workers Union of America, AFL-CIO *(Arthur M. Luby)*

O'DONNELL, Thomas
Baker and McKenzie
815 Connecticut Ave., N.W. Suite 1100, Washington, DC 20006-4078
Telephone: (202) 452-7000

O'DRISCOLL, Mary
Nat'l Press Coordinator, Safe Energy Communication Council
1717 Massachusetts Ave., N.W. Suite LL215, Washington, DC 20036
Telephone: (202) 483-8491

O'DUDEN, Gregory J.
Director, Litigation, Nat'l Treasury Employees Union
1730 K St., N.W., Suite 1100, Washington, DC 20006
Telephone: (202) 785-4411

ODUM, Mark
Project Director, Nat'l Rehabilitation Information Center
8455 Colesville Rd., #935, Silver Spring, MD 20910
Telephone: (301) 588-9284

O'DWYER, Julianne
Exec. Director, Coalition for Government Procurement
1990 M St., N.W., Suite 400, Washington, DC 20036
Telephone: (202) 331-0975

OFFEN, Neil H.
President, Direct Selling Ass'n
1776 K St., N.W., Suite 600, Washington, DC 20006
Telephone: (202) 293-5760
Registered as lobbyist at U.S. Congress.
Background: Also serves as Chairman, Direct Selling Ass'n Political Committee. Also is a member of the Boards of Directors, American Retail Federation, Democratic Nat'l Committee Business Council, American Soc. of Ass'n Executives, the Ethics Resource Center, the American Retail Education Foundation, the Direct Selling Education Foundation and the World Federation of Direct Selling Ass'ns.

OFFUTT, James R.
Sr Counsel, Admin and Legislation, OVERSEAS PRIVATE INVESTMENT CORP.
1615 M St., N.W., Washington, DC 20527
Telephone: (202) 457-7038

O'FLAHERTY, J. Daniel
V. President and Secretary, Nat'l Foreign Trade Council, Inc.
1625 K St., N.W., Suite 1090, Washington, DC 20006
Telephone: (202) 887-0278
Registered as lobbyist at U.S. Congress.

OGAWA, Yoshie
V. President, Internat'l Affrs., Northwest Airlines, Inc.
900 17th St., N.W. Suite 526, Washington, DC 20006
Telephone: (202) 887-5636

OGG, James D.
V. President, Government Relations, Centel Corp.
1350 Eye St., N.W., Suite 500, Washington, DC 20005
Telephone: (202) 778-8700
Background: Responsibilities include Centel Corp. Good Government Fund.

OGG, Jon C.
V. President, State Coordinator, Nat'l Ass'n of Life Companies
1455 Pennsylvania Ave., N.W., Suite 1250, Washington, DC 20004
Telephone: (202) 783-6252
Background: Also represents the Nat'l Ass'n of Life Companies PAC.

OGILVIE, Donald G.
Exec. V. President, American Bankers Ass'n
1120 Connecticut Ave., N.W., Washington, DC 20036
Telephone: (202) 663-5000
Registered as lobbyist at U.S. Congress.

OGLES, George W.
Dir., Public Relations and Membership, Nat'l Security Industrial Ass'n
1025 Connecticut Ave., N.W., Suite 300, Washington, DC 20036
Telephone: (202) 775-1440

OGLESBY, M. G., Jr.
Senior V. President, Government Affairs, RJR Nabisco Washington, Inc.
1455 Pennsylvania Ave., N.W., Suite 525, Washington, DC 20004
Telephone: (202) 626-7200
Registered as lobbyist at U.S. Congress.

O'GRADY, Bridget
Director, Government Affairs, Nat'l Water Resources Ass'n
3800 North Fairfax Dr. Suite 4, Arlington, VA 22203
Telephone: (703) 524-1544
Registered as lobbyist at U.S. Congress.

O'GRADY, Jane
Legislative Representative, AFL-CIO (American Federation of Labor and Congress of Industrial Organizations)
815 16th St., N.W., Washington, DC 20006
Telephone: (202) 637-5393
Registered as lobbyist at U.S. Congress.

O'GRADY, Terri
Political Affairs Liaison, Nat'l Rifle Ass'n of America
1600 Rhode Island Ave., N.W., Washington, DC 20036
Telephone: (202) 828-6353
Registered as lobbyist at U.S. Congress.

OGRODZINSKI, Henry M.
Director of Communications, General Aviation Manufacturers Ass'n
1400 K St., Suite 801, Washington, DC 20005
Telephone: (202) 393-1500

O'HAGAN, Malcolm E.
President, Valve Manufacturers Ass'n of America
1050 17th St., N.W., Washington, DC 20036
Telephone: (202) 331-8105

O'HANLON, Cdr. Rich
Exec Asst, Legis Affrs, DEPARTMENT OF NAVY
The Pentagon, Washington, DC 20350-1300
Telephone: (202) 697-7146

O'HARA, Barbara E.
Director, Government Affairs, American Soc. of Travel Agents
1101 King St., Alexandria, VA 22314
Telephone: (703) 739-2782
Registered as lobbyist at U.S. Congress.
Background: Also represents the American Soc. of Travel Agents PAC.

O'HARA, Bartley M., P.C.
1919 Pennsylvania Ave., N.W., Suite 300, Washington, DC 20006
Telephone: (202) 659-1619
Registered as lobbyist at U.S. Congress.
Organizations represented:
Anheuser-Busch Cos., Inc.
Burlington Northern Railroad
Grocery Manufacturers of America
Internat'l Union of Bricklayers and Allied Craftsmen
MetPath Inc.

O'HARA, James T.
Jones, Day, Reavis and Pogue
1450 G St., N.W., Suite 700, Washington, DC 20005-2088
Telephone: (202) 879-3939
Registered as lobbyist at U.S. Congress.
Background: Section Chief, Reorganization Branch, Internal Revenue Service, 1967-69.

O'HARA, Judith
Executive Director, Agriculture Council of America
1250 I St., N.W., Suite 601, Washington, DC 20005
Telephone: (202) 682-9200

O'HARA, Kathleen
Director, Public Affairs, Fertilizer Institute
501 Second St., N.E., Washington, DC 20002

Telephone: (202) 675-8250

O'HARA, Lorraine
Director, AFSCME Nat'l Public Employees Organized to Promote Legislative Equality (PEOPLE)
Box 65334, Washington, DC 20035
Telephone: (202) 452-4800

O'HARA, Ray
Patton, Boggs and Blow
2550 M St., N.W., Suite 800, Washington, DC 20037
Telephone: (202) 457-6000
Clients:
Smokeless Tobacco Council

O'HARA, Thomas G.
V. President, Prudential Insurance Co. of America
Suite 510, 1140 Connecticut Ave., N.W., Washington, DC 20036
Telephone: (202) 293-1676

O'HARE, Donald L.
Director, Public Affairs, Sea-Land Service, Inc.
1331 Pennsylvania Ave., N.W. Suite 560 National Place, Washington, DC 20004
Telephone: (202) 783-1117
Registered as lobbyist at U.S. Congress.

OHI, Takatsugu
General Manager, Mitsui and Co. (U.S.A.), Inc.
1701 Pennsylvania Ave., N.W., Suite 400, Washington, DC 20006
Telephone: (202) 861-0660

OHLSEN, John W.
Exec. Vice President, Defense Orientation Conference Ass'n
1601 North Kent St., Suite 1012, Arlington, VA 22209-2217
Telephone: (703) 524-1800

OHMANS, Karen
Co-Director, American Labor Education Center
1730 Connecticut Ave., N.W., Washington, DC 20009
Telephone: (202) 387-6780

O'KEEFE, Daniel F., Jr.
Sr. V. President & General Counsel, Nonprescription Drug Manfacturers Ass'n
1150 Connecticut Ave., N.W.,, Washington, DC 20036
Telephone: (202) 429-9260

O'KEEFE, Eileen
Lisboa Associates, Inc.
1317 F St., N.W., Suite 202, Washington, DC 20004
Telephone: (202) 737-2622
Background: Associate, Lisboa Associates, Inc.
Clients:
Virgin Islands, University of the

O'KEEFE, William F.
V. President, Chief Operating Officer, American Petroleum Institute
1220 L St., N.W., Washington, DC 20005
Telephone: (202) 682-8300

O'KEEFFE, Janet
Legislative Affairs Representative, American Psychological Ass'n
1200 17th St., N.W., Washington, DC 20036
Telephone: (202) 955-7600
Registered as lobbyist at U.S. Congress.

O'KELLY, James S.
Barnes, Richardson and Colburn
1819 H St., N.W., Washington, DC 20006
Telephone: (202) 457-0300
Clients:
Asahi Chemical Industry Co.
Mitsui and Co.

OLDAK, Michael D.
Regulatory Counsel, Nat'l Rural Electric Cooperative Ass'n
1800 Massachusetts Ave., N.W., Washington, DC 20036
Telephone: (202) 857-9607
Registered as lobbyist at U.S. Congress.

OLDAKER, William C.
Manatt, Phelps, Rothenberg & Phillips
1200 New Hampshire Ave., N.W., Suite 200, Washington, DC 20036
Telephone: (202) 463-4300
Registered as lobbyist at U.S. Congress.
Registered as Foreign Agent: (#3564).
Background: Special Assistant, Equal Employment Opportunity Commission, 1969-73. Assistant General Counsel for Litigation and Enforcement, Federal Election Commission, 1975-76. General Counsel, Federal Election Commission, 1976-79.
Clients:
AMBASE
American Ass'n of Nurse Anesthetists
Citizen Action
Federal Express Corp.
Nat'l Cable Television Ass'n Political Action Committee
Philip Morris Management Corp.

OLDHAM, Judy
Collier, Shannon & Scott
1055 Thomas Jefferson St., N.W., Suite 300, Washington, DC 20007
Telephone: (202) 342-8400
Clients:
Reynolds Tobacco Co., R. J.

O'LEARY, Bradley
President, American Ass'n of Political Consultants
1211 Connecticut Ave., N.W. Suite 506, Washington, DC 20036
Telephone: (202) 546-1564

O'LEARY, Howard E., Jr.
Dykema Gossett
1752 N St., N.W., 6th Floor, Washington, DC 20036
Telephone: (202) 466-7185
Background: Chief Counsel and Staff Director, U.S. Senate Committee on The Judiciary, Subcommittee on Antitrust and Monopoly, 1969-77.
Clients:
Total Petroleum, Inc.

O'LEARY, John T.
Obadal and O'Leary
1612 K St., N.W. Suite 1400, Washington, DC 20006
Telephone: (202) 457-0260
Registered as lobbyist at U.S. Congress.
Clients:
Associated Equipment Distributors
Associated Equipment Distributors Political Action Committee

O'LEARY, Joseph E.
Consultant, Bishop, Cook, Purcell & Reynolds
1400 L St., N.W., Washington, DC 20005-3502
Telephone: (202) 371-5700
Registered as lobbyist at U.S. Congress.
Background: Held several Congressional staff position, 1969-75.

O'LEARY, Kathleen
Director, Federal Government Affairs, Columbia Gas Transmission Corp.
1250 Eye St., N.W., Suite 703, Washington, DC 20005
Telephone: (202) 842-7400
Registered as lobbyist at U.S. Congress.

O'LEARY, Patrick F.
Tanaka, Ritger and Middleton
1919 Pennsylvania Ave., N.W., Suite 303, Washington, DC 20006
Telephone: (202) 223-1670
Registered as lobbyist at U.S. Congress.
Registered as Foreign Agent: (#0948).
Clients:
Brother Internat'l, Inc.
Flat Glass Ass'n of Japan
Onoda Cement Co., Ltd.

OLIPHANT, C. Frederick, III
Member, Miller & Chevalier, Chartered
Metropolitan Square, 655 15th St., N.W., Washington, DC 20005
Telephone: (202) 626-5800
Clients:
Nat'l Ass'n of Temporary Services

OLIVAS, Ernest, Jr.
Eastern Region Director, Communications Internat'l Inc.
One Thomas Circle, N.W. Suite 975, Washington, DC 20005
Telephone: (202) 429-2900
Background: Responsibilities include government relations. Former Deputy Director for Minority Recruiting, Republican National Committee.

OLIVE, David
Deputy General Manager, Fujitsu Ltd.
1776 Eye St., N.W., Suite 880, Washington, DC 20006
Telephone: (202) 331-8750

OLIVER, Heidi Belz
Director, Briefing Center, Chamber of Commerce of the U.S.A.
1615 H St., N.W., Washington, DC 20062
Telephone: (202) 463-5414

OLIVER, Dr. James
President, Entomological Soc. of America
9301 Annapolis Rd., Lanham, MD 20706-3115
Telephone: (301) 731-4535

OLIVER, John C.
Exec. V. President, Porcelain Enamel Institute
1101 Connecticut Ave., N.W. Suite 700, Washington, DC 20036
Telephone: (202) 857-1134

OLIVER, Nancy
Project Director, Trade & Labor, Citizens for a Sound Economy
470 L'Enfant Plaza East, S.W. Suite 7112, Washington, DC 20024
Telephone: (202) 488-8200

OLIVER, R. Teel
V. President, Government Relations, Merck and Co.
1615 L St., N.W., Suite 1320, Washington, DC 20036
Telephone: (202) 833-8205
Registered as lobbyist at U.S. Congress.

OLIVEREZ, Manuel
President & CEO, Nat'l Image, Inc.
810 First St., N.E., Washington, DC 20002
Telephone: (202) 289-3777

OLLISON, Hague
Cong Liaison Asst, DEPARTMENT OF COMMERCE
14th and Constitution Ave. S.W., Washington, DC 20230
Telephone: (202) 377-5485

OLMER, Lionel H.
Paul, Weiss, Rifkind, Wharton and Garrison
1615 L St., N.W., Suite 1300, Washington, DC 20036
Telephone: (202) 223-7300
Background: Undersecretary of Commerce for International Trade and head of the International Trade Administration, 1981-85; Executive Staff, President's Foreign Intelligence Advisory Board, 1973-77.
Clients:
Itoh (America), Inc., C.
McDonnell Douglas Corp.
Nat'l Music Publishers' Ass'n

OLMSTEAD, Cecil J.
Of Counsel, Steptoe and Johnson
1330 Connecticut Ave. N.W., Washington, DC 20036
Telephone: (202) 429-3000
Background: Assistant to Legal Advisor, State Department, 1951-53. U.S. Delegate, United Nations Committee on Law of Sea, 1972.

OLNEY, Austin P.
LeBoeuf, Lamb, Leiby, and MacRae
1333 New Hampshire Ave., N.W. Suite 1100, Washington, DC 20036
Telephone: (202) 457-7500
Registered as lobbyist at U.S. Congress.
Registered as Foreign Agent: (#2868).
Background: Counsel, U.S. House of Representatives Committee on Merchant Marine and Fisheries, 1975-77.
Clients:
Maritrans Operating Partners, L.P.

OLSEN, George G.
Williams and Jensen, P.C.
1101 Connecticut Ave., N.W., Suite 500, Washington, DC 20036
Telephone: (202) 659-8201
Clients:
Nat'l Ass'n of Rehabilitation Agencies

OLSEN, Kimberly
Assistant Director, Nat'l Ass'n of Solvent Recyclers
1333 New Hampshire Ave., N.W., Suite 1100, Washington, DC 20036
Telephone: (202) 463-6956

OLSEN, Terryle
Confidential Asst, Legis Affrs, EXECUTIVE OFFICE OF THE PRESIDENT - Office of Management and Budget
Old Executive Office Bldg., Washington, DC 20500
Telephone: (202) 395-4790

OLSEN, Van R.
V. President, United States Beet Sugar Ass'n
1156 15th St., N.W., Washington, DC 20005
Telephone: (202) 296-4820
Registered as lobbyist at U.S. Congress.
Background: Serves also as Treasurer, Beet Sugar Political Action Committee.

OLSON & ASSOC., Richard
2000 Edmund Halley Drive, Reston, VA 22091
Telephone: (703) 264-9204
Members of firm representing listed organizations:
Olson, Richard C., President
Background: Former Admin. Assistant to Rep. Morris K. Udall (D-AZ), 1961-71; Former leadership aide to Rep. Jim Wright (D-TX), 1977-82.
Organizations represented:
Citibank, N.A. *(Richard C. Olson)*
DynCorp *(Richard C. Olson)*
DynCorp Federal Political Action Committee *(Richard C. Olson)*
Hydrocarbon Research, Inc. *(Richard C. Olson)*

OLSON, Erik
Counsel, Nat'l Wildlife Federation
1400 16th St., N.W., Washington, DC 20036-2266
Telephone: (202) 797-6800
Registered as lobbyist at U.S. Congress.

OLSON, John F.
Gibson, Dunn and Crutcher
1050 Connecticut Ave. N.W. Suite 900, Washington, DC 20036-5303
Telephone: (202) 955-8500

OLSON, Lisa M.
V. President, Keene, Shirley & Associates, Inc.
919 Prince St., Alexandria, VA 22314
Telephone: (703) 684-0550
Registered as lobbyist at U.S. Congress.
Registered as Foreign Agent: (#3997).
Clients:
AXS
Kendall and Associates, John

OLSON, Mattie
Director, Public Relations, Nat'l Rural Electric Cooperative Ass'n
1800 Massachusetts Ave., N.W., Washington, DC 20036
Telephone: (202) 857-9534

OLSON, Richard C.
President, Olson & Assoc., Richard
2000 Edmund Halley Drive, Reston, VA 22091
Telephone: (703) 264-9204
Registered as lobbyist at U.S. Congress.
Background: Former Admin. Assistant to Rep. Morris K. Udall (D-AZ), 1961-71; Former leadership aide to Rep. Jim Wright (D-TX), 1977-82.
Organizations represented:
Citibank, N.A.
DynCorp
DynCorp Federal Political Action Committee
Hydrocarbon Research, Inc.

OLSON, Sydney
Director, Governmental Affairs Dept., American Speech-Language-Hearing Ass'n
10801 Rockville Pike, Rockville, MD 20852

Telephone: (301) 897-5700
Registered as lobbyist at U.S. Congress.

OLSON, Thomas P.
Wilmer, Cutler and Pickering
2445 M St., N.W., Washington, DC 20037-1420
Telephone: (202) 663-6000
Clients:
Public Broadcasting Service

OLSON, William J.
Gilman, Olson & Pangia
1815 H St., N.W. Suite 600, Washington, DC 20005
Telephone: (202) 466-5100
Clients:
Industry Council for Tangible Assets

OLSSON, FRANK AND WEEDA, P.C.
1400 16th St., N.W. Suite 400, Washington, DC 20036-2220
Telephone: (202) 789-1212
Registered as lobbyist at U.S. Congress.
Members of firm representing listed organizations:
Bode, John
Background: Former Assistant Secretary for Food and Consumer Services, U.S. Department of Agriculture.
Frank, Richard L.
Clients:
Duramed Pharmaceuticals, Inc. *(John Bode)*
Nat'l-American Wholesale Grocers' Ass'n *(John Bode, Richard L. Frank)*
Pillsbury Co. *(Richard L. Frank)*
San Tomo Group *(John Bode)*
Schwan's Sales Enterprises *(John Bode)*
U.S. Surgical Corp. *(John Bode)*
VICAM *(John Bode)*
Western States Meat Ass'n *(John Bode)*

OLSZEWSKI, Gerald B.
V. President, Ketchum Public Relations
1201 Connecticut Ave., N.W. Suite 300, Washington, DC 20036
Telephone: (202) 835-8800
Clients:
Dow Chemical

OLWINE, CONNELLY, CHASE, O'DONNELL AND WEYHER
1701 Pennsylvania Ave., N.W. Suite 1000, Washington, DC 20006
Telephone: (202) 835-0500
Background: Washington office of a New York City-based law firm.
Members of firm representing listed organizations:
Gaines, Frank W. (Jr.)
Hoegle, Robert L.
Sachs, John L.
Wellford, W. Harrison
Background: Chief Legislative Assistant to Senator Philip Hart (D-MI), 1973-76. Exec. Associate Director, White House Office of Management and Budget, 1977-80. Director, President's Reorganization Project, 1977-81.
Clients:
Ad Hoc Committee for Small Hydro Power *(W. Harrison Wellford)*
Alexander & Alexander Inc. *(W. Harrison Wellford)*
Catalyst Energy Corp. *(John L. Sachs. W. Harrison Wellford)*
Companhia de Navagacao Maritima NETUMAR *(Robert L. Hoegle)*
Energy Factors *(W. Harrison Wellford)*
Intercontinental Energy Corp. *(W. Harrison Wellford)*
Liberty Mutual Insurance Co. *(Robert L. Hoegle)*
Long Lake Energy Corp. *(W. Harrison Wellford)*
Nat'l for Housing Partnerships *(W. Harrison Wellford)*
Nat'l Independent Energy Producers *(W. Harrison Wellford)*
Sithe Energies USA *(W. Harrison Wellford)*
United Way of America *(W. Harrison Wellford)*
YMCA of the USA *(W. Harrison Wellford)*

O'MALLEY, Sharon
Director of Public Affairs, Electronic Data Systems Corp.
1331 Pennsylvania Ave., N.W., Suite 1300 North, Washington, DC 20004
Telephone: (202) 637-6700

O'MELIA, Kevin M.
Assistant V. President/Corp. Secretary, Vinnell Corp.
10530 Rosehaven St., Suite 600, Fairfax, VA 22030
Telephone: (703) 385-4544

O'MELVENY AND MYERS
555 13th St., N.W., Suite 500 West, Washington, DC 20004
Telephone: (202) 383-5300
Registered as Foreign Agent: (#3346)
Background: Washington office of a Los Angeles law firm.
Members of firm representing listed organizations:
Almstedt, Kermit W.
Benjamin, Ben E.
Bliss, Donald T. (Jr.)
Background: Assistant to the Secretary of HEW, 1969-73. Special Assistant to the Administrator, EPA, 1973-74. Deputy General Counsel, Department of Transporation, 1975-77. Acting General Counsel, Department of Transportation, 1976-77.
Christopher, Warren
Background: Law Clerk to Mr. Justice Douglas, U.S. Supreme Court, 1949-50. Deputy Attorney General of the U.S., 1967-69. Deputy Secretary of State, 1977-81.
Coleman, William T. (Jr.)
Background: Chief Legislative Assistant to U.S. Senator Howard H. Baker of Tennessee, 1973-76. Member, Board of Directors, CIGNA Corp.
DeBusk, F. Amanda
Holum, John D.
Horlick, Gary N.
Masin, Michael T.
Parker, Richard G.
Valentine, Debra
Warmer, Richard C.
Clients:
Alaska Airlines *(William T. Coleman, Jr.)*
Amax Inc.
Baldwin Co., D. H. *(Richard G. Parker)*
Baldwin United Corp. *(Richard G. Parker)*
Brewers Ass'n of Canada
Broken Hill Proprietary Co., Ltd.
Canada, Government of
Cargill, Inc. *(Kermit W. Almstedt)*
Conseil Europeen des Federations de l'Industrie Chimique (CEFIC)
Emergency Committee for American Trade *(Gary N. Horlick)*
Ford Motor Co. *(Donald T. Bliss, Jr., William T. Coleman, Jr., Gary N. Horlick, Debra Valentine)*
Nippon Zeon *(F. Amanda DeBusk)*
O'Melveny and Myers Political Action Committee *(Ben E. Benjamin)*
Pan American World Airways *(William T. Coleman, Jr.)*
Persico Pizzamiglio, S.A.
Philadelphia Electric Co.
Security Pacific Nat'l Bank *(William T. Coleman, Jr.)*
Southern California Edison Co. *(Warren Christopher)*

OMLIE, Lynne
Secretary and General Counsel, Distilled Spirits Council of the United States
1250 Eye St., N.W., Suite 900, Washington, DC 20005
Telephone: (202) 628-3544

ONDECK, Thomas P.
Baker and McKenzie
815 Connecticut Ave., N.W. Suite 1100, Washington, DC 20006-4078
Telephone: (202) 452-7000
Clients:
Acindar Industria Argentina de Aceros
Camara Argentina de la Alumino y Metales Afines
Melamine Chemicals
Minnesota Mining and Manufacturing Co. (3M Co.)
Mitsubishi Electric Corp.
Nat'l Club Ass'n

ONDER, Ms. Sedef
Director, Media Relations, Citizens for a Sound Economy
470 L'Enfant Plaza East, S.W. Suite 7112, Washington, DC 20024
Telephone: (202) 488-8200

The listings in this directory are available as *Mailing Labels*. See last page.

ONDERS, Stacy
Public Affairs Director, Nat'l Coalition to Ban Handguns
100 Maryland Ave., N.E., Washington, DC 20002
Telephone: (202) 544-7190

O'NEAL, John F.
O'Neal Law Offices, John F.
1455 Pennsylvania Ave., N.W. Suite 1200, Washington,
DC 20004
Telephone: (202) 628-0210
Registered as lobbyist at U.S. Congress.
Organizations represented:
    Nat'l Rural Telecom Ass'n

O'NEAL LAW OFFICES, John F.
1455 Pennsylvania Ave., N.W. Suite 1200, Washington,
DC 20004
Telephone: (202) 628-0210
Members of firm representing listed organizations:
    O'Neal, John F.
Organizations represented:
    Nat'l Rural Telecom Ass'n *(John F. O'Neal)*

O'NEIL, Daniel
Ass't Dir., Congress'l & Agency Relat'ns, American
Nurses' Ass'n
1101 14th St., N.W., Suite 200, Washington, DC 20005
Telephone: (202) 789-1800
Registered as lobbyist at U.S. Congress.

O'NEIL, J. Timothy
Legis Mgr, DEPARTMENT OF TREASURY
15th and Pennsylvania Ave. N.W., Washington, DC 20220
Telephone: (202) 566-2037

O'NEIL, Joseph F.
Exec. Director, American Council of Independent Laboratories
1725 K St., N.W., Washington, DC 20006
Telephone: (202) 887-5872

O'NEIL, Joseph W.
Dir., DOD and Congressional Liaison, ITT Defense, Inc.
1000 Wilson Blvd. Suite 3000, Arlington, VA 22209
Telephone: (703) 276-8300

O'NEIL, R. S.
Senior V. President, DeLeuw, Cather and Co.
1133 15th St., N.W. Suite 800, Washington, DC 20005
Telephone: (202) 775-3300

O'NEIL, William B., Jr.
Pettit & Martin
1800 Massachusetts Ave., N.W., Washington, DC 20036
Telephone: (202) 785-5153
Background: Heads lobbying operations of the law firm of
Pettit & Martin. Former Legislative Director to Rep. Joe
Kolter (D-PA).

O'NEILL AND ATHY, P.C.
1310 19th St., N.W., Washington, DC 20036
Telephone: (202) 466-6555
Members of firm representing listed organizations:
    Athy, Andrew (Jr.)
    Background: Counsel, Committee on Interstate and
    Foreign Commerce, U.S. House of Representatives,
    1977-81.
    Casey, Martha L.
    Background: Legislative Assistant to Rep. Joseph Early
    (D-MA), 1977-79. Counsel to Rep. Brian Donnelly
    (D-MA), 1982-87.
    O'Neill, Christopher R.
    Background: Counsel to U.S. Senate Committee on
    Commerce, Science and Transportation, 1976-77.
    Williams, Thomas C.
    Background: Assistant Counsel, Senate Subcommittee
    on Antitrust and Monopoly, 1958-68. Staff Counsel
    to the late Sen. Philip A. Hart, 1969-72.
Clients:
    Allegheny County, Pennsylvania *(Martha L. Casey)*
    American Bankers Ass'n *(Andrew Athy, Jr.)*
    Bank of New England *(Andrew Athy, Jr.)*
    Beth Israel Hospital *(Martha L. Casey)*
    Boston Bruins, Inc. *(Andrew Athy, Jr.)*
    Brandeis University *(Andrew Athy, Jr.)*
    Coalition of Boston Teaching Hospitals *(Martha L. Casey)*
    Compu Chem Corp. *(Martha L. Casey)*

Connecticut Bank and Trust Corp. *(Andrew Athy, Jr.)*
    Cruise America Line, Inc. *(Andrew Athy, Jr.)*
    Glass Packaging Institute *(Andrew Athy, Jr.)*
    Marathon Oil Co. *(Andrew Athy, Jr.)*
    Massachusetts General Hospital *(Martha L. Casey)*
    Massachusetts Hospital Ass'n *(Martha L. Casey)*
    Nat'l Football League *(Thomas C. Williams)*
    New England Deaconess Hospital *(Martha L. Casey)*
    New England Medical Center *(Martha L. Casey)*
    Northeastern University *(Andrew Athy, Jr.)*
    Northwestern Mutual Life Insurance Co. *(Andrew Athy, Jr.)*
    Pyrotechnic Signal Manufacturers Ass'n *(Thomas C. Williams)*
    Texas Utilities *(Andrew Athy, Jr.)*
    USX Corp. *(Andrew Athy, Jr.)*
    Viacom Internat'l, Inc. *(Andrew Athy, Jr.)*

O'NEILL, Brian
President, Insurance Institute for Highway Safety
1005 North Glebe Rd. Suite 800, Arlington, VA 22201
Telephone: (703) 247-1500

O'NEILL, Christopher R.
O'Neill and Athy, P.C.
1310 19th St., N.W., Washington, DC 20036
Telephone: (202) 466-6555
Background: Counsel to U.S. Senate Committee on Commerce, Science and Transportation, 1976-77.

O'NEILL, Edward S.
Bryan, Cave, McPheeters and McRoberts
1015 15th St., N.W., Suite 1000, Washington, DC 20005
Telephone: (202) 289-6100

O'NEILL, Eileen Creamer
V. President, Direct Selling Ass'n
1776 K St., N.W., Suite 600, Washington, DC 20006
Telephone: (202) 293-5760

O'NEILL, John V.
Administrator, Professional Programs, Institute of Electrical
and Electronics Engineers, Inc.
1828 L St., N.W. Suite 1202, Washington, DC 20036-5104
Telephone: (202) 785-0017
Registered as lobbyist at U.S. Congress.

O'NEILL, Joseph E.
Dir, Legis Affrs & Publ Info Staff (Act), DEPARTMENT OF
AGRICULTURE - Farmers Home Administration
14th and Independence Ave. S.W., Washington, DC 20250
Telephone: (202) 447-6903

O'NEILL, Joseph P.
President, American Retail Federation
1616 H St., N.W. 6th Floor, Washington, DC 20006
Telephone: (202) 783-7971
Registered as lobbyist at U.S. Congress.
Background: Serves as Secretary-Treasurer, Retail Political
Action Committee and as Coordinator for the Retail Industry Trade Action Coalition. Formerly Admininstrative
Assistant to Senator Lloyd Bentsen (D-TX), 1980-84.

O'NEILL, Timothy Patrick
Government Affairs Representative, Internat'l Brotherhood
of Teamsters, Chauffeurs, Warehousemen and Helpers
of America
25 Louisiana Ave., N.W., Washington, DC 20001
Telephone: (202) 624-6800

ONEK, Joseph N.
Onek, Klein & Farr
2550 M St., N.W. Suite 350, Washington, DC 20037
Telephone: (202) 775-0184
Background: Law Clerk to Justice William J. Brennan, U.S.
Supreme Court, 1968-69. Associate Director for Health,
Domestic Policy Staff, The White House, 1977-79. Deputy Counsel to the President, 1979-80.
Clients:
    American Medical Peer Review Ass'n
    Major League Baseball Players Ass'n

ONEK, KLEIN & FARR
2550 M St., N.W. Suite 350, Washington, DC 20037
Telephone: (202) 775-0184
Members of firm representing listed organizations:
    Klein, Joel I.
    Background: Law Clerk to Justice Lewis F. Powell,
    U.S. Supreme Court, 1974-75.

Onek, Joseph N.
Background: Law Clerk to Justice William J. Brennan,
U.S. Supreme Court, 1968-69. Associate Director for
Health, Domestic Policy Staff, The White House,
1977-79. Deputy Counsel to the President, 1979-80.
Clients:
    American College of Psychiatrists, The
    American Medical Peer Review Ass'n *(Joseph N. Onek)*
    American Psychiatric Ass'n *(Joel I. Klein)*
    Major League Baseball Players Ass'n *(Joseph N. Onek)*

ONLEY-CAMPBELL, Diana
Program Coordinator, Nat'l Coalition Against Domestic Violence
P.O. Box 34103, Washington, DC 20043-4103
Telephone: (202) 638-6388

ONSTAD, Clark H.
V. President, Texas Air Corp.
901 15th St., N.W. Suite 500, Washington, DC 20005
Telephone: (202) 289-6060
Registered as lobbyist at U.S. Congress.
Background: Was Chief Counsel, Federal Aviation Administration, 1977-81. Also represents Continental Air
Lines.

ONSTED, William G.
President & CEO, Private Sector Council
1101 16th St., N.W., Suite 500, Washington, DC 20036
Telephone: (202) 822-3910

ONTO, John C.
Director, Center for Internat'l Business and Trade
Georgetown University 1242 35th St., N.W., Suite 501,
Washington, DC 20057
Telephone: (202) 687-6993

OOSTERHUIS, Paul W.
Skadden, Arps, Slate, Meagher and Flom
1440 New York Ave. N.W., Washington, DC 20005
Telephone: (202) 371-7000
Registered as lobbyist at U.S. Congress.
Clients:
    Computer and Business Equipment Manufacturers Ass'n
    Council on Research and Technology (CORE-TECH)

OPPENHEIMER, Jerry L.
Mayer, Brown and Platt
2000 Pennsylvania Ave., N.W. Suite 6500, Washington,
DC 20006
Telephone: (202) 463-2000
Registered as lobbyist at U.S. Congress.
Registered as Foreign Agent: (#3076).
Background: Treasury Department, Associate Tax Legislative Counsel, 1970-71; Deputy Tax Legislative Counsel,
1972; Acting Tax Legislative Counsel, 1973.
Clients:
    Accountant's Liability Assurance Co., Ltd.
    Attorneys' Liability Assurance Soc.
    Cabot, Cabot & Forbes Realty Advisors
    COMDISCO, Inc.
    Continental Illinois Nat'l Bank and Trust Co.
    Dome Petroleum Ltd.
    First Chicago Corp.
    FMC Corp.
    Household Commercial Financial Services, Inc.
    LaSalle Partners Inc.
    Lehndorff & Babson Real Estate Counsel
    Nalco Chemical Co.
    Sara Lee Corp.
    Shearson Lehman Hutton
    Smith Barney, Harris Upham and Co.
    TeleCommunications, Inc.

OPPENHEIMER WOLFF AND DONNELLY
1020 19th St., N.W., Suite 400, Washington, DC 20036
Telephone: (202) 293-5096
Members of firm representing listed organizations:
    Gantz, David A.
    Background: Attorney, Office of the Legal Adviser,
    Department of State, 1970-73. Assistant Legal Adviser: Inter-American Affairs, 1974-76; European Affairs, 1976-77, Department of State.
Clients:
    Daewoo Electronics Co. *(David A. Gantz)*

OPPENHEIMER WOLFF AND DONNELLY (Cont'd)
Korea Footwear Exporters Ass'n *(David A. Gantz)*
Nishika Corp. *(David A. Gantz)*

OPPERMAN, HEINS & PASQUIN
1300 Eye St., N.W. Suite 480 East Tower, Washington, DC 20005
Telephone: (202) 962-3860
Clients:
West Publishing Co.

ORAM, Frank
Exec. Director, World Population Soc.
1333 H St., N.W., Suite 760, Washington, DC 20005
Telephone: (202) 898-1303

ORASIN, Charles J.
President, Handgun Control, Inc.
1225 Eye St., N.W., Suite 1100, Washington, DC 20005
Telephone: (202) 898-0792
Registered as lobbyist at U.S. Congress.

ORBAN, Susan A.
V. President, Nat'l Realty Committee
1250 Connecticut Ave., N.W. Suite 630, Washington, DC 20036
Telephone: (202) 785-0808
Background: Also serves as Assistant Treasurer, Nat'l Realty Political Action Committee.

ORDWAY, Nancy J.
Fed. Budget Liaison, Wash. Office of Gov, California, State of
444 North Capitol St., N.W., Suite 305, Washington, DC 20001
Telephone: (202) 347-6891

ORLANS, F. Barbara, Ph.D.
Research Fellow, Scientists Center for Animal Welfare
4805 St. Elmo Ave., Bethesda, MD 20814
Telephone: (301) 654-6390
Background: Served in the Nat'l Heart, Lung and Blood Institute, Nat'l Institutes of Health, 1956-60 and 1975-84.

ORNDORFF, Charles
V. Chairman, Conservative Caucus, The
450 Maple Ave. East, Suite 309, Vienna, VA 22180
Telephone: (703) 893-1550

ORNOFF EXECUTIVE SERVICES
2000 N St., N.W. Suite 731, Washington, DC 20036
Telephone: (202) 861-0818
Members of firm representing listed organizations:
Ornoff, Lynne H., President

ORNOFF, Lynne H.
President, Ornoff Executive Services
2000 N St., N.W. Suite 731, Washington, DC 20036
Telephone: (202) 861-0818

O'ROURKE, John T.
V. President and Legislative Counsel, Securities Industry Ass'n
1850 M St., N.W., Suite 550, Washington, DC 20036
Telephone: (202) 296-9410
Registered as lobbyist at U.S. Congress.
Background: Also represents the Municipal Security Industry PAC.

O'ROURKE, Robert W.
Public Relations Deputy Director, American Petroleum Institute
1220 L St., N.W., Washington, DC 20005
Telephone: (202) 682-8124

O'ROURKE, Thomas J.
Neill, Mullenholz and Shaw
815 Connecticut Ave., N.W. Suite 800, Washington, DC 20006
Telephone: (202) 463-8400
Background: Office of Chief Counsel, Internal Revenue Service 1974-83. Specializes in tax law.

ORR, Beverly
Business Manager, Center for Study of Responsive Law
Box 19367, Washington, DC 20036
Telephone: (202) 387-8030

ORR, Capt. Bud
Senate Liaison, Legis Affrs, DEPARTMENT OF NAVY
The Pentagon, Washington, DC 20350-1300
Telephone: (202) 697-7146

ORRICK, Frederick J.
Executive Director, Ass'n of Naval Aviation
5205 Leesburg Pike, Suite 200, Falls Church, VA 22041
Telephone: (703) 998-7733

ORTIZ-DALIOT, Jose
V. President, Inter-American Affairs, Jefferson Group, The
1341 G St., N.W., Suite 1100, Washington, DC 20005
Telephone: (202) 638-3535
Background: Former Director, Puerto Rico Federal Affairs Administration.

ORTMANS, Jonathan F.
Director, Columbia Institute
8 E St., S.E., Washington, DC 20003
Telephone: (202) 547-2470
Background: Legislative Ass't to U.S. Rep. Robert Matsui (D-CA) 1984-87.

ORWIG, Martha
Sr Asst, Cong Rels, Legis & Cong Rels, DEPARTMENT OF HOUSING AND URBAN DEVELOPMENT
451 Seventh St., S.W., Washington, DC 20410
Telephone: (202) 755-7380

OSANN, Edward
Dir. & Legis. Rep., Water Resources Div., Nat'l Wildlife Federation
1400 16th St., N.W., Washington, DC 20036-2266
Telephone: (202) 797-6800
Registered as lobbyist at U.S. Congress.

OSBORN, Timothy R.
Manager, Government Affairs, Asea Brown Boveri, Inc.
1101 15th St., N.W. Suite 500, Washington, DC 20005
Telephone: (202) 429-9180

OSHINSKY, Jerold
Anderson, Kill, Olick and Oshinsky
2000 Pennsylvania Ave., N.W., Suite 7500, Washington, DC 20006
Telephone: (202) 728-3100
Clients:
Keene Corp.

OSSOLA, Charles D.
Hunton and Williams
2000 Pennsylvania Ave., N.W., Washington, DC 20006
Telephone: (202) 955-1500
Registered as lobbyist at U.S. Congress.
Clients:
American Soc. of Magazine Photographers
Copyright Justice Coalition

OSTAR, Allan W.
President, American Ass'n of State Colleges and Universities
One Dupont Circle, N.W. Suite 700, Washington, DC 20036
Telephone: (202) 293-7070

OSTBERG, Kay
Deputy Director, HALT-An Organization of Americans for Legal Reform
1319 F St., N.W., Suite 300, Washington, DC 20004
Telephone: (202) 347-9600

O'STEEN, David N., Ph.D.
Exec. Director, Nat'l Right to Life Committee
419 7th St., N.W. Suite 500, Washington, DC 20004
Telephone: (202) 626-8820
Background: Also serves as contact, Nat'l Right to Life PAC.

OSTERHOUT, David S.
V. President, Legislative Affairs, Lockheed Corp.
1825 Eye St., N.W. Suite 1100, Washington, DC 20006
Telephone: (202) 955-3300
Registered as lobbyist at U.S. Congress.

OSTERWEIS, Marian
V. President, Ass'n of Academic Health Centers
1400 16th St., N.W. Suite 410, Washington, DC 20036
Telephone: (202) 265-9600

OSTRONIC, John
Cong Liaison Asst, DEPARTMENT OF COMMERCE
14th and Constitution Ave. S.W., Washington, DC 20230
Telephone: (202) 377-5485

OSTROVSKY, Eric
Assoc. Dir., Commerce & Transportation, Alaska, State of
444 N. Capitol St., N.W. Suite 518, Washington, DC 20001
Telephone: (202) 624-5858

O'SULLIVAN, Marianne
Apprpriations and Budget Committees, AGENCY FOR INTERNAT'L DEVELOPMENT
320 21st St., N.W., Washington, DC 20523
Telephone: (202) 647-8441

OTERO, Jack F.
Internat'l V. Pres. and Polit. Dir., Transportation, Communications Internat'l Union
815 16th St., N.W. Suite 511, Washington, DC 20036
Telephone: (202) 783-3660
Registered as lobbyist at U.S. Congress.

O'TOOLE, Carole J.
Manager, Science Policy, American Industrial Health Council
1330 Connecticut Ave., N.W. Suite 300, Washington, DC 20036-1702
Telephone: (202) 659-0060

O'TOOLE, J. Denis
Exec. V. President, Government Affairs, United States League of Savings Institutions
1709 New York Ave., N.W., Suite 801, Washington, DC 20006
Telephone: (202) 637-8900
Registered as lobbyist at U.S. Congress.

O'TOOLE, John E.
President, American Ass'n of Advertising Agencies
1899 L St., N.W., Suite 700, Washington, DC 20036
Telephone: (202) 331-7345
Registered as lobbyist at U.S. Congress.

O'TOOLE, Robert M.
Sr Staff V.P., Resid Fin/Gov't Agncy Rel, Mortgage Bankers Ass'n of America
1125 15th St., N.W., Suite 700, Washington, DC 20005
Telephone: (202) 861-6500
Background: Served in the Veterans Administration, 1963-87.

O'TOOLE, Stephen E.
Senior Washington Representative, General Motors Corp.
1660 L St., N.W., Washington, DC 20036
Telephone: (202) 775-5056
Registered as lobbyist at U.S. Congress.

OTT, Alan R.
Federal Legislative Representative, American Bankers Ass'n
1120 Connecticut Ave., N.W., Washington, DC 20036
Telephone: (202) 663-5000
Registered as lobbyist at U.S. Congress.

OTT, Judith A.
Pillsbury, Madison and Sutro
1667 K St., N.W., Suite 1100, Washington, DC 20006
Telephone: (202) 887-0300
Registered as Foreign Agent: (# 4212).
Clients:
Korea Foreign Trade Ass'n

OTT, Kathleen G.
Manager, Government Relations Research, TRW Inc.
Suite 2700, 1000 Wilson Blvd., Arlington, VA 22209
Telephone: (703) 276-5016
Registered as lobbyist at U.S. Congress.

OTT, Louise
Public Affairs Director, Women in Communications
2101 Wilson Blvd., Suite 417, Arlington, VA 22201
Telephone: (703) 528-4200

OTTLEY, William H.
Exec. Director, United States Parachute Ass'n
1440 Duke St., Alexandria, VA 22314
Telephone: (703) 836-3495

OTTOSEN AND ASSOCIATES
208 G St., N.E., 2nd Floor, Washington, DC 20002
Telephone: (202) 543-9339
Background: A government relations, political consulting and fundraising firm.
Members of firm representing listed organizations:
Ottosen, Karl J.
Saunders, Carla L.
Clients:
Baroid Corp. *(Karl J. Ottosen, Carla L. Saunders)*
Contran Corp. *(Karl J. Ottosen)*
Kronos, Inc. *(Karl J. Ottosen, Carla L. Saunders)*
NL Industries *(Karl J. Ottosen, Carla L. Saunders)*
OTI, Inc. *(Karl J. Ottosen, Carla L. Saunders)*
U.S. Federation of Small Businesses, Inc. *(Karl J. Ottosen, Carla L. Saunders)*
U.S. Federation of Small Businesses PAC *(Carla L. Saunders)*
Valhi, Inc. *(Karl J. Ottosen)*

OTTOSEN, Karl J.
Ottosen and Associates
208 G St., N.E., 2nd Floor, Washington, DC 20002
Telephone: (202) 543-9339
Registered as lobbyist at U.S. Congress.
Clients:
Baroid Corp.
Contran Corp.
Kronos, Inc.
NL Industries
OTI, Inc.
U.S. Federation of Small Businesses, Inc.
Valhi, Inc.

OUSE, Clifford
Senior Legislative Representative, Nat'l Rural Electric Co-operative Ass'n
1800 Massachusetts Ave., N.W., Washington, DC 20036
Telephone: (202) 857-9558
Registered as lobbyist at U.S. Congress.

OUSLANDER, Arthur R.
Director, Federal Relations, Consolidated Rail Corp. (CONRAIL)
990 L'Enfant Plaza, S.W., Washington, DC 20024
Telephone: (202) 789-5885
Registered as lobbyist at U.S. Congress.

OUTMAN, William D., II
Baker and McKenzie
815 Connecticut Ave., N.W. Suite 1100, Washington, DC 20006-4078
Telephone: (202) 452-7000
Clients:
General Electric Co.
Mitsubishi Electric Corp.
Samsonite Corp.

OVERKAMP, Sunshine
V. President, Communications, United Way of America
701 N. Fairfax St., Alexandria, VA 22314-2045
Telephone: (703) 836-7100
Background: Former Director of Communiciations, White House Office of Private Sector Initiatives.

OVERLY, Cathy
Director, Legislative Field Operations, Nat'l Treasury Employees Union
1730 K St., N.W., Suite 1100, Washington, DC 20006
Telephone: (202) 785-4411
Registered as lobbyist at U.S. Congress.

OVERMAN, Dean L.
Winston and Strawn
2550 M St., N.W., Suite 500, Washington, DC 20037
Telephone: (202) 828-8400
Background: White House Fellow, Assistant to Vice President Nelson Rockefeller, 1975-76. Associate Director, White House Domestic Council, 1976-77.

OVERSTREET, Col. Jack
Weapons Syst Liaison, Cong Liaison, DEPARTMENT OF AIR FORCE
The Pentagon, Washington, DC 20330
Telephone: (202) 697-8153

OVERSTREET, John
Fleishman-Hillard, Inc
1301 Connecticut Ave., N.W., Washington, DC 20036

Telephone: (202) 659-0330
Registered as lobbyist at U.S. Congress.
Clients:
Citizens for a Drug Free America
Coastal Barrier Relief Fund
Eveready
Spectacor Management Group

OWEN, Jeffrey S.
Exec. Director, Banking Organizations, American Bankers Ass'n
1120 Connecticut Ave., N.W., Washington, DC 20036
Telephone: (202) 663-5000

OWEN, Mary Jane
Director, Disability Focus, Inc.
1010 Vermont Ave., N.W., Suite 1100, Washington, DC 20005
Telephone: (202) 483-8582

OWEN, Nicholas, M.D.
President, American Medical Directors Ass'n
325 S. Patrick St., Alexandria, VA 22314
Telephone: (703) 549-5822

OWEN, Roberts B.
Covington and Burling
1201 Pennsylvania Ave., N.W., Box 7566, Washington, DC 20044
Telephone: (202) 662-6000
Background: Legal Advisor, U.S. Department of State, 1979-81.

OWEN, Stephen F., Jr.
Loomis, Owen, Fellman and Howe
2020 K St., N.W. Suite 800, Washington, DC 20006
Telephone: (202) 296-5680
Background: Attorney, Division of Corporate Finance, Securities Exchange Commission, 1962-64. Serves as General Counsel, Classroom Publishers Ass'n.
Clients:
Classroom Publishers Ass'n

OWENS, Christine
Newman and Newell
1920 N St., N.W., Suite 430 Suite 400, Washington, DC 20036
Telephone: (202) 857-5650

OWENS, David K.
V. President, Power Supply Policy, Edison Electric Institute
1111 19th St., N.W., Washington, DC 20036
Telephone: (202) 777-6527

OWENS, Joseph H., Jr.
Exec. Director, Council of State Administrators of Vocational Rehabilitation
P.O. Box 3776, Washington, DC 20007
Telephone: (202) 638-4634
Background: Served as Assistant to Senator Robert Byrd (D-WV), 1966-1973.

OWENS, Loretta A.
Chief, Legis Staff, DEPARTMENT OF AGRICULTURE - Agricultural Research Service
12th and Independence Ave. S.W., Washington, DC 20250
Telephone: (202) 447-7141

OWENS, Russell
Director, Nat'l Policy Institute, Joint Center for Political Studies
1301 Pennsylvania Ave., N.W., Washington, DC 20004
Telephone: (202) 626-3500

OWENS, Dr. Susan Weir
Capital Consultants
643 Pennsylvania Ave., S.E., Suite 200, Washington, DC 20003
Telephone: (202) 546-2277

OWENS, Thomas E.
Congressional Relations Representative, American Dental Ass'n
1111 14th St., N.W. Suite 1200, Washington, DC 20005
Telephone: (202) 898-2400
Registered as lobbyist at U.S. Congress.

OWENS, William H., Jr.
President, Capital Consultants
643 Pennsylvania Ave., S.E., Suite 200, Washington, DC 20003
Telephone: (202) 546-2277

OWENS, William "Joe"
V. President, Finance, Manufactured Housing Institute
1745 Jefferson Davis Hwy. Suite 511, Arlington, VA 22202
Telephone: (703) 979-6620
Registered as lobbyist at U.S. Congress.

OXAAL, John G.
President, Ferroalloys Ass'n
1505 Crystal Drive, Suite 708, Arlington, VA 22202
Telephone: (703) 418-0333
Registered as lobbyist at U.S. Congress.

OXFELD, Eric J.
Counsel, American Insurance Ass'n
1130 Connecticut Ave., N.W., Suite 1000, Washington, DC 20036
Telephone: (202) 828-7100

OXLEY, Joanne
Ass'n Advocates
3312 Camden St., Silver Spring, MD 20902
Telephone: (301) 869-5800
Clients:
Alliance for Fair Competition
Associated Specialty Contractors

OYER, Dr. Paul
President, SCIA - Smart Card Industry Ass'n
2026C Opitz Blvd., Woodbridge, VA 22191
Telephone: (703) 490-3300
Background: Also manages SCAT - Smart Card Applications and Technologies Conference. Prior government service included Census Bureau, Internal Revenue Service and Department of Treasury.

OYLER, Gregory K.
Hopkins and Sutter
888 16th St., N.W., Suite 700, Washington, DC 20006
Telephone: (202) 835-8000
Registered as lobbyist at U.S. Congress.
Background: Law Clerk, U.S. Tax Court, 1978-80.

OZER, Kathy
Policy Coordinator, Nat'l Family Farm Coalition
80 F St., N.W. Suite 714, Washington, DC 20001
Telephone: (202) 737-2215
Registered as lobbyist at U.S. Congress.

PAABO, Ray
P.O. Box 20519, Washington, DC 20007
Telephone: (202) 469-5934
Organizations represented:
Santa Fe Pacific Pipelines, Inc.
Sierra Pacific Industries

PACE, John A.
Pace, Weil and Associates, Internat'l
1606 17th St., N.W., Washington, DC 20009
Telephone: (202) 232-0077

PACE, WEIL AND ASSOCIATES, INTERNAT'L
1606 17th St., N.W., Washington, DC 20009
Telephone: (202) 232-0077
Members of firm representing listed organizations:
Pace, John A.
Weil, Alan M., President

PACHECO, Alex
Chairperson, People for the Ethical Treatment of Animals (PETA)
4980 Wyaconda Road, Rockville, MD 20852
Telephone: (301) 770-7444

PACIFIC ISLANDS WASHINGTON OFFICE
1615 New Hampshire Ave., N.W., Suite 400, Washington, DC 20009-9998
Telephone: (202) 387-8100
Members of firm representing listed organizations:
Radewagen, Fred
Background: Director, Pacific Islands Washington Office. Former employee, U.S. Department of Interior, 1969-75.
Clients:

PACIFIC ISLANDS WASHINGTON OFFICE (Cont'd)

American Samoa, Government of *(Fred Radewagen)*

PACKER, Dr. James S.
Exec. Director, American Institute of Ultrasound Medicine
4405 East-West Hwy., Suite 504, Bethesda, MD 20814
Telephone: (301) 656-6117

PACKER, Joel
Legislative Specialist, Nat'l Education Ass'n of the U.S.
1201 16th St., N.W., Washington, DC 20026
Telephone: (202) 822-7329

PADGETT, Casey Scott
Legislative Rep., Toxics Project, Environmental Action
1525 New Hampshire Ave., N.W., Washington, DC 20036
Telephone: (202) 745-4870
Registered as lobbyist at U.S. Congress.

PADILLA, Oscar
Manager, Internat'l Programs, Bechtel Group, Inc.
1620 Eye St., N.W., Suite 703, Washington, DC 20006
Telephone: (202) 393-4747

PADILLA, Tony
Ass't to the Nat'l Legislative Director, Transportation, Communications Internat'l Union
815 16th St., N.W. Suite 511, Washington, DC 20036
Telephone: (202) 783-3660

PADO, Denise
Operations Manager, American Wind Energy Ass'n
1730 N. Lynn St., Suite 610, Arlington, VA 22209
Telephone: (703) 276-8334
Registered as lobbyist at U.S. Congress.

PAGAN INTERNAT'L INC.
1925 N. Lynn St. Suite 903, Washington, DC 22209
Telephone: (703) 528-4177
Background: Consultancy in public relations, issue management and investments.
Members of firm representing listed organizations:
Cato, Phillip C., Senior V. President
Pagan, Rafael D. (Jr.), Chairman, CEO
Background: Served in Dept. of Defense, 1948-70.
Whipple, Davis, Exec. V. President
Clients:
Issues Management Ass'n *(Rafael D. Pagan, Jr.)*
Puerto Rico, Commonwealth of

PAGAN, Rafael D., Jr.
Chairman, CEO, Pagan Internat'l Inc.
1925 N. Lynn St. Suite 903, Washington, DC 22209
Telephone: (703) 528-4177
Background: Served in Dept. of Defense, 1948-70.
Clients:
Issues Management Ass'n

PAGE, Nancy R.
Spiegel and McDiarmid
1350 New York Ave., N.W., Suite 1100, Washington, DC 20005
Telephone: (202) 879-4000
Registered as lobbyist at U.S. Congress.
Clients:
South Hadley, Massachusetts, Town of

PAGONIS AND DONNELLY GROUP
1620 Eye St., N.W., Suite 603, Washington, DC 20006
Telephone: (202) 452-8811
Members of firm representing listed organizations:
Donnelly, Thomas R. (Jr.)
Background: Former Special Assistant to the President, The White House.
Grisso, Michael E., Director, Legislative Affairs
Background: Former legislative assistant to House Speaker Jim Wright (D-TX).
Henderson, David
Lambert, Blanche
Pagonis, George G.
Robertson, William B.
Clients:
Air Products and Chemicals, Inc. *(Thomas R. Donnelly, Jr.)*
Americans for Nat'l Dividend Act *(David Henderson)*
Asea Brown Boveri, Inc. *(Thomas R. Donnelly, Jr., George G. Pagonis)*

Ass'n of High Medicare Hospitals *(Thomas R. Donnelly, Jr.)*
Burroughs Wellcome Co. *(Thomas R. Donnelly, Jr., Michael E. Grisso)*
Dow Chemical *(Thomas R. Donnelly, Jr., Michael E. Grisso)*
Harrah's *(Thomas R. Donnelly, Jr., Michael E. Grisso)*
Holiday Corp. *(Thomas R. Donnelly, Jr., Michael E. Grisso)*
Nord Resources Corp. *(Thomas R. Donnelly, Jr., George G. Pagonis)*
Transkei, Government of *(Thomas R. Donnelly, Jr., William B. Robertson)*

PAGONIS, George G.
Pagonis and Donnelly Group
1620 Eye St., N.W., Suite 603, Washington, DC 20006
Telephone: (202) 452-8811
Registered as lobbyist at U.S. Congress.
Clients:
Asea Brown Boveri, Inc.
Nord Resources Corp.

PAI MANAGEMENT CORP.
5530 Wisconsin Ave., N.W., Suite 1149, Washington, DC 20815
Telephone: (301) 656-4224
Members of firm representing listed organizations:
Jones, Ronald W.
Lewis, David A.
Background: Serves as Executive Director, American Academy of Optometry, American Soc. for Adolescent Psychiatry and American College of Internat'l Physicians.
Price, Randall C.
Clients:
American Academy of Optometry *(David A. Lewis)*
American College of Internat'l Physicans
American Soc. for Adolescent Psychiatry *(David A. Lewis)*
Ophthalmic Research Institute *(Ronald W. Jones)*
Phlebology Soc. of America, The *(Randall C. Price)*
Physicians for Social Responsibility *(David A. Lewis)*

PAILET, Janet L.
Director, Government Affairs, American Soc. for Medical Technology
2021 L St., N.W. Suite 400, Washington, DC 20036
Telephone: (202) 785-3311

PALACIOS, Alejandro J.
Director, Congressional Relations, U.S. Committee for UNICEF
110 Maryland Ave., N.E. Suite 304, Washington, DC 20002
Telephone: (202) 547-7946
Registered as lobbyist at U.S. Congress.

PALAST, Geri D.
Director, Politics & Legislation Dept., Service Employees Internat'l Union
1313 L St., N.W., Washington, DC 20005
Telephone: (202) 898-3200
Background: Serves as contact for the Service Employees Internat'l Union COPE Political Action Committee.

PALATIELLO & ASSOC., John M.
12020 Sunrise Valley Drive, Reston, VA 22091
Telephone: (703) 391-2739
Members of firm representing listed organizations:
Benson, Daniel L.
Palatiello, John M.
Background: Former Legislative Assistant to Rep. Bill Hendon (R-NC) and Legislative Aide to Rep. John Myers (R-IN).
Organizations represented:
Management Ass'n for Private Photogrammetric Surveyors *(John M. Palatiello)*
Management Ass'n for Private Photogrammetric Surveyors Political Action Committee *(John M. Palatiello)*
Meyer and Associates, Inc., Vernon F. *(John M. Palatiello)*

PALATIELLO, John M.
Palatiello & Assoc., John M.
12020 Sunrise Valley Drive, Reston, VA 22091
Telephone: (703) 391-2739
Registered as lobbyist at U.S. Congress.

Background: Former Legislative Assistant to Rep. Bill Hendon (R-NC) and Legislative Aide to Rep. John Myers (R-IN).
Organizations represented:
Management Ass'n for Private Photogrammetric Surveyors
Management Ass'n for Private Photogrammetric Surveyors Political Action Committee
Meyer and Associates, Inc., Vernon F.

PALAU, Capt. Henry S., USN (Ret.)
Secretary and General Counsel, Retired Officers Ass'n, The (TROA)
201 N. Washington St., Alexandria, VA 22314
Telephone: (703) 549-2311
Registered as lobbyist at U.S. Congress.

PALAZIO, Ernesto
Washington Representative, Nicaraguan Resistance- U.S-.A.
44880 Falcon Place Suite 104, Sterling, VA 22070
Telephone: (703) 328-1133

PALE MOON, Princess
President, American Indian Heritage Foundation
6051 Arlington Blvd., Falls Church, VA 22044
Telephone: (202) 237-7500

PALENSKI, Ronald

General Counsel, ADAPSO, the Computer Software & Services Industry Ass'n
1300 North 17th St. Suite 300, Arlington, VA 22209
Telephone: (703) 522-5055

PALEY, Barbara
Legis. Rep., Energy & Environment, Nat'l Ass'n of Counties
440 First St., N.W., Washington, DC 20001
Telephone: (202) 393-6226

PALK, Roy
Exec. Director, Operations, Nat'l Rural Electric Cooperative Ass'n
1800 Massachusetts Ave., N.W., Washington, DC 20036
Telephone: (202) 857-9520

PALMER, Craig A.
Director, Communications, American Dental Ass'n
1111 14th St., N.W. Suite 1200, Washington, DC 20005
Telephone: (202) 898-2400

PALMER, Fredrick D.
General Manager & CEO, Western Fuels Ass'n
1625 M St., N.W. Magruder Bldg., Washington, DC 20036-3264
Telephone: (202) 463-6580

PALMER, Michael
Director, Professional Relations, College of American Pathologists
1101 Vermont Ave., N.W., Washington, DC 20005
Telephone: (202) 371-6617

PALMETER, N. David
Mudge Rose Guthrie Alexander and Ferdon
2121 K St., N.W., Suite 700, Washington, DC 20037
Telephone: (202) 429-9355
Background: Trial Attorney, Civil Division, U.S. Department of Justice, 1966-68.
Clients:
Altos Hornos de Mexico, S.A.
China Nat'l Metals and Minerals Import and Export Corp.
Cho Heung Chemical Ind. Co., Ltd.
Dai Lim Trading Co., Ltd.
Daicel Chemical Industries, Ltd.
Federation of European Bearing Manufacturers Ass'ns
Grip-Rite, Ltd.
Korea Iron and Steel Works, Ltd.
Korea Leather and Fur Exporters Ass'n
Korea Metal Flatware Exporters Ass'n
Korea Metal Industry Cooperative
Miwon Trading and Shipping Co., Ltd.
Nippon Synthetic Chemical Industry Co.
Norseland Foods
Norske Fiskeoppdretternes Salgslag (FO)
Norwegian Dairies Ass'n
Occidental Coating Co.

Sidermex Internat'l, Inc.
Siderurgica Lazaro Cardenas, S.A.
Toshiba America, Inc.

PALMIERI, Victor H.
Chairman, Overseas Development Council
1717 Massachusetts Ave., N.W., Washington, DC 20036
Telephone: (202) 234-8701

PALUMBO, Benjamin L.
President, Palumbo & Cerrell, Inc.
1629 K St., N.W., Suite 1100, Washington, DC 20006
Telephone: (202) 785-6705
Registered as lobbyist at U.S. Congress.
Background: Admin. Ass't to Senator Harrison Williams (D-NJ), 1971-73. National Campaign Director, Lloyd Bentsen for President, 1973-75. Staff Director, House Democratic Caucus, 1975-77. Staff Director, House Subcommittee on Government Activities, 1977-78.
Clients:
American Institute of Architects, The
American Insurance Ass'n
American Soc. of Composers, Authors and Publishers
ARCO
ARCO Chemical Co.
Order of Sons of Italy in America
Palmer Associates, G. H.
Southern California Rapid Transit District

PALUMBO & CERRELL, INC.
1629 K St., N.W., Suite 1100, Washington, DC 20006
Telephone: (202) 785-6705
Members of firm representing listed organizations:
Deitz, William T., V. Pres., Legislat. & Regul. Affairs
Background: Former Administrative Assistant to Rep. Frank Thompson, Jr. (D-NJ) and Special Counsel to the House of Representatives Public Works and Transportation Committee.
Doranz, Jeffrey D., General Counsel
Background: Special Counsel, Senate Committee on Labor and Public Welfare, 1973-75. Counsel, Office of the Solicitor, U.S. Department of Labor, 1976-86.
Palumbo, Benjamin L., President
Background: Admin. Ass't to Senator Harrison Williams (D-NJ), 1971-73. National Campaign Director, Lloyd Bentsen for President, 1973-75. Staff Director, House Democratic Caucus, 1975-77. Staff Director, House Subcommittee on Government Activities, 1977-78.
Skrabut, Paul A. (Jr.), V. President, Gov't Relations
Background: Former Crisis Management Specialist, Federal Emergency Management Agency and former Administrative Assistant and Legislative Director to former U.S. Senator Harrison A. Williams (D-NJ).
Clients:
American Institute of Architects, The *(Benjamin L. Palumbo, Paul A. Skrabut, Jr.)*
American Insurance Ass'n *(Jeffrey D. Doranz, Benjamin L. Palumbo, Paul A. Skrabut, Jr.)*
American Soc. of Composers, Authors and Publishers *(Benjamin L. Palumbo, Paul A. Skrabut, Jr.)*
ARCO *(Benjamin L. Palumbo)*
ARCO Chemical Co. *(Jeffrey D. Doranz, Benjamin L. Palumbo, Paul A. Skrabut, Jr.)*
Order of Sons of Italy in America *(Jeffrey D. Doranz, Benjamin L. Palumbo, Paul A. Skrabut, Jr.)*
Palmer Associates, G. H. *(Jeffrey D. Doranz, Benjamin L. Palumbo, Paul A. Skrabut, Jr.)*
Rockport Fine Arts Council *(Paul A. Skrabut, Jr.)*
Southern California Rapid Transit District *(Benjamin L. Palumbo)*

PANARO, Gerard Paul
Webster, Chamberlain and Bean
1747 Pennsylvania Ave., N.W., Suite 1000, Washington, DC 20006
Telephone: (202) 785-9500
Background: Serves as General Counsel, Nat'l Candy Wholesalers Ass'n.
Clients:
Retail Bakers of America

PANCAKE, Robbins
Manager, Internat'l Trade Relations, Hewlett-Packard Co.
900 17th St., N.W. Suite 1100, Washington, DC 20006

Telephone: (202) 785-7943

PANCRATZ, Christopher
Exec Dir, Physcn/Alt Care & Hosp Mkt Grp, Health Industry Distributors Ass'n
225 Reinekers Lane, Suite 650, Alexandria, VA 22314
Telephone: (703) 549-4432

PANGBURN & ASSOCIATES
727 15th St., N.W., Suite 1200, Washington, DC 20005
Telephone: (202) 638-1957
Members of firm representing listed organizations:
Pangburn, Wendy S., President

PANGBURN, Wendy S.
President, Pangburn & Associates
727 15th St., N.W., Suite 1200, Washington, DC 20005
Telephone: (202) 638-1957

PANKONIN, Scootch
308 Constitution Ave., N.E., Washington, DC 20002
Telephone: (202) 546-1808
Organizations represented:
DST Systems, Inc.
Kansas City Southern Industries
Nat'l Forest Recreation Ass'n
Tuolumne River Expeditions, Inc.
Western Forest Industries Ass'n
Western River Guides Ass'n

PANTELIS, Jorge
General Coordinator, Casa del Pueblo
1459 Columbia Road, N.W., Washington, DC 20009
Telephone: (202) 332-1082

PANTOS, George J.
Vedder, Price, Kaufman, Kammholz and Day
1919 Pennsylvania Ave., N.W., Washington, DC 20006
Telephone: (202) 828-5000
Background: Special Assistant to the Under Secretary of Commerce, 1970; Special Counsel to the White House Council on International Economic Policy, 1971; Special Assistant to the Secretary of Commerce, 1972; Deputy Under Secretary of Commerce, 1973-1974.
Clients:
Professional Insurance Mass-Marketing Ass'n
Self-Insurance Institute of America, Inc.

PANTUSO, Peter
Director, Legislative Affairs, Rubber Manufacturers Ass'n
1400 K St., N.W., Washington, DC 20005
Telephone: (202) 682-4800
Registered as lobbyist at U.S. Congress.

PANUZIO, Nicholas A.
Chairman of the Board, Black, Manafort, Stone and Kelly Public Affairs Co.
211 N. Union St., Third Floor, Alexandria, VA 22314
Telephone: (703) 683-6612
Registered as lobbyist at U.S. Congress.
Registered as Foreign Agent: (#3600).
Clients:
Casino Ass'n of New Jersey
Edison Electric Institute
Large Public Power Council
NOVA University
Revlon Group
Somalia, Government of
South Carolina Economic Development Board
Trump Organization, The

PAOLINI, Angela J.
Akin, Gump, Strauss, Hauer and Feld
1333 New Hampshire Ave., N.W., Suite 400, Washington, DC 20036
Telephone: (202) 887-4000
Clients:
Lone Star Steel Co.

PAPA, Gail
Director, Communications, Publicat. & PR, American Congress on Surveying and Mapping
5410 Grosvenor Lane, Suite 100, Bethesda, MD 20814-2122
Telephone: (301) 493-0200

PAPE-DANIELS, Marcia M.
Governmental Affairs Director, CH2M HILL
Metropolitan Square, 655 15th St., N.W., Suite 444, Washington, DC 20005
Telephone: (202) 393-2426
Registered as lobbyist at U.S. Congress.

PAPE, Stuart M.
Patton, Boggs and Blow
2550 M St., N.W., Suite 800, Washington, DC 20037
Telephone: (202) 457-6000
Registered as lobbyist at U.S. Congress.
Registered as Foreign Agent: (#2165).
Background: Former Special Assistant to the Commissioner, Food and Drug Administration.
Clients:
American Stock Exchange
Avon Products, Inc.
Biogen
Duty Free Shoppers Group Limited
Immune Response Corp.
Nat'l Soft Drink Ass'n

PAPE, Virginia
V. President, Government Relations, American Stock Exchange
888 17th St., N.W., Suite 308, Washington, DC 20006
Telephone: (202) 887-6880
Registered as lobbyist at U.S. Congress.

PAPKIN, Robert D.
Squire, Sanders and Dempsey
1201 Pennsylvania Ave., N.W. P.O. Box 407, Washington, DC 20044
Telephone: (202) 626-6600
Clients:
Aerolineas Argentinas
Ansett Transport Industries
Avianca Airlines
Compania Mexicana de Aviacion
Lineas Aereas Costarricicenes (Lasca Airlines)
Polynesian Airlines
Transportes Aeros Nacionales (TAN)
VASP Airlines
VIASA
White Consolidated Industries

PARADIS, Kenneth A.
V. President, Labor Relations & Safety, Nat'l Constructors Ass'n
1730 M St., N.W., Suite 900, Washington, DC 20036-4571
Telephone: (202) 466-8880

PARADISE, Stephen J.
Sr. V.P., Congressional/Regulatory Rltns, New York Stock Exchange
1800 K St., N.W., Suite 1100, Washington, DC 20006
Telephone: (202) 293-5740
Registered as lobbyist at U.S. Congress.
Background: Former Chief Counsel and Staff Director, Senate Labor and Human Resourses Committee.

PARCELLS, Harriet Ellen
Transportation Associate, Nat'l Ass'n of Railroad Passengers
236 Massachusetts Ave., N.E., Suite 603, Washington, DC 20002
Telephone: (202) 546-1550
Registered as lobbyist at U.S. Congress.

PARDE, Duane A.
Legislative Director, American Legislative Exchange Council
214 Massachusetts Ave., N.W., Washington, DC 20002
Telephone: (202) 547-4646

PARET, Jonathan R.
V. President and Legislative Counsel, Securities Industry Ass'n
1850 M St., N.W., Suite 550, Washington, DC 20036
Telephone: (202) 296-9410
Registered as lobbyist at U.S. Congress.

PARK, Chang Saeng
V. President, Korea Foreign Trade Ass'n
1800 K St., N.W.,, Washington, DC 20006
Telephone: (202) 408-0100
Registered as Foreign Agent: (#3636).

PARK, Jack H.
V. President, Governmental Relations, Crowley Maritime Corp.
1500 K St., Suite 425, Washington, DC 20005
Telephone: (202) 737-4728

PARK, Judith E.
Director of Legislation, Nat'l Ass'n of Retired Federal Employees
1533 New Hampshire Ave., N.W., Washington, DC 20036
Telephone: (202) 234-0832
Registered as lobbyist at U.S. Congress.
Background: Serves as contact for the Nat'l Ass'n of Retired Federal Employees PAC.

PARK, Robert L.
Director, Public Affairs, American Physical Soc.
2000 Florida Ave., N.W., Washington, DC 20009
Telephone: (202) 232-0189

PARKE, Nancy L.
Joint Government Affairs Director, American Congress on Surveying and Mapping
5410 Grosvenor Lane, Suite 100, Bethesda, MD 20814-2122
Telephone: (301) 493-0200
Registered as lobbyist at U.S. Congress.
Background: Serves also as Treasurer, ACSM-NSPS Political Action Committee.

PARKER, Alan A.
Deputy Exec. Director for Public Affairs, Ass'n of Trial Lawyers of America
1050 31st St., N.W., Washington, DC 20007
Telephone: (202) 965-3500
Registered as lobbyist at U.S. Congress.
Background: Formerly General Counsel, House of Representatives Judiciary Committee.

PARKER, Allison
Exec. Director, Fiberglass Fabrication Ass'n
3299 K St., N.W., 7th Floor, Washington, DC 20007
Telephone: (202) 337-3322

PARKER, Bonnie
Legislative Representative, Tobacco Institute
1875 Eye St., N.W., Suite 800, Washington, DC 20006
Telephone: (202) 457-4800
Registered as lobbyist at U.S. Congress.
Background: Former Staff Administrator, Senate Ethics Committee.

PARKER, Craig
V. President for Public Affairs, Grand Canyon Trust
1400 16th St. N.W., Suite 300, Washington, DC 20036
Telephone: (202) 797-5429

PARKER, David N.
President, Aluminum Ass'n
900 19th St., N.W., Suite 300, Washington, DC 20006
Telephone: (202) 862-5100

PARKER, Demetrius M.
Manager, Program Support and Development, Public Affairs Council
1019 19th St., N.W., Suite 200, Washington, DC 20036
Telephone: (202) 872-1790

PARKER, Douglas L.
Director, Institute for Public Representation
600 New Jersey Ave., N.W., Washington, DC 20001
Telephone: (202) 662-9535
Background: Serves as Director, Citizens Communication Center.

PARKER, Elissa
Director of Research, Environmental Law Institute
1616 P St., N.W., Suite 200, Washington, DC 20036
Telephone: (202) 328-5150

PARKER, Erich
Director, Public Relations, American Academy of Actuaries
1720 Eye St., N.W., 7th Floor, Washington, DC 20006
Telephone: (202) 223-8196

PARKER, Frank R.
Director, Voting Rights Project, Lawyers' Committee for Civil Rights Under Law
1400 Eye St., N.W., Suite 400, Washington, DC 20005
Telephone: (202) 371-1212

PARKER, John N.
Mgr, Gov't Reltns/Internat'l Mktg & Rfng, Mobil Corp.
1100 Connecticut Ave., N.W., Suite 620, Washington, DC 20036
Telephone: (202) 862-1318
Registered as lobbyist at U.S. Congress.

PARKER, Kimberly C.
Legislative Consultant to the President, American Postal Workers Union
1300 L St., N.W., Washington, DC 20005
Telephone: (202) 842-4200
Registered as lobbyist at U.S. Congress.

PARKER, Lynn
Nutrition Consultant, Food Research and Action Center
1319 F St., N.W. Suite 500, Washington, DC 20004
Telephone: (202) 393-5060
Registered as lobbyist at U.S. Congress.

PARKER, Margaret
Program Director/Research Assistant, Piper Pacific Internat'l
2055 North 15th St. Suite 300, Arlington, VA 22201
Telephone: (703) 524-7556
Registered as Foreign Agent: (#4244).
Clients:
Fuji Heavy Industries Ltd.
Nissan Motor Co., Ltd.

PARKER, Richard G.
O'Melveny and Myers
555 13th St., N.W., Suite 500 West, Washington, DC 20004
Telephone: (202) 383-5300
Clients:
Baldwin Co., D. H.
Baldwin United Corp.

PARKER, Sharon
Washington Representative, Girls Clubs of America, Inc.
1301 20th St., N.W. Suite 702, Washington, DC 20036
Telephone: (202) 296-2665
Background: Also serves as Chair of the Board for Women for Meaningful Summits.

PARKER, Thomas, Jr.
Associate Director, Energy, Chemical Manufacturers Ass'n
2501 M St., N.W., Washington, DC 20037
Telephone: (202) 887-1100
Registered as lobbyist at U.S. Congress.

PARKHURST, Muriel Sue
Exec. Director, Veterans of World War I of the U.S.A.
941 North Capitol St., N.E. Suite 1201-C, Washington, DC 20002
Telephone: (202) 275-1388

PARKIN, Penny L.
Federal Information Manager, Dow Chemical
1776 Eye St., N.W., Suite 575, Washington, DC 20006
Telephone: (202) 429-3400
Registered as lobbyist at U.S. Congress.

PARKIN, Scott L.
Director, Communications, American Ass'n of Homes for the Aging
1129 20th St., N.W., Suite 400, Washington, DC 20036
Telephone: (202) 296-5960

PARKINSON, Charles R.
Cong and Public Affrs, DEPARTMENT OF TREASURY - United States Customs Service
1301 Constitution Ave., N.W., Washington, DC 20229
Telephone: (202) 566-9102

PARKINSON, Leonard
Group Dir., Gov't Relations, Atlantic Research Corp.
5390 Cherokee Ave., Alexandria, VA 22312-2302
Telephone: (703) 642-4000

PARKS, Prudence H., Esq.
11301 Popes Head Road, Fairfax, VA 22030
Telephone: (703) 278-9272
Organizations represented:
Washington Gas Light Co.

PARMAN, Ann M.
Director, Government Relations, Nat'l Manufactured Housing Federation
1701 K St., N.W., Suite 400, Washington, DC 20006
Telephone: (202) 822-6470
Registered as lobbyist at U.S. Congress.

PARMELEE, Ken
V. President of Governmental Affairs, Nat'l Rural Letter Carriers' Ass'n
1448 Duke St., Alexandria, VA 22314
Telephone: (703) 684-5545
Registered as lobbyist at U.S. Congress.
Background: Administrative Assistant to Rep. James J. Florio of New Jersey, 1977-80. Exec. Assistant to Sen. Vance Hartke of Indiana, 1975-77.

PARMER, Carolyn L.
V. President for Health Finance, District of Columbia Hospital Ass'n
1250 Eye St., N.W., Suite 700, Washington, DC 20005-3922
Telephone: (202) 682-1581
Registered as lobbyist at U.S. Congress.

PARNELL, Dr. Dale
President, American Ass'n of Community and Junior Colleges
One Dupont Circle, N.W. Suite 410, Washington, DC 20036
Telephone: (202) 293-7050

PAROBEK, Dennis
Cong Affrs, DEPARTMENT OF TRANSPORTATION - Federal Aviation Administration
800 Independence Ave., S.W., Washington, DC 20591
Telephone: (202) 267-3277

PARQUERI, Penny
State & Local Gov't Relatns Coordinator, Electronic Data Systems Corp.
1331 Pennsylvania Ave., N.W., Suite 1300 North, Washington, DC 20004
Telephone: (202) 637-6700

PARRA, Victor S.
Exec. V. President, Nat'l Computer Graphics Ass'n
2722 Merrilee Drive, Suite 200, Fairfax, VA 22031
Telephone: (703) 698-9600

PARRILLO, Douglas F.
Sr. V. President, Communications, Nat'l Ass'n of Securities Dealers (NASDAQ)
1735 K St., N.W., Washington, DC 20006
Telephone: (202) 728-8000

PARRISH AND CO., INC.
1825 I St., N.W., Suite 400, Washington, DC 20006
Telephone: (202) 429-2099
Background: A government relations consulting firm.
Members of firm representing listed organizations:
Parrish, Max R., President

PARRISH, Donald
V. President, Snavely, King and Associates
1220 L St., N.W., Suite 410, Washington, DC 20005
Telephone: (202) 371-1111

PARRISH, Max R.
President, Parrish and Co., Inc.
1825 I St., N.W., Suite 400, Washington, DC 20006
Telephone: (202) 429-2099
Registered as lobbyist at U.S. Congress.

PARRISH, Robert
Staff Attorney, Center for Science in the Public Interest
1501 16th St., N.W., Washington, DC 20036
Telephone: (202) 332-9110

PARRISH, Theda A.
Manager, Corporate Communications, Atlantic Research Corp.
5390 Cherokee Ave., Alexandria, VA 22312-2302
Telephone: (703) 642-4216

PARRY AND ROMANI ASSOCIATES INC.
233 Constitution Ave., N.E., Washington, DC 20002
Telephone: (202) 547-4000
Registered as Foreign Agent: (#3814)

Members of firm representing listed organizations:
Lowrey, Carmen G.
Mehl, Ted
Parry, Tom
Romani, Romano, President
Clients:
American Family Corp. *(Romano Romani)*
Bell Helicopter Textron *(Romano Romani)*
Blue Sea Corp. *(Romano Romani)*
Care Enterprises *(Romano Romani)*
Cessna Aircraft Co. *(Ted Mehl)*
Genentech, Inc.
Generic Pharmaceutical Industry Ass'n *(Romano Romani)*
Herbalife Internat'l *(Romano Romani)*
Industrial Biotechnology Ass'n *(Romano Romani)*
Lockheed Corp.
Motion Picture Ass'n of America *(Romano Romani)*
Nat'l Ass'n of Independent Insurers *(Romano Romani)*
Pfizer, Inc.
Research Corporation Technologies, Inc. *(Romano Romani)*
Schering-Plough Corp. *(Romano Romani)*
Systech Environmental Corp.
Telephonics, CSD *(Romano Romani)*
Upjohn Co.
Warner-Lambert Co. *(Romano Romani)*
Won Door Corp. *(Romano Romani)*
World Chiropractic Alliance

PARRY, Tom
Parry and Romani Associates Inc.
233 Constitution Ave., N.E., Washington, DC 20002
Telephone: (202) 547-4000
Registered as Foreign Agent: (# 3814).

PARSKY, Gerald L.
Gibson, Dunn and Crutcher
1050 Connecticut Ave., N.W. Suite 900, Washington, DC 20036-5303
Telephone: (202) 955-8500
Background: Assistant Secretary of the Treasury for International Affairs, 1974-77.

PARSON, Amber
Legislative Analyst, NMTBA - The Ass'n for Manufacturing Technology
7901 Westpark Dr., McLean, VA 22102
Telephone: (703) 893-2900
Registered as lobbyist at U.S. Congress.

PARSONS, Alvin L.
V. President, Public Affairs, American Insurance Ass'n
1130 Connecticut Ave., N.W., Suite 1000, Washington, DC 20036
Telephone: (202) 828-7100

PARSONS, Richard N.
Ass't to the Dir. of Federal Legislation, Handgun Control, Inc.
1225 Eye St., N.W., Suite 1100, Washington, DC 20005
Telephone: (202) 898-0792
Registered as lobbyist at U.S. Congress.

PARTRIDGE, Col. Charles C., (Ret)
Legislative Counsel, Nat'l Ass'n for Uniformed Services
5535 Hempstead Way, Springfield, VA 22151
Telephone: (703) 750-1342
Registered as lobbyist at U.S. Congress.

PARVER, Alan
Powell, Goldstein, Frazer and Murphy
1001 Pennsylvania, N.W., Sixth Fl., Washington, DC 20004
Telephone: (202) 347-0066
Registered as lobbyist at U.S. Congress.

PARVER, Corrine Propas
Dir., Government and Legal Affairs, Nat'l Ass'n of Medical Equipment Suppliers
625 Slaters Lane, Suite 200, Alexandria, VA 22314
Telephone: (703) 836-6263

PASCALE, Gwen
Confidential Asst, Legis Affrs, DEPARTMENT OF TREASURY
15th and Pennsylvania Ave. N.W., Washington, DC 20220
Telephone: (202) 566-2037

PASCO, James O.
Asst Dir, Cong and Media Affrs, DEPARTMENT OF TREASURY - Bureau of Alcohol, Tobacco and Firearms
1200 Pennsylvania Ave., N.W., Washington, DC 20226
Telephone: (202) 566-7376

PASCO, Richard E.
V. President, Government Affairs, Nat'l Pork Producers Council
501 School St., N.W. Suite 400, Washington, DC 20024
Telephone: (202) 552-3600
Registered as lobbyist at U.S. Congress.
Background: Legislative Ass't to Sen. Edward Zorinski (D-NE).

PASTER, Howard G.
Exec. V. President, Timmons and Co., Inc.
1850 K St., N.W., Suite 850, Washington, DC 20006
Telephone: (202) 331-1760
Background: Former Legis. Director, United Automobile Workers. Former Legis. Assistant to Senator Birch Bayh (D-IN).

PASTER, Mary
Special Assistant to the President, Consortium of Universities of the Washington Metropolitan Area
1717 Massachusetts Ave., N.W., Suite 101, Washington, DC 20036
Telephone: (202) 265-1313

PASTRE, Peter R.
Manager, Congressional Relations, Nat'l Soc. of Professional Engineers
1420 King St., Alexandria, VA 22314-2715
Telephone: (703) 684-2841
Registered as lobbyist at U.S. Congress.
Background: Former legislative aide to Senator Alan Simpson (R-WY). Serves as Contact, Nat'l Soc. of Professional Engineers PAC.

PASTRICK, R. Scott
Senior V. President, Black, Manafort, Stone and Kelly Public Affairs Co.
211 N. Union St., Third Floor, Alexandria, VA 22314
Telephone: (703) 683-6612
Registered as lobbyist at U.S. Congress.
Registered as Foreign Agent: (# 3600).
Background: Former Special Ass't to the Ass't Secretary for Legislative Affairs (1978-80); Staff Director, Subcommittee on Census and Population (1983); Deputy Nat'l Financial Director for Democratic Presidential Nominee Walter F. Mondale (1984).

PATACK, Melissa B.
Legislative Liaison, American Israel Public Affairs Committee
440 First St., N.W. Suite 600, Washington, DC 20001
Telephone: (202) 639-5200
Registered as lobbyist at U.S. Congress.
Background: Former Minority Counsel, U.S. Senate Judiciary Committee.

PATCHAN, Bryan
Exec. Dir, Nat'l Remodelers Council, Nat'l Ass'n of Home Builders of the U.S.
15th and M Streets, N.W., Washington, DC 20005
Telephone: (202) 822-0470

PATE, Leigh
Evergreen Associates, Ltd.
206 G St., N.E., Washington, DC 20002
Telephone: (202) 543-3383
Registered as lobbyist at U.S. Congress.
Clients:
Suffolk County, New York

PATE, Michael L.
Bracewell and Patterson
2000 K St., N.W., Suite 500, Washington, DC 20006-1809
Telephone: (202) 828-5800
Registered as lobbyist at U.S. Congress.
Background: Former Legislative Director for Senator Lloyd Bentsen (D-TX), 1980-86.
Clients:
Massachusetts Mutual Life Insurance Co.

PATRICK, M. Stephanie
Public Affairs Counselor, Cargill, Inc.
1101 15th St., N.W., Suite 205, Washington, DC 20005

Telephone: (202) 785-3060
Registered as lobbyist at U.S. Congress.

PATRICK, Ralph C.
Wigman and Cohen
1735 Jefferson Davis Hwy. Crystal Sq. 3, Suite 200, Arlington, VA 22202
Telephone: (703) 892-4300

PATRIZIA, Charles A.
Paul, Hastings, Janofsky and Walker
1050 Connecticut Ave., N.W. Suite 1200, Washington, DC 20036-5331
Telephone: (202) 223-9000
Registered as lobbyist at U.S. Congress.
Clients:
Allegheny Power Systems
American Electric Power Co.
Central and South West Services, Inc.
Eastern Utilities Associates
Middle South Utilities, Inc.
New England Electric System
Northeast Utilities Service Co.

PATTERSON, Harold
Nat'l Accounts Manager, GTE Government Systems
1001 19th St. North Suite 1100, Arlington, VA 22209
Telephone: (703) 284-1770

PATTERSON, Kathleen
Director of Communications, American Public Welfare Ass'n
810 First St., N.E., Suite 300, Washington, DC 20002
Telephone: (202) 682-0100

PATTERSON, Kathleen F.
Kaplan, Russin and Vecchi
1215 17th St., N.W., Washington, DC 20036
Telephone: (202) 887-0353

PATTERSON, Laird D.
Counsel, Bethlehem Steel Corp.
1667 K St., N.W., Suite 600, Washington, DC 20006
Telephone: (202) 775-6200

PATTERSON, Mary-Margaret
Director, Media Relations, Defenders of Wildlife
1244 19th St., N.W., Washington, DC 20036
Telephone: (202) 659-9510

PATTERSON, Richard M.
Government Relations Manager, Dow Chemical
1776 Eye St., N.W., Suite 575, Washington, DC 20006
Telephone: (202) 429-3400
Registered as lobbyist at U.S. Congress.

PATTERSON, Sally
Senior V. President, Hamilton & Staff
1019 19th St., N.W., Suite 1300, Washington, DC 20036
Telephone: (202) 857-1980
Background: Also serves as President, Women in Government Relations.

PATTI, C. James
President, Maritime Institute for Research and Industrial Development
1133 15th St., N.W. Suite 600, Washington, DC 20005
Telephone: (202) 463-6505
Registered as lobbyist at U.S. Congress.
Background: Also serves as Washington Representative for Masters, Mates and Pilots Political Contribution Fund.

PATTIE, Kenton
Exec. V. President, Internat'l Communications Industries Ass'n (ICIA)
3150 Spring St., Fairfax, VA 22031-2399
Telephone: (703) 273-7200
Registered as lobbyist at U.S. Congress.
Background: Co-Founder and member of the Coalition for Government Procurement. Co-founder of the Business Coalition for Fair Competition. Charter member of the Committee for Education Funding. Co-founded the Copyright Remedies Coalition and the Committee for America's Copyright Community. Represents the Coalition for State Prompt Pay and the Coalition for Prompt Pay.

WASHINGTON REPRESENTATIVES

PATTISON, David J.
Asst. Washington Counsel & Corp. Sec'y, Health Insurance Ass'n of America
1025 Connecticut Ave., N.W. Suite 1200, Washington, DC 20036
Telephone: (202) 223-7780
Registered as lobbyist at U.S. Congress.
Background: Also serves as Treasurer, Health Insurance Ass'n PAC.

PATTOK, Joseph M.
Director, State Government Affairs, Soc. of the Plastics Industry
1275 K St., N.W., Suite 400, Washington, DC 20005
Telephone: (202) 371-5200

PATTON, BOGGS AND BLOW
2550 M St., N.W., Suite 800, Washington, DC 20037
Telephone: (202) 457-6000
Registered as Foreign Agent: (#2165)
Members of firm representing listed organizations:
  Arbuckle, J. Gordon
  Blow, George
  Boggs, Thomas Hale (Jr.)
  Background: Special U.S. Representative to Internat'l Maritime Conference 1965. Serves as Special Counsel to the American Soc. of Ass'n Executives. Member, Board of Directors, Eastern Air Lines.
  Boyce, Katharine R.
  Background: Legislative Aide to Rep. James G. O'Hara (D-MI), 1972-73. Legislative Assistant and Press Secretary to Rep. Brock Adams (D-WA), 1973-77.
  Brady, Robert P.
  Background: Exec. Ass't to the Commissioner, Food and Drug Administration, 1981-83.
  Brand, Joseph L.
  Christian, Ernest S. (Jr.)
  Background: Tax Legislative Counsel, U.S. Treasury Department, 1973-74. Deputy Assistant Secretary of Treasury for Tax Policy, 1974-75.
  Christian, James B. (Jr.)
  Background: Legislative Counsel and Professional Staff Member, Senate Appropriations Committee, 1975-77.
  Davis, Lanny J.
  Dunn, David E. (III)
  Background: Assistant Attorney General, State of Alabama, 1975-76. Assistant to President, Overseas Private Investment Corp., 1977.
  Esch, Michael D.
  Farthing, Penelope S.
  Background: Staff Attorney, Federal Communications Commission, 1970-72. Congressional Liaison, Federal Trade Commission, 1974-77. Special Assistant to the Administrator, USDA Food Safety and Quality Service, 1977-78.
  Fisher, Bart S.
  Fishman, Ira
  Fithian, John F.
  Flores, Dan
  Foster, William C.
  Background: Deputy Director, Alaska Legislative Council and Legislative Counsel to Senator E. L. Bartlett, 1961-64. Counsel, U.S. Senate Commerce Committee, 1964-66.
  Hathaway, William D.
  Background: Member U.S. House of Representatives (D-ME), 1965-72. Member U.S. Senate (D-ME), 1973-78.
  Hills, Laura H.
  Inman, Harry A.
  Jonas, John
  Background: Tax Counsel, Committee on Ways and Means, U.S. House of Representatives, 1981-86.
  Kendrick, Martha M.
  Koehler, Robert H.
  Background: Legal Advisor, U.S. Army Procurement Agency, Vietnam, 1970-71. Trial Attorney, Contract Appeals Division, Office of the Judge Advocate General, 1971-73.
  Kronmiller, Theodore G.
  Background: Counsel, Subcommittee on Oceanography, U.S. House of Representatives, 1978-79. Counsel, House Subcommittee on Fisheries and Wildlife Conservation and the Environment, 1979-81. Deputy Assistant Secretary of State for Ocean and Fisheries Affairs, 1982-83.
  Lachter, Stephen, Of Counsel

Background: Trial Attorney, Civil Aeronautics Board, 1969-1975. Supervisory Trial Attorney, Antitrust Division, U.S. Department of Justice, 1975-1978. Executive Assistant to CAB Member, 1978-1982. Deputy Director and Associate Director, Legal Affairs, Bureau of Domestic Aviation, CAB, 1982-1985 . Special Aviation Counsel, U.S. Department of Transportation, 1985.
  Laws, Elliott P.
  Background: Attorney, U.S. Dept. of Justice, head of Natural Resources Division, 1985-87; Attorney, Environmental Protection Agency, Office of Enforcement and Compliance Monitoring, 1984-85.
  Lee, Lansing B.
  Background: Administrative Ass't to Gov. Jimmy Carter (D-GA), 1970-72, Exec. Director, Democratic Party of Georgia, 1983-85.
  Liebman, Ronald S.
  Background: Assistant U.S. Attorney, District of Maryland, 1972-78.
  Massa, Cliff (III)
  May, Timothy J.
  Background: Law Clerk, U.S. Court of Appeals, D.C. Circuit 1957-58. Consultant, Executive Office of the President 1961-62. Acting Chief Counsel, U.S. Senate National Stockpile Investigating Committee 1962-63. Managing Director Federal Maritime Commission 1963-66. U.S. Representative to International Maritime Conferences 1964-66.
  Messick, Richard
  Background: Chief Counsel, U.S. Senate Foreign Relations Committee, 1985-86.
  Moag, John (Jr.)
  Moorehead, Donald V.
  Background: Chief Minority Counsel, Committee on Finance, U.S. Senate, 1975-76.
  Neipris, Deborah
  Oberdorfer, John L.
  Background: Attorney, Office of the General Counsel, U.S. Department of Transportation, 1971-74.
  O'Hara, Ray
  Pape, Stuart M.
  Background: Former Special Assistant to the Commissioner, Food and Drug Administration.
  Patton, James R. (Jr.)
  Prioleau, Florence W.
  Background: Assistant Director, Domestic Policy Staff, White House, 1979-81. Member, Professional Staff, House of Representatives Committee on Ways and Means, 1976-79.
  Raboy, David G., Cheif Economic Consultant
  Background: Former Legislative Director for Senator William V. Roth, Jr. (R-DE).
  Reeder, Joe Robert
  Background: Trial Attorney, Litigation Division, Office of the Army Judge Advocate General, 1976-78. Contract Appeals Division, Office of Judge Advocate General, 1978-79.
  Robertson, Peter
  Background: Legislative Assistant to Rep. James R. Jones (D-OK), 1979-81. Professional Staff Member, House Budget Committee, 1981-86.
  Robinson, David B.
  Robinson, Phillip L.
  Background: Professional Staff Member, Office of Technology Assessment, U.S. Congress, 1979-81.
  Rowan, Eugene F.
  Samolis, Frank R.
  Background: Legislative Assistant to Rep. Charles A. Vanik (D-OH), 1976. Professional Staff, Committee on Ways and Means, Subcommittee on Trade, U.S. House of Representatives, 1977-80.
  Schneebaum, Steven
  Schutzer, George J.
  Stolbach, Richard H.
  Background: Assistant General Counsel, 1976-77, and Special Counsel to the Exec. Director, 1978, Appalachian Regional Commission.
  Todd, David C.
  Background: Serves as General Counsel, Mail Order Ass'n of America.
  Turner, Jeff
  Tuttle, Alan A.
  Background: Assistant U.S. Attorney, Southern District of New York, 1969-71. Assistant to the Solicitor General, 1971-75. Solicitor, Federal Power Commission, 1975-77.
  Vogel, John H.

  Wade, J. Kirk
  Background: Attorney Advisor, Interpretative Division, Chief Counsel of the Internal Revenue Service, 1972-76. Attorney-Advisor, Tax Legislative Counsel, Department of the Treasury, 1976-77.
Clients:
Advanced Technology, Inc. *(Joe Robert Reeder)*
Agri-Energy Roundtable *(Bart S. Fisher)*
Air Products and Chemicals, Inc. *(Ernest S. Christian, Jr.)*
Aiwa America, Inc.
Alaska Crab Coalition *(James B. Christian, Jr.)*
Alexander & Baldwin, Inc. *(David B. Robinson)*
ALTA Technology *(Lanny J. Davis)*
American Ass'n of Equipment Lessors *(Ernest S. Christian, Jr.)*
American Ass'n of Exporters and Importers
American Congress on Surveying and Mapping *(Joe Robert Reeder)*
American Internat'l Automobile Dealers Ass'n *(George Blow)*
American Logistics Ass'n *(Joe Robert Reeder)*
American Maritime Ass'n *(Alan A. Tuttle)*
American Stock Exchange *(Stuart M. Pape)*
Ass'n of Professional Flight Attendants *(Thomas Hale Boggs, Jr.)*
Ass'n of Trial Lawyers of America *(Thomas Hale Boggs, Jr.)*
Auto Dealers and Drivers for Free Trade PAC *(George Blow)*
Avon Products, Inc. *(Timothy J. May, Stuart M. Pape)*
B.A.T. Industries, PLC
BATUS, Inc. *(Thomas Hale Boggs, Jr.)*
Beckett Packaging, Ltd. *(Timothy J. May)*
Bethlehem Steel Corp. *(James B. Christian, Jr.)*
Biogen *(Stuart M. Pape)*
Bristol-Myers Squibb Co. *(Robert H. Koehler)*
Cargolux Airlines Internat'l *(Timothy J. May)*
Chemfix Technologies, Inc. *(J. Gordon Arbuckle)*
Cherokee Nation Industries, Inc. *(Ernest S. Christian, Jr.)*
Cherokee Nation of Oklahoma *(Katharine R. Boyce)*
Chicago Board Options Exchange *(Thomas Hale Boggs, Jr.)*
CIGNA Corp. *(Lansing B. Lee)*
Citizens for a Sound Economy
Coalition on State Use Taxes *(Timothy J. May)*
College Savings Bank *(James B. Christian, Jr.)*
Columbia Farm Credit District *(John H. Vogel)*
Columbia, Inc.
Costa Rican Foreign Trade Committee *(Frank R. Samolis)*
Council of Graduate Schools *(John Jonas)*
Cryolife Inc. *(Ronald S. Liebman, Deborah Neipris)*
Dealer Action Ass'n *(George Blow)*
Denver, Colorado, City and County of
Dole Fresh Fruit Co. *(Joseph L. Brand)*
Doyon, Ltd. *(Thomas Hale Boggs, Jr.)*
Dredging Industry Size Standard Committee (DISSC) *(Joe Robert Reeder)*
Duty Free Shoppers Group Limited *(Stuart M. Pape)*
Egypt, Embassy of
Fiart Cantieri Italiani S.p.A. *(Katharine R. Boyce, David E. Dunn, III)*
Fidelity Investors *(William D. Hathaway)*
Fishing Vessel Owners Ass'n *(Theodore G. Kronmiller)*
Flexi-Van Leasing *(James B. Christian, Jr.)*
Freedom to Advertise Coalition *(Thomas Hale Boggs, Jr.)*
Fuji Photo Film U.S.A.
Fundacion de Defensa del Comercio Exterior *(Frank R. Samolis)*
Fundacion Pro-Imagen de Colombia en el Exterior *(James B. Christian, Jr., David E. Dunn, III)*
Gana-A' Yoo, Ltd. *(James B. Christian, Jr.)*
Halogenated Solvents Industry Alliance
Hitachi Sales Corp. of America
Hobby Industries Ass'n *(Lanny J. Davis)*
Home Recording Rights Coalition
Iceland, Government of *(Theodore G. Kronmiller)*
Immune Response Corp. *(Stuart M. Pape)*
Incorporated Research Institutions for Seismology *(Penelope S. Farthing)*
Institute of Scrap Recycling Industries, Inc. *(John L. Oberdorfer)*
Internat'l Fabricare Institute
Internat'l Thomson *(Thomas Hale Boggs, Jr.)*

Itel Containers Internat'l Corp. *(James B. Christian, Jr.)*
James Co., T. L. *(J. Gordon Arbuckle)*
Kaiser Aluminum and Chemical Corp. *(Donald V. Moorehead)*
Kenwood U.S.A. Corp.
LOOP, Inc. *(J. Gordon Arbuckle)*
M&M/Mars, Inc. *(James R. Patton, Jr.)*
Magnuson Act Coalition *(James B. Christian, Jr.)*
Marathon Oil Co. *(Thomas Hale Boggs, Jr.)*
Marshall Islands, Government of *(Theodore G. Kronmiller)*
Massachusetts Mutual Life Insurance Co. *(John Jonas)*
Matson Navigation Co. *(Alan A. Tuttle)*
Matsushita Electric Corp. of America
Maxell Corp. of America
May Department Stores Co. *(Cliff Massa, III)*
MCI Communications Corp. *(Thomas Hale Boggs, Jr.)*
Metropolitan Insurance Cos. *(John Jonas)*
Milk Industry Foundation
Minerals Marketing Corp. of Zimbabwe *(Frank R. Samolis)*
Mitsubishi Electric Sales America
Mocatta Metals Corp. *(Thomas Hale Boggs, Jr.)*
Mutual Benefit Life Insurance Co. *(John Jonas)*
Mutual Life Insurance Co. Tax Committee *(John Jonas)*
Mutual Life Insurance Legislative Committee *(John Jonas)*
Nakajima All Co. *(Thomas Hale Boggs, Jr.)*
Nakamichi U.S.A. Corp.
Nat'l Ass'n of Life Underwriters *(John Jonas)*
Nat'l Ass'n of Postal Supervisors *(Timothy J. May)*
Nat'l Ass'n of Postal Supervisors Political Action Committee *(Timothy J. May)*
Nat'l Ass'n of Retail Druggists *(Thomas Hale Boggs, Jr.)*
Nat'l Ass'n of Wholesaler-Distributors *(Cliff Massa, III)*
Nat'l Intergroup, Inc. *(Ernest S. Christian, Jr.)*
Nat'l Marine Manufacturers Ass'n *(James B. Christian, Jr.)*
Nat'l Soft Drink Ass'n *(Stuart M. Pape)*
Navajo Nation, The *(Richard H. Stolbach)*
NCNB Texas Nat'l Bank *(James B. Christian, Jr.)*
NEC Home Electronics (USA) Inc.
New Process Co. *(Timothy J. May)*
New York Life Insurance Co. *(Thomas Hale Boggs, Jr.)*
Northwestern Mutual Life Insurance Co. *(John Jonas)*
Olympic Fibers *(James B. Christian, Jr.)*
Oman, Embassy of the Sultanate of *(David E. Dunn, III)*
Onkyo U.S.A. Corp.
Options Clearing Corp., The *(Thomas Hale Boggs, Jr.)*
OSG Bulk Ships, Inc. *(Alan A. Tuttle)*
Paine Webber Group *(Thomas Hale Boggs, Jr.)*
Parcel Shippers Ass'n Political Action Committee *(Timothy J. May)*
Pioneer Electronics
Reinsurance Ass'n of America *(John Jonas)*
Retail Industry Trade Action Coalition *(Thomas Hale Boggs, Jr., Frank R. Samolis)*
Retail Tax Committee *(Thomas Hale Boggs, Jr.)*
Rice Millers' Ass'n *(Bart S. Fisher)*
Royal Trustco Ltd. *(James B. Christian, Jr.)*
Sansui Electronics Corp.
Sanyo Electronics
Save Chanute Committee *(James B. Christian, Jr.)*
Sharp Electronics Corp.
Smokeless Tobacco Council *(Thomas Hale Boggs, Jr., James B. Christian, Jr., Ray O'Hara)*
Sony Corp. of America
Spain, Government of *(David E. Dunn, III)*
Speciality Seafoods *(James B. Christian, Jr.)*
Standard Federal Savings Bank *(James B. Christian, Jr.)*
TDK U.S.A. Corp.
TEAC Corp. of America
TEKNIKA Electronics Corp.
Toshiba America, Inc.
Trans Ocean Ltd. *(James B. Christian, Jr.)*
Transamerica Leasing, Inc. *(James B. Christian, Jr.)*
Triton Container Co. *(James B. Christian, Jr.)*
U.S. JVC Corp.
University of Arizona *(John Moag, Jr.)*

USAir Group Inc. *(Stephen Lachter)*
Waste Management, Inc. *(Katharine R. Boyce)*
Wayne County, Michigan *(James B. Christian, Jr.)*
XTRA Corp. *(James B. Christian, Jr.)*
Yamaha Electronics Corp., U.S.A.

PATTON, Denise J.
V. President, Public Relations, Nat'l Ass'n of Life Underwriters
1922 F St., N.W., Washington, DC 20006
Telephone: (202) 331-6000

PATTON, James R., Jr.
Patton, Boggs and Blow
2550 M St., N.W., Suite 800, Washington, DC 20037
Telephone: (202) 457-6000
Registered as lobbyist at U.S. Congress.
Registered as Foreign Agent: (#2165).
Clients:
    M&M/Mars, Inc.

PATTON, Thomas B.
V. President, Government Relations, North American Philips Corp.
1300 Eye St., N.W., Washington, DC 20005
Telephone: (202) 962-8550
Registered as lobbyist at U.S. Congress.

PAUL, Andrew R.
Director, Government Relations, Paramount Communications, Inc.
1875 Eye St., N.W., Suite 1225, Washington, DC 20006
Telephone: (202) 429-9690
Registered as lobbyist at U.S. Congress.

PAUL, HASTINGS, JANOFSKY AND WALKER
1050 Connecticut Ave., N.W. Suite 1200, Washington, DC 20036-5331
Telephone: (202) 223-9000
Background: Washington office of a Los Angeles law firm.
Members of firm representing listed organizations:
    Dickson, R. Bruce
    Emery, N. Beth
        Background: Attorney, Electric and Telephone Division, Office of the General Counsel, Department of Agriculture, 1977-79. Legal Advisor to Commissioner Matthew Holden, Jr., Federal Energy Regulatory Commission, 1979-81.
    Everett, Ralph B.
        Background: Special Assistant to Senator Ernest Hollings (D-SC), 1977-78. Legislative Assistant to Senator Hollings, 1979-82. Minority Chief Counsel and Staff Director, Senate Commerce, Science and Transportation Committee, 1983-86; Chief Counsel and Staff Director, same Committee, 1987-89.
    Fairbanks, Richard M. (III)
        Background: Associate Director, White House Domestic Council, 1972-74. Assistant Secretary of State, 1981-82; Special Negotiator, Middle East Peace Process, 1982-83; Ambassador at Large, 1984-85.
    Gerchick, Mark L.
    Hope, Judith Richards
        Background: Associate Director, The Domestic Council, The White House, 1975-77. Member, Nat'l Highway Traffic Safety Commission, 1977-78. Member, President's Commission on Organized Crime, 1985-86.
    Loeb, G. Hamilton
    Patrizia, Charles A.
    Winston, Deborah F., Gov't Affairs Coordinator
Clients:
    Allegheny Power Systems *(Charles A. Patrizia)*
    Amdahl Corp. *(G. Hamilton Loeb)*
    American Electric Power Co. *(Charles A. Patrizia)*
    American Trucking Ass'ns *(Ralph B. Everett)*
    Ameritech (American Information Technologies) *(Ralph B. Everett)*
    Aspirin Foundation of America, Inc. *(R. Bruce Dickson)*
    Bell Atlantic *(Ralph B. Everett)*
    BellSouth Corp. *(Ralph B. Everett)*
    CalMat Co. *(Judith Richards Hope)*
    Central and South West Services, Inc. *(Charles A. Patrizia)*
    Eastern Utilities Associates *(Charles A. Patrizia)*
    Government Affairs Policy Council of the Regional Bell Operating Companies *(Ralph B. Everett, Judith Richards Hope)*

Iraq, Embassy of *(Richard M. Fairbanks, III)*
Kawasaki Motors Corp., USA *(Mark L. Gerchick)*
Koito Manufacturing Co. *(Richard M. Fairbanks, III, G. Hamilton Loeb)*
Middle South Utilities, Inc. *(Charles A. Patrizia)*
New England Electric System *(Charles A. Patrizia)*
Northeast Utilities Service Co. *(Charles A. Patrizia)*
NYNEX *(Ralph B. Everett)*
Pacific Telesis Group-Washington *(Ralph B. Everett)*
Paul, Hastings, Janofsky and Walker Political Action Committee *(Ralph B. Everett)*
Security Life Insurance Co. of Denver *(Judith Richards Hope, Deborah F. Winston)*
Southwestern Bell Corp. *(Ralph B. Everett)*
Telequest, Inc. *(G. Hamilton Loeb)*
Tobacco Institute
Tubos de Acero de Mexico, S.A. *(G. Hamilton Loeb)*
US WEST, Inc. *(Ralph B. Everett)*

PAUL, Joel M.
Director, Communications, Nat'l Pest Control Ass'n
8100 Oak St., Dunn Loring, VA 22027
Telephone: (703) 573-8330

PAUL, Lawrence
Assistant Manager, Mitsubishi Internat'l Corp.
655 15th St., N.W., Suite 860, Washington, DC 20005
Telephone: (202) 638-1101

PAUL, WEISS, RIFKIND, WHARTON AND GARRISON
1615 L St., N.W., Suite 1300, Washington, DC 20036
Telephone: (202) 223-7300
Members of firm representing listed organizations:
    Fortune, Terence J.
        Background: Assistant Legal Adviser, Department of State, 1977-83.
    Montgomery, Robert E. (Jr.)
        Background: Assistant to General Counsel, Department of the Army, 1969-1971; General Counsel, Office of Consumer Affairs, Exec. Office of the President, 1971-1972; Ass't General Counsel, Federal Trade Commission, 1973; General Counsel, Federal Energy Administration, 1974-1975.
    Olmer, Lionel H.
        Background: Undersecretary of Commerce for International Trade and head of the International Trade Administration, 1981-85; Executive Staff, President's Foreign Intelligence Advisory Board, 1973-77.
    Trias, Jose E.
Clients:
    Itoh (America), Inc., C. *(Lionel H. Olmer)*
    McDonnell Douglas Corp. *(Robert E. Montgomery, Jr., Lionel H. Olmer)*
    Nat'l Music Publishers' Ass'n *(Lionel H. Olmer)*
    NEC America *(Terence J. Fortune, Robert E. Montgomery, Jr.)*
    NEC Corp. *(Terence J. Fortune, Robert E. Montgomery, Jr.)*

PAUL, William F.
Sr. V. President, Washington Office, United Technologies Corp.
1825 Eye St., N.W. Suite 700, Washington, DC 20006
Telephone: (202) 785-7400

PAUL, William M.
Covington and Burling
1201 Pennsylvania Ave., N.W., Box 7566, Washington, DC 20044
Telephone: (202) 662-6000
Registered as lobbyist at U.S. Congress.
Clients:
    Maui Land and Pineapple Co., Inc.

PAULEY, Kay
Manager, Gov't Information Services, Direct Marketing Ass'n
1101 17th St., N.W., Suite 900, Washington, DC 20036
Telephone: (202) 347-1222

PAULEY, Roger
Dir, Office of Legislation, DEPARTMENT OF JUSTICE - Criminal Division
10th and Constitution Ave. N.W., Washington, DC 20530
Telephone: (202) 633-3202

The listings in this directory are available as *Mailing Labels*. See last page.

PAULOVIC, Karl
V. President, Snavely, King and Associates
1220 L St., N.W., Suite 410, Washington, DC 20005
Telephone: (202) 371-1111

PAULSON, S. Lawrence
V. President, Public Affairs, Interstate Natural Gas Ass'n
of America
555 13th St., N.W. Suite 300 West, Washington, DC
20004
Telephone: (202) 626-3200

PAYNE, Joyce
Director, Office for Advancement of Public Black Colleges
One Dupont Circle, N.W., Suite 710, Washington, DC
20036-1191
Telephone: (202) 778-0818

PAYNE, Dr. Keith
President, Nat'l Institute for Public Policy
3031 Javier Road Suite 300, Fairfax, VA 22031
Telephone: (703) 698-0563

PAYNE, Kenneth E.
Finnegan, Henderson, Farabow, Garrett and Dunner
1300 I St., N.W., Suite 600, Washington, DC 20005
Telephone: (202) 293-6850
Registered as Foreign Agent: (#3236).
Background: Assistant General Counsel, U.S. Department
of Commerce, 1971-73.
Clients:
Reserve Bank of Australia

PAYNE, Michael L.
V. President, Smith, Bucklin and Associates
1101 Connecticut Ave., N.W., Suite 700, Washington, DC
20036
Telephone: (202) 857-1100
Background: Serves as President, Anti-Friction Bearing
Manufacturers Ass'n and Exec. Director, Financial Sta-
tioners Ass'n.
Clients:
Anti-Friction Bearing Manufacturers Ass'n
Financial Stationers Ass'n

PAYNE, Nell
Spec Asst to Pres, Legis Affrs (Senate), EXECUTIVE OF-
FICE OF THE PRESIDENT - The White House
1600 Pennsylvania Ave., N.W. 107 East Wing, Washing-
ton, DC 20500
Telephone: (202) 456-6782

PAYNE, Tommy J.
Director, Federal Gov't Affairs, RJR Nabisco Washington,
Inc.
1455 Pennsylvania Ave., N.W., Suite 525, Washington, DC
20004
Telephone: (202) 626-7200
Registered as lobbyist at U.S. Congress.

PEABODY FITZPATRICK COMMUNICATIONS
1400 K St., N.W., Suite 1212, Washington, DC 20005
Telephone: (202) 842-5000
Members of firm representing listed organizations:
Fitzpatrick, Joyce, Partner
Koelemay, J. Douglas, Senior Associate
Background: Legislative Assistant to Rep. Robert Mol-
lohan (D-WV), 1980-82. Legislative Assistant to
Senator Frank Lautenberg (D-NJ), 1983-84.
Peabody, Myra B., President
Clients:
American Ass'n of Retired Persons *(J. Douglas Ko-
elemay, Myra B. Peabody)*
Nature Conservancy, The *(Joyce Fitzpatrick, J. Douglas
Koelemay)*
Pennsylvania State System of Higher Education
(J. Douglas Koelemay, Myra B. Peabody)
Pew Health Professions Commission *(Joyce Fitzpa-
trick, J. Douglas Koelemay)*
University of North Carolina *(Joyce Fitzpatrick)*

PEABODY, Myra B.
President, Peabody Fitzpatrick Communications
1400 K St., N.W., Suite 1212, Washington, DC 20005
Telephone: (202) 842-5000
Clients:
American Ass'n of Retired Persons
Pennsylvania State System of Higher Education

PEAGLER, Owen
V. President, Communications, 70001 Training & Employment Institute
501 School St., S.W. Suite 600, Washington, DC 20024
Telephone: (202) 484-0103

PEARCE ASSOCIATES
1730 K St., N.W., Suite 304, Washington, DC 20006
Telephone: (202) 785-0048
Members of firm representing listed organizations:
Pearce, C. Jack
Background: Dep't of Justice, Antitrust Division 1962-
64, 1966-70. Agency for Internat'l Development,
1962-64. White House Office of Consumer Affairs,
1970-71. Serves as General Counsel to the Nat'l Ag-
ricultural Transportation Ass'n.
Clients:
ACR, Inc. *(C. Jack Pearce)*

PEARCE, C. Jack
Pearce Associates
1730 K St., N.W., Suite 304, Washington, DC 20006
Telephone: (202) 785-0048
Registered as lobbyist at U.S. Congress.
Registered as Foreign Agent: (#2750).
Background: Dep't of Justice, Antitrust Division 1962-64,
1966-70. Agency for Internat'l Development, 1962-64.
White House Office of Consumer Affairs, 1970-71. Serves
as General Counsel to the Nat'l Agricultural Transporta-
tion Ass'n.
Clients:
ACR, Inc.

PEARCE, Susan M.
Public Affairs V. President, Ford Aerospace Corp.
1235 Jefferson Davis Hwy. Suite 1300, Arlington, VA
22202
Telephone: (703) 685-5500

PEARS, Don R.
Legislative Director, Veterans of World War I of the U.S.A.
941 North Capitol St., N.E. Suite 1201-C, Washington, DC
20002
Telephone: (202) 275-1388

PEARSE, Warren H., M.D.
Exec. Director, American College of Obstetricians and
Gynecologists
409 12th St., S.W., Washington, DC 20024
Telephone: (202) 638-5577

PEARSON, Cindy
Acting Director, Nat'l Women's Health Network
1325 G St., N.W. Lower Level, Washington, DC 20005
Telephone: (202) 347-1140

PEARSON, Didge
Director of State Affairs, Nat'l Pharmaceutical Council
1894 Preston White Drive, Reston, VA 22091
Telephone: (703) 620-6390

PEARSON, Frederick
Congressional Liaison Director, Nat'l Ass'n of Chiefs of
Police
1000 Connecticut Ave., N.W. Suite 9, Washington, DC
20036
Telephone: (202) 293-9088
Background: Also serves as Congressional Liaison Director
for the American Federation of Police.

PEARSON, Judy Costello
Director, Marketing & Public Relations, Nat'l Ass'n of the
Deaf
814 Thayer Ave., Silver Spring, MD 20910
Telephone: (301) 587-1788

PEARSON, Norman E.
National Exec. Secretary, Fleet Reserve Ass'n
1303 New Hampshire Ave., N.W., Washington, DC 20036
Telephone: (202) 785-2768
Registered as lobbyist at U.S. Congress.

PEARSON & PIPKIN, INC.
422 First St., S.E., Suite 208, Washington, DC 20003
Telephone: (202) 547-7177
Background: A government relations, political and issues
management firm.
Members of firm representing listed organizations:
Pearson, Ronald W., President

Background: Exec. Director, Conservative Victory
Fund. Former aide to former Rep. John Ashbrook
(R-OH).
Pipkin, Robert R. (Jr.), V. President
Clients:
South Africa, Embassy of *(Ronald W. Pearson, Robert
R. Pipkin, Jr.)*

PEARSON, Roger
Director, Council for Social and Economic Studies
1133 13th St., N.W., Suite C-2, Washington, DC 20005
Telephone: (202) 789-0231

PEARSON, Ronald W.
President, Pearson & Pipkin, Inc.
422 First St., S.E., Suite 208, Washington, DC 20003
Telephone: (202) 547-7177
Registered as lobbyist at U.S. Congress.
Registered as Foreign Agent: (#3727).
Background: Exec. Director, Conservative Victory Fund.
Former aide to former Rep. John Ashbrook (R-OH).
Clients:
South Africa, Embassy of

PEARSON, Russell H.
Senior Federal Legislative Manager, Penney Co., J. C.
Suite 1015, 1156 15th St., N.W., Washington, DC 20005
Telephone: (202) 862-4820
Registered as lobbyist at U.S. Congress.

PECARICH, Pamela
Partner, Tax Policy Group, Coopers and Lybrand
1800 M St., N.W., Suite 400, Washington, DC 20036
Telephone: (202) 822-4000
Background: Former staff member, House of Representa-
tives Ways and Means Committee.

PECK, Joe P., Jr.
Congressional Representative, Nat'l Ass'n of Home Build-
ers of the U.S.
15th and M Streets, N.W., Washington, DC 20005
Telephone: (202) 822-0470
Registered as lobbyist at U.S. Congress.
Background: Former aide to Rep. Christopher Smith (R-
NJ).

PECK, Jonathan
Associate Director, Institute for Alternative Futures
108 North Alfred St., Alexandria, VA 22314
Telephone: (703) 684-5880

PECK, Shelley
Program Associate, Children's Defense Fund
122 C St., N.W., Washington, DC 20001
Telephone: (202) 628-8787
Registered as lobbyist at U.S. Congress.

PECKARSKY, Lee
Exec. V. President, Government Affairs, Nat'l Council of
Savings Institutions
1101 15th St., N.W. Suite 400, Washington, DC 20005
Telephone: (202) 857-3100
Registered as lobbyist at U.S. Congress.
Background: Former Staff Director, House Committee on
Banking, Finance and Urban Affairs.

PECKINPAUGH, Tim L.
Preston Gates Ellis & Rouvelas Meeds
1735 New York Ave., N.W., Suite 500, Washington, DC
20006-4759
Telephone: (202) 628-1700
Registered as lobbyist at U.S. Congress.
Background: Professional Staff, Committee on Science and
Technology, 1985; Legislative Assistant, Rep. Sid Morri-
son, 1982-84.
Clients:
American Nuclear Insurers
Earthquake Project, The
Fusion Power Associates
Mutual Atomic Energy Liability Underwriters
Stone and Webster Engineering Corp.
Tri-City Industrial Development Council
Westinghouse Hanford Co.

PECQUEX, Frank
Legislative Director, Seafarers Internat'l Union of North
America
5201 Auth Way, Camp Springs, MD 20746
Telephone: (301) 899-0675

WASHINGTON REPRESENTATIVES

Registered as lobbyist at U.S. Congress.

PEDERSEN HOLUM, Barbara
Director, Nat'l Endowment for Soil and Water Conservation
321 D St., N.E., Washington, DC 20002
Telephone: (202) 546-7407

PEDERSEN, Wes
Dir. of Communications & Public Relats., Public Affairs Council
1019 19th St., N.W., Suite 200, Washington, DC 20036
Telephone: (202) 872-1790

PEDERSON, Bill
Perkins Coie
1110 Vermont Ave., N.W., Suite 1200, Washington, DC 20005
Telephone: (202) 887-9030
Clients:
   Boeing Co.

PEDERSON, Steven R.
Director, elemarketing, Bassin Assoc., Inc., Robert H.
499 South Capitol St., S.W. Suite 407, Washington, DC 20003
Telephone: (202) 863-2611

PEEDO, Endel
Exec. V. President, American Nat'l Heritage Ass'n
P.O. Box 9340, Alexandria, VA 22304-0340
Telephone: (703) 370-3750

PEELE, B. Thomas, III
Baker and McKenzie
815 Connecticut Ave., N.W. Suite 1100, Washington, DC 20006-4078
Telephone: (202) 452-7000
Clients:
   Camara Argentina de la Alumino y Metales Afines

PEELER, Ms. Alexandra
Director of Communications, Catholic Charities USA
1319 F St., N.W., Suite 400, Washington, DC 20004
Telephone: (202) 639-8400

PEHRSON, Gordon O., Jr.
Sutherland, Asbill and Brennan
1275 Pennsylvania, N.W., Washington, DC 20004-2404
Telephone: (202) 383-0100
Registered as lobbyist at U.S. Congress.
Clients:
   Anglo-American Clays Corp.
   China Clay Producers Political Action Committee
   Huber Corp., J. M.
   Minnesota Mutual Life Insurance Co.
   Nord Resources Corp.
   Thiele Kaolin Co.

PELAVIN, Mark J.
Washington Representative, American Jewish Congress
2027 Massachusetts Ave., N.W., Washington, DC 20036
Telephone: (202) 332-4001
Registered as lobbyist at U.S. Congress.

PELETKA, James R.
Exec. Director, ADAPSO Foundation
1300 North 17th St. Suite 300, Arlington, VA 22209
Telephone: (703) 522-5055

PELIZZARI, Patricia
Administrative Coordinator, Washington Area Lawyers for the Arts
2025 Eye St., N.W. Suite 1114, Washington, DC 20006
Telephone: (202) 861-0055

PELKEY, John M.
Haley, Bader and Potts
2000 M St., N.W. Suite 600, Washington, DC 20036
Telephone: (202) 331-0606
Registered as lobbyist at U.S. Congress.
Clients:
   American Electronics Ass'n

PELLETIER, Ann W.
Legislative Analyst, Bell Communications Research, Inc.
2101 L St., N.W. Suite 600, Washington, DC 20037
Telephone: (202) 955-4600

PELLETIER, Stephen G.
Director of Public Affairs, Council of Independent Colleges
One Dupont Circle, N.W. Suite 320, Washington, DC 20036
Telephone: (202) 466-7230

PELTZ, Elin
Assistant Washington Representative, Hawaiian Sugar Planters' Ass'n
1511 K St., N.W., Suite 723, Washington, DC 20005
Telephone: (202) 628-6372
Registered as lobbyist at U.S. Congress.

PEMBLETON, Edward F.
Director of Water Resources Program, Nat'l Audubon Soc.
801 Pennsylvania Ave., S.E., Washington, DC 20003
Telephone: (202) 547-9009
Registered as lobbyist at U.S. Congress.

PEMBROKE, James D.
Duncan, Weinberg, Miller & Pembroke, P.C.
1615 M St., N.W., Suite 800, Washington, DC 20036-3203
Telephone: (202) 467-6370
Clients:
   Arkansas Public Service Commission
   Auburn, Avilla, Bluffton, Columbia City and Other Indiana Municipalities
   Cajun Rural Electric Power Cooperative, Inc.
   Central Montana Electric Power Cooperative, Inc.
   Indiana and Michigan Municipal Distributors Ass'n
   Modesto Irrigation District
   Montana Electric Power Cooperatives Ass'n
   Niles, Michigan, Utilities Department of
   Santa Clara, California, City of
   Sturgis, Michigan, Municipality of
   Transmission Agency of Northern California

PENCAK, Lawrence C.
Exec. Director, Mainstream
1030 15th St., N.W. Suite 1010, Washington, DC 20005
Telephone: (202) 898-1400

PENCE, Randall G.
Director, Government Relations, Nat'l Concrete Masonry Ass'n
P.O. Box 781, Herndon, VA 22070
Telephone: (703) 435-4900
Registered as lobbyist at U.S. Congress.
Background: Former Legislative Director to Senator David Karnes (R-NE). Serves as contact for Nat'l Concrete Masonry Ass'n Political Action Committee.

PENDERGAST, Lee A.
Government Affairs Manager, Upjohn Co.
1455 F St., N.W., Suite 450, Washington, DC 20005
Telephone: (202) 393-6040
Background: Former Deputy Press Secretary to Speaker Thomas P. O'Neill, U.S. House of Representatives.

PENDERGAST, William R.
Arent, Fox, Kintner, Plotkin & Kahn
1050 Connecticut Ave., N.W., Washington, DC 20036-5339
Telephone: (202) 857-6000

PENDILL, Dr. C. Grant, Jr.
Exec. Director, Organization for American-Soviet ExchangeS (OASES-DC)
1302 R St., N.W., Washington, DC 20009
Telephone: (202) 332-1145

PENDLETON, Andrea
Director, Communications, Optical Soc. of America
1816 Jefferson Place, N.W., Washington, DC 20036
Telephone: (202) 223-8130

PENDLETON, Edmund E.
Anderson and Pendleton, C.A.
1000 Connecticut Ave., N.W., Suite 1220, Washington, DC 20036
Telephone: (202) 659-2334
Registered as lobbyist at U.S. Congress.

PENDLETON, John
Exec Asst, Cong Liaison, DEPARTMENT OF JUSTICE - Bureau of Prisons
320 First St., N.W., Washington, DC 20534
Telephone: (202) 724-3198

PENN, Candis Brown
Exec. Director, Southern Governors Ass'n
444 North Capitol St., N.W., Suite 240, Washington, DC 20001
Telephone: (202) 624-5897

PENNA, Richard A.
Schnader, Harrison, Segal and Lewis
1111 19th St., N.W. Suite 1000, Washington, DC 20036
Telephone: (202) 463-2900
Clients:
   Mack Trucks, Inc.
   Toyota Motor Corporate Services U.S.A.

PENNER, Rudolph G.
Senior Fellow, Urban Institute, The
2100 M St., N.W., Washington, DC 20037
Telephone: (202) 833-7200

PENNING, Nicholas J.
Legislative Specialist, American Ass'n of School Administrators
1801 North Moore St., Arlington, VA 22209
Telephone: (703) 528-0700
Registered as lobbyist at U.S. Congress.

PENNINGTON, Maj. Gen. James C., (Ret.)
Exec. V. President, Nat'l Ass'n for Uniformed Services
5535 Hempstead Way, Springfield, VA 22151
Telephone: (703) 750-1342
Registered as lobbyist at U.S. Congress.

PENNINGTON, Thomas W.
V. President & General Counsel, Cogema, Inc.
7401 Wisconsin Ave., Bethesda, MD 20814
Telephone: (301) 986-8585

PENOT, Joseph M.
Dir., Wash. Office, Legis. & Res. Affrs., Radio Officers' Union
100 Indiana Ave., N.W. Suite 311, Washington, DC 20001
Telephone: (202) 737-5109
Registered as lobbyist at U.S. Congress.

PENZER, Susan
Exec. Director, Nat'l Family Farm Coalition
80 F St., N.W. Suite 714, Washington, DC 20001
Telephone: (202) 737-2215

PEPE, Donald
Project Director, Community Development, Nat'l Ass'n of Counties
440 First St., N.W., Washington, DC 20001
Telephone: (202) 393-6226
Background: Serves as contact for the Nat'l Ass'n of County Planning Directors and the Nat'l Ass'n of County Community Development Directors.

PEPPER, Beth
Staff Attorney, Mental Health Law Project
2021 L St., N.W., Washington, DC 20036
Telephone: (202) 467-5730

PEPPER AND CORAZZINI
1776 K St., N.W., Suite 700, Washington, DC 20006
Telephone: (202) 296-0600
Members of firm representing listed organizations:
   Corazzini, Robert F.
Clients:
   KAUT
   KPOB-TV
   KWHB
   Satellite Syndicated Systems, Inc. *(Robert F. Corazzini)*
   WBNA
   WEAU-TV
   WLUC-TV
   WOKR
   WSIL-TV

PERDUE, Robert
Andrews and Kurth
1701 Pennsylvania Ave., N.W., Suite 200, Washington, DC 20006
Telephone: (202) 662-2700
Clients:
Texas Gas Transmission Corp.

PEREZ JOHNSON, Mary
President, Hispanic Elected Local Officials Caucus
1301 Pennsylvania Ave., N.W., Washington, DC 20004
Telephone: (202) 626-3130

PERITO, Paul L.
Laxalt, Washington, Perito & Dubuc
1120 Connecticut Ave., N.W., Suite 1000, Washington, DC 20036
Telephone: (202) 857-4000
Registered as lobbyist at U.S. Congress.
Background: Assistant U.S. Attorney, Department of Justice, 1966-70. Chief Counsel and Staff Director, House Select Committee on Crime, 1970-71. General Counsel and Deputy Director, Special Action Office for Drug Abuse Prevention, Executive Office of the President, 1971-73.
Clients:
Puerto Rico Department of Health

PERKINS, Carol B.
Director, Media Services, Ass'n of American Railroads
50 F Street, N.W., Washington, DC 20001
Telephone: (202) 639-2100

PERKINS COIE
1110 Vermont Ave., N.W., Suite 1200, Washington, DC 20005
Telephone: (202) 887-9030
Background: Washington office of a Seattle law firm.
Members of firm representing listed organizations:
Bauer, Robert F.
Martin, Fred
Background: President, The Bancroft Group, the lobbying affiliate of Perkins Coie.
Martin, Guy R.
Background: Assistant Secretary of the Interior for Land and Water Resources, 1977-81.
Pederson, Bill
Steingold, Stuart G.
Thompson, Anthony J.
Background: Legal Assistant to Chairman, Federal Communications Commission, 1973-74.
Clients:
American Mining Congress *(Anthony J. Thompson)*
Arctic Alaska Fishing Corp. *(Guy R. Martin)*
Boeing Co. *(Guy R. Martin, Bill Pederson)*
Burlington Resources, Inc. *(Guy R. Martin)*
Democrats for the 90s *(Robert F. Bauer)*
General Electric Co. *(Anthony J. Thompson)*
Geothermal Resources Ass'n *(Guy R. Martin)*
James River Corp. *(Guy R. Martin)*
Kootznoowoo, Inc. *(Guy R. Martin)*
Ormat Energy Systems *(Guy R. Martin)*
Perkins Coie Political Action Committee *(Guy R. Martin)*
Wood Heating Alliance *(Guy R. Martin)*

PERKINS, John
Director, AFL-CIO Committee on Political Education/Political Contributions Committee (COPE)
815 16th St., N.W., Washington, DC 20006
Telephone: (202) 637-5101

PERKINS, Robert A.
V. President, Washington Affairs, Chrysler Corp.
1100 Connecticut Ave., N.W., Washington, DC 20036
Telephone: (202) 862-5408
Registered as lobbyist at U.S. Congress.

PERKINSON & ASSOCIATES, INC.
453 New Jersey Ave., S.E., Washington, DC 20003
Telephone: (202) 646-1260
Background: A legislative consulting firm.
Members of firm representing listed organizations:
Bertelsen, Michael J., V. President, Counsel
Background: Served in the federal government, 1985-89.
Blaha, David R., Associate
Perkinson, Gary J., President
Clients:

Alliance for America's Homeowners *(Michael J. Bertelsen, David R. Blaha, Gary J. Perkinson)*
Beneficial Management Corp. of America *(Michael J. Bertelsen, Gary J. Perkinson)*
Nat'l Coalition for Fair Bankruptcy Laws *(Michael J. Bertelsen, Gary J. Perkinson)*
Nat'l Second Mortgage Ass'n *(Michael J. Bertelsen, Gary J. Perkinson)*

PERKINSON, Gary J.
President, Perkinson & Associates, Inc.
453 New Jersey Ave., S.E., Washington, DC 20003
Telephone: (202) 646-1260
Registered as lobbyist at U.S. Congress.
Clients:
Alliance for America's Homeowners
Beneficial Management Corp. of America
Nat'l Coalition for Fair Bankruptcy Laws
Nat'l Second Mortgage Ass'n

PERLE, Linda
Senior Staff Attorney, Center for Law and Social Policy
1616 P St., N.W., Suite 350, Washington, DC 20036
Telephone: (202) 328-5140

PERLIK, William R.
Wilmer, Cutler and Pickering
2445 M St., N.W., Washington, DC 20037-1420
Telephone: (202) 663-6000
Registered as lobbyist at U.S. Congress.

PERLMAN, Jeffry L.
Director, Legal and Regulatory Affairs, Chamber of Commerce of the U.S.A.
1615 H St., N.W., Washington, DC 20062
Telephone: (202) 463-5500
Registered as lobbyist at U.S. Congress.

PERLMAN, Martin
President, Nat'l Ass'n of Home Builders of the U.S.
15th and M Streets, N.W., Washington, DC 20005
Telephone: (202) 822-0470

PERLSTEIN, William J.
Wilmer, Cutler and Pickering
2445 M St., N.W., Washington, DC 20037-1420
Telephone: (202) 663-6000
Clients:
Internat'l Swap Dealers Ass'n

PERMUT, Philip V.
Wiley, Rein & Fielding
1776 K St., N.W., Tenth Floor, Washington, DC 20006-2359
Telephone: (202) 429-7000
Background: Served as Trial Attorney: Broadcast Bureau, 1968-73; General Counsel's Office, 1973-74. Special Assistant to Bureau Chief, 1974-76, Chief, Policy and Rules Division, 1976-77 and Deputy Chief, Common Carrier Bureau, Federal Communications Commission, 1977-78.
Clients:
United Telecommunications

PERNELL, Kathi D.
Director, Public Affairs, Club Managers Ass'n of America
1733 King St., Alexandria, VA 22314
Telephone: (703) 739-9500

PERRELL, Beverly S.
Exec. Director, American Soc. of Professional Estimators
6911 Richmond Hwy., Suite 230, Alexandria, VA 22306
Telephone: (703) 765-2700

PERRONE, Michela
President and Chief Exec. Officer, Kennedy Institute, Lt. Joseph P.
801 Buchanan St., N.E., Washington, DC 20017
Telephone: (202) 529-7600

PERRY, Daniel
Exec. Director, Alliance for Aging Research
2021 K St., N.W. Suite 305, Washington, DC 20006
Telephone: (202) 293-2856
Background: Special Assistant to Senator Alan Cranston (D-CA) from 1972 to 1985.

PERRY, Steve
Partner, V. President, Dutko & Associates
412 First St., S.E. Suite 100, Washington, DC 20003

Telephone: (202) 484-4884
Registered as lobbyist at U.S. Congress.
Background: Former Legis. Ass't to Senator John Heinz (R-PA), 1980-83.
Clients:
Communications Satellite Corp. (COMSAT)
DSC Communications Corp.
Internat'l Telecharge, Inc.
Nat'l Cellular Resellers Ass'n
Yavapai Telephone Exchange

PERRY, Susan
Sr. V. Pres., Government Relations, American Bus Ass'n
1015 15th St., N.W. Suite 250, Washington, DC 20005
Telephone: (202) 842-1645
Registered as lobbyist at U.S. Congress.

PERRY, Thomas J., P.E.
Interim Exec. Director, American Soc. for Engineering Education
11 Dupont Circle, N.W., Suite 200, Washington, DC 20036
Telephone: (202) 293-7080

PERRY, Todd E.
Director for Policy, Physicians for Social Responsibility
1000 16th St., N.W., Suite 810, Washington, DC 20036
Telephone: (202) 785-3777

PERRY, William
Neill and Co.
815 Connecticut Ave., N.W. Suite 800, Washington, DC 20006
Telephone: (202) 463-8877
Registered as lobbyist at U.S. Congress.
Registered as Foreign Agent: (#3320).
Background: Professional Staff Member, Senate Foreign Relations Committee, 1985-86. Director, Latin American Affairs, Nat'l Security Council, 1986-87.

PERRY, William D.
Director, Government Relations, Johnson Wax
900 17th St., N.W., Suite 506, Washington, DC 20006
Telephone: (202) 331-1186

PERRY, William E.
Skadden, Arps, Slate, Meagher and Flom
1440 New York Ave., N.W., Washington, DC 20005
Telephone: (202) 371-7000
Clients:
Fuji Photo Film U.S.A.
Hechinger Co.

PERSKY, Thomas
Senior Manager, Price Waterhouse
1801 K St., N.W., Suite 700, Washington, DC 20006
Telephone: (202) 296-0800
Registered as lobbyist at U.S. Congress.
Background: Formerly in congressional liaison, U.S. Internal Revenue Service.

PERTA, Joseph M.
Weaver & Associates, Robert A.
915 15th St., N.W., Suite 402, Washington, DC 20005
Telephone: (202) 347-3697
Registered as Foreign Agent: (#3916).
Clients:
Zaire, Government of the Republic of

PERTSCHUK, Michael
Co-director, Advocacy Institute, The
1730 Rhode Island Ave., N.W. Suite 600, Washington, DC 20036
Telephone: (202) 659-8475
Background: Former Chairman of the Federal Trade Commission.

PERUGINO, Roxanne
Bannerman and Associates, Inc.
888 16th St., N.W., Washington, DC 20006
Telephone: (202) 835-8188
Registered as lobbyist at U.S. Congress.
Registered as Foreign Agent: (#3964).
Background: Former Staff Member, House Foreign Affairs Committee.
Clients:
Beirut University College
Tunisia, Embassy of

PETER, Phillips S.
V. Pres., Corporate Gov't Relations, General Electric Co.
1331 Pennsylvania Ave., N.W. Suite 800S, Washington, DC 20004
Telephone: (202) 637-4000
Registered as lobbyist at U.S. Congress.

PETERPAUL, John F.
General V. President, Transportation, Internat'l Ass'n of Machinists and Aerospace Workers
1300 Connecticut Ave., N.W. Suite 404, Washington, DC 20036
Telephone: (202) 857-5200

PETERS, Donna F.
Treasurer, Administrator, Republican Majority Fund
503 Capitol Court, N.E., Suite 100, Washington, DC 20002
Telephone: (202) 547-6200

PETERS, Mary Frances
Director, Washington Office, Girl Scouts of the U.S.A.
1025 Connecticut Ave., N.W. Suite 309, Washington, DC 20036
Telephone: (202) 659-3780
Registered as lobbyist at U.S. Congress.

PETERS, Sid R.
Exec. V. President, Nat'l Ass'n of Industrial and Office Parks
1215 Jefferson Davis Hwy., Suite 100, Arlington, VA 22202
Telephone: (703) 979-3400
Registered as lobbyist at U.S. Congress.

PETERS, Terry L.
Exec. Director, Soc. for Marketing Professional Services
99 Canal Center Plaza Suite 320, Alexandria, VA 22314
Telephone: (703) 549-6117

PETERSDORF, Dr. Robert G.
President, Ass'n of American Medical Colleges
One Dupont Circle, N.W., Suite 200, Washington, DC 20036
Telephone: (202) 828-0400

PETERSEN, Dennis L.
Internat'l Technical Expertise, Ltd.
150 South Washington St., Suite 403, Falls Church, VA 22046
Telephone: (703) 536-4500

PETERSEN, Robert E.
President, Columbia Typographical Union - CWA
4626 Wisconsin Ave., N.W. 3rd Floor, Washington, DC 20016
Telephone: (202) 362-9413
Registered as lobbyist at U.S. Congress.

PETERSEN, Robert R.
President, Nat'l Grain Trade Council
1030 15th St., N.W., Suite 1020, Washington, DC 20005
Telephone: (202) 842-0400
Registered as lobbyist at U.S. Congress.

PETERSON, Carolyn
President, Internat'l Ass'n of Psychosocial Rehabilitation Services
5550 Sterrett Place, Suite 214, Columbia, MD 21044
Telephone: (301) 730-7190

PETERSON, Douglas D.
Senior Policy Analyst, Nat'l League of Cities
1301 Pennsylvania Ave., N.W., Washington, DC 20004
Telephone: (202) 626-3000

PETERSON, Gale
Dep Dir, Legis Affrs, DEPARTMENT OF TREASURY
15th and Pennsylvania Ave. N.W., Washington, DC 20220
Telephone: (202) 566-2037

PETERSON, Geoffrey G.
Director, Federal Government Relations, Distilled Spirits Council of the United States
1250 Eye St., N.W., Suite 900, Washington, DC 20005
Telephone: (202) 628-3544
Registered as lobbyist at U.S. Congress.
Background: Serves as contact person for the Distilled Spirits Political Action Committee.

PETERSON, George
Senior Fellow, Urban Institute, The
2100 M St., N.W., Washington, DC 20037
Telephone: (202) 833-7200

PETERSON, Helena Hutton
Manager, Government Relations, Minnesota Mining and Manufacturing Co. (3M Co.)
1101 15th St., N.W., Washington, DC 20005
Telephone: (202) 331-6976
Registered as lobbyist at U.S. Congress.

PETERSON, Dr. Irvin L.
Secretary-Treasurer, World's Poultry Science Ass'n, U.S.-A. Branch
USDA-APHIS, VS, Room 771, Fed. Bldg., 6505 Belcrest Rd., Hyattsville, MD 20782
Telephone: (301) 436-7768

PETERSON, J. William
Director of Government Affairs, Construction Industry Manufacturers Ass'n
525 School St., S.W. Suite 303, Washington, DC 20024
Telephone: (202) 479-2666

PETERSON, Jack
Director, Political Affairs, Nat'l Ass'n of Manufacturers
1331 Pennsylvania Ave., N.W. Suite 1500 North, Washington, DC 20004-1703
Telephone: (202) 637-3000

PETERSON, Lars E.
Sr. Government Relations Representative, Food Marketing Institute
1750 K St., N.W., Washington, DC 20006
Telephone: (202) 452-8444
Registered as lobbyist at U.S. Congress.

PETERSON, Marilyn Kay
Legis Asst, Legis & Public Affrs, DEPARTMENT OF AGRI-CULTURE - Animal and Plant Health Inspection Service
14th and Independence Ave. S.W., Room 1147 South Bldg., Washington, DC 20250
Telephone: (202) 447-2511

PETERSON, Mary Jo
Legislative Representative, Nat'l Automobile Dealers Ass'n
412 First St., S.E., Washington, DC 20003
Telephone: (202) 547-5500
Registered as lobbyist at U.S. Congress.

PETERSON, R. Max
Exec. V. President, Internat'l Ass'n of Fish and Wildlife Agencies
444 North Capitol St., N.W. Suite 534, Washington, DC 20001
Telephone: (202) 624-7890
Background: U.S. Dept. of Agriculture, Forest Service, 1965-78.

PETERSON, Ronald K.
Chief, Res, Def & Int'l Br, Legis Ref, EXECUTIVE OFFICE OF THE PRESIDENT - Office of Management and Budget
Old Executive Office Bldg., Washington, DC 20500
Telephone: (202) 395-4790

PETERSON, Sheryl L.
Assistant Director, Legislative Affairs, American Financial Services Ass'n
1101 14th St., N.W., Washington, DC 20005
Telephone: (202) 289-0400
Registered as lobbyist at U.S. Congress.

PETETE, Dayna R.
Government Relations Director, Population - Environment Balance
1325 G St., N.W., Suite 1003, Washington, DC 20005-3104
Telephone: (202) 879-3000
Registered as lobbyist at U.S. Congress.

PETITO, Joseph P.
Mgr., Professional & Governmental Affrs., Coopers and Lybrand
1800 M St., N.W., Suite 400, Washington, DC 20036
Telephone: (202) 822-4000

PETITO, Margaret L.
Director, Public Affairs, Chambers Development Co., Inc.
1150 17th St., N.W., Suite 307, Washington, DC 20036
Telephone: (202) 463-0306

PETNIUNAS, Susan
Manager, U.S. Government Affairs, Manville Corp.
1625 K St., N.W., Suite 750, Washington, DC 20006
Telephone: (202) 785-4940
Registered as lobbyist at U.S. Congress.

PETRASH, Jeffrey M.
Dickinson, Wright, Moon, Van Dusen and Freeman
1901 L St., N.W. Suite 800, Washington, DC 20036
Telephone: (202) 457-0160
Registered as lobbyist at U.S. Congress.

PETRILLO & HORDELL
915 15th St., N.W. 7th Fl., Washington, DC 20005
Telephone: (202) 783-9150
Members of firm representing listed organizations:
 Petrillo, Joseph J.
 Clients:
  Nat'l Ass'n of Aircraft and Communications Suppliers, Inc. *(Joseph J. Petrillo)*

PETRILLO, Joseph J.
Petrillo & Hordell
915 15th St., N.W. 7th Fl., Washington, DC 20005
Telephone: (202) 783-9150
Registered as lobbyist at U.S. Congress.
Clients:
 Nat'l Ass'n of Aircraft and Communications Suppliers, Inc.

PETRINA, Michael J., Jr.
V. President, Legislative Relations, Cosmetic, Toiletry and Fragrance Ass'n
1110 Vermont Ave., N.W. Suite 800, Washington, DC 20005
Telephone: (202) 331-1770
Registered as lobbyist at U.S. Congress.

PETROSKEY, Dale A.
Director, Public Affairs, Nat'l Geographic Soc.
1145 17th St., N.W., Washington, DC 20036
Telephone: (202) 857-7000
Background: Formerly Assistant Secretary of Transportation for Public Affairs.

PETROVIC, Nikolaj M., CAE
President and Chief Exec. Officer, American Dental Trade Ass'n
4222 King St., Alexandria, VA 22302
Telephone: (703) 379-7755

PETROVICH, Dr. Janice
National Exec. Director, ASPIRA Ass'n, Inc.
1112 16th St., N.W., Suite 340, Washington, DC 20036
Telephone: (202) 835-3600

PETRUTSAS, George
Fletcher, Heald and Hildreth
1225 Connecticut Ave., N.W. Suite 400, Washington, DC 20036
Telephone: (202) 828-5700

PETRY, Stephan
Legislative Representative, Nat'l Rural Electric Cooperative Ass'n
1800 Massachusetts Ave., N.W., Washington, DC 20036
Telephone: (202) 857-9666
Registered as lobbyist at U.S. Congress.

PETTA, Ralph A.
Industry Services Manager, American Ass'n of Equipment Lessors
1300 North 17th St. Suite 1010, Arlington, VA 22209
Telephone: (703) 527-8655
Background: Former Legislative Assistant to Senator Sam Nunn (D-GA).

PETTEY, Laura M.
Tax Manager, Government Relations, Dow Chemical
1776 Eye St., N.W., Suite 575, Washington, DC 20006
Telephone: (202) 429-3400
Registered as lobbyist at U.S. Congress.

PETTEY, Susan M.
Director, Health Policy, American Ass'n of Homes for the Aging
1129 20th St., N.W., Suite 400, Washington, DC 20036
Telephone: (202) 296-5960
Registered as lobbyist at U.S. Congress.

PETTIT, C. L.
Analyst, Nat'l Solid Wastes Management Ass'n
1730 Rhode Island Ave., N.W., 10th Floor, Washington, DC 20036
Telephone: (202) 659-4613
Registered as lobbyist at U.S. Congress.

PETTIT, John W.
Hopkins and Sutter
888 16th St., N.W., Suite 700, Washington, DC 20006
Telephone: (202) 835-8000
Registered as lobbyist at U.S. Congress.
Background: General Counsel, Federal Communications Commission, 1972-74.
Clients:
Rubber Manufacturers Ass'n
Tandy Corp.

PETTIT & MARTIN
1800 Massachusetts Ave., N.W., Washington, DC 20036
Telephone: (202) 785-5153
Registered as Foreign Agent: (#3815)
Members of firm representing listed organizations:
Cladouhos, Harry W.
Background: Legal Assistant, Office of Commissioner, Federal Communications Commission, 1954-55. Foreign Service Officer, Secretary in the Diplomatic Service and Vice Consul, Department of State, 1955-57. Senior Trial Attorney, Trial Section, Antitrust Division, Department of Justice, 1957-69.
Korns, John H.
Background: Law Clerk to Chief Justice Warren E. Burger, U.S. Supreme Court, 1971-72. Assistant U.S. Attorney for District of Columbia, 1976-80.
O'Neil, William B. (Jr.)
Background: Heads lobbying operations of the law firm of Pettit & Martin. Former Legislative Director to Rep. Joe Kolter (D-PA).
Wheeler, Thomas C.
Clients:
Suzuki Motors Co., Ltd. *(Harry W. Cladouhos)*
United States Suzuki Motor Corp. *(Harry W. Cladouhos)*

PETTUS, Drew D.
Preston Gates Ellis & Rouvelas Meeds
1735 New York Ave., N.W., Suite 500, Washington, DC 20006-4759
Telephone: (202) 628-1700
Registered as lobbyist at U.S. Congress.
Background: Former Administrative Assistant and Legal Counsel to Rep. Al Swift (D-WA).
Clients:
TeleCommunications, Inc.

PETTY, Brian T.
V. President, Federal Affairs, Internat'l Ass'n of Drilling Contractors
1901 L St., N.W. Suite 702, Washington, DC 20036
Telephone: (202) 293-0670
Registered as lobbyist at U.S. Congress.

PETTY, Charles W., Jr.
Hopkins and Sutter
888 16th St., N.W., Suite 700, Washington, DC 20006
Telephone: (202) 835-8000
Registered as lobbyist at U.S. Congress.

PETTY, Gary Frank
President and CEO, Nat'l Moving and Storage Ass'n
1500 North Beauregard St. Suite 320, Alexandria, VA 22311
Telephone: (703) 671-8813
Background: Also represents the Nat'l Moving and Storage Ass'n Political Action Committee, the Nat'l Institute of Certified Moving Consultants, and the Nat'l Moving and Storage Technical Foundation.

PEWETT, James W.
Kirlin, Campbell and Keating
One Farragut Square South 2nd Floor, Washington, DC 20006

Telephone: (202) 639-8000

PEYSER ASSOCIATES, INC.
1000 Vermont Ave., N.W. Suite 400, Washington, DC 20005
Telephone: (202) 842-4545
Background: A government relations consulting firm.
Members of firm representing listed organizations:
Howarth, Thomas J.
Background: Former Legis. Ass't to Senator Frank Lautenberg (D-NJ); Former Washington Representative, City of New York.
Martin, Caroline
Background: Former Legislative Aide to Rep. Byron Dorgan (D-ND).
Peyser, Peter A. (Jr.), President
Background: Former Washington Rep., City of New York; former Admin. Assistant to Rep. Geraldine Ferraro of New York; former Legislative Assistant to Rep. James T. Delaney and Rep. P. H. Kostmayer.
Clients:
Ass'n for the Advancement of Health Education
Chicago Regional Transit Authority *(Peter A. Peyser, Jr.)*
Gerald D. Hines Interests
Lazard Freres
Metropolitan Toledo Consortium
Mothers Against Drunk Driving (MADD) *(Thomas J. Howarth, Caroline Martin, Peter A. Peyser, Jr.)*
Nat'l School Health Education Coalition *(Peter A. Peyser, Jr.)*
Philadelphia, Pennsylvania, City of
SAB Engineering and Construction
Seattle Metro
Southeastern Pennsylvania Transit Authority
United States Conference of Mayors

PEYSER, Peter A., Jr.
President, Peyser Associates, Inc.
1000 Vermont Ave., N.W. Suite 400, Washington, DC 20005
Telephone: (202) 842-4545
Registered as lobbyist at U.S. Congress.
Background: Former Washington Rep., City of New York; former Admin. Assistant to Rep. Geraldine Ferraro of New York; former Legislative Assistant to Rep. James T. Delaney and Rep. Peter H. Kostmayer.
Clients:
Chicago Regional Transit Authority
Mothers Against Drunk Driving (MADD)
Nat'l School Health Education Coalition

PFAUTCH, Roy
President, Civic Service, Inc.
1050 Connecticut Ave., N.W. Suite 870, Washington, DC 20036
Telephone: (202) 785-2070
Registered as Foreign Agent: (#3385).
Clients:
Internat'l Public Relations Co.
Mitsubishi Trust and Banking Corp.
Nippon Telephone and Telegraph Corp.
PR Service Co., Ltd.

PFEIFER, Eugene M.
King and Spalding
1730 Pennsylvania Ave., N.W. Suite 1200, Washington, DC 20006-4706
Telephone: (202) 737-0500
Background: Trial Attorney, 1968-73 and Associate Chief Counsel for Enforcement, 1975-79, Office of General Counsel, Food and Drug Administration. Attorney, Office of General Counsel, Federal Trade Commission, 1974.
Clients:
Nat'l Pharmaceutical Alliance
Superpharm Corp.

PFEIFFER, Margaret K.
Sullivan and Cromwell
1701 Pennsylvania Ave., N.W. Suite 800, Washington, DC 20006
Telephone: (202) 956-7500
Clients:
Imo Industries
N.V. Philips Gloeilampenfabrieken

PFISTER, Steven J.
Director, Political Affairs, Nat'l Retail Merchants Ass'n
1000 Connecticut Ave., N.W., Washington, DC 20036
Telephone: (202) 223-8250
Registered as lobbyist at U.S. Congress.

PFLAUM CO., INC., William C.
11800 Sunrise Valley Dr. Suite 212, Reston, VA 22091
Telephone: (703) 620-3773
Members of firm representing listed organizations:
Pflaum, William C., President
Background: Also serves as Executive Director of the Packing Education Foundation and of the Soc. of Packaging Professional.
Organizations represented:
IoPP, the Institute of Packaging Professionals *(William C. Pflaum)*
Packing Education Foundation *(William C. Pflaum)*

PFLAUM, William C.
President, Pflaum Co., Inc., William C.
11800 Sunrise Valley Dr. Suite 212, Reston, VA 22091
Telephone: (703) 620-3773
Background: Also serves as Executive Director of the Packing Education Foundation and of the Soc. of Packaging Professional.
Organizations represented:
IoPP, the Institute of Packaging Professionals
Packing Education Foundation

PFUNDER, Malcolm R.
Hopkins and Sutter
888 16th St., N.W., Suite 700, Washington, DC 20006
Telephone: (202) 835-8000
Background: Associate Director, 1977-78, and Assistant Director, 1978-81, Bureau of Competition, Federal Trade Commission.
Clients:
Tandy Corp.

PHELPS, Francie
Washington Representative, UNOCAL Corp.
1050 Connecticut Ave., N.W., Suite 760, Washington, DC 20036
Telephone: (202) 659-7600
Registered as lobbyist at U.S. Congress.

PHELPS, Laura
Government Relations Consultant, McLeod & Pires
2501 M St., N.W., Suite 400, Washington, DC 20037
Telephone: (202) 861-1234
Registered as lobbyist at U.S. Congress.
Clients:
American Ass'n of Crop Insurers
Mushroom Council

PHELPS, Marshall C.
IBM Director, Governmental Programs, Internat'l Business Machines Corp.
1801 K St., N.W., Suite 1200, Washington, DC 20006
Telephone: (202) 778-5000

PHIFER, James
Manager, Congressional Affairs, Magnavox Government and Industrial Electronics Co.
1700 North Moore St. Suite 820, Arlington, VA 22209
Telephone: (703) 522-9610
Registered as lobbyist at U.S. Congress.

PHILIP MANUEL RESOURCE GROUP LTD.
1747 Pennsylvania Ave., N.W. Suite 701, Washington, DC 20006
Telephone: (202) 861-0651
Members of firm representing listed organizations:
Boggs, Andrea
Manuel, Philip R.
Clients:
Compania Peruana de Vapores *(Andrea Boggs, Philip R. Manuel)*

PHILLIPS, Barbara L.
Legislative Affairs Director, GTE Corp.
Suite 1200, 1850 M St., N.W., Washington, DC 20036
Telephone: (202) 463-5228

PHILLIPS, Deborah M.
Sr. Representative, Government Affairs, General Instrument Corp.
1155 21st St., N.W., Suite 400, Washington, DC 20036

Telephone: (202) 833-9700
Registered as lobbyist at U.S. Congress.

PHILLIPS, Howard J.
Chairman, Policy Analysis, Inc.
9520 Bent Creek Lane, Vienna, VA 22180
Telephone: (703) 759-3975
Background: Chairman, The Conservative Caucus. Represents Conservative Caucus Research, Analysis and Education Foundation. Also directs the Conservative Nat'l Campaign Committee and is Co-Chair of the Anti-Appeasement Alliance. Formerly was Acting Exec. Director, President's Council on Youth Opportunity, 1969-70; and as Acting Director, U.S. Office of Economic Opportunity, 1973.

PHILLIPS, James A.
Deputy Director, Foreign Policy Studies, Heritage Foundation
214 Massachusetts Ave., N.E., Washington, DC 20002
Telephone: (202) 546-4400

PHILLIPS, James M.
Exec. Director, Accrediting Commission, Ass'n of Independent Colleges and Schools
One Dupont Circle, N.W., Suite 350, Washington, DC 20036
Telephone: (202) 659-2460

PHILLIPS, Kate
Assistant Exec. Director, Council on Governmental Relations
1 Dupont Circle, N.W. Suite 670, Washington, DC 20036
Telephone: (202) 861-2595

PHILLIPS, Pam
Assoc. Director, Gov't Relations, American Physical Therapy Ass'n
1111 North Fairfax St., Alexandria, VA 22314
Telephone: (703) 684-2782
Background: President, Washington Area State Relations Group for 1989.

PHILLIPS, Richard M.
Kirkpatrick & Lockhart
1800 M St., N.W., Suite 900 South Lobby, Washington, DC 20036-5891
Telephone: (202) 778-9000
Registered as lobbyist at U.S. Congress.
Background: Securities and Exchange Commission, 1960-68: Legal Asst. to Commissioner, 1962-1964; Special Counsel, 1964-1966; Assistant General Counsel, 1966-1968; Staff Director, Disclosure Study, 1968.

PHILLIPS, Roberta N.
Director of Development, Internat'l Ass'n for Continuing Education and Training
P.O. Box 27043, Washington, DC 20038
Telephone: (301) 384-1059

PHILLIPS, Ron
V. President, Public Affairs, Fertilizer Institute
501 Second St., N.E., Washington, DC 20002
Telephone: (202) 675-8250

PHILLIPS, Willard, Bill Jr.
Washington Representative, Tennessee Valley Authority
412 First St., S.E., Suite 300, Washington, DC 20444
Telephone: (202) 479-4412

PHILLIPS, William D.
Hopkins and Sutter
888 16th St., N.W., Suite 700, Washington, DC 20006
Telephone: (202) 835-8000
Registered as lobbyist at U.S. Congress.
Registered as Foreign Agent: (#3955).
Background: Chief of Staff to Senator Ted Stevens (R-AK), 1983-86; Legislative Director and Legislative Assistant, 1981-83.
Clients:
Alaska Joint Venture Seafoods, Inc.
Infinite Research, Inc.
Korean Air Lines
Martel Laboratory Services, Inc.
United Video Inc.

PHILP, John M.
Regional Director, Public Affairs, United Airlines
1707 L St., N.W., Suite 300, Washington, DC 20036

Telephone: (703) 892-7410

PHIPPS, John G.
Account Executive, Hill and Knowlton Public Affairs Worldwide
Washington Harbour, 901 31st St., N.W., Washington, DC 20007
Telephone: (202) 333-7400

PHYTHYON, Daniel B.
V. President, Congressional Liaison, Nat'l Ass'n of Broadcasters
1771 N St., N.W., Washington, DC 20036
Telephone: (202) 429-5300
Registered as lobbyist at U.S. Congress.
Background: Former Legislative Assistant to Vice President George Bush.

PICARD, B. Donovan
Baker and Botts
555 13th St., N.W., Suite 500 East, Washington, DC 20004-1109
Telephone: (202) 639-7700
Registered as lobbyist at U.S. Congress.
Registered as Foreign Agent: (#4293).
Clients:
Bundesverband der Deutschen Industrie
NMTBA - The Ass'n for Manufacturing Technology
Rhone-Poulenc Inc.
US WEST, Inc.

PICARD, Donald S.
Counsel, Electronic Data Systems Corp.
1331 Pennsylvania Ave., N.W., Suite 1300 North, Washington, DC 20004
Telephone: (202) 637-6700
Registered as lobbyist at U.S. Congress.

PICCOLO, Joann
Manager, Legislative Affairs, Motorola, Inc.
1350 Eye St., N.W., Suite 400, Washington, DC 20005-3306
Telephone: (202) 371-6900
Registered as lobbyist at U.S. Congress.

PICKERING, John H.
Wilmer, Cutler and Pickering
2445 M St., N.W., Washington, DC 20037-1420
Telephone: (202) 663-6000
Clients:
Grand Metropolitan PLC
Wendell Investments Ltd.

PICKERING, Judith
General Counsel-Secretary, Woodward and Lothrop
1025 F St., N.W., Washington, DC 20013
Telephone: (202) 347-5300

PICKITT, John L.
President, Computer and Business Equipment Manufacturers Ass'n
311 First St., N.W. Suite 500, Washington, DC 20001
Telephone: (202) 737-8888
Background: Former Director, Defense Nuclear Agency, U.S. Department of Defense.

PIDCOCK, Paulette C.
Director, Federal Affairs, Baltimore Gas and Electric Co.
1100 Connecticut Ave., N.W., Suite 530, Washington, DC 20036
Telephone: (202) 861-0830
Registered as lobbyist at U.S. Congress.

PIEPER, Janice E.
Ass't Director, Gov't Affairs, United Food and Commercial Workers Internat'l Union
1775 K St., N.W., Washington, DC 20006
Telephone: (202) 223-3111
Registered as lobbyist at U.S. Congress.

PIERCE, James M.
President, Nat'l Federation of Federal Employees
1016 16th St., N.W., Suite 400, Washington, DC 20036
Telephone: (202) 862-4400
Registered as lobbyist at U.S. Congress.

PIERCE, Theodore M.
Legislative Coordinator, Nat'l Ass'n of Surety Bond Producers
6931 Arlington Road, Suite 308, Bethesda, MD 20814
Telephone: (301) 986-4166
Registered as lobbyist at U.S. Congress.

PIERCE, Wayne
Dir. of Legis. and Gen. Treas., United Brotherhood of Carpenters and Joiners of America
101 Constitution Ave., N.W., Washington, DC 20001
Telephone: (202) 546-6206
Registered as lobbyist at U.S. Congress.
Background: Serves as Treasurer, Carpenters' Legislative Improvement Committee.

PIERCE, William L.
President and Chief Exec. Officer, Nat'l Committee for Adoption
1930 17th St., N.W., Washington, DC 20009-6207
Telephone: (202) 328-1200

PIERSON, Jeff
Spec Asst, Legis Affrs (House), EXECUTIVE OFFICE OF THE PRESIDENT - Office of Management and Budget
Old Executive Office Bldg., Washington, DC 20500
Telephone: (202) 395-4790

PIERSON, SEMMES, AND FINLEY
1054 31st St., N.W. Suite 300, Washington, DC 20007
Telephone: (202) 333-4000
Registered as Foreign Agent: (#2988)
Members of firm representing listed organizations:
Finley, William T. (Jr.)
Background: Law Clerk to Mr. Justice Brennan, 1964; Chief Counsel, Subcommittee on Improvements in Judicial Machinery, Committee on the Judiciary, U.S. Senate, 1965-1967; Associate Deputy Attorney General, Department of Justice, 1968-1969.
Pierson, W. DeVier
Background: Chief Counsel, Joint Committee on the Organization of the Congress, 1965-67. Associate Special Counsel to the President of the United States and Counselor of the White House Office, 1967-68. Special Counsel to the President of the United States, 1968-69.
Ryberg, Paul (Jr.)
Semmes, David H.
Clients:
Grand Council of the Cress
Mauritius, Chamber of Agriculture of *(W. DeVier Pierson, Paul Ryberg, Jr.)*
Mauritius Sugar Syndicate *(W. DeVier Pierson, Paul Ryberg, Jr.)*
Oklahoma Natural Gas Co. *(W. DeVier Pierson, Paul Ryberg, Jr.)*
Six Flags, Inc. *(William T. Finley, Jr.)*

PIERSON, W. DeVier
Pierson, Semmes, and Finley
1054 31st St., N.W. Suite 300, Washington, DC 20007
Telephone: (202) 333-4000
Registered as Foreign Agent: (#2988).
Background: Chief Counsel, Joint Committee on the Organization of the Congress, 1965-67. Associate Special Counsel to the President of the United States and Counselor of the White House Office, 1967-68. Special Counsel to the President of the United States, 1968-69.
Clients:
Mauritius, Chamber of Agriculture of
Mauritius Sugar Syndicate
Oklahoma Natural Gas Co.

PIFEL, Bruce
Director Member Services, Nat'l Officers Ass'n
1304 Vincent Place, McLean, VA 22101
Telephone: (703) 821-0555

PIGG, B. J. 'Bob'
President, Asbestos Information Ass'n/North America
1745 Jefferson Davis Hwy. Suite 509, Arlington, VA 22202
Telephone: (703) 979-1150

PIGOTT, Mary C.
Assoc. Director, Environmental Quality, Nat'l Ass'n of Manufacturers
1331 Pennsylvania Ave., N.W. Suite 1500 North, Washington, DC 20004-1703
Telephone: (202) 637-3000

PIGOTT, Mary C. (Cont'd)
Registered as lobbyist at U.S. Congress.
Background: Former Legislative Assistant to Rep. Robert Wise (D-WV).

PIKE, John E.
Associate Director, Space Policy, Federation of American Scientists
307 Massachusetts Ave., N.E., Washington, DC 20002
Telephone: (202) 546-3300

PIKRALLIDAS, Susan G.
Director, Tourism Affairs, American Automobile Ass'n
500 E St. S.W., Suite 950, Washington, DC 20024
Telephone: (202) 554-6060
Registered as lobbyist at U.S. Congress.

PILCHER, John H.
Director, Corporate Finance, Nat'l Ass'n of Manufacturers
1331 Pennsylvania Ave., N.W. Suite 1500 North, Washington, DC 20004-1703
Telephone: (202) 637-3000
Registered as lobbyist at U.S. Congress.

PILENZO, Ronald C.
President, Soc. for Human Resources Management
606 N. Washington St., Alexandria, VA 22314
Telephone: (703) 548-3440

PILIERO, Daniel J., II
Piliero, Tobin & Mazza
888 17th St., N.W. Suite 1100, Washington, DC 20006
Telephone: (202) 857-1000
Registered as lobbyist at U.S. Congress.
Clients:
Fujitec America, Inc.

PILIERO, TOBIN & MAZZA
888 17th St., N.W. Suite 1100, Washington, DC 20006
Telephone: (202) 857-1000
Members of firm representing listed organizations:
Piliero, Daniel J. (II)
Clients:
Fujitec America, Inc. *(Daniel J. Piliero, II)*

PILK, Emily Galloway
Asst. to the President, Communications, Bureau of Nat'l Affairs, Inc., The
1231 25th St., N.W., Washington, DC 20037
Telephone: (202) 452-4200

PILLSBURY, MADISON AND SUTRO
1667 K St., N.W., Suite 1100, Washington, DC 20006
Telephone: (202) 887-0300
Registered as Foreign Agent: (#4212)
Background: Washington office of a San Francisco law firm.
Members of firm representing listed organizations:
Atkin, James
Byington, S. John
deKieffer, Donald E.
Mendelson, Keith J.
Morse, Anne R.
Ott, Judith A.
Sullivan, Kevin R.
Vandergrift, Benjamin M., Partner
Clients:
Chevron Corp. *(Benjamin M. Vandergrift)*
Intermedia Partners *(Benjamin M. Vandergrift)*
Internat'l Anti-Counterfeiting Coalition *(Donald E. deKieffer)*
Korea Foreign Trade Ass'n *(Keith J. Mendelson, Anne R. Morse, Judith A. Ott)*
Masters Championship, Inc.
Nat'l Semiconductor Corp. *(Donald E. deKieffer)*
Titanium Metals Corp. (TIMET) *(Donald E. deKieffer)*
United Telecommunications *(Kevin R. Sullivan)*

PILON, Roger
Senior Fellow, Constitutional Studies, Cato Institute
224 Second St., S.E., Washington, DC 20003
Telephone: (202) 546-0200

PILTZ, Rick
Associate Exec. Director, Renew America Project
1400 16th St., N.W. Suite 710, Washington, DC 20036
Telephone: (202) 232-2252

PINCO, Robert G.
Baker and Hostetler
1050 Connecticut Ave., N.W. Suite 1100, Washington, DC 20036
Telephone: (202) 861-1500
Background: Attorney, Department of Justice, 1969-72. Assistant General Counsel, White House Special Action Office for Drug Abuse Prevention, 1972-74. Director, Over-the-Counter Drugs, Food and Drug Administration, 1974-77.
Clients:
Johnson & Johnson

PINES, Burton Y.
Sr. V. President & Director of Research, Heritage Foundation
214 Massachusetts Ave., N.E., Washington, DC 20002
Telephone: (202) 546-4400

PINES, Patricia L.
V. President, Educational Services, Nat'l Grocers Ass'n
1825 Samuel Morse Drive, Reston, VA 22090
Telephone: (703) 437-5300

PINES, Wayne L.
Exec. V. Pres. & Dir. of Medical Issues, Burson-Marsteller
1850 M St., N.W., Suite 900, Washington, DC 20036
Telephone: (202) 833-8550
Clients:
American Paper Institute
GPU Service Corp.
Pfizer, Inc.

PINNIGER, Simon
V. Presidnet, West African Millers Ass'n
1025 Thomas Jefferson St. N.W., Suite 303 W, Washington, DC 20007
Telephone: (202) 342-0007
Registered as Foreign Agent: (#4240)
Background: Registered as foreign agent for IFACO, S.A., Geneva, Switzerland.

PINSON-MILLBURN, Dr. Nancy
Assistant Exec. Director, American Ass'n for Counseling and Development
5999 Stevenson Ave., Alexandria, VA 22304
Telephone: (703) 823-9800
Registered as lobbyist at U.S. Congress.

PINSON, Valerie
Director, Government Relations, Nat'l Cable Television Ass'n
1724 Massachusetts Ave., N.W., Washington, DC 20036
Telephone: (202) 775-3550
Registered as lobbyist at U.S. Congress.

PINTO, John E.
Exec. V. President for Compliance, Nat'l Ass'n of Securities Dealers (NASDAQ)
1735 K St., N.W., Washington, DC 20006
Telephone: (202) 728-8000

PIPER, Emily C.
Legislative Assistant, American Meat Institute
Box 3556, Washington, DC 20007
Telephone: (703) 841-2400
Registered as lobbyist at U.S. Congress.

PIPER AND MARBURY
1200 19th St., N.W., Washington, DC 20036
Telephone: (202) 861-3900
Background: Washington office of a Baltimore/Washington law firm.
Members of firm representing listed organizations:
Abeles, Charles C.
Hartley, H. Benjamin
Kaseman, A. Carl (III)
Plesser, Ronald L.
Stodghill, LaBrenda G.
Truitt, Thomas H.
  Background: Director, Legal Support Division, Environmental Protection Agency, 1971-72.
Clients:
Cominco, Ltd.
Information Industry Ass'n
Mead Data Central, Inc. *(Ronald L. Plesser)*
Nat'l Ass'n of Independent Colleges and Universities *(H. Benjamin Hartley)*

Nat'l Rural Electric Cooperative Ass'n *(Charles C. Abeles)*

PIPER PACIFIC INTERNAT'L
2055 North 15th St. Suite 300, Arlington, VA 22201
Telephone: (703) 524-7556
Registered as Foreign Agent: (#4244)
Members of firm representing listed organizations:
Parker, Margaret, Program Director/Research Assistant
Piper, W. Stephen, Owner
Winslow, Sara, Program Assistant/Research Assistant
Clients:
Fuji Heavy Industries Ltd. *(Margaret Parker, W. Stephen Piper, Sara Winslow)*
Nissan Motor Co., Ltd. *(Margaret Parker, W. Stephen Piper, Sara Winslow)*

PIPER, W. Stephen
Owner, Piper Pacific Internat'l
2055 North 15th St. Suite 300, Arlington, VA 22201
Telephone: (703) 524-7556
Registered as Foreign Agent: (#4244).
Clients:
Fuji Heavy Industries Ltd.
Nissan Motor Co., Ltd.

PIPKIN, Robert R., Jr.
V. President, Pearson & Pipkin, Inc.
422 First St., S.E., Suite 208, Washington, DC 20003
Telephone: (202) 547-7177
Registered as lobbyist at U.S. Congress.
Registered as Foreign Agent: (#3727).
Clients:
South Africa, Embassy of

PIRAGES, Dr. Suellen
Director, Hazardous Waste Programs, Nat'l Solid Wastes Management Ass'n
1730 Rhode Island Ave., N.W., 10th Floor, Washington, DC 20036
Telephone: (202) 659-4613

PISANO, Susan
Director of Communication & Information, Group Health Ass'n of America
1129 20th St., N.W. Suite 600, Washington, DC 20036
Telephone: (202) 778-3200

PITKIN, Capt. Roger
Legislation, Legis Affrs, DEPARTMENT OF NAVY
The Pentagon, Washington, DC 20350-1300
Telephone: (202) 697-7146

PITKIN, William W.
Exec. V. President, Nat'l Insulation Contractors Ass'n
99 Canal Center Plaza, Suite 222, Alexandria, VA 22314
Telephone: (703) 683-6422

PITLICK, Francis A., Ph.D.
Exec. Officer, American Ass'n of Pathologists
9650 Rockville Pike, Bethesda, MD 20814
Telephone: (301) 530-7130
Background: Serves also as Exec. Officer, Universities Associated for Research and Education in Pathology.

PITT, Harvey L.
Fried, Frank, Harris, Shriver & Jacobson
1001 Pennsylvania Ave., N.W., Suite 800, Washington, DC 20004-2505
Telephone: (202) 639-7000
Background: Special Counsel, Office of the General Counsel, 1971-72; Chief Counsel, Division of Market Regulation, 1972-73; Exec. Assistant to the Chairman, 1973-75; and General Counsel, 1975-78, Securities Exchange Commission.

PITTMAN, C. Juliet
V. President, SENSE, INC.
1511 K St., N.W., Suite 1033, Washington, DC 20005
Telephone: (202) 628-1151
Registered as lobbyist at U.S. Congress.

PITTMAN, Steuart L.
Shaw, Pittman, Potts and Trowbridge
2300 N St., N.W., Washington, DC 20037
Telephone: (202) 663-8000
Registered as Foreign Agent: (#2580).

Background: Assistant General Counsel, Foreign Operations Administration, 1953-54; Assistant Secretary of Defense, 1961-64.
Clients:
Manhurin, S.A.

PITTS, S. Donald
V. President, Technical, Aluminum Ass'n
900 19th St., N.W., Suite 300, Washington, DC 20006
Telephone: (202) 862-5121

PITTS, William P.
Government Affairs Representative, Amdahl Corp.
1667 K St., N.W., Suite 300, Washington, DC 20006
Telephone: (202) 835-2220
Registered as lobbyist at U.S. Congress.

PIZZO, Peggy
Senior Program Associate, Nat'l Center for Clinical Infant Programs
733 15th St., N.W., Suite 912, Washington, DC 20005
Telephone: (202) 347-0308
Registered as lobbyist at U.S. Congress.

PIZZOLI, Anne
Legislative Representative, Reid & Priest
1111 19th St., N.W., Washington, DC 20036
Telephone: (202) 828-0100

PLAIA, Paul, Jr.
Howrey and Simon
1730 Pennsylvania Ave., N.W., Washington, DC 20006-4793
Telephone: (202) 783-0800
Clients:
Amgen, Inc.
SKF USA, Inc.

PLAINE, Daniel J.
Steptoe and Johnson
1330 Connecticut Ave., N.W., Washington, DC 20036
Telephone: (202) 429-3000
Clients:
Nippon Steel Corp.

PLANTE, Charles L.
Washington Representative, American Ass'n of Neurological Surgeons/Congress of Neurological Surgeons
One Farragut Square South, Ninth Floor, Washington, DC 20006
Telephone: (202) 628-7171

PLASTER, Henry
Dir, Cong Correspondence, EXECUTIVE OFFICE OF THE PRESIDENT - The White House
1600 Pennsylvania Ave., N.W., 102 East Wing, Washington, DC 20500
Telephone: (202) 456-7500

PLATT, Alan
Potomac Partners
1250 24th St., N.W. Suite 875, Washington, DC 20037
Telephone: (202) 466-0560

PLATT, Geoffrey, Jr.
Director of Government Affairs, American Ass'n of Museums
1225 Eye St., N.W., Washington, DC 20005
Telephone: (202) 289-1818
Background: Former Administrative Ass't to Rep. Michael L. Strang (R-CO).

PLATT, Ronald L.
Camp, Barsh, Bates and Tate
2550 M St., N.W., Suite 275, Washington, DC 20037
Telephone: (202) 887-5160
Registered as lobbyist at U.S. Congress.
Background: Former aide to Senator Lloyd Bentsen (D-TX), Rep. Jack Brooks (D-TX), and Rep. Glenn English (D-OK).
Clients:
Advance Petroleum, Inc.
ARA Services
Associated Financial Corp.
Blue Cross and Blue Shield of Missouri
Campbell Soup Co.
CIC Enterprises, Inc.
CITGO Petroleum Corp.
Home Intensive Care, Inc.

Invacare Corp.
K mart Corp.
NATCO
Russ Berrie Corp.
Southland Corp., The
World Airways

PLEASANT, Sonya
Staff Asst, Legis Affrs (House), EXECUTIVE OFFICE OF THE PRESIDENT - The White House
1600 Pennsylvania Ave., N.W. 112 East Wing, Washington, DC 20500
Telephone: (202) 456-7030

PLEGER, Wyll W.
Director, Federal Affairs, Brown & Root, Inc.
1150 Connecticut Ave., N.W., Suite 205, Washington, DC 20036-4104
Telephone: (202) 223-0820
Registered as lobbyist at U.S. Congress.
Background: Also represents the Halliburton Co.

PLENGE, William H.
Washington Manager, Government Products, Deere & Co.
1667 K St., N.W., Suite 1230, Washington, DC 20006
Telephone: (202) 223-4817

PLESSER, Ronald L.
Piper and Marbury
1200 19th St., N.W., Washington, DC 20036
Telephone: (202) 861-3900
Registered as lobbyist at U.S. Congress.
Clients:
Mead Data Central, Inc.

PLIHCIK, Suzanne
President, Ass'n of Junior Leagues, Internat'l
1319 F St., N.W., Suite 604, Washington, DC 20004
Telephone: (202) 393-3364

PLOCHER, David
Staff Attorney, OMB Watch
1731 Connecticut Ave., N.W., Washington, DC 20009-1146
Telephone: (202) 234-8494

PLOG, Henry J., Jr.
Cleary, Gottlieb, Steen and Hamilton
1752 N St., N.W., Washington, DC 20036
Telephone: (202) 728-2700
Registered as lobbyist at U.S. Congress.
Clients:
UNOCAL Corp.

PLOTKIN, Harry M.
Arent, Fox, Kintner, Plotkin & Kahn
1050 Connecticut Ave., N.W., Washington, DC 20036-5339
Telephone: (202) 857-6000
Background: Assistant General Counsel, Federal Communications Commission, 1943-51. Special Counsel to the Senate Committee on Interstate and Foreign Commerce, 1954-55. Member, Board of Directors, Viacom Internat'l, Inc.

PLOTT, Curtis E.
Exec. V. President, American Soc. for Training and Development
1630 Duke St., Box 1443, Alexandria, VA 22313
Telephone: (703) 683-8100

PLOURD, E. R.
Legislative Representative, United Transportation Union
400 First St., N.W., Suite 704, Washington, DC 20001
Telephone: (202) 783-3939
Registered as lobbyist at U.S. Congress.

PLUNK, Daryl M.
Director, AEA Washington, Ltd.
905 16th St., N.W., Washington, DC 20006
Registered as Foreign Agent: (#4307).
Clients:
Korean Overseas Information Service

PLUNKETT & COONEY , P.C.
2715 M St., N.W., Suite 300, Washington, DC 20007-3710
Telephone: (202) 333-8803
Members of firm representing listed organizations:
Brodhead, William M.

Background: Member, U.S. House of Representatives from Michigan, 1974-82.
Clients:
Boysville of Michigan *(William M. Brodhead)*
Detroit Educational TV Foundation *(William M. Brodhead)*
Detroit, Michigan, City of *(William M. Brodhead)*
Michigan Humane Soc. *(William M. Brodhead)*

PLUNKETT, Glenn M.
Governmental Relations Specialist, American Foundation for the Blind (Government Relations Department)
1615 M St., N.W., Suite 250, Washington, DC 20036
Telephone: (202) 457-1487

PODELL, Lynn B.
Exec. Director, American Soc. for Medical Technology
2021 L St., N.W. Suite 400, Washington, DC 20036
Telephone: (202) 785-3311

PODESTA, Anthony T.
President, Podesta Associates
424 C St., N.E., Washington, DC 20002
Telephone: (202) 544-6906

PODESTA ASSOCIATES
424 C St., N.E., Washington, DC 20002
Telephone: (202) 544-6906
Members of firm representing listed organizations:
Bell, Richard C., V. President, Research Studies
Grundman, Stacey
Podesta, Anthony T., President
Podesta, John D., V. President
Background: Former Chief Counsel, U.S. Senate Agriculture, Nutrition, and Forestry Committee; Former Chief Counsel, Senate Judiciary Subcommittee on Patents, Copyrights, and Trademarks.
Scher, Michael
Background: Legislative Aide to Senator Daniel P. Moynihan (D-NY), 1984-85. Legislative Assistant to Senator Patrick Leahy (D-VT), 1985-89.
Stern, Todd D., V. President
Clients:
American Newspaper Publishers Ass'n *(John D. Podesta)*
Computer and Business Equipment Manufacturers Ass'n *(John D. Podesta)*
Digital Equipment Corp. *(John D. Podesta)*
Genentech, Inc. *(John D. Podesta)*
Nat'l Artists Equity Ass'n *(John D. Podesta)*
Nat'l Conference of Bankruptcy Judges *(John D. Podesta)*
Puerto Rico Federal Affairs Administration *(John D. Podesta)*

PODESTA, John D.
V. President, Podesta Associates
424 C St., N.E., Washington, DC 20002
Telephone: (202) 544-6906
Registered as lobbyist at U.S. Congress.
Background: Former Chief Counsel, U.S. Senate Agriculture, Nutrition, and Forestry Committee; Former Chief Counsel, Senate Judiciary Subcommittee on Patents, Copyrights, and Trademarks.
Clients:
American Newspaper Publishers Ass'n
Computer and Business Equipment Manufacturers Ass'n
Digital Equipment Corp.
Genentech, Inc.
Nat'l Artists Equity Ass'n
Nat'l Conference of Bankruptcy Judges
Puerto Rico Federal Affairs Administration

POGACH, Shari
Director of Member Services, Soc. of Independent Gasoline Marketers of America
1730 K St., N.W., Suite 907, Washington, DC 20006
Telephone: (202) 429-9333

POGUE, C. Richard
Senior V. President, Management, Investment Company Institute
1600 M St., N.W. Suite 600, Washington, DC 20036
Telephone: (202) 293-7700
Background: Also serves as Treasurer, Investment Management Political Action Committee.

POHLEN, Jerry
Director, Government Relations (Cessna), General Dynamics Corp.
1745 Jefferson Davis Hwy., Suite 1000, Arlington, VA 22202
Telephone: (703) 553-1200

POHORLYES, Louis
Thompson, Hine and Flory
1920 N St., N.W., Washington, DC 20036
Telephone: (202) 331-8800
Clients:
Nat'l Bank of Washington, The

POIREY, Thierry
V. President & CFO, Cogema, Inc.
7401 Wisconsin Ave., Bethesda, MD 20814
Telephone: (301) 986-8585
Registered as Foreign Agent: (#3587)

POIRIER, Marc R.
Spiegel and McDiarmid
1350 New York Ave., N.W., Suite 1100, Washington, DC 20005
Telephone: (202) 879-4000
Registered as lobbyist at U.S. Congress.
Clients:
Manassas, Virginia, City of

POISSON, David
Exec. Director, Government Affairs, Electronic Industries Ass'n
2001 Pennsylvania Ave., N.W., Washington, DC 20006
Telephone: (202) 457-4900
Registered as lobbyist at U.S. Congress.
Background: Former aide to Rep. Richard Durbin (D-IL) and Senator Terry Sanford (D-NC).

POJE, Gerry
Environmental Toxicologist, Nat'l Wildlife Federation
1400 16th St., N.W., Washington, DC 20036-2266
Telephone: (202) 797-6800
Registered as lobbyist at U.S. Congress.

POLACHECK, Laura
Staff Attorney, Center for Auto Safety
2001 S St., N.W., Room 410, Washington, DC 20009
Telephone: (202) 328-7700
Registered as lobbyist at U.S. Congress.

POLANSKY, Jane
Deputy Director, Public Relations, Nat'l Federation of Federal Employees
1016 16th St., N.W., Suite 400, Washington, DC 20036
Telephone: (202) 862-4400
Registered as lobbyist at U.S. Congress.

POLATSEK, Jean
Assoc. Director, Div. of Legislation, American Hospital Ass'n
50 F St., N.W., Suite 1100, Washington, DC 20001
Telephone: (202) 638-1100
Registered as lobbyist at U.S. Congress.

POLICY ANALYSIS, INC.
9520 Bent Creek Lane, Vienna, VA 22180
Telephone: (703) 759-3975
Background: Offers strategic planning and representation for corporations and individuals involved in public policy advocacy, with emphasis on opinion leadership campaigns.
Members of firm representing listed organizations:
Phillips, Howard J., Chairman
Background: Chairman, The Conservative Caucus. Represents Conservative Caucus Research, Analysis and Education Foundation. Also directs the Conservative Nat'l Campaign Committee and is Co-Chair of the Anti-Appeasement Alliance. Formerly was Acting Exec. Director, President's Council on Youth Opportunity, 1969-70; and as Acting Director, U.S. Office of Economic Opportunity, 1973.

POLICY COMMUNICATIONS INC.
1615 L St., N.W., Suite 650, Washington, DC 20036
Telephone: (202) 659-1023
Background: A firm which provides policy analysis, lobbying and communications services.
Members of firm representing listed organizations:
Lilley, William (III), President

Background: Dep. Ass't Sec'y, Housing and Urban Development, 1973-75. Director, Council on Wage and Price Stability, 1975-77. Minority Staff Director, House Budget Committee, 1977-78.

POLICY ECONOMICS GROUP OF KPMG PEAT MARWICK
2001 M St., N.W., Washington, DC 20036
Telephone: (202) 467-3818
Background: A national firm of tax and economics consultants whose clients include law firms, trade associations and Federal and state governmental agencies. The Group was acquired by Peat, Marwick, Mitchell & Co. in December 1986.
Members of firm representing listed organizations:
Johnson, Darwin G.
Background: Former Chief, Fiscal Analysis Branch, Office of Management and Budget.
Samuelson, Lior

POLITICS INC.
1920 L St., N.W., Suite 700, Washington, DC 20036
Telephone: (202) 331-7654
Background: A political affairs consulting firm which is an offshoot of The Kamber Group. Lesley Israel of The Kamber Group is President and Chief Executive of Politics Inc. Victor Kamber is Chairman of the Board.
Members of firm representing listed organizations:
Davenport, Rory, Political Director
Clients:
Democratic Nat'l Committee

POLIVY, Gail
Legal, GTE Corp.
Suite 1200, 1850 M St., N.W., Washington, DC 20036
Telephone: (202) 463-5214

POLK, Joe
Exec. Secretary, Friends Committee on Nat'l Legislation
245 Second St., N.E., Washington, DC 20002
Telephone: (202) 547-6000
Registered as lobbyist at U.S. Congress.

POLLACK, Irving M.
13010 Carney, Wheaton, MD 20906
Telephone: (301) 946-5304
Background: A public affairs consultant. Former Commissioner, Securities and Exchange Commission, 1974-80.
Organizations represented:
Merrill Lynch and Co., Inc.

POLLACK, Richard J.
V. Pres. & Dep. Dir., Washington Office, American Hospital Ass'n
50 F St., N.W., Suite 1100, Washington, DC 20001
Telephone: (202) 638-1100
Registered as lobbyist at U.S. Congress.

POLLACK, Ronald F.
Exec. Director, Families U.S.A.
1334 G St., N.W. Suite 300, Washington, DC 20005
Telephone: (202) 737-6340

POLLAK, Mark A.
V. President, Member Relations, Cosmetic, Toiletry and Fragrance Ass'n
1110 Vermont Ave., N.W. Suite 800, Washington, DC 20005
Telephone: (202) 331-1770

POLLAK, Michele
Legislative Representative, American Ass'n of Retired Persons
1909 K St., N.W., Washington, DC 20049
Telephone: (202) 728-4729
Registered as lobbyist at U.S. Congress.

POLLARD, Alfred M.
Senior V. Pres., Federal Gov't Relations, Security Pacific Nat'l Bank
1701 K St., N.W., Suite 503, Washington, DC 20006
Telephone: (202) 293-8440
Registered as lobbyist at U.S. Congress.

POLLARD, Bob
Nuclear Safety Engineer, Union of Concerned Scientists
1616 P St., N.W., Suite 310, Washington, DC 20036
Telephone: (202) 332-0900
Registered as lobbyist at U.S. Congress.

POLLITT, Joan
Director and Treasurer, Ass'n of Trial Lawyers Political Action Committee
1050 31st St., N.W., Washington, DC 20007
Telephone: (202) 965-3500

POLSON, Lee
Exec. Director & General Counsel, North American Securities Administrators Ass'n
555 New Jersey Ave., N.W., Suite 750, Washington, DC 20001-2029
Telephone: (202) 737-0900
Background: Former Member, U.S. House of Representatives (D-NJ), 1974-80.

POMERANCE, Rafe
Senior Associate, World Resources Institute
1709 New York Ave., N.W., Washington, DC 20006
Telephone: (202) 638-6300

POMERANZ, John
Legislative Representative, HALT-An Organization of Americans for Legal Reform
1319 F St., N.W., Suite 300, Washington, DC 20004
Telephone: (202) 347-9600
Registered as lobbyist at U.S. Congress.
Background: Former Executive Assistant to Rep. Charles Schumer (D-NY).

POMEROY, Harlan
Baker and Hostetler
1050 Connecticut Ave., N.W. Suite 1100, Washington, DC 20036
Telephone: (202) 861-1500
Registered as lobbyist at U.S. Congress.

POMPLIN, Amy L.
Political Program Assistant, American Veterinary Medical Ass'n
1023 15th St., N.W., Suite 300, Washington, DC 20005
Telephone: (202) 659-2040
Registered as lobbyist at U.S. Congress.
Background: Responsibilities include the American Veterinary Medical Ass'n Political Action Committee.

POOLE, Jay
Regional Manager, Mid-Atlantic Region, Philip Morris Management Corp.
1341 G St., N.W., Suite 900, Washington, DC 20005
Telephone: (202) 637-1500
Registered as lobbyist at U.S. Congress.

POOLE, William T.
Director of Research, Capitol Research Center
1612 K St., N.W., Suite 704, Washington, DC 20006
Telephone: (202) 822-8666

POOLER, Susanne J.
V. President, Nat'l Ass'n of Government Employees
1313 L St., N.W., 2nd Floor, Washington, DC 20005
Telephone: (202) 371-6644
Background: Also represents the Nat'l Ass'n of Government Employees Political Action Committee.

POORE, Steve
Dep Dir, Legis & Public Affrs, DEPARTMENT OF AGRICULTURE - Animal and Plant Health Inspection Service
14th and Independence Ave. S.W., Room 1147 South Bldg., Washington, DC 20250
Telephone: (202) 447-2511

POPEO, Daniel J.
Chairman, Washington Legal Foundation
1705 N St., N.W., Washington, DC 20036
Telephone: (202) 857-0240

POPHAM, HAIK, SCHNOBRICH & KAUFMAN, LTD.
1800 M St., N.W. Suite 300 South, Washington, DC 20036
Telephone: (202) 828-5300
Registered as Foreign Agent: (#4247)
Members of firm representing listed organizations:
Casselman, William E. (II)
Background: Legislative Assistant to Rep. Robert McClory (R-IL), 1965-69. Deputy Special Assistant to the President (Congressional Relations), 1969-71. General Counsel, General Services Administration, 1971-73. Legal Counsel to the Vice President of the U.S. and Deputy Assistant for Executive Branch Liaison, 1973-74. Counsel to the President of the U.S.,

1974-75.

Clients:
Japan Steel Works, Ltd. *(William E. Casselman, II)*
Ova Noss Family Partnership *(William E. Casselman, II)*

POPHAM, James
V. President, General Counsel, Ass'n of Independent Television Stations
1200 18th St., N.W. Suite 502, Washington, DC 20036
Telephone: (202) 887-1970
Registered as lobbyist at U.S. Congress.

POPKIN, Richard A.
Swidler & Berlin, Chartered
3000 K St., N.W., Suite 300, Washington, DC 20007
Telephone: (202) 944-4300
Registered as lobbyist at U.S. Congress.
Background: Confidential Assistant to the Under Secretary of Commerce for International Trade, 1984-85. Deputy Assistant Secretary of Commerce for Trade Administration, 1985-87.

PORCARO, Edward T.
Assistant V. President, Metropolitan Insurance Cos.
1615 L St., N.W., Suite 1210, Washington, DC 20036
Telephone: (202) 659-3575
Registered as lobbyist at U.S. Congress.

PORTASIC, Linda
Wright and Talisman
1050 17th St., N.W. Suite 600, Washington, DC 20036
Telephone: (202) 331-1194
Background: Assistant to the Chairman, Federal Power Commission, 1952-53.

PORTE, Phillip L.
Porte, Stafford and Associates
1050 17th St., N.W., Suite 840, Washington, DC 20036
Telephone: (202) 785-1196
Registered as lobbyist at U.S. Congress.
Clients:
American Dietetic Ass'n
American Medical Record Ass'n
Council on Accreditation of Services for Families and Children
Dietary Managers Ass'n
Nat'l Dialysis Ass'n

PORTE, STAFFORD AND ASSOCIATES
1050 17th St., N.W., Suite 840, Washington, DC 20036
Telephone: (202) 785-1196
Background: A legislative consulting firm.
Members of firm representing listed organizations:
Porte, Phillip L.
Stafford, Michael
Background: Legislative Consultant, Porte, Stafford, and Associates.
Clients:
American Dietetic Ass'n *(Phillip L. Porte)*
American Medical Record Ass'n *(Phillip L. Porte)*
Council on Accreditation of Services for Families and Children *(Phillip L. Porte)*
Dietary Managers Ass'n *(Phillip L. Porte)*
Nat'l Ass'n of Medical Directors of Respiratory Care *(Michael Stafford)*
Nat'l Dialysis Ass'n *(Phillip L. Porte)*

PORTER, Bruce D., Dr.
Exec. Director, Board for Internat'l Broadcasting
1201 Connecticut Ave., N.W. Suite 400, Washington, DC 20036
Telephone: (202) 254-8040

PORTER, Catherine T.
Member, Miller & Chevalier, Chartered
Metropolitan Square, 655 15th St., N.W., Washington, DC 20005
Telephone: (202) 626-5800
Registered as lobbyist at U.S. Congress.
Background: Tax Counsel, House Committee on Small Business, 1979-80. Assistant Counsel, Oversight Subcommittee, House Committee on Ways and Means, 1981-82. Tax and Trade Legislative Aide to Senator John Chafee (R-RI), 1983-88.
Clients:
Export Source Rule Coalition
Hewlett-Packard Co.
Office of Fair Treatment of Internat'l Investment

Organization for Fair Treatment of Internat'l Investment

PORTER, J. Robert, Jr.
President, Earth Satellite Corp.
7222 47th St., Chevy Chase, MD 20815
Telephone: (301) 951-0104

PORTER, Mildred
Administrative Director, Progressive Policy Institute
316 Pennsylvania Ave., S.E. Suite 516, Washington, DC 20003
Telephone: (202) 547-0001

PORTER/NOVELLI
1001 30th St., N.W., Washington, DC 20007
Telephone: (202) 342-7000
Members of firm representing listed organizations:
Druckenmiller, Robert
Franz, Jerry
Gibson, Thomas, V. President, Government Affairs
Background: Former Special Assistant and Director of Public Affairs, The White House in the Reagan Administration.
Hoffman, Melane Kinney, V. President
Murphy, Robin, V. President
Rose, Merrill, Senior V. President
Waller, Karen
Clients:
Akademie Fur Fuhrunskrafte der Deutschen Bundespost
Internat'l Apple Institute *(Jerry Franz, Karen Waller)*
Minpeco, S.A.

PORTER, Robert
Secretary-Treasurer, American Federation of Teachers
555 New Jersey Ave., N.W., Washington, DC 20001
Telephone: (202) 879-4415

PORTER, Robert W.
Legislative Representative, Collier, Shannon & Scott
1055 Thomas Jefferson St., N.W., Suite 300, Washington, DC 20007
Telephone: (202) 342-8400
Registered as lobbyist at U.S. Congress.

PORTER, William A.
V. President, Public Affairs & Devel't., Youth For Understanding Internat'l Exchange
3501 Newark St., N.W., Washington, DC 20016
Telephone: (202) 895-1125

PORTER, WRIGHT, MORRIS AND ARTHUR
1233 20th St., N.W., Suite 400, Washington, DC 20005
Telephone: (202) 778-3000
Background: Washington office of an Ohio-based law firm.
Members of firm representing listed organizations:
Dowd, Michael G.
Finkel, E. Jay, Of Counsel
Background: U.S. Member, Board of Directors, Inter-American Development Bank, 1977-80; Asst. Secretary, Development Committee, World Bank and International Monetary Fund, 1975-77; U.S. Treasury, International Finance, 1952-1974.
Kessler, Judd L., Of Counsel
Background: Asst. General Counsel, U.S. Agency for Internat'l Development; Chief Counsel for Middle East Programs, 1980-82; Chief Counsel for Latin America and the Caribbean, 1976-80.
Martin, David H.
Background: Former Chief Counsel, U.S. Secret Service, 1974-77. Former Director, U.S. Office of Government Ethics, 1983-87.
Clients:
Coalition for Environmental-Energy Balance *(Michael G. Dowd)*
Harza Engineering Co. *(E. Jay Finkel)*
Huntington Nat'l Bank *(E. Jay Finkel)*
Maryland People's Counsel *(E. Jay Finkel)*

PORTMAN, Robert J.
Dep Asst to the Pres, Legis Affrs, EXECUTIVE OFFICE OF THE PRESIDENT - The White House
1600 Pennsylvania Ave., N.W., Washington, DC 20500
Telephone: (202) 456-2230

PORTNEY, Paul R.
V. President, Resources for the Future
1616 P St., N.W., Washington, DC 20036
Telephone: (202) 328-5000
Background: Senior Staff Economist, Council on Environmental Quality, 1979-80.

PORTNOY, David Alan
Repesentative, Civil Programs, General Electric Co.
1331 Pennsylvania Ave., N.W. Suite 800S, Washington, DC 20004
Telephone: (202) 637-4000
Registered as lobbyist at U.S. Congress.

POSADA, Ricardo
Account Representative, Internat'l Public Strategies, Inc.
1030 15th St., N.W., Suite 408, Washington, DC 20005
Telephone: (202) 371-5604
Registered as Foreign Agent: (#4200).

POSEY, James Q.
Director, Government Communications, FMC Corp.
1627 K St., N.W., Suite 500, Washington, DC 20006
Telephone: (202) 956-5200
Background: Also serves as Program Coordinator, FMC Corp. Good Government Program.

POSEY, Tyler S.
Dep Asst Admin, Legis Affrs, AGENCY FOR INTERNAT'L DEVELOPMENT
320 21st St., N.W., Washington, DC 20523
Telephone: (202) 647-9080

POSSNER, Karen B.
Director, Legislative Policy, BellSouth Corp.
1133 21st St., N.W., Suite 900, Washington, DC 20036
Telephone: (202) 463-4100

POTEET, Alonzo M.
Dep Asst Secy, Cong Affrs, DEPARTMENT OF VETERANS AFFAIRS
810 Vermont Ave., N.W., Washington, DC 20420
Telephone: (202) 233-2482

POTEMKEN, Donna
Assoc. Director, Div. of Regulatory Afrs, American Hospital Ass'n
50 F St., N.W., Suite 1100, Washington, DC 20001
Telephone: (202) 638-1100
Registered as lobbyist at U.S. Congress.

POTOMAC PARTNERS
1250 24th St., N.W. Suite 875, Washington, DC 20037
Telephone: (202) 466-0560
Background: Harris Miller and Ann Sullivan, of Holt, Miller & Associates, are also consultants for Potomac Partners.
Members of firm representing listed organizations:
Holt, James
Leet, Rebecca
Lehrfeld, Betsy
Platt, Alan
Turesky, Stanley F., Managing Partner
Turner, James
Clients:
Center for Foreign Policy Options
Organic Food Alliance
United States-New Zealand Council, The *(Stanley F. Turesky)*
Washington Insurance Bureau

POTOMAC SURVEY RESEARCH
7940 Norfolk Ave., Bethesda, MD 20814
Telephone: (301) 656-7900
Background: An opinion and market research firm serving the media, business and political organizations and candidates.
Members of firm representing listed organizations:
Haller, Keith, President

POTOMAC VISIONS LIMITED
1111 14th St., N.W. Suite 1001, Washington, DC 20005
Telephone: (202) 289-3684
Background: A government affairs/political consulting firm.
Members of firm representing listed organizations:
Smith, G. Wayne, President
Background: Former Administrative Assistant and Staff Director to Senator John Breaux (D-LA) and Deputy to the Chairman, Democratic Senatorial Campaign Committee.

POTTER, Philip H.
Senior V. President, Walker Associates, Charls E.
1730 Pennsylvania Ave., N.W. Suite 200, Washington, DC
20006
Telephone: (202) 393-4760
Registered as Foreign Agent: (#4180).
Organizations represented:
Atchison, Topeka and Santa Fe Railway Co., The
Lone Star Steel Co.

POTTER, Thomas L.
Exec. Director, Nat'l Lime Ass'n
3601 North Fairfax Drive, Arlington, VA 22201
Telephone: (703) 243-5463

POTTS, Ramsay D.
Shaw, Pittman, Potts and Trowbridge
2300 N St., N.W., Washington, DC 20037
Telephone: (202) 663-8000
Registered as lobbyist at U.S. Congress.
Clients:
Emerson Electric Co.
Investment Counsel Ass'n of America

POTTS, Stephen D.
Shaw, Pittman, Potts and Trowbridge
2300 N St., N.W., Washington, DC 20037
Telephone: (202) 663-8000
Background: Member of the Board of Directors, Overseas
Nat'l Airways.
Clients:
Overseas Nat'l Airways

POULOS, Bill
Manager, Government Affairs, Apple Computer, Inc.
1550 M St., N.W. Suite 1000, Washington, DC 20005
Telephone: (202) 872-6260
Registered as lobbyist at U.S. Congress.

POUND, William T.
Exec. Director, Nat'l Conference of State Legislatures
444 North Capitol St., N.W. Suite 500, Washington, DC
20001
Telephone: (202) 624-5400

POUNIAN, Lynn C.
President and Chief Executive Officer, Reese Communications Companies
2111 Wilson Ave., Suite 900, Arlington, VA 22201
Telephone: (703) 528-4400

POUSSARD, Rayne G.
Manager, Public Affairs, United Parcel Service
316 Pennsylvania Ave., S.E. Suite 304, Washington, DC
20003
Telephone: (202) 675-4220

POWELL, ADAMS & RINEHART
1901 L St., N.W., 3rd Floor, Washington, DC 20036
Telephone: (202) 466-7590
Background: A total communications and issues manage-
ment firm. Owned by the WPP Group on London, Eng-
land.
Members of firm representing listed organizations:
Comer, Suzanne, Senior Account Executive
Costello, Paul, V. President
Downing, Mary Louise, V. President
Garfinkel, Steve, Account Executive
Gross, Beth, Senior Account Executive
Johnson, Jerry, Director of Research
Kaiser, Harry, Senior Account Executive
Background: Former Press Secretary and Special As-
sistant to Rep. Marcy Kaptur (D-OH).
Kell, Bonnie, Account Executive
Leibach, Dale
Background: Former aide to Senator Tom Harkin (D-
IA) and Assistant Press Secretary to President Jimmy
Carter.
Madison, Alan
Background: Senior Account Executive, Ogilvy &
Mather Public Affairs, Inc.
Marcus, Richard, Senior V. President
Moeller, James, Account Executive
Neuman, Robert A., V. President
Background: Former Chief of Staff to Rep. Morris
Udall (D-AZ).
Powell, Jody, Chairman and CEO
Background: Press Secretary to President Jimmy Cart-
er, 1977-81.

Rabin, Steve, President
Rafshoon, Jerry, Senior Communiation\S Consul-
tant
Raines, Elvoy
Savarese, Jim, Director of Research
Silverman, Marcia, Chief Operating Officer
Wahle, Thomas, Sr. Account Executive
Clients:
Aircraft Owners and Pilots Ass'n
American Federation of Teachers
American Iron and Steel Institute *(Dale Leibach,
Jody Powell)*
Amgen, Inc. *(Robert A. Neuman)*
Australia, Commonwealth of
BATUS, Inc.
British Tourist Authority
France, Government of
Glass Packaging Institute
Institute for Educational Leadership
Internat'l Union of Bricklayers and Allied Crafts-
men
Lufthansa German Airlines
March of Dimes
Tobacco Institute

POWELL, Ann
Data Services Coordinator, Nat'l Ass'n of Counties
440 First St., N.W., Washington, DC 20001
Telephone: (202) 393-6226

POWELL, David T.
President, Nat'l Weather Service Employees Organization
400 North Capitol St., N.W. Suite 326, Washington, DC
20001
Telephone: (202) 783-3131

POWELL, GOLDSTEIN, FRAZER AND MURPHY
1001 Pennsylvania, N.W., Sixth Fl., Washington, DC
20004
Telephone: (202) 347-0066
Background: Washington office of an Atlanta law firm.
Members of firm representing listed organizations:
Chanin, Michael H.
Background: Special Assistant, Office of the Secretary
of Commerce, 1977-78. Deputy Assistant to the
President of the U.S., 1978-81.
Eizenstat, Stuart E.
Background: Formerly Assistant to the President for
Domestic Affairs and Policy under President Jimmy
Carter. Member, Board of Directors, Hercules, Inc.,
Public Service Co. of Indiana and Israel Discount
Bank of New York. Serves as Adjunct Lecturer, JFK
School of Government, Harvard University.
Freedman, Anthony S.
Background: Deputy Director, Legislation, U.S. Envi-
ronmental Protection Agency, 1977-78. Deputy As-
sistant Secretary, Housing Policy and Budget, U.S.
Department of Housing and Urban Development,
1979-81.
Gage, Larry S.
Background: Legal Counsel to Commissioner Nicholas
Johnson, Federal Communications Commission,
1972-73. Counsel, U.S. Senate Subcommittee on Em-
ployment, Poverty and Migratory Labor, 1973-75.
Staff Director, U.S. Senate Subcommittee on Al-
coholism and Drug Abuse, 1975-77. Special Assistant
and Deputy Assistant Secretary, Health Legislation,
Department of Health and Human Services, 1977-81.
Serves as President and General Counsel of the Nat'l
Ass'n of Public Hospitals.
Lazarus, Simon (III)
Background: Legal Assistant to Federal Communica-
tions Commissioner Nicholas Johnson, 1967-68. As-
sociate Director, White House Domestic Policy Staff,
1977-81.
Marzulla, Roger J.
Background: Served in the U.S. Department of Justice,
1983-89. Held positions of Special Litigation Coun-
sel, 1982-83, Deputy Assistant Attorney General,
1984-87, and Assistant Attorney General, 1987-89,
in the Land and Natural Resources Division.
Parver, Alan
Simons, Lawrence B.
Background: Assistant Secretary for Housing/FHA
Commissioner, 1977-81.
Suchman, Peter
Background: Lieutenant, U.S. Coast Guard, 1960-64.
U.S. Foreign Service Officer, 1964-70. Director, Of-
fice of Trade Policy, U.S. Treasury Department,

1972-74. Deputy Assistant Secretary, Tariff Affairs,
Treasury Department, 1974-78.
Clients:
American Ass'n of Exporters and Importers *(Peter
Suchman)*
American Koyo Corp. *(Peter Suchman)*
Ass'n of Bank Holding Companies
Bayley Seton Hospital *(Lawrence B. Simons)*
Belz Investment Co.
Caterpillar Inc. *(Peter Suchman)*
Coalition for Equitable Compensation
Committee for Equitable Compensation *(Stuart E.
Eizenstat)*
Computer and Business Equipment Manufactur-
ers Ass'n *(Simon Lazarus, III)*
Council on Research and Technology (CORE-
TECH) *(Stuart E. Eizenstat)*
Davis Walker Corp. *(Peter Suchman)*
Federal Nat'l Mortgage Ass'n *(Lawrence B. Simons)*
Flood Control Advisory Committee *(Stuart E. Eizen-
stat)*
Fluor Corp. *(Stuart E. Eizenstat)*
Hadson Corp. *(Stuart E. Eizenstat)*
Hayes Microcomputer Products, Inc. *(Simon Laza-
rus, III)*
Hercules, Inc. *(Stuart E. Eizenstat)*
Hewlett-Packard Co. *(Stuart E. Eizenstat)*
Hitachi America Ltd.
Hitachi Ltd. *(Stuart E. Eizenstat)*
Hitachi Sales Corp. of America *(Stuart E. Eizenstat)*
Hoogovens Group BV *(Peter Suchman)*
Internat'l Telecommunications Satellite Organiza-
tion (INTELSAT) *(Stuart E. Eizenstat)*
Koyo Seiko *(Peter Suchman)*
Massachusetts Housing Finance Agency *(Anthony
S. Freedman)*
Minorco Societe Anonyme
Nat'l Ass'n of Public Hospitals *(Larry S. Gage)*
Nat'l Latex Products Co. *(Peter Suchman)*
Nat'l Multi Housing Council *(Lawrence B. Simons)*
Nat'l Multi Housing Council Political Action
Committee *(Lawrence B. Simons)*
NVW (USA) *(Peter Suchman)*
Palau, Government of *(Michael H. Chanin)*
Public Service Co. of Indiana *(Roger J. Marzulla)*
Starrett Housing Corp. *(Lawrence B. Simons)*
Stride Rite Corp., The *(Stuart E. Eizenstat)*
Sunbelt Corp.
Union of Councils for Soviet Jews *(Stuart E. Eizen-
stat)*
Weizman Institute of Science *(Stuart E. Eizenstat)*

POWELL, Janet L.
Director, Public Affairs, Anden Group, The
1908 Mt. Vernon Ave. P.O. Box 2449, Alexandria, VA
22301
Telephone: (703) 684-6650
Registered as lobbyist at U.S. Congress.

POWELL, Jennifer
Admin. Asst., Gov't Relats. & Public Aff, Nat'l Federation
of Business and Professional Women's Clubs
2012 Massachusetts Ave., N.W., Washington, DC 20036
Telephone: (202) 293-1100
Registered as lobbyist at U.S. Congress.

POWELL, Jody
Chairman and CEO, Powell, Adams & Rinehart
1901 L St., N.W., 3rd Floor, Washington, DC 20036
Telephone: (202) 466-7590
Background: Press Secretary to President Jimmy Carter,
1977-81.
Clients:
American Iron and Steel Institute

POWELL, Lt. Col. Michael
Manpower, Health & Reserve, Legis Affrs, DEPARTMENT
OF DEFENSE
The Pentagon, Washington, DC 20301
Telephone: (202) 697-6210

POWELL, Paul L.
Dir, Office of Cong Affrs, DEPARTMENT OF COMMERCE
- Internat'l Trade Administration
14th and Constitution Ave. N.W., Washington, DC 20230
Telephone: (202) 377-3015

POWELL, R. Jack
Exec. Director, Paralyzed Veterans of America
801 18th St., N.W., Washington, DC 20006
Telephone: (202) 872-1300

POWER & COLEMAN
1919 Pennsylvania Ave., N.W. Suite 504, Washington, DC 20006
Telephone: (202) 659-9061
Members of firm representing listed organizations:
Power, Thomas W.
Clients:
ARA Services *(Thomas W. Power)*
Denny's, Inc. *(Thomas W. Power)*
Foodservice and Lodging Institute *(Thomas W. Power)*
Foodservice and Lodging Institute Political Action Committee *(Thomas W. Power)*
Hardee's Food Systems
Morrison Inc. *(Thomas W. Power)*
Nat'l Bowling Council *(Thomas W. Power)*
Pizza Inn, Inc. *(Thomas W. Power)*
Saga Corp. *(Thomas W. Power)*

POWER, John 'Jay'
Legislative Representative, AFL-CIO (American Federation of Labor and Congress of Industrial Organizations)
815 16th St., N.w., Washington, DC 20006
Telephone: (202) 637-5084
Registered as lobbyist at U.S. Congress.

POWER, Thomas W.
Power & Coleman
1919 Pennsylvania Ave., N.W. Suite 504, Washington, DC 20006
Telephone: (202) 659-9061
Clients:
ARA Services
Denny's, Inc.
Foodservice and Lodging Institute
Foodservice and Lodging Institute Political Action Committee
Morrison Inc.
Nat'l Bowling Council
Pizza Inn, Inc.
Saga Corp.

POWER, William H.
V. President, Government Affairs, Nat'l Air Transportation Ass'n
4226 King St., Alexandria, VA 22302
Telephone: (703) 845-9000

POWERS, Charles H.
Senior V. President, Public Affairs, Tobacco Institute
1875 Eye St., N.W., Suite 800, Washington, DC 20006
Telephone: (202) 457-4800
Background: Former Deputy Assistant Secretary for Public Affairs, U.S. Treasury Department.

POWERS, E. Lloyd
Petrochemical Director, Nat'l Petroleum Refiners Ass'n
1899 L St., N.W., Suite 1000, Washington, DC 20036
Telephone: (202) 457-0480

POWERS GRISSO, Cindy J.
Gold and Liebengood, Inc.
1455 Pennsylvania Ave., N.W. Suite 950, Washington, DC 20004
Telephone: (202) 639-8899
Background: Former Aide to U.S. Representative Michael A. Andrews and Congressman Lloyd Benton (both D-TX).

POWERS, Pamela M.
Coord., Political and Community Affairs, Contel Corp.
555 13th St. Suite 480 West, Washington, DC 20004
Telephone: (202) 383-3700

POWERS, Patricia
Senior Policy Analyst, American Ass'n of Retired Persons
1909 K St., N.W., Washington, DC 20049
Telephone: (202) 728-4337

POZEN, Walter
Stroock & Stroock & Lavan
1150 17th St., N.W. Sixth Floor, Washington, DC 20036
Telephone: (202) 452-9250
Registered as lobbyist at U.S. Congress.

Registered as Foreign Agent: (#3816).
Background: Assistant to Senator Harrison Williams, Jr., 1958. Assistant to the Secretary of the Interior, 1961-67.
Clients:
Dreyfus Corp.

PPED, INC.
1620 Eye St., N.W., Suite 509, Washington, DC 20006
Telephone: (202) 659-2187
Members of firm representing listed organizations:
Kochan, Richard S., President
Clients:
Benton Harbor, Michigan, City of *(Richard S. Kochan)*
Richmond, California, City of *(Richard S. Kochan)*
San Lorenzo Guaynabo, Puerto Rico, City of *(Richard S. Kochan)*

PRAGER, Rollinde
Murray, Scheer & Montgomery
2715 M St., N.W., Suite 300, Washington, DC 20037
Telephone: (202) 333-8830
Registered as lobbyist at U.S. Congress.
Registered as Foreign Agent: (#2927).
Clients:
Nat'l Federation of Coffee Growers of Colombia

PRASKE, Gregory J.
V. President, Finance and Administration, Nat'l Air Transportation Ass'n
4226 King St., Alexandria, VA 22302
Telephone: (703) 845-9000
Background: Also serves as Treasurer, Nat'l Air Transportation Ass'n Political Action Committee.

PRATHER, Alfred V. J.
Prather, Seeger, Doolittle and Farmer
1600 M St., N.W., Washington, DC 20036
Telephone: (202) 296-0500
Clients:
American Mining Congress
Kennecott

PRATHER, SEEGER, DOOLITTLE AND FARMER
1600 M St., N.W., Washington, DC 20036
Telephone: (202) 296-0500
Members of firm representing listed organizations:
Blase, Kurt E.
Connell, Lawrence
   Background: Chairman, Nat'l Credit Union Administration, 1977-81.
Doolittle, J. William
   Background: Clerk to Justice Felix Frankfurter, U.S. Supreme Court, 1957-58. Assistant to Solicitor General of the U.S., 1961-63. First Assistant, Civil Division, Department of Justice, 1963-66. General Counsel, 1966-68 and Assistant Secretary, 1968-69, Department of the Air Force.
Farmer, Thomas L.
   Background: Chairman, Advisory Board, National Capital Transportation Agency, 1961-1964. Gen. Counsel, Agency for Internat'l Development, 1964-1968. Director and Gen. Counsel, Overseas Development Council, 1968- . Chairman, President's Intelligence Oversight Board, 1977-81.
Nelson, Carl B. (Jr.)
Prather, Alfred V. J.
Seeger, Edwin H.
Welsh, Gary M.
Wilson, D. Edward (Jr.)
   Background: Served as Acting General Counsel for the Treasury Department.
Clients:
American Airlines *(Carl B. Nelson, Jr., Edwin H. Seeger)*
American Mining Congress *(Alfred V. J. Prather)*
Bankers' Ass'n for Foreign Trade *(Thomas L. Farmer)*
Bremer Lagerhaus-Gesellschaft *(Thomas L. Farmer, Carl B. Nelson, Jr., Edwin H. Seeger)*
Cadmium Council *(Kurt E. Blase, Edwin H. Seeger)*
Casalee America Corp. *(D. Edward Wilson, Jr.)*
Comite Textil de la Sociedad Nacional
Elsevier U.S. Holdings, Inc. *(J. William Doolittle)*
Empresa de Transporte Aereo del Peru *(Edwin H. Seeger)*
Flores Esmeralda, Ltda. *(Edwin H. Seeger, Gary M. Welsh)*
Flores Esmeralda, S.R.L. *(Edwin H. Seeger, Gary M. Welsh)*

General Electric Co. *(Kurt E. Blase, D. Edward Wilson, Jr.)*
Greens Creek Mining Co. *(Kurt E. Blase)*
Greenwood Press *(J. William Doolittle)*
Gulf Resources & Chemical Corp. *(Edwin H. Seeger)*
John Hancock Mutual Life Insurance Co. *(Thomas L. Farmer, Gary M. Welsh)*
Kennecott *(Alfred V. J. Prather)*
Lead Industries Ass'n *(Kurt E. Blase, Edwin H. Seeger)*
Nigeria, Government of *(Thomas L. Farmer)*
North Rhine Westphalia, Government of *(Thomas L. Farmer)*
QIT, Inc. *(Kurt E. Blase)*
Ridgeway Mining Co. *(Kurt E. Blase)*
Royal Bank of Canada *(Thomas L. Farmer)*
Salzgitter AG *(Thomas L. Farmer)*
Sima-Peru *(Edwin H. Seeger)*
Sociedad de Industrias "Comite Textil" *(Edwin H. Seeger, Gary M. Welsh)*

PRATS, Lisa M.
V. President, Internat'l Bottled Water Ass'n
113 North Henry St., Alexandria, VA 22314
Telephone: (703) 683-5213

PRATT, David J.
V. President, Federal Affairs, American Insurance Ass'n
1130 Connecticut Ave., N.W., Suite 1000, Washington, DC 20036
Telephone: (202) 828-7100
Registered as lobbyist at U.S. Congress.
Background: Secretary for the Minority, U.S. Senate, 1985-87. Secretary for the Majority, 1987.

PRATT, Kelly
Manager, of Corporate Planning, Designers & Planners, Inc.
2611 Jefferson Davis Highway, Suite 3000, Arlington, VA 22202
Telephone: (703) 418-3800

PRATT, Lawrence D.
Exec. Director, Gun Owners of America
8001 Forbes Place, Suite 102, Springfield, VA 22151
Telephone: (703) 321-8585
Registered as lobbyist at U.S. Congress.
Background: Serves also as President of the Committee to Protect the Family. Registered to lobby for English First.

PRATT, Paul H.
Director of International Issues, Manufacturers' Alliance for Productivity and Innovation (MAPI)
1200 18th St., N.W. Suite 400, Washington, DC 20036
Telephone: (202) 331-8430

PRATT, Sarah J.
Government Affairs Representative, Nat'l Ocean Industries Ass'n
1050 17th St., N.W. Suite 700, Washington, DC 20036
Telephone: (202) 785-5116
Registered as lobbyist at U.S. Congress.

PRENDERGAST, Joseph T.
President, American Ski Federation
207 Constitution Ave., N.E., Washington, DC 20002
Telephone: (202) 543-1595
Registered as lobbyist at U.S. Congress.
Background: Serves as Treasurer, American Ski Federation Political Action Committee and represents the Nat'l Ski Areas Ass'n and Ski Industries of America.

PRENDERGAST, Richard H.
Anderson, Benjamin, Read & Haney
1020 19th St., N.W., Suite 500, Washington, DC 20036
Telephone: (202) 659-5656
Registered as lobbyist at U.S. Congress.
Background: Former Special Assistant to the President for Legislative Affairs, House under President Reagan.

PRENDERGAST, Ruth
Director, Membership Services, American Legislative Exchange Council
214 Massachusetts Ave., N.W., Washington, DC 20002
Telephone: (202) 547-4646

PRENDERGAST, William B.
Dir, Cong Relations, FEDERAL TRADE COMMISSION
6th and Pennsylvania Ave. N.W., Washington, DC 20580
Telephone: (202) 326-2195

PRENNIG, Frank, III
Director, Administration & Development, Lupus Foundation of America
1717 Massachusetts Ave., N.W., Suite 203, Washington, DC 20036
Telephone: (202) 328-4550

PRESCOTT, Donald E.
Assistant to the President, Nat'l Soft Drink Ass'n
1101 16th St., N.W., Washington, DC 20036
Telephone: (202) 463-6745

PRESLAR, Lloyd T.
V. President, DGA Internat'l
1133 Connecticut Ave., N.W. Suite 700, Washington, DC 20036
Telephone: (202) 223-4001
Registered as lobbyist at U.S. Congress.

PRESTI, Susan
StMaxens and Co.
1140 Connecticut Ave., N.W., Suite 201, Washington, DC 20036
Telephone: (202) 833-4466
Background: Former economist, U.S. Department of Commerce.
Clients:
Motorola, Inc.

PRESTON, Cindy
Director, State and Agency Relations, BellSouth Corp.
1133 21st St., N.W., Suite 900, Washington, DC 20036
Telephone: (202) 463-4100

PRESTON GATES ELLIS & ROUVELAS MEEDS
1735 New York Ave., N.W., Suite 500, Washington, DC 20006-4759
Telephone: (202) 628-1700
Registered as Foreign Agent: (# 3567)
Background: Law firm with offices in Seattle, Anchorage, Spokane and Portland.
Members of firm representing listed organizations:
Barnes, Richard L.
Background: Professional staff member, U.S. House of Representatives Government Operations Committee, 1977-79.
Blank, Jonathan
Bloom, John L.
Broderick, Kathryn P.
DeVierno, John A.
Background: Office of General Counsel, U.S. Department of Transportation, 1977-81.
Erenbaum, Allen
Garvie, Pamela J.
Background: Former Chief Counsel to the Subcommittees on Aviation, Surface Transportation and Business, Trade and Tourism of the Senate Commerce Committee, 1986. Counsel to the Subcommittee on Surface Transportation, 1981-86. Assistant Legislative Counsel, Interstate Commerce Commission, 1978-80, Counsel to Rep. Robert Duncan (D-OR), 1976-78.
Gehring, Craig J.
Background: Counsel, Committee on Government Operations, Subcommittee on Legislation and National Security, 1976-79.
Geiger, Susan B.
Background: Senior staff, Office of Management and Budget, 1970-80.
Heiman, Bruce J.
Background: Legislative Director and Trade Counsel to Senator Daniel P. Moynihan, 1984-87.
Ivey, Glenn F.
Background: Former Legislative Assistant to Rep, John Conyers, Jr. (D-MI).
Kay, Kenneth R.
Background: Legislative Director to Sen. Max Baucus, 1982-84. Counsel, Senate Judiciary Committee, 1979-82. Legislative Assistant, Cong. Ed Koch, 1976-77. Serves as Exec. Director, Council on Research and Technology.
Longstreth, John L.
Background: Clerk for U.S. District Court for the Eastern District of Pennsylvania.
Lowry, Suellen
Meeds, Lloyd
Background: Member, U.S. House of Representatives from Washington State's 2nd District, 1965-79.

Mosher, Sol, Sr. Advisor and Fed. Afrs. & Int'l Trade
Background: Former Assistant U.S. Trade Representative.
Myhre, William N.
Peckinpaugh, Tim L.
Background: Professional Staff, Committee on Science and Technology, 1985; Legislative Assistant, Rep. Sid Morrison, 1982-84.
Pettus, Drew D.
Background: Former Administrative Assistant and Legal Counsel to Rep. Al Swift (D-WA).
Rouvelas, Emanuel L.
Background: Counsel, Senate Commerce Committee, 1969-1973; Chief Counsel, Senate Merchant Marine Subcommittee, 1969-1973; Foreign Commerce and Tourism Subcommittee, 1969-1973.
Schaffer, William Gray
Background: Former Special Litigation Counsel, U.S. Department of Justice.
Shook, William A.
Background: Legislative Investigator, Senate Judiciary Committee, 1979-85, and Special Assistant on the House Oversight and Investigations Subcommittee of the Interstate and Foreign Commerce Committee, 1977-79.
Weiss, James R.
Background: Former Chief, Transportation, Energy and Agriculture Section, Antitrust Division, U.S. Department of Justice.
Clients:
Alaska Loggers Ass'n *(Richard L. Barnes, Lloyd Meeds)*
Albion, Michigan, City of *(Allen Erenbaum, Craig J. Gehring)*
American Forest Resource Alliance *(Richard L. Barnes)*
American Nuclear Insurers *(Lloyd Meeds, Tim L. Peckinpaugh)*
American Plywood Ass'n *(Richard L. Barnes, Bruce J. Heiman)*
American President Companies *(Bruce J. Heiman, Emanuel L. Rouvelas)*
Arctic Sounder Enterprises, Inc. *(William N. Myhre)*
Aurora Fisheries, Inc. *(John L. Bloom, William N. Myhre)*
Bellingham Cold Storage *(John L. Bloom, William N. Myhre)*
Birmingham, Alabama, City of *(Craig J. Gehring)*
Boeing Co. *(Lloyd Meeds)*
Burlington Northern Railroad *(Pamela J. Garvie, Emanuel L. Rouvelas)*
Calista Corp. *(Susan B. Geiger, Lloyd Meeds)*
Clyde Hill, Washington, Town of *(Allen Erenbaum, Craig J. Gehring)*
Coastal Transportation, Inc. *(William N. Myhre)*
Council on Research and Technology (CORE-TECH) *(Kenneth R. Kay, Suellen Lowry)*
Data General Corp. *(Kenneth R. Kay, John L. Longstreth)*
Delta Air Lines
Earthquake Project, The *(Lloyd Meeds, Tim L. Peckinpaugh)*
Fluke Manufacturing Co., John *(Lloyd Meeds, William A. Shook)*
Fusion Power Associates *(Tim L. Peckinpaugh)*
Go-Video *(Bruce J. Heiman)*
Golden Alaska Seafoods, Inc. *(John L. Bloom, William N. Myhre)*
Grand Haven, Michigan, City of *(Allen Erenbaum, Craig J. Gehring)*
Hewlett-Packard Co. *(Kenneth R. Kay)*
Instituto Latinoamericano del Fierro y el Acero (ILAFA) *(Bruce J. Heiman)*
Interlake Holding Corp. *(Susan B. Geiger, Emanuel L. Rouvelas)*
Internat'l Council of Containerships Operators *(Emanuel L. Rouvelas)*
Internat'l Telecommunications Satellite Organization (INTELSAT) *(Craig J. Gehring, Bruce J. Heiman, Lloyd Meeds)*
Loudoun County, Virginia *(Allen Erenbaum, Craig J. Gehring)*
Ludington, Michigan, City of *(Craig J. Gehring)*
Marine Management, Inc. *(John L. Bloom, William N. Myhre)*
Maryland, Aviation Administration of the State of *(Susan B. Geiger)*

Mormac Marine Group, Inc. *(Susan B. Geiger, Emanuel L. Rouvelas)*
Mutual Atomic Energy Liability Underwriters *(Lloyd Meeds, Tim L. Peckinpaugh)*
Nat'l Business Aircraft Ass'n *(Pamela J. Garvie)*
Nat'l Council on Compensation Insurance *(Susan B. Geiger, Kenneth R. Kay)*
Nat'l Forest Products Ass'n *(Richard L. Barnes, William A. Shook)*
Nat'l Private Truck Council *(John A. DeVierno)*
Nelbro Packing Co. *(Richard L. Barnes, William N. Myhre)*
Northwest Marine Terminal Ass'n *(William N. Myhre)*
OMI Corp. *(Jonathan Blank, Susan B. Geiger, Emanuel L. Rouvelas)*
Orange, Texas, City of *(Allen Erenbaum, Craig J. Gehring)*
Pitney-Bowes, Inc. *(Lloyd Meeds)*
Sacramento, California, City of *(Allen Erenbaum, Craig J. Gehring)*
SeaHarvest, Inc. *(John L. Bloom, William N. Myhre)*
Seatrain Tankers Corp. *(Jonathan Blank, Emanuel L. Rouvelas)*
Seattle Organizing Committee, 1990 Goodwill Games *(Lloyd Meeds)*
Seattle, Washington, Port of *(Emanuel L. Rouvelas)*
Simpson Investment Co. *(Richard L. Barnes)*
Somerville, Massachusetts, City of *(Allen Erenbaum, Craig J. Gehring)*
South Dakota Department of Transportation *(John A. DeVierno)*
Southeast Alaska Regional Health Corp. (SEARHC) *(Susan B. Geiger, Lloyd Meeds)*
Southfield, Michigan, City of *(Craig J. Gehring)*
Spokane, Washington, City of *(Allen Erenbaum, Craig J. Gehring)*
Stone and Webster Engineering Corp. *(Tim L. Peckinpaugh)*
Sunmar Shipping, Inc. *(John L. Bloom, William N. Myhre)*
TeleCommunications, Inc. *(Bruce J. Heiman, Lloyd Meeds, Drew D. Pettus)*
Transportation Institute *(Jonathan Blank, Emanuel L. Rouvelas)*
Tri-City Industrial Development Council *(Tim L. Peckinpaugh)*
United States Cruises, Inc. *(John L. Bloom, William N. Myhre)*
University of Washington *(Susan B. Geiger, Lloyd Meeds)*
Westinghouse Hanford Co. *(Tim L. Peckinpaugh)*
Wickes Manufacturing Co. *(Richard L. Barnes, Craig J. Gehring)*

PRESTON, Leigh Anne
Newell-Payne Companies, Inc.
2011 Eye St., N.W., 5th Floor, Washington, DC 20006
Telephone: (202) 223-3217
Background: Serves as Acting Exec. Director, Truck Renting and Leasing Ass'n.
Clients:
Truck Renting and Leasing Ass'n

PRESTOWITZ, Clyde, Jr.
President, Economic Strategy Institute
1100 Connecticut Ave., N.W. Suite 330, Washington, DC 20036
Telephone: (202) 728-0993
Background: Former Counselor on Japanese affairs, U.S. Department of Commerce, 1983-86.

PRETANIK, J. Stephen
Director of Science and Technology, Nat'l Broiler Council
1155 15th St., N.W. Suite 614, Washington, DC 20005
Telephone: (202) 296-2622

PRETTYMAN, E. Barrett, Jr.
Hogan and Hartson
555 13th St., N.W., Suite 1200, Washington, DC 20004-1109
Telephone: (202) 637-5600
Background: Law Clerk to U.S. Supreme Court Justices Robert Jackson (1953-54), Felix Frankfurter (1954-55) and John Harlan (1955). Special Assistant to the Attorney General of the U.S.(1963) and to the White House (1963-64). Special Counsel to the House of Representatives Committee on Standards of Official Conduct, 1980-82.

Clients:
Denver and Rio Grande Western Railroad Co.

PRICE, Bill
Director, World Peacemakers
2025 Massachusetts Ave., N.W., Washington, DC 20036
Telephone: (202) 265-7582

PRICE, Bill
Cong Liaison Officer, DEPARTMENT OF COMMERCE
14th and Constitution Ave. S.W., Washington, DC 20230
Telephone: (202) 377-5485

PRICE, Charles F.
Linton, Mields, Reisler and Cottone
1225 Eye St., N.W., Suite 300, Washington, DC 20005
Telephone: (202) 682-3901
Clients:
Nat'l Ass'n of Activity Professionals

PRICE, Gary W.
Director, Government Relations, American College of Radiology
1891 Preston White Drive, Reston, VA 22091
Telephone: (703) 648-8900

PRICE, Harold
National V. President, Nat'l Ass'n of Retired Federal Employees
1533 New Hampshire Ave., N.W., Washington, DC 20036
Telephone: (202) 234-0832

PRICE, JoAnn H.
President, Nat'l Ass'n of Investment Companies
1111 14th St., N.W. Suite 700, Washington, DC 20005
Telephone: (202) 289-4336

PRICE, Joseph H.
Gibson, Dunn and Crutcher
1050 Connecticut Ave., N.W. Suite 900, Washington, DC 20036-5303
Telephone: (202) 955-8500
Background: Law Clerk to Supreme Court Justice Hugo L. Black, 1967-68. Vice President for Insurance, Overseas Private Investment Corp., 1971-73.

PRICE, Maria-Helena
Exec. Officer, American Conference of Academic Deans
1818 R St., N.W., Washington, DC 20009
Telephone: (202) 387-3760

PRICE, Randall C.
PAI Management Corp.
5530 Wisconsin Ave., N.W., Suite 1149, Washington, DC 20815
Telephone: (301) 656-4224
Clients:
Phlebology Soc. of America, The

PRICE, William
Acting Exec. Director, Independent Living for the Handicapped
1301 Belmont St., N.W., Washington, DC 20009
Telephone: (202) 797-9803

PRICE, William C.
Counsel, American Insurance Ass'n
1130 Connecticut Ave., N.W., Suite 1000, Washington, DC 20036
Telephone: (202) 828-7100

PRICE, Woodruff M.
Vice President, Government Relations, CSX Corp.
1331 Pennsylvania Ave., N.W., Suite 560, Washington, DC 20004
Telephone: (202) 783-8124
Registered as lobbyist at U.S. Congress.
Background: Executive Director, Nat'l Ass'n of Railroad Passengers, 1969-71. Former Special Assistant to the Secretary of Transportation.

PRIDE, Patricia
Government Relations Manager, Financial Accounting Foundation
1350 Connecticut Ave., N.W. Suite 620, Washington, DC 20036
Telephone: (202) 466-8016
Registered as lobbyist at U.S. Congress.
Background: Also represents the Financial Accounting Standards Board and the Governmental Standards Accounting Board, operating arms of the Financial Accounting Foundation.

PRIEBE, Louis V.
Director, Public Policy, Salt Institute
700 North Fairfax St. Suite 600, Alexandria, VA 22314
Telephone: (703) 549-4648

PRINCE, Benjamin
President, Boeing Computer Support Srvcs, Boeing Computer Services
7980 Boeing Court, CV-83, Vienna, VA 22182
Telephone: (703) 827-4390

PRINCE, Jeffrey
Senior Director, Communications, Nat'l Restaurant Ass'n
1200 17th St., N.W., Washington, DC 20036-3097
Telephone: (202) 331-5900

PRINCETON PUBLIC AFFAIRS GROUP
3333 K St., N.W., Suite 110, Washington, DC 20007
Telephone: (202) 785-2203
Background: A state government relations consulting firm with offices in Princeton, New Jersey and Washington, DC.
Members of firm representing listed organizations:
Florio, Dale J., Partner
McDonough, Peter, Partner

PRINCIPATO, Gregory O.
Director, Programs, Citizens Network for Foreign Affairs
1616 H St., N.W., Washington, DC 20006
Telephone: (202) 639-8889

PRINDLE, William
Sr. Program Manager, Alliance to Save Energy
1725 K St., N.W., Suite 914, Washington, DC 20006
Telephone: (202) 857-0666
Registered as lobbyist at U.S. Congress.

PRINSEN, Martha
Manager, Domestic Policy Issues, Computer and Business Equipment Manufacturers Ass'n
311 First St., N.W. Suite 500, Washington, DC 20001
Telephone: (202) 737-8888
Registered as lobbyist at U.S. Congress.

PRINTZ, Albert C., Jr.
Neill and Co.
815 Connecticut Ave., N.W. Suite 800, Washington, DC 20006
Telephone: (202) 463-8877
Registered as lobbyist at U.S. Congress.
Registered as Foreign Agent: (#3320).
Background: U.S. Department of Health, Education and Welfare, 1961-69. Chief, Federal Activities, Department of Interior, 1969-70. Director, Permit Program, Environmental Protection Agency, 1970-76. Environmental Coordinator, A.I.D., 1976-86.
Clients:
Adobe Forms
AT&T Technologies, Inc.
Rhone-Poulenc Ag Co.

PRIOLEAU, Florence W.
Patton, Boggs and Blow
2550 M St., N.W., Suite 800, Washington, DC 20037
Telephone: (202) 457-6000
Registered as lobbyist at U.S. Congress.
Background: Assistant Director, Domestic Policy Staff, White House, 1979-81. Member, Professional Staff, House of Representatives Committee on Ways and Means, 1976-79.

PRIOR, Paul
Treasurer, United States League of Savings Institutions Savings Assns Political Elections Committee
1709 New York Ave., N.W., Suite 801, Washington, DC 20006
Telephone: (202) 637-8900

PRITCHARD, Paul C.
President, Nat'l Parks and Conservation Ass'n
1015 31st St., N.W., Washington, DC 20007
Telephone: (202) 944-8530

PRITCHARD, Wayne
Research Analyst, Panhandle Eastern Corp.
1025 Connecticut Ave., N.W., Suite 404, Washington, DC 20036

Telephone: (202) 331-8090

PRITCHETT, Jerry C.
Deputy V. President, Mechanical Contractors Ass'n of America
1385 Piccard Drive, Rockville, MD 20850
Telephone: (301) 869-5800

PRITTS, George W., Jr.
Senior Legislative Affairs Specialist, Rockwell Internat'l
1745 Jefferson Davis Hwy. Suite 1200, Arlington, VA 22202
Telephone: (703) 553-6600
Registered as lobbyist at U.S. Congress.

PRITTS, Joy
Environmental Enforcement Attorney, Trial Lawyers for Public Justice
2000 P St., N.W., Suite 611, Washington, DC 20036
Telephone: (202) 463-8600

PROBST, Sydney
Asst. Director, Federal Gov't Relations, Distilled Spirits Council of the United States
1250 Eye St., N.W., Suite 900, Washington, DC 20005
Telephone: (202) 628-3544
Registered as lobbyist at U.S. Congress.

PROCTOR, Stuart E., Jr.
Exec. V. President and CEO, Nat'l Turkey Federation
11319 Sunset Hills Road, Reston, VA 22090
Telephone: (703) 435-7206
Registered as lobbyist at U.S. Congress.
Background: Also serves as Treasurer, Nat'l Turkey Federation Political Action Committee.

PROFESSIONAL LOBBYING AND CONSULTING CENTER
1111 14th St., N.W., Suite 1001, Washington, DC 20005
Telephone: (202) 898-0084
Background: An association of 265 professional lobbyists and consultants with diversified lobbying skills who provide a multi-faceted approach to legislative and regulatory problems faced by business, associations and the general public. Lobbying services include: counseling on lobbying needs and strategy; finding the right professional for lobbying or consulting; drafting and evaluating legislation; providing political and legislative information; building grass-roots programs; establishing political action committees; and lobbying seminars and congressional surveys. Serves the needs of associations, cities and towns, and medium and small corporations requiring Washington representation. G. Wayne Smith serves as Senior V. President, Senate Liaison; Arthur Cameron, Senior V. President, House Liaison; John Gabusi, Senior V. President, Marketing; and John Reed, Senior V. President, International.
Members of firm representing listed organizations:
Campbell, James I. (Jr.), General Counsel
Gabusi, John, Senior V. President, Marketing
Zorack, John L., President and Chairman
Clients:
Campbell-Mithun *(John L. Zorack)*
Federal Express Corp. *(John L. Zorack)*

PROKOP, John A.
President, Independent Liquid Terminals Ass'n
1133 15th St., N.W. Suite 204, Washington, DC 20005
Telephone: (202) 659-2301

PROKOP-SHORT, Susan
Assoc. Dir., Public Policy & Regul. Afts, American Soc. of Internal Medicine
1101 Vermont Ave., N.W. Suite 500, Washington, DC 20005
Telephone: (202) 289-1700

PROSSER, Norville S.
V. President, Sport Fishing Institute
1010 Massachusetts Ave., N.W., Suite 100, Washington, DC 20001
Telephone: (202) 898-0770

PROTHERO, Michael B.
Adjutant General, Military Order of the Purple Heart of the U.S.A.
5413-B Backlick Rd., Springfield, VA 22151
Telephone: (703) 642-5360

PROTHRO, Pamela
Burson-Marsteller
1850 M St., N.W., Suite 900, Washington, DC 20036
Telephone: (202) 833-8550

PROTULIS, Steve
National Coordinator, Nat'l AFL-CIO Retired Workers Program
815 16th St., N.W., Sixth Floor, Washington, DC 20006
Telephone: (202) 637-5124

PROUT, Deborah M.
Director, Department of Public Policy, American College of Physicians
700 13th St., N.W., Suite 250, Washington, DC 20005
Telephone: (202) 393-1650

PROUT, Gerald R.
Director, Regulatory Affairs, FMC Corp.
1627 K St., N.W., Suite 500, Washington, DC 20006
Telephone: (202) 956-5200
Registered as lobbyist at U.S. Congress.

PROVORNY, Frederick A.
Provorny, Jacoby & Robinson
1350 Connecticut Ave., Suite 502, Washington, DC 20036
Telephone: (202) 223-4200
Clients:
Mycogen Corp.

PROVORNY, JACOBY & ROBINSON
1350 Connecticut Ave., Suite 502, Washington, DC 20036
Telephone: (202) 223-4200
Members of firm representing listed organizations:
Jacoby, Paul B.
Background: Staff Counsel, Office of the Chairman, Occupational Safety and Health Review Commission, 1972-76.
Provorny, Frederick A.
Clients:
Mycogen Corp. *(Paul B. Jacoby, Frederick A. Provorny)*

PROWITT, Nancy Gibson
Alcalde & Rousselot
1901 North Fort Myer Dr., Suite 1204, Rosslyn, VA 22209
Telephone: (703) 841-0626
Clients:
Alliance for Clean Energy (ACE)

PROWITT, Peter D.
Director, Government Affairs, American President Companies
1101 17th St., N.W. Suite 400, Washington, DC 20036
Telephone: (202) 331-1424
Registered as lobbyist at U.S. Congress.

PRUITT, James C.
V. President, Washington Office, Texaco U.S.A.
1050 17th St., N.W., Suite 500, Washington, DC 20036
Telephone: (202) 331-1427
Registered as lobbyist at U.S. Congress.

PRUITT, Steven
Legislative Consultant, Laxalt, Washington, Perito & Dubuc
1120 Connecticut Ave., N.W., Suite 1000, Washington, DC 20036
Telephone: (202) 857-4000
Background: Special Assistant to Senator Howard Metzenbaum, (D-OH), 1977-79. Staff Director, Census and Population Subcommittee, House Committeee on Post Office and Civil Service, 1984. Exec. Director, House Committee on the Budget, 1985-88.

PRUTTING, Janmarie
Asst. V.P. & Mgr., Internat'l Gov't Aff., Coca-Cola Co.
1627 K St., N.W., Suite 800, Washington, DC 20006
Telephone: (202) 466-5310

PRYTULA, George
Director, Grumman Corp.
1000 Wilson Blvd., Suite 2800, Arlington, VA 22209-2280
Telephone: (703) 875-8412

PUBLIC AFFAIRS GROUP, INC.
1629 K St., N.W., Suite 1100, Washington, DC 20006
Telephone: (202) 785-6713
Members of firm representing listed organizations:
Boege, Robert S., Consultant
Background: Former Associate Director, White House Conference on Small Business.

Fraser, Edie, President and CEO
Background: Government service, 1965-73.
Hayden, Samuel, Senior Counsel, International
Vaughn, Cindy, Executive Assistant
Clients:
Ass'n of the Wall and Ceiling Industries-Internat'l *(Edie Fraser)*
Braddock Communications *(Robert S. Boege, Edie Fraser)*
Center for the Study of the Presidency *(Edie Fraser)*
Community Foundation of Greater Washington *(Edie Fraser)*
MTI Export Management, Inc. *(Robert S. Boege, Edie Fraser)*
Novophalt America, Inc. *(Edie Fraser)*
STRATCO, Inc. *(Robert S. Boege, Edie Fraser)*
Strategic Leadership, Inc. *(Robert S. Boege, Edie Fraser)*
Youth in Philanthropy *(Edie Fraser)*

PUBLIC AFFAIRS SERVICES, INC.
1155 15th St., N.W., Suite 710, Washington, DC 20005
Telephone: (202) 659-9101
Members of firm representing listed organizations:
Hagerty, Kenneth C. O.
Clients:
Nat'l Venture Capital Ass'n *(Kenneth C. O. Hagerty)*

PUCCIANO, John G.
President, Ass'n of Independent Colleges and Schools
One Dupont Circle, N.W., Suite 350, Washington, DC 20036
Telephone: (202) 659-2460
Background: Former Deputy Assistant Secretary of Education.

PUCIE, Charles R., Jr.
Sr. V.P., Grp. Dir., Corp & Int'l Couns., Hill and Knowlton Public Affairs Worldwide
Washington Harbour, 901 31st St., N.W., Washington, DC 20007
Telephone: (202) 333-7400
Registered as lobbyist at U.S. Congress.
Registered as Foreign Agent: (#3301).
Clients:
Bureau National Interprofessionel du Cognac
Turkey, Embassy of
Turkey, Government of
Yemen Arab Republic, Government of

PUGH, Keith E., Jr.
Howrey and Simon
1730 Pennsylvania Ave., N.W., Washington, DC 20006-4793
Telephone: (202) 783-0800
Clients:
Heinz Co., H. J.
Hershey Foods Corp.
Royal Dutch Shell Group
Sun Refining and Marketing Co.

PUGH, Theresa
Director, Environmental Quality, Nat'l Ass'n of Manufacturers
1331 Pennsylvania Ave., N.W. Suite 1500 North, Washington, DC 20004-1703
Telephone: (202) 637-3000
Registered as lobbyist at U.S. Congress.

PULIDO, Anna
Braun & Company
1201 Connecticut Ave., N.W. Suite 300, Washington, DC 20036
Telephone: (202) 835-8880

PULIZZI, Philip N., Jr.
Director - Legislative Affairs, Bethlehem Steel Corp.
1667 K St., N.W., Suite 600, Washington, DC 20006
Telephone: (202) 775-6200
Registered as lobbyist at U.S. Congress.

PULLEN, David E.
Director, Public Affairs, Manville Corp.
1625 K St., N.W., Suite 750, Washington, DC 20006
Telephone: (202) 785-4940
Registered as lobbyist at U.S. Congress.

PULLEY, Brenda A.
Exec. Director, Nat'l Ass'n of Solvent Recyclers
1333 New Hampshire Ave., N.W., Suite 1100, Washington, DC 20036
Telephone: (202) 463-6956
Background: Legislative Assistant to Cong. Ike Skelton (D-MO), 1980-82, 1988-89; Legislative Ass't, Small Business Subcommittee on Energy, Environment, and Safety, 1983-85; Small Business Sub Committee on Exports and Special Problems, 1985-87.

PULLIAM, Jennifer L.
Transportation Liaison, Kentucky, Commonwealth of
400 N. Capitol St., N.W., Suite 330, Washington, DC 20001
Telephone: (202) 624-7741

PUMP, Ronald E.
Federal Gov't Affrs. Director & Attorney, AT&T
Suite 1000, 1120 20th St., N.W., Washington, DC 20036
Telephone: (202) 457-3872

PURCELL, Donald E.
President, Portable Power Equipment Manufacturers Ass'n
4720 Montgomery Lane, Suite 812, Bethesda, MD 20814
Telephone: (301) 652-0774
Registered as lobbyist at U.S. Congress.

PURCELL, Graham B., Jr.
Of Counsel, Bishop, Cook, Purcell & Reynolds
1400 L St., N.W., Washington, DC 20005-3502
Telephone: (202) 371-5700
Registered as lobbyist at U.S. Congress.
Registered as Foreign Agent: (#3050).
Background: Former Member, U.S. House of Representatives (D-TX), and former Chairman, House Committee on Agriculture.
Clients:
Colonial Sugar Refineries, Ltd.

PURCELL, John R.
V. President, Giuffrida Associates, Inc.
204 E St., N.E., Washington, DC 20002
Telephone: (202) 547-6340
Registered as lobbyist at U.S. Congress.
Clients:
Nat'l Frozen Food Ass'n

PURCELL, Thomas W.
Director, Environmental Programs, Printing Industries of America
1730 North Lynn St., Arlington, VA 22209
Telephone: (703) 841-8100
Registered as lobbyist at U.S. Congress.

PURVIS, Sue
Federal Affairs Representative, Florida Power Corp.
1725 K St., N.W., Suite 414, Washington, DC 20006
Telephone: (202) 429-9824
Registered as lobbyist at U.S. Congress.

PUTNAM, Earle W.
General Counsel, Amalgamated Transit Union
5025 Wisconsin Ave., N.W., Washington, DC 20016
Telephone: (202) 537-1645
Background: Nat'l Labor Relations Board, 1958-1962.

PUTNAM, Mark C.
Creative Director, Fenn & King Communications
1043 Cecil Place, N.W., Washington, DC 20007
Telephone: (202) 337-6995

PYLE & ASSOCIATES, Robert N.
3222 N St., N.W., Washington, DC 20007
Telephone: (202) 333-8190
Background: A public affairs representation firm.
Members of firm representing listed organizations:
Pyle, Nicholas A.
Pyle, Robert N., President
Background: Seves as President, Independent Bakers Ass'n.
Stoudt, Ashley
Organizations represented:
Accion Medica
ASA Limited
BAKE PAC
Barlow Corp., The
Cathy's Brownies
Elkem Metals Co.

Home Automation Ass'n *(Nicholas A. Pyle)*
Home Oxygen Systems, Inc.
Independent Bakers Ass'n *(Robert N. Pyle)*
Kier English Confectionery, Josephine
Long Co. Bakery Cooperative, The W. E.
Mary Jane Bakeries
Nat'l Council of Career Women *(Ashley Stoudt)*
Nat'l Grape Growers Cooperative
Ort's, Inc. *(Robert N. Pyle)*
Recontec
Refractory Metals Ass'n
Rowley-Scher Reprographics, Inc.
Stratcor *(Robert N. Pyle)*
Tasty Kake, Inc.
Van Eck Funds
Welch's Foods, Inc. *(Robert N. Pyle)*

PYLE, Cassandra A.
Exec. Director, Council for the Internat'l Exchange of Scholars
3400 International Dr., N.W. Suite M-500, Washington, DC 20008
Telephone: (202) 686-4000

PYLE, Howard
Director, Federal Relations, Houston Power and Lighting Co.
1050 17th St., N.W. Suite 550, Washington, DC 20036
Telephone: (202) 467-5040
Registered as lobbyist at U.S. Congress.
Background: Also represents the parent company, Houston Industries, and serves as Treasurer, Western Coal Traffic League Political Action Committee.

PYLE, Nicholas A.
Pyle & Associates, Robert N.
3222 N St., N.W., Washington, DC 20007
Telephone: (202) 333-8190
Organizations represented:
Home Automation Ass'n

PYLE, Robert N.
President, Pyle & Associates, Robert N.
3222 N St., N.W., Washington, DC 20007
Telephone: (202) 333-8190
Registered as lobbyist at U.S. Congress.
Background: Seves as President, Independent Bakers Ass'n.
Organizations represented:
Independent Bakers Ass'n
Ort's, Inc.
Stratcor
Welch's Foods, Inc.

PYLPEC, Nestor N.
V. President, Industry Services, Air Transport Ass'n of America
1709 New York Ave., N.W., Washington, DC 20006-5206
Telephone: (202) 626-4000

QUADRINO, George A.
Warren and Associates
1100 Connecticut Ave., N.W. Suite 440, Washington, DC 20036
Telephone: (202) 293-2165
Clients:
ABC Containerline, N.V.
Barber Blue Sea Line
East Asiatic Co. Ltd.
Hapag-Lloyd AG
Korea Maritime Transport Co.
Mitsui O.S.K. Lines, Ltd.
Nippon Yusen Kaisha (NYK) Line

QUALLS, John
V. President, GRC Economics Group, Hill and Knowlton Public Affairs Worldwide
Washington Harbour, 901 31st St., N.W., Washington, DC 20007
Telephone: (202) 333-7400
Clients:
Citicorp Acceptance Corp.

QUARLES, James L.
Senior Partner, Hale and Dorr
1455 Pennsylvania Ave., N.W. Suite 1000, Washington, DC 20004
Telephone: (202) 393-0800
Registered as lobbyist at U.S. Congress.
Clients:

Mashpee, Massachusetts, Town of

QUARLES, John R., Jr.
Morgan, Lewis and Bockius
1800 M St., N.W., Washington, DC 20036
Telephone: (202) 467-7000
Registered as lobbyist at U.S. Congress.
Clients:
Nat'l Environmental Development Ass'n
Ralston Purina Co.

QUARLES, Steven P.
Crowell and Moring
1001 Pennsylvania Ave., N.W., Washington, DC 20004-2505
Telephone: (202) 624-2500
Registered as lobbyist at U.S. Congress.
Background: Deputy Under Secretary, Department of the Interior, 1979-81.
Clients:
American Forest Resource Alliance
Burlington Resources, Inc.
Cook Inlet Region Inc.
North Miami, City of

QUASHA, WESSELY & SCHNEIDER
1150 17th St., N.W., Suite 400, Washington, DC 20036
Telephone: (202) 293-5304
Members of firm representing listed organizations:
Schneider, Thomas J.
Clients:
AFL-CIO Maritime Committee *(Thomas J. Schneider)*

QUASNEY, Tom
Manager, Advanced Unmanned Systems, Canadair Challenger, Inc. Advanced Unmanned Systems Directorate
1215 Jefferson Davis Highway Suite 901, Arlington, VA 22202
Telephone: (703) 486-5850

QUEALY, Patricia A.
Special Counsel, Eckert Seamans Cherin & Mellott
1818 N St., N.W., Suite 700, Washington, DC 20036
Telephone: (202) 452-1074
Registered as lobbyist at U.S. Congress.
Background: Counsel, 1980-81; Deputy Chief Counsel, 1982-85; and Chief Counsel, 1986-89, U.S. House of Representatives Committee on the Budget.
Clients:
Blockbuster Entertainment Corp.
Blue Cross and Blue Shield Ass'n
Continental Medical Systems, Inc.

QUEEN, Lillian
Legislative Dir., Office of Soc. Devel., Archdiocese of Washington
Box 29260, Washington, DC 20017
Telephone: (301) 853-3800
Registered as lobbyist at U.S. Congress.

QUEHL, Dr. Gary
President, Council for Advancement and Support of Education
11 Dupont Circle Suite 400, Washington, DC 20036
Telephone: (202) 328-5900

QUICK, FINAN AND ASSOCIATES
1133 21st. N.W. Suite 200, Washington, DC 20036
Telephone: (202) 223-4044
Members of firm representing listed organizations:
Finan, William F.
Background: Former Special Assistant to the Undersecretary of Commerce for International Trade.

QUIGGLE, James
Director, Public Relations, Nat'l Ass'n of Professional Insurance Agents
400 North Washington St., Alexandria, VA 22314
Telephone: (703) 836-9340

QUIGLEY, Thomas J.
Squire, Sanders and Dempsey
1201 Pennsylvania Ave., N.W. P.O. Box 407, Washington, DC 20044
Telephone: (202) 626-6600
Clients:
Belgian American Chamber of Commerce

QUINLAN, Pierce A.
Exec. V. President, Nat'l Alliance of Business
1201 New York Ave., N.W., Suite 700, Washington, DC 20005
Telephone: (202) 289-2888

QUINLAN, William A.
3045 Riva Road, Riva, MD 21140
Telephone: (301) 261-4294
Background: An attorney at law. Served with the National Recovery Administration, 1933-35.
Organizations represented:
Retail Bakers of America

QUINN, Harold P.
Counsel & Dir., Surface Mining & Leasing, Nat'l Coal Ass'n
1130 17th St., N.W., Washington, DC 20036
Telephone: (202) 463-2636
Registered as lobbyist at U.S. Congress.

QUINN, Dr. Jarus W.
Exec. Director, Optical Soc. of America
1816 Jefferson Place, N.W., Washington, DC 20036
Telephone: (202) 223-8130

QUINN, John J.
Senior V. President, Ansell Inc.
1001 Pennsylvania Ave., N.W. Suite 790 North, Washington, DC 20004
Telephone: (202) 783-2655
Registered as lobbyist at U.S. Congress.

QUINN, John M.
Arnold & Porter
1200 New Hampshire Ave., N.W., Washington, DC 20036
Telephone: (202) 872-6700
Registered as lobbyist at U.S. Congress.
Registered as Foreign Agent: (#1750).
Background: Chief Legislative Assistant, Senator Floyd Haskell, 1974-75. Special Counsel, Senate Select Committee on Nutrition and Human Needs, 1976.
Clients:
Arnold & Porter Political Action Committee
Earthquake Project, The
Grain and Feed Trade Ass'n, The
Internat'l Commodities Clearing House, Ltd.
London Commodity Exchange Co., Ltd.
State Farm Insurance Cos.

QUINN, Patrick H.
Assoc Admin, Cong and Legis Affrs, ENVIRONMENTAL PROTECTION AGENCY
401 M St., S.W., Washington, DC 20460
Telephone: (202) 382-5200

QUINN, Paul S.
Wilkinson, Barker, Knauer and Quinn
1735 New York Ave., N.W., Suite 600, Washington, DC 20006
Telephone: (202) 783-4141
Registered as lobbyist at U.S. Congress.
Background: Legislative Assistant to Senator Claiborne Pell of Rhode Island, 1961-62. Member of Democratic Senatorial Campaign Committee Leadership Circle and Business Roundtable since 1983.
Clients:
Security Pacific Nat'l Bank
Solano Water Authority

QUINN, Thomas H.
O'Connor & Hannan
1919 Pennsylvania Ave., N.W., Suite 800, Washington, DC 20006
Telephone: (202) 887-1400
Registered as lobbyist at U.S. Congress.
Registered as Foreign Agent: (#2972).
Background: Attorney, Office of the Controller of the Currency, U.S. Treasury Department, 1963-1967. Member, U.S. Government Board for Internat'l Broadcasting, 1974-80.
Clients:
American Institute of Certified Public Accountants
American Soc. of Cataract and Refractive Surgery
China External Trade Development Council
Forstmann, Little & Co.
Healthcare Financing Study Group

QUINN, Thomas H. (Cont'd)
Morgan Grenfell and Co., Ltd.
Nat'l Apartment Ass'n
Nat'l Club Ass'n
Pacific Telesis Group-Washington
Perpetual Savings Bank
Prudential Insurance Co. of America
Securities Industry Ass'n

QUIRK, Daniel
Exec. Director, Nat'l Ass'n of State Units on Aging
2033 K St., N.W. Suite 304, Washington, DC 20006
Telephone: (202) 785-0707

QUIRK, Sherry A.
Verner, Liipfert, Bernhard, McPherson and Hand, Chartered
901 15th St., N.W., Suite 700, Washington, DC 20005
Telephone: (202) 371-6000
Registered as lobbyist at U.S. Congress.
Registered as Foreign Agent: (#3712).

QUIST, Earl C.
State Government Affairs Manager, Toyota Motor Sales, U.S.A.
1850 M St., N.W., Suite 600, Washington, DC 20036
Telephone: (202) 775-1700
Registered as lobbyist at U.S. Congress.

QUIST, Janet
Legislative Counsel, Nat'l League of Cities
1301 Pennsylvania Ave., N.W., Washington, DC 20004
Telephone: (202) 626-3000
Background: Former Legislative Assistant to Rep. Nancy Johnson (R-CT).

RAAB, George Gregory
Director, Public Affairs, Medtronic, Inc.
2000 L St., N.W., Suite 200, Washington, DC 20036
Telephone: (202) 293-7035
Registered as lobbyist at U.S. Congress.

RAABE, Mark J.
Exec. Director & Counsel, Gov't Rtns., Merck and Co.
1615 L St., N.W., Suite 1320, Washington, DC 20036
Telephone: (202) 833-8205
Registered as lobbyist at U.S. Congress.

RABBEN, Robert G.
Asst Gen Couns, Legis, DEPARTMENT OF ENERGY
1000 Independence Ave., S.W., Washington, DC 20585
Telephone: (202) 586-6718

RABEL, Theresa
Director, Government Relations, Nat'l Ass'n of Broadcasters
1771 N St., N.W., Washington, DC 20036
Telephone: (202) 429-5300
Registered as lobbyist at U.S. Congress.
Background: Former aide to Sen. Jennings Randolph (D-WV).

RABIN, Ken
Sr. V.P. & Nat'l Pract. Dir, Health Care, Hill and Knowlton Public Affairs Worldwide
Washington Harbour, 901 31st St., N.W., Washington, DC 20007
Telephone: (202) 333-7400
Clients:
Boots Co.
Chugai Pharmaceutical Co., Ltd.
Intermedics, Inc.
Merck and Co.
Nat'l Cancer Institute
Nat'l Institute on Mental Health
Wyeth-Ayerst Internat'l, Inc.

RABIN, Philip
Public Education Director, Paralyzed Veterans of America
801 18th St., N.W., Washington, DC 20006
Telephone: (202) 872-1300

RABIN, Steve
President, Powell, Adams & Rinehart
1901 L St., N.W., 3rd Floor, Washington, DC 20036
Telephone: (202) 466-7590
Registered as lobbyist at U.S. Congress.

RABINOVITZ, Bruce H.
Ginsburg, Feldman and Bress
1250 Connecticut Ave., N.W. Suite 800, Washington, DC 20036
Telephone: (202) 637-9000
Background: Attorney-Advisor, Procurement Division, General Services Administration, 1971-72. Rates and Agreements Division, Office of General Counsel, Civil Aeronautics Board, 1972-76.

RABINOWITZ, Julie M.
Groom and Nordberg
1701 Pennsylvania Ave., N.W., Suite 1200, Washington, DC 20006
Telephone: (202) 857-0620
Registered as lobbyist at U.S. Congress.
Clients:
True Oil Co.

RABON-SUMMERS, Kathy
Director, Industry Studies, Investment Company Institute
1600 M St., N.W. Suite 600, Washington, DC 20036
Telephone: (202) 293-7700
Background: Formerly employed at the Securities and Exchange Commission.

RABOY, David G.
Cheif Economic Consultant, Patton, Boggs and Blow
2550 M St., N.W., Suite 800, Washington, DC 20037
Telephone: (202) 457-6000
Background: Former Legislative Director for Senator William V. Roth, Jr. (R-DE).

RACLIN, Victoria R.
Keck, Mahin and Cate
1201 New York Ave., N.W., Penthouse Suite, Washington, DC 20005
Telephone: (202) 347-7006
Registered as lobbyist at U.S. Congress.

RADD, Anne
Exec. Vice President, Nat'l Ass'n for Human Development
1424 16th St., N.W., Suite 102, Washington, DC 20036
Telephone: (202) 328-2191

RADECIC, Peri Jude
Lobbyist, Nat'l Gay and Lesbian Task Force
1517 U St., N.W., Washington, DC 20009
Telephone: (202) 332-6483
Registered as lobbyist at U.S. Congress.

RADER, Nancy
Energy Policy Analyst, Public Citizen
2000 P St., N.W., Suite 610, Washington, DC 20036
Telephone: (202) 293-9142

RADER, Robert M.
Conner and Wetterhahn, P.C.
1747 Pennsylvania Ave., N.W. Suite 1050, Washington, DC 20006
Telephone: (202) 833-3500
Background: Trial Attorney, Civil Division, U.S. Department of Justice, 1973-78.
Clients:
U.S. Ecology

RADEWAGEN, Fred
Pacific Islands Washington Office
1615 New Hampshire Ave., N.W., Suite 400, Washington, DC 20009-9998
Telephone: (202) 387-8100
Background: Director, Pacific Islands Washington Office. Former employee, U.S. Department of Interior, 1969-75.
Clients:
American Samoa, Government of

RADFORD, Barbara
Exec. Director, Nat'l Abortion Federation
1436 U St., N.W., Suite 103, Washington, DC 20009
Telephone: (202) 667-5881

RADIN, Alex
President, Radin & Associates, Inc.
1200 New Hampshire Ave., N.W. Suite 507, Washington, DC 20036
Telephone: (202) 785-7213
Registered as lobbyist at U.S. Congress.
Clients:
Northwest Public Power Ass'n

Tennessee Valley Public Power Ass'n
Washington Public Power Supply System (WPPSS)
Washington Public Utility Districts Ass'n

RADIN & ASSOCIATES, INC.
1200 New Hampshire Ave., N.W. Suite 507, Washington, DC 20036
Telephone: (202) 785-7213
Registered as lobbyist at U.S. Congress.
Background: A firm consulting on government energy policy.
Members of firm representing listed organizations:
Radin, Alex, President
Clients:
Northwest Public Power Ass'n *(Alex Radin)*
Tennessee Valley Public Power Ass'n *(Alex Radin)*
Washington Public Power Supply System (WPPSS) *(Alex Radin)*
Washington Public Utility Districts Ass'n *(Alex Radin)*

RADONSKI, Gilbert C.
President, Sport Fishing Institute
1010 Massachusetts Ave., N.W., Suite 100, Washington, DC 20001
Telephone: (202) 898-0770

RADZIEWICZ, W. A.
V. President, Brotherhood of Railroad Signalmen
400 First St., N.W. Suite 708, Washington, DC 20001
Telephone: (202) 628-5935
Registered as lobbyist at U.S. Congress.

RAE, Mark N.
Stroock & Stroock & Lavan
1150 17th St., N.W. Sixth Floor, Washington, DC 20036
Telephone: (202) 452-9250
Registered as lobbyist at U.S. Congress.
Background: Attorney, Office of General Counsel, Commodity Futures Trading Commission, 1977-81.
Clients:
Goldman, Sachs and Co.

RAE, Tess A.
Federal Legislative Representative, American Council of Life Insurance
1001 Pennsylvania Ave., N.W., Washington, DC 20004-2599
Telephone: (202) 624-2112
Registered as lobbyist at U.S. Congress.

RAFFAELLI, John D.
McAuliffe, Kelly, Raffaelli & Siemens
1341 G St., N.W. Suite 200, Washington, DC 20005
Telephone: (202) 783-1800
Registered as lobbyist at U.S. Congress.
Registered as Foreign Agent: (#4332).
Background: Tax and Trade Counsel to Senator Lloyd Bentsen (D-TX), 1980-84.
Clients:
Browning-Ferris Industries (D.C.), Inc.
Council of South Texas Economic Progress
Dallas/Fort Worth RAILTRAN
Dean Witter Realty
Lloyd's U.S.
Nat'l Telephone Services, Inc.
Philip Morris Cos., Inc.
Philip Morris Management Corp.
Turkey, Government of

RAFFENSPERGER, Juliette
Associate, Dutko & Associates
412 First St., S.E. Suite 100, Washington, DC 20003
Telephone: (202) 484-4884
Registered as lobbyist at U.S. Congress.
Background: Former Professional Staff member, Senate Commerce Committee, 1984-87.

RAFFERTY, Ellen M.
Cong Liaison Specialist, FEDERAL COMMUNICATIONS COMMISSION
1919 M St., N.W., Washington, DC 20554
Telephone: (202) 632-6405

RAFSHOON, Jerry
Senior CommuniationS Consultant, Powell, Adams & Rinehart
1901 L St., N.W., 3rd Floor, Washington, DC 20036

Telephone: (202) 466-7590
Registered as lobbyist at U.S. Congress.

RAGAN AND MASON
1156 15th St., N.W., Suite 800, Washington, DC 20005
Telephone: (202) 296-4750
Members of firm representing listed organizations:
  Ragan, William F.
  Shea, Edward M.
Clients:
  American Bureau of Shipping *(William F. Ragan)*
  American Ship Building Co. *(William F. Ragan)*
  Bermuda, Government of *(William F. Ragan)*
  Marco Shipyard - Seattle *(William F. Ragan)*
  Nat'l Bulk Carriers *(William F. Ragan)*
  Ponce, Puerto Rico, Port of *(Edward M. Shea)*
  Reynolds Tobacco Co., R. J. *(William F. Ragan)*
  RJR Nabisco Washington, Inc.
  Sea-Land Service, Inc. *(William F. Ragan)*
  Security Pacific Nat'l Bank
  Security Pacific Nat'l Leasing
  Stimson Lumber Co. *(William F. Ragan)*
  Territorial Savings and Loan Ass'n *(William F. Ragan)*
  United States Telephone Ass'n *(William F. Ragan)*

RAGAN, Robert H.
Manager, Nat'l Security & Space Programs, Bechtel Group, Inc.
1620 Eye St., N.W., Suite 703, Washington, DC 20006
Telephone: (202) 393-4747

RAGAN, William F.
Ragan and Mason
1156 15th St., N.W., Suite 800, Washington, DC 20005
Telephone: (202) 296-4750
Registered as lobbyist at U.S. Congress.
Registered as Foreign Agent: (#1678).
Clients:
  American Bureau of Shipping
  American Ship Building Co.
  Bermuda, Government of
  Marco Shipyard - Seattle
  Nat'l Bulk Carriers
  Reynolds Tobacco Co., R. J.
  Sea-Land Service, Inc.
  Stimson Lumber Co.
  Territorial Savings and Loan Ass'n
  United States Telephone Ass'n

RAGLAND, James W.
Economic Analyst, Arabian American Oil Co.
1667 K St., N.W., Suite 1200, Washington, DC 20006
Telephone: (202) 223-7750

RAGONESE, Clifford
Assistant Exec. Director, United States Nat'l Committee for Pacific Economic Cooperation
1755 Massachusetts Ave., N.W., Suite 420, Washington, DC 20036
Telephone: (202) 745-7444

RAHAL, Pierre
Director of Communications, DSP Internat'l Consultants
777 14th St., N.W., Suite 700, Washington, DC 20005
Telephone: (202) 638-1789
Clients:
  Ass'n for Research on Cancer

RAHALL, Tanya A.
Exec. Director, American Task Force for Lebanon
2550 M St., N.W., Suite 305, Washington, DC 20037
Telephone: (202) 223-9333
Registered as lobbyist at U.S. Congress.

RAHN, Dr. Richard W.
V. President and Chief Economist, Chamber of Commerce of the U.S.A.
1615 H St., N.W., Washington, DC 20062
Telephone: (202) 659-6160
Registered as lobbyist at U.S. Congress.
Background: Serves also as Exec. V. President, Nat'l Chamber Foundation.

RAILSBACK, Thomas F.
Graham and James
2000 M St., N.W., Suite 700, Washington, DC 20036
Telephone: (202) 463-0800
Registered as lobbyist at U.S. Congress.

Background: Member, U.S. House of Representatives (R-IL), 1967-82.
Clients:
  American Hawaii Cruises
  Disney Productions, Walt
  Federal Administrative Law Judges' Conference
  Federal Judges Ass'n
  Holland America Line Westours Inc.
  Illinois Health Facilities Authority
  Mutual of Omaha Insurance Companies
  Nat'l Council of U.S. Magistrates
  Sierra Pacific Resources
  Stock Information Group

RAIMAN, Gail A.
V. President, Public Affairs, Nat'l Ass'n of Independent Colleges and Universities
122 C St., N.W. Suite 750, Washington, DC 20001
Telephone: (202) 347-7512

RAINES, Elvoy
Powell, Adams & Rinehart
1901 L St., N.W., 3rd Floor, Washington, DC 20036
Telephone: (202) 466-7590

RAINES, Lisa J.
Director, Government Relations, Industrial Biotechnology Ass'n
1625 K St., N.W., Suite 1100, Washington, DC 20006
Telephone: (202) 857-0244
Registered as lobbyist at U.S. Congress.

RAINEY, Jean
Senior V. President, Edelman, Inc., Daniel J.
1420 K St., N.W., Washington, DC 20005
Telephone: (202) 371-0200
Organizations represented:
  Hall-Kimbrell
  Nat'l Coffee Ass'n
  Nat'l Dairy Promotion and Research Board
  Nat'l Fish and Seafood Promotion Council
  Sugar Ass'n, Inc.

RAINS, Alan T.
Exec. Director, Future Homemakers of America
1910 Association Drive, Reston, VA 22091
Telephone: (703) 476-4900

RAISBECK, Elizabeth L.
Sr. V. Pres., Gov't Rels. & Reg'l Affrs., Nat'l Audubon Soc.
801 Pennsylvania Ave., S.E., Washington, DC 20003
Telephone: (202) 547-9009
Registered as lobbyist at U.S. Congress.
Background: Executive Assistant, 1984-85 and Administrative Assistant, 1985-87 to Rep. Claudine Schneider (R-RI).

RAISH, Leonard R.
Fletcher, Heald and Hildreth
1225 Connecticut Ave., N.W. Suite 400, Washington, DC 20036
Telephone: (202) 828-5700

RAISLER, Kenneth M.
Rogers and Wells
1737 H St., N.W., Washington, DC 20006
Telephone: (202) 331-7760
Clients:
  Futures Industry Ass'n

RAITANO, Ida M.
President, Parkinson Support Groups of America
11376 Cherry Hill Road, Suite 204, Beltsville, MD 20705
Telephone: (301) 937-1545

RALEY, Gordon A.
Ass't Exec. Dir., Government Relations, American Vocational Ass'n
1410 King St., Alexandria, VA 22314
Telephone: (703) 683-3111
Background: Formerly with U.S. House Committee on Education and Labor.

RALL, Lloyd L.
Director, ITEK Washington Operations, Itek Optical Systems
1700 North Moore St. Suite 1910, Arlington, VA 22209
Telephone: (703) 522-2030

RAMMINGER, Scott
Manager, Public Relations, Nat'l Concrete Masonry Ass'n
P.O. Box 781, Herndon, VA 22070
Telephone: (703) 435-4900

RAMONAS, George A.
Associate, Cassidy and Associates, Inc.
655 15th St., N.W., Suite 1100, Washington, DC 20005
Telephone: (202) 347-0773
Registered as lobbyist at U.S. Congress.
Background: Legislative Director to Sen. Pete V. Domenici (R-NM), 1977-85.
Clients:
  Arizona State University
  Atlantic Financial
  NeoRx, Inc.
  University Hospital of Cleveland
  University of Bridgeport
  University of Kentucky Foundation
  University of Utah

RAMSAY, Diana
Legis. Specialist, Legis. & Polit. Affrs, American Occupational Therapy Ass'n
1383 Piccard Drive, Suite 300 P.O. Box 1725, Rockville, MD 20850
Telephone: (301) 948-9626

RAMSEY, Joe F., Jr.
Exec. Director, Nat'l Svc. Fdn., American Veterans of World War II, Korea and Vietnam (AMVETS)
4647 Forbes Blvd., Lanham, MD 20706
Telephone: (301) 459-9600

RAMSEY, Kathleen Marie
V. Pres., Legislation and Administration, Grocery Manufacturers of America
1010 Wisconsin Ave., N.W., Suite 800, Washington, DC 20007
Telephone: (202) 337-9400
Registered as lobbyist at U.S. Congress.

RANBOM, Shepard
Director, Education Projects, Gallagher-Widmeyer Group Inc., The
1110 Vermont Ave., N.W., Suite 1020, Washington, DC 20005
Telephone: (202) 659-1606
Background: Formerly served on the Congressional Advisory Committee on Student Financial Aid.

RAND, Kristen M.
Attorney, Consumers Union of the United States
2001 S St., N.W., Suite 520, Washington, DC 20009
Telephone: (202) 462-6262
Registered as lobbyist at U.S. Congress.

RANDALL, Albert B.
Asst Chief Counsel, Legislation, DEPARTMENT OF TRANSPORTATION - Federal Aviation Administration
800 Independence Ave., S.W., Washington, DC 20591
Telephone: (202) 267-3217

RANDALL, Donald A.
321 D St., N.E., Washington, DC 20002
Telephone: (202) 543-1440
Background: U.S. Senate Judiciary Committee Counsel on Subcommittee on Antitrust and Monopoly, 1967-73. Attorney, Federal Trade Commission, 1961-67.
Organizations represented:
  Automotive Service Ass'n
  Nat'l Independent Dairy-Food Ass'n

RANDALL, Randy
Managing Editor, Washington Inquirer, Council for the Defense of Freedom
1275 K St., N.W., Suite 1150, Washington, DC 20005
Telephone: (202) 789-4294

RANDALL, Robert
President, Alliance for Cannabis Therapeutics
Box 53318, Washington, DC 20009
Telephone: (202) 483-8595
Registered as lobbyist at U.S. Congress.

RANDI, Thomas
V. President, Tuna Research Foundation
1101 17th St., N.W., Suite 609, Washington, DC 20036
Telephone: (202) 857-0610

RANDLETT, R. Ray
Asst Admin, Legis Affrs, AGENCY FOR INTERNAT'L DE-
VELOPMENT
320 21st St., N.W., Washington, DC 20523
Telephone: (202) 647-8264

RANDOLPH, Suzanne
President, Ass'n of Black Psychologists
Box 55999, Washington, DC 20040
Telephone: (202) 722-0808

RANDS, Jeffrey
Asst, Cong Rels, Legis & Cong Rels, DEPARTMENT OF
HOUSING AND URBAN DEVELOPMENT
451 Seventh St., S.W., Washington, DC 20410
Telephone: (202) 755-7380

RANGE, James D.
Staff V. President, Government Affairs, Waste Management, Inc.
1155 Connecticut Ave., N.W., Suite 800, Washington, DC
20036
Telephone: (202) 467-4480
Registered as lobbyist at U.S. Congress.

RANGE, Rebecca G.
Staff V. President, Government Affairs, Texas Air Corp.
901 15th St., N.W. Suite 500, Washington, DC 20005
Telephone: (202) 289-6060
Registered as lobbyist at U.S. Congress.
Background: Formerly headed White House Office of Pub-
lic Liaison, 1987.

RANKIN, Dennis R.
Assistant V. President, McNair Group Inc.
1155 15th St., N.W., Washington, DC 20005
Telephone: (202) 659-8866
Clients:
Defense Group, Inc.
Texas Instruments, Industrial Automation
Westinghouse Environmental Services

RANKIN, Paul W.
President, Hazardous Materials Advisory Council
1012 14th St., N.W. Suite 907, Washington, DC 20005
Telephone: (202) 783-7460

RANKIN, Robert Allen, Jr.
V. President, Corporate Relations, Marriott Corp.
One Marriott Drive, Washington, DC 20058
Telephone: (301) 380-9000

RANSOM, Betty
Program Manager, Nat'l Council on the Aging
600 Maryland Ave., S.W. West Wing 100, Washington, DC
20024
Telephone: (202) 479-1200
Background: Represents the Nat'l Voluntary Organizations
for Independent Living for the Aging.

RANSOPHER, Ivan
Dep Asst Secy, Legislation, DEPARTMENT OF HOUSING
AND URBAN DEVELOPMENT
451 Seventh St., S.W., Washington, DC 20410
Telephone: (202) 755-5005

RAO, Kishore
President & CEO, Services Group, The
1815 N. Lynn St. Suite 200, Arlington, VA 22209
Telephone: (702) 528-7486

RAPHAEL, David M.
Exec. Director, Community Transportation Ass'n of America
725 15th St., N.W. Suite 900, Washington, DC 20005
Telephone: (202) 628-1480

RAPOZA ASSOCIATES, ROBERT A.
122 C St., N.W., Suite 875, Washington, DC 20001
Telephone: (202) 393-5225
Members of firm representing listed organizations:
Kaiman, Sherry F.
Rapoza, Robert A., President
Background: Serves also as Legislative Director, Nat'l
Rural Housing Coalition.
Clients:
Nat'l Rural Health Ass'n *(Sherry F. Kaiman)*

RAPOZA, Robert A.
President, Rapoza Associates, Robert A.
122 C St., N.W., Suite 875, Washington, DC 20001
Telephone: (202) 393-5225
Registered as lobbyist at U.S. Congress.
Background: Serves also as Legislative Director, Nat'l Ru-
ral Housing Coalition.

RASENBERGER, Raymond J.
Zuckert, Scoutt and Rasenberger
888 17th St., N.W., Suite 600, Washington, DC 20006-
3959
Telephone: (202) 298-8660
Registered as lobbyist at U.S. Congress.
Clients:
Nat'l Business Aircraft Ass'n
Nat'l Committee of Cities and States for Airline
Service

RASKIN, Marcus G.
Senior Fellow, Institute for Policy Studies
1601 Connecticut Ave., N.W. 5th Floor, Washington, DC
20009
Telephone: (202) 234-9382

RASKIN, Nancy
Director, Professions Division, United Jewish Appeal Federation of Greater Washington
6101 Montrose Rd., Rockville, MD 20852
Telephone: (301) 230-7200

RASLEY, George K., Jr.
Asst Dir for Legis and Cong Affrs, DEPARTMENT OF IN-
TERIOR - Nat'l Park Service
18th and C Sts., N.W., Washington, DC 20240
Telephone: (202) 343-5883

RASMUSSEN, Dana
Assistant V. Pres. & Attorney, US WEST, Inc.
1020 19th St., N.W., Suite 700, Washington, DC 20036
Telephone: (202) 429-3100

RASSEL, Edith
Research Associate, Economic Policy Institute
1424 16th St., N.W., Suite 501, Washington, DC 20036
Telephone: (202) 667-0400

RATCHFORD, J. Thomas
Associate Exec. Officer, American Ass'n for the Advancement of Science
1333 H St., N.W., Washington, DC 20005
Telephone: (202) 326-6400

RATCHFORD, William R.
Gold and Liebengood, Inc.
1455 Pennsylvania Ave., N.W. Suite 950, Washington, DC
20004
Telephone: (202) 639-8899
Registered as lobbyist at U.S. Congress.
Background: Former U.S. Representative (D-CT).
Clients:
Energy Research Corp.

RATHBUN, Dennis K.
Dir, Cong Affairs, NUCLEAR REGULATORY COMMIS-
SION
1 White Flint North, Rockville, MD 20850
Telephone: (301) 492-1776

RATHBUN, Frank H.
Manager, Public Information, Aluminum Ass'n
900 19th St., N.W., Suite 300, Washington, DC 20006
Telephone: (202) 862-5163

RAU, Michael C.
Senior V. President, Nat'l Ass'n of Broadcasters
1771 N St., N.W., Washington, DC 20036
Telephone: (202) 429-5300

RAUBER, John W., Jr.
Legislative Affairs Director, American Paper Institute
1250 Connecticut Ave., N.W. Suite 210, Washington, DC
20036
Telephone: (202) 463-2420
Registered as lobbyist at U.S. Congress.

RAULSTON, Carol
V. President, Government Affairs, American Paper Institute
1250 Connecticut Ave., N.W. Suite 210, Washington, DC
20036

Telephone: (202) 463-2420
Registered as lobbyist at U.S. Congress.

RAVEN, Robert
Chairman, State and Federal Associates
1101 King St., Suite 600, Alexandria, VA 22314
Telephone: (703) 739-0200
Registered as lobbyist at U.S. Congress.

RAVITZ, Ruth B.
Manager, Legislative Affairs, Aerospace Industries Ass'n
of America
1250 Eye St., N.W., Suite 1100, Washington, DC 20005
Telephone: (202) 371-8400

RAVIV, Sheila
Sr. V. Pres., Dir., Media Relations, Burson-Marsteller
1850 M St., N.W., Suite 900, Washington, DC 20036
Telephone: (202) 833-8550
Clients:
American Podiatric Medical Ass'n
McNeil Consumer Products Co.
Nat'l Urban Coalition
NutraSweet Co.
Shell Chemical Co.

RAVNHOLT, Eiler C.
V. President & Washington Representative, Hawaiian Sug-
ar Planters' Ass'n
1511 K St., N.W., Suite 723, Washington, DC 20005
Telephone: (202) 628-6372
Registered as lobbyist at U.S. Congress.

RAWDING, Nancy
Exec. Director, Nat'l Ass'n of County Health Officials
440 First St., N.W., Washington, DC 20001
Telephone: (202) 783-5550

RAWLS, W. Lee
Partner, Baker, Worthington, Crossley, Stansberry &
Woolf
1001 Pennsylvania Ave., N.W., Suite 1201, Washington,
DC 20004
Telephone: (202) 347-4360
Registered as lobbyist at U.S. Congress.
Background: Legislative Director and Administrative As-
sistant to Senator Pete Domenici (R-NM), 1975-81,
1982-85.
Clients:
DKT Memorial Fund
Dunigan Companies
Federal Express Corp.
Occidental Petroleum Corp.
Pennzoil Co.
Philip Morris Management Corp.
Public Service Co. of New Mexico
Schering-Plough Corp.
Southern California Edison Co.
Warner-Lambert Co.

RAWSON, Edward
Administrative Director, World Federalist Ass'n
418 Seventh St., S.E., Washington, DC 20003
Telephone: (202) 546-3950
Background: Served with Agency for International Devel-
opment, 1948-76.

RAWSON, W. Randall
Assistant Exec. Director, American Boiler Manufacturers
Ass'n
950 North Glebe Road, Suite 160, Arlington, VA 22203
Telephone: (703) 522-7350
Registered as lobbyist at U.S. Congress.

RAY, Bruce A.
Ray & Company, Bruce
420 C St., N.E., Washington, DC 20002
Telephone: (202) 543-4935
Registered as lobbyist at U.S. Congress.
Organizations represented:
United Gerer Institutions

RAY, Charles G.
Exec. Director, Nat'l Council of Community Mental Health
Centers
12300 Twinbrook Parkway Suite 320, Rockville, MD
20852
Telephone: (301) 984-6200

RAY & COMPANY, Bruce
420 C St., N.E., Washington, DC 20002
Telephone: (202) 543-4935
Members of firm representing listed organizations:
Ray, Bruce A.
Organizations represented:
United Gerer Institutions *(Bruce A. Ray)*

RAY, Dave
Public Relations/Press Secretary, Federation for American Immigration Reform (FAIR)
1666 Connecticut Ave., N.W., Suite 400, Washington, DC 20009
Telephone: (202) 328-7004

RAY, James S.
Connerton, Ray and Simon
1920 L St., N.W., Washington, DC 20036-5004
Telephone: (202) 466-6790

RAY, Jerry
Senior Counsel, Media Relations, Burson-Marsteller
1850 M St., N.W., Suite 900, Washington, DC 20036
Telephone: (202) 833-8550
Background: Former press secretary to Senator Howell Heflin (D-AL).

RAY, Oakley M.
President, American Feed Industry Ass'n
1701 Fort Myer Dr. Suite 1200, Arlington, VA 22209
Telephone: (703) 524-0810

RAYBURN, Dorothy
Bur for Asia and the Near East, AGENCY FOR INTERNAT'L DEVELOPMENT
320 21st St., N.W., Washington, DC 20523
Telephone: (202) 647-8190

RAYBURN, John K.
V. President, Government Programs, Westinghouse Electric Corp.
1801 K St., N.W., Washington, DC 20006
Telephone: (202) 835-2328
Registered as lobbyist at U.S. Congress.

RAYDER, Helene
Manager, Government Affairs, American Express Co.
1020 19th St., N.W., Suite 600, Washington, DC 20036
Telephone: (202) 822-6680
Registered as lobbyist at U.S. Congress.

RAYMER, Steve
Director, News Service, Nat'l Geographic Soc.
1145 17th St., N.W., Washington, DC 20036
Telephone: (202) 857-7000

RAYMOND, David A.
Director, International Programs, ENSERCH Corp.
1025 Connecticut Ave., N.W., Suite 1014, Washington, DC 20036
Telephone: (202) 872-1352
Registered as lobbyist at U.S. Congress.

RAYMOND, John M.
Director of Communications, Washington Gas Light Co.
1100 H St., N.W., Washington, DC 20080
Telephone: (202) 624-6091

RAYMOND, Rosalind Price
Dir., Public Relations & Communications, Sheet Metal and Air Conditioning Contractors' Nat'l Ass'n
8224 Old Courthouse Rd., Vienna, VA 22182
Telephone: (703) 790-9890

RAYMOND, Sharon
Mgr., Member Banker/Grass Roots Program, American Bankers Ass'n
1120 Connecticut Ave., N.W., Washington, DC 20036
Telephone: (202) 663-5000

RAYWID, Alan
Cole, Raywid, and Braverman
1919 Pennsylvania Ave., N.W. Suite 200, Washington, DC 20006
Telephone: (202) 659-9750
Background: Trial Attorney, Admiralty and Shipping Section, U.S. Department of Justice, 1957-63; 1965. Special Assistant to the Assistant Attorney General of the U.S., Civil Division, 1963-66.

RAZZANO, Frank C.
Shea and Gould
1775 Pennsylvania Ave., N.W., Suite 700, Washington, DC 20006
Telephone: (202) 833-9850

RBC ASSOCIATES, INC.
324 Fourth St., N.E., Washington, DC 20002
Telephone: (202) 543-0038
Background: A government relations consulting firm.
Members of firm representing listed organizations:
Chambers, Ray B., Chairman
Background: Administrative Assistant to Rep. Phil Ruppe (R-MI), 1967-71. Deputy Assistant Secretary for Field Administration, U.S. Department of Health, Education and Welfare, 1971-73. Director, Congressional Relations, Department of Transportation, 1973-75.
Hartwell, Keith O., President
Background: Former Administrative Assistant to Rep. Marvin Esch (R-MI), 1971-76. Director, State Senate Legislative Staff, 1978-80.
Clients:
Bangor and Aroostook Railroad *(Ray B. Chambers)*
Chicago and Northwestern Transportation Co. *(Ray B. Chambers)*
Dakota, Minnesota & Eastern *(Keith O. Hartwell)*
Delaware Otsego System *(Ray B. Chambers)*
Genesee and Wyoming Corp. *(Ray B. Chambers)*
Long Island Rail Road Co. *(Ray B. Chambers)*
Pinsly Railroad Co. *(Keith O. Hartwell)*
Regional Railroads of America *(Keith O. Hartwell)*
Turbomeca Engine Corp. *(Keith O. Hartwell)*

RCF GROUP, THE
1200 19th St., N.W. Suite 606, Washington, DC 20036
Telephone: (202) 659-8967
Registered as Foreign Agent: (#4273)
Members of firm representing listed organizations:
Andrae, Charles N. (III), V. President
Background: Former Administrative Assistant to Senator Richard Lugar (R-IN).

REA, Bryce, Jr.
Rea, Cross & Auchincloss
1920 N St., N.W., Suite 420, Washington, DC 20036
Telephone: (202) 785-3700
Background: Counsel, Transportation, Public Utilities and Fuels, Office of Price Stabilization, 1951-53, Antitrust.
Clients:
Middle Atlantic Conference
New England Motor Rate Bureau

REA, CROSS & AUCHINCLOSS
1920 N St., N.W., Suite 420, Washington, DC 20036
Telephone: (202) 785-3700
Members of firm representing listed organizations:
McEligot, Patrick
Rea, Bryce (Jr.)
Background: Counsel, Transportation, Public Utilities and Fuels, Office of Price Stabilization, 1951-53, Antitrust.
Clients:
Middle Atlantic Conference *(Bryce Rea, Jr.)*
New England Motor Rate Bureau *(Patrick McEligot, Bryce Rea, Jr.)*

READ, Todd
Associate, Gilberg & Kurent
1250 I St., N.W. Suite 600, Washington, DC 20005
Telephone: (202) 842-3222

READE, Claire
Arnold & Porter
1200 New Hampshire Ave., N.W., Washington, DC 20036
Telephone: (202) 872-6700
Registered as Foreign Agent: (#1750).
Clients:
Aruba, Government of
ASOCOLFLORES (Colombia Flower Growers Ass'n)
Korea Foreign Trade Ass'n

REAGAN, Joanna E.
Asst. to the Pres. for Gov't Relations, Internat'l Union of Bricklayers and Allied Craftsmen
815 15th St., N.W., 2nd Floor, Washington, DC 20005
Telephone: (202) 783-3788
Registered as lobbyist at U.S. Congress.

REAGAN, Kinsey S.
Kleinfeld, Kaplan and Becker
1140 19th St., N.W., Suite 700, Washington, DC 20036
Telephone: (202) 223-5120
Background: Attorney, U.S. Department of Health and Human Services, 1975-80.
Clients:
SmithKline Animal Health Products
Squibb and Sons, Inc., E. R.

REAL TRENDS
9200 Centerway Road, Gaithersburg, MD 20879
Telephone: (301) 840-6642
Members of firm representing listed organizations:
Nye, Zhi Marie, President
Clients:
Nat'l Military Intelligence Ass'n *(Zhi Marie Nye)*

REAM, Kathleen A.
Head, Dept. of Gov't Rels. & Sci. Policy, American Chemical Soc.
1155 16th St., N.W., Washington, DC 20036
Telephone: (202) 872-4477

REARDON, Mary
Director, Washington Communications, Credit Union Nat'l Ass'n
805 15th St., N.W. Suite 300, Washington, DC 20005
Telephone: (202) 682-4200

REARICK, Linda S.
Tax Legislative Representative, American Bankers Ass'n
1120 Connecticut Ave., N.W., Washington, DC 20036
Telephone: (202) 663-5000
Registered as lobbyist at U.S. Congress.

REAVES, John D.
Baker and Hostetler
1050 Connecticut Ave., N.W. Suite 1100, Washington, DC 20036
Telephone: (202) 861-1500

RECORD, Jeffrey
Sr. Research Fellow, Hudson Institute
4401 Ford Ave. Suite 200, Alexandria, VA 22302
Telephone: (703) 824-2048

RECTOR, Clark E.
Director, Government Relations, American Advertising Federation
1400 K St., N.W., Suite 1000, Washington, DC 20005
Telephone: (202) 898-0089
Registered as lobbyist at U.S. Congress.
Background: Former Legislative Assistant to Rep. Thomas Luken (D-OH).

RECTOR, John M.
V. Pres., Gov't. Affairs & Gen. Counsel, Nat'l Ass'n of Retail Druggists
205 Daingerfield Road, Alexandria, VA 22314
Telephone: (703) 683-8200
Registered as lobbyist at U.S. Congress.
Background: Serves also as contact for Nat'l Ass'n of Pharmacists Political Action Committee (NARD-PAC).

RECTOR, Robert
Policy Analyst, Welfare & Family, Heritage Foundation
214 Massachusetts Ave., N.E., Washington, DC 20002
Telephone: (202) 546-4400

REDDY, BEGLEY AND MARTIN
2033 M St., N.W., Suite 500, Washington, DC 20036
Telephone: (202) 659-5700
Clients:
KIFI
KPAX-TV
KTVH
WBLN
WFBN
WHTN
WJET-TV
WLJC-TV
WNDS
WTWS
WTZH

WASHINGTON REPRESENTATIVES

REDFOOT, Donald L.
Legislative Rep., Federal Affairs, American Ass'n of
Retired Persons
1909 K St., N.W., Washington, DC 20049
Telephone: (202) 872-4700
Registered as lobbyist at U.S. Congress.

REDICKER, Jane
Fleishman-Hillard, Inc
1301 Connecticut Ave., N.W., Washington, DC 20036
Telephone: (202) 659-0330

REDMON, Tim
Director, Regulatory Affairs, Nat'l Ass'n of Medical Equipment Suppliers
625 Slaters Lane, Suite 200, Alexandria, VA 22314
Telephone: (703) 836-6263

REECE, Beverly
Senior Account Supervisor, Hill and Knowlton Public Af-
fairs Worldwide
Washington Harbour, 901 31st St., N.W., Washington, DC
20007
Telephone: (202) 333-7400

REECE, Paul
Exec. Director, Internat'l Military Club Executives Ass'n
1438 Duke St., Alexandria, VA 22314
Telephone: (703) 548-0093

REED, Bruce
Policy Director, Democratic Leadership Council
316 Pennsylvania Ave., S.E., Suite 500, Washington, DC
20003
Telephone: (202) 546-0007
Registered as Foreign Agent: (#000₇)

REED, Campbell
Exec. Dir., Nat'l Commer. B'ldrs Council, Nat'l Ass'n of
Home Builders of the U.S.
15th and M Streets, N.W., Washington, DC 20005
Telephone: (202) 822-0470

REED, David S.
Reed Public Policy
1250 24th St., N.W. Suite 600, Washington, DC 20037
Telephone: (202) 466-0566
Registered as lobbyist at U.S. Congress.
Background: Served in the Federal Communications Com-
mission, 1980-82; in the Executive Office of the Presi-
dent, 1982-86.

REED, Dwight C.
Consultant, Nat'l Soft Drink Ass'n
1101 16th St., N.W., Washington, DC 20036
Telephone: (202) 463-6732
Registered as lobbyist at U.S. Congress.

REED, Jo
Senior Coordinator, American Ass'n of Retired Persons
1909 K St., N.W., Washington, DC 20049
Telephone: (202) 728-4734
Registered as lobbyist at U.S. Congress.

REED, Mary
Legislative Representative, Nat'l Federation of Independent
Business
600 Maryland Ave., S.W., Suite 700, Washington, DC
20024
Telephone: (202) 554-9000
Registered as lobbyist at U.S. Congress.
Background: Former legislative aide to Senator Chic Hecht
(R-NV).

REED, Michael L.
V. President, Government Relations, Pharmaceutical
Manufacturers Ass'n
1100 15th St., N.W., Washington, DC 20005
Telephone: (202) 835-3480
Registered as lobbyist at U.S. Congress.

REED, Pris I.
Administrative Director, American Leprosy Foundation
11600 Nebel St., Suite 210, Rockville, MD 20852
Telephone: (301) 984-1336

REED PUBLIC POLICY
1250 24th St., N.W. Suite 600, Washington, DC 20037
Telephone: (202) 466-0566
Registered as lobbyist at U.S. Congress.
Background: A public policy consultant.

Members of firm representing listed organizations:
Reed, David S.
Background: Served in the Federal Communications
Commission, 1980-82; in the Executive Office of the
President, 1982-86.

REED, Rex H.
Exec. V. Pres., Secy. and Legal Dir., Nat'l Right to Work
Legal Defense Foundation
8001 Braddock Road, Springfield, VA 22160
Telephone: (703) 321-8510

REED SMITH SHAW & MCCLAY
1200 18th St., N.W., Washington, DC 20036
Telephone: (202) 457-6100
Registered as Foreign Agent: (#4227)
Members of firm representing listed organizations:
Bleicher, Beatrice, Counsel, Government Rela-
tions
Buckles, Mary
Colborn, Carol
Evans, David C.
Geoghegan, William A.
Background: Assistant Deputy Attorney General, De-
partment of Justice, 1961-65.
Lawton, Stephan E.
Background: Chief Counsel, Subcommittee on Health
and the Environment, U.S. House of Representatives,
1971-78.
Rowan, Carl (Jr.)
Ryan, T. Timothy (Jr.)
Background: Solicitor of Labor, U.S. Department of
Labor, 1981-83.
Scharff, J. Laurent
St. Ledger-Roty, Judith
Clients:
American Academy of Pediatrics *(Stephan E. Lawton)*
American College of Osteopathic Surgeons *(Ste-
phan E. Lawton)*
Amgen, Inc. *(Mary Buckles, Carol Colborn, Stephan E.
Lawton, T. Timothy Ryan, Jr.)*
Ass'n of Independent Television Stations
Ass'n of Schools of Public Health *(Stephan E. Law-
ton)*
Brick Institute of America *(David C. Evans)*
Building Owners and Managers Ass'n Internat'l
(David C. Evans)
Coalition for Equitable Compensation
Damon Corp.
Dun & Bradstreet *(William A. Geoghegan)*
Genentech, Inc.
Goldman, Sachs and Co. *(T. Timothy Ryan, Jr.)*
Infectious Disease Soc. of America *(Stephan E. Law-
ton)*
Internat'l Telecommunications Satellite Organiza-
tion (INTELSAT) *(T. Timothy Ryan, Jr.)*
Nat'l Ass'n of Dental Laboratories
Nat'l Ass'n of Minority Contractors *(Carl Rowan,
Jr.)*
Nat'l Cellular Resellers Ass'n *(Judith St. Ledger-Roty,
Carl Rowan, Jr.)*
Nat'l Rifle Ass'n of America *(Carl Rowan, Jr.)*
Owens-Illinios *(Beatrice Bleicher)*
Radio-Television News Directors Ass'n *(J. Laurent
Scharff)*
Securities Industry Ass'n *(William A. Geoghegan)*
Soc. of Critical Care Medicine *(Stephan E. Lawton)*

REED, Talmadge
Cong Liaison Officer, DEPARTMENT OF INTERIOR - U.S.
Geological Survey
12201 Sunrise Valley Drive MS 112, Reston, VA 22092
Telephone: (703) 648-4455

REEDER, Joe Robert
Patton, Boggs and Blow
2550 M St., N.W., Suite 800, Washington, DC 20037
Telephone: (202) 457-6000
Registered as lobbyist at U.S. Congress.
Background: Trial Attorney, Litigation Division, Office of
the Army Judge Advocate General, 1976-78. Contract
Appeals Division, Office of Judge Advocate General,
1978-79.
Clients:
Advanced Technology, Inc.
American Congress on Surveying and Mapping
American Logistics Ass'n

Dredging Industry Size Standard Committee
(DISSC)

REEPING, Pauline B.
Director of Public Affairs, New York Shipping Ass'n
6907 Wilson Lane, Bethesda, MD 20817
Telephone: (301) 320-4520
Registered as lobbyist at U.S. Congress.

REES, Jerry
Senior V. President, Nat'l Ass'n of Wheat Growers
415 Second St., N.E. Suite 300, Washington, DC 20002
Telephone: (202) 547-7800
Registered as lobbyist at U.S. Congress.

REES, Joseph M.
FMR Group Inc., The
1000 Potomac St., N.W. Suite 401, Washington, DC
20007
Telephone: (202) 333-2533
Registered as lobbyist at U.S. Congress.
Clients:
Nat'l Coalition of Burn Center Hospitals
United Hospital Fund of New York

REES, Morgan
Policy Plng & Legis Affrs Dep, Civil Wks, DEPARTMENT
OF ARMY
The Pentagon, Washington, DC 20310-0101
Telephone: (202) 697-6767

REES, Susan
Exec. Director, Coalition on Human Needs
1000 Wisconsin Ave., N.W., Washington, DC 20007
Telephone: (202) 342-0726

REESE COMMUNICATIONS COMPANIES
2111 Wilson Ave., Suite 900, Arlington, VA 22201
Telephone: (703) 528-4400
Background: Provides strategic communications consulting,
grassroots organizing and volunteer recruitment designed
to involve a variety of key constituents in critical public
issues. Also provides direct mail and telephone contact
for corporate public affairs and marketing activities.
Works for clients on legislative, regulatory or administrative issues at federal, state and local levels. Additionally
designs innovative commercial direct marketing programs
and corporate communications programs for a variety of
clients. Operates Targeting Systems, Inc., a survey re-
search firm.
Members of firm representing listed organizations:
Bloomberg, Mary Beth, Senior V. President for
Client Services
Background: Senior Special Assistant to the Secretary,
U.S. Department of Health and Human Services,
1983-86.
Buckley, David, Senior Account Executive
Chidester, Becky, V. President for Client Services
Graham, Michael N., Exec. V. President and
COO
Hooley, James L., Senior V. President for Mar-
keting
Background: Assistant to the President, The White
House, 1981-89.
Kopit, Neil R., V. President of Client Services
Mann, Robert W., Senior Associate
Background: Former Administrative Assistant to Rep.
Robert C. Smith (R-NH).
Mitchell, Katherine, Senior Account Executive
Pounian, Lynn C., President and Chief Executive
Officer
Welsh, Charles B., President, Targeting Systems,
Inc.
Background: Also serves as President, Targeting Sys-
tems, Inc.
Clients:
Citizens for Sensible Control of Acid Rain
Electronic Industries Ass'n of Japan
Miller Brewing Co.
Nat'l Ass'n of Securities Dealers (NASDAQ)
Palm-Aire Spa Resort/Katzoff Development
Corp.
Paper Industry of Maine
Philip Morris Cos., Inc.
Philip Morris Internat'l

REESE, J. Mitchell
Consultant - Coal, Chevron, U.S.A.
1700 K St., N.W., Suite 1200, Washington, DC 20006

Telephone: (202) 457-5800
Registered as lobbyist at U.S. Congress.

REESE, Robert S., Jr.
Director, Washington Relations, Philip Morris Management Corp.
1341 G St., N.W., Suite 900, Washington, DC 20005
Telephone: (202) 637-1500
Registered as lobbyist at U.S. Congress.

REESE, William
President, Partners of the Americas
1424 K St., N.W. Suite 700, Washington, DC 20005
Telephone: (202) 628-3300

REEVES, Benjamin F.
Vice President and Managing Director, Burley and Dark Leaf Tobacco Export Ass'n
1100 17th St., N.W., Washington, DC 20036
Telephone: (202) 296-6820
Registered as lobbyist at U.S. Congress.
Background: Exec. Director, Nat'l Cigar Leaf Tobacco Ass'n.

REEVES, Evelyn
President, Nat'l Ass'n of Real Estate Brokers
1629 K St., N.W. Suite 605, Washington, DC 20006
Telephone: (202) 785-4477

REEVES, J. Ronald
V. President, Government Affairs, USAir Group Inc.
2345 Crystal Drive, Arlington, VA 22227
Telephone: (703) 418-5111
Registered as lobbyist at U.S. Congress.

REEVES, Robert
General Counsel, Newbold & Assoc., Bill
1355 Beverly Rd., Suite 200, McLean, VA 22101
Telephone: (703) 243-3100
Registered as lobbyist at U.S. Congress.

REFFALT, Bill
Director, Wildlife Refuge Program, Wilderness Soc.
1400 Eye St., N.W., 10th Floor, Washington, DC 20005
Telephone: (202) 842-3400
Registered as lobbyist at U.S. Congress.

REFFE, Paige E.
Of Counsel, Cutler and Stanfield
1850 M St., N.W. Suite 1000, Washington, DC 20036
Telephone: (202) 822-6400
Background: Special Assistant, Office of Management and Budget, 1977. Special Assistant to the Administrator, General Services Administration, 1978. Trial Attorney, Tax Division, Department of Justice, 1979-83. Chief of Staff to Rep/Senator Timothy Wirth (D-CO), 1985-87.

REFFKIN, Alan D.
HHL Financial Services, Inc.
2000 L St., N.W. Suite 200, Washington, DC 20036
Telephone: (202) 785-2735
Registered as lobbyist at U.S. Congress.

REGALIA, Martin A.
V. Pres. and Dir. of Research & Econ., Nat'l Council of Savings Institutions
1101 15th St., N.W. Suite 400, Washington, DC 20005
Telephone: (202) 857-3100
Registered as lobbyist at U.S. Congress.
Background: Principal Analyst, Fiscal Analysis Division, Congressional Budget Office, 1984-87.

REGAN, James J.
Of Counsel, Crowell and Moring
1001 Pennsylvania Ave., N.W., Washington, DC 20004-2505
Telephone: (202) 624-2500
Background: Chief Counsel and Hearing Examiner, General Services Administration Board of Contract Appeals, 1982-86.
Clients:
United Telecommunications

REGAN, John J.
I and J Associates
648 Anderson Hall 4400 Massachusetts Ave., N.W., Washington, DC 20016-8101
Telephone: (202) 885-7953
Registered as lobbyist at U.S. Congress.
Clients:

Mixmor, Inc.
Public Image Printing
Public Images
T and J Electronics

REGAN, R. Brent
V. President, Federal Relations, Southwestern Bell Corp.
1667 K St., N.W., Suite 1000, Washington, DC 20006
Telephone: (202) 293-8550
Registered as lobbyist at U.S. Congress.

REGAN, R. Michael
Verner, Liipfert, Bernhard, McPherson and Hand, Chartered
901 15th St., N.W., Suite 700, Washington, DC 20005
Telephone: (202) 371-6000
Registered as lobbyist at U.S. Congress.
Registered as Foreign Agent: (#3712).
Background: Counsel to Senate Judiciary Committee 1986-87.

REGAN, Timothy J.
Director, of Public Policy, Corning
1455 Pennsylvania Ave., N.W. Suite 500, Washington, DC 20004
Telephone: (202) 347-2270
Registered as lobbyist at U.S. Congress.
Background: As international economist held staff positions for White House Council on International Economic Policy, the Economic Policy Board and the Office of the U.S. Trade Representative. Most recently served as Deputy Assistant U.S. Trade Representative for Industrial Trade Policy.

REGELBRUGGE, Craig J.
Dir, Regulatory Affrs & Grower Svcs, American Ass'n of Nurserymen
1250 Eye St., N.W., Suite 500, Washington, DC 20005
Telephone: (202) 789-2900

REGNERY, Alfred S.
Leighton and Regnery
1667 K St., N.W., Suite 801, Washington, DC 20006
Telephone: (202) 955-3900
Registered as lobbyist at U.S. Congress.
Clients:
Visiting Nurses Ass'n of America

REHM, John B.
Dorsey & Whitney
1330 Connecticut Ave., N.W., Suite 200, Washington, DC 20036
Telephone: (202) 857-0700
Registered as lobbyist at U.S. Congress.
Registered as Foreign Agent: (#2923).
Background: Office of the Legal Advisor, Department of State, 1953-1963. General Counsel, Office of the Special Representative for Trade Negotiations, 1963-1969.

REHR, David K.
Ass't Dir., Federal Gov't Affairs, House, Nat'l Federation of Independent Business
600 Maryland Ave., S.W., Suite 700, Washington, DC 20024
Telephone: (202) 554-9000
Registered as lobbyist at U.S. Congress.

REICH, Alan A.
President, Nat'l Organization on Disability
910 16th St., N.W., Suite 600, Washington, DC 20006
Telephone: (202) 293-5960

REICH, Otto J.
Partner, Brock Group, The
1130 Connecticut Ave., N.W. Suite 350, Washington, DC 20036
Telephone: (202) 296-1901
Background: Assistant Administrator, U.S. Agency for International Development, 1981-83. Special Advisor to the Secretary of State, 1983-86. U.S. Ambassador to Venezuela, 1986-89.

REICH, Seymour D.
President, B'nai B'rith Internat'l
1640 Rhode Island Ave., N.W., Washington, DC 20036
Telephone: (202) 857-6600

REICHARD, John F.
Exec. V. President, Nat'l Ass'n for Foreign Student Affairs
1860 19th St., N.W., Washington, DC 20009
Telephone: (202) 462-4811

REICHARDT, Glenn R.
Kirkpatrick & Lockhart
1800 M St., N.W., Suite 900 South Lobby, Washington, DC 20036-5891
Telephone: (202) 778-9000
Clients:
American Chipper Knife Coalition

REICHENBERG, Neil
Director, Government Affairs, Internat'l Personnel Management Ass'n
1617 Duke St., Alexandria, VA 22314
Telephone: (703) 549-7100

REICHER, Dan W.
Attorney, Natural Resources Defense Council
1350 New York Ave., N.W. Suite 300, Washington, DC 20005
Telephone: (202) 783-7800

REICHERTZ, Peter S.
Arent, Fox, Kintner, Plotkin & Kahn
1050 Connecticut Ave., N.W., Washington, DC 20036-5339
Telephone: (202) 857-6000

REICHLER APPELBAUM AND WIPPMAN
1701 K St., N.W. Suite 700, Washington, DC 20006
Telephone: (202) 429-0800
Members of firm representing listed organizations:
   Appelbaum, Judith C.
      Background: Attorney Advisor to the Chairman, Federal Trade Commission, 1978-81.
   Reichler, Paul S.
      Background: Member, Commission on United States-Central American Relations, 1982-present.
   Wippman, David
   Clients:
   Bazar San Jorge, S.A. *(Judith C. Appelbaum)*
   Guatemala, Government of *(Paul S. Reichler)*
   Nicaragua, Government of *(Judith C. Appelbaum, Paul S. Reichler, David Wippman)*
   Philippines, Government of the
   United Coconut Ass'n of the Philippines *(Judith C. Appelbaum)*

REICHLER, Paul S.
Reichler Appelbaum and Wippman
1701 K St., N.W. Suite 700, Washington, DC 20006
Telephone: (202) 429-0800
Registered as lobbyist at U.S. Congress.
Background: Member, Commission on United States-Central American Relations, 1982-present.
Clients:
Guatemala, Government of
Nicaragua, Government of

REID, Ambrose B., II
Director, Federal Relations, American Home Products Corp.
1726 M St., N.W., Suite 1001, Washington, DC 20036
Telephone: (202) 659-8320

REID, Herbert O., Sr.
Legal Counsel, Nat'l Ass'n for Equal Opportunity in Higher Education
400 12th St., N.E. 2nd Floor, Washington, DC 20002
Telephone: (202) 543-9111
Background: Professor of Law, Howard University Law School.

REID, Michael W.
Special Assistant to the President, American Postal Workers Union
1300 L St., N.W., Washington, DC 20005
Telephone: (202) 842-4211
Registered as lobbyist at U.S. Congress.

REID & PRIEST
1111 19th St., N.W., Washington, DC 20036
Telephone: (202) 828-0100
Background: Washington Office of a New York law firm.
Members of firm representing listed organizations:
   Bates, John C. (Jr.)

REID & PRIEST (Cont'd)

Background: Special Assistant for Tax Policy, Treasury Department, 1973-76.

Berkoff, Barry I., Legislative Representative

Bowman, Peyton G. (III)

Dacek, Raymond F.

Duncan, Charles T., Counsel

Background: General Counsel, U.S. Equal Employment Opportunity Commission, 1965-66. Corporation Counsel, District of Columbia, 1966-70.

Faber, Michael W.

Background: Attorney Advisor to Commissioner, Federal Communications Commission, 1971.

Healy, Patricia M.

Jacobson, David E.

Junn, S. Chull

Krupin, Jay P.

Leidl, Richard J.

Merriman, Richard M.

Meyers, Tedson J.

Background: Assistant to Chairman, Federal Communications Commission, 1961-62.

Minikes, Stephan M.

Background: Senior V. President, Export-Import Bank, 1974-77. Counsel to the Special Consultant to the President of the United States for Energy, 1973. Counsel and Special Assistant to the Chief of Naval Operations, 1972-74.

Norton, Floyd L.

Pizzoli, Anne, Legislative Representative

Schaefgen, John R.

Waters, Robert S.

Zarin, Donald

Clients:

Arkansas Power and Light Co.

BDM Internat'l, Inc.

Broadcast Music Inc. *(Charles T. Duncan)*

Bunker-Ramo-Eltra Corp.

Carolina Power and Light Co.

CIAC Group, The *(Raymond F. Dacek)*

Cincinnati Gas and Electric Co.

Citicorp

Committee of Corporate Telecommunications Users *(Michael W. Faber)*

Dallas Power and Light Co.

Dayton Power and Light Co.

Delmarva Power and Light Co.

Derecktor of Rhode Island, Robert E. *(Stephan M. Minikes)*

Edison Electric Institute *(Raymond F. Dacek)*

Entergy Corp. *(Richard M. Merriman)*

Florida Power and Light Co.

Florida Progress Corp. *(Raymond F. Dacek)*

Foster Co., L. B.

Great Plains Natural Gas Co. *(Peyton G. Bowman, III)*

Green Mountain Power Corp. *(Richard M. Merriman)*

Gulf States Utilities Co. *(Raymond F. Dacek)*

Halecrest Co. *(Peyton G. Bowman, III)*

Huber Corp., J. M.

Idaho Power Co.

Korea, Embassy of *(S. Chull Junn)*

Korea Foreign Trade Ass'n *(S. Chull Junn)*

Korea, Ministry of Trade and Industry

Louisiana Power and Light Co.

MDU Resources Group, Inc.

Minnesota Power

Mississippi Power and Light Co.

Montana Power Co.

New Orleans Public Service Inc.

Niagara Mohawk Power Corp.

Ohio Edison Co.

Philadelphia Electric Co. *(Peyton G. Bowman, III)*

Philadelphia Industrial Development Corp. *(Stephan M. Minikes)*

Philadelphia, Pennsylvania, City of *(Stephan M. Minikes)*

Pinnacle West Capital Corp.

Potomac Electric Power Co.

Pride Refining, Inc. *(Richard J. Leidl)*

Public Service Electric and Gas Co.

Samsung Electronics Co., Ltd.

Sierra Pacific Resources

Southern California Edison Co.

SPD Technologies *(Stephan M. Minikes)*

Texas Electric Service Co.

Texas Power and Light Co.

Union Electric Co.

Upper Peninsula Power Co.

Utility Decommissioning Tax Group *(Raymond F. Dacek, Patricia M. Healy)*

Washington Water Power Co.

REIDER, Alan E.

Arent, Fox, Kintner, Plotkin & Kahn

1050 Connecticut Ave., N.W., Washington, DC 20036-5339

Telephone: (202) 857-6000

Registered as lobbyist at U.S. Congress.

Background: Analyst, Department of Health, Education and Welfare, 1975-79. Chief, Review Policy Branch, Office of Special Standards Review Organization, Health Care Financing Administration, Department of Health and Human Services, 1979-80.

Clients:

American Ass'n of Bioanalysts

American Medical Imaging Corp.

Mercy Hospital of Des Moines, Iowa

Mobile Diagnostic Systems

Salem Medical Laboratory

REIF, Dee

Exec. Dir., Sales & Marketing Council, American Trucking Ass'ns

2200 Mill Road, Alexandria, VA 22314

Telephone: (703) 838-1926

REIG, Carol D.

Ass't Director, Field Coordination, Nat'l Committee for a Human Life Amendment

1511 K St., N.W., Suite 335, Washington, DC 20005

Telephone: (202) 393-0703

REILLY, Burke G.

Internat'l Associate, Washington Affairs, Ford Motor Co.

1350 Eye St., N.W. Suite 1000, Washington, DC 20005

Telephone: (202) 962-5400

Registered as lobbyist at U.S. Congress.

REILLY, John R.

Winston and Strawn

2550 M St., N.W., Suite 500, Washington, DC 20037

Telephone: (202) 828-8400

Background: Assistant to Deputy Attorney General, Chief of Executive Office for U.S. Attorney, then Asst. Commissioner, Federal Trade Commission, 1964-67. Former adviser to Democratic Presidential nominee Walter F. Mondale.

REILLY, Lynn

Legislative Director, Neighborhood Housing Services of America

1325 G St., N.W., Suite 1010, Washington, DC 20005

Telephone: (202) 376-2576

Registered as lobbyist at U.S. Congress.

REILLY, Mary Jo

Senior V. President, American Soc. of Hospital Pharmacists

4630 Montgomery Ave., Bethesda, MD 20814

Telephone: (301) 657-3000

REIMERS, Mark A.

Assoc Dep Chief, Prog and Legis, DEPARTMENT OF AGRICULTURE - Forest Service

12th and Independence Ave. S.W., Washington, DC 20250

Telephone: (202) 447-4071

REINBURG, Kathleen

V. President, CEHP, Inc.

1333 Connecticut Ave., N.W. Suite 400, Washington, DC 20036

Telephone: (202) 293-1774

Registered as lobbyist at U.S. Congress.

REINERTSON, William W.

Director, Vision Care Benefits Center, American Optometric Ass'n

1505 Prince Street, Suite 300, Alexandria, VA 22314

Telephone: (703) 739-9200

REINFRIED, Robert A.

Lloyd and Associates, Inc.

932 Hungerford Drive, Suite 36, Rockville, MD 20850

Telephone: (301) 738-2448

Background: Serves as Exec. Director, Mechanical Power Transmission Ass'n.

Clients:

Mechanical Power Transmission Ass'n

REINHARDT, Thomas T.

Dir., Cong Relations, DEPARTMENT OF JUSTICE

10th and Constitution Ave., Washington, DC 20530

Telephone: (202) 633-3752

REIS, Diane

Director, Gov't Relats. & Public Affairs, Nat'l Federation of Business and Professional Women's Clubs

2012 Massachusetts Ave., N.W., Washington, DC 20036

Telephone: (202) 293-1100

Registered as lobbyist at U.S. Congress.

REIS, Harold F.

Newman & Holtzinger, P.C.

1615 L St., N.W., 10th Floor, Washington, DC 20005

Telephone: (202) 955-6600

Background: Chief, Legal Branch, Office of Alien Property (1949-52), First Assistant, Office of Legal Counsel (1960-64), and Executive Assistant to the Attorney General (1964-67), U.S. Department of Justice.

Clients:

Florida Power and Light Co.

REISER, Martin G.

Consultant, Government Affairs, Xerox Corp.

490 L'Enfant Plaza East, S.W., Suite 4200, Washington, DC 20024

Telephone: (202) 646-8285

Background: Former Congressional Liaison Ass't, U.S. Dept. of Commerce.

REISLER, Irwin

Linton, Mields, Reisler and Cottone

1225 Eye St., N.W., Suite 300, Washington, DC 20005

Telephone: (202) 682-3901

REISS, Robert N.

V. Pres., Sys. Techn. & Prod. Dvlmnt., Nat'l Ass'n of Securities Dealers (NASDAQ)

1735 K St., N.W., Washington, DC 20006

Telephone: (202) 728-8000

REITER, Harvey L.

McCarthy, Sweeney and Harkaway, P.C.

1750 Pennsylvania Ave. N.W. Suite 1105, Washington, DC 20006

Telephone: (202) 393-5710

Background: Trial Attorney, Federal Power Commission, 1975-78. Special Assistant to the Deputy General Counsel for Litigation, Federal Energy Regulatory Commission, 1979-84.

Clients:

Vermont Department of Public Service

REITH, John L.

Dir., Dept. of Economics and Taxation, American Trucking Ass'ns

2200 Mill Road, Alexandria, VA 22314

Telephone: (703) 838-1788

REMBA, Zev

Government Relations Manager, Academy of General Dentistry

1111 14th St., N.W., Suite 1100, Washington, DC 20005

Telephone: (202) 842-1130

Registered as lobbyist at U.S. Congress.

RENDON CO., THE

1802 T St., N.W., Washington, DC 20009

Telephone: (202) 745-4900

Registered as Foreign Agent: (#3906)

Background: A political consulting firm. President is John W. Rendon, Jr. and Account Exec. is Thomas J. Wolf, both of Capital Services, Inc.

RENDON, John W., Jr.

President, Capital Services, Inc.

1802 T St., N.W., Washington, DC 20009

Telephone: (202) 745-4900

Registered as Foreign Agent: (#4175).

RENNERT, Diane

Congressional Liaison, Ass'n of American Publishers

1718 Connecticut Ave., N.W. Suite 700, Washington, DC 20009-1148

Telephone: (202) 232-3335

Registered as lobbyist at U.S. Congress.

Background: Serves as Manager, American Book Publishers Political Action Committee.

RENO, CAVANAUGH & HORNIG

122 C St., N.W., Suite 875, Washington, DC 20001
Telephone: (202) 783-5120
Members of firm representing listed organizations:
Cavanaugh, Gordon
Background: Administrator, Farmers Home Administration, Department of Agriculture, 1977-81.
Reno, Lee P.
Clients:
Amerind Risk Management Corp. *(Lee P. Reno)*
Council of Large Public Housing Authorities *(Gordon Cavanaugh)*
Housing Authority Risk Retention Group *(Lee P. Reno)*
Nat'l American Indian Housing Council

RENO, Lee P.

Reno, Cavanaugh & Hornig
122 C St., N.W., Suite 875, Washington, DC 20001
Telephone: (202) 783-5120
Registered as lobbyist at U.S. Congress.
Clients:
Amerind Risk Management Corp.
Housing Authority Risk Retention Group

RENSBERGER, Judy

Federal Regulatory Analyst, Nat'l Committee to Preserve Social Security and Medicare
2000 K St., N.W. Suite 800, Washington, DC 20006
Telephone: (202) 822-9459
Registered as lobbyist at U.S. Congress.

REPASS, Capt. Donald, USN (Ret)

Public Relations Officer, Retired Officers Ass'n, The (TROA)
201 N. Washington St., Alexandria, VA 22314
Telephone: (703) 549-2311

REPETTO, Robert

Director, Economic Research Program, World Resources Institute
1709 New York Ave., N.W., Washington, DC 20006
Telephone: (202) 638-6300

REPKO, Riley

Director, Government Affairs, Oracle Corp.
1627 Eye St., N.W., Suite 880, Washington, DC 20006
Telephone: (202) 657-7844
Registered as lobbyist at U.S. Congress.

REPPERT, Linda P.

Dorsey & Whitney
1330 Connecticut Ave., N.W., Suite 200, Washington, DC 20036
Telephone: (202) 857-0700

REPRESENTATIVE FOR GERMAN INDUSTRY AND TRADE

One Farragut Square South 1634 Eye St., N.W., Washington, DC 20006
Telephone: (202) 347-0247
Registered as Foreign Agent: (#4274)
Members of firm representing listed organizations:
Griessbach, (Dr.) Lothar, President and CEO
Schneider, Hartmut
Vaughan, John Heath (Jr,)
Welschke, Bernhard M., Deputy Exec. Officer
Clients:
Bundesverband der Deutschen Industrie *(Dr. Lothar Griessbach, Hartmut Schneider, John Heath Vaughan, Jr,, Bernhard M. Welschke)*
Deutscher Industrie und Handelstag *(Dr. Lothar Griessbach, Hartmut Schneider, John Heath Vaughan, Jr,, Bernhard M. Welschke)*

RESEARCH & MANAGEMENT ASSOCIATES

832 S. 20th St., Arlington, VA 22202-2614
Telephone: (703) 979-8941
Members of firm representing listed organizations:
Shaw, Jerry A.
Clients:
Bio National Corp. *(Jerry A. Shaw)*

RESER, Galen

Asst Secy, Gov't'l Affrs, DEPARTMENT OF TRANSPORTATION
400 Seventh St., S.W., Washington, DC 20590
Telephone: (202) 366-4573

RESLER, Barclay T.

Asst. Manager, Governmental Relations, Coca-Cola Co.
1627 K St., N.W., Suite 800, Washington, DC 20006
Telephone: (202) 466-5310
Registered as lobbyist at U.S. Congress.

RESNICK, Michael A.

Assoc. Exec. Director, Federal Relations, Nat'l School Boards Ass'n
1680 Duke St., Alexandria, VA 22314
Telephone: (703) 838-6722

RESOURCES DEVELOPMENT, INC.

412 First St., S.E., Washington, DC 20003
Telephone: (202) 484-8969
Members of firm representing listed organizations:
Zion, Roger H.
Background: U.S. House of Representatives, 1966-74; Chairman, Republican Task Force on Energy and Resources.
Clients:
Independent Oil Producers Ass'n-Tri State *(Roger H. Zion)*
Industry General Corp. *(Roger H. Zion)*
Morrison, Hecker, Curtis, Kuder & Parrish *(Roger H. Zion)*
Nat'l Ass'n of Professional Educators *(Roger H. Zion)*
Public Service Research Council *(Roger H. Zion)*
Toborg Associates, Inc. *(Roger H. Zion)*

RESOURCES FOR GROUP MANAGEMENT, INC.

1350 New York Ave., N.W. Suite 615, Washington, DC 20005
Telephone: (202) 393-1780
Members of firm representing listed organizations:
McDermott, Marianne
Background: Serves as Exec. V. President, Greeting Card Ass'n and Nat'l Candle Ass'n and as Treasurer, Committee Assisting Republicans and Democrats (CARD-PAC).
Riviere, Nancy
Background: Serves as Director of Communications, Greeting Card Ass'n.
Clients:
Committee Assisting Republicans and Democrats (CARD-PAC) *(Marianne McDermott)*
Greeting Card Ass'n *(Marianne McDermott)*
Greeting Card Creative Network *(Nancy Riviere)*
Nat'l Ass'n of Legal Search Consultants *(Marianne McDermott)*
Nat'l Candle Ass'n *(Marianne McDermott)*
Purchasing Management Ass'n of Washington *(Marianne McDermott)*

RETKE, Wolfgang C.

Assoc Dep Asst Secy, Cong & Intergovt'l, DEPARTMENT OF ENERGY
1000 Independence Ave. S.W., Washington, DC 20585
Telephone: (202) 586-5450

RETTIG, Paul C.

Exec. V. Pres. and Dir., Wash. Office, American Hospital Ass'n
50 F St., N.W., Suite 1100, Washington, DC 20001
Telephone: (202) 638-1100
Registered as lobbyist at U.S. Congress.

REUSING, Vincent P.

Senior Vice-President, Metropolitan Insurance Cos.
1615 L St., N.W., Suite 1210, Washington, DC 20036
Telephone: (202) 659-3575
Registered as lobbyist at U.S. Congress.

REUSS, Pat

Legislative Director, Nat'l Women's Political Caucus
1275 K St., N.W., Suite 750, Washington, DC 20005
Telephone: (202) 898-1100
Registered as lobbyist at U.S. Congress.
Background: Former legislative counsel to the U.S. House Post Office, Civil Service Subcommittee on Human Resources.

REUTER, Peter

Co-Director, Drug Policy Research Center, RAND Corp.
2100 M St., N.W., 8th Floor, Washington, DC 20037
Telephone: (202) 296-5000

REUTHER, Alan V.

Associate General Counsel, United Automobile, Aerospace and Agricultural Implement Workers of America (UAW)
1757 N St., N.W., Washington, DC 20036
Telephone: (202) 828-8500
Registered as lobbyist at U.S. Congress.

REVER, Philip R.

Treasurer, Higher Education Management and Resources Foundation Political Action Committee (HEMAR/HEAF)
1023 15th St, N.W., Suite 1000, Washington, DC 20005
Telephone: (202) 289-4500

REXINGER, Allan R.

Asst. Gen. Counsel and Dir., Con. Rels., Nonprescription Drug Manfacturers Ass'n
1150 Connecticut Ave., N.W.,, Washington, DC 20036
Telephone: (202) 429-9260
Registered as lobbyist at U.S. Congress.
Background: Serves also as Treasurer, Proprietary Industry Political Action Committee.

REY, Mark E.

Exec. Director, American Forest Resource Alliance
1250 Connecticut Ave., N.W. Suite 200, Washington, DC 20036
Telephone: (202) 463-2747
Registered as lobbyist at U.S. Congress.

REYES, Lilia M.

Assistant Exec. Director, United States Conference of City Human Services Officials
1620 Eye St., N.W., Suite 400, Washington, DC 20006
Telephone: (202) 293-7330

REYMOND, Renee

Director, Legislative Affairs, Nat'l Ass'n of Manufacturers
1331 Pennsylvania Ave., N.W., Suite 1500 North, Washington, DC 20004-1703
Telephone: (202) 637-3132
Registered as lobbyist at U.S. Congress.
Background: Serves also as Director, Business Coalition Against Plant Closing Legislation.

REYNOLDS, John R.

Director, Marketing & Public Relations, Internat'l Franchise Ass'n
1350 New York Ave., N.W. Suite 900, Washington, DC 20005
Telephone: (202) 628-8000

REYNOLDS, Margaret W.

Exec. Director, Linguistic Soc. of America
1325 18th St., N.W., Suite 211, Washington, DC 20036-6501
Telephone: (202) 835-1714

REYNOLDS, Nancy Clark

V. Chairman, Wexler, Reynolds, Fuller, Harrison and Schule, Inc.
1317 F St., N.W., Suite 600, Washington, DC 20004
Telephone: (202) 638-2121
Registered as lobbyist at U.S. Congress.
Clients:
Allied-Signal Inc.
American Institute for Foreign Study
Columbia Hospital for Women Medical Center
Manhattan Building Cos., Inc.
Simon Wiesenthal Center/Museum of Tolerance

REYNOLDS, Robert

Cong Liaison Specialist, DEPARTMENT OF COMMERCE
14th and Constitution Ave. S.W., Washington, DC 20230
Telephone: (202) 377-5485

REYNOLDS, Wm. Bradford

Ross and Hardies
888 16th St., N.W., Washington, DC 20006
Telephone: (202) 296-8600
Background: Former Assistant Attorney General (Civil Rights Division), U.S. Department of Justice.
Clients:
Citicorp

REZNECK, Daniel A.
Arnold & Porter
1200 New Hampshire Ave., N.W., Washington, DC 20036
Telephone: (202) 872-6700
Registered as Foreign Agent: (#1750).

REZNICK, Robert P.
Clifford & Warnke
815 Connecticut Ave., N.W., Washington, DC 20006
Telephone: (202) 828-4200

REZNIK, Bruce A.
P.O. Box 1998, Washington, DC 20013
Telephone: (703) 525-1786
Registered as lobbyist at U.S. Congress.
Registered as Foreign Agent: (#3748)
Organizations represented:
    Bangladesh, People's Republic of

RHATICAN, William F.
Senior V. President, Davis Companies, The Susan
1146 19th St., N.W., Washington, DC 20036
Telephone: (202) 775-8881
Background: Special Assistant to President Nixon, 1970-73; Special Assistant/Director of Communications - Treasury, Commerce and Interior, 1974-75; Special Assistant to President Ford, 1976.
Organizations represented:
    Nat'l Ass'n of Home Builders of the U.S.

RHEA, Marsha
Director of Communications, American Subcontractors Ass'n
1004 Duke St., Alexandria, VA 22314
Telephone: (703) 684-3450

RHETT, John T.
Washington Representative, Harding Lawson Associates
3175 North 21st St., Arlington, VA 22201
Telephone: (703) 528-5809
Background: Deputy Ass't Administrator, Water Programs, Environmental Protection Agency, 1973-79; Federal Inspector, Natural Gas Pipeline, 1979-85.

RHINEHART, Raymond P.
V. President, AIA Foundation, American Institute of Architects, The
1735 New York Ave., N.W., Washington, DC 20006
Telephone: (202) 626-7300

RHINELANDER, John B.
Shaw, Pittman, Potts and Trowbridge
2300 N St., N.W., Washington, DC 20037
Telephone: (202) 663-8000
Registered as lobbyist at U.S. Congress.
Background: Law Clerk to Associate Justice John M. Harlan, U.S. Supreme Court, 1961-2. Special Civilian Assistant to Secretary of the Navy, 1966-68. Chief Counsel, Acting Deputy Director, Office of Foreign Direct Investments, Dept. of Commerce, 1968-9. Legal Adviser to U.S. SALT Delegation 1971-2. General Counsel, Dept. of HEW, 1973-5. Under Secretary, Dept. of HUD, 1975-77.

RHODES, Annie C.
Dir., Spec. Projects/Development, Sheehan Associates, Inc.
727 15th St., N.W., Suite 1200, Washington, DC 20005
Telephone: (202) 347-0044
Clients:
    Nat'l Law Enforcement Officers' Memorial Fund
    Nat'l Order of Women Legislators

RHODES, Dr. Donna
Exec. Director, Nat'l Foundation for the Improvement of Education
1201 16th St., N.W., Washington, DC 20036
Telephone: (202) 822-7840

RHODES, Frederick W.
V. President, Legislative Relations, Loral/Fairchild Systems
1111 Jefferson Davis Hwy. Suite 811, Arlington, VA 22202
Telephone: (703) 685-5300
Registered as lobbyist at U.S. Congress.
Background: Professional Staff Member, U.S. Senate Committee on Appropriations, 1973-84.

RHODES, John J.
Of Counsel, Hunton and Williams
2000 Pennsylvania Ave., N.W., Washington, DC 20006
Telephone: (202) 955-1500
Registered as lobbyist at U.S. Congress.
Background: Member, U.S. House of Representatives (R-AZ). House Minority Leader, 1973-81.
Clients:
    Committee for a Responsible Federal Budget

RHODES, Theodore E.
Steptoe and Johnson
1330 Connecticut Ave., N.W., Washington, DC 20036
Telephone: (202) 429-3000
Registered as lobbyist at U.S. Congress.
Background: Attorney-Advisor, Office of Tax Legislative Counsel, U.S. Treasury Department, 1973-76. Consultant to Administrator, Pension and Welfare Benefit Programs, Department of Labor, 1976-77.
Clients:
    Ass'n of Private Pension and Welfare Plans

RHOME, Anne M.
Sr. Staff Specialist, Gov't Affairs, American Ass'n of Colleges of Nursing
One Dupont Circle, N.W., Suite 530, Washington, DC 20036
Telephone: (202) 463-6930

RHYMES, Fisher Ames
V. President, Public Affairs, American Fiber Manufacturers Ass'n
1150 17th St., N.W., Suite 310, Washington, DC 20036
Telephone: (202) 296-6508

RHYNE, Charles S.
President, World Peace Through Law Center
Suite 800, 1000 Connecticut Ave., N.W., Washington, DC 20036
Telephone: (202) 466-5420
Background: An attorney, partner in the firm of Rhyne and Rhyne. Serves also as Of Counsel to the Nat'l Institute of Municipal Law Officers and World President of the World Peace Through Law Center.

RIBICOFF, Abraham A.
Kaye, Scholer, Fierman, Hays and Handler
The McPherson Building 901 15th St., N.W., #1100, Washington, DC 20005
Telephone: (202) 682-3500
Registered as lobbyist at U.S. Congress.
Registered as Foreign Agent: (#3221).
Background: U.S. Senator from Connecticut, 1963-81. Secretary of Health, Education and Welfare, 1961-63.

RIBLER, Karen J.
Exec. V. Pres., Educ. & Trng. Foundation, Nat'l Food Brokers Ass'n
1010 Massachusetts Ave., N.W., Washington, DC 20001
Telephone: (202) 789-2844

RICCHETTI, Steve
Exec. Dir., Congressional Communications, Blue Cross and Blue Shield Ass'n
655 15th St., N.W., Suite 350, Washington, DC 20005
Telephone: (202) 626-4780
Registered as lobbyist at U.S. Congress.
Background: Serves also as Treasurer, CarePAC.

RICE, David
Exec. V. President, Nat'l Business League
4324 Georgia Ave., N.W., Washington, DC 20011
Telephone: (202) 829-5900

RICE, Grace Ellen
Associate Director, Washington Office, American Farm Bureau Federation
600 Maryland Ave., S.W., Washington, DC 20024
Telephone: (202) 484-3600
Registered as lobbyist at U.S. Congress.

RICE, John
Acting Exec. Director, Federation of American Societies for Experimental Biology
9650 Rockville Pike, Bethesda, MD 20814
Telephone: (301) 530-7000

RICE, Lois D.
Sr. V. President for Gov't Affairs, Control Data Corp.
1201 Pennsylvania Ave., N.W., Suite 370, Washington, DC 20004
Telephone: (202) 789-6517
Registered as lobbyist at U.S. Congress.

RICE, Richard E.
Resource Economist, Wilderness Soc.
1400 Eye St., N.W., 10th Floor, Washington, DC 20005
Telephone: (202) 842-3400

RICE, Robert
Kilpatrick & Cody
2501 M St., N.W., Suite 500, Washington, DC 20037
Telephone: (202) 463-2500
Background: Former Special Counsel for Litigation, General Services Administration.

RICE, Roman
Treasurer, Public Service Political Action Committee
8330 Old Courthouse Rd. Suite 600, Vienna, VA 22182
Telephone: (703) 790-0700

RICH, Barbara A.
Exec. V. President, Nat'l Ass'n for Biomedical Research
818 Connecticut Ave., N.W. Third Floor, Washington, DC 20006
Telephone: (202) 857-0540

RICH, Bruce
Director, International Program, Environmental Defense Fund
1616 P St., N.W., Suite 150, Washington, DC 20036
Telephone: (202) 387-3500

RICH, James E., Jr.
Washington Representative, Shell Oil Co.
Suite 200, 1025 Connecticut Ave., N.W., Washington, DC 20036
Telephone: (202) 466-1425
Registered as lobbyist at U.S. Congress.

RICHARD, John
Assistant to the Managing Trustee, Center for Study of Responsive Law
Box 19367, Washington, DC 20036
Telephone: (202) 387-8030

RICHARD, Robert A.
V. Pres. & Director, Regulatory Services, Conference of State Bank Supervisors
1015 18th St., N.W Suite 1100, Washington, DC 20036
Telephone: (202) 296-2840
Background: Full Title is V. President for Supervisory Procedures and State Banking Department Services.

RICHARDS, Alan K., Jr.
Asst Wash Couns, Admin/Regulatory Affrs., Health Insurance Ass'n of America
1025 Connecticut Ave., N.W. Suite 1200, Washington, DC 20036
Telephone: (202) 223-7780
Registered as lobbyist at U.S. Congress.

RICHARDS, Andrea
Govt Affrs Asst, INTERSTATE COMMERCE COMMISSION
12th and Constitution Ave. N.W., Washington, DC 20423
Telephone: (202) 275-7231

RICHARDS, Barbara
Staff Assistant, Progressive Policy Institute
316 Pennsylvania Ave., S.E. Suite 516, Washington, DC 20003
Telephone: (202) 547-0001

RICHARDS, Cory
V. President, Public Policy, Alan Guttmacher Institute, The
2010 Massachusetts Ave., N.W., 5th floor, Washington, DC 20036
Telephone: (202) 296-4012

RICHARDS, Gordon
Asst. V. Pres., Taxation & Fiscal Policy, Nat'l Ass'n of Manufacturers
1331 Pennsylvania Ave., N.W. Suite 1500 North, Washington, DC 20004-1703
Telephone: (202) 637-3000

RICHARDS LAW OFFICES, Richard
1025 Thomas Jefferson St., NW Suite 105, Washington, DC 20007
Telephone: (202) 342-3830
Organizations represented:
British Aerospace, Inc.
Pratt & Whitney
Sunrider Internat'l

RICHARDS, Richard
President, Commerce Consultants Internat'l Ltd.
1025 Thomas Jefferson St, N.W. Suite 105, Washington, DC 20007
Telephone: (202) 342-9610
Registered as Foreign Agent: (#4248).
Clients:
Hughes Aircraft Co.
Thailand, Office of the Prime Minister

RICHARDSON, Alan H.
Assistant Exec. Director, American Public Power Ass'n
2301 M St., N.W., Washington, DC 20037
Telephone: (202) 775-8300
Registered as lobbyist at U.S. Congress.

RICHARDSON, Cleolis
President, Nat'l Beauty Culturists' League
25 Logan Circle, N.W., Washington, DC 20005
Telephone: (202) 332-2695

RICHARDSON, Rep. David P., Jr.
President, Nat'l Black Caucus of State Legislators
444 North Capitol St., N.W. Suite 206, Washington, DC 20001
Telephone: (202) 624-5457

RICHARDSON, Donna Rae
Director, Congress'l & Agency Relat'ns, American Nurses' Ass'n
1101 14th St., N.W., Suite 200, Washington, DC 20005
Telephone: (202) 789-1800
Registered as lobbyist at U.S. Congress.
Background: Serves also as Co-Chair of the Executive Committee, Women and Health Roundtable.

RICHARDSON, Doug
Director, Washington Office, Illinois, State of
444 N. Capitol St., N.W. Suite 210, Washington, DC 20001
Telephone: (202) 624-7760

RICHARDSON, Elliot L.
Milbank, Tweed, Hadley & McCloy
1825 Eye St., N.W. Suite 900, Washington, DC 20006
Telephone: (202) 835-7500
Background: Assistant Secretary for Legislation, Dept. of Health, Education and Welfare, 1957-59. United States Attorney, Massachusetts, 1959-61. Special Assistant to the Attorney General of the U.S., 1961. Lieutenant Governor, 1965-67 and Attorney General, 1967-69, Commonwealth of Massachusetts. Under Secretary, U.S. Department of State, 1969-70. Secretary of Health, Education and Welfare, 1970-73. Secretary of Defense, 1973. Attorney General of the U.S., 1973. Ambassador to the Court of St. James, 1975-76. Secretary of Commerce, 1976-77. Ambassador at Large for the Law of the Sea, 1977-80.
Clients:
Ass'n for Internat'l Investment
Midland Bank plc

RICHARDSON, Prof. Gilbert P., Sr.
President & Dean, USWA Institute, American Ass'n for Study of the United States in World Affairs
3813 Annandale Road, Annandale, VA 22003
Telephone: (703) 256-8761

RICHARDSON, John
Counselor, United States Institute for Peace
1550 M St., N.W. Suite 700, Washington, DC 20005-1708
Telephone: (202) 457-1700
Background: Assistant Secretary of State, 1969-77.

RICHARDSON, Col. John
Senate Affrs Dir, Legis Affrs, DEPARTMENT OF DEFENSE
The Pentagon, Washington, DC 20301
Telephone: (202) 697-6210

RICHARDSON, John G.
V. President, Governmental Affairs, Southern Company, The
1130 Connecticut Ave., N.W., Suite 830, Washington, DC 20036
Telephone: (202) 775-0944
Registered as lobbyist at U.S. Congress.

RICHARDSON, Kenneth O.
Nat'l Legislative Director, Transportation, Communications Internat'l Union
815 16th St., N.W. Suite 511, Washington, DC 20036
Telephone: (202) 783-3660
Registered as lobbyist at U.S. Congress.

RICHARDSON, Kevin C.
Staff V. President, Government Relations, Electronic Industries Ass'n
2001 Pennsylvania Ave., N.W., Washington, DC 20006
Telephone: (202) 457-4900
Registered as lobbyist at U.S. Congress.

RICHARDSON, Mark E.
Exec. Director, Business Council on the Reduction of Paperwork
1625 Eye St., N.W. Suite 903, Washington, DC 20006
Telephone: (202) 331-1915

RICHARDSON, Robert
Exec. Director, Seaplane Pilots Ass'n
421 Aviation Way, Frederick, MD 21701
Telephone: (301) 695-2083

RICHARDSON, Brig. General Robert C., USAF (Ret)
Vice Chairman, Americans for the High Frontier
2800 Shirlington Road Suite 405 A, Arlington, VA 22206
Telephone: (703) 671-4111

RICHARDSON, Warren S.
Washington Lobby Group, The
325 Pennsylvania Ave., S.E., Washington, DC 20003
Telephone: (202) 543-9400
Registered as lobbyist at U.S. Congress.

RICHARDSON, Wesley S.
Washington Lobby Group, The
325 Pennsylvania Ave., S.E., Washington, DC 20003
Telephone: (202) 543-9400
Registered as lobbyist at U.S. Congress.

RICHERSON, Lois
Director, Government Relations, Nat'l Cable Television Ass'n
1724 Massachusetts Ave., N.W., Washington, DC 20036
Telephone: (202) 775-3550
Registered as lobbyist at U.S. Congress.

RICHLAND, Jordan H.
Deputy Director, Public Health Foundation
1220 L St., N.W., Suite 350, Washington, DC 20005
Telephone: (202) 898-5600
Background: Supervisory Program Evaluator, Human Resources Division, General Accounting Office, 1979-87.

RICHMAN, Charles
Exec. Director, American Horticultural Therapy Ass'n
9220 Wightman Road, Suite 300, Gaithersburg, MD 20879
Telephone: (301) 948-3010

RICHMAN, Gerald L.
LaRoe, Winn, Moerman & Donovan
1120 G St., N.W., Suite 800, Washington, DC 20005
Telephone: (202) 628-2788
Registered as lobbyist at U.S. Congress.
Clients:
Pennwalt Corp.
Western Transportation Co.

RICHMAN, Teri F.
Sr. V. President, Public Affairs, Nat'l Ass'n of Convenience Stores
1605 King St., Alexandria, VA 22314
Telephone: (703) 684-3600
Registered as lobbyist at U.S. Congress.
Background: Serves also as contact for the Nat'l Ass'n of Convenience Stores Political Action Committee.

RICHTER, Stephan-Gotz
President, TransAtlantic Futures, Inc.
2311 Connecticut Ave., N.W. Suite 604, Washington, DC 20008
Telephone: (202) 462-1222
Clients:
ABD Securities Corp.
Deutsche Bank AG
Siemens Corp.

RICHTMAN, Max
Director, Government Relations Dept., Nat'l Committee to Preserve Social Security and Medicare
2000 K St., N.W. Suite 800, Washington, DC 20006
Telephone: (202) 822-9459
Registered as lobbyist at U.S. Congress.

RICKARD, Al
Director, Communications, Snack Food Ass'n
1711 King St., Suite One, Alexandria, VA 22314
Telephone: (703) 836-4500

RICKARD, Claire A.
C & M Internat'l L.P.
1001 Pennsylvania Ave., N.W., Washington, DC 20004-2505
Telephone: (202) 624-2895
Registered as Foreign Agent: (#3988).

RICKARDS, Larry, Ph.D.
Assistant Director, Nat'l Ass'n of Area Agencies on Aging
600 Maryland Ave., S.W. Suite 208 West Wing, Washington, DC 20024
Telephone: (202) 484-7520
Registered as lobbyist at U.S. Congress.

RIDDIOUGH, Christine
Field Coordntr, Climate Chng/Energy Prgm, Union of Concerned Scientists
1616 P St., N.W., Suite 310, Washington, DC 20036
Telephone: (202) 332-0900

RIDEOUT, Thomas P.
Exec. Director, Bank Capital Markets Ass'n
Nat'l Press Building Second Floor, Washington, DC 20045
Telephone: (202) 347-5510
Registered as lobbyist at U.S. Congress.

RIDGWAY, Roseanne
President, Atlantic Council of the United States
1616 H St., N.W. 3rd Floor, Washington, DC 20006
Telephone: (202) 347-9353

RIEDEL, E. George
Dir., Business/Government Relations, ITT Defense, Inc.
1000 Wilson Blvd. Suite 3000, Arlington, VA 22209
Telephone: (703) 276-8300

RIEDLIN, Fritz
Director, Federal Operations, Datapoint Corp.
1655 North Fort Myer Drive, Arlington, VA 22209
Telephone: (703) 841-7600

RIEDY, Dr. Mark J.
President, Nat'l Council of Savings Institutions
1101 15th St., N.W. Suite 400, Washington, DC 20005
Telephone: (202) 857-3100
Registered as lobbyist at U.S. Congress.

RIEDY, Mark J.
Shea and Gould
1775 Pennsylvania Ave., N.W., Suite 700, Washington, DC 20006
Telephone: (202) 833-9850

RIEGEL, Quentin
Asst. V. Pres. & Deputy General Counsel, Nat'l Ass'n of Manufacturers
1331 Pennsylvania Ave., N.W. Suite 1500 North, Washington, DC 20004-1703
Telephone: (202) 637-3000

RIFKIN, Jeremy R.
President, Foundation on Economic Trends
1130 17th St., N.W. Suite 630, Washington, DC 20026
Telephone: (202) 466-2823

RIGER, Paul
Exec. Director, VNA, Inc.
5151 Wisconsin Ave., N.W. Suite 400, Washington, DC 20016
Telephone: (202) 686-2862

RIGGIN, E. Philip
Director, Nat'l Legislative Commission, American Legion
1608 K St., N.W., Washington, DC 20006
Telephone: (202) 861-2740
Registered as lobbyist at U.S. Congress.

RIGGOTT, Charles R.
Exec. V. President, Internat'l Fabricare Institute
12251 Tech Road, Silver Spring, MD 20904
Telephone: (301) 622-1900

RIGGS, Channing W.
Assistant, Special Issues, Nestle Enterprises, Inc.
1511 K St., N.W., Suite 1100, Washington, DC 20005
Telephone: (202) 639-8894

RIGGS, Judith Assmus
Director, Federal Issues, Alzheimer's Ass'n
1334 G St., N.W. Suite 500, Washington, DC 20005
Telephone: (202) 393-7737
Registered as lobbyist at U.S. Congress.

RIGNEY, P. Robert, Jr.
Assoc. Exec. Director, Public Affairs, American Ass'n of Blood Banks
1117 North 19th St. Suite 600, Arlington, VA 22209
Telephone: (703) 528-8200
Registered as lobbyist at U.S. Congress.
Background: District Field Representative for Cong. John Brademas (D-IN), 1976-79; Chief Counsel, Subcommittee on General Oversight, Committee on Small Business, U.S. House of Reps., 1982-83; Staff Director and Chief Counsel, Subcommittee on Compensation and Employee Benefits, Committee on Post Office and Civil Service, U.S. House of Reps., 1983-84.

RIKER, Ellen
MARC Associates, Inc.
1030 15th St., N.W. Suite 468, Washington, DC 20005
Telephone: (202) 371-8090
Registered as lobbyist at U.S. Congress.
Clients:
   American Soc. of Anesthesiologists
   American Soc. of Clinical Pathologists
   Merck Sharp and Dohme
   Nat'l Ass'n of Epilepsy Centers

RIKER, Wesley J.
Deputy National Service Director, American Veterans of World War II, Korea and Vietnam (AMVETS)
4647 Forbes Blvd., Lanham, MD 20706
Telephone: (301) 459-9600
Registered as lobbyist at U.S. Congress.

RIKSEN, Michael R.
Director, Federal Affairs, Harris Corp.
1201 East Abingdon Drive Suite 300, Alexandria, VA 22314
Telephone: (703) 548-9200
Registered as lobbyist at U.S. Congress.

RILEY, Chris
Legislative Assistant, Connecticut, State of
444 North Capitol St., N.W. Suite 317, Washington, DC 20001
Telephone: (202) 347-4535

RILEY AND FOX
1101 17th St., N.W., Suite 606, Washington, DC 20036
Telephone: (202) 223-9800
Members of firm representing listed organizations:
   Fox, Albert A., V. President
   Riley, Stephen
Clients:
   South Africa, Chamber of Mines of *(Stephen Riley)*
   South Africa, Government of

RILEY, James E.
Senior V. President and General Counsel, Electronic Industries Ass'n
2001 Pennsylvania Ave., N.W., Washington, DC 20006
Telephone: (202) 457-4900

RILEY, James P.
Fletcher, Heald and Hildreth
1225 Connecticut Ave., N.W. Suite 400, Washington, DC 20036
Telephone: (202) 828-5700

RILEY, Patrick
Attorney, Internat'l Brotherhood of Teamsters, Chauffeurs, Warehousemen and Helpers of America
25 Louisiana Ave., N.W., Washington, DC 20001
Telephone: (202) 624-6800

RILEY, Stephen
Riley and Fox
1101 17th St., N.W., Suite 606, Washington, DC 20036
Telephone: (202) 223-9800
Registered as Foreign Agent: (#3813).
Clients:
   South Africa, Chamber of Mines of

RILEY, Susan
Evans Group, Ltd., The
1010 Wisconsin Ave., N.W. Suite 810, Washington, DC 20007
Telephone: (202) 333-8777
Registered as lobbyist at U.S. Congress.
Clients:
   Matteson Investment Corp.
   Mortgage Bankers Ass'n of America
   Nat'l Multi Housing Council
   New York State Mortgage Loan Enforcement and Administrative Corp.

RILEY, William
Policy and Legislation Div, DEPARTMENT OF HEALTH AND HUMAN SERVICES - Human Development Services
200 Independence Ave. S.W., Washington, DC 20201
Telephone: (202) 245-7027

RINDAL, Karin
Corp. Mgr., Internat'l Trade Regulation, EG&G, Inc.
1850 K St., N.W., Suite 1190, Washington, DC 20006
Telephone: (202) 887-5570

RING, Carlyle C., Jr.
V. President and General Counsel, Atlantic Research Corp.
5390 Cherokee Ave., Alexandria, VA 22312-2302
Telephone: (703) 642-4000

RING, Russell C.
Legislative Representative, Mutual of Omaha Insurance Companies
1700 Pennsylvania Ave., N.W. Suite 500, Washington, DC 20006
Telephone: (202) 393-6200
Registered as lobbyist at U.S. Congress.
Background: Former aide to Rep. Stan Parris (R-VA).

RINGWOOD, Irene
Bogle and Gates
One Thomas Circle, N.W., Suite 900, Washington, DC 20005
Telephone: (202) 293-3600
Registered as lobbyist at U.S. Congress.
Clients:
   American Dehydrated Onion and Garlic Ass'n
   American Fishing Tackle Manufacturers Ass'n
   Basic American Foods
   Puget Sound Cruiseship Alliance
   Washington Agriculture GATT Coalition

RINTYE, Peter R.
V. President, Sheehan Associates, Inc.
727 15th St., N.W., Suite 1200, Washington, DC 20005
Telephone: (202) 347-0044
Registered as lobbyist at U.S. Congress.
Background: Regional Political Director, Republican Nat'l Committee, 1983-84; Deputy Campaign Director and Director, Campaign Finance, Nat'l Republican Congressional Committee, 1987-89.

RIORDAN, Dale P.
Exec. V. President, Marketing, Federal Nat'l Mortgage Ass'n
3900 Wisconsin Ave., N.W., Washington, DC 20016
Telephone: (202) 752-6740
Registered as lobbyist at U.S. Congress.

RIORDAN, Mary Beth
Director, Tax Legislation, Verner, Liipfert, Bernhard, McPherson and Hand, Chartered
901 15th St., N.W., Suite 700, Washington, DC 20005
Telephone: (202) 371-6000
Background: Legislative Assistant to Rep. Raymond McGrath (R-NY), 1981-82. Technical Consultant, House Committee on Science and Technology, 1982-84. Legislative Director and Tax Aide to Rep. McGrath, 1984-89.

RIPPEY, John S.
Senior V. President & Legis. Director, Ass'n of Bank Holding Companies
730 15th St., N.W., Suite 820, Washington, DC 20005
Telephone: (202) 393-1158
Registered as lobbyist at U.S. Congress.
Background: Bureau of Federal Credit Unions, 1966-1970; Federal Reserve Board staff, 1971-75.

RIS, William K., Jr.
Principal, Wexler, Reynolds, Fuller, Harrison and Schule, Inc.
1317 F St., N.W., Suite 600, Washington, DC 20004
Telephone: (202) 638-2121
Registered as lobbyist at U.S. Congress.
Background: Former Counsel, Senate Committee on Commerce, Science and Transportation, 1978-83.
Clients:
   American Airlines
   American Public Transit Ass'n
   MCI Communications Corp.

RISHE, Melvin
Fried, Frank, Harris, Shriver & Jacobson
1001 Pennsylvania Ave., N.W., Suite 800, Washington, DC 20004-2505
Telephone: (202) 639-7000
Registered as Foreign Agent: (#3473).
Background: Deputy General Counsel, Claims and Litigation, Office of the General Counsel, Dept. of the Navy, 1967-74. Counsel, Navy Contract Adjustment Board, 1967-74.
Clients:
   Israel, Embassy of
   Israel, Government of

RISHER, Carol A.
Director of Copyright and New Technology, Ass'n of American Publishers
1718 Connecticut Ave., N.W. Suite 700, Washington, DC 20009-1148
Telephone: (202) 232-3335
Registered as lobbyist at U.S. Congress.

RISSING, Edward W.
Director, Federal Affairs, Edison Electric Institute
1111 19th St., N.W., Washington, DC 20036
Telephone: (202) 778-6400
Registered as lobbyist at U.S. Congress.

RISSLER, Jane
Biotechnology Specialist, Nat'l Wildlife Federation
1400 16th St., N.W., Washington, DC 20036-2266
Telephone: (202) 797-6800

RITA, Margaret A.
Issue Analyst, Tobacco Institute
1875 Eye St., N.W., Suite 800, Washington, DC 20006
Telephone: (202) 457-4800

RITCHIE, Jeanne M.
Political Programs Director, American Council of Life Insurance
1001 Pennsylvania Ave., N.W., Washington, DC 20004-2599
Telephone: (202) 624-2157
Registered as lobbyist at U.S. Congress.
Background: Responsibilities also include the American Council of Life Insurance Political Action Committee.

RITLEY, Dominque
Capitol Associates, Inc.
426 C St., N.E., Washington, DC 20002
Telephone: (202) 544-1880
Registered as lobbyist at U.S. Congress.

RITTINGHAM, William
Director, Federal Relations, Pacific Telesis Group-Washington
1275 Pennsylvania Ave., N.W. Suite 400, Washington, DC 20004
Telephone: (202) 383-6400
Registered as lobbyist at U.S. Congress.

RITTS, Leslie Sue
Morgan, Lewis and Bockius
1800 M St., N.W., Washington, DC 20036
Telephone: (202) 467-7000
Registered as lobbyist at U.S. Congress.
Clients:
Nat'l Environmental Development Ass'n

RITZ, William R.
Director, Public Affairs, Nat'l Committee to Preserve Social Security and Medicare
2000 K St., N.W. Suite 800, Washington, DC 20006
Telephone: (202) 822-9459
Registered as lobbyist at U.S. Congress.
Background: Former chief press aide to Senator Herbert H. Kohl (D-WI).

RIVA, Valentin J.
V. President, Government Affairs, Nat'l Stone Ass'n
1415 Elliot Place, N.W., Washington, DC 20007
Telephone: (202) 342-1100
Registered as lobbyist at U.S. Congress.

RIVERA, Ivette E.
Legislative Representative, Nat'l Automobile Dealers Ass'n
412 First St., S.E., Washington, DC 20003
Telephone: (202) 547-5500
Registered as lobbyist at U.S. Congress.

RIVERS, John S.
Asst Dir, Cong and Intergovt'l Affrs, SELECTIVE SERVICE SYSTEM
1023 31st St., N.W., Washington, DC 20435
Telephone: (202) 724-0413

RIVERS, Father Joseph
President, Orphan Foundation of America
14261 Ben Franklin Station, N.W., Washington, DC 20044-4261
Telephone: (202) 861-0762

RIVERS, Larry W.
Exec. Director, Veterans of Foreign Wars of the U.S.
200 Maryland Ave., N.E., Washington, DC 20002
Telephone: (202) 543-2239

RIVERS, Richard
Akin, Gump, Strauss, Hauer and Feld
1333 New Hampshire Ave., N.W., Suite 400, Washington, DC 20036
Telephone: (202) 887-4000
Registered as Foreign Agent: (#3492).
Background: General Counsel of the Office of the Special Trade Representative for Trade Negotiations in the Executive Office of the President, 1977-79.
Clients:
Fujitsu Ltd.
Levi Strauss and Co.
Oil, Chemical and Atomic Workers Internat'l Union

RIVIERE, Nancy
Resources for Group Management, Inc.
1350 New York Ave., N.W. Suite 615, Washington, DC 20005
Telephone: (202) 393-1780
Background: Serves as Director of Communications, Greeting Card Ass'n.
Clients:
Greeting Card Creative Network

RIVKIN, RADLER, DUNNE AND BAYH
1575 Eye St., N.W. Suite 1025, Washington, DC 20005
Telephone: (202) 289-8660
Background: Washington office of a Uniondale, New York law firm.
Members of firm representing listed organizations:
Bayh, Birch (Jr.)
Background: Former Senator, (D-IN), 1963-81.
Connaughton, Thomas A.

Background: Former Administrative Assistant to Senator Birch Bayh of Indiana.
Faley, Kevin O.
Background: Counsel, U.S. Senate Subcommittee on Juvenile Delinquency, 1974-77. General Counsel, Senate Subcommittee on the Constitution, 1977-78. Chief Counsel and Exec. Director, Senate Subcommittee on the Constitution, 1978-80.
Harris, Sheldon J.
Clients:
ALC Communications Corp. *(Thomas A. Connaughton)*
Chemical Bank *(Thomas A. Connaughton, Sheldon J. Harris)*
Cook Group *(Thomas A. Connaughton)*
Merrill Lynch and Co., Inc.
Milk Industry Foundation
Nat'l Basketball Ass'n *(Birch Bayh, Jr., Thomas A. Connaughton, Kevin O. Faley)*
Nat'l Foreign Trade Council, Inc. *(Birch Bayh, Jr., Kevin O. Faley)*
Nat'l Soft Drink Ass'n *(Thomas A. Connaughton)*
RRD & B Good Government Committee *(Thomas A. Connaughton)*
Seagram & Sons, Inc., Joseph E. *(Birch Bayh, Jr.)*

RIVLIN, Alice M.
Senior Fellow, Economic Studies Program, Brookings Institution
1775 Massachusetts Ave., N.W., Washington, DC 20036
Telephone: (202) 797-6000
Background: Director, Congressional Budget Office (1975-83); Asst. Secretary for Planning and Evaluation, Health, Education and Welfare (1966-69).

RIZZO, Joseph J.
Exec. Director, Better Hearing Institute
5021B Backlick Road, Annandale, VA 22003
Telephone: (703) 642-0580

ROACH, Arvid E., II
Covington and Burling
1201 Pennsylvania Ave., N.W., Box 7566, Washington, DC 20044
Telephone: (202) 662-6000

ROACH, J. Robert
Exec. Director, Operations, Sheet Metal and Air Conditioning Contractors' Nat'l Ass'n
8224 Old Courthouse Rd., Vienna, VA 22182
Telephone: (703) 790-9890

ROBART, Andre W.
Director, Legislative Affairs (Envir.), Edison Electric Institute
1111 19th St., N.W., Washington, DC 20036
Telephone: (202) 828-7671
Background: U.S. Public Health Service, 1951-1973, Assistant Surgeon General. Director, Stationary Source Enforcement, Environmental Protection Agency, 1970-1973.

ROBART, Andrew W.
Dir., Environmental Legislative Affairs, Edison Electric Institute
1111 19th St., N.W., Washington, DC 20036
Telephone: (202) 778-6400
Registered as lobbyist at U.S. Congress.

ROBB, Edmund W., Jr.
Chairman, Institute on Religion and Democracy
729 15th St., N.W., Suite 900, Washington, DC 20005
Telephone: (202) 393-3200

ROBBINS ASSOCIATES, Liz
420 7th St., S.E., Washington, DC 20003
Telephone: (202) 544-6093
Background: A government affairs consulting firm.
Members of firm representing listed organizations:
Brown, Alvin S., Lobbyist
Background: Tax Attorney and Manager, Internal Revenue Service National Office, 1960-89.
Edwards, Sharon
Lucas, Michael J., Lobbyist
Robbins, Liz, President
Organizations represented:
Associated Church Press/Evangelical Press Ass'n *(Liz Robbins)*
Authors Guild, The *(Michael J. Lucas, Liz Robbins)*
Babcock and Brown *(Alvin S. Brown, Liz Robbins)*

Carlan Homes *(Michael J. Lucas, Liz Robbins)*
Coalition of Religious Press Ass'ns *(Michael J. Lucas, Liz Robbins)*
Deleuw/Greeley/Hyman *(Sharon Edwards)*
Dramatists Guild *(Michael J. Lucas, Liz Robbins)*
Gaymar Industries, Inc. *(Sharon Edwards, Liz Robbins)*
Montifiore Medical Center *(Liz Robbins)*
New York Medical Care Facilities Finance Agency *(Sharon Edwards, Liz Robbins)*
New York Public Library *(Sharon Edwards, Liz Robbins)*
New York State Housing Finance Agency *(Sharon Edwards, Liz Robbins)*
Phoenix House *(Liz Robbins)*
Songwriters Guild, The *(Michael J. Lucas, Liz Robbins)*
Southern Baptist Press Ass'n *(Michael J. Lucas, Liz Robbins)*
Spectrascan Imaging Services *(Sharon Edwards, Michael J. Lucas)*
Standard Pacific Corp. *(Alvin S. Brown, Liz Robbins)*
Vail Valley Associates *(Sharon Edwards)*
Warburg Pincus & Co., E. M. *(Alvin S. Brown, Liz Robbins)*

ROBBINS, Liz
President, Robbins Associates, Liz
420 7th St., S.E., Washington, DC 20003
Telephone: (202) 544-6093
Registered as lobbyist at U.S. Congress.
Organizations represented:
Associated Church Press/Evangelical Press Ass'n
Authors Guild, The
Babcock and Brown
Carlan Homes
Coalition of Religious Press Ass'ns
Dramatists Guild
Gaymar Industries, Inc.
Montifiore Medical Center
New York Medical Care Facilities Finance Agency
New York Public Library
New York State Housing Finance Agency
Phoenix House
Songwriters Guild, The
Southern Baptist Press Ass'n
Standard Pacific Corp.
Warburg Pincus & Co., E. M.

ROBBINS, Michelle
Manager, Legislative Affairs, Lockheed Corp.
1825 Eye St., N.W., Suite 1100, Washington, DC 20006
Telephone: (202) 955-3357
Registered as lobbyist at U.S. Congress.

ROBERSON, Floyd I.
First Associates Inc.
4320 Lorcom Lane, Arlington, VA 22207
Telephone: (703) 276-0091
Registered as Foreign Agent: (#3941).
Clients:
Toa Nenryo Kogyo Kabushiki Kaisha

ROBERTS, Anne Marie
Assistant Account Executive, Gallagher-Widmeyer Group Inc., The
1110 Vermont Ave., N.W., Suite 1020, Washington, DC 20005
Telephone: (202) 659-1606

ROBERTS, Carole T.
2nd V. President, Federal Gov't Affairs, Travelers, The
901 15th St., N.W. Suite 520, Washington, DC 20005
Telephone: (202) 789-1380
Registered as lobbyist at U.S. Congress.

ROBERTS & CO.
402 8th St., N.E., Washington, DC 20002
Telephone: (202) 546-0555
Members of firm representing listed organizations:
Roberts, Richard R.
Background: Serves as President, American Council of Highway Advertisers.
Clients:
American Council of Highway Advertisers *(Richard R. Roberts)*
Eagle Canyon Ranch *(Richard R. Roberts)*
South Seas Charter Service *(Richard R. Roberts)*

ROBERTS, Gordon
Director of Communications, American Public Power Ass'n
2301 M St., N.W., Washington, DC 20037
Telephone: (202) 775-8300

ROBERTS, Howard R.
Sr. V. President, Science and Technology, Nat'l Soft Drink
Ass'n
1101 16th St., N.W., Washington, DC 20036
Telephone: (202) 463-6750
Background: Former Acting Director, Bureau of Foods,
Food and Drug Administration.

ROBERTS, Maj. Gen. J. Milnor, AUS (Ret.)
President, Americans for the High Frontier
2800 Shirlington Road Suite 405 A, Arlington, VA 22206
Telephone: (703) 671-4111
Registered as lobbyist at U.S. Congress.

ROBERTS, Karen
Director, Washington Office, North Carolina, State of
444 N. Capitol St., N.W. Suite 320, Washington, DC
20001
Telephone: (202) 624-5830

ROBERTS, Laura
Deputy Director, Coalition Development, Madison Group/
Earle Palmer Brown, The
2033 M St., N.W., 9th Floor, Washington, DC 20036
Telephone: (202) 223-0030

ROBERTS, Michael A.
Washington Representative, American Academy of Ophthalmology
1101 Vermont Ave., N.W., Suite 300, Washington, DC
20005
Telephone: (202) 737-6662
Registered as lobbyist at U.S. Congress.

ROBERTS, Michael J.
Verner, Liipfert, Bernhard, McPherson and Hand, Chart-
ered
901 15th St., N.W., Suite 700, Washington, DC 20005
Telephone: (202) 371-6000
Registered as lobbyist at U.S. Congress.
Background: Member of Staff of Congressman Carlton R.
Sickles of Maryland, 1963-64.

ROBERTS, Paula
Senior Staff Attorney, Center for Law and Social Policy
1616 P St., N.W., Suite 350, Washington, DC 20036
Telephone: (202) 328-5140

ROBERTS, Richard R.
Roberts & Co.
402 8th St., N.E., Washington, DC 20002
Telephone: (202) 546-0555
Registered as lobbyist at U.S. Congress.
Background: Serves as President, American Council of
Highway Advertisers.
Clients:
    American Council of Highway Advertisers
    Eagle Canyon Ranch
    South Seas Charter Service

ROBERTS, Dr. Robert
V. President, Research, Institute for Defense Analyses
1801 North Beauregard St., Alexandria, VA 22311
Telephone: (703) 845-2300

ROBERTS, Robin D.
Black, Manafort, Stone and Kelly Public Affairs Co.
211 N. Union St., Third Floor, Alexandria, VA 22314
Telephone: (703) 683-6612
Registered as lobbyist at U.S. Congress.
Registered as Foreign Agent: (#3927).

ROBERTS, Roslyn D.
Exec. Director, Student Nat'l Medical Ass'n
1012 10th St., N.W., Washington, DC 20001
Telephone: (202) 371-1616

ROBERTS, William A.
Senior V. President, Keefe Co., The
444 North Capitol St., N.W., Suite 711, Washington, DC
20001
Telephone: (202) 638-7030
Registered as lobbyist at U.S. Congress.
Clients:

Broward County Governmental Center
Dallas Area Rapid Transit Authority
Fairfax County, Virginia
Hillsborough Area Regional Transit Authority
Seminole Tribe of Florida
Spillis Candela & Partners, Inc.
Tampa, Florida, City of
University of Miami
Westinghouse Transportation Division

ROBERTS, William A., III
Howrey and Simon
1730 Pennsylvania Ave., N.W., Washington, DC 20006-
4793
Telephone: (202) 783-0800
Clients:
    MCI Communications Corp.

ROBERTS, William J.
Senior Attorney, Environmental Defense Fund
1616 P St., N.W., Suite 150, Washington, DC 20036
Telephone: (202) 387-3500
Background: Former Administrative Assistant to former
Rep. James J. Florio (D-NJ).

ROBERTSON, Linda
Dickstein, Shapiro and Morin
2101 L St., N.W., Washington, DC 20037
Telephone: (202) 785-9700
Clients:
    Iroquois Gas, Inc.

ROBERTSON, Mark
V. President, Hill and Knowlton Public Affairs Worldwide
Washington Harbour, 901 31st St., N.W., Washington, DC
20007
Telephone: (202) 333-7400
Registered as lobbyist at U.S. Congress.
Registered as Foreign Agent: (#3301).
Background: Former Staff Assistant to Senator David Pry-
or (D-AR).
Clients:
    Hecht's

ROBERTSON, MONAGLE AND EASTAUGH
1050 Thomas Jefferson St., NW Sixth Floor, Washington,
DC 20007
Telephone: (202) 333-4400
Members of firm representing listed organizations:
    Gilman, Brad
    Silver, Steven W.
Clients:
    Alaska Loggers Ass'n *(Steven W. Silver)*
    Amselco Minerals, Inc. *(Steven W. Silver)*
    Anchorage School District *(Brad Gilman, Steven W.
        Silver)*
    Atlantic Richfield Company (ARCO) Transporta-
        tion Co. *(Steven W. Silver)*
    Bristol Bay Native Corp. *(Steven W. Silver)*
    Coastal Coalition *(Brad Gilman)*
    Crowley Maritime Corp.
    General Communication Incorporated *(Steven W.
        Silver)*
    Liberty Shipping Group *(Steven W. Silver)*
    Puget Sound Cruiseship Alliance
    Reeve Aleutian Airways *(Brad Gilman)*
    Sea-Land Service, Inc.

ROBERTSON, Peter
Patton, Boggs and Blow
2550 M St., N.W., Suite 800, Washington, DC 20037
Telephone: (202) 457-6000
Registered as lobbyist at U.S. Congress.
Background: Legislative Assistant to Rep. James R. Jones
(D-OK), 1979-81. Professional Staff Member, House Bud-
get Committee, 1981-86.

ROBERTSON, Raymond J.
V. President, Internat'l Ass'n of Bridge, Structural and Ornamental Iron Workers
1750 New York Ave., N.W. Suite 400, Washington, DC
20006
Telephone: (202) 383-4800

ROBERTSON, Reuben B.
Dow, Lohnes and Albertson
1255 23rd St., N.W., Suite 500, Washington, DC 20037
Telephone: (202) 857-2500
Clients:

Colonial Village, Inc.
Virginia Beach Federal Savings Bank

ROBERTSON, Steve A.
Asst. Dir., Nat'l Legislative Commission, American Legion
1608 K St., N.W., Washington, DC 20006
Telephone: (202) 861-2700
Registered as lobbyist at U.S. Congress.

ROBERTSON, William B.
Pagonis and Donnelly Group
1620 Eye St., N.W., Suite 603, Washington, DC 20006
Telephone: (202) 452-8811
Clients:
    Transkei, Government of

ROBESON, Robert E., Jr.
V. President, Civil Aviation, Aerospace Industries Ass'n of
America
1250 Eye St., N.W., Suite 1100, Washington, DC 20005
Telephone: (202) 371-8400

ROBINS, KAPLAN, MILLER & CIRESI
1627 Eye St., N.W., Suite 610, Washington, DC 20006
Telephone: (202) 861-6800
Registered as lobbyist at U.S. Congress.
Members of firm representing listed organizations:
    Deese, Pamela M.
    Hunnicutt, Charles A.
Clients:
    Ad Hoc Granite Trade Group *(Pamela M. Deese)*
    Cold Spring Granite Co. *(Pamela M. Deese)*
    Ecolab *(Pamela M. Deese)*
    Polaris Industries
    St. Paul, Minnesota, City of

ROBINSON, Anthony W.
President, Minority Business Enterprise Legal Defense and
Education Fund
300 Eye St., N.E., Suite 200, Washington, DC 20002
Telephone: (202) 543-0040
Registered as lobbyist at U.S. Congress.

ROBINSON, Carlton C.
Exec. V. President, Highway Users Federation for Safety
and Mobility
1776 Massachusetts Ave., N.W., Washington, DC 20036
Telephone: (202) 857-1200

ROBINSON, Cleveland
Exec. V. President, Coalition of Black Trade Unionists
Box 73055, Washington, DC 20056
Telephone: (202) 429-1203

ROBINSON, Court
Policy Analyst, United States Committee for Refugees
1025 Vermont Ave., N.W. Suite 920, Washington, DC
20005
Telephone: (202) 347-3507

ROBINSON, David B.
Patton, Boggs and Blow
2550 M St., N.W., Suite 800, Washington, DC 20037
Telephone: (202) 457-6000
Clients:
    Alexander & Baldwin, Inc.

ROBINSON, Earl C.
Ass't Director, Machinists Non-Partisan Political League
1300 Connecticut Ave., N.W. Suite 404, Washington, DC
20036
Telephone: (202) 857-5295

ROBINSON, Ernestine S.
Adminstrative Ass't, Gov't Affairs, American Soc. of Ass'n
Executives
1575 Eye St., N.W., Washington, DC 20005-1168
Telephone: (202) 626-2723
Registered as lobbyist at U.S. Congress.

ROBINSON, Frank L.
Exec. Director, American Horticultural Soc.
Box 0105, Mount Vernon, VA 22121
Telephone: (703) 768-5700

ROBINSON, Gilbert A.
Chairman, Robinson, Inc., Gilbert A.
1146 19th St., N.W., Washington, DC 20036
Telephone: (202) 728-9500
Background: Former Ambassador at Large and Deputy Di-
rector of the U.S. Information Agency.

Organizations represented:
Entertainment America
Fontaine Group, Inc.
Marmon Group
Net Equity
Union Tank Car Co.
21st Century Space Foundation

ROBINSON, INC., Gilbert A.
1146 19th St., N.W., Washington, DC 20036
Telephone: (202) 728-9500
Members of firm representing listed organizations:
Robinson, Gilbert A., Chairman
Background: Former Ambassador at Large and Deputy
Director of the U.S. Information Agency.
Organizations represented:
Entertainment America *(Gilbert A. Robinson)*
Fontaine Group, Inc. *(Gilbert A. Robinson)*
Marmon Group *(Gilbert A. Robinson)*
Net Equity *(Gilbert A. Robinson)*
Union Tank Car Co. *(Gilbert A. Robinson)*
21st Century Space Foundation *(Gilbert A. Robinson)*

ROBINSON, J. Lawrence
Exec. V. President, Dry Color Manufacturers Ass'n
Box 20839, Alexandria, VA 22320
Telephone: (703) 684-4044

ROBINSON, Kenneth
President, Nat'l Ass'n of Federal Credit Unions
3138 N. 10th St., Arlington, VA 22201
Telephone: (703) 522-4770
Registered as lobbyist at U.S. Congress.

ROBINSON, LAKE, LERER & MONTGOMERY
1667 K St., N.W., Suite 900, Washington, DC 20006
Telephone: (202) 457-9270
Registered as Foreign Agent: (#3911)
Members of firm representing listed organizations:
Blee, David C., V. President
Background: Director of Public Affairs, 1983-87; Direc-
tor, External Affairs, 1987-88; and Deputy Assistant
Secretary for Congressional, Intergovernmental and
Public Affairs, 1988-89, U.S. Department of Energy.
Buckley, John, V. President
Chambers, Mary, Senior Associate
Background: Former Chief of Staff to Rep. Robert
Matsui (D-CA).
Cheney, Carolyn, V. President
Helmke, Mark
Background: Press Secretary to Senator Richard G. Lu-
gar (R-IN), 1981-86.
Lake, James H., Chairman
Morgan, Lance I., V. President
Background: Former Press Sec'y to Senate Select Com-
mittee on Secret Military Assistance for Iran and the
Nicaraguan Opposition and former Press Secretary to
Sen. Daniel Patrick Moynihan (D-NY).
Robinson, Linda, President and CEO
Background: Deputy Press Secretary to Ronald Reagan
in the 1979-80 Presidential campaign.
Schnoor, Kim
Thompson, Mary Helen
Background: Associate, Robinson, Lake, Lerer & Mont-
gomery. Former Press Secretary to Senator Paul
Tsongas (D-MA).
Clients:
Atari Games Corp. *(Mark Helmke, James H. Lake, Lance
I. Morgan)*
California Prune Board *(James H. Lake)*
California Walnut Commission *(James H. Lake)*
Connell Rice and Sugar Co. *(James H. Lake)*
Guam Commission on Self-Determination *(Mark
Helmke)*
Illinois Power Co. *(David C. Blee)*
Japan Auto Parts Industry Ass'n *(James H. Lake)*
Mitsubishi Electric Corp. *(James H. Lake)*
Napa Flood Control and Water Conservation
District *(James H. Lake, Kim Schnoor)*
Nat'l Venture Capital Ass'n *(Mark Helmke)*
Rice Growers Ass'n of California *(James H. Lake)*
Staley Manufacturing Co., A. E. *(Carolyn Cheney)*
Sun Diamond Growers of California *(James H. Lake)*
Tri-Valley Growers of California *(James H. Lake)*

ROBINSON, Laurine D.
Ass't Exec. Director, American Ass'n of Collegiate Regis-
trars and Admissions Officers
One Dupont Circle, N.W., Suite 330, Washington, DC
20036
Telephone: (202) 293-9161

ROBINSON, Linda
President and CEO, Robinson, Lake, Lerer & Montgomery
1667 K St., N.W., Suite 900, Washington, DC 20006
Telephone: (202) 457-9270
Background: Deputy Press Secretary to Ronald Reagan in
the 1979-80 Presidential campaign.

ROBINSON, Mary Beth
Director, Public Relations, Nat'l Automobile Dealers Ass'n
8400 Westpark Dr., McLean, VA 22102
Telephone: (703) 821-7000

ROBINSON, Michelle
Legislative Representative, Council for a Livable World
100 Maryland Ave., N.E. Suite 211, Washington, DC
20002
Telephone: (202) 543-4100
Registered as lobbyist at U.S. Congress.

ROBINSON, Phillip L.
Patton, Boggs and Blow
2550 M St., N.W., Suite 800, Washington, DC 20037
Telephone: (202) 457-6000
Registered as lobbyist at U.S. Congress.
Background: Professional Staff Member, Office of Tech-
nology Assessment, U.S. Congress, 1979-81.

ROBINSON, Randall
Exec. Director, TransAfrica
545 Eighth St., S.E. Suite 200, Washington, DC 20003
Telephone: (202) 547-2550

ROBINSON, Ron
President, Young America's Foundation
11800 Sunrise Valley Drive, Reston, VA 22090
Telephone: (703) 620-5270

ROBINSON, Roscoe R.
Chairman, Ass'n of Academic Health Centers
1400 16th St., N.W. Suite 410, Washington, DC 20036
Telephone: (202) 265-9600

ROBINSON, Lt. Gen. Wallace H., Jr.
President, Nat'l Security Industrial Ass'n
1025 Connecticut Ave., N.W., Suite 300, Washington, DC
20036
Telephone: (202) 775-1440

ROBINSON, Will
Coordinated Campaign Director, Democratic Nat'l Committee
430 South Capitol St., S.E., Washington, DC 20003
Telephone: (202) 863-8000

ROBISON, Bob John
President, Robison Internat'l, Inc.
2300 N St., N.W., Suite 600, Washington, DC 20037
Telephone: (202) 663-9048
Registered as lobbyist at U.S. Congress.
Registered as Foreign Agent: (#3950).

ROBISON INTERNAT'L, INC.
2300 N St., N.W., Suite 600, Washington, DC 20037
Telephone: (202) 663-9048
Registered as Foreign Agent: (#3950)
Background: A public and legislative affairs firm specializ-
ing in defense matters.
Members of firm representing listed organizations:
Ladd, Richard B., V. President
Robison, Bob John, President
Clients:
British Aerospace, Inc./Defense Programs Office
FMC Corp.
General Atomics
McDonnell Douglas Corp.
McDonnell Douglas Helicopter Co. *(Richard B.
Ladd)*
Royal Ordnance, Inc.

ROBISON, W. Churchill
Washington Representative, Port Authority of New York
and New Jersey
1001 Connecticut Ave., N.W. Suite 610, Washington, DC
20036
Telephone: (202) 887-5240
Background: Formerly on Congressional Relations Staff,
International Trade Administration.

ROCHMAN, Julie
Federal Affairs Specialist, Insurance Information Institute
1101 17th St, N.W., Suite 408, Washington, DC 20036
Telephone: (202) 833-1580

ROCK, James
Exec. Assistant to the General President, Sheet Metal
Workers' Internat'l Ass'n
1750 New York Ave., N.W. Sixth Floor, Washington, DC
20006
Telephone: (202) 783-5880
Registered as lobbyist at U.S. Congress.

ROCK, James A.
Washington Representative, Montana Power Co.
1730 M St., N.W., Suite 607, Washington, DC 20036
Telephone: (202) 296-3060
Registered as lobbyist at U.S. Congress.
Background: Consultant, Public Lands; House Interior
Committee, Public Lands Subcommittee 1973-76; Legisla-
tive Ass't to Sen. John Melcher (D-MT) 1977-83. Also
represents the Washington Power Co.

ROCK, James W.
Concord Associates, Inc.
1455 Pennsylvania Ave., N.W. Suite 560, Washington, DC
20004
Telephone: (202) 737-9300
Background: Former House Ways and Means Committee
Assistant to Rep. Ed Jenkins (D-GA), 1984-88, and to
Rep. Kent Hance (D-TX), 1980-84.

ROCK, Mike
Sr. Assoc. Director, Div. of Legislation, American Hospital
Ass'n
50 F St., N.W., Suite 1100, Washington, DC 20001
Telephone: (202) 638-1100
Registered as lobbyist at U.S. Congress.

ROCKE, Susan
Administrative Coordinator, Nat'l Ass'n of Development
Organizations
400 North Capitol St., N.W. Suite 372, Washington, DC
20001
Telephone: (202) 624-7806

ROCKEFELLER, Edwin S.
Schiff Hardin & Waite
1101 Connecticut Ave., N.W. Suite 600, Washington, DC
20036
Telephone: (202) 857-0600
Background: Assistant to General Counsel, Federal Trade
Commission, 1958-59. Exec. Assistant to the Chairman,
FTC, 1959-61.

ROCKLER, Walter J.
Arnold & Porter
1200 New Hampshire Ave., N.W., Washington, DC 20036
Telephone: (202) 872-6700
Registered as lobbyist at U.S. Congress.

ROCKWELL, H. William, Jr.
Director, Resource Policy, Soc. of American Foresters
5400 Grosvenor Lane, Bethesda, MD 20814
Telephone: (301) 897-8720

RODDY, Carolyn Tatum
Attorney Advisor, Legis Affrs, FEDERAL COMMUNICA-
TIONS COMMISSION
1919 M St., N.W., Washington, DC 20554
Telephone: (202) 632-6405

RODENBERG, Lt. Col. James C., USAF (Ret)
Legislative Counsel, Reserve Officers Ass'n of the U.S.
1 Constitution Ave., N.E., Washington, DC 20002
Telephone: (202) 479-2200
Background: Legislative Assistant to Senator Paula Haw-
kins (R-FL), 1982-86.

RODENBERG, Phillip L.
Director, Legislative Affairs, General Aviation Manufacturers Ass'n
1400 K St., Suite 801, Washington, DC 20005
Telephone: (202) 393-1500
Registered as lobbyist at U.S. Congress.
Background: Former Technical Consultant to the House Subcommittee on Trasnportation, Aviation and Materials and former Legislative Assistant to Rep. Dave McCurdy (D-OK).

RODGERS, Mark W.
Dep Dir, Office of Cong Relations, OFFICE OF PERSONNEL MANAGEMENT
1900 E St., N.W., Washington, DC 20415
Telephone: (202) 632-6514

RODGERS, Michael F.
Senior V. President, American Ass'n of Homes for the Aging
1129 20th St., N.W., Suite 400, Washington, DC 20036
Telephone: (202) 296-5960
Registered as lobbyist at U.S. Congress.
Background: Former Staff Director, House Select Committee on Aging; Professional Staff Member, Senate Special Committee on Aging.

RODGERS, Paul
Admin. Director and General Counsel, Nat'l Ass'n of Regulatory Utility Commissioners
Box 684, I.C.C. Bldg., Washington, DC 20044-0684
Telephone: (202) 898-2200

RODGERS, Quincy
Director, Government Affairs, General Instrument Corp.
1155 21st St., N.W., Suite 400, Washington, DC 20036
Telephone: (202) 833-9700
Registered as lobbyist at U.S. Congress.
Background: Also represents the General Instrument Corp. Political Action Committee.

RODGERS, Ruth
Exec. Director, Home Recording Rights Coalition
P.O. Box 33705, Washington, DC 20033
Telephone: (202) 663-8452

RODINE, Sharon
President, Nat'l Women's Political Caucus
1275 K St., N.W., Suite 750, Washington, DC 20005
Telephone: (202) 898-1100

RODMAN, Veronique
V. President, Cosmetic, Toiletry and Fragrance Ass'n
1110 Vermont Ave., N.W. Suite 800, Washington, DC 20005
Telephone: (202) 331-1770

RODRIGUEZ, Raul R.
Leventhal, Senter & Lerman
2000 K St., N.W., Suite 600, Washington, DC 20006
Telephone: (202) 429-8970
Registered as lobbyist at U.S. Congress.
Clients:
Aeronautical Radio, Inc.

RODRIGUEZ ROJAS, Dr. Rene F.
President, InterAmerican College of Physicians and Surgeons
1101 15th St., N.W. Suite 602, Washington, DC 20005
Telephone: (202) 467-4756

RODRIQUEZ, Gloria
Washington Representative, Nat'l Puerto Rican Forum
1511 K St., N.W., Suite 600, Washington, DC 20005
Telephone: (202) 638-2211

ROE, David A.
V. President, Publishing, Chamber of Commerce of the U.S.A.
1615 H St., N.W., Washington, DC 20062
Telephone: (202) 463-5652

ROE, Randall B.
Director, Washington Operations, Burns and Roe Enterprises, Inc.
1400 K St., N.W., Washington, DC 20005
Telephone: (202) 898-1500

ROEDER, Henry J.
Senior V. President, Nat'l Ass'n of Broadcasters
1771 N St., N.W., Washington, DC 20036
Telephone: (202) 429-5300

ROEMER, Jane
Exec. Director, Public Policy, Nat'l Safety Council
1050 17th St., N.W. Suite 770, Washington, DC 20036
Telephone: (202) 293-2270

ROENIGK, William P.
Dir., Econ. Research & Membership Svcs., Nat'l Broiler Council
1155 15th St., N.W. Suite 614, Washington, DC 20005
Telephone: (202) 296-2622

ROETHEL, David A. H.
Exec. Director, American Institute of Chemists
7315 Wisconsin Ave., Bethesda, MD 20814
Telephone: (301) 652-2447
Background: Also represents the American Institute of Chemists Foundation and the Nat'l Certification Commission in Chemistry and Chemical Engineering.

ROFF, Charles L.
Attorney, Sonat Inc.
1100 15th St., N.W. Suite 700, Washington, DC 20005
Telephone: (202) 775-0840
Registered as lobbyist at U.S. Congress.

ROFF, Peter
Liaison Officer, Cong & Intergov'l Affrs, DEPARTMENT OF LABOR
200 Constitution Ave., N.W., Washington, DC 20210
Telephone: (202) 523-6141

ROGERS & COWAN, INC.
2233 Wisconsin Ave., N.W. Suite 500, Washington, DC 20007
Telephone: (202) 338-1900
Members of firm representing listed organizations:
Hirshberg, Jennefer
Background: As Exec. V. President, Kaufman Public Relations, handles public relations for Rogers & Cowan, Inc. Both firms are units of Shandwick PLC.
Clients:
Canada, Embassy of

ROGERS, George M., Jr.
Shaw, Pittman, Potts and Trowbridge
2300 N St., N.W., Washington, DC 20037
Telephone: (202) 663-8000
Background: Member of the Board of Directors, B.F. Saul Real Estate Investment Trust.
Clients:
Saul Real Estate Investment Trust, B. F.

ROGERS INTERNAT'L, INC.
2018 Gunnell Farms Drive, Vienna, VA 22181
Members of firm representing listed organizations:
Rogers, Joe O.
Background: Exec. Director, House Republican Conference, 1983-84. U.S. Ambassador, Asian Development Bank, 1984-86.
Clients:
Anzonia Hotel Corp., N.A. *(Joe O. Rogers)*
Industrial Insulations of Texas, Inc. *(Joe O. Rogers)*
Korea Insulation Co., Ltd. *(Joe O. Rogers)*
Oil Dri Corp. of America *(Joe O. Rogers)*
Pittsburgh Corning Corp. *(Joe O. Rogers)*

ROGERS, James A.
V. President, United Parcel Service
316 Pennsylvania Ave., S.E. Suite 304, Washington, DC 20003
Telephone: (202) 675-4220
Registered as lobbyist at U.S. Congress.

ROGERS, Joe O.
Rogers Internat'l, Inc.
2018 Gunnell Farms Drive, Vienna, VA 22181
Background: Exec. Director, House Republican Conference, 1983-84. U.S. Ambassador, Asian Development Bank, 1984-86.
Clients:
Anzonia Hotel Corp., N.A.
Industrial Insulations of Texas, Inc.
Korea Insulation Co., Ltd.
Oil Dri Corp. of America

Pittsburgh Corning Corp.

ROGERS, Karen S.
Director, Federal Regulatory Affairs, Southwestern Bell Corp.
1667 K St., N.W., Suite 1000, Washington, DC 20006
Telephone: (202) 293-8550

ROGERS-KINGBURY, Linda
President, Citizens to Protect the Constitution
1156 15th St., N.W., Suite 1212, Washington, DC 20005
Telephone: (202) 785-2936

ROGERS, Margaret
Manager, Government Relations, Dow Chemical
1776 Eye St., N.W., Suite 575, Washington, DC 20006
Telephone: (202) 429-3400
Registered as lobbyist at U.S. Congress.

ROGERS, Mary
President, Nat'l Ass'n of Reimbursement Officers
1101 King St., Suite 160, Alexandria, VA 22314
Telephone: (703) 739-9333

ROGERS, Paul G.
Hogan and Hartson
555 13th St., N.W., Suite 1200, Washington, DC 20004-1109
Telephone: (202) 637-5600
Background: Member of Congress (D-FL) 1955-1979. Chairman, Subcommittee on Health and the Environment, U.S. House of Representatives, 1971-79. Member, Board of Directors, Merck and Co. and of Mutual Life Insurance Co. of New York.

ROGERS, Rod
Oil, Chemical and Atomic Workers Internat'l Union
1126 16th St., N.W., Suite 411, Washington, DC 20036
Telephone: (202) 223-5770

ROGERS, Terrence L.
Director, Legis. and Polit. Activities, American Federation of Government Employees
80 F St., N.W., Washington, DC 20001
Telephone: (202) 737-8700
Registered as lobbyist at U.S. Congress.

ROGERS, Wanda
Treasurer, Helicopter Ass'n Internat'l Political Action Committee
1619 Duke St., Alexandria, VA 22314-3406
Telephone: (703) 683-4646

ROGERS AND WELLS
1737 H St., N.W., Washington, DC 20006
Telephone: (202) 331-7760
Registered as Foreign Agent: (#3428)
Background: Washington office of a New York-based law firm.
Members of firm representing listed organizations:
Essaye, Anthony F.
Background: Office of the General Counsel, 1963-65; Deputy General Counsel, 1965-66, Peace Corps.
Gilberg, David J.
Morris, William
Background: General Counsel to Committee on Finance, U.S. Senate, 1972-80.
Raisler, Kenneth M.
Rossides, Eugene T.
Background: Special Asst. to Under Secretary, U.S. Treasury Department, 1958-1961. Asst. Secretary, U.S. Treasury Department, 1969-1973.
Clients:
American Express Co. *(William Morris)*
Claiborne, Inc., Liz *(Eugene T. Rossides)*
Compagnie Financiere de Paris et des Pays Bas *(Anthony F. Essaye, Eugene T. Rossides)*
Dreyfus Corp. *(William Morris)*
Futures Industry Ass'n *(David J. Gilberg, Kenneth M. Raisler)*
Investment Partnership Ass'n *(William Morris)*
Kamehameha Schools
Liga Agricola Industrial de la Cana de Azucar (LAICA) *(Eugene T. Rossides)*
Merrill Lynch and Co., Inc. *(William Morris, Eugene T. Rossides)*
Nat'l Ass'n of Beverage Importers *(William Morris)*
Republic Nat'l Bank of New York *(Eugene T. Rossides)*

Rutgers, The State University of New Jersey *(William Morris)*
Shearson Lehman Hutton *(William Morris)*
Teachers Insurance and Annuity Ass'n *(Eugene T. Rossides)*
Turner Corp., The *(William Morris)*
Wine and Spirits Wholesalers of America *(William Morris)*

ROGERS, William D.
Arnold & Porter
1200 New Hampshire Ave., N.W., Washington, DC 20036
Telephone: (202) 872-6700
Registered as lobbyist at U.S. Congress.
Registered as Foreign Agent: (#1750).
Background: Law Clerk to Justice Stanley Reed, U.S. Supreme Court, 1952-53. Special Counsel, U.S. Coordinator, Alliance for Progress, 1962-63. Deputy U.S. Coordinator, Alliance for Progress and Deputy Assistant Administrator, AID, 1963-65. Alternate U.S. Representative, Inter-American Economic and Social Council, 1964-65. Assistant Secretary of State for Inter-American Affairs, U.S. Coordinator, Alliance for Progress, 1974-76. Under Secretary of State for Economic Affairs, 1976.
Clients:
   Chile, Embassy of
   Panama, Government of

ROGGENSACK, Margaret E.
Arent, Fox, Kintner, Plotkin & Kahn
1050 Connecticut Ave., N.W., Washington, DC 20036-5339
Telephone: (202) 857-6000
Registered as Foreign Agent: (#2661).

ROGIN, Carole M.
Exec. V. President, Hauck and Associates
1255 23rd St., N.W., Washington, DC 20037
Telephone: (202) 452-8100
Registered as lobbyist at U.S. Congress.
Background: Serves as Exec. Director, Hearing Industries Ass'n and Exec. Director, State Governmental Affairs Council.
Clients:
   Hearing Industries Ass'n
   State Governmental Affairs Council

ROGOVIN, Lori S., M.S.W.
Government Relations Specialist, American Ass'n for Counseling and Development
5999 Stevenson Ave., Alexandria, VA 22304
Telephone: (703) 823-9800
Registered as lobbyist at U.S. Congress.

ROGSTAD, Barry K.
President, American Business Conference
1730 K St., N.W. Suite 1200, Washington, DC 20006
Telephone: (202) 822-9300
Registered as lobbyist at U.S. Congress.

ROHDE, Barbara
Director, Washington Office, Minnesota, State of
400 North Capitol St., N.W. Suite 322, Washington, DC 20001
Telephone: (202) 624-5308

ROHN, David W.
Director, Member Programs, Nat'l Ass'n of Manufacturers
1331 Pennsylvania Ave., N.W. Suite 1500 North, Washington, DC 20004-1703
Telephone: (202) 637-3000

ROHRER, Judy
Cong Liaison Div, ENVIRONMENTAL PROTECTION AGENCY
401 M St., S.W., Washington, DC 20460
Telephone: (202) 382-5200

ROHRKEMPER, Stephen F.
Internat'l Technical Expertise, Ltd.
150 South Washington St., Suite 403, Falls Church, VA 22046
Telephone: (703) 536-4500
Registered as lobbyist at U.S. Congress.

ROLAND, Robert A.
President, Chemical Manufacturers Ass'n
2501 M St., N.W., Washington, DC 20037
Telephone: (202) 887-1100

ROLAPP, R. Richards
President, American Horse Council
1700 K St., N.W. Suite 300, Washington, DC 20006
Telephone: (202) 296-4031
Background: Also serves as Treasurer, American Horse Council Committee on Legislation and Taxation.

ROLDON, RaeAnn
TARPAC Coordinator, Nat'l Ass'n of Broadcasters Television and Radio Political Action Committee (TARPAC)
1771 N St., N.W., Washington, DC 20036
Telephone: (202) 429-5319

ROLL, Charles R.
Director, Washington Office, RAND Corp.
2100 M St., N.W., 8th Floor, Washington, DC 20037
Telephone: (202) 296-5000

ROLLINS, Edward J.
Co-Chairman, Nat'l Republican Congressional Committee
320 First St., S.E., Washington, DC 20003
Telephone: (202) 479-7000

ROLLINS, Royce L.
Treasurer, Pathology Practice Ass'n Federal Political Action Committee
1301 Connecticut Ave., N.W., Washington, DC 20036
Telephone: (202) 659-4593

ROLLYSON, Mikel M.
Davis Polk & Wardwell
1300 Eye St., N.W. 11th Fl. East, Washington, DC 20005
Telephone: (202) 962-7000
Registered as lobbyist at U.S. Congress.
Clients:
   Kohlberg Kravis Roberts & Co.
   Morgan Stanley and Co.

ROLNICK, Michael
Legislative Associate, U.S. English
818 Connecticut Ave., N.W. Suite 200, Washington, DC 20006
Telephone: (202) 833-0100
Registered as lobbyist at U.S. Congress.

ROLPH, John F., III
V. President, Tax Legislation, Citicorp
1275 Pennsylvania Ave., N.W., Suite 503, Washington, DC 20004
Telephone: (202) 879-6800

ROMANI, Romano
President, Parry and Romani Associates Inc.
233 Constitution Ave., N.E., Washington, DC 20002
Telephone: (202) 547-4000
Registered as lobbyist at U.S. Congress.
Registered as Foreign Agent: (#3814).
Clients:
   American Family Corp.
   Bell Helicopter Textron
   Blue Sea Corp.
   Care Enterprises
   Generic Pharmaceutical Industry Ass'n
   Herbalife Internat'l
   Industrial Biotechnology Ass'n
   Motion Picture Ass'n of America
   Nat'l Ass'n of Independent Insurers
   Research Corporation Technologies, Inc.
   Schering-Plough Corp.
   Telephonics, CSD
   Warner-Lambert Co.
   Won Door Corp.

ROMANSKY, Michael A.
McDermott, Will and Emery
1850 K St., N.W., Suite 500, Washington, DC 20006-2296
Telephone: (202) 887-8000
Registered as lobbyist at U.S. Congress.
Clients:
   American Imaging Ass'n

ROMER, Joseph D.
V. President, Governmental Affairs, Nat'l Easter Seal Soc.
1350 New York Ave., N.W., Suite 415, Washington, DC 20005
Telephone: (202) 347-3066
Background: Served as Legislative Counsel to U.S. Representative Andrew Jacobs, Jr. (D-IN), 1975-78.

ROMIG, Michael J.
Senior Counsel, American Council of Life Insurance
1001 Pennsylvania Ave., N.W., Washington, DC 20004-2599
Telephone: (202) 624-2135
Registered as lobbyist at U.S. Congress.

RONCKETTI, Nancy E.
Administrative Officer, Internat'l Ass'n of Counseling Services
5999 Stevenson Ave., 3rd Floor, Alexandria, VA 22304
Telephone: (703) 823-9840

RONDOU, Rene
Secretary-Treasurer, Bakery, Confectionery and Tobacco Workers Internat'l Union
10401 Connecticut Ave., Kensington, MD 20895
Telephone: (301) 933-8600

RONEY, John C.
Special Projects Associate, Hawaiian Sugar Planters' Ass'n
1511 K St., N.W., Suite 723, Washington, DC 20005
Telephone: (202) 628-6372
Registered as lobbyist at U.S. Congress.

RONSICK, Col. Gene
House Liaison, Legis Liaison, DEPARTMENT OF AIR FORCE
The Pentagon, Washington, DC 20330
Telephone: (202) 697-8153

ROONEY, Francis P.
President, Biscuit and Cracker Manufacturers Ass'n
1400 L St., N.W. Suite 400, Washington, DC 20005
Telephone: (202) 898-1636
Registered as lobbyist at U.S. Congress.

ROONEY, Fred B.
1050 Connecticut Ave., N.W. Suite 1200, Washington, DC 20036
Telephone: (202) 457-9494
Registered as lobbyist at U.S. Congress.
Background: A government relations consultant. Former Congressman from Pennsylvania.
Organizations represented:
   American Iron and Steel Institute
   Ass'n of American Railroads
   CalMat Co.
   Kawasaki Motors Corp., USA
   Lone Star Industries
   Security Life Insurance Co. of Denver
   Specialty Vehicle Institute of America

ROONEY, Tom
Program Director, Convention II, Inc.
Box 1987, Washington, DC 20013-1987
Telephone: (202) 544-1789

ROOS, Kristi
Government Affairs Representative, Maersk Inc.
1667 K St., N.W., Suite 350, Washington, DC 20006
Telephone: (202) 887-6770

ROOSE, Don
Exec. Director, Registry of Interpreters for the Deaf
8719 Colesville Rd., Suite 310, Silver Spring, MD 20910
Telephone: (301) 608-0050

ROOT, Kenneth E.
Exec. Director, Nat'l AgriChemical Retailers Ass'n
Box 65493, Washington, DC 20035-5493
Telephone: (202) 467-0825

ROOT MORAN, Cynthia
Dir., Office of Governmental Relations, American Academy of Ophthalmology
1101 Vermont Ave., N.W., Suite 300, Washington, DC 20005
Telephone: (202) 737-6662
Registered as lobbyist at U.S. Congress.

ROPER, Ray
President, Printing Industries of America
1730 North Lynn St., Arlington, VA 22209
Telephone: (703) 841-4814

ROPES AND GRAY
1001 Pennsylvania Ave., N.W., Washington, DC 20004
Telephone: (202) 626-3900

ROPES AND GRAY (Cont'd)

Registered as Foreign Agent: (#4251)
Background: Washington office of a Boston law firm.
Members of firm representing listed organizations:
DeAmicis, Don S.
McDowell, Suzanne Ross
  Background: Attorney-Advisor, 1983-85, Associate Tax Legislative Counsel, 1985-87, U.S. Department of the Treasury.
Shay, Stephen E.
  Background: International Tax Counsel, U.S. Department of the Treasury, 1982-87.
Susman, Thomas M.
  Background: Chief Counsel, Senate Administrative Practice and Procedure Subcommittee, 1972-76. General Counsel, Senate Antitrust and Monopoly Subcommittee, 1977-78. General Counsel, Senate Judiciary Committee, 1979-80.
Clients:
  Butler Capital Corp. *(Suzanne Ross McDowell, Stephen E. Shay, Thomas M. Susman)*
  Digital Equipment Corp. *(Thomas M. Susman)*
  Dunkin' Donuts *(Thomas M. Susman)*
  Eastern Enterprises *(Thomas M. Susman)*
  Ireland, Industrial Development Authority of *(Stephen E. Shay)*
  Nat'l Ass'n of Independent Schools *(Thomas M. Susman)*

ROPOZA, Robert A.

Exec. Secretary/Legislative Director, Nat'l Rural Housing Coalition
122 C St., N.W., Washington, DC 20001
Telephone: (202) 393-5229

ROSADO, Edwin S.

Chicago Washington Office, City of
499 South Capitol St., S.E., Washington, DC 20003
Telephone: (202) 554-7900

ROSAPEPE, James C.

Rosapepe and Spanos
1400 Eye St., N.W., Suite 1150, Washington, DC 20005
Telephone: (202) 842-1880
Background: Legislative Assistant to Senator Fred Harris of Oklahoma, 1971-73. Legislative Assistant to Rep. Andrew Maguire of New Jersey, 1975.
Clients:
  Multistate Tax Commission
  North American Securities Administrators Ass'n

ROSAPEPE AND SPANOS

1400 Eye St., N.W., Suite 1150, Washington, DC 20005
Telephone: (202) 842-1880
Members of firm representing listed organizations:
Rosapepe, James C.
  Background: Legislative Assistant to Senator Fred Harris of Oklahoma, 1971-73. Legislative Assistant to Rep. Andrew Maguire of New Jersey, 1975.
Clients:
  Multistate Tax Commission *(James C. Rosapepe)*
  North American Securities Administrators Ass'n *(James C. Rosapepe)*

ROSCHWALB, Jerald

Dir., Office of Fed. Rtns - Higher Educ., Nat'l Ass'n of State Universities and Land-Grant Colleges
One Dupont Circle, N.W., Suite 710, Washington, DC 20036-1191
Telephone: (202) 778-0818

ROSCHWALB, Mila

Legislative Assistant, American Ass'n of Dental Schools
1625 Massachusetts Ave., N.W., Washington, DC 20036
Telephone: (202) 667-9433

ROSCOE, Wilma J.

V. President, Nat'l Ass'n for Equal Opportunity in Higher Education
400 12th St., N.E. 2nd Floor, Washington, DC 20002
Telephone: (202) 543-9111

ROSE, C. Peter

V. President, Goldman, Sachs and Co.
1101 Pennsylvania Ave., N.W. Suite 900, Washington, DC 20004
Telephone: (202) 637-3700
Registered as lobbyist at U.S. Congress.

ROSE COMMUNICATIONS

901 15th St., N.W., Suite 570, Washington, DC 20036
Telephone: (202) 371-0764
Registered as Foreign Agent: (#4003)
Members of firm representing listed organizations:
Rose, Robert R.
Clients:
  Johnson Matthey PLC *(Robert R. Rose)*

ROSE, David

Export/Import Manager, Intel Corporation
1825 Eye St., N.W., Suite 400, Washington, DC 20006
Telephone: (202) 429-2054

ROSE, Dr. Frank A.

Senior Consultant, Cassidy and Associates, Inc.
655 15th St., N.W., Suite 1100, Washington, DC 20005
Telephone: (202) 347-0773
Registered as lobbyist at U.S. Congress.
Clients:
  Cardinal Hill Hospital
  Challenger Center for Space Science Education
  Infirmary Health System, Inc.
  Louisiana Public Facilities Authority

ROSE, Frederic B.

Marks Murase and White
2001 L St., N.W., Suite 750, Washington, DC 20036
Telephone: (202) 955-4900
Registered as Foreign Agent: (#4141).
Clients:
  Japan Steel Works, Ltd.

ROSE, John

Exec. V. President, Organization for the Protection and Advancement of Small Telephone Cos.
2000 K St., N.W., Suite 205, Washington, DC 20006
Telephone: (202) 659-5990
Background: Also represents OPASTCO Political Action Committee. Formerly Director, Telecommunications Management Division, Rural Electrification Administration.

ROSE, Jonathan C.

Jones, Day, Reavis and Pogue
1450 G St., N.W., Suite 700, Washington, DC 20005-2088
Telephone: (202) 879-3939
Registered as lobbyist at U.S. Congress.
Background: White House Staff Assistant, 1969-71. Special Assistant to the President, 1971-72. General Counsel, Council on International Economic Policy, 1972-74. Associate Deputy Attorney General, 1974-75. Director, Office of Justice Policy and Planning, 1974-75. Deputy Assistant Attorney General, Antitrust Division, Department of Justice, 1975-77. Assistant Attorney General, Office of Legal Policy, 1981-84.

ROSE, Leslie A.

Legislative Director, Group Health Ass'n of America
1129 20th St., N.W. Suite 600, Washington, DC 20036
Telephone: (202) 778-3200
Registered as lobbyist at U.S. Congress.
Background: Serves as Deputy Legislative Director for the Ass'n PAC.

ROSE, Merrill

Senior V. President, Porter/Novelli
1001 30th St., N.W., Washington, DC 20007
Telephone: (202) 342-7000
Registered as Foreign Agent: (#000-,).

ROSE, Michael

Exec. Editor, News Operations, Prentice Hall Information Services
1819 L St., N.W. Suite 400, Washington, DC 20036
Telephone: (202) 293-0707

ROSE, Robert R.

Rose Communications
901 15th St., N.W., Suite 570, Washington, DC 20036
Telephone: (202) 371-0764
Registered as Foreign Agent: (#4003).
Clients:
  Johnson Matthey PLC

ROSE, SCHMIDT, HASLEY & DISALLE

1701 Pennsylvania Ave., N.W., Suite 1040, Washington, DC 20006
Telephone: (202) 293-8600

Members of firm representing listed organizations:
Kushnick, Michael G.
  Background: Army Judge Advocate, 1958-61. Trial Attorney, Federal Trade Commission, 1961-64. Principal Legal Assistant to Federal Trade Commissioner Mary Gardiner Jones, 1964-66.
Sturtevant, Albert D.
Clients:
  Equimark Corp. *(Michael G. Kushnick)*
  Federation of the Swiss Watch Industry *(Michael G. Kushnick)*
  Joy Technologies Inc. *(Michael G. Kushnick)*
  Social Security Protection Bureau *(Michael G. Kushnick)*
  Southwire Co.

ROSE, Dr. Wil

Chief Executive Officer, American Indian Heritage Foundation
6051 Arlington Blvd., Falls Church, VA 22044
Telephone: (202) 237-7500

ROSEN, Burt E.

Director, Federal Legislative Affairs, Bristol-Myers Squibb Co.
655 15th St., N.W., Suite 410, Washington, DC 20005
Telephone: (202) 783-0900
Registered as lobbyist at U.S. Congress.

ROSEN, Hilary B.

V. President, Government Relations, Recording Industry Ass'n of America
1020 19th St., N.W., Suite 200, Washington, DC 20036
Telephone: (202) 775-0101
Registered as lobbyist at U.S. Congress.
Background: Represents the Recording Industry Ass'n of America PAC.

ROSEN, Mark A.

V. President, Labor Bureau, Inc., The
1101 15th St., N.W., Suite 1010, Washington, DC 20005
Telephone: (202) 296-7420

ROSENAUER, David B.

Gibson, Dunn and Crutcher
1050 Connecticut Ave., N.W. Suite 900, Washington, DC 20036-5303
Telephone: (202) 955-8500

ROSENAUER, Kathleen V.

Manager of Public Information, Air Transport Ass'n of America
1709 New York Ave., N.W., Washington, DC 20006-5206
Telephone: (202) 626-4000

ROSENBAUM, Albert B., III

V. President, Allwaste, Inc.
499 S. Capitol St., S.W. Suite 520, Washington, DC 20003
Telephone: (202) 488-4887
Registered as lobbyist at U.S. Congress.

ROSENBAUM, Daniel B.

Caplin and Drysdale
One Thomas Circle, N.W. Suite 1100, Washington, DC 20005
Telephone: (202) 862-5000
Registered as lobbyist at U.S. Congress.
Background: Attorney, U.S. Department of Justice, Tax Division, 1968-72.

ROSENBAUM, Nelson M.

President, CRG Marketing Group
1000 16th St., N.W. Suite 500, Washington, DC 20036
Telephone: (202) 223-2400

ROSENBAUM, Robert D.

Arnold & Porter
1200 New Hampshire Ave., N.W., Washington, DC 20036
Telephone: (202) 872-6700

ROSENBAUM, Sara

Director, Programs and Policy, Children's Defense Fund
122 C St., N.W., Washington, DC 20001
Telephone: (202) 628-8787
Registered as lobbyist at U.S. Congress.

ROSENBERG, Arnold

President, Rosenberg Company, Arnold
1800 Old Meadow Road, McLean, VA 22102

The listings in this directory are available as *Mailing Labels*. See last page.

Telephone: (703) 827-0840

ROSENBERG COMPANY, Arnold
1800 Old Meadow Road, McLean, VA 22102
Telephone: (703) 827-0840
Background: Consultants on marketing to companies in the defense industry.
Members of firm representing listed organizations:
  Rosenberg, Arnold, President

ROSENBERG, Ernest S.
Dir, Envir'l and Health Legis & Reg Afrs, Occidental Petroleum Corp.
1747 Pennsylvania Ave., N.W., Suite 375, Washington, DC 20006
Telephone: (202) 857-3000

ROSENBERG, Marc H.
V. President, Federal Affairs, Insurance Information Institute
1101 17th St, N.W., Suite 408, Washington, DC 20036
Telephone: (202) 833-1580
Background: Sr. Legislative Staff for U.S. Representatives Charles A. Mosher and Charles W. Whalen (both R-OH), 1974-78; Subcommittee Staff Director, House, Small Business Committee, 1979-83.

ROSENBERG, Marvin
Fletcher, Heald and Hildreth
1225 Connecticut Ave., N.W. Suite 400, Washington, DC 20036
Telephone: (202) 828-5700

ROSENBERG, Robert
Manager, State Government Affairs, Nat'l Pest Control Ass'n
8100 Oak St., Dunn Loring, VA 22027
Telephone: (703) 573-8330
Registered as lobbyist at U.S. Congress.

ROSENBERG, Sarah Z.
Exec. Director, American Institute for Conservation of Historic and Artistic Works
1400 16th St., N.W. Suite 340, Washington, DC 20036
Telephone: (202) 232-6636

ROSENBERRY, Margaret
Exec. Director, Human Environment Center
1001 Connecticut Ave., N.W. Suite 827, Washington, DC 20036
Telephone: (202) 331-8387

ROSENBLATT, Daniel
Exec. Director, Internat'l Ass'n of Chiefs of Police
1110 N. Glebe Road Suite 200, Arlington, VA 22201
Telephone: (703) 243-6500

ROSENBLATT, Maurice
President, Nat'l Counsel Associates
421 New Jersey Ave., S.E., Washington, DC 20003
Telephone: (202) 547-5000

ROSENBLATT, Peter R.
1001 Connecticut Ave., N.W. Suite 707, Washington, DC 20036
Telephone: (202) 466-4700
Background: Deputy Ass't General Counsel, Agency for Internat'l Development, 1966; White House Staff, 1966-68; Judicial Officer, Chairman, Board of Contract Appeals, U.S. Post Office Dept., 1968-69; Special Counsultant to Sen. Edmund Muskie (D-ME), 1970-72; Personal Representative of the President to the negotiations on the future political status of the Trust Territory of the Pacific Islands, 1977-81. Serves as President of the Coalition for a Democratic Majority; Secretary-Treasurer, U.S. Nat'l Committee for Pacific Economic Co-operation.
Organizations represented:
  China, Foreign Trade Board of the Republic of
  China, Government of the Republic of

ROSENBLATT, Samuel M.
President, Ass'n for Internat'l Investment
1825 Eye St., N.W., Suite 940, Washington, DC 20006
Telephone: (202) 331-7880
Registered as lobbyist at U.S. Congress.

ROSENBLEETH, Col. Herb
Nat'l Legislative Director, Jewish War Veterans of the U.S.A.
1811 R St., N.W., Washington, DC 20009
Telephone: (202) 265-6280
Registered as lobbyist at U.S. Congress.

ROSENBLOOM, H. David
Caplin and Drysdale
One Thomas Circle, N.W. Suite 1100, Washington, DC 20005
Telephone: (202) 862-5000
Registered as lobbyist at U.S. Congress.
Registered as Foreign Agent: (# 3821).
Background: Special Assistant to U.S. Ambassador to United Nations, 1966-67; Law Clerk, U.S. Supreme Court, 1967-68; International Tax Counsel, U.S. Treasury Department, 1978-81.

ROSENBLOOM, Joel
Wilmer, Cutler and Pickering
2445 M St., N.W., Washington, DC 20037-1420
Telephone: (202) 663-6000
Registered as lobbyist at U.S. Congress.
Clients:
  Capital Cities/ABC Inc.
  Cook Inlet Communications

ROSENBLOOM, Morris Victor
American Surveys Internat'l
2000 N St., N.W., Washington, DC 20036
Telephone: (202) 331-1711

ROSENBLUM, Annette T.
Manager, Science Policy Analysis, American Chemical Soc.
1155 16th St., N.W., Washington, DC 20036
Telephone: (202) 872-4383

ROSENBURG, Gregory
Director of Communications, Mechanical Contractors Ass'n of America
1385 Piccard Drive, Rockville, MD 20850
Telephone: (301) 869-5800
Registered as lobbyist at U.S. Congress.

ROSENDAHL, Jennifer E.
Neill and Co.
815 Connecticut Ave., N.W. Suite 800, Washington, DC 20006
Telephone: (202) 463-8877
Registered as lobbyist at U.S. Congress.
Registered as Foreign Agent: (# 3320).
Background: Office of Congressman Don Bonker, 1981. Member, U.S. House of Representatives Export Task Force, 1982-83.

ROSENFELD, Allen
Director, Agricultural Policy, Public Voice for Food and Health Policy
1001 Connecticut Ave., N.W. Suite 522, Washington, DC 20036
Telephone: (202) 659-5930

ROSENFIELD, Harry N.
1050 17th St., N.W., Suite 740, Washington, DC 20036
Telephone: (202) 457-0202
Background: An attorney in independent practice. Serves as Washington Counsel for the American Chiropractic Ass'n and Consultant to the National Safety Council.
Organizations represented:
  Nat'l Safety Council

ROSENKER, Mark V.
V. President of Public Affairs, Electronic Industries Ass'n
2001 Pennsylvania Ave., N.W., Washington, DC 20006
Telephone: (202) 457-4980

ROSENTHAL, Bruce
Director of Communications, Nat'l Ass'n of Towns and Townships
1522 K St., N.W. Suite 730, Washington, DC 20005
Telephone: (202) 737-5200

ROSENTHAL, Donald L.
Seyfarth, Shaw, Fairweather and Geraldson
815 Connecticut Ave., N.W., Washington, DC 20006-4004
Telephone: (202) 463-2400

Background: Deputy Solicitor of the Department of Labor and Chief of Staff and Counselor to the Secretary of Labor, 1981-82.
Clients:
  Agricultural Producers, Inc.
  Flxible Corp., The
  Pitney-Bowes, Inc.

ROSENTHAL, Eric
Political Director, Human Rights Campaign Fund
1012 14th St., N.W. Suite 607, Washington, DC 20005
Telephone: (202) 628-4160

ROSENTHAL, Herbert A.
2033 M St., N.W., Suite 400, Washington, DC 20036
Telephone: (202) 785-9773
Background: Trial Attorney, Bureau of Operating Rights, Civil Aeronautics Board, 1967-69.
Organizations represented:
  DHL Airways, Inc.
  Dominicana Airlines
  ICB Internat'l Airlines

ROSENTHAL, Jacob W.
Ginsburg, Feldman and Bress
1250 Connecticut Ave., N.W. Suite 800, Washington, DC 20036
Telephone: (202) 637-9000
Background: Counsel to Bureau of Safety Regulation, 1947-49; Assistant Chief, Opinion Writing Division, 1950-56; Chief, Special Authorities Division, 1957-61; Chief, Routes and Agreements Division, 1961-65; and Director, Bureau of Operating Rights, 1966-67, all of the Civil Aeronautics Board. Member, Board of Directors, Systems Automation Corp.
Clients:
  Executive Air Fleet Corp.
  Midway Airlines
  Northern Pacific Transport, Inc.

ROSENTHAL, Paul C.
Collier, Shannon & Scott
1055 Thomas Jefferson St., N.W., Suite 300, Washington, DC 20007
Telephone: (202) 342-8400
Registered as lobbyist at U.S. Congress.
Background: Counsel, U.S. Senate Committee on Governmental Affairs, 1975-81.
Clients:
  American Couplings Coalition
  Ferrous Scrap Consumers Coalition
  Lykes Brothers, Inc.
  Municipal Castings Fair Trade Council
  Nat'l Juice Products Ass'n
  Tropicana Products Inc.

ROSENTHAL, Roger C.
Exec. Director, Migrant Legal Action Program
2001 S St., N.W., Suite 310, Washington, DC 20009
Telephone: (202) 462-7744
Registered as lobbyist at U.S. Congress.

ROSENTHAL, Steven S.
Morrison & Foerster
2000 Pennsylvania Ave., N.W., Suite 5500, Washington, DC 20006
Telephone: (202) 887-1500
Registered as lobbyist at U.S. Congress.
Clients:
  Nat'l Electrical Manufacturers Ass'n

ROSENZWEIG, Richard
Partner, Madison Group/Earle Palmer Brown, The
2033 M St., N.W., 9th Floor, Washington, DC 20036
Telephone: (202) 223-0030
Registered as lobbyist at U.S. Congress.
Clients:
  Keystone Center, The
  Northern States Power Co.
  STRATCO, Inc.

ROSENZWEIG, Robert M.
President, Ass'n of American Universities
One Dupont Circle, N.W. Suite 730, Washington, DC 20036
Telephone: (202) 466-5030

The listings in this directory are available as *Mailing Labels*. See last page.

ROSEWATER, Annemarie G.
Exec. Director, Foundation of American College of Health Care Administrators
325 South Patrick St., Alexandria, VA 22314
Telephone: (703) 549-5822

ROSIER, Dr. Ronald
Administrative Officer, Conference Board of the Mathematical Sciences
1529 18th St., N.W., Washington, DC 20036
Telephone: (202) 293-1170

ROSIN, Carol
President, Institute for Security and Cooperation in Outer Space
1336A Corcoran St., N.W., Washington, DC 20009-4311
Telephone: (202) 462-8886

ROSS, E. Clarke
Ass't Exec. Director, Fed. Relations, Nat'l Ass'n of State Mental Health Program Directors
1101 King St., Suite 160, Alexandria, VA 22314
Telephone: (703) 739-9333

ROSS, Elisabeth
Birch, Horton, Bittner and Cherot
1155 Connecticut Ave., N.W., Suite 1200, Washington, DC 20036
Telephone: (202) 659-5800

ROSS, Gary M.
Congressional Liaison, General Conference of Seventh-day Adventists
6840 Eastern Ave., N.W., Washington, DC 20012
Telephone: (202) 722-6688

ROSS AND HARDIES
888 16th St., N.W., Washington, DC 20006
Telephone: (202) 296-8600
Members of firm representing listed organizations:
Caramango, Salvatore E.
Danner, Pamela
Howell, John C.
Reynolds, Wm. Bradford
Background: Former Assistant Attorney General (Civil Rights Division), U.S. Department of Justice.
Stenger, James A.
Clients:
Association Professionnelle de l'Acier Moule de France *(James A. Stenger)*
Bowman Webber Ltd. *(James A. Stenger)*
Citicorp *(Wm. Bradford Reynolds)*
Nat'l Hand Tool Corp. *(Salvatore E. Caramango)*

ROSS, Jerilyn
President, Phobia Soc. of America
6000 Executive Blvd. Suite 200, Rockville, MD 20852
Telephone: (301) 231-9350

ROSS, Lynne
Deputy Director and Legislative Director, Nat'l Ass'n of Attorneys General
444 North Capitol St., N.W., Suite 403, Washington, DC 20001
Telephone: (202) 628-0435

ROSS MARSH FOSTER MYERS & QUIGGLE
888 16th St., N.W., Suite 400, Washington, DC 20006
Telephone: (202) 822-8888
Background: The information below was obtained from public records and submitted for confirmation to this firm, which declined to confirm or correct the information and asked to be omitted from the book.
Members of firm representing listed organizations:

Clients:
Church Alliance
Colorado Interstate Gas Co.

ROSS, Michelle
Constituency Relations Manager, American Petroleum Institute
1220 L St., N.W., Washington, DC 20005
Telephone: (202) 682-8291

ROSS, Nancy
Exec. Director, Rainbow Lobby
1660 L St., N.W. Suite 204, Washington, DC 20036
Telephone: (202) 457-0700
Registered as lobbyist at U.S. Congress.

ROSS, Stanford G.
Arnold & Porter
1200 New Hampshire Ave., N.W., Washington, DC 20036
Telephone: (202) 872-6700
Registered as lobbyist at U.S. Congress.
Clients:
Mutual of America

ROSS, Stephen R.
Fletcher, Heald and Hildreth
1225 Connecticut Ave., N.W. Suite 400, Washington, DC 20036
Telephone: (202) 828-5700

ROSSANDA, Caroline L.
Communications Coordinator, American Bankruptcy Institute
107 Second St., N.E., Washington, DC 20002
Telephone: (202) 543-1234

ROSSER, Dr. Richard F.
President and C.E.O., Nat'l Ass'n of Independent Colleges and Universities
122 C St., N.W. Suite 750, Washington, DC 20001
Telephone: (202) 347-7512
Registered as lobbyist at U.S. Congress.

ROSSIDES, Eugene T.
Rogers and Wells
1737 H St., N.W., Washington, DC 20006
Telephone: (202) 331-7760
Registered as lobbyist at U.S. Congress.
Registered as Foreign Agent: (#3428).
Background: Special Asst. to Under Secretary, U.S. Treasury Department, 1958-1961. Asst. Secretary, U.S. Treasury Department, 1969-1973.
Clients:
Claiborne, Inc., Liz
Compagnie Financiere de Paris et des Pays Bas
Liga Agricola Industrial de la Cana de Azucar (LAICA)
Merrill Lynch and Co., Inc.
Republic Nat'l Bank of New York
Teachers Insurance and Annuity Ass'n

ROSSITER, Caleb
Staff Consultant, Arms Control and Foreign Policy Caucus
House Annex 2 Room 501, Washington, DC 20515
Telephone: (202) 226-3440

ROSSMILLER, George E.
Dir., Nat'l Ctr. for Food & Agric. Pol., Resources for the Future
1616 P St., N.W., Washington, DC 20036
Telephone: (202) 328-5000
Background: Agricultural Attache, Foreign Agricultural Service, USDA, 1978-79. Assistant Administrator, International Trade Policy, 1979-81 and Senior Economic Advisor, Foreign Agricultural Service, USDA, 1981-86.

ROSSO, Joseph L.
Senior Legislative Representative, American Trucking Ass'ns
430 First St., S.E., Washington, DC 20003
Telephone: (202) 544-6245
Registered as lobbyist at U.S. Congress.

ROSTER, Michael
Morrison & Foerster
2000 Pennsylvania Ave., N.W., Suite 5500, Washington, DC 20006
Telephone: (202) 887-1500
Clients:
Federal Home Loan Bank of Seattle
First Nationwide Bank
Ford Motor Co.

ROTENBERG, Marc
Director, Computer Professionals for Social Responsibility
1025 Connecticut Ave., N.W. Suite 1015, Washington, DC 20036
Telephone: (202) 775-1588
Background: Former Counsel, Senate Judiciary Committee, Subcommittee on Technology and the Law.

ROTH, Alan J.
Spiegel and McDiarmid
1350 New York Ave., N.W., Suite 1100, Washington, DC 20005
Telephone: (202) 879-4000

ROTH, Batya
Admin. Law Atty, Legal & Regul. Affrs., Chamber of Commerce of the U.S.A.
1615 H St., N.W., Washington, DC 20062
Telephone: (202) 659-6000
Registered as lobbyist at U.S. Congress.

ROTH, Mark D.
General Counsel, American Federation of Government Employees
80 F St., N.W., Washington, DC 20001
Telephone: (202) 737-8700

ROTH, Rhond Rudolph
V. President, Nat'l Multi Housing Council
1250 Connecticut Ave., N.W., Suite 620, Washington, DC 20036
Telephone: (202) 659-3381
Registered as lobbyist at U.S. Congress.

ROTH, Thomas R.
President, Labor Bureau, Inc., The
1101 15th St., N.W., Suite 1010, Washington, DC 20005
Telephone: (202) 296-7420

ROTHAAR, Jessica
Craig Associates
1701 K St., N.W., Suite 200, Washington, DC 20006
Telephone: (202) 466-0001

ROTHENBERG, Stuart
Director, Political Division, Institute for Government and Politics
717 Second St., N.E., Washington, DC 20002
Telephone: (202) 546-3004

ROTHER, John C.
Dir., Legis. Res. & Public Policy Div., American Ass'n of Retired Persons
1909 K St., N.W., Washington, DC 20049
Telephone: (202) 728-4780
Registered as lobbyist at U.S. Congress.
Background: Associate Labor Counsel, 1977-78 and Special Counsel for Health, 1978-79, U.S. Senate Committee on Labor and Human Resources. Legislative Assistant to Sen. Jacob Javits (R-NY), 1980. Staff Director and Chief Counsel, Senate Special Committee on Aging, 1981-84.

ROTHFARB, Lauren J.
Legislative Assistant, Internat'l Union of Electronic, Electrical, Salaried, Machine, and Furniture Workers, AFL-CIO
1126 16th St., N.W., Washington, DC 20036
Telephone: (202) 296-1200
Registered as lobbyist at U.S. Congress.

ROTHKOPF, Arthur J.
Hogan and Hartson
555 13th St., N.W., Suite 1200, Washington, DC 20004-1109
Telephone: (202) 637-5600
Registered as lobbyist at U.S. Congress.
Registered as Foreign Agent: (#2244).
Background: Attorney, Securities and Exchange Commission, 1960-63. Associate Tax Legislative Counsel (International), U.S. Treasury Department, 1963-66.
Clients:
Lloyds of London, Underwriters at
Manufacturers Hanover Trust Co.

ROTHLEDER ASSOCIATES, INC.
655 15th St., N.W., Suite 300, Washington, DC 20904
Telephone: (202) 639-4020
Background: Government and Congressional relations consultants.
Members of firm representing listed organizations:
Rothleder, Linda, President
Clients:
Cincinnati Electronics Inc. *(Linda Rothleder)*
Marconi Communications Inc. *(Linda Rothleder)*

ROTHLEDER, Linda
President, Rothleder Associates, Inc.
655 15th St., N.W., Suite 300, Washington, DC 20904

Telephone: (202) 639-4020
Registered as lobbyist at U.S. Congress.
Clients:
  Cincinnati Electronics Inc.
  Marconi Communications Inc.

ROTHMAN, Helen
Legis Affrs Specialist, NAT'L AERONAUTICS AND
  SPACE ADMINISTRATION
400 Maryland Ave, S.W., Washington, DC 20546
Telephone: (202) 453-1055

ROTHROCK, Emily
Associate Director, Government Affairs, American Internat'l Group
1455 Pennsylvania Ave., N.W. Suite 900, Washington, DC
  20004
Telephone: (202) 783-5690
Registered as lobbyist at U.S. Congress.

ROTHSCHILD, Edwin S.
Director, Energy & Environmental Policy, Citizen Action
1300 Connecticut Ave., N.W. Suite 401, Washington, DC
  20036
Telephone: (202) 857-5153
Registered as lobbyist at U.S. Congress.

ROTHSCHILD, Monique
Coordinator, Mental Health Coalition
P.O. Box 11641, Washington, DC 20008
Telephone: (202) 529-1745

ROUNTREE, G. Glynn
Director, Environmental Affairs, Aerospace Industries
  Ass'n of America
1250 Eye St., N.W., Suite 1100, Washington, DC 20005
Telephone: (202) 371-8400

ROUNTREE, Martha
President, Leadership Foundation
P.O. Box 280, Cabin John, MD 20818
Telephone: (301) 229-8400

ROUNTREE, William C.
V. President, Federal Government Affairs, BP America Inc.
1776 Eye St., N.W., Suite 1000, Washington, DC 20006
Telephone: (202) 785-4888
Registered as lobbyist at U.S. Congress.

ROUSH, Michael O.
Asst. Dir., Federal Gov't Rels./Senate, Nat'l Federation of
  Independent Business
600 Maryland Ave., S.W., Suite 700, Washington, DC
  20024
Telephone: (202) 554-9000
Registered as lobbyist at U.S. Congress.

ROUSON, Brigette M.
Manager, Legal and Regulatory Affairs, American News-
  paper Publishers Ass'n
The Newspaper Center 11600 Sunrise Valley Drive, Res-
  ton, VA 22091
Telephone: (703) 648-1000
Registered as lobbyist at U.S. Congress.

ROUSSELOT, Peter F.
Hogan and Hartson
555 13th St., N.W., Suite 1200, Washington, DC 20004-
  1109
Telephone: (202) 637-5600
Clients:
  Denver and Rio Grande Western Railroad Co.

ROUVELAS, Emanuel L.
Preston Gates Ellis & Rouvelas Meeds
1735 New York Ave., N.W., Suite 500, Washington, DC
  20006-4759
Telephone: (202) 628-1700
Registered as lobbyist at U.S. Congress.
Registered as Foreign Agent: (#3567)
Background: Counsel, Senate Commerce Committee,
  1969-1973; Chief Counsel, Senate Merchant Marine Sub-
  committee, 1969-1973; Foreign Commerce and Tourism
  Subcommittee, 1969-1973.
Clients:
  American President Companies
  Burlington Northern Railroad
  Interlake Holding Corp.
  Internat'l Council of Containerships Operators

Mormac Marine Group, Inc.
OMI Corp.
Seatrain Tankers Corp.
Seattle, Washington, Port of
Transportation Institute

ROUX, Christine
Public Affairs and Research Coordinator, Nestle Enterprises, Inc.
1511 K St., N.W., Suite 1100, Washington, DC 20005
Telephone: (202) 639-8894

ROVELSTAD, Dr. Gordon H.
Exec. Director, American College of Dentists
7315 Wisconsin Ave. Suite 352-N, Bethesda, MD 20814
Telephone: (301) 986-0555

ROWAN & BLEWITT, INC.
1000 Vermont Ave., N.W. Suite 1000, Washington, DC
  20005
Telephone: (202) 842-1010
Members of firm representing listed organizations:
  McLain, Patrick M.
Clients:
  Cosmetic, Toiletry and Fragrance Ass'n (Patrick M.
    McLain)

ROWAN, Carl, Jr.
Reed Smith Shaw & McClay
1200 18th St., N.W., Washington, DC 20036
Telephone: (202) 457-6100
Registered as lobbyist at U.S. Congress.
Clients:
  Nat'l Ass'n of Minority Contractors
  Nat'l Cellular Resellers Ass'n
  Nat'l Rifle Ass'n of America

ROWAN, Eugene F.
Patton, Boggs and Blow
2550 M St., N.W., Suite 800, Washington, DC 20037
Telephone: (202) 457-6000
Registered as lobbyist at U.S. Congress.

ROWAN, George R., Jr.
Exec. V. President, Armed Forces Marketing Council
1750 New York Ave., N.W., Suite 340, Washington, DC
  20006
Telephone: (202) 783-8228
Registered as lobbyist at U.S. Congress.

ROWDEN, Marcus A.
Fried, Frank, Harris, Shriver & Jacobson
1001 Pennsylvania Ave., N.W., Suite 800, Washington, DC
  20004-2505
Telephone: (202) 639-7000
Registered as lobbyist at U.S. Congress.
Clients:
  General Electric Co.

ROWE, James W.
President and CEO, Defense Credit Union Council
805 15th St., N.W., Washington, DC 20005-2207
Telephone: (202) 682-5993

ROWE, Sylvia
V. President, Public Relations, Sugar Ass'n, Inc.
1101 15th St., N.W., Suite 600, Washington, DC 20005
Telephone: (202) 785-1122

ROWLAND, J. Patrick
Partner, Rowland & Sellery
1023 15th St., N.W. 7th Fl., Washington, DC 20005
Telephone: (202) 289-1780
Registered as lobbyist at U.S. Congress.
Background: Former Special Assistant for Legislation to
  President Gerald Ford.
Clients:
  Baker Industries, Inc.
  Borg-Warner Automotive, Inc.
  Coalition for Uniform Product Liability Law
  Drugfree Workplace Coalition
  General Electric Plastics
  Labor Policy Ass'n

ROWLAND & SELLERY
1023 15th St., N.W. 7th Fl., Washington, DC 20005
Telephone: (202) 289-1780
Members of firm representing listed organizations:
  Denton, Susan T., Consultant

Dort, Terrie, Legislative Director
Kimball, Amy B., Government Affairs Representa-
  tive
Rowland, J. Patrick, Partner
  Background: Former Special Assistant for Legislation
    to President Gerald Ford.
Sabbath, Lawrence E., V. President
  Background: Staff Director, House Small Business
    Committee- Antitrust, 1983-86. Staff Director, House
    Subcommittee on Transportation and Hazardous Ma-
    terials, 1987-89.
Sellery, William C. (Jr.), Partner
Clients:
  Baker Industries, Inc. (J. Patrick Rowland)
  Borg-Warner Automotive, Inc. (Terrie Dort, J. Patrick
    Rowland)
  Coalition for Uniform Product Liability Law (Ter-
    rie Dort, J. Patrick Rowland)
  Committee of Nat'l Security Companies (Lawrence
    E. Sabbath)
  Drugfree Workplace Coalition (Terrie Dort, J. Patrick
    Rowland)
  Fire Equipment Manufacturers and Services
    Ass'n (Terrie Dort)
  Forest Industries Committee on Timber Valuation
    and Taxation (William C. Sellery, Jr.)
  General Electric Plastics (J. Patrick Rowland, Lawrence
    E. Sabbath)
  Independent Armored Car Operators Ass'n (Law-
    rence E. Sabbath)
  Job Opportunities Business Symposium (Terrie Dort)
  Labor Policy Ass'n (J. Patrick Rowland)
  Libbey-Owens-Ford Co. (Amy B. Kimball, William C.
    Sellery, Jr.)
  Nat'l Armored Car Ass'n (Lawrence E. Sabbath)
  Nat'l Burglar and Fire Alarm Ass'n (Lawrence E.
    Sabbath)
  Nat'l Check Cashers Ass'n (Lawrence E. Sabbath)
  Nat'l Council of Invesigative and Security Ser-
    vices (Lawrence E. Sabbath)
  Northern Textile Ass'n (William C. Sellery, Jr.)
  Pilkington Holdings, Inc. (William C. Sellery, Jr.)
  Product Liability Coordinating Committee (Susan
    T. Denton, William C. Sellery, Jr.)
  Security Companies Organized for Legislative
    Action (Lawrence E. Sabbath)

ROWTON, Charles
Washington Representative, Exxon Corp.
Suite 1100, 1899 L St., N.W., Washington, DC 20036
Telephone: (202) 862-0275
Registered as lobbyist at U.S. Congress.

ROXTON, INC.
2000 S. Eads St., Suite 1003, Arlington, VA 22202
Telephone: (703) 920-0564
Background: A political affairs consulting company.
Members of firm representing listed organizations:
  Bernier, J. Paul, President

ROYAL, Robert
V. President for Research, Ethics and Public Policy Center
1030 15th St., N.W. Suite 300, Washington, DC 20005
Telephone: (202) 682-1200

ROYER, Bill
Fleishman-Hillard, Inc
1301 Connecticut Ave., N.W., Washington, DC 20036
Telephone: (202) 659-0330
Background: Former Member, U.S. House of Representa-
  tives (R-CA).

ROYER, MEHLE & BABYAK
1747 Pennsylvania Ave., N.W. Suite 900, Washington, DC
  20006
Telephone: (202) 296-0784
Registered as Foreign Agent: (#3818)
Members of firm representing listed organizations:
  Babyak, Gregory R.
  Royer, Robert Stewart
    Background: Former staff member, House Administra-
      tion Committee.
Clients:
  Chrysler Military Sales Corp. (Robert Stewart Royer)
  Citizens Savings Bank (Robert Stewart Royer)
  Contact Lens Institute (Gregory R. Babyak)
  Financial Security Assurance, Inc. (Robert Stewart
    Royer)

ROYER, MEHLE & BABYAK (Cont'd)
  Internat'l Futures Exchange (Bermuda) Ltd. *(Robert Stewart Royer)*
  Intex Holdings (Bermuda) Ltd. *(Robert Stewart Royer)*
  Long Island Savings Bank *(Robert Stewart Royer)*
  Michigan Trade Exchange *(Robert Stewart Royer)*
  Morgan Stanley and Co. *(Robert Stewart Royer)*
  Municipal Finance Industry Ass'n *(Gregory R. Babyak)*
  Nuveen & Co., Inc., John *(Gregory R. Babyak, Robert Stewart Royer)*
  Overseas Military Sales Group *(Robert Stewart Royer)*
  Phillips Petroleum Co. *(Robert Stewart Royer)*
  Securities Industry Ass'n *(Gregory R. Babyak, Robert Stewart Royer)*
  Swiss Bankers Ass'n *(Robert Stewart Royer)*

ROYER, Robert Stewart
  Royer, Mehle & Babyak
  1747 Pennsylvania Ave., N.W. Suite 900, Washington, DC 20006
  Telephone: (202) 296-0784
  Registered as lobbyist at U.S. Congress.
  Registered as Foreign Agent: (#3818).
  Background: Former staff member, House Administration Committee.
  Clients:
    Chrysler Military Sales Corp.
    Citizens Savings Bank
    Financial Security Assurance, Inc.
    Internat'l Futures Exchange (Bermuda) Ltd.
    Intex Holdings (Bermuda) Ltd.
    Long Island Savings Bank
    Michigan Trade Exchange
    Morgan Stanley and Co.
    Nuveen & Co., Inc., John
    Overseas Military Sales Group
    Phillips Petroleum Co.
    Securities Industry Ass'n
    Swiss Bankers Ass'n

ROYLANCE, Nancy
  Exec. Director, Opticians Ass'n of America
  10341 Democracy Lane, Box 10110, Fairfax, VA 22030
  Telephone: (703) 691-8355
  Background: Also represents the American Board of Opticianry and Nat'l Contact Lens Examiners. Serves as Assistant Secretary-Treasurer of the Opticians Committee for Political Education.

ROZEN, Tobi Z.
  Director, Marketing, Internat'l Ice Cream Ass'n
  888 16th St., N.W., Washington, DC 20006
  Telephone: (202) 296-4250
  Registered as lobbyist at U.S. Congress.
  Background: Also represents the Milk Industry Foundation.

ROZETT, William
  Field Programs Manager, American Petroleum Institute
  1220 L St., N.W., Washington, DC 20005
  Telephone: (202) 682-8288

ROZYNSKI, Edward M.
  V. President, Internat'l, Health Industry Manufacturers Ass'n
  1030 15th St., N.W. Suite 1100, Washington, DC 20005
  Telephone: (202) 452-8240

RPH & ASSOCIATES
  7268 Evans Mill Road, McLean, VA 22101
  Telephone: (703) 448-0931
  Members of firm representing listed organizations:
  Hanrahan, Robert P., President
    Background: Former Superintendent of Schools, Cook County, Illinois, 1967-71. Member of U.S. House of Representatives (R-IL), 1973-75. Deputy Assistant Secretary of Education, 1975-77. Lake County, Illinois, Commissioner, 1980-82.
  Clients:
    Diversified Realty Corp. and Financial Group *(Robert P. Hanrahan)*
    Elligson Review Seminars, Inc.

RUANA, Rudolph M.
  Director, Washington Office, Jeppesen Sanderson, Inc.
  1725 K St., N.W., Suite 1107, Washington, DC 20006
  Telephone: (202) 331-7727

RUANE, Dr T. Peter
  President, American Road and Transportation Builders Ass'n
  501 School St., S.W. Suite 800, Washington, DC 20024
  Telephone: (202) 488-2722
  Registered as lobbyist at U.S. Congress.

RUBASHKIN, David
  Director, Federal Relations, US WEST, Inc.
  1020 19th St., N.W., Suite 700, Washington, DC 20036
  Telephone: (202) 429-3100

RUBENSTEIN, Leonard S.
  Director, Mental Health Law Project
  2021 L St., N.W., Washington, DC 20036
  Telephone: (202) 467-5730

RUBENSTEIN, Lori
  Exec. Director, Partnership for Democracy
  2335 18th St., N.W., Washington, DC 20009
  Telephone: (202) 483-0030

RUBIN, Alan A.
  President, Nat'l Park Foundation
  P.O. Box 57473, Washington, DC 20037
  Telephone: (202) 785-4500

RUBIN, Barry
  Senior Research Fellow, Washington Institute for Near East Policy
  50 F St., N.W., Suite 8800, Washington, DC 20001
  Telephone: (202) 783-0226

RUBIN, Barry
  General Counsel, Advocacy Institute, The
  1730 Rhode Island Ave., N.W. Suite 600, Washington, DC 20036
  Telephone: (202) 659-8475

RUBIN, Blake D.
  Steptoe and Johnson
  1330 Connecticut Ave., N.W., Washington, DC 20036
  Telephone: (202) 429-3000
  Registered as lobbyist at U.S. Congress.
  Clients:
    Christie's Internat'l
    Nat'l Antique and Art Dealers Ass'n of America
    Sotheby's Holdings, Inc.

RUBIN, Burt
  General Counsel, American Soc. of Travel Agents
  1101 King St., Alexandria, VA 22314
  Telephone: (703) 739-2782

RUBIN, Cheryl
  Manager of Public Relations, Heritage Foundation
  214 Massachusetts Ave., N.E., Washington, DC 20002
  Telephone: (202) 546-4400

RUBIN, Eric M.
  Rubin, Winston and Diercks
  1730 M St., N.W., Suite 412, Washington, DC 20036
  Telephone: (202) 861-0870
  Registered as lobbyist at U.S. Congress.
  Background: Trial Attorney, Department of Justice, 1967-69. Staff Assoc. for Environmental Programs, President's Council on Executive Reorganization, 1969-70. Deputy Assistant Director, 1972-74, Assistant Director, 1974-77, and Associate Director, 1978, Bureau of Consumer Protection, Federal Trade Commission.
  Clients:
    Outdoor Advertising Ass'n of America

RUBIN, Jason
  V. President, Biotechnology Group, Hill and Knowlton Public Affairs Worldwide
  Washington Harbour, 901 31st St., N.W., Washington, DC 20007
  Telephone: (202) 333-7400
  Clients:
    Lederle Laboratories, American Cyanamid Co. Subsidiary

RUBIN, Laura
  Ocean Ecology Specialist, Greenpeace, U.S.A.
  1436 U St., N.W., Washington, DC 20009
  Telephone: (202) 462-1177

RUBIN, Seymour J.
  Senior Consultant, American Soc. of Internat'l Law
  2223 Massachusetts Ave., N.W., Washington, DC 20008
  Telephone: (202) 265-4313

RUBIN, WINSTON AND DIERCKS
  1730 M St., N.W., Washington, DC 20036
  Telephone: (202) 861-0870
  Members of firm representing listed organizations:
  Diercks, Walter E.
    Background: Staff Attorney (1972-76) and Deputy Assistant Director (1976-77), Bureau of Consumer Protection, Federal Trade Commission.
  Rubin, Eric M.
    Background: Trial Attorney, Department of Justice, 1967-69. Staff Assoc. for Environmental Programs, President's Council on Executive Reorganization, 1969-70. Deputy Assistant Director, 1972-74, Assistant Director, 1974-77, and Associate Director, 1978, Bureau of Consumer Protection, Federal Trade Commission.
  Winston, James L.
    Background: Legal Assistant to Commissioner Robert E. Lee, Federal Communications Commission, 1978-80.
  Clients:
    KCBA
    KGET
    KKTV
    KVOS-TV
    Nat'l Ass'n of Black Owned Broadcasters *(James L. Winston)*
    Outdoor Advertising Ass'n of America *(Walter E. Diercks, Eric M. Rubin)*
    WIXT

RUBINOFF, Edward L.
  Akin, Gump, Strauss, Hauer and Feld
  1333 New Hampshire Ave., N.W., Suite 400, Washington, DC 20036
  Telephone: (202) 887-4000
  Clients:
    Amerada Hess Corp.
    Oil, Chemical and Atomic Workers Internat'l Union

RUBINSTEIN, Gwen
  Program Associate, OMB Watch
  1731 Connecticut Ave., N.W., Washington, DC 20009-1146
  Telephone: (202) 234-8494

RUBINSTEIN, Joel S.
  Sadur, Pelland & Rubinstein
  2000 L St., N.W. Suite 612, Washington, DC 20036
  Telephone: (202) 872-8383
  Background: Attorney, Office of the General Counsel, General Accounting Office, 1973-75; Office of the General Counsel, Department of the Air Force, 1975-77.
  Clients:
    A to Z Maintenance Corp.
    Shirley Contracting Corp.

RUCKER, J. Eldon
  Deputy Director, Health & Envir. Affairs, American Petroleum Institute
  1220 L St., N.W., Washington, DC 20005
  Telephone: (202) 682-8313

RUCKERT, Edward
  McDermott, Will and Emery
  1850 K St., N.W., Suite 500, Washington, DC 20006-2296
  Telephone: (202) 887-8000
  Clients:
    California Table Grape Commission
    Internat'l Apple Institute
    Nat'l Potato Council

RUDD, Tamera
  Director, State Affairs, Nat'l Ass'n of Professional Insurance Agents
  400 North Washington St., Alexandria, VA 22314
  Telephone: (703) 836-9340
  Background: Former Legislative Analyst, Federal Energy Regulatory Commission.

RUDDER, Dr. Catherine E.
  Exec. Director, American Political Science Ass'n
  1527 New Hampshire Ave., N.W., Washington, DC 20036

WASHINGTON REPRESENTATIVES

Telephone: (202) 483-2512

RUDDICK, Richard E.
V. President, CNA Insurance Cos.
7361 Calhoun Place, Rockville, MD 20855
Telephone: (301) 738-1216

RUDEN, Paul M.
Wilner and Scheiner
1200 New Hampshire Ave., N.W., Suite 300, Washington, DC 20036
Telephone: (202) 861-7800
Background: Trial Attorney, Civil Aeronautics Board, 1967-68.

RUDMAN, Gloria Cataneo
Legislative Director, American Maritime Congress
444 N. Capitol St., N.W., Suite 801, Washington, DC 20001
Telephone: (202) 877-4477
Registered as lobbyist at U.S. Congress.

RUDOLPH, Barbara A.
Director, Government Relations, Beverly Enterprises
1901 N. Fort Myer Drive Suite 302, Arlington, VA 22209
Telephone: (703) 276-0808
Registered as lobbyist at U.S. Congress.

RUDOLPH, Deborah Karen
Manager, Public Affairs Programs, Institute of Electrical and Electronics Engineers, Inc.
1828 L St., N.W. Suite 1202, Washington, DC 20036-5104
Telephone: (202) 785-0017
Registered as lobbyist at U.S. Congress.

RUDOLPH, John
Hall, Estill, Hardwick, Gable, Golden & Nelson
1120 20th St., N.W., Suite 750 - South Bldg., Washington, DC 20036
Telephone: (202) 822-9100
Clients:
Arkla, Inc.

RUECKEL, Dr. Patricia A.
Exec. Director, Nat'l Ass'n for Women Deans, Administrators, and Counselors
1325 18th St., N.W., Suite 210, Washington, DC 20036
Telephone: (202) 659-9330

RUEMPLER, Henry C.
Director, Tax Office, American Bankers Ass'n
1120 Connecticut Ave., N.W., Washington, DC 20036
Telephone: (202) 663-5000
Registered as lobbyist at U.S. Congress.
Background: Minority Counsel, U.S. Senate Subcommittee on Commerce, Consumer and Monetary Affairs, 1976-79. Judiciary Committee Counsel to Sen. Thad Cochran (R-MS), 1979-80. Legislative Director to Sen. Cochran, 1981-83.

RUFF, Charles
Covington and Burling
1201 Pennsylvania Ave., N.W., Box 7566, Washington, DC 20044
Telephone: (202) 662-6000

RUGGIERI, Nicholas L.
Director, Washington Affairs, Johnson & Johnson
1667 K St., N.W., Suite 410, Washington, DC 20006
Telephone: (202) 293-2620
Registered as lobbyist at U.S. Congress.

RUGH, Timothy
Smith, Bucklin and Associates
1101 Connecticut Ave., N.W., Suite 700, Washington, DC 20036
Telephone: (202) 857-1100
Background: Serves as Director for the Porcelain Enamel Institute and Director, Regulatory Affairs for the Pet Food Institute.
Clients:
Pet Food Institute
Porcelain Enamel Institute

RULAND ASSOCIATES, INC.
415 Church St. Suite 203, Vienna, VA 22180
Telephone: (703) 237-4572
Background: Washington representation, government relations and strategic planning services.

Members of firm representing listed organizations:
Ruland, James K., President
Background: Special Assistant, Programming and Budgeting, Office of the Secretary of the Navy, 1982-84; Special Assistant, Congressional Liaison, Deputy Chief of Naval Operations, 1984-86.
Clients:
Environmental Design Corp. *(James K. Ruland)*
PAI, Inc. *(James K. Ruland)*

RULAND, James K.
President, Ruland Associates, Inc.
415 Church St. Suite 203, Vienna, VA 22180
Telephone: (703) 237-4572
Background: Special Assistant, Programming and Budgeting, Office of the Secretary of the Navy, 1982-84; Special Assistant, Congressional Liaison, Deputy Chief of Naval Operations, 1984-86.
Clients:
Environmental Design Corp.
PAI, Inc.

RUMBARGER, Charles D.
President, Ass'n Management Group
3299 K St., N.W., 7th Floor, Washington, DC 20007
Telephone: (202) 965-7510
Clients:
Nat'l Ass'n of Independent Life Brokerage Agencies

RUMPH, Alan D.
Ivins, Phillips and Barker
1700 Pennsylvania Ave., N.W., Suite 600, Washington, DC 20006
Telephone: (202) 393-7600
Clients:
Employee Relocation Council

RUMPLER, Holly
American Ass'n of Physics Teachers
5112 Berwyn Road, College Park, MD 20740
Telephone: (301) 345-4200

RUMSFELD, Kurt
Legislative Representative, Soc. for Human Resources Management
606 N. Washington St., Alexandria, VA 22314
Telephone: (703) 548-3440
Registered as lobbyist at U.S. Congress.

RUNKLE, Scott
1100 17th St., N.W. Suite 847, Washington, DC 20036
Telephone: (202) 293-3615
Background: A public relations consultant.
Organizations represented:
Puerto Rico Economic Development Administration
Puerto Rico Federal Affairs Administration

RUNYAN, John C.
Director, Political Affairs, Printing Industries of America
1730 North Lynn St., Arlington, VA 22209
Telephone: (703) 841-8196
Registered as lobbyist at U.S. Congress.

RUNYON, Rex A.
V. President, PR - Membership Services, American Feed Industry Ass'n
1701 Fort Myer Dr. Suite 1200, Arlington, VA 22209
Telephone: (703) 524-0810

RUOCCO, Stefano P.
President, Italian Aerospace Industries (USA), Inc.
1235 Jefferson Davis Hwy. Suite 500, Arlington, VA 22202
Telephone: (703) 271-9200
Registered as Foreign Agent: (# 3399)
Background: Represents Finmeccanica Group and Aeritalia S.A.I.p.A.

RUSBULDT, Robert A.
Assistant V. President, Federal Affairs, Independent Insurance Agents of America
600 Pennsylvania Ave., S.E., Suite 200, Washington, DC 20003
Telephone: (202) 544-5833
Registered as lobbyist at U.S. Congress.

RUSCH, Wayne H.
Berliner and Maloney
1101 17th St., N.W., Suite 1004, Washington, DC 20036-4798
Telephone: (202) 293-1414
Registered as Foreign Agent: (# 3512).

RUSCIO, Domenic R.
CR Associates
317 Massachusetts Ave., N.E., Suite 100, Washington, DC 20002
Telephone: (202) 546-4732
Registered as lobbyist at U.S. Congress.
Background: Former Staff Member, U. S. Senate Committee on Appropriations and Deputy Assistant Secretary of Management and Budget, U.S. Department of Health, Education and Welfare.
Clients:
Alzheimer's Ass'n
American Ass'n of Colleges of Podiatric Medicine
Ass'n of University Programs in Health Administration
Conjoint Committee on Diagnostic Radiology
Seton Hall School of Law

RUSE, Laura
Asst, Cong Rels, Legis & Cong Rels, DEPARTMENT OF HOUSING AND URBAN DEVELOPMENT
451 Seventh St., S.W., Washington, DC 20410
Telephone: (202) 755-7380

RUSH, Tonda
Director, Industry Affairs, American Newspaper Publishers Ass'n
The Newspaper Center 11600 Sunrise Valley Drive, Reston, VA 22091
Telephone: (703) 648-1000

RUSHIN, R. K.
Director, Chemical Industries Affairs, Eastman Kodak Co.
1776 Eye St., N.W., Suite 1050, Washington, DC 20006
Telephone: (202) 857-3400
Registered as lobbyist at U.S. Congress.

RUSIN, Michael
Policy Analysis Deputy Director, American Petroleum Institute
1220 L St., N.W., Washington, DC 20005
Telephone: (202) 682-8533

RUSSELL, Barry
General Counsel, Independent Petroleum Ass'n of America
1101 16th St., N.W., Washington, DC 20036
Telephone: (202) 857-4735
Registered as lobbyist at U.S. Congress.

RUSSELL, Cheryl
Dir., Environ'l & Occupat'l Health, American Electronics Ass'n
1225 Eye St., N.W., Suite 950, Washington, DC 20005
Telephone: (202) 682-9110

RUSSELL, Christine A.
Director, Small Business Center, Chamber of Commerce of the U.S.A.
1615 H St., N.W., Washington, DC 20062
Telephone: (202) 659-6000
Registered as lobbyist at U.S. Congress.

RUSSELL, Harold S.
V. President, Government Affairs, FMC Corp.
1627 K St., N.W., Suite 500, Washington, DC 20006
Telephone: (202) 956-5200

RUSSELL, Randy M.
Lesher & Russell, Inc.
517 C St., N.E., Washington, DC 20002
Telephone: (202) 546-6501
Registered as lobbyist at U.S. Congress.
Clients:
Agricultural Policy Working Group

RUSSELL, Rush
Legislative Representative, American Health Care Ass'n
1201 L St., N.W., Washington, DC 20005
Telephone: (202) 842-4444

RUSSELL, Shannon
Legislative Representative, Ashland Oil, Inc.
1025 Connecticut Ave., N.W., Suite 507, Washington, DC 20036
Telephone: (202) 223-8290
Background: Former Staff Member to Sen. Wendell Ford (D-KY).

RUSSELL, William J.
Exec. Officer, American Educational Research Ass'n
1230 17th St., N.W., Washington, DC 20036
Telephone: (202) 223-9485
Background: Also serves as Exec. Officer, Nat'l Council on Measurement in Education.

RUSSIN, Jonathan
Kaplan, Russin and Vecchi
1215 17th St., N.W., Washington, DC 20036
Telephone: (202) 887-0353
Background: With Office of the Gen. Counsel, Agency for Internat'l Development, Dep't of State, 1964-1969 (Regional Legal Adviser, Dominican Republic, 1967-1969).
Clients:
Caribbean Trade and Apparel Coalition (C-TAC)

RUSSMAN, Linda
Director, Communications, Women in Communications
2101 Wilson Blvd., Suite 417, Arlington, VA 22201
Telephone: (703) 528-4200

RUST-TIERNEY, Diann
Legislative Counsel, American Civil Liberties Union
122 Maryland Ave., N.E., Washington, DC 20002
Telephone: (202) 544-1681
Registered as lobbyist at U.S. Congress.

RUSTAD, Wallace
Director, Government Relations Dept., Nat'l Rural Electric Cooperative Ass'n
1800 Massachusetts Ave., N.W., Washington, DC 20036
Telephone: (202) 857-9556
Registered as lobbyist at U.S. Congress.

RUTHERFORD & ASSOC., J. T.
1301 North Courthouse Road Room 1802, Arlington, VA 22201
Telephone: (703) 525-5424
Members of firm representing listed organizations:
Lavanty, Don
Rutherford, J. T., President
Organizations represented:
American College of Radiology *(Don Lavanty)*
American Optometric Ass'n *(Don Lavanty)*

RUTHERFORD, J. T.
President, Rutherford & Assoc., J. T.
1301 North Courthouse Road Room 1802, Arlington, VA 22201
Telephone: (703) 525-5424
Registered as lobbyist at U.S. Congress.

RUTTA, Randall L.
Assistant V. President, Gov't'l Affairs, Nat'l Easter Seal Soc.
1350 New York Ave., N.W., Suite 415, Washington, DC 20005
Telephone: (202) 347-3066

RYAN, Charles J., II
Director of Governmental Affairs, Apartment and Office Building Ass'n of Metropolitan Washington
Suite 600, 1413 K St., N.W., Washington, DC 20005
Telephone: (202) 289-1717
Registered as lobbyist at U.S. Congress.

RYAN, Frank T.
Director, State and Regulatory Affairs, Goodyear Tire and Rubber Co.
901 15th St., N.W. Suite 350, Washington, DC 20005
Telephone: (202) 682-9250

RYAN, Jerry W.
Crowell and Moring
1001 Pennsylvania Ave., N.W., Washington, DC 20004-2505
Telephone: (202) 624-2500
Registered as Foreign Agent: (#3058).
Clients:
Aer Lingus

Pan American World Airways

RYAN, John G.
Director, Government Affairs, Bristol-Myers Squibb Co.
655 15th St., N.W., Suite 410, Washington, DC 20005
Telephone: (202) 783-0900
Registered as lobbyist at U.S. Congress.
Background: Serves as Treasurer, Squibb Good Government Fund.

RYAN, John R.
V. President, Air Traffic Management, Air Transport Ass'n of America
1709 New York Ave., N.W., Washington, DC 20006-5206
Telephone: (202) 626-4000

RYAN, Lawrence B.
V. President, Washington Operations, Bell Aerospace Textron
1090 Vermont Ave., N.W., Suite 1100, Washington, DC 20005
Telephone: (202) 289-5833

RYAN, Lee
Treasurer, Cosmetic, Toiletry and Fragrance Ass'n Political Action Committee
1110 Vermont Ave., N.W., Suite 800, Washington, DC 20005
Telephone: (202) 331-1770

RYAN-MCGINN
1110 Vermont Ave., N.W. Suite 820, Washington, DC 20005
Telephone: (202) 775-4370
Members of firm representing listed organizations:
Fulton, C. Michael, Sr. Ass't Gov't Relations Specialist
McCaleb, Brent
McGinn, Daniel, V. President
Clients:
Ashland Coal *(Daniel McGinn)*
Batman Corp. *(Daniel McGinn)*
Cabot Oil & Gas *(Daniel McGinn)*
Concord College *(C. Michael Fulton)*
Health Industry Manufacturers Ass'n *(Daniel McGinn)*
Humana, Inc. *(Daniel McGinn)*
Independent Oil and Gas Ass'n of West Virginia *(C. Michael Fulton, Daniel McGinn)*
Massey Coal Services *(Daniel McGinn)*
Midwest Corp. *(Daniel McGinn)*
Oregon Ass'n of Hospitals *(Daniel McGinn)*
St. Vincent Hospital and Medical Center *(Brent McCaleb)*
Texas A & M College of Medicine *(Daniel McGinn)*
West Virginia Bankers Ass'n *(Daniel McGinn)*
West Virginia Hospital Ass'n *(Daniel McGinn)*
Wheeling Hospital *(Daniel McGinn)*
Wheeling Jesuit College *(C. Michael Fulton)*

RYAN, Patricia E.
Associate Director, Congressional Affrs., Nat'l Ass'n of Private Psychiatric Hospitals
1319 F St., N.W., Suite 1000, Washington, DC 20004
Telephone: (202) 393-6700
Registered as lobbyist at U.S. Congress.
Background: Responsibilities include the Ass'n Political Action Committee.

RYAN, Paul D.
Manager, Government and Public Affairs, Nissan Motor Corp. in U.S.A.
750 17th St., N.W. Suite 901, Washington, DC 20006
Telephone: (202) 862-5523
Registered as lobbyist at U.S. Congress.

RYAN, T. L.
Director, State and Veterans Affairs, Non Commissioned Officers Ass'n of the U.S.A.
225 North Washington St., Alexandria, VA 22314
Telephone: (703) 549-0311
Registered as lobbyist at U.S. Congress.

RYAN, T. Timothy, Jr.
Reed Smith Shaw & McClay
1200 18th St., N.W., Washington, DC 20036
Telephone: (202) 457-6100
Registered as Foreign Agent: (#4227).
Background: Solicitor of Labor, U.S. Department of Labor, 1981-83.

Clients:
Amgen, Inc.
Goldman, Sachs and Co.
Internat'l Telecommunications Satellite Organization (INTELSAT)

RYAN, Thomas M.
Wunder, Ryan, Cannon & Thelen
1615 L St., N.W., Suite 650, Washington, DC 20036
Telephone: (202) 659-3005
Registered as lobbyist at U.S. Congress.
Registered as Foreign Agent: (#3971).
Background: Staff member and Chief Counsel, House Committee on Energy and Commerce, 1977-87.
Clients:
American Internat'l Group
American Iron and Steel Institute
Ass'n of American Railroads
Burlington Resources, Inc.
Investment Company Institute
Pfizer, Inc.
Philip Morris Management Corp.
Wheelabrator Technologies‡ Inc.

RYAN, Vince
Chairman of the Board of Policy, Liberty Lobby
300 Independence Ave., S.E., Washington, DC 20003
Telephone: (202) 546-5611
Registered as lobbyist at U.S. Congress.

RYAN, Wendy
Director, Division of Communications, Baptist World Alliance
6733 Curran St., McLean, VA 22101-6005
Telephone: (703) 790-8980

RYBERG, Paul, Jr.
Pierson, Semmes, and Finley
1054 31st St., N.W. Suite 300, Washington, DC 20007
Telephone: (202) 333-4000
Registered as lobbyist at U.S. Congress.
Registered as Foreign Agent: (#2988).
Clients:
Mauritius, Chamber of Agriculture of
Mauritius Sugar Syndicate
Oklahoma Natural Gas Co.

RYMAN, Kermit W.
Washington Representative, Chevron, U.S.A.
1700 K St., N.W., Suite 1200, Washington, DC 20006
Telephone: (202) 457-5800
Registered as lobbyist at U.S. Congress.

SABBATH, Lawrence E.
V. President, Rowland & Sellery
1023 15th St., N.W. 7th Fl., Washington, DC 20005
Telephone: (202) 289-1780
Registered as lobbyist at U.S. Congress.
Background: Staff Director, House Small Business Committee- Antitrust, 1983-86. Staff Director, House Subcommittee on Transportation and Hazardous Materials, 1987-89.
Clients:
Committee of Nat'l Security Companies
General Electric Plastics
Independent Armored Car Operators Ass'n
Nat'l Armored Car Ass'n
Nat'l Burglar and Fire Alarm Ass'n
Nat'l Check Cashers Ass'n
Nat'l Council of Invesigative and Security Services
Security Companies Organized for Legislative Action

SABLACK, Lillian
Exec. Director, American Medical Writers Ass'n
9650 Rockville Pike, Bethesda, MD 20814
Telephone: (301) 493-0003

SABLE, Ronald K.
Staff V. President, Legislative Affairs, McDonnell Douglas Corp.
1735 Jefferson Davis Hwy., Arlington, VA 22202
Telephone: (703) 553-3805
Registered as lobbyist at U.S. Congress.

SABO, Kevin
Senior Technical Associate, Financial Executives Institute
1100 17th St., N.W., Suite 1203, Washington, DC 20036
Telephone: (202) 659-3700

Registered as lobbyist at U.S. Congress.

SABORIO, Sylvia
Sr. Trade Fellow, Overseas Development Council
1717 Massachusetts Ave., N.W., Washington, DC 20036
Telephone: (202) 234-8701

SABSHIN, Dr. Melvin
Medical Director, American Psychiatric Ass'n
1400 K St., N.W., Washington, DC 20005
Telephone: (202) 682-6083

SACCO, Samuel R.
Exec. Vice President, Nat'l Ass'n of Temporary Services
119 South St. Asaph St., Alexandria, VA 22314
Telephone: (703) 549-6287
Background: Responsibilities include the Nat'l Ass'n of
Temporary Services Political Action Committee.

SACHER, Steven J.
Johnson & Gibbs, P.C.
1001 Pennsylvania Ave., N.W. Suite 745, Washington, DC
20004
Telephone: (202) 682-4500
Registered as lobbyist at U.S. Congress.
Background: Associate Solicitor of Labor, ERISA, 1974-77.
Special Counsel for ERISA, 1977-80 and General Coun-
sel, 1980-81 U.S. Senate Committee on Labor and Hu-
man Resources.
Clients:
Redmond Industries

SACHS GREENEBAUM AND TAYLER
1140 Connecticut Ave., N.W., Washington, DC 20036
Telephone: (202) 828-8200
Members of firm representing listed organizations:
Zimmerman, Joseph J.
Clients:
Giant Industries *(Joseph J. Zimmerman)*

SACHS, John L.
Olwine, Connelly, Chase, O'Donnell and Weyher
1701 Pennsylvania Ave., N.W. Suite 1000, Washington,
DC 20006
Telephone: (202) 835-0500
Clients:
Catalyst Energy Corp.

SACHSE, Harry R.
Sonosky, Chambers and Sachse
1250 Eye St., N.W., Suite 1000, Washington, DC 20005
Telephone: (202) 682-0240

SACK, James M.
Leva, Hawes, Mason and Martin
1220 19th St., N.W. Suite 700, Washington, DC 20036
Telephone: (202) 775-0725

SACKLER, Arthur B.
Director, Publishing Policy Development, Time Warner Inc.
1050 Connecticut Ave., N.W., Suite 850, Washington, DC
20036
Telephone: (202) 861-4058

SACKS, Stephen M.
Arnold & Porter
1200 New Hampshire Ave., N.W., Washington, DC 20036
Telephone: (202) 872-6700
Background: Assistant to the General Counsel, Department
of the Army, 1967-1970.

SADD, William
Exec. V. President, Nat'l Spa and Pool Institute
2111 Eisenhower Ave., Alexandria, VA 22314
Telephone: (703) 838-0083

SADLER, Linda C.
Dir,Industry/Gov't Rltns-Rockwell Commns, Rockwell Internat'l
1745 Jefferson Davis Hwy. Suite 1200, Arlington, VA
22202
Telephone: (703) 553-6600

SADOFF, David
Legislative Ass't, APCO Associates
1155 21st St., N.W., Suite 1000, Washington, DC 20036
Telephone: (202) 778-1000

SADTLER, Susan L.
Sr. Government Affairs Representative, Nat'l Telephone
Cooperative Ass'n
2626 Pennsylvania Ave., N.W., Washington, DC 20037
Telephone: (202) 298-2300
Registered as lobbyist at U.S. Congress.

SADUR, Marvin P.
Sadur, Pelland & Rubinstein
2000 L St., N.W. Suite 612, Washington, DC 20036
Telephone: (202) 872-8383
Clients:
Shirley Contracting Corp.

SADUR, PELLAND & RUBINSTEIN
2000 L St., N.W. Suite 612, Washington, DC 20036
Telephone: (202) 872-8383
Members of firm representing listed organizations:
Rubinstein, Joel S.
Background: Attorney, Office of the General Counsel,
General Accounting Office, 1973-75; Office of the
General Counsel, Department of the Air Force,
1975-77.
Sadur, Marvin P.
Clients:
A to Z Maintenance Corp. *(Joel S. Rubinstein)*
Shirley Contracting Corp. *(Joel S. Rubinstein, Marvin P.
Sadur)*

SAFIR, Peter O.
Kleinfeld, Kaplan and Becker
1140 19th St., N.W., Suite 700, Washington, DC 20036
Telephone: (202) 223-5120
Clients:
Carter-Wallace, Inc.
Squibb and Sons, Inc., E. R.

SAGAMORE ASSOCIATES, INC.
1701 K St., N.W., Suite 400, Washington, DC 20006
Telephone: (202) 223-0964
Members of firm representing listed organizations:
Gogol, David U., President
Background: Legislative Assistant to Senator Richard
Lugar (R-IN), 1978-81. Assistant to the Chairman,
Senate Subcommittee on Housing and Urban Affairs,
1981-83. Legislative Director to Senator Lugar,
1983-85.
Kraft, Michael B., Exec. V. President
Background: Press Secretary to Senator Vance Hartke
(D-IN), 1963-65. Director, Nat'l Advisory Council
on Small Business, 1979-81. Administrative Assistant
to Rep. Phil Sharp (D-IN), 1981-89.
Clients:
Columbus, Indiana, City of *(David U. Gogol)*
Comprehensive Marketing Systems, Inc. *(David U.
Gogol)*
Indiana Electric Ass'n *(Michael B. Kraft)*
Indiana State University *(David U. Gogol)*
Indianapolis Center for Advanced Research *(David
U. Gogol)*
Indianapolis, Indiana, City of *(David U. Gogol)*
Manufacturers Hanover Trust Co. *(David U. Gogol)*
Nat'l Institute for Fitness and Sport *(Michael B.
Kraft)*
Nobelsville, Indiana, City of *(David U. Gogol)*
North Las Vegas, Nevada, City of *(David U. Gogol)*
Seattle Organizing Committee, 1990 Goodwill
Games *(David U. Gogol)*
South Bend, Indiana, City of *(David U. Gogol)*
1993 World University Games *(David U. Gogol, Mi-
chael B. Kraft)*

SAGER, William H.
Staff Legal Counsel, Nat'l Soc. of Public Accountants
1010 N. Fairfax St., Alexandria, VA 22314
Telephone: (703) 549-6400

SAILER, Henry P.
Covington and Burling
1201 Pennsylvania Ave., N.W., Box 7566, Washington, DC
20044
Telephone: (202) 662-6000

SAINT-ANDREW, Philip P.
President, Total American Cooperation
2000 Pennsylvania Ave., N.W., Suite 7150, Washington,
DC 20006
Telephone: (202) 822-8365

SAIPE, Robin
Community Relations Coordinator, Nat'l Conference on
Soviet Jewry
1522 K St., N.W., Suite 1100, Washington, DC 20005
Telephone: (202) 898-2500

SAITO, Yoshihiro
Graham and James
2000 M St., N.W., Suite 700, Washington, DC 20036
Telephone: (202) 463-0800
Clients:
Hitachi Zosen Corp.
Nippon Benkan Kogyo Co., Ltd.
Nippon Mining Co.

SAIZOW, Hildy
Exec. Director, Criminal Justice Statistics Ass'n
444 North Capitol St., N.W., Suite 606, Washington, DC
20001
Telephone: (202) 624-8560

SAKURAI, Motoatsu
Deputy General Manager, Mitsubishi Internat'l Corp.
655 15th St., N.W., Suite 860, Washington, DC 20005
Telephone: (202) 638-1101

SALAMA, Samir Y.
Assistant V. President, Policy Anal., Interstate Natural Gas
Ass'n of America
555 13th St., N.W. Suite 300 West, Washington, DC
20004
Telephone: (202) 626-3200

SALAVANTIS, Pete
Saunders and Company
1015 Duke St., Alexandria, VA 22314
Telephone: (703) 549-1555
Clients:
Electronic Industries Ass'n of Japan
Seiko Epson Corp.

SALE, Haida
Acting Director, Community Foundation of Greater Washington
1002 Wisconsin Ave., N.W., Washington, DC 20007
Telephone: (202) 338-8993

SALE, Stephen
Fehrenbacher, Sale, Quinn, and Deese
910 16th St., N.W., 5th Floor, Washington, DC 20006
Telephone: (202) 833-4170
Clients:
CSC Credit Services, Inc.

SALEM, George
Thompson, Mann and Hutson
3000 K St., N.W. Suite 600, Washington, DC 20007
Telephone: (202) 783-1900
Background: Former Solicitor, U.S. Department of Labor.

SALEM, Irving
Latham and Watkins
1001 Pennsylvania Ave., N.W., Suite 1300, Washington,
DC 20004
Telephone: (202) 637-2200
Background: Attorney, Office of Chief Counsel, Internal
Revenue Service, 1960-62. Office of Tax Legislative
Counsel, Treasury Department, 1962-64. Technical As-
sistant to Chief Counsel, Internal Revenue Service, 1964-
65.

SALINGER, Frank Max
V. Pres., Gen. Counsel & Dir. Gov't Aff., American Finan-
cial Services Ass'n
1101 14th St., N.W., Washington, DC 20005
Telephone: (202) 289-0400
Registered as lobbyist at U.S. Congress.

SALISBURY, Dallas L.
President, Employee Benefit Research Institute
2121 K St., N.W., Suite 600, Washington, DC 20037-2121
Telephone: (202) 659-0670

SALISBURY, Franklin C.
President, Nat'l Foundation for Cancer Research
7315 Wisconsin Ave. Suite 332 West, Bethesda, MD
20814
Telephone: (301) 654-1250

SALKIND, Chester J.
Exec. Director, American Soc. of Pension Actuaries
2029 K St., N.W., 4th Floor, Washington, DC 20006
Telephone: (202) 659-3620

SALLET, Jonathan
Miller, Cassidy, Larroca and Lewin
2555 M St., N.W. Suite 500, Washington, DC 20037
Telephone: (202) 293-6400
Clients:
Independent Insurance Agents of America
Nat'l Ass'n of Casualty and Surety Agents

SALMON, John J.
Dewey, Ballantine, Bushby, Palmer and Wood
1775 Pennsylvania Ave., N.W. Suite 200, Washington, DC 20006
Telephone: (202) 862-1000
Registered as lobbyist at U.S. Congress.
Registered as Foreign Agent: (#3759).
Background: Former Chief Counsel, House of Representatives Ways and Means Committee.
Clients:
Edgcomb Corp.
Federation of American Health Systems
Hanschell Iniss Ltd.
Hospital Corp. of America
Household Internat'l
Household Internat'l Political Action Committee
Integrated Resources, Inc.
Seagram & Sons, Inc., Joseph E.
Semiconductor Industry Ass'n
Tribune Broadcasting Co.
West Indies Rum and Spirits Producers' Ass'n
Wickes Companies, Inc.
Xerox Corp.

SALOMON, Kenneth D.
Partner, Dow, Lohnes and Albertson
1255 23rd St., N.W., Suite 500, Washington, DC 20037
Telephone: (202) 857-2500
Registered as lobbyist at U.S. Congress.
Clients:
Agricultural Satellite Corp.
Nat'l Technological University

SALONEN, Neil Albert
Director, Washington Institute for Values in Public Policy
1015 18th St., N.W. Suite, Washington, DC 20036
Telephone: (202) 293-7440

SALTA, Joseph
President, Nat'l Ass'n of Dental Assistants
900 S. Washington St., Falls Church, VA 22046
Telephone: (703) 237-8616
Background: Serves also as President, Nat'l Ass'n of Physician Nurses.

SALVATORI, Vincent L.
Exec. V. President, Government Relations, QuesTech, Inc.
7600A Leesburg Pike, Falls Church, VA 22043
Telephone: (703) 760-1000

SAM BAI, Sanyung
Dorsey & Whitney
1330 Connecticut Ave., N.W., Suite 200, Washington, DC 20036
Telephone: (202) 857-0700

SAMMIS, Jack C.
President, Foundation for Internat'l Meetings
4200 Wilson Blvd. Suite 1100, Arlington, VA 22203
Telephone: (703) 243-3288

SAMOLIS, Frank R.
Patton, Boggs and Blow
2550 M St., N.W., Suite 800, Washington, DC 20037
Telephone: (202) 457-6000
Registered as lobbyist at U.S. Congress.
Registered as Foreign Agent: (#2165).
Background: Legislative Assistant to Rep. Charles A. Vanik (D-OH), 1976. Professional Staff, Committee on Ways and Means, Subcommittee on Trade, U.S. House of Representatives, 1977-80.
Clients:
Costa Rican Foreign Trade Committee
Fundacion de Defensa del Comercio Exterior
Minerals Marketing Corp. of Zimbabwe
Retail Industry Trade Action Coalition

SAMORS, Robert J.
Legislative Associate, APCO Associates
1155 21st St., N.W., Suite 1000, Washington, DC 20036
Telephone: (202) 778-1000
Registered as Foreign Agent: (#3597).

SAMP, Richard A.
Chief Counsel, Washington Legal Foundation
1705 N St., N.W., Washington, DC 20036
Telephone: (202) 857-0240

SAMPSON, Arthur F.
Kirkland and Ellis
655 15th St., N.W. Suite 1200, Washington, DC 20005
Telephone: (202) 879-5000

SAMPSON, Dr. Barbara M.
Exec. Director, American Ass'n for Leisure and Recreation
1900 Association Dr., Reston, VA 22091
Telephone: (703) 476-3471

SAMPSON, R. Neil
Exec. V. President, American Forestry Ass'n
P.O. Box 2000, Washington, DC 20013
Telephone: (202) 667-3300
Background: Served with Soil Conservation Service, U.S. Department of Agriculture, 1960-78.

SAMUEL, Howard D.
President, AFL-CIO - Industrial Union Department
815 16th St., N.W., Washington, DC 20006
Telephone: (202) 842-7842

SAMUEL, Wendy
V. President, General Counsel, Nat'l Council of Savings Institutions
1101 15th St., N.W. Suite 400, Washington, DC 20005
Telephone: (202) 857-3100

SAMUEL, William H.
Legislative Director, United Mine Workers of America
900 15th St., N.W., Washington, DC 20005
Telephone: (202) 842-7250
Registered as lobbyist at U.S. Congress.

SAMUELS, Ambassador Michael A.
Sr. V.P. & Nat'l Pract. Dir, Int'l Trade, Hill and Knowlton Public Affairs Worldwide
Washington Harbour, 901 31st St., N.W., Washington, DC 20007
Telephone: (202) 333-7400
Background: Former Deputy U.S. Trade Representative.

SAMUELS, Sheldon W.
Dir. of Health, Safety and Environment, AFL-CIO - Industrial Union Department
815 16th St., N.W., Washington, DC 20006
Telephone: (202) 842-7800

SAMUELSON, Lior
Policy Economics Group of KPMG Peat Marwick
2001 M St. N.W., Washington, DC 20036
Telephone: (202) 467-3818

SAN JULIAN, Gary
V. President, Research and Education, Nat'l Wildlife Federation
1400 16th St., N.W., Washington, DC 20036-2266
Telephone: (202) 797-6800

SANASACK, David
Exec. V. President, Internat'l Management Group, Inc.
1101 14th St., N.W. Suite 1100, Washington, DC 20005
Telephone: (202) 371-2200
Background: Serves also as Exec. V. President, Institute of Ass'n Management Companies; Exec. Director, Soc. of Environmental Toxicology and Chemistry; and Exec. Director, Internat'l Soc. of Transport Aircraft Traders.

SANCHEZ, Felix
Director, Congressional Relations, American Gas Ass'n
1515 Wilson Blvd., Arlington, VA 22209
Telephone: (703) 841-8592
Registered as lobbyist at U.S. Congress.
Background: Former Legislative Assistant to Senator Lloyd Bentsen (D-TX).

SANCHEZ, Rodolfo Balli
President and Chief Executive Officer, Hispanic America, Inc.
1511 K St., N.W., Suite 1026, Washington, DC 20005
Telephone: (202) 393-7836

SANCHIS, Frank
V. Pres., Stewardship/His. Properties, Nat'l Trust for Historic Preservation
1785 Massachusetts Ave., N.W., Washington, DC 20036
Telephone: (202) 673-4000

SAND, Christine M.
Legislative Assistant, Nat'l-American Wholesale Grocers' Ass'n
201 Park Washington Court, Falls Church, VA 22046
Telephone: (703) 532-9400

SAND, Susan Bianchi
President, Ass'n of Flight Attendants
1625 Massachusetts Ave., N.W. 3rd Floor, Washington, DC 20036
Telephone: (202) 328-5400

SANDERS, Brenda G.
Manager, Policy Development, American Soc. of Civil Engineers
1015 15th St., N.W. Suite 600, Washington, DC 20005
Telephone: (202) 789-2200

SANDERS, David G.
National Field Director, Conservative Caucus, The
450 Maple Ave. East, Suite 309, Vienna, VA 22180
Telephone: (703) 893-1550

SANDERS, Gary
Counsel, Nat'l Ass'n of Life Underwriters
1922 F St., N.W., Washington, DC 20006
Telephone: (202) 331-6000

SANDERS, James C.
President, Beer Institute
1225 Eye St., N.W., Suite 825, Washington, DC 20005
Telephone: (202) 737-2337
Registered as lobbyist at U.S. Congress.
Background: Former Administrator, Small Business Administration.

SANDERS, Jane
Technical Services Director, Nat'l Accounting and Finance Council
2200 Mill Road, Second Floor, Alexandria, VA 22314
Telephone: (703) 838-1915

SANDERS, John W.
Director, Washington Office, Nat'l Ass'n of Independent Schools
1749 P St., N.W., Washington, DC 20036
Telephone: (202) 462-3886
Background: Also serves as Exec. V. President of the Independent Education Foundation.

SANDERS, Petronella C.
Assistant Manager, Government Relations, Nat'l Business Aircraft Ass'n
1200 18th St., N.W. Suite 200, Washington, DC 20036
Telephone: (202) 783-9000
Registered as lobbyist at U.S. Congress.

SANDERS, Rose Marie
Legislative Representative/Patents, Chemical Manufacturers Ass'n
2501 M St., N.W., Washington, DC 20037
Telephone: (202) 887-1100
Registered as lobbyist at U.S. Congress.

SANDERS, SCHNABEL & BRANDENBURG, P.C.
1110 Vermont Ave., N.W., Suite 600, Washington, DC 20005
Telephone: (202) 638-2241
Members of firm representing listed organizations:
Brandenburg, Dan S.
Clients:
American Soc. of Ass'n Executives *(Dan S. Brandenburg)*

SANDERSON, Stuart A.
Senior Counsel, American Mining Congress
1920 N St., N.W. Suite 300, Washington, DC 20036
Telephone: (202) 861-2800

Registered as lobbyist at U.S. Congress.

SANDGREN, Amy J.
Food PAC Administrator, Food Marketing Institute Political
Action Committee
1750 K St., N.W. Suite 700, Washington, DC 20006
Telephone: (202) 452-8444

SANDIFER, Myron G., III
McDonald Co., Jack
1001 Pennsylvania Ave., N.W., Suite 625 South, Washington, DC 20004
Telephone: (202) 624-7269
Registered as lobbyist at U.S. Congress.
Registered as Foreign Agent: (#3956).
Background: Former Staff Assistant to Senator Walter D.
Huddleston (D-KY).
Organizations represented:
Dow Corning Corp.
Hitachi America Ltd.
Hitachi Sales Corp. of America
Planeta North America, Inc.
Tuteur Associates, Inc.
WMW Machinery, Inc.

SANDLER, Charles E.
V. President, Government Affairs, American Petroleum Institute
1220 L St., N.W., Washington, DC 20005
Telephone: (202) 682-8400
Registered as lobbyist at U.S. Congress.

SANDLER, Joseph E.
Arent, Fox, Kintner, Plotkin & Kahn
1050 Connecticut Ave., N.W., Washington, DC 20036-
5339
Telephone: (202) 857-6000
Registered as lobbyist at U.S. Congress.
Clients:
San Diego, California, City of

SANDLER, Neil W.
Director of Communications, Nat'l Institute of Building
Sciences
1201 L St., N.W., Suite 400, Washington, DC 20005
Telephone: (202) 289-7800

SANDLER, TRAVIS & ROSENBERG. P.A.
1120 19th St., N.W. Suite 420, Washington, DC 20036
Telephone: (202) 457-0078
Members of firm representing listed organizations:
Gerdes, Ronald W.
Background: U.S. Customs Service: Assistant Chief
Counsel, Administration and Legislation, 1980-85;
Senior Attorney, Office of Regulation and Rulings,
1973-1980.
Travis, Thomas G.
Clients:
American Ass'n of Exporters and Importers *(Ronald W. Gerdes, Thomas G. Travis)*
Florida Customs Brokers and Forwarders *(Ronald W. Gerdes, Thomas G. Travis)*
Florida District Export Council *(Ronald W. Gerdes, Thomas G. Travis)*
Florida Exporters and Importers Ass'n *(Ronald W. Gerdes, Thomas G. Travis)*
Nat'l Bonded Warehouse Ass'n *(Thomas G. Travis)*
U.S. Apparel Industry Council *(Thomas G. Travis)*

SANDLUND, Peter G.
Washington Representative, Council of European and
Japanese Nat'l Shipowners' Ass'ns
1725 Eye St., N.W. Suite 315, Washington, DC 20006
Telephone: (202) 293-1717
Registered as lobbyist at U.S. Congress.
Registered as Foreign Agent: (#2485).

SANDMAN, Jeffrey M.
V. President and General Counsel, Kamber Group, The
1920 L St., N.W., Washington, DC 20036
Telephone: (202) 223-8700
Organizations represented:
Kamber Group Political Action Fund (TKG
PAC)
United Food and Commercial Workers Internat'l
Union

SANDOVAL, Alicia
Director, Communications Services, Nat'l Education Ass'n
of the U.S.
1201 16th St., N.W., Washington, DC 20036
Telephone: (202) 822-7200
Registered as lobbyist at U.S. Congress.

SANDOVAL, Dr. Miguel
President, Nat'l Alliance of Spanish-Speaking People for
Equality
1701 16th St., N.W., Suite 601, Washington, DC 20009
Telephone: (202) 234-8198

SANDS, Dawn
Administrator, Campaign America
511 Capitol Court N. E. Suite 100, Washington, DC 20002
Telephone: (202) 543-5016
Background: Executive Assistant, Nat'l Republican
Senatorial Committee.

SANDSTROM, Mark Roy
Thompson, Hine and Flory
1920 N St., N.W., Washington, DC 20036
Telephone: (202) 331-8800
Registered as lobbyist at U.S. Congress.
Registered as Foreign Agent: (#3365).
Clients:
American Tie Fabric Ass'n
Nat'l Pork Producers Council
Yale Materials Handling Corp.

SANDUSKY, Vincent R.
Exec. Director, Painting and Decorating Contractors of
America
3913 Old Lee Highway Suite 33B, Fairfax, VA 22030
Telephone: (703) 359-0826

SANER, Robert J., II
White, Fine, and Verville
1156 15th St., N.W. Suite 1100, Washington, DC 20005
Telephone: (202) 659-2900
Clients:
Ass'n of Metropolitan Water Agencies
Medical Group Management Ass'n

SANNER, Harvey
Nat'l President, American Agriculture Movement, Inc.
100 Maryland Ave., N.E. Suite 500A, Washington, DC
20002
Telephone: (202) 544-5750
Background: Also represents the Political Action Committee.

SANSEVERO, Vincent
Legis Affrs Specialist, NAT'L AERONAUTICS AND
SPACE ADMINISTRATION
400 Maryland Ave, S.W., Washington, DC 20546
Telephone: (202) 453-1055

SANSOM, Leslie
Media Relations, Women in Communications
2101 Wilson Blvd., Suite 417, Arlington, VA 22201
Telephone: (703) 528-4200

SANTARELLI, Donald E.
Santarelli, Smith, Kraut and Carroccio
1155 Connecticut Ave., N.W., Washington, DC 20036
Telephone: (202) 466-6800
Background: Assistant U.S. Attorney, Department of Justice, 1966-67. Minority Counsel, Judiciary Committee,
House of Representatives, 1967-68. Special Counsel,
Judiciary Committee on Constitutional Rights, U.S. Senate, 1968-69; Associate Deputy Attorney General, Department of Justice, 1969-73; Administrator, Law Enforcement Assistance Administration, 1973-74.
Clients:
Embraer S.A.

SANTARELLI, SMITH, KRAUT AND CARROCCIO
1155 Connecticut Ave., N.W., Washington, DC 20036
Telephone: (202) 466-6800
Members of firm representing listed organizations:
Carroccio, A. Thomas
Santarelli, Donald E.
Background: Assistant U.S. Attorney, Department of
Justice, 1966-67. Minority Counsel, Judiciary Committee, House of Representatives, 1967-68. Special
Counsel, Judiciary Committee on Constitutional
Rights, U.S. Senate, 1968-69; Associate Deputy Attorney General, Department of Justice, 1969-73; Administrator, Law Enforcement Assistance Administration, 1973-74.
Clients:
Embraer S.A. *(Donald E. Santarelli)*
KJAZ-FM *(A. Thomas Carroccio)*
Performing Arts Network of New Jersey *(A. Thomas Carroccio)*

SANTIESTEVAN, Stina
V. President for Communications, Hispanic Policy Development Project
1001 Connecticut Ave., N.W. Suite 310, Washington, DC
20036
Telephone: (202) 822-8414

SANTINI CHARTERED
1101 King St. Suite 350, Alexandria, VA 22314
Telephone: (703) 684-0755
Members of firm representing listed organizations:
Santini, James, President
Background: Former Member, U.S. House of Representatives (R-NV).

SANTINI, James
President, Santini Chartered
1101 King St. Suite 350, Alexandria, VA 22314
Telephone: (703) 684-0755
Background: Former Member, U.S. House of Representatives (R-NV).

SANTOS, Barbara J.
Government Relations Assistant, Southern California Edison Co.
1001 Pennsylvania Ave., N.W. Suite 450N, Washington,
DC 20004
Telephone: (202) 393-3075

SANTY, Robert
Director, Government Relations, Deloitte & Touche Washington Services Group
1001 Pennsylvania Ave., N.W. Suite 350N, Washington,
DC 20004
Telephone: (202) 879-5600
Registered as lobbyist at U.S. Congress.

SAPERSTEIN, Rabbi David
Director, Religious Action Center, Union of American Hebrew Congregations
2027 Massachusetts Ave., N.W., Washington, DC 20036
Telephone: (202) 387-2800

SAPIRSTEIN, Eric
ENS Resources, Inc.
1333 H St., N.W., Suite 400, Washington, DC 20005
Telephone: (202) 789-1226
Registered as lobbyist at U.S. Congress.
Clients:
In-Situ, Inc.
Orange County Sanitation Districts

SAPP, Betty O.
Exec. V. President, Soc. of American Florists
1601 Duke St., Alexandria, VA 22314
Telephone: (703) 836-8700
Registered as lobbyist at U.S. Congress.

SARASIN, Leslie G.
Director, Government Relations, American Frozen Food
Institute
1764 Old Meadow Lane Suite 350, McLean, VA 22102
Telephone: (703) 821-0770
Registered as lobbyist at U.S. Congress.

SARASIN, Ronald A.
President, Nat'l Beer Wholesalers Ass'n
5205 Leesburg Pike, Suite 1600, Falls Church, VA 22041
Telephone: (703) 578-4300
Registered as lobbyist at U.S. Congress.

SARDAN, Julia M.
Washington Assistant, Space Services Inc.
600 Water St., S.W., Suite 207, Washington, DC 20024
Telephone: (202) 646-1025

SARTI, Riccardo
Manager, Business Development, Italian Aerospace Industries (USA), Inc.
1235 Jefferson Davis Hwy. Suite 500, Arlington, VA 22202
Telephone: (703) 271-9200

SARTI, Riccardo (Cont'd)
Registered as Foreign Agent: (#3399)

SARVIS, Aubrey L.
V. Pres., Federal Legislative Relations, Bell Atlantic
Suite 1200, 1710 Rhode Island Ave., N.W., Washington,
DC 20036
Telephone: (202) 392-1382

SASSAMAN, Virginia
Communications Manager, Women's Legal Defense Fund
2000 P St., N.W., Suite 400, Washington, DC 20036
Telephone: (202) 887-0364

SASSO, John A.
Exec. Secretary, Nat'l Community Development Ass'n
522 21st St., N.W., Suite 120, Washington, DC 20006
Telephone: (202) 293-7587

SATAGAJ, John S.
London and Satagaj, Attorneys-at-Law
1025 Vermont Ave., N.W. Suite 1201, Washington, DC
20005
Telephone: (202) 639-8888
Registered as lobbyist at U.S. Congress.
Background: Also serves as President of the Small Business
Legislative Council.
Clients:
  American Floorcovering Ass'n
  American Hardware Manufacturers Ass'n
  American Supply and Machinery Manufacturers'
    Ass'n
  Hand Tools Institute
  Jewelers of America
  Nat'l Ass'n of Exposition Managers
  Nat'l Home Furnishings Ass'n
  Photo Marketing Ass'n-Internat'l
  Small Business Legislative Council
  Wood Machinery Manufacturers of America

SATTEN, Kenneth E.
Wilkinson, Barker, Knauer and Quinn
1735 New York Ave., N.W., Suite 600, Washington, DC
20006
Telephone: (202) 783-4141
Clients:
  Bonneville Pacific Corp.

SATTERWHITE, Ernie J.
Prog. Mgr., Public Sector, Industry Mktg, Internat'l Business Machines Corp.
1801 K St., N.W., Suite 1200, Washington, DC 20006
Telephone: (202) 778-5000

SAUBER, Richard
Fried, Frank, Harris, Shriver & Jacobson
1001 Pennsylvania Ave., N.W., Suite 800, Washington, DC
20004-2505
Telephone: (202) 639-7000

SAUER, Edward W.
Squire, Sanders and Dempsey
1201 Pennsylvania Ave., N.W. P.O. Box 407, Washington,
DC 20044
Telephone: (202) 626-6600
Registered as Foreign Agent: (#0746).
Clients:
  Ansett Transport Industries
  Lineas Aereas Costaricicenes (Lasca Airlines)
  Polynesian Airlines
  VASP Airlines
  VIASA

SAUER, Lawrence M.
Legis Div, Plng, Eval & Legislation, DEPARTMENT OF
HEALTH AND HUMAN SERVICES - Health Resources
and Services Administration
5600 Fishers Lane, Rockville, MD 20857
Telephone: (301) 443-2460

SAUER, Richard J.
President and C.E.O., Nat'l 4-H Council
7100 Connecticut Ave., Chevy Chase, MD 20815
Telephone: (301) 961-2800

SAUNDERS, Albert C.
Legislative Counsel, Pharmaceutical Manufacturers Ass'n
1100 15th St., N.W., Washington, DC 20005
Telephone: (202) 835-3480

Registered as lobbyist at U.S. Congress.

SAUNDERS, Carla L.
Ottosen and Associates
208 G St., N.E., 2nd Floor, Washington, DC 20002
Telephone: (202) 543-9339
Clients:
  Baroid Corp.
  Kronos, Inc.
  NL Industries
  OTI, Inc.
  U.S. Federation of Small Businesses, Inc.
  U.S. Federation of Small Businesses PAC

SAUNDERS, Charles B., Jr.
Sr. V. President, American Council on Education
One Dupont Circle, N.W., Washington, DC 20036
Telephone: (202) 939-9355

SAUNDERS, Charles P.
Manager, Industry Structure Issues, Southern Company
Services, Inc.
1130 Connecticut Ave., N.W., Suite 830, Washington, DC
20036
Telephone: (202) 775-0944
Registered as lobbyist at U.S. Congress.

SAUNDERS AND COMPANY
1015 Duke St., Alexandria, VA 22314
Telephone: (703) 549-1555
Members of firm representing listed organizations:
  Brown, Kim
  Edmondson, Eric
  Goins, Jace
  Salavantis, Pete
  Saunders, Steven R., President
    Background: Chief Legis. Ass't to Rep. Norman F.
    Lent (R-NY), 1975-77. Communications Director,
    Nat'l Republican Senatorial Committee, 1977-79.
    Staff Director, Republican Conference of the Senate,
    1979-81. Assistant U.S. Trade Representative, Executive Office of the President, 1981-82.
  Yonkin, Pam
Clients:
  Electronic Industries Ass'n of Japan *(Pete Salavantis)*
  Internat'l Public Relations Co. *(Eric Edmondson, Steven R. Saunders)*
  Japan, Embassy of *(Eric Edmondson, Steven R. Saunders)*
  Japan Times Corp. *(Steven R. Saunders, Pam Yonkin)*
  Mitsubishi Electric Corp. *(Eric Edmondson, Steven R. Saunders)*
  Mitsubishi Internat'l Corp. *(Kim Brown, Steven R. Saunders)*
  Ohbayashi Corp. *(Eric Edmondson, Steven R. Saunders)*
  Seiko Epson Corp. *(Pete Salavantis, Steven R. Saunders)*
  Taiwan Textile Federation *(Kim Brown)*

SAUNDERS, Dr. Joseph F.
Exec. Officer, American Ass'n of Immunologists
9650 Rockville Pike, Bethesda, MD 20814
Telephone: (301) 530-7178

SAUNDERS, Mary Jane
General Counsel, Software Publishers Ass'n
1101 Connecticut Ave., N.W. Suite 901, Washington, DC
20036
Telephone: (202) 452-1600

SAUNDERS, Steven R.
President, Saunders and Company
1015 Duke St., Alexandria, VA 22314
Telephone: (703) 549-1555
Registered as Foreign Agent: (#3440).
Background: Chief Legis. Ass't to Rep. Norman F. Lent
(R-NY), 1975-77. Communications Director, Nat'l
Republican Senatorial Committee, 1977-79. Staff Director, Republican Conference of the Senate, 1979-81. Assistant U.S. Trade Representative, Executive Office of the
President, 1981-82.
Clients:
  Internat'l Public Relations Co.
  Japan, Embassy of
  Japan Times Corp.
  Mitsubishi Electric Corp.
  Mitsubishi Internat'l Corp.
  Ohbayashi Corp.
  Seiko Epson Corp.

SAUNDERS, William J.
Exec. Director, Nat'l Alliance of Black School Educators
2816 Georgia Ave., N.W., Washington, DC 20001
Telephone: (202) 483-1549

SAVAGE, Carroll J.
Ivins, Phillips and Barker
1700 Pennsylvania Ave., N.W., Suite 600, Washington, DC
20006
Telephone: (202) 393-7600
Registered as lobbyist at U.S. Congress.

SAVAGE, Helen
Senior Analyst, American Ass'n of Retired Persons
1909 K St., N.W., Washington, DC 20049
Telephone: (202) 872-4700

SAVAGE, Robbi J.
Exec. Director/Secretary Treasurer, Ass'n of State and
Interstate Water Pollution Control Administrators
444 North Capitol St., N.W. Suite 330, Washington, DC
20001
Telephone: (202) 624-7782

SAVARESE, Jim
Director of Research, Powell, Adams & Rinehart
1901 L St., N.W., 3rd Floor, Washington, DC 20036
Telephone: (202) 466-7590

SAVARESE, Ralph J.
Howrey and Simon
1730 Pennsylvania Ave., N.W., Washington, DC 20006-
4793
Telephone: (202) 783-0800
Clients:
  General Mills
  Heublein, Inc.
  Timex Corp.

SAVINO, Catherine
Exec. Secretary, World Federation of Public Health Ass'ns
c/o Amer. Public Health Ass'n 1015 15th St., N.W., Washington, DC 20005
Telephone: (202) 789-5600

SAWAYA-BARNES, Diane A.
Attorney, Penney Co., J. C.
Suite 1015, 1156 15th St., N.W., Washington, DC 20005
Telephone: (202) 862-4824

SAWAYA, Richard N.
Director, Federal Government Tax Affairs, ARCO
1333 New Hampshire Ave., N.W., Suite 1001, Washington,
DC 20036
Telephone: (202) 457-6215
Registered as lobbyist at U.S. Congress.

SAWHILL, Isabel V.
Director, Domestic Priorities Program, Urban Institute, The
2100 M St., N.W., Washington, DC 20037
Telephone: (202) 833-7200

SAWHILL, John D.
President, Nature Conservancy, The
1815 N. Lynn St, Arlington, VA 22209
Telephone: (703) 841-5300
Background: Associate Director of Energy & Natural Resources, Office of Management and Budget (1972-74);
Head of Federal Energy Administration (1973-75); Deputy Secretary of Energy (1979-80).

SAWYER, C. T.
V. President, Industry Affairs, American Petroleum Institute
1220 L St., N.W., Washington, DC 20005
Telephone: (202) 682-8140

SAYER, Marcia V.
Staff Dir/Legis Affrs, EQUAL EMPLOYMENT OPPORTUNITY COMMISSION
1801 L St., N.W., Washington, DC 20507
Telephone: (202) 663-4900

SAYLER, Robert N.
Covington and Burling
1201 Pennsylvania Ave., N.W., Box 7566, Washington, DC
20044
Telephone: (202) 662-6000
Clients:
  Armstrong World Industries, Inc.

SCALLET, Edward A.
Thompson and Mitchell
1120 Vermont Ave., N.W. Suite 1000, Washington, DC 20005
Telephone: (202) 857-0350
Registered as lobbyist at U.S. Congress.
Background: Assistant Counsel for Litigation, Department of Labor, 1978-82.
Clients:
Midland Enterprises
Mutual Fairness Taxation Ass'n

SCAMMON, Richard M.
Director, Elections Research Center
5508 Greystone St., Chevy Chase, MD 20815
Telephone: (301) 654-3540

SCANLAN, Mark
Confidential Asst, Cong Rels, DEPARTMENT OF AGRICULTURE
14th and Independence Ave. S.W., Room 234-E, Washington, DC 20205
Telephone: (202) 447-7095

SCANLON, John
Policy Analyst, Housing, Heritage Foundation
214 Massachusetts Ave., N.E., Washington, DC 20002
Telephone: (202) 546-4400

SCANLON, Kerry
Assistant Counsel, NAACP Legal Defense and Educational Fund, Inc.
1275 K St., N.W. Suite 301, Washington, DC 20005
Telephone: (202) 682-1300

SCANLON, Melissa
Jones, Day, Reavis and Pogue
1450 G St., N.W., Suite 700, Washington, DC 20005-2088
Telephone: (202) 879-3939

SCANLON, Patrick M.
General Counsel, Communications Workers of America
1925 K St., N.W., Washington, DC 20006
Telephone: (202) 728-2453

SCANLON, Terrence M.
V. President and Treasurer, Heritage Foundation
214 Massachusetts Ave., N.E., Washington, DC 20002
Telephone: (202) 546-4400
Background: Former Chairman, Consumer Product Safety Commission.

SCANLON, Thomas J.
Benchmarks, Inc.
3248 Prospect St., N.W., Washington, DC 20007
Telephone: (202) 965-3983
Clients:
Chicago Ass'n of Commerce and Industry

SCANLON, William
Co-director, Center for Health Policy Studies
c/o Georgetown University, 2233 Wisconsin Ave., N.W., Washington, DC 20007
Telephone: (202) 342-0107

SCANNELL, Raymond F.
Director of Research and Education, Bakery, Confectionery and Tobacco Workers Internat'l Union
10401 Connecticut Ave., Kensington, MD 20895
Telephone: (301) 933-8600

SCARBOROUGH, Keith
Legislative Counsel, Independent Bankers Ass'n of America
One Thomas Circle, N.W., Suite 950, Washington, DC 20005
Telephone: (202) 659-8111
Registered as lobbyist at U.S. Congress.
Background: Legislative Assistant to Sen. J. James Exon (D-NE), 1983-86.

SCARCELLI, Pat
Int'l V. President, Dir. Women's Affairs, United Food and Commercial Workers Internat'l Union
1775 K St., N.W., Washington, DC 20006
Telephone: (202) 223-3111

SCATENA, Mara
Administrator, Nat'l Ass'n of Private Schools for Exceptional Children
1625 Eye St., N.W., Suite 506, Washington, DC 20006
Telephone: (202) 223-2192

SCHAAF, Jeanne
Director, Legislative Affairs, Sprint International
1850 M St., N.W. Suite 1110, Washington, DC 20036
Telephone: (202) 857-1030

SCHAAF, Thomas W., Jr.
Exec. Director, Mozambique Research Center
1995 National Capital Station, Washington, DC 20013
Telephone: (202) 625-6443

SCHABACKER, William
Director, Public Affairs, American Newspaper Publishers Ass'n
The Newspaper Center 11600 Sunrise Valley Drive, Reston, VA 22091
Telephone: (703) 648-1000

SCHAEFER, Adele L.
Manager, Membership & Office Services, American Ass'n of Pastoral Counselors
9508A Lee Hwy., Fairfax, VA 22031-2303
Telephone: (703) 385-6967

SCHAEFFER, Eric V.
Morgan, Lewis and Bockius
1800 M St., N.W., Washington, DC 20036
Telephone: (202) 467-7000
Clients:
Nat'l Lime Ass'n
Safety-Kleen Corp.
USG Corporation

SCHAEFFER, Esther F.
V. President, Policy, Nat'l Alliance of Business
1201 New York Ave., N.W., Suite 700, Washington, DC 20005
Telephone: (202) 289-2888
Background: Former Executive Assistant to the Assistant Secretary of Employment and Training, Department of Labor.

SCHAEFFER, Capt. Thomas
Chief, Cong and Gov't'l Affrs, DEPARTMENT OF TRANSPORTATION - United States Coast Guard
400 Seventh St., S.W., Washington, DC 20590
Telephone: (202) 366-4280

SCHAEFGEN, John R.
Reid & Priest
1111 19th St., N.W., Washington, DC 20036
Telephone: (202) 828-0100
Registered as lobbyist at U.S. Congress.

SCHAFER, Dr. Paul W.
Exec. Director, Nat'l Ass'n of VA Physicians
3400 Internat'l Drive, N.W. Pod K-2, Washington, DC 20008-3098
Telephone: (202) 363-3838

SCHAFFER, Mark L.
Ashcraft and Gerel
2000 L St., N.W. Suite 700, Washington, DC 20036
Telephone: (202) 783-6400
Registered as lobbyist at U.S. Congress.
Clients:
AFL-CIO (American Federation of Labor and Congress of Industrial Organizations)

SCHAFFER, Rebecca
Keck, Mahin and Cate
1201 New York Ave., N.W., Penthouse Suite, Washington, DC 20005
Telephone: (202) 347-7006
Registered as lobbyist at U.S. Congress.
Clients:
American Petroleum Institute
Arkla Exploration Co.
Williams Companies, The

SCHAFFER, William Gray
Preston Gates Ellis & Rouvelas Meeds
1735 New York Ave., N.W., Suite 500, Washington, DC 20006-4759

Telephone: (202) 628-1700
Background: Former Special Litigation Counsel, U.S. Department of Justice.

SCHAGRIN ASSOCIATES
1112 16th St., N.W. Suite 1000, Washington, DC 20036
Telephone: (202) 223-1700
Members of firm representing listed organizations:
Colza, Carol A.
Background: Former Legislative Director for Rep. Adam Benjamin, Jr., 1978-82.
Jameson, Paul
Luberda, R. Alan
Schagrin, Roger B.
Clients:
Copperweld Corp. *(Carol A. Colza, Roger B. Schagrin)*
Cyclops Industries *(Carol A. Colza, Roger B. Schagrin)*
Grinnell Corp. *(Carol A. Colza, Roger B. Schagrin)*
LTV Tubular *(Carol A. Colza, Roger B. Schagrin)*
Maverick Tube Corp. *(Carol A. Colza, Roger B. Schagrin)*
NEPTCO *(R. Alan Luberda, Roger B. Schagrin)*
Quanex Corp. *(Carol A. Colza, Roger B. Schagrin)*
Weirton Steel Corp.
Wheatland Tube Co. *(Carol A. Colza, Roger B. Schagrin)*

SCHAGRIN, Roger B.
Schagrin Associates
1112 16th St., N.W. Suite 1000, Washington, DC 20036
Telephone: (202) 223-1700
Registered as lobbyist at U.S. Congress.
Clients:
Copperweld Corp.
Cyclops Industries
Grinnell Corp.
LTV Tubular
Maverick Tube Corp.
NEPTCO
Quanex Corp.
Wheatland Tube Co.

SCHAITBERGER, Harold A.
Exec. Assistant to the President, Internat'l Ass'n of Fire Fighters
1750 New York Ave., N.W., Washington, DC 20006
Telephone: (202) 737-8484
Registered as lobbyist at U.S. Congress.

SCHAMBERG WILLIS, Nancy
Director, Government Affairs, American Planning Ass'n
1776 Massachusetts Ave., N.W., Washington, DC 20036
Telephone: (202) 872-0611

SCHANER, Kenneth I.
Swidler & Berlin, Chartered
3000 K St., N.W., Suite 300, Washington, DC 20007
Telephone: (202) 944-4300
Registered as lobbyist at U.S. Congress.
Background: Attorney, Internal Revenue Service, 1966-70.
Clients:
Internat'l Service Agencies
Nat'l Council of Community Hospitals

SCHAPAUGH, William T.
Exec. V. President, American Seed Trade Ass'n
1030 15th St., N.W. Suite 964, Washington, DC 20005
Telephone: (202) 223-4080
Registered as lobbyist at U.S. Congress.
Background: Exec. V. President, Nat'l Council of Commercial Plant Breeders.

SCHARDT, Arlie W.
Editor, Council on Foundations
1828 L St., N.W. Suite 300, Washington, DC 20036
Telephone: (202) 466-6512

SCHARF, Eric G.
Exec. Director, Nat'l Ass'n of Passenger Vessel Owners
1511 K St., N.W., Suite 715, Washington, DC 20005
Telephone: (202) 638-5310

SCHARFF, J. Laurent
Reed Smith Shaw & McClay
1200 18th St., N.W., Washington, DC 20036
Telephone: (202) 457-6100
Registered as lobbyist at U.S. Congress.
Clients:
Radio-Television News Directors Ass'n

SCHARPF, Norman W.
President, Graphic Communications Ass'n
1730 North Lynn St. Suite 604, Arlington, VA 22209
Telephone: (703) 841-8160

SCHATZ, Thomas A.
V. President, Gov't Affairs Director, Citizens Against Government Waste
1301 Connecticut Ave., N.W. Suite 400, Washington, DC 20036
Telephone: (202) 467-5300
Registered as lobbyist at U.S. Congress.

SCHAUBEL, C. A. "Jim", Jr.
V. Pres., Fed. Gov't & Internat'l Rels., Bell Atlantic
Suite 1200, 1710 Rhode Island Ave., N.W., Washington, DC 20036
Telephone: (202) 392-6985

SCHAUER, Carole
President, Mental Health Coalition
P.O. Box 11641, Washington, DC 20008
Telephone: (202) 529-1745

SCHAUFFLER, Peter
Coordinator, Committee on the Constitutional System
1755 Massachusetts Ave., N.W. Suite 416, Washington, DC 20036
Telephone: (202) 387-8787

SCHAW, Walter A.
Exec. V. President, Ass'n of Physical Plant Administrators of Universities and Colleges
1446 Duke St., Alexandria, VA 22314
Telephone: (703) 684-1446

SCHECHTER, Sue
Staff Attorney, Nat'l Ass'n for Public Interest Law
1666 Connecticut Ave., N.W., Suite 424, Washington, DC 20009
Telephone: (202) 462-0120

SCHECKELHOFF, Mary A.
Director, Women's Rights, American Federation of State, County and Municipal Employees
1625 L St., N.W., Washington, DC 20036
Telephone: (202) 429-1000

SCHECTER, Barbara W.
Director of Development, Committee for the Study of the American Electorate
421 New Jersey, Ave., S.E., Washington, DC 20003
Telephone: (202) 546-3221

SCHEER, Julian
Senior Vice President, Corporate Affairs, LTV Corp.
1025 Thomas Jefferson St., N.W., Suite 511 West, Washington, DC 20007
Telephone: (202) 944-5700
Background: Assistant Administrator for Public Affairs, National Aeronautics and Space Administration, 1962-1971.

SCHEERSCHMIDT, Robert H.
V. President, Government Affairs, Xerox Corp.
490 L'Enfant Plaza East, S.W., Suite 4200, Washington, DC 20024
Telephone: (202) 646-8285
Registered as lobbyist at U.S. Congress.

SCHEFER, Leo J.
President, Washington Airports Task Force
P.O. Box 17349, Washington Dulles Internat'l Airport, Washington, DC 20041
Telephone: (703) 661-8040

SCHEIB, Lauren B.
Public Relations Specialist, American Ass'n for Counseling and Development
5999 Stevenson Ave., Alexandria, VA 22304
Telephone: (703) 823-9800

SCHEIDER, Susan E.
Assistant General Counsel, Nat'l Ass'n of Government Employees
1313 L St., N.W., 2nd Floor, Washington, DC 20005
Telephone: (202) 371-6644
Registered as lobbyist at U.S. Congress.

SCHEINESON, Marc J.
Laxalt, Washington, Perito & Dubuc
1120 Connecticut Ave., N.W., Suite 1000, Washington, DC 20036
Telephone: (202) 857-4000
Background: Tax Counsel and Legislative Assistant to Rep. Willis D. Gradison, Jr. (R-OH), 1980-82.
Clients:
Appraisal Foundation
AVW Electronics Systems, Inc.
BTS Development Corp.
Cohen Flax Investments
Greenbaum & Rose Associates
OPTUR - La Sociedad Mercantil Operaciones Turisticas
Soc. of Real Estate Appraisers
Southwest Gas Corp.

SCHELDRUP, Jill L.
Associate Manager, Employee Relations, Chamber of Commerce of the U.S.A.
1615 H St., N.W., Washington, DC 20062
Telephone: (202) 659-6000
Registered as lobbyist at U.S. Congress.

SCHELLHARDT, Donald J.
Dir., State, Local & Coalition Relations, American Gas Ass'n
1515 Wilson Blvd., Arlington, VA 22209
Telephone: (703) 841-8464
Background: Former Legislative Analyst, House Republican Research Committee; Legislative Counsel to Rep. Matthew J. Rinaldo (R-NJ).

SCHELLIN, Eric P.
Exec. V. President, Nat'l Patent Council
2121 Crystal Dr., 2 Crystal Pk Suite 704, Arlington, VA 22202
Telephone: (703) 521-1669

SCHENK, Martha
Ass't ot the President & Corp. Sec'y, Adams Associates, John
1825 K St., N.W. Suite 210, Washington, DC 20006
Telephone: (202) 466-8320

SCHEPPACH, Raymond C.
Exec. Director, Nat'l Governors' Ass'n
444 North Capitol St., N.W., Suite 250, Washington, DC 20001
Telephone: (202) 624-5300

SCHER, Barry F.
V. President, Public Affairs, Giant Food Inc.
6300 Sheriff Road, Landover, MD 20785
Telephone: (301) 341-4100

SCHER, Michael
Podesta Associates
424 C St., N.E., Washington, DC 20002
Telephone: (202) 544-6906
Background: Legislative Aide to Senator Daniel P. Moynihan (D-NY), 1984-85. Legislative Assistant to Senator Patrick Leahy (D-VT), 1985-89.

SCHER, William B., Jr.
V. President, Law, Nat'l Ass'n of Life Underwriters
1922 F St., N.W., Washington, DC 20006
Telephone: (202) 331-6000

SCHERCINGER, J. M.
Manager, Rail-Highway Programs, Ass'n of American Railroads
50 F St., N.W., Suite 6903, Washington, DC 20001
Telephone: (202) 639-2207

SCHEREN, Janet K.
Director of Communications, Nat'l Wholesale Druggists' Ass'n
105 Oronoco St., Alexandria, VA 22314
Telephone: (202) 684-6400

SCHERER, Dr. Joseph J.
Exec. Director, Nat'l School Public Relations Ass'n
1501 Lee Hwy. Suite 201, Arlington, VA 22209
Telephone: (703) 528-5840

SCHERER, Robert D.
President and CEO, Nat'l Cooperative Business Ass'n
1401 New York Ave., N.W. Suite 1100, Washington, DC 20005
Telephone: (202) 638-6222

SCHERI, William L.
Air Transportation Coordinator, Internat'l Ass'n of Machinists and Aerospace Workers
1300 Connecticut Ave., N.W. Suite 404, Washington, DC 20036
Telephone: (202) 857-5200

SCHERR, S. Jacob
Senior Staff Attorney, Natural Resources Defense Council
1350 New York Ave., N.W. Suite 300, Washington, DC 20005
Telephone: (202) 783-7800
Registered as lobbyist at U.S. Congress.

SCHIAFFINO, Dr. S. Stephen
Executive Officer, American Soc. for Clinical Nutrition
9650 Rockville Pike, Room 4500, Bethesda, MD 20814
Telephone: (301) 530-7110

SCHIAPPA, Gerard F.
2300 M St., N.W., Suite 800, Washington, DC 20037
Telephone: (202) 223-0770
Registered as Foreign Agent: (#4284)
Organizations represented:
Guam-Uranao Development Co., Ltd.

SCHICK, Wendy
Legislative Assistant, Ass'n of Private Pension and Welfare Plans
1212 New York Ave., N.W. 12th Floor, Washington, DC 20005
Telephone: (202) 737-6666
Registered as lobbyist at U.S. Congress.
Background: Serves also as Assistant Treasurer of the Ass'n of Private Pension and Welfare Plans Political Action Committee.

SCHIERING, G. David
Taft, Stettinius and Hollister
1620 Eye St., N.W., Suite 800, Washington, DC 20006
Telephone: (202) 785-1620

SCHIFF HARDIN & WAITE
1101 Connecticut Ave., N.W. Suite 600, Washington, DC 20036
Telephone: (202) 857-0600
Background: The Washington office of a Chicago law firm.
Members of firm representing listed organizations:
Journey, Drexel D.
  Background: Member, 1952-77, and General Counsel, 1974-77, Federal Power Commission.
Klein, Andrew M.
  Background: Director, Division of Market Regulation, Securities and Exchange Commission, 1977-79. Special Counsel, Assistant Director, and Associate Director of Division of Market Regulation, 1973-77.
Knowles, Gearold L.
  Background: Attorney, Division of Corporate Regulation, Securities and Exchange Commission, 1973-76. Senior Attorney, Office of the General Counsel, U.S. Railway Ass'n, 1976-77.
Rockefeller, Edwin S.
  Background: Assistant to General Counsel, Federal Trade Commission, 1958-59. Exec. Assistant to the Chairman, FTC, 1959-61.
Clients:
Chicago Board Options Exchange *(Andrew M. Klein)*
China, Directorate General of Telecommunications, Ministry of Communications of Republic of *(Gearold L. Knowles)*

SCHIFF, Jeffrey H.
Exec. Director, Nat'l Ass'n of Towns and Townships
1522 K St., N.W. Suite 730, Washington, DC 20005
Telephone: (202) 737-5200

SCHIFFBAUER, William G.
Groom and Nordberg
1701 Pennsylvania Ave., N.W., Suite 1200, Washington, DC 20006
Telephone: (202) 857-0620
Registered as lobbyist at U.S. Congress.
Clients:

Nebraska Public Power District
Sunflower Electric Cooperative, Inc.

SCHIFFER, H. Michael
Assistant V. President, Federal Affairs, CIGNA Corp.
1825 Eye St., N.W., Suite 750, Washington, DC 20006
Telephone: (202) 296-7174

SCHILLER, Dr. Bradley
President, Potomac Institute for Economic Research
4323 Hawthorne St., N.W., Washington, DC 20016
Telephone: (202) 364-1138

SCHILLERSTROM, David O.
Assistant V. President, Communications, Aerospace Industries Ass'n of America
1250 Eye St., N.W., Suite 1100, Washington, DC 20005
Telephone: (202) 371-8400
Background: Former Deputy Director, Public Affairs, U.S. Department of the Air Force.

SCHIMMEL, Eric J.
V. President, Telecommunications Industry Ass'n
1722 Eye St., N.W., Suite 440, Washington, DC 20006
Telephone: (202) 457-4912

SCHIPPER, Dr. William
Exec. Director, Nat'l Ass'n of State Directors of Special Education
2021 K St., N.W., Suite 315, Washington, DC 20006
Telephone: (202) 296-1800

SCHIRALLI, Ella M.
Staff Associate, Government Relations, Electronic Industries Ass'n
2001 Pennsylvania Ave., N.W., Washington, DC 20006
Telephone: (202) 457-4900
Registered as lobbyist at U.S. Congress.

SCHLEE, G. Michael
Director, Nat'l Security/Foreign Relats., American Legion
1608 K St., N.W., Washington, DC 20006
Telephone: (202) 861-2730

SCHLEFER, Mark P.
Fort and Schlefer
1401 New York Ave., N.W. Twelfth Floor, Washington, DC 20005
Telephone: (202) 467-5900
Clients:
  Crowley Maritime Corp.

SCHLEGEL, John F.
Exec. V. President, American Academy of Facial Plastic and Reconstructive Surgery
1101 Vermont Ave., N.W. Suite 404, Washington, DC 20005
Telephone: (202) 842-4500

SCHLEICHER, Carl
Director, Foundation for Blood Irradiation
1315 Apple Ave., Silver Spring, MD 20910
Telephone: (301) 587-8686
Background: Serves also as President, Society for the Application of Free Energy.

SCHLICHT, James P.
Manager, Government Affairs, Bristol-Myers Squibb Co.
655 15th St., N.W., Suite 410, Washington, DC 20005
Telephone: (202) 783-0900
Registered as lobbyist at U.S. Congress.

SCHLICKER, Sandra A.
McMahon and Associates
1331 Pennsylvania Ave., N.W., Suite 909, Washington, DC 20004
Telephone: (202) 662-7400
Registered as lobbyist at U.S. Congress.
Background: Formerly with the U.S. Dept. of Agriculture, Food and Nutrition Service.
Clients:
  Rodale Press, Inc.

SCHLICKMAN, Stephen E.
Director, Chicago Washington Office, City of
499 South Capitol St., S.E., Washington, DC 20003
Telephone: (202) 554-7900

SCHLOMAN, Kenneth D.
Washington Counsel, Nat'l Ass'n of Independent Insurers
499 South Capitol St., S.W. Suite 401, Washington, DC 20003
Telephone: (202) 484-2350
Registered as lobbyist at U.S. Congress.

SCHLOSS, Howard M.
Communications Director, Democratic Congressional Campaign Committee
430 South Capitol St., S.E. 2nd Floor, Washington, DC 20003
Telephone: (202) 863-1500

SCHLOSSBERG ASSOC., Ken
317 Massachusetts Ave., N.E. Suite 200, Washington, DC 20002
Telephone: (202) 544-6796
Members of firm representing listed organizations:
  Schlossberg, Kenneth, President
  Silveira, Mary, V. President
  Smith, William C., V. President
Organizations represented:
  Alliance for Maritime Heritage Foundation *(William C. Smith)*
  Bowman Gray School of Medicine of Wake Forest University *(Kenneth Schlossberg, William C. Smith)*
  Marine Biological Laboratory *(Kenneth Schlossberg, Mary Silveira)*
  Nat'l Shipwreck Alliance *(William C. Smith)*
  US Tall Ship Foundation *(William C. Smith)*

SCHLOSSBERG, Kenneth
President, Schlossberg Assoc., Ken
317 Massachusetts Ave., N.E. Suite 200, Washington, DC 20002
Telephone: (202) 544-6796
Registered as lobbyist at U.S. Congress.
Organizations represented:
  Bowman Gray School of Medicine of Wake Forest University
  Marine Biological Laboratory

SCHLOTTERBECK, Beverly A.
County News Editor, Nat'l Ass'n of Counties
440 First St., N.W., Washington, DC 20001
Telephone: (202) 393-6226
Background: Serves as contact for Nat'l Ass'n of County Information Officials.

SCHMELTZER, APTAKER AND SHEPPARD
The Watergate, 2600 Virginia Ave., N.W., Washington, DC 20037
Telephone: (202) 333-8800
Background: The information was obtained from public records and submitted for confirmation to this firm, which did not confirm or correct the information and asked to be omitted from the book.
Members of firm representing listed organizations:
  Aptaker, Edward
    Background: Counsel. Attorney, Interstate Commerce Commission, 1949-51. U.S. Maritime Administration, 1951-70.
  Dudley, Deana Francis
  Esslinger, J. Thomas
  Langford Sanford, Suzanne
  Schmeltzer, Edward
    Background: Trial Attorney, Federal Maritime Board, Maritime Administration, 1955-60. Director, Bureau of Domestic Regulation, 1961-66, and Managing Director, 1966-69, Federal Maritime.
  Sheppard, Edward J. (IV)
Clients:
  Alabama State Docks Department *(Edward J. Sheppard, IV)*
  American Honda Motor Co.
  Cargill, Inc. *(Edward Schmeltzer, Edward J. Sheppard, IV)*
  Gulf Seaports Marine Terminals Conference *(Edward J. Sheppard, IV)*
  Lake Charles Harbor and Terminal District *(Edward J. Sheppard, IV)*
  Maritima Transligra *(Deana Francis Dudley, Suzanne Langford Sanford)*
  Massachusetts Port Authority *(Edward J. Sheppard, IV)*
  South Carolina State Port Authority *(J. Thomas Esslinger, Edward J. Sheppard, IV)*
  Tampa Port Authority *(Edward J. Sheppard, IV)*

SCHMELTZER, Edward
Schmeltzer, Aptaker and Sheppard
The Watergate, 2600 Virginia Ave., N.W., Washington, DC 20037
Telephone: (202) 333-8800
Registered as Foreign Agent: (#3925).
Background: Trial Attorney, Federal Maritime Board, Maritime Administration, 1955-60. Director, Bureau of Domestic Regulation, 1961-66, and Managing Director, 1966-69, Federal Maritime.
Clients:
  Cargill, Inc.

SCHMERTZ CO., THE
555 13th St. N.W. Suite 1220 East, Washington, DC 20004
Telephone: (202) 637-6680
Background: A public relations/lobbying firm.
Members of firm representing listed organizations:
  Foer, Esther
  Lewis, Caroline

SCHMICK, John E.
V. President, Washington Office, Boeing Co.
1700 North Moore St., Arlington, VA 22209
Telephone: (703) 558-9600
Registered as lobbyist at U.S. Congress.

SCHMIDT ASSOC., INC., Leslie J.
Box 5934, Bethesda, MD 20814
Telephone: (301) 656-7464
Members of firm representing listed organizations:
  Schmidt, Leslie J.
Organizations represented:
  San Miguel Corp. *(Leslie J. Schmidt)*

SCHMIDT, Christy
Dir, Off of Analysis & Eval (Act), DEPARTMENT OF AGRICULTURE - Food and Nutrition Service
3101 Park Center Drive, Alexandria, VA 22302
Telephone: (703) 756-3039

SCHMIDT, Dale R.
Manager, Legal Services, Nat'l Electrical Manufacturers Ass'n
2101 L St., N.W., Washington, DC 20037
Telephone: (202) 457-8400

SCHMIDT, David B.
Dir, Info & Legis Affrs Staff, DEPARTMENT OF AGRICULTURE - Food Safety and Inspection Service
14th and Independence Ave. S.W., Washington, DC 20250
Telephone: (202) 447-7943

SCHMIDT, Leslie J.
Schmidt Assoc., Inc., Leslie J.
Box 5934, Bethesda, MD 20814
Telephone: (301) 656-7464
Organizations represented:
  San Miguel Corp.

SCHMIDT, Patrick L.
Winston and Strawn
2550 M St., N.W., Suite 500, Washington, DC 20037
Telephone: (202) 828-8400

SCHMIDT-PERKINS, Drusilla
Environmental Action
1525 New Hampshire Ave., N.W., Washington, DC 20036
Telephone: (202) 745-4870

SCHMIDT, Richard M., Jr.
Cohn and Marks
1333 New Hampshire Ave., N.W., Suite 600, Washington, DC 20036
Telephone: (202) 293-3860
Registered as lobbyist at U.S. Congress.
Background: Counsel, Special Investigating Subcommittee, U.S. Senate, 1959-60. General Counsel, U.S.A., 1965-68.
Clients:
  American Soc. of Newspaper Editors
  Nat'l Ass'n of Trade and Technical Schools
  Nat'l Electric Sign Ass'n

SCHMIDT, Robert L.
President, Wireless Cable Ass'n, Inc.
Des Moines, IA
Background: Of Counsel, Gold & Liebengood.

SCHMITT, Robert
Exec. Director, Public Interest Computer Ass'n
1025 Connecticut Ave., N.W. Suite 1015, Washington, DC 20036
Telephone: (202) 775-1588

SCHMITZ, Herbert K.
Director, Government Relations, ICI Americas Inc.
1600 M St., N.W., Suite 702, Washington, DC 20036
Telephone: (202) 775-9722
Registered as lobbyist at U.S. Congress.

SCHNABEL, Pamela M.
Assistant Director, Compliance, Chrysler Technologies Corp.
1100 Connecticut Ave., N.W. 7th Floor, Washington, DC 20036
Telephone: (202) 862-3460
Background: Responsibilities include Chrysler Technologies Political Support Committee.

SCHNADER, HARRISON, SEGAL AND LEWIS
1111 19th St., N.W. Suite 1000, Washington, DC 20036
Telephone: (202) 463-2900
Background: Washington office of a Philadelphia law firm.
Members of firm representing listed organizations:
  Penna, Richard A.
Clients:
  Mack Trucks, Inc. *(Richard A. Penna)*
  Toyota Motor Corporate Services U.S.A. *(Richard A. Penna)*

SCHNEEBAUM, Steven
Patton, Boggs and Blow
2550 M St., N.W., Suite 800, Washington, DC 20037
Telephone: (202) 457-6000
Registered as lobbyist at U.S. Congress.
Registered as Foreign Agent: (#2165).

SCHNEEBERGER, Dana L.
Legislative Representative, Collier, Shannon & Scott
1055 Thomas Jefferson St., N.W., Suite 300, Washington, DC 20007
Telephone: (202) 342-8400
Registered as lobbyist at U.S. Congress.
Registered as Foreign Agent: (#3694).

SCHNEIDER, Hartmut
Representative for German Industry and Trade
One Farragut Square South 1634 Eye St., N.W., Washington, DC 20006
Telephone: (202) 347-0247
Registered as Foreign Agent: (#4274).
Clients:
  Bundesverband der Deutschen Industrie
  Deutscher Industrie und Handelstag

SCHNEIDER, Jan, Esq.
1133 Connecticut Ave., N.W., Washington, DC 20036
Telephone: (202) 457-0008
Background: An attorney and consultant in international affairs.
Organizations represented:
  Canada, Government of

SCHNEIDER, Lawrence A.
Arnold & Porter
1200 New Hampshire Ave., N.W., Washington, DC 20036
Telephone: (202) 872-6700
Registered as lobbyist at U.S. Congress.

SCHNEIDER, Matthew R.
Willkie Farr and Gallagher
1155 21st St., N.W., 6th Fl., Washington, DC 20036-3302
Telephone: (202) 328-8000
Registered as lobbyist at U.S. Congress.
Clients:
  American Institute of Certified Public Accountants
  Nat'l Ass'n of Independent Fee Appraisers
  Shearson Lehman Hutton
  Standard Commerical Tobacco Co.
  Time Warner Inc.
  Westinghouse Electric Corp.
  Yamaha Motor Corp. U.S.A.

SCHNEIDER, Robert V.
V. President, Hill and Knowlton Public Affairs Worldwide
Washington Harbour, 901 31st St., N.W., Washington, DC 20007
Telephone: (202) 333-7400
Registered as lobbyist at U.S. Congress.
Registered as Foreign Agent: (#4170).
Clients:
  Frontec Logistics Corp.
  SNA Canada Inc.

SCHNEIDER, Thomas J.
Quasha, Wessely & Schneider
1150 17th St., N.W., Suite 400, Washington, DC 20036
Telephone: (202) 293-5304
Clients:
  AFL-CIO Maritime Committee

SCHNEIDER, Zoe
Environmental Lobbyist, U.S. Public Interest Research Group
215 Pennsylvania Ave., S.E., Washington, DC 20003
Telephone: (202) 546-9707
Registered as lobbyist at U.S. Congress.

SCHNEIER, Abraham L.
V. President, McKevitt Group, The
1101 16th St., N.W., Suite 333, Washington, DC 20036
Telephone: (202) 822-0604
Registered as lobbyist at U.S. Congress.
Background: Legislative Representative and Tax Counsel for the Nat'l Federation of Independent Business. Advisor to the Securities and Exchange Commission. Past member of the American Legislative Exchange Council and of its Editorial Board on the Impact of Tax Reform on States.

SCHNELLER, Frank
Exec. Dir., Int'l & Construct. Educ. Svc, Associated General Contractors of America
1957 E St., N.W., Washington, DC 20006
Telephone: (202) 393-2040
Registered as lobbyist at U.S. Congress.

SCHNIBBE, Harry C.
Exec. Director, Nat'l Ass'n of State Mental Health Program Directors
1101 King St., Suite 160, Alexandria, VA 22314
Telephone: (703) 739-9333

SCHNOOR, Kim
Robinson, Lake, Lerer & Montgomery
1667 K St., N.W., Suite 900, Washington, DC 20006
Telephone: (202) 457-9270
Registered as lobbyist at U.S. Congress.
Clients:
  Napa Flood Control and Water Conservation District

SCHOCHET, P.C., Kenneth Barry
1129 20th St., N.W., Suite 500, Washington, DC 20036
Telephone: (202) 293-0150
Registered as Foreign Agent: (#4033)
Organizations represented:
  Free Angola Information Service

SCHOELLHAMER, Paul
V. President, Government Affrs., Northwest Airlines, Inc.
900 17th St., N.W. Suite 526, Washington, DC 20006
Telephone: (202) 887-5636

SCHOENBECK, Lynne E.
Administrative Assistant, Ass'n of Oil Pipe Lines
1725 K St., N.W., Washington, DC 20006
Telephone: (202) 331-8228

SCHOENBRUN, Lois
Deputy Director, American Medical Women's Ass'n
801 North Fairfax St., Suite 400, Alexandria, VA 22314
Telephone: (703) 838-0500

SCHOENI, Patricia Q.
Director, Communications, Health Insurance Ass'n of America
1025 Connecticut Ave., N.W. Suite 1200, Washington, DC 20036
Telephone: (202) 223-7780

SCHOLICK, Howard D.
Director, Government Affairs, Abbott Laboratories
1710 Rhode Island Ave. N.W. Suite 300, Washington, DC 20036
Telephone: (202) 659-8524

SCHOLL, Kathleen
Senior Coordinator, American Ass'n of Retired Persons
1909 K St., N.W., Washington, DC 20049
Telephone: (202) 872-4700

SCHOLTE, Sandy
Exec. Director, Nat'l Conservative Political Action Committee
618 S. Alfred St., Alexandria, VA 22314
Telephone: (703) 684-1800

SCHOONOVER, Martha J.
Fulbright & Jaworski
1150 Connecticut Ave., N.W., Suite 400, Washington, DC 20036
Telephone: (202) 452-6800
Registered as lobbyist at U.S. Congress.
Clients:
  Merichem Co.

SCHORR, Lori
Assoc. Director, Political Affairs, American Hospital Ass'n
50 F St., N.W., Suite 1100, Washington, DC 20001
Telephone: (202) 638-1100

SCHOTLAND, Sara D.
Cleary, Gottlieb, Steen and Hamilton
1752 N St., N.W., Washington, DC 20036
Telephone: (202) 728-2700
Registered as lobbyist at U.S. Congress.
Clients:
  Electricity Consumers Resource Council

SCHOUMACHER, Stephanie
Director, Public Affairs, Council on Competitiveness
1331 Pennsylvania Ave., N.W. Suite 900 North, Washington, DC 20004
Telephone: (202) 662-8760

SCHOWALTER, John
President, Soc. of Professors of Child Psychiatry
3615 Wisconsin Ave., N.W., Washington, DC 20016
Telephone: (202) 966-7300

SCHRAMM, Carl J., Ph.D.
President, Health Insurance Ass'n of America
1025 Connecticut Ave., N.W. Suite 1200, Washington, DC 20036
Telephone: (202) 223-7780
Registered as lobbyist at U.S. Congress.

SCHREFT, Tracey
Assoc. Mgr., Community Resources, Chamber of Commerce of the U.S.A.
1615 H St., N.W., Washington, DC 20062
Telephone: (202) 659-6000

SCHREIBER, Charles G.
Director, Legislative Affairs, Nat'l Guard Ass'n of the U.S.
One Massachusetts Ave., N.W., Washington, DC 20001
Telephone: (202) 789-0031
Registered as lobbyist at U.S. Congress.

SCHREIBERG, Sheldon L.
Brownstein Zeidman and Schomer
1401 New York Ave., N.W., Suite 900, Washington, DC 20005
Telephone: (202) 879-5700
Registered as lobbyist at U.S. Congress.
Background: Counsel, Committee on Banking, Finance and Urban Affairs, Subcommittee on Housing and Community Development, U.S. House of Representatives; Exec. Asst. to Asst. Secretary for Housing, Federal Housing Commission, 1977-78. Counsel, Nat'l Housing and Rehabilitation Ass'n, 1980-present.
Clients:
  Schochet Associates

SCHRICHTE, A. Kolbet
Exec. Vice President, American Logistics Ass'n
1133 15th St., N.W. Suite 640, Washington, DC 20005
Telephone: (202) 466-2520
Registered as lobbyist at U.S. Congress.

SCHROEDER, H. B. W.
V. President, Governmental Affairs, Consumers Power Co.
1016 16th St., N.W. 5th Floor, Washington, DC 20036
Telephone: (202) 293-5794
Registered as lobbyist at U.S. Congress.

SCHROEDER, James W.
Kaplan, Russin and Vecchi
1215 17th St., N.W., Washington, DC 20036
Telephone: (202) 887-0353

SCHROEDER, Leah Webb
V. President, Government Affairs, Health Industry Manu-
facturers Ass'n
1030 15th St., N.W. Suite 1100, Washington, DC 20005
Telephone: (202) 452-8240
Registered as lobbyist at U.S. Congress.

SCHROEDER, Mark C.
Dep Gen Couns, Envir, Conserv & Legis, DEPARTMENT
OF ENERGY
1000 Independence Ave., S.W., Washington, DC 20585
Telephone: (202) 586-6732

SCHROTH, Robert D.
V. President, Bendixen and Schroth
1029 Vermont Ave., N.W., Suite 505, Washington, DC
20005
Telephone: (202) 628-4245
Registered as lobbyist at U.S. Congress.

SCHUB, Judy
Senior Coordinator, American Ass'n of Retired Persons
1909 K St., N.W., Washington, DC 20049
Telephone: (202) 728-4740
Registered as lobbyist at U.S. Congress.

SCHUBERT, Lynn M.
Counsel, American Insurance Ass'n
1130 Connecticut Ave., N.W., Suite 1000, Washington, DC
20036
Telephone: (202) 828-7100

SCHUESSLER, Janet L.
V. President, Bonner & Associates
1625 K St., N.W., Suite 300, Washington, DC 20006
Telephone: (202) 463-8880
Background: Former Director of Legislation, Rep. Adam
Benjamin, Jr. (D-IN), 1978-81.

SCHUKER, Jill
Senior V. President, Hill and Knowlton Public Affairs
Worldwide
Washington Harbour, 901 31st St., N.W., Washington, DC
20007
Telephone: (202) 333-7400
Registered as Foreign Agent: (#3301).
Background: Former Press and Public Affairs Counselor,
U.S. Mission, United Nations.
Clients:
Chase Enterprises
Nat'l Cancer Institute

SCHULE, Robert M.
Senior V. President, Wexler, Reynolds, Fuller, Harrison
and Schule, Inc.
1317 F St., N.W., Suite 600, Washington, DC 20004
Telephone: (202) 638-2121
Registered as lobbyist at U.S. Congress.
Registered as Foreign Agent: (#3306).
Background: Former Special Assistant for Congressional
Liaison in the White House under President Jimmy Cart-
er.
Clients:
Coopers and Lybrand
General Motors Corp.
Nat'l Gypsum Co.
Oregon, State of

SCHULTE, Larry
National Secretary, Air Line Pilots Ass'n Internat'l
1625 Massachusetts Ave., N.W., Washington, DC 20036
Telephone: (202) 797-4003

SCHULTHEISS, Patricia
Dir., Policy Coordination & Legal Affrs., American
Pharmaceutical Ass'n
2215 Constitution Ave., N.W., Washington, DC 20037
Telephone: (202) 628-4410

Background: Former Attorney, Bureau of Consumer Protection, Federal Trade Commission.

SCHULTZ, Herb K.
Manager, Congressional Affairs, FHP, Inc.
1225 19th St., N.W., Washington, DC 20036
Telephone: (202) 223-5718
Registered as lobbyist at U.S. Congress.

SCHULTZ, Mark
President, Professional Services Council
918 16th St., N.W, Suite 406, Washington, DC 20006
Telephone: (202) 296-2030
Registered as lobbyist at U.S. Congress.

SCHULTZE, Charles L.
Director, Economic Studies Program, Brookings Institution
1775 Massachusetts Ave., N.W., Washington, DC 20036
Telephone: (202) 797-6000
Background: Chairman, Council of Economic Advisers
(1977-80); Director, U.S. Bureau of the Budget (1965-67);
Asst. Director (1961-64).

SCHULZ, William
Managing Editor, Reader's Digest Ass'n
1730 Rhode Island Ave., N.W. Suite 406, Washington, DC
20036
Telephone: (202) 223-9520

SCHUM, Richard M.
Assoc. Director, Gov't Affairs, Gas Appliance Manufactur-
ers Ass'n
1901 North Moore St., Arlington, VA 22209
Telephone: (703) 525-9565
Registered as lobbyist at U.S. Congress.

SCHUMACHER, Barry J.
Senior Associate, APCO Associates
1155 21st St., N.W., Suite 1000, Washington, DC 20036
Telephone: (202) 778-1000
Registered as Foreign Agent: (#3597).
Clients:
ASOCOLFLORES (Colombia Flower Growers
Ass'n)
Profilo Holding A.S.
State Farm Insurance Cos.

SCHUMACHER, Randal
V. Pres., Occ. Safety, Health & Environ., Jefferson Group,
The
1341 G St., N.W., Suite 1100, Washington, DC 20005
Telephone: (202) 638-3535
Clients:
Georgia-Pacific Corp.
Minnesota Mining and Manufacturing Co. (3M
Co.)
Simpson Paper Co.

SCHUMACK, Ralph D.
V. Pres., Gov't Relations & Public Affrs, Dow Corning
Corp.
1800 M St., N.W., Suite 325 South, Washington, DC
20036
Telephone: (202) 785-0585
Registered as lobbyist at U.S. Congress.

SCHUST, Sunny Mays
Director, Communications & Publications, American Ass'n
of State Highway and Transportation Officials
444 N. Capitol St., N.W., Suite 225, Washington, DC
20001
Telephone: (202) 624-5800

SCHUSTER, Ben
Dir., Fed. Gov't Rels. (ARCO Chemical), ARCO
1333 New Hampshire Ave., N.W., Washington, DC 20036
Telephone: (202) 457-6260
Registered as lobbyist at U.S. Congress.

SCHUSTER, Neil D.
Exec. Director, Internat'l Bridge, Tunnel and Turnpike
Ass'n
2120 L St., N.W. Suite 305, Washington, DC 20037
Telephone: (202) 659-4620

SCHUTZER, George J.
Patton, Boggs and Blow
2550 M St., N.W., Suite 800, Washington, DC 20037
Telephone: (202) 457-6000

Registered as lobbyist at U.S. Congress.

SCHUYLER, James H.
Mintz, Levin, Cohn, Ferris, Glovsky and Popeo, P.C.
1825 Eye St., N.W. 12th Floor, Washington, DC 20006
Telephone: (202) 293-0500
Registered as lobbyist at U.S. Congress.
Clients:
Mortgage Insurance Companies of America

SCHWABE, WILLIAMSON AND WYATT
2000 Pennsylvania Ave., N.W., Suite 8335, Washington,
DC 20006
Telephone: (202) 785-5960
Background: Washington Office of a law firm based in
Portland, Oregon.
Members of firm representing listed organizations:
Boothe, Jeffrey F.
Hitz, Frederick P.
Background: Deputy Assistant Secretary of Defense for
Legislative Affairs, 1975-77. Member, Energy Policy
and Planning Staff, Exec Office of the President,
1977. Director of Congressional Affairs, U.S. Depart-
ment of Energy, 1977-78. Legislative Counsel to the
Director of Central Intelligence, 1978-81.
Clients:
Eugene Water and Electric Board *(Frederick P. Hitz)*
Grant County P.U.D. *(Frederick P. Hitz)*
Multnomah County, Oregon *(Frederick P. Hitz)*
Oregon METRO *(Frederick P. Hitz)*
Oregon, State of *(Frederick P. Hitz)*
Oregon Steel Mills, Inc. *(Frederick P. Hitz)*
Physicians Medical Laboratories *(Frederick P. Hitz)*
Portland Metropolitan Service District *(Frederick P.
Hitz)*
Portland, Oregon, City of *(Frederick P. Hitz)*
Public Generating Pool *(Frederick P. Hitz)*
Tri-County Metropolitan Transportation District
of Oregon *(Frederick P. Hitz)*

SCHWANINGER, James C.
Sr. Gov't. Relations Representative, Penney Co., J. C.
1156 15th St., N.W., Suite 1015, Washington, DC 20005
Telephone: (202) 862-4800

SCHWARTZ, Adam D.
Director, Political Affairs, Nat'l Council of Savings Institu-
tions
1101 15th St., N.W. Suite 400, Washington, DC 20005
Telephone: (202) 857-3100
Registered as lobbyist at U.S. Congress.
Background: Also serves as contact for the Nat'l Council
of Savings Institutions THRIFTPAC

SCHWARTZ, Arthur E.
General Counsel, Nat'l Soc. of Professional Engineers
1420 King St., Alexandria, VA 22314-2715
Telephone: (703) 684-2841
Registered as lobbyist at U.S. Congress.

SCHWARTZ, Daniel C.
Bryan, Cave, McPheeters and McRoberts
1015 15th St., N.W., Suite 1000, Washington, DC 20005
Telephone: (202) 289-6100
Registered as lobbyist at U.S. Congress.
Background: Assistant to the Director, 1973-75; Assistant
Director for Evaluation, 1975-77, and Deputy Director,
1977-79, Bureau of Competition, Federal Trade Commis-
sion.

SCHWARTZ, David M.
Sullivan and Worcester
1025 Connecticut Ave., N.W. Suite 806, Washington, DC
20036
Telephone: (202) 775-8190
Background: Attorney-Advisor to Commissioner Howard
Freas, Interstate Commerce Commission, 1960-65.
Consultant, Department of Commerce, 1965-66. Assistant
Director for Transportation Program Policy, Department
of Commerce, 1966-67. Director, Office of Policy Review
and Coordination, Department of Transportation, 1967-
70.
Clients:
Kansas City Southern Industries

WASHINGTON REPRESENTATIVES

SCHWARTZ, Eleanor
Legislation and Regulatory Mgmt., DEPARTMENT OF IN-TERIOR - Bureau of Land Management
18th and C Sts., N.W. Room 5558, Washington, DC 20240
Telephone: (202) 343-5101

SCHWARTZ, Elinor
318 South Abington St., Arlington, VA 22204
Telephone: (703) 920-5389
Registered as lobbyist at U.S. Congress.
Background: A Washington representation consultant.
Organizations represented:
California State Lands Commission
Washington State Commissioner of Public Lands
Western States Land Commissioners Ass'n

SCHWARTZ, Elizabeth Nash
Manager, Congressional Affairs, Boeing Co.
1700 North Moore St., Arlington, VA 22209
Telephone: (703) 558-9600
Registered as lobbyist at U.S. Congress.

SCHWARTZ, Eric
Washington Director, Asia Watch, Human Rights Watch
1522 K St., N.W., Suite 910, Washington, DC 20005
Telephone: (202) 371-6592

SCHWARTZ, Gilbert
Skadden, Arps, Slate, Meagher and Flom
1440 New York Ave., N.W., Washington, DC 20005
Telephone: (202) 371-7000
Clients:
MacAndrews & Forbes Holdings, Inc.

SCHWARTZ, Jeffrey H.
Jellinek, Schwartz, Connolly & Freshman, Inc.
1015 15th St., N.W. Suite 500, Washington, DC 20005
Telephone: (202) 789-8181
Registered as lobbyist at U.S. Congress.
Clients:
ASARCO Incorporated
Nat'l Independent Energy Producers

SCHWARTZ, Michael
Director, Government Affairs, Federal Home Loan Mort-gage Corp.
1759 Business Center Drive, Reston, VA 22090
Telephone: (703) 789-4700
Registered as lobbyist at U.S. Congress.

SCHWARTZ, Michael
Director, Catholic Policy, Free Congress Foundation
717 2nd St., N.E., Washington, DC 20002
Telephone: (202) 546-3000

SCHWARTZ, Michael H.
Energy Resources Internat'l
1015 18th St., N.W. Suite 500, Washington, DC 20036
Telephone: (202) 785-8833
Clients:
Utility Nuclear Waste Transportation Program

SCHWARTZ, Richard
President, Boat Owners Ass'n of The United States (BOAT/U.S.)
880 South Pickett St., Alexandria, VA 22304
Telephone: (703) 823-9550
Registered as lobbyist at U.S. Congress.

SCHWARTZ, Robert S.
McDermott, Will and Emery
1850 K St., N.W., Suite 500, Washington, DC 20006-2296
Telephone: (202) 887-8000
Registered as lobbyist at U.S. Congress.
Background: Trial Attorney, Antitrust Division, Intellectual Property Section, U.S. Department of Justice, 1975-79.
Clients:
Electronic Industries Ass'n of Japan
Hitachi America Ltd.
Hitachi Ltd.

SCHWARTZ, Robert T.
Exec. Director and COO, Industrial Designers Soc. of America
1142-E Walker Road, Great Falls, VA 22066
Telephone: (703) 759-0100

SCHWARTZ, Stephen I.
Legislative Coordinator, Nuclear, Greenpeace, U.S.A.
1436 U St., N.W., Washington, DC 20009
Telephone: (202) 462-1177
Registered as lobbyist at U.S. Congress.

SCHWARTZ, Tamar R.
Morrison & Foerster
2000 Pennsylvania Ave., N.W., Suite 5500, Washington, DC 20006
Telephone: (202) 887-1500
Registered as Foreign Agent: (#4282).
Clients:
Fujitsu Ltd.

SCHWARTZ, Victor E.
Of Counsel, Crowell and Moring
1001 Pennsylvania Ave., N.W., Washington, DC 20004-2505
Telephone: (202) 624-2500
Registered as lobbyist at U.S. Congress.
Background: Chairman, Federal Interagency Task Force on Product Liability, 1976-80. Exec. Director, Federal Inter-agency Council on Insurance, 1978-80.
Clients:
Eagle-Picher Industries
Minnesota Mining and Manufacturing Co. (3M Co.)
Nat'l Ass'n of Wholesaler-Distributors
Product Liability Alliance, The
Product Liability Coordinating Committee
Product Liability Information Bureau

SCHWARTZMAN, Andrew J.
Exec. Director, Media Access Project
2000 M St., N.W., Suite 400, Washington, DC 20036
Telephone: (202) 232-4300

SCHWARZ, Carl W.
McDermott, Will and Emery
1850 K St., N.W., Suite 500, Washington, DC 20006-2296
Telephone: (202) 887-8000
Background: Trial Attorney, U.S. Department of Justice, 1961-69.
Clients:
Hitachi America Ltd.
Hitachi Ltd.

SCHWARZE, Robert C.
President and CEO, Nat'l Food Brokers Ass'n
1010 Massachusetts Ave., N.W., Washington, DC 20001
Telephone: (202) 789-2844

SCHWEIGER, Larry
V. Pres., Affiliate & Regional Programs, Nat'l Wildlife Fed-eration
1400 16th St., N.W., Washington, DC 20036-2266
Telephone: (202) 797-6800

SCHWEIKER, Richard S.
President, American Council of Life Insurance
1001 Pennsylvania Ave., N.W., Washington, DC 20004-2599
Telephone: (202) 624-2300
Registered as lobbyist at U.S. Congress.
Background: Secretary of Health and Human Services in the Reagan Administration and former U.S. Senator from Pennsylvania.

SCHWEITZER, James J.
Cuneo Law Offices, Jonathan W.
1300 Eye St., N.W. Suite 480 East Tower, Washington, DC 20005
Telephone: (202) 962-3860
Organizations represented:
Songwriters Guild, The

SCHWEITZER, Richard P.
Zuckert, Scoutt and Rasenberger
888 17th St., N.W., Suite 600, Washington, DC 20006-3959
Telephone: (202) 298-8660
Registered as lobbyist at U.S. Congress.
Clients:
Nat'l Welding Supply Ass'n

SCHWEITZER, William H.
Baker and Hostetler
1050 Connecticut Ave., N.W. Suite 1100, Washington, DC 20036
Telephone: (202) 861-1500
Registered as lobbyist at U.S. Congress.
Background: Assistant United States Attorney, Washing-ton, DC 1970-73.

SCHWEIZER, Eric
Treasurer, Woodward and Lothrop Federal Political Action Committee
2800 Eisenhower Ave., Alexandria, VA 22314
Telephone: (703) 329-5457

SCHWENSEN, Carl F.
Exec. V. President, Nat'l Ass'n of Wheat Growers
415 Second St., N.E. Suite 300, Washington, DC 20002
Telephone: (202) 547-7800
Registered as lobbyist at U.S. Congress.
Background: Serves also as Treasurer, Nat'l Ass'n of Wheat Growers Political Action Committee.

SCIULLA, Michael
V. President and Lobbyist, Boat Owners Ass'n of The United States (BOAT/U.S.)
880 South Pickett St., Alexandria, VA 22304
Telephone: (703) 823-9550
Registered as lobbyist at U.S. Congress.

SCOCOZZA, Matthew
McNair Law Firm, P.A.
1155 15th St., N.W. Suite 400, Washington, DC 20005
Telephone: (202) 659-3900
Registered as lobbyist at U.S. Congress.
Background: Senior Counsel, U.S. Senate Committee on Commerce, Science and Transportation, 1977-82. Deputy Assistant Secretary for Transportation and Telecommuni-cations, U.S. Department of State, 1982-83. Assistant Secretary for Policy and and International Affairs, U.S. Department of Transportation, 1984-88.
Clients:
Gateway Freight Services Inc.
Hawaii Department of Transportation

SCOGGINS, Harold B.
President, Independent Petroleum Ass'n of America
1101 16th St., N.W., Washington, DC 20036
Telephone: (202) 857-4701
Registered as lobbyist at U.S. Congress.

SCOTT, Charles
General Agent Manager, Federal Employees Ass'n
929 2nd St., N.E.,, Washington, DC 20002
Telephone: (202) 543-4304

SCOTT, David A.
Washington Representative, American Petroleum Institute
1220 L St., N.W., Washington, DC 20005
Telephone: (202) 682-8406
Registered as lobbyist at U.S. Congress.

SCOTT, Delia
Cong Liaison Div, ENVIRONMENTAL PROTECTION AGENCY
401 M St., S.W., Washington, DC 20460
Telephone: (202) 382-5200

SCOTT, Douglas
Director, Public Policy, Christian Action Council
701 W. Broad St., Suite 405, Falls Church, VA 22046
Telephone: (703) 237-2100

SCOTT, Edward M.
Staff Associate, Nat'l Ass'n of State Aviation Officials
8401 Colesville Road., Suite 505, Silver Spring, MD 20910
Telephone: (301) 588-0587

SCOTT, Gregory
Nat'l Strategies Inc.
818 17th St., N.W., Washington, DC 20006
Telephone: (202) 429-8744
Clients:
Alliance for Capital Access

SCOTT, Gregory R.
Washington Representative, Philip Morris Management Corp.
1341 G St., N.W., Suite 900, Washington, DC 20005

Telephone: (202) 637-1500
Registered as lobbyist at U.S. Congress.

SCOTT, James L.
President and CEO, AmHS Institute
1919 Pennsylvania Ave., N.W., Suite 703, Washington, DC 20006
Telephone: (202) 293-2840

SCOTT, John H.
Ass't Director, Congressional Affairs, American Medical Ass'n
1101 Vermont Ave., N.W., Washington, DC 20005
Telephone: (202) 789-7400
Registered as lobbyist at U.S. Congress.

SCOTT, Karen R.
Executive Director, Federally Employed Women, Inc.
1400 Eye St., N.W. Suite 425, Washington, DC 20005
Telephone: (202) 898-0994

SCOTT, Lisa
Manager, PAC Administration, Nat'l Federation of Independent Business
600 Maryland Ave., S.W., Suite 700, Washington, DC 20024
Telephone: (202) 554-9000

SCOTT, Michael
Squire, Sanders and Dempsey
1201 Pennsylvania Ave., N.W. P.O. Box 407, Washington, DC 20044
Telephone: (202) 626-6600
Registered as lobbyist at U.S. Congress.
Clients:
  American Soc. of Anesthesiologists
  Nat'l Collegiate Athletic Ass'n
  Samaritan Health Services

SCOTT, R. Denny
Collective Bargaining Specialist, United Brotherhood of Carpenters and Joiners of America
101 Constitution Ave., N.W., Washington, DC 20001
Telephone: (202) 546-6206
Registered as lobbyist at U.S. Congress.

SCOTT, Richard W., Jr.
Washington Representative, Space Services Inc.
600 Water St., S.W., Suite 207, Washington, DC 20024
Telephone: (202) 646-1025

SCOTT, Dr. Roland B.
Director, Center for Sickle Cell Disease
c/o Howard University, 2121 Georgia Ave., N.W., Washington, DC 20059
Telephone: (202) 636-7930

SCOTT, Susan J.
Senior Legislative Consultant, American Occupational Therapy Ass'n
1383 Piccard Drive, Suite 300 P.O. Box 1725, Rockville, MD 20850
Telephone: (301) 948-9626
Registered as lobbyist at U.S. Congress.
Background: Serves as contact for American Occupational Therapy Political Action Committee.

SCOTT, Lt. Gen. Willard W., Jr. (Ret.)
Exec. Director, Ass'n of Military Colleges and Schools of the U.S.
9115 McNair Drive, Alexandria, VA 22309
Telephone: (703) 360-1678

SCOTT, William A.
President of the Board, Nat'l Lesbian and Gay Health Foundation
1638 R St., N.W., Suite 2, Washington, DC 20009
Telephone: (202) 797-3708

SCOTT, William W.
Collier, Shannon & Scott
1055 Thomas Jefferson St., N.W., Suite 300, Washington, DC 20007
Telephone: (202) 342-8400
Registered as lobbyist at U.S. Congress.
Registered as Foreign Agent: (#3694).
Clients:
  American Textile Machinery Ass'n
  Independent Lubricant Manufacturers Ass'n

Petroleos de Venezuela, S.A.
Soc. of Independent Gasoline Marketers of America

SCOUTT, Jerrold, Jr.
Zuckert, Scoutt and Rasenberger
888 17th St., N.W., Suite 600, Washington, DC 20006-3959
Telephone: (202) 298-8660
Background: Member, Board of Directors, World Airways.

SCOVILLE, Thomas W.
Director, Policy and Planning, American Maritime Congress
444 N. Capitol St., N.W., Suite 801, Washington, DC 20001
Telephone: (202) 877-4477
Registered as lobbyist at U.S. Congress.

SCOVOTTO, Lawrence E.
Exec. V. President, American Ass'n of Nurserymen
1250 Eye St., N.W., Suite 500, Washington, DC 20005
Telephone: (202) 789-2900
Background: Also serves as Exec. V. President of Wholesale Nursery Growers of America, Nat'l Landscape Ass'n, Garden Centers of America, and Horticultural Research Institute.

SCRIBNER, HALL AND THOMPSON
1850 K St., N.W. Suite 1100, Washington, DC 20006-2201
Telephone: (202) 331-8585
Registered as Foreign Agent: (#4253)
Members of firm representing listed organizations:
  Kelly, Biruta P.
    Background: Attorney, Interpretative Division, Chief Counsel's Office, Internal Revenue Service, 1982-83.
  Thompson, Thomas C. (Jr.)
    Background: Attorney, Appeals Division of Chief Counsel's Office, 1951-53, Legal Advisory Staff, Treasury Department, 1953-55. Staff of Joint Committee on Internal Revenue Taxation, U.S. Congress, 1955-57.
  Willetts, E. Victor (Jr.)
    Background: Chief Counsel's Office, Internal Revenue Service, 1965-70. Legislation Counsel, Staff of Joint Committee on Internal Revenue Taxation, U.S. Congress, 1965-68.
  Winslow, Peter H.
    Background: Attorney, Interpretative and Refund Litigation Divisions, Chief Counsel's Office, Internal Revenue Service, 1975-79.
  Clients:
    CNA Financial Corp. *(Thomas C. Thompson, Jr.)*
    Provident Life and Accident Insurance Co. *(Thomas C. Thompson, Jr.)*
    Security Life Insurance Co. of Denver *(E. Victor Willetts, Jr.)*
    Transamerica Corp.

SCRIVNER, Kerrill
Director, Federal Relations, ENSERCH Corp.
1025 Connecticut Ave., N.W., Suite 1014, Washington, DC 20036
Telephone: (202) 872-1352
Registered as lobbyist at U.S. Congress.

SCRUGGS, John F.
Gold and Liebengood, Inc.
1455 Pennsylvania Ave., N.W. Suite 950, Washington, DC 20004
Telephone: (202) 639-8899
Registered as lobbyist at U.S. Congress.
Background: Former Assistant Secretary for Legislation, U.S. Department of Health and Human Services.
Clients:
  American Academy of Ophthalmology
  British Airports Authority (BAA plc)
  Electronic Data Systems Corp.
  Eye Bank Ass'n of America

SCULLY, Anne
Dir., Fed Budget & Fin. Inst., Gov't Rtns, Nat'l Ass'n of REALTORS
777 14th St., N.W., Washington, DC 20005
Telephone: (202) 383-1000
Registered as lobbyist at U.S. Congress.
Background: Former legislative director for Sen. John Heinz (R-PA).

SCULLY, John C.
Counsel, Washington Legal Foundation
1705 N St., N.W., Washington, DC 20036
Telephone: (202) 857-0240

SCULLY, Thomas A.
Assoc Dir, Legis Affrs, EXECUTIVE OFFICE OF THE PRESIDENT - Office of Management and Budget
Old Executive Office Bldg., Washington, DC 20500
Telephone: (202) 395-4790

SCULLY, Timothy H., Jr.
Legislative Representative, Internat'l Brotherhood of Teamsters, Chauffeurs, Warehousemen and Helpers of America
25 Louisiana Ave., N.W., Washington, DC 20001
Telephone: (202) 624-6890
Registered as lobbyist at U.S. Congress.

SCUREMAN, Murray S.
V. President, Government Affairs, Amdahl Corp.
1667 K St., N.W., Suite 300, Washington, DC 20006
Telephone: (202) 835-2220

SCUTT, Jim
Legislative Director, Nat'l Sheriffs' Ass'n
1450 Duke St., Alexandria, VA 22314
Telephone: (703) 836-7827

SCZUDLO, Walter
Washington Representative, Shell Oil Co.
1025 Connecticut Ave., N.W., Suite 200, Washington, DC 20036
Telephone: (202) 466-1405
Registered as lobbyist at U.S. Congress.
Background: Legislative Director for Senator Frank Murkowski (D-AK), 1982-84.

SEAMON, Harold P.
Deputy Exec. Director, Nat'l School Boards Ass'n
1680 Duke St., Alexandria, VA 22314
Telephone: (703) 838-6722

SEAMON, Theodore I.
Seamon, Wasko and Ozment
1015 18th St., N.W. Suite 800, Washington, DC 20036
Telephone: (202) 331-0770
Clients:
  Pilgrim Airlines
  Wien Air Alaska

SEAMON, WASKO AND OZMENT
1015 18th St., N.W. Suite 800, Washington, DC 20036
Telephone: (202) 331-0770
Members of firm representing listed organizations:
  Feldman, Howard G.
    Background: Attorney, Senior Attorney and Assistant Chief, Legal Division, Bureau of Operating Rights, Civil Aeronautics Board, 1958-67. Chief, Agreements Division, Civil Aeronautics Board, 1967-69.
  Seamon, Theodore I.
  Wasko, Lawrence D.
    Background: Air Transport Examiner, Civil Aeronautics Board, 1958-62.
  Clients:
    Arrow Air *(Lawrence D. Wasko)*
    Northeastern Airlines *(Howard G. Feldman)*
    Pilgrim Airlines *(Theodore I. Seamon)*
    Wien Air Alaska *(Theodore I. Seamon)*

SEARS, John P.
Sears Law Offices, John P.
2021 K St., N.W., Suite 750, Washington, DC 20006
Telephone: (202) 331-3300
Registered as Foreign Agent: (#3584).
Background: Deputy Counsel to the President of the United States, 1968-69. Served as campaign manager for Ronald Reagan in the Presidential election campaigns, 1976 and 1980 (through the New Hampshire Primary).
Organizations represented:
  Japan Air Lines
  Japan Automobile Manufacturers Ass'n
  South Africa, Embassy of

SEARS LAW OFFICES, John P.
2021 K St., N.W., Suite 750, Washington, DC 20006
Telephone: (202) 331-3300
Members of firm representing listed organizations:
  Kelley, Robert
    Background: Former deputy legal counsel, U.S. Senate.

SEARS LAW OFFICES, John P. (Cont'd)
  Sears, John P.
    Background: Deputy Counsel to the President of the United States, 1968-69. Served as campaign manager for Ronald Reagan in the Presidential election campaigns, 1976 and 1980 (through the New Hampshire Primary).
    Organizations represented:
      Japan Air Lines *(John P. Sears)*
      Japan Automobile Manufacturers Ass'n *(John P. Sears)*
      South Africa, Embassy of *(Robert Kelley, John P. Sears)*

SEARS, Mary Helen
  Ginsburg, Feldman and Bress
  1250 Connecticut Ave., N.W. Suite 800, Washington, DC 20036
  Telephone: (202) 637-9000
  Clients:
    Genetics Institute Inc.

SEARS, Robert C.
  Exec. V. President, Irrigation Ass'n
  1911 N. Fort Myer Drive Suite 1009, Arlington, VA 22209
  Telephone: (703) 524-1200
  Background: Also serves as Chairman, Water Resources Export Council and Contractors Pump Bureau.

SEASE, Debbie
  Washington Dir., Public Lands Program, Sierra Club
  408 C St., N.E., Washington, DC 20002
  Telephone: (202) 547-1141
  Registered as lobbyist at U.S. Congress.

SEAY, Douglas
  Political Analyst, East European Affairs, Heritage Foundation
  214 Massachusetts Ave., N.E., Washington, DC 20002
  Telephone: (202) 546-4400

SECREST, David W.
  Whalen Company, Inc., The
  1717 K St., N.W. Suite 706, Washington, DC 20006
  Telephone: (202) 293-5540
  Organizations represented:
    Equitable Life Assurance Soc. of the U.S.
    Toyota Motor Sales, U.S.A.

SECURA GROUP, THE
  1155 21st St., N.W., Washington, DC 20036
  Telephone: (202) 728-4920
  Background: A consulting firm specializing in guidance to banks and other financial institutions in dealings with federal regulatory agencies. Linked to the Washington law firm of Arnold and Porter.
  Members of firm representing listed organizations:
    Boyd, Robert, Managing Director
    Danforth, John, Managing Director
    Fair, Rita, Managing Director
    Fitzgerald, Mary Clare, Senior V. President
      Background: V. President, Chase Manhattan Bank. Serves also as Treasurer, SecuraPAC.
    Golembe, Carter, Chairman of the Board/Managing Director
    Isaac, William M., Managing Director and COO
      Background: Also a partner in the law firm of Arnold and Porter. Chairman, Federal Deposit Insurance Corp., 1981-85.
    Maguire, Margaret, Managing Director
      Background: Also a partner in the law firm of Arnold and Porter.
    Mancusi, Michael, Managing Director
      Background: Former Senior Deputy Comptroller of the Currency.
    Tasker, Janet A.
  Clients:
    Chase Manhattan Bank *(Mary Clare Fitzgerald, William M. Isaac)*
    SecuraPAC *(Mary Clare Fitzgerald)*

SEDAM, Glenn J., Jr.
  Sedam and Shearer
  1700 Pennsylvania Ave., N.W. Suite 620, Washington, DC 20006
  Telephone: (703) 691-2010
  Clients:
    American Public Policy Institute
    Center for the Study of Public Choice Foundation

Tomen Corp.

SEDAM AND SHEARER
  1700 Pennsylvania Ave., N.W. Suite 620, Washington, DC 20006
  Telephone: (703) 691-2010
  Registered as Foreign Agent: (#3350)
  Members of firm representing listed organizations:
    McMahon, Patrick J.
    Sedam, Glenn J. (Jr.)
  Clients:
    American Public Policy Institute *(Glenn J. Sedam, Jr.)*
    Center for the Study of Public Choice Foundation *(Glenn J. Sedam, Jr.)*
    Nat'l Soc. of Fund Raising Executives *(Patrick J. McMahon)*
    Tomen Corp. *(Patrick J. McMahon, Glenn J. Sedam, Jr.)*

SEDERHOLM, Pamela
  Exec. Director, Foodservice and Lodging Institute
  1919 Pennsylvania Ave., N.W., Suite 504, Washington, DC 20006
  Telephone: (202) 659-9060
  Registered as lobbyist at U.S. Congress.
  Background: Also represents the Foodservice and Lodging Institute Political Action Committee.

SEDGWICK, Kathy
  Exec. Director, Foundation of the Wall and Ceiling Industry
  1600 Cameron St., Alexandria, VA 22314-2705
  Telephone: (703) 548-0374

SEDILLO, Pablo, Jr.
  Exec. Director, United States Catholic Conference/Secretariat for Hispanic Affairs
  3211 Fourth St., N.E., Washington, DC 20017
  Telephone: (202) 541-3150

SEEGER, Charles M., III
  Counsel - Government, Chicago Mercantile Exchange
  2000 Pennsylvania Ave., N.W. Suite 6200, Washington, DC 20006
  Telephone: (202) 223-6965
  Registered as lobbyist at U.S. Congress.
  Background: U.S. House of Representatives Agriculture Committee, 1970-73; Appropriations Committee, 1973-75.

SEEGER, Edwin H.
  Prather, Seeger, Doolittle and Farmer
  1600 M St., N.W., Washington, DC 20036
  Telephone: (202) 296-0500
  Registered as lobbyist at U.S. Congress.
  Registered as Foreign Agent: (#1815).
  Clients:
    American Airlines
    Bremer Lagerhaus-Gesellschaft
    Cadmium Council
    Empresa de Transporte Aereo del Peru
    Flores Esmeralda, Ltda.
    Flores Esmeralda, S.R.L.
    Gulf Resources & Chemical Corp.
    Lead Industries Ass'n
    Sima-Peru
    Sociedad de Industrias "Comite Textil"

SEELEY, James F.
  Nat'l Center for Municipal Development
  1620 Eye St., N.W., Suite 300, Washington, DC 20006
  Telephone: (202) 429-0160
  Clients:
    Los Angeles, California, City of

SEELY, Richard L.
  V. President, Dutko & Associates
  412 First St., S.E. Suite 100, Washington, DC 20003
  Telephone: (202) 484-4884
  Registered as lobbyist at U.S. Congress.
  Background: Former Coordinator of Plans and Programs, World Tourism Organization, 1980-83; Consultant to U.S. Travel and Tourism Administration, 1984; Assistant Secretary of Commerce, 1985-88.
  Clients:
    Council of Great Lakes Governors
    Jewish Nat'l Fund
    Puerto Rico, Senate of

SEES, Milton R.
  President, Wire Reinforcement Institute
  1760 Reston Pkwy., Reston, VA 22090

Telephone: (703) 709-9207

SEGAL, David
  Senior Research Analyst, Washington Institute for Near East Policy
  50 F St., N.W., Suite 8800, Washington, DC 20001
  Telephone: (202) 783-0226

SEGAL, Ed
  V. President, Madison Group/Earle Palmer Brown, The
  2033 M St., N.W., 9th Floor, Washington, DC 20036
  Telephone: (202) 223-0030
  Clients:
    American Federation for Clinical Research
    DO IT Coalition

SEGAL, Jerome M., Ph.D.
  President, Jewish Peace Lobby
  Suite 141 4431 Lehigh Rd., College Park, MD 20740
  Telephone: (301) 589-8764
  Registered as lobbyist at U.S. Congress.

SEGAL, Peter W.
  Colton and Boykin
  1025 Thomas Jefferson St., N.W., Suite 500 East, Washington, DC 20007
  Telephone: (202) 342-5400
  Background: Serves as General Counsel, Nat'l Ass'n of Home Builders of the U.S.
  Clients:
    Countrywide Credit Industries
    Nat'l Ass'n of Home Builders of the U.S.

SEGAL, Ruth L.
  Director, Government Affairs, Outdoor Advertising Ass'n of America
  1212 New York Ave., N.W., Suite 1210, Washington, DC 20005
  Telephone: (202) 371-5566
  Registered as lobbyist at U.S. Congress.

SEGAL, Scott H.
  Bracewell and Patterson
  2000 K St., N.W., Suite 500, Washington, DC 20006-1809
  Telephone: (202) 828-5800
  Registered as lobbyist at U.S. Congress.

SEGALL, Harold L.
  Beveridge & Diamond, P.C.
  1350 Eye St., N.W. Suite 700, Washington, DC 20005
  Telephone: (202) 789-6000
  Registered as lobbyist at U.S. Congress.
  Clients:
    Bluefield, West Virginia, City of
    Morgantown, West Virginia, City of

SEGERMARK CO., THE
  25 E. St., N.W., Suite 800, Washington, DC 20001
  Telephone: (202) 783-2200
  Background: An economic and legislative consulting firm.
  Members of firm representing listed organizations:
    Segermark, Howard
      Background: Serves also as President of the Industry Council for Tangible Assets and Managing Director, Free the Eagle. Former aide to Senator Jesse Helms (R-NC).
  Clients:
    Continental Insurance Investment Management
    Fidelity Investors
    Free the Eagle *(Howard Segermark)*
    Lazard Freres

SEGERMARK, Howard
  Segermark Co., The
  25 E. St., N.W., Suite 800, Washington, DC 20001
  Telephone: (202) 783-2200
  Registered as lobbyist at U.S. Congress.
  Background: Serves also as President of the Industry Council for Tangible Assets and Managing Director, Free the Eagle. Former aide to Senator Jesse Helms (R-NC).
  Clients:
    Free the Eagle

SEGHERS, Frances
  Exec. Director, Federal Affairs, Motion Picture Ass'n of America
  1600 Eye St., N.W., Washington, DC 20006
  Telephone: (202) 293-1966
  Registered as lobbyist at U.S. Congress.

SEHER, Jake
V. President, Federal Government Affairs, UST Public Affairs, Inc.
1825 Eye St., N.W., Suite 400, Washington, DC 20006
Telephone: (202) 429-2010
Registered as lobbyist at U.S. Congress.

SEIBERLICH, Carl J.
Director, Military Programs, American President Companies
1101 17th St., N.W. Suite 400, Washington, DC 20036
Telephone: (202) 331-1424
Registered as lobbyist at U.S. Congress.

SEIBERT, H. Richard, Jr.
V. President, Resources and Technology, Nat'l Ass'n of Manufacturers
1331 Pennsylvania Ave., N.W. Suite 1500 North, Washington, DC 20004-1703
Telephone: (202) 637-3000
Registered as lobbyist at U.S. Congress.

SEIBERT, Mary Beth
V. President, American Recreation Coalition
1331 Pennsylvania Ave., N.W., Suite 726, Washington, DC 20004
Telephone: (202) 662-7420

SEIDEN, Elliott M.
V. President, Assoc. General Counsel, Texas Air Corp.
901 15th St., N.W. Suite 500, Washington, DC 20005
Telephone: (202) 289-6060

SEIDEN, Matthew J.
Arnold & Porter
1200 New Hampshire Ave., N.W., Washington, DC 20036
Telephone: (202) 872-6700

SEIDERS, David F.
Sr. Staff V. Pres. & Chief Economist, Nat'l Ass'n of Home Builders of the U.S.
15th and M Streets, N.W., Washington, DC 20005
Telephone: (202) 822-0470
Background: Full title is Senior Staff V. President and Chief Economist for Economics, Mortgage Finance and Housing Policy Division.

SEIDMAN & ASSOCIATES, P.C.
2828 Pennsylvania Ave., N.W. Suite 304, Washington, DC 20007
Telephone: (202) 298-7360
Registered as lobbyist at U.S. Congress.
Members of firm representing listed organizations:
Seidman, Paul J.
Background: Assistant Counsel, Claims and Litigation Support, Naval Sea Systems Command, 1974-76. Acting Director, Freedom of Information and Privacy, 1978-79 and Assistant Chief Counsel for Procurement, Office of Chief Counsel for Advocacy, 1979-81, Small Business Administration. Member of Staff, White House Conference on Small Business, 1980.

SEIDMAN, Paul J.
Seidman & Associates, P.C.
2828 Pennsylvania Ave., N.W. Suite 304, Washington, DC 20007
Telephone: (202) 298-7360
Background: Assistant Counsel, Claims and Litigation Support, Naval Sea Systems Command, 1974-76. Acting Director, Freedom of Information and Privacy, 1978-79 and Assistant Chief Counsel for Procurement, Office of Chief Counsel for Advocacy, 1979-81, Small Business Administration. Member of Staff, White House Conference on Small Business, 1980.

SEIFER, Sarena
Director, Legislative Affairs, American Medical Student Ass'n
1890 Preston White Drive, Reston, VA 22091
Telephone: (703) 620-6600

SEIFERT, Carol
Deputy Director, Alliance for Justice
1601 Connecticut Ave., N.W. Suite 600, Washington, DC 20009
Telephone: (202) 332-3224

SEIGLER, Jane
Government Affairs Counsel, Waste Management, Inc.
1155 Connecticut Ave., N.W., Suite 800, Washington, DC 20036
Telephone: (202) 467-4480
Registered as lobbyist at U.S. Congress.

SEILER, Dean B.
Exec. Director, World Service Office, Salvation Army
1025 Vermont Ave., N.W., Washington,, DC
Telephone: (202) 737-3330

SEISLER, Jeffery
Exec. Director, Natural Gas Vehicle Coalition
2 Lafayette Center 1133 21st St., N.W., Suite 500, Washington, DC 20036
Telephone: (202) 466-9038
Registered as lobbyist at U.S. Congress.

SEKER, Mrs. Jo
Director, Concerned Educators Against Forced Unionism
8001 Braddock Road, Springfield, VA 22160
Telephone: (703) 321-8519

SEKLECKI, Mark
Director, Political Affairs, American Hospital Ass'n
50 F St., N.W., Suite 1100, Washington, DC 20001
Telephone: (202) 638-1100

SELADONES, Susan
Director, Public Affairs, Nat'l Conference of State Legislatures
444 North Capitol St., N.W. Suite 500, Washington, DC 20001
Telephone: (202) 624-5400

SELBY, Steven
Campbell, Falk & Selby
1101 30th St., N.W. Suite 500, Washington, DC 20007
Telephone: (202) 298-0427
Clients:
Puerto Rico, Commonwealth of
Puerto Rico Federal Affairs Administration

SELCI, Larry E.
President, Bombardier Corp.
2000 K St., N.W., Suite 301, Washington, DC 20006
Telephone: (202) 331-3350

SELDMAN, Dr. Neil N.
President, Institute for Local Self-Reliance
2425 18th St., N.W., Washington, DC 20009
Telephone: (202) 232-4108

SELIGSON, Paul Y.
Wilner and Scheiner
1200 New Hampshire Ave., N.W., Suite 300, Washington, DC 20036
Telephone: (202) 861-7800
Background: Trial Attorney and Senior Attorney, Civil Aeronautics Board, 1958-1962. Chief, Legal Staff, Routes and Agreements Division, Civil Aeronautics Board, 1962-1964.

SELLA, Joseph Thomas
Legislative Director, Nat'l Postal Mail Handlers Union
One Thomas Circle, N.W. Suite 525, Washington, DC 20005
Telephone: (202) 833-9095
Registered as lobbyist at U.S. Congress.
Background: Serves also as Chairman, Nat'l Postal Mail Handlers Union MAILPAC.

SELLERS, Barney
Exec. Director, American Soc. for Parenteral and Enteral Nutrition
8630 Fenton St., Silver Spring, MD 20910
Telephone: (301) 587-6315

SELLERS CO.
413 First St., S.E., Washington, DC 20003
Members of firm representing listed organizations:
Sellers, Richard D.
Clients:
Concerned Citizens Foundation (*Richard D. Sellers*)

SELLERS, Joseph M.
Dir., EEO/Intake & Litigation Project, Washington Lawyers' Committee for Civil Rights Under Law
1400 Eye St., N.W., Suite 450, Washington, DC 20005

Telephone: (202) 682-5900

SELLERS, Richard D.
Sellers Co.
413 First St., S.E., Washington, DC 20003
Registered as lobbyist at U.S. Congress.
Clients:
Concerned Citizens Foundation

SELLERS, Tom
Washington Representative, du Pont de Nemours and Co., E. I.
1701 Pennsylvania Ave., N.W., Suite 900, Washington, DC 20006
Telephone: (202) 728-3600
Registered as lobbyist at U.S. Congress.

SELLERY, William C., Jr.
Partner, Rowland & Sellery
1023 15th St., N.W. 7th Fl., Washington, DC 20005
Telephone: (202) 289-1780
Registered as lobbyist at U.S. Congress.
Clients:
Forest Industries Committee on Timber Valuation and Taxation
Libbey-Owens-Ford Co.
Northern Textile Ass'n
Pilkington Holdings, Inc.
Product Liability Coordinating Committee

SELLS, William H.
Director, Government Relations, Computer Dealers and Lessors Ass'n
1212 Potomac St., N.W., Washington, DC 20007
Telephone: (202) 333-0102

SEMAN, Jep
V.P., Public Affrs., State & Local Govt, Hill and Knowlton Public Affairs Worldwide
Washington Harbour, 901 31st St., N.W., Washington, DC 20007
Telephone: (202) 333-7400

SEMERAD, Samantha
Bayless & Boland, Inc.
1072 Thomas Jefferson St., N.W., Washington, DC 20007
Telephone: (202) 342-0040

SEMINARIO, Margaret
Dir., Soc. Secur., Pension & Health Iss., AFL-CIO (American Federation of Labor and Congress of Industrial Organizations)
815 16th St., N.W., Washington, DC 20006
Telephone: (202) 637-5075

SEMMES, David H.
Pierson, Semmes, and Finley
1054 31st St., N.W. Suite 300, Washington, DC 20007
Telephone: (202) 333-4000
Registered as Foreign Agent: (#2988).

SEMPLE, Nathaniel M.
V.P. & Sec'y, Research & Policy Cttee., Committee for Economic Development
1700 K St., N.W., Suite 700, Washington, DC 20006
Telephone: (202) 296-5860
Background: Counsel, House of Representatives Committee on Education and Labor, 1973-81.

SENCHAK, Marlisa
Director of Congressional Relations, Federal Nat'l Mortgage Ass'n
3900 Wisconsin Ave., N.W., Washington, DC 20016
Telephone: (202) 752-7960
Registered as lobbyist at U.S. Congress.

SENDER, Stanton P.
Morgan, Lewis and Bockius
1800 M St., N.W., Washington, DC 20036
Telephone: (202) 467-7000
Background: Heads the firm's government relations practice.
Clients:
Sears, Roebuck and Co.

SENDEROWITZ, Judith
Exec. Director, Center for Population Options
1012 14th St., N.W. Suite 1200, Washington, DC 20005
Telephone: (202) 347-5700

WASHINGTON REPRESENTATIVES

SENG, John
V. President, Kaufman & Associates, Henry J.
2233 Wisconsin Ave., N.W., Washington, DC 20007
Telephone: (202) 333-0700
Organizations represented:
Financial Services Council
Generic Pharmaceutical Industry Ass'n
Healthcare Compliance Packaging Council
Nat'l Dairy Promotion and Research Board

SENKOWSKI, R. Michael
Wiley, Rein & Fielding
1776 K St., N.W., Tenth Floor, Washington, DC 20006-2359
Telephone: (202) 429-7000
Clients:
Telocator

SENOR, Wendy
Legislative Liaison, American Israel Public Affairs Committee
440 First St., N.W. Suite 600, Washington, DC 20001
Telephone: (202) 639-5200
Registered as lobbyist at U.S. Congress.

SENSE, INC.
1511 K St., N.W., Suite 1033, Washington, DC 20005
Telephone: (202) 628-1151
Members of firm representing listed organizations:
Pittman, C. Juliet, V. President
Tallakson, Joe, President
Clients:
Colville Confederated Tribes *(Joe Tallakson)*
Jamestown-Klallam Indian Tribe *(Joe Tallakson)*
Lummi Indian Tribe *(Joe Tallakson)*
Quileute Indian Tribe *(Joe Tallakson)*
Quinault Indian Nation *(Joe Tallakson)*
Squaxin Island Indian Tribe *(Joe Tallakson)*
Suquamish Indian Tribe *(Joe Tallakson)*

SENTER, David L.
Nat'l Director, American Agriculture Movement, Inc.
100 Maryland Ave., N.E. Suite 500A, Washington, DC 20002
Telephone: (202) 544-5750
Registered as lobbyist at U.S. Congress.

SERCHAK, Bridget
Ass't for Gov't Information Services, EG&G, Inc.
1850 K St., N.W., Suite 1190, Washington, DC 20006
Telephone: (202) 887-5570

SEREPCA, Mark
Public Relations, American Bankers Ass'n
1120 Connecticut Ave., N.W., Washington, DC 20036
Telephone: (202) 663-5000

SERIE, Terry L.
Dir, Transportation & State Gov't Reltns, American Paper Institute
1250 Connecticut Ave., N.W. Suite 210, Washington, DC 20036
Telephone: (202) 463-2420
Registered as lobbyist at U.S. Congress.

SERKIN, Stuart D.
Exec. Director, Coal & Slurry Technology Ass'n
1156 15th St., N.W., Suite 525, Washington, DC 20005
Telephone: (202) 296-1133
Registered as lobbyist at U.S. Congress.

SERUMGARD, John R.
V. President, Tire Division, Rubber Manufacturers Ass'n
1400 K St., N.W., Washington, DC 20005
Telephone: (202) 682-4800

SERWER, David
Jefferson Group, The
1341 G St., N.W., Suite 1100, Washington, DC 20005
Telephone: (202) 638-3535
Clients:
Bridgeway Plan for Health
Direct Health, Inc.
Health Management Strategies, Internat'l
HIP Network of Florida
Tidewater Health Care
Total Health Plan

SETTLES, Trudy Y.
Governmental Affairs Assistant, Southern California Gas Co.
1150 Connecticut Ave., N.W., Suite 717, Washington, DC 20036
Telephone: (202) 822-3718

SETTON, Sarah
V. President, Public Affairs, Sugar Ass'n, Inc.
1101 15th St., N.W., Suite 600, Washington, DC 20005
Telephone: (202) 785-1122
Registered as lobbyist at U.S. Congress.

SEWELL, John W.
President, Overseas Development Council
1717 Massachusetts Ave., N.W., Washington, DC 20036
Telephone: (202) 234-8701
Background: A former U.S. Department of State and Foreign Service Officer.

SEYFARTH, SHAW, FAIRWEATHER AND GERALDSON
815 Connecticut Ave., N.W., Washington, DC 20006-4004
Telephone: (202) 463-2400
Members of firm representing listed organizations:
Erlenborn, John N.
Background: U.S. Representative (R-IL), 1965-1985. Serves as government affairs consultant to the American Soc. of Pension Actuaries.
Haley, Timothy F.
Johnson, Richard C.
Background: Member, Office of the General Counsel, Department of the Air Force, 1962-66. Assistant Executive Director, Federal Power Commission, 1966-68.
McHale, James M.
Rosenthal, Donald L.
Background: Deputy Solicitor of the Department of Labor and Chief of Staff and Counselor to the Secretary of Labor, 1981-82.
Wilson, Thomas E.
Clients:
Agricultural Producers, Inc. *(Donald L. Rosenthal)*
American Soc. of Pension Actuaries *(John N. Erlenborn)*
Employers Council on Flexible Compensation *(John N. Erlenborn)*
Flxible Corp., The *(Donald L. Rosenthal)*
Pitney-Bowes, Inc. *(Donald L. Rosenthal)*

SEYMOUR, Marlin K.
Research Associate, Bechtel Group, Inc.
1620 Eye St., N.W., Suite 703, Washington, DC 20006
Telephone: (202) 393-4747

SEYMOUR, Paul
Export Coordination Manager, Smith Industries
1225 Jefferson Davis Hwy., Suite 402, Arlington, VA 22202
Telephone: (703) 920-7640

SEYMOUR, Richard
Dir., Employment Discrimination Project, Lawyers' Committee for Civil Rights Under Law
1400 Eye St., N.W., Suite 400, Washington, DC 20005
Telephone: (202) 371-1212

SHABECOFF, Alice
Director, Community Information Exchange
1029 Vermont Ave. Suite 710, Washington, DC 20005
Telephone: (202) 628-2981

SHACKFORD, Jay
Staff V. President, Public Affairs, Nat'l Ass'n of Home Builders of the U.S.
15th and M Streets, N.W., Washington, DC 20005
Telephone: (202) 822-0470

SHAFFER, Joan
Communications, Democrats for the 90s
Box 3797 3038 N St., N.W., Washington, DC 20007
Telephone: (202) 338-9092

SHAFFER, Stephen C.
Director, Government Relations, U.S. English
818 Connecticut Ave., N.W. Suite 200, Washington, DC 20006
Telephone: (202) 833-0100
Registered as lobbyist at U.S. Congress.

Background: Former Senior Legislative Assistant to Rep. John Myers (R-IN).

SHAFROTH, Frank H.
Director of Federal Relations, Nat'l League of Cities
1301 Pennsylvania Ave., N.W., Washington, DC 20004
Telephone: (202) 626-3020

SHAH, Navin
Legislative Chairman, American College of Internat'l Physicans
5530 Wisconsin Ave., N.W. Suite 1149, Washington, DC 20815
Telephone: (301) 652-8741

SHALLOW, Thomas
Tax Counsel, American Petroleum Institute
1220 L St., N.W., Washington, DC 20005
Telephone: (202) 682-8463

SHAMBERGER, James M.
Senior Vice President, Reinsurance Ass'n of America
1819 L St., N.W., Suite 700, Washington, DC 20036
Telephone: (202) 293-3335
Registered as lobbyist at U.S. Congress.

SHAMEL, Charles D.
President and Chief Executive Officer, Sugar Ass'n, Inc.
1101 15th St., N.W., Suite 600, Washington, DC 20005
Telephone: (202) 785-1122

SHANAHAN, James R.
Partner, Washington Nat'l Tax Svc, Price Waterhouse
1801 K St., N.W., Suite 700, Washington, DC 20006
Telephone: (202) 296-0800
Registered as lobbyist at U.S. Congress.

SHANAHAN, Kathleen M.
Senior Associate, Wexler, Reynolds, Fuller, Harrison and Schule, Inc.
1317 F St., N.W., Suite 600, Washington, DC 20004
Telephone: (202) 638-2121
Background: Served with the National Security Council, 1982-85, and the Office of the Vice President, 1985-89.

SHAND, Fred E.
V. President, Membership Relations, Manufacturers' Alliance for Productivity and Innovation (MAPI)
1200 18th St., N.W. Suite 400, Washington, DC 20036
Telephone: (202) 331-8430

SHANE, Larry I.
Exec. Director, American Academy of Podiatric Sports Medicine
1729 Glastonberry Road, Potomac, MD 20854
Telephone: (301) 424-7440

SHANKER, Albert
President, American Federation of Teachers
555 New Jersey Ave., N.W., Washington, DC 20001
Telephone: (202) 879-4440

SHANLEY, Claire E.
Account Executive, Brownstein & Assoc., C. M.
791 Woodmont Ave., Suite 1208, Bethessda, MD 20814-3015
Telephone: (301) 913-0010
Organizations represented:
American Soc. of Access Professionals

SHANNON, Deborah
Federal Legislative Representative, American Bankers Ass'n
1120 Connecticut Ave., N.W., Washington, DC 20036
Telephone: (202) 663-5000
Registered as lobbyist at U.S. Congress.

SHANNON, John
Senior Fellow, Urban Institute, The
2100 M St., N.W., Washington, DC 20037
Telephone: (202) 833-7200

SHANNON, Kevin J.
Senior Staff Associate, Gov't Rlations, Electronic Industries Ass'n
2001 Pennsylvania Ave., N.W., Washington, DC 20006
Telephone: (202) 457-4900
Registered as lobbyist at U.S. Congress.

SHANNON, Maura
Manager, Communication Department, Air-Conditioning and Refrigeration Institute
1501 Wilson Blvd., Suite 600, Arlington, VA 22209
Telephone: (703) 524-8800

SHANNON, Rick
National Programs Director, American Veterans of World War II, Korea and Vietnam (AMVETS)
4647 Forbes Blvd., Lanham, MD 20706
Telephone: (301) 459-9600

SHANNON, Thomas A.
Exec. Director, Nat'l School Boards Ass'n
1680 Duke St., Alexandria, VA 22314
Telephone: (703) 838-6722

SHANNON, Thomas F.
Collier, Shannon & Scott
1055 Thomas Jefferson St., N.W., Suite 300, Washington, DC 20007
Telephone: (202) 342-8400
Registered as lobbyist at U.S. Congress.
Registered as Foreign Agent: (#3694).
Background: Legislative Counsel to Senator Styles Bridges, 1955-1957. Chief Minority Counsel, Committee on Appropriations, U. S. Senate, 1957-1958.
Clients:
American Couplings Coalition
American Flint Glass Workers Union
American Iron and Steel Institute
Armco Inc.
Bicycle Manufacturers Ass'n of America
Committee of American Ammunition Manufacturers
Footwear Industries of America
Footwear Industry Political Action Committee
Leather Industries of America
Magnavox Consumer Electronics Co.
Outdoor Power Equipment Institute
Petroleos de Venezuela, S.A.
Specialty Steel Industry of the United States
Stanley Bostitch Inc.

SHANOWER, Robert L.
Manager, Washington Operations, Pratt & Whitney
1825 Eye St., N.W., Suite 700, Washington, DC 20006
Telephone: (202) 785-7430

SHAPIRO, Bernard M.
Partner, Price Waterhouse
1801 K St., N.W., Suite 700, Washington, DC 20006
Telephone: (202) 296-0800
Registered as lobbyist at U.S. Congress.
Background: Former staff chief, Congressional Joint Committee on Taxation.

SHAPIRO, Gary J.
V. President and General Counsel, Electronic Industries Ass'n
2001 Pennsylvania Ave., N.W., Washington, DC 20006
Telephone: (202) 457-4900

SHAPIRO, Ira S.
Winthrop, Stimson, Putnam & Roberts
1133 Connecticut Ave., N.W. Suite 1000, Washington, DC 20036
Telephone: (202) 775-9800
Registered as lobbyist at U.S. Congress.
Registered as Foreign Agent: (#3873).
Background: Minority Staff Director and Chief Counsel, Senate Gov't Affairs Committee, 1981-84; Chief of Staff, U.S. Senator John D. Rockefeller IV, 1985-87.
Clients:
America West Airlines
BASF Corp.
Grocery Manufacturers of America
Macrovision
Metallverken AB
Queen City Home Health Care Co.

SHAPIRO, Lauren
Account Supervisor, Nordlinger Associates
1620 Eye St., N.W. 7th Floor, Washington, DC 20006
Telephone: (202) 785-0440

SHAPIRO, Lester G.
Director, Public Affairs, Philipp Brothers, Inc.
1455 Pennsylvania Ave., N.W., Suite 350, Washington, DC 20006
Telephone: (202) 879-4141

SHAPIRO, Richard H.
Exec. Director, Congressional Management Foundation
513 Capitol Court, N.E. Suite 100, Washington, DC 20002
Telephone: (202) 546-0100

SHAPIRO, Robert B.
Bernstein Law Off., George K.
1730 K St., N.W. Suite 313, Washington, DC 20006
Telephone: (202) 452-8010
Registered as Foreign Agent: (#4269).
Organizations represented:
Jauch & Hubener, O.H.G.

SHAPIRO, Robert J.
V. President for Economic Studies, Progressive Policy Institute
316 Pennsylvania Ave., S.E. Suite 516, Washington, DC 20003
Telephone: (202) 547-0001
Background: Former Legislative Director and Economic Counsel to Senator Daniel P. Moynihan (D-NY) and Deputy National Issues Director for the 1988 Democratic Presidential campaign.

SHARBAUGH, John
Dir, Communications/State Society Rltns., American Institute of Certified Public Accountants
1455 Pennsylvania Ave., N.W. Suite 400, Washington, DC 20004
Telephone: (202) 737-6600

SHARK, Alan R., CAE
Assoc. Exec. Dir., Mktg./Communications, Water Pollution Control Federation
601 Wythe Street, Alexandria, VA 22314
Telephone: (703) 684-2400

SHARON, Dennis P.
V. President, Eastern Region, McDonnell Douglas Corp.
1735 Jefferson Davis Hwy., Arlington, VA 22202
Telephone: (703) 553-3801

SHARP, Charles R., Esq.
Counsel, Industry-Government Relations, General Motors Corp.
1660 L St., N.W., Washington, DC 20036
Telephone: (202) 775-5005

SHARP, Gregory L.
Director of Government Affairs, Ferranti Defense and Space Group
1111 Jefferson Davis Hwy, Suite 800, Arlington, VA 22202
Telephone: (703) 979-0005

SHARP, John Hunter
Counsel and Dir., Congressional Affairs, Natural Gas Supply Ass'n
1129 20th St., N.W. Suite 300, Washington, DC 20036
Telephone: (202) 331-8900
Registered as lobbyist at U.S. Congress.
Background: Former Trial Attorney, Federal Energy Regulatory Commission.

SHARP, Larry D.
McGuire, Woods, Battle and Boothe
1627 Eye St., N.W. Suite 1000, Washington, DC 20006
Telephone: (202) 857-1700
Clients:
Viobin Corp.

SHARP, Marcia
Chairman, Hager Sharp Inc.
1101 17th St., N.W., Suite 1001, Washington, DC 20036
Telephone: (202) 466-5430
Clients:
Women's College Coalition

SHARP, Mark J.
Manager, Government Affairs, Matsushita Electric Corp. of America
1001 Pennsylvania Ave., N.W. Suite 1355 North, Washington, DC 20004
Telephone: (202) 347-7592

Registered as lobbyist at U.S. Congress.

SHARP, Nancy J., R.N.
Director of Practice and Legislation, Nurses Ass'n of the American College of Obstetricians and Gynecologists
409 12th St., S.W., Washington, DC 20024
Telephone: (202) 638-0026

SHARP, Norman F.
President, Cigar Ass'n of America
1100 17th St., N.W., Suite 504, Washington, DC 20036
Telephone: (202) 223-8204
Registered as lobbyist at U.S. Congress.
Background: Also responsible for the Cigar Political Action Committee.

SHARPE, Maitland S.
Assoc. Exec. Dir. & Conservation Dir., Izaak Walton League of America
1401 Wilson Blvd., Level B, Arlington, VA 22209
Telephone: (703) 528-1818

SHARRETTS, PALEY, CARTER AND BLAUVELT
1707 L St., N.W., Suite 725, Washington, DC 20036
Telephone: (202) 223-4433
Background: Washington office of a New York law firm.
Members of firm representing listed organizations:
Baskin, Peter Jay
Brickell, Beatrice A.
McCauley, Alfred R.
Clients:
AM&S/BHAS *(Alfred R. McCauley)*
American Ass'n of Exporters and Importers
An Mau Steel Ltd. *(Beatrice A. Brickell)*
Argentina, Government of *(Beatrice A. Brickell)*
Givaudan Corp. *(Beatrice A. Brickell)*
Hamilton Copper and Steel Corp. *(Beatrice A. Brickell)*
SAE Electric *(Alfred R. McCauley)*
Sambo Copper Co., Ltd. *(Beatrice A. Brickell)*
Tandy Corp. *(Peter Jay Baskin)*
Thyssen Inc. *(Beatrice A. Brickell, Alfred R. McCauley)*

SHAW, Col. Edward W.
Senate Liaison, Legis Liaison, DEPARTMENT OF ARMY
The Pentagon, Washington, DC 20310-0101
Telephone: (202) 697-6767

SHAW, G. Jerry, Jr.
Neill, Mullenholz and Shaw
815 Connecticut Ave., N.W. Suite 800, Washington, DC 20006
Telephone: (202) 463-8400
Registered as lobbyist at U.S. Congress.
Registered as Foreign Agent: (#3384).
Background: Director, General Legal Services Division, Office of the Chief Counsel, Internal Revenue Service, 1975-81. President, Senior Executive Ass'n, 1980-82. General Counsel, Senior Executive Ass'n, 1982-present. Chairman, Public Employees Roundtable, 1982-present.
Clients:
Nat'l Ass'n of Chapter Thirteen Bankruptcy Trustees
Nat'l Council of Social Security Management Ass'ns
PHH-Homequity
Public Employees Roundtable
Senior Executives Ass'n

SHAW, Gregory M.
Account Executive, Ketchum Public Relations
1201 Connecticut Ave., N.W. Suite 300, Washington, DC 20036
Telephone: (202) 835-8800
Clients:
Road Information Program, The (TRIP)

SHAW, Ishmael L.
Interim General Secretary, Progressive Nat'l Baptist Convention
601 50th St., N.E., Washington, DC 20019
Telephone: (202) 396-0558

SHAW, Jerry A.
Research & Management Associates
832 S. 20th St., Arlington, VA 22202-2614
Telephone: (703) 979-8941
Registered as lobbyist at U.S. Congress.
Clients:

The listings in this directory are available as *Mailing Labels*. See last page.

379

WASHINGTON REPRESENTATIVES

SHAW, Jerry A. (Cont'd)
Bio National Corp.

SHAW, Judith M.
Research Analyst, Gov't Affairs, Nat'l Easter Seal Soc.
1350 New York Ave., N.W., Suite 415, Washington, DC 20005
Telephone: (202) 347-3066

SHAW, Michael
V. President and Secretary, Internat'l Ass'n of Refrigerated Warehouses
7315 Wisconsin Ave., Suite 1200N, Bethesda, MD 20814
Telephone: (301) 652-5674

SHAW, PITTMAN, POTTS AND TROWBRIDGE
2300 N St., N.W., Washington, DC 20037
Telephone: (202) 663-8000
Members of firm representing listed organizations:
   Aulick, Dean D.
   Baxter, Thomas A.
      Background: Special Assistant for Litigation, Price Commission and Cost of Living Council, 1972-73.
   Blake, Ernest L. (Jr.)
   Breed, Nathaniel P. (Jr.)
   Brown, Winthrop N.
   Burnley, James H. (IV)
   Carr, John L. (Jr.)
   Charnoff, Gerald
      Background: Atomic Energy Commission, 1957-60.
   Cohn, Robert E.
   Drasner, Fred, Counsel
   Ferrara, Peter J.
   Hanlon, R. Timothy
      Background: Honors Program, Office of the General Counsel, Department of the Air Force, 1961-64.
   House, William Mike
      Background: Former Administrative Assistant to Senator Howell Heflin (D-AL).
   Jones, Carleton S.
   Lucas, Steven M.
      Background: Attorney, Office of the Judge Advocate General, Dept. of the Army, 1974-5. Legal Adviser, Panama Canal Negotiations Working Group, Dept. of Defense, 1975-77.
   Pittman, Steuart L.
      Background: Assistant General Counsel, Foreign Operations Administration, 1953-54; Assistant Secretary of Defense, 1961-64.
   Potts, Ramsay D.
   Potts, Stephen D.
      Background: Member of the Board of Directors, Overseas Nat'l Airways.
   Rhinelander, John B.
      Background: Law Clerk to Associate Justice John M. Harlan, U.S. Supreme Court, 1961-2. Special Civilian Assistant to Secretary of the Navy, 1966-68. Chief Counsel, Acting Deputy Director, Office of Foreign Direct Investments, Dept. of Commerce, 1968-9. Legal Adviser to U.S. SALT Delegation 1971-2. General Counsel, Dept. of HEW, 1973-5. Under Secretary, Dept. of HUD, 1975-77.
   Rogers, George M. (Jr.)
      Background: Member of the Board of Directors, B.F. Saul Real Estate Investment Trust.
   Silberg, Jay E.
      Background: Attorney, Office of The General Counsel, Atomic Energy Commission, 1966-69.
   Trowbridge, G. F.
Clients:
   ADDSCO Industries *(William Mike House)*
   Alabama Power Co. *(William Mike House)*
   American Coke and Coal Chemicals Institute *(William Mike House)*
   American Hellenic Institute *(William Mike House)*
   American Savings and Loan of Florida *(William Mike House)*
   Auburn University *(William Mike House)*
   Cape Verde, Embassy of the Republic of
   Carolina Power and Light Co. *(Thomas A. Baxter)*
   Centerior Energy Corp. *(Jay E. Silberg)*
   Cleveland Electric Illuminating Co. *(Jay E. Silberg)*
   Colebrand Ltd. *(James H. Burnley, IV)*
   Drummond Co., Inc. *(William Mike House)*
   Duquesne Light Co. *(Gerald Charnoff, Jay E. Silberg)*
   Eastern Air Lines
   Emerson Electric Co. *(Ramsay D. Potts)*

Energy Efficient Insulation Manufacturers *(William Mike House)*
Federal Express Corp.
Florida Citrus Mutual *(William Mike House)*
French-American Chamber of Commerce in the U.S.
Georgia Power Co. *(William Mike House)*
GPU Service Corp. *(Ernest L. Blake, Jr.)*
Home Recording Rights Coalition
INCO U.S. *(William Mike House)*
Indiana and Michigan Electric Co. *(Gerald Charnoff)*
Indiana Michigan Power Co. *(Gerald Charnoff)*
Institute of Internat'l Bankers *(Steven M. Lucas)*
Intergraph Corp. *(William Mike House)*
Investment Counsel Ass'n of America *(Ramsay D. Potts)*
Jersey Central Power and Light Co. *(Ernest L. Blake, Jr.)*
Kansas Gas & Electric Co. *(Jay E. Silberg)*
Louisiana Power and Light Co. *(Ernest L. Blake, Jr.)*
Manhurin, S.A. *(Steuart L. Pittman)*
Metropolitan Edison Co.
Michelin Tire Co. *(William Mike House)*
Mortgage Insurance Companies of America
Munitions Carrier Conference *(William Mike House)*
Nat'l Air Transportation Ass'n *(Carleton S. Jones)*
Nat'l Industries, Inc. *(William Mike House)*
Northern States Power Co. *(Gerald Charnoff, Jay E. Silberg)*
Northern States Power Co. (Wisconsin)
Overseas Nat'l Airways *(Stephen D. Potts)*
Pennsylvania Electric Co.
Pennsylvania Power and Light Co. *(Jay E. Silberg)*
Public Service Co. of New Hampshire *(Gerald Charnoff)*
Royal Air Maroc *(Dean D. Aulick)*
Rust Engineering *(William Mike House)*
Saul Real Estate Investment Trust, B. F. *(George M. Rogers, Jr.)*
South Central Bell *(William Mike House)*
Southern Company Services, Inc. *(William Mike House)*
Sumitomo Bank Ltd.
Taiwan Power Co. *(R. Timothy Hanlon)*
Toledo Edison Co. *(Gerald Charnoff)*
Union Electric Co. *(Thomas A. Baxter, Gerald Charnoff)*
Utility Nuclear Waste Transportation Program *(Jay E. Silberg)*
Vulcan Materials Co. *(William Mike House)*
Walter Corp., Jim *(William Mike House)*
Wisconsin Electric Power Co. *(Gerald Charnoff)*
Wisconsin Power and Light Co.
Wisconsin Public Service Corp.
Wolf Creek Nuclear Operating Corp. *(Jay E. Silberg)*

SHAW, Sallye B., R.N., M.N.
Exec. Director, Nurses Ass'n of the American College of Obstetricians and Gynecologists
409 12th St., S.W., Washington, DC 20024
Telephone: (202) 638-0026

SHAW, Steve
Nat'l Exec. Director, Jewish War Veterans of the U.S.A.
1811 R St., N.W., Washington, DC 20009
Telephone: (202) 265-6280

SHAW, Susan
Legislative Liaison, Nat'l Treasury Employees Union
1730 K St., N.W., Suite 1100, Washington, DC 20006
Telephone: (202) 785-4411
Registered as lobbyist at U.S. Congress.

SHAW, Sydney
Manager, Media Relations, BellSouth Corp.
1133 21st St., N.W., Suite 900, Washington, DC 20036
Telephone: (202) 463-4100

SHAW, W. Anthony
Manager, Regulatory Affairs, Hoechst-Celanese Corp.
919 18th St., N.W., Suite 700, Washington, DC 20006
Telephone: (202) 296-2890

SHAWHAN, Samuel F., Jr.
Vice President-Government Affairs, GTE Corp.
Suite 1200, 1850 M St., N.W., Washington, DC 20036
Telephone: (202) 463-5201

SHAWN, BERGER, AND MANN
1850 M St., N.W., Suite 280, Washington, DC 20036

Telephone: (202) 778-0680
Clients:
   Mexico, Government of

SHAY, Richard
Internat'l Corporate Affairs, Asia Pacific Space and Communciations
1655 North Fort Myer Drive Suite 1120, Arlington, VA 22209
Telephone: (703) 525-2772

SHAY, Stephen E.
Ropes and Gray
1001 Pennsylvania Ave., N.W., Washington, DC 20004
Telephone: (202) 626-3900
Registered as lobbyist at U.S. Congress.
Registered as Foreign Agent: (#4251).
Background: International Tax Counsel, U.S. Department of the Treasury, 1982-87.
Clients:
   Butler Capital Corp.
   Ireland, Industrial Development Authority of

SHEA, David J.
Manager of Communications, Hughes Aircraft Co.
1100 Wilson Blvd. 20th Floor, Arlington, VA 22209
Telephone: (703) 525-1550

SHEA, Donald B.
Exec. V. President, Council for Solid Waste Solutions
1275 K St., N.W. Suite 400, Washington, DC 20005
Telephone: (202) 371-5319

SHEA, Edward M.
Ragan and Mason
1156 15th St., N.W., Suite 800, Washington, DC 20005
Telephone: (202) 296-4750
Clients:
   Ponce, Puerto Rico, Port of

SHEA, Ernest C.
Exec. V. President, Nat'l Ass'n of Conservation Districts
509 Capitol Court, N.E., Washington, DC 20002
Telephone: (202) 547-6223

SHEA AND GARDNER
1800 Massachusetts Ave., N.W., Washington, DC 20036
Telephone: (202) 828-2000
Registered as Foreign Agent: (#3901)
Members of firm representing listed organizations:
   Aldock, John D.
   Basseches, Robert T.
   Cook, David B.
   Kramer, Franklin D.
      Background: Special Assistant to the Assistant Secretary of Defense for International Security Affairs, 1977-79. Principal Deputy Assistant Secretary of Defense for International Security Affairs, 1979-81. Undersecretary of Defense for Policy, 1981.
Clients:
   American President Companies *(Robert T. Basseches, David B. Cook)*
   SGS Government Programs, Inc.
   SGS North America, Inc.
   Societe Generale de Surveillance

SHEA AND GOULD
1775 Pennsylvania Ave., N.W., Suite 700, Washington, DC 20006
Telephone: (202) 833-9850
Registered as lobbyist at U.S. Congress.
Background: Washington office of a New York law firm.
Members of firm representing listed organizations:
   Conti, William J.
   Mills, Wilbur D.
      Background: Former Member, House of Representatives (D-AR).
   Mirabelli, Mario V.
      Background: Trial Attorney, Bureau of Deceptive Practices, Federal Trade Commission, 1967-69; Division of Corporation Finance, Branch of Administrative Proceedings, Securities and Exchange Commission, 1969-73.
   Razzano, Frank C.
   Riedy, Mark J.
Clients:
   Group Health, Inc.

WASHINGTON REPRESENTATIVES

SHEA, James T.
Neill and Co.
815 Connecticut Ave., N.W. Suite 800, Washington, DC 20006
Telephone: (202) 463-8877
Registered as lobbyist at U.S. Congress.
Registered as Foreign Agent: (#3320).
Background: U.S. Embassy, Nouakchott, Mauretania, 1981-82.

SHEA, Kathleen H.
Newman & Holtzinger, P.C.
1615 L St., N.W., 10th Floor, Washington, DC 20005
Telephone: (202) 955-6600
Background: Attorney, Office of the General Counsel, Atomic Energy Commission, 1957-69, 1972-73. Legal Advisor, U.S. Mission to the European Atomic Energy Community, 1964-68.
Clients:
Iowa Electric Light and Power Co.
Iowa Power and Light Co.

SHEA, Timothy B.
General Counsel, Legal Services Corp.
400 Virginia Ave., S.W., Washington, DC 20024
Telephone: (202) 863-2751

SHEAN, Margaret
Thompson and Co.
1001 G St., N.W. 7th Floor, Washington, DC 20001
Telephone: (202) 383-5590
Registered as lobbyist at U.S. Congress.
Clients:
CareerCom Corp.

SHEARER, Gail E.
Manager, Policy Analysis, Consumers Union of the United States
2001 S St., N.W., Suite 520, Washington, DC 20009
Telephone: (202) 462-6262
Registered as lobbyist at U.S. Congress.

SHEARMAN AND STERLING
1001 30th St., N.W., Suite 400, Washington, DC 20007
Telephone: (202) 337-8200
Registered as Foreign Agent: (#4208)
Members of firm representing listed organizations:
Bransilver, Edward
Daly, William J., Senior Legislative Representative
Epstein, Anita, Legislative Director
Background: Legislative Director, Shearman and Sterling.
Herzstein, Robert
Springer, Gary L., Sr. Legis Rep., Internat'l Trade
Wilner, Thomas B.
Clients:
Chilean Exporters Ass'n
Citicorp *(Edward Bransilver)*
Claro y Cia *(Anita Epstein, Robert Herzstein)*
Compania Sud Americana de Vapores
Confederacion de Federaciones y Asociaciones Gremiales de Agricultores de Chile
Komatsu Ltd. *(Robert Herzstein, Thomas B. Wilner)*

SHEEHAN, Arline M.
Associate, Morgan, Lewis and Bockius
1800 M St., N.W., Washington, DC 20036
Telephone: (202) 467-7000
Registered as lobbyist at U.S. Congress.
Clients:
Safety-Kleen Corp.

SHEEHAN ASSOCIATES, INC.
727 15th St., N.W., Suite 1200, Washington, DC 20005
Telephone: (202) 347-0044
Members of firm representing listed organizations:
Billman, Paul, Director, Political Programs
Maloney, Gary W., Director, Legislative Services
Background: Former aide to Rep. Elton Gallegly (R-CA), 1987-88, and to Rep. Jim McCrery (R-LA), 1988.
Rhodes, Annie C., Dir., Spec. Projects/Development
Rintye, Peter R., V. President
Background: Regional Political Director, Republican Nat'l Committee, 1983-84; Deputy Campaign Director and Director, Campaign Finance, Nat'l Republican Congressional Committee, 1987-89.

Sheehan, Denise L.
Background: Serves as Treasurer, American Ass'n of Politically Active Citizens.
Sheehan, John Thomas, President
Background: Formerly Administrative Assistant to Representative Dan Coats (R-IN), 1981. PAC Director, National Republican Senatorial Committee, 1983-87.
Clients:
American Ass'n of Politically Active Citizens
(Paul Billman, Denise L. Sheehan)
Nat'l Law Enforcement Officers' Memorial Fund
(Annie C. Rhodes, John Thomas Sheehan)
Nat'l Order of Women Legislators *(Annie C. Rhodes, John Thomas Sheehan)*
Searle Co., G. D. *(Gary W. Maloney, John Thomas Sheehan)*
T.M.P. Inc. *(Denise L. Sheehan)*
UST Public Affairs, Inc. *(John Thomas Sheehan)*

SHEEHAN, Daniel
General Counsel, Christic Institute
1324 N. Capitol St., N.W., Washington, DC 20002
Telephone: (202) 797-8106
Registered as lobbyist at U.S. Congress.

SHEEHAN, Denise L.
Sheehan Associates, Inc.
727 15th St., N.W., Suite 1200, Washington, DC 20005
Telephone: (202) 347-0044
Background: Serves as Treasurer, American Ass'n of Politically Active Citizens.
Clients:
American Ass'n of Politically Active Citizens
T.M.P. Inc.

SHEEHAN, John J.
Legislative Director, United Steelworkers of America
815 16th St., N.W. Suite 706, Washington, DC 20006
Telephone: (202) 638-6929
Registered as lobbyist at U.S. Congress.

SHEEHAN, John Thomas
President, Sheehan Associates, Inc.
727 15th St., N.W., Suite 1200, Washington, DC 20005
Telephone: (202) 347-0044
Registered as lobbyist at U.S. Congress.
Background: Formerly Administrative Assistant to Representative Dan Coats (R-IN), 1981. PAC Director, National Republican Senatorial Committee, 1983-87.
Clients:
Nat'l Law Enforcement Officers' Memorial Fund
Nat'l Order of Women Legislators
Searle Co., G. D.
UST Public Affairs, Inc.

SHEEHAN, Kathleen M.
Director of Public Policy, American Home Economics Ass'n
1555 King St., Alexandria, VA 22314
Telephone: (703) 706-4600

SHEEHAN, Monica M.
Assoc. Director, Div. of Legislation, American Hospital Ass'n
50 F St., N.W., Suite 1100, Washington, DC 20001
Telephone: (202) 638-1100

SHEEHAN, Peggy A.
V. President, Food Policy & Market Dev., Nat'l Cooperative Business Ass'n
1401 New York Ave., N.W. Suite 1100, Washington, DC 20005
Telephone: (202) 638-6222
Registered as lobbyist at U.S. Congress.

SHEEHAN, Shaun M.
V. President, Washington Office, Tribune Broadcasting Co.
1111 19th St., N.W., Suite 1000, Washington, DC 20036
Telephone: (202) 775-7750
Registered as lobbyist at U.S. Congress.

SHEEHY, Terrence C.
Howrey and Simon
1730 Pennsylvania Ave., N.W., Washington, DC 20006-4793
Telephone: (202) 783-0800
Clients:
Anheuser-Busch Cos., Inc.

VSI Corp.

SHEEKEY, Kathleen
Legislative Director, Common Cause
2030 M St., N.W., Washington, DC 20036
Telephone: (202) 833-1200
Registered as lobbyist at U.S. Congress.
Background: Former Director of Congressional Relations, Federal Trade Commission.

SHEFFER, Kenneth E., Jr.
Director, AEA Washington, Ltd.
905 16th St., N.W., Washington, DC 20006
Registered as Foreign Agent: (#4307).
Clients:
Korean Overseas Information Service

SHEHAB, Alfred
President, Nat'l Ass'n of Arab Americans
2033 M St., N.W., Suite 300, Washington, DC 20036
Telephone: (202) 467-4800
Registered as lobbyist at U.S. Congress.

SHELBY, Rick
Political Director, Nat'l Republican Senatorial Committee
425 Second St., N.E., Washington, DC 20002
Telephone: (202) 675-6000
Background: Deputy Director, White House Office of Presidential Personnel, 1981.

SHELDON, Karin
Senior Counsel, Wilderness Soc.
1400 Eye St., N.W., 10th Floor, Washington, DC 20005
Telephone: (202) 842-3400

SHELDON, Stuart A.
Dow, Lohnes and Albertson
1255 23rd St., N.W., Suite 500, Washington, DC 20037
Telephone: (202) 857-2500
Clients:
Salomon Brothers Inc.

SHELLEY, Herbert C.
Howrey and Simon
1730 Pennsylvania Ave., N.W., Washington, DC 20006-4793
Telephone: (202) 783-0800
Background: Attorney-Advisor, U.S Internat'l Trade Commission, 1973-74; Ass't Director, office of Tariff Affairs, U.S. Dept. of Treasury, 1974-76; Member, U.S. Delegation to the Multilateral Trade Negotiations, 1976-79.
Clients:
Taiwan Transportation Vehicle Manufacturing Ass'n

SHELLEY, Zack H., Jr.
Mgr., Aerospace Congressional Relations, General Electric Co.
1331 Pennsylvania Ave., N.W., Washington, DC 20004
Telephone: (202) 637-4346
Registered as lobbyist at U.S. Congress.

SHELLHAAS, Philip A.
Program Director, Governmental Programs, Internat'l Business Machines Corp.
Suite 1200, 1801 K St., N.W., Washington, DC 20006
Telephone: (202) 778-5069

SHEPARDSON, Fran
Federal Regulatory Representative, Ashland Oil, Inc.
1025 Connecticut Ave., N.W., Suite 507, Washington, DC 20036
Telephone: (202) 223-8290

SHEPARDSON, Monty
Legislative Assistant, Nat'l Ass'n of Casualty and Surety Agents
600 Pennsylvania Ave., S.E., Suite 211, Washington, DC 20003
Telephone: (202) 547-6616

SHEPHERD, Ritchenya
Public Relations Assistant, American Ass'n of Homes for the Aging
1129 20th St., N.W., Suite 400, Washington, DC 20036
Telephone: (202) 296-5960

The listings in this directory are available as *Mailing Labels*. See last page.

381

SHEPLER, Dr. Monte
President & CEO, Consortium of Universities of the Washington Metropolitan Area
1717 Massachusetts Ave., N.W., Suite 101, Washington, DC 20036
Telephone: (202) 265-1313

SHEPPARD, Carol
Senior Editor, American Mining Congress
1920 N St., N.W. Suite 300, Washington, DC 20036
Telephone: (202) 861-2800

SHEPPARD, Edward J., IV
Schmeltzer, Aptaker and Sheppard
The Watergate, 2600 Virginia Ave., N.W., Washington, DC 20037
Telephone: (202) 333-8800
Clients:
Alabama State Docks Department
Cargill, Inc.
Gulf Seaports Marine Terminals Conference
Lake Charles Harbor and Terminal District
Massachusetts Port Authority
South Carolina State Port Authority
Tampa Port Authority

SHER, Stanley O.
Dow, Lohnes and Albertson
1255 23rd St., N.W., Suite 500, Washington, DC 20037
Telephone: (202) 857-2500
Clients:
Compania Trasatlantica Espanola, S.A.
Hapag-Lloyd AG
Hertz Corp.

SHERBILL, Raymond J.
Leva, Hawes, Mason and Martin
1220 19th St., N.W. Suite 700, Washington, DC 20036
Telephone: (202) 775-0725
Clients:
Ass'n of the United States Army

SHERIDAN, Thomas
Director, Public Policy, AIDS Action Council
2033 M St., N.W., Suite 801, Washington, DC 20036
Telephone: (202) 293-2886
Registered as lobbyist at U.S. Congress.

SHERLINE, Lee S.
Leighton and Sherline
1010 Massachusetts Ave., N.W., Suite 101, Washington, DC 20001-5402
Telephone: (202) 898-1122
Clients:
Idaho Power Co.
PacifiCorp
Utah Power and Light Co.
Washington Water Power Co.

SHERMAN, Dianne
Director of Communications, Zero Population Growth, Inc.
1400 16th St., N.W., Suite 320, Washington, DC 20036
Telephone: (202) 332-2200

SHERMAN, DUNN, COHEN, LEIFER AND COUNTS
1125 15th St., N.W. Suite 801, Washington, DC 20005
Telephone: (202) 785-9300
Background: The information below was obtained from public records and submitted for confirmation to this firm, which declined to confirm or correct the information.
Members of firm representing listed organizations:
Cohen, Laurence J.
Background: Legal Assistant and Supervising Attorney, 1964-67, Nat'l Labor Relations Board. Alternate Member, Chairman's Task force on the NLRB, 1976-77.
Leifer, Elihu I.
Background: Attorney, Civil Rights Division, U.S. Department of Justice, 1964-67.
Clients:
AFL-CIO - Building and Construction Trades Department
Internat'l Brotherhood of Electrical Workers *(Laurence J. Cohen)*

SHERMAN, Gerald H.
Silverstein and Mullens
1776 K St., N.W., Suite 800, Washington, DC 20006
Telephone: (202) 452-7900
Registered as lobbyist at U.S. Congress.
Background: Counsel, Ass'n for Advanced Life Underwriting.
Clients:
Ass'n for Advanced Life Underwriting

SHERMAN, Dr. John F.
Exec. V. President, Ass'n of American Medical Colleges
One Dupont Circle, N.W., Suite 200, Washington, DC 20036
Telephone: (202) 828-0400

SHERMAN, Judith C.
Congressional Relations Representative, American Dental Ass'n
1111 14th St., N.W. Suite 1200, Washington, DC 20005
Telephone: (202) 898-2400
Registered as lobbyist at U.S. Congress.

SHERMAN, Leslie
Public Relations Coordinator, Organization for American-Soviet ExchangeS (OASES-DC)
1302 R St., N.W., Washington, DC 20009
Telephone: (202) 332-1145

SHERMAN, Michael D.
Collier, Shannon & Scott
1055 Thomas Jefferson St., N.W., Suite 300, Washington, DC 20007
Telephone: (202) 342-8400
Registered as lobbyist at U.S. Congress.
Registered as Foreign Agent: (#3694).
Clients:
Siemens Corp.

SHERMAN, Nancy J.
V. President, Public Affairs, Foodservice & Packaging Institute, Inc.
1025 Connecticut Ave., N.W., Suite 513, Washington, DC 20036
Telephone: (202) 822-6420
Registered as lobbyist at U.S. Congress.

SHERMAN, Norman
V. President, Hoving Group, The
910 17th St., N.W. Suite 318, Washington, DC 20006
Telephone: (202) 429-0120
Registered as lobbyist at U.S. Congress.

SHERMAN, Patricia A.
Counsel, Internat'l Trade Pol. & Export, General Electric Co.
1331 Pennsylvania Ave., N.W., Washington, DC
Telephone: (202) 637-4251

SHERMAN, Wendy R.
Exec. Director, EMILY'S List
2000 P St., N.W., Suite 412, Washington, DC 20036
Telephone: (202) 887-1957

SHERRY, Susan
Director, State Health Affairs, Nat'l Health Care Campaign
1334 G St., N.W. LL, Washington, DC 20005
Telephone: (202) 639-8833

SHERZER, Harvey G.
Howrey and Simon
1730 Pennsylvania Ave., N.W., Washington, DC 20006-4793
Telephone: (202) 783-0800
Clients:
Teledyne Industries Inc.

SHEY, Jane E.
Director, Government Affairs, Corn Refiners Ass'n
1100 Connecticut Ave., N.W. Suite 1120, Washington, DC 20036
Telephone: (202) 331-1634
Registered as lobbyist at U.S. Congress.
Background: Former Legislative Ass't to U.S. Rep. Tim Penny (D-MN).

SHIELDS, Nelson T.
Chairman Emeritus, Handgun Control, Inc.
1225 Eye St., N.W., Suite 1100, Washington, DC 20005
Telephone: (202) 898-0792
Registered as lobbyist at U.S. Congress.

SHIELDS, Sonya
Assistant to the President, Soc. of Eye Surgeons
c/o Internat'l Eye Foundation 7801 Norfolk Ave., Bethesda, MD 20814
Telephone: (301) 986-1830

SHILLINGLAW, Ellen
Director, Government Relations, American Soc. of Clinical Oncology
750 17th St., N.W. Suite 1100, Washington, DC 20006
Telephone: (202) 778-2396
Registered as lobbyist at U.S. Congress.
Background: Former Director, Office of Legislation and Policy, Health Care Financing Administration, Department of Health and Human Services.

SHIMER, R. Philip
Washington Representative, Western Governors' Ass'n
444 North Capitol St., Suite 526, Washington, DC 20001
Telephone: (202) 624-5402
Registered as lobbyist at U.S. Congress.

SHINN, Dr. Allen
Dep Dir, Legis and Public Affrs, NAT'L SCIENCE FOUNDATION
1800 G St., N.W., Washington, DC 20550
Telephone: (202) 357-9838

SHIPP, Daniel K.
V. President of Public Affairs, Nat'l Electrical Manufacturers Ass'n
2101 L St., N.W., Washington, DC 20037
Telephone: (202) 457-8452

SHIPP, William Jeffry
Director of Legislation, Farm Credit Council
50 F St., N.W., Suite 900, Washington, DC 20001
Telephone: (202) 626-8710
Registered as lobbyist at U.S. Congress.
Background: Serves as contact for the Farm Credit Council PAC.

SHIRLEY, Craigan P.
Keene, Shirley & Associates, Inc.
919 Prince St., Alexandria, VA 22314
Telephone: (703) 684-0550
Registered as lobbyist at U.S. Congress.
Registered as Foreign Agent: (#3997).
Clients:
Australian Barley Board
Boston Capital Partners, Inc.
Marine Engineers Beneficial Ass'n
Nat'l Farmers' Federation of Australia
The Limited, Inc.
World Freedom Foundation

SHIRLEY, Kimberly
Meyers & Associates
412 First St., S.E., Suite 100, Washington, DC 20003
Telephone: (202) 484-2773

SHLAES, John
Director of Planning, Gov't Affairs, Edison Electric Institute
1111 19th St., N.W., Washington, DC 20036
Telephone: (202) 778-6456
Registered as lobbyist at U.S. Congress.

SHOAF, David C.
Director, Advanced Programs, Westinghouse Electric Corp.
1801 K St., N.W., Washington, DC 20006
Telephone: (202) 835-2345

SHOCAS, Elaine
Associate Director, American Federation of Teachers
555 New Jersey Ave., N.W., Washington, DC 20001
Telephone: (202) 879-4452
Registered as lobbyist at U.S. Congress.

SHOEMAKER, Janet
Assistant Director, Public Affairs, American Soc. for Microbiology
1325 Massachusetts Ave., N.W., Washington, DC 20005
Telephone: (202) 737-3600

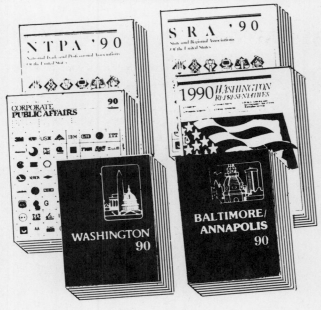

SHOGAN, Cindy
Activist Coordinator, Defenders of Wildlife
1244 19th St., N.W., Washington, DC 20036
Telephone: (202) 659-9510

SHOLES, Juanita R.
Treasurer, Conservative Victory Committee
111 South Columbus St., Alexandria, VA 22316
Telephone: (703) 684-6603

SHOOK, William A.
Preston Gates Ellis & Rouvelas Meeds
1735 New York Ave., N.W., Suite 500, Washington, DC
20006-4759
Telephone: (202) 628-1700
Registered as lobbyist at U.S. Congress.
Background: Legislative Investigator, Senate Judiciary
Committee, 1979-85, and Special Assistant on the House
Oversight and Investigations Subcommittee of the Inter-
state and Foreign Commerce Committee, 1977-79.
Clients:
Fluke Manufacturing Co., John
Nat'l Forest Products Ass'n

SHORR, Ira
Program Coordinator, SANE/FREEZE
1819 H St., N.W., Suite 1000, Washington, DC 20006
Telephone: (202) 862-9740

SHORT, Laurence
Steptoe and Johnson
1330 Connecticut Ave., N.W., Washington, DC 20036
Telephone: (202) 429-3000
Clients:
Atlantic Container Line
Swissair

SHORTLEY, Maiselle Dolan
Chairman, Nat'l Conservative Political Action Committee
618 S. Alfred St., Alexandria, VA 22314
Telephone: (703) 684-1800
Background: Served in the office of Senator James
McClure (R-ID), 1972-73. Confidential Assistant, The
White House, 1981-84. Director, Office of Communica-
tions and Community Relations, Department of Defense,
1984-85. Deputy Director, Office for Volunteer Liaison,
ACTION, 1985-86. Commission on Judicial, Legislative
and Executive Salaries, 1986-87. Department of Educa-
tion, Drug Abuse Policy Working Group, 1987. National
Advisory Council on Adult Education, 1988.

SHORTRIDGE, John G.
Manager, Governmental Affairs, USX Corp.
818 Connecticut Ave., N.W., Washington, DC 20006
Telephone: (202) 331-1340
Registered as lobbyist at U.S. Congress.

SHOTWELL, Scott
V. President, Government Affairs, Nat'l Forest Products
Ass'n
1250 Connecticut Ave., N.W., Washington, DC 20036
Telephone: (202) 463-2740
Registered as lobbyist at U.S. Congress.

SHOUP, Hal
Exec. V. President, American Ass'n of Advertising Agen-
cies
1899 L St., N.W., Suite 700, Washington, DC 20036
Telephone: (202) 331-7345
Registered as lobbyist at U.S. Congress.

SHOWELL, Jill
Analysts, Government Affairs, Federal Home Loan Mort-
gage Corp.
1759 Business Center Drive, Reston, VA 22090
Telephone: (703) 789-4700
Registered as lobbyist at U.S. Congress.

SHREVE, Larry W.
V. President, Field Operations, Emerson Electric Co.
1235 Jefferson Davis Hwy., Suite 305, Arlington, VA
22202
Telephone: (703) 920-7600
Background: Former Deputy Assistant Secretary of Defense for Legislative Affairs.

SHRINER, Robert D.
Managing Partner, Shriner-Midland Co.
6432 Quincy Place, Falls Church, VA 22042

Telephone: (703) 795-4356

SHRINSKY, Jason
Kaye, Scholer, Fierman, Hays and Handler
The McPherson Building 901 15th St., N.W., #1100,
Washington, DC 20005
Telephone: (202) 682-3500
Clients:
Adams Communications Corp.
Barnstable Broadcasting
Golden West Broadcasters
H & D Communications Group
Holt Communications Corp.
Katz Communications, Inc.
Keymarket Communications, Inc.
Lincoln Group, The
Malrite Communications Group, Inc.
Metroplex Communications, Inc.
NewCity Communications, Inc.
Saga Communications, Inc.
Sage Communications Corp.
Spanish Broadcasting System, Inc.
Westwood One, Inc.

SHRIVER, Eunice Kennedy
Chairman of the Board, Special Olympics Internat'l, Inc.
1350 New York Ave., N.W., Suite 500, Washington, DC
20005
Telephone: (202) 628-3630

SHRIVER, Sargent
Fried, Frank, Harris, Shriver & Jacobson
1001 Pennsylvania Ave., N.W., Suite 800, Washington, DC
20004-2505
Telephone: (202) 639-7000
Background: Director, Peace Corps, 1961-1966; Director,
Office of Economic Opportunity, 1964-1968; United
States Ambassador to France, 1968-1970.

SHRUM, Robert M.
Doak, Shrum & Associates
1200 Eaton Court, Washington, DC 20007
Telephone: (202) 333-7901

SHULL, Leon
Interim Exec. Director, Nat'l Committee for Full Employment
815 16th St., N.W., Suite 301, Washington, DC 20006
Telephone: (202) 393-7415

SHULMAN, Eric
Dir. of Legis. Liaison and Research, Nat'l Council of Sen-
ior Citizens
925 15th St., N.W., Washington, DC 20005
Telephone: (202) 347-8800
Registered as lobbyist at U.S. Congress.

SHULMAN, Kathy
Grassroots Coordinator, League of Women Voters of the
United States
1730 M St., N.W., Tenth Floor, Washington, DC 20036
Telephone: (202) 429-1965
Registered as lobbyist at U.S. Congress.

SHULTZ, David G.
Manager, Federal Governmental Affairs, Varian Associates Inc.
2101 Wilson Blvd., Suite 832, Arlington, VA 22201
Telephone: (703) 522-8002

SHUMANN, William A.
Media Relations Representative, General Electric Co.
1331 Pennsylvania Ave., N.W., Washington, DC
Telephone: (202) 637-4555

SHUTE, William H.
Director, Federal Relations, Southwestern Bell Corp.
1667 K St., N.W., Suite 1000, Washington, DC 20006
Telephone: (202) 293-8550
Registered as lobbyist at U.S. Congress.

SHYMANSKY, Patricia
Government Affairs Staff Member, Hughes Aircraft Co.
1100 Wilson Bvld., Arlington, VA 22209
Telephone: (703) 284-4270

SICLARI, Tricia
Asst. V. Pres., Professional Affairs, American Osteopathic
Hospital Ass'n
1454 Duke St., Alexandria, VA 22314
Telephone: (703) 684-7700

SIDES, Stephen R.
Director, Health and Safety, Nat'l Paint and Coatings
Ass'n
1500 Rhode Island Ave., N.W., Washington, DC 20005
Telephone: (202) 462-6272

SIDLEY AND AUSTIN
1722 Eye St., N.W. Sixth Floor, Washington, DC 20006
Telephone: (202) 429-4000
Background: The information below was obtained from
public records and submitted for confirmation to this
firm, which declined to correct the information and asked
to be omitted from the book.
Members of firm representing listed organizations:
Bello, Judith
Background: Former General Counsel. Office of the
U.S. Trade Representative.
Buckhold, Virginia M., Legislative Coordinator
Fant, Lester C. (III)
Flagg, Ronald S.
Flynn, Richard J.
Lee, Rex E.
Background: Assistant Attorney General of the U.S.,
1975-77. Solicitor General of the U.S., 1981-85.
Levy, David
MacBeth, Angus
Background: Chief Pollution Control Section, 1977-79
and Deputy Assistant Attorney General, 1979-81,
Land and Natural Resources Division, Department of
Justice.
Martin, R. Eden
Moates, G. Paul
Nemeroff, Michael A.
Tompkins, Joseph B. (Jr.)
Waxman, Margery
Background: General Counsel, Office of Personnel
Management, 1979-81; Dipputy General Counsel,
Dept. of Treasury, 1981-85.
Clients:
Alliance of Nonprofit Mailers *(David Levy)*
Barclays Bank PLC *(Margery Waxman)*
Cayman Islands, Government of *(Lester C. Fant, III,
Joseph B. Tompkins, Jr.)*
Commerce Clearing House *(Virginia M. Buckhold)*
Federal Home Loan Bank of Chicago *(Margery
Waxman)*
Moscow Narodny Bank
North West Timber Ass'n *(Judith Bello)*
Pohang Iron & Steel Co., Ltd.
Tootsie Roll Industries *(Judith Bello)*

SIDMAN, Mark H.
Weiner, McCaffrey, Brodsky, Kaplan & Levin
1350 New York Ave., N.W., Suite 800, Washington, DC
20005-4797
Telephone: (202) 628-2000

SIDOR, John M.
Exec. Director, Council of State Community Affairs Agencies
444 North Capitol St., N.W., Suite 251, Washington, DC
20001
Telephone: (202) 393-6435

SIEGEL, Allen G.
Arent, Fox, Kintner, Plotkin & Kahn
1050 Connecticut Ave., N.W., Washington, DC 20036-
5339
Telephone: (202) 857-6000
Background: With National Labor Relations Board 1962-
64.
Clients:
Nat'l Parking Ass'n

SIEGEL, Andrew
Legislative Representative, Council for a Livable World
100 Maryland Ave., N.E. Suite 211, Washington, DC
20002
Telephone: (202) 543-4100
Registered as lobbyist at U.S. Congress.

SIEGEL & ASSOCIATES, Mark A.
1030 15th St., N.W., Suite 408, Washington, DC 20005

WASHINGTON REPRESENTATIVES

SIEGEL & ASSOCIATES, Mark A. (Cont'd)
Telephone: (202) 371-5600
Registered as lobbyist at U.S. Congress.
Registered as Foreign Agent: (#3865)
Background: Officers include Mark A. Siegel, also of Internat'l Public Strategies, Inc., the Internat'l wing of the firm.
Members of firm representing listed organizations:
Nolan, Michael J.
   Background: Also serves with Internat'l Public Strategies, Inc., the international arm of Mark A. Siegel & Associates.
Siegel, Mark A.
Organizations represented:
   Money Store, The
   New York Power Authority
   Puerto Rico, Commonwealth of
   Puerto Rico Federal Affairs Administration *(Mark A. Siegel)*
   Puerto Rico, Popular Democratic Party of
   Stevens Institute of Technology

SIEGEL, Elisa K.
Manager, Public Affairs, American Insurance Ass'n
1130 Connecticut Ave., N.W., Suite 1000, Washington, DC 20036
Telephone: (202) 828-7100

SIEGEL, HOUSTON AND ASSOCIATES
1707 L St., N.W., Suite 333, Washington, DC 20036
Telephone: (202) 296-2606
Members of firm representing listed organizations:
Houston, Betsy, Exec. V. President
Siegel, (Dr.) Martin, President
Clients:
   American Institute of Chemical Engineers *(Dr. Martin Siegel)*
   Federation of Materials Societies *(Betsy Houston)*
   Nat'l Ass'n of Career Development Consultants *(Betsy Houston)*

SIEGEL, Kenneth E.
Associate General Counsel, American Trucking Ass'ns
2200 Mill Road, Alexandria, VA 22314
Telephone: (703) 838-1857
Background: Also represents Nat'l Accounting and Finance Council and Nat'l Freight Claims Council.

SIEGEL, Mark A.
Siegel & Associates, Mark A.
1030 15th St., N.W., Suite 408, Washington, DC 20005
Telephone: (202) 371-5600
Organizations represented:
   Puerto Rico Federal Affairs Administration

SIEGEL, Dr. Martin
President, Siegel, Houston and Associates
1707 L St., N.W., Suite 333, Washington, DC 20036
Telephone: (202) 296-2606
Clients:
   American Institute of Chemical Engineers

SIEGEL, Nancy E.
Attorney, American Insurance Ass'n
1130 Connecticut Ave., N.W., Suite 1000, Washington, DC 20036
Telephone: (202) 828-7100

SIEGEL, Richard D.
1400 16th St., N.W., Washington, DC 20036-2220
Telephone: (202) 234-0500
Registered as lobbyist at U.S. Congress.
Background: An attorney in independent practice. Deputy Assistant Secretary of Agriculture for Natural Resources and Environment, 1981-87.
Organizations represented:
   Business Committee for Fair Civil RICO Legislation

SIEGEL, Ronald A.
Cohn and Marks
1333 New Hampshire Ave., N.W., Suite 600, Washington, DC 20036
Telephone: (202) 293-3860
Registered as Foreign Agent: (#4303).
Clients:
   Maclean Hunter Cable TV

SIEMER, Deanne C.
Partner, Wilmer, Cutler and Pickering
2445 M St., N.W., Washington, DC 20037-1420
Telephone: (202) 663-6000
Background: Economist, Office of Management and Budget, 1964-67. General Counsel, Department of Defense, 1977-79. Special Assistant to the Secretary of Energy, 1979-80.
Clients:
   Ford Motor Co.

SIEMIETKOWSKI, Susan Marie
Legislative Assistant, Printing Industries of America
1730 North Lynn St., Arlington, VA 22209
Telephone: (703) 841-8100
Registered as lobbyist at U.S. Congress.

SIERCK, Alexander W.
Beveridge & Diamond, P.C.
1350 Eye St., N.W. Suite 700, Washington, DC 20005
Telephone: (202) 789-6000
Registered as Foreign Agent: (#3772).
Background: Director of Trade Policy, Antitrust Division, U.S. Department of Justice, 1978-80.
Clients:
   Airbus Industrie
   British Independent Steel Producers Ass'n
   Dana Corp.
   Ingersoll Products Co.

SIGAL, Jill Lea
Webster and Sheffield
2000 Pennsylvania Ave., N.W., Suite 7400, Washington, DC 20006
Telephone: (202) 785-8222
Registered as lobbyist at U.S. Congress.
Background: Served in the U.S. Department of Energy, 1985-89.

SIGLER, Christine
Manager, Member Relations, Nat'l Committee to Preserve Social Security and Medicare
2000 K St., N.W. Suite 800, Washington, DC 20006
Telephone: (202) 822-9459
Registered as lobbyist at U.S. Congress.

SIGNER, William A.
Keefe Co., The
444 North Capitol St., N.W., Suite 711, Washington, DC 20001
Telephone: (202) 638-7030
Registered as lobbyist at U.S. Congress.
Clients:
   Foodservice and Lodging Institute
   Glick & Glick
   Greater New York Hospital Ass'n
   Nat'l Burglar and Fire Alarm Ass'n
   NATJ and NATE
   New York Hospital
   RJR Nabisco Washington, Inc.

SIKES, Lucinda
Staff Attorney, U.S. Public Interest Research Group
215 Pennsylvania Ave., S.E., Washington, DC 20003
Telephone: (202) 546-9707
Registered as lobbyist at U.S. Congress.

SILAS, C. J.
Chairman, Business-Industry Political Action Committee
1747 Pennsylvania Ave., N.W. Suite 250, Washington, DC 20006-4697
Telephone: (202) 833-1880

SILBERBERG, Donna
Director, Public Relations, American Arbitration Ass'n
1730 Rhode Island Ave., N.W., Suite 509, Washington, DC 20036
Telephone: (202) 296-8510

SILBERFARB, Stephen
Legislative Liaison, American Israel Public Affairs Committee
440 First St., N.W. Suite 600, Washington, DC 20001
Telephone: (202) 639-5200
Registered as lobbyist at U.S. Congress.

SILBERG, Jay E.
Shaw, Pittman, Potts and Trowbridge
2300 N St., N.W., Washington, DC 20037
Telephone: (202) 663-8000
Background: Attorney, Office of The General Counsel, Atomic Energy Commission, 1966-69.
Clients:
   Centerior Energy Corp.
   Cleveland Electric Illuminating Co.
   Duquesne Light Co.
   Kansas Gas & Electric Co.
   Northern States Power Co.
   Pennsylvania Power and Light Co.
   Utility Nuclear Waste Transportation Program
   Wolf Creek Nuclear Operating Corp.

SILBERGELD, Dr. Ellen
Chairperson, Toxics Program, Environmental Defense Fund
1616 P St., N.W., Suite 150, Washington, DC 20036
Telephone: (202) 387-3500
Background: Also serves as President, Soc. for Occupational and Environmental Health.

SILBERGELD, Mark
Washington Office Director, Consumers Union of the United States
2001 S St., N.W., Suite 520, Washington, DC 20009
Telephone: (202) 462-6262
Registered as lobbyist at U.S. Congress.

SILCOX, Clark R.
Steele & Fornaciari
2020 K St., N.W. Suite 850, Washington, DC 20006-1857
Telephone: (202) 887-1779
Clients:
   Business Council on the Reduction of Paperwork

SILLS & BRODSKY, P.C.
1016 16th St., N.W., Sixth Floor, Washington, DC 20036
Telephone: (202) 955-1000
Members of firm representing listed organizations:
Geske, Alvin J.
   Background: Attorney, Legislation and Regulation Division, Office of Chief Counsel, Internal Revenue Service, 1970-72, and Assistant Branch Chief, 1972-74. Legislation Attorney, Joint Committee on Taxation, U.S. Congress, 1975-77, and Assistant Legislation Counsel, 1978-81.
Clients:
   Grupo Industrial Alfa, S.A. *(Alvin J. Geske)*
   Renewable Fuels Ass'n *(Alvin J. Geske)*

SILLS, Dr. Donald
President, Coalition for Religious Freedom
515 Wythe St., Suite 201, Alexandria, VA 22314
Telephone: (703) 684-9010

SILLS, Hilary
V. President, Hill and Knowlton Public Affairs Worldwide
Washington Harbour, 901 31st St., N.W., Washington, DC 20007
Telephone: (202) 333-7400
Registered as Foreign Agent: (#4170).
Background: Staff Representative to Rep. William Whitehurst (R-VA), 1970-71.
Clients:
   ARCO
   Exxon Co., U.S.A.
   Public Affairs Internat'l

SILVEIRA, Mary
V. President, Schlossberg Assoc., Ken
317 Massachusetts Ave., N.E. Suite 200, Washington, DC 20002
Telephone: (202) 544-6796
Registered as lobbyist at U.S. Congress.
Organizations represented:
   Marine Biological Laboratory

SILVER, Bruce S.
Exec. Director, Nat'l Housing Endowment
15th and M Sts., N.W., Washington, DC 20005
Telephone: (202) 822-0226

SILVER, Daniel B.
Cleary, Gottlieb, Steen and Hamilton
1752 N St., N.W., Washington, DC 20036
Telephone: (202) 728-2700
Registered as Foreign Agent: (#0508).
Background: General Counsel, National Security Agency, 1978-79; Central Intelligence Agency, 1979-81.
Clients:

La Metalli Industriale S.p.A.

SILVER, David
President, Investment Company Institute
1600 M St., N.W. Suite 600, Washington, DC 20036
Telephone: (202) 293-7700
Registered as lobbyist at U.S. Congress.

SILVER, FREEDMAN & TAFF
1735 Eye St., N.W., Washington, DC 20006
Telephone: (202) 429-6100
Members of firm representing listed organizations:
Freedman, Robert L.
Jacobs, Lois G.
Metheny, Earl L.
Stiles, Nancy M.
Clients:
Hiawatha Savings and Loan Ass'n *(Robert L. Freedman, Lois G. Jacobs, Nancy M. Stiles)*
Nat'l Homeowners Ass'n *(Earl L. Metheny)*

SILVER, Howard J.
Exec. Director, Consortium of Social Science Ass'ns
1522 K St., N.W., Suite 836, Washington, DC 20005
Telephone: (202) 842-3525
Registered as lobbyist at U.S. Congress.

SILVER, Linda G.
Director, Legislative Analysis, Korea Economic Institute of America
1030 15th St., N.W. Suite 662, Washington, DC 20005
Telephone: (202) 371-0690
Registered as lobbyist at U.S. Congress.
Registered as Foreign Agent: (#3327)

SILVER, Sarah
Director, Leadership Circle, Democratic Senatorial Campaign Committee
430 South Capitol St., S.E., Washington, DC 20003
Telephone: (202) 224-2447

SILVER, Steven W.
Robertson, Monagle and Eastaugh
1050 Thomas Jefferson St., NW Sixth Floor, Washington, DC 20007
Telephone: (202) 333-4400
Registered as lobbyist at U.S. Congress.
Clients:
Alaska Loggers Ass'n
Amselco Minerals, Inc.
Anchorage School District
Atlantic Richfield Company (ARCO) Transportation Co.
Bristol Bay Native Corp.
General Communication Incorporated
Liberty Shipping Group

SILVER, Taury
V. President, Communication & Education, Air-Conditioning and Refrigeration Institute
1501 Wilson Blvd., Suite 600, Arlington, VA 22209
Telephone: (703) 524-8800

SILVERBERG, Beverly R.
Director of Public Affairs, Washington Metropolitan Area Transit Authority
600 5th St., N.W., Washington, DC 20001
Telephone: (202) 962-1000

SILVERGLADE, Bruce A.
Director of Legal Affairs, Center for Science in the Public Interest
1501 16th St., N.W., Washington, DC 20036
Telephone: (202) 332-9110
Registered as lobbyist at U.S. Congress.

SILVERMAN, Arthur H.
Dow, Lohnes and Albertson
1255 23rd St., N.W., Suite 500, Washington, DC 20037
Telephone: (202) 857-2500
Registered as Foreign Agent: (#3452).
Clients:
California Wine Commission
Chamber of Commerce of the U.S.A.
Hercules, Inc.
Product Liability Coordinating Committee
SOFICIA
Sporicidin Co., The

SILVERMAN, Harold
Sr. V. President, Health Care, Hill and Knowlton Public Affairs Worldwide
Washington Harbour, 901 31st St., N.W., Washington, DC 20007
Telephone: (202) 333-7400
Clients:
American Meat Institute

SILVERMAN, Marcia
Chief Operating Officer, Powell, Adams & Rinehart
1901 L St., N.W., 3rd Floor, Washington, DC 20036
Telephone: (202) 466-7590
Registered as lobbyist at U.S. Congress.

SILVERMAN, Richard S.
General Counsel, American Peanut Product Manufacturers, Inc.
555 13th St., N.W., Washington, DC 20004
Telephone: (202) 637-5600

SILVERMAN, William
Dow, Lohnes and Albertson
1255 23rd St., N.W., Suite 500, Washington, DC 20037
Telephone: (202) 857-2500
Registered as lobbyist at U.S. Congress.
Registered as Foreign Agent: (#3452).
Clients:
Algoma Steel Corp., Ltd.
Campolonghi Italia S.p.A.
Dofasco, Inc.
Envases de Plastico, S.A. de C.V.
Euromarble, S.p.A.
Flyer Industries Ltd.
GoldStar Co., Ltd.
Henraux S.p.A.
OEL/Norfin S.p.A.
PLIVA Pharmaceutical and Chemical Works
Savema S.p.A.
Stelco, Inc.

SILVERS, Curtis
Bannerman and Associates, Inc.
888 16th St., N.W., Washington, DC 20006
Telephone: (202) 835-8188
Registered as lobbyist at U.S. Congress.
Registered as Foreign Agent: (#3964).
Background: Former staff member, Senate Foreign Relations Committee.
Clients:
Bangladesh, People's Republic of
Philippines, Government of the

SILVERSTEIN, Leonard L.
Silverstein and Mullens
1776 K St., N.W., Suite 800, Washington, DC 20006
Telephone: (202) 452-7900
Registered as lobbyist at U.S. Congress.
Registered as Foreign Agent: (#3352).
Background: Attorney, Office of Chief Counsel, Internal Revenue Service and Member, Legal Advisory Staff, Treasury Dep't 1951-1954.
Clients:
Cushman & Wakefield, Inc.
Rolls-Royce, Inc.

SILVERSTEIN AND MULLENS
1776 K St., N.W., Suite 800, Washington, DC 20006
Telephone: (202) 452-7900
Members of firm representing listed organizations:
Corman, James C.
Background: Member, U.S. House of Representatives (D-CA), 1961-81. Member, House Committee on Ways and Means, 1968-81. Chairman, House Democratic Campaign Committee, 1976-81.
Kirk, William A. (Jr.)
Background: Professional staff, U.S. House of Representatives Committee on Ways and Means, 1980-84. Staff Director, House Subcommittee on Oversight, 1982-84. Legislative aide, Capitol Hill, 1975-80.
Sherman, Gerald H.
Background: Counsel, Ass'n for Advanced Life Underwriting.
Silverstein, Leonard L.
Background: Attorney, Office of Chief Counsel, Internal Revenue Service and Member, Legal Advisory Staff, Treasury Dep't 1951-1954.
Clients:

American Newspaper Publishers Ass'n *(William A. Kirk, Jr.)*
Ass'n for Advanced Life Underwriting *(Gerald H. Sherman)*
Cushman & Wakefield, Inc. *(Leonard L. Silverstein)*
Kelso & Co. *(William A. Kirk, Jr.)*
Majestic Realty Co. *(James C. Corman)*
MCA Inc. *(James C. Corman)*
Nat'l Ass'n of Home Builders of the U.S.
Nat'l Structured Settlements Trade Ass'n *(James C. Corman)*
Republic Nat'l Bank of New York *(William A. Kirk, Jr.)*
Rolls-Royce, Inc. *(Leonard L. Silverstein)*
Tropicana Energy Co. *(William A. Kirk, Jr.)*
United States League of Savings Institutions *(James C. Corman)*

SILVERSTONE, Alan
V. President and Regional Manager, Kaiser Foundation Health Plan, Inc.
4200 Wisconsin Ave., N.W., Suite 300, Washington, DC 20016
Telephone: (202) 364-6747

SIMCOX, David E.
Director, Center for Immigration Studies
1424 16th St., N.W. Suite 603, Washington, DC 20036
Telephone: (202) 328-7228
Background: Career Foreign Service Officer, U.S. Department of State, 1956-85.

SIMMENS, Lance R.
Assistant Exec. Director, Legislation, United States Conference of Mayors
1620 Eye St., N.W., Washington, DC 20006
Telephone: (202) 293-7330

SIMMONS, Althea T. L.
Director, Washington Bureau, Nat'l Ass'n for the Advancement of Colored People
1025 Vermont Ave., N.W. Suite 730, Washington, DC 20005
Telephone: (202) 638-2269
Registered as lobbyist at U.S. Congress.

SIMMONS, Deborah S.
Director of Federal Relations, American Ass'n for Marriage and Family Therapy
1717 K St., N.W. Suite 407, Washington, DC 20006
Telephone: (202) 429-1825
Registered as lobbyist at U.S. Congress.
Background: Former Legislative Assistant to Rep. Dante Fascell (D-FL).

SIMMONS, Joan
Director of Communications, Nat'l Committee for Quality Health Care
1500 K St., N.W., Suite 360, Washington, DC 20005
Telephone: (202) 347-5731
Background: Director, Intergovernmental Affairs, Federal Energy Regulatory Commission, 1981-87; Research Director, President's Commission on Privatization, 1987-88.

SIMMONS, Patricia E.
General Manager, Government Relations, Centel Corp.
1350 Eye St., N.W., Suite 500, Washington, DC 20005
Telephone: (202) 778-8700
Registered as lobbyist at U.S. Congress.

SIMMONS, Samuel
President, Nat'l Caucus and Center on Black Aged
1424 K St., N.W. Suite 500, Washington, DC 20005
Telephone: (202) 637-8400

SIMMS, Gary D.
General Counsel & Director, Operations, American Academy of Actuaries
1720 Eye St., N.W., 7th Floor, Washington, DC 20006
Telephone: (202) 223-8196
Registered as lobbyist at U.S. Congress.

SIMMS, William J.
Manager, Strategic Business Development, Solarex Corp.
1335 Piccard Drive, Rockville, MD 20850
Telephone: (301) 948-0202

SIMON, The Rev. Arthur
President, Bread for the World
802 Rhode Island Ave., N.E., Washington, DC 20018
Telephone: (202) 269-0200

SIMON & CO., INC.
1001 Connecticut Ave., N.W. Suite 435, Washington, DC 20005
Telephone: (202) 659-2229
Members of firm representing listed organizations:
Hyde, Floyd H., Consultant
Background: Former Ass't Sec'y, Community Development, U.S. Department of Housing and Urban Dvlmt. (HUD) 1971-73, Under Secretary HUD, 1973-74.
McCleskey, James S., Legislative Director
Background: Staff Assistant to Senator Daniel P. Moynihan (D-NY), 1986-87.
Simon, Leonard S., President
Clients:
Elkhart, Indiana, City of *(Leonard S. Simon)*
Erie, Pennsylvania, City of *(Leonard S. Simon)*
Fresno, California, City of *(Leonard S. Simon)*
Gary, Indiana, City of *(Leonard S. Simon)*
Newark, California, City of
Portland, Oregon, City of *(Leonard S. Simon)*
San Bernardino, California, City of *(Leonard S. Simon)*
San Leandro, California, City of *(Leonard S. Simon)*
Tacoma, Washington, City of *(Leonard S. Simon)*

SIMON, David J.
Coordinator, Parks Preservation, Nat'l Parks and Conservation Ass'n
1015 31st St., N.W., Washington, DC 20007
Telephone: (202) 944-8530
Registered as lobbyist at U.S. Congress.

SIMON, Leonard S.
President, Simon & Co., Inc.
1001 Connecticut Ave., N.W. Suite 435, Washington, DC 20005
Telephone: (202) 659-2229
Registered as lobbyist at U.S. Congress.
Clients:
Elkhart, Indiana, City of
Erie, Pennsylvania, City of
Fresno, California, City of
Gary, Indiana, City of
Portland, Oregon, City of
San Bernardino, California, City of
San Leandro, California, City of
Tacoma, Washington, City of

SIMON, Marsha J.
Director of Legislation, Families U.S.A.
1334 G St., N.W. Suite 300, Washington, DC 20005
Telephone: (202) 737-6340
Registered as lobbyist at U.S. Congress.

SIMON, Michael E.
Mng. Partner, Office of Federal Services, Andersen and Co., Arthur
1666 K St., N.W., Washington, DC 20006
Telephone: (202) 862-3394
Registered as lobbyist at U.S. Congress.

SIMON, Neil A.
Counsel, Director, Government Relations, Internat'l Franchise Ass'n
1350 New York Ave., N.W. Suite 900, Washington, DC 20005
Telephone: (202) 628-8000
Registered as lobbyist at U.S. Congress.
Background: Also serves as Treasurer of the Franchising Political Action Committee.

SIMON, Richard
Director, Family Therapy Network
7703 13th St., N.W., Washington, DC 20012
Telephone: (202) 829-2452

SIMON, Samuel A.
President, Issue Dynamics Inc.
901 15th St., N.W. Suite 230, Washington, DC 20005
Telephone: (202) 408-1400

SIMON, Susan C.
V. President, Shearson Lehman Hutton
1627 I St., N.W., Suite 1100, Washington, DC 20006
Telephone: (202) 452-4700

SIMONETTI, Gilbert, Jr.
Partner-in-Charge, Washington Liaison, Price Waterhouse
1801 K St., N.W., Suite 700, Washington, DC 20006
Telephone: (202) 296-0800
Background: Also serves as Treasurer, Price Waterhouse Partners' Political Action Committee.

SIMONS, David C.
Manager, Congressional Relations, Eaton Corp.
1100 Connecticut Ave., N.W., Suite 410, Washington, DC 20036
Telephone: (202) 955-6444
Registered as lobbyist at U.S. Congress.
Background: Former Legislative Assistant to Rep. Phil Crane (R-IL).

SIMONS, Lawrence B.
Powell, Goldstein, Frazer and Murphy
1001 Pennsylvania, N.W., Sixth Fl., Washington, DC 20004
Telephone: (202) 347-0066
Registered as lobbyist at U.S. Congress.
Background: Assistant Secretary for Housing/FHA Commissioner, 1977-81.
Clients:
Bayley Seton Hospital
Federal Nat'l Mortgage Ass'n
Nat'l Multi Housing Council
Nat'l Multi Housing Council Political Action Committee
Starrett Housing Corp.

SIMONSON, David C.
Exec. V. President, Nat'l Newspaper Ass'n
1627 K St., N.W. Suite 400, Washington, DC 20006
Telephone: (202) 466-7200
Registered as lobbyist at U.S. Congress.

SIMONSON, Kenneth D.
V. President, American Trucking Ass'ns
2200 Mill Road, Alexandria, VA 22314
Telephone: (703) 838-1800

SIMPKINS, Talmage E.
Exec. Director, AFL-CIO Maritime Committee
444 North Capitol St., N.W., Suite 820, Washington, DC 20001
Telephone: (202) 347-5980
Registered as lobbyist at U.S. Congress.
Background: Also serves as Exec. V. President and Treasurer of Labor-Management Maritime Committee, Inc.

SIMPSON & ASSOC., Bill
1155 15th St., N.W. Suite 504, Washington, DC 20005
Telephone: (202) 452-1003
Members of firm representing listed organizations:
Simpson, William G.
Background: Serves as Washington Representative for the State of Mississippi.
Organizations represented:
Mississippi, State of *(William G. Simpson)*

SIMPSON, Charles J., Jr.
Zuckert, Scoutt and Rasenberger
888 17th St., N.W., Suite 600, Washington, DC 20006-3959
Telephone: (202) 298-8660
Registered as lobbyist at U.S. Congress.
Clients:
Advance Petroleum, Inc.
LADECO
Malaysian Airline System

SIMPSON, Charles W.
Sr. Director, Government Affairs, Lipsen Whitten & Diamond
1725 DeSales St., N.W., Suite 800, Washington, DC 20036
Telephone: (202) 659-6540
Registered as lobbyist at U.S. Congress.
Background: Former Adm. Assistant to Senator Lloyd Bentsen (1984-87), and Charles Wilson (1973-84).

SIMPSON, Mary Ann
Assistant Washington Representative, Tennessee Valley Authority
412 First St., S.E., Suite 300, Washington, DC 20444
Telephone: (202) 479-4412

SIMPSON, Thomas D.
V. President, Railway Progress Institute
700 North Fairfax St., Alexandria, VA 22314
Telephone: (703) 836-2332
Registered as lobbyist at U.S. Congress.

SIMPSON, William G.
Simpson & Assoc., Bill
1155 15th St., N.W. Suite 504, Washington, DC 20005
Telephone: (202) 452-1003
Registered as lobbyist at U.S. Congress.
Background: Serves as Washington Representative for the State of Mississippi.
Organizations represented:
Mississippi, State of

SIMS, Helena G.
Director, Nat'l Ass'n of State Auditors, Comptrollers and Treasurers
444 North Capitol St., N.W. Suite 523, Washington, DC 20001
Telephone: (202) 624-5451

SIMS, Joe
Jones, Day, Reavis and Pogue
1450 G St., N.W., Suite 700, Washington, DC 20005-2088
Telephone: (202) 879-3939
Registered as lobbyist at U.S. Congress.

SIMS, Robert B.
Senior V. President, Nat'l Geographic Soc.
1145 17th St., N.W., Washington, DC 20036
Telephone: (202) 857-7000

SINCLAIR-SMITH, Susanne
Director, Washington Legal Clinic for the Homeless
1800 Massachusetts Ave., N.W., Washington, DC 20036
Telephone: (202) 872-1494

SINCLAIR, Warren K.
President, Nat'l Council on Radiation Protection and Measurement
7910 Woodmont Ave. Suite 800, Bethesda, MD 20814
Telephone: (301) 657-2652

SINEL, Norman M.
Arnold & Porter
1200 New Hampshire Ave., N.W., Washington, DC 20036
Telephone: (202) 872-6700
Registered as lobbyist at U.S. Congress.
Clients:
New York City Board of Estimate

SINGER, Christopher A.
Manager, Regulatory Affairs, Pfizer, Inc.
1455 Pennsylvania Ave., N.W., Suite 925, Washington, DC 20004
Telephone: (202) 783-7070

SINGER, James W., III
Legislative Counsel, Pharmaceutical Manufacturers Ass'n
1100 15th St., N.W., Washington, DC 20005
Telephone: (202) 835-3482
Registered as lobbyist at U.S. Congress.

SINGER, Linda R.
Exec. Director, Center for Dispute Settlement
1666 Connecticut Ave., N.W. Suite 501, Washington, DC 20009
Telephone: (202) 265-9572

SINGER, Nancy
V. President, Food and Drug Law Institute
1000 Vermont Ave., N.W., Suite 1200, Washington, DC 20005
Telephone: (202) 371-1420

SINGER, Richard
Director, Mangement Education, Merit Shop Foundation
729 15th St., N.W., Washington, DC 20005
Telephone: (202) 637-8800

SINGER, Ronald
Manager, Internat'l Programs Operation, General Electric Co.
1331 Pennsylvania Ave., N.W. Suite 800S, Washington, DC 20004
Telephone: (202) 637-4000

SINGER, Terry
Exec. Director, Nat'l Ass'n of Energy Service Companies
1440 New York Ave., N.W., Washington, DC 20005
Telephone: (202) 371-7980

SINGER, William S.
Kirkland and Ellis
655 15th St., N.W. Suite 1200, Washington, DC 20005
Telephone: (202) 879-5000
Background: Former Member, Chicago City Council.

SINGLETARY, Donna L.
Legislative Representative, Nat'l Federation of Independent Business
600 Maryland Ave., S.W., Suite 700, Washington, DC 20024
Telephone: (202) 554-9000
Registered as lobbyist at U.S. Congress.

SINGLETARY, Dr. Otis A., Jr.
Sr. Consultant, Cassidy and Associates, Inc.
655 15th St., N.W., Suite 1100, Washington, DC 20005
Telephone: (202) 347-0773
Registered as lobbyist at U.S. Congress.
Clients:
Universal Medical Center

SINGLEY, Elizabeth
Govt'l Affairs Specialist, Lipsen Whitten & Diamond
1725 DeSales St., N.W., Suite 800, Washington, DC 20036
Telephone: (202) 659-6540
Registered as lobbyist at U.S. Congress.
Background: Ass't for Legislative Affairs, The White House, 1981-84; Administrative Officer, National Commission on Air Quality, 1979-81.

SINICK, Marshall S.
Squire, Sanders and Dempsey
1201 Pennsylvania Ave., N.W. P.O. Box 407, Washington, DC 20044
Telephone: (202) 626-6600
Background: Trial Attorney, Bureau of Operating Rights, Civil Aeronautics Board, 1968-71.
Clients:
Air India
Alaska Airlines
Aloha Airlines
Fast Air Carrier
Forestal Venecia Ltda.

SINKIN, Lanny
Director of Litigation, Christic Institute
1324 N. Capitol St., N.W., Washington, DC 20002
Telephone: (202) 797-8106

SINNOTT, Richard L.
President, Century Public Affairs
1752 N St., N.W., Suite 800, Washington, DC 20036
Telephone: (202) 828-2375
Registered as lobbyist at U.S. Congress.
Clients:
Oakland, California, Port of
Transcontinental Development Corp.

SINROD & TASH
2201 Wisconsin Ave., N.W., Suite 250, Washington, DC 20007
Telephone: (202) 965-7956
Members of firm representing listed organizations:
Strupp, Werner
Clients:
American Podiatric Medical Ass'n *(Werner Strupp)*

SIRIGOS, Constantine
Legislative Assistant, American Hellenic Institute Public Affairs Committee
1730 K St., N.W. Suite 1005, Washington, DC 20006
Telephone: (202) 659-4608
Registered as lobbyist at U.S. Congress.

SIRMON, Jeff M.
Dep Chief, Prog & Legis, DEPARTMENT OF AGRICULTURE - Forest Service
12th and Independence Ave. S.W., Washington, DC 20250
Telephone: (202) 447-6663

SISSON, Hall
Legislative Representative, Communications Workers of America
1925 K St., N.W., Washington, DC 20006
Telephone: (202) 728-2467
Registered as lobbyist at U.S. Congress.

SIVE, PAGET & RIESEL
1055 Thomas Jefferson St, N.W. Suite 501, Washington, DC 20007
Telephone: (202) 965-1500
Members of firm representing listed organizations:
Hall, Richard
Background: Former Assistant Director, Surface Mining Reclamation and Enforcement, U.S. Department of Interior.
Clients:
ARCO

SIZEMORE, O. Lou
Cong Liaison Specialist, FEDERAL COMMUNICATIONS COMMISSION
1919 M St., N.W., Washington, DC 20554
Telephone: (202) 632-6405

SJS ADVANCED STRATEGIES INC.
1330 Connecticut Ave., N.W., Washington, DC 20036
Telephone: (202) 429-5500
Members of firm representing listed organizations:
Bennett, B. Timothy
Background: Former Exec. Director, U.S. Generalized System of Preferences, 1980-81. U.S. Trade Attache to the EEC, 1981-85. Deputy Assistant U.S. Trade Representative for Mexico, 1985-88.
Smith, Michael B., President
Background: Former Deputy U.S. Trade Representative and Chief, U.S. Textile Negotiator. Former U.S. Ambassador to GATT.

SKADDEN, ARPS, SLATE, MEAGHER AND FLOM
1440 New York Ave., N.W., Washington, DC 20005
Telephone: (202) 371-7000
Members of firm representing listed organizations:
Coleman, Lynn R.
Background: Serves also as Treasurer, Skadden Arps Political Action Committee. General Counsel, U.S. Department of Energy, 1978-80. Deputy Secretary, U.S. Department of Energy, 1980-81.
Cutrone, Roseann
Goldstein, Jeffery M.
Graham, Thomas R.
Background: Deputy General Counsel, Office of the United States Trade Representative, Executive Office of the President, 1974-79.
Gross, Kenneth A.
Background: Former Associate General Counsel, Federal Election Commission.
Guzick, William J.
Lighthizer, Robert E.
Background: Chief Minority Counsel, Senate Committee on Finance, 1978-81. Chief Counsel and Staff Director, Senate Committee on Finance, 1981-83. Deputy United States Trade Representative, Ambassador, 1983-85.
Naeve, Mike
Background: Legislative Director for Senator Lloyd Bentsen (D-TX), 1978-80. Commissioner, Federal Energy Regulatory Commission, 1985-88.
Oosterhuis, Paul W.
Perry, William E.
Schwartz, Gilbert
Clients:
Akzo America, Inc. *(Robert E. Lighthizer)*
American Electronics Ass'n *(Roseann Cutrone)*
Amoco Corp. *(Mike Naeve)*
Anadarko Petroleum Corp. *(Mike Naeve)*
Anheuser-Busch Cos., Inc. *(Robert E. Lighthizer)*
ATMOS Energy Corp. *(Mike Naeve)*
Bethlehem Steel Corp. *(Robert E. Lighthizer)*
Carson, Pirie, Scott & Co.
Chain Pharmacy Ass'n of New York State *(William J. Guzick)*

COMDISCO, Inc.
Computer and Business Equipment Manufacturers Ass'n *(Paul W. Oosterhuis)*
Council on Research and Technology (CORE-TECH) *(Paul W. Oosterhuis)*
Enron Corp. *(Lynn R. Coleman, Mike Naeve)*
Fuji Photo Film U.S.A. *(Thomas R. Graham, William E. Perry)*
General Development Corp. *(Robert E. Lighthizer)*
General Mills *(Robert E. Lighthizer)*
Hechinger Co. *(William E. Perry)*
Hoylake Investments Ltd. *(Robert E. Lighthizer)*
MacAndrews & Forbes Holdings, Inc. *(Gilbert Schwartz)*
MacMillan Publishing Co. *(Jeffery M. Goldstein)*
Merrill Lynch and Co., Inc. *(Robert E. Lighthizer)*
Mesa Limited Partnership *(Robert E. Lighthizer, Mike Naeve)*
Natural Gas Alliance for Generative Electricity *(Lynn R. Coleman, Mike Naeve)*
Natural Gas Supply Ass'n *(Lynn R. Coleman, Mike Naeve)*
Oryx Energy Co. *(Mike Naeve)*
Public Service Co. of Indiana *(Mike Naeve)*
Questar Corp. *(Robert E. Lighthizer)*
Sara Lee Corp. *(Robert E. Lighthizer)*
Sonat Inc. *(Mike Naeve)*

SKADDEN, Donald H.
V. President, Taxation, American Institute of Certified Public Accountants
1455 Pennsylvania Ave., N.W. Suite 400, Washington, DC 20004
Telephone: (202) 737-6600

SKALL, Gregg P.
Baker and Hostetler
1050 Connecticut Ave., N.W. Suite 1100, Washington, DC 20036
Telephone: (202) 861-1500
Registered as lobbyist at U.S. Congress.
Clients:
Bell Canada

SKARDON, Steve
Nat'l Strategies Inc.
818 17th St., N.W., Washington, DC 20006
Telephone: (202) 429-8744
Background: Exec. Floor Assistant, Office of the Chief Deputy Majority Whip, U.S. House of Representatives, 1983-87.

SKELTIS, Dianne
Director of Public Affairs, Council of Better Business Bureaus
4200 Wilson Blvd. Suite 800, Arlington, VA 22203
Telephone: (703) 276-0100

SKERNOLIS, Edmund J.
Regulatory Affairs Manager, Waste Management, Inc.
1155 Connecticut Ave., N.W., Suite 800, Washington, DC 20036
Telephone: (202) 467-4480
Registered as lobbyist at U.S. Congress.

SKIADOS, Don
Director, Communications, Air Line Pilots Ass'n Internat'l
1625 Massachusetts Ave., N.W., Washington, DC 20036
Telephone: (202) 797-4003

SKIBBIE, LTG. Lawrence F., USA (Ret.)
President, American Defense Preparedness Ass'n
2101 Wilson Blvd. Suite 400, Arlington, VA 22201-3061
Telephone: (703) 522-1820

SKILES, James
Associate General Counsel, Cosmetic, Toiletry and Fragrance Ass'n
1110 Vermont Ave., N.W. Suite 800, Washington, DC 20005
Telephone: (202) 331-1770
Background: Former Assistant Director, Division of Advertising Practices, Federal Trade Commission.

SKILLEN, James W.
Exec. Director, Ass'n for Public Justice
806 15th St., N.W., Suite 440, Washington, DC 20005
Telephone: (202) 737-2110

WASHINGTON REPRESENTATIVES

SKILLMAN, Richard W.
Caplin and Drysdale
One Thomas Circle, N.W. Suite 1100, Washington, DC 20005
Telephone: (202) 862-5000
Registered as lobbyist at U.S. Congress.
Background: Law Clerk to the Chief Justice of the U.S. Supreme Court, 1971-72.

SKINNER, Audrey L.
Administrative Secretary, Internat'l Ass'n of Official Human Rights Agencies
444 North Capitol St., Suite 249, Washington, DC 20001
Telephone: (202) 624-5410

SKINNER, William J.
751 Rockville Pike, Suite 27B, Rockville, MD 20852
Telephone: (301) 762-3784
Background: An attorney in independent practice.
Organizations represented:
United States Pharmacopeial Convention

SKLADANY, Barney J., Jr.
Mgr., Gov't Relats., Chem., Mining & Min., Mobil Corp.
1100 Connecticut Ave., N.W., Suite 620, Washington, DC 20036
Telephone: (202) 862-1326
Registered as lobbyist at U.S. Congress.

SKLADONY, Thomas
Director of Communications, American Enterprise Institute for Public Policy Research
1150 17th St., N.W., Washington, DC 20036
Telephone: (202) 862-5800

SKLAR, Scott
Exec. Director, Solar Energy Industries Ass'n
777 N. Capitol St., N.W. 8th Fl., Washington, DC 20001
Telephone: (703) 524-6100
Registered as lobbyist at U.S. Congress.
Background: Also serves as the part-time Exec. Director of the U.S. Export Council for Renewable Energy, an umbrella group of nine national renewable energy trade associations.

SKLAR, Stephanie C.
V. President, Public Affairs, Nat'l Wildlife Federation
1400 16th St., N.W., Washington, DC 20036-2266
Telephone: (202) 797-6800

SKLAR, William E.
V. President, Burson-Marsteller
1850 M St., N.W., Suite 900, Washington, DC 20036
Telephone: (202) 833-8550

SKLAROW, Mark
Director, Curriculum and Programs, Presidential Classroom for Young Americans
441 N. Lee St., Alexandria, VA 22314
Telephone: (703) 683-5400

SKONBERG, Steven A.
Director, Legislative Affairs, Nat'l Ass'n of Federal Credit Unions
3138 N. 10th St., Arlington, VA 22201
Telephone: (703) 522-4770
Registered as lobbyist at U.S. Congress.
Background: Former aide to Rep. James Scheuer (D-NY).

SKRABUT, Kathleen M.
Legislative Representative, Service Employees Internat'l Union
1313 L St., N.W., Washington, DC 20005
Telephone: (202) 898-3200
Registered as lobbyist at U.S. Congress.

SKRABUT, Paul A., Jr.
V. President, Gov't Relations, Palumbo & Cerrell, Inc.
1629 K St., N.W., Suite 1100, Washington, DC 20006
Telephone: (202) 785-6705
Registered as lobbyist at U.S. Congress.
Background: Former Crisis Management Specialist, Federal Emergency Management Agency and former Administrative Assistant and Legislative Director to former U.S. Senator Harrison A. Williams (D-NJ).
Clients:
American Institute of Architects, The
American Insurance Ass'n

American Soc. of Composers, Authors and Publishers
ARCO Chemical Co.
Order of Sons of Italy in America
Palmer Associates, G. H.
Rockport Fine Arts Council

SKREDYNSKI, Michael P.
Principal and Dir., West Coast Opns., U.S. Strategies Corp.
1321 Duke St., Suite 200, Alexandria, VA 22314-3563
Telephone: (703) 739-7999
Clients:
Cities in Schools, Inc.
GMS/Partners

SLADE, David C.
General Counsel, Coastal States Organization
444 North Capitol St., N.W. Suite 312, Washington, DC 20001
Telephone: (202) 628-9636

SLADE, Jonathon A.
Keefe Co., The
444 North Capitol St., N.W., Suite 711, Washington, DC 20001
Telephone: (202) 638-7030
Registered as lobbyist at U.S. Congress.
Registered as Foreign Agent: (#4228).
Clients:
Adler Group
Cuban American Foundation
Seminole Tribe of Florida

SLADE, Stephen J.
V. President, Government Affairs, Trans World Airlines
808 17th St., N.W., Suite 520, Washington, DC 20006
Telephone: (202) 457-4754

SLATER, G. Bryan
Asst, Cong Rels, Legis & Cong Rels, DEPARTMENT OF HOUSING AND URBAN DEVELOPMENT
451 Seventh St., S.W., Washington, DC 20410
Telephone: (202) 755-7380

SLATON, Sally
Gold and Liebengood, Inc.
1455 Pennsylvania Ave., N.W. Suite 950, Washington, DC 20004
Telephone: (202) 639-8899

SLATTERY, John M.
Curator, Heli Archive, Helicopter Foundation Internat'l
1619 Duke St., Alexandria, VA 22314-3406
Telephone: (703) 683-4646

SLATTERY, William F.
V. President and General Manager, Ceco Corp.
1801 McCormick Place, Landover, MD 20785
Telephone: (301) 322-2326

SLAUGHTER, Denise
Assistant to the President, Nat'l Press Foundation
National Press Bldg. Suite 1282, Washington, DC 20045
Telephone: (202) 662-7350

SLAUGHTER, Robert G.
Sr. Government Affairs Representative, Amoco Corp.
1615 M St., N.W., Suite 200, Washington, DC 20036
Telephone: (202) 857-5306
Registered as lobbyist at U.S. Congress.

SLAYTON, Gus
Exec. Director, Ass'n of Old Crows
1000 North Payne St., Alexandria, VA 22314
Telephone: (703) 549-1600

SLECHTER, Albert J.
Federal Gov't Affairs Director, Chrysler Corp.
1100 Connecticut Ave., N.W., Washington, DC 20036
Telephone: (202) 862-5448
Registered as lobbyist at U.S. Congress.

SLEIGHT, Barry
President, Chronic Fatigue Syndrome Information Institute
5840 Cameron Run Terrace Suite 1413, Alexandria, VA 22303
Telephone: (703) 960-1749

SLESINGER, Cathy L.
Exec. Director - International, NYNEX
1828 L St., N.W., Suite 1000, Washington, DC 20036
Telephone: (202) 416-0100

SLIDER, William T.
Staff Director, Legislative Affairs, Nat'l Ass'n of Home Builders of the U.S.
15th and M Streets, N.W., Washington, DC 20005
Telephone: (202) 822-0470
Registered as lobbyist at U.S. Congress.

SLIZ, Deborah R.
Director, Energy Services, APCO Associates
1155 21st St., N.W., Suite 1000, Washington, DC 20036
Telephone: (202) 778-1000
Background: Former Counsel to the House Interior and Insular Affairs Subcommittee on Energy and Environment.
Clients:
Excess Deferred Tax Coalition
Sacramento Municipal Utility District
Springfield, Missouri, City Utilities of
Tennessee Valley Public Power Ass'n

SLOAN, Catherine Reiss
Director, Legislative Affairs, Competitive Telecommunications Ass'n (COMPTEL)
120 Maryland Ave., N.E., Washington, DC 20002
Telephone: (202) 546-9022
Registered as lobbyist at U.S. Congress.

SLOAN, John, Jr.
President and C.E.O., Nat'l Federation of Independent Business
600 Maryland Ave., S.W., Suite 700, Washington, DC 20024
Telephone: (202) 554-9000
Registered as lobbyist at U.S. Congress.

SLOAN, Judith W.
Director, Washington Office, Asia Society, The
1785 Massachusetts Ave., N.W., Washington, DC 20036
Telephone: (202) 387-6500

SLOAN, Richard S.
President, Challenge America, Inc.
1700 K St., N.W., Suite 1100, Washington, DC 20006
Telephone: (202) 429-9400
Clients:
American Federation of Teachers
Internat'l Ass'n of Machinists and Aerospace Workers
Service Employees Internat'l Union

SLOANE, David P.
Spec Asst to Pres, Legis Affrs (Senate), EXECUTIVE OFFICE OF THE PRESIDENT - The White House
1600 Pennsylvania Ave., N.W. 107 East Wing, Washington, DC 20500
Telephone: (202) 456-6493

SLOBODIN, Alan
President, Legal Studies Division, Washington Legal Foundation
1705 N St., N.W., Washington, DC 20036
Telephone: (202) 857-0240

SLOBODOW, Arlen
Exec. Director, Public Interest Video Network
1642 R St., N.W., Washington, DC 20009
Telephone: (202) 797-8997

SLONE, Kelly A.
Manager, Legislative Affairs, Baxter Internat'l Inc.
1667 K St., N.W., Suite 710, Washington, DC 20006
Telephone: (202) 223-4016
Registered as lobbyist at U.S. Congress.

SLONE, Peter B.
Gold and Liebengood, Inc.
1455 Pennsylvania Ave., N.W. Suite 950, Washington, DC 20004
Telephone: (202) 639-8899
Registered as lobbyist at U.S. Congress.
Background: Former U.S. House Appropriations Committee Associate Staff.
Clients:
Nat'l School Transportation Ass'n

The listings in this directory are available as *Mailing Labels*. See last page.

SLOVER AND LOFTUS
1224 17th St., N.W., Washington, DC 20036
Telephone: (202) 347-7170
Members of firm representing listed organizations:
  Loftus, C. Michael
  McKeever, Ira E.
  Slover, William L.
Clients:
  Central Power and Light Co. *(William L. Slover)*
  Eastern Coal Transportation Conference
  Houston Power and Lighting Co. *(William L. Slover)*
  Kansas City Power & Light Co. *(William L. Slover)*
  Kentucky Utilities Co. *(William L. Slover)*
  Minnesota Power *(William L. Slover)*
  Western Coal Traffic League *(C. Michael Loftus, Ira E. McKeever)*
  Western Coal Traffic League Political Action Committee

SLOVER, William L.
Slover and Loftus
1224 17th St., N.W., Washington, DC 20036
Telephone: (202) 347-7170
Clients:
  Central Power and Light Co.
  Houston Power and Lighting Co.
  Kansas City Power & Light Co.
  Kentucky Utilities Co.
  Minnesota Power

SMALL, Karna
Senior Consultant, Hill and Knowlton Public Affairs Worldwide
Washington Harbour, 901 31st St., N.W., Washington, DC 20007
Telephone: (202) 333-7400
Registered as Foreign Agent: (#3301).
Background: Former Special Assistant to the President and Senior Director of Public Affairs, Nat'l Security Council in the Reagan Administration.

SMALL, Michael E.
Wright and Talisman
1050 17th St., N.W. Suite 600, Washington, DC 20036
Telephone: (202) 331-1194
Background: Attorney, Federal Energy Regulatory Commission, 1979-85.

SMALL, Stephan K.
V. Pres. and Dir. of Cong. Rel., Securities Industry Ass'n
1850 M St., N.W., Suite 550, Washington, DC 20036
Telephone: (202) 296-9410
Registered as lobbyist at U.S. Congress.

SMALL, William E.
Deputy Exec. Director, American Academy of Otolaryngology-Head and Neck Surgery
One Prince St., Alexandria, VA 22314
Telephone: (703) 836-4444
Background: Staff Member, Senate Committee on Public Works, 1969-70. Chief of Information Services, Nat'l Bureau of Standards, 1972-76.

SMALLS, Douglas T.
V. President, United Parcel Service
316 Pennsylvania Ave., S.E. Suite 304, Washington, DC 20003
Telephone: (202) 675-4220

SMART, Andrew W.
Manager, Media Relations, Nat'l Ass'n of Manufacturers
1331 Pennsylvania Ave., N.W. Suite 1500 North, Washington, DC 20004-1703
Telephone: (202) 637-3000

SMART, S. Bruce
Senior Counselor, World Resources Institute
1709 New York Ave., N.W., Washington, DC 20006
Telephone: (202) 638-6300
Background: Former Undersecretary of Commerce for International Trade, 1985-88.

SMATHERS, George A.
Smathers, Hickey and Smathers
1050 Connecticut Ave., N.W. Suite 1230, Washington, DC 20036
Telephone: (202) 862-5510
Background: Member of Congress from Dade County, Florida, 1947-50 and U.S. Senator, 1951-68. Member, Board of Directors, Gulf and Western Industries.

SMATHERS, HICKEY AND SMATHERS
1050 Connecticut Ave., N.W. Suite 1230, Washington, DC 20036
Telephone: (202) 862-5510
Members of firm representing listed organizations:
  Smathers, George A.
    Background: Member of Congress from Dade County, Florida, 1947-50 and U.S. Senator, 1951-68. Member, Board of Directors, Gulf and Western Industries.

SMEAGE, Dennis
Smith, Bucklin and Associates
1101 Connecticut Ave., N.W., Suite 700, Washington, DC 20036
Telephone: (202) 857-1100
Clients:
  American Guild of Patient Account Management

SMEAL, Eleanor
President, Fund for a Feminist Majority
1600 Wilson Blvd., Suite 704, Arlington, VA 22209
Telephone: (202) 522-2214

SMEAL, Paul L.
Chairperson, Public Relations Committee, American Soc. for Horticultural Science
113 South West St., Alexandria, VA 22314-2824
Telephone: (703) 836-4606

SMEALLIE, Shawn M.
Spec Asst, Legis Affrs (Senate), EXECUTIVE OFFICE OF THE PRESIDENT - Office of Management and Budget
Old Executive Office Bldg., Washington, DC 20500
Telephone: (202) 395-4790

SMEDLEY, Lawrence T.
Exec. Director, Nat'l Council of Senior Citizens
925 15th St., N.W., Washington, DC 20005
Telephone: (202) 347-8800

SMERKO, Robert G.
President, Chlorine Institute
2001 L St., N.W., Suite 506, Washington, DC 20036
Telephone: (202) 775-2790
Registered as lobbyist at U.S. Congress.

SMICK, David M.
Smick Medley Internat'l Inc.
1050 Connecticut Ave., N.W., Washington, DC 20036
Telephone: (202) 861-0770

SMICK MEDLEY INTERNAT'L INC.
1050 Connecticut Ave., N.W., Washington, DC 20036
Telephone: (202) 861-0770
Background: An economic consulting firm.
Members of firm representing listed organizations:
  Lavin, Franklin L.
  Medley, Richard
  Smick, David M.

SMIGEL, Diane
Manager, Washington Public Affairs, LTV Aircraft Products Group
1725 Jefferson Davis Hwy. Suite 900, Arlington, VA 22202
Telephone: (703) 521-6560

SMILEY, Donald E.
Vice President, Washington Office, Exxon Corp.
Suite 1100, 1899 L St., N.W., Washington, DC 20036
Telephone: (202) 862-0235
Registered as lobbyist at U.S. Congress.

SMITH, Barry W.
V. President, Southern Technical Services
Suite 610 Three Metro Center, Bethesda, MD 20814
Telephone: (301) 652-2500

SMITH, Bea Pace
Director, Federal Relations, Nat'l Ass'n for Equal Opportunity in Higher Education
400 12th St., N.E. 2nd Floor, Washington, DC 20002
Telephone: (202) 543-9111

SMITH, Becky J.
Exec. Director, Ass'n for the Advancement of Health Education
1900 Association Drive, Reston, VA 22091
Telephone: (703) 476-3437

SMITH, Bemis
Legis Officer, Legis & Cong Rels, DEPARTMENT OF HOUSING AND URBAN DEVELOPMENT
451 Seventh St., S.W., Washington, DC 20410
Telephone: (202) 755-5005

SMITH, Brenda
Attorney, Nat'l Women's Law Center
1616 P St., N.W., Washington, DC 20036
Telephone: (202) 328-5160

SMITH, Brian P.
Exec. V. President, Dep., Chicago Optns., United States League of Savings Institutions
1709 New York Ave., N.W., Suite 801, Washington, DC 20006
Telephone: (202) 637-8900

SMITH, BUCKLIN AND ASSOCIATES
1101 Connecticut Ave., N.W., Suite 700, Washington, DC 20036
Telephone: (202) 857-1100
Background: A Chicago-based association management firm.
Members of firm representing listed organizations:
  Brown, Melissa P.
  Cantor, Donna F.
    Background: Exec. Director, Ass'n for Hospital Medical Education, Council on Continuing Education Unit, and Nat'l Certification Agency for Medical Personnel.
  Chancler, Robert T., V. President
    Background: Serves as Exec. Director of Commercial Refrigerator Manufacturers Ass'n, American Wire Producers Ass'n, Internat'l Ass'n of Airport Duty Free Shops and of the Nat'l Ass'n of Corporate Treasurers.
  DelPolito, Carolyn M. (Ph.D.)
    Background: Exec. Director, American Soc. of Allied Health Professions.
  Ekedahl, Duane H.
    Background: Serves as Exec. Manager, Regional Airline Ass'n and Exec. Director, Pet Food Institute.
  Finn, Susan Kudla
    Background: Serves as Director of Legislative Affairs, Pet Food Institute and Exec. Director, American Women in Radio and Television.
  Fredericksen, John S.
    Background: Serves as President, Regional Airline Ass'n.
  Griffiths, Mark N.
    Background: Serves as Director of Government Relations, Nat'l Ass'n of Metal Finishers and Adhesive Manufacturers Ass'n.
  Hamm, Michael
    Background: Serves as Exec. Director, American Ass'n for Medical Systems and Informatics and Exec. Director, Nat'l Organization for Competency Assurance.
  Hobson, David
    Background: Administrative Director, Internat'l District Heating and Cooling Ass'n and Exec. Director, Ass'n for Governmental Leasing and Financing.
  Horner, Patricia I.
    Background: Serves as Exec. Director of Alliance for Engineering in Medicine and Biology, Rehabilitation Engineering Society of North America, Society of Non-Invasive Vascular Technology and Ass'n for the Advancement of Rehabilitative Technology.
  Keithley, Carter E., V. President
    Background: Serves as Exec. Director, Wood Heating Alliance, and Exec. Director, Regulatory Affairs Professionals Soc.
  Ladomirak, Deborah
    Background: Serves as V. President, Director of Public Affairs, Regional Airline Ass'n.
  Lively, Carol A.
    Background: V. President, Smith, Bucklin and Associates. Serves as Exec. Director, Nat'l Ass'n of Hospital Admitting Managers; Exec. Director, Forum for Health Care Planning; and Exec. Director, American College of Nuclear Physicians.
  McComas, Harry G. (Skip)
    Background: Account Executive for Chain Link Fence Manufacturers Institute, Independent Electrical Contractors and Internat'l Slurry Seal Ass'n.
  Murphy, John C.
    Background: Serves as Exec. Director, Ass'n of Local Housing Finance Agencies and Privatization Council.

SMITH, BUCKLIN AND ASSOCIATES (Cont'd)

Payne, Michael L., V. President
Background: Serves as President, Anti-Friction Bearing Manufacturers Ass'n and Exec. Director, Financial Stationers Ass'n.

Rugh, Timothy
Background: Serves as Director for the Porcelain Enamel Institute and Director, Regulatory Affairs for the Pet Food Institute.

Smeage, Dennis
Terwilliger, James, Director of Gov't Affairs
Walker, Judith
Background: Exec. Director, Museum Trustee Ass'n and American Soc. of Nephrology.

Wilbur, Robert H., V. President, Government Relations
Background: Serves as Exec. Director, Ass'n of Professors of Medicine; V. President, Government Relations of the Health Industry Distributors Ass'n; Director of Government Relations of the Battery Council Internat'l, Amusement and Music Operators Ass'n, the Nat'l Ass'n of Food Equipment Manufacturers and the Popcorn Institute.

Wood, Victoria
Clients:
Adhesives Manufacturers Ass'n *(Mark N. Griffiths, Robert H. Wilbur)*
American Ass'n for Medical Systems and Informatics (AAMSI) *(Michael Hamm)*
American College of Nuclear Physicians *(Carol A. Lively)*
American Guild of Patient Account Management *(Dennis Smeage)*
American Soc. of Allied Health Professions *(Carolyn M. DelPolito, Ph.D.)*
American Soc. of Nephrology *(Judith Walker)*
American Wire Producers Ass'n *(Robert T. Chancler)*
American Women in Radio and Television *(Susan Kudla Finn)*
Amusement and Music Operators Ass'n *(Robert H. Wilbur)*
Amusement and Music Operators Ass'n Political Action Committee *(Robert H. Wilbur)*
Anti-Friction Bearing Manufacturers Ass'n *(Michael L. Payne)*
Ass'n for Governmental Leasing and Financing *(David Hobson)*
Ass'n for Hospital Medical Education *(Donna F. Cantor)*
Ass'n of Local Housing Finance Agencies *(John C. Murphy)*
Ass'n of Professors of Medicine *(James Terwilliger)*
Commercial Refrigerator Manufacturers Ass'n *(Robert T. Chancler)*
Council on Continuing Education Unit *(Donna F. Cantor)*
Financial Stationers Ass'n *(Michael L. Payne)*
Forum for Health Care Planning *(Carol A. Lively)*
Health Industry Distributors Ass'n *(Robert H. Wilbur)*
Health Industry Distributors Ass'n Political Action Committee *(Robert H. Wilbur)*
Internat'l Ass'n of Airport Duty Free Stores *(Robert T. Chancler)*
Internat'l District Heating and Cooling Ass'n *(David Hobson)*
Internat'l Slurry Seal Ass'n *(Harry G., Skip McComas)*
Museum Trustee Ass'n *(Victoria Wood)*
Nat'l Ass'n of Corporate Treasurers *(Robert T. Chancler)*
Nat'l Ass'n of Food Equipment Manufacturers *(Robert H. Wilbur)*
Nat'l Ass'n of Hospital Admitting Managers *(Carol A. Lively)*
Nat'l Ass'n of Metal Finishers *(Mark N. Griffiths)*
Nat'l Ass'n of Metal Finishers Political Action Committee
Nat'l Commission Certifying Agencies *(Michael Hamm)*
Nat'l Organization for Competency Assurance *(Michael Hamm)*
Pet Food Institute *(Duane H. Ekedahl, Susan Kudla Finn, Timothy Rugh)*
Popcorn Institute *(Robert H. Wilbur)*
Porcelain Enamel Institute *(Timothy Rugh)*
Privatization Council *(John C. Murphy)*
Regional Airline Ass'n *(Duane H. Ekedahl, Deborah Ladomirak)*

Regional Airlines Ass'n Political Action Committee *(Duane H. Ekedahl)*
Regulatory Affairs Professionals Soc. *(Carter E. Keithley)*
RESNA *(Patricia I. Horner)*
Soc. of Vascular Technology *(Patricia I. Horner)*
Southern Cemetery Ass'n *(Harry G., Skip McComas)*
Wood Heating Alliance *(Carter E. Keithley)*

SMITH, C. Douglas
Corporate Manager, Gov't & Indus. Rtns., Toyota Motor Sales, U.S.A.
1850 M St., N.W., Suite 600, Washington, DC 20036
Telephone: (202) 775-1700
Registered as lobbyist at U.S. Congress.

SMITH, Caroline A.
Staff Attorney, Congress Watch
215 Pennsylvania Ave., S.E., Washington, DC 20003
Telephone: (202) 546-4996
Registered as lobbyist at U.S. Congress.

SMITH, Catherine S.
V. President, Dev'lpmnt & Public Affairs, Cato Institute
224 Second St., S.E., Washington, DC 20003
Telephone: (202) 546-0200

SMITH, Capt. Charles J., USN (Ret.)
Exec. Director, American Soc. of Naval Engineers
1452 Duke St., Alexandria, VA 22314
Telephone: (703) 836-6727

SMITH CO., Gordon L.
1030 15th St., N.W., Suite 920, Washington, DC 20005
Telephone: (202) 842-1479
Members of firm representing listed organizations:
Smith, Gordon L., President

SMITH CO., INC., Wayne
1300 L St., N.W. Suite 1050, Washington, DC 20005
Telephone: (202) 484-5623
Members of firm representing listed organizations:
Smith, Wayne J., President
Background: Chairman, Small Business Legislative Council, 1988-89.
Organizations represented:
United Bus Owners of America *(Wayne J. Smith)*

SMITH, Creg
External Liaison Representative, American Petroleum Institute
1220 L St., N.W., Washington, DC 20005
Telephone: (202) 682-8292

SMITH, Daniel C.
Arent, Fox, Kintner, Plotkin & Kahn
1050 Connecticut Ave., N.W., Washington, DC 20036-5339
Telephone: (202) 857-6000
Registered as lobbyist at U.S. Congress.
Background: Attorney, Federal Trade Commission, 1966-1969.
Clients:
Nat'l Field Selling Ass'n

SMITH, David S.
Smith, Heenan and Althen
1110 Vermont Ave., N.W., Suite 400, Washington, DC 20005
Telephone: (202) 887-0800
Clients:
Lone Star Industries

SMITH DAWSON & ANDREWS, INC.
1000 Connecticut Ave., N.W., Suite 304, Washington, DC 20036
Telephone: (202) 835-0740
Background: A government affairs consulting firm.
Members of firm representing listed organizations:
Andrews, Gregory B.
Dawson, Thomas C.
Smith, James P., President
Clients:
Bank St. College *(Thomas C. Dawson, James P. Smith)*
Clarke & Co. *(Gregory B. Andrews)*
Eugene, Oregon, City of *(Gregory B. Andrews, Thomas C. Dawson, James P. Smith)*
Illinois Diversatech Corp. *(James P. Smith)*

New York Metropolitan Transportation Authority *(Thomas C. Dawson, James P. Smith)*
Power Packaging Inc. *(Gregory B. Andrews, James P. Smith)*
S & F Warehouses, Inc. *(Gregory B. Andrews, James P. Smith)*
San Francisco, California, City of *(Thomas C. Dawson)*
San Francisco Public Utilities Commission *(Thomas C. Dawson, James P. Smith)*

SMITH, Donald P.
Sr. Assoc. & Director of Legis. Affairs, Cassidy and Associates, Inc.
655 15th St., N.W., Suite 1100, Washington, DC 20005
Telephone: (202) 347-0773
Background: Staff Ass't to the House Committee on Appropriations, 1975-87. Budget Examiner, Office of Management and Budget, 1972-75.
Clients:
Boston University
Catholic University of America
Challenger Center for Space Science Education
Children's Hospital Nat'l Medical Center
Children's Hospital of Michigan
Loma Linda University
Louisiana Public Facilities Authority
Michigan Biotechnology Institute
Michigan Technological University
Mount Sinai Medical Center of Greater Miami
Pennsylvania Turnpike Commission
University of Nebraska
University of Nebraska Foundation
West Virginia University
Western Townships Utilities Authority

SMITH, E. Del
President, Smith, Inc., E. Del
905 16th St., N.W., Suite 310, Washington, DC 20006
Telephone: (202) 638-5023
Registered as lobbyist at U.S. Congress.

SMITH, Elaine W.
Dir., Communications & Public Relations, Air Conditioning Contractors of America
1513 16th St., N.W., Washington, DC 20036
Telephone: (202) 483-9370

SMITH, Eleanor
Staff Attorney, Public Citizen Litigation Group
2000 P St., N.W., Suite 700, Washington, DC 20036
Telephone: (202) 785-3704
Background: Serves as contact for the Freedom of Information Clearinghouse.

SMITH, Elizabeth C.
Manager, HWAC Government Affairs, American Consulting Engineers Council
1015 15th St., N.W., Suite 802, Washington, DC 20005
Telephone: (202) 347-7474
Registered as lobbyist at U.S. Congress.

SMITH, Elizabeth M.
Legislative and Political Director, Amalgamated Clothing and Textile Workers Union
815 16th St., N.W., Suite 507, Washington, DC 20006
Telephone: (202) 628-0214
Registered as lobbyist at U.S. Congress.

SMITH, Ellen S.
Assistant Director, Government Relations, American Psychiatric Ass'n
1400 K St., N.W., Washington, DC 20005
Telephone: (202) 682-6194
Registered as lobbyist at U.S. Congress.

SMITH, Foster C., Jr.
Sr. V. Pres., Marketing/Communications, Nat'l Alliance of Business
1201 New York Ave., N.W., Suite 700, Washington, DC 20005
Telephone: (202) 289-2888

SMITH, Frances B.
V. Pres. & Director, Public Affairs, American Financial Services Ass'n
1101 14th St., N.W., Washington, DC 20005
Telephone: (202) 289-0400

SMITH, Frank P.
President, Systems Technology & Applied Research Corp.
Two Skyline Place, 5203 Leesburg Pike, Suite 1201, Falls Church, VA 22041
Telephone: (703) 931-7773

SMITH, Fred L., Jr.
President, Competitive Enterprise Institute
233 Pennsylvania Ave., S.E., Suite 200, Washington, DC 20003
Telephone: (202) 547-1010
Registered as lobbyist at U.S. Congress.
Background: Former Senior Policy Analyst, Environmental Protection Agency.

SMITH, Frederick P., Jr.
President, Institute of Makers of Explosives
1120 19th St., N.W., Suite 310, Washington, DC 20036-3605
Telephone: (202) 429-9280
Registered as lobbyist at U.S. Congress.
Background: Serves also as Treasurer, Institute of Makers of Explosives Political Action Committee.

SMITH, G. Wayne
President, Potomac Visions Limited
1111 14th St., N.W. Suite 1001, Washington, DC 20005
Telephone: (202) 289-3684
Registered as lobbyist at U.S. Congress.
Background: Former Administrative Assistant and Staff Director to Senator John Breaux (D-LA) and Deputy to the Chairman, Democratic Senatorial Campaign Committee.

SMITH, Georgiana B.
Manager, Public Affairs, American Insurance Ass'n
1130 Connecticut Ave., N.W., Suite 1000, Washington, DC 20036
Telephone: (202) 828-7100

SMITH, Gerard A.
V. President, Washington Operations, Raytheon Co.
1215 Jefferson Davis Hwy., Suite 1500, Arlington, VA 22202
Telephone: (703) 486-5400

SMITH, Gordon L.
President, Smith Co., Gordon L.
1030 15th St., N.W., Suite 920, Washington, DC 20005
Telephone: (202) 842-1479

SMITH AND HARROFF
11 Canal Center Plaza Suite 104, Alexandria, VA 22314
Telephone: (703) 683-8512
Clients:
  Centerior Energy Corp.

SMITH, HEENAN AND ALTHEN
1110 Vermont Ave., N.W., Suite 400, Washington, DC 20005
Telephone: (202) 887-0800
Members of firm representing listed organizations:
  Althen, William I.
    Background: Serves as General Counsel, American League of Lobbyists, 1983.
  Heenan, Michael T.
    Background: Trial Attorney, Division of Mine Health and Safety, Office of the Solicitor, U.S. Department of Interior, 1973-74.
  Lee, Kathryn
  Smith, David S.
Clients:
  American Institute of Biological Sciences
  American League of Lobbyists *(Kathryn Lee)*
  Barnes and Tucker Co. *(Michael T. Heenan)*
  General Portland Inc. *(Michael T. Heenan)*
  Hulcher Quarry, Inc. *(Michael T. Heenan)*
  Internat'l Electronic Facsimile Users Ass'n *(William I. Althen)*
  Lone Star Florida, Inc. *(Michael T. Heenan)*
  Lone Star Industries *(Michael T. Heenan, David S. Smith)*
  Nat'l Ass'n of Computer Stores *(William I. Althen)*
  Nemacolin Mines Corp. *(Michael T. Heenan)*
  New York Trap Rock Co.
  Olga Coal Co.
  Peter White Coal Mining Co. *(Michael T. Heenan)*
  Pittston Co., The
  Youngstown Mines Corp. *(Michael T. Heenan)*

SMITH, Hon. Henry P., III
Chairman, Ass'n to Unite the Democracies
1506 Pennsylvania Ave., S.E., Washington, DC 20003
Telephone: (202) 544-5150

SMITH AND HOWARD ASSOCIATES, INC.
P.O. Box 9406, McLean, VA 22102-0406
Telephone: (703) 356-3777
Members of firm representing listed organizations:
  Smith, Irving P., President
Clients:
  American Seating Co. *(Irving P. Smith)*
  Bergen Auto Upholstery Co. *(Irving P. Smith)*
  Cubic Western Data Corp. *(Irving P. Smith)*
  Escrow Institute of California *(Irving P. Smith)*

SMITH, INC., E. Del
905 16th St., N.W., Suite 310, Washington, DC 20006
Telephone: (202) 638-5023
Background: Government relations consulting.
Members of firm representing listed organizations:
  Smith, E. Del, President
Organizations represented:
  American Ass'n of Petroleum Geologists *(E. Del Smith)*
  Anaheim, California, City of *(E. Del Smith)*
  Cement Free Trade Ass'n *(E. Del Smith)*
  Dalan/Jupiter, Inc. *(E. Del Smith)*
  Houston Airlines *(E. Del Smith)*
  Laguna Beach, California, City of *(E. Del Smith)*
  Long Beach, California, City of *(E. Del Smith)*
  Long Beach, California, Port of *(E. Del Smith)*
  Long Beach Naval Shipyard Employees Ass'n *(E. Del Smith)*
  Los Angeles Community Redevelopment Agency *(E. Del Smith)*
  Los Angeles County, California *(E. Del Smith)*
  Northern California Power Agency *(E. Del Smith)*
  Santa Cruz, California, Port of *(E. Del Smith)*
  Santa Monica, California, City of *(E. Del Smith)*
  Signal Landmark *(E. Del Smith)*
  U.S. Escrow *(E. Del Smith)*

SMITH, Irving P.
President, Smith and Howard Associates, Inc.
P.O. Box 9406, McLean, VA 22102-0406
Telephone: (703) 356-3777
Clients:
  American Seating Co.
  Bergen Auto Upholstery Co.
  Cubic Western Data Corp.
  Escrow Institute of California

SMITH, J. Daniel
Exec. V. President, Propeller Club of the United States, The
3927 Old Lee Highway Suite 101A, Fairfax, VA 22030
Telephone: (703) 691-2777

SMITH, James E.
President, Walker Associates, Charls E.
1730 Pennsylvania Ave., N.W. Suite 200, Washington, DC 20006
Telephone: (202) 393-4760
Registered as lobbyist at U.S. Congress.
Registered as Foreign Agent: (#4180).
Background: Former Comptroller of the Currency.
Organizations represented:
  Federal Home Loan Mortgage Corp.

SMITH, James K.
Dir.-Federal Relations (Regulatory), Ameritech (American Information Technologies)
1050 Connecticut Ave., N.W., Suite 730, Washington, DC 20036
Telephone: (202) 955-3050

SMITH, James L.
Director of Market Relations, Nat'l Pork Board
501 School St., S.W. Suite 400, Washington, DC 20024
Telephone: (202) 554-3601
Background: Deputy Administrator of Packers & Stockyards, U.S. Dept. of Agriculture, 1979-87.

SMITH, James M.
President, Competitive Telecommunications Ass'n (COMP-TEL)
120 Maryland Ave., N.E., Washington, DC 20002
Telephone: (202) 546-9022

Registered as lobbyist at U.S. Congress.
Background: Also represents the Competitive Telecommunications Ass'n Political Action Committee (COMPTELPAC).

SMITH, James N.
V. President, Chambers Associates Incorporated
1625 K St., N.W. Suite 200, Washington, DC 20006
Telephone: (202) 857-0670
Background: Former Ass't Administrator, EPA; Deputy Director, National Commission on Water Quality.
Clients:
  Infrastructure Bond Coalition
  Manville Corp.
  Southwest Realty, Inc.

SMITH, James P.
President, Smith Dawson & Andrews, Inc.
1000 Connecticut Ave., N.W., Suite 304, Washington, DC 20036
Telephone: (202) 835-0740
Registered as lobbyist at U.S. Congress.
Clients:
  Bank St. College
  Eugene, Oregon, City of
  Illinois Diversatech Corp.
  New York Metropolitan Transportation Authority
  Power Packaging Inc.
  S & F Warehouses, Inc.
  San Francisco Public Utilities Commission

SMITH, Jay H.
Hill Group, Inc.
1200 17th St., N.W., Suite 400, Washington, DC 20036
Telephone: (202) 296-9200
Background: Serves as Exec. V. President, Nat'l Ass'n of Hose and Accessories Distributors.
Clients:
  Nat'l Ass'n of Hose and Accessories Distributors

SMITH, Jean
Executive Assistant, Corporate Relations, Alexander & Alexander Inc.
555 13th St., N.W. Suite 1180E, Washington, DC 20004-1109
Telephone: (202) 783-2550

SMITH, Jean
Exec. Associate, Population Ass'n of America
1429 Duke St., Alexandria, VA 22314-3402
Telephone: (703) 684-1221

SMITH, Jeffrey A.
V. President, Public Affairs, American Waterways Operators
1600 Wilson Blvd. Suite 1000, Arlington, VA 22209
Telephone: (703) 841-9300
Registered as lobbyist at U.S. Congress.

SMITH, Jeffrey C.
President, Washington Policy Advocates
312 Massachusetts Ave., N.E., Washington, DC 20002
Telephone: (202) 828-1977
Registered as lobbyist at U.S. Congress.
Clients:
  Commercial Weather Services Ass'n
  Committee for Private Offshore Rescue and Towing (C-PORT)
  Marine Contractors Alliance
  Spill-Net, Inc.

SMITH, Lt. Gen. Jeffrey G., USA (Ret.)
Director of Government Relations, Ethyl Corp.
1155 15th St., N.W., Suite 611, Washington, DC 20005
Telephone: (202) 223-4411

SMITH, Jeffrey H.
Arnold & Porter
1200 New Hampshire Ave., N.W., Washington, DC 20036
Telephone: (202) 872-6700
Registered as lobbyist at U.S. Congress.
Background: Member, Office of the Legal Adviser, U.S. Department of State, 1975-84. Staff, U.S. Senate Armed Services Committee, 1984-88.
Clients:
  Honeywell, Inc.

SMITH, Jennifer
Masaoka Associates, Mike
900 17th St., N.W., Suite 520, Washington, DC 20006
Telephone: (202) 296-4484
Registered as lobbyist at U.S. Congress.

SMITH, John
Comptroller, Air Force Ass'n
1501 Lee Hwy., Arlington, VA 22209-1198
Telephone: (703) 247-5800

SMITH, John T., II
Covington and Burling
1201 Pennsylvania Ave., N.W., Box 7566, Washington, DC 20044
Telephone: (202) 662-6000

SMITH, Joyce
Ass't for Congressional Affairs, Howard University
2400 6th St., N.W., Washington, DC 20059
Telephone: (202) 806-2150

SMITH, Kevin
Director, Federal Relations, US WEST, Inc.
1020 19th St., N.W., Suite 700, Washington, DC 20036
Telephone: (202) 429-3100
Registered as lobbyist at U.S. Congress.

SMITH, Larry E.
Griffin, Johnson & Associates
1211 Connecticut Ave., N.W., Suite 700, Washington, DC 20036
Telephone: (202) 775-8116
Registered as lobbyist at U.S. Congress.
Background: Former Minority Staff Director, Senate Committee on Rules and Administration. Deputy Sergeant at Arms, U.S. Senate, 1981-83. Sergeant at Arms, U.S. Senate, 1983-85.

SMITH, Dr. Marilyn M.
Exec. Director, Nat'l Ass'n for the Education of Young Children
1834 Connecticut Ave., N.W., Washington, DC 20009
Telephone: (202) 232-8777

SMITH, Michael
Steptoe and Johnson
1330 Connecticut Ave., N.W., Washington, DC 20036
Telephone: (202) 429-3000
Background: Former Deputy U.S. Trade Representative.

SMITH, Michael B.
President, SJS Advanced Strategies Inc.
1330 Connecticut Ave., N.W., Washington, DC 20036
Telephone: (202) 429-5500
Background: Former Deputy U.S. Trade Representative and Chief, U.S. Textile Negotiator. Former U.S. Ambassador to GATT.

SMITH, Michael C.
President, American Constitution Committee
7777 Leesburg Pike Suite 300 South, Falls Church, VA 22043
Telephone: (703) 790-5580

SMITH, Michael J., Jr.
Dir, Gov't Spend./Taxat'n, State & Munic, Nat'l Ass'n of REALTORS
777 14th St., N.W., Washington, DC 20005
Telephone: (202) 383-1000
Registered as lobbyist at U.S. Congress.

SMITH, Nancy
Cong Liaison, DEPARTMENT OF INTERIOR - Surface Mining
1951 Constitution Ave. N.W., Washington, DC 20240
Telephone: (202) 343-2165

SMITH, Patricia P.
Senior Coordinator, Health, American Ass'n of Retired Persons
1909 K St., N.W., Washington, DC 20049
Telephone: (202) 728-4612
Registered as lobbyist at U.S. Congress.

SMITH, Patrick F., Jr.
Director of Legislation, Nat'l Treasury Employees Union
1730 K St., N.W., Suite 1100, Washington, DC 20006
Telephone: (202) 785-4411
Registered as lobbyist at U.S. Congress.

Background: Responsibilities include the Nat'l Treasury Employees Political Action Committee.

SMITH, Paul
Federal Adminstrative Counsel, American Bankers Ass'n
1120 Connecticut Ave., N.W., Washington, DC 20036
Telephone: (202) 663-5000

SMITH, Paul
Manager, ATC Services, Nat'l Business Aircraft Ass'n
1200 18th St., N.W. Suite 200, Washington, DC 20036
Telephone: (202) 783-9000

SMITH, Paul C.
Wiley, Rein & Fielding
1776 K St., N.W., Tenth Floor, Washington, DC 20006-2359
Telephone: (202) 429-7000
Registered as lobbyist at U.S. Congress.
Clients:
Marine Mammal Coalition
Nat'l Ass'n of Public Television Stations
Public Broadcasting Service
United Parcel Service

SMITH, Peter
Director of Public Affairs, Ass'n of American Universities
One Dupont Circle, N.W. Suite 730, Washington, DC 20036
Telephone: (202) 466-5030
Background: Former Press Secretary to Senator Joseph Biden (D-DE).

SMITH, Philip A.
Director of Communications, Nat'l School Boards Ass'n
1680 Duke St., Alexandria, VA 22314
Telephone: (703) 838-6722

SMITH, Richard F.
Director, Government Affairs, Textron Inc.
1090 Vermont Ave., N.W., Suite 1100, Washington, DC 20005
Telephone: (202) 289-5800
Registered as lobbyist at U.S. Congress.

SMITH, Richard M.
Mayer, Brown and Platt
2000 Pennsylvania Ave., N.W. Suite 6500, Washington, DC 20006
Telephone: (202) 463-2000
Background: Special Counsel, Federal Power Commission, 1977. Member, White House Energy, Policy and Planning Staff, 1978. Director, Office of Policy Coordination, Department of Energy, 1978-79.

SMITH, Rita
Admin. Director, Nat'l Taxpayers Union
713 Maryland Ave., N.E., Washington, DC 20002
Telephone: (202) 543-1300

SMITH, Robert E.
Director, Federal Gov't Relations, Olin Corp.
1730 K St., N.W., Suite 1300, Washington, DC 20006
Telephone: (202) 331-7400
Registered as lobbyist at U.S. Congress.
Background: Also serves as Vice Chairman, Olin Corp. Good Gov't Fund.

SMITH, Robert L., Jr.
Exec. Director, Videotex Industry Ass'n
8403 Colesville Road Suite 865, Silver Spring, MD 20910
Telephone: (301) 495-4955

SMITH, Robert M.
President, Targeted Communications Corp.
1807 Michael Faraday Court, Reston, VA 22090
Telephone: (703) 742-7888

SMITH, Sandra G.
Dir., Business and Industry Relations, Nat'l Ass'n of Trade and Technical Schools
2251 Wisconsin Ave., N.W. Suite 200, Washington, DC 20007
Telephone: (202) 333-1021

SMITH, Sara Hope
Director, Federal Relations, Pacific Telesis Group-Washington
1275 Pennsylvania Ave., N.W. Suite 400, Washington, DC 20004

Telephone: (202) 383-6400
Registered as lobbyist at U.S. Congress.

SMITH, Steven
Legislative Counsel, Human Rights Campaign Fund
1012 14th St., N.W. Suite 607, Washington, DC 20005
Telephone: (202) 628-4160
Registered as lobbyist at U.S. Congress.

SMITH, Susan A.
Associate Legislative Director, Nat'l Right to Life Committee
419 7th St., N.W. Suite 500, Washington, DC 20004
Telephone: (202) 626-8820
Registered as lobbyist at U.S. Congress.

SMITH, Susan J.
Program Manager, Nat'l Collaboration for Youth
1319 F St., N.W., Suite 601, Washington, DC 20004
Telephone: (202) 347-2080

SMITH, Susan Snyder
Director, Public and Legislative Affairs, Chocolate Manufacturers Ass'n of the U.S.A.
7900 Westpark Drive Suite A320, McLean, VA 22101
Telephone: (703) 790-5011
Registered as lobbyist at U.S. Congress.

SMITH, Thomas B.
Director of Research, American Security Council Foundation
733 15th St., N.W. Suite 700, Washington, DC 20005
Telephone: (202) 484-1676

SMITH, Timothy E.
General Counsel, American Nuclear Energy Council
410 First St., S.E. Third Floor, Washington, DC 20003
Telephone: (202) 484-2670
Registered as lobbyist at U.S. Congress.

SMITH, Vaughan A.
President, American Ass'n of Healthcare Consultants
11208 Waples Mill Road, Suite 109, Fairfax, VA 22030
Telephone: (703) 691-2242

SMITH, Velma
Dir., Ground Water Protection Project, Friends of the Earth
218 D St., S.E., Washington, DC 20003
Telephone: (202) 544-2600
Registered as lobbyist at U.S. Congress.

SMITH, Walter R.
Director, Communications, GEICO Corp.
GEICO Plaza, Washington, DC 20076
Telephone: (301) 986-3000

SMITH, Wayne J.
President, Smith Co., Inc., Wayne
1300 L St., N.W. Suite 1050, Washington, DC 20005
Telephone: (202) 484-5623
Background: Chairman, Small Business Legislative Council, 1988-89.
Organizations represented:
United Bus Owners of America

SMITH, William A.
Exec. V. President, Academy for Educational Development
1255 23rd St., N.W., Washington, DC 20037
Telephone: (202) 862-1900

SMITH, William C.
V. President, Schlossberg Assoc., Ken
317 Massachusetts Ave., N.E. Suite 200, Washington, DC 20002
Telephone: (202) 544-6796
Registered as lobbyist at U.S. Congress.
Organizations represented:
Alliance for Maritime Heritage Foundation
Bowman Gray School of Medicine of Wake Forest University
Nat'l Shipwreck Alliance
US Tall Ship Foundation

SMITH, William G.
Director, Public Affairs, Veterans of Foreign Wars of the U.S.
200 Maryland Ave., N.E., Washington, DC 20002
Telephone: (202) 543-2239

SMITH, Gen. William Y.
President, Institute for Defense Analyses
1801 North Beauregard St., Alexandria, VA 22311
Telephone: (703) 845-2300
Background: Also serves on the Board of Directors, American Council on Germany.

SMOCK, David
Exec. Director, Internat'l Voluntary Services
1424 16th St., N.W. Suite 204, Washington, DC 20036
Telephone: (202) 387-5533

SMOOT, Oliver R.
Exec. V. President and Treasurer, Computer and Business Equipment Manufacturers Ass'n
311 First St., N.W. Suite 500, Washington, DC 20001
Telephone: (202) 737-8888

SMOOTS, Carol A.
Director, Government Relations, MidCon Corp.
1747 Pennsylvania Ave., N.W. Suite 300, Washington, DC 20006
Telephone: (202) 857-3075

SMUCKER, Robert M.
V. President, Government Relations, Independent Sector
1828 L St., N.W., Washington, DC 20036
Telephone: (202) 223-8100

SMULYAN, Deb
Deputy Director, Democratic Leadership Council
316 Pennsylvania Ave., S.E., Suite 500, Washington, DC 20003
Telephone: (202) 546-0007

SMYTH, Matthew D.
V. President, Jar-Mon Consultants, Inc.
214 Massachusetts Ave., N.E. Suite 300, Washington, DC 20002
Telephone: (202) 547-7150
Clients:
American Council for Free Asia

SNAPE, Dale
Principal, Wexler, Reynolds, Fuller, Harrison and Schule, Inc.
1317 F St., N.W., Suite 600, Washington, DC 20004
Telephone: (202) 638-2121
Registered as lobbyist at U.S. Congress.
Clients:
Motion Picture Ass'n of America
Nat'l Gypsum Co.

SNAVELY, KING AND ASSOCIATES
1220 L St., N.W., Suite 410, Washington, DC 20005
Telephone: (202) 371-1111
Members of firm representing listed organizations:
Majoros, Michael, V. President
O'Connor, Tom, V. President
  Background: Economist, Interstate Commerce Commission, 1973-75. Manager, Local Rail Planning, United States Railroad Administration, 1975-77.
Parrish, Donald, V. President
Paulovic, Karl, V. President
Clients:
Burlington Northern Railroad
Canadian Pacific
Dow Jones & Co., Inc.
New York Transit Authority
Puerto Rico Telephone Co.
Wall Street Journal

SNEED, James
McDermott, Will and Emery
1850 K St., N.W., Suite 500, Washington, DC 20006-2296
Telephone: (202) 887-8000
Clients:
Illinois Cereal Mills

SNELL, Peter Leigh
V. President, Vienna & Associates, David
401 Wythe St., Suite 2-A, Alexandria, VA 22314
Telephone: (703) 684-5236
Registered as lobbyist at U.S. Congress.
Background: Former Legislative Counsel to Senator Sam Nunn (D-GA).
Organizations represented:
California Board of Equalization
California Franchise Tax Board

California State Senate
Pacific Stock Exchange, Inc., The

SNOW, Eric P.
Legislative Assistant, American Maritime Congress
444 N. Capitol St., N.W., Suite 801, Washington, DC 20001
Telephone: (202) 877-4477
Registered as lobbyist at U.S. Congress.

SNOW, Gerard C.
Director of Federal Affairs, Transportation Institute
5201 Auth Way, Camp Springs, MD 20746
Telephone: (301) 423-3335
Registered as lobbyist at U.S. Congress.

SNYDER BALL KRISER AND ASSOCIATES, INC.
499 S. Capitol St., S.W., Suite 520, Washington, DC 20003
Telephone: (202) 488-4960
Background: A firm of government operations consultants.
Members of firm representing listed organizations:
Ball, Thomas J., Associate
Kriser, Lou, President
Snyder, Edwin K., Associate
Clients:
Alloy Surfaces, Inc. *(Lou Kriser)*
General Motors (Allison Gas Turbines Division) *(Lou Kriser)*
Service Engineering Co. *(Lou Kriser)*

SNYDER, Bradley J.
President, Army & Air Force Mutual Aid Ass'n
Fort Myer, Bldg. #468, Arlington, VA 22211-3307
Telephone: (703) 522-3060

SNYDER, David F.
Counsel, American Insurance Ass'n
1130 Connecticut Ave., N.W., Suite 1000, Washington, DC 20036
Telephone: (202) 828-7100
Registered as lobbyist at U.S. Congress.

SNYDER, Edwin K.
Associate, Snyder Ball Kriser and Associates, Inc.
499 S. Capitol St., S.W., Suite 520, Washington, DC 20003
Telephone: (202) 488-4960
Registered as lobbyist at U.S. Congress.
Registered as Foreign Agent: (#3655).

SNYDER, George T., Jr.
Chief Executive, American Bus Ass'n
1015 15th St., N.W. Suite 250, Washington, DC 20005
Telephone: (202) 842-1645

SNYDER, Jeffrey L.
Graham and James
2000 M St., N.W., Suite 700, Washington, DC 20036
Telephone: (202) 463-0800
Clients:
ICI Americas Inc.
TDK U.S.A. Corp.

SNYDER, John M.
Public Affairs Director, Citizens Committee for the Right to Keep and Bear Arms
600 Pennsylvania Ave., S.E. Suite 205, Washington, DC 20003
Telephone: (202) 543-3363
Registered as lobbyist at U.S. Congress.

SNYDER, Keith D.
Coordinator, Veterans Education Project
Box 42130, Washington, DC 20015
Telephone: (202) 547-8387

SNYDER, Lynn S.
Epstein Becker and Green
1227 25th St., N.W., Suite 700, Washington, DC 20037
Telephone: (202) 861-0900
Clients:
American Managed Care and Review Ass'n

SNYDER, Richard D.
Exec. V. President and General Manager, Asphalt Roofing Manufacturers Ass'n
6288 Montrose Road, Rockville, MD 20852
Telephone: (301) 231-9050

Registered as lobbyist at U.S. Congress.

SNYDER, Russell K.
Assistant to the Exec. V. President, Asphalt Roofing Manufacturers Ass'n
6288 Montrose Road, Rockville, MD 20852
Telephone: (301) 231-9050

SNYDER, Shelly R.
Asst. to the Director of Communication, General Aviation Manufacturers Ass'n
1400 K St., Suite 801, Washington, DC 20005
Telephone: (202) 393-1500

SNYDER, Wallace S.
Sr. V. Pres., Gov't Rels./Gen. Counsel, American Advertising Federation
1400 K St., N.W., Suite 1000, Washington, DC 20005
Telephone: (202) 898-0089
Registered as lobbyist at U.S. Congress.
Background: Former Associate Director, Advertising Practices, Bureau of Consumer Protection, Federal Trade Commission. Serves as Treasurer, American Advertising Federation Political Action Committee.

SOBBA, Alan C.
Director, Taxes and Credit, Nat'l Cattlemen's Ass'n
1301 Pennsylvania Ave., N.W., Suite 300, Washington, DC 20004
Telephone: (202) 347-0228
Registered as lobbyist at U.S. Congress.

SOBOTA, Lisa J.
Legislative Assistant, Ass'n of American Railroads
50 F St., N.W., Suite 12802, Washington, DC 20001
Telephone: (202) 639-2532

SOCIETY AND ASSOCIATION SERVICES CORP.
8000 Westpark Drive Suite 130, McLean, VA 22102
Telephone: (703) 790-1745
Background: A multiple association management firm.
Members of firm representing listed organizations:
Burk, Richard J. (Jr.), President
Clients:
American Board of Health Physics *(Richard J. Burk, Jr.)*
American Soc. for Photobiology *(Richard J. Burk, Jr.)*
Health Physics Soc. *(Richard J. Burk, Jr.)*
Soc. for Risk Analysis *(Richard J. Burk, Jr.)*

SOCKBESON, Henry J.
Directing Attorney, Native American Rights Fund
1712 N St., N.W., Washington, DC 20036
Telephone: (202) 785-4166

SODOLSKI, John
President, United States Telephone Ass'n
900 19th St., N.W., Suite 800, Washington, DC 20006-2102
Telephone: (202) 835-3100

SOFFER, Lynn
Physician, Public Citizen Health Research Group
2000 P St., N.W., Suite 700, Washington, DC 20036
Telephone: (202) 872-0320
Registered as lobbyist at U.S. Congress.

SOHN, Gigi B.
Staff Attorney, Media Access Project
2000 M St., N.W., Suite 400, Washington, DC 20036
Telephone: (202) 232-4300

SOHN, Michael N.
Arnold & Porter
1200 New Hampshire Ave., N.W., Washington, DC 20036
Telephone: (202) 872-6700
Background: Attorney and Supervising Attorney, General Counsel's Office, National Labor Relations Board, 1964-69. General Counsel, Federal Trade Commission, 1977-80.

SOKLER, Bruce D.
Mintz, Levin, Cohn, Ferris, Glovsky and Popeo, P.C.
1825 Eye St., N.W. 12th Floor, Washington, DC 20006
Telephone: (202) 293-0500
Clients:
Chain Pharmacy Ass'n of New York State

WASHINGTON REPRESENTATIVES

SOLDOVERE, Francis J.
Exec. Director, American Kidney Fund
6110 Executive Blvd., Rockville, MD 20852
Telephone: (301) 881-3052

SOLES, Thomas J., Jr.
Director, Insurance and Safety, Sheet Metal and Air Conditioning Contractors' Nat'l Ass'n
8224 Old Courthouse Rd., Vienna, VA 22182
Telephone: (703) 790-9890
Registered as lobbyist at U.S. Congress.

SOLEY, Mary
V. President, National Programs, Foreign Policy Ass'n
1726 M St., N.W., Suite 800, Washington, DC 20036
Telephone: (202) 293-0046

SOLHEIM, Linda
Dir, Legis Affrs, FEDERAL COMMUNICATIONS COMMISSION
1919 M St., N.W., Washington, DC 20554
Telephone: (202) 632-6405

SOLL, Joy A.
V. President, Travel and Tourism Group, Harrison Co., E. Bruce
1440 New York Ave., N.W. Suite 300, Washington, DC 20005
Telephone: (202) 638-1200

SOLLEE, William
Ivins, Phillips and Barker
1700 Pennsylvania Ave., N.W., Suite 600, Washington, DC 20006
Telephone: (202) 393-7600

SOLOMON, Benna Ruth
Chief Counsel, Academy for State and Local Government
444 North Capitol St., N.W., Suite 349, Washington, DC 20001
Telephone: (202) 638-1445
Background: Responsibilities include the State and Local Legal Center.

SOLOMON, Karen
Regul & Legis Div, Office of Chief Couns, DEPARTMENT OF TREASURY - Thrift Supervision Office
1700 G St., N.W., Washington, DC 20552
Telephone: (202) 906-6804

SOLOMON, Larry
Deputy Director, Nat'l Institute of Corrections
320 First St., N.W. Room 200, Washington, DC 20534
Telephone: (202) 724-3106

SOLOMON, Michael F.
Ivins, Phillips and Barker
1700 Pennsylvania Ave., N.W., Suite 600, Washington, DC 20006
Telephone: (202) 393-7600
Registered as lobbyist at U.S. Congress.
Clients:
  The Limited, Inc.

SOLOMON, Richard A.
Wilner and Scheiner
1200 New Hampshire Ave., N.W., Suite 300, Washington, DC 20036
Telephone: (202) 861-7800
Background: Assistant General Counsel, Federal Communications Commission, 1952-58. Chief, Appellate Section, Antitrust Division, Department of Justice, 1960-62. General Counsel, Federal Power Commission, 1962-69.
Clients:
  Consolidated Edison Co. of New York
  Nat'l Distillers and Chemical Corp.

SOLOWIEJ, Sandra M.
Associated General Contractors of America
1957 E St., N.W., Washington, DC 20006
Telephone: (202) 393-2040
Registered as lobbyist at U.S. Congress.

SOLT, Barbara
Director, Lutheran Social Services Community Justice Ministries
2635 16th St., N.W., Washington, DC 20009
Telephone: (202) 232-6373

SOLTERS, Joseph J.
Manager, Government Affairs, Panhandle Eastern Corp.
1025 Connecticut Ave., N.W., Suite 404, Washington, DC 20036
Telephone: (202) 331-8090

SOMBROTTO, Vincent R.
President, Nat'l Ass'n of Letter Carriers of the United States of America
100 Indiana Ave., N.W., Washington, DC 20001
Telephone: (202) 393-4695
Registered as lobbyist at U.S. Congress.

SOME ASSOCIATES, Steven E.
2000 M St., N.W., Suite 380, Washington, DC 20036
Telephone: (202) 659-0295
Members of firm representing listed organizations:
  Some, Steven E., President
    Background: Former Special Ass't to the Sec. of Labor, Special Ass't to the Assistant Secretary of Labor for Employment and Training and Special Assistant to the Director of Congressional and Legislative Affairs in the Department of Interior.
  Organizations represented:
    Coastal Corp., The/ANR Pipeline Co.
    Potomac Hotel Group *(Steven E. Some)*

SOME, Steven E.
President, Some Associates, Steven E.
2000 M St., N.W., Suite 380, Washington, DC 20036
Telephone: (202) 659-0295
Registered as lobbyist at U.S. Congress.
Background: Former Special Ass't to the Sec. of Labor, Special Ass't to the Assistant Secretary of Labor for Employment and Training and Special Assistant to the Director of Congressional and Legislative Affairs in the Department of Interior.
Organizations represented:
  Potomac Hotel Group

SOMERS, Frederick P.
Director, Legislat. & Political Affairs, American Occupational Therapy Ass'n
1383 Piccard Drive, Suite 300 P.O. Box 1725, Rockville, MD 20850
Telephone: (301) 948-9626
Registered as lobbyist at U.S. Congress.

SOMERS, Pamela E.
Legis Counsel, DEPARTMENT OF INTERIOR
18th and C Sts., N.W., Washington, DC 20240
Telephone: (202) 343-7693

SOMERVILLE, Nancy C.
Sr. Director, State/Local Gov't Afrs., American Institute of Architects, The
1735 New York Ave., N.W., Washington, DC 20006
Telephone: (202) 626-7300
Registered as lobbyist at U.S. Congress.

SOMERVILLE, Ronald J.
Director, National Affairs, Wildlife Legislative Fund of America
1000 Connecticut Ave., N.W., Suite 1202, Washington, DC 20036
Telephone: (202) 466-4407
Registered as lobbyist at U.S. Congress.

SOMMER, A. A., Jr.
Morgan, Lewis and Bockius
1800 M St., N.W., Washington, DC 20036
Telephone: (202) 467-7000
Background: Commissioner, Securities and Exchange Commission, 1973-76. Member, Board of Directors, Consolidated Natural Gas Co.
Clients:
  Consolidated Natural Gas Co.

SOMMER, John F.
Director, National Veterans Affairs, American Legion
1608 K St., N.W., Washington, DC 20006
Telephone: (202) 861-2700

SOMMER, Judah C.
V. President and Manager, Goldman, Sachs and Co.
1101 Pennsylvania Ave., N.W. Suite 900, Washington, DC 20004
Telephone: (202) 637-3700
Registered as lobbyist at U.S. Congress.

Background: Serves also as Chariman, GSMMI Holdings Inc. PAC.

SOMMERHAUSER, James E.
President, Internat'l Federation of Professional and Technical Engineers
8701 Georgia Ave., Suite 701, Silver Spring, MD 20910
Telephone: (301) 565-9016
Registered as lobbyist at U.S. Congress.

SOMMERS, George A.
Manager, Federal Government Affairs, Marion Merrell Dow, Inc.
1776 Eye St., N.W. Suite 575, Washington, DC 20006
Telephone: (202) 429-3400

SONNEMAN, Jean
Attorney, Interstate Natural Gas Ass'n of America
555 13th St., N.W. Suite 300 West, Washington, DC 20004
Telephone: (202) 626-3200

SONNENBERG, Martin J.
V. President and Producer, Kamber Group, The
1920 L St., N.W., Washington, DC 20036
Telephone: (202) 223-8700

SONNENFELDT, Marjorie
Fleishman-Hillard, Inc
1301 Connecticut Ave., N.W., Washington, DC 20036
Telephone: (202) 659-0330

SONNENSCHEIN NATH & ROSENTHAL
1201 Pennsylvania Ave., N.W. Suite 700, Washington, DC 20004
Telephone: (202) 637-2000
Members of firm representing listed organizations:
  Frank, Susan M.
  Clients:
    Geneva Steel Co. *(Susan M. Frank)*

SONNENSTRAHL, Alfred
Exec. Director, Telecommunications for the Deaf
814 Thayer Ave., Silver Spring, MD 20910
Telephone: (301) 589-3786

SONOSKY, CHAMBERS AND SACHSE
1250 Eye St., N.W., Suite 1000, Washington, DC 20005
Telephone: (202) 682-0240
Members of firm representing listed organizations:
  Chambers, Reid Peyton
  Sachse, Harry R.
  Sonosky, Marvin J.
  Clients:
    Assiniboine and Sioux Tribes (Fort Peck Reservation)
    Hopi Tribe
    Multi-Housing Laundry Ass'n
    Puyallup Tribe of Indians
    Seneca Nation
    Standing Rock Sioux Tribe

SONOSKY, Jerome N.
Hogan and Hartson
555 13th St., N.W., Suite 1200, Washington, DC 20004-1109
Telephone: (202) 637-5600
Registered as lobbyist at U.S. Congress.
Background: Special Assistant to the Assistant Secretary for Legislation, Department of Health, Education and Welfare, 1961-63. Legislative Assistant to Senator Abraham Ribicoff of Connecticut 1963-65. Staff Director and General Counsel, Senate Subcommittee on Executive Reorganization, 1965-67.

SONOSKY, Marvin J.
Sonosky, Chambers and Sachse
1250 Eye St., N.W., Suite 1000, Washington, DC 20005
Telephone: (202) 682-0240

SOPHOS, Mary C.
Dep Asst Secy, Legis Affrs (House), DEPARTMENT OF TREASURY
15th and Pennsylvania Ave. N.W., Washington, DC 20220
Telephone: (202) 566-2037

SORG ASSOCIATES, Walter Larke
19110 Montgomery Village Ave. Suite 225, Gaithersburg, MD 20879

Telephone: (301) 330-9586

SOSNIK, Douglas B.
Political Director, Democratic Congressional Campaign Committee
430 South Capitol St., S.E. 2nd Floor, Washington, DC 20003
Telephone: (202) 863-1500

SOTOMAYOR, Dr. Marta
President, Nat'l Hispanic Council on Aging
2713 Ontario Road, N.W. Suite 200, Washington, DC 20009
Telephone: (202) 265-1288

SOUBY, James M.
Exec. Director, Council of State Policy and Planning Agencies
400 North Capitol St., N.W. Suite 285, Washington, DC 20001
Telephone: (202) 624-5386

SOUCY, Diane A.
V. President, Gov't & Internat'l Affairs, Mid-America Committee
1201 Connecticut Ave., N.W. Suite 300, Washington, DC 20036
Telephone: (202) 835-8813

SOUCY, Philip
Manager, Public Affairs - Defense Progs., British Aerospace, Inc./Defense Programs Office
1101 Wilson Blvd. Suite 1200, Arlington, VA 22209
Telephone: (703) 243-3939
Background: Former media spokesman, U.S. Department of Army. U.S. Army officer for 20 years.

SOUERS, Robert T.
V. President, Corporate Information, Marriott Corp.
One Marriott Drive, Washington, DC 20058
Telephone: (301) 380-9000

SOUK, Fred S.
Crowell and Moring
1001 Pennsylvania Ave., N.W., Washington, DC 20004-2505
Telephone: (202) 624-2500

SOUTH/NORTH DEVELOPMENT GROUP, LTD.
610 Fourth Place, S.W., Washington, DC 20024
Telephone: (202) 554-7032
Registered as Foreign Agent: (#4219)
Background: A consulting, lobbying and public relations firm.
Members of firm representing listed organizations:
Cooks, Shirley, Director
Cooks, Stoney, President
  Background: Administrative Assistant, U.S. Congress, 5th District, Georgia, 1973-77. Exec. Assistant to U.S. Ambassador to the United Nations, 1977-79.
Clients:
  Minorco Societe Anonyme *(Stoney Cooks)*

SOUTHWICK, Everett
Dep Asst Admin, Cong Relations, NAT'L AERONAUTICS AND SPACE ADMINISTRATION
400 Maryland Ave, S.W., Washington, DC 20546
Telephone: (202) 453-1055

SOUZA, Bonnie
Development Dir., Central American Proj., Friends of the Earth
218 D St., S.E., Washington, DC 20003
Telephone: (202) 544-2600
Registered as lobbyist at U.S. Congress.

SPAGNOLE, James
Dir, Cong and Legis Affrs, DEPARTMENT OF INTERIOR
18th and C Sts., N.W., Washington, DC 20240
Telephone: (202) 343-7693

SPAHR, Dr. Frederick T.
Exec. Director, American Speech-Language-Hearing Ass'n
10801 Rockville Pike, Rockville, MD 20852
Telephone: (301) 897-5700

SPAIN, Catherine L.
Director, Federal Liaison Center, Government Finance Officers Ass'n
1750 K St., N.W. Suite 200, Washington, DC 20006

Telephone: (202) 429-2750

SPAK, Walter J.
Willkie Farr and Gallagher
1155 21st St., N.W., 6th Fl., Washington, DC 20036-3302
Telephone: (202) 328-8000
Clients:
  Amalgamated Industrial Steel Mills of Malaysia
  Amalgamated Steel Mills of Malaysia
  Brazil Ministry of Finance
  Cementos de Chihuahua
  Duferco Ltd.
  Malaysia Ministry of Trade
  Minbea Singapore
  Nat'l Iron and Steel of Singapore
  Power Electronics
  Singapore Trade Development Board
  Southern Iron and Steel Works

SPANGLER, Susan E.
Assistant Exec. Director, Business Roundtable
1615 L St., N.W., Suite 1350, Washington, DC 20036
Telephone: (202) 872-1260
Registered as lobbyist at U.S. Congress.

SPANGLER, Thomas J.
Legislative Liaison, Nat'l Treasury Employees Union
1730 K St., N.W., Suite 1100, Washington, DC 20006
Telephone: (202) 785-4411
Registered as lobbyist at U.S. Congress.

SPARBER AND ASSOCIATES
1325 Pennsylvania Ave., N.W. Suite 500, Washington, DC 20006
Telephone: (202) 393-3240
Registered as lobbyist at U.S. Congress.
Members of firm representing listed organizations:
Sparber, Peter G.
Clients:
  Appleton Papers, Inc. *(Peter G. Sparber)*
  Nat'l Volunteer Fire Council *(Peter G. Sparber)*
  Tobacco Institute *(Peter G. Sparber)*

SPARBER, Peter G.
Sparber and Associates
1325 Pennsylvania Ave., N.W. Suite 500, Washington, DC 20006
Telephone: (202) 393-3240
Registered as lobbyist at U.S. Congress.
Clients:
  Appleton Papers, Inc.
  Nat'l Volunteer Fire Council
  Tobacco Institute

SPARKMAN AND COLE, INC.
1925 North Lynn St. Suite 308, Arlington, VA 22209
Telephone: (703) 522-7555
Background: Transportation consultants.
Members of firm representing listed organizations:
Cole, Timothy R.
Sparkman, D. Dean, Partner
Clients:
  Air Transport Ass'n of America *(Timothy R. Cole, D. Dean Sparkman)*
  Delta Air Lines *(Timothy R. Cole, D. Dean Sparkman)*
  Embry-Riddle Aeronautical University *(D. Dean Sparkman)*
  Nat'l Business Aircraft Ass'n *(Timothy R. Cole, D. Dean Sparkman)*
  Regional Airport Authority of Louisville *(Timothy R. Cole)*

SPARKMAN, D. Dean
Partner, Sparkman and Cole, Inc.
1925 North Lynn St. Suite 308, Arlington, VA 22209
Telephone: (703) 522-7555
Registered as lobbyist at U.S. Congress.
Clients:
  Air Transport Ass'n of America
  Delta Air Lines
  Embry-Riddle Aeronautical University
  Nat'l Business Aircraft Ass'n

SPARKMAN, John S.
Federal Affairs Representative, Baltimore Gas and Electric Co.
1100 Connecticut Ave., N.W., Suite 530, Washington, DC 20036
Telephone: (202) 861-0830

Registered as lobbyist at U.S. Congress.

SPARKS, Rear Adm. Bennett S., USCGR
Deputy Exec. Director, Reserve Officers Ass'n of the U.S.
1 Constitution Ave., N.E., Washington, DC 20002
Telephone: (202) 479-2200

SPARKS, David
V. President & Sr. Associate, Mahe Company, The Eddie
900 Second St., N.E. Suite 200, Washington, DC 20002
Telephone: (202) 842-4100

SPARKS, Philip L.
Co-Director, Communications Consortium
1333 H St., N.W., 11th Floor, Washington, DC 20005
Telephone: (202) 682-1270

SPATZ, Ian D.
Director, Ctr. for Pres. Policy Studies, Nat'l Trust for Historic Preservation
1785 Massachusetts Ave., N.W., Washington, DC 20036
Telephone: (202) 673-4000
Registered as lobbyist at U.S. Congress.

SPEAKS, Charles E., Ph.D.
Chair, Council on Professional Standards in Speech-Language Pathology and Audiology
10801 Rockville Pike, Rockville, MD 20852
Telephone: (301) 897-5700

SPEAR, Jonathan B.
Legislative Counsel, Pharmaceutical Manufacturers Ass'n
1100 15th St., N.W., Washington, DC 20005
Telephone: (202) 835-3400
Registered as lobbyist at U.S. Congress.

SPEAR, Sandra L.
Covington and Burling
1201 Pennsylvania Ave., N.W., Box 7566, Washington, DC 20044
Telephone: (202) 662-6000
Clients:
  Campbell Soup Co.

SPECIALTY CONTRACTORS MANAGEMENT, INC.
P.O. Box 42558, Northwest Station, Washington, DC 20015-0458
Telephone: (301) 933-7430
Members of firm representing listed organizations:
Kardy, Walter M., President
  Background: Serves as Exec. Director, Instrument Constructing and Engineering Ass'n, Inc.; Exec. Director, Quality Control Council of America; Exec. Director, Internat'l Council of Employers of Bricklayers and Allied Craftsmen; Director, Special Events, Foundation of Internat'l Meetings.
Clients:
  Instrument Constructing and Engineering Ass'n, Inc. *(Walter M. Kardy)*
  Instrument Technicians Labor-Management Cooperation Fund *(Walter M. Kardy)*
  Quality Control Council of America, Inc. *(Walter M. Kardy)*

SPECTOR, Phillip L.
Goldberg & Spector
1229 19th St., N.W., Washington, DC 20036
Telephone: (202) 429-4900
Registered as lobbyist at U.S. Congress.

SPEIDEL, J. Joseph
President, Population Crisis Committee
1120 19th St., N.W., Washington, DC 20036
Telephone: (202) 659-1833

SPEIGEL, Paul
Attorney, Legislation Div, DEPARTMENT OF HEALTH AND HUMAN SERVICES
200 Independence Ave., S.W., Washington, DC 20201
Telephone: (202) 245-7773

SPEISER, KRAUSE, MADOLE & LEAR
1216 16th St., N.W., Washington, DC 20036
Telephone: (202) 223-8501
Clients:
  Internat'l Soc. of Air Safety Investigators

SPELLANE, C. James
V. President, Kamber Group, The
1920 L St., N.W., Washington, DC 20036

SPELLANE, C. James (Cont'd)
Telephone: (202) 223-8700

SPENCE GROUP, THE
1776 Massachusetts Ave., N.W., Washington, DC 20036
Telephone: (202) 659-0600
Members of firm representing listed organizations:
Spence, Sandra
Clients:
Fire Equipment Manufacturers and Services
Ass'n *(Sandra Spence)*

SPENCE, Sandra
Exec. Director, Ass'n for Commuter Transportation
1776 Massachusetts Ave., N.W., Suite 521, Washington,
DC 20036
Telephone: (202) 659-0602
Registered as lobbyist at U.S. Congress.

SPENCE, Sandra
Spence Group, The
1776 Massachusetts Ave., N.W., Washington, DC 20036
Telephone: (202) 659-0600
Clients:
Fire Equipment Manufacturers and Services
Ass'n

SPENCER, Stuart K.
Hecht, Spencer & Associates
499 South Capitol St., S.W., Suite 507, Washington, DC
20003
Telephone: (202) 554-2881
Registered as Foreign Agent: (#3740).
Background: Chairman of the Board, Hecht, Spencer & Associates.

SPENCER, Virginia E.
Exec. Director, Nat'l American Indian Housing Council
122 C St., N.W., Suite 280, Washington, DC 20001
Telephone: (202) 783-2667

SPENCER, William B.
Washington Representative, Govt Affrs, Associated Builders and Contractors
729 15th St., N.W., Washington, DC 20005
Telephone: (202) 637-8800
Registered as lobbyist at U.S. Congress.

SPERLING, Gilbert
Katten, Muchin, Zavis & Dombroff
1275 Pennsylvania Ave., N.W. Suite 301, Washington, DC
20004
Telephone: (202) 626-6400
Clients:
Cogeneration and Independent Power Coalition
of America

SPESER, Dr. Philip
Chairman, Foresight Science & Technology, Inc.
2000 P St., N.W. Suite 305, Washington, DC 20036
Telephone: (202) 833-2322
Registered as lobbyist at U.S. Congress.

SPETH, James Gustave
President, World Resources Institute
1709 New York Ave., N.W., Washington, DC 20006
Telephone: (202) 638-6300
Background: Former Member and Chairman, U.S. Council
on Environmental Quality, 1977-81.

SPICKLER, Ray L.
Exec. V. President, Nat'l Air Traffic Controller Ass'n
444 N. Capitol St., Suite 845, Washington, DC 20001
Telephone: (202) 347-4572
Registered as lobbyist at U.S. Congress.

SPIEGEL, Daniel
Akin, Gump, Strauss, Hauer and Feld
1333 New Hampshire Ave., N.W., Suite 400, Washington,
DC 20036
Telephone: (202) 887-4000
Registered as Foreign Agent: (#3492).
Background: Special Trade Representative of the U.S.,
1977-79. Member, Board of Directors, PepsiCo, Inc.
1971-76. Special Assistant to Secretary of State Cyrus
Vance, 1977-78. State Department Policy Planning Staff,
1978-79.
Clients:
Grand Met USA

SPIEGEL AND MCDIARMID
1350 New York Ave., N.W., Suite 1100, Washington, DC
20005
Telephone: (202) 879-4000
Members of firm representing listed organizations:
Corbett, John J. (Jr.)
Davidson, Daniel I.
Background: Law Clerk, U.S. Court of Appeals, Second
Circuit, 1959-60. U.S. Department of State, 1965-68.
Delegate to Paris Peace Talks on Viet Nam, 1968.
Senior Staff, Nat'l Security Council, 1969.
Finkelstein, Ben
Francis, Frances E.
Background: Assistant to Federal Power Commission
Commissioner, 1965-68. Attorney, Federal Power
Commissioner, 1965-68.
Guttman, Daniel, Special Counsel
Background: Subcommittee on Civil Service and General Services, U.S. Senate Committee on Governmental Affairs, 1980.
Jablon, Robert A.
Matt, Peter K.
McDiarmid, Robert C.
Background: Attorney, Civil Division, Appellate Section, Department of Justice 1964-68. Assistant to the
General Counsel, Federal Power Commission, 1968-70.
Page, Nancy R.
Poirier, Marc R.
Roth, Alan J.
Van Eaton, Joseph
Clients:
Airline Passengers of America *(John J. Corbett, Jr.)*
Centralia, Pennsylvania, Former Residents of
Colorado Aviation Department (City and County
of Denver) *(John J. Corbett, Jr.)*
Connecticut Municipal Electric Energy Cooperative *(Frances E. Francis)*
Florida High Speed Rail Commission *(John J. Corbett, Jr.)*
Government Refuse Collection and Disposal
Ass'n
Manassas, Virginia, City of *(Marc R. Poirier)*
Northern California Power Agency *(Robert C. McDiarmid)*
Palo Alto, California, City of *(Joseph Van Eaton)*
Richmond Power and Light Co. *(Frances E. Francis)*
Sacramento Municipal Utility District *(Frances E. Francis, Peter K. Matt)*
Service Employees Internat'l Union
South Hadley, Massachusetts, Town of *(Ben Finkelstein, Nancy R. Page)*

SPIEGELMAN, James M.
Director of Research and Programs, Center for Internat'l
Business and Trade
Georgetown University 1242 35th St., N.W., Suite 501,
Washington, DC 20057
Telephone: (202) 687-6993

SPIELMAN, Alan P.
Exec. Dir., Gov't Programs Legislation, Blue Cross and
Blue Shield Ass'n
655 15th St., N.W., Suite 350, Washington, DC 20005
Telephone: (202) 626-4780
Registered as lobbyist at U.S. Congress.
Background: Former policy official with the Health Care
Financing Administration.

SPIELMANN, Solveig B.
Chairman and CEO, Internat'l Business-Government
Counsellors, Inc.
818 Connecticut Ave., N.W. Suite 1200, Washington, DC
20006
Telephone: (202) 872-8181
Clients:
Allen-Bradley Corp.

SPIEVACK, Edwin B.
President and Exec. Director, North American Telecommunications Ass'n
2000 M Street, N.W., Suite 550, Washington, DC 20036
Telephone: (202) 296-9800
Background: Responsible for North American Telecommunications Ass'n Political Action Committee.

SPILHAUS, Dr. Athelstan F., Jr.
Exec. Director, American Geophysical Union
2000 Florida Ave., N.W., Washington, DC 20009
Telephone: (202) 462-6900

SPILLER, Larry
Director of Special Projects, American Consulting Engineers Council
1015 15th St., N.W., Suite 802, Washington, DC 20005
Telephone: (202) 347-7474

SPIRO, Rear Adm. Robert H., USNR-Ret.
V. President, American Security Council
733 15th St., N.W. Suite 700, Washington, DC 20005
Telephone: (202) 484-1676
Background: Former Undersecretary of the Army in the
Carter Administration.

SPITZER, Arthur B.
Legal Director, American Civil Liberties Union of the Nat'l
Capital Area
1400 20th St., N.W. Suite 119, Washington, DC 20036
Telephone: (202) 457-0800

SPIVAK, Alvin A.
Corp. Dir., Public Affairs-Washington, General Dynamics
Corp.
1745 Jefferson Davis Hwy., Suite 1000, Arlington, VA
22202
Telephone: (703) 553-1224

SPIVY-WEBER, Frances
Director, Internat'l Program, Nat'l Audubon Soc.
801 Pennsylvania Ave., S.E., Washington, DC 20003
Telephone: (202) 547-9009
Registered as lobbyist at U.S. Congress.

SPLETE, Allen P.
President, Council of Independent Colleges
One Dupont Circle, N.W. Suite 320, Washington, DC
20036
Telephone: (202) 466-7230

SPODAK, William M.
Director, Government Relations, Westinghouse Electric
Corp.
1801 K St., N.W., Washington, DC
Telephone: (202) 835-2327
Registered as lobbyist at U.S. Congress.

SPOTTED ELK, Clara
Funke and Associates, Karl A.
729 2nd St., N.E., Washington, DC 20002
Telephone: (202) 544-4166

SPRADLIN, Thomas Richard
Stovall & Spradlin
2600 Virginia Ave., N.W., Suite 820, Washington, DC
20037
Telephone: (202) 333-8181
Background: Assistant to U.S. Senator Mike Monroney of
Oklahoma, 1956-63.

SPRAGUE, Lisa M.
Manager, Employee Benefits Policy, Chamber of Commerce of the U.S.A.
1615 H St., N.W., Washington, DC 20062
Telephone: (202) 659-6000
Registered as lobbyist at U.S. Congress.

SPRAGUE, Robin
Exec. Director, Young Republican Nat'l Federation
310 First St., S.E., Washington, DC 20003
Telephone: (202) 662-1340

SPRIGGS & HOLLINGSWORTH
1350 Eye St., N.W. 9th Floor, Washington, DC 20005-3304
Telephone: (202) 898-5800
Members of firm representing listed organizations:
Hollingsworth, Joe G.
Nellis, Joseph L., Of Counsel
Background: Chief Counsel, Senate Committee to Investigate Crime in Interstate Commerce, 1949-51.
Special Counsel, Senate Antitrust Subcommittee,
1963-64. Chief Counsel, Investigations Subcommittee,
House Select Business Committee, 1967-68. Special
Counsel, House Crime Committee, 1969-70. Chief
Counsel, House Narcotics Committee and General
Counsel House Judiciary Committee, 1976-81.

Spriggs, William J.
Clients:
Armstrong World Industries, Inc. *(Joe G. Hollingsworth)*
Eagle-Picher Industries *(William J. Spriggs)*

SPRIGGS, William J.
Spriggs & Hollingsworth
1350 Eye St., N.W. 9th Floor, Washington, DC 20005-3304
Telephone: (202) 898-5800
Registered as lobbyist at U.S. Congress.
Clients:
Eagle-Picher Industries

SPRING, Herbert Baker
Policy Analyst, Foreign Policy & Defense, Heritage Foundation
214 Massachusetts Ave., N.E., Washington, DC 20002
Telephone: (202) 546-4400
Background: Former Legislative Assistant to Senator David Karnes (R-NE).

SPRINGER, Gary L.
Sr. Legis Rep., Internat'l Trade, Shearman and Sterling
1001 30th St., N.W., Suite 400, Washington, DC 20007
Telephone: (202) 337-8200

SPROLES, M. R.
Senior V. President, DeLeuw, Cather and Co.
1133 15th St., N.W. Suite 800, Washington, DC 20005
Telephone: (202) 775-3300
Background: Responsibilities include the Deleuw Cather and Co. Political Action Committee.

SPUDIS, Martha Ann
Director, Professional Procurement, American Consulting Engineers Council
1015 15th St., N.W., Suite 802, Washington, DC 20005
Telephone: (202) 347-7474
Registered as lobbyist at U.S. Congress.

SPURRIER, Dr. Earl
V. President, Director, State Affairs, Nat'l Agricultural Chemicals Ass'n
Madison Bldg., 1155 15th St., Suite 900, Washington, DC 20005
Telephone: (202) 296-1585

SQUADRON, William F.
Morrison & Foerster
2000 Pennsylvania Ave., N.W., Suite 5500, Washington, DC 20006
Telephone: (202) 887-1500
Clients:
Coca-Cola Co.

SQUIER & ESKEW COMMUNICATIONS, INC.
511 2nd St., N.E., Washington, DC 20002
Telephone: (202) 547-4970
Registered as Foreign Agent: (#4237)
Members of firm representing listed organizations:
Ochs, Thomas, V. President
Squier, Robert, Partner
Clients:
Venezuela, Government of *(Thomas Ochs, Robert Squier)*

SQUIER, Robert
Partner, Squier & Eskew Communications, Inc.
511 2nd St., N.E., Washington, DC 20002
Telephone: (202) 547-4970
Registered as Foreign Agent: (#4237).
Clients:
Venezuela, Government of

SQUIRE, SANDERS AND DEMPSEY
1201 Pennsylvania Ave., N.W. P.O. Box 407, Washington, DC 20044
Telephone: (202) 626-6600
Background: Washington office of a national law firm.
Members of firm representing listed organizations:
Anderson, Kenneth C.
Background: Chief, Special Regulated Industries Section, Antitrust Division, Department of Justice, 1975-80.
Casserly, James L.
Cerar, Jeffrey O.
Background: Deputy Associate General Counsel, U.S. Environmental Protection Agency, 1978-79.

Collishaw, William C.
Geltman, Edward A.
Background: Trial Attorney, Federal Trade Commission, 1971-73.
Hawkins, Edward J.
Background: Chief Tax Counsel, Senate Finance Committee, 1979-80. Minority Tax Counsel, Senate Finance Committee, 1981.
Huey, Robert H.
Kramer, William D.
LaFrance, Ann J.
Markoski, Joseph P.
Marks, Herbert E.
Papkin, Robert D.
Quigley, Thomas J.
Sauer, Edward W.
Scott, Michael
Sinick, Marshall S.
Background: Trial Attorney, Bureau of Operating Rights, Civil Aeronautics Board, 1968-71.
Stein, Dana
Thomas, Ritchie T.
Background: Office of General Counsel, U.S. Tariff Commission, 1964-67.
Vanik, Charles A.
Background: Former Member, U.S. House of Representatives (D-OH), 1954-80.
Young, Glenn M.
Clients:
ADAPSO, the Computer Software & Services Industry Ass'n *(Joseph P. Markoski, Herbert E. Marks)*
Aerolineas Argentinas *(Robert D. Papkin)*
Air India *(Marshall S. Sinick)*
Alaska Airlines *(Marshall S. Sinick)*
Aloha Airlines *(Marshall S. Sinick)*
American Chamber of Commerce in Germany *(Ritchie T. Thomas)*
American Soc. of Anesthesiologists *(Michael Scott)*
Ansett Transport Industries *(Robert D. Papkin, Edward W. Sauer)*
Ass'n of Research Libraries *(Ritchie T. Thomas)*
Avianca Airlines *(Robert D. Papkin)*
Belgian American Chamber of Commerce *(Thomas J. Quigley)*
Belgium, Embassy of
Bessemer and Lake Erie Railroad Co. *(Kenneth C. Anderson)*
California Steel Industries Inc. *(Robert H. Huey)*
Coalition for North American Trade and Investment *(Charles A. Vanik)*
Compania Mexicana de Aviacion *(Robert D. Papkin)*
Fast Air Carrier *(Marshall S. Sinick)*
Ferro Corp. *(Jeffrey O. Cerar)*
Ferroalloys Ass'n *(Ritchie T. Thomas)*
Forestal Venecia Ltda. *(Marshall S. Sinick)*
Independent Data Communications Manufacturers Ass'n *(James L. Casserly, Herbert E. Marks)*
Lineas Aereas Costarricicenes (Lasca Airlines) *(Robert D. Papkin, Edward W. Sauer)*
McGraw-Hill, Inc. *(Ann J. LaFrance)*
Nat'l Collegiate Athletic Ass'n *(William D. Kramer, Michael Scott)*
Northeast Ohio Regional Sewer District *(Jeffrey O. Cerar)*
Philipp Brothers, Inc. *(Charles A. Vanik)*
Polynesian Airlines *(Robert D. Papkin, Edward W. Sauer)*
Population Crisis Committee *(William C. Collishaw)*
Public Securities Ass'n
Samaritan Health Services *(Michael Scott)*
Transportes Aeros Nacionales (TAN) *(Robert D. Papkin)*
United Technologies Carrier *(Edward A. Geltman)*
VASP Airlines *(Robert D. Papkin, Edward W. Sauer)*
VIASA *(Robert D. Papkin, Edward W. Sauer)*
White Consolidated Industries *(Jeffrey O. Cerar, Edward J. Hawkins, Robert D. Papkin)*

SREDL, Diane
Legislative Aide, Nat'l Organization for Women
1000 16th St., N.W., Suite 700, Washington, DC 20036
Telephone: (202) 331-0066

SRODES, Cecile
Counsel Legislative Affairs, New York Stock Exchange
1800 K St., N.W., Suite 1100, Washington, DC 20006
Telephone: (202) 293-5740
Registered as lobbyist at U.S. Congress.

SROKA, John
Exec. V. President, Sheet Metal and Air Conditioning Contractors' Nat'l Ass'n
8224 Old Courthouse Rd., Vienna, VA 22182
Telephone: (703) 790-9890
Registered as lobbyist at U.S. Congress.

SROUFE, Gerald
Dir., Governmnt'l & Professional Liaison, American Educational Research Ass'n
1230 17th St., N.W., Washington, DC 20036
Telephone: (202) 223-9485

ST. DENIS, Cathy
Account Executive, Gallagher-Widmeyer Group Inc., The
1110 Vermont Ave., N.W., Suite 1020, Washington, DC 20005
Telephone: (202) 659-1606
Background: Formerly served as Deputy Communications Director, Democratic Senatorial Committee and as Deputy Press Secretary to Senator Tom Daschle (D-SD).

ST. GERMAIN, Fernand J.
St. Germain, Rodio & Ursillo, Ltd.
2550 M St., N.W., Suite 250, Washington, DC 20037
Telephone: (202) 785-8752
Registered as lobbyist at U.S. Congress.
Background: Member, U.S. House of Representatives (D-RI), 1961-88.

ST. GERMAIN, RODIO & URSILLO, LTD.
2550 M St., N.W., Suite 250, Washington, DC 20037
Telephone: (202) 785-8752
Members of firm representing listed organizations:
St. Germain, Fernand J.
Background: Member, U.S. House of Representatives (D-RI), 1961-88.
Clients:
American Child Care Foundation *(Fernand J. St. Germain)*
Globaldebt *(Fernand J. St. Germain)*
Hamilton Scientific and Development *(Fernand J. St. Germain)*
Internat'l Ass'n of Firefighters, Local 799 *(Fernand J. St. Germain)*
Newman Group, The *(Fernand J. St. Germain)*
Old Stone Federal Savings Bank *(Fernand J. St. Germain)*
Startron Industries, Inc. *(Fernand J. St. Germain)*
United Ass'n of Steamfitters, Local 476 *(Fernand J. St. Germain)*

ST. LEDGER-ROTY, Judith
Reed Smith Shaw & McClay
1200 18th St., N.W., Washington, DC 20036
Telephone: (202) 457-6100
Registered as lobbyist at U.S. Congress.

ST. PIERRE, Jim
Maine Woods Project Director, Wilderness Soc.
1400 Eye St., N.W., 10th Floor, Washington, DC 20005
Telephone: (202) 842-3400
Registered as lobbyist at U.S. Congress.

STACEY, James H.
Dir., Dept. of Media & Info. Svcs., American Medical Ass'n
1101 Vermont Ave., N.W., Washington, DC 20005
Telephone: (202) 789-7400

STACK, Clinton J.
Internat'l Development Systems
733 15th St., N.W., Suite 520, Washington, DC 20005
Telephone: (202) 783-0720
Registered as lobbyist at U.S. Congress.
Registered as Foreign Agent: (#4012).
Background: Former Deputy Director, Implementation Division, Office of Textiles, U.S. Department of Commerce.

STACK, E. Gifford
V. President, Solid Waste Programs, Nat'l Soft Drink Ass'n
1101 16th St., N.W., Washington, DC 20036
Telephone: (202) 463-6732

STACK, Michael J.
Exec. Director, American Production and Inventory Control Soc.
500 West Annandale Road, Falls Church, VA 22046

STACK, Michael J. (Cont'd)
Telephone: (703) 237-8344

STACK, Richard
V. President, Apter and Associates, David
1706 R St., N.W., Washington, DC 20009
Telephone: (202) 265-1212

STACK, Vivian Escobar
Legislative Representative, Planned Parenthood Federation of America
2010 Massachusetts Ave., N.W. Fifth Floor, Washington, DC 20036
Telephone: (202) 785-3351
Registered as lobbyist at U.S. Congress.

STACY, Mike
V. President, Advanced Unmanned Systems, Canadair Challenger, Inc. Advanced Unmanned Systems Director-ate
1215 Jefferson Davis Highway Suite 901, Arlington, VA 22202
Telephone: (703) 486-5850

STAFFIER, John R.
McHenry and Staffier, P.C.
1300 19th St., N.W. Suite 408, Washington, DC 20036
Telephone: (202) 467-5880
Registered as lobbyist at U.S. Congress.
Background: Staff Attorney, Federal Power Commission, Office of the Solicitor, 1972-75.
Clients:
Foothills Pipe Lines (Yukon), Ltd.
NOVA, An Alberta Corp.
Westcoast Transmission Co.

STAFFORD, BURKE AND HECKER
1006 Cameron St., Alexandria, VA 22314
Telephone: (703) 836-2696
Background: A government and international affairs consulting firm.
Members of firm representing listed organizations:
Burke, Kelly H.
Hecker, Guy L.
Stafford, Thomas P.
Clients:
Construcciones Aeronauticas, S.A. *(Kelly H. Burke, Guy L. Hecker, Thomas P. Stafford)*
Sumitomo Corp. *(Kelly H. Burke, Guy L. Hecker, Thomas P. Stafford)*

STAFFORD, Michael
Porte, Stafford and Associates
1050 17th St., N.W., Suite 840, Washington, DC 20036
Telephone: (202) 785-1196
Background: Legislative Consultant, Porte, Stafford, and Associates.
Clients:
Nat'l Ass'n of Medical Directors of Respiratory Care

STAFFORD, Thomas P.
Stafford, Burke and Hecker
1006 Cameron St., Alexandria, VA 22314
Telephone: (703) 836-2696
Registered as Foreign Agent: (#3625).
Clients:
Construcciones Aeronauticas, S.A.
Sumitomo Corp.

STAHL, David E.
Exec. V. President, Urban Land Institute
1090 Vermont Ave., N.W. Suite 300, Washington, DC 20005
Telephone: (202) 289-8500

STAHL, Melvin R.
Sr. V. President, Government Relations, Motorcycle Industry Council
1235 Jefferson Davis Hwy. Suite 600, Arlington, VA 22202
Telephone: (703) 521-0444
Registered as lobbyist at U.S. Congress.
Background: Also serves as Lobbyist, Specialty Vehicle Institute of America.

STAHR, Dr. Elvis J., Jr.
Senior Consultant, Cassidy and Associates, Inc.
655 15th St., N.W., Suite 1100, Washington, DC 20005
Telephone: (202) 347-0773

Registered as lobbyist at U.S. Congress.
Background: Former Secretary of the Army.
Clients:
West Virginia University

STALEY, Mary T.
Collier, Shannon & Scott
1055 Thomas Jefferson St., N.W., Suite 300, Washington, DC 20007
Telephone: (202) 342-8400
Clients:
Chase Brass and Copper
Hussey Copper Ltd.
Miller Co.

STALKNECHT, Paul T.
V. President, State Relations, American Trucking Ass'ns
430 First St., S.E., Washington, DC 20003-1826
Telephone: (202) 544-6245

STAMBAUGH, Dottie
Legislative Assistant, Nat'l School Boards Ass'n
1680 Duke St., Alexandria, VA 22314
Telephone: (703) 838-6722

STANDA, Joseph
Political Specialist, Nat'l Education Ass'n of the U.S.
1201 16th St., N.W., Washington, DC 20036
Telephone: (202) 822-7300
Background: Serves also as Representative, Nat'l Education Ass'n Political Action Committee.

STANFIELD, Jeffrey L.
Cutler and Stanfield
1850 M St., N.W. Suite 1000, Washington, DC 20036
Telephone: (202) 822-6400
Registered as lobbyist at U.S. Congress.
Background: Assistant to the Secretary, 1977-79 and Associate Under Secretary, 1979-80, U.S. Department of Energy. Assistant to the General Counsel, Federal Administration, 1977.
Clients:
General Atomics
University of Colorado, Office of the President

STANG, David P.
Stang, P.C., David P.
1629 K St., N.W. Suite 601, Washington, DC 20006
Telephone: (202) 223-5730
Registered as lobbyist at U.S. Congress.
Organizations represented:
Polar Gas

STANG, P.C., David P.
1629 K St., N.W. Suite 601, Washington, DC 20006
Telephone: (202) 223-5730
Registered as Foreign Agent: (#4320)
Background: A firm specializing in legislative and administrative law.
Members of firm representing listed organizations:
Stang, David P.
Organizations represented:
Polar Gas *(David P. Stang)*

STANGER, Richard B.
Partner, Employee Benefits, Price Waterhouse
1801 K St., N.W., Suite 700, Washington, DC 20006
Telephone: (202) 296-0800

STANGO, Janice
Sr. Staff V. Pres., Admin. & Operations, Mortgage Bankers Ass'n of America
1125 15th St., N.W., Suite 700, Washington, DC 20005
Telephone: (202) 861-6500

STANION, Theresa
Director, Government Relations, Internat'l Communications Industries Ass'n (ICIA)
3150 Spring St., Fairfax, VA 22031-2399
Telephone: (703) 273-7200
Registered as lobbyist at U.S. Congress.
Background: Director of State Activities for the Business Coalition for Fair Competition.

STANISLAWSKI, Howard J.
Fried, Frank, Harris, Shriver & Jacobson
1001 Pennsylvania Ave., N.W., Suite 800, Washington, DC 20004-2505
Telephone: (202) 639-7000

STANLEY, Robert W.
Exec. Director, Nat'l Ass'n of Dental Laboratories
3801 Mt. Vernon Ave., Alexandria, VA 22305
Telephone: (703) 683-5263
Background: Also serves as Executive Director of the Nat'l Board for Certification in Dental Laboratory Technology and as Executive Director of the Nat'l Board of Certification of Dental Laboratories.

STANTON & ASSOCIATES
1310 19th St., N.W. Lower Level, Washington, DC 20036
Telephone: (202) 467-4333
Members of firm representing listed organizations:
Stanton, James V.
Background: Former member U.S. House of Representatives (D-OH).
Clients:
Anheuser-Busch Cos., Inc. *(James V. Stanton)*
Donaldson, Lufkin & Jenrette *(James V. Stanton)*
Nat'l Spa and Pool Institute *(James V. Stanton)*
Philip Morris Cos., Inc. *(James V. Stanton)*
United HealthCare Corp. *(James V. Stanton)*

STANTON, James V.
Stanton & Associates
1310 19th St., N.W. Lower Level, Washington, DC 20036
Telephone: (202) 467-4333
Registered as lobbyist at U.S. Congress.
Background: Former member U.S. House of Representatives (D-OH).
Clients:
Anheuser-Busch Cos., Inc.
Donaldson, Lufkin & Jenrette
Nat'l Spa and Pool Institute
Philip Morris Cos., Inc.
United HealthCare Corp.

STANTON, John S.
Hogan and Hartson
555 13th St., N.W., Suite 1200, Washington, DC 20004-1109
Telephone: (202) 637-5600
Registered as lobbyist at U.S. Congress.
Background: Member, Professional Staff, House Banking Committee, U.S. Congress, 1974-77.
Clients:
American Medical Internat'l
Lloyds of London, Underwriters at Manufacturers Hanover Trust Co.
SouthernNet, Inc.

STANTON, Joseph M.
Congressional Representative, Nat'l Ass'n of Home Builders of the U.S.
15th and M Streets, N.W., Washington, DC 20005
Telephone: (202) 822-0470
Registered as lobbyist at U.S. Congress.

STANTON, Michael J.
Director, State Relations, Motor Vehicle Manufacturers Ass'n of the United States
1620 Eye St., N.W. Suite 1000, Washington, DC 20006
Telephone: (202) 775-2700
Registered as lobbyist at U.S. Congress.

STAPLETON, Phil
Director, Issue Analysis, Soc. of the Plastics Industry
1275 K St., N.W., Suite 400, Washington, DC 20005
Telephone: (202) 371-5200

STARK, Richard C.
Johnson & Gibbs, P.C.
1001 Pennsylvania Ave., N.W. Suite 745, Washington, DC 20004
Telephone: (202) 682-4500
Registered as lobbyist at U.S. Congress.
Clients:
Permanente Medical Group, Inc., The

STARKE, Jane Sutter
Eckert Seamans Cherin & Mellott
1818 N St., N.W., Suite 700, Washington, DC 20036
Telephone: (202) 452-1074
Registered as lobbyist at U.S. Congress.
Background: Minority Counsel, Committee on Energy and Commerce, U.S. House of Representatives, 1981-87.
Clients:
Blockbuster Entertainment Corp.

New York Metropolitan Transportation Authority

STARKEY, Lois A.
V. President, Government Relations, Manufactured Housing Institute
1745 Jefferson Davis Hwy. Suite 511, Arlington, VA 22202
Telephone: (703) 979-6620
Registered as lobbyist at U.S. Congress.
Background: Also represents the Manufactured Housing Institute Political Action Committee.

STARKS, Ora
Cong Inquiries Analyst, DEPARTMENT OF TREASURY
15th and Pennsylvania Ave. N.W., Washington, DC 20220
Telephone: (202) 566-2037

STARKWEATHER, Kendall N.
Exec. Director, Internat'l Technology Education Ass'n
1914 Association Drive, Reston, VA 22091
Telephone: (703) 860-2100

STARLING, Kenneth G.
Sutherland, Asbill and Brennan
1275 Pennsylvania, N.W., Washington, DC 20004-2404
Telephone: (202) 383-0100
Clients:
Chain Pharmacy Ass'n of New York State

STARR, David
Williams and Jensen, P.C.
1101 Connecticut Ave., N.W., Suite 500, Washington, DC 20036
Telephone: (202) 659-8201
Background: Legislative Director to Senator Howard Metzenbaum (D-OH), 1981-89.
Clients:
Nat'l Board for Professional Training Standards

STARR, Michael
General Counsel, Ass'n of Trial Lawyers of America
1050 31st St., N.W., Washington, DC 20007
Telephone: (202) 965-3500

STATE AND FEDERAL ASSOCIATES
1101 King St., Suite 600, Alexandria, VA 22314
Telephone: (703) 739-0200
Members of firm representing listed organizations:
Miller, Martin, President
Mitchell, Michael
Raven, Robert, Chairman

STATE & LOCAL RESOURCES
901 Sixth St., S.W., Suite 503A, Washington, DC 20024
Telephone: (202) 488-1460
Background: A consulting firm specializing in corporate/government liaison; representing clients with private sector, federal and state governments by designing and implementing pro-active strategies.
Members of firm representing listed organizations:
Henderson, Bruce D., V. President, State & Local Resources
Background: Formerly with Environmental Protection Agency, 1982-83.
McCullough, Kim, Media Consultant
Murphy, Patrick M., President
Background: Democractic Nat'l Committee, 1974-80. U.S. Dept. of Housing and Urban Development, 1980-81. Former Director, State and Local Government Relations, U.S. Synthetic Fuels Corp.
Thibeau, Donald D.
Background: V. President, Marketing, State & Local Resources. U.S. Department of Labor/U.S. SFC, 1983-85.
Clients:
G. W. Electronics *(Bruce D. Henderson, Patrick M. Murphy)*
Mid-American Network *(Bruce D. Henderson, Patrick M. Murphy)*
Nat'l Academy of Engineering *(Bruce D. Henderson, Patrick M. Murphy)*
Nevada Development Authority *(Bruce D. Henderson, Patrick M. Murphy)*
Nevada, State of *(Bruce D. Henderson, Patrick M. Murphy)*
T. M. Community College *(Bruce D. Henderson, Patrick M. Murphy)*

STATESIDE ASSOCIATES
Courthouse Plaza II, Suite 407 2300 Clarendon Blvd., Arlington, VA 22201
Telephone: (703) 525-7466
Background: A state government relations management firm. Chairman of the Board is Martin F. Connor of the American Tort Reform Ass'n.
Members of firm representing listed organizations:
Campanella, Constance, President
Hixson, Sheila E., V. President
Clients:
Monsanto Co.
Nat'l Restaurant Ass'n
Rent A Center
Working Group Coalition, The *(Constance Campanella)*

STATLER, Jean C.
V. President, Communications, Council for Solid Waste Solutions
1275 K St., N.W. Suite 400, Washington, DC 20005
Telephone: (202) 371-5319
Background: Former Director, Public Affairs for the Environmental Protection Agency.

STATLER, Stuart M.
Deputy Exec. Director, Communications, Ass'n of Trial Lawyers of America
1050 31st St., N.W., Washington, DC 20007
Telephone: (202) 965-3500

STATMAN, Alan J.
Wright and Talisman
1050 17th St., N.W. Suite 600, Washington, DC 20036
Telephone: (202) 331-1194
Registered as lobbyist at U.S. Congress.

STATON, Cliff
V. Pres. & Director, West Coast Office, Kamber Group, The
1920 L St., N.W., Washington, DC 20036
Telephone: (202) 223-8700

STATON, James D.
Exec. Director, Air Force Sergeants Ass'n
P.O. Box 50, Temple Hills, MD 20748
Telephone: (301) 899-3500
Registered as lobbyist at U.S. Congress.

STAUFFER, Robert F.
V. President and General Counsel, Nat'l Coal Ass'n
1130 17th St., N.W.., Washington, DC 20036
Telephone: (202) 463-2643

STAWICK, David
Ass't V. President, Nat'l Corn Growers Ass'n
201 Massachusetts Ave., N.E., Suite C4, Washington, DC 20002
Telephone: (202) 546-7611
Registered as lobbyist at U.S. Congress.

STAYIN, Randolph J.
Barnes and Thornburg
1815 H St., N.W., Suite 800, Washington, DC 20006
Telephone: (202) 955-4500
Background: Administrative Assistant and Director of Legislation to Senator Robert Taft, Jr. (R-OH), 1973-76.
Clients:
Headwear Institute of America
Nat'l Candle Ass'n
Special Committee for Workplace Product Liability Reform

STEADLEY, Daniel M.
Argyle & Associates
1117 G St., S.E., Washington, DC 20003
Registered as lobbyist at U.S. Congress.
Clients:
Nat'l Council of Savings Institutions

STEADMAN, Kenneth A.
Director, Nat'l Security & For. Affairs, Veterans of Foreign Wars of the U.S.
200 Maryland Ave., N.E., Washington, DC 20002
Telephone: (202) 543-2239

STEAKLEY, Barbara E.
Dir., Congressional & Regulatory Affairs, American Furniture Manufacturers Ass'n
918 16th St., N.W., Suite 402, Washington, DC 20006
Telephone: (202) 466-7362
Registered as lobbyist at U.S. Congress.

STEARMAN, Stanley H.
Exec. V. President, Nat'l Soc. of Public Accountants
1010 N. Fairfax St., Alexandria, VA 22314
Telephone: (703) 549-6400

STECKELBERG, Kathryn A.
Legislative Representative, Edison Electric Institute
1111 19th St., N.W., Washington, DC 20036
Telephone: (202) 778-6400
Registered as lobbyist at U.S. Congress.

STEEL, Dean E.
V. President, Washington Office, Figgie Internat'l
1735 Jefferson Davis Highway, Suite 705, Arlington, VA 22202
Telephone: (703) 892-1400

STEELE, Lt. Col. Donald
Cong Affrs Coord, Res Devel & Acq (SARD), DEPARTMENT OF ARMY
The Pentagon, Washington, DC 20310-0101
Telephone: (202) 697-6767

STEELE & FORNACIARI
2020 K St., N.W. Suite 850, Washington, DC 20006-1857
Telephone: (202) 887-1779
Members of firm representing listed organizations:
Fornaciari, John R.
Hebda, Robert E.
Silcox, Clark R.
Steele, Robert W.
Clients:
Business Council on the Reduction of Paperwork *(Clark R. Silcox)*
K mart Corp. *(John R. Fornaciari, Robert E. Hebda, Robert W. Steele)*

STEELE, Jeffery V.
Director, Government Affairs, Nat'l Ass'n of Arab Americans
2033 M St., N.W., Suite 300, Washington, DC 20036
Telephone: (202) 467-4800
Registered as lobbyist at U.S. Congress.

STEELE, Robert W.
Steele & Fornaciari
2020 K St., N.W. Suite 850, Washington, DC 20006-1857
Telephone: (202) 887-1779
Registered as lobbyist at U.S. Congress.
Clients:
K mart Corp.

STEELE, William N.
Deputy Director, Congressional Affairs, Boeing Co.
1700 North Moore St., Arlington, VA 22209
Telephone: (703) 558-9600
Registered as lobbyist at U.S. Congress.

STEELMAN, Deborah
Epstein Becker and Green
1227 25th St., N.W., Suite 700, Washington, DC 20037
Telephone: (202) 861-0900
Background: Legislative Director to Sen. John Heinz (R-PA) 1982-83; Director, State Relations, Environmental Protection Agency 1983-84; Deputy Ass't to the President for Intergovernmental Affairs 1985; Assoc. Director for Human Resources Veterans and Labor, Office of Management and Budget, 1986-87.
Clients:
American Academy of Dermatology
Blue Cross and Blue Shield of Missouri
Doctors Nat'l Homecare Corp.
Pfizer, Inc.
Pharmaceutical Manufacturers Ass'n
Professional Ass'n for Quality Home Respiratory Care

STEEN, J. C.
412 First St., S.E. Suite 301, Washington, DC 20003
Telephone: (202) 488-1939
Registered as lobbyist at U.S. Congress.

STEEN, J. C. (Cont'd)

Background: A government affairs consultant. Former Administrative Assistant to Rep. William L. Dickinson (R-AL) and Legislative Assistant/Press Secretary to Rep. Armistead Selden.

Organizations represented:
General Atomics
PEMCO AEROPLEX, Inc.

STEEN, James

Spec Asst, Foreign Affrs, Legis Affrs, DEPARTMENT OF DEFENSE
The Pentagon, Washington, DC 20301
Telephone: (202) 697-6210

STEENLAND, Douglas M.

Verner, Liipfert, Bernhard, McPherson and Hand, Chartered
901 15th St., N.W., Suite 700, Washington, DC 20005
Telephone: (202) 371-6000
Registered as lobbyist at U.S. Congress.
Registered as Foreign Agent: (#3712).
Clients:
Boston Mass Transit Authority
Consolidated Grain and Barge Co.
Irving Ltd., J.D.
Travelers, The

STEENLAND, Sally

Director of Media Programs, Wider Opportunities for Women
1325 G St., N.W. Lower Level, Washington, DC 20005
Telephone: (202) 638-3143

STEENSTRA, Henry J., Jr.

Manager, Congressional Relations, TRW Inc.
Suite 2600, 1000 Wilson Blvd., Arlington, VA 22209
Telephone: (703) 276-5125
Registered as lobbyist at U.S. Congress.

STEGER, Holly

Princ Staff Asst, Legis Affrs (Senate), EXECUTIVE OFFICE OF THE PRESIDENT - The White House
1600 Pennsylvania Ave., N.W. 107 East Wing, Washington, DC 20500
Telephone: (202) 456-7054

STEICH, Thomas J.

General Counsel, American Occupational Therapy Ass'n
1383 Piccard Drive, Suite 300 P.O. Box 1725, Rockville, MD 20850
Telephone: (301) 948-9626

STEIN, Allan

Counsel, American Insurance Ass'n
1130 Connecticut Ave., N.W., Suite 1000, Washington, DC 20036
Telephone: (202) 828-7100
Registered as lobbyist at U.S. Congress.

STEIN, Dana

Squire, Sanders and Dempsey
1201 Pennsylvania Ave., N.W. P.O. Box 407, Washington, DC 20044
Telephone: (202) 626-6600

STEIN, Daniel A.

Exec. Director, Federation for American Immigration Reform (FAIR)
1666 Connecticut Ave., N.W., Suite 400, Washington, DC 20009
Telephone: (202) 328-7004

STEIN, John Hollister

Deputy Director, Nat'l Organization for Victim Assistance
1757 Park Road, N.W., Washington, DC 20010
Telephone: (202) 232-6682

STEIN, Dr. Martin M.

Abt Associates Inc.
4800 Montgomery Lane, Bethesda, MD 20814
Telephone: (301) 913-0500
Background: Director, Transportation Research Department (Business Strategy Division), Abt Associates. Formerly, economist, U.S. Department of Transportation; and an officer in the U.S. Departments of Interior and Commerce.

STEIN, Michael H.

Dewey, Ballantine, Bushby, Palmer and Wood
1775 Pennsylvania Ave., N.W. Suite 200, Washington, DC 20006
Telephone: (202) 862-1000
Background: Former General Counsel, U.S. International Trade Commission.
Clients:
Coalition for Fair Lumber Imports
Inland Steel Co.
Nat'l Forest Products Ass'n
Semiconductor Industry Ass'n

STEIN, Sherwin B.

Ehrlich-Manes and Associates
4901 Fairmont Ave., Bethesda, MD 20814
Telephone: (301) 657-1800
Clients:
Fokker B.V.

STEINBACH, Sheldon Elliott

V. President and General Counsel, American Council on Education
One Dupont Circle, N.W., Washington, DC 20036
Telephone: (202) 939-9355

STEINBRUNER, John D.

Director, Foreign Policy Studies Program, Brookings Institution
1775 Massachusetts Ave., N.W., Washington, DC 20036
Telephone: (202) 797-6000

STEINEN, Margaret

Director of Survey Research, Targeting Systems, Inc.
2111 Wilson Blvd., Suite 900, Arlington, VA 22201
Telephone: (703) 528-7555

STEINER, Bruce A.

V. President, Environment and Energy, American Iron and Steel Institute
1133 15th St., N.W. Suite 300, Washington, DC 20005
Telephone: (202) 452-7271

STEINGOLD, Stuart G.

Perkins Coie
1110 Vermont Ave., N.W., Suite 1200, Washington, DC 20005
Telephone: (202) 887-9030
Registered as Foreign Agent: (#3753).

STEINHILBER, August W.

Assoc. Exec. Director & General Counsel, Nat'l School Boards Ass'n
1680 Duke St., Alexandria, VA 22314
Telephone: (703) 838-6722
Background: Formerly Deputy Assistant Commissioner for Legislation, U.S. Office of Education, Dep't of Health, Education and Welfare. Also represents the Educators' Ad Hoc Committee on Copyright Law.

STEINKULLER, William P.

Internat'l Management Group, Inc.
1101 14th St., N.W. Suite 1100, Washington, DC 20005
Telephone: (202) 371-2200
Background: V. President, Internat'l Management Group. Also serves as Exec. Director, Automotive Dismantlers and Recyclers Ass'n.
Clients:
Auto Dismantlers & Recyclers Ass'n
Automotive Dismantlers and Recyclers Ass'n

STEINWURTZEL, Robert N.

Andrews and Kurth
1701 Pennsylvania Ave., N.W. Suite 200, Washington, DC 20006
Telephone: (202) 662-2700
Registered as lobbyist at U.S. Congress.
Clients:
Secondary Lead Smelters Ass'n

STEITZ, Mark E.

Research Director, Democratic Nat'l Committee
430 South Capitol St., S.E., Washington, DC 20003
Telephone: (202) 863-8000

STEKETEE, Drew

Director, Partnership for Improved Air Travel
1709 New York Ave., N.W. 5th Floor, Washington, DC 20006

Telephone: (202) 626-4200

STELCK, Kristin

Assistant Director, Legislative Affairs, American Ass'n of University Women
2401 Virginia Ave., N.W., Washington, DC 20037
Telephone: (202) 785-7700
Registered as lobbyist at U.S. Congress.

STELLAR, Charles W.

Exec. Vice President, American Managed Care and Review Ass'n
1227 25th St., N.W. Suite 610, Washington, DC 20037
Telephone: (202) 728-0506
Registered as lobbyist at U.S. Congress.
Background: Also represents the Nat'l Committee for Quality Assurance.

STEMMLER, Dr. Edward J.

Exec. V. President, Ass'n of American Medical Colleges
One Dupont Circle, N.W., Suite 200, Washington, DC 20036
Telephone: (202) 828-0400
Background: Dr. Stemmler becomes Exec. V. Pres. effective July 1, 1990.

STEMPLER, Jack L.

V. President, Washington Operations, LTV Aircraft Products Group
1725 Jefferson Davis Hwy. Suite 900, Arlington, VA 22202
Telephone: (703) 521-6560
Registered as lobbyist at U.S. Congress.

STENGER, James A.

Ross and Hardies
888 16th St., N.W., Washington, DC 20006
Telephone: (202) 296-8600
Clients:
Association Professionnelle de l'Acier Moule de France
Bowman Webber Ltd.

STENSON, Jane

Director for Aging Services, Catholic Charities USA
1319 F St., N.W., Suite 400, Washington, DC 20004
Telephone: (202) 639-8400

STENT, Michelle D.

V. President of Government Affairs, United Negro College Fund
2100 M St., N.W., Suite 405, Washington, DC 20037
Telephone: (202) 785-8632

STENZEL, Sam

Exec. Director, Nat'l Vocational Agricultural Teachers Ass'n
Box 15440, Alexandria, VA 22309
Telephone: (703) 780-1862

STENZEL, Thomas E.

Exec. Director, Internat'l Food Information Council
1100 Connecticut Ave. N.W., Suite 430, Washington, DC 20036
Telephone: (202) 296-6540

STEPHENS & GRAHAM

1800 Old Meadow Road, Box 1096, McLean, VA 22101
Telephone: (703) 821-8700
Background: Also maintains an office in the District of Columbia at Two LaFayette Centre, 1331 21st St., N.W., Washington, DC 20036-3002. Tel: (202) 331-8200.
Members of firm representing listed organizations:
Stephens, William T.
Background: Serves as General Counsel and Washington representative for various national trade associations, professional societies and other not-for-profit organiations.
Clients:
American Rental Ass'n *(William T. Stephens)*

STEPHENS, J. Gordon, Jr.

Burson-Marsteller
1850 M St., N.W., Suite 900, Washington, DC 20036
Telephone: (202) 833-8550
Registered as lobbyist at U.S. Congress.
Registered as Foreign Agent: (#2469).
Background: Senior V. President, Burson-Marsteller. Legislative Assistant to former Speaker of the House of Representatives Carl Albert (D-OK), 1973-77.
Clients:

Emhart Corp.
Lever Brothers Co.

STEPHENS, William T.
Stephens & Graham
1800 Old Meadow Road, Box 1096, McLean, VA 22101
Telephone: (703) 821-8700
Background: Serves as General Counsel and Washington representative for various national trade associations, professional societies and other not-for-profit organiations.
Clients:
American Rental Ass'n

STEPHENSON, David
State Legislative Analyst, Nat'l Federation of Independent Business
600 Maryland Ave., S.W., Suite 700, Washington, DC 20024
Telephone: (202) 554-9000

STEPONKUS AND ASSOCIATES
888 16th St., N.W. Suite 300, Washington, DC 20006
Telephone: (202) 331-7060
Background: A government and public relations firm.
Members of firm representing listed organizations:
Steponkus, William P.
Background: Administrative Asst. to U.S. Representative Charles W. Whalen, Jr. of Ohio, 1967-79. White House Speech Writer under President Gerald Ford, 1974.
Clients:
Dublin-McCarter & Associates *(William P. Steponkus)*
Federal Sources, Inc. *(William P. Steponkus)*
USAA *(William P. Steponkus)*

STEPONKUS, William P.
Steponkus and Associates
888 16th St., N.W. Suite 300, Washington, DC 20006
Telephone: (202) 331-7060
Background: Administrative Asst. to U.S. Representative Charles W. Whalen, Jr. of Ohio, 1967-79. White House Speech Writer under President Gerald Ford, 1974.
Clients:
Dublin-McCarter & Associates
Federal Sources, Inc.
USAA

STEPTOE AND JOHNSON
1330 Connecticut Ave., N.W., Washington, DC 20036
Telephone: (202) 429-3000
Registered as Foreign Agent: (#3975)
Background: The following information was obtained from public records and submitted to this firm for confirmation. The firm stated that it does not divulge client information and declined to amend the listing.
Members of firm representing listed organizations:
Bailey, Arthur L.
Baker, Stewart A.
Background: Law Clerk for Associate Justice John Paul Stevens, United States Supreme Court, 1977-78. Special Assistant to Secretary of Education, 1979-80. Deputy General Counsel, Department of Education, 1980-81.
Barshefsky, Charlene
Berg, Gracia M.
Brosch, Kevin J.
Brown, Tyrone
Background: Law Clerk to Chief Justice Earl Warren, U.S. Supreme Court, 1967-68. Staff Director, Intergovernmental Relations Committee, U.S. Senate, 1970-71. Commissioner, Federal Communications Commission, 1977-81.
Carey, Sarah
Christian, Betty Jo
Background: Attorney, Interstate Commerce Commission, 1961-68. Associate General Counsel, Interstate Commerce Commission, 1971-76. Commissioner, 1976-79 and Vice Chairman, 1976-78.
Collier, Thomas C. (Jr.)
Background: Special Assistant to the General Counsel. Department of Housing and Urban Development (HUD), 1979-80. Deputy Assistant Secretary for Regulatory Functions and Interstate Land Sales Administrator, HUD, 1980-81.
Collins, John T.
Background: General Counsel, U.S. Senate Committee on Banking, Housing and Urban Affairs, 1982-85.
Condrell, William K.

Corber, Robert J.
Background: Commissioner, Interstate Commerce Commission, 1975-76.
Cunningham, Richard O.
Esserman, Susan G.
Fleishman, Robert W.
Grandison, W. George
Holden, James P.
Background: Member, Advisory Group to Commissioner of Internal Revenue, 1979-80.
Hopkins, Bruce R.
Horning, Mark F.
Jordan, Robert E. (III)
Background: Special Assistant for Civil Rights, Office of the Secretary of Defense, 1963-64. Assistant U.S. Attorney for the District of Columbia, 1964-65. Executive Assistant for Law Enforcement, Office of the Secretary of the Treasury, 1965-67. General Counsel of the Army and Special Assistant to the Secretary of the Army for Civil Functions, 1967-71.
Karas, William
Leigh, Monroe
Background: Assistant Gen. Counsel for Internat'l Affairs, Office of Secretary of Defense, 1955-1959. Legal Adviser, Dep't of State, 1975-1977. Member on the part of the U.S. of the Permanent Court on Arbitration, 1975-80.
Moran, Mark A.
Nolan, John E. (Jr.)
Background: Law Clerk to Mr. Justice Clark, U.S. Supreme Court, 1955-56. Administrative Assistant to U.S. Attorney General Robert F. Kennedy, 1963-64.
Nussdorf, Melanie Franco
Olmstead, Cecil J., Of Counsel
Background: Assistant to Legal Advisor, State Department, 1951-53. U.S. Delegate, United Nations Committee on Law of Sea, 1972.
Plaine, Daniel J.
Rhodes, Theodore E.
Background: Attorney-Advisor, Office of Tax Legislative Counsel. U.S. Treasury Department, 1973-76. Consultant to Administrator, Pension and Welfare Benefit Programs, Department of Labor, 1976-77.
Rubin, Blake D.
Short, Laurence
Smith, Michael
Background: Former Deputy U.S. Trade Representative.
Taylor, Richard P.
Wallick, Robert D.
Wethington, Olin L.
Zinn, Matthew J.
Clients:
Aerolineas Nacionales del Ecuador *(Richard P. Taylor)*
Alliance for Cannabis Therapeutics
Aluminum Co. of America *(Susan G. Esserman, Mark A. Moran)*
American Ass'n of Colleges for Teacher Education *(Bruce R. Hopkins)*
American Tunaboat Ass'n
Anaconda Minerals Co.
Ass'n of Private Pension and Welfare Plans *(Melanie Franco Nussdorf, Theodore E. Rhodes)*
Atlantic Container Line *(William Karas, Laurence Short)*
Ausimont U.S.A. *(Olin L. Wethington)*
Blue Bell, Inc. *(Richard P. Taylor)*
British Steel Corp. *(Charlene Barshefsky, Richard O. Cunningham)*
Burlington Northern Railroad *(Betty Jo Christian)*
Canadian Sugar Institute *(Susan G. Esserman)*
Cargill, Inc. *(Richard O. Cunningham, Susan G. Esserman)*
Chile, Embassy of *(Monroe Leigh)*
Christie's Internat'l *(Blake D. Rubin)*
Citizens Savings Financial Corp. *(John T. Collins)*
Clean Sound
CNG Transmission Corp.
Coalition for Government Procurement *(Robert D. Wallick)*
Coalition to Promote America's Trade *(Charlene Barshefsky)*
Coast Savings and Loan Ass'n *(John T. Collins)*
Commercial Federal Savings and Loan Ass'n *(John T. Collins)*
Consolidated Natural Gas Co.
Cooperative Central Bank *(John T. Collins)*
CSO Co. *(John T. Collins)*
Cyprus Minerals Corp.

Dart Industries
Evergreen Internat'l Aviation *(Richard P. Taylor)*
Glendale Federal Savings and Loan Ass'n *(John T. Collins)*
Green Olive Trade Ass'n
Gulf Container Line *(William Karas)*
Harley-Davidson, Inc. *(Richard O. Cunningham)*
Independent Insurance Agents of America *(Mark F. Horning)*
Inspiration Consolidated Copper Co.
Inter-City Gas, Ltd.
Islip, New York, City of *(Richard P. Taylor)*
Japan Iron and Steel Exporters Ass'n
Kennecott
Magma Copper Corp.
MeraBank *(John T. Collins)*
Mitsui and Co. *(Charlene Barshefsky, Richard O. Cunningham, Susan G. Esserman)*
Nashua Corp. *(Gracia M. Berg)*
Nat'l Antique and Art Dealers Ass'n of America *(Blake D. Rubin)*
Nat'l Forest Products Ass'n
Nat'l Institute of Building Sciences
Nat'l Oilseed Processors Ass'n *(Kevin J. Brosch)*
New York Life Insurance Co. *(Arthur L. Bailey, Matthew J. Zinn)*
NI Industries *(Olin L. Wethington)*
Nippon Steel Corp. *(W. George Grandison, Daniel J. Plaine)*
Norfolk Port and Industrial Authority *(Richard P. Taylor)*
Outboard Marine Corp. *(Stewart A. Baker)*
Pioneer Financial *(John T. Collins)*
Puerto Rico Telephone Co. *(Matthew J. Zinn)*
Sotheby's Holdings, Inc. *(Blake D. Rubin)*
South Central Air
Swissair *(William Karas, Laurence Short)*
Western Financial Savings Bank *(John T. Collins)*
WNNE-TV

STERN, Jason L.
President, Braddock Communications
909 North Washington St., Alexandria, VA 22314
Telephone: (702) 549-6500

STERN, Jeffrey B.
Dow, Lohnes and Albertson
1255 23rd St., N.W., Suite 500, Washington, DC 20037
Telephone: (202) 857-2500
Clients:
Century Property Fund
Wilmington Savings Fund Soc.

STERN, John P.
V. President, Asia, American Electronics Ass'n
1225 Eye St., N.W., Suite 950, Washington, DC 20005
Telephone: (202) 682-9110

STERN, Leonard W.
Exec. Director, Nat'l Assembly of Nat'l Voluntary Health and Social Welfare Organizations
1319 F St., N.W., Suite 601, Washington, DC 20004
Telephone: (202) 347-2080

STERN, Michael
Wall and Associates, R. Duffy
1317 F St., N.W., Suite 400, Washington, DC 20004
Telephone: (202) 737-0100
Registered as lobbyist at U.S. Congress.
Registered as Foreign Agent: (#3737).
Organizations represented:
American Academy of Dermatology
Bell Atlantic
Footwear Distributors and Retailers of America
Hong Kong Trade Development Council
Pharmaceutical Manufacturers Ass'n
Torchmark Corp.
United Way of America

STERN, Philip M.
Co-Chairman and Founder, Citizens Against PACs
2000 P St., N.W. Suite 408, Washington, DC 20036
Telephone: (202) 463-0465
Background: Former Legislative Aide to Senator Henry M. Jackson of Washington and Senator Paul H. Douglas of Illinois.

STERN, Richard H.
1300 19th St., N.W., Suite 300, Washington, DC 20036

WASHINGTON REPRESENTATIVES

STERN, Richard H. (Cont'd)
Telephone: (202) 659-2690
Background: An attorney. Law Clerk to Mr. Justice Byron White, U.S. Supreme Court, 1962-63. Attorney-Advisor and Trial Attorney, Bureau of Restraint of Trade, Federal Trade Commission, 1963-66. Director, Compliance Division, Office of Federal Direct Investments, U.S. Department of Commerce, 1968-69. Chief, Patent Section, 1970-77 and Chief, Intellectual Property Section, 1977-78, Antitrust Division, U.S. Department of Justice.
Organizations represented:
Semiconductor Industry Ass'n

STERN, Todd D.
V. President, Podesta Associates
424 C St., N.E., Washington, DC 20002
Telephone: (202) 544-6906

STERNBERG, Richard W.
Fuels Coordinator, Nat'l Rural Electric Cooperative Ass'n
1800 Massachusetts Ave., N.W., Washington, DC 20036
Telephone: (202) 857-9606
Registered as lobbyist at U.S. Congress.

STERNBERGER, Rabbi Richard
Director, Mid-Atlantic Council, Union of American Hebrew Congregations
2027 Massachusetts Ave., N.W., Washington, DC 20036
Telephone: (202) 232-4242

STERNFELS, Urvan R.
President, Nat'l Petroleum Refiners Ass'n
1899 L St., N.W., Suite 1000, Washington, DC 20036
Telephone: (202) 457-0480

STERTZER, David
Exec. V. President, Ass'n for Advanced Life Underwriting
1922 F St., N.W., Washington, DC 20006
Telephone: (202) 331-6081

STERUD, Eugene L.
Exec. Director, American Anthropological Ass'n
1703 New Hampshire Ave., N.W., Washington, DC 20009
Telephone: (202) 232-8800

STETSON, Wayne W.
Staff V. President, Conventions, Nat'l Ass'n of Home Builders of the U.S.
15th and M Streets, N.W., Washington, DC 20005
Telephone: (202) 822-0470

STEUART, George C.
Miller & Steuart
1825 I St., N.W. Suite 400, Washington, DC 20006
Telephone: (202) 429-2017
Registered as lobbyist at U.S. Congress.
Clients:
Coastal Corp., The/ANR Pipeline Co.
Squibb and Sons, Inc., E. R.

STEUERLE, C. Eugene
Senior Fellow, Urban Institute, The
2100 M St., N.W., Washington, DC 20037
Telephone: (202) 833-7200

STEVENS, Cynthia
Director, Public Affairs, Chamber of Commerce of the U.S.A.
1615 H St., N.W., Washington, DC 20062
Telephone: (202) 659-6000

STEVENS, Douglas R.
2550 M St., N.W. Suite 405, Washington, DC 20037
Telephone: (202) 775-0500
Background: An attorney.

STEVENS, Joann
Dir., Media Relations, Education Progs., Nat'l Urban Coalition
8601 Georgia Ave., Suite 500, Silver Spring, MD 20910
Telephone: (301) 495-4999

STEVENS, John C.
Ashby and Associates
1140 Connecticut Ave., N.W., Suite 503, Washington, DC 20036
Telephone: (202) 296-3840
Clients:
Internat'l Microwave Systems Corp. (IMSCO)
INTERSECT Corp.

Phase Two Industries
Physical Optics Corp.

STEVENS, John L., Jr.
Director, State Relations, Internat'l Council of Shopping Centers
1199 North Fairfax St. Suite 204, Alexandria, VA 22314
Telephone: (703) 549-7404

STEVENS, Patricia J.
V. President, Member Services, Nat'l Ass'n of Federal Credit Unions
3138 N. 10th St., Arlington, VA 22201
Telephone: (703) 522-4770

STEVENS, Roger G.
President, Nat'l Center for Housing Management
1275 K St., N.W., Suite 700, Washington, DC 20005
Telephone: (202) 872-1717

STEVENSON, Robert E.
Director, American Type Culture Collection
12301 Parklawn Drive, Rockville, MD 20852
Telephone: (301) 881-2600
Background: Also represents Bioresources Laboratories.

STEVENSON, Dr. Robert J.
Exec. Director, Ass'n of Teacher Educators
1900 Association Drive, Reston, VA 22091
Telephone: (703) 620-3110

STEWART, Eugene L.
Stewart and Stewart
808 17th St., N.W. Suite 301, Washington, DC 20006
Telephone: (202) 785-4185
Registered as lobbyist at U.S. Congress.
Clients:
Bethlehem Steel Corp.
Monsanto Co.
Monsanto Industrial Chemicals Co.
Roses, Inc.
Timken Co.

STEWART, Kenneth
Housing Policy Analyst, American Ass'n of Homes for the Aging
1129 20th St., N.W., Suite 400, Washington, DC 20036
Telephone: (202) 296-5960

STEWART, Leigh
Exec. Director, Ass'n of Federal Investigators
3299 K St., N.W. 7th Floor, Washington, DC 20007
Telephone: (202) 337-5234

STEWART, Marise Rene
Director, Washington Office, Missouri, State of
400 N. Capitol St., N.W. Suite 374, Washington, DC 20001
Telephone: (202) 624-7720

STEWART, Robert B.
V. President, Nat'l Ocean Industries Ass'n
1050 17th St., N.W. Suite 700, Washington, DC 20036
Telephone: (202) 785-5116
Registered as lobbyist at U.S. Congress.
Background: Responsibilities include Nat'l Ocean Industries Ass'n Political Action Committee.

STEWART AND STEWART
808 17th St., N.W. Suite 301, Washington, DC 20006
Telephone: (202) 785-4185
Members of firm representing listed organizations:
Nance, David Scott
Stewart, Eugene L.
Stewart, Terrence P.
Clients:
Bethlehem Steel Corp. *(Eugene L. Stewart)*
Cabot Corp. *(Terrence P. Stewart)*
Floral Trade Council *(Terrence P. Stewart)*
Gates Corp. *(Terrence P. Stewart)*
Goodyear Tire and Rubber Co. *(Terrence P. Stewart)*
Hudson Industries Corp. *(Terrence P. Stewart)*
Kimble Glass *(Terrence P. Stewart)*
Libbey Glass *(Terrence P. Stewart)*
Monsanto Co. *(Eugene L. Stewart)*
Monsanto Industrial Chemicals Co. *(Eugene L. Stewart)*
PPG Industries *(David Scott Nance, Terrence P. Stewart)*
Roses, Inc. *(Eugene L. Stewart)*

Smith Corona Corp.
Timken Co. *(Eugene L. Stewart)*
Torrington Co. *(Terrence P. Stewart)*
Trade Relations Council of the U.S.

STEWART, Terrence P.
Stewart and Stewart
808 17th St., N.W. Suite 301, Washington, DC 20006
Telephone: (202) 785-4185
Registered as lobbyist at U.S. Congress.
Clients:
Cabot Corp.
Floral Trade Council
Gates Corp.
Goodyear Tire and Rubber Co.
Hudson Industries Corp.
Kimble Glass
Libbey Glass
PPG Industries
Torrington Co.

STEWART, Brig. Gen. Wilbert T.
Director, Air Activities, Nat'l Guard Ass'n of the U.S.
One Massachusetts Ave., N.W., Washington, DC 20001
Telephone: (202) 789-0031

STICHMAN, Barton
Director, Vietnam Veterans Of America Legal Services Program
c/o Nat'l Veterans Legal Svc. 2001 S St., N.W., Suite 610, Washington, DC 20016
Telephone: (202) 265-8305

STICKLE & ASSOC., Warren E.
1220 19th St., N.W., Suite 300, Washington, DC 20036
Telephone: (202) 785-2732
Members of firm representing listed organizations:
Stickle, Warren E.
Background: Serves also as President, Chemical Producers and Distributors Ass'n.
Organizations represented:
Chemical Producers and Distributors Ass'n *(Warren E. Stickle)*
Cheminova *(Warren E. Stickle)*
Internat'l Sanitary Supply Ass'n *(Warren E. Stickle)*

STICKLE, Warren E.
Stickle & Assoc., Warren E.
1220 19th St., N.W., Suite 300, Washington, DC 20036
Telephone: (202) 785-2732
Registered as lobbyist at U.S. Congress.
Background: Serves also as President, Chemical Producers and Distributors Ass'n.
Organizations represented:
Chemical Producers and Distributors Ass'n
Cheminova
Internat'l Sanitary Supply Ass'n

STIEGLITZ, Perry J.
Director, Gibraltar Information Bureau
1155 15th St., N.W., Washington, DC 20005
Telephone: (202) 452-1108
Registered as Foreign Agent: (#4182)

STILES, Nancy M.
Silver, Freedman & Taff
1735 Eye St., N.W., Washington, DC 20006
Telephone: (202) 429-6100
Registered as lobbyist at U.S. Congress.
Clients:
Hiawatha Savings and Loan Ass'n

STILLER, Phillip
Dep Assoc Commissioner, Legis Affrs, DEPARTMENT OF HEALTH AND HUMAN SERVICES - Food and Drug Administration
5600 Fishers Lane, Rockville, MD 20857
Telephone: (301) 443-3793

STILLMAN, Don
Dir. of Gov't and Internat'l Affairs, United Automobile, Aerospace and Agricultural Implement Workers of America (UAW)
1757 N St., N.W., Washington, DC 20036
Telephone: (202) 828-8500
Registered as lobbyist at U.S. Congress.

STILLWELL, Lee J.
V. President, Public Affairs Group, American Medical
Ass'n
1101 Vermont Ave., N.W., Washington, DC 20005
Telephone: (202) 789-7400
Registered as lobbyist at U.S. Congress.
Background: Special Assistant to Senator Abraham Ribicoff
(D-CT), 1977-1979. Press Secretary for William Arm-
strong, (R-CO) 1979-1987.

STINCHCOMB, Larry
Director, Youth in Philanthropy
P.O. Box 500 20th Floor, Tower 1, Washington, DC 20044
Telephone: (202) 276-3444

STINE, Neal
Manager, Trade/Business Affairs, Baxter Internat'l Inc.
1667 K St., N.W., Suite 710, Washington, DC 20006
Telephone: (202) 223-4016
Registered as lobbyist at U.S. Congress.

STINE, William
Manager, International Services, Nat'l Business Aircraft
Ass'n
1200 18th St., N.W. Suite 200, Washington, DC 20036
Telephone: (202) 783-9000

STINEBERT, Chris S.
Exec. V. President, American Subcontractors Ass'n
1004 Duke St., Alexandria, VA 22314
Telephone: (703) 684-3450

STINGER, Kenneth F.
Director, Government Affairs, American Trucking Ass'ns
430 First St., S.E., Washington, DC 20003
Telephone: (202) 544-6245
Registered as lobbyist at U.S. Congress.

STINNETT, Lee
Exec. Director, American Soc. of Newspaper Editors
11600 Sunrise Valley Drive, Reston, VA 22091
Telephone: (703) 684-1144

STINSON, John M., III
Director, Government Affairs, Nat'l Intergroup, Inc.
1575 Eye St., N.W., Suite 1100, Washington, DC 20005
Telephone: (202) 638-7707

STINSON, Kaye L.
Assistant Director, Government Affairs, American Cyana-
mid Co.
1575 Eye St., N.W., Suite 200, Washington, DC 20005
Telephone: (202) 789-1222
Registered as lobbyist at U.S. Congress.

STIPE, W. H., II
Internat'l Liaison Officer, Internat'l Business Aviation Council (USA Office)
1200 18th St., N.W. Suite 200, Washington, DC 20036-
2598
Telephone: (202) 783-9000
Background: Serves also as Manager, Plans and International Aviation, Nat'l Business Aircraft Ass'n.

STIRK, John J.
Staff V. Pres., Congressional Relations, General Dynamics
Corp.
1745 Jefferson Davis Hwy., Suite 1000, Arlington, VA
22202
Telephone: (703) 553-1292
Registered as lobbyist at U.S. Congress.

STIRPE, David J.
Legislative and Regulatory Affairs Rep., Air-Conditioning
and Refrigeration Institute
1501 Wilson Blvd., Suite 600, Arlington, VA 22209
Telephone: (703) 524-8800
Registered as lobbyist at U.S. Congress.

STIRRUP, Heidi H.
Dir., Cong'l Rel./Small Business & Proc., Associated Gen-
eral Contractors of America
1957 E St., N.W., Washington, DC 20006
Telephone: (202) 393-2040
Registered as lobbyist at U.S. Congress.

STMAXENS AND CO.
1140 Connecticut Ave. N.W., Suite 201, Washington, DC
20036
Telephone: (202) 833-4466

Members of firm representing listed organizations:
Presti, Susan
Background: Former economist, U.S. Department of
Commerce.
StMaxens, Thomas F. (II)
Background: Former Executive Director, Office of the
United States Trade Representative.
Clients:
Corning *(Thomas F. StMaxens, II)*
Daewoo Internat'l (America) Corp. *(Thomas F.
StMaxens, II)*
Internat'l Hardwood Products Ass'n *(Thomas F.
StMaxens, II)*
Kenner Products *(Thomas F. StMaxens, II)*
Mattel, Inc. *(Thomas F. StMaxens, II)*
Motorola, Inc. *(Susan Presti, Thomas F. StMaxens, II)*
Singapore, Embassy of *(Thomas F. StMaxens, II)*
Thailand, Department of Foreign Trade of *(Thomas
F. StMaxens, II)*
Timex Corp. *(Thomas F. StMaxens, II)*
Warner-Lambert Co. *(Thomas F. StMaxens, II)*

STMAXENS, Thomas F., II
StMaxens and Co.
1140 Connecticut Ave., N.W., Suite 201, Washington, DC
20036
Telephone: (202) 833-4466
Background: Former Executive Director, Office of the
United States Trade Representative.
Clients:
Corning
Daewoo Internat'l (America) Corp.
Internat'l Hardwood Products Ass'n
Kenner Products
Mattel, Inc.
Motorola, Inc.
Singapore, Embassy of
Thailand, Department of Foreign Trade of
Timex Corp.
Warner-Lambert Co.

STOCK, Stuart C.
Covington and Burling
1201 Pennsylvania Ave., N.W., Box 7566, Washington, DC
20044
Telephone: (202) 662-6000
Clients:
Washington Area Bankers Ass'n

STOCKEL, Mary
Associate, Gilberg & Kurent
1250 I St., N.W. Suite 600, Washington, DC 20005
Telephone: (202) 842-3222

STOCKER, Frederick T.
Counsel, Manufacturers' Alliance for Productivity and Innovation (MAPI)
1200 18th St., N.W. Suite 400, Washington, DC 20036
Telephone: (202) 331-8430

STOCKER, John J.
President, Shipbuilders Council of America
1110 Vermont Ave., N.W. Suite 1250, Washington, DC
20005
Telephone: (202) 775-9060
Registered as lobbyist at U.S. Congress.

STOCKMEYER & CO.
499 S. Capitol St., S.W. Suite 103, Washington, DC 20003
Telephone: (202) 479-0531
Registered as lobbyist at U.S. Congress.
Members of firm representing listed organizations:
Stockmeyer, Steven F.
Background: Administrative Ass't to Cong. Marvin Es-
cat, 1967-69; Director, Congressional Affairs, Envi-
ronmental Protection Agency, 1971-75; Exec. Direc-
tor, Nat'l Republican Congressional Committee,
1975-80.
Vanderbush, Darlene
Background: Personal Assistant to U.S. Rep. Cliff
Stearns, 1989.
Clients:
Manville Corp. *(Steven F. Stockmeyer)*
Nat'l Ass'n of Business Political Action Commit-
tees *(Steven F. Stockmeyer, Darlene Vanderbush)*
Nat'l Republican Congressional Committee *(Steven
F. Stockmeyer)*
Springs Industries, Inc. *(Steven F. Stockmeyer)*

STOCKMEYER, Steven F.
Stockmeyer & Co.
499 S. Capitol St., S.W. Suite 103, Washington, DC 20003
Telephone: (202) 479-0531
Registered as lobbyist at U.S. Congress.
Background: Administrative Ass't to Cong. Marvin Escat,
1967-69; Director, Congressional Affairs, Environmental
Protection Agency, 1971-75; Exec. Director, Nat'l Repub-
lican Congressional Committee, 1975-80.
Clients:
Manville Corp.
Nat'l Ass'n of Business Political Action Commit-
tees
Nat'l Republican Congressional Committee
Springs Industries, Inc.

STODDARD, Gerard
Curry and Associates, Richard
P.O. Box 66, McLean, VA 22101
Telephone: (703) 821-1404
Organizations represented:
Coastal Reports, Inc.
Long Island Coastal Alliance

STODGHILL, LaBrenda G.
Piper and Marbury
1200 19th St., N.W., Washington, DC 20036
Telephone: (202) 861-3900

STOEL, RIVES, BOLEY, JONES & GREY
1350 New York Ave., N.W., Suite 600A, Washington, DC
20005
Telephone: (202) 347-7744
Background: Washington office of a Portland, Oregon law
firm.
Members of firm representing listed organizations:
Van Brocklin, Robert D.
Clients:
Ass'n of O & C Counties
PacifiCorp *(Robert D. Van Brocklin)*

STOLAR, Michael
Director, Health Sciences, American Diabetes Ass'n
Nat'l Service Center, 1660 Duke St., Alexandria, VA
22314
Telephone: (703) 549-1500

STOLBACH, Richard H.
Patton, Boggs and Blow
2550 M St., N.W., Suite 800, Washington, DC 20037
Telephone: (202) 457-6000
Registered as lobbyist at U.S. Congress.
Registered as Foreign Agent: (#2165).
Background: Assistant General Counsel, 1976-77, and Spe-
cial Counsel to the Exec. Director, 1978, Appalachian
Regional Commission.
Clients:
Navajo Nation, The

STOLGITIS, William C.
Exec. Director and Counsel, Soc. for Technical Communication
901 North Stuart St., Arlington, VA 22203
Telephone: (703) 522-4114

STOLLER, Mitchell R.
Executive Director, Nat'l Sudden Infant Death Syndrome
Foundation
10500 Little Patuxent Pkwy. Suite 420, Columbia, MD
21044
Telephone: (800) 221-7437

STOLLMAN, Israel
Exec. Director, American Planning Ass'n
1776 Massachusetts Ave., N.W., Washington, DC 20036
Telephone: (202) 872-0611
Background: Also represents the American Institute of
Certified Planners.

STOLTE, Darwin E.
President, U.S. Feed Grains Council
1400 K St., N.W., Suite 1200, Washington, DC 20005
Telephone: (202) 789-0789

STOLTE, Dennis C.
Asst. Director, Nat'l Affairs Division, American Farm Bureau Federation
600 Maryland Ave., S.W., Washington, DC 20024
Telephone: (202) 484-3600

STOLTE, Dennis C. (Cont'd)
Registered as lobbyist at U.S. Congress.

STOLTENBERG, Lisa
Legis Mgr, DEPARTMENT OF TREASURY
15th and Pennsylvania Ave. N.W., Washington, DC 20220
Telephone: (202) 566-2037

STOMBLER, Robin E.
Washington Associate, American College of Surgeons
1640 Wisconsin Ave., N.W., Washington, DC 20007
Telephone: (202) 337-2701
Registered as lobbyist at U.S. Congress.

STONE, Ann E. W.
President, Stone and Associates, Ann E. W.
1315 Duke St., Alexandria, VA 22314
Telephone: (703) 836-7717
Registered as lobbyist at U.S. Congress.
Registered as Foreign Agent: (#3914).
Background: Chairman of the Conservative Alliance.

STONE AND ASSOCIATES, Ann E. W.
1315 Duke St., Alexandria, VA 22314
Telephone: (703) 836-7717
Registered as Foreign Agent: (#3914)
Background: A direct response marketing and advertising firm.
Members of firm representing listed organizations:
Herge, J. Curtis, Secretary
Jones, Lora Lynn, V. President
Stone, Ann E. W., President
   Background: Chairman of the Conservative Alliance.
Weintraub, Michael, Director of Marketing
Organizations represented:
Conservative Alliance *(Lora Lynn Jones)*
Nicaraguan Resistance- U.S.A. *(Michael Weintraub)*

STONE, Howard E., Sr.
Exec. Director, Self Help for Hard of Hearing People
7800 Wisconsin Ave., Bethesda, MD 20814
Telephone: (301) 657-2248

STONE, Jeremy J.
President, Federation of American Scientists
307 Massachusetts Ave., N.E., Washington, DC 20002
Telephone: (202) 546-3300

STONE, Judith Lee
Exec. Director, Advocates for Highway and Auto Safety

STONE, Martin E.
PAC Director, Democratic Congressional Campaign Committee
430 South Capitol St., S.E. 2nd Floor, Washington, DC 20003
Telephone: (202) 863-1500

STONE, Roger J.
Black, Manafort, Stone and Kelly Public Affairs Co.
211 N. Union St., Third Floor, Alexandria, VA 22314
Telephone: (703) 683-6612
Registered as lobbyist at U.S. Congress.
Registered as Foreign Agent: (#3600).

STONER, Dena G.
Exec. Director, Council for Educational Development and Research
1201 16th St., N.W. Suite 305, Washington, DC 20036
Telephone: (202) 223-1593

STONER, Floyd E.
Dir., Office of Federal Legis Operations, American Bankers Ass'n
1120 Connecticut Ave., N.W., Washington, DC 20036
Telephone: (202) 663-5000
Registered as lobbyist at U.S. Congress.
Background: Former Legislative Director for Rep. Timothy J. Penny of Minnesota, U.S. House of Representatives.

STONEWALL, Alan J.
President, American Soc. of Pension Actuaries
2029 K St., N.W., 4th Floor, Washington, DC 20006
Telephone: (202) 659-3620

STORCH, Stephen E.
V. President, Government Affairs, Commodity Exchange, Inc. (COMEX)
1331 Pennsylvania Ave., N.W. Suite 550, Washington, DC 20004

Telephone: (202) 662-8770
Registered as lobbyist at U.S. Congress.

STORCK, K.
Public Affairs, Resources for the Future
1616 P St., N.W., Washington, DC 20036
Telephone: (202) 328-5006

STOREY, Deborah
Dep Assoc Admin, Cong and Legis Affrs, ENVIRONMENTAL PROTECTION AGENCY
401 M St., S.W., Washington, DC 20460
Telephone: (202) 382-5200

STOTTLEMYER, Todd A.
Manager, Government Relations, BDM Internat'l, Inc.
7915 Jones Branch Drive, McLean, VA 22102
Telephone: (703) 821-5000
Registered as lobbyist at U.S. Congress.

STOUDT, Ashley
Pyle & Associates, Robert N.
3222 N St., N.W., Washington, DC 20007
Telephone: (202) 333-8190
Organizations represented:
Nat'l Council of Career Women

STOUT, Anna
Director, Legislative Affairs, American League for Exports and Security Assistance (ALESA)
122 C St., N.W., Suite 740, Washington, DC 20001
Telephone: (202) 783-0051
Registered as lobbyist at U.S. Congress.

STOUT, Jan W.
V. President, Development, World Wildlife Fund/The Conservation Foundation
1250 24th St., N.W., Washington, DC 20037
Telephone: (202) 293-4800

STOUT, Mary R.
President, Vietnam Veterans of America, Inc.
2001 S St., N.W., Washington, DC 20009
Telephone: (202) 332-2700
Registered as lobbyist at U.S. Congress.

STOVALL, James T., III
Stovall & Spradlin
2600 Virginia Ave., N.W., Suite 820, Washington, DC 20037
Telephone: (202) 333-8181
Registered as lobbyist at U.S. Congress.
Registered as Foreign Agent: (#3940).
Clients:
Micronesia, Government of the Federated States of

STOVALL & SPRADLIN
2600 Virginia Ave., N.W., Suite 820, Washington, DC 20037
Telephone: (202) 333-8181
Registered as Foreign Agent: (#3940)
Members of firm representing listed organizations:
Spradlin, Thomas Richard
   Background: Assistant to U.S. Senator Mike Monroney of Oklahoma, 1956-63.
Stovall, James T. (III)
Clients:
Advanced Energy Technology, Inc.
Benguela Inc.
Classic Motor Carriages, Inc.
Fredrickson Associates, Inc., D. S.
Gary Aircraft Corp.
Holk Development, Inc.
Micronesia, Government of the Federated States of *(James T. Stovall, III)*
Morocco, Kingdom of
Schick Division (Warner-Lambert Co.)
Tanner Resources Corp.
Warner-Lambert Co.

STOVER, James E.
President, Health Industry Distributors Ass'n
225 Reinekers Lane, Suite 650, Alexandria, VA 22314
Telephone: (703) 549-4432

STOVER, William
V. President, Government Relations, Chemical Manufacturers Ass'n
2501 M St., N.W., Washington, DC 20037
Telephone: (202) 887-1122
Registered as lobbyist at U.S. Congress.

STOW, Ralph
Public Affairs Coordinator, Amoco Corp.
1615 M St., N.W., Suite 200, Washington, DC 20036
Telephone: (202) 857-5324

STOWE, Robert C.
V. President, Citizens Network for Foreign Affairs
1616 H St., N.W., Washington, DC 20006
Telephone: (202) 639-8889

STOWE, Ronald F.
V. President, Washington Operations, Pacific Telesis Group-Washington
1275 Pennsylvania Ave., N.W. Suite 400, Washington, DC 20004
Telephone: (202) 383-6400

STOWELL, John L.
Director, Federal Affairs, Public Service Co. of Indiana
1800 K St., N.W., Suite 1018, Washington, DC 20006
Telephone: (202) 887-0497
Registered as lobbyist at U.S. Congress.

STRACHAN, David E., CAE
Exec. V. President, Nat'l Candy Wholesalers Ass'n
1120 Vermont Ave., N.W., Suite 1120, Washington, DC 20005
Telephone: (202) 463-2124

STRACKBEIN, William
Exec. Director, Lab Products Ass'n, SAMA Group of Ass'ns
225 Reinekers Lane Suite 625, Washington, DC 22314
Telephone: (703) 836-1360

STRAM, Kenneth M.
Bracy Williams & Co.
1000 Connecticut Ave., N.W., Suite 304, Washington, DC 20036
Telephone: (202) 659-4805
Registered as lobbyist at U.S. Congress.
Clients:
Batman Corp.
Daishowa America Co. Ltd.
Fieldstone Co.
Rocky Co., The

STRANAHAN, Robert P., Jr.
Wilmer, Cutler and Pickering
2445 M St., N.W., Washington, DC 20037-1420
Telephone: (202) 663-6000
Clients:
Scripps League Newspaper, Inc.

STRANDQUIST, John H.
Exec. Director, American Ass'n of Motor Vehicle Administrators
4200 Wilson Blvd., Suite 600, Arlington, VA 22203
Telephone: (703) 522-4200

STRANGE, Luther J., III
Director, Federal Government Affairs, Sonat Inc.
1100 15th St., N.W. Suite 700, Washington, DC 20005
Telephone: (202) 775-0840
Registered as lobbyist at U.S. Congress.

STRANO, Richard
President, American Osteopathic Hospital Ass'n
1454 Duke St., Alexandria, VA 22314
Telephone: (703) 684-7700

STRAS, Marcela B.
Barnes and Thornburg
1815 H St., N.W., Suite 800, Washington, DC 20006
Telephone: (202) 955-4500
Clients:
Headwear Institute of America
Nat'l Candle Ass'n

STRASS, Stephanie A.
Director, Public Affairs (Mid-Atlantic), Kaiser Foundation Health Plan, Inc.
4200 Wisconsin Ave., N.W. Suite 300, Washington, DC 20016
Telephone: (202) 364-6747

STRASSBURGER, Raymond
Dir, Gov't Relations/Telecommun. Policy, Northern Telecom Inc..
600 Maryland Ave., S.W. Suite 607, Washington, DC 20024
Telephone: (202) 554-1520
Registered as lobbyist at U.S. Congress.

STRATEGIC POLICY, INC.
1615 L St., N.W., Suite 650, Washington, DC 20036
Telephone: (202) 659-0878
Registered as Foreign Agent: (#4206)
Background: A consulting subsidiary of the law firm of Wunder, Ryan, Cannon & Thelen.
Members of firm representing listed organizations:
  Merkin, William S., Senior V. President, International
  Clients:
  Grey, Clark, Shih and Associates, Ltd. *(William S. Merkin)*
  Labatt Limited, John *(William S. Merkin)*

STRATEGIC RESOURCES CORP.
3000 K St., N.W., Suite 300, Washington, DC 20007
Telephone: (202) 944-4772
Background: A consulting firm associated with the law firm of Swidler and Berlin.
Members of firm representing listed organizations:
  Goldfield, H. P.
  Clients:
  Bermuda, Government of *(H. P. Goldfield)*
  China External Trade Development Council *(H. P. Goldfield)*
  Hyundai Motor Co. *(H. P. Goldfield)*
  Matsushita Electric Corp. of America

STRAUB, Terrence D.
General Manager - Gov't'l Affairs, Energy, USX Corp.
818 Connecticut Ave., N.W., Washington, DC 20006
Telephone: (202) 331-1340
Registered as lobbyist at U.S. Congress.
Background: Former Special Assistant for Congressional Liaison (House) at the White House under President Jimmy Carter.

STRAUS, Ira L.
Exec. Director, Ass'n to Unite the Democracies
1506 Pennsylvania Ave., S.E., Washington, DC 20003
Telephone: (202) 544-5150

STRAUS, Jerry C.
Hobbs, Straus, Dean and Wilder
1819 H St., N.W., Suite 800, Washington, DC 20006
Telephone: (202) 783-5100
Registered as lobbyist at U.S. Congress.
Background: Attorney, Civil Division, Appellate Section, U.S. Department of Justice, 1961-63. Member, Washington D.C. Regional Selection Panel, President's Commission on White House Fellows, 1973.
Clients:
  Aroostook Bank of Micmacs
  Menominee Indian Tribe
  Seminole Tribe of Florida

STRAUS, Julie Brink
Dir., Washington Affairs - Political, Union Pacific Corp.
555 13th St., N.W., Suite 450 West Columbia Square, Washington, DC 20004
Telephone: (202) 662-0100
Background: Serves as assistant treasurer, Union Pacific Fund for Effective Government.

STRAUS, P.C., V. Michael
1001 Connecticut Ave., N.W., Suite 335, Washington, DC 20036
Telephone: (202) 785-2242
Background: A private attorney.
Organizations represented:
  Air Charter (SAFA)
  Air France
  Air Guadeloupe
  Aviation Associates, Inc.

Chaparral Airlines, Inc.
Guyana Airways Corp.
Hyannis Air Service, Inc.
Metro Airlines, Inc.
Metro Express, Inc.
Southern Jersey Airways

STRAUSS, Robert S.
Akin, Gump, Strauss, Hauer and Feld
1333 New Hampshire Ave., N.W., Suite 400, Washington, DC 20036
Telephone: (202) 887-4000
Background: Special Trade Representative of the United States, 1977-79 and former Chairman, Democratic National Committee.

STRAWHORN, Larry
Director, Engineering Department, American Trucking Ass'ns
2200 Mill Road, Alexandria, VA 22314
Telephone: (703) 838-1845

STRAWN, Robert
Exec. V. President, Recreation Vehicle Dealers Ass'n of North America
3251 Old Lee Hwy. Suite 500, Fairfax, VA 22030
Telephone: (703) 591-7130
Background: Also represents the Recreation Vehicle Rental Ass'n.

STRAYER, John W.
Director, Government Relations, Nat'l Ass'n of Convenience Stores
1605 King St., Alexandria, VA 22314
Telephone: (703) 684-3600
Registered as lobbyist at U.S. Congress.

STRECK, Ronald J.
V. President, Gov't & Public Affairs, Nat'l Wholesale Druggists' Ass'n
105 Oronoco St., Alexandria, VA 22314
Telephone: (202) 684-6400

STRIBLING, Jess H.
King and Spalding
1730 Pennsylvania Ave., N.W. Suite 1200, Washington, DC 20006-4706
Telephone: (202) 737-0500
Clients:
  GPIA Animal Drug Alliance

STRICKLAND, Dennis
Legislation & Spec Projects, Legis Affrs, DEPARTMENT OF HEALTH AND HUMAN SERVICES - Food and Drug Administration
5600 Fishers Lane, Rockville, MD 20857
Telephone: (301) 443-3793

STRICKLAND, Stephen P.
President, Nat'l Peace Institute Foundation
110 Maryland Ave., N.E., Suite 409, Washington, DC 20002
Telephone: (202) 546-9500
Registered as lobbyist at U.S. Congress.

STRICKLAND, Suzette
Bergman Associates, William S.
1001 Connecticut Ave., N.W., Suite 800, Washington, DC 20036
Telephone: (202) 452-1520

STRINGER, William L.
V. President, Chambers Associates Incorporated
1625 K St., N.W. Suite 200, Washington, DC 20006
Telephone: (202) 857-0670
Background: Formerly Deputy Treasurer, State of New Jersey; Chief Economist, Senate Budget Committee; and Assistant to the Chairman, Federal Home Loan Bank Board.
Clients:
  Ben Franklin Advanced Technology Center
  Nat'l Ass'n of Home Builders of the U.S.
  North Jersey District Water Supply Commission
  Utah League of Cities and Towns

STROM, Cynthia
Director of Public Education, Christic Institute
1324 N. Capitol St., N.W., Washington, DC 20002
Telephone: (202) 797-8106

STROMBERG, R. Erik
President, American Ass'n of Port Authorities
1010 Duke St., Alexandria, VA 22314
Telephone: (703) 684-5700

STRONG, Wendy
Dep Asst Secy, Cong Liaison, DEPARTMENT OF HEALTH AND HUMAN SERVICES
200 Independence Ave. S.W., Washington, DC 20201
Telephone: (202) 245-7627

STRONGIN, Robin J.
Reseach Associate, Nat'l Health Policy Forum
2011 Eye St., N.W. Suite 200, Washington, DC 20006
Telephone: (202) 872-1390

STROOCK & STROOCK & LAVAN
1150 17th St., N.W. Sixth Floor, Washington, DC 20036
Telephone: (202) 452-9250
Members of firm representing listed organizations:
  McCarthy, Matthew H.
  Pozen, Walter
  Background: Assistant to Senator Harrison Williams, Jr., 1958. Assistant to the Secretary of the Interior, 1961-67.
  Rae, Mark N.
  Background: Attorney, Office of General Counsel, Commodity Futures Trading Commission, 1977-81.
  Clients:
  Dreyfus Corp. *(Walter Pozen)*
  Goldman, Sachs and Co. *(Mark N. Rae)*

STROPP, Robert, Jr.
General Counsel, United Mine Workers of America
900 15th St., N.W., Washington, DC 20005
Telephone: (202) 842-7330

STROTHER AND HOSKING ASSOCIATES
6301 Stevenson Ave., Suite 1, Alexandria, VA 22304
Telephone: (703) 823-1732
Members of firm representing listed organizations:
  Hosking, James H.
  Strother, Michael E.
  Background: Serves as Treasurer, Land and Water Political Action Commitee, Exec. V. President, Power and Communicaions Contractors Ass'n.
  Clients:
  Land Improvement Contractors of America *(Michael E. Strother)*
  Power and Communications Contractors Ass'n *(Michael E. Strother)*

STROTHER, Michael E.
Strother and Hosking Associates
6301 Stevenson Ave., Suite 1, Alexandria, VA 22304
Telephone: (703) 823-1732
Registered as lobbyist at U.S. Congress.
Background: Serves as Treasurer, Land and Water Political Action Commitee, Exec. V. President, Power and Communicaions Contractors Ass'n.
Clients:
  Land Improvement Contractors of America
  Power and Communications Contractors Ass'n

STROUP, Thomas
V. President/General Counsel, Telocator
2000 M St., N.W., Suite 230, Washington, DC 20036
Telephone: (202) 467-4770

STRUMPF, George
Director, Government Relations, Health Insurance Plan of Greater New York
1150 17th St., N.W., Suite 600, Washington, DC 20036
Telephone: (202) 659-9460
Registered as lobbyist at U.S. Congress.
Background: Associate Director, Office of Health Maintenance Organizations, Dept. of Health and Human Services, 1972-79.

STRUPP, Werner
Sinrod & Tash
2201 Wisconsin Ave., N.W., Suite 250, Washington, DC 20007
Telephone: (202) 965-7956
Clients:
American Podiatric Medical Ass'n

STRUYK, Raymond
Director, Internat'l Activities Center, Urban Institute, The
2100 M St., N.W., Washington, DC 20037
Telephone: (202) 833-7200

STUBBS, Anne D.
Exec. Director, Coalition of Northeastern Governors
400 North Capitol St., N.W. Suite 382, Washington, DC 20001
Telephone: (202) 783-6674

STUCKE, Dorothy
Legislative Director, Nat'l Apartment Ass'n
1111 14th St., N.W., 9th Floor, Washington, DC 20005
Telephone: (202) 842-4050
Registered as lobbyist at U.S. Congress.

STUDLEY, Jamienne S.
Exec. Director, Nat'l Ass'n for Law Placement
1666 Connecticut Ave., N.W. Suite 450, Washington, DC 20009
Telephone: (202) 667-1666
Background: Served as Special Assistant to Secretary Harris, Department of Health and Human Services, 1980-81.

STUDLEY, Janet R.
Holland and Knight
888 17th St., N.W. Suite 900, Washington, DC 20006
Telephone: (202) 955-5550
Registered as lobbyist at U.S. Congress.
Registered as Foreign Agent: (#3718).
Background: Former Chief Counsel, Senate Subcommittee on Federal Spending Practices/Senator Lawton Chiles (D-FL).
Clients:
General Development Corp.
Holland and Knight Committee for Effective Government
Pan American Satellite Corp.

STUDZINSKI, James A.
V. Pres. & COO, Rehab. Facilities Svcs., Nat'l Ass'n of Rehabilitation Facilities
Box 17675, Washington, DC 20041-0675
Telephone: (703) 648-9300

STURDIVANT, John N.
National President, American Federation of Government Employees
80 F St., N.W., Washington, DC 20001
Telephone: (202) 737-8700
Registered as lobbyist at U.S. Congress.

STURM, John F.
V. President, Government Affairs, CBS, Inc.
1800 M St., N.W. Suite 300 North, Washington, DC 20036
Telephone: (202) 457-4501

STURTEVANT, Albert D.
Rose, Schmidt, Hasley & DiSalle
1701 Pennsylvania Ave., N.W., Suite 1040, Washington, DC 20006
Telephone: (202) 293-8600
Registered as lobbyist at U.S. Congress.
Registered as Foreign Agent: (#2275).

STUTTMAN, Burton
Treasurer, Third Class Mail Ass'n Political Action Committee
1333 F St., N.W., Suite 710, Washington, DC 20004-1108
Telephone: (202) 347-0055

SUAZO, Vicky M.
Public Affairs Manager, Dow Chemical
1776 Eye St., N.W., Suite 575, Washington, DC 20006
Telephone: (202) 429-3400

SUCHMAN, Peter
Powell, Goldstein, Frazer and Murphy
1001 Pennsylvania, N.W., Sixth Fl., Washington, DC 20004

Telephone: (202) 347-0066
Background: Lieutenant, U.S. Coast Guard, 1960-64. U.S. Foreign Service Officer, 1964-70. Director, Office of Trade Policy, U.S. Treasury Department, 1972-74. Deputy Assistant Secretary, Tariff Affairs, Treasury Department, 1974-78.
Clients:
American Ass'n of Exporters and Importers
American Koyo Corp.
Caterpillar Inc.
Davis Walker Corp.
Hoogovens Group BV
Koyo Seiko
Nat'l Latex Products Co.
NVW (USA)

SUCHMANN, Donna
President, Federation of Organizations for Professional Women
2001 S St., N.W., Suite 540, Washington, DC 20009
Telephone: (202) 328-1415

SUDOW, William E.
Jones, Day, Reavis and Pogue
1450 G St., N.W., Suite 700, Washington, DC 20005-2088
Telephone: (202) 879-3939
Registered as lobbyist at U.S. Congress.
Background: Assistant to Staff Director, U.S. Commission on Civil Rights, 1970-71. Special Assistant and Counsel to Rep. John Brademas of Indiana, 1972-75.

SUGAMELI, Glenn
Counsel, Public Lands and Energy Div., Nat'l Wildlife Federation
1400 16th St., N.W., Washington, DC 20036-2266
Telephone: (202) 797-6800
Registered as lobbyist at U.S. Congress.

SUGANUMA, Kiichi
Manager, Tokyo Electric Power Co.
1901 L St., N.W., Suite 720, Washington, DC 20036
Telephone: (202) 457-0790

SUGARMAN, Jule
Exec. Director, Special Olympics Internat'l, Inc.
1350 New York Ave., N.W., Suite 500, Washington, DC 20005
Telephone: (202) 628-3630

SUGIURA, Komonsuke
Director and General Manager, Tokyo Electric Power Co.
1901 L St., N.W., Suite 720, Washington, DC 20036
Telephone: (202) 457-0790

SULC, Lawrence B.
President, Hale Institute, The Nathan
422 First St., S.E.,, Washington, DC 20003
Telephone: (202) 546-2293
Background: Serves also as President, The Hale Foundation.

SULLIVAN, Ann L.
Director, Wash. Office of the Governor, Connecticut, State of
444 North Capitol St., N.W. Suite 317, Washington, DC 20001
Telephone: (202) 347-4535

SULLIVAN, Ann M.
V. President, Holt, Miller & Associates
2111 Wilson Blvd., Suite 531, Arlington, VA 22201-3008
Telephone: (703) 276-8009
Registered as lobbyist at U.S. Congress.
Background: Former aide to Senators George Mitchell (D-ME) and Carl Levin (D-MI) and to Rep. Philip Sharp (D-IN).
Clients:
Interstate Natural Gas Ass'n of America
Natural Gas Vehicle Coalition

SULLIVAN, Anne
Legislative Representative, Collier, Shannon & Scott
1055 Thomas Jefferson St., N.W., Suite 300, Washington, DC 20007
Telephone: (202) 342-8400
Registered as lobbyist at U.S. Congress.

SULLIVAN, Arthur E., Jr.
Requirement Analyst, Diagnostic Retrieval Systems, Inc.
1215 South Jefferson Davis Hwy., Suite 1004, Arlington, VA 22202
Telephone: (703) 521-8000
Registered as lobbyist at U.S. Congress.

SULLIVAN, Brandi
Davis/Replogle & Associates, Inc.
335 Commerce St., Alexandria, VA 22314
Telephone: (703) 548-5016
Clients:
City & Regional Magazine Ass'n

SULLIVAN, Brendan V., Jr.
Williams and Connolly
839 17th St., N.W. 1000 Hill Bldg., Washington, DC 20006
Telephone: (202) 331-5000
Clients:
Omni Internat'l

SULLIVAN, Carl R.
Exec. Director, American Fisheries Soc.
5410 Grosvenor Lane, Bethesda, MD 20814
Telephone: (301) 897-8616

SULLIVAN, Catherine
Manager, Government Relations, Nat'l Club Ass'n
1625 Eye St., N.W., Suite 609, Washington, DC 20006
Telephone: (202) 466-8424

SULLIVAN, Cathie
Associate Director, Communications, Center for Population Options
1012 14th St., N.W. Suite 1200, Washington, DC 20005
Telephone: (202) 347-5700

SULLIVAN AND CROMWELL
1701 Pennsylvania Ave., N.W. Suite 800, Washington, DC 20006
Telephone: (202) 956-7500
Background: A Washington office of a New York law firm.
Members of firm representing listed organizations:
Akers, James E.
Craft, Robert H. (Jr.)
Background: Special Assistant to Under Secretary of State, 1974-76. Exec. Assistant to Chairman, Securities and Exchange Commission, 1976.
Pfeiffer, Margaret K.
Clients:
Ford Motor Co.
Imo Industries *(Margaret K. Pfeiffer)*
N.V. Philips Gloeilampenfabrieken *(Margaret K. Pfeiffer)*
Securities Industry Ass'n
Solvay et Cie

SULLIVAN, Dr. Donald F.
Exec. Director, Nat'l Conference of Christians and Jews
2041 Martin Luther King Jr. Ave., S.E., Suite 302, Washington, DC 20020
Telephone: (202) 678-9400

SULLIVAN, Dr. Frank J.
Dir., Div of Legis Analysis, DEPARTMENT OF HEALTH AND HUMAN SERVICES - Nat'l Institutes of Health
Bldg. 1, 9000 Rockville Pike, Bethesda, MD 20892
Telephone: (301) 496-3152

SULLIVAN, Gael M.
Director, Federal Relations, LTV Corp.
1025 Thomas Jefferson St., N.W., Suite 511 West, Washington, DC 20007
Telephone: (202) 944-5700
Registered as lobbyist at U.S. Congress.
Background: Former Deputy Assistant Secretary for Congressional Affairs, U.S. Department of Commerce. Member, White House Budget Taskforce, 1979-80. Serves as contact for LTV Corp. Active Citizenship Campaign.

SULLIVAN, Harry
Sr. V. President and General Counsel, Food Marketing Institute
1750 K St., N.W., Washington, DC 20006
Telephone: (202) 452-8444
Registered as lobbyist at U.S. Congress.
Background: Also serves as Treasurer, Food Marketing Institute Political Action Committee.

WASHINGTON REPRESENTATIVES

SULLIVAN, Helen
Kaufman & Associates, Henry J.
2233 Wisconsin Ave., N.W., Washington, DC 20007
Telephone: (202) 333-0700
Organizations represented:
Internat'l Sleep Products Ass'n

SULLIVAN, Janet
Administrator, Washington Office, Telephone Pioneers of
America
930 H St., N.W., 9th Floor, Washington, DC 20001
Telephone: (202) 392-2889

SULLIVAN, Jay R.
Chief, Div of Cong Affrs, DEPARTMENT OF INTERIOR -
Bureau of Land Management
18th and C Sts., N.W. Room 5558, Washington, DC
20240
Telephone: (202) 343-5101

SULLIVAN, John H.
Deputy Exec. Director, American Water Works Ass'n
1010 Vermont Ave., N.W., Suite 810, Washington, DC
20005
Telephone: (202) 628-8303

SULLIVAN, Judy M.
Director of Government Relations, Nat'l Ass'n of Housing
Cooperatives
1614 King St., Alexandria, VA 22314
Telephone: (703) 549-5201
Registered as lobbyist at U.S. Congress.

SULLIVAN, Kevin R.
Pillsbury, Madison and Sutro
1667 K St., N.W., Suite 1100, Washington, DC 20006
Telephone: (202) 887-0300
Clients:
United Telecommunications

SULLIVAN, Marcia Z.
Senior Government Relations Counsel, Consumer Bank-
ers Ass'n
1000 Wilson Blvd., 30th Floor, Arlington, VA 22209-3908
Telephone: (703) 276-1750
Registered as lobbyist at U.S. Congress.

SULLIVAN, Margaret Cox
President, Stockholders of America
1625 Eye St., N.W. Suite 724A, Washington, DC 20006
Telephone: (202) 783-3430
Registered as lobbyist at U.S. Congress.

SULLIVAN, Paul E.
Wunder, Ryan, Cannon & Thelen
1615 L St., N.W., Suite 650, Washington, DC 20036
Telephone: (202) 659-3005
Background: Assistant Legal Counsel, Nat'l Republican
Congressional Committee, 1981-82. Executive Assistant
to Commissioner, Federal Election Commission, 1982-85.
Clients:
Nat'l Council of Savings Institutions THRIFT-
PAC
Nat'l Federation of Independent Business PAC
Nat'l Security Political Action Committee
NutraSweet Co.
Pan American Life
PepsiCo PAC
Restaurant Ass'n of Metropolitan Washington
PAC
State Compliance Systems
VINTA Mineral and Financial, Inc.

SULLIVAN, Richard
Exec. V.P. & Sr. Partner, Fleishman-Hillard, Inc
1301 Connecticut Ave., N.W., Washington, DC 20036
Telephone: (202) 659-0330
Registered as lobbyist at U.S. Congress.

SULLIVAN, Roger K.
President, Ass'n for Information and Image Management
1100 Wayne Ave. Suite 1100, Silver Spring, MD 20910
Telephone: (301) 587-8202

SULLIVAN, Roger W.
President, U.S.-China Business Council
1818 N St., N.W., Suite 500, Washington, DC 20036
Telephone: (202) 429-0340

SULLIVAN, Sean
V. President, New Directions for Policy
1101 Vermont Ave., N.W. Suite 400, Washington, DC
20005
Telephone: (202) 289-3907

SULLIVAN, Timothy
Dykema Gossett
1752 N St., N.W., 6th Floor, Washington, DC 20036
Telephone: (202) 466-7185

SULLIVAN AND WORCESTER
1025 Connecticut Ave., N.W. Suite 806, Washington, DC
20036
Telephone: (202) 775-8190
Background: Washington office of a Boston law firm.
Members of firm representing listed organizations:
Calhoun, Robert L.
Background: Attorney-Advisor to Commissioner
Charles A. Webb, 1963-67 and Legislative Counsel,
1967-69, Interstate Commerce Commission. Deputy
Director, Office of Policy Review, Department of
Transportation, 1969-71.
Fishman, William L.
Background: Deputy Associate Administrator for Poli-
cy, 1974-77, and Senior Policy Advisor, 1979-80,
National Telecommunications and Information Ad-
ministration, U.S. Department of Commerce.
Schwartz, David M.
Background: Attorney-Advisor to Commissioner How-
ard Freas, Interstate Commerce Commission, 1960-
65. Consultant, Department of Commerce, 1965-66.
Assistant Director for Transportation Program Policy,
Department of Commerce, 1966-67. Director, Office
of Policy Review and Coordination, Department of
Transportation, 1967-70.
Clients:
Kansas City Southern Industries *(Robert L. Calhoun,
David M. Schwartz)*
Marion Merrell Dow, Inc.

SULTAN, Peter L.
Barnes, Richardson and Colburn
1819 H St., N.W., Washington, DC 20006
Telephone: (202) 457-0300
Registered as lobbyist at U.S. Congress.
Clients:
Miles, Inc.

SUMBERG, Dr. Alfred D.
Director of Government Relations, American Ass'n of University Professors
1012 14th St., N.W., Suite 500, Washington, DC 20005
Telephone: (202) 737-5900

SUMBERG, Jeffrey
Staff Attorney, Nat'l Federation of Federal Employees
1016 16th St., N.W., Suite 400, Washington, DC 20036
Telephone: (202) 862-4400
Registered as lobbyist at U.S. Congress.

SUMMERTON, Allison B.
Project Manager, Chambers Associates Incorporated
1625 K St., N.W. Suite 200, Washington, DC 20006
Telephone: (202) 857-0670

SUMPTER, Suzanne E.
Assistant Director, Media Relations, Nat'l Ass'n of Life Un-
derwriters
1922 F St., N.W., Washington, DC 20006
Telephone: (202) 331-6000
Background: Former aide to Rep. Gus Yatron (D-PA).

SUNDWALL, David N., M.D.
V. President and Medical Director, AmHS Institute
1919 Pennsylvania Ave., N.W., Suite 703, Washington, DC
20006
Telephone: (202) 293-2840

SUNLEY, Emil
Director of Tax Analysis, Deloitte & Touche Washington
Services Group
1001 Pennsylvania Ave., N.W. Suite 350, Washington, DC
20004
Telephone: (202) 879-4945

SUPER, David A.
Legal Director, Food Research and Action Center
1319 F St., N.W. Suite 500, Washington, DC 20004

Telephone: (202) 393-5060
Registered as lobbyist at U.S. Congress.

SUPLIZIO ASSOCIATES, Paul
5152 Woodmire Lane, Alexandria, VA 22311
Telephone: (703) 931-0103
Registered as Foreign Agent: (# 3802)
Background: A government relations consulting firm.
Members of firm representing listed organizations:
Bobbitt, Timothy, Associate
Miller, Jeanne, Associate
Suplizio, Paul E., President
Organizations represented:
Coalition for North American Trade and Invest-
ment *(Paul E. Suplizio)*
Internat'l Reciprocal Trade Ass'n *(Jeanne Miller, Paul
E. Suplizio)*
Internat'l Reciprocal Trade Ass'n Political Action
Committee *(Paul E. Suplizio)*
M.A.R.S. Inc. *(Paul E. Suplizio)*
Management Insights, Inc. *(Paul E. Suplizio)*
Mintax, Inc. *(Paul E. Suplizio)*
S.R.C. Services, Inc. *(Paul E. Suplizio)*
Targeted Jobs Tax Credit Coalition *(Timothy Bobbitt,
Jeanne Miller, Paul E. Suplizio)*

SUPLIZIO, Paul E.
President, Suplizio Associates, Paul
5152 Woodmire Lane, Alexandria, VA 22311
Telephone: (703) 931-0103
Registered as lobbyist at U.S. Congress.
Registered as Foreign Agent: (# 3802).
Organizations represented:
Coalition for North American Trade and Invest-
ment
Internat'l Reciprocal Trade Ass'n
Internat'l Reciprocal Trade Ass'n Political Action
Committee
M.A.R.S. Inc.
Management Insights, Inc.
Mintax, Inc.
S.R.C. Services, Inc.
Targeted Jobs Tax Credit Coalition

SUSMAN, Julie
V. President, Jefferson Group, The
1341 G St., N.W., Suite 1100, Washington, DC 20005
Telephone: (202) 638-3535
Clients:
Boonestroo, Rosene, Anderlik & Associates
H.S.I.
Planning Research Corp.

SUSMAN, Thomas M.
Ropes and Gray
1001 Pennsylvania Ave., N.W., Washington, DC 20004
Telephone: (202) 626-3900
Registered as lobbyist at U.S. Congress.
Background: Chief Counsel, Senate Administrative Practice
and Procedure Subcommittee, 1972-76. General Counsel,
Senate Antitrust and Monopoly Subcommittee, 1977-78.
General Counsel, Senate Judiciary Committee, 1979-80.
Clients:
Butler Capital Corp.
Digital Equipment Corp.
Dunkin' Donuts
Eastern Enterprises
Nat'l Ass'n of Independent Schools

SUSSER, Peter A.
Keller and Heckman
1150 17th St., N.W. Suite 1000, Washington, DC 20036
Telephone: (202) 956-5600
Clients:
Nat'l-American Wholesale Grocers' Ass'n

SUSSMAN, Robert M.
Latham and Watkins
1001 Pennsylvania Ave., N.W., Suite 1300, Washington,
DC 20004
Telephone: (202) 637-2200

SUSSWEIN, Donald B.
Thacher, Proffitt and Wood
1500 K St., N.W., Suite 200, Washington, DC 20005
Telephone: (202) 347-8400

SUTHERLAND, ASBILL AND BRENNAN
1275 Pennsylvania, N.W., Washington, DC 20004-2404

SUTHERLAND, ASBILL AND BRENNAN (Cont'd)
Telephone: (202) 383-0100
Members of firm representing listed organizations:
  Abramowitz, George R.
  Andrews, Wright H. (Jr.)
    Background: Chief Legislative Assistant to Senator Sam Nunn (D-GA), 1973-75.
  Asbill, Mac (Jr.)
    Background: Law Clerk to Justice Stanley Reed, U.S. Supreme Court, 1948-49.
  Cohen, N. Jerold
    Background: Chief Counsel, Internal Revenue Service, 1979-81.
  Gregory, Francis M. (Jr.)
    Background: Law Clerk to U.S. Supreme Court Justice William J. Brennan, 1967-68.
  Grenier, Edward J. (Jr.)
  Hoffman, Joel E.
    Background: Trial Attorney, Appellate Section, Antitrust Division, U.S. Department of Justice, 1960-63.
  Howard, Glen S.
  Jones, Anne P.
    Background: Attorney, 1968-77 and Director, Division of Investment Management, 1976-77, Securities and Exchange Commission. General Counsel, Federal Home Loan Bank Board, 1978-79. Commissioner, Federal Communications Commission, 1979-83.
  Libin, Jerome B.
    Background: Law Clerk to Justice Charles E. Whittaker, U.S. Supreme Court, 1959-60.
  Morrow, Robert R.
  O'Donnell, Earle H.
  Pehrson, Gordon O. (Jr.)
  Starling, Kenneth G.
  Vlcek, Jan Benes
    Background: Trial Attorney, Civil Aeronautics Board, 1968-69. Attorney-Advisor, Environmental Protection Agency, 1971-73. Associate Minority Counsel, U.S. House of Representatives Committee on Interstate and Foreign Commerce, 1973-78. Counsel for Regulatory Policy, House Ad Hoc Committee on Energy, 1977-78.
Clients:
  Acacia Mutual Life Insurance Co. *(Wright H. Andrews, Jr.)*
  Acacia Mutual Political Action Committee
  Ad Hoc Committee for a Competitive Electric Supply System (ACCESS) *(Earle H. O'Donnell, Jan Benes Vlcek)*
  American Industrial Clay Co. *(Edward J. Grenier, Jr.)*
  Anglo-American Clays Corp. *(Gordon O. Pehrson, Jr.)*
  Argo Communications Corp. *(Anne P. Jones)*
  Armco Inc. *(Edward J. Grenier, Jr., Earle H. O'Donnell, Jan Benes Vlcek)*
  Bank of Baltimore *(Wright H. Andrews, Jr.)*
  Chain Pharmacy Ass'n of New York State *(Kenneth G. Starling)*
  China Clay Producers Political Action Committee *(Gordon O. Pehrson, Jr.)*
  Columbia Federal Savings and Loan *(Anne P. Jones)*
  Committee Against Revising Staggers *(Jan Benes Vlcek)*
  Council of Industrial Boiler Owners *(Jan Benes Vlcek)*
  Duke University
  Equifax Inc. *(Wright H. Andrews, Jr., Francis M. Gregory, Jr.)*
  First Financial Management Corp. *(Wright H. Andrews, Jr.)*
  GAF Corp.
  Georgia Kaolin Co. *(Edward J. Grenier, Jr.)*
  Huber Corp., J. M. *(Gordon O. Pehrson, Jr.)*
  Kaiser Aluminum and Chemical Corp. *(Jan Benes Vlcek)*
  KN Energy Inc.
  Lederle Laboratories, American Cyanamid Co. Subsidiary *(Joel E. Hoffman)*
  Minnesota Mutual Life Insurance Co. *(Gordon O. Pehrson, Jr.)*
  Nevada, State of *(Wright H. Andrews, Jr.)*
  New England Digital Distribution Corp. *(Anne P. Jones)*
  Nord Resources Corp. *(Gordon O. Pehrson, Jr.)*
  Pacific Telesis Group-Washington *(Anne P. Jones)*
  Philip Morris Cos., Inc. *(Wright H. Andrews, Jr.)*
  Process Gas Consumers Group *(Edward J. Grenier, Jr., Glen S. Howard, Robert R. Morrow, Jan Benes Vlcek)*
  Questar Corp.

Springs Industries, Inc.
Thiele Kaolin Co. *(Gordon O. Pehrson, Jr.)*
Washington, State of *(Wright H. Andrews, Jr.)*
WNHT
WSYT

SUTHERLAND, Scott
Director, Federal Relations, Ducks Unlimited Inc.
1155 Connecticut Ave., N.W., Suite 800, Washington, DC 20036
Telephone: (202) 452-8824
Background: Former Assistant Director-Public Liaison for Presidents Reagan and Bush.

SUTLEY, Nancy
Policy Director, Nat'l Independent Energy Producers
601 13th St., N.W. Suite 320S, Washington, DC 20004
Telephone: (202) 783-2244

SUTO, Eugene
Exec. Secretary, Nat'l Classification Management Soc.
6116 Roseland Drive, Rockville, MD 20852
Telephone: (301) 231-9191

SUTTER, Leonard L.
Chief, Div of Legis, Off of Gen Counsel, DEPARTMENT OF TRANSPORTATION - Maritime Administration
400 Seventh St., S.W., Washington, DC 20590
Telephone: (202) 366-5724

SUTTLE, W. Thomas
Assoc. Staff Dir., Prof. Activities, Institute of Electrical and Electronics Engineers, Inc.
1828 L St., N.W. Suite 1202, Washington, DC 20036-5104
Telephone: (202) 785-0017
Registered as lobbyist at U.S. Congress.

SUTTON, Sharon
Manager, Marketing and Communications, Nat'l Computer Graphics Ass'n
2722 Merrilee Drive, Suite 200, Fairfax, VA 22031
Telephone: (703) 698-9600

SUTTON, Stephen
Director, Congressional Relations, Grumman Corp.
1000 Wilson Blvd., Suite 2800, Arlington, VA 22209
Telephone: (703) 875-8400
Registered as lobbyist at U.S. Congress.

SUZUKI, Yutaka
Vice President, External Relations, Nissan Motor Corp. in U.S.A.
750 17th St., N.W. Suite 901, Washington, DC 20006
Telephone: (202) 862-5523
Registered as lobbyist at U.S. Congress.

SVEC, Milan
Fellow, United States Institute for Peace
1550 M St., N.W. Suite 700, Washington, DC 20005-1708
Telephone: (202) 457-1700

SVENDSON, Douglass W., Jr.
1730 Rhode Island Ave., N.W. Suite 417-19, Washington, DC 20036
Telephone: (202) 293-3411
Registered as lobbyist at U.S. Congress.
Organizations represented:
  Eastern Central Motor Carriers Ass'n
  Hollywood Marine Service, Inc.
  Middle Atlantic Conference

SWALBACH, Robert
Congressional Liaison, Northern Mariana Islands, Commonwealth of
2121 R St., N.W., Washington, DC 20008
Telephone: (202) 673-5869

SWANN, Lance B.
V. President, Gov't Relations, Computer Sciences Corp.
3160 Fairview Park Drive, MC/410, Falls Church, VA 22042
Telephone: (703) 641-2560

SWANN, STEPHEN L., LAW OFFICES OF
1005 N. Glebe Road, Suite 250, Arlington, VA 22201
Telephone: (703) 276-4820
Background: Attorney, U.S. Coast Guard, 1975-85; Legislative Counsel, Department of Transporatation, Congressional Affairs Staff, U.S. Coast Guard, 1985-88.
Clients:

Science Industries (S.A.R.L.)

SWANSON, David L.
Craft and Loesch
1050 Thomas Jefferson St, N.W. 6th Floor, Washington, DC 20007
Telephone: (202) 965-6290

SWANSON, Lisa
Legal Research Coordinator, Nat'l Abortion Rights Action League
1101 14th St., N.W., Suite 500, Washington, DC 20005
Telephone: (202) 371-0779

SWANSON, Cdr. Ronald
Legal and Legis Matters, DEPARTMENT OF NAVY - Chief of Naval Operations Office
The Pentagon, Washington, DC 20350-2000
Telephone: (202) 695-3480

SWANSON, Sylvia E.
V. President, Public Affairs, Glass Packaging Institute
1801 K St., N.W., Suite 1105L, Washington, DC 20006
Telephone: (202) 887-4850
Registered as lobbyist at U.S. Congress.

SWARD, Marcia P.
Exec. Director, Mathematical Ass'n of America
1529 18th St., N.W., Washington, DC 20036
Telephone: (202) 387-5200

SWARTZ, Deborah
Director, Government Relations, Economic Consulting Services Inc.
1225 19th St. N.W., Suite 210, Washington, DC 20036
Telephone: (202) 466-7720
Registered as lobbyist at U.S. Congress.
Clients:
  Amalgamated Clothing and Textile Workers Union
  Footwear Industries of America
  Goody Products, Inc.
  Internat'l Leather Goods, Plastics and Novelty Workers Union, AFL-CIO
  Luggage and Leather Goods Manufacturers of America
  Neckwear Ass'n of America
  Outboard Marine Corp.
  Work Glove Manufacturers Ass'n

SWARTZ, Rick
Director, Coalition of Advocates for Immigrants and Refugees (CAIR)

SWECKER, Dale
Director, Communications, Gypsum Ass'n
810 First St., N.E., Suite 510, Washington, DC 20002
Telephone: (202) 289-5440

SWEDIN, Kris
Deputy Exec. Director, Democratic Senatorial Campaign Committee
430 South Capitol St., S.E., Washington, DC 20003
Telephone: (202) 224-2447

SWEENEY, Daniel J.
McCarthy, Sweeney and Harkaway, P.C.
1750 Pennsylvania Ave. N.W. Suite 1105, Washington, DC 20006
Telephone: (202) 393-5710
Clients:
  Nat'l Small Shipments Traffic Conference - NASSTRAC

SWEENEY, David A.
Director, Legislative Department, Internat'l Brotherhood of Teamsters, Chauffeurs, Warehousemen and Helpers of America
25 Louisiana Ave., N.W., Washington, DC 20001
Telephone: (202) 624-6890
Registered as lobbyist at U.S. Congress.

SWEENEY, John J.
Internat'l President, Service Employees Internat'l Union
1313 L St., N.W., Washington, DC 20005
Telephone: (202) 898-3200

SWEENEY, Robert E.
Senior Consultant, Southern Technical Services
Suite 610 Three Metro Center, Bethesda, MD 20814

WASHINGTON REPRESENTATIVES

Telephone: (301) 652-2500

SWEENEY, Robert H.
President, Nat'l Ass'n of Children's Hospitals and Related
Institutions
401 Wythe St., Alexandria, VA 22314
Telephone: (703) 684-1355

SWEENEY, Rosemarie
Director, Washington Office, American Academy of Family
Physicians
600 Maryland Ave., S.W., Suite 770, Washington, DC
20024
Telephone: (202) 488-7448
Registered as lobbyist at U.S. Congress.

SWEENEY, William R., Jr.
Washington Resources and Strategy, Inc.
536 7th St., S.E., Washington, DC 20003
Telephone: (202) 544-1988
Registered as lobbyist at U.S. Congress.
Registered as Foreign Agent: (# 3989).
Background: Former Deputy Chairman, Democratic National Committee. Former Executive Director, Democratic Congressional Campaign Committee.
Clients:
American Challenge Today Political Action Committee
American Medical Ass'n
China External Trade Development Council
Electronic Data Systems Corp.
Japan, Embassy of
Kelso Political Action Committee

SWEET, Frederic H.
V. President, Legislative Affairs, Northwestern Mutual Life
Insurance Co.
1133 20th St., N.W., Suite 600, Washington, DC 20036
Telephone: (202) 296-1020
Background: Has offices in Washington and Milwaukee.

SWEET, Paul E.
Dir., Federal Governmental Relations, University of California
1523 New Hampshire Ave., N.W., Washington, DC 20036
Telephone: (202) 785-2666

SWEET, Stuart J.
Black, Manafort, Stone and Kelly Public Affairs Co.
211 N. Union St., Third Floor, Alexandria, VA 22314
Telephone: (703) 683-6612
Registered as lobbyist at U.S. Congress.
Registered as Foreign Agent: (# 3600).

SWEGLE, Harry W.
Washington Liaison, Nat'l Center for State Courts
444 N. Capitol St., N.W., Suite 608, Washington, DC
20001
Telephone: (202) 347-5924

SWEITZER, Donald R.
V. President, Black, Manafort, Stone and Kelly Public Affairs Co.
211 N. Union St., Third Floor, Alexandria, VA 22314
Telephone: (703) 683-6612
Background: Former Finance Director, Democratic National Committee.

SWENSON, Diane K.
V. President, American Tort Reform Ass'n
1212 New York Ave., N.W. Suite 515, Washington, DC
20005
Telephone: (202) 682-1163

SWEZEY, Robert D., Jr.
Director, Federal Relations, MCI Communications Corp.
1133 19th St., N.W., Washington, DC 20036
Telephone: (202) 872-1600
Registered as lobbyist at U.S. Congress.

SWIDLER & BERLIN, CHARTERED
3000 K St., N.W., Suite 300, Washington, DC 20007
Telephone: (202) 944-4300
Registered as Foreign Agent: (#4079)
Members of firm representing listed organizations:
Berlin, Edward
Background: Attorney, Department of Justice, 1961-66.
Assistant General Counsel, Federal Power Commission, 1966-69.

Blake, Francis S.
Background: Deputy Counsel to the Vice President,
1981-83. General Counsel, Environmental Protection
Agency, 1985-88.
Direnfeld, Barry
Gifford, Dawn
Background: Former Administrative Assistant to Senator Robert Kasten (R-WI).
Hoff, John S.
Hyman, Lester S.
Background: Attorney, Securities and Exchange Commission, 1955-56.
Legato, Carmen D.
Background: Law Clerk to Justice William J. Brennan,
U.S. Supreme Court, 1977-78.
Lehman, Bruce A.
Background: Counsel, Committee on the Judiciary,
1974-83 and Chief Counsel, Subcommittee on Courts,
Civil Liberties and the Administration of Justice,
1977-83, U.S. House of Representatives.
Malter, Barry L.
Background: Attorney, Federal Trade Commission,
1973-76. Acting Deputy Associate General Counsel,
Environmental Protection Agency, 1976-80.
Popkin, Richard A.
Background: Confidential Assistant to the Under Secretary of Commerce for International Trade, 1984-85.
Deputy Assistant Secretary of Commerce for Trade
Administration, 1985-87.
Schaner, Kenneth I.
Background: Attorney, Internal Revenue Service,
1966-70.
Swidler, Joseph C.
Background: Assistant Solicitor, Department of Interior, 1933. Office of the General Counsel, TVA, 1933-57. Chairman, Federal Power Commission, 1961-65.
Clients:
Aldus *(Bruce A. Lehman)*
American Bakers Ass'n *(Barry Direnfeld)*
American Gas Ass'n *(Francis S. Blake)*
American Iron and Steel Institute *(Francis S. Blake)*
Ashton-Tate *(Bruce A. Lehman)*
Autodesk, Inc. *(Bruce A. Lehman)*
Bermuda, Government of *(Lester S. Hyman)*
Browning-Ferris Industries (D.C.), Inc.
BSA - Business Software Alliance *(Bruce A. Lehman)*
Business Coalition for RICO Reform *(Barry Direnfeld)*
China External Trade Development Council *(Dawn Gifford)*
China, Foreign Trade Board of the Republic of
Design Protection Coalition *(Bruce A. Lehman)*
External Tanks Corp. *(Dawn Gifford)*
Hyundai Motor Co. *(Lester S. Hyman)*
Intercontinental Energy Corp. *(Carmen D. Legato)*
Internat'l Environmental Policy Coalition *(Dawn Gifford, Barry L. Malter)*
Internat'l Service Agencies *(Kenneth I. Schaner)*
Laidlaw, Inc. *(Barry Direnfeld, Barry L. Malter)*
Lotus Development Corp. *(Bruce A. Lehman)*
MacAndrews & Forbes Holdings, Inc.
Merrill Lynch and Co., Inc. *(Barry Direnfeld)*
Microsoft *(Bruce A. Lehman)*
Motor Vehicle Manufacturers Ass'n of the United
States
Nat'l Council of Community Hospitals *(John S. Hoff, Kenneth I. Schaner)*
New England Power Co. *(Edward Berlin)*
Product Liability Alliance, The *(Dawn Gifford)*
Software Publishers Ass'n *(Bruce A. Lehman)*
Swidler & Berlin Political Action Committee
Typeface Design Coalition
United States Trademark Ass'n *(Bruce A. Lehman)*
WordPerfect *(Bruce A. Lehman)*

SWIDLER, Joseph C.
Swidler & Berlin, Chartered
3000 K St., N.W., Suite 300, Washington, DC 20007
Telephone: (202) 944-4300
Registered as lobbyist at U.S. Congress.
Background: Assistant Solicitor, Department of Interior,
1933. Office of the General Counsel, TVA, 1933-57.
Chairman, Federal Power Commission, 1961-65.

SWIFT, Carol A.
Director of Domestic Policy Issues, Computer and Business Equipment Manufacturers Ass'n
311 First St., N.W. Suite 500, Washington, DC 20001

Telephone: (202) 737-8888
Registered as lobbyist at U.S. Congress.

SWIFT CONSULTING CO., LTD., THE
P.O. Box 607, Courthouse Station, Arlington, VA 22216
Telephone: (703) 528-5807
Background: A government and public relations consulting
firm.
Members of firm representing listed organizations:
Swift, Ivan (Red), President
Background: Ass't to former Senator John Sherman
Cooper (R-KY); Administrative Assistant to former
Rep. Carl D. Perkins (D-KY) and Senior Professional
Staff member, House Committee on Education and
Labor; former Administrative Assistant to Rep.
Charles Rose (D-NC) and staff member, House Committee on Administration.
Clients:
Delta Marine, Inc. *(Ivan, Red Swift)*
New England Anti-Vivisection Soc. *(Ivan, Red Swift)*
People for the Ethical Treatment of Animals
(PETA) *(Ivan, Red Swift)*
PressNet Systems, Inc. *(Ivan, Red Swift)*
Shaw Food Services Co., Inc. *(Ivan, Red Swift)*

SWIFT, Ivan, Red
President, Swift Consulting Co., Ltd., The
P.O. Box 607, Courthouse Station, Arlington, VA 22216
Telephone: (703) 528-5807
Registered as lobbyist at U.S. Congress.
Background: Ass't to former Senator John Sherman Cooper (R-KY); Administrative Assistant to former Rep. Carl
D. Perkins (D-KY) and Senior Professional Staff member,
House Committee on Education and Labor; former Administrative Assistant to Rep. Charles Rose (D-NC) and
staff member, House Committee on Administration.
Clients:
Delta Marine, Inc.
New England Anti-Vivisection Soc.
People for the Ethical Treatment of Animals
(PETA)
PressNet Systems, Inc.
Shaw Food Services Co., Inc.

SWIGART, Richard P.
Director, External Communications, Council for Solid
Waste Solutions
1275 K St., N.W. Suite 400, Washington, DC 20005
Telephone: (202) 371-5319

SWINDLE, Jonathan C.
V. President, Operations and Secretary, Saul Real Estate
Investment Trust, B. F.
8401 Connecticut Ave., Chevy Chase, MD 20815
Telephone: (301) 986-6282

SWIRLING, Scott R.
Exec. Director, Nat'l Family Planning and Reproductive
Health Ass'n
122 C St., N.W., Suite 380, Washington, DC 20001
Telephone: (202) 628-3535
Registered as lobbyist at U.S. Congress.

SWISHER, Randall S.
Exec. Director, American Wind Energy Ass'n
1730 N. Lynn St., Suite 610, Arlington, VA 22209
Telephone: (703) 276-8334
Background: Serves as Treasurer, American Wind Energy
Ass'n Political Action Committee.

SWISHER, Ron
President, Nat'l League of Postmasters of the U.S.
1023 North Royal St., Alexandria, VA 22314
Telephone: (703) 548-5922
Registered as lobbyist at U.S. Congress.

SYER, Nora
Education Associate, Employee Benefit Research Institute
2121 K St., N.W., Suite 600, Washington, DC 20037-2121
Telephone: (202) 659-0670

SYKES, Ronald G.
Senior Washington Representative, General Motors Corp.
1660 L St., N.W., Washington, DC 20036
Telephone: (202) 775-5024
Registered as lobbyist at U.S. Congress.

SYLVESTER, Nancy
Nat'l Coordinator, NETWORK
806 Rhode Island Ave., N.E., Washington, DC 20018
Telephone: (202) 526-4070
Registered as lobbyist at U.S. Congress.

SYMINGTON, James W.
O'Connor & Hannan
1919 Pennsylvania Ave., N.W., Suite 800, Washington, DC 20006
Telephone: (202) 887-1400
Registered as lobbyist at U.S. Congress.
Background: United States Chief of Protocol, 1966; United States Congressman (D-MO), 1969-77.

SYMONS, Hugh W.
Sr. V. Pres., Research & Technical Svcs., American Frozen Food Institute
1764 Old Meadow Lane Suite 350, McLean, VA 22102
Telephone: (703) 821-0770
Background: Serves as Assistant Director General, Internat'l Frozen Food Ass'n.

SZABAT, Mary Eleanor
Jones, Day, Reavis and Pogue
1450 G St., N.W., Suite 700, Washington, DC 20005-2088
Telephone: (202) 879-3939

SZABAT, Ronald
Washington Legislative Attorney, American Medical Ass'n
1101 Vermont Ave., N.W., Washington, DC 20005
Telephone: (202) 789-7400
Registered as lobbyist at U.S. Congress.

SZABO, Robert G.
Van Ness, Feldman & Curtis
1050 Thomas Jefferson St., 7th Floor, Washington, DC 20007
Telephone: (202) 298-1800
Registered as lobbyist at U.S. Congress.
Background: Legislative Assistant to Senator J. Bennett Johnston of Louisiana, 1975-78. Serves as Exec. Director, Consumers United for Rail Equity.
Clients:
  Consumers United for Rail Equity
  Nat'l Nutrition Coalition
  Seneca Resources, Inc.
  Van Ness, Feldman & Curtis Political Action Committee

SZANTON, Eleanor
Exec. Director, Nat'l Center for Clinical Infant Programs
733 15th St., N.W., Suite 912, Washington, DC 20005
Telephone: (202) 347-0308

SZEJK, Leslie
Director, Wall and Ceiling Political Action Committee
1600 Cameron St., Alexandria, VA 22314
Telephone: (703) 684-2924

SZPAK, Carole
Director, Communications, Nat'l Ass'n of Private Psychiatric Hospitals
1319 F St., N.W., Suite 1000, Washington, DC 20004
Telephone: (202) 393-6700

SZYMANSKI, John J., CPA
V.Pres., Dir., Federal Legislat. Affrs., Rouse Company, The
10275 Little Patuxent Pkwy., Columbia, MD 21044
Telephone: (301) 992-6468

TABB, M. Amanda
Adm. Ass't, Internat'l Trade Services, Control Data Corp.
1201 Pennsylvania Ave., N.W. Suite 370, Washington, DC 20004
Telephone: (202) 796-6798

TABOR, Janis
Ass't Director, Federal Gov't Relations, American Soc. of Mechanical Engineers
1825 K St., N.W., Suite 218, Washington, DC 20006
Telephone: (202) 785-3756
Registered as lobbyist at U.S. Congress.

TABOR, Mary L.
Editorial and Special Issues Director, American Petroleum Institute
1220 L St., N.W., Washington, DC 20005

Telephone: (202) 682-8081

TABOR, Ralph
Director, Legislative Staff, Nat'l Ass'n of Counties
440 First St., N.W., Washington, DC 20001
Telephone: (202) 393-6226

TADCO ENTERPRISES
Box 65498, Washington, DC 20035-5498
Telephone: (202) 639-4787
Members of firm representing listed organizations:
  Allen, Katherine E., President
  Clients:
    ADM Milling Co. *(Katherine E. Allen)*
    American River Transport Co. *(Katherine E. Allen)*
    Archer-Daniels-Midland Co. *(Katherine E. Allen)*
    Corn Sweeteners, Inc. *(Katherine E. Allen)*

TAFFER, Sheri
Communicaqtions Coordinator, Nat'l Ass'n of Convenience Stores
1605 King St., Alexandria, VA 22314
Telephone: (703) 684-3600

TAFT, Robert, Jr.
Taft, Stettinius and Hollister
1620 Eye St., N.W., Suite 800, Washington, DC 20006
Telephone: (202) 785-1620
Registered as lobbyist at U.S. Congress.
Background: Member, U.S. House of Representatives, 1963-64 and 1967-70. U.S. Senator from Ohio, 1971-76.
Clients:
  Great American Broadcasting Co.
  Kings Entertainment Co.
  Telephone and Data Systems, Inc.
  Westland Oil Development Corp.

TAFT, Shirley
President, Ex-Partners of Servicemen/Women for Equality
Box 11191, Alexandria, VA 22312
Telephone: (703) 941-5844

TAFT, STETTINIUS AND HOLLISTER
1620 Eye St., N.W., Suite 800, Washington, DC 20006
Telephone: (202) 785-1620
Background: Washington office of a Cincinnati law firm. Also has offices in Columbus, Ohio and Ft. Thomas, Kentucky.
Members of firm representing listed organizations:
  Hopkins, Virginia E.
  Schiering, G. David
  Taft, Robert (Jr.)
    Background: Member, U.S. House of Representatives, 1963-64 and 1967-70. U.S. Senator from Ohio, 1971-76.
Clients:
  Abitibi-Price, Inc.
  Great American Broadcasting Co. *(Virginia E. Hopkins, Robert Taft, Jr.)*
  Kings Entertainment Co. *(Virginia E. Hopkins, Robert Taft, Jr.)*
  Telephone and Data Systems, Inc. *(Virginia E. Hopkins, Robert Taft, Jr.)*
  Wald Manufacturing Co. *(Virginia E. Hopkins)*
  Westland Oil Development Corp. *(Robert Taft, Jr.)*

TAGG, George C.
Managing Director, Government Affairs, Federal Express Corp.
300 Maryland Ave., N.E., Washington, DC 20002
Telephone: (202) 546-1631
Registered as lobbyist at U.S. Congress.

TAGGART AND ASSOCIATES, INC.
1155 15th St., N.W., Suite 1108, Washington, DC 20005
Telephone: (202) 429-1940
Members of firm representing listed organizations:
  Cook, Judith Wise
  Taggart, William A.
  Clients:
    Animal Health Institute *(William A. Taggart)*
    Ass'n of American Railroads *(William A. Taggart)*
    Telephone and Data Systems, Inc. *(William A. Taggart)*

TAGGART, Judith F.
President, J T & A, Inc.
1000 Connecticut Ave., N.W., Suite 300, Washington, DC 20036

Telephone: (202) 833-3380
Clients:
  North American Lake Management Soc.

TAGGART, William A.
Taggart and Associates, Inc.
1155 15th St., N.W., Suite 1108, Washington, DC 20005
Telephone: (202) 429-1940
Registered as lobbyist at U.S. Congress.
Clients:
  Animal Health Institute
  Ass'n of American Railroads
  Telephone and Data Systems, Inc.

TAITANO, Francisco I.
Federal Programs Coordinator, Northern Mariana Islands, Commonwealth of
2121 R St., N.W., Washington, DC 20008
Telephone: (202) 673-5869

TALAREK, Walter G.
Weinberg & Green
10480 Little Patuxent Pkwy., Columbia, MD 21044-3506
Telephone: (301) 740-8500
Clients:
  Chemical Specialties, Inc.
  Mooney Chemicals, Inc.
  Trenton Sales, Inc.

TALBERT, Phyllis
Associate Exec. Director, American College of Obstetricians and Gynecologists
409 12th St., S.W., Washington, DC 20024
Telephone: (202) 638-5577

TALBOT, Maurice P., Jr.
Director, Federal Regulatory Affairs, BellSouth Corp.
1133 21st St., N.W., Suite 900, Washington, DC 20036
Telephone: (202) 463-4100

TALBOTT, Lt. Gen. C. M., USAF (Ret)
Chief of Staff, Military Order of the World Wars
435 North Lee St., Alexandria, VA 22314
Telephone: (703) 683-4911

TALISMAN, Harold L.
Wright and Talisman
1050 17th St., N. W., Suite 600, Washington, DC 20036
Telephone: (202) 331-1194

TALISMAN, Mark E.
Director, Washington Action Office, Council of Jewish Federations
227 Massachusetts Ave., N.E., Suite 220, Washington, DC 20002
Telephone: (202) 547-0020

TALLAKSON, Joe
President, SENSE, INC.
1511 K St., N.W., Suite 1033, Washington, DC 20005
Telephone: (202) 628-1151
Registered as lobbyist at U.S. Congress.
Clients:
  Colville Confederated Tribes
  Jamestown-Klallam Indian Tribe
  Lummi Indian Tribe
  Quileute Indian Tribe
  Quinault Indian Nation
  Squaxin Island Indian Tribe
  Suquamish Indian Tribe

TALLEY, Bruce
Exec. Director, Coalition for Employment through Exports
1801 K St., N.W., 8th Floor, Washington, DC 20006
Telephone: (202) 296-6107

TALLIA, Eugene J.
V. President, Washington, Pratt & Whitney
1825 Eye St., N.W., Washington, DC 20006
Telephone: (202) 785-7427

TALMADGE, William C.
King and Spalding
1730 Pennsylvania Ave., N.W. Suite 1200, Washington, DC 20006-4706
Telephone: (202) 737-0500
Registered as lobbyist at U.S. Congress.
Background: Legislative Assistant to U.S. Senator Herman Talmadge. Administrative Assistant to Congressman Richard Ray.

TAMAN, Martin B.
Federal Programs Coordinator, Northern Mariana Islands, Commonwealth of
2121 R St., N.W., Washington, DC 20008
Telephone: (202) 673-5869

TAMMEN GROUP, THE
1750 Pennsylvania Ave., N.W. Suite 1201, Washington, DC 20006
Telephone: (202) 347-0273
Background: A government relations/lobbying firm specializing in banking, agriculture and environmental issues.
Members of firm representing listed organizations:
Tammen, Ronald L., President
Background: Former Chief of Staff to former Sen. William Proxmire (D-WI).
Clients:
Cray Research, Inc. *(Ronald L. Tammen)*
Decision Insights, Inc. *(Ronald L. Tammen)*
Organic Food Alliance *(Ronald L. Tammen)*
Population - Environment Balance *(Ronald L. Tammen)*
Standard Federal Savings Bank *(Ronald L. Tammen)*

TAMMEN, Melanie S.
Policy Analyst, Trade, Competitive Enterprise Institute
233 Pennsylvania Ave., S.E., Suite 200, Washington, DC 20003
Telephone: (202) 547-1010

TAMMEN, Ronald L.
President, Tammen Group, The
1750 Pennsylvania Ave., N.W. Suite 1201, Washington, DC 20006
Telephone: (202) 347-0273
Registered as lobbyist at U.S. Congress.
Background: Former Chief of Staff to former Sen. William Proxmire (D-WI).
Clients:
Cray Research, Inc.
Decision Insights, Inc.
Organic Food Alliance
Population - Environment Balance
Standard Federal Savings Bank

TANAKA, H. William
Tanaka, Ritger and Middleton
1919 Pennsylvania Ave., N.W., Suite 303, Washington, DC 20006
Telephone: (202) 223-1670
Registered as lobbyist at U.S. Congress.
Registered as Foreign Agent: (#0948).
Clients:
Brother Internat'l, Inc.
Electronic Industries Ass'n of Japan
Flat Glass Ass'n of Japan
Japan Bearing Industrial Ass'n
Japan, Embassy of
Japan Export Metal Flatware Industry Ass'n
Japan General Merchandise Exporters Ass'n
Japan, Government of
Japan Pottery Exporters Ass'n
Japan Trade Center
New Hampshire Ball Bearings, Inc.
Onoda Cement Co., Ltd.

TANAKA, Michele N.
Tanaka, Ritger and Middleton
1919 Pennsylvania Ave., N.W., Suite 303, Washington, DC 20006
Telephone: (202) 223-1670
Registered as lobbyist at U.S. Congress.
Registered as Foreign Agent: (#0948).
Clients:
Japan Automobile Tire Manufacturers Ass'n
Minebea Co.

TANAKA, RITGER AND MIDDLETON
1919 Pennsylvania Ave., N.W., Suite 303, Washington, DC 20006
Telephone: (202) 223-1670
Members of firm representing listed organizations:
Davenport, James
Middleton, B. Jenkins
O'Leary, Patrick F.
Tanaka, H. William
Tanaka, Michele N.
Clients:

Brother Internat'l, Inc. *(Patrick F. O'Leary, H. William Tanaka)*
Electronic Industries Ass'n of Japan *(B. Jenkins Middleton, H. William Tanaka)*
Fasteners Institute of Japan
Flat Glass Ass'n of Japan *(Patrick F. O'Leary, H. William Tanaka)*
Japan Automobile Tire Manufacturers Ass'n *(James Davenport, B. Jenkins Middleton, Michele N. Tanaka)*
Japan Bearing Industrial Ass'n *(James Davenport, H. William Tanaka)*
Japan, Embassy of *(H. William Tanaka)*
Japan Export Metal Flatware Industry Ass'n *(James Davenport, H. William Tanaka)*
Japan General Merchandise Exporters Ass'n *(James Davenport, H. William Tanaka)*
Japan, Government of *(H. William Tanaka)*
Japan Pottery Exporters Ass'n *(H. William Tanaka)*
Japan Trade Center *(James Davenport, B. Jenkins Middleton, H. William Tanaka)*
Minebea Co. *(Michele N. Tanaka)*
New Hampshire Ball Bearings, Inc. *(H. William Tanaka)*
Onoda Cement Co., Ltd. *(Patrick F. O'Leary, H. William Tanaka)*

TANAKA, Takeo
Sr. V. President, Marubeni America Inc.
1615 L St., N.W., Suite 1215, Washington, DC 20036
Telephone: (202) 331-1167

TANNENBAUM, Susan M.
Senior Lobbyist, Common Cause
2030 M St., N.W., Washington, DC 20036
Telephone: (202) 833-1200
Registered as lobbyist at U.S. Congress.

TANNER, Doug
Deputy Director, Project Vote!
1424 16th St., N.W., Suite 101, Washington, DC 20005
Telephone: (202) 328-1500

TANNER, Michael
Legislative Director, American Legislative Exchange Council
214 Massachusetts Ave., N.W., Washington, DC 20002
Telephone: (202) 547-4646

TANNER, William E.
10803 Norman Ave., Fairfax, VA 22030
Telephone: (703) 273-7233
Organizations represented:
Coalition for Environmental-Energy Balance

TAP, Lt. Col. James
Senate Liaison, Legis Liaison, DEPARTMENT OF AIR FORCE
The Pentagon, Washington, DC 20330
Telephone: (202) 697-8153

TAPIA, M. Isabelle
Member, Legialtive Services Group, Van Ness, Feldman & Curtis
1050 Thomas Jefferson St., 7th Floor, Washington, DC 20007
Telephone: (202) 298-1800
Background: Serves as Exec. Director, Coalition for American Energy Security.
Clients:
Coalition for American Energy Security

TAPPER, James B.
Dep Asst Secy, Senate Liaison, DEPARTMENT OF ENERGY
1000 Independence Ave. S.W., Washington, DC 20585
Telephone: (202) 586-5450

TARGETED COMMUNICATIONS CORP.
1807 Michael Faraday Court, Reston, VA 22090
Telephone: (703) 742-7888
Background: A direct communications consulting firm that specializes in constutuency mobilization, corporate communications, product and service marketing and membership development. Acquired by Ogilvy & Mather Worldwide in 1986.
Members of firm representing listed organizations:
Burch, Michael, V. President,Public Policy
Smith, Robert M., President
Clients:

Aircraft Owners and Pilots Ass'n
American Council for Capital Formation
American Council of Life Insurance
American Insurance Ass'n
American Medical Ass'n
American Psychological Ass'n
CIBA-GEIGY Corp.
Hardee's Food Systems
Nat'l Federation of Independent Business - Tennessee
Schering-Plough Corp.
WNET/Channel 13

TARGETING SYSTEMS, INC.
2111 Wilson Blvd., Suite 900, Arlington, VA 22201
Telephone: (703) 528-7555
Background: Provides message development, demographic and geographic targeting for public policy, public relations, and advertising campaigns. Also provides custom designed survey research for corporate and political clients. An affiliate of Reese Communications Companies, President is Charles B. Welsh of Reese Communications Companies, former V. President of Democratic polling firm Hamilton and Staff.
Members of firm representing listed organizations:
Barron, Kevin, Research and Demographic Analyst
Cohen, Maura S., Marketing and Sales Manager
Steinen, Margaret, Director of Survey Research
Clients:
Drug Policy Foundation
Humana, Inc.
Japan, Ministry of International Trade and Industry
Miller Brewing Co.
Missouri Hospital Ass'n
Nat'l Ass'n of Securities Dealers (NASDAQ)
Palm-Aire Spa Resort/Katzoff Development Corp.
Paper Industry of Maine
Philip Morris USA

TARNAPOL, Paula
Director, Public Affairs, Soc. of American Foresters
5400 Grosvenor Lane, Bethesda, MD 20814
Telephone: (301) 897-8720

TARNORE, Lorraine
Exec. Director, American Medical Directors Ass'n
325 S. Patrick St., Alexandria, VA 22314
Telephone: (703) 549-5822

TARPEY, Mike P.
Director, Public Relations, Washington, AT&T
2000 L St., N.W., Suite 815, Washington, DC
Telephone: (202) 457-4138

TARR-WHELAN, Keith
Director, Long Term Care Campaign
1334 G St., N.W., Suite 300, Washington, DC 20005
Telephone: (202) 628-3030

TARR-WHELAN, Linda
Director, Nat'l Center for Policy Alternatives
2000 Florida Ave., N.W. 4th Floor, Washington, DC 20009
Telephone: (202) 387-6030
Background: Former Deputy Assistant to Jimmy Carter for Women's Concerns. Serves as Treasurer, Women's Campaign Fund. Also represents Women's Economic Justice Center.

TASKER, Janet A.
Secura Group, The
1155 21st St., N.W., Washington, DC 20036
Telephone: (202) 728-4920

TASSAN, Vickie
V. President, Public Affairs, American Security Bank
1501 Pennsylvania Ave., N.W., Washington, DC 20013
Telephone: (202) 624-4695
Background: Responsibilities include serving as Treasurer, American Security Bank Political Action Committee.

TATE, Dan C.
Camp, Barsh, Bates and Tate
2550 M St., N.W., Suite 275, Washington, DC 20037
Telephone: (202) 887-5160
Registered as lobbyist at U.S. Congress.

TATE, Dan C. (Cont'd)
Background: Legislative Assistant to Senator Herman (D-GA), 1969-76. Chief Legislative Representative (Senate) for President Jimmy Carter, 1977-80.
Clients:
California Pipe Trades Council
PGA Tour

TATE, M. Louise
Secretary-Treasurer, United States Defense Committee
3238 Wynford Drive, Fairfax, VA 22031
Telephone: (703) 914-2010
Registered as lobbyist at U.S. Congress.

TATE, Sheila B.
V. Chairman, Communications, Cassidy and Associates, Inc.
655 15th St., N.W., Suite 1100, Washington, DC 20005
Telephone: (202) 347-0773
Registered as lobbyist at U.S. Congress.
Background: White House Press Secretary to Nancy Reagan, 1981-85. Campaugn and Transition Press Secretary to President Bush, 1988.
Clients:
Internat'l Data Corp.

TATE, Thomas N.
V. President, Legislative Affairs, Aerospace Industries Ass'n of America
1250 Eye St., N.W., Suite 1100, Washington, DC 20005
Telephone: (202) 371-8400
Registered as lobbyist at U.S. Congress.
Background: Former senior staff member, House Committee on Science and Technology.

TAUBENBLATT, Sy A.
Executive Consultant, Bechtel Group, Inc.
1620 Eye St., N.W., Suite 703, Washington, DC 20006
Telephone: (202) 393-4747

TAVENNER, Mary T.
Senior Director, Government Relations, Nat'l Ass'n of Wholesaler-Distributors
1725 K St., N.W. Suite 710, Washington, DC 20006
Telephone: (202) 872-0885
Registered as lobbyist at U.S. Congress.
Background: Also serves as Exec. Director of the Concerned Alliance of Responsible Employees (CARE), an employment-issues coalition.

TAYLOR ASSOC, INC., Gene
453 New Jersey Ave., S.E., Washington, DC 20003
Telephone: (202) 488-3581
Members of firm representing listed organizations:
Taylor, Gene
Background: Member U.S. House of Representatives (R-MO), 1973-89.
Organizations represented:
Associated Electric Cooperative *(Gene Taylor)*
Eagle-Picher Industries *(Gene Taylor)*
Empire District Electric Co. *(Gene Taylor)*
Empire Gas Corp. *(Gene Taylor)*
FAG Bearings Corp. *(Gene Taylor)*
Nat'l Ass'n of Postmasters of the U.S. *(Gene Taylor)*

TAYLOR, Charles A., III
Ass't V. President, Gov't Relations, Nat'l Ass'n of Independent Insurers
499 South Capitol St., S.W. Suite 401, Washington, DC 20003
Telephone: (202) 484-2350
Registered as lobbyist at U.S. Congress.

TAYLOR, Jr. Chester
Hogan and Hartson
555 13th St., N.W., Suite 1200, Washington, DC 20004-1109
Telephone: (202) 637-5600
Registered as lobbyist at U.S. Congress.
Clients:
Whitman Distributing Co.

TAYLOR, David
Legis Asst, EXECUTIVE OFFICE OF THE PRESIDENT - Office of Management and Budget
Old Executive Office Bldg., Washington, DC 20500
Telephone: (202) 395-4790

TAYLOR, Donald
Director of International Affairs, Pan American World Airways
1200 17th St., N.W., Suite 500, Washington, DC 20036
Telephone: (202) 659-7805

TAYLOR, Elizabeth L.
Director, Government Affairs, McNair Group Inc.
1155 15th St., N.W., Washington, DC 20005
Telephone: (202) 659-8866
Registered as lobbyist at U.S. Congress.
Clients:
Clemson University
Nat'l Composites Consortium, Inc.
Sotheby's Holdings, Inc.
South Carolina State College
Virginia Polytechnic Institute and State University

TAYLOR, Frank
Director, Government Relations, Lucas Aerospace Inc.
11150 Sunrise Valley Drive, Reston, VA 22091-4399
Telephone: (703) 264-1704

TAYLOR, Gene
Taylor Assoc, Inc., Gene
453 New Jersey Ave., S.E., Washington, DC 20003
Telephone: (202) 488-3581
Registered as lobbyist at U.S. Congress.
Background: Member U.S. House of Representatives (R-MO), 1973-89.
Organizations represented:
Associated Electric Cooperative
Eagle-Picher Industries
Empire District Electric Co.
Empire Gas Corp.
FAG Bearings Corp.
Nat'l Ass'n of Postmasters of the U.S.

TAYLOR, Gregory W.
Federal Gov't Affairs Director, AT&T
Suite 1000, 1120 20th St., N.W., Washington, DC 20036
Telephone: (202) 457-3818

TAYLOR, Jr. James
Dorsey & Whitney
1330 Connecticut Ave., N.W., Suite 200, Washington, DC 20036
Telephone: (202) 857-0700

TAYLOR, Jefferson D.
Legis. Director, Congressional Affairs, Nat'l Ass'n of REALTORS
777 14th St., N.W., Washington, DC 20005
Telephone: (202) 383-1000
Registered as lobbyist at U.S. Congress.

TAYLOR, Jeremy B.
V. President, American Ass'n of Equipment Lessors
1300 North 17th St. Suite 1010, Arlington, VA 22209
Telephone: (703) 527-8655

TAYLOR, Jerry
Legislative Assistant, American Legislative Exchange Council
214 Massachusetts Ave., N.W., Washington, DC 20002
Telephone: (202) 547-4646

TAYLOR, Margaret J.
V. President, Legislative Affairs, Burlington Resources, Inc.
50 F St., N.W., Suite 1080, Washington, DC 20001
Telephone: (202) 383-4960
Registered as lobbyist at U.S. Congress.

TAYLOR, Marie
Asst. to Dir., Government Relations, Goodrich Co., BF
1825 Eye St., N.W., Suite 400, Washington, DC 20006
Telephone: (202) 429-2060
Registered as lobbyist at U.S. Congress.

TAYLOR, Marjorie N.
Director of Communications, ERISA Industry Committee (ERIC), The
1726 M St., N.W., Suite 1101, Washington, DC 20036
Telephone: (202) 833-2800

TAYLOR, Mary Ellen
Evans Group, Ltd., The
1010 Wisconsin Ave., N.W. Suite 810, Washington, DC 20007
Telephone: (202) 333-8777
Registered as lobbyist at U.S. Congress.
Clients:
Federal Home Loan Bank of Pittsburgh
Mortgage Bankers Ass'n of America

TAYLOR, Melinda
Deputy Counsel, Nat'l Audubon Soc.
801 Pennsylvania Ave., S.E., Washington, DC 20003
Telephone: (202) 547-9009
Registered as lobbyist at U.S. Congress.

TAYLOR, Michael
Exec. Director, Nat'l Committee for a Human Life Amendment
1511 K St., N.W., Suite 335, Washington, DC 20005
Telephone: (202) 393-0703

TAYLOR, Patricia
Dir. for Alchohol Policies Project, Center for Science in the Public Interest
1501 16th St., N.W., Washington, DC 20036
Telephone: (202) 332-9110
Registered as lobbyist at U.S. Congress.

TAYLOR, Peggy
Assoc. Director, Legislative Dept., AFL-CIO (American Federation of Labor and Congress of Industrial Organizations)
815 16th St., N.W., Washington, DC 20006
Telephone: (202) 637-5090
Registered as lobbyist at U.S. Congress.

TAYLOR, R. William, CAE
President, American Soc. of Ass'n Executives
1575 Eye St., N.W., Washington, DC 20005-1168
Telephone: (202) 626-2723
Registered as lobbyist at U.S. Congress.

TAYLOR, Richard
Legislative Assistant, Consolidated Natural Gas Co.
1819 L St., N.W. Suite 900, Washington, DC 20036
Telephone: (202) 833-3900
Registered as lobbyist at U.S. Congress.

TAYLOR, Richard P.
Steptoe and Johnson
1330 Connecticut Ave., N.W., Washington, DC 20036
Telephone: (202) 429-3000
Clients:
Aerolineas Nacionales del Ecuador
Blue Bell, Inc.
Evergreen Internat'l Aviation
Islip, New York, City of
Norfolk Port and Industrial Authority

TAYLOR, Sandra E.
Government Relations Specialist, ICI Americas Inc.
1600 M St., N.W., Suite 702, Washington, DC 20036
Telephone: (202) 775-9722
Registered as lobbyist at U.S. Congress.

TAYLOR, Sid
Research Director, Nat'l Taxpayers Union
713 Maryland Ave., N.E., Washington, DC 20002
Telephone: (202) 543-1300

TAYLOR, Sunny
V. President, Government Affiars, Collins & Associates
6269 Franconia Road, Alexandria, VA 22310
Telephone: (703) 971-1900
Registered as lobbyist at U.S. Congress.
Background: Legislative Assistant and Chief Legislative Director to Rep. Dan Mica (D-FL), 1982-87.
Clients:
First Page
New Era Communications
Pompano Beach, Florida, City of
USA Telecommunications

TAYLOR, Warren P.
McNair Law Firm, P.A.
1155 15th St., N.W. Suite 400, Washington, DC 20005
Telephone: (202) 659-3900
Registered as lobbyist at U.S. Congress.

Background: Command Judge Advocate, Delta Regional Assistance Command, Republic of Vietnam, 1972-73. Legislative Counsel, Office of the Secretary of the Army, 1976. Staff Judge Advocate, 2nd Infantry Division, 1981. Team Chief and Senior Trial Attorney, U.S. Army, 1982-83. Legislative Assistant to the Secretary of Defense, 1983-87.

TAYLOR, William J.
V. Pres., Internat'l Security Programs, Center for Strategic and Internat'l Studies
1800 K St., N.W., Washington, DC 20006
Telephone: (202) 887-0200

TCI WASHINGTON GROUP
3701 Connecticut Ave., N.W., Washington, DC 20008
Telephone: (202) 363-2800
Background: The Washington office of TCI Corp., a Cleveland, Ohio corporation.
Members of firm representing listed organizations:
   Williams, Merrill
   Clients:
      Freshwater Press *(Merrill Williams)*
      Galactica Biochemical *(Merrill Williams)*
      Nat'l Credit Improvement Group *(Merrill Williams)*
      Technology Transfer *(Merrill Williams)*

TEACH, Randy L.
Sr. V. Pres., Health Policy & Gov't Aff., Nat'l Ass'n of Chain Drug Stores
Box 1417-D49, Alexandria, VA 22313
Telephone: (703) 549-3001
Registered as lobbyist at U.S. Congress.

TEAGUE, Randal C.
Of Counsel, Vorys, Sater, Seymour and Pease
1828 L St., N.W., Suite 1111, Washington, DC 20036
Telephone: (202) 822-8200
Registered as lobbyist at U.S. Congress.
Background: Administrative Assistant and Legislative Counsel to Representative Jack F. Kemp of New York, 1973-79.
Clients:
   Citizens Network for Foreign Affairs
   Committee of Publicly Owned Companies
   Fraternal Order of Police (Nat'l Lodge)
   Ohio Broadcasters Ass'n
   Toledo Zoological Gardens
   Wendy's Internat'l, Inc.
   World Council on Free Zones

TEAMWORKS
1117 North 19th St., Suite 900, Arlington, VA 22209
Telephone: (703) 528-7967
Members of firm representing listed organizations:
   Berger, Renee A., President

TEARE, G. William
Exec. V. President, Printing Industries of America
1730 North Lynn St., Arlington, VA 22209
Telephone: (703) 841-4814
Background: Also serves as Exec. Director for the Nat'l Ass'n of Lithographic Plate Manufacturers.

TEARNO, T. Daniel
Director, Federal Government Affairs, Miller Brewing Co.
1341 G St., N.W., Suite 900, Washington, DC 20005
Telephone: (202) 637-1520
Registered as lobbyist at U.S. Congress.

TECHLAW
14500 Avion Pkwy. Suite 300, Chantilly, VA 22021
Telephone: (703) 263-7327
Background: A consulting firm.
Members of firm representing listed organizations:
   Jackson, Benjamin R.
      Background: Formerly Deputy Assistant Administrator, U.S. Environmental Protection Agency.

TECTON, Michael
President, Thomas Jefferson Equal Tax Soc.
1469 Spring Vale Ave., McLean, VA 22101
Telephone: (703) 356-5800

TEEL, Keith A.
Covington and Burling
1201 Pennsylvania Ave., N.W., Box 7566, Washington, DC 20044
Telephone: (202) 662-6000

TEELEY & ASSOCIATES, Peter
1815 Connecticut Ave., N.W., Suite 1100, Washington, DC 20006
Telephone: (202) 452-7019
Members of firm representing listed organizations:
   Teeley, Peter
   Organizations represented:
      Amgen, Inc. *(Peter Teeley)*
      California Steel Industries Inc.
      Motion Picture Ass'n of America *(Peter Teeley)*

TEELEY, Peter
Teeley & Associates, Peter
1815 Connecticut Ave., N.W., Suite 1100, Washington, DC 20006
Telephone: (202) 452-7019
Organizations represented:
   Amgen, Inc.
   Motion Picture Ass'n of America

TEICH, Albert H.
Director, Science & Policy Programs, American Ass'n for the Advancement of Science
1333 H St., N.W., Washington, DC 20005
Telephone: (202) 326-6400

TEITZ, Louise E.
Akin, Gump, Strauss, Hauer and Feld
1333 New Hampshire Ave., N.W., Suite 400, Washington, DC 20036
Telephone: (202) 887-4000
Clients:
   Revlon Group

TEMENAK, James M.
V. President, Washington Operations, Nat'l Steel and Shipbuilding Co.
2301 South Jefferson Davis Hwy Suite 501, Arlington, VA 22202
Telephone: (703) 418-1195
Registered as lobbyist at U.S. Congress.

TEMKO, Stanley L.
Covington and Burling
1201 Pennsylvania Ave., N.W., Box 7566, Washington, DC 20044
Telephone: (202) 662-6000
Clients:
   Merck and Co.
   SmithKline Beecham
   Upjohn Co.

TEMPLE, Riley K.
Verner, Liipfert, Bernhard, McPherson and Hand, Chartered
901 15th St., N.W., Suite 700, Washington, DC 20005
Telephone: (202) 371-6000
Registered as lobbyist at U.S. Congress.
Registered as Foreign Agent: (#3712).
Background: Legislative Assistant to Senator Charles Mathias (R-MD), 1977-78. Communications Counsel, U.S. Senate Committee on Commerce, Science and Transportation,1981-83.
Clients:
   NYNEX

TEMPLETON AND CO.
1925 North Lynn St., Arlington, VA 22209
Telephone: (703) 525-3888
Members of firm representing listed organizations:
   Birdsong, John G., Associate
   Templeton, Patrick A., President
      Background: Associate Administrator for External Relations, Nat'l Aeronautics and Space Administration, 1981-84.
   Clients:
      Beggs Associates, J. M. *(John G. Birdsong, Patrick A. Templeton)*
      Bionetics Corp., The *(John G. Birdsong, Patrick A. Templeton)*
      Brooks Brothers *(Patrick A. Templeton)*
      Greenbrier Companies *(Patrick A. Templeton)*
      Intertrade Capital Group, Inc. *(Patrick A. Templeton)*

TEMPLETON, Patrick A.
President, Templeton and Co.
1925 North Lynn St., Arlington, VA 22209
Telephone: (703) 525-3888
Registered as lobbyist at U.S. Congress.

Background: Associate Administrator for External Relations, Nat'l Aeronautics and Space Administration, 1981-84.
Clients:
   Beggs Associates, J. M.
   Bionetics Corp., The
   Brooks Brothers
   Greenbrier Companies
   Intertrade Capital Group, Inc.

TENDLER, GOLDBERG & BIGGINS, CHTD.
1090 Vermont Ave., N.W., Suite 1200, Washington, DC 20005-4905
Telephone: (202) 682-9000
Members of firm representing listed organizations:
   Goldberg, James M.
   Tendler, Paul M., President
      Background: Serves as Exec. Director, American Licensed Practical Nurses Ass'n.
   Clients:
      American Licensed Practical Nurses Ass'n *(Paul M. Tendler)*
      American Soc. for Biotechnology *(James M. Goldberg)*
      Geodesco *(Paul M. Tendler)*
      Hugo Boss Fashions, Inc. *(Paul M. Tendler)*
      Joseph and Feiss Inc. *(Paul M. Tendler)*
      Mears Internat'l Sales Co. *(Paul M. Tendler)*
      Michigan Retailers Ass'n *(James M. Goldberg)*
      Nat'l Alcoholic Beverage Control Ass'n *(James M. Goldberg)*
      Nat'l Ass'n of Meat Purveyors *(James M. Goldberg)*
      Nat'l Ass'n of Music Merchants *(James M. Goldberg)*
      Nat'l Ass'n of Retail Dealers of America *(James M. Goldberg)*
      Nat'l Ass'n of School Music Dealers *(James M. Goldberg)*
      Nat'l Incorporation of Tenants *(Paul M. Tendler)*
      Nat'l Peanut Council *(James M. Goldberg)*
      Nat'l Shoe Retailers Ass'n *(James M. Goldberg)*
      Nat'l Wine Distributors Ass'n *(James M. Goldberg)*
      Prescription Footwear Ass'n *(James M. Goldberg)*
      Rasch Elektronik *(Paul M. Tendler)*
      Solargistics Corp. *(Paul M. Tendler)*
      TDCC: The Electronic Data Interchange Ass'n *(James M. Goldberg)*

TENDLER, Paul M.
President, Tendler, Goldberg & Biggins, Chtd.
1090 Vermont Ave., N.W., Suite 1200, Washington, DC 20005-4905
Telephone: (202) 682-9000
Registered as lobbyist at U.S. Congress.
Registered as Foreign Agent: (#3181).
Background: Serves as Exec. Director, American Licensed Practical Nurses Ass'n.
Clients:
   American Licensed Practical Nurses Ass'n
   Geodesco
   Hugo Boss Fashions, Inc.
   Joseph and Feiss Inc.
   Mears Internat'l Sales Co.
   Nat'l Incorporation of Tenants
   Rasch Elektronik
   Solargistics Corp.

TENUTA, Joshua P.
Federal Legislative Representative, American Bankers Ass'n
1120 Connecticut Ave., N.W., Washington, DC 20036
Telephone: (202) 663-5348
Registered as lobbyist at U.S. Congress.

TER HORST, Jerald F.
Director of Nat'l Public Affairs Office, Ford Motor Co.
1350 Eye St., N.W. Suite 1000, Washington, DC 20005
Telephone: (202) 962-5400
Background: Former Press Secretary to President Gerald Ford, 1974.

TERIO, Cheryl
Associated General Contractors of America
1957 E St., N.W., Washington, DC 20006
Telephone: (202) 393-2040
Registered as lobbyist at U.S. Congress.

TERLECKYJ, Nestor E.
V. President, Nat'l Planning Ass'n
1424 16th St., N.W. Suite 700, Washington, DC 20036

TERLECKYJ, Nestor E. (Cont'd)
Telephone: (202) 265-7685

TERPSTRA, Betty-Grace
Washington Corporate Affairs Rep., Scott Paper Co.
1726 M St., N.W., Suite 901, Washington, DC 20036
Telephone: (202) 331-0730
Registered as lobbyist at U.S. Congress.
Background: Serves also as Administrator, Scott Paper Co.
Political Action Committee.

TERRELL, Joseph L. S.
V. President, Public & Member Relations, Farm Credit
Council
50 F St., N.W., Suite 900, Washington, DC 20001
Telephone: (202) 626-8710
Registered as lobbyist at U.S. Congress.

TERRY, Daniel G.
V. President (Grumman Data Systems), Grumman Corp.
6862 Elm St., McLean, VA 22101
Telephone: (703) 556-7400

TERRY, Gary A.
President, American Resort and Residential Development
Ass'n
1220 L St., N.W. Suite 510, Washington, DC 20005
Telephone: (202) 371-6700
Background: Also represents the six councils of ARRDA.

TERRY, W. Grey
News Relations Manager - Washington, General Motors
Corp.
1660 L St., N.W., 4th Floor, Washington, DC 20036
Telephone: (202) 775-5027
Background: Former Special Assistant to President Reagan
and Deputy Director, Presidential Advance Office.

TERWILLIGER, James
Director of Gov't Affairs, Smith, Bucklin and Associates
1101 Connecticut Ave., N.W., Suite 700, Washington, DC
20036
Telephone: (202) 857-1100
Clients:
Ass'n of Professors of Medicine

TERZANO, Virginia M.
Press Secretary, Democratic Nat'l Committee
430 South Capitol St., S.E., Washington, DC 20003
Telephone: (202) 863-8000

TESKE, Richard Paul
Dir., Federal Relations & Public Policy, Burroughs Well-
come Co.
1500 K St., N.W., Suite 625, Washington, DC 20005
Telephone: (202) 393-1420
Registered as lobbyist at U.S. Congress.
Background: Deputy Assistant Secretary, Health and Hu-
man Services, 1985-86; Associate Administrator, Health
Care Financing Administration, 1984-85; Director, Public
and Intergovernmental Affairs, HCFA, 1981-84; Special
Assistant to Sen. David Durenberger (R-MN), 1980-81.

TESLIK, Kennan L.
Manager, Internat'l Government Affairs, Asea Brown
Boveri, Inc.
1101 15th St., N.W. Suite 500, Washington, DC 20005
Telephone: (202) 429-9180

TESLIK, Sarah A. B.
Exec. Director, Council of Institutional Investors
1420 16th St., N.W., Suite 405, Washington, DC 20036
Telephone: (202) 745-0800
Registered as lobbyist at U.S. Congress.

TESTA, Robert D.
Mgr., Federal Governmental Relations, Pacific Gas and
Electric Co.
1726 M St., N.W., Suite 1100, Washington, DC 20036-
4502
Telephone: (202) 466-7980
Registered as lobbyist at U.S. Congress.

TESTA, Capt. Ronald F.
Principal Dep Chief, Legis Affrs, DEPARTMENT OF NAVY
The Pentagon, Washington, DC 20350-1300
Telephone: (202) 697-7146

TETELMAN, Alice
Director, Washington Office, New Jersey, State of
444 N. Capitol St., N.W. Suite 236, Washington, DC
20001
Telephone: (202) 638-0631

TETIRICK, J. Guy
Manager, State/Local Gov't Relations, Penney Co., J. C.
Suite 1015, 1156 15th St., N.W., Washington, DC 20005
Telephone: (202) 862-4861
Registered as lobbyist at U.S. Congress.

TETZ, Rayond D.
V. President for Communications, Adventist Development
and Relief Agency Internat'l
12501 Old Columbia Pike, Silver Spring, MD 20904
Telephone: (301) 680-6380

THACHER, PROFFITT AND WOOD
1500 K St., N.W., Suite 200, Washington, DC 20005
Telephone: (202) 347-8400
Members of firm representing listed organizations:
Benton, Hu A., Associate
Brown, Virginia W.
Buckley, Jeremiah S.
Background: Assistant Counsel, Committee on Govern-
ment Operations, U.S. House of Representatives,
1971-73. Minority Counsel, Subcommittee on Hous-
ing, Committee on Banking, Housing, and Urban Af-
fairs, U.S. Senate, 1973-77. Minority Staff Director,
Committee on Banking, Housing, and Urban Affairs,
U.S. Senate, 1977-79.
Judah, Jeffrey N., Government Affairs
Kolar, Joseph M.
Leahy, Edward R.
Nevins, Louis H., Partner
Background: Attorney, Federal Housing Administra-
tion, 1963-67.
Susswein, Donald B.
Clients:
Apple Bank for Savings *(Louis H. Nevins)*
Binghampton Savings Bank *(Louis H. Nevins)*
Boston Five Cents Savings Bank, FSB *(Louis H. Ne-
vins)*
Castine Partners *(Virginia W. Brown)*
Chicago Board Options Exchange *(Edward R. Leahy)*
Citicorp *(Jeffrey N. Judah, Edward R. Leahy)*
Citicorp Mortgage Finance, Inc. *(Virginia W. Brown,
Jeremiah S. Buckley)*
Dollar Bank *(Louis H. Nevins)*
Federal Home Loan Mortgage Corp. *(Virginia W.
Brown, Louis H. Nevins)*
General Electric Mortgage Insurance Co. *(Virginia
W. Brown, Louis H. Nevins)*
Great Western Financial Corp. *(Louis H. Nevins)*
Massachusetts Bankers Ass'n *(Jeremiah S. Buckley)*
Mutual Savings Central Fund *(Jeremiah S. Buckley)*
New Hampshire Savings Bank *(Louis H. Nevins)*
Peoples Westchester Savings Bank *(Louis H. Nevins)*
Ranieri-Wilson *(Hu A. Benton, Joseph M. Kolar, Louis H.
Nevins)*
River Bank America *(Louis H. Nevins)*
Rochester Community Savings Bank *(Louis H. Ne-
vins)*
Savings Banks Ass'n of Massachusetts *(Jeremiah S.
Buckley)*
Standard Federal Savings Bank *(Virginia W. Brown,
Louis H. Nevins)*

THARPE, Don I.
Exec. Director, Ass'n of School Business Officials Internat'l
11401 North Shore Drive, Reston, VA 22090
Telephone: (703) 478-0405

THATCHER, Mary Kay
Asst. Director, Nat'l Affairs Division, American Farm Bu-
reau Federation
600 Maryland Ave., S.W., Washington, DC 20024
Telephone: (202) 484-3600
Registered as lobbyist at U.S. Congress.

THAYER, Richard
District Manager, Federal Gov't Affairs, AT&T
Suite 1000, 1120 20th St., N.W., Washington, DC 20036
Telephone: (202) 457-2405

THEIS, Roger
Hyman, Phelps and McNamera
1120 G St., N.W., Suite 1040, Washington, DC 20005
Telephone: (202) 737-5600
Clients:
Lederle Laboratories, American Cyanamid Co.
Subsidiary

THEISEN, Patrick M.
Director of Government Affairs, Water Quality Ass'n
1001 Connecticut Ave., N.W., Suite 407, Washington, DC
20036
Telephone: (202) 452-7855
Registered as lobbyist at U.S. Congress.

THELEN, Dennis C.
Wunder, Ryan, Cannon & Thelen
1615 L St., N.W., Suite 650, Washington, DC 20036
Telephone: (202) 659-3005
Registered as lobbyist at U.S. Congress.
Background: Deputy Chief Counsel, U.S. Senate Subcom-
mittee on Criminal Laws and Procedures, 1975-76. Coun-
sel to Senate Majority Leader, 1977-78.
Clients:
Bristol-Myers Squibb Co.
Cosmetic, Toiletry and Fragrance Ass'n
HDTV 1125/60 Group
Sony Corp. of America

THELIAN, Lorraine
Sr. V. Pres., Assoc. Director, Ketchum Public Relations
1201 Connecticut Ave., N.W. Suite 300, Washington, DC
20036
Telephone: (202) 835-8800
Clients:
American Industrial Health Council
Aspirin Foundation of America, Inc.

THEROUX, Eugene A.
Baker and McKenzie
815 Connecticut Ave., N.W. Suite 1100, Washington, DC
20006-4078
Telephone: (202) 452-7000
Clients:
China Nat'l Chemical Import and Export Corp.
Pizza Hut, Inc.

THEUS, Dana
Government Affairs Representative, Electronic Data Systems Corp.
1331 Pennsylvania Ave., N.W., Suite 1300 North, Washington, DC 20004
Telephone: (202) 637-6700

THEVENOT, E. Wayne
Concord Associates, Inc.
1455 Pennsylvania Ave., N.W. Suite 560, Washington, DC
20004
Telephone: (202) 737-9300
Registered as lobbyist at U.S. Congress.
Background: Former Executive Assistant to Senator Rus-
sell B. Long (D-LA), 1963-75.

THEVENOT, Laura Ison
Federal Legislative Representative, Principal Financial
Group, The
655 15th St., N.W., Suite 950, Washington, DC 20005
Telephone: (202) 737-5930
Background: Senate Select Committee on Secret Military
Assistance to Iran and the Nicaraguan Opposition, 1987.

THIBAU, Janelle C. M.
Government Relations Representative, Merrill Lynch and
Co., Inc.
1828 L St., N.W., Suite 906, Washington, DC 20036
Telephone: (202) 822-3600
Registered as lobbyist at U.S. Congress.

THIBEAU, Donald D.
State & Local Resources
901 Sixth St., S.W., Suite 503A, Washington, DC 20024
Telephone: (202) 488-1460
Background: V. President, Marketing, State & Local Re-
sources. U.S. Department of Labor/U.S. SFC, 1983-85.

THIBODEAU, Catherine
Cong. Correspondence, DEPARTMENT OF STATE
2201 C St., N.W., Washington, DC 20520
Telephone: (202) 647-4204

THIERWECHTER, Douglas E.
Manager, Governmental Affairs, USX Corp.
818 Connecticut Ave., N.W., Washington, DC 20006
Telephone: (202) 331-1340
Registered as lobbyist at U.S. Congress.

THOM, Edlu J.
Assoc. Director, Environmental Affairs, Grace and Co., W.
R.
919 18th St., N.W., Suite 400, Washington, DC 20006
Telephone: (202) 452-6700

THOMA, Robert G.
V. President, Government Relations, BASF Corp.
2100 Pennsylvania Ave., N.W. Suite 755, Washington, DC
20037
Telephone: (202) 296-4894
Registered as lobbyist at U.S. Congress.

THOMAS, Cindy
Attorney, Kent & O'Connor, Incorp.
1825 K St., N.W., Suite 305, Washington, DC 20006
Telephone: (202) 223-6222
Background: Served in the federal government, 1973-77.

THOMAS, David C.
President and CEO, American Institute of Cooperation
50 F St., N.W., Suite 900, Washington, DC 20001
Telephone: (202) 626-8740

THOMAS, Diane Kay
V. President, Nat'l Ass'n of Investment Companies
1111 14th St., N.W. Suite 700, Washington, DC 20005
Telephone: (202) 289-4336
Background: Contact for the Nat'l Ass'n of Investment
Companies PAC

THOMAS, Doris I.
Senior Congressional Liaison, Nat'l Ass'n of Home Build-
ers of the U.S.
15th and M Streets, N.W., Washington, DC 20005
Telephone: (202) 822-0470
Registered as lobbyist at U.S. Congress.

THOMAS, Gordon M.
Director, Government Affairs, Textron Inc.
1090 Vermont Ave., N.W., Suite 1100, Washington, DC
20005
Telephone: (202) 289-5800
Registered as lobbyist at U.S. Congress.

THOMAS, James M., Jr.
President, Amalgamated Transit Union, Local 689
2001 9th St., N.W., Suite 300, Washington, DC 20001
Telephone: (202) 232-4734
Registered as lobbyist at U.S. Congress.

THOMAS, Joel T.
General Counsel, Nat'l Wildlife Federation
1412 16th St., N.W., Washington, DC 20036
Telephone: (703) 790-4321

THOMAS, John H.
V. President, Communications, Independent Sector
1828 L St., N.W., Washington, DC 20036
Telephone: (202) 223-8100

THOMAS, John P.
Exec. Director, Nat'l Ass'n of Counties
440 First St., N.W., Washington, DC 20001
Telephone: (202) 393-6226
Background: Serves also as contact for the Nat'l Ass'n of
Counties Research Foundation.

THOMAS, John W.
Senior Counsel, Animal Health Institute
119 Oronoco St., Box 1417-D50, Alexandria, VA 22313-
1480
Telephone: (703) 684-0011
Registered as lobbyist at U.S. Congress.
Background: Also serves as Treasurer of the Animal
Health Institute Political Action Committee.

THOMAS, Karl C.
Assoc. Director, Chief Information Off., American Type
Culture Collection
12301 Parklawn Drive, Rockville, MD 20852
Telephone: (301) 881-2600

THOMAS, Larry L.
President, Soc. of the Plastics Industry
1275 K St., N.W., Suite 400, Washington, DC 20005
Telephone: (202) 371-5200

THOMAS, Meshall
Manager, Emerg. Domestic Rels. Project, Women's Legal
Defense Fund
2000 P St., N.W., Suite 400, Washington, DC 20036
Telephone: (202) 887-0364
Registered as lobbyist at U.S. Congress.

THOMAS, Nancy
Office Manager, Nat'l Pork Producers Council
501 School St., N.W. Suite 400, Washington, DC 20024
Telephone: (202) 552-3600

THOMAS, Oliver
Director of Research and General Counsel, Baptist Joint
Committee on Public Affairs
200 Maryland Ave., N.E. Suite 303, Washington, DC
20002
Telephone: (202) 544-4226

THOMAS, Osceola F.
Federal Gov't Affairs Director, AT&T
Suite 1000, 1120 20th St., N.W., Washington, DC 20036
Telephone: (202) 457-2404

THOMAS, Peter W.
Consumer V. President, American State of the Art Pros-
thetic Ass'n
403 1st St., S.E., Washington, DC 20003
Telephone: (202) 544-4441
Registered as lobbyist at U.S. Congress.
Background: Also a member of the Board of Directors.

THOMAS, Ralph C., III
Exec. Director, Nat'l Ass'n of Minority Contractors
806 15th St., N.W., Suite 340, Washington, DC 20005
Telephone: (202) 347-8259

THOMAS, Ritchie T.
Squire, Sanders and Dempsey
1201 Pennsylvania Ave., N.W. P.O. Box 407, Washington,
DC 20044
Telephone: (202) 626-6600
Background: Office of General Counsel, U.S. Tariff Com-
mission, 1964-67.
Clients:
American Chamber of Commerce in Germany
Ass'n of Research Libraries
Ferroalloys Ass'n

THOMAS, Robert L.
Exec. Director, Nat'l Ass'n of Private Psychiatric Hospitals
1319 F St., N.W., Suite 1000, Washington, DC 20004
Telephone: (202) 393-6700
Registered as lobbyist at U.S. Congress.

THOMAS, Roberta
Exec. Director, American Soc. for Deaf Children
814 Thayer Ave., Silver Spring, MD 20910
Telephone: (301) 585-5400

THOMAS, Stephen G.
Washington Project Manager, Nat'l Center for Appropriate
Technology
1212 New York Ave.,, N.W. Suite 340, Washington, DC
20005
Telephone: (202) 289-6657

THOMAS, Thomas L.
Sr. V. President/Treasurer, American Financial Services
Ass'n
1101 14th St., N.W., Washington, DC 20005
Telephone: (202) 289-0400
Background: Serves as Treasurer, AFSA PAC.

THOMAS, Virginia
Legis Officer, Cong & Intergovt'l Affrs, DEPARTMENT OF
LABOR
200 Constitution Ave., N.W., Washington, DC 20210
Telephone: (202) 523-6141

THOMAS, W. Dennis
V. President, Internat'l Paper Co.
1620 Eye St., N.W., Suite 700, Washington, DC 20006
Telephone: (202) 785-3666
Registered as lobbyist at U.S. Congress.

THOMASSON, Sara L.
Director, Congressional Affairs, Glaxo, Inc.
1500 K St., N.W., Suite 650, Washington, DC 20005
Telephone: (202) 783-1277
Registered as lobbyist at U.S. Congress.

THOMPSON, Amy
Director, Special Projects/Press, Nat'l Defense Council
Foundation
228 S. Washington St., Suite 230, Alexandria, VA 22314-
3626
Telephone: (703) 836-3443

THOMPSON, Andrew
Director of Development, Competitive Enterprise Institute
233 Pennsylvania Ave., S.E., Suite 200, Washington, DC
20003
Telephone: (202) 547-1010

THOMPSON, Anthony J.
Perkins Coie
1110 Vermont Ave., N.W., Suite 1200, Washington, DC
20005
Telephone: (202) 887-9030
Background: Legal Assistant to Chairman, Federal Com-
munications Commission, 1973-74.
Clients:
American Mining Congress
General Electric Co.

THOMPSON AND ASSOCIATES
7015 Old Keene Mill Road Suite 203, Springfield, VA
22150
Telephone: (703) 451-6943
Members of firm representing listed organizations:
Thompson, Michael W.
Clients:
Conservative Republican Committee *(Michael W.
Thompson)*

THOMPSON, Barbara J.
Director, Government Affairs, Nat'l Council of State Housing Agencies
444 N. Capitol St., N.W., Suite 118, Washington, DC
20001
Telephone: (202) 624-7710

THOMPSON, Bruce E., Jr.
V. President, Dir. of Gov't Rels., Merrill Lynch and Co.,
Inc.
1828 L St., N.W., Suite 906, Washington, DC 20036
Telephone: (202) 822-3600
Registered as lobbyist at U.S. Congress.

THOMPSON AND CO.
1001 G St., N.W. 7th Floor, Washington, DC 20001
Telephone: (202) 383-5590
Members of firm representing listed organizations:
Meuser, Robert L.
Nasrallah, Karen
Shean, Margaret
Thompson, Robert J.
Weggeland, Ted
Clients:
CareerCom Corp. *(Robert L. Meuser, Karen Nasrallah,
Margaret Shean, Robert J. Thompson, Ted Weggeland)*
Intermedia Partners *(Robert J. Thompson)*
Mitsubishi Electronics America, Inc. *(Robert J.
Thompson)*
Morse/Diesel *(Robert J. Thompson)*
United States Suzuki Motor Corp. *(Robert J. Thomp-
son)*

THOMPSON, Dana S.
Asst. for Legislative/Political Affairs, Sheet Metal and Air
Conditioning Contractors' Nat'l Ass'n
305 4th St., N.E., Washington, DC 20002
Telephone: (202) 547-8202
Registered as lobbyist at U.S. Congress.
Background: Contact for the Ass'n PAC.

THOMPSON, Daniel R.
Thompson, P.C., Daniel R.
1620 I St., N.W. Suite 925, Washington, DC 20006
Telephone: (202) 293-5800
Organizations represented:
Certified Color Manufacturers Ass'n
Flavor and Extract Manufacturers Ass'n

WASHINGTON REPRESENTATIVES

THOMPSON, Doug
Div. V. Pres, Gov't & Polit. Rtns Admin., Nat'l Ass'n of REALTORS
777 14th St., N.W., Washington, DC 20005
Telephone: (202) 383-1000

THOMPSON, Duane R.
Ass't Director, Government Relations, Internat'l Franchise Ass'n
1350 New York Ave., N.W. Suite 900, Washington, DC 20005
Telephone: (202) 628-8000
Registered as lobbyist at U.S. Congress.

THOMPSON GROUP, INC.
1919 Pennsylvania Ave., N.W. Suite 800, Washington, DC 20006
Telephone: (202) 887-1450
Members of firm representing listed organizations:
   Thompson, Kenneth W.
Clients:
   American Health Care Ass'n *(Kenneth W. Thompson)*
   BellSouth Corp. *(Kenneth W. Thompson)*
   Nat'l Funeral Directors Ass'n *(Kenneth W. Thompson)*

THOMPSON, HINE AND FLORY
1920 N St., N.W., Washington, DC 20036
Telephone: (202) 331-8800
Background: Washington office of a Cleveland law firm.
Members of firm representing listed organizations:
   Kelly, Jon F.
   Madan, Rafael A.
      Background: Foreign language specialist with firm.
   Martin, Lewe B.
   Pohorlyes, Louis
   Sandstrom, Mark Roy
Clients:
   American Cutlery Manufacturers Ass'n *(Lewe B. Martin)*
   American Tie Fabric Ass'n *(Mark Roy Sandstrom)*
   Bicycle Wholesale Distributors Ass'n *(Lewe B. Martin)*
   Interface Group, Inc., The *(Lewe B. Martin)*
   Manufacturing Jewelers and Silversmiths of America, Inc. *(Lewe B. Martin)*
   Nat'l Bank of Washington, The *(Louis Pohorlyes)*
   Nat'l Pork Producers Council *(Mark Roy Sandstrom)*
   Yale Materials Handling Corp. *(Rafael A. Madan, Mark Roy Sandstrom)*

THOMPSON, Jeff
Finance Director, Democratic Congressional Campaign Committee
430 South Capitol St., S.E. 2nd Floor, Washington, DC 20003
Telephone: (202) 863-1500

THOMPSON, Kathleen O.
Chief Washington Counsel, Credit Union Nat'l Ass'n
805 15th St., N.W. Suite 300, Washington, DC 20005
Telephone: (202) 682-4200

THOMPSON, Kenneth W.
Thompson Group, Inc.
1919 Pennsylvania Ave., N.W. Suite 800, Washington, DC 20006
Telephone: (202) 887-1450
Clients:
   American Health Care Ass'n
   BellSouth Corp.
   Nat'l Funeral Directors Ass'n

THOMPSON, Kirstin
Manager, Public Policy & Gov't Affairs, Seagram & Sons, Inc., Joseph E.
1455 Pennsylvania Ave., N.W., Suite 600, Washington, DC 20004
Telephone: (202) 638-3090

THOMPSON, Louis M.
President & Chief Operating Officer, Nat'l Investor Relations Institute
2000 L St., N.W. Suite 701, Washington, DC 20036
Telephone: (202) 861-0630

THOMPSON, MANN AND HUTSON
3000 K St., N.W. Suite 600, Washington, DC 20007
Telephone: (202) 783-1900

Members of firm representing listed organizations:
   Coxson, Harold P.
   Salem, George
      Background: Former Solicitor, U.S. Department of Labor.
Clients:
   Bechtel Civil & Minerals, Inc. *(Harold P. Coxson)*
   Construction Industry Labor Law Coalition *(Harold P. Coxson)*
   Fluor-Daniel Corp. *(Harold P. Coxson)*
   Milliken and Co. *(Harold P. Coxson)*

THOMPSON, Mary Helen
Robinson, Lake, Lerer & Montgomery
1667 K St., N.W., Suite 900, Washington, DC 20006
Telephone: (202) 457-9270
Background: Associate, Robinson, Lake, Lerer & Montgomery. Former Press Secretary to Senator Paul Tsongas (D-MA).

THOMPSON, Michael A.
Legislative Assistant, Clark & Associates, Vern
1730 M St., N.W. Suite 911, Washington, DC 20036
Telephone: (202) 737-1123
Organizations represented:
   Vern Clark & Associates, Inc. PAC

THOMPSON, Michael F.
Assoc. Dir. for State Legislative Affrs., Chemical Specialties Manufacturers Ass'n
1913 Eye St., N.W., Washington, DC 20006
Telephone: (202) 872-8110
Registered as lobbyist at U.S. Congress.

THOMPSON, Michael J.
Wright and Talisman
1050 17th St., N.W. Suite 600, Washington, DC 20036
Telephone: (202) 331-1194
Background: Attorney, U.S. Environmental Protection Agency, 1981.

THOMPSON, Michael W.
Thompson and Associates
7015 Old Keene Mill Road Suite 203, Springfield, VA 22150
Telephone: (703) 451-6943
Clients:
   Conservative Republican Committee

THOMPSON AND MITCHELL
1120 Vermont Ave., N.W. Suite 1000, Washington, DC 20005
Telephone: (202) 857-0350
Members of firm representing listed organizations:
   Belman, Murray J.
      Background: Deputy Legal Advisor, U.S. Department of State, 1967-69.
   Myers, Robert H.
   Scallet, Edward A.
      Background: Assistant Counsel for Litigation, Department of Labor, 1978-82.
Clients:
   Cold Finished Steel Bar Institute *(Murray J. Belman)*
   Midland Enterprises *(Edward A. Scallet)*
   Mutual Fairness Taxation Ass'n *(Edward A. Scallet)*

THOMPSON, Nancy
Director, Office Administration, Motion Picture Ass'n of America
1600 Eye St., N.W., Washington, DC 20006
Telephone: (202) 293-1966
Registered as lobbyist at U.S. Congress.

THOMPSON, Otis N., Jr.
Exec. Director, Organization of Professional Employees of the U.S. Dep't of Agriculture (OPEDA)
Box 381, Washington, DC 20044
Telephone: (202) 447-4898
Registered as lobbyist at U.S. Congress.

THOMPSON, P.C., Daniel R.
1620 I St., N.W. Suite 925, Washington, DC 20006
Telephone: (202) 293-5800
Background: A law firm specializing in administrative, Food and Drug and trade association law.
Members of firm representing listed organizations:
   Thompson, Daniel R.
Organizations represented:

Certified Color Manufacturers Ass'n *(Daniel R. Thompson)*
Flavor and Extract Manufacturers Ass'n *(Daniel R. Thompson)*

THOMPSON, Philip C.
Dow, Lohnes and Albertson
1255 23rd St., N.W., Suite 500, Washington, DC 20037
Telephone: (202) 857-2500
Clients:
   Masstock Internat'l Limited
   Sefri Construction Internat'l

THOMPSON, Randell
Exec. Director, Coalition for Acid Rain Equity (CARE)
P.O. Box 33924, Washington, DC 20033-0924
Registered as lobbyist at U.S. Congress.

THOMPSON, Richard L.
V. President, Government Affairs, Bristol-Myers Squibb Co.
655 15th St., N.W., Suite 410, Washington, DC 20005
Telephone: (202) 783-0900
Registered as lobbyist at U.S. Congress.

THOMPSON, Robert J.
Thompson and Co.
1001 G St., N.W. 7th Floor, Washington, DC 20001
Telephone: (202) 383-5590
Registered as lobbyist at U.S. Congress.
Registered as Foreign Agent: (#4094).
Clients:
   CareerCom Corp.
   Intermedia Partners
   Mitsubishi Electronics America, Inc.
   Morse/Diesel
   United States Suzuki Motor Corp.

THOMPSON, Thomas C., Jr.
Scribner, Hall and Thompson
1850 K St., N.W. Suite 1100, Washington, DC 20006-2201
Telephone: (202) 331-8585
Registered as lobbyist at U.S. Congress.
Registered as Foreign Agent: (#4253).
Background: Attorney, Appeals Division of Chief Counsel's Office, 1951-53, Legal Advisory Staff, Treasury Department, 1953-55. Staff of Joint Committee on Internal Revenue Taxation, U.S. Congress, 1955-57.
Clients:
   CNA Financial Corp.
   Provident Life and Accident Insurance Co.

THOMPSON, William D.
V. President, Government Affairs, Nat'l Intergroup, Inc.
1575 Eye St., N.W., Suite 1100, Washington, DC 20005
Telephone: (202) 638-7707

THOMSON, Campbell
Deputy Director, Communications, Federation of American Health Systems
1111 19th St., N.W. Suite 402, Washington, DC 20036
Telephone: (202) 833-3090
Background: Also represents FEDPAC, the political action committee sponsored by the Federation.

THOMSON, Marcia
Director, Public Affairs/Gov't Relations, Industrial Fabrics Ass'n Internat'l
2000 L St., N.W., Suite 200, Washington, DC 20036-4907
Telephone: (202) 861-0981
Background: Serves as contact for the Industrial Fabrics Ass'n PAC. Serves also as Exec. Director, U.S. Industrial Fabrics Institution.

THORMAN, Judith
Deputy Director, Illinois, State of
444 N. Capitol St., N.W. Suite 210, Washington, DC 20001
Telephone: (202) 624-7760

THORNBURG, Richard
Director, Government Relations, Flexible Packaging Ass'n
1090 Vermont Ave., N.W Suite 500, Washington, DC 20005
Telephone: (202) 842-3880

THORNDIKE, Joseph
Executive Associate, Consortium of Social Science Ass'ns
1522 K St., N.W., Suite 836, Washington, DC 20005

Telephone: (202) 842-3525
Registered as lobbyist at U.S. Congress.

THORNE, James L.
Director, Government Relations, Tenneco Inc.
490 L'Enfant Plaza East, S.W. Suite 2202, S.W., Washington, DC 20024
Telephone: (202) 554-2850
Registered as lobbyist at U.S. Congress.

THORNER, John A.
Director, Gov't Affairs & Gen. Counsel, Water Pollution Control Federation
601 Wythe Street, Alexandria, VA 22314
Telephone: (703) 684-2400

THORNING, Dr. Margo
Chief Economist, American Council for Capital Formation
1850 K St., N.W. Suite 400, Washington, DC 20006
Telephone: (202) 293-5811
Registered as lobbyist at U.S. Congress.

THORNTON, John F.
Sr. Director, Legislative Affairs, Nat'l Air Traffic Controller Ass'n
444 N. Capitol St., Suite 845, Washington, DC 20001
Telephone: (202) 347-4572
Registered as lobbyist at U.S. Congress.

THORNTON, Olen
Exec. Director, Manufacturers Standardization Soc. of the Valve and Fitting Industry
127 Park St., N.E., Vienna, VA 22180
Telephone: (703) 281-6613

THORPE, Gordon L.
Exec. Director, Washington Office, Textron Marine Systems
1090 Vermont Ave., N.W., Suite 1100, Washington, DC 20005
Telephone: (202) 289-5800

THORPE, Merle, Jr.
President, Foundation for Middle East Peace
555 13th St., N.W. 8th Floor, Washington, DC 20005
Telephone: (202) 637-6558

THORPE, Richard L.
Exec. V. Pres. and CEO, American College of Health Care Administrators
325 South Patrick St., Alexandria, VA 22314
Telephone: (703) 549-5822
Background: Responsibilities include the Foundation of the American College of Health Care Administrators.

THORPE, Richard W.
V. President, Export Activities, Shipbuilders Council of America
1110 Vermont Ave., N.W. Suite 1250, Washington, DC 20005
Telephone: (202) 775-9060

THORUD, Gary D.
Exec. V. President, World Mercy Fund
121 S. Saint Asaph St., Alexandria, VA 22314
Telephone: (703) 548-4646

THRIFT, Dr. Julianne Still
Exec. V. President, Nat'l Ass'n of Independent Colleges and Universities
122 C St., N.W. Suite 750, Washington, DC 20001
Telephone: (202) 347-7512
Registered as lobbyist at U.S. Congress.

THURM, Gil
Of Counsel, Arent, Fox, Kintner, Plotkin & Kahn
1050 Connecticut Ave., N.W., Washington, DC 20036-5339
Telephone: (202) 857-6000
Clients:
Ass'n of Global Real Estate Executives (AGREE)
Nat'l Moving and Storage Ass'n

THURSZ, Daniel
President, Nat'l Council on the Aging
600 Maryland Ave., S.W. West Wing 100, Washington, DC 20024
Telephone: (202) 479-1200

THYKEN, Joanne M.
V. President, General Manager, American Ass'n for Clinical Chemistry
2029 K St., N.W., 7th Floor, Washington, DC 20006
Telephone: (202) 857-0717

TICE, R. Dean
Exec. Director, Nat'l Recreation and Park Ass'n
3101 Park Center Drive, Alexandria, VA 22302
Telephone: (703) 820-4940

TICHENOR, Donald K.
Exec. Director, Internat'l Personnel Management Ass'n
1617 Duke St., Alexandria, VA 22314
Telephone: (703) 549-7100

TIDD, Thomas J.
V. Pres. and General Counsel, Law Dept., Ass'n of American Railroads
50 F St., N.W., Suite 12102, Washington, DC 20001
Telephone: (202) 639-2502

TIDWELL, Robert L.
Director, Government Relations, Hawker Pacific
1225 Jefferson Davis Hwy. Suite 600, Arlington, VA 22202
Telephone: (703) 486-5696

TIEGER, Carolyn
Sr. V. President, Burson-Marsteller
1850 M St., N.W., Suite 900, Washington, DC 20036
Telephone: (202) 833-8550
Background: Former Communications and Special Projects Director, Office of Private Sector Initiatives, The White House.
Clients:
American Handicapped Employers Ass'n
Asbestos Claims Facility
du Pont de Nemours and Co., E. I.
Ridgeview Institute
Safe Buildings Alliance

TIERNEY, John L.
Tierney & Swift
1200 18th St., N.W., Suite 210, Washington, DC 20036
Telephone: (202) 293-7979
Clients:
KCSM-TV
KDSM-TV
KOCE-TV
KVCR-TV
WCBB-TV

TIERNEY & SWIFT
1200 18th St., N.W., Suite 210, Washington, DC 20036
Telephone: (202) 293-7979
Members of firm representing listed organizations:
Tierney, John L.
Clients:
KCSM-TV (John L. Tierney)
KDSM-TV (John L. Tierney)
KOCE-TV (John L. Tierney)
KVCR-TV (John L. Tierney)
WCBB-TV (John L. Tierney)

TIERNEY, Timothy B.
Exec. Director, Automotive Refrigeration Products Institute
5100 Forbes Blvd., Lanham, MD 20706
Telephone: (301) 731-5195
Registered as lobbyist at U.S. Congress.

TIFFANY, Curran
Consultant, Nat'l Ass'n of Evangelicals
1023 15th St., N.W., Suite 500, Washington, DC 20005
Telephone: (202) 789-1011

TILL, Susan K.
Legislative Assistant, Nat'l Water Resources Ass'n
3800 North Fairfax Dr. Suite 4, Arlington, VA 22203
Telephone: (703) 524-1544
Registered as lobbyist at U.S. Congress.

TILLMAN, Jacqueline
Exec. Director, Cuban-American Nat'l Foundation
1000 Thomas Jefferson St. N.W. Suite 601, Washington, DC 20007
Telephone: (202) 265-2822

TILLMAN, Wallace F.
Chief Regulatory Counsel, Nat'l Rural Electric Cooperative Ass'n
1800 Massachusetts Ave., N.W., Washington, DC 20036
Telephone: (202) 857-9595
Registered as lobbyist at U.S. Congress.
Background: Attorney, Federal Trade Commission, 1969-1975.

TILLY, Jane
Senior Analyst, American Ass'n of Retired Persons
1909 K St., N.W., Washington, DC 20049
Telephone: (202) 872-4700

TILSON, Patti A.
Masaoka Associates, Mike
900 17th St., N.W., Suite 520, Washington, DC 20006
Telephone: (202) 296-4484
Registered as lobbyist at U.S. Congress.
Organizations represented:
Toyota Motor Sales, U.S.A.

TILSON, Theresa M.
Congressional Affairs, Boeing Co.
1700 North Moore St., Arlington, VA 22209
Telephone: (703) 558-9600

TIMKEN, Harold A.
Exec. V. President & Treasurer, Internat'l Health Evaluation Ass'n
90 West Montgomery Ave., Suite 340, Rockville, MD 20850
Telephone: (301) 762-6050

TIMKO, David
Exec. Director, National Capital Area, Leukemia Soc. of America
2900 Eisenhower Ave. Suite 419, Alexandria, VA 22314
Telephone: (703) 960-1100

TIMMELL, Sally
Director, Washington Office, Church Women United
110 Maryland Ave., N.E. Suite 108, Washington, DC 20003
Telephone: (202) 544-8747

TIMMONS, Becky
Director of Congressional Liaison, American Council on Education
One Dupont Circle, N.W., Washington, DC 20036
Telephone: (202) 939-9300

TIMMONS AND CO., INC.
1850 K St., N.W., Suite 850, Washington, DC 20006
Telephone: (202) 331-1760
Registered as lobbyist at U.S. Congress.
Background: A lobbying consultant firm. Owned by the WPP Group of London, England.
Members of firm representing listed organizations:
Bates, Michael J., V. President
Cable, William H., V. President and General Counsel
Background: Former Counsel to the House Committee on Education and Labor and Staff Director, House Administration Committee; Deputy Assistant (Legislative Affairs) to President Jimmy Carter, 1977-81.
Korologos, Tom C., President
Background: Dep. Ass't, Legis. to Presidents Nixon and Ford, 1970-74. Former Assistant to Sen. Wallace F. Bennett.
Paster, Howard G., Exec. V. President
Background: Former Legis. Director, United Automobile Workers. Former Legis. Assistant to Senator Birch Bayh (D-IN).
Timmons, William E.
Background: Chairman, Executive Committee, Timmons and Co. Assistant to Sen. Alexander Wiley, 1955-62; Administrative Assistant to Rep. William Brock, 1963-69; Assistant to President Nixon, 1969-74; Assistant to President Ford, 1974.
Clients:
American Petroleum Institute
American Trucking Ass'ns
Amoco Corp.
Anheuser-Busch Cos., Inc.
Ass'n of Trial Lawyers of America
Capital Cities/ABC Inc.
Chrysler Corp.
Heinz Co., H. J.

The listings in this directory are available as *Mailing Labels*. See last page.

417

TIMMONS AND CO., INC. (Cont'd)
Major League Baseball
Morgan Stanley and Co.
Mutual Fairness Taxation Ass'n
Nat'l Rifle Ass'n of America
Northern Telecom Inc..
Northrop Corp.
NutraSweet Co.
Searle Co., G. D.

TIMMONS, Frank E.
Deputy Director, Tire Division, Rubber Manufacturers Ass'n
1400 K St., N.W., Washington, DC 20005
Telephone: (202) 628-4800

TIMMONS, Gary G.
Legislative Specialist, Nat'l Education Ass'n of the U.S.
1201 16th St., N.W., Washington, DC 20036
Telephone: (202) 822-7300
Registered as lobbyist at U.S. Congress.

TIMMONS, William E.
Timmons and Co., Inc.
1850 K St., N.W., Suite 850, Washington, DC 20006
Telephone: (202) 331-1760
Background: Chairman, Executive Committee, Timmons and Co. Assistant to Sen. Alexander Wiley, 1955-62; Administrative Assistant to Rep. William Brock, 1963-69; Assistant to President Nixon, 1969-74; Assistant to President Ford, 1974.

TIMOTHY, Alan R.
Director, Federal Government Affairs, Coors Brewing Company
601 Pennsylvania Ave., N.W., Suite 500, Washington, DC 20004
Telephone: (202) 737-4444
Registered as lobbyist at U.S. Congress.

TIMPERLAKE, Edward T.
Asst Secy for Cong and Public Affrs, DEPARTMENT OF VETERANS AFFAIRS
810 Vermont Ave., N.W., Washington, DC 20420
Telephone: (202) 233-2817

TINDALL, Barry
Director, Public Affairs, Nat'l Recreation and Park Ass'n
3101 Park Center Drive, Alexandria, VA 22302
Telephone: (703) 820-4940

TINER & ASSOCIATES, Michael L.
1112 16th St., N.W. Suite 750, Washington, DC 20004
Telephone: (202) 822-0193
Members of firm representing listed organizations:
Tiner, Michael L., President
Organizations represented:
Seagram & Sons, Inc., Joseph E. *(Michael L. Tiner)*
United Food and Commercial Workers Internat'l Union *(Michael L. Tiner)*

TINER, Michael L.
President, Tiner & Associates, Michael L.
1112 16th St., N.W. Suite 750, Washington, DC 20004
Telephone: (202) 822-0193
Registered as lobbyist at U.S. Congress.
Organizations represented:
Seagram & Sons, Inc., Joseph E.
United Food and Commercial Workers Internat'l Union

TINGLE, G. Wayne
Director, Legislative Affairs, LTV Aircraft Products Group
1725 Jefferson Davis Hwy. Suite 900, Arlington, VA 22202
Telephone: (703) 521-6560
Registered as lobbyist at U.S. Congress.

TINGLING-CLEMMONS, Michele
Staff Coordinator, Nat'l Anti-Hunger Coalition
1319 F St., N.W. Suite 500, Washington, DC 20004
Telephone: (202) 393-5060

TINKLEPAUGH, William C.
V. President, Economics, Internat'l Ice Cream Ass'n
888 16th St., N.W., Washington, DC 20006
Telephone: (202) 296-4250
Registered as lobbyist at U.S. Congress.
Background: Also represents Milk Industry Foundation.

TINSLEY, Mary
Asst Trade Rep, Cong Affrs, EXECUTIVE OFFICE OF THE PRESIDENT - US Trade Representative
600 17th St., N.W., Washington, DC 20506
Telephone: (202) 395-6951

TIPPENS, Julie
Legislative Representative, Nat'l Abortion Rights Action League
1101 14th St., N.W., Suite 500, Washington, DC 20005
Telephone: (202) 371-0779
Registered as lobbyist at U.S. Congress.
Background: Former aide to Rep. Ron Wyden (D-OR).

TIPPING, William M.
Exec. V. President, American Cancer Soc. (Public Affairs Office)
316 Pennsylvania Ave., S.E. Suite 200, Washington, DC 20003
Telephone: (202) 546-4011

TIPTON, Constance E.
V. President, Public Affairs, Internat'l Ice Cream Ass'n
888 16th St., N.W., Washington, DC 20006
Telephone: (202) 296-4250
Registered as lobbyist at U.S. Congress.
Background: Also represents Milk Industry Foundation and the Internat'l Ice Cream Ass'n Political Action Committee.

TIPTON, E. Linwood
President, Internat'l Ice Cream Ass'n
888 16th St., N.W., Washington, DC 20006
Telephone: (202) 296-4250
Registered as lobbyist at U.S. Congress.
Background: Also President, Milk Industry Foundation.

TIPTON, Rev. Paul S., S.J.
President, Ass'n of Jesuit Colleges and Universities
1424 16th St., N.W. Suite 504, Washington, DC 20036
Telephone: (202) 667-3889

TIPTON, Ronald
Deputy, Field Operations, Wilderness Soc.
1400 Eye St., N.W., 10th Floor, Washington, DC 20005
Telephone: (202) 842-3400

TISDALE, Eben S.
General Manager, Government Affairs, Hewlett-Packard Co.
900 17th St., N.W. Suite 1100, Washington, DC 20006
Telephone: (202) 785-7943
Registered as lobbyist at U.S. Congress.

TISHMAN, Primrose Prapt
Coordinator, Government Affairs, Federal Express Corp.
300 Maryland Ave., N.E., Washington, DC 20002
Telephone: (202) 546-1631

TITUS, C. Richard
Exec. V. President, Nat'l Kitchen Cabinet Ass'n
6711 Lee Hwy., Arlington, VA 22205
Telephone: (703) 237-7580

TKC INTERNAT'L, INC.
444 North Capitol St., N.W., Suite 711, Washington, DC 20001
Telephone: (202) 638-7030
Background: The internat'l consulting arm of The Keefe Co. Formerly known as Interface Internat'l, Inc.
Clients:
Aruba, Government of
Capital Hill Group, Inc., The
Fideicomiso ProMexico
Good Relations
Hitachi Ltd.
Internat'l Public Relations Co.
Japan Trade Center
Nippon Telephone and Telegraph Corp.
Toyota Motor Corp.
Uniao Nacional Para Independencia Total de Angola (UNITA)
Union Industrial de Argentina

TOBIAS, Robert
Nat'l President, Nat'l Treasury Employees Union
1730 K St., N.W., Suite 1100, Washington, DC 20006
Telephone: (202) 785-4411

TOBIN AND ASSOCIATES, William J.
3612 Bent Branch Court, Falls Church, VA 22041
Telephone: (703) 941-4329
Background: Provides government, Congressional and public relations services for clients in deversified industries.
Members of firm representing listed organizations:
Tobin, William J., President
Background: Special Assistant to the Assistant Secretary of Defense (C3I), 1976-77. Special Assistant to the Acting Chairman, U.S. Consumer Product Safety Commission, 1986.
Organizations represented:
American Ass'n of Early Childhood Educators *(William J. Tobin)*
Business Coalition for Fair Competition *(William J. Tobin)*
Engel Publications *(William J. Tobin)*
Nat'l Ass'n of Early Childhood Educators *(William J. Tobin)*
Nat'l Center for Ass'n Resources *(William J. Tobin)*
Nat'l Child Care Ass'n *(William J. Tobin)*
Nat'l Child Care Parents Ass'n *(William J. Tobin)*
Nat'l Hearing Aid Soc. *(William J. Tobin)*
Open Court Publishing Co. *(William J. Tobin)*

TOBIN, Kenneth R.
V. Pres., Gov't Relations & Nat'l Affrs., Nat'l Aggregates Ass'n
900 Spring St., Silver Spring, MD 20910
Telephone: (301) 587-1400
Background: Also represents the Nat'l Ready Mixed Concrete Ass'n as V. President, Government Relations and National Affairs and the Nat'l Industrial Sand Ass'n as Director of Government Relations and National Affairs. Serves also as contact for Nat'l Ready Mixed Concrete Ass'n Political Action Committee and the Nat'l Aggregates Ass'n Political Action Committee.

TOBIN, William J.
President, Tobin and Associates, William J.
3612 Bent Branch Court, Falls Church, VA 22041
Telephone: (703) 941-4329
Registered as lobbyist at U.S. Congress.
Background: Special Assistant to the Assistant Secretary of Defense (C3I), 1976-77. Special Assistant to the Acting Chairman, U.S. Consumer Product Safety Commission, 1986.
Organizations represented:
American Ass'n of Early Childhood Educators
Business Coalition for Fair Competition
Engel Publications
Nat'l Ass'n of Early Childhood Educators
Nat'l Center for Ass'n Resources
Nat'l Child Care Ass'n
Nat'l Child Care Parents Ass'n
Nat'l Hearing Aid Soc.
Open Court Publishing Co.

TODD, David C.
Patton, Boggs and Blow
2550 M St., N.W., Suite 800, Washington, DC 20037
Telephone: (202) 457-6000
Registered as lobbyist at U.S. Congress.
Registered as Foreign Agent: (#2165).
Background: Serves as General Counsel, Mail Order Ass'n of America.

TODD, James S., MD
Acting Exec. V. President, American Medical Ass'n
1101 Vermont Ave., N.W., Washington, DC 20005
Telephone: (202) 789-7400
Registered as lobbyist at U.S. Congress.

TODD, John J.
V. President, Smith Industries
1225 Jefferson Davis Hwy., Suite 402, Arlington, VA 22202
Telephone: (703) 920-7640

TOKER, Mary Catherine
Washington Representative, General Mills
555 13th St., N.W., Suite 490 West, Washington, DC 20004
Telephone: (202) 737-8200
Registered as lobbyist at U.S. Congress.
Background: Former Special Assistant to Senator George Mitchell (D-ME).

TOLLERTON, Kathryn R.
Associate Conservation Dir., Defenders of Wildlife
1244 19th St., N.W., Washington, DC 20036
Telephone: (202) 659-9510
Registered as lobbyist at U.S. Congress.

TOLLET, Erica
Policy Advocate, Center for Law and Social Policy
1616 P St., N.W., Suite 350, Washington, DC 20036
Telephone: (202) 328-5140

TOLLETT, Jacqueline
Director, Legislation, Nat'l Alliance for Political Action
1628 11th St., N.W., Washington, DC 20001
Telephone: (202) 939-6325

TOM, Maeley L.
Washington Representative, Nat'l Democratic Council of
Asian and Pacific Americans
1118 22nd St., N.W. Suite 204, Washington, DC 20037
Telephone: (202) 659-4037
Registered as lobbyist at U.S. Congress.

TOMAN, Mildred
Admin Asst, Govt and Public Affrs, INTERSTATE COM-
MERCE COMMISSION
12th and Constitution Ave. N.W., Washington, DC 20423
Telephone: (202) 275-7231

TOMASKY, Susan
Van Ness, Feldman & Curtis
1050 Thomas Jefferson St., 7th Floor, Washington, DC
20007
Telephone: (202) 298-1800
Clients:
Collier County, Florida

TOMCZAK, Judy
Public Information Officer, American Ass'n of Community
and Junior Colleges
One Dupont Circle, N.W. Suite 410, Washington, DC
20036
Telephone: (202) 293-7050
Background: Former Assistant Press Secretary to Senator
Lawton Chiles (D-FL).

TOMENGA, Michael K.
McKenna, Conner and Cuneo
1575 Eye St., N.W. Suite 800, Washington, DC 20005
Telephone: (202) 789-7500
Clients:
Southwire Co.

TOMPKINS, Joseph B., Jr.
Sidley and Austin
1722 Eye St., N.W. Sixth Floor, Washington, DC 20006
Telephone: (202) 429-4000
Registered as Foreign Agent: (#3731).
Clients:
Cayman Islands, Government of

TONER, Hugh Patrick
Director, Tech. and Regulatory Affairs, Soc. of the Plas-
tics Industry
1275 K St., N.W., Suite 400, Washington, DC 20005
Telephone: (202) 371-5200
Registered as lobbyist at U.S. Congress.

TONJES, Ann
Director, Special Projects, Ass'n of Flight Attendants
1625 Massachusetts Ave., N.W. 3rd Floor, Washington,
DC 20036
Telephone: (202) 328-5400

TONNER, Susan
Legislative to the President, Nat'l Security Industrial Ass'n
1025 Connecticut Ave., N.W., Suite 300, Washington, DC
20036
Telephone: (202) 775-1440

TONYA, INC.
1620 Eye St., N.W., Suite 515, Washington, DC 20006
Telephone: (202) 835-3300
Members of firm representing listed organizations:
Jones, Anthony L., President
Clients:
Birmingham, Alabama, City of *(Anthony L. Jones)*

TOOHEY, Jean R.
Manager, Government Relations, Rhone-Poulenc Inc.
Metropolitan Square, Suite 225 655 15th St., N.W., Wash-
ington, DC 20005
Telephone: (202) 628-0500
Registered as lobbyist at U.S. Congress.
Registered as Foreign Agent: (#4188)

TOOHEY, Michael J.
Senior Washington Representative, Ashland Oil, Inc.
1025 Connecticut Ave., N.W., Suite 507, Washington, DC
20036
Telephone: (202) 223-8290
Registered as lobbyist at U.S. Congress.
Background: Former Minority Staff Director, House Public
Works and Transportation Committee.

TOOKER, Peter W.
Technical Analyst, American Mining Congress
1920 N St., N.W. Suite 300, Washington, DC 20036
Telephone: (202) 861-2800
Registered as lobbyist at U.S. Congress.

TOOLE, John E.
Senior Manager, Government Relations, Ernst & Young
1200 19th St., N.W., Suite 400, Washington, DC 20036
Telephone: (202) 862-9300

TOPEL, Lt. Col. Robert
Air Opns Officer, Legis Liaison, DEPARTMENT OF AIR
FORCE
The Pentagon, Washington, DC 20330
Telephone: (202) 697-8153

TOPELIUS, Kathleen E.
Morgan, Lewis and Bockius
1800 M St., N.W., Washington, DC 20036
Telephone: (202) 467-7000
Registered as Foreign Agent: (#3794).
Background: Attorney, Office of General Counsel, Federal
Home Loan Bank Board, 1978-80.
Clients:
Banco de Santander, S.A.d.c.

TOPOL, Allan J.
Covington and Burling
1201 Pennsylvania Ave., N.W., Box 7566, Washington, DC
20044
Telephone: (202) 662-6000
Clients:
General Electric Co.

TOPPIN, Dr. Edgar A.
President, Associated Publishers, Inc.
1407 14th St., N.W., Washington, DC 20005-3704
Telephone: (202) 265-1441

TOPPING, John C., Jr.
President, Climate Institute
316 Pennsylvania Ave., S.E., Suite 403, Washington, DC
20003
Telephone: (202) 547-0104

TORCHIA, Marion
Sr. Assoc. Director, Regulatory Affairs, American Hospital
Ass'n
50 F St., N.W., Suite 1100, Washington, DC 20001
Telephone: (202) 638-1100

TOREGAS, Costis
President, Public Technology Inc.
1301 Pennsylvania Ave., N.W. Suite 704, Washington, DC
20004
Telephone: (202) 626-2400

TORGERSON, James E.
Spec. Asst. Atty. General, Off. of Gov., Alaska, State of
444 N. Capitol St., N.W. Suite 518, Washington, DC
20001
Telephone: (202) 624-5858

TORGERSON, William T.
V. President and General Counsel, Potomac Electric Pow-
er Co.
1900 Pennsylvania Ave., N.W., Washington, DC 20068
Telephone: (202) 872-2000
Registered as lobbyist at U.S. Congress.

TORRES, Alicia
Exec. Director, Cuban-American Committee
1010 Vermont Ave., N.W. Suite 620, Washington, DC
20005
Telephone: (202) 783-6637

TORRES, Ivette A.
President, Nat'l Conference of Puerto Rican Women
5 Thomas Circle, N.W., Washington, DC 20036
Telephone: (202) 387-4716

TOSINI, Paula A.
Director, Futures Industry Institute, Futures Industry Ass'n
1825 Eye St., N.W., Suite 1040, Washington, DC 20006
Telephone: (202) 466-5460
Background: Former Director, Division of Economic Anal-
ysis, Commodity Futures Trading Commission.

TOTH, Stephen J.
Manager - Washington Office, CBI Industries, Inc.
1101 17th St., N.W., Suite 812, Washington, DC 20036
Telephone: (202) 466-3706

TOTMAN, Timothy
Asst. V. Pres., Federal Regulatory Affrs, Contel Corp.
555 13th St. Suite 480 West, Washington, DC 20004
Telephone: (202) 383-3700

TOUR, Jeffrey H.
Johnson & Gibbs, P.C.
1001 Pennsylvania Ave., N.W. Suite 745, Washington, DC
20004
Telephone: (202) 682-4500
Registered as lobbyist at U.S. Congress.

TOURIGNY, Ann Ward, Ph.D.
Exec. Director, American Soc. for Psychoprophylaxis in
Obstetrics (ASPO/Lamaze)
1840 Wilson Blvd. Suite 204, Arlington, VA 22201
Telephone: (703) 524-7802

TOWLE, Ray
Project Manager, Bonner & Associates
1625 K St., N.W., Suite 300, Washington, DC 20006
Telephone: (202) 463-8880
Background: Staff member to Senator Carl Levin (D-MI),
1984. Aide to Rep. John Dingell (D-MI), 1984-88.

TOWNSEND, Wanda
Director, Government Relations, Nat'l Cable Television
Ass'n
1724 Massachusetts Ave., N.W., Washington, DC 20036
Telephone: (202) 775-3675
Registered as lobbyist at U.S. Congress.

TOZZI, James J.
Director, Multinational Business Services, Inc.
11 Dupont Circle, N.W. Suite 700, Washington, DC 20003
Telephone: (202) 293-5886
Background: Former Dep. Administrator, Office of Man-
agement and Budget.
Clients:
General Motors Corp.
Goodyear Tire and Rubber Co.

TRACHTENBERG, David J.
Senior Defense Analyst, Committee on the Present Danger
905 16th St., N.W., Washington, DC 20006
Telephone: (202) 628-2409

TRACHTMAN, Richard L.
Director, Dept. of Federal Affairs, American Soc. of Internal Medicine
1101 Vermont Ave., N.W. Suite 500, Washington, DC
20005
Telephone: (202) 289-1700
Registered as lobbyist at U.S. Congress.

TRAIN, Russell E.
Chairman of the Board, World Wildlife Fund/The Conservation Foundation
1250 24th St., N.W., Washington, DC 20037
Telephone: (202) 293-4800
Background: Former Administrator, Environmental Protection Agency. Serves also as Chairman, Clean Sites, Inc.

TRAINOR, J. P.
400 First St., N.W. Suite 804, Washington, DC 20001
Telephone: (202) 737-1541

TRAINOR, J. P. (Cont'd)
Registered as lobbyist at U.S. Congress.
Organizations represented:
Nat'l Ass'n of Retired and Veteran Railway Employees, Inc.
Railway Labor Executives' Ass'n

TRAINUM, SNOWDON, HOLLAND, HYLAND & DEANE
888 17th St., N.W., Suite 500, Washington, DC 20006
Telephone: (202) 835-0900
Members of firm representing listed organizations:
Deane, John Russell (II)
Background: Staff Assistant to the President of the U.S., 1971-72 Deputy Assistant General Counsel, Federal Energy Administration, 1974-75. Serves as Counsel for the Specialty Equipment Market Ass'n, Performance Warehouse Ass'n, Nat'l Hot Rod Ass'n, and Coalition of Automotive Ass'ns.

TRAMMELL, Jeffrey B.
V.P., Gov't Rels./State & Local Affairs, Hill and Knowlton Public Affairs Worldwide
Washington Harbour, 901 31st St., N.W., Washington, DC 20007
Telephone: (202) 333-7400
Registered as lobbyist at U.S. Congress.
Clients:
Blue Cross and Blue Shield Ass'n
Hertz Corp.

TRANSATLANTIC FUTURES, INC.
2311 Connecticut Ave., N.W. Suite 604, Washington, DC 20008
Telephone: (202) 462-1222
Background: A political communications firm.
Members of firm representing listed organizations:
Richter, Stephan-Gotz, President
Zuschlag, W. Alan, Senior V. President
Clients:
ABD Securities Corp. *(Stephan-Gotz Richter, W. Alan Zuschlag)*
Deutsche Bank AG *(Stephan-Gotz Richter, W. Alan Zuschlag)*
European Communities, Commission of the *(W. Alan Zuschlag)*
Siemens Corp. *(Stephan-Gotz Richter, W. Alan Zuschlag)*

TRANSNATIONAL, INC.
1511 K St., N.W., Suite 1100, Washington, DC 20005
Telephone: (202) 393-7690
Registered as Foreign Agent: (#3779)
Members of firm representing listed organizations:
Levine, Peter J.
Clients:
Associacao das Industrias de Calcados do Rio Grande do Sul *(Peter J. Levine)*
Companhia Siderurgica de Tubarao *(Peter J. Levine)*

TRAUBERMAN, Jeffrey
Washington Manager, Space Systems Div., Boeing Co.
1700 North Moore St., Arlington, VA 22209
Telephone: (703) 558-9600

TRAVESKY, Paul D.
V. President, Strategic Technology, Loral/Fairchild Systems
1111 Jefferson Davis Hwy. Suite 811, Arlington, VA 22202
Telephone: (703) 685-5300

TRAVIS & GOOCH
1100 15th St., N.W. Suite 1200, Washington, DC 20005
Telephone: (202) 457-9100
Members of firm representing listed organizations:
Gooch, R. Gordon
Background: General Counsel, Federal Power Commission, 1969-72.
Clients:
Anadarko Petroleum Corp. *(R. Gordon Gooch)*
Coalition to Oppose Energy Taxes *(R. Gordon Gooch)*
Petrochemical Energy Group

TRAVIS, Thomas G.
Sandler, Travis & Rosenberg. P.A.
1120 19th St., N.W. Suite 420, Washington, DC 20036
Telephone: (202) 457-0078
Clients:
American Ass'n of Exporters and Importers
Florida Customs Brokers and Forwarders
Florida District Export Council
Florida Exporters and Importers Ass'n
Nat'l Bonded Warehouse Ass'n
U.S. Apparel Industry Council

TRAYERS, Paul E.
Exec. Director, Federal Managers Ass'n
1000 16th St., N.W., Suite 701, Washington, DC 20006
Telephone: (202) 778-1500
Registered as lobbyist at U.S. Congress.

TREANOR, William W.
Exec. Director, American Youth Work Center, The
1751 N St., N.W., Suite 302, Washington, DC 20036
Telephone: (202) 785-0764

TREBACH, Arnold S.
President, Drug Policy Foundation
4801 Massachusetts Ave., N.W. Suite 400, Washington, DC 20016
Telephone: (202) 895-1634

TREFREY, Charles S.
President, Nat'l Wholesale Druggists' Ass'n
105 Oronoco St., Alexandria, VA 22314
Telephone: (202) 684-6400

TREICHEL, Janet M.
Exec. Director, Nat'l Business Education Ass'n
1914 Association Dr., Reston, VA 22091
Telephone: (703) 860-8300

TREICHLER, Ray
Research Analyst, Hudson Manufacturing Co., H. D.
1130 17th St., N.W. Suite 500, Washington, DC 20036
Telephone: (202) 331-1245

TREMPER, Dr. Paul
Exec. Director, Nat'l Soc. for Performance and Instruction
1126 16th St., N.W., Suite 102, Washington, DC 20036
Telephone: (202) 861-0777

TRENT, Judith M.
Global Aviation Associates, Ltd.
1800 K St., N.W. Suite 1104, Washington, DC 20006
Telephone: (202) 457-0212
Clients:
Huntsville-Madison County Airport
Phoenix Sky Harbour Internat'l Airport

TREVINO, Steven A.F.
Senior Associate for Stategy Affairs, Internat'l Security Council
818 Connecticut Ave., N.W. Suite 600, Washington, DC 20006
Telephone: (202) 828-0802

TRIAS, Jose E.
Paul, Weiss, Rifkind, Wharton and Garrison
1615 L St., N.W., Suite 1300, Washington, DC 20036
Telephone: (202) 223-7300

TRIBLE, Paul S.
Laxalt, Washington, Perito & Dubuc
1120 Connecticut Ave., N.W. Suite 1000, Washington, DC 20036
Telephone: (202) 857-4000
Background: Member, U.S. House of Representatives (R-VA), 1977-83. Member, U.S. Senate (R-VA), 1983-89. Member, U.S. Delegation to the United Nations, 1989.

TRILLING, Helen R.
Hogan and Hartson
555 13th St., N.W., Suite 1200, Washington, DC 20004-1109
Telephone: (202) 637-5600
Registered as lobbyist at U.S. Congress.
Clients:
American Physical Therapy Ass'n
Dianon Systems

TRIMBLE, Bernard
Exec. Director, CUE, Nat'l Ass'n of Manufacturers
1331 Pennsylvania Ave., N.W. Suite 1500 North, Washington, DC 20004-1703
Telephone: (202) 637-3000

TRIMBLE, Margaret
Legislative Assistant, Fireman's Fund Insurance Cos.
1730 Rhode Island Ave., N.W. Suite 1117, Washington, DC 20036
Telephone: (202) 785-3575

TRINCA, Carl E.
Exec. Director, American Ass'n of Colleges of Pharmacy
1426 Prince St., Alexandria, VA 22314
Telephone: (703) 739-2330

TRINDER, Rachel B.
Zuckert, Scoutt and Rasenberger
888 17th St., N.W., Suite 600, Washington, DC 20006-3959
Telephone: (202) 298-8660
Clients:
Dragonair
Martinair Holland
Transportation Research Forum

TROCCHI, Deborah
Exec. Director, Nat'l Ass'n of Government Communicators
80 South Early St., Alexandria, VA 22304
Telephone: (703) 823-4821

TROCCHIO, Julie
Government Liaison, Catholic Health Ass'n of the United States
1776 K St., N.W. Suite 204, Washington, DC 20006
Telephone: (202) 296-3993

TROJAK, Gary F.
V. Pres., Packaging & Technical Services, Chlorine Institute
2001 L St., N.W., Suite 506, Washington, DC 20036
Telephone: (202) 775-2790

TROLL, J. Richard
Exec. V. President, Ass'n of Independent Corrugated Converters
801 N. Fairfax St., Alexandria, VA 22314
Telephone: (703) 836-2422

TROMBETTI, Steve
Director, Communications, American Hotel and Motel Ass'n
1201 New York Ave., N.W. Suite 600, Washington, DC 20005
Telephone: (202) 289-3100

TROOBOFF, Peter D.
Covington and Burling
1201 Pennsylvania Ave., N.W., Box 7566, Washington, DC 20044
Telephone: (202) 662-6000
Registered as lobbyist at U.S. Congress.

TROOP, Michael G.
Sr. V. President & Legislative Rep., United States League of Savings Institutions
1709 New York Ave., N.W., Suite 801, Washington, DC 20006
Telephone: (202) 637-8900
Registered as lobbyist at U.S. Congress.

TROPP, Richard A.
Nat'l Strategies Inc.
818 17th St., N.W., Washington, DC 20006
Telephone: (202) 429-8744
Background: Special Assistant to the Administrator, U.S. Agency for International Development, 1982-88. Earlier served in four Executive Branch agencies, the White House and as Legislative Assistant to a U.S. Senator from New York.

TROUTMAN, George G.
V. President, Washington Operations, Bell Helicopter Textron
1090 Vermont Ave., N.W. Suite 1100, Washington, DC 20005
Telephone: (202) 289-5850
Registered as lobbyist at U.S. Congress.

WASHINGTON REPRESENTATIVES

TROWBRIDGE, G. F.
Shaw, Pittman, Potts and Trowbridge
2300 N St., N.W., Washington, DC 20037
Telephone: (202) 663-8000

TROXELL, Gregory A.
Director, Regulatory & Environ. Affairs, Public Service Co. of Indiana
1800 K St., N.W., Suite 1018, Washington, DC 20006
Telephone: (202) 887-0497
Registered as lobbyist at U.S. Congress.

TROY, Michael H.
Director - Government Relations, GTE Corp.
1850 M St., N.W., Suite 1200, Washington, DC 20036
Telephone: (202) 463-5200
Background: Former Legislative Director to Rep. Buddy MacKay (D-FL).

TROYER, Thomas A.
Caplin and Drysdale
One Thomas Circle, N.W. Suite 1100, Washington, DC 20005
Telephone: (202) 862-5000
Registered as lobbyist at U.S. Congress.
Background: Tax Division, Department of Justice, 1962-64; Office of Assistant Secretary of the Treasury for Tax Policy, 1964-66; Associate Tax Legislative Counsel, 1966-67.

TRUITT, Thomas H.
Piper and Marbury
1200 19th St., N.W., Washington, DC 20036
Telephone: (202) 861-3900
Background: Director, Legal Support Division, Environmental Protection Agency, 1971-72.

TRULL, Frankie
Capitol Associates, Inc.
426 C St., N.E., Washington, DC 20002
Telephone: (202) 544-1880
Registered as lobbyist at U.S. Congress.

TRULUCK, Phillip N.
Exec. V. President, Heritage Foundation
214 Massachusetts Ave., N.E., Washington, DC 20002
Telephone: (202) 546-4400

TRUMKA, Richard L.
President, United Mine Workers of America
900 15th St., N.W., Washington, DC 20005
Telephone: (202) 842-7280

TRYENS, Jeffrey
Associate Director, Nat'l Center for Policy Alternatives
2000 Florida Ave., N.W. 4th Floor, Washington, DC 20009
Telephone: (202) 387-6030

TRYFIATES, P. George
Exec. Director, English First
8001 Forbes Place, Suite 102, Springfield, VA 22151
Telephone: (703) 321-8818

TSONGAS, Paul
Foley, Hoag and Eliot
1615 L St., N.W., Suite 950, Washington, DC 20036
Telephone: (202) 775-0600
Clients:
Humane Soc. of the United States

TSUI, Pauline
Exec. Director, Organization of Chinese American Women
1300 N St., N.W., Suite 100, Washington, DC 20005
Telephone: (202) 638-0330

TUBBESING, Carl
Director, Washington Office, Nat'l Conference of State Legislatures
444 North Capitol St., N.W. Suite 500, Washington, DC 20001
Telephone: (202) 624-5400

TUCCILLO, Dr. John A.
Chief Economist and Sr. V. President, Nat'l Ass'n of REALTORS
777 14th St., N.W., Washington, DC 20005
Telephone: (202) 383-1000

TUCHOW, Genevieve W.
Director, Federal Gov't Affairs, Columbia Gas Distribution Cos.
1250 Eye St., N.W., Suite 703, Washington, DC 20005
Telephone: (202) 842-7424

TUCKER & ASSOCIATES
1701 Pennsylvania Ave., N.W., Suite 1000, Washington, DC 20006
Telephone: (202) 835-0744
Registered as Foreign Agent: (#4292)
Background: An international trade, public relations and public affairs firm.
Members of firm representing listed organizations:
Tucker, William, President
Background: Served in the White House counsel's Office, 1981-82.
Clients:
Alexander & Alexander Inc. *(William Tucker)*
Denver Regional Transportation District *(William Tucker)*
Korea, Embassy of *(William Tucker)*
New York Life Insurance Co. *(William Tucker)*
Taiwan Ass'n of Machinery Industries *(William Tucker)*

TUCKER, FLYER, SANGER & LEWIS
1615 L St., N.W. Suite 400, Washington, DC 20036
Telephone: (202) 452-8600
Members of firm representing listed organizations:
Tucker, Stefan F.
Clients:
Nat'l Realty Committee *(Stefan F. Tucker)*

TUCKER, Kitty
Exec. Director, Health and Energy Institute
P.O. Box 5357, Takoma Park, MD 20912
Telephone: (301) 585-5541

TUCKER, Stefan F.
Tucker, Flyer, Sanger & Lewis
1615 L St., N.W. Suite 400, Washington, DC 20036
Telephone: (202) 452-8600
Clients:
Nat'l Realty Committee

TUCKER, Stuart K.
Fellow, Overseas Development Council
1717 Massachusetts Ave., N.W., Washington, DC 20036
Telephone: (202) 234-8701

TUCKER, William
President, Tucker & Associates
1701 Pennsylvania Ave., N.W., Suite 1000, Washington, DC 20006
Telephone: (202) 835-0744
Registered as lobbyist at U.S. Congress.
Registered as Foreign Agent: (#4292).
Background: Served in the White House counsel's Office, 1981-82.
Clients:
Alexander & Alexander Inc.
Denver Regional Transportation District
Korea, Embassy of
New York Life Insurance Co.
Taiwan Ass'n of Machinery Industries

TUEL, Shannon B.
Legislative Representative, Nat'l Restaurant Ass'n
1200 17th St., N.W., Washington, DC 20036-3097
Telephone: (202) 331-5900

TUFTY, Hal
Nat'l Director of Federal Liaison, Soc. of American Value Engineers
Nat'l Press Bldg., Room 1199, Washington, DC 20045
Telephone: (202) 347-8998
Background: Also represents the Value Foundation.

TULLY, Paul R.
Director, Political Operations, Democratic Nat'l Committee
430 South Capitol St., S.E., Washington, DC 20003
Telephone: (202) 863-8000

TURE, Dr. Norman B.
President, Institute for Research on the Economics of Taxation (IRET)
1331 Pennsylvania Ave., N.W. Suite 515, Washington, DC 20004
Telephone: (202) 347-9570

TURENNE, William J.
Director of Government Relations, Lilly and Co., Eli
1901 L. St., N.W. Suite 705, Washington, DC 20036
Telephone: (202) 955-5350
Registered as lobbyist at U.S. Congress.

TURESKY, Stanley F.
Managing Partner, Potomac Partners
1250 24th St., N.W. Suite 875, Washington, DC 20037
Telephone: (202) 466-0560
Clients:
United States-New Zealand Council, The

TURNBULL, Bruce H.
Weil, Gotshal & Manges
1615 L St., N.W., Suite 700, Washington, DC 20036
Telephone: (202) 682-7000
Registered as lobbyist at U.S. Congress.

TURNBULL, Lowell D.
Leva, Hawes, Mason and Martin
1220 19th St., N.W. Suite 700, Washington, DC 20036
Telephone: (202) 775-0725
Registered as lobbyist at U.S. Congress.
Registered as Foreign Agent: (#3881).
Clients:
British Embassy
Electro- & Electronik Appartebau Gesellschaft mbH

TURNER, Audrey S.
Mercer, Inc., William M.
1001 22nd St., N.W. Suite 400, Washington, DC 20037
Telephone: (202) 293-9422
Registered as lobbyist at U.S. Congress.

TURNER, Brian
Executive Ass't to the President, AFL-CIO - Industrial Union Department
815 16th St., N.W., Washington, DC 20006
Telephone: (202) 842-7845
Registered as lobbyist at U.S. Congress.

TURNER, Caren
Fleishman-Hillard, Inc
1301 Connecticut Ave., N.W., Washington, DC 20036
Telephone: (202) 659-0330
Registered as lobbyist at U.S. Congress.
Clients:
American Ambulance Ass'n
Pathology Practice Ass'n

TURNER, Debbie
Director, Washington Office, Utah, State of
444 N. Capitol St., N.W., Suite 204, Washington, DC 20001
Telephone: (202) 624-7704

TURNER, Garry R.
Government Relations Associate, Federation for American Immigration Reform (FAIR)
1666 Connecticut Ave., N.W., Suite 400, Washington, DC 20009
Telephone: (202) 328-7004
Registered as lobbyist at U.S. Congress.

TURNER, J. Terry
Exec. Director, Interstate Truckload Carriers Conference
2200 Mill Road Suite 600, Alexandria, VA 22314
Telephone: (703) 838-1950
Registered as lobbyist at U.S. Congress.

TURNER, James
Potomac Partners
1250 24th St., N.W. Suite 875, Washington, DC 20037
Telephone: (202) 466-0560

TURNER, Jane
Congressional Representative, Nat'l Forest Products Ass'n
1250 Connecticut Ave., N.W., Suite 200, Washington, DC 20036

TURNER, Jane (Cont'd)
Telephone: (202) 463-2700
Registered as lobbyist at U.S. Congress.

TURNER, Jeff
Patton, Boggs and Blow
2550 M St., N.W., Suite 800, Washington, DC 20037
Telephone: (202) 457-6000
Registered as lobbyist at U.S. Congress.
Registered as Foreign Agent: (#2165).

TURNER, John H.
Associate Counsel, Nat'l Solid Wastes Management Ass'n
1730 Rhode Island Ave., N.W., 10th Floor, Washington, DC 20036
Telephone: (202) 659-4613
Registered as lobbyist at U.S. Congress.

TURNER, John M.
Corp. Director, Government Affairs, Georgia-Pacific Corp.
1875 Eye St., N.W. Suite 775, Washington, DC 20006
Telephone: (202) 659-3600
Registered as lobbyist at U.S. Congress.

TURNER, Pamela J.
V. President, Government Relations, Nat'l Cable Television Ass'n
1724 Massachusetts Ave., N.W., Washington, DC 20036
Telephone: (202) 775-3550
Registered as lobbyist at U.S. Congress.
Background: Former Chief Legislative Ass't to Sen. John Tower (R-TX), Deputy Ass't for Legislative Affairs to President Ronald Reagan, 1982-89.

TURNER, Samuel D.
Fox, Bennett and Turner
750 17th St., N.W., Suite 1100, Washington, DC 20006
Telephone: (202) 778-2300
Background: Deputy General Counsel, U.S. Department of Health and Human Services, 1981-84.
Clients:
Lederle Laboratories, American Cyanamid Co. Subsidiary
New MediCo Associates, Inc.

TURNER, Susan M.
Manager, Legislative Regulatory Programs, American Chemical Soc.
1155 16th St., N.W., Washington, DC 20036
Telephone: (202) 872-4466

TURNER, Walter
Associate Exec. Director, American Ass'n of School Administrators
1801 North Moore St., Arlington, VA 22209
Telephone: (703) 528-0700

TURNEY, Richard F.
Courtney, McCamant and Turney
1725 K St., N.W., Washington, DC 20006
Telephone: (202) 331-9825
Registered as lobbyist at U.S. Congress.
Background: Washington Representative, Automotive Service Industry Ass'n.
Clients:
Automotive Service Industry Ass'n
Interstate Taxation Coalition
Nat'l Ass'n of Chain Manufacturers

TURNIPSEED, Max L.
Asst. Director of Government Relations, Ethyl Corp.
1155 15th St., N.W., Suite 611, Washington, DC 20005
Telephone: (202) 223-4411
Registered as lobbyist at U.S. Congress.

TURPIN, Jim
Manager, State Affairs, Nat'l Solid Wastes Management Ass'n
1730 Rhode Island Ave., N.W., 10th Floor, Washington, DC 20036
Telephone: (202) 659-4613

TURZA, Peter
Gibson, Dunn and Crutcher
1050 Connecticut Ave., N.W. Suite 900, Washington, DC 20036-5303
Telephone: (202) 955-8500

TUTTLE, Alan A.
Patton, Boggs and Blow
2550 M St., N.W., Suite 800, Washington, DC 20037
Telephone: (202) 457-6000
Registered as lobbyist at U.S. Congress.
Background: Assistant U.S. Attorney, Southern District of New York, 1969-71. Assistant to the Solicitor General, 1971-75. Solicitor, Federal Power Commission, 1975-77.
Clients:
American Maritime Ass'n
Matson Navigation Co.
OSG Bulk Ships, Inc.

TUTTLE, Baldwin B.
Milbank, Tweed, Hadley & McCloy
1825 Eye St., N.W. Suite 900, Washington, DC 20006
Telephone: (202) 835-7500
Background: Assistant General Counsel, 1973-76 and Deputy General Counsel, 1976-77, Board of Governors of the Federal Reserve System.

TUTTLE, Beth
V. President, Communications, People for the American Way
2000 M St., N.W., Suite 400, Washington, DC 20036
Telephone: (202) 467-4999

TUTTLE, Jon F.
Dorsey & Whitney
1330 Connecticut Ave., N.W., Suite 200, Washington, DC 20036
Telephone: (202) 857-0700

TUVIN ASSOCIATES
2805 Washington Ave., Chevy Chase, MD 20815
Telephone: (202) 667-2400
Members of firm representing listed organizations:
Tuvin, Carl R., President
Clients:
Nat'l Ass'n of State Veterans Nursing Homes *(Carl R. Tuvin)*
Nat'l Telecommunications Network *(Carl R. Tuvin)*

TUVIN, Carl R.
President, Tuvin Associates
2805 Washington Ave., Chevy Chase, MD 20815
Telephone: (202) 667-2400
Registered as lobbyist at U.S. Congress.
Clients:
Nat'l Ass'n of State Veterans Nursing Homes
Nat'l Telecommunications Network

TWAITS, Alan R.
Corporate Counsel, Crowley Maritime Corp.
1500 K St., Suite 425, Washington, DC 20005
Telephone: (202) 737-4728

TWEEDIE, St. Clair J.
Director, Government Relations, American Cyanamid Co.
1575 Eye St., N.W., Suite 200, Washington, DC 20005
Telephone: (202) 789-1222
Registered as lobbyist at U.S. Congress.
Background: Serves as Chairman, American Cyanamid Good Government Fund.

TYDINGS, John R.
Exec. V. President, Greater Washington Board of Trade
1129 20th St., N.W., Washington, DC 20036
Telephone: (202) 857-5910
Registered as lobbyist at U.S. Congress.

TYDINGS, Joseph D.
Anderson, Kill, Olick and Oshinsky
2000 Pennsylvania Ave., N.W., Suite 7500, Washington, DC 20006
Telephone: (202) 728-3100
Registered as lobbyist at U.S. Congress.
Background: Member, Maryland House of Delegates, 1955-61. U.S. Attorney, District of Maryland, 1961-63. U.S. Senator from Maryland, 1965-71.
Clients:
Population Crisis Committee

TYERYAR, Clay D.
Ass'n and Society Management Internat'l Inc.
7297 Lee Highway, Unit N, Falls Church, VA 22042
Telephone: (703) 533-0251
Clients:
Meat Industry Suppliers Ass'n

Textile Machinery Good Government Committee
Wire Industry Suppliers Ass'n

TYLE, Craig
Ass't General Counsel, Investment Company Institute
1600 M St., N.W. Suite 600, Washington, DC 20036
Telephone: (202) 293-7700
Registered as lobbyist at U.S. Congress.

TYROLER, Charles, II
Director, Committee on the Present Danger
905 16th St., N.W., Washington, DC 20006
Telephone: (202) 628-2409

TYRRELL, Patrick J.
Weaver & Associates, Robert A.
915 15th St., N.W., Suite 402, Washington, DC 20005
Telephone: (202) 347-3697
Registered as Foreign Agent: (#3916).
Clients:
Zaire, Government of the Republic of

TYSON, James N.
Exec. Director, Nat'l Pharmaceutical Ass'n
Box 934, Howard University, Washington, DC 20059
Telephone: (202) 328-9229

TYSON, Patricia
Exec. Director, Religious Coalition for Abortion Rights
100 Maryland Ave., N.E., Washington, DC 20002
Telephone: (202) 543-7032

TYSSE, G. John
McGuiness and Williams
1015 15th St., N.W., Suite 1200, Washington, DC 20005
Telephone: (202) 789-8600
Registered as lobbyist at U.S. Congress.
Background: Director of Labor Law, U.S. Chamber of Commerce, 1980-84.
Clients:
Internat'l Theatrical Agencies Ass'n
Nat'l Ass'n of Orchestra Leaders
Nat'l Club Ass'n

U.S. STRATEGIES CORP.
1321 Duke St., Suite 200, Alexandria, VA 22314-3563
Telephone: (703) 739-7999
Members of firm representing listed organizations:
Hanson, Eric R., Chairman, CEO and President
Hanson, Heidi A., V. President, Public Affairs
Background: Ass't to U.S. Rep. John Buchanan, 1976; Special Ass't, U.S. Dept. of State, 1977-79; Special Ass't to the Secretary, Dept. of Health and Human Services, 1979-80.
Matthews, K. Michael, V. President, Government Relations
Miltenberger, Joseph H., Director, Government Relations
Skredynski, Michael P., Principal and Dir., West Coast Opns.
Wilson, Quentin C., Dir., Midwest Region
Clients:
American Medical EEG Ass'n *(Joseph H. Miltenberger)*
BioMed Services, Inc. *(K. Michael Matthews)*
Cities in Schools, Inc. *(Heidi A. Hanson, Michael P. Skredynski)*
Economy Fastners, Inc. *(Joseph H. Miltenberger)*
Envirotech Operating Services, Inc. *(K. Michael Matthews)*
GMS/Partners *(Michael P. Skredynski)*
HealthSouth Rehabilitation Corp. *(K. Michael Matthews, Joseph H. Miltenberger)*
Nat'l Alliance of Outpatient Cancer Therapy Centers *(Joseph H. Miltenberger)*
O'Brien Energy Systems, Inc. *(K. Michael Matthews)*
Oncology Services, Inc. *(Joseph H. Miltenberger)*
Service Employees Internat'l Union *(K. Michael Matthews)*
Ultrasystems Development Corp. *(K. Michael Matthews)*
USSI, Inc. *(K. Michael Matthews)*

UCELLI, Loretta M.
Communications Director, Nat'l Abortion Rights Action League
1101 14th St., N.W., Suite 500, Washington, DC 20005
Telephone: (202) 371-0779

UDALL, Lori
Staff Attorney, Environmental Defense Fund
1616 P St., N.W., Suite 150, Washington, DC 20036
Telephone: (202) 387-3500

UDALL, Stewart L.
Of Counsel, Kirkpatrick & Lockhart
1800 M St., N.W., Suite 900 South Lobby, Washington, DC 20036-5891
Telephone: (202) 778-9000
Background: Member, U.S. House of Representatives (D-AZ), 1955-61. Secretary of the Interior, 1961-69.

UDELL, Jerry G.
Vice President, American Retail Federation
1616 H St., N.W. 6th Floor, Washington, DC 20006
Telephone: (202) 783-7971
Registered as lobbyist at U.S. Congress.

UDWIN, Gerald E.
V. President, Westinghouse Broadcasting Co., Inc.
1025 Connecticut Ave., N.W., Washington, DC 20036
Telephone: (202) 429-0196

UEHARA, Jo
Associate Director, Government Relations, Independent Sector
1828 L St., N.W., Washington, DC 20036
Telephone: (202) 223-8100

UEHLEIN, E. Carl, Jr.
Morgan, Lewis and Bockius
1800 M St., N.W., Washington, DC 20036
Telephone: (202) 467-7000
Registered as lobbyist at U.S. Congress.
Clients:
　　Scotch Whiskey Ass'n

UGORETZ, Mark J.
Exec. Director, ERISA Industry Committee (ERIC), The
1726 M St., N.W., Suite 1101, Washington, DC 20036
Telephone: (202) 833-2800
Registered as lobbyist at U.S. Congress.

UHLENHOPP, Cletus R.
Cong Liaison Officer, DEPARTMENT OF INTERIOR - Bureau of Mines
2401 E St., N.W., Washington, DC 20241
Telephone: (202) 634-1282

UHLER, Lewis K.
President, Nat'l Tax Limitation Committee
201 Massachusetts Ave., N.E., Suite C-7, Washington, DC 20002
Telephone: (202) 547-4196

UHRE, Curtis B.
President, Coalition for Affordable Home Financing
1350 New York Ave., N.W. Suite 800, Washington, DC 20005
Telephone: (202) 628-2015
Registered as lobbyist at U.S. Congress.

ULLMANN, Maximilian
V. President, Defense Systems, Fiat Washington
1776 Eye St., N.W. Suite 775, Washington, DC 20006
Telephone: (202) 862-1610

ULMER, Elizabeth
Asssociate Director, Development, Sierra Club Legal Defense Fund
1531 P St., N.W. Suite 200, Washington, DC 20005
Telephone: (202) 667-4500
Registered as lobbyist at U.S. Congress.

ULRICH, Craig
General Counsel, Consumer Bankers Ass'n
1000 Wilson Blvd., 30th Floor, Arlington, VA 22209-3908
Telephone: (703) 276-1750
Registered as lobbyist at U.S. Congress.

UMANSKY, Barry
Deputy General Counsel, Nat'l Ass'n of Broadcasters
1771 N St., N.W., Washington, DC 20036
Telephone: (202) 429-5300

UMANSKY, David J.
Sr. V.P./Director, Grass Roots Mobiliztn, Burson-Marsteller
1850 M St., N.W., Suite 900, Washington, DC 20036

Telephone: (202) 833-8550

UMPHREY, Robert, Jr.
Manager, Congressional Affairs, Hoechst-Celanese Corp.
919 18th St., N.W., Suite 700, Washington, DC 20006
Telephone: (202) 296-2890
Registered as lobbyist at U.S. Congress.
Background: Legislative Assistant, Sen. William S. Cohen (R-ME), 1979-84.

UNGER, Charles K.
Ass't Exec. Director, American Orthotic and Prosthetic Ass'n
717 Pendleton St., Alexandria, VA 22314
Telephone: (703) 836-7116
Registered as lobbyist at U.S. Congress.

UNGER, Peter S.
V. President, American Ass'n for Laboratory Accreditation
656 Quince Orchard Road, Suite 704, Gaithersburg, MD 20878
Telephone: (301) 670-1377

UNGERER, Richard A.
Exec. Director, Nat'l Institute for Work and Learning
1255 23rd St., N.W., Suite 400, Washington, DC 20037
Telephone: (202) 862-8845
Background: Special Assistant, U.S. Office of Education, 1975-76.

UNITED INTERNAT'L CONSULTANTS
1800 Diagonal Rd., Alexandria, VA 22314
Telephone: (703) 684-4450
Members of firm representing listed organizations:
　　Baldwin, Joan B.
Clients:
　　South Africa, Embassy of *(Joan B. Baldwin)*
　　South Africa, Government of

UNWIN, Andrew F.G.
V. President, Int'l Development Program, Fiat Washington
1776 Eye St., N.W. Suite 775, Washington, DC 20006
Telephone: (202) 862-1610

UPSHAW, Gene
Exec. Director, Nat'l Football League Players Ass'n
2021 L St., N.W., Washington, DC 20036
Telephone: (202) 463-2200

UPSON, Cynthia
Director, Communications, Consumer Group, Electronic Industries Ass'n
2001 Pennsylvania Ave., N.W., Washington, DC 20006
Telephone: (202) 457-4900

UPSTON, John
Jefferson Group, The
1341 G St., N.W., Suite 1100, Washington, DC 20005
Telephone: (202) 638-3535
Clients:
　　Si.A.C./Italy

URBAN, Anne I.
Director, International Issues, Computer and Business Equipment Manufacturers Ass'n
311 First St., N.W. Suite 500, Washington, DC 20001
Telephone: (202) 737-8888
Registered as lobbyist at U.S. Congress.
Background: Former Legislative Assistant to Rep. Barbara Kennelly (D-CT).

URBANCHUK, John
V. President, Hill and Knowlton Public Affairs Worldwide
Washington Harbour, 901 31st St., N.W., Washington, DC 20007
Telephone: (202) 333-7400
Background: Desk Officer, Soviet Union/Eastern Europe, Politico-Military Division, Strategic Plans and Policy Directorate, Office of the Deputy Chief of Staff for Operations and Plans, Department of the Army, 1982-86.
Clients:
　　Monsanto Co.
　　Rohm and Haas Co.
　　USF&G

URBANCZYK, Steve
Williams and Connolly
839 17th St., N.W. 1000 Hill Bldg., Washington, DC 20006
Telephone: (202) 331-5000
Clients:

Nat'l Committee to Preserve Social Security and Medicare

URIBE, Ernesto
Director, Congressional Hispanic Caucus Institute
504 C St., N.E., Washington, DC 20002
Telephone: (202) 543-1771

URSOMARSO, Anthony
Treasurer, Dealers Election Action Committee of the Nat'l Automobile Dealers Ass'n (DEAC)
8400 Westpark Drive, McLean, VA 22102
Telephone: (703) 821-7110

URWITZ, Jay P.
Senior Partner, Hale and Dorr
1455 Pennsylvania Ave., N.W. Suite 1000, Washington, DC 20004
Telephone: (202) 393-0800
Registered as lobbyist at U.S. Congress.
Background: Legislative Assistant to Senator Edward Kennedy (D-MA), 1977-81.
Clients:
　　Boston Museum of Science
　　Dakota Wesleyan University
　　Gay Head Taxpayers' Ass'n
　　Genetics Institute Inc.
　　Metalor USA Refining Corp.
　　Northeastern University
　　Prime Computer, Inc.
　　USS Constitution Museum

USDAN, Michael D.
President, Institute for Educational Leadership
1001 Connecticut Ave., N.W. Suite 310, Washington, DC 20036
Telephone: (202) 822-8405

USERA, J. Andrew
White, Fine, and Verville
1156 15th St., N.W. Suite 1100, Washington, DC 20005
Telephone: (202) 659-2900
Background: Legislative Assistant to Hon. Jaime Benitez, Resident Commissioner from Puerto Rico, 1977-79; Legislative Assistant to Hon. Baltasar Corrada, Resident Commissioner from Puerto Rico, 1977-79. Deputy Director, Legislative Liaison, Community Services Administration, 1980-81.

UTRECHT, Lyn
Manatt, Phelps, Rothenberg & Phillips
1200 New Hampshire Ave., N.W., Suite 200, Washington, DC 20036
Telephone: (202) 463-4300
Registered as lobbyist at U.S. Congress.

UTT, Dr. Ronald D.
V. President, Nat'l Chamber Foundation
1615 H St., N.W., Washington, DC 20062
Telephone: (202) 463-5552

UYEDA, Mary
Director, County Health Policy Center, Nat'l Ass'n of Counties
440 First St., N.W., Washington, DC 20001
Telephone: (202) 393-6226
Background: Serves as contact for the Nat'l Ass'n of County Health Officials and the Nat'l Ass'n of County Health Facility Administrators.

VACCA, Francis J.
V. President for Government Relations, Mid-America Dairymen, Inc.
100 North Carolina Ave., S.E. Suite 1, Washington, DC 20003
Telephone: (202) 546-8987

VADNEY, Susan M.
Director, Media Relations, Council for Solid Waste Solutions
1275 K St., N.W. Suite 400, Washington, DC 20005
Telephone: (202) 371-5319

VAGLEY, Robert E.
President, American Insurance Ass'n
1130 Connecticut Ave., N.W., Suite 1000, Washington, DC 20036
Telephone: (202) 828-7100
Registered as lobbyist at U.S. Congress.

VAHOUNY, Karen
Director, Corporate Communications, Planning Research
Corp.
1500 Planning Research Drive, McLean, VA 22102
Telephone: (703) 556-1500

VAID, Urvashi
Exec. Director, Nat'l Gay and Lesbian Task Force
1517 U St., N.W., Washington, DC 20009
Telephone: (202) 332-6483

VALADEZ, Stanley
Exec. Director, Hispanic Organization of Professionals and
Executives
87 Catoctin Court, Silver Spring, MD 20906
Telephone: (301) 234-2351

VALANZANO, Anthony
Chief Counsel, Federal Relations, American Council of
Life Insurance
1001 Pennsylvania Ave., N.W., Washington, DC 20004-
2599
Telephone: (202) 624-2160
Registered as lobbyist at U.S. Congress.

VALDEZ, Abelardo L.
Laxalt, Washington, Perito & Dubuc
1120 Connecticut Ave., N.W., Suite 1000, Washington, DC
20036
Telephone: (202) 857-4000
Background: Attorney-Advisor, U.S. Overseas Private In-
vestment Corp., 1971-73. General Counsel, Inter-Ameri-
can Foundation, 1973-75. Assistant Administrator for
Latin America and the Caribbean, U.S. Agency for Inter-
national Dvelopment, 1977-79. Ambassador, Chief of
Protocol, U.S. Department of State, 1979-81.
Clients:
Asociacion de Empresas RENFE/Patentes TAL-
GO, S.A.

VALDIVIESO, Rafael
V. President for Program and Research, Hispanic Policy
Development Project
1001 Connecticut Ave., N.W. Suite 310, Washington, DC
20036
Telephone: (202) 822-8414

VALENTE, Mark, III
Dir, Cong Relations, OFFICE OF PERSONNEL MANAGE-
MENT
1900 E St., N.W., Washington, DC 20415
Telephone: (202) 632-6514

VALENTI, Jack J.
President, Motion Picture Ass'n of America
1600 Eye St., N.W., Washington, DC 20006
Telephone: (202) 293-1966
Registered as lobbyist at U.S. Congress.
Background: Special Assistant to the President of the Unit-
ed States, 1963-1966.

VALENTINE, Debra
O'Melveny and Myers
555 13th St., N.W., Suite 500 West, Washington, DC
20004
Telephone: (202) 383-5300
Clients:
Ford Motor Co.

VALENTINE, Ellen
Regulatory Assistant, MidCon Corp.
1747 Pennsylvania Ave. N.W. Suite 300, Washington, DC
20006
Telephone: (202) 857-3075

VALENTINE, Mark
Issues Director, Earth Day
1301-1A Connecticut Ave., N.W., Washington, DC 20036
Telephone: (202) 331-3329

VALENTINO, Ellen
Government Relations, Greater Washington/Maryland
Service Station and Automotive Repair Ass'n
9420 Annapolis Road, Suite 307, Lanham, MD 20706
Telephone: (301) 577-2875
Registered as lobbyist at U.S. Congress.

VALIS ASSOCIATES
1747 Pennsylvania Ave., N.W., Suite 1201, Washington,
DC 20006
Telephone: (202) 833-5055
Background: A government relations and public affairs
consulting firm.
Members of firm representing listed organizations:
Hillen, Cheryl E., V. President
Lynch, Jennifer C., Associate
Valis, Wayne H., President
Background: Served on White House staffs of Former
Presidents Richard Nixon, Gerald Ford and Ronald
Reagan.
Clients:
Coalition for Open Markets and Expanded Trade
(Wayne H. Valis)
Nat'l Ass'n of Wholesaler-Distributors *(Wayne H.
Valis)*
Nat'l Paint and Coatings Ass'n *(Wayne H. Valis)*
Transportation Reform Alliance *(Cheryl E. Hillen,
Wayne H. Valis)*

VALIS, Wayne H.
President, Valis Associates
1747 Pennsylvania Ave., N.W., Suite 1201, Washington,
DC 20006
Telephone: (202) 833-5055
Background: Served on White House staffs of Former
Presidents Richard Nixon, Gerald Ford and Ronald Rea-
gan.
Clients:
Coalition for Open Markets and Expanded Trade
Nat'l Ass'n of Wholesaler-Distributors
Nat'l Paint and Coatings Ass'n
Transportation Reform Alliance

VALLIERE, Reginald T.
Director, Government Relations, Nat'l Ass'n of Postmas-
ters of the U.S.
8 Herbert St., Alexandria, VA 22305-2600
Telephone: (703) 683-9027
Registered as lobbyist at U.S. Congress.
Background: Serves as a contact for Political Education for
Postmasters, the Political Action Committee of the Ass'n.

VAN AGT, Andreas A. M.
Head of Delegation, European Communities, Commission
of the
2100 M St., N.W., 7th Floor, Washington, DC 20037
Telephone: (202) 862-9500

VAN ARSDALL, R. Thomas
V. Pres., Agricultural Inputs & Services, Nat'l Council of
Farmer Cooperatives
50 F St., N.W., Suite 900, Washington, DC 20001
Telephone: (202) 626-8700
Registered as lobbyist at U.S. Congress.

VANBRAKLE, Tina
Congressional Affrs Officer, FEDERAL ELECTION COM-
MISSION
999 E St., N.W., Washington, DC 20463
Telephone: (202) 376-5136

VAN BROCKLIN, Robert D.
Stoel, Rives, Boley, Jones & Grey
1350 New York Ave., N.W., Suite 600A, Washington, DC
20005
Telephone: (202) 347-7744
Registered as lobbyist at U.S. Congress.
Clients:
PacifiCorp

VANCE, Andrew P.
Barnes, Richardson and Colburn
1819 H St., N.W., Washington, DC 20006
Telephone: (202) 457-0300
Registered as lobbyist at U.S. Congress.

VANCE, John A.
Wash. Counsel, Fed. Gov't Relations, Pacific Gas and
Electric Co.
1726 M St., N.W., Suite 1100, Washington, DC 20036-
4502
Telephone: (202) 466-7980
Registered as lobbyist at U.S. Congress.

VAN COVERDEN, Thomas
Exec. Director, Nat'l Ass'n of Community Health Centers
1330 New Hampshire Ave., N.W. Suite 122, Washington,
DC 20036
Telephone: (202) 659-8008

VAN DEHEI, Diane
Exec. Director, Ass'n of Metropolitan Water Agencies
1717 K St., N.W. Suite 1006, Washington, DC 20036
Telephone: (202) 331-2820

VANDERBILT, Marjorie
Ass't Dir., Congress'l & Agency Relat'ns, American
Nurses' Ass'n
1101 14th St., N.W., Suite 200, Washington, DC 20005
Telephone: (202) 789-1800
Registered as lobbyist at U.S. Congress.

VANDERBUSH, Darlene
Stockmeyer & Co.
499 S. Capitol St., S.W. Suite 103, Washington, DC 20003
Telephone: (202) 479-0531
Background: Personal Assistant to U.S. Rep. Cliff Stearns,
1989.
Clients:
Nat'l Ass'n of Business Political Action Commit-
tees

VANDERGRIFT, Benjamin M.
Partner, Pillsbury, Madison and Sutro
1667 K St., N.W., Suite 1100, Washington, DC 20006
Telephone: (202) 887-0300
Registered as lobbyist at U.S. Congress.
Clients:
Chevron Corp.
Intermedia Partners

VANDERSLICE, E. Lane
Public Policy Analyst, Nat'l Council for Internat'l Health
1701 K St., N.W. Suite 600, Washington, DC 20006
Telephone: (202) 833-5900

VAN DER VOORT ASSOCIATES, LTD.
1134 Westmoreland Road, Alexandria, VA 22308
Telephone: (703) 660-8959
Members of firm representing listed organizations:
van der Voort, Thomas L., President
Clients:
Pharmaceutical Manufacturers Ass'n *(Thomas L. van
der Voort)*

VAN DER VOORT, Thomas L.
President, van der Voort Associates, Ltd.
1134 Westmoreland Road, Alexandria, VA 22308
Telephone: (703) 660-8959
Registered as lobbyist at U.S. Congress.
Clients:
Pharmaceutical Manufacturers Ass'n

VAN DONGEN, Dirk
President, Nat'l Ass'n of Wholesaler-Distributors
1725 K St., N.W. Suite 710, Washington, DC 20006
Telephone: (202) 872-0885
Background: Also serves as Treasurer of Wholesaler-Dis-
tributor Political Action Committee.

VANDORN, Bonnie
Exec. Director, Ass'n of Science-Technology Centers
1413 K St., N.W. 10th Floor, Washington, DC 20005
Telephone: (202) 371-1171

VAN DRESSER, William
Director, Government Relations Division, American Veteri-
nary Medical Ass'n
1023 15th St., N.W., Suite 300, Washington, DC 20005
Telephone: (202) 659-2040
Registered as lobbyist at U.S. Congress.

VAN DUYNE, Nancy
Manager, Federal Legislation, Air Transport Ass'n of
America
1709 New York Ave., N.W., Washington, DC 20006-5206
Telephone: (202) 626-4000
Registered as lobbyist at U.S. Congress.

VAN DYK ASSOCIATES, INC.
1250 24th St., N.W. Suite 600, Washington, DC 20037
Telephone: (202) 223-4880
Registered as Foreign Agent: (#4201)

Background: A public policy/public affairs consulting firm. Publisher of Washington Intelligence Report, a joint venture with Financial World magazine.

Members of firm representing listed organizations:
Dickenson, Jim
Gwirtzman, Milton
Hamrin, Robert
Van Dyk, Ted, President
  Background: Former assistant to the late Senator and Vice President Hubert H. Humphrey (D-MN). Also held policy positions in past Democratic Administrations and Presidential campaigns.

Clients:
American Gas Ass'n
Autranet, Inc. *(Ted Van Dyk)*
Boston Co., The *(Milton Gwirtzman, Ted Van Dyk)*
Browning-Ferris Industries (D.C.), Inc. *(Jim Dickenson, Milton Gwirtzman, Ted Van Dyk)*
Council on United States Internat'l Trade Policy *(Robert Hamrin)*
Financial World Partners *(Ted Van Dyk)*
Insurance Information Institute *(Jim Dickenson, Ted Van Dyk)*
New Zealand, Embassy of *(Ted Van Dyk)*
Newmet Steel Co. *(Ted Van Dyk)*
Star Tribune Co, *(Jim Dickenson, Ted Van Dyk)*
USF&G *(Ted Van Dyk)*

VAN DYK, Ted
President, Van Dyk Associates, Inc.
1250 24th St., N.W., Suite 600, Washington, DC 20037
Telephone: (202) 223-4880
Registered as lobbyist at U.S. Congress.
Registered as Foreign Agent: (#4201).
Background: Former assistant to the late Senator and Vice President Hubert H. Humphrey (D-MN). Also held policy positions in past Democratic Administrations and Presidential campaigns.
Clients:
Autranet, Inc.
Boston Co., The
Browning-Ferris Industries (D.C.), Inc.
Financial World Partners
Insurance Information Institute
New Zealand, Embassy of
Newmet Steel Co.
Star Tribune Co,
USF&G

VAN EATON, Joseph
Spiegel and McDiarmid
1350 New York Ave., N.W., Suite 1100, Washington, DC 20005
Telephone: (202) 879-4000
Clients:
Palo Alto, California, City of

VAN ETTEN, Laura
V. President & Associate Counsel, Equitable Life Assurance Soc. of the U.S.
1700 Pennsylvania Ave., N.W., Suite 525, Washington, DC 20006
Telephone: (202) 393-3210
Registered as lobbyist at U.S. Congress.

VAN FLEET, METZNER & MEREDITH
499 South Capitol St., S.W. Suite 520, Washington, DC 20003
Telephone: (202) 488-1749
Members of firm representing listed organizations:
Meredith, Bruce

VAN FOSSEN, Sandra
Director, National Programs, Nat'l Commission on Working Women
1325 G St., N.W. Lower Level, Washington, DC 20005
Telephone: (202) 737-5764

VAN GELDER, Susan
Assoc. Dir., Policy Developt. & Research, Health Insurance Ass'n of America
1025 Connecticut Ave., N.W. Suite 1200, Washington, DC 20036
Telephone: (202) 223-7780

VAN GIESON, Henry B.
Deputy Director, Congressional Affairs, Boeing Co.
1700 North Moore St., Arlington, VA 22209
Telephone: (703) 558-9600

Registered as lobbyist at U.S. Congress.

VAN HEUVEN, Gerard J.
Exec. V. President, United States-Mexico Chamber of Commerce
1900 L St., N.W., Suite 612, Washington, DC 20036
Telephone: (202) 296-5198

VAN HOLLEN, Christopher
V. President and Coordinator, Middle East Institute
1761 N St., N.W., Washington, DC 20036
Telephone: (202) 785-1141
Background: Former U.S. Ambassador to Sri Lanka and the Republic of the Maldives and Deputy Assistant Secretary of State for Near Eastern and South Asian Affairs.

VAN HOOK, Matthew
Senior Environmental Counsel, American Paper Institute
1250 Connecticut Ave., N.W. Suite 210, Washington, DC 20036
Telephone: (202) 463-2420
Registered as lobbyist at U.S. Congress.

VANIK, Charles A.
Squire, Sanders and Dempsey
1201 Pennsylvania Ave., N.W. P.O. Box 407, Washington, DC 20044
Telephone: (202) 626-6600
Background: Former Member, U.S. House of Representatives (D-OH), 1954-80.
Clients:
Coalition for North American Trade and Investment
Philipp Brothers, Inc.

VAN, Jeff
Director of Media Communications, Chemical Manufacturers Ass'n
2501 M St., N.W., Washington, DC 20037
Telephone: (202) 887-1100

VAN KIRK, Burkett
Webster, Chamberlain and Bean
1747 Pennsylvania Ave., N.W., Suite 1000, Washington, DC 20006
Telephone: (202) 785-9500
Registered as lobbyist at U.S. Congress.
Background: Counsel, Senate Rules Committee, 1962-73. Senior Counsel, Senate Appropriations Committee, 1973-83.
Clients:
Commercial Law League of America
INTERARMS

VAN KLOBERG AND ASSOCIATES
1900 L St., N.W. Suite 500, Washington, DC 20036
Telephone: (202) 463-7820
Members of firm representing listed organizations:
van Kloberg, Edward J. (III), President
Ventry, Lance T.
Clients:
Burundi, Embassy of *(Edward J. van Kloberg, III)*
Cameroon, Government of *(Edward J. van Kloberg, III)*
Cape Verde, Embassy of the Republic of *(Edward J. van Kloberg, III)*
Equitable Life Assurance Soc. of the U.S. *(Edward J. van Kloberg, III)*
Grenada, Government of *(Edward J. van Kloberg, III)*
Haiti, Government of *(Edward J. van Kloberg, III)*
Iraq, Embassy of *(Edward J. van Kloberg, III)*
Lesotho, Government of *(Edward J. van Kloberg, III)*
Mongolia People's Republic, Embassy of *(Edward J. van Kloberg, III)*
Nigeria, Embassy of *(Edward J. van Kloberg, III)*
Occidental Petroleum Corp. *(Edward J. van Kloberg, III)*
Picker Internat'l *(Edward J. van Kloberg, III)*
Romania, Embassy of the Socialist Republic of *(Edward J. van Kloberg, III)*
Royal Nepalese Embassy *(Lance T. Ventry)*
Suriname, Government of *(Edward J. van Kloberg, III)*
Universal Shipping *(Edward J. van Kloberg, III)*
Zaire, Government of the Republic of *(Edward J. van Kloberg, III)*

VAN KLOBERG, Edward J., III
President, van Kloberg and Associates
1900 L St., N.W. Suite 500, Washington, DC 20036
Telephone: (202) 463-7820

Registered as Foreign Agent: (#3466).
Clients:
Burundi, Embassy of
Cameroon, Government of
Cape Verde, Embassy of the Republic of
Equitable Life Assurance Soc. of the U.S.
Grenada, Government of
Haiti, Government of
Iraq, Embassy of
Lesotho, Government of
Mongolia People's Republic, Embassy of
Nigeria, Embassy of
Occidental Petroleum Corp.
Picker Internat'l
Romania, Embassy of the Socialist Republic of
Suriname, Government of
Universal Shipping
Zaire, Government of the Republic of

VAN KOEVERING, Dyck
Manatos & Manatos, Inc.
1750 New York Ave., N.W. Suite 210, Washington, DC 20006
Telephone: (202) 393-7790
Clients:
American Hellenic Alliance, Inc.
Hellenic American Council of Southern California
Pancyprian Ass'n of America

VAN LOHUIVEN, Jan
Market Opinion Research, Inc.
1400 L St., N.W., Suite 650, Washington, DC 20005
Telephone: (202) 289-0420

VAN METER, Wanda
Secretary-Treasurer, Nat'l Rural Letter Carriers' Ass'n
1448 Duke St., Alexandria, VA 22314
Telephone: (703) 684-5545
Background: Serves as Treasurer, Nat'l Rural Letter Carriers' Ass'n Political Action Committee.

VAN NESS, Daniel W.
President, Justice Fellowship
Box 17152, Washington, DC 20041
Telephone: (703) 759-9400
Registered as lobbyist at U.S. Congress.

VAN NESS, FELDMAN & CURTIS
1050 Thomas Jefferson St., 7th Floor, Washington, DC 20007
Telephone: (202) 298-1800
Members of firm representing listed organizations:
Ain, Ross D.
  Background: Member, Office of the Legislative Counsel, U.S. House of Representatives 1971-76; Committee on Interstate and Foreign Commerce, U.S. House of Representatives, 1976-79. Federal Energy Regulatory Commission, 1979-80.
Bachman, Gary
Crawford, Milly, Member Legislative Services
Curtis, Charles B.
  Background: Supervisory Attorney, Comptroller of the Currency, Department of the Treasury, 1965-67. Special Counsel, Chief Branch of Market Regulation, and Inspection, Securities and Exchange Commission, 1967-71. Counsel, House Committee on Interstate and Foreign Commerce, 1971-76. Chairman, Federal Power Commission, 1977. Federal Energy Regulatory Commission, 1977-81.
Feldman, Howard J.
  Background: Attorney, Tax Division, U.S. Department of Justice, 1964-1968. Chief Counsel, U.S. Senate Permanent Committee on Investigations, 1973-1977.
Garside, Grenville
  Background: Special Assistant to the Secretary of Interior, 1967-68. Staff Director and Counsel, Senate Committee on Energy and Natural Resources, 1975-78.
Hultman, Dwight Eric
Lew, Jacob J.
Macan, Nancy, Member, Legislative Services Group
Mintz, Alan L.
  Background: Senior Attorney, Office of Exceptions and Appeals, Federal Energy Administration, 1974-77.
Nordhaus, Robert R.
Szabo, Robert G.

VAN NESS, FELDMAN & CURTIS (Cont'd)

Background: Legislative Assistant to Senator J. Bennett Johnston of Louisiana, 1975-78. Serves as Exec. Director, Consumers United for Rail Equity.

Tapia, M. Isabelle, Member, Legialtive Services Group

Background: Serves as Exec. Director, Coalition for American Energy Security.

Tomasky, Susan

Van Ness, William J. (Jr.)

Background: Special Counsel, 1966-69, and Chief Counsel, 1970-76, U.S. Senate Interior and Insular Affairs Committee.

Yamagata, Ben

Background: Counsel and Staff Director, Senate Subcommittee on Energy Research and Development, 1975-77. Legislative Counsel to the late Senator Frank Church of Idaho, 1974-75. Professional Staff Member, Senate Special Committee on Aging, 1973-74. Serves as Exec. Director, Clean Coal Technology Coalition.

Clients:

America First Companies *(Dwight Eric Hultman)*

American Institute of Certified Public Accountants *(Charles B. Curtis)*

Arctic Slope Regional Corp. *(Alan L. Mintz, William J. Van Ness, Jr.)*

Bumble Bee Seafoods, Inc. *(Howard J. Feldman)*

Clean Coal Technology Coalition *(Ben Yamagata)*

Coalition for American Energy Security *(M. Isabelle Tapia)*

Collier County, Florida *(Alan L. Mintz, Susan Tomasky)*

Committee of Hydroelectric Dam Owners *(Gary Bachman)*

Consumers United for Rail Equity *(Grenville Garside, Nancy Macan, Robert G. Szabo)*

Energy Fuels Nuclear, Inc. *(Alan L. Mintz)*

Geothermal Resources Ass'n *(Milly Crawford, Ben Yamagata)*

Los Angeles, California, Department of Water and Power *(Ben Yamagata)*

Lower Colorado River Authority *(Robert R. Nordhaus)*

LUZ Internat'l *(Ross D. Ain, Jacob J. Lew)*

McKesson Corp. *(Howard J. Feldman)*

Nat'l Nutrition Coalition *(Robert G. Szabo)*

Seneca Resources, Inc. *(Robert G. Szabo)*

Southern California Edison Co. *(Ben Yamagata)*

Uranium Producers of America *(Grenville Garside)*

Van Ness, Feldman & Curtis Political Action Committee *(Robert G. Szabo)*

Wagner and Brown *(Howard J. Feldman)*

VAN NESS, William J., Jr.

Van Ness, Feldman & Curtis
1050 Thomas Jefferson St., 7th Floor, Washington, DC 20007
Telephone: (202) 298-1800
Registered as lobbyist at U.S. Congress.
Background: Special Counsel, 1966-69, and Chief Counsel, 1970-76, U.S. Senate Interior and Insular Affairs Committee.
Clients:
Arctic Slope Regional Corp.

VAN NOORD, John

Manager, Energy Resource Development, American Gas Ass'n
1515 Wilson blvd., Arlington, VA 22209
Telephone: (703) 841-8653

VAN NOSTRAND, Lyman

Dep Assoc Admin, Plng, Eval & Legislat, DEPARTMENT OF HEALTH AND HUMAN SERVICES - Health Resources and Services Administration
5600 Fishers Lane, Rockville, MD 20857
Telephone: (301) 443-2460

VAN NOTE, Craig

Exec. V. President, Monitor
1506 19th St., N.W., Washington, DC 20036
Telephone: (202) 234-6576

VAN PELT, Karen

Director of Administration, Air Transport Ass'n of America
1709 New York Ave., N.W., Washington, DC 20006-5206
Telephone: (202) 626-4000

VAN PRAET, Connie

Director, Institute for Security and Cooperation in Outer Space
1336A Corcoran St., N.W., Washington, DC 20009-4311
Telephone: (202) 462-8886

VANSCOYOC, H. Stewart

Winburn, VanScoyoc, and Hooper
453 New Jersey Ave., S.E., Washington, DC 20003
Telephone: (202) 488-3581
Registered as lobbyist at U.S. Congress.
Clients:
Coalition of EPSCoR States
du Pont de Nemours and Co., E. I.
Internat'l Paper Co.
Quanex Corp.
Scott Paper Co.
University of Alabama System
USF&G

VAN TINE, Kirk K.

Baker and Botts
555 13th St., N.W., Suite 500 East, Washington, DC 20004-1109
Telephone: (202) 639-7700

VAN VLACK, Charles W.

V. President and Secretary, Chemical Manufacturers Ass'n
2501 M St., N.W., Washington, DC 20037
Telephone: (202) 887-1100

VAONAIS, Arlene

Communications Director, NTEA/Bankers Committee, The
1629 K St., N.W., Suite 1000, Washington, DC 20036
Telephone: (202) 466-8308

VARBLOW, Carl R.

Treasurer, Veda PAC, Veda Inc. Employees Political Action Committee
11 Canal Center Plaza Suite 300, Alexandria, VA 22314
Telephone: (703) 684-8005

VARDAMAN, John W., Jr.

Williams and Connqlly
839 17th St., N.W. 1000 Hill Bldg., Washington, DC 20006
Telephone: (202) 331-5000
Background: Law Clerk to Justice Hugo L. Black, U.S. Supreme Court, 1965-66.

VARGAS, Ellen

Attorney, Nat'l Women's Law Center
1616 P St., N.W., Washington, DC 20036
Telephone: (202) 328-5160

VARNER, Theresa

Health Policy Analyst, Pub. Pol. Inst., American Ass'n of Retired Persons
1909 K St., N.W., Washington, DC 20049
Telephone: (202) 728-4747
Registered as lobbyist at U.S. Congress.

VARNEY, Christine L.

General Counsel, Democratic Nat'l Committee
430 South Capitol St., S.E., Washington, DC 20003
Telephone: (202) 863-8000

VARON, Jay N.

Foley & Lardner
1775 Pennsylvania Ave., N.W., Suite 1000, Washington, DC 20006-4680
Telephone: (202) 862-5300
Registered as lobbyist at U.S. Congress.
Clients:
Coldwell Banker

VARTIAN, Ross P.

Exec. Director, Armenian Assembly of America
122 C St., N.W., Suite 350, Washington, DC 20001
Telephone: (202) 393-3434
Registered as lobbyist at U.S. Congress.

VASILOFF, Jennifer

Program Director, Physicians for Social Responsibility
1000 16th St., N.W., Suite 810, Washington, DC 20036
Telephone: (202) 785-3777

VAUGHAN, David A.

Mudge Rose Guthrie Alexander and Ferdon
2121 K St., N.W., Suite 700, Washington, DC 20037

Telephone: (202) 429-9355
Registered as lobbyist at U.S. Congress.
Background: Assistant General Counsel, Federal Energy Administration, 1974-76.
Clients:
Mercedes-Benz of North America, Inc.
Toshiba Corp.
Western Union Corp.

VAUGHAN, John Heath, Jr,

Representative for German Industry and Trade
One Farragut Square South 1634 Eye St., N.W., Washington, DC 20006
Telephone: (202) 347-0247
Registered as Foreign Agent: (#4274).
Clients:
Bundesverband der Deutschen Industrie
Deutscher Industrie und Handelstag

VAUGHN, Christine L.

Vinson and Elkins
Willard Office Building, 1455 Pennsylvania Ave., N.W., Washington, DC 20004-1007
Telephone: (202) 639-6500
Registered as lobbyist at U.S. Congress.
Background: Special Assistant to Assistant Secretary for Tax Policy, U.S. Treasury Department, 1981-84.
Clients:
Warburg Pincus & Co., E. M.

VAUGHN, Cindy

Executive Assistant, Public Affairs Group, Inc.
1629 K St., N.W., Suite 1100, Washington, DC 20006
Telephone: (202) 785-6713

VAUGHN, Eric

President, Renewable Fuels Ass'n
201 Massachusetts Ave., N.E. Suite C-4, Washington, DC 20002
Telephone: (202) 543-3802
Registered as lobbyist at U.S. Congress.

VAUGHN, Philip

Government Relations Counselor, Internat'l Business-Government Counsellors, Inc.
818 Connecticut Ave., N.W. Suite 1200, Washington, DC 20006
Telephone: (202) 872-8181

VAUGHN, Robert

V. Pres. of Membership and Conferences, Radio-Television News Directors Ass'n
1717 K St., N.W. Suite 615, Washington, DC 20006
Telephone: (202) 659-6510

VEACH, John B., III

Baker and Botts
555 13th St., N.W., Suite 500 East, Washington, DC 20004-1109
Telephone: (202) 639-7700
Registered as Foreign Agent: (#2930).
Clients:
Bundesverband der Deutschen Industrie

VEATCH, Robert M.

Director, Kennedy Institute of Ethics
Georgetown University, Washington, DC 20057
Telephone: (202) 687-6774

VEDDER, PRICE, KAUFMAN, KAMMHOLZ AND DAY

1919 Pennsylvania Ave., N.W., Washington, DC 20006
Telephone: (202) 828-5000
Background: Washington office of a Chicago law firm.
Members of firm representing listed organizations:
Pantos, George J.
Background: Special Assistant to the Under Secretary of Commerce, 1970; Special Counsel to the White House Council on International Economic Policy, 1971; Special Assistant to the Secretary of Commerce, 1972; Deputy Under Secretary of Commerce, 1973-1974.
Clients:
Professional Insurance Mass-Marketing Ass'n *(George J. Pantos)*
Self-Insurance Institute of America, Inc. *(George J. Pantos)*

VEGA, Yvonne M.
Exec. Director, AYUDA, Inc.
1736 Columbia Road, N.W., Washington, DC 20009
Telephone: (202) 387-4848

VEHAR, Nila A.
Exec. Director, Presidential Classroom for Young Americans
441 N. Lee St., Alexandria, VA 22314
Telephone: (703) 683-5400

VEHRS, Kristin L.
KLV Associates
1110 Vermont Ave., N.W., Suite 1160, Washington, DC 20005
Telephone: (202) 429-0949
Registered as lobbyist at U.S. Congress.
Clients:
American Ass'n of Zoological Parks and Aquariums
Texas Shrimp Ass'n

VEILLEUX, Nicole
Editor, Wetlands Newsletter, Nat'l Wetlands Technical Council
1616 P St., N.W., Washington, DC 20036
Telephone: (202) 328-5150

VELEY, Jennifer D.
Legislative Assistant, American Maritime Congress
444 N. Capitol St., N.W., Suite 801, Washington, DC 20001
Telephone: (202) 877-4477
Registered as lobbyist at U.S. Congress.

VELIOTES, Nicholas A.
President, Ass'n of American Publishers
1718 Connecticut Ave., N.W. Suite 700, Washington, DC 20009-1148
Telephone: (202) 232-3335
Registered as lobbyist at U.S. Congress.
Background: Formerly Assistant Secretary of State for Near Eastern and South Asian Affairs and U.S. Ambassador to Egypt.

VENABLE, BAETJER, HOWARD AND CIVILETTI
1201 New York Ave., N.W., Suite 1000, Washington, DC 20005
Telephone: (202) 962-4800
Background: Washington office of a Baltimore law firm.
Members of firm representing listed organizations:
Ames, Robert G.
Baskin, Maurice
Bass, Kenneth C. (III)
Background: Former law clerk to Supreme Court Justice Black, 1969-70; legislative assistant to a Member of Congress; Counsel for Intelligence Policy, U.S. Department of Justice, 1979-81.
Civiletti, Benjamin R.
Background: Deputy Attorney General and Attorney General in the Administration of President Jimmy Carter.
Dunn, Jeffrey A.
Hogan, Ilona M.
Madden, Thomas J.
Background: Deputy General Counsel, Department of Justice, Law Enforcement Assistance Administration, 1970-71. General Counsel, Law Enforcement Assistance Administration, 1972-79. Office of Justice Assistance, Research and Statistics, Department of Justice, 1980. Director, National Advisory Commission on Criminal Justice Standards and Goals, 1971-73.
Meyer, Lindsay
Clients:
Alliance of Metalworking Industries *(Ilona M. Hogan)*
Associated Builders and Contractors *(Maurice Baskin, Benjamin R. Civiletti)*
Nat'l Council of Juvenile and Family Court Judges
Nat'l Criminal Justice Ass'n

VENKATESWARAN, Indira
Market Opinion Research, Inc.
1400 L St., N.W., Suite 650, Washington, DC 20005
Telephone: (202) 289-0420

VENTRY, Lance T.
van Kloberg and Associates
1900 L St., N.W. Suite 500, Washington, DC 20036
Telephone: (202) 463-7820
Registered as Foreign Agent: (# 3466).
Clients:
Royal Nepalese Embassy

VENTURA, Rick
Exec. V. President, Urban Land Institute
1090 Vermont Ave., N.W. Suite 300, Washington, DC 20005
Telephone: (202) 289-8500

VERBY, Carol
Congressional Relations Representative, CNA Insurance Cos.
1800 M St., N.W., Washington, DC 20036
Telephone: (202) 785-9425
Registered as lobbyist at U.S. Congress.
Background: Former staffer to Congressman William Ford (MI).

VERDIER, Stephen J.
Senior Legislative Counsel, Independent Bankers Ass'n of America
One Thomas Circle, N.W., Suite 950, Washington, DC 20005
Telephone: (202) 659-8111
Registered as lobbyist at U.S. Congress.
Background: Counsel, House Banking Committee, 1976-83.

VERDISCO, Robert J.
V. President, Government Relations, Internat'l Mass Retail Ass'n
1901 Pennsylvania Ave., N.W. Suite 200, Washington, DC 20006
Telephone: (202) 861-0774
Registered as lobbyist at U.S. Congress.

VERDON, William P.
President, United Shipowners of America
1627 K St., N.W., Suite 1200, Washington, DC 20006
Telephone: (202) 466-5388
Registered as lobbyist at U.S. Congress.

VERKLER, Jerry T.
Senior Vice President, Interstate Natural Gas Ass'n of America
555 13th St., N.W. Suite 300 West, Washington, DC 20004
Telephone: (202) 626-3200
Registered as lobbyist at U.S. Congress.
Background: Serves also as Treasurer, Interstate Natural Gas Ass'n Political Action Committee.

VERNBERG, Lori S.
Manager, BREAD Political Action Committee
1111 14th St., N.W., Washington, DC 20005
Telephone: (202) 296-5800

VERNER, LIIPFERT, BERNHARD, MCPHERSON AND HAND, CHARTERED
901 15th St., N.W., Suite 700, Washington, DC 20005
Telephone: (202) 371-6000
Members of firm representing listed organizations:
Bernhard, Berl
Background: Supervisory General Attorney, U.S. Civil Rights Commission, 1959; Deputy Director, 1959-1960; Director, 1961-1963. General Counsel, Democratic Senatorial Campaign Committee, 1967-71. Special Counsel, Democratic Nat'l Committee, 1969-70. Senior advisor to the Secretary of State, 1980.
Bondurant, Amy L.
Background: Legislative Assistant to Senator Wendell Ford (D-KY), 1975-78; Consumer Counsel/Senior Counsel, U.S. Senate Committee on Commerce, Science and Transportation, 1978- 1987.
Cartwright, Suzanne, Director of Legislative Affairs
Background: Legislative Assistant to Rep. Jim Moody (D-WI), 1983-85.
Darneille, Hopewell H. (III)
Drogula, Fred W.
Background: Law Clerk to the Chief Judge of the U.S. Court of Appeals, District of Columbia, 1961-63; Trial Attorney with the U.S. Dept. of Justice, 1963-67; Special Ass't to the Deputy Attorney General of the U.S., 1967-69.

Eskin, Andrew D.
Background: Legislative Aide to Rep. James Santini (D-NV), 1977-78. Attorney, Federal Trade Commission, 1985-86. Legislative Director to Senator Richard Bryan (D-NV), 1989-90.
Gould, Rebecca M.J.
Grant, Andrea
Background: Attorney on the Oil Import Appeals Board, 1974-76.
Hand, Lloyd N.
Background: Assistant to Senate Majority Leader and Vice President Lyndon B. Johnson, 1957-61. U.S. Chief of Protocol, 1965-66.
Keller, Thomas J.
Klein, Gary
Background: Legislative ass't to Sen. Jacob Javits (R-NY), 1973-75; Minority Counsel to the Energy Subcommittee of the Senate Government Affairs Committee, 1975-77.
Kramerich, Leslie
Background: Professional Staff Member, Senate Committee on Aging, 1984-86. Aide to Senator Dave Durenberger (R-MN), 1986-87. Staff Member, House Appropriations Committee, 1987-89.
Krumholtz, Jack
Lewis, Rita
McPherson, Harry C.
Background: General Counsel, Senate Democratic Policy Committee, 1956-63. Deputy Undersecretary of the Army, 1963-64. Assistant Secretary of State for Educational and Cultural Affairs, 1964-65. Special Counsel to the President, 1965-69. General Counsel for the John F. Kennedy Center.
Merrigan, John A.
Background: Staff of Sen. Russell Long (D-LA), 1971.
Quirk, Sherry A.
Regan, R. Michael
Background: Counsel to Senate Judiciary Committee 1986-87.
Riordan, Mary Beth, Director, Tax Legislation
Background: Legislative Assistant to Rep. Raymond McGrath (R-NY), 1981-82. Technical Consultant, House Committee on Science and Technology, 1982-84. Legislative Director and Tax Aide to Rep. McGrath, 1984-89.
Roberts, Michael J.
Background: Member of Staff of Congressman Carlton R. Sickles of Maryland, 1963-64.
Steenland, Douglas M.
Temple, Riley K.
Background: Legislative Assistant to Senator Charles Mathias (R-MD), 1977-78. Communications Counsel, U.S. Senate Committee on Commerce, Science and Transportation,1981-83.
Vince, Clinton A.
Vincent, William E.
Zentay, John H.
Background: Legislative Ass't to Sen. Stewart Symington, 1958-63; Member of the Legislative Presentation Staff of the Agency for Internat'l Development, Dept. of State, 1963-66.
Clients:
Alcatel *(Lloyd N. Hand)*
ARCO *(Harry C. McPherson)*
Bell Atlantic *(Lloyd N. Hand)*
Boston Mass Transit Authority *(Harry C. McPherson, Douglas M. Steenland)*
Burlington Northern Railroad *(Berl Bernhard)*
Central Gulf Lines *(John A. Merrigan)*
Consolidated Grain and Barge Co. *(Harry C. McPherson, John A. Merrigan, Douglas M. Steenland)*
Continental Airlines *(Berl Bernhard)*
Coopers and Lybrand *(John A. Merrigan)*
Fairchild Space & Defense Corp.
GenCorp *(Lloyd N. Hand)*
General Aviation Manufacturers Ass'n *(Amy L. Bondurant)*
General Dynamics Corp. *(Amy L. Bondurant)*
Indiana Port Commission *(Hopewell H. Darneille, III)*
Investment Company Institute *(John A. Merrigan)*
Irving Ltd., J.D. *(Berl Bernhard, Lloyd N. Hand, Harry C. McPherson, John A. Merrigan, Douglas M. Steenland)*
Matra Aerospace, Inc.
McDonnell Douglas Corp. *(Amy L. Bondurant)*
Nat'l Wildlife Federation *(Lloyd N. Hand)*
NYNEX *(Riley K. Temple)*
Oerlikon-Buhrle Ltd.

VERNER, LIIPFERT, BERNHARD, MCPHERSON AND HAND, CHARTERED (Cont'd)

Puerto Rico, New Progressive Party Of (*Harry C. McPherson, John A. Merrigan*)
Rayburn County Electric Cooperative (*Harry C. McPherson, Clinton A. Vince*)
Southeastern Power Resource Committee (*Clinton A. Vince*)
Southwestern Power Resource Ass'n (*Clinton A. Vince*)
Travelers, The (*John A. Merrigan, Douglas M. Steenland*)
TRW Inc. (*Lloyd N. Hand*)
UNC Incorporated (*Berl Bernhard, John A. Merrigan*)
Verner, Liipfert, Bernhard, McPherson and Hand Political Action Committee (*John A. Merrigan*)
Wings Holdings Inc. (*Berl Bernhard*)

VERNETTI, Michael

V. President, Public Relations, Telocator
2000 M St., N.W., Suite 230, Washington, DC 20036
Telephone: (202) 467-4770

VERRASTRO, Frank A.

V. President, Government Relations, Pennzoil Co.
1155 15th St., N.W., Suite 600, Washington, DC 20005
Telephone: (202) 331-0212
Registered as lobbyist at U.S. Congress.

VERSAGE, Vincent M.

Associate, Cassidy and Associates, Inc.
655 15th St., N.W., Suite 1100, Washington, DC 20005
Telephone: (202) 347-0773
Registered as lobbyist at U.S. Congress.
Registered as Foreign Agent: (#4259).
Background: Legislative Director to Rep. Timothy Wirth (D-CO), 1984-85. Senior Legislative Assistant to Senator Spark Matsunaga (D-HI), 1976-84.
Clients:
Clark Atlanta University
Hawaii State Department of Business and Economic Development
Hawaii, University of
Lehigh University
Loyola College
Massachusetts Corp. for Educational Telecommunications
Michigan Technological University
Mount Sinai Medical Center
Nat'l Jewish Center for Immunology and Respiratory Medicine
Pirelli Cable Corp.
Polytechnic University of New York
Rochester Institute of Technology
Societa Cavi Pirelli S.p.A.
St. Joseph's University

VERSTANDIG AND ASSOCIATES, INC.

1455 Pennsylvania Ave., N.W. Suite 1180, Washington, DC 20004
Telephone: (202) 628-4800
Members of firm representing listed organizations:
Verstandig, Lee L.
Background: Legislative Director (1977) and Administrative Assistant to Senator John Chafee (R-RI), 1978-81. Assistant Secretary for Government Affairs, U.S. Department of Transportation, 1981-83. Acting Administrator, U.S. Environmental Protection Agency, 1983. Assistant to the President for Intergovernmental Affairs, The White House, 1983-85. Under Secretary, U.S. Department of Housing and Urban Development, 1985-86.

VERSTANDIG, Lee L.

Verstandig and Associates, Inc.
1455 Pennsylvania Ave., N.W. Suite 1180, Washington, DC 20004
Telephone: (202) 628-4800
Registered as lobbyist at U.S. Congress.
Background: Legislative Director (1977) and Administrative Assistant to Senator John Chafee (R-RI), 1978-81. Assistant Secretary for Government Affairs, U.S. Department of Transportation, 1981-83. Acting Administrator, U.S. Environmental Protection Agency, 1983. Assistant to the President for Intergovernmental Affairs, The White House, 1983-85. Under Secretary, U.S. Department of Housing and Urban Development, 1985-86.

VERTIZ, Dr. Virginia C.

Government Relations Specialist, American Ass'n of School Administrators
1801 North Moore St., Arlington, VA 22209
Telephone: (703) 528-0700

VERVEER, Melanne

Exec. V. Pres. & Dir., Public Policy, People for the American Way
2000 M St., N.W., Suite 400, Washington, DC 20036
Telephone: (202) 467-4999
Registered as lobbyist at U.S. Congress.

VERVEER, Philip L.

Willkie Farr and Gallagher
1155 21st St., N.W., 6th Fl., Washington, DC 20036-3302
Telephone: (202) 328-8000
Clients:
Cable and Wireless North America
Cellular Telecommunications Industry Ass'n
Dun & Bradstreet
Network Equipment Technologies
Telecommunications Industry Ass'n
Time Warner Inc.

VERVILLE, Richard E.

White, Fine, and Verville
1156 15th St., N.W. Suite 1100, Washington, DC 20005
Telephone: (202) 659-2900
Background: Special Assistant to the Secretary, HEW 1970; Deputy Assistant Secretary, HEW 1971-73.
Clients:
American Academy of Physical Medicine and Rehabilitation
American Ass'n of Nurse Anesthetists
American Congress of Rehabilitation Medicine
Helen Keller Internat'l
Joint Council on Allergy and Immunology
Nat'l Multiple Sclerosis Soc.

VETTER, Betty M.

Exec. Director, Commission on Professionals in Science and Technology
1500 Massachusetts Ave., N.W. Suite 831, Washington, DC 20005
Telephone: (202) 223-6995

VIAR, David

Exec. Director, Ass'n of Community College Trustees
1740 N St., N.W., Washington, DC 20036
Telephone: (202) 347-1740

VICK, Kathy

Secretary, Democratic Nat'l Committee
430 South Capitol St., S.E., Washington, DC 20003
Telephone: (202) 863-8000

VICKERMAN, John C.

Exec. Director, Business Records Manufacturers Ass'n
1000 Connecticut Ave., N.W. Suite 1035, Washington, DC 20036
Telephone: (202) 296-7400

VICKERS, Eugene B.

Vickers & Vickers
1706 23rd St. South, Arlington, VA 22202
Telephone: (202) 486-1548
Registered as Foreign Agent: (#4050).
Clients:
Australian Wheat Board
Elders Grain, Inc.
Mitsui Grain Corp
NorOats, Inc.
Rice Growers Ass'n of California

VICKERS, Linda

Vickers & Vickers
1706 23rd St. South, Arlington, VA 22202
Telephone: (202) 486-1548
Registered as lobbyist at U.S. Congress.
Clients:
Communicating for Agriculture
Nat'l Ass'n of Crop Insurance Agents Political Action Committee

VICKERS & VICKERS

1706 23rd St. South, Arlington, VA 22202
Telephone: (202) 486-1548
Members of firm representing listed organizations:
Vickers, Eugene B.
Vickers, Linda
Clients:
Australian Wheat Board (*Eugene B. Vickers*)
Communicating for Agriculture (*Linda Vickers*)
Elders Grain, Inc. (*Eugene B. Vickers*)
Mitsui Grain Corp (*Eugene B. Vickers*)
Nat'l Ass'n of Crop Insurance Agents Political Action Committee (*Linda Vickers*)
NorOats, Inc. (*Eugene B. Vickers*)
Rice Growers Ass'n of California (*Eugene B. Vickers*)

VICKERY, Ann Morgan

Hogan and Hartson
555 13th St., N.W., Suite 1200, Washington, DC 20004-1109
Telephone: (202) 637-5600
Registered as lobbyist at U.S. Congress.
Clients:
American Physical Therapy Ass'n
Amgen, Inc.
Caremark/Home Health Care of America

VICTOR, A. Paul

Weil, Gotshal & Manges
1615 L St., N.W., Suite 700, Washington, DC 20036
Telephone: (202) 682-7000
Clients:
Matsushita Electronic Corp.
Mitsubishi Corp.

VIEHE-NAESS, Brenda

Partner, Lord Day & Lord, Barrett Smith
1201 Pennsylvania Ave., N.W., Suite 821, Washington, DC 20004
Telephone: (202) 393-5024
Registered as Foreign Agent: (#4168).

VIENNA & ASSOCIATES, David

401 Wythe St., Suite 2-A, Alexandria, VA 22314
Telephone: (703) 684-5236
Background: Public affairs consultants.
Members of firm representing listed organizations:
Snell, Peter Leigh, V. President
Background: Former Legislative Counsel to Senator Sam Nunn (D-GA).
Vienna, Cheryl, V. President
Background: Former Legislative Director for Senator Sam Nunn (D-GA).
Vienna, David P., President
Background: Former Professional Staff, U.S. Senate Permanent Subcommittee on Investigations.
Organizations represented:
California Board of Equalization (*Peter Leigh Snell*)
California Franchise Tax Board (*Peter Leigh Snell, Cheryl Vienna*)
California Public Employees' Retirement System (*David P. Vienna*)
California State Controller (*Cheryl Vienna*)
California State Senate (*Peter Leigh Snell, Cheryl Vienna*)
Pacific Stock Exchange, Inc., The (*Peter Leigh Snell, David P. Vienna*)

VIENNA, Cheryl

V. President, Vienna & Associates, David
401 Wythe St., Suite 2-A, Alexandria, VA 22314
Telephone: (703) 684-5236
Registered as lobbyist at U.S. Congress.
Background: Former Legislative Director for Senator Sam Nunn (D-GA).
Organizations represented:
California Franchise Tax Board
California State Controller
California State Senate

VIENNA, David P.

President, Vienna & Associates, David
401 Wythe St., Suite 2-A, Alexandria, VA 22314
Telephone: (703) 684-5236
Registered as lobbyist at U.S. Congress.
Background: Former Professional Staff, U.S. Senate Permanent Subcommittee on Investigations.
Organizations represented:
California Public Employees' Retirement System
Pacific Stock Exchange, Inc., The

VIERRA ASSOCIATES, INC.
1825 Eye St., N.W. Suite 400, Washington, DC 20006
Telephone: (202) 429-6830
Background: A government and public relations consulting firm.
Members of firm representing listed organizations:
Vierra, Dennis C., President
   Background: With the Urban Mass Transportation Administration 1977-83.
   Clients:
      Dallas Area Rapid Transit Authority *(Dennis C. Vierra)*
      Hillsborough Area Regional Transit Authority *(Dennis C. Vierra)*
      Jacksonville Transportation Authority *(Dennis C. Vierra)*
      Lipton Internat'l Players Championships *(Dennis C. Vierra)*
      Metro-Dade County *(Dennis C. Vierra)*
      New York Metropolitan Transportation Authority *(Dennis C. Vierra)*
      Niagara Frontier Transportation Authority *(Dennis C. Vierra)*
      Westinghouse Transportation Division *(Dennis C. Vierra)*

VIERRA, Dennis C.
President, Vierra Associates, Inc.
1825 Eye St., N.W. Suite 400, Washington, DC 20006
Telephone: (202) 429-6830
Registered as lobbyist at U.S. Congress.
Background: With the Urban Mass Transportation Administration 1977-83.
Clients:
   Dallas Area Rapid Transit Authority
   Hillsborough Area Regional Transit Authority
   Jacksonville Transportation Authority
   Lipton Internat'l Players Championships
   Metro-Dade County
   New York Metropolitan Transportation Authority
   Niagara Frontier Transportation Authority
   Westinghouse Transportation Division

VIETH, G. Duane
Arnold & Porter
1200 New Hampshire Ave., N.W., Washington, DC 20036
Telephone: (202) 872-6700
Background: Member of the Board of Directors of Mortgage Investors of Washington.

VIETS, Richard N.
Aspen Hill Enterprises, Ltd.
815 Connecticut Ave.,, N.W. Suite 800, Washington, DC 20006
Telephone: (202) 785-2525
Registered as Foreign Agent: (#4158).
Clients:
   Jordan, Hashemite Kingdom of

VIGNONE, Rudolph A.
V. President, Governmental Relations, Goodyear Tire and Rubber Co.
901 15th St., N.W. Suite 350, Washington, DC 20005
Telephone: (202) 682-9250
Registered as lobbyist at U.S. Congress.

VIGUERIE CO., THE
7777 Leesburg Pike, Falls Church, VA 22043
Telephone: (703) 356-0440
Background: A very conservative political consulting firm specializing in direct mail, grass-roots mobilization.
Members of firm representing listed organizations:
   Viguerie, Richard

VIGUERIE, Richard
Viguerie Co., The
7777 Leesburg Pike, Falls Church, VA 22043
Telephone: (703) 356-0440

VIHSTADT, Mary
Washington Representative, Greyhound Corp., The
2000 K St., N.W., Suite 203, Washington, DC 20006
Telephone: (202) 223-8630

VILHAUER, Robert J.
Manager, Congressional Affairs, Boeing Co.
1700 North Moore St., Arlington, VA 22209
Telephone: (703) 558-9600

Registered as lobbyist at U.S. Congress.

VILLASTRIGO, Edith
Nat'l Legislative Coordinator, Women Strike for Peace
105 2nd St., N.E., Washington, DC 20002
Telephone: (202) 543-2660

VINCE, Clinton A.
Verner, Liipfert, Bernhard, McPherson and Hand, Chartered
901 15th St., N.W., Suite 700, Washington, DC 20005
Telephone: (202) 371-6000
Clients:
   Rayburn County Electric Cooperative
   Southeastern Power Resource Committee
   Southwestern Power Resource Ass'n

VINCENT, Jo
Director, Business Roundtable, Democratic Senatorial Campaign Committee
430 South Capitol St., S.E., Washington, DC 20003
Telephone: (202) 224-2447

VINCENT, William E.
Verner, Liipfert, Bernhard, McPherson and Hand, Chartered
901 15th St., N.W., Suite 700, Washington, DC 20005
Telephone: (202) 371-6000
Registered as lobbyist at U.S. Congress.

VINE, Howard A.
Dyer, Ellis, Joseph & Mills
600 New Hampshire Ave., N.W., Suite 1000, Washington, DC 20037
Telephone: (202) 944-3040
Registered as lobbyist at U.S. Congress.
Registered as Foreign Agent: (#4121).
Clients:
   Ace Frosty Shipping Co., Ltd.
   Alliance for Corporate Growth
   Bobbie Brooks
   Competitive Health Care Coalition
   PubCo Corp.
   Smith Corona Corp.
   Torrington Co.

VINE, John M.
Covington and Burling
1201 Pennsylvania Ave., N.W., Box 7566, Washington, DC 20044
Telephone: (202) 662-6000
Registered as lobbyist at U.S. Congress.
Clients:
   Amoco Corp.
   ERISA Industry Committee (ERIC), The

VINOVICH, Ralph
V. President, Legislative Affairs, Tobacco Institute
1875 Eye St., N.W., Suite 800, Washington, DC 20006
Telephone: (202) 457-4854
Registered as lobbyist at U.S. Congress.

VINSON AND ELKINS
Willard Office Building, 1455 Pennsylvania Ave., N.W., Washington, DC 20004-1007
Telephone: (202) 639-6500
Registered as lobbyist at U.S. Congress.
Registered as Foreign Agent: (#4277)
Background: Washington office of a Houston law firm.
Members of firm representing listed organizations:
   Buxton, C. Michael
      Background: Attorney-Advisor, Office of Legal Counsel, U.S. Department of Justice, 1971-73. Special Assistant U.S. Attorney, District of Columbia, 1972.
   Chapoton, John E.
      Background: Tax Legislative Counsel, U.S. Treasury Department, 1970-72. Assistant Secretary of the Treasury for Tax Policy, 1981-84.
   Ewing, Ky P. (Jr.)
      Background: Deputy Assistant Attorney General, Antitrust Division, U.S. Department of Justice, 1978-80.
   Gould, James C.
      Background: Legislative Assistant to Senator Lloyd Bentsen (D-TX), 1984-86. Chief Tax Counsel, 1987, and Staff Director and Chief Counsel, 1988, Senate Finance Committee.
   Kassinger, Theodore W.
      Background: Attorney, Office of the Legal Adviser, Department of State, 1980-81. International Trade Counsel, Senate Committee on Finance, 1981-85.

   Lewis, Cathy A.
      Background: Assistant to Counsel to Chairman, 1974-78 and Attorney, 1978-79, Board of Governors of the Federal Reserve System.
   Mathews, Colin D.
   Vaughn, Christine L.
      Background: Special Assistant to Assistant Secretary for Tax Policy, U.S. Treasury Department, 1981-84.
   Clients:
      Arkla, Inc.
      Citizens Utilities Co.
      ENSERCH Corp. *(John E. Chapoton)*
      Federal Express Corp.
      Fiat Washington
      Goldman, Sachs and Co. *(John E. Chapoton)*
      Merrill Lynch and Co., Inc. *(John E. Chapoton)*
      Modar, Inc. *(James C. Gould)*
      Nat'l Refrigerants, Inc. *(James C. Gould)*
      Panhandle Eastern Corp.
      Pennsylvania Engineering Co. *(James C. Gould)*
      Sterling Group, Inc., The *(James C. Gould)*
      Trammell Crow, Inc. *(James C. Gould)*
      Travelers, The *(Ky P. Ewing, Jr.)*
      United Savings of Texas, FSB *(Cathy A. Lewis)*
      Vitro, S.A. *(John E. Chapoton, Theodore W. Kassinger)*
      Warburg Pincus & Co., E. M. *(Christine L. Vaughn)*

VINYARD, Walter D., Jr.
Zuckert, Scoutt and Rasenberger
888 17th St., N.W., Suite 600, Washington, DC 20006-3959
Telephone: (202) 298-8660
Registered as lobbyist at U.S. Congress.
Background: Attorney, Securities and Exchange Commission, 1968-72.
Clients:
   Continental Corp., The
   Nat'l Fraternal Congress of America
   Resource Deployment, Inc.

VISCIDO, Dr. Anthony J.
Exec. Director, Academy for Implants and Transplants
Box 223, Springfield, VA 22150
Telephone: (703) 451-0001

VISHNY, Paul
Legal Counsel, Telecommunications Industry Ass'n
1722 Eye St., N.W., Suite 440, Washington, DC 20006
Telephone: (202) 457-4912

VISSCHER, Dr. Harrison C.
Director, Education, Council on Resident Education in Obstetrics and Gynecology
409 12th St., S.W., Washington, DC 20024-2588
Telephone: (202) 638-5577

VITALI, Andrew
Interlocke Associates
117 C St., S.E., Washington, DC 20003
Telephone: (202) 546-7973
Registered as Foreign Agent: (#3954).

VITALIANO, Peter
Director, Policy Analysis, Nat'l Milk Producers Federation
1840 Wilson Blvd., Arlington, VA 22201
Telephone: (703) 243-6111

VIVERETTE, George A., Jr.
Director, Highway Transportation, American Automobile Ass'n
500 E St. S.W., Suite 950, Washington, DC 20024
Telephone: (202) 554-6060
Registered as lobbyist at U.S. Congress.

VIZZA, Paul J.
Director, Media Relations, American Enterprise Institute for Public Policy Research
1150 17th St., N.W., Washington, DC 20036
Telephone: (202) 862-5800

VLADECK, David
Staff Attorney, Public Citizen Litigation Group
2000 P St., N.W., Suite 700, Washington, DC 20036
Telephone: (202) 785-3704

VLCEK, Jan Benes
Sutherland, Asbill and Brennan
1275 Pennsylvania, N.W., Washington, DC 20004-2404
Telephone: (202) 383-0100

The listings in this directory are available as *Mailing Labels.* See last page.

429

VLCEK, Jan Benes (Cont'd)
Registered as lobbyist at U.S. Congress.
Background: Trial Attorney, Civil Aeronautics Board, 1968-69. Attorney-Advisor, Environmental Protection Agency, 1971-73. Associate Minority Counsel, U.S. House of Representatives Committee on Interstate and Foreign Commerce, 1973-78. Counsel for Regulatory Policy, House Ad Hoc Committee on Energy, 1977-78.
Clients:
Ad Hoc Committee for a Competitive Electric Supply System (ACCESS)
Armco Inc.
Committee Against Revising Staggers
Council of Industrial Boiler Owners
Kaiser Aluminum and Chemical Corp.
Process Gas Consumers Group

VODRA, William W.
Arnold & Porter
1200 New Hampshire Ave., N.W., Washington, DC 20036
Telephone: (202) 872-6700
Background: Attorney, U.S. Department of Justice, Bureau of Narcotics and Dangerous Drugs/Drug Enforcement Administration, 1971-74. U.S. Department of Health, Education and Welfare, Office of General Counsel, Food and Drug Division, 1974-79.

VOGEL, John H.
Patton, Boggs and Blow
2550 M St., N.W., Suite 800, Washington, DC 20037
Telephone: (202) 457-6000
Clients:
Columbia Farm Credit District

VOGELSINGER, Bruce E., P.E.
V. President, Planning and Development, Nat'l Institute of Building Sciences
1201 L St., N.W., Suite 400, Washington, DC 20005
Telephone: (202) 289-7800
Registered as Foreign Agent: (#000,)

VOGT, Carl W.
Fulbright & Jaworski
1150 Connecticut Ave., N.W., Suite 400, Washington, DC 20036
Telephone: (202) 452-6800
Clients:
Nat'l Cottonseed Products Ass'n
Textile Fibers and By-Products Ass'n (TFBA)

VOGT, John
Legis Mgr - Tax, DEPARTMENT OF TREASURY
15th· and Pennsylvania Ave. N.W., Washington, DC 20220
Telephone: (202) 566-2037

VOLK, Mary Jane
Kurz & Volk
733 15th St., N.W., Suite 700, Washington, DC 20005
Telephone: (202) 783-5233

VOLLMER, Douglas K.
Acting Assoc Exec. Dir., Gov't Relations, Paralyzed Veterans of America
801 18th St., N.W., Washington, DC 20006
Telephone: (202) 872-1300
Registered as lobbyist at U.S. Congress.

VOLNER, Ian D.
Cohn and Marks
1333 New Hampshire Ave., N.W., Suite 600, Washington, DC 20036
Telephone: (202) 293-3860
Registered as lobbyist at U.S. Congress.
Registered as Foreign Agent: (#4303).
Background: Serves as General Counsel, Third Class Mail Ass'n. Staff Attorney, Federal Communications Commission Review Board, 1968-70.
Clients:
Direct Marketing Ass'n
Maclean Hunter Cable TV
Nat'l Ass'n of Trade and Technical Schools
Third Class Mail Ass'n

VOLPE, BOSKEY AND LYONS
918 16th St., N.W., Washington, DC 20006
Telephone: (202) 737-6580
Members of firm representing listed organizations:
Lyons, Ellis
Clients:

American Ass'n of Equipment Lessors
American Ass'n of Equipment Lessors Capital Investment Political Action Committee *(Ellis Lyons)*
American Automotive Leasing Ass'n
American Optometric Ass'n

VOLPE, John
Exec. Director, Nat'l Wine Coalition
1575 Eye St., N.W. Suite 325, Washington, DC 20005
Telephone: (202) 408-1120

VOM EIGEN, Ann Hadley
Associate Legislative Counsel, Mortgage Bankers Ass'n of America
1125 15th St., N.W., Suite 700, Washington, DC 20005
Telephone: (202) 861-6500
Registered as lobbyist at U.S. Congress.

VOM EIGEN, Robert P.
Hopkins and Sutter
888 16th St., N.W., Suite 700, Washington, DC 20006
Telephone: (202) 835-8000
Registered as lobbyist at U.S. Congress.

VON BERGEN, Drew
Director, Public Relations, Nat'l Ass'n of Letter Carriers of the United States of America
100 Indiana Ave., N.W., Washington, DC 20001
Telephone: (202) 393-4695

VON CONRAD, Gunter
Barnes, Richardson and Colburn
1819 H St., N.W., Washington, DC 20006
Telephone: (202) 457-0300
Registered as lobbyist at U.S. Congress.
Registered as Foreign Agent: (#2751).
Clients:
Case Co., J. I.
Consolidated Diesel Corp.
Meat Importers Council of America

VONK, Jeffrey
Legis Asst, DEPARTMENT OF AGRICULTURE - Soil Conservation Service
12th and Independence Ave. S.W., Washington, DC 20250
Telephone: (202) 447-2771

VON KANN, Maj. Gen. Clifton F., USA (Ret.)
Chairman of the Board, Nat'l Aeronautic Ass'n of the U.S-.A.
1763 R St., N.W., Washington, DC 20009
Telephone: (202) 265-8720

VON KESZYCKI, Alexine I.
Jones, Day, Reavis and Pogue
1450 G St., N.W., Suite 700, Washington, DC 20005-2088
Telephone: (202) 879-3939

VON ROTHKIRCH, Dr. Edward
Exec. Director, Internat'l Ass'n of Independent Producers
Box 2801, Washington, DC 20013
Telephone: (202) 775-1113

VON SALZEN, Eric A.
Hogan and Hartson
555 13th St., N.W., Suite 1200, Washington, DC 20004-1109
Telephone: (202) 637-5600
Clients:
Denver and Rio Grande Western Railroad Co.

VON SCHILCHER, Johanes
Exec. Director, Internat'l Anti-Counterfeiting Coalition
818 Connecticut Ave., N.W. 12th Floor, Washington, DC 20036
Telephone: (202) 223-5728

VON UNWERTH, Frederick H.
Counsel, Kilpatrick & Cody
2501 M St., N.W., Suite 500, Washington, DC 20037
Telephone: (202) 463-2500
Registered as lobbyist at U.S. Congress.
Background: Staff Director and Legislative Counsel to Rep. Wyche Fowler, Jr., U.S. House of Representatives, 1981-84.
Clients:
Eye Bank Ass'n of America
First Carolina Communications
Frito-Lay, Inc.

Furniture Rental Ass'n of America
Scientific-Atlanta, Inc.

VOORHEES, Ingrid A.
Director of Domestic Policy Issues, Computer and Business Equipment Manufacturers Ass'n
311 First St., N.W. Suite 500, Washington, DC 20001
Telephone: (202) 737-8888
Registered as lobbyist at U.S. Congress.

VOORHES, Amy
Director of Communications, Business Executives for Nat'l Security
601 Pennsylvania Ave., N.W. Suite 700, Washington, DC 20004
Telephone: (202) 737-1090

VORHIS, Donald G.
Exec. Director, Nat'l Registry in Clinical Chemistry
1155 16th St., N.W., Washington, DC 20036
Telephone: (202) 745-1698

VORNDRAN, Kurt
Legislative Liaison and Research, Nat'l Council of Senior Citizens
925 15th St., N.W., Washington, DC 20005
Telephone: (202) 347-8800
Registered as lobbyist at U.S. Congress.

VORYS, SATER, SEYMOUR AND PEASE
1828 L St., N.W., Suite 1111, Washington, DC 20036
Telephone: (202) 822-8200
Background: Washington office of a Columbus, Ohio law firm.
Members of firm representing listed organizations:
Brown, Stephen H., Associate
Teague, Randal C., Of Counsel
Background: Administrative Assistant and Legislative Counsel to Representative Jack F. Kemp of New York, 1973-79.
Clients:
American Ass'n of Enterprise Zones
Bell Communications Research, Inc. *(Stephen H. Brown)*
Bobbie Brooks
Business Computing Internat'l
Citizens Network for Foreign Affairs *(Randal C. Teague)*
Committee of Publicly Owned Companies *(Randal C. Teague)*
Competitive Health Care Coalition
Fraternal Order of Police (Nat'l Lodge) *(Randal C. Teague)*
Grocery Manufacturers of America
Ohio Advanced Technology Center *(Stephen H. Brown)*
Ohio Broadcasters Ass'n *(Randal C. Teague)*
Ohio Deposit Guaranty Fund
Ohio Forestry Ass'n *(Stephen H. Brown)*
Ohio Manufacturers Ass'n
Ohio Soft Drink Ass'n
Snow Aviation Internat'l *(Stephen H. Brown)*
Toledo Zoological Gardens *(Randal C. Teague)*
Wendy's Internat'l, Inc. *(Randal C. Teague)*
World Council on Free Zones *(Randal C. Teague)*

VOYACK, Frank J.
Legislative and Political Assistant, Internat'l Ass'n of Bridge, Structural and Ornamental Iron Workers
1750 New York Ave., N.W. Suite 400, Washington, DC 20006
Telephone: (202) 383-4800
Registered as lobbyist at U.S. Congress.

VROOM, Jay J.
President, Nat'l Agricultural Chemicals Ass'n
Madison Bldg., 1155 15th St., Suite 900, Washington, DC 20005
Telephone: (202) 296-1585
Registered as lobbyist at U.S. Congress.

VUKMER, Pamela
Exec. Assistant, Equitable Life Assurance Soc. of the U.S.
1700 Pennsylvania Ave., N.W., Suite 525, Washington, DC 20006
Telephone: (202) 393-3210
Background: Scheduler for Sen. Jay Rockefeller (D-VW), 1987-89.

WASHINGTON REPRESENTATIVES

WACHTER, Donna D.
Exec. Director, Ass'n of Professors of Gynecology and Obstetrics
409 12th St., S.W., Washington, DC 20024
Telephone: (202) 863-2545

WACHTMEISTER, Count Wilhelm
Senior International Advisor, Coudert Brothers
1627 Eye St., N.W. 12th Floor, Washington, DC 20006
Telephone: (202) 775-5100
Background: Former Swedish Ambassador to the United States.

WACKER, Thomas
Government Affairs Representative, Nat'l Telephone Cooperative Ass'n
2626 Pennsylvania Ave., N.W., Washington, DC 20037
Telephone: (202) 298-2300
Registered as lobbyist at U.S. Congress.

WADE, J. Kirk
Patton, Boggs and Blow
2550 M St., N.W., Suite 800, Washington, DC 20037
Telephone: (202) 457-6000
Registered as lobbyist at U.S. Congress.
Registered as Foreign Agent: (#2165).
Background: Attorney Advisor, Interpretative Division, Chief Counsel of the Internal Revenue Service, 1972-76. Attorney-Advisor, Tax Legislative Counsel, Department of the Treasury, 1976-77.

WADE, Kenneth W.
Washington Representative, Alameda County, California
440 First St., N.W. Suite 502, Washington, DC 20001
Telephone: (202) 737-9696

WADE, Robert J.
National Industry Affairs Manager, Toyota Motor Sales, U.S.A.
1850 M St., N.W., Suite 600, Washington, DC 20036
Telephone: (202) 775-1700
Registered as lobbyist at U.S. Congress.

WADE, T. Rogers
Ginn, Edington, Moore and Wade
803 Prince St., Alexandria, VA 22314
Telephone: (703) 836-3328
Registered as lobbyist at U.S. Congress.
Registered as Foreign Agent: (#4134).

WAFFLE, Robert
Director, State/Local Gov't Affairs, American Institute of Architects, The
1735 New York Ave., N.W., Washington, DC 20006
Telephone: (202) 626-7300
Registered as lobbyist at U.S. Congress.

WAGENHAUSER, David
Exec. Director, Telecommunications Research and Action Center
Box 12038, Washington, DC 20005
Telephone: (202) 462-2520
Background: Also represents Citizens Television System. Former senior attorney, Federal Trade Commission.

WAGER, Robert J.
Manatt, Phelps, Rothenberg & Phillips
1200 New Hampshire Ave., N.W., Suite 200, Washington, DC 20036
Telephone: (202) 463-4300
Registered as lobbyist at U.S. Congress.
Background: General Counsel and Staff Director, House Subcommittee on Reorganization, Research and International Operations, 1970-74.
Clients:
American Institute of Real Estate Appraisers
Northrop Corp.

WAGES, Robert G.
V. President, Oil, Chemical and Atomic Workers Internat'l Union
1126 16th St., N.W., Suite 411, Washington, DC 20036
Telephone: (202) 223-5770

WAGGONER, Daniel
Davis Wright Tremaine
1752 N St., N.W., Suite 800, Washington, DC 20036
Telephone: (202) 822-9775
Clients:

McCaw Cellular Communications Cos.

WAGNER, Carl
Director, Strategic Planning, Democratic Nat'l Committee
430 South Capitol St., S.E., Washington, DC 20003
Telephone: (202) 863-8000

WAGNER, HINES AND AVARY
1899 L St., N.W., Suite 500, Washington, DC 20036
Telephone: (202) 659-0930
Registered as Foreign Agent: (#3845)
Members of firm representing listed organizations:
  Avary, Robert P. (Jr.)
  Hines, William J.
  Juliana, James N.
  Miller, Michael V.
  Wagner, Paul F.
Clients:
  American Heavy Lift Shipping Co. *(Robert P. Avary, Jr., William J. Hines)*
  H. E. Ventures, Inc. *(Robert P. Avary, Jr., William J. Hines, James N. Juliana)*
  Holmes & Narver, Inc. *(Robert P. Avary, Jr., William J. Hines, Paul F. Wagner)*

WAGNER, Marvin
Legal Counsel, Heckler & Koch
21480 Pacific Blvd., Sterling, VA 22170
Telephone: (703) 450-1900
Registered as lobbyist at U.S. Congress.

WAGNER, Nancy E.
Director, Safety and Gov't Affairs, Gypsum Ass'n
810 First St., N.E., Suite 510, Washington, DC 20002
Telephone: (202) 289-5440

WAGNER, Paul
Director of Administration & Budget, Agriculture Council of America
1250 I St., N.W., Suite 601, Washington, DC 20005
Telephone: (202) 682-9200
Background: Partner in the law firm of Popham, Haik, Schnobrich, Kaufman & Doty, Ltd. Former Governor of Minnesota, 1955-61. U.S. Secretary of Agriculture, 1961-69.

WAGNER, Paul F.
Wagner, Hines and Avary
1899 L St., N.W., Suite 500, Washington, DC 20036
Telephone: (202) 659-0930
Registered as lobbyist at U.S. Congress.
Registered as Foreign Agent: (#3845).
Clients:
  Holmes & Narver, Inc.

WAGNER, William H.
Exec. Director, Labor Institute of Public Affairs
815 16th St., N.W., Suite 206, Washington, DC 20006
Telephone: (202) 637-5334

WAHL, Fred
Chairman, Melpar Division Political Action Committee
7700 Arlington Blvd., Falls Church, VA 22046
Telephone: (703) 560-5000

WAHLE, Thomas
Sr. Account Executive, Powell, Adams & Rinehart
1901 L St., N.W., 3rd Floor, Washington, DC 20036
Telephone: (202) 466-7590

WAHLQUIST, Andrew
President, Wahlquist Associates, Andrew
1701 Pennsylvania Ave., N.W. Suite 1000, Washington, DC 20007
Telephone: (202) 835-0929
Registered as lobbyist at U.S. Congress.
Organizations represented:
  McDonnell Douglas Corp.

WAHLQUIST ASSOCIATES, Andrew
1701 Pennsylvania Ave., N.W. Suite 1000, Washington, DC 20007
Telephone: (202) 835-0929
Members of firm representing listed organizations:
  Wahlquist, Andrew, President
Organizations represented:
  McDonnell Douglas Corp. *(Andrew Wahlquist)*

WAHLQUIST, Richard A.
V. President, Nat'l Ass'n of Temporary Services
119 South St. Asaph St., Alexandria, VA 22314
Telephone: (703) 549-6287

WAIDMANN, Brian K.
Spec Asst to Pres, Legis Affrs (Senate), EXECUTIVE OFFICE OF THE PRESIDENT - The White House
1600 Pennsylvania Ave., N.W. 107 East Wing, Washington, DC 20500
Telephone: (202) 456-7557

WAIKART, Douglas O.
Wright and Talisman
1050 17th St., N.W. Suite 600, Washington, DC 20036
Telephone: (202) 331-1194

WAIT, Robert A.
V. President, Federal Government Affairs, Kraft General Foods, Inc.
1341 G St., N.W., 9th Floor, Washington, DC 20005
Telephone: (202) 637-1540
Registered as lobbyist at U.S. Congress.

WAITE, Herbert R.
Washington Representative, Bank of Boston
1515 S. Jefferson Davis Hwy., Suite 1623, Arlington, VA 22202
Telephone: (703) 979-9606

WAITS, John A.
Bishop, Cook, Purcell & Reynolds
1400 L St., N.W., Washington, DC 20005-3502
Telephone: (202) 371-5700
Registered as lobbyist at U.S. Congress.
Background: Administrative Assistant to Rep. David R. Bowen (D-MS), 1980-82, and Counsel to House Agriculture Subcommittee on Cotton, Rice and Sugar, 1979-80.
Clients:
  Mississippi Department of Economic and Community Development

WAKEFIELD, Dean M.
Director, Public Affairs, American Podiatric Medical Ass'n
9312 Old Georgetown Road, Bethesda, MD 20814
Telephone: (301) 571-9200
Background: Also publisher of APMA News.

WAKEFORD, Ronald C.
Exec. Director, Council for Export Trading Cos., Inc.
1900 19th St., N.W. Suite 605, Washington, DC 20036
Telephone: (202) 861-4705

WAKELYN, P. J.
Mgr., Environmental Health and Safety, Nat'l Cotton Council of America
1110 Vermont Ave., N.W. Suite 430, Washington, DC 20005
Telephone: (202) 833-2943

WAKS, Donna
Legislative Aide, Rainbow Lobby
1660 L St., N.W. Suite 204, Washington, DC 20036
Telephone: (202) 457-0700
Registered as lobbyist at U.S. Congress.

WALDEN, Susan S.
Manager, Federal Relations, Johnson & Johnson
1667 K St., N.W., Suite 410, Washington, DC 20006
Telephone: (202) 293-2620
Registered as lobbyist at U.S. Congress.

WALDERS, Lawrence R.
Graham and James
2000 M St., N.W., Suite 700, Washington, DC 20036
Telephone: (202) 463-0800
Clients:
  Komatsu Ltd.

WALDMAN, Benjamin S.
Exec. Director, Nat'l Jewish Coalition
415 Second St., N.E., Washington, DC 20002
Telephone: (202) 547-7701

WALDMAN, Byron
Principal, Anderson, Hibey, Nauheim and Blair
1708 New Hampshire Ave., N.W., Washington, DC 20009
Telephone: (202) 483-1900
Registered as lobbyist at U.S. Congress.

WALDMAN, Daniel
Arnold & Porter
1200 New Hampshire Ave., N.W., Washington, DC 20036
Telephone: (202) 872-6700
Registered as lobbyist at U.S. Congress.
Clients:
   Grain and Feed Trade Ass'n, The
   Internat'l Commodities Clearing House, Ltd.
   London Commodity Exchange Co., Ltd.

WALDMAN, Michael
Director, Congress Watch
215 Pennsylvania Ave., S.E., Washington, DC 20003
Telephone: (202) 546-4996
Registered as lobbyist at U.S. Congress.

WALKER, Allen
Manager, Public Affairs, Japan Automobile Manufacturers
Ass'n
1050 17th St., N.W. Suite 410, Washington, DC 20036
Telephone: (202) 296-8537

WALKER ASSOCIATES, Charls E.
1730 Pennsylvania Ave., N.W. Suite 200, Washington, DC
20006
Telephone: (202) 393-4760
Background: A Washington lobbying firm partially owned
   by Ogilvy & Mather.
Members of firm representing listed organizations:
   Englert, Roy T.
   Free, James C.
      Background: Former Congressional Liaison, The White
      House, under President Jimmy Carter.
   Fuller, Lee O.
      Background: Former Minority Staff Director and
      Majority Staff Director, Senate Committee on Envi-
      ronment and Public Works.
   Meuser, Kenneth G.
   Northup, Clifford, V. President
      Background: Former Legislative Ass't to Sen. Wm.
      Armstrong (R-CO).
   Potter, Philip H., Senior V. President
   Smith, James E., President
      Background: Former Comptroller of the Currency.
   Walker, Charls E., President and Chairman of
   the Board
      Background: Formerly Assistant to Secretary of the
      Treasury, 1959-61. Under Secretary of the Treasury,
      1969-72. Deputy Secretary of the Treasury, 1972-73.
      Serves also as Chairman, American Council for Capi-
      tal Formation.
Organizations represented:
   American Institute of Certified Public Account-
      ants
   Anheuser-Busch Cos., Inc.
   AT&T *(Charls E. Walker)*
   Atchison, Topeka and Santa Fe Railway Co., The
      (Lee O. Fuller, Kenneth G. Meuser, Philip H. Potter)
   Broadcast Music Inc. *(James C. Free)*
   CBS Records Group *(James C. Free)*
   Coalition for Competitive Capital
   Columbia Pictures Entertainment, Inc.
   CSX Corp. *(James C. Free)*
   Enron Corp.
   Federal Home Loan Mortgage Corp. *(James E.
      Smith)*
   Goodyear Tire and Rubber Co.
   HealthTrust, Inc.
   Lone Star Steel Co. *(Philip H. Potter)*
   Mid-Continent Oil and Gas Ass'n
   Mitsubishi Corp.
   Northwestern Mutual Life Insurance Co.

WALKER, Barbara J.
Legislative Counsel, Animal Health Institute
119 Oronoco St., Box 1417-D50, Alexandria, VA 22313-
1480
Telephone: (703) 684-0011
Registered as lobbyist at U.S. Congress.

WALKER, Beverley
Director, Federal Affairs, Ryder System, Inc.
1275 K St., N.W. 10th Floor, Washington, DC 20005
Telephone: (202) 783-1229

WALKER, Cary
Wash. Rep, CA State World Trade Commiss., California,
State of
444 North Capitol St., N.W., Suite 305, Washington, DC
20001
Telephone: (202) 347-6891

WALKER, Catherine L.
Manager, Government Affairs, Warner-Lambert Co.
1667 K St., N.W., Suite 1270, Washington, DC 20006
Telephone: (202) 862-3840

WALKER, Charls E.
President and Chairman of the Board, Walker Associates,
Charls E.
1730 Pennsylvania Ave., N.W. Suite 200, Washington, DC
20006
Telephone: (202) 393-4760
Registered as lobbyist at U.S. Congress.
Registered as Foreign Agent: (#4180).
Background: Formerly Assistant to Secretary of the Treas-
   ury, 1959-61. Under Secretary of the Treasury, 1969-72.
   Deputy Secretary of the Treasury, 1972-73. Serves also as
   Chairman, American Council for Capital Formation.
Organizations represented:
   AT&T

WALKER, Gerald S.
CounterTerrorism Consultants L.P.
1800 Diagonal Road, Suite 230, Alexandria, VA 22314
Telephone: (703) 683-6988
Registered as Foreign Agent: (#4294).
Clients:
   Jamaica, Government of

WALKER, H. Laird
V. President, Federal Relations, US WEST, Inc.
1020 19th St., N.W., Suite 700, Washington, DC 20036
Telephone: (202) 429-3100

WALKER, Jerry A.
Exec. Director, Gypsum Ass'n
810 First St., N.E., Suite 510, Washington, DC 20002
Telephone: (202) 289-5440

WALKER, Joseph L., III
Director, Public & Member Communications, Chlorine Institute
2001 L St., N.W., Suite 506, Washington, DC 20036
Telephone: (202) 775-2790

WALKER, Judith
Smith, Bucklin and Associates
1101 Connecticut Ave., N.W., Suite 700, Washington, DC
20036
Telephone: (202) 857-1100
Background: Exec. Director, Museum Trustee Ass'n and
   American Soc. of Nephrology.
Clients:
   American Soc. of Nephrology

WALKER, Kevin
Exec. Director and Treasurer, American Medical Ass'n
Political Action Committee
1101 Vermont Ave., N.W., Washington, DC 20005
Telephone: (202) 789-7400

WALKER, Lynda K.
Counsel, Nat'l Realty Committee
1250 Connecticut Ave., N.W. Suite 630, Washington, DC
20036
Telephone: (202) 785-0808

WALKER, Philip M.
V. President, Internat'l Affairs, Sprint International
12490 Sunrise Valley Drive, Reston, VA 22096
Telephone: (703) 689-6000

WALKER, Stevenson T.
Director, Government Relations, Reynolds Metals Co.
1620 Eye St., N.W., Washington, DC 20006
Telephone: (202) 833-3760
Registered as lobbyist at U.S. Congress.

WALKER, William N.
Mudge Rose Guthrie Alexander and Ferdon
2121 K St., N.W., Suite 700, Washington, DC 20037
Telephone: (202) 429-9355
Registered as Foreign Agent: (#3200).

Background: General Counsel, Cost of Living Council,
   1972-74. Federal Energy Office, 1974. Deputy U.S. Spe-
   cial Trade Representative, serving as Ambassador and
   Head of U.S. Delegation to Multilateral Trade Negotia-
   tions in Geneva, Switzerland, 1975-77.
Clients:
   C.V.G. Siderurgica del Orinoco Ca. (SIDOR)
   Electronic Industries Ass'n of Japan
   Japan Aluminum Federation

WALL AND ASSOCIATES, R. Duffy
1317 F St., N.W., Suite 400, Washington, DC 20004
Telephone: (202) 737-0100
Registered as lobbyist at U.S. Congress.
Members of firm representing listed organizations:
   Folsom, R. D.
   Harman, John R.
   Massie, James
   Stern, Michael
   Wall, R. Duffy
   Wilmer, Charlotte
Organizations represented:
   American Academy of Dermatology *(Michael Stern)*
   Bell Atlantic *(Michael Stern, R. Duffy Wall)*
   BHP Holdings (USA) Inc. *(R. Duffy Wall)*
   Coal Industry Tax Committee *(R. Duffy Wall, Char-
      lotte Wilmer)*
   Footwear Distributors and Retailers of America
      (R. D. Folsom, Michael Stern, R. Duffy Wall)
   Glaxo, Inc. *(R. D. Folsom)*
   Hong Kong Trade Development Council *(R. D. Fol-
      som, Michael Stern, R. Duffy Wall, Charlotte Wilmer)*
   Peabody Holding Co. *(R. Duffy Wall)*
   Pennsylvania Engineering Co. *(R. Duffy Wall)*
   Pharmaceutical Manufacturers Ass'n *(R. D. Folsom,
      Michael Stern, R. Duffy Wall)*
   Pittston Co., The *(R. Duffy Wall)*
   R. Duffy Wall and Associates Inc. Political Ac-
      tion Committee *(R. Duffy Wall)*
   Securities Industry Ass'n *(R. Duffy Wall)*
   Torchmark Corp. *(Michael Stern, R. Duffy Wall)*
   United Company, The *(R. Duffy Wall)*
   United Way of America *(Michael Stern)*

WALL, Christopher R.
Winthrop, Stimson, Putnam & Roberts
1133 Connecticut Ave., N.W. Suite 1000, Washington, DC
20036
Telephone: (202) 775-9800
Registered as Foreign Agent: (#3873).
Clients:
   Swedish Steelproducers' Ass'n (Jernkontoret)

WALL, Martin A.
Senior V. President, American Osteopathic Hospital Ass'n
1454 Duke St., Alexandria, VA 22314
Telephone: (703) 684-7700

WALL, R. Duffy
Wall and Associates, R. Duffy
1317 F St., N.W., Suite 400, Washington, DC 20004
Telephone: (202) 737-0100
Registered as lobbyist at U.S. Congress.
Registered as Foreign Agent: (#3737).
Organizations represented:
   Bell Atlantic
   BHP Holdings (USA) Inc.
   Coal Industry Tax Committee
   Footwear Distributors and Retailers of America
   Hong Kong Trade Development Council
   Peabody Holding Co.
   Pennsylvania Engineering Co.
   Pharmaceutical Manufacturers Ass'n
   Pittston Co., The
   R. Duffy Wall and Associates Inc. Political Ac-
      tion Committee
   Securities Industry Ass'n
   Torchmark Corp.
   United Company, The

WALLACE, A. Lee, III
Dir./Counsel, Regulatory & Leg. Affairs, Gas Research Institute
1331 Pennsylvania Ave., N.W., Suite 730 North, Washington, DC 20004
Telephone: (202) 662-8989

WALLACE, Donald L., Jr.
Wallace & Edwards
1150 Connecticut Ave., N.W., Suite 507, Washington, DC 20036
Telephone: (202) 331-4331
Registered as lobbyist at U.S. Congress.
Background: Chairman, Wallace & Edwards.
Clients:
Alabama Farmers Federation
American Sugar Cane League of the U.S.A.
Cotton Warehouse Ass'n of America
Cotton Warehouse Government Relations Committee
Service Corporation Internat'l
U.S. Canola Ass'n

WALLACE & EDWARDS
1150 Connecticut Ave., N.W., Suite 507, Washington, DC 20036
Telephone: (202) 331-4331
Background: A government relations/public affairs consulting firm specializing in clients with agricultural interests.
Members of firm representing listed organizations:
  Davis, (Rebecca) McPherson
    Background: Serves as Treasurer, Cotton Warehouse Government Relations Committee.
  Edwards, Macon T., President
  Humphreys, Allison
  Wallace, Donald L. (Jr.)
    Background: Chairman, Wallace & Edwards.
Clients:
Alabama Farmers Federation *(Donald L. Wallace, Jr.)*
American Soc. of Farm Managers and Rural Appraisers *(Macon T. Edwards)*
American Sugar Cane League of the U.S.A. *(Donald L. Wallace, Jr.)*
Cotton Warehouse Ass'n of America *(Donald L. Wallace, Jr.)*
Cotton Warehouse Government Relations Committee *(Allison Humphreys, Donald L. Wallace, Jr.)*
Federal Compress and Warehouse Co.
Fiber, Fabric and Apparel Coalition for Trade *(Macon T. Edwards)*
Flue-Cured Tobacco Cooperative Stabilization Corp. *(Macon T. Edwards)*
Service Corporation Internat'l *(Donald L. Wallace, Jr.)*
U.S. Canola Ass'n *(Donald L. Wallace, Jr.)*

WALLACE, Nancy
Washington Director, Population Program, Sierra Club
408 C St., N.E., Washington, DC 20002
Telephone: (202) 547-1141
Registered as lobbyist at U.S. Congress.

WALLACE, Robert B.
Wilson, Elser, Moskowitz, Edelman & Dicker
1341 G St., N.W. 5th Floor, Washington, DC 20005
Telephone: (202) 626-7660
Registered as Foreign Agent: (#3908).
Clients:
Morgan Grenfell and Co., Ltd.

WALLACE, Sondra
Attorney, Legislation Div, DEPARTMENT OF HEALTH AND HUMAN SERVICES
200 Independence Ave., S.W., Washington, DC 20201
Telephone: (202) 245-7773

WALLER, Claudia C.
Exec. Director, American Ass'n of Children's Residential Centers
440 First St., N.W., Suite 310, Washington, DC 20001
Telephone: (202) 638-1604

WALLER, John D.
Lachelli, Waller and Associates
600 Maryland Ave., S.W., Suite 200A East Wing, Washington, DC 20024
Telephone: (202) 863-1472
Clients:
Advanced Management & Technologies
Aurora University
Inter Tribal Council of Nevada
Sierra Press
Silent Partner

WALLER, Karen
Porter/Novelli
1001 30th St., N.W., Washington, DC 20007
Telephone: (202) 342-7000
Clients:
Internat'l Apple Institute

WALLGREN, Robert A.
Exec. Dir., Banking Professions Group, American Bankers Ass'n
1120 Connecticut Ave., N.W., Washington, DC 20036
Telephone: (202) 663-5000

WALLICK, Robert D.
Steptoe and Johnson
1330 Connecticut Ave., N.W., Washington, DC 20036
Telephone: (202) 429-3000
Clients:
Coalition for Government Procurement

WALLIN, R. Douglas, Jr.
Director, Cong. Affrs., Aerosp. Programs, Allied-Signal Inc.
1001 Pennsylvania Ave., N.W. Suite 700, Washington, DC 20004
Telephone: (202) 662-2650
Registered as lobbyist at U.S. Congress.

WALLIS, Jim
Editor, Sojourners
P.O. Box 29272, Washington, DC 20017
Telephone: (202) 636-3637

WALLIS, Norman E.
Exec. Director, Nat'l Board of Examiners in Optometry
5530 Wisconsin Ave., N.W. Suite 805, Washington, DC 20815
Telephone: (202) 652-5192

WALLISON, Frieda K.
Jones, Day, Reavis and Pogue
1450 G St., N.W., Suite 700, Washington, DC 20005-2088
Telephone: (202) 879-3939
Registered as lobbyist at U.S. Congress.
Background: Special Counsel, Securities and Exchange Commission, 1975. Executive Director and General Counsel, Municipal Securities Rulemaking Board, 1975-78.
Clients:
Los Angeles County, California
Nat'l Ass'n of State Auditors, Comptrollers and Treasurers
State Ass'n of County Retirement Systems

WALLOP, French C.
President, Corporate Consulting Internat'l Ltd.
1700 North Moore St., Suite 1610, Arlington, VA 22209
Telephone: (703) 524-8957

WALLS, Janice
Director, State Programs, Institute of Scrap Recycling Industries, Inc.
1627 K St., N.W. Suite 700, Washington, DC 20006
Telephone: (202) 466-4050

WALLS, Richard A.
Senior Associate, Morgan Casner Associates, Inc.
1332 Independence Ave., S.E., Washington, DC 20003
Telephone: (202) 543-4600

WALSH, Alexandra
Dir., Communications and Education, Wine and Spirits Wholesalers of America
1023 15th St., N.W., 4th Floor, Washington, DC 20005
Telephone: (202) 371-9792

WALSH, Ann Marie
Assistant Washington Counsel, Health Insurance Ass'n of America
1025 Connecticut Ave., N.W. Suite 1200, Washington, DC 20036
Telephone: (202) 223-7780
Registered as lobbyist at U.S. Congress.

WALSH, Charles S.
Fleischman and Walsh, P.C.
1400 16th St., N.W. Suite 600, Washington, DC 20036
Telephone: (202) 939-7900
Registered as lobbyist at U.S. Congress.
Background: Serves as Treasurer, Nat'l Cable Television Political Action Committee.

WALSH, Dorothy A.
Director-Federal Relations-Congressional, Ameritech (American Information Technologies)
1050 Connecticut Ave., N.W., Suite 730, Washington, DC 20036
Telephone: (202) 955-3050

WALSH, James P.
Of Counsel, Davis Wright Tremaine
1752 N St., N.W., Suite 800, Washington, DC 20036
Telephone: (202) 822-9775
Registered as lobbyist at U.S. Congress.
Background: Staff Counsel, Senate Committee on Commerce, 1972-77. General Counsel, Senate Committee on Commerce, Science and Transportation, 1977-78. Deputy Administrator, National Oceanic and Atmospheric Administration, 1978-81.
Clients:
American Tunaboat Ass'n
F/V American Empire
Klukwan Forest Products, Inc.

WALSH, Molly
Liaison Officer, Cong & Intergov'l Affrs, DEPARTMENT OF LABOR
200 Constitution Ave., N.W., Washington, DC 20210
Telephone: (202) 523-8201

WALSH, Thomas
General Counsel, People-to-People Health Foundation (Project HOPE)
2 Wisconsin Circle, Suite 500, Chevy Chase, MD 20815
Telephone: (301) 656-7401

WALSH, Thomas M.
Director, Government Relations, Nat'l Club Ass'n
1625 Eye St., N.W., Suite 609, Washington, DC 20006
Telephone: (202) 466-8424

WALSH, Dr. William B.
President, People-to-People Health Foundation (Project HOPE)
2 Wisconsin Circle, Suite 500, Chevy Chase, MD 20815
Telephone: (301) 656-7401

WALSTON, Dennis
Sr. V. Pres., and Director, Art Dept., Kamber Group, The
1920 L St., N.W., Washington, DC 20036
Telephone: (202) 223-8700
Organizations represented:
American University, The
Nat'l Ass'n of Social Workers
Police Foundation
Wyatt Communications

WALTER, Daniel G.
President, Associated Specialty Contractors
7315 Wisconsin Ave. Suite 1300W, Bethesda, MD 20814
Telephone: (301) 657-3110

WALTER, Frank J.
V. President, Technical Activities, Manufactured Housing Institute
1745 Jefferson Davis Hwy. Suite 511, Arlington, VA 22202
Telephone: (703) 979-6620

WALTER, J. Jackson
President, Nat'l Trust for Historic Preservation
1785 Massachusetts Ave., N.W., Washington, DC 20036
Telephone: (202) 673-4105

WALTER, Lew
Special Asst, Cong Rels, DEPARTMENT OF AGRICULTURE
14th and Indepence Ave. S.W., Room 235-E, Washington, DC 20205
Telephone: (202) 447-7095

WALTER, Michael J.
General Counsel, Corporation for Open Systems
1750 Old Meadow Road, McLean, VA 22102
Telephone: (703) 883-2700

WALTER, Susan
Mgr., State Gov't Relations Operations, General Electric Co.
1331 Pennsylvania Ave., N.W. Suite 800S, Washington, DC 20004
Telephone: (202) 637-4000

WALTER, Velva
Cong and Public Affrs Deputy Director, DEPARTMENT OF JUSTICE - Office of Justice Programs
633 Indiana Ave., N.W., Washington, DC 20531
Telephone: (202) 724-7694

WALTERS, J. P.
Exec. Director, American Maritime Congress
444 N. Capitol St., N.W., Suite 801, Washington, DC 20001
Telephone: (202) 877-4477
Registered as lobbyist at U.S. Congress.

WALTHER, Henry L.
President, United States Defense Committee
3238 Wynford Drive, Fairfax, VA 22031
Telephone: (703) 914-2010
Registered as lobbyist at U.S. Congress.

WALTON, John C.
1401 North Oak St., #302, Arlington, VA 22209
Telephone: (703) 527-2240
Registered as lobbyist at U.S. Congress.
Organizations represented:
    Chance and Associates, John E.
    Ferranti Defense and Space Group

WALTON, June L.
Manatt, Phelps, Rothenberg & Phillips
1200 New Hampshire Ave., N.W., Suite 200, Washington, DC 20036
Telephone: (202) 463-4300
Registered as lobbyist at U.S. Congress.
Registered as Foreign Agent: (#3736).
Clients:
    American Ass'n of Nurse Anesthetists
    American Institute of Real Estate Appraisers
    Edison Electric Institute

WALVICK, Walter J.
Dickstein, Shapiro and Morin
2101 L St., N.W., Washington, DC 20037
Telephone: (202) 785-9700
Registered as Foreign Agent: (#3028).
Clients:
    Kuwait Airways
    Middle East Airlines

WAMPLER AND ASSOCIATES
655 15th St., N.W. Suite 300, Washington, DC 20005
Telephone: (202) 639-4027
Clients:
    Louisiana Land and Exploration Co.

WAMSLEY, Herbert C.
Exec. Director, Intellectual Property Owners, Inc.
1255 23rd St., N.W., Suite 850, Washington, DC 20037
Telephone: (202) 466-2396
Registered as lobbyist at U.S. Congress.
Background: Formerly at U.S. Patent and Trademark Office as: Director of Trademark Examining, 1980-82; Executive Assistant to the Commissioner, 1974-80; Legislative and International Affairs Attorney, 1969-74.

WAN, Bonnie B.
Staff V. President, Kimberly-Clark Corp.
1201 Pennsylvania Ave., N.W. Suite 730, Washington, DC 20004
Telephone: (202) 393-8280
Registered as lobbyist at U.S. Congress.

WARD, Alan S.
Baker and Hostetler
1050 Connecticut Ave., N.W. Suite 1100, Washington, DC 20036
Telephone: (202) 861-1500
Background: Antitrust Division, Dep't of Justice 1956-61; Federal Trade Commission 1970-73.
Clients:
    Aluminum Ass'n
    PPG Industries

WARD, Curtis A.
7603 Georgia Ave., N.W. Suite 301, Washington, DC 20012
Telephone: (202) 829-8530
Registered as Foreign Agent: (#3938).
Organizations represented:
    People's National Party

WARD, Gregg
Group V. President, External Affairs, American Institute of Architects, The
1735 New York Ave., N.W., Washington, DC 20006
Telephone: (202) 626-7300
Registered as lobbyist at U.S. Congress.

WARD, Justin R.
Assistant to Staff Attorney, Natural Resources Defense Council
1350 New York Ave., N.W. Suite 300, Washington, DC 20005
Telephone: (202) 783-7800
Registered as lobbyist at U.S. Congress.

WARD, Morris, Bud
Exec. Director, Environmental Health Ctr, Nat'l Safety Council
1050 17th St., N.W. Suite 770, Washington, DC 20036
Telephone: (202) 293-2270

WARD, Richard S.
V. President, Government Affairs, ITT Corp.
1600 M St., N.W., Washington, DC 20036
Telephone: (202) 775-7373

WARD, Stephen D.
V. President, Campaign Performance Group
507 Capital Court, N.E., Washington, DC 20002
Telephone: (202) 546-3170

WARD, Stephen E.
V. President, Mid-Continent Oil and Gas Ass'n
1919 Pennsylvania Ave., N.W. Suite 503, Washington, DC 20006
Telephone: (202) 785-3515
Registered as lobbyist at U.S. Congress.

WARDEN, Barbara F.
Legislative Director, AFL-CIO - Industrial Union Department
815 16th St., N.W., Washington, DC 20006
Telephone: (202) 842-7820
Registered as lobbyist at U.S. Congress.

WARDEN, Richard D.
Legislative Director, United Automobile, Aerospace and Agricultural Implement Workers of America (UAW)
1757 N St., N.W., Washington, DC 20036
Telephone: (202) 828-8540
Registered as lobbyist at U.S. Congress.

WARDEN, Robert A.
McDermott, Will and Emery
1850 K St., N.W., Suite 500, Washington, DC 20006-2296
Telephone: (202) 887-8000
Registered as lobbyist at U.S. Congress.
Background: Assistant Legislation Counsel, 1975-79; Legislation Counsel, 1977 and Assistant Chief of Staff, 1978, Joint Committee on Taxation, U.S. Congress.
Clients:
    Globe Corp.
    Public Employees' Retirement Ass'n of Colorado

WARE, Michael O.
Director, Legislative Affairs, du Pont de Nemours and Co., E. I.
1701 Pennsylvania Ave., N.W., Suite 900, Washington, DC 20006
Telephone: (202) 728-3600
Registered as lobbyist at U.S. Congress.

WARING, Michael A.
Director, Political Communications, Nat'l Ass'n of Broadcasters
1771 N St., N.W., Washington, DC 20036
Telephone: (202) 429-5300
Registered as lobbyist at U.S. Congress.
Background: Former Press Secretary to Rep. Harold Rogers (R-KY).

WARKER, Peter F.
Director, International Affairs, TRW Inc.
Suite 2700, 1000 Wilson Blvd., Arlington, VA 22209
Telephone: (703) 276-5050
Registered as lobbyist at U.S. Congress.

WARMER, Richard C.
O'Melveny and Myers
555 13th St., N.W., Suite 500 West, Washington, DC 20004
Telephone: (202) 383-5300
Registered as lobbyist at U.S. Congress.
Registered as Foreign Agent: (#3346).

WARNE, W. Robert
President, Korea Economic Institute of America
1030 15th St., N.W. Suite 662, Washington, DC 20005
Telephone: (202) 371-0690
Registered as Foreign Agent: (#3327).
Background: Also represents the Korea Development Institute of Seoul, Korea.

WARNER, Barbara
Sr. Political Economist, Japan Economic Institute of America
1000 Connecticut Ave., N.W. Suite 211, Washington, DC 20036
Telephone: (202) 296-5633
Registered as Foreign Agent: (#0929)

WARNER, Ernest R., Jr.
DGA Internat'l
1133 Connecticut Ave., N.W. Suite 700, Washington, DC 20036
Telephone: (202) 223-4001
Registered as lobbyist at U.S. Congress.

WARNER, Harland, apr
Exec. V. President & Deputy Mng. Dir., Manning, Selvage & Lee/Washington
1250 Eye St., N.W., Suite 300, Washington, DC 20005
Telephone: (202) 682-1660

WARNER, Jack
President, ACEC Research and Management Foundation
1015 15th St., N.W., Washington, DC 20005
Telephone: (202) 347-7474

WARNER, Robert T.
Exec. V. President, Nat'l Ass'n of State Aviation Officials
8401 Colesville Road., Suite 505, Silver Spring, MD 20910
Telephone: (301) 588-0587

WARNER, William
V. Pres., Mktg. & Public Communications, ADAPSO, the Computer Software & Services Industry Ass'n
1300 North 17th St. Suite 300, Arlington, VA 22209
Telephone: (703) 522-5055

WARNKE, Paul C.
Clifford & Warnke
815 Connecticut Ave., N.W., Washington, DC 20006
Telephone: (202) 828-4200
Background: General Counsel, Department of Defense, 1966-67. Assistant Secretary of Defense, International Security Affairs, 1967-69. Director, Arms Control and Disarmament Agency and Chief U.S. Strategic Arms Negotiator, 1977-78.

WARREN AND ASSOCIATES
1100 Connecticut Ave., N.W. Suite 440, Washington, DC 20036
Telephone: (202) 293-2165
Members of firm representing listed organizations:
    Quadrino, George A.
    Warren, Charles F., President
Clients:
    ABC Containerline, N.V. *(George A. Quadrino)*
    Air-Compack Inc.
    Barber Blue Sea Line *(George A. Quadrino, Charles F. Warren)*
    East Asiatic Co. Ltd. *(George A. Quadrino, Charles F. Warren)*
    Hapag-Lloyd AG *(George A. Quadrino, Charles F. Warren)*
    Japan/Korea-Atlantic and Gulf Freight Conference
    Japan/Puerto Rico and Virgin Islands Freight Conference *(Charles F. Warren)*
    Kawasaki Kisen Kaisha, Ltd. *(Charles F. Warren)*
    Korea Maritime Transport Co. *(George A. Quadrino, Charles F. Warren)*
    Mitsui O.S.K. Lines, Ltd. *(George A. Quadrino, Charles F. Warren)*

Nippon Yusen Kaisha (NYK) Line *(George A. Quadrino, Charles F. Warren)*
Trans-Pacific Freight Conference of Japan/Korea

WARREN, Charles F.
President, Warren and Associates
1100 Connecticut Ave., N.W. Suite 440, Washington, DC 20036
Telephone: (202) 293-2165
Clients:
Barber Blue Sea Line
East Asiatic Co. Ltd.
Hapag-Lloyd AG
Japan/Puerto Rico and Virgin Islands Freight Conference
Kawasaki Kisen Kaisha, Ltd.
Korea Maritime Transport Co.
Mitsui O.S.K. Lines, Ltd.
Nippon Yusen Kaisha (NYK) Line

WARREN, Edward W.
Kirkland and Ellis
655 15th St., N.W. Suite 1200, Washington, DC 20005
Telephone: (202) 879-5000

WARREN, Jacqueline
Senior Attorney, Natural Resources Defense Council
1350 New York Ave., N.W. Suite 300, Washington, DC 20005
Telephone: (202) 783-7800

WARREN, Richard F.
Co-ordinator of Government Affairs, Nat'l Electrical Manufacturers Ass'n
2101 L St., N.W., Washington, DC 20037
Telephone: (202) 457-8400

WARRINGTON, Julie
Administrative Secretary, Church of the Brethren
110 Maryland Ave., N.E., Washington, DC 20002
Telephone: (202) 546-3202

WARSLEY, Daniel P.
Director, Member Services, Helicopter Ass'n Internat'l
1619 Duke St., Alexandria, VA 22314-3406
Telephone: (703) 683-4646

WASCH, Kenneth A.
Exec. Director, Software Publishers Ass'n
1101 Connecticut Ave., N.W. Suite 901, Washington, DC 20036
Telephone: (202) 452-1600
Background: Also represents the Software Publishers Ass'n PAC.

WASHBURN, Barbara J.
Senior Washington Representative, General Motors Corp.
1660 L St., N.W., 4th Floor, Washington, DC 20036
Telephone: (202) 775-5027
Registered as lobbyist at U.S. Congress.
Background: Former Legislative Assistant to Senator Dave Durenberger (R-MN).

WASHINGTON COMMUNICATIONS GROUP/RUDER FINN
1615 M St., N.W., Suite 220, Washington, DC 20036
Telephone: (202) 466-7800
Registered as Foreign Agent: (#4315)
Members of firm representing listed organizations:
Berry, Mark, Director, Media Relations
Background: Former deputy press secretary for the presidential campaign of Rep. Jack Kemp (R-NY).
Butterfield, Jane, V. President
Collins, Carrie, V. President
Harff, James W., Senior V. President
Clients:
Axa Midi Assurances *(James W. Harff)*

WASHINGTON CONSULTING GROUP
1625 Eye St., N.W. Suite 214, Washington, DC 20006
Telephone: (202) 457-0233
Members of firm representing listed organizations:
Barquin, Ramon C., Exec. V. President and COO

WASHINGTON FINANCIAL INFORMATION SERVICES, INC.
406 3rd St., S.E., Washington, DC 20003
Members of firm representing listed organizations:
Feinberg, Robert S., President
Clients:

Downey Savings and Loan *(Robert S. Feinberg)*

WASHINGTON INDUSTRIAL TEAM, INC.
499 South Capitol St., S.W. Suite 520, Washington, DC 20003
Telephone: (202) 347-0633
Background: A government relations consulting firm.
Members of firm representing listed organizations:
Ichord, Richard H.
Background: Member, U.S. House of Representatives from Missouri, 1961-81. Serves as Co-Chairman, American Freedom Coalition.
Wilson, Robert C.
Background: Member, U.S. House of Representatives from California, 1953-81. Serves as Co-Chairman, American Freedom Coalition.

WASHINGTON LOBBY GROUP, THE
325 Pennsylvania Ave., S.E., Washington, DC 20003
Telephone: (202) 543-9400
Background: A government relations/lobbying firm.
Members of firm representing listed organizations:
Richardson, Warren S.
Richardson, Wesley S.
Clients:
Preston Trucking Co.

WASHINGTON POLICY ADVOCATES
312 Massachusetts Ave., N.E., Washington, DC 20002
Telephone: (202) 828-1977
Members of firm representing listed organizations:
Smith, Jeffrey C., President
Clients:
Commercial Weather Services Ass'n *(Jeffrey C. Smith)*
Committee for Private Offshore Rescue and Towing (C-PORT) *(Jeffrey C. Smith)*
Marine Contractors Alliance *(Jeffrey C. Smith)*
Spill-Net, Inc. *(Jeffrey C. Smith)*

WASHINGTON POLICY & ANALYSIS
655 15th St., N.W., Ninth Floor, Washington, DC 20005-5701
Telephone: (202) 626-5800
Registered as Foreign Agent: (#4211)
Background: A government relations consulting firm.
Members of firm representing listed organizations:
Campbell, Scott L.
Martin, William F.
Clients:
Statoil North America, Inc. *(Scott L. Campbell, William F. Martin)*
Tohoku Electric Power Co. *(Scott L. Campbell, William F. Martin)*

WASHINGTON RESOURCES AND STRATEGY, INC.
536 7th St., S.E., Washington, DC 20003
Telephone: (202) 544-1988
Background: A public relations, government relations and political consulting firm.
Members of firm representing listed organizations:
Conroy, Amy S., Senior Account Executive
Sweeney, William R. (Jr.)
Background: Former Deputy Chairman, Democratic National Committee. Former Executive Director, Democratic Congressional Campaign Committee.
Clients:
American Challenge Today Political Action Committee *(William R. Sweeney, Jr.)*
American Medical Ass'n *(William R. Sweeney, Jr.)*
China External Trade Development Council *(William R. Sweeney, Jr.)*
Electronic Data Systems Corp. *(William R. Sweeney, Jr.)*
Japan, Embassy of *(William R. Sweeney, Jr.)*
Kelso Political Action Committee *(William R. Sweeney, Jr.)*

WASHINGTON, Robert B., Jr.
Laxalt, Washington, Perito & Dubuc
1120 Connecticut Ave., N.W., Suite 1000, Washington, DC 20036
Telephone: (202) 857-4000
Registered as lobbyist at U.S. Congress.
Registered as Foreign Agent: (#4107).
Background: Counsel, Committee on the District of Columbia, U.S. Senate, 1971-1972. Chief Counsel and Staff Director, Committee on the District of Columbia, U.S. House of Representatives, 1973-1975.

Clients:
Angola, Government of the People's Republic of
Antigua and Barbuda, Government of
Home Group, The
Laxalt Washington Perito and Dubuc PAC

WASHINGTON SPECIAL EVENTS
329 F St., N.E., Washington, DC 20002
Telephone: (202) 544-4286
Members of firm representing listed organizations:
Copperthite, Michael C., President
Background: Former Deputy Political Director, Gephardt for President Committee.

WASHIO, Kota
General Manager, Washington Office, Nomura Research Institute (America), Inc.
1001 Connecticut Ave., N.W., Suite 625, Washington, DC 20036
Telephone: (202) 822-9431

WASKO, Lawrence D.
Seamon, Wasko and Ozment
1015 18th St., N.W. Suite 800, Washington, DC 20036
Telephone: (202) 331-0770
Background: Air Transport Examiner, Civil Aeronautics Board, 1958-62.
Clients:
Arrow Air

WASSERMAN, William B.
Field Director, People for the American Way
2000 M St., N.W., Suite 400, Washington, DC 20036
Telephone: (202) 467-4999

WATARU, Yasuo
Sr. V. President, General Manager, Nissho-Iwai American Corp.
1825 K St., N.W. Suite 1103, Washington, DC 20006
Telephone: (202) 429-0280

WATERMAN & ASSOCIATES
900 2nd St., N.E., Suite 109, Washington, DC 20002
Telephone: (202) 898-1444
Members of firm representing listed organizations:
Waterman, Ron, President

WATERMAN, Ron
President, Waterman & Associates
900 2nd St., N.E., Suite 109, Washington, DC 20002
Telephone: (202) 898-1444

WATERS, Alexis B.
Director, Public Relations, American Physical Therapy Ass'n
1111 North Fairfax St., Alexandria, VA 22314
Telephone: (703) 684-2782

WATERS, Dr. Jerry B.
Washington Representative, Farmland Industries
777 14th St., N.W., Suite 680, Washington, DC 20005
Telephone: (202) 783-5330
Registered as lobbyist at U.S. Congress.

WATERS, Mary Kirtley
Assistant Director, Washington Office, ConAgra, Inc.
888 17th St., N.W., Suite 300, Washington, DC 20006
Telephone: (202) 223-5115
Registered as lobbyist at U.S. Congress.
Background: Agricultural Task Force Director for Rep. Edward Madigan (R-IL), 1981 and Legislative Assistant to Rep. Larry J. Hopkins (R-KY), 1982-86.

WATERS, Michael J.
Director of Public Relations, Natural Gas Supply Ass'n
1129 20th St., N.W. Suite 300, Washington, DC 20036
Telephone: (202) 331-8900

WATERS, Robert J.
Arent, Fox, Kintner, Plotkin & Kahn
1050 Connecticut Ave., N.W., Washington, DC 20036-5339
Telephone: (202) 857-6000
Registered as lobbyist at U.S. Congress.

WATERS, Robert S.
Reid & Priest
1111 19th St., N.W., Washington, DC 20036
Telephone: (202) 828-0100

WATKIN, Virginia G.
Covington and Burling
1201 Pennsylvania Ave., N.W., Box 7566, Washington, DC
20044
Telephone: (202) 662-6000

WATKINS, Lucy R.
Education Advocate, Center for Law and Education
236 Massachusetts Ave., N.E. Suite 504, Washington, DC
20002
Telephone: (202) 546-5300
Registered as lobbyist at U.S. Congress.

WATKINS, Robert D.
Director, Public Affairs/Relations, American Soc. for Microbiology
1325 Massachusetts Ave., N.W., Washington, DC 20005
Telephone: (202) 737-3600

WATKINS, Robert P.
Williams and Connolly
839 17th St., N.W. 1000 Hill Bldg., Washington, DC 20006
Telephone: (202) 331-5000
Background: Civil Rights Division, Department of Justice, 1965-66. Hearing Counsel, Federal Maritime Commission, 1967. Assistant U.S. Attorney, Washington, DC, 1968-72.
Clients:
General Motors Corp.

WATKINSON, Wayne R.
Partner, McLeod & Pires
2501 M St., N.W., Suite 400, Washington, DC 20037
Telephone: (202) 861-1234
Clients:
American Soybean Ass'n
Cattlemen's Beef Promotion and Research Board
Nat'l Dairy Promotion and Research Board

WATROUS, David S.
Exec. Director, Radio Technical Commission for Aeronautics
One McPherson Sq. 1425 K St., N.W. Suite 500, Washington, DC 20005
Telephone: (202) 682-0266

WATSON, Austen W.
V. President, Government Relations, Plessey Electronic Systems Corp.
1725 Jefferson Davis Hwy., Suite 206, Arlington, VA
22202
Telephone: (703) 486-1288

WATSON, Jay
Forest Issues Specialist, Wilderness Soc.
1400 Eye St., N.W., 10th Floor, Washington, DC 20005
Telephone: (202) 842-3400
Registered as lobbyist at U.S. Congress.

WATSON, Leroy, Jr.
Legislative Representative, Nat'l Grange
1616 H St., N.W., Washington, DC 20006
Telephone: (202) 628-3507
Registered as lobbyist at U.S. Congress.

WATSON, Susan
Exec. Director, Foundation for Critical Care
1001 Connecticut Ave., N.W, Suite 428, Washington, DC
20036
Telephone: (202) 775-0721

WATT, Carl E., Jr.
Manager, Legislative Programs, Rockwell Internat'l
1745 Jefferson Davis Hwy. Suite 1200, Arlington, VA
22202
Telephone: (703) 553-6600
Registered as lobbyist at U.S. Congress.

WATT, James B.
President & CEO, Conference of State Bank Supervisors
1015 18th St., N.W Suite 1100, Washington, DC 20036
Telephone: (202) 296-2840
Registered as lobbyist at U.S. Congress.

WATTENBERG, Ben J.
Chairman, Coalition for a Democratic Majority
1001 Connecticut Ave., N.W., Suite 707, Washington, DC
20036
Telephone: (202) 466-4702

Background: Assistant to President Lyndon B. Johnson, 1966-68. Aide to Vice President Hubert Humphrey, Minneapolis, 1970. Campaign Advisor to Senator Henry Jackson (D-WA), 1972 and 1976.

WATTS, Adrian
Director of Marketing and Communications, Nat'l School
Supply and Equipment Ass'n
2020 North 14th St., Arlington, VA 22201
Telephone: (703) 524-8819

WATTS, Carolyn Herr
Legislative Representative, Nat'l Rural Electric Cooperative Ass'n
1800 Massachusetts Ave., N.W., Washington, DC 20036
Telephone: (202) 857-9559
Registered as lobbyist at U.S. Congress.

WATTS, Douglas R.
Legislative Counsel, Nat'l Cable Television Ass'n
1724 Massachusetts Ave., N.W., Washington, DC 20036
Telephone: (202) 775-3550
Registered as lobbyist at U.S. Congress.

WATTS, George B.
President, Nat'l Broiler Council
1155 15th St., N.W. Suite 614, Washington, DC 20005
Telephone: (202) 296-2622
Registered as lobbyist at U.S. Congress.
Background: Also serves as Treasurer, Nat'l Broiler Council Political Action Committee.

WATTS, Ralph S., Jr.
President, Adventist Development and Relief Agency Internat'l
12501 Old Columbia Pike, Silver Spring, MD 20904
Telephone: (301) 680-6380

WATZMAN, Bruce H.
Dir., Safety, Health, & Human Resources, Nat'l Coal Ass'n
1130 17th St., N.W., Washington, DC 20036
Telephone: (202) 463-2657
Registered as lobbyist at U.S. Congress.
Background: Former Legislative Assistant to Rep. Nick J. Rahall, II of West Virginia.

WAXMAN, Judith G.
Managing Attorney, Nat'l Health Law Program
2025 M St., N.W., Suite 400, Washington, DC 20036
Telephone: (202) 887-5310

WAXMAN, Laura DeKoven
Deputy Exec. Director, United States Conference of City Human Services Officials
1620 Eye St., N.W., Suite 400, Washington, DC 20006
Telephone: (202) 293-7330

WAXMAN, Margery
Sidley and Austin
1722 Eye St., N.W. Sixth Floor, Washington, DC 20006
Telephone: (202) 429-4000
Background: General Counsel, Office of Personnel Management, 1979-81; Dupufy General Counsel, Dept. of Treasury, 1981-85.
Clients:
Barclays Bank PLC
Federal Home Loan Bank of Chicago

WAY, George H.
V. Pres., Research and Test Dept., Ass'n of American Railroads
50 F St., N.W., Suite 7200, Washington, DC 20001
Telephone: (202) 639-2250

WAY, Kathryn
Director, Washington Office, Delaware, State of
400 North Capitol St., N.W. Suite 378, Washington, DC
20001
Telephone: (202) 624-7724

WAYNE, Claudia E.
Exec. Director, Nat'l Committee on Pay Equity
1201 16th St., N.W., Suite 422, Washington, DC 20036
Telephone: (202) 822-7304

WAYNE, Kirk
President, Tobacco Associates
1725 K St., N.W. Suite 512, Washington, DC 20006
Telephone: (202) 828-9144

WAZ, Joseph W., Jr.
Principal and General Counsel, Wexler, Reynolds, Fuller, Harrison and Schule, Inc.
1317 F St., N.W., Suite 600, Washington, DC 20004
Telephone: (202) 638-2121
Registered as lobbyist at U.S. Congress.
Background: Responsibilities include Treasurer, Wexler, Reynolds, Fuller, Harrison & Schule Political Action Committee.
Clients:
Committee for America's Copyright Community
Communications Satellite Corp. (COMSAT)
MCI Communications Corp.
Motion Picture Ass'n of America
Training Media Distributors Ass'n

WEALTH MANAGEMENT CORP.
Washington Harbour 3000 K St., N.W., P.H. 3-A, Washington, DC 20007
Telephone: (202) 944-4920
Members of firm representing listed organizations:
Curtin, Wayne T., Assistant Director
Mousseau, Paul W., Director
Clients:
Finryan Internat'l Ltd. *(Paul W. Mousseau)*
Motorcycle Riders Foundation *(Wayne T. Curtin)*

WEAR, Terrance J.
President, Legal Services Corp.
400 Virginia Ave., S.W., Washington, DC 20024
Telephone: (202) 863-1820
Background: Former Counsel to the Senate Agriculture Committee.

WEATHERLY & CO.
1155 15th St., N.W., Suite 302, Washington, DC 20005
Telephone: (202) 775-8130
Background: International business development consultants.
Members of firm representing listed organizations:
Weatherly, Jin-Hyun
Clients:
FRISA *(Jin-Hyun Weatherly)*
Kia Motor Corp. *(Jin-Hyun Weatherly)*

WEATHERLY, Jin-Hyun
Weatherly & Co.
1155 15th St., N.W., Suite 302, Washington, DC 20005
Telephone: (202) 775-8130
Registered as Foreign Agent: (#4160).
Clients:
FRISA
Kia Motor Corp.

WEAVER & ASSOCIATES, ROBERT A.
915 15th St., N.W., Suite 402, Washington, DC 20005
Telephone: (202) 347-3697
Registered as Foreign Agent: (#3916)
Members of firm representing listed organizations:
Perta, Joseph M.
Tyrrell, Patrick J.
Weaver, Robert A. (Jr.)
Clients:
Zaire, Government of the Republic of *(Joseph M. Perta, Patrick J. Tyrrell, Robert A. Weaver, Jr.)*

WEAVER, David
Ass't Director, State Legislation, Handgun Control, Inc.
1225 Eye St., N.W., Suite 1100, Washington, DC 20005
Telephone: (202) 898-0792
Registered as lobbyist at U.S. Congress.

WEAVER, David A.
President, Mail Advertising Service Ass'n Internat'l
1421 Prince St. Suite 200, Alexandria, VA 22314-2814
Telephone: (703) 836-9200
Registered as lobbyist at U.S. Congress.

WEAVER, Gerald
Evergreen Associates, Ltd.
206 G St., N.E., Washington, DC 20002
Telephone: (202) 543-3383
Registered as lobbyist at U.S. Congress.
Clients:
Gundle Lining Systems, Inc.
United Video Inc.
Zambelli Internationale

WEAVER, Kathy
Government Relations Specialist, SEMATECH
1825 Eye St., N.W. Suite 400, Washington, DC 20006
Telephone: (202) 429-2021

WEAVER, Rebecca A.
Field Director, Professionals' Coalition for Nuclear Arms
Control
1616 P St., N.W., Suite 320, Washington, DC 20036
Telephone: (202) 332-4823
Registered as lobbyist at U.S. Congress.

WEAVER, Robert A., Jr.
Weaver & Associates, Robert A.
915 15th St., N.W., Suite 402, Washington, DC 20005
Telephone: (202) 347-3697
Registered as Foreign Agent: (#3916).
Clients:
    Zaire, Government of the Republic of

WEAVER, Susan
Cong Affrs Officer, DEPARTMENT OF COMMERCE -
Nat'l Marine Fisheries Service
1335 East-West Hwy., Silver Spring, MD 20917
Telephone: (301) 427-2263

WEBB, C. Edwin
Director, Professional Affairs, American Pharmaceutical
Ass'n
2215 Constitution Ave., N.W., Washington, DC 20037
Telephone: (202) 628-4410
Background: Serves also as Staff Liaison, Academy of
Pharmacy Practice and Management.

WEBB, David O.
Sr. V. Pres., Policy & Regulatory Affrs., Gas Research Institute
1331 Pennsylvania Ave., N.W., Suite 730 North, Washington, DC 20004
Telephone: (202) 662-8989

WEBB, Morrison DeS.
V. President, Government Affairs, NYNEX
1828 L St., N.W., Suite 1000, Washington, DC 20036
Telephone: (202) 416-0100

WEBB, Ralph A.
General Manager, Contract Research Div., Babcock and
Wilcox Co.
c/o McDermott Internat'l Inc. 1850 K St., N.W., Suite 950,
Washington, DC 20006
Telephone: (202) 296-0390

WEBBER, Andrew H.
Exec. V. President, American Medical Peer Review Ass'n
810 First St., N.E., Suite 410, Washington, DC 20002
Telephone: (202) 371-5610
Registered as lobbyist at U.S. Congress.

WEBBER, Frederick L.
President & CEO, United States League of Savings Institutions
1709 New York Ave., N.W., Suite 801, Washington, DC
20006
Telephone: (202) 637-8900
Registered as lobbyist at U.S. Congress.
Background: Former Special Assistant for Legislative Affairs to President Gerald Ford.

WEBER & ASSOCIATES, J. Arthur
1140 23rd St., N.W., Suite 806, Washington, DC 20037
Telephone: (202) 293-7187
Members of firm representing listed organizations:
    Weber, Joseph A., President
Organizations represented:
    Citizens Against Research Bans *(Joseph A. Weber)*
    Coalition for Reliable Energy *(Joseph A. Weber)*
    Terio Internat'l *(Joseph A. Weber)*
    Westinghouse Electric Corp. *(Joseph A. Weber)*

WEBER, Cheryl
Exec Asst, Legis & Cong Rels, DEPARTMENT OF HOUS-
ING AND URBAN DEVELOPMENT
451 Seventh St., S.W., Washington, DC 20410
Telephone: (202) 755-5005

WEBER, James D.
Senior Associate, Mahe Company, The Eddie
900 Second St., N.E. Suite 200, Washington, DC 20002

Telephone: (202) 842-4100
Background: Managed the Virginia gubernatorial primary
campaign of Rep. Stan Parris (R-VA), 1989.

WEBER, Joseph A.
President, Weber & Associates, J. Arthur
1140 23rd St., N.W., Suite 806, Washington, DC 20037
Telephone: (202) 293-7187
Organizations represented:
    Citizens Against Research Bans
    Coalition for Reliable Energy
    Terio Internat'l
    Westinghouse Electric Corp.

WEBER, Lt. Gen. LaVern E.
Exec. Director, Nat'l Guard Ass'n of the U.S.
One Massachusetts Ave., N.W., Washington, DC 20001
Telephone: (202) 789-0031

WEBER, Michael
V. President for Programs, Center for Marine Conserva-
tion
1725 DeSales St., N.W. Suite 500, Washington, DC 20036
Telephone: (202) 429-5609
Registered as lobbyist at U.S. Congress.

WEBER, Susan
Exec. Director, Zero Population Growth, Inc.
1400 16th St., N.W., Suite 320, Washington, DC 20036
Telephone: (202) 332-2200
Registered as lobbyist at U.S. Congress.

WEBSTER, CHAMBERLAIN AND BEAN
1747 Pennsylvania Ave., N.W., Suite 1000, Washington,
DC 20006
Telephone: (202) 785-9500
Members of firm representing listed organizations:
    Chamberlain, Charles E.
        Background: Member, U.S. House of Representatives
        from Michigan, 1957-74.
    Dye, Alan P.
    Hazard, John W. (Jr.)
    Herold, Arthur L.
        Background: Trial Attorney, Federal Trade Commis-
        sion 1967-70.
    Panaro, Gerard Paul
        Background: Serves as General Counsel, Nat'l Candy
        Wholesalers Ass'n.
    Van Kirk, Burkett
        Background: Counsel, Senate Rules Committee, 1962-
        73. Senior Counsel, Senate Appropriations Commit-
        tee, 1973-83.
    Webster, George D.
        Background: Special U.S. Ambassador, 1972; Member,
        Advisor Group to Commissioner's Exempt Organiza-
        tion, 1987-88. Serves as General Counsel to the
        American Soc. of Ass'n Executives.
Clients:
    Amana Refrigeration, Inc. *(Arthur L. Herold)*
    American Academy of Optometry *(John W. Hazard,
    Jr.)*
    American College of Cardiology
    American Financial Services Ass'n *(Arthur L. He-
    rold)*
    American Financial Services Ass'n Political Ac-
    tion Committee *(Arthur L. Herold)*
    American Fishing Tackle Manufacturers Ass'n
    American Soc. of Ass'n Executives *(George D. Web-
    ster)*
    Associated Landscape Contractors of America
    Ass'n of School Business Officials Internat'l
    Commercial Law League of America *(Burkett Van
    Kirk)*
    Committee for Production Sharing *(Charles E. Cham-
    berlain)*
    Dairy and Food Industries Supply Ass'n *(George D.
    Webster)*
    INTERARMS *(Burkett Van Kirk)*
    Internat'l Taxicab Ass'n *(Arthur L. Herold)*
    Nat'l Ass'n of Temporary Services *(Arthur L. Herold)*
    Nat'l Candy Wholesalers Ass'n
    Nat'l Center for Homeopathy
    Nat'l Right to Work Committee *(George D. Webster)*
    Nat'l Tooling and Machining Ass'n *(Alan P. Dye)*
    Packaging Machinery Manufacturers Institute
    (George D. Webster)
    Power Tool Institute *(Arthur L. Herold)*
    Retail Bakers of America *(Gerard Paul Panaro)*

Soc. of American Wood Preservers, Inc.
Vocational Industrial Clubs of America *(Arthur L.
Herold)*

WEBSTER AND FREDRICKSON
1819 H St., N.W., Suite 300, Washington, DC 20006
Telephone: (202) 659-8510
Members of firm representing listed organizations:
    Webster, Wendell W.
Clients:
    Student Nat'l Medical Ass'n *(Wendell W. Webster)*

WEBSTER, George D.
Webster, Chamberlain and Bean
1747 Pennsylvania Ave., N.W., Suite 1000, Washington,
DC 20006
Telephone: (202) 785-9500
Registered as lobbyist at U.S. Congress.
Background: Special U.S. Ambassador, 1972; Member, Ad-
visor Group to Commissioner's Exempt Organization,
1987-88. Serves as General Counsel to the American Soc.
of Ass'n Executives.
Clients:
    American Soc. of Ass'n Executives
    Dairy and Food Industries Supply Ass'n
    Nat'l Right to Work Committee
    Packaging Machinery Manufacturers Institute

WEBSTER, R. Timothy
Exec. Director, American Soc. of Consultant Pharmacists
2300 9th St., South, Arlington, VA 22204
Telephone: (703) 920-8492

▶**WEBSTER AND SHEFFIELD**
2000 Pennsylvania Ave., N.W., Suite 7400, Washington,
DC 20006
Telephone: (202) 785-8222
Background: Washington office of a New York law firm.
Members of firm representing listed organizations:
    Sigal, Jill Lea
        Background: Served in the U.S. Department of Energy,
        1985-89.
    Zausner, L. Andrew
        Background: Served in the U.S. Department of Energy,
        1977-79.
Clients:
    ASARCO Incorporated *(L. Andrew Zausner)*
    Liggett Group, Inc. *(L. Andrew Zausner)*
    Magma Copper Corp. *(L. Andrew Zausner)*
    Mazda Motor Manufacturing Corp. *(L. Andrew
    Zausner)*
    PG&E-Bechtel Generating Co. *(L. Andrew Zausner)*
    Tobacco Institute *(L. Andrew Zausner)*

WEBSTER, Wendell W.
Webster and Fredrickson
1819 H St., N.W., Suite 300, Washington, DC 20006
Telephone: (202) 659-8510
Clients:
    Student Nat'l Medical Ass'n

WEBSTER, Wendy A.
Account Supervisor and Dir., Media Rtns., Abramson Associates
1275 K St., N.W., Washington, DC 20005
Telephone: (202) 289-6900

WECHSLER, Steven A.
President, Nat'l Realty Committee
1250 Connecticut Ave., N.W. Suite 630, Washington, DC
20036
Telephone: (202) 785-0808
Background: Also serves as Treasurer, Nat'l Realty Political Action Committee.

WECKER, Miranda
Associate Director, Council on Ocean Law
1709 New York Ave., N.W. Suite 700, Washington, DC
20006
Telephone: (202) 347-3766

WECKSTEIN, Paul
District of Columbia Director, Center for Law and Education
236 Massachusetts Ave., N.E. Suite 504, Washington, DC
20002
Telephone: (202) 546-5300
Registered as lobbyist at U.S. Congress.

WEDDIG, Lee
Exec. V. President, Nat'l Fisheries Institute
1525 Wilson Blvd., Suite 500, Arlington, VA 22209
Telephone: (703) 524-8880
Registered as lobbyist at U.S. Congress.
Background: Also represents the Nat'l Fisheries Institute PAC.

WEDDLE, Karl G.
Exec. Director, American Home Economics Ass'n
1555 King St., Alexandria, VA 22314
Telephone: (703) 706-4600

WEEKLY, Larry
Director, Public Relations, American Bankers Ass'n
1120 Connecticut Ave., N.W., Washington, DC 20036
Telephone: (202) 663-5000

WEGER, Bill
Communications Director, Hardwood Plywood Manufacturers Ass'n
1825 Michael Faraday Dr., Reston, VA 22090
Telephone: (703) 435-2900

WEGGELAND, Ted
Thompson and Co.
1001 G St., N.W. 7th Floor, Washington, DC 20001
Telephone: (202) 383-5590
Registered as lobbyist at U.S. Congress.
Clients:
CareerCom Corp.

WEGMAN, Richard A.
Garvey, Schubert & Barer
1000 Potomac St., N.W. Suite 500, Washington, DC 20007
Telephone: (202) 965-7880
Registered as lobbyist at U.S. Congress.
Background: Appellate Attorney, Antitrust Division, U.S. Department of Justice, 1965-68. Staff Director, Senate Subcommittee on Executive Reorganization, and Legislative Counsel to Senator William Proxmire (D-WI), 1968-74. Exec. Director, President's Commission on a National Agenda for the 80's, 1979-81. Chief Counsel and Staff Director, Senate Committee on Government Affairs, 1975-81.
Clients:
American Iron and Steel Institute
Canada, Embassy of
Canada, Government of
Dade County Aviation Department
Manitoba, Province of
Miami Internat'l Airport
Ontario, Province of

WEIDLEIN, John
President, Nat'l Homeowners Ass'n
1906 Sunderland Place, N.W., Washington, DC 20036
Telephone: (202) 223-1453

WEIDMAN, Jim
Manager, State Media Relations, Nat'l Federation of Independent Business
600 Maryland Ave., S.W., Suite 700, Washington, DC 20024
Telephone: (202) 554-9000

WEIGEND, Robert E.
Chwat/Weigend Associates
400 First St., N.W. Suite 100, Washington, DC 20001
Telephone: (202) 638-6400
Registered as lobbyist at U.S. Congress.
Registered as Foreign Agent: (#4320).
Clients:
American Home Sewing Ass'n
American Radio Relay League
Associated Locksmiths of America
Lockwood Trade Journal
Nat'l Exchange Carriers Ass'n
Nat'l Licensed Beverage Ass'n
Nat'l Weather Service Employees Organization
Nat'l Weather Service Employees Organization Political Action Committee

WEIL, Alan M.
President, Pace, Weil and Associates, Internat'l
1606 17th St., N.W., Washington, DC 20009
Telephone: (202) 232-0077

WEIL, GOTSHAL & MANGES
1615 L St., N.W., Suite 700, Washington, DC 20036
Telephone: (202) 682-7000
Background: Washington office of a New York law firm.
Members of firm representing listed organizations:
Bialos, Jeffrey P.
Buc, Nancy L.
Background: Assistant General Counsel, Department of Health and Human Services, and Chief Counsel, Food and Drug Administration, 1980-81. Attorney, Federal Trade Commission, 1969-72.
Hird, David B.
Krakovec, Laura L.
Odle, Robert C. (Jr.)
Background: Staff Assistant to the President of the U.S., 1969-71. Deputy Assistant Secretary, Department of Housing and Urban Development, 1973-76. Assistant Secretary, Department of Energy, 1981-85.
Turnbull, Bruce H.
Victor, A. Paul
Clients:
Marine Shale Processors, Inc. *(Robert C. Odle, Jr.)*
Matsushita Electronic Corp. *(Jeffrey P. Bialos, A. Paul Victor)*
Mitsubishi Corp. *(Jeffrey P. Bialos, A. Paul Victor)*
Noranda, Inc. *(Robert C. Odle, Jr.)*
Schering Internat'l *(Nancy L. Buc, David B. Hird, Laura L. Krakovec)*

WEIL, Patricia E.
V. President, Communications, Aircraft Owners and Pilots Ass'n
421 Aviation Way, Frederick, MD 21701
Telephone: (301) 695-2000

WEIL, Russell T.
Kirlin, Campbell and Keating
One Farragut Square South 2nd Floor, Washington, DC 20006
Telephone: (202) 639-8000
Registered as lobbyist at U.S. Congress.
Registered as Foreign Agent: (#3472).
Clients:
Council of European and Japanese Nat'l Shipowners' Ass'ns

WEIMAN, David M.
517 Albany Ave., Takoma Park, MD 20912
Telephone: (202) 797-9119
Registered as Foreign Agent: (#4316)
Organizations represented:
Rongelap Atoll Local Government

WEIN, Steven A.
Manager, Legislative Affairs, Textron Inc.
1090 Vermont Ave., N.W., Suite 1100, Washington, DC 20005
Telephone: (202) 289-5800
Registered as lobbyist at U.S. Congress.

WEINBERG, Barbi
President, Washington Institute for Near East Policy
50 F St., N.W., Suite 8800, Washington, DC 20001
Telephone: (202) 783-0226

WEINBERG, Edward
Duncan, Weinberg, Miller & Pembroke, P.C.
1615 M St., N.W., Suite 800, Washington, DC 20036-3203
Telephone: (202) 467-6370
Registered as lobbyist at U.S. Congress.
Background: Dep't of the Interior, Attorney, 1944-1951 and Assistant Chief Counsel, 1951-54 Bureau of Reclamation; Assistant Solicitor, Branch of Power, 1955-1961; Associate Solicitor, Water and Power, 1961-1963; Deputy Solicitor, 1963-1968; Solicitor, 1968-1969. Principal Consultant, The Nat'l Water Commission, 1969-1973.
Clients:
Basin Electric Power Cooperative
Beard Oil Co.
Colorado River Commission of Nevada
Kenai Natives Ass'n, Inc.
Lake Andes-Wagner Water Systems, Inc.
Mid-West Electric Consumers Ass'n
Transmission Agency of Northern California
Web Water Development Ass'n
Western Fuels Ass'n

WEINBERG & GREEN
10480 Little Patuxent Pkwy., Columbia, MD 21044-3506

Telephone: (301) 740-8500
Background: An attorney.
Members of firm representing listed organizations:
Talarek, Walter G.
Clients:
Chemical Specialties, Inc. *(Walter G. Talarek)*
Mooney Chemicals, Inc. *(Walter G. Talarek)*
Trenton Sales, Inc. *(Walter G. Talarek)*

WEINBERG, Larry P.
Kirschner, Weinberg & Dempsey
1615 L St., N.W., Suite 1360, Washington, DC 20036
Telephone: (202) 775-5900
Clients:
American Federation of State, County and Municipal Employees

WEINBERG, N. Myrl
Director of Government Relations, American Diabetes Ass'n
Nat'l Service Center, 1660 Duke St., Alexandria, VA 22314
Telephone: (703) 549-1500

WEINBERG, Nancy A.
Director, Environmental Affairs, Grocery Manufacturers of America
1010 Wisconsin Ave., N.W., Suite 800, Washington, DC 20007
Telephone: (202) 337-9400

WEINBERG, Richard A.
Comptroller, Nat'l League of Postmasters Political Action Committee
1023 North Royal St., Alexandria, VA 22314
Telephone: (202) 548-5922

WEINBERG, Robert
Duncan, Weinberg, Miller & Pembroke, P.C.
1615 M St., N.W., Suite 800, Washington, DC 20036-3203
Telephone: (202) 467-6370
Clients:
Allegheny Electric Cooperative, Inc.
Bentonville, Arkansas, City of
Cajun Rural Electric Power Cooperative, Inc.
Central Virginia Electric Cooperative, Inc.
Craig-Botetourt Electric Cooperative
Lubbock, Brownfield, Floyada and Tulia, Texas, Municipalities of
Lubbock Power and Light
Southern Maryland Electric Cooperative, Inc.

WEINBLATT, Rabbi Stuart
Admin. Dir., Louis D. Brandeis District, Zionist Organization of America
11710 Hunters Lane, Rockville, MD 20852-2367
Telephone: (301) 468-3900

WEINER, Deborah Feldman
Associate Director, Government Relations, American Soc. for the Prevention of Cruelty to Animals Legislative Office
1755 Massachusetts Ave., N.W. Suite 418, Washington, DC 20036
Telephone: (202) 232-5020
Registered as lobbyist at U.S. Congress.

WEINER, Fred S.
Director, Program Development & Services, Nat'l Ass'n of the Deaf
814 Thayer Ave., Silver Spring, MD 20910
Telephone: (301) 587-1788

WEINER, Harvey E.
Weiner, McCaffrey, Brodsky, Kaplan & Levin
1350 New York Ave., N.W., Suite 800, Washington, DC 20005-4797
Telephone: (202) 628-2000
Registered as lobbyist at U.S. Congress.
Background: Office of General Counsel, Dept. of Housing and Urban Development (HUD), 1969-74; Special Ass't to Ass't Secretary for Housing Production and Mortgage Credit FHA Commissioner, HUD, 1974-76; Deputy Ass't Secretary for Regulatory Programs - Interstate Land Sales Administrator, HUD, 1976-77.

WEINER, MCCAFFREY, BRODSKY, KAPLAN & LEVIN
1350 New York Ave., N.W., Suite 800, Washington, DC 20005-4797
Telephone: (202) 628-2000
Members of firm representing listed organizations:
Avrakotos, Gus
Brodsky, James A.
Background: Patent Examiner, U.S. Patent Office, 1968-72. Special Assistant to Commissioner Newman, U.S. Consumer Product Safety Commission, 1974-76. Deputy Assistant Secretary for Consumer Affairs, HUD, 1976-77.
Gilbertson, Peter A.
Levin, Mark M.
Background: Trial Attorney, Public Counsel Section, Antitrust Division, U.S. Department of Justice, 1973-77.
McCaffrey, R. Lawrence
Background: Attorney Advisor, Office of General Counsel, U.S. Department of Housing and Urban Development, 1971-74. Special Assistant to the General Counsel, U.S. Department of Transportation, 1974-75. Chief Counsel, Federal Railroad Administration, 1975-77.
Sidman, Mark H.
Weiner, Harvey E.
Background: Office of General Counsel, Dept. of Housing and Urban Development (HUD), 1969-74; Special Ass't to Ass't Secretary for Housing Production and Mortgage Credit FHA Commissioner, HUD, 1974-76; Deputy Ass't Secretary for Regulatory Programs - Interstate Land Sales Administrator, HUD, 1976-77.
Clients:
Nat'l Manufactured Housing Finance Ass'n

WEINER, Michael
Public Information Specialist, Nat'l Computer Graphics Ass'n
2722 Merrilee Drive, Suite 200, Fairfax, VA 22031
Telephone: (703) 698-9600

WEINER, Ronald H.
President, Automotive Information Council
13505 Dulles Technology Drive, Herndon, VA 22071
Telephone: (703) 904-0700

WEINER, Roslyne
Legislative Policy Analyst, American Group Practice Ass'n
1422 Duke St., Alexandria, VA 22314
Telephone: (703) 838-0033
Registered as lobbyist at U.S. Congress.

WEINERT, Donald G.
Exec. Director, Nat'l Soc. of Professional Engineers
1420 King St., Alexandria, VA 22314-2715
Telephone: (703) 684-2841
Registered as lobbyist at U.S. Congress.

WEINROTH, Anna
Legislative Assistant, Federation for American Immigration Reform (FAIR)
1666 Connecticut Ave., N.W., Suite 400, Washington, DC 20009
Telephone: (202) 328-7004
Registered as lobbyist at U.S. Congress.

WEINSTEIN, Dr. Allen
President and CEO, Center for Democracy
1101 15th St., N.W., Suite 505, Washington, DC 20005
Telephone: (202) 429-9141

WEINSTEIN, Elaine B.
Legislative Assistant, New Jersey, State of
444 N. Capitol St., N.W. Suite 236, Washington, DC 20001
Telephone: (202) 638-0631

WEINTRAUB, Frederick J.
Asst. Exec. Dir., Communications, Council for Exceptional Children
1920 Association Drive, Reston, VA 22091

Telephone: (703) 620-3660

WEINTRAUB, Michael
Director of Marketing, Stone and Associates, Ann E. W.
1315 Duke St., Alexandria, VA 22314
Telephone: (703) 836-7717
Registered as Foreign Agent: (#3914).
Organizations represented:
Nicaraguan Resistance- U.S.A.

WEIR, Ellen
Research Coordinator, Nat'l Broadcasting Co.
1331 Pennsylvania Ave., N.W. Suite 700S, Washington, DC 20004
Telephone: (202) 637-4534

WEISMAN, David E.
Meyer, Faller, Weisman and Greenburg
4400 Jennifer St., N.W., Suite 380, Washington, DC 20015
Telephone: (202) 362-1100
Clients:
Nat'l Ass'n of Business and Educational Radio

WEISMAN, Leslie
President, American Soc. of Access Professionals
7910 Woodmont Ave. Suite 1208, Bethesda, MD 20814
Telephone: (301) 913-0030

WEISMILLER, Toby
Sr. Staff Associate for Political Action, Nat'l Ass'n of Social Workers
7981 Eastern Ave., Silver Spring, MD 20910
Telephone: (301) 565-0333
Background: Responsible for the Nat'l Ass'n of Social Workers Political Action Committee for Candidate Action.

WEISS, Arnold H.
Arent, Fox, Kintner, Plotkin & Kahn
1050 Connecticut Ave., N.W., Washington, DC 20036-5339
Telephone: (202) 857-6000
Background: Attorney, Office for International Finance and Congressional Liaison, U.S. Treasury Department, 1952-60.

WEISS, Daniel
Wash. Dir., Pollution & Toxics Program, Sierra Club
408 C St., N.E., Washington, DC 20002
Telephone: (202) 547-1141
Registered as lobbyist at U.S. Congress.

WEISS, Debra
News Director, Interstate Natural Gas Ass'n of America
555 13th St., N.W. Suite 300 West, Washington, DC 20004
Telephone: (202) 626-3200
Registered as lobbyist at U.S. Congress.

WEISS, James R.
Preston Gates Ellis & Rouvelas Meeds
1735 New York Ave., N.W., Suite 500, Washington, DC 20006-4759
Telephone: (202) 628-1700
Background: Former Chief, Transportation, Energy and Agriculture Section, Antitrust Division, U.S. Department of Justice.

WEISS, Mark A.
Covington and Burling
1201 Pennsylvania Ave., N.W., Box 7566, Washington, DC 20044
Telephone: (202) 662-6000
Registered as lobbyist at U.S. Congress.

WEISS, Richard
V. President, Public Affairs, Nat'l Dairy Promotion and Research Board
2111 Wilson Blvd., Suite 600, Arlington, VA 22201
Telephone: (703) 528-4800

WEISS, Richard A.
Senior V. President, Kamber Group, The
1920 L St., N.W., Washington, DC 20036
Telephone: (202) 223-8700
Organizations represented:
American Federation of Musicians
Retail, Wholesale and Department Store Workers Union

WEISS, Rick
Congressional Liaison, American Foreign Service Ass'n
2101 E St., N.W., Washington, DC 20037
Telephone: (202) 338-4045
Registered as lobbyist at U.S. Congress.

WEISS, Stanley A.
Board Chairman, Business Executives for Nat'l Security
601 Pennsylvania Ave., N.W. Suite 700, Washington, DC 20004
Telephone: (202) 737-1090
Registered as lobbyist at U.S. Congress.

WEISS, Suzanne
Health Reimbursement Analyst, American Ass'n of Homes for the Aging
1129 20th St., N.W., Suite 400, Washington, DC 20036
Telephone: (202) 296-5960
Registered as lobbyist at U.S. Congress.

WEISSBRODT, I. S.
1614 20th St., N.W., Washington, DC 20009
Telephone: (202) 265-1933
Organizations represented:
State Farm Insurance Cos.
Travelers, The

WEISSMAN, Rozanne
V. President, Corporate Communications, Corporation for Public Broadcasting
901 E St., N.W. Suite 2209, Washington, DC 20004-2006
Telephone: (202) 879-9712

WEITZ, Peter R.
Director of Programs, German Marshall Fund of the United States
11 Dupont Circle, N.W., Suite 750, Washington, DC 20036
Telephone: (202) 745-3950

WEITZMAN, James M.
Kaye, Scholer, Fierman, Hays and Handler
The McPherson Building 901 15th St., N.W., #1100, Washington, DC 20005
Telephone: (202) 682-3500

WEIZMANN, Howard C.
Exec. Director, Ass'n of Private Pension and Welfare Plans
1212 New York Ave., N.W. 12th Floor, Washington, DC 20005
Telephone: (202) 737-6666
Registered as lobbyist at U.S. Congress.
Background: Serves also as Treasurer and principal contact for the Ass'n of Private Pension and Welfare Plans Political Action Committee.

WELBURN, Brenda L.
Deputy Exec. Director, Nat'l Ass'n of State Boards of Education
1012 Cameron St., Alexandria, VA 22314
Telephone: (703) 684-4000
Background: Formerly Legislative Assistant to Sen. Paul Tsongas (D-MA).

WELCH, Bryant L.
Exec. Dir., Professional Practice, American Psychological Ass'n
1200 17th St., N.W., Washington, DC 20036
Telephone: (202) 955-7600
Registered as lobbyist at U.S. Congress.

WELCH, John Frederick
President, Safe Buildings Alliance
655 15th St., N.W., Suite 1200, Washington, DC 20005
Telephone: (202) 879-5120
Registered as lobbyist at U.S. Congress.

WELCH, Monica
Government Affairs Representative, Electronic Data Systems Corp.
1331 Pennsylvania Ave., N.W., Suite 1300 North, Washington, DC 20004
Telephone: (202) 637-6700

WELCH, Suzanne
Manager, Information Industry Affairs, Eastman Kodak Co.
1776 Eye St., N.W Suite 1050, Washington, DC 20006
Telephone: (202) 857-3472
Registered as lobbyist at U.S. Congress.

WELCOME, Jerry, Jr
Director, Legislative Affairs, American Meat Institute
Box 3556, Washington, DC 20007
Telephone: (703) 841-2400
Registered as lobbyist at U.S. Congress.

WELDON, Sara
Bergman Associates, William S.
1001 Connecticut Ave., N.W., Suite 800, Washington, DC 20036
Telephone: (202) 452-1520
Background: Serves as Director of Administration, Internat'l Ass'n of Cooking Professionals.
Organizations represented:
Internat'l Ass'n of Cooking Professionals

WELLBORN, Stanley N.
Director, Public Affairs, Brookings Institution
1775 Massachusetts Ave., N.W., Washington, DC 20036
Telephone: (202) 797-6000

WELLEN, Robert H.
Fulbright & Jaworski
1150 Connecticut Ave., N.W., Suite 400, Washington, DC 20036
Telephone: (202) 452-6800
Registered as lobbyist at U.S. Congress.
Clients:
Memorial Hospital System

WELLER, Mark W.
Director, Corporate Government Affairs, Ball Corp.
2200 Clarendon Blvd. Suite 1006, Arlington, VA 22201
Telephone: (703) 284-5400

WELLER, Paul S., Jr.
President, Agri/Washington
1629 K St., N.W., Suite 1100, Washington, DC 20006
Telephone: (202) 785-6710
Registered as lobbyist at U.S. Congress.
Clients:
Agricultural Relations Council
American Agricultural Editors Ass'n
American Ass'n of Grain Inspection and Weighing Agencies
Apple Processors Ass'n

WELLFORD, W. Harrison
Olwine, Connelly, Chase, O'Donnell and Weyher
1701 Pennsylvania Ave., N.W. Suite 1000, Washington, DC 20006
Telephone: (202) 835-0500
Registered as lobbyist at U.S. Congress.
Background: Chief Legislative Assistant to Senator Philip Hart (D-MI), 1973-76. Exec. Associate Director, White House Office of Management and Budget, 1977-80. Director, President's Reorganization Project, 1977-81.
Clients:
Ad Hoc Committee for Small Hydro Power
Alexander & Alexander Inc.
Catalyst Energy Corp.
Energy Factors
Intercontinental Energy Corp.
Long Lake Energy Corp.
Nat'l Corp. for Housing Partnerships
Nat'l Independent Energy Producers
Sithe Energies USA
United Way of America
YMCA of the USA

WELLING, Brad
Asst. Federal Administrative Counsel, American Bankers Ass'n
1120 Connecticut Ave., N.W., Washington, DC 20036
Telephone: (202) 663-5000

WELLMAN, Arnold F.
Manager, Public Affairs, United Parcel Service
316 Pennsylvania Ave., S.E. Suite 304, Washington, DC 20003
Telephone: (202) 675-4220

WELLS, Jack
Director of Internat'l Marketing, American Seed Trade Ass'n
1030 15th St., N.W. Suite 964, Washington, DC 20005
Telephone: (202) 223-4080

WELLS, Kent M.
Exec. Director, Federal Relations, Southwestern Bell Corp.
1667 K St., N.W., Suite 1000, Washington, DC 20006
Telephone: (202) 293-8550
Registered as lobbyist at U.S. Congress.

WELLS, L. H.
Senior Staff Representative, Shell Oil Co.
Suite 200, 1025 Connecticut Ave., N.W., Washington, DC 20036
Telephone: (202) 466-1400
Registered as lobbyist at U.S. Congress.

WELLS, Milton T.
Director, Federal Relations, Nat'l Ass'n of State Treasurers
400 N. Capitol St., N.W. Suite 320 S, Washington, DC 20001
Telephone: (202) 624-8595
Background: Serves also as representative for the Nat'l Ass'n of State Auditors Comptrollers and Treasurers.

WELLS, Nan S.
Director, Office of Governmental Affairs, Princeton University
1156 15th St., N.W., Suite 1102, Washington, DC 20005
Telephone: (202) 429-8719

WELLS, Robert C.
Director, Internat'l Govt't Relations, Citicorp
1275 Pennsylvania Ave., N.W., Suite 503, Washington, DC 20004
Telephone: (202) 879-6800
Registered as lobbyist at U.S. Congress.

WELSCHKE, Bernhard M.
Deputy Exec. Officer, Representative for German Industry and Trade
One Farragut Square South 1634 Eye St., N.W., Washington, DC 20006
Telephone: (202) 347-0247
Registered as Foreign Agent: (#4274).
Clients:
Bundesverband der Deutschen Industrie
Deutscher Industrie und Handelstag

WELSH, Charles B.
President, Targeting Systems, Inc., Reese Communications Companies
2111 Wilson Ave., Suite 900, Arlington, VA 22201
Telephone: (703) 528-4400
Background: Also serves as President, Targeting Systems, Inc.

WELSH, David P.
President, United States Army Warrant Officers Ass'n
Box 2040, Reston, VA 22090
Telephone: (703) 620-3986

WELSH, Gary M.
Prather, Seeger, Doolittle and Farmer
1600 M St., N.W., Washington, DC 20036
Telephone: (202) 296-0500
Registered as lobbyist at U.S. Congress.
Clients:
Flores Esmeralda, Ltda.
Flores Esmeralda, S.R.L.
John Hancock Mutual Life Insurance Co.
Sociedad de Industrias "Comite Textil"

WELSH, Peggy
Government Relations Rep., Dickstein, Shapiro and Morin
2101 L St., N.W., Washington, DC 20037
Telephone: (202) 785-9700

WELTMANN, Allen J.
Partner in Charge, Government Relations, Coopers and Lybrand
1800 M St., N.W., Washington, DC 20036
Telephone: (202) 822-4222
Background: Serves also as Secretary and Treasurer of the Coopers and Lybrand Political Action Committee.

WENDORF & ASSOCIATES
53 D St., S.E., Washington, DC 20003
Telephone: (202) 488-4782
Registered as lobbyist at U.S. Congress.
Background: A lobbying/consulting firm.

Members of firm representing listed organizations:
Wendorf, Frederick C.
Clients:
Central and South West Services, Inc. *(Frederick C. Wendorf)*
Oklahoma Gas and Electric Co. *(Frederick C. Wendorf)*

WENDORF, Frederick C.
Wendorf & Associates
53 D St., S.E., Washington, DC 20003
Telephone: (202) 488-4782
Registered as lobbyist at U.S. Congress.
Clients:
Central and South West Services, Inc.
Oklahoma Gas and Electric Co.

WENGER, Michael R.
Washington Representative, Appalachian Regional Commission, States' Washington Representative of
1666 Connecticut Ave., N.W. 7th Floor, Washington, DC 20235
Telephone: (202) 673-7842

WENNING, Thomas F.
Sr. V. President and General Counsel, Nat'l Grocers Ass'n
1825 Samuel Morse Drive, Reston, VA 22090
Telephone: (703) 437-5300
Registered as lobbyist at U.S. Congress.

WENTWORTH, Eric
Senior V. President, Public Affairs, Council for Advancement and Support of Education
11 Dupont Circle Suite 400, Washington, DC 20036
Telephone: (202) 328-5900

WERGELES, Amy S.
Mintz, Levin, Cohn, Ferris, Glovsky and Popeo, P.C.
1825 Eye St., N.W. 12th Floor, Washington, DC 20006
Telephone: (202) 293-0500
Clients:
Chain Pharmacy Ass'n of New York State

WERNEKE, Diane
Cong Liaison, FEDERAL RESERVE SYSTEM
20th and C Sts., N.W., Washington, DC 20551
Telephone: (202) 452-3456

WERNER, Michele
Legislative Assistant, Soc. of American Florists
1601 Duke St., Alexandria, VA 22314
Telephone: (703) 836-8700

WERNER, Nicole
Research Assistant, Center for Clean Air Policy
444 N. Capitol St., Suite 526, Washington, DC 20001
Telephone: (202) 624-7709

WERTHEIMER, Fred
President, Common Cause
2030 M St., N.W., Washington, DC 20036
Telephone: (202) 833-1200
Registered as lobbyist at U.S. Congress.

WERTHEIMER, Wendy J.
Director of Public & Government Affairs, American Social Health Ass'n
311 Massachusetts Ave., N.E., Washington, DC 20002
Telephone: (202) 593-9129
Background: Legislative Assistant to Sen. Jacob Javits on the Senate Human Resources Committee, 1974-79.

WERTIME, Jacqueline G.
Staff V. President, Communications, Mortgage Bankers Ass'n of America
1125 15th St., N.W., Suite 700, Washington, DC 20005
Telephone: (202) 861-6500

WESSON, Sheldon
Director of Press Relations, American Iron and Steel Institute
1133 15th St., N.W., Suite 300, Washington, DC 20005-2701
Telephone: (202) 452-7115

WEST, Charles M.
Exec. Vice President, Nat'l Ass'n of Retail Druggists
205 Daingerfield Road, Alexandria, VA 22314
Telephone: (703) 683-8200

WASHINGTON REPRESENTATIVES

Registered as lobbyist at U.S. Congress.

WEST, Ford B.
V. President, Government Relations, Fertilizer Institute
501 Second St., N.E., Washington, DC 20002
Telephone: (202) 675-8250
Registered as lobbyist at U.S. Congress.
Background: Also serves as Treasurer, Fertilizer Institute
Political Action Committee (FERT PAC).

WEST, G. Frank
53 D St., S.E., Washington, DC 20003
Telephone: (202) 488-8562
Registered as lobbyist at U.S. Congress.
Organizations represented:
Church Alliance
Marine Resources Development Foundation
Oklahoma Natural Gas Co.

WEST, Gail Berry
Director, Government Affairs, Bell Communications Research, Inc.
2101 L St., N.W., Washington, DC 20036
Telephone: (202) 955-4653
Background: Formerly Deputy Assistant Secretary of the
Air Force, Manpower and Reserve Affairs.

WEST, Pete
V. President, Government & Public Affrs., Nat'l Business
Aircraft Ass'n
1200 18th St., N.W. Suite 200, Washington, DC 20036
Telephone: (202) 783-9000
Registered as lobbyist at U.S. Congress.
Background: Former Legislative Assistant to Rep. Doug
Barnard, Jr. (D-GA).

WEST, Dr. Peter A.
President, Federal Physicians Ass'n
P.O. Box 45150, Washington, DC 20026
Telephone: (703) 455-5947

WESTENDORF, William
Director, State Affairs, Chemical Manufacturers Ass'n
2501 M St., N.W., Washington, DC 20037
Telephone: (202) 887-1100

WESTER, Shirley H.
Exec. Director, American Soc. for Public Administration
1120 G St., N.W. Suite 500, Washington, DC 20005
Telephone: (202) 393-7878

WESTERFIELD, Mark G.
Associate, Gilberg & Kurent
1250 I St., N.W. Suite 600, Washington, DC 20005
Telephone: (202) 842-3222

WESTERMANN, Edith E.
Westermann and Hendricks, Inc.
1225 Jefferson Davis Hwy., Suite 600, Arlington, VA
22202
Telephone: (703) 486-5659
Registered as lobbyist at U.S. Congress.
Clients:
Partnerships in Education
Young Astronaut Council

WESTERMANN AND HENDRICKS, INC.
1225 Jefferson Davis Hwy., Suite 600, Arlington, VA
22202
Telephone: (703) 486-5659
Registered as lobbyist at U.S. Congress.
Background: A government relations consulting firm.
Members of firm representing listed organizations:
Hendricks, Diane
Background: Second Vice President, American League
of Lobbyists, 1990.
Westermann, Edith E.
Clients:
Partnerships in Education *(Diane Hendricks, Edith E.
Westermann)*
Young Astronaut Council *(Diane Hendricks, Edith E.
Westermann)*

WESTNER, Joe
Director, Federal Relations, Bell Telephone Co. of Pennsylvania
c/o Bell Atlantic, 1710 Rhode Island Ave., 12th Floor,
Washington, DC 20036
Telephone: (202) 392-6982

WESTON INC., Roy F.
955 L'Enfant Plaza, S.W. North Bldg. Sixth Floor, Washington, DC 20024
Telephone: (202) 646-6800
Background: Washington office of a Pennsylvania consulting firm.
Organizations represented:
Interstate Conference on Water Policy

WESTON, Richard
Senior Writer and Editor, Public Affairs, American Trucking
Ass'ns
2200 Mill Road, Alexandria, VA 22314
Telephone: (703) 838-1873

WESTOVER, Michelle M.
Legislative Assistant, Nat'l Trust for Historic Preservation
1785 Massachusetts Ave., N.W., Washington, DC 20036
Telephone: (202) 673-4000
Registered as lobbyist at U.S. Congress.
Background: Former Legislative Assistant to the late Rep.
Claude Pepper (D-FL).

WESTWATER, Joseph
Government Relations Consultant, McLeod & Pires
2501 M St., N.W., Suite 400, Washington, DC 20037
Telephone: (202) 861-1234
Registered as lobbyist at U.S. Congress.

WETHINGTON, Olin L.
Steptoe and Johnson
1330 Connecticut Ave., N.W., Washington, DC 20036
Telephone: (202) 429-3000
Registered as lobbyist at U.S. Congress.
Clients:
Ausimont U.S.A.
NI Industries

WETMORE, Thomas E.
Johns and Carson
12501 Old Columbia Pike, Silver Spring, MD 20904
Telephone: (301) 680-6320

WETTERHAHN, Mark J.
Conner and Wetterhahn, P.C.
1747 Pennsylvania Ave., N.W. Suite 1050, Washington,
DC 20006
Telephone: (202) 833-3500
Clients:
Cincinnati Gas and Electric Co.
Gulf States Utilities Co.
Niagara Mohawk Power Corp.
Public Service Electric and Gas Co.
U.S. Ecology

WETZEL, John F.
Assistant to the V. President, Ass'n of American Railroads
50 F Street, N.W., Washington, DC 20001
Telephone: (202) 639-2100
Registered as lobbyist at U.S. Congress.

WEWER, William
American Tax Reduction Movement
2113 National Press Building, Washington, DC 20045
Telephone: (202) 232-7443
Registered as lobbyist at U.S. Congress.

WEXLER, Anne
Chairwoman, Wexler, Reynolds, Fuller, Harrison and
Schule, Inc.
1317 F St., N.W., Suite 600, Washington, DC 20004
Telephone: (202) 638-2121
Registered as lobbyist at U.S. Congress.
Registered as Foreign Agent: (#3306).
Background: Former Assistant to President Jimmy Carter
for public liaison.
Clients:
Allied-Signal Inc.
Columbia Hospital for Women Medical Center
Foothills Pipe Lines (Yukon), Ltd.
General Motors Corp.
New England Electric System
NOVA, An Alberta Corp.
Novacor Chemicals, Ltd.

**WEXLER, REYNOLDS, FULLER, HARRISON AND
SCHULE, INC.**
1317 F St., N.W., Suite 600, Washington, DC 20004
Telephone: (202) 638-2121

Background: A government relations and public affairs
consulting firm.
Members of firm representing listed organizations:
Ames, Kristen, Junior Assoicate
Background: Staff Assistant, House Energy and Commerce Committee, 1985-88.
Bevels, Terry D., President
Carter, David W., Associate
Background: Former staff member, House Appropriations Committee.
Fuller, Craig L., President
Background: Former Chief of Staff to Vice President
George Bush.
Gaskill, Stephen, Associate
Harrison, Gail, Senior V. President
Herlihy-Gearan, Mary H., Associate
Ingle, R. Edward, Associate
Background: Former Senior Budget Examiner, Office of
Management and Budget.
Kinard, Lisa P., Associate
Background: Former Legislative Assistant to Rep.
Augustus F. Hawkins (D-CA).
Reynolds, Nancy Clark, V. Chairman
Ris, William K. (Jr.), Principal
Background: Former Counsel, Senate Committee on
Commerce, Science and Transportation, 1978-83.
Schule, Robert M., Senior V. President
Background: Former Special Assistant for Congressional Liaison in the White House under President Jimmy Carter.
Shanahan, Kathleen M., Senior Associate
Background: Served with the National Security Council, 1982-85, and the Office of the Vice President,
1985-89.
Snape, Dale, Principal
Waz, Joseph W. (Jr.), Principal and General
Counsel
Background: Responsibilities include Treasurer, Wexler,
Reynolds, Fuller, Harrison & Schule Political Action
Committee.
Wexler, Anne, Chairwoman
Background: Former Assistant to President Jimmy
Carter for public liaison.
Wolpe, Bruce, Principal
Clients:
Aetna Life & Casualty Co.
Allied-Signal Inc. *(Nancy Clark Reynolds, Anne Wexler)*
American Airlines *(William K. Ris, Jr.)*
American Institute for Foreign Study *(Nancy Clark
Reynolds, Bruce Wolpe)*
American Public Transit Ass'n *(Terry D. Bevels, William K. Ris, Jr.)*
Columbia Hospital for Women Medical Center
(Gail Harrison, Nancy Clark Reynolds, Anne Wexler)
Committee for America's Copyright Community
(Joseph W. Waz, Jr.)
Communications Satellite Corp. (COMSAT) *(Joseph W. Waz, Jr., Bruce Wolpe)*
Consortium of State Maritime Schools *(Terry D.
Bevels)*
Coopers and Lybrand *(Robert M. Schule, Bruce Wolpe)*
Foothills Pipe Lines (Yukon), Ltd. *(Gail Harrison,
Anne Wexler, Bruce Wolpe)*
General Motors Corp. *(Robert M. Schule, Anne Wexler)*
Manhattan Building Cos., Inc. *(Nancy Clark Reynolds)*
Massachusetts Maritime Academy *(Terry D. Bevels)*
MCI Communications Corp. *(William K. Ris, Jr., Joseph W. Waz, Jr., Bruce Wolpe)*
Monarch Capital Corp.
Motion Picture Ass'n of America *(Dale Snape, Joseph
W. Waz, Jr.)*
Nat'l Ass'n of Social Workers *(Kristen Ames)*
Nat'l Gypsum Co. *(Robert M. Schule, Dale Snape)*
New England Aquarium *(Terry D. Bevels)*
New England Electric System *(Anne Wexler)*
NOVA, An Alberta Corp. *(Anne Wexler, Bruce Wolpe)*
Novacor Chemicals, Ltd. *(Anne Wexler, Bruce Wolpe)*
Oceanic Institute *(Terry D. Bevels)*
Oregon, State of *(Terry D. Bevels, Robert M. Schule)*
Simon Wiesenthal Center/Museum of Tolerance
(Nancy Clark Reynolds)
Training Media Distributors Ass'n *(Joseph W. Waz,
Jr.)*
Wexler, Reynolds, Fuller, Harrison and Schule
Political Action Committee

WEYL, Nancy Katherine
Legis. Analyst, Government Relations, Nat'l Ass'n of
REALTORS
777 14th St., N.W., Washington, DC 20005
Telephone: (202) 383-1000
Registered as lobbyist at U.S. Congress.

WEYRICH, Paul M.
National Chairman, Free Congress Political Action Committee
717 2nd St., N.E., Washington, DC 20002
Telephone: (202) 546-3000
Background: A former aide to Senator Gordon Allott of
Colorado and a founder of the Heritage Foundation. Also
serves as President, Free Congress Foundation, and President, Coalitions for America.

WHALEN COMPANY, INC., The
1717 K St., N.W. Suite 706, Washington, DC 20006
Telephone: (202) 293-5540
Background: Public affairs and communications consul-
tants.
Members of firm representing listed organizations:
Secrest, David W.
Whalen, Joan M.
Whalen, R. Christopher, Senior V. President
Whalen, Richard J., Chairman
Organizations represented:
Chile, Embassy of *(Richard J. Whalen)*
Equitable Life Assurance Soc. of the U.S. *(David
W. Secrest, Richard J. Whalen)*
Toshiba America, Inc. *(Richard J. Whalen)*
Toyota Motor Sales, U.S.A. *(David W. Secrest, Richard
J. Whalen)*

WHALEN, Curtis E.
V. President, Governmental Affairs, Transco Energy Co.
555 13th St., N.W., Suite 430 West, Washington, DC
20004
Telephone: (202) 628-3060
Registered as lobbyist at U.S. Congress.

WHALEN, Joan M.
Whalen Company, Inc., The
1717 K St., N.W. Suite 706, Washington, DC 20006
Telephone: (202) 293-5540

WHALEN, Mary L.
Williams and Jensen, P.C.
1101 Connecticut Ave., N.W., Suite 500, Washington, DC
20036
Telephone: (202) 659-8201
Background: Formerly a legislative staff member, U.S. Sen-
ate Committee on Veterans' Affairs and a legislative ana-
lyst with the Library of Congress Congresional Research
Service.
Clients:
Bass Group, Robert M.
Century 21 Political Action Committee
Century 21 Real Estate Corp.
Financial Security Assurance, Inc.
First Boston Corp.

WHALEN, R. Christopher
Senior V. President, Whalen Company, Inc., The
1717 K St., N.W. Suite 706, Washington, DC 20006
Telephone: (202) 293-5540

WHALEN, Richard J.
Chairman, Whalen Company, Inc., The
1717 K St., N.W. Suite 706, Washington, DC 20006
Telephone: (202) 293-5540
Organizations represented:
Chile, Embassy of
Equitable Life Assurance Soc. of the U.S.
Toshiba America, Inc.
Toyota Motor Sales, U.S.A.

WHALEN, Thomas J.
Condon and Forsyth
1100 15th St., N.W., Suite 300, Washington, DC 20005
Telephone: (202) 289-0500
Clients:
Air Pacific Ltd.
British Airtours Ltd.
Qantas Airways

WHARTON, Ellan K.
Washington Counsel, du Pont de Nemours and Co., E. I.
1701 Pennsylvania Ave., N.W., Suite 900, Washington, DC
20006
Telephone: (202) 728-3600
Registered as lobbyist at U.S. Congress.

WHARTON, Jody
Exec. Director, Business Coalition for Fair Competition
1725 K St., N.W. Suite 412, Washington, DC 20006
Telephone: (202) 887-5872
Background: Former staff member, House Small Business
Committee.

WHATLEY, George C.
Carmen Group, The
1667 K St., N.W., Suite 700, Washington, DC 20006
Telephone: (202) 785-0500
Registered as Foreign Agent: (#4233).
Clients:
Committee for Free Elections and Democracy in
Nicaragua

WHEAT, Leonard P.
Director, Government Relations, American Dental Ass'n
1111 14th St., N.W. Suite 1200, Washington, DC 20005
Telephone: (202) 898-2400
Registered as lobbyist at U.S. Congress.

WHEATON, George R.
V. President, American Institutes for Research
3333 K St., N.W., Suite 300, Washington, DC 20007
Telephone: (202) 342-5000

WHEELER AND ASSOC., Ed
1629 K St., N.W. Suite 1100, Washington, DC 20006
Telephone: (202) 785-6707
Background: Consultants specializing in government affairs.
Members of firm representing listed organizations:
Wheeler, Edwin M.

WHEELER, Douglas
Executive V. President/Conservation F'dn, World Wildlife
Fund/The Conservation Foundation
1250 24th St., N.W., Washington, DC 20037
Telephone: (202) 293-4800

WHEELER, Edward K.
Wheeler and Wheeler
808 17th St., N.W. Suite 400, Washington, DC 20006
Telephone: (202) 467-0500
Registered as Foreign Agent: (#3262).

WHEELER, Edwin M.
Wheeler and Assoc., Ed
1629 K St., N.W. Suite 1100, Washington, DC 20006
Telephone: (202) 785-6707
Registered as lobbyist at U.S. Congress.

WHEELER, Gordon B.
Director, Public Affairs, Health Insurance Ass'n of America
1025 Connecticut Ave., N.W. Suite 1200, Washington, DC
20036
Telephone: (202) 223-7780
Registered as lobbyist at U.S. Congress.
Background: Former Special Assistant to the President for
Legislative Affairs and Director, Congressional Relations.

WHEELER, Larry M.
Director, Congressional Affairs, Hughes Aircraft Co.
1100 Wilson Blvd. 20th Floor, Arlington, VA 22209
Telephone: (703) 525-1550

WHEELER, Porter
V. President, Jefferson Group, The
1341 G St., N.W., Suite 1100, Washington, DC 20005
Telephone: (202) 638-3535
Clients:
Investment Partnership Ass'n

WHEELER, Sandra
Grassroots Coordinator, Nat'l Committee to Preserve So-
cial Security and Medicare
2000 K St., N.W. Suite 800, Washington, DC 20006
Telephone: (202) 822-9459
Registered as lobbyist at U.S. Congress.

WHEELER, Thomas C.
Pettit & Martin
1800 Massachusetts Ave., N.W., Washington, DC 20036

Telephone: (202) 785-5153

WHEELER AND WHEELER
808 17th St., N.W. Suite 400, Washington, DC 20006
Telephone: (202) 467-0500
Members of firm representing listed organizations:

Wheeler, Edward K.
Clients:
Chicago and Northwestern Transportation Co.

WHELER, Brad
President, Merit Shop Foundation
729 15th St., N.W., Washington, DC 20005
Telephone: (202) 637-8800

WHIPPLE, David D.
Exec. Director, Ass'n of Former Intelligence Officers
6723 Whittier Ave. Suite 303A, McLean, VA 22101
Telephone: (703) 790-0320

WHIPPLE, Davis
Exec. V. President, Pagan Internat'l Inc.
1925 N. Lynn St. Suite 903, Washington, DC 22209
Telephone: (703) 528-4177

WHITAKER, A. Duncan
Howrey and Simon
1730 Pennsylvania Ave., N.W., Washington, DC 20006-
4793
Telephone: (202) 783-0800
Background: Trial Attorney, Antitrust Division, Depart-
ment of Justice, 1957-59.
Clients:
Mobil Corp.
Sun Pipe Line Co.

WHITAKER, John C.
V. President, Public Affairs, Union Camp Corp.
2021 L St., N.W., Suite 320, Washington, DC 20036-4909
Telephone: (202) 785-0320
Registered as lobbyist at U.S. Congress.

WHITAKER, L. Paige
Lachelli, Waller and Associates
600 Maryland Ave., S.W., Suite 200A East Wing, Washington, DC 20024
Telephone: (202) 863-1472

WHITE AND ASSOCIATES
207 Pennsylvania Ave., S.E., Washington, DC 20003
Telephone: (202) 547-5557
Members of firm representing listed organizations:
White, Eric B., CEO
Will, Paulette
Clients:
American Democratic Political Action Commit-
tee *(Eric B. White)*
Pro-Choice Fund *(Paulette Will)*

WHITE-CALL, Elizabeth
Ass't Director of Public Affairs, Independent Insurance
Agents of America
600 Pennsylvania Ave., S.E., Suite 200, Washington, DC
20003
Telephone: (202) 544-5833

WHITE & CASE
1747 Pennsylvania Ave., N.W., Suite 500, Washington, DC
20006
Telephone: (202) 872-0013
Background: The information below was obtained from
public records and submitted for confirmation to this
firm, which declined to confirm or correct the informa-
tion.
Members of firm representing listed organizations:
Barnum, John W.
Background: General Counsel, 1971-73; Under Secre-
tary, 1973-74; Deputy Secretary, 1974-77; U.S. De-
partment of Transportation.
Lamm, Carolyn B.
McAvoy, John J.
Clients:
Costa Rica, Central Bank of
Federal Paper Board Co. *(John W. Barnum)*
Gabon, Republic of
George Washington Corp. *(Carolyn B. Lamm)*

Guinea, Government of
Honduras, Government of
Indonesia, Bank of
Indonesia, Government of
Morocco, Kingdom of
Parker Drilling Co. *(Carolyn B. Lamm)*
Peru, Government of
RIV-SKF Industrie S.p.A. *(John W. Barnum)*
Singapore, Embassy of
Sri Lanka, Government of
Suriname, Government of
Thailand, Embassy of
Tunisia, Embassy of
Turkey, Central Bank of
Turkey, Government of *(Carolyn B. Lamm, John J. McAvoy)*
Zaire, Bank of

WHITE, Deborah A.
Director, Federal Government Relations, ARCO
1333 New Hampshire Ave., N.W., Suite 1001, Washington, DC 20036
Telephone: (202) 457-6265
Registered as lobbyist at U.S. Congress.

WHITE, Deborah A.
Exec. Assistant, Nat'l Ass'n of Conservation Districts
509 Capitol Court, N.E., Washington, DC 20002
Telephone: (202) 547-6223

WHITE, Eric B.
CEO, White and Associates
207 Pennsylvania Ave., S.E., Washington, DC 20003
Telephone: (202) 547-5557
Clients:
American Democratic Political Action Committee

WHITE, FINE, AND VERVILLE
1156 15th St., N.W. Suite 1100, Washington, DC 20005
Telephone: (202) 659-2900
Members of firm representing listed organizations:
Fulton, Richard A.
Background: Assistant to Senator Allen J. Ellender of Louisiana, 1960-62.
Havens, Arnold I.
Leyton, Peter S.
Marvin, Michael L., Legislative Director
Background: Legislative Director/Press Secretary to Rep. Frank Horton (R-NY), 1985-88. Administrative Assistant to Rep. Silvio Conte (R-MA), 1988-89.
Saner, Robert J. (II)
Usera, J. Andrew
Background: Legislative Assistant to Hon. Jaime Benitez, Resident Commissioner from Puerto Rico, 1977-79; Legislative Assistant to Hon. Baltasar Corrada, Resident Commissioner from Puerto Rico, 1977-79. Deputy Director, Legislative Liaison, Community Services Administration, 1980-81.
Verville, Richard E.
Background: Special Assistant to the Secretary, HEW 1970; Deputy Assistant Secretary, HEW 1971-73.
White, Lee C.
Background: Attorney, Division of Law, TVA, 1950-54; Legislative Assistant to Senator John F. Kennedy, 1954-57; Counsel, U.S. Senate Select Committee on Small Business, 1957-58; Admin. Assistant to Senator John Cooper, 1958-61; Assistant Special Counsel to President Kennedy, 1961-63. Special Counsel to President Johnson, 1963-66; Chairman, Federal Power Commission, 1966-69. Campaign Manager for Sargent Shriver, 1972.
Clients:
American Academy of Physical Medicine and Rehabilitation *(Richard E. Verville)*
American Ass'n of Nurse Anesthetists *(Richard E. Verville)*
American Chiropractic Registry of Radiologic Technologists *(Richard A. Fulton)*
American Congress of Rehabilitation Medicine *(Richard E. Verville)*
Armstrong World Industries, Inc. *(Arnold I. Havens)*
Ass'n of American Railroads *(Arnold I. Havens)*
Ass'n of Metropolitan Sewerage Agencies *(Lee C. White)*
Ass'n of Metropolitan Water Agencies *(Robert J. Saner, II)*

Ass'n of Theological Schools in the United States and Canada, The *(Richard A. Fulton)*
Burlington Northern Railroad *(Arnold I. Havens)*
CSX Corp. *(Arnold I. Havens, Michael L. Marvin)*
Helen Keller Internat'l *(Richard E. Verville)*
Illinois Ass'n of Colleges and Schools *(Richard A. Fulton)*
Joint Council on Allergy and Immunology *(Richard E. Verville)*
Marketing Education Ass'n *(Richard A. Fulton)*
Medical Group Management Ass'n *(Robert J. Saner, II)*
MetPath Inc. *(Arnold I. Havens)*
Nat'l Ass'n of Health Career Schools *(Richard A. Fulton)*
Nat'l Multiple Sclerosis Soc. *(Richard E. Verville)*

WHITE, Frances
Assoc Gen Couns, Legislation Div, DEPARTMENT OF HEALTH AND HUMAN SERVICES
200 Independence Ave., S.W., Washington, DC 20201
Telephone: (202) 245-7760

WHITE, George A.
Secretary, Rubber Manufacturers Ass'n
1400 K St., N.W., Washington, DC 20005
Telephone: (202) 682-4800

WHITE, Jack
Exec. Director, Coalition for the Homeless
2824 Sherman Ave., N.W., Washington, DC 20001
Telephone: (202) 328-1184

WHITE, Jeffrey
Staff Attorney, Ass'n of Trial Lawyers of America
1050 31st St., N.W., Washington, DC 20007
Telephone: (202) 965-3500

WHITE, Jennifer J.
Senior Associate, Center for Security Policy
1250 24th St., N.W., Washington, DC 20037
Telephone: (202) 466-0515
Background: Special Ass't to the Director General, Dept. of Commerce, 1983-84; House Foreign Affairs Committee, Subcommittee on Internat'l Economic Policy and Trade, 1984-89.

WHITE, Jocelyn
V. President, Gov't Relations, APCO Associates
1155 21st St., N.W., Suite 1000, Washington, DC 20036
Telephone: (202) 778-1000
Clients:
Outboard Marine Corp.

WHITE, John Thomas, III
Washington Representative, Tenneco Inc.
490 L'Enfant Plaza East, S.W. Suite 2202, S.W., Washington, DC 20024
Telephone: (202) 554-2850
Registered as lobbyist at U.S. Congress.

WHITE, Justus P.
V. President, Cambridge Internat'l, Inc.
1600 Wilson Blvd., Suite 713, Arlington, VA 22209
Telephone: (703) 524-1068
Registered as lobbyist at U.S. Congress.
Clients:
Eastern Technologies, Ltd.
General Dynamics Corp.
General Dynamics Valley Systems Division
McDonnell Douglas Helicopter Co.
Optic-Electronic Corp.
Textron Inc.

WHITE, Kazuko
Assistant Manager, Mitsubishi Internat'l Corp.
655 15th St., N.W., Suite 860, Washington, DC 20005
Telephone: (202) 638-1101

WHITE, Keith
Meyers & Associates
412 First St., S.E., Suite 100, Washington, DC 20003
Telephone: (202) 484-2773
Registered as lobbyist at U.S. Congress.
Clients:
American Beekeeping Federation

WHITE, Larry
Legislative Representative, American Ass'n of Retired Persons
1909 K St., N.W., Washington, DC 20049
Telephone: (202) 872-4700
Registered as lobbyist at U.S. Congress.

WHITE, Lee C.
White, Fine, and Verville
1156 15th St., N.W. Suite 1100, Washington, DC 20005
Telephone: (202) 659-2900
Background: Attorney, Division of Law, TVA, 1950-54; Legislative Assistant to Senator John F. Kennedy, 1954-57; Counsel, U.S. Senate Select Committee on Small Business, 1957-58; Admin. Assistant to Senator John Cooper, 1958-61; Assistant Special Counsel to President Kennedy, 1961-63. Special Counsel to President Johnson, 1963-66; Chairman, Federal Power Commission, 1966-69. Campaign Manager for Sargent Shriver, 1972.
Clients:
Ass'n of Metropolitan Sewerage Agencies

WHITE, Leland J.
Government Relations Representative, Nat'l Utility Contractors Ass'n
1235 Jefferson Davis Hwy. Suite 606, Arlington, VA 22202
Telephone: (703) 486-2100
Registered as lobbyist at U.S. Congress.

WHITE, Margita E.
President, Ass'n of Maximum Service Telecasters, Inc.
1400 16th St., N.W. Suite 610, Washington, DC 20036
Telephone: (202) 462-4351
Registered as lobbyist at U.S. Congress.

WHITE, Ray
Director, Congressional Relations, Harris Corp.
1201 East Abingdon Drive Suite 300, Alexandria, VA 22314
Telephone: (703) 548-9200
Registered as lobbyist at U.S. Congress.

WHITE, Richard H.
V. Pres., Legis. Affrs., Federal Relats., Tobacco Institute
1875 Eye St., N.W., Suite 800, Washington, DC 20006
Telephone: (202) 457-4821
Registered as lobbyist at U.S. Congress.

WHITE, Robert E.
President, Internat'l Center for Development Policy
731 Eighth St., S.E., Washington, DC 20003
Telephone: (202) 547-3800

WHITE, Robert L., Jr.
Manager, Government Affairs, Nat'l Electrical Contractors Ass'n
13th floor, 7315 Wisconsin Ave., Bethesda, MD 20814
Telephone: (301) 657-3110
Background: Serves as Chairman, Legislative Committee, Nat'l Construction Industry Council and represents the Associated Specialty Contractors and the Electrical Contractors Political Action Committee.

WHITE, Rosanne T.
Exec. Director, Technology Student Ass'n
1914 Association Drive, Reston, VA 22091
Telephone: (703) 860-9000

WHITE, Stephanie A.
Fincke & White
1900 L St., N.W., Suite 500, Washington, DC 20036
Telephone: (202) 331-8414
Registered as lobbyist at U.S. Congress.
Background: Attorney Advisor to Assistant Secretary for Civil Rights, U.S. Department of Education. Minority Counsel, House Committee on the District of Columbia, 1986-87.
Clients:
Magnetic Technologies Corp.
Pitney-Bowes, Inc.

WHITE, Dr. Steven C.
Dir., Reimb'rsmnt P'lcy Div., Gov't Afrs, American Speech-Language-Hearing Ass'n
10801 Rockville Pike, Rockville, MD 20852
Telephone: (301) 897-5700
Registered as lobbyist at U.S. Congress.

WHITE, Susan J.
Legis. Rep., Taxation & Finance, Nat'l Ass'n of Counties
440 First St., N.W., Washington, DC 20001
Telephone: (202) 393-6226
Background: Also serves as contact for the Nat'l Ass'n of County Treasurers and Finance Officers.

WHITE, Toni D.
Legislative Liaison (Def. Syst. & Elec.), Texas Instruments
1745 Jefferson Davis Hwy. Suite 605, Arlington, VA 22202
Telephone: (703) 892-9333
Registered as lobbyist at U.S. Congress.

WHITE, Valerie
Degnon Associates, Inc.
6728 Old McLean Village Drive, McLean, VA 22101
Telephone: (703) 556-9222
Clients:
Ass'n of State and Territorial Health Officials

WHITE, Ward H.
V. Pres., Government and Public Affairs, United States Telephone Ass'n
900 19th St., N.W., Suite 800, Washington, DC 20006-2102
Telephone: (202) 835-3100
Registered as lobbyist at U.S. Congress.

WHITE, William R.
Kaplan, Russin and Vecchi
1215 17th St., N.W., Washington, DC 20036
Telephone: (202) 887-0353
Registered as lobbyist at U.S. Congress.
Registered as Foreign Agent: (#4092).
Background: Administrative Assistant to Senator John Glenn (D-OH), 1975-84.
Clients:
Caribbean Trade and Apparel Coalition (C-TAC)

WHITEHEAD, Alfred K.
President, Internat'l Ass'n of Fire Fighters
1750 New York Ave., N.W., Washington, DC 20006
Telephone: (202) 737-8484

WHITEHEAD, Donald
Anderson and Pendleton, C.A.
1000 Connecticut Ave., N.W., Suite 1220, Washington, DC 20036
Telephone: (202) 659-2334
Registered as lobbyist at U.S. Congress.
Clients:
Appalachian Regional Commission, States' Washington Representative of
Emergent Technologies, Inc.

WHITEHOUSE, Theodore C.
Willkie Farr and Gallagher
1155 21st St., N.W., 6th Fl., Washington, DC 20036-3302
Telephone: (202) 328-8000
Clients:
Cable and Wireless North America
Dun & Bradstreet

WHITFIELD, Dennis E.
Managing Partner, Brock Group, The
1130 Connecticut Ave., N.W. Suite 350, Washington, DC 20036
Telephone: (202) 296-1901
Background: Director of Political Affairs, Director of Education and Training, and Regional Political Director for the Southeast, Republican National Committee, 1977-80. Chief of Staff, Office of the U.S. Trade Representative, 1981-85. Deputy Secretary of Labor, 1985-89.

WHITFILL, Aileen
Senior Health Specialist, Children's Defense Fund
122 C St., N.W., Washington, DC 20001
Telephone: (202) 628-8787
Registered as lobbyist at U.S. Congress.

WHITING, Fred
Director, Public Affairs, American Occupational Therapy Ass'n
1383 Piccard Drive, Suite 300 P.O. Box 1725, Rockville, MD 20850
Telephone: (301) 948-9626

WHITING, Richard M.
General Counsel and Secretary, Ass'n of Bank Holding Companies
730 15th St., N.W., Suite 820, Washington, DC 20005
Telephone: (202) 393-1158
Registered as lobbyist at U.S. Congress.
Background: Serves as contact for Ass'n of Bank Holding Companies Political Action Committee.

WHITLEY, Elizabeth
Asst. Dir., Nat'l Affairs Division, American Farm Bureau Federation
600 Maryland Ave., S.W., Washington, DC 20024
Telephone: (202) 484-3600
Registered as lobbyist at U.S. Congress.

WHITMAN, Cameron
Field Director, U.S. English
818 Connecticut Ave., N.W. Suite 200, Washington, DC 20006
Telephone: (202) 833-0100
Registered as lobbyist at U.S. Congress.

WHITMAN, James A.
Manager, Agency & Reg. Afrs/Gen. Counsel, Nat'l Ass'n of Chain Drug Stores
Box 1417-D49, Alexandria, VA 22313
Telephone: (703) 549-3001
Registered as lobbyist at U.S. Congress.
Background: Contact for the Ass'n Political Action Committee.

WHITMIRE, Robert L.
Corp. Mgr., Legislative Affairs-Navy, General Dynamics Corp.
1745 Jefferson Davis Hwy., Suite 1000, Arlington, VA 22202
Telephone: (703) 553-1226
Registered as lobbyist at U.S. Congress.

WHITMORE, Susan
Director, Communications, Handgun Control, Inc.
1225 Eye St., N.W., Suite 1100, Washington, DC 20005
Telephone: (202) 898-0792

WHITNEY, Steven C.
Director, Nat'l Parks Program, Wilderness Soc.
1400 Eye St., N.W., 10th Floor, Washington, DC 20005
Telephone: (202) 842-3400
Registered as lobbyist at U.S. Congress.
Background: Legislative Assistant to Rep. Leon E. Panetta (D-CA), 1984-85.

WHITSITT, William F.
V. President, Government Relations, Oryx Energy Co.
1212 New York Ave., N.W. Suite 1200, Washington, DC 20005-3987
Telephone: (202) 682-1212
Registered as lobbyist at U.S. Congress.

WHITT, Mickki
Program Coordinator, University of Oklahoma
1 Dupont Circle, N.W. Suite 340, Washington, DC 20036
Telephone: (202) 223-9147

WHITTAKER, Patricia A.
Associate Director, Gov't Affairs, Bell Communications Research, Inc.
2101 L St., N.W. Suite 600, Washington, DC 20037
Telephone: (202) 955-4600

WHITTED, Pamela J.
Manager, Federal Government Affairs, Pacific Resources, Inc.
1700 K St., N.W., Suite 502, Washington, DC 20006
Telephone: (202) 223-4623
Registered as lobbyist at U.S. Congress.

WHITTEMORE, Ilsa
Associate Exec. Director, Hotel Sales and Marketing Ass'n Internat'l
1300 L St., N.W., Suite 800, Washington, DC 20005
Telephone: (202) 789-0089

WHITTEN, Jamie L.
Lipsen Whitten & Diamond
1725 DeSales St., N.W., Suite 800, Washington, DC 20036
Telephone: (202) 659-6540

Registered as lobbyist at U.S. Congress.
Background: Trial Attorney, Office of U.S. Attorney, Miami, 1966-70. Trial Attorney, U.S. Department of Justice, 1970-73.

WHITTLE, Robin
Director of Communications, Air Force Ass'n
1501 Lee Hwy., Arlington, VA 22209-1198
Telephone: (703) 247-5800

WHITTLESEY, Judy
Davis Companies, The Susan
1146 19th St., N.W., Washington, DC 20036
Telephone: (202) 775-8881
Registered as lobbyist at U.S. Congress.
Background: Exec. V. President, The Susan Davis Communications Group. Former Chief of Staff, Press Secretary to Joan Mondale. Former Chief of Staff to B.A. Bentsen, Dukakis-Bentsen Campaign, 1988.
Organizations represented:
MayCenters, Inc.

WHITWORTH & ASSOCIATES
1455 Pennsylvania Ave., N.W., Suite 985, Washington, DC 20004
Telephone: (202) 393-0692
Background: A legislative and political affairs consulting firm.
Members of firm representing listed organizations:
Whitworth, Ralph V.
Background: A former aide to Senator Paul Laxalt (R-NV).
Clients:
Mesa Limited Partnership *(Ralph V. Whitworth)*

WHITWORTH, Ralph V.
Whitworth & Associates
1455 Pennsylvania Ave., N.W., Suite 985, Washington, DC 20004
Telephone: (202) 393-0692
Background: A former aide to Senator Paul Laxalt (R-NV).
Clients:
Mesa Limited Partnership

WHOOLEY, Barbara
Capitol Associates, Inc.
426 C St., N.E., Washington, DC 20002
Telephone: (202) 544-1880
Registered as lobbyist at U.S. Congress.

WHORTON, Ronald E.
Exec. V. President, American Ass'n for Clinical Chemistry
2029 K St., N.W., 7th Floor, Washington, DC 20006
Telephone: (202) 857-0717

WHYTE, Kathleen M.
V. President, Government Affairs, Sterling Drug Inc.
1776 Eye St., N.W. Suite 1060, Washington, DC 20006
Telephone: (202) 857-3450
Registered as lobbyist at U.S. Congress.

WHYTE, Sandra Butler
Exec. Director, Nat'l Perinatal Ass'n
101 1/2 South Union St., Alexandria, VA 22314-3323
Telephone: (703) 549-5523

WIACEK, Raymond J.
Jones, Day, Reavis and Pogue
1450 G St., N.W., Suite 700, Washington, DC 20005-2088
Telephone: (202) 879-3939
Registered as lobbyist at U.S. Congress.
Clients:
Pfizer, Inc.

WIBLE, Robert C.
Exec. Director, Nat'l Conference of States on Building Codes and Standards
481 Carlisle Drive, Herndon, VA 22070
Telephone: (703) 437-0100

WICE, Jeffrey M.
O'Connor & Hannan
1919 Pennsylvania Ave., N.W., Suite 800, Washington, DC 20006
Telephone: (202) 887-1400
Registered as lobbyist at U.S. Congress.
Clients:
Democratic State Legislative Leaders Ass'n
New York State Assembly

WICKENDEN, David
V. President, Fleishman-Hillard, Inc
1301 Connecticut Ave., N.W., Washington, DC 20036
Telephone: (202) 659-0330

WICKER, Cynthia
Associate General Counsel, American Trucking Ass'ns
2200 Mill Road, Alexandria, VA 22314
Telephone: (703) 838-1800
Background: Former Federal Trade Commission lawyer.

WICKERT, William E., Jr.
V. President, Federal Gov't Affairs, Bethlehem Steel Corp.
1667 K St., N.W., Suite 600, Washington, DC 20006
Telephone: (202) 775-6203
Registered as lobbyist at U.S. Congress.

WICKHAM, John A., Jr.
President, Armed Forces Communications and Electronics Ass'n Headquarters
4400 Fair Lakes Court, Fairfax, VA 22033
Telephone: (703) 631-6100
Background: General (USA-Ret.).

WICKWIRE GAVIN, P.C.
8230 Boone Blvd. Suite 400, Vienna, VA 22182
Telephone: (703) 790-8750
Clients:
Cogeneration and Independent Power Coalition of America
KN Energy Inc.

WIDENER, Wayne
Secretary-Treasurer, Nat'l Ass'n of Postmasters of the U.S.
8 Herbert St., Alexandria, VA 22305-2600
Telephone: (703) 683-9027

WIDES, Burton V.
Arent, Fox, Kintner, Plotkin & Kahn
1050 Connecticut Ave., N.W., Washington, DC 20036-5339
Telephone: (202) 857-6000
Registered as lobbyist at U.S. Congress.
Background: Legislative Counsel, Sen. Philip A. Hart, 1970-76; Legislative Director and Administrative Assistant, Sen. Paul Sarbanes, 1976-77. Counsel, President's Intelligence Oversight Board, 1977-79. Legislative Counsel, 1979-80, and Counsel, 1981-84, U.S. Senate Committee on the Judiciary.
Clients:
Nat'l Ass'n of College Stores
Nat'l Nutrition Coalition
San Diego, California, City of
Toyota Motor Corp.
Video Software Dealers Ass'n

WIDMEYER, Scott D.
Gallagher-Widmeyer Group Inc., The
1110 Vermont Ave., N.W., Suite 1020, Washington, DC 20005
Telephone: (202) 659-1606
Background: Deputy Press Secretary in the 1980 Presidential campaign of Jimmy Carter and also served in press aide roles in the 1984 campaigns of Walter Mondale and Geraldine Ferraro.
Clients:
American Ass'n for the Advancement of Science
American Federation of Teachers
Carnegie Council on Adolescent Development
Education Commission of the States
Education Week
Edunetics
Grant Foundation, W. T.
Institute for Educational Leadership
Nat'l Alliance of Business
Nat'l Ass'n of Trade and Technical Schools
Nat'l Board of Professional Teaching Standards
Nat'l Center on Education and the Economy
Pelavin Associates
RJR Nabisco Washington, Inc.
United Automobile, Aerospace and Agricultural Implement Workers of America (UAW)
Whittle Communications

WIEDEMER, Anne Marie
Executive Assistant, Ralston Purina Co.
2000 L St., N.W., Suite 801, Washington, DC 20036
Telephone: (202) 223-5302

WIEDERHORN, Helen C.
Legis. Assoc., Corp. & Financial Srvcs., Ford Motor Co.
1350 Eye St., N.W. Suite 1000, Washington, DC 20005
Telephone: (202) 962-5400
Registered as lobbyist at U.S. Congress.

WIEGAND, Douglas W.
Exec. Director, Menswear Retailers of America
2011 Eye St., N.W. Suite 600, Washington, DC 20006
Telephone: (202) 347-1932
Background: Also represents Western/English Retailers of America.

WIELAND, Henry, Jr.
Exec. Director for Special Events, United States Telephone Ass'n
900 19th St., N.W., Suite 800, Washington, DC 20006-2102
Telephone: (202) 835-3100

WIENER, Joshua M.
Senior Fellow, Brookings Institution
1775 Massachusetts Ave., N.W., Washington, DC 20036
Telephone: (202) 797-6000

WIERZYNSKI, Barbara
Gen. Counsel & V.P., Regulatory Affairs, Futures Industry Ass'n
1825 Eye St., N.W., Suite 1040, Washington, DC 20006
Telephone: (202) 466-5460
Registered as lobbyist at U.S. Congress.

WIESE, Arthur E.
V. President, Public Affairs, American Petroleum Institute
1220 L St., N.W., Washington, DC 20005
Telephone: (202) 682-8060

WIESSNER, Andy
V. President, Kogovsek & Associates, Inc.
1455 Pennsylvania Ave., N.W., Suite 950, Washington, DC 20004
Telephone: (202) 639-8899
Registered as lobbyist at U.S. Congress.
Background: Former Counsel, U.S. House of Representatives Interior Subcommittee on Public Lands.

WIGGLESWORTH, Margaret S.
Exec. Director, Coalition of Service Industries
2001 M St., N.W. 4th Floor, Washington, DC 20036
Telephone: (202) 467-3054
Background: Former staff member in the office of Sen. Charles Mc Mathias (R-MD), 1977-82.

WIGHT, William J.
V. President, Government Relations, Imo Industries
727 23rd St. South, Arlington, VA 22202
Telephone: (703) 920-4500

WIGMAN AND COHEN
1735 Jefferson Davis Hwy. Crystal Sq. 3, Suite 200, Arlington, VA 22202
Telephone: (703) 892-4300
Members of firm representing listed organizations:
Cohen, Herbert, Chairman of the Board
Patrick, Ralph C.
Wigman, Victor M., President
Clients:
Southwire Co. *(Victor M. Wigman)*

WIGMAN, Victor M.
President, Wigman and Cohen
1735 Jefferson Davis Hwy. Crystal Sq. 3, Suite 200, Arlington, VA 22202
Telephone: (703) 892-4300
Clients:
Southwire Co.

WILBER, W. Scott
Director, Dept. of Congressional Affairs, American Medical Ass'n
1101 Vermont Ave., N.W., Washington, DC 20005
Telephone: (202) 789-7400
Registered as lobbyist at U.S. Congress.

Telephone: (202) 857-1100

WILBUR, Phil
Director, Health Advoc. Resource Center, Advocacy Institute, The
1730 Rhode Island Ave., N.W. Suite 600, Washington, DC 20036
Telephone: (202) 659-8475

WILBUR, Robert H.
V. President, Government Relations, Smith, Bucklin and Associates
1101 Connecticut Ave., N.W., Suite 700, Washington, DC 20036
Telephone: (202) 857-1100
Background: Serves as Exec. Director, Ass'n of Professors of Medicine; V. President, Government Relations of the Health Industry Distributors Ass'n; Director of Government Relations of the Battery Council Internat'l, Amusement and Music Operators Ass'n, the Nat'l Ass'n of Food Equipment Manufacturers and the Popcorn Institute.
Clients:
Adhesives Manufacturers Ass'n
Amusement and Music Operators Ass'n
Amusement and Music Operators Ass'n Political Action Committee
Health Industry Distributors Ass'n
Health Industry Distributors Ass'n Political Action Committee
Nat'l Ass'n of Food Equipment Manufacturers
Popcorn Institute

WILBUR, W. Allan
Exec. Director, Public Affairs, Nat'l Automobile Dealers Ass'n
8400 Westpark Dr., McLean, VA 22102
Telephone: (703) 821-7000

WILBURN, Mary
Chairwoman, DC Chapter, Nat'l Ass'n of Black Women Attorneys
3711 Macomb St., N.W., Washington, DC 20016
Telephone: (202) 966-9693
Background: Formerly with U.S. Department of Labor.

WILCHER, Frank E., Jr.
President, Industrial Safety Equipment Ass'n
1901 North Moore St., Suite 501, Arlington, VA 22209
Telephone: (703) 525-1695

WILCHER, Shirley J.
Director, State Relations & Counsel, Nat'l Ass'n of Independent Colleges and Universities
122 C St., N.W. Suite 750, Washington, DC 20001
Telephone: (202) 347-7512
Registered as lobbyist at U.S. Congress.
Background: Assoc. Counsel, House Education and Labor Committee 1985-90.

WILCOX, Caren A.
Director, Government Relations, Hershey Foods Corp.
Hershey Foods Corp. Administrative Center, Hershey, PA
Telephone: (717) 534-7547

WILCOX, Thomas D.
Exec. Director and General Counsel, Nat'l Ass'n of Stevedores
2011 Eye St., N.W., Washington, DC 20006
Telephone: (202) 296-2810

WILDE, Alexander
Exec. Director, Washington Office on Latin America
110 Maryland Ave., N.E. Suite 404, Washington, DC 20002
Telephone: (202) 544-8045

WILDER, James
Director, External Affairs, Kettering Foundation
444 North Capitol St., N.W. Suite 408, Washington, DC 20001
Telephone: (202) 393-4478

WILDER, Timothy E.
Account Representative, Internat'l Public Strategies, Inc.
1030 15th St., N.W., Suite 408, Washington, DC 20005
Telephone: (202) 371-5604
Registered as Foreign Agent: (#4200).

The listings in this directory are available as *Mailing Labels*. See last page.

WILDEROTTER, James A.
Jones, Day, Reavis and Pogue
1450 G St., N.W., Suite 700, Washington, DC 20005-2088
Telephone: (202) 879-3939
Registered as lobbyist at U.S. Congress.
Background: Special Assistant to the Under Secretary, Department of Commerce, 1971-73. Exec. Assistant to the Secretary, Department of Housing and Urban Development, 1973-74. Associate Deputy Attorney General, Department of Justice, 1974-75. Associate Counsel to the President, 1975-76. General Counsel, Energy Research and Development Administration, 1976-77.
Clients:
Laurel Industries
Morgan Grenfell and Co., Ltd.

WILES, Harry G., II
V. Pres., Federal Government Relations, Wine and Spirits Wholesalers of America
1023 15th St., N.W., 4th Floor, Washington, DC 20005
Telephone: (202) 371-9792
Registered as lobbyist at U.S. Congress.

WILES, Lanny F.
Hecht, Spencer & Associates
499 South Capitol St., S.W., Suite 507, Washington, DC 20003
Telephone: (202) 554-2881
Registered as lobbyist at U.S. Congress.
Clients:
Jacksonville, Florida, City of

WILEY, REIN & FIELDING
1776 K St., N.W., Tenth Floor, Washington, DC 20006-2359
Telephone: (202) 429-7000
Background: The information below was collected from public records and submitted to the firm for confirmation or correction. The firm declined to review the information and asked that it not be listed in this directory.
Members of firm representing listed organizations:
Baran, Jan
  Background: Exec. Assistant to the Chairman, Federal Election Commission, 1977-79.
Brunner, Thomas W.
Dawson, Mimi Weyforth, Lobbyist
  Background: Former Deputy Secretary of Transportation.
Hodges, John A.
Permut, Philip V.
  Background: Served as Trial Attorney: Broadcast Bureau, 1968-73; General Counsel's Office, 1973-74. Special Assistant to Bureau Chief, 1974-76, Chief, Policy and Rules Division, 1976-77 and Deputy Chief, Common Carrier Bureau, Federal Communications Commission, 1977-78.
Senkowski, R. Michael
Smith, Paul C.
Wiley, Richard E.
  Background: General Counsel, 1970-72, Commissioner, 1972-74 and Chairman, 1974-77, Federal Communications Commission.
Clients:
American Newspaper Publishers Ass'n *(Richard E. Wiley)*
BMW of North America *(Mimi Weyforth Dawson)*
Certified Color Manufacturers Ass'n
Communications Satellite Corp. (COMSAT)
CSX Transportation Inc. Political Action Committee
General Electric Information Services *(Mimi Weyforth Dawson)*
GTE Corp.
Information Industry Ass'n
Marine Mammal Coalition *(John A. Hodges, Paul C. Smith)*
Nat'l Ass'n of Public Television Stations *(Paul C. Smith)*
Nat'l Health Care Anti-Fraud Ass'n *(Thomas W. Brunner)*
Nat'l Republican Congressional Committee *(Jan Baran)*
Nat'l Republican Senatorial Committee *(Jan Baran)*
Public Broadcasting Service *(Paul C. Smith)*
Steel Manufacturers Ass'n
Telocator *(R. Michael Senkowski)*
United Parcel Service *(Paul C. Smith)*
United Telecommunications *(Philip V. Permut)*

Western Union Corp.

WILEY, Richard E.
Wiley, Rein & Fielding
1776 K St., N.W., Tenth Floor, Washington, DC 20006-2359
Telephone: (202) 429-7000
Background: General Counsel, 1970-72, Commissioner, 1972-74 and Chairman, 1974-77, Federal Communications Commission.
Clients:
American Newspaper Publishers Ass'n

WILFINGER, Rebecca
Director, Public Information, American Soc. of Hospital Pharmacists
4630 Montgomery Ave., Bethesda, MD 20814
Telephone: (301) 657-3000

WILHELM, Guenther O.
Deputy Manager, Washington Office, Exxon Corp.
Suite 1100, 1899 L St., N.W., Washington, DC 20036
Telephone: (202) 862-0245
Registered as lobbyist at U.S. Congress.

WILHIDE, Lee
Treasurer, Soc. of American Florists Political Action Committee
1601 Duke St., Alexandria, VA 22314
Telephone: (703) 836-8400

WILHOIT, Gene
Exec. Director, Nat'l Ass'n of State Boards of Education
1012 Cameron St., Alexandria, VA 22314
Telephone: (703) 684-4000

WILKERSON, Carl B.
Senior Counsel, American Council of Life Insurance
1001 Pennsylvania Ave., N.W., Washington, DC 20004-2599
Telephone: (202) 624-2118
Registered as lobbyist at U.S. Congress.

WILKES, ARTIS, HEDRICK AND LANE, CHARTERED
1666 K St., N.W., Suite 1100, Washington, DC 20006
Telephone: (202) 457-7800
Background: The information shown below was obtained from public records and submitted to the firm for confirmation or correction. The firm declined to do so and, commenting that much of the information was incorrect, asked to be omitted from the book.
Members of firm representing listed organizations:
Lane, John D.
McKaig, J. Carter
Clients:
Chesapeake and Potomac Telephone Co. of Maryland
Motorola, Inc.
Westinghouse Broadcasting Co., Inc. *(John D. Lane)*

WILKIE, Edith B.
Exec. Director, Arms Control and Foreign Policy Caucus
House Annex 2 Room 501, Washington, DC 20515
Telephone: (202) 226-3440
Background: Serves also as Exec. Director, Peace Through Law Education Fund.

WILKINS, Gail B.
Davis & Harman
1455 Pennsylvania Ave., N.W. Suite 1200, Washington, DC 20004
Telephone: (202) 347-2230
Registered as lobbyist at U.S. Congress.
Registered as Foreign Agent: (# 4018).
Clients:
Associated Electric and Gas Insurance Services, Ltd.
Dresser Industries
Lloyds of London, Underwriters at

WILKINS, Horace, Jr.
V. President, Gov't & Industry Affairs, Southwestern Bell Corp.
1667 K St., N.W., Suite 1000, Washington, DC 20006
Telephone: (202) 293-8550
Registered as lobbyist at U.S. Congress.

WILKINS, John G.
Dir., Tax Policy for Economic Analysis, Coopers and Lybrand
1800 M St., N.W., Suite 400, Washington, DC 20036
Telephone: (202) 822-4000
Background: Legislative Director for Cong. Robert Torricelli (D-NJ), 1985-86.

WILKINS, Marge L.
Legis Specialist, DEPARTMENT OF INTERIOR - Indian Affairs
18th and C Sts., N.W. Room 4641, Washington, DC 20240
Telephone: (202) 343-5706

WILKINS, Suzanne C.
Director, River Protection, American Rivers
801 Pennsylvania Ave., S.E. Suite 303, Washington, DC 20003-2155
Telephone: (202) 547-6900
Registered as lobbyist at U.S. Congress.

WILKINS, Will
Executive Director, Road Information Program, The (TRIP)
1200 18th St., N.W. Suite 314, Washington, DC 20036
Telephone: (202) 466-6706

WILKINS, William J.
Partner, Wilmer, Cutler and Pickering
2445 M St., N.W., Washington, DC 20037-1420
Telephone: (202) 663-6000
Registered as lobbyist at U.S. Congress.
Background: Former Staff Director and Chief Counsel, U.S. Senate Finance Committee.
Clients:
Bankers Trust Co.
Common Fund, The
Dow Chemical
McDonald's Corp.
PepsiCo, Inc.
Shearson Lehman Hutton
Unisys Corp.

WILKINSON, BARKER, KNAUER AND QUINN
1735 New York Ave., N.W., Suite 600, Washington, DC 20006
Telephone: (202) 783-4141
Members of firm representing listed organizations:
Hein, Werner J.
Knauer, Leon T.
Quinn, Paul S.
  Background: Legislative Assistant to Senator Claiborne Pell of Rhode Island, 1961-62. Member of Democratic Senatorial Campaign Committee Leadership Circle and Business Roundtable since 1983.
Satten, Kenneth E.
Clients:
Akademie Fur Fuhrunskrafte der Deutschen Bundespost
Asociacion Nacional de Fabricantes de Acumuladores, A.C.
BellSouth Corp.
Bonneville Pacific Corp. *(Kenneth E. Satten)*
Empire Blue Cross and Blue Shield
Germany, Ministry of Posts and Communications of the Federal Republic of
KIRO-TV
KSL-TV
Penney Co., J. C.
Security Pacific Nat'l Bank *(Paul S. Quinn)*
Solano Water Authority *(Paul S. Quinn)*

WILKINSON, David A.
General Electric Co.
1331 Pennsylvania Ave., N.W. Suite 800S, Washington, DC 20004
Telephone: (202) 637-4000
Registered as lobbyist at U.S. Congress.

WILKINSON, Theodore S.
President, American Foreign Service Ass'n
2101 E St., N.W., Washington, DC 20037
Telephone: (202) 338-4045

WILKS, Laurice F.
Director, Nat'l Center for Religious Involvement
1115 P. St., N.W., Washington, DC 20005
Telephone: (202) 667-2338

WILL & MUYS, P.C.
1825 Eye St., N.W., Suite 920, Washington, DC 20006
Telephone: (202) 429-4344
Registered as lobbyist at U.S. Congress.
Background: An attorney.
Members of firm representing listed organizations:
   Will, Robert P.
Clients:
   Central Arizona Water Conservation District *(Robert P. Will)*
   Coachella Valley Water District *(Robert P. Will)*
   PHH Corp. *(Robert P. Will)*
   Santa Ana Watershed Project Authority *(Robert P. Will)*
   Signal Landmark *(Robert P. Will)*
   Transmission Agency of Northern California

WILL, Paulette
White and Associates
207 Pennsylvania Ave., S.E., Washington, DC 20003
Telephone: (202) 547-5557
Clients:
   Pro-Choice Fund

WILL, Robert P.
Will & Muys, P.C.
1825 Eye St., N.W., Suite 920, Washington, DC 20006
Telephone: (202) 429-4344
Clients:
   Central Arizona Water Conservation District
   Coachella Valley Water District
   PHH Corp.
   Santa Ana Watershed Project Authority
   Signal Landmark

WILLARD, Lori
Public Relations Representative, Dairy and Food Industries Supply Ass'n
6245 Executive Blvd., Rockville, MD 20852
Telephone: (301) 984-1444

WILLCOX, Alfred B.
Head, Office of Gov'tl & Public Affairs, Mathematical Ass'n of America
1529 18th St., N.W., Washington, DC 20036
Telephone: (202) 387-5200

WILLENS, Howard P.
Wilmer, Cutler and Pickering
2445 M St., N.W., Washington, DC 20037-1420
Telephone: (202) 663-6000
Background: Deputy Assistant Attorney General, Criminal Division, 1961-65.
Clients:
   American Honda Motor Co.
   Ford Motor Co.

WILLENZ, June A.
Exec. Director, American Veterans Committee
1717 Massachusetts Ave., N.W. Suite 203, Washington, DC 20036
Telephone: (202) 667-0090

WILLER, Dr. Barbara A.
Public Affairs Director, Nat'l Ass'n for the Education of Young Children
1834 Connecticut Ave., N.W., Washington, DC 20009
Telephone: (202) 232-8777

WILLER, Jay D.
Manager, Program Coordination, Institute of Gas Technology
1825 K St., N.W. Suite 503, Washington, DC 20006
Telephone: (202) 785-3511

WILLETTS, E. Victor, Jr.
Scribner, Hall and Thompson
1850 K St., N.W. Suite 1100, Washington, DC 20006-2201
Telephone: (202) 331-8585
Registered as lobbyist at U.S. Congress.
Background: Chief Counsel's Office, Internal Revenue Service, 1965-70. Legislation Counsel, Staff of Joint Committee on Internal Revenue Taxation, U.S. Congress, 1965-68.
Clients:
   Security Life Insurance Co. of Denver

WILLHAM, Ralph E.
Director of Governmental Affairs, Sheet Metal Workers' Internat'l Ass'n
1750 New York Ave., N.W. Sixth Floor, Washington, DC 20006
Telephone: (202) 783-5880
Registered as lobbyist at U.S. Congress.
Background: Responsible contact for the Sheet Metal Workers' Internat'l Ass'n Political Action League.

WILLIAMS, Andrew W.
V. President, Energy Policy & Develop't., Potomac Electric Power Co.
1900 Pennsylvania Ave., N.W., Washington, DC 20068
Telephone: (202) 872-2000

WILLIAMS, Arlene
Communications Director, Nat'l Organization of Black Law Enforcement Executives
908 Pennsylvania Ave., S.E., Washington, DC 20003
Telephone: (202) 546-8811

WILLIAMS ASSOCIATES, Cindy
1155 15th St., N.W., Suite 1100, Washington, DC 20005
Telephone: (202) 659-2443
Background: A consultant/lobbyist firm specializing in health care issues.
Members of firm representing listed organizations:
   Williams, Lucinda L., President
Organizations represented:
   Centerra Group, The *(Lucinda L. Williams)*
   HillHaven Corp. *(Lucinda L. Williams)*
   Huskey Realty *(Lucinda L. Williams)*
   Nat'l Medical Enterprises, Inc. *(Lucinda L. Williams)*
   Psychiatric Institutes of America *(Lucinda L. Williams)*
   Vaupel Artistry *(Lucinda L. Williams)*

WILLIAMS, Cindy Deacon
Legislative Representative, Nat'l Wildlife Federation
1400 16th St., N.W., Washington, DC 20036-2266
Telephone: (202) 797-6800
Registered as lobbyist at U.S. Congress.

WILLIAMS AND CONNOLLY
839 17th St., N.W. 1000 Hill Bldg., Washington, DC 20006
Telephone: (202) 331-5000
Members of firm representing listed organizations:
   Aufhauser, David D.
   Baine, Kevin
   Barnett, Robert B.
      Background: Law clerk to U.S. Supreme Court Justice Byron R. White, 1972-73. Legislative Assistant to Senator Walter F. Mondale, 1973-75.
   Collins, Jeremiah C.
   Craig, Gregory
   Daniel, Aubrey M. (III)
   Galbraith, J. Alan
   Genderson, Bruce R.
   Kendall, David E.
      Background: Law Clerk to U.S. Supreme Court Justice Byron R. White, 1971-72.
   Kester, John
   Lucchino, Lawrence
      Background: Counsel, Impeachment Inquiry, U.S. House of Representatives Committee on the Judiciary.
   Sullivan, Brendan V. (Jr.)
   Urbanczyk, Steve
   Vardaman, John W. (Jr.)
      Background: Law Clerk to Justice Hugo L. Black, U.S. Supreme Court, 1965-66.
   Watkins, Robert P.
      Background: Civil Rights Division, Department of Justice, 1965-66. Hearing Counsel, Federal Maritime Commission, 1967. Assistant U.S. Attorney, Washington, DC, 1968-72.
Clients:
   Baltimore Orioles *(Lawrence Lucchino)*
   Catholic University of America
   General Motors Corp. *(Aubrey M. Daniel, III, Robert P. Watkins)*
   Loral/Fairchild Systems *(David D. Aufhauser, John Kester)*
   MCA Inc. *(David E. Kendall)*
   McKechnie Brothers (South Africa) Ltd. *(David D. Aufhauser, Bruce R. Genderson)*
   Motion Picture Ass'n of America

   Nat'l Committee to Preserve Social Security and Medicare *(Steve Urbanczyk)*
   Navistar Internat'l Corp. *(Aubrey M. Daniel, III, J. Alan Galbraith)*
   Omni Internat'l *(Brendan V. Sullivan, Jr.)*
   Washington Post Co. *(Kevin Baine, David E. Kendall)*

WILLIAMS, Coquese
Program Manager, Nat'l Council on the Aging
600 Maryland Ave., S.W. West Wing 100, Washington, DC 20024
Telephone: (202) 479-1200
Background: Serves also as contact, Nat'l Ass'n of Older Worker Employment.

WILLIAMS, Daren R.
Public Relations Associate, Agri/Washington
1629 K St., N.W., Suite 1100, Washington, DC 20006
Telephone: (202) 785-6710
Clients:
   Agricultural Relations Council
   American Agricultural Editors Ass'n
   American Ass'n of Grain Inspection and Weighing Agencies

WILLIAMS, David O., Jr.
Director, Federal Relations, BellSouth Corp.
1133 21st St., N.W., Suite 900, Washington, DC 20036
Telephone: (202) 463-4100

WILLIAMS, DeWitt S.
Exec. Director, Narcotics Education
12501 Old Columbia Pike, Silver Spring, MD 20904
Telephone: (301) 680-6732

WILLIAMS, Eddie N.
President, Joint Center for Political Studies
1301 Pennsylvania Ave., N.W., Washington, DC 20004
Telephone: (202) 626-3500

WILLIAMS, Eliazer A.
Cramer and Haber
1029 Vermont Ave., N.W. 4th Floor, Washington, DC 20005
Telephone: (202) 872-8103
Registered as Foreign Agent: (# 3688).
Clients:
   China, Administration of Shantou Special Economic Zone of

WILLIAMS, Faith M.
Senior Legislative Consultant, New York Life Insurance Co.
600 New Hampshire Ave., N.W., Suite 200, Washington, DC 20037
Telephone: (202) 331-8733
Registered as lobbyist at U.S. Congress.

WILLIAMS, Floyd
Staff V. Pres./Legislative Counsel, Nat'l Ass'n of Home Builders of the U.S.
15th and M Streets, N.W., Washington, DC 20005
Telephone: (202) 822-0470
Registered as lobbyist at U.S. Congress.

WILLIAMS, Francis G.
Exec. V. President, Administration, American Frozen Food Institute
1764 Old Meadow Lane Suite 350, McLean, VA 22102
Telephone: (703) 821-0770
Background: Serves as Exec. Director, Nat'l Frozen Pizza Institute and Treasurer, American Frozen Food Institute Political Action Committee.

WILLIAMS, Hubert
President, Police Foundation
1001 22nd St., N.W., Suite 200, Washington, DC 20037
Telephone: (202) 833-1460

WILLIAMS, J. D.
Chairman of the Board, Williams and Jensen, P.C.
1101 Connecticut Ave., N.W., Suite 500, Washington, DC 20036
Telephone: (202) 659-8201
Background: Former Assistant to the late Senator Robert Kerr of Oklahoma, 1959-61.
Clients:
   Pharmaceutical Manufacturers Ass'n
   Texaco U.S.A.

WILLIAMS, Jack L.
451 New Jersey Ave., S.E., Washington, DC 20003
Telephone: (202) 547-6078
Registered as lobbyist at U.S. Congress.
Organizations represented:
Arkansas Best Corp.
Arkla, Inc.
Cooper Communities
ElectroCom Automation, Inc.
Riceland Foods
Tyson Foods, Inc.

WILLIAMS AND JENSEN, P.C.
1101 Connecticut Ave., N.W., Suite 500, Washington, DC
20036
Telephone: (202) 659-8201
Registered as Foreign Agent: (#3112)
Background: A professional corporation engaged in general
federal practice with activities in the areas of tax, anti-
trust, securities regulation, economic stabilization, trans-
portation, energy, insurance, banking, health, food, drug,
cosmetics, agriculture and related legislative matters.
Members of firm representing listed organizations:
  Baker, George D.
    Background: Former Attorney, Office of Hearings and
    Appeals, U.S. Department of Energy.
  Brack, William T.
  Costello, Ann
  Crigler, Winfield P.
  Edmondson, June E.
  Glennon, Robert E. (Jr.)
  Hart, J. Steven, President
    Background: Former Ass't to the Chair, President's
    Task Force on ERISA Reorganization, Office of
    Management and Budget, 1978-79. Special Assistant
    to the Assistant Attorney General for Legal Policy,
    Department of Justice, 1981-82.
  Jensen, Robert E.
  Martinez, Robert J., Of Counsel
  McMackin, John J. (Jr.)
  Olsen, George G.
  Starr, David
    Background: Legislative Director to Senator Howard
    Metzenbaum (D-OH), 1981-89.
  Whalen, Mary L.
    Background: Formerly a legislative staff member, U.S.
    Senate Committee on Veterans' Affairs and a legisla-
    tive analyst with the Library of Congress Congresion-
    al Research Service.
  Williams, J. D., Chairman of the Board
    Background: Former Assistant to the late Senator Rob-
    ert Kerr of Oklahoma, 1959-61.
  Zall, Barnaby, Of Counsel
Clients:
American Home Products Corp. *(John J. McMackin, Jr.)*
Ass'n of Family Farmers *(Robert E. Glennon, Jr.)*
Bass Group, Robert M. *(Robert E. Glennon, Jr., Mary L. Whalen)*
Century 21 Political Action Committee *(Mary L. Whalen)*
Century 21 Real Estate Corp. *(Mary L. Whalen)*
CIGNA Corp. *(Robert E. Glennon, Jr.)*
College Construction Loan Insurance Ass'n *(William T. Brack)*
Executive Life Insurance Co.
Federation for American Immigration Reform (FAIR) *(Barnaby Zall)*
Financial Security Assurance, Inc. *(Mary L. Whalen)*
First Boston Corp. *(Mary L. Whalen)*
Gamma Corp. *(George D. Baker)*
Goldome FSB *(William T. Brack)*
GTE Corp. *(William T. Brack)*
Higher Education Assistance Foundation *(Winfield P. Crigler)*
Keystone Provident Life Insurance Co. *(Robert E. Glennon, Jr.)*
Lauder Inc., Estee *(George D. Baker)*
Mustang Fuel Corp. *(George D. Baker)*
Nat'l Ass'n of Rehabilitation Agencies *(George G. Olsen)*
Nat'l Board for Professional Training Standards *(J. Steven Hart, David Starr)*
Nat'l Realty Political Action Committee (REAL-PAC) *(June E. Edmondson)*
Nippon Cargo Airlines *(John J. McMackin, Jr.)*
Pharmaceutical Manufacturers Ass'n *(J. D. Williams)*
Pittston Co., The *(J. Steven Hart)*

Recording Industry Ass'n of America *(J. Steven Hart)*
Southern Pacific Transportation Co. *(John J. McMackin, Jr.)*
Southwest Airlines *(John J. McMackin, Jr.)*
Southwestern Bell Corp. *(William T. Brack)*
Student Loan Marketing Ass'n *(Winfield P. Crigler)*
Texaco U.S.A. *(J. D. Williams)*
Texas Air Corp. *(J. Steven Hart)*
Trailer Train Co. *(John J. McMackin, Jr.)*
Turner Broadcasting System, Inc. *(J. Steven Hart)*
United States Telephone Ass'n *(William T. Brack)*
Universal Foods Corp. *(George D. Baker)*
USAA *(Ann Costello)*
Williams and Jensen P.C. Political Action Committee

WILLIAMS, John B.
Collier, Shannon & Scott
1055 Thomas Jefferson St., N.W., Suite 300, Washington,
DC 20007
Telephone: (202) 342-8400

WILLIAMS, Karen Hastie
Of Counsel, Crowell and Moring
1001 Pennsylvania Ave., N.W., Washington, DC 20004-
2505
Telephone: (202) 624-2500
Registered as lobbyist at U.S. Congress.
Background: Administrator, Office of Federal Procurement
Policy, Office of Management and Budget, 1980-81.
Clients:
Crowell and Moring PAC
Design Professionals Coalition

WILLIAMS, Kathy J.
Director, Internat'l & Gov't Affairs, Federal Express Corp.
300 Maryland Ave., N.E., Washington, DC 20002
Telephone: (202) 546-1631

WILLIAMS, Kevin Michael
General Counsel, Regular Common Carrier Conference
2200 Mill Road, Suite 350, Alexandria, VA 22314
Telephone: (703) 838-1971

WILLIAMS, Larry
Washington Dir., Internat'l Program, Sierra Club
408 C St., N.E., Washington, DC 20002
Telephone: (202) 547-1141
Registered as lobbyist at U.S. Congress.

WILLIAMS, Lee
Senior Vice President, American Retail Federation
1616 H St., N.W. 6th Floor, Washington, DC 20006
Telephone: (202) 783-7971
Registered as lobbyist at U.S. Congress.

WILLIAMS, Leonard B.
Director - Legislative Affairs, Bethlehem Steel Corp.
1667 K St., N.W., Suite 600, Washington, DC 20006
Telephone: (202) 775-6200
Registered as lobbyist at U.S. Congress.

WILLIAMS, Lucinda L.
President, Williams Associates, Cindy
1155 15th St., N.W., Suite 1100, Washington, DC 20005
Telephone: (202) 659-2443
Registered as lobbyist at U.S. Congress.
Organizations represented:
Centerra Group, The
HillHaven Corp.
Huskey Realty
Nat'l Medical Enterprises, Inc.
Psychiatric Institutes of America
Vaupel Artistry

WILLIAMS, Maggie
Director of Communications, Children's Defense Fund
122 C St., N.W., Washington, DC 20001
Telephone: (202) 628-8787

WILLIAMS, Marci
Senior V. President and Unit Manager, Hill and Knowlton
Public Affairs Worldwide
Washington Harbour, 901 31st St., N.W., Washington, DC
20007
Telephone: (202) 333-7400
Clients:
Apple Computer, Inc.

David Sarnoff Research Center
Thomson Consumer Electronics, Inc.

WILLIAMS, Marcia E.
Div. V. Pres., Envir. Policy & Planning, Browning-Ferris Industries (D.C.), Inc.
1150 Connecticut Ave., N.W. Suite 500, Washington, DC
20036
Telephone: (202) 223-8151
Registered as lobbyist at U.S. Congress.
Background: Former Director, Office of Solid Waste, Environmental Protection Agency.

WILLIAMS, Margie R.
V. President, Public Affairs, Nat'l Ass'n of Wheat Growers
415 Second St., N.E. Suite 300, Washington, DC 20002
Telephone: (202) 547-7800
Registered as lobbyist at U.S. Congress.

WILLIAMS, Merrill
TCI Washington Group
3701 Connecticut Ave., N.W., Washington, DC 20008
Telephone: (202) 363-2800
Registered as lobbyist at U.S. Congress.
Clients:
Freshwater Press
Galactica Biochemical
Nat'l Credit Improvement Group
Technology Transfer

WILLIAMS, Nathaniel E.
V. President, Government Relations, Nature Conservancy,
The
1815 N. Lynn St, Arlington, VA 22209
Telephone: (703) 841-5300

WILLIAMS, Brig. Gen. P. D.
Legis Asst, DEPARTMENT OF NAVY - United States Ma-
rine Corps
Navy Annex, Arlington Ridge Road, Washington, DC
20380-0001
Telephone: (202) 694-1686

WILLIAMS, Patrick H.
Director, Government Relations, Telecommunications In-
dustry Ass'n
1722 Eye St., N.W., Suite 440, Washington, DC 20006
Telephone: (202) 457-4912
Registered as lobbyist at U.S. Congress.
Background: Former legislative aide to Rep. Dennis Hertel
(D-MI).

WILLIAMS, Paul A.
Chasey Organization, The William
1015 33rd St., N.W., Suite 509, Washington, DC 20007
Telephone: (202) 333-1968

WILLIAMS, Peter
President, Royal Ordnance, Inc.
1101 Wilson Blvd., Suite 1200, Alexandria, VA 22209
Telephone: (703) 516-2731

WILLIAMS, Peter M.
Executive Director of Common Cause of DC, Common
Cause
2030 M St., N.W., Washington, DC 20036
Telephone: (202) 833-1200
Registered as lobbyist at U.S. Congress.

WILLIAMS, Richard T.
Ass't Grassroots Manager, Chemical Manufacturers Ass'n
2501 M St., N.W., Washington, DC 20037
Telephone: (202) 887-1100
Registered as lobbyist at U.S. Congress.

WILLIAMS, Robert
Policy Assoc., Governmental Activities, United Cerebral
Palsy Ass'ns
1522 K St., N.W., Suite 1112, Washington, DC 20005
Telephone: (202) 842-1266

WILLIAMS, Robert E.
Director, Legislative Affairs, United Airlines
1707 L St., N.W., Suite 300, Washington, DC 20036
Telephone: (703) 892-7410
Registered as lobbyist at U.S. Congress.

WASHINGTON REPRESENTATIVES

WILLIAMS, Robin L.
Associate Director, Government Relations, Rohm and Haas Co.
1667 K St., N.W., Suite 210, Washington, DC 20006
Telephone: (202) 872-0660
Registered as lobbyist at U.S. Congress.

WILLIAMS, Ronald L.
Director of Communications, American Pharmaceutical Ass'n
2215 Constitution Ave., N.W., Washington, DC 20037
Telephone: (202) 628-4410

WILLIAMS, Ruby
Assistant Exec. Dir. for Public Affairs, Nat'l Education Ass'n of the U.S.
1201 16th St., N.W., Washington, DC 20036
Telephone: (202) 822-7300
Registered as lobbyist at U.S. Congress.

WILLIAMS, Susan J.
President, Bracy Williams & Co.
1000 Connecticut Ave., N.W., Suite 304, Washington, DC 20036
Telephone: (202) 659-4805
Registered as lobbyist at U.S. Congress.
Background: Former Assistant Secretary for Congressional and Governmental Affairs, U.S. Department of Transportation.
Clients:
American Home Satellite Ass'n
American Southwest Financial Corp.
Batman Corp.
Daishowa America Co. Ltd.
Energy Absorption Systems, Inc.
Fieldstone Co.
Millicom Inc.
Rocky Co., The
Tucson, Arizona, City of

WILLIAMS, Thomas C.
O'Neill and Athy, P.C.
1310 19th St., N.W., Washington, DC 20036
Telephone: (202) 466-6555
Registered as lobbyist at U.S. Congress.
Background: Assistant Counsel, Senate Subcommittee on Antitrust and Monopoly, 1958-68. Staff Counsel to the late Sen. Philip A. Hart, 1969-72.
Clients:
Nat'l Football League
Pyrotechnic Signal Manufacturers Ass'n

WILLIAMS, Timothy
Legislative Representative, Marlowe and Co.
1667 K St., N.W., Suite 480, Washington, DC 20006
Telephone: (202) 775-1796
Registered as lobbyist at U.S. Congress.

WILLIAMS, Wade S.
Sr. Manager, Washington Service Center, Deloitte & Touche Washington Services Group
1001 Pennsylvania Ave., N.W. Suite 350, Washington, DC 20004
Telephone: (202) 879-4973
Registered as lobbyist at U.S. Congress.
Background: President, American League of Lobbyists, 1990.

WILLIAMSON, Darla
Director, Closure Manufacturers Ass'n
1801 K St., N.W., Suite 1105L, Washington, DC 20006
Telephone: (202) 223-9050

WILLIAMSON, Joel V.
Mayer, Brown and Platt
2000 Pennsylvania Ave. N.W. Suite 6500, Washington, DC 20006
Telephone: (202) 463-2000
Registered as lobbyist at U.S. Congress.
Clients:
Nestle, S.A.

WILLIAMSON, John L.
V. President, Hannaford Co., Inc., The
655 15th St., N.W. Suite 200, Washington, DC 20005
Telephone: (202) 638-4600
Registered as lobbyist at U.S. Congress.

WILLIAMSON, Lonnie L.
Vice President, Wildlife Management Institute
1101 14th St., N.W., Suite 725, Washington, DC 20005
Telephone: (202) 371-1808

WILLIAMSON, Thomas S., Jr.
Partner, Covington and Burling
1201 Pennsylvania Ave., N.W., Box 7566, Washington, DC 20044
Telephone: (202) 662-6000
Registered as lobbyist at U.S. Congress.
Clients:
Cranston, Rhode Island, Department of Human Services
Lansing, Michigan, Department of Social Services

WILLIFORD, Frederick L.
Exec. Director/Chief Exec. Officer, Distributive Education Clubs of America
1908 Association Dr., Reston, VA 22091
Telephone: (703) 860-5000
Background: Also represents the DECA Foundation.

WILLIS, Betty E.
Director, Washington Office, Georgia, State of
444 N. Capitol St., N.W. Suite 240, Washington, DC 20001
Telephone: (202) 624-5437

WILLIS, David K.
Senior V. Pres., ATA Foundation, American Trucking Ass'ns
2200 Mill Road, Alexandria, VA 22314
Telephone: (703) 838-1800
Background: Also holds position of Exec. V. President, Trucking Research Institute.

WILLIS, Tommy
Treasurer, American Agriculture Movement Political Action Committee
100 Maryland Ave., N.E. Box 69, Washington, DC 20002
Telephone: (202) 544-5750

WILLIS, Wayne D.
Manager, Technical Liaison/Defense, General Atomics
1100 17th St., N.W., Suite 1200, Washington, DC 20036
Telephone: (202) 659-3140
Registered as lobbyist at U.S. Congress.

WILLKE, John C., M.D.
President, Nat'l Right to Life Committee
419 7th St., N.W. Suite 500, Washington, DC 20004
Telephone: (202) 626-8820

WILLKIE FARR AND GALLAGHER
1155 21st St., N.W., 6th Fl., Washington, DC 20036-3302
Telephone: (202) 328-8000
Background: Washington office of a New York law firm.
Members of firm representing listed organizations:
Barringer, William H.
Blumenfeld, Sue D.
Craco, Louis A.
Dunn, Christopher A.
Hennessy, Ellen A.
Schneider, Matthew R.
Spak, Walter J.
Verveer, Philip L.
Whitehouse, Theodore C.
Clients:
Amalgamated Industrial Steel Mills of Malaysia *(Walter J. Spak)*
Amalgamated Steel Mills of Malaysia *(Walter J. Spak)*
American Institute of Certified Public Accountants *(Louis A. Craco, Matthew R. Schneider)*
AOC Internat'l, Inc. *(Christopher A. Dunn)*
ASEAN Federation of Textile Industries *(William H. Barringer)*
Associacao das Industrias de Calcados do Rio Grande do Sul *(William H. Barringer)*
Automobile Importers of America
Brazil Ministry of Finance *(Walter J. Spak)*
Brazilian Iron and Steel Institute *(William H. Barringer)*
Cable and Wireless North America *(Sue D. Blumenfeld, Philip L. Verveer, Theodore C. Whitehouse)*
Cellular Telecommunications Industry Ass'n *(Sue D. Blumenfeld, Philip L. Verveer)*
Cementos de Chihuahua *(Walter J. Spak)*

Duferco Ltd. *(Walter J. Spak)*
Dun & Bradstreet *(Sue D. Blumenfeld, Philip L. Verveer, Theodore C. Whitehouse)*
Frutropic, S.A. *(Christopher A. Dunn)*
Fuji Heavy Industries Ltd. *(William H. Barringer)*
Instituto Brasileira de Siderugia *(William H. Barringer)*
Japan Iron and Steel Exporters Ass'n *(William H. Barringer)*
Japan Machinery Exporters Ass'n *(William H. Barringer)*
Kobe Steel Co. *(Christopher A. Dunn)*
Louis Dreyfus Corp. *(Christopher A. Dunn)*
Malaysia Ministry of Trade *(Walter J. Spak)*
Minbea Singapore *(Walter J. Spak)*
Nat'l Ass'n of Independent Fee Appraisers *(Matthew R. Schneider)*
Nat'l Iron and Steel of Singapore *(Walter J. Spak)*
Network Equipment Technologies *(Sue D. Blumenfeld, Philip L. Verveer)*
New York State Employees Retirement System *(Ellen A. Hennessy)*
Nippon Kokan K.K. *(William H. Barringer)*
Power Electronics *(Walter J. Spak)*
Prudential Insurance Co. of America *(Sue D. Blumenfeld)*
Sampo Corp. *(Christopher A. Dunn)*
Sharon Steel Co. *(Ellen A. Hennessy)*
Shearson Lehman Hutton *(Matthew R. Schneider)*
Siderbras *(William H. Barringer)*
Silver Reed America *(Christopher A. Dunn)*
Singapore Trade Development Board *(Walter J. Spak)*
Southern Iron and Steel Works *(Walter J. Spak)*
Standard Commerical Tobacco Co. *(Christopher A. Dunn, Matthew R. Schneider)*
Stelco, Inc. *(Christopher A. Dunn)*
Subaru-Isuzu Automotive Inc.
Sucocitrico Cutrale *(William H. Barringer, Christopher A. Dunn)*
Sun Moon Star Group *(Christopher A. Dunn)*
Tatung Co. *(Christopher A. Dunn)*
Telecommunications Industry Ass'n *(Philip L. Verveer)*
Time Warner Inc. *(Sue D. Blumenfeld, Matthew R. Schneider, Philip L. Verveer)*
Westinghouse Electric Corp. *(Matthew R. Schneider)*
Yamaha Corp. of America *(William H. Barringer)*
Yamaha Motor Corp. U.S.A. *(William H. Barringer, Matthew R. Schneider)*

WILMER, Charlotte
Wall and Associates, R. Duffy
1317 F St., N.W., Suite 400, Washington, DC 20004
Telephone: (202) 737-0100
Registered as lobbyist at U.S. Congress.
Registered as Foreign Agent: (# 3737).
Organizations represented:
Coal Industry Tax Committee
Hong Kong Trade Development Council

WILMER, Cindy J.
Associate Director, Government Affairs, American Internat'l Group
1455 Pennsylvania Ave., N.W. Suite 900, Washington, DC 20004
Telephone: (202) 783-5690
Registered as lobbyist at U.S. Congress.

WILMER, CUTLER AND PICKERING
2445 M St., N.W., Washington, DC 20037-1420
Telephone: (202) 663-6000
Members of firm representing listed organizations:
Berman, Bruce M.
Black, Timothy N.
Campbell, James S.
Background: Special Assistant, Antitrust Division, Department of Justice, 1967-68. General Counsel, Nat'l Commission pn Causes and Prevention of Violence, 1968-69. Counsel, Office of the Secretary, Department of Housing and Urban Development, 1977-78.
Cass, Richard W.
Cassidy, Robert C. (Jr.)
Background: International Trade Counsel, Senate Finance Committee, 1975-79. General Counsel, Office of the U.S. Trade Representative, Exec. Office of the President, 1979-81.
Cutler, Lloyd N.
Background: Counsel to the President under President Jimmy Carter.

WILMER, CUTLER AND PICKERING (Cont'd)

Doyle, Stephen P.
Gardiner, Arthur Z. (Jr.)
Greene, Ronald J.
Greenwald, John D.
Helfer, Michael S.
Jetton, C. Loring (Jr.)
Katzen, Sally
  Background: General Counsel, Council on Wage and Price Stability, Exec. Office of the President, 1979-81.
King, Neil J.
Lake, F. David (Jr.)
Lake, William T.
  Background: Deputy Legal Adviser, Department of State, 1980-81. Counsel, Council on Environmental Quality, 1970-73.
Lange, Dieter G. F.
Lee, Carol F., Partner
Lerman, Arnold M.
Marcus, Daniel
  Background: Deputy General Counsel, Department of Health, Education and Welfare, 1977-79. General Counsel, Department of Agriculture, 1979-80.
Mayers, Daniel K.
Mode, Paul J. (Jr.)
Olson, Thomas P.
Perlik, William R.
Perlstein, William J.
Pickering, John H.
Rosenbloom, Joel
Siemer, Deanne C., Partner
  Background: Economist, Office of Management and Budget, 1964-67. General Counsel, Department of Defense, 1977-79. Special Assistant to the Secretary of Energy, 1979-80.
Stranahan, Robert P. (Jr.)
Wilkins, William J., Partner
  Background: Former Staff Director and Chief Counsel, U.S. Senate Finance Committee.
Willens, Howard P.
  Background: Deputy Assistant Attorney General, Criminal Division, 1961-65.
Witten, Roger M.
Wollenberg, J. Roger
  Background: Lieutenant, U.S. Navy, 1942-46. Law Clerk to Justice William O. Douglas, U.S. Supreme Court, 1946-47. Assistant Chief, Antitrust Division, Department of Justice, 1947-52. Assistant Chief Counsel for Litigation, Federal Communications Commission, 1952-54.
Clients:
Aetna Life & Casualty Co.
AM Internat'l
Amerada Hess Corp. *(Sally Katzen)*
American Honda Motor Co. *(Ronald J. Greene, Howard P. Willens)*
American Petroleum Institute *(Stephen P. Doyle)*
Bank Capital Markets Ass'n *(Michael S. Helfer)*
Bankers Trust Co. *(William J. Wilkins)*
Capital Cities/ABC Inc. *(Joel Rosenbloom)*
Citicorp *(Arnold M. Lerman)*
Columbia Gas Transmission Corp. *(Timothy N. Black)*
Common Cause *(Roger M. Witten)*
Common Fund, The *(William J. Wilkins)*
Communications Satellite Corp. (COMSAT) *(Sally Katzen)*
Cook Inlet Communications *(Joel Rosenbloom)*
Dow Chemical *(William J. Wilkins)*
du Pont de Nemours and Co., E. I. *(John D. Greenwald, Daniel Marcus)*
Educational Testing Service
Federal Home Loan Bank of San Francisco *(Sally Katzen)*
Ford Motor Co. *(Robert C. Cassidy, Jr., Lloyd N. Cutler, Neil J. King, Deanne C. Siemer, Howard P. Willens)*
Grand Metropolitan PLC *(John H. Pickering)*
Greenpeace, U.S.A.
Handgun Control, Inc. *(James S. Campbell)*
Howard, Meedles, Tammen & Bergendoff *(Bruce M. Berman)*
Internat'l Business Machines Corp. *(J. Roger Wollenberg)*
Internat'l Metals Reclamation Co. *(Neil J. King)*
Internat'l Swap Dealers Ass'n *(William J. Perlstein)*
Lederle Laboratories, American Cyanamid Co. Subsidiary *(Ronald J. Greene)*

Long Island Savings Bank *(Lloyd N. Cutler, Michael S. Helfer)*
Lufthansa German Airlines *(James S. Campbell, Robert C. Cassidy, Jr., Dieter G. F. Lange, Carol F. Lee)*
Marianas Political Status Commission
McDonald's Corp. *(William J. Wilkins)*
Peoples Heritage Savings Bank *(Michael S. Helfer)*
PepsiCo, Inc. *(William J. Wilkins)*
Polaroid Corp. *(Richard W. Cass)*
Public Broadcasting Service *(Thomas P. Olson)*
RKO General, Inc. *(J. Roger Wollenberg)*
Scripps League Newspaper, Inc. *(Robert P. Stranahan, Jr.)*
Shearson Lehman Hutton *(William J. Wilkins)*
Sony Corp.
Southeast Banking Corp. *(Michael S. Helfer)*
Superpharm Corp. *(Daniel Marcus)*
Tibet, Government of (in Exile) *(William T. Lake)*
Trans-Alaska Pipeline Liability Fund *(Sally Katzen)*
Trans Ocean Leasing Corp. *(Ronald J. Greene)*
Unisys Corp. *(William J. Wilkins)*
UNOCAL Corp. *(Paul J. Mode, Jr.)*
Washington Post Co.
Wendell Investments Ltd. *(John H. Pickering)*
Yamaha Motor Corp. U.S.A. *(Robert C. Cassidy, Jr.)*

WILMOT, David W.

Harmon and Wilmot
1010 Vermont Ave., N.W., Suite 310, Washington, DC 20005
Telephone: (202) 783-9100
Clients:
Anheuser-Busch Cos., Inc.
Hotel Ass'n of Washington

WILMOT, Luis A.

Assoc. People's Counsel (Gov't Relats), District of Columbia Office of the People's Counsel
1101 14th St., N.W., Suite 900, Washington, DC 20005
Telephone: (202) 727-3071

WILNER, Carol W.

Federal Gov't Affairs Director, AT&T
Suite 1000, 1120 20th St., N.W., Washington, DC 20036
Telephone: (202) 457-7435

WILNER, Frank N.

Ass't V. Pres., Information & Publ. Aff., Ass'n of American Railroads
50 F Street, N.W., Washington, DC 20001
Telephone: (202) 639-2100

WILNER AND SCHEINER

1200 New Hampshire Ave., N.W., Suite 300, Washington, DC 20036
Telephone: (202) 861-7800
Members of firm representing listed organizations:
Braden, Susan G.
  Background: Senior Trial Attorney, Antitrust Division, Department of Justice, 1978-80. Senior Attorney Advisor to Commissioner and Acting Chairman, 1980-83 and Special Counsel to the Chairman, 1984-85, Federal Trade Commission.
Kneisley, Robert W.
  Background: Attorney/Advisor, Office of General Counsel, Civil Aeronautics Board, 1976-78. Trial Attorney, Bureau of Internat'l Aviation and Bureau of Consumer Protection, Antitrust Division, Civil Aeronautics Board, 1978-80.
Lane, Dennis
  Background: Trial Attorney, Rate Section, Federal Power Commission, 1975-77.
Lessenco, Gilbert B.
Ruden, Paul M.
  Background: Trial Attorney, Civil Aeronautics Board, 1967-68.
Seligson, Paul Y.
  Background: Trial Attorney and Senior Attorney, Civil Aeronautics Board, 1958-1962. Chief, Legal Staff, Routes and Agreements Division, Civil Aeronautics Board, 1962-1964.
Solomon, Richard A.
  Background: Assistant General Counsel, Federal Communications Commission, 1952-58. Chief, Appellate Section, Antitrust Division, Department of Justice, 1960-62. General Counsel, Federal Power Commission, 1962-69.
Clients:

Consolidated Edison Co. of New York *(Richard A. Solomon)*
General Mills *(Gilbert B. Lessenco)*
Graco, Inc. *(Gilbert B. Lessenco)*
Midwest Energy Inc.
Nat'l Distillers and Chemical Corp. *(Richard A. Solomon)*

WILNER, Thomas B.

Shearman and Sterling
1001 30th St., N.W., Suite 400, Washington, DC 20007
Telephone: (202) 337-8200
Registered as lobbyist at U.S. Congress.
Clients:
Komatsu Ltd.

WILSON, Benet

Publication Manager, Ass'n of Farmworker Opportunity Programs
408 7th St., S.E., Washington, DC 20003
Telephone: (202) 543-3443

WILSON, Chapin E., Jr.

Legislative Representative, American Federation of Government Employees
80 F St., N.W., Washington, DC 20001
Telephone: (202) 737-8700
Registered as lobbyist at U.S. Congress.

WILSON, D. Edward, Jr.

Prather, Seeger, Doolittle and Farmer
1600 M St., N.W., Washington, DC 20036
Telephone: (202) 296-0500
Background: Served as Acting General Counsel for the Treasury Department.
Clients:
Casalee America Corp.
General Electric Co.

WILSON, Dena L.

V. President, Legislative Affairs, American Waterways Operators
1600 Wilson Blvd. Suite 1000, Arlington, VA 22209
Telephone: (703) 841-9300
Registered as lobbyist at U.S. Congress.
Background: Serves as contact for American Waterways Operators Political Action Committee.

WILSON, Col. Donald E.

Director, Army Activities, Nat'l Guard Ass'n of the U.S.
One Massachusetts Ave., N.W., Washington, DC 20001
Telephone: (202) 789-0031

WILSON, Donald T.

Director, Government Relations Division, Nat'l Tire Dealers and Retreaders Ass'n
1250 I St., N.W. Suite 400, Washington, DC 20005
Telephone: (202) 789-2300
Registered as lobbyist at U.S. Congress.

WILSON, Dorothea

Exec. Officer, American Soc. for Cell Biology
9650 Rockville Pike, Bethesda, MD 20814
Telephone: (301) 530-7153

WILSON, Edie

V. President, Burson-Marsteller
1850 M St., N.W., Suite 900, Washington, DC 20036
Telephone: (202) 833-8550

WILSON, ELSER, MOSKOWITZ, EDELMAN & DICKER

1341 G St., N.W. 5th Floor, Washington, DC 20005
Telephone: (202) 626-7660
Registered as Foreign Agent: (#3908)
Members of firm representing listed organizations:
Wallace, Robert B.
Clients:
Morgan Grenfell and Co., Ltd. *(Robert B. Wallace)*

WILSON, Frank J.

Exec. V. President, Legal & Compliance, Nat'l Ass'n of Securities Dealers (NASDAQ)
1735 K St., N.W., Washington, DC 20006
Telephone: (202) 728-8000
Background: Former Legislative Aide to Senator John Marshall Butler of Maryland.

WILSON, Gerald
Exec. Director, Citizens for Public Action on Cholesterol
7200 Wisconsin Ave. Suite 1002, Bethesda, MD 20814
Telephone: (301) 907-7790
Background: Also represents Citizens for the Treatment of High Blood Pressure and the New York State Committee for the Treatment of High Blood Pressure.

WILSON, James D.
V. President, Health Policy, American Industrial Health Council
1330 Connecticut Ave., N.W. Suite 300, Washington, DC 20036-1702
Telephone: (202) 659-0060

WILSON, Joy Johnson
Sr. Prog. Dir., Health & Human Svcs., Nat'l Conference of State Legislatures
444 North Capitol St., N.W. Suite 500, Washington, DC 20001
Telephone: (202) 624-5400

WILSON, Kerrie B.
Coordinator of Cancer Care Policy, American Cancer Soc. (Public Affairs Office)
316 Pennsylvania Ave., S.E. Suite 200, Washington, DC 20003
Telephone: (202) 546-4011

WILSON, Michael G.
Policy Analyst, Latin America, Heritage Foundation
214 Massachusetts Ave., N.E., Washington, DC 20002
Telephone: (202) 546-4400

WILSON, Michael J.
Legislative Representative, Amalgamated Clothing and Textile Workers Union
815 16th St., N.W., Suite 507, Washington, DC 20006
Telephone: (202) 628-0214
Registered as lobbyist at U.S. Congress.
Background: Former Legislative Aide and Press Ass't to Rep. Charles Hayes (D-IL).

WILSON, Nancy L.
Asst. V. President, Government Relations, Ass'n of American Railroads
50 F St., N.W., Suite 12500, Washington, DC 20001
Telephone: (202) 639-2401

WILSON, Patricia M.
Manager, Governmental Affairs, USX Corp.
818 Connecticut Ave., N.W., Washington, DC 20006
Telephone: (202) 331-1340
Registered as lobbyist at U.S. Congress.

WILSON, Peter
Director, Government Relations, Nat'l Ass'n of Children's Hospitals and Related Institutions
401 Wythe St., Alexandria, VA 22314
Telephone: (703) 684-1355

WILSON, Quentin C.
Dir., Midwest Region, U.S. Strategies Corp.
1321 Duke St., Suite 200, Alexandria, VA 22314-3563
Telephone: (703) 739-7999

WILSON, Reid
Political Director, Sierra Club
408 C St., N.E., Washington, DC 20002
Telephone: (202) 547-1141
Registered as lobbyist at U.S. Congress.

WILSON, Robert C.
Washington Industrial Team, Inc.
499 South Capitol St., S.W. Suite 520, Washington, DC 20003
Telephone: (202) 347-0633
Registered as lobbyist at U.S. Congress.
Background: Member, U.S. House of Representatives from California, 1953-81. Serves as Co-Chairman, American Freedom Coalition.

WILSON, Robert Dale
Wilson & Wilson
1900 L St., N.W., Suite 500, Washington, DC 20036
Telephone: (202) 835-1571
Registered as lobbyist at U.S. Congress.
Background: Director, Strategic Resources, U.S. Department of Commerce, 1981-86. Exec. Director, White House Materials Council, 1986-88.

Clients:
Hecla Mining Co.

WILSON, Robert Gary
Director, Corporate Government Affairs, PPG Industries
1730 Rhode Island Ave., N.W., Suite 715, Washington, DC 20036
Telephone: (202) 659-9894
Registered as lobbyist at U.S. Congress.

WILSON, Ronald
Of Counsel, Sierra Club Legal Defense Fund
1531 P St., N.W. Suite 200, Washington, DC 20005
Telephone: (202) 667-4500

WILSON, Scott A.
Maupin Taylor Ellis & Adams, P.C.
1130 Connecticut Ave., N.W. Suite 750, Washington, DC 20036
Telephone: (202) 429-8910
Registered as Foreign Agent: (#4242).
Background: Chief Legislative Assistant for Domestic Policy to Senator Jesse Helms (R-NC), 1979-85.
Clients:
Glaxo Australia Pty, Ltd.

WILSON, Sharon Cockayne
Wilson & Wilson
1900 L St., N.W., Suite 500, Washington, DC 20036
Telephone: (202) 835-1571
Background: Director, House of Representatives Mining Committee, 1977-85.

WILSON, Shelley
Meyers & Associates
412 First St., S.E., Suite 100, Washington, DC 20003
Telephone: (202) 484-2773
Clients:
Texas A & M University Research Foundation

WILSON, Dr. Stephanie
V. Pres. & Magr., Internat'l Area, Abt Associates Inc.
4800 Montgomery Lane, Bethesda, MD 20814
Telephone: (301) 913-0500

WILSON, Thomas E.
Seyfarth, Shaw, Fairweather and Geraldson
815 Connecticut Ave., N.W., Washington, DC 20006-4004
Telephone: (202) 463-2400

WILSON, W. Gerald
President, Internat'l Road Federation
525 School St., S.W., Washington, DC 20024
Telephone: (202) 554-2106

WILSON, William J.
Director, Public Relations, Vision Council of America
1800 North Kent St. Suite 1210, Arlington, VA 22209
Telephone: (703) 243-1508

WILSON & WILSON
1900 L St., N.W., Suite 500, Washington, DC 20036
Telephone: (202) 835-1571
Background: Law and government relations.
Members of firm representing listed organizations:
Wilson, Robert Dale
Background: Director, Strategic Resources, U.S. Department of Commerce, 1981-86. Exec. Director, White House Materials Council, 1986-88.
Wilson, Sharon Cockayne
Background: Director, House of Representatives Mining Committee, 1977-85.
Clients:
Hecla Mining Co. *(Robert Dale Wilson)*

WILSON, Winston L.
President, U.S. Wheat Associates, Inc.
1620 Eye St., N.W., Suite 801, Washington, DC 20006
Telephone: (202) 463-0999

WINBURN, John P.
Winburn, VanScoyoc, and Hooper
453 New Jersey Ave., S.E., Washington, DC 20003
Telephone: (202) 488-3581
Registered as lobbyist at U.S. Congress.
Clients:
American Ass'n of Equipment Lessors
American Ass'n of Equipment Lessors Capital Investment Political Action Committee

American Automotive Leasing Ass'n
Burlington Northern Railroad
Burlington Resources, Inc.
FAG Bearings Corp.
Hartford Insurance Group
Leggett & Platt
Nat'l Ass'n of County Office Employees
Pennzoil Co.
Philip Morris Management Corp.
Quanex Corp.
University of Michigan

WINBURN, VANSCOYOC, AND HOOPER
453 New Jersey Ave., S.E., Washington, DC 20003
Telephone: (202) 488-3581
Members of firm representing listed organizations:
Hooper, Linsay D.
VanScoyoc, H. Stewart
Winburn, John P.
Clients:
American Ass'n of Equipment Lessors *(John P. Winburn)*
American Ass'n of Equipment Lessors Capital Investment Political Action Committee *(John P. Winburn)*
American Automotive Leasing Ass'n *(John P. Winburn)*
Burlington Northern Railroad *(John P. Winburn)*
Burlington Resources, Inc. *(John P. Winburn)*
Coalition of EPSCoR States *(H. Stewart VanScoyoc)*
du Pont de Nemours and Co., E. I. *(H. Stewart VanScoyoc)*
FAG Bearings Corp. *(John P. Winburn)*
Hallmark Cards, Inc. *(Linsay D. Hooper)*
Hartford Insurance Group *(John P. Winburn)*
Internat'l Paper Co. *(H. Stewart VanScoyoc)*
Jackson Nat'l Life Insurance Co. *(Linsay D. Hooper)*
Kansas City Southern Industries *(Linsay D. Hooper)*
Leggett & Platt *(John P. Winburn)*
Nat'l Ass'n of County Office Employees *(John P. Winburn)*
Pennzoil Co. *(John P. Winburn)*
Philip Morris Management Corp. *(John P. Winburn)*
Quanex Corp. *(H. Stewart VanScoyoc, John P. Winburn)*
Scott Paper Co. *(H. Stewart VanScoyoc)*
University of Alabama System *(H. Stewart VanScoyoc)*
University of Michigan *(John P. Winburn)*
USF&G *(H. Stewart VanScoyoc)*

WINCEK, Mark D.
Kilpatrick & Cody
2501 M St., N.W., Suite 500, Washington, DC 20037
Telephone: (202) 463-2500
Registered as lobbyist at U.S. Congress.
Background: Member of Staff, U.S. House of Representatives Committee on Ways and Means, Subcommittee on Oversight, 1976-81; Senior Subcommittee Counsel, 1980-81.
Clients:
Bank South
Frito-Lay, Inc.
PepsiCo, Inc.
Zayre Corp.

WINDELS, MARX, DAVIES AND IVES
1701 Pennsylvania Ave., N.W. Suite 940, Washington, DC 20006
Telephone: (202) 775-5980
Members of firm representing listed organizations:
Moore, Jonathon R.
Clients:
Crown Controls Corp. *(Jonathon R. Moore)*

WINDER STRANGE, Ms. RoseMary
Director for Social Services, Catholic Charities USA
1319 F St., N.W., Suite 400, Washington, DC 20004
Telephone: (202) 639-8400

WINE, L. Mark
Kirkland and Ellis
655 15th St., N.W. Suite 1200, Washington, DC 20005
Telephone: (202) 879-5000
Background: Member, Land and Natural Resources Division, U.S. Department of Justice, 1972-78.
Clients:
Safe Buildings Alliance

WINES, Stephen H.
Special Assistant, Maritime Institute for Research and Industrial Development
1133 15th St., N.W. Suite 600, Washington, DC 20005
Telephone: (202) 463-6505
Registered as lobbyist at U.S. Congress.

WINGER, Jim
Cong Liaison Officer, DEPARTMENT OF COMMERCE
14th and Constitution Ave. S.W., Washington, DC 20230
Telephone: (202) 377-5485

WINGERTER, Eugene J.
Exec. Director, Nat'l Solid Wastes Management Ass'n
1730 Rhode Island Ave., N.W., 10th Floor, Washington, DC 20036
Telephone: (202) 659-4613
Background: Serves also as Treasurer, Nat'l Solid Wastes Management Ass'n Political Action Committee.

WINIK, Peter L.
Latham and Watkins
1001 Pennsylvania Ave., N.W., Suite 1300, Washington, DC 20004
Telephone: (202) 637-2200

WINKELMAN, Eileen M.
Legislative Rep., Health & Safety, Chemical Manufacturers Ass'n
2501 M St., N.W., Washington, DC 20037
Telephone: (202) 887-1100
Registered as lobbyist at U.S. Congress.

WINKELMANN & ASSOCIATES, INC.
1250 Connecticut Ave. NW Suite 620, Washington, DC 20036
Telephone: (202) 466-7263
Members of firm representing listed organizations:
  Harty, Christopher E.
  Winkelmann, Joe
Clients:
  American Resort and Residential Development Ass'n *(Joe Winkelmann)*
  Nat'l Ass'n of Industrial and Office Parks *(Joe Winkelmann)*

WINKELMANN, Joe
Winkelmann & Associates, Inc.
1250 Connecticut Ave. NW Suite 620, Washington, DC 20036
Telephone: (202) 466-7263
Registered as lobbyist at U.S. Congress.
Clients:
  American Resort and Residential Development Ass'n
  Nat'l Ass'n of Industrial and Office Parks

WINN, Allan R.
Colton and Boykin
1025 Thomas Jefferson St., N.W., Suite 500 East, Washington, DC 20007
Telephone: (202) 342-5400

WINN, Donald J.
Asst to the Board, FEDERAL RESERVE SYSTEM
20th and C Sts., N.W., Washington, DC 20551
Telephone: (202) 452-3456

WINNER, Sonya D.
Covington and Burling
1201 Pennsylvania Ave., N.W., Box 7566, Washington, DC 20044
Telephone: (202) 662-6000
Clients:
  Internat'l Minerals and Chemical Corp.

WINNICK, Jeanne M.
Davis Companies, The Susan
1146 19th St., N.W., Washington, DC 20036
Telephone: (202) 775-8881
Background: Director, Los Angeles Office, The Susan Davis Companies. Former Staff Assistant, Press Secretary's Office, The White House, under President Ronald Reagan.

WINNIK, Joel S.
Hogan and Hartson
555 13th St., N.W., Suite 1200, Washington, DC 20004-1109
Telephone: (202) 637-5600

Registered as lobbyist at U.S. Congress.

WINOY, Lars
Director, Federal Liaison, American Institute of Architects, The
1735 New York Ave., N.W., Washington, DC 20006
Telephone: (202) 626-7300
Registered as lobbyist at U.S. Congress.

WINSLOW, Anne
Director, Food Policy & Public Affairs, Nat'l Cattlemen's Ass'n
1301 Pennsylvania Ave., N.W., Suite 300, Washington, DC 20004
Telephone: (202) 347-0228

WINSLOW, Peter H.
Scribner, Hall and Thompson
1850 K St., N.W. Suite 1100, Washington, DC 20006-2201
Telephone: (202) 331-8585
Registered as Foreign Agent: (#4253).
Background: Attorney, Interpretative and Refund Litigation Divisions, Chief Counsel's Office, Internal Revenue Service, 1975-79.

WINSLOW, Sara
Program Assistant/Research Assistant, Piper Pacific Internat'l
2055 North 15th St. Suite 300, Arlington, VA 22201
Telephone: (703) 524-7556
Registered as Foreign Agent: (#4244).
Clients:
  Fuji Heavy Industries Ltd.
  Nissan Motor Co., Ltd.

WINSTON, David A.
Associate General Counsel, Nat'l Ass'n of Life Underwriters
1922 F St., N.W., Washington, DC 20006
Telephone: (202) 331-6025
Registered as lobbyist at U.S. Congress.

WINSTON, Deborah F.
Gov't Affairs Coordinator, Paul, Hastings, Janofsky and Walker
1050 Connecticut Ave., N.W., Suite 1200, Washington, DC 20036-5331
Telephone: (202) 223-9000
Registered as lobbyist at U.S. Congress.
Clients:
  Security Life Insurance Co. of Denver

WINSTON, James L.
Rubin, Winston and Diercks
1730 M St., N.W., Suite 412, Washington, DC 20036
Telephone: (202) 861-0870
Registered as lobbyist at U.S. Congress.
Background: Legal Assistant to Commissioner Robert E. Lee, Federal Communications Commission, 1978-80.
Clients:
  Nat'l Ass'n of Black Owned Broadcasters

WINSTON, Judith
Deputy Director, Public Policy, Women's Legal Defense Fund
2000 P St., N.W., Suite 400, Washington, DC 20036
Telephone: (202) 887-0364
Registered as lobbyist at U.S. Congress.

WINSTON AND STRAWN
2550 M St., N.W., Suite 500, Washington, DC 20037
Telephone: (202) 828-8400
Background: Washington office of a Chicago law firm.
Members of firm representing listed organizations:
  Fiduccia, Paul C.
  Maeder, Edward C.
    Background: Legislative Assistant to Sen. William B. Spong, 1967-70. Counsel, Senate Committee on the District of Columbia, 1970-71.
  Meltzer, Richard
  Milliken, John G.
    Background: Exec. Assistant, Congressman Joseph L. Fisher of Virginia, 1975-78.
  Overman, Dean L.
    Background: White House Fellow, Assistant to Vice President Nelson Rockefeller, 1975-76. Associate Director, White House Domestic Council, 1976-77.
  Reilly, John R.

Background: Assistant to Deputy Attorney General, Chief of Executive Office for U.S. Attorney, 1961-64. Commissioner, Federal Trade Commission, 1964-67. Former adviser to Democratic Presidential nominee Walter F. Mondale.
  Schmidt, Patrick L.
Clients:
  American Appraisal Associates, Inc. *(John G. Milliken)*
  American Ass'n of Museums *(Richard Meltzer)*
  CNA Financial Corp. *(Richard Meltzer)*
  Gillett Group Management, Inc. *(John G. Milliken)*
  Internat'l Council of Shopping Centers *(Edward C. Maeder)*
  Nat'l Council of Health Facilities Finance Authorities *(Paul C. Fiduccia)*
  Tucson, Arizona, City of *(Richard Meltzer)*

WINTER, Roger
Director, United States Committee for Refugees
1025 Vermont Ave., N.W. Suite 920, Washington, DC 20005
Telephone: (202) 347-3507
Background: Also represents the American Council for Nationalities Service.

WINTER, Thomas S.
Treasurer, Conservative Victory Fund
422 First St., S.E., Suite 208, Washington, DC 20003
Telephone: (202) 546-5833

WINTER, William L.
Director, American Press Institute
11690 Sunrise Valley Drive, Reston, VA 22090
Telephone: (703) 620-3611

WINTERS-HAZELTON, Carolynn
Deputy Director, Washington Office on Latin America
110 Maryland Ave., N.E. Suite 404, Washington, DC 20002
Telephone: (202) 544-8045

WINTHROP, STIMSON, PUTNAM & ROBERTS
1133 Connecticut Ave., N.W. Suite 1000, Washington, DC 20036
Telephone: (202) 775-9800
Members of firm representing listed organizations:
  Arky, M. Elizabeth
    Background: Staff, House Telecommunications and Finance Subcommittee, 1986.
  Atkins, G. Lawrence, Director, Employee Benefit Policy
    Background: Minority Staff Director, Senate Special Committee on Aging, 1981-89.
  Berlin, Kenneth
  Calamaro, Raymond S.
    Background: Legislative Director for Sen. Gaylord Nelson, 1973-75. Deputy Assistant U.S. Attorney General, 1976-79.
  Carr, Donald A., Of Counsel
    Background: Acting Assistant Attorney General, Land and Natural Resources Division, U.S. Department of Justice, 1989.
  Dolan, Michael W.
    Background: Deputy Ass't Attorney General, Office of Legislative Affairs, U.S. Dept. of Justice 1979-85.
  Freiberg, Ronna A., Director, Legislative Affairs
    Background: Admin. Ass't to U.S. Rep. Peter Rodino, Jr., 1975-76; Congressional Liaison, The White House, 1976-80.
  Gillick, John E., Of Counsel
  Gold, Peter F.
    Background: Legislative Director, U.S. Senator Gary Hart (D-CO), 1975-81.
  Gray, Robert Reed, Of Counsel
    Background: Staff of General Counsel, Civil Aeronautics Board, 1951-52 and Assistant Chief, International and Rules Division, CAB, 1953-55. Legal Advisor, DCNO (Air), 1952-53.
  Kaswell, Stuart
    Background: Served with Securities and Exchange Commission, 1979-86, including as Special Counsel, 1983-84, and Branch Chief, OTC Regulation, 1984-86. Minority Counsel, House Energy and Commerce Committee, 1986-90.
  Kurrelmeyer, Louis H.
  Lang, Jeffrey M., Of Counsel

Background: Deputy General Counsel, International Trade Commission, 1976-79. Senate Finance Committee Staff, 1979-90, including Chief, International Trade Counsel, 1987-90.

Monborne, Mark A.

Morgan, Gerald D. (Jr.)

Background: Attorney, 1971-74, Deputy Vice President for Insurance, 1974-75, Vice President and General Counsel, 1975-76, Overseas Private Investment Corp. General Counsel, Agency for International Development, 1976-77.

Shapiro, Ira S.

Background: Minority Staff Director and Chief Counsel, Senate Gov't Affairs Committee, 1981-84; Chief of Staff, U.S. Senator John D. Rockfeller IV, 1985-87.

Wall, Christopher R.

Clients:

America West Airlines *(Ronna A. Freiberg, John E. Gillick, Ira S. Shapiro)*

Amoco Performance Products, Inc. *(Peter F. Gold)*

BASF Corp. *(Ronna A. Freiberg, Peter F. Gold, Ira S. Shapiro)*

BASF Structural Materials, Inc. *(Peter F. Gold)*

Bowater, Inc. *(Raymond S. Calamaro, Michael W. Dolan)*

Brown and Bain *(Peter F. Gold)*

Connecticut Liquidity Investment Fund, Inc. *(Raymond S. Calamaro, Michael W. Dolan, Ronna A. Freiberg)*

CP Air *(Robert Reed Gray)*

El Al Israel Airlines, Ltd. *(Robert Reed Gray)*

Fiberite Corp. *(Peter F. Gold)*

Grocery Manufacturers of America *(Ira S. Shapiro)*

Hercules Aerospace Co. (Aerospace Products Group) *(Peter F. Gold)*

IBJ Schroder Bank and Trust Co. *(Raymond S. Calamaro)*

Israel Aircraft Industries *(Robert Reed Gray)*

Macrovision *(Ronna A. Freiberg, Ira S. Shapiro)*

Metallverken AB *(Raymond S. Calamaro, Ira S. Shapiro)*

Nat'l Vehicle Leasing Ass'n *(Michael W. Dolan, Ronna A. Freiberg, John E. Gillick)*

Navajo Nation, The *(M. Elizabeth Arky, Peter F. Gold)*

Nigeria Airways *(Robert Reed Gray)*

Polskie Linie Lotnicze *(Robert Reed Gray)*

Quebecair *(Robert Reed Gray)*

Queen City Home Health Care Co. *(Ronna A. Freiberg, Ira S. Shapiro)*

Saab-Scania of America *(John E. Gillick, Robert Reed Gray)*

Scandinavian Airlines System (SAS) *(Robert Reed Gray)*

Snappy Car Rental *(Michael W. Dolan, Ronna A. Freiberg, Peter F. Gold)*

Swedish Steelproducers' Ass'n (Jernkontoret) *(Raymond S. Calamaro, Louis H. Kurrelmeyer, Christopher R. Wall)*

Thrifty Rent-A-Car System, Inc. *(Michael W. Dolan, Ronna A. Freiberg, Peter F. Gold)*

Transportes Aereos Mercantiles Panamericanos *(Robert Reed Gray)*

Varig Brazilian Airlines *(Robert Reed Gray)*

Westinghouse Electric Corp. *(G. Lawrence Atkins)*

WINTZ, Leigh
Exec. Director, General Federation of Women's Clubs
1734 N St., N.W., Washington, DC 20036
Telephone: (202) 347-3168

WINWOOD, Christine
Exec. Director, Internat'l Newspaper Promotion Ass'n
11600 Sunrise Valley Dr., Reston, VA 22091
Telephone: (703) 648-1094

WIPPMAN, David
Reichler Appelbaum and Wippman
1701 K St., N.W. Suite 700, Washington, DC 20006
Telephone: (202) 429-0800
Clients:
Nicaragua, Government of

WIRG, Lyle
Treasurer, SANE/FREEZEPAC
1819 H St., N.W. Suite 1000, Washington, DC 20006
Telephone: (202) 862-9740

WISE ASSOCIATES, Jim
1707 Duke St., Suite 300, Alexandria, VA 22314
Telephone: (703) 548-6295

Members of firm representing listed organizations:
Wise, James W., President
Organizations represented:
Nat'l Ass'n of Credit Management *(James W. Wise)*
San Francisco Bar Pilots Ass'n *(James W. Wise)*

WISE, Donna
Director, Policy Affairs, World Resources Institute
1709 New York Ave., N.W., Washington, DC 20006
Telephone: (202) 638-6300

WISE, Gail Alexander
Staff Dir., Public Relations, American Bar Ass'n
1800 M St., N.W., Washington, DC 20036
Telephone: (202) 331-2293

WISE, James W.
President, Wise Associates, Jim
1707 Duke St., Suite 300, Alexandria, VA 22314
Telephone: (703) 548-6295
Registered as lobbyist at U.S. Congress.
Organizations represented:
Nat'l Ass'n of Credit Management
San Francisco Bar Pilots Ass'n

WISEMAN, Alan M.
Howrey and Simon
1730 Pennsylvania Ave., N.W., Washington, DC 20006-4793
Telephone: (202) 783-0800
Clients:
Mead Corp.

WISEMAN, Laurence
President, American Forest Council
1250 Connecticut Ave., N.W. Suite 320, Washington, DC 20036
Telephone: (202) 463-2455

WISNIEWSKI, Raymond F., Jr.
Secretary, Concrete Plant Manufacturers Bureau
900 Spring St., Silver Spring, MD 20910
Telephone: (301) 587-1400
Background: Also represents the Truck Mixer Manufacturers Bureau as its Secretary.

WISOR, Russell C.
Director, Government Affairs, Aluminum Co. of America
1615 M St., N.W., Suite 500, Washington, DC 20036
Telephone: (202) 956-5300

WISS, Marcia A.
Kaplan, Russin and Vecchi
1215 17th St., N.W., Washington, DC 20036
Telephone: (202) 887-0353
Registered as lobbyist at U.S. Congress.
Clients:
Canned and Cooked Meat Importers Ass'n

WITECK, Robert
Sr. V. Pres and Creative Director, Hill and Knowlton Public Affairs Worldwide
Washington Harbour, 901 31st St., N.W., Washington, DC 20007
Telephone: (202) 333-7400
Background: Former Communications Director to Senator Bob Packwood (R-OR).

WITEK, Walt
V. Pres., Political Field Operations, Nat'l Ass'n of REALTORS
777 14th St., N.W., Washington, DC 20005
Telephone: (202) 383-1000
Registered as lobbyist at U.S. Congress.

WITHERS, Claudia A.
Deputy Director, Employment Programs, Women's Legal Defense Fund
2000 P St., N.W., Suite 400, Washington, DC 20036
Telephone: (202) 887-0364
Registered as lobbyist at U.S. Congress.

WITHEY, Lyn M.
Assoc. Director, Federal Corp. Affairs, Internat'l Paper Co.
1620 Eye St., N.W., Suite 700, Washington, DC 20006
Telephone: (202) 785-3666
Registered as lobbyist at U.S. Congress.
Background: Former Special Assistant to the President for Legislative Affairs, House under President Reagan.

WITHNELL, David D.
Wright and Talisman
1050 17th St., N.W. Suite 600, Washington, DC 20036
Telephone: (202) 331-1194

WITHWORTH, Ralph V.
Director, United Shareholders Ass'n
1667 K St., N.W., Suite 770, Washington, DC 20006
Telephone: (202) 393-4600

WITIAK, Diane
Asst Dir, Communication/Political Action, American Federation of Government Employees Political Action Committee
80 F St., N.W., Washington, DC 20001
Telephone: (202) 737-8700

WITKIN, Cynthia D.
Director, Congressional Relations/Labor, Associated General Contractors of America
1957 E St., N.W., Washington, DC 20006
Telephone: (202) 393-2040
Registered as lobbyist at U.S. Congress.

WITKOWSKI, Christopher J.
Exec. Director, Aviation Consumer Action Project
P.O. Box 19029, Washington, DC 20036
Telephone: (202) 785-3704
Registered as lobbyist at U.S. Congress.

WITT, Daniel A.
V. President, Tax Foundation, Citizens for a Sound Economy
470 L'Enfant Plaza East, S.W. Suite 7112, Washington, DC 20024
Telephone: (202) 488-8200

WITTEN, Roger M.
Wilmer, Cutler and Pickering
2445 M St., N.W., Washington, DC 20037-1420
Telephone: (202) 663-6000
Clients:
Common Cause

WITTENBERG, Ernest
V. Chairma, Harrison Co., E. Bruce
1440 New York Ave., N.W. Suite 300, Washington, DC 20005
Telephone: (202) 638-1200

WITTENBERG, Hope R.
Ass't Director, Congressional Relations, College of American Pathologists
1101 Vermont Ave., N.W., Washington, DC 20005
Telephone: (202) 371-6617
Registered as lobbyist at U.S. Congress.

WITTIG, Judith A.
Corporate Secretary, Defense Products Marketing Inc.
1213 Jefferson Davis Hwy., Suite 1414, Arlington, VA 22202
Telephone: (703) 486-2288
Registered as lobbyist at U.S. Congress.

WITTIG, Richard J.
President, Defense Products Marketing Inc.
1213 Jefferson Davis Hwy., Suite 1414, Arlington, VA 22202
Telephone: (703) 486-2288
Registered as lobbyist at U.S. Congress.

WOBBE, Sandra W.
Ass't. V. President, Policy & Planning, Aerospace Industries Ass'n of America
1250 Eye St., N.W., Suite 1100, Washington, DC 20005
Telephone: (202) 371-8400
Registered as lobbyist at U.S. Congress.

WODDER, Rebecca
V. President, Membership & Development, Wilderness Soc.
1400 Eye St., N.W., 10th Floor, Washington, DC 20005
Telephone: (202) 842-3400

WOELFER, Kathy
NAS, USIA Interpreting Coordinator, Organization for American-Soviet ExchangeS (OASES-DC)
1302 R St., N.W., Washington, DC 20009
Telephone: (202) 332-1145

WOESSNER, William M.
President, Youth For Understanding Internat'l Exchange
3501 Newark St., N.W., Washington, DC 20016
Telephone: (202) 895-1125

WOHLBRUCK, Aliceann
Exec. Director, Nat'l Ass'n of Development Organizations
400 North Capitol St., N.W. Suite 372, Washington, DC 20001
Telephone: (202) 624-7806

WOHLSTETTER, Alan F.
Denning and Wohlstetter
1700 K St., N.W., Washington, DC 20006
Telephone: (202) 833-8884
Background: Trial Attorney for Federal Maritime Board and Maritime Administration 1951-52.
Clients:
Central Freight Forwarding
Household Goods Forwarders Ass'n of America
Karlander Kangaroo Lines
Mobley Inc., E. L.
Richmond Transfer and Storage Co.

WOHLSTETTER, John C.
Attorney/Dir., Special Federal Projects, Contel Corp.
555 13th St. Suite 480 West, Washington, DC 20004
Telephone: (202) 383-3700

WOJCIK, Paul N.
V. President and General Counsel, Bureau of Nat'l Affairs, Inc., The
1231 25th St., N.W., Washington, DC 20037
Telephone: (202) 452-4200

WOLDEHAWARIAT, Alem
Treasurer, CSX Transportation Inc. Political Action Committee
1331 Pennsylvania Ave., N.W., Suite 560, Washington, DC 20004
Telephone: (202) 783-8124

WOLF, James E.
V. President, Government Affairs, American Standard Inc.
2020 14th St., North Suite 408, Arlington, VA 22201
Telephone: (703) 525-4015
Registered as lobbyist at U.S. Congress.

WOLF, James L.
Exec. Director, Alliance to Save Energy
1725 K .St., N.W., Suite 914, Washington, DC 20006
Telephone: (202) 857-0666
Registered as lobbyist at U.S. Congress.

WOLF, James W.
V. President, Jefferson Group, The
1341 G St., N.W., Suite 1100, Washington, DC 20005
Telephone: (202) 638-3535
Background: Legislative Director to then-Senator Dan Quayle (R-IN), 1981-83.

WOLF, Kenneth L.
Account Executive, Gov't Relations, Hill and Knowlton Public Affairs Worldwide
Washington Harbour, 901 31st St., N.W., Washington, DC 20007
Telephone: (202) 333-7400
Registered as lobbyist at U.S. Congress.
Clients:
Hertz Corp.

WOLF, Linda
Deputy Director, American Public Welfare Ass'n
810 First St., N.E., Suite 300, Washington, DC 20002
Telephone: (202) 682-0100

WOLFE, Dr. Leslie R.
Exec. Director, Center for Women Policy Studies
2000 P St., N.W. Suite 508, Washington, DC 20036
Telephone: (202) 872-1770

WOLFE, Dr. Sidney M.
Director, Public Citizen Health Research Group
2000 P St., N.W., Suite 700, Washington, DC 20036
Telephone: (202) 872-0320
Registered as lobbyist at U.S. Congress.

WOLFE, Tom
Manager, Nat'l Restaurant Ass'n Political Action Committee
1200 Seventh St., N.W., Washington, DC 20036
Telephone: (202) 638-6100

WOLFF, Alan W.
Dewey, Ballantine, Bushby, Palmer and Wood
1775 Pennsylvania Ave., N.W. Suite 200, Washington, DC 20006
Telephone: (202) 862-1000
Registered as lobbyist at U.S. Congress.
Background: Attorney, Office of General Counsel, Internat'l Affairs Section, U.S. Treasury Department, 1968-73. Deputy General Counsel, 1973-74. General Counsel, 1974-76, and Deputy Special Representative for Trade Negotiations , 1977-79, Office of Special Representative for Trade Negotiations.
Clients:
Coalition for Fair Lumber Imports
Intel Corporation
Labor-Industry Coalition for Internat'l Trade
Nat'l Forest Products Ass'n
Semiconductor Industry Ass'n

WOLFMAN, Brian
Staff Attorney, Public Citizen Litigation Group
2000 P St., N.W., Suite 700, Washington, DC 20036
Telephone: (202) 785-3704

WOLFORD, Melissa
Director, Federal Affairs, American Insurance Ass'n
1130 Connecticut Ave., N.W., Suite 1000, Washington, DC 20036
Telephone: (202) 828-7100
Registered as lobbyist at U.S. Congress.
Background: Former Legislative Assistant to Senator Robert Byrd (D-WV).

WOLFSOHN, Venlo J.
Newell-Payne Companies, Inc.
2011 Eye St., N.W., 5th Floor, Washington, DC 20006
Telephone: (202) 223-3217
Background: Serves as Exec. Director, Nat'l Corrugated Steel Pipe Ass'n.
Clients:
Nat'l Corrugated Steel Pipe Ass'n

WOLK, Susan T.
Exec. Director, Ass'n for Information and Image Management
1100 Wayne Ave. Suite 1100, Silver Spring, MD 20910
Telephone: (301) 587-8202

WOLLACK, Leslie
Legislative Counsel, Nat'l League of Cities
1301 Pennsylvania Ave., N.W., Washington, DC 20004
Telephone: (202) 626-3000

WOLLENBERG, J. Roger
Wilmer, Cutler and Pickering
2445 M St., N.W., Washington, DC 20037-1420
Telephone: (202) 663-6000
Background: Lieutenant, U.S. Navy, 1942-46. Law Clerk to Justice William O. Douglas, U.S. Supreme Court, 1946-47. Assistant Chief, Antitrust Division, Department of Justice, 1947-52. Assistant Chief Counsel for Litigation, Federal Communications Commission, 1952-54.
Clients:
Internat'l Business Machines Corp.
RKO General, Inc.

WOLLOCK, Andrea J.
Regional Mgr., State Government Affairs, Abbott Laboratories
1710 Rhode Island Ave., N.W. Suite 300, Washington, DC 20036
Telephone: (202) 659-8524
Registered as lobbyist at U.S. Congress.

WOLPE, Bruce
Principal, Wexler, Reynolds, Fuller, Harrison and Schule, Inc.
1317 F St., N.W., Suite 600, Washington, DC 20004
Telephone: (202) 638-2121
Registered as lobbyist at U.S. Congress.
Clients:
American Institute for Foreign Study
Communications Satellite Corp. (COMSAT)

Coopers and Lybrand
Foothills Pipe Lines (Yukon), Ltd.
MCI Communications Corp.
NOVA, An Alberta Corp.
Novacor Chemicals, Ltd.

WOLSEY, Ronald W.
Washington Representative, Amoco Corp.
1615 M St., N.W., Suite 200, Washington, DC 20036
Telephone: (202) 857-5307
Registered as lobbyist at U.S. Congress.

WOMACK, Don
V. President, TU Services
1825 K St., N.W., Suite 303, Washington, DC 20006
Telephone: (202) 822-9745
Registered as lobbyist at U.S. Congress.

WOMACK, John
Legis Section, DEPARTMENT OF TRANSPORTATION - Nat'l Highway Traffic Safety Administration
400 Seventh St., S.W., Washington, DC 20590
Telephone: (202) 366-5265

WOMACK, Richard Marvin
V. President,. Nat'l Gov't Relations, Procter and Gamble Mfg. Co.
801 18th St., N.W., Suite 400, Washington, DC 20006
Telephone: (202) 833-9500
Registered as lobbyist at U.S. Congress.

WOMACK, Stephanie
McBride Assoc, Inc., Charlie
1101 Connecticut Ave., N.W., Suite 906, Washington, DC 20036
Telephone: (202) 466-4210
Registered as lobbyist at U.S. Congress.
Organizations represented:
Louisiana Energy Services

WOOD, Bruce C.
Counsel, American Insurance Ass'n
1130 Connecticut Ave., N.W., Suite 1000, Washington, DC 20036
Telephone: (202) 828-7100

WOOD, Burton C.
Consultant, Mortgage Bankers Ass'n of America
1125 15th St., N.W., Suite 700, Washington, DC 20005
Telephone: (202) 861-6500

WOOD, Douglass G.
V. President, Military Marketing, Gulfstream Aerospace Corp.
1000 Wilson Blvd., Suite 2701, Arlington, VA 22209
Telephone: (703) 276-9500

WOOD, Frederic L.
Donelan, Cleary, Wood and Maser, P.C.
1275 K St., N.W., Suite 850, Washington, DC 20005
Telephone: (202) 371-9500
Clients:
American Frozen Food Institute
Minnesota Power

WOOD, G. Dean
President, Nat'l Coffee Service Ass'n
4000 Williamsburg Square, Fairfax, VA 22032
Telephone: (703) 273-9008

WOOD, Gordon
Sr. V. President, Government Relations, Synthetic Organic Chemical Manufacturers Ass'n
1330 Connecticut Ave., N.W. Suite 300, Washington, DC 20036
Telephone: (202) 659-0060

WOOD, Joel, Jr.
Assistant V. Pres., Government Affairs, Nat'l Ass'n of Professional Insurance Agents
400 North Washington St., Alexandria, VA 22314
Telephone: (703) 836-9340
Registered as lobbyist at U.S. Congress.
Background: Former Legislative Assistant and Press Secretary to Rep. Donald Sundquist (R-TN).

WOOD, John H.
V. President, Public Affairs, Sterling Drug Inc.
1776 Eye St., N.W. Suite 1060, Washington, DC 20006
Telephone: (202) 857-3450

WASHINGTON REPRESENTATIVES

WOOD, Mildred
Income Policy Analyst, Nat'l Committee to Preserve Social Security and Medicare
2000 K St., N.W. Suite 800, Washington, DC 20006
Telephone: (202) 822-9459
Registered as lobbyist at U.S. Congress.

WOOD, Victoria
Smith, Bucklin and Associates
1101 Connecticut Ave., N.W., Suite 700, Washington, DC 20036
Telephone: (202) 857-1100
Clients:
  Museum Trustee Ass'n

WOODALL, S. Roy, Jr.
President, Nat'l Ass'n of Life Companies
1455 Pennsylvania Ave., N.W., Suite 1250, Washington, DC 20004
Telephone: (202) 783-6252
Registered as lobbyist at U.S. Congress.

WOODALL, W. Robert
Southern Company Services, Inc.
1130 Connecticut Ave., N.W., Suite 830, Washington, DC 20036
Telephone: (202) 775-0944
Registered as lobbyist at U.S. Congress.

WOODHAM, David H.
Treasurer, Andersen and Co. Political Action Committee, Arthur
1666 K St., N.W., Washington, DC 20006
Telephone: (202) 862-3100

WOODLE, Clyde E.
Exec. Dir., Trucking Research Institute, American Trucking Ass'ns
2200 Mill Road, Alexandria, VA 22314
Telephone: (703) 838-1800
Background: Served for several years on the staff of the House of Representatives Committee on Public Works and Transportation, most recently as Chief Engineer.

WOODMAN, G. Kent
Eckert Seamans Cherin & Mellott
1818 N St., N.W., Suite 700, Washington, DC 20036
Telephone: (202) 452-1074
Registered as lobbyist at U.S. Congress.
Background: Formerly served in the Office of the Legislative Counsel, U.S. House of Representatives, 1974-81; and in the Urban Mass Transportation Administration, 1981-84.
Clients:
  New York Metropolitan Transportation Authority

WOODRUFF, C. Roy, Ph.D.
Exec. Director, American Ass'n of Pastoral Counselors
9508A Lee Hwy., Fairfax, VA 22031-2303
Telephone: (703) 385-6967

WOODRUFF, James
Legis Analysis, Office of General Couns, OFFICE OF PERSONNEL MANAGEMENT
1900 E St., N.W., Washington, DC 20415
Telephone: (202) 632-6514

WOODS AND ASSOCIATES
P.O. Box 521, The Plains, VA 22171-0521
Telephone: (703) 253-9621
Members of firm representing listed organizations:
  Woods, Irvin M., President
Clients:
  Maule Air, Inc. *(Irvin M. Woods)*
  OTL, Inc. *(Irvin M. Woods)*
  Woods Research Associates *(Irvin M. Woods)*

WOODS, Irvin M.
President, Woods and Associates
P.O. Box 521, The Plains, VA 22171-0521
Telephone: (703) 253-9621
Registered as lobbyist at U.S. Congress.
Clients:
  Maule Air, Inc.
  OTL, Inc.
  Woods Research Associates

WOODS, Jeanne
Legislative Counsel, American Civil Liberties Union
122 Maryland Ave., N.E., Washington, DC 20002
Telephone: (202) 544-1681
Registered as lobbyist at U.S. Congress.
Background: Serves also as a legislative counsel for the Center for Nat'l Security Studies.

WOODS, Jennifer
V. President, Asia Pacific Space and Communciations
1655 North Fort Myer Drive Suite 1120, Arlington, VA 22209
Telephone: (703) 525-2772

WOODS, Col. Jerry
House Liaison, Legis Liaison, DEPARTMENT OF AIR FORCE
The Pentagon, Washington, DC 20330
Telephone: (202) 697-8153

WOODS, Stephen P.
Director, State Government Relations, Nat'l Federation of Independent Business
600 Maryland Ave., S.W., Suite 700, Washington, DC 20024
Telephone: (202) 554-9000

WOODSIDE, Cynthia
Associate, Federal Gov't Relations, United Way of America
701 N. Fairfax St., Alexandria, VA 22314-2045
Telephone: (703) 836-7100
Registered as lobbyist at U.S. Congress.

WOODSON, Robert L.
Congressional Liaison, Nat'l Center for Neighborhood Enterprise
1367 Connecticut Ave., N.W., 2nd Floor, Washington, DC 20036
Telephone: (202) 331-1103

WOODWARD, Michele T.
Sr. Specialist, Government Relations, COMSAT General Corp.
950 L'Enfant Plaza, S.W., Washington, DC 20024
Telephone: (202) 863-6000
Registered as lobbyist at U.S. Congress.

WOODWARD, Robert
Regional Director, Dataproducts Corp.
12200 Sunrise Valley Drive Suite 230, Reston, VA 22091
Telephone: (703) 648-0930

WOODWORTH, Donald C.
MacMeekin & Woodworth
1776 Massachusetts Ave., N.W. Suite 604, Washington, DC 20036
Telephone: (202) 223-1717
Background: Former General Counsel to the Resident Representative for the Northern Mariana Islands.

WOODY, Robert J.
Lane and Mittendorf
919 18th St., N.W., Suite 800, Washington, DC 20006
Telephone: (202) 785-4949
Background: Legislative Assistant to Sen. James B. Pearson, 1969-71. Counsel, Senate Committee on Commerce, 1971-73.

WOOFTER, Perry W.
Sr. V. President, Government Relations, Tesoro Petroleum Corp.
1800 K St., N.W. Suite 530, Washington, DC 20006
Telephone: (202) 775-8840
Registered as lobbyist at U.S. Congress.

WOOLLEY, Howard E.
Director, Government Relations, Nat'l Ass'n of Broadcasters
1771 N St., N.W., Washington, DC 20036
Telephone: (202) 429-5300
Registered as lobbyist at U.S. Congress.

WOOLLEY, Linda A.
Director, Public Affairs, ITT Corp.
1600 M St., N.W., Washington, DC 20036
Telephone: (202) 775-7367
Registered as lobbyist at U.S. Congress.

WOOLSEY, Noel C.
National Service Director, American Veterans of World War II, Korea and Vietnam (AMVETS)
4647 Forbes Blvd., Lanham, MD 20706
Telephone: (301) 459-9600

WOOTTON, James M.
Director, Policy Develpmnt & Communic., Legal Services Corp.
400 Virginia Ave., S.W., Washington, DC 20024
Telephone: (202) 863-1820

WOOTTON, Robert
Tax Legis Counsel (Act), DEPARTMENT OF TREASURY
15th and Pennsylvania Ave. N.W., Washington, DC 20220
Telephone: (202) 566-2316

WORDEN, George M.
Senior Consultant, Hill and Knowlton Public Affairs Worldwide
Washington Harbour, 901 31st St., N.W., Washington, DC 20007
Telephone: (202) 333-7400
Registered as lobbyist at U.S. Congress.

WORDEN, Joan
V. President, Hill and Knowlton Public Affairs Worldwide
Washington Harbour, 901 31st St., N.W., Washington, DC 20007
Telephone: (202) 333-7400
Clients:
  Peat Marwick

WORK, Dr. Jane
V. President, Legislative Analysis, Nat'l Ass'n of Manufacturers
1331 Pennsylvania Ave., N.W. Suite 1500 North, Washington, DC 20004-1703
Telephone: (202) 637-3000

WORK, Peter B.
Crowell and Moring
1001 Pennsylvania Ave., N.W., Washington, DC 20004-2505
Telephone: (202) 624-2500

WORKINGS, Steve
Consultant, Federation for American Immigration Reform (FAIR)
1666 Connecticut Ave., N.W., Suite 400, Washington, DC 20009
Telephone: (202) 328-7004
Registered as lobbyist at U.S. Congress.

WORKMAN, Willard
Dir, Programs and Policy, Internat'l Div, Chamber of Commerce of the U.S.A.
1615 H St., N.W., Washington, DC 20062
Telephone: (202) 659-6000
Registered as lobbyist at U.S. Congress.

WORLD TRADE LINK
One Thomas Circle, N.W. Suite 900, Washington, DC 20005
Telephone: (202) 293-0616
Registered as Foreign Agent: (#4317)
Clients:
  Continental Manufacturing Corp.
  Lembaga Bantuan Pemesaran & Manajemen

WORLDWIDE ASSOCIATES, INC
1155 15th St., N.W. Suite 800, Washington, DC 20005
Telephone: (202) 429-9788
Members of firm representing listed organizations:
  Goldberg, Sherwood D., Director
  Haig, Alexander M. (Jr.), President

WORSHAM, Wanda
Confidential Asst, Cong Rels, DEPARTMENT OF AGRICULTURE
14th and Independence Ave. S.W., Room 209-E, Washington, DC 20205
Telephone: (202) 447-7095

WORSTELL, Mary E.
Exec. V. President, Asthma and Allergy Foundation of America
1717 Massachusetts Ave., N.W., Suite 305, Washington, DC 20036

WORSTELL, Mary E. (Cont'd)
Telephone: (202) 265-0265

WORTH, Douglas C.
IBM Director of Public Affairs, Internat'l Business Machines Corp.
Suite 1200, 1801 K St., N.W., Washington, DC 20006
Telephone: (202) 778-5064

WORTHINGTON, Barry K.
Exec. Director, United States Energy Ass'n
1620 Eye St., N.W., Suite 615, Washington, DC 20006
Telephone: (202) 331-0415
Background: Also serves as Executive Director of the Member Committee of the U.S., World Energy Conference.

WORTHINGTON, John R.
Sr. V. Pres. and General Counsel, MCI Communications Corp.
1133 19th St., N.W., Washington, DC 20036
Telephone: (202) 872-1600

WORTHY, K. Martin
Hopkins and Sutter
888 16th St., N.W., Suite 700, Washington, DC 20006
Telephone: (202) 835-8000
Background: Chief Counsel, Internal Revenue Service, 1969-72. Member, Board of Directors, Beneficial Corp.

WOSCHITZ, Frank
Director of Public Relations, Federation of Professional Athletes
2021 L St., N.W., Suite 600, Washington, DC 20036
Telephone: (202) 463-2200

WOTRING, Thomas K.
Morgan, Lewis and Bockius
1800 M St., N.W., Washington, DC 20036
Telephone: (202) 467-7000
Clients:
Florida Public Utilities Co.
Harsco Corp.

WRENN, Grover
President, Environ Corp.
4350 North Fairfax Drive Suite 300, Arlington, VA 22203
Telephone: (703) 516-2300

WRIGHT, Andrew S.
Senior Counsel, Federal Affairs, American Insurance Ass'n
1130 Connecticut Ave., N.W., Suite 1000, Washington, DC 20036
Telephone: (202) 828-7100
Registered as lobbyist at U.S. Congress.

WRIGHT, Dennis
V. President, Operations, Nat'l Business Aircraft Ass'n
1200 18th St., N.W. Suite 200, Washington, DC 20036
Telephone: (202) 783-9000

WRIGHT, Elizabeth L.
Manager, Llegislative Affairs, Texas Instruments
1455 Pennsylvania Ave., N.W., Suite 230, Washington, DC 20004
Telephone: (202) 628-3133

WRIGHT, F. Leo
V. President, Government Affairs, Westinghouse Electric Corp.
1801 K St., N.W., Washington, DC 20006
Telephone: (202) 835-2324

WRIGHT, Rev. Francis W.
National Director, Holy Childhood Ass'n
1720 Massachusetts Ave., N.W., Washington, DC 20036
Telephone: (202) 775-8637

WRIGHT, Jeffrey
National Chairman, Young Americans for Freedom
380 Maple Ave. West Suite 303, Vienna, VA 22180
Telephone: (703) 938-3305

WRIGHT, Lloyd
President and Exec. Director, Nat'l Senior Sports Ass'n
10560 Main St., Suite 205, Fairfax, VA 22030
Telephone: (703) 385-7540

WRIGHT, Marion
Nat'l Secretary-Treasurer, Nat'l Postal Mail Handlers Union
One Thomas Circle, N.W. Suite 525, Washington, DC 20005
Telephone: (202) 833-9095

WRIGHT, Pat A.
Director, Governmental Affairs, Disability Rights Education and Defense Fund
1616 P St., N.W., Suite 100, Washington, DC 20036
Telephone: (202) 328-5185

WRIGHT, Paul E.
Chairman, Chrysler Technologies Corp.
1100 Connecticut Ave., N.W. 7th Floor, Washington, DC 20036
Telephone: (202) 862-3460

WRIGHT, Paul R.
Exec. Director, American Medical Student Ass'n
1890 Preston White Drive, Reston, VA 22091
Telephone: (703) 620-6600
Registered as lobbyist at U.S. Congress.

WRIGHT, Roberta Y.
V. President and General Counsel, Nat'l Urban Coalition
8601 Georgia Ave., Suite 500, Silver Spring, MD 20910
Telephone: (301) 495-4999

WRIGHT AND TALISMAN
1050 17th St., N.W. Suite 600, Washington, DC 20036
Telephone: (202) 331-1194
Members of firm representing listed organizations:
  Benna, Robert H.
  Davidson, Richard H.
    Background: Attorney, Federal Energy Regulatory Commission, 1985-86.
  Flynn, Paul M.
  Fryxell, Joseph O.
  Grady, Gregory
    Background: Attorney, Federal Power Commission, 1973-74.
  Kern, Robert G.
  Ketcham, John T.
  McManus, James T.
    Background: Attorney, Federal Power Commission, 1975-77.
  Portasic, Linda
    Background: Assistant to the Chairman, Federal Power Commission, 1952-53.
  Small, Michael E.
    Background: Attorney, Federal Energy Regulatory Commission, 1979-85.
  Statman, Alan J.
  Talisman, Harold L.
  Thompson, Michael J.
    Background: Attorney, U.S. Environmental Protection Agency, 1981.
  Waikart, Douglas O.
  Withnell, David D.
Clients:
Alabama Gas Corp.
Arizona Power Authority
Bangor Hydro-Electric Co.
East Tennessee Natural Gas Co.
Five Flags
Maine Public Service Co.
Midwestern Gas Transmission Co.
North Carolina Natural Gas Corp.
Northwest Pipeline Corp.
Public Service Co. of North Carolina
Southwestern Public Service Co.
Williams Companies, The

WRIGLEY, Pat R.
Director, Administration, Nat'l Petroleum Refiners Ass'n
1899 L St., N.W., Suite 1000, Washington, DC 20036
Telephone: (202) 457-0480

WUERTHNER ASSOCIATES
6700 Emporia, Suite 200, Springfield, VA 22152
Telephone: (703) 569-4840
Members of firm representing listed organizations:
  Wuerthner, J. J. (Jr.), President

WUERTHNER, J. J., Jr.
President, Wuerthner Associates
6700 Emporia, Suite 200, Springfield, VA 22152

Telephone: (703) 569-4840

WUNDER, Bernard J.
Wunder, Ryan, Cannon & Thelen
1615 L St., N.W., Suite 650, Washington, DC 20036
Telephone: (202) 659-3005
Registered as lobbyist at U.S. Congress.
Registered as Foreign Agent: (#3971).
Background: Aide to Rep. James Broyhill (R-NC), 1975-81, and Chief Counsel to House Subcommittee on Communications. Assistant Secretary of Commerce for Communications and Information, 1981-83.
Clients:
BellSouth Corp.
Industrial Equity (Pacific) Ltd.
Mylan Laboratories, Inc.
Polaris Industries
Shared Medical Systems
United Financial Group
United States Telephone Ass'n

WUNDER, RYAN, CANNON & THELEN
1615 L St., N.W., Suite 650, Washington, DC 20036
Telephone: (202) 659-3005
Registered as Foreign Agent: (#3971)
Members of firm representing listed organizations:
  Bliss, John S.
    Background: Legislative Aide to Senator Arlen Specter (R-PA), 1981-84.
  Cannon, W. Stephen
    Background: Trial Attorney, Antitrust Division, Department of Justice, 1977-81; Chief Antitrust Counsel to the Senate Judiciary Committee, 1981-85; Deputy Assistant Attorney General, Antitrust Division, Department of Justice, 1985-86.
  Forscey, Michael A.
    Background: Counsel, U.S. Senate Subcommittee on Labor, 1977-80. Special Assistant to the Majority Whip of the U.S. House of Representatives, 1980-81. Chief Minority Counsel, U.S. Senate Committee on Labor and Human Resources, 1981-85.
  Gibson, Joseph
    Background: Research Assistant, Senate Judiciary Committee, 1983-84. Law Clerk to the Hon. R. Lanier Anderson, III, 1987-88.
  Higgins, Lawrence P.
    Background: Chief Counsel, Federal Taxes and Pension, American Council of Life Insurance, 1982-84.
  Koch, Patrick C.
  Levine, Kenneth S.
    Background: Director, Office of Congressional Consumer and Public Affairs, Federal Energy Regulatory Commission, 1979-81. Deputy Assistant Secretary for Legislation, U.S. Department of Health, Education and Welfare, 1977-79. Administrative Assistant to Rep. Bob Eckhardt (D-TX), 1975-76.
  McGovern, John J. (Jr.)
    Background: Legislative Assistant to Senator Richard Lugar (R-IN), 1977-83. Legislative Assistant to Chairman John S. R. Shad, Securities and Exchange Commission, 1983-85.
  Ryan, Thomas M.
    Background: Staff member and Chief Counsel, House Committee on Energy and Commerce, 1977-87.
  Sullivan, Paul E.
    Background: Assistant Legal Counsel, Nat'l Republican Congressional Committee, 1981-82. Executive Assistant to Commissioner, Federal Election Commission, 1982-85.
  Thelen, Dennis C.
    Background: Deputy Chief Counsel, U.S. Senate Subcommittee on Criminal Laws and Procedures, 1975-76. Counsel to Senate Majority Leader, 1977-78.
  Wunder, Bernard J.
    Background: Aide to Rep. James Broyhill (R-NC), 1975-81, and Chief Counsel to House Subcommittee on Communications. Assistant Secretary of Commerce for Communications and Information, 1981-83.
Clients:
Aermacchi, S.p.A. *(John J. McGovern, Jr.)*
Airship Industries, Ltd. *(John J. McGovern, Jr.)*
American Internat'l Group *(Kenneth S. Levine, Thomas M. Ryan)*
American Iron and Steel Institute *(Michael A. Forscey, Thomas M. Ryan)*
Ass'n of American Railroads *(Thomas M. Ryan)*
BellSouth Corp. *(Bernard J. Wunder)*

The listings in this directory are available as *Mailing Labels*. See last page.

Bermuda, Government of *(Kenneth S. Levine)*
Bond Internat'l Gold *(John J. McGovern, Jr.)*
Bristol-Myers Squibb Co. *(Dennis C. Thelen)*
Burlington Resources, Inc. *(Thomas M. Ryan)*
Cosmetic, Toiletry and Fragrance Ass'n *(Dennis C. Thelen)*
Dresser Industries *(W. Stephen Cannon)*
Environmental Air Control Inc. *(Kenneth S. Levine)*
Falcon Safety Products *(Kenneth S. Levine)*
FFA Fluzeugwerke *(John J. McGovern, Jr.)*
Finanziaria Mirabella SpA *(John J. McGovern, Jr.)*
Gesamtverband der Deutschen Versicherung-swirtschaft e.V. *(Kenneth S. Levine)*
Grocery Manufacturers of America *(W. Stephen Cannon, Patrick C. Koch)*
HDTV 1125/60 Group *(Dennis C. Thelen)*
Hook-SupeRx, Inc. *(Kenneth S. Levine)*
Industrial Equity (Pacific) Ltd. *(Bernard J. Wunder)*
Intermarine S.p.A. *(John J. McGovern, Jr.)*
Investment Company Institute *(Thomas M. Ryan)*
Kelly Services, Inc. *(Michael A. Forscey)*
Kohlberg Kravis Roberts & Co. *(Kenneth S. Levine)*
KRC Research and Consulting *(Michael A. Forscey)*
Manville Corp. *(Michael A. Forscey)*
Metropolitan Insurance Cos. *(Michael A. Forscey, Lawrence P. Higgins)*
Mirabella *(John J. McGovern, Jr.)*
Mutual Life Insurance Co. Tax Committee *(Lawrence P. Higgins)*
Mylan Laboratories, Inc. *(Michael A. Forscey, Bernard J. Wunder)*
Nat'l Ass'n of Temporary Services *(Michael A. Forscey)*
Nat'l Council of Savings Institutions THRIFT-PAC *(Paul E. Sullivan)*
Nat'l Federation of Independent Business PAC *(Paul E. Sullivan)*
Nat'l Security Political Action Committee *(Paul E. Sullivan)*
NEC Home Electronics (USA) Inc. *(W. Stephen Cannon)*
North American Philips Corp. *(W. Stephen Cannon)*
Northwestern Mutual Life Insurance Co. *(Lawrence P. Higgins)*
NutraSweet Co. *(Paul E. Sullivan)*
NYNEX *(W. Stephen Cannon)*
Pan American Life *(Paul E. Sullivan)*
PepsiCo PAC *(Paul E. Sullivan)*
Pfizer, Inc. *(Kenneth S. Levine, Thomas M. Ryan)*
Philip Morris Management Corp. *(Kenneth S. Levine, Thomas M. Ryan)*
Polaris Industries *(Bernard J. Wunder)*
Restaurant Ass'n of Metropolitan Washington PAC *(Paul E. Sullivan)*
Rohm and Haas Co. *(W. Stephen Cannon)*
Section 8 Coalition *(W. Stephen Cannon)*
Shared Medical Systems *(Bernard J. Wunder)*
Sony Corp. of America *(Dennis C. Thelen)*
State Compliance Systems *(Paul E. Sullivan)*
Tobacco Industry Labor Management Committee *(Michael A. Forscey)*
Trailer Train Co. *(W. Stephen Cannon)*
United Financial Group *(Bernard J. Wunder)*
United States Telephone Ass'n *(Patrick C. Koch, Bernard J. Wunder)*
VINTA Mineral and Financial, Inc. *(Paul E. Sullivan)*
Westinghouse Airship *(John J. McGovern, Jr.)*
Westinghouse Electric Corp. *(John J. McGovern, Jr.)*
Wheelabrator Technologies‡ Inc. *(Thomas M. Ryan)*

WURFEL, Walter R.
Sr. V. Pres., Public Affrs. & Commo., Nat'l Ass'n of Broadcasters
1771 N St., N.W., Washington, DC 20036
Telephone: (202) 429-5300

WURZEL, Mary
Immediate Past President, Ex-Partners of Servicemen/Women for Equality
Box 11191, Alexandria, VA 22312
Telephone: (703) 941-5844

WYATT, Lisa
Director, Public Affairs, American Psychological Ass'n
1200 17th St., N.W., Washington, DC 20036
Telephone: (202) 955-7600

WYERMAN, James K.
Dir., Internat'l Wildlife Trade Program, Defenders of Wildlife
1244 19th St., N.W., Washington, DC 20036
Telephone: (202) 659-9510

WYLIE, Thomas L.
V. President, Government Affairs, Sun Co.
555 13th St., N.W., Suite 1010 East, Washington, DC 20004
Telephone: (202) 628-1010
Registered as lobbyist at U.S. Congress.

WYMAN, BAUTZER, CHRISTENSEN, KUCHEL AND SILBERT
1919 Pennsylvania Ave., N.W., Suite 800, Washington, DC 20006
Telephone: (202) 887-5236
Background: Washington office of a Los Angeles law firm. The following information was obtained from public records and submitted to this firm for confirmation; the firm did not respond.
Members of firm representing listed organizations:
Miron, George
Background: Assistant Chief, General Litigation Section and Trial Attorney, Anti-trust Division, Dep't of Justice, 1959-1965. Special Assistant to the Solicitor and Associate Solicitor for Reclamation and Power, Dep't of the Interior, 1965-1968.
Clients:
American Boiler Manufacturers Ass'n *(George Miron)*
Eklutna, Inc.
Korea Textile Manufacturers Ass'n
Southern Bell Telephone and Telegraph Co.
Southwestern Bell Telephone Co.

WYNETT, David S.
Manager, Legislative Affairs, Delta Air Lines
1629 K St., N.W., Suite 501, Washington, DC 20006
Telephone: (202) 296-6464
Registered as lobbyist at U.S. Congress.

WYNN, William H.
Internat'l President, United Food and Commercial Workers Internat'l Union
1775 K St., N.W., Washington, DC 20006
Telephone: (202) 223-3111
Registered as lobbyist at U.S. Congress.

WYNNE, Brian P.
Sr. Manager, Internat'l Trade Affairs, American Electronics Ass'n
1225 Eye St., N.W., Suite 950, Washington, DC 20005
Telephone: (202) 682-9110

WYNNE, George
Director, Internat'l Center, Academy for State and Local Government
444 North Capitol St., N.W., Suite 349, Washington, DC 20001
Telephone: (202) 638-1445
Background: Responsibilities include the International Center of the Academy.

YABLONSKI, BOTH & EDELMAN
1140 Connecticut Ave., N.W. Suite 800, Washington, DC 20036
Telephone: (202) 833-9060
Members of firm representing listed organizations:
Edelman, Daniel B.
Background: Law Clerk to Justice Harry A. Blackmun, U.S. Supreme Court, 1970-71.
Clients:
United Mine Workers of America *(Daniel B. Edelman)*

YACKER, Marc D.
Director, Congressional Affairs, American Paper Institute
1250 Connecticut Ave., N.W. Suite 210, Washington, DC 20036
Telephone: (202) 463-2420
Registered as lobbyist at U.S. Congress.
Background: Former Administrative Assistant to Rep. Peter A. Peyser of New York.

YAGER, Brenda
Asst Admin, Govt and Industry Affrs, DEPARTMENT OF TRANSPORTATION - Federal Aviation Administration
800 Independence Ave., S.W., Washington, DC 20591
Telephone: (202) 267-3277

YAGER, Milan P.
Senior Legislative Representative, Nat'l Ass'n of Home Builders of the U.S.
15th and M Streets, N.W., Washington, DC 20005
Telephone: (202) 822-0470
Registered as lobbyist at U.S. Congress.

YAGI, Tatsuo
Chief Representative, Chubu Electric Power Co.
900 17th St., N.W., Suite 1220, Washington, DC 20006
Telephone: (202) 775-1960

YAKEMOWICZ, Anthony J.
V. Pres. and Interim Legis. Director, Internat'l Brotherhood of Boilermakers, Iron Shipbuilders, Blacksmiths, Forgers and Helpers
400 First St., N.W., Suite 814, Washington, DC 20001
Telephone: (202) 638-5768
Registered as lobbyist at U.S. Congress.

YAKSICH, Nick
Policy Analyst, Nat'l League of Cities
1301 Pennsylvania Ave., N.W., Washington, DC 20004
Telephone: (202) 626-3000

YAMADA, Deborah K.
Manager, Government Affairs, American Express Co.
1020 19th St., N.W., Suite 600, Washington, DC 20036
Telephone: (202) 822-6680
Registered as lobbyist at U.S. Congress.

YAMADA, Masayuki
Senior Representative, Hitachi Ltd.
1850 K St., N.W., Suite 475, Washington, DC 20006
Telephone: (202) 828-9272
Registered as Foreign Agent: (# 3855)

YAMADA, T. Albert
President, Masaoka Associates, Mike
900 17th St., N.W., Suite 520, Washington, DC 20006
Telephone: (202) 296-4484
Registered as lobbyist at U.S. Congress.
Organizations represented:
Toyota Motor Sales, U.S.A.
West Mexico Vegetable Distributors Ass'n

YAMAGATA, Ben
Van Ness, Feldman & Curtis
1050 Thomas Jefferson St., 7th Floor, Washington, DC 20007
Telephone: (202) 298-1800
Registered as lobbyist at U.S. Congress.
Background: Counsel and Staff Director, Senate Subcommittee on Energy Research and Development, 1975-77. Legislative Counsel to the late Senator Frank Church of Idaho, 1974-75. Professional Staff Member, Senate Special Committee on Aging, 1973-74. Serves as Exec. Director, Clean Coal Technology Coalition.
Clients:
Clean Coal Technology Coalition
Geothermal Resources Ass'n
Los Angeles, California, Department of Water and Power
Southern California Edison Co.

YAMAMOTO, Toshiaki
Chief Representative, New Energy and Industrial Technology Development Organization
1800 K St., N.W. Suite 924, Washington, DC 20006
Telephone: (202) 822-9298

YANCEY, F. Dalton
Exec. V. President, Florida Sugar Cane League
910 16th St., N.W., Suite 402, Washington, DC 20006
Telephone: (202) 785-4070
Registered as lobbyist at U.S. Congress.

YANDRICK, Rudy
Communications Director, Ass'n of Labor-Management Administrators and Consultants on Alcoholism
4601 N. Fairfax Drive Suite 1001, Arlington, VA 22203
Telephone: (703) 522-6272

WASHINGTON REPRESENTATIVES

YANICH, Beverly
Associate Director, American Public Welfare Ass'n
810 First St., N.E., Suite 300, Washington, DC 20002
Telephone: (202) 682-0100

YANISH, Nancy Foster
Director, Agricultural Relations, Food Marketing Institute
1750 K St., N.W., Washington, DC 20006
Telephone: (202) 452-8444
Registered as lobbyist at U.S. Congress.

YANNITELL, David M.
Mgr., Nucl. Energy Proj., GE Nucl. Energy, General Electric Co.
12300 Twinbrook Pkwy Suite 315, Rockville, MD 20852
Telephone: (202) 637-4567

YANNUCCI, Thomas D.
Kirkland and Ellis
655 15th St., N.W. Suite 1200, Washington, DC 20005
Telephone: (202) 879-5000
Background: Former Law Clerk to Hon. John A Danaher, U.S. Court of Appeals for the District of Columbia.

YARBOROUGH, William Glenn, Jr.
Manager, Ford Aerospace Corp.
Suite 1300, 1235 Jefferson Davis Hwy., Arlington, VA 22202
Telephone: (703) 685-5531

YARD, Molly
President, Nat'l Organization for Women
1000 16th St., N.W., Suite 700, Washington, DC 20036
Telephone: (202) 331-0066

YARRINGTON, Mary J.
Senior Policy Analyst, Nat'l Committee to Preserve Social Security and Medicare
2000 K St., N.W. Suite 800, Washington, DC 20006
Telephone: (202) 822-9459
Registered as lobbyist at U.S. Congress.
Background: Former Staff Assistant to Rep. James Oberstar (D-MN).

YARWOOD, Bruce
Legislative Counsel, American Health Care Ass'n
1201 L St., N.W., Washington, DC 20005
Telephone: (202) 842-4444

YAWN, Edward R.
Sr. Legislative Affairs Representative, Edison Electric Institute
1111 19th St., N.W., Washington, DC 20036
Telephone: (202) 778-6481
Registered as lobbyist at U.S. Congress.

YEADON, Eric
President, American Wood Preservers Bureau
7962 Conell Court, Lorton, VA 22079
Telephone: (703) 339-6660

YEAGER, Brooks B.
V. President, Government Relations, Nat'l Audubon Soc.
801 Pennsylvania Ave., S.E., Washington, DC 20003
Telephone: (202) 547-9009
Registered as lobbyist at U.S. Congress.

YEAGER, J. R.
Administrative Director, Greenpeace, U.S.A.
1436 U St., N.W., Washington, DC 20009
Telephone: (202) 462-1177

YEE, Melinda C.
Exec. Director, Organization of Chinese Americans
2025 Eye St., N.W. Suite 926, Washington, DC 20006
Telephone: (202) 223-5500

YELTON, Kim
Director, Government Relations, Americans United for Separation of Church and State
8120 Fenton St., Silver Spring, MD 20910
Telephone: (301) 589-3707
Registered as lobbyist at U.S. Congress.

YELVERTON, Jack
Exec. Director, Nat'l District Attorneys Ass'n
1033 N. Fairfax St., Suite 200, Alexandria, VA 22314
Telephone: (703) 549-9222

YEP, Richard K.
Director of Government Relations, American Ass'n for Counseling and Development
901 East Capitol St, S.E., 2nd Floor, Washington, DC 20003
Telephone: (202) 543-0030
Registered as lobbyist at U.S. Congress.
Background: Responsibilities include the Ass'n for Religious and Value Issues in Counseling and the American School Counselors Ass'n.

YERKES, Sara C.
Ass't to the Washington Representative, Nat'l Fire Protection Ass'n
1110 North Glebe Road, Suite 560, Arlington, VA 22201
Telephone: (703) 524-3505

YERMAN, Robert N.
Treasurer, Deloitte & Touche Federal PAC
P.O. Box 18174, Washington, DC 20036
Telephone: (202) 638-7850

YERRICK, Mary
Senior V. President, Kaufman & Associates, Henry J.
2233 Wisconsin Ave., N.W., Washington, DC 20007
Telephone: (202) 333-0700

YINGLING, Edward L.
Exec. Director of Government Relations, American Bankers Ass'n
1120 Connecticut Ave., N.W., Washington, DC 20036
Telephone: (202) 663-5000
Registered as lobbyist at U.S. Congress.
Background: Former Legislative Assistant to Senator J. W. Fulbright (D-AR).

YINGST, Jeanne L.
Assistant Director, American Bankers Ass'n BankPac
1120 Connecticut Ave., N.W., Washington, DC 20036
Telephone: (202) 663-5076

YOCHELSON, John N.
V. President, Corporate Affairs, Center for Strategic and Internat'l Studies
1800 K St., N.W., Washington, DC 20006
Telephone: (202) 887-0200
Background: Also holds the position of Director, International Business and Economics Program.

YODICE, John S.
Washington Counsel, Aircraft Owners and Pilots Ass'n
500 E St., S.W., Suite 920, Washington, DC 20024
Telephone: (202) 479-4050
Registered as lobbyist at U.S. Congress.

YOHAY, Stephen C.
McGuiness and Williams
1015 15th St., N.W., Suite 1200, Washington, DC 20005
Telephone: (202) 789-8600
Background: Attorney, Enforcement Division, National Labor Relations Board, 1971-74. Supervisory Attorney, OSHA Division, U.S. Department of Labor, 1974-75.

YOHE, D. Scott
V. President, Gov't Affairs, Delta Air Lines
1629 K St., N.W., Suite 501, Washington, DC 20006
Telephone: (202) 296-6464
Registered as lobbyist at U.S. Congress.

YOHO, Lisa
Federal Relations Representative, Panhandle Eastern Corp.
1025 Connecticut Ave., N.W., Suite 404, Washington, DC 20036
Telephone: (202) 331-8090

YOLLES, Bryan Jay
Clifford & Warnke
815 Connecticut Ave., N.W., Washington, DC 20006
Telephone: (202) 828-4200
Background: Trial Attorney, Civil Aeronautics Board, 1977-79.

YOLTON, Rev. L. William
Exec. Director, Nat'l Interreligious Service Board for Conscientious Objectors
1601 Connecticut Ave., N.W. Suite 750, Washington, DC 20009
Telephone: (202) 293-5962

YONKIN, Pam
Saunders and Company
1015 Duke St., Alexandria, VA 22314
Telephone: (703) 549-1555
Clients:
Japan Times Corp.

YONTZ, Caryl
Legislative Affairs Specialist, American Federation of State, County and Municipal Employees
1625 L St., N.W., Washington, DC 20036
Telephone: (202) 429-1000
Registered as lobbyist at U.S. Congress.

YOOD, Andrew
Taxation Director, American Petroleum Institute
1220 L St., N.W., Washington, DC 20005
Telephone: (202) 682-8465

YOSIE, Terry F.
V. President, Health and Environment, American Petroleum Institute
1220 L St., N.W., Washington, DC 20005
Telephone: (202) 682-8090

YOST, Nicholas C.
Dickstein, Shapiro and Morin
2101 L St., N.W., Washington, DC 20037
Telephone: (202) 785-9700
Background: General Counsel, Council on Environmental Quality, Executive Office of the President, 1977-81.

YOUNG, Amy
Exec. Director, Internat'l Human Rights Law Group
1601 Connecticut Ave., N.W. Suite 700, Washington, DC 20009
Telephone: (202) 232-8500

YOUNG, Emily
Senior Associate, Dutko & Associates
412 First St., S.E. Suite 100, Washington, DC 20003
Telephone: (202) 484-4884
Registered as lobbyist at U.S. Congress.
Background: Former Special Assistant to U.S. Senate Energy and Natural Resources Committee, 1984-85; Legislative Assistant to Rep. Billy Tauzin (D-LA), 1985-89.
Clients:
American Iron and Steel Institute
Ass'n of Oil Pipe Lines
Council for Solid Waste Solutions
Creditors Alliance to Preserve Freight Undercharge Assets
McDonald's Corp.
Pacificare Health Systems, Inc.
Satellite Broadcasting and Communications Ass'n

YOUNG, Francis L.
Partner, Young & Jatlow
2300 N St., N.W., Suite 600, Washington, DC 20037
Telephone: (202) 663-9000
Background: Served formerly as Attorney-Advisor, Legal Assistant to the Chairman, and Legal Assistant to a Commissioner, Federal Communications Commission, 1976-82.
Clients:
Alascom, Inc.
Bay Area Teleport

YOUNG, Glenn M.
Squire, Sanders and Dempsey
1201 Pennsylvania Ave., N.W. P.O. Box 407, Washington, DC 20044
Telephone: (202) 626-6600

YOUNG-HORVATH, Dr. Viola M.
Exec. Director, Federation of Organizations for Professional Women
2001 S St., N.W., Suite 540, Washington, DC 20009
Telephone: (202) 328-1415

YOUNG, James A.
Manager, Industry & Economic Affairs, Nissan Motor Corp. in U.S.A.
750 17th St., N.W. Suite 901, Washington, DC 20006
Telephone: (202) 862-5523
Registered as lobbyist at U.S. Congress.

YOUNG & JATLOW
2300 N St., N.W., Suite 600, Washington, DC 20037

The listings in this directory are available as *Mailing Labels*. See last page.

Telephone: (202) 663-9080
Background: A law firm.
Members of firm representing listed organizations:
Young, Francis L., Partner
  Background: Served formerly as Attorney-Advisor, Legal Assistant to the Chairman, and Legal Assistant to a Commissioner, Federal Communications Commission, 1976-82.
  Clients:
  Alascom, Inc. *(Francis L. Young)*
  Bay Area Teleport *(Francis L. Young)*

YOUNG, Joanne W.
Partner, Lord Day & Lord, Barrett Smith
1201 Pennsylvania Ave., N.W., Suite 821, Washington, DC 20004
Telephone: (202) 393-5024
Clients:
  Aeromexico
  Aeroservicios Ecuatorianos, C.A.
  American Trans Air
  Bangor Internat'l Airport
  Iceland Air
  Iceland Steamship Co.
  Lineas Aereas del Caribe
  Miami Internat'l Airport
  Tradewinds Airways Ltd.
  Transbrasil
  Worldways Canada, Ltd.

YOUNG, Kenneth
Exec. Assistant to the President, AFL-CIO (American Federation of Labor and Congress of Industrial Organizations)
815 16th St., N.W., Washington, DC 20006
Telephone: (202) 637-5368

YOUNG, Malcolm C.
Exec. Director, Sentencing Project, The
918 F St., N.W. Suite 501, Washington, DC 20004
Telephone: (202) 628-0871

YOUNG, Mark D.
Kirkland and Ellis
655 15th St., N.W. Suite 1200, Washington, DC 20005
Telephone: (202) 879-5000
Background: Former Assistant General Counsel, Commodity Futures Trading Commission.

YOUNG, Marlene
Exec. Director, Nat'l Organization for Victim Assistance
1757 Park Road, N.W., Washington, DC 20010
Telephone: (202) 232-6682

YOUNG, Nina M.
Director, Marine Mammal Protection Fund
1725 DeSales St., N.W. Suite 500, Washington, DC 20036
Telephone: (202) 429-5609
Background: Also represents the Seal Rescue Fund.

YOUNG, Patricia
Editor, Retail Bakers of America
Presidential Bldg. 6525 Belcrest Rd., Suite 250, Hyattsville, MD 20782
Telephone: (301) 277-0990

YOUNG, Susan J.
Exec. Director, Nat'l Ass'n of Executive Secretaries
900 S. Washington St., Falls Church, VA 22046
Telephone: (703) 237-8616

YOUNG, Thane
Ferguson Co., The
1730 Rhode Island Ave., N.W., Suite 400, Washington, DC 20036
Telephone: (202) 331-8500
Registered as lobbyist at U.S. Congress.
Organizations represented:
  Alhambra, California, City of
  Berg-Revoir Corp.
  Imperial Irrigation District
  Inglewood, California, City of
  Irvine Co., The
  Long Beach Transit
  Oceanside, California, City of
  Oceanside Redevelopment Agency
  Provo, Utah, City of
  Redondo Beach, California, City of
  Santa Ana, California, City of

Santa Cruz Properties, Inc.
South Salt Lake, Utah, City of

YOUNG, William C.
Dir., Consumer Affairs & Public Liaison, Nat'l Ass'n of Home Builders of the U.S.
15th and M Streets, N.W., Washington, DC 20005
Telephone: (202) 822-0470

YOUNGBLOOD, Thomas F.
Director, Federal Affairs, American Hotel and Motel Ass'n
1201 New York Ave., N.W. Suite 600, Washington, DC 20005
Telephone: (202) 289-3100
Registered as lobbyist at U.S. Congress.

YOUNKINS, Betsy
Washington Representative, American Petroleum Institute
1220 L St., N.W., Washington, DC 20005
Telephone: (202) 682-8410
Registered as lobbyist at U.S. Congress.

YOUNT, David
President, Nat'l Press Foundation
National Press Bldg. Suite 1282, Washington, DC 20045
Telephone: (202) 662-7350

YOUNTS, George R.
Ashby and Associates
1140 Connecticut Ave., N.W., Suite 503, Washington, DC 20036
Telephone: (202) 296-3840

YSLA, Elizabeth
Hunt Management Systems
2033 M St., N.W., Suite 605, Washington, DC 20036
Telephone: (202) 223-6413
Background: Serves as Director of Government Relations, Soc. of Professional Benefit Administrators.
Clients:
  Soc. of Professional Benefit Administrators

YUDIN, ATT'Y-AT-LAW, David E.
1225 Eye St., N.W. Suite 300, Washington, DC 20005
Telephone: (202) 682-4092
Registered as lobbyist at U.S. Congress.
Background: An attorney.
Members of firm representing listed organizations:
Yudin, David E.
  Background: Legislative Counsel, Urban Mass Transportation Administration, U.S. Department of Transportation, 1975-78. Counsel, U.S. Senate Committee on Banking, Housing and Urban Affairs, 1978-83.
Organizations represented:
  Denver Regional Transportation District *(David E. Yudin)*

YUDIN, David E.
Yudin, Att'y-at-Law, David E.
1225 Eye St., N.W. Suite 300, Washington, DC 20005
Telephone: (202) 682-4092
Background: Legislative Counsel, Urban Mass Transportation Administration, U.S. Department of Transportation, 1975-78. Counsel, U.S. Senate Committee on Banking, Housing and Urban Affairs, 1978-83.
Organizations represented:
  Denver Regional Transportation District

YUI, Ellen Moulton
Account Supervisor, Edelman, Inc., Daniel J.
1420 K St., N.W., Washington, DC 20005
Telephone: (202) 371-0200

YUILLE, Julia E.
Legis Information Center, EXECUTIVE OFFICE OF THE PRESIDENT - Office of Management and Budget
Old Executive Office Bldg., Washington, DC 20500
Telephone: (202) 395-4790

YUSPEH, Alan R.
Member, Miller & Chevalier, Chartered
Metropolitan Square, 655 15th St., N.W., Washington, DC 20005
Telephone: (202) 626-5800
Registered as lobbyist at U.S. Congress.
Background: Legislative Assistant and Administrative Assistant to Senator J. Bennett Johnston (D-LA), 1974-78. General Counsel, Committee on the Armed Services, U.S. Senate, 1982-85.
Clients:

Boeing Co.
McDonnell Douglas Corp.
Pacific Medical Center
Professional Services Council
Varian Associates Inc.

YZAGUIRRE, Raul
President, Nat'l Council of La Raza
810 1st St., N.E., Suite 300, Washington, DC 20002
Telephone: (202) 289-1380

ZACHARIADIS, Christofer P.
Exec. Director, Ass'n for Community Based Education
1806 Vernon St., N.W., Washington, DC 20009
Telephone: (202) 462-6333

ZADINA, Barbara C.
Manager, Government & External Relations, Orbital Sciences Corp.
12500 Fair Lakes Circle, Fairfax, VA 22033
Telephone: (703) 631-3600
Registered as lobbyist at U.S. Congress.

ZAGAME ASSOCIATES, John R.
211 N. Union St. Suite 210, Alexandria, VA 22314
Telephone: (703) 739-0122
Background: A business consulting firm.
Members of firm representing listed organizations:
Zagame, John R., President
Organizations represented:
  Nat'l Music Publishers' Ass'n *(John R. Zagame)*

ZAGAME, John R.
President, Zagame Associates, John R.
211 N. Union St. Suite 210, Alexandria, VA 22314
Telephone: (703) 739-0122
Registered as lobbyist at U.S. Congress.
Organizations represented:
  Nat'l Music Publishers' Ass'n

ZAHLER, Eric J.
Fried, Frank, Harris, Shriver & Jacobson
1001 Pennsylvania Ave., N.W., Suite 800, Washington, DC 20004-2505
Telephone: (202) 639-7000

ZAINA, Lisa M.
General Counsel, Organization for the Protection and Advancement of Small Telephone Cos.
2000 K St., N.W., Suite 205, Washington, DC 20006
Telephone: (202) 659-5990

ZAINALDIN, Jamil S.
President, Federation of State Humanities Councils
1012 14th St., N.W., Suite 1007, Washington, DC 20005
Telephone: (202) 393-5400

ZAKRZESKI, Paulette
Sr. Government Relations Representative, Nat'l Cotton Council of America
1110 Vermont Ave., N.W. Suite 430, Washington, DC 20005
Telephone: (202) 833-2943
Registered as lobbyist at U.S. Congress.
Background: Former legislative aide to the House Agriculture Committee.

ZAKUPOWSKY, Alexander, Jr.
Member, Miller & Chevalier, Chartered
Metropolitan Square, 655 15th St., N.W., Washington, DC 20005
Telephone: (202) 626-5800
Registered as lobbyist at U.S. Congress.
Background: Advisor on Tax Accounting Matters, Office of Tax Policy, Department of Treasury, 1976-78.
Clients:
  Aerospace Industries Ass'n of America

WASHINGTON REPRESENTATIVES

ZALL, Barnaby
Of Counsel, Williams and Jensen, P.C.
1101 Connecticut Ave., N.W., Suite 500, Washington, DC 20036
Telephone: (202) 659-8201
Clients:
Federation for American Immigration Reform (FAIR)

ZAMBA, Michael J.
Director, Washington Office, Nat'l Ass'n of Latino Elected and Appointed Officials (NALEO)
708 G St., S.E., Washington, DC 20003
Telephone: (202) 546-2536

ZAPANTA, Albert C.
Director, Federal Government Relations, ARCO
1333 New Hampshire Ave., N.W. Suite 1001, Washington, DC 20036
Telephone: (202) 457-6200
Registered as lobbyist at U.S. Congress.

ZAPP, Dr. John S.
Director, Government Affairs Division, American Medical Ass'n
1101 Vermont Ave., N.W., Washington, DC 20005
Telephone: (202) 789-7400
Registered as lobbyist at U.S. Congress.

ZARIN, Donald
Reid & Priest
1111 19th St., N.W., Washington, DC 20036
Telephone: (202) 828-0100

ZARO, Joan
Senior V. President and COO, American Pharmaceutical Ass'n
2215 Constitution Ave., N.W., Washington, DC 20037
Telephone: (202) 628-4410

ZAUCHA, Thomas K.
President, Nat'l Grocers Ass'n
1825 Samuel Morse Drive, Reston, VA 22090
Telephone: (703) 437-5300
Registered as lobbyist at U.S. Congress.
Background: Also represents the Nat'l Grocers Ass'n Political Action Committee.

ZAUSNER, L. Andrew
Webster and Sheffield
2000 Pennsylvania Ave., N.W., Suite 7400, Washington, DC 20006
Telephone: (202) 785-8222
Registered as lobbyist at U.S. Congress.
Background: Served in the U.S. Department of Energy, 1977-79.
Clients:
ASARCO Incorporated
Liggett Group, Inc.
Magma Copper Corp.
Mazda Motor Manufacturing Corp.
PG&E-Bechtel Generating Co.
Tobacco Institute

ZAVADOWSKI, Richard A.
Mtkg. Mgr., Wash. Liaison, Contract Resrc, Babcock and Wilcox Co.
c/o McDermott Internat'l Inc. 1850 K St., N.W., Suite 950, Washington, DC 20006
Telephone: (202) 296-0390

ZAX, Leonard A.
Partner, Fried, Frank, Harris, Shriver & Jacobson
1001 Pennsylvania Ave., N.W., Suite 800, Washington, DC 20004-2505
Telephone: (202) 639-7000
Registered as lobbyist at U.S. Congress.
Clients:
Forstmann, Little & Co.

ZDENEK, Robert
President, Nat'l Congress for Community Economic Development
1612 K St., N.W. Suite 510, Washington, DC 20006
Telephone: (202) 659-8411

ZEDD, Sherri G.
V. President, American Wood Preservers Institute
1945 Old Gallows Road Suite 550, Vienna, VA 22182

Telephone: (703) 893-4005
Registered as lobbyist at U.S. Congress.
Background: Former Legislative Director for Rep. Newt Gingrich (R-GA).

ZEE, Robin J.
Exec. V. President, Nat'l Institute of Governmental Purchasing
115 Hillwood Ave., Falls Church, VA 22046
Telephone: (703) 533-7300

ZEESE, Kevin B.
V. President, Drug Policy Foundation
4801 Massachusetts Ave., N.W. Suite 400, Washington, DC 20016
Telephone: (202) 895-1634

ZEFERETTI, Leo C.
Legislative Director, AFL-CIO - Building and Construction Trades Department
815 16th St., N.W., Suite 603, Washington, DC 20006
Telephone: (202) 347-1461
Background: Member, U.S. House of Representatives (D-NY), 1975-82.

ZEIDMAN, Philip F.
Brownstein Zeidman and Schomer
1401 New York Ave., N.W., Suite 900, Washington, DC 20005
Telephone: (202) 879-5700
Registered as lobbyist at U.S. Congress.
Background: Federal Trade Commission, 1960-61. Staff Assistant, White House Committee on Small Business, 1961-63. General Counsel, Small Business Administration, 1961-68. Special Assistant to the Vice President of the U.S., 1968. General Counsel, Internat'l Franchise Ass'n. Washington Counsel, American Business Conference.

ZEIFMAN, Jerome M.
General Counsel & Exec. Director, Nat'l Council for Industrial Defense
417 6th St., S.E., Washington, DC 20003
Telephone: (202) 543-7592

ZEIGLER, Sharon
Federal Government Relations Specialist, Kimberly-Clark Corp.
1201 Pennsylvania Ave., N.W. Suite 730, Washington, DC 20004
Telephone: (202) 393-8280

ZEISZLER, Eugene J.
Industrial Preparedness Assistant, NMTBA - The Ass'n for Manufacturing Technology
7901 Westpark Dr., McLean, VA 22102
Telephone: (703) 893-2900
Registered as lobbyist at U.S. Congress.

ZELKO, Renate
Manager, Corporate Communications, Lucas Aerospace Inc.
11150 Sunrise Valley Drive, Reston, VA 22091-4399
Telephone: (703) 264-1704

ZELLER, Don J.
Sr. Government Affairs Representative, Amoco Corp.
1615 M St., N.W., Suite 200, Washington, DC 20036
Telephone: (202) 857-5325
Registered as lobbyist at U.S. Congress.

ZELLER, F.C. Duke
Communications Director, Internat'l Brotherhood of Teamsters, Chauffeurs, Warehousemen and Helpers of America
25 Louisiana Ave., N.W., Washington, DC 20001
Telephone: (202) 624-6800

ZENKEL, Norman
First V. President, Federal Administrative Law Judges' Conference
424 Nat'l Lawyers Club, 1815 H St., N.W., Washington, DC 20006
Telephone: (202) 633-0525

ZENOR, Stanley D.
Exec. Director, Ass'n for Educational Communications and Technology
1025 Vermont Ave., N.W. Suite 820, Washington, DC 20005

Telephone: (202) 347-7834

ZENTAY, John H.
Verner, Liipfert, Bernhard, McPherson and Hand, Chartered
901 15th St., N.W., Suite 700, Washington, DC 20005
Telephone: (202) 371-6000
Registered as lobbyist at U.S. Congress.
Background: Legislative Ass't to Sen. Stewart Symington, 1958-63; Member of the Legislative Presentation Staff of the Agency for Internat'l Development, Dept. of State, 1963-66.

ZERKEL, Fred H.
V. President, Washington Opns., Institute of Gas Technology
1825 K St., N.W. Suite 503, Washington, DC 20006
Telephone: (202) 785-3511

ZEVNIK, Paul A.
Kaye, Scholer, Fierman, Hays and Handler
The McPherson Building 901 15th St., N.W., #1100, Washington, DC 20005
Telephone: (202) 682-3500
Registered as lobbyist at U.S. Congress.
Clients:
GAF Corp.

ZHANG, Samuel X.
Graham and James
2000 M St., N.W., Suite 700, Washington, DC 20036
Telephone: (202) 463-0800

ZIEGLER, Ronald L.
President and CEO, Nat'l Ass'n of Chain Drug Stores
Box 1417-D49, Alexandria, VA 22313
Telephone: (703) 549-3001
Registered as lobbyist at U.S. Congress.

ZIEMBA, Elaine M.
Director, Congressional Relations, American Gas Ass'n
1515 Wilson Blvd., Arlington, VA 22209
Telephone: (703) 841-8591
Registered as lobbyist at U.S. Congress.
Background: Former Legislative Director for Rep. Bill Richardson (D-NM)

ZIEWACZ, Judy
Director of Member Services, Nat'l Milk Producers Federation
1840 Wilson Blvd., Arlington, VA 22201
Telephone: (703) 243-6111
Registered as lobbyist at U.S. Congress.

ZIFF, Bradley P.
3841 Newark St., N.W. Apt. A451, Washington, DC 20016
Telephone: (202) 966-7769
Registered as lobbyist at U.S. Congress.
Background: Serves as Exec. Director, Internat'l Swap Dealers Ass'n.
Organizations represented:
Internat'l Swap Dealers Ass'n

ZIGAS, Barry
President, Nat'l Low Income Housing Coalition
1012 14th St., N.W. Suite 1500, Washington, DC 20005
Telephone: (202) 662-1530
Registered as lobbyist at U.S. Congress.

ZIGEL, Jim
Legal Counsel, Lucas Aerospace Inc.
11150 Sunrise Valley Drive, Reston, VA 22091-4399
Telephone: (703) 264-1704

ZIGLAR-CLAY, Kelly
Legislative & Regulatory Representative, Mortgage Insurance Companies of America
805 15th St., N.W., Suite 1110, Washington, DC 20005
Telephone: (202) 371-2899
Registered as lobbyist at U.S. Congress.

ZILL, Anne B.
President, Fund for Constitutional Government
122 Maryland Ave., N.E. 3rd Floor, Washington, DC 20002
Telephone: (202) 546-3732

ZILLINGER, Fred E.
Director, Government Affairs, Fertilizer Institute
501 Second St., N.E., Washington, DC 20002

The listings in this directory are available as *Mailing Labels.* See last page.

Telephone: (202) 675-8250
Registered as lobbyist at U.S. Congress.
Background: Former press aide to Rep. Pat Roberts (R-KS).

ZIMMERMAN, Edward J.
Deputy Chief Counsel, State Relations, American Council of Life Insurance
1001 Pennsylvania Ave., N.W., Washington, DC 20004-2599
Telephone: (202) 624-2180
Registered as lobbyist at U.S. Congress.

ZIMMERMAN, Fred
Director of Communications, Cooperative League of the USA Political Action Committee (Nat'l Coop Business PAC)
1401 New York Ave., N.W., Suite 1100, Washington, DC 20005
Telephone: (202) 638-6222

ZIMMERMAN, John B.
Ordnance Div. Dir., Washington Office, Olin Corp.
1730 K St., N.W., Suite 1300, Washington, DC 20006
Telephone: (202) 331-7400

ZIMMERMAN, John H.
Associate Director, Legislative Affairs, Nat'l Ass'n of Federal Credit Unions
3138 N. 10th St., Arlington, VA 22201
Telephone: (703) 522-4770
Registered as lobbyist at U.S. Congress.

ZIMMERMAN, John H.
Sr. V. President, MCI Communications Corp.
1133 19th St., N.W., Washington, DC 20036
Telephone: (202) 872-1600

ZIMMERMAN, Joseph J.
Sachs Greenebaum and Tayler
1140 Connecticut Ave., N.W., Washington, DC 20036
Telephone: (202) 828-8200
Registered as lobbyist at U.S. Congress.
Clients:
Giant Industries

ZIMMERMAN, Kate
Counsel, Public Lands and Energy Div., Nat'l Wildlife Federation
1400 16th St., N.W., Washington, DC 20036-2266
Telephone: (202) 797-6800
Registered as lobbyist at U.S. Congress.

ZIMMERMAN, Teresa M.
Sr. Staff Associate, Nat'l Ass'n of Homes for Children
1701 K St., N.W., Suite 200, Washington, DC 20006
Telephone: (202) 223-3447

ZIMMERMANN, Mary Erb
Director, Communications, Special Libraries Ass'n
1700 18th St., N.W., Washington, DC 20009
Telephone: (202) 234-4700

ZINN, Matthew J.
Steptoe and Johnson
1330 Connecticut Ave., N.W., Washington, DC 20036
Telephone: (202) 429-3000
Clients:
New York Life Insurance Co.
Puerto Rico Telephone Co.

ZION, Roger H.
Resources Development, Inc.
412 First St., S.E., Washington, DC 20003
Telephone: (202) 484-8969
Background: U.S. House of Representatives, 1966-74; Chairman, Republican Task Force on Energy and Resources.
Clients:
Independent Oil Producers Ass'n-Tri State
Industry General Corp.
Morrison, Hecker, Curtis, Kuder & Parrish
Nat'l Ass'n of Professional Educators
Public Service Research Council
Toborg Associates, Inc.

ZIZKA, Gary M.
Government Affairs, Nat'l Beer Wholesalers Ass'n
5205 Leesburg Pike, Suite 1600, Falls Church, VA 22041

Telephone: (703) 578-4300
Registered as lobbyist at U.S. Congress.

ZOGBY, James J.
Exec. Director, Arab American Institute
918 16th St., N.W., Suite 601, Washington, DC 20006
Telephone: (202) 429-9210
Background: Also represents the Arab American Leadership Political Action Committee.

ZOGLIO, Kim R.
Manager, Public Relations, Printing Industries of America
1730 North Lynn St., Arlington, VA
Telephone: (703) 841-8153

ZOLL, David F.
V. President and General Counsel, Chemical Manufacturers Ass'n
2501 M St., N.W., Washington, DC 20037
Telephone: (202) 887-1350

ZOLLAR, Carolyn C.
Gen. Counsel, Dir., Governmental Affairs, Nat'l Ass'n of Rehabilitation Facilities
Box 17675, Washington, DC 20041-0675
Telephone: (703) 648-9300

ZOLLMAN, Sarah
Public Affairs Assistant, Soc. of American Foresters
5400 Grosvenor Lane, Bethesda, MD 20814
Telephone: (301) 897-8720

ZOOMERS, Yvonne E.T.G.B.
Assistant V. President, Federal Affairs, CIGNA Corp.
1825 Eye St., N.W., Suite 750, Washington, DC 20006
Telephone: (202) 296-7174

ZORACK, John L.
President and Chairman, Professional Lobbying and Consulting Center
1111 14th St., N.W., Suite 1001, Washington, DC 20005
Telephone: (202) 898-0084
Clients:
Campbell-Mithun
Federal Express Corp.

ZORTHIAN ASSOCIATES
4201 Cathedral Ave. N.W. #405E, Washington, DC 20016
Telephone: (202) 244-1984
Members of firm representing listed organizations:
Zorthian, Barry

ZORTHIAN, Barry
Zorthian Associates
4201 Cathedral Ave. N.W. #405E, Washington, DC 20016
Telephone: (202) 244-1984

ZUCK, Alfred M.
Exec. Director, Nat'l Ass'n of Schools of Public Affairs and Administration
1120 G St. N.W. Suite 520, Washington, DC 20005
Telephone: (202) 628-8965

ZUCKERT, SCOUTT AND RASENBERGER
888 17th St., N.W., Suite 600, Washington, DC 20006-3959
Telephone: (202) 298-8660
Members of firm representing listed organizations:
Callaway, William H. (Jr.)
Costello, Frank J.
Devall, James L.
Keeling, J. Michael
Kissick, Ralph L.
Rasenberger, Raymond J.
Schweitzer, Richard P.
Scoutt, Jerrold (Jr.)
Background: Member, Board of Directors, World Airways.
Simpson, Charles J. (Jr.)
Trinder, Rachel B.
Vinyard, Walter D. (Jr.)
Background: Attorney, Securities and Exchange Commission, 1968-72.
Clients:
Advance Petroleum, Inc. *(Charles J. Simpson, Jr.)*
Air Afrique *(William H. Callaway, Jr.)*
Air Aruba *(Frank J. Costello)*

Air-Sea Forwarders, Inc. *(Frank J. Costello)*
All Nippon Airways Co. *(James L. Devall)*
Challenge Air Cargo *(William H. Callaway, Jr.)*
Continental Corp., The *(Walter D. Vinyard, Jr.)*
Dragonair *(Rachel B. Trinder)*
Employee Stock Ownership Ass'n *(J. Michael Keeling)*
Empresa Consolidada Cubana de Aviacion *(James L. Devall)*
Korean Air Lines *(James L. Devall)*
LADECO *(Charles J. Simpson, Jr.)*
Malaysian Airline System *(Charles J. Simpson, Jr.)*
Martinair Holland *(Frank J. Costello, Rachel B. Trinder)*
Nat'l Ass'n of Royalty Owners *(J. Michael Keeling)*
Nat'l Business Aircraft Ass'n *(Raymond J. Rasenberger)*
Nat'l Committee of Cities and States for Airline Service *(Raymond J. Rasenberger)*
Nat'l Fraternal Congress of America *(Walter D. Vinyard, Jr.)*
Nat'l Welding Supply Ass'n *(Richard P. Schweitzer)*
Nippon Cargo Airlines *(James L. Devall)*
Pakistan Internat'l Airlines *(James L. Devall)*
Resource Deployment, Inc. *(Walter D. Vinyard, Jr.)*
Small Business Council of America *(J. Michael Keeling)*
Transportation Research Forum *(Rachel B. Trinder)*

ZUGSCHWERT, John F.
Exec. Director, American Helicopter Soc.
217 N. Washington St., Alexandria, VA 22314
Telephone: (703) 684-6777
Background: Also represents the Vertical Flight Foundation.

ZUSCHLAG, W. Alan
Senior V. President, TransAtlantic Futures, Inc.
2311 Connecticut Ave., N.W. Suite 604, Washington, DC 20008
Telephone: (202) 462-1222
Clients:
ABD Securities Corp.
Deutsche Bank AG
European Communities, Commission of the
Siemens Corp.

ZUVER, Charles O.
Senior V. Pres. & Dir., Gov't Affrs., Credit Union Nat'l Ass'n
805 15th St., N.W. Suite 300, Washington, DC 20005
Telephone: (202) 682-4200
Registered as lobbyist at U.S. Congress.
Background: Serves also as Administrator, Credit Union Legislative Council.

ZWEBEN, Murray
Nossaman, Guthner, Knox and Elliott
1227 25th St., N.W., Suite 700, Washington, DC 20037
Telephone: (202) 223-9100
Registered as lobbyist at U.S. Congress.
Background: Assistant Parliamentarian (1963-75), Parliamentarian (1975-81), Parliamentarian Emeritus, 1986-present, U.S. Senate.
Clients:
Advo-Systems, Inc.
Anheuser-Busch Cos., Inc.
California Co-Compost Systems
Edison Electric Institute
General Cellular Corp.
Nat'l Shorthand Reporters Ass'n
Southern California Edison Co.
Sun Microsystems

ZWERDLING, PAUL, LEIBIG & THOMPSON
1025 Connecticut Ave., N.W. Suite 307, Washington, DC 20036
Telephone: (202) 857-5000
Members of firm representing listed organizations:
Leibig, Michael
Clients:
Internat'l Union of Police Ass'ns *(Michael Leibig)*

ZWICK, David
Exec. Director, Clean Water Action Project
317 Pennsylvania Ave., S.E., Washington, DC 20003
Telephone: (202) 547-1196

20/20 VISION NAT'L PROJECT
1000 16th St., N.W., Washington, DC 20036

20/20 VISION NAT'L PROJECT (Cont'd)
Telephone: (202) 728-1157
Members of firm representing listed organizations:
Mark, Richard F., Director, Research and Communications

WASHINGTON REPRESENTATIVES

1990

ORGANIZATIONS REPRESENTED

The following organizations may be headquartered anywhere in the United States (including Washington) or abroad. They appear here because they either maintain a Washington office or retain someone in Washington to represent their interests. Details on their Washington representatives are set forth in the preceding section.

A/E Pronet
1213 Prince St., Alexandria, VA 22314
Telephone: (703) 836-1329
Counsel or consultant:
Adams, Adams & Assoc. (Ann Allen Adams)

A-PAC
1575 Eye St., N.W., Washington, DC 20005
Telephone: (202) 626-2723
Background: The political arm of the American Soc. of Ass'n Executives. Formed in 1982. Supports political candidates who favor the activities of trade and professional organizations. Contact is J. Reese Meisinger of the American Soc. of Ass'n Executives.

A/S Ivarans Rederi
Oslo, Norway
Counsel or consultant:
Graham and James

A to Z Maintenance Corp.
Atlantic City, NJ
Counsel or consultant:
Sadur, Pelland & Rubinstein (Joel S. Rubinstein)

AAAE Good Government Committee
4212 King St., Alexandria, VA 22302
Telephone: (703) 824-0500
Background: The political action committee of the American Ass'n of Airport Executives. Contact is Charles Barclay. (See American Ass'n of Airport Executives.)

AB Bofors
Bofors, Sweden
Counsel or consultant:
Coudert Brothers
Ginn, Edington, Moore and Wade

AB Electronics Group Ltd.
Mid-Glamorgan, United Kington
Counsel or consultant:
Lonington, Inc. (Alan G. Gray)

AB Hagglund & Soner
Ornskoldsvik, Sweden
Counsel or consultant:
Fierce and Associates (Donald L. Fierce)
O'Brien and Associates, David (David D. O'Brien)

AB SKF, Inc.
Goteborg, Switzerland
Counsel or consultant:
Akin, Gump, Strauss, Hauer and Feld

Abbott Laboratories
1710 Rhode Island Ave., N.W. Suite 300, Washington, DC 20036
Telephone: (202) 659-8524

Represented by:
Joseph S. Jenckes, Vice President, Washington
David W. Landsidle, Director, Washington Affairs
Victoria McKenzie Shain, Director, Federal Health Policy
Howard D. Scholick, Director, Government Affairs
Andrea J. Wollock, Regional Mgr., State Government Affairs
Counsel or consultant:
Hill and Knowlton Public Affairs Worldwide (Dale Lawson)
Holland and Knight (Marshall L. Matz)
Lee, Toomey & Kent

Abbott Laboratories Better Government Fund
North Chicago, IL
Background: Washington contact is Joseph S. Jenckes. (See Abbott Laboratories.)

ABC Containerline, N.V.
Antwerp, Belgium
Counsel or consultant:
Warren and Associates (George A. Quadrino)

ABC-PAC
729 15th St., N.W., Washington, DC 20005
Telephone: (202) 637-8800
Background: A political action committee supported by Associated Builders and Contractors. Contacts are Marra Harris and Charles E. Hawkins, III of the Associated Builders and Contractors.

ORGANIZATIONS REPRESENTED

ABD Securities Corp.
New York, NY
Counsel or consultant:
Dickstein, Shapiro and Morin (Henry C. Cashen, II)
TransAtlantic Futures, Inc. (Stephan-Gotz Richter, W. Alan Zuschlag)

Aberdeen, Washington, City of
Aberdeen, WA
Counsel or consultant:
Garvey, Schubert & Barer (Alan A. Butchman)

Abitibi-Price, Inc.
Toronto, Ontario
Counsel or consultant:
Taft, Stettinius and Hollister

Acacia Mutual Life Insurance Co.
51 Louisiana Ave., N.W., Washington, DC 20001
Telephone: (202) 628-4506
Represented by:
C. Lawrence Evans, Jr., V. President, Government Relations
Charles T. Nason, Chairman of the Board
Counsel or consultant:
Sutherland, Asbill and Brennan (Wright H. Andrews, Jr.)

Acacia Mutual Political Action Committee
51 Louisiana Ave., N.W., Washington, DC 20001
Telephone: (202) 628-4506
Background: Responsible contact is C. Lawrence Evans, Jr. of Acacia Mutual Life Insurance Co.
Counsel or consultant:
Sutherland, Asbill and Brennan

Academy for Educational Development
1255 23rd St., N.W., Washington, DC 20037
Telephone: (202) 862-1900
Background: An independent, nonprofit organization that addresses human development needs through information, communication and education. Under grants and contracts, AED operates programs for government and international agencies, educational institutions, foundations and corporations.
Represented by:
Stephen F. Moseley, President
William A. Smith, Exec. V. President

Academy for Implants and Transplants
Box 223, Springfield, VA 22150
Telephone: (703) 451-0001
Represented by:
Dr. Anthony J. Viscido, Exec. Director

Academy for State and Local Government
444 North Capitol St., N.W., Suite 349, Washington, DC 20001
Telephone: (202) 638-1445
Represented by:
Enid Beaumont, Director
Carol Garner, Director, Election Center
Benna Ruth Solomon, Chief Counsel
George Wynne, Director, Internat'l Center

Academy of General Dentistry
1111 14th St., N.W., Suite 1100, Washington, DC 20005
Telephone: (202) 842-1130
Represented by:
Zev Remba, Government Relations Manager

Academy of Model Aeronautics
1810 Samuel Morse Drive, Reston, VA 22090
Telephone: (703) 435-0750
Background: Represented by Everett W. Langworthy of the Nat'l Aeronautic Ass'n of the U.S.A..
Counsel or consultant:
Blooston, Mordkofsky, Jackson & Dickens (Jeremiah Courtney)

Academy of Pharmaceutical Research and Science
2215 Constitution Ave., N.W., Washington, DC 20037
Telephone: (202) 628-4410
Background: A subdivision of the American Pharmaceutical Ass'n. Dr. Arthur H. Kibbe of the American Pharmaceutical Ass'n serves as Director, Scientific Affairs.

Academy of Pharmacy Practice and Management
2215 Constitution Ave., N.W., Washington, DC 20037

Telephone: (202) 628-4410
Background: Staff Liaison is C. Edwin Webb of the American Pharmaceutical Ass'n.

Accion Medica
Miami, FL
Counsel or consultant:
Robert N. Pyle & Associates

Accountant's Liability Assurance Co., Ltd.
Hamilton, Bermuda
Counsel or consultant:
Mayer, Brown and Platt (Jerry L. Oppenheimer)

Accreditation Ass'n for Ambulatory Healthcare, Inc.
Skokie, IL
Counsel or consultant:
McDermott, Will and Emery

Accrediting Commission on Education for Health Services Administration
1911 North Fort Myer Drive Suite 503, Arlington, VA 22209
Telephone: (703) 524-0511
Represented by:
Sherril B. Gelman, Exec. Director

Accuracy in Academia
1275 K St., N.W., Suite 1150, Washington, DC 20005
Telephone: (202) 789-4076
Background: Encourages students on college and university campuses to challenge professors who 'misinform' or 'propagandize' during the course of lectures and to report such incidents to its monthly newspaper, The Campus Report. A politically conservative organization which perceives a liberal and radical bias on college faculties, AIA asserts that it was founded 'to promote accuracy, fairness and balance in higher education.'
Represented by:
Leslie Carbone, Exec. Director

Accuracy in Media
1275 K St., N.W., Suite 1150, Washington, DC 20005
Telephone: (202) 371-6710
Background: Conservative critics of news organizations. Organized in 1969.
Represented by:
Joseph C. Goulden, Director of Media Analysis
Reed J. Irvine, Chairman of the Board

Ace Frosty Shipping Co., Ltd.
London, England
Counsel or consultant:
Dyer, Ellis, Joseph & Mills (Thomas M. Dyer, James B. Ellis, II, Michael Joseph, Thomas L. Mills, Howard A. Vine)

ACEC Research and Management Foundation
1015 15th St., N.W., Washington, DC 20005
Telephone: (202) 347-7474
Background: Associated with the American Consulting Engineers Council.
Represented by:
Jack Warner, President

Aceitunas de Mesa, S.A.
Seville, Spain
Background: A table olive export association.
Counsel or consultant:
George V. Egge, Jr.

Acerinox, S.A.
Madrid, Spain
Background: Spanish exporter of stainless steel sheet product.
Counsel or consultant:
George V. Egge, Jr.

Acindar Industria Argentina de Aceros
Buenos Aires, Argentina
Background: The Center of the Steel Industry of Argentina.
Counsel or consultant:
Baker and McKenzie (Thomas P. Ondeck)

ACORN (Ass'n of Community Organizations for Reform Now)
522 8th St., S.E., Washington, DC 20003
Telephone: (202) 547-9292

Background: A neighborhood-based organization of low and moderate income people in twenty-six states who are concerned with such issues as taxes, utility rates, housing and employment.
Represented by:
Steven Kest, Exec. Director

Acorn Data Systems, Inc.
Covina, CA
Counsel or consultant:
Cassidy and Associates, Inc. (Thomas M. Gannon)

ACR, Inc.
Pittsburgh, PA
Counsel or consultant:
Pearce Associates (C. Jack Pearce)

Acrylonitrile Group, Inc., The
1815 H St., N.W., Suite 1000, Washington, DC 20006-3604
Telephone: (202) 296-6300
Background: Address given is that of the offices of the law firm of Hadley and McKenna. Exec. Director and Legal Counsel of the Group is Joseph E. Hadley, Jr. of Hadley and McKenna.
Counsel or consultant:
Hadley and McKenna (Joseph E. Hadley, Jr.)

ACSM-NSPS Political Action Committee
5410 Grosvenor Lane, Suite 100, Bethesda, MD 20814-2122
Telephone: (301) 493-0200
Background: A political action committee formed by the American Congress on Surveying and Mapping and the Nat'l Soc. of Professional Surveyors, one of its member groups. Treasurer and contact is Nancy L. Parke of the American Congress on Surveying and Mapping.

Action Committee for Rural Electrification
1800 Massachusetts Ave., N.W., Washington, DC 20036
Telephone: (202) 857-9500
Background: Represents the legislative and political interests of the Nat'l Rural Electric Cooperative Ass'n. Contact person is Robert M. Dawson of the parent association.

Action for Boston Community Development
Boston, MA
Counsel or consultant:
Cassidy and Associates, Inc. (James P. Collins)

Action on Smoking and Health
2013 H St. N.W., Washington, DC 20006
Telephone: (202) 659-4310
Background: A national, non-profit contributor organization utilizing legal action and education to reduce the hazards of smoking and protect the rights of the non-smoking majority.
Represented by:
John F. Banzhaf, III, Exec. Director and Chief Counsel
Athena Mueller, General Counsel

Active Ballot Club
1775 K St., N.W., c/o UFCW, Washington, DC 20006
Telephone: (202) 223-3111
Background: A political action committee sponsored by the United Food and Commercial Workers Internat'l Union.
Represented by:
Jerry Menapace, Secretary-Treasurer

Acton Corp.
Raleigh, NC
Counsel or consultant:
Dow, Lohnes and Albertson (Robert M. Chasnow)

Acurex Corp.
1725 K St., N.W., Suite 1111, Washington, DC 20006
Telephone: (202) 296-8498
Represented by:
Charles H. S. Eaton, Manager, Washington Operations
Counsel or consultant:
Dunlap & Browder, Inc.

Ad Hoc Committee for a Competitive Electric Supply System (ACCESS)
c/o Sutherland Asbill & Brenn. 1275 Pennsylvania Ave., N.W., Washington, DC 20004
Telephone: (202) 383-0100
Background: An ad hoc group of large electricity consumers.

ORGANIZATIONS REPRESENTED

Counsel or consultant:
Sutherland, Asbill and Brennan (Earle H. O'Donnell, Jan Benes Vlcek)

Ad Hoc Committee for Small Hydro Power
New York, NY
Counsel or consultant:
Olwine, Connelly, Chase, O'Donnell and Weyher (W. Harrison Wellford)

Ad Hoc Committee for Western Utilities
Washington, DC
Counsel or consultant:
Bishop, Cook, Purcell & Reynolds (H. Lawrence Fox)

Ad Hoc Committee in Defense of Life
1187 Nat'l Press Bldg., Washington, DC 20045
Telephone: (202) 347-8686
Background: A group headquartered in New York City concerned with abortion and euthanasia issues.
Represented by:
Robert McFadden, Director, Washington Information Bureau

Ad Hoc Committee of Producers of Metal Castings
Taipei, Taiwan
Counsel or consultant:
Ablondi and Foster, P.C. (Italo H. Ablondi)

Ad Hoc Granite Trade Group
c/o Robins Kaplan Miller & Ciresi, 1627 Eye St., N.W. 610, Washington, DC 20006
Telephone: (202) 861-6800
Counsel or consultant:
Robins, Kaplan, Miller & Ciresi (Pamela M. Deese)

Ad Hoc MGA Group
New York, NY
Counsel or consultant:
Groom and Nordberg (Theodore R. Groom)

Ada Software Alliance (ASA)
2111 Wilson Boulevard Suite 531, Arlington, VA 22201-3008
Telephone: (703) 276-9068
Counsel or consultant:
Holt, Miller & Associates (Harris N. Miller)

Adams Communications Corp.
Clearwater, FL
Counsel or consultant:
Kaye, Scholer, Fierman, Hays and Handler (Jason Shrinsky)

ADAPSO Foundation
1300 North 17th St. Suite 300, Arlington, VA 22209
Telephone: (703) 522-5055
Represented by:
James R. Peletka, Exec. Director

ADAPSO-PAC
1300 North 17th St., Suite 300, Arlington, VA 22209
Telephone: (703) 522-5055
Background: Represented by Luanne James, Exec. Director of the Ass'n, and Olga Grkavac, its Senior V. President.

ADAPSO, the Computer Software & Services Industry Ass'n
1300 North 17th St. Suite 300, Arlington, VA 22209
Telephone: (703) 522-5055
Background: Formerly the Ass'n of Data Processing Service Organizations.
Represented by:
Bob Cohen, Director, Communications
Olga Grkavac, Sr. V. President, Government Relations
Luanne James, Exec. Director
Ronald Palenski, General Counsel
William Warner, V. Pres., Mktg. & Public Communications
Counsel or consultant:
Squire, Sanders and Dempsey (Joseph P. Markoski, Herbert E. Marks)

ADDSCO Industries
Mobile, AL
Counsel or consultant:
Shaw, Pittman, Potts and Trowbridge (William Mike House)

Adhesive and Sealant Council
1627 K St., N.W., Washington, DC 20006
Telephone: (202) 452-1500
Background: A trade association representing manufacturers of adhesives and sealants and suppliers to the industry.
Represented by:
Kerry L. Lake, Exec. V. President
Michael J. O'Connor, Director, Government Relations
Counsel or consultant:
Jenner and Block (Jerald A. Jacobs)

Adhesives Manufacturers Ass'n
1101 Connecticut Ave., N.W. Suite 700, Washington, DC 20036
Telephone: (202) 857-1100

Counsel or consultant:
Smith, Bucklin and Associates (Mark N. Griffiths, Robert H. Wilbur)

Adidas U.S.A.
Warren, NJ
Counsel or consultant:
Cole, Corette & Abrutyn (R. Christian Berg)

ADIG-Investment GmbH
Frankfurt, West Germany
Counsel or consultant:
Hill and Knowlton Public Affairs Worldwide (Dr. Ira P. Kaminow)

Adjutants General Ass'n of the United States
One Massachusetts Ave., N.W., Washington, DC 20001
Telephone: (202) 789-0031
Represented by:
Major General T. Eston Marchant, President

Adler Group
Miami, FL
Counsel or consultant:
Keefe Co., The (Jonathon A. Slade)

ADM Milling Co.
Shawnee Mission, KS
Counsel or consultant:
TADCO Enterprises (Katherine E. Allen)

Adobe Forms
Santa Fe, NM
Counsel or consultant:
Neill and Co. (Denis M. Neill, Albert C. Printz, Jr.)

Adria Laboratories, Inc.
Columbus, OH
Counsel or consultant:
Kleinfeld, Kaplan and Becker (Alan H. Kaplan)

Advance Petroleum, Inc.
Miami Springs, FL
Counsel or consultant:
Camp, Barsh, Bates and Tate (Ronald L. Platt)
Zuckert, Scoutt and Rasenberger (Charles J. Simpson, Jr.)

Advance Publications, Inc.
New York, NY
Counsel or consultant:
Dickstein, Shapiro and Morin (Leonard Garment)
Dow, Lohnes and Albertson (Bernard J. Long, Jr.)

Advanced Energy Technology, Inc.
Boston, MA
Counsel or consultant:
Stovall & Spradlin

Advanced Management & Technologies
600 Maryland Ave., S.W., Suite 200A - East Wing, Washington, DC 20024
Telephone: (202) 863-1472
Counsel or consultant:
Lachelli, Waller and Associates (John D. Waller)

Advanced Technology, Inc.
12005 Sunrise Valley Drive, Reston, VA 22091
Telephone: (703) 620-8000
Counsel or consultant:
Patton, Boggs and Blow (Joe Robert Reeder)

Advanced Technology Inc. Political Action Committee
12005 Sunrise Valley Drive, Reston, VA 22091

Telephone: (703) 620-8000
Represented by:
John Gall, Treasurer

Advanced Transit Ass'n
9019 Hamilton Drive, Fairfax, VA 22031
Telephone: (703) 591-8328
Background: Seeks encouragement and application of advanced technology and planning to meet the public transportation needs of metropolitan complexes.
Represented by:
Dr. Jarold A. Kieffer, Secretary/Treasurer

Adventist Development and Relief Agency Inter-nat'l
12501 Old Columbia Pike, Silver Spring, MD 20904
Telephone: (301) 680-6380
Represented by:
R. I. Gainer, V. President for Finance
Mario Ochoa, Exec. V. President
Raynod D. Tetz, V. President for Communications
Ralph S. Watts, Jr., President
Counsel or consultant:
Johns and Carson

Adventist Health System/United States
Arlington, TX
Counsel or consultant:
Johns and Carson

Advisory Council on Historic Preservation
1100 Pennsylvania Ave., N.W. Suite 809, Washington, DC 20004
Telephone: (202) 786-0503
Represented by:
Robert D. Bush, Exec. Director

Advo-Systems, Inc.
Hartford, CT
Counsel or consultant:
Daniel J. Edelman, Inc. (Leslie Dach, Michelle Feichgraeber)
Nossaman, Guthner, Knox and Elliott (Murray Zweben)

Advocacy Institute, The
1730 Rhode Island Ave., N.W. Suite 600, Washington, DC 20036
Telephone: (202) 659-8475
Background: A center for learning about public interest advocacy, providing counseling and teaching on lobbying, media, and public policy advocacy strategies.
Represented by:
David Cohen, Co-director
Michael Pertschuk, Co-director
Barry Rubin, General Counsel
Phil Wilbur, Director, Health Advoc. Resource Center

Advocates for Highway and Auto Safety
Background: An advocacy group supported by the insurance industry and several public interest groups dedicated to such goals as speed limit enforcement, mandatory helmet use by motocyclists and control of drunken and drugged driving.
Represented by:
Judith Lee Stone, Exec. Director

Adwell Corp.
Jacksonville, FL
Counsel or consultant:
McNair Law Firm, P.A. (James McIntyre, Jr.)

AECL Research Co.
Rockville, MD
Counsel or consultant:
Durante Associates

AEG Aktiengesellschaft
West Germany
Counsel or consultant:
Ballard, Spahr, Andrews and Ingersoll (Frederic L. Ballard, Jr.)

Aer Lingus
New York, NY
Counsel or consultant:
Crowell and Moring (Jerry W. Ryan)

Aeritalia
Rome, Italy
Background: Represented by Stefano P. Ruocco and Frank D. Moruzzi of Italian Aerospace Industries (U.S.A.), Inc.

ORGANIZATIONS REPRESENTED

Aermacchi, S.p.A.
Italy
Counsel or consultant:
Hogan and Hartson (Clifford S. Gibbons)
Wunder, Ryan, Cannon & Thelen (John J. McGovern, Jr.)

Aero B
Caracas, Venezuela
Counsel or consultant:
Bowen & Atkin (Harry A. Bowen)

Aero Consultants
Nanikon, Switzerland
Counsel or consultant:
DGM Internat'l Inc. (Donald E. Ellison)

Aerojet
1025 Connecticut Ave., N.W. Suite 1107, Washington, DC 20036
Telephone: (202) 828-6826
Represented by:
Don Brownlee, Director, Public Affairs
Hal W. Howes, V. President, Washington Operations
Terry King, Director, Congressional Relations

Aerolineas Argentinas
New York, NY
Counsel or consultant:
Squire, Sanders and Dempsey (Robert D. Papkin)

Aerolineas Nacionales del Ecuador
Quito, Ecuador
Counsel or consultant:
Steptoe and Johnson (Richard P. Taylor)

Aeromexico
Mexico City, Mexico
Counsel or consultant:
Lord Day & Lord, Barrett Smith (Joanne W. Young)

Aeronautical Radio, Inc.
Annapolis, MD
Counsel or consultant:
Leventhal, Senter & Lerman (Raul R. Rodriguez)

Aeronautical Repair Station Ass'n
1612 K St., N.W., Suite 1400, Washington, DC 20006
Telephone: (202) 293-2511
Counsel or consultant:
Obadal and O'Leary (Sarah MacLeod)

Aeroservicios Ecuatorianos, C.A.
Guyaquil, Ecuador
Counsel or consultant:
Lord Day & Lord, Barrett Smith (Joanne W. Young)

Aerospace Education Foundation
1501 Lee Hwy., Arlington, VA 22209
Telephone: (703) 247-5839
Background: An educational-outreach organization established by the Air Force Ass'n in 1956. Promotes greater understanding of technological advancements and aerospace education and encourages higher education in technological career fields.
Represented by:
Steve Lee, Director

Aerospace Industries Ass'n of America
1250 Eye St., N.W., Suite 1100, Washington, DC 20005
Telephone: (202) 371-8400
Background: The trade association representing the nation's major manufacturers of commercial, military and business aircraft; helicopters; aircraft engines; missiles; spacecraft; and related components and equipment.

Represented by:
Alexis B. Allen, Manager, Media Relations
John P. Amatetti, Manager, Civil Aviation Affairs
Don Fuqua, President
Robert D. Hackett, Director, Contract Policies
Leroy J. Haugh, V. President, Procurement and Finance
Herbert E. Hetu, V. President, Communications
Joel L. Johnson, V. President, International
Ellen I. Kelly, Manager, Member Relations
Virginia C. Lopez, Exec Director, Aerospace Research Center
Ruth B. Ravitz, Manager, Legislative Affairs
Robert E. Robeson, Jr., V. President, Civil Aviation
G. Glynn Rountree, Director, Environmental Affairs
David O. Schillerstrom, Assistant V. President, Communications
Thomas N. Tate, V. President, Legislative Affairs
Sandra W. Wobbe, Ass't. V. President, Policy & Planning
Counsel or consultant:
Dunaway & Cross (Mac S. Dunaway)
Miller & Chevalier, Chartered (Alexander Zakupowsky, Jr.)

Aerospace Industries Ass'n of Canada
Ottawa, Ontario
Background: Represented in Washington by Matthew Abrams of CANAMCO.

Aerospace Medical Ass'n
320 South Henry St., Alexandria, VA 22314
Telephone: (703) 739-2240
Background: Founded in 1929. A professional organization of medical specialists, life scientists and engineers in the fields of aviation, space and environmental medicine. Seeks to stimulate study, exchange of information and cooperation among those involved in these disciplines.
Represented by:
Rufus R. Hessberg, M.D., Exec. V. President

AES Corporation, The
Arlington, VA
Counsel or consultant:
Chadbourne and Parke

Aetna Life & Casualty Co.
1667 K St., N.W., Suite 400, Washington, DC 20006
Telephone: (202) 223-2821
Represented by:
Peter J. Connell, Vice President and Washington Counsel
Jack Ericksen, Director of Federal Relations
Counsel or consultant:
Black, Manafort, Stone and Kelly Public Affairs Co. (Peter G. Kelly)
Duberstein Group, Inc., The
Foreman & Heidepriem (Carol Tucker Foreman, Nikki Heidepriem)
Nossaman, Guthner, Knox and Elliott (Warren G. Elliott)
Wexler, Reynolds, Fuller, Harrison and Schule, Inc.
Wilmer, Cutler and Pickering

AFE, Inc.
4440 Sedgwick St., N.W., Washington, DC 20016
Telephone: (202) 244-0987
Background: Founded in 1981 by A. R. Ferguson to influence and to increase public knowledge about the economic effects of political decisions and to provide advice and counselling in litigation and government relations.
Represented by:
Allen R. Ferguson, President

Affiliated Leadership League of and for the Blind of America
c/o MARC Assoc., 1030 15th St. N.W., Suite 468, Washington, DC 20005
Telephone: (202) 775-8261
Counsel or consultant:
MARC Associates, Inc. (Robert R. Humphreys)

Affordable Housing Preservation Center
1225 Eye St., N.W., Washington, DC 20005
Telephone: (202) 326-8402
Counsel or consultant:
Linda Parke Gallagher & Assoc. (Linda Parke Gallagher)

AFL-CIO (American Federation of Labor and Congress of Industrial Organizations)
815 16th St., N.W., Washington, DC 20006
Telephone: (202) 637-5075
Background: AFL-CIO was established in 1955 through a merger of the American Federation of Labor (1881) and the Congress of Industrial Organizations (1935). Labor's

voice in Washington, it consists of 51 state organizations and 740 local units broken into 90 separate unions with 14,100,000 members.
Represented by:
Dennis Beal, Assistant to the President for Commo.
William J. Cunningham, Jr., Legislative Representative
Ernest DuBester, Legislative Representative
Michael W. Gildea, Assistant to the Director, Legislation
Laurence Gold, General Counsel
Robert F. Guthrie, Asst. Dir., Dept. for Prof. Employees
Karen Ignagni, Dir., Occ. Safety & Health Issues
Calvin P. Johnson, Legislative Representative
Charles S. McDonald, Assistant to the Secretary-Treasurer
Robert M. McGlotten, Director, Dept. of Legislation
Meredith Miller, Employee Benefit Specialist
Jane O'Grady, Legislative Representative
John 'Jay' Power, Legislative Representative
Margaret Seminario, Dir., Soc. Secur., Pension & Health Iss.
Peggy Taylor, Assoc. Director, Legislative Dept.
Kenneth Young, Exec. Assistant to the President
Counsel or consultant:
Ashcraft and Gerel (Mark L. Schaffer)
Bregman, Abell & Kay (Stanley I. Bregman)
Chambers Associates Incorporated (Letitia Chambers)
Marlowe and Co.
Nordlinger Associates

AFL-CIO - Building and Construction Trades Department
815 16th St., N.W., Suite 603, Washington, DC 20006
Telephone: (202) 347-1461
Represented by:
Robert A. Georgine, President
Joseph F. Maloney, Secretary-Treasurer
Leo C. Zeferetti, Legislative Director
Counsel or consultant:
Arnold & Porter
Bredhoff and Kaiser
The Kamber Group (Victor S. Kamber)
Sherman, Dunn, Cohen, Leifer and Counts

AFL-CIO Committee on Political Education/Political Contributions Committee (COPE)
815 16th St., N.W., Washington, DC 20006
Telephone: (202) 637-5101
Background: The political action arm of the AFL-CIO.
Represented by:
Ben Albert, Director of Public Relations
Thomas R. Donahue, Secretary/ Treasurer
John Perkins, Director

AFL-CIO - Food and Allied Service Trades Department
815 16th St., N.W., Suite 408, Washington, DC 20006
Telephone: (202) 737-7200
Represented by:
John A. Boardman, Director, Publc Affairs
Cynthia Coleman, Legislative Representative
Jeff Fiedler, Director, Corporate Affairs
Robert F. Harbrant, President
Keith Mestrich, Director, Health and Safety
Counsel or consultant:
Robert E. Juliano Associates

AFL-CIO - Industrial Union Department
815 16th St., N.W., Washington, DC 20006
Telephone: (202) 842-7800
Represented by:
Elmer Chatak, Secretary-Treasurer
Allegra P. McManus, Associate Legislative Representative
Howard D. Samuel, President
Sheldon W. Samuels, Dir. of Health, Safety and Environment
Brian Turner, Executive Ass't to the President
Barbara F. Warden, Legislative Director
Counsel or consultant:
Bredhoff and Kaiser (Elliot Bredhoff, Jeffrey L. Gibbs)
The Kamber Group (Lesley Israel)

AFL-CIO - Industrial Union Department Voluntary Fund
815 16th St., N.W., Washington, DC 20006
Telephone: (202) 842-7820
Background: Represented by Barbara F. Warden of the AFL-CIO - Industrial Union Department.

ORGANIZATIONS REPRESENTED

AFL-CIO - Labor Heritage Foundation
815 16th St., N.W., Washington, DC 20005
Telephone: (202) 637-5100
Counsel or consultant:
Nordlinger Associates

AFL-CIO Maritime Committee
444 North Capitol St., N.W., Suite 820, Washington, DC 20001
Telephone: (202) 347-5980
Background: Represents a group of seamen's unions in legislative matters.
Represented by:
Robert B. Leventhal, Counsel
Talmage E. Simpkins, Exec. Director
Counsel or consultant:
Quasha, Wessely & Schneider (Thomas J. Schneider)

AFL-CIO - Martime Trades Department
815 16th St., N.W., Suite 510, Washington, DC 20006
Telephone: (202) 628-6300
Represented by:
Jean F. Ingrao, Exec. Secretary-Treasurer

AFL-CIO - Public Employee Department
815 16th St., N.W., Suite 308, Washington, DC 20006
Telephone: (202) 393-2820
Represented by:
Al Bilik, President
John F. Leyden, Secretary-Treasurer
Paula D. Lucak, Legislative Coordinator

African American Institute
1625 Massachusetts Ave., N.W. Suite 210, Washington, DC 20036
Telephone: (202) 667-5636
Represented by:
Jerry Drew, V. Pres. & Director, Washington Office

African Methodist Episcopal Church
1134 11th St., N.W., Washington, DC 20001
Telephone: (202) 371-8700
Represented by:
Dr. Joseph C. McKinney, Treasurer

Africare
440 R St., N.W., Washington, DC 20001
Telephone: (202) 462-3614
Background: Established in 1971 in Washington, D.C., where the organization's headquarters are located. A private, non-profit African development organization with field offices in Chad, Mali, Niger, Senegal, Somalia, Angola, Zambia, Zimbabwe, Guinea-Bissau, Malawi, Mozambique, Burkina Faso, Central Africa Republic, Ethiopia, Guinea, Nigeria and Rwanda. Supported by private foundations, corporations, small businesses, churches, private voluntary organizations, the U.S. Agency for International Development, the United Nations High Commission for Refugees and many thousands of individuals.
Represented by:
Mary Ann Larkin, Director, Major Donor Relations
C. Payne Lucas, Exec. Director

AFSCME Nat'l Public Employees Organized to Promote Legislative Equality (PEOPLE)
Box 65334, Washington, DC 20035
Telephone: (202) 452-4800
Background: A political action committee sponsored by the American Federation of State, County, and Municipal Employees.
Represented by:
Lorraine O'Hara, Director

Agri-Energy Roundtable
2550 M St., N.W., Suite 300, Washington, DC 20037
Telephone: (202) 887-0528
Represented by:
Nicholas E. Hollis, Exec. Director
Counsel or consultant:
Patton, Boggs and Blow (Bart S. Fisher)

Agribusiness Council, The
2550 M St., N.W., Suite 405, Washington, DC 20037
Telephone: (202) 296-4563
Background: President is Nicholas E. Hollis (see Agri-Energy Roundtable). ABC is a private, non-profit organization emerging countries through agro-food and allied industries.

Agricultural Policy Working Group
517 C St., N.E., Washington, DC 20002

Telephone: (202) 546-6501
Background: A coalition of agribusiness firms opposed to mandatory production controls in farm programs.
Counsel or consultant:
Lesher & Russell, Inc. (William Lesher, Randy M. Russell)

Agricultural Producers, Inc.
Valencia, CA
Counsel or consultant:
Holt, Miller & Associates (Harris N. Miller)
Seyfarth, Shaw, Fairweather and Geraldson (Donald L. Rosenthal)

Agricultural Relations Council
1629 K St., N.W. Suite 1100, Washington, DC 20006
Telephone: (202) 785-6710
Counsel or consultant:
Agri/Washington (Paul S. Weller, Jr., Daren R. Williams)

Agricultural Research Institute
9650 Rockville Pike, Bethesda, MD 20814
Telephone: (301) 530-7122
Represented by:
Stan Cath, Exec. Director

Agricultural Satellite Corp.
Lincoln, NE
Counsel or consultant:
Dow, Lohnes and Albertson (Kenneth D. Salomon)

Agriculture Council of America
1250 I St., N.W., Suite 601, Washington, DC 20005
Telephone: (202) 682-9200
Background: Established in 1973. An umbrella organization of farmers and ranchers, agribusinesses, major farm and commodity organizations, which focuses on agricultural and trade issues. Provides educational materials and conducts programs to demonstrate the food and fiber industry's role in the world economy and its contribution to America's prosperity as the nation's second largest industry.
Represented by:
Judith O'Hara, Executive Director
Paul Wagner, Director of Administration & Budget
Counsel or consultant:
Leslae Grubb

Agriculture Ocean Transportation Coalition
1225 19th St., N.W. Suite 200, Washington, DC 20036
Telephone: (202) 347-2060
Counsel or consultant:
Lindsay, Hart, Neil & Weigler (Peter Friedmann)

Agusta Group, The
1735 Jefferson Davis Highway, Arlington, VA 22202
Telephone: (703) 920-4220
Counsel or consultant:
Ginn, Edington, Moore and Wade

Ahmanson & Co., H. F.
Los Angeles, CA
Counsel or consultant:
Kirkpatrick & Lockhart

AIDA Engineering Ltd.
Tokyo, Japan
Counsel or consultant:
Arent, Fox, Kintner, Plotkin & Kahn (Stephen L. Gibson)

AIDS Action Council
2033 M St., N.W., Suite 801, Washington, DC 20036
Telephone: (202) 293-2886
Represented by:
Jean F. McGuire, Exec. Director
Thomas Sheridan, Director, Public Policy

Air Afrique
Abidjan, Ivory Coast
Counsel or consultant:
Zuckert, Scoutt and Rasenberger (William H. Callaway, Jr.)

Air Aruba
Queen Beatrice Airport, Aruba
Counsel or consultant:
Zuckert, Scoutt and Rasenberger (Frank J. Costello)

Air BVI
Road Town, Tortola, British Virgin Islands

Boros and Garofalo (Gary B. Garofalo)

Air Charter (SAFA)
Paris, France
Counsel or consultant:
V. Michael Straus, P.C.

Air China Internat'l Corp., Ltd.
Beijing, China
Counsel or consultant:
Laxalt, Washington, Perito & Dubuc (Carroll E. Dubuc)

Air-Compack Inc.
Melbourne, FL
Counsel or consultant:
Warren and Associates

Air Conditioning Contractors of America
1513 16th St., N.W., Washington, DC 20036
Telephone: (202) 483-9370
Represented by:
Christine Ayotte, Director, Government Relations
James P. Norris, Exec. Vice President
Elaine W. Smith, Dir., Communications & Public Relations

Air Conditioning Contractors of America Political Action Committee
1513 16th St., N.W., Washington, DC 20036
Telephone: (202) 483-9370
Background: Responsible contacts are Christine Ayotte and James P. Norris. (See Air Conditioning Contractors of America.)

Air-Conditioning and Refrigeration Institute
1501 Wilson Blvd., Suite 600, Arlington, VA 22209
Telephone: (703) 524-8800
Represented by:
Arnold W. Braswell, President
Renee S. Hancher, Manager, International Trade
Marvin W. Heininger, Dir. of Communications & Public Relats.
Joseph M. McGuire, Sr. V. President, Policy & Gov't Affairs
Maura Shannon, Manager, Communication Department
Taury Silver, V. President, Communication & Education
David J. Stirpe, Legislative and Regulatory Affairs Rep.

Air-Conditioning and Refrigeration Institute Political Action Committee
1501 Wilson Blvd., Suite 600, Arlington, VA 22209
Telephone: (703) 524-8800
Background: The political action committee of the Air-Conditioning and Refrigeration Institute. Represented by Joseph M. McGuire of the Institute.

Air Force Ass'n
1501 Lee Hwy., Arlington, VA 22209-1198
Telephone: (703) 247-5800
Represented by:
Kenneth A. Goss, Director, National Defense Issues
General John O. Gray, (Ret.), Exec. Director
Brian Green, Director, Legislative Research
James A. McDonnell, Director, Military Relations
John Smith, Comptroller
Robin Whittle, Director of Communications

Air Force Sergeants Ass'n
P.O. Box 50, Temple Hills, MD 20748
Telephone: (301) 899-3500
Background: Represents some 150,000 active and retired Air Force enlisted members in more than 300 chapters worldwide before congressional and military decisionmakers, voicing their concerns over pay, benefits, advancement, retirement and living conditions.
Represented by:
Rudy I. Clark, Director, Military & Gov't Relations
Nelson L. Fink, Legislative Assistant, Gov't & Mil. Rel.
Dale Nelson, Director, Support Operations
James D. Staton, Exec. Director

Air France
Paris, France
Counsel or consultant:
V. Michael Straus, P.C.

Air Freight Ass'n of America
1710 Rhode Island Ave., N.W. 2nd Floor, Washington, DC 20036
Telephone: (202) 293-1030

ORGANIZATIONS REPRESENTED

Air Freight Ass'n of America (Cont'd)
Counsel or consultant:
Meyers and Alterman (Stephen A. Alterman)

Air Guadeloupe
Guadeloupe, French West Indies
Counsel or consultant:
V. Michael Straus, P.C.

Air Haiti
Port-au-Prince, Haiti
Counsel or consultant:
Bowen & Atkin (Harry A. Bowen)

Air India
Bombay, India
Counsel or consultant:
Squire, Sanders and Dempsey (Marshall S. Sinick)

Air Jamaica
Kingston, Jamaica
Counsel or consultant:
Galland, Kharasch, Morse and Garfinkle (Morris R. Garfinkle, Susan B. Jollie, Mark S. Kahan)

Air Line Pilots Ass'n Internat'l
1625 Massachusetts Ave., N.W., Washington, DC 20036
Telephone: (202) 797-4003
Represented by:
Gerald E. Baker, Senior Legislative Representative
Henry A. Duffy, President
Julia D. Graves Reneau, Manager, Communications
Gary Green, Director, Legal Department
Roger Hall, First V. President
Paul Hallisay, Director, Legislative Affairs
Brendan M. Kenny, Legislative Representative
John Mazor, Communications Specialist
John E. O'Brien, Director, Engineering and Air Safety
Larry Schulte, National Secretary
Don Skiados, Director, Communications

Air Line Pilots Ass'n Political Action Committee
1625 Massachusetts Ave., N.W., Washington, DC 20036
Telephone: (703) 689-2270
Background: Supported by the Air Lines Pilots Ass'n Internat'l. Contact is Paul L. Hallisay.

Air-Log Ltd.
1730 M St., N.W., Suite 515, Washington, DC 20036
Telephone: (202) 466-2885
Counsel or consultant:
Charles G. Botsford Office (Charles G. Botsford)

Air Pacific Ltd.
Suva, Fiji
Counsel or consultant:
Condon and Forsyth (Thomas J. Whalen)

Air Products and Chemicals, Inc.
805 15th St., N.W. Southern Bldg., Washington, DC 20006
Telephone: (202) 289-4110
Represented by:
James T. Christy, Director, Federal Government Relations
Peg Hughes, Exec. Secretary, Federal Gov't Relations
Counsel or consultant:
Cadwalader, Wickersham & Taft (Donald C. Alexander)
Covington and Burling (Nicholas W. Fels)
Pagonis and Donnelly Group (Thomas R. Donnelly, Jr.)
Patton, Boggs and Blow (Ernest S. Christian, Jr.)

Air-Sea Forwarders, Inc.
San Francisco, CA
Counsel or consultant:
Zuckert, Scoutt and Rasenberger (Frank J. Costello)

Air Traffic Control Ass'n
2020 North 14th St., Arlington, VA 22201
Telephone: (703) 522-5717
Represented by:
Gabriel A. Hartl, President
Counsel or consultant:
Suzette Matthews

Air Transport Ass'n Employees Political Action Committee
1156 15th St., N.W. Suite 1212, Washington, DC 20005-5206
Telephone: (202) 223-2900
Background: The political action committee of the Air Transport Ass'n of America. The above address is that of the law firm of Bregman, Abell & Kay.

Counsel or consultant:
Bregman, Abell & Kay (Stanley I. Bregman)

Air Transport Ass'n of America
1709 New York Ave., N.W., Washington, DC 20006-5206
Telephone: (202) 626-4000
Represented by:
Robert J. Aaronson, President
Patrice Allen-Gifford, Exec. Assistant to the President
Larry P. Barnett, V. President, Government Affairs
Zemphria R. Baskin, Director, Government Affairs
James L. Casey, Assistant General Counsel
Guy Clough, Director, Federal Legislation
Roger Cohen, Ass't. to the V. Pres. Gov't Affairs
Walter S. Coleman, V. President, Operations
Donald C. Comlish, V. President, Internat'l Affairs
Mary E. Downs, Asst. General Counsel and Secretary
J. Roger Fleming, Sr. V. President, Tech. Services
Angelynn Hall, Director, Federal Legislation
Stephen D. Hayes, V. President, Public Information
William W. Hoover, Exec. V. Pres., Operations and Safety
William E. Jackman, Asst. V. President, Public Information
Richard F. Lally, V. President, Security
James E. Landry, Sr. V. President and General Counsel
Robert L. Mandel, Director of Taxation
Edward Merlis, V. President, Policy and Planning
Tim Neale, Director of Public Information
Nestor N. Pylpec, V. President, Industry Services
Kathleen V. Rosenauer, Manager of Public Information
John R. Ryan, V. President, Air Traffic Management
Nancy Van Duyne, Manager, Federal Legislation
Karen Van Pelt, Director of Administration
Counsel or consultant:
Bregman, Abell & Kay
Cadwalader, Wickersham & Taft (Donald C. Alexander)
Griffin, Johnson & Associates
Hogan and Hartson
Sparkman and Cole, Inc. (Timothy R. Cole, D. Dean Sparkman)

Airbus Industrie of North America
1825 Eye St., N.W., Suite 400, Washington, DC 20006
Telephone: (202) 429-2052
Represented by:
Alan Boyd, Chairman

Aircraft Owners and Pilots Ass'n
421 Aviation Way, Frederick, MD 21701
Telephone: (301) 695-2000
Background: Represents the interests of over 280,000 pilots and aircraft owners who fly general aviation aircraft. Works with the Federal Aviation Administration, the Department of Transportation, the National Transportation Safety Board, the U.S. Congress and other local and national aviation organizations to ensure that the interests of its members and the entire general aviation community are well represented.
Represented by:
John L. Baker, President
Stephen R. Bassett, Sr. V. President, Gov't & Technical Afrs
Steven J. Brown, V. Pres., Strategic Planning & Policy
Robert G. Carter, V. President, Technical Analysis
Tom Chapman, V. Pres., Legislative Affairs & Counsel
William R. Deere, Director, Congressional Affairs
Donald D. Engen, President, Air Safety Foundation
Cheri L. Farha, Director, Media and Public Relations
Ann C. Hodges, Director, Congressional Affairs
David Kennedy, Assoc. Dir, State Legislative Affairs
Gail W. Lewis, V. President, Regional Affairs
Patricia E. Weil, V. President, Communications
John S. Yodice, Washington Counsel
Counsel or consultant:
Powell, Adams & Rinehart
Targeted Communications Corp.

Aircraft Owners and Pilots Ass'n Political Action Committee
500 E St., S.W., Suite 920, Washington, DC 20024

Telephone: (202) 479-4050
Background: Represented by Bill Deere of the Aircraft Owners and Pilots Ass'n.

Airline Industrial Relations Conference
1920 N St., N.W., Suite 250, Washington, DC 20036
Telephone: (202) 861-7550
Background: Also known as AIR Conference. Used by its members as an information exchange on such matters as industrial and personnel relations and related issues.
Represented by:
Robert Delucia, V. President and Treasurer

Airline Passengers of America
4212 King St., Alexandria, VA 22302
Telephone: (703) 824-0505
Background: A non-profit consumer advocacy group representing the interests of airline passengers before the federal government and aviation industry.
Represented by:
David Jeffrey, Public Affairs Director
Counsel or consultant:
Spiegel and McDiarmid (John J. Corbett, Jr.)

Airlines Reporting Corp. (ARC)
Counsel or consultant:
David Apter and Associates

Airport Operators Council Internat'l
1220 19th St., N.W. Suite 200, Washington, DC 20036
Telephone: (202) 293-8500
Represented by:
Robert A. Bunnell, V. President, External Affairs
Howard George, Exec. Director
Deborah Lunn, Exec. V. President

Airship Industries, Ltd.
London, United Kingdom
Counsel or consultant:
Ginsburg, Feldman and Bress (David Ginsburg, Robert W. Hawkins)
Wunder, Ryan, Cannon & Thelen (John J. McGovern, Jr.)

AIRTRAX
Burbank, CA
Counsel or consultant:
Hecht, Spencer & Associates (William H. Hecht, Walter D. Huddleston, W. Timothy Locke)

Aiwa America, Inc.
Mooachie, NJ
Counsel or consultant:
Patton, Boggs and Blow

Akademie Fur Fuhrunskrafte der Deutschen Bundespost
Bad Honnef, West Germany
Counsel or consultant:
Porter/Novelli
Wilkinson, Barker, Knauer and Quinn

Akhiok-Kaguyak, Inc.
Anchorage, AK
Counsel or consultant:
Bishop, Cook, Purcell & Reynolds (Marlow W. Cook)
Manatt, Phelps, Rothenberg & Phillips (Robert T. Herbolsheimer)

Akin, Gump, Strauss, Hauer and Feld Civic Action Committee
1333 New Hampshire Ave., N.W., Suite 400, Washington, DC 20036
Telephone: (202) 887-4000
Counsel or consultant:
Akin, Gump, Strauss, Hauer and Feld (Malcolm Lassman)

Akzo America, Inc.
New York, NY
Counsel or consultant:
Skadden, Arps, Slate, Meagher and Flom (Robert E. Lighthizer)

Alabama Farmers Federation
Montgomery, AL
Counsel or consultant:
Wallace & Edwards (Donald L. Wallace, Jr.)

Alabama Gas Corp.
Birmingham, AL

ORGANIZATIONS REPRESENTED

Counsel or consultant:
Wright and Talisman

Alabama Hospital Ass'n
Montgomery, AL
Counsel or consultant:
Robert Betz Associates, Inc (Robert B. Betz)

Alabama Power Co.
Birmingham, AL
Background: A subsidiary of Southern Co.
Counsel or consultant:
C. V. & R. V. Maudlin (Robert V. Maudlin)
Shaw, Pittman, Potts and Trowbridge (William Mike House)

Alabama State Docks Department
Montgomery, AL
Counsel or consultant:
Schmeltzer, Aptaker and Sheppard (Edward J. Sheppard, IV)

Alameda County, California
440 First St., N.W. Suite 502, Washington, DC 20001
Telephone: (202) 737-9696
Represented by:
Kenneth W. Wade, Washington Representative
Counsel or consultant:
McAuliffe, Kelly, Raffaelli & Siemens (James M. Copeland, Jr.)

Alamo Rent-a-Car
Fort Lauderdale, FL
Counsel or consultant:
Anderson, Hibey, Nauheim and Blair (Stanton D. Anderson, Robert A. Blair)
Galland, Kharasch, Morse and Garfinkle (Susan B. Jollie)
Gardner, Carton and Douglas (J. Curtis Moffat)

Alan Guttmacher Institute, The
2010 Massachusetts Ave., N.W., 5th floor, Washington, DC 20036
Telephone: (202) 296-4012
Background: A private, nonprofit corporation for research, policy analysis and public education in the fields of reproductive health. Founded in 1968 as the Center for Family Planning Program Development, it is an independent special affiliate of Planned Parenthood Federation of America. Maintains offices in New York City and Washington, DC.
Represented by:
Cory Richards, V. President, Public Policy

Alascom, Inc.
1726 M St., N.W., Suite 801, Washington, DC 20036
Telephone: (202) 223-5200
Background: A subsidiary of Pacific Telecom, Inc. Represented by Alexander F. Karman of Pacific Telecom, Inc.
Counsel or consultant:
Koteen and Naftalin (Margot Smiley Humphrey, Alan Y. Naftalin)
Young & Jatlow (Francis L. Young)

Alaska Airlines
Seattle, WA
Counsel or consultant:
O'Melveny and Myers (William T. Coleman, Jr.)
Squire, Sanders and Dempsey (Marshall S. Sinick)

Alaska Crab Coalition
Seattle, WA
Counsel or consultant:
C. Deming Cowles, IV
Patton, Boggs and Blow (James B. Christian, Jr.)

Alaska Joint Venture Seafoods, Inc.
Anchorage, AK
Counsel or consultant:
Hopkins and Sutter (William D. Phillips)

Alaska Loggers Ass'n
Juneau, AK
Counsel or consultant:
Gold and Liebengood, Inc. (Martin B. Gold)
Preston Gates Ellis & Rouvelas Meeds (Richard L. Barnes, Lloyd Meeds)
Robertson, Monagle and Eastaugh (Steven W. Silver)

Alaska Pacific Refining, Inc.
Santa Barbara, CA

Counsel or consultant:
Birch, Horton, Bittner and Cherot (Joseph M. Chomski)

Alaska, State of
444 N. Capitol St., N.W. Suite 518, Washington, DC 20001
Telephone: (202) 624-5858
Represented by:
Suzanne Iudicello, Assoc. Dir., Fisheries & the Environ.
John W. Katz, Director of State/Federal Relations
Margaret A. Moran, Spec. Ass't, Arctic Nat'l Wildlife Ref.
Eric Ostrovsky, Assoc. Dir., Commerce & Transportation
James E. Torgerson, Spec. Asst. Atty. General, Off. of Gov.
Counsel or consultant:
O'Connor & Hannan (George J. Mannina, Jr.)

Alaska Teamster-Employer Pension Trust
Anchorage, AK
Counsel or consultant:
Birch, Horton, Bittner and Cherot (Joseph M. Chomski)

Alaskan Loggers Ass'n
Ketchikan, AK
Counsel or consultant:
Jack Ferguson Associates (Jack Ferguson)

Albanian American Civic League
1220 19th St., N.W. Suite 400, Washington, DC 20036
Telephone: (202) 452-8060
Background: Political Director is Kieran Mahoney of the DC firm Capitol Strategies.
Counsel or consultant:
Capitol Strategists Group (Kieran Mahoney)

Alberta Petroleum Marketing Commission
Edmonton, Alberta, Canada
Counsel or consultant:
Brady and Berliner

Albion, Michigan, City of
Counsel or consultant:
Preston Gates Ellis & Rouvelas Meeds (Allen Erenbaum, Craig J. Gehring)

Albuquerque, New Mexico, City of
Counsel or consultant:
Nat'l Center for Municipal Development (John R. O'Donnell)

ALC Communications Corp.
Chicago, IL
Counsel or consultant:
Kendall and Associates (William T. Kendall)
Rivkin, Radler, Dunne and Bayh (Thomas A. Connaughton)

Alcan Aluminum Corp.
918 16th St., N.W. Suite 304, Washington, DC 20006
Telephone: (202) 785-3018
Represented by:
James P. Monaghan, Vice President, Government Affairs

Alcatel
Paris, France
Counsel or consultant:
Verner, Liipfert, Bernhard, McPherson and Hand, Chartered (Lloyd N. Hand)

Alcide de Gasperi Foundation
c/o Hogan & Hartson 555 13th St., N.W., Washington, DC 20004
Telephone: (202) 637-5600
Counsel or consultant:
Hogan and Hartson (Deborah T. Ashford)

Alcohol and Drug Problems Ass'n of North America
444 N. Capitol St., N.W., Washington, DC 20001
Telephone: (202) 737-4340
Background: Acts to develop policies which offer possible solutions to the problem of addiction. Serves as a forum for members to join in improving the quality of prevention and treatment services.
Represented by:
Karst Besteman, Exec. Director

Alcoma Packing Co.
Lake Wells, FL

Counsel or consultant:
Davis & Harman (Thomas A. Davis)

Aldus
Seattle, WA
Counsel or consultant:
Swidler & Berlin, Chartered (Bruce A. Lehman)

Alexander & Alexander Inc.
555 13th St., N.W. Suite 1180E, Washington, DC 20004-1109
Telephone: (202) 783-2550
Represented by:
Laurie E. Londoner, Ass't V.P./ Dir., Gov't & Industry Affrs
Robert H. Moore, Senior V. President, Corp. Relations
Jean Smith, Executive Assistant, Corporate Relations
Counsel or consultant:
Newmyer Associates, Inc. (Sidney Booth, A. G. Newmyer, III)
Olwine, Connelly, Chase, O'Donnell and Weyher (W. Harrison Wellford)
Tucker & Associates (William Tucker)

Alexander & Baldwin, Inc.
Honolulu, HI
Background: A shipping and agricultural concern.
Counsel or consultant:
Patton, Boggs and Blow (David B. Robinson)

Alexander Graham Bell Ass'n for the Deaf
3417 Volta Place, N.W., Washington, DC 20007
Telephone: (202) 337-5220
Background: Founded by Alexander Graham Bell in 1890. A nonprofit organization with membership in 38 countries which exists to promote the study, understanding and early detection of hearing loss in adults and children, as well as to work for better educational opportunities and teacher training for the hearing-impaired.
Represented by:
Dr. Donna McCord Dickman, Exec. Director
Counsel or consultant:
Cassidy and Associates, Inc. (James P. Fabiani)

Alexander Hamilton Life Insurance Co. of America
Farmington Hills, MI
Background: A subsidiary of Household Internat'l. Represented by H. A. Doersam of the parent company office.

Alexander Laing & Cruickshank
London, England
Counsel or consultant:
Hill and Knowlton Public Affairs Worldwide (Dr. Ira P. Kaminow)

Alfa Romeo, Inc.
Italy
Counsel or consultant:
Barnes, Richardson and Colburn (Rufus E. Jarman, Jr.)

Algoma Steel Corp., Ltd.
Sault Ste. Marie, Ontario
Counsel or consultant:
Dow, Lohnes and Albertson (William Silverman)

Algonquin Gas Transmission Co.
Boston, MA
Counsel or consultant:
Campbell-Raupe, Inc. (Jeanne M. Campbell)

Alhambra, California, City of
Counsel or consultant:
The Ferguson Co. (William Ferguson, Jr., Patricia Jordan, Thane Young)

Alitalia Airlines
Rome, Italy
Counsel or consultant:
Dickstein, Shapiro and Morin (Henry C. Cashen, II)

All American Nat'l Bank
Virginia Gardens, FL
Counsel or consultant:
Warren W. Koffler

All Nippon Airways Co.
Tokyo, Japan
Counsel or consultant:
Global USA, Inc. (John M. Nugent, Jr.)
Zuckert, Scoutt and Rasenberger (James L. Devall)

ORGANIZATIONS REPRESENTED

Allegheny County, Pennsylvania
Pittsburgh, PA
Counsel or consultant:
O'Neill and Athy, P.C. (Martha L. Casey)

Allegheny Electric Cooperative, Inc.
Harrisburg, PA
Counsel or consultant:
Duncan, Weinberg, Miller & Pembroke, P.C. (Robert Weinberg)

Allegheny Power Systems
New York, NY
Counsel or consultant:
Paul, Hastings, Janofsky and Walker (Charles A. Patrizia)

Allen-Bradley Corp.
Milwaukee, WI
Counsel or consultant:
Internat'l Business-Government Counsellors, Inc. (Solveig B. Spielmann)

Allergan
Irvine, CA
Counsel or consultant:
Hill and Knowlton Public Affairs Worldwide (Susan Cohen)

Alliance for Acid Rain Control
444 North Capitol St., N.W., Suite 526, Washington, DC 20001
Telephone: (202) 624-5475
Represented by:
Edward A. 'Ned' Helme, Director

Alliance for Aging Research
2021 K St., N.W. Suite 305, Washington, DC 20006
Telephone: (202) 293-2856
Background: A non-profit, tax-exempt, bipartisan forum seeking to increase the visibility and priority of aging research as a goal of national science policy. Founded in 1986; includes scientists, corporate exeutives, and members of congress.
Represented by:
Sharon L. Cohen, Director, Health Policy
Paul DelPonte, Director, Communications
Daniel Perry, Exec. Director

Alliance for America's Homeowners
50 E St., S.E., Washington, DC 20003
Telephone: (202) 646-1263
Background: A coalition monitoring mortgage interest legislation.
Counsel or consultant:
Perkinson & Associates, Inc. (Michael J. Bertelsen, David R. Blaha, Gary J. Perkinson)

Alliance for Better Child Care
c/o Children's Defense Fund 122 C St., N.W., Washington, DC 20001
Telephone: (202) 628-8787
Background: A coalition of child advocacy groups, women's organizations, labor unions and religious and minority assistance groups lobbying for increased federal funding of day care for children of low income families. Helen Blank of the Children's Defense Fund is a leading organizer.

Alliance for Cannabis Therapeutics
Box 53318, Washington, DC 20009
Telephone: (202) 483-8595
Background: An educational organization to promote the use of marijuana for legitimate medical, therapeutic, scientific and research purposes.
Represented by:
Robert Randall, President
Counsel or consultant:
Steptoe and Johnson

Alliance for Capital Access
1919 Pennsylvania Ave., N.W., Suite 701, Washington, DC 20006
Telephone: (202) 429-9628
Background: An association of more than 60 companies that issue or invest in high yield securities to fund their growth. Primary mission is to educate members of Congress and regulatory agencies on the need to preserve free access to capital markets. Also works on other matters affecting growth companies, including tax policy, merger and acquisition issues and finance issues. Exec. Director is David K. Aylward and Vice Presidents are Douglas Lowenstein and Gregory Scott (see Nat'l Strategies Inc.)

Counsel or consultant:
Collier, Shannon & Scott (R. Timothy Columbus)
King and Spalding (Richard D'Avino)
Nat'l Strategies Inc. (David K. Aylward, Douglas Lowenstein, Gregory Scott)

Alliance for Clean Energy (ACE)
c/o Alcalde & Rousselot 1901 N. Ft. Myer Dr., 12th Fl., Rosslyn, VA 22209
Telephone: (703) 841-1781
Counsel or consultant:
Alcalde & Rousselot (Nancy Gibson Prowitt)

Alliance for Corporate Growth
600 New Hampshire Ave., N.W., Suite 1000, Washington, DC 20037
Telephone: (202) 944-3000
Background: A coalition of mid-sized corporations supporting disparate voting rights in corporate governance.
Counsel or consultant:
Dyer, Ellis, Joseph & Mills (Howard A. Vine)

Alliance for Fair Competition
7315 Wisconsin Ave., Bethesda, MD 20814
Telephone: (301) 657-3110
Counsel or consultant:
Ass'n Advocates (Joanne Oxley)

Alliance for Justice
1601 Connecticut Ave., N.W. Suite 600, Washington, DC 20009
Telephone: (202) 332-3224
Background: Founded in 1975 as the Council for Public Interest Law to promote and assist public interest law firms. Worked for citizen participation in administrative agency and court proceedings and for awards of equitable attorney fees in public interest law cases. Became the Alliance for Justice in 1981 as a coalition of 28 public interest and civil rights groups including Nat'l Organization of Women Legal Defense Fund, Natural Resources Defense Council and the Consumers Union.
Represented by:
Nan Aron, Exec. Director
George Kassouf, Director, Judicial Selection Project
Carol Seifert, Deputy Director

Alliance for Maritime Heritage Foundation
317 Massachusetts Ave., N.E., Washington, DC 20002
Telephone: (202) 544-6798
Background: Seeks to promote responsible archaeological shipwreck salvage.
Counsel or consultant:
Ken Schlossberg Assoc. (William C. Smith)

Alliance for Responsible CFC Policy
2011 Eye St., N.W. Suite 500, Washington, DC 20006
Telephone: (202) 429-1614
Background: A coalition of approximately 500 companies which produce or use chlorofluorcarbons, the gas used as propellants in aerosol cans. Established in 1980 to coordinate the industry's effort to resist over-regulation in response to environmental concerns.
Represented by:
Kevin J. Fay, Exec. Director
Peter Likes, Chairman

Alliance for Traffic Safety
2200 Mill Road, Alexandria, VA 22314
Telephone: (703) 838-1840
Background: Represented by William E. Johns of the American Trucking Ass'ns.

Alliance of American Insurers
1629 K St., N.W. Suite 1010, Washington, DC 20006
Telephone: (202) 822-8811
Background: A national property-casualty insurance trade ass'n representing more than 175 insurance companies in dealing with problems of common interest in the fields of legislation, regulation, litigation and public information.
Represented by:
Sara Clary, Senior Washington Representative
David M. Farmer, V. President, Federal Affairs
Thomas A. O'Day, Associate V. President
Counsel or consultant:
Bonner & Associates

Alliance of Metalworking Industries
1155 Connecticut Ave., N.W. 3rd Floor, Washington, DC 20036
Telephone: (202) 429-6545

Background: Composed of seven associations representing 20,000 metalworking firms: Precision Metal Forming Ass'n, Forging Industry Association, National Screw Machine Products Association, Spring Manufacturers' Institute, Metal Treating Institute, the Industrial Fasteners Institute, and the Nat'l Tooling and Machining Ass'n.
Counsel or consultant:
Venable, Baetjer, Howard and Civiletti (Ilona M. Hogan)

Alliance of Nonprofit Mailers
2001 S St., N.W., Suite 301, Washington, DC 20009
Telephone: (202) 462-5132
Background: A national coalition of nonprofit organizations seeking to maintain reasonable and stable nonprofit mail rates.
Represented by:
Robert Neal Denton, Assistant Director
Daniel P. Doherty, Exec. Director
Counsel or consultant:
Sidley and Austin (David Levy)

Alliance to Save Energy
1725 K St., N.W., Suite 914, Washington, DC 20006
Telephone: (202) 857-0666
Background: Founded in 1977 by Senators Charles H. Percy and Hubert Humphrey, and now chaired by Sen. Tim Wirth (D-CO), the Alliance is a non-profit coalition of government, business, consumer and labor leaders dedicated to increasing the efficiency of energy use. Conducts research and pilot projects to stimulate investment in energy efficiency, formulates policy initiatives and conducts educational programs.
Represented by:
Mark Hopkins, Director of Corporate Relations
William Prindle, Sr. Program Manager
James L. Wolf, Exec. Director

Allied-Signal Inc.
1001 Pennsylvania Ave., N.W. Suite 700, Washington, DC 20004
Telephone: (202) 662-2650
Represented by:
John E. Bonitt, Legislative and Regulatory Affairs
Richard Buek, Treasurer, Allied-Signal PAC
Kenneth W. Cole, Corp. V. Pres., Government Relations
Thomas D. Hart, Dir., Legislative and Regulatory Affairs
M. L. Hefti, V.P. & Chief, Cong. Rtns., Aerosp. Prgms
Michael W. Naylor, Dir., Legislative and Regulatory Affairs
E. Archie NeSmith, Jr., V.P., Congressional Afrs, Aerosp. Prgrams
R. Douglas Wallin, Jr., Director, Cong. Affrs., Aerosp. Programs
Counsel or consultant:
Black, Manafort, Stone and Kelly Public Affairs Co.
Ginn, Edington, Moore and Wade
McNair Law Firm, P.A.
Wexler, Reynolds, Fuller, Harrison and Schule, Inc. (Nancy Clark Reynolds, Anne Wexler)

Allnet Communications Services Inc. Good Government Fund
1990 M St., N.W., Suite 500, Washington, DC 20036
Telephone: (202) 293-0593
Represented by:
Janice Loichle, Treasurer

Alloy Surfaces, Inc.
Wilmington, DE
Counsel or consultant:
Denny Miller Associates
Snyder Ball Kriser and Associates, Inc. (Lou Kriser)

Allstate Insurance Co.
633 Pennsylvania Ave., N.W., Suite 600, Washington, DC 20004
Telephone: (202) 737-4900
Represented by:
J. Charles Bruse, Asst. V. Pres. & Asst. General Counsel
Counsel or consultant:
Hopkins and Sutter (Francis O. McDermott)

Allwaste, Inc.
499 S. Capitol St., S.W. Suite 520, Washington, DC 20003
Telephone: (202) 488-4887
Represented by:
Albert B. Rosenbaum, III, V. President

Allwaste Political Action Committee
499 S. Capitol St., S.W. Suite 520, Washington, DC 20003

The listings in this directory are available as *Mailing Labels*. See last page.

ORGANIZATIONS REPRESENTED

Telephone: (202) 488-4887
Background: Represented by Albert B. Rosenbaum III of Allwaste, Inc.

Alnor Oil Co.
Valley Stream, NY
Background: A castor oil importer.
Counsel or consultant:
Meyers & Associates (Rick Meyers)

Aloha Airlines
Honolulu, HI
Counsel or consultant:
Squire, Sanders and Dempsey (Marshall S. Sinick)

Alpha Environmental, Inc.
Austin, TX
Counsel or consultant:
Kuykendall Co. (Dan H. Kuykendall)

Alpha 21 Corp.
Midland, TX
Counsel or consultant:
Kuykendall Co. (Dan H. Kuykendall)

Alpo Pet Foods, Inc.
Allentown, PA
Counsel or consultant:
Leighton and Regnery (Richard J. Leighton)

ALTA Technology
Stamford, CT
Background: A manufacturer of automated fare collection equipment.
Counsel or consultant:
Patton, Boggs and Blow (Lanny J. Davis)

Alternative Materials Institute
1440 New York Ave., N.W., Suite 300, Washington, DC 20005
Telephone: (202) 638-1200
Background: Address given is that of the consulting firm E. Bruce Harrison Co.
Counsel or consultant:
E. Bruce Harrison Co.

Alternative Schools Network
Chicago, IL
Counsel or consultant:
Capitol Pespectives (Mary Elise DeGonia)

Altos Hornos de Mexico, S.A.
Mexico City, Mexico
Counsel or consultant:
Mudge Rose Guthrie Alexander and Ferdon (N. David Palmeter)

Alumax, Inc.
Norcross, GA
Counsel or consultant:
Jefferson Group, The (Robert L. Harris)

Aluminum Ass'n
900 19th St., N.W., Suite 300, Washington, DC 20006
Telephone: (202) 862-5100
Background: Members represent virtually all domestic primary producers and about 85% of the semi-fabricated aluminum shipped in this country.
Represented by:
John Dickinson, Director, Statistical Services
Seymour G. Epstein, Tech. Dir.-Env. Res'ch, Health & Safety
Jack H. Goldman, Manager, Technical Services
M. Barry Meyer, V.P., Gov't Rel. & Assoc. Gen'l Counsel
David N. Parker, President
S. Donald Pitts, V. President, Technical
Frank H. Rathbun, Manager, Public Information
Counsel or consultant:
Baker and Hostetler (Alan S. Ward)

Aluminum Ass'n Political Action Committee
900 19th St., N.W., Suite 300, Washington, DC 20006
Telephone: (202) 862-5100
Background: Contact person is M. Barry Meyer of the Aluminum Ass'n.

Aluminum Co. of America
1615 M St., N.W., Suite 500, Washington, DC 20036
Telephone: (202) 956-5300

Represented by:
J. Mel Bass, Manager, Government Affairs
Marcia Bresee Dalrymple, Manager, Government Affairs
Frank P. Jones, Jr., V. President, Government Affairs
Russell C. Wisor, Director, Government Affairs
Counsel or consultant:
Steptoe and Johnson (Susan G. Esserman, Mark A. Moran)

Alyeska Pipeline Service Co.
10009 Kensington Parkway, Kensington, MD 20895
Telephone: (301) 942-6121
Represented by:
Anne Banville, Public Affairs Representative
Counsel or consultant:
Gibson, Dunn and Crutcher (Cynthia C. Lebow, Robert A. McConnell)
Holland and Hart (Lauren E. Brown, Quinn O'Connell)

Alzheimer's Ass'n
1334 G St., N.W. Suite 500, Washington, DC 20005
Telephone: (202) 393-7737
Represented by:
Stephen R. McConnell, Director, Washington Office
Erica Neale, Legislative Assistant
Judith Assmus Riggs, Director, Federal Issues
Counsel or consultant:
CR Associates (Nicholas G. Cavarocchi, Domenic R. Ruscio)

AM Internat'l
Chicago, IL
Counsel or consultant:
Wilmer, Cutler and Pickering

AM&S/BHAS
Melbourne, Australia
Counsel or consultant:
Sharretts, Paley, Carter and Blauvelt (Alfred R. McCauley)

Amalgamated Clothing and Textile Workers Union
815 16th St., N.W., Suite 507, Washington, DC 20006
Telephone: (202) 628-0214
Represented by:
Eric Frumin, Health and Safety Director
Elizabeth M. Smith, Legislative and Political Director
Michael J. Wilson, Legislative Representative
Counsel or consultant:
Economic Consulting Services Inc. (Mark W. Love, Deborah Swartz)
Marlowe and Co.

Amalgamated Industrial Steel Mills of Malaysia
Malaysia
Counsel or consultant:
Willkie Farr and Gallagher (Walter J. Spak)

Amalgamated Metal Corp. PLC
London, England
Counsel or consultant:
Chadbourne and Parke (Cornelius Golden, Jr.)

Amalgamated Steel Mills of Malaysia
Kuala Lumpur, Malaysia
Counsel or consultant:
Willkie Farr and Gallagher (Walter J. Spak)

Amalgamated Transit Union
5025 Wisconsin Ave., N.W., Washington, DC 20016
Telephone: (202) 537-1645
Represented by:
Ellis B. Franklin, Internat'l Exec. V. President
Oliver W. Green, Internat'l Secretary-Treasurer
Joseph N. Jaquay, Research Director
Robert A. Molofsky, Legislative Director
Earle W. Putnam, General Counsel
Counsel or consultant:
Marlowe and Co.

Amalgamated Transit Union Committee on Political Education
5025 Wisconsin Ave., N.W., Washington, DC 20016
Telephone: (202) 537-1645
Background: Represented by Oliver Green of the Amalgamated Transit Union.

Amalgamated Transit Union, Local 689
2001 9th St., N.W., Suite 300, Washington, DC 20001
Telephone: (202) 232-4734

Represented by:
James M. Thomas, Jr., President

Amana Refrigeration, Inc.
Amana, IA
Counsel or consultant:
Webster, Chamberlain and Bean (Arthur L. Herold)

Amarillo/Pantex
Amarillo, TX
Counsel or consultant:
Lipsen Whitten & Diamond

Amax Inc.
1819 L St., N.W., Suite 300, Washington, DC 20036-3895
Telephone: (202) 466-6966
Represented by:
Dorothy J. Gusler, Sr. Federal Affairs Representative
Donald F. Kratz, Senior Counsel
Counsel or consultant:
Richard W. Bliss
O'Melveny and Myers

AmBase Corp.
New York, NY
Counsel or consultant:
Burchette & Associates
Holt, Miller & Associates (Harris N. Miller)

Manatt, Phelps, Rothenberg & Phillips (William C. Oldaker)

Ambulatory Pediatric Ass'n
6728 Old McLean Village, McLean, VA 22101
Telephone: (703) 556-9222
Counsel or consultant:
Degnon Associates, Inc. (Marge Degnon)

Amdahl Corp.
1667 K St., N.W., Suite 300, Washington, DC 20006
Telephone: (202) 835-2220
Represented by:
R. J. Collins, Government Affairs Representative
Robert F. Lockhart, Jr., Government Affairs Representative
William P. Pitts, Government Affairs Representative
Murray S. Scureman, V. President, Government Affairs
Counsel or consultant:
Baker and McKenzie
Paul, Hastings, Janofsky and Walker (G. Hamilton Loeb)

Amerace Corp. (Stimsonite Division)
Niles, IL
Counsel or consultant:
Arthur E. Cameron

Amerada Hess Corp.
New York, NY
Counsel or consultant:
Akin, Gump, Strauss, Hauer and Feld (Edward L. Rubinoff)
Wilmer, Cutler and Pickering (Sally Katzen)

Ameri-Cable Internat'l, Inc.
Miami, FL
Counsel or consultant:
Keefe Co., The (Clarence L. James, Jr., Robert J. Keefe, Terry M. O'Connell)

Ameribanc Investors Group
P.O. Box 36 7630 Little River Turnpike, Annandale, VA 22003
Telephone: (703) 658-2720
Counsel or consultant:
Miller & Chevalier, Chartered (Leonard Bickwit, Jr.)

America First Companies
Omaha, NE
Counsel or consultant:
Van Ness, Feldman & Curtis (Dwight Eric Hultman)

America the Beautiful Fund
219 Shoreham Bldg., Washington, DC 20005
Telephone: (202) 638-1649
Background: Provides encouragement and technical and financial support to individuals and groups undertaking projects to improve the quality of their local environment.

The listings in this directory are available as *Mailing Labels.* See last page.

471

ORGANIZATIONS REPRESENTED

America the Beautiful Fund (Cont'd)
Represented by:
Paul Bruce Dowling, Exec. Director

America West Airlines
Phoenix, AZ
Counsel or consultant:
Winthrop, Stimson, Putnam & Roberts (Ronna A. Freiberg, John E. Gillick, Ira S. Shapiro)

American Academy of Actuaries
Schaumburg, IL
Telephone: (202) 223-8196
Represented by:
Gary Hendricks, Director of Gov't Info & Chief Economist
James J. Murphy, Exec. V. President
Christine E. Nickerson, Director, Standards Program
Erich Parker, Director, Public Relations
Gary D. Simms, General Counsel & Director, Operations
Counsel or consultant:
Daniel J. Edelman, Inc. (Elizabeth Kelley)

American Academy of Child and Adolescent Psychiatry
3615 Wisconsin Ave., N.W., Washington, DC 20016
Telephone: (202) 966-7300
Represented by:
Virginia Q. Anthony, Exec. Director
Mary Crosby, Assistant Director for Gov't Affairs

American Academy of Dermatology
Evanston, IL
Counsel or consultant:
Epstein Becker and Green (Deborah Steelman)
Dr. John T. Grupenhoff
R. Duffy Wall and Associates (Michael Stern)

American Academy of Facial Plastic and Reconstructive Surgery
1101 Vermont Ave., N.W. Suite 404, Washington, DC 20005
Telephone: (202) 842-4500
Represented by:
Judith C. Marden, Director of Communications
John F. Schlegel, Exec. V. President

American Academy of Family Physicians
600 Maryland Ave., S.W., Suite 770, Washington, DC 20024
Telephone: (202) 488-7448
Represented by:
Lois Holwerda-Hoyt, Assistant Director
Charlie Huntington, Legislative Representative
Rosemarie Sweeney, Director, Washington Office
Counsel or consultant:
Health and Medicine Counsel of Washington (Dale P. Dirks)

American Academy of Nurse Practitioners
8904 1st Ave., Silver Spring, MD 20910
Telephone: (301) 726-3794
Background: Represents almost 21,000 nurse practitioners who work as employees of healthcare institutions and in independent practice. Lobbies for direct reimbursement for services under medicaid and medicare and all health insurance plans.
Counsel or consultant:
Carole P. Jennings, Ph.D.

American Academy of Ophthalmology
1101 Vermont Ave., N.W., Suite 300, Washington, DC 20005
Telephone: (202) 737-6662
Represented by:
Lori A. Bounds, Washigton Representative
Stephanie C. Mensh, Washington Representative
David J. Noonan, Deputy Exec. Vice President
Michael A. Roberts, Washington Representative
Cynthia Root Moran, Dir., Office of Governmental Relations
Counsel or consultant:
Gold and Liebengood, Inc. (John F. Scruggs)

American Academy of Optometry
5530 Wisconsin Ave., N.W. Suite 1149, Washington, DC 20815
Telephone: (301) 652-0905

Counsel or consultant:
PAI Management Corp. (David A. Lewis)
Webster, Chamberlain and Bean (John W. Hazard, Jr.)

American Academy of Orthopaedic Surgeons
317 Massachusetts Ave., N.E., Suite 100, Washington, DC 20002
Telephone: (202) 546-4430
Background: A member organization of the Coalition of Health Funding in Washington.
Represented by:
Joyce Hooper, Legislative Assistant
Counsel or consultant:
CR Associates (Nicholas G. Cavarocchi)

American Academy of Otolaryngic Allergy
8455 Colesville Road Suite 745, Silver Spring, MD 20910-9998
Telephone: (301) 588-1800
Represented by:
Donald J. Clark, Exec. Director

American Academy of Otolaryngology-Head and Neck Surgery
One Prince St., Alexandria, VA 22314
Telephone: (703) 836-4444
Represented by:
Karin Bierstein, J.D., M.S., Director, Socio-Economic Affairs
Dr. Harry W. McCurdy, Exec. V. President
William E. Small, Deputy Exec. Director
Counsel or consultant:
Dr. John T. Grupenhoff

American Academy of Pediatrics
1331 Pennsylvania Ave., N.W., Suite 721 North, Washington, DC 20004-1703
Telephone: (202) 662-7460
Background: A member organization of the Coalition for Health Funding in Washington.
Represented by:
Graham H. Newsom, Assistant Director, Government Liaison
Elizabeth J. Noyes, Director, Government Liaison
Counsel or consultant:
Reed Smith Shaw & McClay (Stephan E. Lawton)

American Academy of Physical Medicine and Rehabilitation
Chicago, IL
Counsel or consultant:
White, Fine, and Verville (Richard E. Verville)

American Academy of Physician Assistants
950 North Washington St., Alexandria, VA 22314
Telephone: (703) 836-2272
Background: Provides public education on the physician assistants profession and lobbies on federal legislation of importance to physician assistants.
Represented by:
William A. Finerfrock, Director of Federal Affairs
John Friedman, Public Affairs Administrator
Nicole Gara, Director, Gov't and Professional Affairs
F. Lynn May, Exec. V. President

American Academy of Physician Assistants Political Action Committee
950 North Washington St., Alexandria, VA 22314
Telephone: (703) 836-2272
Background: Represented by William A. Finerfrock of the American Academy of Physician Assistants.

American Academy of Podiatric Sports Medicine
1729 Glastonberry Road, Potomac, MD 20854
Telephone: (301) 424-7440
Represented by:
Larry I. Shane, Exec. Director

American Advertising Federation
1400 K St., N.W., Suite 1000, Washington, DC 20005
Telephone: (202) 898-0089
Background: Established in 1905. Represents all facets of the advertising industry: corporations, advertisers, advertising agencies, media, suppliers and related trade associations. Seeks to represent the industry's views, to prevent overregulation and promote a better understanding in government, education and the general public.

Represented by:
Howard Hughes Bell, President
Dennis Brown, Director, State Advertising Coalition
Julie A. Dolan, V. President, Communications
Clark E. Rector, Director, Government Relations
Wallace S. Snyder, Sr. V. Pres., Gov't Rels./Gen. Counsel
Counsel or consultant:
Davidson Colling Group, Inc., The (James H. Davidson)

American Advertising Federation Political Action Committee
1400 K St., N.W., Suite 1000, Washington, DC 20005
Telephone: (202) 898-0089
Represented by:
James Baker, PAC Contact

American Agenda
Background: A bipartisan policy advisory organization funded by the Times-Mirror Foundation. Co-Chairs are former Presidents Jimmy Carter and Gerald Ford. Co-Exec. Directors are James M. Cannon and Stuart E. Eizenstat, domestic policy advisors to Presidents Ford and Carter, respectively.
Represented by:
James M. Cannon, Co-Exec. Director

American Agricultural Editors Ass'n
1629 K St., N.W. Suite 1100, Washington, DC 20006
Telephone: (202) 785-6709
Counsel or consultant:
Agri/Washington (Paul S. Weller, Jr., Daren R. Williams)

American Agriculture Movement, Inc.
100 Maryland Ave., N.E. Suite 500A, Washington, DC 20002
Telephone: (202) 544-5750
Background: Founded in 1979 as a farm organization and lobbying group of family farm producers from all producing sectors of agriculture.
Represented by:
Lawrence W. Mitchell, Director, Federal & State Relations
Harvey Sanner, Nat'l President
David L. Senter, Nat'l Director

American Agriculture Movement Political Action Committee
100 Maryland Ave., N.E. Box 69, Washington, DC 20002
Telephone: (202) 544-5750
Represented by:
Tommy Willis, Treasurer

American Airlines
1101 17th St., N.W. Suite 600, Washington, DC 20036
Telephone: (202) 857-4221
Represented by:
William J. Burhop, V. President, Federal Affairs
Edward Faberman, Associate General Counsel
Mary A. Kennedy, Managing Director, Government Affairs
Diane J. Koller, Managing Director, Gov't Affairs
Counsel or consultant:
Baker, Worthington, Crossley, Stansberry & Woolf (Edward R. Hamberger)
Campbell-Raupe, Inc. (Jeanne M. Campbell)
Hill and Knowlton Public Affairs Worldwide (Robert Keith Gray)
Prather, Seeger, Doolittle and Farmer (Carl B. Nelson, Jr., Edwin H. Seeger)
Wexler, Reynolds, Fuller, Harrison and Schule, Inc. (William K. Ris, Jr.)

American Airlines Political Action Committee
1101 17th St., N.W., Washington, DC 20036
Telephone: (202) 857-4204
Background: The political action committee sponsored by American Airlines. Responsible contact is Diane Koller.

American Alliance for Health, Physical Education, Recreation and Dance
1900 Association Drive, Reston, VA 22091
Telephone: (703) 476-3400
Represented by:
Charles H. Hartman, Exec. V. President

American Alliance for Rights and Responsibilities
1819 H St., N.W., Suite 500, Washington, DC 20006
Telephone: (202) 785-7844

The listings in this directory are available as *Mailing Labels*. See last page.

Background: Engages in public interest litigation and public education regarding the balance of individualism and commitment in American life.
Represented by:
Roger L. Conner, Exec. Director

American Ambulance Ass'n
Sacramento, CA
Counsel or consultant:
Fleishman-Hillard, Inc (Paul Johnson, Caren Turner)

American Amusement Machine Ass'n
12731 Directors Loop, Woodbridge, VA 22192
Telephone: (703) 548-8044
Represented by:
Robert C. Fay, Exec. V. President

American Anthropological Ass'n
1703 New Hampshire Ave., N.W., Washington, DC 20009
Telephone: (202) 232-8800
Represented by:
Judith Lisansky, Director, Programs
Eugene L. Sterud, Exec. Director

American Apparel Manufacturers Ass'n
2500 Wilson Blvd., Suite 301, Arlington, VA 22201
Telephone: (703) 524-1864
Represented by:
G. Stewart Boswell, President and Chief Operating Officer
Stephanie Godley, Director, Legislative Services
Larry K. Martin, Director, Government Relations

American Apparel Manufacturers Political Action Committee
2500 Wilson Blvd., Suite 301, Arlington, VA 22201
Telephone: (703) 524-1864
Background: Contact is Larry K. Martin of American Apparel Manufacturers Ass'n.

American Appraisal Associates, Inc.
Milwaukee, WI
Counsel or consultant:
Winston and Strawn (John G. Milliken)

American-Arab Affairs Council
1730 M St., N.W. Suite 512, Washington, DC 20036
Telephone: (202) 296-6767
Background: A nonprofit organization to acquaint Americans with the civilization, peoples, culture and history of the Arab World. Seeks to foster improved understanding between the United States and the Arabs and to expand public debate on U.S. Middle East policy through its publications, conferences and state committee programs.
Represented by:
George A. Naifeh, President

American-Arab Anti-Discrimination Committee
4201 Connecticut Ave., N.W. Suite 500, Washington, DC 20009
Telephone: (202) 244-2990
Background: Dedicated to fighting the negative stereotyping of Arabs in the U.S. media and in political life. Has 22,000 members, 60 chapters and nine regional offices across the country.
Represented by:
James G. Abourezk, National Chairman
Barbara Shahin Batlouni, Exec. Director
Abdeen Jabara, President

American Arbitration Ass'n
1730 Rhode Island Ave., N.W., Suite 509, Washington, DC 20036
Telephone: (202) 296-8510
Represented by:
Thomas R. Colosi, Vice President, National Affairs
Ms. Garylee Cox, Regional V. President
Donna Silberberg, Director, Public Relations

American Arts Alliance
1319 F St., N.W., Suite 307, Washington, DC 20004-1182
Telephone: (202) 737-1727
Background: A consortium of about 400 artistic organizations formed in 1977 to strengthen public support of the arts.
Represented by:
Lee Kessler, Deputy Director
Anne G. Murphy, Exec. Director

American Ass'n for Adult and Continuing Education
1112 16th St., N.W., Suite 420, Washington, DC 20036
Telephone: (202) 463-6333
Background: An international education association serving the field of adult and continuing education through advocacy, professional development and public information programs.
Represented by:
Judith Ann Koloski, Exec. Director

American Ass'n for Clinical Chemistry
2029 K St., N.W., 7th Floor, Washington, DC 20006
Telephone: (202) 857-0717
Represented by:
Pamela A. Nash, Director, Government Affairs
Joanne M. Thyken, V. President, General Manager
Ronald E. Whorton, Exec. V. President

American Ass'n for Counseling and Development
5999 Stevenson Ave., Alexandria, VA 22304
Telephone: (703) 823-9800
Represented by:
William Hunter, Acting Director
Dr. Nancy Pinson-Millburn, Assistant Exec. Director
Lori S. Rogovin, M.S.W., Government Relations Specialist
Lauren B. Scheib, Public Relations Specialist
Richard K. Yep, Director of Government Relations

American Ass'n for Dental Research
1111 14th St., N.W. Suite 1000, Washington, DC 20005
Telephone: (202) 898-1050
Background: A member organization of the Coalition for Health Funding in Washington.
Represented by:
John J. Clarkson, Exec. Director
Counsel or consultant:
CR Associates (Nicholas G. Cavarocchi)

American Ass'n for Geriatric Psychiatry
Box 376A, Greenbelt, MD 20768
Telephone: (301) 220-0952
Background: Represented in Washington by Alice Conde Martinez of The American College of Psychiatrists.

American Ass'n for Higher Education
One Dupont Circle, N.W. Suite 600, Washington, DC 20036
Telephone: (202) 293-6440
Represented by:
Russell Edgerton, President

American Ass'n for Internat'l Aging
1511 K St., N.W., Suite 443, Washington, DC 20005
Telephone: (202) 638-6815
Background: An international organization concerned about older people. Formed in response to the U.N.'s World Assembly on Aging.
Represented by:
Helen K. Kerschner, Ph.D., Exec. Director
Counsel or consultant:
EMJ Consultants (Frances F. Butler)

American Ass'n for Laboratory Accreditation
656 Quince Orchard Road, Suite 704, Gaithersburg, MD 20878
Telephone: (301) 670-1377
Represented by:
John W. Locke, President
Peter S. Unger, V. President
Counsel or consultant:
Kirkland and Ellis (James S. Hostetler)

American Ass'n for Leisure and Recreation
1900 Association Dr., Reston, VA 22091
Telephone: (703) 476-3471
Represented by:
Dr. Barbara M. Sampson, Exec. Director

American Ass'n for Marriage and Family Therapy
1717 K St., N.W. Suite 407, Washington, DC 20006
Telephone: (202) 429-1825

Michael Bowers, Assoc Exec Dir for Professional Practice
Mark R. Ginsberg, Ph.D., Executive Director
Deborah S. Simmons, Director of Federal Relations
Counsel or consultant:
Keck, Mahin and Cate

American Ass'n for Marriage and Family Therapy PAC
1717 K St., N.W., Suite 407, Washington, DC 20006
Telephone: (202) 429-1825
Represented by:
Evelyn Hight, Treasurer

American Ass'n for Medical Systems and Informatics (AAMSI)
1101 Connecticut Ave., N.W., Suite 700, Washington, DC 20036
Telephone: (202) 857-1189
Background: A multi-disciplinary group promoting technological systems in medicine and health care.
Counsel or consultant:
Smith, Bucklin and Associates (Michael Hamm)

American Ass'n for Study of the United States in World Affairs
3813 Annandale Road, Annandale, VA 22003
Telephone: (703) 256-8761
Background: Founded in 1948 by Dr. Samuel E. Burr, Jr. at American University, Washington, D.C. A non-profit educational organization which is independent of government, party or any other domestic or foreign interest group. Describes its purpose as 'to put a mirror on the position of the U.S. in world affairs' through graduate level studies, seminars, lectures and contributions to publications.
Represented by:
Prof. Gilbert P. Richardson, Sr., President & Dean, USWA Institute

American Ass'n for the Advancement of Science
1333 H St., N.W., Washington, DC 20005
Telephone: (202) 326-6400
Represented by:
Richard S. Nicholson, Exec. Officer
J. Thomas Ratchford, Associate Exec. Officer
Albert H. Teich, Director, Science & Policy Programs
Counsel or consultant:
Gallagher-Widmeyer Group Inc., The (Scott D. Widmeyer)

American Ass'n of Advertising Agencies
1899 L St., N.W., Suite 700, Washington, DC 20036
Telephone: (202) 331-7345
Represented by:
Glenda Leggitt Etchison, Senior Staff Executive
John F. Kamp, V. President
John E. O'Toole, President
Hal Shoup, Exec. V. President
Counsel or consultant:
Campbell-Raupe, Inc. (Jeanne M. Campbell)
Davidson Colling Group, Inc., The (James H. Davidson)

American Ass'n of Airport Executives
4212 King St., Alexandria, VA 22302
Telephone: (703) 824-0500
Represented by:
Charles Barclay, Exec. V. President
Linda Daschle, V. President, Federal Affairs
J. Spencer Dickerson, Senior V. President

American Ass'n of Bioanalysts
St. Louis, MO
Counsel or consultant:
Arent, Fox, Kintner, Plotkin & Kahn (Alan E. Reider)

American Ass'n of Blacks in Energy
1220 L St., N.W., Suite 605, Washington, DC 20005
Telephone: (202) 898-0828
Represented by:
Cheryl Dobbins, Consulting Director

American Ass'n of Blood Banks
1117 North 19th St. Suite 600, Arlington, VA 22209
Telephone: (703) 528-8200

ORGANIZATIONS REPRESENTED

American Ass'n of Blood Banks (Cont'd)
Represented by:
Gilbert M. Clark, Exec. Director
Cynthia K. Kelly, Manager, Government and Legal Affairs
Marcia S. Lane, Dir., Communications & Public Relations
P. Robert Rigney, Jr., Assoc. Exec. Director, Public Affairs

American Ass'n of Children's Residential Centers
440 First St., N.W., Suite 310, Washington, DC 20001
Telephone: (202) 638-1604
Background: A national organization of agency and individual members concerned with residential treatment of children with emotional problems.
Represented by:
Claudia C. Waller, Exec. Director

American Ass'n of Clinical Urologists
Baltimore, MD
Counsel or consultant:
MARC Associates, Inc. (Randolph B. Fenninger)

American Ass'n of Colleges for Teacher Education
One Dupont Circle, N.W., Suite 610, Washington, DC 20036
Telephone: (202) 293-2450
Represented by:
Penelope Earley, Director, Governmental Relations
David G. Imig, Exec. Director
Counsel or consultant:
Steptoe and Johnson (Bruce R. Hopkins)

American Ass'n of Colleges of Nursing
One Dupont Circle, N.W., Suite 530, Washington, DC 20036
Telephone: (202) 463-6930
Background: A member organization of the Coalition for Health Funding in Washington.
Represented by:
Geraldine Polly Bednash, Exec. Director
G. Brockwell Heylin, Director, Government Affairs
Anne M. Rhome, Sr. Staff Specialist, Gov't'l Affairs

American Ass'n of Colleges of Osteopathic Medicine
1620 Eye St., N.W., Suite 220, Washington, DC 20006
Telephone: (202) 467-4131
Represented by:
Sherry R. Arnstein, Exec. Director
Roger C. Courtney, Director of Government Relations
Counsel or consultant:
MARC Associates, Inc. (Randolph B. Fenninger)

American Ass'n of Colleges of Pharmacy
1426 Prince St., Alexandria, VA 22314
Telephone: (703) 739-2330
Background: A member organization of the Federation of Associations of Schools of the Health Professions and the Coalition for Health Funding in Washington.
Represented by:
Jacqueline Eng, Director of Public Affairs
Carl E. Trinca, Exec. Director

American Ass'n of Colleges of Podiatric Medicine
6110 Executive Blvd. Suite 204, Rockville, MD 20852
Telephone: (301) 984-9350
Represented by:
Anthony McNevin, President
Counsel or consultant:
CR Associates (Domenic R. Ruscio)

American Ass'n of Collegiate Registrars and Admissions Officers
One Dupont Circle, N.W., Suite 330, Washington, DC 20036
Telephone: (202) 293-9161
Represented by:
Wayne E. Becraft, Exec. Director
Laurine D. Robinson, Ass't Exec. Director

American Ass'n of Community and Junior Colleges
One Dupont Circle, N.W. Suite 410, Washington, DC 20036
Telephone: (202) 293-7050

Represented by:
Phillip English, V. President, Communications Services
Dr. James F. Gollattscheck, Exec. V. President
John R. McGill, Executive Assistant to the President
James McKenney, Ass't V. President, Federal Relations
Frank Mensel, V. President for Federal Relations
Dr. Dale Parnell, President
Judy Tomczak, Public Information Officer

American Ass'n of Crop Insurers
2501 M St., N.W., Suite 430, Washington, DC 20037
Telephone: (202) 463-0541
Counsel or consultant:
McLeod & Pires (Michael R. McLeod, Margaret R. Murray, Laura Phelps)

American Ass'n of Crop Insurers Political Action Committee
2501 M St., N.W., Suite 400, Washington, DC 20037
Telephone: (202) 463-0541
Counsel or consultant:
McLeod & Pires (Michael R. McLeod)

American Ass'n of Dental Schools
1625 Massachusetts Ave., N.W., Washington, DC 20036
Telephone: (202) 667-9433
Background: Represents all dental schools in the U.S., as well as advanced education, hospital and allied dental institutions. Monitors relevant federal legislative and regulatory activities and maintains liaison with Congress, federal agencies, and other health and education ass'ns.
Represented by:
Martha Liggett, Asst. Exec. Dir., Government Affairs
Scott Litch, Legislative Counsel
Richard D. Mumma, Jr., Exec. Director
Mila Roschwalb, Legislative Assistant
Counsel or consultant:
Burson-Marsteller (Rebecca L. Halkias)

American Ass'n of Early Childhood Educators
3612 Bent Branch Court, Falls Church, VA 22041
Telephone: (703) 941-4329
Counsel or consultant:
William J. Tobin and Associates (William J. Tobin)

American Ass'n of Electromyography and Electrodiagnosis
Rochester, MN
Counsel or consultant:
Jenner and Block

American Ass'n of Engineering Societies
415 2nd St., N.E., Suite 200, Washington, DC 20002
Telephone: (202) 546-2237
Background: A multidisciplinary organization of professional engineering societies. Membership is over 500,000.
Represented by:
Mitchell Bradley, Exec. Director
M. Melissa Moore, Director, Communications & Public Affrs.

American Ass'n of Enterprise Zones
1730 K St., N.W., Suite 915, Washington, DC 20006
Telephone: (202) 466-2687
Represented by:
Dick Cowden, Exec. Director
Counsel or consultant:
Vorys, Sater, Seymour and Pease

American Ass'n of Equipment Lessors
1300 North 17th St. Suite 1010, Arlington, VA 22209
Telephone: (703) 527-8655
Represented by:
Michael J. Fleming, President
Katherine George, Communications Manager
Ralph A. Petta, Industry Services Manager
Jeremy B. Taylor, V. President
Counsel or consultant:
Patton, Boggs and Blow (Ernest S. Christian, Jr.)
Volpe, Boskey and Lyons
Winburn, VanScoyoc, and Hooper (John P. Winburn)

American Ass'n of Equipment Lessors Capital Investment Political Action Committee
1300 North 17th St. Suite 1010, Arlington, VA 22209
Telephone: (703) 527-8655
Background: Represented by Michael J. Fleming of the Association.

Counsel or consultant:
Volpe, Boskey and Lyons (Ellis Lyons)
Winburn, VanScoyoc, and Hooper (John P. Winburn)

American Ass'n of Exporters and Importers
New York, NY
Counsel or consultant:
Patton, Boggs and Blow
Powell, Goldstein, Frazer and Murphy (Peter Suchman)
Sandler, Travis & Rosenberg. P.A. (Ronald W. Gerdes, Thomas G. Travis)
Sharretts, Paley, Carter and Blauvelt

American Ass'n of Eye and Ear Hospitals
Dallas, TX
Counsel or consultant:
Robert Betz Associates, Inc (Robert B. Betz)

American Ass'n of Fastener Importers
Sayreville, NJ
Counsel or consultant:
Barnes, Richardson and Colburn (Matthew T. McGrath)
Kessler and Associates

American Ass'n of Gastroenterology
4222 King St., Alexandria, VA 22302
Telephone: (703) 549-4440
Counsel or consultant:
Ass'n Resources Management, Inc. (Thomas Fise)
Health and Medicine Counsel of Washington (Dale P. Dirks)

American Ass'n of Grain Inspection and Weighing Agencies
1629 K St., N.W. Suite 100, Washington, DC 20006
Telephone: (202) 785-6740
Counsel or consultant:
Agri/Washington (Paul S. Weller, Jr., Daren R. Williams)

American Ass'n of Healthcare Consultants
11208 Waples Mill Road, Suite 109, Fairfax, VA 22030
Telephone: (703) 691-2242
Represented by:
Vaughan A. Smith, President

American Ass'n of Homes for the Aging
1129 20th St., N.W., Suite 400, Washington, DC 20036
Telephone: (202) 296-5960
Background: An organization representing the nation's nonprofit nursing homes and housing projects for the elderly.
Represented by:
Deborah A. Cloud, Manager of Public Relations
Sheldon L. Goldberg, President
Patricia G. Kallsen, Senior V. President
Larry McNickle, Director, Housing and Tax Policy
Evelyn Fieman Munley, Health Policy Analyst
Scott L. Parkin, Director, Communications
Susan M. Pettey, Director, Health Policy
Michael F. Rodgers, Senior V. President
Ritchenya Shepherd, Public Relations Assistant
Kenneth Stewart, Housing Policy Analyst
Suzanne Weiss, Health Reimbursement Analyst

American Ass'n of Immunologists
9650 Rockville Pike, Bethesda, MD 20814
Telephone: (301) 530-7178
Represented by:
Dr. Joseph F. Saunders, Exec. Officer

American Ass'n of Motor Vehicle Administrators
4200 Wilson Blvd., Suite 600, Arlington, VA 22203
Telephone: (703) 522-4200
Represented by:
John H. Strandquist, Exec. Director

American Ass'n of Museums
1225 Eye St., N.W., Washington, DC 20005
Telephone: (202) 289-1818
Represented by:
Edward H. Able, Jr., Exec. Director
Geoffrey Platt, Jr., Director of Government Affairs
Counsel or consultant:
Winston and Strawn (Richard Meltzer)

American Ass'n of Neurological Surgeons/Congress of Neurological Surgeons
One Farragut Square South, Ninth Floor, Washington, DC 20006
Telephone: (202) 628-7171

ORGANIZATIONS REPRESENTED

Represented by:
  Charles L. Plante, Washington Representative

American Ass'n of Nurse Anesthetists
Park Ridge, IL
Counsel or consultant:
  Capitol Associates, Inc. (Karen Bodenhorn, Debra M. Hardy-Havens)
  Manatt, Phelps, Rothenberg & Phillips (William C. Oldaker, June L. Walton)
  White, Fine, and Verville (Richard E. Verville)

American Ass'n of Nurserymen
1250 Eye St., N.W., Suite 500, Washington, DC 20005
Telephone: (202) 789-2900
Represented by:
  Joel Albizo, Director, Public Relations
  Benjamin C. Bolusky, Director, Government Affairs
  Craig J. Regelbrugge, Dir, Regulatory Affrs & Grower Svcs
  Lawrence E. Scovotto, Exec. V. President

American Ass'n of Pastoral Counselors
9508A Lee Hwy., Fairfax, VA 22031-2303
Telephone: (703) 385-6967
Represented by:
  Adele L. Schaefer, Manager, Membership & Office Services
  C. Roy Woodruff, Ph.D., Exec. Director

American Ass'n of Pathologists
9650 Rockville Pike, Bethesda, MD 20814
Telephone: (301) 530-7130
Represented by:
  Francis A. Pitlick, Ph.D., Exec. Officer

American Ass'n of Petroleum Geologists
Wichita Falls, TX
Counsel or consultant:
  E. Del Smith, Inc. (E. Del Smith)

American Ass'n of Physics Teachers
5112 Berwyn Road, College Park, MD 20740
Telephone: (301) 345-4200
Counsel or consultant:
  Holly Rumpler

American Ass'n of Political Consultants
1211 Connecticut Ave., N.W. Suite 506, Washington, DC 20036
Telephone: (202) 546-1564
Represented by:
  Bradley O'Leary, President

American Ass'n of Politically Active Citizens
3617 N. John Marshall Drive, Arlington, VA 22207
Telephone: (703) 534-1440
Background: A political action committee.
Counsel or consultant:
  Sheehan Associates, Inc. (Paul Billman, Denise L. Sheehan)

American Ass'n of Port Authorities
1010 Duke St., Alexandria, VA 22314
Telephone: (703) 684-5700
Represented by:
  W. Patrick Jones, V. President, Government Relations
  R. Erik Stromberg, President

American Ass'n of Private Railroad Car Owners, Inc.
Somerville, NJ
Counsel or consultant:
  Elliott Associates (M. Diane Elliott)

American Ass'n of Retired Persons
1909 K St., N.W., Washington, DC 20049
Telephone: (202) 872-4700

Represented by:
  Alex Armendaris, Exec. Assistant to the Exec. Director
  Myriam Bailey, Senior Analyst
  Howard Bedlin, Legislative Representative
  Laurel Beedon, Senior Analyst
  William Kent Brunette, Legislative Representative
  David Certner, Legislative Representative
  Gary Clayton, Senior Analyst
  Martin C. Corry, Director, Federal Affairs
  Horace B. Deets, Exec. Director
  Kevin J. Donnellan, Legislative Counsel
  Larry Fenster, Senior Analyst
  George Gaberlavage, Senior Analyst
  John Gist, Senior Analyst
  James R. Holland, Director, Office of Communications
  Judy Hushbeck, Senior Analyst
  Shelah Leader, Policy Analyst
  Cheryl Matheis, Legislative Representative
  Marion R. Mayer, Legislative Representative
  Evelyn Morton, Legislative Representative
  Michele Pollak, Legislative Representative
  Patricia Powers, Senior Policy Analyst
  Donald L. Redfoot, Legislative Rep., Federal Affairs
  Jo Reed, Senior Coordinator
  John C. Rother, Dir., Legis. Res. & Public Policy Div.
  Helen Savage, Senior Analyst
  Kathleen Scholl, Senior Coordinator
  Judy Schub, Senior Coordinator
  Patricia P. Smith, Senior Coordinator, Health
  Jane Tilly, Senior Analyst
  Theresa Varner, Health Policy Analyst, Pub. Pol. Inst.
  Larry White, Legislative Representative
Counsel or consultant:
  Capitol Associates, Inc. (Gwen Gampel)
  Chambers Associates Incorporated (Craig E. Bury)
  Peabody Fitzpatrick Communications (J. Douglas Koelemay, Myra B. Peabody)

American Ass'n of School Administrators
1801 North Moore St., Arlington, VA 22209
Telephone: (703) 528-0700
Represented by:
  Lu Fulbright, Manager, Communications Projects
  Bruce Hunter, Assoc. Exec. Director, Gov't Relations
  Dr. Effie Jones, Assoc. Exec. Director, Minority Affairs
  Gary Marx, Associate Exec. Director, Communications
  Raymond Melton, Assoc. Exec. Dir. and Dir, NASE
  Richard D. Miller, Exec. Director
  Nicholas J. Penning, Legislative Specialist
  Walter Turner, Associate Exec. Director
  Dr. Virginia C. Vertiz, Government Relations Specialist

American Ass'n of Small Research Companies
Upper Darby, PA
Counsel or consultant:
  Bowytz, Sherman and Mitchell (Robert B. Bowytz)

American Ass'n of State Colleges and Universities
One Dupont Circle, N.W. Suite 700, Washington, DC 20036
Telephone: (202) 293-7070
Represented by:
  Gay Clyburn, Director of Public Affairs
  Edward Elmendorf, V. President, Governmental Relations
  Allan W. Ostar, President

American Ass'n of State Highway and Transportation Officials
444 N. Capitol St., N.W., Suite 225, Washington, DC 20001
Telephone: (202) 624-5800
Represented by:
  Francis B. Francois, Exec. Director
  Billy K. Higgins, Congressional Liaison
  Sunny Mays Schust, Director, Communications & Publications
Counsel or consultant:
  Barksdale Ballard & Co. (D. Michael Ballard, Walter E. Duka)
  Loomis, Owen, Fellman and Howe (James E. Anderson)

American Ass'n of Surgeons Assistants
1600 Wilson Blvd., Suite 905, Arlington, VA 22209
Telephone: (703) 525-1191
Background: Richard Guggolz of Drohan Management Group serves as the Exec. Director.
Counsel or consultant:
  Drohan Management Group (Richard A. Guggolz)

American Ass'n of Tissue Banks
1350 Beverly Road, Suite 220A, McLean, VA 22101
Telephone: (703) 827-9582
Represented by:
  Jeanne C. Mowe, Exec. Director

American Ass'n of University Affiliated Programs
8630 Fenton St., Suite 410, Silver Spring, MD 20910
Telephone: (301) 588-8252
Background: A member organization of the Coalition for Health Funding in Washington.
Represented by:
  William Jones, Exec. Director

American Ass'n of University Professors
1012 14th St., N.W., Suite 500, Washington, DC 20005
Telephone: (202) 737-5900
Represented by:
  Ernst Benjamin, General Secretary
  Dr. Alfred D. Sumberg, Director of Government Relations

American Ass'n of University Women
2401 Virginia Ave., N.W., Washington, DC 20037
Telephone: (202) 785-7700
Represented by:
  Dr. Anne L. Bryant, Exec. Director
  Ann Chipley, Director of Program and Policy
  Kristin Stelck, Assistant Director, Legislative Affairs

American Ass'n of Zoological Parks and Aquariums
1110 Vermont Ave., N.W., Suite 1160, Washington, DC 20005
Telephone: (202) 429-0949
Represented by:
  Karen Asis, Public Relations Director
Counsel or consultant:
  KLV Associates (Kristin L. Vehrs)

American Ass'n on Mental Retardation
1719 Kalorama Road, N.W., Washington, DC 20009
Telephone: (202) 387-1968
Represented by:
  M. Doreen Croser, Exec. Director

American Astronautical Soc.
6352 Rolling Mill Place Suite 102, Springfield, VA 22152
Telephone: (703) 866-0020
Represented by:
  Carolyn Brown, Exec. Director

American Astronomical Soc.
2000 Florida Ave., N.W., Suite 300, Washington, DC 20009
Telephone: (202) 328-2010
Represented by:
  Dr. Peter B. Boyce, Exec. Officer

American Automar, Inc.
1025 Thomas Jefferson St., N.W., Suite 308, Washington, DC 20007
Telephone: (202) 342-2410
Represented by:
  J. William Charrier, President

American Automobile Ass'n
500 E St. S.W., Suite 950, Washington, DC 20024
Telephone: (202) 554-6060
Represented by:
  John Archer, Managing Director, Government Affairs
  William R. Berman, Director, Environment and Energy Dept.
  John F. Haifley, Director of Federal Relations
  Ronald W. Kosh, General Manager, AAA Potomac
  Robert S. Krebs, Dir., Public & Gov't Affrs., AAA Potomac
  Susan G. Pikrallidas, Director, Tourism Affairs
  George A. Viverette, Jr., Director, Highway Transportation
Counsel or consultant:
  Anderson and Quinn (Quentin R. Corrie)

American Automotive Leasing Ass'n
1001 Connecticut Ave., N.W., Suite 1201, Washington, DC 20036
Telephone: (202) 223-2600

ORGANIZATIONS REPRESENTED

American Automotive Leasing Ass'n (Cont'd)
Represented by:
John H. Fitch, Jr., Exec. Director
Counsel or consultant:
Volpe, Boskey and Lyons
Winburn, VanScoyoc, and Hooper (John P. Winburn)

American Bakers Ass'n
1111 14th St., N.W., Suite 300, Washington, DC 20005
Telephone: (202) 296-5800
Represented by:
Paul C. Abenante, President
Lee Becker, Legislative Representative
Kevin M. Burke, Dir., Industrial & Regulatory Affairs
Lorraine Champ, Controller
Ira H. Dorfman, V. President, Government Affairs
Counsel or consultant:
Swidler & Berlin, Chartered (Barry Direnfeld)

American Bankers Ass'n
1120 Connecticut Ave., N.W., Washington, DC 20036
Telephone: (202) 663-5000
Represented by:
Joanne Ames, Assistant Tax Counsel
Peter Blocklin, Senior Legislative Representative-Senate
John J. Byrne, Senior Legislative Counsel
Philip S. Corwin, Dir., Office of Optns. & Retail Banking
Virginia Dean, Director, Gov't and Membership Relations
Robert H. Dugger, Chief Economist. Dir., Policy Develop't
Nessa Feddis, Fed. Couns., Gov't Rels./Retail Banking
Gary W. Fields, Director, State Ass'n Division
John J. Gill, General Counsel
C. G. Holthus, President
James E. Lodge, Exec. Dir., Communications
Judith A. McCormick, Assistant Federal Counsel
Gail McGowan, Corporate Secretary
James D. McLaughlin, Dir., Agency Relations, Trust/Securities
Mary-Liz Meany, Manager, Public Relations
Sarah Miller, Senior Government Relations Counsel
Donald G. Ogilvie, Exec. V. President
Alan R. Ott, Federal Legislative Representative
Jeffrey S. Owen, Exec. Director, Banking Organizations
Sharon Raymond, Mgr., Member Banker/Grass Roots Program
Linda S. Rearick, Tax Legislative Representative
Henry C. Ruempler, Director, Tax Office
Mark Serepca, Public Relations
Deborah Shannon, Federal Legislative Representative
Paul Smith, Federal Adminstrative Counsel
Floyd E. Stoner, Dir., Office of Federal Legis Operations
Joshua P. Tenuta, Federal Legislative Representative
Robert A. Wallgren, Exec. Dir., Banking Professions Group
Larry Weekly, Director, Public Relations
Brad Welling, Asst. Federal Administrative Counsel
Edward L. Yingling, Exec. Director of Government Relations
Counsel or consultant:
Dionne Davies
O'Neill and Athy, P.C. (Andrew Athy, Jr.)

American Bankers Ass'n BankPac
1120 Connecticut Ave., N.W., Washington, DC 20036
Telephone: (202) 663-5076
Background: The political action committee sponsored by the American Bankers Ass'n.
Represented by:
Brian M. Meyer, Director
Jeanne L. Yingst, Assistant Director

American Bankruptcy Institute
107 Second St., N.E., Washington, DC 20002
Telephone: (202) 543-1234
Background: A professional association of attorneys, accountants, educators and others focusing on bankruptcy reorganization and insolvency matters.
Represented by:
Louis J. Brune, III, Exec. Director
Caroline L. Rossanda, Communications Coordinator

American Bar Ass'n
1800 M St., N.W., Washington, DC 20036
Telephone: (202) 331-2200

Represented by:
Craig H. Baab, Staff Director for Governmental Liaison
Denise A. Cardman, Legislative Counsel
Kevin J. Driscoll, Staff Director for Bar Liaison
Irene R. Emsellem, Staff Director for Member Liaison
Robert D. Evans, Director, ABA Washington Office
Lillian B. Gaskin, Legislative Counsel
Bruce Nicholson, Legislative Counsel
Gail Alexander Wise, Staff Dir., Public Relations

American Beekeeping Federation
Jesup, GA
Counsel or consultant:
Meyers & Associates (Keith White)

American Blind Lawyers Ass'n
1010 Vermont Ave., N.W. Suite 1100, Washington, DC 20036
Telephone: (202) 393-3666
Background: Represented by Roberta Douglas of the American Council of the Blind.

American Blood Commission
1600 Wilson Blvd., Suite 905, Arlington, VA 22209
Telephone: (703) 525-1191
Counsel or consultant:
Drohan Management Group (William M. Drohan)

American Board of Health Physics
8000 Westpark Drive Suite 130, McLean, VA 22102
Telephone: (703) 790-1745
Counsel or consultant:
Society and Association Services Corp. (Richard J. Burk, Jr.)

American Board of Opticianry
10341 Democracy Lane, Fairfax, VA 22030
Telephone: (703) 691-8356
Background: Represented by Nancy Roylance of the Opticians Ass'n of America.

American Boiler Manufacturers Ass'n
950 North Glebe Road, Suite 160, Arlington, VA 22203
Telephone: (703) 522-7350
Represented by:
Russell N. Mosher, Exec. Director
W. Randall Rawson, Assistant Exec. Director
Counsel or consultant:
Wyman, Bautzer, Christensen, Kuchel and Silbert (George Miron)

American Book Publishers Political Action Committee
1718 Connecticut Ave., N.W. Suite 700, Washington, DC 20009
Telephone: (202) 232-3335
Background: Represents the legislative and political interests of the Ass'n of American Publishers. Contact person is Diane Rennert of the Ass'n of American Publishers.

American Bureau of Shipping
Paramus, NJ
Counsel or consultant:
Ragan and Mason (William F. Ragan)

American Bus Ass'n
1015 15th St., N.W. Suite 250, Washington, DC 20005
Telephone: (202) 842-1645
Background: Represents the intercity bus industry in its relations with the Congress, other elements of the transportation industry and the government. Formerly Nat'l Ass'n of Motor Bus Owners.
Represented by:
Susan Perry, Sr. V. Pres., Government Relations
George T. Snyder, Jr., Chief Executive
Counsel or consultant:
O'Connor & Hannan (Timothy M. Haake)

American Business Conference
1730 K St., N.W. Suite 1200, Washington, DC 20006
Telephone: (202) 822-9300
Background: An organization limited to the Chief Executive Officers of midsize, high growth companies.
Represented by:
W. L. Lyons Brown, Jr., Chairman
Howard John Endean, V. President, Policy
Frances B. Frazier, Director, Government/Corporate Relations
Rhonda Lee Halverson, V. President, Administration
Peggy Roth Murray, V. President, Communications
Barry K. Rogstad, President

American Butter Institute
888 16th St., N.W., Washington, DC 20006
Telephone: (202) 659-1454
Background: Exec. Director is Floyd D. Gaibler, who is also Exec. Director of the Nat'l Cheese Institute.

American Cancer Soc. (Public Affairs Office)
316 Pennsylvania Ave., S.E. Suite 200, Washington, DC 20003
Telephone: (202) 546-4011
Represented by:
Alan C. Davis, V. President for Public Affairs
Nancy Hailpern, Legislative Assistant
John H. Madigan, Jr., Asst. V. President for Public Affairs
Gerard P. Murphy, MD, Senior V. President, Medical Affairs
William M. Tipping, Exec. V. President
Kerrie B. Wilson, Coordinator of Cancer Care Policy

American Car Rental Ass'n
2011 Eye St., N.W., 5th Floor, Washington, DC 20006
Telephone: (202) 223-2118
Background: ACRA is a voluntary, non-profit trade association dedicated to serving the interests of those in the business of short term automobile rental. Jan Armstrong of the DC firm Payne, Murch, and Assocs. serves as Exec. Director.
Counsel or consultant:
Collier, Shannon & Scott (R. Timothy Columbus)
Newell-Payne Companies, Inc. (Jan M. Armstrong)

American Cast Iron Pipe Co.
Birmingham, AL
Counsel or consultant:
Edward D. Heffernan

American Cast Metals Ass'n
918 16th St., N.W., Suite 403, Washington, DC 20006
Telephone: (202) 833-1316
Background: Established in 1987 by the merger of the National Foundry Ass'n and the Metal Casting Soc.
Represented by:
Carol Green, Associate Director
Walter M. Kiplinger, Jr., V. President, Government Affairs

American Cement Alliance
1331 Pennsylvania Ave., N.W. Suite 910, Washington, DC 20004
Telephone: (202) 662-7416
Represented by:
Richard C. Creighton, President
David S. Hubbard, Legislative Director
Counsel or consultant:
Howrey and Simon (John F. Bruce)
Murphy and Associates (William T. Murphy, Jr.)

American Cement Alliance Political Action Committee
1331 Pennsylvania Ave., N.W. Suite 910, Washington, DC 20004
Telephone: (202) 662-7416
Background: Treasurer and principal contact is Richard C. Creighton, of the American Cement Alliance.

American Cemetery Ass'n
Three Skyline Place 5201 Leesburg Pike, Suite 1111, Falls Church, VA 22041
Telephone: (703) 379-5838
Represented by:
Stephen L. Morgan, Exec. V. President

American Chain Ass'n
932 Hungerford Drive, Suite 36, Rockville, MD 20850
Telephone: (301) 738-2448
Counsel or consultant:
Lloyd and Associates, Inc. (Raymond J. Lloyd)

American Challenge Today Political Action Committee
536 Seventh St., S.E., Washington, DC 20003
Telephone: (202) 544-1988
Counsel or consultant:
Washington Resources and Strategy, Inc. (William R. Sweeney, Jr.)

American Chamber of Commerce Executives
4232 King St., Alexandria, VA 22302
Telephone: (703) 998-0072

The listings in this directory are available as *Mailing Labels*. See last page.

ORGANIZATIONS REPRESENTED

Represented by:
John De Lellis, V. Pres., Communications & Member Svcs.
Paul J. Greeley, Jr., CAE, President
Rosemary Harper, V. President, Ass'n Services

American Chamber of Commerce Executives Communications Council
4232 King St., Alexandria, VA 22302
Telephone: (703) 998-0072
Background: Responsible contact is Rosemary Harper. (See American Chamber of Commerce Executives.)

American Chamber of Commerce in Germany
Frankfurt, West Germany
Counsel or consultant:
Squire, Sanders and Dempsey (Ritchie T. Thomas)

American Chemical Soc.
1155 16th St., N.W., Washington, DC 20036
Telephone: (202) 872-4600
Represented by:
John Kistler Crum, Exec. Director
Nancy Enright, Head, Public Communication
Robert H. Marks, Director, Publications
Patrick McCurdy, Director of Communications
Ann Messmore, Director, Administration
Terri L. Nally, Manager, Office of College Chemistry
Kathleen A. Ream, Head, Dept. of Gov't Rels. & Sci. Policy
Annette T. Rosenblum, Manager, Science Policy Analysis
Susan M. Turner, Manager, Legislative Regulatory Programs

American Child Care Foundation
1801 Robert Fulton Drive Suite 400, Reston, VA 22091
Telephone: (703) 758-3583
Counsel or consultant:
St. Germain, Rodio & Ursillo, Ltd. (Fernand J. St. Germain)

American Chipper Knife Coalition
1800 M St., N.W. Suite 900 South Lobby, Washington, DC 20036-5891
Telephone: (202) 778-9000
Counsel or consultant:
Kirkpatrick & Lockhart (Glenn R. Reichardt)

American Chiropractic Ass'n
1701 Clarendon Blvd., Arlington, VA 22209
Telephone: (703) 276-8800
Represented by:
Thomas R. Daly, Legal Counsel
Joseph Michael Hogan, Jr., Asst. Director, Governmental Relations
Paul T. Kelly, Director of Governmental Relations
J. Ray Morgan, Exec. V. President
Counsel or consultant:
Marlowe and Co.

American Chiropractic Ass'n Political Action Committee
1701 Clarendon Blvd., Arlington, VA 22209
Telephone: (703) 276-8800
Background: Contact is J. Michael Hogan, Jr. of the Association.

American Chiropractic Registry of Radiologic Technologists
Kalamazoo, MI
Counsel or consultant:
White, Fine, and Verville (Richard A. Fulton)

American Civil Liberties Union
122 Maryland Ave., N.E., Washington, DC 20002
Telephone: (202) 544-1681
Represented by:
Jerry J. Berman, Dir., Proj. Technology & Civil Liberties
Anthony J. Califa, Legislative Counsel
Judy C. Crockett, Legislative Representative
Chai R. Feldblum, Legislative Counsel
Janlori Goldman, Legislative Counsel
Gene Guerrero, Field Coordinator & Legislative Rep.
Morton H. Halperin, Director, Washington Office
Leslie Harris, Chief Legislative Counsel
Wade J. Henderson, Associate Director
Barry W. Lynn, Legislative Counsel
Diann Rust-Tierney, Legislative Counsel
Jeanne Woods, Legislative Counsel

American Civil Liberties Union of the Nat'l Capital Area
1400 20th St., N.W. Suite 119, Washington, DC 20036
Telephone: (202) 457-0800
Represented by:
Arthur B. Spitzer, Legal Director

American Clinical Laboratory Ass'n
1919 Pennsylvania Ave., N.W., Washington, DC 20006
Telephone: (202) 887-1400
Counsel or consultant:
O'Connor & Hannan (Hope S. Foster)

American Clinical Laboratory Ass'n Political Action Committee
1919 Pennsylvania Ave., N.W. Suite 800, Washington, DC 20006
Telephone: (202) 887-1400
Counsel or consultant:
O'Connor & Hannan (Hope S. Foster)

American Coal Ash Ass'n
1000 16th St., N.W., Suite 507, Washington, DC 20036
Telephone: (202) 659-2303
Represented by:
Erast Borissoff, Exec. Director
Counsel or consultant:
Griffin, Johnson & Associates

American Cocoa Research Institute
7900 Westpark Dr. Suite A-320, McLean, VA 22102
Telephone: (703) 790-5011
Background: The research institution of the Chocolate Manufacturers Ass'n of the U.S.A. Represented by Richard T. O'Connell of the Chocolate Manufacturers Ass'n of the U.S.A.

American Coke and Coal Chemicals Institute
1255 23rd St., N.W., Washington, DC 20037
Telephone: (202) 452-1140
Background: President is Mark T. Engle (see Hauck and Associates).
Counsel or consultant:
Hauck and Associates (David C. Ailor, Mark T. Engle)
Shaw, Pittman, Potts and Trowbridge (William Mike House)

American College Health Ass'n
1300 Piccard Drive Suite 200, Rockville, MD 20850
Telephone: (301) 963-1100
Represented by:
Stephen D. Blom, Exec. Director

American College of Cardiology
9111 Old Georgetown Road, Bethesda, MD 20814
Telephone: (301) 897-5400
Represented by:
Karen Collishaw, Director, Government Relations
Dr. Marie E. Michnich, Assoc. Exec. V. Pres. for Health Policy
William D. Nelligan, CAE, Exec. V. President
Counsel or consultant:
Webster, Chamberlain and Bean

American College of Dentists
7315 Wisconsin Ave. Suite 352-N, Bethesda, MD 20814
Telephone: (301) 986-0555
Represented by:
Dr. Gordon H. Rovelstad, Exec. Director

American College of Emergency Physicians
900 17th St., N.W., Suite 1250, Washington, DC 20006
Telephone: (202) 728-0610
Background: Headquartered in Dallas, Texas.
Represented by:
Paulette Kellogg, Regulatory Representative
Stephanie A. Kennan, Legislative Representative
Thomas P. Nickels, Director, Government Affairs

American College of Health Care Administrators
325 South Patrick St., Alexandria, VA 22314
Telephone: (703) 549-5822
Background: The national professional society for long-term health care administrators.
Represented by:
Richard L. Thorpe, Exec. V. Pres. and CEO

American College of Healthcare Marketing
4200 Wisconsin Ave., N.W. Suite 106, Box 340, Washington, DC 20016
Telephone: (202) 331-1223

Represented by:
Raymond H. Geisler, Exec. Director

American College of Internat'l Physicians
5530 Wisconsin Ave., N.W. Suite 1149, Washington, DC 20815
Telephone: (301) 652-8741
Represented by:
Navin Shah, Legislative Chairman
Counsel or consultant:
PAI Management Corp.

American College of Neuropsychopharmacology
Nashville, TN
Counsel or consultant:
Laxalt, Washington, Perito & Dubuc (Michael F. Cole)

American College of Nuclear Physicians
1101 Connecticut Ave., N.W. Suite 700, Washington, DC 20036
Telephone: (202) 857-1135
Counsel or consultant:
MARC Associates, Inc. (Randolph B. Fenninger)
Smith, Bucklin and Associates (Carol A. Lively)

American College of Nurse-Midwives
1522 K St., N.W., Suite 1000, Washington, DC 20005
Telephone: (202) 289-0171
Represented by:
Karen S. Fennell, Government Relations Coordinator
Ronald E. Nitzsche, Chief Operating Officer

American College of Obstetricians and Gynecologists
409 12th St., S.W., Washington, DC 20024
Telephone: (202) 638-5577
Represented by:
Kathy Bryant, J.D., Associate Director, Government Relations
Florence Foelak, Special Asst. for Public Information
Morton A. Lebow, Assoc. Director of Public Information
Susan A. Lightfoot, Government Relations Representative
Warren H. Pearse, M.D., Exec. Director
Phyllis Talbert, Associate Exec. Director

American College of Occupational Medicine
Chicago, IL
Counsel or consultant:
Kent & O'Connor, Incorp. (Patrick C. O'Connor)

American College of Osteopathic Internists
300 5th St., N.E., Washington, DC 20002
Telephone: (202) 546-0095
Represented by:
Brian Donadio, Executive Director

American College of Osteopathic Surgeons
123 North Henry St., Alexandria, VA 22314
Telephone: (703) 684-0416
Background: Has over 1,200 members and represents osteopathic surgeons practicing in the specialities of general surgery, orthopedic surgery, urology, cardiothoracic and vascular surgery, neurosurgery, and plastic and reconstructive surgery.
Represented by:
Guy D. Beaumont, Exec. Director
Counsel or consultant:
Reed Smith Shaw & McClay (Stephan E. Lawton)

American College of Physicians
700 13th St., N.W., Suite 250, Washington, DC 20005
Telephone: (202) 393-1650
Represented by:
Deborah M. Prout, Director, Department of Public Policy

American College of Preventive Medicine
Suite 403, 1015 15th St., N.W, Washington, DC 20005
Telephone: (202) 789-0003
Represented by:
Hazel Keimowitz, Acting Exec. Director

American College of Psychiatrists, The
Box 365, Greenbelt, MD 20768
Telephone: (301) 345-3534
Represented by:
Alice Conde Martinez, Exec. Director
Counsel or consultant:
Onek, Klein & Farr

American College of Radiology
1891 Preston White Drive, Reston, VA 22091

ORGANIZATIONS REPRESENTED

American College of Radiology (Cont'd)
Telephone: (703) 648-8900
Represented by:
John J. Curry, Exec. Director
Rebecca L. Kupper, Ass't Director, Government Relations
Otha W. Linton, Associate Exec. Director
Gary W. Price, Director, Government Relations
Counsel or consultant:
J. T. Rutherford & Assoc. (Don Lavanty)

American College of Surgeons
1640 Wisconsin Ave., N.W., Washington, DC 20007
Telephone: (202) 337-2701
Background: A voluntary educational and scientific organization that was established in 1913 to raise the standards of surgical practice and to improve the care of the surgical patient; has over 50,000 Fellows in this country and abroad.
Represented by:
Cynthia A. Brown, Manager, Washington Office
Robin E. Stombler, Washington Associate

American College Personnel Ass'n
5999 Stevenson Ave., Alexandria, VA 22304
Telephone: (703) 823-9800
Background: Represented by William Hunter, Lauren Scheib and Richard Yep of the American Ass'n for Counseling and Development, of which ACPA is a division.

American Committee on U.S.-Soviet Relations
109 11th St., S.E., Washington, DC 20003
Telephone: (202) 546-1700
Background: A nonpartisan, tax-exempt educational organization of prominent individuals interested in improving U.S.-Soviet relations through strengthening public understanding of diplomatic efforts, arms control initiatives, nonmilitary trade, and cultural, scientific and educational exchanges.
Represented by:
William Green Miller, President

American Community TV Ass'n
Montgomery, AL
Counsel or consultant:
Gardner, Carton and Douglas (M. Scott Johnson)

American Concrete Pipe Ass'n
8300 Boone Blvd., Suite 400, Vienna, VA 22182-2689
Telephone: (703) 821-1990
Represented by:
Richard E. Barnes, CAE, President
Cyril I. Malloy, Vice President, Government Relations

American Conference of Academic Deans
1818 R St., N.W., Washington, DC 20009
Telephone: (202) 387-3760
Represented by:
Maria-Helena Price, Exec. Officer

American Congress of Rehabilitation Medicine
Chicago, IL
Background: A member organization of the Coalition for Health Funding in Washington.
Counsel or consultant:
White, Fine, and Verville (Richard E. Verville)

American Congress on Surveying and Mapping
5410 Grosvenor Lane, Suite 100, Bethesda, MD 20814-2122
Telephone: (301) 493-0200
Represented by:
Richard F. Dorman, Exec. Director
Joan Martin, Director of Communication
Gail Papa, Director, Communications, Publicat. & PR
Nancy L. Parke, Joint Government Affairs Director
Counsel or consultant:
Patton, Boggs and Blow (Joe Robert Reeder)

American Conservative Union
38 Ivy St., S.E., Washington, DC 20003
Telephone: (202) 546-6555
Background: A lobbying organization with a membership of over 100,000; composed of people from all walks of life. Engages in political activity at the national level to advance conservative interests and views.
Represented by:
Robert D. Billings, Legislative Director
Daniel L. Casey, Exec. Director

American Conservative Union Political Action Committee
38 Ivy St., S.E., Washington, DC 20003
Telephone: (202) 546-6555
Background: Contacts is Daniel L. Casey and Robert Billings of the American Conservative Union.

American Constitution Committee
7777 Leesburg Pike Suite 300 South, Falls Church, VA 22043
Telephone: (703) 790-5580
Represented by:
Michael C. Smith, President

American Consulting Engineers Council
1015 15th St., N.W., Suite 802, Washington, DC 20005
Telephone: (202) 347-7474
Represented by:
Edward R. Bajer, Director of Energy
Terre H. Belt, Exec. Dir., Hazardous Waste Act Coalit.
Laurence D. Bory, Managing Director, Governmental Affairs
Mark Anthony Casso, Gen. Counsel & Mng. Dir., Administration
Thomas B. Dobbins, Director, Legislative Services
Murray Keene, Mng. Dir., Communications & Member Svcs.
Howard M. Messner, Exec. V. Pres., Chief Operating Officer
Lori A. Moran, Governmental Affairs Representative
Elizabeth C. Smith, Manager, HWAC Government Affairs
Larry Spiller, Director of Special Projects
Martha Ann Spudis, Director, Professional Procurement

American Consulting Engineers Council Political Action Committee
1015 15th St., N.W. Suite 802, Washington, DC 20005
Telephone: (202) 347-7474
Background: Represented by Thomas B. Dobbins of the American Consulting Engineers Council.

American Continental Corp.
Phoenix, AZ
Counsel or consultant:
Miller & Chevalier, Chartered (Leonard Bickwit, Jr.)

American Cordage and Netting Manufacturers
1667 K St., N.W., Suite 801, Washington, DC 20006
Telephone: (202) 955-3900
Counsel or consultant:
Leighton and Regnery (Ann Ottoson King)

American Corn Millers Federation
6707 Old Dominion Drive Suite 240, McLean, VA 22101
Telephone: (703) 821-3025
Represented by:
Betsy Faga, President

American Corporate Counsel Ass'n
1225 Connecticut Ave., N.W., Suite 302, Washington, DC 20036
Telephone: (202) 296-4523
Represented by:
Nancy Ann Nord, Exec. Director

American Correctional Ass'n
8025 Laurel Lakes Court, Laurel, MD 20707
Telephone: (301) 206-5100
Represented by:
Kenneth J. Aud, Membership Administrator, Legis. Liaison
Counsel or consultant:
Fehrenbacher, Sale, Quinn, and Deese (C. Michael Deese)

American Cotton Growers
Counsel or consultant:
Highley & Associates (Vern F. Highley)

American Cotton Shippers Ass'n
1725 K St., N.W. Suite 1210, Washington, DC 20006
Telephone: (202) 296-7116
Represented by:
Neal P. Gillen, General Counsel

American Council for an Energy-Efficient Economy
1001 Connecticut Ave., N.W., Suite 535, Washington, DC 20036
Telephone: (202) 429-8873
Background: A non-profit research organization which gathers, evaluates and disseminates information to stimulate use of energy-efficient technologies and practices.
Represented by:
Howard S. Geller, Associate Director
Marc Ledbetter, Senior Associate
Steve Nadel, Senior Associate

American Council for Capital Formation
1850 K St., N.W. Suite 400, Washington, DC 20006
Telephone: (202) 293-5811
Background: A non-profit, tax-exempt organization established in 1973. Seeks to eliminate the bias in the tax code against saving and investment. Maintains economic education programs to encourage public awareness of capital formation issues and advocates policy changes that would increase saving and investment.
Represented by:
Mark A. Bloomfield, President
Mari Lee Dunn, Vice President
Dr. Margo Thorning, Chief Economist
Counsel or consultant:
Targeted Communications Corp.

American Council for Drug Education
204 Monroe St., Rockville, MD 20850
Telephone: (301) 294-0600
Background: A national, non-profit organization dedicated to educating the public about the perils of drug and alcohol use.
Represented by:
Trina Brugger, Associate Director
Lee I. Dogoloff, Exec. Director

American Council for Free Asia
214 Massachusetts Ave., N.E. Suite 120, Washington, DC 20002
Telephone: (202) 547-7528
Background: A conservative group favoring measures to "increase U.S. aid for non-communist countries and to increase aid for Southeast Asia refugees.'
Counsel or consultant:
Jar-Mon Consultants, Inc. (Matthew D. Smyth)

American Council for Nationalities Service
1025 Vermont Ave., N.W. Suite 920, Washington, DC 20005
Telephone: (202) 347-3507
Background: Represented by Roger Winter of the United States Committee for Refugees.

American Council for the Arts
New York, NY
Counsel or consultant:
Duncan and Associates

American Council of Blind Lions
1010 Vermont Ave., N.W. Suite 1100, Washington, DC 20005
Telephone: (202) 393-3666
Background: Represented by Roberta Douglas of the American Council of the Blind.

American Council of Highway Advertisers
402 8th St., N.E., Washington, DC 20002
Telephone: (202) 546-0555
Counsel or consultant:
Roberts & Co. (Richard R. Roberts)

American Council of Independent Laboratories
1725 K St., N.W., Washington, DC 20006
Telephone: (202) 887-5872
Represented by:
Joseph F. O'Neil, Exec. Director
Counsel or consultant:
Allan Associates (Roger D. Allan)
Kirkland and Ellis

American Council of Independent Laboratories Political Action Committee
1725 K St., N.W., Washington, DC 20006
Telephone: (202) 887-5872
Background: Represented by Joseph F. O'Neil of the Council of Independent Laboratories.

American Council of Life Insurance
1001 Pennsylvania Ave. N.W., Washington, DC 20004-2599
Telephone: (202) 624-2000

The listings in this directory are available as *Mailing Labels*. See last page.

ORGANIZATIONS REPRESENTED

Represented by:
Richard E. Barnsback, Chief Counsel, State Relations
Douglas P. Bates, Director, Tax Analysis
Barbara Bey, Managing Director, External Affairs
John K. Booth, V. President and Chief Actuary
Allen R. Caskie, Senior Counsel
William T. Gibb, Chief Counsel, Federal Taxes & Pensions
Gene Grabowski, Director, Media Relations
Carol J. Gray, Federal Legislative Representative
Beverly L. Groom, Federal Legislative Representative
Shawn Hausman, Director, External Affairs
John W. Holt, Senior Counsel
Gary E. Hughes, Chief Counsel, Securities
John E. Kane, Director, Federal Relations
William E. Kingsley, Exec. V. President, Public Affairs
Stephen W. Kraus, Senior Counsel - Pensions
Roger J. LeMaster, Dep. Dir., Fed. Relations & Sr. Counsel
Anthony Manzanares, Jr., Senior Counsel
Robert S. McConnaughey, Senior Counsel
Daniel A. Mica, Exec. V. President, Federal Affairs
Richard V. Minck, Exec. V. President
Tess A. Rae, Federal Legislative Representative
Jeanne M. Ritchie, Political Programs Director
Michael J. Romig, Senior Counsel
Richard S. Schweiker, President
Anthony Valanzano, Chief Counsel, Federal Relations
Carl B. Wilkerson, Senior Counsel
Edward J. Zimmerman, Deputy Chief Counsel, State Relations
Counsel or consultant:
Targeted Communications Corp.

American Council of Life Insurance Political Action Committee
1001 Pennsylvania Ave., N.W., Washington, DC 20004
Telephone: (202) 624-2000
Background: Contact is Jeanne Ritchie of the American Council of Life Insurance.

American Council of the Blind
1010 Vermont Ave., N.W. Suite 1100, Washington, DC 20005
Telephone: (202) 393-3666
Represented by:
Stephanie Cooper, Coordinator, Member and Student Services
Roberta Douglas, Director of Development
Oral O. Miller, Director

American Council of the Blind Federal Employees
1010 Vermont Ave., N.W. Suite 1100, Washington, DC 20005
Telephone: (202) 393-3666
Represented by:
Charles Hodge, President

American Council of the Blind Parents
1010 Vermont Ave., N.W. Suite 1100, Washington, DC 20005
Telephone: (202) 393-3666
Background: Represented by Roberta Douglas of the American Council of the Blind.

American Council of the Blind Radio Amateurs
1010 Vermont Ave., N.W. Suite 1100, Washington, DC 20005
Telephone: (202) 393-3666
Background: Represented by Roberta Douglas of the American Council of the Blind.

American Council of Young Political Leaders
1000 Connecticut Ave., N.W. Suite 208, Washington, DC 20036
Telephone: (202) 857-0999
Background: A bi-partisan council which selects emerging politcal leaders under the age of 41 to participate in bilateral educational study tours with other nations.
Represented by:
Elizabeth R. Haskell, Exec. Director
Counsel or consultant:
Hogan and Hartson

American Council on Education
One Dupont Circle, N.W., Washington, DC 20036
Telephone: (202) 939-9300

Represented by:
Robert H. Atwell, President
David R. Merkowitz, Director, Public Affairs
Charles B. Saunders, Jr., Sr. V. President
Sheldon Elliott Steinbach, V. President and General Counsel
Becky Timmons, Director of Congressional Liaison
Counsel or consultant:
Bracewell and Patterson

American Council on Internat'l Personnel
New York, NY
Counsel or consultant:
Holt, Miller & Associates (Harris N. Miller)

American Council on Science and Health
New York, NY
Background: A national association of scientists from a variety of disciplines headquartered in New York City. Reports to policymakers and consumers on nutritional and environmental issues, drawing on current, reliable research to promote sound personal decisions and public health policies.
Counsel or consultant:
Ketchum Public Relations

American Council on the Environment
1301 20th St., N.W. Suite 113, Washington, DC 20036
Telephone: (202) 659-1900
Background: Advocates of a "balanced" approach to environmental issues, especially the clean water problem and waterways projects, which gives greater weight to economic development and business interests as opposed to what is perceived as the excessively protectionist views of the environmentalists.
Represented by:
John Gullett, Exec. Director

American Council on Transplantation
700 North Fairfax St., Suite 505, Alexandria, VA 22314
Telephone: (703) 836-4301
Represented by:
Nancy R. Holland, Exec. Director

American Couplings Coalition
1055 Thomas Jefferson St., N.W., Suite 306, Washington, DC 20007
Telephone: (202) 342-8400
Counsel or consultant:
Collier, Shannon & Scott (David A. Hartquist, Paul C. Rosenthal, Thomas F. Shannon)

American Cutlery Manufacturers Ass'n
1101 14th St., N.Ww. Suite 1100, Washington, DC 20005
Telephone: (202) 371-1262
Background: David W. Barrack, of Internat'l Management Group, serves as Exec. Director.
Counsel or consultant:
Internat'l Management Group, Inc. (David W. Barrack)
Thompson, Hine and Flory (Lewe B. Martin)

American Cyanamid Co.
1575 Eye St., N.W., Suite 200, Washington, DC 20005
Telephone: (202) 789-1222
Represented by:
Nancy C. Benson, Dir., Agricultural Legislative Affairs
Jerry L. Chambers, Assistant Director, Government Relations
Dack Dalrymple, Director, Medical Government Affairs
John T. Engelen, Ass't Dir., Agricultural Legis. Affairs
Bronwen A. Kaye, Assistant Director, Medical Gov't Affrs.
Kaye L. Stinson, Assistant Director, Government Affairs
St. Clair J. Tweedie, Director, Government Relations
Counsel or consultant:
Cleary, Gottlieb, Steen and Hamilton (Donald L. Morgan)
Covington and Burling
Denny Miller Associates

American Cyanamid Co. (Agricultural Division)
Wayne, NJ
Counsel or consultant:
McMillan and Farrell Associates (C. W. McMillan)

American Cyanamid Company Good Government Fund
1575 Eye St., N.W. Suite 200, Washington, DC 20005
Telephone: (202) 789-1222
Background: Contact is St. Clair J. Tweedie of American Cyanamid Co.

American Cyanamid Employee Political Action Committee
1575 Eye St., N.W., Suite 200, Washington, DC 20005
Telephone: (202) 789-1222
Background: Chairman is Jerry Chambers of American Cyanamid Co.

American Dairy Products Institute
Chicago, IL
Counsel or consultant:
Leighton and Regnery (Richard J. Leighton)

American Defense Foundation
214 Massachusetts Ave., N.E. Suite 200, Washington, DC 20002
Telephone: (202) 544-4704
Background: Promotes strong national defense legislation and, through its American Defense Institute, works to increase young Americans' awareness of the threat to freedom.
Represented by:
Capt. Eugene B. McDaniel, President/Founder

American Defense Preparedness Ass'n
2101 Wilson Blvd. Suite 400, Arlington, VA 22201-3061
Telephone: (703) 522-1820
Background: Seeks "to increase weapons technology, improve defense management and maintain a strong science-industry defense team that is responsive to the needs of the development, production, logistics and management phases of national preparedness."
Represented by:
Col. DeForrest Ballou, Editor, National Defense
LTG. Lawrence F. Skibbie, USA (Ret.), President

American Dehydrated Onion and Garlic Ass'n
Gilroy, CA
Counsel or consultant:
Bogle and Gates (Robert G. Hayes, Irene Ringwood)

American Democratic Political Action Committee
207 Pennsylvania Ave., S.E., Washington, DC 20003
Telephone: (202) 547-8683
Counsel or consultant:
White and Associates (Eric B. White)

American Dental Ass'n
1111 14th St., N.W. Suite 1200, Washington, DC 20005
Telephone: (202) 898-2400
Represented by:
Carole L. Frings, Federal Relations Representative
Dr. Enid Neidle, Director, Scientific Affairs
John F. O'Donnell, Dir., Legislation and Legislative Policy
Thomas E. Owens, Congressional Relations Representative
Craig A. Palmer, Director, Communications
Judith C. Sherman, Congressional Relations Representative
Leonard P. Wheat, Director, Government Relations

American Dental Hygienists' Ass'n
Chicago, IL
Counsel or consultant:
McDermott, Will and Emery

American Dental Trade Ass'n
4222 King St., Alexandria, VA 22302
Telephone: (703) 379-7755
Represented by:
Nikolaj M. Petrovic, CAE, President and Chief Exec. Officer
Counsel or consultant:
Jenner and Block

American Design Drafting Ass'n
5522 Noreck Road, Suite 391, Rockville, MD 20853
Telephone: (301) 460-6875
Represented by:
Rachel Howard, Exec. Director

American Diabetes Ass'n
Nat'l Service Center, 1660 Duke St., Alexandria, VA 22314
Telephone: (703) 549-1500

ORGANIZATIONS REPRESENTED

American Diabetes Ass'n (Cont'd)
Represented by:
Robert S. Bolan, Executive V. President
Amy Danzig, Director of Communications
Michael Stolar, Director, Health Sciences
N. Myrl Weinberg, Director of Government Relations
Counsel or consultant:
Jenner and Block

American Dietetic Ass'n
1667 K St., N.W., Suite 430, Washington, DC 20006
Telephone: (202) 296-3956
Represented by:
Patti R. Blumer, Asst. Exec. Director for Gov't Affairs
Counsel or consultant:
Porte, Stafford and Associates (Phillip L. Porte)

American Dietetic Ass'n Political Action Committee
1667 K St., N.W., Suite 430, Washington, DC 20006
Telephone: (202) 293-3956
Background: Represented by Patti R. Blumer of the Association.

American Dredging Co.
Camden, NJ
Counsel or consultant:
Cassidy and Associates, Inc. (Robert K. Dawson, Thomas M. Gannon)

American Driver and Traffic Safety Education Ass'n
239 Florida Ave., Salisbury, MD 21801
Telephone: (301) 860-0075
Background: Represents secondary school teachers of driver education, state supervisors of driver and traffic safety and educators of driver education teachers as well as institutional supporters and corporate suppliers.
Represented by:
Jefferson D. Keith, Exec. Director

American Ecology Corp.
P.O. Box 3600, Gaithersburg, MD 20878
Telephone: (301) 590-9056
Represented by:
Joanne M. Buehler, Director, Governmental Affairs

American Educational Research Ass'n
1230 17th St., N.W., Washington, DC 20036
Telephone: (202) 223-9485
Represented by:
Jamie Hitchcock, Exec. Assistant
William J. Russell, Exec. Officer
Gerald Sroufe, Dir., Governmn'l & Professional Liaison

American Electric Power Co.
Columbus, OH
Counsel or consultant:
Charlie McBride Assoc, Inc. (Charlie McBride)
Paul, Hastings, Janofsky and Walker (Charles A. Patrizia)

American Electric Power Service Corp.
1667 K St., N.W. Suite 450, Washington, DC 20006
Telephone: (202) 659-0454
Background: A subsidiary of the American Electric Power Co.
Represented by:
Bruce A. Beam, V. President, Governmental Affairs
Dale E. Heydlauff, Director, Federal Agency Affairs
Counsel or consultant:
Dunaway & Cross (Mac S. Dunaway)

American Electronics Ass'n
1225 Eye St., N.W., Suite 950, Washington, DC 20005
Telephone: (202) 682-9110

Represented by:
Jon Englund, Manager, Government Affairs
Edgar Hatcher, Senior Manager, Tax Policy
Pat Hill Hubbard, V. President, Education & Science Policy
J. R. Iverson, President and CEO
William K. Krist, V. President, Internat'l Affairs
John Mancini, V. President, Domestic Public Affairs
D. Bruce Merrifield, Consultant
Cheryl Russell, Dir., Environ'l & Occupat'l Health
John P. Stern, V. President, Asia
Brian P. Wynne, Sr. Manager, Internat'l Trade Affairs
Counsel or consultant:
Haley, Bader and Potts (John M. Pelkey)
Skadden, Arps, Slate, Meagher and Flom (Roseann Cutrone)

American Electronics Ass'n Electro PAC
1225 Eye St., N.W. Suite 950, Washington, DC 20005
Telephone: (202) 682-9110
Background: A political action committee sponsored by the American Electronics Ass'n. Represented by J. R. Iverson of the Association.

American Electronics Laboratories
Lansdale, PA
Counsel or consultant:
Dawson and Associates, Mathis (Dawson Mathis)

American Enterprise Institute for Public Policy Research
1150 17th St., N.W., Washington, DC 20036
Telephone: (202) 862-5800
Background: A nonpartisan, nonprofit, research and educational organization founded in 1943. Conducts research, sponsors conferences and seminars, and publishes books and periodicals in economic policy, foreign policy, and social and political policy.
Represented by:
Christopher C. DeMuth, President
David B. Gerson, Exec. V. President
Jeane J. Kirkpatrick, Counselor, Foreign Policy Studies
Marvin H. Kosters, Director, Economic Policy Studies
Michael Novak, Dir., Social & Political Studies
Thomas Skladony, Director of Communications
Paul J. Vizza, Director, Media Relations

American Express Co.
1020 19th St., N.W., Suite 600, Washington, DC 20036
Telephone: (202) 822-6680
Represented by:
Paula J. Collins, Director, Government Affairs
Denise G. Ferguson, V. President, Government Affairs
Laurel Kamen, V. President, Government Affairs
Richard M. Moose, Sr. V. President, Government Affairs
Valerie T. Morse, V. President, Government Affairs
Helene Rayder, Manager, Government Affairs
Deborah K. Yamada, Manager, Government Affairs
Counsel or consultant:
Rogers and Wells (William Morris)

American Express Committee for Responsible Government
1020 19th St., N.W., Suite 600, Washington, DC 20036
Telephone: (202) 822-6680
Background: Represented by Richard M. Moose, Senior V. President for Government Affairs for the American Express Co.

American Express Travel Related Services Co., Inc.
New York, NY
Counsel or consultant:
Morrison Associates (James W. Morrison, Jr.)

American Family Corp.
Columbus, GA
Counsel or consultant:
Evans & Associates, P.C.
O'Connor & Hannan (Thomas R. Jolly)
Parry and Romani Associates Inc. (Romano Romani)

American Farm Bureau Federation
600 Maryland Ave., S.W., Washington, DC 20024
Telephone: (202) 484-3600
Background: An independent, non-governmental, voluntary organization of farm and ranch families to analyze their common problems and formulate action to achieve educational improvement, economic opportunity, social advancement, and, thereby, to promote the national welfare.

Represented by:
George L. Berg, Jr., Asst. Director, Nat'l Affairs Division
John C. Datt, Executive & Director, Washington Office
Paul A. Drazek, Asst. Director, Nat'l Affairs Division
John R. Keeling, Ass't Director, Nat'l Affairs Division
Mark A. Maslyn, Asst. Director, Nat'l Affairs Division
Robert I. Nooter, Asst. Director, Nat'l Affairs Division
Grace Ellen Rice, Associate Director, Washington Office
Dennis C. Stolte, Asst. Director, Nat'l Affairs Division
Mary Kay Thatcher, Asst. Director, Nat'l Affairs Division
Elizabeth Whitley, Asst. Dir., Nat'l Affairs Division
Counsel or consultant:
Mayer, Brown and Platt (Simeon M. Kriesberg, Charles S. Levy)

American Farmland Trust
1920 N St., N.W., Suite 400, Washington, DC 20036
Telephone: (202) 659-5170
Background: Works to preserve agricultural resources through public education, policy development and private land conservancy transactions.
Represented by:
Ralph E. Grossi, President

American Federal Savings Bank
Jacksonville, FL
Counsel or consultant:
Bregman, Abell & Kay (Stanley I. Bregman)

American Federation for Clinical Research
50 F St., N.W., Suite 1040, Washington, DC 20001
Telephone: (202) 628-3954
Counsel or consultant:
Madison Group/Earle Palmer Brown, The (Ed Segal)

American Federation of Government Employees
80 F St., N.W., Washington, DC 20001
Telephone: (202) 737-8700
Represented by:
Allen H. Kaplan, Secretary-Treasurer
Janice R. Lachance, Director, Commun. & Political Action
Beth Moten, Legislative Representative
Terrence L. Rogers, Director, Legis. and Polit. Activities
Mark D. Roth, General Counsel
John N. Sturdivant, National President
Chapin E. Wilson, Jr., Legislative Representative

American Federation of Government Employees Political Action Committee
80 F St., N.W., Washington, DC 20001
Telephone: (202) 737-8700
Represented by:
Diane Witiak, Asst Dir, Communication/Political Action

American Federation of Home Health Agencies
1320 Fenwick Lane, Suite 100, Silver Spring, MD 20910
Telephone: (301) 588-1454
Represented by:
Ann B. Howard, Exec. Director

American Federation of Home Health Agencies Political Action Committee
1320 Fenwick Lane, Suite 500, Silver Spring, MD 20910
Telephone: (301) 588-1454
Represented by:
John G. Beard, Legal Specialist

American Federation of Information Processing Societies
1899 Preston White Drive, Reston, VA 22091-4366
Telephone: (703) 620-8900
Represented by:
John R.B. Clement, Chairman Government Activities

American Federation of Musicians
New York, NY
Counsel or consultant:
The Kamber Group (Richard A. Weiss)

American Federation of Police
1000 Connecticut Ave., N.W., Suite 9, Washington, DC 20036
Telephone: (202) 293-9088
Background: Represented by Frederick Pearson, Congressional Liaison Director (see Nat'l Ass'n of Chiefs of Police).
Represented by:
Gerald S. Arenberg, Exec. Director

ORGANIZATIONS REPRESENTED

American Federation of State, County and Municipal Employees
1625 L St., N.W., Washington, DC 20036
Telephone: (202) 429-1000
Represented by:
Marjorie D. Allen, Legislative Affairs Specialist
Diane B. Burke, Legislative Affairs Specialist
Robert E. Harman, Director, Public Affairs
T. Michael Kerr, Assistant Director of Legislation
Jerry D. Klepner, Director of Legislation
Iris J. Lav, Assistant Director for Economic Policy
Charles M. Loveless, Associate Director, Legislation
William Lucy, Secretary-Treasurer
Gerald W. McEntee, President
Patricia C. Murdock, Legislative Affairs Specialist
Mary A. Scheckelhoff, Director, Women's Rights
Caryl Yontz, Legislative Affairs Specialist
Counsel or consultant:
Kirschner, Weinberg & Dempsey (Craig Becker, Richard Kirschner, Larry P. Weinberg)

American Federation of Teachers
555 New Jersey Ave., N.W., Washington, DC 20001
Telephone: (202) 879-4400
Represented by:
Rachelle Horowitz, Political Director
Jamie Horwitz, Assistant Director, Public Relations
Gregory A. Humphrey, Legislative Director
Kate Krell, Public Relations Director
Gerald Morris, Deputy Director
Robert Porter, Secretary-Treasurer
Albert Shanker, President
Elaine Shocas, Associate Director
Counsel or consultant:
Challenge America, Inc. (Richard S. Sloan)
Gallagher-Widmeyer Group Inc., The (Scott D. Widmeyer)
Powell, Adams & Rinehart

American Federation of Teachers Committee on Political Education
555 New Jersey Ave., N.W., Washington, DC 20001
Telephone: (202) 879-4400
Background: Represented by Rachelle Horowitz, Political Director of the Federation.

American Federation of Teachers Staff Union Committee on Political Education
555 New Jersey Ave., N.W., Washington, DC 20001
Telephone: (202) 879-4471
Represented by:
Kim Harkness, Treasurer

American Feed Industry Ass'n
1701 Fort Myer Dr. Suite 1200, Arlington, VA 22209
Telephone: (703) 524-0810
Represented by:
Mark Anderson, Government Affairs Specialist
Steven Kopperud, V. President, Legislation
Oakley M. Ray, President
Rex A. Runyon, V. President, PR - Membership Services

American Fertility Soc.
409 12th St., S.W. Suite 110, Washington, DC 20024
Telephone: (202) 863-2576
Background: A voluntary, non-profit organization of 11,000 physicians and scientists interested in reproductive healthcare.
Represented by:
Lynne Lawrence, Director, Government Relations

American Fiber Manufacturers Ass'n
1150 17th St., N.W., Suite 310, Washington, DC 20036
Telephone: (202) 296-6508
Represented by:
Robert H. Barker, V. Pres., Technical & Legislative Affrs.
David A. Brody, Attorney
Paul T. O'Day, President
Fisher Ames Rhymes, V. President, Public Affairs

American Film Marketing Ass'n
Los Angeles, CA
Counsel or consultant:
The Hoving Group (John H. F. Hoving)
Jenner and Block (Jerald A. Jacobs)

American Financial Corp.
Cincinnati, OH

Counsel or consultant:
Bond Donatelli Inc. (Frank Donatelli)
Cadwalader, Wickersham & Taft (Donald C. Alexander)

American Financial Services Ass'n
1101 14th St., N.W., Washington, DC 20005
Telephone: (202) 289-0400
Represented by:
Robert B. Evans, President
Charles 'Andy' Harkey, Federal Legislative Representative
Robert McKew, Assoc. Counsel, Ass't Dir., Regul. Affrs
Sheryl L. Peterson, Assistant Director, Legislative Affairs
Frank Max Salinger, V. Pres., Gen. Counsel & Dir. Gov't Aff.
Frances B. Smith, V. Pres. & Director, Public Affairs
Thomas L. Thomas, Sr. V. President/Treasurer
Counsel or consultant:
Webster, Chamberlain and Bean (Arthur L. Herold)

American Financial Services Ass'n Political Action Committee
1101 14th St., N.W., Washington, DC 20005
Telephone: (202) 289-0400
Background: Contacts are Frank Max Salinger and Thomas L. Thomas of the Association.
Counsel or consultant:
Webster, Chamberlain and Bean (Arthur L. Herold)

American Fisheries Soc.
5410 Grosvenor Lane, Bethesda, MD 20814
Telephone: (301) 897-8616
Represented by:
Paul Brouha, Deputy Director
Carl R. Sullivan, Exec. Director

American Fishing Tackle Manufacturers Ass'n
Arlington Height, IL
Counsel or consultant:
Bogle and Gates (Robert G. Hayes, Irene Ringwood)
Webster, Chamberlain and Bean

American Flint Glass Workers Union
Toledo, OH
Counsel or consultant:
Collier, Shannon & Scott (Paul D. Cullen, David A. Hartquist, Thomas F. Shannon)

American Floorcovering Ass'n
Chicago, IL
Counsel or consultant:
London and Satagaj, Attorneys-at-Law (Sheldon I. London, John S. Satagaj)

American Foreign Service Ass'n
2101 E St., N.W., Washington, DC 20037
Telephone: (202) 338-4045
Represented by:
Robert M. Beers, Congressional Liaison Officer
Susan Z. Holik, Legislative Representative
Rick Weiss, Congressional Liaison
Theodore S. Wilkinson, President

American Forest Council
1250 Connecticut Ave., N.W. Suite 320, Washington, DC 20036
Telephone: (202) 463-2455
Represented by:
Richard Scott Berg, V. President, Forest Policy & Research
Timothy S. McCarthy, Director, Communications
Laurence Wiseman, President

American Forest Resource Alliance
1250 Connecticut Ave., N.W. Suite 200, Washington, DC 20036
Telephone: (202) 463-2747
Represented by:
Heidi Biggs, Government Affairs Representative
William R. Murray, Natural Resources Counsel
Mark E. Rey, Exec. Director
Counsel or consultant:
Crowell and Moring (Steven P. Quarles)
Preston Gates Ellis & Rouvelas Meeds (Richard L. Barnes)

American Forestry Ass'n
P.O. Box 2000, Washington, DC 20013
Telephone: (202) 667-3300

Represented by:
Deborah Gangloff, V. President for Program Services
Gerald Gray, Director of Resource Policy
R. Neil Sampson, Exec. V. President
Counsel or consultant:
Bernard H. Ehrlich

American Foundation for the Blind (Government Relations Department)
1615 M St., N.W., Suite 250, Washington, DC 20036
Telephone: (202) 457-1487
Represented by:
Alan M. Dinsmore, Legislative Network Coordinator
Scott Marshall, Director, Governmental Relations Dept.
Glenn M. Plunkett, Governmental Relations Specialist

American Free Trade Ass'n
One Thomas Circle, N.W., Suite 800, Washington, DC 20005
Telephone: (202) 223-7200
Counsel or consultant:
Nixon, Hargrave, Devans and Doyle (Stephen Kurzman)

American Freedom Coalition
1001 Pennsylvania Ave., N.W., Suite 850, Washington, DC 20004
Telephone: (202) 393-1333
Background: A 300,000-member grass roots coalition dedicated to preserving traditional values and constitutional government with incorporated chapters in 46 states. Co-Chairmen of the organization are The Hon. Richard H. Ichord and The Hon. Robert C. Wilson (see Washington Industrial Team). President is Dr. Robert G. Grant of Christian Voice.

American Friends Service Committee
1822 R St., N.W., Washington, DC 20009
Telephone: (202) 483-3341
Background: An organization of the Society of Friends (Quakers) which seeks to bring together persons holding key positions in government and others influential in the formulation of US policies and public opinion to explore points of view on domestic and international issues and to share AFSC's field experience in humanitarian aid, development, peace and social justice programs.
Represented by:
Jim Matlack, Director, Washington Office

American Frozen Food Institute
1764 Old Meadow Lane Suite 350, McLean, VA 22102
Telephone: (703) 821-0770
Represented by:
Steven C. Anderson, President
Thomas B. House, CAE, President Emeritus
Leslie G. Sarasin, Director, Government Relations
Hugh W. Symons, Sr. V. Pres., Research & Technical Svcs.
Francis G. Williams, Exec. V. President, Administration
Counsel or consultant:
Donelan, Cleary, Wood and Maser, P.C. (John F. Donelan, Frederic L. Wood)
Hogan and Hartson (Gary J. Kushner)

American Frozen Food Institute Political Action Committee
1764 Old Meadow Lane Suite 350, McLean, VA 22102
Telephone: (703) 821-0770
Background: Represented by Steven C. Anderson and Leslie G. Sarasin of the American Frozen Food Institute.

American Furniture Manufacturers Ass'n
918 16th St., N.W., Suite 402, Washington, DC 20006
Telephone: (202) 466-7362
Represented by:
Joseph G. Gerard, Vice President, Government Affairs
Barbara E. Steakley, Dir., Congressional & Regulatory Affairs

American Gas Ass'n
1515 Wilson Blvd., Arlington, VA 22209
Telephone: (703) 841-8400

ORGANIZATIONS REPRESENTED

American Gas Ass'n (Cont'd)
Represented by:
Michael Baly, III, Exec. V. President and COO
Robert E. Berry, Legislative Representative
Phillip Borish, V. President and Treasurer
David Cerotzke, Manager, Regulatory Affairs
Bill Cope, Manager, Federal Financial Relations
S. Lorraine Cross, Director, Executive Branch Relations
Dennis Eshman, Counsel, Legislat. & Regulatory Affairs
Michael I. German, Senior V. President
Jack Hawks, Director, Public Information
Robert L. Hill, V. Pres., Consumer and Community Affairs
Andrea Riddle Hilliard, Dir., Leg. & Reg. Affrs. & AGC
Richard Irby, III, V. President, Government Relations
Russell T. Keene, Assistant the Exec. V.P. and COO
Richard R. Kolodziej, Senior V. President
George H. Lawrence, President
Phyllis Levine, Counsel, Legis. & Regulatory Affairs
Hugh McCastlian, Manager, Energy Technology Development
John Mitchell, Manager, Federal Marketing Relations
Donald I. Moritz, Chairman, Gov't Relations Committee
David J. Muchow, Gen. Counsel/Corporate Secretary
Felix Sanchez, Director, Congressional Relations
Donald J. Schellhardt, Dir., State, Local & Coalition Relations
John Van Noord, Manager, Energy Resource Development
Elaine M. Ziemba, Director, Congressional Relations
Counsel or consultant:
Swidler & Berlin, Chartered (Francis S. Blake)
Van Dyk Associates, Inc.

American Gear Manufacturers Ass'n
1500 King St., Suite 201, Alexandria, VA 22314
Telephone: (703) 684-0211
Background: A national trade association of 330 manufacturers and users of gears and gearing products.
Represented by:
William Bradley, Manager, Technical Division
Susan Herrenbruck, Manager, Public & Economic Affairs
Richard B. Norment, Exec. Director

American Gear Political Action Committee
1500 King St., Suite 201, Alexandria, VA 22209
Telephone: (703) 684-0211
Background: The political action committee of the American Gear Manufacturers Ass'n.
Represented by:
Thomas Kling, Treasurer

American General Corp.
Houston, TX
Counsel or consultant:
Davis & Harman
Hill and Knowlton Public Affairs Worldwide (Larry I. Good)

American General Investment Corp.
Houston, TX
Counsel or consultant:
Akin, Gump, Strauss, Hauer and Feld

American Geological Institute
4220 King St., Alexandria, VA 22302
Telephone: (703) 379-2480
Represented by:
Marvin E. Kauffman, Exec. Director

American Geophysical Union
2000 Florida Ave., N.W., Washington, DC 20009
Telephone: (202) 462-6900
Background: A scientific society seeking to advance knowledge in the atmospheric, oceanic, solid-earth, and hydrologic sciences.
Represented by:
Dr. Leslie H. Meredith, Group Director
Dr. Athelstan F. Spilhaus, Jr., Exec. Director

American Great Lakes Ports
1911 North Fort Meyer Drive, Arlington, VA 22209
Telephone: (703) 276-9093
Represented by:
Lewis Gulick, President

American Greyhound Track Operators Ass'n
North Miami, FL

Counsel or consultant:
Dickstein, Shapiro and Morin (Henry C. Cashen, II, John C. Dill)

American Group Practice Ass'n
1422 Duke St., Alexandria, VA 22314
Telephone: (703) 838-0033
Represented by:
Dr. Donald W. Fisher, CAE, Exec. Vice President
Brent Miller, Director, Government Relations
Roslyne Weiner, Legislative Policy Analyst

American Guild of Patient Account Management
1101 Connecticut Ave., N.W., Suite 700, Washington, DC 20036
Telephone: (202) 857-1179
Counsel or consultant:
Smith, Bucklin and Associates (Dennis Smeage)

American Handicapped Employers Ass'n
Nashville, TN
Counsel or consultant:
Burson-Marsteller (Carolyn Tieger)

American Hardware Manufacturers Ass'n
Schaumburg, IL
Counsel or consultant:
London and Satagaj, Attorneys-at-Law (Sheldon I. London, John S. Satagaj)

American Hawaii Cruises
San Fransisco, CA
Counsel or consultant:
Graham and James (J. Michael Cavanaugh, Thomas F. Railsback)

American Health Assistance Foundation
15825 Shady Grove Road, Rockville, MD 20850
Telephone: (301) 948-3244
Represented by:
Katherine Dodson, Director, Public Relations

American Health Care Advisory Ass'n
Ft. Worth, TX
Counsel or consultant:
Jefferson Group, The (Frederick J. Hannett)

American Health Care Ass'n
1201 L St., N.W., Washington, DC 20005
Telephone: (202) 842-4444
Background: Represents nursing homes throughout the United States. Formerly (1974) American Nursing Home Ass'n.
Represented by:
Norma Blankenship, Legislative Representative
Winthrop Cashdollar, Legislative Representative
Richard Miller, Legislative Representative
Rush Russell, Legislative Representative
Bruce Yarwood, Legislative Counsel
Counsel or consultant:
O'Connor & Hannan (Timothy M. Haake)
Thompson Group, Inc. (Kenneth W. Thompson)

American Health Care Ass'n Political Action Committee
1201 L St., N.W., Washington, DC 20005
Telephone: (202) 842-4444
Represented by:
Nancey Kaplan, PAC Director

American Heart Ass'n
1250 Connecticut Ave., N.W., Suite 360, Washington, DC 20036
Telephone: (202) 822-9380
Represented by:
Scott D. Ballin, V. President and Legislative Counsel
Mary Crane, Legislative Representative
Claudia Louis, Legislative Representative

American Heartworm Soc.
808 17th St., N.W., Suite 200, Washington, DC 20006
Telephone: (202) 223-9669
Counsel or consultant:
Bostrom Corp. (Ramon A. Estrada)

American Heavy Lift Shipping Co.
Houston, TX
Counsel or consultant:
Wagner, Hines and Avary (Robert P. Avary, Jr., William J. Hines)

American Helicopter Soc.
217 N. Washington St., Alexandria, VA 22314
Telephone: (703) 684-6777
Represented by:
John F. Zugschwert, Exec. Director

American Hellenic Alliance, Inc.
11730 Bowman Green Drive, Reston, VA 22090
Telephone: (703) 834-5541
Counsel or consultant:
Manatos & Manatos, Inc. (Andrew E. Manatos, Dyck Van Koevering)

American Hellenic Educational Progressive Ass'n (AHEPA)
1707 L St., N.W., Suite 200, Washington, DC 20036
Telephone: (202) 785-9284
Background: A cultural organization for Americans of Greek extraction.
Represented by:
Constantine W. Gekas, Exec. Director

American Hellenic Educational Progressive Ass'n Political Action Committee
1707 L St., N.W., Suite 200, Washington, DC 20036
Telephone: (202) 785-9284
Represented by:
Michael Firilas, Treasurer

American Hellenic Institute
1730 K St., N.W., Washington, DC 20006
Telephone: (202) 785-8430
Background: Formed in August 1974 immediately following the invasion of Cyprus by Turkey to strengthen trade and commerce between the U.S. and Greece and Cyprus. Complements the work of the AHI Public Affairs Committee. Incorporated in the District of Columbia.
Represented by:
Linda Avraamides, Office Manager
Counsel or consultant:
Shaw, Pittman, Potts and Trowbridge (William Mike House)

American Hellenic Institute Public Affairs Committee
1730 K St., N.W. Suite 1005, Washington, DC 20006
Telephone: (202) 659-4608
Background: Monitors activity affecting trade, commerce and related public policy matters between the U.S. and Greece and Cyprus, as well as trade and related issues within the U.S. Hellenic community.
Represented by:
Nicholas Larigakis, Special Projects Coordinator
Constantine Sirigos, Legislative Assistant

American Hiking Soc.
1015 31st St., N.W., Washington, DC 20007
Telephone: (202) 385-3252
Represented by:
Susan A. Henley, Exec. Director

American Hispanic PAC
c/o ZGS, 2300 Clarendon Blvd., Arlington, VA 22201
Telephone: (703) 351-5656
Represented by:
Ronald Gordon, Director

American Historical Ass'n
400 A St., S.E., Washington, DC 20003
Telephone: (202) 544-2422
Represented by:
Samuel R. Gammon, Exec. Director

American Home Economics Ass'n
1555 King St., Alexandria, VA 22314
Telephone: (703) 706-4600
Represented by:
Kathleen M. Sheehan, Director of Public Policy
Karl G. Weddle, Exec. Director

American Home Products Corp.
1726 M St., N.W., Suite 1001, Washington, DC 20036
Telephone: (202) 659-8320
Represented by:
Robin F. Callicott, Washington Affairs Representative
Leo C. Jardot, Sr. Director and Counsel, Fed. Relations
Ambrose B. Reid, II, Director, Federal Relations
Counsel or consultant:
Lee, Toomey & Kent
Williams and Jensen, P.C. (John J. McMackin, Jr.)

ORGANIZATIONS REPRESENTED

American Home Satellite Ass'n
Bellevue, WA
Counsel or consultant:
Bracy Williams & Co. (Kenneth S. Birnbaum, Terrence L. Bracy, Thomas J. Hennessey, Jr., Susan J. Williams)

American Home Sewing Ass'n
New York, NY
Counsel or consultant:
Chwat/Weigend Associates (John S. Chwat, Robert E. Weigend)

American Honda Motor Co.
955 L'Enfant Plaza Suite 5300, Washington, DC 20024
Telephone: (202) 554-1650
Represented by:
Eiji Amito, Senior V. President
Counsel or consultant:
Davis Wright Tremaine (Edward B. Cohen)
Schmeltzer, Aptaker and Sheppard
Wilmer, Cutler and Pickering (Ronald J. Greene, Howard P. Willens)

American Horse Council
1700 K St., N.W. Suite 300, Washington, DC 20006
Telephone: (202) 296-4031
Background: The trade association of the equine industry established in 1969 to keep its members informed of developments affecting taxation, funding of livestock research, import-export restrictions and similar matters affecting those who live by horses.
Represented by:
James J. Hickey, Jr., Counsel & Director, Government Relations
R. Richards Rolapp, President
Counsel or consultant:
Davis & Harman (Thomas A. Davis)

American Horse Council Committee on Legislation and Taxation
1700 K St., N.W. Suite 300, Washington, DC 20006
Telephone: (202) 296-4031
Background: Supported by the American Horse Council. R. Richards Rolapp, President of the American Horse Council, serves as Treasurer.

American Horse Protection Ass'n
1000 29th St., N.W., Suite T-100, Washington, DC 20007
Telephone: (202) 965-0500
Represented by:
Robin C. Lohnes, Exec. Director

American Horse Racing Federation
1700 K St., N.W., Suite 300, Washington, DC 20006
Telephone: (202) 296-4031
Represented by:
James P. Heffernan, Exec. Director

American Horticultural Soc.
Box 0105, Mount Vernon, VA 22121
Telephone: (703) 768-5700
Represented by:
Frank L. Robinson, Exec. Director

American Horticultural Therapy Ass'n
9220 Wightman Road, Suite 300, Gaithersburg, MD 20879
Telephone: (301) 948-3010
Represented by:
Charles Richman, Exec. Director

American Hospital Ass'n
50 F St., N.W., Suite 1100, Washington, DC 20001
Telephone: (202) 638-1100
Represented by:
Eileen M. Collins, Sr. Assoc, Director, Div. of Legislation
Gaelyn DeMartino, Washington Counsel
Dona De Sanctis, Ass't Dir., Communications & Public Rel.
Patricia R. Goldman, Sr. Assoc. Director, Div. of Legislation
Steven Kroll, Assoc. Director, Political Affairs
Herb B. Kuhn, Sr Assoc. Director, Div. of Leg. Affairs
Carla Lunetta, Assoc. Dir, Div. of Legislative Affairs
Linda Magno, Director, Regulatory Affairs
James T. Marrinan, Director, Federal Agency Affairs
Christine W. McEntee, Director, Div. of Membership Relations
Janis A. Nero, Ass't Director, Div. of Regulatory Afrs.
Neal I. Neuberger, Assoc. Director, Div. of Legislation
Anne Nicoll, Assoc. Director, Division of Legislation
Jean Polatsek, Assoc. Director, Div. of Legislation
Richard J. Pollack, V. Pres. & Dep. Dir., Washington Office
Donna Potemken, Assoc. Director, Div. of Regulatory Afrs
Paul C. Rettig, Exec. V. Pres. and Dir., Wash. Office
Mike Rock, Sr. Assoc. Director, Div. of Legislation
Lori Schorr, Assoc. Director, Political Affairs
Mark Seklecki, Director, Political Affairs
Monica M. Sheehan, Assoc. Director, Div. of Legislation
Marion Torchia, Sr. Assoc. Director, Regulatory Affairs

American Hospital in Shanghai Foundation
Washington, DC
Counsel or consultant:
Cassidy and Associates, Inc. (Gerald S. J. Cassidy, William M. Cloherty, Elliott M. Fiedler)

American Hotel and Motel Ass'n
1201 New York Ave., N.W. Suite 600, Washington, DC 20005
Telephone: (202) 289-3100
Represented by:
Kenneth F. Hine, Exec. V. President and CEO
Brian Kinsella, Manager, Government Affairs
Richard C. Nelson, Secretary/Treasurer
Steve Trombetti, Director, Communications
Thomas F. Youngblood, Director, Federal Affairs

American Hotel Motel Political Action Committee
1201 New York Ave., N.W. 6th Floor, Washington, DC 20005
Telephone: (202) 289-3120
Background: Contact is Brian Kinsella of the American Hotel and Motel Ass'n.

American Imaging Ass'n
Nashville, TN
Counsel or consultant:
McDermott, Will and Emery (Michael A. Romansky)

American Immigration Institute
4401 Ford Ave., Suite 200, Alexandria, VA 22302
Telephone: (703) 824-2048
Background: A pro-immigration think tank affiliated with the Hudson Institute.
Represented by:
Stephen J. Moore, Exec. Director

American Immigration Lawyers Ass'n
1000 16th St., N.W. Suite 604, Washington, DC 20036
Telephone: (202) 331-0046
Represented by:
Warren R. Leiden, Exec. Director

American Import Shippers Ass'n
Counsel or consultant:
Mudge Rose Guthrie Alexander and Ferdon (Martin J. Lewin)

American Importers Meat Products Group
3213 O St., N.W., Washington, DC 20007
Telephone: (202) 298-6134
Counsel or consultant:
Max N. Berry Law Offices (Max N. Berry)

American Independent Refiners Ass'n
1275 Pennsylvania Ave., N.W. Suite 301, Washington, DC 20004
Telephone: (202) 626-6490
Counsel or consultant:
Legislative Strategies Inc. (Raymond F. Bragg, Jr.)

American Independent Refiners Ass'n PAC
1275 Pennsylvania Ave., N.W. Suite 301, Washington, DC 20004
Telephone: (202) 626-6490
Counsel or consultant:
Legislative Strategies Inc. (Raymond F. Bragg, Jr.)

American Indian Healthcare Ass'n
St. Paul, MN
Counsel or consultant:
Evergreen Associates, Ltd. (Jo Ann Kauffman)

American Indian Heritage Foundation
6051 Arlington Blvd., Falls Church, VA 22044
Telephone: (202) 237-7500
Background: Shares the cultural diversity of the American Indian with the non-Indian, and sponsors numerous special programs to benefit Indians. Has attracted more than 250,000 donors.
Represented by:
Princess Pale Moon, President
Dr. Wil Rose, Chief Executive Officer

American Indian Trade Development Council
Everett, WA
Counsel or consultant:
APCO Associates (Don Bonker)

American Industrial Clay Co.
Sandersville, GA
Counsel or consultant:
Sutherland, Asbill and Brennan (Edward J. Grenier, Jr.)

American Industrial Health Council
1330 Connecticut Ave., N.W. Suite 300, Washington, DC 20036-1702
Telephone: (202) 659-0060
Background: A coalition of corporations operating in the U.S. and U.S. industrial trade ass'ns concerned with ensuring the quality of the scientific bases for regulatory decision making. AIHC advocates and promotes implementation of the most advanced, sound scientific methods as a basis for the review, risk assessment and regulation (where warranted) of the substances which may pose significant chronic health risks to people. AIHC does not act as an advocate for any specific product or substance. The group's President is Ronald A. Lang (also of the Synthetic Organic Chemical Manufacturers Ass'n).
Represented by:
Marcia G. Lawson, Manager, Communications
Gaylen Millard, Director, Science and Health Policy
Carole J. O'Toole, Manager, Science Policy
James D. Wilson, V. President, Health Policy
Counsel or consultant:
Ketchum Public Relations (Lorraine Thelian)

American Institute for Conservation of Historic and Artistic Works
1400 16th St., N.W. Suite 340, Washington, DC 20036
Telephone: (202) 232-6636
Background: Founded in 1959 as the American Group of the Internat'l Institute for Conservation of Historic and Artistic Works. A nonprofit professional organization whose purpose is to advance the knowledge and practice of conservation of cultural property.
Represented by:
Sarah Z. Rosenberg, Exec. Director

American Institute for Foreign Study
Greenwich, CT
Counsel or consultant:
Wexler, Reynolds, Fuller, Harrison and Schule, Inc. (Nancy Clark Reynolds, Bruce Wolpe)

American Institute for Free Labor Development
1015 20th St., N.W., Washington, DC 20036
Telephone: (202) 659-6300
Represented by:
William C. Doherty, Jr., Exec. Director

American Institute for Shippers' Ass'ns
Box 33457, Washington, DC 20033
Telephone: (202) 628-0933
Background: Represents the cooperative shipping industry.
Represented by:
Glenn R. Cella, Exec. Director
Counsel or consultant:
Grove, Jaskiewicz, Gilliam and Cobert (Ronald N. Cobert)

ORGANIZATIONS REPRESENTED

American Institute of Aeronautics and Astronautics
370 L'Enfant Promenade, Washington, DC 20004
Telephone: (202) 646-7400
Background: A non-profit professional society for aerospace engineers and scientists. Membership (1990): 43,000.
Represented by:
Gayle Armstrong, Manager, Communications
Johan T. Benson, Administrator, Public Policy
Cort Durocher, Exec. Director
Mike Lewis, Director, Communications

American Institute of Architects' Quality Government Fund
1735 New York Ave., N.W., Washington, DC 20006
Telephone: (202) 626-7556
Background: Represented by James P. Cramer of the American Institute of Architects.

American Institute of Architects, The
1735 New York Ave., N.W., Washington, DC 20006
Telephone: (202) 626-7300
Represented by:
James P. Cramer, Exec V. President/Chief Exec. Officer
Fred R. DeLuca, CFO, Group Executive
Albert C. Eisenberg, Senior Director, Federal Liaison
Kevin Fry, Senior Director, Public Affairs
Norman L. Koonce, President, AIA Foundation
Ann Looper, Ass't Dir., Gov't Afrs./Federal Liaison
Alice Malloy, Exec. Ass't to Group V.P., Ext. Affairs
Raymond P. Rhinehart, V. President, AIA Foundation
Nancy C. Somerville, Sr. Director, State/Local Gov't Afrs.
Robert Waffle, Director, State/Local Gov't Affairs
Gregg Ward, Group V. President, External Affairs
Lars Winoy, Director, Federal Liaison
Counsel or consultant:
The Susan Davis Companies (Susan A. Davis)
Palumbo & Cerrell, Inc. (Benjamin L. Palumbo, Paul A. Skrabut, Jr.)

American Institute of Biological Sciences
730 11th St., N.W., Washington, DC 20001-4521
Telephone: (202) 628-1500
Background: Fosters research and education in the biological sciences, including the medical, agricultural and environmental sciences for the advance of their applications to human welfare through meetings, publications and assistance to and cooperation with other science, health and environmental organizations.
Represented by:
Dr. Charles M. Chambers, Exec. Director
Jennie L. Moehlmann, Special Assistant for Policy Development
Counsel or consultant:
Smith, Heenan and Althen

American Institute of Certified Planners
1776 Massachusetts Ave., N.W. Suite 704, Washington, DC 20036
Telephone: (202) 872-0611
Background: Exec. Director is Israel Stollman, also Exec. Director of the American Planning Ass'n.

American Institute of Certified Public Accountants
1455 Pennsylvania Ave., N.W. Suite 400, Washington, DC 20004
Telephone: (202) 737-6600
Represented by:
J. Thomas Higginbotham, V. President, Legislative Affairs
Bernard Z. Lee, Deputy Chairman, Federal Affairs
Joseph Moraglio, V. President, Federal Government
John Sharbaugh, Dir, Communications/State Society Rltns.
Donald H. Skadden, V. President, Taxation
Counsel or consultant:
Arnold & Porter (Geoffrey Aranow)
Davis Polk & Wardwell (Richard Moe)
O'Connor & Hannan (Thomas H. Quinn)
Van Ness, Feldman & Curtis (Charles B. Curtis)
Charls E. Walker Associates
Willkie Farr and Gallagher (Louis A. Craco, Matthew R. Schneider)

American Institute of Chemical Engineers
New York, NY

Counsel or consultant:
Siegel, Houston and Associates (Dr. Martin Siegel)

American Institute of Chemists
7315 Wisconsin Ave., Bethesda, MD 20814
Telephone: (301) 652-2447
Represented by:
David A. H. Roethel, Exec. Director

American Institute of Chemists Foundation
7315 Wisconsin Ave., Bethesda, MD 20814
Telephone: (301) 652-8634
Background: Represented by David A. H. Roethel, Exec. Director of the Institute.

American Institute of Cooperation
50 F St., N.W., Suite 900, Washington, DC 20001
Telephone: (202) 626-8740
Background: A non-profit, educational organization to promote the idea of cooperatives. Publishes a yearbook and newsletter and sponsors the National Institute on Cooperative Education.
Represented by:
David C. Thomas, President and CEO

American Institute of Merchant Shipping
1000 16th St., N.W., Suite 511, Washington, DC 20036-5705
Telephone: (202) 775-4399
Background: Represents owners and/or operators of American flag crude, product and chemical tankers, bulk carriers and dry cargo vessels.
Represented by:
Ernest J. Corrado, President
Joseph J. Cox, V. President
Lawrence M. Hadley, Director of Marine Affairs

American Institute of Nutrition
9650 Rockville Pike, Bethesda, MD 20814
Telephone: (301) 530-7050
Represented by:
Richard G. Allison, Exec. Officer

American Institute of Professional Geologists
Arvada, CO
Background: A professional organization of about 5,000 practicing geologists. Washington Representative is Elizabeth G. Newton (see E. G. Newton & Associates, Inc.).
Counsel or consultant:
E. G. Newton & Assoc. (Elisabeth G. Newton)

American Institute of Real Estate Appraisers
Chicago, IL
Counsel or consultant:
Manatt, Phelps, Rothenberg & Phillips (Robert J. Kabel, Robert J. Wager, June L. Walton)

American Institute of Ultrasound Medicine
4405 East-West Hwy., Suite 504, Bethesda, MD 20814
Telephone: (301) 656-6117
Represented by:
Dr. James S. Packer, Exec. Director

American Institutes for Research
3333 K St., N.W., Suite 300, Washington, DC 20007
Telephone: (202) 342-5000
Background: A private, non-profit organization that conducts research in the behavioral sciences.
Represented by:
George W. Bohrnstedt, V. President and Director
Dr. David A. Goslin, President and Chief Exec. Officer
George R. Wheaton, V. President

American Insurance Ass'n
1130 Connecticut Ave., N.W., Suite 1000, Washington, DC 20036
Telephone: (202) 828-7100

Represented by:
Debra T. Ballen, V. President, Policy Development/ Rsrch.
Craig A. Berrington, General Counsel
Rene Carter, Manager, Public Affairs
Marilyn Cheek, Manager, Public Affairs
Grover E. Czech, V. President, State Affairs
Ronald S. Gass, Senior Counsel
Kenneth F. Hacker, Manager, Public Affairs
Martha R. Hamby, Director, Federal Affairs
Stacy L. Hennessey, Assistant Counsel
George H. Henry, Senior Counsel
James L. Kimble, Senior Counsel
George R. Klotzbaugh, Senior Counsel
Amy Jill Layton, Manager, Public Affairs
Michael Lovendusky, Counsel
Eric J. Oxfeld, Counsel
Alvin L. Parsons, V. President, Public Affairs
David J. Pratt, V. President, Federal Affairs
William C. Price, Counsel
Lynn M. Schubert, Counsel
Elisa K. Siegel, Manager, Public Affairs
Nancy E. Siegel, Attorney
Georgiana B. Smith, Manager, Public Affairs
David F. Snyder, Counsel
Allan Stein, Counsel
Robert E. Vagley, President
Melissa Wolford, Director, Federal Affairs
Bruce C. Wood, Counsel
Andrew S. Wright, Senior Counsel, Federal Affairs
Counsel or consultant:
Foreman & Heidepriem (Carol Tucker Foreman, Nikki Heidepriem)
Palumbo & Cerrell, Inc. (Jeffrey D. Doranz, Benjamin L. Palumbo, Paul A. Skrabut, Jr.)
Targeted Communications Corp.

American Insurance Ass'n Political Action Committee
1130 Connecticut Ave., N.W., Suite 1000, Washington, DC 20036
Telephone: (202) 828-7100
Background: Represented by Robert E. Vagley, President of the Association.

American Integrity Insurance Co.
Philadelphia, PA
Counsel or consultant:
Dow, Lohnes and Albertson (Richard S. Belas)

American Intellectual Property Law Ass'n
2001 Jefferson Davis Hwy. Suite 203, Arlington, VA 22202
Telephone: (703) 521-1680
Represented by:
Michael W. Blommer, Exec. Director
Martha R. Morales, Assoc. Exec. Director

American Internat'l Automobile Dealers Ass'n
1128 16th St., N.W., Washington, DC 20036
Telephone: (202) 659-2561
Represented by:
Walter E. Huizenga, Exec. V. President
Ben Machinist, V. President
Kathleen Mordini, V. President, Public Affairs
Counsel or consultant:
Patton, Boggs and Blow (George Blow)

American Internat'l Automobile Dealers Ass'n Political Action Committee
1128 16th St., N.W., Washington, DC 20036
Telephone: (202) 659-2561
Represented by:
Fred Miller, Treasurer

American Internat'l Group
1455 Pennsylvania Ave., N.W. Suite 900, Washington, DC 20004
Telephone: (202) 783-5690
Represented by:
Susan F. Delaney, Exec. Asst.
L. Oakley Johnson, V. President, Corporate Affairs
Richard P. Merski, Director, Government Affairs
Emily Rothrock, Associate Director, Government Affairs
Cindy J. Wilmer, Associate Director, Government Affairs
Counsel or consultant:
Wunder, Ryan, Cannon & Thelen (Kenneth S. Levine, Thomas M. Ryan)

The listings in this directory are available as *Mailing Labels*. See last page.

ORGANIZATIONS REPRESENTED

American Iron and Steel Institute
1133 15th St., N.W., Suite 300, Washington, DC 20005-2701
Telephone: (202) 452-7100
Represented by:
Milton Deaner, President
George T. Esherick, Vice President, Government Relations
Frank Fenton, Senior V. President, Public Policy
Barton C. Green, Sr. V. Pres., Gen. Counsel & Secy-Treas.
Peter A. Hernandez, V. President, Employee Relations
James J. Hughes, V. Pres., Communications & Admin. Svcs.
Bruce A. Steiner, V. President, Environment and Energy
Sheldon Wesson, Director of Press Relations
Counsel or consultant:
Collier, Shannon & Scott (Pamela Allen, Thomas F. Shannon)
Dewey, Ballantine, Bushby, Palmer and Wood (Joseph K. Dowley)
Dutko & Associates (Emily Young)
Garvey, Schubert & Barer (Richard A. Wegman)
Powell, Adams & Rinehart (Dale Leibach, Jody Powell)
Fred B. Rooney
Swidler & Berlin, Chartered (Francis S. Blake)
Wunder, Ryan, Cannon & Thelen (Michael A. Forscey, Thomas M. Ryan)

American Israel Public Affairs Committee
440 First St., N.W. Suite 600, Washington, DC 20001
Telephone: (202) 639-5200
Background: A domestic, American organization of about 50,000 members which lobbies on behalf of legislation effecting US-Israel relations. Formerly (1954) American Zionist Council Public Affairs Committee.
Represented by:
Dan Cohen, Legislative Liaison
Thomas A. Dine, Exec. Director
Ester Kurz, Legislative Director
Edward Levy, Jr., President
Melissa B. Patack, Legislative Liaison
Wendy Senor, Legislative Liaison
Stephen Silberfarb, Legislative Liaison

American Jewish Committee
2027 Massachusetts Ave., N.W., Washington, DC 20036
Telephone: (202) 265-2000
Background: Founded in 1906 by upper middle class German Jews. Now claims about 50,000 members and maintains offices in 30 U.S. cities and Jerusalem, Paris and Latin America. Generally supports pro-Israel policies, but takes independent positon on some specific issues. Domestic program covers broad range of human rights, civil liberties, social welfare and education issues. Affiliated with Leadership Conference on Civil Rights and other coalitional groups in furtherance of a democratic, pluralist society.
Represented by:
Judy Golub, Associate Washington Representative
David A. Harris, Washington Representative

American Jewish Congress
2027 Massachusetts Ave., N.W., Washington, DC 20036
Telephone: (202) 332-4001
Background: National Jewish community relations and civil liberties membership organization dedicated to the preservation of all religious, racial and gender rights. It seeks to combat anti-Semitism and other forms of discrimination in the areas of employment, education, housing and voting. Areas of activity include: Church-State relations; government involvement in parochial schools; public school prayer; constitutional, minority and women's rights; Arab boycotts; Middle East peace; and world Jewry. Headquartered in New York City.
Represented by:
Jane P. Merkin, Exec. Director, National Capital Region
Mark J. Pelavin, Washington Representative

American Kidney Fund
6110 Executive Blvd., Rockville, MD 20852
Telephone: (301) 881-3052
Background: Provides direct financial assistance to kidney patients, educational programs for health professionals and for the public, and actively supports organ donation.
Represented by:
Judith Kari, Director of Programs
Francis J. Soldovere, Exec. Director

American Koyo Corp.
Westlake, OH
Counsel or consultant:
Powell, Goldstein, Frazer and Murphy (Peter Suchman)

American Labor Education Center
1730 Connecticut Ave., N.W., Washington, DC 20009
Telephone: (202) 387-6780
Represented by:
Debbie Duke, Co-Director
Karen Ohmans, Co-Director

American Land Title Ass'n
1828 L St., N.W., Suite 705, Washington, DC 20036
Telephone: (202) 296-3671
Represented by:
Gary L. Garrity, Vice President, Public Affairs
Robin E. Keeney, Director, Government Relations
James R. Maher, Exec. V. President

American League for Exports and Security Assistance (ALESA)
122 C St., N.W., Suite 740, Washington, DC 20001
Telephone: (202) 783-0051
Background: Founded in 1976. An association of major U.S. defense contractor corporations and three labor unions.
Represented by:
Henry J. Kenny, V. President
James E. McInerney, Jr., Exec. V. President
Anna Stout, Director, Legislative Affairs
Counsel or consultant:
Ginn, Edington, Moore and Wade

American League of Financial Institutions
1709 New York Ave., N.W. Suite 801, Washington, DC 20006
Telephone: (202) 628-5624
Represented by:
John W. Harshaw, President

American League of Lobbyists
P.O. Box 30005, Alexandria, VA 22310
Telephone: (703) 960-3011
Background: President is Wade S. Williams of Deloitte & Touche.
Represented by:
Patti Jo Baber, Exec. Director
Counsel or consultant:
Smith, Heenan and Althen (Kathryn Lee)

American Legion
1608 K St., N.W., Washington, DC 20006
Telephone: (202) 861-2700
Background: A major, influential veterans organization established in 1919. Adopts resolutions, offers suggestions and presents testimony to Congress on foreign affairs and defense issues.
Represented by:
Mylio S. Kraja, Exec. Director, Washington Office
E. Philip Riggin, Director, Nat'l Legislative Commission
Steve A. Robertson, Asst. Dir., Nat'l Legislative Commission
G. Michael Schlee, Director, Nat'l Security/Foreign Relats.
John F. Sommer, Director, National Veterans Affairs

American Legislative Exchange Council
214 Massachusetts Ave., N.W., Washington, DC 20002
Telephone: (202) 547-4646
Background: Established in 1973; it is the largest individual membership organization of state legislators. Provides research and legislative analysis to state lawmakers and other state policy leaders. Serves as legislative liaison for its members.
Represented by:
Tim Beauchemin, Legislative Director
Robert Bennett, Chief of Staff
Samuel A. Brunelli, Exec. Director
Lining Burnet, Programs Director
Michael Fletcher, Conference Manager
Richard Gowdy, Legislative Director
Garland McCoy, Director of Development
Roop Mohunlall, Legislative Director
Duane A. Parde, Legislative Director
Ruth Prendergast, Director, Membership Services
Michael Tanner, Legislative Director
Jerry Taylor, Legislative Assistant

American Leprosy Foundation
11600 Nebel St., Suite 210, Rockville, MD 20852
Telephone: (301) 984-1336
Represented by:
Pris I. Reed, Administrative Director

American Library Ass'n
110 Maryland Ave., N.E., Suite 101, Washington, DC 20002
Telephone: (202) 547-4440
Represented by:
Eileen D. Cooke, Director, Washington Office
Anne A. Heanue, Associate Director
Carol C. Henderson, Deputy Director, Washington Office

American Licensed Practical Nurses Ass'n
1090 Vermont Ave., N.W., Suite 1200, Washington, DC 20005-4905
Telephone: (202) 682-5800
Counsel or consultant:
Tendler, Goldberg & Biggins, Chtd. (Paul M. Tendler)

American Life League
P.O. Box 1350, Stafford, VA 22554
Telephone: (703) 659-4171
Background: A 150,000 member, grassroots, Christian pro-life organization.
Represented by:
Judie Brown, President
Robert G. Marshall, Director of Research

American Logistics Ass'n
1133 15th St., N.W. Suite 640, Washington, DC 20005
Telephone: (202) 466-2520
Background: Lobbies for an improved military resale system.
Represented by:
Carol Bok, Director, Gov't Relations, Exchange Aff.
Marsha Herzstein, Government Liaison
William Irwin, Director of Operations
A. Kolbet Schrichte, Exec. Vice President
Counsel or consultant:
Diuguid and Epstein
Patton, Boggs and Blow (Joe Robert Reeder)

American Lung Ass'n/American Thoracic Soc.
1726 M St., N.W. Suite 902, Washington, DC 20005
Telephone: (202) 785-3355
Background: A member organization of the Coalition for Health Funding, the Nat'l Clean Air Coalition in Washington and the Coalition on Smoking or Health.
Represented by:
Fran DuMelle, Director of Government Relations
Counsel or consultant:
Health and Medicine Counsel of Washington (Dale P. Dirks)

American Machine Tool Distributors Ass'n
1335 Rockville Pike Suite 300, Rockville, MD 20852
Telephone: (301) 738-1200
Represented by:
Robert A. Gale, President
Ralph J. Nappi, Director, Communication and Education

American Machine Tool Distributors Political Action Committee
1335 Rockville Pike, Rockville, MD 20852
Telephone: (301) 738-1200
Background: Responsible contact is Ralph J. Nappi of the American Machine Tool Distributors Ass'n.

American Managed Care Pharmacy Ass'n
2300 9th St. South, Suite 210, Arlington, VA 22204
Telephone: (703) 920-8480
Background: Represents companies providing home-delivered pharmacy services to patients.
Represented by:
Delbert D. Konnor, Exec. V. President

American Managed Care and Review Ass'n
1227 25th St., N.W. Suite 610, Washington, DC 20037
Telephone: (202) 728-0506
Background: The national trade association for health care groups focusing on prepaid care, utilization review and quality of patient service.
Represented by:
Charles W. Stellar, Exec. Vice President
Counsel or consultant:
Epstein Becker and Green (Lynn S. Snyder)

The listings in this directory are available as *Mailing Labels*. See last page.

485

ORGANIZATIONS REPRESENTED

American Managed Care and Review Ass'n Political Action Committee (AMCRA PAC)
1227 25th St., N.W. Suite 610, Washington, DC 20037
Telephone: (202) 728-0506
Represented by:
Ronald A. Hurst, Exec. V. President
Counsel or consultant:
Epstein Becker and Green

American Maritime Ass'n
Iselin, NJ
Counsel or consultant:
Patton, Boggs and Blow (Alan A. Tuttle)

American Maritime Congress
444 N. Capitol St., N.W., Suite 801, Washington, DC 20001
Telephone: (202) 877-4477
Represented by:
Mary Aukofer, Editor
Jan Clarke, Legislative Analyst
Gloria Cataneo Rudman, Legislative Director
Thomas W. Scoville, Director, Policy and Planning
Eric P. Snow, Legislative Assistant
Jennifer D. Veley, Legislative Assistant
J. P. Walters, Exec. Director
Counsel or consultant:
Keene, Shirley & Associates, Inc.

American Maritime Officers Service
490 L'Enfant Plaza East, S.W., Suite 490, Washington, DC 20024
Telephone: (202) 479-1133
Represented by:
Karen A. Hoover, Asst. Legislative Director

American Maritime Transport, Inc.
Tarrytown, NY
Counsel or consultant:
O'Connor & Hannan (George J. Mannina, Jr.)

American Meat Institute
Box 3556, Washington, DC 20007
Telephone: (703) 841-2400
Represented by:
Dr. A. Dewey Bond, Special Assistant to the President
J. Patrick Boyle, President and CEO
Jerome J. Breiter, President, Hides, Skins & Leather
Michael J. Copps, Sr. V. Pres., Public & Congress'l Affrs.
Sara Lilygren, Director of Public Relations
Emily C. Piper, Legislative Assistant
Jerry Welcome, Jr, Director, Legislative Affairs
Counsel or consultant:
Hill and Knowlton Public Affairs Worldwide (Harold Silverman)

American Meat Institute Political Action Committee
Box 3556, Washington, DC 20007
Telephone: (703) 778-0535
Background: Contact is Jerry Welcome, Jr. of the American Meat Institute.

American Medical Ass'n
1101 Vermont Ave., N.W., Washington, DC 20005
Telephone: (202) 789-7400
Represented by:
Richard A. Deem, Asst. Director, Dept. of Federal Affairs
James E. Drake, Ass't Dir., Dept. of Congress'l Affairs
Stephen C. Duffy, Asst. Dir., Dept. of Congress'l Affairs
Jack M. Emery, Assistant Director, Federal Affairs
Jayne A. Hart, Ass't Dir., Dept. of Congress'l Affairs
Fanny L. Haslebacher, Washington Legislative Counsel
Robin L. Kropf, Assistant Director, Federal Affairs
Leslie C. Ludwick, Ass't Director, Congressional Affairs
Dorothy J. Moss, Director, Dept. of Federal Affairs
John H. Scott, Ass't Director, Congressional Affairs
James H. Stacey, Dir., Dept. of Media & Info. Svcs.
Lee J. Stillwell, V. President, Public Affairs Group
Ronald Szabat, Washington Legislative Attorney
James S. Todd, MD, Acting Exec. V. President
W. Scott Wilber, Director, Dept. of Congressional Affairs
Dr. John S. Zapp, Director, Government Affairs Division
Counsel or consultant:
Gold and Liebengood, Inc. (Martin B. Gold)
Targeted Communications Corp.
Washington Resources and Strategy, Inc. (William R. Sweeney, Jr.)

American Medical Ass'n Political Action Committee
1101 Vermont Ave., N.W., Washington, DC 20005
Telephone: (202) 789-7400
Represented by:
Kevin Walker, Exec. Director and Treasurer

American Medical Directors Ass'n
325 S. Patrick St., Alexandria, VA 22314
Telephone: (703) 549-5822
Background: Consists of doctors who provide care to patients of long term care facilities either as Medical Directors or attending physicians.
Represented by:
Nicholas Owen, M.D., President
Lorraine Tarnore, Exec. Director

American Medical EEG Ass'n
Elm Grove, IL
Counsel or consultant:
U.S. Strategies Corp. (Joseph H. Miltenberger)

American Medical Imaging Corp.
Doylestown, PA
Counsel or consultant:
Arent, Fox, Kintner, Plotkin & Kahn (Alan E. Reider)

American Medical Internat'l
Beverly Hills, CA
Counsel or consultant:
Hogan and Hartson (Clifford S. Gibbons, John S. Stanton)

American Medical Peer Review Ass'n
810 First St., N.E., Suite 410, Washington, DC 20002
Telephone: (202) 371-5610
Represented by:
Lisa Looper, Associate Exec. V. President
Dr. William H. Moncrief, President
Andrew H. Webber, Exec. V. President
Counsel or consultant:
Onek, Klein & Farr (Joseph N. Onek)

American Medical Record Ass'n
Chicago, IL
Counsel or consultant:
Porte, Stafford and Associates (Phillip L. Porte)

American Medical Student Ass'n
1890 Preston White Drive, Reston, VA 22091
Telephone: (703) 620-6600
Background: Nat'l organization representing physicans in training.
Represented by:
Sharon McHale, Public Affairs Officer
Sarena Seifer, Director, Legislative Affairs
Paul R. Wright, Exec. Director

American Medical Women's Ass'n
801 North Fairfax St., Suite 400, Alexandria, VA 22314
Telephone: (703) 838-0500
Represented by:
Lois Schoenbrun, Deputy Director

American Medical Writers Ass'n
9650 Rockville Pike, Bethesda, MD 20814
Telephone: (301) 493-0003
Represented by:
Lillian Sablack, Exec. Director

American Mental Health Counselors Ass'n
5999 Stevenson Ave., Alexandria, VA 22304
Telephone: (703) 823-9800
Background: A division of American Ass'n for Counseling and Development. Responsible contact is William Hunter.
Represented by:
Danielle LeMoal, Director, Administrative Services

American Mental Health Fund
2735 Hartland Road, Suite 302, Falls Church, VA 22043
Telephone: (703) 573-2200
Represented by:
John David George, President

American Methanol Institute
815 Connecticut Ave., N.W. Suite 800, Washington, DC 20006
Telephone: (202) 467-5050
Counsel or consultant:
Neill and Co. (George A. Dalley, Denis M. Neill)

American Mining Congress
1920 N St., N.W. Suite 300, Washington, DC 20036
Telephone: (202) 861-2800
Represented by:
James Beizer, Director of Communications
Kevin R. Burns, Counsel
Michael J. Chakarun, Tax Analyst
Roderick T. Dwyer, Assistant V. President
Mark G. Ellis, Counsel
George F. Fenton, Jr., V. President - Government Affairs
James E. Gilchrist, V. President - Environmental Affairs
Ann M. Gosier, V. President, Manufacturers Services
Edward M. Green, Chief Counsel
Alma P. Hale, Legislative and Regulatory Analyst
Bobby J. Jackson, V. President, Human Resources
Joseph A. Jeffrey, Vice President, Taxation
John A. Knebel, President
Keith R. Knoblock, V.P., Minerals Avail'ty & Public Lands
E. Joyce Morgan, Managing Editor
Stuart A. Sanderson, Senior Counsel
Carol Sheppard, Senior Editor
Peter W. Tooker, Technical Analyst
Counsel or consultant:
Dunaway & Cross (Mac S. Dunaway)
Hill and Knowlton Public Affairs Worldwide (Tamara Cox)
Miller & Chevalier, Chartered
Perkins Coie (Anthony J. Thompson)
Prather, Seeger, Doolittle and Farmer (Alfred V. J. Prather)

American Movers Conference
2200 Mill Road, Alexandria, VA 22314
Telephone: (703) 838-1930
Represented by:
George E. Bennett, Public Relations Director
Nathan R. Berkley, Director, Government Traffic
Jane L. Downey, General Counsel
Charles C. Irions, President
John Moehring, Director of Tax Policy

American Museum of Natural History
New York, NY
Counsel or consultant:
Chernikoff and Co. (Larry Chernikoff)

American Narcolepsy Ass'n
511 Capitol Court, N.E. Suite 300, Washington, DC 20002
Telephone: (202) 544-7499
Counsel or consultant:
Health and Medicine Counsel of Washington (Dale P. Dirks)

American Nat'l Heritage Ass'n
P.O. Box 9340, Alexandria, VA 22304-0340
Telephone: (703) 370-3750
Represented by:
Endel Peedo, Exec. V. President

American Nat'l Metric Council
1620 I St., N.W., Suite 220, Washington, DC 20006
Telephone: (202) 628-5757
Represented by:
James M. Meredith, President

American Near East Refugee Aid
1522 K St., N.W. Suite 202, Washington, DC 20005
Telephone: (202) 347-2558
Background: A charitable organization founded in 1968 in the aftermath of the Six-Day War to provide assistance to Palestinians and civilian victims of war in the Middle East.
Represented by:
Peter A. Gubser, President

American Newspaper Publishers Ass'n
The Newspaper Center 11600 Sunrise Valley Drive, Reston, VA 22091
Telephone: (703) 648-1000

The listings in this directory are available as *Mailing Labels*. See last page.

ORGANIZATIONS REPRESENTED

Represented by:
Leslie A. Barhyte, Legislative Assistant
Paul J. Boyle, Government Affairs Representative
Robert L. Burke, Senior V. President
Jerry W. Friedheim, President
Kevin Grant, Manager, State Affairs
Mark W. Ingham, Exec. Dir., Newspaper Pers. Relat. Ass'n
Claudia M. James, V. President/Legal & Governmental Afrs.
W. Terry Maguire, Senior V. President
Rene P. Milam, Counsel
Brigette M. Rouson, Manager, Legal and Regulatory Affairs
Tonda Rush, Director, Industry Affairs
William Schabacker, Director, Public Affairs
Counsel or consultant:
Davidson Colling Group, Inc., The (James H. Davidson)
Podesta Associates (John D. Podesta)
Silverstein and Mullens (William A. Kirk, Jr.)
Wiley, Rein & Fielding (Richard E. Wiley)

American Nuclear Energy Council
410 First St., S.E. Third Floor, Washington, DC 20003
Telephone: (202) 484-2670
Represented by:
Mary Bresnahan, Director, Finance and Management
Edward M. Davis, President
Andrea N. Dravo, Vice President
Diane S. Holmes, Director, Special Programs
Joseph T. Kelliher, Legislative Programs Director
K. P. Lau, V. President, Technical
Paul MacMurdy, Legislative Programs Director
Timothy E. Smith, General Counsel
Counsel or consultant:
Direct Impact Co., The
Dutko & Associates (Daniel A. Dutko)
Flanagan Group, Inc. (Theodore J. Garrish)
Griffin, Johnson & Associates
McAuliffe, Kelly, Raffaelli & Siemens (Edward E. Allison)
Charlie McBride Assoc, Inc. (Charlie McBride)
Miller & Chevalier, Chartered (Leonard Bickwit, Jr.)

American Nuclear Insurers
Farmington, CT
Counsel or consultant:
Preston Gates Ellis & Rouvelas Meeds (Lloyd Meeds, Tim L. Peckinpaugh)

American Nuclear Soc.
1129 20th St., N.W. Suite 500, Washington, DC 20036
Telephone: (202) 822-1713
Counsel or consultant:
Durante Associates

American Nurses' Ass'n
1101 14th St., N.W., Suite 200, Washington, DC 20005
Telephone: (202) 789-1800
Represented by:
Christine deVries, Ass't Dir., Congressional & Agency Rtns.
Judith A. Huntington, Director, Washington Office
Cathy Koeppen, Senior Staff Specialist/Communications
Patricia McGill, Ass't Dir., Congress'l & Agency Relat'ns
Kathleen Michels, Ass't Dir., Congress'l & Agency Relat'ns
Pamela Mittelstat, Ass't Dir., Congress'l & Agency Relat'ns
Daniel O'Neil, Ass't Dir., Congress'l & Agency Relat'ns
Donna Rae Richardson, Director, Congress'l & Agency Relat'ns
Marjorie Vanderbilt, Ass't Dir., Congress'l & Agency Relat'ns
Counsel or consultant:
Health Policy Alternatives

American Nurses' Ass'n Political Action Committee (ANA-PAC)
1101 14th St., N.W. Suite 200, Washington, DC 20005
Telephone: (202) 789-1800
Background: The American Nurses Ass'n Political Action Committee.
Represented by:
Pat Ford-Roegner, R.N., Director

American Occupational Therapy Ass'n
1383 Piccard Drive, Suite 300 P.O. Box 1725, Rockville, MD 20850
Telephone: (301) 948-9626
Represented by:
Francis Aquaviva, Assoc. Exec. Dir., Member Services
Jeanette Bair, Exec. Director
William J. Graves, Assoc. Exec. Dir., Finan., Bus. Adm.
Howard Holland, Program Manager, External Affairs
Stephanie Hoover, Associate Exec. Director
Diana Ramsay, Legis. Specialist, Legis. & Polit. Affrs
Susan J. Scott, Senior Legislative Consultant
Frederick P. Somers, Director, Legislat. & Political Affairs
Thomas J. Steich, General Counsel
Fred Whiting, Director, Public Affairs

American Occupational Therapy Political Action Committee
Suite 300, 1383 Piccard Drive, P.O. Box 1725, Rockville, MD 20850-4375
Telephone: (301) 948-9626
Background: Represented by Frederick Somers, and William J. Graves of the American Occupational Therapy Ass'n.

American Optometric Ass'n
1505 Prince Street, Suite 300, Alexandria, VA 22314
Telephone: (703) 739-9200
Represented by:
Kelly Brand, Assistant Director, Government Relations
David S. Danielson, Assistant Director, Gov't Relations
Nancy Garland, Government Relations Counsel
Millicent Gorham, Assistant Director, Gov't Relations
Jeffrey G. Mays, Director, Government Relations
William W. Reinertson, Director, Vision Care Benefits Center
Counsel or consultant:
J. T. Rutherford & Assoc. (Don Lavanty)
Volpe, Boskey and Lyons

American Optometric Ass'n Political Action Committee
1505 Prince St. Suite 300, Alexandria, VA 22314
Telephone: (703) 739-9200
Represented by:
Noel Brazil, Director

American Orthotic and Prosthetic Ass'n
717 Pendleton St., Alexandria, VA 22314
Telephone: (703) 836-7116
Represented by:
Charles K. Unger, Ass't Exec. Director
Counsel or consultant:
O'Connor & Hannan (Timothy M. Haake)

American Orthotic and Prosthetic Ass'n Political Action Committee
717 Pendleton St., Alexandria, VA 22314
Telephone: (703) 836-7116
Background: Represented by Dr. Ian R. Horen of the Orthotic and Prosthetic Nat'l Office.

American Osteopathic Ass'n
300 5th St., N.E., Washington, DC 20002
Telephone: (202) 544-5060
Represented by:
Elizabeth W. Beckwith, Director, Gov't Relations
Paul Eyer, Assoc. Director,
Mary T. McSorley, Associate Director, Government Relations

American Osteopathic Hospital Ass'n
1454 Duke St., Alexandria, VA 22314
Telephone: (703) 684-7700
Represented by:
Catherine D. Cahill, Asst. V. Pres., Government Affairs
Tricia Siclari, Asst. V. Pres., Professional Affairs
Richard Strano, President
Martin A. Wall, Senior V. President

American Paper Institute
1250 Connecticut Ave., N.W. Suite 210, Washington, DC 20036
Telephone: (202) 463-2420

Represented by:
Michael C. Farrar, V. Pres., Environmental & Health Affairs
John L. Festa, Director, Chemical Control Programs
Marilyn Beth Haugen, Mgr., Groundwater/Drinking Water Prgrms
Patricia K. Hill, Dir., Water Quality & Waste Disposal Pgm
Robert C. Kaufmann, Director, Air Quality Program
Ann H. Mattheis, Manager, Government Relations
Robert T. McKernan, V. President, Policy Planning & Commun.
John W. Rauber, Jr., Legislative Affairs Director
Carol Raulston, V. President, Government Affairs
Terry L. Serie, Dir, Transportation & State Gov't Reltns
Matthew Van Hook, Senior Environmental Counsel
Marc D. Yacker, Director, Congressional Affairs
Counsel or consultant:
Burson-Marsteller (Wayne L. Pines)
Chadbourne and Parke
Donelan, Cleary, Wood and Maser, P.C. (John F. Donelan)

American Paper Machinery Ass'n
5313 38th St., N.W., Washington, DC 20015
Telephone: (202) 362-6034
Represented by:
Frank M. McManus, Jr., Exec. Director

American Peanut Product Manufacturers, Inc.
555 13th St., N.W., Washington, DC 20004
Telephone: (202) 637-5600
Represented by:
Richard S. Silverman, General Counsel

American Pediatric Soc.
St. Louis, MO
Background: A member organization of the Coalition for Health Funding in Washington.
Counsel or consultant:
Bryan, Cave, McPheeters and McRoberts (James J. Murphy)

American Petroleum Institute
1220 L St., N.W., Washington, DC 20005
Telephone: (202) 682-8000
Background: Established in 1919 as non-profit tax-exempt foundation, API has become the trade association and chief lobbying arm for over 200 corporations.

ORGANIZATIONS REPRESENTED

American Petroleum Institute (Cont'd)
Represented by:
Betty Anthony, Federal Agencies
Martha Beauchamp, Health & Environmental Affairs Director
Edward A. Beck, III, Washington Representative
Dr. Leonard G. Bower, Policy Analysis Director
Barbara Bush, Taxation Deputy Director
Dr. Michael E. Canes, V. President, Fin. Analysis & Statistics
Stephen J. Cloud, Legislative Research Manager
Jim C. Craig, Public Relations Director
Charles J. DiBona, President
Paula Dietz, External Liaison Associate
Robert T. Drew, Health & Environmental Sciences Director
Thomas B. Farley, II, Washington Representative
Becky Fowler, Staff Assistant, State Gov't Rels.
G. William Frick, V. President, General Counsel & Sec'y
E. June Garvin, Director, State Government Relations
Carlton Jackson, External Liaison Director
Frank J. Jandrowitz, V. President, Field Operations
Mary Ellen Joyce, Federal Agencies
Margaret Kelley, External Liaison Representative
P. Richard Long, External Liaison Representative
Michael J. Mason, Washington Representative
William F. O'Keefe, V. President, Chief Operating Officer
Robert W. O'Rourke, Public Relations Deputy Director
Michelle Ross, Constituency Relations Manager
William Rozett, Field Programs Manager
J. Eldon Rucker, Deputy Director, Health & Envir. Affairs
Michael Rusin, Policy Analysis Deputy Director
Charles E. Sandler, V. President, Government Affairs
C. T. Sawyer, V. President, Industry Affairs
David A. Scott, Washington Representative
Thomas Shallow, Tax Counsel
Creg Smith, External Liaison Representative
Mary L. Tabor, Editorial and Special Issues Director
Arthur E. Wiese, V. President, Public Affairs
Andrew Yood, Taxation Director
Terry F. Yosie, V. President, Health and Environment
Betsy Younkins, Washington Representative
Counsel or consultant:
Bond Donatelli Inc. (Frank Donatelli)
Direct Impact Co., The (John Brady, Tom Herrity)
Groom and Nordberg (Carl A. Nordberg, Jr.)
Keck, Mahin and Cate (Rebecca Schaffer)
Kirkland and Ellis
Miller & Chevalier, Chartered (Donald B. Craven)
Timmons and Co., Inc.
Wilmer, Cutler and Pickering (Stephen P. Doyle)

American Pharmaceutical Ass'n
2215 Constitution Ave., N.W., Washington, DC 20037
Telephone: (202) 628-4410
Represented by:
John A. Gans, Exec. V. President and CEO
William M. Hermelin, Director, Government Affairs
Brian M. Hyps, Government Affairs Assistant
Arthur H. Kibbe, Dir., Scientific Affairs, Policy Div.
Patricia Schultheiss, Dir., Policy Coordination & Legal Affrs.
C. Edwin Webb, Director, Professional Affairs
Ronald L. Williams, Director of Communications
Joan Zaro, Senior V. President and COO
Counsel or consultant:
O'Brien, Birney and Butler (Paul L. O'Brien)

American Pharmaceutical Ass'n Political Action Committee
2215 Constitution Ave., N.W., Washington, DC 20037
Telephone: (202) 628-4410
Background: Represented by William Hermelin of the American Pharmaceutical Ass'n.

American Pharmaceutical Institute
2215 Constitution Ave., N.W., Washington, DC 20037
Telephone: (202) 429-7514
Background: A non-profit research and education organization established by the American Pharmaceutical Ass'n. Mission is to support and disseminate the findings of public policy research on the value of pharmaceuticals and professional pharmacy services in the delivery of health care.
Represented by:
Ginny L. Graybill, Assistant to the Exec. Director
Robert B. Helms, Exec. Director

American Physical Soc.
2000 Florida Ave., N.W., Washington, DC 20009
Telephone: (202) 232-0189
Represented by:
Robert L. Park, Director, Public Affairs

American Physical Therapy Ass'n
1111 North Fairfax St., Alexandria, VA 22314
Telephone: (703) 684-2782
Represented by:
Barbara L. Bryant, Exec. Dir., Private Practice Section
William D. Coughlan, Exec. V. President and CEO
R. Charles Harker, Director, Government Affairs
Sherry Keramidas, Assoc. Exec. V. President
Francis J. Mallon, Assoc. Exec. V. Pres., Prof. Rel. Dept.
Johnette L. Meadows, Director, Minority Affairs
Pam Phillips, Assoc. Director, Gov't Relations
Alexis B. Waters, Director, Public Relations
Counsel or consultant:
Hogan and Hartson (Helen R. Trilling, Ann Morgan Vickery)

American Physical Therapy Congressional Action Committee
1111 North Fairfax St., Alexandria, VA 22314
Telephone: (703) 684-2782
Background: Represented by Charles Harker of the American Physical Therapy Ass'n.

American Physiological Soc.
9650 Rockville Pike, Bethesda, MD 20814
Telephone: (301) 530-7164
Represented by:
Dr. Martin Frank, Exec. Director

American Pilots Ass'n
1055 Thomas Jefferson St, N.W. Suite 404, Washington, DC 20007
Telephone: (202) 333-9377
Represented by:
Capt. Pat Neely, President
Counsel or consultant:
Kurrus and Kirchner (Paul G. Kirchner)

American Pilots Ass'n Political Action Committee
1055 Thomas Jefferson St, N.W. Suite 404, Washington, DC 20007
Telephone: (202) 333-9377
Background: The political action arm of the American Pilots Ass'n. Treasurer and contact is Pat Neely of the Ass'n.

American Pipe Fittings Ass'n
6203 Old Keene Mill Court, Springfield, VA 22152
Telephone: (703) 644-0001
Represented by:
Paul H. Engle, Jr., Exec. Director
Counsel or consultant:
McKenna, Conner and Cuneo (Peter Buck Feller)

American Planning Ass'n
1776 Massachusetts Ave., N.W., Washington, DC 20036
Telephone: (202) 872-0611
Represented by:
Karen Finucan, Director, Public Information
George Marcou, Deputy Exec. Director
Nancy Schamberg Willis, Director, Government Affairs
Israel Stollman, Exec. Director

American Plywood Ass'n
Tacoma, WA
Counsel or consultant:
Preston Gates Ellis & Rouvelas Meeds (Richard L. Barnes, Bruce J. Heiman)

American Podiatric Medical Ass'n
9312 Old Georgetown Road, Bethesda, MD 20814
Telephone: (301) 571-9200
Represented by:
John R. Carson, Director of Governmental Affairs
Faye B. Frankfort, Ass't Director, Government Affairs
Frank J. Malouff, Exec. Director
Dean M. Wakefield, Director, Public Affairs
Counsel or consultant:
Burson-Marsteller (Sheila Raviv)
Sinrod & Tash (Werner Strupp)

American Podiatric Medical Students Ass'n
9312 Old Georgetown Road, Bethesda, MD 20814
Telephone: (301) 493-9667

Represented by:
Betsy M. Herman, Exec. Director

American Political Science Ass'n
1527 New Hampshire Ave., N.W., Washington, DC 20036
Telephone: (202) 483-5212
Represented by:
Dr. Catherine E. Rudder, Exec. Director

American Postal Workers Union
1300 L St., N.W., Washington, DC 20005
Telephone: (202) 842-4200
Represented by:
Mike Benner, Special Ass't to the President
Moe Biller, President
Roy Braunstein, Legislative Aide
William Burrus, V. President
Douglas C. Holbrook, Secretary-Treasurer
Thomas Neill, Director, Industrial Relations
Patrick J. Nilan, Director of Legislation
Kimberly C. Parker, Legislative Consultant to the President
Michael W. Reid, Special Assistant to the President
Counsel or consultant:
Chambers Associates Incorporated (Craig E. Bury)
O'Donnell, Schwartz & Anderson (Darryl Anderson)

American President Companies
1101 17th St., N.W. Suite 400, Washington, DC 20036
Telephone: (202) 331-1424
Represented by:
Douglas Cole, Manager, Government Sales/Service
John R. McLaurin, Director, Federal Affairs
Michael M. Murphy, V. President, Government Affairs
Peter D. Prowitt, Director, Government Affairs
Carl J. Seiberlich, Director, Military Programs
Counsel or consultant:
Preston Gates Ellis & Rouvelas Meeds (Bruce J. Heiman, Emanuel L. Rouvelas)
Shea and Gardner (Robert T. Basseches, David B. Cook)

American Press Institute
11690 Sunrise Valley Drive, Reston, VA 22090
Telephone: (703) 620-3611
Represented by:
William L. Winter, Director

American Production and Inventory Control Soc.
500 West Annandale Road, Falls Church, VA 22046
Telephone: (703) 237-8344
Represented by:
Michael J. Stack, Exec. Director

American Protestant Health Ass'n
Schaumburg, IL
Counsel or consultant:
Baker and Hostetler

American Psychiatric Ass'n
1400 K St., N.W., Washington, DC 20005
Telephone: (202) 682-6000
Represented by:
Jay B. Cutler, Dir. of Gov't Relations & Special Couns.
Frederick Fedeli, Assistant Director, Government Relations
Phyllis Greenberger, Ass't Dir., Political Ed. Coord.
Karen E. Howard, Assistant Director, Government Relations
Dr. Melvin Sabshin, Medical Director
Ellen S. Smith, Assistant Director, Government Relations
Counsel or consultant:
Onek, Klein & Farr (Joel I. Klein)

American Psychological Ass'n
1200 17th St., N.W., Washington, DC 20036
Telephone: (202) 955-7600

The listings in this directory are available as *Mailing Labels*. See last page.

ORGANIZATIONS REPRESENTED

Represented by:
  William A. Altman, Legislative Counsel
  William A. Bailey, Legislative and Federal Affairs Officer
  Elizabeth Baldwin, Research Ethics Officer
  Barbara J. Calkins, Director of Legis. and Federal Affairs
  Wayne J. Camara, Testing and Assessment
  Donna Daley, Director, Federal Advocacy
  William D. Echols, Federal and Legislative Affairs Officer
  Patricia Kobor, Legislative & Federal Affairs Officer
  Sarah Lynn, Legislative Counsel
  Janet O'Keeffe, Legislative Affairs Representative
  Bryant L. Welch, Exec. Dir., Professional Practice
  Lisa Wyatt, Director, Public Affairs
Counsel or consultant:
  Dow, Lohnes and Albertson (William B. Ingersoll)
  Griffin, Johnson & Associates
  Nordlinger Associates
  Targeted Communications Corp.

American Psychosomatic Soc.
6728 Old McLean Village Drive, McLean, VA 22101
Telephone: (703) 556-9222
Counsel or consultant:
  Degnon Associates, Inc. (George K. Degnon, Carol Ann
  Kiner)

American Public Gas Ass'n
Box 1426, Vienna, VA 22183
Telephone: (703) 281-2910
Represented by:
  Robert S. Cave, Exec. Director
Counsel or consultant:
  Miller, Balis and O'Neil (Stanley W. Balis, Mark C. Dar-
  rell, Susan N. Kelly, William T. Miller)

American Public Health Ass'n
1015 15th St., N.W. Third Floor, Washington, DC 20005
Telephone: (202) 789-5600
Background: A member organization of the Coalition for
  Health Funding in Washington.
Represented by:
  Richard Gilbert, Dir., State & Local Affrs., Gov't Relat.
  Jeffrey P. Jacobs, Congressional Liaison
  Barbara W. Levine, Dir., Federal Affairs, Gov't Relations
  Dr. William H. McBeath, Exec. Director
  Katherine McCarter, Assoc. Exec. Director, Gov't Rela-
  tions

American Public Land Exchange Co.
Missoula, MT
Counsel or consultant:
  Kogovsek & Associates, Inc.

American Public Policy Institute
11800 Sunrise Valley Drive Suite 812, Reston, VA 22091
Telephone: (703) 620-5270
Counsel or consultant:
  Sedam and Shearer (Glenn J. Sedam, Jr.)

American Public Power Ass'n
2301 M St., N.W., Washington, DC 20037
Telephone: (202) 775-8300
Represented by:
  Charles Acquard, Legislative Representative
  Madalyn Cafruny, Director of Public Information
  Linda Church Ciocci, Legislative Representative
  Paul Fry, Deputy Exec. Director
  Anne Marie Gibbons, Legislative Representative
  Ruth Gonze, Policy Analyst
  Lawrence S. Hobart, Exec. Director
  Martin B. Kanner, Director of Government Relations
  Lilian Ann Newby, Legislative Representative
  Alan H. Richardson, Assistant Exec. Director
  Gordon Roberts, Director of Communications

American Public Transit Ass'n
1201 New York Ave., N.W.,, Washington, DC 20005
Telephone: (202) 898-4000

Represented by:
  Robert W. Batchelder, Chief Cnsl/Dep Exec V. Pres,
  Govt'al Affr
  Charles O. Bishop, Jr., Director, Public Relations
  Arcadio R. de la Cruz, Exec. Director, Policy and Pro-
  grams
  Albert Engelken, Deputy Exec. Director
  Jack R. Gilstrap, Exec. V. President
  Robert L. Healy, Jr., Government Affairs Director
  Dennis Kouba, Director, Communications
Counsel or consultant:
  Wexler, Reynolds, Fuller, Harrison and Schule, Inc. (Ter-
  ry D. Bevels, William K. Ris, Jr.)

American Public Welfare Ass'n
810 First St., N.E., Suite 300, Washington, DC 20002
Telephone: (202) 682-0100
Background: A non-profit ass'n providing professional con-
  sultation to Congress and an active program of legislative
  monitoring and analysis.
Represented by:
  Rick A. Ferreira, Policy Associate
  A. Sidney Johnson, III, Exec. Director
  Kathleen Patterson, Director of Communications
  Linda Wolf, Deputy Director
  Beverly Yanich, Associate Director

American Public Works Ass'n
1301 Pennsylvania Ave., N.W. Suite 501, Washington, DC
  20004
Telephone: (202) 393-2792
Represented by:
  Charles A. Byrley, Director, Washington Office

American Pulpwood Ass'n
1025 Vermont Ave., N.W., Suite 1020, Washington, DC
  20005
Telephone: (202) 347-2900
Represented by:
  Douglas Domenech, Director, Forestry Programs
  Richard Lewis, President

American Pyrotechnics Ass'n
P.O. Box 213, Chestertown, MD 21620
Telephone: (301) 778-6825
Background: Fireworks importers, distributors, suppliers
  and manufacturers.
Counsel or consultant:
  John Adams Associates

American Radio Relay League
Newington, CT
Counsel or consultant:
  Chwat/Weigend Associates (John S. Chwat, Robert E.
  Weigend)

American Railway Car Institute
Olympia Fields, IL
Counsel or consultant:
  Harris & Ellsworth (Herbert E. Harris, II)

American Railway Engineering Ass'n
50 F St., N.W., Suite 7702, Washington, DC 20001
Telephone: (202) 639-2190
Represented by:
  Louis T. Cerny, Exec. Director

American Real Estate Group
Irvine, CA
Counsel or consultant:
  Dow, Lohnes and Albertson (Stuart Marshall Bloch)

American Recreation Coalition
1331 Pennsylvania Ave., N.W., Suite 726, Washington, DC
  20004
Telephone: (202) 662-7420
Represented by:
  Derrick A. Crandall, President
  Mary Beth Seibert, V. President

American Red Cross
2025 E St., N.W., Washington, DC 20006-5099
Telephone: (202) 639-3000
Represented by:
  Lynn Martenstein, Director, Media Coordination
Counsel or consultant:
  Foley & Lardner (Paul E. Cooney)

American Ref-Fuel Co.
Houston, TX

Counsel or consultant:
  Bonner & Associates

American Rehabilitation Counseling Ass'n
5999 Stevenson Ave., Alexandria, VA 22304
Telephone: (703) 823-9800
Background: Represented by William Hunter, Lauren
  Scheib and Richard Yep of the American Ass'n for Coun-
  seling and Development.

American Rental Ass'n
Moline, IL
Counsel or consultant:
  Stephens & Graham (William T. Stephens)

American Resort and Residential Development Ass'n
1220 L St., N.W. Suite 510, Washington, DC 20005
Telephone: (202) 371-6700
Background: Represents developers of recreation, resort
  and residential real estate projects.
Represented by:
  Thomas C. Franks, V. President for Government Rela-
  tions
  Gary A. Terry, President
Counsel or consultant:
  Concord Associates, Inc.
  Dow, Lohnes and Albertson (William B. Ingersoll)
  Winkelmann & Associates, Inc. (Joe Winkelmann)

American Resort and Residential Development Ass'n Political Action Committee
1220 L St., N.W., Fifth Floor, Washington, DC 20005
Telephone: (202) 371-6700
Background: Treasurer is Thomas C. Franks of the Ameri-
  can Resort and Residential Development Ass'n.
Counsel or consultant:
  Baker and Hostetler (Kenneth J. Kies)

American Retail Federation
1616 H St., N.W. 6th Floor, Washington, DC 20006
Telephone: (202) 783-7971
Background: Will be merging with the Nat'l Retail Mer-
  chants Ass'n to form the Nat'l Retail Federation.
Represented by:
  William Kay Daines, Exec. V. President and General
  Counsel
  Katherine T. Mance, Vice President
  Joseph P. O'Neill, President
  Jerry G. Udell, Vice President
  Lee Williams, Senior Vice President

American River Transport Co.
Decatur, IL
Counsel or consultant:
  TADCO Enterprises (Katherine E. Allen)

American Rivers
801 Pennsylvania Ave., S.E. Suite 303, Washington, DC
  20003-2155
Telephone: (202) 547-6900
Background: A public interest group working to preserve
  the free-flowing rivers of the United States.
Represented by:
  Kevin J. Coyle, President
  John D. Echeverria, Gen. Cous./Dir, Nat'l Hydro-Pwr
  Plcy Ctr
  Patricia Munoz, Director, Donor & Foundation Relations
  Suzanne C. Wilkins, Director, River Protection

American Road and Transportation Builders Ass'n
501 School St., S.W. Suite 800, Washington, DC 20024
Telephone: (202) 488-2722
Represented by:
  Richard M. Harris, Exec. V. President
  Dr T. Peter Ruane, President

American Road and Transportation Builders Ass'n PAC
501 School St., S.W., Washington, DC 20024
Telephone: (202) 488-2722
Background: Contact is Richard M. Harris of the American Road and Transportation Builders Ass'n PAC.

American Running and Fitness Ass'n
9310 Old Georgetown Rd., Bethesda, MD 20814
Telephone: (301) 897-0197
Background: Founded in 1968 as the Nat'l Jogging Ass'n.
  Main goals include encouraging Americans to exercise
  and keeping health professionals up-to-date on the latest
  in sports medicine.

ORGANIZATIONS REPRESENTED

American Running and Fitness Ass'n (Cont'd)
Represented by:
Lisa Gundling, Public Information Specialist
Susan Kalish, Exec. Director

American Samoa, Government of
Pago Pago, American Samoa
Counsel or consultant:
Cotten, Day and Selfon
Pacific Islands Washington Office (Fred Radewagen)

American Savings Bank, F.A.
Irvine, CA
Counsel or consultant:
Dow, Lohnes and Albertson (Stuart Marshall Bloch)

American Savings and Loan of Florida
Miami, FL
Counsel or consultant:
Shaw, Pittman, Potts and Trowbridge (William Mike House)

American School Counselors Ass'n
5999 Stevenson Ave., Alexandria, VA 22304
Telephone: (703) 823-9800
Background: Represented by William Hunter, Lauren Scheib and Richard Yep of the American Ass'n for Counseling and Development.

American School Food Service Ass'n
1600 Duke St., 7th Floor, Alexandria, VA 22314
Telephone: (703) 739-3900
Represented by:
Patricia Bayer, Exec. Director

American Science & Engineering Inc.
Cambridge, MA
Counsel or consultant:
Cassidy and Associates, Inc. (Thomas M. Gannon, Pete W. Glavas)

American Seating Co.
Grand Rapids, MI
Counsel or consultant:
Smith and Howard Associates, Inc. (Irving P. Smith)

American Security Bank
1501 Pennsylvania Ave., N.W., Washington, DC 20013
Telephone: (202) 624-4000
Represented by:
Vickie Tassan, V. President, Public Affairs
Counsel or consultant:
Dow, Lohnes and Albertson (David F. Bantleon)

American Security Bank Political Action Committee
1501 Pennsylvania Ave., N.W., Washington, DC 20013
Telephone: (202) 624-4695
Background: Represented by Vickie Tassan of American Security Bank.

American Security Council
733 15th St., N.W. Suite 700, Washington, DC 20005
Telephone: (202) 484-1676
Background: The nation's largest pro-defense lobbying group, with a membership of over 265,000. Serves as administrative coordinator for the National Security Caucus. President is U.S. House of Representatives Member Duncan Hunter (R-CA).
Represented by:
John M. Fisher, Chairman
Gregg Hilton, Exec. Director
Rear Adm. Robert H. Spiro, USNR-Ret., V. President

American Security Council Foundation
733 15th St., N.W. Suite 700, Washington, DC 20005
Telephone: (202) 484-1676
Background: Exec. Director of the Foundation is Gregg Hilton of the American Security Council.
Represented by:
Col. Philip Cox, USAF (Ret), Military Analyst
Col. Samuel T. Dickens, USAF (Ret), Director, Inter-American Affairs
Ann Kruger, Seminar Director
Thomas B. Smith, Director of Research

American Security Council Political Action Committee
499 South Capitol St., S.W., Washington, DC 20003
Telephone: (202) 484-1677

Represented by:
May Johnson, Treasurer

American Security Fence Corp.
Phoenix, AZ
Counsel or consultant:
Foley & Co. (Joseph P. Foley)

American Security Resources, Inc.
Bethesda, MD
Counsel or consultant:
Ashby and Associates (William B. Montano)

American Seed Research Foundation
1030 15th St., N.W. Suite 964, Washington, DC 20005
Telephone: (202) 223-4080
Background: Represented by Robert J. Falasca of the American Seed Trade Ass'n.

American Seed Trade Ass'n
1030 15th St., N.W. Suite 964, Washington, DC 20005
Telephone: (202) 223-4080
Represented by:
Robert J. Falasca, Assistant to the Exec. V. President
David R. Lambert, Director of Government Affairs
William T. Schapaugh, Exec. V. President
Jack Wells, Director of Internat'l Marketing

American Seed Trade Ass'n Political Action Committee
1030 15th St., N.W. Suite 964, Washington, DC 20005
Telephone: (202) 223-4080
Background: Principal contact is David R. Lambert, Director of Government Affairs for the Ass'n.

American Sheep Industry Ass'n
412 1st St., S.E., Suite 100, Washington, DC 20003
Telephone: (202) 484-2778
Counsel or consultant:
Meyers & Associates (Rick Meyers)

American Sheep Industry Ass'n RAMSPAC
412 First St., S.E., Washington, DC 20003
Telephone: (202) 484-2778
Counsel or consultant:
Meyers & Associates (Larry D. Meyers)

American Ship Building Co.
Tampa, FL
Counsel or consultant:
Ragan and Mason (William F. Ragan)

American Shooting Sports Coalition
Background: A coalition representing foreign gun manufacturers and U.S. firearm importers and manufacturers. Opposes legislation to restrict the importation and sale of firearms. members include Smith & Wesson, Sigarms, Heckler & Koch, Glock Inc., Action Arms, Interarms and Gun South Inc.
Represented by:
Emanuel Kapelsohn, Exec. Director

American Short Line Railroad Ass'n
2000 Massachusetts Ave., N.W., Washington, DC 20036
Telephone: (202) 785-2250
Background: Provides representation for small railroads before federal agencies, the Congress, and the courts.
Represented by:
William E. Loftus, President

American Ski Federation
207 Constitution Ave., N.E., Washington, DC 20002
Telephone: (202) 543-1595
Represented by:
Caroline Bowers, Director, Legislative Affairs
Joseph T. Prendergast, President

American Ski Federation Political Action Committee
207 Constitution Ave., N.E., Washington, DC 20002
Telephone: (202) 543-1595
Background: Joseph T. Prendergast, President of the Federation, serves as Treasurer.

American Sleep Disorders Ass'n
511 Capitol St., N.E. Suite 300, Washington, DC 20001
Telephone: (202) 544-7499
Counsel or consultant:
Health and Medicine Counsel of Washington

American Soc. for Adolescent Psychiatry
5530 Wisconsin Ave., N.W. Suite 1149, Washington, DC 20815
Telephone: (301) 652-0646
Counsel or consultant:
PAI Management Corp. (David A. Lewis)

American Soc. for Biochemistry and Molecular Biology
9650 Rockville Pike, B-22, Bethesda, MD 20814
Telephone: (301) 530-7145
Represented by:
Peter Farnham, Public Affairs Officer
Charles C. Hancock, Exec. Officer

American Soc. for Biotechnology
Sausalito, CA
Counsel or consultant:
Tendler, Goldberg & Biggins, Chtd. (James M. Goldberg)

American Soc. for Bone and Mineral Research
Kelseyville, CA
Counsel or consultant:
MARC Associates, Inc. (Daniel C. Maldonado)

American Soc. for Cell Biology
9650 Rockville Pike, Bethesda, MD 20814
Telephone: (301) 530-7153
Represented by:
Dorothea Wilson, Exec. Officer

American Soc. for Clinical Nutrition
9650 Rockville Pike, Room 4500, Bethesda, MD 20814
Telephone: (301) 530-7110
Represented by:
Dr. S. Stephen Schiaffino, Executive Officer

American Soc. for Deaf Children
814 Thayer Ave., Silver Spring, MD 20910
Telephone: (301) 585-5400
Represented by:
Roberta Thomas, Exec. Director

American Soc. for Engineering Education
11 Dupont Circle, N.W., Suite 200, Washington, DC 20036
Telephone: (202) 293-7080
Background: A professional society of institutions and faculty involved in engineering education. Activities include monitoring federal legislation affecting engineering education and management of federal government faculty and post-doctoral fellowship programs.
Represented by:
Ann Leigh, Manager, Federal Liaison Office
Thomas J. Perry, P.E., Interim Exec. Director

American Soc. for Extra-Corporeal Technology
11480 Sunset Hills Road Suite 100E, Reston, VA 22090
Telephone: (703) 435-8556
Counsel or consultant:
Cate Corp., The (George M. Cate)

American Soc. for Gastrointestinal Endoscopy
Manchester, MA
Counsel or consultant:
MARC Associates, Inc. (Randolph B. Fenninger)

American Soc. for Horticultural Science
113 South West St., Alexandria, VA 22314-2824
Telephone: (703) 836-4606
Represented by:
Skip McAfee, Exec. Director
Cary A. Mitchell, Chairperson, Science Priorities Cmte.
Paul L. Smeal, Chairperson, Public Relations Committee

American Soc. for Industrial Security
1655 N. Ft. Myer Drive Suite 1200, Arlington, VA 22209
Telephone: (703) 522-5800
Represented by:
Ernest J. Criscuoli, Jr., Exec. Vice President

American Soc. for Information Science
1424 16th St., N.W. Suite 404, Washington, DC 20036
Telephone: (202) 462-1000
Represented by:
Richard B. Hill, Exec. Director

American Soc. for Medical Technology
2021 L St., N.W. Suite 400, Washington, DC 20036
Telephone: (202) 785-3311

The listings in this directory are available as *Mailing Labels*. See last page.

ORGANIZATIONS REPRESENTED

Represented by:
Janet L. Pailet, Director, Government Affairs
Lynn B. Podell, Exec. Director

American Soc. for Medical Technology Political Action Committee
2021 L St., N.W., Washington, DC 20036
Telephone: (202) 785-3311
Represented by:
Joan Longberry, Chairman, ASMT-PAC
Counsel or consultant:
McDermott, Will and Emery

American Soc. for Microbiology
1325 Massachusetts Ave., N.W., Washington, DC 20005
Telephone: (202) 737-3600
Background: A membership organization established in 1899 to promote scientific knowledge and research in the field of microbiology; its Public and Scientific Affairs Board monitors federal, state and local laws and informs the Society's members of the potential impact of proposed legislation and regulation.
Represented by:
Michael I. Goldberg, Exec. Director
Martin Hight, Staff Assistant, Public Affairs
Janet Shoemaker, Assistant Director, Public Affairs
Robert D. Watkins, Director, Public Affairs/Relations

American Soc. for Parenteral and Enteral Nutrition
8630 Fenton St., Silver Spring, MD 20910
Telephone: (301) 587-6315
Represented by:
Barney Sellers, Exec. Director

American Soc. for Pharmacology and Experimental Therapeutics
9650 Rockville Pike, Bethesda, MD 20814
Telephone: (301) 530-7060
Represented by:
Mrs. Kay A. Croker, Exec. Officer
Anthony J. Mazzaschi, Public Affairs Officer

American Soc. for Photobiology
8000 Westpark Drive Suite 130, McLean, VA 22102
Telephone: (703) 790-1745
Counsel or consultant:
Society and Association Services Corp. (Richard J. Burk, Jr.)

American Soc. for Photogrammetry and Remote Sensing
5410 Grovsenor Lane, Suite 210, Bethesda, MD 20814-2160
Telephone: (301) 493-0290
Counsel or consultant:
Cranwell & O'Connell (George E. Cranwell)

American Soc. for Psychoprophylaxis in Obstetrics (ASPO/Lamaze)
1840 Wilson Blvd. Suite 204, Arlington, VA 22201
Telephone: (703) 524-7802
Background: A non-profit organization consisting of professional, provider, and family coalition members whose purpose is to promote an optimal childbirth and early-parenting experience for famiies through education, advocacy, and reform.
Represented by:
Ann Ward Tourigny, Ph.D., Exec. Director

American Soc. for Public Administration
1120 G St., N.W. Suite 500, Washington, DC 20005
Telephone: (202) 393-7878
Represented by:
Shirley H. Wester, Exec. Director

American Soc. for the Prevention of Cruelty to Animals Legislative Office
1755 Massachusetts Ave., N.W. Suite 418, Washington, DC 20036
Telephone: (202) 232-5020
Represented by:
Deborah Feldman Weiner, Associate Director, Government Relations

American Soc. for Training and Development
1630 Duke St., Box 1443, Alexandria, VA 22313
Telephone: (703) 683-8100

Represented by:
Helen Frank Bensimon, Director, Public Relations
Anthony P. Carnevale, Chief Economist and V.P., Nat'l Affrs.
Alicia G. Kleckley, Nat'l Affairs Representative
Curtis E. Plott, Exec. V. President

American Soc. of Access Professionals
7910 Woodmont Ave. Suite 1208, Bethesda, MD 20814
Telephone: (301) 913-0030
Background: An independent professional organization working to enhance effective methods, techniques, and procedures for administering access statutes.
Represented by:
Leslie Weisman, President
Counsel or consultant:
C. M. Brownstein & Assoc. (Claire E. Shanley)

American Soc. of Agricultural Consultants
8301 Greensboro Drive Suite 260, McLean, VA 22102
Telephone: (703) 356-2455
Represented by:
Russell F. Frazier, Exec. V. President

American Soc. of Agricultural Consultants Internat'l Political Action Committee
8301 Greensboro Drive, Suite 260, McLean, VA 22102
Telephone: (703) 356-2455
Background: Principal contact is Russell F. Frazier of the Society.

American Soc. of Allied Health Professions
1101 Connecticut Ave., N.W. Suite 700, Washington, DC 20036
Telephone: (202) 857-1150
Counsel or consultant:
Smith, Bucklin and Associates (Carolyn M. DelPolito, Ph.D.)

American Soc. of Anesthesiologists
1111 14th St., N.W., Suite 501, Washington, DC 20005
Telephone: (202) 289-2222
Background: Washington office of a professional society based in Park Ridge, IL.
Represented by:
Adrienne Lang, Director of Governmental Affairs
Counsel or consultant:
MARC Associates, Inc. (Daniel C. Maldonado, Ellen Riker)
Squire, Sanders and Dempsey (Michael Scott)

American Soc. of Appraisers
535 Herndon Parkway, Suite 150, Herndon, VA 22070
Telephone: (703) 478-2228
Represented by:
A. W. Carson, Exec. Director
William C. Middlebrook, International Secretary
Counsel or consultant:
O'Brien, Birney and Butler (Paul L. O'Brien)

American Soc. of Appraisers PAC
535 Herndon Pkwy., Herndon, VA 22070
Telephone: (703) 478-2228
Represented by:
Gregory A. Gilbert, Treasurer

American Soc. of Ass'n Executives
1575 Eye St., N.W., Washington, DC 20005-1168
Telephone: (202) 626-2723
Background: Supports A-PAC.
Represented by:
Thomas A. Gorski, Director, Public Relations & Market Res.
Jon P. Grove, CAE, Exec. Vice President
G. Harris Jordan, Director, Government Affairs
Malcolm S. Karl, Director of Finance
J. Reese Meisinger, Manager, Government Relations
Ernestine S. Robinson, Adminstrative Ass't, Gov't Affairs
R. William Taylor, CAE, President
Counsel or consultant:
O'Connor & Hannan (Timothy M. Haake)
Sanders, Schnabel & Brandenburg, P.C. (Dan S. Brandenburg)
Webster, Chamberlain and Bean (George D. Webster)

American Soc. of Cataract and Refractive Surgery
3702 Pender Drive, Suite 250, Fairfax, VA 22030
Telephone: (703) 591-2220

Represented by:
David A. Karcher, Exec. Director
Andrea Katsenes, Director of Communications
Counsel or consultant:
Jenner and Block (Jerald A. Jacobs)
O'Connor & Hannan (Thomas H. Quinn)

American Soc. of Cataract and Refractive Surgery Political Action Committee
3702 Pender Drive, Suite 250, Fairfax, VA 22033
Telephone: (703) 591-2220
Represented by:
Dr. John Hunkeler, Treasurer

American Soc. of Civil Engineers
1015 15th St., N.W. Suite 600, Washington, DC 20005
Telephone: (202) 789-2200
Represented by:
Jeffrey L. Beard, Manager, Regulatory Affairs
Curtis C. Deane, Managing Director
Casey Dinges, Legislative Affairs Manager
Brenda G. Sanders, Manager, Policy Development

American Soc. of Clinical Oncology
750 17th St., N.W. Suite 1100, Washington, DC 20006
Telephone: (202) 778-2396
Represented by:
Ellen Shillinglaw, Director, Government Relations
Counsel or consultant:
Dr. John T. Grupenhoff

American Soc. of Clinical Pathologists
1101 Vermont Ave., N.W. 6th Floor, Washington, DC 20005
Telephone: (202) 371-0515
Represented by:
Catherine Grealy Cohen, Director, Washington Office
Cheri McNett, Legislative Assistant
Counsel or consultant:
MARC Associates, Inc. (Randolph B. Fenninger, Ellen Riker)

American Soc. of Composers, Authors and Publishers
New York, NY
Counsel or consultant:
Palumbo & Cerrell, Inc. (Benjamin L. Palumbo, Paul A. Skrabut, Jr.)

American Soc. of Consultant Pharmacists
2300 9th St., South, Arlington, VA 22204
Telephone: (703) 920-8492
Background: Represents pharmacists who provide pharmacy and consultant services to nursing homes, home health and many other long-term care settings.
Represented by:
Maude A. Babington, Associate Exec. Director
Paul G. Cano, Director, Government Affairs
Joanne Kaldy, Director of Communications
R. Timothy Webster, Exec. Director

American Soc. of Consultant Pharmacists Political Action Committee
2300 9th St., South, Arlington, VA 22204
Telephone: (703) 920-8492
Background: Represented by R. Timothy Webster of the American Soc. of Consultant Pharmacists.

American Soc. of Electroplated Plastics
1101 14th St, N.W. Suite 1100, Washington, DC 20005
Telephone: (202) 371-1323
Background: David W. Barrack, of Internat'l Management Group, serves as Exec. Director.
Counsel or consultant:
Internat'l Management Group, Inc. (David W. Barrack)

American Soc. of Farm Managers and Rural Appraisers
Denver, CO
Counsel or consultant:
Wallace & Edwards (Macon T. Edwards)

American Soc. of Heating, Refrigerating and Air Conditioning Engineers
1825 K St., N.W., Suite 215, Washington, DC 20006-1202
Telephone: (202) 833-1830
Represented by:
Dr. James E. Cox, Director of Government Affairs

American Soc. of Home Inspectors
3299 K St., N.W., 7th Floor, Washington, DC 20007

ORGANIZATIONS REPRESENTED

American Soc. of Home Inspectors (Cont'd)
Telephone: (202) 842-3096
Counsel or consultant:
Ass'n Management Group (Robert J. Dolibois)

American Soc. of Hospital Pharmacists
4630 Montgomery Ave., Bethesda, MD 20814
Telephone: (301) 657-3000
Represented by:
David D. Almquist, V. Pres, Membership/Organization Liaison
Thomas P. Bruderle, Director, Federal Legislative Affairs
Robert Greenberg, Vice President and General Counsel
Charles M. King, Jr., Exec. V. Pres., Res. & Educ. Foundation
Fern Z. Liang, Director, Gov't Affairs Division
Joseph A. Oddis, Exec. Vice President
Mary Jo Reilly, Senior V. President
Rebecca Wilfinger, Director, Public Information

American Soc. of Internal Medicine
1101 Vermont Ave., N.W. Suite 500, Washington, DC 20005
Telephone: (202) 289-1700
Represented by:
Laura L. Allendorf, Government Affairs Representative
Jane M. Anderson, Director, Public Relations
Dr. Joseph F. Boyle, Exec. Vice President
Robert B. Doherty, V. Pres., Gov't'l Affrs. & Public Policy
Dawn Hauercamp, Director of Federation Relations
S. J. Kalian, V. President
Mark Leasure, Deputy Exec. V. President
Susan Prokop-Short, Assoc. Dir., Public Policy & Regul. Affs
Richard L. Trachtman, Director, Dept. of Federal Affairs

American Soc. of Internat'l Law
2223 Massachusetts Ave., N.W., Washington, DC 20008
Telephone: (202) 265-4313
Represented by:
John Lawrence Hargrove, Exec. Director
Seymour J. Rubin, Senior Consultant

American Soc. of Interpreters
P.O. Box 9603, Washington, DC 20016
Telephone: (703) 998-8636
Background: Professional conference and federally certified court interpreters.
Represented by:
Eva Desrosiers, FASI, Secretary
Mario A. Montenegro, FASI, President

American Soc. of Landscape Architects
4401 Connecticut Ave., N.W., Washington, DC 20008
Telephone: (202) 686-2752
Represented by:
Betsy A. Cuthbertson, Dir. of Gov't Affairs & Public Relats.
Raymond L. Freeman, Government Affairs Consultant
Deborah Mattar, Government Affairs & Public Rtns. Ass't.
Counsel or consultant:
Burson-Marsteller (Michelle Hartz)

American Soc. of Magazine Photographers
New York, NY
Counsel or consultant:
Hunton and Williams (Charles D. Ossola)

American Soc. of Mechanical Engineers
1825 K St., N.W., Suite 218, Washington, DC 20006
Telephone: (202) 785-3756
Represented by:
Sharon R. Cowan, Federal Government Relations Manager
Philip W. Hamilton, Managing Director, Public Affairs
Judith Krauthamer, Manager, State Government Relations
Nelson L. Milder, Assistant Director, Government Relations
Janis Tabor, Ass't Director, Federal Gov't Relations

American Soc. of Military Comptrollers
Box 338, Burgess, VA 22432-0338
Telephone: (703) 462-5637
Represented by:
Lawrence O. Mann, Exec. Director

American Soc. of Naval Engineers
1452 Duke St., Alexandria, VA 22314
Telephone: (703) 836-6727

Represented by:
Capt. Charles J. Smith, USN (Ret.), Exec. Director

American Soc. of Nephrology
1101 Connecticut Ave., N.W., Suite 700, Washington, DC 20036
Telephone: (202) 857-1190
Counsel or consultant:
Capitol Associates, Inc. (Terry Lierman)
Smith, Bucklin and Associates (Judith Walker)

American Soc. of Newspaper Editors
11600 Sunrise Valley Drive, Reston, VA 22091
Telephone: (703) 684-1144
Represented by:
Mireille Grangenois, Director, Minority Affairs
Lee Stinnett, Exec. Director
Counsel or consultant:
Cohn and Marks (Richard M. Schmidt, Jr.)

American Soc. of Notaries
918 16th St., N.W., Washington, DC 20006
Telephone: (202) 955-6162
Represented by:
Eugene E. Hines, Exec. Director

American Soc. of Outpatient Surgeons
San Diego, CA
Counsel or consultant:
McDermott, Will and Emery

American Soc. of Pension Actuaries
2029 K St., N.W., 4th Floor, Washington, DC 20006
Telephone: (202) 659-3620
Represented by:
Chester J. Salkind, Exec. Director
Alan J. Stonewall, President
Counsel or consultant:
Seyfarth, Shaw, Fairweather and Geraldson (John N. Erlenborn)

American Soc. of Plant Physiologists
15501 Monona Drive, Rockville, MD 20855
Telephone: (301) 251-0560
Represented by:
Melvin Josephs, Exec. Director

American Soc. of Plastic and Reconstructive Surgeons
Arlington Hgts., IL
Counsel or consultant:
Kent & O'Connor, Incorp. (J. H. Kent)

American Soc. of Professional Estimators
6911 Richmond Hwy., Suite 230, Alexandria, VA 22306
Telephone: (703) 765-2700
Represented by:
Beverly S. Perrell, Exec. Director

American Soc. of Therapeutic Radiologists
Chicago, IL
Background: Represented by Otha W. Linton of the American College of Radiology.

American Soc. of Travel Agents
1101 King St., Alexandria, VA 22314
Telephone: (703) 739-2782
Represented by:
John Charles Bennison, V. President, Government Affairs
Robin B. Gray, Jr., V. President, Admin. & Mbr. Svcs.
Ray Greenly, V. President, Public Relations
Barbara E. O'Hara, Director, Government Affairs
Burt Rubin, General Counsel

American Soc. of Travel Agents Political Action Committee
1101 King St., Alexandria, VA 22314
Telephone: (703) 739-2782
Background: Represented by Barbara E. O'Hara of the Society.

American Soc. of Tropical Medicine and Hygiene
Shreveport, LA
Counsel or consultant:
Capitol Associates, Inc. (Marguerite Donoghue)

American Social Health Ass'n
311 Massachusetts Ave., N.E., Washington, DC 20002
Telephone: (202) 593-9129
Background: A national voluntary health organization focused on sexually transmitted diseases, including AIDS.

Represented by:
Wendy J. Wertheimer, Director of Public & Government Affairs
Counsel or consultant:
Fox, Bennett and Turner (Allan M. Fox)

American Sociological Ass'n
1722 N St., N.W., Washington, DC 20036
Telephone: (202) 833-3410
Represented by:
Dr. William V. D'Antonio, Exec. Officer

American Southwest Financial Corp.
Phoenix, AZ
Counsel or consultant:
Bracy Williams & Co. (Kenneth S. Birnbaum, Terrence L. Bracy, Susan J. Williams)

American Soybean Ass'n
1300 L St., N.W., Suite 950, Washington, DC 20005-4107
Telephone: (202) 371-5511
Background: A national single-commodity association organized to assure a profitable soybean industry. Has approximately 30,000 dues-paying soybean-producer members; programs supported by over 450,000 soybean producers.
Represented by:
Nancy E. Foster, Staff V. Pres., Public Affairs Dept.
Mark Nestlen, Director, Congressional Relations
Counsel or consultant:
Hogan and Hartson (Gary J. Kushner)
McLeod & Pires (Michael R. McLeod, Wayne R. Watkinson)

American Specialty Chemical Corp.
Gloucester City, NJ
Counsel or consultant:
Mica, Dudinsky & Associates (John Dudinsky, Jr., John L. Mica)

American Speech-Language-Hearing Ass'n
10801 Rockville Pike, Rockville, MD 20852
Telephone: (301) 897-5700
Background: A professional, scientific and accrediting organization representing 57,000 professionals in the field of speech and hearing. A member organization of the Committee for Education Funding, the Consortium for Citizens with Disabilities, the Nat'l Rehabilitation Coalition, and the Washington Health Issues Forum.
Represented by:
Dr. Roger P. Kingsley, Director, Congressional Relations Div.
Constance E. Lynch, Director, State Liaison
Sydney Olson, Director, Governmental Affairs Dept.
Dr. Frederick T. Spahr, Exec. Director
Dr. Steven C. White, Dir., Reimb'rsmnt P'lcy Div., Gov't Afrs
Counsel or consultant:
Melrod, Redman and Gartlan, A Professional Corporation

American Speech-Language-Hearing Ass'n Political Action Committee
10801 Rockville Pike, Rockville, MD 20852
Telephone: (301) 897-5700
Background: Represented by Dr. Frederick T. Spahr, Treasurer, and Dr. Roger P. Kingsley, Staff Director, of the Ass'n.

American Standard Inc.
2020 14th St., North Suite 408, Arlington, VA 22201
Telephone: (703) 525-4015
Represented by:
James E. Wolf, V. President, Government Affairs

American State of the Art Prosthetic Ass'n
403 1st St., S.E., Washington, DC 20003
Telephone: (202) 544-4441
Background: A consumer-based organization which, with the collaboration of innovative prosthetists and orthotists, seeks to improve the general level of sophistication of artificial limb technology.
Represented by:
George W. Breece, Exec. Director
Peter W. Thomas, Consumer V. President

American Statistical Ass'n
1429 Duke St., Alexandria, VA 22314-3402
Telephone: (703) 684-1221
Background: Advocates the development of statistical methodology, and professional standards in statistics.

ORGANIZATIONS REPRESENTED

Represented by:
Barbara A. Bailar, Exec. Director
Marilyn J. Humm, Director, Scientific and Public Affairs

American Stock Exchange
888 17th St., N.W., Suite 308, Washington, DC 20006
Telephone: (202) 887-6880
Represented by:
Tamara Hirschfeld, Manager, Gov't Relations
Virginia Pape, V. President, Government Relations
Counsel or consultant:
Patton, Boggs and Blow (Stuart M. Pape)

American Subcontractors Ass'n, Inc. Political Action Committee
1004 Duke St., Alexandria, VA 22314
Telephone: (703) 684-3450
Background: Treasurer is E. Colette Nelson of the American Subcontractors Ass'n.

American Subcontractors Ass'n
1004 Duke St., Alexandria, VA 22314
Telephone: (703) 684-3450
Represented by:
E. Colette Nelson, V. President of Government Relations
Marsha Rhea, Director of Communications
Chris S. Stinebert, Exec. V. President

American Sugar Beet Growers Ass'n
1156 15th St., N.W. Suite 1020, Washington, DC 20005
Telephone: (202) 833-2398
Represented by:
Ruthann Geib, Administrative Assistant
Luther Markwart, Exec. Vice President

American Sugar Beet Growers Ass'n Political Action Committee
1156 15th St., N.W. Suite 1020, Washington, DC 20005
Telephone: (202) 833-2398
Background: Represented by Luther Markwart of the American Sugar Beet Growers Ass'n.

American Sugar Cane League of the U.S.A.
Thibodaux, LA
Counsel or consultant:
Wallace & Edwards (Donald L. Wallace, Jr.)

American Supply Ass'n
Chicago, IL
Counsel or consultant:
Kent & O'Connor, Incorp. (J. H. Kent, Patrick C. O'Connor)

American Supply and Machinery Manufacturers' Ass'n
Cleveland, OH
Counsel or consultant:
London and Satagaj, Attorneys-at-Law (Sheldon I. London, John S. Satagaj)

American Surety Ass'n
1029 Vermont Ave., N.W., Suite 800, Washington, DC 20005
Telephone: (202) 737-2696
Counsel or consultant:
Magnotti Enterprises, Inc. (Dr. John F. Magnotti, Jr.)

American Suzuki Motor Corp.
Brea, CA
Counsel or consultant:
Dorsey & Whitney

American Symphony Orchestra League
777 14th St., N.W., Suite 500, Washington, DC 20005
Telephone: (202) 628-0099
Represented by:
Catherine French, Exec. Vice President and CEO
Toby Halliday, Director, Government Affairs

American Task Force for Lebanon
2550 M St., N.W., Suite 305, Washington, DC 20037
Telephone: (202) 223-9333
Background: A membership organization representing Americans of Lebanese ancestry.
Represented by:
Tanya A. Rahall, Exec. Director

American Tax Reduction Movement
2113 National Press Building, Washington, DC 20045
Telephone: (202) 232-7443

Represented by:
Landis Neal, Exec. Director
Counsel or consultant:
William Wewer

American Tennis Federation
1625 K St., N.W., Suite 900, Washington, DC 20006
Telephone: (202) 775-1762
Background: Represented by Jan Kinney of the Sporting Goods Manufacturers Ass'n.

American Textile Machinery Ass'n
7297 Lee Highway, Suite N, Falls Church, VA 22042
Telephone: (703) 533-9251
Counsel or consultant:
Ass'n and Society Management Internat'l Inc. (Harry W. Buzzerd, Jr.)
Collier, Shannon & Scott (William W. Scott)

American Textile Manufacturers Institute
1801 K St., N.W. Suite 900, Washington, DC 20006
Telephone: (202) 862-0500
Represented by:
Deborah E. Anderson, Assistant Director, Public Relations
Victor Bryant, Alex, Government Relations Associate
Douglas W. Bulcao, Deputy Exec. V. President
Robert F. DuPree, Jr., Government Relations Associate
Carlos Moore, Exec. V. President
James A. Morrissey, Director, Communications
O'Jay Niles, Director, Product Services Division
Counsel or consultant:
Ivins, Phillips and Barker (Jay W. Glasmann, Philip D. Morrison)

American Textile Manufacturers Institute Committee for Good Government
1801 K St., N.W. Suite 900, Washington, DC 20006
Telephone: (202) 862-0500
Background: The political action arm of the American Textile Manufacturers Institute. Responsible contact is Douglas W. Bulcao.

American Tie Fabric Ass'n
New York, NY
Counsel or consultant:
Thompson, Hine and Flory (Mark Roy Sandstrom)

American Tort Reform Ass'n
1212 New York Ave., N.W. Suite 515, Washington, DC 20005
Telephone: (202) 682-1163
Represented by:
Martin F. Connor, President
Diane K. Swenson, V. President

American Traffic Safety Services Ass'n
ATSSA Building 5440 Jefferson Davis Highway, Fredericksburg, VA 22401
Telephone: (703) 898-5400
Represented by:
Caroline Carver, Director, Legis. and Gov't Activities
Robert M. Garrett, Exec. Director

American Trans Air
Indianapolis, IN
Counsel or consultant:
Lord Day & Lord, Barrett Smith (Joanne W. Young)

American Trucking Ass'ns
430 First St., S.E., Washington, DC 20003-1826
Telephone: (202) 544-6245

Represented by:
Daniel Barney, Director, Litigation Center
Lana R. Batts, Sr. V. President, Government Affairs
William Busker, Sr. V. President, Law and Finance
Steve Campbell, Director, Safety Department
Joanne Casey, Exec. Director, Intermodal Council
John Collins, V. President
Robert Digges, Jr., Law Department
Thomas J. Donohue, President and CEO
Robert E. Farris, V. President, Policy
Richard L. Few, Senior V. President, Federation Relats.
Mark D. French, Sr. V. President, Development
David F. Gordon, Director, Public Affairs
J. R. Halladay, Counselor to the President
Leslie Wheeler Hortum, V. President, Communications
Allan R. Jones, Manager, Legislative Affairs
Kevin H. Kruke, V. President, Public & Int'l Affairs
Jai Kundu, Exec. Dir., Safety Management Council
John E. Lynn, Sr. Director, Congressional Relations
Gerald J. McKiernan, V. President, Legislative Affairs
Mary Runkel Moehring, Director of State Laws
Dee Reif, Exec. Dir., Sales & Marketing Council
John L. Reith, Dir., Dept. of Economics and Taxation
Joseph L. Rosso, Senior Legislative Representative
Kenneth E. Siegel, Associate General Counsel
Kenneth D. Simonson, V. President
Paul T. Stalknecht, V. President, State Relations
Kenneth F. Stinger, Director, Government Affairs
Larry Strawhorn, Director, Engineering Department
Richard Weston, Senior Writer and Editor, Public Affairs
Cynthia Wicker, Associate General Counsel
David K. Willis, Senior V. Pres., ATA Foundation
Clyde E. Woodle, Exec. Dir., Trucking Research Institute
Counsel or consultant:
Paul, Hastings, Janofsky and Walker (Ralph B. Everett)
Timmons and Co., Inc.

American Tunaboat Ass'n
San Diego, CA
Counsel or consultant:
Davis Wright Tremaine (James P. Walsh)
McAuliffe, Kelly, Raffaelli & Siemens (Frederick W. Hatfield)
Steptoe and Johnson

American Type Culture Collection
12301 Parklawn Drive, Rockville, MD 20852
Telephone: (301) 881-2600
Represented by:
Robert E. Stevenson, Director
Karl C. Thomas, Assoc. Director, Chief Information Off.

American University of Beirut
Beirut, Lebanon
Counsel or consultant:
William L. Hoffman

American University, The
4400 Massachusetts Ave., N.W., Washington, DC 20016
Telephone: (202) 885-1000
Counsel or consultant:
The Kamber Group (Dennis Walston)

American Urological Ass'n
Baltimore, MD
Counsel or consultant:
MARC Associates, Inc. (Randolph B. Fenninger)

American Veterans Committee
1717 Massachusetts Ave., N.W. Suite 203, Washington, DC 20036
Telephone: (202) 667-0090
Background: A membership organization of veterans who share the philosophy, 'Citizens first, veterans second.' Affiliated with the World Veterans Federation.
Represented by:
June A. Willenz, Exec. Director

American Veterans of World War II, Korea and Vietnam (AMVETS)
4647 Forbes Blvd., Lanham, MD 20706
Telephone: (301) 459-9600

The listings in this directory are available as *Mailing Labels*. See last page.

ORGANIZATIONS REPRESENTED

American Veterans of World War II, Korea and Vietnam (AMVETS) (Cont'd)
Represented by:
Warren Eagles, Sr., National Commander
Richard Flanagan, National Public Relations Director
Gregory V. Floberg, National Membership Director
Frank T. Huray, Ass't. Exec. Director, Nat'l Svc. Fdn.
Robert L. Jones, National Exec. Director
Joe F. Ramsey, Jr., Exec. Director, Nat'l Svc. Fdn.
Wesley J. Riker, Deputy National Service Director
Rick Shannon, National Programs Director
Noel C. Woolsey, National Service Director

American Veterinary Medical Ass'n
1023 15th St., N.W., Suite 300, Washington, DC 20005
Telephone: (202) 659-2040
Represented by:
Marcia D. Brody, Legislative Assistant
John B. McCarthy, Senior Program Specialist
Amy L. Pomplin, Political Program Assistant
William Van Dresser, Director, Government Relations Division

American Veterinary Medical Ass'n Political Action Committee
1023 15th St., N.W., Washington, DC 20005
Telephone: (202) 659-2040
Background: Represented by Amy Pomplin of the Association.

American Vocational Ass'n
1410 King St., Alexandria, VA 22314
Telephone: (703) 683-3111
Background: A federation of state vocational education associations.
Represented by:
Charles H. Buzzell, Exec. Director
Gordon A. Raley, Ass't Exec. Dir., Government Relations

American War Mothers
2615 Woodley Place, N.W., Washington, DC 20008
Telephone: (202) 462-2791
Represented by:
Louise Caldwell, Nat'l President

American Warehousemen's Ass'n
Chicago, IL
Counsel or consultant:
Kent & O'Connor, Incorp. (Patrick C. O'Connor)

American Watch Ass'n
1201 Pennsylvania Ave., N.W. P.O. Box 464, Washington, DC 20044
Telephone: (703) 759-3377
Background: A trade association of watch importers.
Represented by:
Emilio G. Collado, III, Exec. Director
Counsel or consultant:
Covington and Burling

American Water Works Ass'n
1010 Vermont Ave., N.W., Suite 810, Washington, DC 20005
Telephone: (202) 628-8303
Represented by:
John H. Sullivan, Deputy Exec. Director

American Waterways Operators
1600 Wilson Blvd. Suite 1000, Arlington, VA 22209
Telephone: (703) 841-9300
Background: The national trade ass'n representing coastal and inland tugboat, towboat and barge operators and shipyards.
Represented by:
Thomas A. Allegretti, V. President, Operations
Jennifer Evans, Assistant to the President
Joseph A. Farrell, III, President
KayLynn Goelzer, Government Relations Associate
Cornel Martin, Director, Shipyard Operations
Jeffrey A. Smith, V. President, Public Affairs
Dena L. Wilson, V. President, Legislative Affairs
Counsel or consultant:
Leva, Hawes, Mason and Martin (Harold E. Mesirow)

American Waterways Operators Political Action Committee
1600 Wilson Blvd., Suite 1000, Arlington, VA 22209
Telephone: (703) 841-9300
Background: Contact is Dena L. Wilson of the American Waterways Operators.

American Wind Energy Ass'n
1730 N. Lynn St., Suite 610, Arlington, VA 22209
Telephone: (703) 276-8334
Represented by:
Earl Kelly, Director, Governmental Affairs
Denise Pado, Operations Manager
Randall S. Swisher, Exec. Director

American Wind Energy Ass'n Wind PAC
1730 N. Lynn St., Suite 610, Arlington, VA 22209
Telephone: (703) 276-8334
Background: Represented by Randall S. Swisher of the American Wind Energy Ass'n.

American Wire Producers Ass'n
1101 Connecticut Ave., N.W., Suite 700, Washington, DC 20036
Telephone: (202) 857-1155
Counsel or consultant:
Davis, Graham and Stubbs
Smith, Bucklin and Associates (Robert T. Chancler)

American Women in Radio and Television
1101 Connecticut Ave., N.W. Suite 700, Washington, DC 20036
Telephone: (202) 429-5102
Counsel or consultant:
Smith, Bucklin and Associates (Susan Kudla Finn)

American Wood Council
1250 Connecticut Ave., N.W., Suite 230, Washington, DC 20036
Telephone: (202) 833-1595
Represented by:
Carl E. Darrow, President

American Wood Preservers Ass'n
P.O. Box 849, Stevensville, MD 21666
Telephone: (301) 643-4163
Counsel or consultant:
J. D. Ferry Associates (John D. Ferry)

American Wood Preservers Bureau
7962 Conell Court, Lorton, VA 22079
Telephone: (703) 339-6660
Represented by:
Eric Yeadon, President

American Wood Preservers Institute
1945 Old Gallows Road Suite 550, Vienna, VA 22182
Telephone: (703) 893-4005
Represented by:
John F. Hall, President
Patricia Hamilton, Director, Communications
Victor E. Lindenheim, V. President, Regulatory Affairs
Sherri G. Zedd, V. President

American Wood Preservers Institute Political Action Committee
1945 Gallows Road, Suite 550, Vienna, VA 22182
Telephone: (703) 893-4005
Background: Contact is John F. Hall of the Institute.

American Youth Work Center, The
1751 N St., N.W., Suite 302, Washington, DC 20036
Telephone: (202) 785-0764
Background: Established in 1984 to advocate youth service programs.
Represented by:
Virginia K. Hines, Deputy Director
William W. Treanor, Exec. Director

Americans Against Union Control of Government
1761 Business Center Drive Suite 230, Vienna, VA 22090
Telephone: (703) 438-3966
Background: Founded in 1973 by Carol Applegate, a Michigan public school teacher. Reports a current membership of 65,000. Operates as a division of the Public Service Research Council. Opposes collective bargaining for public employee unions. Represented by David Y. Denholm of the Public Service Research Council.

Americans for Constitutional Action
955 L'Enfant Plaza North, S.W. Suite 1000, Washington, DC 20024
Telephone: (202) 484-5525
Background: Established in August 1958 as a counter-organization to offset the work of the liberal ADA (Americans for Democratic Action). Works to elect candidates to the House of Representatives and Senate who have allegiance to the original spirit and principles of the Con-

stitution.
Represented by:
Charlene Baker Craycraft, Chairman of the Board
Counsel or consultant:
Cederberg and Associates (Elford A. Cederberg)

Americans for Democratic Action
1511 K St., N.W. Suite 941, Washington, DC 20005
Telephone: (202) 638-6447
Background: An independent political action group concerned with liberal domestic and foreign policies. Established in 1947.
Represented by:
Donita Hicks, Deputy Director
Amy Isaacs, National Director

Americans for Democratic Action Political Action Committee
1511 K St., N.W., Suite 941, Washington, DC 20005
Telephone: (202) 638-6447
Background: Treasurer is Eric Rosenthal of the Human Rights Campaign Fund.

Americans for Energy Independence
1629 K St., N.W., Washington, DC 20006
Telephone: (202) 466-2105
Background: AFEI describes itself as a non-profit, public policy and educational organization concerned with energy policies that enhance economic well-being and national security.
Represented by:
Dr. Elihu Bergman, Exec. Director

Americans for Immigration Control
721 2nd St., N.E., Suite 307, Washington, DC 20002
Telephone: (202) 543-3719
Represented by:
Robert H. Goldsborough, Legislative Director

Americans for Indian Opportunity
3508 Garfield St., N.W., Washington, DC 20007
Telephone: (202) 338-8809
Background: An advocacy organization concerned with the governance and self-sufficiency of American Indian tribes.
Represented by:
LaDonna Harris, President/ Exec. Director

Americans for Nat'l Dividend Act
1620 Eye St., N.W., Suite 202, Washington, DC 20006
Telephone: (202) 452-8811
Counsel or consultant:
Pagonis and Donnelly Group (David Henderson)

Americans for Nuclear Energy
2525 Wilson Blvd., Arlington, VA 22201
Telephone: (703) 528-4430
Background: An independent citizens group which favors the safe utilization of nuclear energy as well as the development of new sources of energy. Supported solely by individual members' contributions.
Represented by:
Douglas O. Lee, Chairman

Americans for the High Frontier
2800 Shirlington Road Suite 405 A, Arlington, VA 22206
Telephone: (703) 671-4111
Background: A lobbying organization promoting legislation in support of the development of space for both military and commercial purposes.
Represented by:
Lt. Gen. Daniel Graham, USA (Ret.), Chairman
Daniel O. Graham, Jr., Exec. Director
Brig. General Robert C. Richardson, USAF (Ret), Vice Chairman
Maj. Gen. J. Milnor Roberts, AUS (Ret.), President

Americans for the Nat'l Voter Initiative Amendment
3115 N St., N.W., Washington, DC 20007
Telephone: (202) 333-4846
Represented by:
Edward A. Dent, Director

Americans for the Supercollider
Dallas, TX
Background: A Dallas-based group promoting the superconducting supercollider to be contructed in Texas.
Counsel or consultant:
Lipsen Whitten & Diamond

ORGANIZATIONS REPRESENTED

Americans United for Separation of Church and State
8120 Fenton St., Silver Spring, MD 20910
Telephone: (301) 589-3707
Background: A non-profit, non-sectarian, non-partisan organization founded in 1947 with the sole purpose of maintaining the Constitutional guarantee of religious freedom in the First Amendment. Opposes the support of church-related schools or other church-related activities with tax money.
Represented by:
Lee Boothby, General Counsel
Joseph L. Conn, Mng. Edit., Church and State Magazine
Rev. Robert L. Maddox, Exec. Director
Kim Yelton, Director, Government Relations

Americans United Research Foundation
900 Silver Spring Ave., Silver Spring, MD 20910
Telephone: (301) 588-2282
Background: Established by Americans United for Separation of Church and State. Represented by Dr. Robert L. Maddox of that organization.
Represented by:
Dr. Charles C. Haynes, Project Director

Americares Foundation
New Canaan, CT
Counsel or consultant:
John Adams Associates

Americas Society
1625 K St., N.W., Suite 1200, Washington, DC 20006
Telephone: (202) 659-1547
Background: Above address also serves as Washington office for the Council of the Americas. Ludlow Flower, Managing Director for the Council, also serves as V. President.

Amerijet Internat'l Inc.
Counsel or consultant:
Hill and Knowlton Public Affairs Worldwide

Amerind Risk Management Corp.
122 C St., N.W., Suite 280, Washington, DC 20001
Telephone: (202) 783-2667
Counsel or consultant:
Reno, Cavanaugh & Hornig (Lee P. Reno)

Ameritech (American Information Technologies)
1050 Connecticut Ave., N.W., Suite 730, Washington, DC 20036
Telephone: (202) 955-3050
Background: Provides communications products and services in the Midwest through its five Bell operating companies. Other subsidiaries provide a variety of telecommunications-related services
Represented by:
Anthony Alessi, Mgr.-Federal Relations (Regulatory)
John J. Connarn, V. President-Federal Relations
Bruce J. Eggers, Dir.-Federal Relations (Congressional)
Peter M. Lincoln, Director-Corporate Communications
Renee M. Martin, Attorney
James K. Smith, Dir.-Federal Relations (Regulatory)
Dorothy A. Walsh, Director-Federal Relations-Congressional
Counsel or consultant:
Bonner & Associates
Jack McDonald Co. (Jack McDonald)
Paul, Hastings, Janofsky and Walker (Ralph B. Everett)

AmeriTrust Co. N.A.
Cleveland, OH
Counsel or consultant:
Jones, Day, Reavis and Pogue (C. Thomas Long)

Amexco
West Germany
Counsel or consultant:
Ballard, Spahr, Andrews and Ingersoll (Frederic L. Ballard, Jr.)

Amgen, Inc.
Thousand Oaks, CA
Counsel or consultant:
Hogan and Hartson (Ann Morgan Vickery)
Howrey and Simon (Cecilia Gonzalez, Paul Plaia, Jr.)
Powell, Adams & Rinehart (Robert A. Neuman)
Reed Smith Shaw & McClay (Mary Buckles, Carol Colborn, Stephan E. Lawton, T. Timothy Ryan, Jr.)
Peter Teeley & Associates (Peter Teeley)

AmHS Institute
1919 Pennsylvania Ave., N.W., Suite 703, Washington, DC 20006
Telephone: (202) 293-2840
Represented by:
James L. Scott, President and CEO
David N. Sundwall, M.D., V. President and Medical Director

Amnesty Internat'l U.S.A.
304 Pennsylvania Ave., S.E., Washington, DC 20003
Telephone: (202) 544-0200
Represented by:
James O'Dea, Director, Washington Office
Counsel or consultant:
The Kamber Group (Mary Roddy Betzler)

Amoco Corp.
1615 M St., N.W., Suite 200, Washington, DC 20036
Telephone: (202) 857-5300
Represented by:
Stephen A. Elbert, Director, Federal Relations
Richard L. Fischer, V. Pres., Gov't Affairs, Washington
Robert G. Slaughter, Sr. Government Affairs Representative
Ralph Stow, Public Affairs Coordinator
Ronald W. Wolsey, Washington Representative
Don J. Zeller, Sr. Government Affairs Representative
Counsel or consultant:
Bonner & Associates
Covington and Burling (John M. Vine)
Hopkins and Sutter (William H. Bradford, Jr.)
Kirkland and Ellis
Murphy and Associates (William T. Murphy, Jr.)
Skadden, Arps, Slate, Meagher and Flom (Mike Naeve)
Timmons and Co., Inc.

Amoco Performance Products, Inc.
Richfield, CT
Counsel or consultant:
Winthrop, Stimson, Putnam & Roberts (Peter F. Gold)

Ampco-Pittsburgh Co.
Pittsburgh, PA
Counsel or consultant:
Manchester Associates, Ltd. (John V. Moller)

AMR Corp.
Dallas-Ft. Worth, TX
Counsel or consultant:
Hill and Knowlton Public Affairs Worldwide (Robert Keith Gray, Gary Hymel)

Amselco Minerals, Inc.
Denver, CO
Counsel or consultant:
Robertson, Monagle and Eastaugh (Steven W. Silver)

AMTRAK (Nat'l Rail Passenger Corp.)
60 Massachusetts Ave., N.E., Washington, DC 20002
Telephone: (202) 383-3000
Background: A quasi-governmental corporation.
Represented by:
David J. Carol, Senior Director, Government Affairs
T. J. Gillespie, Jr., Asst. V. Pres., Gov't & Public Affairs
John L. Jacobsen, Director, Government and Public Affairs
Sue Martin, Senior Director, Public Affairs

Amusement and Music Operators Ass'n
1101 Connecticut Ave., N.W., Suite 700, Washington, DC 20036
Telephone: (202) 857-1100
Counsel or consultant:
Smith, Bucklin and Associates (Robert H. Wilbur)

Amusement and Music Operators Ass'n Political Action Committee
1101 Connecticut Ave., N.W., Suite 700, Washington, DC 20036
Telephone: (202) 857-1100
Counsel or consultant:
Smith, Bucklin and Associates (Robert H. Wilbur)

Amway Corp.
214 Massachusetts Ave., N.E., Suite 210, Washington, DC 20002
Telephone: (202) 547-5005

Represented by:
John C. Gartland, Director, Washington Office
Counsel or consultant:
Arter & Hadden (Bruce Goodman)

An Mau Steel Ltd.
Taipei, Taiwan
Counsel or consultant:
Sharretts, Paley, Carter and Blauvelt (Beatrice A. Brickell)

Anaconda Minerals Co.
Denver, CO
Counsel or consultant:
Steptoe and Johnson

Anadarko Petroleum Corp.
Houston, TX
Counsel or consultant:
Skadden, Arps, Slate, Meagher and Flom (Mike Naeve)
Travis & Gooch (R. Gordon Gooch)

Anaheim, California, City of
Anaheim, CA
Counsel or consultant:
E. Del Smith, Inc. (E. Del Smith)

Anchor Industries, Inc.
Tulsa, OK
Counsel or consultant:
Dutko & Associates (L. L. Hank Hankla)

Anchorage School District
Anchorage, AK
Counsel or consultant:
Robertson, Monagle and Eastaugh (Brad Gilman, Steven W. Silver)

Anden Group, The
1908 Mt. Vernon Ave. P.O. Box 2449, Alexandria, VA 22301
Telephone: (703) 684-6650
Background: Washington office of a Los Angeles-based land development company.
Represented by:
Janet L. Powell, Director, Public Affairs

Andersen and Co., Arthur
1666 K St., N.W., Washington, DC 20006
Telephone: (202) 862-3100
Represented by:
Byrle M. Abbin, Mng. Dir., Office of Federal Tax Svcs.
Rachelle Bernstein, Tax Manager
Fred Brinkman, Area Managing Partner
George N. Carlson, Partner, Office of Federal Tax Services
Bruce F. Davie, Manager, Federal Tax Services
Michael E. Simon, Mng. Partner, Office of Federal Services
Counsel or consultant:
Burson-Marsteller
Griffin, Johnson & Associates
O'Connor & Hannan

Andersen and Co. Political Action Committee, Arthur
1666 K St., N.W., Washington, DC 20006
Telephone: (202) 862-3100
Represented by:
David H. Woodham, Treasurer

Andrew Corporation
Orland Park, IL
Counsel or consultant:
Gardner, Carton and Douglas (J. Curtis Moffat)

ANG Coal Gasification Co.
Bismarck, ND
Counsel or consultant:
W. J. William Harsh (J. William W. Harsch)

Anglo-American Auto Auctions Inc.
Nashville, TN
Counsel or consultant:
Murphy and Demory, Ltd. (Jerry W. Cox)

Anglo-American Clays Corp.
Sandersville, GA
Counsel or consultant:
Sutherland, Asbill and Brennan (Gordon O. Pehrson, Jr.)

ORGANIZATIONS REPRESENTED

Angola, Government of the People's Republic of
Luanda, Angola
Counsel or consultant:
Fenton Communications, Inc. (David Fenton)
Laxalt, Washington, Perito & Dubuc (Robert B. Washington, Jr.)

Anheuser-Busch Cos., Inc.
1776 I St., Suite 200, Washington, DC 20006
Telephone: (202) 293-9494
Represented by:
Wiley C. Harrell, Jr., Director, National Affairs
Richard F. Keating, V. President, Nat'l Affairs
Counsel or consultant:
Harmon and Wilmot (David W. Wilmot)
Howrey and Simon (Terrence C. Sheehy)
Nossaman, Guthner, Knox and Elliott (Murray Zweben)
Bartley M. O'Hara, P.C.
Skadden, Arps, Slate, Meagher and Flom (Robert E. Lighthizer)
Stanton & Associates (James V. Stanton)
Timmons and Co., Inc.
Charls E. Walker Associates

Animal Health Institute
119 Oronoco St., Box 1417-D50, Alexandria, VA 22313-1480
Telephone: (703) 684-0011
Represented by:
Fred H. Holt, President
John W. Thomas, Senior Counsel
Barbara J. Walker, Legislative Counsel
Counsel or consultant:
Covington and Burling (Eugene I. Lambert)
McDermott, Will and Emery (Robert B. Nicholas)
Taggart and Associates, Inc. (William A. Taggart)

Animal Health Institute Political Action Committee
P.O. Box 1417-D50, Alexandria, VA 22313
Telephone: (703) 684-0011
Background: Represented by John W. Thomas of the Animal Health Institute.

Animal Industry Foundation
1701 Fort Myer Drive, Suite 1200, Arlington, VA 22209
Telephone: (703) 524-0810
Background: A national education/research foundation dedicated to developing information on livestock and poultry production for consumer eduction. Steven Kopperud of the American Feed Industry Ass'n serves as Exec. Director.

Animal Legal Defense Fund
San Rafael, CA
Counsel or consultant:
Galvin, Stanley & Hazard

Animas-La Plata Water Conservancy District
Durango, CO
Counsel or consultant:
Kogovsek & Associates, Inc.

Ann Richards for Governor Committee '90
322 Massachusetts Ave., N.E., Washington, DC 20002
Telephone: (202) 546-4204
Background: A Democratic primary candidate in Texas.
Counsel or consultant:
Cynthia Friedman Assoc. Inc. (Cynthia Friedman, Ellen McCabe)

Anodyne, Inc.
San Angelo, TX
Counsel or consultant:
Meyers & Associates (Rick Meyers)

ANR Pipeline, Inc.
Houston, TX
Counsel or consultant:
Lipsen Whitten & Diamond

ANSAC
Westport, CT
Counsel or consultant:
Internat'l Business-Government Counsellors, Inc. (John F. McDermid)

Ansell Inc.
1001 Pennsylvania Ave., N.W. Suite 790 North, Washington, DC 20004
Telephone: (202) 783-2655

Represented by:
John J. Quinn, Senior V. President
Counsel or consultant:
Gardner, Carton and Douglas (J. Curtis Moffat)

Ansell Inc. Political Action Committee
1001 Pennsylvania Ave., N.W. Suite 790 North, Washington, DC 20004
Telephone: (202) 783-2655
Background: Represented by John J. Quinn, Senior V. President, Ansell Inc.

Ansett Transport Industries
Melbourne, Australia
Counsel or consultant:
Squire, Sanders and Dempsey (Robert D. Papkin, Edward W. Sauer)

Anti-Defamation League of B'nai B'rith
1100 Connecticut Ave., N.W., Washington, DC 20036
Telephone: (202) 452-8320
Background: A division of the Jewish service organization focusing on civil rights, individual liberty and U.S. foreign policy, particularly the Middle East. Actively opposes anti-semitism and racism.
Represented by:
Jess N. Hordes, Director, Washington Office
Michael Lieberman, Washington Counsel/Associate Director
Mark Medin, Ass't Director

Anti-Friction Bearing Manufacturers Ass'n
1101 Connecticut Ave., N.W., Suite 700, Washington, DC 20036
Telephone: (202) 429-5155
Counsel or consultant:
Smith, Bucklin and Associates (Michael L. Payne)

Antigua and Barbuda, Government of
St. Johns, Antigua
Counsel or consultant:
Laxalt, Washington, Perito & Dubuc (Robert B. Washington, Jr.)

Antimony Products of America
Chadds Ford, PA
Counsel or consultant:
Mica, Dudinsky & Associates (John Dudinsky, Jr., John L. Mica)

Anzonia Hotel Corp., N.A.
St. Maarten, Netherlands Antilles
Counsel or consultant:
Rogers Internat'l, Inc. (Joe O. Rogers)

AOC Internat'l, Inc.
Taipei, Taiwan
Counsel or consultant:
Willkie Farr and Gallagher (Christopher A. Dunn)

Aon Corp.
Chicago, IL
Counsel or consultant:
Cadwalader, Wickersham & Taft (Donald C. Alexander)

Apartment and Office Building Ass'n of Metropolitan Washington
1413 K St., N.W. Suite 600, Washington, DC 20005
Telephone: (202) 289-1717
Represented by:
Margaret O. Jeffers, Exec. Director
Charles J. Ryan, II, Director of Governmental Affairs
Counsel or consultant:
King and Nordlinger

Apartment Political Committee of the Nat'l Apartment Ass'n
1111 14th St., N.W. Suite 900, Washington, DC 20005
Telephone: (202) 842-4050
Background: Treasurer and contact is Colleen Fisher of the Nat'l Apartment Ass'n.

Apex Ltd.
Hamilton, Bermuda
Counsel or consultant:
Arnold & Porter (Paul S. Berger)

Apex Marine Co.
Lake Success, NY

Counsel or consultant:
Dyer, Ellis, Joseph & Mills (Thomas L. Mills)
Fierce and Associates

Appalachian Regional Commission, States' Washington Representative of
1666 Connecticut Ave., N.W. 7th Floor, Washington, DC 20235
Telephone: (202) 673-7842
Represented by:
Michael R. Wenger, Washington Representative
Counsel or consultant:
Anderson and Pendleton, C.A. (Donald Whitehead)

Apple Bank for Savings
New York, NY
Counsel or consultant:
Thacher, Proffitt and Wood (Louis H. Nevins)

Apple Computer, Inc.
1550 M St., N.W. Suite 1000, Washington, DC 20005
Telephone: (202) 872-6260
Represented by:
Bill Fasig, Manager, Government Affairs
Chuck Jacob, Manager, Government Affairs
James A. R. Johnson, Director of Government Affairs
Bill Poulos, Manager, Government Affairs
Counsel or consultant:
Hill and Knowlton Public Affairs Worldwide (Marci Williams)

Apple & Eve
Roslyn, NY
Counsel or consultant:
Fleishman-Hillard, Inc (W. Douglas Campbell, Paul Johnson)

Apple Processors Ass'n
1629 K St., N.W., Suite 1100, Washington, DC 20006
Telephone: (202) 785-6715
Counsel or consultant:
Agri/Washington (Paul S. Weller, Jr.)

Appleton Papers, Inc.
Appleton, WI
Counsel or consultant:
Sparber and Associates (Peter G. Sparber)

Applied Expertise
2002 North Kenmore St., Arlington, VA 22207
Telephone: (703) 527-8382
Counsel or consultant:
Lachelli, Waller and Associates

Applied Recovery Technologies, Inc.
Fairfax Station, VA
Counsel or consultant:
Hill and Knowlton Public Affairs Worldwide

Appraisal Foundation
1029 Vermont Ave., N.W. Suite 900, Washington, DC 20005
Telephone: (202) 347-7722
Counsel or consultant:
Laxalt, Washington, Perito & Dubuc (Marc J. Scheineson)

ARA Services
Philadelphia, PA
Counsel or consultant:
Camp, Barsh, Bates and Tate (Ronald L. Platt)
Morrison Associates (James W. Morrison, Jr.)
Power & Coleman (Thomas W. Power)

Arab American Institute
918 16th St., N.W., Suite 601, Washington, DC 20006
Telephone: (202) 429-9210
Background: The AAI was founded in 1985 to advance Arab American access to the political parties, participation in electoral politics, and to develop a political strategy with ethnic leaders nationwide to empower Arab Americans and their domestic concerns.
Represented by:
James J. Zogby, Exec. Director

Arab American Leadership Political Action Committee
918 16th St., N.W., Suite 601, Washington, DC 20006
Telephone: (202) 429-9210
Background: Represented by James J. Zogby of the Arab American Institute.

ORGANIZATIONS REPRESENTED

Arab Information Center
1100 17th St., N.W., Suite 602, Washington, DC 20036
Telephone: (202) 265-3210
Represented by:
  Marwan Al-Gharably, Financial/Administrative Officer

Arabian American Oil Co.
1667 K St., N.W., Suite 1200, Washington, DC 20006
Telephone: (202) 223-7750
Represented by:
  Majed Elass, Vice President, U.S. Office
  E. Taylor Kelsch, Senior Planning and Programs Analyst
  Robert L. Norberg, Assistant to the V. President
  James W. Ragland, Economic Analyst

Archdiocese of Washington
Box 29260, Washington, DC 20017
Telephone: (301) 853-3800
Represented by:
  Lillian Queen, Legislative Dir., Office of Soc. Devel.

Archer-Daniels-Midland Co.
Decatur, IL
Counsel or consultant:
  F. Nordy Hoffmann & Assoc. (F. Nordy Hoffmann)
  TADCO Enterprises (Katherine E. Allen)

Archery Manufacturers Organization
1625 K St., N.W., Suite 900, Washington, DC 20006
Telephone: (202) 775-1762
Background: Represented by Jan Kinney of the Sporting Goods Manufacturers Ass'n.

Architectural Woodwork Institute
2310 South Walter Reed Dr., Arlington, VA 22206
Telephone: (703) 671-9100
Represented by:
  H. Keith Judkins, Exec. V. President

ARCO
1333 New Hampshire Ave., N.W. Suite 1001, Washington, DC 20036
Telephone: (202) 457-6200
Represented by:
  Judith L. Baird, Director, Federal Government Relations
  Patricia M. Boinski, Director, Federal Government Relations
  Janet S. Fisher, Director, Federal Government Relations
  James E. Ford, Director, Federal Government Relations
  Dr. Robert Healy, Washington Representative
  E. F. Livaudais, Jr., Manager, Federal Government Relations
  Mary A. Naughton, Office Mgr/TV Conf. Coordinator
  Richard N. Sawaya, Director, Federal Government Tax Affairs
  Ben Schuster, Dir., Fed. Gov't Rels. (ARCO Chemical)
  Deborah A. White, Director, Federal Government Relations
  Albert C. Zapanta, Director, Federal Government Relations
Counsel or consultant:
  John G. Campbell, Inc. (John G. Campbell)
  Hill and Knowlton Public Affairs Worldwide (Hilary Sills)
  Murphy and Associates (William T. Murphy, Jr.)
  Palumbo & Cerrell, Inc. (Benjamin L. Palumbo)
  Sive, Paget & Riesel
  Verner, Liipfert, Bernhard, McPherson and Hand, Chartered (Harry C. McPherson)

ARCO Chemical Co.
1333 New Hampshire Ave., N.W. Suite 1001, Washington, DC 20036
Telephone: (202) 457-6200
Counsel or consultant:
  Palumbo & Cerrell, Inc. (Jeffrey D. Doranz, Benjamin L. Palumbo, Paul A. Skrabut, Jr.)

ARCO Oil & Gas Co.
Dallas, TX
Counsel or consultant:
  Camp, Barsh, Bates and Tate (Harry E. Barsh, Jr.)

Arctic Alaska Fishing Corp.
Seattle, WA
Counsel or consultant:
  Perkins Coie (Guy R. Martin)

Arctic Slope Regional Corp.
Barrow, AK
Background: A largely Eskimo-owned Alaskan land company which has leased oil rights to its lands to some major petroleum producers.

Counsel or consultant:
  Van Ness, Feldman & Curtis (Alan L. Mintz, William J. Van Ness, Jr.)

Arctic Sounder Enterprises, Inc.
Seattle, WA
Counsel or consultant:
  Phyllis D. Carnilla
  Preston Gates Ellis & Rouvelas Meeds (William N. Myhre)

Ares-Serono, Inc.
Boston, MA
Counsel or consultant:
  Fox, Bennett and Turner (Alan R. Bennett, Allan M. Fox)

Argentina, Government of
Buenos Aires, Argentina
Counsel or consultant:
  Sharretts, Paley, Carter and Blauvelt (Beatrice A. Brickell)

Argo Communications Corp.
New Rochelle, NY
Counsel or consultant:
  Sutherland, Asbill and Brennan (Anne P. Jones)

Arizona Power Authority
Phoenix, AZ
Counsel or consultant:
  Wright and Talisman

Arizona, State of
Phoenix, AZ
Counsel or consultant:
  Hartz/Meek Internat'l (Jim Hartz, John Meek)
  Laxalt, Washington, Perito & Dubuc

Arizona State University
Tempe, AZ
Counsel or consultant:
  Cassidy and Associates, Inc. (George A. Ramonas)

Arkansas Best Corp.
Fort Smith, AR
Counsel or consultant:
  Jack L. Williams

Arkansas Electric Cooperative Corp.
Little Rock, AR
Counsel or consultant:
  · Mayer, Brown and Platt (William L. Massey)

Arkansas Power and Light Co.
Blytheville, AR
Counsel or consultant:
  Hunton and Williams
  Reid & Priest

Arkansas Public Service Commission
Little Rock, AR
Background: Law firm of Duncan, Weinberg, Miller & Pembroke represents public service commission before federal agencies and courts.
Counsel or consultant:
  Duncan, Weinberg, Miller & Pembroke, P.C. (Wallace L. Duncan, Janice L. Lower, James D. Pembroke)

Arkansas, State of
Little Rock, AR
Counsel or consultant:
  Dickstein, Shapiro and Morin (Andrew P. Miller, Bernard Nash)

Arkla Exploration Co.
Shreveport, LA
Counsel or consultant:
  Keck, Mahin and Cate (Rebecca Schaffer)

Arkla, Inc.
1150 Connecticut Ave,m N.W. Suite 1125, Washington, DC 20036
Telephone: (202) 331-7175

Represented by:
  James H. Bailey, V. President, Federal Regulatory Affairs
  Nancy U. Etkin, Legislative Affairs Specialist
Counsel or consultant:
  Bassman, Mitchell & Alfano, Chartered
  Bracy Williams & Co.
  Hall, Estill, Hardwick, Gable, Golden & Nelson (John Rudolph)
  Jones, Day, Reavis and Pogue
  Keck, Mahin and Cate
  Vinson and Elkins
  Jack L. Williams

Armco Employees' Political Action Committee
1667 K St., N.W., Suite 650, Washington, DC 20006
Telephone: (202) 223-5370
Background: Washington contact is John L. Bauer, Jr. of Armco, Inc.

Armco Inc.
1667 K St., N.W., Suite 650, Washington, DC 20006
Telephone: (202) 223-5370
Represented by:
  John L. Bauer, Jr., Manager, Legislative Affairs
Counsel or consultant:
  Collier, Shannon & Scott (David A. Hartquist, Thomas F. Shannon)
  Davis & Harman (Thomas A. Davis)
  Dewey, Ballantine, Bushby, Palmer and Wood
  Sutherland, Asbill and Brennan (Edward J. Grenier, Jr., Earle H. O'Donnell, Jan Benes Vlcek)

Armed Forces Communications and Electronics Ass'n Headquarters
4400 Fair Lakes Court, Fairfax, VA 22033
Telephone: (703) 631-6100
Represented by:
  Brig. Gen. Kirby Lamar, USA (Ret.), V. President & Treasurer
  John A. Wickham, Jr., President

Armed Forces Marketing Council
1750 New York Ave., N.W., Suite 340, Washington, DC 20006
Telephone: (202) 783-8228
Represented by:
  George R. Rowan, Jr., Exec. V. President

Armed Forces Relief and Benefit Ass'n
909 N. Washington St., Alexandria, VA 22314
Telephone: (703) 659-5140
Represented by:
  Lt. Gen. Charles C. Blanton, USAF (Ret), President

Armenian Assembly of America
122 C St., N.W., Suite 350, Washington, DC 20001
Telephone: (202) 393-3434
Background: Acts as a conduit of information between the Armenian- American community and the federal government. Through its public affairs, government affairs, grants and student affairs programs, the Assembly seeks to protect the interests and welfare of Armenian-Americans and to encourage greater participation in the nation's democratic process.
Represented by:
  R. Kyle Horst, Director, Refugee Affairs
  Van Z. Krikorian, Government and Legal Affairs Director
  Carole Long, Public Affairs Director
  Ross P. Vartian, Exec. Director

Armenian Assembly of America Political Action Committee
122 C St., N.W., Suite 350, Washington, DC 20001
Telephone: (202) 393-3434
Represented by:
  Adrienne Berenson, Treasurer

Armenian Nat'l Committee of America
1901 Pennsylvania Ave., N.W., Suite 206, Washington, DC 20006
Telephone: (202) 775-1918
Background: Pursues restitution of Armenian political rights and territorial claims from Turkey. Seeks recognition by the international community (including Turkey itself) of the genocidal character of the Turkish massacres of Armenians in 1915. Also concerned about current fate of Armenian people internationally and the rights of people of Armenian origin in the U. S.
Represented by:
  Seto Boyadjian, Exec. Director

ORGANIZATIONS REPRESENTED

Arms Control Ass'n
11 Dupont Circle, N.W., Washington, DC 20036
Telephone: (202) 797-6450
Background: A national membership organization promoting public education on arms control and disarmament. Not a lobbying organization.
Represented by:
  Lee A. Feinstein, Senior Research Analyst
  Spurgeon M. Keeny, Jr., President and Exec. Director
  Jack Mendelsohn, Deputy Director

Arms Control and Foreign Policy Caucus
House Annex 2 Room 501, Washington, DC 20515
Telephone: (202) 226-3440
Background: Establised in 1967. A bi-cameral, bi-partisan body comprising over one-third of the Congress made up of members concerned with U.S. foreign and military policy.
Represented by:
  Margaret Ellis, Exec. Assistant
  Jordan Goldstein, Staff Consultant
  Caleb Rossiter, Staff Consultant
  Edith B. Wilkie, Exec. Director

Armstrong World Industries, Inc.
1025 Connecticut Ave., N.W., Suite 1007, Washington, DC 20036
Telephone: (202) 296-2830
Represented by:
  Camilla L. Collova, Deputy Director, Government Relations
  John N. Jordin, V.P. & Dir., Human Resources/Gov't Affrs
  William B. King, Director, Government Relations
Counsel or consultant:
  Covington and Burling (Robert N. Sayler)
  McGuire, Woods, Battle and Boothe (Robert H. Lamb)
  Spriggs & Hollingsworth (Joe G. Hollingsworth)
  White, Fine, and Verville (Arnold I. Havens)

Army & Air Force Mutual Aid Ass'n
Fort Myer, Bldg. #468, Arlington, VA 22211-3307
Telephone: (703) 522-3060
Background: Provides aid to families of deceased career army officers by immediate payment of a fixed life insurance benefit, assistance with claims for federal compensation and similar matters.
Represented by:
  Bradley J. Snyder, President

Arnold & Porter Political Action Committee
1200 New Hampshire Ave., N.W., Washington, DC 20036
Telephone: (202) 872-6700
Counsel or consultant:
  Arnold & Porter (John M. Quinn)

Aroostook Bank of Micmacs
Presque Isle, ME
Counsel or consultant:
  Hobbs, Straus, Dean and Wilder (Jerry C. Straus)

ARROW (Americans for Restitution, Righting Old Wrongs)
1000 Connecticut Ave., N.W. Suite 401, Washington, DC 20036
Telephone: (202) 296-0685
Background: Founded in 1949, provides needy American Indians crucial health care; direct aid; programs to help prevent AIDS and drug abuse; support of tribal law and justice; pride in American Indian heritage.
Represented by:
  E. Thomas Colosimo, Exec. Director

Arrow Air
Miami, FL
Counsel or consultant:
  Allan W. Markham
  Seamon, Wasko and Ozment (Lawrence D. Wasko)

Art Dealers Ass'n of America
New York, NY
Counsel or consultant:
  Jack Ferguson Associates (Jack Ferguson)

Art PAC
707 8th St., S.E., Suite 200, Washington, DC 20003
Telephone: (202) 546-1821
Background: A political action committee organized to support the arts and the rights of artists before Congress and to aid the elected friends of the arts in Congress.

Represented by:
  Robert Bedard, Treasurer

Art Supply Labeling Coalition
Boston, MA
Background: A coalition of trade associations involved with art and craft materials.
Counsel or consultant:
  Keller and Heckman (Mary Martha McNamara)

Aruba, Government of
Oranjestad, Aruba
Counsel or consultant:
  Arnold & Porter (Claire Reade)
  Internat'l Public Strategies, Inc. (C. Grayson Fowler)
  Keefe Co., The (Clarence L. James, Jr., Robert J. Keefe, Terry M. O'Connell)
  TKC Internat'l, Inc.

ASA Limited
Floral Park, NJ
Counsel or consultant:
  Robert N. Pyle & Associates

Asahi Chemical Industry Co.
Tokyo, Japan
Counsel or consultant:
  Barnes, Richardson and Colburn (James S. O'Kelly)

ASARCO Incorporated
New York, NY
Background: Formerly known as the American Smelting and Refining Co.
Counsel or consultant:
  Hill and Knowlton Public Affairs Worldwide (Tom Hoog)
  Jellinek, Schwartz, Connolly & Freshman, Inc. (Jeffrey H. Schwartz)
  Lee, Toomey & Kent
  James J. Magner & Assoc. Inc. (James J. Magner)
  Webster and Sheffield (L. Andrew Zausner)

Asbestos Claims Facility
Princeton, NJ
Counsel or consultant:
  Burson-Marsteller (Carolyn Tieger)

Asbestos Information Ass'n/North America
1745 Jefferson Davis Hwy. Suite 509, Arlington, VA 22202
Telephone: (703) 979-1150
Represented by:
  B. J. 'Bob' Pigg, President
Counsel or consultant:
  Kirkland and Ellis

ASDC Democratic Victory Fund
430 South Capitol St., S.E., Washington, DC 20003
Telephone: (202) 863-8000
Background: A political action committee affiliated with the Democratic Nat'l Committee.
Represented by:
  Ann Fishman, Treasurer

Asea Brown Boveri, Inc.
1101 15th St., N.W. Suite 500, Washington, DC 20005
Telephone: (202) 429-9180
Represented by:
  C. B. Brinkman, Manager, Washington Nuclear Operations
  Thomas P. Crowley, Director, Internat'l Business Support
  Dr. Fruzsina M. Harsanyi, V. President, Gov't & Internat'l Affairs
  Timothy R. Osborn, Manager, Government Affairs
  Kennan L. Teslik, Manager, Internat'l Government Affairs
Counsel or consultant:
  Pagonis and Donnelly Group (Thomas R. Donnelly, Jr., George G. Pagonis)

ASEAN Federation of Textile Industries
Counsel or consultant:
  Willkie Farr and Gallagher (William H. Barringer)

ASFE
8811 Colesville Rd. Suite G106, Silver Spring, MD 20910
Telephone: (301) 565-2733
Counsel or consultant:
  Bachner Communications, Inc. (John P. Bachner)

Ashland Coal
Huntington, WV

Counsel or consultant:
  Ryan-McGinn (Daniel McGinn)

Ashland Exploration, Inc.
Ashland, KY
Counsel or consultant:
  Baker and Botts (Charles M. Darling, IV, John P. Mathis)

Ashland Oil, Inc.
1025 Connecticut Ave., N.W., Suite 507, Washington, DC 20036
Telephone: (202) 223-8290
Represented by:
  Doris J. Dewton, Assoc. Director, Federal Gov't Relations
  William G. Haddeland, Director, Federal Gov't Relations
  Clifton T. Hilderley, Jr., Assoc. Director, Federal Gov't Relations
  Shannon Russell, Legislative Representative
  Fran Shepardson, Federal Regulatory Representative
  Michael J. Toohey, Senior Washington Representative

Ashton-Tate
Torrence, CA
Counsel or consultant:
  Swidler & Berlin, Chartered (Bruce A. Lehman)

Asia Foundation, The
2301 E St., N.W., Suite 713, Washington, DC 20037
Telephone: (202) 223-5268
Represented by:
  N. Cinnamon Dornsife, Washington Representative

Asia Pacific Space and Communications
1655 North Fort Myer Drive Suite 1120, Arlington, VA 22209
Telephone: (703) 525-2772
Represented by:
  Richard Shay, Internat'l Corporate Affairs
  Jennifer Woods, V. President

Asia Society, The
1785 Massachusetts Ave., N.W., Washington, DC 20036
Telephone: (202) 387-6500
Represented by:
  Judith W. Sloan, Director, Washington Office

Asian American Nat'l Bank
Miami, FL
Counsel or consultant:
  Warren W. Koffler

Asociacion de Bancos de Ahorro Puerto Rico
San Juan, Puerto Rico
Counsel or consultant:
  Kirkpatrick & Lockhart (Garry E. Brown)

Asociacion de Empresas RENFE/Patentes TALGO, S.A.
Madrid, Spain
Counsel or consultant:
  Laxalt, Washington, Perito & Dubuc (Abelardo L. Valdez)

Asociacion Nacional de Fabricantes de Acumuladores, A.C.
Mexico
Counsel or consultant:
  Wilkinson, Barker, Knauer and Quinn

Asociacion Nacional de Industriales (ANDI)
Medellin, Columbia
Counsel or consultant:
  Internat'l Business and Economic Research Corp. (Wally Lenahan)
  Mudge Rose Guthrie Alexander and Ferdon (Michael P. Daniels)

Asociacion Nacional de la Empresa Privada de El Salvador
San Salvador, El Salvador
Counsel or consultant:
  O'Connor & Hannan (Joseph H. Blatchford, Patrick E. O'Donnell)

ASOCOLFLORES (Colombia Flower Growers Ass'n)
Bogota, Colombia
Counsel or consultant:
  APCO Associates (Barry J. Schumacher)
  Arnold & Porter (Patrick F. J. Macrory, Claire Reade)

ORGANIZATIONS REPRESENTED

Aspen Technology, Inc.
Cambridge, MA
Counsel or consultant:
W. J. William Harsh (J. William W. Harsch)

Asphalt Emulsion Manufacturers Ass'n
3 Church Circle, Suite 250, Annapolis, MD 21401
Telephone: (301) 267-0023
Counsel or consultant:
Krissoff & Associates, Inc.

Asphalt Institute
Lexington, KY
Counsel or consultant:
Covington and Burling (Peter Barton Hutt)

Asphalt Recycling and Reclaiming Ass'n
3 Church Circle, Suite 250, Annapolis, MD 21401
Telephone: (301) 267-0023
Counsel or consultant:
Krissoff & Associates, Inc. (Michael Krissoff)

Asphalt Roofing Manufacturers Ass'n
6288 Montrose Road, Rockville, MD 20852
Telephone: (301) 231-9050
Represented by:
Richard D. Snyder, Exec. V. President and General
Manager
Russell K. Snyder, Assistant to the Exec. V. President

ASPIRA Ass'n, Inc.
1112 16th St., N.W., Suite 340, Washington, DC 20036
Telephone: (202) 835-3600
Background: A nonprofit organization dedicated to en-
couraging education and leadership development among
Hispanic youth.
Represented by:
Dr. Janice Petrovich, National Exec. Director

Aspirin Foundation of America, Inc.
1330 Connecticut Ave., N.W., Suite 300, Washington, DC
20036
Telephone: (202) 659-0060
Background: A nonprofit organization made up of companies engaged in the manufacture, preparation, propaga-
tion, compounding or processing of aspirin and aspirin
products. It informs members of scientific developments
relating to aspirin and encourages an understanding of the
potential health benefits of aspirin.
Represented by:
John Kneiss, Exec. Director
Counsel or consultant:
Ketchum Public Relations (Lorraine Thelian)
Paul, Hastings, Janofsky and Walker (R. Bruce Dickson)

Assassination Archive and Research Center
918 F St., N.W., Suite 510, Washington, DC 20004
Telephone: (202) 393-1917
Counsel or consultant:
Fensterwald & Alcorn, P.C. (Bernard Fensterwald, Jr.)

**Assiniboine and Sioux Tribes (Fort Peck Reser-
vation)**
Poplar, MT
Counsel or consultant:
Sonosky, Chambers and Sachse

**Associacao Brasileira dos Exportadores de Ci-
tricos**
Sao Paulo, Brazil
Counsel or consultant:
L. A. Motley and Co. (Langhorne A. Motley)

**Associacao das Industrias de Calcados do Rio
Grande do Sul**
Novo Hamburgo, Brazil
Counsel or consultant:
L. A. Motley and Co. (Claud L. Gingrich, Harry Kopp,
Langhorne A. Motley)
TransNational, Inc. (Peter J. Levine)
Willkie Farr and Gallagher (William H. Barringer)

Associacao Nacional das Industrias de Citricos
Sao Paulo, Brazil
Counsel or consultant:
L. A. Motley and Co. (Claud L. Gingrich, Harry Kopp,
Langhorne A. Motley)

**Associacao Nacional dos Fabricantes de Papel
e Celulose**
Rio de Janeiro, Brazil

Counsel or consultant:
L. A. Motley and Co. (Langhorne A. Motley)

Associated Builders and Contractors
729 15th St., N.W., Washington, DC 20005
Telephone: (202) 637-8800
Represented by:
Daniel J. Bennet, Exec. V. President
Michael Bolen, Assistant Director, Federal Legislation
Marc Freedman, Director, Federal Regulation
Richard T. Haas, V. President, Public Affairs
Marra Harris, Director, Political Affairs
Charles E. Hawkins, III, V. President, Government Af-
fairs
Susan E. Howe, Asst. to the Dir., Federal Legislation
Jenifer Loon, Washington Representative
Jeffrey P. Noah, Director, Government Relations
William B. Spencer, Washington Representative, Govt
Affrs
Counsel or consultant:
Venable, Baetjer, Howard and Civiletti (Maurice Baskin,
Benjamin R. Civiletti)

**Associated Church Press/Evangelical Press
Ass'n**
Grand Rapids, MI
Counsel or consultant:
Liz Robbins Associates (Liz Robbins)

Associated Credit Bureaus, Inc.
1090 Vermont Ave., N.W., Suite 501, Washington, DC
20005
Telephone: (202) 371-0910
Represented by:
Steven I. Fier, Dir., Gov't Relations & Legis. Counsel

Associated Direct Marketing Services
P.O. Box 3296, Falls Church, VA 22043
Telephone: (703) 284-3651
Represented by:
Peter B. Gemma, Jr., President

Associated Electric Cooperative
Springfield, MO
Counsel or consultant:
Gene Taylor Assoc, Inc. (Gene Taylor)

**Associated Electric and Gas Insurance Services,
Ltd.**
Hamilton, Bermuda
Counsel or consultant:
Davis & Harman (Thomas A. Davis, Gail B. Wilkins)

Associated Enterprises, Inc.
Annapolis, MD
Counsel or consultant:
Jere W. Glover

Associated Equipment Distributors
1612 K St., N.W., Suite 1400, Washington, DC 20005
Telephone: (202) 785-5585
Counsel or consultant:
Obadal and O'Leary (Anthony J. Obadal, John T. O'Lea-
ry)

**Associated Equipment Distributors Political Ac-
tion Committee**
1612 K St., N.W., Suite 1400, Washington, DC 20006
Telephone: (202) 785-5585
Counsel or consultant:
Obadal and O'Leary (John T. O'Leary)

Associated Financial Corp.
Los Angeles, CA
Counsel or consultant:
Camp, Barsh, Bates and Tate (Ronald L. Platt)

Associated Gas Distributors
1001 Pennsylvania Ave., N.W., Washington, DC 20004
Telephone: (202) 624-2500
Counsel or consultant:
Crowell and Moring (Dana C. Contratto)

Associated General Contractors of America
1957 E St., N.W., Washington, DC 20006
Telephone: (202) 393-2040

Represented by:
Hubert Beatty, Exec. V. President
Christopher M. Blessington, Ass't. Director, Highway
Division
Sally M. Brain, Director, Construction Economics
Terry M. Chamberlain, Director, Internat'l Construction
Richard Chriss, Dir., Cong. Rels., PACs & Fiscal Affrs.
Brian Deery, Director, Municipal Utilities Division
Christopher Engquist, Director, Manpower Training Divi-
sion
John R. Gentille, Exec. Director, Market Services
Edmund C. Graber, Dir., Cong. Rel./Public Works/Inter-
nat'l
Craig N. Grimm, Asst. Dir., Manpower & Training Svcs.
John Heffner, Assoc. Dir., Manpower & Training Div.
Damian P. Hill, Assistant Director, Highway Division
William A. Isokait, Ass't. Director, Open Shop
Ernest W. Jones, Dir., Construction Education Services
Michael E. Kennedy, Director, Equal Employment Op-
portunity
Joan H. LaVor, Director, Cong'l Relations/PAC Manager
Susan J. Loomis, Exec. Director, Congressional Relations
David R. Lukens, Director, Highway Division
Christopher S. Monek, Director, Building Division
Karen O'Donnell, Director, Taxation & Fiscal Affairs
Frank Schneller, Exec. Dir., Int'l & Construct. Educ. Svc
Heidi H. Stirrup, Dir., Cong'l Rel./Small Business & Proc.
Cynthia D. Witkin, Director, Congressional Relations/La-
bor
Counsel or consultant:
Stuart Binstock
Tim E. More
Sandra M. Solowiej
Cheryl Terio

**Associated General Contractors Political Action
Committee**
1957 E St., N.W., Washington, DC 20006
Telephone: (202) 393-2040
Background: Sponsored by the Associated General Con-
tractors of America. Washington contacts include John
Gentille, Susan J. Loomis and Joan H. LaVor of the spon-
soring organization.

Associated Information Managers
2026-C Opitz Blvd., Woodbridge, VA 22191
Telephone: (703) 490-4246
Background: Founded by the Information Industry Ass'n;
independent since 1981. Dedicated to the integration of
information techniques and content for mid- and top-level
executives and managers. Exec. Director is Dr. Paul Oyer
of SCIA - Smart Card Industry Ass'n.

Associated Landscape Contractors of America
405 North Washington St. Suite 104, Falls Church, VA
22046
Telephone: (703) 241-4004
Represented by:
Debra H. Dennis, Exec. Director
Martha Lindaur, Director, Communications
Counsel or consultant:
Webster, Chamberlain and Bean

Associated Locksmiths of America
Dallas, TX
Counsel or consultant:
Chwat/Weigend Associates (John S. Chwat, Robert E.
Weigend)

Associated Merchandising Corp.
1615 L St., N.W. Suite 700, Washington, DC 20036
Telephone: (202) 682-7098
Represented by:
Julia K. Hughes, Director of Government Relations

Associated Publishers, Inc.
1407 14th St., N.W., Washington, DC 20005-3704
Telephone: (202) 265-1441
Background: Publishes Afro-American history materials.
Represented by:
W. Leanna Miles, Managing Director
Dr. Edgar A. Toppin, President

Associated Specialty Contractors
7315 Wisconsin Ave. Suite 1300W, Bethesda, MD 20814
Telephone: (301) 657-3110
Represented by:
Daniel G. Walter, President
Counsel or consultant:
Ass'n Advocates (Joanne Oxley)

ORGANIZATIONS REPRESENTED

Associated Universities
Upton, NY
Background: Administers national laboratories.
Counsel or consultant:
Jerome A. Ambro Associates (Jerome A. Ambro)

Ass'n for Advanced Life Underwriting
1922 F St., N.W., Washington, DC 20006
Telephone: (202) 331-6081
Background: A trade ass'n of highly qualified life insurance underwriters who wish to present to Congress and government agencies their position on estate and gift taxes, taxation of small business, retirement and employee benefit plans and other subjects related to formation of capital for security.
Represented by:
Mary Dreape Hanagan, Director, Government Affairs
Thomas Korb, Coordinator, Legislative Issues
David Stertzer, Exec. V. President
Counsel or consultant:
Silverstein and Mullens (Gerald H. Sherman)

Ass'n for Childhood Education Internat'l
11141 Georgia Ave., Suite 200, Wheaton, MD 20902
Telephone: (301) 942-2443
Background: A non-profit professional organization devoted to the education and well-being of children from infancy through early adolescence. Members include teachers, teacher educators, school administrators, students of education, parents and librarians. Through publications, conferences and other programs, it seeks to foster the professional growth of members and to inform members and the larger community on issues of concern to children. Affiliate structure includes over 200 local, state, and national branches.
Represented by:
A. Gilson Brown, Executive Director
Mary Louise Burger, President

Ass'n for Community Based Education
1806 Vernon St., N.W., Washington, DC 20009
Telephone: (202) 462-6333
Background: Formerly the Clearinghouse for Community Based Free Standing Educational Institutions. Dedicated to meeting the needs of non-traditional learners, the disadvantaged and minorities.
Represented by:
Christofer P. Zachariadis, Exec. Director

Ass'n for Commuter Transportation
1776 Massachusetts Ave., N.W., Suite 521, Washington, DC 20036
Telephone: (202) 659-0602
Background: Advocates car, van and bus pooling and public transit; and equitable tax treatment for commute-to-work benefits.
Represented by:
Sandra Spence, Exec. Director

Ass'n for Computing Machinery
New York, NY
Background: A Washington contact is John Clement of the American Federation of Information Processing Societies.

Ass'n for Counselor Education and Supervision
5999 Stevenson Ave., Alexandria, VA 22304
Telephone: (703) 823-9800
Background: Represented by William Hunter, Lauren Scheib Reichard Yep of the American Ass'n for Counseling and Development.

Ass'n for Education & Rehabilitation of the Blind & Visually Impaired
206 North Washington St., Suite 320, Alexandria, VA 22314
Telephone: (703) 548-1884
Background: An international organization formed in 1984 as a result of the consolidation of the American Ass'n of Workers for the Blind and the Ass'n for Education of the Visually Handicapped. Primary purpose is to promote quality services for blind children and adults.
Represented by:
Kathleen Megivern, Exec. Director

Ass'n for Educational Communications and Technology
1025 Vermont Ave., N.W. Suite 820, Washington, DC 20005
Telephone: (202) 347-7834
Background: National affiliates include: Community College Ass'n for Instruction and Technology, Federal Education Technology Ass'n, Health Sciences Communications Ass'n., Internat'l Visual Literacy Ass'n, Minorities in Media, Nat'l Ass'n of Regional Media Centers, New England Educational Media Ass'n, State University of New York Educational Communications Center, and the Southeastern Media Leadership Council.
Represented by:
Stanley D. Zenor, Exec. Director

Ass'n for Governmental Leasing and Financing
1101 Connecticut Ave., N.W., Suite 700, Washington, DC 20036
Telephone: (202) 429-5135
Counsel or consultant:
Smith, Bucklin and Associates (David Hobson)

Ass'n for Health Services Research
2100 M St., N.W., Suite 402, Washington, DC 20037
Telephone: (202) 223-2477
Represented by:
Alice S. Hersh, Exec. Director

Ass'n for Hospital Medical Education
1101 Connecticut Ave., N.W. Suite 700, Washington, DC 20036
Telephone: (202) 857-1196
Counsel or consultant:
Smith, Bucklin and Associates (Donna F. Cantor)

Ass'n for Humanistic Education and Development
5999 Stevenson Ave., Alexandria, VA 22304
Telephone: (703) 823-9800
Background: Represented by William Hunter, Lauren Scheib and Richard Yep of the American Ass'n for Counseling and Development.

Ass'n for Information and Image Management
1100 Wayne Ave. Suite 1100, Silver Spring, MD 20910
Telephone: (301) 587-8202
Background: The industry deals with the storage, retrieval, and manipulation of images of documents (business records, engineering drawings, etc.). The ass'n monitors laws and regulations in these disciplines which could affect its members.
Represented by:
James E. Breuer, Director of Communications
Marilyn Courtot, Director, Standard & Technology
Roger K. Sullivan, President
Susan T. Wolk, Exec. Director
Counsel or consultant:
Kidd and Co.

Ass'n for Internat'l Investment
1825 Eye St., N.W., Suite 940, Washington, DC 20006
Telephone: (202) 331-7880
Background: Organized in 1988 to fight legislation that would restrict foreign investment in the U.S. General Counsel is Elliot Richardson of the law firm of Milbank, Tweed, Hadley and McCloy.
Represented by:
Samuel M. Rosenblatt, President
Counsel or consultant:
Milbank, Tweed, Hadley & McCloy (Elliot L. Richardson)

Ass'n for Multicultural Counseling and Development
5999 Stevenson Ave., Alexandria, VA 22304
Telephone: (703) 823-9800
Background: Represented by William Hunter, Lauren Scheib and Richard Yep of the American Ass'n for Counseling and Development.

Ass'n for Persons with Severe Handicaps
1511 King St., Alexandria, VA 22314
Telephone: (703) 683-5586
Represented by:
Celane McWhorter, Director of Government Relations

Ass'n for Public Justice
806 15th St., N.W., Suite 440, Washington, DC 20005
Telephone: (202) 737-2110
Background: A Christian citizens movement that seeks to promote active and responsible citizenship and just public policies both domestically and internationally.
Represented by:
James W. Skillen, Exec. Director

Ass'n for Regulatory Reform
1331 Pennsylvania Ave., N.W., Suite 508, Washington, DC 20004
Telephone: (202) 783-4087
Background: A trade association of about 20 companies which produce manufactured housing. Dedicated to reform of the regulatory framework as it affects the housing and building industries.
Represented by:
Daniel D. Ghorbani, President

Ass'n for Religious and Value Issues in Counseling
5999 Stevenson Ave., Alexandria, VA 22304
Telephone: (703) 823-9800
Background: A division of the American Association for Counseling and Development. A non-profit organization dedicated to the growth and enhancement of the counseling and human development profession. Represented by William Hunter, Lauren Scheib and Richard Yep of the American Ass'n for Counseling and Development.

Ass'n for Research, Administration, Professional Councils and Societies
1900 Association Drive, Reston, VA 22091
Telephone: (703) 476-3430
Background: Affiliated with the American Alliance for Health, Physical Education, Recreation and Dance.
Represented by:
Dr. Raymond Ciszek, Exec. Director

Ass'n for Research on Cancer
777 14th St., N.W., Suite 700, Washington, DC 20005
Telephone: (202) 639-8807
Counsel or consultant:
DSP Internat'l Consultants (Jean Claude Dubost, Pierre Rahal)

Ass'n for Retarded Citizens of the U.S.
1522 K St., N.W. Suite 516, Washington, DC 20005
Telephone: (202) 785-3388
Background: A governmental affairs office of volunteers, parents, educators, and professionals who are devoted to improving the welfare of retarded persons--regardless of race, creed, geographic location or degree of education.
Represented by:
Martha Ford, Assistant Director, Government Affairs
Paul Marchand, Director of Governmental Affairs

Ass'n for Specialists in Group Work
5999 Stevenson Ave., Alexandria, VA 22304
Telephone: (703) 823-9800
Background: Represented by William Hunter, Lauren Scheib and Richard Yep of the American Ass'n for Counseling and Development. ASGW is a division of American Ass'n for Counseling and Development.

Ass'n for Supervision and Curriculum Development
1250 North Pitt Street, Alexandria, VA 22314
Telephone: (703) 549-9110
Represented by:
Dr. Gordon Cawelti, Exec. Director

Ass'n for the Advancement of Health Education
1900 Association Drive, Reston, VA 22091
Telephone: (703) 476-3437
Represented by:
Becky J. Smith, Exec. Director
Counsel or consultant:
Peyser Associates, Inc.

Ass'n for the Advancement of Medical Instrumentation
3330 Washington Blvd. Suite 400, Arlington, VA 22201
Telephone: (703) 525-4890
Represented by:
Michael J. Miller, Exec. Director

Ass'n for the Behavioral Sciences and Medical Education
6728 Old McLean Village Drive, McLean, VA 22101
Telephone: (703) 556-9222
Counsel or consultant:
Degnon Associates, Inc. (George K. Degnon, Carol Ann Kiner)

Ass'n for the Care of Children's Health
3615 Wisconsin Ave., N.W., Washington, DC 20016
Telephone: (202) 244-1801

ORGANIZATIONS REPRESENTED

Represented by:
Beverley Johnson, Exec. Director

Ass'n for the Safe Handling of Medical Waste
Tulsa, OK
Counsel or consultant:
Cassidy and Associates, Inc. (Thomas M. Gannon)

Ass'n for Unmanned Vehicle Systems
1101 14th St., N.W., Washington, DC 20005
Telephone: (202) 371-1170
Counsel or consultant:
Internat'l Management Group, Inc. (John L. Fiegel)

Ass'n for Women in Science
1522 K St., N.W. Suite 820, Washington, DC 20005
Telephone: (202) 408-0742
Background: Works to promote equal opportunity for women and girls to enter scientific professions and achieve their career goals.
Represented by:
Stephanie J. Bird, President
Dr. Torry D. Dickinson, Exec. Director

Ass'n Management Corp.
Rockford, IL
Counsel or consultant:
Hopkins and Sutter (Francis O. McDermott)

Ass'n of Academic Health Centers
1400 16th St., N.W. Suite 410, Washington, DC 20036
Telephone: (202) 265-9600
Background: Organization of American and Canadian Academic Health Centers (university components which bring together schools of medicine, other health profession schools and teaching hospitals).
Represented by:
Roger J. Bulger, President
Marian Osterweis, V. President
Roscoe R. Robinson, Chairman

Ass'n of American Chambers of Commerce in Latin America
1615 H St., N.W., Washington, DC 20062
Telephone: (202) 463-5485
Represented by:
Keith L. Miceli, Exec. V. President

Ass'n of American Colleges
1818 R St., N.W., Washington, DC 20009
Telephone: (202) 387-3760
Background: Promotes liberal learning in the undergraduate curriculum.
Represented by:
Dr. John W. Chandler, President
Dr. Sherry Levy-Reiner, Director, Public Info & Publications

Ass'n of American Geographers
1710 16th St., N.W., Washington, DC 20009
Telephone: (202) 234-1450
Represented by:
Ronald F. Abler, Exec. Director

Ass'n of American Law Schools
1201 Connecticut Ave., N.W. Suite 800, Washington, DC 20036
Telephone: (202) 296-8851
Represented by:
Betsy Levin, Exec. Director
Carl C. Monk, Deputy Director

Ass'n of American Medical Colleges
One Dupont Circle, N.W., Suite 200, Washington, DC 20036
Telephone: (202) 828-0400
Background: Composed of 127 medical schools, 436 teaching hospitals, 82 academic societies and the Organization of Student Representatives. Works with medical schools in developing national policies and goals in medical education, biomedical research and patient care.
Represented by:
James D. Bentley, V. Pres., Division of Clinical Services
Joseph A. Keyes, Jr., General Counsel
Dr. Richard M. Knapp, Senior V. President
Elizabeth M. Martin, V. President, Communications
Joan Hartman Moore, Director, Public Relations
Dr. Robert G. Petersdorf, President
Dr. John F. Sherman, Exec. V. President
Dr. Edward J. Stemmler, Exec. V. President

Ass'n of American Publishers
1718 Connecticut Ave., N.W. Suite 700, Washington, DC 20009-1148
Telephone: (202) 232-3335
Represented by:
Virginia Antos, Assistant Director, Copyright
Diane Rennert, Congressional Liaison
Carol A. Risher, Director of Copyright and New Technology
Nicholas A. Veliotes, President
Counsel or consultant:
Cohn and Marks
McClure and Trotter

Ass'n of American Publishers Political Action Committee
1718 Connecticut Ave., N.W., Washington, DC 20009
Telephone: (202) 232-3335
Background: Contact is Diane Rennert of the Ass'n of American Publishers.

Ass'n of American Railroads
50 F Street, N.W., Washington, DC 20001
Telephone: (202) 639-2100
Represented by:
Robert W. Blanchette, Special Counsel
Harvey H. Bradley, V. President, Operations and Maintenance
Richard E. Briggs, Exec. V. President
Joseph L. Carter, Jr., V. President - Legislative
William H. Dempsey, President and Chief Exec. Officer
Hollis G. Duensing, General Solicitor
William G. Handfield, Assistant V. President
Charles L. Keller, Director, Bureau of Explosives
L. Lee Lane, Exec. Dir., Intermodal Policy Division
Katherine E. Martin, Asst. to V. President, Legislative Dept.
John B. Norton, General Attorney
Paul C. Oakley, Exec. Director, State Rail Programs
Hubert K. O'Bannon, Jr., Assistant V. President - Legislation
Carol B. Perkins, Director, Media Services
J. M. Schercinger, Manager, Rail-Highway Programs
Lisa J. Sobota, Legislative Assistant
Thomas J. Tidd, V. Pres. and General Counsel, Law Dept.
George H. Way, V. Pres., Research and Test Dept.
John F. Wetzel, Assistant to the V. President
Frank N. Wilner, Ass't V. Pres., Information & Publ. Aff.
Nancy L. Wilson, Asst. V. President, Government Relations
Counsel or consultant:
Joseph S. Miller
Morgan, Lewis and Bockius
Fred B. Rooney
Taggart and Associates, Inc. (William A. Taggart)
White, Fine, and Verville (Arnold I. Havens)
Wunder, Ryan, Cannon & Thelen (Thomas M. Ryan)

Ass'n of American Universities
One Dupont Circle, N.W. Suite 730, Washington, DC 20036
Telephone: (202) 466-5030
Represented by:
Robert M. Rosenzweig, President
Peter Smith, Director of Public Affairs

Ass'n of American Veterinary Medical Colleges
1023 15th St., N.W., 3rd Floor, Washington, DC 20005
Telephone: (202) 371-9195
Background: A member organization of the Coalition for Health Funding in Washington. Represents the interests of departments of veterinary science and colleges of veterinary medicine.
Represented by:
Dr. Billy E. Hooper, Exec. Director

Ass'n of Bank Holding Companies
730 15th St., N.W., Suite 820, Washington, DC 20005
Telephone: (202) 393-1158
Represented by:
Thomas L. Ashley, President
John F. Betar, Legislative Counsel
John S. Rippey, Senior V. President & Legis. Director
Richard M. Whiting, General Counsel and Secretary
Counsel or consultant:
Bonner & Associates
Powell, Goldstein, Frazer and Murphy

Ass'n of Big Eight Universities
Box 9513, Arlington, VA 22209
Telephone: (202) 479-0651
Represented by:
Owen Cylke, President

Ass'n of Biotechnology Companies
1120 Vermont Ave., N.W., Suite 601, Washington, DC 20005
Telephone: (202) 842-2229
Represented by:
Pamela Bridgen, Exec. Director
Frank J. Lessen, Director, Legislative Affairs & Press
Counsel or consultant:
Mackler and Gibbs

Ass'n of Bituminous Contractors
2020 K St., N.W., Washington, DC 20036
Telephone: (202) 296-5680
Counsel or consultant:
Loomis, Owen, Fellman and Howe (William H. Howe)

Ass'n of Black Psychologists
Box 55999, Washington, DC 20040
Telephone: (202) 722-0808
Background: Established in 1968, an organization of Black professionals and students in psychology working to improve the psychological health of Black people.
Represented by:
Dr. Ruth E.G. King, Nat'l Office Administrator
Suzanne Randolph, President

Ass'n of British Insurers
London, England
Counsel or consultant:
Lord Day & Lord, Barrett Smith (Brenda Viehe-Naess)

Ass'n of Chocolate, Biscuit and Confectionery Industries of the EEC
Brussels, Belgium
Counsel or consultant:
Max N. Berry Law Offices (Max N. Berry)

Ass'n of Collegiate Schools of Architecture
1735 New York Ave., N.W. Seventh Floor, Washington, DC 20006
Telephone: (202) 785-2324
Represented by:
Richard E. McCommons, Exec. Director

Ass'n of Community Cancer Centers
11600 Nebel St., Suite 201, Rockville, MD 20852
Telephone: (301) 984-9496
Represented by:
Lee E. Mortenson, Exec. Director

Ass'n of Community College Trustees
1740 N St., N.W., Washington, DC 20036
Telephone: (202) 347-1740
Represented by:
David Viar, Exec. Director

Ass'n of Engineering Geologists
Sudbury, MA
Counsel or consultant:
E. G. Newton & Assoc. (Elisabeth G. Newton)

Ass'n of Family Farmers
Little Rock, AR
Counsel or consultant:
Williams and Jensen, P.C. (Robert E. Glennon, Jr.)

Ass'n of Farmworker Opportunity Programs
408 7th St., S.E., Washington, DC 20003
Telephone: (202) 543-3443
Background: A national federation of 37 non-profit organizations and state agencies using federal dollars (under title 14, section 402 of the JTPA Act of 1982) to provide training leading to full-time employment for eligible migrant and seasonal farmworkers in 47 states and Puerto Rico. Founded in 1971.
Represented by:
I. Regina Borkoski, Administrative Secretary
Lynda D. Mull, Exec. Director
Benet Wilson, Publication Manager

Ass'n of Federal Investigators
3299 K St., N.W. 7th Floor, Washington, DC 20007
Telephone: (202) 337-5234
Background: Members are active employees of the federal government with investigation and law enforcement functions.

ORGANIZATIONS REPRESENTED

Ass'n of Federal Investigators (Cont'd)
Represented by:
Leigh Stewart, Exec. Director

Ass'n of Flight Attendants
1625 Massachusetts Ave., N.W. 3rd Floor, Washington,
DC 20036
Telephone: (202) 328-5400
Represented by:
Jo Ellen Deutsch, Manager, Government Affairs
Matthew H. Finucane, Director, Air Safety
Susan Bianchi Sand, President
Ann Tonjes, Director, Special Projects
Counsel or consultant:
Gallagher-Widmeyer Group Inc., The (Mary Jane Gallagher)
Marlowe and Co.

Ass'n of Flight Attendants Political Action Committee/Flight PAC
1625 Massachusetts Ave., N.W., Washington, DC 20036
Telephone: (202) 328-5400

Ass'n of Floral Importers of Florida
Miami, FL
Counsel or consultant:
Arnold & Porter

Ass'n of Food Industries, Inc.
New York, NY
Counsel or consultant:
Harris & Ellsworth (Herbert E. Harris, II)

Ass'n of Foreign Investors in U.S. Real Estate
2300 M St., N.W., Washington, DC 20037
Telephone: (202) 887-0937
Background: Organized in 1987 under the leadership of former U.S. Ambassador to the European Community, J. William Middendorf. Aim is 'to establish a dialogue between foreign investors and (U.S.) government officials on interests of mutual importance.' Founding members include Fuji Bank and Mitsubishi Trust of Japan, Banque Indo-Suez of France and Philips Pension Fund of The Netherlands.
Represented by:
James P. Low, Exec. V. President and CEO

Ass'n of Former Intelligence Officers
6723 Whittier Ave. Suite 303A, McLean, VA 22101
Telephone: (703) 790-0320
Represented by:
David D. Whipple, Exec. Director

Ass'n of Former Members of Congress
1755 Massachusetts Ave., N.W., Suite 412, Washington,
DC 20036
Telephone: (202) 332-3532
Represented by:
Jed Johnson, Jr., Exec. Director

Ass'n of Freestanding Radiation Oncology Centers
San Diego, CA
Counsel or consultant:
McDermott, Will and Emery

Ass'n of Global Real Estate Executives (AGREE)
1620 Eye St., N.W., Suite 350, Washington, DC 20006
Telephone: (703) 284-2324
Background: Membership consists of real estate professionals involved in international real estate matters.
Counsel or consultant:
Arent, Fox, Kintner, Plotkin & Kahn (Gil Thurm)

Ass'n of Governing Boards of Universities and Colleges
One Dupont Circle, N.W. Suite 400, Washington, DC 20036
Telephone: (202) 296-8400
Represented by:
Robert L. Gale, President

Ass'n of Government Accountants
601 Wythe St., Suite 204, Alexandria, VA 22314
Telephone: (703) 684-6931
Represented by:
Mary Jane Kolar, CAE, Exec. Director
Counsel or consultant:
Curtis, Mallet-Prevost, Colt & Mosle

Ass'n of Government Guaranteed Lenders Political Action Committee
1666 K St., N.W., Suite 901, Washington, DC 20006
Telephone: (202) 331-1112
Background: The political action arm of the Regional Ass'n of Small Business Lending.
Represented by:
David J. Gladstone, President

Ass'n of High Medicare Hospitals
1015 18th St., N.W., Suite 900, Washington, DC 20026
Telephone: (202) 785-9670
Represented by:
Bartlett S. Fleming, President
Counsel or consultant:
Pagonis and Donnelly Group (Thomas R. Donnelly, Jr.)

Ass'n of Home Appliance Manufacturers
200 Dangerfield Road, Alexandria, VA 22314
Telephone: (703) 683-8822
Represented by:
Robert M. Gants, Vice President, Government Relations

Ass'n of Home Appliance Manufacturers Political Action Committee
200 Dangerfield Road, Alexandria, VA 22314
Telephone: (703) 683-8822
Background: Responsible contact is Robert M. Gants of the Ass'n of Home Appliance Manufacturers.

Ass'n of Independent Colleges and Schools
One Dupont Circle, N.W., Suite 350, Washington, DC 20036
Telephone: (202) 659-2460
Represented by:
Dr. James Foran, V. President, Educational Affairs
Coleman Furr, Chairman of the Board
D. Lynn Harloe, Government Relations Representative
James M. Phillips, Exec. Director, Accrediting Commission
John G. Pucciano, President
Counsel or consultant:
Clohan & Dean (William C. Clohan, Jr.)

Ass'n of Independent Colleges and Schools Political Action Committee
One Dupont Circle, N.W. Suite 350, Washington, DC 20036
Telephone: (202) 659-2460
Background: D. Lynn Harloe, of the ass'n, serves as contact.
Counsel or consultant:
Clohan & Dean

Ass'n of Independent Corrugated Converters
801 N. Fairfax St., Alexandria, VA 22314
Telephone: (703) 836-2422
Represented by:
J. Richard Troll, Exec. V. President

Ass'n of Independent Television Stations
1200 18th St., N.W. Suite 502, Washington, DC 20036
Telephone: (202) 887-1970
Represented by:
David L. Donovan, V. President, Legal & Legislat. Affairs
James B. Hedlund, President
James Popham, V. President, General Counsel
Counsel or consultant:
McNair Law Firm, P.A. (Michael S. Gelacek)
Reed Smith Shaw & McClay

Ass'n of Independent Television Stations Political Action Committee
1200 18th St., N.W. Suite 502, Washington, DC 20036
Telephone: (202) 887-1970
Background: Responsible contact is James Hedlund. (See Ass'n of Independent Television Stations.)

Ass'n of Jesuit Colleges and Universities
1424 16th St., N.W., Suite 504, Washington, DC 20036
Telephone: (202) 667-3889
Represented by:
Rev. Paul S. Tipton, S.J., President

Ass'n of Junior Leagues, Internat'l
1319 F St., N.W., Suite 604, Washington, DC 20004
Telephone: (202) 393-3364
Represented by:
Anne Dalton, Dir. of Commun. Research & Policy Group
Karen M. Hendricks, Director of Government Affairs
Suzanne Plihcik, President

Ass'n of Labor-Management Administrators and Consultants on Alcoholism
4601 N. Fairfax Drive Suite 1001, Arlington, VA 22203
Telephone: (703) 522-6272
Represented by:
Thomas J. Delaney, Exec. Director
Rudy Yandrick, Communications Director

Ass'n of Local Air Pollution Control Officials
444 North Capitol St., N.W. Suite 306, Washington, DC 20001
Telephone: (202) 624-7864
Background: Represented by S. William Becker of the State and Territorial Air Pollution Program Administrators.

Ass'n of Local Housing Finance Agencies
1101 Connecticut Ave., N.W., Suite 700, Washington, DC 20036
Telephone: (202) 857-1197
Counsel or consultant:
Brownstein Zeidman and Schomer
Smith, Bucklin and Associates (John C. Murphy)

Ass'n of Major City Building Officials
481 Carlisle Drive, Herndon, VA 22070
Telephone: (703) 437-0100
Background: Building officials of 31 major cities in the U.S. Represented by Marla McIntyre of the Nat'l Conference of States on Building Codes and Standards.

Ass'n of Maximum Service Telecasters, Inc.
1400 16th St., N.W. Suite 610, Washington, DC 20036
Telephone: (202) 462-4351
Represented by:
Gregory L. DePriest, V. President
Margita E. White, President
Counsel or consultant:
Covington and Burling (Jonathan D. Blake)

Ass'n of Metropolitan Sewerage Agencies
1000 Connecticut Ave., N.W. Suite 1006, Washington, DC 20036
Telephone: (202) 833-2672
Represented by:
Paula Dannenfeldt, Legislative & Public Affairs Director
Ken Kirk, Exec. Director
Counsel or consultant:
White, Fine, and Verville (Lee C. White)

Ass'n of Metropolitan Water Agencies
1717 K St., N.W. Suite 1006, Washington, DC 20036
Telephone: (202) 331-2820
Represented by:
Diane van DeHei, Exec. Director
Counsel or consultant:
White, Fine, and Verville (Robert J. Saner, II)

Ass'n of Military Colleges and Schools of the U.S.
9115 McNair Drive, Alexandria, VA 22309
Telephone: (703) 360-1678
Represented by:
Lt. Gen. Willard W. Scott, Jr. (Ret.), Exec. Director

Ass'n of Military Surgeons of the U.S.
9320 Old Georgetown Rd., Bethesda, MD 20814
Telephone: (301) 897-8800
Represented by:
Lt. General Max B. Bralliar, USAF (Ret), Exec. Director

Ass'n of Minority Health Professions Schools
511 Capitol Court, N.E. Suite 300, Washington, DC 20002
Telephone: (202) 544-7499
Background: Comprised of eight minority health professions schools in the U.S. whose mission is to help career development of health care professionals who come from disadvantaged backgrounds.
Counsel or consultant:
Health and Medicine Counsel of Washington (Dale P. Dirks)

Ass'n of Nat'l Advertisers
1725 K St., N.W., Suite 601, Washington, DC 20006
Telephone: (202) 785-1525
Represented by:
McNair Bishop, Legislative Analyst
DeWitt F. Helm, Jr., President
Daniel L. Jaffe, Exec. V. President
Counsel or consultant:
Davidson Colling Group, Inc., The (James H. Davidson)

The listings in this directory are available as *Mailing Labels*. See last page.

ORGANIZATIONS REPRESENTED

Ass'n of Navajo Community Controlled School Boards
Window Rock, AR
Counsel or consultant:
Hobbs, Straus, Dean and Wilder (S. Bobo Dean)

Ass'n of Naval Aviation
5205 Leesburg Pike, Suite 200, Falls Church, VA 22041
Telephone: (703) 998-7733
Represented by:
Rear Adm. C. A. Hill, USN (Ret.), V. President for Government Affairs
Frederick J. Orrick, Executive Director

Ass'n of O & C Counties
Roseburg, OR
Counsel or consultant:
Stoel, Rives, Boley, Jones & Grey

Ass'n of Official Analytical Chemists
2200 Wilson Blvd. Suite 400, Arlington, VA 22201-3301
Telephone: (703) 522-3032
Represented by:
Rita Bahner, Assistant Exec. Director
Ronald R. Christensen, Exec. Director

Ass'n of Oil Pipe Lines
1725 K St., N.W., Washington, DC 20006
Telephone: (202) 331-8228
Represented by:
Carole L. Beeman, Secretary and Director of Research
Patrick H. Corcoran, Exec. Director
Lynne E. Schoenbeck, Administrative Assistant
Counsel or consultant:
Dutko & Associates (Emily Young)

Ass'n of Old Crows
1000 North Payne St., Alexandria, VA 22314
Telephone: (703) 549-1600
Background: An association promoting electronic defense.
Represented by:
Gus Slayton, Exec. Director

Ass'n of Outplacement Consulting Firms
Parsippany, NJ
Counsel or consultant:
Delaney and Associates, Edward N. (Edward N. Delaney)

Ass'n of Part-Time Professionals
7700 Leesburg Pike, Suite 216, Falls Church, VA 22043-2615
Telephone: (703) 734-7975
Represented by:
Maria Laqueur, Exec. Director

Ass'n of Physical Fitness Centers
600 Jefferson St., Suite 202, Rockville, MD 20852
Telephone: (301) 424-7744
Represented by:
Dr. Jimmy D. Johnson, President

Ass'n of Physical Plant Administrators of Universities and Colleges
1446 Duke St., Alexandria, VA 22314
Telephone: (703) 684-1446
Represented by:
Colleen Conner, Exec. Secretary
Wayne E. Leroy, Associate V. President
Walter A. Schaw, Exec. V. President

Ass'n of Physician Assistant Programs
950 N. Washington St., Alexandria, VA 22314
Telephone: (703) 836-2272
Background: A member organization of the Coalition for Health Funding in Washington.
Represented by:
Mr. Lynn May, Exec. Director

Ass'n of Practicing CPAs
7910 Woodmont Ave., Suite 1208, Bethesda, MD 20814-3015
Telephone: (301) 913-0010
Counsel or consultant:
C. M. Brownstein & Assoc. (Clifford M. Brownstein)

Ass'n of Private Pension and Welfare Plans
1212 New York Ave., N.W. 12th Floor, Washington, DC 20005
Telephone: (202) 737-6666

Represented by:
Ellen Goldstein, Director, Health & Public Affairs
James A. Klein, Deputy Exec. Director
Wendy Schick, Legislative Assistant
Howard C. Weizmann, Exec. Director
Counsel or consultant:
Steptoe and Johnson (Melanie Franco Nussdorf, Theodore E. Rhodes)

Ass'n of Private Pension and Welfare Plans Political Action Committee
1212 New York Ave., N.W., 12th Floor, Washington, DC 20005
Telephone: (202) 737-6666
Background: Treasurer and principal contact is Howard Weizmann of the Ass'n of Private Pension and Welfare Plans.

Ass'n of Professional Flight Attendants
Arlington, VA
Background: The union of American Airlines flight attendants.
Counsel or consultant:
Arent, Fox, Kintner, Plotkin & Kahn (David J. Aronofsky, Michael D. Barnes, John C. Culver)
Patton, Boggs and Blow (Thomas Hale Boggs, Jr.)

Ass'n of Professors of Gynecology and Obstetrics
409 12th St., S.W., Washington, DC 20024
Telephone: (202) 863-2545
Represented by:
Donna D. Wachter, Exec. Director

Ass'n of Professors of Medicine
1101 Connecticut Ave., N.W., Suite 700, Washington, DC 20036
Telephone: (202) 857-1158
Counsel or consultant:
Smith, Bucklin and Associates (James Terwilliger)

Ass'n of Progressive Rental Organizations
Austin, TX
Counsel or consultant:
Dutko & Associates

Ass'n of Publicly Traded Companies
1707 L St., N.W., Suite 950, Washington, DC 20036
Telephone: (202) 785-9200
Background: Formerly (until May 1, 1990) Nat'l Ass'n of OTC Companies. Members are companies that trade their stock on the NASDAQ market system.
Represented by:
Douglas L. Crow, V. President
Lloyd J. Derrickson, Legal Counsel
John F. Guion, President

Ass'n of Reproduction Materials Manufacturers
901 North Washington St., Alexandria, VA 22314
Telephone: (703) 548-7500
Represented by:
Philip P. Nowers, Exec. Director

Ass'n of Research Libraries
1527 New Hampshire Ave., N.W., Washington, DC 20036
Telephone: (202) 232-2466
Represented by:
Prudence Adler, Federal Relations Officer
Counsel or consultant:
Squire, Sanders and Dempsey (Ritchie T. Thomas)

Ass'n of Reserve City Bankers
1710 Rhode Island Ave., N.W. Suite 500, Washington, DC 20036
Telephone: (202) 296-5709
Represented by:
Dr. Anthony Cluff, Exec. Director

Ass'n of School Business Officials Internat'l
11401 North Shore Drive, Reston, VA 22090
Telephone: (703) 478-0405
Represented by:
Don I. Tharpe, Exec. Director
Counsel or consultant:
Webster, Chamberlain and Bean

Ass'n of Schools and Agencies for the Handicapped
Robbinsville, NJ

Counsel or consultant:
Montgomery, McCracken, Walker & Rhoads (David F. Norcross)

Ass'n of Schools and Colleges of Optometry
6110 Executive Blvd., Suite 514, Rockville, MD 20852
Telephone: (301) 231-5944
Background: A member organization of the Federation of Associations of Schools of Health Professions in Washington.
Represented by:
Robert J. Boerner, Exec. Director

Ass'n of Schools of Public Health
Suite 404, 1015 15th St., N.W., Washington, DC 20005
Telephone: (202) 842-4668
Background: A member organization representing the 24 accredited schools of Public Health in the U.S. and Puerto Rico. It's mission is to serve the collective needs of the Schools of Public Health as they pursue the education and training of public health professionals.
Represented by:
Michael Gemmell, Exec. Director
Counsel or consultant:
Reed Smith Shaw & McClay (Stephan E. Lawton)

Ass'n of Science-Technology Centers
1413 K St., N.W. 10th Floor, Washington, DC 20005
Telephone: (202) 371-1171
Represented by:
Ellen Griffee, Government Relations Director
Bonnie VanDorn, Exec. Director

Ass'n of Small Business Development Centers
1050 17th St., N.W., Suite 810, Washngton, DC 20036
Telephone: (202) 887-5599
Counsel or consultant:
Neece, Cator and Associates (Allen Neece, Jr.)

Ass'n of Small Research, Engineering and Technical Services Companies
450 Maple Ave., East Suite 204, Vienna, VA 22180
Telephone: (703) 255-5011
Represented by:
Rose R. Downes, Exec. Administrator

Ass'n of Specialists in Cleaning and Restoration (ASCR Internat'l)
10830 Annapolis Junction Road, Suite 312, Annapolis Jct., MD 20701
Telephone: (301) 604-4411
Background: Member institutes are Nat'l Institute of Fire Restoration, Carpet and Upholstery Cleaning Institute, Nat'l Institute of Rug Cleaning and Drapery Specialists Institute.
Represented by:
C. Martin Berry, Exec. V. President

Ass'n of State and Interstate Water Pollution Control Administrators
444 North Capitol St., N.W. Suite 330, Washington, DC 20001
Telephone: (202) 624-7782
Represented by:
Robbi J. Savage, Exec. Director/Secretary Treasurer

Ass'n of State and Territorial Health Officials
6728 Old McLean Village Drive, McLean, VA 22101
Telephone: (703) 556-9222
Counsel or consultant:
Degnon Associates, Inc. (George K. Degnon, Valerie White)

Ass'n of State and Territorial Solid Waste Management Officials
444 North Capitol St., N.W., Suite 388, Washington, DC 20001
Telephone: (202) 624-5828
Represented by:
Thomas Kennedy, Exec. Director

Ass'n of Systematics Collections
730 11th St., N.W., 2nd Floor, Washington, DC 20001
Telephone: (202) 347-2850
Represented by:
K. Elaine Hoagland, Exec. Director

Ass'n of Teacher Educators
1900 Association Drive, Reston, VA 22091
Telephone: (703) 620-3110

ORGANIZATIONS REPRESENTED

Ass'n of Teacher Educators (Cont'd)
Represented by:
Dr. Robert J. Stevenson, Exec. Director

Ass'n of Telemessaging Services Internat'l
1150 South Washington St. Suite 150, Alexandria, VA 22314
Telephone: (703) 684-0016
Represented by:
Mark J. Golden, V. President
Joseph N. Laseau, Exec. V. President

Ass'n of Telemessaging Services Internat'l Political Action Committee
1150 South Washington St. Suite 150, Alexandria, VA 22314
Telephone: (703) 684-0016
Background: Represented by Joseph N. Laseau of the Ass'n of Telemessaging Services Internat'l.

Ass'n of the United States Army
2425 Wilson Blvd., Arlington, VA 22201
Telephone: (703) 841-4300
Represented by:
General Jack N. Merritt, USA (Ret), Exec. V. President
Counsel or consultant:
Leva, Hawes, Mason and Martin (Arthur K. Mason, Raymond J. Sherbill)

Ass'n of the Wall and Ceiling Industries-Internat'l
1600 Cameron St., Alexandria, VA 22314
Telephone: (703) 684-2924
Background: Formed by a consolidation, in July, 1976, of the Gypsum Drywall Contracters Internat'l and the Internat'l Ass'n of Wall and Ceiling Contractors. Current name assumed July 1979.
Represented by:
Joe M. Baker, Jr., Exec. V. President
Janet Oppenheim McMullen, Exec. Dir., Asbestos Abatement Council
Counsel or consultant:
Public Affairs Group, Inc. (Edie Fraser)

Ass'n of Theological Schools in the United States and Canada, The
Vandalia, OH
Counsel or consultant:
White, Fine, and Verville (Richard A. Fulton)

Ass'n of Thrift Holding Companies
888 17th St., N.W., Suite 312, Washington, DC 20006
Telephone: (202) 223-6575
Background: Founded in 1985. 40 member organizations are thrift holding companies and savings and loan associations that plan to become thrift holding companies, i.e. firms that control at least 25% of the stock of a savings and loan association. A lobbying group that serves as liaison between members and the banking committees of the House and Senate, the Federal Deposit Insurance Corp., the Federal Home Loan Bank Board, the Federal Reserve System, the Securities and Exchange Commission and the Treasury Department.
Represented by:
Patrick A. Forte, President
Counsel or consultant:
Allan Associates (Roger D. Allan)

Ass'n of Thrift Holding Companies Political Action Committee
888 17th St., N.W., Suite 312, Washington, DC 20006
Telephone: (202) 223-6575
Background: Represented by Patrick A. Forte of the Association.

Ass'n of Transportation Practitioners
1725 K St., N.W. Suite 301, Washington, DC 20006
Telephone: (202) 466-2080
Represented by:
E. Dale Jones, Exec. Director

Ass'n of Trial Lawyers of America
1050 31st St., N.W., Washington, DC 20007
Telephone: (202) 965-3500

Represented by:
Daniel L. Cohen, Director, National Affairs
Thomas H. Henderson, Exec. Director
Bob Lembo, Director, State Relations
Alan A. Parker, Deputy Exec. Director for Public Affairs
Michael Starr, General Counsel
Stuart M. Statler, Deputy Exec. Director, Communications
Jeffrey White, Staff Attorney
Counsel or consultant:
Patton, Boggs and Blow (Thomas Hale Boggs, Jr.)
Timmons and Co., Inc.

Ass'n of Trial Lawyers Political Action Committee
1050 31st St., N.W., Washington, DC 20007
Telephone: (202) 965-3500
Background: A political action committee sponsored by the Ass'n of Trial Lawyers of America.
Represented by:
Joan Pollitt, Director and Treasurer

Ass'n of U.S. Night Vision Manufacturers
918 16th St., N.W., Suite 702, Washington, DC 20006
Telephone: (202) 638-3707
Counsel or consultant:
James Michael Bailey
Cove Associates (John F. Cove)

Ass'n of University Programs in Health Administration
1911 N. Fort Myer Dr. Suite 503, Arlington, VA 22209
Telephone: (703) 524-5500
Represented by:
Gary L. Filerman, President
Counsel or consultant:
CR Associates (Domenic R. Ruscio)

Ass'n of University Radiologists
Chicago, IL
Background: Represented by Otha W. Linton of the American College of Radiology.

Ass'n of Urban Universities
501 I St., S.W., Washington, DC 20024
Telephone: (202) 863-2027
Background: Established in 1976 by about 20 universities to work for passage and funding of the Urban Grant Act. (now Title XI, Higher Education Act) and to represent the legislative and regulatory interests of the nation's urban universities.
Represented by:
Jim Harrison, President

Ass'n on Third World Affairs
1629 K St., N.W., Suite 802, Washington, DC 20006
Telephone: (202) 331-8455
Represented by:
Lorna Hahn, Exec. Director

Association Professionnelle de l'Acier Moule de France
Paris, France
Counsel or consultant:
Ross and Hardies (James A. Stenger)

Ass'n to Unite the Democracies
1506 Pennsylvania Ave., S.E., Washington, DC 20003
Telephone: (202) 544-5150
Background: Promotes a federation of industrial democracies to secure peace and world order, and integrate and stabilize emerging Soviet-bloc democracies, including the development of a common market and currency.
Represented by:
Hon. Henry P. Smith, III, Chairman
Ira L. Straus, Exec. Director

Association Trends
4948 St. Elmo Ave., Suite 306, Bethesda, MD 20814
Telephone: (301) 652-8666
Background: A weekly newspaper carrying news and articles of value to national trade and professional association executives.
Represented by:
Jill Cornish, Publisher
Frank Martineau, CAE, Chairman

Asthma and Allergy Foundation of America
1717 Massachusetts Ave., N.W., Suite 305, Washington, DC 20036
Telephone: (202) 265-0265

Represented by:
Mary E. Worstell, Exec. V. President

Asturiana de Zinc, S.A.
Madrid, Spain
Counsel or consultant:
George V. Egge, Jr.

AT&T
1120 20th St., N.W., Suite 1000, Washington, DC 20036
Telephone: (202) 457-3810
Represented by:
Terry M. Banks, Federal Gov't Affrs V. Pres. & Attorney
Michael D. Baudhuin, Corporate V. President
J. Michael Brown, Federal Gov't Affrs V. Pres. & Attorney
W. V. Catucci, Corporate V. President
Thomas E. Chilcott, Federal Gov't Affairs V. President
Rhonda Crane, District Manager, Federal Gov't Affairs
James W. Davis, Federal Gov't Affairs Director
Nathaniel L. Friends, Regulatory Affrs. V. Pres. & Attorney
Jan Gentry, District Manager, Public Affairs
John W. Gray, Jr., Corp. V. Pres., Federal Gov't Affairs
Katherine Ann Hagen, Federal Gov't Affairs Director
Eric Lee, Federal Gov't Affrs Director & Attorney
Gerald M. Lowrie, Sr. V. President, Federal Gov't Affairs
Randolph C. Lumb, Federal Gov't Affairs V. President
Albert J. McGann, Federal Gov't Affairs V. President
Charles H. Miller, Federal Gov't Affairs V. President
Gregory T. Millert, Federal Gov't Affrs. V. Pres. & Attorney
T. H. Norris, Corporate V. President
Ronald E. Pump, Federal Gov't Affrs. Director & Attorney
Mike P. Tarpey, Director, Public Relations, Washington
Gregory W. Taylor, Federal Gov't Affairs Director
Richard Thayer, District Manager, Federal Gov't Affairs
Osceola F. Thomas, Federal Gov't Affairs Director
Carol W. Wilner, Federal Gov't Affairs Director
Counsel or consultant:
Akin, Gump, Strauss, Hauer and Feld
Covington and Burling (Harvey M. Applebaum, Jr. O. Thomas Johnson)
Charls E. Walker Associates (Charls E. Walker)

AT&T PAC
1120 20th St., N.W. Suite 1000, Washington, DC 20036
Telephone: (202) 457-3841
Background: Represented by Thomas Chilcott of AT&T.

AT&T Technologies, Inc.
Morristown, NJ
Counsel or consultant:
Neill and Co. (Denis M. Neill, Albert C. Printz, Jr.)

Atalanta Corp.
Elizabeth, NJ
Counsel or consultant:
Max N. Berry Law Offices (Max N. Berry)

Atari Games Corp.
Milipitas, CA
Counsel or consultant:
Robinson, Lake, Lerer & Montgomery (Mark Helmke, James H. Lake, Lance I. Morgan)

Atchison, Topeka and Santa Fe Railway Co., The
1001 Pennsylvania Ave., N.W., Suite 675 North, Washington, DC 20004
Telephone: (202) 637-1250
Represented by:
Alan J. Moore, Representative of the President
Counsel or consultant:
Baker and Hostetler (Robert J. Casey)
Charls E. Walker Associates (Lee O. Fuller, Kenneth G. Meuser, Philip H. Potter)

Atlanta Falcons
Atlanta, GA
Counsel or consultant:
Dow, Lohnes and Albertson (Marion H. Allen, III)

Atlantic Container Line
New York, NY
Counsel or consultant:
Steptoe and Johnson (William Karas, Laurence Short)

Atlantic Council of the United States
1616 H St., N.W. 3rd Floor, Washington, DC 20006
Telephone: (202) 347-9353

ORGANIZATIONS REPRESENTED

Background: Promotes greater understanding of and among the United States and its Atlantic and Pacific allies. Gen. Andrew J. Goodpaster, USA (Retired), President of the Institute for Defense Analyses, serves as Chairman.
Represented by:
Roseanne Ridgway, President

Atlantic Financial
Bala Cynwyd, PA
Counsel or consultant:
Cassidy and Associates, Inc. (Gerald S. J. Cassidy, Pete W. Glavas, George A. Ramonas)

Atlantic Lines and Navigation Co., Ltd.
Houston, TX
Counsel or consultant:
Morgan, Lewis and Bockius (Dennis N. Barnes)

Atlantic Research Corp.
5390 Cherokee Ave., Alexandria, VA 22312-2302
Telephone: (703) 642-4000
Background: A subsidiary of Sequa Corp., New York, NY.
Represented by:
Robert Lieg, V. Pres., Admin. & Contracts
Leonard Parkinson, Group Dir., Gov't Relations
Theda A. Parrish, Manager, Corporate Communications
Carlyle C. Ring, Jr., V. President and General Counsel

Atlantic Research Corp. Political Action Committee
5390 Cherokee Ave., Alexandria, VA 22314
Telephone: (703) 642-4000
Represented by:
Daniel Eyob, Treasurer

Atlantic Richfield Company (ARCO) Marine Co.
Long Beach, CA
Counsel or consultant:
Dyer, Ellis, Joseph & Mills (Thomas L. Mills)

Atlantic Richfield Company (ARCO) Transportation Co.
Long Beach, CA
Counsel or consultant:
Robertson, Monagle and Eastaugh (Steven W. Silver)

Atlantic-Southeast Airlines
Atlanta, GA
Counsel or consultant:
Kilpatrick & Cody (Joseph W. Dorn, C. Randall Nuckolls)

ATMOS Energy Corp.
Dallas, TX
Counsel or consultant:
Skadden, Arps, Slate, Meagher and Flom (Mike Naeve)

Atomic Energy of Canada Ltd.
Ontario
Counsel or consultant:
Durante Associates

Attorneys' Liability Assurance Soc.
Hamilton, Bermuda
Counsel or consultant:
Mayer, Brown and Platt (Jerry L. Oppenheimer)

ATU COPE Political Contributors Committee
5025 Wisconsin Ave., N.W., Washington, DC 20016
Telephone: (202) 537-1645
Background: The political action committee of the Amalgamated Transit Union and its Committee on Political Education. Contact person is Raymond C. Wallace of the Amalgamated Transit Union.

Auburn, Avilla, Bluffton, Columbia City and Other Indiana Municipalities
Background: Full list of municipalities includes: Auburn, Avilla, Bluffton, Columbia City, Garrett, Gas City, Mishawaka, New Carlisle, South Haven and Warren, Indiana.
Counsel or consultant:
Duncan, Weinberg, Miller & Pembroke, P.C. (Janice L. Lower, James D. Pembroke)

Auburn University
Auburn, AL
Counsel or consultant:
Shaw, Pittman, Potts and Trowbridge (William Mike House)

Aurora Fisheries, Inc.
Seattle, WA

Counsel or consultant:
Preston Gates Ellis & Rouvelas Meeds (John L. Bloom, William N. Myhre)

Aurora Health Care, Inc.
Milwaukee, WI
Counsel or consultant:
Foley & Lardner (Paul E. Cooney)

Aurora University
Aurora, IL
Counsel or consultant:
Lachelli, Waller and Associates (John D. Waller)

Ausimont U.S.A.
Ausimont, NV
Counsel or consultant:
Steptoe and Johnson (Olin L. Wethington)

Australia, Commonwealth of
Canberra, Australia
Counsel or consultant:
Coudert Brothers (Sherman E. Katz)
Gregory Co., The (Neal Gregory)
Powell, Adams & Rinehart

Australia, Department of Industry, Technology and Resources of
Melbourne, Australia
Counsel or consultant:
Burson-Marsteller

Australia, Embassy of
1601 Massachusetts Ave., N.W., Washington, DC 20036
Telephone: (202) 797-3000
Counsel or consultant:
Gregory Co., The (Neal Gregory)

Australia-New Zealand Direct Line
Long Beach, CA
Counsel or consultant:
Fort and Schlefer (William H. Fort)

Australian Barley Board
Adelaide, Australia
Counsel or consultant:
Keene, Shirley & Associates, Inc. (Darrel Choat, David A. Keene, Craigan P. Shirley)

Australian Meat and Livestock Corp.
Sydney, Australia
Counsel or consultant:
Clifford & Warnke

Australian Wheat Board
Melbourne, Australia
Counsel or consultant:
Vickers & Vickers (Eugene B. Vickers)

Australian Wool Corp.
Parkville, Australia
Counsel or consultant:
Barnes, Richardson and Colburn (Rufus E. Jarman, Jr.)

Austrian Airlines
Vienna, Austria
Counsel or consultant:
Baker, Worthington, Crossley, Stansberry & Woolf (III J. E. Murdock)
Global Aviation Associates, Ltd. (Jon F. Ash)

Authors Guild, The
New York, NY
Counsel or consultant:
Liz Robbins Associates (Michael J. Lucas, Liz Robbins)

Autism Soc. of America
1234 Massachusetts Ave., N.W., Suite C-1017, Washington, DC 20005
Telephone: (202) 783-0125
Background: Promotes research and provides information to assist professionals and parents working for the welfare and education of all person with autism. Washington advocacy activities focus on protecting and securing rights and services in education, vocational training, community living and related needs.
Represented by:
Thomas Nerney, Director

Auto Dealers and Drivers for Free Trade PAC
Jamaica, NY

Counsel or consultant:
Patton, Boggs and Blow (George Blow)

Auto Dismantlers & Recyclers Ass'n
10400 Eaton Place Suite 203, Fairfax, VA 22030-2208
Telephone: (703) 385-1001
Counsel or consultant:
Internat'l Management Group, Inc. (William P. Steinkuller)

Autodesk, Inc.
Sausalito, CA
Counsel or consultant:
Swidler & Berlin, Chartered (Bruce A. Lehman)

Automobile Importers of America
1725 Jefferson Davis Hwy., Suite 1002, Arlington, VA 22202
Telephone: (703) 979-5550
Represented by:
Anna J. Baldwin, State Legislative Specialist
Charles H. Lockwood, V. President and General Counsel
George C. Nield, President
Counsel or consultant:
Bonner & Associates
Willkie Farr and Gallagher

Automotive Consumer Action Program
8400 Westpark Drive, McLean, VA 22102
Telephone: (202) 821-7144
Represented by:
Deborah M. Hopkins, Manager, Consumer Affairs

Automotive Dismantlers and Recyclers Ass'n
10400 Eaton Place, Fairfax, VA 22030-2208
Telephone: (703) 385-1001
Background: Supports the ADRA Scholarship Foundation and the ADRA Educational Foundation, same address.
Counsel or consultant:
Internat'l Management Group, Inc. (William P. Steinkuller)

Automotive Information Council
13505 Dulles Technology Drive, Herndon, VA 22071
Telephone: (703) 904-0700
Represented by:
Ronald H. Weiner, President

Automotive Parts and Accessories Ass'n
5100 Forbes Blvd., Lanham, MD 20706
Telephone: (301) 459-9110
Represented by:
Linda J. Hoffman, V. President, Gov't Affairs and Trade
Lee Kadrich, Managing Dir., Gov't Affairs & Trade
Julian C. Morris, President

Automotive Parts Rebuilders Ass'n
6849 Old Dominion Drive, Suite 352, McLean, VA 22101
Telephone: (703) 790-1050
Represented by:
William C. Gager, Exec. V. President
Counsel or consultant:
Conlon, Frantz, Phelan & Knapp (Michael J. Conlon)

Automotive Refrigeration Products Institute
5100 Forbes Blvd., Lanham, MD 20706
Telephone: (301) 731-5195
Represented by:
Timothy B. Tierney, Exec. Director
Counsel or consultant:
Conlon, Frantz, Phelan & Knapp (Michael J. Conlon)
Fleishman-Hillard, Inc (Paul Johnson, Elizabeth C. McLean)

Automotive Service Ass'n
Bedford, TX
Counsel or consultant:
Donald A. Randall

Automotive Service Industry Ass'n
Chicago, IL
Counsel or consultant:
Courtney, McCamant and Turney (Richard F. Turney)

Automotive Trade Ass'n Executives
8400 Westpark Dr., McLean, VA 22102
Telephone: (703) 821-7072
Represented by:
C. Alan Marlette, Exec. Director

ORGANIZATIONS REPRESENTED

Autranet, Inc.
New York, NY
Counsel or consultant:
Van Dyk Associates, Inc. (Ted Van Dyk)

Avac Systems, Inc.
Atlanta, GA
Counsel or consultant:
Durante Associates

AVCO Financial Services
Newport Beach, CA
Counsel or consultant:
Ballard, Spahr, Andrews and Ingersoll (Frederic L. Ballard, Jr.)

Avco Research Lab, Inc.
Everett, MA
Counsel or consultant:
Brown, Coates and McCarthy (Vincent J. Coates, Jr.)

Avia Footwear, Inc.
Portland, OR
Counsel or consultant:
Fort and Schlefer
Lindsay, Hart, Neil & Weigler (Peter Friedmann)

Avianca Airlines
Bogota, Colombia
Counsel or consultant:
Bergner, Boyette & Bockorny, Inc. (Van R. Boyette)
Dunaway & Cross (Mac S. Dunaway)
Holland and Knight
Squire, Sanders and Dempsey (Robert D. Papkin)

Aviation Associates, Inc.
St. Croix, VI
Counsel or consultant:
V. Michael Straus, P.C.

Aviation Consumer Action Project
P.O. Box 19029, Washington, DC 20036
Telephone: (202) 785-3704
Background: Represents the interests of air passengers and other members of the public in improved air safety, lower fares, elimination of unfair consumer practices, the reduction of jet noise and the open formulation of regulatory decisions. Founded by Ralph Nader.
Represented by:
Christopher J. Witkowski, Exec. Director

Avis Rent A Car Systems, Inc.
Garden City, NY
Counsel or consultant:
Dow, Lohnes and Albertson (David F. Bantleon)
Fulbright & Jaworski (Warren Belmar)

Avon Products, Inc.
New York, NY
Counsel or consultant:
Crowell and Moring (Harold J. Heltzer)
Lee, Toomey & Kent
Patton, Boggs and Blow (Timothy J. May, Stuart M. Pape)

Avondale Industries, Inc.
2711 Jefferson Davis Hwy., Suite 903, Arlington, VA 22202
Telephone: (703) 920-6403
Counsel or consultant:
Dickstein, Shapiro and Morin (John C. Dill, James R. Jones)

AVW Electronics Systems, Inc.
Inglewood, CA
Counsel or consultant:
Laxalt, Washington, Perito & Dubuc (Marc J. Scheineson)

Axa Midi Assurances
Paris, France
Counsel or consultant:
Washington Communications Group/Ruder Finn (James W. Harff)

AXS
Carrollton, TX
Counsel or consultant:
Keene, Shirley & Associates, Inc. (Lisa M. Olson)

AYUDA, Inc.
1736 Columbia Road, N.W., Washington, DC 20009
Telephone: (202) 387-4848
Background: A nonprofit, apolitical organization offering free legal services to low income members of the Hispanic community in the Washington area.
Represented by:
Rebecca Cusic, Deputy Director
Yvonne M. Vega, Exec. Director

B.A.T. Industries, PLC
London, England
Counsel or consultant:
Andrews' Associates, Inc. (Mark Andrews, Jacqueline Balk-Tusa)
Dawson and Associates, Mathis (Dawson Mathis)
Patton, Boggs and Blow

B E & K Daycare
Birmingham, AL
Counsel or consultant:
Jefferson Group, The (Ron Eisenberg)

Babcock and Brown
San Francisco, CA
Counsel or consultant:
Liz Robbins Associates (Alvin S. Brown, Liz Robbins)

Babcock and Wilcox Co.
c/o McDermott Internat'l Inc. 1850 K St., N.W., Suite 950, Washington, DC 20006
Telephone: (202) 296-0390
Background: A wholly owned subsidiary of McDermott Inc. Government operations representation includes Edward S. Gaffney of McDermott Internat'l, Inc. Legislative affairs handled by John H. Henry, also of McDermott Internat'l, Inc. Also represented by Mark W. Miller of McDermott Internat'l.
Represented by:
Samuel H. Esleeck, Mgr. Wash. Liaison, Contract Resrch Div.
Larry Lauderdale, Sr. Mktg. Speclst, Contract Research Div
Ralph A. Webb, General Manager, Contract Research Div.
Richard A. Zavadowski, Mtkg. Mgr, Wash. Liaison, Contract Resrc

Baden-Wuerttemberg, State of, Development Corp.
Stuttgart, West Germany
Counsel or consultant:
Hill and Knowlton Public Affairs Worldwide (Mary C. Foerster)

Bahamas, Government of the
Nassau, Bahamas
Counsel or consultant:
Hogan and Hartson

BAKE PAC
Box 3731, Washington, DC 20007
Telephone: (202) 333-8190
Background: Political action arm of the Independent Bakers Ass'n.
Counsel or consultant:
Robert N. Pyle & Associates

Baker Industries, Inc.
Parsippany, NJ
Counsel or consultant:
Rowland & Sellery (J. Patrick Rowland)

Bakery, Confectionery and Tobacco Workers Internat'l Union
10401 Connecticut Ave., Kensington, MD 20895
Telephone: (301) 933-8600
Represented by:
John DeConcini, President
Rene Rondou, Secretary-Treasurer
Raymond F. Scannell, Director of Research and Education
Counsel or consultant:
Bredhoff and Kaiser (Julia Penny Clark, Jeffrey L. Gibbs)

Bakery, Confectionery and Tobacco Workers Internat'l Union Political Action Committee
10401 Connecticut Ave., Kensington, MD 20895
Telephone: (301) 933-8600
Represented by:
Caroline Jacobson, Contact

Baking Industry and Teamster Labor Conference
4950 MacArthur Blvd., N.W. Suite 200, Washington, DC 20007
Telephone: (202) 337-1502
Counsel or consultant:
Hartnett & Associates (Cynthia Kunz)

Baldt, Inc.
Chester, PA
Counsel or consultant:
Ervin Technical Associates, Inc. (ETA) (James L. Ervin)

Baldwin Co., D. H.
Cincinnati, OH
Counsel or consultant:
Elias, Matz, Tiernan and Herrick
O'Melveny and Myers (Richard G. Parker)

Baldwin United Corp.
Cincinnati, OH
Counsel or consultant:
Morgan, Lewis and Bockius
O'Melveny and Myers (Richard G. Parker)

Ball Brothers, Inc.
Anchorage, AK
Counsel or consultant:
Ginsburg, Feldman and Bress (Alfred J. Eichenlaub)

Ball Corp.
2200 Clarendon Blvd. Suite 1006, Arlington, VA 22201
Telephone: (703) 284-5400
Background: A manufacturer of packaging, industrial, and technical products.
Represented by:
Robert W. Dean, Senior V. Pres., Washington Operations
Mark W. Weller, Director, Corporate Government Affairs
Counsel or consultant:
Burson-Marsteller
Klein & Saks, Inc.

Baltimore Gas and Electric Co.
1100 Connecticut Ave., N.W., Suite 530, Washington, DC 20036
Telephone: (202) 861-0830
Represented by:
Paulette C. Pidcock, Director, Federal Affairs
John S. Sparkman, Federal Affairs Representative

Baltimore, Maryland, City of
Counsel or consultant:
Kelley, Drye and Warren (Michael R. Lemov)

Baltimore Orioles
Baltimore, MD
Counsel or consultant:
Williams and Connolly (Lawrence Lucchino)

Banco Central do Brasil
Rio de Janeiro, Brazil
Counsel or consultant:
Arnold & Porter

Banco Cooperativo
San Juan, PR
Counsel or consultant:
Warren W. Koffler

Banco de Santander, S.A.d.c.
Santander, Spain
Counsel or consultant:
Morgan, Lewis and Bockius (Kathleen E. Topelius)

Banco Nacional, N.A.
Hato Rey, PR
Counsel or consultant:
Warren W. Koffler

Bangladesh Garment Manufacturers and Exporters Ass'n
Dacca, Bangladesh
Counsel or consultant:
Internat'l Development Systems (C. Donald Brasher, Jr.)

Bangladesh, People's Republic of
Dacca, Bangladesh
Counsel or consultant:
Bannerman and Associates, Inc. (M. Graeme Bannerman, Curtis Silvers)
Bruce A. Reznik

The listings in this directory are available as *Mailing Labels.* See last page.

ORGANIZATIONS REPRESENTED

Bangor and Aroostook Railroad
Bangor, ME
Counsel or consultant:
RBC Associates, Inc. (Ray B. Chambers)

Bangor Hydro-Electric Co.
Bangor, ME
Counsel or consultant:
Wright and Talisman

Bangor Internat'l Airport
Bangor, ME
Counsel or consultant:
Lord Day & Lord, Barrett Smith (Joanne W. Young)

Bank Capital Markets Ass'n
Nat'l Press Building Second Floor, Washington, DC 20045
Telephone: (202) 347-5510
Background: The trade association for commercial banks engaged in underwriting of and dealing in public securities.
Represented by:
Richard K. Liggitt, Deputy Director
Thomas P. Rideout, Exec. Director
Counsel or consultant:
Wilmer, Cutler and Pickering (Michael S. Helfer)

Bank Capital Markets Ass'n Political Action Committee
Nat'l Press Building, Suite 200, Washington, DC 20045
Telephone: (202) 347-5510
Background: Administrator is Thomas P. Rideout of the Bank Capital Markets Ass'n. Treasurer is Richard K. Liggitt, also of the Ass'n.

Bank Card Servicers Ass'n
1001 Connecticut Ave., N.W. Suite 800, Washington, DC 20026
Telephone: (202) 452-1520
Counsel or consultant:
William S. Bergman Associates (Valerie H. Bergman)

Bank of America NT & SA
1800 K St., N.W., Suite 900, Washington, DC 20006
Telephone: (202) 778-0535
Represented by:
Patrick S. Antrim, Senior Counsel
Nancy Camm, V. President and Washington Rep.
Joyce Kinney, Office Manager
Fred J. Martin, Jr., Sr. V. Pres. & Director, Gov't Relations

Bank of Baltimore
Baltimore, MD
Counsel or consultant:
James J. Butera, Chartered
Sutherland, Asbill and Brennan (Wright H. Andrews, Jr.)

Bank of Boston
1515 S. Jefferson Davis Hwy., Suite 1623, Arlington, VA 22202
Telephone: (703) 979-9606
Represented by:
Herbert R. Waite, Washington Representative

Bank of Hungary
Budapest, Hungary
Counsel or consultant:
Hill and Knowlton Public Affairs Worldwide (Mary C. Foerster, Frank Mankiewicz)

Bank of New England
Boston, MA
Counsel or consultant:
O'Neill and Athy, P.C. (Andrew Athy, Jr.)

Bank of Nova Scotia
Toronto, Canada
Counsel or consultant:
Akin, Gump, Strauss, Hauer and Feld (Joel Jankowsky)

Bank of Oklahoma
Tulsa, OK
Counsel or consultant:
Dickstein, Shapiro and Morin (James R. Jones)

Bank of Tokyo Trust Co.
New York, NY
Counsel or consultant:
Epstein Becker and Green

Bank South
Atlanta, GA
Counsel or consultant:
Kilpatrick & Cody (Mark D. Wincek)

Bank St. College
New York, NY
Counsel or consultant:
Smith Dawson & Andrews, Inc. (Thomas C. Dawson, James P. Smith)

BankAmerica Federal Election Fund
1800 K St., N.W., Suite 900, Washington, DC 20006
Telephone: (202) 778-0535
Background: Represented by Fred J. Martin, Jr. of Bank of America.

Bankcard Holders of America
560 Herndon Parkway Suite 120, Herndon, VA 22070
Telephone: (703) 481-1110
Background: Founded in 1980. Seeks lower interest rates on credit cards.
Represented by:
Elgie Holstein, Director

Bankers' Ass'n for Foreign Trade
1600 M St., N.W., Washington, DC 20036
Telephone: (202) 452-0952
Background: A trade association, established in 1921, of commercial banks with international departments dedicated to promoting international trade and finance.
Represented by:
Mary Condeelis, Exec. Director
Counsel or consultant:
Prather, Seeger, Doolittle and Farmer (Thomas L. Farmer)

Bankers Trust Co.
New York, NY
Counsel or consultant:
Dewey, Ballantine, Bushby, Palmer and Wood (Lawrence F. O'Brien, III)
Wilmer, Cutler and Pickering (William J. Wilkins)

Banner Industries
New York, NY
Counsel or consultant:
Nat'l Strategies Inc. (David K. Aylward)

Banner Life Insurance Co.
1701 Research Blvd., Rockville, MD 20850
Telephone: (301) 279-4800
Background: Formerly Government Employees Life Insurance Co.
Represented by:
Edward J. Bove, Staff Attorney
Gene Gilbertson, Exec. V. President
Dave Lenaburg, CEO and President

Baptist Joint Committee on Public Affairs
200 Maryland Ave., N.E. Suite 303, Washington, DC 20002
Telephone: (202) 544-4226
Background: Staffed in Washington, DC in 1946. A joint effort of nine major Baptist denominations with 25 million members to promote religious liberty and separation of church and state.
Represented by:
James M. Dunn, Exec. Director
Oliver Thomas, Director of Research and General Counsel

Baptist World Alliance
6733 Curran St., McLean, VA 22101-6005
Telephone: (703) 790-8980
Background: Founded in 1905 in London. An international alliance of 144 national Baptist unions with 36 million members worldwide.
Represented by:
Denton Lotz, General Secretary-Treasurer
Wendy Ryan, Director, Division of Communications

Barbados, Government of
Bridgetown, Barbados
Counsel or consultant:
Berliner and Maloney

Barber Blue Sea Line
New York, NY

Counsel or consultant:
Warren and Associates (George A. Quadrino, Charles F. Warren)

Barclays Bank PLC
1722 Eye St., N.W., 5th Floor, Washington, DC 20006
Telephone: (202) 429-4298
Represented by:
Marlene Nicholson, Director, Government Relations
Counsel or consultant:
Sidley and Austin (Margery Waxman)

Barlow Corp., The
5454 Wisconsin Ave., Chevy Chase, MD 20815
Telephone: (301) 657-8450
Counsel or consultant:
Robert N. Pyle & Associates

Barnes and Tucker Co.
Haverford, PA
Counsel or consultant:
The Hoving Group
Smith, Heenan and Althen (Michael T. Heenan)

Barnstable Broadcasting
Waltham, MA
Counsel or consultant:
Kaye, Scholer, Fierman, Hays and Handler (Jason Shrinsky)

Baroid Corp.
208 G St., N.E. 2nd Fl., Washington, DC 20002
Telephone: (202) 546-0125
Background: Director of Government Relations in Washington, DC is Karl J. Ottosen of Ottosen & Associates.
Counsel or consultant:
Ottosen and Associates (Karl J. Ottosen, Carla L. Saunders)

Barrier Beach Preservation Ass'n
Westhamptn Beach, NY
Counsel or consultant:
Richard Curry and Associates (Richard C. Curry)

Barry University
Miami, FL
Counsel or consultant:
Cassidy and Associates, Inc. (Gerald S. J. Cassidy, C. Frank Godfrey, Jr.)

BASF Corp.
2100 Pennsylvania Ave., N.W. Suite 755, Washington, DC 20037
Telephone: (202) 296-4894
Represented by:
Alyson A. Emanuel, Manager, Government Relations
Joan M. Kovalic, Manager, Government Relations
Robert G. Thoma, V. President, Government Relations
Counsel or consultant:
James E. Guirard, Jr.
Winthrop, Stimson, Putnam & Roberts (Ronna A. Freiberg, Peter F. Gold, Ira S. Shapiro)

BASF Structural Materials, Inc.
Charlotte, NC
Counsel or consultant:
Winthrop, Stimson, Putnam & Roberts (Peter F. Gold)

Basic American Foods
San Francisco, CA
Counsel or consultant:
Bogle and Gates (Robert G. Hayes, Irene Ringwood)

Basic Industry Coalition
c/o Armco, Inc. 1667 K St., N.W., Suite 650, Washington, DC 20006
Telephone: (202) 223-5370
Background: A coalition of companies seeking to ensure more consideration of international competitiveness concerns in tax reforms proposed by the Reagan Administration in 1985. John Bauer of Armco, Inc. serves as contact.
Counsel or consultant:
LeBoeuf, Lamb, Leiby, and MacRae (John K. Meagher)

Basin Electric Power Cooperative
Bismarck, ND
Counsel or consultant:
Duncan, Weinberg, Miller & Pembroke, P.C. (Richmond F. Allan, Edward Weinberg)

ORGANIZATIONS REPRESENTED

Bass Group, Robert M.
Ft. Worth, TX
Counsel or consultant:
Williams and Jensen, P.C. (Robert E. Glennon, Jr., Mary L. Whalen)

Bata Shoe Co.
Belcamp, MD
Counsel or consultant:
Hudson, Creyke, Koehler and Tacke

Bath Iron Works Corp.
2341 Jefferson Davis Highway Suite 1100, Arlington, VA 22202
Telephone: (703) 979-2030
Represented by:
Kaylene H. Green, Director, Washington Operations
Gerard F. Lamb, Director, Government Affairs

Bath Iron Works Corp. Political Action Committee
2341 Jefferson Davis Hwy., Suite 1035, Arlington, VA 22202
Telephone: (703) 979-2030
Background: Contact is Kaylene H. Green of the Washington office of Bath Iron Works.

Batman Corp.
300 West Service Road, #200 Wash/Dulles Internat'l Airport, Washington, DC 20041
Telephone: (202) 478-5720
Counsel or consultant:
Bracy Williams & Co. (Kenneth S. Birnbaum, Terrence L. Bracy, Kenneth M. Stram, Susan J. Williams)
Dickstein, Shapiro and Morin (John C. Dill)
Ryan-McGinn (Daniel McGinn)

Battelle Memorial Institute
370 L'Enfant Promenade S.W. 901 D St., S.W., Suite 900, Washington, DC 20004-2115
Telephone: (202) 479-0500
Represented by:
John F. Bagley, Director, External Relations
David W. Dragnich, Director, Program Development
Betty Hall Fimiani, Manager, Information

BATUS, Inc.
Louisville, KY
Counsel or consultant:
B. L. Evans & Assoc. Inc. (Billy Lee Evans)
French & Company (Mark M. Ellison, Verrick O. French)
Hecht, Spencer & Associates (Bronwyn R. Bachrach, William H. Hecht, Walter D. Huddleston, W. Timothy Locke)
Patton, Boggs and Blow (Thomas Hale Boggs, Jr.)
Powell, Adams & Rinehart

Bausch & Lomb, Inc.
Rochester, NY
Counsel or consultant:
Gold and Liebengood, Inc. (Martin B. Gold)
Nixon, Hargrave, Devans and Doyle (Stephen Kurzman)

Baxter Internat'l Inc.
1667 K St., N.W., Suite 710, Washington, DC 20006
Telephone: (202) 223-4016
Background: Based in Deerfield, IL.
Represented by:
David J. Aho, Corp. V. Pres., Government Affairs
Donna Bower, Manager, State Affairs
Sarah Massengal Gregg, Manager, Health Affairs
Susan McNally, Manager, Alternate Site & Reimbursement
Kelly A. Slone, Manager, Legislative Affairs
Neal Stine, Manager, Trade/Business Affairs

Bay Area Rapid Transit District
Oakland, CA
Counsel or consultant:
Anderson, Hibey, Nauheim and Blair (Robert A. Blair)
McAuliffe, Kelly, Raffaelli & Siemens (James M. Copeland, Jr.)

Bay Area Renal Stone Center
St. Petersburg, FL
Counsel or consultant:
Dyer, Ellis, Joseph & Mills (Thomas L. Mills)

Bay Area Teleport
Alameda, CA

Counsel or consultant:
Young & Jatlow (Francis L. Young)

Bay State Gas Co.
Canton, MA
Counsel or consultant:
Gallagher, Boland, Meiburger and Brosnan (Thomas F. Brosnan)

Bayamon Federal Savings and Loan Ass'n
San Juan, PR
Counsel or consultant:
Elias, Matz, Tiernan and Herrick

Bayley Seton Hospital
Staten Island, NY
Counsel or consultant:
Powell, Goldstein, Frazer and Murphy (Lawrence B. Simons)

Bayonne Board of Education
Bayonne, NJ
Counsel or consultant:
Krivit and Krivit (Daniel H. Krivit)

Bayonne, New Jersey, City of
Counsel or consultant:
Krivit and Krivit (Daniel H. Krivit)

Bazar San Jorge, S.A.
Tegucigalpa, Honduras
Counsel or consultant:
Reichler Appelbaum and Wippman (Judith C. Appelbaum)

BDM Internat'l, Inc.
7915 Jones Branch Drive, McLean, VA 22102
Telephone: (703) 821-5000
Represented by:
Stephanie C. Bolick, Director, Public Affairs
Phillip A. Karber, Sr. V. Pres., Nat'l Security Programs
George S. Newman, V. President, Gov't and Public Affairs
Todd A. Stottlemyer, Manager, Government Relations
Counsel or consultant:
John G. Campbell, Inc. (John G. Campbell)
Reid & Priest

BDM Political Action Committee
7915 Jones Branch Drive, McLean, VA 22102
Telephone: (703) 848-5000
Background: A political action committee sponsored by the BDM Internat'l, Inc. Contact is George Newman, V. President of Government and Public Affairs of the corporation.

Bear, Stearns and Co.
New York, NY
Counsel or consultant:
Dickstein, Shapiro and Morin (Charles H. Morin)
Murray, Scheer & Montgomery (D. Michael Murray)

Beard Oil Co.
Oklahoma City, OK
Background: Law firm of Duncan, Weinberg, Miller & Pembroke represents Beard Oil Co. in administrative matters regarding oil and gas leasing on U.S. land.
Counsel or consultant:
Duncan, Weinberg, Miller & Pembroke, P.C. (Richmond F. Allan, Edward Weinberg)

Beaumont, Texas, City of
Counsel or consultant:
Nat'l Center for Municipal Development (Carolyn Chaney)

Bechtel Aviation Services
Vienna, VA
Counsel or consultant:
Baker, Worthington, Crossley, Stansberry & Woolf (III J. E. Murdock)

Bechtel Civil & Minerals, Inc.
San Francisco, CA
Counsel or consultant:
Keefe Co., The (Clarence L. James, Jr., Robert J. Keefe, Terry M. O'Connell)
Thompson, Mann and Hutson (Harold P. Coxson)

Bechtel Group, Inc.
1620 Eye St., N.W., Suite 703, Washington, DC 20006
Telephone: (202) 393-4747

Represented by:
Leon Awerbuch, Manager, Business Development
Robert C. Branick, Senior Program Analyst
William D. Craig, Manager, Energy Programs
John J. Gersuk, Congressional Affairs Manager
Earline A. Keyser, Domestic Issues Manager
Jack W. Lillywhite, Manager, Federal Programs
Thomas L. Mack, Manager and V. President
Oscar Padilla, Manager, Internat'l Programs
Robert H. Ragan, Manager, Nat'l Security & Space Programs
Marlin K. Seymour, Research Associate
Sy A. Taubenblatt, Executive Consultant
Counsel or consultant:
Cadwalader, Wickersham & Taft (Donald C. Alexander)

Bechtel Investments, Inc.
San Francisco, CA
Counsel or consultant:
Cadwalader, Wickersham & Taft (Donald C. Alexander)

Beckett Packaging, Ltd.
Mississauga, Canada
Counsel or consultant:
Patton, Boggs and Blow (Timothy J. May)

Bedford Group
Lafayette, CA
Counsel or consultant:
Dutko & Associates (L. L. Hank Hankla)

Bedford Stuyvesant Restoration Corp.
New York, NY
Counsel or consultant:
McMahon and Associates

Beech Aircraft Corp.
1215 Jefferson Davis Hwy., 15th Floor, Arlington, VA 22202-4302
Telephone: (703) 521-2020
Background: A subsidiary of the Raytheon Co.
Represented by:
Bill Butler, Director, Government Relations

Beer Institute
1225 Eye St., N.W., Suite 825, Washington, DC 20005
Telephone: (202) 737-2337
Represented by:
Leonard J. Goldstein, Chairman
Philip C. Katz, V. President, Research Services
Gary M. Nateman, V. President and General Counsel
James C. Sanders, President

Beet Sugar Political Action Committee
1156 15th St., N.W. Suite 1019, Washington, DC 20005
Telephone: (202) 296-4820
Background: Sponsored by the United States Beet Sugar Ass'n. Van R. Olsen of the Ass'n serves as Treasurer.

Beggs Associates, J. M.
Arlington, VA
Counsel or consultant:
Templeton and Co. (John G. Birdsong, Patrick A. Templeton)

Beirut University College
New York, NY
Counsel or consultant:
Bannerman and Associates, Inc. (M. Graeme Bannerman, Roxanne Perugino)

Belgian American Chamber of Commerce
New York, NY
Counsel or consultant:
Squire, Sanders and Dempsey (Thomas J. Quigley)

Belgium, Embassy of
3330 Garfield St., N.W., Washington, DC 20008
Telephone: (202) 333-6900
Counsel or consultant:
Squire, Sanders and Dempsey

Belin and Associates
Houston, TX
Counsel or consultant:
Dow, Lohnes and Albertson (Stuart Marshall Bloch)

Belk Stores Services, Inc.
Charlotte, NC
Counsel or consultant:
Chambers Associates Incorporated (Mary S. Lyman)

The listings in this directory are available as *Mailing Labels*. See last page.

ORGANIZATIONS REPRESENTED

Bell Aerospace Textron
1090 Vermont Ave., N.W., Suite 1100, Washington, DC 20005
Telephone: (202) 289-5833
Background: A division of Textron, Inc.
Represented by:
Lawrence B. Ryan, V. President, Washington Operations

Bell Atlantic
1710 Rhode Island Ave., N.W. Suite 1200, Washington, DC 20036
Telephone: (202) 392-6977
Represented by:
Trudi Blair, Exec. Director
Barbara Butler, Exec. Director
Rita Hankins, Exec. Director
Kathryn F. Hauser, Exec. Director
Myricks E. McGee, Manager
Aubrey L. Sarvis, V. Pres., Federal Legislative Relations
C. A. "Jim" Schaubel, Jr., V. Pres., Fed. Gov't & Internat'l Rels.
Counsel or consultant:
Bergner, Boyette & Bockorny, Inc. (David A. Bockorny)
Jefferson Group, The (Frederick J. Hannett)
Lee, Toomey & Kent
Paul, Hastings, Janofsky and Walker (Ralph B. Everett)
Verner, Liipfert, Bernhard, McPherson and Hand, Chartered (Lloyd N. Hand)
R. Duffy Wall and Associates (Michael Stern, R. Duffy Wall)

Bell Canada
Montreal, Quebec, Canada
Counsel or consultant:
Baker and Hostetler (Gregg P. Skall)

Bell Communications Research, Inc.
2101 L St., N.W. Suite 600, Washington, DC 20037
Telephone: (202) 955-4600
Represented by:
Joseph K. Lautieri; Ass't Manager
Ann W. Pelletier, Legislative Analyst
Gail Berry West, Director, Government Affairs
Patricia A. Whittaker, Associate Director, Gov't Affairs
Counsel or consultant:
Vorys, Sater, Seymour and Pease (Stephen H. Brown)

Bell Helicopter Textron
1090 Vermont Ave., N.W. Suite 1100, Washington, DC 20005
Telephone: (202) 289-5850
Represented by:
George G. Troutman, V. President, Washington Operations
Counsel or consultant:
Parry and Romani Associates Inc. (Romano Romani)

Bell and Howell (Business Equipment Division)
Chicago, IL
Counsel or consultant:
Daly Associates, Inc. (John Jay Daly)

Bell Telephone Co. of Pennsylvania
c/o Bell Atlantic, 1710 Rhode Island Ave., 12th Floor, Washington, DC 20036
Telephone: (202) 392-6982
Background: A telephone operating company of Bell Atlantic.
Represented by:
Joe Westner, Director, Federal Relations

Bellingham Cold Storage
Bellingham, WA
Counsel or consultant:
Preston Gates Ellis & Rouvelas Meeds (John L. Bloom, William N. Myhre)

Bellingham, Port of
Bellingham, WA
Counsel or consultant:
Garvey, Schubert & Barer (Alan A. Butchman)

BellSouth Corp.
1133 21st St., N.W., Suite 900, Washington, DC 20036
Telephone: (202) 463-4100
Represented by:
Robert Blau, Director, Regulatory Policy Analysis
Hugh S. Brady, Director, Legislative Affairs
Gary Dennis, Director, Federal Regulatory Affairs
Mary J. Pepper English, Director, Congressional Relations
Lynn R. Holmes, Director, Legislative Affairs
Kathleen Hughes, Director, Media Relations
Whit Jordan, Director, Federal Regulatory Affairs
David J. Markey, V. Pres., Federal Regulatory Affairs
Daniel J. Mattoon, Director, Congressional Affairs
William McCloskey, Manager, Media Relations
Raymond L. McGuire, Exec. V. President, Governmental Affairs
Lisa McKenzie, Staff Manager, Congressional Relations
Daniel H. Murray, Director, Congressional Affairs
Raymond K. Nolin, V. President, Federal Relations
Karen B. Possner, Director, Legislative Policy
Cindy Preston, Director, State and Agency Relations
Sydney Shaw, Manager, Media Relations
Maurice P. Talbot, Jr., Director, Federal Regulatory Affairs
David O. Williams, Jr., Director, Federal Relations
Counsel or consultant:
Camp, Barsh, Bates and Tate (John C. Camp)
Paul, Hastings, Janofsky and Walker (Ralph B. Everett)
Thompson Group, Inc. (Kenneth W. Thompson)
Wilkinson, Barker, Knauer and Quinn
Wunder, Ryan, Cannon & Thelen (Bernard J. Wunder)

Belmont Development
151 Spring St., Suite 300, Herndon, VA 22070
Telephone: (703) 742-7730
Counsel or consultant:
H. John Elliott

Belz Investment Co.
Memphis, TN
Counsel or consultant:
Powell, Goldstein, Frazer and Murphy

Ben Franklin Advanced Technology Center
Philadelphia, PA
Counsel or consultant:
Chambers Associates Incorporated (William L. Stringer)

Ben Franklin Savings Institution
Houston, TX
Counsel or consultant:
Bryan, Cave, McPheeters and McRoberts

Bender Shipbuilding & Repair Co., Inc.
Mobile, AL
Counsel or consultant:
Dyer, Ellis, Joseph & Mills (Thomas L. Mills)

Beneficial Corp.
Peapack, NJ
Counsel or consultant:
Dewey, Ballantine, Bushby, Palmer and Wood (Lawrence F. O'Brien, III)
Elias, Matz, Tiernan and Herrick
Lee, Toomey & Kent

Beneficial Management Corp. of America
Peapack, NJ
Counsel or consultant:
Ballard, Spahr, Andrews and Ingersoll (Frederic L. Ballard, Jr.)
Perkinson & Associates, Inc. (Michael J. Bertelsen, Gary J. Perkinson)

Benevolent and Protective Order of Elks (BPOE)
Chicago, IL
Counsel or consultant:
Gregory Co., The (Neal Gregory)

Benguela Inc.
Lagos, Nigeria
Counsel or consultant:
Stovall & Spradlin

Benjamin Moore & Co.
Montvale, NJ
Counsel or consultant:
Kaye, Scholer, Fierman, Hays and Handler (Christopher R. Brewster)

Bennett Lumber Products, Inc.
Princeton, ID

Counsel or consultant:
F. H. Hutchison and Co. (Fred H. Hutchison)

Benton Harbor, Michigan, City of
Counsel or consultant:
PPED, Inc. (Richard S. Kochan)

Bentonville, Arkansas, City of
Counsel or consultant:
Duncan, Weinberg, Miller & Pembroke, P.C. (Robert Weinberg)

Beretta U.S.A. Corp.
Accokeek, MD
Counsel or consultant:
Gold and Liebengood, Inc. (Howard S. Liebengood)

Berg-Revoir Corp.
Novato, CA
Counsel or consultant:
The Ferguson Co. (William Ferguson, Jr., Patricia Jordan, Thane Young)

Bergen Auto Upholstery Co.
Rutherford, NJ
Counsel or consultant:
Smith and Howard Associates, Inc. (Irving P. Smith)

Bering Sea Fishermen's Ass'n
Anchorage, AK
Counsel or consultant:
C. Deming Cowles, IV

Bermuda, Government of
Hamilton, Bermuda
Counsel or consultant:
Ragan and Mason (William F. Ragan)
Strategic Resources Corp. (H. P. Goldfield)
Swidler & Berlin, Chartered (Lester S. Hyman)
Wunder, Ryan, Cannon & Thelen (Kenneth S. Levine)

Bernard Johnson, Inc.
Houston, TX
Counsel or consultant:
Korth and Korth (Fred Korth)

Bessemer and Lake Erie Railroad Co.
Monroeville, PA
Counsel or consultant:
Squire, Sanders and Dempsey (Kenneth C. Anderson)

Best Western Internat'l, Inc.
Phoenix, AZ
Counsel or consultant:
David Apter and Associates

Beth Israel Hospital
Boston, MA
Counsel or consultant:
O'Neill and Athy, P.C. (Martha L. Casey)

Bethlehem Steel Corp.
1667 K St., N.W., Suite 600, Washington, DC 20006
Telephone: (202) 775-6200
Represented by:
Maurice E. Carino, Manager, Government Programs
Laird D. Patterson, Counsel
Philip N. Pulizzi, Jr., Director - Legislative Affairs
William E. Wickert, Jr., V. President, Federal Gov't Affairs
Leonard B. Williams, Director - Legislative Affairs
Counsel or consultant:
Black, Manafort, Stone and Kelly Public Affairs Co. (Charles R. Black)
Burson-Marsteller (Timothy G. Brosnahan)
Collier, Shannon & Scott (David A. Hartquist)
Davis & Harman (Thomas A. Davis)
Dewey, Ballantine, Bushby, Palmer and Wood
Morrison & Foerster
Patton, Boggs and Blow (James B. Christian, Jr.)
Skadden, Arps, Slate, Meagher and Flom (Robert E. Lighthizer)
Stewart and Stewart (Eugene L. Stewart)

Better Hearing Institute
5021B Backlick Road, Annandale, VA 22003
Telephone: (703) 642-0580
Background: A non-profit organization founded in 1973 in Washington whose principal purpose is to educate the public and provide hearing information through the mass media.

ORGANIZATIONS REPRESENTED

Better Hearing Institute (Cont'd)
Represented by:
   Joseph J. Rizzo, Exec. Director

Better Working Environments, Inc.
Carson City, NV
Counsel or consultant:
   Fehrenbacher, Sale, Quinn, and Deese (C. Michael Deese)

Beverly Enterprises
1901 N. Fort Myer Drive Suite 302, Arlington, VA 22209
Telephone: (703) 276-0808
Background: A California-based health care company.
Represented by:
   Jack A. MacDonald, V. President
   Barbara A. Rudolph, Director, Government Relations

BHC, Inc.
New York, NY
Counsel or consultant:
   Clarence J. Brown & Co. (Robert B. Giese)

BHP Holdings (USA) Inc.
San Francisco, CA
Counsel or consultant:
   R. Duffy Wall and Associates (R. Duffy Wall)

BHP-Utah Internat'l Inc.
1700 K St., N.W., Suite 502, Washington, DC 20006
Telephone: (202) 775-1389
Background: An international mining company.
Represented by:
   Barbara W. Johnston, Washington Representative

Bibby-Ste. Croix Foundries, Inc.
Ontario, Canada
Counsel or consultant:
   Marks Murase and White

Bicycle Manufacturers Ass'n of America
1055 Thomas Jefferson St. N.W. Suite 300, Washington, DC 20007
Telephone: (202) 333-4052
Counsel or consultant:
   Collier, Shannon & Scott (Lauren R. Howard, Thomas F. Shannon)

Bicycle Wholesale Distributors Ass'n
Philadelphia, PA
Counsel or consultant:
   Thompson, Hine and Flory (Lewe B. Martin)

Binghampton Savings Bank
Binghampton, NY
Counsel or consultant:
   Thacher, Proffitt and Wood (Louis H. Nevins)

Bio National Corp.
Bakersfield, CA
Counsel or consultant:
   Research & Management Associates (Jerry A. Shaw)

Biogen
Cambridge, MA
Counsel or consultant:
   Patton, Boggs and Blow (Stuart M. Pape)

BioMed Services, Inc.
Counsel or consultant:
   U.S. Strategies Corp. (K. Michael Matthews)

Bionetics Corp., The
Hampton, VA
Counsel or consultant:
   Templeton and Co. (John G. Birdsong, Patrick A. Templeton)

Bionox, Inc.
Charlotte, NC
Counsel or consultant:
   O'Connor & Hannan

Biopure Corp.
Boston, MA
Counsel or consultant:
   Cassidy and Associates, Inc. (Thomas M. Gannon)

Bioresources Laboratories
12301 Parklawn Drive, Rockville, MD 20852
Telephone: (301) 881-2600
Background: President is Robert E. Stevenson (see American Type Culture Collection.)

Bird and Son
East Walpole, MA
Counsel or consultant:
   Morgan, Lewis and Bockius (Caswell O. Hobbs, III)

Birmingham, Alabama, City of
Counsel or consultant:
   Preston Gates Ellis & Rouvelas Meeds (Craig J. Gehring)
   Tonya, Inc. (Anthony L. Jones)

Birting Fisheries
Seattle, WA
Counsel or consultant:
   Phyllis D. Carnilla

Biscuit and Cracker Manufacturers Ass'n
1400 L St., N.W. Suite 400, Washington, DC 20005
Telephone: (202) 898-1636
Represented by:
   Linda Chapman, Director, Government Affairs
   Francis P. Rooney, President

Bituminous Coal Operators Ass'n
918 16th St., N.W. Suite 303, Washington, DC 20006
Telephone: (202) 783-3195
Represented by:
   Joseph P. Brennan, President

Bixby Ranch
Los Angeles, CA
Counsel or consultant:
   Hecht, Spencer & Associates (Bronwyn R. Bachrach, William H. Hecht)

Black and Decker Corp., The
Towson, MD
Counsel or consultant:
   Dorsey & Whitney
   Miles and Stockbridge (Richard W. Bowe)

Blacks in Government
1424 K St., N.W. Suite 604, Washington, DC 20005
Telephone: (202) 638-7767
Represented by:
   Mrs. Rubye S. Fields, President

Blinded Veterans Ass'n
477 H St., N.W., Washington, DC 20001
Telephone: (202) 371-8880
Represented by:
   Ronald L. Miller, Ph.D., Exec. Director
   Thomas H. Miller, Dir., Govt'l & Community Relations

Block, H. & R.
1641 Rt. 3 North, Suite 101, Crofton, MD 21114
Telephone: (301) 858-1210
Represented by:
   Al James Golato, Corporate Director of Public Affairs

Blockbuster Entertainment Corp.
Fort Lauderdale, FL
Counsel or consultant:
   Eckert Seamans Cherin & Mellott (Patricia A. Quealy, Jane Sutter Starke)

Blue Bell, Inc.
Greensboro, NC
Counsel or consultant:
   Steptoe and Johnson (Richard P. Taylor)

Blue Cross and Blue Shield Ass'n
655 15th St., N.W., Suite 350, Washington, DC 20005
Telephone: (202) 626-4780
Background: The Association serves as the coordinating agency for the nation's 77 locally-based Blue Cross and Blue Shield plans.

Represented by:
   Paul W. Dennett, Wash. Rep./Legislative Policy Analyst
   Alissa Fox, Senior Washington Representative
   Diana Jost, Exec. Dir., Private Market Programs
   Mary Nell Lehnhard, V. President, Office of Gov't Relations
   Robert Mulligan, Senior Washington Representative
   Steve Ricchetti, Exec. Dir., Congressional Communications
   Alan P. Spielman, Exec. Dir., Gov't Programs Legislation
Counsel or consultant:
   Eckert Seamans Cherin & Mellott (Patricia A. Quealy)
   Griffin, Johnson & Associates (David E. Johnson)
   Hill and Knowlton Public Affairs Worldwide (Jeffrey B. Trammell)
   Morrison Associates (James W. Morrison, Jr.)

Blue Cross and Blue Shield of Chicago
Chicago, IL
Counsel or consultant:
   Morrison Associates (James W. Morrison, Jr.)

Blue Cross and Blue Shield of Colorado
Denver, CO
Counsel or consultant:
   Kogovsek & Associates, Inc.

Blue Cross and Blue Shield of Maryland
Baltimore, MD
Counsel or consultant:
   Dow, Lohnes and Albertson (Arnold P. Lutzker)

Blue Cross and Blue Shield of Missouri
St. Louis, MO
Counsel or consultant:
   Camp, Barsh, Bates and Tate (Ronald L. Platt)
   Epstein Becker and Green (Deborah Steelman)

Blue Cross and Blue Shield of Nevada
Reno, NV
Counsel or consultant:
   Kogovsek & Associates, Inc.

Blue Cross and Blue Shield of New Mexico
Albuquerque, NM
Counsel or consultant:
   Kogovsek & Associates, Inc.

Blue Cross and Blue Shield of the National Capital Area
550 12th St., S.W., Washington, DC 20065
Telephone: (202) 479-8000
Represented by:
   Raymond D. Freson, Director, Public Relations & Advertising

Blue Cross of Pennsylvania
Philadelphia, PA
Counsel or consultant:
   Burson-Marsteller (Rebecca L. Halkias)

Blue Sea Corp.
Houston, TX
Counsel or consultant:
   Parry and Romani Associates Inc. (Romano Romani)

Bluefield, West Virginia, City of
Counsel or consultant:
   Beveridge & Diamond, P.C. (Richard S. Davis, Harold L. Segall)

BMW of North America
Montvale, NJ
Counsel or consultant:
   Dorsey & Whitney
   Wiley, Rein & Fielding (Mimi Weyforth Dawson)

B'nai B'rith Internat'l
1640 Rhode Island Ave., N.W., Washington, DC 20036
Telephone: (202) 857-6600
Represented by:
   Warren W. Eisenberg, Director
   Bezalel Gordon, Director, Press Relations
   Daniel S. Mariaschin, Director, Public Affairs
   Seymour D. Reich, President

B'nai B'rith Women
1828 L St., N.W., Suite 250, Washington, DC 20036
Telephone: (202) 857-1310

ORGANIZATIONS REPRESENTED

Represented by:
Elaine Kotell Binder, Exec. Director
Aileen Cooper, Director, Program & Public Affairs

Board for Internat'l Broadcasting
1201 Connecticut Ave., N.W. Suite 400, Washington, DC 20036
Telephone: (202) 254-8040
Represented by:
Bruce D. Porter, Dr., Exec. Director

Boat Owners Ass'n of the U.S. Political Action Committee
880 South Pickett St., Alexandria, VA 22304
Telephone: (703) 823-9550
Background: Treasurer and contact is Michael Sciulla of Boat Owners Ass'n of the United States.

Boat Owners Ass'n of The United States (BOAT/U.S.)
880 South Pickett St., Alexandria, VA 22304
Telephone: (703) 823-9550
Background: The largest organization of recreational boat owners, serving 350,000 members, specializing in federal legislative and consumer affairs.
Represented by:
Elaine Dickinson, Associate Editor, Public Affairs
Richard Schwartz, President
Michael Sciulla, V. President and Lobbyist

Bobbie Brooks
Cleveland, OH
Counsel or consultant:
Dyer, Ellis, Joseph & Mills (Howard A. Vine)
Vorys, Sater, Seymour and Pease

Boeing Co.
1700 North Moore St., Arlington, VA 22209
Telephone: (703) 558-9600
Represented by:
Dale R. Babione, Director, Government Business Relations
E. W. Baragar, Manager, Congressional Affairs
Edward N. Bond, V. President, Congressional Affairs
Jane H. Cicala, Director, Boeing Commercial Airplane Co.
Paul Fang, Director, Public Relations
Christopher W. Hansen, Deputy Director, Congressional Affairs
James W. Kanouse, Manager, Congressional Affairs
Robert Lange, Manager, Congressional Affairs
Judith Morehouse, Manager, Government Business Relations
John E. Schmick, V. President, Washington Office
Elizabeth Nash Schwartz, Manager, Congressional Affairs
William N. Steele, Deputy Director, Congressional Affairs
Theresa M. Tilson, Congressional Affairs
Jeffrey Trauberman, Washington Manager, Space Systems Div.
Henry B. Van Gieson, Deputy Director, Congressional Affairs
Robert J. Vilhauer, Manager, Congressional Affairs
Counsel or consultant:
Hill and Knowlton Public Affairs Worldwide
Denny Miller Associates
Miller & Chevalier, Chartered (Alan R. Yuspeh)
Perkins Coie (Guy R. Martin, Bill Pederson)
Preston Gates Ellis & Rouvelas Meeds (Lloyd Meeds)

Boeing Computer Services
7980 Boeing Court, CV-83, Vienna, VA 22182
Telephone: (703) 827-4390
Represented by:
Sheldon R. Bentley, Director, Government Affairs
James L. Francalangria, FTS2000 Program Manager
Benjamin Prince, President, Boeing Computer Support Srvcs

Boise Cascade Corp.
Boise, ID
Counsel or consultant:
Lee, Toomey & Kent

Boise, Idaho, City of
Counsel or consultant:
F. H. Hutchison and Co. (Fred H. Hutchison)

Bollinger Machine Shop and Shipyard, Inc.
Lockport, LA

Counsel or consultant:
Fierce and Associates (Donald L. Fierce)
Fort and Schlefer

Bolova System and Instrument Division
Long Island, NY
Counsel or consultant:
Interlocke Associates

Bolt, Beranek and Newman
Cambridge, MA
Counsel or consultant:
Cassidy and Associates, Inc. (C. Frank Godfrey, Jr.)

Bombardier Corp.
2000 K St., N.W., Suite 301, Washington, DC 20006
Telephone: (202) 331-3350
Background: Serves its U.S. business groups and represents Bombardier Inc., the parent company, a Quebec based internat'l transportation and aerospace equipment manufacturer.
Represented by:
Larry E. Selci, President

Bond Internat'l Gold
Denver, CO
Counsel or consultant:
Wunder, Ryan, Cannon & Thelen (John J. McGovern, Jr.)

Bonneville Pacific Corp.
Salt Lake City, UT
Counsel or consultant:
Kogovsek & Associates, Inc.
Wilkinson, Barker, Knauer and Quinn (Kenneth E. Satten)

Boone Co.
Amarillo, TX
Counsel or consultant:
Akin, Gump, Strauss, Hauer and Feld (Joel Jankowsky, Edward S. Knight)
The Laxalt Corp. (Michelle D. Laxalt)

Boonestroo, Rosene, Anderlik & Associates
St. Paul, MN
Counsel or consultant:
Jefferson Group, The (Mark D. Cowan, Julie Susman)

Boots Co.
Lincolnshire, IL
Counsel or consultant:
Hill and Knowlton Public Affairs Worldwide (Ken Rabin)

Bophuthatswana, Government of
Mmbatho, Bophuthatswana
Counsel or consultant:
Allpoints Internat'l, Ltd. (James L. Denson)

Borden Internat'l
New York, NY
Background: A subsidiary of Borden, Inc.
Counsel or consultant:
Dross and Levenstein (William Levenstein)

Borg-Warner Automotive, Inc.
Detroit, MI
Counsel or consultant:
Rowland & Sellery (Terrie Dort, J. Patrick Rowland)

Bosch Corporation, Robert
Broadview, IL
Counsel or consultant:
Kaye, Scholer, Fierman, Hays and Handler (Christopher R. Brewster)

Boston Bruins, Inc.
Boston, MA
Counsel or consultant:
O'Neill and Athy, P.C. (Andrew Athy, Jr.)

Boston Capital Partners, Inc.
Boston, MA
Counsel or consultant:
Keene, Shirley & Associates, Inc. (Brent Bahler, Craigan P. Shirley)

Boston Carmen's Union, Local 589
Boston, MA
Counsel or consultant:
Cassidy and Associates, Inc. (James P. Collins, Thomas M. Gannon)

Boston Co., The
Boston, MA
Counsel or consultant:
Van Dyk Associates, Inc. (Milton Gwirtzman, Ted Van Dyk)

Boston College
Chestnut Hill, MA
Counsel or consultant:
Cassidy and Associates, Inc. (James P. Fabiani, C. Frank Godfrey, Jr.)

Boston Edison Co.
Boston, MA
Counsel or consultant:
Bruder, Gentile & Marcoux (George F. Bruder)

Boston Five Cents Savings Bank, FSB
Boston, MA
Counsel or consultant:
Thacher, Proffitt and Wood (Louis H. Nevins)

Boston Mass Transit Authority
Boston, MA
Counsel or consultant:
Verner, Liipfert, Bernhard, McPherson and Hand, Chartered (Harry C. McPherson, Douglas M. Steenland)

Boston, Massachusetts, City of
Counsel or consultant:
Nat'l Center for Municipal Development (Kevin Flanagan)

Boston Museum of Science
Boston, MA
Counsel or consultant:
Hale and Dorr (Jay P. Urwitz)

Boston University
Boston, MA
Counsel or consultant:
Cassidy and Associates, Inc. (Gerald S. J. Cassidy, James P. Collins, C. Frank Godfrey, Jr., Donald P. Smith)

Boundary Gas
Boston, MA
Counsel or consultant:
Dickstein, Shapiro and Morin (Frederick M. Lowther)

Bowater, Inc.
Darien, CT
Counsel or consultant:
Winthrop, Stimson, Putnam & Roberts (Raymond S. Calamaro, Michael W. Dolan)

Bowe Maschinenfabrik GmbH
Augsburg, Germany
Counsel or consultant:
Barnes, Richardson and Colburn (Rufus E. Jarman, Jr.)

Bowling and Billiard Institute of America
1625 K St., N.W., Washington, DC 20006
Telephone: (202) 775-1762
Background: Represented by Jan Kinney of the Sporting Goods Manufacturers Ass'n.

Bowling Proprietors' Ass'n of America
Arlington, TX
Counsel or consultant:
Manatt, Phelps, Rothenberg & Phillips (Robert T. Herbolsheimer)

Bowman Gray School of Medicine of Wake Forest University
Winston-Salem, NC
Counsel or consultant:
Ken Schlossberg Assoc. (Kenneth Schlossberg, William C. Smith)

Bowman Webber Ltd.
London, England
Counsel or consultant:
Ross and Hardies (James A. Stenger)

Boy Scouts of America
Irving, TX
Counsel or consultant:
Hecht, Spencer & Associates (Bronwyn R. Bachrach, William H. Hecht, W. Timothy Locke)

Boys Clubs of America
611 Rockville Pike, Suite 230, Rockville, MD 20852

ORGANIZATIONS REPRESENTED

Boys Clubs of America (Cont'd)
Telephone: (301) 251-6676
Represented by:
Robbie Callaway, Director, Government Relations

Boys Town Nat'l Research Hospital
Omaha, NE
Counsel or consultant:
MARC Associates, Inc. (Robert R. Humphreys)

Boysville of Michigan
Clinton, MI
Counsel or consultant:
Plunkett & Cooney , P.C. (William M. Brodhead)

BP America Inc.
1776 Eye St., N.W., Suite 1000, Washington, DC 20006
Telephone: (202) 785-4888
Represented by:
Larry D. Burton, Ass't. Director, Federal Gov't. Affairs
Felicia B. Coppola, Legislative Assistant
John C. Gore, V. President, Internat'l Affairs
Mary Lyn Herdt, Associate Director, Fed. Gov't. Affairs
Michael J. McAdams, Ass't Director, Federal Gov't Affairs
Janice I. Milazzo, Washington Representative
Kimberley A. Music, Legislative Assistant
William C. Rountree, V. President, Federal Government Affairs
Counsel or consultant:
Bonner & Associates

Bracewell and Patterson Political Action Committee
2000 K St., N.W., Suite 500, Washington, DC 20006-1809
Telephone: (202) 828-5800
Counsel or consultant:
Bracewell and Patterson (Gene E. Godley)

Braddock Communications
909 North Washington St., Alexandria, VA 22314
Telephone: (702) 549-6500
Represented by:
Jason L. Stern, President
Counsel or consultant:
Public Affairs Group, Inc. (Robert S. Boege, Edie Fraser)

Braille Revival League
1010 Vermont Ave., N.W. Suite 1100, Washington, DC 20005
Telephone: (202) 393-3666
Background: Represented by Roberta Douglas of the American Council of the Blind.

Brambles USA, Inc.
Chicago, IL
Counsel or consultant:
Mayer, Brown and Platt (William L. Massey)

Brand and Lowell Political Action Committee
923 15th St., N.W., Washington, DC 20005
Telephone: (202) 662-9700
Counsel or consultant:
Brand and Lowell, P.C.

Brandeis University
Waltham, MA
Counsel or consultant:
O'Neill and Athy, P.C. (Andrew Athy, Jr.)

Branigar Organization
Savannah, GA
Counsel or consultant:
Dow, Lohnes and Albertson (William B. Ingersoll)

Brazil Ministry of Finance
Brasilia, Brazil
Counsel or consultant:
Willkie Farr and Gallagher (Walter J. Spak)

Brazil, Secretariat of Waterborne Transportation (STA)
New York, NY
Counsel or consultant:
Hoppel, Mayer and Coleman (Neal M. Mayer)

Brazil-U.S. Business Council
Rio de Janeiro, Brazil
Counsel or consultant:
Bishop, Cook, Purcell & Reynolds

Brazilian Iron and Steel Institute
Rio de Janeiro, Brazil
Counsel or consultant:
Willkie Farr and Gallagher (William H. Barringer)

Bread for the World
802 Rhode Island Ave., N.E., Washington, DC 20018
Telephone: (202) 269-0200
Background: A Christian citizen's lobbying movement which seeks government policies that address the causes of hunger.
Represented by:
Larry Hollar, Department Director, Issues
The Rev. Arthur Simon, President

BREAD Political Action Committee
1111 14th St., N.W., Washington, DC 20005
Telephone: (202) 296-5800
Background: Represents the legislative and political interests of the American Bakers Ass'n. Paul Abenante, President of the Ass'n, serves as Treasurer.
Represented by:
Lori S. Vernberg, Manager

Bremer Lagerhaus-Gesellschaft
Bremen, West Germany
Background: The port authority of the German port of Bremen.
Counsel or consultant:
Prather, Seeger, Doolittle and Farmer (Thomas L. Farmer, Carl B. Nelson, Jr., Edwin H. Seeger)

Brennan Research Internat'l, Inc.
2300 M St., N.W., Suite 800, Washington, DC 20037
Telephone: (202) 466-5544
Background: A foreign trade consulting firm.
Represented by:
John V. Brennan, President

Brenton Banks
Des Moines, IA
Counsel or consultant:
Warren W. Koffler

Brewers Ass'n of Canada
Ottawa, Ontario
Counsel or consultant:
O'Melveny and Myers

Brewster Heights Packing Co.
Brewster, MA
Counsel or consultant:
Hill and Knowlton Public Affairs Worldwide (Tamara Cox)

Brick Institute of America
11490 Commerce Park Drive, Reston, VA 22091
Telephone: (703) 620-0010
Represented by:
Nelson J. Cooney, President
Charles Farley, Marketing Director
Counsel or consultant:
Reed Smith Shaw & McClay (David C. Evans)

Bridgeport and Port Jefferson Steamboat Co.
Bridegport, CT
Counsel or consultant:
Holland and Knight (David H. Baker)

Bridgeway Plan for Health
San Francisco, CA
Counsel or consultant:
Jefferson Group, The (David Serwer)

Bristol Bay Health Corp.
Dillingham, AK
Counsel or consultant:
Hobbs, Straus, Dean and Wilder (S. Bobo Dean)

Bristol Bay Native Corp.
Anchorage, AK
Counsel or consultant:
Dyer, Ellis, Joseph & Mills (Thomas L. Mills)
Robertson, Monagle and Eastaugh (Steven W. Silver)

Bristol-Myers Squibb Co.
655 15th St., N.W., Suite 410, Washington, DC 20005
Telephone: (202) 783-0900
Background: Formed with the acquisition of Squibb Co. by Bristol-Myers Co. Squibb is now a wholly-owned division of the new company.

Represented by:
Michael Carozza, Manager, Reimbursement Policy
Burt E. Rosen, Director, Federal Legislative Affairs
John G. Ryan, Director, Government Affairs
James P. Schlicht, Manager, Government Affairs
Richard L. Thompson, V. President, Government Affairs
Counsel or consultant:
Covington and Burling
Dewey, Ballantine, Bushby, Palmer and Wood (Joseph K. Dowley)
Patton, Boggs and Blow (Robert H. Koehler)
Wunder, Ryan, Cannon & Thelen (Dennis C. Thelen)

British Aerospace, Inc.
13873 Park Center Road, Herndon, VA 22071
Telephone: (703) 478-9420
Represented by:
George Dahlman, Manager, Press Office
Michael Jolley, V. President, Public Affairs
Counsel or consultant:
Hyman Fine & Associates Ltd.
Richard Richards Law Offices

British Aerospace, Inc./Defense Programs Office
1101 Wilson Blvd. Suite 1200, Arlington, VA 22209
Telephone: (703) 243-3939
Background: Marketing representatives of British Aerospace's defense business interests in the U.S.
Represented by:
Peter Boxer, Senior V. President
Philip Soucy, Manager, Public Affairs - Defense Progs.
Counsel or consultant:
Robison Internat'l, Inc.

British Airports Authority (BAA plc)
London, England
Counsel or consultant:
Gold and Liebengood, Inc. (David W. Bushong, Howard S. Liebengood, John F. Scruggs)

British Airtours Ltd.
London, England
Counsel or consultant:
Condon and Forsyth (Thomas J. Whalen)

British Ass'n of Investment Trust Companies
London, England
Counsel or consultant:
Alcalde & Rousselot (Hector Alcalde)

British Columbia, Canada, Government of
Victoria, British Columbia
Counsel or consultant:
Covington and Burling (Harvey M. Applebaum)

British Columbia Raspberry Growers Ass'n
Vancouver, British Columbia
Counsel or consultant:
Cameron and Hornbostel (William K. Ince)

British Consortium, The
Chicago, IL
Counsel or consultant:
O'Connor & Hannan (Timothy M. Haake)

British Embassy
3100 Massachusetts Ave., N.W., Washington, DC 20008
Telephone: (202) 462-1340
Counsel or consultant:
Leva, Hawes, Mason and Martin (Lowell D. Turnbull)

British Independent Steel Producers Ass'n
London, England
Counsel or consultant:
Beveridge & Diamond, P.C. (Alexander W. Sierck)

British Petroleum Oil Marketers Ass'n
GA
Counsel or consultant:
Bassman, Mitchell & Alfano, Chartered

British Steel Corp.
London, England
Counsel or consultant:
Steptoe and Johnson (Charlene Barshefsky, Richard O. Cunningham)

British Telecom plc
London, England

ORGANIZATIONS REPRESENTED

Counsel or consultant:
  Murphy and Malone (Terence R. Murphy)

British Tourist Authority
Woodside, NY
Counsel or consultant:
  Powell, Adams & Rinehart

Broad, Inc.
Los Angeles, CA
Counsel or consultant:
  Concord Associates, Inc.

Broadcast Education Ass'n
1771 N St., N.W., Washington, DC 20036
Telephone: (202) 429-5355
Represented by:
  Louisa A. Nielsen, Exec. Director

Broadcast Music Inc.
New York, NY
Counsel or consultant:
  Reid & Priest (Charles T. Duncan)
  Charls E. Walker Associates (James C. Free)

Broken Hill Proprietary Co., Ltd.
Melbourne, Australia
Counsel or consultant:
  O'Melveny and Myers

Bromon Aircraft Corp.
Las Vegas, NV
Counsel or consultant:
  Kilpatrick & Cody (Joseph W. Dorn, C. Randall Nuckolls)

Brookings Institution
1775 Massachusetts Ave., N.W., Washington, DC 20036
Telephone: (202) 797-6000
Background: A private, non-profit organization devoted to research, education and publication in economics, politics, government and foreign policy. Non partisan as an institution, it has attracted scholars and senior officials of both parties to its staff and had major impact on development of government policies and programs.
Represented by:
  Henry J. Aaron, Senior Fellow, Economic Studies Program
  Richard K. Betts, Defense Analyst
  Gary Burtless, Senior Fellow, Economic Studies Program
  Robert L. Faherty, Program Director, Publications Program
  Jane G. Fishkin, Dir., Social Science Computation Center
  Raymond L. Garthoff, Senior Fellow, Foreign Studies Program
  Stephen Hess, Sr. Fellow, Governmental Studies Program
  Edward A. Hewett, Senior Fellow
  John M. Hills, V. President, External Affairs
  Lawrence J. Korb, Dir., Center for Public Policy Education
  Robert E. Litan, Dir., Ctr. For Econ. Progress & Employ.
  Barbara Littell, Assoc. Dir., Ctr. for Public Pol. Educ.
  Bruce K. MacLaury, President
  Thomas E. Mann, Director, Governmental Studies Program
  Barbara Mathias, Assistant Director, Public Affairs
  Alice M. Rivlin, Senior Fellow, Economic Studies Program
  Charles L. Schultze, Director, Economic Studies Program
  John D. Steinbruner, Director, Foreign Policy Studies Program
  Stanley N. Wellborn, Director, Public Affairs
  Joshua M. Wiener, Senior Fellow
Counsel or consultant:
  Bruce G. Blair

Brooklyn Union Gas Co.
1225 19th St., N.W., Suite 320, Washington, DC 20036
Telephone: (202) 659-4716
Represented by:
  Brian M. Dolan, Director, Federal Government Relations
Counsel or consultant:
  Crowell and Moring (Dana C. Contratto)
  Cullen and Dykman (Michael W. Hall)

Brooks Brothers
New York, NY
Counsel or consultant:
  Templeton and Co. (Patrick A. Templeton)

Brother Internat'l, Inc.
Tokyo, Japan
Counsel or consultant:
  Tanaka, Ritger and Middleton (Patrick F. O'Leary, H. William Tanaka)

Brotherhood of Locomotive Engineers
400 First St., N.W., Suite 819, Washington, DC 20001
Telephone: (202) 347-7936
Represented by:
  Donald Lindsey, V. Pres. and Nat'l Legislative Rep.

Brotherhood of Maintenance of Way Employees
400 First St., N.W., Room 801, Washington, DC 20001
Telephone: (202) 638-2135
Represented by:
  Michael De Emilio, Assistant to the President
  Andrew T. Malleck, Nat'l Legislative Representative

Brotherhood of Railroad Signalmen
400 First St., N.W. Suite 708, Washington, DC 20001
Telephone: (202) 628-5935
Represented by:
  W. A. Radziewicz, V. President

Brotherhood of Railway Carmen of the U.S. and Canada
400 First St., N.W., Suite 804, Washington, DC 20001
Telephone: (202) 737-1541
Represented by:
  James E. Allred, General V. Pres & Nat'l Legislative Rep.

Broward County Governmental Center
Fort Lauderdale, FL
Counsel or consultant:
  Keefe Co., The (Clarence L. James, Jr., William A. Roberts)

Broward County, Office of the Sheriff
Fort Lauderdale, FL
Counsel or consultant:
  Mica, Dudinsky & Associates (John Dudinsky, Jr., John L. Mica)

Brown and Bain
Phoenix, AZ
Counsel or consultant:
  Winthrop, Stimson, Putnam & Roberts (Peter F. Gold)

Brown Bridgman & Co Retiree Health Care Group
1016 16th St. N.W. Suite 100, Washington, DC 20036
Telephone: (202) 659-3507
Background: Employee benefits consulting firm specializing in corporate America's retiree health care liability and its prefunding.
Represented by:
  Helen M. Ball, Director, Government Affairs

Brown Brothers Harriman & Co.
New York, NY
Counsel or consultant:
  Kaye, Scholer, Fierman, Hays and Handler (Christopher R. Brewster)

Brown & Root, Inc.
1150 Connecticut Ave., N.W., Suite 205, Washington, DC 20036-4104
Telephone: (202) 223-0820
Background: A wholly-owned subsidiary of the Halliburton Co.
Represented by:
  Wyll W. Pleger, Director, Federal Affairs

Brown and Williamson Tobacco Corp.
Louisville, KY
Counsel or consultant:
  B. L. Evans & Assoc. Inc. (Billy Lee Evans)
  Hecht, Spencer & Associates (Bronwyn R. Bachrach, William H. Hecht, Walter D. Huddleston, W. Timothy Locke)

Browning-Ferris Industries (D.C.), Inc.
1150 Connecticut Ave., N.W. Suite 500, Washington, DC 20036
Telephone: (202) 223-8151
Background: A waste services company.

Represented by:
  Phillip S. Angell, Consultant
  Richard F. Goodstein, Div. V. Pres, Nat'l Government Affairs
  Jon Greenberg, Manager, Environmental Policy
  Dolores Gregory, Consultant
  Lynette Lenard, Director of Federal Relations
  Mary Ellen Lynch, Manager, Environmental Planning
  Marcia E. Williams, Div. V. Pres., Envir. Policy & Planning
Counsel or consultant:
  Bonner & Associates
  Hill and Knowlton Public Affairs Worldwide
  McAuliffe, Kelly, Raffaelli & Siemens (John D. Raffaelli)
  McCutchen, Doyle, Brown & Enersen (Philip T. Cummings)
  Swidler & Berlin, Chartered
  Van Dyk Associates, Inc. (Jim Dickenson, Milton Gwirtzman, Ted Van Dyk)

Bruker Meerestechnik GmbH
Karlsruhe, Germany
Counsel or consultant:
  Forster & Associates (Johann R. Forster)

Brunei, Embassy of
2600 Virginia Ave., N.W., Suite 300, Washington, DC 20037
Telephone: (202) 342-0159
Counsel or consultant:
  Henry J. Kaufman & Associates (Michael G. Carberry, Sarah M. Goewey)
  Marshall, Tenzer, Greenblatt, Fallon and Kaplan (Sylvan M. Marshall)

Brunswick Corp. Defense Division
1745 Jefferson Davis Hwy. Suite 410, Arlington, VA 22202
Telephone: (703) 521-5650
Represented by:
  Thomas R. Flynn, V. President

BSA - Business Software Alliance
1201 Pennsylvania Ave., N.W. Suite 250, Washington, DC 20004
Telephone: (202) 737-7060
Represented by:
  Pilar M. Cloud, Director of Operations
Counsel or consultant:
  Covington and Burling (James R. Atwood)
  Swidler & Berlin, Chartered (Bruce A. Lehman)

BSN Groupe
Paris, France
Counsel or consultant:
  Max N. Berry Law Offices (Max N. Berry)

BTS Development Corp.
Sanibel Island, FL
Counsel or consultant:
  Laxalt, Washington, Perito & Dubuc (Marc J. Scheineson)

Buckeye Pipe Line Co.
Emmaus, PA
Counsel or consultant:
  Akin, Gump, Strauss, Hauer and Feld (Joel Jankowsky)

Budd Co.
Troy, MI
Counsel or consultant:
  Barnes, Richardson and Colburn (James H. Lundquist, Matthew T. McGrath)

Buenaventura Industrial Free Zone
Buenaventura, Colombia
Counsel or consultant:
  MacKenzie McCheyne, Inc. (I. R. MacKenzie)

BUILD-Political Action Committee
15th and M Sts., N.W., Washington, DC 20005
Telephone: (202) 822-0470
Background: Supported by the Nat'l Ass'n of Home Builders of the U.S.
Represented by:
  Jerry G. Malloy, Treasurer
Counsel or consultant:
  Baker and Hostetler

Building Industry Ass'n of Southern California
Irvine, CA
Counsel or consultant:
  Dutko & Associates (L. L. Hank Hankla)

ORGANIZATIONS REPRESENTED

Building Owners and Managers Ass'n Internat'l
1201 New York Ave., N.W. Suite 300, Washington, DC 20005
Telephone: (202) 289-7000
Represented by:
Henry Chamberlain, V. President, Communications
James C. Dinegar, V. President, Gov't & Industry Affairs
Mark W. Hurwitz, Exec. V. President
Michael A. Jawer, Legislative Director
Patricia L. Kosciuszko, Manager, Public Relations
Counsel or consultant:
Reed Smith Shaw & McClay (David C. Evans)

Building Owners and Managers Ass'n Political Action Committee
1201 New York Ave., N.W. Suite 300, Washington, DC 20005
Telephone: (202) 408-2662
Background: Contact is James C. Dinegar of the Association.

Building Service Contractors Ass'n, Internat'l
10201 Lee Hwy. Suite 225, Fairfax, VA 22030
Telephone: (703) 359-7090
Represented by:
Carol A. Dean, Exec. V. President

Bulgaria, Embassy of
1621 22nd St., N.W., Washington, DC 20008
Telephone: (202) 387-7969
Counsel or consultant:
Marshall, Tenzer, Greenblatt, Fallon and Kaplan (Sylvan M. Marshall)

Bulk Carrier Conference, Inc.
8007 Cryden Way, Forestville, MD 20747
Telephone: (301) 736-5515
Counsel or consultant:
Grove, Jaskiewicz, Gilliam and Cobert (Leonard A. Jaskiewicz)

Bumble Bee Seafoods, Inc.
San Diego, CA
Counsel or consultant:
Van Ness, Feldman & Curtis (Howard J. Feldman)

Bundesverband der Deutschen Industrie
Cologne, Germany
Counsel or consultant:
Baker and Botts (John P. Babb, Paul Freedenberg, B. Donovan Picard, John B. Veach, III)
Representative for German Industry and Trade (Dr. Lothar Griessbach, Hartmut Schneider, John Heath Vaughan, Jr,, Bernhard M. Welschke)

Bundesvereiningung der Deutschen Ernahrangsindustrie
West Germany
Counsel or consultant:
Coudert Brothers (Robert A. Lipstein)

Bunge Corp.
1101 15th St., N.W., Suite 503, Washington, DC 20005
Telephone: (202) 785-3885
Represented by:
Charles A. Nelson, V. President & Washington Representative

Bunker-Ramo-Eltra Corp.
Morristown, NJ
Counsel or consultant:
Reid & Priest

Bureau National Interprofessionel du Cognac
Cognac, France
Counsel or consultant:
Hill and Knowlton Public Affairs Worldwide (Charles R. Pucie, Jr.)

Bureau of Nat'l Affairs, Inc., The
1231 25th St., N.W., Washington, DC 20037
Telephone: (202) 452-4200
Background: Publishes legal, economic, labor, tax, financial, environmental, safety and energy information for business and professional users.
Represented by:
William A. Beltz, President and Editor-in-Chief
Emily Galloway Pilk, Asst. to the President, Communications
Paul N. Wojcik, V. President and General Counsel

Bureau of Wholesale Sales Representatives
Atlanta, GA
Counsel or consultant:
McKevitt Group, The

Burger King
Miami, FL
Counsel or consultant:
Richard B. Berman and Co.,Inc. (Richard B. Berman)

Burley and Dark Leaf Tobacco Export Ass'n
1100 17th St., N.W., Washington, DC 20036
Telephone: (202) 296-6820
Represented by:
Benjamin F. Reeves, Vice President and Managing Director

Burlington Industries Inc.
1001 Connecticut Ave., N.W. Suite 701, Washington, DC 20036
Telephone: (202) 223-3167
Represented by:
Donna Lee McGee, Director, Government Relations

Burlington Northern Railroad
50 F St., N.W., Suite 1080, Washington, DC 20001
Telephone: (202) 383-4980
Represented by:
Catharine R. Batky, Director, Legislative Affairs
Counsel or consultant:
Bartley M. O'Hara, P.C.
Preston Gates Ellis & Rouvelas Meeds (Pamela J. Garvie, Emanuel L. Rouvelas)
Snavely, King and Associates
Steptoe and Johnson (Betty Jo Christian)
Verner, Liipfert, Bernhard, McPherson and Hand, Chartered (Berl Bernhard)
White, Fine, and Verville (Arnold I. Havens)
Winburn, VanScoyoc, and Hooper (John P. Winburn)

Burlington Resources, Inc.
50 F St., N.W., Suite 1080, Washington, DC 20001
Telephone: (202) 383-4960
Represented by:
Randall I. Cole, Director, Legislative Affairs
Michael D. Moore, Director, Federal Agency Relations
Margaret J. Taylor, V. President, Legislative Affairs
Counsel or consultant:
Crowell and Moring (Steven P. Quarles)
Laxalt, Washington, Perito & Dubuc
Perkins Coie (Guy R. Martin)
Winburn, VanScoyoc, and Hooper (John P. Winburn)
Wunder, Ryan, Cannon & Thelen (Thomas M. Ryan)

Burnett & Hallamshire Holdings, PLC
London, England
Counsel or consultant:
Chadbourne and Parke

Burns and Roe Enterprises, Inc.
1400 K St., N.W., Washington, DC 20005
Telephone: (202) 898-1500
Represented by:
Randall B. Roe, Director, Washington Operations

Burroughs Wellcome Co.
1500 K St., N.W., Suite 625, Washington, DC 20005
Telephone: (202) 393-1420
Background: An international pharmaceutical manufacturer of prescription and over-the-counter drugs such as Actifed, Sudafed, Retrovir and Zovirex.
Represented by:
Dorothy A. Keville, Regional Government Affairs Manager
Richard Paul Teske, Dir., Federal Relations & Public Policy
Counsel or consultant:
Pagonis and Donnelly Group (Thomas R. Donnelly, Jr., Michael E. Grisso)

Burson-Marsteller Political Action Committee
1850 M St., N.W., Suite 900, Washington, DC 20036
Telephone: (202) 833-8550
Counsel or consultant:
Burson-Marsteller

Burundi, Embassy of
2233 Wisconsin Ave., N.W. Suite 212, Washington, DC 20007
Telephone: (202) 342-2574

Counsel or consultant:
van Kloberg and Associates (Edward J. van Kloberg, III)

Business Coalition for Fair Competition
1725 K St., N.W. Suite 412, Washington, DC 20006
Telephone: (202) 887-5872
Represented by:
James Lovell, Chairman
Jody Wharton, Exec. Director
Counsel or consultant:
William J. Tobin and Associates (William J. Tobin)

Business Coalition for RICO Reform
c/o Swidler & Berlin 3000 K St., N.W., Suite 300, Washington, DC 20007
Telephone: (202) 944-4300
Counsel or consultant:
Swidler & Berlin, Chartered (Barry Direnfeld)

Business Committee for Fair Civil RICO Legislation
c/o Richard Siegel 1400 16th St., N.W., Washington, DC 20036-2220
Telephone: (202) 234-0500
Background: A coalition opposing retroactivity provisions in legislation proposed to amend the Racketeer Influenced and Corrupt Organizations Act.
Counsel or consultant:
Richard D. Siegel

Business Computing Internat'l
New York, NY
Counsel or consultant:
Vorys, Sater, Seymour and Pease

Business Council
888 17th St., N.W., Suite 506, Washington, DC 20006
Telephone: (202) 298-7650
Background: A forum for the exchange of ideas between top corporate executives and government officials. Established originally as the Business Advisory Council to the Department of Commerce, it assumed its present name in 1961.
Represented by:
Jean H. Carter, Exec. Director

Business Council on the Reduction of Paperwork
1625 Eye St., N.W. Suite 903, Washington, DC 20006
Telephone: (202) 331-1915
Background: Works with business and the Federal Government to reduce regulatory complience paperwork and to improve the quality and timeliness of Federal statistics.
Represented by:
Mark E. Richardson, Exec. Director
Counsel or consultant:
Steele & Fornaciari (Clark R. Silcox)

Business Executives for Nat'l Security
601 Pennsylvania Ave., N.W. Suite 700, Washington, DC 20004
Telephone: (202) 737-1090
Background: Concerned with military planning and spending issues and use of sound business practices in national security policy.
Represented by:
Michael Burns, Senior Fellow
Mary Dent Crisp, Senior Political Advisor
James W. Morrison, V. President for Policy
Amy Voorhes, Director of Communications
Stanley A. Weiss, Board Chairman

Business-Higher Education Forum
One Dupont Circle, N.W., Suite 800, Washington, DC 20036
Telephone: (202) 939-9345
Represented by:
Don M. Blandin, Director

Business-Industry Political Action Committee
1747 Pennsylvania Ave., N.W. Suite 250, Washington, DC 20006-4697
Telephone: (202) 833-1880
Background: Founded in 1963. Supported by over 1,000 associations and corporations. Publishes The BIPAC Action Report (q.), Politikit (m.), and Politics (q.).

ORGANIZATIONS REPRESENTED

Represented by:
  Bernadette A. Budde, V. President, Political Education
  Joseph J. Fanelli, President
  C. J. Silas, Chairman
Counsel or consultant:
  Miller & Chevalier, Chartered

Business Men's Assurance Co. of America
Kansas City, MO
Counsel or consultant:
  Covington and Burling

Business Records Manufacturers Ass'n
1000 Connecticut Ave., N.W. Suite 1035, Washington, DC 20036
Telephone: (202) 296-7400
Represented by:
  John C. Vickerman, Exec. Director

Business Roundtable
1615 L St., N.W., Suite 1350, Washington, DC 20036
Telephone: (202) 872-1260
Background: An association of business executives of major corporations which examines and develops positions on public issues that affect the economy.
Represented by:
  Patricia H. Engman, Deputy Exec. Director
  Samuel L. Maury, Exec. Director
  Susan E. Spangler, Assistant Exec. Director
Counsel or consultant:
  Mayer, Brown and Platt

Business Software Ass'n
1201 Pennsylvania Ave., N.W. Suite 250, Washington, DC 20044
Telephone: (202) 737-7060
Represented by:
  Lori Forte, Director, Public Affairs

BUSPAC-Political Action Committee of the American Bus Ass'n
1015 15th St., N.W. Suite 250, Washington, DC 20005
Telephone: (202) 842-1645
Background: Represented by Susan Perry, Sr. V. President of Government Relations for the American Bus Ass'n.

Butler Capital Corp.
New York, NY
Counsel or consultant:
  Ropes and Gray (Suzanne Ross McDowell, Stephen E. Shay, Thomas M. Susman)

Buyers Up
P.O. Box 33757, Washington, DC 20009
Telephone: (202) 328-3800
Background: Affiliated with Public Citizen, Buyers Up purchases and provides low-cost home heating oil for consumers, and conducts residential conservation and radon gas measurement programs.
Represented by:
  Paul Israel, Director, Washington Office

C F Industries, Inc.
805 15th St., N.W., Washington, DC 20005
Telephone: (202) 371-9279
Represented by:
  Lori A. Comeau, Washington Representative
  Rosemary L. O'Brien, V. President, Public Affairs
Counsel or consultant:
  Kirkland and Ellis

C.V.G. Sideurgica del Orinoco Ca. (SIDOR)
Caracas, Venezuela
Counsel or consultant:
  Mudge Rose Guthrie Alexander and Ferdon (David P. Houlihan, William N. Walker)

Cable Television Administration and Marketing Soc.
635 Slaters Lane, Suite 250, Alexandria, VA 22314
Telephone: (703) 549-4200
Represented by:
  Margaret C. Durborow, President, Chief Operating Officer

Cable Television Ass'n of Maryland, Delaware and the District of Columbia
Annapolis, MD
Counsel or consultant:
  Arthur J. Gregg

Cable and Wireless North America
1919 Gallows Road, Vienna, VA 22182
Telephone: (703) 790-5300
Background: A subsidiary of Cable and Wireless plc of London, England.
Represented by:
  Keith E. Bernard, V. Pres., Internat'l & Regulatory Affrs.
  Carol Lynne Butler, Director, Regulatory Affairs
  Mark Richard Esherick, Manager, Legislative Affairs
Counsel or consultant:
  Willkie Farr and Gallagher (Sue D. Blumenfeld, Philip L. Verveer, Theodore C. Whitehouse)

Cablevision System Development Co.
Woodbury, NY
Counsel or consultant:
  Mintz, Levin, Cohn, Ferris, Glovsky and Popeo, P.C.

Cabot, Cabot & Forbes Realty Advisors
Boston, MA
Counsel or consultant:
  Mayer, Brown and Platt (Jerry L. Oppenheimer)

Cabot Corp.
Waltham, MA
Counsel or consultant:
  Baker and Botts (James A. Baker, IV)
  Stewart and Stewart (Terrence P. Stewart)

Cabot Oil & Gas
Houston, TX
Counsel or consultant:
  Ryan-McGinn (Daniel McGinn)

Cadmium Council
New York, NY
Counsel or consultant:
  Prather, Seeger, Doolittle and Farmer (Kurt E. Blase, Edwin H. Seeger)

CAE-LINK Corp.
1213 Jefferson Davis Hwy. Suite 1400, Gateway 4, Arlington, VA 22202
Telephone: (703) 553-0084
Represented by:
  Robert W. Harrison, Director, Washington Operations

Cain Hoy Plantation
Wando, SC
Counsel or consultant:
  Evans Group, Ltd., The (L. A., Skip Bafalis, Thomas B. Evans, Jr.)

Caisse des Depots et Consignations
Paris, France
Counsel or consultant:
  Hill and Knowlton Public Affairs Worldwide (Dr. Ira P. Kaminow)

Cajun Rural Electric Power Cooperative, Inc.
Baton Rouge, LA
Background: Law firm of Duncan, Weinberg, Miller & Pembroke represents rural electric cooperative in electric power matters.
Counsel or consultant:
  Duncan, Weinberg, Miller & Pembroke, P.C. (James D. Pembroke, Robert Weinberg)

California Ass'n of Sanitation Agencies
Sacramento, CA
Counsel or consultant:
  ENS Resources, Inc.

California Bankers Ass'n
San Francisco, CA
Counsel or consultant:
  Manatt, Phelps, Rothenberg & Phillips (Robert J. Kabel, Charles T. Manatt)

California Bankers Clearinghouse Ass'n
San Francisco, CA
Counsel or consultant:
  Morrison & Foerster (L. Richard Fischer, Robert M. Kurucza)

California Board of Equalization
Sacramento, CA
Counsel or consultant:
  David Vienna & Associates (Peter Leigh Snell)

California Co-Compost Systems
Playa del Ray, CA

California Department of Commerce
Sacramento, CA
Counsel or consultant:
  Braun & Company

California Department of Education
1000 Potomac St., N.W. Suite 401, Washington, DC 20007
Telephone: (202) 333-0349
Background: The listed member of The FMR Group, Inc. serves as a Federal Liaison Officer for the California Department of Educationn.
Counsel or consultant:
  FMR Group Inc., The (Patricia G. McGinnis)

California Desert Coalition
Riverside, CA
Counsel or consultant:
  Flanagan Group, Inc. (Theodore J. Garrish)

California Energy Co.
c/o Murphy & Demory 2300 M St., N.W. Suite 800, Washington, DC 20037
Telephone: (202) 785-3323
Counsel or consultant:
  Murphy and Demory, Ltd. (Admiral Daniel J. Murphy, USN (Ret.), Willard L. Demory, Jeffrey J. Grieco)

California Franchise Tax Board
Sacramento, CA
Counsel or consultant:
  David Vienna & Associates (Peter Leigh Snell, Cheryl Vienna)

California Instiute of Technology
Pasadena, CA
Counsel or consultant:
  Akin, Gump, Strauss, Hauer and Feld (Joel Jankowsky)

California Pipe Trades Council
San Mateo, CA
Counsel or consultant:
  Camp, Barsh, Bates and Tate (Dan C. Tate)

California Pistachio Commission
Fresno, CA
Counsel or consultant:
  Fried, Frank, Harris, Shriver & Jacobson (David E. Birenbaum)

California Prune Board
San Francisco, CA
Counsel or consultant:
  Robinson, Lake, Lerer & Montgomery (James H. Lake)

California Public Employees' Retirement System
Sacramento, CA
Counsel or consultant:
  David Vienna & Associates (David P. Vienna)

California Shipping Line, Inc.
Counsel or consultant:
  Galland, Kharasch, Morse and Garfinkle

California State Controller
Sacramento, CA
Counsel or consultant:
  Josiah Beeman
  David Vienna & Associates (Cheryl Vienna)

California State Lands Commission
Sacramento, CA
Counsel or consultant:
  Elinor Schwartz

California, State of
444 North Capitol St., N.W., Suite 305, Washington, DC 20001
Telephone: (202) 347-6891

The listings in this directory are available as *Mailing Labels*. See last page.

ORGANIZATIONS REPRESENTED

California, State of (Cont'd)
Represented by:
Michael Byrne, Washington Rep/Administrative Officer
Kathy Hoffman, Washington Rep, Transportation
Judy Jaussi, Washington Rep, Health & Welfare
Margaret McCarthy, Public Information Officer
Mary McDonald, Washington Rep, Natural Resources
Robert Moore, Director
John Nakamura, Washington Representative, Agriculture
Nancy J. Ordway, Fed. Budget Liaison, Wash. Office of Gov
Cary Walker, Wash. Rep, CA State World Trade Commiss.

California State Senate
Sacramento, CA
Counsel or consultant:
David Vienna & Associates (Peter Leigh Snell, Cheryl Vienna)

California Steel Industries Inc.
Fontana, CA
Counsel or consultant:
Arent, Fox, Kintner, Plotkin & Kahn (Michael D. Barnes)
Squire, Sanders and Dempsey (Robert H. Huey)
Peter Teeley & Associates

California Table Grape Commission
CA
Counsel or consultant:
McDermott, Will and Emery (Edward Ruckert)

California Walnut Commission
Sacramento, CA
Counsel or consultant:
Robinson, Lake, Lerer & Montgomery (James H. Lake)

California Wine Commission
San Francisco, CA
Counsel or consultant:
Dow, Lohnes and Albertson (Arthur H. Silverman)

Calista Corp.
Anchorage, AK
Counsel or consultant:
Preston Gates Ellis & Rouvelas Meeds (Susan B. Geiger, Lloyd Meeds)

CalMat Co.
Los Angeles, CA
Counsel or consultant:
Paul, Hastings, Janofsky and Walker (Judith Richards Hope)
Fred B. Rooney

Camara Argentina de la Alumino y Metales Afines
Buenos Aires, Brazil
Counsel or consultant:
Baker and McKenzie (Thomas P. Ondeck, B. Thomas Peele, III)

Camara de la Industria Curtidora Argentina
Buenos Aires, Argentina
Counsel or consultant:
Mudge Rose Guthrie Alexander and Ferdon (David P. Houlihan, Julie C. Mendoza)

Cambridge Information Group
7200 Wisconsin Ave. Suite 601, Bethesda, MD 20814
Telephone: (301) 961-6700
Counsel or consultant:
Akin, Gump, Strauss, Hauer and Feld (Joel Jankowsky)

Camera de la Industria Aceitara de la Republica
Buenos Aires, Argentina
Counsel or consultant:
Mudge Rose Guthrie Alexander and Ferdon

Cameroon, Government of
Yaounde, Cameroon
Counsel or consultant:
van Kloberg and Associates (Edward J. van Kloberg, III)

Campaign America
511 Capitol Court N. E. Suite 100, Washington, DC 20002
Telephone: (202) 543-5016
Background: A political action committee founded to increase Republican representation at all levels of the ballot. Founded by Sen. Robert Dole (R-KS).

Represented by:
JoAnne Coe, President & Exec. Director
Mark L. Miller, Finance Director
Dawn Sands, Administrator

Campaign Finance Reform Coalition
c/o Fred Wertheimer, Common Cause, 2030 M St., N.W., Washington, DC 20036
Telephone: (202) 833-1200
Background: A coalition of over 50 organizations working for new legislation to reform election campaign financing laws. Supporting groups include Common Cause, Public Citizen, the American Ass'n of Retired Persons, the National Farmers Union and the National Community Action Foundation.

Campaign for United Nations Reform
418 7th St., S.E., Washington, DC 20003
Telephone: (202) 546-3956
Background: A bi-partisan political organization working to create support for an upgraded U.N. through legislation, lobbying, electioneering, and publications. Also conducts a rating system for House and Senate and operates a PAC.
Represented by:
Eric Cox, Exec. Director

Campbell-Mithun
Minneapolis, MN
Counsel or consultant:
Professional Lobbying and Consulting Center (John L. Zorack)

Campbell Soup Co.
Camden, NJ
Counsel or consultant:
Camp, Barsh, Bates and Tate (Ronald L. Platt)
Covington and Burling (Sandra L. Spear)
McMillan and Farrell Associates (C. W. McMillan)

Campolonghi Italia S.p.A.
Montignoro, Italy
Counsel or consultant:
Dow, Lohnes and Albertson (William Silverman)

Can Manufacturers Institute
1625 Massachusetts Ave., N.W., Suite 500, Washington, DC 20036
Telephone: (201) 232-4677
Represented by:
Leslie Brown, V. President, Marketing & Communications
Robert Budway, General Counsel
J. Michael Dunn, President
John A. McIntyre, Exec. V. President

Canada, Embassy of
501 Pennsylvania Ave., N.W., Washington, DC 20001
Telephone: (202) 682-1740
Counsel or consultant:
Max N. Berry Law Offices (Max N. Berry)
Garvey, Schubert & Barer (Richard A. Wegman)
Rogers & Cowan, Inc.

Canada, Government of
Ottawa, Ontario
Counsel or consultant:
Coudert Brothers
Garvey, Schubert & Barer (Richard A. Wegman)
Miller & Chevalier, Chartered
O'Melveny and Myers
Jan Schneider, Esq.

Canada-United States Environmental Council
1244 19th St., N.W., Washington, DC 20036
Telephone: (202) 659-9510
Represented by:
James G. Deane, Co-Chairman

Canadair Challenger, Inc. Advanced Unmanned Systems Directorate
1215 Jefferson Davis Highway Suite 901, Arlington, VA 22202
Telephone: (703) 486-5850
Represented by:
Michael Hughes, Manager, Advanced Unmanned Systems
Tom Quasney, Manager, Advanced Unmanned Systems
Mike Stacy, V. President, Advanced Unmanned Systems
Counsel or consultant:
Fried, Frank, Harris, Shriver & Jacobson

Canadian Cattlemen's Ass'n

Counsel or consultant:
Bronz and Farrell (Edward J. Farrell)

Canadian Pacific
Montreal, Quebec
Counsel or consultant:
Snavely, King and Associates

Canadian Petroleum Ass'n
Calgary, Alberta
Counsel or consultant:
Brady and Berliner (Roger A. Berliner, Jerry M. Brady)

Canadian Pork Council
Ottawa, Ontario
Counsel or consultant:
Cameron and Hornbostel (William K. Ince)

Canadian Sugar Institute
Toronto, Ontario
Counsel or consultant:
Steptoe and Johnson (Susan G. Esserman)

Canai Inc.
Tokyo, Japan
Counsel or consultant:
Dorsey & Whitney

CANAMCO (The Canadian-American Company)
1220 19th St., N.W., Suite 202, Washington, DC 20036
Telephone: (202) 822-0707
Background: Represents American, Canadian and foreign firms and governments in Washington and U.S. firms with interests in Canada and abroad.
Represented by:
Matthew J. Abrams, President

Canaveral Port Authority
FL
Counsel or consultant:
Cramer and Haber

Canned and Cooked Meat Importers Ass'n
1215 17th St., N.W., Washington, DC 20036
Telephone: (202) 887-0353
Background: Incorporated in the District of Columbia in 1971. Primarily a legislative interest group whose members import meat from South America.
Counsel or consultant:
Kaplan, Russin and Vecchi (Marcia A. Wiss)

Cape Verde, Embassy of the Republic of
3415 Massachusetts Ave., N.W., Washington, DC 20007
Telephone: (202) 965-6820
Counsel or consultant:
Graham and James
Shaw, Pittman, Potts and Trowbridge
van Kloberg and Associates (Edward J. van Kloberg, III)

Capital Cities/ABC Inc.
2445 M St., N.W., Suite 480, Washington, DC 20037-1420
Telephone: (202) 887-7777
Represented by:
Deborah H. Gum, Office Supervisor, Government Relations
Mark M. MacCarthy, V. President, Government Affairs
Counsel or consultant:
Timmons and Co., Inc.
Wilmer, Cutler and Pickering (Joel Rosenbloom)

Capital Group
Los Angeles, CA
Counsel or consultant:
Newmyer Associates, Inc.

Capital Hill Group, Inc., The
Ottawa, Ontario
Counsel or consultant:
Keefe Co., The (Robert J. Keefe, Terry M. O'Connell)
TKC Internat'l, Inc.

Capital Markets Assurance Corp.
New York, NY
Counsel or consultant:
Kutak Rock & Campbell (Nancy L. Granese)

Capitol Research Center
1612 K St., N.W., Suite 704, Washington, DC 20006
Telephone: (202) 822-8666
Background: A research organization focusing on philanthropy, specializing in public interest groups, what they believe, how they are financed and how they and their financial supporters are affecting the political process and

ORGANIZATIONS REPRESENTED

society.
Represented by:
Thom Golab, Director Development
Willa Ann Johnson, Chairman
William T. Poole, Director of Research

Car Audio Specialists Ass'n
2101 L St., N.W., Suite 800, Washington, DC 20037
Telephone: (202) 828-2270
Represented by:
Cheryl J. Hollins, Exec. V. President
Counsel or consultant:
Dickstein, Shapiro and Morin (Sidney Dickstein)

Car Rental Coalition
2011 Eye St., N.W. Suite 500, Washington, DC 20006
Telephone: (202) 223-2118
Counsel or consultant:
Bregman, Abell & Kay (Stanley I. Bregman)

Carborundum Co.
Niagara Falls, NY
Counsel or consultant:
Dross and Levenstein (William Levenstein)

Cardinal Hill Hospital
Lexington, KY
Counsel or consultant:
Cassidy and Associates, Inc. (Andrea W. Bolling, C. Frank Godfrey, Jr., Dr. Frank A. Rose)

CARE
2025 I St., N.W., Suite 1003, Washington, DC 20006
Telephone: (202) 296-5696
Represented by:
Ronwyn Ingraham, Director, Washington Office

Care Enterprises
Los Angeles, CA
Counsel or consultant:
Parry and Romani Associates Inc. (Romano Romani)

Career Communications
Baltimore, MD
Counsel or consultant:
The Susan Davis Companies (Michael Cryor)

CareerCom Corp.
LeMoyne, PA
Counsel or consultant:
Carmen Group, The (Page C. Lee)
O'Connor & Hannan (Thomas R. Jolly)
Thompson and Co. (Robert L. Meuser, Karen Nasrallah, Margaret Shean, Robert J. Thompson, Ted Weggeland)

Caremark/Home Health Care of America
Newport Beach, CA
Counsel or consultant:
Hogan and Hartson (Bob Glen Odle, Ann Morgan Vickery)

CarePAC, The Blue Cross and Blue Shield Ass'n Political Action Committee
655 15th St., N.W. Suite 350, Washington, DC 20005
Telephone: (202) 626-4780
Background: Treasurer is Steve Ricchetti of the Association.
Represented by:
Brenda Larsen Becker, Director
Joyce Litz, CarePac Coordinator

Cargill, Inc.
1101 15th St., N.W., Suite 205, Washington, DC 20005
Telephone: (202) 785-3060
Represented by:
Robert R. Fahs, V. President & Washington Representative
W. Brendan Harrington, Public Affairs Counselor
Robert W. Kohlmeyer, Public Affairs Counselor
M. Stephanie Patrick, Public Affairs Counselor
Counsel or consultant:
O'Melveny and Myers (Kermit W. Almstedt)
Schmeltzer, Aptaker and Sheppard (Edward Schmeltzer, Edward J. Sheppard, IV)
Steptoe and Johnson (Richard O. Cunningham, Susan G. Esserman)

Cargolux Airlines Internat'l
Luxembourg
Counsel or consultant:
Patton, Boggs and Blow (Timothy J. May)

Caribbean/Central American Action
1211 Connecticut Ave., N.W. Suite 510, Washington, DC 20036
Telephone: (202) 466-7464
Background: Seeks to encourage the American private sector to play a more active role in helping Caribbean countries develop their economies. Supported financially by several major U.S. corporations.
Represented by:
Peter B. Johnson, Exec. Director

Caribbean Investment Group
Sarasota, FL
Counsel or consultant:
Lachelli, Waller and Associates

Caribbean Trade and Apparel Coalition (C-TAC)
1215 17th St., N.W., Washington, DC 20036
Telephone: (202) 887-0353
Background: Address above is that of Kaplan, Russin, & Vecchi, a Washington law firm.
Counsel or consultant:
Kaplan, Russin and Vecchi (Jonathan Russin, William R. White)

Carlan Homes
Tustin, CA
Counsel or consultant:
Liz Robbins Associates (Michael J. Lucas, Liz Robbins)

Carlon Co.
Beachwood, OH
Counsel or consultant:
Kaye, Scholer, Fierman, Hays and Handler (Christopher R. Brewster)

Carlon Electrical Sciences, Inc.
Cleveland, OH
Counsel or consultant:
Marlowe and Co.

Carlucci Construction Co.
Pittsburgh, PA
Counsel or consultant:
Durante Associates

Carlyle Group, The
1001 Pennsylvania Ave., N.W. Suite 220, Washington, DC 20004
Telephone: (202) 347-2626
Counsel or consultant:
Dow, Lohnes and Albertson (Jeffrey Kurzweil)
Hill and Knowlton Public Affairs Worldwide (Charles Francis)

Carnegie Council on Adolescent Development
11 Dupont Circle, N.W., Washington, DC 20036
Telephone: (202) 265-9080
Counsel or consultant:
Gallagher-Widmeyer Group Inc., The (Scott D. Widmeyer)

Carnival Cruise Lines
Miami, FL
Counsel or consultant:
Alcalde & Rousselot (Hector Alcalde)
Holland and Knight (Marshall L. Matz)

Carolina Power and Light Co.
Raleigh, NC
Counsel or consultant:
Donelan, Cleary, Wood and Maser, P.C. (John F. Donelan)
Howrey and Simon (Ray S. Bolze)
Charlie McBride Assoc, Inc. (Charlie McBride)
Reid & Priest
Shaw, Pittman, Potts and Trowbridge (Thomas A. Baxter)

Carolina, Puerto Rico, City of
Counsel or consultant:
Jefferson Group, The (Jose Ortiz-Daliot)

Carpenter Labs
Willowstreet, PA
Counsel or consultant:
Montgomery, McCracken, Walker & Rhoads (Linda Long, David F. Norcross)

Carpenter Technology Corp.
Reading, PA

Collier, Shannon & Scott (David A. Hartquist)

Carpenters' Legislative Improvement Committee
101 Constitution Ave., N.W., Washington, DC 20001
Telephone: (202) 546-6206
Background: A political action committee sponsored by the United Brotherhood of Carpenters and Joiners of America. Wayne Pierce of the parent association serves as Treasurer.

Carr Company, The Oliver
1700 Pennsylvania Ave., N.W., Washington, DC 20006
Telephone: (202) 624-1700
Counsel or consultant:
Burson-Marsteller (Sharon Natanblut)

Carson, Pirie, Scott & Co.
Chicago, IL
Counsel or consultant:
Skadden, Arps, Slate, Meagher and Flom

Carter-Wallace, Inc.
New York, NY
Counsel or consultant:
Kleinfeld, Kaplan and Becker (Robert H. Becker, Alan H. Kaplan, Peter O. Safir)
Lee, Toomey & Kent

CASA (Church Alliance of South Africa)
Irene, South Africa
Counsel or consultant:
The William Chasey Organization (Virginia Chasey)

Casa del Pueblo
1459 Columbia Road, N.W., Washington, DC 20009
Telephone: (202) 332-1082
Background: A community-oriented organization serving the Hispanic community in the metropolitian Washington area.
Represented by:
Jorge Pantelis, General Coordinator

Casalee America Corp.
Winston-Salem, NC
Counsel or consultant:
Prather, Seeger, Doolittle and Farmer (D. Edward Wilson, Jr.)

Cascade Natural Gas Corp.
Seattle, WA
Counsel or consultant:
Donelan, Cleary, Wood and Maser, P.C. (Ted P. Gerarden)

Case Co., J. I.
Racine, WI
Counsel or consultant:
Barnes, Richardson and Colburn (Robert E. Burke, Matthew T. McGrath, Gunter Von Conrad)

Casino
Paris, France
Counsel or consultant:
Hill and Knowlton Public Affairs Worldwide (Dr. Ira P. Kaminow)

Casino Ass'n of New Jersey
Atlantic City, NJ
Counsel or consultant:
Black, Manafort, Stone and Kelly Public Affairs Co. (Nicholas A. Panuzio)

Cast Iron Pipefittings Committee
1575 Eye St., N.W., Suite 800, Washington, DC 20005
Telephone: (202) 789-7510
Counsel or consultant:
McKenna, Conner and Cuneo (Peter Buck Feller)

Castine Partners
New York, NY
Counsel or consultant:
Dow, Lohnes and Albertson (Stuart Marshall Bloch)
Thacher, Proffitt and Wood (Virginia W. Brown)

Castle-Harlan, Inc.
New York, NY
Counsel or consultant:
Jones, Day, Reavis and Pogue (Randall E. Davis)

Catalyst Energy Corp.
New York, NY

ORGANIZATIONS REPRESENTED

Catalyst Energy Corp. (Cont'd)
Counsel or consultant:
Olwine, Connelly, Chase, O'Donnell and Weyher (John L. Sachs, W. Harrison Wellford)

Caterpillar Inc.
1730 Pennsylvania Ave., N.W., Suite 750, Washington, DC 20006
Telephone: (202) 879-3050
Represented by:
William W. Beddow, Governmental Affairs, Washington Manager
Douglas P. Crew, Washington Representative
Counsel or consultant:
Hogan and Hartson (Samuel R. Berger)
Howrey and Simon (Richard T. Colman, David C. Murchison)
Powell, Goldstein, Frazer and Murphy (Peter Suchman)

Catholic Charities USA
1319 F St., N.W., Suite 400, Washington, DC 20004
Telephone: (202) 639-8400
Background: Mission is to provide service to those in need, to be an advocate for justice in societal structures and to call the entire Church and other people of good will to do the same. Represents Catholic social philosophy to government and private agencies.
Represented by:
Brother Joseph Berg, Director for Special Programs
Lisa Carr, Legislative Assistant
Lynn B. Carroll, Director for Development
Rev. Thomas J. Harvey, Exec. Director
Ms. Alexandra Peeler, Director of Communications
Jane Stenson, Director for Aging Services
Ms. RoseMary Winder Strange, Director for Social Services

Catholic Health Ass'n of the United States
1776 K St., N.W. Suite 204, Washington, DC 20006
Telephone: (202) 296-3993
Represented by:
William J. Cox, V. President, Div. of Gov't Services
Julie Trocchio, Government Liaison

Catholic Indian Missions, Bureau of
2021 H St., N.W., Washington, DC 20006
Telephone: (202) 331-8542
Represented by:
Msgr. Paul A. Lenz, Exec. Director

Catholic University of America
620 Michigan Ave., N.E., Washington, DC 20017
Telephone: (202) 635-5100
Counsel or consultant:
Cassidy and Associates, Inc. (Gerald S. J. Cassidy, Donald P. Smith)
Williams and Connolly

Catholic War Veterans of the U.S.A.
419 N. Lee St., Alexandria, VA 22314
Telephone: (703) 549-3622
Represented by:
Chet Ellisage, Nat'l Commander
William Gill, Exec. Director

Catholics for a Free Choice
1436 U St., N. W. Suite 301, Washington, DC 20009
Telephone: (202) 638-1706
Background: A group of Catholics who are working for reproductive freedom and who support the Supreme Court decision on abortion.
Represented by:
Mary Jean Collins, Director, Public Affairs
Margaret Conway, Director, State and Local Projects
Frances Kissling, President

Cathy's Brownies
P.O. Box 3731, Washington, DC 20007
Telephone: (202) 333-8190
Counsel or consultant:
Robert N. Pyle & Associates

Cato Institute
224 Second St., S.E., Washington, DC 20003
Telephone: (202) 546-0200
Background: A public policy research institution which tends to favor a "classical liberal" approach to political and economic issues.
Represented by:
Doug Bandow, Senior Fellow
David D. Boaz, Exec. V. President
Ted Galen Carpenter, Director, Foreign Policy Studies
Edward H. Crane, President
James A. Dorn, V. President, Academic Affairs
Catherine England, Director, Regulatory Studies
Peter Ferrara, Senior Fellow
Sandra H. McCluskey, Director of Public Affairs
William A. Niskanen, Jr., Chairman
Roger Pilon, Senior Fellow, Constitutional Studies
Catherine S. Smith, V. President, Dev'lpmnt & Public Affairs

Cattlemen's Beef Promotion and Research Board
Englewood, CO
Counsel or consultant:
McLeod & Pires (Wayne R. Watkinson)

Cayman Airways Ltd.
Grand Cayman, Cayman Islands
Counsel or consultant:
Bishop, Cook, Purcell & Reynolds

Cayman Islands, Government of
Grand Cayman, Cayman Islands
Counsel or consultant:
Berliner and Maloney
Sidley and Austin (Lester C. Fant, III, Joseph B. Tompkins, Jr.)

CBI Industries, Inc.
1101 17th St., N.W., Suite 812, Washington, DC 20036
Telephone: (202) 466-3706
Represented by:
Stephen J. Toth, Manager - Washington Office

CBS, Inc.
1800 M St., N.W. Suite 300 North, Washington, DC 20036
Telephone: (202) 457-4501
Represented by:
Martin D. Franks, V. President, Washington
John F. Sturm, V. President, Government Affairs
Counsel or consultant:
Griffin, Johnson & Associates
Lee, Toomey & Kent

CBS Records Group
New York, NY
Counsel or consultant:
Charls E. Walker Associates (James C. Free)

CDM/Federal Programs Corp.
Faifax, VA
Counsel or consultant:
Daniel J. Edelman, Inc. (Stephen K. Cook, Christine Fillip)

Ceco Corp.
1801 McCormick Place, Landover, MD 20785
Telephone: (301) 322-2326
Represented by:
William F. Slattery, V. President and General Manager

Cellular Telecommunications Industry Ass'n
1133 21St., N.W., Third Floor, Washington, DC 20036
Telephone: (202) 785-0081
Represented by:
Jo-Anne R. Basile, Director, Federal Relations
Kevin J. Kelley, V. President
Robert W. Maher, President
Elizabeth F. Maxfield, V. President
Counsel or consultant:
Willkie Farr and Gallagher (Sue D. Blumenfeld, Philip L. Verveer)

Cement Free Trade Ass'n
Los Angeles, CA
Counsel or consultant:
E. Del Smith, Inc. (E. Del Smith)

Cementos de Chihuahua
Mexico
Counsel or consultant:
Willkie Farr and Gallagher (Walter J. Spak)

Centel Corp.
1350 Eye St., N.W., Suite 500, Washington, DC 20005
Telephone: (202) 778-8700
Represented by:
Nancy R. McCabe, Assistant Manager, Government Relations
James D. Ogg, V. President, Government Relations
Patricia E. Simmons, General Manager, Government Relations

Centel Corp. Good Government Fund
1350 Eye St., N.W. Suite 500, Washington, DC 20005
Telephone: (202) 778-8700
Background: Contact is James Ogg of Centel Corp.

Center for Auto Safety
2001 S St., N.W., Room 410, Washington, DC 20009
Telephone: (202) 328-7700
Represented by:
Clarence M. Ditlow, Exec. Director
Gerald A. Donaldson, Highway Safety Project Director
Laura Polacheck, Staff Attorney
Counsel or consultant:
Howard A. Heffron

Center for Clean Air Policy
444 N. Capitol St., Suite 526, Washington, DC 20001
Telephone: (202) 624-7709
Background: Created with a desire to inform decision-makers of the underlying environmental and economic implications of air pollution controls with the hope of advancing the air pollution debate beyond traditionally polarizing perspectives. Edward A. Helme serves as Exec. Director.
Represented by:
Chris Neme, Senior Policy Analyst
Nicole Werner, Research Assistant

Center for Community Change
1000 Wisconsin Ave., N.W., Washington, DC 20007
Telephone: (202) 342-0519
Background: Renders assistance and advice on community investment and related issues of particular concern to minority groups and low and moderate income community organizations.
Represented by:
Pablo Eisenberg, President
Allen Fishbein, Dir., Neighborhood Revitalization Proj.

Center for Constitutional Rights
New York, NY
Counsel or consultant:
Maggio and Kattar, P.C. (Michael Maggio)

Center for Corporate Public Involvement
1001 Pennsylvania Ave., N.W., Washington, DC 20004
Telephone: (202) 624-2425
Background: Sponsored by the American Council of Life Insurance and the Health Insurance Association of America to assist member insurance companies to broaden participation and improve their effectiveness in social responsibility activities and community programs.
Represented by:
Stanley G. Karson, Director

Center for Defense Information
1500 Massachusetts Ave., N.W., Washington, DC 20005
Telephone: (202) 862-0700
Background: Founded in 1972, CDI exists "to make independent, informed analyses of U. S. defense policies available to journalists, scholars, government officials and the executive branch." It proposes options for obtaining equal or greater security at reduced expense; a particular concern is the danger of nuclear war. Publishes Defense Monitor (10/yr.); each edition is devoted to a single military issue.
Represented by:
James T. Bush, Associate Director
Rear Admiral Eugene J. Carroll, USN (Ret), Deputy Director
David T. Johnson, Research Director
Rear Admiral Gene R. La Rocque, USN (Ret), Founder and Director

Center for Democracy
1101 15th St., N.W., Suite 505, Washington, DC 20005
Telephone: (202) 429-9141

ORGANIZATIONS REPRESENTED

Background: A non-profit, non-partisan and tax-exempt institute founded in 1985 to undertake interdisciplinary programs and studies on major issues confronting democratic societies. Board of Directors includes a range of national political, congressional, business and educational leaders, including the chairmen of the Democratic and Republican parties. Active programs abroad include projects in Central and South America, Western Europe, Southern Africa, the Philippines and Hong Kong. Enjoys a close working relationship with the U.S. Congress, the Council of Europe, the European Parliament and legislatures throughout the Americas. It has undertaken electoral monitoring missions in the Philippines, Panama and Nicaragua. Its U.S. programs include the Bipartisan Commission on National Political Conventions and 'Democracy Hall', a national museum of the democratic experience.
Represented by:
Dr. Allen Weinstein, President and CEO
Counsel or consultant:
Hogan and Hartson (Anthony Harrington)
Montgomery, McCracken, Walker & Rhoads (David F. Norcross)

Center for Dispute Settlement
1666 Connecticut Ave., N.W. Suite 501, Washington, DC 20009
Telephone: (202) 265-9572
Background: Designs, implements and evaluates alternative methods of resolving disputes.
Represented by:
Linda R. Singer, Exec. Director

Center for Economic Organizing
1522 K St., N.W., Suite 406, Washington, DC 20005
Telephone: (202) 775-9072
Background: Founded in 1972 as the People's Bicentennial Commission, CEO promotes "economic democracy", a goal which entails greater labor union and public sector control of capital and the work place through, among other things, investment of $800 billion in pension fund assets.
Represented by:
Randy Barber, Director

Center for Foreign Journalists
11690-A Sunrise Valley Drive, Reston, VA 22091
Telephone: (703) 620-5984
Represented by:
George A. Krimsky, V. President and Exec. Director

Center for Foreign Policy Options
Counsel or consultant:
Potomac Partners

Center for Health Policy Studies
c/o Georgetown University, 2233 Wisconsin Ave., N.W., Washington, DC 20007
Telephone: (202) 342-0107
Represented by:
Jack Hadely, Co-director
William Scanlon, Co-director

Center for Historic Houses
1785 Massachusetts Ave., N.W., Washington, DC 20036
Telephone: (202) 673-4025
Represented by:
Maureen McKasy-Donlin, Director

Center for Immigration Studies
1424 16th St., N.W. Suite 603, Washington, DC 20036
Telephone: (202) 328-7228
Background: Founded to encourage original thinking about immigration and its relation to the national interest.
Represented by:
David E. Simcox, Director

Center for Individual Rights
2300 N St., N.W. Suite 600, Washington, DC 20037
Telephone: (202) 663-9041
Represented by:
Michael Greve, Exec. Director

Center for Internat'l Business and Trade
Georgetown University 1242 35th St., N.W., Suite 501, Washington, DC 20057
Telephone: (202) 687-6993
Represented by:
John C. Onto, Director
James M. Spiegelman, Director of Research and Programs

Center for Internat'l Development and Environment
1709 New York Ave., N.W. 7th Floor, Washington, DC 20006
Telephone: (202) 638-6300
Background: A center within the World Resources Institute which serves as a catalyst for action on environment and development issues.
Represented by:
Thomas H. Fox, Director

Center for Internat'l Policy
1755 Massachusetts Ave., N.W., Suite 500, Washington, DC 20036
Telephone: (202) 232-3317
Background: A private, non-profit research and public education organization concerned with the impact of U.S. foreign policies, particularly economic and military assistance, on human rights and social and economic needs in the Third World. A project of the Fund for Peace.
Represented by:
William C. Goodfellow, Director

Center for Internat'l Private Enterprise
1615 H St., N.W., Washington, DC 20062
Telephone: (202) 463-5901
Background: An arm of the Chamber of Commerce of the U.S.A. William T. Archey, of the Chamber of Commerce as V. President and Exec. Director.
Represented by:
Donald R. Norland, Program Director

Center for Investigative Reporting
309 Pennsylvania Ave., S.E. 3rd Floor, Washington, DC 20003
Telephone: (202) 546-1880
Background: An organization dedicated to the principle of freedom of expression and the need for close and critical examination of influential individuals and public and private institutions. Funded by foundations and other private sources.
Represented by:
William Kistner, Staff Writer

Center for Judicial Studies
Box 15499, Washington, DC 20003
Telephone: (202) 544-1776
Background: A conservative 'think tank' devoted to the study and reform of the Constitution and the courts. National office is located in Richmond, Virginia.
Represented by:
Dr. James McClellan, President

Center for Law and Education
236 Massachusetts Ave., N.E. Suite 504, Washington, DC 20002
Telephone: (202) 546-5300
Represented by:
Lucy R. Watkins, Education Advocate
Paul Weckstein, District of Columbia Director

Center for Law and Social Policy
1616 P St., N.W., Suite 350, Washington, DC 20036
Telephone: (202) 328-5140
Background: Represents the interests of the poor before federal agencies, Congress and courts on family policy and law and represents legal service programs on legal and regulatory issues.
Represented by:
Mark Greenberg, Senior Staff Attorney
Alan W. Houseman, Director
Jodie Levin-Epstein, State Policy Advocate
Linda Perle, Senior Staff Attorney
Paula Roberts, Senior Staff Attorney
Erica Tollet, Policy Advocate

Center for Marine Conservation
1725 DeSales St., N.W. Suite 500, Washington, DC 20036
Telephone: (202) 429-5609
Background: Tax exempt organization founded in 1972 which seeks to mobilize public concern for protecting the marine environment. Sponsors programs on habitat conservation, pollution prevention, protected species, fisheries management, and citizen education.
Represented by:
Roger E. McManus, President
Michael Weber, V. President for Programs
Counsel or consultant:
O'Connor & Hannan (George J. Mannina, Jr.)

Center for Media and Public Affairs
2101 L St., N.W., Suite 505, Washington, DC 20037
Telephone: (202) 223-2942
Background: A research institute devoted to scientific analysis of news and entertainment media.
Represented by:
Antoinette Grueninger, Manager, Public Relations
Linda S. Lichter, Co-Director
S. Robert Lichter, Co-Director

Center for Nat'l Policy
317 Massachusetts Ave., N.E. Suite 300, Washington, DC 20002
Telephone: (202) 546-9300
Background: A nonprofit research and education organization focused on public policy issues. Seeks a discussion and re-evaluation of policies and problems through publications, sponsored studies and conferences and symposia. Former Secretary of State Edmund S. Muskie is Board Chairman. Until 1982 known as the Center for Democratic Policy.
Represented by:
Madeleine K. Albright, President

Center for Nat'l Security Studies
122 Maryland Ave., N.E., Washington, DC 20002
Telephone: (202) 544-1681
Background: A project of the American Civil Liberties Union Foundation and the Fund for Peace which has focused on what it believes have been violation of individual citizens rights in the name of nat'l security and on the public's right to know. Director is Morton Halperin of the ACLU Washington Office.
Represented by:
Kate Martin, Director, Nat'l Security Litigation Proj

Center for Peace and Freedom
214 Massachusetts Ave., N.E., Suite 360, Washington, DC 20002
Telephone: (202) 547-5607
Background: Provides information on human rights, defense and foreign policy. Takes particular interest in the Strategic Defense Initiative, which it supports.
Represented by:
John D. Kwapisz, Exec. Director

Center for Population Options
1012 14th St., N.W. Suite 1200, Washington, DC 20005
Telephone: (202) 347-5700
Background: Seeks to assist professionals and to educate adolescents about family planning, reproductive health and life options to reduce the incidence of teenage pregnancy.
Represented by:
Judith Senderowitz, Exec. Director
Cathie Sullivan, Associate Director, Communications

Center for Privatization
2000 Pennsylvania Ave., N.W. Suite 2500, Washington, DC 20006
Telephone: (202) 872-9250
Background: A consulting organization created by AID to promote privatization in developing countries.
Represented by:
Paul H. Elicker, Exec. Director

Center for Public Integrity
P.O. Box 18134, Washington, DC 20036
Telephone: (202) 223-0299
Background: A non-partisan group of investigative reporters concerned about public ethics.
Represented by:
Charles Lewis, Exec. Director

Center for Responsive Politics
1320 19th St., N.W., Washington, DC 20036
Telephone: (202) 857-0044
Background: Founded in 1983, the Center for Responsive Politics is a non-profit, bi-partisan organization which examines congressional issues and trends.
Represented by:
Ellen S. Miller, Director

Center for Science in the Public Interest
1501 16th St., N.W., Washington, DC 20036
Telephone: (202) 332-9110
Background: A tax-exempt public interest organization set up to clarify the relationship between scientific issues and the public's health and safety. Its major thrust is to increase public awareness of food and nutrition problems and it is critical of certain food industry and government

ORGANIZATIONS REPRESENTED

Center for Science in the Public Interest (Cont'd)
policies and practices.
Represented by:
Roger Blobaum, Dir., Americans for Safe Food Project
Dr. Michael F. Jacobson, Exec. Director
Charles P. Mitchell, Staff Attorney
Robert Parrish, Staff Attorney
Bruce A. Silverglade, Director of Legal Affairs
Patricia Taylor, Dir. for Alchohol Policies Project

Center for Security Policy
1250 24th St., N.W., Washington, DC 20037
Telephone: (202) 466-0515
Background: A non-partisan policy information network serving those in government, industry, and the press desiring an understanding of the strategically significant developments related to national defense and foreign policy.
Represented by:
Rinelda Bliss-Walters, Special Assistant and Corp. Secretary
Frank J. Gaffney, Jr., President and Director
Sven F. Kraemer, Deputy Director
Jennifer J. White, Senior Associate

Center for Sickle Cell Disease
c/o Howard University, 2121 Georgia Ave., N.W., Washington, DC 20059
Telephone: (202) 636-7930
Represented by:
Dr. Roland B. Scott, Director

Center for Strategic and Internat'l Studies
1800 K St., N.W., Washington, DC 20006
Telephone: (202) 887-0200
Background: An independent research organization. Was affiliated with Georgetown University from 1962-87. Exerts key influence over foreign policy thinking within government, government-connected circles in Washington, academia and the corporate community through its research, publications and seminars.
Represented by:
David M. Abshire, President and CEO
Stanton Burnett, Director of Studies
Robert E. Hunter, V. Pres., Regional Programs
Douglas M. Johnston, Jr., Exec. V. President and COO
William J. Taylor, V. Pres., Internat'l Security Programs
John N. Yochelson, V. President, Corporate Affairs

Center for Studies in Health Policy
1155 Connecticut Ave., N.W. Suite 500, Washington, DC 20036
Telephone: (202) 659-3270
Background: Offers research and advisory service to those who formulate and implement health policy in both the public and private sectors of the economy.
Represented by:
Dr. Meredith A. Gonyea, President

Center for Study of Responsive Law
Box 19367, Washington, DC 20036
Telephone: (202) 387-8030
Background: The first Nader organization to be established, in 1968, as a tax-exempt study group to conduct research and produce reports for public education on consumer, environmental, tax, health and other problems.
Represented by:
Ralph Nader, Managing Trustee
Beverly Orr, Business Manager
John Richard, Assistant to the Managing Trustee

Center for the Study of Public Choice Foundation
Faifax, VA
Counsel or consultant:
Sedam and Shearer (Glenn J. Sedam, Jr.)

Center for the Study of Social Policy
1250 Eye St., N.W., Suite 503, Washington, DC 20005
Telephone: (202) 371-1565
Represented by:
Tom Joe, Director, Washington Office

Center for the Study of the Presidency
New York, NY
Counsel or consultant:
Public Affairs Group, Inc. (Edie Fraser)

Center for Women Policy Studies
2000 P St., N.W. Suite 508, Washington, DC 20036
Telephone: (202) 872-1770
Background: A non-profit, policy and research-oriented organization that works on specific issues affecting women, particularly women and girls of color.
Represented by:
Dr. Leslie R. Wolfe, Exec. Director

Center of Industries of the State of San Paulo (CIESP)
Sao Paulo, Brazil
Counsel or consultant:
Bishop, Cook, Purcell & Reynolds (Royal Daniel, III)

Center on Budget and Policy Priorities
236 Massachusetts Ave., N.E., Suite 305, Washington, DC 20002
Telephone: (202) 544-0591
Background: An independent, non-profit research organization which studies the impact of federal and state budget and policy proposals on low and moderate income Americans. Publishes reports, fact sheets, analyses and monographs for use by policymakers and legislators and others.
Represented by:
Robert Greenstein, Exec. Director
Paul A. Leonard, Budget/Housing Analyst
Ellen Nissenbaum, Legislative Director

Center on Children and the Law
1800 M St., N.W., Washington, DC 20036
Telephone: (202) 331-2250
Represented by:
Howard Davidson, Director

Center on Nat'l Labor Policy
5211 Port Royal Rd. Suite 400, Springfield, VA 22151
Telephone: (703) 321-9180
Background: Supports employees, employers and consumers in legal and regulatory action opposing abuses of labor union power.
Represented by:
Michael Avakian, General Counsel

Center on Social Welfare Policy and Law
1029 Vermont Ave., N.W. Suite 850, Washington, DC 20005
Telephone: (202) 347-5615
Background: A public interest law office.
Represented by:
Adele Blong, Associate Director

Centergas, Inc.
Amarillo, TX
Counsel or consultant:
Meyers & Associates (Larry D. Meyers)

Centerior Energy Corp.
Cleveland, OH
Background: Formed from a merger of Cleveland Electric Illuminating and Toledo Edison.
Counsel or consultant:
Shaw, Pittman, Potts and Trowbridge (Jay E. Silberg)
Smith and Harroff

Centerra Group, The
Heathrow, FL
Counsel or consultant:
Cindy Williams Associates (Lucinda L. Williams)

Centex Corp.
Dallas, TX
Counsel or consultant:
Bracewell and Patterson (Gene E. Godley)
Johnson & Gibbs, P.C. (David G. Glickman)
Jones, Day, Reavis and Pogue (Randall E. Davis)

Central Arizona Water Conservation District
Phoenix, AZ
Counsel or consultant:
Will & Muys, P.C. (Robert P. Will)

Central Bank of Tampa
Tampa, FL
Counsel or consultant:
Foley & Lardner (Paul E. Cooney)

Central Bureau for Fruit and Vegetable Auctions in Holland
Counsel or consultant:
Hill and Knowlton Public Affairs Worldwide

Central Freight Forwarding
Miami, FL
Counsel or consultant:
Denning and Wohlstetter (Alan F. Wohlstetter)

Central Gulf Lines
New Orleans, LA
Counsel or consultant:
Verner, Liipfert, Bernhard, McPherson and Hand, Chartered (John A. Merrigan)

Central Montana Electric Power Cooperative, Inc.
Billings, MT
Counsel or consultant:
Duncan, Weinberg, Miller & Pembroke, P.C. (Janice L. Lower, James D. Pembroke)

Central Nebraska Public Power and Irrigation District
Holdrege, NE
Counsel or consultant:
Crowell and Moring (Dana C. Contratto)

Central Power and Light Co.
Corpus Christi, TX
Counsel or consultant:
Slover and Loftus (William L. Slover)

Central and South West Services, Inc.
Dallas, TX
Counsel or consultant:
McCamish, Martin, Brown & Loeffler (Tom Loeffler)
Paul, Hastings, Janofsky and Walker (Charles A. Patrizia)
Wendorf & Associates (Frederick C. Wendorf)

Central Station Electrical Protection Ass'n
7101 Wisconsin Ave. Suite 1390, Bethesda, MD 20814
Telephone: (301) 907-3202
Background: Represented by its Exec. Director and CAE, Charles B. Lavin, Jr. (See also Nat'l Burglar & Fire Alarm Ass'n).
Counsel or consultant:
Blooston, Mordkofsky, Jackson & Dickens (Benjamin Dickens)

Central Union of Agricultural Cooperatives (ZEN-CHU)
Tokyo, Japan
Counsel or consultant:
Arter & Hadden (Georgia H. Burke, William K. Dabaghi)

Central Vermont Public Service Corp.
Rutland, VT
Counsel or consultant:
Bruder, Gentile & Marcoux

Central Virginia Electric Cooperative, Inc.
Lovingston, VA
Counsel or consultant:
Duncan, Weinberg, Miller & Pembroke, P.C. (Robert Weinberg)

Central Virginia Health Systems Agency
Richmond, VA
Counsel or consultant:
Epstein Becker and Green (William G. Kopit)

Centrale Marketinggesellschaft der Deutschen Agrarwirtschaft
West Germany
Background: Represents the West German mushroom industry.
Counsel or consultant:
Coudert Brothers (Milo C. Coerper, Robert A. Lipstein)

Centralia, Pennsylvania, Former Residents of
Counsel or consultant:
Spiegel and McDiarmid

Centre for Development and Population Activity
1717 Massachusetts Ave., N.W., Washington, DC 20036
Telephone: (202) 667-1142
Represented by:
Peggy Curlin, President and CEO

Centre National Interprofessionel de L'Economie Laitiere (French Dairy Ass'n)
Paris, France
Counsel or consultant:
Max N. Berry Law Offices (Max N. Berry)

ORGANIZATIONS REPRESENTED

Centre Point Associates
Charleston, SC
Counsel or consultant:
Manatt, Phelps, Rothenberg & Phillips (Robert T. Herbolsheimer)

Century Internat'l
Montreal, Quebec
Counsel or consultant:
Lipsen Whitten & Diamond

Century Property Fund
Counsel or consultant:
Dow, Lohnes and Albertson (Jeffrey B. Stern)

Century 21 Political Action Committee
1101 Connecticut Ave., N.W., Suite 500, Washington, DC 20036
Telephone: (202) 463-8850
Background: Represented by Robin Dole of Century 21 Real Estate Corp.
Counsel or consultant:
Williams and Jensen, P.C. (Mary L. Whalen)

Century 21 Real Estate Corp.
1101 Connecticut Ave., N.W., Suite 500, Washington, DC 20036
Telephone: (202) 463-8850
Represented by:
Robin Dole, Director of Government Relations
Counsel or consultant:
Williams and Jensen, P.C. (Mary L. Whalen)

Ceramic Tile Marketing Federation
1200 17th St., N.W., Suite 400, Washington, DC 20036
Telephone: (202) 296-9200
Counsel or consultant:
Hill Group, Inc. (J. Craig Barnes)

Certified Color Manufacturers Ass'n
1620 Eye St., N.W., Suite 925, Washington, DC 20005
Telephone: (202) 293-5800
Counsel or consultant:
Daniel R. Thompson, P.C. (Daniel R. Thompson)
Wiley, Rein & Fielding

Cessna Aircraft Co.
1745 Jefferson Davis Hwy., Arlington, VA 22202
Telephone: (703) 553-1281
Counsel or consultant:
Parry and Romani Associates Inc. (Ted Mehl)

Cetus Corp.
Emeryville, CA
Counsel or consultant:
Hill and Knowlton Public Affairs Worldwide

Chain Link Fence Manufacturers Ass'n
1776 Massachusetts Ave., N.W. Suite 521, Washington, DC 20036
Telephone: (202) 659-3536
Represented by:
Mark Levin, Exec. V. President

Chain Pharmacy Ass'n of New York State
New York, NY
Counsel or consultant:
Mintz, Levin, Cohn, Ferris, Glovsky and Popeo, P.C. (Bruce D. Sokler, Amy S. Wergeles)
Skadden, Arps, Slate, Meagher and Flom (William J. Guzick)
Sutherland, Asbill and Brennan (Kenneth G. Starling)

Challenge Air Cargo
Miami, FL
Counsel or consultant:
Zuckert, Scoutt and Rasenberger (William H. Callaway, Jr.)

Challenger Center for Space Science Education
1101 King St. Suite 190, Alexandria, VA 22314
Telephone: (703) 683-9740
Represented by:
Doug King, President
Counsel or consultant:
Cassidy and Associates, Inc. (Dr. Frank A. Rose, Donald P. Smith)

Chamber of Commerce of the U.S.A.
1615 H St., N.W., Washington, DC 20062
Telephone: (202) 659-6000

Background: Organized in Washington in 1912, the Chamber is now generally regarded as the spokesman for U.S. business. It is the world's largest federation of businessmen with a membership of over 180,000 companies and chambers of commerce and trade and professional organizations. It is a potent voice in the nation's councils.
Represented by:
Robert J. Aagre, Manager, Legislative Department
Dr. Harvey Alter, Manager, Resources Policy Department
William T. Archey, V. President, International Division
Tia Armstrong, Assoc. Manager, Environmental Policy
Mary E. Bernhard, Manager, Environmental Policy
Stephen Bokat, V. President and General Counsel
Richard L. Breault, Group V. President for Policy
Karen A. Brigham, Assoc. Manager, Business & Gov't Policy
Dr. Wolf Brueckmann, Director, Internat'l Investment Policy
David Burton, Manager, Tax Policy
John K. Carson, Tax Specialist
Meryl Comer, V. President, Communications Development
Robin S. Conrad, Dir. of Litigat., Nat'l Chamb. Lit. Ctr.
Daniel Costello, Director of House Liaison
Susan M. Cousins, Associate Manager, Legislation
Ivan C. Elmer, Director, Small Business Programs
Nancy Reed Fulco, Human Resource Attorney
Dr. Carl Grant, Group V. President, Communications
Dr. Stuart B. Hardy, Manager, Food and Agriculture Policy
Donald J. Hasfurther, Director, East-West Internat'l Division
Marian E. Hopkins, Director of Senate Liaison
John Howard, Director, Internat'l Finance
Larry Hunter, Deputy Chief Economist
Jeffrey H. Joseph, V. President, Domestic Policy
William D. Kelleher, Manager, Community Development
Barrett T. King, Director, Media Relations
Joanne Marie Kling, Coalition Coordinator
Frederick L. Krebs, Manager, Business- Government Policy
Donald J. Kroes, V.P., Federation Develop't & Field Opns.
Daniel M. Kush, BizNet Congressional Correspondent
Lorraine Lavet, Dir., Procurement Policy, Bus-Gov't Pol.
Dr. Richard L. Lesher, President
Ted Maness, Director of Political Affairs
Jeffery D. Marcoe, Editor/Spec. Ass't Cong. Relations Div.
Robert L. Martin, Dir., Employee Relations Policy Center
Hugh McCahey, Manager, Association Department
John J. Meehan, V. President, Corporate Relations
Roger E. Middleton, Antitrust and Corporate Policy Attorney
Billy P. Mitchell, Mgr., Office of Chamber of Commerce Rtns
Susan Moya, Mgr., Energy & Natural Resources Policy
Heidi Belz Oliver, Director, Briefing Center
Jeffry L. Perlman, Director, Legal and Regulatory Affairs
Dr. Richard W. Rahn, V. President and Chief Economist
David A. Roe, V. President, Publishing
Batya Roth, Admin. Law Atty, Legal & Regul. Affrs.
Christine A. Russell, Director, Small Business Center
Jill L. Scheldrup, Associate Manager, Employee Relations
Tracey Schreft, Assoc. Mgr., Community Resources
Lisa M. Sprague, Manager, Employee Benefits Policy
Cynthia Stevens, Director, Public Affairs
Willard Workman, Dir, Programs and Policy, Internat'l Div
Counsel or consultant:
Dow, Lohnes and Albertson (Arthur H. Silverman)

Chambers Development Co., Inc.
1150 17th St., N.W., Suite 307, Washington, DC 20036
Telephone: (202) 463-0306
Represented by:
Martin G. Hamberger, Counsel, Corp, Devel. & Public Affairs
Margaret L. Petito, Director, Public Affairs

Chambre Syndicale des Producteurs d'Aciers Fins et Speciaux
Paris, France
Counsel or consultant:
Covington and Burling (Harvey M. Applebaum)

Champion Internat'l Corp.
1875 Eye St., N.W., Suite 540, Washington, DC 20006
Telephone: (202) 785-9888

Represented by:
Jeanne K. Connelly, V. President, Government Affairs
David Frankil, Director, Federal Government Affairs
Donna Akers Harman, Director, Government Affairs

Champon Flavors & Fragrances
Boca Raton, FL
Counsel or consultant:
Hogan and Hartson (Edward L. Korwek)
Mica, Dudinsky & Associates (John Dudinsky, Jr., John L. Mica)

Champon Pet Products
Boca Raton, FL
Counsel or consultant:
Mica, Dudinsky & Associates (John Dudinsky, Jr., John L. Mica)

Chance and Associates, John E.
Lafayette, LA
Counsel or consultant:
John C. Walton

Chaparral Airlines, Inc.
Abilene, TX
Counsel or consultant:
V. Michael Straus, P.C.

Charming Shops
Bensalem, PA
Counsel or consultant:
Lachelli, Waller and Associates

Chase Brass and Copper
Solon, OH
Counsel or consultant:
Collier, Shannon & Scott (Jeffrey S. Beckington, David A. Hartquist, Mary T. Staley)

Chase Enterprises
Hartford, CT
Counsel or consultant:
Hill and Knowlton Public Affairs Worldwide (Jill Schuker)

Chase Manhattan Bank
New York, NY
Counsel or consultant:
Bonner & Associates
Braun & Company
Hill and Knowlton Public Affairs Worldwide (John Doherty, David Miller)
Secura Group, The (Mary Clare Fitzgerald, William M. Isaac)

Chater Medical Corp.
Macon, GA
Counsel or consultant:
King and Spalding

Cheese Importers Ass'n of America
New York, NY
Counsel or consultant:
Chwat/Weigend Associates (John S. Chwat)
Harris & Ellsworth (Herbert E. Harris, II)

Chemed Corp.
Cincinnati, OH
Counsel or consultant:
Baker and Hostetler (Kenneth J. Kies)

Chemfix Technologies, Inc.
Kenner, LA
Counsel or consultant:
Patton, Boggs and Blow (J. Gordon Arbuckle)

Chemical Bank
New York, NY
Counsel or consultant:
Rivkin, Radler, Dunne and Bayh (Thomas A. Connaughton, Sheldon J. Harris)

Chemical Manufacturers Ass'n
2501 M St., N.W., Washington, DC 20037
Telephone: (202) 887-1100
Background: Has some 180 U.S. and Canadian member companies who seek to provide responsibility for the chemical needs of society.

The listings in this directory are available as *Mailing Labels*. See last page.

ORGANIZATIONS REPRESENTED

Chemical Manufacturers Ass'n (Cont'd)
Represented by:
R. Garrity Baker, Director, Internat'l Affairs
Claude P. Boudrias, Legislative Rep., Tax and Trade
Bradly A. Broadwell, Grassroots Manager
Timothy F. Burns, Director Federal Legislative Affairs
David W. Carroll, Director of Environmental Programs
Dr. Geraldine V. Cox, Vice President, Technical Director
Donald D. Evans, Deputy General Counsel
Robert B. Flagg, Legis Rep, Hazardous Waste & Groundwater
Robert B. Hill, Legislative Tax Representative
Jon C. Holtzman, Vice President, Communications
Allen J. Lenz, Director, Trade and Economics
Karen J. Neale, Legislative Manager/Environment
K. James O'Connor, Associate Director, Internat'l Trade
Thomas Parker, Jr., Associate Director, Energy
Robert A. Roland, President
Rose Marie Sanders, Legislative Representative/Patents
William Stover, V. President, Government Relations
Jeff Van, Director of Media Communications
Charles W. Van Vlack, V. President and Secretary
William Westendorf, Director, State Affairs
Richard T. Williams, Ass't Grassroots Manager
Eileen M. Winkelman, Legislative Rep., Health & Safety
David F. Zoll, V. President and General Counsel
Counsel or consultant:
Bracewell and Patterson (Gene E. Godley)
Direct Impact Co., The (John Brady, Tom Herrity)

Chemical Producers and Distributors Ass'n
1220 19th St., N.W., Suite 202, Washington, DC 20036
Telephone: (202) 785-2732
Represented by:
Diane J. Molchon, Exec. Assistant
Cindy O'Connor, Manager, Regulatory Affairs
Counsel or consultant:
Warren E. Stickle & Assoc. (Warren E. Stickle)

Chemical Producers and Distributors Ass'n Political Action Committee
1225 19th St., N.W., Suite 300, Washington, DC 20036
Telephone: (202) 785-2732
Background: Contact is Cindy O'Connor of the Association.

Chemical Specialties, Inc.
Charlotte, NC
Counsel or consultant:
Weinberg & Green (Walter G. Talarek)

Chemical Specialties Manufacturers Ass'n
1913 Eye St., N.W., Washington, DC 20006
Telephone: (202) 872-8110
Represented by:
F. H. Brewer, III, Director Legislative Affairs
Ralph Engel, President
Stephen S. Kellner, Vice President, Legal Affairs
Connie Neuman, Director, Communications
Michael F. Thompson, Assoc. Dir. for State Legislative Affrs.
Counsel or consultant:
Ketchum Public Relations
McKenna, Conner and Cuneo

Chemical Specialties Manufacturers Ass'n Political Action Committee
1001 Connecticut Ave., N.W. Suite 1120, Washington, DC 20036
Telephone: (202) 872-8110
Background: Responsible contact is Stephen S. Kellner. (See Chemical Specialties Manufacturers Ass'n.)

Chemical Waste Management, Inc.
Oak Brook, IL
Counsel or consultant:
Hill and Knowlton Public Affairs Worldwide (Tom Hoog)

Cheminova
Bloomfield, NJ
Counsel or consultant:
Warren E. Stickle & Assoc. (Warren E. Stickle)

Cherokee Nation Industries, Inc.
Stilwell, OK
Counsel or consultant:
Patton, Boggs and Blow (Ernest S. Christian, Jr.)

Cherokee Nation of Oklahoma
Tahlequan, OK

Counsel or consultant:
Patton, Boggs and Blow (Katharine R. Boyce)

Chesapeake and Potomac Telephone Co.
1710 H St., N.W. 5th Floor, Washington, DC 20006
Telephone: (202) 392-1904
Represented by:
R. Webster Chamberlin, Director, Public/Media Relations
William A. Grove, Jr., Exec. Director - Congressional Relations

Chesapeake and Potomac Telephone Co. Federal Political Action Committee
1710 H St., N.W., Washington, DC 20006
Telephone: (202) 392-1905
Background: Represented by its Vice Chairman, William A. Grove, Jr. (see Chesapeake and Potomac Telephone Co. listing).

Chesapeake and Potomac Telephone Co. of Maryland
Baltimore, MD
Counsel or consultant:
Wilkes, Artis, Hedrick and Lane, Chartered

Chevron Corp.
San Francisco, CA
Counsel or consultant:
Groom and Nordberg (Robert B. Harding, Carl A. Nordberg, Jr.)
Pillsbury, Madison and Sutro (Benjamin M. Vandergrift)

Chevron Petroleum Marketers Ass'n
UT
Counsel or consultant:
Bassman, Mitchell & Alfano, Chartered

Chevron, U.S.A.
1700 K St., N.W., Suite 1200, Washington, DC 20006
Telephone: (202) 457-5800
Background: Subsidiary of Chevron Corp.
Represented by:
Thomas M. Bresnahan, III, Manager, Federal Government Affairs
Dale E. Brooks, Washington Representative
Paul S. Caskey, Wash. Rep. (Taxation & Natural Gas)
Dan L. Fager, Washington Representative
Gary K. Fisher, Washington Representative (Marketing)
Clair Ghylin, V. President
Chris W. Howe, Washington Representative
Katherine L. Judd, Area Representative (Chevron Chem)
Richard W. Lewis, Washington Representative
Mary R. Ludke, Washington Representative
J. Mitchell Reese, Consultant - Coal
Kermit W. Ryman, Washington Representative
Counsel or consultant:
Alvarado Group, The (Susan Alvarado)
Bayless & Boland, Inc. (James L. Bayless, Jr., Michael J. P. Boland)

Chevy Chase Savings Bank
Chevy Chase, MD
Counsel or consultant:
Jones, Day, Reavis and Pogue (Randall E. Davis)
Miller & Chevalier, Chartered (Leonard Bickwit, Jr.)

Cheyenne River Sioux Tribe
Eagle Butte, SD
Counsel or consultant:
Karl A. Funke and Associates (Clara Spotted Elk)

Chicago Ass'n of Commerce and Industry
Chicago, IL
Counsel or consultant:
Benchmarks, Inc. (Thomas J. Scanlon)

Chicago Board of Trade
1455 Pennsylvania Ave., N.W. Suite 1225, Washington, DC 20004
Telephone: (202) 783-1190
Represented by:
Celesta S. Jurkovich, V. President, Government Relations
Counsel or consultant:
Davis & Harman (Thomas A. Davis)
Kirkland and Ellis
McLeod & Pires (Michael R. McLeod)

Chicago Board Options Exchange
Chicago, IL

Counsel or consultant:
Edward D. Heffernan
Patton, Boggs and Blow (Thomas Hale Boggs, Jr.)
Schiff Hardin & Waite (Andrew M. Klein)
Thacher, Proffitt and Wood (Edward R. Leahy)

Chicago Mercantile Exchange
2000 Pennsylvania Ave., N.W. Suite 6200, Washington, DC 20006
Telephone: (202) 223-6965
Background: The world's leading financial futures and options exchange with offices in Chicago, Washington, London, Tokyo and New York.
Represented by:
Deborah A. Fischione, Director, Government Relations
Kathy Gagnon, Asst. to the Sr. V.P., Gov't Relations
C. Dayle Henington, Sr. V. President, Government Relations
Charles M. Seeger, III, Counsel - Government
Counsel or consultant:
Hopkins and Sutter (Francis O. McDermott)
McAuliffe, Kelly, Raffaelli & Siemens (James M. Copeland, Jr.)

Chicago and Northwestern Transportation Co.
Chicago, IL
Counsel or consultant:
RBC Associates, Inc. (Ray B. Chambers)
Wheeler and Wheeler

Chicago Regional Transit Authority
Chicago, IL
Counsel or consultant:
Black, Manafort, Stone and Kelly Public Affairs Co. (Charles R. Black)
Peyser Associates, Inc. (Peter A. Peyser, Jr.)

Chicago Washington Office, City of
499 South Capitol St., S.E., Washington, DC 20003
Telephone: (202) 554-7900
Represented by:
Stephen E. Schlickman, Director
Counsel or consultant:
Jay E. Michad
Edwin S. Rosado

Child Nutrition Forum
1319 F St., N.W. Suite 500, Washington, DC 20004
Telephone: (202) 393-5060
Background: Represented by Edward Cooney of the Food Research and Action Center.

Child Welfare League of America
440 First St., N.W., Suite 310, Washington, DC 20001
Telephone: (202) 638-2952
Represented by:
Linda Greenan, Director of Public Policy
David S. Liederman, Exec. Director
Counsel or consultant:
Capitol Associates, Inc. (Gwen Gampel)

Children's Defense Fund
122 C St., N.W., Washington, DC 20001
Telephone: (202) 628-8787
Background: An organization concerned with promoting preventive investment policies for children and youth. Major program areas are: education, child health and mental health, child welfare, child care and family support, and adolescent pregnancy prevention. Through research, public education, litigation, monitoring federal administrative policies and assistance to state and community organizations and parents, CDF seeks to improve policies and practices resulting in the neglect or mistreatment of children of all races and classes.
Represented by:
Helen K. Blank, Director, Child Care
Mary M. Bourdette, Director of Governmental Affairs
Marian Wright Edelman, President
Kati Haycock, V. President
Cliff Johnson, Director, Family Support
Kay Johnson, Director, Child Health
Debra J. Lipson, Assistant Dir., Program & Policy
Molly McNulty, Senior Health Specialist
Shelley Peck, Program Associate
Sara Rosenbaum, Director, Programs and Policy
Aileen Whitfill, Senior Health Specialist
Maggie Williams, Director of Communications

Children's Foundation
725 15th St., N.W., Washington, DC 20005

The listings in this directory are available as *Mailing Labels*. See last page.

Telephone: (202) 347-3300
Background: A national, nonprofit, children's advocacy organization. Seeks improvement and expansion of federal food assistance programs with emphasis on the Child Care Food Program for family day care homes and day care centers.
Represented by:
Kay Hollestelle, Exec. Director

Children's Health System, Inc.
Norfolk, VA
Counsel or consultant:
Jefferson Group, The (Frederick J. Hannett)

Children's Hospice Internat'l
1101 King St., Suite 131, Alexandria, VA 22314
Telephone: (703) 684-0330
Represented by:
Ann Armstrong Dailey, Founding Director
Counsel or consultant:
The Susan Davis Companies

Children's Hospital (Pittsburgh)
Pittsburgh, PA
Counsel or consultant:
Cassidy and Associates, Inc. (James P. Fabiani)

Children's Hospital and Health Center
San Diego, CA
Counsel or consultant:
Cassidy and Associates, Inc.

Children's Hospital Nat'l Medical Center
111 Michigan Ave., N.E., Washington, DC 20010
Telephone: (202) 745-5000
Represented by:
Jacqueline E. Bowens-Jones, Director, Gov't and Community Affairs
Counsel or consultant:
Cassidy and Associates, Inc. (James P. Fabiani, Thomas M. Gannon, Donald P. Smith)

Children's Hospital of Michigan
Detroit, MI
Counsel or consultant:
Cassidy and Associates, Inc. (Gerald S. J. Cassidy, John R. Hogness, M.D., Donald P. Smith)

Children's Survival Plan
Glendale, CA
Counsel or consultant:
Jefferson Group, The (John Coy)

Children's World Learning Centers
Golden, CO
Counsel or consultant:
Morrison Associates (James W. Morrison, Jr.)

Chile, Army Procurement Mission
Santiago, Chile
Counsel or consultant:
Anderson and Pendleton, C.A.
Brownrigg and Muldoon

Chile, Embassy of
1732 Massachusetts Ave., N.W., Washington, DC 20006
Telephone: (202) 785-1746
Counsel or consultant:
Arnold & Porter (William D. Rogers)
Steptoe and Johnson (Monroe Leigh)
The Whalen Company, Inc. (Richard J. Whalen)

Chilean Exporters Ass'n
Santiago, Chile
Counsel or consultant:
Akin, Gump, Strauss, Hauer and Feld (Lawrence D. Levien)
Fleishman-Hillard, Inc
Lepon, McCarthy, Jutkowitz & Holzworth (David A. Holzworth, Jeffrey M. Lepon)
Shearman and Sterling

Chilean Nitrate Sales Corp.
Santiago, Chile
Counsel or consultant:
Dorsey & Whitney

Chili's
Dallas, TX
Counsel or consultant:
Richard B. Berman and Co.,Inc. (Richard B. Berman)

China, Administration of Shantou Special Economic Zone of
Beijing, China
Counsel or consultant:
Cramer and Haber (William C. Cramer, Eliazer A. Williams)

China Airlines, Ltd.
Taipei, Taiwan
Counsel or consultant:
Alcalde & Rousselot (Hector Alcalde)

China Clay Producers Political Action Committee
1275 Pennsylvania Ave., N.W., Washington, DC 20004
Telephone: (202) 383-0169
Background: A group of kaolin producers established in 1978 concerned with various state and federal laws affecting their mining industry.
Counsel or consultant:
Sutherland, Asbill and Brennan (Gordon O. Pehrson, Jr.)

China, Directorate General of Telecommunications, Ministry of Communications of Republic of
Taipei, Taiwan
Counsel or consultant:
Schiff Hardin & Waite (Gearold L. Knowles)

China, Embassy of the People's Republic of
2300 Connecticut Ave., N.W., Washington, DC 20008
Telephone: (202) 328-2500
Counsel or consultant:
Jones, Day, Reavis and Pogue
Marshall, Tenzer, Greenblatt, Fallon and Kaplan (Sylvan M. Marshall)

China External Trade Development Council
Taipei, Taiwan
Background: Organization to promote sales of products made in Taiwan.
Counsel or consultant:
Bergner, Boyette & Bockorny, Inc. (Jeffrey T. Bergner)
Internat'l Trade and Development Agency
Neill and Co. (Robert L. Downen, Denis M. Neill)
O'Connor & Hannan (Michael Colopy, Thomas H. Quinn)
Strategic Resources Corp. (H. P. Goldfield)
Swidler & Berlin, Chartered (Dawn Gifford)
Washington Resources and Strategy, Inc. (William R. Sweeney, Jr.)

China, Foreign Trade Board of the Republic of
Taipei, Taiwan
Counsel or consultant:
Ablondi and Foster, P.C. (Italo H. Ablondi)
C & M Internat'l L.P. (Doral S. Cooper)
Peter R. Rosenblatt
Swidler & Berlin, Chartered

China, Government Information Office of the Republic of
Taipei, Taiwan
Counsel or consultant:
The Hannaford Co., Inc.

China, Government of the People's Republic of
Beijing, China
Counsel or consultant:
Baker and McKenzie
Coudert Brothers
Jones, Day, Reavis and Pogue

China, Government of the Republic of
Taipei, Taiwan
Counsel or consultant:
Peter R. Rosenblatt

China Nat'l Chemical Import and Export Corp.
Beijing, China
Counsel or consultant:
Baker and McKenzie (Eugene A. Theroux)
Mudge Rose Guthrie Alexander and Ferdon

China Nat'l Machinery and Equipment Import and Export Corp.
Beijing, China
Counsel or consultant:
Graham and James

China Nat'l Metals and Minerals Import and Export Corp.
Beijing, China
Counsel or consultant:
Mudge Rose Guthrie Alexander and Ferdon (N. David Palmeter)

China Nat'l Textiles Import and Export Corp.
Beijing, China
Counsel or consultant:
Mudge Rose Guthrie Alexander and Ferdon (Michael P. Daniels, Martin J. Lewin)

China Ocean Shipping Co.
Shanghai, China
Counsel or consultant:
Garvey, Schubert & Barer (Stanley H. Barer)

China West
Tuscon, AZ
Counsel or consultant:
McAuliffe, Kelly, Raffaelli & Siemens (Lynnette R. Jacquez)

Chitimacha Tribe of Louisiana
Charenton, LA
Counsel or consultant:
Karl A. Funke and Associates (Jane B. Esterly)

Chlorine Institute
2001 L St., N.W., Suite 506, Washington, DC 20036
Telephone: (202) 775-2790
Represented by:
Arthur E. Dungan, V. Pres., Safety, Health & Environment
Diane R. Dungan, Director, Government Relations
Michael E. Lyden, V. Pres., Storage and Transportation
Robert G. Smerko, President
Gary F. Trojak, V. Pres., Packaging & Technical Services
Joseph L. Walker, III, Director, Public & Member Communications
Counsel or consultant:
Hill and Knowlton Public Affairs Worldwide (Josephine S. Cooper)

Cho Heung Chemical Ind. Co., Ltd.
Seoul, Korea
Counsel or consultant:
Mudge Rose Guthrie Alexander and Ferdon (N. David Palmeter)

Chocolate Manufacturers Ass'n of the U.S.A.
7900 Westpark Drive Suite A320, McLean, VA 22101
Telephone: (703) 790-5011
Represented by:
Richard T. O'Connell, CAE, President
Susan Snyder Smith, Director, Public and Legislative Affairs

Chocolate Political Action Committee
7900 Westpark Dr., Suite A-320, McLean, VA 22102
Telephone: (703) 790-5011
Background: The political action committee of the Chocolate Manufacturers Ass'n of the U.S.A. Represented by Richard T. O'Connell, President of the Ass'n.

CHP
New Hyde Park, NY
Background: A medical group associated with the Long Island Jewish Medical Center.
Counsel or consultant:
Alan M. Gnessin Law Offices (Alan M. Gnessin)

Chris-Craft Industries Inc.
New York, NY
Counsel or consultant:
Clarence J. Brown & Co. (Robert B. Giese)

Christian Action Council
701 W. Broad St., Suite 405, Falls Church, VA 22046
Telephone: (703) 237-2100
Background: A pro-life organization.
Represented by:
Douglas Scott, Director, Public Policy

Christian College Coalition
327 8th St., N.E., Washington, DC 20002
Telephone: (202) 293-6177
Background: A nat'l ass'n of approximately 80 Christ-centered liberal arts colleges committed to hiring only Christians as faculty members and administrators and to making the Christian faith relevant to all academic disciplines

Christian College Coalition (Cont'd)

and daily life on campus. The Coalition publishes 'Consider a Christian College', 'Christian College News' and other public relations materials. Monitors legislation and litigation of special concern to Christian colleges and coordinates an internship/seminar American Studies Program for students in Washington, D.C. and a Latin American Studies Program in San Jose, Costa Rica.
Represented by:
Myron S. Augsburger, President

Christian Democrat Internat'l
Brussels, Belgium
Counsel or consultant:
DC Internat'l, Inc. (Andres R. Hernandez)

Christian Democrat Organization of the Americas
Caracas, Venezuela
Counsel or consultant:
DC Internat'l, Inc. (Andres R. Hernandez)

Christic Institute
1324 N. Capitol St., N.W., Washington, DC 20002
Telephone: (202) 797-8106
Background: An interfaith public interest law and policy center currently prosecuting a civil racketeering case against many of the major figures in the Iran-Contra affair, with a particular focus on criminal activity as part of 'covert operations'. Also involved in litigation challenging the regulatory processes of the Nuclear Regulatory Commission.
Represented by:
Dick Billings, Coordinator of Investigations
Mary Cassell, Director of Outreach
Rick Emrich, Director of Communications
Sara Nelson, Exec. Director
Daniel Sheehan, General Counsel
Lanny Sinkin, Director of Litigation
Cynthia Strom, Director of Public Education

Christie's Internat'l
New York, NY
Counsel or consultant:
Jack Ferguson Associates (Jack Ferguson)
Steptoe and Johnson (Blake D. Rubin)

Chromalloy Gas Turbine Corp.
1155 Connecticut Ave., N.W. Suite 500, Washington, DC 20036
Telephone: (202) 659-4280
Represented by:
Peter H. Hahn, Legislative Representative

Chronic Fatigue Syndrome Information Institute
5840 Cameron Run Terrace Suite 1413, Alexandria, VA 22303
Telephone: (703) 960-1749
Background: Represents interests of patients with Chronic Fatigue Syndrome and Chronic Epstein-Barr Virus Syndrome.
Represented by:
Barry Sleight, President

Chrysler Corp.
1100 Connecticut Ave., N.W. Suite 900, Washington, DC 20036
Telephone: (202) 862-5400
Represented by:
Robert J. Conner, Director, Federal Relations
Brenda T. Day, Director, Environmental Affairs
Robert T. Griffin, Staff Executive, Washington Office
John E. Guiniven, Director, Washington Public Relations
Alisa J. Learner, Issue Analyst/Policy Develmnt. Director
Robert G. Liberatore, Exec Dir, Public Policy/Legisltv. Affrs
Walter B. Maher, Dir., Fed. Rtns./Human Resources Office
Richard J. Muller, Public Affairs Consultant
Robert A. Perkins, V. President, Washington Affairs
Albert J. Slechter, Federal Gov't Affairs Director
Counsel or consultant:
Dewey, Ballantine, Bushby, Palmer and Wood (Joseph A. Califano, Jr.)
FMR Group Inc., The
Ginn, Edington, Moore and Wade
Timmons and Co., Inc.

Chrysler Military Sales Corp.
Woodbury, NY

Counsel or consultant:
Royer, Mehle & Babyak (Robert Stewart Royer)

Chrysler Technologies Corp.
1100 Connecticut Ave., N.W. 7th Floor, Washington, DC 20036
Telephone: (202) 862-3460
Background: A subsidiary pf Chrysler Corp.
Represented by:
Pamela M. Schnabel, Assistant Director, Compliance
Paul E. Wright, Chairman

Chrysler Technologies Political Support Committee
1100 Connecticut Ave., N.W. Suite 730, Washington, DC 20036
Telephone: (202) 862-3460
Background: Represented by Pamela M. Schnabel of Chrysler Technologies Corp.

Chubb Corp., The
New York, NY
Counsel or consultant:
Baker and Hostetler (Kenneth J. Kies)

Chubu Electric Power Co.
900 17th St., N.W., Suite 1220, Washington, DC 20006
Telephone: (202) 775-1960
Represented by:
Tatsuo Yagi, Chief Representative

Chugach Alaska Corp.
Anchorage, AK
Counsel or consultant:
Birch, Horton, Bittner and Cherot (Joseph M. Chomski)

Chugai Pharmaceutical Co., Ltd.
Tokyo, Japan
Counsel or consultant:
Hill and Knowlton Public Affairs Worldwide (Ken Rabin)

Church Alliance
Dallas, TX
Counsel or consultant:
Johnson & Gibbs, P.C. (David G. Glickman)
Ross Marsh Foster Myers & Quiggle
G. Frank West

Church of the Brethren
110 Maryland Ave., N.E., Washington, DC 20002
Telephone: (202) 546-3202
Represented by:
Melva Jimerson, Legislative Associate
Julie Warrington, Administrative Secretary

Church Women United
110 Maryland Ave., N.E. Suite 108, Washington, DC 20003
Telephone: (202) 544-8747
Background: A liberal ecumenical organization.
Represented by:
Sally Timmell, Director, Washington Office

Church World Service/Lutheran World Relief
110 Maryland Ave., N.E. Building Box #45, Washington, DC 20002-5694
Telephone: (202) 543-6336
Represented by:
Carol Capps, Associate for Development Policy
Larry Minear, Representative for Development Policy

Churches' Center for Theology and Public Policy
4500 Massachusetts Ave., N.W., Washington, DC 20016
Telephone: (202) 885-9100
Background: An ecumenical study center whose purpose is to strengthen Christian leadership and involvement in public issues such as arms control and disarmament, urban policy, health care, and political/economic problems.
Represented by:
James A. Nash, Exec. Director

Churfine-Central Corp.
Northlake, IL
Counsel or consultant:
McDermott, Will and Emery (Ronald A. Bloch)

CH2M HILL
Metropolitan Square, 655 15th St., N.W., Suite 444, Washington, DC 20005
Telephone: (202) 393-2426

Background: An employee-owned firm with 60 offices worldwide. Established in 1946 to provide comprehensive services in engineering, planning, economics and environmental sciences to government and the private sector. Specialists in water, wastewater and hazardous waste.
Represented by:
Richard L. Corrigan, Vice President, Government Affairs
Marcia M. Pape-Daniels, Governmental Affairs Director
Counsel or consultant:
Ball, Janik and Novack

CIAC Group, The
c/o Reid & Priest, 1111 19th St., N.W., Washington, DC 20026
Telephone: (202) 828-0100
Counsel or consultant:
Reid & Priest (Raymond F. Dacek)

CIBA-GEIGY Corp.
1747 Pennsylvania Ave., N.W., Suite 700, Washington, DC 20006
Telephone: (202) 293-3019
Represented by:
David P. Drake, Jr., Manager, Federal Government Relations
Marge Lyons, Manager, Washington Office
William T. Lyons, Director, Federal Government Relations
Counsel or consultant:
Targeted Communications Corp.

CIC Enterprises, Inc.
Indianapolis, IN
Background: An employment consulting firm.
Counsel or consultant:
Camp, Barsh, Bates and Tate (Ronald L. Platt)

Cigar Ass'n of America
1100 17th St., N.W., Suite 504, Washington, DC 20036
Telephone: (202) 223-8204
Represented by:
Norman F. Sharp, President
Counsel or consultant:
McKenna, Conner and Cuneo (Peter Buck Feller)

Cigar Political Action Committee
1100 17th St., N.W., Suite 504, Washington, DC 20036
Telephone: (202) 223-8204
Background: Represented by Norman F. Sharp, President of the Cigar Ass'n of America.

Cigarette Export Ass'n
New York, NY
Counsel or consultant:
Burson-Marsteller

CIGNA Corp.
1825 Eye St., N.W., Suite 750, Washington, DC 20006
Telephone: (202) 296-7174
Background: A major insurance company formed by the merger of Connecticut General Life Insurance Co. and INA.
Represented by:
A. J. Harris, II, V. President, Federal Affairs
Lynn S. Jacobs, Assistant V. President, Federal Affairs
K. Michael Miller, Assistant V. President, Federal Affairs
H. Michael Schiffer, Assistant V. President, Federal Affairs
Yvonne E.T.G.B. Zoomers, Assistant V. President, Federal Affairs
Counsel or consultant:
Baker and Hostetler
Davis & Harman
Patton, Boggs and Blow (Lansing B. Lee)
Williams and Jensen, P.C. (Robert E. Glennon, Jr.)

Cincinnati Electronics Inc.
Cincinnati, OH
Counsel or consultant:
Rothleder Associates, Inc. (Linda Rothleder)

Cincinnati Gas and Electric Co.
Cincinnati, OH
Counsel or consultant:
Conner and Wetterhahn, P.C. (Troy B. Conner, Jr., Mark J. Wetterhahn)
Reid & Priest

CITGO Petroleum Corp.
Tulsa, OK

ORGANIZATIONS REPRESENTED

Counsel or consultant:
Camp, Barsh, Bates and Tate (Ronald L. Platt)
Dutko & Associates (Daniel A. Dutko)

Citibank, N.A.
New York, NY
Counsel or consultant:
Dow, Lohnes and Albertson (Ralph W. Hardy, Jr.)
Richard Olson & Assoc. (Richard C. Olson)

Citicorp
1275 Pennsylvania Ave., N.W., Suite 503, Washington, DC 20004
Telephone: (202) 879-6800
Represented by:
Jeffery A. Abrahamson, League Analyst
Martha A. Golden, V. President, Support Programs
Peter Gray, V. President, Domestic Government Rltns.
William S. Haraf, V. President, Policy Analysis
F. William Hawley, III, V. President, Internat'l Gov't Relations
Stephen A. Hopkins, V. President, Domestic Government Rltns.
David C. Jory, V. President, Government Relations
Robert Y. Lider, V. President, Tax Dept.
Charles E. Long, Exec. V. President and Secretary
John F. Rolph, III, V. President, Tax Legislation
Robert C. Wells, Director, Internat'l Govt't Relations
Counsel or consultant:
Bonner & Associates
Loeffler Group, The
Newmyer Associates, Inc.
Reid & Priest
Ross and Hardies (Wm. Bradford Reynolds)
Shearman and Sterling (Edward Bransilver)
Thacher, Proffitt and Wood (Jeffrey N. Judah, Edward R. Leahy)
Wilmer, Cutler and Pickering (Arnold M. Lerman)

Citicorp Acceptance Corp.
St. Louis, MO
Counsel or consultant:
Ballard, Spahr, Andrews and Ingersoll (Frederic L. Ballard, Jr.)
Hill and Knowlton Public Affairs Worldwide (John Qualls)

Citicorp Mortgage Finance, Inc.
St. Louis, MO
Counsel or consultant:
Thacher, Proffitt and Wood (Virginia W. Brown, Jeremiah S. Buckley)

Citicorp Voluntary Political Fund - Federal
1275 Pennsylvania Ave., N.W., Suite 503, Washington, DC 20004
Telephone: (202) 879-6800
Background: Treasurer is Martha A. Golden.

Cities in Schools, Inc.
1023 15th St., N.W., Washington, DC 20005
Telephone: (202) 861-0230
Counsel or consultant:
U.S. Strategies Corp. (Heidi A. Hanson, Michael P. Skredynski)

Citizen Action
1300 Connecticut Ave., N.W. Suite 401, Washington, DC 20036
Telephone: (202) 857-5153
Background: A national citizens' action organization representing 1.75 million members in 24 states espousing a stronger citizen voice in economic and political decisions.
Represented by:
Lorraine Driscoll, Legislative Director
Edwin S. Rothschild, Director, Energy & Environmental Policy
Counsel or consultant:
Manatt, Phelps, Rothenberg & Phillips (William C. Oldaker)

Citizen/Labor Energy Coalition Project
1300 Connecticut Ave., N.W. Suite 401, Washington, DC 20036
Telephone: (202) 857-5153
Background: A national alliance of over 270 labor, senior citizen and other community organizations working for energy policies that reflect fair and affordable prices, promote economic health by preserving and creating jobs and seek to break up concentrated power in the industry.

Represented by:
Robert M. Brandon, Exec. Director
Counsel or consultant:
Miller, Balis and O'Neil

Citizens Against Government Waste
1301 Connecticut Ave., N.W. Suite 400, Washington, DC 20036
Telephone: (202) 467-5300
Background: A non-partisan, non-profit foundation which educates the American people about the findings of the Grace Commission and government waste. Board Members include J. Peter Grace, national columnist Jack Anderson, and former Secretary of the Treasury William Simon. Also supports the Council for Citizens Against Government Waste (CCAGW), a grassroots lobby whose members actively pursue enactment of waste-cutting recommendations to reduce the federal deficit. Combined membership exceeds 250,000.
Represented by:
Allan Keyes, President
Thomas A. Schatz, V. President, Gov't Affairs Director

Citizens Against PACs
2000 P St., N.W. Suite 408, Washington, DC 20036
Telephone: (202) 463-0465
Background: A national organization seeking to eliminate political action committees as fundraising instruments for candidates in Federal elections. Established in 1984.
Represented by:
Philip M. Stern, Co-Chairman and Founder

Citizens Against Research Bans
1140 23rd St., N.W., Suite 806, Washington, DC 20037
Telephone: (202) 293-7187
Background: An advocacy organization which opposes referendums to impose nuclear research bans and freezes.
Counsel or consultant:
J. Arthur Weber & Associates (Joseph A. Weber)

Citizens Clearinghouse for Hazardous Wastes
P.O. Box 926, Arlington, VA 22216
Telephone: (703) 276-7070
Background: Serves more than 7,000 affiliated grassroots organizations combatting toxic polluters and other threats to the environment.
Represented by:
Will Collette, Organizing Director
Lois Marie Gibbs, Exec. Director

Citizens Committee for the Right to Keep and Bear Arms
600 Pennsylvania Ave., S.E. Suite 205, Washington, DC 20003
Telephone: (202) 543-3363
Background: A conservative group which opposes registration of firearms. Based in Bellevue, Washington.
Represented by:
John M. Snyder, Public Affairs Director

Citizens Communications Center
Georgetown Univ. Law Center, 600 New Jersey Ave., N.W., Washington, DC 20001
Telephone: (202) 662-9535
Background: A non-profit public interest communications law firm that represents citizens groups and other members of the public in proceedings before the FCC and the courts involving mass media and telecommunications issues.
Represented by:
Angela J. Campbell, Associate Director

Citizens for a Drug Free America
2230 George C. Marshall Drive, Falls Church, VA 22042
Telephone: (703) 207-9300
Represented by:
Nancy Baker-Smith, Exec. Director
Roger Chapin, President & Founder
Counsel or consultant:
Fleishman-Hillard, Inc (Thomas L. Buckmaster, W. Douglas Campbell, Paul Johnson, John Overstreet)

Citizens for a Sound Economy
470 L'Enfant Plaza East, S.W. Suite 7112, Washington, DC 20024
Telephone: (202) 488-8200
Background: A non-profit, non-partisan citizen action organization promoting free market alternatives to government rules, regulations and programs. Supported by individuals, foundations and corporations. Present membership is 250,000.

Represented by:
Michael Becker, Director, Research
Becky Norton Dunlop, Sr. Fellow, Envir. & Natural Res. Policy
Wayne E. Gable, President
Stephen Gold, Director of Public Policy
Brian Lopina, Director of Government Relations
David A. Makarechian, Project Director, Tax and Budget
James C. Miller, III, Distinguished Fellow, Chairman
Phillip S. Mink, Gen. Couns., Legal & Reg. Reform Project
Michael Monroney, Senior Advisor
Nancy Oliver, Project Director, Trade & Labor
Ms. Sedef Onder, Director, Media Relations
Daniel A. Witt, V. President, Tax Foundation
Counsel or consultant:
Patton, Boggs and Blow

Citizens for America
214 Massachusetts Ave., N.E. Suite 480, Washington, DC 20002
Telephone: (202) 544-7888
Background: A lobbying and education organization formed in 1983 to promote the policies of the Reagan Administration. Chairman is Alan Keyes, also President of the Council for Citizens Against Waste.
Represented by:
Donald J. Devine, Consultant

Citizens for Educational Freedom
927 S. Walter Reed Drive, Suite 1, Arlington, VA 22204
Telephone: (703) 486-8311
Represented by:
Robert S. Marlowe, Exec. Director

Citizens for Public Action on Cholesterol
7200 Wisconsin Ave. Suite 1002, Bethesda, MD 20814
Telephone: (301) 907-7790
Background: A member organization of the Coalition for Health Funding in Washington.
Represented by:
Gerald Wilson, Exec. Director

Citizens for Safe Drivers Against Drunk Drivers and Chronic Offenders (CSD)
7401 MacKenzie Court, Bethesda, MD 20817
Telephone: (301) 469-6282
Background: Oldest national non-profit, public interest membership organization working to prevent highway deaths and injuries caused by drunk drivers and other chronic offenders. Conducts public information and education campaigns, works for state and federal legislation and enforcement and acts as an information clearinghouse and communications network. Also works to improve the National Driver Register and to help implement the federal law mandating a single national license for drivers of trucks and buses. Acts as a self-help group for families of highway crash victime.
Represented by:
Kenneth L. Nathanson, Representative

Citizens for Sensible Control of Acid Rain
1301 Connecticut Ave., N.W. Suite 700, Washington, DC 20036
Telephone: (202) 659-0330
Background: A grassroots citizens coalition supported by utility companies and other business interests to promote public education and awareness in the debate over the control of acid rain. The above address is that of Fleishman-Hillard, Inc., a public relations firm; Thomas L. Buckmaster serves as Exec. Director.
Counsel or consultant:
Fleishman-Hillard, Inc (Martha L. Miller)
Reese Communications Companies

Citizens for Tax Justice
1311 L St., N.W. 4th Floor, Washington, DC 20005
Telephone: (202) 626-3780
Background: A coalition of national public interest organizations, labor unions and state and local groups seeking tax reform, with particular concern for low and medium income citizens.
Represented by:
Michael P. Ettlinger, State Tax Policy Director
Bruce L. Fisher, Research Director
Doug Kelly, Policy Analyst
Robert S. McIntyre, Director
Edward R. Meyers, Program Director

ORGANIZATIONS REPRESENTED

Citizens for the Treatment of High Blood Pressure
7200 Wisconsin Ave. Suite 1002, Bethesda, MD 20814
Telephone: (301) 907-7790
Background: A member organization of the Coalition for Health Funding in Washington. Represented by Gerald Wilson, (See Citizens for Public Action on Cholesterol.)
Counsel or consultant:
Capitol Associates, Inc. (Karen Bodenhorn, Terry Lierman)

Citizens Network for Foreign Affairs
1616 H St., N.W., Washington, DC 20006
Telephone: (202) 639-8889
Background: Works 'to build a broader understanding among the American public of the growing importance of America's international relationships, especially those with developing countries, to the security and economic and environmental well-being of the United States.'
Represented by:
John H. Costello, President
Wendy Sears Grassi, Director, Communications
Gregory O. Principato, Director, Programs
Robert C. Stowe, V. President
Counsel or consultant:
Vorys, Sater, Seymour and Pease (Randal C. Teague)

Citizens Savings Bank
Providence, RI
Counsel or consultant:
Royer, Mehle & Babyak (Robert Stewart Royer)

Citizens Savings Financial Corp.
Miami, FL
Counsel or consultant:
Steptoe and Johnson (John T. Collins)

Citizens and Southern Corp.
Atlanta, GA
Counsel or consultant:
Akin, Gump, Strauss, Hauer and Feld (Joel Jankowsky)

Citizens to Protect the Constitution
1156 15th St., N.W., Suite 1212, Washington, DC 20005
Telephone: (202) 785-2936
Background: A private, non-partisan coalition of over 150 national organizations with the primary goal of informing the public and state legislators of the 'serious potential dangers' of holding a new constitutional convention. Kevin Faley, of Rivkin Rakler Dunne and Bayh, serves as General Counsel.
Represented by:
Linda Rogers-Kingbury, President

Citizens Utilities Co.
Stamford, CT
Counsel or consultant:
Vinson and Elkins

City & Regional Magazine Ass'n
335 Commerce St., Alexandria, VA 22314
Telephone: (703) 548-5016
Background: Exec. Director is Brandi Sullivan.
Counsel or consultant:
Davis/Replogle & Associates, Inc. (Brandi Sullivan)

City University
Seattle, WA
Counsel or consultant:
The William Chasey Organization (Virginia Chasey)

Civil Pilots for Regulatory Reform
Austin, TX
Background: A national organization of pilots concerned with the FAA's airman medical certification regulations.
Counsel or consultant:
Joseph, Gajarsa, McDermott and Reiner, P.C. (Mark T. McDermott)

Clackamas County, Oregon
Oregon City, OR
Counsel or consultant:
Ball, Janik and Novack (James A. Beall, Michelle E. Giguere)

Claiborne, Inc., Liz
New York, NY
Counsel or consultant:
Rogers and Wells (Eugene T. Rossides)

Clark Atlanta University
Atlanta, GA
Counsel or consultant:
Cassidy and Associates, Inc. (James P. Fabiani, Vincent M. Versage)

Clark County, Nevada
Las Vegas, NV
Counsel or consultant:
Marcus G. Faust
McAuliffe, Kelly, Raffaelli & Siemens (Edward E. Allison)

Clark Equipment Co.
South Bend, IN
Counsel or consultant:
Baker and McKenzie (Bruce E. Clubb)

Clarke/Bardes Organization, Inc.
Dallas, TX
Counsel or consultant:
Akin, Gump, Strauss, Hauer and Feld

Clarke & Co.
Boston, MA
Counsel or consultant:
Smith Dawson & Andrews, Inc. (Gregory B. Andrews)

Claro y Cia
Santiago, Chile
Counsel or consultant:
Shearman and Sterling (Anita Epstein, Robert Herzstein)

Classic Motor Carriages, Inc.
Miami, FL
Counsel or consultant:
Stovall & Spradlin

Classroom Publishers Ass'n
2020 K St., N.W., Washington, DC 20036
Telephone: (202) 296-5680
Counsel or consultant:
Loomis, Owen, Fellman and Howe (Stephen F. Owen, Jr.)

Clayton & Dubilier, Inc.
New York, NY
Counsel or consultant:
Cadwalader, Wickersham & Taft (Linda E. Carlisle, J. Roger Mentz)

Clean Air Act Project
1440 New York Ave., N.W., Suite 300, Washington, DC 20005
Telephone: (202) 638-1230
Background: A project of the Nat'l Environmental Development Ass'n.
Counsel or consultant:
Alvarado Group, The (Susan Alvarado)
E. Bruce Harrison Co. (Jeffrey B. Conley, Steven B. Hellem)

Clean Air Working Group
818 Connecticut Ave., N.W., Suite 900, Washington, DC 20006
Telephone: (202) 857-0370
Background: An alliance of nearly 2,000 large and small companies and trade associations united for effective, affordable air quality improvements. Administrator and contact for the group is William D. Fay of the National Coal Ass'n.

Clean Coal Technology Coalition
1050 Thomas Jefferson St., N.W., Washington, DC 20007
Telephone: (202) 298-1800
Background: An ad-hoc group of electric utilities, coal companies, architect & engineering firms and others interested in advancing the use of clean coal technologies.
Counsel or consultant:
Van Ness, Feldman & Curtis (Ben Yamagata)

Clean Fuels Development Coalition
1129 20th St., N.W. Suite 500, Washington, DC 20036
Telephone: (202) 822-1715
Counsel or consultant:
Durante Associates

Clean Sites, Inc.
1199 North Fairfax St., Alexandria, VA 22314
Telephone: (703) 739-1275

Background: Established by several leaders of the chemical industry and environmental groups as a private effort to hasten cleanup of toxic chemical dumps throughout the country. Russell Train of the Conservation Foundation serves as Chairman.
Represented by:
Joan Ebzery, Director, Public Affairs
Thomas P. Grumbly, President

Clean Sound
Seattle, WA
Background: A cooperative of petroleum producing, shipping and pipeline companies concerned about oil spills.
Counsel or consultant:
Steptoe and Johnson

Clean Water Action Project
317 Pennsylvania Ave., S.E., Washington, DC 20003
Telephone: (202) 547-1196
Background: A national citizen organization working for clean and safe water at an affordable cost, control of toxic chemicals and preservation of natural resources.
Represented by:
Ken Brown, Campaigns Director
Dr. Henry S. Cole, Research and Science Director
David Zwick, Exec. Director

Clearinghouse on Educational Choice
927 S. Walter Reed Drive, Suite 1, Arlington, VA 22204
Telephone: (703) 486-8311
Background: A public policy organization which seeks to educate the public and decision makers on such issues as tuition tax credits, educational vouchers and magnet schools. Exec. Director is Robert S. Marlowe, of Citizens for Educational Freedom.

Cleartel Communication
1232 22nd St., N.W. Suite 100, Washington, DC 20037
Telephone: (202) 463-8500
Counsel or consultant:
Jefferson Group, The (Ron Eisenberg)

Clemson University
Clemson, SC
Counsel or consultant:
McNair Group Inc. (Elizabeth L. Taylor)

Cleveland-Cliffs Iron Co.
Cleveland, OH
Counsel or consultant:
Murray, Scheer & Montgomery (D. Michael Murray)

Cleveland Clinic Foundation
2000 L St., N.W., Suite 200, Washington, DC 20036
Telephone: (202) 861-0955
Represented by:
Daniel E. Nickelson, Director, Government Affairs
Counsel or consultant:
Baker and Hostetler (Frederick H. Graefe, Kenneth J. Kies)

Cleveland Electric Illuminating Co.
Cleveland, OH
Counsel or consultant:
Shaw, Pittman, Potts and Trowbridge (Jay E. Silberg)

Clifton, New Jersey, City of
Counsel or consultant:
Krivit and Krivit (Daniel H. Krivit)

Climate Institute
316 Pennsylvania Ave., S.E., Suite 403, Washington, DC 20003
Telephone: (202) 547-0104
Background: An organization which advocates societal action to respond to climate change and ozone depletion.
Represented by:
John C. Topping, Jr., President

Climax Paper Converters Ltd.
Hong Kong
Counsel or consultant:
Mudge Rose Guthrie Alexander and Ferdon (Donald B. Cameron, Jr.)

Clopay Corp.
Cincinnati, OH
Counsel or consultant:
Arent, Fox, Kintner, Plotkin & Kahn (John D. Hushon)

ORGANIZATIONS REPRESENTED

Clorox Co., The
Oakland, CA
Counsel or consultant:
Leighton and Regnery (Richard J. Leighton)

Close Up Foundation
1235 Jefferson Davis Hwy., Arlington, VA 22202
Telephone: (703) 892-5400
Represented by:
Cindy Bank, Congressional Liaison
Deborah L. Horan, Director, Congressional Relations
Stephen A. Janger, President
Robert A. Malson, Exec. V. President and COO

Closure Manufacturers Ass'n
1801 K St., N.W., Suite 1105L, Washington, DC 20006
Telephone: (202) 223-9050
Background: An affiliate of the Glass Packaging Institute.
Represented by:
Darla Williamson, Director

Clover Park School District
Tacoma, WA
Counsel or consultant:
Evergreen Associates, Ltd. (Robert M. Brooks)

Club Managers Ass'n of America
1733 King St., Alexandria, VA 22314
Telephone: (703) 739-9500
Background: A professional association for managers of private membership clubs. It represents over 4,000 professional managers of country, city, yacht, faculty, military and golf clubs worldwide.
Represented by:
Bonnie Fedchock, Assistant Manager, Governmental Affairs
Kathi D. Pernell, Director, Public Affairs

Clyde Hill, Washington, Town of
Counsel or consultant:
Preston Gates Ellis & Rouvelas Meeds (Allen Erenbaum, Craig J. Gehring)

CNA Financial Corp.
Chicago, IL
Counsel or consultant:
Baker and Hostetler (Kenneth J. Kies)
Bishop, Cook, Purcell & Reynolds (Marlow W. Cook)
O'Connor & Hannan (Thomas R. Jolly)
Scribner, Hall and Thompson (Thomas C. Thompson, Jr.)
Winston and Strawn (Richard Meltzer)

CNA Insurance Cos.
7361 Calhoun Place, Rockville, MD 20855
Telephone: (301) 738-1216
Represented by:
Thomas R. DeYulia, V. President, Program & Support Services
Richard E. Ruddick, V. President
Carol Verby, Congressional Relations Representative
Counsel or consultant:
O'Connor & Hannan (Thomas R. Jolly)

CNG Transmission Corp.
Clarksburg, WV
Counsel or consultant:
Newman & Holtzinger, P.C.
Steptoe and Johnson

Coachella Valley Water District
Coachella, CA
Counsel or consultant:
Will & Muys, P.C. (Robert P. Will)

Coal Exporters Ass'n of the U.S.
1130 17th St., N.W. 9th Floor, Washington, DC 20036
Telephone: (202) 463-2654
Represented by:
Betsy Kraft, Exec. Director

Coal Industry Tax Committee
1317 F Street, N.W., Suite 400, Washington, DC 20004
Telephone: (202) 737-0100
Background: The above address is that of the consulting firm R. Duffy Wall & Associates, Inc.
Counsel or consultant:
R. Duffy Wall and Associates (R. Duffy Wall, Charlotte Wilmer)

Coal Miners Political Action Committee
900 15th St., N.W., Washington, DC 20005
Telephone: (202) 842-7200
Background: The political action committee of the United Mine Workers of America.
Represented by:
Matthew Miller, Administrator

Coal & Slurry Technology Ass'n
1156 15th St., N.W., Suite 525, Washington, DC 20005
Telephone: (202) 296-1133
Background: Organized in Houston, August, 1975 as the Slurry Transport Ass'n. Took present name in 1987. Pipeline and mining companies and suppliers interested in slurry bulk transport and coal slurry fuels. Coal and utility interests that back slurry pipelines favor legislation giving them eminent domain powers to acquire rights-of-way.
Represented by:
George H. Eatman, Executive Consultant
Stuart D. Serkin, Exec. Director

Coalition Against Regressive Taxation
430 First St., S.E., Washington, DC 20003
Telephone: (202) 544-6245
Background: A coalition of business interests whose members and customers pay the bulk of federal excise taxes. Opposes increases in excise levies. Member groups include the American Trucking Ass'ns, Air Transport Ass'n, Beer Institute, Distilled Spirits Council of the U.S., Tobacco Institute, Wine and Spirits Wholesalers of America, the American Petroleum Institute, RJR Nabisco Inc., Joseph E. Seagram and Sons and Brown and Williams Tobacco Corp. President of the Coalition is Thomas J. Donohue, the President and CEO of the American Trucking Ass'ns. The Secretary of the Coalition is Kenneth F. Stinger, Director of Government Affairs of the American Trucking Ass'ns.
Counsel or consultant:
Patricia Bario Associates (Patricia Bario)
Burson-Marsteller (Leonard Biegel)

Coalition for a Democratic Majority
1001 Connecticut Ave., N.W., Suite 707, Washington, DC 20036
Telephone: (202) 466-4702
Background: A not-for-profit organization of centrist Democrats dedicated to promoting a strong defense, an assertive U.S. foreign policy and the effective use of government power to improve the lives of Americans. President is Peter R. Rosenblatt.
Represented by:
Penn Kemble, Chairman, Executive Committee
Ben J. Wattenberg, Chairman

Coalition for Acid Rain Equity (CARE)
P.O. Box 33924, Washington, DC 20033-0924
Represented by:
Randell Thompson, Exec. Director

Coalition for Affordable Home Financing
1350 New York Ave., N.W. Suite 800, Washington, DC 20005
Telephone: (202) 628-2015
Represented by:
Curtis B. Uhre, President
Counsel or consultant:
McAuliffe, Kelly, Raffaelli & Siemens (Frederick W. Hatfield)
O'Connor & Hannan

Coalition for American Energy Security
1050 Thomas Jefferson St., N.W., 6th Floor, Washington, DC 20007
Telephone: (202) 333-7484
Counsel or consultant:
Morris J. Amitay, P.C.
Van Ness, Feldman & Curtis (M. Isabelle Tapia)

Coalition for Capital Import Neutrality
1333 New Hampshire Ave., N.W., Washington, DC 20036
Telephone: (202) 862-2200
Counsel or consultant:
Cadwalader, Wickersham & Taft (J. Roger Mentz)

Coalition for Competitive Capital
2001 L St., N.W. Suite 304, Washington, DC 20036
Telephone: (202) 785-9700
Background: Contact is John Dill of the DC Firm Dickstein, Shapiro and Morin, and the above address is that of the frim.

Counsel or consultant:
Dickstein, Shapiro and Morin (John C. Dill)
Charls E. Walker Associates

Coalition for Competitive Imports
c/o Nixon, Hargrave, et al One Thomas Circle, N.W., Washington, DC 20005
Telephone: (202) 223-7200
Background: A coalition of U.S. importers, distributors and retailers seeking continued ability to import name-brand goods for sale at a discount in the U.S. without permission from the American trademark owner.
Counsel or consultant:
Nixon, Hargrave, Devans and Doyle (Stephen Kurzman)

Coalition for Employment through Exports
1801 K St., N.W., 8th Floor, Washington, DC 20006
Telephone: (202) 296-6107
Background: An organization of business and labor leaders and state governors interested in foreign trade and the competitive position of U.S. exports, especially as the problems relate to programs of the U.S. Export-Import Bank.
Represented by:
Bruce Talley, Exec. Director

Coalition for Environmental-Energy Balance
c/o Porter, Wright et al 1233 20th St., N.W., Washington, DC 20036
Telephone: (202) 778-3000
Counsel or consultant:
Murphy and Associates (William T. Murphy, Jr.)
Porter, Wright, Morris and Arthur (Michael G. Dowd)
William E. Tanner

Coalition for Equitable Compensation
1200 18th St., N.W. First Floor, Washington, DC 20036
Telephone: (202) 457-6100
Background: A coalition of former asbestos manufacturers seeking a more efficient and equitable alternative to the litigation of asbeston-related lawsuits in tort. Address above is that of the D.C. firm of Reed, Smith, Shaw & McClay.
Counsel or consultant:
Camp, Barsh, Bates and Tate (John C. Camp, Kate Moss)
Collier, Shannon & Scott
Frank, Bernstein, Conaway & Goldman
The Hoving Group
Powell, Goldstein, Frazer and Murphy
Reed Smith Shaw & McClay

Coalition for Fair Lumber Imports
1775 Pennsylvania Ave., N.W., Suite 600, Washington, DC 20006
Telephone: (202) 862-4505
Counsel or consultant:
Dewey, Ballantine, Bushby, Palmer and Wood (Michael H. Stein, Alan W. Wolff)

Coalition for FDA Resources
c/o Fleishman-Hillard Inc. 1301 Connecticut Ave., N.W., Washington, DC 20036
Telephone: (202) 659-0330
Background: A coalition of nine trade, consumer and medical organizations seeking increased funding of the Food and Drug Administration. A pro bono organization located at the offices of the DC firm Fleishman-Hillard.
Counsel or consultant:
Fleishman-Hillard, Inc (W. Douglas Campbell)

Coalition for Government Procurement
1990 M St., N.W., Suite 400, Washington, DC 20036
Telephone: (202) 331-0975
Background: A nonprofit membership organization composed of small and large businesses which sell commercial products to the Federal Government. Concerned about preserving the Multiple Award Schedule contracting system and other policies affecting federal commercial product procurement. Backed by several trade associations.
Represented by:
Paul J. Caggiano, President
Julianne O'Dwyer, Exec. Director
Counsel or consultant:
Steptoe and Johnson (Robert D. Wallick)

Coalition for High Definition Television 1125/60 Production
New York, NY

The listings in this directory are available as *Mailing Labels.* See last page.

527

ORGANIZATIONS REPRESENTED

Coalition for High Definition Television 1125/60 Production (Cont'd)
Counsel or consultant:
Mintz, Levin, Cohn, Ferris, Glovsky and Popeo, P.C. (Charles D. Ferris)

Coalition for North American Trade and Investment
5152 Woodmire Lane, Alexandria, VA 22311
Telephone: (703) 931-0104
Background: An ad hoc coalition formed in 1986 to advocate legislation to promote mutually beneficial trade and investment among the United States, Canada, Mexico and the Caribbean nations; economic development of the U.S.-Mexico border region; to uphold free capital movement and global production sharing; to support the maquiladora (twin-plan) system; to uphold items 9802.00.60 and 9802.00.80 of the tariff code; and to stimulate business investment in Mexico and the Caribbean region. Director is Paul Suplizio of Suplizio Associates. Counsel is Charles A. Vanik of Squire, Sanders, and Dempsey.
Counsel or consultant:
Squire, Sanders and Dempsey (Charles A. Vanik)
Paul Suplizio Associates (Paul E. Suplizio)

Coalition for Open Markets and Expanded Trade
c/o Valis Associates, 1747 Pennsylvania Ave., N.W. #1201, Washington, DC 20006
Telephone: (202) 833-5055
Background: A grassroots coalition that advocates the elimination of barriers to exports and imports, and urges internat'l market opening agreements.
Counsel or consultant:
Valis Associates (Wayne H. Valis)

Coalition for Prompt Pay
3150 Spring Street, Fairfax, VA 22031-2399
Telephone: (703) 273-7200
Background: A coalition of trade associations representing businesses and manufacturers who contract with the U.S. government to provide goods and services. Represented by Kenton Pattie of the Internat'l Communications Industries Ass'n.

Coalition for Regional Banking and Economic Development
1919 Pennsylvania Ave., N.W. Suite 400, Washington, DC 20006
Telephone: (202) 775-7100
Background: Favors individual state's rights under federal banking laws.
Counsel or consultant:
Arter & Hadden (William K. Dabaghi)

Coalition for Reliable Energy
Lexington, MA
Counsel or consultant:
J. Arthur Weber & Associates (Joseph A. Weber)

Coalition for Religious Freedom
515 Wythe St., Suite 201, Alexandria, VA 22314
Telephone: (703) 684-9010
Background: A 'First Amendment' organization composed of Americans of all faiths defending the free exercise of religion against unconstitutional government encroachment.
Represented by:
Daniel C. Holdgreiwe, Exec. Director
Dr. Donald Sills, President

Coalition for Retirement Income Security
c/o AT&T 1120 20th St., N.W., #1000, Washington, DC 20036
Telephone: (202) 457-3838
Background: A coalition of some 30 large companies lobbying on a variety of pension issues, including seeking tax breaks to help companies bear the expense of proposed accounting requirements for health cost benefits for retired employees. Members include AT&T, W. R. Grace and Co., IBM, Eastman Kodak, GTE, Ford, General Electric, Southwestern Bell, TRW, Ameritech, Bell Atlantic, BellSouth and du Pont. Contact is Katherine Hagen, Public Affairs Director in Washington of AT&T.

Coalition for Safe Ceramicware
Yor, PA
Counsel or consultant:
Collier, Shannon & Scott (David A. Hartquist)

Coalition for State Prompt Pay
3150 Spring St., Fairfax, VA 22031-2399
Telephone: (703) 273-7200
Background: An organization of 26 national, state and regional trade associations united to get state governments and the organizations they subsidize to pay their bills promptly. Represented by Kenton Pattie of the Internat'l Communications Industries Ass'n (ICIA).

Coalition for the Homeless
2824 Sherman Ave., N.W., Washington, DC 20001
Telephone: (202) 328-1184
Background: Operates centers and second stage houses for the homeless. Provides a program by which homeless individuals can realize independent living status and become economically contributing members of the community.
Represented by:
Jack White, Exec. Director

Coalition for the Promotion of Costa Rica Abroad
San Jose, Costa Rica
Counsel or consultant:
The William Chasey Organization (William C. Chasey, Ph.D.)

Coalition for Uniform Product Liability Law
c/o Rowland & Sellery 1023 15th St., N.W., Washington, DC 20005
Telephone: (202) 289-1780
Counsel or consultant:
Rowland & Sellery (Terrie Dort, J. Patrick Rowland)

Coalition for Women's Appointments
1275 K St., N.W., Suite 750, Washington, DC 20005
Telephone: (202) 898-1100
Background: A bi-partisan network focused on increasing the number of women elected and appointed to public office and advancing issues of concern to women and their families. Linda Kaplan, Exec. Director of the Nat'l Women's Political Caucus, serves as Coordinator.

Coalition of Advocates for Immigrants and Refugees (CAIR)
Background: An activist organization in support of immigrants' and refugees' rights.
Represented by:
Rick Swartz, Director

Coalition of ARBA Licensees
Washington, DC
Background: Manufacturers licensed by the American Revolution Bicentennial Administration.
Counsel or consultant:
F. H. Hutchison and Co. (Fred H. Hutchison)

Coalition of Black Trade Unionists
Box 73055, Washington, DC 20056
Telephone: (202) 429-1203
Background: Founded in 1972 to bring more Blacks into active trade union participation. President is William Lucy of the American Federation of State, County and Municipal Employees.
Represented by:
Cleveland Robinson, Exec. V. President

Coalition of Boston Teaching Hospitals
Boston, MA
Counsel or consultant:
O'Neill and Athy, P.C. (Martha L. Casey)

Coalition of EPSCoR States
453 New Jersey Ave., S.E., Washington, DC 20003
Telephone: (202) 488-3581
Counsel or consultant:
Winburn, VanScoyoc, and Hooper (H. Stewart VanScoyoc)

Coalition of Higher Education Assistance Organizations
1101 Vermont Ave., N.W. Suite 400, Washington, DC 20005
Telephone: (202) 289-3900
Counsel or consultant:
Clohan & Dean (John E. Dean)

Coalition of Labor Union Women
New York, NY
Counsel or consultant:
The Kamber Group (John W. Leslie)

Coalition of Northeastern Governors
400 North Capitol St., N.W. Suite 382, Washington, DC 20001
Telephone: (202) 783-6674
Background: A non-profit organization conducting regional research and programs for the Northeastern Governors. It does limited monitoring of federal issues.
Represented by:
Anne D. Stubbs, Exec. Director

Coalition of Publicly Traded Partnerships
1625 K St., N.W., Suite 200, Washington, DC 20006
Telephone: (202) 857-0670
Background: A trade ass'n representing publicly traded partnerships, corporations which are general partners of PTPs, and attorneys, accountants, and investment bankers who work with them. Letitia Chambers and Mary S. Lyman, of Chambers Asociates Inc., serve as President and Tax Counsel.
Counsel or consultant:
Chambers Associates Incorporated (Letitia Chambers, Mary S. Lyman)

Coalition of Publicly Traded Partnerships Political Action Committee
1625 K St., N.W., Suite 200, Washington, DC 20006
Telephone: (202) 857-0670
Background: Contact is Letitia Chambers of Chambers Associates.
Counsel or consultant:
Chambers Associates Incorporated (Letitia Chambers)

Coalition of Religious Press Ass'ns
Jefferson City, MO
Counsel or consultant:
Liz Robbins Associates (Michael J. Lucas, Liz Robbins)

Coalition of Service Industries
2001 M St., N.W. 4th Floor, Washington, DC 20036
Telephone: (202) 467-3054
Background: Represents 17 major service corporations on foreign and economic policy matters.
Represented by:
Margaret S. Wigglesworth, Exec. Director

Coalition on Human Needs
1000 Wisconsin Ave., N.W., Washington, DC 20007
Telephone: (202) 342-0726
Background: An alliance of over 100 national organizations and hundreds of grass-roots groups concerned about the needs of the poor, minorities, children, women, the aged and the disabled. Major issues include federal budget priorities, welfare reform, tax policy and block grants/federalism questions.
Represented by:
Susan Rees, Exec. Director

Coalition on Smoking or Health
1615 New Hampshire Ave., N.W. Second Floor, Washington, DC 20009
Telephone: (202) 234-9375
Counsel or consultant:
Asbill, Junkin, Myers & Buffone (Matthew L. Myers)

Coalition on State Use Taxes
2550 M St., N.W., Suite 800, Washington, DC 20037
Telephone: (202) 457-6000
Counsel or consultant:
Patton, Boggs and Blow (Timothy J. May)

Coalition to End the Permanent Congress
Kansas City, MO
Background: A bipartisan organization of individuals who have been unsuccessful candidates for Congress in past elections.
Counsel or consultant:
James L. Kenworthy, Esq.

Coalition to Keep Alaska Oil
1667 K St., N.W., Suite 480, Washington, DC 20006
Telephone: (202) 775-1796
Counsel or consultant:
Marlowe and Co. (Howard Marlowe)

Coalition to Oppose Energy Taxes
1100 15th St., N.W. Suite 1200, Washington, DC 20005
Telephone: (202) 457-9100
Counsel or consultant:
Travis & Gooch (R. Gordon Gooch)

The listings in this directory are available as *Mailing Labels*. See last page.

ORGANIZATIONS REPRESENTED

Coalition to Preserve the Integrity of American Trademarks
c/o Covington & Burling, 1201 Pennsylvania Ave., N.W., Washington, DC 20044
Telephone: (202) 662-6000
Background: A group of U.S. manufacturers opposed to the importation by discounters of name brand goods. The address given is that of the Washington law firm of Covington and Burling.
Counsel or consultant:
Covington and Burling (Scott D. Gilbert, Eugene A. Ludwig)
Foreman & Heidepriem (Carol Tucker Foreman, Nikki Heidepriem)

Coalition to Preserve the Low Income Housing Tax Credit
2300 M St., N.W., Washington, DC 20037
Telephone: (202) 955-9790
Counsel or consultant:
Kelley, Drye and Warren (Charles L. Edson)

Coalition to Promote America's Trade
1101 15th St., N.W., Suite 205, Washington, DC 20005
Telephone: (202) 785-3060
Counsel or consultant:
Steptoe and Johnson (Charlene Barshefsky)

Coalitions for America
717 2nd St., N.E., Washington, DC 20002
Telephone: (202) 546-3003
Background: A conservative lobbying organization which brings together a wide range of organizations for the purpose of coordinating strategy and organizing grass roots participation in the political process. Paul M. Weyrich is Founder and Nat'l Chairman. Curt Anderson directs the organization's activities.
Represented by:
Eric Licht, President
Patrick B. McGuigan, Sr. Scholar, Ctr for Law and Democracy

COALPAC
1130 17th St., N.W., Washington, DC 20036
Telephone: (202) 463-2645
Background: The political action committee of the National Coal Association. Represented by Andrea L. Innes of the Nat'l Coal Ass'n.

Coast Federal Savings and Loan Ass'n
Sarasota, FL
Counsel or consultant:
Elias, Matz, Tiernan and Herrick

Coast Savings and Loan Ass'n
Los Angeles, CA
Counsel or consultant:
Steptoe and Johnson (John T. Collins)

Coastal Airlines, Inc.
Jacksonville, FL
Counsel or consultant:
Allan W. Markham

Coastal Barrier Relief Fund
Tavernier, FL
Counsel or consultant:
Fleishman-Hillard, Inc (Paul Johnson, John Overstreet)

Coastal Coalition
Anchorage, AK
Counsel or consultant:
Robertson, Monagle and Eastaugh (Brad Gilman)

Coastal Conservation Ass'n
Houston, TX
Background: A group of recreational fisheries.
Counsel or consultant:
Bogle and Gates (Robert G. Hayes)

Coastal Corp., The/ANR Pipeline Co.
2000 M St., N.W., Suite 500, Washington, DC 20036
Telephone: (202) 466-7430
Represented by:
Margaret H. Bryant, Director, Federal Affairs
Robert E. Moss, V. President, Federal Affairs
Counsel or consultant:
Miller & Steuart (Judith M. Greenberg, Marshall V. Miller, George C. Steuart)
Steven E. Some Associates

Coastal Reports, Inc.
New York, NY
Counsel or consultant:
Richard Curry and Associates (Richard C. Curry, Gerard Stoddard)

Coastal Soc.
3202 Tower Oaks Blvd., Rockville, MD 20852
Telephone: (301) 231-5250
Background: An international non-profit organization dedicated to the protection and wise use of coastal areas.
Represented by:
Anthony Lee, President

Coastal States Organization
444 North Capitol St., N.W. Suite 312, Washington, DC 20001
Telephone: (202) 628-9636
Background: Membership consists of delegates appointed by the governors of 35 states, commonwealths and territories of the U.S. which have an ocean, gulf or Great Lakes boundary. Serves as clearinghouse and spokesman on national coastal and ocean resource issues of interest to its member jurisdictions.
Represented by:
R. Gary Magnuson, Director
David C. Slade, General Counsel

Coastal Transportation, Inc.
Seattle, WA
Counsel or consultant:
Preston Gates Ellis & Rouvelas Meeds (William N. Myhre)

Coca-Cola Co.
1627 K St., N.W., Suite 800, Washington, DC 20006
Telephone: (202) 466-5310
Represented by:
Janmarie Prutting, Asst. V.P. & Mgr., Internat'l Gov't Aff.
Barclay T. Resler, Asst. Manager, Governmental Relations
Counsel or consultant:
Akin, Gump, Strauss, Hauer and Feld (Andrew G. Berg, Owen Johnson)
F. Nordy Hoffmann & Assoc. (F. Nordy Hoffmann)
Morrison & Foerster (Philip D. Bartz, Ronald G. Carr, Scott D. Livingston, William F. Squadron)
O'Connor & Hannan (Patrick E. O'Donnell)

Coca-Cola Enterprises Inc.
Atlanta, GA
Counsel or consultant:
McClure and Trotter

Coca-Cola Foods
Houston, TX
Counsel or consultant:
Fierce and Associates (Donald L. Fierce)

Coeur d'Alene Mines
Coeur d'Alene, ID
Counsel or consultant:
Denny Miller Associates

Coffee, Sugar and Cocoa Exchange
New York, NY
Counsel or consultant:
Lord Day & Lord, Barrett Smith (Mahlon Frankhauser, Ellen S. Levinson)

Cogema, Inc.
7401 Wisconsin Ave., Bethesda, MD 20814
Telephone: (301) 986-8585
Background: Formerly known as French-American Metals Corp. Owns Pathfinder Mines, Inc. in the U.S. Cogema provides supplies and services for all stages of nuclear fuel cycle.
Represented by:
Amour Kouakou, Manager, Public Information
Michael A. McMurphy, President and CEO
Thomas W. Pennington, V. President & General Counsel
Thierry Poirey, V. President & CFO

Cogeneration and Independent Power Coalition of America
1133 21st St., N.W. Suite 420, Washington, DC 20036
Telephone: (202) 785-8776

Represented by:
Christine L. Nolin, Exec. Director
Counsel or consultant:
Katten, Muchin, Zavis & Dombroff (Gilbert Sperling)
Wickwire Gavin, P.C.

Cogentrix, Inc.
Charlotte, NC
Counsel or consultant:
Concord Associates, Inc.

Cohen Flax Investments
Bethesda, MD
Counsel or consultant:
Laxalt, Washington, Perito & Dubuc (Marc J. Scheineson)

Coin Coalition, The
1000 Connecticut Ave., N.W., Suite 304, Washington, DC 20036
Telephone: (202) 659-4805
Background: A lobbying group calling for a newly-designed one dollar coin and phasing out of the dollar bill and the penny.
Counsel or consultant:
Bracy Williams & Co. (James C. Benfield)

Cold Finished Steel Bar Institute
1120 Vermont Ave., N.W. Suite 1000, Washington, DC 20005
Telephone: (202) 857-0059
Represented by:
Stephanie D. Nore, Administrative Secretary
Counsel or consultant:
Thompson and Mitchell (Murray J. Belman)

Cold Spring Granite Co.
Cold Spring, MN
Counsel or consultant:
Baker and McKenzie (Bruce E. Clubb)
Robins, Kaplan, Miller & Ciresi (Pamela M. Deese)

Coldwell Banker
Chicago, IL
Counsel or consultant:
Foley & Lardner (Jay N. Varon)

Colebrand Ltd.
London, England
Counsel or consultant:
Lipsen Whitten & Diamond
Shaw, Pittman, Potts and Trowbridge (James H. Burnley, IV)

Colgate-Palmolive Co.
New York, NY
Counsel or consultant:
Dorsey & Whitney
Lee, Toomey & Kent

Collagen Corp.
Palo Alto, CA
Counsel or consultant:
Akin, Gump, Strauss, Hauer and Feld (John F. Markus, Kirk O'Donnell)
Daniel J. Edelman, Inc. (Leslie Dach, Christopher Gidez)

College Construction Loan Insurance Ass'n
2445 M St., N.W., Suite 450, Washington, DC 20037
Telephone: (202) 835-0090
Counsel or consultant:
Williams and Jensen, P.C. (William T. Brack)

College Football Ass'n
Boulder, CO
Counsel or consultant:
Baraff, Koerner, Olender and Hochberg (Philip R. Hochberg)

College of American Pathologists
1101 Vermont Ave., N.W., Washington, DC 20005
Telephone: (202) 371-6617
Represented by:
Norman D. Burch, Ass't Dir., Dir., Congressional Rltns.
Jane Carlile, Asst. Director, Professional Relations
Julia Ciorletti, Keyman Coordinator
Alfred S. Ercolano, Director, Washington Office
Michael Palmer, Director, Professional Relations
Hope R. Wittenberg, Ass't Director, Congressional Relations
Counsel or consultant:
Gold and Liebengood, Inc. (Martin B. Gold)

The listings in this directory are available as *Mailing Labels*. See last page.

ORGANIZATIONS REPRESENTED

College of Property Management, The
8811 Coleville Road, Suite G106, Silver Spring, MD 20910
Telephone: (301) 587-6543
Counsel or consultant:
  Bachner Communications, Inc. (John P. Bachner)

College Republican Nat'l Committee
310 First St., S.E., Washington, DC 20003
Telephone: (202) 662-1330
Background: Promotes the Republican Party on college campuses.
Represented by:
  Jason Miko, Exec. Director

College Savings Bank
Princeton, NJ
Counsel or consultant:
  Patton, Boggs and Blow (James B. Christian, Jr.)

College and University Personnel Ass'n
1233 20th St., N.W., Suite 503, Washington, DC 20036
Telephone: (202) 429-0311
Represented by:
  Richard C. Creal, Exec. Director

Collier County, Florida
FL
Counsel or consultant:
  Van Ness, Feldman & Curtis (Alan L. Mintz, Susan Tomasky)

Colombia, Embassy of
2118 Leroy Place, N.W., Washington, DC 20008
Telephone: (202) 387-8338
Counsel or consultant:
  Coudert Brothers

Colonial Sugar Refineries, Ltd.
Sydney, Australia
Background: The marketing agent for Australian raw sugar.
Counsel or consultant:
  Bishop, Cook, Purcell & Reynolds (Graham B. Purcell, Jr.)
  Cleary, Gottlieb, Steen and Hamilton

Colonial Village, Inc.
Reston, VA
Counsel or consultant:
  Dow, Lohnes and Albertson (Reuben B. Robertson)

Color Marketing Group
4001 N. 9th St., Suite 102, Arlington, VA 22203
Telephone: (703) 528-7666
Represented by:
  Nancy A. Burns, Exec. Director

Colorado Aviation Department (City and County of Denver)
Denver, CO
Counsel or consultant:
  Spiegel and McDiarmid (John J. Corbett, Jr.)

Colorado Bankers Ass'n
Denver, CO
Counsel or consultant:
  Bonner & Associates

Colorado Interstate Gas Co.
Colorado Springs, CO
Background: A subsidiary of the Coastal Corp.
Counsel or consultant:
  Ross Marsh Foster Myers & Quiggle

Colorado River Commission of Nevada
Las Vegas, NV
Background: Concerned with Hoover Dam power matters.
Counsel or consultant:
  Duncan, Weinberg, Miller & Pembroke, P.C. (Frederick L. Miller, Jr., Edward Weinberg)

Colorado State University
Fort Collins, CO
Counsel or consultant:
  Hill and Knowlton Public Affairs Worldwide (Tom Hoog)

Columbia Communications Corp.
Honolulu, HI
Counsel or consultant:
  Camp, Barsh, Bates and Tate (Harry E. Barsh, Jr.)

Columbia Farm Credit District
Columbia, SC

Counsel or consultant:
  Patton, Boggs and Blow (John H. Vogel)

Columbia Federal Savings and Loan
Westport, CT
Counsel or consultant:
  Sutherland, Asbill and Brennan (Anne P. Jones)

Columbia Gas Distribution Cos.
1250 Eye St., N.W., Suite 703, Washington, DC 20005
Telephone: (202) 842-7400
Background: A subsidiary of The Columbia Gas System, Inc.
Represented by:
  Genevieve W. Tuchow, Director, Federal Gov't Affairs

Columbia Gas System
Wilmington, DE
Counsel or consultant:
  Camp, Barsh, Bates and Tate (Harry E. Barsh, Jr.)

Columbia Gas System Service Corp.
1250 Eye St., N.W., Suite 703, Washington, DC 20005
Telephone: (202) 842-7400
Represented by:
  Richard A. Casali, Vice President
  Suzanne N. Cook, Regulatory Assistant
  Pamela Gottfried, Manager, Government Affairs
  Ronald P. Johnsen, Legislative Representative
  Gilbert A. Martin, V. President, Regulatory Affairs

Columbia Gas Transmission Corp.
1250 Eye St., N.W., Suite 703, Washington, DC 20005
Telephone: (202) 842-7400
Background: A subsidiary of Columbia Gas System.
Represented by:
  Kathleen O'Leary, Director, Federal Government Affairs
Counsel or consultant:
  Wilmer, Cutler and Pickering (Timothy N. Black)

Columbia Gulf Transmission Corp.
Houston, TX
Background: A subsidiary of Columbia Gas System. Represented by Richard A. Casali of Columbia Gas System Service Corp.

Columbia Hospital for Women Medical Center
2425 L St., N.W., Washington, DC 20037
Telephone: (202) 293-2048
Counsel or consultant:
  Foreman & Heidepriem (Carol Tucker Foreman, Nikki Heidepriem)
  Wexler, Reynolds, Fuller, Harrison and Schule, Inc. (Gail Harrison, Nancy Clark Reynolds, Anne Wexler)

Columbia, Inc.
Fairfield, NJ
Counsel or consultant:
  Patton, Boggs and Blow

Columbia Institute
8 E St., S.E., Washington, DC 20003
Telephone: (202) 547-2470
Background: An independent, non-partisan organization whose activities deal primarily with communication between the public and private sectors on public policy issues. Services include coordinating public policy conferences, overseas trade missions and congressional surveys.
Represented by:
  Orval Hansen, President
  Jonathan F. Ortmans, Director

Columbia LNG Corp.
Wilmington, DE
Background: A subsidiary of Columbia Gas System. Represented by Richard A. Casali of Columbia Gas System Service Corp.

Columbia Pictures Entertainment, Inc.
New York, NY
Counsel or consultant:
  Charls E. Walker Associates

Columbia Presbyterian Hospital
New York, NY
Counsel or consultant:
  Direct Impact Co., The (John Brady, Tom Herrity)

Columbia Savings and Loan Ass'n
Beverly Hills, CA

Counsel or consultant:
  Cleary, Gottlieb, Steen and Hamilton (Kenneth L. Bachman, Jr.)

Columbia, South Carolina, City of
Counsel or consultant:
  Nat'l Center for Municipal Development (Barbara T. McCall)

Columbia Typographical Union - CWA
4626 Wisconsin Ave., N.W. 3rd Floor, Washington, DC 20016
Telephone: (202) 362-9413
Represented by:
  Robert E. Petersen, President

Columbia University
New York, NY
Counsel or consultant:
  Cassidy and Associates, Inc. (Gerald S. J. Cassidy, Thomas M. Gannon, C. Frank Godfrey, Jr.)

Columbus, Indiana, City of
Columbus, IN
Counsel or consultant:
  Sagamore Associates, Inc. (David U. Gogol)

Columbus and Southern Ohio Electric Co.
Columbus, OH
Counsel or consultant:
  Conner and Wetterhahn, P.C.

Colville Confederated Tribes
WA
Counsel or consultant:
  SENSE, INC. (Joe Tallakson)

COMDISCO, Inc.
Rosemont, IL
Background: Leases computer equipment.
Counsel or consultant:
  Coffield Ungaretti Harris & Slavin (Andrea S. Kramer, Robert Macari, Howard Menell)
  Hopkins and Sutter (Donald G. Brotzman)
  Mayer, Brown and Platt (Jerry L. Oppenheimer)
  Skadden, Arps, Slate, Meagher and Flom

Cominco, Ltd.
Toronto, Canada
Counsel or consultant:
  Bogle and Gates
  Counselors For Management, Inc. (Richard M. Cooperman)
  Piper and Marbury

Comite Textil de la Sociedad Nacional
Lima, Peru
Counsel or consultant:
  Prather, Seeger, Doolittle and Farmer

Commerce Clearing House
Riverwood, IL
Counsel or consultant:
  Sidley and Austin (Virginia M. Buckhold)

Commercial Federal Savings and Loan Ass'n
Omaha, NE
Counsel or consultant:
  Steptoe and Johnson (John T. Collins)

Commercial Law League of America
Millburn, NJ
Counsel or consultant:
  Webster, Chamberlain and Bean (Burkett Van Kirk)

Commercial Metals Co.
Dallas, TX
Counsel or consultant:
  Marlowe and Co.

Commercial Refrigerator Manufacturers Ass'n
1101 Connecticut Ave., N.W., Suite 700, Washington, DC 20036
Telephone: (202) 857-1145
Counsel or consultant:
  Smith, Bucklin and Associates (Robert T. Chancler)

Commercial Solvents Corp.
New York, NY
Counsel or consultant:
  Dross and Levenstein (William Levenstein)

ORGANIZATIONS REPRESENTED

Commercial Weather Services Ass'n
312 Massachusetts Ave., N.E., Washington, DC 20002
Telephone: (202) 828-1977
Background: A trade association promoting private weather-related companies and services. Exec. Director is Jeffrey C. Smith of Washington Policy Advocates.
Counsel or consultant:
  Washington Policy Advocates (Jeffrey C. Smith)

Commission for the Advancement of Public Interest Organizations
P.O. Box 53424, Washington, DC 20009
Telephone: (202) 462-0505
Background: Founded in 1974 to promote and strengthen public interest organizations.
Represented by:
  Samuel S. Epstein, M.D., Chairperson

Commission of Accredited Truck Driving Schools (CATDS)
1899 L St., N.W. Suite 500, Washington, DC 20036
Telephone: (202) 331-8866
Represented by:
  James J. McAlpin, Exec. Director
Counsel or consultant:
  Bernard H. Ehrlich

Commission on Minority Business Development
730 Jackson Place, N.W., Washington, DC 20006
Telephone: (202) 523-0030
Counsel or consultant:
  Jensen & Co. (Michael G. Brown, Ronald R. Jensen)

Commission on Professionals in Science and Technology
1500 Massachusetts Ave., N.W. Suite 831, Washington, DC 20005
Telephone: (202) 223-6995
Background: A private, non-profit corporation formed by fourteen scientific societies to focus attention on common manpower problems. It is concerned with the recruitment, training and utilization of scientific manpower.
Represented by:
  Eleanor L. Babco, Associate Director
  Betty M. Vetter, Exec. Director

Commissioned Officers Ass'n of the U.S. Public Health Service
1400 Eye St., N.W., Suite 725, Washington, DC 20005
Telephone: (202) 289-6400
Represented by:
  William J. Lucca, Jr., Exec. Director
Counsel or consultant:
  Forrest Gerard & Associates (Forrest J. Gerard)

Committee Against Revising Staggers
c/o Sutherland, Asbill 1275 Pennsylvania Ave., N.W., Washington, DC 20004
Telephone: (202) 383-0100
Counsel or consultant:
  Sutherland, Asbill and Brennan (Jan Benes Vlcek)

Committee Assisting Republicans and Democrats (CARD-PAC)
1350 New York Ave., N.W., Suite 615, Washington, DC 20005
Telephone: (202) 393-1778
Background: The political action committee of the Greeting Card Ass'n.
Counsel or consultant:
  Resources for Group Management, Inc. (Marianne McDermott)

Committee for a Free Afghanistan
214 Massachusetts Ave., N.E. Suite 480, Washington, DC 20002
Telephone: (202) 546-7577
Represented by:
  Henry Kriegel, Executive Director

Committee for a Responsible Federal Budget
220 1/2 E St., N.E., Washington, DC 20002
Telephone: (202) 547-4484
Represented by:
  Carol G. Cox, President
Counsel or consultant:
  Hunton and Williams (John J. Rhodes)
  Nossaman, Guthner, Knox and Elliott (Robert N. Giaimo)

Committee for America's Copyright Community

Leventhal, Senter & Lerman (Michael R. Klipper)
Wexler, Reynolds, Fuller, Harrison and Schule, Inc. (Joseph W. Waz, Jr.)

Committee for Citizen Awareness
1750 New York Ave., N.W., Washington, DC 20006
Telephone: (202) 393-8553
Background: A non-profit, non-partisan organization seeking to enhance public awareness of the legislative process and increase voter participation.
Counsel or consultant:
  Manatos & Manatos, Inc. (Andrew E. Manatos, Kimberley A. Matthews)

Committee for Dulles
P.O. Box 17053-Washington/ Dulles Airport, Washington, DC 20041
Telephone: (703) 481-4278
Represented by:
  Katherine Hooper, Exec. Director

Committee for Economic Development
1700 K St., N.W., Suite 700, Washington, DC 20006
Telephone: (202) 296-5860
Background: An independent research and educational organization whose 250 trustees formulate business and public policies that can help solve the nation's most critical economic and social problems. Unique policy making process centers on the active participation of these corporate and university leaders. Current study topics include tax policy, demography and public policy, education reform, trade policy, foreign investment in the United States, and child care in the workplace.
Represented by:
  William J. Beeman, V. Pres. and Dir., Macroeconomic Studies
  R. Scott Fosler, V. Pres., & Director, Government Studies
  Dr. Robert C. Holland, President
  Nathaniel M. Semple, V.P. & Sec'y, Research & Policy Cttee.

Committee For Education Funding
505 Capitol Court, N.E. Suite 200, Washington, DC 20002
Telephone: (202) 543-6300
Background: A coalition of 100 educational institutions, associations, and state departments of education interested in federal funding for education.
Represented by:
  Susan Frost, Exec. Director
  Bonnie D. Kraus, Legislative Ass't

Committee for Environmentally Effective Packaging
c/o Bracy Williams & Co. 1000 Connecticut Ave., N.W., Washington, DC 20036
Telephone: (202) 659-4805
Counsel or consultant:
  Bracy Williams & Co. (James C. Benfield)

Committee for Equitable Compensation
1055 Thomas Jefferson St, N.W., Washington, DC 20007
Telephone: (202) 342-8400
Counsel or consultant:
  Camp, Barsh, Bates and Tate (John C. Camp, Kate Moss)
  Chambers Associates Incorporated (Letitia Chambers)
  O'Bannon & Co. (Dona O'Bannon)
  Powell, Goldstein, Frazer and Murphy (Stuart E. Eizenstat)

Committee for Free Elections and Democracy in Nicaragua
Miami, FL
Background: Opposed to the Sandanista regime.
Counsel or consultant:
  Burgum & Grimm, Ltd. (Thomas L. Burgum, Rodman D. Grimm, Cynthia Lebrun-Yaffe)
  Carmen Group, The (Willie W. Bledsoe, David M. Carmen, Carol Boyd Hallett, George C. Whatley)

Committee for Humane Legislation
1506 19th St., N.W. Suite 3, Washington, DC 20036
Telephone: (202) 483-8998
Represented by:
  Leslie Fain, Legislative Director

Committee for Nat'l Health Insurance
1757 N St., N.W., Washington, DC 20036
Telephone: (202) 223-9685
Background: Director is Melvin Glasser (see Health Security Action Council).

Committee for Nat'l Security
1601 Connecticut Ave., N.W. Suite 302, Washington, DC 20009
Telephone: (202) 745-2450
Background: Seeks to foster new foreign and security policy approaches which do not rely excessively on military solutions to international problems.
Represented by:
  Susan Cancade, Deputy Director
  Robert Edgar, Director
Counsel or consultant:
  Cynthia Friedman Assoc. Inc. (Keith F. Abbott)

Committee for Private Offshore Rescue and Towing (C-PORT)
312 Massachusetts Ave., N.E., Washington, DC 20002
Telephone: (202) 828-1977
Background: A trade group representing the private towing, salvage and rescue industry.
Counsel or consultant:
  Washington Policy Advocates (Jeffrey C. Smith)

Committee for Pro-Life Activities
3211 4th St., N.E., Washington, DC 20017
Telephone: (202) 541-3070
Background: Sponsored by The Nat'l Conference of Catholic Bishops.
Represented by:
  Rev. John W. Gouldrick, C.M., Exec. Director

Committee for Production Sharing
1629 K St., N.W., Suite 802, Washington, DC 20006
Telephone: (202) 223-6270
Background: A trade organization committed to enhancing the competitiveness of U.S. industry by promoting and fostering the growth of production sharing options such as tariff items 806.30/807.00, the GSP, and the CBI.
Represented by:
  Carolyn C. Miller, Exec. Secretary
Counsel or consultant:
  Webster, Chamberlain and Bean (Charles E. Chamberlain)

Committee for Purchase from the Blind and Other Severely Handicapped
1755 Jeff Davis Hwy., Crystal Square 5, Rm. 1107, Arlington, VA 22202-3509
Telephone: (703) 557-1145
Represented by:
  Beverly Lyford Milkman, Exec. Director

Committee for the Advancement of Cotton
Memphis, TN
Background: Represents the legislative and political interests of the Nat'l Cotton Council of America. Washington Representative is A. John Maguire of the Nat'l Cotton Council.

Committee for the Study of the American Electorate
421 New Jersey, Ave., S.E., Washington, DC 20003
Telephone: (202) 546-3221
Represented by:
  Curtis B. Gans, Exec. Director
  Barbara W. Schecter, Director of Development

Committee of American Ammunition Manufacturers
c/o Collier, Shannon, & Scott 1055 Thomas Jefferson St., NW, Washington, DC 20007
Telephone: (202) 342-8400
Counsel or consultant:
  Collier, Shannon & Scott (Lauren R. Howard, Thomas F. Shannon)

Committee of American Axle Producers
c/o Harris & Ellsworth 1101 30th St., N.W., Suite 103, Washington, DC 20007
Telephone: (202) 337-8338
Counsel or consultant:
  Harris & Ellsworth (Herbert E. Harris, II)

Committee of Annuity Insurers
1455 Pennsylvania Ave., N.W. Suite 1200, Washington, DC 20004
Telephone: (202) 347-2230
Background: The address given is that of the law firm Davis & Harman
Counsel or consultant:
  Davis & Harman

ORGANIZATIONS REPRESENTED

Committee of Corporate Telecommunications Users
1111 19th St., N.W., Washington, DC 20036
Telephone: (202) 828-0100
Counsel or consultant:
  Reid & Priest (Michael W. Faber)

Committee of Domestic Steel Wire Rope and Specialty Cable Manufacturers
1101 30th St., N.W. Suite 103, Washington, DC 20007
Telephone: (202) 337-8338
Counsel or consultant:
  Harris & Ellsworth (Herbert E. Harris, II)

Committee of Hydroelectric Dam Owners
1050 Thomas Jefferson St., N.W., 7th Floor, Washington, DC 20007
Telephone: (202) 298-1800
Counsel or consultant:
  Van Ness, Feldman & Curtis (Gary Bachman)

Committee of Nat'l Security Companies
Memphis, TN
Counsel or consultant:
  Rowland & Sellery (Lawrence E. Sabbath)

Committee of Publicly Owned Companies
New York, NY
Counsel or consultant:
  Vorys, Sater, Seymour and Pease (Randal C. Teague)

Committee on Human Rights for the People of Nicaragua
11400 Falls Road, Potomac, MD 20854
Telephone: (301) 983-9333
Background: Established in 1977 to monitor and publicize violations of human rights committed against the people of Nicaragua.
Represented by:
  Carlos Anzoategui, Exec. Director

Committee on Letter Carriers' Political Education
100 Indiana Ave., N.W., Washington, DC 20001
Telephone: (202) 393-4695
Background: Represented by George B. Gould of the Nat'l Ass'n of Letter Carriers of the United States of America.

Committee on Political Action of the American Postal Workers Union, AFL-CIO
1300 L St., N.W., Washington, DC 20005
Telephone: (202) 842-4210
Background: The political action arm of the American Postal Workers Union. Secretary-Treasurer is Patrick J. Nilan, Director of Legislation of the Union.

Committee on Political Education of the Columbia Typographical Union
4626 Wisconsin Ave., N.W. 3rd Floor, Washington, DC 20016
Telephone: (202) 362-9413
Background: Represented by Robert E. Petersen of the Columbia Typographical Union.

Committee on Problems of Drug Dependence
Boston, MA
Background: Associated with the Department of Pharmacology, Boston University School of Medicine.
Counsel or consultant:
  Baker and Hostetler
  Laxalt, Washington, Perito & Dubuc (Michael F. Cole)

Committee on the Constitutional System
1755 Massachusetts Ave., N.W. Suite 416, Washington, DC 20036
Telephone: (202) 387-8787
Background: Advocates consideration of structural changes in the Constitution and other measures to improve the working relationship between the President and Congress and among the various levels of government. Seeks to make the government more responsive to current problems.
Represented by:
  Peter Schauffler, Coordinator

Committee on the Present Danger
905 16th St., N.W., Washington, DC 20006
Telephone: (202) 628-2409
Background: A nonprofit, nonpartisan educational organization founded in November 1976 by a group of private individuals who believe that "the principal threat to our nation, to world peace, and to the cause of human freedom is the Soviet drive for dominance based on an unparalleled military buildup."
Represented by:
  David J. Trachtenberg, Senior Defense Analyst
  Charles Tyroler, II, Director

Committee Organized for the Trading of Cotton (COTCO)
1725 K St., N.W. Suite 1210, Washington, DC 20006
Telephone: (202) 296-7116
Background: Political Action Committee supported by The American Cotton Shippers Ass'n. Treasurer and contact is Neal P. Gillen of the American Cotton Shippers Ass'n.

Committee to Assure the Availability of Casein
3213 O St., N.W., Washington, DC 20007
Telephone: (202) 298-6134
Background: Operates from the law offices of Max N. Berry. Opposes legislation restricting imports of casein, a protein found in milk used in both edible and inedible forms.
Counsel or consultant:
  Max N. Berry Law Offices (Max N. Berry)

Committee to Eliminate Equipment Giveaways
2011 Eye St., N.W., Washington, DC 20006
Telephone: (202) 223-3217
Background: Represented by Pamela Boyajiam of the Nat'l Beverage Dispensing Equipment Ass'n.
Counsel or consultant:
  Bregman, Abell & Kay (Stanley I. Bregman)

Committee to Support the Antitrust Laws
1400 Eye St., N.W. Suite 480 East Tower, Washington, DC 20005
Telephone: (202) 962-3862
Counsel or consultant:
  Jonathan W. Cuneo Law Offices (Jonathan W. Cuneo)

Committee to Support U.S. Trade Laws
c/o USBIC, 220 Nat'l Press Bldg., Washington, DC 20045
Telephone: (202) 662-8744
Background: A coalition of companies supporting strong U.S. anti-dumping laws. Spokesman is John Cregan of the United States Business and Industrial Council. Attorneys active on the Committee include David Hartquist and Paul Rosenthal of Collier, Shannon & Scott; Michael Stein of Dewey, Ballantine, Bushby, Palmer & Wood; Gilbert Kaplan of Morrison & Foerster; and Howard Vine of Dyer, Ellis, Joseph & Mills.

Commodity Exchange, Inc. (COMEX)
1331 Pennsylvania Ave., N.W. Suite 550, Washington, DC 20004
Telephone: (202) 662-8770
Represented by:
  Stephen E. Storch, V. President, Government Affairs

Commodity Storage, Ltd.
1300 North 17th St., Suite 1400, Arlington, VA 22209
Telephone: (703) 527-6700
Counsel or consultant:
  Johnson & Associates, Inc. (James H. Johnson)

Common Cause
2030 M St., N.W., Washington, DC 20036
Telephone: (202) 833-1200
Background: Established in 1969 as the Urban Coalition Council. A non-partisan citizens' lobby whose purpose is to "make the system work" by organizing its membership to participate in the legislative process.
Represented by:
  Rebecca Avila, Political Organizer
  Elizabeth Bernstein, Rsrch. Asst, Campaign Finance Monitoring
  Dorothy D. Cecelski, Director, State Communications
  Archibald Cox, Chairman
  Edwin H. Davis, Associate Director, Issues Development
  Jeff Denny, Research Associate
  Marcy Frosh, Senior Research Associate
  Suzanne Greenfield, Political Organizer
  Jay Hedlund, Director, Grassroots Lobbying
  Randy Huwa, V. President, Membership & Media Commun.
  Amy Judy, Political Organizer
  Jennifer Layman-Heitman, Coord. & Res. Assoc., State Issues Dev.
  Susan Manes, V. President, Issue Development
  Michael Mawby, Lobbyist
  Ann McBride, Senior V. President
  Meredith McGehee, Lobbyist
  Jane Mentzinger, Spokeswoman
  Katharine Mountcastle, Director, Campaign Finance Monitoring
  Kathleen Sheekey, Legislative Director
  Susan M. Tannenbaum, Senior Lobbyist
  Fred Wertheimer, President
  Peter M. Williams, Executive Director of Common Cause of DC
Counsel or consultant:
  Wilmer, Cutler and Pickering (Roger M. Witten)

Common Fund, The
Fairfield, CT
Counsel or consultant:
  Wilmer, Cutler and Pickering (William J. Wilkins)

Commonwealth Edison Co.
1722 Eye St., N.W., Suite 600, Washington, DC 20006
Telephone: (202) 452-6278
Represented by:
  John S. Maxson, Director, Governmental Affairs
Counsel or consultant:
  Charlie McBride Assoc, Inc. (Charlie McBride)

Communicating for Agriculture
Fergus Falls, MN
Counsel or consultant:
  Vickers & Vickers (Linda Vickers)

Communication Industries Ass'n of Japan
Tokyo, Japan
Background: A trade association of Japanese telecommunications firms.
Counsel or consultant:
  Anderson, Hibey, Nauheim and Blair (Stanton D. Anderson)
  Mintz, Levin, Cohn, Ferris, Glovsky and Popeo, P.C. (Charles D. Ferris)

Communications Consortium
1333 H St., N.W., 11th Floor, Washington, DC 20005
Telephone: (202) 682-1270
Background: A non-profit media center.
Represented by:
  Kathy Bonk, Co-Director
  Philip L. Sparks, Co-Director

Communications Internat'l Inc.
One Thomas Circle, N.W. Suite 975, Washington, DC 20005
Telephone: (202) 429-2900
Represented by:
  Ernest Olivas, Jr., Eastern Region Director

Communications Satellite Corp. (COMSAT)
950 L'Enfant Plaza, S.W., Washington, DC 20024
Telephone: (202) 863-6000

ORGANIZATIONS REPRESENTED

Represented by:
   Kathleen Q. Abernathy, Director, Federal Affairs
   James A. Amdur, Corp Tax Counsel-Assoc General
      Counsel
   Robert W. Hunter, Director of Corporate Communica-
      tions
   Ernest B. Kelly, III, Director, Government Relations
   Richard L. McGraw, V. President, Corporate Affairs
   Willard R. Nichols, V. President and General Counsel
Counsel or consultant:
   Akin, Gump, Strauss, Hauer and Feld
   Crowell and Moring (Harold J. Heltzer)
   Dutko & Associates (Steve Perry)
   Griffin, Johnson & Associates
   The Eddie Mahe Company
   Morgan, Lewis and Bockius
   Wexler, Reynolds, Fuller, Harrison and Schule, Inc. (Jo-
      seph W. Waz, Jr., Bruce Wolpe)
   Wiley, Rein & Fielding
   Wilmer, Cutler and Pickering (Sally Katzen)

Communications Workers of America
   1925 K St., N.W., Washington, DC 20006
   Telephone: (202) 728-2300
   Represented by:
   Morton Bahr, President
   Dina Beaumont, Exec. Assistant to the President
   James B. Booe, Secretary-Treasurer
   Loretta Bowen, Director of Political Affairs
   Barbara J. Easterling, Exec. V. President
   Louis M. Gerber, Legislative Representative
   Leslie Loble, Legislative Representative
   John Morgan, Asst. to Exec. V.P., Legis./Gov't Affrs.
   Patrick M. Scanlon, General Counsel
   Hall Sisson, Legislative Representative

Community Action Program Political Action Committee
   2100 M St., N.W., Suite 604A, Washington, DC 20037
   Telephone: (202) 775-0223
   Background: Represented by David Bradley of the Nat'l
      Community Action Foundation.

Community Antenna Television Ass'n
   Box 1005, Fairfax, VA 22030-1005
   Telephone: (703) 691-8875
   Counsel or consultant:
   Stephen R. Effros, P.C. (Stephen R. Effros)

Community Ass'ns Institute
   1423 Powhatan St., Suite 7, Alexandria, VA 22314
   Telephone: (703) 548-8600
   Background: Owners, builders and managers of condomini-
      ums. Organized by the Nat'l Ass'n of Home Builders and
      the Urban Land Institute.
   Represented by:
   C. James Dowden, Exec. V. President

Community Enterprise Development Corp. of Alaska
   Anchorage, AK
   Background: Represented by Robert Rapoza of the Nat'l
      Rural Housing Coalition.

Community Foundation of Greater Washington
   1002 Wisconsin Ave., N.W., Washington, DC 20007
   Telephone: (202) 338-8993
   Background: A public non-profit organization which re-
      cieves, administers and distributes charitable funds for the
      Metro DC area.
   Represented by:
   Haida Sale, Acting Director
   Counsel or consultant:
   Public Affairs Group, Inc. (Edie Fraser)

Community Information Exchange
   1029 Vermont Ave. Suite 710, Washington, DC 20005
   Telephone: (202) 628-2981
   Background: Provides information and technical services to
      low-income communities.
   Represented by:
   Alice Shabecoff, Director

Community Nutrition Institute
   2001 S St., N.W. Suite 530, Washington, DC 20009
   Telephone: (202) 462-4700
   Background: A non-profit organization that supports the
      development of a national food or nutrition policy serving
      consumer needs at the community level.

Represented by:
   Rodney E. Leonard, Exec. Director

Community Public Service Co.
   Ft. Worth, TX
   Counsel or consultant:
   Goldberg, Fieldman and Letham

Community Transportation Ass'n of America
   725 15th St., N.W. Suite 900, Washington, DC 20005
   Telephone: (202) 628-1480
   Background: A national membership organization to indi-
      vidual mobility and public transit in rural and urban com-
      munities. Formerly (1989) known as Rural America.
   Represented by:
   David M. Raphael, Exec. Director

Compagnie d'Affretement et de Transport USA
   New York, NY
   Counsel or consultant:
   Denning and Wohlstetter (Joseph F. Mullins, Jr.)

Compagnie Financiere de Paris et des Pays Bas
   Paris, France
   Counsel or consultant:
   Rogers and Wells (Anthony F. Essaye, Eugene T. Ros-
      sides)

Companhia de Navagacao Maritima NETUMAR
   Rio de Janeiro, Brazil
   Counsel or consultant:
   Hoppel, Mayer and Coleman (Neal M. Mayer)
   L. A. Motley and Co. (Langhorne A. Motley)
   Olwine, Connelly, Chase, O'Donnell and Weyher (Robert
      L. Hoegle)

Companhia de Navagacao Lloyd Brasileiro
   Rio de Janeiro, Brazil
   Counsel or consultant:
   Hoppel, Mayer and Coleman (Neal M. Mayer)

Companhia Siderurgica de Tubarao
   Espirito Santo, Brazil
   Counsel or consultant:
   TransNational, Inc. (Peter J. Levine)

Compania Mexicana de Aviacion
   Mexico City, Mexico
   Counsel or consultant:
   Squire, Sanders and Dempsey (Robert D. Papkin)

Compania Peruana de Vapores
   New York, NY
   Counsel or consultant:
   Alvord and Alvord
   Philip Manuel Resource Group Ltd. (Andrea Boggs, Phi-
      lip R. Manuel)

Compania Sud Americana de Vapores
   Santiago, Chile
   Counsel or consultant:
   Shearman and Sterling

Compania Trasatlantica Espanola, S.A.
   Madrid, Spain
   Counsel or consultant:
   Dow, Lohnes and Albertson (Stanley O. Sher)

Compaq Computer
   Houston, TX
   Counsel or consultant:
   Johnson & Gibbs, P.C. (David G. Glickman)

Compass Internat'l Inc.
   1730 M St., N.W., Suite 911, Washington, DC 20036
   Telephone: (202) 785-3066
   Background: A Washington-based public relations, advertis-
      ing and Washington representation firm established in
      1974. Represented by Walter L. Frankland, Jr. (see Silver
      Users Ass'n).

Competitive Enterprise Institute
   233 Pennsylvania Ave., S.E., Suite 200, Washington, DC
      20003
   Telephone: (202) 547-1010
   Background: A free-market oriented, non-profit, public
      policy group.

Represented by:
   Sam Kazman, Dir., Free Market Legal Prog. & GC
   Tom Miller, Policy Analyst, Cong. Ratings/Antitrust
   Fred L. Smith, Jr., President
   Melanie S. Tammen, Policy Analyst, Trade
   Andrew Thompson, Director of Development

Competitive Health Care Coalition
   600 New Hampshire Ave., N.W., Suite 1000, Washington,
      DC 20037
   Telephone: (202) 944-3040
   Background: Represents firms which repackage prescription
      drugs for doctors to sell to their patients. Opposed by
      pharmacists and the drug store industry.
   Counsel or consultant:
   Dyer, Ellis, Joseph & Mills (Thomas L. Mills, Howard A.
      Vine)
   Kostmayer Communications, Inc. (Harry Frazier)
   O'Brien and Associates, David (David D. O'Brien)
   Vorys, Sater, Seymour and Pease

Competitive Telecommunications Ass'n (COMP-TEL)
   120 Maryland Ave., N.E., Washington, DC 20002
   Telephone: (202) 546-9022
   Background: Formed by a merger of the Ass'n of Long
      Distance Telephone Companies and the American Coun-
      cil for Competitive Telecommunications in 1984.
   Represented by:
   Genevieve Morelli, General Counsel
   Catherine Reiss Sloan, Director, Legislative Affairs
   James M. Smith, President

Competitive Telecommunications Ass'n Political Action Committee (COMPTELPAC)
   120 Maryland Ave., N.E., Washington, DC 20002
   Telephone: (202) 546-9022
   Background: Represented by James M. Smith of the Com-
      petitive Telecommunications Ass'n.

Composite Can and Tube Institute
   1818 N St., N.W. Suite T-10, Washington, DC 20036
   Telephone: (202) 223-4840
   Represented by:
   Kristine Garland, Exec. V. President and CEO

Comprehensive Marketing Systems, Inc.
   Counsel or consultant:
   Sagamore Associates, Inc. (David U. Gogol)

Compressed Gas Ass'n
   1235 Jefferson Davis Hwy., Arlington, VA 22202
   Telephone: (703) 979-0900
   Represented by:
   Robert C. Gilardi, Staff Manager
   Carl T. Johnson, President

Compu Chem Corp.
   Rsrch. Tri. Park, NC
   Counsel or consultant:
   O'Neill and Athy, P.C. (Martha L. Casey)

CompuServe Inc.
   Columbus, OH
   Counsel or consultant:
   Bishop, Cook, Purcell & Reynolds (Randolph J. May)

Computer and Business Equipment Manufactur-ers Ass'n
   311 First St., N.W. Suite 500, Washington, DC 20001
   Telephone: (202) 737-8888

ORGANIZATIONS REPRESENTED

Computer and Business Equipment Manufacturers Ass'n (Cont'd)
Represented by:
William F. Hanrahan, Sr. Dir., Standards/Technology Program
Ted A. Heydinger, V. President, Domestic Issues
Maryann Karinch, Director, Communications
William A. Maxwell, V. President, International Issues
John L. Pickitt, President
Martha Prinsen, Manager, Domestic Policy Issues
Oliver R. Smoot, Exec. V. President and Treasurer
Carol A. Swift, Director of Domestic Policy Issues
Anne I. Urban, Director, International Issues
Ingrid A. Voorhees, Director of Domestic Policy Issues
Counsel or consultant:
The Susan Davis Companies (Timothy Gay)
Dorsey & Whitney
Podesta Associates (John D. Podesta)
Powell, Goldstein, Frazer and Murphy (Simon Lazarus, III)
Skadden, Arps, Slate, Meagher and Flom (Paul W. Oosterhuis)

Computer and Communications Industry Ass'n
666 Eleventh St., N.W., Sixth Floor, Washington, DC 20001
Telephone: (202) 783-0070
Background: Manufacturers of computers, terminals and peripheral devices; software and service houses; leasing and maintenance organizations; and telecommunications equipment and services providers, including common carriers.
Represented by:
A. G. W. Biddle, President
Counsel or consultant:
Cohen and White (David S. Cohen)

Computer and Communications Industry Ass'n Political Action Committee
666 Eleventh St., N.W., Sixth Floor, Washington, DC 20001
Telephone: (202) 783-0070
Represented by:
Stephanie Biddle, Treasurer

Computer Dealers and Lessors Ass'n
1212 Potomac St., N.W., Washington, DC 20007
Telephone: (202) 333-0102
Represented by:
Kenneth A. Bouldin, President and COO
Greg M. Carroll, Exec. Director
Douglas B. McAllister, Director, Communications
William H. Sells, Director, Government Relations
Counsel or consultant:
Bracewell and Patterson (Gene E. Godley)

Computer Professionals for Social Responsibility
1025 Connecticut Ave., N.W. Suite 1015, Washington, DC 20036
Telephone: (202) 775-1588
Background: Former Counsel, Senate Judiciary Committee, Subcommittee on Technology and the Law.
Represented by:
Marc Rotenberg, Director

Computer Sciences Corp.
3160 Fairview Park Drive, MC/410, Falls Church, VA 22042
Telephone: (703) 641-2560
Represented by:
Lance B. Swann, V. President, Gov't Relations
Counsel or consultant:
Alcalde & Rousselot (Hector Alcalde)

Computer Sciences Corp. (Systems Group)
3160 Fairview Park Drive, Falls Church, VA 22042
Telephone: (703) 876-1000
Represented by:
Milton Cooper, V. President, Program Development

Computer Society, The
1730 Massachusetts Ave., N.W., Washington, DC 20036
Telephone: (202) 371-0101
Background: An international organization with offices in Washington, California, Brussels, Belgium, and Tokyo, Japan.
Represented by:
Dr. T. Michael Elliott, Exec. Director

Computerized Machine Tools, Inc.
Farmington Hills, MI
Counsel or consultant:
Douglas Bloomfield Assoc. (Douglas M. Bloomfield)

Computerized Medical Imaging Soc.
Georgetown Medical Center Pre-Clinical Sci. Bldg. LR3, Washington, DC 20007
Telephone: (202) 687-2121
Background: Radiologists interested in computerized tomography, an X-ray technique. Represented by Robert S. Ledley of the Pattern Recognition Soc.

COMSAT General Corp.
950 L'Enfant Plaza, S.W., Washington, DC 20024
Telephone: (202) 863-6000
Represented by:
William Coulter, V. President, Policy and Affairs
Michele T. Woodward, Sr. Specialist, Government Relations

COMSATPAC
950 L'Enfant Plaza, S.W., Washington, DC 20024
Telephone: (202) 863-6000
Background: The political action arm of the Communications Satellite Corp.
Represented by:
Dennis Furhwirth, Treasurer

ConAgra, Inc.
888 17th St., N.W., Suite 300, Washington, DC 20006
Telephone: (202) 223-5115
Represented by:
Paul A. Korody, V. President, Government Affairs
Jean Muth, Regulatory Affairs
Mary Kirtley Waters, Assistant Director, Washington Office

Concern, Inc.
1794 Columbia Road, N.W., Washington, DC 20009
Telephone: (202) 328-8160
Background: A nonprofit tax exempt organization concerned with increasing public awareness of environmental problems and their management.
Represented by:
Susan Boyd, Exec. Director

Concerned Alliance of Responsible Employers (CARE)
1725 K St., N.W., Suite 710, Washington, DC 20006
Telephone: (202) 872-0885
Background: A coalition of about 200 corporations and trade associations to lobby against mandated employee benefits. Mary Tavenner, Director of Government Relations for the Nat'l Ass'n of Wholesaler-Distributors, serves as principal contact for the Coalition. The above address is that of the Nat'l Ass'n of Wholesaler-Distributors.

Concerned Citizens Foundation
Capitol Hill Office Bldg. 412 First St., S.E., Suite 301, Washington, DC 20003
Telephone: (202) 479-9068
Background: A public interest educational organization of individuals pursuing policies of peace and prosperity. Offices also in Alabama and California.
Represented by:
Allison Barr, Staff Assistant
Cindy Brock, Staff Assistant
Chanlee Collins, Staff Assistant
Tino Giordino, Staff Assistant
Patricia L. Johnson, Administrative Assistant
Counsel or consultant:
Sellers Co. (Richard D. Sellers)

Concerned Educators Against Forced Unionism
8001 Braddock Road, Springfield, VA 22160
Telephone: (703) 321-8519
Represented by:
Mrs. Jo Seker, Director

Concerned Federal Railroad Administration Employees
Burke, VA
Counsel or consultant:
Fensterwald & Alcorn, P.C. (Bernard Fensterwald, III)

Concerned Women for America
370 L'Enfant Promenade, S.W., Suite 800, Washington, DC 20024
Telephone: (202) 488-7000
Background: Acts to preserve, protect and promote traditional and Judeo-Christian values through education, legal defense, legislative programs, humanitarian aid and other activities.
Represented by:
Karen Geers, Congressional Liaison
Rebecca Hegelin, Communications Coordinator
Karen K. Kohl, Congressional Liaison
Beverly LaHaye, President

Concord College
Athens, WV
Counsel or consultant:
Ryan-McGinn (C. Michael Fulton)

Concrete Pipe Ass'ns, Inc.
8300 Boone Blvd., Suite 400, Vienna, VA 22182-2689
Telephone: (703) 821-1990
Background: Represented by Richard E. Barnes of the American Concrete Pipe Ass'n.
Counsel or consultant:
Obadal and O'Leary (Anthony J. Obadal)

Concrete Plant Manufacturers Bureau
900 Spring St., Silver Spring, MD 20910
Telephone: (301) 587-1400
Represented by:
Raymond F. Wisniewski, Jr., Secretary

Confederacion de Federaciones y Asociaciones Gremiales de Agricultores de Chile
Santiago, Chile
Counsel or consultant:
Shearman and Sterling

Conference Board
1755 Massachusetts Ave., N.W., Suite 312, Washington, DC 20036
Telephone: (202) 483-0580
Background: A business, trade, labor and academic membership institution which researches, analyzes, and reports on the US economy, business management and public affairs.
Represented by:
Meredith Armstrong Whiting, Director, Congressional Assistant Prgm.
Ellen Boyers, Development Director - Southeast Region

Conference Board of the Mathematical Sciences
1529 18th St., N.W., Washington, DC 20036
Telephone: (202) 293-1170
Background: Fourteen mathematical societies united to provide "a two-way channel of communication between the mathematical community and the Washington scene, and to serve as a focus for projects of broad concern to the mathematical sciences."
Represented by:
Dr. Ronald Rosier, Administrative Officer

Conference of Chief Justices
444 N. Capitol St., N.W., Suite 608, Washington, DC 20001
Telephone: (202) 347-5924
Background: Represented by Harry W. Swegle, Washington Liaison for the Nat'l Center for State Courts.

Conference of Educational Administrators Serving the Deaf
West Hartford, CT
Counsel or consultant:
Duncan and Associates

Conference of Major Superiors of Men of the U.S.A.
8808 Cameron St., Silver Spring, MD 20910
Telephone: (301) 588-4030
Represented by:
Roland Faley, TOR, Exec. Director

Conference of State Bank Supervisors
1015 18th St., N.W Suite 1100, Washington, DC 20036
Telephone: (202) 296-2840
Background: Organization's goals are (1) to improve and maintain capabilities of state banking departments and (2) maintain for states the right to determine their financial structure as best suits their needs and to exercise proper control over their financial resource base.

ORGANIZATIONS REPRESENTED

Represented by:
Doyle C. Bartlett, V. Pres & Director, Federal Legis. Srvcs
Ellen C. Lamb, Ass't Dir., Federal Legislative Services
Robert A. Richard, V. Pres. & Director, Regulatory Services
James B. Watt, President & CEO

Congo, Office of the President of the
Brazzaville, Congo
Counsel or consultant:
Garrett and Company (Thaddeus A. Garrett, Jr.)

Congo, People's Republic of the
Brazzaville, Congo
Counsel or consultant:
The Hannaford Co., Inc.

Congress Watch
215 Pennsylvania Ave., S.E., Washington, DC 20003
Telephone: (202) 546-4996
Background: The research and lobbying arm on Capitol Hill of Public Citizen, Inc., the Nader organization. Works for the enactment of legislation for consumer protection and other matters, such as environmental, tax, government reform, nuclear and campaign financing issues. Advocates reforms to increase citizen participation in government and corporate decision-making. Above address also serves as second office of Public Citizen.
Represented by:
Anne W. Bloom, Staff Attorney
Cindy Campbell, Field Organizer
David Eppler, Staff Attorney
Sherry E. Ettleson, Staff Attorney
Pamela Gilbert, Legislative Director, Congress Watch
Karen Hobart, Field Organizer
Steven Johnson, Field Organizer
Michael McCauley, Field Organizer
Craig McDonald, Director, Clean Up Congress Campaign
Caroline A. Smith, Staff Attorney
Michael Waldman, Director

Congressional Black Caucus Foundation
1004 Pennsylvania Ave., S.E., Washington, DC 20003
Telephone: (202) 675-6730
Represented by:
Karen A. McRae, Interim Adminstrator

Congressional Economic Leadership Institute
1000 Wilson Blvd., Suite 2700, Arlington, VA 22209
Telephone: (703) 276-5007
Background: A private, non-profit organization that serves as a link between Congress and the public sector on nat'l policy issues. Pat Choate of TRW serves as Chairman.
Represented by:
Nancy LeaMond, President and Exec. Director

Congressional Hispanic Caucus Institute
504 C St., N.E., Washington, DC 20002
Telephone: (202) 543-1771
Represented by:
Marina Laverdy, Deputy Director
Ernesto Uribe, Director

Congressional Institute for the Future
412 First St., S.E., Washington, DC 20003
Telephone: (202) 544-7994
Background: A nonprofit research and education group which works regularly with the Congressional Clearinghouse on the Future, a bi-partisan coalition of over 100 Members of Congress. Drawing together private and public policy leaders, the Institute addresses the policy implications of emerging technological, demographic, and economic trends.
Represented by:
Rob McCord, Exec. Director

Congressional Management Foundation
513 Capitol Court, N.E. Suite 100, Washington, DC 20002
Telephone: (202) 546-0100
Background: A nonprofit, non-partisan organization which provides management training and consulting for Members of Congress and their staffs. Also offers training and consulting services to foreign governments, state governments, corporations, trade associations and nonprofit groups on how Congress operates.
Represented by:
Ira Chalef, President
Richard H. Shapiro, Exec. Director

Conjoint Committee on Diagnostic Radiology
c/o CR Associates 317 Massachusetts Ave., N.E.,, Washington, DC 20002
Telephone: (202) 546-4732
Counsel or consultant:
CR Associates (Domenic R. Ruscio)

Connaught Laboratories, Inc.
Swiftwater, PA
Counsel or consultant:
O'Connor & Hannan (Timothy M. Haake)

Connecticut Ass'n of REALTORS
Hartford, CT
Counsel or consultant:
Marlowe and Co.

Connecticut Bank and Trust Corp.
Hartford, CT
Counsel or consultant:
O'Neill and Athy, P.C. (Andrew Athy, Jr.)

Connecticut Liquidity Investment Fund, Inc.
Hartford, CT
Counsel or consultant:
Winthrop, Stimson, Putnam & Roberts (Raymond S. Calamaro, Michael W. Dolan, Ronna A. Freiberg)

Connecticut Municipal Electric Energy Cooperative
Groton, CT
Counsel or consultant:
Spiegel and McDiarmid (Frances E. Francis)

Connecticut Mutual Life Insurance Co.
Hartford, CT
Counsel or consultant:
Murray, Scheer & Montgomery (D. Michael Murray)

Connecticut, State of
444 North Capitol St., N.W. Suite 317, Washington, DC 20001
Telephone: (202) 347-4535
Represented by:
Matthew Cooksin, Legislative Specialist
Chris Riley, Legislative Assistant
Ann L. Sullivan, Director, Wash. Office of the Governor

Connell Rice and Sugar Co.
Westfield, NJ
Counsel or consultant:
Robinson, Lake, Lerer & Montgomery (James H. Lake)

Conoco, Inc.
Houston, TX
Counsel or consultant:
Jack Ferguson Associates

Conquest Tours Ltd.
Toronto, Ontario
Counsel or consultant:
Hewes, Morella, Gelband and Lamberton, P.C.

Conseil Europeen des Federations de l'Industrie Chimique (CEFIC)
Brussels, Belgium
Counsel or consultant:
O'Melveny and Myers

Conservation Foundation
1250 24th St., N.W., Washington, DC 20037
Telephone: (202) 293-4800
Represented by:
Richard E. Benedick, Senior Fellow
Michael A. Mantell, General Counsel

Conservation Internat'l Foundation
1015 18th St., N.W. Suite 1000, Washington, DC 20036
Telephone: (202) 429-5660
Background: A private, non-profit organization dedicated to the protection and Preservation of natural ecosystems and the species that rely on these habitats for their survival. CI has 40,000 members.
Represented by:
Russell A. Mittermeier, President

Conservative Alliance
1315 Duke St., Alexandria, VA 22314
Telephone: (703) 683-4329

Represented by:
J. Barry Bitzer, Exec. Director
Counsel or consultant:
Ann E. W. Stone and Associates (Lora Lynn Jones)

Conservative Caucus Research, Analysis and Education Foundation
450 Maple Ave. East, Suite 309, Vienna, VA 22180
Telephone: (703) 281-6782
Background: Contact is Howard J. Phillips of The Conservative Caucus and Policy Analysis Inc.

Conservative Caucus, The
450 Maple Ave. East, Suite 309, Vienna, VA 22180
Telephone: (703) 893-1550
Background: Organized in 1974 by Howard J. Phillips, who continues to serve as its Chairman. A national activist group promoting conservative causes. Lobbying activities specialize in organizing grass roots support.
Represented by:
Charles Orndorff, V. Chairman
David G. Sanders, National Field Director

Conservative Democratic PAC
c/o Bracewell & Patterson 2000 K St., N.W., Suite 500, Washington, DC 20006-1809
Telephone: (202) 828-5800
Counsel or consultant:
Bracewell and Patterson (Gene E. Godley)

Conservative Nat'l Committee
450 Maple Ave. East, Vienna, VA 22180
Telephone: (703) 893-1550
Background: A political action committee directed by Howard Phillips of The Conservative Caucus and Policy Analysis Inc.

Conservative Political Action Conference
919 Prince St., Alexandria, VA 22314
Telephone: (703) 739-2550
Background: Chairman is David A. Keene of Keene, Shirley & Associates, of the same address.
Counsel or consultant:
Keene, Shirley & Associates, Inc. (David A. Keene)

Conservative Republican Committee
7015 Old Keene Mill Road Suite 203, Springfield, VA 22150
Telephone: (703) 451-6943
Background: Support political candidates who advocate a strong national defense position.
Counsel or consultant:
Thompson and Associates (Michael W. Thompson)

Conservative Victory Committee
111 South Columbus St., Alexandria, VA 22316
Telephone: (703) 684-6603
Background: A conservative political action group monitoring press and other media activity.
Represented by:
Leif E. Noren, Chairman
Juanita R. Sholes, Treasurer
Counsel or consultant:
Keene, Shirley & Associates, Inc. (Gregory R. Mueller)

Conservative Victory Fund
422 First St., S.E., Suite 208, Washington, DC 20003
Telephone: (202) 546-5833
Background: A political action committee.
Represented by:
Thomas S. Winter, Treasurer

Consolidated Diesel Corp.
Whitakers, NC
Counsel or consultant:
Barnes, Richardson and Colburn (Robert E. Burke, Matthew T. McGrath, Gunter Von Conrad)

Consolidated Edison Co. of New York
2100 Pennsylvania Ave., N.W., Suite 695, Washington, DC 20037
Telephone: (202) 331-2020
Represented by:
Anthony P. Kavanagh, Government Affairs Representative
Counsel or consultant:
Charlie McBride Assoc., Inc. (Charlie McBride)
McCarthy, Sweeney and Harkaway, P.C. (William I. Harkaway)
Wilner and Scheiner (Richard A. Solomon)

ORGANIZATIONS REPRESENTED

Consolidated Freightways Corp.
Menlo Park, CA
Counsel or consultant:
Alcalde & Rousselot (Hector Alcalde)

Consolidated Gas Supply Corp.
Clarksburg, WV
Background: A subsidiary of the Consolidated Natural Gas Co. Represented by Beverly E. Jones of the parent company.

Consolidated Grain and Barge Co.
St. Louis, MO
Counsel or consultant:
Verner, Liipfert, Bernhard, McPherson and Hand, Chartered (Harry C. McPherson, John A. Merrigan, Douglas M. Steenland)

Consolidated Natural Gas Co.
1819 L St., N.W. Suite 900, Washington, DC 20036
Telephone: (202) 833-3900
Background: A public utility holding company.
Represented by:
Dwight A. Howes, Legislative Counsel
Beverly E. Jones, V. President, Government Affairs
Mark G. Magnuson, Assistant General Counsel-Washington
Colleen M. Moore, Legislative Specialist
Richard Taylor, Legislative Assistant
Counsel or consultant:
Legislative Strategies Inc. (Raymond F. Bragg, Jr.)
Morgan, Lewis and Bockius (A. A. Sommer, Jr.)
Steptoe and Johnson

Consolidated Rail Corp. (CONRAIL)
990 L'Enfant Plaza, S.W., Washington, DC 20024
Telephone: (202) 789-5885
Represented by:
William B. Newman, Jr., Vice President and Washington Counsel
Arthur R. Ouslander, Director, Federal Relations
Counsel or consultant:
Duberstein Group, Inc., The

Consolidation Coal Co.
1701 Pennsylvania Ave., N.W. Suite 900, Washington, DC 20006
Telephone: (202) 728-3660
Background: A subsidiary of Du Pont. Mark D. Nelson of the parent organization serves as Director, Legislative Affairs.

Consortium of Social Science Ass'ns
1522 K St., N.W., Suite 836, Washington, DC 20005
Telephone: (202) 842-3525
Background: Advocates increased federal funding for the social and behavioral sciences.
Represented by:
Stacey Beckhardt, Government Liaison
Howard J. Silver, Exec. Director
Joseph Thorndike, Executive Associate

Consortium of State Maritime Schools
Bronx, NY
Counsel or consultant:
Wexler, Reynolds, Fuller, Harrison and Schule, Inc. (Terry D. Bevels)

Consortium of Universities of the Washington Metropolitan Area
1717 Massachusetts Ave., N.W., Suite 101, Washington, DC 20036
Telephone: (202) 265-1313
Background: Represents The American University, The Catholic University of America, George Washington University, Georgetown University, Howard University, University of the District of Columbia, University of Maryland (College Park), Gallaudet University, Mount Vernon College, Trinity College, Marymount University, and George Mason University.
Represented by:
Mary Paster, Special Assistant to the President
Dr. Monte Shepler, President & CEO

Construcciones Aeronauticas, S.A.
Madrid, Spain
Counsel or consultant:
Stafford, Burke and Hecker (Kelly H. Burke, Guy L. Hecker, Thomas P. Stafford)

Construction Industry Labor Law Coalition
3000 K St., N.W. Suite 600, Washington, DC 20007
Telephone: (202) 783-1900
Counsel or consultant:
Thompson, Mann and Hutson (Harold P. Coxson)

Construction Industry Manufacturers Ass'n
525 School St., S.W. Suite 303, Washington, DC 20024
Telephone: (202) 479-2666
Represented by:
J. William Peterson, Director of Government Affairs

Construction Labor Research Council
1730 M St., N.W., Suite 900B, Washington, DC 20036
Telephone: (202) 223-8045
Represented by:
Robert Gasperow, Exec. Director

Construction Management Ass'n of America
12355 Sunrise Valley Drive Suite 640, Reston, VA 22091
Telephone: (703) 391-1200
Represented by:
Karl F. Borgstrom, Exec. Director
Albert W. Heyer, III, President

Construction Specifications Institute
601 Madison St., Alexandria, VA 22314-1791
Telephone: (703) 684-0300
Represented by:
Joseph A. Gascoigne, Exec. Director

Consulting Engineers Council of Metropolitan Washington
8811 Colesville Rd. Suite G106, Silver Spring, MD 20910
Telephone: (301) 588-6616
Counsel or consultant:
Bachner Communications, Inc. (John P. Bachner)

Consumer Bankers Ass'n
1000 Wilson Blvd., 30th Floor, Arlington, VA 22209-3908
Telephone: (703) 276-1750
Represented by:
Joe Belew, President
Fritz M. Elmendorf, V. President - Communications
Barbara L. Munson, V. Pres./Manager, Congressional Affairs
Marcia Z. Sullivan, Senior Government Relations Counsel
Craig Ulrich, General Counsel

Consumer Bankers Ass'n Political Action Committee
1300 North 17th St., Arlington, VA 22209
Telephone: (703) 276-1750
Represented by:
Jayne E. Hunt, Treasurer

Consumer Energy Council of America Research Foundation
2000 L St., N.W., Suite 802, Washington, DC 20036
Telephone: (202) 659-0404
Background: The nation's oldest public interest energy policy organization, founded in 1973. Provides a leading national resource pool of information, analysis and technical expertise on a variety of energy initiatives. Emphasizes conservation and energy efficiency as the cornerstone of a sound energy economy. Has expertise in forging successful partnerships among public and private sector organizations, state and local groups, businesses, utilities, consumers, environmentalists and government agencies in furtherance of consumer interests.
Represented by:
Ellen Berman, Exec. Director

Consumer Federation of America
1424 16th St., N.W. Suite 604, Washington, DC 20036
Telephone: (202) 387-6121
Background: A federation of national, state, regional and community consumer organizations dedicated to consumer action through legislation, information and education.
Represented by:
Stephen Brobeck, Exec. Director
Mark N. Cooper, Research Director
Mary Ellen Fise, Product Safety Director
Barbara J. Katz, Legislative Counsel
Gene Kimmelman, Legislative Director
Peggy Miller, Legislative Representative

Consumer Federation of America Political Action Fund
1424 16th St., N.W. Suite 604, Washington, DC 20036
Telephone: (202) 387-6121

Background: Sponsored by the Consumer Federation of America. Treasurer and senior contact is Stephen Brobeck of the Federation.

Consumers for Competitive Fuels
c/o Amoco Oil 1615 M St., N.W., Suite 200, Washington, DC 20036
Telephone: (202) 879-3939
Counsel or consultant:
Jones, Day, Reavis and Pogue (Randall E. Davis)

Consumers for World Trade
1001 Connecticut Ave., N.W. Suite 800, Washington, DC 20036
Telephone: (202) 785-4835
Background: In the interests of consumers, favors an open trading system, opposes the imposition of tariffs, quotas and other trade barriers and favors the elimination of export disincentives.
Represented by:
Doreen L. Brown, President
Counsel or consultant:
William S. Bergman Associates (William S. Bergman, CAE, Laura Devlin)

Consumers Power Co.
1016 16th St., N.W. 5th Floor, Washington, DC 20036
Telephone: (202) 293-5794
Represented by:
Jane W. Bergwin, Federal Governmental Affairs Rep.
John A. Howes, Director of Federal Governmental Affairs
Mona M. Janopanl, Attorney
William M. Lange, Assistant General Counsel
H. B. W. Schroeder, V. President, Governmental Affairs

Consumers Union of the United States
2001 S St., N.W., Suite 520, Washington, DC 20009
Telephone: (202) 462-6262
Background: An influential, nonpartisan consumer organization founded in 1936. Maintains a public interest law office in Washington. Publishes Consumer Reports providing information and evaluations of consumer products and services nationally.
Represented by:
Linda A. Lipsen, Legislative/Regulatory Counsel
Michelle Meier, Counsel for Governmental Affairs
Kristen M. Rand, Attorney
Gail E. Shearer, Manager, Policy Analysis
Mark Silbergeld, Washington Office Director
Counsel or consultant:
Lobel, Novins, Lamont and Flug (James F. Flug)

Consumers United for Rail Equity
1050 Thomas Jefferson St, N.W., Washington, DC 20007
Telephone: (202) 333-7481
Background: Robert G. Szabo serves as Exec. Director.
Counsel or consultant:
Van Ness, Feldman & Curtis (Grenville Garside, Nancy Macan, Robert G. Szabo)

Contact Lens Institute
1747 Pennsylvania Ave., N.W. Suite 900, Washington, DC 20006
Telephone: (202) 296-0784
Counsel or consultant:
Royer, Mehle & Babyak (Gregory R. Babyak)

Contact Lens Manufacturers Ass'n
2000 M St., N.W., Washington, DC 20036
Telephone: (202) 872-1698
Counsel or consultant:
Graham and James (Daniel J. Manelli)

Contact Lens Manufacturers Ass'n Political Action Committee
1120 Vermont Ave., N.W., Suite 1000, Washington, DC 20005
Telephone: (202) 857-0350
Counsel or consultant:
Graham and James (Daniel J. Manelli)

Contel Corp.
555 13th St. Suite 480 West, Washington, DC 20004
Telephone: (202) 383-3700
Background: A telecommunications company headquartered in Atlanta, Georgia.

ORGANIZATIONS REPRESENTED

Represented by:
James E. Graf, II, V. President, Governmental Relations
Glenn S.'Steve' Meader, Jr., Asst. V. Pres., Governmental Relations
Pamela M. Powers, Coord., Political and Community Affairs
Timothy Totman, Asst. V. Pres., Federal Regulatory Affrs
John C. Wohlstetter, Attorney/Dir., Special Federal Projects
Counsel or consultant:
Baker, Worthington, Crossley, Stansberry & Woolf (Edward R. Hamberger)

Contel Corp. Political Action Committee (CON-TELPAC)
555 13th St., N.W. Suite 480W, Washington, DC 20004
Telephone: (202) 383-8700
Background: A political action committee sponsored by Contel Corp. Secretary-Treasurer is Pamela M. Powers of Contel.

Continental Airlines
901 15th St., N.W. Suite 500, Washington, DC 20004
Telephone: (202) 629-6060
Background: Represented by Clark H. Onstad, V. President of Texas Air Corp.
Counsel or consultant:
Marshall S. Filler, P.C.
Verner, Liipfert, Bernhard, McPherson and Hand, Chartered (Berl Bernhard)

Continental Ass'n of Funeral and Memorial Societies
7910 Woodmont Ave., Suite 1208, Washington, DC 20814-3015
Telephone: (301) 913-0030
Background: An association of non-profit consumer cooperatives that works to obtain low-cost, dignified, simple funerals; lobbies for funeral reform and works in consumer education. Exec. Director is Clifford Brownstein of C. M. Brownstein and Associates.
Counsel or consultant:
C. M. Brownstein & Assoc. (Clifford M. Brownstein)

Continental Corp., The
New York, NY
Counsel or consultant:
Arnold & Porter (Thomas R. Dwyer)
Zuckert, Scoutt and Rasenberger (Walter D. Vinyard, Jr.)

Continental Grain Co.
818 Connecticut Ave., N.W., 8th Floor, Washington, DC 20006
Telephone: (202) 331-1922
Represented by:
Richard Goodman, V. President, Government Affairs
Counsel or consultant:
Arent, Fox, Kintner, Plotkin & Kahn (Samuel Efron, Lewis E. Leibowitz)
Paul H. DeLaney Law Offices

Continental Illinois Nat'l Bank and Trust Co.
Chicago, IL
Counsel or consultant:
Mayer, Brown and Platt (Charles F. Levy, Jerry L. Oppenheimer)

Continental Insurance Investment Management
New York, NY
Counsel or consultant:
Baker and Hostetler (Kenneth J. Kies)
Segermark Co., The

Continental Manufacturing Corp.
Manilla, Philippines
Counsel or consultant:
World Trade Link

Continental Medical Systems, Inc.
Mechanicsburg, PA
Counsel or consultant:
Eckert Seamans Cherin & Mellott (Patricia A. Quealy)

Contraco, Inc.
Stamford, CT
Counsel or consultant:
Evans Group, Ltd., The (L. A., Skip Bafalis, Thomas B. Evans, Jr.)

Contract Services Ass'n of America
1350 New York Ave., N.W., Suite 200, Washington, DC 20005
Telephone: (202) 347-0600
Background: Membership consists of companies that contract services with the government. One of the association's functions is to serve companies that provide operations and maintenance for government agencies.
Represented by:
Gary D. Engebretson, President
Kevin Frankovich, Director of Government Relations

Contract Services Ass'n Political Action Committee
1350 New York Ave., N.W., Suite 200, Washington, DC 20005
Telephone: (202) 347-0600
Background: Gary D. Engebretson, of the Contract Services Ass'n, serves as the Treasurer.

Contractors Pump Bureau
P.O. Box 5858, Rockville, MD 20855
Telephone: (301) 340-2094
Represented by:
Walter D. Anderson, Exec. Director
Counsel or consultant:
Keller and Heckman (Malcolm D. MacArthur)

Contran Corp.
Dallas, TX
Counsel or consultant:
Ottosen and Associates (Karl J. Ottosen)

Contraves Italiana S.p.A.
Rome, Italy
Counsel or consultant:
Neill and Co. (John E. Bircher, III, Denis M. Neill)

Control Data Corp.
1201 Pennsylvania Ave., N.W., Suite 370, Washington, DC 20004
Telephone: (202) 789-6518
Represented by:
Mary H. Budd, Manager, Government Affairs
Joseph S. Lester, Jr., Assistant General Counsel
James J. O'Connell, Director, Int'l Trade Services
Lois D. Rice, Sr. V. President for Gov't Affairs
M. Amanda Tabb, Adm. Ass't, Internat'l Trade Services

Conundrum Joint Venture
Denver, CO
Counsel or consultant:
Jefferson Group, The (Robert Carlstrom, Jr.)

Convention II, Inc.
Box 1987, Washington, DC 20013-1987
Telephone: (202) 544-1789
Background: Directs model constitutional convention of high school students; experiential education in politics; active in bicentennial commemoration of U.S. constitution. President is G. Timothy Leighton of Capital Dimension, Inc.
Represented by:
Linda Henberger, Director, Operations
Tom Rooney, Program Director

Conveyor Equipment Manufacturers Ass'n
932 Hungerford Drive, Suite 36, Rockville, MD 20850
Telephone: (301) 738-2448
Counsel or consultant:
Lloyd and Associates, Inc. (Raymond J. Lloyd)

Cook Group
Bloomington, IN
Counsel or consultant:
Rivkin, Radler, Dunne and Bayh (Thomas A. Connaughton)

Cook Inlet Communications
Los Angeles, CA
Counsel or consultant:
Wilmer, Cutler and Pickering (Joel Rosenbloom)

Cook Inlet Region Inc.
Anchorage, AK
Counsel or consultant:
Crowell and Moring (Steven P. Quarles)

Cookware Manufacturers Ass'n
Walworth, WI

Counsel or consultant:
Kilpatrick & Cody (Joseph W. Dorn)

Cooley's Anemia Foundation
New York, NY
Counsel or consultant:
Dr. John T. Grupenhoff

Cooney Enterprises, Gerry
Garden City, NY
Counsel or consultant:
Birch, Horton, Bittner and Cherot (Joseph M. Chomski)

Cooper Communities
Bella Vista, AR
Counsel or consultant:
Jack L. Williams

Cooperative Central Bank
Boston, MA
Counsel or consultant:
Steptoe and Johnson (John T. Collins)

Cooperative Housing Foundation
1010 Wayne Ave., Suite 240, Silver Spring, MD 20910
Telephone: (301) 587-4700
Background: Non-profit, tax-exempt organization to promote low-to-moderate income cooperative housing homeownership.
Represented by:
Shirley Boden, Chairman, Board of Trustees

Cooperative League of the USA Political Action Committee (Nat'l Coop Business PAC)
1401 New York Ave., N.W., Suite 1100, Washington, DC 20005
Telephone: (202) 638-6222
Represented by:
Leta Mach, Director of Communications
Fred Zimmerman, Director of Communications

Coopers and Lybrand
1800 M St., N.W., Suite 400, Washington, DC 20036
Telephone: (202) 822-4000
Represented by:
Viveca M. Carroll, Government Relations Specialist
William P. McHenry, Manager, Government Relations
Pamela Pecarich, Partner, Tax Policy Group
Joseph P. Petito, Mgr., Professional & Governmental Affrs.
Allen J. Weltmann, Partner in Charge, Government Relations
John G. Wilkins, Dir., Tax Policy for Economic Analysis
Counsel or consultant:
Hughes Hubbard and Reed
Mica, Dudinsky & Associates (John Dudinsky, Jr., John L. Mica)
Verner, Liipfert, Bernhard, McPherson and Hand, Chartered (John A. Merrigan)
Wexler, Reynolds, Fuller, Harrison and Schule, Inc. (Robert M. Schule, Bruce Wolpe)

Coopers and Lybrand Political Action Committee
1800 M St., N.W., Suite 200, Washington, DC 20036
Telephone: (202) 822-4222
Background: A political action committee sponsored by the accounting firm of Coopers and Lybrand. Allen J. Weltmann, Partner in Charge of Government Relations, serves as the Secretary and Treasurer of the PAC.

Coordinating Committee of the Hungarian Organizations of North America
4101 Blackpool Road, Rockville, MD 20853
Telephone: (301) 871-7018
Represented by:
Istvan B. Gereben, Exec. Secretary

Coordination Council for North American Affairs
4201 Wisconsin Ave., N.W., Washington, DC 20016
Telephone: (202) 895-1800
Background: The diplomatic mission of the Republic of China.
Counsel or consultant:
Corcoran, Youngman and Rowe (Thomas G. Corcoran, Jr.)
The Hannaford Co., Inc.
Hugh C. Newton & Assoc. (Hugh C. Newton)

ORGANIZATIONS REPRESENTED

Coors Brewing Company
601 Pennsylvania Ave., N.W., Suite 500, Washington, DC 20004
Telephone: (202) 737-4444
Represented by:
Alan R. Timothy, Director, Federal Government Affairs
Counsel or consultant:
Jellinek, Schwartz, Connolly & Freshman, Inc. (John D. Freshman)
Kilpatrick & Cody (Linda E. Christenson)

Copper and Brass Fabricators Council
1050 17th St., N.W. Suite 440, Washington, DC 20036
Telephone: (202) 833-8575
Represented by:
Joseph L. Mayer, President
Counsel or consultant:
Collier, Shannon & Scott (David A. Hartquist)
Covington and Burling

Copperweld Corp.
Pittsburgh, PA
Counsel or consultant:
Schagrin Associates (Carol A. Colza, Roger B. Schagrin)

Copyright Justice Coalition
c/o Hunton & Williams 2000 Pennsylvania Ave., N.W., Washington, DC 20006
Telephone: (202) 955-1500
Background: An ad-hoc group of 50 organizations representing artists, photographers, illustrators, cartoonists, writers and other creators, formed to secure changes in federal copyright laws through legislation and litigation.
Counsel or consultant:
Hunton and Williams (Charles D. Ossola)

Copyright Remedies Coalition
2000 K St., N.W., Suite 600, Washington, DC 20006-1809
Telephone: (202) 429-8970
Counsel or consultant:
Leventhal, Senter & Lerman (Michael R. Klipper)

Corcoran Gallery of Art, The
17th and New York Ave., N.W., Washington, DC 20006
Telephone: (202) 638-3211
Counsel or consultant:
Chernikoff and Co. (Larry Chernikoff)
Hill and Knowlton Public Affairs Worldwide (Frank Mankiewicz, Lauri J. Fitz-Pegado)

Cord Laboratories
Broomfield, CO
Counsel or consultant:
Kleinfeld, Kaplan and Becker (Robert H. Becker, Alan H. Kaplan, Richard S. Morey)

Cordage Institute
Framingham, MA
Counsel or consultant:
Economic Consulting Services Inc. (Mark W. Love)

Cordova District Fishermen United
Cordova, AK
Counsel or consultant:
C. Deming Cowles, IV
Dickstein, Shapiro and Morin (John C. Dill)

COREPAC
Corning, NY
Background: A political action committee sponsored by Corning Inc. Represented in Washington by Allan D. Cors of Corning.

Corn Refiners Ass'n
1100 Connecticut Ave., N.W. Suite 1120, Washington, DC 20036
Telephone: (202) 331-1634
Represented by:
Robert C. Liebenow, President
Jane E. Shey, Director, Government Affairs

Corn Sweeteners, Inc.
Cedar Rapids, IA
Counsel or consultant:
TADCO Enterprises (Katherine E. Allen)

Corning
1455 Pennsylvania Ave., N.W. Suite 500, Washington, DC 20004
Telephone: (202) 347-2270

Represented by:
Allan D. Cors, Sr. V. Pres. and Dir. of Gov't Affairs
Carolyn Kim McCarthy, Legis. Couns. & Dir., Fed. Gov't Affairs
Timothy J. Regan, Director, of Public Policy
Counsel or consultant:
StMaxens and Co. (Thomas F. StMaxens, II)

Corporate Property Investors
New York, NY
Counsel or consultant:
Carl F. Arnold

Corporation for Enterprise Development
1725 K St., N.W. Suite 1401, Washington, DC 20006
Telephone: (202) 293-7963
Represented by:
Robert E. Friedman, President

Corporation for Open Systems
1750 Old Meadow Road, McLean, VA 22102
Telephone: (703) 883-2700
Represented by:
Michael J. Walter, General Counsel

Corporation for Public Broadcasting
901 E St., N.W. Suite 2209, Washington, DC 20004-2006
Telephone: (202) 879-9712
Represented by:
Gerald F. Hogan, V. President, Government Relations
Mary F. Maguire, Director, External Communications
Rozanne Weissman, V. President, Corporate Communications

Corpus Christi, Nueces County, Port Authority of
Corpus Christi, TX
Counsel or consultant:
Dale Miller

Cosmetic, Toiletry and Fragrance Ass'n
1110 Vermont Ave., N.W. Suite 800, Washington, DC 20005
Telephone: (202) 331-1770
Represented by:
Thomas J. Donegan, Jr., V. President and General Counsel
Dick Fisher, V. President, Administration
Marsha W. Gardner, V. President, International Affairs
E. Edward Kavanaugh, President
Irene L. Malbin, V. President, Public Affairs
Dr. Gerald N. McEwen, Jr., V. President, Science
Michael J. Petrina, Jr., V. President, Legislative Relations
Mark A. Pollak, V. President, Member Relations
Veronique Rodman, V. President
James Skiles, Associate General Counsel
Counsel or consultant:
Bonner & Associates
Rowan & Blewitt, Inc. (Patrick M. McLain)
Wunder, Ryan, Cannon & Thelen (Dennis C. Thelen)

Cosmetic, Toiletry and Fragrance Ass'n Political Action Committee
1110 Vermont Ave., N.W., Suite 800, Washington, DC 20005
Telephone: (202) 331-1770
Represented by:
Lee Ryan, Treasurer

Costa Rica, Central Bank of
San Jose, Costa Rica
Counsel or consultant:
White & Case

Costa Rica Shirt Manufacturers
San Jose, Costa Rica
Counsel or consultant:
Internat'l Development Systems

Costa Rican Foreign Trade Committee
San Jose, Costa Rica
Counsel or consultant:
Patton, Boggs and Blow (Frank R. Samolis)

Cotton Cooperatives
Lubbock, TX
Counsel or consultant:
Highley & Associates (Vern F. Highley)

Cotton Council Internat'l
1110 Vermont Ave., N.W. Suite 430, Washington, DC 20005
Telephone: (202) 833-2909
Background: The overseas operating arm of the Nat'l Cotton Council of America.
Represented by:
Adrian Hunnings, Exec. Director

Cotton Warehouse Ass'n of America
1150 Connecticut Ave., N.W., Suite 507, Washington, DC 20036
Telephone: (202) 331-4337
Background: Donald L. Wallace Jr., of Wallace & Edwards, serves as the Exec. V. President.
Counsel or consultant:
Wallace & Edwards (Donald L. Wallace, Jr.)

Cotton Warehouse Government Relations Committee
1150 Connecticut Ave., N.W., Suite 507, Washington, DC 20036
Telephone: (202) 331-4337
Background: Represents the legislative and political interests of the Cotton Warehouse Ass'n of America.
Counsel or consultant:
Wallace & Edwards (Allison Humphreys, Donald L. Wallace, Jr.)

Cottongrowers Warehouse Ass'n
Counsel or consultant:
Highley & Associates (Vern F. Highley)

Council for a Livable World
100 Maryland Ave., N.E. Suite 211, Washington, DC 20002
Telephone: (202) 543-4100
Background: Registered national political lobbying organization working for 'an end to the nuclear arms race and greatly scaled down military expenditures by the major powers". Raises funds and otherwise assists sympathetic candidates, lobbies chiefly in the Senate, and publishes reports advocating its objectives. Sponsors PEACE PAC.
Represented by:
John D. Isaacs, Legislative Director
Michelle Robinson, Legislative Representative
Andrew Siegel, Legislative Representative

Council for Advancement and Support of Education
11 Dupont Circle Suite 400, Washington, DC 20036
Telephone: (202) 328-5900
Background: An organization of college and university public relations, alumni and development officers concerned with educational legislation.
Represented by:
Dr. Gary Quehl, President
Eric Wentworth, Senior V. President, Public Affairs

Council for American Private Education
1726 M St., N.W. Suite 1102, Washington, DC 20036
Telephone: (202) 659-0016
Background: Comprised of 13 national organizations of private secondary and elementary schools and school personnel.
Represented by:
Joyce G. McCray, Exec. Director

Council for Basic Education
725 15th St., N.W., Suite 801, Washington, DC 20005
Telephone: (202) 347-4171
Represented by:
A. Graham Down, Exec. Director

Council for Court Excellence
1025 Vermont Ave., N.W., Suite 510, Washington, DC 20005
Telephone: (202) 783-7736
Background: A civic group seeking reforms and improvement in the administration of justice at the federal, state and local levels.
Represented by:
Samuel Harahan, Exec. Director

Council for Educational Development and Research
1201 16th St., N.W. Suite 305, Washington, DC 20036
Telephone: (202) 223-1593

The listings in this directory are available as *Mailing Labels*. See last page.

ORGANIZATIONS REPRESENTED

Represented by:
Dena G. Stoner, Exec. Director
Counsel or consultant:
Cashdollar-Jones & Co. (Robert Cashdollar)

Council for Excellence in Government
1775 Pennsylvania Ave., N.W. Suite 750, Washington, DC 20006
Telephone: (202) 728-0418
Background: A nonprofit, educational organization drawing on the experience of 500 business leaders with government experience to promote and support excellence in public service and government management.
Represented by:
Mark A. Abramson, President

Council for Exceptional Children
1920 Association Drive, Reston, VA 22091
Telephone: (703) 620-3660
Represented by:
B. Joseph Ballard, Associate Dir., Governmental Relations
Frederick J. Weintraub, Asst. Exec. Dir., Communications

Council for Export Trading Cos., Inc.
1900 19th St., N.W. Suite 605, Washington, DC 20036
Telephone: (202) 861-4705
Represented by:
Ronald C. Wakeford, Exec. Director

Council for Inter-American Security
122 C St., N.W., Suite 710, Washington, DC 20001
Telephone: (202) 393-6622
Background: A research and education organization specializing in foreign policy and defense issues affecting Western Hemisphere Security.
Represented by:
L. Francis Bouchey, President
Stephen R. Edelen, Exec. V. President
David Hirschmann, Director, Research and Liaison
Joe Loconte, Director, Communications

Council for Internat'l Development
1000 Potomac St., N.W. Plaza 100, Washington, DC 20007
Telephone: (703) 965-0900
Represented by:
Antony L. Campaigne, Chairman

Council for Responsible Nutrition
1300 19th St., N.W. Suite 310, Washington, DC 20036
Telephone: (202) 872-1488
Background: A trade association of suppliers, manufacturers and distributors of nutritional supplements.
Represented by:
J. B. Cordaro, President

Council for Rural Housing and Development
2300 M St., N.W., Suite 260, Washington, DC 20037
Telephone: (202) 955-9715
Represented by:
Anna M. Moser, Exec. Director
Counsel or consultant:
Kelley, Drye and Warren (Charles L. Edson)

Council for Social and Economic Studies
1133 13th St., N.W., Suite C-2, Washington, DC 20005
Telephone: (202) 789-0231
Represented by:
Roger Pearson, Director

Council for Solid Waste Solutions
1275 K St., N.W. Suite 400, Washington, DC 20005
Telephone: (202) 371-5319
Background: Established by the Soc. of the Plastics Industry. Through technical research, government relations and communications programs, the Council seeks to offer guidance of the entire solid waste issue.

Represented by:
Roger D. Bernstein, Director, State Government Affairs
Catharine M. DeLacy, Director, Federal Government Affairs
Ronald N. Liesemer, Ph.D., V. President, Technology
Rodney W. Lowman, V. President, Government Affairs
Donald B. Shea, Exec. V. President
Jean C. Statler, V. President, Communications
Richard P. Swigart, Director, External Communications
Susan M. Vadney, Director, Media Relations
Counsel or consultant:
Dutko & Associates (Emily Young)
Holland and Hart (Lauren E. Brown, William F. Demarest, Jr.)
Madison Group/Earle Palmer Brown, The (Richard Bagin)

Council for the Advancement of Citizenship
1724 Massachusetts Ave., N.W., Suite 300, Washington, DC 20036
Telephone: (202) 857-0578
Represented by:
Diane U. Eisenberg, Exec. Director

Council for the Defense of Freedom
1275 K St., N.W., Suite 1150, Washington, DC 20005
Telephone: (202) 789-4294
Background: A conservative group dedicated to 'educate the public about the threat of communism.' Publishes the Washington Inquirer.
Represented by:
Marx Lewis, Chairman
Randy Randall, Managing Editor, Washington Inquirer

Council for the Internat'l Exchange of Scholars
3400 International Dr., N.W. Suite M-500, Washington, DC 20008
Telephone: (202) 686-4000
Represented by:
Cassandra A. Pyle, Exec. Director

Council of American Building Officials
5203 Leesburg Pike, Falls Church, VA 22041
Telephone: (703) 931-4533
Represented by:
Richard P. Kuchnicki, President

Council of Better Business Bureaus
4200 Wilson Blvd. Suite 800, Arlington, VA 22203
Telephone: (703) 276-0100
Represented by:
Steven J. Cole, V. President and Senior Counsel
Robert E. Gibson, V. Pres., Gen. Mgr., Alt. Dispute Resol.
Stephen R. Jones, V. President, Law and Policy
James H. McIlhenny, President
Dianne Skeltis, Director of Public Affairs

Council of Chief State School Officers
400 North Capitol St., N.W., Suite 379, Washington, DC 20001
Telephone: (202) 393-8161
Background: A nationwide non-profit organization representing the public officials who head departments of elementary and secondary education in 57 jurisdiction.
Represented by:
Gordon M. Ambach, Exec. Director
Carnie Hayes, Director, Federal-State Relations

Council of Citizens with Low Vision
1010 Vermont Avenue, N.W. Suite 1100, Washington, DC 20005
Telephone: (202) 393-3666
Background: Represented by Roberta Douglas of the American Council of the Blind.

Council of Defense and Space Industry Ass'ns
1722 Eye St., N.W., Suite 300, Washington, DC 20006
Telephone: (202) 457-8713
Background: An organization established in 1964, composed of ten industry ass'ns having common interests in the defense and space fields: Aerospace Industries Ass'n of America, Electronic Industries Ass'n, Motor Vehicle Manufacturers Ass'n, Nat'l Security Industrial Ass'n, Shipbuilders Council of America, American Electronics Ass'n, Computer and Business Equipment Manufacturers Ass'n, the Professional Services Council, Contract Services Ass'n, and the Manufacturers' Alliance for Productivity and Innovation.

Represented by:
Ruth W. Franklin, Admin. Officer

Council of Energy Resource Tribes
Denver, CO
Counsel or consultant:
Karl A. Funke and Associates (Karl A. Funke)

Council of European and Japanese Nat'l Shipowners' Ass'ns
1725 Eye St., N.W. Suite 315, Washington, DC 20006
Telephone: (202) 293-1717
Background: A worldwide trade association of national shipowners associations from 12 European countries and Japan, and of individual liner ship operators in these countries.
Represented by:
Peter G. Sandlund, Washington Representative
Counsel or consultant:
Kirlin, Campbell and Keating (Russell T. Weil)

Council of Graduate Schools
One Dupont Circle, N.W. Suite 430, Washington, DC 20036
Telephone: (202) 223-3791
Represented by:
Dr. Jules B. LaPidus, President
Counsel or consultant:
Patton, Boggs and Blow (John Jonas)

Council of Great City Schools
1413 K St., N.W. Suite 400, Washington, DC 20005
Telephone: (202) 371-0163
Represented by:
Michael Casserly, Senior Associate, Legislative

Council of Great Lakes Governors
c/o Rosemary Freeman 444 N. Capitol St., N.W. #390, Washington, DC 20001
Telephone: (202) 624-5840
Counsel or consultant:
Dutko & Associates (Richard L. Seely)

Council of Independent Colleges
One Dupont Circle, N.W. Suite 320, Washington, DC 20036
Telephone: (202) 466-7230
Background: The nonprofit, national service association for independent liberal arts colleges and universities. Develops programs and provides practical services that strengthen and advance independent colleges in these major areas: Leadership Development and Educational Development and Curriculum Reform. CIC also assists independent colleges in their efforts to promote and market themselves.
Represented by:
Howard E. Holcomb, Government Affairs Counsel
Stephen G. Pelletier, Director of Public Affairs
Allen P. Splete, President

Council of Industrial Boiler Owners
6035 Burke Centre Pkwy. Suite 360, Burke, VA 22015
Telephone: (703) 250-9042
Represented by:
William B. Marx, President
Counsel or consultant:
Sutherland, Asbill and Brennan (Jan Benes Vlcek)

Council of Industrial Development Bond Issuers
1225 Eye St., NW, Suite 300, Washington, DC 20005
Telephone: (202) 682-3764
Background: Membership open to any state, city, county, public agency or special authority whose primary purpose is the provision of economic development financing through the issuance of IDBs.
Counsel or consultant:
Linton, Mields, Reisler and Cottone (Kevin McCarty)

Council of Infrastructure Financing Authorities
655 15th St., N.W., Suite 300, Washington, DC 20005
Telephone: (202) 347-6333
Represented by:
George F. Ames, Exec. Director

Council of Institutional Investors
1420 16th St., N.W., Suite 405, Washington, DC 20036
Telephone: (202) 745-0800
Background: Founded in 1985, the Council has some 40 institutional members, mostly state or municipal pension funds. Seeks a more active role for public pension fund managers in decision of corporations in which their funds are invested.

ORGANIZATIONS REPRESENTED

Council of Institutional Investors (Cont'd)
Represented by:
Sarah A. B. Teslik, Exec. Director

Council of Jewish Federations
227 Massachusetts Ave., N.E., Suite 220, Washington, DC 20002
Telephone: (202) 547-0020
Background: Assists 200 Jewish federations to keep informed of federal programs and to apply for and obtain appropriate federal assistance for their programs.
Represented by:
Mark E. Talisman, Director, Washington Action Office

Council of Large Public Housing Authorities
122 C St., S.E. Suite 865, Washington, DC 20001
Telephone: (202) 638-1300
Background: A non-profit public housing interest organization.
Represented by:
Robert E. McKay, Exec. Director
Counsel or consultant:
Reno, Cavanaugh & Hornig (Gordon Cavanaugh)

Council of Mutual Savings Institutions
New York, NY
Background: A New York based group of depositor-owned savings institutions united to oppose the spread of stockholder-owned savings institutions beyond the states in which they are now permitted.
Counsel or consultant:
Morgan, Lewis and Bockius

Council of Rehabilitation Specialists
1010 Vermont Ave., N.W. Suite 1100, Washington, DC 20036
Telephone: (202) 393-3666
Background: Represented by Roberta Douglas of the American Council of the Blind.

Council of South Texas Economic Progress
MCallen, TX
Counsel or consultant:
McAuliffe, Kelly, Raffaelli & Siemens (John D. Raffaelli)

Council of State Administrators of Vocational Rehabilitation
P.O. Box 3776, Washington, DC 20007
Telephone: (202) 638-4634
Represented by:
Joseph H. Owens, Jr., Exec. Director

Council of State Chambers of Commerce
122 C St., N.W. Suite 330, Washington, DC 20001
Telephone: (202) 484-8103
Represented by:
William R. Brown, President
Mark Cahoon, V. President

Council of State Community Affairs Agencies
444 North Capitol St., N.W., Suite 251, Washington, DC 20001
Telephone: (202) 393-6435
Represented by:
John M. Sidor, Exec. Director

Council of State Governments
444 North Capitol St., N.W., Washington, DC 20001
Telephone: (202) 624-5460
Background: A joint agency created and supported by the states to promote inter-governmental cooperation. Conducts research, publishes reports and assists in state-federal liaison.
Represented by:
Ben Jones, Director, Washington Office

Council of State Policy and Planning Agencies
400 North Capitol St., N.W. Suite 285, Washington, DC 20001
Telephone: (202) 624-5386
Background: A nonprofit membership organization comprised of key executive aides in the fifty states and U.S. Territories. Founded in 1968, this nonpartisan think tank focuses on such state policy issues as economic development, human resources and natural resources. Conducts research, stages conferences and publishes proceedings and policy studies.
Represented by:
Lauren A. Cook, Coordinator, State Scanning Network
James M. Souby, Exec. Director

Council of the Americas
1625 K St., N.W., Suite 1200, Washington, DC 20006
Telephone: (202) 659-1547
Background: A business association of 200 corporations doing business in Latin America. The U.S. private sector vehicle for promoting positive change and future private sector-led development in the hemisphere.
Represented by:
Ludlow Flower, Managing Director

Council of the Great City Schools
1413 K St., N.W. 4th Floor, Washington, DC 20006
Telephone: (202) 371-0163
Represented by:
Samuel B. Husk, Exec. Director

Council on Accreditation of Services for Families and Children
New York, NY
Counsel or consultant:
Porte, Stafford and Associates (Phillip L. Porte)

Council on Competitiveness
1331 Pennsylvania Ave., N.W. Suite 900 North, Washington, DC 20004
Telephone: (202) 662-8760
Background: A nonpartisan group concerned with American Industry's position in world trade. Action arm of Foundation for American Economic Competitiveness. Seeks to increase public awareness of competitiveness issues, and, working with business, labor and universities, to develop comprehensive approaches for private and public actions on the problem, to increase American competitiveness.
Represented by:
Daniel F. Burton, Jr., Exec. V. President
Kent H. Hughes, President
Stephanie Schoumacher, Director, Public Affairs
Counsel or consultant:
Guttenberg & Company (John P. Guttenberg, Jr.)

Council on Continuing Education Unit
1101 Connecticut Ave., N.W., Suite 300, Washington, DC 20036
Telephone: (202) 857-1122
Counsel or consultant:
Smith, Bucklin and Associates (Donna F. Cantor)

Council on Education of the Deaf
c/o Gallaudet, EMG Room 206 800 Florida Ave., N.E., Washington, DC 20002
Telephone: (202) 651-5020
Represented by:
Doin Hicks, Ed.D., Exec. Director

Council on Foreign Relations
2400 N St., N.W., Washington, DC 20037
Telephone: (202) 862-7780
Represented by:
Alton Frye, V. President and Washington Director

Council on Foundations
1828 L St., N.W. Suite 300, Washington, DC 20036
Telephone: (202) 466-6512
Represented by:
Anne H. Babcock, Director, Legislative Affairs
John Edie, General Counsel
James A. Joseph, President
Louis J. Knowles, Director, Planning & Internat'l Affairs
Arlie W. Schardt, Editor

Council on Governmental Relations
1 Dupont Circle, N.W. Suite 670, Washington, DC 20036
Telephone: (202) 861-2595
Background: An organization consisting of 125 major research-oriented universities that deals with executive agencies of the federal government with regard to policies, regulations and practices which affect university research.
Represented by:
Milton Goldberg, Exec. Director
Kate Phillips, Assistant Exec. Director

Council on Hemispheric Affairs
724 9th St., N.W., Washington, DC 20001
Telephone: (202) 393-3322
Background: Founded in 1975. A non-profit research and information organization which seeks to promote a more balanced U.S. policy towards Latin America and increase respect for strong human rights standards, raise the visibility of the inter-American relationship and encourage a rational and constructive Latin America policy for the United States and Canada.
Represented by:
Laurence R. Birns, Director

Council on Hotel, Restaurant & Institutional Education
1200 17th St., N.W. 7th Floor, Washington, DC 20036
Telephone: (202) 331-5990
Represented by:
Douglas E. Adair, Exec. Director

Council on Internat'l Non-Theatrical Events
1001 Connecticut Ave., N.W., Suite 1016, Washington, DC 20036
Telephone: (202) 785-1136
Represented by:
Richard Calkins, Exec. Director

Council on Legal Education Opportunity
1800 M St., N.W. Suite 290, N. Lobby, Washington, DC 20036
Telephone: (202) 785-4840
Background: The Council works to increase the opportunity for disadvantaged persons - principally minorities - to become lawyers by annually sponsoring pre-law summer institutes and providing financial assistance to those institute participants who enroll in law school.
Represented by:
Yolanda Nyerges, Exec. Director

Council on Ocean Law
1709 New York Ave., N.W. Suite 700, Washington, DC 20006
Telephone: (202) 347-3766
Background: Promotes the development of a stable and balanced regime of law for the world's oceans, and educates the public about the importance of widely acceptable international agreement on rules to govern the expansion of ocean uses.
Represented by:
Lee A. Kimball, Exec. Director
Miranda Wecker, Associate Director

Council on Podiatric Medical Education
9312 Old Georgetown Road, Bethesda, MD 20015
Telephone: (301) 571-9200
Represented by:
Jay Levrio, Director

Council on Postsecondary Accreditation
One Dupont Circle, N.W., Suite 305, Washington, DC 20036
Telephone: (202) 452-1433
Background: Works to support, coordinate and improve all non-governmental accrediting activities conducted at the postsecondary education level.
Represented by:
Thurston E. Manning, President

Council on Professional Standards in Speech-Language Pathology and Audiology
10801 Rockville Pike, Rockville, MD 20852
Telephone: (301) 897-5700
Represented by:
Charles E. Speaks, Ph.D., Chair

Council on Research and Technology (CORE-TECH)
1735 New York Ave., N.W., Suite 500, Washington, DC 20006
Telephone: (202) 628-1700
Background: A coalition seeking improved national support for industrial and university research and development. Operates from the offices of the law firm Preston Gates Ellis & Rouvelas Meeds. Kenneth R. Kay serves as Exec. Director.
Counsel or consultant:
Powell, Goldstein, Frazer and Murphy (Stuart E. Eizenstat)
Preston Gates Ellis & Rouvelas Meeds (Kenneth R. Kay, Suellen Lowry)
Skadden, Arps, Slate, Meagher and Flom (Paul W. Oosterhuis)

Council on Resident Education in Obstetrics and Gynecology
409 12th St., S.W., Washington, DC 20024-2588
Telephone: (202) 638-5577

The listings in this directory are available as *Mailing Labels.* See last page.

Represented by:
Dr. Harrison C. Visscher, Director, Education

Council on United States Internat'l Trade Policy
c/o Van Dyk Assoc., 1250 24th St., N.W., Suite 600,
Washington, DC 20037
Telephone: (202) 223-4880
Counsel or consultant:
Van Dyk Associates, Inc. (Robert Hamrin)

Countrywide Credit Industries
Pasadena, CA
Counsel or consultant:
Colton and Boykin (Peter W. Segal)

County Supervisors Ass'n of California
440 First St., N.W., Suite 503, Washington, DC 20001
Telephone: (202) 783-7575
Represented by:
Jack W. Merelman, Washington Representative

County Welfare Directors of California
Sacramento, CA
Counsel or consultant:
Craig Associates (Patricia Johnson Craig)

Covenant House
1331 Pennsylvania Ave., N.W., Suite 909, Washington, DC
20004
Telephone: (202) 662-7482
Counsel or consultant:
McMahon and Associates

Cox Enterprises, Inc.
Atlanta, GA
Counsel or consultant:
Dow, Lohnes and Albertson (Richard L. Braunstein)

Cox-Matthews
10520 Warwick, Fairfax, VA 22030
Telephone: (703) 385-2981
Counsel or consultant:
Patricia Bario Associates (Patricia Bario)

CP Air
Vancouver, British Columbia
Counsel or consultant:
Winthrop, Stimson, Putnam & Roberts (Robert Reed
Gray)

Craig-Botetourt Electric Cooperative
New Castle, VA
Counsel or consultant:
Duncan, Weinberg, Miller & Pembroke, P.C. (Robert
Weinberg)

Cranberry Institute, The
1101 15th St., N.W., Washington, DC 20005
Telephone: (202) 785-3232
Counsel or consultant:
Robert H. Kellen Co. (Andrew Ebert, Robert H. Kellen)

Cranston, Rhode Island, City of
Counsel or consultant:
W. J. William Harsh (J. William W. Harsch)

**Cranston, Rhode Island, Department of Human
Services**
Cranston, RI
Counsel or consultant:
Covington and Burling (Thomas S. Williamson, Jr.)

Cray Research, Inc.
1331 Pennsylvania Ave., N.W., Suite 1331 North, Wash-
ington, DC 20004
Telephone: (202) 638-6000
Represented by:
P. W. Dillingham, Jr., V. President, Government Opera-
tions
Counsel or consultant:
Tammen Group, The (Ronald L. Tammen)

Credit Union Legislative Action Council
805 15th St., N.W., Suite 300, Washington, DC 20005
Telephone: (202) 628-2862
Background: The political action committee of the Credit
Union Nat'l Ass'n. Contact is John J. McKechnie of the
Ass'n.

Credit Union Nat'l Ass'n
805 15th St., N.W. Suite 300, Washington, DC 20005
Telephone: (202) 682-4200

Represented by:
Richard Beach, V. President, Governmental Affairs
Larry Blanchard, Director, Public Affairs
Sara Cummer, Federal Compliance Counsel
Mary Mitchell Dunn, Federal Regulatory Counsel
Karen McGee, Federal Legislative Representative
John J. McKechnie, III, Director, Political Action
Jeanne Marie Murphy, V. President, Congressional Af-
fairs
Mary Reardon, Director, Washington Communications
Kathleen O. Thompson, Chief Washington Counsel
Charles O. Zuver, Senior V. Pres. & Dir., Gov't Affrs.
Counsel or consultant:
Campbell-Raupe, Inc. (Jeanne M. Campbell)

**Creditors Alliance to Preserve Freight Under-
charge Assets**
c/o Sims, Walker & Steinfeld 1275 K St., N.W., #875,
Washington, DC 20005
Telephone: (202) 842-1741
Counsel or consultant:
Dutko & Associates (Emily Young)

Crest Hotels, Internat'l
London, England
Counsel or consultant:
David Apter and Associates

Crestar
Richmond, VA
Background: Formerly United Virginia Bank.
Counsel or consultant:
Hunton and Williams

Creusot Loire Steel Products Co.
Bloomfield, NY
Counsel or consultant:
Mudge Rose Guthrie Alexander and Ferdon

CRG Marketing Group
1000 16th St., N.W. Suite 500, Washington, DC 20036
Telephone: (202) 223-2400
Represented by:
Milton Kotler, V. President
Nelson M. Rosenbaum, President

Criminal Justice Statistics Ass'n
444 North Capitol St., N.W., Suite 606, Washington, DC
20001
Telephone: (202) 624-8560
Background: Members are heads of state criminal justice
statistical units.
Represented by:
Hildy Saizow, Exec. Director

Cristal Services, Inc.
London, England
Counsel or consultant:
Marye T. Miller

Critical Languages Consortium
Brattleboro, VT
Counsel or consultant:
Cassidy and Associates, Inc. (William M. Cloherty, Elliott
M. Fiedler)

Crop Insurance Research Bureau
Indianapolis, IN
Counsel or consultant:
Collier, Shannon & Scott (David A. Hartquist)

Crossland Savings Bank
Falls Church, VA
Counsel or consultant:
Dow, Lohnes and Albertson (Stuart Marshall Bloch)

Crowell and Moring PAC
1001 Pennsylvania Ave., N.W., Washington, DC 20004-
2505
Telephone: (202) 624-2500
Background: The political action committee of the law firm
Crowell and Moring.
Counsel or consultant:
Crowell and Moring (Karen Hastie Williams)

Crowley Maritime Corp.
1500 K St., Suite 425, Washington, DC 20005
Telephone: (202) 737-4728
Background: Headquartered in San Francisco, CA.

Represented by:
Jack H. Park, V. President, Governmental Relations
Alan R. Twaits, Corporate Counsel
Counsel or consultant:
Dawson and Associates, Mathis (Dawson Mathis)
Dyer, Ellis, Joseph & Mills (Thomas L. Mills)
Fort and Schlefer (Mark P. Schlefer)
Lindsay, Hart, Neil & Weigler (Peter Friedmann)
Robertson, Monagle and Eastaugh

Crown Central Petroleum Corp.
Baltimore, MD
Counsel or consultant:
Hoppel, Mayer and Coleman (Paul D. Coleman)

Crown Controls Corp.
New Bremen, OH
Counsel or consultant:
Dunaway & Cross (Mac S. Dunaway)
Windels, Marx, Davies and Ives (Jonathon R. Moore)

CRSS Constructors, Inc.
1201 New York Ave., N.W., Suite 1250, Washington, DC
20005
Telephone: (202) 898-1110
Background: An international architecture, engineering,
construction and construction management firm.
Represented by:
Robert Holt, V. President
Counsel or consultant:
Akin, Gump, Strauss, Hauer and Feld (Joel Jankowsky)

Cruise America Line, Inc.
Fort Lauderdale, FL
Counsel or consultant:
O'Neill and Athy, P.C. (Andrew Athy, Jr.)

Crum and Forster Corp.
1025 Connecticut Ave., N.W. Suite 414, Washington, DC
20036
Telephone: (202) 296-5850
Represented by:
Leslie Cheek, III, Senior V. President, Federal Affairs

Cryo-Chem Internat'l, Inc.
St Simons Island, GA
Counsel or consultant:
Hogan and Hartson (Clifford S. Gibbons, Laurie Michel)

Cryolife Inc.
Marietta, GA
Counsel or consultant:
Patton, Boggs and Blow (Ronald S. Liebman, Deborah
Neipris)

Crysen Corp.
Santa Ana, CA
Counsel or consultant:
Fulbright & Jaworski (Warren Belmar)

Crystal Cruises, Inc.
Los Angeles, CA
Counsel or consultant:
Jack Ferguson Associates (Jack Ferguson)

Crystal Globe Ltd.
Alesund, Norway
Counsel or consultant:
Bogle and Gates

CSC Credit Services, Inc.
Houston, TX
Counsel or consultant:
Fehrenbacher, Sale, Quinn, and Deese (Stephen Sale)

CSO Co.
Omaha, NE
Counsel or consultant:
Steptoe and Johnson (John T. Collins)

CSX Corp.
1331 Pennsylvania Ave., N.W., Suite 560, Washington, DC
20004
Telephone: (202) 783-8124
Background: A corporation formed by the merger of Seaboard Coast Line Industries, Inc. and Chessie Systems,
Inc.

ORGANIZATIONS REPRESENTED

CSX Corp. (Cont'd)
Represented by:
Diane S. Liebman, V. Pres., Legislative & Media Relations
Woodruff M. Price, Vice President, Government Relations
Counsel or consultant:
Edward D. Heffernan
Charls E. Walker Associates (James C. Free)
White, Fine, and Verville (Arnold I. Havens, Michael L. Marvin)

CSX Transportation Inc. Political Action Committee
1331 Pennsylvania Ave., N.W., Suite 560, Washington, DC 20004
Telephone: (202) 783-8124
Represented by:
Alem Woldehawariat, Treasurer
Counsel or consultant:
Wiley, Rein & Fielding

Cuban-American Committee
1010 Vermont Ave., N.W. Suite 620, Washington, DC 20005
Telephone: (202) 783-6637
Background: Addresses the rights and welfare of the Cuban-American community in the U.S. and its members' relationships with relatives in Cuba.
Represented by:
Alicia Torres, Exec. Director

Cuban American Foundation
Miami, FL
Counsel or consultant:
Keefe Co., The (Jonathon A. Slade)

Cuban-American Nat'l Foundation
1000 Thomas Jefferson St. N.W. Suite 601, Washington, DC 20007
Telephone: (202) 265-2822
Represented by:
Jacqueline Tillman, Exec. Director

Cuban Patriotic Council
Miami, FL
Counsel or consultant:
MacKenzie McCheyne, Inc. (Ana Colomar O'Brien)

Cubic Western Data Corp.
San Diego, CA
Counsel or consultant:
Smith and Howard Associates, Inc. (Irving P. Smith)

Cummins Engine Co., Inc.
Columbus, IN
Counsel or consultant:
Lee, Toomey & Kent

Curacao Internat'l Trust Co.
New York, NY
Counsel or consultant:
Anderson, Hibey, Nauheim and Blair (Stephen A. Nauheim)

Cushman & Wakefield, Inc.
New York, NY
Counsel or consultant:
Kelley, Drye and Warren
Silverstein and Mullens (Leonard L. Silverstein)

CWA-COPE Political Contributions Committee
1925 K St., N.W., Washington, DC 20006
Telephone: (202) 728-2465
Background: The political action committee sponsored by the Communications Workers of America. Treasurer is James B. Booe, Secretary-Treasurer of the Communications Workers of America. Political contact is Loretta Bowen, Director of Political Affairs. Chair is Barbara J. Easterling, Exec. V. President of the CWA.

Cyclops Industries
Pittsburgh, PA
Counsel or consultant:
Schagrin Associates (Carol A. Colza, Roger B. Schagrin)

Cyprus, Embassy of the Republic of
2111 R St., N.W., Washington, DC 20008
Telephone: (202) 462-5772

Counsel or consultant:
Evans Group, Ltd., The (Thomas B. Evans, Jr., James R. Meltsner)

Cyprus, Government of the Republic of
Nicosia, Cyprus
Counsel or consultant:
Evans Group, Ltd., The

Cyprus Minerals Corp.
Denver, CO
Counsel or consultant:
Thomas D. Campbell & Assoc. (Thomas D. Campbell)
Steptoe and Johnson

Cystic Fibrosis Foundation
6931 Arlington Road Suite 200, Bethesda, MD 20814
Telephone: (301) 951-4422
Represented by:
Robert J. Beall, Exec. V. President, Medical Affairs
Robert K. Dresing, President
Counsel or consultant:
Capitol Associates, Inc. (Debra M. Hardy-Havens, Terry Lierman)

Czechoslovakia, Chamber of Commerce and Industry of
Prague, Czechoslovakia
Counsel or consultant:
Bryan, Cave, McPheeters and McRoberts (J. Michael Cooper)

Dade County Aviation Department
Miami, FL
Counsel or consultant:
Garvey, Schubert & Barer (Richard A. Wegman)

Dade County Internat'l Airport
Miami, FL
Counsel or consultant:
Cramer and Haber (William C. Cramer)

Daewoo Electronics Co.
Seoul, Korea
Counsel or consultant:
Oppenheimer Wolff and Donnelly (David A. Gantz)

Daewoo Internat'l
Seoul, Korea
Counsel or consultant:
Latham and Watkins (Richard J. Danzig)

Daewoo Internat'l (America) Corp.
1120 19th St., N.W., Suite 500, Washington, DC 20036
Telephone: (202) 293-8030
Background: The Washington office of Daewoo Corp.
Represented by:
Jae Ho Kim, Managing Director
Counsel or consultant:
StMaxens and Co. (Thomas F. StMaxens, II)

Dai Lim Trading Co., Ltd.
Seoul, Korea
Counsel or consultant:
Mudge Rose Guthrie Alexander and Ferdon (N. David Palmeter)

Daicel Chemical Industries, Ltd.
Tokyo, Japan
Counsel or consultant:
Mudge Rose Guthrie Alexander and Ferdon (N. David Palmeter)

Daimler-Berry A.G.
Stuggart, West Germany
Counsel or consultant:
Hogan and Hartson

Dairy and Food Industries Supply Ass'n
6245 Executive Blvd., Rockville, MD 20852
Telephone: (301) 984-1444
Represented by:
Bruce D'Agostino, Public Relations Director
John M. Martin, Exec. V. President
Lori Willard, Public Relations Representative
Counsel or consultant:
Webster, Chamberlain and Bean (George D. Webster)

Dairy Industry Committee
6245 Executive Blvd., Rockville, MD 20852
Telephone: (301) 984-1444

Background: Composed of main executives of all the dairy and food industry ass'ns (American Butter Institute, American Dairy Products Institute, Dairy and Food Industries Supply Ass'n Evaporated Milk Ass'n, Internat'l Ice Cream Ass'n, Milk Industry Ass'n, Nat'l Cheese Institute,) and interested in legislation affecting the environment, sanitation standards, ect. Represented by John M. Martin of the Dairy and Food Industries Supply Ass'n.

Dairyland Power Cooperative
La Crosse, WI
Counsel or consultant:
Newman & Holtzinger, P.C. (Kevin P. Gallen)

Daishowa America Co. Ltd.
Port Angeles, WA
Counsel or consultant:
Bracy Williams & Co. (Kenneth S. Birnbaum, Terrence L. Bracy, Thomas J. Hennessey, Jr., Kenneth M. Stram, Susan J. Williams)

Dakota County, Minnesota
Hastings, MN
Counsel or consultant:
Craig Associates (Patricia Johnson Craig)

Dakota, Minnesota & Eastern
Brookings, SD
Counsel or consultant:
RBC Associates, Inc. (Keith O. Hartwell)

Dakota Wesleyan University
Mitchell, SD
Counsel or consultant:
Hale and Dorr (Jay P. Urwitz)

Dalan/Jupiter, Inc.
Chicago, IL
Counsel or consultant:
E. Del Smith, Inc. (E. Del Smith)

Dallas Area Rapid Transit Authority
Dallas, TX
Counsel or consultant:
Keefe Co., The (William A. Roberts)
Vierra Associates, Inc. (Dennis C. Vierra)

Dallas County Utility and Reclamation District
Irving, TX
Counsel or consultant:
Lipsen Whitten & Diamond

Dallas/Fort Worth RAILTRAN
Fort Worth, TX
Counsel or consultant:
McAuliffe, Kelly, Raffaelli & Siemens (Steven C. Halsey, John D. Raffaelli)

Dallas-Ft. Worth Internat'l Airport
TX
Counsel or consultant:
Century Public Affairs

Dallas Power and Light Co.
Dallas, TX
Counsel or consultant:
Reid & Priest

Dalmine Siderica
Buenos Aires, Argentina
Counsel or consultant:
Mudge Rose Guthrie Alexander and Ferdon (David P. Houlihan, Julie C. Mendoza)

Dalton Construction Co.
Las Vegas, NV
Counsel or consultant:
McAuliffe, Kelly, Raffaelli & Siemens (Edward E. Allison)

Daly City, California, City of
Counsel or consultant:
John McE. Atkisson, P.C.

Damon Corp.
Needham, MA
Counsel or consultant:
Reed Smith Shaw & McClay

Dana Corp.
Toledo, OH

The listings in this directory are available as *Mailing Labels*. See last page.

ORGANIZATIONS REPRESENTED

Counsel or consultant:
Beveridge & Diamond, P.C. (Alexander W. Sierck)
Newmyer Associates, Inc.

Darome, Inc.
Chicago, IL
Counsel or consultant:
Mica, Dudinsky & Associates (John Dudinsky, Jr., John L. Mica)
Murphy and Associates (William T. Murphy, Jr.)

Dart Industries
Los Angeles, CA
Counsel or consultant:
Steptoe and Johnson

Data General Corp.
Westboro, MA
Counsel or consultant:
Preston Gates Ellis & Rouvelas Meeds (Kenneth R. Kay, John L. Longstreth)

Data Processing Management Ass'n
Park Ridge, IL
Background: A Washington contact is John Clement of the American Federation of Information Processing Societies.

DataCom Systems Corp.
Boston, MA
Counsel or consultant:
Cassidy and Associates, Inc. (James P. Collins, Thomas M. Gannon)

Datapoint Corp.
1655 North Fort Myer Drive, Arlington, VA 22209
Telephone: (703) 841-7600
Represented by:
Fritz Riedlin, Director, Federal Operations

Dataproducts Corp.
12200 Sunrise Valley Drive Suite 230, Reston, VA 22091
Telephone: (703) 648-0930
Background: A manufacturer of computer printers and related equipment and supplies. Based in California.
Represented by:
Robert Woodward, Regional Director

Daughters of the American Revolution
1776 D St., N.W., Washington, DC 20006-5392
Telephone: (202) 628-1776
Background: A non-governmental, non-profit, historic, educational, and patriotic organization whose members are women whose lineage can be traced back to a Revolutionary patriot who aided in the cause of American Independence.
Represented by:
Mrs. Eldred Martin Yochim, President General

David Sarnoff Research Center
Princeton, NJ
Counsel or consultant:
Hill and Knowlton Public Affairs Worldwide (Jackson Bain, Marci Williams)

Davis Walker Corp.
Los Angeles, CA
Counsel or consultant:
Powell, Goldstein, Frazer and Murphy (Peter Suchman)

Davis Wright Political Action Committee
1752 N St., N.W., Suite 800, Washington, DC 20007
Telephone: (202) 822-9775
Background: A political action committee of the law firm of Davis Wright Tremaine.
Counsel or consultant:
Davis Wright Tremaine (Edward B. Cohen)

Day-Glo Color Corp.
Cleveland, OH
Counsel or consultant:
Cleary, Gottlieb, Steen and Hamilton (Richard deC. Hinds)

Day Kimball Hospital
Putnam, CT
Counsel or consultant:
Jones, Day, Reavis and Pogue (Randall E. Davis)

Day & Zimmerman
Philadelphia, PA

Counsel or consultant:
Baker, Worthington, Crossley, Stansberry & Woolf (Edward R. Hamberger)

Dayton Hudson Corp.
Minneapolis, MN
Counsel or consultant:
Flack Inc. (Susan Garber Flack)

Dayton Power and Light Co.
Dayton, OH
Counsel or consultant:
Conner and Wetterhahn, P.C.
Keller and Heckman
Reid & Priest

DCL Industries
Marietta, GA
Counsel or consultant:
Evergreen Associates, Ltd. (Robert M. Brooks)

Deafpride
1350 Potomac Ave., S.E., Washington, DC 20003
Telephone: (202) 675-6700
Represented by:
Ann Champ-Wilson, Exec. Director

Dealer Action Ass'n
Bethesda, MD
Counsel or consultant:
Patton, Boggs and Blow (George Blow)

Dealers Election Action Committee of the Nat'l Automobile Dealers Ass'n (DEAC)
8400 Westpark Drive, McLean, VA 22102
Telephone: (703) 821-7110
Background: The political action committee sponsored by the Nat'l Automobile Dealers Ass'n.
Represented by:
William E. Hancock, Jr., Chairman
Gregory V. Knopp, DEAC Director
Anthony Ursomarso, Treasurer

Dean Witter Financial Services Group
633 Pennsylvania Ave., N.W., Washington, DC 20004
Telephone: (202) 737-4900
Represented by:
Christine A. Edwards, Sr. V. President/Director, Gov'tl Affrs.
Kathryn 'Kelly' McNamara, Manager, Federal Government Affairs
Counsel or consultant:
Keller and Heckman (Mary Martha McNamara)

Dean Witter Realty
New York, NY
Counsel or consultant:
McAuliffe, Kelly, Raffaelli & Siemens (John D. Raffaelli)

DECA Foundation
1908 Association Dr., Reston, VA 22091
Telephone: (703) 860-5000
Background: The Distributive Education Clubs of America Foundation. Represented by Frederick L. Williford.

Decision Insights, Inc.
Reston, VA
Counsel or consultant:
Tammen Group, The (Ronald L. Tammen)

Decorative Window Coverings Ass'n
St. Louis, MO
Counsel or consultant:
Fehrenbacher, Sale, Quinn, and Deese (C. Michael Deese)

Deere & Co.
1667 K St., N.W., Suite 1230, Washington, DC 20006
Telephone: (202) 223-4817
Represented by:
Dean R. Dort, II, Washington Counsel
Brian T. Hanson, Government Affairs Representative
William H. Plenge, Washington Manager, Government Products
Counsel or consultant:
Bell, Boyd & Lloyd
Lee, Toomey & Kent

Defenders of Wildlife
1244 19th St., N.W., Washington, DC 20036
Telephone: (202) 659-9510

Background: A non-profit national educational organization with a membership of 80,000 working for the natural abundance and diversity of wildlife and for the protection of wildlife habitat through education, litigation, research and advocacy. Publishes the bi-monthly magazine 'Defenders'.
Represented by:
M. Rupert Cutler, President
Cathy Dirksen, Manager, Special Activities
John M. Fitzgerald, Esq., Counsel for Wildlife Policy
Jennifer Jones, Assistant Development Director
Albert M Manville, II, Ph.D., Senior Staff Wildlife Biologist
Mary-Margaret Patterson, Director, Media Relations
Cindy Shogan, Activist Coordinator
Kathryn R. Tollerton, Associate Conservation Dir.
James K. Wyerman, Dir., Internat'l Wildlife Trade Program

Defense Budget Project
236 Massachusetts Ave., N.E., Suite 401, Washington, DC 20002
Telephone: (202) 546-9737
Background: Seeks to promote better understanding of the U.S. military budget and the impact of defense spending on the American economy.
Represented by:
Gordon Adams, Director
Stephen Alexis Cain, Senior Budget Analyst

Defense Credit Union Council
805 15th St., N.W., Washington, DC 20005-2207
Telephone: (202) 682-5993
Represented by:
James W. Rowe, President and CEO

Defense Group, Inc.
1901 North Moore St. Suite 1000, Arlington, VA 22209
Telephone: (703) 524-5800
Counsel or consultant:
McNair Group Inc. (Kathy E. Gallegos, Dennis R. Rankin)

Defense Orientation Conference Ass'n
1601 North Kent St., Suite 1012, Arlington, VA 22209-2217
Telephone: (703) 524-1800
Background: Composed of individuals interested in defense issues. Offers tours of defense installations and provides speakers for membership.
Represented by:
John W. Ohlsen, Exec. Vice President

Defense Products Marketing Inc.
1213 Jefferson Davis Hwy., Suite 1414, Arlington, VA 22202
Telephone: (703) 486-2288
Represented by:
Judith A. Wittig, Corporate Secretary
Richard J. Wittig, President

Delaware Municipal Electric Corp. (DEMEC)
New Castle, DE
Background: A municipal electric joint action agency. Represented by Duncan, Weinberg, Miller & Pembroke before federal and state commissions.
Counsel or consultant:
Duncan, Weinberg, Miller & Pembroke, P.C. (Wallace L. Duncan, Janice L. Lower)

Delaware Otsego System
Cooperstown, NY
Counsel or consultant:
RBC Associates, Inc. (Ray B. Chambers)

Delaware River and Bay Pilots Ass'n
Philadelphia, PA
Counsel or consultant:
Montgomery, McCracken, Walker & Rhoads (David F. Norcross)

Delaware State Department of Transportation
Dover, DE
Counsel or consultant:
Cassidy and Associates, Inc. (Thomas M. Gannon)

Delaware, State of
400 North Capitol St., N.W. Suite 378, Washington, DC 20001
Telephone: (202) 624-7724

ORGANIZATIONS REPRESENTED

Delaware, State of (Cont'd)
Represented by:
Kathryn Way, Director, Washington Office
Counsel or consultant:
Dickstein, Shapiro and Morin (Andrew P. Miller, Bernard Nash)

Delegation General pour l' Armement (DRI)
Paris, France
Counsel or consultant:
DGA Internat'l (Sandra K. Meredith)

DeLeuw, Cather and Co.
1133 15th St., N.W. Suite 800, Washington, DC 20005
Telephone: (202) 775-3300
Represented by:
Michael D. Coleman, V. President, International Operations
C. C. Eby, V. President
David S. Gedney, President
James Lockwood, Legal Counsel
R. S. O'Neil, Senior V. President
M. R. Sproles, Senior V. President

DeLeuw, Cather and Co. Political Action Committee
1133 15th St., N.W. Suite 900, Washington, DC 20005
Telephone: (202) 775-3300
Background: Chairman is M. R. Sproles of the parent organization.

Deleuw/Greeley/Hyman
1133 15th St., N.W., Washington, DC 20005
Telephone: (202) 775-3300
Counsel or consultant:
Liz Robbins Associates (Sharon Edwards)

Delmarva Power and Light Co.
Wilmington, DE
Counsel or consultant:
Hunton and Williams
Reid & Priest

Del Monte-USA
San Francisco, CA
Background: A subsidiary of RJR Nabisco, Inc. Represented in Washington by Alan C. Caldwell, Director, Federal Government Relations (See RJR Nabisco Washington, Inc. listing.)

Del Norte Technology
Euless, TX
Counsel or consultant:
Korth and Korth (Fritz-Alan Korth)

Deloitte & Touche Federal PAC
P.O. Box 18174, Washington, DC 20036
Telephone: (202) 638-7850
Represented by:
Robert N. Yerman, Treasurer

Deloitte & Touche Washington Services Group
1001 Pennsylvania Ave., N.W. Suite 350N, Washington, DC 20004
Telephone: (202) 879-5600
Represented by:
John T. Connor, Managing Partner
Hal Daub, Director, Government Affairs
Robert Santy, Director, Government Relations
Emil Sunley, Director of Tax Analysis
Wade S. Williams, Sr. Manager, Washington Service Center

Delta Air Lines
1629 K St., N.W., Suite 501, Washington, DC 20006
Telephone: (202) 296-6464
Represented by:
Richard J. Doubrava, Manager, Government Affairs
David S. Wynett, Manager, Legislative Affairs
D. Scott Yohe, V. President, Gov't Affairs
Counsel or consultant:
Preston Gates Ellis & Rouvelas Meeds
Sparkman and Cole, Inc. (Timothy R. Cole, D. Dean Sparkman)

Delta Dental Plans Ass'n
Chicago, IL
Counsel or consultant:
CR Associates

Delta Marine, Inc.
Wilmington, NC
Counsel or consultant:
Swift Consulting Co., Ltd., The (Ivan, Red Swift)

Democratic Congressional Campaign Committee
430 South Capitol St., S.E. 2nd Floor, Washington, DC 20003
Telephone: (202) 863-1500
Represented by:
Richard Bates, Exec. Director
Ginnie Kontnik, Director, Harriman Communun. Center
Debra Levin-Jardot, Deputy Exec. Director
Robert Norris, Research Director
Howard M. Schloss, Communications Director
Douglas B. Sosnik, Political Director
Martin E. Stone, PAC Director
Jeff Thompson, Finance Director

Democratic Governors Ass'n
430 South Capitol St., S.E., Washington, DC 20003
Telephone: (202) 863-8096
Represented by:
Mark D. Gearan, Exec. Director

Democratic Leadership Council
316 Pennsylvania Ave., S.E., Suite 500, Washington, DC 20003
Telephone: (202) 546-0007
Represented by:
Alvin From, President & Exec. Director
Andrea Mietus, Administrative Director
Linda Moore, Director of Field Operations
Bruce Reed, Policy Director
Deb Smulyan, Deputy Director

Democratic Nat'l Committee
430 South Capitol St., S.E., Washington, DC 20003
Telephone: (202) 863-8000
Represented by:
Joan N. Baggett, Dir., Congressional & Organizat'l Relats
Joe L. Barrow, Jr., Deputy Director, Communications
Ronald H. Brown, Chairman
Daniel S. Carol, Director, Opposition Research
Lynn Cutler, V. Chairwoman
Alexis M. Herman, Chief of Staff
Phillip J. Jones, Southern Regional Political Director
Jack Martin, Senior Adviser
Michael D. McCurry, Communications Director
Will Robinson, Coordinated Campaign Director
Mark E. Steitz, Research Director
Virginia M. Terzano, Press Secretary
Paul R. Tully, Director, Political Operations
Christine L. Varney, General Counsel
Kathy Vick, Secretary
Carl Wagner, Director, Strategic Planning
Counsel or consultant:
Politics Inc.

Democratic-Republican-Independent Voter Education (DRIVE) Committee
25 Louisiana Ave., N.W., Washington, DC 20001
Telephone: (202) 624-8741
Background: A political action committee sponsored by the Internat'l Brotherhood of Teamsters, Chauffeurs, Warehousemen and Helpers of America.
Represented by:
William J. McCarthy, Chairman

Democratic Senatorial Campaign Committee
430 South Capitol St., S.E., Washington, DC 20003
Telephone: (202) 224-2447
Represented by:
Anita B. Dunn, Communications Director
Noel Gould, Exec. Director
Larry Harrington, Political Director
Sarah Silver, Director, Leadership Circle
Kris Swedin, Deputy Exec. Director
Jo Vincent, Director, Business Roundtable

Democratic State Legislative Leaders Ass'n
430 South Capitol St., S.E., Washington, DC 20003
Telephone: (202) 863-8172
Background: The official national Democratic Party organizations for state legislature speakers, senate presidents and minority leaders.
Counsel or consultant:
O'Connor & Hannan (Jeffrey M. Wice)

Democratic Unionist Party of Northern Ireland
Belfast, N. Ireland
Counsel or consultant:
Jack E. Buttram Co. (Jack E. Buttram)

Democrats for the 90s
Box 3797 3038 N St., N.W., Washington, DC 20007
Telephone: (202) 338-9092
Background: A political action committee founded in 1980 to assist in strengthening the Democratic Party and to elect Democratic candidates.
Represented by:
Pamela Harriman, Chairperson
Janet A. Howard, Director
Joan Shaffer, Communications
Counsel or consultant:
Perkins Coie (Robert F. Bauer)

Denny's, Inc.
La Mirada, CA
Counsel or consultant:
Power & Coleman (Thomas W. Power)

Dental Gold Institute
Boston, MA
Counsel or consultant:
Jenner and Block

Denver, Colorado, City and County of
Denver, CO
Counsel or consultant:
Andrews' Associates, Inc. (Mark Andrews)
Patton, Boggs and Blow

Denver Regional Transportation District
Denver, CO
Counsel or consultant:
Tucker & Associates (William Tucker)
David E. Yudin, Att'y-at-Law (David E. Yudin)

Denver and Rio Grande Western Railroad Co.
Denver, CO
Counsel or consultant:
Hogan and Hartson (Thomas B. Leary, George W. Mayo, Jr., E. Barrett Prettyman, Jr., Peter F. Rousselot, Eric A. Von Salzen)

Derby Line, Vermont, Town of
Counsel or consultant:
Duncan, Weinberg, Miller & Pembroke, P.C. (Richmond F. Allan)

Derecktor of Rhode Island, Robert E.
Coddington Cove, RI
Counsel or consultant:
Reid & Priest (Stephan M. Minikes)

Desert Research Institute
Reno, NV
Counsel or consultant:
Marcus G. Faust

Design Cuisine
Washington, DC
Counsel or consultant:
Holman Communications

Design Professionals Coalition
1015 15th St., N.W., Suite 802, Washington, DC 20005
Telephone: (202) 347-7474
Counsel or consultant:
Crowell and Moring (Karen Hastie Williams)
Neece, Cator and Associates

Design Protection Coalition
Peoria, IL
Counsel or consultant:
Timothy X. Moore and Co. (Timothy X. Moore)
Swidler & Berlin, Chartered (Bruce A. Lehman)

Designers & Planners, Inc.
2611 Jefferson Davis Highway, Suite 3000, Arlington, VA 22202
Telephone: (703) 418-3800
Background: An engineering consulting firm that provides design, engineering computing and logistics services, specialized training programs, and safety and environmental protection programs for the U.S. Navy, Coast Guard, and other government clients.

The listings in this directory are available as *Mailing Labels*. See last page.

ORGANIZATIONS REPRESENTED

Represented by:
Dennis Jeffrey, President
Kelly Pratt, Manager, of Corporate Planning
Counsel or consultant:
Coffey, McGovern and Noel, Ltd. (James H. Falk)

Detachable Container Ass'n
1730 Rhode Island Ave., N.W., Suite 1000, Washington, DC 20036
Telephone: (202) 659-4613
Represented by:
Karen Bishop, Exec. Secretary

Detroit Edison Co.
1990 M St., N.W., Suite 480, Washington, DC 20036
Telephone: (202) 466-5495
Represented by:
Barbara Bauman, Washington Representative
Robert J. Horn, Asst. V. Pres. and Mgr., Federal Affairs

Detroit Educational TV Foundation
Detroit, MI
Counsel or consultant:
Plunkett & Cooney , P.C. (William M. Brodhead)

Detroit, Michigan, City of
Counsel or consultant:
Plunkett & Cooney , P.C. (William M. Brodhead)

Deutsche Bank AG
Frankfurt, West Germany
Counsel or consultant:
TransAtlantic Futures, Inc. (Stephan-Gotz Richter, W. Alan Zuschlag)

Deutscher Industrie und Handelstag
Bonn, Germany
Counsel or consultant:
Representative for German Industry and Trade (Dr. Lothar Griessbach, Hartmut Schneider, John Heath Vaughan, Jr,, Bernhard M. Welschke)

Development Group for Alternative Policies
1400 Eye St., N.W., Suite 520 Suite 520, Washington, DC 20005
Telephone: (202) 898-1566
Background: A development policy resource organization which involves addressing international economic policies that affect them.
Represented by:
Douglas Hellinger, Managing Director
Stephen Hellinger, Exec. Director

DHL Airways, Inc.
Redwood City, CA
Counsel or consultant:
Herbert A. Rosenthal

Diagnostic Retrieval Systems, Inc.
1215 South Jefferson Davis Hwy., Suite 1004, Arlington, VA 22202
Telephone: (703) 521-8000
Represented by:
Jackson Kemper, Jr., V. President, Washington Operations
Cynthia L. Martin, Director, Government Relations
Arthur E. Sullivan, Jr., Requirement Analyst
Counsel or consultant:
Donald Baldwin Associates (Donald Baldwin)

Dianon Systems
Stratford, CT
Counsel or consultant:
Hogan and Hartson (Helen R. Trilling)

Dickstein, Shapiro and Morin Political Action Committee
2101 L St., N.W., Washington, DC 20037
Telephone: (202) 785-9700
Counsel or consultant:
Dickstein, Shapiro and Morin (John C. Dill)

Dictaphone Corp.
8260 Greensboro Drive A-32, Mclean, VA 22102
Telephone: (703) 893-2390
Represented by:
Walter Boss, Director, Federal Government Division

Dietary Managers Ass'n
Lombard, IL

Counsel or consultant:
Porte, Stafford and Associates (Phillip L. Porte)

Dietary Supplement Coalition
Farmingdale, NY
Counsel or consultant:
Morris J. Amitay, P.C.

Digestive Disease Nat'l Coalition
511 Capitol Court, N.E. Suite 300, Washington, DC 20002
Telephone: (202) 544-7497
Counsel or consultant:
Health and Medicine Counsel of Washington (Dale P. Dirks)

Digital Equipment Corp.
1331 Pennsylvania Ave., N.W. Suite 600, Washington, DC 20004
Telephone: (202) 383-5600
Represented by:
Michael A. Aisenberg, Manager, Federal Government Relations
Grace L. Hinchman, Manager, Public Affairs
Counsel or consultant:
Dewey, Ballantine, Bushby, Palmer and Wood (R. Michael Gadbaw)
Ivins, Phillips and Barker (Jay W. Glasmann, Philip D. Morrison)
Podesta Associates (John D. Podesta)
Ropes and Gray (Thomas M. Susman)

Dillingham Construction N.A., Inc.
Pleasanton, CA
Counsel or consultant:
Jack Ferguson Associates

Dillingham Construction Pacific, Ltd.
Honolulu, HI
Counsel or consultant:
Jack Ferguson Associates

Dillingham Corp.
San Francisco, CA
Counsel or consultant:
Hudson, Creyke, Koehler and Tacke

Dime Savings Bank of New York
New York, NY
Counsel or consultant:
James J. Butera, Chartered

DINAMO
Pittsburgh, PA
Counsel or consultant:
Baker, Worthington, Crossley, Stansberry & Woolf (Edward R. Hamberger)

Diplomatic and Consular Officers, Retired (Dacor)
1801 F St., N.W., Washington, DC 20006
Telephone: (202) 682-0500
Represented by:
William B. Cobb, Jr., Exec. Director

Direct Health, Inc.
Bethesda, MD
Counsel or consultant:
Jefferson Group, The (David Serwer)

Direct Marketing Ass'n
1101 17th St., N.W., Suite 900, Washington, DC 20036
Telephone: (202) 347-1222
Represented by:
Richard A. Barton, Senior V. President, Government Affairs
Margaret Gottlieb, Director, State Government Affairs
Robert J. Levering, V.P., Gov't Affrs. & Legislative Couns.
Kay Pauley, Manager, Gov't Information Services
Counsel or consultant:
Cohn and Marks (Ian D. Volner)
Covington and Burling
Davidson Colling Group, Inc., The (James H. Davidson)

Direct Marketing Ass'n Political Action Committee
1101 17th St., N.W., Suite 705, Washington, DC 20036
Telephone: (202) 347-1222
Background: Represented by Richard Barton of the Direct Marketing Ass'n.

Direct Marketing Guaranty Trust
Nashua, NH
Counsel or consultant:
Daly Associates, Inc. (John Jay Daly)

Direct Selling Ass'n
1776 K St., N.W., Suite 600, Washington, DC 20006
Telephone: (202) 293-5760
Represented by:
Mario Brossi, Counsel & V. President, Gov't Relations
Janice L. Caldwell, Attorney/Government Relations
George C. Hescock, Exec. V. President
Joseph N. Mariano, Associate Counsel & Mgr., Gov't Affairs
Neil H. Offen, President
Eileen Creamer O'Neill, V. President

Direct Selling Ass'n Political Action Committee
1776 K St., N.W., Suite 600, Washington, DC 20006
Telephone: (202) 293-5760
Background: Treasurer and contact is George C. Hescock of the Direct Selling Ass'n.

Direct Selling Education Foundation
1776 K St., N.W., Washington, DC 20006
Telephone: (202) 293-5760
Background: The public service arm of the Direct Selling Ass'n. Provides educational information and research activities on matters of interest to the consumer, marketing professors and the public on consumer and marketplace matters.
Represented by:
Marlene W. Futterman, Exec. Director

Directors Guild of America
Los Angeles, CA
Counsel or consultant:
Chernikoff and Co. (Larry Chernikoff)
Dow, Lohnes and Albertson (Arnold P. Lutzker)

Disability Focus, Inc.
1010 Vermont Ave., N.W., Suite 1100, Washington, DC 20005
Telephone: (202) 483-8582
Background: Seeks to provide a 'disability perspective' on all social policy.
Represented by:
Mary Jane Owen, Director
Counsel or consultant:
Charles Goldman

Disability Rights Education and Defense Fund
1616 P St., N.W., Suite 100, Washington, DC 20036
Telephone: (202) 328-5185
Represented by:
Pat A. Wright, Director, Governmental Affairs

Disabled American Veterans
807 Maine Ave., S.W., Washington, DC 20024
Telephone: (202) 554-3501
Represented by:
Denvel D. Adams, National Adjutant
Paul J. Breuer, Associate National Legislative Director
John F. Heilman, National Legislative Director
Counsel or consultant:
Morgan, Lewis and Bockius

Disney Productions, Walt
Burbank, CA
Counsel or consultant:
Dewey, Ballantine, Bushby, Palmer and Wood (Lawrence F. O'Brien, III)
Graham and James (Eileen Shannon Carlson, Thomas F. Railsback)

Distilled Spirits Council of the United States
1250 Eye St., N.W., Suite 900, Washington, DC 20005
Telephone: (202) 628-3544

ORGANIZATIONS REPRESENTED

Distilled Spirits Council of the United States (Cont'd)
Represented by:
Tim Dudgeon, Asst. Director, Federal Gov't Relations
Janet Flynn, Director, Public Affairs
Paul F. Gavaghan, V. President, Research and Education
F. A. Meister, President and CEO
Lynne Omlie, Secretary and General Counsel
Geoffrey G. Peterson, Director, Federal Government Relations
Sydney Probst, Asst. Director, Federal Gov't Relations
Counsel or consultant:
Hill and Knowlton Public Affairs Worldwide (Josephine S. Cooper)
O'Connor & Hannan (Thomas R. Jolly, Patrick E. O'Donnell)

Distilled Spirits Political Action Committee
1250 Eye St., N.W. Suite 900, Washington, DC 20005
Telephone: (202) 628-3544
Background: Supported by the Distilled Spirits Council of the United States. Contact person is Geoffrey Peterson of the Council.

Distributive Education Clubs of America
1908 Association Dr., Reston, VA 22091
Telephone: (703) 860-5000
Represented by:
Frederick L. Williford, Exec. Director/Chief Exec. Officer

District of Columbia Armory Board
2001 East Capitol St. S.E., Washington, DC 20003
Telephone: (202) 547-9077
Counsel or consultant:
Laxalt, Washington, Perito & Dubuc

District of Columbia Chamber of Commerce
1411 K St., N.W., Suite 500, Washington, DC 20005
Telephone: (202) 347-7202
Represented by:
Lynn C. Clark, Deputy Director

District of Columbia Hospital Ass'n
1250 Eye St., N.W., Suite 700, Washington, DC 20005-3922
Telephone: (202) 682-1581
Represented by:
Howard T. Jessamy, President
Carolyn L. Parmer, V. President for Health Finance

District of Columbia League for Nursing
5100 Wisconsin Ave., N.W. Suite 306, Washington, DC 20016
Telephone: (202) 244-0628
Represented by:
Johnella Banks, President

District of Columbia Office of Intergovernmental Relations
1350 Pennsylvania Ave., N.W., Room 416, Washington, DC 20004
Telephone: (202) 727-6265
Represented by:
Luis Burgillo, Jr., Assoc Dir, Congressional & Federal Affrs
Dwight S. Cropp, Director

District of Columbia Office of the People's Counsel
1101 14th St., N.W., Suite 900, Washington, DC 20005
Telephone: (202) 727-3071
Background: The statutorily created advocate for District of Columbia utility ratepayers.
Represented by:
Frederick D. Dorsey, People's Counsel
Marlene Johnson, Public Affairs Specialist
Elizabeth A. Noel, Deputy People's Counsel
Luis A. Wilmot, Assoc. People's Counsel (Gov't Relats)

District of Columbia Special Olympics
220 Eye St., N.E., Suite 280, Washington, DC 20002
Telephone: (202) 544-7770
Represented by:
Stephen A. Hocker, Exec. Director

Diversified Realty Corp. and Financial Group
Counsel or consultant:
RPH & Associates (Robert P. Hanrahan)

Diving Equipment Manufacturers Ass'n
1625 K St., N.W., Suite 900, Washington, DC 20006
Telephone: (202) 775-1762
Background: Represented by Jan Kinney of the Sporting Goods Manufacturers Ass'n.

DKT Memorial Fund
1120 19th St., N.W. Suite 600, Washington, DC 20036
Counsel or consultant:
Baker, Worthington, Crossley, Stansberry & Woolf (W. Lee Rawls)

DNA Plant Technology Corp.
Oakland, CA
Counsel or consultant:
McCutchen, Doyle, Brown & Enersen (David Andrews, Philip T. Cummings)

DO IT Coalition
1129 20th St., N.W. Suite 200, Washington, DC 20036
Telephone: (202) 857-5990
Counsel or consultant:
Madison Group/Earle Palmer Brown, The (Ed Segal)

Doctors Nat'l Homecare Corp.
Reno, NV
Counsel or consultant:
Epstein Becker and Green (Deborah Steelman)

Doe Run Co.
St. Louis, MO
Background: Owned jointly by Fluor Corp. and Homestake Mining Co.
Counsel or consultant:
Jefferson Group, The (Robert L. Harris)
McGuire, Woods, Battle and Boothe (Robert H. Lamb)

Dofasco, Inc.
Hamilton, Ontario
Counsel or consultant:
Dow, Lohnes and Albertson (William Silverman)

Dole Foundation for Employment of People with Disabilities, The
1819 H St., N.W., Suite 850, Washington, DC 20006
Telephone: (202) 457-0318
Background: Chaired by Senator Robert Dole. Vice Chairman is Robert S. Strauss.
Represented by:
Paul G. Hearne, President

Dole Fresh Fruit Co.
Boca Raton, FL
Counsel or consultant:
Patton, Boggs and Blow (Joseph L. Brand)

Dollar Bank
Pittsburgh, PA
Counsel or consultant:
Thacher, Proffitt and Wood (Louis H. Nevins)

Dollar Drydock Savings Bank
White Plains, NY
Counsel or consultant:
Gibson, Dunn and Crutcher (Peter L. Baumbusch)

Dome Petroleum Ltd.
Calgary, Alberta
Counsel or consultant:
Mayer, Brown and Platt (Joan P. Fread, Charles S. Levy, Jerry L. Oppenheimer)

Dominican Republic Internat'l Sugar Policy Coordinating Commission
Santo Domingo, Dominican Republic
Counsel or consultant:
McClure and Trotter

Dominican Sugar Institute
Santo Domingo, Dominican Republic
Counsel or consultant:
McClure and Trotter

Dominicana Airlines
Santo Domingo, Dominican Republic
Counsel or consultant:
Herbert A. Rosenthal

Dominion Marine Ass'n
Ottawa, Ontario
Background: Represented in Washington by Matthew Abrams of CANAMCO.

Dominion Resources, Inc.
Richmond, VA
Counsel or consultant:
Flanagan Group, Inc. (Daniel V. Flanagan, Jr.)

Domtar, Inc.
Montreal, Quebec
Counsel or consultant:
Covington and Burling (Harvey M. Applebaum)

Donaldson, Lufkin & Jenrette
New York, NY
Counsel or consultant:
Cassidy and Associates, Inc. (Gerald S. J. Cassidy)
Stanton & Associates (James V. Stanton)

Dong Sung Steel Industries Co., Ltd.
Seoul, Korea
Counsel or consultant:
Mudge Rose Guthrie Alexander and Ferdon (Donald B. Cameron, Jr., Julie C. Mendoza)

Donnelley & Sons, R. R.
3141 Fairview Park Drive Suite 550, Falls Church, VA 22042
Telephone: (703) 204-2170
Counsel or consultant:
Beckerman Associates (George Beckerman)

Door and Hardware Institute
7711 Old Springhouse Road, McLean, VA 22102-3474
Telephone: (703) 556-3990
Represented by:
Jerry Heppes, Assistant to the Exec. V. President
Richard M. Hornaday, CAE, Exec. V. President

Door and Hardware Institute Political Action Committee
7711 Old Springhouse Road, McLean, VA 22102-3474
Telephone: (703) 556-3990
Background: Represented by Richard M. Hornaday of the Door and Hardware Institute.

Doris Day Animal League
111 Massachusetts Ave., N.W. Suite 200, Washington, DC 20001
Telephone: (202) 842-3325
Background: Exec. Director is Holly Elizabeth Hazard of Galvin, Stanley & Hazard.
Counsel or consultant:
Galvin, Stanley & Hazard (Holly Eliz. Hazard)

Dorr-Oliver, Inc.
Stamford, CT
Counsel or consultant:
Hudson, Creyke, Koehler and Tacke

Dow Chemical
1776 Eye St., N.W., Suite 575, Washington, DC 20006
Telephone: (202) 429-3400
Represented by:
C. Thomas Campbell, Manager, Government Relations
Frank J. Farfone, Manager, Government Affairs
Lewis F. Gayner, Director, Regulatory & Legis. Affairs
David W. Graham, Environmental Issues Manager
F. Milton Hunt, Gov't Relats. Mgr., Agricultural Product
Charles T. Marck, V. President & Director, Gov't Relations
Penny L. Parkin, Federal Information Manager
Richard M. Patterson, Government Relations Manager
Laura M. Pettey, Tax Manager, Government Relations
Margaret Rogers, Manager, Government Relations
Vicky M. Suazo, Public Affairs Manager
Counsel or consultant:
Ketchum Public Relations (Gerald B. Olszewski)
Pagonis and Donnelly Group (Thomas R. Donnelly, Jr., Michael E. Grisso)
Wilmer, Cutler and Pickering (William J. Wilkins)

Dow Corning Corp.
1800 M St., N.W., Suite 325 South, Washington, DC 20036
Telephone: (202) 785-0585

ORGANIZATIONS REPRESENTED

Represented by:
Faye A. Gorman, Government Relations Representative
Ralph D. Schumack, V. Pres., Gov't Relations & Public Affrs
Counsel or consultant:
Hill and Knowlton Public Affairs Worldwide (Dale Lawson)
Jack McDonald Co. (Jack McDonald, Myron G. Sandifer, III)

Dow Jones & Co., Inc.
New York, NY
Counsel or consultant:
Snavely, King and Associates

Downey Savings and Loan
Newport Beach, CA
Counsel or consultant:
Washington Financial Information Services, Inc. (Robert S. Feinberg)

Doyon, Ltd.
Fairbanks, AK
Counsel or consultant:
Patton, Boggs and Blow (Thomas Hale Boggs, Jr.)

Dragonair
Hong Kong
Counsel or consultant:
Zuckert, Scoutt and Rasenberger (Rachel B. Trinder)

Dramatists Guild
New York, NY
Counsel or consultant:
Liz Robbins Associates (Michael J. Lucas, Liz Robbins)

Dredging Industry Size Standard Committee (DISSC)
c/o Patton, Boggs & Blow, 2550 M St., N.W., Washington, DC 20037
Telephone: (202) 457-6000
Background: A coalition of smaller dredging companies.
Counsel or consultant:
Patton, Boggs and Blow (Joe Robert Reeder)

Dresdnerbank
Frankfurt, Weste Germany
Counsel or consultant:
Hill and Knowlton Public Affairs Worldwide (Dr. Ira P. Kaminow)

Dresser Industries
1100 Connecticut Ave., N.W. Suite 310, Washington, DC 20036
Telephone: (202) 296-3070
Background: Manufacturers of all types of equipment in the energy field.
Represented by:
Diane Crawford, Government Affairs Representative
Barbara Jones, Legislative Representative
Ardon B. Judd, Jr., Staff V. President, Washington Counsel
Counsel or consultant:
Davis & Harman (Gail B. Wilkins)
Wunder, Ryan, Cannon & Thelen (W. Stephen Cannon)

Drexel University
Philadelphia, PA
Counsel or consultant:
Cassidy and Associates, Inc. (Gerald S. J. Cassidy, Charles F. Dougherty, C. Frank Godfrey, Jr.)

Dreyfus Corp.
New York, NY
Counsel or consultant:
Rogers and Wells (William Morris)
Stroock & Stroock & Lavan (Walter Pozen)

Drug Policy Foundation
4801 Massachusetts Ave., N.W. Suite 400, Washington, DC 20016
Telephone: (202) 895-1634
Background: A research and educational organization which favors legalization of certain currently illicit drugs.
Represented by:
Arnold S. Trebach, President
Kevin B. Zeese, V. President
Counsel or consultant:
Targeting Systems, Inc.

Drugfree Workplace Coalition
1023 15th St., N.W. 7th Floor, Washington, DC 20005
Telephone: (202) 289-1780
Counsel or consultant:
Rowland & Sellery (Terrie Dort, J. Patrick Rowland)

Drum Reconditioners Environmental Committee
1030 15th St., N.W., Washington, DC 20005
Telephone: (202) 296-8028
Background: The political action committee of NABADA. Contact is Daniel W. Barber of NABADA.

Drummond Co., Inc.
Birmingham, AL
Counsel or consultant:
Shaw, Pittman, Potts and Trowbridge (William Mike House)

Dry Color Manufacturers Ass'n
Box 20839, Alexandria, VA 22320
Telephone: (703) 684-4044
Represented by:
J. Lawrence Robinson, Exec. V. President

DSC Communications Corp.
Plano, TX
Counsel or consultant:
Dutko & Associates (Steve Perry)

DST Systems, Inc.
Kansas City, MO
Counsel or consultant:
Scootch Pankonin

Dublin-McCarter & Associates
San Antonio, TX
Counsel or consultant:
Steponkus and Associates (William P. Steponkus)

Ducks Unlimited Inc.
1155 Connecticut Ave., N.W., Suite 800, Washington, DC 20036
Telephone: (202) 452-8824
Represented by:
Scott Sutherland, Director, Federal Relations

Duferco Ltd.
New York, NY
Counsel or consultant:
Willkie Farr and Gallagher (Walter J. Spak)

Duke Power Co.
Charlotte, NC
Counsel or consultant:
Donelan, Cleary, Wood and Maser, P.C. (John F. Donelan)

Duke University
Durham, NC
Counsel or consultant:
Sutherland, Asbill and Brennan

Dulles Area Rapid Transit, Inc.
McLean, VA
Counsel or consultant:
Direct Impact Co., The (John Brady, Tom Herrity)

Dulles Area Transportation Ass'n
13873 Park Center Road, Herndon, VA 22071
Telephone: (703) 689-9589
Background: Represented by Katherine Hooper of the Committee for Dulles.

Duluth, Minnesota, City of
Counsel or consultant:
Nat'l Center for Municipal Development (Richard C. Johnson)

Dump Transport Industries Ass'n
1001 Connecticut Ave., N.W. Suite 528, Washington, DC 20036
Telephone: (202) 296-2207
Counsel or consultant:
Dan Botkiss and Assoc. (Daniel A. Botkiss)

Dun & Bradstreet
600 Maryland Ave., S.W., Suite 240, Washington, DC 20024
Telephone: (202) 484-7381

Represented by:
Michael F. Brewer, V. President, Government Affairs
Jean Cantrell, Manager, Government Affairs
Gary Friend, Director, Corporate Government Services
Counsel or consultant:
Beckerman Associates (George Beckerman)
Reed Smith Shaw & McClay (William A. Geoghegan)
Willkie Farr and Gallagher (Sue D. Blumenfeld, Philip L. Verveer, Theodore C. Whitehouse)

Dunigan Companies
Abilene, TX
Counsel or consultant:
Baker, Worthington, Crossley, Stansberry & Woolf (W. Lee Rawls)

Dunkin' Donuts
Randolph, MA
Counsel or consultant:
Ropes and Gray (Thomas M. Susman)

du Pont de Nemours and Co., E. I.
1701 Pennsylvania Ave., N.W., Suite 900, Washington, DC 20006
Telephone: (202) 728-3600
Represented by:
Robert Heine, Sr. Washington Representative
Kenneth Jacobson, Public Affairs Manager
Nancie Johnson, Manager, Internat'l Trade & Investment
Stacey J. Mobley, V. President, Federal Affairs
Mark D. Nelson, Washington Counsel
Tom Sellers, Washington Representative
Michael O. Ware, Director, Legislative Affairs
Ellan K. Wharton, Washington Counsel
Counsel or consultant:
Burson-Marsteller (Carolyn Tieger)
Covington and Burling (Daniel M. Gribbon)
Daniel J. Edelman, Inc. (Joanna Hanes)
Jefferson Group, The (John Coy)
Wilmer, Cutler and Pickering (John D. Greenwald, Daniel Marcus)
Winburn, VanScoyoc, and Hooper (H. Stewart VanScoyoc)

Duquesne Light Co.
Pittsburgh, PA
Counsel or consultant:
Shaw, Pittman, Potts and Trowbridge (Gerald Charnoff, Jay E. Silberg)

Duracell Inc.
Bethel, CT
Counsel or consultant:
Foley & Lardner (James N. Bierman)

Duramed Pharmaceuticals, Inc.
Cincinnati, OH
Counsel or consultant:
Olsson, Frank and Weeda, P.C. (John Bode)

Duty Free Shoppers Group Limited
San Francisco, CA
Counsel or consultant:
Patton, Boggs and Blow (Stuart M. Pape)

DynCorp
2000 Edmund Halley Dr., Reston, VA 22091
Telephone: (703) 264-0330
Counsel or consultant:
Richard Olson & Assoc. (Richard C. Olson)

DynCorp Federal Political Action Committee
2000 Edmund Halley Drive, Reston, VA 22091
Telephone: (703) 264-9202
Counsel or consultant:
Richard Olson & Assoc. (Richard C. Olson)

E-Systems, Inc.
1901 North Moore St. Suite 609, Arlington, VA 22209
Telephone: (703) 524-2310
Represented by:
W. R. McClain, V. President, Gov't and Int'l Operations
Michael M. McMillan, V. President, Internat'l Operations

E Z America Ltd.
Irvine, CA
Counsel or consultant:
APCO Associates (Kevin G. Nealer)

Eagle Canyon Ranch
Jacksonville, OR

ORGANIZATIONS REPRESENTED

Eagle Canyon Ranch (Cont'd)
Counsel or consultant:
Roberts & Co. (Richard R. Roberts)

Eagle Forum
316 Pennsylvania Ave., S.E. Suite 203, Washington, DC 20003
Telephone: (202) 544-0353
Background: Organization headed by Phyllis Schlafly which promotes policies to support and protect the family, homemakers' benefits, better education and a strong national defense.
Represented by:
Susan Brackin, Exec. Director
Counsel or consultant:
Griffin Communications (Frances Griffin)

Eagle-Picher Industries
Cincinnati, OH
Counsel or consultant:
Chambers Associates Incorporated (Letitia Chambers)
Crowell and Moring (Victor E. Schwartz)
The Hoving Group (John H. F. Hoving)
Spriggs & Hollingsworth (William J. Spriggs)
Gene Taylor Assoc, Inc. (Gene Taylor)

Early Winters Resort
Methow, WA
Counsel or consultant:
Garvey, Schubert & Barer (Alan A. Butchman)

Earth Corps
750 17th St., N.W., Suite 1100, Washington, DC 20006
Telephone: (202) 778-2371
Counsel or consultant:
Jensen & Co. (Michael G. Brown, Ronald R. Jensen)

Earth Day
1301-1A Connecticut Ave., N.W., Washington, DC 20036
Telephone: (202) 331-3329
Represented by:
Mark Valentine, Issues Director

Earth Observation Satellite Co.
Lanham, MD
Counsel or consultant:
Global USA, Inc. (George S. Kopp)

Earth Satellite Corp.
7222 47th St., Chevy Chase, MD 20815
Telephone: (301) 951-0104
Represented by:
J. Robert Porter, Jr., President

Earthquake Project, The
Boston, MA
Counsel or consultant:
Arnold & Porter (John M. Quinn)
David A. Jewell & Associates (David A. Jewell)
Preston Gates Ellis & Rouvelas Meeds (Lloyd Meeds, Tim L. Peckinpaugh)

East Asiatic Co. Ltd.
San Francisco, CA
Counsel or consultant:
Warren and Associates (George A. Quadrino, Charles F. Warren)

East Ohio Gas Co.
Cleveland, OH
Background: A subsidiary of the Consolidated Natural Gas Co. Represented by Beverly E. Jones of the parent company.

East Tennessee Natural Gas Co.
Knoxville, TN
Counsel or consultant:
Wright and Talisman

Eastern Air Lines
Miami, FL
Counsel or consultant:
Akin, Gump, Strauss, Hauer and Feld (Joel Jankowsky)
Anderson, Hibey, Nauheim and Blair (Stanton D. Anderson)
Marshall S. Filler, P.C.
Kaye, Scholer, Fierman, Hays and Handler (Christopher R. Brewster)
Shaw, Pittman, Potts and Trowbridge

Eastern Band of Cherokee Indians
Cherokee, NC
Counsel or consultant:
Karl A. Funke and Associates (Karl A. Funke)

Eastern Caribbean Investment Promotion Service
1730 M St., N.W., Suite 901, Washington, DC 20036
Telephone: (202) 659-8689
Background: A joint economic development promotion effort of the Organization of Eastern Caribbean States: Antigua and Barbuda, Dominica, Grenada, Montserrat, St. Kitts/Nevis, St. Lucia, St. Vincent and the Grenadines and the British Virgin Islands.
Represented by:
Swinburne A.S. Lestrade, Exec. Director

Eastern Central Motor Carriers Ass'n
Akron, OH
Counsel or consultant:
Douglass W. Svendson, Jr.

Eastern Coal Transportation Conference
1224 17th St., N.W., Washington, DC 20036
Telephone: (202) 347-7170
Background: An association of eastern coal producers, sellers, and exporters.
Counsel or consultant:
Slover and Loftus

Eastern Enterprises
Weston, MA
Counsel or consultant:
Ropes and Gray (Thomas M. Susman)

Eastern Michigan University
Ypsilanti, MI
Counsel or consultant:
O'Connor & Hannan (Thomas R. Jolly)

Eastern Shore Natural Gas Co.
Salisbury, MD
Counsel or consultant:
Morgan, Lewis and Bockius

Eastern Technologies, Ltd.
Lynnfield, MA
Counsel or consultant:
Cambridge Internat'l, Inc. (Justus P. White)

Eastern Utilities Associates
Bridgewater, MA
Counsel or consultant:
Paul, Hastings, Janofsky and Walker (Charles A. Patrizia)

Eastman Kodak Co.
1776 Eye St., N.W., Suite 1050, Washington, DC 20006
Telephone: (202) 857-3400
Represented by:
John J. Coogan, Director, Health Affairs
Wells Denyes, Director, Federal Gov't Rtns & V. Pres.
David B. Hickerson, Washington Rep., Human Resource Affairs
David M. Kiser, Manager Environmental Affairs
Sandra Masur, Director, Public Policy Analysis
R. K. Rushin, Director, Chemical Industries Affairs
Suzanne Welch, Manager, Information Industry Affairs
Counsel or consultant:
The Susan Davis Companies

Eastman Savings & Loan Ass'n
Rochester, NY
Counsel or consultant:
Nixon, Hargrave, Devans and Doyle (Stephen Kurzman)

Eaton Corp.
1100 Connecticut Ave., N.W., Suite 410, Washington, DC 20036
Telephone: (202) 955-6444
Represented by:
Jon A. Anderson, Director, Federal Affairs
John W. Hushen, V. President, Government Relations
David C. Simons, Manager, Congressional Relations

Ebasco Services, Inc.
1025 Connecticut Ave., N.W. Suite 1014, Washington, DC 20036
Telephone: (202) 872-1352
Background: Ebasco provides energy, environment, infrastructure, advanced technology, and quality assurance services to government and industry.

Represented by:
Robert J. Blackwell, Dir., Fed. Relats. & Mktg. -Mil & Space
James U. DeFrancis, V. President, Corporate Relations
Counsel or consultant:
Baker, Worthington, Crossley, Stansberry & Woolf (III J. E. Murdock)

Eberhard Manufacturing
Cleveland, OH
Counsel or consultant:
Interlocke Associates

ECO Corp.
Toronto, Ontario
Counsel or consultant:
Anderson, Hibey, Nauheim and Blair (Robert A. Blair)

Ecolab
St. Paul, MN
Counsel or consultant:
Robins, Kaplan, Miller & Ciresi (Pamela M. Deese)

Ecological and Toxicological Ass'n of the Dyestuffs Manufacturing Industry
1330 Connecticut Ave., N.W., Washington, DC 20036-1702
Telephone: (202) 659-0060
Background: Formed to address health and environmental issues associated with dyes.
Represented by:
Dr. C. Tucker Helmes, Exec. Director

Ecology & Environment, Inc.
Lancaster, NY
Counsel or consultant:
Braun & Company

Ecomarine, Inc.
New York, NY
Counsel or consultant:
O'Connor & Hannan (George J. Mannina, Jr.)

Economic Policy Institute
1424 16th St., N.W., Suite 501, Washington, DC 20036
Telephone: (202) 667-0400
Background: An economics think-tank described as a liberal alternative to such conservative organizations as the Heritage Foundation.
Represented by:
Robert Blecker, Research Economist
Jeff Faux, President
Roger Hickey, V. President, Public Affairs
Lawrence R. Mishel, Research Director
Edith Rassel, Research Associate

Economic Strategy Institute
1100 Connecticut Ave., N.W. Suite 330, Washington, DC 20036
Telephone: (202) 728-0993
Represented by:
Kevin L. Kearns, Fellow
Clyde Prestowitz, Jr., President

Economy Fastners, Inc.
Hauppauge, NY
Counsel or consultant:
U.S. Strategies Corp. (Joseph H. Miltenberger)

Edelstahlwerke Buderus AG
Germany
Counsel or consultant:
Coudert Brothers (Milo C. Coerper)

Edgcomb Corp.
Bensalem, PA
Counsel or consultant:
Dewey, Ballantine, Bushby, Palmer and Wood (John J. Salmon)

Edgell Communications
Cleveland, OH
Counsel or consultant:
Dunaway & Cross (Mac S. Dunaway)

Edison Electric Institute
1111 19th St., N.W., Washington, DC 20036
Telephone: (202) 778-6400

ORGANIZATIONS REPRESENTED

Represented by:
Eric Ackerman, Manager, Regulatory Policy
Edwin Anthony, V. Pres., Corp. Affairs & Member Rtns.
Robert Beck, Director, Environmental Programs
Julia Blankenship, Legislative Affairs Representative
Judith Ann Boddie, Senior Legislative Representative
M. William Brier, V. President, Communications
Fred G. Davis, Director, Legislative Affairs (Nuclear)
Bruce S. Edelston, Director, Public Policy
Gordon H. Fry, Manager, State-Local Gov't Relations
Bruce G. Humphrey, Assistant to the President, Strat.
 Plng.
Peter B. Kelsey, V. President, Law & Coprorate Secretary
Mary Kenkel, Public Information Representative
Thomas R. Kuhn, President
Loring E. Mills, V. President, Nuclear Activities
Walker F. Nolan, Sr. V. President, Government Affairs
David K. Owens, V. President, Power Supply Policy
Edward W. Rissing, Director, Federal Affairs
Andre W. Robart, Director, Legislative Affairs (Envir.)
Andrew W. Robart, Dir., Environmental Legislative Af-
 fairs
John Shlaes, Director of Planning, Gov't Affairs
Kathryn A. Steckelberg, Legislative Representative
Edward R. Yawn, Sr. Legislative Affairs Representative
Counsel or consultant:
Andrews' Associates, Inc. (Mark Andrews, Jacqueline
 Balk-Tusa)
Black, Manafort, Stone and Kelly Public Affairs Co.
 (Nicholas A. Panuzio)
George H. Denison
Manatt, Phelps, Rothenberg & Phillips (June L. Walton)
Marlowe and Co.
McNair Law Firm, P.A. (James McIntyre, Jr.)
Nossaman, Guthner, Knox and Elliott (Murray Zweben)
Reid & Priest (Raymond F. Dacek)

EDO Corp.
2001 Jefferson Davis Hwy. Suite 1000, Arlington, VA
 22202
Telephone: (703) 521-5260
Counsel or consultant:
Charles H. Cromwell Inc. (Charles H. Cromwell)

EDU-DYNE Systems, Inc.
Matawan, NJ
Counsel or consultant:
Manatt, Phelps, Rothenberg & Phillips (Robert T. Herbol-
 sheimer)

Education Commission of the States
444 North Capitol St., N.W. Suite 248, Washington, DC
 20001
Telephone: (202) 624-5838
Background: The Washington office of a Denver-based
 state compact.
Represented by:
Caroline Hickey, Washington Liaison
Counsel or consultant:
Gallagher-Widmeyer Group Inc., The (Scott D. Widmey-
 er)

Education Funding Research Council
1611 North Kent St. Suite 508, Arlington, VA 22209
Telephone: (703) 528-1082
Represented by:
James J. Marshall, President

Education and Research Institute
800 Maryland Ave., N.W., Washington, DC 20002
Telephone: (202) 546-1710
Represented by:
Whitney L. Ball, Finance Director
M. Stanton Evans, Chairman

Education Week
4301 Connecticut Ave., N.W. Suite 250, Washington, DC
 20008
Telephone: (202) 364-4114
Counsel or consultant:
Gallagher-Widmeyer Group Inc., The (Scott D. Widmeyer)

Educational Clinics Inc.
Seattle, WA
Counsel or consultant:
Denny Miller Associates

Educational Fund to End Handgun Violence
100 Maryland Ave., N.E., Washington, DC 20002

Telephone: (202) 544-7227
Represented by:
Joshua M. Horwitz, Legal Director

Educational Media
Oklahoma City, OK
Counsel or consultant:
Kaye, Scholer, Fierman, Hays and Handler (Christopher
 R. Brewster)

Educational Testing Service
Princeton, NJ
Counsel or consultant:
Wilmer, Cutler and Pickering

Educators' Ad Hoc Committee on Copyright Law
1680 Duke St., Alexandria, VA 22314
Telephone: (703) 838-6722
Background: Represented by August W. Steinhilber of the
 Nat'l School Boards Ass'n.

Edunetics
1611 N. Kent St. Suite 805, Arlington, VA 22209
Telephone: (703) 243-2602
Counsel or consultant:
Gallagher-Widmeyer Group Inc., The (Scott D. Widmey-
 er)

EG&G, Inc.
1850 K St., N.W., Suite 1190, Washington, DC 20006
Telephone: (202) 887-5570
Represented by:
Roger Arias, Corp. Dir., Gov't Business Development
Philip C. Kautt, V. President
Karin Rindal, Corp. Mgr., Internat'l Trade Regulation
Bridget Serchak, Ass't for Gov't Information Services

Egypt, Embassy of
2310 Decatur Pl., N.W., Washington, DC 20008
Telephone: (202) 232-5400
Counsel or consultant:
Bannerman and Associates, Inc.
Brownrigg and Muldoon
Patton, Boggs and Blow

Egypt, Government of
Cairo, Egypt
Counsel or consultant:
Bannerman and Associates, Inc. (M. Graeme Bannerman)

Eklutna, Inc.
Anchorage, AK
Counsel or consultant:
Wyman, Bautzer, Christensen, Kuchel and Silbert

El Al Israel Airlines, Ltd.
Tel Aviv, Israel
Counsel or consultant:
Winthrop, Stimson, Putnam & Roberts (Robert Reed
 Gray)

El Paso Natural Gas Co.
El Paso, TX
Counsel or consultant:
Andrews and Kurth (Richard Green, Rush Moody, Jr.)

El Salvador Freedom Foundation
San Salvador, El Salvador
Counsel or consultant:
MacKenzie McCheyne, Inc. (I. R. MacKenzie, Ana Colo-
 mar O'Brien)

El Salvador, Government of
San Salvador, El Salvador
Counsel or consultant:
O'Connor & Hannan (Joseph H. Blatchford)

Elanco Products Co.
Indianapolis, IN
Counsel or consultant:
McMillan and Farrell Associates (C. W. McMillan)

Elbit Inc./Inframetrics, Inc.
Boston, MA
Background: A manufacturer of military computers and in-
 fared sensors.
Counsel or consultant:
Morris J. Amitay, P.C.

Elders Grain, Inc.
Overland Park, KS

Counsel or consultant:
Arent, Fox, Kintner, Plotkin & Kahn (Eugene J. Meigher)
Vickers & Vickers (Eugene B. Vickers)

Elections Research Center
5508 Greystone St., Chevy Chase, MD 20815
Telephone: (301) 654-3540
Represented by:
Richard M. Scammon, Director

Electric Power Development Co., Ltd.
1825 K St., N.W., Suite 1205, Washington, DC 20006
Telephone: (202) 429-0670
Represented by:
Tadahisa Miyasaka, Chief Representative

Electric Power Research Institute
1019 19th St., N.W., Washington, DC 20036
Telephone: (202) 872-9222
Represented by:
James R. Johnson, Acting Manager, Washington Office

Electrical Construction PAC-Nat'l Electrical Con-
tractors As'n (ECPAC)
7315 Wisconsin Ave., 13th Fl., Bethesda, MD 20814
Telephone: (301) 657-3110
Background: Represented by Robert L. White, Jr. of the
 Ass'n.

Electricity Consumers Resource Council
1333 H St., N.W., West Tower - 8th Fl., Washington, DC
 20005
Telephone: (202) 466-4686
Background: Established in January, 1976 by a number of
 industrial consumers of electricity who support regulatory
 practices that assure adequate supplies of electricity at
 prices based on cost of service.
Represented by:
John A. Anderson, Exec. Director
John Hughes, Technical Affairs Director
Counsel or consultant:
Cleary, Gottlieb, Steen and Hamilton (Sara D. Schotland)
E. Bruce Harrison Co. (Steven B. Hellem)

Electro- & Electronik Appartebau Gesellschaft
mbH
Nachrodt, West Germany
Counsel or consultant:
Leva, Hawes, Mason and Martin (Lowell D. Turnbull)

ElectroCom Automation, Inc.
Arlington, TX
Counsel or consultant:
Jack L. Williams

Electromagnetic Energy Policy Alliance
1255 23rd St., N.W. Suite 850, Washington, DC 20037
Telephone: (202) 452-8100
Background: Founding members include AT&T Bell Labs,
 GTE Corp., MCI Corp., Motorola, Raytheon, RCA,
 Rockwell International and the National Association of
 Broadcasters.
Counsel or consultant:
Hauck and Associates (Richard H. Ekfelt)

Electronic Data Interchange Ass'n
225 Reinekers Lane Suite 550, Alexandria, VA 22314
Telephone: (703) 838-8042
Represented by:
Catherine A. Kachurik, Director, Internat'l & Gov't Rela-
 tions

Electronic Data Processing Auditors Ass'n
Carol Stream, IL
Counsel or consultant:
O'Connor & Hannan (Timothy M. Haake)

Electronic Data Systems Corp.
1331 Pennsylvania Ave., N.W., Suite 1300 North, Washington, DC 20004
Telephone: (202) 637-6700

The listings in this directory are available as *Mailing Labels.* See last page.

ORGANIZATIONS REPRESENTED

Electronic Data Systems Corp. (Cont'd)
Represented by:
Stephen E. Chertoff, Government Affairs Representative
Alexandra Cook, Government Affairs Representative
Carla M. Dancy, International Affairs Representative
Fred Gebler, III, Government Affairs Representative
Chuck Jiggetts, Government Affairs Representative
John D. Lacopo, V. Pres., Office of Government Affairs
John Lynn, Government Affairs Representative
Allen Miller, Government Affairs Representative
Karen Magee Myers, Government Affairs Representative
Sharon O'Malley, Director of Public Affairs
Penny Parqueri, State & Local Gov't Relatns Coordinator
Donald S. Picard, Counsel
Dana Theus, Government Affairs Representative
Monica Welch, Government Affairs Representative
Counsel or consultant:
Gold and Liebengood, Inc. (John F. Scruggs)
O'Connor & Hannan
Washington Resources and Strategy, Inc. (William R. Sweeney, Jr.)

Electronic Funds Transfer Ass'n
1421 Prince St., Suite 310, Alexandria, VA 22314
Telephone: (703) 549-9800
Represented by:
Sean W. Kennedy, President and CEO

Electronic Industries Ass'n
2001 Pennsylvania Ave., N.W., Washington, DC 20006
Telephone: (202) 457-4900
Represented by:
Jean A. Caffiaux, Senior V. President, Government Div.
Jeanne N. Chircop, Mgr., Communications, Consumer Group
Tom Friel, Group V. President, Consumer Group
Suzanne M. Heaton, Staff Dir., Gov't Affairs, Consumer Grp.
Dan C. Heinemeier, Exec. Director, Government Relations
Kim King, Communications Coordinator, Consumer Grp
John M. Kinn, Staff V. Pres., Engineering Department
Lisa K. Kjaer, Exec. Director, Government Relations
Tom Lauterback, Staff V. Pres., Commo., Consumer Group
Kathryn A. McCarl, Mgr. Gov't Affairs, Consumer Group
Peter F. McCloskey, President
David Poisson, Exec. Director, Government Affairs
Kevin C. Richardson, Staff V. President, Government Relations
James E. Riley, Senior V. President and General Counsel
Mark V. Rosenker, V. President of Public Affairs
Ella M. Schiralli, Staff Associate, Government Relations
Kevin J. Shannon, Senior Staff Associate, Gov't Rlations
Gary J. Shapiro, V. President and General Counsel
Cynthia Upson, Director, Communications, Consumer Group
Counsel or consultant:
Miller & Chevalier, Chartered (Anne E. Moran)

Electronic Industries Ass'n of Japan
Tokyo, Japan
Counsel or consultant:
Anderson, Hibey, Nauheim and Blair (Stanton D. Anderson)
Hill and Knowlton Public Affairs Worldwide (Mary C. Foerster)
McDermott, Will and Emery (Robert S. Schwartz)
Mudge Rose Guthrie Alexander and Ferdon (William N. Walker)
Reese Communications Companies
Saunders and Company (Pete Salavantis)
Tanaka, Ritger and Middleton (B. Jenkins Middleton, H. William Tanaka)

Electronic Industries Ass'n of Korea
Seoul, Korea
Counsel or consultant:
Hill and Knowlton Public Affairs Worldwide (Stephen H. Meeter)

Electronic Mail Ass'n
1555 Wilson Blvd., Suite 555, Arlington, VA 22209
Telephone: (703) 522-7111
Represented by:
Michael F. Cavanagh, Exec. Director

Eliminate the Nat'l Debt (END)
P.O. Box 1807, Washington, DC 20013

Telephone: (202) 546-7000
Background: A volunteer effort to encourage reduction of the national debt.
Counsel or consultant:
Bonsib, Inc. (L. W. "Bill" Bonsib)

Elkem Metals Co.
Pittsburgh, PA
Counsel or consultant:
Robert N. Pyle & Associates

Elkhart, Indiana, City of
Elkhart, IN
Counsel or consultant:
Simon & Co., Inc. (Leonard S. Simon)

Ellerbe-Becket Architects, Inc.
Bloomington, MN
Counsel or consultant:
Charles G. Botsford Office (Charles G. Botsford)

Elligson Review Seminars, Inc.
P.O. Box 10621, Rockville, MD 20850
Telephone: (301) 340-0066
Counsel or consultant:
RPH & Associates

Elmont AG
St. Gallen, Switzerland
Counsel or consultant:
Berliner and Maloney (Clemens J. Kochinke)

Elsevier U.S. Holdings, Inc.
4520 East-West Highway Suite 800, Bethesda, MD 20814
Telephone: (301) 654-1550
Represented by:
Paul P. Massa, President
Counsel or consultant:
Prather, Seeger, Doolittle and Farmer (J. William Doolittle)

Eluma S/A Industria e Comercio
Sao Paolo, Brazil
Counsel or consultant:
L. A. Motley and Co.

Elyria Memorial Hospital and Medical Center
Elyria, OH
Counsel or consultant:
Baker and Hostetler (Frederick H. Graefe)

Embraer S.A.
Sao Paolo, Brazil
Background: A manufacturer and exporter of aviation products, 51 per cent owned by the Brazilian Government.
Counsel or consultant:
Santarelli, Smith, Kraut and Carroccio (Donald E. Santarelli)

Embry-Riddle Aeronautical University
Daytona Beach, FL
Counsel or consultant:
Sparkman and Cole, Inc. (D. Dean Sparkman)

Emergency Committee for American Trade
1211 Connecticut Ave., N.W. Suite 801, Washington, DC 20036
Telephone: (202) 659-5147
Background: A lobby for expanded international trade and investment composed of 65 chairmen of companies operating internationally.
Represented by:
Calman J. Cohen, Vice President
Robert L. McNeill, Exec. Vice Chairman
Counsel or consultant:
O'Melveny and Myers (Gary N. Horlick)

Emergency Medical Services Associates
Counsel or consultant:
Evans Group, Ltd., The (L. A., Skip Bafalis, Thomas B. Evans, Jr.)

Emergent Technologies, Inc.
San Jose, CA
Counsel or consultant:
Anderson and Pendleton, C.A. (Donald Whitehead)

Emerson Electric Co.
1235 Jefferson Davis Hwy., Suite 305, Arlington, VA 22202
Telephone: (703) 920-7600

Represented by:
Larry R. Brewer, Director, Legislative Affairs
John D. Cuaderes, Manager, Legislative Projects
Larry W. Shreve, V. President, Field Operations
Counsel or consultant:
Shaw, Pittman, Potts and Trowbridge (Ramsay D. Potts)

Emery Worldwide
Wilton, CT
Counsel or consultant:
Crowell and Moring (R. Bruce Keiner, Jr.)

Emhart Corp.
Hartford, CT
Counsel or consultant:
Burson-Marsteller (Paul T. Heilig, J. Gordon Stephens, Jr.)

Emhart Political Action Committee
1500 Planning Research Drive, McLean, VA 22102
Telephone: (703) 556-1520
Background: Responsible contact is Bert Concklin of Planning Research Corp.

EMILY'S List
2000 P St., N.W., Suite 412, Washington, DC 20036
Telephone: (202) 887-1957
Background: An acronym for Early Money Is Like Yeast, the group is a political action committee supporting Democratic women candidates.
Represented by:
Deborah Davis Hicks, Communications Director
Ellen R. Malcolm, President
Wendy R. Sherman, Exec. Director

Empire Blue Cross and Blue Shield
New York, NY
Counsel or consultant:
Paul Arneson, P.C. (Paul Arneson)
Wilkinson, Barker, Knauer and Quinn

Empire District Electric Co.
Joplin, MO
Counsel or consultant:
Dana W. Haas
Gene Taylor Assoc, Inc. (Gene Taylor)

Empire Gas Corp.
Lebanon, MO
Counsel or consultant:
Gene Taylor Assoc, Inc. (Gene Taylor)

Employee Benefit Research Institute
2121 K St., N.W., Suite 600, Washington, DC 20037-2121
Telephone: (202) 659-0670
Background: A private, non profit organization sponsored by corporations, associations and unions that conducts research and educational programs on employee benefit issues.
Represented by:
Laura Bos, Director, Education
Dallas L. Salisbury, President
Nora Syer, Education Associate
Counsel or consultant:
Arnold & Porter

Employee Relocation Council
1720 N St., N.W., Washington, DC 20036
Telephone: (202) 857-0857
Background: Organized in 1964 by a small group of companies who wished to lessen the impact of relocation on their employees' productivity, efficiency and morale. Now has about 13,000 members.
Represented by:
H. Cris Collie, Exec. V. President
Counsel or consultant:
Ivins, Phillips and Barker (Jay W. Glasmann, Alan D. Rumph)

Employee Stock Ownership Ass'n
1100 17th St., N.W. Suite 1207, Washington, DC 20036
Telephone: (202) 293-2971
Represented by:
David M. Binns, Exec. Director
Counsel or consultant:
Zuckert, Scoutt and Rasenberger (J. Michael Keeling)

Employee Stock Ownership Ass'n (ESOP) Political Action Committee
1100 17th St., N.W. Suite 1207, Washington, DC 20036
Telephone: (202) 293-2971

The listings in this directory are available as *Mailing Labels*. See last page.

ORGANIZATIONS REPRESENTED

Background: Represented by David M. Binns of the Employee Stock Ownership Ass'n.

Employers Council on Flexible Compensation
927 15th St., N.W., Suite 1000, Washington, DC 20005
Telephone: (202) 659-4300
Background: Established in 1981. Represents interests of 400 employers who favor retention of flexible compensation programs whereby employees are offered a variety of compensation and benefit arrangements from which they can select those most suitable to their needs.
Represented by:
Kenneth E. Feltman, Director
Counsel or consultant:
Seyfarth, Shaw, Fairweather and Geraldson (John N. Erlenborn)

Empresa Consolidada Cubana de Aviacion
Havana, Cuba
Counsel or consultant:
Zuckert, Scoutt and Rasenberger (James L. Devall)

Empresa de Transporte Aereo del Peru
Lima, Peru
Counsel or consultant:
Prather, Seeger, Doolittle and Farmer (Edwin H. Seeger)

End Notch Discrimination, Inc.
Arcadia, CA
Counsel or consultant:
Marlowe and Co.

Endicott, New York, Municipality of
Counsel or consultant:
Duncan, Weinberg, Miller & Pembroke, P.C. (Wallace L. Duncan, Jeffrey C. Genzer)

Endocrine Soc.
9650 Rockville Pike, Bethesda, MD 20814
Telephone: (301) 571-1802
Represented by:
Scott Hunt, Exec. Director
Counsel or consultant:
Capitol Associates, Inc. (Amy Kardell, Terry Lierman)

Energy Absorption Systems, Inc.
Chicago, IL
Counsel or consultant:
Bracy Williams & Co. (Susan J. Williams)

Energy Conservation Coalition
1525 New Hampshire Ave., N.W., Washington, DC 20036
Telephone: (202) 745-4870
Background: A project of Environmental Action Foundation. Through research and education, ECC promotes energy efficiency as part of an environmentally sound and cost effective solution to such problems as acid rain, global warming, smog and loss of wilderness areas. Exec. Director is Ruth Caplan of Environmental Action.
Represented by:
Nick Fedourk, Policy Director

Energy Contractors Price-Anderson Group
1752 N St., N.W., Suite 800, Washington, DC 20036
Telephone: (202) 822-9775
Background: An ad hoc group of government contractors. The address given is that of the law firm of Davis Wright Tremaine.
Counsel or consultant:
Davis Wright Tremaine (Omer F. Brown, II)

Energy Efficient Insulation Manufacturers
Clark, NJ
Counsel or consultant:
Shaw, Pittman, Potts and Trowbridge (William Mike House)

Energy Factors
San Diego, CA
Counsel or consultant:
Olwine, Connelly, Chase, O'Donnell and Weyher (W. Harrison Wellford)

Energy Fuels Nuclear, Inc.
Denver, CO
Counsel or consultant:
Van Ness, Feldman & Curtis (Alan L. Mintz)

Energy Research Corp.
1627 K St., N.W. Suite 403, Washington, DC 20006
Telephone: (202) 785-9321

Represented by:
Jack T. Brown, Director of Marketing
Donald R. Glenn, V. President
Counsel or consultant:
Gold and Liebengood, Inc. (William R. Ratchford)

Energy Research Corp. PAC
1627 K St., N.W., Suite 403, Washington, DC 20006
Telephone: (202) 955-9321
Background: PAC contact is Donald R. Glenn of the Energy Research Corp.

Engel Publications
West Trenton, NJ
Counsel or consultant:
William J. Tobin and Associates (William J. Tobin)

Engineers and Architects Ass'n
Los Angeles, CA
Counsel or consultant:
Lipsen Whitten & Diamond

Engineers' Political and Education Committee
1125 17th St., N.W., Washington, DC 20036
Telephone: (202) 429-9100
Background: Political action committee of the Internat'l Union of Operating Engineers.
Represented by:
Matt DeConcini, Legislative Representative

English First
8001 Forbes Place, Suite 102, Springfield, VA 22151
Telephone: (703) 321-8818
Represented by:
P. George Tryfiates, Exec. Director

Enid Joint Industrial Foundation
Enid, OK
Counsel or consultant:
Cassidy and Associates, Inc. (Pete W. Glavas)

Enron Corp.
1020 16th St., N.W., Washington, DC 20036-5754
Telephone: (202) 828-3360
Background: Formerly HNG/Internorth.
Represented by:
Cynthia C. Anderson, Director, Federal Government Affairs
Ellen Gay Baker, Mgr., Regul. Affrs. (Enron/Interstate)
Donna Fulton, Regulatory Specialist (Enron/Interstate)
Edward J. Hillings, V. President, Fed. Gov't Affairs
Counsel or consultant:
Akin, Gump, Strauss, Hauer and Feld
Bracewell and Patterson (Gene E. Godley)
Gallagher, Boland, Meiburger and Brosnan (Frank X. Kelly, George J. Meiburger)
Nancy Whorton George & Associates, P.C. (Nancy Whorton George)
Skadden, Arps, Slate, Meagher and Flom (Lynn R. Coleman, Mike Naeve)
Charls E. Walker Associates

Ensco Fund for Safer Waste Treatment
211 North Union St., Suite 100, Alexandria, VA 22314
Telephone: (703) 549-5528
Background: The political action arm of Ensco-Environmental Systems Co.
Represented by:
Douglas MacMillan, Treasurer

ENSERCH Corp.
1025 Connecticut Ave., N.W., Suite 1014, Washington, DC 20036
Telephone: (202) 872-1352
Represented by:
Robert E. Ebel, V. President International Affairs
David A. Raymond, Director, International Programs
Kerrill Scrivner, Director, Federal Relations
Counsel or consultant:
Edward H. Forgotson
Lipsen Whitten & Diamond
Vinson and Elkins (John E. Chapoton)

Entergy Corp.
1776 Eye St., N.W., Suite 275, Washington, DC 20006
Telephone: (202) 785-8444

Represented by:
S.M. Henry Brown, Jr., V. President, Governmental Affairs
Jana R. Oakley, Director, Federal Governmental Affairs
Counsel or consultant:
Birch, Horton, Bittner and Cherot (William M. Bumpers)
Mayer, Brown and Platt (William L. Massey)
Reid & Priest (Richard M. Merriman)

Enterprise Bank
Fairfax, VA
Counsel or consultant:
Elias, Matz, Tiernan and Herrick (Allin P. Baxter)

Entertainment America
New York, NY
Counsel or consultant:
Gilbert A. Robinson, Inc. (Gilbert A. Robinson)

Entex, Inc.
Houston, TX
Counsel or consultant:
Elias, Matz, Tiernan and Herrick

Entomological Soc. of America
9301 Annapolis Rd., Lanham, MD 20706-3115
Telephone: (301) 731-4535
Represented by:
W. Darryl Hansen, Exec. Director
Dr. James Oliver, President

Envases de Plastico, S.A. de C.V.
Mexico City, Mexico
Counsel or consultant:
Dow, Lohnes and Albertson (William Silverman)

Envelope Manufacturers Ass'n
1600 Duke St., Suite 440, Alexandria, VA 22314-3421
Telephone: (703) 739-2200
Represented by:
Maynard H. Benjamin, Exec. V. President

Environmental Action
1525 New Hampshire Ave., N.W., Washington, DC 20036
Telephone: (202) 745-4870
Background: A non-profit lobbying organization, founded by the organizers of Earth Day in April 1970, active in legislative areas of clean air, the greenhouse effect, nuclear energy, solid waste management, toxic substances, energy conservation and pollution control and clean up.
Represented by:
Ruth Caplan, Exec. Director
David Goeller, Media Coordinator
Scott Hempling, Legislative Representative
Leon Lowery, Legislative Representative
Casey Scott Padgett, Legislative Rep., Toxics Project
Counsel or consultant:
Drusilla Schmidt-Perkins

Environmental Action Foundation
1525 New Hampshire Ave., N.W., Washington, DC 20036
Telephone: (202) 745-4870
Background: An independent, tax-exempt organization founded by the organizers of the first Earth Day in 1970 to promote environmental protection through research, public education, grass roots organizing assistance and legal action. Work is focused in five major areas: toxic pollution, safe energy, plastics waste, recycling and energy conservation. Services include working with citizens and community organizations and developing public policy analysis, research and background materials on a variety of related topics. Exec. Director is Ruth Caplan of Environmental Action.

Environmental Action's Political Action Committee (ENACT/PAC)
1525 New Hampshire Ave., N.W., Washington, DC 20036
Telephone: (202) 745-4870
Background: Works to elect pro-environment candidates. Designates the 'Dirty Dozen', a list of office holders who have harmed the environment. Treasurer of the PAC is Leon Lowery of Environmental Action.
Represented by:
Paul A. Friedman, Political Director

Environmental Air Control Inc.
Hagerstown, MD
Counsel or consultant:
Wunder, Ryan, Cannon & Thelen (Kenneth S. Levine)

ORGANIZATIONS REPRESENTED

Environmental Business Ass'n, The
4400 Jennifer St, N.W. Suite 310, Washington, DC 20015
Telephone: (202) 966-0006
Background: A trade association of business or professional service firms which are involved in consulting or contracting work related to environmental clean-up or preserving a healthy environment.
Counsel or consultant:
William Bode and Associates (William Bode)

Environmental Defense Fund
1616 P St., N.W., Suite 150, Washington, DC 20036
Telephone: (202) 387-3500
Background: A national membership organization staffed by scientists, economists and attorneys whose purpose is to protect environmental quality and public health. EDF'S efforts are concentrated in four main areas: energy, toxic chemicals, water resources, and wildlife. Offices are maintained in New York City; Berkeley, CA; Boulder, CO; and Richmond, VA. Methods include scientific research, litigation, public education, and community organization.
Represented by:
Michael Bean, Director, Wildlife Program
Karen Florini, Senior Staff Attorney, Toxics Program
Bruce Rich, Director, International Program
William J. Roberts, Senior Attorney
Dr. Ellen Silbergeld, Chairperson, Toxics Program
Lori Udall, Staff Attorney

Environmental Design Corp.
Manassas, VA
Counsel or consultant:
Ruland Associates, Inc. (James K. Ruland)

Environmental and Energy Study Institute
122 C St., N.W., Suite 700, Washington, DC 20001
Telephone: (202) 628-1400
Represented by:
Ken Murphy, Exec. Director
Counsel or consultant:
Hartnett & Associates (Douglas Hartnett)

Environmental Federation of America
3007 Tilden St., N.W. Suite 4L, Washington, DC 20008
Telephone: (202) 537-7100
Background: A coalition of 18 environment groups formed to increase their share of on-the-job fund raising campaigns.
Represented by:
Melissa Hippler, Secretary

Environmental Industry Council
1825 K St., N.W. Suite 210, Washington, DC 20006
Telephone: (202) 331-7706
Background: An organization representing all industries that produce environment protection equipment such as catalytic converters, scrubbers, and water pollution control equipment.
Counsel or consultant:
John Adams Associates

Environmental Law Institute
1616 P St., N.W., Suite 200, Washington, DC 20036
Telephone: (202) 328-5150
Background: Maintains a program of research into current developments in environmental law and policy, provides a legal document service, and publishes journals for the bar, scholars, managers, public officials and other environmental affairs professionals.
Represented by:
Barry Breen, Director of Publications
J. William Futrell, President
Peter Gray, Economist and Policy Analyst
Erik J. Meyers, General Counsel
Dan Moshavi, Director, Communications
Elissa Parker, Director of Research

Environmental Power Corp.
Boston, MA
Counsel or consultant:
Legislative Strategies Inc. (Raymond F. Bragg, Jr.)

Environmental Research Center, University of Nervada/Las Vegas
Las Vegas, NV
Counsel or consultant:
McAuliffe, Kelly, Raffaelli & Siemens (Edward E. Allison)

Environmental Sciences Ass'n
511 Capitol Court, N.E. Suite 300, Washington, DC 20002
Telephone: (202) 544-7499
Counsel or consultant:
Health and Medicine Counsel of Washington (Dale P. Dirks)

Envirotech Operating Services, Inc.
Birmingham, AL
Counsel or consultant:
U.S. Strategies Corp. (K. Michael Matthews)

EPIC Healthcare Group, Inc.
Irving, TX
Counsel or consultant:
Johnson & Gibbs, P.C. (David G. Glickman)

Epilepsy Foundation of America
4351 Garden City Drive, Landover, MD 20785
Telephone: (301) 459-3700
Represented by:
William M. McLin, Exec. V. President
Richard Nugent, Director of Government Liaison

Episcopal Church, Washington Office of the
110 Maryland Ave., N.E. Suite 309, Washington, DC 20002
Telephone: (202) 547-7300
Represented by:
Father Robert J. Brooks, Presiding Bishop's Staff Officer
Dr. Betty A. Coats, Presiding Bishop's Staff Officer

Epoc Water, Inc.
Fresno, CA
Counsel or consultant:
McAuliffe, Kelly, Raffaelli & Siemens (Lynnette R. Jacquez)

Epstein Becker and Green Political Committee
1227 25th St., N.W., Suite 700, Washington, DC 20037
Telephone: (202) 861-0900
Counsel or consultant:
Epstein Becker and Green

Equal Employment Advisory Council
1015 15th St., N.W. Suite 1200, Washington, DC 20005
Telephone: (202) 789-8650
Background: Organized in 1976 with a membership of companies and trade and business associations to present the views of employers in the development and implementation by the government of "equal opportunity" policies and procedures.
Counsel or consultant:
McGuiness and Williams (Lorence L. Kessler, Douglas S. McDowell, Jeffrey A. Norris)

Equifax Inc.
Atlanta, GA
Counsel or consultant:
Ginn, Edington, Moore and Wade
Sutherland, Asbill and Brennan (Wright H. Andrews, Jr., Francis M. Gregory, Jr.)

Equimark Corp.
Pittsburgh, PA
Counsel or consultant:
Rose, Schmidt, Hasley & DiSalle (Michael G. Kushnick)

Equitable Life Assurance Soc. of the U.S.
1700 Pennsylvania Ave., N.W., Suite 525, Washington, DC 20006
Telephone: (202) 393-3210
Represented by:
Carolyn A. Boyer, V. President & Associate Counsel
Kimberly R. Kynoch, PAC Director
Laura Luther, Legislative Assistant
William C. Mattox, V. President and Dir., Federal Relations
Susan Maxim, Staff Assistant
Laura Van Etten, V. President & Associate Counsel
Pamela Vukmer, Exec. Assistant
Counsel or consultant:
Gold and Liebengood, Inc. (Denise A. Bode)
van Kloberg and Associates (Edward J. van Kloberg, III)
The Whalen Company, Inc. (David W. Secrest, Richard J. Whalen)

Erie Islands Resort and Marina
Youngstown, OH
Counsel or consultant:
Dow, Lohnes and Albertson (Robert M. Chasnow)

Erie Lackawanna Railway Co.
Cleveland, OH
Counsel or consultant:
Mudge Rose Guthrie Alexander and Ferdon

Erie, Pennsylvania, City of
Counsel or consultant:
Simon & Co., Inc. (Leonard S. Simon)

ERISA Industry Committee (ERIC), The
1726 M St., N.W., Suite 1101, Washington, DC 20036
Telephone: (202) 833-2800
Background: Represents the employee benefit and retirement security interests of America's major enterprises. Members administer private sector retirement, health plans and other benefits for some 10 million active and retired workers and their beneficiaries.
Represented by:
Janice M. Gregory, Legislative Director
Marjorie N. Taylor, Director of Communications
Mark J. Ugoretz, Exec. Director
Counsel or consultant:
Covington and Burling (John M. Vine)

Eritrean People's Liberation Front
1418 15th St., N.W., Suite 1, Washington, DC 20005
Telephone: (202) 234-9282
Represented by:
Hagos Ghebrehiwep, Exec. Director

Ernst & Whinney Political Action Committee
1200 19th St., N.W., Suite 400, Washington, DC 20036
Telephone: (202) 862-9395
Background: A political action committee of Ernst & Young. Assistant Treasurer is John E. Toole of Ernst & Young's Washington government relations office.

Ernst & Young
1200 19th St., N.W., Suite 400, Washington, DC 20036
Telephone: (202) 862-9300
Represented by:
David Franasiak, Senior Manager, Government Relations
Thomas V. Fritz, V. Chairman, Government Relations
John E. Toole, Senior Manager, Government Relations
Counsel or consultant:
Daniel J. Edelman, Inc. (Christopher Gidez)

Escrow Institute of California
Irvine, CA
Counsel or consultant:
Smith and Howard Associates, Inc. (Irving P. Smith)

Espanola del Zinc, S.A.
Madrid, Spain
Counsel or consultant:
George V. Egge, Jr.

Ethics and Public Policy Center
1030 15th St., N.W. Suite 300, Washington, DC 20005
Telephone: (202) 682-1200
Background: An independent research and education organization established in 1976 and affiliated with Georgetown University until 1980. Does research and publishes studies on major national and international issues while affirming political relevance of fundamental Western ethical standards and giving special attention to the role of religious organizations in public policy formulation.
Represented by:
Raymond English, Senior Vice President
Robert Royal, V. President for Research

Ethics Resource Center Inc.
600 New Hampshire Ave., N.W. Suite 400, Washington, DC 20037
Telephone: (202) 333-3419
Background: Founded in 1977, the Ethics Resource Center is a non-profit, nonpartisan, nonsectarian educational organization working to strengthen public trust and confidence in business, government, and education.
Represented by:
Gary Edwards, Exec. Director

Ethyl Corp.
1155 15th St., N.W., Suite 611, Washington, DC 20005
Telephone: (202) 223-4411

The listings in this directory are available as *Mailing Labels*. See last page.

Represented by:
Barbara A. Little, Sr. Government Relations Representative
Lt. Gen. Jeffrey G. Smith, USA (Ret.), Director of Government Relations
Max L. Turnipseed, Asst. Director of Government Relations
Counsel or consultant:
Hunton and Williams

Eugene, Oregon, City of
Counsel or consultant:
Smith Dawson & Andrews, Inc. (Gregory B. Andrews, Thomas C. Dawson, James P. Smith)

Eugene Water and Electric Board
Eugene, OR
Background: Produces electrical energy.
Counsel or consultant:
Schwabe, Williamson and Wyatt (Frederick P. Hitz)

Eurofer
Brussels, Belgium
Background: A federation of European steelmakers.
Counsel or consultant:
JCLD Consultancy (John C. L. Donaldson)

Euromarble, S.p.A.
Carrara Avenza, Italy
Counsel or consultant:
Dow, Lohnes and Albertson (William Silverman)

European Communities, Commission of the
2100 M St., N.W., 7th Floor, Washington, DC 20037
Telephone: (202) 862-9500
Represented by:
Andreas A. M. van Agt, Head of Delegation
Counsel or consultant:
Kroloff Marshall and Associates (George M. Kroloff)
TransAtlantic Futures, Inc. (W. Alan Zuschlag)

European Council of American Chambers of Commerce in Europe
1615 H St., N.W., Washington, DC 20062
Telephone: (202) 463-5487
Represented by:
J. Philip Hinson, Dir, West Europe & Near East/US C of C

European Investment Bank
Luxembourg
Counsel or consultant:
Hill and Knowlton Public Affairs Worldwide (Dr. Ira P. Kaminow)

European Space Agency
Paris, France
Counsel or consultant:
John B. Gantt

European Union of Christian Democrats/European People'sParty
Brussels, Belgium
Counsel or consultant:
DC Internat'l, Inc. (Andres R. Hernandez)

Eveready
St. Louis, MO
Counsel or consultant:
Fleishman-Hillard, Inc (Jack Gregory, John Overstreet)

Evergreen Forest Products, Inc.
New Meadows, ID
Counsel or consultant:
F. H. Hutchison and Co. (Fred H. Hutchison)

Evergreen Internat'l Aviation
1629 K St., N.W., Suite 503, Washington, DC 20036
Telephone: (202) 466-2929
Background: A total aviation capabilities company specializing in airplane and helicopter operations, including sales, leasing, ground services, maintenance and storage.
Counsel or consultant:
Charles G. Botsford Office (Charles G. Botsford)
Steptoe and Johnson (Richard P. Taylor)

Ex-Partners of Servicemen/Women for Equality
Box 11191, Alexandria, VA 22312
Telephone: (703) 941-5844
Background: Members are former spouses of military personnel and other persons supporting the cause. Seeks federal laws to restore to ex-spouses and dependents military benefits lost through divorce. Disseminates information on federal laws and Department of Defense regulations impacting on military personnel divorces.
Represented by:
Shirley Taft, President
Mary Wurzel, Immediate Past President

Excess Deferred Tax Coalition
Counsel or consultant:
APCO Associates (Deborah R. Sliz)

Executive Air Fleet Corp.
Teterboro, NJ
Counsel or consultant:
Ginsburg, Feldman and Bress (Jacob W. Rosenthal)

Executive Leadership Council
444 North Capitol St., N.W. Suite 715, Washington, DC 20001
Telephone: (202) 783-6339
Counsel or consultant:
Keefe Co., The (C. L. James, III)

Executive Life Insurance Co.
Englewood, CA
Counsel or consultant:
Williams and Jensen, P.C.

Experiment in Internat'l Living
Brattleboro, VT
Counsel or consultant:
Cassidy and Associates, Inc. (Elliott M. Fiedler)

Export-Import Bank of Japan
Tokyo, Japan
Counsel or consultant:
Dechert Price & Rhoads (Allan S. Mostoff)

Export Source Rule Coalition
1710 Rhode Island Ave., N.W. Suite 300, Washington, DC 20036
Telephone: (202) 737-4461
Counsel or consultant:
Miller & Chevalier, Chartered (Catherine T. Porter)

Express Foods Co., Inc.
Louisville, KY
Counsel or consultant:
Leighton and Regnery (Richard J. Leighton)

Express Forwarding and Storage, Inc.
New York, NY
Counsel or consultant:
Denning and Wohlstetter

External Tanks Corp.
Boulder, CO
Counsel or consultant:
Swidler & Berlin, Chartered (Dawn Gifford)

Exxon Co., U.S.A.
Houston, TX
Background: A division of Exxon Corp.
Counsel or consultant:
Covington and Burling (Harvey M. Applebaum)
Hill and Knowlton Public Affairs Worldwide (Hilary Sills)
Howrey and Simon (Robert G. Abrams)

Exxon Corp.
1899 L St., N.W., Suite 1100, Washington, DC 20036
Telephone: (202) 862-0200
Represented by:
Bev D. Blackwood, Washington Representative
Amy R. Hammer, Washington Representative
James D. McMillan, Washington Representative
Charles Rowton, Washington Representative
Donald E. Smiley, Vice President, Washington Office
Guenther O. Wilhelm, Deputy Manager, Washington Office
Counsel or consultant:
Bogle and Gates
Bonner & Associates
Camp, Barsh, Bates and Tate (Harry E. Barsh, Jr.)

Eye Bank Ass'n of America
1725 Eye St., N.W., Washington, DC 20006-2403
Telephone: (202) 775-4999

Represented by:
Patricia Aiken-O'Neill, President-CEO
Counsel or consultant:
Gold and Liebengood, Inc. (John F. Scruggs)
Kilpatrick & Cody (Frederick H. von Unwerth)

Eye Care
1319 F St., N.W., Suite 905, Washington, DC 20004
Telephone: (202) 628-3816
Represented by:
Donna A. Fujiwara, Exec. Director

F&C Management Ltd.
London, England
Counsel or consultant:
Hill and Knowlton Public Affairs Worldwide (Dr. Ira P. Kaminow)

F/V American Empire
Seattle, WA
Counsel or consultant:
Davis Wright Tremaine (James P. Walsh)

FAG Bearings Corp.
Stamford, CT
Counsel or consultant:
Gene Taylor Assoc., Inc. (Gene Taylor)
Winburn, VanScoyoc, and Hooper (John P. Winburn)

Fairbanks/North Star Borough
Fairbanks, AK
Counsel or consultant:
C. Deming Cowles, IV

Fairchild Political Action Committee
300 West Service Road Dulles Internat'l Airport, Chantilly, VA 22021-9998
Telephone: (703) 478-5800
Background: Headed by Steven Flajser, Director of Government Relations of Fairchild Space and Defense Corp.
Represented by:
Robert H. Kelley, Jr., Treasurer

Fairchild Space & Defense Corp.
20301 Century Blvd, G-17, Germantown, MD 20874
Telephone: (301) 428-6325
Background: Includes: Fairchild Communications and Electronics Co., Fairchild Space Co., Fairchild Control Systems Co.
Represented by:
Steven H. Flajser, Director, Government Relations
Counsel or consultant:
Verner, Liipfert, Bernhard, McPherson and Hand, Chartered

Fairfax County, Virginia
4100 Chain Bridge Road, Fairfax, VA 22030
Telephone: (703) 246-2000
Counsel or consultant:
Government Relations, Inc. (Thomas J. Bulger)
Keefe Co., The (William A. Roberts)

Fairfield Communities, Inc.
Little Rock, AR
Counsel or consultant:
Jones, Day, Reavis and Pogue (Randall E. Davis)
Manatt, Phelps, Rothenberg & Phillips (Robert T. Herbolsheimer)

Falcon Safety Products
Somerville, NJ
Counsel or consultant:
Wunder, Ryan, Cannon & Thelen (Kenneth S. Levine)

Falconbridge Ltd.
Toronto, Ontario
Counsel or consultant:
Dickstein, Shapiro and Morin (I. Lewis Libby)

Families U.S.A.
1334 G St., N.W. Suite 300, Washington, DC 20005
Telephone: (202) 737-6340
Background: A nonprofit advocacy organization for low-income elderly people.
Represented by:
Ronald F. Pollack, Exec. Director
Marsha J. Simon, Director of Legislation

Family Health Plan, Inc.
Miami Lakes, FL
Background: A health maintenance organization.

ORGANIZATIONS REPRESENTED

Family Health Plan, Inc. (Cont'd)
Counsel or consultant:
Alan M. Gnessin Law Offices (Alan M. Gnessin)

Family Holding Co. Advocacy Group
1700 Pennsylvania Ave., N.W. Suite 600, Washington, DC
20006
Telephone: (202) 662-3414
Counsel or consultant:
Ivins, Phillips and Barker (Philip D. Morrison)

Family Life Insurance Co.
Seattle, WA
Counsel or consultant:
Cadwalader, Wickersham & Taft (Donald C. Alexander)

Family Research Council, Inc.
601 Pennsylvania Ave., N.W., Suite 901, Washington, DC
20004
Telephone: (202) 393-2100
Background: A research and lobbying organization founded
in 1982. Now a division of Focus on the Family, an orga-
nization based in Pomona, CA.
Represented by:
Gary L. Bauer, President
Elizabeth Y. Kepley, Director, Government Relations
Counsel or consultant:
Charles Donovan

Family Service America
1319 F St., N.W., Suite 606, Washington, DC 20004
Telephone: (202) 347-1124
Background: An organization with 300 member family and
child service agencies throughout North America. Head-
quartered in Milwaukee, WI.
Represented by:
Patricia Langley, Director, Washington Office

Family Therapy Network
7703 13th St., N.W., Washington, DC 20012
Telephone: (202) 829-2452
Represented by:
Richard Simon, Director

Fanuc, Ltd.
Yamanashi, Japan
Counsel or consultant:
Global USA, Inc. (Dr. Bohdan Denysyk)

Far East Machinery Co. Ltd.
Taipei, Taiwan
Counsel or consultant:
Ablondi and Foster, P.C. (Italo H. Ablondi, F. David
Foster)

Farberware
Bronx, NY
Counsel or consultant:
Kilpatrick & Cody (Joseph W. Dorn)

Farley Industries
1455 Pennsylvania Ave., N.W. Suite 1170, Washington,
DC 20004
Telephone: (202) 737-1930
Represented by:
Evelyn V. Keyes, Government Affairs Director

Farm Animal Reform Movement
P.O. Box 30654, Bethesda, MD 20824
Telephone: (301) 530-1737
Background: A national public interest organization dedi-
cated to exposing animal abuse and other adverse impacts
of animal agriculture on human health and the environ-
ment. Critical of the meat industry and its practices.
Represented by:
Alex Hershaft, President

Farm Credit Council
50 F St., N.W., Suite 900, Washington, DC 20001
Telephone: (202) 626-8710
Background: Protects and promotes the business conditions
and interests of cooperative farm lending institutions. Af-
filiated with the National Council of Farmer Coopera-
tives.
Represented by:
Kenneth E. Auer, Acting President
Paul B. Darby, Director of Information
William Jeffry Shipp, Director of Legislation
Joseph L. S. Terrell, V. President, Public & Member Rela-
tions

Farm Credit Council Political Action Committee
50 F St., N.W., Suite 900, Washington, DC 20001
Telephone: (202) 626-8710
Background: Represented by Kenneth E. Auer (Treasurer
of the PAC) of the Farm Credit Council.

Farmland Industries
777 14th St., N.W., Suite 680, Washington, DC 20005
Telephone: (202) 783-5330
Represented by:
Dr. Jerry B. Waters, Washington Representative
Counsel or consultant:
Bryan, Cave, McPheeters and McRoberts
Hill and Knowlton Public Affairs Worldwide

Farmworker Justice Fund
2001 S St., N.W., Suite 210, Washington, DC 20009
Telephone: (202) 462-8192
Background: A human rights advocacy organization repre-
senting the interests of migrant farmworkers.
Represented by:
Garry Geffert, Counsel
Michael Hancock, Exec. Director
Isabel Kaldenbach, Director, Public & Governmental Af-
fairs
Counsel or consultant:
Hogan and Hartson (George Mernick, III)

Fast Air Carrier
Santiago, Chile
Counsel or consultant:
Squire, Sanders and Dempsey (Marshall S. Sinick)

Fasteners Institute of Japan
Tokyo, Japan
Counsel or consultant:
Tanaka, Ritger and Middleton

FDA Council
c/o Capitol Associates 426 C St., N.E., Washington, DC
20002
Telephone: (202) 544-1880
Background: A coalition pharmaceutical and food compa-
nies and non-profit groups seeking increases in the budget
of the Food and Drug Administration.
Counsel or consultant:
Capitol Associates, Inc. (Marguerite Donoghue, Terry
Lierman)

Federal Administrative Law Judges' Conference
424 Nat'l Lawyers Club, 1815 H St., N.W., Washington,
DC 20006
Telephone: (202) 633-0525
Represented by:
Norman Zenkel, First V. President
Counsel or consultant:
Graham and James (Eileen Shannon Carlson, Thomas F.
Railsback)

Federal Agricultural Mortgage Corp.
Washington, DC
Counsel or consultant:
McMillan and Farrell Associates (C. W. McMillan)

Federal Bar Ass'n
1815 H St., N.W., Suite 408, Washington, DC 20006
Telephone: (202) 638-0252
Represented by:
John G. Blanche, III, Exec. Director
Keith Kelley, Staff Director for Public Relations

**Federal Commerce and Industry Political Action
Committee**
1129 20th St., N.W. Suite 200, Washington, DC 20036
Telephone: (202) 857-5934
Background: A political action committee of the Greater
Washington Board of Trade.
Represented by:
William Calomiris, Treasurer

Federal Compress and Warehouse Co.
Memphis, TN
Counsel or consultant:
Wallace & Edwards

Federal Construction Council
c/o Nat'l Academy of Sciences 2101 Constitution Ave.,
N.W., Washington, DC 20418
Telephone: (202) 334-3378
Background: Encourages cooperation among several federal
construction agencies.

Represented by:
Henry A. Borger, Exec. Secretary

Federal Criminal Investigators Ass'n
1140 Connecticut Ave., N.W., Suite 804, Washington, DC
20036
Telephone: (202) 223-6850
Counsel or consultant:
Donald Baldwin Associates (Donald Baldwin)

Federal Data Corp.
One Bethesda Center Suite 1100, Bethesda, MD 20814
Telephone: (301) 986-0800
Counsel or consultant:
Guttenberg & Company (John P. Guttenberg, Jr.)

Federal Deposit Insurance Corp.
550 17th St., N.W., Washington, DC 20429
Telephone: (202) 393-8400
Counsel or consultant:
Baker and Hostetler (Kenneth J. Kies)

Federal Employees Ass'n
929 2nd St., N.E., Washington, DC 20002
Telephone: (202) 543-4304
Background: Provides various discounts and services to
federal workers nationwide.
Represented by:
Charles Scott, General Agent Manager

Federal Express Corp.
300 Maryland Ave., N.E., Washington, DC 20002
Telephone: (202) 546-1631
Represented by:
Ann Sanders Dickey, Senior Manager, State & Federal
Affairs
Melanie A. Kutska, Administrative Secretary
George C. Tagg, Managing Director, Government Affairs
Primrose Prapt Tishman, Coordinator, Government Af-
fairs
Kathy J. Williams, Director, Internat'l & Gov't Affairs
Counsel or consultant:
Baker, Worthington, Crossley, Stansberry & Woolf (W.
Lee Rawls)
Hill and Knowlton Public Affairs Worldwide (Charles
Francis)
Keefe Co., The (Robert J. Keefe, Terry M. O'Connell)
Kilpatrick & Cody (Elliott H. Levitas, C. Randall Nuck-
olls)
Manatt, Phelps, Rothenberg & Phillips (Robert J. Kabel,
William C. Oldaker)
Mudge Rose Guthrie Alexander and Ferdon (Richard H.
Abbey)
Professional Lobbying and Consulting Center (John L.
Zorack)
Shaw, Pittman, Potts and Trowbridge
Vinson and Elkins

Federal Home Loan Bank of Boston
Boston, MA
Counsel or consultant:
James J. Butera, Chartered
Kirkland & Lockhart (Garry E. Brown)

Federal Home Loan Bank of Chicago
Chicago, IL
Counsel or consultant:
Sidley and Austin (Margery Waxman)

Federal Home Loan Bank of Cincinnati
Cincinnati, OH
Counsel or consultant:
Kirkpatrick & Lockhart (Garry E. Brown)

Federal Home Loan Bank of Dallas
Dallas, TX
Counsel or consultant:
Fulbright & Jaworski (Warren Belmar)

Federal Home Loan Bank of Des Moines
Des Moines, IA
Counsel or consultant:
Morrison & Foerster (L. Richard Fischer)
O'Connor & Hannan

Federal Home Loan Bank of New York
New York, NY
Counsel or consultant:
James J. Butera, Chartered
Kirkpatrick & Lockhart

ORGANIZATIONS REPRESENTED

Federal Home Loan Bank of Pittsburgh
Pittsburgh, PA
Counsel or consultant:
Evans Group, Ltd., The (Thomas B. Evans, Jr., Mary Ellen Taylor)

Federal Home Loan Bank of San Francisco
San Francisco, CA
Counsel or consultant:
Bregman, Abell & Kay (Stanley I. Bregman)
Wilmer, Cutler and Pickering (Sally Katzen)

Federal Home Loan Bank of Seattle
Seattle, WA
Counsel or consultant:
Morrison & Foerster (William S. Eckland, Michael Roster)
O'Connor & Hannan

Federal Home Loan Bank of Topeka
Topeka, KS
Counsel or consultant:
Morrison & Foerster (L. Richard Fischer)
O'Connor & Hannan

Federal Home Loan Mortgage Corp.
1759 Business Center Drive, Reston, VA 22090
Telephone: (703) 789-4700
Represented by:
Jeanne Broyhill, Regional Director
Helen Dalton, Director, Public Relations
Daniel J. Driscoll, V. President, Corporate Communications
Barbara Fox, Manager, Government Affairs
Terri Freeman, Director, Community Communications
Charles Fritts, Director, Government Affairs
Lee B. Holmes, Exec. V. President, Corporate Relations
Judith A. Kennedy, V. President, Government Affairs
Michael Schwartz, Director, Government Affairs
Jill Showell, Analysts, Government Affairs
Counsel or consultant:
Thacher, Proffitt and Wood (Virginia W. Brown, Louis H. Nevins)
Charls E. Walker Associates (James E. Smith)

Federal Judges Ass'n
Atlanta, GA
Counsel or consultant:
Graham and James (Eileen Shannon Carlson, Thomas F. Railsback)

Federal Managers Ass'n
1000 16th St., N.W., Suite 701, Washington, DC 20006
Telephone: (202) 778-1500
Represented by:
Pamela D. Frank, Legislative Representative
Bruce Moyer, Legislative Counsel
Paul E. Trayers, Exec. Director

Federal Managers Ass'n Political Action Committee
1000 16th St., N.W., Washington, DC 20006
Telephone: (202) 778-1500
Background: Contact for the PAC is Bruce Moyer of the Federal Managers Ass'n.

Federal Nat'l Mortgage Ass'n
3900 Wisconsin Ave., N.W., Washington, DC 20016
Telephone: (202) 752-7000
Represented by:
David W. Berson, V. President and Chief Economist
James H. Carr, V. President, Housing Policy Research
Annette P. Fribourg, V. President for Congressional Relations
Ed Greelegs, Director, Government Relations
Gwenn Hibbs, V. President, Legislative Analysis
Robert Maloney, Director, Government Relations
William R. Maloni, Sr. V. Pres., Policy & Public Affrs.
Gerald R. McMurray, V. President, Housing Initiatives
Dale P. Riordan, Exec. V. President, Marketing
Marlisa Senchak, Director of Congressional Relations
Counsel or consultant:
Dewey, Ballantine, Bushby, Palmer and Wood (Joseph A. Califano, Jr., Lawrence F. O'Brien, III)
Dickstein, Shapiro and Morin (John C. Dill)
Newmyer Associates, Inc.
Powell, Goldstein, Frazer and Murphy (Lawrence B. Simons)

Federal Nat'l Mortgage Ass'n Political Action Committee (FANNIA PAC)
3900 Wisconsin Ave., N.W., Washington, DC 20016
Telephone: (202) 752-7120
Background: Represented by William R. Maloni of the Federal Nat'l Mortgage Ass'n.

Federal Paper Board Co.
Montvale, NJ
Counsel or consultant:
White & Case (John W. Barnum)

Federal Physicians Ass'n
P.O. Box 45150, Washington, DC 20026
Telephone: (703) 455-5947
Represented by:
Dennis W. Boyd, Exec. Director
Dr. Peter A. West, President

Federal Record Service Corp.
N. Miami Beach, FL
Counsel or consultant:
Lipsen Whitten & Diamond

Federal Sources, Inc.
Vienna, VA
Counsel or consultant:
Steponkus and Associates (William P. Steponkus)

Federalist Soc. for Law
1700 K St., N.W. Suite 901, Washington, DC 20006
Telephone: (202) 822-8138
Represented by:
Eugene B. Meyer, Exec. Director

Federally Employed Women, Inc.
1400 Eye St., N.W. Suite 425, Washington, DC 20005
Telephone: (202) 898-0994
Represented by:
Lynn Eppard, Legislative Director
Karen R. Scott, Executive Director

Federated Ambulatory Surgery Ass'n
700 N. Fairfax St., Suite 520, Alexandria, VA 22314
Telephone: (703) 836-8808
Represented by:
Gail D. Durant, Exec. Director

Federated Cash Management Systems
Pittsburgh, PA
Counsel or consultant:
Dickstein, Shapiro and Morin (Charles H. Morin)

Federated Investors, Inc.
Pittsburgh, PA
Counsel or consultant:
Gold and Liebengood, Inc. (William F. Hildenbrand)

Federation for American Immigration Reform (FAIR)
1666 Connecticut Ave., N.W., Suite 400, Washington, DC 20009
Telephone: (202) 328-7004
Background: A national, nonprofit, membership organization working to stop illegal immigration and conform U.S. legal immigration policy to reasonable levels.
Represented by:
Jim Dorcy, Sr. Government Relations Associate
Cynthia W. McConnell, Field Director
Ira Mehlman, Public Relations Director
Alan C. Nelson, Consultant
Dave Ray, Public Relations/Press Secretary
Daniel A. Stein, Exec. Director
Garry R. Turner, Government Relations Associate
Anna Weinroth, Legislative Assistant
Steve Workings, Consultant
Counsel or consultant:
Williams and Jensen, P.C. (Barnaby Zall)

Federation of American Health Systems
1111 19th St., N.W. Suite 402, Washington, DC 20036
Telephone: (202) 833-3090

Represented by:
Michael D. Bromberg, Exec. Director
Mary R. Grealy, Deputy Director and Executive Counsel
Lynn S. Hart, Director, Federal Legislation
Samuel Mitchell, Director, Research and Federal Relations
Campbell Thomson, Deputy Director, Communications
Counsel or consultant:
Dewey, Ballantine, Bushby, Palmer and Wood (John J. Salmon)

Federation of American Health Systems Political Action Committee
1111 19th St., N.W., Suite 402, Washington, DC 20036
Telephone: (202) 833-3090
Background: Represented by Lynn S. Hart, Director of Federal Legislation of the Federation.

Federation of American Scientists
307 Massachusetts Ave., N.E., Washington, DC 20002
Telephone: (202) 546-3300
Background: Organized in 1945 for the purpose of lobbying to help insure civilian control of atomic energy. Conducts research on arms control and other issues of science and society.
Represented by:
David H. Albright, Senior Scientist
Gordon Burck, Staff Assoc., Chem./Biological Warfare
Thomas Longstreth, Assoc. Dir., Strategic Weapons Policy
John E. Pike, Associate Director, Space Policy
Jeremy J. Stone, President

Federation of American Societies for Experimental Biology
9650 Rockville Pike, Bethesda, MD 20814
Telephone: (301) 530-7000
Represented by:
Roger Johnson, Public Information Officer
Gar Kaganowich, Director, Office of Public Affairs
John Rice, Acting Exec. Director

Federation of Behavioral, Psychological and Cognitive Sciences
1200 17th St., N.W., Room 517, Washington, DC 20036
Telephone: (202) 955-7758
Background: Seeks to encourage policy and legislation that enhance training and research on behavioral, psychological and cognitive processes and works to educate the public and private and public agencies on the need for such research.
Represented by:
Dr. David H. Johnson, Exec. Director

Federation of European Bearing Manufacturers Ass'ns
West Germany
Counsel or consultant:
Mudge Rose Guthrie Alexander and Ferdon (N. David Palmeter)

Federation of Internat'l Trade Ass'ns
1851 Alexander Bell Drive, Reston, VA 22091
Telephone: (703) 391-6106
Background: Represents 150 world trade clubs and international trade associations located across the United States.
Represented by:
Nelson T. Joyner, Chairman

Federation of Japan Tuna Fisheries Cooperative Ass'ns
Japan
Counsel or consultant:
Anderson and Pendleton, C.A. (Francis G. McKenna)

Federation of Materials Societies
1707 L St., N.W. Suite 333, Washington, DC 20036
Telephone: (202) 296-9282
Counsel or consultant:
Siegel, Houston and Associates (Betsy Houston)

Federation of Nurses and Health Professionals/ AFT
555 New Jersey Ave., N.W., Washington, DC 20001
Telephone: (202) 879-4491
Represented by:
Katherine Kany, Professional Issues Coordinator

Federation of Organizations for Professional Women
2001 S St., N.W., Suite 540, Washington, DC 20009

ORGANIZATIONS REPRESENTED

Federation of Organizations for Professional Women (Cont'd)
Telephone: (202) 328-1415
Represented by:
Donna Suchmann, President
Dr. Viola M. Young-Horvath, Exec. Director

Federation of Professional Athletes
2021 L St., N.W., Suite 600, Washington, DC 20036
Telephone: (202) 463-2200
Background: An umbrella organization through which such professional athlete unions as the Nat'l Football League Players Ass'n and the Major Indoor Soccer Ass'n are linked to the AFL-CIO.
Represented by:
Frank Woschitz, Director of Public Relations

Federation of State Humanities Councils
1012 14th St., N.W., Suite 1007, Washington, DC 20005
Telephone: (202) 393-5400
Represented by:
Jamil S. Zainaldin, President
Counsel or consultant:
Duncan and Associates

Federation of Tax Administrators
444 North Capitol St., N.W., Suite 334, Washington, DC 20001
Telephone: (202) 624-5890
Represented by:
Harley T. Duncan, Exec. Director
John Gambill, Sr. Res. Assoc, Dir. of Publications

Federation of the Swiss Watch Industry
Bienne, Switzerland
Counsel or consultant:
Rose, Schmidt, Hasley & DiSalle (Michael G. Kushnick)

Federation of Wine and Spirits Exporters of France
Paris, France
Counsel or consultant:
Max N. Berry Law Offices (Max N. Berry)

Feed Industry Political Action Committee
1701 Fort Myer Drive Suite 1200, Arlington, VA 22209
Telephone: (703) 524-0810
Background: The political action arm of the American Feed Industry Ass'n. Represented by Steven Kopperud of the Ass'n.

Fellowship Square Foundation
11718 Bowman Green Drive, Reston, VA 22090
Telephone: (703) 471-5370
Background: Interested in housing and related services for the elderly physically handicapped.
Represented by:
Dr. C. David Hartmann, President

Ferranti Defense and Space Group
1111 Jefferson Davis Hwy, Suite 800, Arlington, VA 22202
Telephone: (703) 979-0005
Represented by:
J. D. Gould, V. President, Washington Operations
C. B. Higgins, Jr., Chief Marketing Officer
Gregory L. Sharp, Director of Government Affairs
Counsel or consultant:
John C. Walton

Ferro Corp.
Cleveland, OH
Counsel or consultant:
Squire, Sanders and Dempsey (Jeffrey O. Cerar)

Ferroalloys Ass'n
1505 Crystal Drive, Suite 708, Arlington, VA 22202
Telephone: (703) 418-0333
Represented by:
John G. Oxaal, President
Counsel or consultant:
APCO Associates (Kevin G. Nealer)
Edward J. Kinghorn & Assoc., Jr.
Squire, Sanders and Dempsey (Ritchie T. Thomas)

Ferrous Scrap Consumers Coalition
1055 Thomas Jefferson St. N.W. Suite 300, Washington, DC 20007
Telephone: (202) 342-8400
Counsel or consultant:
Collier, Shannon & Scott (Paul C. Rosenthal)

Fertilizer Institute
501 Second St., N.E., Washington, DC 20002
Telephone: (202) 675-8250
Represented by:
Diane Bateman, Assistant V. President, Gov't Relations
Donald J. Casey, Director, Regulatory Programs
Gary D. Myers, President
Kathleen O'Hara, Director, Public Affairs
Ron Phillips, V. President, Public Affairs
Ford B. West, V. President, Government Relations
Fred E. Zillinger, Director, Government Affairs
Counsel or consultant:
McKenna, Conner and Cuneo (Richard A. Flye)

Fertilizer Institute Political Action Committee (FERT PAC)
501 2nd St., N.E., Washington, DC 20002
Telephone: (202) 675-8250
Background: Represented by Ford B. West, Vice President, Government Relations of the Fertilizer Institute.

FFA Fluzeugwerke
Altenrhein, Switzerland
Counsel or consultant:
Wunder, Ryan, Cannon & Thelen (John J. McGovern, Jr.)

FHP, Inc.
1225 19th St., N.W., Washington, DC 20036
Telephone: (202) 223-5718
Represented by:
Janet G. Newport, Manager, Federal Affairs
Herb K. Schultz, Manager, Congressional Affairs

Fiart Cantieri Italiani S.p.A.
Naples, Italy
Counsel or consultant:
Patton, Boggs and Blow (Katharine R. Boyce, David E. Dunn, III)

Fiat Washington
1776 Eye St., N.W. Suite 775, Washington, DC 20006
Telephone: (202) 862-1610
Background: Represents Fiat S.p.A. interests in the United States.
Represented by:
Mario Locatelli, President
Maximilian Ullmann, V. President, Defense Systems
Andrew F.G. Unwin, V. President, Int'l Development Program
Counsel or consultant:
Gold and Liebengood, Inc. (Howard S. Liebengood)
Vinson and Elkins

Fiber, Fabric and Apparel Coalition for Trade
1801 K St., N.W., Suite 900, Washington, DC 20006
Telephone: (202) 862-0517
Background: A coalition whose members include the American Textile Manufacturers Institute, the Internat'l Ladies' Garment Workers Union, the Nat'l Cotton Council of America and the Industrial Fabrics Association. Seeks import controls on foreign textiles and apparel.
Counsel or consultant:
Wallace & Edwards (Macon T. Edwards)

Fiberglass Fabrication Ass'n
3299 K St., N.W., 7th Floor, Washington, DC 20007
Telephone: (202) 337-3322
Represented by:
Allison Parker, Exec. Director
Counsel or consultant:
Ass'n Management Group (Robert F. Lederer, Jr.)

Fiberite Corp.
Orange, CA
Counsel or consultant:
Winthrop, Stimson, Putnam & Roberts (Peter F. Gold)

Fibreboard Corp.
Concord, CA
Counsel or consultant:
F. H. Hutchison and Co. (Fred H. Hutchison)

Fideicomiso ProMexico
Mexico City, Mexico
Counsel or consultant:
TKC Internat'l, Inc.

Fidelity Investors
Boston, MA

Counsel or consultant:
Patton, Boggs and Blow (William D. Hathaway)
Segermark Co., The

Fidelity Television, Inc.
Los Angeles, CA
Counsel or consultant:
Mullin, Rhyne, Emmons and Topel, P.C.

Field Museum of Natural History, The
Chicago, IL
Counsel or consultant:
Chernikoff and Co. (Larry Chernikoff)

Fieldstone Co.
Newport Beach, CA
Counsel or consultant:
Bracy Williams & Co. (Kenneth S. Birnbaum, Terrence L. Bracy, Kenneth M. Stram, Susan J. Williams)

Figgie Internat'l
1735 Jefferson Davis Highway, Suite 705, Arlington, VA 22202
Telephone: (703) 892-1400
Represented by:
Dean E. Steel, V. President, Washington Office
Counsel or consultant:
Richard W. Bliss

Film, Air and Package Carriers Conference
2200 Mill Road, Alexandria, VA 22314
Telephone: (703) 838-1887
Background: Umbrella organization of the Air & Expedited Motor Carriers Conference, Nat'l Film Carriers, American Package Express Carriers Ass'n, and Messenger Courier Ass'n of America
Represented by:
George H. Mundell, Exec. Director

Financial Accounting Foundation
1350 Connecticut Ave., N.W. Suite 620, Washington, DC 20036
Telephone: (202) 466-8016
Represented by:
Patricia Pride, Government Relations Manager

Financial Accounting Standards Board
1350 Connecticut Ave., N.W. Suite 620, Washington, DC 20036
Telephone: (202) 466-8016
Background: Represented by Patricia Pride of the Financial Accounting Foundation.

Financial Corp. of America
Los Angeles, CA
Counsel or consultant:
Elias, Matz, Tiernan and Herrick

Financial Executives Institute
1100 17th St., N.W., Suite 1203, Washington, DC 20036
Telephone: (202) 659-3700
Background: A professional organization of individuals who are senior financial and administrative officers in business organizations throughout the U.S. FEI has over 13,000 members, affiliated with 6,000 companies in virtually all segments of the economy, who represent a broad cross section of American business.
Represented by:
James A. Kaitz, Director - Government Relations
Gina Shea Mitchell, Senior Technical Associate
Kevin Sabo, Senior Technical Associate

Financial Northeastern Corp.
Fairfield, NJ
Counsel or consultant:
The William Chasey Organization (Virginia Chasey)

Financial Security Assurance, Inc.
New York, NY
Counsel or consultant:
Black, Manafort, Stone and Kelly Public Affairs Co. (Paul J. Manafort)
Kutak Rock & Campbell (Nancy L. Granese)
Royer, Mehle & Babyak (Robert Stewart Royer)
Williams and Jensen, P.C. (Mary L. Whalen)

Financial Services Council
1225 19th St., N.W., Suite 410, Washington, DC 20036
Telephone: (202) 785-1500

The listings in this directory are available as *Mailing Labels*. See last page.

ORGANIZATIONS REPRESENTED

Represented by:
Samuel J. Baptista, President
Daniel J. McDermott, Legislative Counsel
Counsel or consultant:
Henry J. Kaufman & Associates (John Seng)

Financial Stationers Ass'n
1101 Connecticut Ave., N.W., Suite 700, Washington, DC 20036
Telephone: (202) 857-1144
Counsel or consultant:
Smith, Bucklin and Associates (Michael L. Payne)

Financial World Partners
New York, NY
Counsel or consultant:
Van Dyk Associates, Inc. (Ted Van Dyk)

Finanziaria Mirabella SpA
Caserta, Italy
Counsel or consultant:
Wunder, Ryan, Cannon & Thelen (John J. McGovern, Jr.)

Fine Arts Museums of San Francisco
San Francisco, CA
Counsel or consultant:
Chernikoff and Co. (Larry Chernikoff)

Fine Hardwood Veneer Ass'n
Indianapolis, IN
Counsel or consultant:
F. H. Hutchison and Co. (Fred H. Hutchison)

Finland, Embassy of
3216 New Mexico Ave., N.W., Washington, DC 20016
Telephone: (202) 363-8233
Counsel or consultant:
Marshall, Tenzer, Greenblatt, Fallon and Kaplan (Sylvan M. Marshall)

Finryan Internat'l Ltd.
New York, NY
Counsel or consultant:
Wealth Management Corp. (Paul W. Mousseau)

Fire Equipment Manufacturers and Services Ass'n
1776 Massachusetts Ave., N.W. Suite 521, Washington, DC 20036
Telephone: (202) 659-0602
Background: Founded in 1966, FEMSA members are manufacturers of all types of equipment used by fire departments. Represented by Sandra Spence of The Spence Group.
Counsel or consultant:
Rowland & Sellery (Terrie Dort)
Spence Group, The (Sandra Spence)

Fire Island Ass'n, Inc.
New York, NY
Background: An association of 17 coastal community associations.
Counsel or consultant:
Richard Curry and Associates (Richard C. Curry)

FIRE-PAC
1750 New York Ave., N.W., Washington, DC 20006
Telephone: (202) 737-8484
Background: A political action committee sponsored by the Internat'l Ass'n of Fire Fighters. Represented by Frederick H. Nesbitt, Legislative and Political Director of the Ass'n, Barry Kasinitz and David B. Billy, also of the ass'n.

Fireman's Fund Insurance Cos.
1730 Rhode Island Ave., N.W. Suite 1117, Washington, DC 20036
Telephone: (202) 785-3575
Represented by:
Peter A. Lefkin, Asst. V. Pres. & Dir., Fed. Relations
Margaret Trimble, Legislative Assistant
Counsel or consultant:
Baker and Hostetler
Dow, Lohnes and Albertson (Richard S. Belas)
Lee, Toomey & Kent

First Annapolis Savings Bank F.S.B.
Annapolis, MD
Counsel or consultant:
Dickstein, Shapiro and Morin (John C. Dill)

First Boston Corp.
New York, NY
Counsel or consultant:
Bergner, Boyette & Bockorny, Inc. (David A. Bockorny)
Dow, Lohnes and Albertson (Richard S. Belas, Jeffrey Kurzweil)
Williams and Jensen, P.C. (Mary L. Whalen)

First Carolina Communications
Rocky Mount, NC
Counsel or consultant:
Kilpatrick & Cody (Frederick H. von Unwerth)

First Chicago Corp.
Chicago, IL
Counsel or consultant:
Hopkins and Sutter (Francis O. McDermott)
Mayer, Brown and Platt (Jerry L. Oppenheimer)

First Church of Christ-Scientist
Boston, MA
Counsel or consultant:
Jones, Day, Reavis and Pogue (Lawrence P. Lataif)

First City Bancorporation of Texas
Houston, TX
Counsel or consultant:
Akin, Gump, Strauss, Hauer and Feld (Joel Jankowsky)

First Co.
Dallas, TX
Counsel or consultant:
Loomis, Owen, Fellman and Howe

First Co-operative Airlines
Santa Monica, CA
Counsel or consultant:
Allan W. Markham

First Construction Fund
Rochester, NY
Counsel or consultant:
Kuykendall Co. (Dan H. Kuykendall)

First Federal Savings Bank
Santurce, PR
Counsel or consultant:
Hopkins and Sutter (Joaquin A. Marquez)
Kirkpatrick & Lockhart (Garry E. Brown)

First Federal Savings Bank of Western Maryland
Cumberland, MD
Counsel or consultant:
Covington and Burling

First Federal Savings and Loan Ass'n (Inverness)
Inverness, FL
Counsel or consultant:
Warren W. Koffler

First Federal Savings and Loan Ass'n of Raleigh
Raleigh, NC
Counsel or consultant:
Elias, Matz, Tiernan and Herrick

First Financial Corp.
El Paso, TX
Counsel or consultant:
Korth and Korth (Fred Korth)

First Financial Management Corp.
Atlanta, GA
Counsel or consultant:
Sutherland, Asbill and Brennan (Wright H. Andrews, Jr.)

First Hawaiian Bank
Honolulu, HI
Counsel or consultant:
Edwin T. C. Ing

First Media Corp.
Semmes Bldg., Suite 304 10220 River Road, Potomac, MD 20854
Telephone: (301) 441-3561
Counsel or consultant:
Dow, Lohnes and Albertson (Ralph W. Hardy, Jr.)

First Nat'l Bank of Chicago
Chicago, IL
Counsel or consultant:
Dow, Lohnes and Albertson (Bernard J. Long, Jr.)

First Nat'l Bank of Douglasville
Douglasville, GA
Counsel or consultant:
Warren W. Koffler

First Nat'l Bank of Hollywood
Hollywood, FL
Counsel or consultant:
Warren W. Koffler

First Nationwide Bank
San Francisco, CA
Counsel or consultant:
Morrison & Foerster (William S. Eckland, Michael Roster)

First Page
6180 Grovedale Drive, Alexandria, VA 22310
Telephone: (703) 922-2000
Counsel or consultant:
Collins & Associates (Sunny Taylor)

First Republic Bank Corp.
Dallas, TX
Counsel or consultant:
Gibson, Dunn and Crutcher (Cynthia C. Lebow)

First Savings and Loan
El Paso, TX
Counsel or consultant:
Korth and Korth

Fischbach and Moore
New York, NY
Counsel or consultant:
Hudson, Creyke, Koehler and Tacke

Fishing Vessel Owners Ass'n
Seattle, WA
Counsel or consultant:
Patton, Boggs and Blow (Theodore G. Kronmiller)

Five Flags
Birmingham, AL
Counsel or consultant:
Wright and Talisman

Flachglas A.G.
West Germany
Counsel or consultant:
Mudge Rose Guthrie Alexander and Ferdon (David P. Houlihan)

Flat Glass Ass'n of Japan
Tokyo, Japan
Background: An association of three major Japanese glass manufacturers: Asahi Glass Co., Central Glass Co., and Nippon Sheet Glass Co.
Counsel or consultant:
Tanaka, Ritger and Middleton (Patrick F. O'Leary, H. William Tanaka)

Flavor and Extract Manufacturers Ass'n
1620 Eye St., N.W. Suite 925, Washington, DC 20006
Telephone: (202) 293-5800
Counsel or consultant:
Daniel R. Thompson, P.C. (Daniel R. Thompson)

Fleet Nat'l Bank
Providence, RI
Counsel or consultant:
W. J. William Harsh (J. William W. Harsch)

Fleet Reserve Ass'n
1303 New Hampshire Ave., N.W., Washington, DC 20036
Telephone: (202) 785-2768
Represented by:
Norman E. Pearson, National Exec. Secretary
Counsel or consultant:
Thomas Morton Gittings, Jr.

Fleisher-Smythe Co.
Boulder, CO
Counsel or consultant:
Lipsen Whitten & Diamond

FLEX Land Exchange, Inc.
Las Vegas, NV
Counsel or consultant:
Kogovsek & Associates, Inc.

ORGANIZATIONS REPRESENTED

Flexi-Van Leasing
Hackensack, NJ
Counsel or consultant:
Patton, Boggs and Blow (James B. Christian, Jr.)

Flexible Packaging Ass'n
1090 Vermont Ave., N.W Suite 500, Washington, DC 20005
Telephone: (202) 842-3880
Background: A national trade association which represents 200 manufacturers, converters and suppliers of paper, metal foil, and plastic or cellulose film for packaging.
Represented by:
Powell W. Berger, Manager, Government Relations
Glenn Braswell, President
Melanie P. Gness, Assistant Director, Government Relations
Richard Thornburg, Director, Government Relations

Flight Engineers' Internat'l Ass'n
905 16th St., N.W. Suite 201, Washington, DC 20006
Telephone: (202) 347-4511
Represented by:
Jerry L. Austin, President

Flight Safety Foundation
2200 Wilson Blvd., Suite 500, Arlington, VA 22201
Telephone: (703) 522-8300
Background: An international organization of airlines, aerospace manufacturers and others interested in flight safety.
Represented by:
John H. Enders, President
Ralph F. Nelson, V. President and Ass't to the President

FlightSafety Internat'l
655 15th St., N.W., Suite 300, Washington, DC 20005-5701
Telephone: (202) 639-4066
Background: Company provides classroom, simulator, and flight training for aircraft pilots and maintenance technicians. MarineSafety subsidiary provides classroom and simulator training for deck and engineering officers in ship handling operations and procedures. Simulation Systems Division manufactures simulators and training aids. PowerSafety Internat'l provides in-depth training programs to improve power plant performance and reliability.
Represented by:
Elmer G. Gleske, V. President, Governmental Affairs

Flo-Sun Land Corp.
Palm Beach, FL
Counsel or consultant:
Bergner, Boyette & Bockorny, Inc. (Van R. Boyette)

Flood Control Advisory Committee
Minneapolis, MN
Background: Operates from the law offices of Chestnut and Brooks, Minneapolis.
Counsel or consultant:
Powell, Goldstein, Frazer and Murphy (Stuart E. Eizenstat)

Floral Trade Council
Davis, CA
Counsel or consultant:
Stewart and Stewart (Terrence P. Stewart)

Flores Esmeralda, Ltda.
Medellin, Colombia
Counsel or consultant:
Prather, Seeger, Doolittle and Farmer (Edwin H. Seeger, Gary M. Welsh)

Flores Esmeralda, S.R.L.
Lima, Peru
Counsel or consultant:
Prather, Seeger, Doolittle and Farmer (Edwin H. Seeger, Gary M. Welsh)

Florida Bankshares
Hollywood, FL
Counsel or consultant:
Warren W. Koffler

Florida Celery Exchange
Orlando, FL
Counsel or consultant:
Holland and Knight (John M. Himmelberg)

Florida Citrus Mutual
Lakeland, FL

Counsel or consultant:
Barnes, Richardson and Colburn (James H. Lundquist, Matthew T. McGrath)
Shaw, Pittman, Potts and Trowbridge (William Mike House)

Florida Commercial Developers Ass'n
Tampa, FL
Counsel or consultant:
Direct Impact Co., The (John Brady, Gloria Dittus, Tom Herrity)

Florida Crushed Orange, Inc.
Weirsdale, FL
Counsel or consultant:
C. Deming Cowles, IV

Florida Customs Brokers and Forwarders
Miami, FL
Counsel or consultant:
Sandler, Travis & Rosenberg. P.A. (Ronald W. Gerdes, Thomas G. Travis)

Florida District Export Council
Miami, FL
Counsel or consultant:
Sandler, Travis & Rosenberg. P.A. (Ronald W. Gerdes, Thomas G. Travis)

Florida East Coast Railway Co.
St. Augustine, FL
Counsel or consultant:
Neill, Mullenholz and Shaw (John J. Mullenholz)

Florida Exporters and Importers Ass'n
Miami, FL
Counsel or consultant:
Sandler, Travis & Rosenberg. P.A. (Ronald W. Gerdes, Thomas G. Travis)

Florida Fruit and Vegetable Ass'n
Orlando, FL
Counsel or consultant:
Holland and Knight (John M. Himmelberg)

Florida High Speed Rail Commission
Tallahassee, FL
Counsel or consultant:
Spiegel and McDiarmid (John J. Corbett, Jr.)

Florida Lime & Avocado Commission, Trustees of
Homestead, FL
Counsel or consultant:
McLeod & Pires (Harold W. Furman, II)

Florida Power Corp.
1725 K St., N.W., Suite 414, Washington, DC 20006
Telephone: (202) 429-9824
Represented by:
Sue Purvis, Federal Affairs Representative
Counsel or consultant:
Bruder, Gentile & Marcoux
Morgan, Lewis and Bockius

Florida Power and Light Co.
1800 K St., N.W. Suite 1110, Washington, DC 20006
Telephone: (202) 872-0451
Counsel or consultant:
Davis & Harman
Dunaway & Cross (Mac S. Dunaway)
Newman & Holtzinger, P.C. (Harold F. Reis)
Reid & Priest

Florida Progress Corp.
St. Petersburg, FL
Counsel or consultant:
Reid & Priest (Raymond F. Dacek)

Florida Public Utilities Co.
West Palm Beach, FL
Counsel or consultant:
Gallagher, Boland, Meiburger and Brosnan (Thomas F. Brosnan)
Morgan, Lewis and Bockius (Thomas K. Wotring)

Florida State Department of Citrus
Lakeland, FL
Counsel or consultant:
Max N. Berry Law Offices (Max N. Berry)
McLeod & Pires (Michael R. McLeod)

Florida Sugar Cane League
910 16th St., N.W., Suite 402, Washington, DC 20006
Telephone: (202) 785-4070
Background: Serves as Washington Representative for the Rio Grande Valley Sugar Growers.
Represented by:
Michael L. Morton, V. President
F. Dalton Yancey, Exec. V. President

Florida Tomato Exchange
Orlando, FL
Counsel or consultant:
Holland and Knight (John M. Himmelberg)

Florida Washington Office, State of
444 N. Capitol St., Suite 287, Washington, DC 20001
Telephone: (202) 624-5885
Represented by:
Dr. Lynda Davis, Director, Washington Office

Florida West Indies Airlines
Miami Springs, FL
Counsel or consultant:
Bowen & Atkin (Harry A. Bowen)

Florists Transworld Delivery Ass'n
216 7th St., S.E., Washington, DC 20003
Telephone: (202) 546-1090
Background: A cooperative acting as a clearing house for wire service orders and advertising.
Represented by:
Elaine Acevedo, Director, Government Affairs
Kelley O'Conor, Governmental Affairs Representative
Counsel or consultant:
Dorsey & Whitney

Flue-Cured Tobacco Cooperative Stabilization Corp.
Raleigh, NC
Counsel or consultant:
Wallace & Edwards (Macon T. Edwards)

Fluke Manufacturing Co., John
Everett, WA
Counsel or consultant:
Preston Gates Ellis & Rouvelas Meeds (Lloyd Meeds, William A. Shook)

Fluor Corp.
1627 K St., N.W., Suite 300, Washington, DC 20006
Telephone: (202) 955-9300
Represented by:
Betty L. Hudson, V. President, Government Relations
Timothy C. Kernan, Director, Congressional Relations
Counsel or consultant:
Arnold & Porter
Richard W. Bliss
Powell, Goldstein, Frazer and Murphy (Stuart E. Eizenstat)

Fluor-Daniel Corp.
Greenville, SC
Counsel or consultant:
Thompson, Mann and Hutson (Harold P. Coxson)

Flxible Corp., The
Delaware, OH
Counsel or consultant:
Seyfarth, Shaw, Fairweather and Geraldson (Donald L. Rosenthal)

Flyer Industries Ltd.
Winnipeg, Manitoba
Counsel or consultant:
Dow, Lohnes and Albertson (William Silverman)

FMC Corp.
1627 K St., N.W., Suite 500, Washington, DC 20006
Telephone: (202) 956-5200

ORGANIZATIONS REPRESENTED

Represented by:
Lizanne Hefferon Davis, Manager, Regulatory Affairs
Michael J. Johnson, V. President, International Affairs
John A. Mullett, Director, Legislative Affairs
James Q. Posey, Director, Government Communications
Gerald R. Prout, Director, Regulatory Affairs
Harold S. Russell, V. President, Government Affairs
Counsel or consultant:
Beveridge & Diamond, P.C.
Bond Donatelli Inc. (Frank Donatelli)
Bonner & Associates
Cambridge Internat'l, Inc.
Direct Impact Co., The (John Brady, Gloria Dittus, Tom Herrity)
Hill and Knowlton Public Affairs Worldwide (Josephine S. Cooper)
Mayer, Brown and Platt (Jerry L. Oppenheimer)
Robison Internat'l, Inc.

FMC Corp. Good Government Program
1627 K St., N.W. Suite 500, Washington, DC 20006
Telephone: (202) 956-5207
Background: The political action committee of FMC Corp. James Q. Posey of the Corp. serves as Program Coordinator.

Fokker Aircraft U.S.A., Inc.
1199 North Fairfax St. Suite 500, Alexandria, VA 22314
Telephone: (703) 838-0100
Represented by:
Robert M. Hawk, Dir., Public Relations & Advertising
Stuart Matthews, President & Chief Exec. Officer

Fokker B.V.
Amsterdam, Netherlands
Counsel or consultant:
Ehrlich-Manes and Associates (Sherwin B. Stein)

Fontaine Group, Inc.
Birmingham, AL
Counsel or consultant:
Gilbert A. Robinson, Inc. (Gilbert A. Robinson)

Food and Drug Law Institute
1000 Vermont Ave., N.W., Suite 1200, Washington, DC 20005
Telephone: (202) 371-1420
Represented by:
Margaret Deegan, Director of Publications
Frank A. Duckworth, President
Nancy Singer, V. President
Counsel or consultant:
Hill and Knowlton Public Affairs Worldwide

Food Marketing Institute
1750 K St., N.W., Washington, DC 20006
Telephone: (202) 452-8444
Background: Formed Jan. 3, 1977, by a merger of the Nat'l Ass'n of Food Chains and the Super Market Institute. A nonprofit association conducting programs in research, education and public affairs. Members are food retailers and wholesalers and their customers.
Represented by:
Robert O. Aders, President
Andrea Bilson, Manager, State Issues
Laura L. Bourne, Manager, Legislative Information
Karen H. Brown, Vice President, Communications
Anne McGhee Curry, Sr. Government Relations Representative
Dagmar T. Farr, V. President, Consumer Affairs
George R. Green, V. President and Asst. General Counsel
J. Tyrone Kelley, Government Relations Representative
William S. Kies, Jr., Sr V. Pres, Marketing & Field Services
Karen Theibert Knobloch, Government Relations Representative
Peter J. Larkin, Director, State Government Relations
Hardy L. Nathan, Director, Government Relations
Lars E. Peterson, Sr. Government Relations Representative
Harry Sullivan, Sr. V. President and General Counsel
Nancy Foster Yanish, Director, Agricultural Relations
Counsel or consultant:
Collier, Shannon & Scott
John M. Martin, Jr.

Food Marketing Institute Political Action Committee
1750 K St., N.W. Suite 700, Washington, DC 20006
Telephone: (202) 452-8444

Background: Treasurer is Harry Sullivan, Fundraising Coordinator is Karen Theibert Knobloch, and Disbursements Coordinator is Hardy L. Nathan, all of the Food Marketing Institute.
Represented by:
Amy J. Sandgren, Food PAC Administrator

Food Processing Machinery and Supplies Ass'n
200 Daingerfield Road, Alexandria, VA 22314
Telephone: (703) 684-1080
Background: Sponsers various programs, including the Beverage Industry Advisory Council.
Represented by:
Nancy Breed, Director, Administration
George O. Melnykovich, President and CEO

Food Processors Institute, The
1401 New York Ave., N.W., Washington, DC 20005
Telephone: (202) 393-0890
Background: The educational arm of the Nat'l Food Processors Ass'n.
Represented by:
Drusilla Cunningham, Program Assistant

Food Research and Action Center
1319 F St., N.W. Suite 500, Washington, DC 20004
Telephone: (202) 393-5060
Background: A national advocacy center and public interest law center working to reduce hunger among low-income people in the United States.
Represented by:
Edward Cooney, Deputy Director
Robert J. Fersh, Exec. Director
Lynn Parker, Nutrition Consultant
David A. Super, Legal Director

Foodservice and Lodging Institute
1919 Pennsylvania Ave., N.W., Suite 504, Washington, DC 20006
Telephone: (202) 659-9060
Background: Trade industry group of major multi-unit, multi-state restaurant and hotel companies.
Represented by:
Pamela Sederholm, Exec. Director
Counsel or consultant:
Keefe Co., The (Camilla A. McGhee, William A. Signer)
Power & Coleman (Thomas W. Power)

Foodservice and Lodging Institute Political Action Committee
1919 Pennsylvania Ave., N.W., Suite 504, Washington, DC 20006
Telephone: (202) 659-9060
Background: Represented by Pamela Sederholm of the Institute.
Counsel or consultant:
Power & Coleman (Thomas W. Power)

Foodservice & Packaging Institute, Inc.
1025 Connecticut Ave., N.W., Suite 513, Washington, DC 20036
Telephone: (202) 822-6420
Background: Manufacturers of disposable products for food service and packaging.
Represented by:
Joseph W. Bow, CAE, President
Nancy J. Sherman, V. President, Public Affairs

Foothills Pipe Lines (Yukon), Ltd.
Calgary, Alberta
Background: A diversified company which is parent company of Novacor Chemicals Ltd., a petrochemical manufacturer.
Counsel or consultant:
McHenry and Staffier, P.C. (George W. McHenry, Jr., John R. Staffier)
Wexler, Reynolds, Fuller, Harrison and Schule, Inc. (Gail Harrison, Anne Wexler, Bruce Wolpe)

Footwear Distributors and Retailers of America
1319 F St., N.W. Suite 700, Washington, DC 20004
Telephone: (202) 737-5660
Represented by:
Peter T. Mangione, President
Counsel or consultant:
Mudge Rose Guthrie Alexander and Ferdon (Michael P. Daniels)
R. Duffy Wall and Associates (R. D. Folsom, Michael Stern, R. Duffy Wall)

Footwear Industries of America
1420 K St., N.W., Suite 600, Washington, DC 20005
Telephone: (202) 789-1420
Represented by:
Fawn K. Evenson, President
Counsel or consultant:
Collier, Shannon & Scott (Lauren R. Howard, Thomas F. Shannon)
Economic Consulting Services Inc. (Deborah Swartz)

Footwear Industry Political Action Committee
1420 K St., N.W. St., Suite 600, Washington, DC 20005
Telephone: (202) 789-1420
Background: Responsible contact is Fawn K. Evenson of the Footwear Industries of America.
Counsel or consultant:
Collier, Shannon & Scott (Pamela Allen, Lauren R. Howard, Thomas F. Shannon)

Ford Aerospace Corp.
1235 Jefferson Davis Hwy. Suite 1300, Arlington, VA 22202
Telephone: (703) 685-5500
Background: A subsidiary of Ford Motor Co.
Represented by:
Norman Black, Manager, News and Information
Robert W. Davis, Aerospace Progam Development
Kenneth N. Hollander, V. President, Marketing
Peter Iovino, Manager, Corporate Programs
Susan M. Pearce, Public Affairs V. President
William Glenn Yarborough, Jr., Manager

Ford Motor Co.
1350 Eye St., N.W. Suite 1000, Washington, DC 20005
Telephone: (202) 962-5400
Represented by:
Mabel Brandon, Muffie, Dir. Corp. Programming & Cultural Affrs.
Charles W. Day, Manager, Washigton Public Affairs
James A. Dupree, Director, National Affairs Office
Elliott S. Hall, V. President, Washington Affairs
Wendell M. Holloway, Corp. & Financial Legis. Mgr, Wash. Afrs
Robert M. Howard, Legs. Mgr., Washington Afrs (Automotive)
Paul A. Kelly, Jr., Plant Safety and Energy Manager
William K. King, Reg. Mgr, Auto Sfty, Emissns & Fuel Econ
William F. Little, Legislative Assoc., Washington Affrs.
Barbara I. Mansfield, Ass't Manager, Washington Public Affairs
Jay Railton Morgan, Legislative Rep., Automotive Group
Burke G. Reilly, Internat'l Associate, Washington Affairs
Jerald F. ter Horst, Director of Nat'l Public Affairs Office
Helen C. Wiederhorn, Legis. Assoc., Corp. & Financial Srvcs.
Counsel or consultant:
Bonner & Associates
FMR Group Inc., The
Gold and Liebengood, Inc.
Morrison & Foerster (William S. Eckland, Michael Roster)
O'Melveny and Myers (Donald T. Bliss, Jr., William T. Coleman, Jr., Gary N. Horlick, Debra Valentine)
Sullivan and Cromwell
Wilmer, Cutler and Pickering (Robert C. Cassidy, Jr., Lloyd N. Cutler, Neil J. King, Deanne C. Siemer, Howard P. Willens)

Ford's Theater
511 10th St., N.W., Washington, DC 20009
Telephone: (202) 638-2941
Counsel or consultant:
Chernikoff and Co. (Larry Chernikoff)

Foreign Policy Ass'n
1726 M St., N.W., Suite 800, Washington, DC 20036
Telephone: (202) 293-0046
Represented by:
Mary Soley, V. President, National Programs

Foreign Student Service Council
2337 18th St., N.W., Washington, DC 20009
Telephone: (202) 232-4979
Represented by:
Frances W. Bremer, Exec. Director

Forest Farmers Ass'n
Albany, GA

The listings in this directory are available as *Mailing Labels*. See last page.

ORGANIZATIONS REPRESENTED

Forest Farmers Ass'n (Cont'd)
Counsel or consultant:
  Kilpatrick & Cody (C. Randall Nuckolls)

Forest Industries Committee on Timber Valuation and Taxation
1250 Connecticut Ave., N.W. Suite 320, Washington, DC 20036
Telephone: (202) 463-2477
Counsel or consultant:
  Rowland & Sellery (William C. Sellery, Jr.)

Forest Industries Political Action Committee
1250 Connecticut Ave., N.W. Suite 200, Washington, DC 20036
Telephone: (202) 463-2741
Background: The political action committee of the Nat'l Forest Products Ass'n. Contact is Debra Barwick of the Ass'n.

Forest Products Trucking Council
1025 Vermont Ave., N.W., Suite 1020, Washington, DC 20005
Telephone: (202) 347-2900
Background: Represented by Richard Lewis, President, American Pulpwood Ass'n.

Forestal Venecia Ltda.
Santiago, Chile
Counsel or consultant:
  Squire, Sanders and Dempsey (Marshall S. Sinick)

Formaldehyde Institute
1330 Connecticut Ave., N.W. Suite 300, Washington, DC 20036
Telephone: (202) 659-0060
Represented by:
  John F. Murray, Exec. Director

Forstmann, Little & Co.
New York, NY
Counsel or consultant:
  Fried, Frank, Harris, Shriver & Jacobson (Leonard A. Zax)
  O'Connor & Hannan (Thomas H. Quinn)

Fort Howard Corp.
Green Bay, WI
Counsel or consultant:
  Concord Associates, Inc.

Fort Worth, Texas, City of
Counsel or consultant:
  Nat'l Center for Municipal Development (Thomas N. Duffy)

Forum for Health Care Planning
1101 Connecticut Ave., N.W. Suite 700, Washington, DC 20036
Telephone: (202) 857-1162
Counsel or consultant:
  Smith, Bucklin and Associates (Carol A. Lively)

Forum Group, Inc.
Indianapolis, IN
Counsel or consultant:
  Bergner, Boyette & Bockorny, Inc. (Van R. Boyette)

Foss Maritime Co.
Seattle, WA
Counsel or consultant:
  Garvey, Schubert & Barer (Alan A. Butchman)
  Leva, Hawes, Mason and Martin (Harold E. Mesirow)

Foster Co., L. B.
Pittsburgh, PA
Counsel or consultant:
  Reid & Priest

Foster Wheeler Internat'l Corp.
1701 Pennsylvania Ave., N.W. Suite 460, Washington, DC 20006
Telephone: (202) 298-7750
Represented by:
  R. N. Bery, Vice President

Foundation Center
1001 Connecticut Ave., N.W. Suite 938, Washington, DC 20036
Telephone: (202) 331-1400
Represented by:
  Margot Brinkley, Director, Washington Office

Foundation for Blood Irradiation
1315 Apple Ave., Silver Spring, MD 20910
Telephone: (301) 587-8686
Represented by:
  Carl Schleicher, Director

Foundation for Change
310 Pennsylvania Ave., S.E., Washington, DC 20003
Telephone: (202) 546-8410
Represented by:
  Mark H. Gitenstein, Exec. Director

Foundation for Chiropractic Education and Research
1701 Clarendon Blvd., Arlington, VA 22209
Telephone: (703) 276-7445
Represented by:
  Brian E. Cartier, Exec. Director

Foundation for Critical Care
1001 Connecticut Ave., N.W., Suite 428, Washington, DC 20036
Telephone: (202) 775-0721
Represented by:
  Susan Watson, Exec. Director

Foundation for Democracy in Namibia
Windhoek, Namibia
Counsel or consultant:
  Commonwealth Consulting Corp. (Christopher M. Lehman)

Foundation for Eye Research
Tampa, FL
Counsel or consultant:
  Casson, Harkins & LaPallo

Foundation for Internat'l Human Relations
P.O. Box 18206, Washington, DC 20036
Telephone: (202) 659-5552
Represented by:
  Dr. Raymond H. Hamden, Chairman of the Board

Foundation for Internat'l Meetings
4200 Wilson Blvd. Suite 1100, Arlington, VA 22203
Telephone: (703) 243-3288
Background: An organization composed of executives whose ass'ns and corporations meet outside the United States on an ongoing basis.
Represented by:
  April L. Noland, V. President, Operations
  Jack C. Sammis, President

Foundation for Middle East Peace
555 13th St., N.W. 8th Floor, Washington, DC 20005
Telephone: (202) 637-6558
Background: A privately funded organization seeking to promote a peaceful solution to the Israeli-Palestinian conflict which takes into account the security of both Israelis and Palestinians and is in accord with U.S. national interests.
Represented by:
  Merle Thorpe, Jr., President

Foundation for the Advancement of Chiropractic Tenets and Science
1110 North Glebe Road Suite 1000, Arlington, VA 22201
Telephone: (703) 528-5000

Foundation for the Advancement of Hispanic Americans
P.O. Box 66012, Washington, DC 20035
Telephone: (703) 866-1578
Background: A nonprofit organization working to extend the role of Hispanic culture, enhanced educational opportunities for Hispanics, more active participation in civic and social affairs and increased economic opportunites for Hispanics.
Represented by:
  Dr. Pedro de Mesones, President

Foundation for Women's Resources
700 North Fairfax St., Suite 302, Alexandria, VA 22314
Telephone: (703) 549-1102
Represented by:
  Martha P. Farmer, National Exec. Director

Foundation Health Corp.
Sacramento, CA
Counsel or consultant:
  Dixon Arnett Associates (Dixon Arnett)

Foundation of American College of Health Care Administrators
325 South Patrick St., Alexandria, VA 22314
Telephone: (703) 549-5822
Represented by:
  Annemarie G. Rosewater, Exec. Director

Foundation of the Wall and Ceiling Industry
1600 Cameron St., Alexandria, VA 22314-2705
Telephone: (703) 548-0374
Background: Disseminates information to the public on the wall and ceiling industry, including asbestos, lead-based paint, plaster, drywall, and exterior insulation.
Represented by:
  Kathy Sedgwick, Exec. Director

Foundation on Economic Trends
1130 17th St., N.W. Suite 630, Washington, DC 20026
Telephone: (202) 466-2823
Background: Seeks to 'encourage the examination of emerging technologies in their full social and economic context, taking both benefits and potential adverse impacts into consideration.'
Represented by:
  Andrew Kimbrell, Policy Director
  Jeremy R. Rifkin, President

Fountain Trading Co., Ltd.
Taipei, Taiwan
Counsel or consultant:
  Alcalde & Rousselot (Hector Alcalde)

Fourdrinier Wire Council
Box 849, Stevensville, MD 21666
Telephone: (301) 643-4161
Counsel or consultant:
  J. D. Ferry Associates (John D. Ferry)

Fox Broadcasting Inc.
5151 Wisconsin Ave., N.W., Washington, DC 20016
Telephone: (202) 244-5151
Counsel or consultant:
  Bergner, Boyette & Bockorny, Inc. (David A. Bockorny)
  Hogan and Hartson

France, Government of
Paris, France
Counsel or consultant:
  Powell, Adams & Rinehart

Franchising Political Action Committee
1350 New York Ave., N.W. Suite 900, Washington, DC 20005
Telephone: (202) 628-8000
Background: The political action committee of the Internat'l Franchise Ass'n. Treasurer is Neil Simon of the Ass'n.

Franklin Federal Bancorp
Austin, TX
Counsel or consultant:
  Dow, Lohnes and Albertson (Stuart Marshall Bloch)

Fraternal Order of Police (Nat'l Lodge)
Louisville, KY
Counsel or consultant:
  Vorys, Sater, Seymour and Pease (Randal C. Teague)

Fredrickson Associates, Inc., D. S.
Bethesda, MD
Counsel or consultant:
  Stovall & Spradlin

Free Angola Information Service
One Thomas Circle, N.W. Suite 1250, Washington, DC 20005
Telephone: (202) 775-0958
Counsel or consultant:
  Griffin Communications (Frances Griffin)
  Kenneth Barry Schochet, P.C.

Free Congress Center for State Policy
721 2nd St., N.E., Washington, DC 20002
Telephone: (202) 546-3004
Represented by:
  William C. Myers, Director

Free Congress Foundation
717 2nd St., N.E., Washington, DC 20002
Telephone: (202) 546-3000

The listings in this directory are available as *Mailing Labels*. See last page.

ORGANIZATIONS REPRESENTED

Represented by:
Michael Schwartz, Director, Catholic Policy

Free Congress Political Action Committee
717 2nd St., N.E., Washington, DC 20002
Telephone: (202) 546-3000
Background: An ultraconservative political action group founded in 1974.
Represented by:
Ed Ceol, PAC Director
Paul M. Weyrich, National Chairman

Free the Eagle
25 E St., N.W., 8th Floor, Washington, DC 20001
Telephone: (202) 638-0080
Background: Seeks to limit government regulation of the American economy and banking industry. Advocates a return to the gold standard and favors reformation of the Federal Reserve System. Advocates U.S. assistance to anti-communist guerrillas in Africa, Asia and Central America. Managing Director is Howard Segermark of the Segermark Co.
Counsel or consultant:
Segermark Co., The (Howard Segermark)

Freedom of Information Clearinghouse
2000 P St., N.W. Suite 700, Washington, DC 20036
Telephone: (202) 785-3704
Background: A project of Ralph Nader's Center for Study of Responsive Law which assists citizens in making Freedom of Information Act requests from the U.S. Government and, less often, in litigation of cases arising therefrom. Contact is Eleanor Smith of the Public Citizen Litigation Group.

Freedom to Advertise Coalition
c/o Patton, Boggs & Blow 2550 M St., N.W., Washington, DC 20037
Telephone: (202) 457-6000
Counsel or consultant:
Patton, Boggs and Blow (Thomas Hale Boggs, Jr.)

Freeport-McMoRan Inc.
50 F St., N.W., Suite 1050, Washington, DC 20001
Telephone: (202) 737-1400
Represented by:
W. Russell King, President, Freeport-McMoRan D.C.

Freeport-McMoRan Inc. Citizenship Committee
50 F St., N.W., Suite 1050, Washington, DC 20001
Telephone: (202) 737-1400
Background: Represented by W. Russell King of Freeport-McMoRan D.C. Inc.

Freeport, New York, Village of
Background: Law firm of Duncan, Weinberg, Miller & Pembroke represents the municipal utility of Freeport, NY.
Counsel or consultant:
Duncan, Weinberg, Miller & Pembroke, P.C. (Wallace L. Duncan, Jeffrey C. Genzer)

Freight-Savers Shipping Co. Ltd.
Rutherford, NJ
Counsel or consultant:
Galland, Kharasch, Morse and Garfinkle

Freightliner Corp.
1155 Connecticut Ave., N.W. Suite 420, Washington, DC 20036
Telephone: (202) 467-8530
Counsel or consultant:
Hogan and Hartson

French-American Chamber of Commerce in the U.S.
New York, NY
Background: Represents about 200 French companies doing business with the United States.
Counsel or consultant:
Shaw, Pittman, Potts and Trowbridge

Freshwater Press
Cleveland, OH
Counsel or consultant:
TCI Washington Group (Merrill Williams)

Fresno, California, City of
Counsel or consultant:
Simon & Co., Inc. (Leonard S. Simon)

Fresno, California, County of
Fresno, CA
Counsel or consultant:
Ball, Janik and Novack (M. Victoria Cram)

Fresno Surgery and Recovery Care Center
Fresno, CA
Counsel or consultant:
Dixon Arnett Associates (Dixon Arnett)

Friends Committee on Nat'l Legislation
245 Second St., N.E., Washington, DC 20002
Telephone: (202) 547-6000
Background: Quaker peace lobby, founded 1943, carrying to Congress the Friends' concerns for peace and justice at home and abroad.
Represented by:
Nancy L. Alexander, Legislative Secretary
Jay Fikes, Legislative Secretary
Ruth Flower, Legislative Secretary
Joe Polk, Exec. Secretary

Friends-in-Art of ACB, Inc.
1010 Vermont Ave., N.W., Suite 1100, Washington, DC 20005
Telephone: (202) 393-3666
Background: Represented by Roberta Douglas of the American Council of the Blind.

Friends of Free China
1629 K St., N.W., Washington, DC 20006
Telephone: (202) 296-5056
Background: Advocates U.S. Support of the Republic of China.
Counsel or consultant:
Jack E. Buttram Co.

Friends of the Earth
218 D St., S.E., Washington, DC 20003
Telephone: (202) 544-2600
Background: A public interest group committed to the preservation, restoration and rational use of the ecosphere. Established in 1969 with headquarters in Washington. Merged with the Environmental Policy Institute.
Represented by:
James E. Beard, Dir., Nuclear Weapons Production Project
Brent Blackwelder, Dir., Water Resources/Internat'l & V.P.
Michael S. Clark, President
Liz Cook, Ozone Campaign Director
Jack Doyle, Agricultural & Biotechnology Director
Chuck Fox, Director of Legislative Affairs
Keiki Kehoe, Dir., Nuclear Accoun./Global Warming
Jennifer M. McAdoo, Dir., Community Involvement/GroundWater
Fred Millar, Wash Rep., Nuclear & Hazardous Waste
Velma Smith, Dir., Ground Water Protection Project
Bonnie Souza, Development Dir., Central American Proj.
Counsel or consultant:
Communications Management Associates (David K. Martin)

Friends' Provident Life Office
London, England
Counsel or consultant:
Hill and Knowlton Public Affairs Worldwide (Dr. Ira P. Kaminow)

Friendship in Freedom Ass'n
Hamburg, Germany
Background: An association of German Business Leaders founded to monitor legislation affecting U.S.-German relations.
Counsel or consultant:
Bergner, Boyette & Bockorny, Inc. (Jeffrey T. Bergner)

Friendswood Development Corp.
Houston, TX
Counsel or consultant:
Daniel J. Edelman, Inc. (Christopher Gidez)

FRISA
Mexico
Counsel or consultant:
Weatherly & Co. (Jin-Hyun Weatherly)

Frito-Lay, Inc.
Dallas, TX

Counsel or consultant:
Kilpatrick & Cody (C. Randall Nuckolls, Frederick H. von Unwerth, Mark D. Wincek)

Fritz Companies, The
San Francisco, CA
Counsel or consultant:
Flanagan Group, Inc. (Daniel V. Flanagan, Jr.)

Frontec Logistics Corp.
Ottawa, Ontario
Counsel or consultant:
Hill and Knowlton Public Affairs Worldwide (Robert V. Schneider)

Frontier Express Inc.
Torrance, CA
Counsel or consultant:
Graham and James (Eliot J. Halperin)

Frozen Potato Products Institute
1764 Old Meadow Lane Suite 350, McLean, VA 22102
Telephone: (703) 821-0770
Background: Represented by Steven C. Anderson of the American Frozen Food Institute.

Frutropic, S.A.
Rio de Janeiro, Brazil
Counsel or consultant:
Willkie Farr and Gallagher (Christopher A. Dunn)

Fudan Foundation
Washington, DC
Counsel or consultant:
Cassidy and Associates, Inc. (Gerald S. J. Cassidy, William M. Cloherty, Elliott M. Fiedler)

Fuji Heavy Industries Ltd.
Tokyo, Japan
Counsel or consultant:
Piper Pacific Internat'l (Margaret Parker, W. Stephen Piper, Sara Winslow)
Willkie Farr and Gallagher (William H. Barringer)

Fuji Photo Film U.S.A.
Elmsford, NY
Counsel or consultant:
Daniel J. Edelman, Inc. (Leslie Dach)
Patton, Boggs and Blow
Skadden, Arps, Slate, Meagher and Flom (Thomas R. Graham, William E. Perry)

Fujitec America, Inc.
Lebanon, OH
Counsel or consultant:
Piliero, Tobin & Mazza (Daniel J. Piliero, II)

Fujitsu America, Inc.
San Jose, CA
Counsel or consultant:
Akin, Gump, Strauss, Hauer and Feld (Warren E. Connelly, Joel Jankowsky)
Daniel J. Edelman, Inc. (Leslie Dach)

Fujitsu Ltd.
1776 Eye St., N.W., Suite 880, Washington, DC 20006
Telephone: (202) 331-8750
Represented by:
Kuniaki Nozoe, General Manager
David Olive, Deputy General Manager
Counsel or consultant:
Akin, Gump, Strauss, Hauer and Feld (Warren E. Connelly, Richard Rivers)
Morrison & Foerster (Jonathan Band, Philip D. Bartz, Ronald G. Carr, Tamar R. Schwartz)

Fujitsu Microelectronics, Inc.
Tokyo, Japan
Counsel or consultant:
Ball, Janik and Novack (James A. Beall)

Fund for a Feminist Majority
1600 Wilson Blvd., Suite 704, Arlington, VA 22209
Telephone: (202) 522-2214
Represented by:
Eleanor Smeal, President

Fund for Assuring an Independent Retirement
100 Indiana Ave., N.W., Washington, DC 20001
Telephone: (202) 393-4695
Background: An ad-hoc coalition organized by 28 active and retired federal and postal employee organizations. Chairman is Vincent R. Sombrotto of the Nat'l Ass'n of

ORGANIZATIONS REPRESENTED

Fund for Assuring an Independent Retirement (Cont'd)
Letter Carriers of the United States of America.

Fund for Constitutional Government
122 Maryland Ave., N.E. 3rd Floor, Washington, DC 20002
Telephone: (202) 546-3732
Background: A funding organization for supporting the investigation of government corruption and the abuse of constitutional power.
Represented by:
Anne B. Zill, President

Fund for Freedom
1001 Pennsylvania Ave., N.W. Suite 275N, Washington, DC 20503
Telephone: (202) 624-5914
Background: A political action committee.
Represented by:
Martin Mendelsohn, Treasurer

Fund for New Leadership
1110 Vermont Ave., N.W. Suite 1020, Washington, DC 20005
Telephone: (202) 659-1606
Background: A political action committee for young Democrats. Founder and contact is Julie Anbender of the public relations firm of Gallagher-Widmeyer.

Fundacion de Defensa del Comercio Exterior
San Jose, Costa Rica
Counsel or consultant:
Patton, Boggs and Blow (Frank R. Samolis)

Fundacion Pro-Imagen de Colombia en el Exterior
Bogota, Colombia
Counsel or consultant:
Patton, Boggs and Blow (James B. Christian, Jr., David E. Dunn, III)

Fur Institute of Canada
Toronto, Ontario
Counsel or consultant:
Corporate CPR

Furniture Rental Ass'n of America
Westerville, OH
Counsel or consultant:
Kilpatrick & Cody (Frederick H. von Unwerth)

Fusion Power Associates
Gaithersburg, MD
Counsel or consultant:
Preston Gates Ellis & Rouvelas Meeds (Tim L. Peckinpaugh)

Fusion Systems Corp.
7600 Standish Place, Rockville, MD 20855
Telephone: (301) 251-0300
Represented by:
Nancy Chasen, Director, Public Affairs

Futaba Corp.
Tokyo, Japan
Counsel or consultant:
Mudge Rose Guthrie Alexander and Ferdon (Donald B. Cameron, Jr., David P. Houlihan)

Future Business Leaders of America
P.O. Box 17417-Dulles, Washington, DC 20041
Telephone: (703) 860-3334
Represented by:
Douglas L. Barber, Exec. V. President
Dr. Edward D. Miller, Chief Exec. Officer

Future Farmers of America
Box 15160, Alexandria, VA 22309-0160
Telephone: (703) 360-3600
Represented by:
Dr. Larry D. Case, National Adviser
C. Coleman Harris, Exec. Secretary

Future Homemakers of America
1910 Association Drive, Reston, VA 22091
Telephone: (703) 476-4900
Represented by:
Warren Clayton, Exec. Director, Foundation
Alan T. Rains, Exec. Director

Futures Industry Ass'n
1825 Eye St., N.W., Suite 1040, Washington, DC 20006
Telephone: (202) 466-5460
Represented by:
John M. Damgard, President
Paula A. Tosini, Director, Futures Industry Institute
Barbara Wierzynski, Gen. Counsel & V.P., Regulatory Affairs
Counsel or consultant:
Rogers and Wells (David J. Gilberg, Kenneth M. Raisler)

Futures Industry Political Action Committee
1825 Eye St., N.W., Suite 1040, Washington, DC 20006
Telephone: (202) 466-5460
Background: Represented by John Damgard of the Futures Industry Ass'n.

G. W. Electronics
Sacramento, CA
Counsel or consultant:
State & Local Resources (Bruce D. Henderson, Patrick M. Murphy)

Gabon, Republic of
Libreville, Gabon
Counsel or consultant:
White & Case

GAF Corp.
New York, NY
Counsel or consultant:
Kaye, Scholer, Fierman, Hays and Handler (Paul A. Zevnik)
Sutherland, Asbill and Brennan

Galactica Biochemical
Counsel or consultant:
TCI Washington Group (Merrill Williams)

Gallard-Schlesinger Chemical Manufacturing Corp.
Carle Place, NY
Counsel or consultant:
Max N. Berry Law Offices (Max N. Berry)

Gallatin Institute
1620 Eye St., N.W., Washington, DC 20006
Telephone: (202) 965-4717
Counsel or consultant:
Nordlinger Associates

Gamma Corp.
Austin, TX
Counsel or consultant:
Williams and Jensen, P.C. (George D. Baker)

Gana-A' Yoo, Ltd.
Galena, AK
Counsel or consultant:
Patton, Boggs and Blow (James B. Christian, Jr.)

Gannett Co., Inc.
1100 Wilson Blvd., Arlington, VA 22234
Telephone: (703) 284-6046
Background: A nationwide news and information company. Publishes 83 daily newspapers, including USA TODAY; 52 publications, including USA WEEKEND, a newspaper magazine. Operates 10 TV and 16 radio stations, Gannett News Services and the largest outdoor advertising company in N. America.
Represented by:
Mimi A. Feller, V. Pres., Public Affrs. & Gov't Relats.
Sheila J. Gibbons, Director, Public Affairs
Counsel or consultant:
Dow, Lohnes and Albertson (Arnold P. Lutzker)

Garden Centers of America
1250 Eye St., N.W., Suite 500, Washington, DC 20005
Telephone: (202) 789-2900
Background: Represented by Lawrence E. Scovotto of the American Ass'n of Nurserymen.

Garden State Paper Co.
Garfield, NJ
Background: A recycler of newsprint.
Counsel or consultant:
Davidson Colling Group, Inc., The (Terese Colling)

Garuda Indonesian Airways
Jakarta, Indonesia

Counsel or consultant:
Burwell, Hansen, Peters and Houston (Walter D. Hansen)

Garvey, Schubert & Barer Political Action Committee
1000 Potomac St., N.W., Washington, DC 20007
Telephone: (202) 965-7880
Counsel or consultant:
Garvey, Schubert & Barer (Alan A. Butchman)

Gary Aircraft Corp.
Hondo, TX
Counsel or consultant:
Stovall & Spradlin

Gary, Indiana, City of
Counsel or consultant:
Simon & Co., Inc. (Leonard S. Simon)

Gas Appliance Manufacturers Ass'n
1901 North Moore St., Arlington, VA 22209
Telephone: (703) 525-9565
Represented by:
C. Reuben Autery, President
Joseph M. Mattingly, Director, Gov't Affrs & General Counsel
Richard M. Schum, Assoc. Director, Gov't Affairs

Gas Employees Political Action Committee
1515 Wilson Blvd., 12th Floor, Arlington, VA 22209
Telephone: (703) 841-8400
Background: The Political Action Committee of the American Gas Ass'n. Represented by Russell T. Keene of the Association.

Gas Research Institute
1331 Pennsylvania Ave., N.W., Suite 730 North, Washington, DC 20004
Telephone: (202) 662-8989
Represented by:
Daniel A. Dreyfus, V. Pres., Strat. Analysis & Energy Fcstn
Richard H. Hilt, Ass't Dir., Energy Analysis & Forcasting
Thomas T. Leuchtenburg, Dir, Gov't Rels. & Public Communications
Gail C. McDonald, Manager, Regulatory Affairs
Michelle McElroy, Manager, Public Information
A. Lee Wallace, III, Dir./Counsel, Regulatory & Leg. Affairs
David O. Webb, Sr. V. Pres., Policy & Regulatory Affrs.
Counsel or consultant:
Gallagher, Boland, Meiburger and Brosnan (James M. Broadstone)

Gasoline Alliance to Preserve Competition
Washington, DC
Counsel or consultant:
McNair Law Firm, P.A. (Thomas H. Barksdale, Jr.)

Gates Corp.
Denver, CO
Counsel or consultant:
Stewart and Stewart (Terrence P. Stewart)

Gateway Freight Services Inc.
Los Angeles, CA
Counsel or consultant:
McNair Group Inc. (Denis J. Dwyer)
McNair Law Firm, P.A. (Matthew Scocozza)

Gay Head Taxpayers' Ass'n
Gay Head, MA
Counsel or consultant:
Hale and Dorr (Jay P. Urwitz)

Gay and Lesbian Activists Alliance
1517 U St., N.W., Suite 1A, Washington, DC 20009
Telephone: (202) 667-5139
Represented by:
Roger Doughty, President

Gaymar Industries, Inc.
Orchard Park, NY
Counsel or consultant:
Liz Robbins Associates (Sharon Edwards, Liz Robbins)

GE Nuclear Energy
12300 Twinbrook Pkwy., Rockville, MD 20852
Telephone: (301) 770-9650
Represented by:
Laurence S. Gifford, Manager, Regulatory Operations

The listings in this directory are available as *Mailing Labels*. See last page.

ORGANIZATIONS REPRESENTED

GEICO Corp.
GEICO Plaza, Washington, DC 20076
Telephone: (301) 986-3000
Represented by:
August P. Alegi, V. Pres. and Legislative Counsel
Andrea M. Covell, Asst. V. Pres. & Asst. Legislat. Counsel
G. D. Gertz, Ass't Counsel
Walter R. Smith, Director, Communications
Counsel or consultant:
Hartz/Meek Internat'l

GEICO Political Action Committee
Geico Plaza, Washington, DC 20076
Telephone: (202) 986-2657
Background: August P. Alegi of GEICO Corp. is the Chairman.

GenCorp
Akron, OH
Counsel or consultant:
Verner, Liipfert, Bernhard, McPherson and Hand, Chartered (Lloyd N. Hand)

Genentech, Inc.
1747 Pennsylvania Ave., N.W. Suite 1223, Washington, DC 20006
Telephone: (202) 296-7272
Represented by:
David Beier, V. President, Government Affairs
John P. McLaughlin, V. President, General Counsel
Counsel or consultant:
Bracewell and Patterson (Gene E. Godley)
Parry and Romani Associates Inc.
Podesta Associates (John D. Podesta)
Reed Smith Shaw & McClay

General Atomics
1100 17th St., N.W., Suite 1200, Washington, DC 20036
Telephone: (202) 659-3140
Represented by:
Kathryne M. Bruner, Mgr., Energy Development Technologies
Norval E. Carey, Sr. V. President, Government Operations
Wayne D. Willis, Manager, Technical Liaison/Defense
Counsel or consultant:
Cutler and Stanfield (Jeffrey L. Stanfield)
Charlie McBride Assoc, Inc. (Charlie McBride)
Robison Internat'l, Inc.
J. C. Steen

General Aviation Manufacturers Ass'n
1400 K St., Suite 801, Washington, DC 20005
Telephone: (202) 393-1500
Represented by:
James D. Gormley, President
Stanley J. Green, V. President-General Counsel
Henry M. Ogrodzinski, Director of Communications
Phillip L. Rodenberg, Director, Legislative Affairs
Shelly R. Snyder, Asst. to the Director of Communication
Counsel or consultant:
Dow, Lohnes and Albertson (Richard S. Belas)
Verner, Liipfert, Bernhard, McPherson and Hand, Chartered (Amy L. Bondurant)

General Aviation Manufacturers Ass'n Political Action
1400 K St., N.W. Suite 801, Washington, DC 20005
Telephone: (202) 393-1500
Background: Supported by the General Aviation Manufacturers Ass'n. James D. Gormley of the Association serves as Secretary-Treasurer.

General Cellular Corp.
San Francisco, CA
Counsel or consultant:
Nossaman, Guthner, Knox and Elliott (Murray Zweben)

General Chemical Corp.
Parsippany, NJ
Counsel or consultant:
Concord Associates, Inc.

General Communication Incorporated
Anchorage, AK
Counsel or consultant:
Robertson, Monagle and Eastaugh (Steven W. Silver)

General Conference of Seventh-day Adventists
12501 Old Columbia Pike, Silver Spring, MD 20904

Telephone: (301) 680-6320
Represented by:
Bert B. Beach, Director of Public Affairs
Shirley Burton, Director of Communication
Gary M. Ross, Congressional Liaison
Counsel or consultant:
Johns and Carson

General Development Corp.
Miami, FL
Counsel or consultant:
Hill and Knowlton Public Affairs Worldwide
Holland and Knight (Janet R. Studley)
Lee, Toomey & Kent
Skadden, Arps, Slate, Meagher and Flom (Robert E. Lighthizer)

General Dynamics Corp.
1745 Jefferson Davis Hwy., Suite 1000, Arlington, VA 22202
Telephone: (703) 553-1200
Represented by:
Ellen B. Brown, Corp. Dir, Procure. & Acquisition Policy
Peter J. Gossens, Corporate Manager, Legislative Affairs
Karl F. Lauenstein, Corp. Dir., Legis. Affairs - Internat'l
William W. Maurer, Corporate Director, Legislative Affairs
W. H. L. Mullins, Corp. V. President, Government Relations
Jerry Pohlen, Director, Government Relations (Cessna)
Alvin A. Spivak, Corp. Dir., Public Affairs-Washington
John J. Stirk, Staff V. Pres., Congressional Relations
Robert L. Whitmire, Corp. Mgr., Legislative Affairs-Navy
Counsel or consultant:
Cambridge Internat'l, Inc. (Justus P. White)
Dressendorfer-Laird, Inc. (John H. Dressendorfer)
Neill and Co. (John E. Bircher, III, Denis M. Neill)
Verner, Liipfert, Bernhard, McPherson and Hand, Chartered (Amy L. Bondurant)

General Dynamics Valley Systems Division
Ontario, CA
Counsel or consultant:
Cambridge Internat'l, Inc. (Justus P. White)

General Dynamics Voluntary Political Contribution Plan
1745 Jefferson Davis Hwy. Suite 1000, Arlington, VA 22202
Telephone: (703) 553-1290
Background: A political action committee sponsored by General Dynamics Corp. Represented by W. H. L. Mullins of General Dynamics Corp.

General Electric Co.
1331 Pennsylvania Ave., N.W. Suite 800S, Washington, DC 20004
Telephone: (202) 637-4000

Represented by:
Robert W. Barrie, Mgr., Federal Legis. Relations
B. A. Barron, Mgr., Fin. Anal. & Regulatory Opns.
Kristina M. Beach, Manager, Congressional Relations
Anne C. Canfield, Washington Rep., Government Relations
K. Richard Cook, Wash. Representative, Gov't Relations
John W. Davis, Manager, Congressional Relations
D. B. Denning, V. President, Government Services
Mary Ann Freeman, Mgr., Congressional & Industry Relations
Clifford C. LaPlante, Mgr., Cong. & Exec. Aircraft Engineering
William F. McManus, Washington Rep., Gov't Relations
Neil T. Messick, Washington Rep., Government Relations
Robert M. Moliter, Manager, Gov't Prog. Op'tns, Medical Sy.
Phillips S. Peter, V. Pres., Corporate Gov't Relations
David Alan Portnoy, Repesentative, Civil Programs
Zack H. Shelley, Jr., Mgr., Aerospace Congressional Relations
Patricia A. Sherman, Counsel, Internat'l Trade Pol. & Export
William A. Shumann, Media Relations Representative
Ronald Singer, Manager, Internat'l Programs Operation
Susan Walter, Mgr., State Gov't Relations Operations
David M. Yannitell, Mgr, Nucl. Energy Proj., GE Nucl. Energy
Counsel or consultant:
Baker and McKenzie (William D. Outman, II)
John G. Campbell, Inc.
Cohn and Marks (Stanley B. Cohen)
Covington and Burling (Patricia Anne Barald, Allan J. Topol)
Fierce and Associates (Donald L. Fierce)
Fried, Frank, Harris, Shriver & Jacobson (Marcus A. Rowden)
Hill and Knowlton Public Affairs Worldwide (Dale Lawson)
Frederick L. Ikenson, P.C. (Frederick L. Ikenson)
Madison Group/Earle Palmer Brown, The (Edward M. Gabriel)
McCutchen, Doyle, Brown & Enersen
Neill and Co. (Denis M. Neill)
Perkins Coie (Anthony J. Thompson)
Prather, Seeger, Doolittle and Farmer (Kurt E. Blase, D. Edward Wilson, Jr.)
David A. Wilkinson

General Electric Information Services
New York, NY
Counsel or consultant:
Wiley, Rein & Fielding (Mimi Weyforth Dawson)

General Electric Mortgage Insurance Co.
Raleigh, NC
Counsel or consultant:
Thacher, Proffitt and Wood (Virginia W. Brown, Louis H. Nevins)

General Electric Pension Trust
Stamford, CT
Counsel or consultant:
Dewey, Ballantine, Bushby, Palmer and Wood

General Electric Plastics
Pittsfield, MA
Counsel or consultant:
Rowland & Sellery (J. Patrick Rowland, Lawrence E. Sabbath)

General Federation of Women's Clubs
1734 N St., N.W., Washington, DC 20036
Telephone: (202) 347-3168
Represented by:
Gail Collins, Legislative Director
Alice C. Donahue, Internat'l President
Sally Kranz, Director, Public Relations
Leigh Wintz, Exec. Director

General Foods Foundation
White Plains, NY
Counsel or consultant:
Daniel J. Edelman, Inc. (Elizabeth Kelley)

General Housewares Corp.
Terra Haute, IN
Counsel or consultant:
Kilpatrick & Cody (Joseph W. Dorn)

The listings in this directory are available as *Mailing Labels.* See last page.

563

ORGANIZATIONS REPRESENTED

General Instrument Corp.
1155 21st St., N.W., Suite 400, Washington, DC 20036
Telephone: (202) 833-9700
Represented by:
Deborah M. Phillips, Sr. Representative, Government Affairs
Quincy Rodgers, Director, Government Affairs
Counsel or consultant:
Keck, Mahin and Cate

General Instrument Corp. Political Action Committee
1155 21st St., N.W., Suite 400, Washington, DC 20036
Telephone: (202) 833-9700
Background: Represented by Quincy Rodgers and Deborah M. Phillips of the General Instrument Corp. Washington office.

General Mills
555 13th St., N.W., Suite 490 West, Washington, DC 20004
Telephone: (202) 737-8200
Represented by:
Robert S. Bird, Director, Washington Office
Mary Catherine Toker, Washington Representative
Counsel or consultant:
Arnold & Porter
Howrey and Simon (Ralph J. Savarese)
Lee, Toomey & Kent
Skadden, Arps, Slate, Meagher and Flom (Robert E. Lighthizer)
Wilner and Scheiner (Gilbert B. Lessenco)

General Motors (Allison Gas Turbines Division)
Indianapolis, IN
Counsel or consultant:
Snyder Ball Kriser and Associates, Inc. (Lou Kriser)

General Motors Corp.
1660 L St., N.W., 4th Floor, Washington, DC 20036
Telephone: (202) 775-5027
Represented by:
John T. Anderson, Media Coordinator, Public Relats. Staff
William L. Ball, Director, Washington Office
Carolyn L. Brehm, Senior Washington Representative
James D. Johnston, V. Pres., Industry & Gov't Relations
Edward M. Kavjian, Washington Representative
Mark L. Kemmer, Senior Washington Representative
Ingolf N. Kiland, Jr., Senior Washington Representative
Freddie H. Lucas, Senior Washington Representative
William H. Noack, Director, Public Relations - Washington
Stephen E. O'Toole, Senior Washington Representative
Charles R. Sharp, Esq., Counsel, Industry-Government Relations
Ronald G. Sykes, Senior Washington Representative
W. Grey Terry, News Relations Manager - Washington
Barbara J. Washburn, Senior Washington Representative
Counsel or consultant:
Bonner & Associates
John G. Campbell, Inc.
Duberstein Group, Inc., The
FMR Group Inc., The
Kirkland and Ellis (Alfred W. Cortese)
Multinational Business Services, Inc. (James J. Tozzi)
Wexler, Reynolds, Fuller, Harrison and Schule, Inc. (Robert M. Schule, Anne Wexler)
Williams and Connolly (Aubrey M. Daniel, III, Robert P. Watkins)

General Portland Inc.
Dallas, TX
Counsel or consultant:
Smith, Heenan and Althen (Michael T. Heenan)

General Railway Signal Co.
Rochester, NY
Background: A unit of General Signal Corp.
Counsel or consultant:
Hudson, Creyke, Koehler and Tacke

General Reinsurance
Stamford, CT
Counsel or consultant:
Dewey, Ballantine, Bushby, Palmer and Wood (Lawrence F. O'Brien, III)

General Signal Corp.
1735 Eye St., N.W., Suite 917, Washington, DC 20006

Telephone: (202) 785-3076
Represented by:
Richard Griffin, Director, Government Relations

General Telephone Co. of California
Santa Monica, CA
Counsel or consultant:
Covington and Burling

Generic Pharmaceutical Industry Ass'n
New York, NY
Counsel or consultant:
Henry J. Kaufman & Associates (John Seng)
King and Spalding
Lobel, Novins, Lamont and Flug (James F. Flug)
Parry and Romani Associates Inc. (Romano Romani)

Genesee and Wyoming Corp.
Greenwich, CT
Counsel or consultant:
RBC Associates, Inc. (Ray B. Chambers)

Genetics Institute Inc.
Cambridge, MA
Counsel or consultant:
Dorsey & Whitney (Will E. Leonard)
Ginsburg, Feldman and Bress (Peter M. Kirby, Mary Helen Sears)
Hale and Dorr (Jay P. Urwitz)

Genetics Soc. of America
9650 Rockville Pike, Bethesda, MD 20814
Telephone: (301) 571-1825
Represented by:
Gerry Gurvitch, Executive Director

Geneva Steel Co.
Provo, UT
Counsel or consultant:
Marcus G. Faust
Sonnenschein Nath & Rosenthal (Susan M. Frank)

Genix Corp.
Palo Alto, CA
Counsel or consultant:
Mica, Dudinsky & Associates (John Dudinsky, Jr., John L. Mica)

Geo-Centers, Inc.
Newton Upper Fls, MA
Counsel or consultant:
Michael Hugo & Associates (F. Michael Hugo)

Geodesco
Northbrook, IL
Counsel or consultant:
Tendler, Goldberg & Biggins, Chtd. (Paul M. Tendler)

GeoProducts Corp.
Walnut Creek, CA
Counsel or consultant:
F. H. Hutchison and Co. (Fred H. Hutchison)

George Mason University Law School
3401 N. Fairfax Drive, Arlington, VA 22201-4498
Telephone: (703) 841-7114
Represented by:
Lauren M. Cook, Director, Public Affairs and Development

George Washington Corp.
Jacksonville, FL
Counsel or consultant:
White & Case (Carolyn B. Lamm)

Georgia Internat'l Investment Coalition
Atlanta, GA
Counsel or consultant:
King and Spalding (Theodore M. Hester)

Georgia Kaolin Co.
Elizabeth, NJ
Counsel or consultant:
Sutherland, Asbill and Brennan (Edward J. Grenier, Jr.)

Georgia-Pacific Corp.
1875 Eye St., N.W. Suite 775, Washington, DC 20006
Telephone: (202) 659-3600

Represented by:
Maggie Dean, Ass't Director, Government Affairs
C. T. "Kip" Howlett, Jr., V. President, Government Affairs
Dave Modi, Director, Federal Government Affairs
Denise O'Donnell, Sr. Government Affairs Representative
John M. Turner, Corp. Director, Government Affairs
Counsel or consultant:
Jefferson Group, The (Randal Schumacher)
Lee, Toomey & Kent
McNair Law Firm, P.A.

Georgia-Pacific Employees Fund
1875 Eye St., N.W., Suite 400, Washington, DC 20006
Telephone: (202) 659-3600
Background: The political action committee of the Georgia-Pacific Corp. Contact is Denise M. O'Donnell of Georgia-Pacific Corp.'s Washington office.

Georgia Power Co.
1130 Connecticut Ave., N.W. Suite 830, Washington, DC 20036
Telephone: (202) 775-0944
Background: A subsidiary of Southern Co.
Represented by:
Craig S. Lesser, Manager, Legislative Affairs - Federal
Counsel or consultant:
Keller and Heckman
Shaw, Pittman, Potts and Trowbridge (William Mike House)

Georgia, State of
444 N. Capitol St., N.W. Suite 240, Washington, DC 20001
Telephone: (202) 624-5437
Represented by:
Betty E. Willis, Director, Washington Office

Georgia Tech Research Corp.
Atlanta, GA
Counsel or consultant:
Kilpatrick & Cody (C. Randall Nuckolls)

Geostar Corp.
1001 22nd St., N.W., Washington, DC 20037
Telephone: (202) 887-0870
Represented by:
Christine Brazeau, Coordinator, Govt'l Affairs
Dr. T. Stephan Ceston, Exec V Pres., Internat'l/ Govt'l Affairs

Geothermal Resources Ass'n
1050 Thomas Jefferson St. N.W. Seventh Floor, Washington, DC 20007
Telephone: (202) 298-1800
Counsel or consultant:
Perkins Coie (Guy R. Martin)
Van Ness, Feldman & Curtis (Milly Crawford, Ben Yamagata)

Gerald D. Hines Interests
Dallas, TX
Counsel or consultant:
Peyser Associates, Inc.

Gerber Products Corp.
Fremont, MI
Counsel or consultant:
Hill and Knowlton Public Affairs Worldwide (Donald F. Massey)

Gerico
Denver, CO
Counsel or consultant:
Collier, Shannon & Scott (Michael R. Kershow)

German Democratic Republic, Embassy of the
1717 Massachusetts Ave., N.W., Washington, DC 20036
Telephone: (202) 232-3134
Counsel or consultant:
Marshall, Tenzer, Greenblatt, Fallon and Kaplan (Sylvan M. Marshall)

German Flatware Manufacturers Ass'n
Frankfurt, West Germany
Counsel or consultant:
Coudert Brothers (Milo C. Coerper)

German Marshall Fund of the United States
11 Dupont Circle, N.W., Suite 750, Washington, DC 20036
Telephone: (202) 745-3950

ORGANIZATIONS REPRESENTED

Represented by:
Frank E. Loy, President
Peter R. Weitz, Director of Programs

German Nat'l Tourist Office
New York, NY
Counsel or consultant:
Hill and Knowlton Public Affairs Worldwide (Mary C. Foerster)

German Specialty Steel Ass'n
West Germany
Counsel or consultant:
Coudert Brothers (Milo C. Coerper)

Germany, Ministry of Posts and Communications of the Federal Republic of
Bonn, West Germany
Counsel or consultant:
Wilkinson, Barker, Knauer and Quinn

Gerontological Soc. of America
1275 K St., N.W., Suite 350, Washington, DC 20005
Telephone: (202) 842-1275
Represented by:
John M. Cornman, Exec. Director

Gerson and Co., L. M.
Middleboro, MA
Counsel or consultant:
Jefferson Group, The (Mark D. Cowan)

Gesamtverband der Deutschen Versicherungswirtschaft e.V.
Bonn, West Germany
Counsel or consultant:
Wunder, Ryan, Cannon & Thelen (Kenneth S. Levine)

Giant Food Inc.
6300 Sheriff Road, Landover, MD 20785
Telephone: (301) 341-4100
Represented by:
Barry F. Scher, V. President, Public Affairs

Giant Industries
Phoenix, AZ
Counsel or consultant:
Sachs Greenebaum and Tayler (Joseph J. Zimmerman)

Gibraltar Information Bureau
1155 15th St., N.W., Washington, DC 20005
Telephone: (202) 452-1108
Represented by:
Perry J. Stieglitz, Director

Gibraltar, P.R., Inc.
San Lorenzo, PR
Counsel or consultant:
Jefferson Group, The (Frederick J. Hannett)

Gifts in Kind, Inc.
700 North Fairfax St., Suite 300, Alexandria, VA 22314
Telephone: (703) 836-2121
Background: Serves as liaison between donor corporations and not-for-profit organizations in distribution of corporate donations to the needy.
Represented by:
Susan Corrigan, Exec. V. President & CEO

Gillett Group Management, Inc.
Nashville, TN
Counsel or consultant:
Winston and Strawn (John G. Milliken)

Gillette Co.
Boston, MA
Counsel or consultant:
Newmyer Associates, Inc.

Gilway Co., Ltd., The
Paramus, NJ
Counsel or consultant:
Max N. Berry Law Offices (Marsha A. Echols)

Girl Scouts of the U.S.A.
1025 Connecticut Ave., N.W. Suite 309, Washington, DC 20036
Telephone: (202) 659-3780
Background: A national organization for all girls ages 5-17, emphasizing service to society, development of values and self-awareness and leadership training.

Represented by:
Mary Frances Peters, Director, Washington Office

Girls Clubs of America, Inc.
1301 20th St., N.W. Suite 702, Washington, DC 20036
Telephone: (202) 296-2665
Represented by:
Sharon Parker, Washington Representative

Gist Brocades
Charlotte, NC
Counsel or consultant:
Max N. Berry Law Offices (Max N. Berry)

Givaudan Corp.
Basel, Switzerland
Counsel or consultant:
Sharretts, Paley, Carter and Blauvelt (Beatrice A. Brickell)

GKN Defense, Plc.
Telford, England
Counsel or consultant:
Interlocke Associates

Glass Packaging Institute
1801 K St., N.W., Suite 1105L, Washington, DC 20006
Telephone: (202) 887-4850
Represented by:
Lewis D. Andrews, Jr., President
R. Roger Fries, Director, Federal and Technical Affairs
Chaz Miller, Recycling Director
Sylvia E. Swanson, V. President, Public Affairs
Counsel or consultant:
O'Neill and Athy, P.C. (Andrew Athy, Jr.)
Powell, Adams & Rinehart

Glaxo Australia Pty, Ltd.
Victoria, Australia
Counsel or consultant:
Maupin Taylor Ellis & Adams, P.C. (Scott A. Wilson)

Glaxo, Inc.
1500 K St., N.W., Suite 650, Washington, DC 20005
Telephone: (202) 783-1277
Represented by:
Katherine D. Ladd, Director, Federal Health Policy
E. Geoffrey Littlehale, V. President, Government Relations
Sara L. Thomasson, Director, Congressional Affairs
Counsel or consultant:
R. Duffy Wall and Associates (R. D. Folsom)

Glendale Federal Savings and Loan Ass'n
Glendale, CA
Counsel or consultant:
Steptoe and Johnson (John T. Collins)

Glick & Glick
Rowlett, TX
Background: Employment consultants.
Counsel or consultant:
Keefe Co., The (Camilla A. McGhee, William A. Signer)

Global Marine, Inc.
Houston, TX
Counsel or consultant:
Jack Ferguson Associates
Leva, Hawes, Mason and Martin (Harold E. Mesirow)

Global Medical Products, Inc.
Miami, FL
Counsel or consultant:
Balsamo & Associates, Chartered (Richard W. Balsamo)

Global Tomorrow Coalition
1325 G St., N.W., Suite 915, Washington, DC 20005-3104
Telephone: (202) 628-4016
Background: A consortium of over 115 organizations whose combined memberships total over 10 million Americans with a common interest in the health of the planet's economic and ecological future. Educates community groups, teachers and policy makers on the interrelationship of population, environmental, natural resource and economic problems and encourages stronger U.S. leadership in the search for solutions.
Represented by:
Donald R. Lesh, President
Diane G. Lowrie, V. President

Globaldebt
1129 20th St., N.W., Washington, DC 20036
Telephone: (202) 331-1369
Counsel or consultant:
St. Germain, Rodio & Ursillo, Ltd. (Fernand J. St. Germain)

Globe Corp.
Scottsdale, AZ
Counsel or consultant:
McDermott, Will and Emery (Robert A. Warden)

Globe Securities System Inc.
Philadelphia, PA
Counsel or consultant:
Kelly and Associates, Inc. (John A. Kelly)

Gloucester County, New Jersey
Counsel or consultant:
Krivit and Krivit (Daniel H. Krivit)

GMS/Partners
Counsel or consultant:
U.S. Strategies Corp. (Michael P. Skredynski)

GNB, Inc.
Mendota Heights, MN
Counsel or consultant:
Edward H. Forgotson

Go-Video
Scottsdale, AZ
Counsel or consultant:
Preston Gates Ellis & Rouvelas Meeds (Bruce J. Heiman)

Gold Institute
1026 16th St., N.W. Suite 101, Washington, DC 20036
Telephone: (202) 783-0500
Counsel or consultant:
Klein & Saks, Inc. (Cindy Joy Arenberg, Michael J. Brown, John H. Lutley)

Goldbelt, Inc.
Juneau, AK
Counsel or consultant:
Camp, Barsh, Bates and Tate

Golden Alaska Seafoods, Inc.
Seattle, WA
Counsel or consultant:
Preston Gates Ellis & Rouvelas Meeds (John L. Bloom, William N. Myhre)

Golden Nugget, Inc.
Las Vegas, NV
Counsel or consultant:
LeBoeuf, Lamb, Leiby, and MacRae (John K. Meagher)

Golden West Broadcasters
Los Angeles, CA
Counsel or consultant:
Kaye, Scholer, Fierman, Hays and Handler (Jason Shrinsky)

Goldman, Sachs and Co.
1101 Pennsylvania Ave., N.W. Suite 900, Washington, DC 20004
Telephone: (202) 637-3700
Represented by:
W. Carter Doswell, V. President
C. Peter Rose, V. President
Judah C. Sommer, V. President and Manager
Counsel or consultant:
Duberstein Group, Inc., The
Kaye, Scholer, Fierman, Hays and Handler (Kenneth R. Feinberg)
Mintz, Levin, Cohn, Ferris, Glovsky and Popeo, P.C. (Francis X. Meaney)
Reed Smith Shaw & McClay (T. Timothy Ryan, Jr.)
Stroock & Stroock & Lavan (Mark N. Rae)
Vinson and Elkins (John E. Chapoton)

Goldome FSB
Buffalo, NY
Counsel or consultant:
Williams and Jensen, P.C. (William T. Brack)

GoldStar Co., Ltd.
Seoul, Korea
Counsel or consultant:
Dow, Lohnes and Albertson (William Silverman)

The listings in this directory are available as *Mailing Labels.* See last page.

565

ORGANIZATIONS REPRESENTED

Golodetz Corp.
New York, NY
Counsel or consultant:
Arnold & Porter (Thomas R. Dwyer)

Gonzaga University
Spokane, WA
Counsel or consultant:
Cassidy and Associates, Inc. (C. Frank Godfrey, Jr.)

Good Relations
London, England
Counsel or consultant:
TKC Internat'l, Inc.

Goodrich Co., BF
1825 Eye St., N.W., Suite 400, Washington, DC 20006
Telephone: (202) 429-2060
Represented by:
Gerrie Bjornson, Director, Government Relations
Marie Taylor, Asst. to Dir., Government Relations

Goodwill Industries of America, Inc.
9200 Wisconsin Ave., Bethesda, MD 20814-3896
Telephone: (301) 530-6500
Represented by:
David Barringer, Director, Communications
David M. Cooney, President
Miriam B. Goulding, Gen. Counsel & Dir. of Gov'tl Affairs

Goody Products, Inc.
Kearny, NJ
Counsel or consultant:
Economic Consulting Services Inc. (Mark W. Love, Deborah Swartz)

Goodyear Tire and Rubber Co.
901 15th St., N.W. Suite 350, Washington, DC 20005
Telephone: (202) 682-9250
Represented by:
Isabel E. Hyde, Director, Federal & Legislative Affairs
Robert G. Mercer, Manager, Public Relations
Frank T. Ryan, Director, State and Regulatory Affairs
Rudolph A. Vignone, V. President, Governmental Relations
Counsel or consultant:
Multinational Business Services, Inc. (James J. Tozzi)
Stewart and Stewart (Terrence P. Stewart)
Charls E. Walker Associates

Government Accountability Project (GAP)
25 E St., N.W. Suite 700, Washington, DC 20001
Telephone: (202) 347-0460
Background: An activity to assist and advise "whistleblowers" in government.
Represented by:
Louis Clark, Exec. Director
Joseph B. Kennedy, Consulting Attorney
Counsel or consultant:
Thomas Devine

Government Affairs Policy Council of the Regional Bell Operating Companies
c/o Laird Walker, US West 1020 19th St., N.W., Suite 700, Washington, DC 20036
Telephone: (202) 429-3100
Counsel or consultant:
Paul, Hastings, Janofsky and Walker (Ralph B. Everett, Judith Richards Hope)

Government Finance Officers Ass'n
1750 K St., N.W. Suite 200, Washington, DC 20006
Telephone: (202) 429-2750
Represented by:
Betsy Dotson, Legislative Rep., Federal Liaison Center
Cathie G. Eitelberg, Ass't Director, Federal Liaison Center
Catherine L. Spain, Director, Federal Liaison Center

Government Refuse Collection and Disposal Ass'n
Silver Spring, MD
Counsel or consultant:
Spiegel and McDiarmid

Governmental Standards Accounting Board
1350 Connecticut Ave., N.W. Suite 620, Washington, DC 20036
Telephone: (202) 466-8016
Background: Represented by Patricia Pride of the Financial Accounting Foundation.

Governors Club Development Corp.
Chapel Hill, NC
Counsel or consultant:
Dow, Lohnes and Albertson (William B. Ingersoll)

GPIA Animal Drug Alliance
New York, NY
Counsel or consultant:
King and Spalding (Theodore M. Hester, Jess H. Stribling)

GPU Service Corp.
600 Maryland Ave., S.W., Suite 520, Washington, DC 20024
Telephone: (202) 554-7616
Background: A utility. The parent company of GPU Nuclear Corp. (operator of Three Mile Island), Jersey Central Power & Light Co., Metropolitan Edison Co., and the Pennsylvania Electric Co.
Represented by:
Darnell K. Horio, Legislative Assistant
Cynthia Mansfield, Director, Government Affairs
Counsel or consultant:
Bishop, Cook, Purcell & Reynolds
Burson-Marsteller (Wayne L. Pines)
Shaw, Pittman, Potts and Trowbridge (Ernest L. Blake, Jr.)

Grace and Co., W. R.
919 18th St., N.W., Suite 400, Washington, DC 20006
Telephone: (202) 452-6700
Represented by:
Donald A. Crane, Assoc. Director, Government Relations
Alan D. Fiers, Corp V. Pres. & Dir., Gov't Relations
Polly S. Hannas, Manager, Legislative Affairs
Jacquelyn M. Johnson, Manager, Environmental Affairs
Joseph B. Kelley, Manager, State and Outreach Affairs
Hugh J. McGillicuddy, Government Marketing Representative
Kenneth Y. Millian, Corp. V. Pres. & Dir., Envirmnt'l Afrs.
Priscilla N. Myerson, Associate Director, Government Marketing
Edlu J. Thom, Assoc. Director, Environmental Affairs

Graco, Inc.
Minneapolis, MN
Counsel or consultant:
Wilner and Scheiner (Gilbert B. Lessenco)

Grain and Feed Trade Ass'n, The
London, England
Counsel or consultant:
Arnold & Porter (Brooksley E. Born, John M. Quinn, Daniel Waldman)

Grand Canyon Chamber Music Festival Inc.
New York, NY
Counsel or consultant:
Richard Curry and Associates (Richard C. Curry)

Grand Canyon Trust
1400 16th St. N.W., Suite 300, Washington, DC 20036
Telephone: (202) 797-5429
Background: An environmental and natural resources conservation organization concerned primarily with the Grand Canyon and other public land land and water resources on the Colorado River and Plateau area.
Represented by:
Hilary Hart, Conservation Associate
Edward M. Norton, Jr., President
Craig Parker, V. President for Public Affairs

Grand Council of the Cress
Quebec City, Canada
Counsel or consultant:
Pierson, Semmes, and Finley

Grand Haven, Michigan, City of
Counsel or consultant:
Preston Gates Ellis & Rouvelas Meeds (Allen Erenbaum, Craig J. Gehring)

Grand Met USA
Montvale, NJ
Counsel or consultant:
Akin, Gump, Strauss, Hauer and Feld (Smith W. Davis, Daniel Spiegel)

Grand Metropolitan PLC
London, England

Counsel or consultant:
Akin, Gump, Strauss, Hauer and Feld
Fort and Schlefer (Leonard Egan)
O'Connor & Hannan
Wilmer, Cutler and Pickering (John H. Pickering)

Grand Targhee Ski Resort
Alta, WY
Counsel or consultant:
Birch, Horton, Bittner and Cherot (Joseph M. Chomski)

Grand Trunk Corp.
Detroit, MI
Background: Subsidiaries include Grand Trunk Western Railroad Co.; Central Vermont Railway, Inc. and Duluth Winnipeg and Pacific Railway Co.
Counsel or consultant:
Hopkins and Sutter (Robert P. vom Eigen)

Granite Industrial Development
Buford, GA
Counsel or consultant:
Kilpatrick & Cody (C. Randall Nuckolls)

Grant County P.U.D.
Ephrata, WA
Counsel or consultant:
Schwabe, Williamson and Wyatt (Frederick P. Hitz)

Grant Foundation, W. T.
1001 Connecticut Ave., N.W. Suite 301, Washington, DC 20036-5541
Telephone: (202) 775-9731
Counsel or consultant:
Gallagher-Widmeyer Group Inc., The (Scott D. Widmeyer)

Graphic Communications Ass'n
1730 North Lynn St. Suite 604, Arlington, VA 22209
Telephone: (703) 841-8160
Represented by:
Norman W. Scharpf, President

Graphic Communications Internat'l Union
1900 L St., N.W., Washington, DC 20036
Telephone: (202) 462-1400
Represented by:
James J. Norton, President

Graphic Communications Internat'l Union Political Contributions Committee
1900 L St., N.W., Washington, DC 20036
Telephone: (202) 462-1400
Represented by:
John M. Greer, Chairman

Grass Roots in Politics (NFO GRIP)
475 L'Enfant Plaza, S.W., Suite 2250, Washington, DC 20024
Telephone: (202) 484-7075
Background: The political action committee of the Nat'l Farmers Organization. Contact is Charles L. Frazier of the Organization.

Gravure Research Institute
Port Washington, NY
Background: Represented by Benjamin Y. Cooper of Printing Industries of America.

Gravure Technical Ass'n
New York, NY
Background: Represented by Benjamin Y. Cooper of Printing Industries of America.

Gray Panthers Nat'l Office in Washington
1424 16th St., N.W., Washington, DC 20036
Telephone: (202) 387-3111
Background: An advocacy organization for the aging which, among other things, has worked to improve nursing home care and to eliminate discrimination in employment on the basis of age.
Represented by:
Frances Humphreys, Director, Washington Office

Great American Broadcasting Co.
Cincinnati, OH
Counsel or consultant:
Taft, Stettinius and Hollister (Virginia E. Hopkins, Robert Taft, Jr.)

Great Lakes Dredge and Dock Co.
Oak Brook, IL

The listings in this directory are available as *Mailing Labels*. See last page.

ORGANIZATIONS REPRESENTED

Counsel or consultant:
  Cassidy and Associates, Inc. (Robert K. Dawson, Thomas M. Gannon)

Great Northern Insured Annuity Corporation
Seattle, WA
Counsel or consultant:
  Miller & Chevalier, Chartered (Anne E. Moran)

Great Northern Nekoosa Corp.
Norwalk, CT
Counsel or consultant:
  Lee, Toomey & Kent

Great Plains Natural Gas Co.
Omaha, NE
Counsel or consultant:
  Reid & Priest (Peyton G. Bowman, III)

Great Western Financial Corp.
Beverly Hills, CA
Counsel or consultant:
  Braun & Company
  B. L. Evans & Assoc. Inc. (Billy Lee Evans)
  Kelley, Drye and Warren (Michael R. Lemov)
  Thacher, Proffitt and Wood (Louis H. Nevins)

Greater Denver Corporation
Denver, CO
Counsel or consultant:
  Kogovsek & Associates, Inc.

Greater New York Hospital Ass'n
New York, NY
Counsel or consultant:
  Baker and Hostetler (Frederick H. Graefe)
  Keefe Co., The (Camilla A. McGhee, William A. Signer)

Greater Orlando Aviation Authority
Orlando, FL
Counsel or consultant:
  Mica, Dudinsky & Associates (John Dudinsky, Jr., John L. Mica)

Greater Washington Board of Trade
1129 20th St., N.W., Washington, DC 20036
Telephone: (202) 857-5910
Represented by:
  Samuel W. Christine, III, Manager, Legislative Bureau
  John R. Tydings, Exec. V. President

Greater Washington Ibero-American Chamber of Commerce
733 15th St., N.W., Suite 315, Washington, DC 20005
Telephone: (202) 737-2676
Background: Founded in 1977 to promote the establishment and growth of the area's Hispanic-owned businesses.
Represented by:
  Walter Divila, President

Greater Washington/Maryland Service Station and Automotive Repair Ass'n
9420 Annapolis Road, Suite 307, Lanham, MD 20706
Telephone: (301) 577-2875
Represented by:
  Roy E. Littlefield, Exec. Director
  Ellen Valentino, Government Relations

Greater Washington/Maryland Service Station and Automotive Repair Ass'n PAC
9420 Annapolis Road, Suite 307, Lanham, MD 20706
Telephone: (301) 577-2875
Background: Contact is Roy E. Littlefield of the Ass'n.
Represented by:
  William Apicella, Treasurer

Greater Washington Soc. of Ass'n Executives
1426 21st St., N.W., Suite 200, Washington, DC 20036
Telephone: (202) 429-9370
Represented by:
  Stephen W. Carey, CAE, Exec. V. President
Counsel or consultant:
  Loomis, Owen, Fellman and Howe (James E. Anderson)

Greece, Embassy of
2221 Massachusetts Ave., N.W., Washington, DC 20008
Telephone: (202) 667-3168
Counsel or consultant:
  Manatos & Manatos, Inc. (Andrew E. Manatos)

Green Bay and Western Railroad Co.
Green Bay, WI

Counsel or consultant:
  McCarthy, Sweeney and Harkaway, P.C.

Green Mountain Power Corp.
Burlington, VT
Counsel or consultant:
  Reid & Priest (Richard M. Merriman)

Green Olive Trade Ass'n
Carlstadt, NJ
Counsel or consultant:
  Steptoe and Johnson

Greenbaum & Rose Associates
Washington, DC
Counsel or consultant:
  Laxalt, Washington, Perito & Dubuc (Marc J. Scheineson)

Greenbrier Companies
Lake Oswego, OR
Counsel or consultant:
  Templeton and Co. (Patrick A. Templeton)

Greenbrier Leasing Corp.
Lake Oswego, OR
Counsel or consultant:
  Ball, Janik and Novack (James A. Beall)

Greenpeace, U.S.A.
1436 U St., N.W., Washington, DC 20009
Telephone: (202) 462-1177
Background: Environmental protection organization concerned with chemical and nuclear waste, endangered species of marine mammals, nuclear weapons testing, Antarctica, acid rain, ocean incineration of hazardous wastes, outercontinental shelf oil exploration.
Represented by:
  William M. Arkin, Nuclear Information Director
  Peter Bahouth, Exec. Director
  Gerald B. Leape, Legislative Director, Wildlife
  Laura Rubin, Ocean Ecology Specialist
  Stephen I. Schwartz, Legislative Coordinator, Nuclear
  J. R. Yeager, Administrative Director
Counsel or consultant:
  Kilpatrick & Cody (J. Vance Hughes)
  Wilmer, Cutler and Pickering

Greens Creek Mining Co.
Counsel or consultant:
  Prather, Seeger, Doolittle and Farmer (Kurt E. Blase)

Greenwich Capital Markets, Inc.
Greenwich, CT
Counsel or consultant:
  Hopkins and Sutter (William H. Bradford, Jr.)

Greenwood Press
Westport, CT
Counsel or consultant:
  Prather, Seeger, Doolittle and Farmer (J. William Doolittle)

Greeting Card Ass'n
1350 New York Ave., N.W., Suite 615, Washington, DC 20005
Telephone: (202) 393-1778
Background: Trade association representing greeting card publishers.
Counsel or consultant:
  Resources for Group Management, Inc. (Marianne McDermott)

Greeting Card Creative Network
1350 New York Ave., N.W. Suite 615, Washington, DC 20005
Telephone: (202) 393-1780
Counsel or consultant:
  Resources for Group Management, Inc. (Nancy Riviere)

Grenada, Government of
St. George's, Grenada
Counsel or consultant:
  Dutko & Associates (L. L. Hank Hankla)
  van Kloberg and Associates (Edward J. van Kloberg, III)

Grey, Clark, Shih and Associates, Ltd.
Ottawa, Ontario
Counsel or consultant:
  Strategic Policy, Inc. (William S. Merkin)

Greyhound Corp., The
2000 K St., N.W., Suite 203, Washington, DC 20006

Telephone: (202) 223-8630
Represented by:
  James T. Corcoran, V. President, Government Affairs
  Mary Vihstadt, Washington Representative

Greyhound Leasing and Financial Corp.
Phoenix, AZ
Counsel or consultant:
  Melrod, Redman and Gartlan, A Professional Corporation

Greyhound Lines, Inc.
1101 14th St., Suite 1201, Washington, DC 20005
Telephone: (202) 347-3827
Represented by:
  Theodore C. Knappen, Senior V. President/Gov't Affairs

Grinnell Corp.
Exeter, NH
Counsel or consultant:
  Schagrin Associates (Carol A. Colza, Roger B. Schagrin)

Grip-Rite, Ltd.
Purchase, NY
Counsel or consultant:
  Mudge Rose Guthrie Alexander and Ferdon (N. David Palmeter)

Grocery Manufacturers of America
1010 Wisconsin Ave., N.W., Suite 800, Washington, DC 20007
Telephone: (202) 337-9400
Represented by:
  Sherwin Gardner, Vice President, Science and Technology
  Allen Goldberg, Sr. Associate, Gov't & Media Relations
  James C. Hassett, Jace, Government Relations Representative
  C. Manly Molpus, President and Chief Executive Officer
  Jeffrey Nedelman, V. President, Public Affairs
  Kathleen Marie Ramsey, V. Pres., Legislation and Administration
  Nancy A. Weinberg, Director, Environmental Affairs
Counsel or consultant:
  Holland and Hart (William F. Demarest, Jr.)
  Kirkpatrick & Lockhart
  Bartley M. O'Hara, P.C.
  Vorys, Sater, Seymour and Pease
  Winthrop, Stimson, Putnam & Roberts (Ira S. Shapiro)
  Wunder, Ryan, Cannon & Thelen (W. Stephen Cannon, Patrick C. Koch)

Groth Air Services, Inc.
Castella, IA
Counsel or consultant:
  Paul H. DeLaney Law Offices (Paul H. DeLaney, Jr.)

Group Health Ass'n of America
1129 20th St., N.W. Suite 600, Washington, DC 20036
Telephone: (202) 778-3200
Background: A national "mother" organization of local Health Maintenance Organizations (HMOs).
Represented by:
  James F. Doherty, President
  Erling Hansen, General Counsel
  Susan Pisano, Director of Communication & Information
  Leslie A. Rose, Legislative Director

Group Health Ass'n of America Political Action Committee
1129 20th St., N.W., Washington, DC 20036
Telephone: (202) 778-3200
Background: Contacts are Leslie Rose of the parent organization

Group Health, Inc.
Counsel or consultant:
  Shea and Gould

Group Hospital and Medical Services, Inc.
Washington, DC
Counsel or consultant:
  Laxalt, Washington, Perito & Dubuc (Michael F. Cole)

Group Practice Political Action Committee
1422 Duke St., Alexandria, VA 22314
Telephone: (703) 838-0033
Background: Sponsored by the American Group Practice Ass'n. Represented by Dr. Donald W. Fisher and Brent V. Miller of the Ass'n.

The listings in this directory are available as *Mailing Labels*. See last page.

ORGANIZATIONS REPRESENTED

Group 1 Software
Greenbelt, MD
Counsel or consultant:
Daly Associates, Inc. (John Jay Daly)

Grumman Aerospace Corp.
Bethpage, NY
Counsel or consultant:
Cederberg and Associates (Elford A. Cederberg)

Grumman Corp.
1000 Wilson Blvd., Suite 2800, Arlington, VA 22209
Telephone: (703) 875-8400
Represented by:
Peter F. Barry, V. President - Washington Operations
George L. Brown, V. President - Washington Operations
Diane Craun-Harper, Director, Congressional Relations
Larry Hamilton, Director, Public Affairs -Wash. Office
William S. Hettinger, Director, Business Programs
John Kendrick, Director, Congressional Relations
Dana McGee, V. President - Congressional Liaison
E. Alan Middleton, Congressional Relations
Richard A. Milburn, V. President, Washington Operations
George Prytula, Director
Stephen Sutton, Director, Congressional Relations
Daniel G. Terry, V. President (Grumman Data Systems)
Counsel or consultant:
Bond Donatelli Inc. (Frank Donatelli)
Cove Associates (John F. Cove)
Fried, Frank, Harris, Shriver & Jacobson
Griffin, Johnson & Associates (David E. Johnson)

Grupo Industrial Alfa, S.A.
Nuevo Leon, Mexico
Counsel or consultant:
Sills & Brodsky, P.C. (Alvin J. Geske)

GSMMI Holdings Inc. Political Action Committee
1101 Pennsylvania Ave., N.W. Suite 900, Washington, DC
20004
Telephone: (202) 637-3700
Background: Also known as Goldman Sachs PAC. Responsible contact is Judah C. Sommer of Goldman, Sachs and Co.

GT-Devices, Inc.
5705-A General Washington Dr., Alexandria, VA 22312
Telephone: (703) 642-8150
Counsel or consultant:
Ashby and Associates (R. Barry Ashby)

GTE Corp.
1850 M St., N.W., Suite 1200, Washington, DC 20036
Telephone: (202) 463-5200
Represented by:
Dan Bart, Legal
C. Russell Campbell, Jr., Asst. Vice President - Legislative Affrs
Dennis Glaves, Director, Legislative Affairs
F. Whitney Hatch, Asst. V. President - Regulatory Affairs
James R. Hobson, Legal
F. James Koch, Director - Government Affairs
Gary Krach, Director, Internat'l Affairs
F. Gordon Maxson, Director - Regulatory Matters
Barbara L. Phillips, Legislative Affairs Director
Gail Polivy, Legal
Samuel F. Shawhan, Jr., Vice President-Government Affairs
Michael H. Troy, Director - Government Relations
Counsel or consultant:
McNair Group Inc. (Kathy E. Gallegos)
Mintz, Levin, Cohn, Ferris, Glovsky and Popeo, P.C.
Wiley, Rein & Fielding
Williams and Jensen, P.C. (William T. Brack)

GTE Corp. Political Action Club (GTE-PAC)
1850 M St., N.W. Suite 1200, Washington, DC 20036
Telephone: (202) 463-5271
Background: F. James Koch, of GTE, is the treasurer.

GTE Government Systems
1001 19th St. North Suite 1100, Arlington, VA 22209
Telephone: (703) 284-1770
Represented by:
Harold Patterson, Nat'l Accounts Manager
Counsel or consultant:
McNair Law Firm, P.A. (John W. Hunter)

GTE Products Corp.
Danvers, MA

Counsel or consultant:
Leighton and Regnery (Richard J. Leighton)

Guam Commission on Self-Determination
Agana, Guam
Counsel or consultant:
Dorsey & Whitney
Robinson, Lake, Lerer & Montgomery (Mark Helmke)

Guam, Office of the Attorney General of
Agana, Guam
Counsel or consultant:
Dorsey & Whitney

Guam, Port Authority of
Agana, Guam
Counsel or consultant:
Dorsey & Whitney

Guam-Uranao Development Co., Ltd.
Tokyo, Japan
Counsel or consultant:
Gerard F. Schiappa

Guan Haur Industries Ltd.
Taipei, Taiwan
Counsel or consultant:
Ablondi and Foster, P.C. (F. David Foster)

Guardian Life Insurance Co. of America
New York, NY
Counsel or consultant:
Arent, Fox, Kintner, Plotkin & Kahn (John D. Hushon)

Guardian Savings and Loan Ass'n
Houston, TX
Counsel or consultant:
Akin, Gump, Strauss, Hauer and Feld (Joel Jankowsky)

Guatemala Freedom Foundation
Guatemala City, Guatemala
Counsel or consultant:
MacKenzie McCheyne, Inc. (I. R. MacKenzie, Ana Colomar O'Brien)

Guatemala, Government of
Guatemala City, Guatemala
Counsel or consultant:
Bruce P. Cameron
DC Internat'l, Inc. (Andres R. Hernandez)
Internat'l Development Systems
Reichler Appelbaum and Wippman (Paul S. Reichler)

Guernsey and Co., C. H.
Oklahoma City, OK
Counsel or consultant:
Ashby and Associates (R. Barry Ashby)

Guess, Inc.
Los Angeles, CA
Counsel or consultant:
Dickstein, Shapiro and Morin (John C. Dill, James R. Jones)

Guggenheim Foundation, The Harry Frank
New York, NY
Counsel or consultant:
Cleary, Gottlieb, Steen and Hamilton (J. Eugene Marans)

Guide Dog Users, Inc.
1010 Vermont Ave., N.W. Suite 1100, Washington, DC
20005
Telephone: (202) 393-3666
Background: Represented by Roberta Douglas of the American Council of the Blind.

Guinea, Government of
Conakry, Guinea
Counsel or consultant:
Neill and Co. (Leslie A. Janka, Denis M. Neill)
White & Case

Guiness Peat Aviation
Stamford, CT
Counsel or consultant:
Baker, Worthington, Crossley, Stansberry & Woolf (III J. E. Murdock)

Guinness PLC
London, England
Counsel or consultant:
Kelley, Drye and Warren

Gulf Atlantic Transport Corp.
Jacksonville, FL
Counsel or consultant:
Denning and Wohlstetter (Joseph F. Mullins, Jr.)

Gulf Container Line
Houston, TX
Counsel or consultant:
Steptoe and Johnson (William Karas)

Gulf Power Co.
1130 Connecticut Ave., N.W. Suite 830, Washington, DC
20036
Telephone: (202) 775-0944
Background: A subsidiary of Southern Co.
Represented by:
Ralf W.K. Czepluch, Manager, Federal Legislative Affairs
Counsel or consultant:
C. V. & R. V. Maudlin (Robert V. Maudlin)

Gulf Resources & Chemical Corp.
Boston, MA
Counsel or consultant:
Prather, Seeger, Doolittle and Farmer (Edwin H. Seeger)

Gulf Seaports Marine Terminals Conference
New Orleans, LA
Counsel or consultant:
Schmeltzer, Aptaker and Sheppard (Edward J. Sheppard, IV)

Gulf States Utilities Co.
Beaumont, TX
Counsel or consultant:
Conner and Wetterhahn, P.C. (Troy B. Conner, Jr., Mark J. Wetterhahn)
Keller and Heckman
Reid & Priest (Raymond F. Dacek)

Gulfstream Aerospace Corp.
1000 Wilson Blvd., Suite 2701, Arlington, VA 22209
Telephone: (703) 276-9500
Represented by:
Douglas E. Ferlin, International Marketing
Douglass G. Wood, V. President, Military Marketing

Gulfstream Aerospace Corp. Political Action Committee
1000 Wilson Blvd., Suite 2701, Arlington, VA 22209
Telephone: (703) 276-9500
Background: Chairman of the Political Action Committee is Douglas E. Ferlin of Gulfstream Aerospace Corp.
Represented by:
Richard A. Krajec, Treasurer

Gun Owners of America
8001 Forbes Place, Suite 102, Springfield, VA 22151
Telephone: (703) 321-8585
Background: A conservative political action group opposing the registration of firearms. Founded in 1976 and based in Sacramento, it has a dues-paying membership of about 250,000 and has a budget of about 2 million dollars.
Represented by:
Lawrence D. Pratt, Exec. Director

Gundle Lining Systems, Inc.
Houston, TX
Counsel or consultant:
Evergreen Associates, Ltd. (Gerald Weaver)

Gurabo, Puerto Rico, City of
Counsel or consultant:
Jefferson Group, The (Jose Ortiz-Daliot)

Guyana Airways Corp.
Georgetown, Guyana
Counsel or consultant:
V. Michael Straus, P.C.

Gypsum Ass'n
810 First St., N.E., Suite 510, Washington, DC 20002
Telephone: (202) 289-5440
Represented by:
Dale Swecker, Director, Communications
Nancy E. Wagner, Director, Safety and Gov't Affairs
Jerry A. Walker, Exec. Director

H.C. Internat'l Trade, Inc.
Dallas, TX
Counsel or consultant:
Dutko & Associates (Daniel A. Dutko)

The listings in this directory are available as *Mailing Labels*. See last page.

ORGANIZATIONS REPRESENTED

H & D Communications Group
Farmington, CT
Counsel or consultant:
Kaye, Scholer, Fierman, Hays and Handler (Jason Shrinsky)

H. E. Ventures, Inc.
Minneapolis, MN
Counsel or consultant:
Wagner, Hines and Avary (Robert P. Avary, Jr., William J. Hines, James N. Juliana)

H.S.I.
West Bloomfield, MI
Counsel or consultant:
Jefferson Group, The (Julie Susman)

Hadson Corp.
1001 30th St., N.W. Suite 340, Washington, DC 20007
Telephone: (202) 337-5430
Represented by:
B. Jeanine Hull, Manager
Counsel or consultant:
Powell, Goldstein, Frazer and Murphy (Stuart E. Eizenstat)

Hadson Gas Systems
1001 30th St., N.W. Suite 340, Washington, DC 20007
Telephone: (202) 337-5430
Represented by:
Susan Woolum Ginsberg, Ass't Manager, Regulatory Affairs
Philip M. Martson, V. President

Haida Corp.
Hydaburg, AK
Counsel or consultant:
Jack Ferguson Associates

Haiti, Government of
Port-au-Prince, Haiti
Counsel or consultant:
Murphy and Demory, Ltd. (Admiral Daniel J. Murphy, USN (Ret.), Jeffrey J. Grieco)
van Kloberg and Associates (Edward J. van Kloberg, III)

Hale Foundation, The
422 First St., S.E. Suite 300, Washington, DC 20003
Telephone: (202) 546-2293
Background: Founded in 1976 to support educational and informational programs to foster greater public understanding and approval of the U.S. intelligence agencies. The President is Lawrence B. Sulc of The Nathan Hale Institute.

Hale Institute, The Nathan
422 First St., S.E., Washington, DC 20003
Telephone: (202) 546-2293
Background: The public information and education arm of The Hale Foundation. Dedicated to promoting better public understanding and support for the U.S. intelligence community.
Represented by:
Lawrence B. Sulc, President

Halecrest Co.
Edison, NJ
Counsel or consultant:
Reid & Priest (Peyton G. Bowman, III)

Hall-Kimbrell
Lawrence, KS
Counsel or consultant:
Daniel J. Edelman, Inc. (Jean Rainey)

Halliburton Co.
1150 Connecticut Ave., N.W. Suite 205, Washington, DC 20036
Telephone: (202) 223-0820
Background: Also represented by Wyll W. Pleger of Brown & Root, Inc.
Represented by:
Larry G. Bowles, Director, Government Relations

Hallmark Cards, Inc.
1615 L St., N.W., Suite 1220, Washington, DC 20036
Telephone: (202) 659-0946

Represented by:
Barbara G. Burchett, National Affairs Manager
Rae Forker Evans, Staff V. President, Nat'l Affairs
Teddi Norman-Quattrone, National Affairs Coordinator
Counsel or consultant:
Winburn, VanScoyoc, and Hooper (Linsay D. Hooper)

Hallssen & Lyon
West Germany
Counsel or consultant:
Ballard, Spahr, Andrews and Ingersoll (Frederic L. Ballard, Jr.)

Halogenated Solvents Industry Alliance
1225 19th St., N.W., Suite 300, Washington, DC 20036
Telephone: (202) 223-5890
Counsel or consultant:
Patton, Boggs and Blow

HALT-An Organization of Americans for Legal Reform
1319 F St., N.W., Suite 300, Washington, DC 20004
Telephone: (202) 347-9600
Background: HALT-An Organization of Americans for Legal Reform, a public interest group working to reduce the costs and improve the quality of legal services through reform of selected laws (eg., probate and divorce law) and the development of alternative systems for resolving legal problems.
Represented by:
Deborah M. Chalfie, Legislative Director
Richard Hebert, Communications Director
George Milco, Staff Attorney
Glenn Nishimura, Exec. Director
Kay Ostberg, Deputy Director
John Pomeranz, Legislative Representative

Hamilton Copper and Steel Corp.
Los Angeles, CA
Counsel or consultant:
Sharretts, Paley, Carter and Blauvelt (Beatrice A. Brickell)

Hamilton Scientific and Development
New York, NY
Counsel or consultant:
St. Germain, Rodio & Ursillo, Ltd. (Fernand J. St. Germain)

Hand Tools Institute
Tarrytown, NY
Counsel or consultant:
Frederick L. Ikenson, P.C. (Frederick L. Ikenson)
Kilpatrick & Cody (Joseph W. Dorn)
London and Satagaj, Attorneys-at-Law (Sheldon I. London, John S. Satagaj)

Handgun Control, Inc.
1225 Eye St., N.W., Suite 1100, Washington, DC 20005
Telephone: (202) 898-0792
Background: A national membership, non-profit citizen lobby working for passage of effective legislation and regulations to keep handguns out of the wrong hands.
Represented by:
Sarah Brady, Chair
David Doi, Director, Law Enforcement Relations
Gail H. Hoffman, Legislative Director
Bernard P. Horn, Director, State Legislation
Phillip McQuire, Law Enforcement Advisor
David Mengebier, Legislative Counsel
Charles J. Orasin, President
Richard N. Parsons, Ass't to the Dir. of Federal Legislation
Nelson T. Shields, Chairman Emeritus
David Weaver, Ass't Director, State Legislation
Susan Whitmore, Director, Communications
Counsel or consultant:
Fried, Frank, Harris, Shriver & Jacobson (David E. Birenbaum)
Wilmer, Cutler and Pickering (James S. Campbell)

Handgun Control, Inc. Political Action Committee
1225 Eye St, N.W., Suite 1100, Washington, DC 20005
Telephone: (202) 898-0792
Background: Represented by Gail H. Hoffman of Handgun Control, Inc.

Hanford-Tridec
Kennewick, WA

Counsel or consultant:
The Eddie Mahe Company

Hannover, City of
Hannover, West Germany
Counsel or consultant:
P. W. Anderson & Partners (Philip W. Anderson)

Hanschell Iniss Ltd.
Bridgetown, Barbados
Counsel or consultant:
Dewey, Ballantine, Bushby, Palmer and Wood (John J. Salmon)

Hapag-Lloyd AG
Hamburg, West Germany
Counsel or consultant:
Dow, Lohnes and Albertson (Stanley O. Sher)
Warren and Associates (George A. Quadrino, Charles F. Warren)

Harbour Group Ltd.
Clayton, MO
Counsel or consultant:
Dickstein, Shapiro and Morin (Sidney Dickstein, John C. Dill)

Harcourt Brace Jovanovich, Inc.
Orlando, FL
Counsel or consultant:
Delaney and Associates, Edward N. (Edward N. Delaney)
Dow, Lohnes and Albertson (Marshall F. Berman)

Hardee's Food Systems
Rocky Mount, NC
Counsel or consultant:
Power & Coleman
Targeted Communications Corp.

Harding Lawson Associates
3175 North 21st St., Arlington, VA 22201
Telephone: (703) 528-5809
Background: An engineering consulting organization.
Represented by:
John T. Rhett, Washington Representative

Hardwood Plywood Manufacturers Ass'n
1825 Michael Faraday Dr., Reston, VA 22090
Telephone: (703) 435-2900
Represented by:
E. T. Altman, President
William J. Groah, Technical Director
Sebert H. Keiffer, General Counsel
Bill Weger, Communications Director

Haribo of America, Inc.
Baltimore, MD
Counsel or consultant:
Ballard, Spahr, Andrews and Ingersoll (Frederic L. Ballard, Jr.)

Harley-Davidson, Inc.
Milwaukee, WI
Counsel or consultant:
O'Brien and Associates, David (David D. O'Brien)
Steptoe and Johnson (Richard O. Cunningham)

Harmon Industries, Inc.
Blue Springs, MO
Counsel or consultant:
McNair Group Inc. (Denis J. Dwyer)

Harmon-Motive
Martinsville, IN
Counsel or consultant:
Dave Evans Associates

Harnischfeger Corp.
2828 Pennsylvania Ave., N.W. Suite 500, Washington, DC 20007
Telephone: (202) 342-0150
Represented by:
Joseph A. Devlin, V. President, Government Affairs

Harrah's
Reno, NV
Counsel or consultant:
Pagonis and Donnelly Group (Thomas R. Donnelly, Jr., Michael E. Grisso)

ORGANIZATIONS REPRESENTED

Harris Corp.
1201 East Abingdon Drive Suite 300, Alexandria, VA 22314
Telephone: (703) 548-9200
Represented by:
Melissa C. Carey, Legislative Representative
Joseph Hall, Manager, Congressional Relations
Frank J. Lewis, Sr. V. P. & Spec. Ass't to the CEO
Michael R. Riksen, Director, Federal Affairs
Ray White, Director, Congressional Relations

Harris County, Metropolitan Transit Authority of
Houston, TX
Counsel or consultant:
Akin, Gump, Strauss, Hauer and Feld (Joel Jankowsky)

Harris Government Systems
Melbourne, FL
Counsel or consultant:
Mica, Dudinsky & Associates (John Dudinsky, Jr., John L. Mica)

Harris RF Communications
Rochester, NY
Counsel or consultant:
Mica, Dudinsky & Associates (John L. Mica)

Harsch Investment Corp.
Portland, OR
Counsel or consultant:
Ball, Janik and Novack (Michelle E. Giguere)

Harsco Corp.
Camp Hill, PA
Counsel or consultant:
Cadwalader, Wickersham & Taft (Donald C. Alexander)
Morgan, Lewis and Bockius (Thomas K. Wotring)

Hartford Insurance Group
1600 M St., N.W., Washington, DC 20036
Telephone: (202) 775-7361
Represented by:
Joel Freedman, V. President & Federal Affairs Counsel
Counsel or consultant:
Winburn, VanScoyoc, and Hooper (John P. Winburn)

Harvard University
499 South Capitol St., S.W., Washington, DC 20003
Telephone: (292) 863-1292
Represented by:
Nan F. Nixon, Washington Representative

Harza Engineering Co.
1060 Leighmill Road, Great Falls, VA 22066
Telephone: (703) 759-6746
Represented by:
Richard J. Hesse, Manager, Washington Office
Counsel or consultant:
Edward D. Heffernan
Porter, Wright, Morris and Arthur (E. Jay Finkel)

Hastings, Nebraska, City of
Counsel or consultant:
Hill and Knowlton Public Affairs Worldwide (Josephine S. Cooper)

Havasupai Tribal Council
Supai, AZ
Counsel or consultant:
William Byler Associates (William Byler)

Haven Federal Savings and Loan Ass'n
Winter Haven, FL
Counsel or consultant:
Elias, Matz, Tiernan and Herrick

Hawaii Department of Transportation
Honolulu, HI
Counsel or consultant:
McNair Group Inc. (Denis J. Dwyer)
McNair Law Firm, P.A. (Matthew Scocozza)

Hawaii State Department of Business and Economic Development
Honolulu, HI
Counsel or consultant:
Cassidy and Associates, Inc. (Thomas M. Gannon, Vincent M. Versage)

Hawaii, University of
Honolulu, HI

Counsel or consultant:
Cassidy and Associates, Inc. (Vincent M. Versage)

Hawaii, Washington Office of
1000 16th St., N.W., Suite 603, Washington, DC 20036
Telephone: (202) 785-0550
Counsel or consultant:
Counselors For Management, Inc. (Janice C. Lipsen)

Hawaiian Airlines
Honolulu, HI
Counsel or consultant:
Dow, Lohnes and Albertson (Jonathan B. Hill)

Hawaiian Sugar Planters' Ass'n
1511 K St., N.W., Suite 723, Washington, DC 20005
Telephone: (202) 628-6372
Represented by:
Elin Peltz, Assistant Washington Representative
Eiler C. Ravnholt, V. President & Washington Representative
John C. Roney, Special Projects Associate
Counsel or consultant:
Edwin T. C. Ing

Hawker Pacific
1225 Jefferson Davis Hwy. Suite 600, Arlington, VA 22202
Telephone: (703) 486-5696
Background: Activities include aircraft sales and service, landing gear and hydraulic component overhaul and manufacture, and a flight control hydraulics distribution network throughout the pacific rim.
Represented by:
Robert L. Tidwell, Director, Government Relations

Hayes Microcomputer Products, Inc.
Norcross, GA
Counsel or consultant:
Powell, Goldstein, Frazer and Murphy (Simon Lazarus, III)

Hazardous Materials Advisory Council
1012 14th St., N.W. Suite 907, Washington, DC 20005
Telephone: (202) 783-7460
Background: Formerly (until 1978) the Hazardous Materials Advisory Committee of the Transportation Ass'n of America.
Represented by:
Paul W. Rankin, President

Hazardous Waste Treatment Council
1440 New York Ave., N.W., Suite 310, Washington, DC 20005
Telephone: (202) 783-0870
Represented by:
Richard C. Fortuna, Executive Director

Hazardous Waste Treatment Council Political Action Committee
1440 New York Ave., N.W. Suite 310, Washington, DC 20005
Telephone: (202) 783-0870
Background: Represented by Richard C. Fortuna.

HDTV 1125/60 Group
1615 L St., N.W., Suite 650, Washington, DC 20036
Telephone: (202) 659-1992
Counsel or consultant:
Wunder, Ryan, Cannon & Thelen (Dennis C. Thelen)

Headwear Institute of America
New York, NY
Counsel or consultant:
Barnes and Thornburg (Randolph J. Stayin, Marcela B. Stras)

Health Education Foundation
600 New Hampshire Ave., N.W., Suite 452, Washington, DC 20037
Telephone: (202) 338-3501
Represented by:
Dr. Morris E. Chafetz, President

Health and Education Resources
4733 Bethesda Ave, Suite 735, Bethesda, MD 20814
Telephone: (301) 656-3178
Represented by:
Dallas Johnson, President

Health and Energy Institute
P.O. Box 5357, Takoma Park, MD 20912

Telephone: (301) 585-5541
Background: A private, non-profit research and education organization seeking to preserve a healthy environment and to promote human health and life. Focused particularly on hazards of irradiated food, nuclear weapons production and nuclear waste and sensitivity of children and the unborn child to toxic chemicals, radiation and similar hazards.
Represented by:
Kitty Tucker, Exec. Director

Health Industry Distributors Ass'n
225 Reinekers Lane, Suite 650, Alexandria, VA 22314
Telephone: (703) 549-4432
Represented by:
Cara C. Bachenheimer, Director, Government Relations
Elizabeth Hilla, Exec. Director, Educational Foundation
Craig S. Jeffries, Exec Dir & Gen Couns, Home Care Mkt Grp
Elizabeth M. Mathes, V. President, Marketing & Communications
Christopher Pancratz, Exec Dir, Physcn/Alt Care & Hosp Mkt Grp
James E. Stover, President
Counsel or consultant:
Smith, Bucklin and Associates (Robert H. Wilbur)

Health Industry Distributors Ass'n Political Action Committee
1701 Pennsylvania Ave., N.W. Suite 470, Washington, DC 20006
Telephone: (202) 659-0050
Counsel or consultant:
Smith, Bucklin and Associates (Robert H. Wilbur)

Health Industry Manufacturers Ass'n
1030 15th St., N.W. Suite 1100, Washington, DC 20005
Telephone: (202) 452-8240
Represented by:
Edwin H. Allen, Gen. Counsel & V. President
Jill A. Eicher, Manager, State Affairs
Samuel A. Genovese, Director, State Affairs
Dolly A. Hanrahan, Manager, Government Affairs
James W. Hawkins, III, Director, Government Affairs
Alan H. Magazine, President
Ted R. Mannen, Sr V. President, Policy & Communications
Edward M. Rozynski, V. President, Internat'l
Leah Webb Schroeder, V. President, Government Affairs
Counsel or consultant:
Guttenberg & Company (John P. Guttenberg, Jr.)
Ryan-McGinn (Daniel McGinn)

Health Industry Manufacturers Ass'n Political Action Committee (HIMAPAC)
1030 15th St., N.W. Suite 1100, Washington, DC 20005
Telephone: (202) 452-8240
Background: Represented by James W. Hawkins, III of the Association.

Health Insurance Ass'n of America
1025 Connecticut Ave., N.W. Suite 1200, Washington, DC 20036
Telephone: (202) 223-7780
Represented by:
Richard E. Curtis, Dir., Policy, Development and Research
James A. Dorsch, Washington Counsel
Linda Jenckes, Vice President, Federal Affairs
Tara L. McMahon, Assistant Washington Counsel
David J. Pattison, Asst. Washington Counsel & Corp. Sec'y
Alan K. Richards, Jr., Asst Wash Couns, Admin/Regulatory Affrs.
Patricia Q. Schoeni, Director, Communications
Carl J. Schramm, Ph.D., President
Susan Van Gelder, Assoc. Dir., Policy Developt. & Research
Ann Marie Walsh, Assistant Washington Counsel
Gordon B. Wheeler, Director, Public Affairs
Counsel or consultant:
Dewey, Ballantine, Bushby, Palmer and Wood (Lawrence F. O'Brien, III)

Health Insurance Plan of Greater New York
1150 17th St., N.W., Suite 600, Washington, DC 20036
Telephone: (202) 659-9460

ORGANIZATIONS REPRESENTED

Represented by:
Martha A. Holbert, Legislative Assistant
George Strumpf, Director, Government Relations

Health Insurance Political Action Committee
1025 Connecticut Ave., N.W. Suite 1200, Washington, DC
20036
Telephone: (202) 223-7780
Background: The political action committee of the Health
Insurance Ass'n. Treasurer is David J. Pattison of the
Ass'n.

Health Management Strategies, Internat'l
Washington, DC
Counsel or consultant:
Jefferson Group, The (David Serwer)

Health Physics Soc.
8000 Westpark Drive Suite 130, McLean, VA 22102
Telephone: (703) 790-1745
Counsel or consultant:
Society and Association Services Corp. (Richard J. Burk,
Jr.)

Health Policy Coalition
Solon, OH
Counsel or consultant:
Jones, Day, Reavis and Pogue

Health Security Action Council
1757 N St., N.W., Washington, DC 20036
Telephone: (202) 223-9685
Background: Organized in 1968, HSAC is a network of organizations representing labor, consumers, business, women, youth, senior citizens, education, religious, and farm
groups.
Represented by:
Melvin Glasser, Director

Healthcare Compliance Packaging Council
c/0 Keller & Heckman 1150 17th St., N.W., Washington,
DC 20036
Telephone: (202) 956-5600
Counsel or consultant:
Henry J. Kaufman & Associates (John Seng)
Keller and Heckman

Healthcare Financial Management Ass'n
1050 17th St., N.W., Suite 510, Washington, DC 20036
Telephone: (202) 296-2920
Background: Represents over 27,000 members with a
professional interest in healthcare financial management,
including chief financial officers of healthcare institutions,
accountants and patient accounts managers.
Represented by:
Wendy W. Herr, Director, Regulatory Issues
R. R. Kovener, Vice President
Joseph A. Kuchler, Director, Federal Issues

Healthcare Financing Study Group
1919 Pennsylvania Ave., N.W., Suite 800, Washington, DC
20006
Telephone: (202) 887-1400
Background: The address given is that of the law firm of
O'Connor and Hannan.
Counsel or consultant:
O'Connor & Hannan (Michael Colopy, Thomas H.
Quinn)

Healthcare Recoveries Inc.
Louisville, KY
Counsel or consultant:
Casson, Harkins & LaPallo

HealthSouth Rehabilitation Corp.
Birmingham, AL
Counsel or consultant:
U.S. Strategies Corp. (K. Michael Matthews, Joseph H.
Miltenberger)

HealthTrust, Inc.
Nashville, TN
Counsel or consultant:
Charls E. Walker Associates

Hearing Industries Ass'n
1255 23rd St., N.W., Washington, DC 20037
Telephone: (202) 833-1411
Counsel or consultant:
Hauck and Associates (Carole M. Rogin)

Heart of America Northwest
Seattle, WA
Counsel or consultant:
APCO Associates (Don Bonker)

Hechinger Co.
3500 Pennsy Dr., Landover, MD 20785
Telephone: (301) 341-1000
Counsel or consultant:
Skadden, Arps, Slate, Meagher and Flom (William E.
Perry)

Hecht's
685 N. Glebe Road, Arlington, VA 22203
Telephone: (703) 558-1414
Represented by:
Peggy L. Disney, Divisional V. Pres., Public Relations
Counsel or consultant:
Hill and Knowlton Public Affairs Worldwide (Mark Rob-
ertson)

Heckler & Koch
21480 Pacific Blvd., Sterling, VA 22170
Telephone: (703) 450-1900
Represented by:
Marvin Wagner, Legal Counsel
Counsel or consultant:
Arent, Fox, Kintner, Plotkin & Kahn (Samuel Efron)

Hecla Mining Co.
Couer d'Alene, ID
Counsel or consultant:
Wilson & Wilson (Robert Dale Wilson)

Heinz Co., H. J.
Pittsburgh, PA
Counsel or consultant:
Howrey and Simon (Keith E. Pugh, Jr.)
Timmons and Co., Inc.

Helen Keller Internat'l
New York, NY
Counsel or consultant:
White, Fine, and Verville (Richard E. Verville)

**Helen Keller Nat'l Center for Deaf-Blind Youths
and Adults**
Sands Point, NY
Counsel or consultant:
MARC Associates, Inc. (Robert R. Humphreys)

Helicopter Ass'n Internat'l
1619 Duke St., Alexandria, VA 22314-3406
Telephone: (703) 683-4646
Represented by:
Frank L. Jensen, Jr., President
Anna Minaya, Legislative Assistant
Daniel P. Warsley, Director, Member Services

**Helicopter Ass'n Internat'l Political Action Com-
mittee**
1619 Duke St., Alexandria, VA 22314-3406
Telephone: (703) 683-4646
Represented by:
Wanda Rogers, Treasurer

Helicopter Foundation Internat'l
1619 Duke St., Alexandria, VA 22314-3406
Telephone: (703) 683-4646
Represented by:
John M. Slattery, Curator, Heli Archive

Hellenic American Council of Southern California
Los Angeles, CA
Counsel or consultant:
Manatos & Manatos, Inc. (Andrew E. Manatos, Dyck
Van Koevering)

Henderson, Nevada, City of
Counsel or consultant:
Nat'l Center for Municipal Development (Barbara T.
McCall)

Henley Group, Inc., The
Hampton, NH
Counsel or consultant:
Concord Associates, Inc.

Hennepin County, Minnesota
Counsel or consultant:
O'Connor & Hannan

Henraux S.p.A.
Lucca, Italy
Counsel or consultant:
Dow, Lohnes and Albertson (William Silverman)

Henry L. Stimson Center
1350 Connecticut Ave., N.W. Suite 304, Washington, DC
20036
Telephone: (202) 223-5956
Represented by:
Barry M. Blechman, Chairman of the Board
Michael Krepon, President

Herbalife Internat'l
Los Angeles, CA
Counsel or consultant:
Parry and Romani Associates Inc. (Romano Romani)

**Hercules Aerospace Co. (Aerospace Products
Group)**
Salt Lake City, UT
Counsel or consultant:
Winthrop, Stimson, Putnam & Roberts (Peter F. Gold)

Hercules, Inc.
1800 K St., N.W., Suite 710, Washington, DC 20006
Telephone: (202) 223-8590
Represented by:
Samuel A. Mabry, Director, Federal Affairs
Counsel or consultant:
Dow, Lohnes and Albertson (Arthur H. Silverman)
Powell, Goldstein, Frazer and Murphy (Stuart E. Eizen-
stat)

Heritage Foundation
214 Massachusetts Ave., N.E., Washington, DC 20002
Telephone: (202) 546-4400
Background: Founded in 1973. Analysts research and pub-
lish studies on major economic and foreign policy issues,
generally, but not invariably, aligned with conservative
views. Also publishes quarterly journal, Policy Review,
conducts scholars program, and provides media with analysis of issues and trends. Claims to be most broadly-based
policy think tank in the U.S. with 140,000 individual, corporate and foundation supporters.

ORGANIZATIONS REPRESENTED

Heritage Foundation (Cont'd)
Represented by:
Jeanne Allen, Education Policy Analyst
Richard V. Allen, Distinguished Fellow
Dr. Leon Aron, Salvatori Fellow in Soviet Studies
Herbert Berkowitz, V. President, Public Relations
Roger A. Brooks, Director, Asian Studies Center
Stuart M. Butler, Director, Domestic Policy Studies
Margo D. B. Carlisle, V. President, Government Relations
Kenneth Conboy, Deputy Director, Asian Studies Center
Caroline Cooney, Public Relations Associate
Thomas Cox, Policy Analyst, Latin America
Edwin J. Feulner, Jr., President
Richard Fisher, Policy Analyst, Asian Studies
Jeffrey Gayner, Counselor for International Relations
Edmund Haislmaier, Policy Analyst, Health Care
Charles L. Heatherly, V. President, Academic Relations
Duane Higgins, Director of House Relations
Barbara Hohbach, Coordinator, Media Relations
Kim R. Holmes, Dir., Foreign Policy & Defense Studies
Robert Huberty, Director, Resource Bank
Edward L. Hudgins, Dir., Center for Internat'l Econ. Growth
Meg Hunt, Director of Senate Relations
Steven Kent Jeffreys, Energy and Environmental Policy Analyst
Michael Johns, Policy Analyst, Third World & Africa
Jay Kosminsky, Deputy Director, Defense Policy Studies
Charles M. Lichenstein, Distinguished Scholar
Michael Lind, Visiting Fellow
David Mason, Director, Executive Branch Liaison
Edwin Meese, III, Distinguished Fellow
Daniel J. Mitchell, Senior Fellow, Political Economy
Kate Walsh O'Beirne, Deputy Dir. for Domestic Policy Studies
James A. Phillips, Deputy Director, Foreign Policy Studies
Burton Y. Pines, Sr. V. President & Director of Research
Robert Rector, Policy Analyst, Welfare & Family
Cheryl Rubin, Manager of Public Relations
John Scanlon, Policy Analyst, Housing
Terrence M. Scanlon, V. President and Treasurer
Douglas Seay, Political Analyst, East European Affairs
Herbert Baker Spring, Policy Analyst, Foreign Policy & Defense
Phillip N. Truluck, Exec. V. President
Michael G. Wilson, Policy Analyst, Latin America
Counsel or consultant:
Hugh C. Newton & Assoc. (Hugh C. Newton)

Hermann Hospital
Houston, TX
Counsel or consultant:
Baker and Hostetler (Frederick H. Graefe)

Heron Internat'l, Ltd.
London, England
Counsel or consultant:
Jones, Day, Reavis and Pogue (C. Thomas Long)

Hershey Foods Corp.
1730 Rhode Island Ave., N.W., Suite 206, Washington, DC 20036
Telephone: (202) 223-9070
Represented by:
Holly Hassett, Manager, Washington Office
Angela Y. Kurtz, Government Relations Represenative
Caren A. Wilcox, Director, Government Relations
Counsel or consultant:
Howrey and Simon (Keith E. Pugh, Jr.)

Hertz Corp.
Park Ridge, NJ
Counsel or consultant:
Dow, Lohnes and Albertson (David F. Bantleon, Stanley O. Sher)
Hill and Knowlton Public Affairs Worldwide (Jeffrey B. Trammell, Kenneth L. Wolf)
Lee, Toomey & Kent

Heublein, Inc.
1825 Eye St., N.W. Suite 400, Washington, DC 20006
Telephone: (202) 429-2003
Counsel or consultant:
Howrey and Simon (Ralph J. Savarese)

Hewlett-Packard Co.
900 17th St., N.W. Suite 1100, Washington, DC 20006
Telephone: (202) 785-7943

Represented by:
Rita E. Downey, Government Affairs Specialist
Bob Hungate, Government Affairs, Health Care Manager
Cynthia Johnson, Washington Government Affairs Manager
Bernard F. McKay, Federal Procurement Policy Manager
Robbins Pancake, Manager, Internat'l Trade Relations
Eben S. Tisdale, General Manager, Government Affairs
Counsel or consultant:
Lee, Toomey & Kent
Mayer, Brown and Platt (Charles S. Levy)
Miller & Chevalier, Chartered (Catherine T. Porter)
Powell, Goldstein, Frazer and Murphy (Stuart E. Eizenstat)
Preston Gates Ellis & Rouvelas Meeds (Kenneth R. Kay)

Hexagon Technical Co. Inc.
New York, NY
Counsel or consultant:
Cassidy and Associates, Inc. (Gerald S. J. Cassidy, Thomas M. Gannon)

Hialeah Hospital
Hialeah, FL
Counsel or consultant:
. Holland and Knight (Ronald A. Fried)

Hiawatha Savings and Loan Ass'n
Hiawatha, KS
Counsel or consultant:
Silver, Freedman & Taff (Robert L. Freedman, Lois G. Jacobs, Nancy M. Stiles)

High Island Offshore Systems
Houston, TX
Counsel or consultant:
Gallagher, Boland, Meiburger and Brosnan (Christopher T. Boland)

High Speed Rail Ass'n
Pittsburgh, PA
Counsel or consultant:
Paul Arneson, P.C. (Paul Arneson)

Higher Education Assistance Foundation
Overland Park, KS
Counsel or consultant:
Williams and Jensen, P.C. (Winfield P. Crigler)

Higher Education Management and Resources Foundation Political Action Committee (HE-MAR/HEAF)
1023 15th St, N.W., Suite 1000, Washington, DC 20005
Telephone: (202) 289-4500
Represented by:
Philip R. Rever, Treasurer

Highway Safety Corp,
Gastonbury, CT
Counsel or consultant:
Arthur E. Cameron

Highway Users Federation for Safety and Mobility
1776 Massachusette Ave., N.W., Washington, DC 20036
Telephone: (202) 857-1200
Background: Members generally include those connected with the automotive industry and other providers and users of highway transportation goods and services who stand to benefit from increased use of the nation's road system.
Represented by:
Neil A. Gray, Director, Government Relations
Lester P. Lamm, President
Mark Norman, Director, Policy Development
Carlton C. Robinson, Exec. V. President

Higman Barge Lines
Houston, TX
Counsel or consultant:
Bracewell and Patterson (Gene E. Godley)

Hill and Knowlton Inc. Political Action Committee
901 31st St., N.W., Washington, DC 20007
Telephone: (202) 333-7400
Counsel or consultant:
Hill and Knowlton Public Affairs Worldwide (Gary Hymel)

HillHaven Corp.
Tacoma, WA
Background: A nursing home chain.
Counsel or consultant:
Cindy Williams Associates (Lucinda L. Williams)

Hillsborough Area Regional Transit Authority
Tampa, FL
Counsel or consultant:
Keefe Co., The (Clarence L. James, Jr., William A. Roberts)
Vierra Associates, Inc. (Dennis C. Vierra)

Hillsborough County Aviation Authority
Tampa, FL
Counsel or consultant:
Alcalde & Rousselot

Hilton Hotels Corp.
Beverly Hills, CA
Counsel or consultant:
Dow, Lohnes and Albertson (David F. Bantleon)

HIP Network of Florida
Fort Lauderdale, FL
Counsel or consultant:
Jefferson Group, The (David Serwer)

Hiram Walker and Sons, Inc.
1331 Pennsylvania Ave., N.W., Suite 720, Washington, DC 20004
Telephone: (202) 628-5877
Represented by:
Nancy H. Jessick, Director of Government Affairs

Hispanic Americana, Inc.
1511 K St., N.W., Suite 1026, Washington, DC 20005
Telephone: (202) 393-7836
Background: A company specializing in public relations, marketing and programs consultation in health and human services serving the Hispanic community, in particular.
Represented by:
Rodolfo Balli Sanchez, President and Chief Executive Officer

Hispanic Ass'n on Corporate Responsibility
2000 L St., N.W. Suite 702, Washington, DC 20036
Telephone: (202) 835-9672
Background: A coalition of organizations whose goal is to secure funding from corporations for enhancing the quality of life for Hispanic-Americans.
Represented by:
Jerry Adopaca, President

Hispanic Elected Local Officials Caucus
1301 Pennsylvania Ave., N.W., Washington, DC 20004
Telephone: (202) 626-3130
Background: A forum for the exchange of information and ideas among Hispanic local governmrnt officials within the framework of the Nat'l League of Cities.
Represented by:
Mary Perez Johnson, President

Hispanic Higher Education Coalition
20 F St., N.W., Suite 108, Washington, DC 20001
Telephone: (202) 638-7339
Background: A coalition of 13 national organizations interested in improving the participation and support of Hispanics in higher education.
Represented by:
Rafael Magallan, Exec. Director

Hispanic Organization of Professionals and Executives
87 Catoctin Court, Silver Spring, MD 20906
Telephone: (301) 234-2351
Background: Seeks to promote Hispanic participation in the free enterprise economy and democratic system in the U.S.
Represented by:
Stanley Valadez, Exec. Director

Hispanic Policy Development Project
1001 Connecticut Ave., N.W. Suite 310, Washington, DC 20036
Telephone: (202) 822-8414
Background: A private, non-profit organization founded in 1982 to provide accurate information about Hispanics and to encourage the analysis of public policies and policy proposals affecting Hispanics.

The listings in this directory are available as *Mailing Labels*. See last page.

ORGANIZATIONS REPRESENTED

Represented by:
Mildred R. Garcia, Director of Adminstration
Stina Santiestevan, V. President for Communications
Rafael Valdivieso, V. President for Program and Research

History Factory, The
2831 15th St., N.W., Washington, DC 20009
Telephone: (202) 387-3228
Counsel or consultant:
Patricia Bario Associates (Pamela Jenkins)

Hitachi America Ltd.
Brisbane, CA
Counsel or consultant:
McDermott, Will and Emery (Robert S. Schwartz, Carl W. Schwartz)
Jack McDonald Co. (Jack McDonald, Myron G. Sandifer, III)
Powell, Goldstein, Frazer and Murphy

Hitachi Ltd.
1850 K St., N.W., Suite 475, Washington, DC 20006
Telephone: (202) 828-9272
Represented by:
Mitsuhiko Harada, Representative
Masayuki Yamada, Senior Representative
Counsel or consultant:
Global USA, Inc. (John M. Nugent, Jr.)
Hill and Knowlton Public Affairs Worldwide (Stephen H. Meeter)
McDermott, Will and Emery (Robert S. Schwartz, Carl W. Schwartz)
Powell, Goldstein, Frazer and Murphy (Stuart E. Eizenstat)
TKC Internat'l, Inc.

Hitachi Research Institute
Tokyo, Japan
Counsel or consultant:
Hill and Knowlton Public Affairs Worldwide (Andrew G. Durant)

Hitachi Sales Corp. of America
Compton, CA
Counsel or consultant:
Jack McDonald Co. (Jack McDonald, Myron G. Sandifer, III)
Patton, Boggs and Blow
Powell, Goldstein, Frazer and Murphy (Stuart E. Eizenstat)

Hitachi Zosen Corp.
Tokyo, Japan
Counsel or consultant:
Graham and James (Brian E. McGill, Yoshihiro Saito)

Hobby Industries Ass'n
Elmwood Park, NJ
Counsel or consultant:
Patton, Boggs and Blow (Lanny J. Davis)

Hoboken, New Jersey, City of
Counsel or consultant:
Krivit and Krivit (Daniel H. Krivit)

Hoechst-Celanese Corp.
919 18th St., N.W., Suite 700, Washington, DC 20006
Telephone: (202) 296-2890
Represented by:
Donald R. Greeley, V. President, Government Relations
W. Anthony Shaw, Manager, Regulatory Affairs
Robert Umphrey, Jr., Manager, Congressional Affairs
Counsel or consultant:
Caplin and Drysdale

Hoffmann-La Roche Inc.
1050 Connecticut Ave., N.W. Suite 401, Washington, DC 20036
Telephone: (202) 223-1975
Represented by:
Kathryn E. Bannan, Federal Government Affairs Associate
Gaston de Bearn, Assistant Director, Government Affairs
Judith A. Buckalew, Manager, Government Affairs
Gerald D. Lore, Asst. V. Pres. & Dir., Gov't Affrs.

Holiday Corp.
Memphis, TN
Counsel or consultant:
Pagonis and Donnelly Group (Thomas R. Donnelly, Jr., Michael E. Grisso)

Holk Development, Inc.
Cleveland, OH
Counsel or consultant:
Stovall & Spradlin

Holland America Line Westours Inc.
New York, NY
Counsel or consultant:
Graham and James (Thomas F. Railsback)

Holland and Knight Committee for Effective Government
888 17th St., N.W., Suite 900, Washington, DC 20006
Telephone: (202) 955-5550
Counsel or consultant:
Holland and Knight (Janet R. Studley)

Hollywood Federal Savings and Loan Ass'n
Hollywood, FL
Counsel or consultant:
Warren W. Koffler

Hollywood Marine Service, Inc.
Houston, TX
Counsel or consultant:
Douglass W. Svendson, Jr.

Holmes & Narver, Inc.
Orange, CA
Counsel or consultant:
Wagner, Hines and Avary (Robert P. Avary, Jr., William J. Hines, Paul F. Wagner)

Holt Communications Corp.
Allentown, PA
Counsel or consultant:
Kaye, Scholer, Fierman, Hays and Handler (Jason Shrinsky)

Holy Childhood Ass'n
1720 Massachusetts Ave., N.W., Washington, DC 20036
Telephone: (202) 775-8637
Represented by:
Edwin P. Fichter, Coordinating Director
Rev. Francis W. Wright, National Director

Holzer, Inc., E.
Englewood Cliffs, NJ
Counsel or consultant:
Balsamo & Associates, Chartered (Richard W. Balsamo)

Home Automation Ass'n
P.O. Box 3731, Washington, DC 20007
Telephone: (202) 333-8190
Counsel or consultant:
Robert N. Pyle & Associates (Nicholas A. Pyle)

Home Box Office
New York, NY
Counsel or consultant:
Dickstein, Shapiro and Morin (Bernard Nash)

Home Economics Education Ass'n
1201 16th St., N.W., Washington, DC 20036
Telephone: (202) 822-7844
Represented by:
Catherine A. Leisher, Exec. Director

Home Federal Savings and Loan Ass'n
Worcester, MA
Counsel or consultant:
Timothy D. Naegele and Assoc. (Timothy D. Naegele)

Home Group, The
New York, NY
Counsel or consultant:
Laxalt, Washington, Perito & Dubuc (Robert B. Washington, Jr.)

Home Intensive Care, Inc.
No. Miami Beach, FL
Counsel or consultant:
Camp, Barsh, Bates and Tate (Ronald L. Platt)

Home Life Insurance Co.
New York, NY
Counsel or consultant:
Murray, Scheer & Montgomery (D. Michael Murray)

Home Owners Warranty Corp.
1110 N. Glebe Road Suite 800, Arlington, VA 22201
Telephone: (703) 516-4100

Represented by:
Terence S. Cooke, Counsel
Counsel or consultant:
Colton and Boykin

Home Oxygen Systems, Inc.
Long Island, NY
Counsel or consultant:
Robert N. Pyle & Associates

Home Recording Rights Coalition
P.O. Box 33705, Washington, DC 20033
Telephone: (202) 663-8452
Represented by:
Ruth Rodgers, Exec. Director
Counsel or consultant:
Mintz, Levin, Cohn, Ferris, Glovsky and Popeo, P.C. (Charles D. Ferris)
Patton, Boggs and Blow
Shaw, Pittman, Potts and Trowbridge

Homedco
Foundation Val., CA
Counsel or consultant:
Baker and Hostetler (Frederick H. Graefe)

Homestead Financial Corp.
San Francisco, CA
Counsel or consultant:
Elias, Matz, Tiernan and Herrick

Homewood Corp.
Columbus, OH
Counsel or consultant:
Keefe Co., The (Clarence L. James, Jr., Terry M. O'Connell)

Honda Motor Co.
Tokyo, Japan
Counsel or consultant:
Covington and Burling (Harvey M. Applebaum)

Honda North America, Inc.
955 L'Enfant Plaza S.W., Suite 5300, Washington, DC 20024
Telephone: (202) 554-1650
Represented by:
Scott A. Gerke, Government Relations Assistant
Toni Harrington, Manager, Government and Industry Rtns.
Shogo Iizuka, Senior V. President
Barbara Nocera, Asst. Manager, Government Relations

Honduras, Government of
Tegucigalpa, Honduras
Counsel or consultant:
White & Case

Honeywell, Inc.
1100 Connecticut Ave., N.W., Suite 710, Washington, DC 20036
Telephone: (202) 872-0495
Represented by:
Linda W. Banton, Governemnt Relations Representative
Pamela K. Ernest, Director, Federal Affairs
Counsel or consultant:
APCO Associates (Margery Kraus)
Arnold & Porter (Jeffrey H. Smith)
Manning, Selvage & Lee/Washington
Mayer, Brown and Platt

Hong Kong Aircraft Engineering Co., Ltd.
Hong Kong
Counsel or consultant:
Galland, Kharasch, Morse and Garfinkle (Morris R. Garfinkle, Susan B. Jollie)

Hong Kong Press Publishers
Hong Kong
Counsel or consultant:
Lachelli, Waller and Associates (Kim M., Lam Lachelli)

Hong Kong Trade Development Council
New York, NY
Counsel or consultant:
R. Duffy Wall and Associates (R. D. Folsom, Michael Stern, R. Duffy Wall, Charlotte Wilmer)

Hong Kong Trade, Industry and Customs Department
Hong Kong

ORGANIZATIONS REPRESENTED

Hong Kong Trade, Industry and Customs Department (Cont'd)
Counsel or consultant:
Internat'l Business and Economic Research Corp.
Mudge Rose Guthrie Alexander and Ferdon (Michael P. Daniels, Martin J. Lewin)

Hoogovens Group BV
Ijmuiden, Netherlands
Counsel or consultant:
Powell, Goldstein, Frazer and Murphy (Peter Suchman)

Hook-SupeRx, Inc.
Cincinnati, OH
Counsel or consultant:
Wunder, Ryan, Cannon & Thelen (Kenneth S. Levine)

Hopi Tribe
Kykotsmoui, AZ
Counsel or consultant:
Gold and Liebengood, Inc. (Howard S. Liebengood)
Sonosky, Chambers and Sachse

Horatio Alger Ass'n of Distinguished Americans
11 Canal Center Plaza Suite 210, Alexandria, VA 22314
Telephone: (703) 684-9444
Represented by:
Terrence J. Giroux, Exec. Director

Horsehead Resource Development Co.
c/o The Jefferson Group 1341 G St., N.W., #1100, Washington, DC 20005-3105
Telephone: (202) 638-3535
Counsel or consultant:
Jefferson Group, The (Robert L. Harris)

Horticultural Research Institute
1250 Eye St., N.W., Suite 500, Washington, DC 20005
Telephone: (202) 789-2900
Background: Exec. V. President is Lawrence E. Scovotto of the American Ass'n of Nurserymen.

Hospice Ass'n of America
519 C St., N.E., Washington, DC 20002
Telephone: (202) 546-4759
Represented by:
Janet Neigh, Exec. Director

Hospice Care, Inc.
Miami, FL
Counsel or consultant:
Holland and Knight

Hospital Corp. of America
Nashville, TN
Counsel or consultant:
Dewey, Ballantine, Bushby, Palmer and Wood (John J. Salmon)

Hospital Council of the Nat'l Capital Area
1250 Eye St., N.W., Suite 700, Washington, DC 20005
Telephone: (202) 789-1500
Represented by:
Anthony J. Monaco, President

Hotel Ass'n of Washington
1201 New York Ave., N.W. Suite 601, Washington, DC 20005
Telephone: (202) 289-3141
Represented by:
Emily F. Durso, Exec. V. President
Counsel or consultant:
Harmon and Wilmot (David W. Wilmot)

Hotel Employees and Restaurant Employees International TIP Union To Insure Progress
1219 28th St., N.W., Washington, DC 20006
Telephone: (202) 393-4373
Background: The political action committee of the Hotel and Restaurant Employees Internat'l Union.
Represented by:
Herman Leavitt, Treasurer

Hotel Employees and Restaurant Employees Internat'l Union
1219 28th St., N.W., Washington, DC 20007
Telephone: (202) 393-4373
Represented by:
Edward T. Hanley, President
Counsel or consultant:
Robert E. Juliano Associates (Robert E. Juliano)

Hotel Sales and Marketing Ass'n Internat'l
1300 L St., N.W., Suite 800, Washington, DC 20005
Telephone: (202) 789-0089
Represented by:
Leonard H. Hoyle, Exec. V. President
Ilsa Whittemore, Associate Exec. Director
Counsel or consultant:
Loomis, Owen, Fellman and Howe (James E. Anderson)

Houghton Mifflin Co.
Boston, MA
Counsel or consultant:
Mintz, Levin, Cohn, Ferris, Glovsky and Popeo, P.C.

Household Banks, F.S.B.
Westminster, CA
Background: A subsidiary of Household Internat'l. Represented by H. A. Doersam of the parent company office.

Household Commercial Financial Services, Inc.
Prospect Heights, IL
Counsel or consultant:
Mayer, Brown and Platt (Jerry L. Oppenheimer)

Household Goods Carrier's Bureau
1611 Duke St., Alexandria, VA 22314
Telephone: (703) 683-7410
Represented by:
Joseph M. Harrison, President

Household Goods Forwarders Ass'n of America
2111 Eisenhower Ave. Suite 404, Alexandria, VA 22314
Telephone: (703) 684-3780
Background: Represents regulated household goods forwarders. Members move both Department of Defense and commercial personal property domestically and internationally.
Represented by:
Donald H. Mensch, Executive Director
Counsel or consultant:
Denning and Wohlstetter (Alan F. Wohlstetter)

Household Internat'l
1000 Connecticut Ave., N.W., Suite 507, Washington, DC 20036
Telephone: (202) 466-3561
Represented by:
Toni A. Bellissimo, Federal Government Relations Manager
Harold A. Doersam, Federal Government Relations Manager
Thomas E. Fitzgerald, Federal Government Relations Manager
J. Thomas Nelson, III, V. Pres., Federal Government Relations
Counsel or consultant:
Dewey, Ballantine, Bushby, Palmer and Wood (John J. Salmon)
Lee, Toomey & Kent

Household Internat'l Political Action Committee
1000 Connecticut Ave., N.W. Suite 507, Washington, DC 20036
Telephone: (202) 466-3561
Counsel or consultant:
Dewey, Ballantine, Bushby, Palmer and Wood (John J. Salmon)

Household Merchandising
Des Plaines, IL
Background: A subsidiary of Household Internat'l. Represented by J. Thomas Nelson of the parent company.

Housing Assistance Council
1025 Vermont Ave., N.W. Suite 606, Washington, DC 20005
Telephone: (202) 842-8600
Background: A non-profit national organization to help provide decent housing and a suitable living environment for the rural poor by using its loan funds, technical assistance and training to supplement the efforts of housing organizations serving these people.
Represented by:
Jon Linfield, Government'l Services Liaison Officer
Moises Loza, Exec. Director

Housing Authority Risk Retention Group
Cheshire, CT
Counsel or consultant:
Reno, Cavanaugh & Hornig (Lee P. Reno)

Housing Study Group
2101 L St., N.W., Suite 210 c/o Krooth & Altman, Washington, DC 20037
Telephone: (202) 293-8200
Counsel or consultant:
Krooth & Altman (Michael E. Mazer)

Houston Agricultural Credit Corp.
Katy, TX
Counsel or consultant:
Bishop, Cook, Purcell & Reynolds (Robert M. Bor)

Houston Airlines
Houston, TX
Counsel or consultant:
E. Del Smith, Inc. (E. Del Smith)

Houston Clearing House Ass'n
Houston, TX
Counsel or consultant:
Arter & Hadden (William K. Dabaghi)

Houston Oilers
Houston, TX
Counsel or consultant:
Akin, Gump, Strauss, Hauer and Feld (Joel Jankowsky)

Houston Lighting & Power Co.
1050 17th St., N.W. Suite 550, Washington, DC 20036
Telephone: (202) 467-5040
Background: A subsidiary of Houston Industries.
Represented by:
Howard Pyle, Director, Federal Relations
Counsel or consultant:
Newman & Holtzinger, P.C. (Jack R. Newman)
Slover and Loftus (William L. Slover)

Houston's
Atlanta, GA
Counsel or consultant:
Richard B. Berman and Co.,Inc. (Richard B. Berman)

Howard Hughes Medical Institute
6701 Rockledge Drive, Bethesda, MD 20817
Telephone: (301) 571-0305
Represented by:
Purnell W. Choppin, President

Howard, Meedles, Tammen & Bergendoff
Kansas City, MO
Counsel or consultant:
Wilmer, Cutler and Pickering (Bruce M. Berman)

Howard University
2400 6th St., N.W., Washington, DC 20059
Telephone: (202) 806-2150
Represented by:
Joyce Smith, Ass't for Congressional Affairs

Howmet/Pechiney Corp.
Greenwich, CT
Background: A manufacturer of turbine blades and engine components.
Counsel or consultant:
Morris J. Amitay, P.C.

Hoylake Investments Ltd.
Hamilton, Bermuda
Counsel or consultant:
Akin, Gump, Strauss, Hauer and Feld (Joel Jankowsky)
Skadden, Arps, Slate, Meagher and Flom (Robert E. Lighthizer)

Huber Corp., J. M.
Edison, NJ
Counsel or consultant:
Reid & Priest
Sutherland, Asbill and Brennan (Gordon O. Pehrson, Jr.)

Hudson County, New Jersey
Counsel or consultant:
Krivit and Krivit (Daniel H. Krivit)

Hudson Industries Corp.
West Orange, NJ
Counsel or consultant:
Stewart and Stewart (Terrence P. Stewart)

The listings in this directory are available as *Mailing Labels*. See last page.

ORGANIZATIONS REPRESENTED

Hudson Institute
4401 Ford Ave. Suite 200, Alexandria, VA 22302
Telephone: (703) 824-2048
Background: An Indianapolis-based 'think tank'.
Represented by:
Dennis T. Avery, Dir., Agricultural Technology Project
Mark N. Blitz, Director, Political and Social Studies
Lt. Gen. William E. Odom, USA (Ret), Director, Nat'l Security Studies
Jeffrey Record, Sr. Research Fellow

Hudson Manufacturing Co., H. D.
1130 17th St., N.W. Suite 500, Washington, DC 20036
Telephone: (202) 331-1245
Represented by:
Ray Treichler, Research Analyst

Hughes Aircraft Co.
1100 Wilson Blvd. 20th Floor, Arlington, VA 22209
Telephone: (703) 525-1550
Represented by:
Julie W. Maccabee, Corporate Manager, Congressional Affairs
Gordon L. Merritt, Asst. Director, Congressional Affairs
William D. Merritt, V. President, Government Operations
David J. Shea, Manager of Communications
Patricia Shymansky, Government Affairs Staff Member
Larry M. Wheeler, Director, Congressional Affairs
Counsel or consultant:
Commerce Consultants Internat'l Ltd. (David M. Hatcher, Richard Richards)
Daniel J. Edelman, Inc. (Stephen K. Cook, Leslie Dach)

Hugo Boss Fashions, Inc.
New York, NY
Counsel or consultant:
Tendler, Goldberg & Biggins, Chtd. (Paul M. Tendler)

Hulcher Quarry, Inc.
Nokomis, IL
Counsel or consultant:
Smith, Heenan and Althen (Michael T. Heenan)

Human Environment Center
1001 Connecticut Ave., N.W. Suite 827, Washington, DC 20036
Telephone: (202) 331-8387
Background: Seeks to promote the common interests of urban, minority and environmental groups through advocating such projects as inner-city parks and recreational facilities and a national conservation corps programs, minority entry into environmental professions and other common-interest initiatives.
Represented by:
Margaret Rosenberry, Exec. Director

Human Relations Institute
P.O. Box 18206, Washington, DC 20036
Telephone: (202) 659-5552
Background: Represented by Dr. Raymond H. Hamden of the Foundation for Internat'l Human Relations.

Human Rights Campaign Fund
1012 14th St., N.W. Suite 607, Washington, DC 20005
Telephone: (202) 628-4160
Background: Supports congressional candidates who favor gay and lesbian civil rights and full funding for AIDS treatment and research. Conducts lobbying in addition to PAC activities.
Represented by:
Karen D. Friedman, Congressional Liaison
Gregory King, Communications Director
Tim McFeeley, Exec. Director
Eric Rosenthal, Political Director
Steven Smith, Legislative Counsel

Human Rights Watch
1522 K St., N.W., Suite 910, Washington, DC 20005
Telephone: (202) 371-6592
Background: The umbrella human rights organization whose components include Americas Watch, Asia Watch, Helsinki Watch, and Middle East Watch. Based in New York, NY.
Represented by:
Holly J. Burkhalter, Washington Director
Catherine Cosman, Washington Representative-Helsinki Watch
Anne Manuel, Research Director, Americas Watch
Juan E. Mendez, Washington Exec Director, Americas Watch
Joyce Mends-Cole, Washington Representative - Africa Watch
Eric Schwartz, Washington Director, Asia Watch

Humana, Inc.
Louisville, KY
Counsel or consultant:
Ryan-McGinn (Daniel McGinn)
Targeting Systems, Inc.

Humane Soc. of the United States
2100 L St., N.W., Washington, DC 20037
Telephone: (202) 452-1100
Background: A private, non-profit organization concerned with the protection of animals, both domestic and wild. Provides consultation and guidance to local animal welfare agencies and conducts investigations into major incidents of animal abuse. Actively pursues implimentation of State and Federal Legislation and engages in litigation on behalf of animal welfare.
Represented by:
Patricia Forkan, Senior V. President
Martha Cole Glenn, Director, Federal Affairs
John A. Hoyt, President
Paul Irwin, Executive V. President
Counsel or consultant:
Foley, Hoag and Eliot (Dennis Kanin, Paul Tsongas)
Nancy E. Gendron

Hungarian Reformed Federation of America
2001 Massachusetts Ave., N.W., Washington, DC 20036
Telephone: (202) 328-2630
Represented by:
Imre Bertalan, President
George Dozsa, V. President

Huntington Nat'l Bank
Columbus, OH
Counsel or consultant:
Porter, Wright, Morris and Arthur (E. Jay Finkel)

Huntsville-Madison County Airport
Huntsville, AL
Counsel or consultant:
Global Aviation Associates, Ltd. (Judith M. Trent)

Huskey Realty
Longwood, FL
Counsel or consultant:
Cindy Williams Associates (Lucinda L. Williams)

Hussey Copper Ltd.
Leetsdale, PA
Counsel or consultant:
Collier, Shannon & Scott (Jeffrey S. Beckington, David A. Hartquist, Mary T. Staley)

Hutchinson Cancer Center
Seattle, WA
Counsel or consultant:
Capitol Associates, Inc. (Marguerite Donoghue, Terry Lierman)

Hutchinson Island Limited, Inc.
Fort Pierce, FL
Counsel or consultant:
O'Connor & Hannan (George J. Mannina, Jr.)

Hvide Shipping, Inc.
Fort Lauderdale, FL
Counsel or consultant:
Mica, Dudinsky & Associates (John Dudinsky, Jr., John L. Mica)

Hyannis Air Service, Inc.
Hyannis, MA
Counsel or consultant:
V. Michael Straus, P.C.

Hydro-Quebec
Montreal, Quebec
Counsel or consultant:
Paul A. London Assoc., Inc. (Paul A. London)

Hydrocarbon Research, Inc.
Lawrenceville, NJ
Counsel or consultant:
Richard Olson & Assoc. (Richard C. Olson)

Hydrocel Corp.
Walnut Creek, CA
Counsel or consultant:
F. H. Hutchison and Co. (Fred H. Hutchison)

HYLSA
Monterrey, Mexico
Counsel or consultant:
Manchester Trade, Inc. (Stephen L. Lande)

Hyster Co.
Portland, OR
Counsel or consultant:
Collier, Shannon & Scott

Hyundai Motor America
Garden Grove, CA
Counsel or consultant:
Dorsey & Whitney
Global USA, Inc. (William H. Morris, Jr.)

Hyundai Motor Co.
Seoul, Korea
Counsel or consultant:
Dorsey & Whitney
Strategic Resources Corp. (H. P. Goldfield)
Swidler & Berlin, Chartered (Lester S. Hyman)

IAMUS/Internat'l Unlimited
Palm Beach, FL
Counsel or consultant:
Mica, Dudinsky & Associates (John Dudinsky, Jr., John L. Mica)

IBJ Schroder Bank and Trust Co.
New York, NY
Counsel or consultant:
Winthrop, Stimson, Putnam & Roberts (Raymond S. Calamaro)

IBP, Inc.
Dakota City, NE
Counsel or consultant:
Bishop, Cook, Purcell & Reynolds (Robert M. Bor)

ICB Internat'l Airlines
Manhattan Beach, CA
Counsel or consultant:
Herbert A. Rosenthal

Ice Cream and Milk PAC
888 16th St., N.W. 2nd Floor, Washington, DC 20006
Telephone: (202) 296-4250
Represented by:
Lynn A. Jalosky, Treasurer

Iceland Air
Reykjavik, Iceland
Counsel or consultant:
Lord Day & Lord, Barrett Smith (Joanne W. Young)

Iceland, Government of
Reykjavik, Iceland
Counsel or consultant:
Patton, Boggs and Blow (Theodore G. Kronmiller)

Iceland Steamship Co.
Reykjavik, Iceland
Counsel or consultant:
Lord Day & Lord, Barrett Smith (Joanne W. Young)

ICI Americas Inc.
1600 M St., N.W., Suite 702, Washington, DC 20036
Telephone: (202) 775-9722
Represented by:
Richard A. Herrett, Government Relations Scientific Liaison
William A. Meaux, Government Relations Specialist
Herbert K. Schmitz, Director, Government Relations
Sandra E. Taylor, Government Relations Specialist
Counsel or consultant:
Graham and James (Jeffrey L. Snyder)
Howrey and Simon (Michael A. Hertzberg)
Lee, Toomey & Kent

Idaho Power Co.
Boise, ID

The listings in this directory are available as *Mailing Labels*. See last page.

575

ORGANIZATIONS REPRESENTED

Idaho Power Co. (Cont'd)
Counsel or consultant:
Leighton and Sherline (Lee S. Sherline)
Reid & Priest

Idapine Mills/Clearwater Forest Industries
Grangeville, ID
Counsel or consultant:
F. H. Hutchison and Co. (Fred H. Hutchison)

Illinois Ass'n of Colleges and Schools
Chicago, IL
Counsel or consultant:
White, Fine, and Verville (Richard A. Fulton)

Illinois Cereal Mills
Paris, IL
Counsel or consultant:
McDermott, Will and Emery (James Sneed)

Illinois Collaboration on Youth
Chicago, IL
Counsel or consultant:
Capitol Associates, Inc. (Debra M. Hardy-Havens)

Illinois Committee on Tort Reform
Wheaton, IL
Counsel or consultant:
Bonner & Associates

Illinois Department of Children and Family Services
Springfield, IL
Counsel or consultant:
Dickstein, Shapiro and Morin (John C. Dill)

Illinois Department of Energy and Natural Resources
Springfield, IL
Counsel or consultant:
Burgum & Grimm, Ltd. (Thomas L. Burgum)
Duncan, Weinberg, Miller & Pembroke, P.C. (Jeffrey C. Genzer)

Illinois Diversatech Corp.
Manteno, IL
Counsel or consultant:
Smith Dawson & Andrews, Inc. (James P. Smith)

Illinois Health Facilities Authority
Chicago, IL
Counsel or consultant:
Graham and James (Eileen Shannon Carlson, Thomas F. Railsback)

Illinois Power Co.
Decatur, IL
Counsel or consultant:
Robinson, Lake, Lerer & Montgomery (David C. Blee)

Illinois, State of
444 N. Capitol St., N.W. Suite 210, Washington, DC 20001
Telephone: (202) 624-7760
Represented by:
Tom Litjen, Associate Director
Ann McCabe, Associate Director
Terri Moreland, Associate Director
Doug Richardson, Director, Washington Office
Judith Thorman, Deputy Director

Imasco
Manila, Philippines
Counsel or consultant:
Lachelli, Waller and Associates (Sam Ballenger)

IMC-PAC
1726 M St., N.W., Suite 701, Washington, DC 20036
Telephone: (202) 659-1750
Background: The political action arm of the International Minerals and Chemical Corp. Responsible contact is Joan T. Bier, Vice President for Government Affairs of the sponsoring Company.

IMC/Pittman Moore
Terre Haute, IN
Counsel or consultant:
McMillan and Farrell Associates (C. W. McMillan)

Immigration Reform Law Institute
1666 Connecticut Ave., N.W. Suite 402, Washington, DC 20009
Telephone: (202) 462-1969
Background: A non-profit public interest law firm which promotes reasoned immigration law and policy by litigation on behalf of American citizens.
Represented by:
Richard Higgins, Exec. Director

Immune Response Corp.
La Jolla, CA
Counsel or consultant:
Patton, Boggs and Blow (Stuart M. Pape)

Imo Industries
727 23rd St. South, Arlington, VA 22202
Telephone: (703) 920-4500
Represented by:
William J. Wight, V. President, Government Relations
Counsel or consultant:
Sullivan and Cromwell (Margaret K. Pfeiffer)

IMPAC 2000
122 C St., N.W., Suite 500A, Washington, DC 20001
Telephone: (202) 628-0617
Represented by:
Katherine A. Meek, Exec. Director

IMPACT
100 Maryland Ave., N.E. Suite 502, Washington, DC 20002
Telephone: (202) 544-8636
Background: Interfaith organization seeking to influence public policy on peace, justice, women's rights, hunger, the federal budget, civil rights and economic issues.
Represented by:
Gretchen C. Eick, Nat'l Director

Imperial Irrigation District
Imperial, CA
Counsel or consultant:
The Ferguson Co. (William Ferguson, Jr., Patricia Jordan, Thane Young)

In-Situ, Inc.
Laramie, WY
Counsel or consultant:
ENS Resources, Inc. (Eric Sapirstein)

INCO U.S.
New York, NY
Background: Formerly the Internat'l Nickel Co.
Counsel or consultant:
Newmyer Associates, Inc.
Shaw, Pittman, Potts and Trowbridge (William Mike House)

Incorporated Research Institutions for Seismology
1616 North Ft. Myer Drive, Suite 1440, Arlington, VA 22209
Telephone: (703) 524-6222
Counsel or consultant:
Patton, Boggs and Blow (Penelope S. Farthing)

INDA, Ass'n of the Nonwoven Fabrics Industry
1150 17th St., N.W., Suite 1000, Washington, DC 20036
Telephone: (202) 956-5631
Background: Founded in 1968, INDA is the recognized international trade association of the nonwoven fabrics industry, including goods such as disposable diapers, tea bags, filters, wall paper and carpet backing, and feminine hygene products. Director of Government Affairs is Peter G. Mayberry, of the DC firm Keller and Heckman.
Counsel or consultant:
Keller and Heckman (Wayne V. Black, Peter G. Mayberry)

Independent Action
1511 K St., N.W. Suite 619, Washington, DC 20005
Telephone: (202) 628-4321
Background: A progressive Democratic political action committee.
Represented by:
Mark A. Ingram, Treasurer
Cheryl C. Kagan, Exec. Director
Counsel or consultant:
Epstein Becker and Green (Leslie Kerman)

Independent Armored Car Operators Ass'n
Broadview, IL
Counsel or consultant:
Rowland & Sellery (Lawrence E. Sabbath)

Independent Bakers Ass'n
Box 3731, Washington, DC 20007
Telephone: (202) 333-8190
Counsel or consultant:
Robert N. Pyle & Associates (Robert N. Pyle)

Independent Bankers Ass'n of America
One Thomas Circle, N.W., Suite 950, Washington, DC 20005
Telephone: (202) 659-8111
Represented by:
Ronald K. Ence, Dir., Agricultural and Rural Affairs
Linda A. Garvelink, Operations Liaison
Dorothy M. Gillman, Legislative Representative
Linda A. Gravelink, Director of Regulation
Kenneth A. Guenther, Exec. V. President
Gary J. Kohn, Legislative Counsel
Keith Scarborough, Legislative Counsel
Stephen J. Verdier, Senior Legislative Counsel

Independent Bankers Political Action Committee
One Thomas Circle, N.W., Suite 950, Washington, DC 20005
Telephone: (202) 659-8111
Represented by:
Alexandra Maroulis-Cronmiller, Administrator

Independent Blue Cross
Philadelphia, PA
Counsel or consultant:
Burson-Marsteller (Rebecca L. Halkias)

Independent Cosmetic Manufacturers and Distributors, Inc.
Bensenville, IL
Counsel or consultant:
Walter E. Byerley Law Offices (Walter E. Byerley)

Independent Data Communications Manufacturers Ass'n
1201 Pennsylvania Ave., N.W. Suite 500, Washington, DC 20004
Telephone: (202) 626-6600
Counsel or consultant:
Squire, Sanders and Dempsey (James L. Casserly, Herbert E. Marks)

Independent Education Fund
1749 P St., N.W., Washington, DC 20036
Telephone: (202) 462-3886
Background: Exec. V. President is John W. Sanders, V. President, Nat'l Ass'n of Independent Schools.
Counsel or consultant:
Bahnsen Communications
Belden and Russonello (Nancy Belden)
Caplin and Drysdale

Independent Health Plan
Buffalo, NY
Counsel or consultant:
Jefferson Group, The (Frederick J. Hannett)

Independent Insurance Agents of America
600 Pennsylvania Ave., S.E., Suite 200, Washington, DC 20003
Telephone: (202) 544-5833
Represented by:
Leonard C. Brevik, Director, State Government Affairs
Ellen K. Dollase, Assistant Director, State Gov't Affairs
Paul A. Equale, V. President, Government Affairs
M. C. Keegan-Ayer, Ass't Director, Federal Affairs
Robert A. Rusbuldt, Assistant V. President, Federal Affairs
Elizabeth White-Call, Ass't Director of Public Affairs
Counsel or consultant:
Miller, Cassidy, Larroca and Lewin (Jonathan Sallet)
Steptoe and Johnson (Mark F. Horning)

Independent Insurance Agents of America, Inc. Political Action Committee
600 Pennsylvania Ave., S.E. Suite 200, Washington, DC 20003
Telephone: (202) 675-6485
Represented by:
Lisa M. Costello, Administrator
Magenta Ishak, Director

Independent Liquid Terminals Ass'n
1133 15th St., N.W. Suite 204, Washington, DC 20005
Telephone: (202) 659-2301

The listings in this directory are available as *Mailing Labels*. See last page.

ORGANIZATIONS REPRESENTED

Represented by:
E. Bruce Calvert, Director of Administration
Cindy Hughes, Technical Director
John A. Prokop, President

Independent Living for the Handicapped
1301 Belmont St., N.W., Washington, DC 20009
Telephone: (202) 797-9803
Represented by:
William Price, Acting Exec. Director

Independent Lubricant Manufacturers Ass'n
651 S. Washington, Alexandria, VA 22314
Telephone: (703) 684-5574
Represented by:
Nancy DeMarco, Exec. Director
Counsel or consultant:
Collier, Shannon & Scott (William W. Scott)

Independent Lubricant Manufacturers Ass'n Political Action Committee
651 S. Washington St., Alexandria, VA 22314
Telephone: (703) 684-5574
Represented by:
Kelly Kephart, Treasurer
Counsel or consultant:
Collier, Shannon & Scott

Independent Oil and Gas Ass'n of West Virginia
Charleston, WV
Counsel or consultant:
Ryan-McGinn (C. Michael Fulton, Daniel McGinn)

Independent Oil Producers Ass'n-Tri State
Evansville, IN
Counsel or consultant:
Resources Development, Inc. (Roger H. Zion)

Independent Petroleum Ass'n of America
1101 16th St., N.W., Washington, DC 20036
Telephone: (202) 857-4704
Represented by:
Bob Avant, Resident Tax Specialist
Douglas L. Francisco, V. President
Barry Russell, General Counsel
Harold B. Scoggins, President

Independent Petroleum Ass'n of Canada
Calgary, Alberta
Counsel or consultant:
Brady and Berliner (Roger A. Berliner, Jerry M. Brady)

Independent Sector
1828 L St., N.W., Washington, DC 20036
Telephone: (202) 223-8100
Background: A coalition of approximately 600 philanthropic organizations and institutions from the former Nat'l Council on Philanthropy and the Coalition of Nat'l Voluntary Organizations. Initial funding for the new coalition was provided by 30 foundations.
Represented by:
Brian Foss, V. President, Assistant to the President
Sandra Trice Gray, V. President, Give Five Program
Virginia Ann Hodgkinson, V. President, Research
Edwin B. Knauft, Exec. V. President
Char Mollison, V. President, Membership
Brian O'Connell, President
Robert M. Smucker, V. President, Government Relations
John H. Thomas, V. President, Communications
Jo Uehara, Associate Director, Government Relations
Counsel or consultant:
Harmon, Curran and Tousley (Gail Harmon)
Marlowe and Co.

Independent Terminal Operators Ass'n
1150 Connecticut Ave., N.W., 9th Floor, Washington, DC 20036
Telephone: (202) 828-4100
Counsel or consultant:
William Bode and Associates (William Bode)

Independent Visually Impaired Enterprisers
1010 Vermont Ave., N.W. Suite 1100, Washington, DC 20005
Telephone: (202) 393-3666
Background: Represented by Roberta Douglas of the American Council of the Blind.

Independent Zinc Alloyers Ass'n, Inc.
1000 16th St., N.W., Suite 603, Washington, DC 20036
Telephone: (202) 785-0558

Counsel or consultant:
Counselors For Management, Inc. (Richard M. Cooperman, Janice C. Lipsen)

Indian River Citrus League
FL
Counsel or consultant:
Holland and Knight (John M. Himmelberg)

Indiana Department of Commerce
Indianapolis, IN
Counsel or consultant:
Cassidy and Associates, Inc. (Thomas M. Gannon)

Indiana Electric Ass'n
Indiana, IN
Counsel or consultant:
Sagamore Associates, Inc. (Michael B. Kraft)

Indiana Gas Co.
Indianapolis, IN
Counsel or consultant:
Barnes and Thornburg

Indiana and Michigan Electric Co.
Fort Wayne, IN
Counsel or consultant:
Shaw, Pittman, Potts and Trowbridge (Gerald Charnoff)

Indiana and Michigan Municipal Distributors Ass'n
Niles, MI
Counsel or consultant:
Duncan, Weinberg, Miller & Pembroke, P.C. (Janice L. Lower, James D. Pembroke)

Indiana Michigan Power Co.
Columbus, OH
Counsel or consultant:
Shaw, Pittman, Potts and Trowbridge (Gerald Charnoff)

Indiana Port Commission
Indianapolis, IN
Counsel or consultant:
Verner, Liipfert, Bernhard, McPherson and Hand, Chartered (Hopewell H. Darneille, III)

Indiana State University
Terre Haute, IN
Counsel or consultant:
Sagamore Associates, Inc. (David U. Gogol)

Indianapolis Center for Advanced Research
Indianapolis, IN
Counsel or consultant:
Sagamore Associates, Inc. (David U. Gogol)

Indianapolis, Indiana, City of
Counsel or consultant:
Sagamore Associates, Inc. (David U. Gogol)

Indo-U.S. Political Action Committee
Los Angeles, CA
Counsel or consultant:
The William Chasey Organization (William C. Chasey, Ph.D.)

Indochina Resource Action Center
1628 16th St., N.W. 3rd Floor, Washington, DC 20037
Telephone: (202) 667-4690
Represented by:
Khoa X. Le, President

Indonesia, Bank of
Jakarta, Indonesia
Counsel or consultant:
White & Case

Indonesia, Government of
Jakarta, Indonesia
Counsel or consultant:
Hill and Knowlton Public Affairs Worldwide (Gary Hymel)
Internat'l Business and Economic Research Corp.
White & Case

Indonesia, Nat'l Development Information Office
Jakarta, Indonesia
Counsel or consultant:
Hill and Knowlton Public Affairs Worldwide (Donald F. Massey)

Indonesian Ass'n of Textile Industries
Jakarta, Indonesia
Counsel or consultant:
Internat'l Business and Economic Research Corp.

Industrial Bank of Japan, Ltd.
Tokyo, Japan
Counsel or consultant:
Wilbur F. Monroe Associates (Wilbur F. Monroe)

Industrial Biotechnology Ass'n
1625 K St., N.W., Suite 1100, Washington, DC 20006
Telephone: (202) 857-0244
Represented by:
Richard D. Godown, President
Alan R. Goldhammer, Director, Technical Affairs
Lisa J. Raines, Director, Government Relations
Counsel or consultant:
Parry and Romani Associates Inc. (Romano Romani)

Industrial Designers Soc. of America
1142-E Walker Road, Great Falls, VA 22066
Telephone: (703) 759-0100
Represented by:
Robert T. Schwartz, Exec. Director and COO

Industrial Diamond Ass'n of America
Columbia, SC
Counsel or consultant:
Loomis, Owen, Fellman and Howe (James E. Anderson)

Industrial Equity (Pacific) Ltd.
LaJolla, CA
Counsel or consultant:
Wunder, Ryan, Cannon & Thelen (Bernard J. Wunder)

Industrial Fabrics Ass'n Internat'l
2000 L St., N.W., Suite 200, Washington, DC 20036-4907
Telephone: (202) 861-0981
Represented by:
Marcia Thomson, Director, Public Affairs/Gov't Relations
Counsel or consultant:
Fehrenbacher, Sale, Quinn, and Deese (C. Michael Deese)
Kaye, Scholer, Fierman, Hays and Handler (Christopher R. Brewster)

Industrial Fabrics Ass'n Internat'l Political Action Committee
2000 L St., N.W., Suite 200, Washington, DC 20036
Telephone: (202) 861-0981
Background: Contact is Marcia Thomson of the Ass'n.

Industrial Heating Equipment Ass'n
1901 North Moore St., Arlington, VA 22209
Telephone: (703) 525-2513
Counsel or consultant:
Houston Associates, Inc. (James J. Houston)

Industrial Heating Equipment Ass'n Political Action Committee
1901 North Moore St., Arlington, VA 22209
Telephone: (703) 525-2513
Counsel or consultant:
Houston Associates, Inc. (James J. Houston)

Industrial Heating Magazine
Pittsburgh, PA
Counsel or consultant:
Ashby and Associates (R. Barry Ashby)

Industrial Indemnity Financial Corp.
San Francisco, CA
Counsel or consultant:
Akin, Gump, Strauss, Hauer and Feld (Joel Jankowsky)

Industrial Insulations of Texas, Inc.
Houston, TX
Counsel or consultant:
Rogers Internat'l, Inc. (Joe O. Rogers)

Industrial Safety Equipment Ass'n
1901 North Moore St., Suite 501, Arlington, VA 22209
Telephone: (703) 525-1695
Represented by:
Thomas G. Aughteron, Technical Director
Patricia A. Gleason, Director of Communication
Frank E. Wilcher, Jr., President
Counsel or consultant:
Jefferson Group, The (Mark D. Cowan)

ORGANIZATIONS REPRESENTED

Industrial Truck Ass'n
1750 K St., N.W. Suite 210, Washington, DC 20006
Telephone: (202) 296-9880
Represented by:
William J. Montwieler, Exec. Director
Counsel or consultant:
Dunaway & Cross (Mac S. Dunaway)

Industrial Union of Marine and Shipbuilding Workers of America
5101 River Road, Suite 110, Bethesda, MD 20816
Telephone: (301) 951-4266
Represented by:
Arthur E. Batson, Jr., President

Industrias Resistol
Mexico City, Mexico
Counsel or consultant:
Brownstein Zeidman and Schomer

Industry Coalition on Technology Transfer
c/o Bishop, Cook, Purcell & Reynolds, 1400 L St., N.W., Washington, DC 20005
Telephone: (202) 371-5994
Background: A coalition of ten trade associations representing U.S. manufacturers whose products are subject to export controls.
Represented by:
R. Allen Flowers, Deputy Exec. Secretary
Counsel or consultant:
Bishop, Cook, Purcell & Reynolds (Eric L. Hirschhorn)

Industry Council for Tangible Assets
25 E St., N.W. Suite 810, Washington, DC 20001
Telephone: (202) 783-3500
Background: A non-profit trade associaton which lobbies to safeguard rights of industries dealing in "tangible assets", such as rare coins, gold, silver, gemstones, antiques and art.
Counsel or consultant:
Gilman, Olson & Pangia (William J. Olson)
Murray, Scheer & Montgomery (D. Michael Murray)

Industry General Corp.
Memphis, TN
Counsel or consultant:
Resources Development, Inc. (Roger H. Zion)

Infectious Disease Soc. of America
Rochester, NY
Counsel or consultant:
Reed Smith Shaw & McClay (Stephan E. Lawton)

Infinite Research, Inc.
Las Vegas, NV
Counsel or consultant:
Hopkins and Sutter (William D. Phillips)

Infirmary Health System, Inc.
Mobile, AL
Counsel or consultant:
Cassidy and Associates, Inc. (Robert K. Dawson, James P. Fabiani, Dr. Frank A. Rose)

Infomedia Corporation
7700 Leesburg Pike Centre Tower, Falls Church, VA 22042
Telephone: (703) 847-0077
Represented by:
Don Binns, Chairman

Information Industry Ass'n
555 New Jersey Ave., N.W. Suite 800, Washington, DC 20001
Telephone: (202) 639-8262
Represented by:
Kenneth B. Allen, Senior V. President
David C. Fullarton, President
Susan E, Goewey, Director, Public Relations
Stephen J. Metalitz, V. President and Counsel
Counsel or consultant:
Piper and Marbury
Wiley, Rein & Fielding

Infrastructure Bond Coalition
c/o Chambers Assoc., 1625 K St., N.W., Suite 200, Washington, DC 20006
Telephone: (202) 857-0670
Counsel or consultant:
Chambers Associates Incorporated (James N. Smith)

Ingersoll Products Co.
Chicago, IL
Counsel or consultant:
Beveridge & Diamond, P.C. (Alexander W. Sierck)

Ingersoll-Rand Co.
1627 K St., N.W., Suite 900, Washington, DC 20006
Telephone: (202) 955-1450
Represented by:
Robert N. Eakin, Mgr., Government Accounts, New Products
Robert G. Littlefield, Manager, Government Sales

Inglewood, California, City of
Counsel or consultant:
The Ferguson Co. (William Ferguson, Jr., Patricia Jordan, Thane Young)
Laxalt, Washington, Perito & Dubuc (James M. Christian, Sr.)

Inland Steel Co.
Chicago, IL
Counsel or consultant:
Collier, Shannon & Scott
Dewey, Ballantine, Bushby, Palmer and Wood (Michael H. Stein)
Hopkins and Sutter (Francis O. McDermott)
Mayer, Brown and Platt

Innovation Technology, Inc.
1140 Connecticut Ave., N.W., Suite 804, Washington, DC 20036
Telephone: (202) 452-6004
Counsel or consultant:
Offices of V.J. Adduci

Inova Health Systems
8001 Braddock Road, Springfield, VA 22151
Telephone: (703) 321-4213
Represented by:
Maston T. Jacks, V. President, Legal & External Affairs
Counsel or consultant:
Miles and Stockbridge (Richard W. Bowe, Barent L. Fake)

Inspiration Consolidated Copper Co.
Phoenix, AZ
Counsel or consultant:
Steptoe and Johnson

Institut de la Vie
Paris, France
Counsel or consultant:
Laxalt, Washington, Perito & Dubuc (Carroll E. Dubuc)

Institute for a Drug-Free Workplace
P.O. Box 65708, Washington, DC 20035-5708
Telephone: (202) 463-5530
Background: Exec. Director is Mark A. de Bernardo.
Represented by:
Nancy N. Delogu, Associate Director

Institute for Alternative Futures
108 North Alfred St., Alexandria, VA 22314
Telephone: (703) 684-5880
Background: Founders included Alvin Toffler, author of Future Shock and The Third Wave. Established as a research and education organization focused on the future and on new approaches to future problems, including greater citizen involvement in the workplace and government. Directs attention to public and governmental audiences.
Represented by:
Clement Bezold, Ph.D., Exec. Director
Jonathan Peck, Associate Director

Institute for Defense Analyses
1801 North Beauregard St., Alexandria, VA 22311
Telephone: (703) 845-2300
Represented by:
Dr. Robert Roberts, V. President, Research
Gen. William Y. Smith, President

Institute for Educational Affairs
1112 16th St., N.W. Suite 520, Washington, DC 20036
Telephone: (202) 833-1801
Background: Provides editorial and financial assistance to independent student newspapers at approximately 54 U.S. colleges and universities. Sponsors 'Philanthropic Roundtable,' an organization of nearly 200 foundations, corporate grant-makers and others interested in innovative philanthropy.

Represented by:
Peter Frumkin, V. President
Dr. Leslie Lenkowsky, President

Institute for Educational Leadership
1001 Connecticut Ave., N.W. Suite 310, Washington, DC 20036
Telephone: (202) 822-8405
Represented by:
Peter B. Goldberg, Senior Associate
Harold L. Hodgkinson, Director, Center for Demographic Policy
Michael D. Usdan, President
Counsel or consultant:
Gallagher-Widmeyer Group Inc., The (Scott D. Widmeyer)
Powell, Adams & Rinehart

Institute for Government and Politics
717 Second St., N.E., Washington, DC 20002
Telephone: (202) 546-3004
Background: An arm of the Free Congress Foundation.
Represented by:
Stuart Rothenberg, Director, Political Division

Institute for Internat'l Economics
11 Dupont Circle, N.W., Washington, DC 20036
Telephone: (202) 328-0583
Background: Established in 1981 as a nonprofit research institution devoted to the study of international economics and to present its ideas to government policy makers and the public. Board of Directors includes such prominent former government officials as W. Michael Blumenthal, Alan Greenspan, Peter G. Peterson and Andrew Young.
Represented by:
C. Fred Bergsten, Director
William R. Cline, Senior Fellow
C. Randall Henning, Research Fellow

Institute for Local Self-Reliance
2425 18th St., N.W., Washington, DC 20009
Telephone: (202) 232-4108
Background: Provides technical and policy assistance to groups and governments on waste recycling and local economic development.
Represented by:
Dr. Neil N. Seldman, President

Institute for Policy Studies
1601 Connecticut Ave., N.W. 5th Floor, Washington, DC 20009
Telephone: (202) 234-9382
Background: Founded in 1963, IPS describes itself as 'a transnational center for research, education and social invention." Sponsors critical examination of assumptions and policies on domestic and international issues.
Represented by:
Richard J. Barnet, Senior Fellow
Diana de Vegh, Director
Marcus G. Raskin, Senior Fellow

Institute for Professional Health Services Administrators
1101 King St., Suite 601, Alexandria, VA 22314
Telephone: (703) 684-0288
Background: An organization of professional health service supervisors, administrators and managers.
Represented by:
Royce P. Noland, President/ CEO

Institute for Public Representation
600 New Jersey Ave., N.W., Washington, DC 20001
Telephone: (202) 662-9535
Background: Operates out of Georgetown University Law Center; Engages in federal administrative practice, encouraging the federal government to consider the views of otherwise unrepresented, or under-represented, groups and individuals.
Represented by:
Laura Macklin, Associate Director
Douglas L. Parker, Director

Institute for Research on the Economics of Taxation (IRET)
1331 Pennsylvania Ave., N.W. Suite 515, Washington, DC 20004
Telephone: (202) 347-9570

ORGANIZATIONS REPRESENTED

Represented by:
Nancy Craft Baker, V. President, Communications
Steven Lakin, V. President
Cheryl Long, V. President, Corporate Development
Dr. Norman B. Ture, President

Institute for Security and Cooperation in Outer Space
1336A Corcoran St., N.W., Washington, DC 20009-4311
Telephone: (202) 462-8886
Background: Seeks Congressional support for East-West cooperation in space.
Represented by:
Carol Rosin, President
Connie Van Praet, Director

Institute for Soviet-American Relations
1608 New Hampshire Ave., N.W., Washington, DC 20009
Telephone: (202) 387-3034
Background: An organization seeking to improve relations between the U.S. and the USSR by encouraging communication and exchanges, particularly at the non-governmental level.
Represented by:
Harriett Crosby, President
Nancy A. Graham, Senior Associate
Eliza K. Klose, Exec. Director

Institute of Electrical and Electronics Engineers, Inc.
1828 L St., N.W. Suite 1202, Washington, DC 20036-5104
Telephone: (202) 785-0017
Represented by:
Chris Julian Brantley, Administrator, Professional Programs
Leo C. Fanning, Staff Director, Professional Activities
James H. Ferguson, Senior Legislative Specialist
John V. O'Neill, Administrator, Professional Programs
Deborah Karen Rudolph, Manager, Public Affairs Programs
W. Thomas Suttle, Assoc. Staff Dir., Prof. Activities
Counsel or consultant:
Allan Associates (Roger D. Allan)

Institute of Financial and Fiscal Studies of Curacao
Curacao, Netherlands Antilles
Counsel or consultant:
Anderson, Hibey, Nauheim and Blair (Stanton D. Anderson, Stephen A. Nauheim)

Institute of Gas Technology
1825 K St., N.W. Suite 503, Washington, DC 20006
Telephone: (202) 785-3511
Background: A non-profit research and development organization concerned with all forms of energy production other than nuclear. Founded in 1941; headquartered in Chicago.
Represented by:
Mary M. Cremin, Exec. Secretary
Laurence M. Feder, Ass't Director, Program Development
Jay D. Willer, Manager, Program Coordination
Fred H. Zerkel, V. President, Washington Opns.

Institute of Industrial Launderers
1730 M St., N.W. Suite 610, Washington, DC 20036
Telephone: (202) 296-6744
Represented by:
Lawrence T. Graham, Exec. Director

Institute of Internat'l Bankers
New York, NY
Counsel or consultant:
Shaw, Pittman, Potts and Trowbridge (Steven M. Lucas)

Institute of Makers of Explosives
1120 19th St., N.W., Suite 310, Washington, DC 20036-3605
Telephone: (202) 429-9280
Represented by:
Lynn S. Green, Manager, Governmental Services
Frederick P. Smith, Jr., President

Institute of Makers of Explosives Political Action Committee
1120 19th St., N.W., Suite 310, Washington, DC 20036-3605
Telephone: (202) 429-9280

Background: The political action committee sponsored by the Institute of Makers of Explosives. Frederick P. Smith, Jr., President of the Institute, serves as Treasurer.

Institute of Navigation
1026 16th St., N.W., Washington, DC 20036
Telephone: (202) 783-4121
Represented by:
Frank B. Brady, Exec. Director

Institute of Professional Practice, The
8811 Colesville Road Suite G106, Silver Spring, MD 20910
Telephone: (301) 587-6048
Counsel or consultant:
Bachner Communications, Inc. (John P. Bachner)

Institute of Resource Management
Salt Lake City, UT
Counsel or consultant:
C. Deming Cowles, IV

Institute of Scrap Recycling Industries, Inc.
1627 K St., N.W. Suite 700, Washington, DC 20006
Telephone: (202) 466-4050
Background: Formed as the result of the merger of the Nat'l Ass'n of Recycling Industries and the Institute of Scrap Iron and Steel.
Represented by:
Dr. Herschel Cutler, Exec. Director
Vivian Makosky, Assistant Exec. Director and Counsel
Janice Walls, Director, State Programs
Counsel or consultant:
Patton, Boggs and Blow (John L. Oberdorfer)

Institute of Scrap Recycling Industries Political Action Committee
1627 K St., N.W., Washington, DC 20006
Telephone: (202) 466-4050
Background: Sponsored by the Institute of Scrap Recycling Industries. Represented by Dr. Herschel Cutler of the Institute.

Institute of the Ironworking Industry
1750 New York Ave., N.W. Suite 400, Washington, DC 20006
Telephone: (202) 783-3998
Background: Formed in 1977 by the Internat'l Ass'n of Bridge, Structural and Ornamental Iron Workers (AFL-CIO) in equal participation with the various independent regional associations of Iron Workers Employers. Activities are targeted to expand contract and work opportunities for the industry and to represent the industry in code and standards review and development.
Represented by:
John J. McMahon, Jr., Exec. Director

Institute of Transportation Engineers
525 School St., S.W., Suite 410, Washington, DC 20024
Telephone: (202) 554-8050
Represented by:
Thomas W. Brahms, Exec. Director

Institute on Religion and Democracy
729 15th St., N.W., Suite 900, Washington, DC 20005
Telephone: (202) 393-3200
Background: An interdenominational, non-partisan organization founded in 1981 to promote balanced and constructive church involvement in foreign policy issues. Opposes compromising basic Christian beliefs by linking them with partisan political positions and affirms democracy as the political system most consistent with these Christian values.
Represented by:
Lawrence Adams, Internat'l Affairs & Economics Associate
Kent R. Hill, Exec. Director
Diane L. Knippers, Deputy Director
Edmund W. Robb, Jr., Chairman
Counsel or consultant:
Gammon and Grange

Institutional and Municipal Parking Congress
P.O. Box 7167, Fredericksburg, VA 22404
Telephone: (703) 371-7535
Represented by:
David L. Ivey, Exec. V. President
Counsel or consultant:
David E. Fox

Instituto Brasileira de Siderugia
Rio de Janeiro, Brazil
Counsel or consultant:
Willkie Farr and Gallagher (William H. Barringer)

Instituto Latinoamericano del Fierro y el Acero (ILAFA)
Santiago, Chile
Counsel or consultant:
Preston Gates Ellis & Rouvelas Meeds (Bruce J. Heiman)

Instrument Constructing and Engineering Ass'n, Inc.
P.O. Box 42558, Northwest Station, Washington, DC 20015-0458
Telephone: (301) 933-7430
Counsel or consultant:
Specialty Contractors Management, Inc. (Walter M. Kardy)

Instrument Soc. of America
Res. Triangle Pk, NC
Background: A Washington contact is John Clement of the American Federation of Information Processing Societies.

Instrument Technicians Labor-Management Cooperation Fund
P.O. Box 42558, Northwest Station, Washington, DC 20015
Telephone: (301) 933-7430
Counsel or consultant:
Specialty Contractors Management, Inc. (Walter M. Kardy)

Instrumentation Testing Ass'n
1225 Eye St., NW, Suite 300, Washington, DC 20005
Telephone: (202) 683-3760
Background: Membership is open to public or private agencies utilizing instrumentation for the conduct or enhancement of water, wastewater, or industrial waste treatment, or other public works functions.
Counsel or consultant:
Linton, Mields, Reisler and Cottone (Bashar Masri)

Insulation Contractors Ass'n of America
15819 Crabbs Branch Way, Rockville, MD 20855
Telephone: (301) 590-0030
Represented by:
R. Hartley Edes, Exec. Director

Insurance Ass'n of Connecticut
Hartford, CT
Counsel or consultant:
Bonner & Associates

Insurance/Financial Affiliates of America
Denver, CO
Counsel or consultant:
McNair Law Firm, P.A. (James McIntyre, Jr.)

Insurance Information Institute
1101 17th St, N.W., Suite 408, Washington, DC 20036
Telephone: (202) 833-1580
Represented by:
Tim Dove, Federal Affairs Issues Manager
Julie Rochman, Federal Affairs Specialist
Marc H. Rosenberg, V. President, Federal Affairs
Counsel or consultant:
Van Dyk Associates, Inc. (Jim Dickenson, Ted Van Dyk)

Insurance Institute for Highway Safety
1005 North Glebe Rd. Suite 800, Arlington, VA 22201
Telephone: (703) 247-1500
Background: A non-profit public service organization working to reduce injury, death and property loss on the highways.
Represented by:
Chuck Hurkey, V. President, Communications
Brian O'Neill, President

Insurance Services Office
1666 K St., N.W. Suite 915, Washington, DC 20006
Telephone: (202) 466-2800
Represented by:
Deborah Bindeman, Federal Affairs Representative
Ann Ferrill Lavie, Director, Federal Affairs

InTecTran, Inc.
1129 20th St., N.W., Suite 500, Washington, DC 20036-3403
Telephone: (202) 293-0154

ORGANIZATIONS REPRESENTED

InTecTran, Inc. (Cont'd)
Represented by:
Thomas Blau, President

Integrated Resources, Inc.
New York, NY
Counsel or consultant:
Dewey, Ballantine, Bushby, Palmer and Wood (John J. Salmon)

Intel Corporation
1825 Eye St., N.W., Suite 400, Washington, DC 20006
Telephone: (202) 429-2054
Represented by:
Michael C. Maibach, Government Affairs Director
David Rose, Export/Import Manager
Counsel or consultant:
Dewey, Ballantine, Bushby, Palmer and Wood (R. Michael Gadbaw, Alan W. Wolff)

Intellectual Property Owners, Inc.
1255 23rd St., N.W., Suite 850, Washington, DC 20037
Telephone: (202) 466-2396
Background: A nonprofit association representing patent, trademark and copyright owners. Founded in 1972. Members include large corporations, small businesses, universities and inventors.
Represented by:
Donald W. Banner, President
Herbert C. Wamsley, Exec. Director
Counsel or consultant:
Communications Management Associates (David K. Martin)

Intellectual Property Political Action Committee
2001 Jefferson Davis Hwy. Suite 203, Arlington, VA 22202
Telephone: (703) 521-1680
Background: A political action committee sponsored by the American Intellectual Property Law Ass'n. Contact is Michael W. Blommer of that organization.

Inter-American Bar Ass'n
1889 F St., N.W. Suite LL2, Washington, DC 20006
Telephone: (202) 789-2747
Represented by:
Donald Duvall, President
Grover Prevatte Hopkins, Secretary General

Inter-American Bar Foundation
1819 H St., N.W., Washington, DC 20006
Telephone: (202) 293-1455
Background: Contact is Donald Duvall of the ass'n.

Inter-American Dialogue
1333 New Hampshire Ave., N.W., Washington, DC 20036
Telephone: (202) 466-6410
Represented by:
Peter Hakim, Staff Director
Richard A. Nuccio, Senior Associate

Inter-American University
Hato Rey, PR
Counsel or consultant:
Jefferson Group, The (Jose Ortiz-Daliot)

Inter-City Gas, Ltd.
Winnipeg, Manitoba
Counsel or consultant:
Steptoe and Johnson

Inter-Industry Log Export Action Committee
Indianapolis, IN
Counsel or consultant:
F. H. Hutchison and Co. (Fred H. Hutchison)

Inter-Power of New York
Albany, NY
Counsel or consultant:
Chadbourne and Parke

Inter Tribal Council of Nevada
Reno, NV
Counsel or consultant:
Lachelli, Waller and Associates (John D. Waller)

InterAmerican College of Physicians and Surgeons
1101 15th St., N.W. Suite 602, Washington, DC 20005
Telephone: (202) 467-4756
Background: A nonprofit group working to increase the exchange of medical knowledge between Latin America and the U.S., to strengthen the number of Hispanic physicians

in the U.S. and to improve relations with Latin America in general.
Represented by:
Dr. Gonzalo Lopez, Washington Director
Dr. Rene F. Rodriguez Rojas, President

INTERARMS
10 Prince St., Alexandria, VA 22313
Telephone: (704) 548-1400
Counsel or consultant:
Webster, Chamberlain and Bean (Burkett Van Kirk)

Intercontinental Energy Corp.
Counsel or consultant:
Olwine, Connelly, Chase, O'Donnell and Weyher (W. Harrison Wellford)
Swidler & Berlin, Chartered (Carmen D. Legato)

Interface Group, Inc., The
Needham, MA
Counsel or consultant:
Thompson, Hine and Flory (Lewe B. Martin)

Interfaith Action for Economic Justice
110 Maryland Ave., N.E. Suite 509, Washington, DC 20002
Telephone: (202) 543-2800
Background: Interreligious advocacy organization working on domestic poverty, international development and food and agriculture.
Represented by:
Arthur Keys, Executive Director

Interfaith Forum on Religion, Art and Architecture
1777 Church St., N.W., Washington, DC 20036
Telephone: (202) 387-8333
Represented by:
Doris Justis, Exec. Secretary

Intergovernmental Health Policy Project
2011 Eye St., N.W. Suite 200, Washington, DC 20006
Telephone: (202) 872-1445
Background: A George Washington University-based program of research on the health law and programs of the 50 states. Provides assistance to state executive officials, legislative staff and others who need to know about important developments in health programs and policies in other states.
Represented by:
Richard Merritt, Director

Intergraph Corp.
Huntsville, AL
Counsel or consultant:
Shaw, Pittman, Potts and Trowbridge (William Mike House)

Interlake Corp.
1730 M St., N.W., Suite 911, Washington, DC 20036
Telephone: (202) 659-1601
Represented by:
Joseph J. Meder, Washington Representative

Interlake Holding Corp.
Stamford, CT
Counsel or consultant:
Preston Gates Ellis & Rouvelas Meeds (Susan B. Geiger, Emanuel L. Rouvelas)

Intermarine S.p.A.
Savannah, GA
Counsel or consultant:
Wunder, Ryan, Cannon & Thelen (John J. McGovern, Jr.)

Intermec Corp.
Lynnwood, WA
Counsel or consultant:
Century Public Affairs

Intermedia Partners
San Francisco, CA
Counsel or consultant:
Pillsbury, Madison and Sutro (Benjamin M. Vandergrift)
Thompson and Co. (Robert J. Thompson)

Intermedics, Inc.
Freeport, TX

Counsel or consultant:
Hill and Knowlton Public Affairs Worldwide (Susan Cohen, Ken Rabin)

Intermodal Marketing Ass'n
2111 Wilson Blvd., Suite 700, Arlington, VA 22201
Telephone: (703) 875-8665
Represented by:
John A. McQuaid, Exec. Director
Counsel or consultant:
Allan Associates (Roger D. Allan)
Grove, Jaskiewicz, Gilliam and Cobert

Intermodal Transportation Ass'n
6410 Kenilworth Ave. Suit 108, Riverdale, MD 20737
Telephone: (301) 864-2661
Represented by:
Albert J. Mascaro, Exec. Director
Counsel or consultant:
Grove, Jaskiewicz, Gilliam and Cobert (Leonard A. Jaskiewicz)

Internat'l Air Transport Ass'n
1001 Pennsylvania Ave., N.W. Suite 285, Washington, DC 20004
Telephone: (202) 624-2977
Background: The international organization which promotes cooperation among world airlines with the objectives of providing safe and economical air transportation, fostering air commerce and studying problems connected therewith.
Represented by:
David M. O'Connor, Regional Director, United States

Internat'l Anti-Counterfeiting Coalition
818 Connecticut Ave., N.W. 12th Floor, Washington, DC 20036
Telephone: (202) 223-5728
Represented by:
Johanes Von Schilcher, Exec. Director
Counsel or consultant:
Pillsbury, Madison and Sutro (Donald E. deKieffer)

Internat'l Apple Institute
Box 1137, McLean, VA 22101
Telephone: (703) 442-8850
Represented by:
Derl I. Derr, President
Counsel or consultant:
McDermott, Will and Emery (Edward Ruckert)
Porter/Novelli (Jerry Franz, Karen Waller)

Internat'l Ass'n for Continuing Education and Training
P.O. Box 27043, Washington, DC 20038
Telephone: (301) 384-1059
Background: Provides Congressional relations, Washington representation and developmental and administrative assistance to non-profit organizations.
Represented by:
Michael A. Enders, V. President
G. Timothy Leighton, President
David A. Nichols, Legislative Director
Roberta N. Phillips, Director of Development

Internat'l Ass'n for Dental Research
1111 14th St., N.W., Suite 1000, Washington, DC 20005
Telephone: (202) 898-1050
Background: Represented by John J. Clarkson of the American Ass'n for Dental Research.

Internat'l Ass'n for Financial Planning
Atlanta, GA
Counsel or consultant:
McNair Law Firm, P.A. (James McIntyre, Jr.)

Internat'l Ass'n of Airport Duty Free Stores
1101 Connecticut Ave., N.W. Suite 700, Washington, DC 20036
Telephone: (202) 857-1184
Counsel or consultant:
Kent & O'Connor, Incorp. (J. H. Kent)
Smith, Bucklin and Associates (Robert T. Chancler)

Internat'l Ass'n of Amusement Parks and Attractions
4230 King St., Alexandria, VA 22302
Telephone: (703) 671-5800
Represented by:
John R. Graff, Exec. Dir., Counsel and Dir., Govt. Rels

ORGANIZATIONS REPRESENTED

Internat'l Ass'n of Amusement Parks and Attractions Political Action Committee
4230 King Street, Alexandria, VA 22302
Telephone: (703) 671-5800
Background: Represented by John Graff of the ass'n.

Internat'l Ass'n of Boards of Examiners in Optometry
5530 Wisconsin Ave. Suite 711, Chevy Chase, MD 20815
Telephone: (301) 951-6330
Represented by:
Kenneth G. Crosby, Ed.D., Exec. Director

Internat'l Ass'n of Bridge, Structural and Ornamental Iron Workers
1750 New York Ave., N.W. Suite 400, Washington, DC 20006
Telephone: (202) 383-4800
Represented by:
Michael J. Brennan, Legislative and Political Director
Raymond J. Robertson, V. President
Frank J. Voyack, Legislative and Political Assistant
Counsel or consultant:
The Kamber Group (Mary Roddy Betzler)

Internat'l Ass'n of Chiefs of Police
1110 N. Glebe Road Suite 200, Arlington, VA 22201
Telephone: (703) 243-6500
Represented by:
Cheryl Anthony Epps, Legislative Analyst
Daniel Rosenblatt, Exec. Director

Internat'l Ass'n of Convention and Visitor Bureaus
Champaign, IL
Counsel or consultant:
O'Connor & Hannan (Timothy M. Haake)

Internat'l Ass'n of Cooking Professionals
1001 Connecticut Ave., N.W., Washington, DC 20036
Telephone: (202) 293-7716
Counsel or consultant:
William S. Bergman Associates (Sara Weldon)

Internat'l Ass'n of Counseling Services
5999 Stevenson Ave., 3rd Floor, Alexandria, VA 22304
Telephone: (703) 823-9840
Represented by:
Nancy E. Roncketti, Administrative Officer

Internat'l Ass'n of Drilling Contractors
1901 L St., N.W. Suite 702, Washington, DC 20036
Telephone: (202) 293-0670
Represented by:
Brian T. Petty, V. President, Federal Affairs

Internat'l Ass'n of Energy Economists
1101 14th St., N.W. Suite 1100, Washington, DC 20005
Telephone: (202) 371-1347
Background: The above address is that of Internat'l Management Group, Inc., an association management firm.
Counsel or consultant:
Internat'l Management Group, Inc. (Joan Walsh Cassedy)

Internat'l Ass'n of Fire Chiefs
1329 18th St., N.W., Washington, DC 20036
Telephone: (202) 833-3420
Represented by:
Garry L. Briese, Exec. Director
Counsel or consultant:
Keller and Heckman

Internat'l Ass'n of Fire Fighters
1750 New York Ave., N.W., Washington, DC 20006
Telephone: (202) 737-8484
Background: Labor union affiliated with AFL-CIO.
Represented by:
David B. Billy, Political Action Assistant
Vincent J. Bollon, Secretary-Treasurer
Richard M. Duffy, Occupatonal Safety and Health Director
Barry Kasinitz, Legislative Assistant
Frederick H. Nesbitt, Legislative and Political Director
Harold A. Schaitberger, Exec. Assistant to the President
Alfred K. Whitehead, President
Counsel or consultant:
The Kamber Group (Robert F. Bonitati)

Internat'l Ass'n of Firefighters, Local 799
Providence, RI

Counsel or consultant:
St. Germain, Rodio & Ursillo, Ltd. (Fernand J. St. Germain)

Internat'l Ass'n of Fish and Wildlife Agencies
444 North Capitol St., N.W. Suite 534, Washington, DC 20001
Telephone: (202) 624-7890
Background: A quasi-governmental organization of public agencies charged with the protection and management of North America's fish and wildlife resources.
Represented by:
George D. LaPointe, Legislative Counsel
R. Max Peterson, Exec. V. President

Internat'l Ass'n of Heat and Frost Insulators and Asbestos Workers
1300 Connecticut Ave., N,W. Suite 505, Washington, DC 20036
Telephone: (202) 785-2388
Represented by:
William G. Bernard, President

Internat'l Ass'n of Heat and Frost Insulators and Asbestos Workers Political Action Committee
1300 Connecticut Ave., N.W. Suite 505, Washington, DC 20036
Telephone: (202) 785-2388
Background: William G. Bernard of the Internat'l Ass'n of Heat and Frost Insulators and Asbestos Workers serves as the contact.

Internat'l Ass'n of Independent Producers
Box 2801, Washington, DC 20013
Telephone: (202) 775-1113
Background: Membership represents all facets of the audio/visual industry from suppliers of equipment and services to end users of audio/visual production. Active members are the producers of audio/visual material.
Represented by:
Dr. Edward Von Rothkirch, Exec. Director
Counsel or consultant:
Edward Jasen

Internat'l Ass'n of Independent Tanker Owners
Oslo, Norway
Counsel or consultant:
Dyer, Ellis, Joseph & Mills
Graham and James (Richard K. Bank, Stuart S. Dye)
Hill, Betts and Nash

Internat'l Ass'n of Machinists and Aerospace Workers
1300 Connecticut Ave., N.W. Suite 404, Washington, DC 20036
Telephone: (202) 857-5200
Represented by:
Maria C. Cordone, Legislative Representative
Dorothy Ellsworth, Assistant Director, Legislative Affairs
Richard Greenwood, Assistant to the President
William J. Holayter, Dir., Legislation & Political Action
Andrew Kenopensky, Automotive Coordinator
George Kourpias, President
Robert McCarthy, Railroad Coordinator
John F. Peterpaul, General V. President, Transportation
William L. Scheri, Air Transportation Coordinator
Counsel or consultant:
Challenge America, Inc. (Richard S. Sloan)
Collier, Shannon & Scott (Paul D. Cullen, Laurence J. Lasoff)

Internat'l Ass'n of Official Human Rights Agencies
444 North Capitol St., Suite 249, Washington, DC 20001
Telephone: (202) 624-5410
Background: Provides support services and training for human rights professionals; prepares comments on techincal papers and proposed legislation which would affect the practice of human rights law enforcement.
Represented by:
Audrey L. Skinner, Administrative Secretary

Internat'l Ass'n of Psychosocial Rehabilitation Services
5550 Sterrett Place, Suite 214, Columbia, MD 21044
Telephone: (301) 730-7190
Represented by:
Ruth A. Hughes, Exec. Director
Carolyn Peterson, President

Internat'l Ass'n of Refrigerated Warehouses
7315 Wisconsin Ave., Suite 1200N, Bethesda, MD 20814
Telephone: (301) 652-5674
Represented by:
J. William Hudson, President
Michael Shaw, V. President and Secretary
Counsel or consultant:
Meyers & Associates (Rick Meyers)

Internat'l Ass'n of Wiping Cloth Manufacturers
7910 Woodmont Ave., Suite 1212, Bethesda, MD 20814
Telephone: (301) 656-1077
Background: Represents the interests of companies involved with used clothing and wiping cloths. Sponsors two conventions, a monthly publication, and a nonprofit shippers association.
Represented by:
Bernard D. Brill, Exec. V. President

Internat'l Banana Ass'n
1101 Vermont Ave., N.W. Suite 306, Washington, DC 20005
Telephone: (202) 371-1620
Represented by:
Robert M. Moore, President

Internat'l Biometric Ass'n
1001 Connecticut Ave., N.W., Washington, DC 20036
Telephone: (202) 429-7479
Counsel or consultant:
William S. Bergman Associates (William S. Bergman, CAE)

Internat'l Bottled Water Ass'n
113 North Henry St., Alexandria, VA 22314
Telephone: (703) 683-5213
Represented by:
Geary Campbell, Manager, Public Relations
William F. Deal, CAE, Exec. Vice President
Lisa M. Prats, V. President

Internat'l Bridge, Tunnel and Turnpike Ass'n
2120 L St., N.W. Suite 305, Washington, DC 20037
Telephone: (202) 659-4620
Background: An autonomous organization to serve the needs of toll-supported bridge, tunnel and turnpike facilities. Concerns itself with member organizations' interest in financing, constructing and managing their facilities.
Represented by:
Neil D. Schuster, Exec. Director

Internat'l Brotherhood of Boilermakers, Iron Shipbuilders, Blacksmiths, Forgers and Helpers
400 First St., N.W., Suite 814, Washington, DC 20001
Telephone: (202) 638-5768
Represented by:
Ande M. Abbott, International Representative
Anthony J. Yakemowicz, V. Pres. and Interim Legis. Director
Counsel or consultant:
The Kamber Group

Internat'l Brotherhood of Electrical Workers
1125 15th St., N.W., Washington, DC 20005
Telephone: (202) 833-7000
Represented by:
Rick Diegel, Political Director
Michael J. Emig, Legislative Director
Tom Hickman, Exec. Assistant to the President
Jack F. Moore, Internat'l Secretary
Counsel or consultant:
The Kamber Group (Mary Roddy Betzler)
Sherman, Dunn, Cohen, Leifer and Counts (Laurence J. Cohen)

Internat'l Brotherhood of Electrical Workers Committee on Political Education
1125 15th St., N.W., Washington, DC 20005
Telephone: (202) 833-7000
Background: The political action arm of the Internat'l Brotherhood of Electrical Workers. Responsible contact is Rick Diegel of that organization.

Internat'l Brotherhood of Painters and Allied Trades
1750 New York Ave., N.W., Washington, DC 20006
Telephone: (202) 637-0700

The listings in this directory are available as *Mailing Labels*. See last page.

581

ORGANIZATIONS REPRESENTED

Internat'l Brotherhood of Painters and Allied Trades (Cont'd)

Represented by:

Francis X. Burkhardt, Special Asst. to the General President

William A. Duval, President

Counsel or consultant:

Barr, Peer & Cohen

Internat'l Brotherhood of Painters and Allied Trades Political Action Committee

1750 New York Ave., N.W., Washington, DC 20006

Telephone: (202) 637-0700

Background: Contact is Francis X. Burkhardt of the parent organization.

Internat'l Brotherhood of Police Officers

1313 L St., N.W., Washington, DC 20005

Telephone: (202) 371-6644

Background: Represented by Edward L. Murphy and Susan E. Scheider of the Nat'l Ass'n of Government Employees.

Internat'l Brotherhood of Teamsters, Chauffeurs, Warehousemen and Helpers of America

25 Louisiana Ave., N.W., Washington, DC 20001

Telephone: (202) 624-6800

Background: Sponsors a political action committee known as DRIVE.

Represented by:

R. V. Durham, Director, Safety and Health Department

Angela M. Hunter, Assistant Legislative Representative

John J. Joyce, Director, Nat'l Housing Program

Weldon L. Mathis, Secretary-Treasurer

Timothy Patrick O'Neill, Government Affairs Representative

Patrick Riley, Attorney

Timothy H. Scully, Jr., Legislative Representative

David A. Sweeney, Director, Legislative Department

F.C. Duke Zeller, Communications Director

Counsel or consultant:

Brand and Lowell, P.C. (Stanley M. Brand)

Internat'l Business Aviation Council (USA Office)

1200 18th St., N.W. Suite 200, Washington, DC 20036-2598

Telephone: (202) 783-9000

Background: IBAC is an alliance of national and regional business aviation organizations. Its represents, promotes and protects the interests of business aviation in international forums.

Represented by:

W. H. Stipe, II, Internat'l Liaison Officer

Internat'l Business Forms Industries

2111 Wilson Blvd., Suite 350, Arlington, VA 22209

Telephone: (703) 841-9191

Represented by:

Christopher R. Bevevino, President

Counsel or consultant:

Loomis, Owen, Fellman and Howe (James E. Anderson)

Internat'l Business Machines Corp.

1801 K St., N.W., Suite 1200, Washington, DC 20006

Telephone: (202) 778-5000

Represented by:

Thomas M. Arrasmith, Program Dir., Federal Government Rtns.

John G. Boyd, Program Director, Public Affairs

Christopher G. Caine, Program Dir., Federal Government Rtns.

Kent T. Cushenberry, Prog. Dir., Federal Government Relations

Lou Durden, Prog. Dir., Community & Ext'l Programs

J. William Howell, IBM Director, Government Relations

Linda Meyer Johnson, Program Manager, Governmental Programs

Kathleen N. Kingscott, Program Dir., Federal Government Relats.

Charles E. McKittrick, Jr., IBM V. President, Governmental Programs

Marshall C. Phelps, IBM Director, Governmental Programs

Ernie J. Satterwhite, Prog. Mgr., Public Sector, Industry Mktg

Philip A. Shellhaas, Program Director, Governmental Programs

Douglas C. Worth, IBM Director of Public Affairs

Counsel or consultant:

Hill and Knowlton Public Affairs Worldwide (Larry I. Good)

Newmyer Associates, Inc.

Wilmer, Cutler and Pickering (J. Roger Wollenberg)

Internat'l Center for Development Policy

731 Eighth St., S.E., Washington, DC 20003

Telephone: (202) 547-3800

Background: A private, non-profit agency which monitors U.S. foreign policy and provides the press, public groups and interested government officials with independent analyses of U.S. foreign policy.

Represented by:

John J. Fitzpatrick, Director of Public Affairs

Lindsay Mattison, Exec. Director

Robert E. White, President

Internat'l Center for Research on Women

1717 Massachusetts Ave., N.W., Suite 302, Washington, DC 20036

Telephone: (202) 797-0007

Background: An organization that works to improve the productivity and incomes of poor women in developing countries.

Represented by:

Mayra Buvinic, Director

Margaret Lycette, Deputy Director

Internat'l Chemical Workers Union

1126 16th St., N.W., Suite 200, Washington, DC 20036

Telephone: (202) 659-3747

Background: Labor union based in Akron, Ohio.

Represented by:

E. Robert Marlow, V. President, Region IV

Internat'l Chiropractors Ass'n

1110 N. Glebe Rd. Suite 1000, Arlington, VA 22201

Telephone: (703) 528-5000

Represented by:

Ron Hendrickson, Exec. Director

Internat'l Chiropractors Ass'n Political Action Committee

1110 N. Glebe Road, Suite 1000, Arlington, VA 22201

Telephone: (202) 528-5000

Background: Represented by Ron Hendrickson of the Internat'l Chiropractors Ass'n.

Internat'l Circulation Managers Ass'n

Newspaper Center, 11600 Sunrise Valley Dr., Reston, VA 22091

Telephone: (703) 620-9555

Represented by:

Joseph B. Forsee, Exec. Director

Internat'l City Management Ass'n

777 North Capitol St., N.E., Suite 500, Washington, DC 20002

Telephone: (202) 289-4262

Background: Professional and educational association for local government administrators.

Represented by:

William H. Hansell, Jr., Exec. Director

Elizabeth Keller, Deputy Director

Internat'l Commission for the Prevention of Alcoholism and Drug Dependency

12501 Old Columbia Pike, Silver Spring, MD 20904-1600

Telephone: (301) 680-6719

Represented by:

Thomas R. Neslund, Exec. Director

Internat'l Committee of Passenger Lines

New York, NY

Counsel or consultant:

Gold and Liebengood, Inc. (Martin B. Gold)

Hogan and Hartson

Internat'l Commodities Clearing House, Ltd.

London, England

Counsel or consultant:

Arnold & Porter (Brooksley E. Born, John M. Quinn, Daniel Waldman)

Internat'l Communications Ass'n

Dallas, TX

Counsel or consultant:

Fisher, Wayland, Cooper and Leader (Brian R. Moir)

Internat'l Communications Industries Ass'n (ICIA)

3150 Spring St., Fairfax, VA 22031-2399

Telephone: (703) 273-7200

Background: ICIA is the internat'l trade ass'n for the professional communications products industry representing over 900 dealers, manufacturers, producers and other firms selling products and services in the video, computer and

Represented by:

Kenton Pattie, Exec. V. President

Theresa Stanion, Director, Government Relations

Internat'l Council of Containerships Operators

Germany

Counsel or consultant:

Preston Gates Ellis & Rouvelas Meeds (Emanuel L. Rouvelas)

Internat'l Council of Shopping Centers

1199 North Fairfax St. Suite 204, Alexandria, VA 22314

Telephone: (703) 549-7404

Represented by:

Judy A. Black, Staff V. President, Government Relations

Brian R. Detter, Director, Federal Relations

John L. Stevens, Jr., Director, State Relations

Counsel or consultant:

Nordlinger Associates

Winston and Strawn (Edward C. Maeder)

Internat'l Council of Societies of Pathology

7001 Georgia St., Chevy Chase, MD 20815

Telephone: (301) 654-0095

Background: Seeks to provide a medium for exchange of information among pathologists, to encourage research and education in the field of pathology, to aid and cooperate in developing uniformity in the criteria for defintion and diagnosis of disease, and to promote relations with related national and international organizations.

Represented by:

F. K. Mostofi, Secretary Treasurer

Internat'l Craniofacial Foundations

Dallas, TX

Counsel or consultant:

Dutko & Associates (Daniel A. Dutko)

Internat'l Data Corp.

Framingham, MA

Counsel or consultant:

Cassidy and Associates, Inc. (Gerald S. J. Cassidy, Thomas M. Gannon, General Paul X. Kelley, USMC-Ret., Sheila B. Tate)

Internat'l District Heating and Cooling Ass'n

1101 Connecticut Ave., N.W., Suite 700, Washington, DC 20036

Telephone: (202) 429-5111

Background: An 80 year old association representing utilities, institutions, consultants, engineers and suppliers of the district heating and cooling industry. Promotes environmentally acceptable concept of supplying heating or cooling centrally to areas via piping networks.

Counsel or consultant:

Smith, Bucklin and Associates (David Hobson)

ORGANIZATIONS REPRESENTED

Internat'l Downtown Ass'n
915 15th St., N.W. Suite 900, Washington, DC 20005-2375
Telephone: (202) 783-4963
Background: Members include executives of downtown revitalization organizations. Public officials, consultants and other qualified individuals engaged in local economic development are associates.
Represented by:
Richard H. Bradley, President

Internat'l Economic Policy Ass'n
12605 Native Daneer Place, Gaithersburg, MD 20878
Telephone: (301) 990-1255
Background: A nonprofit organization which studies problems with foreign trade, foreign investment, taxation, balance of payments, natural resources and foreign policy, and participate in analyses of related public policy issues. IEPA testifies before Congressional committees as invited expert witnesses on these issues.
Represented by:
Ronald L. Danielian, President

Internat'l Electronic Facsimile Users Ass'n
Fort Pierce, FL
Counsel or consultant:
Smith, Heenan and Althen (William I. Althen)

Internat'l Electronics Manufacturers and Consumers of America
1455 Pennsylvania Ave., N.W. Suite 1260, Washington, DC 20004
Telephone: (202) 783-7276
Background: An American trade association composed of the U.S. manufacturing subsidiaries of 18 major overseas electronics companies. Exec. Director is Mark M. Ellison of French & Company.
Counsel or consultant:
Cole, Corette & Abrutyn (Robert T. Cole)
Dorsey & Whitney
French & Company (Mark M. Ellison, Verrick O. French, Sally D. Iskenderian)
Gibson, Dunn and Crutcher (Robert A. McConnell)

Internat'l Environmental Policy Coalition
c/o Swidler & Berlin 3000 K St., N.W., Suite 300, Washington, DC 20007
Telephone: (202) 944-4300
Background: A coalition of major exporters of hazardous waste opposed to legislation which would bar the export of such waste materials to countries where treatment plants do not meet EPA standards.
Counsel or consultant:
Timothy X. Moore and Co. (Timothy X. Moore)
Swidler & Berlin, Chartered (Dawn Gifford, Barry L. Malter)

Internat'l Exhibitors Ass'n
5501 Backlick Road, Suite 200, Springfield, VA 22151
Telephone: (703) 941-3725
Represented by:
Michael J. Bandy, Director, Communications
Peter J. Mangelli, Vice President

Internat'l Eye Foundation/Soc. of Eye Surgeons
7801 Norfolk Ave., Bethesda, MD 20814
Telephone: (301) 986-1830
Represented by:
Jack B. Blanks, Acting Exec. Director

Internat'l Fabricare Institute
12251 Tech Road, Silver Spring, MD 20904
Telephone: (301) 622-1900
Represented by:
John Meijer, Legislative/Joint State Liaison
Charles R. Riggott, Exec. V. President
Counsel or consultant:
Patton, Boggs and Blow

Internat'l Federation of Professional and Technical Engineers
8701 Georgia Ave., Suite 701, Silver Spring, MD 20910
Telephone: (301) 565-9016
Represented by:
Julia L. Akins, Counsel, Fed. Labor Rel. & Legis. Issues
John H. Dunne, Secy.-Treas.
Kathryn JoAnn Hawes, Assistant to the President
James E. Sommerhauser, President
Counsel or consultant:
Barr, Peer & Cohen

Internat'l Federation of Professional and Technical Engineers LEAP-PAC
8701 Georgia Ave. Suite 701, Silver Spring, MD 20910
Telephone: (301) 565-9016
Background: Responsible contact is John H. Dunne. (See Internat'l Federation of Professional and Technical Engineers.)

Internat'l Food Information Council
1100 Connecticut Ave. N.W., Suite 430, Washington, DC 20036
Telephone: (202) 296-6540
Represented by:
Elaine Auld, MPH, Director, Health Communications
Libby Mikesell, Manager, Editorial Services
Thomas E. Stenzel, Exec. Director

Internat'l Food Policy Research Institute
1776 Massachusetts Ave., N.W. Suite 800, Washington, DC 20036
Telephone: (202) 862-5600
Background: Analyzes world food problems, especially in developing countries, and conducts research on policies to increase the availability of food to needy populations.
Represented by:
John W. Mellor, Director

Internat'l Foodservice Distributors Ass'n
201 Park Washington Court, Falls Church, VA 22046
Telephone: (703) 532-9400
Background: Represented by Bruce A. Gates of the Nat'l-American Wholesale Grocers' Ass'n.

Internat'l Franchise Ass'n
1350 New York Ave., N.W. Suite 900, Washington, DC 20005
Telephone: (202) 628-8000
Represented by:
William B. Cherkasky, President
Herbert A. Hedden, Assistant Director, Government Relations
John R. Reynolds, Director, Marketing & Public Relations
Neil A. Simon, Counsel, Director, Government Relations
Duane R. Thompson, Ass't Director, Government Relations

Internat'l Frozen Food Ass'n
1764 Old Meadow Lane, McLean, VA 22102
Telephone: (703) 821-0770
Background: Represented by Thomas B. House of the American Frozen Food Institute.

Internat'l Futures Exchange (Bermuda) Ltd.
Hamilton, Bermuda
Counsel or consultant:
Royer, Mehle & Babyak (Robert Stewart Royer)

Internat'l Hardwood Products Ass'n
Box 1308, Alexandria, VA 22313
Telephone: (703) 836-6696
Represented by:
Wendy J. Baer, Exec. Vice President
Counsel or consultant:
StMaxens and Co. (Thomas F. StMaxens, II)

Internat'l Hardwood Products Ass'n INPAC
Box 1308, Alexandria, VA 22313
Telephone: (703) 836-6696
Background: Also represented by Wendy Baer of the Ass'n.
Represented by:
L. Russell Haan, Treasurer

Internat'l Health Evaluation Ass'n
90 West Montgomery Ave., Suite 340, Rockville, MD 20850
Telephone: (301) 762-6050
Represented by:
Harold A. Timken, Exec. V. President & Treasurer

Internat'l Healthcare Safety Professional Certification Board
5010-A Nicholson Lane, Rockville, MD 20852
Telephone: (301) 984-8969
Represented by:
Harold Gordon, Exec. Director

Internat'l Hospital Federation
50 F St., N.W., Suite 1100, Washington, DC 20001
Telephone: (202) 638-1100

Represented by:
Dr. Jose Gonzalez, Director, International Affairs

Internat'l Human Rights Law Group
1601 Connecticut Ave., N.W. Suite 700, Washington, DC 20009
Telephone: (202) 232-8500
Background: Monitors human rights developments on an international scope and provides both legal assistance to persons deprived of human rights and seeks to educate the public on international human rights issues.
Represented by:
Janelle Diller, Legal Director
Nancy Goodman, Director of Development
Amy Young, Exec. Director

Internat'l Hydrolyzed Protein Council
1625 K St., N.W. Suite 1190, Washington, DC 20006
Telephone: (202) 628-5530
Counsel or consultant:
Walter E. Byerley Law Offices (Walter E. Byerley)

Internat'l Ice Cream Ass'n
888 16th St., N.W., Washington, DC 20006
Telephone: (202) 296-4250
Represented by:
Thomas M. Balmer, Manager, Membership & Special Projects
Dawn M. Brydon, Director, Industry Promotions
Becky L. Davenport, Exec. Asst., Mmbrship & Public Affrs.
Jerome J. Kozak, V. President
Tobi Z. Rozen, Director, Marketing
William C. Tinklepaugh, V. President, Economics
Constance E. Tipton, V. President, Public Affairs
E. Linwood Tipton, President
Counsel or consultant:
Covington and Burling

Internat'l Institute for Women's Political Leadership
1101 14th St., N.W., Suite 200, Washington, DC 20005
Telephone: (202) 842-1523

Internat'l Insurance Council
1212 New York Ave., N.W. Suite 205, Washington, DC 20005
Telephone: (202) 682-2345
Background: An international trade policy advocate organization of U.S. insurance and reinsurance companies that do business in international markets.
Represented by:
Gordon J. Cloney, President

Internat'l Intellectual Property Alliance
1300 19th St., N.W. Suite 350, Washington, DC 20036
Telephone: (202) 833-4198
Background: Carol Risher of the Ass'n of American Publishers serves as Exec. Director. Above address is that of the Ass'n. of American Publishers.

Internat'l Ladies Garment Workers Union
815 16th St., N.W. Suite 103, Washington, DC 20006
Telephone: (202) 347-7417
Represented by:
Evelyn Dubrow, V. President and Legislative Director

Internat'l Law Institute
1615 New Hampshire Ave., N.W., Washington, DC 20009
Telephone: (202) 483-3036
Background: A non-profit organization which conducts training programs in DC and abroad for gov't officials in developing countries.
Represented by:
Stuart Kerr, Exec. Director

Internat'l Lead Zinc Research Organization
Research Tr. Pk., NC
Counsel or consultant:
Jefferson Group, The (Robert Carlstrom, Jr.)

Internat'l Leather Goods, Plastics and Novelty Workers Union, AFL-CIO
New York, NY
Counsel or consultant:
Economic Consulting Services Inc. (Deborah Swartz)

Internat'l Legal Fraternity-Phi Delta Phi
1750 N St., N.W., Washington, DC 20036
Telephone: (202) 628-0148

The listings in this directory are available as *Mailing Labels.* See last page.

ORGANIZATIONS REPRESENTED

Internat'l Legal Fraternity-Phi Delta Phi (Cont'd)
Background: Founded December 13, 1869 at Ann Arbor, Michigan to advance legal ethics, professionalism, and scholarship in the law schools and in the profession at large.
Represented by:
Sam S. Crutchfield, Exec. Director

Internat'l Life Sciences Institute
1126 16th St., N.W. Suite 300, Washington, DC 20036
Telephone: (202) 659-0074
Represented by:
Sherri Lopez, Administrator

Internat'l Life Sciences Institute Nutrition Foundation
1126 16th St., N.W., Suite 300, Washington, DC 20036
Telephone: (202) 659-0074
Background: Represented by Sherri Lopez of the Internat'l Life Sciences Institute.
Represented by:
Robin C. Gray, Director of Public Affairs

Internat'l Llama Ass'n
Boseman, MT
Counsel or consultant:
Bishop, Cook, Purcell & Reynolds (Marlow W. Cook)

Internat'l Longshoremen's Ass'n
815 16th St., N.W., Suite 104, Washington, DC 20006
Telephone: (202) 628-4546
Represented by:
John Bowers, Jr., Legislative Director
Ingolf G. Esders, Assistant to the Director
Robert E. Gleason, Assistant Legislative Director

Internat'l Longshoremen's and Warehousemen's Union
1133 15th St., N.W. Suite 600, Washington, DC 20005
Telephone: (202) 463-6265
Represented by:
Michael R. Lewis, Washington Representative

Internat'l Magnesium Ass'n
2010 Corporate Ridge Suite 700, McLean, VA 22102
Telephone: (703) 442-8888
Background: An international organization made up of the producers, marketers, and users of magnesium.
Represented by:
Byron B. Clow, Exec. V. President
Felicia Garber, Communications Director

Internat'l Management and Development Institute
2600 Virginia Ave., N.W. Suite 905, Washington, DC 20037
Telephone: (202) 337-1022
Background: Provides educational programs to strengthen the ability of business and government to deal with mutual international problems.
Represented by:
Gene E. Bradley, Chairman and President

Internat'l Maritime Associates
2600 Virginia Ave., N.W., Washington, DC 20037
Telephone: (202) 333-8501
Background: A management consulting, market research firm specializing in maritime matters.
Represented by:
James R. McCaul, President

Internat'l Masonry Institute
Suite 1001, 823 15th St., N.W., Washington, DC 20005
Telephone: (202) 783-3908
Represented by:
Phillip Ray Lackey, Exec. V. President

Internat'l Mass Retail Ass'n
1901 Pennsylvania Ave., N.W. Suite 200, Washington, DC 20006
Telephone: (202) 861-0774
Represented by:
Morrison G. Cain, Public Affairs Counsel
Robin Lanier, Sr. Legislative Representative
Robert J. Verdisco, V. President, Government Relations

Internat'l Mass Transit Ass'n
P.O. Box 40247, Washington, DC 20016-0247
Telephone: (202) 362-7960
Background: Manufacturers, consultants, governments and others who promote and develop the world market for urban public transportation systems and equipment.

Represented by:
C. Carter Carter, Exec. Director

Internat'l Metals Reclamation Co.
Ellwood City, PA
Counsel or consultant:
Wilmer, Cutler and Pickering (Neil J. King)

Internat'l Microwave Power Institute
13542 Union Village Circle, Clifton, VA 22024
Telephone: (703) 830-5588
Counsel or consultant:
Executives Consultants, Inc. (Robert C. LaGasse, CAE)

Internat'l Microwave Systems Corp. (IMSCO)
San Diego, CA
Counsel or consultant:
Ashby and Associates (John C. Stevens)

Internat'l Military Club Executives Ass'n
1438 Duke St., Alexandria, VA 22314
Telephone: (703) 548-0093
Represented by:
Paul Reece, Exec. Director

Internat'l Minerals and Chemical Corp.
1726 M St., N.W., Suite 701, Washington, DC 20036
Telephone: (202) 659-1750
Represented by:
Joan T. Bier, Corp. Staff V. President, Gov't Affairs
Counsel or consultant:
Covington and Burling (Harvey M. Applebaum, Jr. O. Thomas Johnson, Sonya D. Winner)

Internat'l Narcotic Enforcement Officers Ass'n
Albany, NY
Counsel or consultant:
Kelly and Associates, Inc. (John A. Kelly)

Internat'l Newspaper Advertising and Marketing Executives
Box 17210, Washington, DC 20041
Telephone: (703) 648-1168
Represented by:
Reggie Hall, Exec. Director

Internat'l Newspaper Promotion Ass'n
11600 Sunrise Valley Dr., Reston, VA 22091
Telephone: (703) 648-1094
Represented by:
Christine Winwood, Exec. Director

Internat'l Paper Co.
1620 Eye St., N.W., Suite 700, Washington, DC 20006
Telephone: (202) 785-3666
Represented by:
Arthur W. Brownell, Assoc. Director, Federal Corp. Affairs
W. Dennis Thomas, V. President
Lyn M. Withey, Assoc. Director, Federal Corp. Affairs
Counsel or consultant:
Winburn, VanScoyoc, and Hooper (H. Stewart VanScoyoc)

Internat'l Paper Co. Volunteers for Better Government
1620 Eye St., N.W., Suite 700, Washington, DC 20006
Telephone: (202) 785-3666
Background: Supported by the Internat'l Paper Co. Treasurer and contact is Arthur Brownell of the company.

Internat'l Personnel Management Ass'n
1617 Duke St., Alexandria, VA 22314
Telephone: (703) 549-7100
Represented by:
Neil Reichenberg, Director, Government Affairs
Donald K. Tichenor, Exec. Director

Internat'l Petroleum Exchange of London
London, England
Counsel or consultant:
Arnold & Porter (Brooksley E. Born)

Internat'l Playtex, Inc.
Stamford, CT
Counsel or consultant:
Bonner & Associates

Internat'l Public Relations Co.
Tokyo, Japan

Counsel or consultant:
Civic Service, Inc. (Roy Pfautch)
Keefe Co., The (Robert J. Keefe, Terry M. O'Connell)
Saunders and Company (Eric Edmondson, Steven R. Saunders)
TKC Internat'l, Inc.

Internat'l Reciprocal Trade Ass'n
5152 Woodmire Lane, Alexandria, VA 22311
Telephone: (703) 931-0105
Background: A trade association representing the commercial barter industry in the U.S. and internationally.
Counsel or consultant:
Paul Suplizio Associates (Jeanne Miller, Paul E. Suplizio)

Internat'l Reciprocal Trade Ass'n Political Action Committee
5152 Woodmire Lane, Alexandria, VA 22311
Telephone: (703) 931-0105
Counsel or consultant:
Paul Suplizio Associates (Paul E. Suplizio)

Internat'l Religious Liberty Ass'n
12501 Old Columbia Ave., Silver Spring, MD 20904
Telephone: (301) 680-6320
Background: The General Conference of Seventh-day Adventists provides salaried personnel for the office.
Counsel or consultant:
Johns and Carson

Internat'l Road Federation
525 School St., S.W., Washington, DC 20024
Telephone: (202) 554-2106
Represented by:
W. Gerald Wilson, President

Internat'l Sanitary Supply Ass'n
Lincolnwood, IL
Counsel or consultant:
Warren E. Stickle & Assoc. (Warren E. Stickle)

Internat'l Security Council
818 Connecticut Ave., N.W. Suite 600, Washington, DC 20006
Telephone: (202) 828-0802
Background: An independent, non-profit public policy institution primarily concerned with security policy issues affecting the national security of the United States. Emphasis is on geopolitical matters related to the Soviet-American strategic balance.
Represented by:
Mark P. Barry, Media Liaison
Dr. Joseph Churba, President
Steven A.F. Trevino, Senior Associate for Stategy Affairs

Internat'l Service Agencies
6000 Executive Blvd, Suite 608, Rockville, MD 20852
Telephone: (301) 881-2468
Background: A federation of American charitable organizations that provide health and welfare services to needy people overseas.
Represented by:
Richard J. Leary, Exec. Director
Richard W. Murphy, Nat'l Coordinator, Combined Fed Campaign
Counsel or consultant:
Swidler & Berlin, Chartered (Kenneth I. Schaner)

Internat'l Sleep Products Ass'n
333 Commerce St., Alexandria, VA 22314
Telephone: (703) 683-8371
Represented by:
Russ Abolt, Exec. V. President
Nancy Butler, V. President, Communications
Gerald P. Nagy, V. President
Counsel or consultant:
Henry J. Kaufman & Associates (Helen Sullivan)

Internat'l Slurry Seal Ass'n
1101 Connecticut Ave., N.W., Suite 700, Washington, DC 20036
Telephone: (202) 857-1160
Counsel or consultant:
Smith, Bucklin and Associates (Harry G., Skip McComas)

Internat'l Snowmobile Industry Ass'n
3975 University Drive Suite 310, Fairfax, VA 22030
Telephone: (703) 273-9606

The listings in this directory are available as *Mailing Labels*. See last page.

ORGANIZATIONS REPRESENTED

Represented by:
Catherine A. Ahern, V. President and Corporate Secretary
Roy W. Muth, President and Chief Exec. Officer

Internat'l Soc. for Hybrid Microelectronics
1861 Wiehle Ave., Suite 260, Box 2698, Reston, VA 22090
Telephone: (703) 471-0066
Represented by:
Walter H. Biddle, CAE, Exec. Director
Counsel or consultant:
Jenner and Block

Internat'l Soc. for Photogrammetry and Remote Sensing
5410 Grosvenor Lane, Suite 210, Bethesda, MD 20814-2160
Telephone: (301) 493-0290
Counsel or consultant:
Cranwell & O'Connell (George E. Cranwell)

Internat'l Soc. of Air Safety Investigators
Technology Trading Park, 5 Export Drive, Sterling, VA 22170-4421
Telephone: (703) 430-9668
Represented by:
Frank S. Del Gandio, Secretary
Capt. Thomas J. Kreamer, V. President
Counsel or consultant:
Speiser, Krause, Madole & Lear

Internat'l Soc. of Transport Aircraft Traders
1101 14th St., N.W., Suite 1100, Washington, DC 20005
Telephone: (202) 371-1237
Counsel or consultant:
Internat'l Management Group, Inc. (Brian Cassedy)

Internat'l Speedway Corp.
Daytona Beach, FL
Counsel or consultant:
Robert E. Juliano Associates (Robert E. Juliano)

Internat'l Swap Dealers Ass'n
New York, NY
Background: An international organization of commercial investment and merchant banks that act as dealers in interest rate and currency exchange transactions.
Counsel or consultant:
Covington and Burling (Eugene A. Ludwig)
Wilmer, Cutler and Pickering (William J. Perlstein)
Bradley P. Ziff

Internat'l Taxicab Ass'n
3849 Farragut Ave., Kensington, MD 20898
Telephone: (301) 946-5701
Represented by:
Alfred B. LaGasse, III, Exec. V. President
Counsel or consultant:
Webster, Chamberlain and Bean (Arthur L. Herold)

Internat'l Taxicab Ass'n Political Action Committee
3849 Farragut Ave., Kensington, MD 20898
Telephone: (301) 946-5701
Background: Treasurer and contact is Alfred B. LaGasse, III of the Internat'l Taxicab Ass'n.

Internat'l Technology Corp.
1233 20th St., N.W. 7th Floor, Washington, DC 20036
Telephone: (202) 778-8760
Represented by:
John E. Daniel, Corp. V. President, Government Affairs
Philip C. Deakin, Director, Defense Programs

Internat'l Technology Education Ass'n
1914 Association Drive, Reston, VA 22091
Telephone: (703) 860-2100
Represented by:
Kendall N. Starkweather, Exec. Director

Internat'l Telecharge, Inc.
Dallas, TX
Counsel or consultant:
Dutko & Associates (Steve Perry)
Jones, Day, Reavis and Pogue (Randall B. Lowe)

Internat'l Telecom Japan
Tokyo, Japan

Counsel or consultant:
Debevoise and Plimpton (Robert R. Bruce, Jeffrey P. Cunard)

Internat'l Telecommunications Satellite Organization (INTELSAT)
3400 International Drive, N.W., Washington, DC 20008-3098
Telephone: (202) 944-6800
Background: INTELSAT, with 114 member countries, provides worldwide voice, TV and data links by satellite. Questions concern deregulation of international telecommunications.
Represented by:
Dean Burch, Director General
Francis Latappi, Director, External Relations
Counsel or consultant:
Powell, Goldstein, Frazer and Murphy (Stuart E. Eizenstat)
Preston Gates Ellis & Rouvelas Meeds (Craig J. Gehring, Bruce J. Heiman, Lloyd Meeds)
Reed Smith Shaw & McClay (T. Timothy Ryan, Jr.)

Internat'l Teleconferencing Ass'n
1299 Woodside Drive, McLean, VA 22102
Telephone: (703) 556-6115
Counsel or consultant:
J. Robert Brouse Associates

Internat'l Televent Inc.
2000 Corporate Ridge Suite 815, McLean, VA 22102
Telephone: (703) 556-7778
Background: A nonprofit telecommunications organization.
Represented by:
Ronald D. Coleman, Chairman & CEO

Internat'l Theatrical Agencies Ass'n
Dallas, TX
Counsel or consultant:
McGuiness and Williams (G. John Tysse)

Internat'l Thomson
New York, NY
Counsel or consultant:
Patton, Boggs and Blow (Thomas Hale Boggs, Jr.)

Internat'l Tool Works Ltd.
Windsor, Ontario
Counsel or consultant:
Barnes, Richardson and Colburn (David O. Elliott)

Internat'l Trade Council
3114 Circle Hill Road, Alexandria, VA 22305
Telephone: (703) 548-1234
Background: A coalition of some 850 companies engaged in international commerce. Maintains contact with Congress and U.S. federal agencies and with foreign embassies and international organizations to promote principles of free trade and corporate/individual economic rights.
Represented by:
Dr. Peter T. Nelsen, President
Sandy Nelsen, Director

Internat'l Trade and Development, Inc.
New York, NY
Counsel or consultant:
Alvord and Alvord

Internat'l Union of Bricklayers and Allied Craftsmen
815 15th St., N.W., 2nd Floor, Washington, DC 20005
Telephone: (202) 783-3788
Represented by:
John T. Joyce, President
Constance A. Lambert, Asst. to the Pres., Administration
Joanna E. Reagan, Asst. to the Pres. for Gov't Relations
Counsel or consultant:
Bartley M. O'Hara, P.C.
Powell, Adams & Rinehart

Internat'l Union of Bricklayers and Allied Craftsmen Political Action Committee
815 15th St., N.W., 2nd Floor, Washington, DC 20005
Telephone: (202) 783-3788
Represented by:
L. Gerald Carlisle, Secretary-Treasurer

Internat'l Union of Electronic, Electrical, Salaried, Machine, and Furniture Workers, AFL-CIO
1126 16th St., N.W., Washington, DC 20036
Telephone: (202) 296-1200

Represented by:
William H. Bywater, President
Robert Friedman, General Counsel
Maria Landolfo, Director, Legislation & Political Action
Douglas Meyer, Director, Research & Internat'l Affairs
Lauren J. Rothfarb, Legislative Assistant

Internat'l Union of Operating Engineers
1125 17th St., N.W., Washington, DC 20036
Telephone: (202) 429-9100
Represented by:
John J. Flynn, Director of Legislation and Politics

Internat'l Union of Police Ass'ns
1016 Duke St., Alexandria, VA 22314
Telephone: (703) 549-7473
Represented by:
Al Angele, Secretary-Treasurer
John A. Gannon, Legislative Liaison
Robert B. Kliesmet, President
Counsel or consultant:
Zwerdling, Paul, Leibig & Thompson (Michael Leibig)

Internat'l Voluntary Services
1424 16th St., N.W. Suite 204, Washington, DC 20036
Telephone: (202) 387-5533
Represented by:
David Smock, Exec. Director

INTERSECT Corp.
Irvine, CA
Counsel or consultant:
Ashby and Associates (John C. Stevens)

Intersociety Committee on Pathology Information
4733 Bethesda Ave., Suite 735, Bethesda, MD 20814
Telephone: (301) 656-2944
Represented by:
Eileen M. Lavine, Information Counsel

Interspace Inns Internat'l
Marina Del Rey, CA
Counsel or consultant:
Lachelli, Waller and Associates (Vincent P. Lachelli)

Interstate Conference of Employment Security Agencies
444 North Capitol St., N.W. Suite 126, Washington, DC 20001-1571
Telephone: (202) 628-5588
Background: The official organization of the administrators who manage the public employment/job services and unemployment insurance programs of the 50 states, the District of Columbia, Puerto Rico and the Virgin Islands.
Represented by:
Robert M. Guttman, Consultant

Interstate Conference on Water Policy
955 L'Enfant Plaza, S.W. Sixth Floor, Washington, DC 20024
Telephone: (202) 466-7287
Background: An organization of state, interstate and intrastate officials with responsibility for water quality and quantity.
Counsel or consultant:
Roy F. Weston Inc.

Interstate Natural Gas Ass'n of America
555 13th St., N.W. Suite 300 West, Washington, DC 20004
Telephone: (202) 626-3200

The listings in this directory are available as *Mailing Labels.* See last page.

585

ORGANIZATIONS REPRESENTED

Interstate Natural Gas Ass'n of America (Cont'd)
Represented by:
John G. Ams, V.P., Financial Affrs. & Administration
Robert L. Beauregard, V. President, Regulatory Affairs
John H. Cheatham, III, Sr. V. Pres., Gen. Counsel and Secretary
David N. Friedman, Manager, Environmental Affairs
Jerald V. Halvorsen, President
Cheryl W. Hoffman, Director of Communications
R. Skip Horvath, V. Pres., Rate and Policy Analysis
Glenn F. Jackson, Asst. V. Pres., Legislative Affairs
Theodore L. Kinne, V. Pres., Safety Environment & Operatns.
S. Lawrence Paulson, V. President, Public Affairs
Samir Y. Salama, Assistant V. President, Policy Anal.
Jean Sonneman, Attorney
Jerry T. Verkler, Senior Vice President
Debra Weiss, News Director
Counsel or consultant:
Andrews' Associates, Inc. (Mark Andrews, Jacqueline Balk-Tusa)
Holt, Miller & Associates (Ann M. Sullivan)

Interstate Natural Gas Political Action Committee
555 13th St., N.W. Suite 300 West, Washington, DC 20004
Telephone: (202) 626-3220
Background: Jerry T. Verkler of the parent association serves as Treasurer.

Interstate Taxation Coalition
Chicago, IL
Counsel or consultant:
Courtney, McCamant and Turney (Richard F. Turney)

Interstate Truckload Carriers Conference
2200 Mill Road Suite 600, Alexandria, VA 22314
Telephone: (703) 838-1950
Background: Formed in 1983 through a merger of the Common Carrier Conference-Irregular Route and the Contract Carrier Conference.
Represented by:
John J. Huber, Staff Attorney
Kris H. Ikejiri, General Counsel
J. Terry Turner, Exec. Director

Interstate Truckload Carriers Conference Political Action Committee
2200 Mill Road, Alexandria, VA 22314
Telephone: (703) 838-1950
Represented by:
Donald Freymiller, Treasurer

Intertrade Capital Group, Inc.
Miami, FL
Counsel or consultant:
Templeton and Co. (Patrick A. Templeton)

Intex Holdings (Bermuda) Ltd.
Hamilton, Bermuda
Counsel or consultant:
Royer, Mehle & Babyak (Robert Stewart Royer)

Invacare Corp.
Cleveland, OH
Counsel or consultant:
Camp, Barsh, Bates and Tate (Ronald L. Platt)

Invention Stores Internat'l
1140 Connecticut Ave., N.W., Suite 804, Washington, DC 20036
Telephone: (202) 452-6004
Counsel or consultant:
Offices of V.J. Adduci

Invest to Compete Alliance
1010 Pennsylvania Ave., S.E., Washington, DC 20003
Telephone: (202) 546-4991
Background: A group of individuals, corporations and trade associations concerned about trade and tax issues. The group's goal is to educate Congress and the public on the need for American business to compete at home and abroad. A 501-C-6 organization.
Counsel or consultant:
Campbell-Raupe, Inc. (Jeanne M. Campbell)

InvestAmerica
1100 Connecticut Ave., N.W. Suite 500, Washington, DC 20036
Telephone: (202) 775-9750

Background: A political action committee. Represented by Christopher L. Davis, President of the Investment Partnership Ass'n.

Investment Company Institute
1600 M St., N.W. Suite 600, Washington, DC 20036
Telephone: (202) 293-7700
Background: The trade association for the mutual fund industry.
Represented by:
Jo Ellen Darcy, Legislative Affairs Associate
Julie Domenick, V. President, Legislative Affairs
Matthew P. Fink, Senior V. President and General Counsel
Betty K. Hart, Public Information Officer
Carol Ann Higgins, Legislative Affairs Representative
L. Eric Kantor, V. President, Public Information
C. Richard Pogue, Senior V. President, Management
Kathy Rabon-Summers, Director, Industry Studies
David Silver, President
Craig Tyle, Ass't General Counsel
Counsel or consultant:
Covington and Burling
Gold and Liebengood, Inc. (Howard S. Liebengood)
O'Connor & Hannan
Verner, Liipfert, Bernhard, McPherson and Hand, Chartered (John A. Merrigan)
Wunder, Ryan, Cannon & Thelen (Thomas M. Ryan)

Investment Counsel Ass'n of America
New York, NY
Counsel or consultant:
Shaw, Pittman, Potts and Trowbridge (Ramsay D. Potts)

Investment Management Political Action Committee
1600 M St., N.W. Suite 600, Washington, DC 20036
Telephone: (202) 293-7700
Background: Sponsored by the Investment Co. Institute. C. Richard Pogue of the Institute serves as Treasurer.

Investment Partnership Ass'n
1100 Connecticut Ave., N.W., Suite 500, Washington, DC 20036-5303
Telephone: (202) 775-9750
Background: Established in 1985, the principal organization representing investors in limited partnerships, trusts, and program sponsors raising capital for real estate, oil and gas, equipment leasing and research & development/venture capital. Its members include the leading sponsors of limited partnerships, REITs, brokerage firms, attorneys, accountants and others interested in the investment partnership industry.
Represented by:
Christopher L. Davis, President
Counsel or consultant:
Jefferson Group, The (Porter Wheeler)
Rogers and Wells (William Morris)

Investors Internat'l
New York, NY
Background: A gold-based mutual fund.
Counsel or consultant:
Freedman, Levy, Kroll and Simonds (John H. Chettle)

Inwood Laboratories, Inc.
Inwood, NY
Counsel or consultant:
Kleinfeld, Kaplan and Becker (Peter R. Mathers)

IoPP, the Institute of Packaging Professionals
11800 Sunrise Valley Dr., Reston, VA 22091
Telephone: (703) 620-9380
Counsel or consultant:
William C. Pflaum Co., Inc. (William C. Pflaum)

Iowa Electric Light and Power Co.
Cedar Rapids, IA
Counsel or consultant:
Newman & Holtzinger, P.C. (Jack R. Newman, Kathleen H. Shea)

Iowa-Illinois Gas and Electric Co.
Davenport, IA
Counsel or consultant:
Donelan, Cleary, Wood and Maser, P.C.

Iowa Power and Light Co.
Des Moines, IA

Counsel or consultant:
Keller and Heckman
Newman & Holtzinger, P.C. (Jack R. Newman, Kathleen H. Shea)

Iowa Public Service Co.
Sioux City, IA
Counsel or consultant:
Donelan, Cleary, Wood and Maser, P.C.

Iowa Southern Utilities Co.
Centerville, IA
Counsel or consultant:
Donelan, Cleary, Wood and Maser, P.C.

Iowa, State of
Des Moines, IA
Counsel or consultant:
Dickstein, Shapiro and Morin (Andrew P. Miller, Bernard Nash)

IPP Working Group
Boston, MA
Counsel or consultant:
Dickstein, Shapiro and Morin (John C. Dill)

IPSCO Inc.
Regina, Saskatchewan
Counsel or consultant:
Barnes, Richardson and Colburn (Rufus E. Jarman, Jr.)

Iraq, Embassy of
1801 P St., N.W., Washington, DC 20036
Telephone: (202) 483-7500
Counsel or consultant:
Paul, Hastings, Janofsky and Walker (Richard M. Fairbanks, III)
van Kloberg and Associates (Edward J. van Kloberg, III)

Ireland, Industrial Development Authority of
Dublin, Ireland
Counsel or consultant:
Ropes and Gray (Stephen E. Shay)

Irish Immigration Reform Movement
New York, NY
Background: Seeks to loosen U.S. immigration laws regarding Irish and other groups seeking U.S. citizenship.
Counsel or consultant:
Holt, Miller & Associates (Michael G. Kirby, Harris N. Miller)

Irish Nat'l Caucus
413 E. Capitol St., S.E., Washington, DC 20003
Telephone: (202) 544-0568
Background: Seeks to educate the public, Congress and the Federal Government about 'injustice and oppression in Northern Ireland and to get America to stand up for Irish justice, freedom and peace'. Also initiated the MacBride Principles, a 'code of conduct for U.S. Companies doing business in Ireland.'
Represented by:
Fr. Sean McManus, Nat'l Director
Rita Mullan, Exec. Director

Irish Nat'l Caucus Political Action Committee (IRISH PAC)
413 E. Capitol St., S.E., Washington, DC 20003
Telephone: (202) 544-0568
Background: Director is Father Sean McManus of the Irish Nat'l Caucus.

Iron Castings Soc.
Des Plaines, IL
Background: Represented by Walter M. Kiplinger, Jr. of the American Cast Metals Ass'n.

Iron Ore Lessors Ass'n, Inc.
St. Paul, MN
Counsel or consultant:
Murray, Scheer & Montgomery (D. Michael Murray)

Iron Workers Political Action League
1750 New York Ave., N.W. Suite 400, Washington, DC 20006
Telephone: (202) 383-4800
Background: The political action committee sponsored by the Internat'l Ass'n of Bridge, Structural and Ornamental Iron Workers. Represented by Michael J. Brennan, Political Director of the Ass'n. (See Internat'l Ass'n of Bridge, Structural and Ornamental Iron Workers.)

The listings in this directory are available as *Mailing Labels*. See last page.

ORGANIZATIONS REPRESENTED

Iroquois Gas, Inc.
New York, NY
Counsel or consultant:
Dickstein, Shapiro and Morin (Linda Robertson)

Irrigation Ass'n
1911 N. Fort Myer Drive Suite 1009, Arlington, VA 22209
Telephone: (703) 524-1200
Represented by:
Robert C. Sears, Exec. V. President

Irvine Co., The
Newport Beach, CA
Counsel or consultant:
The Ferguson Co. (William Ferguson, Jr., Patricia Jordan, Thane Young)

Irving Ltd., J.D.
St. John, New Brunswick
Counsel or consultant:
Verner, Liipfert, Bernhard, McPherson and Hand, Chartered (Berl Bernhard, Lloyd N. Hand, Harry C. McPherson, John A. Merrigan, Douglas M. Steenland)

Irvington, New Jersey, Town of
Counsel or consultant:
Krivit and Krivit (Daniel H. Krivit)

Ishikawajima-Harima Heavy Industries Co.
Tokyo, Japan
Counsel or consultant:
Arent, Fox, Kintner, Plotkin & Kahn

Island Development Corp.
411 8th St., S.E., Washington, DC 20003
Telephone: (202) 547-2207
Counsel or consultant:
The Eddie Mahe Company

Islip, New York, City of
Counsel or consultant:
Steptoe and Johnson (Richard P. Taylor)

Israel Aircraft Industries
Tel Aviv, Israel
Counsel or consultant:
Galland, Kharasch, Morse and Garfinkle (Morris R. Garfinkle, Susan B. Jollie)
Marvin G. Klemow
Winthrop, Stimson, Putnam & Roberts (Robert Reed Gray)

Israel Electric Corp., Ltd.
Haifa, Israel
Counsel or consultant:
Kaplan, Russin and Vecchi (Julius Kaplan)

Israel, Embassy of
3514 International Dr., N.W., Washington, DC 20008
Telephone: (202) 364-5500
Counsel or consultant:
Arnold & Porter (Brooksley E. Born)
Fried, Frank, Harris, Shriver & Jacobson (Melvin Rishe)

Israel, Government of
Jerusalem, Israel
Counsel or consultant:
Fried, Frank, Harris, Shriver & Jacobson (Alan G. Kashdan, Melvin Rishe)
Mudge Rose Guthrie Alexander and Ferdon
O'Connor & Hannan (George J. Mannina, Jr.)

Israel Military Industries
Israel
Counsel or consultant:
Fried, Frank, Harris, Shriver & Jacobson

Israel, Ministry of Defense
Israel
Counsel or consultant:
Fried, Frank, Harris, Shriver & Jacobson

Issues Management Ass'n
1785 Massachusetts Ave., N.W., Washington, DC 20036
Telephone: (202) 775-0180
Counsel or consultant:
Pagan Internat'l Inc. (Rafael D. Pagan, Jr.)

Italian Aerospace Industries (USA), Inc.
1235 Jefferson Davis Hwy. Suite 500, Arlington, VA 22202
Telephone: (703) 271-9200
Background: Represents Aeritalia and the Finmeccanica Group.

Represented by:
M. L. Boswell, Chairman
Stefano P. Ruocco, President
Riccardo Sarti, Manager, Business Development

Itek Optical Systems
1700 North Moore St. Suite 1910, Arlington, VA 22209
Telephone: (703) 522-2030
Represented by:
Lloyd L. Rall, Director, ITEK Washington Operations

Itel Containers Internat'l Corp.
San Francisco, CA
Counsel or consultant:
Patton, Boggs and Blow (James B. Christian, Jr.)

Itoh (America), Inc., C.
1155 21st St., N.W. Suite 710, Washington, DC 20036
Telephone: (202) 822-9082
Represented by:
Takeshi Kondo, Senior V. President
Counsel or consultant:
Paul, Weiss, Rifkind, Wharton and Garrison (Lionel H. Olmer)

ITT Corp.
1600 M St., N.W., Fifth Floor, Washington, DC 20036
Telephone: (202) 296-6000
Represented by:
Jack H. Gardner, Dir., Regul. Affrs. & Asst. Gen. Counsel
Nicholas J. Glakas, Director, Government Affairs
Michael M. Hunter, Director, Corporate Affairs
Roger W. Langsdorf, Dir., Antitrust Compliance & Sr. Counsel
Wingate Lloyd, Director, International Relations
Raymond V. O'Brien, Director, Public Affairs
Richard S. Ward, V. President, Government Affairs
Linda A. Woolley, Director, Public Affairs
Counsel or consultant:
Hill and Knowlton Public Affairs Worldwide (James C. Jennings)

ITT Defense, Inc.
1000 Wilson Blvd. Suite 3000, Arlington, VA 22209
Telephone: (703) 276-8300
Represented by:
A. Robin Battaglini, Dir., DOD and Congressional Liaison
Joseph W. O'Neil, Dir., DOD and Congressional Liaison
E. George Riedel, Dir., Business/Government Relations
Counsel or consultant:
ARB Consultants (Anthony R. Battista)

ITT Gilfillan
Van Nuys, CA
Counsel or consultant:
Cassidy and Associates, Inc. (Thomas M. Gannon)

IUE Committee on Political Education
1126 16th St., N.W., Washington, DC 20036
Telephone: (202) 296-1200
Background: The political action arm of the Internat'l Union of Electronic, Electrical, Salaried, Machine, and Furniture Workers, AFL-CIO. Principal contact is Maria Landolfo, Director of Legislation and Political Action for the Union.

Ivacare Corp.
Elyria, OH
Counsel or consultant:
Baker and Hostetler (Frederick H. Graefe)

Ivory Coast, Government of
Abidjan, Ivory Coast
Counsel or consultant:
Neill and Co. (George A. Dalley, Denis M. Neill)

Izaak Walton League of America
1401 Wilson Blvd., Level B, Arlington, VA 22209
Telephone: (703) 528-1818
Background: A 50,000-member nationwide, non-profit citizen organization dedicated to the wise use of our country's natural resources.
Represented by:
Jack Lorenz, Exec. Director
Maitland S. Sharpe, Assoc. Exec. Dir. & Conservation Dir.

J & B Management Co.
Fort Lee, NJ

Counsel or consultant:
Concord Associates, Inc.
Garvey, Schubert & Barer (Paul S. Hoff)

Jackson Nat'l Life Insurance Co.
Lansing, MI
Counsel or consultant:
Winburn, VanScoyoc, and Hooper (Linsay D. Hooper)

Jacksonville, Florida, City of
Jacksonville, FL
Counsel or consultant:
Hecht, Spencer & Associates (Lanny F. Wiles)

Jacksonville, Florida, Port of
Jacksonville, FL
Counsel or consultant:
Alcalde & Rousselot (Hector Alcalde)

Jacksonville Transportation Authority
Jacksonville, FL
Counsel or consultant:
Vierra Associates, Inc. (Dennis C. Vierra)

Jamaica, Government of
Kingston, Jamaica
Counsel or consultant:
CounterTerrorism Consultants L.P. (L. Carter McCormick, Jr., Gerald S. Walker)
Fenton Communications, Inc. (David Fenton, Leila McDowell-Head)
Holland and Knight
Neill and Co. (George A. Dalley, Denis M. Neill)

Jamaica Nat'l Export Corp.
Kingston, Jamaica
Counsel or consultant:
Holland and Knight (David H. Baker)

James Co., T. L.
Kenner, LA
Counsel or consultant:
Cassidy and Associates, Inc. (Robert K. Dawson, Thomas M. Gannon)
Patton, Boggs and Blow (J. Gordon Arbuckle)

James River Corp.
Richmond, VA
Counsel or consultant:
Lee, Toomey & Kent
McGuire, Woods, Battle and Boothe (Robert H. Lamb)
Perkins Coie (Guy R. Martin)

Jamestown-Klallam Indian Tribe
WA
Counsel or consultant:
SENSE, INC. (Joe Tallakson)

Jamestown, New York, City of
Background: Law firm of Duncan, Weinberg, Miller & Pembroke represents the municipal utility of Jamestown, NY, on environmental and electric utility matters.
Counsel or consultant:
Duncan, Weinberg, Miller & Pembroke, P.C. (Wallace L. Duncan, Jeffrey C. Genzer, Frederick L. Miller, Jr.)

Japan Air Lines
Tokyo, Japan
Counsel or consultant:
John P. Sears Law Offices (John P. Sears)

Japan Aluminum Federation
Tokyo, Japan
Counsel or consultant:
Mudge Rose Guthrie Alexander and Ferdon (William N. Walker)

Japan Auto Parts Industry Ass'n
Tokyo, Japan
Counsel or consultant:
Robinson, Lake, Lerer & Montgomery (James H. Lake)

Japan Automobile Manufacturers Ass'n
1050 17th St., N.W. Suite 410, Washington, DC 20036
Telephone: (202) 296-8537
Represented by:
William C. Duncan, Deputy General Director
Akihiko Miyoshi, General Director, Washington Office
Allen Walker, Manager, Public Affairs
Counsel or consultant:
John P. Sears Law Offices (John P. Sears)

The listings in this directory are available as *Mailing Labels*. See last page.

ORGANIZATIONS REPRESENTED

Japan Automobile Tire Manufacturers Ass'n
Tokyo, Japan
Counsel or consultant:
Tanaka, Ritger and Middleton (James Davenport, B. Jenkins Middleton, Michele N. Tanaka)

Japan Bearing Industrial Ass'n
Tokyo, Japan
Counsel or consultant:
Tanaka, Ritger and Middleton (James Davenport, H. William Tanaka)

Japan Chemical Fibers Ass'n
Tokyo, Japan
Counsel or consultant:
Internat'l Business and Economic Research Corp.

Japan Economic Institute of America
1000 Connecticut Ave., N.W. Suite 211, Washington, DC 20036
Telephone: (202) 296-5633
Represented by:
Gretchen Green, Government Relations Analyst
Barbara Warner, Sr. Political Economist
Counsel or consultant:
Lerch and Co., Inc. (Donald G. Lerch, Jr.)

Japan Electronic Industry Development Ass'n
Tokyo, Japan
Counsel or consultant:
Graham and James

Japan, Embassy of
2520 Massachusetts Ave., N.W., Washington, DC 20008
Telephone: (202) 939-6700
Counsel or consultant:
Davis Wright Tremaine (Walter H. Evans, III)
Dechert Price & Rhoads (Allan S. Mostoff)
Paul H. DeLaney Law Offices (Paul H. DeLaney, Jr.)
Hogan and Hartson
Mike Masaoka Associates
Milbank, Tweed, Hadley & McCloy
Saunders and Company (Eric Edmondson, Steven R. Saunders)
Tanaka, Ritger and Middleton (H. William Tanaka)
Washington Resources and Strategy, Inc. (William R. Sweeney, Jr.)

Japan Export Metal Flatware Industry Ass'n
Tokyo, Japan
Counsel or consultant:
Tanaka, Ritger and Middleton (James Davenport, H. William Tanaka)

Japan External Trade Organization (JETRO)
New York, NY
Counsel or consultant:
Mike Masaoka Associates

Japan Federation of Construction Contractors
Tokyo, Japan
Counsel or consultant:
Global USA, Inc. (Dr. Bohdan Denysyk)

Japan Fisheries Ass'n
Tokyo, Japan
Counsel or consultant:
Frank, Richard A., Law Offices of
Garvey, Schubert & Barer
Ginsburg, Feldman and Bress (David Ginsburg)

Japan General Merchandise Exporters Ass'n
Tokyo, Japan
Counsel or consultant:
Tanaka, Ritger and Middleton (James Davenport, H. William Tanaka)

Japan, Government of
Tokyo, Japan
Counsel or consultant:
Lerch and Co., Inc. (Donald G. Lerch, Jr.)
Wilbur F. Monroe Associates (Wilbur F. Monroe)
Tanaka, Ritger and Middleton (H. William Tanaka)

Japan Iron and Steel Exporters Ass'n
Toyko, Japan
Counsel or consultant:
Steptoe and Johnson
Willkie Farr and Gallagher (William H. Barringer)

Japan/Korea-Atlantic and Gulf Freight Conference
Tokyo, Japan
Counsel or consultant:
Warren and Associates

Japan Lumber Importers Ass'n
Tokyo, Japan
Counsel or consultant:
Internat'l Business and Economic Research Corp.
Mudge Rose Guthrie Alexander and Ferdon (Julia Christine Bliss, David P. Houlihan)

Japan Machine Tool Builders Ass'n
Tokyo, Japan
Counsel or consultant:
Anderson, Hibey, Nauheim and Blair (Stanton D. Anderson)

Japan Machinery Exporters Ass'n
Tokyo, Japan
Counsel or consultant:
Anderson, Hibey, Nauheim and Blair (Stanton D. Anderson)
Willkie Farr and Gallagher (William H. Barringer)

Japan Metal Forming Machine Builders Ass'n
Tokyo, Japan
Counsel or consultant:
Anderson, Hibey, Nauheim and Blair (Stanton D. Anderson)

Japan, Ministry of Foreign Affairs of
Tokyo, Japan
Counsel or consultant:
The Eddie Mahe Company

Japan, Ministry of International Trade and Industry
c/o Japanese Embassy 2520 Massachusetts Ave., N.W., Washington, DC 20008
Telephone: (202) 939-6700
Counsel or consultant:
Targeting Systems, Inc.

Japan Pottery Exporters Ass'n
Tokyo, Japan
Counsel or consultant:
Tanaka, Ritger and Middleton (H. William Tanaka)

Japan Productivity Center
1729 King St., Suite 100, Alexandria, VA 22314
Telephone: (703) 838-0414
Represented by:
Daisaku Harada, Director, U.S. Office

Japan/Puerto Rico and Virgin Islands Freight Conference
Tokyo, Japan
Counsel or consultant:
Warren and Associates (Charles F. Warren)

Japan Soc. of Industrial Machinery Manufacturers
Tokyo, Japan
Counsel or consultant:
Paul A. London Assoc., Inc. (Paul A. London)

Japan Steel Works, Ltd.
Tokyo, Japan
Counsel or consultant:
Marks Murase and White (Matthew J. Marks, Frederic B. Rose)
Popham, Haik, Schnobrich & Kaufman, Ltd. (William E. Casselman, II)

Japan Times Corp.
Tokyo, Japan
Counsel or consultant:
Saunders and Company (Steven R. Saunders, Pam Yonkin)

Japan Tobacco, Inc.
1667 K St., N.W., Suite 330, Washington, DC 20006
Telephone: (202) 293-4289
Background: A private company based in Tokyo, Japan.
Represented by:
Seichi Assako, Chief Representative, Washington Office
Counsel or consultant:
Daniel J. Edelman, Inc. (Stephen K. Cook)
Hoppel, Mayer and Coleman (Neal M. Mayer)

Japan Trade Center
New York, NY
Counsel or consultant:
Hill and Knowlton Public Affairs Worldwide (Andrew G. Durant)
Tanaka, Ritger and Middleton (James Davenport, B. Jenkins Middleton, H. William Tanaka)
TKC Internat'l, Inc.

Japan Tuna Fisheries Cooperative
Tokyo, Japan
Counsel or consultant:
Anderson and Pendleton, C.A. (Francis G. McKenna)

Japan Woolen and Linen Textiles Exporters Ass'n
Osaka, Japan
Counsel or consultant:
Internat'l Business and Economic Research Corp.

Japanese Aero Engines Corp.
Tokyo, Japan
Counsel or consultant:
Global USA, Inc. (Dr. Bohdan Denysyk)

Japanese Aircraft Development Corp.
Tokyo, Japan
Counsel or consultant:
Global USA, Inc. (Dr. Bohdan Denysyk)

Japanese American Citizens League
1730 Rhode Island Ave., N.W., Suite 204, Washington, DC 20036
Telephone: (202) 223-1240
Background: A national, non-profit, educational and civil rights organization. Monitors legislation and other activities which affect civil and constitutional rights.
Represented by:
Paul M. Igasaki, Washington Representative
JoAnne Kagiwada, Acting Exec. Dir., Legis. Educ. Comm.

Jauch & Hubener, O.H.G.
Hamburg, Germany
Counsel or consultant:
George K. Bernstein Law Off. (George K. Bernstein, Robert B. Shapiro)

Jaycees Internat'l
Coral Gables, FL
Counsel or consultant:
Randolph G. Flood and Associates

JEFCO
Chicago, IL
Counsel or consultant:
Burgum & Grimm, Ltd. (Thomas L. Burgum)

Jefferson Bancorp
Miami, FL
Counsel or consultant:
Warren W. Koffler

Jefferson Parish, Louisiana
Harahan, LA
Counsel or consultant:
Nat'l Center for Municipal Development (Dicken Cherry)

Jeppesen Sanderson, Inc.
1725 K St., N.W., Suite 1107, Washington, DC 20006
Telephone: (202) 331-7727
Background: A Times Mirror Co. subsidiary.
Represented by:
Rudolph M. Ruana, Director, Washington Office

Jersey Central Power and Light Co.
Morristown, NJ
Counsel or consultant:
Shaw, Pittman, Potts and Trowbridge (Ernest L. Blake, Jr.)

Jersey City Office of Grants Management
Jersey City, NJ
Counsel or consultant:
Krivit and Krivit (Daniel H. Krivit)

Jesuit Secondary Education Ass'n
1424 16th St., N.W. Suite 300, Washington, DC 20036
Telephone: (202) 667-3888
Represented by:
Rev. Charles P. Costello, S.J., President

ORGANIZATIONS REPRESENTED

Jesuit Social Ministries
1424 16th St., N.W., Suite 300, Washington, DC 20036
Telephone: (202) 462-7008
Represented by:
   Joseph R. Hacala, S. J., Director

Jewelers of America
New York, NY
Counsel or consultant:
   London and Satagaj, Attorneys-at-Law (Sheldon I. London, John S. Satagaj)

Jewish Institute for Nat'l Security Affairs
1100 17th St., N.W., Suite 330, Washington, DC 20036
Telephone: (202) 833-0020
Background: Provides information concerning U.S. defense to the American Jewish community. Supports strong U.S. defense posture. Supports cooperation between U.S. and Israel on defense and security issues.
Represented by:
   Shoshana Bryen, Exec. Director

Jewish Nat'l Fund
New York, NY
Background: A fund raising organization in support of Israel.
Counsel or consultant:
   Dutko & Associates (Daniel A. Dutko, Susan Goodman, Richard L. Seely)

Jewish Peace Lobby
Suite 141 4431 Lehigh Rd., College Park, MD 20740
Telephone: (301) 589-8764
Background: Works for peace in the Middle East by focusing on U.S. foreign policy. Lobbies in congressional districts in over 40 states.
Represented by:
   Jerome M. Segal, Ph.D., President

Jewish Republican PAC
1575 I St., N.W. Suite 800, Washington, DC 20005
Telephone: (202) 789-7520
Background: Previously known as Potomac PAC.
Represented by:
   Jeffrey P. Altman, Chairman and Treasurer

Jewish War Veterans of the U.S.A.
1811 R St., N.W., Washington, DC 20009
Telephone: (202) 265-6280
Represented by:
   Michelle Spivak Kelley, Nat'l Program Director
   Col. Herb Rosenbleeth, Nat'l Legislative Director
   Steve Shaw, Nat'l Exec. Director

Jimmie Heuga Center
Vail, CO
Counsel or consultant:
   Kessler and Associates

Job Opportunities Business Symposium
c/o Rowland & Sellery 1023 15th St., N.W., Washington, DC 20005
Telephone: (202) 289-1780
Counsel or consultant:
   Rowland & Sellery (Terrie Dort)

John Gray Institute
Beaumont, TX
Counsel or consultant:
   Lipsen Whitten & Diamond

John Hancock Mutual Life Insurance Co.
Boston, MA
Counsel or consultant:
   Prather, Seeger, Doolittle and Farmer (Thomas L. Farmer, Gary M. Welsh)

Johnson Controls, Inc.
Milwaukee, WI
Counsel or consultant:
   Hill and Knowlton Public Affairs Worldwide (Roger Lindberg)

Johnson & Johnson
1667 K St., N.W., Suite 410, Washington, DC 20006
Telephone: (202) 293-2620
Represented by:
   Leon B. Gibbs, Dir, Gov't Afrs (Lat Amer & Carib Basin)
   John P. Hall, Jr., V. President, Federal Relations
   Nicholas L. Ruggieri, Director, Washington Affairs
   Susan S. Walden, Manager, Federal Relations
Counsel or consultant:
   Baker and Hostetler (Robert G. Pinco)
   Black, Manafort, Stone and Kelly Public Affairs Co. (James H. Healey)
   Fox, Bennett and Turner (Alan R. Bennett, Allan M. Fox)
   Howrey and Simon (John W. Nields, Jr.)
   Lee, Toomey & Kent

Johnson Matthey PLC
London, England
Counsel or consultant:
   Rose Communications (Robert R. Rose)

Johnson-Simmons Co., The
Clearwater, FL
Counsel or consultant:
   Dow, Lohnes and Albertson (Jeffrey Kurzweil)

Johnson Wax
900 17th St., N.W., Suite 506, Washington, DC 20006
Telephone: (202) 331-1186
Represented by:
   William D. Perry, Director, Government Relations

Joint Baltic American Nat'l Committee
Box 4578, Rockville, MD 20850
Telephone: (301) 340-1954
Background: Represents the American Latvian Ass'n, the Lithuanian American Council and the Estonian American Nat'l Council.
Represented by:
   Sandra M. Aistars, Director of Public Relations

Joint Center for Political Studies
1301 Pennsylvania Ave., N.W., Washington, DC 20004
Telephone: (202) 626-3500
Background: A national nonprofit tax exempt organization which conducts research on issues of special concern to Black Americans and promotes the informed and effective involvement of Blacks in the political process. Provides non-partisan analyses to the public through conferences, publications and other information services.
Represented by:
   Eleanor Farrar, V. President
   Milton D. Morris, Director of Research
   Russell Owens, Director, Nat'l Policy Institute
   Eddie N. Williams, President

Joint Council on Allergy and Immunology
Mt. Prospect, IL
Counsel or consultant:
   Capitol Associates, Inc. (Debra M. Hardy-Havens, Terry Lierman)
   White, Fine, and Verville (Richard E. Verville)

Joint Electron Device Engineering Council (JEDEC)
1722 Eye St., N.W., Washington, DC 20006
Telephone: (202) 457-4971
Background: Represented by John M. Kinn of the Electronic Industries Ass'n, JEDEC is a subgroup of EIA that covers semiconductor standards.

Joint Industry Group
818 Connecticut Ave., N.W., 12th Floor, Washington, DC 20006
Telephone: (202) 466-5490
Background: A coalition of 100 trade associations, manufacturers and business firms, law and other professional firms involved in international trade focusing on Custom matters. Harry Lamar of Monticello Associates serves as Secretariat of the Group.
Counsel or consultant:
   Monticello Associates (Harry Lamar)

Joint Nat'l Committee for Languages
300 I St., N.E., Suite 211, Washington, DC 20002
Telephone: (202) 546-7855
Represented by:
   John David Edwards, Exec. Director

JOMM Limited Partnership
Seattle, WA
Counsel or consultant:
   Phyllis D. Carnilla

Jones Chemicals Political Action Committee
c/o LaRoe, Winn, et al 1120 G St., N.W., Suite 800, Washington, DC 20005
Telephone: (202) 628-2788
Counsel or consultant:
   LaRoe, Winn, Moerman & Donovan (Paul M. Donovan)

Jones, Day, Reavis and Pogue Good Government Fund
1450 G St., N.W. Suite 700, Washington, DC 20005-2088
Telephone: (202) 879-3939
Background: The political action committee of the law firm of Jones, Day, Reavis and Pogue.
Counsel or consultant:
   Jones, Day, Reavis and Pogue

Jones Medical Industries, Inc.
St. Louis, MO
Counsel or consultant:
   Kleinfeld, Kaplan and Becker (Peter R. Mathers)

Jordan, Hashemite Kingdom of
Amman, Jordan
Counsel or consultant:
   Aspen Hill Enterprises, Ltd. (Richard N. Viets)
   Neill and Co. (Leslie A. Janka, Denis M. Neill)

Joseph and Feiss Inc.
New York, NY
Counsel or consultant:
   Tendler, Goldberg & Biggins, Chtd. (Paul M. Tendler)

Joy Technologies Inc.
Pittsburgh, PA
Counsel or consultant:
   Rose, Schmidt, Hasley & DiSalle (Michael G. Kushnick)

Judge Advocates Ass'n
1815 H St., N.W., Suite 408, Washington, DC 20006
Telephone: (202) 628-0979
Background: Affiliated with the American Bar Ass'n. Represents the interests and expresses the viewpoints of the lawyer in uniform. Seeks to guard the rights of military personnel and promote the careers of military lawyers. Represented by Capt. Kevin Barry of the Dept. of Transportation - United States Coast Guard.

Junex Enterprises
Hartsdale, NY
Counsel or consultant:
   Max N. Berry Law Offices (Max N. Berry)

Justice Fellowship
Box 17152, Washington, DC 20041
Telephone: (703) 759-9400
Background: Advocates reform of the criminal justice system.
Represented by:
   Daniel W. Van Ness, President

Juvenile Diabetes Foundation
New York, NY
Counsel or consultant:
   McDermott, Will and Emery

"K" Line Air Service (U.S.A.), Inc.
Tokyo, Japan
Counsel or consultant:
   Robert N. Meiser, P.C.

K-Line Pharmaceuticals, Ltd.
Downsview, Ontario
Counsel or consultant:
   Keller and Heckman (John S. Eldred, Joseph E. Keller)

K mart Corp.
Troy, MI
Counsel or consultant:
   Camp, Barsh, Bates and Tate (Ronald L. Platt)
   Steele & Fornaciari (John R. Fornaciari, Robert E. Hebda, Robert W. Steele)

Ka Pono Hawaii Nei Inc.
Kaneohe, HI
Counsel or consultant:
   Lachelli, Waller and Associates

KABY-TV
Aberdeen, SD
Counsel or consultant:
   Marmet and McCombs, P.C.

ORGANIZATIONS REPRESENTED

KADN
Lafayette, LA
Counsel or consultant:
Fletcher, Heald and Hildreth

KADN-TV
Lafayette, LA
Counsel or consultant:
Mullin, Rhyne, Emmons and Topel, P.C.

Kaempen Internat'l
Orange, CA
Counsel or consultant:
Lachelli, Waller and Associates

Kaibab Industries
Phoenix, AZ
Counsel or consultant:
James J. Magner & Assoc. Inc. (James J. Magner)

KAIL
Fresno, CA
Counsel or consultant:
Miller and Fields

Kaiser Aluminum and Chemical Corp.
900 17th St., N.W. Suite 706, Washington, DC 20006
Telephone: (202) 296-5474
Represented by:
Robert E. Cole, Vice President
Counsel or consultant:
Patton, Boggs and Blow (Donald V. Moorehead)
Sutherland, Asbill and Brennan (Jan Benes Vlcek)

Kaiser Foundation Health Plan, Inc.
1700 K St., N.W. Suite 601, Washington, DC 20006
Telephone: (202) 296-1314
Represented by:
Richard Froh, V. President, Government Relations
JoAnne Glisson, Legislative Representative
John D. Johnson, M.D., Physicians' Representative
Alan Silverstone, V. President and Regional Manager
Stephanie A. Strass, Director, Public Affairs (Mid-Atlantic)

Kaiser Steel Holdings
Rancho Cucamonga, CA
Counsel or consultant:
Braun & Company

KAIT-TV
Jonesboro, AR
Counsel or consultant:
Crowell and Moring

Kajima Corp.
New York, NY
Counsel or consultant:
Armstrong, Byrd and Associates (Russell T. Adise, Rodney E. Armstrong)

KAKE-TV
Wichita, KS
Counsel or consultant:
Fletcher, Heald and Hildreth

Kaman Corp.
Bloomfield, CT
Counsel or consultant:
Black, Manafort, Stone and Kelly Public Affairs Co. (Paul J. Manafort)
Ervin Technical Associates, Inc. (ETA) (James L. Ervin)

Kamber Group Political Action Fund (TKG PAC)
1920 L St., N.W., Washington, DC 20036
Telephone: (202) 223-8700
Counsel or consultant:
The Kamber Group (Victor S. Kamber, Jeffrey M. Sandman)

Kamehameha Schools
Honolulu, HI
Counsel or consultant:
Edwin T. C. Ing
Rogers and Wells

Kansas City Power & Light Co.
1800 K St., N.W., Suite 1018, Washington, DC 20006
Telephone: (202) 887-0497
Background: The above address is that of Dana Haas, a federal affairs representative.
Counsel or consultant:
Dana W. Haas
Slover and Loftus (William L. Slover)

Kansas City Southern Industries
Kansas City, MO
Counsel or consultant:
Elliott Associates (M. Diane Elliott)
Scootch Pankonin
Sullivan and Worcester (Robert L. Calhoun, David M. Schwartz)
Winburn, VanScyoc, and Hooper (Linsay D. Hooper)

Kansas Gas & Electric Co.
Wichita, KS
Counsel or consultant:
Dana W. Haas
Shaw, Pittman, Potts and Trowbridge (Jay E. Silberg)

KARK
Little Rock, AR
Counsel or consultant:
Fletcher, Heald and Hildreth

KARK-TV
Little Rock, AR
Counsel or consultant:
Gammon and Grange

Karlander Kangaroo Lines
San Francisco, CA
Counsel or consultant:
Denning and Wohlstetter (Alan F. Wohlstetter)

KATC
Lafayette, LA
Counsel or consultant:
Marmet and McCombs, P.C.

KATU
Portland, OR
Counsel or consultant:
Fisher, Wayland, Cooper and Leader

Katz Communications, Inc.
New York, NY
Counsel or consultant:
Kaye, Scholer, Fierman, Hays and Handler (Jason Shrinsky)

KAUT
Oklahoma City, OK
Counsel or consultant:
Pepper and Corazzini

Kawasaki Kisen Kaisha, Ltd.
New York, NY
Counsel or consultant:
O'Connor & Hannan (George J. Mannina, Jr.)
Warren and Associates (Charles F. Warren)

Kawasaki Motors Corp., USA
Santa Ana, CA
Counsel or consultant:
Paul, Hastings, Janofsky and Walker (Mark L. Gerchick)
Fred B. Rooney

KBCP
Paradise, CA
Counsel or consultant:
Fletcher, Heald and Hildreth

KBMT
Beaumont, TX
Counsel or consultant:
Cohn and Marks

KBMY
Bismarck, ND
Counsel or consultant:
Marmet and McCombs, P.C.

KBTX-TV
Bryan, TX
Counsel or consultant:
Cordon and Kelly

KCBA
Salinas, CA
Counsel or consultant:
Rubin, Winston and Diercks

KCEN-TV
Temple, TX
Counsel or consultant:
Fisher, Wayland, Cooper and Leader

KCFW-TV
Kalispell, MT
Counsel or consultant:
Cohn and Marks

KCIK
El Paso, TX
Counsel or consultant:
Fisher, Wayland, Cooper and Leader

KCMY
Sacramento, CA
Counsel or consultant:
Fletcher, Heald and Hildreth

KCNA-TV
Kearney, NE
Counsel or consultant:
Koteen and Naftalin

KCOS-TV
El Paso, TX
Counsel or consultant:
Cohn and Marks

KCPQ
Seattle, WA
Counsel or consultant:
Koteen and Naftalin

KCRA-TV
Sacramento, CA
Counsel or consultant:
Koteen and Naftalin

KCSM-TV
San Mateo, CA
Counsel or consultant:
Tierney & Swift (John L. Tierney)

KCSO
Modesto, CA
Counsel or consultant:
Fletcher, Heald and Hildreth

KCTZ-TV
Bozeman, MT
Counsel or consultant:
Cohn and Marks

KCWC-TV
Lander, WY
Counsel or consultant:
Fletcher, Heald and Hildreth

KCWT
Wenatchee, WA
Counsel or consultant:
Fisher, Wayland, Cooper and Leader

KDLH-TV
Duluth, MN
Counsel or consultant:
Crowell and Moring

KDOC-TV
Westminister, CA
Counsel or consultant:
Cohn and Marks

KDRV
Medford, OR
Counsel or consultant:
Fisher, Wayland, Cooper and Leader

KDSM-TV
Des Moines, IA
Counsel or consultant:
Tierney & Swift (John L. Tierney)

KDUH-TV
Scottsbluff, NE

The listings in this directory are available as *Mailing Labels*. See last page.

ORGANIZATIONS REPRESENTED

Counsel or consultant:
Fisher, Wayland, Cooper and Leader

Kearny, New Jersey, Town of
Counsel or consultant:
Krivit and Krivit (Daniel H. Krivit)

KECI-TV
Missoula, MT
Counsel or consultant:
Cohn and Marks

KEDT-TV
Corpus Christi, TX
Counsel or consultant:
Cohn and Marks

Keene Corp.
New York, NY
Counsel or consultant:
Anderson, Kill, Olick and Oshinsky (Jerold Oshinsky)
Clifford & Warnke

Keep America Beautiful
New York, NY
Counsel or consultant:
Kostmayer Communications, Inc. (Christine Dolan)

Kellogg
2000 L St., N.W., Suite 200, Washington, DC 20036
Telephone: (202) 833-2443
Represented by:
John Ford, Director, Government Relations

Kellogg Co., M. W.
1317 F St., N.W., Suite 300, Washington, DC 20004-1105
Telephone: (202) 639-8870
Represented by:
James H. Andrews, V. President, Government Affairs

Kellwood Co.
St. Louis, MO
Counsel or consultant:
George Demougeot

Kelly Press, Inc.
Cheverly, MD
Counsel or consultant:
The Kamber Group

Kelly Services, Inc.
Troy, MI
Counsel or consultant:
McKevitt Group, The
Wunder, Ryan, Cannon & Thelen (Michael A. Forscey)

Kelso & Co.
New York, NY
Counsel or consultant:
Silverstein and Mullens (William A. Kirk, Jr.)

Kelso Political Action Committee
536 7th St., S.E., Washington, DC 20003
Telephone: (202) 544-1988
Background: The above address is that of Washington Resources and Strategy, Inc., a consulting firm.
Counsel or consultant:
Washington Resources and Strategy, Inc. (William R. Sweeney, Jr.)

Kemper Group
600 Pennsylvania Ave., S.E., Suite 206, Washington, DC 20003
Telephone: (202) 547-0120
Represented by:
Michael F. Dineen, Director of Federal Relations
Diann McCormick, Assistant to the Dir., Federal Relations

Kenai Natives Ass'n, Inc.
Kenai, AK
Counsel or consultant:
Duncan, Weinberg, Miller & Pembroke, P.C. (Richmond F. Allan, Edward Weinberg)

Kendall and Associates, John
London, England
Counsel or consultant:
Keene, Shirley & Associates, Inc. (Lisa M. Olson)

KENI-TV
Anchorage, AK

Counsel or consultant:
Fisher, Wayland, Cooper and Leader

Kennecott
Salt Lake City, UT
Counsel or consultant:
Prather, Seeger, Doolittle and Farmer (Alfred V. J. Prather)
Steptoe and Johnson

Kennedy Engine Service Co.
Biloxi, MS
Counsel or consultant:
H. John Elliott

Kennedy Institute, Lt. Joseph P.
801 Buchanan St., N.E., Washington, DC 20017
Telephone: (202) 529-7600
Background: Serves children and adults with developmental disabilities in the Metro region.
Represented by:
Michela Perrone, President and Chief Exec. Officer

Kennedy Institute of Ethics
Georgetown University, Washington, DC 20057
Telephone: (202) 687-6774
Background: Sponsors research on ethical issues in medicine, including the legal and medical definitions of death, allocation of health resources and issues concerning recombinant DNA.
Represented by:
Robert M. Veatch, Director

Kenner Products
Cincinnati, OH
Counsel or consultant:
StMaxens and Co. (Thomas F. StMaxens, II)

Kentucky, Commonwealth of
400 N. Capitol St., N.W., Suite 330, Washington, DC 20001
Telephone: (202) 624-7741
Represented by:
Linda Breathitt, Fed. Liaison, Wash. Office of the Gov.
Jennifer L. Pulliam, Transportation Liaison

Kentucky Utilities Co.
Lexington, KY
Counsel or consultant:
Jones, Day, Reavis and Pogue (Randall E. Davis)
Slover and Loftus (William L. Slover)

Kenwood U.S.A. Corp.
Carson, CA
Background: An electronics products distributor.
Counsel or consultant:
Patton, Boggs and Blow

Kenya, Government of
Nairobi, Kenya
Counsel or consultant:
Black, Manafort, Stone and Kelly Public Affairs Co.
Neill and Co. (Denis M. Neill)

Kern River Gas Transmission Co.
Houston, TX
Counsel or consultant:
Cadwalader, Wickersham & Taft

KERO-TV
Bakersfield, CA
Counsel or consultant:
Koteen and Naftalin

Kerr-McGee Corp.
1667 K St., N.W., Suite 250, Washington, DC 20006
Telephone: (202) 728-9600
Represented by:
Peter M. Frank, Manager, Washington Office
Counsel or consultant:
Cassidy and Associates, Inc. (Thomas M. Gannon)

KETA-TV
Oklahoma City, OK
Counsel or consultant:
Cohn and Marks

Kettering Foundation
444 North Capitol St., N.W. Suite 408, Washington, DC 20001
Telephone: (202) 393-4478

Background: An operating (not grant-making) foundation with research programs on governmental, educational, scientific and technical and international issues. Headquartered in Dayton, Ohio. John H. Buchanan of People for the American Way serves as Senior Associate.
Represented by:
James Wilder, Director, External Affairs

Keuffel and Esser Co.
Morristown, NJ
Counsel or consultant:
Hudson, Creyke, Koehler and Tacke

KEVU
Eugene, OR
Counsel or consultant:
Fletcher, Heald and Hildreth

KEX Nat'l Ass'n
Burlington, NC
Counsel or consultant:
Bernard H. Ehrlich

Keydata Systems, Inc.
6411 Ivy Lane, Suite 604, Greenbelt, MD 20770
Telephone: (301) 474-7740
Counsel or consultant:
Denny Miller Associates

Keymarket Communications, Inc.
North Augusta, SC
Counsel or consultant:
Kaye, Scholer, Fierman, Hays and Handler (Jason Shrinsky)

Keystone Center, The
Keystone, CO
Counsel or consultant:
Madison Group/Earle Palmer Brown, The (Edward M. Gabriel, Richard Rosenzweig)

Keystone Provident Life Insurance Co.
Boston, MA
Counsel or consultant:
Williams and Jensen, P.C. (Robert E. Glennon, Jr.)

KFAR-TV
Fairbanks, AK
Counsel or consultant:
Fisher, Wayland, Cooper and Leader

KFBB-TV
Great Falls, MT
Counsel or consultant:
Fleischman and Walsh, P.C.

KFCB
Concord, CA
Counsel or consultant:
Gammon and Grange

KFDX-TV
Wichita Falls, TX
Counsel or consultant:
Cohn and Marks

KFNB
Casper, WY
Counsel or consultant:
Cordon and Kelly

KFNE
Lander, WY
Counsel or consultant:
Cordon and Kelly

KFNR
Rawlins, WY
Counsel or consultant:
Cordon and Kelly

KFSM-TV
Fort Smith, AR
Counsel or consultant:
Koteen and Naftalin

KFTL
Stockton, CA
Counsel or consultant:
Fletcher, Heald and Hildreth

KFTY
Santa Rosa, CA

ORGANIZATIONS REPRESENTED

KFTY (Cont'd)
Counsel or consultant:
Fletcher, Heald and Hildreth

KGET
Bakersfield, CA
Background: Formerly operated as KPWR-TV.
Counsel or consultant:
Rubin, Winston and Diercks

KGMC
Oklahoma City, OK
Counsel or consultant:
Fisher, Wayland, Cooper and Leader

KGTV
San Diego, CA
Counsel or consultant:
Koteen and Naftalin

KGW-TV
Portland, OR
Counsel or consultant:
Fletcher, Heald and Hildreth

Khalistan, Council of
2025 Eye St., N.W., Suite 901, Washington, DC 20007
Telephone: (202) 833-3262
Background: Represents the interests of the Sikh population of the Punjab in its conflict with the Indian Government.
Represented by:
Dr. Gurmit Singh Aulakh, President

KHAW-TV
Honolulu, HI
Counsel or consultant:
Marmet and McCombs, P.C.

KHNL-TV
Honolulu, HI
Counsel or consultant:
Fletcher, Heald and Hildreth

KHON-TV
Honolulu, HI
Counsel or consultant:
Marmet and McCombs, P.C.

KHSD-TV
Rapid City, SD
Counsel or consultant:
Fisher, Wayland, Cooper and Leader

Kia Motor Corp.
Seoul, Korea
Counsel or consultant:
Weatherly & Co. (Jin-Hyun Weatherly)

Kidder, Peabody & Co., Inc.
New York, NY
Counsel or consultant:
Bishop, Cook, Purcell & Reynolds (H. Lawrence Fox)

Kids Project
1101 Connecticut Ave., N.W. Suite 500, Washington, DC 20036
Telephone: (202) 429-7470
Represented by:
Anne R. Hill, Executive Director

KIEM-TV
Eureka, CA
Counsel or consultant:
Cohn and Marks

Kier English Confectionery, Josephine
Milford, DE
Counsel or consultant:
Robert N. Pyle & Associates

Kiewit Sons, Inc., Peter
Omaha, NE
Counsel or consultant:
Akin, Gump, Strauss, Hauer and Feld (Joel Jankowsky)

KIFI
Idaho Falls, ID
Counsel or consultant:
Reddy, Begley and Martin

KIHS-TV
Ontario, CA

Counsel or consultant:
Fisher, Wayland, Cooper and Leader

KIII
Corpus Christi, TX
Counsel or consultant:
Cohn and Marks

Kimberly-Clark Corp.
1201 Pennsylvania Ave., N.W. Suite 730, Washington, DC 20004
Telephone: (202) 393-8280
Represented by:
Bradford L. Bates, Transportation Counsel
Richard H. Kimberly, Director, Federal Government Relations
Bonnie B. Wan, Staff V. President
Sharon Zeigler, Federal Government Relations Specialist

Kimble Glass
Vineland, NJ
Counsel or consultant:
Stewart and Stewart (Terrence P. Stewart)

KING-TV
Seattle, WA
Counsel or consultant:
Fletcher, Heald and Hildreth

Kings Entertainment Co.
Cincinnati, OH
Counsel or consultant:
Taft, Stettinius and Hollister (Virginia E. Hopkins, Robert Taft, Jr.)

Kintetsu World Express (U.S.A.) Inc.
Tokyo, Japan
Counsel or consultant:
Robert N. Meiser, P.C.

Kirkpatrick & Lockhart Political Action Committee
1800 M St., N.W., Suite 900 South Lobby, Washington, DC 20036
Telephone: (202) 778-9000
Background: The political action committee formed by certain partners of the law firm Kirkpatrick & Lockhart.
Counsel or consultant:
Kirkpatrick & Lockhart (Garry E. Brown)

KIRO-TV
Seattle, WA
Counsel or consultant:
Wilkinson, Barker, Knauer and Quinn

KISU-TV
Pocatello, ID
Counsel or consultant:
Fletcher, Heald and Hildreth

KITN
Minneapolis, MN
Counsel or consultant:
Fletcher, Heald and Hildreth

KIVA-TV
Farmington, MN
Counsel or consultant:
Koteen and Naftalin

KJAC-TV
Port Arthur, TX
Counsel or consultant:
Cohn and Marks

KJAZ-FM
San Francisco, CA
Counsel or consultant:
Santarelli, Smith, Kraut and Carroccio (A. Thomas Carroccio)

KJCT-TV
Grand Junction, CO
Counsel or consultant:
Fletcher, Heald and Hildreth

KJNP
North Pole, AK
Counsel or consultant:
Fletcher, Heald and Hildreth

KKTV
Colorado Springs, CO
Counsel or consultant:
Rubin, Winston and Diercks

KLBK-TV
Lubbock, TX
Counsel or consultant:
Koteen and Naftalin

Kleinfeld, Kaplan and Becker Political Action Committee
1140 19th St., N.W., Suite 700, Washington, DC 20036
Telephone: (202) 223-5120
Counsel or consultant:
Kleinfeld, Kaplan and Becker

KLFY-TV
Lafayette, LA
Counsel or consultant:
Cordon and Kelly

KLNO-TV
Llano, TX
Counsel or consultant:
Cohn and Marks

KLRT
Little Rock, AR
Counsel or consultant:
Crowell and Moring

Klukwan Forest Products, Inc.
Juneau, AK
Counsel or consultant:
Davis Wright Tremaine (James P. Walsh)

Klukwan, Inc.
Haines, AK
Counsel or consultant:
Jack Ferguson Associates (Jack Ferguson)

KMGH-TV
Denver, CO
Counsel or consultant:
Koteen and Naftalin

KMIR-TV
Palm Springs, CA
Counsel or consultant:
Koteen and Naftalin

KMLY
Minot, ND
Counsel or consultant:
Marmet and McCombs, P.C.

KMOM-TV
Odessa, TX
Counsel or consultant:
Koteen and Naftalin

KMOS-TV
Sedalia, MO
Counsel or consultant:
Fisher, Wayland, Cooper and Leader

KMPH
Visalia, CA
Counsel or consultant:
Fletcher, Heald and Hildreth

KMS Industries, Inc.
Ann Arbor, MI
Background: Interested in legislative matters relating to inertial fusion.
Counsel or consultant:
James E. Guirard, Jr.

KMSG
Fresno, CA
Counsel or consultant:
Cohn and Marks

KMSO-TV
Missoula, MT
Counsel or consultant:
Fisher, Wayland, Cooper and Leader

KN Energy Inc.
Lakewood, CO

The listings in this directory are available as *Mailing Labels*. See last page.

ORGANIZATIONS REPRESENTED

Counsel or consultant:
   Sutherland, Asbill and Brennan
   Wickwire Gavin, P.C.

Knappton Corp.
   Portland, OR
   Counsel or consultant:
   Davis Wright Tremaine (Walter H. Evans, III)

Knight-Ridder Newspapers
   Miami, FL
   Counsel or consultant:
   Clifford & Warnke

KNOE-TV
   Monroe, LA
   Counsel or consultant:
   Cohn and Marks

KOB-TV
   Albuquerque, NM
   Counsel or consultant:
   Fletcher, Heald and Hildreth

Kobe Steel Co.
   Kobe, Japan
   Counsel or consultant:
   Willkie Farr and Gallagher (Christopher A. Dunn)

KOBF
   Farmington, NM
   Counsel or consultant:
   Fletcher, Heald and Hildreth

KOCE-TV
   Huntington Beach, CA
   Counsel or consultant:
   Tierney & Swift (John L. Tierney)

Koch Industries
   2000 Pennsylvania Ave., N.W. Suite 3580, Washington,
   DC 20006
   Telephone: (202) 466-2789
   Represented by:
   Leanne J. Abdnor, Director, Federal Government Affairs

KOCV-TV
   Odessa, TX
   Counsel or consultant:
   Cohn and Marks

Kodiak Island Borough
   Kodiak, AK
   Counsel or consultant:
   Birch, Horton, Bittner and Cherot (Joseph M. Chomski)

Kodiak Longline Vessel Owners Ass'n
   Kodiak, AK
   Counsel or consultant:
   C. Deming Cowles, IV

KOED-TV
   Tulsa, OK
   Counsel or consultant:
   Cohn and Marks

KOET-TV
   Eufala, OK
   Counsel or consultant:
   Cohn and Marks

KOGG
   Wailuku, HI
   Counsel or consultant:
   Fletcher, Heald and Hildreth

Kohlberg Kravis Roberts & Co.
   New York, NY
   Counsel or consultant:
   Davis Polk & Wardwell (Mikel M. Rollyson)
   Foley & Lardner (James N. Bierman)
   Wunder, Ryan, Cannon & Thelen (Kenneth S. Levine)

Koito Manufacturing Co.
   Tokyo, Japan
   Counsel or consultant:
   Paul, Hastings, Janofsky and Walker (Richard M. Fair-
   banks, III, G. Hamilton Loeb)

Kollmorgen Corp.
   Box 2306, Falls Church, VA 22042
   Telephone: (703) 573-7050

Represented by:
   Alan Craigue, Regional Manager

Kollsman
   2001 Jefferson Davis Hwy. Suite 807, Arlington, VA 22202
   Telephone: (703) 979-1200
   Background: A division of Sequa Corporation. Manufac-
   tures aircraft instrumentation and electro-optics systems.
   Headquartered in Merrimack, New Hampshire.
   Represented by:
   Albert H. Friedrich, V. President, Washington Operations

Komatsu Ltd.
   Tokyo, Japan
   Background: A heavy construction equipment manufactur-
   er. U.S. office is in Chattanooga, TN.
   Counsel or consultant:
   Global USA, Inc. (William H. Morris, Jr.)
   Graham and James (Lawrence R. Walders)
   Shearman and Sterling (Robert Herzstein, Thomas B. Wil-
   ner)

KOMO-TV
   Seattle, WA
   Counsel or consultant:
   Fisher, Wayland, Cooper and Leader

KOMU-TV
   Columbia, MO
   Counsel or consultant:
   Fisher, Wayland, Cooper and Leader

Konishoruku Photo Industry U.S.A.
   Englewood Cliffs, NJ
   Counsel or consultant:
   Ginsburg, Feldman and Bress

Kootznoowoo, Inc.
   Angoon, AK
   Counsel or consultant:
   Kilpatrick & Cody (J. Vance Hughes, C. Randall Nuck-
   olls)
   Perkins Coie (Guy R. Martin)

Korea Consumer Goods Exporters Ass'n
   Seoul, Korea
   Counsel or consultant:
   Mudge Rose Guthrie Alexander and Ferdon (Donald B.
   Cameron, Jr.)

Korea Deep Sea Fisheries Ass'n
   Seoul, Korea
   Counsel or consultant:
   Armstrong, Byrd and Associates (Hong K. An, Rodney
   E. Armstrong)

Korea Development Institute
   Seoul, Korea
   Background: Represented by John T. Bennett, President of
   the Korea Economic Institute of America.

Korea Economic Institute of America
   1030 15th St., N.W. Suite 662, Washington, DC 20005
   Telephone: (202) 371-0690
   Represented by:
   Linda G. Silver, Director, Legislative Analysis
   W. Robert Warne, President

Korea, Embassy of
   2370 Massachusetts Ave., N.W., Washington, DC 20008
   Telephone: (202) 939-5600
   Counsel or consultant:
   Internat'l Trade and Development Agency
   Reid & Priest (S. Chull Junn)
   Tucker & Associates (William Tucker)

Korea Federation of Footwear Industries
   Seoul, Korea
   Counsel or consultant:
   Internat'l Business and Economic Research Corp.

Korea Footwear Exporters Ass'n
   Seoul, Korea
   Counsel or consultant:
   Oppenheimer Wolff and Donnelly (David A. Gantz)

Korea Foreign Trade Ass'n
   1800 K St., N.W.,, Washington, DC 20006
   Telephone: (202) 408-0100
   Background: Founded in 1946, KFTA collects information
   on U.S. and world trade trends, conducts research and
   surveys on the U.S. economy, and provides facilities to
   support the overseas activities of member companies.

Represented by:
   Nam Hong Cho, President
   Sung K Chung, Manager
   Dae Kyum Kim, Senior Trade Analyst
   Kyoung Sun Min, Ass't Manager
   Chang Saeng Park, V. President
   Counsel or consultant:
   Arnold & Porter (Claire Reade)
   C & M Internat'l L.P. (Doral S. Cooper)
   Daniel J. Edelman, Inc.
   Manchester Trade, Inc. (Stephen L. Lande)
   Pillsbury, Madison and Sutro (Keith J. Mendelson, Anne
   R. Morse, Judith A. Ott)
   Reid & Priest (S. Chull Junn)

Korea Foundry Forging Cooperative Ass'n
   Seoul, Korea
   Counsel or consultant:
   Mudge Rose Guthrie Alexander and Ferdon (Donald B.
   Cameron, Jr.)

Korea, Government of
   Seoul, Korea
   Counsel or consultant:
   Arnold & Porter (Sukhan Kim)

Korea Insulation Co., Ltd.
   Seoul, Korea
   Counsel or consultant:
   Rogers Internat'l, Inc. (Joe O. Rogers)

Korea Iron and Steel Ass'n
   Seoul, Korea
   Counsel or consultant:
   Internat'l Business and Economic Research Corp.
   Mudge Rose Guthrie Alexander and Ferdon (Donald B.
   Cameron, Jr., Julie C. Mendoza)

Korea Iron and Steel Works, Ltd.
   Seoul, Korea
   Counsel or consultant:
   Mudge Rose Guthrie Alexander and Ferdon (N. David
   Palmeter)

Korea Leather and Fur Exporters Ass'n
   Seoul, Korea
   Counsel or consultant:
   Internat'l Business and Economic Research Corp.
   Mudge Rose Guthrie Alexander and Ferdon (N. David
   Palmeter)

Korea Maritime Transport Co.
   Houston, TX
   Counsel or consultant:
   Warren and Associates (George A. Quadrino, Charles F.
   Warren)

Korea Metal Flatware Exporters Ass'n
   Seoul, Korea
   Counsel or consultant:
   Mudge Rose Guthrie Alexander and Ferdon (N. David
   Palmeter)

Korea Metal Industry Cooperative
   Seoul, Korea
   Counsel or consultant:
   Mudge Rose Guthrie Alexander and Ferdon (N. David
   Palmeter)

Korea, Ministry of Trade and Industry
   Seoul, Korea
   Counsel or consultant:
   Reid & Priest

Korea Plastic Goods Exporters Ass'n
   Seoul, Korea
   Counsel or consultant:
   Internat'l Business and Economic Research Corp.

Korea Tacoma Marine Industries Inc.
   Masan, Korea
   Counsel or consultant:
   Murphy and Demory, Ltd. (Admiral Daniel J. Murphy,
   USN (Ret.), Jeffrey J. Grieco)

Korea Textile Manufacturers Ass'n
   Seoul, Korea
   Counsel or consultant:
   Wyman, Bautzer, Christensen, Kuchel and Silbert

Korea Trade Center
   1129 20th St. N.W. 4th Floor, Washington, DC 20036

ORGANIZATIONS REPRESENTED

Korea Trade Center (Cont'd)
Telephone: (202) 857-7919
Background: A Korean governmental agency based in
Seoul with 76 offices worldwide, including 6 U.S. cities.
The Washington office is involved primarily with report-
ing trade policy developments.
Represented by:
Don Young Cho, Director
Robert E. Cunningham, Jr., Legislative Analyst

Korean Air Lines
Seoul, Korea
Counsel or consultant:
Hopkins and Sutter (William D. Phillips)
Zuckert, Scoutt and Rasenberger (James L. Devall)

Korean Overseas Information Service
Seoul, Korea
Counsel or consultant:
AEA Washington, Ltd. (Daryl M. Plunk, Kenneth E.
Sheffer, Jr.)

Korean Soybean Processors Ass'n
Seoul, Korea
Counsel or consultant:
Hogan and Hartson

KOTA-TV
Rapid City, SD
Counsel or consultant:
Fisher, Wayland, Cooper and Leader

Koyo Seiko
Osaka, Japan
Counsel or consultant:
Powell, Goldstein, Frazer and Murphy (Peter Suchman)

KPAX-TV
Missoula, MT
Counsel or consultant:
Reddy, Begley and Martin

KPLR-TV
St. Louis, MO
Counsel or consultant:
Koteen and Naftalin

KPMG Peat Marwick
2001 M St., N.W., Washington, DC 20036
Telephone: (202) 467-3846
Represented by:
Kathy G. Houser, Manager
John E. Hunnicutt, Partner
Counsel or consultant:
Newmyer Associates, Inc.

KPOB-TV
Harrisburg, IL
Counsel or consultant:
Pepper and Corazzini

KPOM-TV
Fort Smith, AR
Counsel or consultant:
Fletcher, Heald and Hildreth

KPRY-TV
Pierre, SD
Counsel or consultant:
Marmet and McCombs, P.C.

KPVI
Pocatello, ID
Counsel or consultant:
Hopkins and Sutter (John P. Bankson, Jr.)

Kraft General Foods, Inc.
1341 G St., N.W., 9th Floor, Washington, DC 20005
Telephone: (202) 637-1540
Represented by:
Linda Leigh Bartlett, Director, Federal Government Af-
fairs
Sally S. Donner, Manager, Federal Government Relations
Robert A. Wait, V. President, Federal Government Af-
fairs

KRBK-TV
Sacramento, CA
Counsel or consultant:
Cohn and Marks

KRC Research and Consulting
New York, NY
Counsel or consultant:
Wunder, Ryan, Cannon & Thelen (Michael A. Forscey)

KRDO-TV
Colorado Springs, CO
Counsel or consultant:
Fletcher, Heald and Hildreth

KREM-TV
Spokane, WA
Counsel or consultant:
Fletcher, Heald and Hildreth

KREN-TV
Reno, NV
Counsel or consultant:
Fletcher, Heald and Hildreth

KREQ
Arcata, CA
Counsel or consultant:
Arter & Hadden

KRGV-TV
Weslaco, TX
Counsel or consultant:
Cohn and Marks

KRLR
Las Vegas, NV
Counsel or consultant:
Miller and Fields

KROC-TV
Rochester, MN
Counsel or consultant:
Cordon and Kelly

KRON-TV
San Francisco, CA
Counsel or consultant:
Fletcher, Heald and Hildreth

Kronos, Inc.
Houston, TX
Counsel or consultant:
Ottosen and Associates (Karl J. Ottosen, Carla L. Saun-
ders)

Krupp Internat'l
West Germany
Counsel or consultant:
Coudert Brothers (Milo C. Coerper)

KSCH-TV
Stockton, CA
Counsel or consultant:
Fletcher, Heald and Hildreth

KSFY-TV
Sioux Falls, SD
Counsel or consultant:
Marmet and McCombs, P.C.

KSGW-TV
Sheridan-Gillett, WY
Counsel or consultant:
Fisher, Wayland, Cooper and Leader

KSL-TV
Salt Lake City, UT
Counsel or consultant:
Wilkinson, Barker, Knauer and Quinn

KSMQ-TV
Austin, TX
Counsel or consultant:
Cohn and Marks

KSMS-TV
Monterey, CA
Counsel or consultant:
Fletcher, Heald and Hildreth

KSNF-TV
Joplin, MO
Counsel or consultant:
Cohn and Marks

KSTP-TV
St. Paul, MN

Counsel or consultant:
Fletcher, Heald and Hildreth

KTBS-TV
Shreveport, LA
Counsel or consultant:
Fletcher, Heald and Hildreth

KTEN
Ada, OK
Counsel or consultant:
Fletcher, Heald and Hildreth

KTKA
Topeka, KS
Counsel or consultant:
Cohn and Marks

KTMA-TV
Minneapolis, MN
Counsel or consultant:
Marmet and McCombs, P.C.

KTNV-TV
Las Vegas, NV
Counsel or consultant:
Crowell and Moring

KTNW
Richland, WA
Counsel or consultant:
Cohn and Marks

KTSP-TV
Phoenix, AZ
Counsel or consultant:
Koteen and Naftalin

KTTY
Chula Vista, CA
Counsel or consultant:
Hopkins and Sutter (John P. Bankson, Jr.)

KTUU
Anchorage, AK
Counsel or consultant:
Fisher, Wayland, Cooper and Leader

KTVB
Boise, ID
Counsel or consultant:
Fisher, Wayland, Cooper and Leader
Fletcher, Heald and Hildreth

KTVH
Hutchinson, KS
Counsel or consultant:
Reddy, Begley and Martin

KTVM
Butte, MT
Counsel or consultant:
Cohn and Marks

KTVN
Reno, NV
Counsel or consultant:
Cohn and Marks

KTVV
Austin, TX
Counsel or consultant:
Koteen and Naftalin

KTXA
Ft. Worth, TX
Counsel or consultant:
Koteen and Naftalin

KTXH
Houston, TX
Counsel or consultant:
Koteen and Naftalin

KTXS-TV
Abilene, TX
Counsel or consultant:
Arter & Hadden

KUAC-TV
Fairbanks, AK
Counsel or consultant:
Cohn and Marks

The listings in this directory are available as *Mailing Labels*. See last page.

Kuehne and Nagel, Inc.
Hamburg, Germany
Counsel or consultant:
Robert N. Meiser, P.C.

KUPK-TV
Garden City, KS
Counsel or consultant:
Fletcher, Heald and Hildreth

KUSI
San Diego, CA
Counsel or consultant:
Fletcher, Heald and Hildreth

KUSK
Phoenix, AZ
Counsel or consultant:
Cohn and Marks

Kutak Rock & Campbell Political Action Committee
1101 Connecticut Ave., N.W., Washington, DC 20036
Telephone: (202) 828-2400
Counsel or consultant:
Kutak Rock & Campbell (Nancy L. Granese)

Kuwait Airways
Safat, Kuwait
Counsel or consultant:
Dickstein, Shapiro and Morin (G. Joseph Minetti, Walter J. Walvick)

Kuwait, Government of
Safat, Kuwait
Counsel or consultant:
Milbank, Tweed, Hadley & McCloy

KVCR-TV
San Bernardino, CA
Counsel or consultant:
Tierney & Swift (John L. Tierney)

KVCT-TV
Victoria, TX
Counsel or consultant:
Cohn and Marks

KVOS-TV
Bellingham, WA
Counsel or consultant:
Rubin, Winston and Diercks

KWAB-TV
Big Spring, TX
Counsel or consultant:
Koteen and Naftalin

KWCH
Wichita, KS
Counsel or consultant:
Marmet and McCombs, P.C.

KWET-TV
Cheyenne, WY
Counsel or consultant:
Cohn and Marks

KWHB
Tulsa, OK
Counsel or consultant:
Pepper and Corazzini

KWHY-TV
Los Angeles, CA
Counsel or consultant:
Cohn and Marks

KWSU-TV
Pullman, WA
Counsel or consultant:
Cohn and Marks

KWTV
Oklahoma City, OK
Counsel or consultant:
Fletcher, Heald and Hildreth

KWTX-TV
Waco, TX
Counsel or consultant:
Cordon and Kelly

KXAS-TV
Ft. Worth, TX
Counsel or consultant:
Koteen and Naftalin

KXII
Ardmore, OK
Counsel or consultant:
Cordon and Kelly

KXLN-TV
Rosenberg, TX
Counsel or consultant:
Mullin, Rhyne, Emmons and Topel, P.C.

KXMA-TV
Dickinson, ND
Counsel or consultant:
Fisher, Wayland, Cooper and Leader

KXMB
Bismarck, ND
Counsel or consultant:
Fisher, Wayland, Cooper and Leader

KXMC-TV
Minot, ND
Counsel or consultant:
Fisher, Wayland, Cooper and Leader

KXMD-TV
Williston, ND
Counsel or consultant:
Fisher, Wayland, Cooper and Leader

KXRM-TV
Colorado Springs, CO
Counsel or consultant:
Cohn and Marks

KXTX-TV
Dallas, TX
Counsel or consultant:
Fisher, Wayland, Cooper and Leader

Kyocera Corp.
Kyoto, Japan
Background: An industrial ceramics manufacturer. U.S. office in San Diego, CA.
Counsel or consultant:
Global USA, Inc. (William H. Morris, Jr.)

K17BA
Eureka, CA
Counsel or consultant:
Fletcher, Heald and Hildreth

K21AG
Wailuku, HI
Counsel or consultant:
Fletcher, Heald and Hildreth

K45AC
Wenatchee, WA
Counsel or consultant:
Fletcher, Heald and Hildreth

Lab Support, Inc.
Counsel or consultant:
McKevitt Group, The

Labatt Limited, John
London, Ontario
Counsel or consultant:
Strategic Policy, Inc. (William S. Merkin)

Labor Council for Latin American Advancement
815 16th St., N.W. Suite 707, Washington, DC 20006
Telephone: (202) 347-4223
Background: A Hispanic trade union association representing about 40 unions in 80 chapters throughout the country. Linked to the AFL-CIO in working for voter registration, education and participation by Hispanic workers.
Represented by:
Alfredo C. Montoya, Exec. Director

Labor-Industry Coalition for Internat'l Trade
1775 Pennsylvania Ave., N.W. Suite 500, Washington, DC 20006
Telephone: (202) 862-1000
Background: A coalition of major industrial companies, including Allied Signal, Corning Glass, BF Goodrich and W.R. Grace - and 11 labor organizations. Seeks trade

policy changes and other measures to help U.S. industry to compete more effectively against foreign industry. The above address is that of the law firm of Dewey, Ballantine, Bushby, Palmer and Wood.
Counsel or consultant:
Dewey, Ballantine, Bushby, Palmer and Wood (Alan W. Wolff)

Labor Institute of Public Affairs
815 16th St., N.W., Suite 206, Washington, DC 20006
Telephone: (202) 637-5334
Background: The television production arm of the AFL-CIO.
Represented by:
William H. Wagner, Exec. Director

Labor Policy Ass'n
1015 15th St., N.W. Suite 1200, Washington, DC 20005
Telephone: (202) 789-8670
Background: President is Jeffrey C. McGuiness (see McGuiness and Williams).
Counsel or consultant:
McGuiness and Williams (Jeffrey C. McGuiness)
Rowland & Sellery (J. Patrick Rowland)

Laborers' Internat'l Union of North America
905 16th St., N.W., Washington, DC 20006
Telephone: (202) 737-8320
Represented by:
Arthur A. Coia, General Secretary - Treasurer
Jack Curran, Legislative Director
Angelo Fosco, General President
Donald Kaniewski, Assistant to the Legislat. Director
Counsel or consultant:
Connerton, Ray and Simon (Robert J. Connerton)

Lac du Flambeau Chippewa Tribe
Lac du Flambeau, MI
Counsel or consultant:
Karl A. Funke and Associates (Karl A. Funke)

Lac Vieux Desert Tribe
Watersmeet, MI
Counsel or consultant:
Karl A. Funke and Associates (Karl A. Funke)

Laclede Gas Co.
St. Louis, MO
Counsel or consultant:
Bryan, Cave, McPheeters and McRoberts (James J. Murphy)

LADECO
Santiago, Chile
Counsel or consultant:
Zuckert, Scoutt and Rasenberger (Charles J. Simpson, Jr.)

Laguna Beach, California, City of
Laguna Beach, CA
Counsel or consultant:
E. Del Smith, Inc. (E. Del Smith)

Laidlaw, Inc.
1155 Connecticut Ave., N.W., Suite 300, Washington, DC 20036
Telephone: (202) 429-6533
Represented by:
John A. King, Director
Counsel or consultant:
Swidler & Berlin, Chartered (Barry Direnfeld, Barry L. Malter)

L'Air Liquide
Paris, France
Counsel or consultant:
Coudert Brothers (Robert A. Lipstein)

Lake Andes-Wagner Water Systems, Inc.
Wagner, SD
Counsel or consultant:
Duncan, Weinberg, Miller & Pembroke, P.C. (Frederick L. Miller, Jr., Edward Weinberg)

Lake Charles Harbor and Terminal District
Lake Charles, LA
Counsel or consultant:
Schmeltzer, Aptaker and Sheppard (Edward J. Sheppard, IV)

Lake County Job Training Corp.
Lake County, IN

Lake County Job Training Corp. (Cont'd)
Counsel or consultant:
Krivit and Krivit (Daniel H. Krivit)

LAM Research Corp.
Fremont, CA
Counsel or consultant:
Ashby and Associates

La Metalli Industriale S.p.A.
Florence, Italy
Counsel or consultant:
Cleary, Gottlieb, Steen and Hamilton (Richard deC. Hinds, Daniel B. Silver)

Land Improvement Contractors of America
Maywood, IL
Counsel or consultant:
Strother and Hosking Associates (Michael E. Strother)

Land O'Lakes, Inc.
Arden Hills, MN
Counsel or consultant:
Leighton and Regnery

Landmark Hotel Corp.
Topeka, KS
Counsel or consultant:
Bergner, Boyette & Bockorny, Inc. (David A. Bockorny, Van R. Boyette)

Landmark Legal Foundation Center for Civil Rights
216 G St., N.E., Washington, DC 20002
Telephone: (202) 546-6045
Background: Known as a conservatively-oriented organization on civil rights issues.
Represented by:
Clint Bolick, Director

Landscape Architecture Foundation
4401 Connecticut Ave., N.W. Suite 500, Washington, DC 20009
Telephone: (202) 686-0068
Represented by:
Mary Hanson, Director

Lansing, Michigan, Department of Social Services
Lansing, MI
Counsel or consultant:
Covington and Burling (Thomas S. Williamson, Jr.)

Laredo, Texas, City of
Counsel or consultant:
Miller and Holbrooke

Large Public Power Council
New York, NY
Background: A coalition of the nation's largest public power entities.
Counsel or consultant:
Black, Manafort, Stone and Kelly Public Affairs Co. (Nicholas A. Panuzio)

Larry Jones Ministries
Oklahoma City, OK
Counsel or consultant:
Hill and Knowlton Public Affairs Worldwide (Diana Aldridge, Tamara Cox)

Las Vegas, Nevada, City of
Counsel or consultant:
Alcalde & Rousselot (Hector Alcalde)

Las Vegas Paiute Indian Tribe
Las Vegas, NV
Counsel or consultant:
Lachelli, Waller and Associates (Vincent P. Lachelli)

LaSalle Partners Inc.
Chicago, IL
Counsel or consultant:
Mayer, Brown and Platt (Jerry L. Oppenheimer)

Latin American Management Ass'n
Washington, DC
Counsel or consultant:
MacKenzie McCheyne, Inc. (I. R. MacKenzie)
McAuliffe, Kelly, Raffaelli & Siemens (Lynnette R. Jacquez)

Latin American Manufacturers Ass'n
419 New Jersey Ave., S.E., Washington, DC 20003
Telephone: (202) 546-3803
Background: National trade association promoting Hispanic enterprise, industry, and technology. Founded in 1973.
Represented by:
Albert S. Jacquez, President

Latin American Manufacturers Ass'n Political Action Committee
419 New Jersy Ave., S.E., Washington, DC 20003
Telephone: (202) 546-3803
Background: Treasurer and contact is Albert S. Jacquez of the Latin American Manufacturers Ass'n.

Lauder Inc., Estee
New York, NY
Counsel or consultant:
Williams and Jensen, P.C. (George D. Baker)

Laurel Industries
Cleveland, OH
Counsel or consultant:
Jones, Day, Reavis and Pogue (James A. Wilderotter)

Law Related Education
Washington, DC
Background: A not-for-profit educational program.
Counsel or consultant:
Kirkpatrick & Lockhart (Robert R. Belair)

Lawler/Wood, Inc.
Knoxville, TN
Counsel or consultant:
Baker, Worthington, Crossley, Stansberry & Woolf (Edward R. Hamberger)

Lawyers Alliance for Nuclear Arms Control
1001 Pennsylvania Ave., N.W.,, Washington, DC 20004
Telephone: (202) 624-2755
Background: Washington chapter of a national group emphasizing the art of negotiation in nuclear arms control. Chairman and contact for the chapter is Phillip Fleming, a partner in the law firm of Crowell and Moring.
Represented by:
Ralph Earle, II, National Policy Director
Counsel or consultant:
Crowell and Moring (Philip A. Fleming)

Lawyers Co-operative Publishing Co.
Rochester, NY
Counsel or consultant:
Nixon, Hargrave, Devans and Doyle (Stephen Kurzman)

Lawyers' Committee for Civil Rights Under Law
1400 Eye St., N.W., Suite 400, Washington, DC 20005
Telephone: (202) 371-1212
Background: A national non-profit organization that works for the elimination of discrimination in areas of education, employment and voting rights through litigation in the courts under constitutional and civil rights laws.
Represented by:
Barbara R. Arnwine, Director
Gay McDougall, Director, Southern Africa Project
Frank R. Parker, Director, Voting Rights Project
Richard Seymour, Dir., Employment Discrimination Project

Lawyers for Civil Justice
1225 19th St., N.W. Suite 470, Washington, DC 20036
Telephone: (202) 479-0045
Background: A group of defense trial lawyers, manufacturers, insurers and traade associations seeking 'tort reform' legislation to protect companies against 'unfair' product liability claims. Members include AT&T, Exxon, General Motors, Ford, Pfizer and 3M. Associations included are the Internat'l Ass'n of Defense Counsel, the Federation of Insurance and Corporate Counsel, Defense Research Institute, and the Ass'n of Defense Trial Attorneys.
Represented by:
Barry H. Bauman, Exec. Director

Lawyers for the Republic
1025 Vermont Ave., N.W. Suite 900, Washington, DC 20005
Telephone: (202) 408-1990
Background: A nonprofit group providing information and advice on political redistricting issues. Has several links to the Republican Party. Principal activist is Robert E. Freer, Jr., an attorney with the law firm of Patterson, Belknap, Webb & Tyler from whose offices the group operates. Other Washington residents on the Board are attorneys Robert J. Horn of Detroit Edison Co. and Daniel J. Swillinger of Alagia, Day, Marshall, Mintmire and Chauvin.

Laxalt Washington Perito and Dubuc PAC
1120 Connecticut Ave., N.W. Suite 1000, Washington, DC 20036
Telephone: (202) 857-4000
Counsel or consultant:
Laxalt, Washington, Perito & Dubuc (Robert B. Washington, Jr.)

Lazard Freres
New York, NY
Counsel or consultant:
Dow, Lohnes and Albertson (Bernard J. Long, Jr.)
Peyser Associates, Inc.
Segermark Co., The

Lazare Kaplan International, Inc.
New York, NY
Counsel or consultant:
Marlowe and Co.

LBG Political Action Committee of Burgum & Grimm Ltd.
106 North Carolina Ave., S.E., Washington, DC 20003
Telephone: (202) 546-3414
Counsel or consultant:
Burgum & Grimm, Ltd. (Cynthia Lebrun-Yaffe)

Lead Industries Ass'n
New York, NY
Counsel or consultant:
Prather, Seeger, Doolittle and Farmer (Kurt E. Blase, Edwin H. Seeger)

Leadership America
700 North Fairfax St., Suite 302, Alexandria, VA 22314
Telephone: (703) 549-1102
Background: Represented by Martha P. Farmer (see Foundation for Women's Resources).

Leadership Conference on Civil Rights
2027 Massachusetts Ave., N.W., Washington, DC 20036
Telephone: (202) 667-1780
Background: Founded in 1950, a coalition of 185 national civil rights, labor, religious, civic, and professional groups that have joined together to work for federal legislation and executive action to assure full equality for all Americans. Particularly active in working for the enactment and enforcement of federal legislation that guarantees the rights of minorities, women, the disabled and senior citizens.
Represented by:
Mimi Mager, Grass Roots Coordinator
Ralph Graham Neas, Exec. Director

Leadership Foundation
P.O. Box 280, Cabin John, MD 20818
Telephone: (301) 229-8400
Background: Founded in 1965. A conservative citizen's organization concerned with the need to revitalize the economy, strengthen national security and defense and halt America's moral decline.
Represented by:
Martha Rountree, President

Leaf Tobacco Exporters Ass'n
Raleigh, NC
Counsel or consultant:
Dorsey & Whitney

League of Conservation Voters
1150 Connecticut Ave., N.W. Suite 501, Washington, DC 20036
Telephone: (202) 785-8683
Background: Established in 1970, LCV is the national, non-partisan arm of the environmental movement. LCV works to elect pro- environmental candidates to Congress. LCV ratings are based on key votes concerning energy, environment, and natural resource issues. The votes are selected by leaders from major national environmental organizations.
Represented by:
Anna Goldrich, Assistant to the Director
James D. Maddy, Exec. Director

League of United Latin American Citizens
777 N. Capitol St., N.E. Suite 305, Washington, DC 20002
Telephone: (202) 408-0060

ORGANIZATIONS REPRESENTED

Background: Founded in 1929 to encourage civic groups to assist underprivileged and unrepresented Hispanic Americans.
Represented by:
Jose Longoria, Exec. Director

League of Women Voters of the United States
1730 M St., N.W., Tenth Floor, Washington, DC 20036
Telephone: (202) 429-1965
Background: A voluntary, non-partisan, grass roots organization established in 1920 "to promote political responsibility through informed and active participation of citizens in government." The League now has over 250,000 members and supporters.
Represented by:
Mary E. Brooks, Senior Lobbyist
Stephanie Drea, Communications Director
Elizabeth Lawson, Senior Lobbyist
Lloyd J. Leonard, Legislative Director
Ellen Mazer, Grassroots Lobbying Specialist
Nancy M. Neuman, President
Kathy Shulman, Grassroots Coordinator
Counsel or consultant:
Arnold & Porter (Brooksley E. Born)

Learjet Corp.
1825 Eye St., Suite 400, Washington, DC 20006
Telephone: (202) 331-1610
Represented by:
James R. Dunbar, Director, Washington Operations

Leather Industries of America
1000 Thomas Jefferson St. N.W., Suite 515, Washington, DC 20007
Telephone: (202) 342-8086
Background: Formerly the Tanners' Council of America.
Represented by:
Charles Myers, President
Counsel or consultant:
Collier, Shannon & Scott (Thomas F. Shannon)

Lebanese Information and Research Center
1730 M St., N.W., Suite 807, Washington, DC 20036
Telephone: (202) 785-6666
Background: Promotes the views of the Christian 'Lebanese Forces' in the Lebanese civil war.
Represented by:
Robert Farah, Exec. Director

Lederle Laboratories, American Cyanamid Co. Subsidiary
1575 Eye St., N.W., Suite 200, Washington, DC 20005
Telephone: (202) 789-1222
Background: Represented by Dack Dalrymple of the American Cyanamid Co. office.
Counsel or consultant:
Bonner & Associates
Fox, Bennett and Turner (Allan M. Fox, Samuel D. Turner)
Hill and Knowlton Public Affairs Worldwide (Jason Rubin)
Hyman, Phelps and McNamera (Roger Theis)
Sutherland, Asbill and Brennan (Joel E. Hoffman)
Wilmer, Cutler and Pickering (Ronald J. Greene)

Lee Company, Thomas H.
Boston, MA
Counsel or consultant:
Cassidy and Associates, Inc. (Thomas M. Gannon)

Leech Lake Reservation Business Committee
Cass Lake, MN
Background: An Indian tribal government.
Counsel or consultant:
Forrest Gerard & Associates (Forrest J. Gerard)

Lees Co, J B & S
West Bromwich, England
Counsel or consultant:
L. A. Motley and Co. (Langhorne A. Motley)

Legal Services Corp.
400 Virginia Ave., S.W., Washington, DC 20024
Telephone: (202) 863-1820
Background: A non-profit organization funded by the federal government that provides attorneys for those who cannot afford private attorneys in civil cases.

Represented by:
James Cardel, Manager of Government Affairs
David Eisner, Public Affairs Manager
Timothy B. Shea, General Counsel
Terrance J. Wear, President
James M. Wootton, Director, Policy Develpmnt & Communic.

Legal Services Reform Coalition
c/o Keene, Shirley & Assoc. 919 Prince St., Alexandria, VA 22314
Telephone: (703) 684-0550
Counsel or consultant:
Keene, Shirley & Associates, Inc. (David A. Keene)

Leggett & Platt
Carthage, MO
Counsel or consultant:
Winburn, VanScoyoc, and Hooper (John P. Winburn)

Lehigh University
Betheleham, PA
Counsel or consultant:
Cassidy and Associates, Inc. (Robert K. Dawson, Vincent M. Versage)

Lehn & Fink Products Group
Montvale, NJ
Counsel or consultant:
Crowell and Moring (Dana C. Contratto)

Lehndorff & Babson Real Estate Counsel
Dallas, TX
Counsel or consultant:
Mayer, Brown and Platt (Jerry L. Oppenheimer)

Lembaga Bantuan Pemesaran & Manajemen
Jakarta, Indonesia
Counsel or consultant:
World Trade Link

Leprino Foods, Inc.
Denver, CO
Counsel or consultant:
Leighton and Regnery (Richard J. Leighton)

Lesotho, Government of
Maseru, Lesotho
Counsel or consultant:
van Kloberg and Associates (Edward J. van Kloberg, III)

Leukemia Soc. of America
2900 Eisenhower Ave. Suite 419, Alexandria, VA 22314
Telephone: (703) 960-1100
Represented by:
David Timko, Exec. Director, National Capital Area

Lever Brothers Co.
New York, NY
Counsel or consultant:
Burson-Marsteller (J. Gordon Stephens, Jr.)

Levi Strauss and Co.
San Francisco, CA
Counsel or consultant:
Akin, Gump, Strauss, Hauer and Feld (Richard Rivers)

Liaison Committee of Cooperating Oil and Gas Ass'ns
5914 Woodley Road, McLean, VA 22101
Telephone: (703) 532-3320
Counsel or consultant:
Elmer L. Hoehn

Libbey Glass
Toledo, OH
Counsel or consultant:
Stewart and Stewart (Terrence P. Stewart)

Libbey-Owens-Ford Co.
Toledo, OH
Counsel or consultant:
Rowland & Sellery (Amy B. Kimball, William C. Sellery, Jr.)

Liberia, Nat'l Bank of
Monrovia, Liberia
Counsel or consultant:
Mitchell, Friedlander & Gittleman (James S. Friedlander, Patrick H. Mitchell)

Liberty Homes, Inc.
Goshen, IN
Counsel or consultant:
Casey, Scott, Canfield & Heggestad (Edward F. Canfield)

Liberty Lobby
300 Independence Ave., S.E., Washington, DC 20003
Telephone: (202) 546-5611
Background: Founded in 1955 by Willis A. Carto and a group of supporters in California. Describes itself as standing for "constitutionalism," "Americanism," "individualism," a "populist" domestic policy and a "nationalist" foreign policy.
Represented by:
Willis A. Carto, Treasurer
Anne Cronin, Secretary of Board of Policy
Vince Ryan, Chairman of the Board of Policy

Liberty Mutual Insurance Co.
Boston, MA
Counsel or consultant:
Olwine, Connelly, Chase, O'Donnell and Weyher (Robert L. Hoegle)

Liberty Shipping Group
Long Island, NY
Counsel or consultant:
Dyer, Ellis, Joseph & Mills
Fierce and Associates (Donald L. Fierce)
Robertson, Monagle and Eastaugh (Steven W. Silver)

Library Users of America
1010 Vermont Ave., N.W., Suite 1100, Washington, DC 20005
Telephone: (202) 393-3666
Background: Represented by Roberta Douglas of the American Council of the Blind.

Licensed Beverage Information Council
1225 Eye St., N.W. Suite 500, Washington, DC 20005
Telephone: (202) 682-4775
Background: A consortium of national trade asociations sponsoring alcohol and health education programs. Chairman is John Burcham of the Nat'l Liquor Stores Ass'n.
Represented by:
Monita W. Fontaine, Exec. Director

Life Card, Inc.
Towson, MD
Counsel or consultant:
Dow, Lohnes and Albertson (Arnold P. Lutzker)

Lifecare Services Co.
Des Moines, IA
Counsel or consultant:
Dow, Lohnes and Albertson (Jeffrey Kurzweil)

Liga Agricola Industrial de la Cana de Azucar (LAICA)
San Jose, Costa Rica
Counsel or consultant:
Rogers and Wells (Eugene T. Rossides)

Liggett Group, Inc.
Durham, NC
Counsel or consultant:
Webster and Sheffield (L. Andrew Zausner)

Lighter Ass'n, Inc.
888 17th St., N.W., Suite 900, Washington, DC 20006
Telephone: (202) 955-5550
Counsel or consultant:
Holland and Knight (David H. Baker)

Lilly and Co., Eli
1901 L. St., N.W. Suite 705, Washington, DC 20036
Telephone: (202) 955-5350
Represented by:
Irene M. Brandt, Government Affairs Associate
William J. Turenne, Director of Government Relations
Counsel or consultant:
Barnes and Thornburg
Bergner, Boyette & Bockorny, Inc. (Jeffrey T. Bergner, Van R. Boyette)
Groom and Nordberg (Robert B. Harding, Carl A. Nordberg, Jr.)

Lin Broadcasting Corp.
New York, NY
Counsel or consultant:
Covington and Burling (Jonathan D. Blake)

ORGANIZATIONS REPRESENTED

Lincoln Group, The
Syracuse, NY
Counsel or consultant:
Kaye, Scholer, Fierman, Hays and Handler (Jason Shrinsky)

Lincoln Nat'l Life Insurance Co.
Fort Wayne, IN
Counsel or consultant:
Baker and Hostetler (Kenneth J. Kies)
Davis & Harman

Lincoln, Nebraska, City of
Counsel or consultant:
Nat'l Center for Municipal Development (Carolyn Chaney)

Lincoln Savings and Loan Ass'n
Phoenix, AZ
Counsel or consultant:
Bryan, Cave, McPheeters and McRoberts

Lineas Aereas Costarricicenes (Lasca Airlines)
San Jose, Costa Rica
Counsel or consultant:
Squire, Sanders and Dempsey (Robert D. Papkin, Edward W. Sauer)

Lineas Aereas del Caribe
Barranquilla, Colombia
Counsel or consultant:
Lord Day & Lord, Barrett Smith (Joanne W. Young)

Lineas Aereas Paraguayes (LAP)
Asuncion, Paraguay
Counsel or consultant:
Boros and Garofalo (Gary B. Garofalo)

Linguistic Soc. of America
1325 18th St., N.W., Suite 211, Washington, DC 20036-6501
Telephone: (202) 835-1714
Represented by:
Margaret W. Reynolds, Exec. Director

Linton, Mields Reisler and Cottone Political Action Committee
1225 Eye St., N.W., Suite 300, Washington, DC 20005
Telephone: (202) 682-3901
Counsel or consultant:
Linton, Mields, Reisler and Cottone (Mello Cottone)

Lipman Hearne
Chicago, IL
Counsel or consultant:
Jefferson Group, The (Ron Eisenberg)

Lipton Internat'l Players Championships
Coral Gables, FL
Counsel or consultant:
Vierra Associates, Inc. (Dennis C. Vierra)

LITEF GmbH
Freiburg, West Germany
Counsel or consultant:
Forster & Associates (Johann R. Forster)

LiTel Telecommunications Corp.
Worthington, OH
Counsel or consultant:
Cassidy and Associates, Inc. (C. Frank Godfrey, Jr.)

Litton Industries
490 L'Enfant Plaza East, S.W., Washington, DC 20024
Telephone: (202) 554-2570
Represented by:
John Georg, Manager, Public Relations
Walter P. Lukens, V. President

Lloyds of London, Underwriters at
London, England
Counsel or consultant:
Davis & Harman (Thomas A. Davis, Gail B. Wilkins)
Hogan and Hartson (Clifford S. Gibbons, Arthur J. Rothkopf, John S. Stanton)
LeBoeuf, Lamb, Leiby, and MacRae (Charles W. Havens, III)
Morgan, Lewis and Bockius

Lloyd's U.S.
Dallas, TX

Counsel or consultant:
McAuliffe, Kelly, Raffaelli & Siemens (John D. Raffaelli)

Lobbyists for Campaign Financing Reform
Care of Arnold & Porter, 1200 New Hampshire Ave., N.W., Washington, DC 20036
Telephone: (202) 872-6700
Background: A group in formation in early 1987 under the leadership of former Federal Trade Commission Chairman Michael Pertschuk to work for reform of campaign financing practices. Members are chiefly Washington lobbyists.
Counsel or consultant:
Arnold & Porter

Lockheed Corp.
1825 Eye St., N.W., Suite 1100, Washington, DC 20006
Telephone: (202) 955-3300
Represented by:
Tom Burbage, V. Pres., Wash. Off. (Aeronaut. Systems)
Hugh P. Burns, Dir., News and Information-Washington
H. Hollister Cantus, Group V. President (Missiles & Space)
Richard K. Cook, Vice President
James E. Kneale, Manager, Legislative Affairs
Donald C. Latham, President, Lockheed C31 Systems Division
Michael C. Mitchell, Legislative Affairs
W. C. Moller, Manager, Legislative Affairs
David S. Osterhout, V. President, Legislative Affairs
Michelle Robbins, Manager, Legislative Affairs
Counsel or consultant:
Ginn, Edington, Moore and Wade
Jefferson Group, The (David T. Crow, Robert L. Harris, Jack O. Nutter)
Parry and Romani Associates Inc.

Lockheed Missiles and Space Co.
Sunnyvale, CA
Counsel or consultant:
Hyman Fine & Associates Ltd.

Lockheed, Sanders Inc.
1735 Jefferson Davis Hwy., Suite 700, Arlington, VA 22202
Telephone: (703) 920-5204
Represented by:
W. George Chamberlin, Manager, Washington Operations
William Gureck, V. President, Field Operations

Lockwood Trade Journal
New York, NY
Counsel or consultant:
Chwat/Weigend Associates (John S. Chwat, Robert E. Weigend)

Loma Linda Foods
Riverside, CA
Counsel or consultant:
Johns and Carson

Loma Linda University
Loma Linda, CA
Counsel or consultant:
Cassidy and Associates, Inc. (Donald P. Smith)
Johns and Carson

London Commodity Exchange Co., Ltd.
London, England
Counsel or consultant:
Arnold & Porter (Brooksley E. Born, John M. Quinn, Daniel Waldman)

London Futures and Options Exchange
London, England
Counsel or consultant:
APCO Associates

London Internat'l Financial Futures Exchange
London England
Counsel or consultant:
Arnold & Porter

London Metal Exchange, Ltd.
London, England
Counsel or consultant:
Mayer, Brown and Platt

Londontown Corp.
Eldersburg, MD

Counsel or consultant:
Kaye, Scholer, Fierman, Hays and Handler (Christopher R. Brewster)

Lone Star Florida, Inc.
Ft. Lauderdale, FL
Background: A subsidiary of Lone Star Industries.
Counsel or consultant:
Smith, Heenan and Althen (Michael T. Heenan)

Lone Star Industries
Greenwich, CT
Counsel or consultant:
Fred B. Rooney
Smith, Heenan and Althen (Michael T. Heenan, David S. Smith)

Lone Star Steel Co.
Dallas, TX
Background: Manufacturer of steel pipe and tube products.
Counsel or consultant:
Akin, Gump, Strauss, Hauer and Feld (Warren E. Connelly, Angela J. Paolini)
Charls E. Walker Associates (Philip H. Potter)

Long Beach, California, City of
Counsel or consultant:
E. Del Smith, Inc. (E. Del Smith)

Long Beach, California, Port of
Long Beach, CA
Counsel or consultant:
E. Del Smith, Inc. (E. Del Smith)

Long Beach Naval Shipyard Employees Ass'n
Long Beach, CA
Counsel or consultant:
E. Del Smith, Inc. (E. Del Smith)

Long Beach Transit
Long Beach, CA
Counsel or consultant:
The Ferguson Co. (William Ferguson, Jr., Patricia Jordan, Thane Young)

Long Co. Bakery Cooperative, The W. E.
Chicago, IL
Counsel or consultant:
Robert N. Pyle & Associates

Long Island Ass'n
Commack, NY
Counsel or consultant:
Miller & Chevalier, Chartered (Leonard Bickwit, Jr.)

Long Island Coastal Alliance
New York, NY
Counsel or consultant:
Richard Curry and Associates (Richard C. Curry, Gerard Stoddard)

Long Island Lighting Co.
Hicksville, NY
Counsel or consultant:
Akin, Gump, Strauss, Hauer and Feld
Hunton and Williams

Long Island Rail Road Co.
Long Island City, NY
Counsel or consultant:
RBC Associates, Inc. (Ray B. Chambers)

Long Island Savings Bank
Melville, NY
Counsel or consultant:
Royer, Mehle & Babyak (Robert Stewart Royer)
Wilmer, Cutler and Pickering (Lloyd N. Cutler, Michael S. Helfer)

Long Lake Energy Corp.
New York, NY
Counsel or consultant:
Dawson and Associates, Mathis (Dawson Mathis)
Olwine, Connelly, Chase, O'Donnell and Weyher (W. Harrison Wellford)

Long Term Care Campaign
1334 G St., N.W., Suite 300, Washington, DC 20005
Telephone: (202) 628-3030

Represented by:
Deborah Briceland-Betts, Deputy Director
Michael Brogiola, Field Coordinator
Molly Daniels, Field Coordinator
Keith Tarr-Whelan, Director

Longview Fibre Co.
Longview, CO
Counsel or consultant:
Kogovsek & Associates, Inc.

Lonza Inc.
Fairlawn, NJ
Counsel or consultant:
Fried, Frank, Harris, Shriver & Jacobson (Henry A. Hubschman)

LOOP, Inc.
New Orleans, LA
Background: A corporation involved in the construction of a deepwater port.
Counsel or consultant:
Patton, Boggs and Blow (J. Gordon Arbuckle)

Lorain Community Hospital
Lorain, OH
Counsel or consultant:
Baker and Hostetler (Frederick H. Graefe)

Loral/Fairchild Systems
1111 Jefferson Davis Hwy. Suite 811, Arlington, VA 22202
Telephone: (703) 685-5300
Represented by:
Lois G. Bailey, Washington Rep., State & Commerce Depts.
John Marks, V. President, Regional Office
Frederick W. Rhodes, V. President, Legislative Relations
Paul D. Travesky, V. President, Strategic Technology
Counsel or consultant:
Akin, Gump, Strauss, Hauer and Feld (Joel Jankowsky)
Williams and Connolly (David D. Aufhauser, John Kester)

Lord Corp.
Erie, PA
Counsel or consultant:
Dunaway & Cross (Mac S. Dunaway)

Los Angeles, California, City of
Counsel or consultant:
Nat'l Center for Municipal Development (James F. Seeley)

Los Angeles, California, Department of Water and Power
Los Angeles, CA
Counsel or consultant:
Van Ness, Feldman & Curtis (Ben Yamagata)

Los Angeles Community Redevelopment Agency
Los Angeles, CA
Counsel or consultant:
Latham and Watkins (William C. Kelly, Jr.)
E. Del Smith, Inc. (E. Del Smith)

Los Angeles County, California
Counsel or consultant:
Jones, Day, Reavis and Pogue (Frieda K. Wallison)
E. Del Smith, Inc. (E. Del Smith)

Los Angeles County Museum of Art
Los Angeles, CA
Counsel or consultant:
Chernikoff and Co. (Larry Chernikoff)

Los Angeles County Museum of Natural History
Los Angeles CA
Counsel or consultant:
Chernikoff and Co. (Larry Chernikoff)

Los Angeles County Sanitation District
Whittier, CA
Counsel or consultant:
Jellinek, Schwartz, Connolly & Freshman, Inc. (John D. Freshman)

Los Angeles County Transportation Commission
Los Angeles, CA
Counsel or consultant:
Baker, Worthington, Crossley, Stansberry & Woolf (Edward R. Hamberger)

Los Angeles Raiders
El Segundo, CA
Counsel or consultant:
Hecht, Spencer & Associates (William H. Hecht)

Lotus Development Corp.
Boston, MA
Counsel or consultant:
Swidler & Berlin, Chartered (Bruce A. Lehman)

Loudoun County, Virginia
Leesburg, VA
Counsel or consultant:
Preston Gates Ellis & Rouvelas Meeds (Allen Erenbaum, Craig J. Gehring)

Louis Dreyfus Corp.
Wilton, CT
Counsel or consultant:
Willkie Farr and Gallagher (Christopher A. Dunn)

Louisiana Energy Services
600 New Hampshire Ave., N.W. Suite 404, Washington, DC 20037
Telephone: (202) 333-3254
Counsel or consultant:
Charlie McBride Assoc, Inc. (Charlie McBride, Stephanie Womack)

Louisiana Land and Exploration Co.
New Orleans, LA
Counsel or consultant:
Bracewell and Patterson (Gene E. Godley)
Cole, Corette & Abrutyn (Edward H. Lieberman)
Wampler and Associates

Louisiana Pacific Corp.
Portland, OR
Counsel or consultant:
Hopkins and Sutter (Steven C. Lambert)

Louisiana Power and Light Co.
New Orleans, LA
Counsel or consultant:
Reid & Priest
Shaw, Pittman, Potts and Trowbridge (Ernest L. Blake, Jr.)

Louisiana Public Facilities Authority
Baton Rouge, LA
Counsel or consultant:
Cassidy and Associates, Inc. (Gerald S. J. Cassidy, Dr. Frank A. Rose, Donald P. Smith)

Louisiana, State of
Baton Rouge, LA
Counsel or consultant:
Dickstein, Shapiro and Morin (Andrew P. Miller, Bernard Nash)

Louisiana Tanners
Baton Rouge, LA
Counsel or consultant:
DGM Internat'l Inc. (Donald E. Ellison)

Lower Colorado River Authority
Austin, TX
Counsel or consultant:
Van Ness, Feldman & Curtis (Robert R. Nordhaus)

Lower Columbia Regional Navy Task Force
Astoria, OR
Counsel or consultant:
Ball, Janik and Novack (Michelle E. Giguere)

Loyola College
Baltimore, MD
Counsel or consultant:
Cassidy and Associates, Inc. (James P. Fabiani, Vincent M. Versage)

Loyola Marymount University
Los Angeles, CA
Counsel or consultant:
Cassidy and Associates, Inc. (Thomas M. Gannon, C. Frank Godfrey, Jr.)

Loyola University of Chicago
Chicago, IL
Counsel or consultant:
Cassidy and Associates, Inc. (Andrea W. Bolling, C. Frank Godfrey, Jr.)

LTV Aircraft Products Group
1725 Jefferson Davis Hwy. Suite 900, Arlington, VA 22202
Telephone: (703) 521-6560
Background: A subsidiary of LTV Corp. Manufactures missiles, rockets, military vehicles, electronics, avionics, space systems and aerostructures for military and commercial aircraft.
Represented by:
Ned Carol, Dir., Washington Opns., Sierra Research
Douglas Crain, Dir., Wash. Office, Aircraft Prod. Grp.
Howard Fish, V. President, International
Paul Goncz, Director, Wash. Operations, AM General
Fred Haynes, V.P., Plng. & Anal., Miss. & Elect. Grp.
John C. McNerney, Dir., Wash. Off., Missiles Division
Grant Miller, Director, Legislative Affairs
Diane Smigel, Manager, Washington Public Affairs
Jack L. Stempler, V. President, Washington Operations
G. Wayne Tingle, Director, Legislative Affairs

LTV Corp.
1025 Thomas Jefferson St., N.W., Suite 511 West, Washington, DC 20007
Telephone: (202) 944-5700
Represented by:
Maxine C. Champion, V. President, Government Relations
Barbara M. Kostuk, Manager, Government Relations
Julian Scheer, Senior Vice President, Corporate Affairs
Gael M. Sullivan, Director, Federal Relations
Counsel or consultant:
Laxalt, Washington, Perito & Dubuc

LTV Corp. Active Citizenship Campaign
1025 Thomas Jefferson St., N.W., Suite 511-W, Washington, DC 20007
Telephone: (202) 944-5700
Background: Contact is Gael M. Sullivan of LTV Corp.

LTV Tubular
Youngstown, OH
Counsel or consultant:
Schagrin Associates (Carol A. Colza, Roger B. Schagrin)

Lubbock, Brownfield, Floyada and Tulia, Texas, Municipalities of
Counsel or consultant:
Duncan, Weinberg, Miller & Pembroke, P.C. (Wallace L. Duncan, Robert Weinberg)

Lubbock Power and Light
Lubbock, TX
Counsel or consultant:
Duncan, Weinberg, Miller & Pembroke, P.C. (Wallace L. Duncan, Janice L. Lower, Robert Weinberg)

Lubrizol Corp.
Wickliffe, OH
Counsel or consultant:
Jones, Day, Reavis and Pogue

Lucas Aerospace Inc.
11150 Sunrise Valley Drive, Reston, VA 22091-4399
Telephone: (703) 264-1704
Represented by:
Frank Taylor, Director, Government Relations
Renate Zelko, Manager, Corporate Communications
Jim Zigel, Legal Counsel

Ludington, Michigan, City of
Counsel or consultant:
Preston Gates Ellis & Rouvelas Meeds (Craig J. Gehring)

Lufthansa German Airlines
1130 Connecticut Ave., N.W., Suite 800, Washington, DC 20037
Telephone: (202) 296-5604
Counsel or consultant:
Powell, Adams & Rinehart
Wilmer, Cutler and Fickering (James S. Campbell, Robert C. Cassidy, Jr., Dieter G. F. Lange, Carol F. Lee)

Luggage and Leather Goods Manufacturers of America
New York, NY
Counsel or consultant:
Economic Consulting Services Inc. (Mark W. Love, Deborah Swartz)

Lukens Steel, Inc. (Flex-0-Lite Div.)
St. Louis, MO

ORGANIZATIONS REPRESENTED

Lukens Steel, Inc. (Flex-0-Lite Div.) (Cont'd)
Counsel or consultant:
Arthur E. Cameron

Lumber Dealers Political Action Committee
40 Ivy St., S.E., Washington, DC 20003
Telephone: (202) 547-2230
Background: Sponsored by the Nat'l Lumber and Building Material Dealers Ass'n. Represented by Mark Gallant of the Association.

Lummi Indian Tribe
WA
Counsel or consultant:
SENSE, INC. (Joe Tallakson)

Lupus Foundation of America
1717 Massachusetts Ave., N.W., Suite 203, Washington, DC 20036
Telephone: (202) 328-4550
Represented by:
Frank Prennig, III, Director, Administration & Development

Lusk Company, The
Irvine, CA
Counsel or consultant:
Dutko & Associates (L. L. Hank Hankla)

Lutheran Office for Governmental Affairs/Evangelical Lutheran Church in America
122 C St., N.W. Suite 300, Washington, DC 20001
Telephone: (202) 783-7508
Represented by:
Kay S. Dowhower, H.H.D., Director
Dennis Frado, Assistant Director for Foreign Affairs
John Fredriksson, Asst. Dir. for Immig. and Refugee Affrs.
Rev. John Lillie, Assistant Director
Sarah Naylor, Assistant Director for Advocacy
Marian Nickelson, Assistant Director for Advocacy

Lutheran Resources Commission
5 Thomas Circle, N.W., Washington, DC 20005
Telephone: (202) 667-9844
Background: An agency of The Evangelical Lutheran Church in America and the Lutheran Church-Missouri Synod, the LRC acts as a central clearinghouse to provide consultation and resource development services for projects on behalf of participating church bodies and agencies. Includes the Presbyterian Church (USA) and the United Methodist Church. Publishes LRC NEWSBRIEFS, a monthly bulletin of grants and other resources.
Represented by:
Lloyd C. Foerster, Director

Lutheran Social Services Community Justice Ministries
2635 16th St., N.W., Washington, DC 20009
Telephone: (202) 232-6373
Represented by:
Barbara Solt, Director

LUZ, International
Los Angeles, CA
Background: A manufacturer of solar industrial equipment.
Counsel or consultant:
Morris J. Amitay, P.C.
Van Ness, Feldman & Curtis (Ross D. Ain, Jacob J. Lew)

Lykes Bros. Steamship Co.
1001 Connecticut Ave., N.W., Suite 1010, Washington, DC 20036
Telephone: (202) 659-3737
Represented by:
William V. Brierre, Jr., Senior V. President

Lykes Brothers, Inc.
Tampa, FL
Counsel or consultant:
Collier, Shannon & Scott (Paul C. Rosenthal)

LymphoMed Inc.
Rosemont, IL
Counsel or consultant:
APCO Associates (Neal M. Cohen)
Arnold & Porter

Lyon Moving and Storage Co.
Los Angeles, CA

Counsel or consultant:
Burwell, Hansen, Peters and Houston

M.A.R.S. Inc.
Missoula, MT
Counsel or consultant:
Paul Suplizio Associates (Paul E. Suplizio)

M&M/Mars, Inc.
6885 Elm St., McLean, VA 22101
Telephone: (703) 821-4900
Counsel or consultant:
Andrews' Associates, Inc. (Mark Andrews, Jacqueline Balk-Tusa)
Patton, Boggs and Blow (James R. Patton, Jr.)

MacAndrews & Forbes Holdings, Inc.
1001 Pennsylvania Ave., N.W. Suite 715 South Concourse, Washington, DC 20004
Telephone: (202) 628-2600
Represented by:
Marydale DeBor, Attorney
William J. Green, V. President, Government Relations
Counsel or consultant:
Akin, Gump, Strauss, Hauer and Feld
Hill and Knowlton Public Affairs Worldwide (Tom Hoog)
Skadden, Arps, Slate, Meagher and Flom (Gilbert Schwartz)
Swidler & Berlin, Chartered

Machine Tool Political Action Committee
7901 Westpark Dr., McLean, VA 22102
Telephone: (703) 893-2900
Background: Political action arm of NMBTA - The Ass'n for Manufacturing Technology. Treasurer and contact is James H. Mack of the Ass'n.

Machinery Dealers Nat'l Ass'n
1110 Spring St., Silver Spring, MD 20910
Telephone: (301) 585-9494
Represented by:
Darryl D. McEwen, Exec. V. President

Machinery Dealers Political Action Committee
1110 Spring St., Silver Spring, MD 20910
Telephone: (301) 585-9494
Background: Treasurer is Darryl D. McEwen of the Machinery Dealers Nat'l Ass'n.

Machinists Non-Partisan Political League
1300 Connecticut Ave., N.W. Suite 404, Washington, DC 20036
Telephone: (202) 857-5295
Background: A political action committee sponsored by the Internat'l Ass'n of Machinists and Aerospace Workers. Represented by William J. Holayter of the Ass'n.
Represented by:
Earl C. Robinson, Ass't Director

Mack Trucks, Inc.
1140 Connecticut Ave., N.W. Suite 804, Washington, DC 20036
Telephone: (202) 452-6004
Counsel or consultant:
Offices of V.J. Adduci (V. J. Adduci)
Donald Baldwin Associates (Donald Baldwin)
Schnader, Harrison, Segal and Lewis (Richard A. Penna)

Maclean Hunter Cable TV
Etobicoke, Ontario
Counsel or consultant:
Cohn and Marks (Allan Robert Adler, Ronald A. Siegel, Ian D. Volner)

MacMillan Publishing Co.
New York, NY
Counsel or consultant:
Skadden, Arps, Slate, Meagher and Flom (Jeffery M. Goldstein)

Macrovision
Mountain View, CA
Counsel or consultant:
Winthrop, Stimson, Putnam & Roberts (Ronna A. Freiberg, Ira S. Shapiro)

Madison Gas and Electric Co.
Madison, WI
Counsel or consultant:
Baker and Botts (Bruce F. Kiely)

Maersk Inc.
1667 K St., N.W., Suite 350, Washington, DC 20006
Telephone: (202) 887-6770
Represented by:
Mark R. Johnson, General Mgr.-Governmental Affairs
Lars T. Nyberg, V. President
Kristi Roos, Government Affairs Representative

Magazine Publishers of America
1211 Connecticut Ave., N.W. Suite 406, Washington, DC 20036
Telephone: (202) 296-7277
Represented by:
George Gross, Exec. V. President, Government Affairs
Counsel or consultant:
Davidson Colling Group, Inc., The (James H. Davidson)
David Minton

Magazine Publishers of America Political Action Committee
1211 Connecticut Ave., N.W. Suite 406, Washington, DC 20036
Telephone: (202) 296-7277
Background: Responsible contact is George Gross, Exec. V. President, Magazine Publishers of America.

Maglev Transit, Inc.
Tallahassee, FL
Counsel or consultant:
Direct Impact Co., The (John Brady, Gloria Dittus, Tom Herrity)

Maglev USA
c/o Concord Associates, Inc. 1455 Pennsylvania Ave., N.W., Washington, DC 20004
Telephone: (202) 737-9300
Counsel or consultant:
Concord Associates, Inc.

Magma Copper Corp.
San Manuel, AZ
Counsel or consultant:
Steptoe and Johnson
Webster and Sheffield (L. Andrew Zausner)

Magnavox Consumer Electronics Co.
Fort Wayne, IN
Counsel or consultant:
Collier, Shannon & Scott (Paul D. Cullen, David A. Hartquist, Thomas F. Shannon)

Magnavox Government and Industrial Electronics Co.
1700 North Moore St. Suite 820, Arlington, VA 22209
Telephone: (703) 522-9610
Represented by:
William Behan, Director, Government Relations
James Phifer, Manager, Congressional Affairs
Counsel or consultant:
Hyman Fine & Associates Ltd.

Magnetic Technologies Corp.
Rochester, NY
Counsel or consultant:
Fincke & White (Stephanie A. White)

Magnuson Act Coalition
Seattle, WA
Counsel or consultant:
Patton, Boggs and Blow (James B. Christian, Jr.)

Mail Advertising Service Ass'n Internat'l
1421 Prince St. Suite 200, Alexandria, VA 22314-2814
Telephone: (703) 836-9200
Represented by:
David A. Weaver, President
Counsel or consultant:
Caplin and Drysdale (Graeme Bush)

Maine Public Service Co.
Presque Isle, ME
Counsel or consultant:
Wright and Talisman

Mainstream
1030 15th St., N.W. Suite 1010, Washington, DC 20005
Telephone: (202) 898-1400
Background: An organization providing information and technical assistance to all concerned with "mainstreaming" handicapped people into the workplace.

ORGANIZATIONS REPRESENTED

Represented by:
Lawrence C. Pencak, Exec. Director

Majestic Realty Co.
City of Industry, CA
Counsel or consultant:
Silverstein and Mullens (James C. Corman)

Major League Baseball
New York, NY
Counsel or consultant:
Timmons and Co., Inc.

Major League Baseball Players Ass'n
New York, NY
Counsel or consultant:
Onek, Klein & Farr (Joseph N. Onek)

Makah Tribal Council
Neah Bay, WA
Counsel or consultant:
Denny Miller Associates

Malaysia, Government of
Kuala Lumpur, Malaysia
Counsel or consultant:
Dickstein, Shapiro and Morin

Malaysia Ministry of Trade
Kuala Lumpur, Malaysia
Counsel or consultant:
Willkie Farr and Gallagher (Walter J. Spak)

Malaysian Airline System
Kuala Lumpur, Malaysia
Counsel or consultant:
Zuckert, Scoutt and Rasenberger (Charles J. Simpson, Jr.)

Malaysian Rubber Bureau
1925 K St., N.W. Suite 204, Washington, DC 20006
Telephone: (202) 452-0544
Represented by:
Paul E. Hurley, President

Mall Properties, Inc.
New York, NY
Counsel or consultant:
Theodore L. Jones

Malrite Communications Group, Inc.
Cleveland, OH
Counsel or consultant:
Kaye, Scholer, Fierman, Hays and Handler (Jason Shrinsky)

Management Ass'n for Private Photogrammetric Surveyors
12020 Sunrise Valley Dr. Suite 100, Reston, VA 22091
Telephone: (703) 391-2739
Counsel or consultant:
John M. Palatiello & Assoc. (John M. Palatiello)

Management Ass'n for Private Photogrammetric Surveyors Political Action Committee
12020 Sunrise Valley Dr. Suite 100, Reston, VA 22091
Telephone: (703) 391-2739
Background: Formed by the Management Ass'n for Private Photogrammetric Surveyors to support candidates with records in support of the free enterprise system and other issues affecting the private surveying and mapping businesses.
Counsel or consultant:
John M. Palatiello & Assoc. (John M. Palatiello)

Management Insights, Inc.
Dallas, TX
Counsel or consultant:
Paul Suplizio Associates (Paul E. Suplizio)

Manassas, Virginia, City of
Counsel or consultant:
Spiegel and McDiarmid (Marc R. Poirier)

Manhattan Building Cos., Inc.
Tulsa, OK
Counsel or consultant:
Wexler, Reynolds, Fuller, Harrison and Schule, Inc. (Nancy Clark Reynolds)

Manhurin, S.A.
Mulhouse, France

Counsel or consultant:
Shaw, Pittman, Potts and Trowbridge (Steuart L. Pittman)

Maniilaq Ass'n
Kotzebue, AK
Counsel or consultant:
Hobbs, Straus, Dean and Wilder (S. Bobo Dean)

Manitoba, Province of
Winnipeg
Counsel or consultant:
Garvey, Schubert & Barer (Richard A. Wegman)

Manor Care
10750 Columbia Pike, Silver Spring, MD 20901
Telephone: (301) 593-9600
Represented by:
Ann McDermott, Director, Government Relations
Counsel or consultant:
Nat'l Strategies Inc.

Manor Healthcare Federal Political Action Committee
10750 Columbia Pike, Silver Spring, MD 20901
Telephone: (301) 593-9600
Background: Contact is Ann McDermott of the parent company, Manor Care.
Counsel or consultant:
Nat'l Strategies Inc.

ManTech Internat'l
2121 Eisenhower Ave., Alexandria, VA 22314
Telephone: (703) 838-5600
Counsel or consultant:
John G. Campbell, Inc.

Manufactured Housing Institute
1745 Jefferson Davis Hwy. Suite 511, Arlington, VA 22202
Telephone: (703) 979-6620
Represented by:
Bruce Butterfield, V. President, Public Affairs
Jerry C. Connors, President
William "Joe" Owens, V. President, Finance
Lois A. Starkey, V. President, Government Relations
Frank J. Walter, V. President, Technical Activities

Manufactured Housing Institute Political Action Committee
1745 Jefferson Davis Hwy., Arlington, VA 22202
Telephone: (703) 979-6620
Background: Responsible contact is Lois A. Starkey of the Manufactured Housing Institute.

Manufacturers' Alliance for Productivity and Innovation (MAPI)
1200 18th St., N.W. Suite 400, Washington, DC 20036
Telephone: (202) 331-8430
Background: The economic research organization and national spokesman for the capital goods and allied products industries. Members include makers of machinery, industrial equipment, tools, farm equipment, printing equipment, instruments and controls and companies in the aerospace, computer, electronics and telecommunications industries. etc.
Represented by:
Francis W. Holman, Jr., V. President and Secretary
Richard R. MacNabb, Senior V. President and Chief Economist
Kenneth McLennan, President
Peggy Morrissette, Director of Public and Gov't Affairs
Paul H. Pratt, Director of International Issues
Fred E. Shand, V. President, Membership Relations
Frederick T. Stocker, Counsel

Manufacturers Hanover Trust Co.
New York, NY
Counsel or consultant:
Hogan and Hartson (Arthur J. Rothkopf, John S. Stanton)
Manatt, Phelps, Rothenberg & Phillips (Robert J. Kabel)
Sagamore Associates, Inc. (David U. Gogol)

Manufacturers Life Insurance Co.
Toronto, Ontario
Counsel or consultant:
Leach, McGreevy, Eliassen & Leach (Daniel E. Leach)

Manufacturers Standardization Soc. of the Valve and Fitting Industry
127 Park St., N.E., Vienna, VA 22180
Telephone: (703) 281-6613

Represented by:
Olen Thornton, Exec. Director

Manufacturing Jewelers and Silversmiths of America, Inc.
Providence, RI
Counsel or consultant:
Thompson, Hine and Flory (Lewe B. Martin)

Manville Corp.
1625 K St., N.W., Suite 750, Washington, DC 20006
Telephone: (202) 785-4940
Represented by:
Joseph L. Lach, Manager, Government Marketing
Susan Petniunas, Manager, U.S. Government Affairs
David E. Pullen, Director, Public Affairs
Counsel or consultant:
Chambers Associates Incorporated (James N. Smith)
Davis Polk & Wardwell (Richard Moe)
Kendall and Associates (William T. Kendall)
Stockmeyer & Co. (Steven F. Stockmeyer)
Wunder, Ryan, Cannon & Thelen (Michael A. Forscey)

Manville Corp. Political Action Committee
1625 K St., N.W. Suite 750, Washington, DC 20006
Telephone: (202) 785-4940
Background: David E. Pullen of Manville Corp. serves as treasurer.

Maple Leaf Fish Co.
Wyandotte, MI
Counsel or consultant:
Barnes, Richardson and Colburn (David O. Elliott, Matthew T. McGrath)

Marathon Oil Co.
818 Connecticut Ave., N.W., Suite 900, Washington, DC 20006
Telephone: (202) 331-1340
Background: A subsidiary of USX Corp. Represented in Washington by Terrence D. Straub, Paula D. Freer, and Patricia M. Wilson, all of USX Corp.
Counsel or consultant:
O'Neill and Athy, P.C. (Andrew Athy, Jr.)
Patton, Boggs and Blow (Thomas Hale Boggs, Jr.)

March of Dimes
White Plains, NY
Counsel or consultant:
Powell, Adams & Rinehart

March of Dimes Birth Defects Foundation
1725 K St., N.W., Suite 814, Washington, DC 20006
Telephone: (202) 659-1800
Background: Works to eliminate the causes of all types of birth defects, including reducing incidence of low birth-weight and infant mortality. A member organization of the Coalition for Health Funding in Washington.
Represented by:
Anne Harrison-Clark, V. President for Public Affairs
Jo Merrill, Deputy Director - State Public Affairs
Loretta Morris Williams, Legislative Analyst

Marco Shipyard - Seattle
Seattle, WA
Counsel or consultant:
Ragan and Mason (William F. Ragan)

Marconi Communications Inc.
1930 Isaac Newton Square, Reston, VA 22090
Telephone: (703) 742-8083
Counsel or consultant:
Rothleder Associates, Inc. (Linda Rothleder)

Marianas Political Status Commission
Saipan, Marianas Islands
Counsel or consultant:
Wilmer, Cutler and Pickering

Marine Biological Laboratory
Woods Hole, MA
Counsel or consultant:
Ken Schlossberg Assoc. (Kenneth Schlossberg, Mary Silveira)

Marine Contractors Alliance
655 15th St., N.W., Suite 310, Washington, DC 20005
Telephone: (202) 828-1977
Counsel or consultant:
Washington Policy Advocates (Jeffrey C. Smith)

The listings in this directory are available as *Mailing Labels.* See last page.

601

Marine Corps League
8626 Lee Highway Suite 201, Fairfax, VA 22031
Telephone: (703) 207-9588
Represented by:
Robert N. Forsyth, Exec. Director

Marine Corps Reserve Officers Ass'n
201 North Washington St. Suite 206, Alexandria, VA 22314
Telephone: (703) 548-7607
Represented by:
Col. Laurence. Gaboury, USMC (Ret), Exec. Director

Marine Engineers Beneficial Ass'n
444 North Capitol St., N.W. Suite 800, Washington, DC 20001
Telephone: (202) 347-8585
Represented by:
C. E. De Fries, President
Carl Landgrebe, Special Assistant to the President
Counsel or consultant:
Dickstein, Shapiro and Morin (John C. Dill, Charles H. Morin)
F. Nordy Hoffmann & Assoc. (F. Nordy Hoffmann)
Keene, Shirley & Associates, Inc. (David A. Keene, Craigan P. Shirley)
Denny Miller Associates
Joseph S. Miller

Marine Engineers Beneficial Ass'n Political Action Fund
444 North Capitol St., N.W. Suite 800, Washington, DC 20001
Telephone: (202) 347-8585
Background: Supported by the Marine Engineers Beneficial Ass'n. Contact is Carl Landgrebe of the Ass'n.

Marine Engineers Beneficial Ass'n Retirees Group Fund
444 North Capitol St. Suite 800, Washington, DC 20001
Telephone: (202) 347-8585
Represented by:
Rauol A. Amador, Treasurer

Marine Mammal Coalition
Noank, CT
Background: An association of aquariums.
Counsel or consultant:
Wiley, Rein & Fielding (John A. Hodges, Paul C. Smith)

Marine Mammal Protection Fund
1725 DeSales St., N.W. Suite 500, Washington, DC 20036
Telephone: (202) 429-5609
Background: A project of the Center for Marine Conservation.
Represented by:
Nina M. Young, Director

Marine Management, Inc.
Seattle, WA
Counsel or consultant:
Preston Gates Ellis & Rouvelas Meeds (John L. Bloom, William N. Myhre)

Marine Midland Banks, Inc.
New York, NY
Counsel or consultant:
Hill and Knowlton Public Affairs Worldwide (John Doherty, David Miller)

Marine Resources Development Foundation
Key Largo, FL
Counsel or consultant:
G. Frank West

Marine Shale Processors, Inc.
Amelia, LA
Counsel or consultant:
Weil, Gotshal & Manges (Robert C. Odle, Jr.)

Marine Transport Overseas Services
New York, NY
Counsel or consultant:
Denning and Wohlstetter (Joseph F. Mullins, Jr.)

Marion Merrell Dow, Inc.
1776 Eye St., N.W. Suite 575, Washington, DC 20006
Telephone: (202) 429-3400
Background: A global, research-intensive pharmaceutical company devoted to the discovery, development, manufacturing and marketing of brand-name prescription and over-the-counter (non-prescription) medicines and other pharmaceutical products.
Represented by:
Ronald F. Docksai, V. President, Government Relations
George A. Sommers, Manager, Federal Government Affairs
Counsel or consultant:
Sullivan and Worcester

Maritima Transligra
Quito, Ecuador
Counsel or consultant:
Schmeltzer, Aptaker and Sheppard (Deana Francis Dudley, Suzanne Langford Sanford)

Maritime Institute for Research and Industrial Development
1133 15th St., N.W. Suite 600, Washington, DC 20005
Telephone: (202) 463-6505
Background: A research organization of the Internat'l Organization of Masters, Mates and Pilots American-flag shipping companies.
Represented by:
Sandra D. Kjellberg, Government Relations
C. James Patti, President
Stephen H. Wines, Special Assistant

Maritrans Operating Partners, L.P.
Philadelphia, PA
Counsel or consultant:
LeBoeuf, Lamb, Leiby, and MacRae (Austin P. Olney)

Marketing Education Ass'n
1908 Association Drive, Reston, VA 22091
Telephone: (703) 476-4299
Counsel or consultant:
White, Fine, and Verville (Richard A. Fulton)

Marlin Group, The
San Diego, CA
Counsel or consultant:
Highley & Associates (Vern F. Highley)

Marmon Group
Chicago, IL
Counsel or consultant:
Gilbert A. Robinson, Inc. (Gilbert A. Robinson)

Marriott Corp.
One Marriott Drive, Washington, DC 20058
Telephone: (301) 380-9000
Represented by:
Sterling D. Colton, Senior V. President and General Counsel
William D. Ladd, V. President, Government Affairs
Robert Allen Rankin, Jr., V. President, Corporate Relations
Robert T. Souers, V. President, Corporate Information
Counsel or consultant:
Dow, Lohnes and Albertson (Jeffrey Kurzweil)

Marriott Political Action Committee
One Marriott Drive, Washington, DC 20058
Telephone: (301) 380-1073
Background: Responsible contact is William D. Ladd of Marriott Corp.

Marshall Islands, Government of
Majuro, Marshall Islands
Counsel or consultant:
Coudert Brothers
Patton, Boggs and Blow (Theodore G. Kronmiller)

Martel Laboratory Services, Inc.
St. Petersburg, FL
Counsel or consultant:
Hopkins and Sutter (William D. Phillips)

Martin Luther King, Jr. Federal Holiday Commission
451 Seventh St, S.W. Suite 5182, Washington, DC 20410
Telephone: (202) 755-1005
Represented by:
Madeline Lawson, Deputy Director

Martin Marietta Corp.
6801 Rockledge Drive, Bethesda, MD 20817
Telephone: (301) 897-6000
Represented by:
K K Bigelow, V. President, Washington Operations
John T. de Visser, Director, Corporate Affairs
Phillip S. Giaramita, Exec. Director, Public Relations
Counsel or consultant:
Akin, Gump, Strauss, Hauer and Feld (Joel Jankowsky)
Ervin Technical Associates, Inc. (ETA) (James L. Ervin)
Griffin, Johnson & Associates
The Paul Laxalt Group (Paul Laxalt)
Laxalt, Washington, Perito & Dubuc

Martin Marietta Corp. Political Action Committee
6801 Rockledge Drive MP 337, Bethesda, MD 20817
Telephone: (301) 897-6164
Background: Represented by K K Bigelow, V. President Washington Operations, Martin Marietta Corp.

Martinair Holland
Amsterdam, Netherlands
Counsel or consultant:
Zuckert, Scoutt and Rasenberger (Frank J. Costello, Rachel B. Trinder)

Marubeni America Inc.
1615 L St., N.W., Suite 1215, Washington, DC 20036
Telephone: (202) 331-1167
Represented by:
Takeo Tanaka, Sr. V. President
Counsel or consultant:
Hill and Knowlton Public Affairs Worldwide

Marwais Steel Co.
Leesburg, VA
Counsel or consultant:
Hecht, Spencer & Associates (Bronwyn R. Bachrach, William H. Hecht, W. Timothy Locke)

Mary Jane Bakeries
Norfolk, VA
Counsel or consultant:
Robert N. Pyle & Associates

Mary Kay Cosmetics
Dallas, TX
Counsel or consultant:
Hill and Knowlton Public Affairs Worldwide (Steven A. Grossman)

Maryland, Aviation Administration of the State of
BWI Airport, MD
Counsel or consultant:
Preston Gates Ellis & Rouvelas Meeds (Susan B. Geiger)

Maryland Nat'l Bank
Baltimore, MD
Counsel or consultant:
Dow, Lohnes and Albertson (David F. Bantleon)

Maryland People's Counsel
Baltimore, MD
Counsel or consultant:
Porter, Wright, Morris and Arthur (E. Jay Finkel)

Maryland Washington Office, State of
444 N. Capitol St., N.W. Suite 315, Washington, DC 20001
Telephone: (202) 638-2215
Represented by:
Monica M. Healy, Director

Mashpee, Massachusetts, Town of
Counsel or consultant:
Hale and Dorr (James L. Quarles)

Massachusetts Ass'n of Community Health Agencies
Boston, MA
Counsel or consultant:
Cassidy and Associates, Inc. (James P. Collins)

Massachusetts Bankers Ass'n
Boston, MA
Counsel or consultant:
Thacher, Proffitt and Wood (Jeremiah S. Buckley)

Massachusetts, Commonwealth of
444 N. Capitol St., Suite 307, Washington, DC 20001
Telephone: (202) 628-1065
Represented by:
Kris M. Balderston, Director, Office of Fed.-State Relations

ORGANIZATIONS REPRESENTED

Massachusetts Corp. for Educational Telecommunications
Boston, MA
Counsel or consultant:
Cassidy and Associates, Inc. (Andrea W. Bolling, Vincent M. Versage)

Massachusetts General Hospital
Boston, MA
Counsel or consultant:
O'Neill and Athy, P.C. (Martha L. Casey)

Massachusetts Hospital Ass'n
Burlington, MA
Counsel or consultant:
O'Neill and Athy, P.C. (Martha L. Casey)

Massachusetts Housing Finance Agency
Boston, MA
Counsel or consultant:
Powell, Goldstein, Frazer and Murphy (Anthony S. Freedman)

Massachusetts League of Community Banks
Boston, MA
Counsel or consultant:
Cassidy and Associates, Inc. (James P. Collins)

Massachusetts Maritime Academy
Buzzards Bay, MA
Counsel or consultant:
Wexler, Reynolds, Fuller, Harrison and Schule, Inc. (Terry D. Bevels)

Massachusetts Mutual Life Insurance Co.
600 Pennsylvania Ave., N.W., Suite 601, Washington, DC 20004
Telephone: (202) 737-0440
Represented by:
Barry H. Gottehrer, Senior V. President, Public Affairs
Counsel or consultant:
Bracewell and Patterson (Michael L. Pate)
Dawson and Associates, Mathis (Dawson Mathis)
Patton, Boggs and Blow (John Jonas)

Massachusetts Port Authority
Boston, MA
Counsel or consultant:
Schmeltzer, Aptaker and Sheppard (Edward J. Sheppard, IV)

Massena, New York, Town of
Background: Duncan, Weinberg, Miller & Pembroke represents the municipal electric utility of Massena, NY.
Counsel or consultant:
Duncan, Weinberg, Miller & Pembroke, P.C. (Wallace L. Duncan, Jeffrey C. Genzer)

Massey Coal Services
Daniels, WV
Counsel or consultant:
Ryan-McGinn (Daniel McGinn)

Massport/Commonwealth of Massachusetts
Boston, MA
Counsel or consultant:
McAuliffe, Kelly, Raffaelli & Siemens (Edward E. Allison)

Masstock Internat'l Limited
Dublin, Ireland
Counsel or consultant:
Dow, Lohnes and Albertson (Philip C. Thompson)

Master Printers of America
1730 North Lynn St., Suite 805, Arlington, VA 22209
Telephone: (703) 841-8130
Background: Open Shop division of the Printing Industries of America.
Represented by:
Brian W. Gill, President

MasterCard Internat'l. Inc.
New York, NY
Counsel or consultant:
Morrison & Foerster (L. Richard Fischer, Robert M. Kurucza)
O'Connor & Hannan

Masters Championship, Inc.
Anchorage, AK

Counsel or consultant:
Pillsbury, Madison and Sutro

Masters, Mates and Pilots Political Contribution Fund
1133 15th St., N.W. Suite 600, Washington, DC 20005
Telephone: (202) 463-6505
Background: Sponsored by the Internat'l Organization of Masters, Mates and Pilots, the Marine Division of the Internat'l Longshoremen's Ass'n. C. James Patti, President of the Maritime Institute for Research and Industrial Development, serves as Washington Representative.

Mathematical Ass'n of America
1529 18th St., N.W., Washington, DC 20036
Telephone: (202) 387-5200
Represented by:
Marcia P. Sward, Exec. Director
Alfred B. Willcox, Head, Office of Gov'tl & Public Affairs

Matlack Systems, Inc.
Wilmington, DE
Counsel or consultant:
Evans Group, Ltd., The (L. A., Skip Bafalis, Thomas B. Evans, Jr., James R. Meltsner)

Matra Aerospace, Inc.
1213 Jefferson Davis Hwy. Crystal City IV, Suite 1102, Arlington, VA 22202
Telephone: (703) 979-3600
Represented by:
Gilbert Croze, President & CEO
Counsel or consultant:
Verner, Liipfert, Bernhard, McPherson and Hand, Chartered

Matson Navigation Co.
444 North Capitol St., Suite 514, Washington, DC 20001
Telephone: (202) 833-3555
Represented by:
Phillip M. Grill, V. President, Government Relations
Counsel or consultant:
Patton, Boggs and Blow (Alan A. Tuttle)

Matsushita Electric Corp. of America
1001 Pennsylvania Ave., N.W. Suite 1355 North, Washington, DC 20004
Telephone: (202) 347-7592
Represented by:
Mary Alexander, Manager, Government Affairs
M. McAllister, Government Affairs Coordinator
Masayuki Nakao, Senior Representative
Hall Northcott, Director, Government and Public Affairs
Mark J. Sharp, Manager, Government Affairs
Counsel or consultant:
Cole, Corette & Abrutyn (Robert T. Cole)
Patton, Boggs and Blow
Strategic Resources Corp.

Matsushita Electronic Corp.
Tokyo, Japan
Counsel or consultant:
Weil, Gotshal & Manges (Jeffrey P. Bialos, A. Paul Victor)

Mattel, Inc.
Hawthorne, CA
Counsel or consultant:
StMaxens and Co. (Thomas F. StMaxens, II)

Matteson Investment Corp.
Menlo Park, CA
Counsel or consultant:
Evans Group, Ltd., The (Thomas B. Evans, Jr., Susan Riley)

Maui Land and Pineapple Co., Inc.
Kahului, HI
Counsel or consultant:
Covington and Burling (William M. Paul)

Maule Air, Inc.
Moultrie, GA
Counsel or consultant:
Woods and Associates (Irvin M. Woods)

Mauritius, Chamber of Agriculture of
Port Louis, Mauritius

Counsel or consultant:
Pierson, Semmes, and Finley (W. DeVier Pierson, Paul Ryberg, Jr.)

Mauritius Sugar Syndicate
Port Louis, Mauritius
Counsel or consultant:
Pierson, Semmes, and Finley (W. DeVier Pierson, Paul Ryberg, Jr.)

Maverick Tube Corp.
Chesterfield, MO
Counsel or consultant:
Schagrin Associates (Carol A. Colza, Roger B. Schagrin)

Maxell Corp. of America
Moonachie, NJ
Background: A distributor of electronic technology.
Counsel or consultant:
Patton, Boggs and Blow

Maxicare HealthPlans, Inc.
Los Angeles, CA
Counsel or consultant:
Jefferson Group, The (Frederick J. Hannett)
Theodore L. Jones

Maxima Corp.
2101 East Jefferson St., Rockville, MD 20852
Telephone: (301) 230-2000
Counsel or consultant:
Jensen & Co. (Michael G. Brown, Ronald R. Jensen)

Maxus Energy
Dallas, TX
Counsel or consultant:
Fulbright & Jaworski

May Department Stores Co.
St. Louis, MO
Counsel or consultant:
Albers and Co.
Hogan and Hartson (Samuel R. Berger, Clifford S. Gibbons, Bob Glen Odle)
Patton, Boggs and Blow (Cliff Massa, III)

MayCenters, Inc.
St. Louis, MO
Background: A shopping center developer.
Counsel or consultant:
The Susan Davis Companies (Judy Whittlesey)

Maytag Corp.
McLean Office Square 1319 Vincent Place, McLean, VA 22101
Telephone: (703) 790-1611
Represented by:
Douglass C. Horstman, Gov't Affairs Counsel and PAC Manager

Mazak Corp.
Nagoya, Japan
Background: U.S. office is in Florence, KY.
Counsel or consultant:
Global USA, Inc. (Dr. Bohdan Denysyk)

Mazda Motor Manufacturing Corp.
Flat Rock, MI
Counsel or consultant:
Webster and Sheffield (L. Andrew Zausner)

MCA Inc.
Universal City, CA
Background: Aka Music Corp. of America.
Counsel or consultant:
Silverstein and Mullens (James C. Corman)
Williams and Connolly (David E. Kendall)

McCann Construction Co., Inc.
Seattle, WA
Counsel or consultant:
Denny Miller Associates

McCaw Cellular Communications Cos.
1250 Connecticut Ave., N.W., Suite 401, Washington, DC 20036
Telephone: (202) 223-9222
Counsel or consultant:
Davis Wright Tremaine (Edward B. Cohen, Daniel Waggoner)
Duberstein Group, Inc., The
Griffin, Johnson & Associates

ORGANIZATIONS REPRESENTED

McCown De Leeuw & Co.
Menlo Park, CA
Counsel or consultant:
Dewey, Ballantine, Bushby, Palmer and Wood (Joseph K. Dowley)

McDermott Inc.
1850 K St., N.W. Suite 950, Washington, DC 20006
Telephone: (202) 296-0390
Represented by:
William A. Cameron, V. Pres., Gov't Optns. - McDermott Int'l
John H. Henry, Manager, Federal Legislative Affairs
Mark W. Miller, Mgr., Int'l Gov't Afrs - McDermott Int'l

McDonald's Corp.
Oak Brook, IL
Counsel or consultant:
The Susan Davis Companies
Dutko & Associates (Emily Young)
Holt, Miller & Associates (Harris N. Miller)
Wilmer, Cutler and Pickering (William J. Wilkins)

McDonnell Douglas Corp.
1735 Jefferson Davis Hwy., Suite 1200, Arlington, VA 22202
Telephone: (703) 553-3800
Represented by:
B. P. Bacheller, Director, Public Relations
F. W. Bloomcamp, Director-Air Force Programs
Robert R. Bocek, Director - Space & Technology Programs
Gregory S. Dole, Director, Commercial Programs
George D. Iverson, Director - Army Programs
Charles M. Kupperman, Dir.-Quality Processes & Strat. Planning
J. P. Monroe, Director-USN/USMC Aircraft Programs
Robert O'Brien, Director, Washington Public Relations
Ronald K. Sable, Staff V. President, Legislative Affairs
Dennis P. Sharon, V. President, Eastern Region
Counsel or consultant:
Akin, Gump, Strauss, Hauer and Feld (Malcolm Lassman)
Bergner, Boyette & Bockorny, Inc. (Jeffrey T. Bergner)
Miller & Chevalier, Chartered (Alan R. Yuspeh)
Paul, Weiss, Rifkind, Wharton and Garrison (Robert E. Montgomery, Jr., Lionel H. Olmer)
Robison Internat'l, Inc.
Verner, Liipfert, Bernhard, McPherson and Hand, Chartered (Amy L. Bondurant)
Andrew Wahlquist Associates (Andrew Wahlquist)

McDonnell Douglas Helicopter Co.
1735 Jefferson Davis Hwy. Suite 1200, Arlington, VA 22202
Telephone: (703) 553-3885
Background: Formerly Hughes Helicopters, Inc.
Represented by:
J. S. 'Stan' Kimmitt, Assistant to the Pres., Gov't Affairs
Counsel or consultant:
Cambridge Internat'l, Inc. (Justus P. White)
Charles H. Cromwell Inc. (Charles H. Cromwell)
Franklin Group (Gen. Charles D. Franklin, USA (Ret))
Robison Internat'l, Inc. (Richard B. Ladd)

McDonnell Douglas Systems Integration
2070 Chain Bridge Rd. Suite 200, Vienna, VA 22182
Telephone: (703) 734-0088
Represented by:
Dan Hutchinson, Director, Federal Systems

McGraw-Hill, Inc.
1750 K St., N.W., Suite 1170, Washington, DC 20006
Telephone: (202) 955-3830
Represented by:
William P. Giglio, Reg. V.P., Wash. & V.P., Wash. Affairs
Counsel or consultant:
Squire, Sanders and Dempsey (Ann J. LaFrance)

MCI Communications Corp.
1133 19th St., N.W., Washington, DC 20036
Telephone: (202) 872-1600

Represented by:
T. Scott Bunton, Senior Policy Advisor, Gov't Relations
Francis J. Cantrel, Jr., Communications Executive
Bernard A. Goodrich, Director, Public Communications
Edwin K. Hall, V. President, Government Relations
Elizabeth A. Hogan, Manager, Congressional Relations
Dr. Daniel Kelley, Director, Regulatory Policy & Analysis
Gail Knapp, V. President, Corporate Communications
Gerald J. Kovach, Senior V. President, External Affairs
Patrick J. Nugent, Director of Finance Taxes
Robert D. Swezey, Jr., Director, Federal Relations
John R. Worthington, Sr. V. Pres. and General Counsel
John H. Zimmerman, Sr. V. President
Counsel or consultant:
Gold and Liebengood, Inc. (Martin B. Gold, Charles L. Merin)
Haley, Bader and Potts (Michael H. Bader, William J. Byrnes, Kenneth A. Cox)
Howrey and Simon (William A. Roberts, III)
Patton, Boggs and Blow (Thomas Hale Boggs, Jr.)
Wexler, Reynolds, Fuller, Harrison and Schule, Inc. (William K. Ris, Jr., Joseph W. Waz, Jr., Bruce Wolpe)

MCI Telecommunications Political Action Committee
1133 19th St., N.W., Washington, DC 20036
Telephone: (202) 872-1600
Background: Contact is Edwin K. Hall of MCI Communications.

McKechnie Brothers (South Africa) Ltd.
South Africa
Counsel or consultant:
Williams and Connolly (David D. Aufhauser, Bruce R. Genderson)

McKesson Corp.
San Francisco, CA
Counsel or consultant:
Lipsen Whitten & Diamond
Van Ness, Feldman & Curtis (Howard J. Feldman)

McNeil Consumer Products Co.
Fort Washington, PA
Counsel or consultant:
Burson-Marsteller (Sheila Raviv)

MDU Resources Group, Inc.
Bismarck, ND
Counsel or consultant:
Reid & Priest

Mead Corp.
1667 K St., N.W., Suite 420, Washington, DC 20006
Telephone: (202) 833-9643
Represented by:
William E. Brown, Senior Consultant
Jane Scherer Haake, Senior Washington Representative
Sidney G. Hawkes, Vice President, Washington Affairs
Counsel or consultant:
Howrey and Simon (Alan M. Wiseman)

Mead Data Central, Inc.
Dayton, OH
Counsel or consultant:
Piper and Marbury (Ronald L. Plesser)

Mead Johnson and Co.
Evansville, IN
Counsel or consultant:
Kleinfeld, Kaplan and Becker (Alan H. Kaplan, Richard S. Morey)

Mears Internat'l Sales Co.
San Francisco, CA
Counsel or consultant:
Tendler, Goldberg & Biggins, Chtd. (Paul M. Tendler)

Meat Importers Council of America
1901 North Ft. Myer Dr. Suite 1110, Arlington, VA 22209
Telephone: (703) 522-1910
Represented by:
William C. Morrison, Exec. Director
Counsel or consultant:
Barnes, Richardson and Colburn (Rufus E. Jarman, Jr., James H. Lundquist, Gunter Von Conrad)

Meat Industry Suppliers Ass'n
7297 Lee Highway, Suite N, Falls Church, VA 22042
Telephone: (703) 533-1159

Counsel or consultant:
Ass'n and Society Management Internat'l Inc. (Harry W. Buzzerd, Jr., Clay D. Tyeryar)

MEBA District II
490 L'Enfant Plaza East, S.W., Suite 3204, Washington, DC 20024
Telephone: (202) 479-1166
Represented by:
John F. Brady, Exec. V. President

Mechanical Contractors Ass'n of America
1385 Piccard Drive, Rockville, MD 20850
Telephone: (301) 869-5800
Represented by:
James R. Noble, Exec. V. President
Jerry C. Pritchett, Deputy V. President
Gregory Rosenburg, Director of Communications

Mechanical Contractors Ass'n of America/PAC
1385 Piccard Drive, Rockville, MD 20850
Telephone: (301) 869-5800
Background: A political action committee sponsored by the Mechanical Contractors Ass'n of America.
Represented by:
Patricia M. Fink, Staff Administrator

Mechanical Power Transmission Ass'n
932 Hungerford Drive Suite 36, Rockville, MD 20850
Telephone: (301) 738-2448
Counsel or consultant:
Lloyd and Associates, Inc. (Robert A. Reinfried)

Mechanical Technology Inc.
Latham, NY
Counsel or consultant:
Bob Lawrence & Assoc. (Bob Lawrence)

Media Access Project
2000 M St., N.W., Suite 400, Washington, DC 20036
Telephone: (202) 232-4300
Background: A public interest, non-profit communications law firm that represents citizen, civil rights, and grass root organizations across the country who are trying to get access to the media under the fairness doctrine and through application of other legal principles.
Represented by:
Andrew J. Schwartzman, Exec. Director
Gigi B. Sohn, Staff Attorney

Media General, Inc.
Richmond, VA
Counsel or consultant:
Davidson Colling Group, Inc., The (Terese Colling)

Media Institute
3017 M St., N.W., Washington, DC 20007
Telephone: (202) 298-7512
Background: A Washington-based, non-profit, research organization which publishes studies, convenes seminars, and conducts other programs on a variety of communications policy issues.
Represented by:
Richard T. Kaplar, V. President
Patrick D. Maines, President

Medical Care Development
Augusta, ME
Counsel or consultant:
W. J. William Harsh (J. William W. Harsch)

Medical Care Internat'l
Dallas, TX
Counsel or consultant:
Dyer, Ellis, Joseph & Mills (Thomas L. Mills)

Medical College of Wisconsin
Milwaukee, WI
Counsel or consultant:
Cassidy and Associates, Inc. (Thomas M. Gannon)

Medical-Dental Hospital Services Bureaus of America
1200 17th St., N.W., Suite 400, Washington, DC 20036
Telephone: (202) 296-9200
Counsel or consultant:
Hill Group, Inc. (Sanford J. Hill)

Medical Group Management Ass'n
Denver, CO

ORGANIZATIONS REPRESENTED

Counsel or consultant:
White, Fine, and Verville (Robert J. Saner, II)

Medical University of South Carolina
Charleston, SC
Counsel or consultant:
Cassidy and Associates, Inc. (Larry F. Ayres, C. Frank
Godfrey, Jr.)

Medicine in the Public Interest
600 New Hampshire Ave., N.W., Suite 720, Washington,
DC 20037
Telephone: (202) 338-8255
Represented by:
Dr. Louis Lasagna, Chairman

Medline Industries
Northbrook, IL
Counsel or consultant:
Barnes, Richardson and Colburn

Medtronic, Inc.
2000 L St., N.W., Suite 200, Washington, DC 20036
Telephone: (202) 293-7035
Represented by:
Dominique Colon, Public Affairs Associate
George Gregory Raab, Director, Public Affairs
Counsel or consultant:
Dickstein, Shapiro and Morin (John C. Dill, Peter J. Kad-
zik, George Kaufmann, Joseph Kolick, Jr., Andrew P.
Miller, Bernard Nash)
Mayer, Brown and Platt (Kenneth Geller)

Melamine Chemicals
Donaldsonville, LA
Background: A subsidiary of First Mississippi Corp.
Counsel or consultant:
Baker and McKenzie (Thomas P. Ondeck)

Melpar Division Political Action Committee
7700 Arlington Blvd., Falls Church, VA 22046
Telephone: (703) 560-5000
Background: Supported by the Melpar Division of E-Sys-
tems, Inc.
Represented by:
Fred Wahl, Chairman

Melrose Co., The
Hilton Head Isl., SC
Counsel or consultant:
Manatt, Phelps, Rothenberg & Phillips (Robert T. Herbol-
sheimer)

**Member Committee of the U.S., World Energy
Conference**
1620 Eye St., N.W. Suite 615, Washington, DC 20006
Telephone: (202) 331-0415
Background: Executive Director is Barry K. Worthington
of the United States Energy Ass'n.

Memorex Corp.
8609 Westwood Center Drive Suite 500, Vienna, VA
22182
Telephone: (703) 761-5600
Represented by:
Jeff Grant, Federal Contracts Manager

Memorial Hospital System
Houston, TX
Counsel or consultant:
Fulbright & Jaworski (Robert H. Wellen)

Memphis-Shelby County Airport Authority
Memphis, TN
Counsel or consultant:
Global Aviation Associates, Ltd. (Jon F. Ash)
Marlowe and Co. (Howard Marlowe)

Mennonite Central Committee, Peace Section
110 Maryland Ave., N.E. Suite 502, Washington, DC
20002
Telephone: (202) 544-6564
Represented by:
Delton Franz, Director, Washington Office

Menominee Indian Tribe
Kenshena, WI
Counsel or consultant:
Hobbs, Straus, Dean and Wilder (Jerry C. Straus)

Menswear Retailers of America
2011 Eye St., N.W. Suite 600, Washington, DC 20006

Telephone: (202) 347-1932
Represented by:
Greg Hetrick, Director of Government Affairs
Douglas W. Wiegand, Exec. Director

**Menswear Retailers of America Political Action
Committee**
2011 Eye St., N.W., Suite 600, Washington, DC 20006
Telephone: (202) 347-1932
Background: The political action committee of Menswear
Retailers of America. Greg Hetrick, Director of Govern-
ment Affairs for Menswear Retailers of America, serves
as contact.

Mental Health Coalition
P.O. Box 11641, Washington, DC 20008
Telephone: (202) 529-1745
Background: An organization of private, community-based
mental health service providers.
Represented by:
Monique Rothschild, Coordinator
Carole Schauer, President

Mental Health Law Project
2021 L St., N.W., Washington, DC 20036
Telephone: (202) 467-5730
Background: A public interest organization which helps to
define, establish, and implement constitutional rights of
the mentally disabled (and those so perceived by society).
Represented by:
Ira A. Burnim, Legal Director
Lee Carty, Administrator
Joseph Manes, Senior Policy Analyst
Bonnie Milstein, Senior Staff Attorney
Beth Pepper, Staff Attorney
Leonard S. Rubenstein, Director
Counsel or consultant:
Covington and Burling (Peter J. Nickles)

MeraBank
Phoenix, AZ
Counsel or consultant:
Steptoe and Johnson (John T. Collins)

Mercedes-Benz of North America, Inc.
Montvale, NJ
Counsel or consultant:
Barnes, Richardson and Colburn (Edgar Thomas Honey)
Cadwalader, Wickersham & Taft (J. Roger Mentz)
Hogan and Hartson (Clifford S. Gibbons)
Mudge Rose Guthrie Alexander and Ferdon (David A.
Vaughan)
O'Connor & Hannan (Patrick E. O'Donnell)

Merck and Co.
1615 L St., N.W., Suite 1320, Washington, DC 20036
Telephone: (202) 833-8205
Represented by:
Marie A. Dray, Director, Regulatory Agency Relations
Janie A. Kinney, Counsel, Congressional Relations
R. Teel Oliver, V. President, Government Relations
Mark J. Raabe, Exec. Director & Counsel, Gov't Rtns.
Counsel or consultant:
Covington and Burling (Herbert Dym, Stanley L. Temko)
Griffin, Johnson & Associates
Hill and Knowlton Public Affairs Worldwide (Ken Rabin)
Hughes Hubbard and Reed

Merck Sharp and Dohme
West Point, PA
Counsel or consultant:
MARC Associates, Inc. (Daniel C. Maldonado, Ellen
Riker)

Mercury Stainless Corp.
305 3rd St., S.E., Washington, DC 20003
Telephone: (202) 546-3538
Represented by:
Mary Cavanagh, Director, Washington Office

Mercy Hospital of Des Moines, Iowa
Des Moines, IA
Counsel or consultant:
Arent, Fox, Kintner, Plotkin & Kahn (Alan E. Reider)

Meredith Corp.
1850 K St., N.W., Suite 275, Washington, DC 20006
Telephone: (202) 223-2406
Background: A printing, broadcasting and franchised real
estate company.

Represented by:
Robert F. Goodwin, Staff V.P., Dir. of Governmental Affairs

Merichem Co.
Houston, TX
Counsel or consultant:
Fulbright & Jaworski (Martha J. Schoonover)

Meridian House Internat'l
1630 Crescent Place, N.W., Washington, DC 20009
Telephone: (202) 667-6800
Represented by:
Walter L. Cutler, President
Richard K. Fox, Senior V. President
Thomas A. O'Coin, Deputy Dir. of Development, Corp,
Affrs.
Counsel or consultant:
Chernikoff and Co. (Larry Chernikoff)

Merit Protection System, Inc.
Philadelphia, PA
Counsel or consultant:
Kelly and Associates, Inc. (John A. Kelly)

Merit Shop Foundation
729 15th St., N.W., Washington, DC 20005
Telephone: (202) 637-8800
Background: Supported by the Associated Builders and
Contractors. Raises funds to promote the merit shop
through education and research.
Represented by:
Richard Singer, Director, Mangement Education
Brad Wheler, President

Merrill Lynch and Co., Inc.
1828 L St., N.W., Suite 906, Washington, DC 20036
Telephone: (202) 822-3600
Represented by:
William R. DeReuter, Government Relations Representa-
tive
John F. Kelly, Government Relations Representative
David A. Lefeve, V. Pres., State & Local Gov't Relations
Janelle C. M. Thibau, Government Relations Representa-
tive
Bruce E. Thompson, Jr., V. President, Dir. of Gov't Rels.
Counsel or consultant:
Irving M. Pollack
Rivkin, Radler, Dunne and Bayh
Rogers and Wells (William Morris, Eugene T. Rossides)
Skadden, Arps, Slate, Meagher and Flom (Robert E.
Lighthizer)
Swidler & Berlin, Chartered (Barry Direnfeld)
Vinson and Elkins (John E. Chapoton)

Merrill Lynch Futures Inc.
New York, NY
Counsel or consultant:
Lord Day & Lord, Barrett Smith (Mahlon Frankhauser)

Merrill Lynch Political Action Committee
1828 L St., N.W. Suite 906, Washington, DC 20036
Telephone: (202) 822-3600
Background: Represented by William R. DeReuter of the
sponsoring organization.

Mesa Limited Partnership
Amarillo, TX
Counsel or consultant:
Akin, Gump, Strauss, Hauer and Feld (Joel Jankowsky)
The Laxalt Corp. (Michelle D. Laxalt)
Skadden, Arps, Slate, Meagher and Flom (Robert E.
Lighthizer, Mike Naeve)
Whitworth & Associates (Ralph V. Whitworth)

Met-Fuel Inc.
Houston, TX
Counsel or consultant:
McClure and Trotter

Metal Construction Ass'n
1101 14th St., N.W. Suite 1100, Washington, DC 20005
Telephone: (202) 371-1243
Counsel or consultant:
Internat'l Management Group, Inc. (David W. Barrack)

Metal Market and Exchange Co. Ltd.
London, England
Counsel or consultant:
Arnold & Porter

ORGANIZATIONS REPRESENTED

Metallverken AB
Vasteras, Sweden
Counsel or consultant:
Winthrop, Stimson, Putnam & Roberts (Raymond S. Calamaro, Ira S. Shapiro)

Metalor USA Refining Corp.
N. Attleborough, MA
Counsel or consultant:
Hale and Dorr (Jay P. Urwitz)

Metcor Inc.
Suite 505, 2000 P St., N.W., Washington, DC 20036
Telephone: (202) 833-9624
Counsel or consultant:
Cook and Associates (Howard L. Cook, Jr.)

Metlakatla Indian Community
Annette Islands, AK
Counsel or consultant:
Hobbs, Straus, Dean and Wilder (S. Bobo Dean)

MetPath Inc.
Teterboro, NJ
Counsel or consultant:
Manatos & Manatos, Inc. (Andrew E. Manatos, Kimberley A. Matthews)
Bartley M. O'Hara, P.C.
White, Fine, and Verville (Arnold I. Havens)

Metro Airlines, Inc.
Dallas, TX
Counsel or consultant:
V. Michael Straus, P.C.

Metro-Dade County
Miami, FL
Counsel or consultant:
Vierra Associates, Inc. (Dennis C. Vierra)

Metro Express, Inc.
Atlanta, GA
Counsel or consultant:
V. Michael Straus, P.C.

Metromedia Co.
New York, NY
Counsel or consultant:
Vern Clark & Associates (Vernon Clark)

Metroplex Communications, Inc.
Cleveland, OH
Counsel or consultant:
Kaye, Scholer, Fierman, Hays and Handler (Jason Shrinsky)

Metropolitan Edison Co.
Reading, PA
Counsel or consultant:
Shaw, Pittman, Potts and Trowbridge

Metropolitan Education and Training Corp.
2000 P St., N.W., Suite 505, Washington, DC 20036
Telephone: (202) 833-9624
Represented by:
James Muldoon, Director

Metropolitan Insurance Cos.
1615 L St., N.W., Suite 1210, Washington, DC 20036
Telephone: (202) 659-3575
Represented by:
Leonard N. Henderson, Senior Washington Representative
Carol A. Kelly, V. President
William F. Mullin, V. President
Edward T. Porcaro, Assistant V. President
Vincent P. Reusing, Senior Vice-President
Counsel or consultant:
Dressendorfer-Laird, Inc. (David M. Laird)
Patton, Boggs and Blow (John Jonas)
Wunder, Ryan, Cannon & Thelen (Michael A. Forscey, Lawrence P. Higgins)

Metropolitan Life Insurance Co.
New York, NY
Counsel or consultant:
Miller & Chevalier, Chartered (John S. Nolan)

Metropolitan Toledo Consortium
Toledo, OH
Background: Members include City of Toledo; Lucas County, Ohio; Toledo Public Schools; Medical College of Ohio; University of Toledo; Toledo-Lucas County Port Authority; and Toledo Area Regional Transportation Authority.
Counsel or consultant:
Peyser Associates, Inc.

Metropolitan Transportation Commission of Oakland
Oakland, CA
Counsel or consultant:
Government Relations, Inc. (Thomas J. Bulger)

Metropolitan Washington Council of Governments
777 N. Capitol St., N.E. Suite 300, Washington, DC 20002-4201
Telephone: (202) 962-3200
Background: A regional organization of the Washington area's major local governments and governing officials. Provides a forum for addressing regional problems through discussion, formal agreement, policy implications and trend assessment.
Represented by:
John J. Bosley, General Counsel

Mexican-American Legal Defense and Educational Fund
1430 K St., N.W., Suite 700, Washington, DC 20005
Telephone: (202) 628-4074
Background: Strives to protect and further the civil rights of Mexican Americans by litigating to ensure equal educational opportunity, non-discriminatory immigration and naturalization laws, voting rights and employment equality.
Represented by:
Jose Garza, Nat'l Director, Political Access Program
G. Mario Moreno, Regional Counsel

Mexican American Women's Nat'l Ass'n
1201 16th St., N.W., Suite 230, Washington, DC 20036
Telephone: (202) 822-7888
Background: Founded in 1974 with the principal objective of advancing the status of women of Hispanic descent.
Represented by:
Irma Maldonado, President

Mexico, Government of
Mexico City, Mexico
Counsel or consultant:
Milbank, Tweed, Hadley & McCloy
Mark E. Moran
Morgan, Lewis and Bockius
Shawn, Berger, and Mann

Mexico, Ministry of Commerce
Mexico City, Mexico
Counsel or consultant:
Fleishman-Hillard, Inc

Mexico, Ministry of Finance and Public Credit
Mexico City, Mexico
Counsel or consultant:
Cleary, Gottlieb, Steen and Hamilton (Douglas E. Kliever)

Mexinox, S.A. de C.V.
San Luis Potosi, Bolivia
Counsel or consultant:
Mudge Rose Guthrie Alexander and Ferdon (Donald B. Cameron, Jr., Julie C. Mendoza)

Meyer and Associates, Inc., Vernon F.
Sulphur, LA
Counsel or consultant:
John M. Palatiello & Assoc. (John M. Palatiello)

MGIC Investment Corp.
Milwaukee, WI
Counsel or consultant:
Brownstein Zeidman and Schomer (Philip N. Brownstein)

MGM/UA Communications Co.
Culver City, CA
Counsel or consultant:
Lee, Toomey & Kent

Miami, Florida, City of
Counsel or consultant:
Nat'l Center for Municipal Development (Mark S. Israel)

Miami Internat'l Airport
Miami, FL

Counsel or consultant:
Garvey, Schubert & Barer (Richard A. Wegman)
Lord Day & Lord, Barrett Smith (Joanne W. Young)

Miccosukee Tribe of Indians of Florida
Miami, FL
Counsel or consultant:
Karl A. Funke and Associates (Karl A. Funke)
Hobbs, Straus, Dean and Wilder (S. Bobo Dean)

Michelin Tire Co.
Greenville, SC
Background: The U.S. subsidiary of Compagnie General des Etablissements Michelin of Clermont-Ferrand, France.
Counsel or consultant:
McNair Law Firm, P.A.
Shaw, Pittman, Potts and Trowbridge (William Mike House)

Michigan Bell Telephone Co.
Detroit, MI
Counsel or consultant:
Bonner & Associates

Michigan Biotechnology Institute
Lansing, MI
Counsel or consultant:
Cassidy and Associates, Inc. (Larry F. Ayres, Donald P. Smith)

Michigan Channel 38
Detroit, MI
Counsel or consultant:
Ginsburg, Feldman and Bress (E. William Henry)

Michigan Humane Soc.
Detroit, MI
Counsel or consultant:
Plunkett & Cooney , P.C. (William M. Brodhead)

Michigan Retailers Ass'n
Lansing, MI
Counsel or consultant:
Tendler, Goldberg & Biggins, Chtd. (James M. Goldberg)

Michigan, State of
444 N. Capitol St., N.W. Suite 390, Washington, DC 20001
Telephone: (202) 624-5840
Represented by:
Douglas Frost, Dir., Wash. Office of the Governor
Counsel or consultant:
Cadwalader, Wickersham & Taft (Ronald D. Eastman)

Michigan Technological University
Houghton, MI
Counsel or consultant:
Cassidy and Associates, Inc. (Thomas M. Gannon, Donald P. Smith, Vincent M. Versage)

Michigan Trade Exchange
Southfield, MI
Background: A barter exchange.
Counsel or consultant:
Royer, Mehle & Babyak (Robert Stewart Royer)

Micron Technology, Inc.
Boise ID
Counsel or consultant:
Morrison & Foerster

Micronesia, Government of the Federated States of
Ponape, Trust Territory
Counsel or consultant:
Stovall & Spradlin (James T. Stovall, III)

Micronesian Telecommunications Corp.
Honolulu, HI
Counsel or consultant:
Murphy and Malone (William R. Malone)

Microsoft
Redmond, WA
Counsel or consultant:
Swidler & Berlin, Chartered (Bruce A. Lehman)

Mid-America Committee
1201 Connecticut Ave., N.W. Suite 300, Washington, DC 20036
Telephone: (202) 835-8813

The listings in this directory are available as *Mailing Labels.* See last page.

ORGANIZATIONS REPRESENTED

Represented by:
Thomas H. Miner, Chairman
Diane A. Soucy, V. President, Gov't & Internat'l Affairs

Mid-America Dairymen, Inc.
100 North Carolina Ave., S.E. Suite 1, Washington, DC 20003
Telephone: (202) 546-8987
Represented by:
Francis J. Vacca, V. President for Government Relations

Mid-American Network
Des Moines, IA
Counsel or consultant:
State & Local Resources (Bruce D. Henderson, Patrick M. Murphy)

Mid-Atlantic Council of Shopping Center Managers
8811 Colesville Rd., Suite G106, Silver Spring, MD 20910
Telephone: (301) 588-8668
Counsel or consultant:
Bachner Communications, Inc. (John P. Bachner)

Mid-Continent Oil and Gas Ass'n
1919 Pennsylvania Ave., N.W. Suite 503, Washington, DC 20006
Telephone: (202) 785-3515
Represented by:
Wayne Gibbens, President
Stephen E. Ward, V. President
Counsel or consultant:
Charls E. Walker Associates

Mid-West Electric Consumers Ass'n
Denver, CO
Background: Duncan, Weinberg, Miller & Pembroke works on water and power issues as well as Congressional and federal administrative representation.
Counsel or consultant:
Duncan, Weinberg, Miller & Pembroke, P.C. (Frederick L. Miller, Jr., Edward Weinberg)

MidCon Corp.
1747 Pennsylvania Ave., N.W. Suite 300, Washington, DC 20006
Telephone: (202) 857-3075
Background: A division of Occidental Petroleum Corp., and the parent company of Natural Gas Pipeline Co. of America and United Gas Pipe Line Co., and United Texas Transmission Co., an intrastate gas transmission company.
Represented by:
Patricia Laws, Legislative Assistant
Carol A. Smoots, Director, Government Relations
Ellen Valentine, Regulatory Assistant

Middle Atlantic Conference
Riverdale, MD
Counsel or consultant:
Rea, Cross & Auchincloss (Bryce Rea, Jr.)
Douglass W. Svendson Jr.

Middle East Airlines
Beirut, Lebanon
Counsel or consultant:
Dickstein, Shapiro and Morin (G. Joseph Minetti, Walter J. Walvick)

Middle East Institute
1761 N St., N.W., Washington, DC 20036
Telephone: (202) 785-1141
Background: Founded in 1946 to foster American understanding of the Middle East through conferences, lectures, education and publications. By charter may not become an instrument of policy nor attempt to influence legislation.
Represented by:
Lucius D. Battle, President
Jean Newsom, Editor, Middle East Journal
Christopher Van Hollen, V. President and Coordinator

Middle South Utilities, Inc.
New Orleans, LA
Counsel or consultant:
Paul, Hastings, Janofsky and Walker (Charles A. Patrizia)

Midland Bank plc
London, England

Milbank, Tweed, Hadley & McCloy (Elliot L. Richardson)

Midland Enterprises
Cincinnati, OH
Counsel or consultant:
Thompson and Mitchell (Edward A. Scallet)

Midway Airlines
Chicago, IL
Counsel or consultant:
Ginsburg, Feldman and Bress (Jacob W. Rosenthal)

Midwest Corp.
Charleston, WV
Counsel or consultant:
Ryan-McGinn (Daniel McGinn)

Midwest Energy Inc.
Great Bend, KS
Counsel or consultant:
Wilner and Scheiner

Midwestern Gas Transmission Co.
Houston, TX
Counsel or consultant:
Wright and Talisman

Migrant Legal Action Program
2001 S St., N.W., Suite 310, Washington, DC 20009
Telephone: (202) 462-7744
Background: A national legal services center that aids migrant and seasonal farm workers with legal representation.
Represented by:
Roger C. Rosenthal, Exec. Director

Miles College
Birmingham, AL
Counsel or consultant:
Clohan & Dean (William A. Blakey)

Miles, Inc.
West Haven, CT
Counsel or consultant:
Barnes, Richardson and Colburn (Matthew T. McGrath, Peter L. Sultan)

Military Boot Manufacturers Ass'n
1752 N St., N.W. - 6th Floor, Washington, DC 20036
Telephone: (202) 466-7185
Counsel or consultant:
Dykema Gossett (Judy P. Jenkins)

Military Chaplains Ass'n of the U.S.
Box 645, Riverdale, MD 20737-0645
Telephone: (301) 674-3306
Represented by:
William F. Emery, Exec. Director

Military Educator and Counselor Ass'n
5999 Stevenson Ave., Alexandria, VA 22304
Telephone: (703) 823-9800
Background: Responsible contact is William Hunter, Lauren Scheib and Richard Yep of the American Ass'n for Counseling and Development.

Military Impacted School Districts Ass'n
c/o Stanley McFarland 11718 Devilwood Drive, Potomac, MD 20854
Telephone: (301) 279-9556
Counsel or consultant:
Evergreen Associates, Ltd. (Robert M. Brooks)

Military Order of the Purple Heart of the U.S.A.
5413-B Backlick Rd., Springfield, VA 22151
Telephone: (703) 642-5360
Represented by:
Robert L. Alvarez, Nat'l Service Director
Michael B. Prothero, Adjutant General

Military Order of the World Wars
435 North Lee St., Alexandria, VA 22314
Telephone: (703) 683-4911
Background: A patriotic group of commissioned officers who have served on active duty in the U.S. armed forces. Founded in 1919 by General Pershing. Now more than 20,000 members. Advocates a strong national defense posture and active support of patriotic education.
Represented by:
Lt. Gen. C. M. Talbott, USAF (Ret), Chief of Staff

Milk Industry Foundation
888 16th St., N.W., Washington, DC 20006
Telephone: (202) 296-4250
Background: Although separate and autonomous trade association, the Milk Industry Foundation shares offices and staff with the Internat'l Ice Cream Ass'n, the American Butter Institute, the Nat'l Cheese Institute and the Marketing and Training Institute.
Counsel or consultant:
Bishop, Cook, Purcell & Reynolds
Covington and Burling
Patton, Boggs and Blow
Rivkin, Radler, Dunne and Bayh

Miller Brewing Co.
1341 G St., N.W., Suite 900, Washington, DC 20005
Telephone: (202) 637-1520
Represented by:
Tod I. Gimbel, Federal Affairs Representative
T. Daniel Tearno, Director, Federal Government Affairs
Counsel or consultant:
Akin, Gump, Strauss, Hauer and Feld (Kirk O'Donnell)
Arnold & Porter
Patricia Bario Associates (Patricia Bario)
Bonner & Associates
Reese Communications Companies
Targeting Systems, Inc.

Miller Co.
Meriden, CT
Counsel or consultant:
Collier, Shannon & Scott (Jeffrey S. Beckington, David A. Hartquist, Mary T. Staley)

Millers' Nat'l Federation
600 Maryland Ave., S.W., Suite 305 West, Washington, DC 20024
Telephone: (202) 484-2200
Represented by:
James A. Bair, Director, Government Relations
Roy M. Henwood, President
Counsel or consultant:
Holland and Knight

Millicom Inc.
New York, NY
Counsel or consultant:
Bracy Williams & Co. (Kenneth S. Birnbaum, Terrence L. Bracy, Thomas J. Hennessey, Jr., Susan J. Williams)

Milliken and Co.
1100 Connecticut Ave., N.W. 13th Floor, Washington, DC 20036
Telephone: (202) 543-9374
Represented by:
Katherine D. Dutilh, Lobbyist
John F. Nash, Jr., Washington Counsel
Counsel or consultant:
The Laxalt Corp. (Michelle D. Laxalt)
Thompson, Mann and Hutson (Harold P. Coxson)

Minbea Singapore
Singapore
Counsel or consultant:
Willkie Farr and Gallagher (Walter J. Spak)

Minebea Co.
Tokyo, Japan
Counsel or consultant:
Tanaka, Ritger and Middleton (Michele N. Tanaka)

Mineral Insulation Manufacturers Ass'n
1420 King St., 4th Floor, Alexandria, VA 22314
Telephone: (703) 684-0084
Represented by:
Kenneth D. Mentzer, Exec. V. President

Mineralogical Soc. of America
1625 Eye St., N.W., Suite 414, Washington, DC 20006
Telephone: (202) 775-4344
Represented by:
Susan L. Myers, Executive Secretary

Minerals Marketing Corp. of Zimbabwe
Harare, Zimbabwe
Counsel or consultant:
Patton, Boggs and Blow (Frank R. Samolis)

Minimum Wage Coalition to Save Jobs
P.O. Box 28261, Washington, DC 20038
Telephone: (202) 463-5970

ORGANIZATIONS REPRESENTED

Minimum Wage Coalition to Save Jobs (Cont'd)
Counsel or consultant:
Richard B. Berman and Co.,Inc. (Richard B. Berman)

Minnesota AFL-CIO
St. Paul, MN
Counsel or consultant:
Gallagher-Widmeyer Group Inc., The (Mary Jane Gallagher)

Minnesota Mining and Manufacturing Co. (Traffic Control Materials Division)
St. Paul, MN
Counsel or consultant:
Arthur E. Cameron

Minnesota Mining and Manufacturing Co. (3M Co.)
1101 15th St., N.W., Washington, DC 20005
Telephone: (202) 331-6900
Represented by:
Andrew J. Donelson, Manager, Regulatory Affairs
John R. Frahm, Manager, Gov't Activities-Internat'l
Dan L. Hitt, V. President, Federal Gov't Affairs
Helena Hutton Peterson, Manager, Government Relations
Counsel or consultant:
Baker and McKenzie (Kevin M. O'Brien, Thomas P. Ondeck)
John G. Campbell, Inc. (John G. Campbell)
Crowell and Moring (Victor E. Schwartz)
Gardner, Carton and Douglas (J. Curtis Moffat)
The Hannaford Co., Inc.
Jefferson Group, The (Mark D. Cowan, Randal Schumacher)
Lee, Toomey & Kent

Minnesota Mutual Life Insurance Co.
St. Paul, MN
Counsel or consultant:
O'Connor & Hannan (Patrick J. O'Connor)
Sutherland, Asbill and Brennan (Gordon O. Pehrson, Jr.)

Minnesota Power
Duluth, MN
Counsel or consultant:
Akin, Gump, Strauss, Hauer and Feld (Joel Jankowsky)
Donelan, Cleary, Wood and Maser, P.C. (John F. Donelan, Frederic L. Wood)
Reid & Priest
Slover and Loftus (William L. Slover)

Minnesota, State of
400 North Capitol St., N.W. Suite 322, Washington, DC 20001
Telephone: (202) 624-5308
Represented by:
Thomas Lehman, Associate Director
Barbara Rohde, Director, Washington Office

Minorco Societe Anonyme
Luxembourg Ville, Luxembourg
Counsel or consultant:
Powell, Goldstein, Frazer and Murphy
South/North Development Group, Ltd. (Stoney Cooks)

Minority Business Enterprise Legal Defense and Education Fund
300 Eye St., N.E., Suite 200, Washington, DC 20002
Telephone: (202) 543-0040
Represented by:
Franklin M. Lee, Exec. V. Pres. and Chief Counsel
Parren Mitchell, Founder and Chairman
Anthony W. Robinson, President

Minpeco, S.A.
Lima, Peru
Counsel or consultant:
Porter/Novelli

Mintax, Inc.
Oldbridge, NJ
Counsel or consultant:
Paul Suplizio Associates (Paul E. Suplizio)

MIP Instandsetzungsbetriebe GmbH
Mainz, Germany
Counsel or consultant:
Ervin Technical Associates, Inc. (ETA) (James L. Ervin)
Morgan, Lewis and Bockius

Mirabella
Caserta, Italy
Counsel or consultant:
Wunder, Ryan, Cannon & Thelen (John J. McGovern, Jr.)

Mississippi Department of Economic and Community Development
Jackson, MS
Counsel or consultant:
Bishop, Cook, Purcell & Reynolds (John A. Waits)

Mississippi Power and Light Co.
Jackson, MS
Counsel or consultant:
Reid & Priest

Mississippi River Transmission Corp.
St. Louis, MO
Counsel or consultant:
Newman & Holtzinger, P.C.

Mississippi, State of
Suite 504, 1155 15th St., N.W., Washington, DC 20005
Telephone: (202) 452-1003
Counsel or consultant:
Bill Simpson & Assoc. (William G. Simpson)

Missouri Ass'n of Private Career Schools
Jefferson City, MO
Counsel or consultant:
Manatt, Phelps, Rothenberg & Phillips (Robert T. Herbolsheimer)

Missouri Hospital Ass'n
St. Louis, MO
Counsel or consultant:
Targeting Systems, Inc.

Missouri Public Service Co.
Kansas City, MO
Counsel or consultant:
McCarthy, Sweeney and Harkaway, P.C.

Missouri Public Service Commission
Jefferson City, MO
Counsel or consultant:
Birch, Horton, Bittner and Cherot (Eric A. Eisen)

Missouri, State of
400 N. Capitol St., N.W. Suite 374, Washington, DC 20001
Telephone: (202) 624-7720
Represented by:
Marise Rene Stewart, Director, Washington Office

Mitsubishi Corp.
Tokyo, Japan
Counsel or consultant:
Barnes, Richardson and Colburn (Edgar Thomas Honey)
Charls E. Walker Associates
Weil, Gotshal & Manges (Jeffrey P. Bialos, A. Paul Victor)

Mitsubishi Electric Corp.
Tokyo, Japan
Counsel or consultant:
Baker and McKenzie (Thomas P. Ondeck, William D. Outman, II)
Robinson, Lake, Lerer & Montgomery (James H. Lake)
Saunders and Company (Eric Edmondson, Steven R. Saunders)

Mitsubishi Electric Sales America
Compton, CA
Counsel or consultant:
Patton, Boggs and Blow

Mitsubishi Electronics America, Inc.
816 Connecticut Ave., N.W. Suite 600, Washington, DC 20036
Telephone: (202) 223-3424
Counsel or consultant:
Thompson and Co. (Robert J. Thompson)

Mitsubishi Internat'l Corp.
655 15th St., N.W., Suite 860, Washington, DC 20005
Telephone: (202) 638-1101

Represented by:
Michael Call, Manager
Gordon Epstein, Manager
Masato Nagase, Manager
Lawrence Paul, Assistant Manager
Motoatsu Sakurai, Deputy General Manager
Kazuko White, Assistant Manager
Counsel or consultant:
Saunders and Company (Kim Brown, Steven R. Saunders)

Mitsubishi Research Institute
655 15th St., N.W. Suite 880, Washington, DC 20005
Telephone: (202) 393-2424
Background: The Washington, DC office of a research institute based in Tokyo, Japan.
Represented by:
Akiyosha Nasu, Chief Representative

Mitsubishi Trust and Banking Corp.
Tokyo, Japan
Counsel or consultant:
Civic Service, Inc. (Roy Pfautch)

Mitsui and Co.
Tokyo, Japan
Counsel or consultant:
Barnes, Richardson and Colburn (James S. O'Kelly)
Marks Murase and White (Matthew J. Marks)
Steptoe and Johnson (Charlene Barshefsky, Richard O. Cunningham, Susan G. Esserman)

Mitsui and Co. (U.S.A.), Inc.
1701 Pennsylvania Ave., N.W., Suite 400, Washington, DC 20006
Telephone: (202) 861-0660
Represented by:
William C. Bell, Research Associate
Kent Bossart, Export License Supervisor
Lawrence Bruser, Deputy General Manager
Jacalyn Douglas, Research Assistant
Takatsugu Ohi, General Manager

Mitsui Grain Corp
Chicago, IL
Counsel or consultant:
Vickers & Vickers (Eugene B. Vickers)

Mitsui O.S.K. Lines, Ltd.
New York, NY
Counsel or consultant:
Warren and Associates (George A. Quadrino, Charles F. Warren)

Miwon Trading and Shipping Co., Ltd.
Seoul, Korea
Counsel or consultant:
Mudge Rose Guthrie Alexander and Ferdon (N. David Palmeter)

Mixmor, Inc.
King of Prussia, PA
Counsel or consultant:
I and J Associates (Ira F. Jersey, Jr., John J. Regan)

Mobil Corp.
1100 Connecticut Ave., N.W., Suite 620, Washington, DC 20036
Telephone: (202) 862-1300
Represented by:
Robert B. Andrews, Mgr., Gov't Relats., Trade Ass'n Liaison
Robert E. Bates, Jr., Mgr., Gov't Relats., US Mktg. & Refg.
Anthony R. Corso, General Mgr., Corp. Government Relations
N. Boyd Ecker, Mgr., Gov't Relats, Expl. & Producing
Sara B. Glenn, Government Relations Advisor
James E. Green, Manager, Government Relations
Timothy A. Hanan, Manager, Federal Government Relations
John N. Parker, Mgr, Gov't Reltns/Internat'l Mktg & Rfng
Barney J. Skladany, Jr., Mgr., Gov't Relats, Chem., Mining & Min.
Counsel or consultant:
Bonner & Associates
Camp, Barsh, Bates and Tate (Harry E. Barsh, Jr., John C. Camp)
Howrey and Simon (A. Duncan Whitaker)

The listings in this directory are available as *Mailing Labels*. See last page.

ORGANIZATIONS REPRESENTED

Mobil Land Development Co.
Reston, VA
Counsel or consultant:
Dow, Lohnes and Albertson (William B. Ingersoll)

Mobile Diagnostic Systems
Dallas, TX
Counsel or consultant:
Arent, Fox, Kintner, Plotkin & Kahn (Alan E. Reider)

Mobley Inc., E. L.
Savannah, GA
Counsel or consultant:
Denning and Wohlstetter (Alan F. Wohlstetter)

Mocatta Metals Corp.
New York, NY
Counsel or consultant:
Patton, Boggs and Blow (Thomas Hale Boggs, Jr.)

Modar, Inc.
Houston, TX
Counsel or consultant:
Vinson and Elkins (James C. Gould)

Modesto Irrigation District
Modesto, CA
Counsel or consultant:
Duncan, Weinberg, Miller & Pembroke, P.C. (Wallace L.
Duncan, James D. Pembroke)

Momentum '88
Spokane, WA
Counsel or consultant:
Denny Miller Associates

Monarch Capital Corp.
Springfield, MA
Counsel or consultant:
Covington and Burling
Wexler, Reynolds, Fuller, Harrison and Schule, Inc.

Monarch Wines
North Brunswick, NJ
Counsel or consultant:
McAuliffe, Kelly, Raffaelli & Siemens (Frederick W. Hatfield)

Money Store, The
Springfield, NJ
Counsel or consultant:
Manatt, Phelps, Rothenberg & Phillips (Robert J. Kabel)
Mark A. Siegel & Associates

Mongolia People's Republic, Embassy of
3636 16th St., N.W., Washington, DC 20010
Telephone: (202) 483-3176
Counsel or consultant:
Marshall, Tenzer, Greenblatt, Fallon and Kaplan (Sylvan
M. Marshall)
van Kloberg and Associates (Edward J. van Kloberg, III)

Monitor
1506 19th St., N.W., Washington, DC 20036
Telephone: (202) 234-6576
Background: A consortium of 35 conservation, environmental and animal welfare organizations for the protection of endangered species, marine mammals and their habitats.
Represented by:
Craig Van Note, Exec. V. President

Monongahela Power Co.
Fairmont, WV
Counsel or consultant:
Keller and Heckman

Monsanto Co.
700 14th St., N.W., Suite 1100, Washington, DC 20005
Telephone: (202) 783-2460

Represented by:
David S. J. Brown, V. President, Government Affairs
Kevin F. Cannon, Manager, Agricultural Affairs
Chester T. Dickerson, Jr., Director, Agricultural Affairs
Thomas M. Helscher, Director, Congressional Affairs
Morton L. Mullins, Director, Regulatory Affairs
Counsel or consultant:
Duberstein Group, Inc., The
Hill and Knowlton Public Affairs Worldwide (John Urbanchuk)
Stateside Associates
Stewart and Stewart (Eugene L. Stewart)

Monsanto Industrial Chemicals Co.
St. Louis, MO
Counsel or consultant:
Stewart and Stewart (Eugene L. Stewart)

Montana Electric Power Cooperatives Ass'n
Helena, MT
Counsel or consultant:
Duncan, Weinberg, Miller & Pembroke, P.C. (Janice L.
Lower, James D. Pembroke)

Montana Power Co.
1730 M St., N.W., Suite 607, Washington, DC 20036
Telephone: (202) 296-3060
Represented by:
James A. Rock, Washington Representative
Counsel or consultant:
Covington and Burling
Keller and Heckman
Lund and O'Brien
McCarthy, Sweeney and Harkaway, P.C.
Reid & Priest

Montaup Electric Co.
Somerset, MA
Counsel or consultant:
Bruder, Gentile & Marcoux (George F. Bruder)

Monterey Institute of Internat'l Studies
Monterey, CA
Counsel or consultant:
Cassidy and Associates, Inc. (C. Frank Godfrey, Jr.)

Montgomery Ward & Co., Inc.
Chicago, IL
Counsel or consultant:
French & Company (Mark M. Ellison, Verrick O.
French)

Montifiore Medical Center
Bronx, NY
Counsel or consultant:
Liz Robbins Associates (Liz Robbins)

Mooney Chemicals, Inc.
Cleveland, OH
Counsel or consultant:
Weinberg & Green (Walter G. Talarek)

Morgan & Co., J. P.
New York, NY
Counsel or consultant:
Dickstein, Shapiro and Morin (John C. Dill, James R.
Jones)
Kelley, Drye and Warren

Morgan Grenfell and Co., Ltd.
London, England
Counsel or consultant:
Jones, Day, Reavis and Pogue (James A. Wilderotter)
O'Connor & Hannan (Thomas H. Quinn)
Wilson, Elser, Moskowitz, Edelman & Dicker (Robert B.
Wallace)

Morgan Guaranty Trust Co.
New York, NY
Counsel or consultant:
Davis Polk & Wardwell (Theodore A. Doremus, Jr., Richard Moe)
Dow, Lohnes and Albertson (Richard S. Belas, Jeffrey
Kurzweil)

Morgan Stanley and Co.
New York, NY

Counsel or consultant:
Akin, Gump, Strauss, Hauer and Feld (Joel Jankowsky)
Davis Polk & Wardwell (Mikel M. Rollyson)
Dewey, Ballantine, Bushby, Palmer and Wood (Joseph K.
Dowley, Lawrence F. O'Brien, III)
Dow, Lohnes and Albertson (Bernard J. Long, Jr.)
Epstein Becker and Green
Royer, Mehle & Babyak (Robert Stewart Royer)
Timmons and Co., Inc.

Morgantown, West Virginia, City of
Counsel or consultant:
Beveridge & Diamond, P.C. (Richard S. Davis, Harold L.
Segall)

Mormac Marine Group, Inc.
Stamford, CT
Counsel or consultant:
Preston Gates Ellis & Rouvelas Meeds (Susan B. Geiger,
Emanuel L. Rouvelas)

Morocco, Kingdom of
Rabat, Morocco
Counsel or consultant:
Ginsburg, Feldman and Bress (David Ginsburg, Lee R.
Marks)
Neill and Co. (John E. Bircher, III, Denis M. Neill)
Stovall & Spradlin
White & Case

Morrison, Hecker, Curtis, Kuder & Parrish
Kansas City, MO
Counsel or consultant:
Resources Development, Inc. (Roger H. Zion)

Morrison Inc.
Mobile, AL
Counsel or consultant:
Power & Coleman (Thomas W. Power)

Morrison-Knudsen Corp.
555 13th St., N.W. Suite 410 West Tower, Washington,
DC 20004-1109
Telephone: (202) 638-6355
Represented by:
Thomas E. Debruycker, Director, Governmental Affairs

Morse/Diesel
San Francisco, CA
Counsel or consultant:
Thompson and Co. (Robert J. Thompson)

Mortgage Bankers Ass'n of America
1125 15th St., N.W., Suite 700, Washington, DC 20005
Telephone: (202) 861-6500
Background: The only national trade association devoted exclusively to real estate finance. Represents more than 2,700 members, including mortgage bankers, savings and loan associations, commercial banks, life insurance companies and others in the mortgage lending field.
Represented by:
Mark P. Bolduc, Assistant Director
Linda Knell Bumbalo, Associate Legislative Counsel
Sharon M. Canavan, Staff V. Pres., Deputy Legis. Counsel
William E. Cumberland, Staff V. President & General
Counsel
Jane M. De Marines, Staff V. Pres., Public Affairs/Marketing
Michael J. Ferrell, Sr. Staff V.P. & Legislative Counsel
James T. Freeman, Legislative Staff Assistant
Lyle E. Gramley, Sr. Staff V. President & Chief Economist
Warren Lasko, Exec. V. President
Robert M. O'Toole, Sr Staff V.P., Resid Fin/Gov't Agncy
Rel
Janice Stango, Sr. Staff V. Pres., Admin. & Operations
Ann Hadley vom Eigen, Associate Legislative Counsel
Jacqueline G. Wertime, Staff V. President, Communications
Burton C. Wood, Consultant
Counsel or consultant:
Evans Group, Ltd., The (Thomas B. Evans, Jr., Susan Riley, Mary Ellen Taylor)

Mortgage Bankers Ass'n of America Political Action Committee
1125 15th St., N.W., Suite 700, Washington, DC 20005
Telephone: (202) 861-6500
Background: Represented by Mark P. Bolduc of the Mortgage Bankers Ass'n.

The listings in this directory are available as *Mailing Labels*. See last page.

609

ORGANIZATIONS REPRESENTED

Mortgage Guaranty Insurance Corp.
Milwaukee, WI
Counsel or consultant:
Cadwalader, Wickersham & Taft (Donald C. Alexander)

Mortgage Insurance Companies of America
805 15th St., N.W., Suite 1110, Washington, DC 20005
Telephone: (202) 371-2899
Represented by:
Suzanne C. Hutchinson, Exec. V. President
Dawn E. Kuykendall, Office Manager
Kelly Ziglar-Clay, Legislative & Regulatory Representative
Counsel or consultant:
Black, Manafort, Stone and Kelly Public Affairs Co.
Dave Evans Associates (David W. Evans)
Mintz, Levin, Cohn, Ferris, Glovsky and Popeo, P.C. (James H. Schuyler)
Shaw, Pittman, Potts and Trowbridge

Mortgage Insurance Political Action Committee
805 15th St., N.W., Suite 1110, Washington, DC 20005
Telephone: (202) 371-2899
Background: Contact is Suzanne C. Hutchinson of the Mortgage Insurance Companies of America.

Morton Internat'l, Inc.
Chicago, IL
Counsel or consultant:
Lee, Toomey & Kent

Moscow Narodny Bank
London, England
Counsel or consultant:
Sidley and Austin

Mothers Against Drunk Driving (MADD)
Hurst, TX
Counsel or consultant:
Kostmayer Communications, Inc. (Harry Frazier)
Peyser Associates, Inc. (Thomas J. Howarth, Caroline Martin, Peter A. Peyser, Jr.)

Motion Picture Ass'n of America
1600 Eye St., N.W., Washington, DC 20006
Telephone: (202) 293-1966
Represented by:
Fritz E. Attaway, Sr. V. President, Government Relations
Barbara A. Dixon, V. President
Matthew T. Gerson, Asst. V. Pres., Congressional Affairs
Mary Knapp, Exec. Secretary to S.V.P., Gov't Relats.
Frances Seghers, Exec. Director, Federal Affairs
Nancy Thompson, Director, Office Administration
Jack J. Valenti, President
Counsel or consultant:
Akin, Gump, Strauss, Hauer and Feld (James P. Denvir, III)
The Laxalt Corp. (Michelle D. Laxalt)
McClure and Trotter (William P. McClure)
Nathan Associates Inc. (Robert R. Nathan)
Parry and Romani Associates Inc. (Romano Romani)
Peter Teeley & Associates (Peter Teeley)
Wexler, Reynolds, Fuller, Harrison and Schule, Inc. (Dale Snape, Joseph W. Waz, Jr.)
Williams and Connolly

Motion Picture Ass'n Political Action Committee
1600 Eye St., N.W., Washington, DC 20006
Telephone: (202) 293-1966
Background: Mary Knapp of the Ass'n serves as Treasurer. (See Motion Picture Ass'n of America.)

Motor and Equipment Manufacturers Ass'n
1325 Pennsylvania Ave., N.W. Suite 600, Washington, DC 20004
Telephone: (202) 393-6362
Represented by:
Christopher M. Bates, Director, Policy Analysis
James J. Conner, Exec. V. President
Paul T. Haluza, Dir., Gov'tal Relations & Public Affairs
Counsel or consultant:
Arent, Fox, Kintner, Plotkin & Kahn (Marc L. Fleischaker)

Motor Vehicle Manufacturers Ass'n of the United States
1620 Eye St., N.W. Suite 1000, Washington, DC 20006
Telephone: (202) 775-2700

Represented by:
Anne E. Carlson, Manager, Federal Liaison Dept.
Stephen J. Collins, Director, Econ. & International Affairs
Anne Edlund, Vice President, Public Affairs
Peter Griskivich, V. President, Motor Truck Mfrs. Division
Ronald P. Hamm, Manager, Federal Liaison Dept.
Thomas H. Hanna, President/Chief Exec. Officer
Edrie Irvine, Sr. Econ. Analyst, Econ. & Int'l Affrs.
Earl R. Kreher, Sr. Econ. Analyst, Econ. & Int'l Afrs.
Timothy C. MacCarthy, Director of Federal Liaison
Robert H. McFadden, Senior Analyst, Fed. Liaison Dept.
Michael J. Stanton, Director, State Relations
Counsel or consultant:
Bonner & Associates
Swidler & Berlin, Chartered

Motorcycle Industry Council
1235 Jefferson Davis Hwy. Suite 600, Arlington, VA 22202
Telephone: (703) 521-0444
Background: Liaison with federal and state governments on behalf of manufacturers and distributors of motorcycles and motorcycle parts and accessories, and of some members of allied trades.
Represented by:
Melvin R. Stahl, Sr. V. President, Government Relations

Motorcycle Riders Foundation
P.O. Box 1808, Washington, DC 20013-1808
Telephone: (202) 944-4920
Counsel or consultant:
Wealth Management Corp. (Wayne T. Curtin)

Motorola Employees' Good Government Committee
1350 Eye St., N.W. Suite 400, Washington, DC 20005-3306
Telephone: (202) 371-6000
Background: A political action committee sponsored by Motorola, Inc. Treasurer is C. Travis Marshall of Motorola, Inc. Bruce C. Ladd, Jr., of Motorola, Inc., serves as PAC Administrator.

Motorola, Inc.
1350 Eye St., N.W., Suite 400, Washington, DC 20005-3306
Telephone: (202) 371-6900
Represented by:
William Borman, V. Pres. & Dir., Internat'l Telecomms.
John B. Copeland, Director of Export Administration
Roni Haggart, V. President, Internat'l Trade
Veronica A. Haggert, V. Pres. & Dir., Internat'l Trade Rels.
Sheila Kern, Manager, International Programs
Mary Lou Lackey, Manager, State Government Relations
Bruce C. Ladd, Jr., V. President of Legislative Affairs
C. Travis Marshall, Sr. V. Pres., Director, Gov't Relations
Joann Piccolo, Manager, Legislative Affairs
Counsel or consultant:
Covington and Burling (Harvey M. Applebaum)
StMaxens and Co. (Susan Presti, Thomas F. StMaxens, II)
Wilkes, Artis, Hedrick and Lane, Chartered

Mount Airy Refining Co.
Houston, TX
Counsel or consultant:
William Bode and Associates (William Bode)

Mount Sinai Medical Center
New York, NY
Counsel or consultant:
Cassidy and Associates, Inc. (Gerald S. J. Cassidy, Vincent M. Versage)

Mount Sinai Medical Center of Greater Miami
Miami Beach, FL
Counsel or consultant:
Cassidy and Associates, Inc. (Thomas M. Gannon, Donald P. Smith)

Mountain Plains Agricultural Service
Casper, WY
Counsel or consultant:
Holt, Miller & Associates (Michael G. Kirby, Harris N. Miller)

Mozambique, Government of
Maputo, Mozambique

Counsel or consultant:
Bruce P. Cameron

Mozambique Research Center
1995 National Capital Station, Washington, DC 20013
Telephone: (202) 625-6443
Background: Conducts research on historic and current events in Mozambique with reference to the situation of human and political rights, cause and effect of the conflict, humanitarian relief and future development and investment.
Represented by:
Thomas W. Schaaf, Jr., Exec. Director

MRJ, Inc.
10455 White Granite Dr. Suite 305, Oakton, VA 22124
Telephone: (703) 385-0703
Represented by:
J. Kenneth Driessen, V. Pres. & Gen. Mgr., Gov't Systems

MSR Public Power Agency
Modesto, CA
Counsel or consultant:
Duncan, Weinberg, Miller & Pembroke, P.C. (Wallace L. Duncan, Frederick L. Miller, Jr.)

MTI Export Management, Inc.
Washington, DC
Counsel or consultant:
Public Affairs Group, Inc. (Robert S. Boege, Edie Fraser)

Multi-Housing Laundry Ass'n
Raleigh, NC
Counsel or consultant:
Sonosky, Chambers and Sachse

Multiprogres
Budapest, Hungary
Counsel or consultant:
DGM Internat'l Inc. (Gordon S. Jones)

Multistate Tax Commission
1400 Eye St., N.W. Suite 1150, Washington, DC 20005
Telephone: (202) 842-1880
Counsel or consultant:
Rosapepe and Spanos (James C. Rosapepe)

Multnomah County, Oregon
Counsel or consultant:
Schwabe, Williamson and Wyatt (Frederick P. Hitz)

Municipal Bond Insurance Ass'n
White Plains, NY
Counsel or consultant:
Kutak Rock & Campbell (Nancy L. Granese)

Municipal Castings Fair Trade Council
Pittsburgh, PA
Counsel or consultant:
Collier, Shannon & Scott (Paul C. Rosenthal)

Municipal Electric Utilities Ass'n of New York State
Albany, NY
Background: Duncan, Weinberg, Miller & Pembroke represents the utilities before federal and state agencies.
Counsel or consultant:
Duncan, Weinberg, Miller & Pembroke, P.C. (Wallace L. Duncan, Jeffrey C. Genzer)

Municipal Finance Industry Ass'n
1747 Pennsylvania Ave., N.W. Suite 900, Washington, DC 20006
Telephone: (202) 296-0784
Background: Address above is that of the DC firm Royer, Mehle &nd Babyak.
Counsel or consultant:
Royer, Mehle & Babyak (Gregory R. Babyak)

Municipal Securities Industry Political Action Committee
1850 M St., N.W., Suite 550, Washington, DC 20036
Telephone: (202) 296-9410
Background: Represented by John T. O'Rourke of the Securities Industry Ass'n.

Municipal Treasurers Ass'n of the United States and Canada
1420 16th St., N.W., Suite 302, Washington, DC 20036
Telephone: (202) 797-7347

The listings in this directory are available as *Mailing Labels*. See last page.

ORGANIZATIONS REPRESENTED

Represented by:
Stacey L. Crane, Exec. Director

Munitions Carrier Conference
7021 Tilden Lane, Rockville, MD 20852
Telephone: (301) 984-1114
Counsel or consultant:
Shaw, Pittman, Potts and Trowbridge (William Mike House)

Murata Machinery, Ltd.
Kyoto, Japan
Counsel or consultant:
Global USA, Inc. (Dr. Bohdan Denysyk)

Murphy Oil U.S.A.
Eldorado, AR
Counsel or consultant:
Groom and Nordberg (Carl A. Nordberg, Jr.)

Murry's, Inc.
8300 Pennsylvania Ave., Forestville, MD 20747-0398
Telephone: (301) 420-6400
Counsel or consultant:
Bergner, Boyette & Bockorny, Inc. (Van R. Boyette)

Muscular Dystrophy Ass'n
5350 Shawnee Rd., Suite 330, Alexandria, VA 22312
Telephone: (703) 941-5001
Represented by:
Melissa Hurtt, District Director
Nancy McGovern, District Director

Museum of Science and Industry
Chicago, IL
Counsel or consultant:
Capitol Associates, Inc. (Gordon P. MacDougall)

Museum Trustee Ass'n
1101 Connecticut Ave., N.W., Suite 700, Washington, DC 20036
Telephone: (202) 857-1180
Counsel or consultant:
Smith, Bucklin and Associates (Victoria Wood)

Mushroom Council
Quincy, FL
Counsel or consultant:
McLeod & Pires (Michael R. McLeod, Laura Phelps)

Music Educators Nat'l Conference
1902 Association Drive, Reston, VA 22091
Telephone: (703) 860-4000
Represented by:
Mary Ann Cameron, Director of Communications
John J. Mahlmann, Exec. Director
Harriet M. Mogge, Director of Meetings and Conventions

Mustang Fuel Corp.
Oklahoma City, OK
Counsel or consultant:
Williams and Jensen, P.C. (George D. Baker)

Mutual Atomic Energy Liability Underwriters
Farmington, CT
Counsel or consultant:
Preston Gates Ellis & Rouvelas Meeds (Lloyd Meeds, Tim L. Peckinpaugh)

Mutual Benefit Life Insurance Co.
Newark, NJ
Counsel or consultant:
Patton, Boggs and Blow (John Jonas)

Mutual Broadcasting System
1755 South Jefferson Davis Hwy., Suite 1200, Arlington, VA 22202
Telephone: (703) 685-2000
Represented by:
Jack Clements, President

Mutual Fairness Taxation Ass'n
1120 Vermont Ave., N.W. Suite 1000, Washington, DC 20005
Telephone: (202) 857-0350
Background: An advocacy coalition of medium-sized mutual insurance companies.
Counsel or consultant:
Thompson and Mitchell (Edward A. Scallet)
Timmons and Co., Inc.

Mutual Interest Transactions
Bronx, NY
Counsel or consultant:
Cassidy and Associates, Inc. (Thomas M. Gannon)

Mutual Life Insurance Co. of New York
New York, NY
Counsel or consultant:
Hogan and Hartson (Clifford S. Gibbons)

Mutual Life Insurance Co. Tax Committee
Milwaukee, WI
Counsel or consultant:
Patton, Boggs and Blow (John Jonas)
Wunder, Ryan, Cannon & Thelen (Lawrence P. Higgins)

Mutual Life Insurance Legislative Committee
1615 L St., N.W., Suite 1210, Washington, DC 20036
Telephone: (202) 785-2211
Counsel or consultant:
Concord Associates, Inc.
Patton, Boggs and Blow (John Jonas)

Mutual of America
New York, NY
Counsel or consultant:
Arnold & Porter (Stanford G. Ross)

Mutual of Omaha Insurance Companies
1700 Pennsylvania Ave., N.W. Suite 500, Washington, DC 20006
Telephone: (202) 393-6200
Represented by:
William W. Bailey, Exec. V.P., Federal Government Affairs
M. Theresa Doyle, Senior Legislative Representative
Joan Albert Dreux, VP, Fed. Legislative & Regulatory Affrs.
Russell C. Ring, Legislative Representative
Counsel or consultant:
Graham and James (Thomas F. Railsback)

Mutual Savings Central Fund
Boston, MA
Counsel or consultant:
Thacher, Proffitt and Wood (Jeremiah S. Buckley)

Mycogen Corp.
San Diego, CA
Counsel or consultant:
Provorny, Jacoby & Robinson (Paul B. Jacoby, Frederick A. Provorny)

Mylan Laboratories, Inc.
Pittsburgh, PA
Counsel or consultant:
Wunder, Ryan, Cannon & Thelen (Michael A. Forscey, Bernard J. Wunder)

N.V. Philips Gloeilampenfabrieken
Netherlands
Counsel or consultant:
Sullivan and Cromwell (Margaret K. Pfeiffer)

NAACP Legal Defense and Educational Fund, Inc.
1275 K St., N.W. Suite 301, Washington, DC 20005
Telephone: (202) 682-1300
Background: Established in 1939 as the legal arm of the Nat'l Ass'n for the Advancement of Colored People. Separated from the NAACP in 1957 at the behest of the IRS. At present the LDF is a civil rights law firm with no connection to the NAACP. Headquarters are at 99 Hudson St., New York, NY 10013.
Represented by:
Elaine R. Jones, Director, Deputy/Counsel
Phyllis McClure, Div. of Policy and Information
Kerry Scanlon, Assistant Counsel

NAATS Political Action Fund
4740 Corridor Place, Suite C, Beltsville, MD 20705-1165
Telephone: (301) 595-2012
Background: The political action committee of the Nat'l Ass'n of Air Traffic Specialists.
Represented by:
David Minton, Contact

NABADA - The Ass'n of Container Reconditioners
1030 15th St., N.W., Washington, DC 20005
Telephone: (202) 296-8028

Represented by:
Daniel W. Barber, President

Naegle Outdoor Advertising
Minneapolis, MN
Counsel or consultant:
O'Connor & Hannan (Mary Scott Guest)

Nakajima All Co.
Tokyo, Japan
Counsel or consultant:
Patton, Boggs and Blow (Thomas Hale Boggs, Jr.)

Nakamichi U.S.A. Corp.
Torrance, CA
Counsel or consultant:
Patton, Boggs and Blow

Nalco Chemical Co.
Naperville, IL
Counsel or consultant:
Mayer, Brown and Platt (Jerry L. Oppenheimer)

Napa Flood Control and Water Conservation District
Napa, CA
Counsel or consultant:
Robinson, Lake, Lerer & Montgomery (James H. Lake, Kim Schnoor)

Napp Chemicals
Lodi, NJ
Counsel or consultant:
Chadbourne and Parke

Narcotics Education
12501 Old Columbia Pike, Silver Spring, MD 20904
Telephone: (301) 680-6732
Represented by:
DeWitt S. Williams, Exec. Director

Nashua Corp.
Nashua, NH
Counsel or consultant:
Crowell and Moring (Brian C. Elmer)
Steptoe and Johnson (Gracia M. Berg)

NATCO
2550 M St., N.W. Suite 275, Washington, DC 20027
Telephone: (202) 887-5160
Counsel or consultant:
Camp, Barsh, Bates and Tate (Ronald L. Platt)

Nat'l Abortion Federation
1436 U St., N.W., Suite 103, Washington, DC 20009
Telephone: (202) 667-5881
Represented by:
Barbara Radford, Exec. Director

Nat'l Abortion Rights Action League
1101 14th St., N.W., Suite 500, Washington, DC 20005
Telephone: (202) 371-0779
Background: Largest national membership organization whose single purpose is to keep abortion safe, legal and available. Works through 40 state affiliates to mobilize "pro-choice" citizens to become politically active and uses its Political Action Committee to bring contributions and volunteers to the campaigns of "pro-choice" Congressional and state legislative candidates.
Represented by:
Robert Bingaman, Jr., Nat'l Field Manager
Dawn Johnsen, Legal Research Director
Ann McGuiness, Development Director
Kate Michelman, Exec. Director
Debra Ness, Associate Director, Programs
Lisa Swanson, Legal Research Coordinator
Julie Tippens, Legislative Representative
Loretta M. Ucelli, Communications Director
Counsel or consultant:
Craver, Mathews, Smith and Co. (Roger M. Craver)
Foreman & Heidepriem (Nikki Heidepriem)
Greer, Margolis, Mitchell & Associates (Frank Greer)
Harmon, Curran and Tousley
Hickman-Maslin Research (Harrison Hickman)

Nat'l Abortion Rights Action League Political Action Committee
1101 14th St., N.W., Suite 500, Washington, DC 20005
Telephone: (202) 371-0779
Background: Exec. Director is Kate Michelman. The PAC's purpose is to provide support to pro-choice candidates at the federal, state and local levels. Makes direct

ORGANIZATIONS REPRESENTED

Nat'l Abortion Rights Action League Political Action Committee (Cont'd)
contributions to campaigns and encourages members of the League to become involved directly in the electoral process. In the 1987-88 election cycle the PAC made approximately $300,000 in direct and indirect contributions to federal and state candidates. and indirect contributions to federal candidates.
Represented by:
Jill Hanaver, PAC Manager
Marcela Howell, PAC Chair

Nat'l Academy of Engineering
2101 Constitution Ave., N.W., Washington, DC 20037
Telephone: (202) 334-2195
Background: A private organization established in 1964 under the Congressional charter of the National Academy of Sciences. An organization of distinguished engineers, autonomous in its administration and selection of members, and sharing with the National Academy of Sciences responsibility for advising the Federal Government. Most activities carried out through the National Research Council.
Represented by:
Carrie Levandoski, Public Awareness Officer
Counsel or consultant:
State & Local Resources (Bruce D. Henderson, Patrick M. Murphy)

Nat'l Academy of Opticianry
10111 Martin Luther King, Jr. Hwy., Suite 112, Bowie, MD 20720
Telephone: (301) 577-4828
Represented by:
Floyd H. Holmgrain, Jr., Ed.D., Exec. Director

Nat'l Academy of Public Administration
1120 G St., N.W. Suite 540, Washington, DC 20005
Telephone: (202) 347-3190
Represented by:
Ray Kline, President

Nat'l Accounting and Finance Council
2200 Mill Road, Second Floor, Alexandria, VA 22314
Telephone: (703) 838-1915
Background: An arm of the American Trucking Ass'ns. Members are chief financial officers, treasurers and higher accounting officials of trucking companies and their suppliers.
Represented by:
Samuel H. Gill, Exec. Director
Jane Sanders, Technical Services Director

Nat'l Advertising Co.
Argo, IL
Counsel or consultant:
Arthur E. Cameron

Nat'l Aeronautic Ass'n of the U.S.A.
1763 R St., N.W., Washington, DC 20009
Telephone: (202) 265-8720
Represented by:
Malvern J. Gross, President
Col. Everett W. Langworthy, USAF (Ret), Exec. V. President
Maj. Gen. Clifton F. von Kann, USA (Ret.), Chairman of the Board

Nat'l AFL-CIO Retired Workers Program
815 16th St., N.W., Sixth Floor, Washington, DC 20006
Telephone: (202) 637-5124
Background: Members are retired union members interested in Social Security and federal health insurance legislation.
Represented by:
Steve Protulis, National Coordinator

Nat'l Aggregates Ass'n
900 Spring St., Silver Spring, MD 20910
Telephone: (301) 587-1400
Background: President is Vincent P. Ahearn, Jr., who is also President of the Nat'l Ready Mixed Concrete Ass'n.
Represented by:
Richard D. Gaynor, Exec. V. President
Richard A. Morris, V. Pres., Gov't Relations & Public Affs.
Kenneth R. Tobin, V. Pres., Gov't Relations & Nat'l Affrs.

Nat'l Aggregates Ass'n Political Action Committee
900 Spring St., Silver Spring, MD 20910
Telephone: (301) 587-1400
Background: Contact is Kenneth R. Tobin of the Association.

Nat'l AgriChemical Retailers Ass'n
Box 65493, Washington, DC 20035-5493
Telephone: (202) 467-0825
Background: A trade association of pesticide dealers.
Represented by:
Kenneth E. Root, Exec. Director
Counsel or consultant:
Christopher A. Myrick

Nat'l Agricultural Aviation Ass'n
1005 E St., S.E., Washington, DC 20003
Telephone: (202) 546-5722
Represented by:
Harold M. Collins, Exec. Director

Nat'l Agricultural Chemicals Ass'n
Madison Bldg., 1155 15th St., Suite 900, Washington, DC 20005
Telephone: (202) 296-1585
Background: The Nat'l Ass'n of U.S. manufacturers, formlators, and distributors of pest control products used in agricultural productions.
Represented by:
W. Scott Ferguson, General Counsel
Dr. Ray McAllister, Director, Regulatory Affairs
Dr. John F. McCarthy, V. Pres., Dir., Scient. & Regul. Affairs
Susan Miller, Director, Communications
Dr. Earl Spurrier, V. President, Director, State Affairs
Jay J. Vroom, President
Counsel or consultant:
Meyers & Associates (Larry D. Meyers)

Nat'l Agricultural Coalition
2111 Wilson Blvd., Suite 531, Arlington, VA 22201-3008
Telephone: (703) 276-8009
Counsel or consultant:
Holt, Miller & Associates (Harris N. Miller)

Nat'l AIDS Network
2033 M St., N.W., Suite 800, Washington, DC 20036
Telephone: (202) 293-2437
Background: Information resource center for AIDS education and services.
Represented by:
Eric Engstrom, Exec. Director
Counsel or consultant:
Noterman and Ward (Peter A. Noterman)

Nat'l Air Carrier Ass'n
1730 M St., N.W. Suite 806, Washington, DC 20036
Telephone: (202) 833-8200
Background: Members are charter airlines.
Represented by:
Edward J. Driscoll, Chairman of the Board, President & CEO

Nat'l Air Traffic Controller Ass'n
444 N. Capitol St., Suite 845, Washington, DC 20001
Telephone: (202) 347-4572
Background: The collective bargaining agent for the nation's more than 13,500 air traffic controllers. Interests include legislation affecting air safety, the FAA and DOT, and federal workers.
Represented by:
R. Steve Bell, President
Anthony V. Dresden, Director, Public Affairs
Ray L. Spickler, Exec. V. President
John F. Thornton, Sr. Director, Legislative Affairs
Counsel or consultant:
Biens, Axelrod, Osborne & Mooney, P.C.

Nat'l Air Traffic Controllers Ass'n PAC
444 N. Capitol St., N.W. Suite 845, Washington, DC 20001
Telephone: (202) 347-4572
Background: Represented by R. Steve Bell of the Nat'l Air Traffic Controllers Ass'n.

Nat'l Air Transportation Ass'n
4226 King St., Alexandria, VA 22302
Telephone: (703) 845-9000

Represented by:
Lawrence L. Burian, President
Andrew V. Cebula, Director, Government Affairs
Mark L. Collatz, Manager, Public Relations
William H. Power, V. President, Government Affairs
Gregory J. Praske, V. President, Finance and Administration
Counsel or consultant:
Shaw, Pittman, Potts and Trowbridge (Carleton S. Jones)

Nat'l Alcoholic Beverage Control Ass'n
4216 King St. West, Alexandria, VA 22302-1507
Telephone: (703) 578-4200
Represented by:
Paul C. Dufek, Exec. V. President and Treasurer
Counsel or consultant:
Tendler, Goldberg & Biggins, Chtd. (James M. Goldberg)

Nat'l Alliance for Animal Legislation
P.O. Box 75116, Washington, DC 20013-5116
Telephone: (703) 684-0654
Represented by:
Peter G. Linck, Exec. Director

Nat'l Alliance for Political Action
1628 11th St., N.W., Washington, DC 20001
Telephone: (202) 939-6325
Background: A political action committee sponsored by the Nat'l Alliance of Postal and Federal Employees.
Represented by:
Jacqueline Tollett, Director, Legislation

Nat'l Alliance for the Mentally Ill
2101 Wilson Blvd., Suite 302, Arlington, VA 22201
Telephone: (703) 524-7600
Background: A national network of 936 local and state affiliates of a self-help movement for families and friends of people with serious mental illnesses and those persons themselves. Membership includes over 80,000 families nationwide.
Represented by:
Lynn Borton, Deputy Director
James Cromwell, Research Advocate
Laurie Flynn, Exec. Director
Charles R. Harman, Director, Public Relations
James Havel, Director, Government Relations
Ron Honberg, Legislative Associate

Nat'l Alliance of Black School Educators
2816 Georgia Ave., N.W., Washington, DC 20001
Telephone: (202) 483-1549
Background: Seeks to improve American educational opportunity and remove racial barriers in the field of education.
Represented by:
William J. Saunders, Exec. Director

Nat'l Alliance of Blind Students
1010 Vermont Ave., N.W. Suite 1100, Washington, DC 20005
Telephone: (202) 393-3666
Background: Represented by Stephanie Cooper of the American Council of the Blind.

Nat'l Alliance of Business
1201 New York Ave., N.W., Suite 700, Washington, DC 20005
Telephone: (202) 289-2888
Background: An independent, business-led, non-profit corporation whose mission is to increase private sector training and job opportunities for the economically disadvantaged and the long-term unemployed by building and strengthening public/private partnerships of business, government, labor, education and community-based organizations.
Represented by:
William H. Kolberg, President and CEO
Thomas A. Lindsley, V. President, Congressional Affairs
Pierce A. Quinlan, Exec. V. President
Esther F. Schaeffer, V. President, Policy
Foster C. Smith, Jr., Sr. V. Pres., Marketing/Communications
Counsel or consultant:
Gallagher-Widmeyer Group Inc., The (Scott D. Widmeyer)

Nat'l Alliance of Outpatient Cancer Therapy Centers
1321 Duke St., Suite 200, Alexandria, VA 22314
Telephone: (703) 739-7999

ORGANIZATIONS REPRESENTED

Counsel or consultant:
  U.S. Strategies Corp. (Joseph H. Miltenberger)

Nat'l Alliance of Postal and Federal Employees
1628 11th St., N.W., Washington, DC 20001
Telephone: (202) 939-6325
Background: Sponsors the Nat'l Alliance for Political Action.
Represented by:
  James McGee, President

Nat'l Alliance of Spanish-Speaking People for Equality
1701 16th St., N.W., Suite 601, Washington, DC 20009
Telephone: (202) 234-8198
Background: A civil rights organization seeking equal rights for Hispanic people, partcularly in employment, education, living conditions and justice.
Represented by:
  Dr. Miguel Sandoval, President

Nat'l Alliance to End Homelessness
1518 K St., N.W., Suite 206, Washington, DC 20005
Telephone: (202) 638-1526
Background: A national non-profit organization formed to reinforce and encourage programs to serve the hungry and homeless and to link government and private resources for that purpose.
Represented by:
  Tom Kenyon, Exec. Director
  Mike Mayer, Editor

Nat'l American Corp.
Atlanta, GA
Counsel or consultant:
  Dow, Lohnes and Albertson (Robert M. Chasnow)

Nat'l American Indian Court Clerks Ass'n
1000 Connecticut Ave., N.W., Washington, DC 20036
Telephone: (202) 296-0685
Background: Represented by E. Thomas Colosimo of ARROW (Americans for Righting and Restitution of Old Wrongs).

Nat'l American Indian Housing Council
122 C St., N.W., Suite 280, Washington, DC 20001
Telephone: (202) 783-2667
Background: A non-profit organization which provides a forum for the discussion of Indian housing issues and concerns on behalf ot its member Indian Housing Authorities. Seeks to support these IHAs in efforts to provide safe and sanitary dwellings to Indian and Alaska Native communities.
Represented by:
  Virginia E. Spencer, Exec. Director
Counsel or consultant:
  Reno, Cavanaugh & Hornig

Nat'l-American Wholesale Grocers' Ass'n
201 Park Washington Court, Falls Church, VA 22046
Telephone: (703) 532-9400
Background: Represents wholesale grocers and foodservice distributors. Includes its division, the Internat'l Foodservice Distributors Ass'n (IFDA), of the same address.
Represented by:
  John R. Block, President
  Stephen P. Bower, Director of Marketing/Communications
  Bruce A. Gates, V. President, Government Relations
  Joyce Hamilton, Director, Government Relations
  Cheri Jacobus, Director, Press and Media
  Gilbert L. Kretzer, V. Pres. & Exec. Dir., IFDA
  Christine M. Sand, Legislative Assistant
Counsel or consultant:
  Bergner, Boyette & Bockorny, Inc. (Van R. Boyette)
  Keller and Heckman (William H. Borghesani, Jr., Peter A. Susser)
  Olsson, Frank and Weeda, P.C. (John Bode, Richard L. Frank)

Nat'l-American Wholesale Grocers' Ass'n Political Action Committee
201 Park Washington Court, Falls Church, VA 22046
Telephone: (703) 532-9400
Background: Represented by Bruce A. Gates of the Association.

Nat'l Anti-Hunger Coalition
1319 F St., N.W. Suite 500, Washington, DC 20004
Telephone: (202) 393-5060

Represented by:
  Michele Tingling-Clemmons, Staff Coordinator

Nat'l Anti-Vivisection Soc.
112 North Carolina Ave., S.E., Washington, DC 20003
Telephone: (202) 543-6601
Background: A non-profit education organization of 50,000 members which seeks to eliminate use of animals in biomedical and behavioral research. Headquartered in Chicago.
Represented by:
  Donald J. Barnes, Director, Washington Office

Nat'l Antique and Art Dealers Ass'n of America
New York, NY
Counsel or consultant:
  Steptoe and Johnson (Blake D. Rubin)

Nat'l Apartment Ass'n
1111 14th St., N.W., 9th Floor, Washington, DC 20005
Telephone: (202) 842-4050
Represented by:
  Colleen Fisher, V. President, Government Relations
  Roddy L. Hiduskey, Director, Public Relations
  Donna A. McCulloch, Legislative Representative
  Dorothy Stucke, Legislative Director
Counsel or consultant:
  O'Connor & Hannan (Thomas H. Quinn)

Nat'l Apparel and Textile Ass'n
Seattle, WA
Counsel or consultant:
  Bogle and Gates

Nat'l Armored Car Ass'n
Seattle, WA
Counsel or consultant:
  Rowland & Sellery (Lawrence E. Sabbath)

Nat'l Art Education Ass'n
1916 Association Dr., Reston, VA 22091
Telephone: (703) 860-8000
Represented by:
  Dr. Thomas A. Hatfield, Exec. Director

Nat'l Arthritis and Musculoskeletal and Skin Diseases Information Clearinghouse
P.O. Box AMS, Bethesda, MD 20892
Telephone: (301) 468-3235
Background: Information Specialist is Phyllis Abramczyk, also of the Nat'l Digestive Diseases Information Clearinghouse.

Nat'l Artists Equity Ass'n
P.O. Box 28068 Central Station, Washington, DC 20038
Telephone: (202) 628-9633
Represented by:
  Catherine Auth, Exec. Director
Counsel or consultant:
  Podesta Associates (John D. Podesta)

Nat'l Asphalt Pavement Ass'n
Box 517, Riverdale, MD 20737
Telephone: (301) 779-4880

Nat'l Assembly of Local Arts Agencies
1420 K St., N.W., Suite 204, Washington, DC 20005
Telephone: (202) 371-2830
Represented by:
  Robert Lynch, President/CEO

Nat'l Assembly of Nat'l Voluntary Health and Social Welfare Organizations
1319 F St., N.W., Suite 601, Washington, DC 20004
Telephone: (202) 347-2080
Represented by:
  Doni G. Blumenstock, Assistant Director
  Leonard W. Stern, Exec. Director

Nat'l Assembly of State Arts Agencies
1010 Vermont Ave., N.W., Suite 920, Washington, DC 20005
Telephone: (202) 347-6352
Represented by:
  Jonathan Katz, Exec. Director

Nat'l Assistance Management Ass'n
Box 57051, Washington, DC 20037
Telephone: (202) 223-1448
Background: An association of persons concerned with the management of financial assistance.

Represented by:
  Gary Dwoskin, President

Nat'l Assisted Housing Management Ass'n
1800 Diagonal Rd. Suite 600, Alexandria, VA 22314
Telephone: (703) 684-4476
Represented by:
  John Bohm, Exec. Director
Counsel or consultant:
  Coan & Lyons (Carl A. S. Coan, Jr.)

Nat'l Ass'n for Ambulatory Care
Dallas, TX
Counsel or consultant:
  Michaels and Wishner, P.C. (Joel L. Michaels)

Nat'l Ass'n for Bilingual Education
810 First St., N.E. 3rd Floor, Washington, DC 20002-4205
Telephone: (202) 898-1829
Background: Founded in 1976 as an association of educators, parents, businessmen and women and professionals to promote bilingual education for the sector of the population with limited proficiency in English.
Represented by:
  James J. Lyons, Exec. Director

Nat'l Ass'n for Biomedical Research
818 Connecticut Ave., N.W. Third Floor, Washington, DC 20006
Telephone: (202) 857-0540
Represented by:
  Barbara A. Rich, Exec. V. President
  Frankie L. Trull, President
Counsel or consultant:
  Covington and Burling

Nat'l Ass'n for County Community and Economic Development
440 First St., N.W., Washington, DC 20001
Telephone: (202) 393-6226
Background: Contact is Donald Pepe of the Nat'l Ass'n of Counties.

Nat'l Ass'n for Equal Opportunity in Higher Education
400 12th St., N.E. 2nd Floor, Washington, DC 20002
Telephone: (202) 543-9111
Represented by:
  Dr. Samuel L. Myers, President
  Herbert O. Reid, Sr., Legal Counsel
  Wilma J. Roscoe, V. President
  Bea Pace Smith, Director, Federal Relations

Nat'l Ass'n for Foreign Student Affairs
1860 19th St., N.W., Washington, DC 20009
Telephone: (202) 462-4811
Represented by:
  Jill Bulthius, Dir, Public Relations & Membership Info.
  Bill Carroll, Staff Director, Government Relations
  John F. Reichard, Exec. V. President

Nat'l Ass'n for Girls and Women in Sport
1900 Association Drive, Reston, VA 22091
Telephone: (703) 476-3450
Represented by:
  Peggy Kellers, Exec. Director

Nat'l Ass'n for Home Care
519 C St., N.E., Washington, DC 20002
Telephone: (202) 547-7424
Background: Represents the nation's home health agencies, homemaker-home health aide organizations and hospices.
Represented by:
  Erica M. Battaglia, Director, State Relations
  Dayle Berke, Director, Government Affairs
  Val J. Halamandaris, President
Counsel or consultant:
  Brand and Lowell, P.C. (Stanley M. Brand)

Nat'l Ass'n for Home Care Congressional Action Committee
P.O. Box 75197, Washington, DC 20013
Telephone: (202) 547-7424
Background: Represented by Val J. Halamandaris of the Association.

Nat'l Ass'n for Hospital Development
112-B East Broad St., Falls Church, VA 22046
Telephone: (703) 532-6243
Represented by:
  Dr. William C. McGinly, President

ORGANIZATIONS REPRESENTED

Nat'l Ass'n for Human Development
1424 16th St., N.W., Suite 102, Washington, DC 20036
Telephone: (202) 328-2191
Background: A self-help, health/education/employment-training organization primarily for older adults; develops and publishes a variety of health/fitness print and audiovisual materials for older adults and professionals who serve them; and conducts training and other special projects for these target groups.
Represented by:
Jules Evan Baker, President
Anne Radd, Exec. Vice President

Nat'l Ass'n for Law Placement
1666 Connecticut Ave., N.W. Suite 450, Washington, DC 20009
Telephone: (202) 667-1666
Represented by:
Jamienne S. Studley, Exec. Director

Nat'l Ass'n for Music Therapy
505 11th St., S.E., Washington, DC 20003
Telephone: (202) 543-6864
Represented by:
Andrea H. Farbman, Exec. Director

Nat'l Ass'n for Professional Saleswomen
712 West Broad St., Suite 5, Falls Church, VA 20046
Telephone: (703) 538-4390
Background: A non-profit organization dedicated to the education and promotion of women in sales and marketing.
Represented by:
Gail Bamford, President

Nat'l Ass'n for Public Interest Law
1666 Connecticut Ave., N.W., Suite 424, Washington, DC 20009
Telephone: (202) 462-0120
Background: Founded in 1986, NAPIL is a resource center for Public Interest Law Foundations, Student Funded Fellowships, local Equal Justice Foundations, and other income-sharing programs. Student and lawyer members of these organizations contribute a portion of their summer or annual legal employment income to fund others working in public interest law. NAPIL organizes new income-sharing programs, provides technical assistance to existing programs, promotes loan forgiveness programs and produce public public interest law career publications.
Represented by:
Michael Caudell-Feagan, Exec. Director
Sue Schechter, Staff Attorney

Nat'l Ass'n for Search and Rescue
Box 3709, Fairfax, VA 22038
Telephone: (703) 352-1349
Represented by:
Greg McDonald, Exec. Director

Nat'l Ass'n for the Advancement of Colored People
1025 Vermont Ave., N.W. Suite 730, Washington, DC 20005
Telephone: (202) 638-2269
Background: The largest civil rights organization seeks to end racial segregation and discrimination in all aspects of American life.
Represented by:
Althea T. L. Simmons, Director, Washington Bureau

Nat'l Ass'n for the Education of Young Children
1834 Connecticut Ave., N.W., Washington, DC 20009
Telephone: (202) 232-8777
Represented by:
Ellen Galinsky, President
Dr. Marilyn M. Smith, Exec. Director
Dr. Barbara A. Willer, Public Affairs Director

Nat'l Ass'n for the Self-Employed
Dallas, TX
Counsel or consultant:
Jere W. Glover

Nat'l Ass'n for the Specialty Food Trade
New York, NY
Counsel or consultant:
Max N. Berry Law Offices (Marsha A. Echols)

Nat'l Ass'n for the Support of Long Term Care - NASL
Austin, TX

Counsel or consultant:
Hecht, Spencer & Associates (Bronwyn R. Bachrach, William H. Hecht, W. Timothy Locke)

Nat'l Ass'n for Uniformed Services
5535 Hempstead Way, Springfield, VA 22151
Telephone: (703) 750-1342
Represented by:
John W. Morrison, Legislative Counsel
Col. Charles C. Partridge, (Ret), Legislative Counsel
Maj. Gen. James C. Pennington, (Ret.), Exec. V. President

Nat'l Ass'n for Uniformed Services Political Action Committee
5535 Hempstead Way, Springfield, VA 22151
Telephone: (703) 750-1342
Background: Formed in 1978. Supported by the Nat'l Ass'n for Uniformed Services.
Represented by:
Col. James W. Bradbury, (Ret), Treasurer

Nat'l Ass'n for Women Deans, Administrators, and Counselors
1325 18th St., N.W., Suite 210, Washington, DC 20036
Telephone: (202) 659-9330
Represented by:
Dr. Patricia A. Rueckel, Exec. Director

Nat'l Ass'n of Accredited Cosmetology Schools
5201 Leesburg Pike, Suite 205, Falls Church, VA 22041
Telephone: (703) 845-1333
Represented by:
Dr. James P. Murphy, Exec. Director

Nat'l Ass'n of Accredited Cosmetology Schools PAC
5201 Leesburg Pike, Suite 205, Falls Church, VA 22041
Telephone: (703) 845-1333
Background: Represented by James P. Murphy of the Nat'l Ass'n of Accredited Cosmetology Schools.

Nat'l Ass'n of Activity Professionals
1225 Eye St., N.W., Suite 300, Washington, DC 20005
Telephone: (202) 289-0722
Background: Formed to advance the professiona;l competence of those who provide long term health care for the elderly.
Counsel or consultant:
Linton, Mields, Reisler and Cottone (Mary E. Birmingham, Charles F. Price)

Nat'l Ass'n of Air Traffic Specialists
4740 Corridor Place, Suite c, Beltsville, MD 20705
Telephone: (301) 595-2012
Represented by:
Sharon Bell, Chairman
Bruce B. Henry, President/Exec. Director

Nat'l Ass'n of Air Traffic Specialists Political Action Fund
4780 Corridor Place, #B, Beltsville, MD 20705
Telephone: (301) 595-2012
Represented by:
Joanne F. Bentz, Treasurer

Nat'l Ass'n of Aircraft and Communications Suppliers, Inc.
North Hollywood, CA
Counsel or consultant:
Petrillo & Hordell (Joseph J. Petrillo)

Nat'l Ass'n of Arab Americans
2033 M St., N.W., Suite 300, Washington, DC 20036
Telephone: (202) 467-4800
Background: A Washington-based political action organization focused primarily on promoting a more balanced U.S. foreign policy in the Middle East.
Represented by:
Jawad F. George, Exec. Director
Khalil E. Jahshan, Associate Exec. Director, Public Affairs
Rebecca Nahas, Director, Media Relations
Alfred Shehab, President
Jeffery V. Steele, Director, Government Affairs

Nat'l Ass'n of Arab Americans Political Action Committee
2033 M St., N.W., Suite 300, Washington, DC 20036
Telephone: (202) 467-4800
Background: Represented by Jawad F. George of the Nat'l Ass'n of Arab Americans.

Nat'l Ass'n of Area Agencies on Aging
600 Maryland Ave., S.W. Suite 208 West Wing, Washington, DC 20024
Telephone: (202) 484-7520
Represented by:
Jonathan D. Linkous, Exec. Director
Larry Rickards, Ph.D., Assistant Director

Nat'l Ass'n of Attorneys General
444 North Capitol St., N.W., Suite 403, Washington, DC 20001
Telephone: (202) 628-0435
Background: Expresses views of state attorneys general through resolutions, communications and testimony on selected subjects to the executive and legislative agencies of state and federal governments.
Represented by:
Christine T. Milliken, Exec. Director and General Counsel
Lynne Ross, Deputy Director and Legislative Director

Nat'l Ass'n of Auctioneers
Overland Park, KS
Counsel or consultant:
Campbell-Raupe, Inc. (Jeanne M. Campbell)

Nat'l Ass'n of Beverage Importers
1025 Vermont Ave., N.W. Suite 1205, Washington, DC 20005
Telephone: (202) 638-1617
Represented by:
David F. Gencarelli, General Counsel & Secretary
Robert J. Maxwell, President
Counsel or consultant:
Rogers and Wells (William Morris)

Nat'l Ass'n of Beverage Importers Political Action Committee
1025 Vermont Ave., N.W. Suite 1205, Washington, DC 20005
Telephone: (202) 638-1617
Background: Represented by Robert J. Maxwell, President of the Association.

Nat'l Ass'n of Biology Teachers
11250 Roger Bacon Dr. Suite 19, Reston, VA 22090
Telephone: (703) 471-1134
Represented by:
Patricia J. McWethy, Exec. Director

Nat'l Ass'n of Black Accountants
900 2nd St., N.E., Suite 205, Washington, DC 20002
Telephone: (202) 682-0222
Represented by:
Beverly Ever-Jones, Exec. Director

Nat'l Ass'n of Black Owned Broadcasters
1730 M St., N.W. Suite 412, Washington, DC 20036
Telephone: (202) 463-8970
Background:
Counsel or consultant:
Rubin, Winston and Diercks (James L. Winston)

Nat'l Ass'n of Black Women Attorneys
3711 Macomb St., N.W., Washington, DC 20016
Telephone: (202) 966-9693
Represented by:
Robin Alexander, Public Relations Director
Mabel Dole Haden, President
Mary Wilburn, Chairwoman, DC Chapter

Nat'l Ass'n of Blind Teachers
1010 Vermont Ave., N.W. Suite 1100, Washington, DC 20005
Telephone: (202) 393-3666
Background: Represented by Roberta Douglas of the American Council of the Blind.

Nat'l Ass'n of Boards of Examiners of Nursing Home Administrators
808 17th St., N.W., Suite 200, Washington, DC 20006
Telephone: (202) 223-9750
Counsel or consultant:
Bostrom Corp. (Jerome A. Miller, CAE)

Nat'l Ass'n of Bond Lawyers
2000 Pennsylvania Ave., N.W., Suite 9000, Washington, DC 20006
Telephone: (202) 778-2244
Represented by:
Amy K. Dunbar, Director, Governmental Affairs

ORGANIZATIONS REPRESENTED

Nat'l Ass'n of Brick Distributors
212 South Henry St., Alexandria, VA 22314
Telephone: (703) 549-2555
Represented by:
Walter E. Galanty, Jr., President

Nat'l Ass'n of Broadcast Employees and Technicians
7101 Wisconsin Ave. Suite 800, Bethesda, MD 20814
Telephone: (301) 657-8420
Represented by:
James P. Nolan, Internat'l President

Nat'l Ass'n of Broadcasters
1771 N St., N.W., Washington, DC 20036
Telephone: (202) 429-5300
Background: Established in 1922 to foster and promote the development of the arts of aural and visual broadcasting in all its forms, to protect its members in every lawful and proper manner from injustices and unjust exactions and to do what is necessary to encourage practices which strengthen and maintain the broadcast industry to the end that it may best serve the public.
Represented by:
Henry L. Baumann, Exec. V. President and General Counsel
Rory Benson, Sr. V. Pres., Assistant to the President
Patricia A. Blood, Legislative Affairs (Senate)
Steven A. Bookshester, Assoc. Gen. Counsel & First Amend. Atty.

Belva B. Brissett, Sr. V. President, Regulatory Affairs
Tristan E. Carter, Legislative Affairs (House)
John C. David, V.P., Broadcaster-Congressional Relats.
Mark Fratrik, V. President/Economist
Edward O. Fritts, President
Vivian A. Hightower, Senior Research Associate
Stephen I. Jacobs, V. President, Congressional Liaison
Gene Jeffers, V. Pres., Public Affrs. & Communications
Susan Kraus, V. President, Media Relations
Teri Lepovitz, Senior V. President
James C. May, Exec. V. President, Government Relations
Daniel B. Phythyon, V. President, Congressional Liaison
Theresa Rabel, Director, Government Relations
Michael C. Rau, Senior V. President
Henry J. Roeder, Senior V. President
Barry Umansky, Deputy General Counsel
Michael A. Waring, Director, Political Communications
Howard E. Woolley, Director, Government Relations
Walter R. Wurfel, Sr. V. Pres., Public Affrs. & Commo.
Counsel or consultant:
Davidson Colling Group, Inc., The (James H. Davidson)

Nat'l Ass'n of Broadcasters Television and Radio Political Action Committee (TARPAC)
1771 N St., N.W., Washington, DC 20036
Telephone: (202) 429-5319
Background: James C. May, of the Nat'l Ass'n of Broadcasters, serves as contact.
Represented by:
RaeAnn Roldon, TARPAC Coordinator

Nat'l Ass'n of Business and Educational Radio
1501 Duke St., Suite 200, Alexandria, VA 22314
Telephone: (703) 739-0300
Represented by:
Emmett B. Kitchen, Jr., President and General Manager
Counsel or consultant:
Bergner, Boyette & Bockorny, Inc. (David A. Bockorny)
Manning, Selvage & Lee/Washington
Meyer, Faller, Weisman and Greenburg (David E. Weisman)

Nat'l Ass'n of Business and Educational Radio Political Action Committee
1501 Duke St., Suite 200, Alexandria, VA 22314
Telephone: (703) 739-0300
Represented by:
Nancy Hahn, Treasurer
Counsel or consultant:
Meyer, Faller, Weisman and Greenburg

Nat'l Ass'n of Business Political Action Committees
499 S. Capitol St., S.W. Suite 103, Washington, DC 20003
Telephone: (202) 479-0531
Counsel or consultant:
Stockmeyer & Co. (Steven F. Stockmeyer, Darlene Vanderbush)

Nat'l Ass'n of Career Development Consultants
1707 L St., N.W., Suite 333, Washington, DC 20036
Telephone: (202) 452-9102
Counsel or consultant:
Siegel, Houston and Associates (Betsy Houston)

Nat'l Ass'n of Casualty and Surety Agents
600 Pennsylvania Ave., S.E., Suite 211, Washington, DC 20003
Telephone: (202) 547-6616
Background: Exec. Director is J. Martin Huber, also of the Nat'l Ass'n of Surety Bond Producers.
Represented by:
Ken A. Crerar, V. President, Government Affairs
Ann L. Garver, Director of Legislative Affairs
Monty Shepardson, Legislative Assistant
Counsel or consultant:
Miller, Cassidy, Larroca and Lewin (Jonathan Sallet)

Nat'l Ass'n of Casualty and Surety Agents Political Action Committee (NACSAPAC)
600 Pennsylvania Ave., S.E. Suite 211, Washington, DC 20003
Telephone: (202) 547-6616
Background: Responsible contact is Ken A. Crerar. (See Nat'l Ass'n of Casualty and Surety Agents.)

Nat'l Ass'n of Chain Drug Stores
Box 1417-D49, Alexandria, VA 22313
Telephone: (703) 549-3001
Represented by:
John Covert, Director, Communications
Leonard J. DeMino, V. Pres., Pharmacy & Professional Affrs.
Kathy J. Gavett, Manager, State Government Affairs
Kathryn M. Lavriha, Manager, State Government Affairs
Randy L. Teach, Sr. V. Pres., Health Policy & Gov't Aff.
James A. Whitman, Manager, Agency & Reg. Afrs/Gen. Counsel
Ronald L. Ziegler, President and CEO
Counsel or consultant:
Flack Inc. (Susan Garber Flack)

Nat'l Ass'n of Chain Drug Stores Political Action Committee
Box 1417-D49, Alexandria, VA 22313
Telephone: (703) 549-3001
Represented by:
R. James Huber, Treasurer

Nat'l Ass'n of Chain Manufacturers
Chicago, IL
Counsel or consultant:
Courtney, McCamant and Turney (Richard F. Turney)

Nat'l Ass'n of Chapter Thirteen Bankruptcy Trustees
Columbia, SC
Counsel or consultant:
Neill, Mullenholz and Shaw (G. Jerry Shaw, Jr.)

Nat'l Ass'n of Chemical Distributors
1200 17th St., N.W., Suite 400, Washington, DC 20036
Telephone: (202) 296-9200
Background: Joseph A. Cook of the DC firm Hill Group, Inc. serves as Exec. V. President.
Counsel or consultant:
Hill Group, Inc. (Joseph A. Cook)

Nat'l Ass'n of Chiefs of Police
1000 Connecticut Ave., N.W. Suite 9, Washington, DC 20036
Telephone: (202) 293-9088
Represented by:
Robert Ferguson, President
Frederick Pearson, Congressional Liaison Director

Nat'l Ass'n of Children's Hospitals and Related Institutions
401 Wythe St., Alexandria, VA 22314
Telephone: (703) 684-1355
Background: Legislative interest includes children's access to health care and child abuse prevention.
Represented by:
Robert H. Sweeney, President
Peter Wilson, Director, Government Relations

Nat'l Ass'n of College Stores
Oberlin, OH

Counsel or consultant:
Arent, Fox, Kintner, Plotkin & Kahn (David J. Aronofsky, Michael D. Barnes, Marc L. Fleischaker, Burton V. Wides)

Nat'l Ass'n of College and University Attorneys
One Dupont Circle, N.W. Suite 620, Washington, DC 20036
Telephone: (202) 833-8390
Represented by:
Phillip M. Grier, Exec. Director

Nat'l Ass'n of College and University Business Officers
One Dupont Circle, N.W., Suite 500, Washington, DC 20036-1178
Telephone: (202) 861-2500
Represented by:
Mary Jane Calais, Director, Public Policy & Mgmt. Programs
John B. Cox, Director of Communications
Phyllis R. Forbes, V. President
Martin S. Green, Program Manager
Anne Gross, Program Manager
Caspa L. Harris, Jr., President
Christine Larger, Program Manager

Nat'l Ass'n of Commissions for Women
YWCA Bldg., Suite M-10, 624 Ninth St., N.W., Washington, DC 20001
Telephone: (202) 628-5030
Background: Membership organization composed of regional, state and local commissions created by government to improve the status of women. Organized in 1970.
Represented by:
Claire Bigelow, Exec. Director

Nat'l Ass'n of Community Action Agencies
1775 T St., N.W.,, Washington, DC 20009
Telephone: (202) 265-7546
Background: Members represent organizations funded under Section 221 of the Economic Opportunity Community Services Act.
Represented by:
Edward L. Block, Exec. Director

Nat'l Ass'n of Community Health Centers
1330 New Hampshire Ave., N.W. Suite 122, Washington, DC 20036
Telephone: (202) 659-8008
Represented by:
Daniel Cardenas, Assoc. Director, Policy Analysis
Alice M. Jackson, Assoc. Director, Policy Analysis
Vincent A. Keane, Special Ass't, Resource Development
Katherine Kiedrowski, Health Services Specialist
Thomas Van Coverden, Exec. Director

Nat'l Ass'n of Computer Stores
Fort Pierce, FL
Counsel or consultant:
Smith, Heenan and Althen (William I. Althen)

Nat'l Ass'n of Conservation Districts
509 Capitol Court, N.E., Washington, DC 20002
Telephone: (202) 547-6223
Represented by:
Eugene Lamb, Programs Analyst
Steven R. Meyer, Director, Governmental Affairs
Ernest C. Shea, Exec. V. President
Deborah A. White, Exec. Assistant

Nat'l Ass'n of Consumer Agency Administrators
1010 Vermont Ave., N.W., Suite 514, Washington, DC 20005
Telephone: (202) 347-7395
Represented by:
Pauline Flynn, Exec. Director

Nat'l Ass'n of Convenience Stores
1605 King St., Alexandria, VA 22314
Telephone: (703) 684-3600
Represented by:
Kerley LeBoeuf, President
Teri F. Richman, Sr. V. President, Public Affairs
John W. Strayer, Director, Government Relations
Sheri Taffer, Communicaqtions Coordinator
Counsel or consultant:
Collier, Shannon & Scott (R. Timothy Columbus)

ORGANIZATIONS REPRESENTED

Nat'l Ass'n of Convenience Stores Political Action Committee
1605 King St., Alexandria, VA 22314
Telephone: (703) 684-3600
Background: Reprsented by Teri F. Richman of the Association.
Counsel or consultant:
　Collier, Shannon & Scott

Nat'l Ass'n of Corporate Directors
1707 L St., N.W., Suite 560, Washington, DC 20036
Telephone: (202) 775-0509
Background: Affiliated with the American Management Ass'ns.
Represented by:
　John M. Nash, President

Nat'l Ass'n of Corporate Treasurers
1101 Connecticut Ave., N.W., Suite 700, Washington, DC 20036
Telephone: (202) 857-1115
Counsel or consultant:
　Smith, Bucklin and Associates (Robert T. Chancler)

Nat'l Ass'n of Counties
440 First St., N.W., Washington, DC 20001
Telephone: (202) 393-6226
Represented by:
　Karen Battle, Legis. Director, Community Development
　Michael L. Benjamin, Legis. Rep., Human Services in Education
　Neil Bomberg, Research Associate for Employment & Tng
　Edward E. Ferguson, Deputy Exec. Director
　Robert Fogel, Legis. Rep., Transp. & Intergov't Afrs.
　Jim Golden, Director of Research
　G. Thomas Goodman, Director, Public Affairs
　Larry Jones, Legis. Rep., Employment/Labor Relations
　Thomas L. Joseph, III, Legislative Representative, Health
　Rick Keister, Legis. Rep., Public Lands
　Jerald McNeil, Sr Proj. Dir., Employment & Training
　Donald Murray, Legis. Rep., Justice/Public Safety
　Barbara Paley, Legis. Rep., Energy & Environment
　Donald Pepe, Project Director, Community Development
　Ann Powell, Data Services Coordinator
　Beverly A. Schlotterbeck, County News Editor
　Ralph Tabor, Director, Legislative Staff
　John P. Thomas, Exec. Director
　Mary Uyeda, Director, County Health Policy Center
　Susan J. White, Legis. Rep., Taxation & Finance

Nat'l Ass'n of Counties Council of Intergovernmental Coordinators
440 First St., N.W., Washington, DC 20001
Telephone: (202) 393-6226
Background: Contact is Robert Fogel of the Nat'l Ass'n of Counties.

Nat'l Ass'n of Counties Research Foundation
440 First St., N.W., Washington, DC 20001
Telephone: (202) 393-6226
Background: Represented by Jim Golden of the Nat'l Ass'n of Counties.

Nat'l Ass'n of County Administrators
440 First St., N.W., Washington, DC 20001
Telephone: (202) 393-6226
Background: Contact is Edward E. Ferguson, Deputy Director of the Nat'l Ass'n of Counties.

Nat'l Ass'n of County Aging Programs
440 First St., N.W., Washington, DC 20001
Telephone: (202) 393-6226
Background: Michael L. Benjamin of the Nat'l Ass'n of Counties and the Nat'l Ass'n of County Services Administrators serves as Staff Liaison.

Nat'l Ass'n of County Association Executives
440 First St., N.W., Washington, DC 20001
Telephone: (202) 393-6226
Background: Contact is Edward E. Ferguson of the Nat'l Ass'n of Counties.

Nat'l Ass'n of County Civil Attorneys
440 First St., N.W., Washington, DC 20001
Telephone: (202) 393-6226
Background: Contact is Donald Murray of the Nat'l Ass'n of Counties.

Nat'l Ass'n of County Data Processing Administrators
440 First St., N.W., Washington, DC 20001
Telephone: (202) 393-6226
Background: Contact is Ann Powell of the Nat'l Ass'n of Counties.

Nat'l Ass'n of County Engineers
440 First St., N.W., Washington, DC 20001
Telephone: (202) 393-6226
Background: Contact is Robert Fogel of the Nat'l Ass'n of Counties.

Nat'l Ass'n of County Health Facility Administrators
440 First St., N.W., Washington, DC 20001
Telephone: (202) 393-6226
Background: Contact is Tom Joseph of the Nat'l Ass'n of Counties.

Nat'l Ass'n of County Health Officials
440 First St., N.W., Washington, DC 20001
Telephone: (202) 783-5550
Background: A member organization of the Coalition for Health Funding in Washington. Liaison with the Nat'l Ass'n of Counties is maintained through Mary Uyeda of the latter organization.
Represented by:
　Nancy Rawding, Exec. Director

Nat'l Ass'n of County Human Services Administrators
440 First St., N.W., Washington, DC 20001
Telephone: (202) 393-6226
Background: Contact is Michael L. Benjamin of the Nat'l Ass'n of Counties.

Nat'l Ass'n of County Information Officials
440 First St., N.W., Washington, DC 20001
Telephone: (202) 393-6226
Background: Contact is Tom Goodman, Public Affairs Director, Nat'l Ass'n of Counties.

Nat'l Ass'n of County Office Employees
Neiphi, UT
Counsel or consultant:
　Winburn, VanScoyoc, and Hooper (John P. Winburn)

Nat'l Ass'n of County Park and Recreation Officials
440 First St., N.W., Washington, DC 20001
Telephone: (202) 393-6226
Background: Contact is Neil Bomberg of the Nat'l Ass'n of Counties.

Nat'l Ass'n of County Planning Directors
440 First St., N.W., Washington, DC 20001
Telephone: (202) 393-6226
Background: Contact is Donald Pepe of the Nat'l Ass'n of Counties.

Nat'l Ass'n of County Training and Employment Professionals
440 First St., N.W., Washington, DC 20001
Telephone: (202) 393-6226
Background: Contact is Jerald McNeil of the Nat'l Ass'n of Counties.

Nat'l Ass'n of County Treasurers and Finance Officers
440 First St., N.W., Washington, DC 20001
Telephone: (202) 393-6226
Background: Contact is Susan White of the Nat'l Ass'n of Counties.

Nat'l Ass'n of Credit Management
8815 Centre Park Drive Suite 200, Columbia, MD 21045-2117
Telephone: (301) 740-5560
Represented by:
　Paul J. Mignini, Jr., President
Counsel or consultant:
　Jim Wise Associates (James W. Wise)

Nat'l Ass'n of Criminal Justice Planners
1511 K St., N.W., Suite 445, Washington, DC 20005
Telephone: (202) 347-0501
Represented by:
　Mark A. Cunniff, Exec. Director

Nat'l Ass'n of Crop Insurance Agents Political Action Committee
1000 16th St., N.W., Suite 702, Washington, DC 20036
Telephone: (202) 223-8074
Counsel or consultant:
　Vickers & Vickers (Linda Vickers)

Nat'l Ass'n of Decorative Architectural Finishes
112 North Alfred St., Alexandria, VA 22314
Telephone: (703) 836-6504
Represented by:
　Wilhelmina T. Loomis, Exec. Director

Nat'l Ass'n of Dental Assistants
900 S. Washington St., Falls Church, VA 22046
Telephone: (703) 237-8616
Represented by:
　Joseph Salta, President

Nat'l Ass'n of Dental Laboratories
3801 Mt. Vernon Ave., Alexandria, VA 22305
Telephone: (703) 683-5263
Represented by:
　Robert W. Stanley, Exec. Director
Counsel or consultant:
　Reed Smith Shaw & McClay

Nat'l Ass'n of Development Companies
1730 Rhode Island Ave., N.W., Suite 209, Washington, DC 20036
Telephone: (202) 785-8484
Represented by:
　Kathy J. Grimes, Exec. Director

Nat'l Ass'n of Development Organizations
400 North Capitol St., N.W. Suite 372, Washington, DC 20001
Telephone: (202) 624-7806
Background: Members, numbering over 225, are mainly regional planning and development organizations. Objectives are to promote community and economic development, primarily in rural areas and small towns, and to provide for communication and education. Updates members on legislative developments through its weekly newsletter, NADO NEWS.
Represented by:
　Adam Krinsky, Legislative Analyst
　Susan Rocke, Administrative Coordinator
　Aliceann Wohlbruck, Exec. Director

Nat'l Ass'n of Developmental Disabilities Councils
1234 Massachusetts Ave., N.W. Suite 103, Washington, DC 20005
Telephone: (202) 347-1234
Represented by:
　Susan Ames-Zierman, Exec. Director

Nat'l Ass'n of Discount Theatres
Tacoma, WA
Counsel or consultant:
　Madison Group/Earle Palmer Brown, The (Peggy L. Martin)

Nat'l Ass'n of Dredging Contractors
1625 Eye St., N.W. Suite 321, Washington, DC 20006
Telephone: (202) 223-4820
Represented by:
　S. Dilworth Hager, Washington Representative

Nat'l Ass'n of Early Childhood Educators
Annandale, VA
Counsel or consultant:
　William J. Tobin and Associates (William J. Tobin)

Nat'l Ass'n of Educational Office Personnel
7223 Lee Highway, #301, Falls Church, VA 22046
Telephone: (703) 533-0810
Represented by:
　Rebecca W. Grim, Exec. Secretary

Nat'l Ass'n of Elected County Executives
440 First St., N.W., Washington, DC 20001
Telephone: (202) 393-6226
Background: Represented by Edward E. Ferguson, Deputy Exec. Director of the Nat'l Ass'n of Counties.

Nat'l Ass'n of Energy Service Companies
1440 New York Ave., N.W., Washington, DC 20005
Telephone: (202) 371-7980

ORGANIZATIONS REPRESENTED

Background: A group of energy service companies (including utilities, equipment manufacturers, financial institutions, and government entities) interested in third party financing of cogeneration, waste-to-energy, and energy efficiency.
Represented by:
Terry Singer, Exec. Director

Nat'l Ass'n of Enrolled Agents
6000 Executive Blvd., #205, Rockville, MD 20852
Telephone: (301) 984-6232
Represented by:
Phyllis Borghese, Director, Government Relations

Nat'l Ass'n of Enrolled Agents PAC
6000 Executive Blvd., #205, Rockville, MD 20852
Telephone: (301) 984-6232
Background: Contact is Phyllis Borghese of the parent organization.

Nat'l Ass'n of Environmental Professionals
Box 15210, Alexandria, VA 22309-0210
Telephone: (703) 660-2364
Represented by:
Robert F. Ehrhardt, V. President
Robert A. McDonald, V. President

Nat'l Ass'n of Epilepsy Centers
Minneapolis, MN
Counsel or consultant:
MARC Associates, Inc. (Ellen Riker)

Nat'l Ass'n of Evangelicals
1023 15th St., N.W., Suite 500, Washington, DC 20005
Telephone: (202) 789-1011
Represented by:
Richard C. Cizik, Policy Analyst
Tim Crater, Special Representative
Robert P. Dugan, Jr., Director, Office of Public Affairs
Forest D. Montgomery, Counsel
Brian F. O'Connell, Peace, Freedom and Security Studies Prgm
Curran Tiffany, Consultant

Nat'l Ass'n of Executive Secretaries
900 S. Washington St., Falls Church, VA 22046
Telephone: (703) 237-8616
Represented by:
Susan J. Young, Exec. Director

Nat'l Ass'n of Exposition Managers
Indianapolis, IN
Counsel or consultant:
London and Satagaj, Attorneys-at-Law (Sheldon I. London, John S. Satagaj)

Nat'l Ass'n of Federal Credit Unions
3138 N. 10th St., Arlington, VA 22201
Telephone: (703) 522-4770
Background: The only national trade association which exclusively serves federally chartered credit unions. Primary purpose is to provide members with strong representation before Congress and the federal regulatory agencies that have an impact on the operations of this type of credit union.
Represented by:
William J. Donovan, V. President, Government Affrs. Counsel
Yvonne Gilmore, Associate Director, Regulatory Affairs
E. Y. Holt, Jr., V. President, Finance and Administration
Patrick Keefe, Director of Communications
Lisa E. Lotter, Director, Regulatory Affairs
Kenneth Robinson, President
Steven A. Skonberg, Director, Legislative Affairs
Patricia J. Stevens, V. President, Member Services
John H. Zimmerman, Associate Director, Legislative Affairs
Counsel or consultant:
Haden & Bisker, P.C.

Nat'l Ass'n of Federal Credit Unions Political Action Committee
3138 North 10th St., Arlington, VA 22201
Telephone: (703) 522-4770
Background: Contact is William J. Donovan of the Nat'l Ass'n of Federal Credit Unions.

Nat'l Ass'n of Federal Education Program Administrators
1801 N. Moore St., Arlington, VA 22209
Telephone: (703) 528-0700

Represented by:
Dr. Richard Miller, Executive Director

Nat'l Ass'n of Federal Veterinarians
1023 15th St., N.W. Suite 300, Washington, DC 20005
Telephone: (202) 289-6334
Represented by:
William G. Hughes, General Counsel
Edward L. Menning, Exec. V. President

Nat'l Ass'n of Federal Veterinarians Political Action Committee
1023 15th St., N.W., Suite 300, Washington, DC 20005
Telephone: (202) 289-6334
Background: Represented by Edward L. Menning of the Ass'n.

Nat'l Ass'n of Federally Impacted Schools
444 North Capitol St., N.W., Suite 405, Washington, DC 20001
Telephone: (202) 624-5455
Background: Education information ass'n which represents those school districts located throughout the U.S. which educate children whose parents live and/or work on some type of federal property e.g. Indian reservations, military bases, federally subsidized housing projects.
Represented by:
John Forkenbrock, Exec. Director

Nat'l Ass'n of Fleet Administrators
Iselin, NJ
Counsel or consultant:
Kent & O'Connor, Incorp. (Patrick C. O'Connor)

Nat'l Ass'n of Flight Instructors
5021 Powell Road, Fairfax, VA 22032
Telephone: (703) 323-8763
Represented by:
Bernard A. Geier, Exec. Director

Nat'l Ass'n of Flood and Stormwater Management Agencies
1225 Eye St., NW, Suite 300, Washington, DC 20005
Telephone: (202) 682-3761
Background: Formed to interact with congress and federal agencies on water resource management issues, flood prevention and damage mitigation in urban environments.
Counsel or consultant:
Linton, Mields, Reisler and Cottone (Kevin McCarty)

Nat'l Ass'n of Food Equipment Manufacturers
1101 Connecticut Ave., N.W., Suite 700, Washington, DC 20036
Telephone: (202) 857-1100
Counsel or consultant:
Smith, Bucklin and Associates (Robert H. Wilbur)

Nat'l Ass'n of Foster Grandparent Program Directors
Orlando, FL
Counsel or consultant:
EMJ Consultants (Frances F. Butler)

Nat'l Ass'n of Government Communicators
80 South Early St., Alexandria, VA 22304
Telephone: (703) 823-4821
Background: Formed by a merger of the Armed Forces Writers League, Federal Editors Ass'n and the Government Information Organization. Furthers professional interests of communicators (writers, editors, public information officers, audiovisual specialists) working in federal, state, county, city, and other governments.
Represented by:
Deborah Trocchi, Exec. Director

Nat'l Ass'n of Government Employees
1313 L St., N.W., 2nd Floor, Washington, DC 20005
Telephone: (202) 371-6644
Represented by:
Kenneth T. Lyons, President
Edward L. Murphy, Legislative Counsel
Susanne J. Pooler, V. President
Susan E. Scheider, Assistant General Counsel

Nat'l Ass'n of Government Employees' Political Action Committee
1313 L St., N.W., 2nd Floor, Washington, DC 20005
Telephone: (202) 371-6644
Background: Represented by Susanne J. Pooler, V. President of the Ass'n.

Nat'l Ass'n of Governors' Highway Safety Representatives
444 North Capitol St., N.W. Suite 530, Washington, DC 20001
Telephone: (202) 624-5877
Represented by:
Barbara Harsha, Exec. Director

Nat'l Ass'n of Health Career Schools
Los Angeles, CA
Counsel or consultant:
White, Fine, and Verville (Richard A. Fulton)

Nat'l Ass'n of Health Underwriters
1000 Connecticut Ave., N.W., Suite 1111, Washington, DC 20036
Telephone: (202) 223-5533
Represented by:
William F. Flood, Exec. V. President

Nat'l Ass'n of Hispanic Journalists
National Press Building Room 634, Washington, DC 20045
Telephone: (202) 783-6228
Represented by:
Jose McMurray, Exec. Director

Nat'l Ass'n of Home Builders of the U.S.
15th and M Streets, N.W., Washington, DC 20005
Telephone: (202) 822-0470
Represented by:
G. Tom Baker, Staff V. President for Political Affairs
Robert D Bannister, Sr. Staff V. Pres., Government Affairs
Mark Benson, Ass't Staff VP, Political Field Operatns
James R. Birdsong, Exec. Dir., Building Systems
Michael S. Carliner, Staff V. Pres., Econ. and Housing Policy
Betty Christy, Asst. Staff V. President, Public Affairs
Kent W. Colton, Exec. V. President and CEO
Ronda Daniels, Associate Regulatory Counsel
William D. Ellingsworth, Sr. Staff V. President, Public Affairs
Nancy Elwood, Senior Legislative Representative
Charles G. Field, Staff V. Pres. Regulatory & Tech. Svcs.
Charles W. Hackney, Senior Congressional Liaison
Thomas Hipple, Political Affairs Director
Gerald Michael Howard, Tax Counsel
John Kinas, Staff Director, Political Affairs
Deborah Imle Miller, Staff VP, Congressional Affairs & Admin.
Michael O'Brien, Direcor, State and Local Affairs
Bryan Patchan, Exec. Dir, Nat'l Remodelers Council
Joe P. Peck, Jr., Congressional Representative
Martin Perlman, President
Campbell Reed, Exec. Dir., Nat'l Commer. B'ldrs Council
David F. Seiders, Sr. Staff V. Pres. & Chief Economist
Jay Shackford, Staff V. President, Public Affairs
William T. Slider, Staff Director, Legislative Affairs
Joseph M. Stanton, Congressional Representative
Wayne W. Stetson, Staff V. President, Conventions
Doris I. Thomas, Senior Congressional Liaison
Floyd Williams, Staff V. Pres./Legislative Counsel
Milan P. Yager, Senior Legislative Representative
William C. Young, Dir., Consumer Affairs & Public Liaison
Counsel or consultant:
Chambers Associates Incorporated (William L. Stringer)
Colton and Boykin (Peter W. Segal)
The Susan Davis Companies (William F. Rhatican)
Silverstein and Mullens

Nat'l Ass'n of Home Builders Political Action Committee
15th and M Sts., N.W., Washington, DC 20005
Telephone: (202) 822-0470
Background: Tom Baker, of the Ass'n, serves as contact for the Political Action Committee.

Nat'l Ass'n of Homes for Children
1701 K St., N.W., Suite 200, Washington, DC 20006
Telephone: (202) 223-3447
Background: An organization of voluntary, not-for-profit agencies providing services to children and their families. An advocate, at the national level, for improved services to children.
Represented by:
Teresa M. Zimmerman, Sr. Staff Associate
Counsel or consultant:
Nordlinger Associates

The listings in this directory are available as *Mailing Labels*. See last page.

ORGANIZATIONS REPRESENTED

Nat'l Ass'n of Hose and Accessories Distributors
1200 17th St., N.W., Suite 400, Washington, DC 20036
Telephone: (202) 296-9200
Counsel or consultant:
  Hill Group, Inc. (Jay H. Smith)

Nat'l Ass'n of Hospital Admitting Managers
1101 Connecticut Ave., N.W. Suite 700, Washington, DC 20036
Telephone: (202) 857-1125
Counsel or consultant:
  Smith, Bucklin and Associates (Carol A. Lively)

Nat'l Ass'n of Housing Cooperatives
1614 King St., Alexandria, VA 22314
Telephone: (703) 549-5201
Represented by:
  Herbert J. Levy, Exec. Director
  Judy M. Sullivan, Director of Government Relations

Nat'l Ass'n of Housing and Redevelopment Officials
1320 18th St., N.W., Washington, DC 20036
Telephone: (202) 429-2960
Represented by:
  Apolonio Flores, President
  Marion Morris, Director of Legislative Services
  Richard Y. Nelson, Jr., Exec. Director

Nat'l Ass'n of Independent Colleges and Universities
122 C St., N.W. Suite 750, Washington, DC 20001
Telephone: (202) 347-7512
Background: An 800-member organization representing independent colleges and universities on public policy issues with all branches of the federal government.
Represented by:
  David Baime, Director for Education Funding
  Linda K. Berkshire, Exec. Director, Education Finance
  Kathleen Curry Santora, Exec. Dir. for Operations
  Sandra H. McMullan, Exec. Dir. for Tax Policy & Gen Counsel
  Gail A. Raiman, V. President, Public Affairs
  Dr. Richard F. Rosser, President and C.E.O.
  Dr. Julianne Still Thrift, Exec. V. President
  Shirley J. Wilcher, Director, State Relations & Counsel
Counsel or consultant:
  Piper and Marbury (H. Benjamin Hartley)

Nat'l Ass'n of Independent Fee Appraisers
St. Louis, MO
Counsel or consultant:
  Willkie Farr and Gallagher (Matthew R. Schneider)

Nat'l Ass'n of Independent Insurers
499 South Capitol St., S.W. Suite 401, Washington, DC 20003
Telephone: (202) 484-2350
Represented by:
  Darrell Coover, Sr. V. President, Government Relations
  Tania Demchuk, Public Affairs Specialist
  Charles H. Fritzel, Asst. V. President, Government Relations
  Kenneth D. Schloman, Washington Counsel
  Charles A. Taylor, III, Ass't V. President, Gov't Relations
Counsel or consultant:
  Delaney and Associates, Edward N. (Edward N. Delaney)
  Parry and Romani Associates Inc. (Romano Romani)

Nat'l Ass'n of Independent Life Brokerage Agencies
3299 K St., N.W., 7th Floor, Washington, DC 20007
Telephone: (202) 965-8998
Counsel or consultant:
  Ass'n Management Group (Charles D. Rumbarger)

Nat'l Ass'n of Independent Schools
1749 P St., N.W., Washington, DC 20036
Telephone: (202) 462-3886
Represented by:
  John W. Sanders, Director, Washington Office
Counsel or consultant:
  Bahnsen Communications
  Caplin and Drysdale
  Ropes and Gray (Thomas M. Susman)

Nat'l Ass'n of Industrial and Office Parks
1215 Jefferson Davis Hwy., Suite 100, Arlington, VA 22202
Telephone: (703) 979-3400
Represented by:
  Thomas J. Bisacquino, Senior V. President
  Jeffrey DeBoer, Chief Legislative Counsel
  Sid R. Peters, Exec. V. President
Counsel or consultant:
  Davidson Colling Group, Inc., The (James H. Davidson)
  Winkelmann & Associates, Inc. (Joe Winkelmann)

Nat'l Ass'n of Industrial and Office Parks American Development PAC
1215 Jefferson Davis Hwy. Suite 100, Arlington, VA 22202
Telephone: (703) 979-3400
Background: Represented by Jeffrey D. DeBoer of the Nat'l Ass'n of Industrial and Office Parks.

Nat'l Ass'n of Insurance Brokers
1401 New York Ave., N.W., Suite 720, Washington, DC 20005
Telephone: (202) 628-6700
Represented by:
  Barbara Haugen, Director, Federal Affairs
  Coletta I. Kemper, Director, Public Affairs

Nat'l Ass'n of Insurance Brokers Political Action Committee
1401 New York Ave., N.W., Suite 720, Washington, DC 20005
Telephone: (202) 628-6700
Background: Contact is Barbara Haugen of the Nat'l Ass'n of Insurance Brokers.

Nat'l Ass'n of Insurance Commissioners
444 N. Capitol St., Suite 316, Washington, DC 20001
Telephone: (202) 624-7790
Represented by:
  Kevin T. Cronin, Washington Counsel
  Julia E. Lynch, Legislative Assistant

Nat'l Ass'n of Investment Companies
1111 14th St., N.W. Suite 700, Washington, DC 20005
Telephone: (202) 289-4336
Represented by:
  JoAnn H. Price, President
  Diane Kay Thomas, V. President

Nat'l Ass'n of Investment Companies Political Action Committee
1111 14th St., N.W. Suite 700, Washington, DC 20005
Telephone: (202) 289-4336
Background: Contact is Diane Kay Thomas of the Ass'n.

Nat'l Ass'n of Latino Elected and Appointed Officials (NALEO)
708 G St., S.E., Washington, DC 20003
Telephone: (202) 546-2536
Background: Non partisan civic affairs and education organization that advocates on behalf of issues relevant to the hispanic community.
Represented by:
  Michael J. Zamba, Director, Washington Office

Nat'l Ass'n of Legal Search Consultants
1350 New York Ave., N.W. Suite 615, Washington, DC 20005
Telephone: (202) 347-1917
Counsel or consultant:
  Resources for Group Management, Inc. (Marianne McDermott)

Nat'l Ass'n of Letter Carriers of the United States of America
100 Indiana Ave., N.W., Washington, DC 20001
Telephone: (202) 393-4695
Represented by:
  Roger Blacklow, Legislative Analyst
  Francis J. Conners, Exec. V. President
  Walter E. Couillard, Director of Retired Members
  George B. Gould, Legis. and Polit. Ass't to the President
  Lawrence G. Hutchins, Vice President
  Vincent R. Sombrotto, President
  Drew Von Bergen, Director, Public Relations
Counsel or consultant:
  Nordlinger Associates

Nat'l Ass'n of Life Companies
1455 Pennsylvania Ave., N.W., Suite 1250, Washington, DC 20004

Telephone: (202) 783-6252
Represented by:
  Elaine Andrews, V. President, Federal Coordinator
  Jon C. Ogg, V. President, State Coordinator
  S. Roy Woodall, Jr., President
Counsel or consultant:
  Davis & Harman

Nat'l Ass'n of Life Companies Political Action Committee
1455 Pennsylvania Ave., N.W., Suite 1250, Washington, DC 20004

Telephone: (202) 783-6252
Background: Represented by Jon C. Ogg of the Association.

Nat'l Ass'n of Life Underwriters
1922 F St., N.W., Washington, DC 20006
Telephone: (202) 331-6000
Represented by:

  William N. Albus, Senior Associate General Counsel
  Timothy Bigelow, Asst. V. President, Conventions/Meetings
  Jack E. Bobo, Exec. V. President
  Francis D. Bouchard, Assistant Director, Public Affairs
  Patricia Briotta, Associate Director, Media Relations
  Lucy Coburn, Director, Legislative Communications
  H. James Douds, Senior V. President and General Counsel
  David E. Hebert, Government Affairs Counsel
  Karen Hurley, Asst. Director, Legislat. Communications
  Danea M. Kehoe, Associate General Counsel
  Michael L. Kerley, V. President, Government Affairs
  Dawn Lindsey, Associate Director, Internal Relations
  Jay H. Morris, Associate Director, Public Affairs
  Denise J. Patton, V. President, Public Relations
  Gary Sanders, Counsel
  William B. Scher, Jr., V. President, Law
  Suzanne E. Sumpter, Assistant Director, Media Relations
  David A. Winston, Associate General Counsel
Counsel or consultant:
  Miller, Cassidy, Larroca and Lewin (Jamie S. Gorelick)
  Patton, Boggs and Blow (John Jonas)

Nat'l Ass'n of Life Underwriters Political Action Committee
1922 F St., N.W., Washington, DC 20006
Telephone: (202) 347-1444
Represented by:
  Austin Adkinson, Exec. Director

Nat'l Ass'n of Lithographic Plate Manufacturers
1730 North Lynn St., Arlington, VA 22209
Telephone: (703) 841-8100
Background: Exec. Director is G. William Teare of the Printing Industries of America.

Nat'l Ass'n of Manufacturers
1331 Pennsylvania Ave., N.W. Suite 1500 North, Washington, DC 20004-1703
Telephone: (202) 637-3000

The listings in this directory are available as *Mailing Labels.* See last page.

ORGANIZATIONS REPRESENTED

Represented by:
Jan S. Amundson, V. President & General Counsel
Michael E. Baroody, Sr. V. Pres, Policy and Communications
Christian N. Braunlich, Exec. Director, Small Mfrs. Forum
Laura L. Brown, Director, Media Relations
Sharon F. Canner, Assistant V. Pres., Industrial Relations
Daniel W. Cannon, Director, Program Development, R & T
James P. Carty, V. Pres., Gov't Relations & Competition
John Cohen, Assoc. Dir., Energy & Natural Resources
Stephen Cooney, Director, Internat'l Investment
Donna J. Costlow, Assoc. Director, Risk Management
Douglas W. Darby, Dir., Spec. Projects, Legislative Anal.
Phyllis Eisen, Director, Risk Management
Lawrence A. Fineran, Director, Regulation and Competition
Diane Generous, Assoc. Director, Employee Relations
Denny Gulino, V. President, Media Relations
Bruce N. Hahn, V. President, Public Affairs
Randolph M. Hale, V. President, Industrial Relations
Lee Hamilton, Sr. V. Pres., Membership & Public Affrs.
Paul R. Huard, V. Pres., Taxation and Fiscal Policy
Jerry J. Jasinowski, President
Mari Konoshima, Assoc. Director, International Trade
Doug Kurkul, Director, Legislative Analysis
Howard K. Lewis, III, V. President, Internat'l Economic Affrs.
Tim Lugbill, Legislative Analyst
Francis M. Lunnie, Jr., Director, Employee Relations
Monica M. McGuire, Director, Fiscal and Monetary Policy
William G. Morin, Dir., High Tech. Couns. & Defense Forum
R. K. Morris, Director, International Trade
Jack Peterson, Director, Political Affairs
Mary C. Pigott, Assoc. Director, Environmental Quality
John H. Pilcher, Director, Corporate Finance
Theresa Pugh, Director, Environmental Quality
Renee Reymond, Director, Legislative Affairs
Gordon Richards, Asst. V. Pres., Taxation & Fiscal Policy
Quentin Riegel, Asst. V. Pres. & Deputy General Counsel
David W. Rohn, Director, Member Programs
H. Richard Seibert, Jr., V. President, Resources and Technology
Andrew W. Smart, Manager, Media Relations
Bernard Trimble, Exec. Director, CUE
Dr. Jane Work, V. President, Legislative Analysis

Nat'l Ass'n of Margarine Manufacturers
1101 15th St., N.W., Suite 202, Washington, DC 20005
Telephone: (202) 785-3232
Counsel or consultant:
Robert H. Kellen Co. (Richard E. Cristol, Belva W. Jones)

Nat'l Ass'n of Meat Purveyors
8365-B Greensboro Drive, McLean, VA 22102-3585
Telephone: (703) 827-5754
Represented by:
Stanley J. Emerling, Exec. V. President
Counsel or consultant:
Tendler, Goldberg & Biggins, Chtd. (James M. Goldberg)

Nat'l Ass'n of Medical Directors of Respiratory Care
1050 17th St., N.W., Suite 840, Washington, DC 20036
Telephone: (202) 785-1196
Counsel or consultant:
Porte, Stafford and Associates (Michael Stafford)

Nat'l Ass'n of Medical Equipment Suppliers
625 Slaters Lane, Suite 200, Alexandria, VA 22314
Telephone: (703) 836-6263
Represented by:
Thomas M. Antone, IV, President
Janet A. Bourne Potter, Exec. V. President
Patrick J. Cacchione, Director, Government Affairs
Corrine Propas Parver, Dir., Government and Legal Affairs
Tim Redmon, Director, Regulatory Affairs

Nat'l Ass'n of Medical Equipment Suppliers Political Action Committee
625 Slaters Lane, Suite 200, Alexandria, VA 22314
Telephone: (703) 836-6263
Background: Contact is Patrick Cacchione of the Association.

Nat'l Ass'n of Metal Finishers
1101 Connecticut Ave., N.W., Suite 700, Washington, DC 20036
Telephone: (202) 857-1127
Counsel or consultant:
Smith, Bucklin and Associates (Mark N. Griffiths)

Nat'l Ass'n of Metal Finishers Political Action Committee
1101 Connecticut Ave., N.W. Suite 700, Washington, DC 20036
Telephone: (202) 857-1127
Counsel or consultant:
Smith, Bucklin and Associates

Nat'l Ass'n of Military Widows
4023 25th Road North, Arlington, VA 22207
Telephone: (703) 527-4565
Represented by:
Jean Arthurs, Legislative Liaison-President

Nat'l Ass'n of Minority Contractors
806 15th St., N.W., Suite 340, Washington, DC 20005
Telephone: (202) 347-8259
Represented by:
Ralph C. Thomas, III, Exec. Director
Counsel or consultant:
Reed Smith Shaw & McClay (Carl Rowan, Jr.)

Nat'l Ass'n of Mirror Manufacturers
9005 Congressional Ct., Potomac, MD 20854
Telephone: (301) 365-4080
Background: James E. Mack of American Trade Ass'n Management serves as Exec. Secretary and General Counsel.
Counsel or consultant:
American Trade Ass'n Management (James E. Mack, CAE)

Nat'l Ass'n of Miscellaneous, Ornamental and Architectural Products Contractors
10382 Main St., Suite 200 Box 280, Fairfax, VA 22030
Telephone: (703) 591-1870
Background: Represented by Fred H. Codding of the Nat'l Ass'n of Reinforcing Steel Contractors.

Nat'l Ass'n of Music Merchants
Carlsbad, CA
Counsel or consultant:
Tendler, Goldberg & Biggins, Chtd. (James M. Goldberg)

Nat'l Ass'n of Mutual Insurance Companies
Indianapolis, IN
Counsel or consultant:
Collier, Shannon & Scott (Pamela Allen, David A. Hartquist)

Nat'l Ass'n of Negro Business & Professional Women's Clubs, Inc.
1806 New Hampshire Ave., N.W., Washington, DC 20009
Telephone: (202) 483-4206
Background: A 10,000 member association of Black business and professional women with a mission of improving the quality of life in American communities. Through seminars, publications and leadership training programs, the Association educates its constituencies about contempoaryy social issues and relevant legislation on the local, state and national levels of government.
Represented by:
Jacquelyn Gates, Nat'l President
Ellen Graves, Exec. Director

Nat'l Ass'n of Neighborhoods
1651 Fuller St., N.W., Washington, DC 20009
Telephone: (202) 332-7766
Background: Urban and rural organizations and coalitions working to strengthen neighborhood rights and responsibilities.
Represented by:
Marla Anderson, Exec. Director

Nat'l Ass'n of NIDSPORT Users
1200 17th St., N.W., Suite 400, Washington, DC 20036
Telephone: (202) 296-9200
Counsel or consultant:
Hill Group, Inc. (Sanford J. Hill)

Nat'l Ass'n of Older Worker Employment Services
600 Maryland Ave., S.W., Washington, DC 20024
Telephone: (202) 479-6641

Background: An organization of the Nat'l Council on the Aging. Promotes expansion of voluntary placement programs to increase job opportunities for older adults. Represented by Coquese Williams of the Nat'l Council on the Aging.

Nat'l Ass'n of Orchestra Leaders
New York, NY
Counsel or consultant:
McGuiness and Williams (G. John Tysse)

Nat'l Ass'n of Partners in Education
601 Wythe St., Suite 200, Alexandria, VA 22314
Telephone: (703) 836-4880
Represented by:
Bently Lipscomb, Deputy Director, Operations
Dan W. Merenda, Exec. Director

Nat'l Ass'n of Passenger Vessel Owners
1511 K St., N.W., Suite 715, Washington, DC 20005
Telephone: (202) 638-5310
Background: Represents the tour, excursion and dinner boat industry. Primary issues are user taxes, safety and liability issues and Coast Guard regulation.
Represented by:
Eric G. Scharf, Exec. Director

Nat'l Ass'n of Pediatric Nurse Associates and Practitioners
Maple Shade, NJ
Counsel or consultant:
Capitol Associates, Inc. (Karen Bodenhorn, Debra M. Hardy-Havens)

Nat'l Ass'n of Personnel Consultants
3133 Mt. Vernon Ave., Alexandria, VA 22305
Telephone: (703) 684-0180
Background: Members are employment agencies.
Represented by:
John Lisack, Jr., Exec. V. President
Counsel or consultant:
J. C. Luman and Assoc. (Joseph C. Luman)

Nat'l Ass'n of Physician Nurses
900 S. Washington St., Falls Church, VA 22046
Telephone: (703) 237-8616
Background: Represented by Joseph Salta, President (see Nat'l Ass'n of Dental Assistants).

Nat'l Ass'n of Plant Patent Owners
1250 Eye St., N.W. Suite 500, Washington, DC 20005
Telephone: (202) 789-2900
Background: Exec. V. President is Lawrence E. Scovotto of the American Ass'n of Nurserymen. Administrator is Craig Regelbrugge also of the Ass'n.

Nat'l Ass'n of Plumbing-Heating-Cooling Contractors
180 South Washington St. Box 6808, Falls Church, VA 22046
Telephone: (703) 237-8100
Represented by:
Robert E. Beck, Director, Government Relations
David M. Goldberg, Director of Communications

Nat'l Ass'n of Plumbing-Heating-Cooling Contractors Political Action Committee
180 South Washington St. Box 6808, Falls Church, VA 22046
Telephone: (703) 237-8100
Represented by:
Allen Inlow, Treasurer

Nat'l Ass'n of Portable X-Ray Providers
Erie, PA
Counsel or consultant:
O'Connor & Hannan (Hope S. Foster)

Nat'l Ass'n of Postal Supervisors
490 L'Enfant Plaza, S.W., Suite 3200, Washington, DC 20024
Telephone: (202) 484-6070
Background: Supports the Supervisors Political Action Committee.
Represented by:
Rubin Handelman, President
Robert E. McLean, Legislative Counsel
Counsel or consultant:
Patton, Boggs and Blow (Timothy J. May)

ORGANIZATIONS REPRESENTED

Nat'l Ass'n of Postal Supervisors Political Action Committee
490 L'Enfant Plaze S.W., Suite 3200, Washington, DC 20024-2120
Telephone: (202) 484-6070
Background: Represented by Robert McLean of the Nat' Ass'n of Postal Supervisors.
Counsel or consultant:
  Patton, Boggs and Blow (Timothy J. May)

Nat'l Ass'n of Postmasters of the U.S.
8 Herbert St., Alexandria, VA 22305-2600
Telephone: (703) 683-9027
Represented by:
  David E. Hyde, President
  Reginald T. Valliere, Director, Government Relations
  Wayne Widener, Secretary-Treasurer
Counsel or consultant:
  N. Isaac Groner (Isaac N. Groner)
  Gene Taylor Assoc, Inc. (Gene Taylor)

Nat'l Ass'n of Postmasters of the U.S. PAC for Postmasters
8 Herbert St., Alexandria, VA 22305
Telephone: (703) 683-9027
Represented by:
  Cora Lee, Treasurer

Nat'l Ass'n of Printers and Lithographers
Teaneck, NJ
Background: Represented by Benjamin Y. Cooper of Printing Industries of America.

Nat'l Ass'n of Private Industry Councils
1201 New York Ave., N.W. Suite 800, Washington, DC 20005
Telephone: (202) 289-2950
Background: Founded in 1979 as a service organization representing local private industry councils created by the Job Training Partnership Act. Focuses on employment and training policy and programming.
Represented by:
  Robert Knight, President

Nat'l Ass'n of Private Psychiatric Hospitals
1319 F St., N.W., Suite 1000, Washington, DC 20004
Telephone: (202) 393-6700
Background: An association of freestanding psychiatric hospitals for the private treatment of mental illness, alcohol and drug dependencies.
Represented by:
  Mark Covall, Director, Congressional Affairs
  Edward Kelly, Director, Regulatory Affairs
  Patricia E. Ryan, Associate Director, Congressional Affrs.
  Carole Szpak, Director, Communications
  Robert L. Thomas, Exec. Director

Nat'l Ass'n of Private Psychiatric Hospitals Political Action Committee
1319 F St., N.W. Suite 1000, Washington, DC 20004
Telephone: (202) 393-6700
Background: Contact is Patricia Ryan of the Ass'n.

Nat'l Ass'n of Private Residential Resources
4200 Evergreen Lane, Suite 315, Annandale, VA 22003
Telephone: (703) 642-6614
Represented by:
  Aase J. Collins, Assistant Exec. Director
  Joni Fritz, Exec. Director
Counsel or consultant:
  Duncan and Associates

Nat'l Ass'n of Private Schools for Exceptional Children
1625 Eye St., N.W., Suite 506, Washington, DC 20006
Telephone: (202) 223-2192
Represented by:
  Mara Scatena, Administrator
Counsel or consultant:
  Montgomery, McCracken, Walker & Rhoads (Linda Long, David F. Norcross)

Nat'l Ass'n of Professional Educators
412 First St., S.E., Washington, DC 20003
Telephone: (202) 484-8969
Background: A small lobby group of classroom teachers opposed to the unionist policies of the National Education Association.
Counsel or consultant:
  Resources Development, Inc. (Roger H. Zion)

Nat'l Ass'n of Professional Insurance Agents
400 North Washington St., Alexandria, VA 22314
Telephone: (703) 836-9340
Represented by:
  Lydia M. Astorga, Research Analyst, Gov't & Industry Afrs.
  Patricia A. Borowski, CPIW, V. President, Gov't and Industry Affairs
  Douglas S. Culkin, Sr. V. President
  Donald K. Gardiner, CAE, Exec. V. President
  Katherine Hoffman, APR, Associate Director
  Dennis Jay, Asst. V. President, Communications
  James Quiggle, Director, Public Relations
  Tamera Rudd, Director, State Affairs
  Joel Wood, Jr., Assistant V. Pres., Government Affairs
Counsel or consultant:
  Baker and Hostetler (Kenneth J. Kies)
  Miller, Cassidy, Larroca and Lewin (Jamie S. Gorelick)

Nat'l Ass'n of Public Hospitals
1212 New York Ave., N.W. Suite 800, Washington, DC 20004
Telephone: (202) 408-0223
Represented by:
  Christine C. Burch, Exec. V. President
Counsel or consultant:
  Powell, Goldstein, Frazer and Murphy (Larry S. Gage)

Nat'l Ass'n of Public Insurance Adjusters
1101 14th St., N.W., Suite 1100, Washington, DC 20005
Telephone: (292) 371-1258
Represented by:
  Paul L. Cornish, Exec. Director
Counsel or consultant:
  Internat'l Management Group, Inc. (David W. Barrack)

Nat'l Ass'n of Public Television Stations
1350 Connecticut Ave., N.W. Suite 200, Washington, DC 20036
Telephone: (202) 887-1700
Background: Represents the nation's public television licensees.
Represented by:
  David J. Brugger, President
  Richard Grefe, V. President
  John M. Lawson, Director, National Affairs
  Chalmers Marquis, Congressional Affairs
Counsel or consultant:
  Garland Associates (Sara G. Garland)
  Media Enterprises Corp.
  Wiley, Rein & Fielding (Paul C. Smith)

Nat'l Ass'n of Railroad Passengers
236 Massachusetts Ave., N.E., Suite 603, Washington, DC 20002
Telephone: (202) 546-1550
Represented by:
  Ross Capon, Exec. Director
  Scott Leonard, Assistant Director
  John R. Martin, President
  Harriet Ellen Parcells, Transportation Associate

Nat'l Ass'n of Real Estate Brokers
1629 K St., N.W. Suite 605, Washington, DC 20006
Telephone: (202) 785-4477
Represented by:
  Evelyn Reeves, President

Nat'l Ass'n of Real Estate Investment Trusts
1129 20th St., N.W. Suite 705, Washington, DC 20036
Telephone: (202) 785-8717
Represented by:
  David L. Brandon, General Counsel
  Mark O. Decker, Exec. V. President

Nat'l Ass'n of REALTORS
777 14th St., N.W., Washington, DC 20005
Telephone: (202) 383-1000

Represented by:
  Desiree Anderson, Director, Gov'tl & Political Relations
  Kenneth J. Beirne, Division V. Pres., Government Relations
  Denise Bell, Legis. Director, Congressional Affairs
  Lisa Blackwell, Legis. Analyst, Gov't Relations
  Richard R. Blake, Jr., Dir, Pol Commun Network, Pol Field Optns
  John B. Blount, Jr., V. President, Congressional Affairs
  Michael D. Chapman, Legis. Director, Congressional Affairs
  Kelly Craven, Polit. Director, Political Field Optns.
  Roy DeLoach, Legis. Analyst, Gov't Relations
  Martin L. DePoy, Legis. Director, Congressional Affairs
  Stephen D. Driesler, Sr. V. Pres, Gov't Affairs & Polit. Rtns
  Linda G. Fitcheard, Manager of Policy and Development
  Lisa A. Friday, Dir, Polit Reforms & Indep. Expenditures
  Mary Fruscello, Divisional V. Pres., Real Estate Finance
  Gerard Giovaniello, Staff V. Pres., Congressional Affairs
  Linda Goold, Dir., Fed. Tax Programs, Gov't Relations
  Robert H. Green, Staff V. Pres, Fed. Taxation, Gov't Rtns
  Anne Greenfield, Polit. Director, Political Field Optns.
  Cynthia A. Hill, Research Specialist
  Sarah Hospodor, Dir, Energy, Envir. & Dvmn't, Gov't Rtns
  Michael F. Hussey, Legis. Director, Congressional Affairs
  Collette Johnson-Schulke, V. President, State and Municipal
  Kenneth J. Kerin, Senior V. President
  Robert D. Landis, Politcal Dir, Political Field Operations
  Barbara Leach, Polit. Director, Political Field Optns.
  Jeff Lubar, V. President, Public Affairs
  David H. Lynch, Polit. Director, Political Field Optns.
  Peter Denis Morgan, Dir, Housing & Commun. Devmt, Gov't Rtns
  Daniel Nadash, Polit. Director, Political Field Optns.
  William D. North, Exec. V. President
  Emily O'Connor, Dir, Land Use/Prop Rights, State & Munic
  Anne Scully, Dir, Fed Budget & Fin. Inst., Gov't Rtns
  Michael J. Smith, Jr., Dir, Gov't Spend./Taxat'n, State & Munic
  Jefferson D. Taylor, Legis. Director, Congressional Affairs
  Doug Thompson, Div. V. Pres, Gov't & Polit. Rtns Admin.
  Dr. John A. Tuccillo, Chief Economist and Sr. V. President
  Nancy Katherine Weyl, Legis. Analyst, Government Relations
  Walt Witek, V. Pres., Political Field Operations

Nat'l Ass'n of REALTORS Political Action Committee
777 14th St., N.W., Washington, DC 20005
Telephone: (202) 383-1000
Background: Represented by Stephen D. Driesler of the Nat'l Ass'n of Realtors.

Nat'l Ass'n of Regional Councils
1700 K St., N.W., Suite 1300, Washington, DC 20006-0011
Telephone: (202) 457-0710
Background: Represents councils of local elected governments for metropolitan and rural regions concerned with federal programs affecting housing; transportation; community, economic and rural development; air, water, solid waste, coastal zone management; criminal justice; health and aging with emphasis on area-wide planning.
Represented by:
  Richard C. Hartman, Exec. Director
  Janet Oakley, Associate for Government Affairs
Counsel or consultant:
  McCutchen, Doyle, Brown & Enersen (Philip T. Cummings)

Nat'l Ass'n of Regulatory Utility Commissioners
Box 684, I.C.C. Bldg., Washington, DC 20044-0684
Telephone: (202) 898-2200
Represented by:
  Caroline M. Chambers, Director, Congressional Relations
  Michael Foley, Director, Financial Analysis
  Charles D. Gray, Assistant General Counsel
  Paul Rodgers, Admin. Director and General Counsel

Nat'l Ass'n of Rehabilitation Agencies
1600 Wilson Blvd., Suite 905, Arlington, VA 22209
Telephone: (703) 525-1191

The listings in this directory are available as *Mailing Labels*. See last page.

ORGANIZATIONS REPRESENTED

Background: Richard A. Guggolz of Drohan Management Group serves as Exec. Director.
Counsel or consultant:
Drohan Management Group (Richard A. Guggolz)
Williams and Jensen, P.C. (George G. Olsen)

Nat'l Ass'n of Rehabilitation Facilities
Box 17675, Washington, DC 20041-0675
Telephone: (703) 648-9300
Represented by:
John A. Doyle, Exec. Director
Karen Machusic, Director, Education & Info. Services
Edmumd McLaughlin, Past President
James A. Studzinski, V. Pres. & COO, Rehab. Facilities Svcs.
Carolyn C. Zollar, Gen. Counsel, Dir., Governmental Affairs

Nat'l Ass'n of Reimbursement Officers
1101 King St., Suite 160, Alexandria, VA 22314
Telephone: (703) 739-9333
Represented by:
Mary Rogers, President

Nat'l Ass'n of Reinforcing Steel Contractors
10382 Main St., Suite 200 Box 280, Fairfax, VA 22030
Telephone: (703) 591-1870
Represented by:
Fred H. Codding, Exec. Director and General Counsel

Nat'l Ass'n of Retail Dealers of America
Lombard, IL
Counsel or consultant:
Tendler, Goldberg & Biggins, Chtd. (James M. Goldberg)

Nat'l Ass'n of Retail Druggists
205 Daingerfield Road, Alexandria, VA 22314
Telephone: (703) 683-8200
Represented by:
John M. Rector, V. Pres., Gov't. Affairs & Gen. Counsel
Charles M. West, Exec. Vice President
Counsel or consultant:
Patricia Bario Associates (Patricia Bario)
Patton, Boggs and Blow (Thomas Hale Boggs, Jr.)

Nat'l Ass'n of Retired Federal Employees
1533 New Hampshire Ave., N.W., Washington, DC 20036
Telephone: (202) 234-0832
Represented by:
H. T. Steve Morrissey, President
Judith E. Park, Director of Legislation
Harold Price, National V. President
Counsel or consultant:
Kator, Scott and Heller (Michael J. Kator)

Nat'l Ass'n of Retired Federal Employees Political Action Committee
1533 New Hampshire Ave., N.W., Washington, DC 20036
Telephone: (202) 234-0832
Background: Responsible contact is Judy Park. (See Nat'l Ass'n of Retired Federal Employees.)

Nat'l Ass'n of Retired Senior Volunteer Program Directors
Patterson, NJ
Counsel or consultant:
EMJ Consultants (Frances F. Butler)

Nat'l Ass'n of Retired and Veteran Railway Employees, Inc.
Kansas City, MO
Counsel or consultant:
J. P. Trainor

Nat'l Ass'n of Royalty Owners
Ada, OK
Counsel or consultant:
Zuckert, Scoutt and Rasenberger (J. Michael Keeling)

Nat'l Ass'n of School Music Dealers
Appleton, WI
Counsel or consultant:
Tendler, Goldberg & Biggins, Chtd. (James M. Goldberg)

Nat'l Ass'n of School Psychologists
808 17th St., N.W., Suite 200, Washington, DC 20006
Telephone: (202) 223-9498
Counsel or consultant:
Bostrom Corp. (John F. Donahue)

Nat'l Ass'n of Schools of Art and Design
11250 Roger Bacon Drive, #21, Reston, VA 22090
Telephone: (703) 437-0700
Background: Exec. Director is Samuel Hope (see Nat'l Ass'n of Schools of Music).

Nat'l Ass'n of Schools of Dance
11250 Roger Bacon Drive, #21, Reston, VA 22090
Telephone: (703) 437-0700
Background: Exec. Director is Samuel Hope (see Nat'l Ass'n of Schools of Music).

Nat'l Ass'n of Schools of Music
11250 Roger Bacon Drive, #21, Reston, VA 22090
Telephone: (703) 437-0700
Represented by:
Samuel Hope, Exec. Director

Nat'l Ass'n of Schools of Public Affairs and Administration
1120 G St., N.W. Suite 520, Washington, DC 20005
Telephone: (202) 628-8965
Represented by:
Alfred M. Zuck, Exec. Director

Nat'l Ass'n of Schools of Theatre
11250 Roger Bacon Drive, #21, Reston, VA 22090
Telephone: (703) 437-0700
Background: Exec. Director is Samuel Hope (see Nat'l Ass'n of Schools of Music).

Nat'l Ass'n of Scissors and Shears Manufacturers
1511 K St., N.W., Suite 535, Washington, DC 20005
Telephone: (202) 628-8777
Counsel or consultant:
C. V. & R. V. Maudlin (Robert V. Maudlin)

Nat'l Ass'n of Secondary School Principals
1904 Association Drive, Reston, VA 22091
Telephone: (703) 860-0200
Represented by:
Lew Armistead, Director of Public Relations
Timothy J. Dyer, Exec. Director
Richard A. Kruse, Assistant Director, Government Relations
George E. Melton, Deputy Exec. Director

Nat'l Ass'n of Securities and Commercial Law Attorneys
1300 Eye St., N.W. Suite 480 East Tower, Washington, DC 20005
Telephone: (202) 962-3863
Counsel or consultant:
Jonathan W. Cuneo Law Offices (Jonathan W. Cuneo)

Nat'l Ass'n of Securities Dealers (NASDAQ)
1735 K St., N.W., Washington, DC 20006
Telephone: (202) 728-8000
Represented by:
Robert E. Aber, V. President, Deputy General Counsel
T. Grant Callery, V. President, Deputy General Counsel
Raymond Cocchi, V. Pres., Congressional & State Liaison
Robert J. Ferri, Jr., Manager, Press Relations
Gene L. Finn, V. President and Chief Economist
Joseph R. Hardiman, President & CEO
Douglas F. Parrillo, Sr. V. President, Communications
John E. Pinto, Exec. V. President for Compliance
Robert N. Reiss, V. Pres., Sys. Techn. & Prod. Dvlmnt.
Frank J. Wilson, Exec. V. President, Legal & Compliance
Counsel or consultant:
Reese Communications Companies
Targeting Systems, Inc.

Nat'l Ass'n of Senior Companion Program Directors
Salt Lake City, UT
Counsel or consultant:
EMJ Consultants (Frances F. Butler)

Nat'l Ass'n of Small Business Investment Companies
1156 15th St., N.W. Suite 1101, Washington, DC 20005
Telephone: (202) 833-8230
Represented by:
Eileen E. Denne, Director, Public Relations
Peter F. McNeish, President
Counsel or consultant:
Brown & Wood (James E. Murray)
Hager Sharp Inc. (Susan Hager)

Nat'l Ass'n of Small Business Investment Companies Political Action Committee
1156 15th St., N.W. Suite 1101, Washington, DC 20005
Telephone: (202) 833-8320
Background: Responsible contact is Peter F. McNeish. (See Nat'l Ass'n of Small Business Investment Companies.)

Nat'l Ass'n of Social Workers
7981 Eastern Ave., Silver Spring, MD 20910
Telephone: (301) 565-0333
Background: A 126,000 member organization that represents its clients on health, mental health, anti-poverty, and social justice issues.
Represented by:
Mark Battle, Exec. Director
Judy A. Hall, Associate Director, Program Division
Sandra K. Harding, Staff Associate for Legislation
Sunny Harris, Staff Associate for Legislation
Susan Hoechstetter, Director, Legislation
Toby Weismiller, Sr. Staff Associate for Political Action
Counsel or consultant:
The Kamber Group (Dennis Walston)
Wexler, Reynolds, Fuller, Harrison and Schule, Inc. (Kristen Ames)

Nat'l Ass'n of Social Workers Political Action Committee for Candidate Action
7981 Eastern Ave., Silver Spring, MD 20910
Telephone: (301) 565-0333
Background: Responsible contact is Toby Weismiller of the Association.

Nat'l Ass'n of Solvent Recyclers
1333 New Hampshire Ave., N.W., Suite 1100, Washington, DC 20036
Telephone: (202) 463-6956
Background: The national organization of 67 companies engaged in solvent recycling and related industries. Promotes beneficial recycling and reuse of solvent waste streams. Educates Congress, regulatory agencies and states on issues affecting recycling industry and environmental concerns.
Represented by:
Kimberly Olsen, Assistant Director
Brenda A. Pulley, Exec. Director

Nat'l Ass'n of State Alcohol and Drug Abuse Directors
444 North Capitol St., N.W. Suite 642, Washington, DC 20001
Telephone: (202) 783-6868
Represented by:
Dr. William Butynski, Exec. Director
Diane Canova, Director of Public Policy

Nat'l Ass'n of State Auditors, Comptrollers and Treasurers
444 North Capitol St., N.W. Suite 523, Washington, DC 20001
Telephone: (202) 624-5451
Represented by:
Helena G. Sims, Director
Counsel or consultant:
Jones, Day, Reavis and Pogue (Frieda K. Wallison)

Nat'l Ass'n of State Aviation Officials
8401 Colesville Road., Suite 505, Silver Spring, MD 20910
Telephone: (301) 588-0587
Background: Seeks to foster cooperation and mutual aid among the states and the federal government in developing national and state air transportation systems that serve the public interest. Washington office serves in dual role of representing the states' interests to federal agencies and vice versa.
Represented by:
Edward M. Scott, Staff Associate
Robert T. Warner, Exec. V. President

Nat'l Ass'n of State Boards of Education
1012 Cameron St., Alexandria, VA 22314
Telephone: (703) 684-4000

ORGANIZATIONS REPRESENTED

Nat'l Ass'n of State Boards of Education (Cont'd)
Represented by:
Brenda L. Welburn, Deputy Exec. Director
Gene Wilhoit, Exec. Director

Nat'l Ass'n of State Budget Officers
400 North Capitol St., N.W. Suite 295, Washington, DC 20001
Telephone: (202) 624-5382
Represented by:
Dr. Gerald H. Miller, Exec. Director

Nat'l Ass'n of State Credit Union Supervisors
1901 North Ft. Myer Dr. Suite 201, Arlington, VA 22209
Telephone: (703) 528-8351
Represented by:
Sheralyn J. Odom, Exec. Director

Nat'l Ass'n of State Departments of Agriculture
1616 H St., N.W., Washington, DC 20006
Telephone: (202) 628-1566
Represented by:
James B. Grant, Exec. Secretary

Nat'l Ass'n of State Development Agencies
444 North Capitol St., N.W. Suite 611, Washington, DC 20001
Telephone: (202) 624-5411
Represented by:
Miles Friedman, Exec. Director

Nat'l Ass'n of State Directors of Special Education
2021 K St., N.W., Suite 315, Washington, DC 20006
Telephone: (202) 296-1800
Represented by:
Dr. William Schipper, Exec. Director

Nat'l Ass'n of State Directors of Veterans Affairs
941 North Capitol St., N.E., Suite 1211-F, Washington, DC 20421
Telephone: (202) 737-5050
Represented by:
Cleveland Jordan, Washington Liaison

Nat'l Ass'n of State Directors of Vocational Technical Education Consortium
1420 16th St., N.W., Washington, DC 20036
Telephone: (202) 328-0216
Represented by:
Madeline B. Hemmings, Exec. Director

Nat'l Ass'n of State Energy Officials
122 C St., N.W., Suite 810, Washington, DC 20001
Telephone: (202) 639-8749
Background: A non-profit corporation promoting a balanced national energy policy including energy conservation, alternative fuels and energy security.
Represented by:
Frank Bishop, Exec. Director
Counsel or consultant:
Duncan, Weinberg, Miller & Pembroke, P.C. (Jeffrey C. Genzer)

Nat'l Ass'n of State Foresters
444 North Capitol St., N.W., Washington, DC 20001
Telephone: (202) 624-5415
Represented by:
Terri Bates, Washington Representative

Nat'l Ass'n of State Mental Health Program Directors
1101 King St., Suite 160, Alexandria, VA 22314
Telephone: (703) 739-9333
Represented by:
E. Clarke Ross, Ass't Exec. Director, Fed. Relations
Harry C. Schnibbe, Exec. Director

Nat'l Ass'n of State Mental Retardation Program Directors
113 Oronoco St., Alexandria, VA 22314
Telephone: (703) 683-4202
Represented by:
Robert M. Gettings, Exec. Director

Nat'l Ass'n of State Treasurers
400 N. Capitol St., N.W. Suite 320 S, Washington, DC 20001
Telephone: (202) 624-8595

Represented by:
Milton T. Wells, Director, Federal Relations

Nat'l Ass'n of State Units on Aging
2033 K St., N.W. Suite 304, Washington, DC 20006
Telephone: (202) 785-0707
Represented by:
Daniel Quirk, Exec. Director

Nat'l Ass'n of State Universities and Land-Grant Colleges
One Dupont Circle, N.W., Suite 710, Washington, DC 20036-1191
Telephone: (202) 778-0818
Represented by:
Robert L. Clodius, President
James W. Cowan, Dir., Fed. Rtns. - Agr./Natural Resouces
Jerald Roschwalb, Dir., Office of Fed. Rtns - Higher Educ.

Nat'l Ass'n of State Veterans Nursing Homes
Norfolk, NE
Counsel or consultant:
Tuvin Associates (Carl R. Tuvin)

Nat'l Ass'n of Steel Pipe Distributors
Houston, TX
Counsel or consultant:
Kent & O'Connor, Incorp. (J. H. Kent)

Nat'l Ass'n of Stevedores
2011 Eye St., N.W., Washington, DC 20006
Telephone: (202) 296-2810
Represented by:
Charles T. Carroll, Assistant General Counsel
Mary A. Dyess, Ass't Exec. Director
Donald J. McCarty, President
Thomas D. Wilcox, Exec. Director and General Counsel

Nat'l Ass'n of Student Financial Aid Administrators
1920 L St., N.W., Suite 200, Washington, DC 20036
Telephone: (202) 785-0453
Represented by:
Dr. A. Dallas Martin, Jr., President

Nat'l Ass'n of Student Personnel Administrators
1700 18th Street, N.W. Suite 301, Washington, DC 20009
Telephone: (202) 265-7500
Represented by:
Dr. Elizabeth Nuss, Executive Director

Nat'l Ass'n of Sugar Cane Growers
Cali, Colombia
Background: Wishes an increased sugar quota allotment.
Counsel or consultant:
Coudert Brothers

Nat'l Ass'n of Surety Bond Producers
6931 Arlington Road, Suite 308, Bethesda, MD 20814
Telephone: (301) 986-4166
Represented by:
J. Martin Huber, Exec. V. President
Theodore M. Pierce, Legislative Coordinator

Nat'l Ass'n of Tax Consultants
Eugene, OR
Background: Represented in Washington by Robert E. Gordon (202) 872-0161.

Nat'l Ass'n of Telecommunications Dealers
1255 23rd St., N.W., Washington, DC 20037
Telephone: (202) 872-8420
Counsel or consultant:
Hauck and Associates (Mark T. Engle)

Nat'l Ass'n of Temporary Services
119 South St. Asaph St., Alexandria, VA 22314
Telephone: (703) 549-6287
Represented by:
Edward A. Lenz, Sr. V. President and General Counsel
Samuel R. Sacco, Exec. Vice President
Richard A. Wahlquist, V. President
Counsel or consultant:
Miller & Chevalier, Chartered (C. Frederick Oliphant, III)
Webster, Chamberlain and Bean (Arthur L. Herold)
Wunder, Ryan, Cannon & Thelen (Michael A. Forscey)

Nat'l Ass'n of Temporary Services Political Action Committee
119 South St. Asaph St., Alexandria, VA 22314
Telephone: (703) 549-6287
Background: Represented by Samuel R. Sacco, Exec. V. President of the Ass'n.

Nat'l Ass'n of the Deaf
814 Thayer Ave., Silver Spring, MD 20910
Telephone: (301) 587-1788
Background: Works to improve the quality of products and services available to deaf and hard of hearing persons. Membership is 20,000. Legislative advocate for equal access to communications and employment opportunities
Represented by:
Marc Charmatz, Counsel
Merv Garretson, Interim Exec. Director
Judy Costello Pearson, Director, Marketing & Public Relations
Fred S. Weiner, Director, Program Development & Services

Nat'l Ass'n of the Remodeling Industry
1901 North Moore St. Suite 808, Arlington, VA 22209
Telephone: (703) 276-7600
Background: Represents professional remodeling contractors, manufacturers of remodeling products, wholesalers, distributors, lenders, utlilities and publishers.
Represented by:
Alan J. Campbell, Exec. Director
Patti Knoff, Director, Government Affairs
Leslie Levine, Director, Communications

Nat'l Ass'n of Theatre Owners
North Hollywood, CA
Counsel or consultant:
Loomis, Owen, Fellman and Howe (Steven John Fellman)

Nat'l Ass'n of Tobacco Distributors
1199 North Fairfax St. Suite 701, Alexandria, VA 22314
Telephone: (703) 683-8336
Represented by:
Terry J. Burns, V. President
Jacqueline A. Cohen, Director, Government Relations

Nat'l Ass'n of Tobacco Distributors Political Action Committee
1199 North Fairfax St. Suite 701, Alexandria, VA 22314
Telephone: (703) 683-8336
Background: The political action committee of the Nat'l Ass'n of Tobacco Distributors. Administrator and contact is Terry J. Burns of the Nat'l Ass'n of Tobacco Distributors.

Nat'l Ass'n of Towns and Townships
1522 K St., N.W. Suite 730, Washington, DC 20005
Telephone: (202) 737-5200
Background: A federation of state associations and direct members representing over 13,000 units of local government. Units are mostly small and rural.
Represented by:
Sharon Lawrence, Director, Federal Affairs
Beverly C. Nykwest, Assoc Dir, Communications/Public./PR
Bruce Rosenthal, Director of Communications
Jeffrey H. Schiff, Exec. Director

Nat'l Ass'n of Trade and Technical Schools
2251 Wisconsin Ave., N.W. Suite 200, Washington, DC 20007
Telephone: (202) 333-1021
Represented by:
Stephen J. Blair, President
Tony Calandro, Director, Governmental Relations
Michael A. Gonzales, V. President
Nancy O'Brien, Associate Dir, Governmental Relations
Sandra G. Smith, Dir., Business and Industry Relations
Counsel or consultant:
Cohn and Marks (Richard M. Schmidt, Jr., Ian D. Volner)
Gallagher-Widmeyer Group Inc., The (Scott D. Widmeyer)

Nat'l Ass'n of Trade and Technical Schools Political Action Committee
2251 Wisconsin Ave., N.W., Washington, DC 20007
Telephone: (202) 333-1021
Background: Contact is Tony Calandro of the Ass'n.

ORGANIZATIONS REPRESENTED

Nat'l Ass'n of Truck Stop Operators
1199 N. Fairfax St. Suite 801, Alexandria, VA 22314
Telephone: (703) 549-2100
Represented by:
  Brian C. Bonnet, Associate Director, Government Relations
  W. Dewey Clower, President
  Howard N. Menaker, General Counsel

Nat'l Ass'n of Truck Stop Operators Political Action Committee
Box 1285, Alexandria, VA 22313
Telephone: (703) 549-2100
Background: Contact is Howard N. Menaker of the Ass'n.

Nat'l Ass'n of VA Physicians
3400 Internat'l Drive, N.W. Pod K-2, Washington, DC 20008-3098
Telephone: (202) 363-3838
Represented by:
  Dr. Paul W. Schafer, Exec. Director

Nat'l Ass'n of Video Distributors
1255 23rd St., N.W., Washington, DC 20037
Telephone: (202) 452-8100
Counsel or consultant:
  Hauck and Associates (Mark T. Engle)

Nat'l Ass'n of Water Companies
1725 K St., N.W. Suite 1212, Washington, DC 20006
Telephone: (202) 833-8383
Background: Formerly (1971) Nat'l Water Co. Conference.
Represented by:
  James B. Groff, Exec. Director
  Elaine M. Krawiec, Director of Government Relations
Counsel or consultant:
  Paul Arneson, P.C. (Paul Arneson)

Nat'l Ass'n of Water Companies Political Action Committee
1725 K St., N.W., Suite 1212, Washington, DC 20006
Telephone: (202) 833-8383
Background: Represented by James B. Groff, Exec. Director of the Association.
Counsel or consultant:
  Paul Arneson, P.C.

Nat'l Ass'n of Wheat Growers
415 Second St., N.E. Suite 300, Washington, DC 20002
Telephone: (202) 547-7800
Represented by:
  Barry L. Jenkins, Director of Communications
  Bruce I. Knight, Dir., Gov't Affairs & Mktg. Svcs.
  Jerry Rees, Senior V. President
  Carl F. Schwensen, Exec. V. President
  Margie R. Williams, V. President, Public Affairs
Counsel or consultant:
  Arent, Fox, Kintner, Plotkin & Kahn (Samuel Efron, Stephen L. Gibson)
  Jellinek, Schwartz, Connolly & Freshman, Inc. (Steven D. Jellinek)

Nat'l Ass'n of Wheat Growers Political Action Committee
415 Second St., N.E. Suite 300, Washington, DC 20002
Telephone: (202) 547-7800
Background: Carl F. Schwensen, Exec. V. President of the Ass'n, serves as Treasurer.

Nat'l Ass'n of Wholesaler-Distributors
1725 K St., N.W. Suite 710, Washington, DC 20006
Telephone: (202) 872-0885
Represented by:
  James A. Anderson, Jr., Senior Director, Government Relations
  Alan M. Kranowitz, Senior V. President, Gov't Relations
  Mary T. Tavenner, Senior Director, Government Relations
  Dirk Van Dongen, President
Counsel or consultant:
  Crowell and Moring (Michael J. Mullen, Victor E. Schwartz)
  Dewey, Ballantine, Bushby, Palmer and Wood (Lawrence F. O'Brien, III)
  McKevitt Group, The
  Patton, Boggs and Blow (Cliff Massa, III)
  Valis Associates (Wayne H. Valis)

Nat'l Ass'n of Women Business Owners
Chicago, IL

Counsel or consultant:
  O'Bannon & Co. (Dona O'Bannon)

Nat'l Audubon Soc.
801 Pennsylvania Ave., S.E., Washington, DC 20003
Telephone: (202) 547-9009
Background: One of the nation's oldest (1905), largest (600,000 members), and most experienced membership organizations dedicated to the conservation of wildlife and other natural resources and to the sound protection of the natural environment. High campaigns - Artic Nat'l Wildlife Refuge, Clean Air, Old-Growth Forests, Platte River, Wetlands Preservation and Global Warming.
Represented by:
  Hope M. Babcock, Counselor, Dir., Public Lands and Waters
  Patricia A. Baldi, Director of Population Programs
  Jan Bayea, Senior Staff Scientist
  Brock Evans, V. President for Nat'l Issues
  Maureen K. Hinkle, Director of Agriculture Policy
  Cynthia R. Lenhart, Wildlife Specialist
  Connie Mahan, Grassroots Coordinator
  Edward F. Pembleton, Director of Water Resources Program
  Elizabeth L. Raisbeck, Sr. V. Pres., Gov't Rels. & Reg'l Affrs.
  Frances Spivy-Weber, Director, Internat'l Program
  Melinda Taylor, Deputy Counsel
  Brooks B. Yeager, V. President, Government Relations

Nat'l Automated Clearing House Ass'n
607 Herndon Parkway Suite 200, Herndon, VA 22070
Telephone: (703) 742-9190
Represented by:
  Elliott C. McEntee, President
  William Nelson, Senior Director

Nat'l Automatic Merchandising Ass'n
11718 Bowman Green Drive, Reston, VA 22090
Telephone: (703) 435-1210
Represented by:
  Thomas McMahon, Eastern Manager and Counsel

Nat'l Automobile Dealers Ass'n
8400 Westpark Dr., McLean, VA 22102
Telephone: (703) 821-7000
Represented by:
  H. Thomas Greene, Exec. Director of Legislative Affairs
  Scott Hughes Lane, Legislative Representative
  Frank E. McCarthy, Exec. V. President
  William A. Newman, Chief Legal Counsel
  Mary Jo Peterson, Legislative Representative
  Ivette E. Rivera, Legislative Representative
  Mary Beth Robinson, Director, Public Relations
  W. Allan Wilbur, Exec. Director, Public Affairs

Nat'l Bakery Suppliers Ass'n
1625 K St., N.W. Suite 1190, Washington, DC 20006
Telephone: (202) 628-5530
Counsel or consultant:
  Walter E. Byerley Law Offices (Wayne K. Hill)

Nat'l Bank for Cooperatives
Denver, CO
Counsel or consultant:
  E. A. Jaenke & Associates (Robert T. Lowerre)

Nat'l Bank of Washington, The
619 14th St., N.W., Washington, DC 20005
Telephone: (202) 537-2000
Represented by:
  Patricia N. Mathews, Sr. V. President, Public Affairs
Counsel or consultant:
  Dickstein, Shapiro and Morin
  Thompson, Hine and Flory (Louis Pohorlyes)

Nat'l Bankers Ass'n
122 C St., N.W. Suite 580, Washington, DC 20001
Telephone: (202) 783-3200
Represented by:
  Bruce Gamble, V. President, External Affairs
  John P. Kelly, Jr., President

Nat'l Bankers Ass'n Political Action Committee
122 C St., N.W. Suite 580, Washington, DC 20001
Telephone: (202) 783-3200
Background: Responsible contact is John P. Kelly, Jr. of the Nat'l Bankers Ass'n.

Nat'l Bar Ass'n
1225 11th St., N.W., Washington, DC 20001

Telephone: (202) 842-3900
Background: Membership consists principally of black lawyers.
Represented by:
  John Crump, Exec. Director
  Thomas A. Duckenfield, President

Nat'l Bark Producers Ass'n
13542 Union Village Circle, Clifton, VA 22024
Telephone: (703) 830-5367
Counsel or consultant:
  Executives Consultants, Inc. (Robert C. LaGasse, CAE)

Nat'l Basketball Ass'n
New York, NY
Counsel or consultant:
  Baraff, Koerner, Olender and Hochberg (Philip R. Hochberg)
  Rivkin, Radler, Dunne and Bayh (Birch Bayh, Jr., Thomas A. Connaughton, Kevin O. Faley)

Nat'l Beauty Culturists' League
25 Logan Circle, N.W., Washington, DC 20005
Telephone: (202) 332-2695
Represented by:
  Cleolis Richardson, President

Nat'l Beer Wholesalers Ass'n
5205 Leesburg Pike, Suite 1600, Falls Church, VA 22041
Telephone: (703) 578-4300
Represented by:
  Robert S. Bludworth, Government Affairs Coordinator
  Jack W. Lewis, V. President, Government Affairs
  Ronald A. Sarasin, President
  Gary M. Zizka, Government Affairs
Counsel or consultant:
  Jones, Day, Reavis and Pogue

Nat'l Beer Wholesalers Ass'n Political Action Committee
5205 Leesburg Pike Suite 1600, Falls Church, VA 22041
Telephone: (703) 578-4300
Background: Contact is Ronald A. Sarasin of the Association.

Nat'l Beverage Dispensing Equipment Ass'n
2011 Eye St., N.W., Fifth Floor, Washington, DC 20006
Telephone: (202) 775-4885
Represented by:
  Pamela Boyajian, Exec. Director

Nat'l Black Caucus of State Legislators
444 North Capitol St., N.W. Suite 206, Washington, DC 20001
Telephone: (202) 624-5457
Background: Established in 1977 as an information resource and network for Black state legislators.
Represented by:
  Rep. David P. Richardson, Jr., President

Nat'l Black Child Development Institute
1463 Rhode Island Ave., N.W., Washington, DC 20005
Telephone: (202) 387-1281
Background: Serves as a national advocacy and service organization concerned with the human development and rights of black children. Provides services in the areas of child development, child welfare and education.
Represented by:
  Evelyn K. Moore, Exec. Director

Nat'l Black Media Coalition
38 New York Ave., N.E., Washington, DC 20002
Telephone: (202) 387-8155
Represented by:
  Carmen Marshall, Exec. Director
  Pluria W. Marshall, Chairman

Nat'l Black Police Ass'n
1100 17th St., N.W., Suite 1000, Washington, DC 20036
Telephone: (202) 457-0563
Background: An organization of over 100 police associations representing some 35,000 individual members. Serves as advocate for minority police officers.
Represented by:
  Ronald E. Hampton, Exec. Director

Nat'l Black Women's Political Leadership Caucus
3005 Bladensburg Road, N.E. Suite 217, Washington, DC 20018
Telephone: (202) 529-2806

The listings in this directory are available as *Mailing Labels*. See last page.

ORGANIZATIONS REPRESENTED

Nat'l Black Women's Political Leadership Caucus (Cont'd)
Background: Seeks to educate and include all black women in the political and economic process through voter registration drives, conferences, seminars, and other activities. Founded in 1971.
Represented by:
Juanita Kennedy Morgan, Exec. Secretary/Org. Director

Nat'l Board for Certification in Dental Laboratory Technology
3801 Mt. Vernon Ave., Alexandria, VA 22305
Telephone: (703) 683-5263
Background: Executive Director is Robert W. Stanley of the Nat'l Ass'n of Dental Laboratories.

Nat'l Board for Certification of Dental Laboratories
3801 Mt. Vernon Ave., Alexandria, VA 22305
Telephone: (703) 683-5263
Background: Represented by Robert Stanley, Exec. Director (see Nat'l Board for Certification in Dental Laboratory Technology).

Nat'l Board for Professional Training Standards
Detroit, MI
Counsel or consultant:
Williams and Jensen, P.C. (J. Steven Hart, David Starr)

Nat'l Board of Examiners in Optometry
5530 Wisconsin Ave., N.W. Suite 805, Washington, DC 20815
Telephone: (202) 652-5192
Represented by:
Norman E. Wallis, Exec. Director

Nat'l Board of Professional Teaching Standards
1320 18th St., N.W. Suite 401, Washington, DC 20036
Telephone: (202) 463-3980
Counsel or consultant:
Gallagher-Widmeyer Group Inc., The (Scott D. Widmeyer)

Nat'l Bonded Warehouse Ass'n
Miami, FL
Counsel or consultant:
Sandler, Travis & Rosenberg. P.A. (Thomas G. Travis)

Nat'l Bowling Council
1919 Pennsylvania Ave., N.W., Washington, DC 20006
Telephone: (202) 659-9070
Represented by:
R. Lance Elliott, Exec. Director
Counsel or consultant:
Power & Coleman (Thomas W. Power)

Nat'l Broadcasting Co.
1331 Pennsylvania Ave., N.W. Suite 700S, Washington, DC 20006
Telephone: (202) 833-3600
Background: A wholly owned subsidiary of the General Electric Co.
Represented by:
Sallie H. Forman, V. President, Government Relations
Robert D. Hynes, Jr., V. President, Washington
Terence P. Mahony, V. President, Government Relations
Howard Monderer, Consultant, Law
Ellen Weir, Research Coordinator
Counsel or consultant:
Hill and Knowlton Public Affairs Worldwide (Jackson Bain)

Nat'l Broiler Council
1155 15th St., N.W. Suite 614, Washington, DC 20005
Telephone: (202) 296-2622
Represented by:
Mary M. Colville, Director of Government Relations
J. Stephen Pretanik, Director of Science and Technology
William P. Roenigk, Dir., Econ. Research & Membership Svcs.
George B. Watts, President
Counsel or consultant:
Mahlon A. Burnette, III
Collier, Shannon & Scott
Hogan and Hartson

Nat'l Broiler Council Political Action Committee
1155 15th St., N.W., Suite 614, Washington, DC 20005
Telephone: (202) 296-2622
Background: Sponsored by the Nat'l Broiler Council. Contacts are George B. Watts and Mary M. Colville of the Council.

Nat'l Bulk Carriers
New York, NY
Counsel or consultant:
Ragan and Mason (William F. Ragan)

Nat'l Burglar and Fire Alarm Ass'n
7101 Wisconsin Ave. Suite 1390, Bethesda, MD 20814-1100
Telephone: (301) 907-3202
Represented by:
Pamela DeSanto, Dir. of Communications, Public Relations
Charles B. Lavin, Jr., Exec. Director
Counsel or consultant:
Keefe Co., The (William A. Signer)
Rowland & Sellery (Lawrence E. Sabbath)

Nat'l Business Aircraft Ass'n
1200 18th St., N.W. Suite 200, Washington, DC 20036
Telephone: (202) 783-9000
Represented by:
Cassandra Bosco, Manager, Public Affairs
Alan Darrow, V. President, Administration
William M. Fanning, Manager, Technical Services
E. H. Haupt, Manager, Airport & Environmental Svcs.
Jonathan Howe, President
Mark Allan Micali, Manager, Government Affairs
Petronella C. Sanders, Assistant Manager, Government Relations
Paul Smith, Manager, ATC Services
William Stine, Manager, International Services
Pete West, V. President, Government & Public Affrs.
Dennis Wright, V. President, Operations
Counsel or consultant:
Baker, Worthington, Crossley, Stansberry & Woolf (III J. E. Murdock)
Dow, Lohnes and Albertson (Richard S. Belas)
Gold and Liebengood, Inc. (David W. Bushong, Howard S. Liebengood)
Preston Gates Ellis & Rouvelas Meeds (Pamela J. Garvie)
Sparkman and Cole, Inc. (Timothy R. Cole, D. Dean Sparkman)
Zuckert, Scoutt and Rasenberger (Raymond J. Rasenberger)

Nat'l Business Education Ass'n
1914 Association Dr., Reston, VA 22091
Telephone: (703) 860-8300
Represented by:
Janet M. Treichel, Exec. Director

Nat'l Business Forms Ass'n
433 East Monroe Ave., Alexandria, VA 22301
Telephone: (703) 836-6225
Represented by:
Peter L. Colaianni, Exec. Director

Nat'l Business League
4324 Georgia Ave., N.W., Washington, DC 20011
Telephone: (202) 829-5900
Background: Formerly the Nat'l Negro Business League. Founded by Booker T. Washington in 1900.
Represented by:
David Rice, Exec. V. President

Nat'l Business Owners Ass'n
7910 Woodmont Ave., Suite 1208, Bethesda, MD 20814-3015
Telephone: (301) 913-0010
Counsel or consultant:
C. M. Brownstein & Assoc. (Clifford M. Brownstein)

Nat'l Cable Television Ass'n
1724 Massachusetts Ave., N.W., Washington, DC 20036
Telephone: (202) 775-3550
Represented by:
Elise Adde, V. President, Industry Communications
Decker Anstrom, Exec. Vice President
Daniel Craig, Director, Legislative Policy
James P. Mooney, President and CEO
Valerie Pinson, Director, Government Relations
Lois Richerson, Director, Government Relations
Wanda Townsend, Director, Government Relations
Pamela J. Turner, V. President, Government Relations
Douglas R. Watts, Legislative Counsel

Nat'l Cable Television Ass'n Political Action Committee
1724 Massachusetts Ave., N.W., Washington, DC 20036
Telephone: (202) 775-3650

Background: Represented by Decker Anstrom of the Association.
Counsel or consultant:
Manatt, Phelps, Rothenberg & Phillips (William C. Oldaker)

Nat'l Campaign for a Peace Tax Fund
2121 Decatur Place, N.W., Washington, DC 20008
Telephone: (202) 483-3751
Background: A citizens' lobby advocating passage of a law permitting people conscientiously opposed to war to have the military portion of their taxes allocated to peace projects instead of for military expenditures.
Represented by:
Marian C. Franz, Exec. Director

Nat'l Campground Owners Ass'n
11307 Sunset Hills Rd. Suite B-7, Reston, VA 22090
Telephone: (703) 471-0143
Represented by:
David Gorin, Exec. V. President
Dawn M. Mancuso, Exec. Director

Nat'l Cancer Institute
c/o Prospect Associates, Inc. 1801 Rockville Pike, #500, Rockville, MD 20852
Telephone: (301) 468-6555
Counsel or consultant:
Hill and Knowlton Public Affairs Worldwide (Ken Rabin, Jill Schuker)

Nat'l Cancer Research Coalition
New York, NY
Counsel or consultant:
Capitol Associates, Inc. (Terry Lierman)

Nat'l Candle Ass'n
1350 New York Ave., N.W. Suite 615, Washington, DC 20005
Telephone: (202) 393-1780
Counsel or consultant:
Barnes and Thornburg (Randolph J. Stayin, Marcela B. Stras)
Resources for Group Management, Inc. (Marianne McDermott)

Nat'l Candy Wholesalers Ass'n
1120 Vermont Ave., N.W., Suite 1120, Washington, DC 20005
Telephone: (202) 463-2124
Background: The major trade association for wholesale distributors of candy, tobacco products, health and beauty aids and allied products.
Represented by:
Dennis Lavallee, CAE, Director, Member & Government Relations
David E. Strachan, CAE, Exec. V. President
Counsel or consultant:
Webster, Chamberlain and Bean

Nat'l Captioning Institute
5203 Leesburg Pike, Suite 1500, Falls Church, VA 22041
Telephone: (703) 998-2400
Represented by:
John Ball, President

Nat'l Career Development Ass'n
5999 Stevenson Ave., Alexandria, VA 22304
Telephone: (703) 823-9800
Represented by:
E. Niel Carey, Exec. Director

Nat'l Catholic Conference for Interracial Justice
3033 Fourth St., N.E., Washington, DC 20017
Telephone: (202) 529-6480
Represented by:
Jerome B. Ernst, Exec. Director

Nat'l Catholic Educational Ass'n
1077 30th St., N.W. Suite 100, Washington, DC 20007
Telephone: (202) 337-6232
Represented by:
Mary V. Burke, Assistant Exec. Director, Secondary
Catherine T. McNamee, CSJ, President

Nat'l Catholic News Service
1312 Massachusetts Ave., N.W., Washington, DC 20005
Telephone: (202) 541-3250
Represented by:
Thomas N. Lorsung, Director and Editor-in-Chief

ORGANIZATIONS REPRESENTED

Nat'l Cattlemen's Ass'n
1301 Pennsylvania Ave., N.W., Suite 300, Washington, DC 20004
Telephone: (202) 347-0228
Background: Non-profit trade association representing all segments of the nation's cattle industry, including cattle breeders, producers and feeders. Services include government affairs, public information and market information.
Represented by:
Thomas M. Cook, Director, Industry Affairs
J. Burton Eller, Jr., Sr. V. President, Government Affairs
Alisa Harrison, Manager, Washington Information
Kathleen Hartnett, Assoc. Dir., Private Lands & Envir Mgmt
G. Chandler Keys, III, Director, Congressional Relations
Patricia A. McDonald, Director, Public Lands
Alan C. Sobba, Director, Taxes and Credit
Anne Winslow, Director, Food Policy & Public Affairs
Counsel or consultant:
The Susan Davis Companies
Davis & Harman
Gold and Liebengood, Inc. (Denise A. Bode)
Hill and Knowlton Public Affairs Worldwide (Barbara Hyde)

Nat'l Caucus and Center on Black Aged
1424 K St., N.W. Suite 500, Washington, DC 20005
Telephone: (202) 637-8400
Represented by:
Samuel Simmons, President

Nat'l Cellular Resellers Ass'n
Cleveland, OH
Counsel or consultant:
Dutko & Associates (Steve Perry)
Reed Smith Shaw & McClay (Judith St. Ledger-Roty, Carl Rowan, Jr.)

Nat'l Center for Advanced Technologies
1250 Eye St., N.W., Suite 1100, Washington, DC 20005
Telephone: (202) 371-8544
Background: A foundation established in December 1988 by the Aerospace Industries of America. Coordinates the development of major technologies which are key to U.S. aerospace competitiveness and to national security.
Represented by:
Thomas F. Faught, Jr., Exec. Director

Nat'l Center for Appropriate Technology
1212 New York Ave.,, N.W. Suite 340, Washington, DC 20005
Telephone: (202) 289-6657
Background: Researches and develops technologies applicable to the special needs of the poor. Transfers information on energy and energy conservation, agriculture, health and housing through technical assistance, training and publications.
Represented by:
Stephen G. Thomas, Washington Project Manager

Nat'l Center for Ass'n Resources
1511 K St., N.W. Suite 715, Washington, DC 20005
Telephone: (202) 628-7144
Background: Organized in 1986 to provide a variety of services and advice to trade associations and governmental entities.
Represented by:
Richard A. Lillquist, CAE, President
Counsel or consultant:
William J. Tobin and Associates (William J. Tobin)

Nat'l Center for Clinical Infant Programs
733 15th St., N.W., Suite 912, Washington, DC 20005
Telephone: (202) 347-0308
Represented by:
David F. Chavkin, Senior Prog. Assoc., Public Pol & Educa.
Peggy Pizzo, Senior Program Associate
Eleanor Szanton, Exec. Director

Nat'l Center for Health Education
New York, NY
Counsel or consultant:
Capitol Associates, Inc. (Karen Bodenhorn, Terry Lierman)

Nat'l Center for Homeopathy
1500 Massachusetts Ave., N.W., Washington, DC 20005
Telephone: (202) 223-6182

Counsel or consultant:
Webster, Chamberlain and Bean

Nat'l Center for Housing Management
1275 K St., N.W., Suite 700, Washington, DC 20005
Telephone: (202) 872-1717
Represented by:
Roger G. Stevens, President

Nat'l Center for Law and the Deaf
Gallaudet University 800 Florida Ave., N.E., Washington, DC 20002
Telephone: (202) 651-5373
Background: Established to provide a variety of services to the deaf community including monitoring legislation, providing testimony, sponsoring conferences, and developing counselling and educational workshops.
Represented by:
Sy DuBow, Legal Director

Nat'l Center for Missing and Exploited Children
2101 Wilson Blvd., Suite 550, Arlington, VA 22201
Telephone: (703) 235-3900
Background: Provides information on missing and exploited child issues and offers direct assistance to parents and law-enforcement agencies investigating such cases. Toll-free hotline number is 1-800-843-5678.
Represented by:
Ernest Allen, President
Julie Cartwright, Media Director
Michael P. Lynch, Director of Administration

Nat'l Center for Neighborhood Enterprise
1367 Connecticut Ave., N.W., 2nd Floor, Washington, DC 20036
Telephone: (202) 331-1103
Background: A black activist organization advocating self-help and private entrepreneurial approaches to community development and relatively less reliance on governmental intervention.
Represented by:
Christina L. Bradshaw, Exec. Asst. to the President
Hedi Butler, Acting Public Relations Director
Robert L. Woodson, Congressional Liaison
Counsel or consultant:
Catherine Ludwig Gayle

Nat'l Center for Policy Alternatives
2000 Florida Ave., N.W. 4th Floor, Washington, DC 20009
Telephone: (202) 387-6030
Background: Provides a forum for analysis and dissemination of progressive policies and programs for application at the state and local level.
Represented by:
Linda Tarr-Whelan, Director
Jeffrey Tryens, Associate Director
Counsel or consultant:
Nordlinger Associates

Nat'l Center for Public Policy Research
300 Eye St., N.E., Suite 3, Washington, DC 20002
Telephone: (202) 543-1286
Represented by:
Amy Moritz, President

Nat'l Center for Religious Involvement
1115 P. St., N.W., Washington, DC 20005
Telephone: (202) 667-2338
Background: A Network/Training organization created to disseminate information on socio-economic and educational programing conducted by black and ethnic churches in low income communities.
Represented by:
LaVern Duckwilder, Secretary/Treasurer
Brenda Harper-Diggs, Chairwoman
Laurice F. Wilks, Director

Nat'l Center for Social Policy and Practice
7981 Eastern Ave., Silver Spring, MD 20910
Telephone: (301) 565-0333
Represented by:
Dr. Karen Orloff Kaplan, Director

Nat'l Center for State Courts
444 N. Capitol St., N.W., Suite 608, Washington, DC 20001
Telephone: (202) 347-5924
Represented by:
Harry W. Swegle, Washington Liaison

Nat'l Center for Urban Ethnic Affairs
20 Cardinal Station, Washington, DC 20064
Telephone: (202) 232-3600
Background: An independent, national, non-profit organization affiliated with the United States Catholic Conference. Concerned with the problems of populations in older industrial cities and particularly with neighorhoods founded by immigrants.
Represented by:
John A. Kromkowski, President

Nat'l Center on Education and the Economy
Rochester, NY
Counsel or consultant:
Gallagher-Widmeyer Group Inc., The (Scott D. Widmeyer)

Nat'l Center on Institutions and Alternatives
635 Slaters Lane Suite G-100, Alexandria, VA 22314
Telephone: (703) 684-0373
Represented by:
Herbert Hoelter, Director
Jerome G. Miller, President

Nat'l Center on Rural Aging
600 Maryland Ave., S.W. West Wing 100, Washington, DC 20024
Telephone: (202) 479-6683
Background: A membership unit of the Nat'l Council on the Aging Represented by Cynthia Creyke of the Nat'l Council on the Aging.

Nat'l Certification Agency for Medical Laboratory Personnel
2021 L St., N.W. Suite 400, Washington, DC 20036
Telephone: (202) 857-1023
Represented by:
Liz Barkley, Administrator

Nat'l Certification Commission in Chemistry and Chemical Engineering
7315 Wisconsin Ave., Bethesda, MD 20814
Telephone: (301) 652-8634
Background: Represented by David A. H. Roethel, Exec. Director of the American Institute of Chemists.

Nat'l Certified Pipe Welding Bureau
1385 Piccard Drive, Rockville, MD 20850
Telephone: (301) 897-0770
Represented by:
Jack Hansmann, Exec. Secretary

Nat'l Chamber Foundation
1615 H St., N.W., Washington, DC 20062
Telephone: (202) 463-5552
Background: The non-profit public policy research institute affiliated with the Chamber of Commerce of the U.S.A. Exec. Vice President is Dr. Richard Rahn of the Chamber. V. President is Dr. Ronald Utt of the Chamber.
Represented by:
Dr. Ronald D. Utt, V. President

Nat'l Check Cashers Ass'n
Clifton, NJ
Counsel or consultant:
Rowland & Sellery (Lawrence E. Sabbath)

Nat'l Check Cashers Coalition
New York, NY
Counsel or consultant:
Montgomery, McCracken, Walker & Rhoads (Linda Long)

Nat'l Cheese Institute
888 16th St., N.W., Washington, DC 20006
Telephone: (202) 659-1454
Background: Represents manufacturers, processors, packagers, and distributors of cheese and cheese products.
Represented by:
Floyd D. Gaibler, Exec. Director

Nat'l Child Care Ass'n
Austin, TX
Counsel or consultant:
William J. Tobin and Associates (William J. Tobin)

Nat'l Child Care Parents Ass'n
Annandale, VA
Counsel or consultant:
William J. Tobin and Associates (William J. Tobin)

ORGANIZATIONS REPRESENTED

Nat'l Child Support Enforcement Ass'n
444 North Capitol St., N.W., Suite 613, Washington, DC 20001
Telephone: (202) 624-8180
Represented by:
Russell F. McKinnon, CAE, Exec. Director

Nat'l Chinese Welfare Council
803 H St., N.W., Washington, DC 20001
Telephone: (202) 638-1041
Background: An umbrella organization of all the Chinese consolidated benevolent associations in the U.S.A. for the purpose of enhancing mutual well being and protecting mutual interests.
Represented by:
William Mak, Executive Director

Nat'l Cigar Leaf Tobacco Ass'n
1100 17th St., N.W., Washington, DC 20036
Telephone: (202) 296-6820
Background: Benjamin F. Reeves, Managing Director of the Burley and Dark Leaf Tobacco Export Ass'n, serves as Exec. Director.

Nat'l Citizens Coalition for Nursing Home Reform
1424 16th St., N.W., Suite L2, Washington, DC 20036
Telephone: (202) 797-0657
Represented by:
Barbara Frank, Associate Director
Elma Holder, Exec. Director
Carleen Joyce, Director, Information Clearinghouse

Nat'l Classification Management Soc.
6116 Roseland Drive, Rockville, MD 20852
Telephone: (301) 231-9191
Represented by:
Eugene Suto, Exec. Secretary

Nat'l Clay Pipe Institute
206 Vassar Place, Alexandria, VA 22314
Telephone: (703) 370-5750
Represented by:
E. Jack Newbould, Counsel

Nat'l Clean Air Coalition
1400 16th St., N.W., Washington, DC 20036
Telephone: (202) 797-5436
Background: A public interest group formed in 1973 to protect the integrity of the 1970 Clean Air Act. Richard E. Ayres of Natural Resources Defense Council.

Nat'l Club Ass'n
1625 Eye St., N.W., Suite 609, Washington, DC 20006
Telephone: (202) 466-8424
Represented by:
Gerard F. Hurley, CAE, Exec. V. President
Catherine Sullivan, Manager, Government Relations
Thomas M. Walsh, Director, Government Relations
Counsel or consultant:
Baker and McKenzie (Thomas P. Ondeck)
Lehrfeld Cantor & Henzke, P.C. (Leonard J. Henzke, Jr., William J. Lehrfeld)
McGuiness and Williams (G. John Tysse)
O'Connor & Hannan (Patrick E. O'Donnell, Thomas H. Quinn)

Nat'l Club Ass'n Political Action Committee (CLUBPAC)
1625 Eye St., N.W., Suite 609, Washington, DC 20006
Telephone: (202) 466-8424
Background: Contact is Thomas M. Walsh of the Nat'l Club Ass'n.

Nat'l Coal Ass'n
1130 17th St., N.W., Washington, DC 20036
Telephone: (202) 463-2625

Represented by:
Thomas H. Altmeyer, Senior V. President, Gov't Affairs
David C. Branand, Counsel, Director, Environmental Affairs
Susan B. Carver, Director, Legislative Affairs
William D. Fay, V. President, Congressional Affairs
Peter A. Gabauer, Jr., Deputy General Counsel
Daniel R. Gerkin, Sr. V. Pres., Public & Constituent Rels.
John L. C. Grasser, Director, Media Relations
Constance D. Holmes, Senior V. President, Policy Analysis
William E. Hynan, Sr. V. President, Law Dept.
Andrea L. Innes, Director, Political Affairs
Richard L. Lawson, President
Joseph E. Lema, V. President, Transportation
Robert Long, Director, Congressional Affairs
Harold P. Quinn, Counsel & Dir., Surface Mining & Leasing
Robert F. Stauffer, V. President and General Counsel
Bruce H. Watzman, Dir., Safety, Health, & Human Resources

Nat'l Coal Council
Box 17370, Arlington, VA 22216
Telephone: (703) 527-1191
Background: An advisory committee to the Executive Branch of the government chartered by the Secy. of Energy under the Federal Advisory Committee Act.
Represented by:
James McAvoy, Exec. Director

Nat'l Coalition Against Domestic Violence
P.O. Box 34103, Washington, DC 20043-4103
Telephone: (202) 638-6388
Background: A national grassroots organization working to end violence in the lives of women and children. Provides support services and shelters for battered women and children, a clearinghouse for information and technical assistance, and a unified voice on public policy issues.
Represented by:
Diana Onley-Campbell, Program Coordinator

Nat'l Coalition Against the Misuse of Pesticides
530 7th St., S.E., Washington, DC 20003
Telephone: (202) 543-5450
Represented by:
Jay Feldman, National Coordinator
Jane Kochersperger, Information and Research Coordinator

Nat'l Coalition for Cancer Research
New York, NY
Counsel or consultant:
Capitol Associates, Inc. (Marguerite Donoghue, Terry Lierman)
Fox, Bennett and Turner (Allan M. Fox)

Nat'l Coalition for Fair Bankruptcy Laws
453 New Jersey Ave., S.E., Washington, DC
Telephone: (202) 646-1260
Counsel or consultant:
Perkinson & Associates, Inc. (Michael J. Bertelsen, Gary J. Perkinson)

Nat'l Coalition for the Homeless
1621 Connecticut Ave., N.W. 4th Fl., Washington, DC 20007
Telephone: (202) 265-2371
Background: A federation of agencies with a nationally-representative board of 66 members.
Represented by:
Mary Ellen Hombs, Director

Nat'l Coalition for Volunteer Protection
426 C St., N.E., Washington, DC 20002
Telephone: (202) 544-1880
Counsel or consultant:
Capitol Associates, Inc. (Gordon P. MacDougall)

Nat'l Coalition of Burn Center Hospitals
Birmingham, AL
Counsel or consultant:
FMR Group Inc., The (Joseph M. Rees)

Nat'l Coalition of Hispanic Health and Human Services
1030 15th St., N.W. Suite 1053, Washington, DC 20005
Telephone: (202) 371-2100

Represented by:
William Bogan, Exec. V. President
Jane L. Delgado, Ph.D., President

Nat'l Coalition of Petroleum Retailers
1300 Eye St., N.W. Suite 480 East Tower, Washington, DC 20005
Telephone: (202) 962-3864
Counsel or consultant:
Jonathan W. Cuneo Law Offices (Jonathan W. Cuneo)

Nat'l Coalition of Title I/Chapter I Parents
Edmond School Bldg., 9th & D Sts., N.E., Rm. 201, Washington, DC 20002
Telephone: (202) 547-9286
Represented by:
Bobby Green, Board Chairman

Nat'l Coalition on Black Voter Participation, Inc.
1101 14th St., N.W., Suite 925, Washington, DC 20005
Telephone: (202) 898-2220
Background: An organization that works to increase black voter registration and turnout with a goal of political empowerment of blacks and other minorities.
Represented by:
Sonia R. Jarvis, Esq., Exec. Director
Leslie McFarland, Deputy Director

Nat'l Coalition on Immune System Disorders
c/o MARC Assoc., 1030 15th St. N.W., Suite 468, Washington, DC 20005
Telephone: (202) 371-8090
Counsel or consultant:
MARC Associates, Inc. (Robert R. Humphreys)

Nat'l Coalition to Ban Handguns
100 Maryland Ave., N.E., Washington, DC 20002
Telephone: (202) 544-7190
Background: Conducts educational, research and lobbying work aimed at banning the manufacture and sale of handguns and assault weapons to private individuals.
Represented by:
Michael K. Beard, President & CEO
Marjolijn Bijlefeld, Associate Director
Jeffrey Y. Muchnick, Political Affairs Director
Stacy Onders, Public Affairs Director

Nat'l Coalition to Ban Handguns Political Action Committee
100 Maryland Ave., N.E., Washington, DC 20002
Telephone: (202) 544-7213
Represented by:
Sanford Horowitt, Political Consultant

Nat'l Coffee Ass'n
New York, NY
Counsel or consultant:
Daniel J. Edelman, Inc. (Jean Rainey)

Nat'l Coffee Service Ass'n
4000 Williamsburg Square, Fairfax, VA 22032
Telephone: (703) 273-9008
Represented by:
Maggie Lyons, Publications Director
G. Dean Wood, President

Nat'l Collaboration for Youth
1319 F St., N.W., Suite 601, Washington, DC 20004
Telephone: (202) 347-2080
Background: Can be contacted through The Nat'l Assembly of Nat'l Voluntary Health and Social Welfare Organizations of which it is an affinity group. Principal contact is Doni G. Blumenstock, Assistant Director.
Represented by:
Susan J. Smith, Program Manager

Nat'l Collegiate Athletic Ass'n
Shawnee Mission, KS
Counsel or consultant:
Squire, Sanders and Dempsey (William D. Kramer, Michael Scott)

Nat'l Commission Against Drunk Driving
1140 Connecticut Ave., N.W. Suite 804, Washington, DC 20036
Telephone: (202) 452-6004
Counsel or consultant:
Offices of V.J. Adduci
Donald Baldwin Associates
J. Thomas Malatesta & Co.

　　　　The listings in this directory are available as *Mailing Labels*. See last page.

ORGANIZATIONS REPRESENTED

Nat'l Commission Certifying Agencies
1101 Connecticut Ave., N.W., Suite 700, Washington, DC 20036
Telephone: (202) 857-1165
Counsel or consultant:
Smith, Bucklin and Associates (Michael Hamm)

Nat'l Commission on Working Women
1325 G St., N.W. Lower Level, Washington, DC 20005
Telephone: (202) 737-5764
Represented by:
Sandra van Fossen, Director, National Programs

Nat'l Commission to Prevent Infant Mortality
330 C St., S.W. Suite 2006 Switzer Bldg., Washington, DC 20201
Telephone: (202) 472-1364
Counsel or consultant:
Gallagher-Widmeyer Group Inc., The (Mary Jane Gallagher)

Nat'l Committee Against Repressive Legislation
236 Massachusetts Ave., N.E., Suite 406, Washington, DC 20002
Telephone: (202) 543-7659
Background: An organization based in Los Angeles established in 1960 to support and coordinate opposition to all threats to the First Amendment rights of freedom of speech and association.
Represented by:
Kit Gage, Washington Representative

Nat'l Committee for a Human Life Amendment
1511 K St., N.W., Suite 335, Washington, DC 20005
Telephone: (202) 393-0703
Represented by:
Carol D. Reig, Ass't. Director, Field Coordination
Michael Taylor, Exec. Director

Nat'l Committee for Adoption
1930 17th St., N.W., Washington, DC 20009-6207
Telephone: (202) 328-1200
Background: A non-profit membership organization for agencies which provide sevices to pregnant adolescents, unmarried parents and infertile couples as well as for individuals who support the promotion of adoption.
Represented by:
William L. Pierce, President and Chief Exec. Officer

Nat'l Committee for an Effective Congress
507 Capitol Court, N.E., Washington, DC 20002
Telephone: (202) 547-1151
Background: Established in 1948 to provide funds and technical campaign services to progressive candidates for Congress. Has helped elect both liberal Republicans and Democrats.
Represented by:
James Byron, Treasurer
Mark H. Gersh, Director, Washington Office
Russell D. Hemenway, National Director

Nat'l Committee for Full Employment
815 16th St., N.W., Suite 301, Washington, DC 20006
Telephone: (202) 393-7415
Background: A coalition of civil rights, labor, religious and other groups which conducts research and education on attainment of a full employment society.
Represented by:
Leon Shull, Interim Exec. Director

Nat'l Committee for Quality Health Care
1500 K St., N.W., Suite 360, Washington, DC 20005
Telephone: (202) 347-5731
Background: A broad-based coalition of hospitals, and related firms which supply goods and services to the health care industry.
Represented by:
Pamela G. Bailey, President
Joan Simmons, Director of Communications

Nat'l Committee for Responsive Philanthropy
2001 S St., N.W., Suite 620, Washington, DC 20009
Telephone: (202) 387-9177
Background: A coalition of about 1000 activist, social action and public interest non-profit organizations working to make United Ways, foundations, and corporate giving programs more accountable, accessible, and responsive to civic needs.
Represented by:
Robert O. Bothwell, Exec. Director

Nat'l Committee of Cities and States for Airline Service
St. Paul, MN
Counsel or consultant:
Zuckert, Scoutt and Rasenberger (Raymond J. Rasenberger)

Nat'l Committee on Pay Equity
1201 16th St., N.W., Suite 422, Washington, DC 20036
Telephone: (202) 822-7304
Background: A coalition working to eliminate sex- and race-based wage discrimination and achieve pay equity.
Represented by:
Claudia E. Wayne, Exec. Director

Nat'l Committee on Public Employee Pension Systems
1221 Connecticut Ave., N.W., 4th Floor, Washington, DC 20036
Telephone: (202) 293-3960
Background: A non-profit, non-partisan, education organization established to address the political, social and economic impact of public employee pension systems.
Represented by:
Olive Hunt, Public Relations Director
Hastings Keith, Co-Chairman

Nat'l Committee to Preserve Social Security and Medicare
2000 K St., N.W. Suite 800, Washington, DC 20006
Telephone: (202) 822-9459
Represented by:
Barbara Allen, Legislative Representative
Bente E. Cooney, Policy Analyst
Susan Dahlquist, Legislative Rep./Asst. PAC Director
Lloyd L. Duxbury, Legislative Representative
Kristen Funk, Grassroots Coordinator
Cheryl Gannon, Legislative Representative
George Allen Johnston, Dir., Grassroots & Member Relations
William J. Lessard, Jr., Director of Policy and Research
Beth Lyle-Durham, Grassroots Coordinator
Jack McDavitt, Director, Publications
Monette McKinnon, Grassroots Coordinator
Martha A. McSteen, President
Martha Mohler, Policy & Research Representative
Dinah Kay O'Berry, Legislative Representative
Judy Rensberger, Federal Regulatory Analyst
Max Richtman, Director, Government Relations Dept.
William R. Ritz, Director, Public Affairs
Christine Sigler, Manager, Member Relations
Sandra Wheeler, Grassroots Coordinator
Mildred Wood, Income Policy Analyst
Mary J. Yarrington, Senior Policy Analyst
Counsel or consultant:
Williams and Connolly (Steve Urbanczyk)

Nat'l Committee to Preserve Social Security and Medicare Political Action Committee
2000 K St., N.W., Suite 800, Washington, DC 20006
Telephone: (202) 822-9459
Represented by:
Mary Kane, PAC Representative

Nat'l Community Action Foundation
2100 M St., N.W. Suite 604, Washington, DC 20037
Telephone: (202) 775-0223
Background: A non-profit legislative organization representing the concerns of 900 community action agencies on human service legislation, including the Community Service Block Grant, Low Income Energy Assistance, Community Food Distribution, Weatherization, Headstart, and other programs for the poor.
Represented by:
David Bradley, Legislative Director

Nat'l Community Development Ass'n
522 21st St., N.W., Suite 120, Washington, DC 20006
Telephone: (202) 293-7587
Represented by:
John A. Sasso, Exec. Secretary

Nat'l Community Education Ass'n
801 N. Farifax St. Suite 209, Alexandria, VA 22314
Represented by:
Starla Jewell-Kelly, Exec. Director

Nat'l Composites Consortium, Inc.
Herndon, VA

Counsel or consultant:
McNair Group Inc. (Elizabeth L. Taylor)

Nat'l Composition and Prepress Ass'n
1730 North Lynn St., Arlington, VA 22209
Telephone: (703) 841-8165
Background: A section of Printing Industries of America.
Represented by:
Tina H. Allman, President

Nat'l Computer Graphics Ass'n
2722 Merrilee Drive, Suite 200, Fairfax, VA 22031
Telephone: (703) 698-9600
Background: An organization of individuals and major companies dedicated to developing and promoting the computer graphics industry and to improving graphics applications in business, government, science and the arts.
Represented by:
Victor S. Parra, Exec. V. President
Sharon Sutton, Manager, Marketing and Communications
Michael Weiner, Public Information Specialist

Nat'l Computer Systems
4601 N. Fairfax Drive, Arlington, VA 22203
Telephone: (703) 516-4306
Represented by:
Karl Doerr, V. President, Federal Government Mktg.
Michael McShane, Manager, Government Relations

Nat'l Concrete Masonry Ass'n
P.O. Box 781, Herndon, VA 22070
Telephone: (703) 435-4900
Represented by:
John A. Heslip, President
Randall G. Pence, Director, Government Relations
Scott Ramminger, Manager, Public Relations

Nat'l Concrete Masonry Ass'n Political Action Committee
P.O. Box 781, Herndon, VA 22070
Telephone: (703) 435-4900
Background: Responsible contact is Randall G. Pence of the Nat'l Concrete Masonry Ass'n.

Nat'l Confectioners Ass'n
7900 Westpark Drive Suite A-320, McLean, VA 22102
Telephone: (703) 790-5750
Represented by:
Philips H. Kimball, Director of Communications
Stephen Lodge, Director, Legislative Affairs

Nat'l Confectioners Ass'n Political Action Committee
7900 Westpark Drive, Suite A-320, McLean, VA 22102
Telephone: (703) 790-5750
Background: Represented by Stephen Lodge of the Nat'l Confectioners Ass'n.

Nat'l Conference of Bankruptcy Judges
Nashville, TN
Counsel or consultant:
Podesta Associates (John D. Podesta)

Nat'l Conference of Catholic Bishops
3211 4th St., N.E., Washington, DC 20017
Telephone: (202) 541-3000
Background: An allied organization of the United States Catholic Conference. General Secretary is Rev. Robert N. Lynch of the United States Catholic Conference.
Represented by:
Richard Doerflinger, Asst. Dir., Office for Pro-Life Activ.

Nat'l Conference of Christians and Jews
2041 Martin Luther King Jr. Ave., S.E., Suite 302, Washington, DC 20020
Telephone: (202) 678-9400
Represented by:
Dr. Donald F. Sullivan, Exec. Director

Nat'l Conference of Puerto Rican Women
5 Thomas Circle, N.W., Washington, DC 20036
Telephone: (202) 387-4716
Represented by:
Ivette A. Torres, President

Nat'l Conference of State Historic Preservation Officers
444 N. Capitol St., N.W. Suite 332, Washington, DC 20001
Telephone: (202) 624-5465

ORGANIZATIONS REPRESENTED

Nat'l Conference of State Historic Preservation Officers (Cont'd)
Represented by:
Eric Hertfelder, Exec. Director

Nat'l Conference of State Legislatures
444 North Capitol St., N.W. Suite 500, Washington, DC 20001
Telephone: (202) 624-5400
Background: A non-partisan organization funded by the states which works to improve the quality and effectiveness of state legislatures, assure states a strong and cohesive voice in the federal decision-making process, and foster inter-governmental communication and cooperation.
Represented by:
Michael Bird, Federal Affairs Counsel
William J. M. Hagan, II, Chief Lobbyist, Congressional Relations
Richard E. May, Federal Affairs Counsel
Larry Morandi, Program Manager, Natural Resources
William T. Pound, Exec. Director
Susan Seladones, Director, Public Affairs
Carl Tubbesing, Director, Washington Office
Joy Johnson Wilson, Sr. Prog. Dir., Health & Human Svcs.

Nat'l Conference of States on Building Codes and Standards
481 Carlisle Drive, Herndon, VA 22070
Telephone: (703) 437-0100
Represented by:
Marla McIntyre, Director of Information
Robert C. Wible, Exec. Director

Nat'l Conference on Soviet Jewry
1522 K St., N.W., Suite 1100, Washington, DC 20005
Telephone: (202) 898-2500
Represented by:
Barbara Gaffin, Congressional Liaison
Mark B. Levin, Assoc. Exec. Director, Washington Office
Robin Saipe, Community Relations Coordinator

Nat'l Congress for Community Economic Development
1612 K St., N.W. Suite 510, Washington, DC 20006
Telephone: (202) 659-8411
Background: A national organization which supports community-based, non-profit economic development corporations known as Community Development Corporations (CDCs).
Represented by:
Robert Zdenek, President

Nat'l Congress of American Indians
900 Pennsylvania Ave., S.E., Washington, DC 20003
Telephone: (202) 546-9404
Background: Founded in 1944 and representing more than 150 Indian tribes, NCAI monitors government developments in Washington and acts as the voice of the Indians on the national level.
Represented by:
A. Gay Kingman, Exec. Director (Interim)

Nat'l Congress of Parents and Teachers
1201 16th St., N.W. Room 621, Washington, DC 20036
Telephone: (202) 822-7878
Represented by:
Arnold F. Fege, Director of Governmental Relations
Carolyn Henrich, Government Relations Specialist
Maribeth Oakes, Policy Analyst/Editor
Counsel or consultant:
Baker and Hostetler

Nat'l Conservative Congressional Committee
P.O. Box 1807, Washington, DC 20003
Telephone: (202) 546-7000
Counsel or consultant:
Bonsib, Inc. (L. W. "Bill" Bonsib)

Nat'l Conservative Political Action Committee
618 S. Alfred St., Alexandria, VA 22314
Telephone: (703) 684-1800
Represented by:
Sandy Scholte, Exec. Director
Maiselle Dolan Shortley, Chairman

Nat'l Consortium for Child Mental Health Services
3615 Wisconsin Ave., N.W., Washington, DC 20016
Telephone: (202) 966-7300

Background: Seeks concerted effort of several national organizations to improve the delivery of services in child mental health.
Represented by:
Richard Gross, Chairperson

Nat'l Constructors Ass'n
1730 M St., N.W., Suite 900, Washington, DC 20036-4571
Telephone: (202) 466-8880
Represented by:
Mark G. Chalpin, V. Pres., Gov't & Internat'l Affrs.
Robert P. McCormick, President
Kenneth A. Paradis, V. President, Labor Relations & Safety

Nat'l Consumer Law Center
236 Massachusetts Ave., N.E. Suite 504, Washington, DC 20002
Telephone: (202) 543-6060
Background: Aids legal services programs and other low-income advocates in matters involving consumer and energy issues.
Represented by:
Helen Gonzalez, Attorney/Legislative Specialist
Charles E. Hill, Managing Attorney

Nat'l Consumers League
815 15th St., N.W., Suite 516, Washington, DC 20005
Telephone: (202) 639-8140
Background: A private, non-profit membership organization, founded in 1899 to bring consumer power to bear on marketplace and workplace issues. NCL investigates, educates and advocates consumer and worker rights through individual citizens, local affiliates and the national office.
Represented by:
Sara Cooper, Director of Public Information
Linda F. Golodner, Exec. Director
Ponder Mary, Deputy Director

Nat'l Contact Lens Examiners
10341 Democracy Lane, Fairfax, VA 22030
Telephone: (703) 691-8357
Background: Represented by Nancy Roylance of the Opticians Ass'n of America.

Nat'l Contract Management Ass'n
1912 Woodford Road, Vienna, VA 22182
Telephone: (703) 448-9231
Represented by:
James Goggins, Exec. Director

Nat'l Cooperative Bank
1630 Connecticut Ave., N.W., Washington, DC 20009-1004
Telephone: (202) 745-4610
Background: A privately-owned financial servces company providing mortage banking, commercial lending, capital markets and depository services to cooperative enterprises nationwide.
Represented by:
Cary A. Brazeman, Assistant V. President, Public Relations
Linda R. Lewis, Corporate V. President
Counsel or consultant:
E. A. Jaenke & Associates (E. A. Jaenke)

Nat'l Cooperative Business Ass'n
1401 New York Ave., N.W. Suite 1100, Washington, DC 20005
Telephone: (202) 638-6222
Represented by:
Paul Hazen, V. President, Government Relations
Russell C. Notar, Senior V. Pres., Domestic Operations
Robert D. Scherer, President and CEO
Peggy A. Sheehan, V. President, Food Policy & Market Dev.

Nat'l Coordinating Committee for Multiemployer Plans
815 16th St., N.W., Suite 603, Washington, DC 20006
Telephone: (202) 347-1461
Background: Interested in legislation and regulations affecting employees who have served or are serving several employers - in particular, multi-employer pension plans. Chairman is Robert A. Georgine of AFL-CIO (Building and Construction Trades Department).
Counsel or consultant:
Arnold & Porter (Paul S. Berger, Stephen L. Hester)
The Kamber Group (Mary Roddy Betzler)

Nat'l Coordinating Council on Emergency Management
7297 Lee Highway, Suite N, Falls Church, VA 22042
Telephone: (703) 533-7672
Background: The national organization of local emergency managers and civil defense coordinators.
Counsel or consultant:
Ass'n and Society Management Internat'l Inc. (Elizabeth A. Buzzerd)

Nat'l Corn Growers Ass'n
201 Massachusetts Ave., N.E., Suite C4, Washington, DC 20002
Telephone: (202) 546-7611
Represented by:
B. Keith Heard, Exec. V. President
David Stawick, Ass't V. President

Nat'l Corp. for Housing Partnerships
1225 Eye St., N.W. Suite 700, Washington, DC 20005
Telephone: (202) 347-6247
Background: A private organization that develops multifamily rental apartments, including housing for low and moderate income families. Also known as The Nat'l Housing Partnership.
Represented by:
Linda G. Davenport, COO, Affordable Housing & Exec. V. Pres.
J. Roderick Heller, III, Chairman, President and CEO
Counsel or consultant:
Olwine, Connelly, Chase, O'Donnell and Weyher (W. Harrison Wellford)

Nat'l Corporation For Housing Partnerships Political Action Committee
1225 Eye St., N.W. Suite700, Washington, DC 20005
Telephone: (202) 347-6247
Represented by:
Joel F. Bonder, Treasurer

Nat'l Corrugated Steel Pipe Ass'n
2011 Eye St., N.W., Fifth Floor, Washington, DC 20006
Telephone: (202) 223-3217
Counsel or consultant:
Newell-Payne Companies, Inc. (Venlo J. Wolfsohn)

Nat'l Cosmetology Ass'n
St. Louis, MO
Counsel or consultant:
Collier, Shannon & Scott

Nat'l Cotton Council of America
1110 Vermont Ave., N.W. Suite 430, Washington, DC 20005
Telephone: (202) 833-2943
Represented by:
Phillip Burnett, Exec. V. President
Carl C. Campbell, Special Projects Representative
Daniel J. Hunter, Sr. Government Relations Representative
A. John Maguire, V. President, Washington Operations
P. J. Wakelyn, Mgr., Environmental Health and Safety
Paulette Zakrzeski, Sr. Government Relations Representative
Counsel or consultant:
Bishop, Cook, Purcell & Reynolds (Robert M. Bor)

Nat'l Cottonseed Products Ass'n
Memphis, TN
Counsel or consultant:
Fulbright & Jaworski (Carl W. Vogt)

Nat'l Council for Accreditation of Teacher Education
2029 K St.,, N.W. Suite 500, Washington, DC 20006
Telephone: (202) 466-7496
Represented by:
Donna M. Gollick, Interim Exec. Director

Nat'l Council for Children's Rights
721 2nd St., N.E. Suite 103, Washington, DC 20002
Telephone: (202) 223-6227
Background: A non-profit organization seeking to strengthen American families and to reduce the trauma of divorce for children. Concerns include the child's right to joint custody, mediation and fair child support and access (visitation) arrangements.
Represented by:
David L. Levy, President

The listings in this directory are available as *Mailing Labels*. See last page.

ORGANIZATIONS REPRESENTED

Nat'l Council for Industrial Defense
417 6th St., S.E., Washington, DC 20003
Telephone: (202) 543-7592
Background: Represents interests of several trade unions and subcontractors in the defense industry.
Represented by:
Jerome M. Zeifman, General Counsel & Exec. Director

Nat'l Council for Internat'l Health
1701 K St., N.W. Suite 600, Washington, DC 20006
Telephone: (202) 833-5900
Represented by:
Dr. Russell E. Morgan, President
E. Lane Vanderslice, Public Policy Analyst

Nat'l Council for Languages and Internat'l Studies
300 I St., N.E., Suite 211, Washington, DC 20002
Telephone: (202) 546-7855
Background: Supported by 36 language and international studies organizations. John David Edwards, of the Joint Nat'l Committee for Languages, is the Exec. Director.

Nat'l Council for the Social Studies
3501 Newark St., N.W., Washington, DC 20016
Telephone: (202) 966-7840
Represented by:
Frances Haley, Exec. Director

Nat'l Council for Urban Economic Development
1730 K St., N.W., Suite 915, Washington, DC 20006
Telephone: (202) 223-4735
Background: Founded in 1967 as an information source on new approaches to urban revitalization, including use of public resources to generate significant private reinvestment in cities.
Represented by:
Jeffrey A. Finkle, Exec. Director

Nat'l Council of Agricultural Employers
1735 Eye St., N.W. Suite 704, Washington, DC 20003
Telephone: (202) 728-0300
Background: A non-profit trade association founded in 1964 to represent the interests of employers of agricultural labor and to ensure an adequate and capable work force for agriculture.
Represented by:
Sharon M. Hughes, Exec. V. President

Nat'l Council of Architectural Registration Boards
1735 New York Ave., N.W. Suite 700, Washington, DC 20006
Telephone: (202) 783-6500
Represented by:
Samuel T. Balen, Exec. Director

Nat'l Council of Career Women
3222 N St., N.W., Suite 32, Washington, DC 20007
Telephone: (202) 333-8190
Counsel or consultant:
Robert N. Pyle & Associates (Ashley Stoudt)

Nat'l Council of Catholic Women
1275 K St., N.W. Suite 975, Washington, DC 20005
Telephone: (202) 682-0334
Represented by:
Beverly Medved, President

Nat'l Council of Coal Lessors, Inc.
Charleston, WV
Counsel or consultant:
Murray, Scheer & Montgomery (D. Michael Murray)

Nat'l Council of Commercial Plant Breeders
1030 15th St., N.W. Suite 964, Washington, DC 20005
Telephone: (202) 223-4080
Background: Represented by Robert J. Falasca and William T. Schapaugh of the American Seed Trade Ass'n.

Nat'l Council of Community Hospitals
1700 K St., N.W. Suite 906, Washington, DC 20006
Telephone: (202) 728-0830
Background: An organization of 110 community hospitals.

Represented by:
Katie M. Bolt, Exec. Director
John F. Horty, President
Counsel or consultant:
Swidler & Berlin, Chartered (John S. Hoff, Kenneth I. Schaner)

Nat'l Council of Community Mental Health Centers
12300 Twinbrook Parkway Suite 320, Rockville, MD 20852
Telephone: (301) 984-6200
Represented by:
James K. Finley, Director of Government Relations
Cynthia Folcarelli, Coordinator, Public Policy Information
Charles G. Ray, Exec. Director

Nat'l Council of Educational Opportunity Ass'ns
1025 Vermont Ave., N.W. Suite 310, Washington, DC 20005
Telephone: (202) 347-7430
Counsel or consultant:
Clohan & Dean (William A. Blakey)

Nat'l Council of Farmer Cooperatives
50 F St., N.W., Suite 900, Washington, DC 20001
Telephone: (202) 626-8700
Represented by:
Terry N. Barr, V. President, Agriculture & Trade Policy
Wayne A. Boutwell, President
Donald K. Hanes, Vice President, Communications
James P. Howell, Director, Legislative Affairs
Randall T. Jones, Sr. V. Pres., Gov't & Public Affairs
James S. Krzyminski, Sr. V. Pres., Corp. Svcs. & Gen. Couns.
Leslie S. Mead, Associate General Counsel
R. Thomas Van Arsdall, V. Pres., Agricultural Inputs & Services

Nat'l Council of Farmer Cooperatives Political Action Committee (Co-op/PAC)
50 F. St., N.W., Suite 900, Washington, DC 20001
Telephone: (202) 626-8700
Background: Represented by Randall T. Jones of the Nat'l Council of Farmer Cooperatives.

Nat'l Council of Health Facilities Finance Authorities
Counsel or consultant:
Winston and Strawn (Paul C. Fiduccia)

Nat'l Council of Higher Education Loan Programs
804 E St., S.E., Washington, DC 20003
Telephone: (202) 547-1571
Represented by:
Jean S. Frohlicher, Exec. Director

Nat'l Council of Investigative and Security Services
P.O. Box 2842, Washington, DC 20013
Telephone: (202) 289-1780
Counsel or consultant:
Rowland & Sellery (Lawrence E. Sabbath)

Nat'l Council of Jewish Women
1101 15th St., N.W., Suite 1012, Washington, DC 20005
Telephone: (202) 296-2588
Represented by:
Sammie S. Moshenberg, Director of Washington Operations

Nat'l Council of Juvenile and Family Court Judges
Reno, NV
Counsel or consultant:
Venable, Baetjer, Howard and Civiletti

Nat'l Council of La Raza
810 1st St., N.E., Suite 300, Washington, DC 20002
Telephone: (202) 289-1380
Background: An advocacy organization for Americans of Hispanic descent. Provides research services and technical assistance for community development groups.
Represented by:
Charles K. Kamasaki, V. Pres, Office of Resrch, Advoc & Legis
Cecelia Munoz, Senior Immigration Policy Analyst
Isabel M. Navarrete, Public Information Director
Raul Yzaguirre, President

Nat'l Council of Negro Women
1211 Connecticut Ave. N.W. Suite 702, Washington, DC 20036
Telephone: (202) 659-0006
Background: A coalition of 27 Black and other minority women's groups established in 1937.
Represented by:
Gayla Cook, Director, International Division
Dr. Dorothy I. Height, Nat'l President

Nat'l Council of Savings Institutions
1101 15th St., N.W. Suite 400, Washington, DC 20005
Telephone: (202) 857-3100
Background: Formed by the consolidation of the Nat'l Ass'n of Mutual Savings Banks and the Nat'l Savings and Loan League.
Represented by:
David Danovitch, Regulatory Counsel
Jean Foster, V. President, Corporate Development
Dr. George Hanc, Exec. V. Pres., Finance & Administration
Peter E. Knight, V. President and Dir., Mortgage Finance
Sally Ann LaHue, Associate Director, Congressional Afrs.
James E. O'Connor, V. President and Dir., Tax Legislation
Lee Peckarsky, Exec. V. President, Government Affairs
Martin A. Regalia, V. Pres., and Dir. of Research & Econ.
Dr. Mark J. Riedy, President
Wendy Samuel, V. President, General Counsel
Adam D. Schwartz, Director, Political Affairs
Counsel or consultant:
Argyle & Associates (Susie Deller, Daniel M. Steadley)

Nat'l Council of Savings Institutions THRIFTPAC
1101 15th St., N.W., Washington, DC 20005
Telephone: (202) 857-3132
Background: The political action committee of the Nat'l Council of Savings Institutions. Contact is Adam D. Schwartz of the Council.
Counsel or consultant:
Wunder, Ryan, Cannon & Thelen (Paul E. Sullivan)

Nat'l Council of Senior Citizens
925 15th St., N.W., Washington, DC 20005
Telephone: (202) 347-8800
Background: Established in July 1961 to work for the enactment of Medicare. It is now a national organization with more than 4.5 million members coming from organized labor, religious and community groups. Promotes the health and economic interests of senior citizens and campaigns for preservation of Social Security, Medicare, long term care facilities for the elderly, elimination of mandatory retirement and food stamp reform. Rates members of Congress on the basis of their support on issues of interest to the Council.
Represented by:
Eugene Glover, President
Ken Hoagland, Spec. Asst. to the Exec. Director
Johnathon Lawniczak, Senior Legislative Assistant
Eric Shulman, Dir. of Legis. Liaison and Research
Lawrence T. Smedley, Exec. Director
Kurt Vorndran, Legislative Liaison and Research

Nat'l Council of Senior Citizens Political Action Committee
925 15th St., N.W., Washington, DC 20005
Telephone: (202) 347-8800
Background: Represented by Lawrence T. Smedley, Exec. Director of the Council.

Nat'l Council of Small Federal Contractors
1029 Vermont Ave., N.W., Suite 500, Washington, DC 20005
Telephone: (202) 737-2696
Counsel or consultant:
Magnotti Enterprises, Inc. (Dr. John F. Magnotti, Jr.)

Nat'l Council of Social Security Management Ass'ns
Grand Rapids, MI
Background: Represents Field Office Managers of the Social Security Administration.
Counsel or consultant:
Neill, Mullenholz and Shaw (G. Jerry Shaw, Jr.)

Nat'l Council of State Education Ass'ns
1201 16th St., N.W., Washington, DC 20036
Telephone: (202) 822-7745

ORGANIZATIONS REPRESENTED

Nat'l Council of State Education Ass'ns (Cont'd)
Represented by:
Larry A. Diebold, Special Assistant, State Relations

Nat'l Council of State Housing Agencies
444 N. Capitol St., N.W., Suite 118, Washington, DC 20001
Telephone: (202) 624-7710
Background: Organization of state agencies financing low and moderate income housing.
Represented by:
John T. McEvoy, Exec. V. Director
Barbara J. Thompson, Director, Government Affairs

Nat'l Council of Teachers of Mathematics
1906 Association Dr., Reston, VA 22091
Telephone: (703) 620-9840
Background: Affiliated with the American Ass'n for the Advancement of Science.
Represented by:
James D. Gates, Exec. Director
Richard Long, Government Relations Specialist

Nat'l Council of the Churches of Christ in the USA
110 Maryland Ave., N.E., Washington, DC 20002
Telephone: (202) 544-2350
Background: A community of national religious organizations including 32 member communions with a combined membership of 40 million people. Convenes policy formulation panels, makes policy statements on public issues, lobbies before Congress and petitions federal agencies.
Represented by:
Mary Anderson Cooper, Acting Director
James A. Hamilton, General Secretary

Nat'l Council of U.S. Magistrates
Indianapolis, IN
Counsel or consultant:
Graham and James (Thomas F. Railsback)

Nat'l Council of University Research Administrators
One Dupont Circle, N.W. Suite 420, Washington, DC 20036
Telephone: (202) 466-3894
Represented by:
Natalie Kirkman, Director, National Office

Nat'l Council of Women of the U.S.
4341 Forest Lane, N.W., Washington, DC 20007
Telephone: (202) 363-2192
Background: A council of women's organizations founded in 1888; affiliated with the International Council of Women.
Represented by:
Pamela Moffat, Washington Representative

Nat'l Council on Alcoholism and Drug Dependence
1511 K St., N.W., Suite 926, Washington, DC 20005
Telephone: (202) 737-8122
Represented by:
Sarah Kayson, Public Policy Associate
Christine B. Lubinski, Director for Public Policy

Nat'l Council on Compensation Insurance
New York, NY
Counsel or consultant:
Preston Gates Ellis & Rouvelas Meeds (Susan B. Geiger, Kenneth R. Kay)

Nat'l Council on Disability
800 Independence Ave., S.W. Suite 814, Washington, DC 20591
Telephone: (202) 267-3846
Represented by:
Ethel D. Briggs, Exec. Director (Acting)

Nat'l Council on Employment Policy
1730 K St., N.W., Suite 701, Washington, DC 20006
Telephone: (202) 833-2532
Background: A private organization specializing in research and assessment of employment and training programs and problems.
Represented by:
Sar Levitan, Chairman, Steering Committee

Nat'l Council on Measurement in Education
1230 17th St., N.W., Washington, DC 20036
Telephone: (202) 223-9318

Background: William J. Russell of the American Educational Research Ass'n serves as Exec. Officer.

Nat'l Council on Patient Information and Education
666 11th St., N.W., Suite 810, Washington, DC 20001
Telephone: (202) 347-6711
Background: A non-profit corporation organized to improve the dialogue between health professionals and patients about prescription medicines. Develops public and health professional campaigns for adoption by its 234 member organizations, conducts 'Talk About Prescriptions' Month, an annual health observance, publishes a newsletter, produces reports on medicine misuse and holds a national meeting.
Represented by:
Robert M. Bachman, Exec. Director
Counsel or consultant:
KAL/PR (Karen A. Lubieniecki)
Charles S. Lerner Associates (Charles S. Lerner)

Nat'l Council on Radiation Protection and Measurement
7910 Woodmont Ave. Suite 800, Bethesda, MD 20814
Telephone: (301) 657-2652
Represented by:
W. Roger Ney, Exec. Director
Warren K. Sinclair, President

Nat'l Council on Rehabilitation Education
1213 29th St., N.W., Washington, DC 20007
Telephone: (202) 333-5841
Counsel or consultant:
Duncan and Associates

Nat'l Council on the Aging
600 Maryland Ave., S.W. West Wing 100, Washington, DC 20024
Telephone: (202) 479-1200
Background: Established in 1950 as the national organization for professionals and volunteers who work to improve the quality of life for older Americans. Serves as central, national resource for planning, training, information dissemination, technical assistance, advocacy program and standards development and publications that relate to all aspects of aging.
Represented by:
Michael Creedon, Director, Corporate Programs
Cynthia Shearin Creyke, Program Manager
Moses Gozonsky, Program Associate
Tanya Hart, Program Manager
Paul Kerschner, Senior V. President
Morton Leeds, Program Associate
Ruth Mayer, Program Manager
Betty Ransom, Program Manager
Daniel Thursz, President
Coquese Williams, Program Manager

Nat'l Credit Improvement Group
Springfield, VA
Counsel or consultant:
TCI Washington Group (Merrill Williams)

Nat'l Crime Prevention Council
1700 K St., N.W. 2nd Floor, Washington, DC 20005
Telephone: (202) 466-6272
Represented by:
John Calhoun, Exec. Director
Counsel or consultant:
Capitol Associates, Inc. (Gordon P. MacDougall)

Nat'l Criminal Justice Ass'n
444 N. Capitol St., N.W., Suite 608, Washington, DC 20001
Telephone: (202) 347-4900
Represented by:
Gwen A. Holden, Exec. V. President
Counsel or consultant:
Venable, Baetjer, Howard and Civiletti

Nat'l Customs Brokers and Forwarders Ass'n of America
New York, NY
Counsel or consultant:
Kent & O'Connor, Incorp. (J. H. Kent)

Nat'l Dairy Promotion and Research Board
2111 Wilson Blvd., Suite 600, Arlington, VA 22201
Telephone: (703) 528-4800

Represented by:
Richard Weiss, V. President, Public Affairs
Counsel or consultant:
Direct Impact Co., The
Daniel J. Edelman, Inc. (Mary Christ-Erwin, Jean Rainey)
Henry J. Kaufman & Associates (Michael G. Carberry, John Seng)
McLeod & Pires (Wayne R. Watkinson)

Nat'l Decorating Products Ass'n
St. Louis, MO
Counsel or consultant:
Fehrenbacher, Sale, Quinn, and Deese (C. Michael Deese)

Nat'l Defense Contractors Expo
Columbus, OH
Counsel or consultant:
Norman G. Cornish

Nat'l Defense Council Foundation
228 S. Washington St., Suite 230, Alexandria, VA 22314-3626
Telephone: (703) 836-3443
Represented by:
F. Andy Messing, Jr., Exec. Director
Amy Thompson, Director, Special Projects/Press

Nat'l Defense Transportation Ass'n
50 S. Pickett St., Suite 220, Alexandria, VA 22304
Telephone: (703) 751-5011
Background: Since its founding in 1944, the NDTA has functioned as a major channel of cooperation and communication between transportation and government executives who must rely upon industry's services; NDTA has undertaken this role because it was recognized early that a full and free partnership between industry and military forces is vital to the security of the free world. The military relies heavily upon private-sector transportation, during both peace and war.
Represented by:
Lt. Gen. Edward Honor, USA (Ret), President

Nat'l Democratic Council of Asian and Pacific Americans
1118 22nd St., N.W. Suite 204, Washington, DC 20037
Telephone: (202) 659-4037
Represented by:
Maeley L. Tom, Washington Representative

Nat'l Democratic Institute for Internat'l Affairs
1717 Massachusetts Ave., N.W. Suite 605, Washington, DC 20036
Telephone: (202) 328-3136
Represented by:
Jean B. Dunn, V. President, Development & Admin.
Mahnaz Ispahani, Research Director
Thomas O. Melia, Program Director

Nat'l Dental Ass'n
5506 Connecticut Ave., N.W. Suite 25, Washington, DC 20015
Telephone: (202) 244-7555
Background: Founded in Virginia in 1913, the largest organization of minority dentists is dedicated to providing quality dental care to the unserved and underserved population. Representing the nation's 5,000 Black dentists, with 50 chapters, the NDA along with its four auxiliaries advocate the inclusion of dental care services in local, state and federal health care programs, foster the integration of minority dental health care providers into the profession and promote dentistry as a viable career for minorities through scholarship and support programs.
Represented by:
Rosita Stevens Holsey, National Office Director

Nat'l Dental Hygienists' Ass'n
5506 Connecticut Ave., N.W., Suite 24-25, Washington, DC 20015
Telephone: (202) 699-3710
Represented by:
Andrea Foster, President

Nat'l Development Council
1025 Connecticut Ave., N.W., Suite 317, Washington, DC 20036
Telephone: (202) 466-3906
Represented by:
Andrea Levere, Director

The listings in this directory are available as *Mailing Labels*. See last page.

Nat'l Dialysis Ass'n
1050 17th St., N.W., Suite 840, Washington, DC 20036
Telephone: (202) 785-1197
Counsel or consultant:
Porte, Stafford and Associates (Phillip L. Porte)

Nat'l Digestive Diseases Information Clearinghouse
P.O. Box NDDIC, Bethesda, MD 20892
Telephone: (301) 468-6344
Represented by:
Phyllis Abramczyk, Information Specialist

Nat'l Distillers and Chemical Corp.
New York, NY
Counsel or consultant:
Wilner and Scheiner (Richard A. Solomon)

Nat'l District Attorneys Ass'n
1033 N. Fairfax St., Suite 200, Alexandria, VA 22314
Telephone: (703) 549-9222
Represented by:
Jack Yelverton, Exec. Director

Nat'l Easter Seal Soc.
1350 New York Ave., N.W., Suite 415, Washington, DC 20005
Telephone: (202) 347-3066
Represented by:
Joseph D. Romer, V. President, Governmental Affairs
Randall L. Rutta, Assistant V. President, Gov't Affairs
Judith M. Shaw, Research Analyst, Gov't Affairs

Nat'l Economists Club
Falls Church, VA
Counsel or consultant:
James L. Kenworthy, Esq.

Nat'l Education Ass'n of the U.S.
1201 16th St., N.W., Washington, DC 20036
Telephone: (202) 822-7300
Represented by:
Don Cameron, Exec. Director
Howard J. Carroll, Manager, Media Relations & Public Rtns.
Robert H. Chanin, General Counsel
John A. Conway, Political Specialist
Debra DeLee, Director, Government Relations
Patsy B. Dix, Legislative Specialist
Michael D. Edwards, Manager, Congressional Relations
Isabelle Garcia, Legislative Specialist
Moses D. Holmes, Jr., Legislative Specialist
Sheri Lanoff, Political Specialist
Dale Lestina, Assistant Director, Special Projects
Kenneth F. Melley, Exec. Manager, Advocacy Programs
Joel Packer, Legislative Specialist
Alicia Sandoval, Director, Communications Services
Joseph Standa, Political Specialist
Gary G. Timmons, Legislative Specialist
Ruby Williams, Assistant Exec. Dir. for Public Affairs
Counsel or consultant:
F. Nordy Hoffmann & Assoc. (Gerald R. Gereau, F. Nordy Hoffmann)
The Kamber Group (Katherine Kinsella)
Nordlinger Associates

Nat'l Education Ass'n Political Action Committee
1201 16th St., N.W., Washington, DC 20036
Telephone: (202) 822-7300
Background: Represents the legislative and political interests of the Nat'l Education Ass'n of the U.S. Responsible contacts are Ken Melley and Debbie DeLee of the Nat'l Education Ass'n.

Nat'l Electric Sign Ass'n
801 North Fairfax St. Suite 205, Alexandria, VA 22314
Telephone: (703) 836-4012
Represented by:
George M. Kopecky, President
Counsel or consultant:
Cohn and Marks (Richard M. Schmidt, Jr.)

Nat'l Electric Sign Ass'n Political Action Committee
801 North Fairfax St. Suite 205, Alexandria, VA 22314
Telephone: (703) 836-4012
Background: Contact is George M. Kopecky, President of the Nat'l Electric Sign Ass'n.

Nat'l Electrical Contractors Ass'n
13th floor, 7315 Wisconsin Ave., Bethesda, MD 20814

Telephone: (301) 657-3110
Represented by:
Bonnie Duncan, Director, Communications
John Grau, Exec. V. President
Robert L. White, Jr., Manager, Government Affairs

Nat'l Electrical Manufacturers Ass'n
2101 L St., N.W., Washington, DC 20037
Telephone: (202) 457-8400
Background: The principal national association representing over 600 American electroindustry companies. A leading developer of US and international standards for electrical products and systems. Issue interests include international trade, energy, environment, safety, and liability.
Represented by:
Janet M. DeSavage, Government Affairs
Bernard H. Falk, President
Dale R. Schmidt, Manager, Legal Services
Daniel K. Shipp, V. President of Public Affairs
Richard F. Warren, Co-ordinator of Government Affairs
Counsel or consultant:
Morrison & Foerster (Steven S. Rosenthal)

Nat'l Employment Counselors Ass'n
5999 Stevenson Ave., Alexandria, VA 22304
Telephone: (703) 823-9800
Background: Represented by William Hunter, Lauren Scheib and Richard Yep of the American Ass'n for Counseling and Development.

Nat'l Endowment for Democracy
1101 15th St., N.W. Suite 203, Washiongton, DC 20005
Telephone: (202) 293-9072
Background: A private, nonprofit organization with substantial federal financial support which seeks to promote the growth of democracy in nondemocratic countries.
Represented by:
Carl Gershman, President

Nat'l Endowment for Soil and Water Conservation
321 D St., N.E., Washington, DC 20002
Telephone: (202) 546-7407
Background: The purpose of the Endowment is to form a partnership between the public and private sectors to conserve our agricultural resource base. Raises tax-deductible money from the private sector to fund agricultural conservation projects.
Represented by:
Barbara Pedersen Holum, Director

Nat'l Energy Management Institute
601 North Fairfax St., Alexandria, VA 22314
Telephone: (703) 739-7100
Represented by:
Donald Lahr, Administrator

Nat'l Environmental Development Ass'n
1440 New York Ave., N.W., Suite 300, Washington, DC 20005
Telephone: (202) 638-1230
Counsel or consultant:
Capital Legislative Services
E. Bruce Harrison Co. (Steven B. Hellem)
Morgan, Lewis and Bockius (John R. Quarles, Jr., Leslie Sue Ritts)

Nat'l Environmental Health Ass'n
Denver, CO
Counsel or consultant:
Dan Botkiss and Assoc. (Daniel A. Botkiss)

Nat'l Erectors Ass'n
1501 Lee Hwy., Suite 202, Arlington, VA 22209
Telephone: (703) 524-3336
Represented by:
Noel C. Borck, Exec. V. President
Counsel or consultant:
Loomis, Owen, Fellman and Howe (Steven John Fellman)

Nat'l Exchange Carriers Ass'n
Whippany, NJ
Counsel or consultant:
Chwat/Weigend Associates (John S. Chwat, Robert E. Weigend)

Nat'l Family Farm Coalition
80 F St., N.W. Suite 714, Washington, DC 20001
Telephone: (202) 737-2215
Background: Seeks to strengthen the family farm system of agriculture by promoting federal policies that benefit family farms, protect the environment, and create economic

stability in rural communities.
Represented by:
Brian Ahlberg, Communications Coordinator
Larry Gray, Legislative Coordinator
Kathy Ozer, Policy Coordinator
Susan Penzer, Exec. Director

Nat'l Family Planning and Reproductive Health Ass'n
122 C St., N.W., Suite 380, Washington, DC 20001-2109
Telephone: (202) 628-3535
Background: NFPRHA represents over 90% of the family planning providers nationwide who receive federal funding under Title X of the Public Health Service Act and who provide health care services to nearly 5 million poor women and teenagers annually.
Represented by:
Lisa Shuger Hublitz, Director, Government Relations
Scott R. Swirling, Exec. Director

Nat'l Farm and Power Equipment Dealers Ass'n
St. Louis, MO
Counsel or consultant:
Neill, Mullenholz and Shaw (John J. Mullenholz)

Nat'l Farmers' Federation of Australia
Canberra, Australia
Counsel or consultant:
Keene, Shirley & Associates, Inc. (David A. Keene, Craigan P. Shirley)

Nat'l Farmers Organization
475 L'Enfant Plaza, S.W., Washington, DC 20024
Telephone: (202) 484-7075
Background: A farm-membership organization which bargains for better commodity prices for farmers and ranchers.
Represented by:
Charles L. Frazier, Director, Washington Office

Nat'l Farmers Union
600 Maryland Ave., S.W., Suite 202W, Washington, DC 20024
Telephone: (202) 554-1600
Background: Also known under the corporate name of Farmers Educational and Cooperative Union of America. Dedicated to promoting and strengthening family farmers and a family farm system of agriculture through policies and programs.
Represented by:
Cheryl Cook, Legislative Assistant
Nancy Danielson, Legislative Assistant
Robert A. Denman, Legislative Assistant
Michael V Dunn, V. President, Legislative Services
Howard T. Lyman, Legislative Assistant

Nat'l Federation of Business and Professional Women's Clubs
2012 Massachusetts Ave., N.W., Washington, DC 20036
Telephone: (202) 293-1100
Represented by:
LaVerne Collins, Nat'l President
Linda Colvard Dorian, Exec. Director
Jennifer Powell, Admin. Asst., Gov't Relats. & Public Aff
Diane Reis, Director, Gov't Relats. & Public Affairs

Nat'l Federation of Business and Professional Women's Clubs Political Action Committee
2012 Massachusetts Ave., N.W., Washington, DC 20036
Telephone: (202) 293-1100
Background: Represented by Diane Reis, Director of Government Relations & Public Affairs for the Nat'l Federation of Business and Women's Clubs.

Nat'l Federation of Coffee Growers of Colombia
Bogota, Colombia
Background: Federacion Nacional de Cafeteros de Colombia
Counsel or consultant:
Murray, Scheer & Montgomery (Rollinde Prager)

Nat'l Federation of Community Broadcasters
666 11th St., N.W. Suite 805, Washington, DC 20001
Telephone: (202) 393-2355
Background: Non-commercial radio stations licensed to community organizations.
Represented by:
Lynn Chadwick, President and CEO

Nat'l Federation of Democratic Women
5422 2nd St., N.W., Washington, DC 20011

ORGANIZATIONS REPRESENTED

Nat'l Federation of Democratic Women (Cont'd)
Telephone: (202) 723-8182
Represented by:
Annette Jones, Liaison

Nat'l Federation of Federal Employees
1016 16th St., N.W., Suite 400, Washington, DC 20036
Telephone: (202) 862-4400
Background: A labor union representing 150,000 federal workers in federal agencies throughout the country.
Represented by:
Charles Bernhardt, Labor Relations Specialist
Alice Bodley, Deputy Gerneral Counsel
Josh Bowers, Staff Attorney
Andreas 'Red' Evans, Dir. of Publications & Public Relations
Robbie G. Exley, CAE, Labor Relations Specialist
H. Stephan Gordon, General Counsel
Julius L. Hall, Legislative Counsel
Ronald Kipke, Secretary-Treasurer
Anne Morgan, Staff Attorney
Joshua Neiman, Legislative Director
James M. Pierce, President
Jane Polansky, Deputy Director, Public Relations
Jeffrey Sumberg, Staff Attorney

Nat'l Federation of Federal Employees Public Affairs Council
1016 16th St., N.W., Washington, DC 20036
Telephone: (202) 862-4400
Represented by:
Stephanie Boteler, Treasurer

Nat'l Federation of Independent Business
600 Maryland Ave., S.W., Suite 700, Washington, DC 20024
Telephone: (202) 554-9000
Represented by:
Leslie C. Aubin, Legislative Representative
David Cullen, V. President of Public Affairs
Sally L. Douglas, Asst. Dir., Fed. Gov't Afrs./Res. & Pol.
David J. Gribbin, IV, Legislative Representative
Terry Hill, Manager, Nat'l Media Relations
Margaret Renken Hudson, Legislative Representative
David R. Jones, President, NFIB Foundation
Wendy Lechner, Legislative Representative
Carolyn E. Miller, Legislative Representative
Carol Ward Mills, Admin. Asst. to the Pres. & Office Mgr.
Joan Moeltner, Associate for Membership Liaison
John J. Motley, V. Pres., Federal Governmental Affairs
Mary Reed, Legislative Repesentative
David K. Rehr, Ass't Dir., Federal Gov't Affairs, House
Michael O. Roush, Asst. Dir., Federal Gov't Rels./Senate
Lisa Scott, Manager, PAC Administration
Donna L. Singletary, Legislative Representative
John Sloan, Jr., President and C.E.O.
David Stephenson, State Legislative Analyst
Jim Weidman, Manager, State Media Relations
Stephen P. Woods, Director, State Government Relations
Counsel or consultant:
McKevitt Group, The

Nat'l Federation of Independent Business PAC
600 Maryland Ave., S.W. Suite 700, Washington, DC 20024
Telephone: (202) 554-9000
Counsel or consultant:
Wunder, Ryan, Cannon & Thelen (Paul E. Sullivan)

Nat'l Federation of Independent Business - Tennessee
Nashville, TN
Counsel or consultant:
Targeted Communications Corp.

Nat'l Federation of Republican Women
310 First St., S.E., Washington, DC 20003
Telephone: (202) 547-9341
Background: Founded in 1938, the Federation now has about 160,000 members and 2,600 clubs in all 50 states. Dedicated to mobilization of women to ensure election of Republican candidates at all levels of government.
Represented by:
Karen Johnson, Director of Communications
Huda Jones, President
Nellie McCormack, Chief of Staff

Nat'l Federation of Societies for Clinical Social Work
New York, NY
Counsel or consultant:
Dickstein, Shapiro and Morin (John C. Dill)

Nat'l Field Selling Ass'n
San Antonio, TX
Counsel or consultant:
Arent, Fox, Kintner, Plotkin & Kahn (Daniel C. Smith)

Nat'l Fire Protection Ass'n
1110 North Glebe Road, Suite 560, Arlington, VA 22201
Telephone: (703) 524-3505
Background: Educates the public with firesafety information through educational programs, and the distribution of the National Fire Codes.
Represented by:
John C. Gerard, Washington Representative
Sara C. Yerkes, Ass't to the Washington Representative

Nat'l Fish and Seafood Promotion Council
Counsel or consultant:
Daniel J. Edelman, Inc. (Mary Christ-Erwin, Jean Rainey)

Nat'l Fisheries Institute
1525 Wilson Blvd., Suite 500, Arlington, VA 22209
Telephone: (703) 524-8880
Represented by:
Richard Gutting, V. President, Government Relations
Lee Weddig, Exec. V. President

Nat'l Fisheries Institute Political Action Committee
2000 M St., N.W., Suite 580, Washington, DC 20036
Telephone: (202) 296-5090
Background: Represented by Lee Weddig of the Nat'l Fisheries Institute.

Nat'l Food Brokers Ass'n
1010 Massachusetts Ave., N.W., Washington, DC 20001
Telephone: (202) 789-2844
Represented by:
Mark W. Baum, Senior V. President
Alan Goldstein, Director, Communications
Isobel Murray, Legislative Counsel
Karen J. Ribler, Exec. V. Pres., Educ. & Trng. Foundation
Robert C. Schwarze, President and CEO

Nat'l Food Processors Ass'n
1401 New York Ave., N.W. Suite 400, Washington, DC 20005
Telephone: (202) 639-5900
Represented by:
John R. Cady, President
Glenn Gamber, Legislative Representative
Counsel or consultant:
Burson-Marsteller

Nat'l Food Processors Ass'n Political Action Committee
1401 New York Ave., N.W. Suite 400, Washington, DC 20005
Telephone: (202) 639-5900
Background: Represented by Glenn Gamber of the Association.

Nat'l Football League
New York, NY
Counsel or consultant:
Akin, Gump, Strauss, Hauer and Feld (Edward S. Knight)
Gold and Liebengood, Inc. (Martin B. Gold)
O'Neill and Athy, P.C. (Thomas C. Williams)

Nat'l Football League Players Ass'n
2021 L St., N.W., Washington, DC 20036
Telephone: (202) 463-2200
Represented by:
Gene Upshaw, Exec. Director

Nat'l Foreign Trade Council, Inc.
1625 K St., N.W., Suite 1090, Washington, DC 20006
Telephone: (202) 887-0278
Background: Established 1914. Represents the foreign trade and investment interests of the 500-plus U.S. corporations who make up its membership. Favors open international economic system and expansion of international trade and investment.

Represented by:
Willard M. Berry, V. President
Charles E. Hugel, Chairman and CEO
Frank D. Kittredge, President
J. Daniel O'Flaherty, V. President and Secretary
Counsel or consultant:
Rivkin, Radler, Dunne and Bayh (Birch Bayh, Jr., Kevin O. Faley)

Nat'l Forest Products Ass'n
1250 Connecticut Ave., N.W. Suite 200, Washington, DC 20036
Telephone: (202) 463-2700
Background: Sponsors the Forest Industries Political Action Committee.
Represented by:
Debra Barwick, Research Assistant, Government Affairs
Barry M. Cullen, President
Cindy Evans, Environmental Counsel
David Ford, V. President, Public Timber
Annelise B. Gillespie, Congressional Representative
Alberto Goetzl, V. Pres., Economics & Info. Services
Robert A. Kirshner, Environmental Counsel
Steve Lovett, V. President, Internat'l Trade Council
Samuel H. Murray, Tax Counsel
Scott Shotwell, V. President, Government Affairs
Jane Turner, Congressional Representative
Counsel or consultant:
Dewey, Ballantine, Bushby, Palmer and Wood (Michael H. Stein, Alan W. Wolff)
Preston Gates Ellis & Rouvelas Meeds (Richard L. Barnes, William A. Shook)
Steptoe and Johnson

Nat'l Forest Recreation Ass'n
Flagstaff, AZ
Counsel or consultant:
Scootch Pankonin

Nat'l Forum on the Future of Children and Their Families
2101 Constitution Ave., N.W. Room HA 172, Washington, DC 20418
Telephone: (202) 334-1935
Counsel or consultant:
Gallagher-Widmeyer Group Inc., The (Mary Jane Gallagher)

Nat'l Foundation for Cancer Research
7315 Wisconsin Ave. Suite 332 West, Bethesda, MD 20814
Telephone: (301) 654-1250
Represented by:
Franklin C. Salisbury, President

Nat'l Foundation for the Handicapped
1850 K St., N.W., Suite 500, Washington, DC 20006
Telephone: (202) 778-8117
Background: Seeks to influence national policy via targeted initiatives such as the Self-Sufficiency Trust, Anna Emery Hanson Canter for the Arts, PBS film series, Imagine This World, highlighting the contributions of people with disabilities.
Represented by:
Paul L. Medlin, Sr. V. President
Counsel or consultant:
McDermott, Will and Emery

Nat'l Foundation for the Improvement of Education
1201 16th St., N.W., Washington, DC 20036
Telephone: (202) 822-7840
Background: A nonprofit organization whose mission is to empower teachers through grants, information exchanges and public awareness programs. Created in 1969 by the Nat'l Education Ass'n.
Represented by:
Dr. Donna Rhodes, Exec. Director

Nat'l Foundry Ass'n
Des Plaines, IL
Background: Represented by Walter M. Kiplinger, Jr. of the American Cast Metals Ass'n.

Nat'l Fraternal Congress of America
Chicago, IL
Background: The trade association for fraternal benefit societies.
Counsel or consultant:
Zuckert, Scoutt and Rasenberger (Walter D. Vinyard, Jr.)

The listings in this directory are available as *Mailing Labels*. See last page.

ORGANIZATIONS REPRESENTED

Nat'l Frozen Food Ass'n
204 E St., N.E., Washington, DC 20002
Telephone: (202) 547-6340
Counsel or consultant:
Giuffrida Associates, Inc. (Mike Giuffrida, John R. Purcell)

Nat'l Frozen Pizza Institute
1764 Old Meadow Lane Suite 350, McLean, VA 22102
Telephone: (703) 821-0770
Background: Francis G. Williams of the American Frozen Food Institute serves as Exec. Director.

Nat'l Funeral Directors Ass'n
Milwaukee, WI
Counsel or consultant:
O'Connor & Hannan (Timothy M. Haake)
Thompson Group, Inc. (Kenneth W. Thompson)

Nat'l Gaucher Foundation
1424 K St., N.W., 4th Floor, Washington, DC 20005
Telephone: (202) 393-2777
Represented by:
Karen Cohen, Exec. Director

Nat'l Gay and Lesbian Task Force
1517 U St., N.W., Washington, DC 20009
Telephone: (202) 332-6483
Represented by:
Peri Jude Radecic, Lobbyist
Urvashi Vaid, Exec. Director

Nat'l Geographic Soc.
1145 17th St., N.W., Washington, DC 20036
Telephone: (202) 857-7000
Represented by:
Gilbert M. Grosvenor, President & Chairman of the Board
Mary Jeanne Jacobsen, Manager, Broadcast Media Relations
Barbara S. Moffet, Manager, Print Media Relations
Dale A. Petroskey, Director, Public Affairs
Steve Raymer, Director, News Service
Robert B. Sims, Senior V. President

Nat'l Glass Ass'n
8200 Greensboro Drive Suite 302, McLean, VA 22102
Telephone: (703) 442-4890
Represented by:
Philip J. James, Group Vice President & CEO
Carolyn Lugbill, Manager, Government & Industry Affairs
Counsel or consultant:
Jenner and Block
Kelley, Drye and Warren (Michael R. Lemov)

Nat'l Glass Ass'n Political Action Committee
8200 Greensboro Drive Suite 302, McLean, VA 22102
Telephone: (703) 442-4890
Background: Contact is Leo M. Cyr of the Ass'n.

Nat'l Governors' Ass'n
444 North Capitol St., N.W., Suite 250, Washington, DC 20001
Telephone: (202) 624-5300
Background: Represents state governors and serves as liaison between state and federal governments. Formerly known as the Nat'l Governors Conference.
Represented by:
Rae Young Bond, Director, Public Affairs
Tom Curtis, Dir., Natural Resources Group
James L. Martin, Legislative Counsel
Raymond C. Scheppach, Exec. Director

Nat'l Grain and Feed Ass'n
1201 New York Ave., N.W. Suite 830, Washington, DC 20005
Telephone: (202) 289-0873
Represented by:
David C. Barrett, Jr., Director, Public Affairs
David M. Brockman, Director, Legislative Affairs
Randall C. Gordon, V.P., Communications and Gov't Relations
Kendell W. Keith, Exec. V. President
Counsel or consultant:
Arent, Fox, Kintner, Plotkin & Kahn (Marc L. Fleischaker)

Nat'l Grain Trade Council
1030 15th St., N.W., Suite 1020, Washington, DC 20005
Telephone: (202) 842-0400

Represented by:
Robert R. Petersen, President

Nat'l Grange
1616 H St., N.W., Washington, DC 20006
Telephone: (202) 628-3507
Background: A civic and fraternal organization with special interest in farm policies and programs. Concerned with legislation relating to agriculture and international trade.
Represented by:
Robert E. Barrow, National Master
Robert M. Frederick, Legislative Director
Judith T. Massabny, Public Relations Director
Leroy Watson, Jr., Legislative Representative

Nat'l Grape Growers Cooperative
Westfield, NY
Counsel or consultant:
Robert N. Pyle & Associates

Nat'l Greyhound Ass'n
Abilene, KS
Counsel or consultant:
Arthur E. Cameron

Nat'l Grocers Ass'n
1825 Samuel Morse Drive, Reston, VA 22090
Telephone: (703) 437-5300
Background: Formed as result of a merger of the Cooperative Food Distributors of America and the Nat'l Ass'n of Retail Grocers of the United States.
Represented by:
Richard A. Brown, Senior V. President, Operations
Richard C. Crawford, Director, Government Relations
Patricia L. Pines, V. President, Educational Services
Thomas F. Wenning, Sr. V. President and General Counsel
Thomas K. Zaucha, President
Counsel or consultant:
McDermott, Will and Emery (Ronald A. Bloch)

Nat'l Grocers Ass'n Political Action Committee
1825 Samuel Morse Drive, Reston, VA 22090
Telephone: (703) 437-5300
Background: Contact is Richard Crawford of the Nat'l Grocers Ass'n.

Nat'l Guard Ass'n of the U.S.
One Massachusetts Ave., N.W., Washington, DC 20001
Telephone: (202) 789-0031
Represented by:
Cpt. Victor Dubina, Director, Public Relations
Maj. Gen. Bruce Jacobs, Asst. Exec. Director
Edward C. Morai, Director, Plns, Policy, and Evaluation
Charles G. Schreiber, Director, Legislative Affairs
Brig. Gen. Wilbert T. Stewart, Director, Air Activities
Lt. Gen. LaVern E. Weber, Exec. Director
Col. Donald E. Wilson, Director, Army Activities

Nat'l Gypsum Co.
Buffalo, NY
Counsel or consultant:
Daniel J. Edelman, Inc. (Stephen K. Cook)
Wexler, Reynolds, Fuller, Harrison and Schule, Inc. (Robert M. Schule, Dale Snape)

Nat'l Hand Tool Corp.
Dallas, TX
Counsel or consultant:
Ross and Hardies (Salvatore E. Caramango)

Nat'l Head Injury Foundation
Southborough, MA
Counsel or consultant:
Duncan and Associates

Nat'l Head Start Ass'n
1220 King St., Suite 200, Alexandria, VA 22314
Telephone: (703) 739-0875
Background: Membership is comprised of staff, parents and friends involved in 1,500 Head Start programs across the country.
Represented by:
Don Bolce, Director, Information Services
Marlene Karwowski, Editor
Jim Matlack, Exec. Director

Nat'l Health Care Anti-Fraud Ass'n
1255 23rd St., N.W., Washington, DC 20037
Telephone: (202) 452-8100

Background: Organized to improve the prevention, detection and prosecution of health care fraud offenders. Board of Governors members include: Aetna Insurance, Travelers, Metropolitan Life, CIGNA, Employers Health Insurance, U.S. Dept. of Health ad Human Services, Nat'l Ass'n of Medicaid Fraud Control Units, Florida Medicaid Fraud Control Unit, and Pennsylvania Blue Shield. Exec. Director is Richard Ekfelt of Hauck and Associates.
Counsel or consultant:
Hauck and Associates (Richard H. Ekfelt)
Wiley, Rein & Fielding (Thomas W. Brunner)

Nat'l Health Care Campaign
1334 G St., N.W. LL, Washington, DC 20005
Telephone: (202) 639-8833
Background: An organization committed to achieving a national health care plan which assures high-quality, affordable health care for all Americans,
Represented by:
Cathy Hurwit, Director, Federal Health Policy
Susan Sherry, Director, State Health Affairs

Nat'l Health Council
1700 K St., N.W. Suite 1005, Washington, DC 20006
Telephone: (202) 785-3913
Background: A sixty-nine year old membership association of the nation's major health organizations, dedicated to promoting and enhancing the health of all Americans.
Represented by:
Joseph C. Isaacs, V. President for Government Relations

Nat'l Health Laboratories
Bridgeport, CT
Counsel or consultant:
Akin, Gump, Strauss, Hauer and Feld (Joel Jankowsky)

Nat'l Health Law Program
2025 M St., N.W., Suite 400, Washington, DC 20036
Telephone: (202) 887-5310
Represented by:
Judith G. Waxman, Managing Attorney

Nat'l Health Lawyers Ass'n
1620 Eye St., N.W. Suite 900, Washington, DC 20006
Telephone: (202) 833-1100
Represented by:
David J. Greenburg, Exec. Director

Nat'l Health Policy Forum
2011 Eye St., N.W. Suite 200, Washington, DC 20006
Telephone: (202) 872-1390
Represented by:
Rheada Michele Black, Associate Director
John F. Hoadley, Senior Research Associate
Judith Miller Jones, Director
Jane Koppelman, Research Associate
Karen Matherlee, Deputy Director
Robin J. Strongin, Reseach Associate

Nat'l Hearing Aid Soc.
Livonia, MI
Counsel or consultant:
William J. Tobin and Associates (William J. Tobin)

Nat'l Hemophilia Foundation
New York, NY
Counsel or consultant:
MARC Associates, Inc. (Randolph B. Fenninger, Daniel C. Maldonado)

Nat'l Hispanic Council on Aging
2713 Ontario Road, N.W. Suite 200, Washington, DC 20009
Telephone: (202) 265-1288
Background: Founded in 1980 as a national voluntary organization to serve the needs of the Hispanic elderly.
Represented by:
Tomasa Gonzales, Community Liaison
Dr. Marta Sotomayor, President

Nat'l Hockey League
New York, NY
Counsel or consultant:
Baraff, Koerner, Olender and Hochberg (Philip R. Hochberg)

Nat'l Home Furnishings Ass'n
Wood Dale, IL
Counsel or consultant:
London and Satagaj, Attorneys-at-Law (Sheldon I. London, John S. Satagaj)

The listings in this directory are available as *Mailing Labels.* See last page.

633

ORGANIZATIONS REPRESENTED

Nat'l Home Study Council
1601 18th St., N.W., Washington, DC 20009
Telephone: (202) 234-5100
Represented by:
William A. Fowler, Exec. Director
Counsel or consultant:
J. C. Luman and Assoc. (Joseph C. Luman)

Nat'l Homeowners Ass'n
1906 Sunderland Place, N.W., Washington, DC 20036
Telephone: (202) 223-1453
Background: Works to promote and enhance the position of American homeowners, looks after their interests on Capitol Hill, monitors federal legislation and regulations affecting home ownership.
Represented by:
Patricia Bradford, Admin. Assistant
John Weidlein, President
Counsel or consultant:
Silver, Freedman & Taff (Earl L. Metheny)

Nat'l Honey Board
Longmont, CO
Counsel or consultant:
Highley & Associates (Vern F. Highley)

Nat'l Honor Soc.
1904 Association Drive, Reston, VA 22091
Telephone: (703) 860-0200
Background: Service organization for secondary school leaders in scholarship, character and service.
Represented by:
Dale Hawley, Exec. Director

Nat'l Hospice Organization
1901 Moore St. Suite 901, Arlington, VA 22209
Telephone: (703) 243-5900
Represented by:
Nina Arback, Director of Communications
John J. Mahoney, President
Counsel or consultant:
Hogan and Hartson

Nat'l Housing Conference
1126 16th St., N.W., Suite 211, Washington, DC 20036
Telephone: (202) 223-4844
Background: Established in 1931, a citizen's lobby which seeks to mobilize support for programs in housing and community development.
Represented by:
Jean Hutter, Director of Legislation
Juliette B. Madison, Exec. Director

Nat'l Housing Endowment
15th and M Sts., N.W., Washington, DC 20005
Telephone: (202) 822-0226
Represented by:
Bruce S. Silver, Exec. Director

Nat'l Housing Partnership
1225 Eye St., N.W. Suite 700, Washington, DC 20005
Telephone: (202) 347-6247
Counsel or consultant:
Linda Parke Gallagher & Assoc. (Linda Parke Gallagher)

Nat'l Housing Rehabilitation Ass'n
1726 18th St., N.W., Washington, DC 20009
Telephone: (202) 328-9171
Represented by:
Peter Bell, Exec. Director

Nat'l Housing Rehabilitation Ass'n Political Action Committee
1726 18th St., N.W., Washington, DC 20009
Telephone: (202) 328-9171
Represented by:
Sharon Dworkin Bell, Treasurer

Nat'l Hydropower Ass'n
555 13th St., N.W. Suite 900 East, Washington, DC 20004
Telephone: (202) 637-8115
Represented by:
Elaine Evans, Exec. Director
Barbara S. Flynn, Director, Public Affairs
Counsel or consultant:
Legislative Strategies Inc. (Raymond F. Bragg, Jr.)

Nat'l Hydropower Ass'n Political Action Committee
1133 21st St., N.W., Suite 500, Washington, DC 20036
Telephone: (202) 887-5200

Background: Represented by Elaine Evans of the Association.

Nat'l Image, Inc.
810 First St., N.E., Washington, DC 20002
Telephone: (202) 289-3777
Background: An organization which seeks to promote employment opportunities for Hispanic Americans in both the public and private sectors.
Represented by:
Manuel Oliverez, President & CEO

Nat'l Incorporation of Tenants
Great Neck, NY
Counsel or consultant:
Tendler, Goldberg & Biggins, Chtd. (Paul M. Tendler)

Nat'l Independent Automobile Dealers Ass'n
Irving, TX
Counsel or consultant:
Kelley, Drye and Warren (Michael R. Lemov)

Nat'l Independent Dairy-Food Ass'n
321 D St., N.E., Washington, DC 20002
Telephone: (202) 543-3838
Counsel or consultant:
Donald A. Randall

Nat'l Independent Energy Producers
601 13th St., N.W. Suite 320S, Washington, DC 20004
Telephone: (202) 783-2244
Background: NIEP represents companies which generate electricity for sale to utilities and develop power generation projects for a variety of users.
Represented by:
Merribel S. Ayres, Exec. Director
Nancy Sutley, Policy Director
Counsel or consultant:
Jellinek, Schwartz, Connolly & Freshman, Inc. (Jeffrey H. Schwartz)
Olwine, Connelly, Chase, O'Donnell and Weyher (W. Harrison Wellford)

Nat'l Independent Energy Producers Political Action Committee (NIEPAC)
601 13th St., N.W. Suite 320S, Washington, DC 20004
Telephone: (202) 783-2244
Background: Represented by Merribel S. Ayres of the Association.

Nat'l Indian Education Ass'n
1819 H St., N.W., Suite 800, Washington, DC 20006
Telephone: (202) 783-5100
Background: Address above is that of Hobbs Straus, et al, a Washington, DC law firm.
Counsel or consultant:
Hobbs, Straus, Dean and Wilder (Karen J. Funk)

Nat'l Indian Impacted Schools
Mission, SD
Counsel or consultant:
Evergreen Associates, Ltd. (Robert M. Brooks)

Nat'l Industrial Council
1331 Pennsylvania Ave., N.W. N. Lobby Suite 1500, Washington, DC 20004-1703
Telephone: (202) 637-3053
Background: A federation of state manufacturers' and employers' ass'ns under the aegis of the Nat'l Ass'n of Manufacturers.
Represented by:
Barry Buzby, Exec. Director, State Ass'ns Group
Argyll C. Campbell, Exec. Dir., Industrial Relations Group

Nat'l Industrial Sand Ass'n
900 Spring St., Silver Spring, MD 20910
Telephone: (301) 587-1400
Background: Represented by Vincent P. Ahearn, Jr., President; Richard A. Morris, V. Pres. of Government Relations and Public Affairs; and Kenneth R. Tobin, V. Pres. of Government Relations and National Affairs.

Nat'l Industrial Transportation League
1090 Vermont Ave., N.W. Suite 410, Washington, DC 20005-4905
Telephone: (202) 842-3870
Background: Presents the viewpoint of the users of transportation services to the Government.

Represented by:
James E. Bartley, Exec. V. President
M. J. Fiocco, Director of Legislative Communications
Counsel or consultant:
Donelan, Cleary, Wood and Maser, P.C. (Nicholas J. DiMichael)

Nat'l Industries for the Severely Handicapped
2235 Cedar Lane, Vienna, VA 22182
Telephone: (703) 560-6800
Represented by:
Eivind H. Johansen, President
Counsel or consultant:
J. C. Luman and Assoc. (Joseph C. Luman)

Nat'l Industries, Inc.
Montgomery, AL
Counsel or consultant:
Shaw, Pittman, Potts and Trowbridge (William Mike House)

Nat'l Inholders Ass'n
4 Library Court, S.E., Washington, DC 20003
Telephone: (202) 544-6156
Background: Formed in 1978 as the National Park Inholders Association by individuals owning property in national parks. Expanded as the National Inholders Association in 1980 to include all persons owning property or some other equity interest within the boundary of any federally managed area or who is impacted by the management, regulation or access of that area. This includes all National Parks, Forests, Fish and Wildlife Areas, Bureau of Land Management and Corps of Engineers/Bureau of Reclamation areas. These people may own, lease or rent property or have a permit to graze, timber, mine or otherwise use federal land.
Represented by:
Myron Ebell, Washington Representative

Nat'l Institute for Automotive Service Excellence
13505 Dulles Technology Drive, Herndon, VA 22071-3415
Telephone: (703) 742-3800
Counsel or consultant:
Patricia Bario Associates (Patricia Bario)
O'Brien, Birney and Butler

Nat'l Institute for Citizen Education in the Law
711 G St., S.E., Washington, DC 20003
Telephone: (202) 662-9620
Represented by:
Edward L. O'Brien, Co-Director
Counsel or consultant:
Kirkpatrick & Lockhart (Robert R. Belair)

Nat'l Institute for Fitness and Sport
Indianapolis, IN
Counsel or consultant:
Sagamore Associates, Inc. (Michael B. Kraft)

Nat'l Institute for Public Policy
3031 Javier Road Suite 300, Fairfax, VA 22031
Telephone: (703) 698-0563
Represented by:
Dr. Keith Payne, President

Nat'l Institute for State Credit Union Examination
1901 North Fort Myer Drive Suite 201, Arlington, VA 22209
Telephone: (703) 528-8351
Background: Represented by Sheralyn J. Odom of the Nat'l Ass'n of State Credit Union Supervisors.

Nat'l Institute for Work and Learning
1255 23rd St., N.W., Suite 400, Washington, DC 20037
Telephone: (202) 862-8845
Background: A nonprofit research and policy organization concerned primarily with the transition between education in the classroom and employment in the workplace.
Represented by:
Richard A. Ungerer, Exec. Director

Nat'l Institute of Building Sciences
1201 L St., N.W., Suite 400, Washington, DC 20005
Telephone: (202) 289-7800
Background: An organization which represents the building community, i.e. home builders, contractors, building trade unions, building-related corporations, research testing laboratories, building code officials, gas and electricity product manufacturers, real estate institutions, architects, engineers, standards organizations, individual design professionals and consumer interests in building construction. Seeks to encourage more rational building regulations and

ORGANIZATIONS REPRESENTED

to facilitate the safe introduction of new technology into building processes.
Represented by:
Gene C. Brewer, President Emeritus
David A. Harris, A.I.A., President
Neil W. Sandler, Director of Communications
Bruce E. Vogelsinger, P.E., V. President, Planning and Development
Counsel or consultant:
Steptoe and Johnson

Nat'l Institute of Certified Moving Consultants
1500 N. Beauregard St., Alexandria, VA 22311-1715
Telephone: (703) 671-8813
Background: President is Gary F. Petty of the Nat'l Moving and Storage Ass'n.

Nat'l Institute of Corrections
320 First St., N.W. Room 200, Washington, DC 20534
Telephone: (202) 724-3106
Represented by:
M. Wayne Huggins, Director
Larry Solomon, Deputy Director

Nat'l Institute of Governmental Purchasing
115 Hillwood Ave., Falls Church, VA 22046
Telephone: (703) 533-7300
Background: A professional society founded in 1944 dedicated to raising the standards of public purchasing and materials management.
Represented by:
Robin J. Zee, Exec. V. President

Nat'l Institute of Municipal Law Officers
1000 Connecticut Ave., N.W. Suite 902, Washington, DC 20036
Telephone: (202) 466-5424
Background: A non-profit organization rendering service, information, and assistance to municipal attorneys nationwide.
Represented by:
Benjamin L. Brown, Exec. Director and Gen. Counsel

Nat'l Institute of Oilseed Products
San Francisco, CA
Counsel or consultant:
Meyers & Associates (Margaret Judson, Rick Meyers)

Nat'l Institute of Senior Centers
600 Maryland Ave., S.W., Washington, DC 20024
Telephone: (202) 479-6683
Background: An organization of the Nat'l Council on the Aging. Established in 1970 to promote professional development of senior center practitioners. Represented by Cynthia Shearin Creyke of the Nat'l Council on the Aging.

Nat'l Institute of Senior Housing
600 Maryland Ave., S.W., Washington, DC 20024
Telephone: (202) 479-6677
Background: A membership unit of the Nat'l Council on the Aging which addresses the growing need for independent housing adapted to the special requirements and interests of older Americans. Represented by Moses Gozonsky and Morton Leeds.

Nat'l Institute on Adult Daycare
West Wing, 600 Maryland Ave., S.W., Washington, DC 20024
Telephone: (202) 479-1200
Background: An organization of the Nat'l Council on the Aging. Represented by Tanya Hart of the Nat'l Council on the Aging.

Nat'l Institute on Community-Based Long-Term Care
600 Maryland Ave., S.W., West Wing 100, Washington, DC 20024
Telephone: (202) 479-1200
Background: A membership unit of the Nat'l Council on the Aging. Represented by Tanya Hart of the Nat'l Council on the Aging.

Nat'l Institute on Mental Health
5600 Fishers Lane, Rockville, MD 20857
Telephone: (301) 443-4515
Counsel or consultant:
Hill and Knowlton Public Affairs Worldwide (Ken Rabin)

Nat'l Insulation Contractors Ass'n
99 Canal Center Plaza, Suite 222, Alexandria, VA 22314

Telephone: (703) 683-6422
Represented by:
William W. Pitkin, Exec. V. President

Nat'l Insurance Consumer Organization
121 North Payne St., Alexandria, VA 22314
Telephone: (703) 549-8050
Background: Provides guidance to consumers of insurance, acts as an advocate for consumers on policy matters and works for of abuses in the insurance industry.
Represented by:
Jay Angoff, Counsel
Linda J. Burnette, Office Manager
Howard Clark, Director
James H. Hunt, Director
J. Robert Hunter, President

Nat'l Intergroup, Inc.
1575 Eye St., N.W., Suite 1100, Washington, DC 20005
Telephone: (202) 638-7707
Represented by:
John M. Stinson, III, Director, Government Affairs
William D. Thompson, V. President, Government Affairs
Counsel or consultant:
Patton, Boggs and Blow (Ernest S. Christian, Jr.)

Nat'l Interreligious Service Board for Conscientious Objectors
1601 Connecticut Ave., N.W. Suite 750, Washington, DC 20009
Telephone: (202) 293-5962
Background: A nonprofit service organization sponsored by a broad coalition of religious groups. Disseminates information on conscription developments and seeks to defend and extend the rights of conscientious objectors to war. Opposes any form of registration, the draft, or compulsory national service.
Represented by:
Charles A. Maresca, Jr., Staff Attorney
Rev. L. William Yolton, Exec. Director

Nat'l Investor Relations Institute
2000 L St., N.W. Suite 701, Washington, DC 20036
Telephone: (202) 861-0630
Represented by:
Louis M. Thompson, President & Chief Operating Officer

Nat'l Iron and Steel of Singapore
Singapore
Counsel or consultant:
Willkie Farr and Gallagher (Walter J. Spak)

Nat'l Jai Alai Ass'n
Miami, FL
Counsel or consultant:
McAuliffe, Kelly, Raffaelli & Siemens (Lynnette R. Jacquez)

Nat'l Jewish Center for Immunology and Respiratory Medicine
Denver, CO
Counsel or consultant:
Cassidy and Associates, Inc. (Gerald S. J. Cassidy, Elliott M. Fiedler, Vincent M. Versage)

Nat'l Jewish Coalition
415 Second St., N.E., Washington, DC 20002
Telephone: (202) 547-7701
Represented by:
Matthew Brooks, Political Director
Benjamin S. Waldman, Exec. Director

Nat'l Judicial College
Reno, NV
Counsel or consultant:
McAuliffe, Kelly, Raffaelli & Siemens (Edward E. Allison)

Nat'l Juice Products Ass'n
Tampa, FL
Counsel or consultant:
Collier, Shannon & Scott (Robin H. Gilbert, Paul C. Rosenthal)

Nat'l Kitchen Cabinet Ass'n
6711 Lee Hwy., Arlington, VA 22205
Telephone: (703) 237-7580
Represented by:
C. Richard Titus, Exec. V. President

Nat'l Kraut Packers Ass'n, Inc.
St. Charles, IL
Counsel or consultant:
Walter E. Byerley Law Offices (Walter E. Byerley)

Nat'l Label Co.
Lafayette Hill, PA
Counsel or consultant:
Baker, Worthington, Crossley, Stansberry & Woolf (Edward R. Hamberger)

Nat'l Labor Relations Board Professional Ass'n
1717 Pennsylvania Ave., N.W., Room 1148, Washington, DC 20570
Telephone: (202) 254-9372
Represented by:
Andrew Brinker, President

Nat'l Landscape Ass'n
1250 Eye St., N.W., Suite 500, Washington, DC 20005
Telephone: (202) 789-2900
Background: Exec. V. President is Lawrence E. Scovotto of the American Ass'n of Nurserymen.

Nat'l Latex Products Co.
Ashland, OH
Counsel or consultant:
Powell, Goldstein, Frazer and Murphy (Peter Suchman)

Nat'l Law Center on Homelessness and Poverty
1575 Eye St., N.W., Suite 1135, Washington, DC 20005
Telephone: (202) 289-1680
Represented by:
Maria Foscarinis, Director

Nat'l Law Enforcement Council
1140 Connecticut Ave., N.W. Suite 804, Washington, DC 20036
Telephone: (202) 223-6850
Counsel or consultant:
Donald Baldwin Associates (Donald Baldwin)

Nat'l Law Enforcement Officers' Memorial Fund
1360 Beverly Road Suite 305, Mclean, VA 22101
Telephone: (703) 827-0518
Counsel or consultant:
Kostmayer Communications, Inc. (Harry Frazier)
Sheehan Associates, Inc. (Annie C. Rhodes, John Thomas Sheehan)

Nat'l League of Cities
1301 Pennsylvania Ave., N.W., Washington, DC 20004
Telephone: (202) 626-3000
Background: Founded in 1924 and known until 1964 as the American Municipal Ass'n, the National League of Cities exists to represent the interests of its more than 1,300 member municipalities and 49 member state municipal leagues before the Federal Government.
Represented by:
Randolph Arndt, Media Relations Director
William Barnes, Research Director
Julio Barreto, Jr., Policy Analyst
Donald J. Borut, Exec. Director
William Davis, Director, Policy Analysis & Development
Donald Jones, Director of State Programs
John R. Joyner, Deputy Exec. Director
Carol Kocheisen, Legislative Counsel
John E. Kyle, Dir., Children & Families in Cities
Marvin A. McGraw, Legislative Counsel
Douglas D. Peterson, Senior Policy Analyst
Janet Quist, Legislative Counsel
Frank H. Shafroth, Director of Federal Relations
Leslie Wollack, Legislative Counsel
Nick Yaksich, Policy Analyst

Nat'l League of Families of American Prisoners and Missing in Southeast Asia
1001 Connecticut Ave., N.W. Suite 219, Washington, DC 20036
Telephone: (202) 223-6846
Background: Seeks to obtain the release of all prisoners, the fullest possible accounting for the missing and repatriation of the remains of those who died in Southeast Asia.
Represented by:
Ann Mills Griffiths, Exec. Director

Nat'l League of Postmasters of the U.S.
1023 North Royal St., Alexandria, VA 22314
Telephone: (703) 548-5922

The listings in this directory are available as *Mailing Labels*. See last page.

ORGANIZATIONS REPRESENTED

Nat'l League of Postmasters of the U.S. (Cont'd)
Represented by:
Ed Bowley, Legislative Consultant
Ron Swisher, President

Nat'l League of Postmasters Political Action Committee
1023 North Royal St., Alexandria, VA 22314
Telephone: (202) 548-5922
Represented by:
Richard A. Weinberg, Comptroller

Nat'l Learning Center, The
800 Third St., N.E., Washington, DC 20002
Telephone: (202) 543-8600
Counsel or consultant:
Chernikoff and Co. (Larry Chernikoff)

Nat'l Leased Housing Ass'n
2300 M St., N.W., Suite 260, Washington, DC 20037
Telephone: (202) 785-8888
Background: Represents more than 800 private and public organizations involved in government-related rental housing.
Represented by:
Denise Muha, Staff Director
Counsel or consultant:
Kelley, Drye and Warren (Charles L. Edson)

Nat'l Legal Aid and Defender Ass'n
1625 K St., N.W., Washington, DC 20006
Telephone: (202) 452-0620
Represented by:
Mary Broderick, Director, Defender Division
Julie Clark, Director, Government Relations
Clinton Lyons, Exec. Director

Nat'l Legal Center for the Public Interest
1000 16th St., N.W., Suite 301, Washington, DC 20036
Telephone: (202) 296-1683
Background: A Washington-based legal foundation, supportive of judicial restraint within the marketplace and within society generally. Established in 1975; thereafter created six independent regional conservative public interest law firms.
Represented by:
Terry H. Eastland, Resident Scholar
Ernest B. Hueter, President
Irene Jacoby, V. President, Administration

Nat'l Lesbian and Gay Health Foundation
1638 R St., N.W., Suite 2, Washington, DC 20009
Telephone: (202) 797-3708
Represented by:
William A. Scott, President of the Board

Nat'l Licensed Beverage Ass'n
4214 King St. West, Alexandria, VA 22302
Telephone: (703) 671-7575
Represented by:
Gerald E. Murphy, Exec. Director
Counsel or consultant:
Chwat/Weigend Associates (John S. Chwat, Robert E. Weigend)

Nat'l Licensed Beverage Ass'n Beverage Alcohol Retailer PAC
4214 King St., Alexandria, VA 22302-1507
Telephone: (703) 671-7575
Represented by:
Carolyn Moore, PAC Contact

Nat'l Lighting Bureau
2101 L St., N.W., Suite 300, Washington, DC 20037
Telephone: (202) 457-8437
Represented by:
Fred Nicholson, Exec. Director

Nat'l Lime Ass'n
3601 North Fairfax Drive, Arlington, VA 22201
Telephone: (703) 243-5463
Represented by:
Harry Francis, Technical Manager
Kenneth A. Gutschick, Technical Director
Thomas L. Potter, Exec. Director
Counsel or consultant:
Morgan, Lewis and Bockius (Eric V. Schaeffer)

Nat'l Liquor Stores Ass'n
5101 River Road Suite 108, Bethesda, MD 20816
Telephone: (301) 656-1494

Represented by:
John B. Burcham, Jr., Exec. Director

Nat'l Low Income Housing Coalition
1012 14th St., N.W. Suite 1500, Washington, DC 20005
Telephone: (202) 662-1530
Represented by:
Christine Harper-Fahey, Legislative Representative
Barry Zigas, President

Nat'l Lumber and Building Material Dealers Ass'n
40 Ivy St., S.E., Washington, DC 20003
Telephone: (202) 547-2230
Represented by:
Harlan Hummel, Exec. V. President
Counsel or consultant:
Mark Gallant

Nat'l Manufactured Housing Federation
1701 K St., N.W., Suite 400, Washington, DC 20006
Telephone: (202) 822-6470
Represented by:
Daniel Gilligan, President
Ann M. Parman, Director, Government Relations

Nat'l Manufactured Housing Federation Political Action Committee
1701 K St., N.W., Suite 400, Washington, DC 20006
Telephone: (202) 822-6470
Background: Assistant Treasurer and contact is Daniel Gilligan of the Federation.

Nat'l Manufactured Housing Finance Ass'n
1350 New York Ave., N.W., Suite 800, Washington, DC 20005
Telephone: (202) 628-2009
Represented by:
Lisa Noel, Government Relations Specialist
Counsel or consultant:
Weiner, McCaffrey, Brodsky, Kaplan & Levin

Nat'l Marine Manufacturers Ass'n
1000 Thomas Jefferson St, N.W. Suite 525, Washington, DC 20007
Telephone: (202) 338-6662
Represented by:
David W. Broome, V. President, Government Relations
John Dane, Manager, State Government Relations
Nancy Linden, Legislative Representative
Mary Mann, Legislative Representative
Counsel or consultant:
Patton, Boggs and Blow (James B. Christian, Jr.)

Nat'l Meat Canners Ass'n
Box 3556, Washington, DC 20007
Telephone: (703) 841-2400
Background: Represented by Dr. A. Dewey Bond of the American Meat Institute.

Nat'l Medical Ass'n
1012 10th St., N.W., Washington, DC 20001
Telephone: (202) 347-1895
Background: Composed primarily of black physicians.
Represented by:
William C. Garrett, Exec. V. President

Nat'l Medical Ass'n Political Action Committee
Box 56241 Brightwood Station, Washington, DC 20011
Telephone: (202) 347-1895
Represented by:
Lucius Earles, M.D., Chairman

Nat'l Medical Care, Inc.
Waltham, MA
Counsel or consultant:
McAuliffe, Kelly, Raffaelli & Siemens (Edward E. Allison)

Nat'l Medical Enterprises, Inc.
Santa Monica, CA
Counsel or consultant:
Cindy Williams Associates (Lucinda L. Williams)

Nat'l Mental Health Ass'n
1021 Prince St., Alexandria, VA 22314
Telephone: (703) 684-7722

Represented by:
John P. Ambrose, Sr. Director, Advocacy
Diane Baranik, Child and Adolescent Mental Health
Pat Franciosi, Nat'l President
Preston J. Garrison, Nat'l Exec. Director
Chris Koyanagi, Sr. Director, Government Affairs

Nat'l Military Intelligence Ass'n
Pentagon Station, Box 46583, Washington, DC 20050-6583
Telephone: (301) 840-6642
Background: Active and retired military and civilian intelligence personnel seeking to promote a stronger U. S. intelligence system through educational means.
Represented by:
Jack Morris, President
Counsel or consultant:
Real Trends (Zhi Marie Nye)

Nat'l Milk Producers Federation
1840 Wilson Blvd., Arlington, VA 22201
Telephone: (703) 243-6111
Background: A national association with membership composed of dairy cooperatives.
Represented by:
John Adams, Director, Milk Safety and Animal Health
James C. Barr, Chief Exec. Officer
Edward T. Coughlin, Director, Regulatory Affairs
Lisa Keller, Communications Specialist
Daniel Lauwers, Legislative Representative
James Mulhern, Director of Legislation
Peter Vitaliano, Director, Policy Analysis
Judy Ziewacz, Director of Member Services
Counsel or consultant:
Thomas J. Oden

Nat'l Minority AIDS Council
Telephone: (202) 544-1076
Represented by:
Mencer D. Edwards, Exec. Director

Nat'l Motor Freight Traffic Ass'n
2200 Mill Road, Alexandria, VA 22314
Telephone: (703) 838-1818
Represented by:
Martin Foley, Exec. Director

Nat'l Moving and Storage Ass'n
1500 North Beauregard St. Suite 320, Alexandria, VA 22311
Telephone: (703) 671-8813
Represented by:
Joyce McDowell, Director of Public Affairs
Gary Frank Petty, President and CEO
Counsel or consultant:
Arent, Fox, Kintner, Plotkin & Kahn (Gil Thurm)

Nat'l Moving and Storage Ass'n Political Action Committee
1500 N. Beauregard St., Alexandria, VA 22311
Telephone: (703) 671-8813
Background: Represented by Dr. Gary F. Petty, President of the Ass'n.

Nat'l Multi Housing Council
1250 Connecticut Ave., N.W., Suite 620, Washington, DC 20036
Telephone: (202) 659-3381
Background: A trade association for multi-family and condominium housing owners, developers, builders, financers, and management.
Represented by:
Jonathan L. Kempner, President
Rhond Rudolph Roth, V. President
Counsel or consultant:
Evans Group, Ltd., The (Thomas B. Evans, Jr., Susan Riley)
Powell, Goldstein, Frazer and Murphy (Lawrence B. Simons)

Nat'l Multi Housing Council Political Action Committee
1250 Connecticut Ave., N.W., Suite 620, Washington, DC 20036
Telephone: (202) 659-3381
Background: Contact is Jonathan L. Kempner, President of the Council.
Counsel or consultant:
Powell, Goldstein, Frazer and Murphy (Lawrence B. Simons)

The listings in this directory are available as *Mailing Labels*. See last page.

ORGANIZATIONS REPRESENTED

Nat'l Multiple Sclerosis Soc.
New York, NY
Counsel or consultant:
Capitol Associates, Inc. (Debra M. Hardy-Havens, Terry Lierman)
White, Fine, and Verville (Richard E. Verville)

Nat'l Museum of Women in the Arts
1250 New York Ave., N.W., Washington, DC 20005
Telephone: (202) 783-5000
Counsel or consultant:
Chernikoff and Co. (Larry Chernikoff)

Nat'l Music Publishers' Ass'n
New York, NY
Counsel or consultant:
Griffin, Johnson & Associates
Paul, Weiss, Rifkind, Wharton and Garrison (Lionel H. Olmer)
John R. Zagame Associates (John R. Zagame)

Nat'l Neighborhood Coalition
810 First St., N.E. 3rd Floor, Washington, DC 20002
Telephone: (202) 289-1551
Background: A membership association of nonprofit organizations working with inner-city groups. Serves as a clearinghouse on federal programs and national public policies.
Represented by:
Bud Kanitz, Exec. Director

Nat'l Network of Runaway and Youth Services
1400 Eye St., N.W., Suite 330, Washington, DC 20005
Telephone: (202) 682-4114
Represented by:
Della Hughes, Exec. Director
Nexus Nichols, Policy Associate

Nat'l Network to Prevent Birth Defects
Box 15309 Southeast Station, Washington, DC 20003
Telephone: (202) 543-5450
Represented by:
Erik T. Jansson, Coordinator

Nat'l Newspaper Ass'n
1627 K St., N.W. Suite 400, Washington, DC 20006
Telephone: (202) 466-7200
Represented by:
Robert J. Brinkmann, General Counsel
Teena M. Harris, Goverment Relations Legislative Ass't
David C. Simonson, Exec. V. President

Nat'l Newspaper Publishers Ass'n
948 National Press Building, Washington, DC 20045
Telephone: (202) 662-7324
Represented by:
Steve G. Davis, Exec. Director

Nat'l Nutrition Coalition
1050 Thomas Jefferson St, N.W. Sixth Floor, Washington, DC 20007
Telephone: (202) 298-1800
Counsel or consultant:
Arent, Fox, Kintner, Plotkin & Kahn (Burton V. Wides)
Van Ness, Feldman & Curtis (Robert G. Szabo)

Nat'l Ocean Industries Ass'n
1050 17th St., N.W. Suite 700, Washington, DC 20036
Telephone: (202) 785-5116
Background: Oil and gas companies, their suppliers and supporting firms, exploring and drilling in the outer continental shelf. Other companies engaged in fishing, shipbuilding, deep sea mining and other developers or users of ocean resources.
Represented by:
William P. DuBose, IV, Government Affairs Representative
Charles D. Matthews, President
Sarah J. Pratt, Government Affairs Representative
Robert B. Stewart, V. President

Nat'l Ocean Industries Ass'n Political Action Committee
1050 17th St., N.W. Suite 700, Washington, DC 20036
Telephone: (202) 785-5116
Background: Sponsored by the Nat'l Ocean Industries Ass'n. Represented by Robert B. Stewart, Charles D. Matthews and William P. DuBose, IV, all of the Association.

Nat'l Office Products Ass'n
301 North Fairfax St., Alexandria, VA 22314

Telephone: (703) 549-9040
Represented by:
Jerry Davis, Senior V. President
Donald P. Haspel, Exec. V. President
Bruce McLellan, Director of Government Relations
Counsel or consultant:
Colton and Boykin (Hamilton Boykin)

Nat'l Office Products Ass'n Political Action Committee
301 North Fairfax St., Alexandria, VA 22314
Telephone: (703) 549-9040
Background: Donald P. Haspel, of the Nat'l Office Products Ass'n, serves as contact for the PAC.

Nat'l Officers Ass'n
1304 Vincent Place, McLean, VA 22101
Telephone: (703) 821-0555
Background: Supports active duty (15%), retired (80%) military officers and widows/former spouses (5%).
Represented by:
Bruce Pifel, Director Member Services

Nat'l Oilseed Processors Ass'n
1255 23rd St., N.W., Washington, DC 20037
Telephone: (202) 452-8040
Counsel or consultant:
Hauck and Associates (Sheldon J. Hauck, Brose A. McVey)
Steptoe and Johnson (Kevin J. Brosch)

Nat'l Order of Women Legislators
727 15th St., N.W. Suite 1200, Washington, DC 20005
Telephone: (202) 347-0044
Counsel or consultant:
Sheehan Associates, Inc. (Annie C. Rhodes, John Thomas Sheehan)

Nat'l Organization Against Invisible Disease Spread
Telephone: (202) 462-8640
Represented by:
Joseph B. Fallon, President

Nat'l Organization for Competency Assurance
1101 Connecticut Ave., N.W., Suite 700, Washington, DC 20036
Telephone: (202) 857-1100
Counsel or consultant:
Smith, Bucklin and Associates (Michael Hamm)

Nat'l Organization for the Reform of Marijuana Laws
2001 S St., N.W., Suite 640, Washington, DC 20009
Telephone: (202) 483-5500
Background: A non-profit educational organization concerned with marijuana, the laws governing its use, and their effect on our society.
Represented by:
Donald B. Fiedler, National Director

Nat'l Organization for Victim Assistance
1757 Park Road, N.W., Washington, DC 20010
Telephone: (202) 232-6682
Represented by:
John Hollister Stein, Deputy Director
Marlene Young, Exec. Director

Nat'l Organization for Women
1000 16th St., N.W., Suite 700, Washington, DC 20036
Telephone: (202) 331-0066
Background: Seeks to insure the equal status and full participation of women in society.
Represented by:
Diane Sredl, Legislative Aide
Molly Yard, President
Counsel or consultant:
Cynthia Friedman Assoc. Inc. (Cynthia Friedman)

Nat'l Organization for Women Political Action Committee (NOW Equality PAC)
1401 New York Ave., N.W., Suite 800, Washington, DC 20005
Telephone: (202) 347-2279
Background: A political action committee organized by the Nat'l Organization for Women in support of feminist issues and candidates. Contact is Barbara Hays-Hamilton (see Nat'l Organization for Women.)

Nat'l Organization of Black Law Enforcement Executives
908 Pennsylvania Ave., S.E., Washington, DC 20003
Telephone: (202) 546-8811
Represented by:
Arlene Williams, Communications Director

Nat'l Organization on Disability
910 16th St., N.W., Suite 600, Washington, DC 20006
Telephone: (202) 293-5960
Represented by:
Mark Lewis, Director of Communications
Alan A. Reich, President

Nat'l Organization to Insure a Sound-Controlled Environment-N.O.I.S.E.
1620 Eye St., N.W., Suite 300, Washington, DC 20006
Telephone: (202) 429-0166
Background: An organization of municipalities, local and regional organizations and citizen groups working to control and reduce aviation noise, focusing on the aircraft itself and on traffic practices at airports.
Counsel or consultant:
Nat'l Center for Municipal Development (Thomas N. Duffy)

Nat'l ORT Project
2626 Pennsylvania Ave., N.W. Suite 201, Washington, DC 20037
Telephone: (202) 338-8700
Counsel or consultant:
Greer, Margolis, Mitchell & Associates

Nat'l Paint and Coatings Ass'n
1500 Rhode Island Ave., N.W., Washington, DC 20005
Telephone: (202) 462-6272
Represented by:
Robert Cunningham, Senior Counsel
J. Andrew Doyle, Exec. Director
Thomas J. Graves, Director Federal Affairs
Bruce Hamill, General Counsel
David Lloyd, Director, State Affairs
Stephen R. Sides, Director, Health and Safety
Counsel or consultant:
Richard W. Bliss
McGuire, Woods, Battle and Boothe (Robert H. Lamb)
Valis Associates (Wayne H. Valis)

Nat'l Park Foundation
P.O. Box 57473, Washington, DC 20037
Telephone: (202) 785-4500
Background: Chartered by Congress in 1967 as a private, nonprofit, philanthropic organization which seeks financial support and other assistance from the private sector for National Park Service activities.
Represented by:
Mary D. Hewes, Director of Projects
Alan A. Rubin, President

Nat'l Parking Ass'n
1112 16th St., N.W., Suite 300, Washington, DC 20036
Telephone: (202) 296-4336
Represented by:
George V. Dragotta, Exec. V. President
Counsel or consultant:
Arent, Fox, Kintner, Plotkin & Kahn (Michael J. Kurman, Allen G. Siegel)

Nat'l Parking Ass'n Political Action Committee
1112 16th St., N.W. Suite 2000, Washington, DC 20036
Telephone: (202) 296-4336
Background: Represented by George V. Dragotta, Exec. Director of the Association.

Nat'l Parks and Conservation Ass'n
1015 31st St., N.W., Washington, DC 20007
Telephone: (202) 944-8530
Background: A non-profit organization whose primary responsibility is protecting the national parks and monuments.
Represented by:
Bruce Craig, Coordinator, Cultural Resources
Elizabeth Fayad, Park Threats Coordinator
William C. Lienesch, Director, Federal Activities
Paul C. Pritchard, President
David J. Simon, Coordinator, Parks Preservation

Nat'l Particleboard Ass'n
18928 Premiere Court, Gaithersburg, MD 20879
Telephone: (301) 670-0604

ORGANIZATIONS REPRESENTED

Nat'l Particleboard Ass'n (Cont'd)
Represented by:
 William H. McCredie, Exec. V. President
Counsel or consultant:
 Keck, Mahin and Cate (Brock R. Landry)

Nat'l Pasta Ass'n
2101 Wilson Blvd. Suite 920, Arlington, VA 22201
Telephone: (703) 841-0818
Represented by:
 Jula J. Kinnaird, V. President, Communications
 Joseph M. Lichtenberg, President
Counsel or consultant:
 Collier, Shannon & Scott
 Fleishman-Hillard, Inc
 Hogan and Hartson (Gary J. Kushner)

Nat'l Patent Council
2121 Crystal Dr., 2 Crystal Pk Suite 704, Arlington, VA 22202
Telephone: (703) 521-1669
Represented by:
 Eric P. Schellin, Exec. V. President

Nat'l Peace Institute Foundation
110 Maryland Ave., N.E., Suite 409, Washington, DC 20002
Telephone: (202) 546-9500
Represented by:
 Kathleen Lansing, Communication Director
 Stephen P. Strickland, President

Nat'l Peanut Council
1500 King St., Suite 301, Alexandria, VA 22314-2730
Telephone: (703) 838-9500
Represented by:
 Jeannette Anderson, Internat'l Marketing Director
 C. Edward Ashdown, President
 Kimberly Cutchins, Director of Industry Services
Counsel or consultant:
 Tendler, Goldberg & Biggins, Chtd. (James M. Goldberg)

Nat'l Peanut Growers Group
Gorman, TX
Counsel or consultant:
 Meyers & Associates (Larry D. Meyers)

Nat'l Perinatal Ass'n
101 1/2 South Union St., Alexandria, VA 22314-3323
Telephone: (703) 549-5523
Represented by:
 Dr. Robert Cicco, Legislative Chairperson
 Sandra Butler Whyte, Exec. Director

Nat'l Pest Control Ass'n
8100 Oak St., Dunn Loring, VA 22027
Telephone: (703) 573-8330
Represented by:
 Harvey S. Gold, Exec. V. President
 A. Jack Grimes, Director of Government Affairs
 Joel M. Paul, Director, Communications
 Robert Rosenberg, Manager, State Government Affairs

Nat'l Petroleum Council
1625 K St., N.W., Suite 600, Washington, DC 20006
Telephone: (202) 393-6100
Represented by:
 John H. Guy, IV, Deputy Exec. Director
 Marshall W. Nichols, Exec. Director

Nat'l Petroleum Refiners Ass'n
1899 L St., N.W., Suite 1000, Washington, DC 20036
Telephone: (202) 457-0480
Represented by:
 Herbert W. Bruch, Technical Director
 Robert L. Dziuban, Director, Convention Services
 Terrence S. Higgins, Assistant Technical Director
 Maurice H. McBride, Attorney
 E. Lloyd Powers, Petrochemical Director
 Urvan R. Sternfels, President
 Pat R. Wrigley, Director, Administration

Nat'l Pharmaceutical Alliance
1730 Pennsylvania Ave., N.W., Suite 1200, Washington, DC 20006
Telephone: (202) 737-0500
Counsel or consultant:
 King and Spalding (Eugene M. Pfeifer)

Nat'l Pharmaceutical Alliance Political Action Committee
1730 Pennsylvania Ave., N.W., Suite 1200, Washington, DC 20006
Telephone: (202) 737-0500
Counsel or consultant:
 King and Spalding

Nat'l Pharmaceutical Ass'n
Box 934, Howard University, Washington, DC 20059
Telephone: (202) 328-9229
Represented by:
 James N. Tyson, Exec. Director

Nat'l Pharmaceutical Council
1894 Preston White Drive, Reston, VA 22091
Telephone: (703) 620-6390
Represented by:
 Mark R. Knowles, President
 Didge Pearson, Director of State Affairs

Nat'l Planning Ass'n
1424 16th St., N.W. Suite 700, Washington, DC 20036
Telephone: (202) 265-7685
Background: A non-profit, non-partisan research organization which brings together key private sector leaders representing business, labor, agriculture and the professions.
Represented by:
 James A. Auerbach, V. President
 Richard S. Belous, V. President, Internat'l Affairs
 Edward E. Masters, President
 Nestor E. Terleckyj, V. President

Nat'l Political Action Committee, The
555 New Jersey Ave., N.W., Suite 718, Washington, DC 20000
Background: A pro-Israel political action organization.
Represented by:
 Richard H. Altman, Exec. Director
 Marvin Josephson, Treasurer

Nat'l Pork Board
501 School St., S.W. Suite 400, Washington, DC 20024
Telephone: (202) 554-3601
Background: Responsible for the collection and disbursement of funds generated by pork producers.
Represented by:
 James L. Smith, Director of Market Relations

Nat'l Pork Producers Council
501 School St., N.W. Suite 400, Washington, DC 20024
Telephone: (202) 552-3600
Represented by:
 Karen Coble, Director of Washington Communications
 Dr. Frank Mulhern, Consultant, Scientific and Gov't Affairs
 Richard E. Pasco, V. President, Government Affairs
 Nancy Thomas, Office Manager
Counsel or consultant:
 Thompson, Hine and Flory (Mark Roy Sandstrom)

Nat'l Postal Mail Handlers Union
One Thomas Circle, N.W. Suite 525, Washington, DC 20005
Telephone: (202) 833-9095
Represented by:
 Glenn Berrien, President
 Howard Linett, Staff Counsel
 Joseph Thomas Sella, Legislative Director
 Marion Wright, Nat'l Secretary-Treasurer

Nat'l Postal Mail Handlers Union 'Mail Handlers PAC'
One Thomas Circle, N.W. Suite 525, Washington, DC 20005
Telephone: (202) 833-9095
Background: Chairman is Joseph Sella of the Nat'l Postal Mail Handlers Union.

Nat'l Potato Council
Englewood, CO
Counsel or consultant:
 McDermott, Will and Emery (Edward Ruckert)

Nat'l Press Foundation
National Press Bldg. Suite 1282, Washington, DC 20045
Telephone: (202) 662-7350
Background: Established in 1975 by former presidents of the National Press Club. Provides grants, awards, and fellowships to journalists, sponsors forums for policy-makers and the public, and underwrites operations of the H.L.

Mencken Library in Washington.
Represented by:
 Denise Slaughter, Assistant to the President
 David Yount, President

Nat'l Printing Equipment and Supply Ass'n
1899 Preston White Drive, Reston, VA 22091
Telephone: (703) 264-7200
Represented by:
 Regis J. Delmontagne, President
 Carol J. Hurlburt, Director of Communications
 Mark J. Nuzzaco, Director of Government Affairs

Nat'l Prison Project
1616 P St., N.W. Suite 340, Washington, DC 20036
Telephone: (202) 331-0500
Background: A project of the American Civil Liberties Union Foundation. Seeks to broaden prisoners' rights, improve overall prison conditions and develop alternatives to incarceration.
Represented by:
 Alvin J. Bronstein, Exec. Director
 Edward Koren, Staff Attorney

Nat'l Private Truck Council
1320 Braddock Place Suite 720, Alexandria, VA 22314
Telephone: (703) 683-1300
Background: An association of companies which ship their products with their own truck fleets.
Represented by:
 Gene S. Bergoffen, Exec. V. President
 Earl B. Eisenhart, V. President, Government Affairs
 Robert A. Hirsch, General Counsel/Dir. of Regulatory Afrs.
Counsel or consultant:
 Preston Gates Ellis & Rouvelas Meeds (John A. DeVierno)

Nat'l Pro-Family Coalition
717 Second St., N.E., Washington, DC 20002
Telephone: (202) 546-3003
Background: Chairman is Eric Licht (see Coalitions for America).

Nat'l Propane Gas Ass'n
1235 Jefferson Davis Hwy., Suite 702, Arlington, VA 22202
Telephone: (703) 979-3560
Background: Formerly (1989) Nat'l LP-Gas Ass'n.
Represented by:
 Lisa Bontempo, Manager, Federal Affairs
 James N. Burroughs, V. Pres., Gov't Relations & Gen. Counsel

Nat'l Public Law Training Center
1441 E. Capitol St., S.E., Washington, DC 20003
Telephone: (202) 544-0180
Background: A non-profit center offering courses in law and community organizing skills to staff of social service agencies.
Represented by:
 William R. Fry, President

Nat'l Public Radio
2025 M St., N.W., Washington, DC 20036
Telephone: (202) 822-2000
Background: A private, non-profit corporation established in 1969 to provide programming and representation for its member non-commercial radio stations. The Ass'n of Public Radio Stations and Nat'l Public Radio voted to merge under the name Nat'l Public Radio in 1977.
Represented by:
 Douglas J. Bennet, President
 Karen Christensen, Assistant General Counsel
 Mary Lou Joseph, Director, National Affairs

Nat'l Puerto Rican Coalition
1700 K St., N.W., Suite 500, Washington, DC 20006
Telephone: (703) 223-3915
Background: Organized in 1977, the Coalition began project operations in 1980. Includes the Nat'l Puerto Rican Forum, the Puerto Rican Legal Defense and Education Fund and more than 90 other educational, religious and social organizations of Puerto Ricans in the United States.
Represented by:
 Ramon Daubon, V. President
 Louis Nunez, President

Nat'l Puerto Rican Forum
1511 K St., N.W., Suite 600, Washington, DC 20005

The listings in this directory are available as *Mailing Labels*. See last page.

ORGANIZATIONS REPRESENTED

Telephone: (202) 638-2211
Background: A community-based social service organization seeking to improve the social and economic status of mainland Puerto Ricans through job training and placement, counseling, English language and high school equivalency instruction and advocacy.
Represented by:
Gloria Rodriquez, Washington Representative

Nat'l Railway Labor Conference
1901 L St., N.W. Suite 500, Washington, DC 20036
Telephone: (202) 862-7200
Represented by:
Charles I. Hopkins, Jr., Chairman

Nat'l Ready Mixed Concrete Ass'n
900 Spring St., Silver Spring, MD 20910
Telephone: (301) 587-1400
Background: Government relations handled by Richard A. Morris, V. President of Government Relations and Public Affairs and Kenneth R. Tobin, V. President of Government Relations and National Affairs.
Represented by:
Vincent P. Ahearn, Jr., President

Nat'l Ready Mixed Concrete Ass'n Political Action Committee
900 Spring St., Silver Spring, MD 20910
Telephone: (301) 587-1400
Background: Contact is Kenneth R. Tobin, V. President of Government Relations and National Affairs of the Association.

Nat'l Realty Committee
1250 Connecticut Ave., N.W. Suite 630, Washington, DC 20036
Telephone: (202) 785-0808
Background: Established in 1969, the NRC represents all facets of income-producing real estate -- development, ownership and finance. NRC addresses nat'l issues of concern to its members including federal tax policy, environmental and land use policy, and capitol flow issues.
Represented by:
Susan A. Orban, V. President
Lynda K. Walker, Counsel
Steven A. Wechsler, President
Counsel or consultant:
Hill and Knowlton Public Affairs Worldwide (Dr. Ira P. Kaminow)
Tucker, Flyer, Sanger & Lewis (Stefan F. Tucker)

Nat'l Realty Political Action Committee (REAL-PAC)
1250 Connecticut Ave., N.W. Suite 630, Washington, DC 20036
Telephone: (202) 785-0808
Background: The political action arm of the National Realty Committee. Treasurer is Steven A. Wechsler and Assistant Treasurer is Susan A. Orban, President and V. President respectively, of the Nat'l Realty Committee.
Counsel or consultant:
Williams and Jensen, P.C. (June E. Edmondson)

Nat'l Recreation and Park Ass'n
3101 Park Center Drive, Alexandria, VA 22302
Telephone: (703) 820-4940
Represented by:
Christine M. Cullinan, Associate for Public Policy
Laurie Kusak, Communication
R. Dean Tice, Exec. Director
Barry Tindall, Director, Public Affairs

Nat'l Refrigerants, Inc.
Plymouth Meeting, PA
Counsel or consultant:
Vinson and Elkins (James C. Gould)

Nat'l Registry in Clinical Chemistry
1155 16th St., N.W., Washington, DC 20036
Telephone: (202) 745-1698
Represented by:
Donald G. Vorhis, Exec. Director

Nat'l Rehabilitation Ass'n
633 S. Washington St., Alexandria, VA 22314
Telephone: (703) 836-0850
Represented by:
Robert E. Brabham, Ph.D., Exec. Director
Counsel or consultant:
Duncan and Associates

Nat'l Rehabilitation Information Center
8455 Colesville Rd., #935, Silver Spring, MD 20910
Telephone: (301) 588-9284
Represented by:
Mark Odum, Project Director

Nat'l Rehabilitation Political Action Committee
1213 29th St., N.W., Washington, DC 20007
Telephone: (202) 333-5841
Counsel or consultant:
Duncan and Associates

Nat'l Renal Administrators Ass'n
Orlando, FL
Counsel or consultant:
Capitol Associates, Inc. (Gwen Gampel)

Nat'l Republican Congressional Committee
320 First St., S.E., Washington, DC 20003
Telephone: (202) 479-7000
Represented by:
Bill Anderson, PAC Director
John G. Maddox, Campaign Director
Teresa L. McFillen, Deputy PAC Director
R. Marc Nuttle, Exec. Director
Edward J. Rollins, Co-Chairman
Counsel or consultant:
Stockmeyer & Co. (Steven F. Stockmeyer)
Wiley, Rein & Fielding (Jan Baran)

Nat'l Republican Heritage Groups Council
310 First St., S.E., Washington, DC 20003
Telephone: (202) 662-1345
Represented by:
Elena Jurgela, Exec. Director

Nat'l Republican Institute for Internat'l Affairs
601 Indiana Ave., N.W., Washington, DC 20004
Telephone: (202) 783-2280
Represented by:
Robert E. Henderson, V. President
Counsel or consultant:
Montgomery, McCracken, Walker & Rhoads (David F. Norcross)

Nat'l Republican Senatorial Committee
425 Second St., N.E., Washington, DC 20002
Telephone: (202) 675-6000
Represented by:
Doyce Boesch, Exec. Director
Steve Bull, PAC and Business Development Director
William B. Canfield, Legal Counsel
Ellen Conaway, Deputy Exec. Director
Wendy M. DeMocker, Communications Director
Al Mitchler, Finance Director
Rick Shelby, Political Director
Counsel or consultant:
Wiley, Rein & Fielding (Jan Baran)

Nat'l Resource Center for Consumers of Legal Services
1444 Eye St., N.W., Eighth Floor, Washington, DC 20005
Telephone: (202) 842-3503
Background: A public interest group which serves as a national clearinghouse for consumer groups, labor unions, and other groups interested in legal service plans.
Represented by:
William A. Bolger, Exec. Director

Nat'l Restaurant Ass'n
1200 17th St., N.W., Washington, DC 20036-3097
Telephone: (202) 331-5900
Represented by:
Colette Coleman, Director, State Relations
William P. Fisher, Exec. V. President
Mark S. Gorman, Senior Director, Government Affairs
Elaine Graham, Director, Federal Relations
Michael E. Hurst, President and Chairman of the Board
Richard C. Johnson, General Counsel
Jeffrey Prince, Senior Director, Communications
Shannon B. Tuel, Legislative Representative
Counsel or consultant:
Gold and Liebengood, Inc. (Charles L. Merin)
Stateside Associates

Nat'l Restaurant Ass'n Political Action Committee
1200 Seventh St., N.W., Washington, DC 20036
Telephone: (202) 638-6100

Represented by:
Tom Wolfe, Manager

Nat'l Retail Hardware Ass'n
Indianapolis, IN
Counsel or consultant:
O'Connor & Hannan (Timothy M. Haake)

Nat'l Retail Merchants Ass'n
1000 Connecticut Ave., N.W., Washington, DC 20036
Telephone: (202) 223-8250
Background: Will be merging with the American Retail Federation to form the Nat'l Retail Federation.
Represented by:
Michael J. Altier, V. President & Legislative Counsel
Tracy Mullin, Exec. V. President, Governmental Affair
Steven J. Pfister, Director, Political Affairs

Nat'l Retail Merchants Ass'n Political Action Committee
1000 Connecticut Ave., N.W., Suite 700, Washington, DC 20036
Telephone: (202) 223-8250
Background: Represented by Tracy Mullin of the Association.

Nat'l Rifle Ass'n of America
1600 Rhode Island Ave., N.W., Washington, DC 20036
Telephone: (202) 828-6000
Represented by:
James Jay Baker, Director, Federal Affairs Division
William B. Binswanger, Treasurer
J. Warren Cassidy, Exec. V. President
Warren L. Cheek, Secretary
David W. Conover, Federal Liaison
Mary Marcotte Corrigan, Dir., Research and Information, ILA
Charles H. Cunningham, State Liaison, Inst. for Legis. Action
Joe Foss, President
Richard Gardiner, Director, State & Local Affairs Division
Mary K. Jolly, Federal Liaison
Wayne R. LaPierre, Jr., Exec. Dir., Inst. For Legis. Action
Anthony V. Madda, Ass't Director, Field Services Division
Michael K. McCabe, General Counsel
Terri O'Grady, Political Affairs Liaison
Counsel or consultant:
Reed Smith Shaw & McClay (Carl Rowan, Jr.)
Timmons and Co., Inc.

Nat'l Rifle Ass'n Political Victory Fund
1600 Rhode Island Ave., N.W., Washington, DC 20036
Telephone: (202) 828-6353
Background: A political action committee sponsored by the Nat'l Rifle Ass'n. Political Director is Wayne R. LaPierre, Jr. of the NRA.

Nat'l Right to Life Committee
419 7th St., N.W. Suite 500, Washington, DC 20004
Telephone: (202) 626-8820
Background: Opposes abortion, infanticide and euthanasia.
Represented by:
Douglas Johnson, Legislative Director
David N. O'Steen, Ph.D., Exec. Director
Susan A. Smith, Associate Legislative Director
John C. Willke, M.D., President

Nat'l Right to Life Political Action Committee
419 7th St., N.W. Suite 500, Washington, DC 20004
Telephone: (202) 626-8820
Background: Contact is David O'Steen of Nat'l Right to Life.

Nat'l Right to Work Committee
8001 Braddock Road, Springfield, VA 22160
Telephone: (703) 321-9820
Background: Established in 1955, NRWC is a single-purpose interest group opposing compulsory union membership. Claims approximately 1.7 million supporters and a budget of about $5 million used in a nationwide educational program in behalf of the open shop.

The listings in this directory are available as *Mailing Labels*. See last page.

ORGANIZATIONS REPRESENTED

Nat'l Right to Work Committee (Cont'd)
Represented by:
Karl Gallant, V.P. & Director, Federal Legislation
Steven C. Kerekes, Director, Public Relations
Reed E. Larson, President
Martin Mayfield, Legislative Assistant
Brooke W. McLeod, Media Relations Specialist
Counsel or consultant:
Webster, Chamberlain and Bean (George D. Webster)

Nat'l Right to Work Legal Defense Foundation
8001 Braddock Road, Springfield, VA 22160
Telephone: (703) 321-9820
Background: "Defending America's working men and women against the injustices of compulsory unionism." Works through the courts, providing free legal aid to employees opposing closed shop abuses and other forms of forced union participation. President is Reed E. Larson.
Represented by:
Edith Hakola, V. President and General Counsel
Rex H. Reed, Exec. V. Pres., Secy. and Legal Dir.

Nat'l Roofing Contractors Ass'n
206 E St., N.E., Washington, DC 20002
Telephone: (202) 546-7584
Represented by:
Craig S. Brightup, Director of Government Relations

Nat'l Rural Development and Finance Corp.
1818 N St., N.W., Suite 410, Washington, DC 20036
Telephone: (202) 429-9017
Represented by:
Neal W. Nathanson, President and Chief Executive Officer

Nat'l Rural Electric Cooperative Ass'n
1800 Massachusetts Ave., N.W., Washington, DC 20036
Telephone: (202) 857-9500
Represented by:
Fred D. Clark, Jr., Legislative Representative - Agriculture
Robert W. Cromartie, Legislative Representative
Rae E. Cronmiller, Environmental Counsel
Robert M. Dawson, Manager, Legis. Research and Information
Morgan D. Dubrow, Chief Engineer
Arthur W. Hartmann, Government Policy Specialist
Dan Kamerman, Community and Econ. Devel't Specialist
Joan F. Keiser, Legislative Representative
Bradley R. Koch, Dir., Energy and Environmental Policy
Richard Larochelle, Legislative Representative
Daniel Lismez, Legislative Representative
Robert W. Lively, Legislative Representative
Meredith McCoy, Staff Counsel
John Neal, Mgr. of Energy Research and Development
Robert W. Nelson, Director, Public & Ass'n Affairs Dept.
Michael D. Oldak, Regulatory Counsel
Mattie Olson, Director, Public Relations
Clifford Ouse, Senior Legislative Representative
Roy Palk, Exec. Director, Operations
Stephan Petry, Legislative Representative
Wallace Rustad, Director, Government Relations Dept.
Richard W. Sternberg, Fuels Coordinator
Wallace F. Tillman, Chief Regulatory Counsel
Carolyn Herr Watts, Legislative Representative
Counsel or consultant:
Piper and Marbury (Charles C. Abeles)

Nat'l Rural Health Ass'n
Kansas City, MO
Counsel or consultant:
Rapoza Associates, Robert A. (Sherry F. Kaiman)

Nat'l Rural Housing Coalition
122 C St., N.W., Washington, DC 20001
Telephone: (202) 393-5229
Background: A non-profit membership organization that works to improve housing conditions and community facilities for people in small towns and rural areas.
Represented by:
Robert Marshall, Chairman
Robert A. Ropoza, Exec. Secretary/Legislative Director

Nat'l Rural Letter Carriers' Ass'n
1448 Duke St., Alexandria, VA 22314
Telephone: (703) 684-5545

Represented by:
William R. Brown, V. President
Scottie B. Hicks, Secretary-Treasurer
Vernon H. Meier, President
Ken Parmelee, V. President of Governmental Affairs
Wanda Van Meter, Secretary-Treasurer
Counsel or consultant:
Lipsen Whitten & Diamond

Nat'l Rural Letter Carriers' Ass'n Political Action Committee
1448 Duke St., Alexandria, VA 22314
Telephone: (703) 684-5545
Background: Treasurer and representative is Wanda Van Meter of the Nat'l Rural Letter Carriers' Ass'n.

Nat'l Rural Telecom Ass'n
Blair, NE
Counsel or consultant:
John F. O'Neal Law Offices (John F. O'Neal)

Nat'l Rural Water Ass'n
Duncan, OK
Counsel or consultant:
Barrett, Montgomery & Murphy (John H. Montgomery)

Nat'l SAFE KIDS Campaign, Children's Hospital Nat'l Medical Center, The
111 Michigan Ave., N.W., Washington, DC 20010
Telephone: (202) 939-4993
Represented by:
Bill Kamela, Public Policy Director

Nat'l Safety Council
1050 17th St., N.W. Suite 770, Washington, DC 20036
Telephone: (202) 293-2270
Background: A non-profit, non-governmental public service organization formed in 1913 and federally chartered by the U.S. Congress in 1953. Works to prevent accidents and occupational illness, to arouse and maintain interest in prevention, and to encourage the adoption and implementation of safety and health methods for all types of individuals and organizations.
Represented by:
Jane Roemer, Exec. Director, Public Policy
Morris Ward, Bud, Exec. Director, Environmental Health Ctr
Counsel or consultant:
Harry N. Rosenfield

Nat'l School Boards Ass'n
1680 Duke St., Alexandria, VA 22314
Telephone: (703) 838-6722
Background: Represents the nation's 97,000 local school board members who determine policy for the more than 15,300 public school districts.
Represented by:
Don Blom, Assoc. Exec. Director, Program Services
David Byer, Exec. Branch Advocate, Federal Relations
Michael Eader, Associate Exec. Director
Jeremiah Floyd, Assoc. Exec. Director, Public Relations
Lynne Glassman, Director, Network Operations
Gwendolyn H. Gregory, Deputy General Counsel
Catharine Herber, Legislative Counsel
Edward Kealy, Director, Federal Programs
Susan P. Merry, Assoc. Exec. Director & Controller
Michael A. Resnick, Assoc. Exec. Director, Federal Relations
Harold P. Seamon, Deputy Exec. Director
Thomas A. Shannon, Exec. Director
Philip A. Smith, Director of Communications
Dottie Stambaugh, Legislative Assistant
August W. Steinhilber, Assoc. Exec. Director & General Counsel
Counsel or consultant:
Manning, Selvage & Lee/Washington

Nat'l School Health Education Coalition
New York, NY
Counsel or consultant:
Peyser Associates, Inc. (Peter A. Peyser, Jr.)

Nat'l School Public Relations Ass'n
1501 Lee Hwy. Suite 201, Arlington, VA 22209
Telephone: (703) 528-5840
Represented by:
Dr. Joseph J. Scherer, Exec. Director

Nat'l School Supply and Equipment Ass'n
2020 North 14th St., Arlington, VA 22201

Telephone: (703) 524-8819
Represented by:
Timothy Holt, Exec. V. President
Adrian Watts, Director of Marketing and Communications

Nat'l School Transportation Ass'n
Box 2639, Springfield, VA 22152
Telephone: (703) 644-0700
Background: Fosters safe and efficient school bus transportation and education of its members in pupil transportation matters.
Represented by:
Karen E. Finkel, Exec. Director
Counsel or consultant:
Gold and Liebengood, Inc. (Charles L. Merin, Peter B. Slone)

Nat'l Science Teachers Ass'n
1742 Connecticut Ave., N.W., Washington, DC 20009
Telephone: (202) 328-5800
Represented by:
Bill G. Aldridge, Exec. Director

Nat'l Second Mortgage Ass'n
Rancho Cucamonga, CA
Counsel or consultant:
Perkinson & Associates, Inc. (Michael J. Bertelsen, Gary J. Perkinson)

Nat'l Security Archive
1755 Massachusetts Ave., N.W. Suite 500, Washington, DC 22036
Telephone: (202) 797-0882
Background: A not-for-profit library, publisher and research organization. Maintains an archive of documents dealing with U.S. Government policy on foreign affairs, national security, and the Freedom of Infromation Act.
Represented by:
Thomas Blanton, Deputy Director

Nat'l Security Industrial Ass'n
1025 Connecticut Ave., N.W., Suite 300, Washington, DC 20036
Telephone: (202) 775-1440
Represented by:
Col. Arlan F. Bond, USA (Ret.), Vice President
Philip J. Cole, Director of Nat'l Activities
George W. Ogles, Dir., Public Relations and Membership
Lt. Gen. Wallace H. Robinson, Jr., President
Susan Tonner, Legislative to the President

Nat'l Security Political Action Committee
Washington Harbor West 3050 K St., N.W., Suite 310, Washington, DC 20007
Telephone: (202) 363-9472
Represented by:
Elizabeth I. Fediay, Exec. Director
Counsel or consultant:
Wunder, Ryan, Cannon & Thelen (Paul E. Sullivan)

Nat'l Semiconductor Corp.
Santa Clara, CA
Counsel or consultant:
Pillsbury, Madison and Sutro (Donald E. deKieffer)

Nat'l Senior Citizens Law Center
2025 M St., N.W. Suite 400, Washington, DC 20036
Telephone: (202) 887-5280
Background: Provides expert representation before agencies of government and the courts on behalf of the elderly poor.
Represented by:
Burton D. Fretz, Exec. Director

Nat'l Senior Sports Ass'n
10560 Main St., Suite 205, Fairfax, VA 22030
Telephone: (703) 385-7540
Background: Conducts recreational and competitive events in golf, tennis and bowling at resorts worldwide, using group purchasing and off-season scheduling to get economical rates.
Represented by:
Lloyd Wright, President and Exec. Director

Nat'l Service Secretariat
5140 Sherrier Place, N.W., Washington, DC 20016
Telephone: (202) 244-5828
Background: Founded in 1966 to stimulate and facilitate consideration of a national service program for the nation's youth.

The listings in this directory are available as *Mailing Labels*. See last page.

ORGANIZATIONS REPRESENTED

Represented by:
Donald J. Eberly, Exec. Director

Nat'l Sheriffs' Ass'n
1450 Duke St., Alexandria, VA 22314
Telephone: (703) 836-7827
Represented by:
Jim Scutt, Legislative Director

Nat'l Shipwreck Alliance
317 Massachusetts Ave., N.W., Washington, DC 20002
Telephone: (202) 231-3666
Background: Represents the interests of individual divers, commercial salvage companies and others who seek to protect the right of private interests in the exploration and recovery of shipwrecks.
Counsel or consultant:
Ken Schlossberg Assoc. (William C. Smith)

Nat'l Shoe Retailers Ass'n
9861 Broken Land Pkwy., Columbia, MD 21046-1148
Telephone: (301) 381-8282
Represented by:
William Boettge, President
Counsel or consultant:
Tendler, Goldberg & Biggins, Chtd. (James M. Goldberg)

Nat'l Shorthand Reporters Ass'n
118 Park St., S.E., Vienna, VA 22180
Telephone: (703) 281-4677
Represented by:
Charles G. Hagee, CAE, Exec. Director
M. S. Jorpeland, Communications Director
Counsel or consultant:
Nossaman, Guthner, Knox and Elliott (Murray Zweben)

Nat'l Shorthand Reporters Ass'n Heritage Foundation
118 Park St., S.E., Vienna, VA 22180
Telephone: (703) 281-4677
Background: Represented by Charles G. Hagee, CAE, of the Nat'l Shorthand Reporters Ass'n.

Nat'l Shorthand Reporters Ass'n Political Action Committee
118 Park St., S.E., Vienna, VA 22180
Telephone: (703) 281-4677
Background: Treasurer and contact is Charles G. Hagee, CAE, of the Nat'l Shorthand Reporters Ass'n.

Nat'l Slag Ass'n
300 South Washington St., Alexandria, VA 22314
Telephone: (703) 549-3111
Represented by:
William E. Mattison, President

Nat'l Small Business United
1155 15th St., N.W. 7th Floor, Washington, DC 20005
Telephone: (202) 293-8830
Represented by:
Marcia Bradford, Communications Director
John Paul Galles, Exec. V. President and COO
Todd McCracken, Legislative Director
Counsel or consultant:
Neece, Cator and Associates (G. Thomas Cator, Allen Neece, Jr.)

Nat'l Small Business United PAC
1155 15th St., N.W. Suite 710, Washington, DC 20005
Telephone: (202) 293-8830
Background: Represented by John P. Galles of Nat'l Small Business United.

Nat'l Small Shipments Traffic Conference - NASSTRAC
1750 Pennsylvania Ave., N.W., Suite 1111, Washington, DC 20006
Telephone: (202) 393-5505
Represented by:
Joseph F. H. Cutrona, Exec. Director
Counsel or consultant:
McCarthy, Sweeney and Harkaway, P.C. (Daniel J. Sweeney)

Nat'l Soc. for Cardiovascular and Pulmonary Technology
1101 Connecticut Ave., N.W. Suite 1100, Washington, DC 20005
Telephone: (202) 371-1267
Background: Above address that of Internat'l Management Group, Inc.

Counsel or consultant:
Internat'l Management Group, Inc. (Brian Cassedy, Peggy McElgunn)

Nat'l Soc. for Histotechnology
5900 Princess Garden Pkwy. Suite 805, Lanham, MD 20706
Telephone: (301) 577-4907
Represented by:
Roberta Mosedale, Exec. Secretary

Nat'l Soc. for Performance and Instruction
1126 16th St., N.W., Suite 102, Washington, DC 20036
Telephone: (202) 861-0777
Represented by:
Dr. Paul Tremper, Exec. Director

Nat'l Soc. for Real Estate Finance
2300 M St., N.W., Suite 800, Washington, DC 20037
Telephone: (202) 466-6015
Represented by:
Lewis O. Kerwood, Exec. V. President

Nat'l Soc. of Accountants for Cooperatives
6320 Augusta Drive, #800C, Springfield, VA 22150
Telephone: (703) 569-3088
Represented by:
Barbara C. Hickey, Exec. Director

Nat'l Soc. of Black Engineers
344 Commerce St., Alexandria, VA 22314
Telephone: (703) 549-2207
Background: An organization dedicated to increasing the participation of blacks in the fields of engineering and the engineering sciences.
Represented by:
James F. Jenkins, Advisory Board Chairperson
Florida Morehead, Exec. Director

Nat'l Soc. of Fund Raising Executives
1101 King St., Suite 3000, Alexandria, VA 22314
Telephone: (703) 684-0410
Represented by:
Gail Clarke, Acting Chief Exec. Officer
Counsel or consultant:
Sedam and Shearer (Patrick J. McMahon)

Nat'l Soc. of Professional Engineers
1420 King St., Alexandria, VA 22314-2715
Telephone: (703) 684-2841
Represented by:
William M. Bennett, Manager, Congressional Relations
Charles O. Campbell, Director, Government Relations
James G. Dalton, Deputy Exec. Director, Programs
Mary Ellen Larson, Manager, Congressional Relations
Peter R. Pastre, Manager, Congressional Relations
Arthur E. Schwartz, General Counsel
Donald G. Weinert, Exec. Director

Nat'l Soc. of Professional Engineers Political Action Committee
1420 King St., Alexandria, VA 22314
Telephone: (703) 684-2841
Background: The PAC for the Nat'l Soc. of Professional Engineers.

Nat'l Soc. of Public Accountants
1010 N. Fairfax St., Alexandria, VA 22314
Telephone: (703) 549-6400
Represented by:
Peter M. Berkery, Jr., Dir., Congressional Relations/Tax Couns.
William H. Sager, Staff Legal Counsel
Stanley H. Stearman, Exec. V. President

Nat'l Soc. of Public Accountants Political Action Committee
1010 N. Fairfax St., Alexandria, VA 22314
Telephone: (703) 549-6400
Represented by:
Samuel A. Braunstein, Treasurer

Nat'l Soft Drink Ass'n
1101 16th St., N.W., Washington, DC 20036
Telephone: (202) 463-6732
Background: Formerly (1966) American Bottlers of Carbonated Beverages.

Represented by:
William L. Ball, III, President
Robert Z. Bohan, Sr. V. President/General Counsel
Thomas A. Daly, Of Counsel
Drew M. Davis, Director, Congressional Affairs
Jim B. Finkelstein, V. President, Communications
Barbara L. Hiden, Legislative Analyst
Brian Leugs, Manager, State & Local Affairs
Virginia McCoy, Legislative Analyst, State & Local Afrs.
Robert L. McKinney, Director, State & Local Affairs
Lorie J. Nevares, Manager, State and Local Affairs
Donald E. Prescott, Assistant to the President
Dwight C. Reed, Consultant
Howard R. Roberts, Sr. V. President, Science and Technology
E. Gifford Stack, V. President, Solid Waste Programs
Counsel or consultant:
Arent, Fox, Kintner, Plotkin & Kahn (Evan R. Berlack)
Bergner, Boyette & Bockorny, Inc. (Jeffrey T. Bergner, David A. Bockorny, Van R. Boyette)
Patton, Boggs and Blow (Stuart M. Pape)
Rivkin, Radler, Dunne and Bayh (Thomas A. Connaughton)

Nat'l Solid Wastes Management Ass'n
1730 Rhode Island Ave., N.W., 10th Floor, Washington, DC 20036
Telephone: (202) 659-4613
Represented by:
Bill Bertera, Managing Director, State Programs
Kent Burton, Resource Recovery Director
Robert Eisenbud, Managing Director, Environmental Policy
Susan McCaffrey, State Analyst
Allen Moore, President
C. L. Pettit, Analyst
Dr. Suellen Pirages, Director, Hazardous Waste Programs
John H. Turner, Associate Counsel
Jim Turpin, Manager, State Affairs
Eugene J. Wingerter, Exec. Director
Counsel or consultant:
Bonner & Associates

Nat'l Solid Wastes Management Ass'n Political Action Committee
1730 Rhode Island Ave., N.W., 10th Floor, Washington, DC 20036
Telephone: (202) 659-4613
Background: Represented by Eugene J. Wingerter of the Nat'l Solid Wastes Management Ass'n.

Nat'l Spa and Pool Institute
2111 Eisenhower Ave., Alexandria, VA 22314
Telephone: (703) 838-0083
Represented by:
Richard F. Ali, Director Goverment Affairs
Jack Cergol, Director, Communications
Joan E. Giblin, Manager, Communications
Elizabeth S. Nelson, Public Relations/Communications Manager
William Sadd, Exec. V. President
Counsel or consultant:
Morgan, Lewis and Bockius (Caswell O. Hobbs, III)
Stanton & Associates (James V. Stanton)

Nat'l Star Route Mail Contractors Ass'n
324 East Capitol St., S.E., Washington, DC 20003
Telephone: (202) 543-1661
Background: Represents highway mail contractors.
Represented by:
John V. Maraney, Exec. Director

Nat'l Star Route Mail Contractors Political Action Committee
324 East Capitol St., S.E., Washington, DC 20003
Telephone: (202) 543-1661
Background: Contact is John V. Maraney of the Ass'n.

Nat'l Steel and Shipbuilding Co.
2301 South Jefferson Davis Hwy Suite 501, Arlington, VA 22202
Telephone: (703) 418-1195
Represented by:
James M. Temenak, V. President, Washington Operations
Counsel or consultant:
Fierce and Associates (Donald L. Fierce)

Nat'l Stone Ass'n
1415 Elliot Place, N.W., Washington, DC 20007
Telephone: (202) 342-1100

The listings in this directory are available as *Mailing Labels*. See last page.

641

ORGANIZATIONS REPRESENTED

Nat'l Stone Ass'n (Cont'd)
Represented by:
  Adele Abrams, Director, Government Affairs
  Robert G. Bartlett, President
  Valentin J. Riva, V. President, Government Affairs

Nat'l Stone Ass'n Political Action Committee
1415 Elliot Place, N.W., Washington, DC 20007
Telephone: (202) 342-1100
Background: Responsible contact is Valentin J. Riva of the Ass'n.

Nat'l Strategy Information Center
1730 Rhode Island Ave., N.W., Washington, DC 20036
Telephone: (202) 429-0129
Background: A nonprofit, nonpartisan education and research organization focused on national security issues.
Represented by:
  Frank R. Barnett, President
  Dr. Roy Godson, Director, Washington Office

Nat'l Structured Settlements Political Action Committee
1001 Connecticut Ave., N.W. Suite 800, Washington, DC 20036
Telephone: (202) 857-4299
Counsel or consultant:
  William S. Bergman Associates (Valerie H. Bergman)

Nat'l Structured Settlements Trade Ass'n
1001 Connecticut Ave., N.W. Suite 800, Washington, DC 20036
Telephone: (202) 857-4299
Counsel or consultant:
  William S. Bergman Associates (William S. Bergman, CAE)
  Silverstein and Mullens (James C. Corman)

Nat'l Student Educational Fund
1012 14th St. N.W., Suite 403, Washington, DC 20005
Telephone: (202) 347-4769
Background: Designed to instill students with a sense of social responsibility and encourage them to improve their educational environment and the world around them.
Represented by:
  Kevin Harris, Project Director

Nat'l Student Speech Language Hearing Ass'n
10801 Rockville Pike, Rockville, MD 20852
Telephone: (301) 897-5700
Represented by:
  Charleen Bloom, Ph.D., Administrative Consultant

Nat'l Sudden Infant Death Syndrome Foundation
10500 Little Patuxent Pkwy. Suite 420, Columbia, MD 21044
Telephone: (800) 221-7437
Represented by:
  Mitchell R. Stoller, Executive Director
Counsel or consultant:
  Health and Medicine Counsel of Washington (Dale P. Dirks)

Nat'l Superconducting Super Collider Coalition
1725 DeSales St., N.W. Suite 800, Washington, DC 20036
Telephone: (202) 659-6568
Background: Supports continued congressional funding for the construction and operation of the Superconducting Super Collider.
Counsel or consultant:
  Hollye Doane

Nat'l Symphony Orchestra, The
Kennedy Center for the Performing Arts, Washington, DC 20566-0002
Telephone: (202) 416-8100
Counsel or consultant:
  Chernikoff and Co. (Larry Chernikoff)

Nat'l Tank Truck Carriers
2200 Mill Road, Suite 601, Alexandria, VA 22314
Telephone: (703) 838-1960
Represented by:
  John Conley, V. President
  Clifford J. Harvison, President

Nat'l Tank Truck Carriers Political Action Committee
2200 Mill Road, Alexandria, VA 22314
Telephone: (703) 838-1960
Background: Treasurer and contact is John Conley of the Nat'l Tank Truck Carriers.

Nat'l Tax Limitation Committee
201 Massachusetts Ave., N.E., Suite C-7, Washington, DC 20002
Telephone: (202) 547-4196
Background: Founded in 1975, the Committee now has approximately 700,000 members and affiliate groups in 50 states. Works to "constitutionally limit spending and taxes at all levels of government". Actively lobbies for a tax limitation/balanced budget constitutional amendment.
Represented by:
  Cliff Christian, Nat'l Field Director
  Al Cors, Jr., Legislative and Political Director
  Lewis K. Uhler, President

Nat'l Taxpayers Union
713 Maryland Ave., N.E., Washington, DC 20002
Telephone: (202) 543-1300
Background: Non-partisan coalition, opposing wasteful spending, promoting tax cuts, and a diminished bureaucracy. Established in 1969. Supports a constitutional amendment requiring a balanced budget. Rates members of Congress on their voting records on government spending.
Represented by:
  David L. Keating, Exec. V. President
  Jill Lancelot, Director of Congressional Affairs
  Sheila MacDonald, Director, Government Relations
  Rita Smith, Admin. Director
  Sid Taylor, Research Director

Nat'l Technical Ass'n
206 N. Washington St., Suite 202, Alexandria, VA 22314
Telephone: (202) 829-6100
Represented by:
  Mildred Johnson, Exec. Director

Nat'l Technological University
Fort Collins, CO
Counsel or consultant:
  Dow, Lohnes and Albertson (Kenneth D. Salomon)

Nat'l Telecommunications Network
804 W. Diamond Ave., Gaithersburg, MD 20878
Telephone: (301) 258-9717
Counsel or consultant:
  Hogan and Hartson (Anthony Harrington)
  Tuvin Associates (Carl R. Tuvin)

Nat'l Telephone Cooperative Ass'n
2626 Pennsylvania Ave., N.W., Washington, DC 20037
Telephone: (202) 298-2300
Background: Established in 1954. Represents both cooperative and commercial independent rural phone companies many of which receive financing from the REA under the Department of Agriculture. Supports the Telephone Education Committee Organization.
Represented by:
  Shirley A. Bloomfield, Director, Government Affairs
  Andrew Brown, Special Counsel
  Michael E. Brunner, Exec. Vice President
  David Cosson, V. President, Legal and Industry
  Julia Jackson, Government Affairs Representative
  Robert J. Leigh, Senior V. President
  Marlee Norton, Public Relations Director
  Susan L. Sadtler, Sr. Government Affairs Representative
  Thomas Wacker, Government Affairs Representative

Nat'l Telephone Cooperative Ass'n Telephone Education Committee Organization
2626 Pennsylvania Ave., N.W., Washington, DC 20037
Telephone: (202) 298-2300
Background: Contact is Shirley Bloomfield of the Ass'n.

Nat'l Telephone Services, Inc.
6100 Executive Blvd., Rockville, MD 20852
Telephone: (301) 770-7657
Counsel or consultant:
  McAuliffe, Kelly, Raffaelli & Siemens (James M. Copeland, Jr., Steven C. Halsey, John D. Raffaelli)

Nat'l Therapeutic Recreation Soc.
3101 Park Center Drive, Alexandria, VA 22302
Telephone: (703) 820-4940
Background: Position of Program Manager vacant at publication date. (See Nat'l Recreation and Park Ass'n.)

Nat'l Tire Dealers and Retreaders Ass'n
1250 I St., N.W. Suite 400, Washington, DC 20005
Telephone: (202) 789-2300

Nat'l Tire Dealers and Retreaders Ass'n (Cont'd)
Represented by:
  Anita Drummond, Legislative Assistant
  Philip P. Friedlander, Jr., Exec. V. President
  K. Wayne Malbon, Associate Director
  Donald T. Wilson, Director, Government Relations Division
Counsel or consultant:
  Keck, Mahin and Cate (Brock R. Landry)

Nat'l Tire Dealers and Retreaders Ass'n Political Action Committee
1250 Eye St., N.W., Suite 400, Washington, DC 20005
Telephone: (202) 789-2300
Represented by:
  Ross Kogel, Treasurer

Nat'l Tooling and Machining Ass'n
9300 Livingston Rd., Fort Washington, MD 20744
Telephone: (301) 248-6200
Represented by:
  Matthew B. Coffey, President and Chief Operating Officer
  John A. Cox, Jr., Manager, Government Affairs
  Jeanne Marie Little, Government Affairs Representative
Counsel or consultant:
  Webster, Chamberlain and Bean (Alan P. Dye)

Nat'l Treasury Employees Union
1730 K St., N.W., Suite 1100, Washington, DC 20006
Telephone: (202) 785-4411
Background: An independent labor union. Formerly (1973) Nat'l Ass'n of Internal Revenue Service Employees. Absorbed Nat'l Ass'n of Alcohol and Tobacco Tax Officers and Nat'l Customs Service Ass'n.
Represented by:
  Frank Ferris, Director of Negotiations
  Maureen Gilman, Assistant Director of Legislation
  Elaine Kaplan, Deputy Director, Litigation
  George King, Director, Public Relations
  Gregory J. O'Duden, Director, Litigation
  Cathy Overly, Director, Legislative Field Operations
  Susan Shaw, Legislative Liaison
  Patrick F. Smith, Jr., Director of Legislation
  Thomas J. Spangler, Legislative Liaison
  Robert Tobias, Nat'l President

Nat'l Treasury Employees Union Political Action Committee
1730 K St., N.W. Suite 1101, Washington, DC 20006
Telephone: (202) 785-4411
Represented by:
  Francis X. McLaughlin, Director

Nat'l Truck Equipment Ass'n
1350 New York Ave., N.W. Suite 800, Washington, DC 20005
Telephone: (202) 628-2010
Background: Also represents the Nat'l Truck Equipment Ass'n PAC.
Represented by:
  Michael E. Kastner, Director of Government Relations

Nat'l Truck Equipment Ass'n PAC
1350 New York Ave., N.W. Suite 800, Washington, DC 20005
Telephone: (202) 628-2010
Background: Represented by Michael E. Kastner of the Association.

Nat'l Trust for Historic Preservation
1785 Massachusetts Ave., N.W., Washington, DC 20036
Telephone: (202) 673-4000
Background: Chartered by act of Congress in 1949 and supported by private contributions and federal grants.
Represented by:
  Peter Brink, V. President, Programs and Services
  David A. Doheny, Vice President, General Counsel
  John L. Heyl, V. President, Resources Development
  Helen D. Hooper, Congressional Liaison
  Mary Finch Hoyt, Director, Public Relations
  Frank Sanchis, V. Pres., Stewardship/His. Properties
  Ian D. Spatz, Director, Ctr. for Pres. Policy Studies
  J. Jackson Walter, President
  Michelle M. Westover, Legislative Assistant

Nat'l Turkey Federation
11319 Sunset Hills Road, Reston, VA 22090
Telephone: (703) 435-7206

The listings in this directory are available as *Mailing Labels*. See last page.

ORGANIZATIONS REPRESENTED

Represented by:
Eddie Aldrete, Director, Public Affairs
Stuart E. Proctor, Jr., Exec. V. President and CEO

Nat'l Turkey Federation Political Action Committee
11319 Sunset Hills Road, Reston, VA 22090
Telephone: (703) 435-7206
Background: Sponsored by the Nat'l Turkey Federation. Stuart E. Proctor Jr. the parent association serves as Treasurer.

Nat'l U.S.-Arab Chamber of Commerce
1825 K St., N.W. Suite 1107, Washington, DC 20006
Telephone: (202) 331-8010
Represented by:
J. R. AbiNader, President
Counsel or consultant:
Kirkpatrick & Lockhart

Nat'l University Continuing Education Ass'n
One Dupont Circle, N.W. Suite 615, Washington, DC 20036-1168
Telephone: (202) 659-3130
Background: A non-profit member organization representing 400 accedited, degree-granting colleges and universities which provide continuing higher education opportunities to part-time students.
Represented by:
J. Noah Brown, Director, Gov't Relations & Public Afrs
Kay J. Kohl, Exec. Director

Nat'l Urban Coalition
8601 Georgia Ave., Suite 500, Silver Spring, MD 20910
Telephone: (301) 495-4999
Background: Founded 1967. A network of 40 affiliate organizations around the country seeking private and government cooperation to help the poor, working class and minority populations of urban areas. Operates 'Say YES to a Youngster's Future', an early education program for African-American and Latino children. Maintains interest in health, housing, economic development and other urban issues.
Represented by:
Ramona H. Edelin, Ph.D., President and CEO
Steve Lembesis, Dir. of Advocacy & Public Affairs
Joann Stevens, Dir., Media Relations, Education Progs.
Roberta Y. Wright, V. President and General Counsel
Counsel or consultant:
Burson-Marsteller (Sheila Raviv)

Nat'l Urban League
1114 14th St., N.W., 6th Floor, Washington, DC 20005
Telephone: (202) 898-1604
Background: An inter-racial, non-profit, community service organization working to secure opportunities for African Americans and other minorities in every sector of American society.
Represented by:
Leslye Cheek, Communications Associate
Robert McAlpine, Director, Policy & Gov't Relations

Nat'l Utility Contractors Ass'n
1235 Jefferson Davis Hwy. Suite 606, Arlington, VA 22202
Telephone: (703) 486-2100
Represented by:
Brian L. Connor, Government Relations Director
William G. Harley, Exec. Director
Leland J. White, Government Relations Representative

Nat'l Utility Contractors Ass'n Legislative and Action Committee
1235 Jefferson Davis Hwy. Suite 606, Arlington, VA 22202
Telephone: (703) 486-2100
Background: Supported by the Nat'l Utility Contractors Ass'n. Represented by William G. Harley of the Association. Treasurer is Brian Connor of the Association.

Nat'l Vehicle Leasing Ass'n
Culver City, CA
Counsel or consultant:
Winthrop, Stimson, Putnam & Roberts (Michael W. Dolan, Ronna A. Freiberg, John E. Gillick)

Nat'l Venture Capital Ass'n
1655 N. Fort Myer Drive Suite 700, Arlington, VA 22209
Telephone: (703) 528-4370

Represented by:
Daniel T. Kingsley, Exec. Director
Counsel or consultant:
Neece, Cator and Associates (Allen Neece, Jr.)
Public Affairs Services, Inc. (Kenneth C. O. Hagerty)
Robinson, Lake, Lerer & Montgomery (Mark Helmke)

Nat'l Venture Capital Ass'n Political Action Committee
1655 N. Fort Myer Drive Suite 700, Arlington, VA 22209
Telephone: (703) 528-4370
Counsel or consultant:
Neece, Cator and Associates (Allen Neece, Jr.)

Nat'l Vietnam Veterans Coalition
1000 Thomas Jefferson St., N.W., Suite 600, Washington, DC 20007
Telephone: (202) 338-6882
Background: A federation of approximately 45 veterans organizations devoted to resolution of eight issues of concern to Vietnam veterans (e.g. live POWs, Agent Orange, judicial review of VA benefits decisions).
Represented by:
William T. Bennett, General Secretary
J. Thomas Burch, Jr., Chairman

Nat'l Vocational Agricultural Teachers Ass'n
Box 15440, Alexandria, VA 22309
Telephone: (703) 780-1862
Represented by:
Sam Stenzel, Exec. Director

Nat'l Voluntary Health Agencies
1660 L St., N.W. Suite 601, Washington, DC 20036
Telephone: (202) 467-5913
Background: Member organizations include such groups as the American Heart Association, American Cancer Society and the March of Dimes.
Represented by:
James L. Barr, Exec. Director

Nat'l Voluntary Organizations for Independent Living for the Aging
600 Maryland Ave., S.W. West Wing 100, Washington, DC 20024
Telephone: (202) 479-1200
Background: An organization of the Nat'l Council on the Aging. An outgrowth of the 1971 White House Conference on Aging. Brings together civic, fraternal, denominational and professional organizations to improve and expand community-based services and opportunities for older persons. Represented by Betty R. Ransom of the Nat'l Council on the Aging.

Nat'l Volunteer Fire Council
1325 Pennsylvania Ave., N.W. Suite 500, Washington, DC 20005
Telephone: (202) 393-3351
Counsel or consultant:
Sparber and Associates (Peter G. Sparber)

Nat'l Water Alliance
1225 Eye St., N.W., Suite 300, Washington, DC 20005
Telephone: (202) 646-0917
Background: A coalition of non-profit organizations, labor unions, trade associations, corporate supporters and politicians seeking to encourage the development of a national water policy and to educate the public on water-related issues and problems. President is Ron Linton of the government relations firm of Linton, Mields, Reisler and Cottone.
Counsel or consultant:
Linton, Mields, Reisler and Cottone (Ron M. Linton)

Nat'l Water Resources Ass'n
3800 North Fairfax Dr. Suite 4, Arlington, VA 22203
Telephone: (703) 524-1544
Represented by:
Thomas F. Donnelly, Exec. V. President
Bridget O'Grady, Director, Government Affairs
Susan K. Till, Legislative Assistant

Nat'l Waterbed Retailers Ass'n
Chicago, IL
Counsel or consultant:
Fehrenbacher, Sale, Quinn, and Deese (C. Michael Deese)

Nat'l Watermelon Ass'n
Morven, GA

Counsel or consultant:
Highley & Associates (Vern F. Highley)

Nat'l Waterways Conference, Inc.
1130 17th St., N.W., Washington, DC 20036
Telephone: (202) 296-4415
Background: A group of shippers, barge lines, shipyards, river valley associations, state water boards and port authorities working to promote a better understanding of the public value of the American waterways system.
Represented by:
Harry N. Cook, President
Robert Freedman, Exec. Assistant
William J. Hull, V. President and Counsel
Counsel or consultant:
Allan Associates (Roger D. Allan)

Nat'l Weather Service Employees Organization
400 North Capitol St., N.W. Suite 326, Washington, DC 20001
Telephone: (202) 783-3131
Background: NWSEO is dedicated to the interests of NWS and NESDIS employees.
Represented by:
Richard J. Hirn, General Counsel
David T. Powell, President
Counsel or consultant:
Chwat/Weigend Associates (John S. Chwat, Robert E. Weigend)

Nat'l Weather Service Employees Organization Political Action Committee
400 North Capitol St. Suite 326, Washington, DC 20001
Telephone: (202) 783-3131
Counsel or consultant:
Chwat/Weigend Associates (Robert E. Weigend)

Nat'l Welding Supply Ass'n
Philadelphia, PA
Counsel or consultant:
Zuckert, Scoutt and Rasenberger (Richard P. Schweitzer)

Nat'l Welfare Rights and Reform Union
1000 Wisconsin Ave., N.W., Washington, DC 20007
Telephone: (202) 775-0925
Represented by:
Kevin M. Aslanian, Chairperson, Legislative Committee

Nat'l Wetlands Technical Council
1616 P St., N.W., Washington, DC 20036
Telephone: (202) 328-5150
Background: An independent scientific committee which advises federal and state governments on wetlands policies and research priorities. Administrative and staff support provided by the Environmental Law Institute.
Represented by:
Nicole Veilleux, Editor, Wetlands Newsletter

Nat'l Wholesale Druggists' Ass'n
105 Oronoco St., Alexandria, VA 22314
Telephone: (202) 684-6400
Represented by:
Sherry J. Haber, Director, Government & Public Affairs
Kate Kulesber, Legislative Analyst
Janet K. Scheren, Director of Communications
Ronald J. Streck, V. President, Gov't & Public Affairs
Charles S. Trefrey, President

Nat'l Wildlife Federation
1400 16th St., N.W., Washington, DC 20036-2266
Telephone: (202) 797-6800
Background: A non-governmental, nationwide conservation education organization with over four million members including affiliates and subsidiaries. Favors legislation for the enhancement of our natural resources. Founded in 1936 as an outgrowth of the first North American Wildlife Conference called to stimulate popular interest in proper management of natural resources and wildlife.

ORGANIZATIONS REPRESENTED

Nat'l Wildlife Federation (Cont'd)
Represented by:
David Albersworth, Director, Public Lands and Energy Div.
S. Elizabeth Birnbaum, Counsel, Water Resources Division
Barbara Bramble, Director, International Program
David Campbell, Economist, Water Resources Division
Catharine A. Carlson, Legislative Representative
David R. Conrad, Water Resource Specialist
Norman L. Dean, Jr., Director, Environmental Quality Division
William E. Deegans, Surface Mining Project Coordinator
John Ernst, Director, Office of Legislative Affairs
J. Scott Feierabend, Director, Fisheries and Wildlife Div.
Janice Goldman-Carter, Counsel
Lynn A. Greenwalt, V. President, Internat'l Affairs
Barbara Haas, Director, Corporate Conservation Council
David K. Hahn-Baker, Environmental Quality Coordinator
Jay D. Hair, Ph.D., President
William W. Howard, Jr., Exec. V. President
Stewart Hudson, Legis. Rep., Internat'l Program
Frances A. Hunt, Resource Specialist, Forestry
Doug Inkley, Wildlife Resource Specialist
William Robert Irvin, Counsel, Fisheries & Wildlife Div.
Philip Kavits, Director, Radio-TV
Lee Keller-Reis, Director, Communications
Bill Klinefelter, Sr. Legislative Representative
Ann Krumboltz, Director, Earth Day Program
Margaret G. Mellon, Director, Nat'l Biotechnology Policy Ctr
Charles R. Miller, Director, Media Relations
Kenneth S. Modzelewski, V. President, Promotional Activities
Steven Moyer, Legislative Representative, Fisheries
Sharon L. Newsome, V. President, Resources Conservation
Erik Olson, Counsel
Edward Osann, Dir. & Legis. Rep., Water Resources Div.
Gerry Poje, Environmental Toxicologist
Jane Rissler, Biotechnology Specialist
Gary San Julian, V. President, Research and Education
Larry Schweiger, V. Pres., Affiliate & Regional Programs
Stephanie C. Sklar, V. President, Public Affairs
Glenn Sugameli, Counsel, Public Lands and Energy Div.
Joel T. Thomas, General Counsel
Cindy Deacon Williams, Legislative Representative
Kate Zimmerman, Counsel, Public Lands and Energy Div.
Counsel or consultant:
Caplin and Drysdale
Verner, Liipfert, Bernhard, McPherson and Hand, Chartered (Lloyd N. Hand)

Nat'l Wine Coalition
1575 Eye St., N.W. Suite 325, Washington, DC 20005
Telephone: (202) 408-1120
Represented by:
John Volpe, Exec. Director

Nat'l Wine Distributors Ass'n
Palos Hills, IL
Counsel or consultant:
Tendler, Goldberg & Biggins, Chtd. (James M. Goldberg)

Nat'l Woman Abuse Prevention Project
2000 P St., N.W., 508, Washington, DC 20036
Telephone: (202) 857-0216
Background: Serves battered and abused women and their advocates, works toward achieving appropriate methods for effective intervention.
Represented by:
Mary Pat Brygger, Director

Nat'l Woman's Party
144 Constitution Ave., N.E., Washington, DC 20002
Telephone: (202) 546-1210
Represented by:
Mary Eastwood, President

Nat'l Women's Economic Alliance
1440 New York Ave., N.W., Suite 300, Washington, DC 20005
Telephone: (202) 638-1200
Background: An organization aimed at educating women entrepreneurs; helping women acquire corporate board directorships; and honoring women in business, government, industry and the arts.

Counsel or consultant:
E. Bruce Harrison Co. (Patricia S. Harrison)

Nat'l Women's Health Network
1325 G St., N.W. Lower Level, Washington, DC 20005
Telephone: (202) 347-1140
Background: Founded in 1976 in Washington, DC to monitor federal health policy pertinent to women's health and to testify before Congress and Federal agencies. Members of the network are consumers, organizations and health centers. Sponsors the Women's Health Clearinghouse.
Represented by:
Cindy Pearson, Acting Director

Nat'l Women's Law Center
1616 P St., N.W., Washington, DC 20036
Telephone: (202) 328-5160
Represented by:
Nancy Duff Campbell, Managing Attorney
Marcia D. Greenberger, Managing Attorney
Ann Kolker, Public Policy Director
Caroline Newkirk, Staff Attorney
Brenda Smith, Attorney
Ellen Vargas, Attorney

Nat'l Women's Political Caucus
1275 K St., N.W., Suite 750, Washington, DC 20005
Telephone: (202) 898-1100
Background: Women's rights group seeking more women in elected and appointed government positions.
Represented by:
Linda Kaplan, Exec. Director
Marie Morse, Political Director
Pat Reuss, Legislative Director
Sharon Rodine, President

Nat'l Women's Political Caucus Campaign Support Committee
1275 K St., N.W., Suite 750, Washington, DC 20005
Telephone: (202) 898-1100
Background: A political action committee sponsored by the Nat'l Women's Political Caucus. Contact Linda Kaplan of the Caucus.

Nat'l Women's Political Caucus Victory Fund
1275 K St., N.W. Suite 750, Washington, DC 20005
Telephone: (202) 898-1100
Represented by:
Sarah Lichtenstein, Treasurer

Nat'l Wood Window and Door Ass'n
1250 Connecticut Ave., N.W. Suite 300, Washington, DC 20036
Telephone: (202) 463-2799
Represented by:
Ward Hitchings, Washington Representative

Nat'l Wooden Pallet and Container Ass'n
1625 Massachusetts Ave., N.W., Washington, DC 20036
Telephone: (202) 667-3670
Represented by:
John J. Healy, Exec. V. President and CEO

Nat'l 4-H Council
7100 Connecticut Ave., Chevy Chase, MD 20815
Telephone: (301) 961-2800
Represented by:
Larry L. Krug, Director of Public Affairs
Richard J. Sauer, President and C.E.O.

Nationwide Auction Co.
Tucson, AZ
Counsel or consultant:
Lachelli, Waller and Associates (Vincent P. Lachelli)

Nationwide Insurance Cos.
Columbus, OH
Counsel or consultant:
George K. Bernstein Law Off. (George K. Bernstein)
Bonner & Associates
Cadwalader, Wickersham & Taft (Donald C. Alexander)

Native American Fish and Wildlife Society
Broomfield, CO
Counsel or consultant:
Karl A. Funke and Associates (Karl A. Funke)

Native American Industrial Trade Ass'n
Phoenix, AZ

Counsel or consultant:
McAuliffe, Kelly, Raffaelli & Siemens (Lynnette R. Jacquez)

Native American Rights Fund
1712 N St., N.W., Washington, DC 20036
Telephone: (202) 785-4166
Represented by:
Henry J. Sockbeson, Directing Attorney

NATJ and NATE
Dallas, TX
Background: Employment consultants.
Counsel or consultant:
Keefe Co., The (Camilla A. McGhee, William A. Signer)

Natural Gas Alliance for Generative Electricity
555 13th St., N.W., Suite 1010, Washington, DC 20004-1109
Telephone: (202) 863-2226
Counsel or consultant:
Nancy Whorton George & Associates, P.C. (Nancy Whorton George)
Skadden, Arps, Slate, Meagher and Flom (Lynn R. Coleman, Mike Naeve)

Natural Gas Consumers Information Center
1440 New York Ave., N.W., Suite 300, Washington, DC 20005
Telephone: (202) 638-1200
Counsel or consultant:
E. Bruce Harrison Co.

Natural Gas Supply Ass'n
1129 20th St., N.W. Suite 300, Washington, DC 20036
Telephone: (202) 331-8900
Background: Chief lobbying arm of the natural gas producers.
Represented by:
Philip M. Budzik, Director, Research and Analysis
Nicholas J. Bush, President
Patricia A. Hammick, V. President
John Paul Johnson, Director of Industry Relations
John Hunter Sharp, Counsel and Dir., Congressional Affairs
Michael J. Waters, Director of Public Relations
Counsel or consultant:
Bergner, Boyette & Bockorny, Inc. (Jeffrey T. Bergner)
Camp, Barsh, Bates and Tate (Harry E. Barsh, Jr.)
Murphy and Associates (William T. Murphy, Jr.)
Skadden, Arps, Slate, Meagher and Flom (Lynn R. Coleman, Mike Naeve)

Natural Gas Vehicle Coalition
2 Lafayette Center 1133 21st St., N.W., Suite 500, Washington, DC 20036
Telephone: (202) 466-9038
Background: Supports federal government programs which encourage the development of natural gas powered vehicles.
Represented by:
Jeffery Seisler, Exec. Director
Counsel or consultant:
Holt, Miller & Associates (Ann M. Sullivan)

Natural Resources Defense Council
1350 New York Ave., N.W. Suite 300, Washington, DC 20005
Telephone: (202) 783-7800
Background: A public interest law firm established in New York City in 1970 supported by about 130,000 dues paying members. Through education and appropriate litigation, NRDC works to preserve the nation's resources and environment for future generations.

ORGANIZATIONS REPRESENTED

Represented by:
Robert Adler, Senior Attorney
Paul J. Allen, Director of Communications
Richard E. Ayres, Staff Attorney
Jane Bloom, Senior Attorney
Dr. Faith Thompson Campbell, Senior Project Staff Officer
Thomas B. Cochran, Senior Scientist
David D. Doniger, Senior Staff Attorney
Janet S. Hathaway, Senior Project Attorney
David G. Hawkins, Attorney
Robert S. Norris, Senior Research Analyst
Dan W. Reicher, Attorney
S. Jacob Scherr, Senior Staff Attorney
Justin R. Ward, Assistant to Staff Attorney
Jacqueline Warren, Senior Attorney
Counsel or consultant:
Harmon, Curran and Tousley (Eric Glitzenstein)

Natural Rubber Shippers Ass'n
1400 K St., N.W. 9th Floor, Washington, DC 20005
Telephone: (202) 682-1325
Represented by:
T. I. Lemon, V. President, General Manager

Nature Conservancy, The
1815 N. Lynn St, Arlington, VA 22209
Telephone: (703) 841-5300
Background: A international nonprofit organization whose primary purpose is to protect ecologically significant natural areas and the life they shelter. Rescues threatened land and acquires outstanding unspoiled acres. Works with local, state and federal governments to help identify and preserve rare species by protecting land.
Represented by:
Geoffrey S. Barnard, V. President, International Program
Ronald J. Geatz, Manager, Media Relations
Lynne Murphy, Director, Communication
John D. Sawhill, President
Nathaniel E. Williams, V. President, Government Relations
Counsel or consultant:
Peabody Fitzpatrick Communications (Joyce Fitzpatrick, J. Douglas Koelemay)

Navajo Nation, The
2033 M St., N.W., Suite 404, Washington, DC 20036
Telephone: (202) 775-0393
Represented by:
Rodger Boyd, Exec. Director
Counsel or consultant:
Patton, Boggs and Blow (Richard H. Stolbach)
Winthrop, Stimson, Putnam & Roberts (M. Elizabeth Arky, Peter F. Gold)

Naval Reserve Ass'n
1619 King St., Alexandria, VA 22314-2793
Telephone: (703) 548-5800
Represented by:
James E. Forrest, Exec. Director

Navistar Internat'l Corp.
Chicago, IL
Background: Formerly Internat'l Harvester.
Counsel or consultant:
Williams and Connolly (Aubrey M. Daniel, III, J. Alan Galbraith)

Navy League of the United States
2300 Wilson Blvd., Arlington, VA 22201
Telephone: (703) 528-1775
Background: Founded in 1902. A patriotic, educational action group supporting a strong defense establishment, especially naval forces, and a foreign policy consistent with maintaining America's security.
Represented by:
V. Adm. Dudley L. Carlson, USN, Ret., Exec. Director
Calvin H. Cobb, Jr., Nat'l President
S. Peter Huhn, Director, Legislative Education

NCNB Texas Nat'l Bank
Dallas, TX
Counsel or consultant:
Patton, Boggs and Blow (James B. Christian, Jr.)

NCR Corporation
1156 15th St., N.W. Suite 1201, Washington, DC 20005
Telephone: (202) 872-0717

Represented by:
Laura W. Moorhead, Legislative Affairs Manager
Counsel or consultant:
Lee, Toomey & Kent

Nebraska Public Power District
Lincoln, NE
Counsel or consultant:
Crowell and Moring (Dana C. Contratto)
Groom and Nordberg (William G. Schiffbauer)

NEC America
Melville, NY
Counsel or consultant:
Paul, Weiss, Rifkind, Wharton and Garrison (Terence J. Fortune, Robert E. Montgomery, Jr.)

NEC Corp.
Tokyo, Japan
Counsel or consultant:
Coudert Brothers (Mark D. Herlach)
Manatt, Phelps, Rothenberg & Phillips (J. Michael Farrell, Charles T. Manatt)
Paul, Weiss, Rifkind, Wharton and Garrison (Terence J. Fortune, Robert E. Montgomery, Jr.)

NEC Home Electronics (USA) Inc.
Wood Dale, IL
Counsel or consultant:
Patton, Boggs and Blow
Wunder, Ryan, Cannon & Thelen (W. Stephen Cannon)

Neckwear Ass'n of America
New York, NY
Counsel or consultant:
Economic Consulting Services Inc. (Deborah Swartz)

Neighborhood Housing Services of America
1325 G St., N.W., Suite 1010, Washington, DC 20005
Telephone: (202) 376-2576
Background: A non-profit low income neighborhood improvement corporation serving over 250 communities.
Represented by:
Lynn Reilly, Legislative Director

Neighborhood Legal Services Program
701 4th St., N.W., Washington, DC 20001
Telephone: (202) 682-2700
Background: Provides free legal assistance to the indigent in the District of Columbia.
Represented by:
Willie E. Cooke, Jr,, Exec. Director

Nelbro Packing Co.
Seattle, WA
Counsel or consultant:
Preston Gates Ellis & Rouvelas Meeds (Richard L. Barnes, William N. Myhre)

Nemacolin Mines Corp.
McMurray, PA
Background: A subsidiary of Lykes Corp.
Counsel or consultant:
Smith, Heenan and Althen (Michael T. Heenan)

NeoRx, Inc.
Seattle, WA
Counsel or consultant:
Cassidy and Associates, Inc. (Gerald S. J. Cassidy, George A. Ramonas)

Nepal, Embassy of
2131 Leroy Place, N.W., Washington, DC 20008
Telephone: (202) 667-4550
Counsel or consultant:
Marshall, Tenzer, Greenblatt, Fallon and Kaplan (Sylvan M. Marshall)

NEPTCO
Pawtucket, RI
Counsel or consultant:
Schagrin Associates (R. Alan Luberda, Roger B. Schagrin)

Neptune Orient Lines
Singapore
Counsel or consultant:
Graham and James

Nestle Enterprises, Inc.
1511 K St., N.W., Suite 1100, Washington, DC 20005
Telephone: (202) 639-8894

Represented by:
John F. Hussey, V. President, Corporate Affairs
Thad M. Jackson, Ph.D., Special Issues Director
Stephen M. MacArthur, Washington Representative
Channing W. Riggs, Assistant, Special Issues
Christine Roux, Public Affairs and Research Coordinator

Nestle, S.A.
Vevey, Switzerland
Counsel or consultant:
Mayer, Brown and Platt (Joel V. Williamson)

Net Equity
Counsel or consultant:
Gilbert A. Robinson, Inc. (Gilbert A. Robinson)

Netherlands Antilles, Government of
Curacao, Netherlands Antilles
Counsel or consultant:
Alcalde & Rousselot (Hector Alcalde)
Cole, Corette & Abrutyn (Robert T. Cole, Steven A. Musher)

NETWORK
806 Rhode Island Ave., N.E., Washington, DC 20018
Telephone: (202) 526-4070
Background: A National Catholic social justice lobby established in 1971.
Represented by:
Nancy Sylvester, Nat'l Coordinator

Network Equipment Technologies
Redwood City, CA
Counsel or consultant:
Willkie Farr and Gallagher (Sue D. Blumenfeld, Philip L. Verveer)

Network in Solidarity with the People of Guatemala
1314 14th St., N.W., 3rd Floor, Washington, DC 20005
Telephone: (202) 483-0050
Background: An organization opposed to U.S. 'intervention' in Guatemala. It is dedicated to building, in the U.S., an understanding of and support for the Guatemalan people's struggle for peace and justice.
Represented by:
Joe Gorin, Coordinator

Nevada Development Authority
Las Vegas, NV
Counsel or consultant:
State & Local Resources (Bruce D. Henderson, Patrick M. Murphy)

Nevada Power Co.
Las Vegas, NV
Counsel or consultant:
Marcus G. Faust

Nevada, State of
Carson City, NV
Counsel or consultant:
State & Local Resources (Bruce D. Henderson, Patrick M. Murphy)
Sutherland, Asbill and Brennan (Wright H. Andrews, Jr.)

New American View
132 Third St., S.E., Washington, DC 20003
Telephone: (202) 547-1036
Background: A semi-monthly publication whose 'purpose is to liberate the U.S. Government from the domination of the Jewish, single-issue, pro-Israeli lobby -- which is subverting the political process of the American democratic system in order to promote the interests of a foreign state.'
Represented by:
Mark Lane, Associate Editor
Victor Marchetti, Editor

New Directions for Policy
1101 Vermont Ave., N.W. Suite 400, Washington, DC 20005
Telephone: (202) 289-3907
Represented by:
Jack A. Meyer, President
Sean Sullivan, V. President

New Directions Group, Inc.
Norwalk, CT
Counsel or consultant:
Norman G. Cornish

ORGANIZATIONS REPRESENTED

New Energy and Industrial Technology Development Organization
1800 K St., N.W. Suite 924, Washington, DC 20006
Telephone: (202) 822-9298
Represented by:
Toshiaki Yamamoto, Chief Representative

New England Anti-Vivisection Soc.
Boston, MA
Counsel or consultant:
Swift Consulting Co., Ltd., The (Ivan, Red Swift)

New England Aquarium
Boston, MA
Counsel or consultant:
Wexler, Reynolds, Fuller, Harrison and Schule, Inc. (Terry D. Bevels)

New England Council, Inc., The
1455 Pennsylvania Ave., N.W. Suite 1000, Washington, DC 20004
Telephone: (202) 639-8955
Represented by:
Elisa M. Lund, Director, Washington Programs

New England Deaconess Hospital
Boston, MA
Counsel or consultant:
O'Neill and Athy, P.C. (Martha L. Casey)

New England Digital Distribution Corp.
Boston, MA
Counsel or consultant:
Sutherland, Asbill and Brennan (Anne P. Jones)

New England Electric System
2100 Pennsylvania Ave. N.W., Suite 695, Washington, DC 20037
Telephone: (202) 488-3789
Represented by:
Bruce Foster, V. President, Washington Affairs
Counsel or consultant:
Paul, Hastings, Janofsky and Walker (Charles A. Patrizia)
Wexler, Reynolds, Fuller, Harrison and Schule, Inc. (Anne Wexler)

New England Medical Center
Boston, MA
Counsel or consultant:
O'Neill and Athy, P.C. (Martha L. Casey)

New England Motor Rate Bureau
Burlington, MA
Counsel or consultant:
Rea, Cross & Auchincloss (Patrick McEligot, Bryce Rea, Jr.)

New England Power Co.
Westborough, MA
Counsel or consultant:
Swidler & Berlin, Chartered (Edward Berlin)

New England, The
Boston, MA
Background: Formerly New England Life.
Counsel or consultant:
Murray, Scheer & Montgomery (D. Michael Murray)

New Era Communications
6273 Franconia Road, Alexandria, VA 22310
Telephone: (703) 971-4285
Counsel or consultant:
Collins & Associates (Sunny Taylor)

New Hampshire Ball Bearings, Inc.
Peterborough, NH
Background: A subsidiary of Minebea Co. Ltd. of Japan.
Counsel or consultant:
Richard W. Bliss
Hill and Knowlton Public Affairs Worldwide
Tanaka, Ritger and Middleton (H. William Tanaka)

New Hampshire Savings Bank
Concord, NH
Counsel or consultant:
Thacher, Proffitt and Wood (Louis H. Nevins)

New Jersey Council of Savings Institutions
West Orange, NJ
Counsel or consultant:
James J. Butera, Chartered

New Jersey Federation of Advocates for Insurance Reform
Trenton, NJ
Counsel or consultant:
Bonner & Associates

New Jersey, Public Advocate of
Trenton, NJ
Counsel or consultant:
Miller, Balis and O'Neil

New Jersey, State of
444 N. Capitol St., N.W. Suite 236, Washington, DC 20001
Telephone: (202) 638-0631
Represented by:
Alice Buchalter, Legislative Assistant
Kevin Kirchner, Legislative Assistant
Stavroula Lambrakopoulos, Deputy Director, Washington Office
Alice Tetelman, Director, Washington Office
Elaine B. Weinstein, Legislative Assistant

New MediCo Associates, Inc.
Boston, MA
Counsel or consultant:
Fox, Bennett and Turner (Samuel D. Turner)

New Mexico Electric Service Co.
Hobbs, NM
Counsel or consultant:
Keller and Heckman

New Orleans, Louisiana, City of
Counsel or consultant:
Nat'l Center for Municipal Development (Dicken Cherry)

New Orleans Public Service Inc.
New Orleans, LA
Counsel or consultant:
Reid & Priest

New Process Co.
Warren, PA
Background: Mail Order House.
Counsel or consultant:
Patton, Boggs and Blow (Timothy J. May)

New United Motor Manufacturing, Inc. (NUMMI)
Fremont, CA
Counsel or consultant:
Century Public Affairs (Philip A. Bangert)

New West Savings and Loan Ass'n
Irvine, CA
Counsel or consultant:
Dow, Lohnes and Albertson (Stuart Marshall Bloch)

New York City (Washington Office)
555 New Jersey Ave., N.W. Suite 700, Washington, DC 20001
Telephone: (202) 393-3903
Background: Legislative interest involves all municipal issues and related matters.
Represented by:
Judy L. Chesser, Director

New York City Board of Education
555 New Jersey Ave., N.W. Suite 702, Washington, DC 20001
Telephone: (202) 783-6262
Represented by:
Fern M. Lapidus, Washington Representative

New York City Board of Estimate
New York, NY
Counsel or consultant:
Arnold & Porter (Norman M. Sinel)

New York City Housing Development Corp.
New York, NY
Counsel or consultant:
Brownstein Zeidman and Schomer (Kenneth G. Lore)

New York Hospital
New York, NY
Counsel or consultant:
Keefe Co., The (Camilla A. McGhee, William A. Signer)
Kelley, Drye and Warren (Charles L. Marinaccio)

New York Life Insurance Co.
600 New Hampshire Ave., N.W., Suite 200, Washington, DC 20037
Telephone: (202) 331-8733
Represented by:
Marilyn S. Koss, Wash. Representative, Ass't V. President
Faith M. Williams, Senior Legislative Consultant
Counsel or consultant:
Patton, Boggs and Blow (Thomas Hale Boggs, Jr.)
Steptoe and Johnson (Arthur L. Bailey, Matthew J. Zinn)
Tucker & Associates (William Tucker)

New York Medical Care Facilities Finance Agency
New York, NY
Counsel or consultant:
Liz Robbins Associates (Sharon Edwards, Liz Robbins)

New York Metropolitan Transportation Authority
New York, NY
Counsel or consultant:
Eckert Seamans Cherin & Mellott (Anthony A. Anderson, Jane Sutter Starke, G. Kent Woodman)
Smith Dawson & Andrews, Inc. (Thomas C. Dawson, James P. Smith)
Vierra Associates, Inc. (Dennis C. Vierra)

New York Power Authority
1030 15th St., N.W. Suite 408, Washington, DC 20005
Telephone: (202) 371-5606
Counsel or consultant:
Mark A. Siegel & Associates

New York Public Library
New York, NY
Counsel or consultant:
Liz Robbins Associates (Sharon Edwards, Liz Robbins)

New York Shipping Ass'n
6907 Wilson Lane, Bethesda, MD 20817
Telephone: (301) 320-4520
Represented by:
Pauline B. Reeping, Director of Public Affairs

New York State Assembly
444 North Capitol St., N.W., Washington, DC 20001
Telephone: (202) 624-5860
Counsel or consultant:
O'Connor & Hannan (Jeffrey M. Wice)

New York State Bankers Ass'n
New York, NY
Counsel or consultant:
McNair Law Firm, P.A.

New York State Employees Retirement System
Albany, NY
Counsel or consultant:
Willkie Farr and Gallagher (Ellen A. Hennessy)

New York State Housing Finance Agency
New York, NY
Counsel or consultant:
Liz Robbins Associates (Sharon Edwards, Liz Robbins)

New York State Mortgage Loan Enforcement and Administrative Corp.
New York, NY
Counsel or consultant:
Brownstein Zeidman and Schomer (Kenneth G. Lore)
Evans Group, Ltd., The (Susan Riley)

New York, State of
444 N. Capitol St., N.W. Suite 301, Washington, DC 20001
Telephone: (202) 638-1311
Represented by:
Steven J. Hoffman, Deputy Dir., Couns., Off. of Fed. Affrs.
Brad C. Johnson, Director, Office of Federal Affairs

New York State Senate
444 North Capitol St., N.W. Suite 340, Washington, DC 20001
Telephone: (202) 624-5880
Represented by:
Richard J. Bartholomew, Exec. Director, Washington Office

New York Stock Exchange
1800 K St., N.W., Suite 1100, Washington, DC 20006

The listings in this directory are available as *Mailing Labels*. See last page.

ORGANIZATIONS REPRESENTED

Telephone: (202) 293-5740
Represented by:
Harry F. Day, Regulatory Counsel
David P. Lambert, Sr. V. President, Public Affairs
Stephen J. Paradise, Sr. V.P., Congressional/Regulatory Rltns
Cecile Srodes, Counsel Legislative Affairs

New York Stock Exchange Political Action Committee
1800 K St., N.W., Suite 1100, Washington, DC 20006
Telephone: (202) 293-5740
Background: Represented by David P. Lambert of the New York Stock Exchange.

New York Telephone Co.
New York, NY
Counsel or consultant:
Bonner & Associates

New York Transit Authority
New York, NY
Counsel or consultant:
Snavely, King and Associates

New York Trap Rock Co.
West Nyack, NY
Background: A subsidiary of Lone Star Industries.
Counsel or consultant:
Smith, Heenan and Althen

New York University
New York, NY
Counsel or consultant:
Burchette & Associates

New Zealand, Embassy of
37 Observatory Circle, N.W., Washington, DC 20008
Telephone: (202) 328-4800
Counsel or consultant:
Van Dyk Associates, Inc. (Ted Van Dyk)

Newark, California, City of
Counsel or consultant:
Simon & Co., Inc.

Newark, Delaware, City of
Counsel or consultant:
Duncan, Weinberg, Miller & Pembroke, P.C. (Janice L. Lower, Frederick L. Miller, Jr.)

Newark, Seaford, Smyrna, Middletown, Dover, Lewes, Clayton, New Castle & Milford, Delaware, Municipalities of
Counsel or consultant:
Duncan, Weinberg, Miller & Pembroke, P.C. (Wallace L. Duncan, Janice L. Lower)

Newburgh, New York, City of
Counsel or consultant:
Nat'l Center for Municipal Development (Barbara T. McCall)

NewCity Communications, Inc.
Bridgeport, CT
Counsel or consultant:
Kaye, Scholer, Fierman, Hays and Handler (Jason Shrinsky)

Newhall Land and Farming Co.
Valencia, CA
Counsel or consultant:
Chambers Associates Incorporated

Newman Group, The
1129 20th St., N.W., Washington, DC 20036
Telephone: (202) 331-1369
Counsel or consultant:
St. Germain, Rodio & Ursillo, Ltd. (Fernand J. St. Germain)

Newmet Steel Co.
New York, NY
Counsel or consultant:
Van Dyk Associates, Inc. (Ted Van Dyk)

Newmont Mining Corp.
1233 20th St., N.W., Suite 200, Washington, DC 20036
Telephone: (202) 659-2080
Represented by:
Mary Beth Donnelly, V. President, Government Relations

Newport Beach, California, City of
Counsel or consultant:
Kaye, Scholer, Fierman, Hays and Handler (Christopher R. Brewster)

Newport Group
Heathrow, FL
Counsel or consultant:
Dickstein, Shapiro and Morin (John C. Dill)

News America
New York, NY
Counsel or consultant:
Akin, Gump, Strauss, Hauer and Feld (Joel Jankowsky)

Newsletter Ass'n, The
1401 Wilson Blvd, Suite 403, Arlington, VA 22209
Telephone: (703) 527-2333
Represented by:
Frederick D. Goss, Exec. Director

Newspaper Guild, The
8611 2nd Ave., Silver Spring, MD 20910
Telephone: (301) 585-2990
Represented by:
Charles Dale, President
Phillip M. Kadis, Education Director
Counsel or consultant:
Barr, Peer & Cohen (David S. Barr)

Nez Perce Tribe
Lapwai, ID
Counsel or consultant:
Evergreen Associates, Ltd. (Jo Ann Kauffman)

NHK (Japanese Broadcasting Corp.)
Toyko, Japan
Counsel or consultant:
Anderson, Hibey, Nauheim and Blair (Stanton D. Anderson)

NI Industries
Los Angeles, CA
Counsel or consultant:
MARC Associates, Inc. (Daniel C. Maldonado)
Steptoe and Johnson (Olin L. Wethington)

Niagara Frontier Transportation Authority
Buffalo, NY
Counsel or consultant:
Vierra Associates, Inc. (Dennis C. Vierra)

Niagara Mohawk Power Corp.
Syracuse, NY
Counsel or consultant:
Conner and Wetterhahn, P.C. (Troy B. Conner, Jr., Mark J. Wetterhahn)
Reid & Priest

Nicaragua, Government of
Managua, Nicaragua
Counsel or consultant:
Reichler Appelbaum and Wippman (Judith C. Appelbaum, Paul S. Reichler, David Wippman)

Nicaraguan Resistance- U.S.A.
44880 Falcon Place Suite 104, Sterling, VA 22070
Telephone: (703) 328-1133
Background: Official representation of the Nicaraguan resistance movement, known as the Contras. Advocates the establishmnet of democracy in Nicaragua.
Represented by:
Ernesto Palazio, Washington Representative
Counsel or consultant:
Ann E. W. Stone and Associates (Michael Weintraub)

Niedermeyer-Martin Co.
Portland, OR
Counsel or consultant:
APCO Associates (Don Bonker)

Nigeria Airways
Lagos, Nigeria
Counsel or consultant:
Winthrop, Stimson, Putnam & Roberts (Robert Reed Gray)

Nigeria, Embassy of
2201 M St., N.W., Washington, DC 20037
Telephone: (202) 822-1500

Land, Lemle & Arnold (Millard W. Arnold, J. Stuart Lemle)
van Kloberg and Associates (Edward J. van Kloberg, III)

Nigeria, Government of
Lagos, Nigeria
Counsel or consultant:
Black, Manafort, Stone and Kelly Public Affairs Co.
Evans Group, Ltd., The (L. A., Skip Bafalis, Thomas B. Evans, Jr.)
Prather, Seeger, Doolittle and Farmer (Thomas L. Farmer)

NIKE, Inc.
507 Second St., N.E., Washington, DC 20002
Telephone: (202) 543-8500
Represented by:
Carl Davis, East Coast Counsel
Counsel or consultant:
Davis Wright Tremaine (Walter H. Evans, III)

Niles, Michigan, Utilities Department of
Background: Representation on utility matters includes development of generation, cogeneration and state and federal committee representation.
Counsel or consultant:
Duncan, Weinberg, Miller & Pembroke, P.C. (Janice L. Lower, James D. Pembroke)

Nintendo
Redmond, WA
Counsel or consultant:
Hill and Knowlton Public Affairs Worldwide (Roger Lindberg, Donald F. Massey)

Nippon Benkan Kogyo Co., Ltd.
Tokyo, Japan
Counsel or consultant:
Graham and James (Yoshihiro Saito)

Nippon Cargo Airlines
888 17th St., N.W., Suite 600, Washington, DC 20006
Telephone: (202) 298-8660
Represented by:
Shun-Ichi Fujimura, Chief Representative
Counsel or consultant:
Williams and Jensen, P.C. (John J. McMackin, Jr.)
Zuckert, Scoutt and Rasenberger (James L. Devall)

Nippon Electric Co., Ltd.
Tokyo, Japan
Counsel or consultant:
Coudert Brothers (Milo C. Coerper)

Nippon Kokan K.K.
Tokyo, Japan
Counsel or consultant:
Willkie Farr and Gallagher (William H. Barringer)

Nippon Mining Co.
Tokyo, Japan
Counsel or consultant:
Graham and James (Brian E. McGill, Yoshihiro Saito)

Nippon Steel Corp.
Tokyo, Japan
Counsel or consultant:
Steptoe and Johnson (W. George Grandison, Daniel J. Plaine)

Nippon Synthetic Chemical Industry Co.
Tokyo, Japan
Counsel or consultant:
Mudge Rose Guthrie Alexander and Ferdon (N. David Palmeter)

Nippon Telephone and Telegraph Corp.
Tokyo, Japan
Counsel or consultant:
Civic Service, Inc. (Roy Pfautch)
TKC Internat'l, Inc.

Nippon Yusen Kaisha (NYK) Line
New York, NY
Counsel or consultant:
Warren and Associates (George A. Quadrino, Charles F. Warren)

Nippon Zeon
Tokyo, Japan

ORGANIZATIONS REPRESENTED

Nippon Zeon (Cont'd)
Counsel or consultant:
O'Melveny and Myers (F. Amanda DeBusk)

Nishika Corp.
Henderson, NV
Counsel or consultant:
Oppenheimer Wolff and Donnelly (David A. Gantz)

Nisqually Indian Tribal Business Committee
Olympia, WA
Counsel or consultant:
Karl A. Funke and Associates (Karl A. Funke)

Nissan Aerospace Division
Tokyo, Japan
Counsel or consultant:
Charles Louis Fishman, P.C. (Charles Louis Fishman)

Nissan Industrial Equipment Co.
Tokyo, Japan
Counsel or consultant:
Arnold & Porter (Patrick F. J. Macrory)

Nissan Motor Co., Ltd.
Tokyo, Japan
Counsel or consultant:
Arnold & Porter (Patrick F. J. Macrory)
Charles Louis Fishman, P.C. (Charles Louis Fishman)
Manchester Associates, Ltd. (John V. Moller)
Piper Pacific Internat'l (Margaret Parker, W. Stephen Piper, Sara Winslow)

Nissan Motor Corp. in U.S.A.
750 K St., N.W. Suite 901, Washington, DC 20006
Telephone: (202) 862-5523
Represented by:
Franklin J. Crawford, Director, Government and Public Affairs
Paul D. Ryan, Manager, Government and Public Affairs
Yutaka Suzuki, Vice President, External Relations
James A. Young, Manager, Industry & Economic Affairs
Counsel or consultant:
Dorsey & Whitney

Nissan Motor Manufacturing Corp. U.S.A.
Smyrna, TN
Counsel or consultant:
Manchester Associates, Ltd. (John V. Moller)

Nissan Research & Development
750 17th St., N.W., Suite 901, Washington, DC 20006
Telephone: (202) 466-5284
Represented by:
Satoshi Nishibori, V. President

Nissho-Iwai American Corp.
1825 K St., N.W. Suite 1103, Washington, DC 20006
Telephone: (202) 429-0280
Represented by:
Yasuo Wataru, Sr. V. President, General Manager
Counsel or consultant:
Donovan Leisure Rogovin Huge & Schiller (William E. Colby)
Dorsey & Whitney

NL Industries
208 G St., N.E., 2nd Floor, Washington, DC 20002
Telephone: (202) 546-0125
Background: Director of Government Relations in Washington, DC is Karl J. Ottosen of Ottosen & Associates.
Counsel or consultant:
Ottosen and Associates (Karl J. Ottosen, Carla L. Saunders)

NMTBA - The Ass'n for Manufacturing Technology
7901 Westpark Dr., McLean, VA 22102
Telephone: (703) 893-2900
Represented by:
Ed Chandler, Legislative Representative
Charles P. Downer, Industrial Preparedness Representative
James H. Mack, V. President, Government Relations
Albert W. Moore, President
Amber Parson, Legislative Analyst
Eugene J. Zeiszler, Industrial Preparedness Assistant
Counsel or consultant:
Baker and Botts (B. Donovan Picard)

No Greater Love
1750 New York Ave., N.W., Washington, DC 20006
Telephone: (202) 783-4665
Background: Advocacy group for families who have lost relatives through war or acts of terrorism. Also serves as a support group for families of those held hostage in the Middle East.
Represented by:
Carmella LaSpada, Chairman of the Board

Nobelsville, Indiana, City of
Counsel or consultant:
Sagamore Associates, Inc. (David U. Gogol)

Nolisair (NationAir Canada)
Montreal, Quebec
Counsel or consultant:
Baker, Worthington, Crossley, Stansberry & Woolf (III J. E. Murdock)

Nomura Research Institute (America), Inc.
1001 Connecticut Ave., N.W., Suite 1022, Washington, DC 20036
Telephone: (202) 822-9431
Represented by:
Kota Washio, General Manager, Washington Office
Counsel or consultant:
Wilbur F. Monroe Associates (Wilbur F. Monroe)

Non Commissioned Officers Ass'n of the U.S.A.
225 North Washington St., Alexandria, VA 22314
Telephone: (703) 549-0311
Represented by:
C. R. Jackson, V. President for Gov't Affairs
Richard W. Johnson, Jr., Director of Legislation
C. A. McKinney, Legislative Counsel
T. L. Ryan, Director, State and Veterans Affairs

Non Ferrous Founders' Soc.
Des Plaines, IL
Background: Represented by Walter M. Kiplinger, Jr. of the American Cast Metals Ass'n.

Non-Ferrous Metals Producers Committee
c/o Economic Consulting Svcs. 1225 19th St., N.W, Suite 210, Washington, DC 20036
Telephone: (202) 466-7720
Counsel or consultant:
Economic Consulting Services Inc. (Kenneth R. Button)

Non-Partisan Transportation Action Committee
Box 2639, Springfield, VA 22152
Telephone: (703) 644-0700
Background: A political action committee promoting legislation favorable to the interests of school transportation. Supported by members of National School Transportation Ass'n and others. Represented by Karen E. Finkel of the Nat'l School Transportation Ass'n.

Non-Powder Gun Products Ass'n
1625 K St., N.W., Suite 900, Washington, DC 20006
Telephone: (202) 775-1762
Background: Represented by Jan Kinney of the Sporting Goods Manufacturers Ass'n.

Nonprescription Drug Manfacturers Ass'n
1150 Connecticut Ave., N.W.,, Washington, DC 20036
Telephone: (202) 429-9260
Background: Manufacturers and distributors of over-the-counter medicines.
Represented by:
James D. Cope, President
Barbara Gleason, Assistant Director, Public Affairs
Daniel F. O'Keefe, Jr., Sr. V. President & General Counsel
Allan R. Rexinger, Asst. Gen. Counsel and Dir., Con. Rels.
Counsel or consultant:
Clifford & Warnke (Robert A. Altman)

Nonprofit Mailers Federation
4351 Garden City Drive Suite 655, Landover, MD 20785
Telephone: (301) 577-6388
Represented by:
Esther Huggins, Member Services Manager

Noranda, Inc.
Toronto, Ontario
Counsel or consultant:
Weil, Gotshal & Manges (Robert C. Odle, Jr.)·

Nord Resources Corp.
Dayton, OH
Counsel or consultant:
Pagonis and Donnelly Group (Thomas R. Donnelly, Jr., George G. Pagonis)
Sutherland, Asbill and Brennan (Gordon O. Pehrson, Jr.)

Nordisk USA
Copenhagen, Denmark
Counsel or consultant:
Laxalt, Washington, Perito & Dubuc (Michael F. Cole)

Norfolk Port and Industrial Authority
Norfolk, VA
Counsel or consultant:
Steptoe and Johnson (Richard P. Taylor)

Norfolk Shipbuilding & Drydock Corp.
Norfolk, VA
Counsel or consultant:
Randolph G. Flood and Associates

Norfolk Southern Corp.
1500 K St., N.W., Suite 375, Washington, DC 20005
Telephone: (202) 383-4166
Represented by:
Edward T. Breathitt, Senior V. President, Public Affairs
John F. Corcoran, Assistant V. President, Public Affairs
James L. Granum, Assistant V. President, Public Affairs
Celia C. Lovell, Washington Representative

NorOats, Inc.
St. Ansgar, IA
Counsel or consultant:
Vickers & Vickers (Eugene B. Vickers)

Norseland Foods
Stamford, CT
Counsel or consultant:
Mudge Rose Guthrie Alexander and Ferdon (N. David Palmeter)

Norske Fiskeoppdretternes Salgslag (FO)
Norway
Counsel or consultant:
Mudge Rose Guthrie Alexander and Ferdon (Jeffrey S. Neeley, N. David Palmeter)

North American Export Grain Ass'n
1030 15th St., N.W. Suite 1020, Washington, DC 20005
Telephone: (202) 682-4030
Represented by:
Steven A. McCoy, President

North American Lake Management Soc.
1000 Connecticut Ave. Suite 300, Washington, DC 20036
Telephone: (202) 833-3380
Background: Address above is of J T & A, Inc., which manages the nat'l office of NALMS. Judith F. Taggart is the Exec. Secretary.
Counsel or consultant:
J T & A, Inc. (Judith F. Taggart)

North American Philips Corp.
1300 Eye St., N.W., Washington, DC 20005
Telephone: (202) 962-8550
Represented by:
Randall B. Moorhead, Director, Government Affairs
Thomas B. Patton, V. President, Government Relations
Counsel or consultant:
Wunder, Ryan, Cannon & Thelen (W. Stephen Cannon)

North American Securities Administrators Ass'n
555 New Jersey Ave., N.W., Suite 750, Washington, DC 20001-2029
Telephone: (202) 737-0900
Represented by:
Lee Polson, Exec. Director & General Counsel
Counsel or consultant:
Elias, Matz, Tiernan and Herrick
Rosapepe and Spanos (James C. Rosapepe)

North American Telecommunications Ass'n
2000 M Street, N.W., Suite 550, Washington, DC 20036
Telephone: (202) 296-9800
Represented by:
Mary Bradshaw, Director, Industry Relations
J. Dent Farr, Director, Government Relations
Eric Nelson, Director, Market Research
Edwin B. Spievack, President and Exec. Director

The listings in this directory are available as *Mailing Labels*. See last page.

ORGANIZATIONS REPRESENTED

North American Telecommunications Ass'n Political Action Committee
2000 M St., N.W. Suite 550, Washington, DC 20036
Telephone: (202) 296-9800
Background: Responsible contact is Mary Bradshaw. (See North American Telecommunications Ass'n.)

North Atlantic Ports Ass'n
Camden, NJ
Counsel or consultant:
LaRoe, Winn, Moerman & Donovan

North Beach Property Owner's Ass'n
Vero Beach, FL
Counsel or consultant:
Manatt, Phelps, Rothenberg & Phillips (Robert T. Herbolsheimer)

North Carolina Department of Natural Resources
Raleigh, NC
Counsel or consultant:
Dickstein, Shapiro and Morin (Bernard Nash)

North Carolina Natural Gas Corp.
Fayetteville, NC
Counsel or consultant:
Wright and Talisman

North Carolina Power Co.
Charlotte, NC
Counsel or consultant:
Flanagan Group, Inc. (Daniel V. Flanagan, Jr.)

North Carolina, State of
444 N. Capitol St., N.W. Suite 320, Washington, DC 20001
Telephone: (202) 624-5830
Represented by:
Karen Roberts, Director, Washington Office

North Dakota, State of ·
Bismarck, ND
Counsel or consultant:
Dickstein, Shapiro and Morin (Andrew P. Miller, Bernard Nash)

North Jersey District Water Supply Commission
Wanaque, NJ
Counsel or consultant:
Chambers Associates Incorporated (William L. Stringer)

North Las Vegas, Nevada, City of
Counsel or consultant:
Sagamore Associates, Inc. (David U. Gogol)

North Miami, City of
North Miami, FL
Counsel or consultant:
Crowell and Moring (Steven P. Quarles)

North Penn Gas Co.
Port Allegany, PA
Counsel or consultant:
Goldberg, Fieldman and Letham

North Rhine Westphalia, Government of
West Germany
Counsel or consultant:
Prather, Seeger, Doolittle and Farmer (Thomas L. Farmer)

North Slope Borough
Barrow, AK
Counsel or consultant:
Birch, Horton, Bittner and Cherot (Ronald G. Birch)

North West Timber Ass'n
Eugene, OR
Counsel or consultant:
Sidley and Austin (Judith Bello)

Northeast-Midwest Institute
218 D St., S.E., Washington, DC 20003
Telephone: (202) 544-5200
Represented by:
Dick Munson, Exec. Director

Northeast Ohio Regional Sewer District
Cleveland, OH
Counsel or consultant:
Squire, Sanders and Dempsey (Jeffrey O. Cerar)

Northeast Utilities Service Co.
Hartford, CT
Counsel or consultant:
Hunton and Williams
Paul, Hastings, Janofsky and Walker (Charles A. Patrizia)

Northeastern Airlines
Scranton, PA
Counsel or consultant:
Seamon, Wasko and Ozment (Howard G. Feldman)

Northeastern University
Boston, MA
Counsel or consultant:
Hale and Dorr (Jay P. Urwitz)
O'Neill and Athy, P.C. (Andrew Athy, Jr.)

Northern Air Cargo
Anchorage, AK
Counsel or consultant:
Jack Ferguson Associates (Jack Ferguson)

Northern California Power Agency
Roseville, CA
Background: Cities of Alameda, Biggs, Gridley, Healdsburg, Lodi, Lompoc, Palo Alto, Redding, Roseville, Santa Clara and Ukiah, associated with the Plumas-Sierra Rural Electric Cooperative.
Counsel or consultant:
E. Del Smith, Inc. (E. Del Smith)
Spiegel and McDiarmid (Robert C. McDiarmid)

Northern Indiana Public Service Co.
Hammond, IN
Counsel or consultant:
Beveridge & Diamond, P.C.
Edward H. Forgotson

Northern Jaeger
Seattle, WA
Counsel or consultant:
Bogle and Gates (Terry L. Leitzell)

Northern Mariana Islands, Commonwealth of
2121 R St., N.W., Washington, DC 20008
Telephone: (202) 673-5869
Background: The constitutionally mandated office serving as the arm for the Government of the Northern Mariana Islands on all official matters relating to the federal government.
Represented by:
Juan N. Barauto, Resident Representative to the U.S.
Alejandro M. Falig, Federal Programs Coordinator
Robert Swalbach, Congressional Liaison
Francisco I. Taitano, Federal Programs Coordinator
Martin B. Taman, Federal Programs Coordinator

Northern Pacific Transport, Inc.
Anchorage, AK
Counsel or consultant:
Ginsburg, Feldman and Bress (Jacob W. Rosenthal)

Northern States Power Co.
655 15th St., N.W., Suite 300, Washington, DC 20005
Telephone: (202) 639-4051
Represented by:
Gay H. Friedmann, Director, Federal Government Affairs
Counsel or consultant:
Bruder, Gentile & Marcoux (George F. Bruder)
Keller and Heckman
Madison Group/Earle Palmer Brown, The (Richard Rosenzweig)
Miller, Balis and O'Neil
Shaw, Pittman, Potts and Trowbridge (Gerald Charnoff, Jay E. Silberg)

Northern States Power Co. (Wisconsin)
Eau Claire, WI
Counsel or consultant:
Shaw, Pittman, Potts and Trowbridge

Northern Telecom Inc..
600 Maryland Ave., S.W. Suite 607, Washington, DC 20024
Telephone: (202) 554-1520

Represented by:
Melanie Carter-Maguire, Director, Government Relations, Int'l
Greg Farmer, Director, Government Relations
Mary S. Gordon, Manager, Government Relations
Paul J. Myer, V. President, Government Relations
Raymond Strassburger, Dir, Gov't Relations/Telecommun. Policy
Counsel or consultant:
Timmons and Co., Inc.

Northern Textile Ass'n
Boston, MA
Counsel or consultant:
Rowland & Sellery (William C. Sellery, Jr.)

Northland Marine Lines
Seattle, WA
Counsel or consultant:
Denning and Wohlstetter

Northrop Corp.
1000 Wilson Blvd., Suite 2300, Arlington, VA 22209
Telephone: (703) 525-6767
Represented by:
Ralph D. Crosby, Jr., V. P. & Manager, Washington Office
Robert W. Helm, V. President, Legislative Affairs
Loye W. Miller, Director, Public Information
Counsel or consultant:
Morris J. Amitay, P.C.
Hand, Arendall, Bedsole, Greaves & Johnston (Jack Edwards)
Manatt, Phelps, Rothenberg & Phillips (Charles T. Manatt, Robert J. Wager)
Timmons and Co., Inc.

Northwest Airlines, Inc.
900 17th St., N.W. Suite 526, Washington, DC 20006
Telephone: (202) 887-5636
Represented by:
Yoshie Ogawa, V. President, Internat'l Affrs.
Paul Schoellhamer, V. President, Government Affrs.
Counsel or consultant:
Cadwalader, Wickersham & Taft (Ronald D. Eastman)
Hughes Hubbard and Reed

Northwest Industrial Gas Users
Woodburn, OR
Counsel or consultant:
Ball, Janik and Novack (James A. Beall)

Northwest Marine Iron Works
Portland, OR
Counsel or consultant:
Ball, Janik and Novack (James A. Beall, Michelle E. Giguere)

Northwest Marine Terminal Ass'n
Portland, OR
Counsel or consultant:
Preston Gates Ellis & Rouvelas Meeds (William N. Myhre)

Northwest Pipeline Corp.
Salt Lake City, UT
Counsel or consultant:
Wright and Talisman

Northwest Public Power Ass'n
Vancouver, WA
Counsel or consultant:
Radin & Associates, Inc. (Alex Radin)

Northwestern Mutual Life Insurance Co.
1133 20th St., N.W., Suite 600, Washington, DC 20036
Telephone: (202) 296-1020
Represented by:
Frederic H. Sweet, V. President, Legislative Affairs
Counsel or consultant:
O'Neill and Athy, P.C. (Andrew Athy, Jr.)
Patton, Boggs and Blow (John Jonas)
Charls E. Walker Associates
Wunder, Ryan, Cannon & Thelen (Lawrence P. Higgins)

Northwestern Nat'l Life Insurance Co.
Minneapolis, MN
Counsel or consultant:
Nossaman, Guthner, Knox and Elliott (Warren G. Elliott)

ORGANIZATIONS REPRESENTED

Norway, Government of
Oslo, Norway
Counsel or consultant:
Burson-Marsteller

Norwegian Caribbean Lines
Miami, FL
Counsel or consultant:
Alcalde & Rousselot (Hector Alcalde)

Norwegian Dairies Ass'n
Norway
Counsel or consultant:
Mudge Rose Guthrie Alexander and Ferdon (N. David Palmeter)

Norwegian Fisheries Ass'n
Trondheim, Norway
Counsel or consultant:
Bogle and Gates (Terry L. Leitzell)

Norwest Corp.
Minneapolis, MN
Counsel or consultant:
Davis Polk & Wardwell (Theodore A. Doremus, Jr.)

NOVA, An Alberta Corp.
Calgary, Alberta
Background: A diversified enterprise, which includes ownership of Novacor Chemicals, Ltd. and the manufacture and sale of petrochemicals in the U.S. and Canada.
Counsel or consultant:
McHenry and Staffier, P.C. (George W. McHenry, Jr., John R. Staffier)
Wexler, Reynolds, Fuller, Harrison and Schule, Inc. (Anne Wexler, Bruce Wolpe)

NOVA University
Ft. Lauderdale, FL
Counsel or consultant:
Black, Manafort, Stone and Kelly Public Affairs Co. (Nicholas A. Panuzio)

Novacor Chemicals, Ltd.
Calgary, Alberta
Counsel or consultant:
Wexler, Reynolds, Fuller, Harrison and Schule, Inc. (Anne Wexler, Bruce Wolpe)

Novelty Manufacturing, Inc.
1140 Connecticut Ave., N.W., Suite 804, Washington, DC 20036
Telephone: (202) 452-6004
Counsel or consultant:
Offices of V.J. Adduci

Novophalt America, Inc.
Sterling, VA
Counsel or consultant:
Public Affairs Group, Inc. (Edie Fraser)

NTEA/Bankers Committee, The
1629 K St., N.W., Suite 1000, Washington, DC 20036
Telephone: (202) 466-8308
Background: An association of 500 banks and businesses concerned about promoting tax reform legislation and fair competition. Opposes taxation of savings and investment capital.
Represented by:
Edward N. Delaney, II, President
Gregory N. Johnson, Legislative Counsel
Arlene Vaonais, Communications Director

NTS Corp.
Louisville, KY
Counsel or consultant:
Dow, Lohnes and Albertson (William B. Ingersoll)

NTT America
New York, NY
Counsel or consultant:
Paul Muroyama & Assoc. (Paul Muroyama)

Nuclear Control Institute
1000 Connecticut Ave., N.W. Suite 704, Washington, DC 20036
Telephone: (202) 822-8444
Background: A non-profit educational organization concerned with the proliferation of nuclear weapons. Opposes the export of sensitive nuclear technology, materials and facilities. Sponsored the International Task Force on Prevention of Nuclear Terrorism.

Represented by:
Paul Leventhal, President
Sharon Leventhal, Exec. Director

Nuclear Information and Resource Service
1424 16th St., N.W. Suite 601, Washington, DC 20036
Telephone: (202) 328-0002
Background: A national clearinghouse for information on nuclear power and safe energy alternatives.
Represented by:
Diane D'Arrigo, Regulatory Oversight Coordinator
Michael Mariotte, Exec. Director

Nursery Industry Political Action Committee
1250 Eye St., N.W. Suite 500, Washington, DC 20005
Telephone: (202) 789-2900
Background: Represents the legislative and political interests of the American Ass'n of Nurserymen, Inc. Lawrence E. Scovotto and Benjamin C. Bolusky, of the Association, serve as contacts.

Nurses Ass'n of the American College of Obstetricians and Gynecologists
409 12th St., S.W., Washington, DC 20024
Telephone: (202) 638-0026
Represented by:
Nancy J. Sharp, R.N., Director of Practice and Legislation
Sallye B. Shaw, R.N., M.N., Exec. Director

Nursing Economics
1511 K St., N.W., Washington, DC 20005
Telephone: (202) 347-2187
Represented by:
Carmella A. Bocchino, Director, Legislative Services Division

NUS Corp.
910 Clopper Road, Gaithersburg, MD 20877-0962
Telephone: (301) 258-6000
Represented by:
John Bradburne, Director, Government Affairs
Counsel or consultant:
Griffin, Johnson & Associates

NutraSweet Co.
Skokie, IL
Counsel or consultant:
Burson-Marsteller (Sheila Raviv)
Timmons and Co., Inc.
Wunder, Ryan, Cannon & Thelen (Paul E. Sullivan)

Nuveen & Co., Inc., John
Chicago, IL
Counsel or consultant:
Royer, Mehle & Babyak (Gregory R. Babyak, Robert Stewart Royer)

NVW (USA)
Scarsdale, NY
Counsel or consultant:
Powell, Goldstein, Frazer and Murphy (Peter Suchman)

Nylo-Flex Manufacturing Co., Inc.
Mobile, AL
Counsel or consultant:
Max N. Berry Law Offices (Max N. Berry)

NYNEX
1828 L St., N.W., Suite 1000, Washington, DC 20036
Telephone: (202) 416-0100
Represented by:
Sue Browning, Director, Fed. Regulatory Matters (FCC)
Peter C. Czekanski, Director, Government Relations
Gordon R. Evans, Exec. Dir, Fed, Regulatory Matters (FCC)
Susanne Guyer, Director, Fed., Regulatory Matters (FCC)
Michael Hickey, Director, Gov't Relations (Agencies)
Robert J. Jasinski, Public Relations Manager
Irwin Litman, Exec. Dir., Legislative Tax Matters
Barbara A. Morris, Exec. Director, Government Relations
Cathy L. Slesinger, Exec. Director - International
Morrison DeS. Webb, V. President, Government Affairs
Counsel or consultant:
Bonner & Associates
Dewey, Ballantine, Bushby, Palmer and Wood (Lawrence F. O'Brien, III)
Paul, Hastings, Janofsky and Walker (Ralph B. Everett)
Verner, Liipfert, Bernhard, McPherson and Hand, Chartered (Riley K. Temple)
Wunder, Ryan, Cannon & Thelen (W. Stephen Cannon)

O and C Counties Ass'n
Roseburg, OR
Counsel or consultant:
Joseph S. Miller

Oak Ridge Nat'l Laboratory
Oak Ridge, TN
Counsel or consultant:
Ashby and Associates

Oakland, California, City of
Oakland, CA
Counsel or consultant:
Laxalt, Washington, Perito & Dubuc (James M. Christian, Sr.)

Oakland, California, Port of
Counsel or consultant:
Century Public Affairs (Philip A. Bangert, Richard L. Sinnott)

Oakland County Board of Supervisors
Pontiac, MI
Counsel or consultant:
Bishop, Cook, Purcell & Reynolds (H. Lawrence Fox)
Government Relations, Inc. (Thomas J. Bulger)

Oberlin College
Oberlin, OH
Counsel or consultant:
Ivins, Phillips and Barker (Philip D. Morrison)

O'Brien Energy Systems, Inc.
Philadelphia, PA
Counsel or consultant:
U.S. Strategies Corp. (K. Michael Matthews)

Occidental Chemical Corporation
1747 Pennsylvania Ave., N.W., Suite 375, Washington, DC 20006
Telephone: (202) 857-3000
Background: A subsidiary of Occidental Petroleum.
Represented by:
R. M. Julie Archuleta, V. President, Government Affairs
William G. Margaritis, Manager, State Government Affairs
Laurie J. Micciche, Manager, Federal Government Affairs

Occidental Coating Co.
Van Nuys, CA
Counsel or consultant:
Mudge Rose Guthrie Alexander and Ferdon (N. David Palmeter)

Occidental Internat'l Corp.
1747 Pennsylvania Ave., N.W., Suite 375, Washington, DC 20006
Telephone: (202) 857-3000
Background: A subsidiary of Occidental Petroleum Corp.
Represented by:
Jack King, Exec. V. President

Occidental Petroleum Corp.
1747 Pennsylvania Ave., N.W., Suite 375, Washington, DC 20006
Telephone: (202) 857-3000
Represented by:
Ernest S. Rosenberg, Dir, Envir'l and Health Legis & Reg Afrs
Counsel or consultant:
Baker, Worthington, Crossley, Stansberry & Woolf (W. Lee Rawls)
Hill and Knowlton Public Affairs Worldwide (Dale Lawson)
Manatt, Phelps, Rothenberg & Phillips (Robert J. Kabel)
van Kloberg and Associates (Edward J. van Kloberg, III)

Occupational Safety and Health Law Center
1536 16th St., N.W., Washington, DC 20036
Telephone: (202) 328-8300
Background: Founded in 1984 to represent workers in lawsuits over safety and health issues where unions can't or won't take action.
Represented by:
J. Davitt McAteer, Director

Ocean Spray Cranberries
Plymouth, MA
Counsel or consultant:
Cassidy and Associates, Inc. (Carol F. Casey, Gerald S. J. Cassidy, James P. Collins, C. Frank Godfrey, Jr.)

Ocean State Power
Boston, MA
Counsel or consultant:
Dickstein, Shapiro and Morin (John C. Dill)

Oceanic Institute
Waimanalo, HI
Counsel or consultant:
Wexler, Reynolds, Fuller, Harrison and Schule, Inc. (Terry D. Bevels)

Oceanside, California, City of
Counsel or consultant:
The Ferguson Co. (William Ferguson, Jr., Patricia Jordan, Thane Young)

Oceanside Redevelopment Agency
Oceanside, CA
Counsel or consultant:
The Ferguson Co. (William Ferguson, Jr., Patricia Jordan, Thane Young)

Oceantrawl, Inc.
Seattle, WA
Counsel or consultant:
Bogle and Gates (Terry L. Leitzell)

O'Connell Management Co.
North Quincy, MA
Counsel or consultant:
Cassidy and Associates, Inc. (Gerald S. J. Cassidy, James P. Fabiani)

O'Connor and Associates
Chicago, IL
Counsel or consultant:
Murphy and Associates (William T. Murphy, Jr.)

OEL/Norfin S.p.A.
Legnano, Italy
Counsel or consultant:
Dow, Lohnes and Albertson (William Silverman)

Oerlikon-Buhrle Ltd.
Quebec, Canada
Counsel or consultant:
Verner, Liipfert, Bernhard, McPherson and Hand, Chartered

Office for Advancement of Public Black Colleges
One Dupont Circle, N.W., Suite 710, Washington, DC 20036-1191
Telephone: (202) 778-0818
Represented by:
Joyce Payne, Director

Office of Fair Treatment of Internat'l Investment
Wilmington, DE
Counsel or consultant:
Miller & Chevalier, Chartered (Catherine T. Porter)

Office and Professional Employees Internat'l Union
815 16th St., N.W., Suite 606, Washington, DC 20006
Telephone: (202) 393-4464
Represented by:
Gilles Beauregard, Secretary-Treasurer

Office and Professional Employees Internat'l Union Voice of the Electorate
815 16th St., N.W., Suite 606, Washington, DC 20006
Telephone: (202) 393-4464
Background: Treasurer is Gilles Beauregard of the Ass'n.

Ogden Martin Systems
Fairfield, NJ
Counsel or consultant:
Nixon, Hargrave, Devans and Doyle

Oglala Sioux Tribe
Pine Ridge, SD
Counsel or consultant:
Hobbs, Straus, Dean and Wilder (S. Bobo Dean)

Oglethorpe Power Corp.
Tucker, GA
Counsel or consultant:
Ginn, Edington, Moore and Wade

Ohbayashi Corp.
New York, NY

Counsel or consultant:
Graham and James
Saunders and Company (Eric Edmondson, Steven R. Saunders)

Ohio Advanced Technology Center
Dayton, OH
Counsel or consultant:
Vorys, Sater, Seymour and Pease (Stephen H. Brown)

Ohio Alliance for Civil Justice
Columbus, OH
Counsel or consultant:
Bonner & Associates

Ohio Broadcasters Ass'n
Columbus, OH
Counsel or consultant:
Vorys, Sater, Seymour and Pease (Randal C. Teague)

Ohio Deposit Guaranty Fund
OH
Counsel or consultant:
Vorys, Sater, Seymour and Pease

Ohio Edison Co.
Akron, OH
Counsel or consultant:
Clarence J. Brown & Co. (Robert B. Giese)
Reid & Priest

Ohio Forestry Ass'n
Worthington, OH
Counsel or consultant:
Vorys, Sater, Seymour and Pease (Stephen H. Brown)

Ohio Manufacturers Ass'n
Columbus, OH
Counsel or consultant:
Vorys, Sater, Seymour and Pease

Ohio Soft Drink Ass'n
Columbus, OH
Counsel or consultant:
Vorys, Sater, Seymour and Pease

Ohio, State of
444 N. Capitol St., N.W., Suite 528, Washington, DC 20001
Telephone: (202) 624-5844
Represented by:
J. Gary Falle, Director, Washington Office
Jacqueline Gillan, Assistant Director

Oil, Chemical and Atomic Workers Internat'l Union
1126 16th St., N.W., Suite 411, Washington, DC 20036
Telephone: (202) 223-5770
Represented by:
Nolan W. Hancock, Citizenship-Legislative Director
Robert G. Wages, V. President
Counsel or consultant:
Akin, Gump, Strauss, Hauer and Feld (Richard Rivers, Edward L. Rubinoff)
Rod Rogers

Oil, Chemical and Atomic Workers Internat'l Union Committee on Political Education Fund
1126 16th St., N.W. Suite 411, Washington, DC 20036
Telephone: (202) 223-5770
Background: Represented by Nolan W. Hancock of the Oil, Chemical and Atomic Workers Union.

Oil Dri Corp. of America
Chicago, IL
Counsel or consultant:
Rogers Internat'l, Inc. (Joe O. Rogers)

OKC Limited Partnership
Dallas, TX
Counsel or consultant:
Korth and Korth (Fritz-Alan Korth)

Okeelanta Corp.
West Palm Beach, FL
Counsel or consultant:
Bergner, Boyette & Bockorny, Inc. (Van R. Boyette)

Oklahoma City, Oklahoma, City of
Counsel or consultant:
Barrett, Montgomery & Murphy (John H. Montgomery)

Oklahoma Department of Human Services
Oklahoma City, OK
Counsel or consultant:
Covington and Burling (Charles A. Miller)

Oklahoma Gas and Electric Co.
Oklahoma City, OK
Counsel or consultant:
Hunton and Williams
Wendorf & Associates (Frederick C. Wendorf)

Oklahoma Natural Gas Co.
Tulsa, OK
Counsel or consultant:
Pierson, Semmes, and Finley (W. DeVier Pierson, Paul Ryberg, Jr.)
G. Frank West

Old Harbor Corp.
Old Harbor, AK
Counsel or consultant:
Birch, Horton, Bittner and Cherot (Joseph M. Chomski)

Old Stone Federal Savings Bank
Providence, RI
Counsel or consultant:
St. Germain, Rodio & Ursillo, Ltd. (Fernand J. St. Germain)

Older Women's League
730 11th St., N.W. Suite 300, Washington, DC 20001
Telephone: (202) 783-6686
Background: Founded in 1980, OWL is a grass-roots organization focusing on issues and problems concerning mid-life older women through a D.C. office and over 100 national chapters.
Represented by:
Joan A. Kuriansky, Exec. Director
Laura Loeb, Public Policy Director

Olga Coal Co.
McMurray, PA
Background: A subsidiary of Lykes Corp.
Counsel or consultant:
Smith, Heenan and Althen

Olin Corp.
1730 K St., N.W., Suite 1300, Washington, DC 20006
Telephone: (202) 331-7400
Represented by:
Lawrence B. Anixt, Ordnance Div., Dir., Internat'l Mktg.
Robert E. Smith, Director, Federal Gov't Relations
John B. Zimmerman, Ordnance Div. Dir., Washington Office
Counsel or consultant:
Denny Miller Associates

Olin Corp. (Aerospace, Brass, Ordnance and Winchester Divisions)
East Alton, IL
Counsel or consultant:
Denny Miller Associates (Denny Miller)

Olin Corp. Good Government Fund
1730 K St., N.W., Suite 1300, Washington, DC 20006
Telephone: (202) 331-7400
Represented by:
Phyllis S. Black, Secretary
D. H. Brewer, Vice Chairman
George H. Nusloch, Chairman

Olivetti, USA
Dallas, TX
Counsel or consultant:
Lipsen Whitten & Diamond

Olympic Fibers
San Jose, Costa Rica
Counsel or consultant:
Patton, Boggs and Blow (James B. Christian, Jr.)

Omaha Public Power District
Omaha, NE
Counsel or consultant:
Hudson, Creyke, Koehler and Tacke

Omak Wood Products Co.
Omak, WA
Counsel or consultant:
Aylward & Finchem

ORGANIZATIONS REPRESENTED

Oman, Embassy of the Sultanate of
2342 Massachusetts Ave., N.W., Washington, DC 20016
Telephone: (202) 387-1980
Counsel or consultant:
Patton, Boggs and Blow (David E. Dunn, III)

OMB Watch
1731 Connecticut Ave., N.W., Washington, DC 20009-
1146
Telephone: (202) 234-8494
Background: A non-profit research and advocacy organization that monitors administrative governance issues, primarily those involving the White House Office of Management and Budget (OMB). Established to call greater
attention to the power of OMB and to promote a more
open and accountable government.
Represented by:
Dr. Gary D. Bass, Exec. Director
Shannon Ferguson, Technical Coordinator
David Plocher, Staff Attorney
Gwen Rubinstein, Program Associate

O'Melveny and Myers Political Action Committee
555 13th St., N.W. Suite 500 West, Washington, DC
20004
Telephone: (202) 383-5300
Counsel or consultant:
O'Melveny and Myers (Ben E. Benjamin)

OMI Corp.
New York, NY
Counsel or consultant:
Lipsen Whitten & Diamond
Preston Gates Ellis & Rouvelas Meeds (Jonathan Blank,
Susan B. Geiger, Emanuel L. Rouvelas)

Omni Internat'l
Rockville, MD
Counsel or consultant:
Williams and Connolly (Brendan V. Sullivan, Jr.)

Omstead Foods Ltd.
Wheatley, Ontario
Counsel or consultant:
Barnes, Richardson and Colburn (David O. Elliott, Mat-
thew T. McGrath)

On the Potomac Productions, Inc.
1221 11th St., N.W., Washington, DC 20001
Telephone: (202) 898-0899
Counsel or consultant:
Alvarado Group, The (Susan Alvarado)

Oncology Services, Inc.
State College, PA
Counsel or consultant:
U.S. Strategies Corp. (Joseph H. Miltenberger)

Onkyo U.S.A. Corp.
Ramsey, NJ
Background: A distributor of electronic products.
Counsel or consultant:
Patton, Boggs and Blow

Onoda Cement Co., Ltd.
Tokyo, Japan
Counsel or consultant:
Tanaka, Ritger and Middleton (Patrick F. O'Leary, H.
William Tanaka)

Ontario, Province of
Toronto, Ontario
Counsel or consultant:
Garvey, Schubert & Barer (Richard A. Wegman)
Hogan and Hartson (Clifford S. Gibbons, Mark S.
McConnell, Bob Glen Odle)

OPASTCO Political Action Committee
2000 K St., N.W. Suite 205, Washington, DC 20006
Telephone: (202) 659-5990
Background: The political action arm of the Organization
for the Protection and Advancement of Small Telephone
Cos. Represented by John Rose of the sponsoring organization.

Open Challenge Candidate Fund
403 First St., S.E., Wasgington, DC 20003
Telephone: (202) 547-4935
Background: Supports Democratic candidates in open seat
and challenger races for the U.S. Congress.

Represented by:
Pamela Davis Needham, President

Open Court Publishing Co.
Peru, IL
Counsel or consultant:
William J. Tobin and Associates (William J. Tobin)

Open Government Institute
2112 C Gallows Road, Vienna, VA 22180
Telephone: (703) 734-0500
Counsel or consultant:
Fensterwald & Alcorn, P.C. (Bernard Fensterwald, III)

OPERA America
777 14th St., N.W. Suite 520, Washington, DC 20005
Telephone: (202) 347-9262
Represented by:
Joanne M. Cooney, Administrative Director

Operaciones Turisticas, S.A.
Tegulcigalpa, Honduras
Counsel or consultant:
Laxalt, Washington, Perito & Dubuc

**Operative Plasterers' and Cement Masons' Inter-
nat'l Ass'n of the U.S. and Canada**
1125 17th St., N.W. 6th Floor, Washington, DC 20036
Telephone: (202) 393-6569
Represented by:
Robert J. Holton, General President

Ophthalmic Research Institute
5530 Wisconsin Ave., N.W. Suite 1149, Washington, DC
20815
Telephone: (301) 656-2214
Counsel or consultant:
PAI Management Corp. (Ronald W. Jones)

Opportunities Industrialization Centers
3224 16th St., N.W., Washington, DC 20010
Telephone: (202) 265-2626
Background: A private, non-profit network of training centers to assist unemployed, underemployed and disadvantaged persons to qualify for jobs. Based in Philadelphia
where the movement was originally established to assist
Black urban unemployed by Rev. Leon Sullivan.
Represented by:
Dr. Edward A. Hailes, Exec. Director, District of Columbia

OPT IN AMERICA
1020 19th St., N.W. Suite 500, Washington, DC 20036
Telephone: (202) 659-5212
Background: Promotes use of fiber optics in the home.
Represented by:
Gregory Owen Lipscomb, National Coordinator

Optic-Electronic Corp.
Dallas, TX
Counsel or consultant:
Cambridge Internat'l, Inc. (Justus P. White)

Optical Laboratories Ass'n
Box 2000, Merrifield, VA 22116-2000
Telephone: (703) 849-8550
Represented by:
Irby N. Hollans, Jr., Exec. Director

Optical Manufacturers Ass'n
6055A Arlington Blvd., Falls Church, VA 22044
Telephone: (703) 237-8433
Represented by:
Eugene Adams Keeney, Exec. V. President
Counsel or consultant:
Loomis, Owen, Fellman and Howe (James E. Anderson)

Optical Soc. of America
1816 Jefferson Place, N.W., Washington, DC 20036
Telephone: (202) 223-8130
Represented by:
Andrea Pendleton, Director, Communications
Dr. Jarus W. Quinn, Exec. Director

Opticians Ass'n of America
10341 Democracy Lane, Box 10110, Fairfax, VA 22030
Telephone: (703) 691-8355
Represented by:
Nancy Roylance, Exec. Director

Opticians Committee for Political Education
10341 Democracy Lane, Box 10110, Fairfax, VA 22030

Telephone: (703) 691-8355
Background: The political action committee of Opticians
Ass'n of America.
Represented by:
Dwayne J. Broe, Treasurer

Options Clearing Corp., The
Chicago, IL
Counsel or consultant:
Patton, Boggs and Blow (Thomas Hale Boggs, Jr.)

Options Policy Ass'n, The
Chicago, IL
Counsel or consultant:
Murphy and Associates (William T. Murphy, Jr.)

**OPTUR - La Sociedad Mercantil Operaciones
Turisticas**
Tegucigalpa, Honduras
Counsel or consultant:
Laxalt, Washington, Perito & Dubuc (Marc J. Scheineson)

Oracle Corp.
1627 Eye St., N.W., Suite 880, Washington, DC 20006
Telephone: (202) 657-7860
Represented by:
Donna S. Dempsey, Government Affairs Exec. Adminis-
trator
Timothy Feldman, Manager, Legislative Affairs
Kate McGee, Manager, Government Affairs
Riley Repko, Director, Government Affairs

Orange, California, County of
Counsel or consultant:
James F. McConnell

Orange County Sanitation Districts
Fountain Valley, CA
Counsel or consultant:
ENS Resources, Inc. (Eric Sapirstein)

Orange County Transit District
Santa Ana, CA
Counsel or consultant:
James F. McConnell

Orange County Transportation Commission
Santa Ana, CA
Counsel or consultant:
James F. McConnell

Orange County Water District
Fountain Valley, CA
Counsel or consultant:
James F. McConnell

Orange & Rockland
Pearl River, NY
Counsel or consultant:
Bergner, Boyette & Bockorny, Inc. (David A. Bockorny,
Van R. Boyette)

Orange, Texas, City of
Counsel or consultant:
Nat'l Center for Municipal Development (Barbara T.
McCall)
Preston Gates Ellis & Rouvelas Meeds (Allen Erenbaum,
Craig J. Gehring)

Orbital Research Fund
12500 Fair Lakes Circle, Fairfax, VA 22033
Telephone: (703) 631-3600
Background: The political action committee of the Orbital
Sciences Corp.; represented by Barbara C. Zadina of Or-
bital Sciences Corp.

Orbital Sciences Corp.
12500 Fair Lakes Circle, Fairfax, VA 22033
Telephone: (703) 631-3600
Represented by:
Barbara C. Zadina, Manager, Government & External Re-
lations

Order of Sons of Italy in America
219 E St., N.E., Washington, DC 20002
Telephone: (202) 547-2900
Counsel or consultant:
Palumbo & Cerrell, Inc. (Jeffrey D. Doranz, Benjamin L.
Palumbo, Paul A. Skrabut, Jr.)

Oregon Ass'n of Hospitals
Lake Oswego, OR

652

The listings in this directory are available as *Mailing Labels*. See last page.

ORGANIZATIONS REPRESENTED

Counsel or consultant:
Ryan-McGinn (Daniel McGinn)

Oregon Caneberry Commission
Salem, OR
Counsel or consultant:
Kilpatrick & Cody (Joseph W. Dorn)

Oregon Economic Development Dept., Ports Division
Portland, OR
Counsel or consultant:
Davis Wright Tremaine (Walter H. Evans, III)
Lindsay, Hart, Neil & Weigler (Peter Friedmann)

Oregon Graduate Institute of Science and Technology
Beaverton, OR
Counsel or consultant:
Ball, Janik and Novack (Michelle E. Giguere)

Oregon METRO
Portland, OR
Counsel or consultant:
Schwabe, Williamson and Wyatt (Frederick P. Hitz)

Oregon, State of
Salem, OR
Counsel or consultant:
Schwabe, Williamson and Wyatt (Frederick P. Hitz)
Wexler, Reynolds, Fuller, Harrison and Schule, Inc. (Terry D. Bevels, Robert M. Schule)

Oregon, State of, Department of Economic Development, Ports Division
Portland, OR
Counsel or consultant:
Davis Wright Tremaine (Walter H. Evans, III)

Oregon Steel Mills, Inc.
Portland, OR
Counsel or consultant:
Schwabe, Williamson and Wyatt (Frederick P. Hitz)

Organic Food Alliance
Arlington, VA
Counsel or consultant:
Potomac Partners
Tammen Group, The (Ronald L. Tammen)

Organization for American-Soviet ExchangeS (OASES-DC)
1302 R St., N.W., Washington, DC 20009
Telephone: (202) 332-1145
Background: A non-profit, non-political organization dedicated to establishing more open communication between citizens of the two superpowers. Facilitates person-to-person exchanges and visits; makes arrangements to host Soviets in the U.S.; provides English/Russian interpreting and translating services.
Represented by:
Elizabeth Gardiner, EPA/Environment Project Manager
Eleanor Gorman, EPA Project Assistant
Dr. C. Grant Pendill, Jr., Exec. Director
Leslie Sherman, Public Relations Coordinator
Kathy Woelfer, NAS, USIA Interpreting Coordinator

Organization for Fair Treatment of Internat'l Investment
Counsel or consultant:
Miller & Chevalier, Chartered (Catherine T. Porter)

Organization for the Protection and Advancement of Small Telephone Cos.
2000 K St., N.W., Suite 205, Washington, DC 20006
Telephone: (202) 659-5990
Background: The national trade association representing independently owned and operated telephone companies and cooperatives in rural America.
Represented by:
Ruth L. Barrens, Director of Education
Linda M. Buckley, Director, Public Relations
John Rose, Exec. V. President
Lisa M. Zaina, General Counsel

Organization of Chinese American Women
1300 N St., N.W., Suite 100, Washington, DC 20005
Telephone: (202) 638-0330
Represented by:
Pauline Tsui, Exec. Director

Organization of Chinese Americans
2025 Eye St., N.W. Suite 926, Washington, DC 20006
Telephone: (202) 223-5500
Background: A national non-profit educational and civic organization of concerned Chinese Americans. Encourages active participation by Chinese Americans in all areas of civic life. Has 45 local chapters in 25 states.
Represented by:
Melinda C. Yee, Exec. Director
Counsel or consultant:
Hopkins and Sutter (William Hou)

Organization of Professional Employees of the U.S. Dep't of Agriculture (OPEDA)
Box 381, Washington, DC 20044
Telephone: (202) 447-4898
Represented by:
Otis N. Thompson, Jr., Exec. Director

Orient Airlines Ass'n
Manila, Philippines
Counsel or consultant:
Galland, Kharasch, Morse and Garfinkle (Morris R. Garfinkle, Susan B. Jollie)

Orion Air
Raleigh, NC
Counsel or consultant:
Hewes, Morella, Gelband and Lamberton, P.C. (Stephen L. Gelband)

Orion Electric Co., Ltd.
Taipei, Taiwan
Counsel or consultant:
Barnes, Richardson and Colburn

Orlando, Florida, City of
Counsel or consultant:
Holland and Knight

Ormat Energy Systems
Sparks, NV
Counsel or consultant:
Chadbourne and Parke
Perkins Coie (Guy R. Martin)

Orphan Foundation of America
14261 Ben Franklin Station, N.W., Washington, DC 20044-4261
Telephone: (202) 861-0762
Background: A nationwide organization championing the rights of orphaned and abandoned youth.
Represented by:
Father Joseph Rivers, President

Orthotic and Prosthetic Nat'l Office
717 Pendleton St., Alexandria, VA 22314
Telephone: (703) 836-7114
Background: The national headquarters for the American Orthotic and Prosthetic Ass'n (AOPA), American Board for Certification in Orthotics and Prosthetics (ABC), American Academy of Orthotists and Prosthetists, and the American Orthotic and Prosthetic Ass'n Political Action Committee.
Represented by:
Dr. Ian R. Horen, Exec. Director

Ort's, Inc.
LaVale, MD
Counsel or consultant:
Robert N. Pyle & Associates (Robert N. Pyle)

Oryx Energy Co.
1212 New York Ave., N.W. Suite 1200, Washington, DC 20005-3987
Telephone: (202) 682-1212
Represented by:
Becky McGee, Senior Attorney
William F. Whitsitt, V. President, Government Relations
Counsel or consultant:
Baker and Botts (Thomas J. Eastment)
Johnson & Gibbs, P.C. (David G. Glickman)
Skadden, Arps, Slate, Meagher and Flom (Mike Naeve)

OSG Bulk Ships, Inc.
New York, NY
Counsel or consultant:
Patton, Boggs and Blow (Alan A. Tuttle)

Oshkosh Truck Corp.
4660 Kenmore Ave. Suite 1018, Alexandria, VA 22304

Telephone: (703) 823-9778
Represented by:
V. P. Grove, V. President, Government Affairs
Counsel or consultant:
McKenna, Conner and Cuneo (Del S. Dameron, Lane L. McVey)

OTI, Inc.
Houston, TX
Counsel or consultant:
Ottosen and Associates (Karl J. Ottosen, Carla L. Saunders)

OTL, Inc.
Las Vegas, NV
Counsel or consultant:
Woods and Associates (Irvin M. Woods)

Outboard Marine Corp.
Waukegan, IL
Counsel or consultant:
APCO Associates (Jocelyn White)
Economic Consulting Services Inc. (Bruce P. Malashevich, Deborah Swartz)
Jack McDonald Co. (Jack McDonald)
Steptoe and Johnson (Stewart A. Baker)

Outdoor Advertising Ass'n of America
1212 New York Ave., N.W., Suite 1210, Washington, DC 20005
Telephone: (202) 371-5566
Represented by:
Myron F. Laible, V. President
Roland McElroy, President
Ruth L. Segal, Director, Government Affairs
Counsel or consultant:
Ginn, Edington, Moore and Wade
Griffin, Johnson & Associates (Patrick J. Griffin, David E. Johnson)
O'Connor & Hannan
Rubin, Winston and Diercks (Walter E. Diercks, Eric M. Rubin)

Outdoor Power Equipment Aftermarket Ass'n
1001 Connecticut Ave., N.W., Washington, DC 20036
Telephone: (202) 775-8605
Counsel or consultant:
William S. Bergman Associates (William S. Bergman, CAE)

Outdoor Power Equipment Institute
341 S. Patrick St., Alexandria, VA 22314
Telephone: (703) 549-7600
Represented by:
Dennis C. Dix, Exec. Director & Chief Operating Officer
Counsel or consultant:
Collier, Shannon & Scott (Thomas F. Shannon)

Outokumpu Oy
Helsinki, Finland
Counsel or consultant:
Arent, Fox, Kintner, Plotkin & Kahn (Jerome P. Akman, Stephen L. Gibson, Lewis E. Leibowitz)

Ova Noss Family Partnership
Counsel or consultant:
Popham, Haik, Schnobrich & Kaufman, Ltd. (William E. Casselman, II)

Overseas Development Council
1717 Massachusetts Ave., N.W., Washington, DC 20036
Telephone: (202) 234-8701
Background: Seeks to promote better understanding of the economic and social problems of the developing nations and greater awareness of their importance to the United States. Serves as a leading forum for discussion of U.S. relations with and policies toward the Third World.
Represented by:
Sheldon Annis, Senior Associate
Christine Contee, Director of Public Affairs/Fellow
Richard E. Feinberg, V. President
Joan M. Nelson, Senior Associate
Victor H. Palmieri, Chairman
Sylvia Saborio, Sr. Trade Fellow
John W. Sewell, President
Stuart K. Tucker, Fellow

Overseas Education Ass'n
1201 16th St., N.W., Washington, DC 20036
Telephone: (202) 822-7850

ORGANIZATIONS REPRESENTED

Overseas Education Ass'n (Cont'd)
Represented by:
Ronald R. Austin, Exec. Director and General Counsel

Overseas Education Fund Internat'l
1815 H St., N.W., 11th Floor, Washington, DC 20006
Telephone: (202) 466-3430
Background: A private, nonprofit organization which addresses the need for programs focused on women in development. Works in over 50 countries to promote understanding of development problems unique to women from low-income backgrounds and single-headed households.
Represented by:
Cynthia Metzler, Exec. Director

Overseas Military Sales Group
Woodbury, NY
Background: A distributor overseas of American automobiles.
Counsel or consultant:
Royer, Mehle & Babyak (Robert Stewart Royer)

Overseas Nat'l Airways
Kingston, Jamaica
Counsel or consultant:
Alvord and Alvord
Shaw, Pittman, Potts and Trowbridge (Stephen D. Potts)

Overseas Shipping Co.
San Francisco, CA
Counsel or consultant:
Graham and James (Eliot J. Halperin)

Owens-Illinios
Toledo, OH
Counsel or consultant:
Reed Smith Shaw & McClay (Beatrice Bleicher)

Owens-Illinois Development Corp.
Toledo, OH
Counsel or consultant:
Dow, Lohnes and Albertson (Stuart Marshall Bloch)

Owner-Operator Independent Drivers Ass'n Political Action Committee
1055 Thomas Jefferson St., N.W., Suite 300, Washington, DC 20007
Telephone: (202) 342-8400
Counsel or consultant:
Collier, Shannon & Scott (K. Michael O'Connell)

Oxbow Power Cprp.
Dedham, MA
Counsel or consultant:
Chadbourne and Parke

Oxford Energy Co.
Santa Rosa, CA
Counsel or consultant:
John McE. Atkisson, P.C.
Leon G. Billings, Inc. (Leon G. Billings)
Charlie McBride Assoc, Inc. (Charlie McBride)

OXY USA Inc.
1747 Pennsylvania Ave., N.W., Suite 300, Washington, DC 20006
Telephone: (202) 857-3080
Background: A subsidiary of Occidental Petroleum Corp.
Represented by:
Jean L. Mestres, Manager, Federal Relations

P & O (TFL) Ltd./Trans Freight Lines
Wayne, NJ
Counsel or consultant:
Hoppel, Mayer and Coleman (Neal M. Mayer)

Pacific Coast Council of Freight Forwarders
Portland, OR
Counsel or consultant:
Lindsay, Hart, Neil & Weigler (Peter Friedmann)

Pacific Coast European Conference
San Francisco, CA
Counsel or consultant:
Graham and James

Pacific Enterprises
Los Angeles, CA
Counsel or consultant:
Gold and Liebengood, Inc. (Martin B. Gold)

Pacific Gas and Electric Co.
1726 M St., N.W., Suite 1100, Washington, DC 20036-4502
Telephone: (202) 466-7980
Represented by:
Patrick G. Golden, Attorney, Law Department
Thomas M. Hill, Director, Federal Legislative Relations
Robert D. Testa, Mgr., Federal Governmental Relations
John A. Vance, Wash. Counsel, Fed. Gov't Relations

Pacific Inland Navigation
Seattle, WA
Counsel or consultant:
Denning and Wohlstetter

Pacific Medical Center
Seattle, WA
Counsel or consultant:
Miller & Chevalier, Chartered (Alan R. Yuspeh)

Pacific Mutual Life Insurance Co.
Newport Beach, CA
Counsel or consultant:
McAuliffe, Kelly, Raffaelli & Siemens (James M. Copeland, Jr.)
Murray, Scheer & Montgomery (D. Michael Murray)

Pacific Nuclear Systems
Federal Way, WA
Counsel or consultant:
Denny Miller Associates

Pacific Power & Light
1350 New York Ave., N.W. Suite 600, Washington, DC 20005-4702
Telephone: (202) 347-5242
Represented by:
Sandra K. McDonough, Federal Affairs Manager

Pacific Press Publishing Ass'n
Boise, ID
Background: A publisher of religious materials, associated with the Seventh-day Adventist Church.
Counsel or consultant:
Johns and Carson

Pacific Resources, Inc.
1700 K St., N.W., Suite 502, Washington, DC 20006
Telephone: (202) 223-4623
Represented by:
John K. Evans, Consultant
Richard F. Hall, V. President, Government Affairs
Pamela J. Whitted, Manager, Federal Government Affairs

Pacific States Marine Fisheries Commission
Portland, OR
Counsel or consultant:
C. Deming Cowles, IV

Pacific Stock Exchange, Inc., The
San Francisco, CA
Counsel or consultant:
David Vienna & Associates (Peter Leigh Snell, David P. Vienna)

Pacific Telecom, Inc.
1726 M St., N.W. Suite 801, Washington, DC 20036
Telephone: (202) 223-5200
Represented by:
Alexander F. Karman, Assistant V. President

Pacific Telesis Group-Washington
1275 Pennsylvania Ave., N.W. Suite 400, Washington, DC 20004
Telephone: (202) 383-6400
Represented by:
W. F. Adler, Exec. Dir., Federal Regulatory Matters
Janet Ann Denton, Director, Federal Relations
Frank Hopwood, Dir., Federal Regulatory Relations
Marian E. McDowell, Director, Federal Relations
Thomas O. Moulton, Jr., V. President, Federal Relations
William Rittingham, Director, Federal Relations
Sara Hope Smith, Director, Federal Relations
Ronald F. Stowe, V. President, Washington Operations
Counsel or consultant:
Bonner & Associates
O'Connor & Hannan (Thomas H. Quinn)
Paul, Hastings, Janofsky and Walker (Ralph B. Everett)
Sutherland, Asbill and Brennan (Anne P. Jones)

Pacific Toxicology Laboratories
Los Angeles, CA
Counsel or consultant:
Bayless & Boland, Inc. (James L. Bayless, Jr., Michael J. P. Boland)

Pacificare Health Systems, Inc.
Cypress, CA
Counsel or consultant:
Dutko & Associates (Emily Young)

PacifiCorp
Portland, OR
Counsel or consultant:
Leighton and Sherline (Lee S. Sherline)
Stoel, Rives, Boley, Jones & Grey (Robert D. Van Brocklin)

Packaging Machinery Manufacturers Institute
1343 L St., N.W., Washington, DC 20005
Telephone: (202) 347-3838
Represented by:
Claude S. Breeden, Jr., Exec. Director
Counsel or consultant:
Webster, Chamberlain and Bean (George D. Webster)

Packing Education Foundation
11800 Sunrise Valley Dr., Reston, VA 22091
Telephone: (703) 620-2155
Background: Establishes and assists college programs in packaging science.
Counsel or consultant:
William C. Pflaum Co., Inc. (William C. Pflaum)

PACO Enterprises
Bayside, NY
Counsel or consultant:
Murphy and Demory, Ltd. (Admiral Daniel J. Murphy, USN (Ret.))

Page Land and Cattle Co.
Phoenix, AZ
Counsel or consultant:
Kogovsek & Associates, Inc.

PAI, Inc.
415 Church St. Suite 203, Vienna, VA 22180
Telephone: (703) 938-3385
Counsel or consultant:
Ruland Associates, Inc. (James K. Ruland)

Paine Webber Group
New York, NY
Counsel or consultant:
McNair Group Inc. (Denis J. Dwyer)
O'Connor & Hannan (Mary Scott Guest)
Patton, Boggs and Blow (Thomas Hale Boggs, Jr.)

Painting and Decorating Contractors of America
3913 Old Lee Highway Suite 33B, Fairfax, VA 22030
Telephone: (703) 359-0826
Represented by:
Vincent R. Sandusky, Exec. Director

Pakistan, Government of
Islamabad, Pakistan
Counsel or consultant:
Internat'l Public Strategies, Inc.

Pakistan Internat'l Airlines
Karachi, Pakistan
Counsel or consultant:
Zuckert, Scoutt and Rasenberger (James L. Devall)

Palau, Government of
Koror, Republic of Palau
Counsel or consultant:
Powell, Goldstein, Frazer and Murphy (Michael H. Chanin)

Palestine Affairs Center
1730 K St., N.W., Suite 703, Washington, DC 20006
Telephone: (202) 785-8394
Background: Represents Palestinian interests at the League of Arab States in the United States.
Represented by:
Hasan Abdel Rahman, Director

Palestinian Congress of North America
4401 East-West Highway Suite 301, Bethesda, MD 20814
Telephone: (301) 652-0052

The listings in this directory are available as *Mailing Labels*. See last page.

ORGANIZATIONS REPRESENTED

Represented by:
Said Arikat, Exec. Director

Palm-Aire Spa Resort/Katzoff Development Corp.
Pamano Beach, FL
Counsel or consultant:
Reese Communications Companies
Targeting Systems, Inc.

Palmer Associates, G. H.
Los Angeles, CA
Counsel or consultant:
Palumbo & Cerrell, Inc. (Jeffrey D. Doranz, Benjamin L. Palumbo, Paul A. Skrabut, Jr.)

Palo Alto, California, City of
Counsel or consultant:
Spiegel and McDiarmid (Joseph Van Eaton)

Palomar/Pomerado Hospital District
San Diego, CA
Counsel or consultant:
The William Chasey Organization (William C. Chasey, Ph.D.)

Pan-Alberta Gas, Ltd.
Calgary, Alberta
Counsel or consultant:
McHenry and Staffier, P.C. (George W. McHenry, Jr.)

Pan Am Political Action Committee
1200 17th St., N.W. Suite 500, Washington, DC 20036
Telephone: (202) 659-7805
Background: Chairman and Assistant Treasurer is William J. Evans of Pan American World Airways.

Pan American Health and Education Foundation
525 23rd St., N.W., Washington, DC 20037
Telephone: (202) 861-3416
Represented by:
Richard P. Marks, Exec. Secretary

Pan American Life
New Orleans, LA
Counsel or consultant:
Wunder, Ryan, Cannon & Thelen (Paul E. Sullivan)

Pan American Satellite Corp.
Greenwich, CT
Background: A satellite communications system.
Counsel or consultant:
Goldberg & Spector
Holland and Knight (Janet R. Studley)

Pan American World Airways
1200 17th St., N.W., Suite 500, Washington, DC 20036
Telephone: (202) 659-7805
Represented by:
William J. Evans, Systems Director, Government Affairs
Richard D. Mathias, Senior V. President, Government Affairs
Donald Taylor, Director of International Affairs
Counsel or consultant:
Crowell and Moring (Jerry W. Ryan)
Morgan, Lewis and Bockius
O'Melveny and Myers (William T. Coleman, Jr.)

Panama, Government of
Panama City, Panama
Counsel or consultant:
Arnold & Porter (Douglas Dworkin, William D. Rogers)

Pancyprian Ass'n of America
New York, NY
Counsel or consultant:
Manatos & Manatos, Inc. (Andrew E. Manatos, Dyck Van Koevering)

Panhandle Eastern Corp.
1025 Connecticut Ave., N.W., Suite 404, Washington, DC 20036
Telephone: (202) 331-8090

Represented by:
Michael E. Costello, Director, Government Affairs
Palmateer Ellie, Research Analyst
Frances M. Turk Granahan, Manager, Government Affairs
Wayne Pritchard, Research Analyst
Joseph J. Solters, Manager, Government Affairs
Lisa Yoho, Federal Relations Representative
Counsel or consultant:
Vinson and Elkins

Paper Industry of Maine
Augusta, ME
Counsel or consultant:
Reese Communications Companies
Targeting Systems, Inc.

Paperboard Packaging Council
1101 Vermont Ave., N.W. Suite 411, Washington, DC 20005
Telephone: (202) 289-4100
Represented by:
Spencer A. Johnson, V. President

Papeteries Bollore, S.A.
France
Counsel or consultant:
Barnes, Richardson and Colburn

Papua New Guinea, Government of
Port Moresby, Papua New Guinea
Counsel or consultant:
Cameron and Hornbostel (Duncan H. Cameron)

Par Pharmaceutical Inc.
Spring Valley, NY
Counsel or consultant:
Kleinfeld, Kaplan and Becker (Alan H. Kaplan)

Paralyzed Veterans of America
801 18th St., N.W., Washington, DC 20006
Telephone: (202) 872-1300
Represented by:
Linda K. C. Mansfield, Assoc. Exec. Director, Communication
Victor McCoy, Assoc. Exec. Director, Veterans Benefits
Robert L. Nelson, General Counsel
R. Jack Powell, Exec. Director
Philip Rabin, Public Education Director
Douglas K. Vollmer, Acting Assoc Exec. Dir., Gov't Relations

Paramount Communications, Inc.
1875 Eye St., N.W., Suite 1225, Washington, DC 20006
Telephone: (202) 429-9690
Represented by:
Lawrence E. Levinson, Sr. V. President, Government Relations
Andrew R. Paul, Director, Government Relations

Parcel Shippers Ass'n
1211 Connecticut Ave., N.W. Suite 406, Washington, DC 20036
Telephone: (202) 296-3690
Represented by:
David A. Bunn, Exec. V. President

Parcel Shippers Ass'n Political Action Committee
1211 Connecticut Ave., N.W., Washington, DC 20036
Telephone: (202) 296-3690
Background: Represented by David A. Bunn, Exec. V. President of the Association.
Counsel or consultant:
Patton, Boggs and Blow (Timothy J. May)

Parker Drilling Co.
Tulsa, OK
Counsel or consultant:
White & Case (Carolyn B. Lamm)

Parkinson Support Groups of America
11376 Cherry Hill Road, Suite 204, Beltsville, MD 20705
Telephone: (301) 937-1545
Represented by:
Ida M. Raitano, President

Parsons Brinkerhoff Quade & Douglas Inc.
555 13th St., N.W. Suite 460 West Tower, Washington, DC 20004
Telephone: (202) 637-8150

Represented by:
Catherine Connor, Manager, Government Relations
Mary Ann Novak, Program Director - Energy

Parsons Corp.
1133 15th St., N.W. Suite 800, Washington, DC 20005
Telephone: (202) 775-6010
Represented by:
Joseph K. Bratton, Jr., Sr. V. Pres., Manager, Washington Opns.
W. Jack Hargett, Manager, Governmental Affairs

Partners for Livable Places
1429 21st St., N.W., Washington, DC 20036
Telephone: (202) 887-5990
Background: Formed in 1977 to work for the economic health and improvement of the quality of life of communities across the country.
Represented by:
Robert H. McNulty, President

Partners of the Americas
1424 K St., N.W. Suite 700, Washington, DC 20005
Telephone: (202) 628-3300
Represented by:
William Reese, President
Counsel or consultant:
Bill Newbold & Assoc. (Bill Newbold)

Partnership for Democracy
2335 18th St., N.W., Washington, DC 20009
Telephone: (202) 483-0030
Represented by:
Bob Nicklas, Deputy Director
Lori Rubenstein, Exec. Director

Partnership for Improved Air Travel
1709 New York Ave., N.W. 5th Floor, Washington, DC 20006
Telephone: (202) 626-4200
Background: A coalition of aviation interests and air passengers seeking to educate the public on the need for more and improved airports and better management of the Federal Aviation Administration.
Represented by:
Jim Brown, Director of Communications
Drew Steketee, Director

Partnerships in Education
Englewood, NJ
Counsel or consultant:
Westermann and Hendricks, Inc. (Diane Hendricks, Edith E. Westermann)

Pasadena, California, City of
Counsel or consultant:
Nat'l Center for Municipal Development (Carolyn Chaney)

Pathology Practice Ass'n
1301 Connecticut Ave., N.W. 7th Floor, Washington, DC 20036
Telephone: (202) 659-0330
Counsel or consultant:
Fleishman-Hillard, Inc (Paul Johnson, Caren Turner)

Pathology Practice Ass'n Federal Political Action Committee
1301 Connecticut Ave., N.W., Washington, DC 20036
Telephone: (202) 659-4593
Represented by:
Royce L. Rollins, Treasurer

Patlex Corp.
Chatsworth, CA
Counsel or consultant:
Garland Associates (Sara G. Garland)

Patten Corp.
Stamford, VT
Counsel or consultant:
Dow, Lohnes and Albertson (William B. Ingersoll)

Pattern Recognition Soc.
Georgetown Medical Ctr. Pre-Clinical Sci. Bldg. LR3, Washington, DC 20007
Telephone: (202) 687-2121
Background: An organization of computer scientists.
Represented by:
Robert S. Ledley, Exec. Director

ORGANIZATIONS REPRESENTED

Paul, Hastings, Janofsky and Walker Political Action Committee
1050 Connecticut Ave., N.W., Suite 1200, Washington, DC 20036-5331
Telephone: (202) 223-9000
Counsel or consultant:
Paul, Hastings, Janofsky and Walker (Ralph B. Everett)

Paulucci Enterprises
Sanford, FL
Counsel or consultant:
Dickstein, Shapiro and Morin (Henry C. Cashen, II)

Pax Americas
122 Maryland Ave., N.E., Third Floor, Washington, DC 20002
Telephone: (202) 546-0116
Background: A political action committee (formerly known as Priorities PAC), co-chaired by Rep. George Miller (D-CA) and Ms. Rosa DeLauro.
Represented by:
Cindy M. Buhl, PAC Director

PCI, Inc.
Richmond Hill, Ontario
Counsel or consultant:
Murphy and Demory, Ltd. (Admiral Daniel J. Murphy, USN (Ret.))

Peabody Holding Co.
122 C St., N.W., Suite 240, Washington, DC 20001
Telephone: (202) 393-4366
Background: The nation's largest producer and marketer of coal.
Represented by:
Christopher G. Farrand, V. President for Government Relations
Jeffrey L. Klinger, Eastern Regional Counsel
Counsel or consultant:
R. Duffy Wall and Associates (R. Duffy Wall)

PEACE PAC
100 Maryland Ave., N.E., Washington, DC 20002
Telephone: (202) 543-4100
Background: Affiliated with Council for a Livable World. Focuses on U.S. House of Representatives.
Represented by:
Jerome Grossman, Jr., Treasurer

Peanut Butter and Nut Processors Ass'n
9005 Congressional Ct., Potomac, MD 20854
Telephone: (301) 365-4080
Background: James E. Mack of American Trade Ass'n Management serves as Managing Director and General Counsel.
Counsel or consultant:
American Trade Ass'n Management (James E. Mack, CAE)

Peanut Butter and Nut Processors Ass'n Political Action Committee
9005 Congressional Court, Potomac, MD 20854
Telephone: (301) 365-4080
Counsel or consultant:
American Trade Ass'n Management (James E. Mack, CAE)

Peat Marwick
Los Angeles, CA
Counsel or consultant:
Hill and Knowlton Public Affairs Worldwide (Joan Worden)
Jefferson Group, The (Frederick J. Hannett)

Pechiney Corp.
Greenwich, CT
Counsel or consultant:
Dorsey & Whitney

Pediatricians for Children Inc.
c/o Reed Smith Shaw & McClay 1200 18th St., N.W., Washington, DC 20036
Telephone: (202) 457-6100
Background: Part of the Coalition for Health Funding. Elizabeth J. Noyes of the American Academy of Pediatrics serves as Treasurer.

Peerless Petrochemicals, Inc.
Peneles, PR
Counsel or consultant:
William Bode and Associates (William Bode)*

Pelavin Associates
2030 M St., N.W., 8th Floor, Washington, DC 20036
Telephone: (202) 785-3308
Counsel or consultant:
Gallagher-Widmeyer Group Inc., The (Scott D. Widmeyer)

PEMCO AEROPLEX, Inc.
Birmingham, AL
Counsel or consultant:
J. C. Steen

Penn Mutual Life Insurance Co.
Philadelphia, PA
Counsel or consultant:
Murray, Scheer & Montgomery (D. Michael Murray)

Penn Yan, New York, Municipality of
Counsel or consultant:
Duncan, Weinberg, Miller & Pembroke, P.C. (Wallace L. Duncan, Jeffrey C. Genzer)

Penney Co., J. C.
1156 15th St., N.W., Suite 1015, Washington, DC 20005
Telephone: (202) 862-4800
Represented by:
Richard C. Darling, Manager, Federal Gov't Relations
Mallory B. Duncan, Attorney
Raymond A. Messina, Attorney
Obie L. Moore, Senior Federal Legislative Manager
Russell H. Pearson, Senior Federal Legislative Manager
Diane A. Sawaya-Barnes, Attorney
James C. Schwaninger, Sr. Gov't. Relations Representative
J. Guy Tetirick, Manager, State/Local Gov't Relations
Counsel or consultant:
O'Connor & Hannan (Patrick E. O'Donnell)
Wilkinson, Barker, Knauer and Quinn

Pennsylvania Ass'n of Nurse Anesthetists
Harrisburg, PA
Counsel or consultant:
Lipsen Whitten & Diamond

Pennsylvania Builders Ass'n
Harrisburg, PA
Counsel or consultant:
Manning, Selvage & Lee/Washington

Pennsylvania, Commonwealth of
444 N. Capitol St., N.W., Suite 700, Washington, DC 20001
Telephone: (202) 624-7828
Represented by:
Philip F. Jehle, Washington Office Director

Pennsylvania Electric Co.
Johnstown, PA
Counsel or consultant:
Shaw, Pittman, Potts and Trowbridge

Pennsylvania Engineering Co.
Philadelphia, PA
Counsel or consultant:
Vinson and Elkins (James C. Gould)
R. Duffy Wall and Associates (R. Duffy Wall)

Pennsylvania Mines Corp.
Ebensburg, PA
Counsel or consultant:
Lund and O'Brien

Pennsylvania Power and Light Co.
Allentown, PA
Counsel or consultant:
Hunton and Williams
Kaye, Scholer, Fierman, Hays and Handler
Lund and O'Brien (James D. O'Brien)
McCarthy, Sweeney and Harkaway, P.C.
Shaw, Pittman, Potts and Trowbridge (Jay E. Silberg)

Pennsylvania State System of Higher Education
Harrisburg, PA
Background: Comprised of 14 state university elements.
Counsel or consultant:
Peabody Fitzpatrick Communications (J. Douglas Koelemay, Myra B. Peabody)

Pennsylvania Turnpike Commission
Harrisburg, PA

Counsel or consultant:
Cassidy and Associates, Inc. (Larry F. Ayres, Charles F. Dougherty, Donald P. Smith)

Pennwalt Corp.
Philadelphia, PA
Counsel or consultant:
Burson-Marsteller
LaRoe, Winn, Moerman & Donovan (Gerald L. Richman)

Pennzoil Co.
1155 15th St., N.W., Suite 600, Washington, DC 20005
Telephone: (202) 331-0212
Represented by:
Karen K. Hillenbrand, Washington Representative
Paul R. Kruse, Senior Washington Representative
Frank A. Verrastro, V. President, Government Relations
Counsel or consultant:
Baker, Worthington, Crossley, Stansberry & Woolf (W. Lee Rawls)
Camp, Barsh, Bates and Tate (Harry E. Barsh, Jr.)
Gold and Liebengood, Inc. (Martin B. Gold, Howard S. Liebengood)
Winburn, VanScoyoc, and Hooper (John P. Winburn)

Pension Rights Center
918 16th St., N.W., Suite 704, Washington, DC 20006
Telephone: (202) 296-3776
Background: Concerned with the rights of individuals. Educates the public and represents pensioner interests.
Represented by:
Karen W. Ferguson, Director

People for the American Way
2000 M St., N.W., Suite 400, Washington, DC 20036
Telephone: (202) 467-4999
Background: A national nonprofit, nonpartisan education organization founded in 1980 to promote First Amendment rights and democratic values. This 200,000 member organization focuses primarily on issues of church-state separation, religious liberty, intellectual freedom, justice and the independent judiciary and access to ideas, information, citizen education, and civic rights. Chairman of the Board is John Buchanan Jr. of the Kettering Foundation.
Represented by:
Marsha Nye Adler, Legislative Representative
Susan Armsby, Legislative Representative
John Buchanan, Chairman
David C. Crane, V. Pres, Issues Development and Research
John S. Gomperts, Legislative Counsel
Arthur Kropp, President
Elliot M. Mincberg, Director, Legal Department
Beth Tuttle, V. President, Communications
Melanne Verveer, Exec. V. Pres. & Dir., Public Policy
William B. Wasserman, Field Director

People for the American Way Action Fund
2000 M St., N.W., Suite 400, Washington, DC 20036
Telephone: (202) 467-4999
Background: Contact is Melanne Verveer of People for the American Way.

People for the Ethical Treatment of Animals (PETA)
4980 Wyaconda Road, Rockville, MD 20852
Telephone: (301) 770-7444
Background: Seeks elimination of the use of animals for experimentation, in the food and clothing industries and for amusement.
Represented by:
Ingrid Newkirk, National Director
Alex Pacheco, Chairperson
Counsel or consultant:
Swift Consulting Co., Ltd., The (Ivan, Red Swift)

People-to-People Health Foundation (Project HOPE)
2 Wisconsin Circle, Suite 500, Chevy Chase, MD 20815
Telephone: (301) 656-7401
Represented by:
Thomas Walsh, General Counsel
Dr. William B. Walsh, President

Peoples Bank
Bridgeport, CT
Counsel or consultant:
James J. Butera, Chartered

People's Committee for Libyan Students
510 N. Washington St. Suite 400, Falls Church, VA 22045
Telephone: (703) 532-6262
Represented by:
Mohammed Bashir, Washington Representative
Counsel or consultant:
Beveridge & Diamond, P.C.

Peoples Energy Corp.
Chicago, IL
Counsel or consultant:
Hopkins and Sutter (Lawrence M. Dubin)

Peoples Heritage Savings Bank
Portland, ME
Counsel or consultant:
Wilmer, Cutler and Pickering (Michael S. Helfer)

People's National Party
Kingston, Jamaica
Counsel or consultant:
Curtis A. Ward

Peoples Natural Gas Co.
Pittsburgh, PA
Background: A subsidiary of the Consolidated Natural Gas
Co. Represented by Beverly E. Jones of the parent com-
pany.

Peoples Westchester Savings Bank
Hawthorne, NY
Counsel or consultant:
Thacher, Proffitt and Wood (Louis H. Nevins)

PEPCO Political Action Committee
1900 Pennsylvania Ave., N.W. Suite 804, Washington, DC
20068
Telephone: (202) 872-2823
Background: A political action committee sponsored by the
Potomac Electric Power Co. Chairman of the Committee
is Martin J. Kmetz of the Company.

PepsiCo, Inc.
Purchase, NY
Counsel or consultant:
Akin, Gump, Strauss, Hauer and Feld
Howrey and Simon (Richard T. Colman, Raymond A.
Jacobsen, Jr.)
Kilpatrick & Cody (C. Randall Nuckolls, Mark D. Win-
cek)
Wilmer, Cutler and Pickering (William J. Wilkins)

PepsiCo PAC
Purchase, NY
Counsel or consultant:
Wunder, Ryan, Cannon & Thelen (Paul E. Sullivan)

Perdue Farms Inc.
Salisbury, MD
Counsel or consultant:
Kelly and Associates, Inc. (John A. Kelly)

Performing Arts Network of New Jersey
Trenton, NJ
Counsel or consultant:
Santarelli, Smith, Kraut and Carroccio (A. Thomas Car-
roccio)

Perkins Coie Political Action Committee
1110 Vermont Ave., N.W. Suite 1200, Washington, DC
20005
Telephone: (202) 887-9030
Background: The political action committee of the law firm
Perkins Coie.
Counsel or consultant:
Perkins Coie (Guy R. Martin)

Permanente Medical Group, Inc., The
Oakland, CA
Counsel or consultant:
Johnson & Gibbs, P.C. (Bryan P. Collins, Lawrence B.
Gibbs, David G. Glickman, Richard C. Stark)

Perot Group, The
Dallas, TX
Counsel or consultant:
Lipsen Whitten & Diamond

Perot Systems Inc.
Vienna, VA
Counsel or consultant:
Lipsen Whitten & Diamond

Perpetual Savings Bank
2034 Eisenhower Ave., Alexandria, VA 22314
Telephone: (703) 838-6000
Counsel or consultant:
O'Connor & Hannan (Thomas H. Quinn)

Perrier Group
Greenwich, CT
Counsel or consultant:
Arent, Fox, Kintner, Plotkin & Kahn

Persico Pizzamiglio, S.A.
Sao Paulo, Brazil
Counsel or consultant:
O'Melveny and Myers

Peru, Government of
Lima, Peru
Counsel or consultant:
White & Case

Pet Food Institute
1101 Connecticut Ave., N.W. Suite 700, Washington, DC
20036
Telephone: (202) 857-1120
Counsel or consultant:
Smith, Bucklin and Associates (Duane H. Ekedahl, Susan
Kudla Finn, Timothy Rugh)

Pet Industry Joint Advisory Council
1710 Rhode Island Ave., N.W. Suite 200, Washington, DC
20036
Telephone: (202) 452-1525
Represented by:
Howard Deardorff, Director, Membership Services
Marshall Meyers, General Counsel
Counsel or consultant:
Meyers and Alterman (N. Marshall Meyers)

Peter White Coal Mining Co.
Bluefield, WV
Background: A subsidiary of Belco Petroleum Corp.
Counsel or consultant:
Smith, Heenan and Althen (Michael T. Heenan)

Petrochemical Energy Group
1100 15th St., N.W. Suite 1200, Washington, DC 20005
Telephone: (202) 452-1880
Background: An ad hoc group of independent petrochemi-
cal producers.
Counsel or consultant:
Travis & Gooch

Petrojam Ltd.
Kingston, Jamaica
Counsel or consultant:
William Bode and Associates (William Bode)
Collier, Shannon & Scott (R. Timothy Columbus)

Petroleos de Venezuela, S.A.
Caracas, Venezuela
Counsel or consultant:
Cleary, Gottlieb, Steen and Hamilton
Collier, Shannon & Scott (Paul D. Cullen, William W.
Scott, Thomas F. Shannon)
Hill and Knowlton Public Affairs Worldwide (Lauri J.
Fitz-Pegado)

Petroleum Marketers Ass'n of America
1120 Vermont Ave., N.W., Suite 1130, Washington, DC
20005
Telephone: (202) 331-1198
Represented by:
Phillip R. Chisholm, Exec. V. President
Alan J. Cobb, V. Pres., Legislative & Political Affrs.
Barbara J. Faulkner, V. Pres. for Policy and Legal Affairs
Amy Graham, Heating Fuels Counsel
David L. Morehead, V. President, Communications

**Petroleum Marketers Ass'n of America Small
Businessmen's Committee**
1120 Vermont Ave., N.W., Suite 1130, Washington, DC
20005
Telephone: (202) 331-1198
Background: The political action arm of the Petroleum
Marketers Ass'n of America. Responsible contact is Phillip R. Chisholm, Exec. V. President of the Association.
Assistant Treasurer of the PAC is Alan J. Cobb, V. President of Legislative and Political Affairs for the Association.

PETROMIN
Riyadh, Saudi Arabia
Background: The government-owned general petroleum
and mineral monopoly.
Counsel or consultant:
Dutton and Dutton, P.C. (Frederick G. Dutton)

Pew Health Professions Commission
Durham, NC
Counsel or consultant:
Peabody Fitzpatrick Communications (Joyce Fitzpatrick,
J. Douglas Koelemay)

PFIC Group
1333 New Hampshire Ave., N.W., Washington, DC 20036
Telephone: (202) 862-2200
Background: A coalition of multinational corporations
seeking revision of the Tax Reform Act of 1986 to remove the overlap between the provision governing 'pas-
sive foreign investment companies and controlled foreign
corporations.' The address given is that of the law firm of
Cadwalader, Wickersham & Taft.
Counsel or consultant:
Cadwalader, Wickersham & Taft (J. Roger Mentz)

Pfizer, Inc.
1455 Pennsylvania Ave., N.W., Suite 925, Washington, DC
20004
Telephone: (202) 783-7070
Represented by:
Catherine P. Bennett, Exec. Director, Government Rela-
tions
M. Kenneth Bowler, V. President, Washington Govt Af-
fairs
Marjorie O. Crawford, Manager, Government Relations
Walter K. Moore, Director, Congressional Relations
Christopher A. Singer, Manager, Regulatory Affairs
Counsel or consultant:
Arnold & Porter (James F. Fitzpatrick)
Burson-Marsteller (Wayne L. Pines)
Dewey, Ballantine, Bushby, Palmer and Wood (Joseph A.
Califano, Jr.)
Epstein Becker and Green (Deborah Steelman)
Jones, Day, Reavis and Pogue (Raymond J. Wiacek)
Lee, Toomey & Kent
Parry and Romani Associates Inc.
Wunder, Ryan, Cannon & Thelen (Kenneth S. Levine,
Thomas M. Ryan)

PG&E-Bechtel Generating Co.
Bethesda, MD
Counsel or consultant:
Webster and Sheffield (L. Andrew Zausner)

PGA Tour
Ponte Vedra, FL
Counsel or consultant:
Camp, Barsh, Bates and Tate (Dan C. Tate)

Pharmaceutical Aerosol CFC Coalition
1001 Pennsylvania Ave., N.W. Suite 750, Washington, DC
20004
Telephone: (202) 347-9200
Counsel or consultant:
Gardner, Carton and Douglas (J. Curtis Moffat)

Pharmaceutical Manufacturers Ass'n
1100 15th St., N.W., Washington, DC 20005
Telephone: (202) 835-3400
Represented by:
Robert F. Allnutt, Exec. V. President
Gerald J. Mossinghoff, President
Lynda L. Nersesian, Deputy V. Pres., Government Rela-
tions
Michael L. Reed, V. President, Government Relations
Albert C. Saunders, Legislative Counsel
James W. Singer, III, Legislative Counsel
Jonathan B. Spear, Legislative Counsel
Counsel or consultant:
Bonner & Associates
Epstein Becker and Green (Deborah Steelman)
Griffin, Johnson & Associates
van der Voort Associates, Ltd. (Thomas L. van der
Voort)
R. Duffy Wall and Associates (R. D. Folsom, Michael
Stern, R. Duffy Wall)
Williams and Jensen, P.C. (J. D. Williams)

The listings in this directory are available as *Mailing Labels*. See last page.

ORGANIZATIONS REPRESENTED

Pharmaceutical Manufacturers Ass'n Better Government Committee
1100 15th St., N.W. Suite 900, Washington, DC 20005
Telephone: (202) 835-3400
Represented by:
Vincent J. Klaus, Treasurer

Pharmakinetics Laboratories, Inc.
Counsel or consultant:
Laxalt, Washington, Perito & Dubuc (Michael F. Cole)

Phase Two Industries
Santa Clara, CA
Counsel or consultant:
Ashby and Associates (John C. Stevens)

Phelps Dodge Corp.
1015 15th St., N.W., Suite 909, Washington, DC 20005
Telephone: (202) 789-1745
Represented by:
Joan Costain Bowyer, Asst. to the V. Pres., Gov't Relations
Charles S. Burns, Vice President, Government Relations

PHH Corp.
Hunt Valley, MD
Counsel or consultant:
Will & Muys, P.C. (Robert P. Will)

PHH-Homequity
Wilton, CT
Background: Represents with federal agencies and Congress relocation services for employees.
Counsel or consultant:
Neill, Mullenholz and Shaw (G. Jerry Shaw, Jr.)

Philadelphia Electric Co.
Philadelphia, PA
Counsel or consultant:
Conner and Wetterhahn, P.C. (Troy B. Conner, Jr.)
O'Melveny and Myers
Reid & Priest (Peyton G. Bowman, III)

Philadelphia Industrial Development Corp.
Philadelphia, PA
Counsel or consultant:
Burson-Marsteller
Reid & Priest (Stephan M. Minikes)

Philadelphia, Pennsylvania, City of
Counsel or consultant:
Burson-Marsteller (Rebecca L. Halkias)
Peyser Associates, Inc.
Reid & Priest (Stephan M. Minikes)

Philadelphia Port Corp.
Philadelphia, PA
Counsel or consultant:
Burson-Marsteller (Rebecca L. Halkias)

Philip Morris Cos., Inc.
New York, NY
Counsel or consultant:
Arnold & Porter
Richard W. Bliss
Bonner & Associates
Burson-Marsteller
The Susan Davis Companies
Madison Group/Earle Palmer Brown, The
McAuliffe, Kelly, Raffaelli & Siemens (John D. Raffaelli)
Reese Communications Companies
Stanton & Associates (James V. Stanton)
Sutherland, Asbill and Brennan (Wright H. Andrews, Jr.)

Philip Morris Internat'l
New York, NY
Counsel or consultant:
Reese Communications Companies

Philip Morris Management Corp.
1341 G St., N.W., Suite 900, Washington, DC 20005
Telephone: (202) 637-1500

Represented by:
James W. Dyer, Director, Washington Relations
David I. Greenberg, Staff V. President, Washington Relations
Kathleen M. Linehan, Senior Director, Washington Relations
Robert Y. Maples, Washington Representative
Amy J. Millman, Washington Representative
Donald M. Nelson, Jr., Director, Internat'l Trade Relations
Jay Poole, Regional Manager, Mid-Atlantic Region
Robert S. Reese, Jr., Director, Washington Relations
Gregory R. Scott, Washington Representative
Counsel or consultant:
APCO Associates (Neal M. Cohen, Margery Kraus)
Baker, Worthington, Crossley, Stansberry & Woolf (W. Lee Rawls)
Gold and Liebengood, Inc. (Martin B. Gold, Howard S. Liebengood)
Manatt, Phelps, Rothenberg & Phillips (Robert J. Kabel, Charles T. Manatt, William C. Oldaker)
McAuliffe, Kelly, Raffaelli & Siemens (John D. Raffaelli)
Winburn, VanScyoc, and Hooper (John P. Winburn)
Wunder, Ryan, Cannon & Thelen (Kenneth S. Levine, Thomas M. Ryan)

Philip Morris USA
New York, NY
Counsel or consultant:
Targeting Systems, Inc.

Philipp Brothers, Inc.
1455 Pennsylvania Ave., N.W., Suite 350, Washington, DC 20006
Telephone: (202) 879-4141
Represented by:
Lester G. Shapiro, Director, Public Affairs
Counsel or consultant:
Dorsey & Whitney
Mudge Rose Guthrie Alexander and Ferdon (Jeffrey S. Neeley)
Squire, Sanders and Dempsey (Charles A. Vanik)

Philippines, Government of the
Manila, Philippines
Counsel or consultant:
Bannerman and Associates, Inc. (M. Graeme Bannerman, Curtis Silvers)
Fidelity Pacific Group (Jack L. Copeland)
Reichler Appelbaum and Wippman

Phillips Collection, The
1600 21st St., N.W., Washington, DC 20009
Telephone: (202) 387-2151
Background: A privately administered museum of 19th and 20th century European and American art.
Counsel or consultant:
Chernikoff and Co. (Larry Chernikoff)

Phillips & Drew
London, England
Counsel or consultant:
Hill and Knowlton Public Affairs Worldwide (Dr. Ira P. Kaminow)

Phillips Petroleum Co.
1776 Eye St., N.W. Suite 700, Washington, DC 20006
Telephone: (202) 833-0900
Represented by:
Earl F. David, Federal Relations Representative
Don R. Duncan, Dir., Federal Tax & Nat. Resource Issues
James W. Godlove, Federal Relations Representative
Olivia C. Mackin, Federal Relations Analyst
Tom C. Morris, Manager, Federal Relations
Counsel or consultant:
Gold and Liebengood, Inc. (Denise A. Bode)
Groom and Nordberg (Robert B. Harding, Carl A. Nordberg, Jr.)
McNair Law Firm, P.A. (John L. Napier)
Royer, Mehle & Babyak (Robert Stewart Royer)

Phlebology Soc. of America, The
5530 Wisconsin Ave., N.W., Suite 1149, Washington, DC 20815
Telephone: (301) 656-2214
Counsel or consultant:
PAI Management Corp. (Randall C. Price)

Phobia Soc. of America
6000 Executive Blvd. Suite 200, Rockville, MD 20852
Telephone: (301) 231-9350
Background: The only national non-profit organization dedicated to the interest of people who suffer from phobias and related anxiety disorders. Members include people with disorders, clinical personnel and researchers.
Represented by:
Jerilyn Ross, President

Phoenix, Arizona, City of
Counsel or consultant:
Nat'l Center for Municipal Development (John R. O'Donnell)

Phoenix House
New York, NY
Counsel or consultant:
Liz Robbins Associates (Liz Robbins)

Phoenix Mutual Life Insurance Co.
Hartford, CT
Counsel or consultant:
Dutko & Associates (Daniel A. Dutko, William R. McKenney)
Lautzenheiser and Associates (Barbara J. Lautzenheiser)

Phoenix Sky Harbour Internat'l Airport
Phoenix, AZ
Counsel or consultant:
Global Aviation Associates, Ltd. (Judith M. Trent)

Phone Medium
Lansing, MI
Counsel or consultant:
Lobel, Novins, Lamont and Flug (James F. Flug)

Photo Marketing Ass'n-Internat'l
Jackson, MI
Counsel or consultant:
London and Satagaj, Attorneys-at-Law (Sheldon I. London, John S. Satagaj)

Physical Optics Corp.
Torrance, CA
Counsel or consultant:
Ashby and Associates (John C. Stevens)

Physician Insurers Ass'n of America
Lawrenceville, NJ
Counsel or consultant:
LeBoeuf, Lamb, Leiby, and MacRae (John K. Meagher)

Physicians for Social Responsibility
1000 16th St., N.W., Suite 810, Washington, DC 20036
Telephone: (202) 785-3777
Background: An alliance of physicians attempting to educate the government and the public about the consequences of nuclear war, and about public policies which could limit nuclear danger.
Represented by:
John W. Loretz, Director, Communications
Todd E. Perry, Director for Policy
Jennifer Vasiloff, Program Director
Counsel or consultant:
PAI Management Corp. (David A. Lewis)

Physicians Medical Laboratories
Portland, OR
Counsel or consultant:
Schwabe, Williamson and Wyatt (Frederick P. Hitz)

Physicians Mutual Insurance Co.
Omaha, NE
Counsel or consultant:
Groom and Nordberg (Theodore R. Groom, Robert B. Harding)

Pickands Mather and Co.
Cleveland, OH
Counsel or consultant:
Bredhoff and Kaiser (Elliot Bredhoff)

Picker Internat'l
Highland Heights, OH
Counsel or consultant:
van Kloberg and Associates (Edward J. van Kloberg, III)

Pickle Packers Internat'l, Inc.
St. Charles, IL
Counsel or consultant:
Walter E. Byerley Law Offices (Walter E. Byerley)

ORGANIZATIONS REPRESENTED

Pilgrim Airlines
New London, CT
Counsel or consultant:
Seamon, Wasko and Ozment (Theodore I. Seamon)

Pilkington Holdings, Inc.
Toledo, OH
Counsel or consultant:
Rowland & Sellery (William C. Sellery, Jr.)

Pillsbury Co.
Minneapolis, MN
Counsel or consultant:
Akin, Gump, Strauss, Hauer and Feld (Joel Jankowsky)
Baker, Worthington, Crossley, Stansberry & Woolf (Edward R. Hamberger)
Richard B. Berman and Co.,Inc. (Richard B. Berman)
Olsson, Frank and Weeda, P.C. (Richard L. Frank)

PIMA (A Trade Association)
Deerfield, IL
Counsel or consultant:
O'Bannon & Co. (Dona O'Bannon)

Pinnacle Data Corp.
San Bruno, CA
Counsel or consultant:
Fierce and Associates (Donald L. Fierce)

Pinnacle West Capital Corp.
1735 Eye St., N.W., Suite 916, Washington, DC 20006
Telephone: (202) 293-2655
Background: A holding company whose subsidiaries are Arizona Public Service Co., SunCor Development, and El Dorado Investment.
Represented by:
Robert S. Aiken, Manager of Federal Affairs
Counsel or consultant:
Reid & Priest

Pinsly Railroad Co.
Westfield, MA
Counsel or consultant:
RBC Associates, Inc. (Keith O. Hartwell)

Pioneer Electronics
Long Beach, CA
Counsel or consultant:
Patton, Boggs and Blow

Pioneer Financial
Malden, MA
Counsel or consultant:
Steptoe and Johnson (John T. Collins)

Pioneer Hi-Bred Seed Internat'l
Johnstown, IA
Counsel or consultant:
Lipsen Whitten & Diamond

Pirelli Cable Corp.
Union, NJ
Counsel or consultant:
Cassidy and Associates, Inc. (James P. Fabiani, Thomas M. Gannon, Vincent M. Versage)

Pitney-Bowes, Inc.
409 12th St., S.W. Suite 701, Washington, DC 20024
Telephone: (202) 488-4464
Counsel or consultant:
Fincke & White (Stephanie A. White)
Preston Gates Ellis & Rouvelas Meeds (Lloyd Meeds)
Seyfarth, Shaw, Fairweather and Geraldson (Donald L. Rosenthal)

Pittsburgh Corning Corp.
Pittsburgh, PA
Counsel or consultant:
Collier, Shannon & Scott (David A. Hartquist)
Rogers Internat'l, Inc. (Joe O. Rogers)

Pittsburgh, Stadium Authority of
Pittsburgh, PA
Counsel or consultant:
Foley, Hoag and Eliot (John L. Burke, Jr.)

Pittston Co., The
Greenwich, CT
Background: Subsidiaries include the Pittston Coal Group of Lebanon, VA.

Counsel or consultant:
Capital Communications Group
Jefferson Group, The (Mark D. Cowan, Jack O. Nutter)
Smith, Heenan and Althen
R. Duffy Wall and Associates (R. Duffy Wall)
Williams and Jensen, P.C. (J. Steven Hart)

Pizza Hut, Inc.
Wichita, KS
Counsel or consultant:
Baker and McKenzie (Eugene A. Theroux)

Pizza Inn, Inc.
Dallas, TX
Counsel or consultant:
Power & Coleman (Thomas W. Power)

PKR Foundation
Kansas City, MO
Background: A foundation for kidney research.
Counsel or consultant:
Nossaman, Guthner, Knox and Elliott (Warren G. Elliott)

Planeta North America, Inc.
Great Neck, NY
Counsel or consultant:
Jack McDonald Co. (Jack McDonald, Myron G. Sandifer, III)

Planned Parenthood Federation of America
2010 Massachusetts Ave., N.W. Fifth Floor, Washington, DC 20036
Telephone: (202) 785-3351
Background: Conducts a nation-wide program of medical services, public education and research to make family planning services universally accessible.
Represented by:
Ellen S. Battistelli, Legislative Representative
Joanne S. Blum, Assistant Director
William W. Hamilton, Jr., Director, Washington Office
Betty J. Means, Field Coordinator
Vivian Escobar Stack, Legislative Representative

Planning Research Corp.
1500 Planning Research Drive, McLean, VA 22102
Telephone: (703) 556-1500
Represented by:
Bert M. Concklin, V. President, Government Relations
Karen Vahouny, Director, Corporate Communications
Counsel or consultant:
Jefferson Group, The (Julie Susman)

Plantation Foods
Waco, TX
Counsel or consultant:
Campbell-Raupe, Inc. (Jeanne M. Campbell)

Plasterers' and Cement Masons' Action Committee
1125 17th St., N.W. 6th Floor, Washington, DC 20036
Telephone: (202) 393-6569
Background: The political action committee of the Operative Plasterers' and Cement Masons' Internat'l Ass'n. Represented by the General President of the Ass'n.
Counsel or consultant:
The Kamber Group (Donovan McClure)

Platte River Whooping Crane Trust
Grand Island, NE
Counsel or consultant:
Brand and Lowell, P.C. (Abbe David Lowell)

Plattsburgh, New York, Municipality of
Counsel or consultant:
Duncan, Weinberg, Miller & Pembroke, P.C. (Wallace L. Duncan, Jeffrey C. Genzer)

Playtex, Inc.
Stamford, CT
Counsel or consultant:
O'Bannon & Co. (Dona O'Bannon)

Plessey Co. PLC, The
London England
Counsel or consultant:
Akin, Gump, Strauss, Hauer and Feld

Plessey Electronic Systems Corp.
1725 Jefferson Davis Hwy., Suite 206, Arlington, VA 22202
Telephone: (703) 486-1288

Represented by:
Austen W. Watson, V. President, Government Relations

Plessey Electronic Systems, Inc.
1215 Jefferson Davis Hwy., Suite 1203, Arlington, VA 22202
Telephone: (703) 920-7575
Background: A defense electronics company for naval, land and avionics systems, including Federal Aviation Administration and NATO programs.
Represented by:
Bryan Barrett, V. President- Marconi Underwater Systems

PLIVA Pharmaceutical and Chemical Works
Zagreb, Yugoslavia
Counsel or consultant:
Dow, Lohnes and Albertson (William Silverman)

Plumbing Manufacturers Institute
1655 N. Ft. Myer Drive Suite 700, Arlington, VA 22209
Telephone: (703) 522-2339
Counsel or consultant:
CM Services, Inc. (David F. Martin)

Podiatry Political Action Committee
9312 Old Georgetown Road, Bethesda, MD 20814
Telephone: (301) 571-9200
Background: Supported by the American Podiatric Medical Ass'n. Manager of the Committee is John R. Carson, Director of Government Affairs of the Ass'n.
Represented by:
Dr. Harvey Lederman, Treasurer

Pogo Producing Co.
Houston, TX
Counsel or consultant:
Baker and Botts (Thomas J. Eastment)

Pohang Iron & Steel Co., Ltd.
1730 Rhode Island Ave., N.W. Suite 1215, Washington, DC 20036
Telephone: (202) 785-5643
Represented by:
K. H. Kim, General Manager
Counsel or consultant:
Sidley and Austin

Poland, Ministry of Finance of
Warsaw, Poland
Counsel or consultant:
Arnold & Porter (Jeffrey A. Burt)
Hogan and Hartson (Joseph C. Bell, Samuel R. Berger)

Polar Gas
Calgary, Alberta
Counsel or consultant:
David P. Stang, P.C. (David P. Stang)

Polaris Industries
Minneapolis, MN
Counsel or consultant:
Robins, Kaplan, Miller & Ciresi
Wunder, Ryan, Cannon & Thelen (Bernard J. Wunder)

Polaroid Corp.
Cambridge, MA
Counsel or consultant:
Wilmer, Cutler and Pickering (Richard W. Cass)

Police Ass'n of the District of Columbia
1441 Pennsylvania Ave., S.E., Washington, DC 20003
Telephone: (202) 543-9557
Represented by:
Earl Cronin, President
Patrick O'Brien, Exec. Director

Police Ass'n of the District of Columbia Political Action Committee
1441 Pennsylvania Ave., S.E., Washington, DC 20020
Telephone: (202) 582-4620
Background: Represented by Patrick O'Brien of the Police Ass'n of the District of Columbia.

Police Executive Research Forum
2300 M St., N.W., Washington, DC 20037
Telephone: (202) 466-7820
Counsel or consultant:
Kostmayer Communications, Inc. (Judy Keyserling)

Police Foundation
1001 22nd St., N.W., Suite 200, Washington, DC 20037
Telephone: (202) 833-1460

The listings in this directory are available as *Mailing Labels*. See last page.

ORGANIZATIONS REPRESENTED

Police Foundation (Cont'd)
Represented by:
Rae M. Hamilton, Director of Communications
Hubert Williams, President
Counsel or consultant:
The Kamber Group (Dennis Walston)

Polish-American Congress
1625 Eye St., N.W., Suite 326, Washington, DC 20006
Telephone: (202) 296-6955
Background: Interested in legislation and government action and practices affecting Americans of Polish origin and heritage. Based in Chicago.
Represented by:
Myra Lenard, Exec. Director

Political Action Committee of the American Osteopathic Hospital Ass'n
1454 Duke St., Alexandria, VA 22314
Telephone: (703) 684-7700
Background: Represented by Catherine D. Cahill, of the American Osteopathic Hospital Ass'n.

Political Action Committee of the Dun & Bradstreet Corporation
600 Maryland Ave., S.W. Suite 545, Washington, DC 20024
Telephone: (202) 479-0860
Background: Contact is Jean Cantrell, Manager, Government Affairs of Dun & Bradstreet.

Political Education Fund of the Building and Construction Trades Department (AFL-CIO)
815 16th St., N.W., Washington, DC 20006
Telephone: (202) 347-1461
Background: The political action committee of the Building and Construction Trades Department of the AFL-CIO. Represented by Joseph F. Maloney of the AFL-CIO (Building and Construction Trades Department).

Polskie Linie Lotnicze
Warsaw, Poland
Counsel or consultant:
Winthrop, Stimson, Putnam & Roberts (Robert Reed Gray)

Polynesian Airlines
Aisa, Western Samoa
Counsel or consultant:
Squire, Sanders and Dempsey (Robert D. Papkin, Edward W. Sauer)

PolyPhaser Corp.
Gardnerville, NV
Counsel or consultant:
Foley & Co. (Kelly A. Crawford, Kathryn A. Delahanty, Joseph P. Foley, Paul C. Lavery)

Polysar Limited
Sarnia, Ontario
Counsel or consultant:
Keefe Co., The (Robert J. Keefe, Terry M. O'Connell)

Polystyrene Packaging Council
1025 Connecticut Ave., N.W., Suite 508, Washington, DC 20036
Telephone: (202) 822-6424
Counsel or consultant:
Madison Group/Earle Palmer Brown, The (Peggy L. Martin)

Polytechnic University of New York
Brooklyn, NY
Counsel or consultant:
Cassidy and Associates, Inc. (James P. Fabiani, Vincent M. Versage)

Pompano Beach, Florida, City of
Counsel or consultant:
Collins & Associates (Sunny Taylor)

Ponce, Puerto Rico, City of
Counsel or consultant:
Krivit and Krivit (Daniel H. Krivit)

Ponce, Puerto Rico, Port of
Ponce, PR
Counsel or consultant:
Ragan and Mason (Edward M. Shea)

Ponds India
India

Counsel or consultant:
Mudge Rose Guthrie Alexander and Ferdon (Julia Christine Bliss)

Pony Express Courier Corp.
Charlotte, NC
Counsel or consultant:
McGuiness and Williams (Jeffrey C. McGuiness)

Popcorn Institute
1101 Connecticut Ave., N.W., Suite 700, Washington, DC 20036
Telephone: (202) 857-1100
Counsel or consultant:
Smith, Bucklin and Associates (Robert H. Wilbur)

Population Ass'n of America
1429 Duke St., Alexandria, VA 22314-3402
Telephone: (703) 684-1221
Background: Founded in 1931 as a scientific and professional society dedicated to the research, study and analysis of demographic patterns, changes and projections for nations, regions and local areas.
Represented by:
Suzanne Bianchi, Secretary/Treasurer
Jean Smith, Exec. Associate

Population Crisis Committee
1120 19th St., N.W., Washington, DC 20036
Telephone: (202) 659-1833
Background: A clearinghouse of information for population and family planning programs and liaison with international population organizations.
Represented by:
Sharon L. Camp, Vice President
J. Joseph Speidel, President
Counsel or consultant:
Anderson, Kill, Olick and Oshinsky (Joseph D. Tydings)
Squire, Sanders and Dempsey (William C. Collishaw)

Population - Environment Balance
1325 G St., N.W., Suite 1003, Washington, DC 20005-3104
Telephone: (202) 879-3000
Background: A non-profit national membership organization dedicated to education and advocacy of measures which would encourage population stabilization in the United States, in order to safeguard the environment.
Represented by:
Rose M. Hanes, Exec. Director
Dayna R. Petete, Government Relations Director
Counsel or consultant:
Tammen Group, The (Ronald L. Tammen)

Population Institute
110 Maryland Ave., N.E. Suite 207, Washington, DC 20002
Telephone: (202) 544-3300
Background: Works to motivate key leaders and groups to help bring population growth into balance with available resources and assists developing nation broadcast systems in producing population programming.
Represented by:
Werner Fornos, President

Population Reference Bureau
777 14th St., N.W. Suite 800, Washington, DC 20005
Telephone: (202) 639-8040
Background: Gathers, interprets and publishes information on population changes and their social, economic and environmental impact.
Represented by:
Carl Haub, Director, Demographic Analysis
Thomas W. Merrick, President

Population Resource Center
1725 K St., N.W., Suite 1102, Washington, DC 20006
Telephone: (202) 467-5030
Background: Established in 1975 as a non-profit organization to inform and educate the public and government leaders on demographic trends which might affect economic and social policies. Administrative headquarters are in New York City.
Represented by:
Nancy Fifield McConnell, Director, Washington Office

Porcelain Enamel Institute
1101 Connecticut Ave., N.W. Suite 700, Washington, DC 20036
Telephone: (202) 857-1134

Represented by:
John C. Oliver, Exec. V. President
Counsel or consultant:
Smith, Bucklin and Associates (Timothy Rugh)

Port Authority of New York and New Jersey
1001 Connecticut Ave., N.W. Suite 610, Washington, DC 20036
Telephone: (202) 887-5240
Represented by:
Paul H. Bea, Jr., Washington Representative, Director
James D. E. Jones, Washington Representative
W. Churchill Robison, Washington Representative

Portable Power Equipment Manufacturers Ass'n
4720 Montgomery Lane, Suite 812, Bethesda, MD 20814
Telephone: (301) 652-0774
Represented by:
Donald E. Purcell, President
Counsel or consultant:
Dunaway & Cross (Mac S. Dunaway)

Portland Cement Ass'n
1620 Eye St., N.W., Suite 520, Washington, DC 20006
Telephone: (202) 293-4260
Represented by:
Fred Armstrong, Director, Government Services
Robert W. Crolius, V. President, Washington Affairs
John P. Gleason, President

Portland Cement Ass'n Political Action Committee
1620 Eye St., N.W., Suite 520, Washington, DC 20006
Telephone: (202) 293-4260
Background: Robert W. Crolius of the Ass'n serves as Treasurer.

Portland Metropolitan Service District
Portland, OR
Counsel or consultant:
Schwabe, Williamson and Wyatt (Frederick P. Hitz)

Portland, Oregon, City of
Counsel or consultant:
Ball, Janik and Novack (M. Victoria Cram)
Schwabe, Williamson and Wyatt (Frederick P. Hitz)
Simon & Co., Inc. (Leonard S. Simon)

Portland, Oregon, Port of
Counsel or consultant:
Bishop, Cook, Purcell & Reynolds (Bill Alberger)
Lindsay, Hart, Neil & Weigler (Peter Friedmann)
Joseph S. Miller

Ports of Philadelphia Maritime Exchange
Philadelphia, PA
Counsel or consultant:
Montgomery, McCracken, Walker & Rhoads (David F. Norcross)

Portsmouth-Kittery Armed Services Committee, Inc.
Portsmouth, NH
Background: Promotes the economic and political interests of the Portsmouth-Kittery Naval Shipyard and surrounding communities.
Counsel or consultant:
Gray and Associates, David C. (David C. Gray)

Potash Corp. of Saskatchewan
Saskatoon, Saskatchewan
Counsel or consultant:
Arent, Fox, Kintner, Plotkin & Kahn

Potomac Electric Power Co.
1900 Pennsylvania Ave., N.W., Washington, DC 20068
Telephone: (202) 872-2000

The listings in this directory are available as _Mailing Labels_. See last page.

ORGANIZATIONS REPRESENTED

Represented by:
Amy Bowling Back, Assistant, Gov't Affairs - Maryland
Harold E. Brazil, Mgr., DC and Federal Government Affairs
Karen B. Brown, Government Affairs Assistant
Rhett B. Dawson, Sr. V. Pres., Law and Public Policy
John M. Derrick, Jr., Exec. V. President & C.O.O.
Jill Downs, Manager, Corp. Affairs
Paul Dragoumis, Exec. V. President
Martin J. Kmetz, Manager, Gov't Affairs - Maryland
John D. McCallum, Assistant Comptroller
Nancy Moses, Manager, Media Relations
William T. Torgerson, V. President and General Counsel
Andrew W. Williams, V. President, Energy Policy & Develop't.
Counsel or consultant:
Reid & Priest

Potomac Hotel Group
1901 N. Fort Myer Drive, Arlington, VA 22209
Telephone: (703) 243-4100
Counsel or consultant:
Steven E. Some Associates (Steven E. Some)

Potomac Institute
1400 20th St., N.W. Suite 5, Washington, DC 20036
Telephone: (202) 331-0087
Background: Conducts research on civil rights, housing and community development issues.
Represented by:
Harold C. Fleming, Pres. Emeritus & Senior Consultant

Potomac Institute for Economic Research
4323 Hawthorne St., N.W., Washington, DC 20016
Telephone: (202) 364-1138
Background: Provides research, evaluation and technical support for public policy formulation and implementation in such fields as employment, job training, social security, welfare and equal opportunity programs.
Represented by:
Dr. Bradley Schiller, President

Potters Industries, Inc.
Parsippany, NJ
Counsel or consultant:
Arthur E. Cameron

Powder Coating Institute
1800 Diagonal Road, Suite 370, Alexandria, VA 22314
Telephone: (703) 684-1770
Represented by:
Gregory J. Bocchi, Exec. Director

Power and Communications Contractors Ass'n
6301 Stevenson Ave., Suite 1, Alexandria, VA 22304
Telephone: (703) 823-1555
Counsel or consultant:
Strother and Hosking Associates (Michael E. Strother)

Power Electronics
Kuala Lumpur, Malaysia
Counsel or consultant:
Willkie Farr and Gallagher (Walter J. Spak)

Power PAC of the Edison Electric Institute
1111 19th St., N.W., Washington, DC 20036
Telephone: (202) 778-6400
Background: The political action committee for the Edison Electric Institute. Contact is Fred G. Davis of the Institute.

Power Packaging Inc.
West Chicago, IL
Counsel or consultant:
Smith Dawson & Andrews, Inc. (Gregory B. Andrews, James P. Smith)

Power Technology Inc.
Biloxi, MS
Counsel or consultant:
H. John Elliott

Power Tool Institute
Arlington Hghts., IL
Counsel or consultant:
Webster, Chamberlain and Bean (Arthur L. Herold)

PPG Industries
1730 Rhode Island Ave., N.W., Suite 715, Washington, DC 20036
Telephone: (202) 659-9894

Represented by:
Edward L. Jaffee, Washington Rep. & Mgr., Wash. Office
Robert Gary Wilson, Director, Corporate Government Affairs
Counsel or consultant:
Baker and Hostetler (Alan S. Ward)
Camp, Barsh, Bates and Tate (Carl E. Bates)
Latham and Watkins (Irwin Goldbloom)
Morgan, Lewis and Bockius (Michael R. Calabrese)
Stewart and Stewart (David Scott Nance, Terrence P. Stewart)

PR Service Co., Ltd.
Tokyo, Japan
Counsel or consultant:
Civic Service, Inc. (Roy Pfautch)

Pratt & Whitney
1825 Eye St., N.W., Suite 700, Washington, DC 20006
Telephone: (202) 785-7430
Background: A division of United Technologies Corp.
Represented by:
Melvin G. Goodweather, Director, Government Relations
Robert L. Shanower, Manager, Washington Operations
Eugene J. Tallia, V. President, Washington
Counsel or consultant:
Bracy Williams & Co. (Terrence L. Bracy)
James R. Calloway
Richard Richards Law Offices

Preferred Health
Wilton CT
Counsel or consultant:
Jefferson Group, The (Frederick J. Hannett)

Premark Internat'l
Deerfield, IL
Counsel or consultant:
Dewey, Ballantine, Bushby, Palmer and Wood (Joseph K. Dowley)
Lee, Toomey & Kent

Prentice Hall Information Services
1819 L St., N.W. Suite 400, Washington, DC 20036
Telephone: (202) 293-0707
Represented by:
Thomas Fritz, Exec. Editor, Tax
Patricia Lenihan, Washington Bureau Chief
Michael Rose, Exec. Editor, News Operations

Presbyterian Church (U.S.A.)
110 Maryland Ave., N.E., Washington, DC 20002
Telephone: (202) 543-1126
Represented by:
Elenora Gidding Ivory, Director, Washington Office

Presbyterian Health Center
Dallas, TX
Counsel or consultant:
Bill Newbold & Assoc. (Bill Newbold)

Presbyterian Hospital/University of Pittsburgh
Pittsburgh, PA
Counsel or consultant:
Cassidy and Associates, Inc. (Gerald S. J. Cassidy, C. Frank Godfrey, Jr.)

Prescription Footwear Ass'n
Columbia, MD
Counsel or consultant:
Tendler, Goldberg & Biggins, Chtd. (James M. Goldberg)

Preservation Action
1350 Connecticut Ave., N.W. Suite 401, Washington, DC 20036
Telephone: (202) 659-0915
Background: Individuals and organizations concerned with historic preservation.
Represented by:
Nellie Longsworth, President

Presidential Classroom for Young Americans
441 N. Lee St., Alexandria, VA 22314
Telephone: (703) 683-5400
Represented by:
Mark Sklarow, Director, Curriculum and Programs
Nila A. Vehar, Exec. Director

President's Drug Advisory Counsel
Exec. Office of the President, Washington, DC 20503

Counsel or consultant:
Direct Impact Co., The

PressNet Systems, Inc.
Baltimore, MD
Counsel or consultant:
Swift Consulting Co., Ltd., The (Ivan, Red Swift)

Preston Gates Ellis & Rouvelas Meeds Political Action Committee
1735 New York Ave., N.W., Suite 500, Washington, DC 20006
Telephone: (202) 628-1700
Represented by:
Rosanne Maroon, Treasurer

Preston Trucking Co.
Preston, MD
Counsel or consultant:
The Eddie Mahe Company
Washington Lobby Group, The

Preuss Foundation, The Peter
Solana Beach, CA
Counsel or consultant:
The William Chasey Organization (William C. Chasey, Ph.D.)

Preussag AG
Hannover, West Germany
Counsel or consultant:
Jones, Day, Reavis and Pogue (Randall E. Davis, Charles McC. Mathias)

Price Waterhouse
1801 K St., N.W., Suite 700, Washington, DC 20006
Telephone: (202) 296-0800
Background: An accounting and government consulting firm.
Represented by:
Andrea Andrews, Sr. Manager/Washington Liaison
Robert R. Bench, Principal, Financial Svcs. Indus. Pract.
Holly Chamberlin, Manager, State Tax Government Relations
Elaine K. Church, Principal, Employee Benefits Svcs.
Stanley E. Collender, Dir, Fed Budget Plcy, Wash Nat'l Tax Svc
Larry L. Dildine, Partner, Wasington Nat'l Tax Svc
Roscoe L. Egger, Jr., Partner, Washington Nat'l Tax Svc
James R. McCarthy, Director, Wash. Energy Tax Practice
Mark McConaghy, Principal, Washington Nat'l Tax Svc
Thomas Persky, Senior Manager
James R. Shanahan, Partner, Washington Nat'l Tax Svc
Bernard M. Shapiro, Partner
Gilbert Simonetti, Jr., Partner-in-Charge, Washington Liaison
Richard B. Stanger, Partner, Employee Benefits

Price Waterhouse Partners' Political Action Committee
1801 K St., N.W., Suite 700, Washington, DC 20006
Telephone: (202) 296-0800
Background: Represented by Gilbert Simonetti, Jr. of Price Waterhouse.

Pride Refining, Inc.
Abilene, TX
Counsel or consultant:
Reid & Priest (Richard J. Leidl)

Prime Computer, Inc.
Natick, MA
Counsel or consultant:
Hale and Dorr (Jay P. Urwitz)

Primerica Corp.
Greenwich, CT
Background: Formerly known as the American Can Co.
Counsel or consultant:
Dewey, Ballantine, Bushby, Palmer and Wood (Joseph A. Califano, Jr., Lawrence F. O'Brien, III)

Prince des Bretagne
Paris, France
Counsel or consultant:
Max N. Berry Law Offices (Max N. Berry)

Prince George's County, Maryland
Counsel or consultant:
Arent, Fox, Kintner, Plotkin & Kahn

ORGANIZATIONS REPRESENTED

Princeton University
1156 15th St., N.W., Suite 1102, Washington, DC 20005
Telephone: (202) 429-8719
Represented by:
Nan S. Wells, Director, Office of Governmental Affairs

Principal Financial Group, The
655 15th St., N.W., Suite 950, Washington, DC 20005
Telephone: (202) 737-5930
Represented by:
Stuart J. Brahs, V. Pres., Federal Government Relations
Laura Ison Thevenot, Federal Legislative Representative
Counsel or consultant:
Groom and Nordberg (Theodore R. Groom, Robert B. Harding)

Printing Industries of America
1730 North Lynn St., Arlington, VA 22209
Telephone: (703) 841-8100
Background: An international graphic arts trade association federation of regional, state and city associations.
Represented by:
Benjamin Y. Cooper, Sr. V. President of Government Affairs
Ron H. Davis, Director, Research and Chief Economist
Mary Fuller, Exec. Dir., Ass'n of Graphic Arts Cons.
Mary Ellen Kenner, Director, Marketing and Communications
Thomas W. Purcell, Director, Environmental Programs
Ray Roper, President
John C. Runyan, Director, Political Affairs
Susan Marie Siemietkowski, Legislative Assistant
G. William Teare, Exec. V. President
Kim R. Zoglio, Manager, Public Relations

Printing Industries of America Political Action Committee (Print PAC)
1730 North Lynn St., Arlington, VA 22209
Telephone: (703) 841-8100
Background: Treasurer and contact is Benjamin Y. Cooper of Printing Industries of America.

Prison Fellowship Ministries
P.O. Box 17500, Washington, DC 20041-0500
Telephone: (703) 478-0100
Represented by:
Charles W. Colson, Chairman of the Board

Prison Industries Reform Council
6609 E. Wakefield Drive Suite A-2, Alexandria, VA 22307
Telephone: (703) 768-7738
Background: Seeks reforms in prison workshop preferences in the federal procurement system.
Counsel or consultant:
Kidd and Co. (Yvonne Kidd)

Private Sector Council
1101 16th St., N.W., Suite 500, Washington, DC 20036
Telephone: (202) 822-3910
Represented by:
William G. Onsted, President & CEO
Counsel or consultant:
McKevitt Group, The

Privatization Council
1101 Connecticut Ave., N.W., Suite 700, Washington, DC 20036
Telephone: (202) 857-1142
Counsel or consultant:
Smith, Bucklin and Associates (John C. Murphy)

Pro-Choice Fund
207 Pennsylvania Ave., S.E., Washington, DC 20003
Telephone: (202) 543-1500
Counsel or consultant:
White and Associates (Paulette Will)

Pro-Trade Group, The
1616 H St., N.W., Washington, DC 20006
Telephone: (202) 783-7971
Background: A coalition of about 50 trade associations and companies lobbying for free trade, i.e., opposing legislation which would restrict imports and favoring measures to expand exports. William Kay Daines of the American Retail Federation and William Maxwell of the Computer & Business Equipment Manufacturers Ass'n are active in this organization.

Process Equipment Manufacturers Ass'n
7297 Lee Highway, Suite N, Falls Church, VA 22042
Telephone: (703) 533-0286

Counsel or consultant:
Ass'n and Society Management Internat'l Inc. (Harry W. Buzzerd, Jr.)

Process Gas Consumers Group
1275 Pennsylvania Ave., N.W., Washington, DC 20004
Telephone: (202) 383-0444
Background: An ad hoc group of gas consuming corporations including Alcan Aluminum, Alcoa, American Nat'l Can, Armco, Inc., Bethlehem Steel, Carpenter Technology, Cone Mills, Corning Inc., Eaton Corp, Ford Motor Co., General Motors Corp., LTV Steel Co., Owens-Corning Fiberglas Corp., Owens-Illinois, Inc, PPG, Procter and Gamble, and Nat'l Steel.
Counsel or consultant:
E. Bruce Harrison Co. (Steven B. Hellem)
Sutherland, Asbill and Brennan (Edward J. Grenier, Jr., Glen S. Howard, Robert R. Morrow, Jan Benes Vlcek)

Processed Apples Institute
Atlanta, GA
Counsel or consultant:
Fleishman-Hillard, Inc (Paul Johnson, Elizabeth C. McLean)

Processed Cherries
MI
Counsel or consultant:
Highley & Associates (Vern F. Highley)

Procter and Gamble Mfg. Co.
801 18th St., N.W., Suite 400, Washington, DC 20006
Telephone: (202) 833-9500
Background: A subsidiary of The Procter and Gamble Co.
Represented by:
Edwin L. Behrens, Assoc Dir, Tech Afrs & Nat'l Gov't Rtns
Jane Fawcett-Hoover, Assoc. Dir., Nat'l Government Relations
Dorothy F. Gevinson, Assoc. Dir., Nat'l Government Relations
Charles Leppert, Jr., Director, Fed. Affairs, Nat'l Gov't Rtns
Richard Marvin Womack, V. President,. Nat'l Gov't Relations
Counsel or consultant:
Dow, Lohnes and Albertson (David A. Hildebrandt)
Foreman & Heidepriem (Carol Tucker Foreman, Nikki Heidepriem)
Hill and Knowlton Public Affairs Worldwide (Barbara Hyde)
McMahon and Associates

Product Liability Alliance, The
1725 K St., N.W., Suite 710, Washington, DC 20006
Telephone: (202) 872-0885
Background: A coalition of over 300 business interests lobbying for reform of product liability laws.
Counsel or consultant:
Crowell and Moring (Victor E. Schwartz)
Swidler & Berlin, Chartered (Dawn Gifford)

Product Liability Coordinating Committee
1575 Eye St., N.E. Suite 200, Washington, DC 20005
Telephone: (202) 371-0088
Counsel or consultant:
Aker Associates, Inc. (G. Colburn Aker)
Crowell and Moring (Victor E. Schwartz)
Dow, Lohnes and Albertson (Arthur H. Silverman)
Rowland & Sellery (Susan T. Denton, William C. Sellery, Jr.)

Product Liability Information Bureau
Counsel or consultant:
Crowell and Moring (Victor E. Schwartz)

Productive Employment Foundation
Chatsworth, CA
Counsel or consultant:
Bettie McCarthy and Assoc. (Bettie S. McCarthy)

PROEXPO/INCOMEX
Bogota, Colombia
Counsel or consultant:
Mudge Rose Guthrie Alexander and Ferdon (Julia Christine Bliss, Michael P. Daniels)

Professional Airways Systems Specialists
444 North Capitol St., N.W., Suite 840, Washington, DC 20001
Telephone: (202) 347-6065

Represented by:
Howard E. Johannssen, President

Professional Ass'n for Quality Home Respiratory Care
Background: A group of physician-owned companies that provide oxygen equipment and home respiratory therapy.
Counsel or consultant:
Epstein Becker and Green (Deborah Steelman)

Professional Engineers in Private Practice
1420 King St., Alexandria, VA 22314
Telephone: (703) 684-2862
Background: A division of the National Soc. of Professional Engineers, the organization represents the interests of individual consulting engineers licensed to offer construction-related engineering services to the public.
Represented by:
Frank Musica, Staff Director

Professional Insurance Agents' Political Action Committee
400 N. Washington St., Alexandria, VA 22314
Telephone: (703) 836-9340
Background: Political Action Committee of the Nat'l Ass'n of Professional Insurance Agents (formerly the Nat'l Ass'n of Mutual Insurance Agents).
Represented by:
Jan Hensley, Director

Professional Insurance Mass-Marketing Ass'n
4733 Bethesda Ave., Suite 33, Bethesda, MD 20814
Telephone: (301) 951-1260
Represented by:
John J. McManus, Exec. V. President
Counsel or consultant:
Vedder, Price, Kaufman, Kammholz and Day (George J. Pantos)

Professional Photographers of America, Inc.
Des Plaines, IL
Counsel or consultant:
Richard O. Bolger

Professional Services Council
918 16th St., N.W., Suite 406, Washington, DC 20006
Telephone: (202) 296-2030
Background: Associations and companies providing professional services to the government and private sector; most members are concerned with federal procurement.
Represented by:
Melanie K. Doon, Manager, Business-Government Policy
Nancy Johnson, Director, Public Affairs and Research
Katherine D. Kiggins, Director, Public Affairs
Mark Schultz, President
Counsel or consultant:
Michael Hugo & Associates (F. Michael Hugo)
Miller & Chevalier, Chartered (Alan R. Yuspeh)

Professional Services Management Ass'n
1213 Prince St., Alexandria, VA 22314
Telephone: (703) 548-4593
Counsel or consultant:
Adams, Adams & Assoc. (Ann Allen Adams)

Professionals' Coalition for Nuclear Arms Control
1616 P St., N.W., Suite 320, Washington, DC 20036
Telephone: (202) 332-4823
Background: David Cohen of The Advocacy Institute serves as President.
Represented by:
Jessica R. Aberly, Field Organizer
Robert Musil, Exec. Director
Rebecca A. Weaver, Field Director

Profilo Holding A.S.
Istanbul, Turkey
Counsel or consultant:
APCO Associates (Barry J. Schumacher)
Arnold & Porter (Patrick F. J. Macrory)

Profit Sharing Council of America
Chicago, IL
Represented by:
Susan M. Noon, Director, Legislative Activities
Counsel or consultant:
Dow, Lohnes and Albertson (David A. Hildebrandt)

Progressive Nat'l Baptist Convention
601 50th St., N.E., Washington, DC 20019

The listings in this directory are available as *Mailing Labels*. See last page.

Telephone: (202) 396-0558
Background: Founded in 1961 the Convention now represents over 1,000 churches. Affiliated with Nat'l Council of Churches and the World Council of Churches.
Represented by:
Ishmael L. Shaw, Interim General Secretary

Progressive Policy Institute
316 Pennsylvania Ave., S.E. Suite 516, Washington, DC 20003
Telephone: (202) 547-0001
Represented by:
Joel Berg, Policy Analyst, Ctr. for Civic Enterpr.
Bert S. Brandenburg, Policy Analyst
Dana Crosby, Exec. Assistant
Will Marshall, President
Mildred Porter, Administrative Director
Barbara Richards, Staff Assistant
Robert J. Shapiro, V. President for Economic Studies

Project on Government Procurement
613 Pennsylvania Ave., S.E. 2nd Floor, Washington, DC 20003
Telephone: (202) 543-0883
Background: A project of the Fund for Constitutional Government. Objective is to "reform the military acquisition system to produce effective, reliable and less expensive national defense." Seeks to uncover and expose waste and other abuses in military procurement.
Represented by:
Liz Galtney, Director

Project Orbis
New York, NY
Counsel or consultant:
Anderson, Hibey, Nauheim and Blair (Robert A. Blair)

Project Vote!
1424 16th St., N.W., Suite 101, Washington, DC 20005
Telephone: (202) 328-1500
Background: Seeks to involve more low-income and minority citizens in voting.
Represented by:
Helen Fleming, Chief Deputy Director
Sanford A. Newman, Exec. Director
Doug Tanner, Deputy Director

Project 500
6 E St., S.E., Washington, DC 20003
Telephone: (202) 543-9200
Background: A political action committee affiliated with the Democratic Nat'l Committee.
Represented by:
Timothy E. Dickson, Exec. Director
Counsel or consultant:
Gallagher-Widmeyer Group Inc., The (Mary Jane Gallagher)

Promodes
Mondeville, France
Counsel or consultant:
Hill and Knowlton Public Affairs Worldwide (Dr. Ira P. Kaminow)

Propeller Club of the United States, The
3927 Old Lee Highway Suite 101A, Fairfax, VA 22030
Telephone: (703) 691-2777
Background: Promotes and supports the American merchant marine in all its segments: ocean, inland waterways and on the Great Lakes; and the maritime industry generally. Consists of about 105 local clubs with 13,000 members in the U.S. and overseas.
Represented by:
J. Daniel Smith, Exec. V. President

Property Management Ass'n of America
8811 Colesville Rd. Suite G106, Silver Spring, MD 20910
Telephone: (301) 587-6543
Counsel or consultant:
Bachner Communications, Inc. (John P. Bachner)

Property Management Ass'n of Metropolitan Washington
8811 Colesville Rd. Suite G106, Silver Spring, MD 20910
Telephone: (301) 587-6543
Counsel or consultant:
Bachner Communications, Inc. (John P. Bachner)

Proprietary Industries Ass'n
Glendale, CA

Counsel or consultant:
Bettie McCarthy and Assoc. (Bettie S. McCarthy)

Propulsora Siderurgica S.A.I.C.
Buenos Aires, Argentina
Counsel or consultant:
Mudge Rose Guthrie Alexander and Ferdon (David P. Houlihan, Julie C. Mendoza)

Protatek Internat'l, Inc.
St. Paul, MN
Counsel or consultant:
McMillan and Farrell Associates (C. W. McMillan)

Providence, Rhode Island, City of
Counsel or consultant:
Nat'l Center for Municipal Development (Richard C. Johnson)

Provident Life and Accident Insurance Co.
Chattanooga, TN
Counsel or consultant:
Scribner, Hall and Thompson (Thomas C. Thompson, Jr.)

Provident Mutual Life Insurance
Philadelphia, PA
Counsel or consultant:
Murray, Scheer & Montgomery (D. Michael Murray)

Provo, Utah, City of
Counsel or consultant:
The Ferguson Co. (William Ferguson, Jr., Patricia Jordan, Thane Young)

Prudential-Bache Securities, Inc.
New York, NY
Counsel or consultant:
Groom and Nordberg (Robert B. Harding)
Hill and Knowlton Public Affairs Worldwide (Tom Hoog)
Lord Day & Lord, Barrett Smith (Mahlon Frankhauser)

Prudential Insurance Co. of America
1140 Connecticut Ave., N.W., Suite 510, Washington, DC 20036
Telephone: (202) 463-0060
Represented by:
J. Laurence McCarty, V. President, Government Relations
M. Kenneth Oboz, V. President, Government Relations
Thomas G. O'Hara, V. President
Counsel or consultant:
Dewey, Ballantine, Bushby, Palmer and Wood (Joseph K. Dowley)
Gibson, Dunn and Crutcher (Cynthia C. Lebow)
Groom and Nordberg (Theodore R. Groom, Robert B. Harding)
O'Connor & Hannan (Thomas H. Quinn)
Willkie Farr and Gallagher (Sue D. Blumenfeld)

Psychemedics Corp.
Boston, MA
Counsel or consultant:
Bayless & Boland, Inc. (James L. Bayless, Jr., Michael J. P. Boland)

Psychiatric Institutes of America
1010 Wisconsin Ave., N.W., Washington, DC 20007
Telephone: (202) 298-3282
Counsel or consultant:
Cindy Williams Associates (Lucinda L. Williams)

PubCo Corp.
Cleveland, OH
Counsel or consultant:
Dyer, Ellis, Joseph & Mills (Howard A. Vine)

Public Advocate
6001 Leesburg Pike, #3, Falls Church, VA 22041
Telephone: (202) 546-3224
Background: A national non-partisan government watchdog and citizen action committee dedicated to limited government, a free market economy, a strong national defense and a reduced tax burden for Americans.
Represented by:
Columbia Eugene Delgaudio, Director

Public Affairs Council
1019 19th St., N.W., Suite 200, Washington, DC 20036
Telephone: (202) 872-1790
Background: A bi-partisan professional organization of corporate public affairs representatives established in 1954 as the Effective Citizens Organization. Associated with the

Foundation for Public Affairs.
Represented by:
Raymond L. Hoewing, President
Peter B. Kennerdell, Exec. Director of Programs
David B. Kinsman, Manager, Program Support and Development
Demetrius M. Parker, Manager, Program Support and Development
Wes Pedersen, Dir. of Communications & Public Relats.

Public Affairs Council of the Nat'l Federation of Federal Employees
1016 16th St., N.W., Suite 400, Washington, DC 20036
Telephone: (202) 862-4400
Background: Principal contact is Red Evans, Director of Public Relations of the Nat'l Federation of Federal Employees.

Public Affairs Internat'l
Ottawa, Ontario
Counsel or consultant:
Hill and Knowlton Public Affairs Worldwide (Richard M. Anderson, Paul J. Fekete, Hilary Sills)

Public Broadcasting Service
1320 Braddock Place, Alexandria, VA 22314
Telephone: (703) 739-5000
Represented by:
Robb Deigh, Director of Corporate Information
Counsel or consultant:
Barksdale Ballard & Co. (D. Michael Ballard)
Wiley, Rein & Fielding (Paul C. Smith)
Wilmer, Cutler and Pickering (Thomas P. Olson)

Public Citizen
2000 P St., N.W., Suite 610, Washington, DC 20036
Telephone: (202) 293-9142
Background: A national public interest group organized by Ralph Nader in 1971 that works for the protection of the consumer. Composed of several subgroups for which it serves as funding agency: Congress Watch, Health Research Group, Litigation Group, Buyers Up, and the Critical Mass Energy Project. Also maintains an office on Capitol Hill.
Represented by:
Joan B. Claybrook, President
Nancy Rader, Energy Policy Analyst

Public Citizen Health Research Group
2000 P St., N.W., Suite 700, Washington, DC 20036
Telephone: (202) 872-0320
Background: Monitors the medical establishment, health-related industries, and government regulators.
Represented by:
Lynn Soffer, Physician
Dr. Sidney M. Wolfe, Director

Public Citizen Litigation Group
2000 P St., N.W., Suite 700, Washington, DC 20036
Telephone: (202) 785-3704
Background: Established in 1972 and supported by Public Citizen, the Nader organization. Initiates and handles litigation for the protection of the consumer.
Represented by:
Arthur L. Fox, II, Staff Attorney
Patti Goldman, Staff Attorney
Cornish F. Hitchcock, Staff Attorney
Paul Alan Levy, Staff Attorney
Alan B. Morrison, Director
Eleanor Smith, Staff Attorney
David Vladeck, Staff Attorney
Brian Wolfman, Staff Attorney

Public Citizen's Critical Mass Energy Project
215 Pennsylvania Ave., S.E., Washington, DC 20003
Telephone: (202) 546-4996
Background: Founded in 1974 by Ralph Nader to serve as a non-profit research and advocacy organization. Primary objective is to promote safe alternatives to nuclear power.
Represented by:
Ken Bossong, Director

Public Employees' Retirement Ass'n of Colorado
Denver, CO
Counsel or consultant:
Kogovsek & Associates, Inc.
McDermott, Will and Emery (Robert A. Warden)

Public Employees Roundtable
Box 6184, Ben Franklin Station, Washington, DC 20044

ORGANIZATIONS REPRESENTED

Public Employees Roundtable (Cont'd)
Telephone: (202) 535-4324
Background: A non-profit educational consortium of 30 professional and management associations with over one million members. Seeks to inform the public and lawmakers of the dedication and quality of the more than 20 million public employees serving this country. Forty-six federal, state and local government units hold associate membership. Chairman is G. Jerry Shaw, Jr. of Neill, Mullenholz and Shaw.
Represented by:
Joan Keston, Exec. Director
Counsel or consultant:
Neill, Mullenholz and Shaw (G. Jerry Shaw, Jr.)

Public Generating Pool
Seattle, WA
Background: Public utilities generating electric power.
Counsel or consultant:
Schwabe, Williamson and Wyatt (Frederick P. Hitz)

Public Health Foundation
1220 L St., N.W., Suite 350, Washington, DC 20005
Telephone: (202) 898-5600
Background: Purpose is to strengthen national, state and local public health activities. Works through five divisions: Education and Training, Environmental Health, Health Services Information, Research and Evaluation and Telecommunications.
Represented by:
James T. Dimas, Exec. Director
Jordan H. Richland, Deputy Director

Public Housing Authorities Directors Ass'n
511 Capitol Court, N.E., Washington, DC 20002-4937
Telephone: (202) 546-5445
Represented by:
Judy Cook, Research Assistant, Public Housing
Wallace Johnson, Exec. Director

Public Image Printing
Hauppauge, NY
Counsel or consultant:
I and J Associates (Ira F. Jersey, Jr., John J. Regan)

Public Images
Medford, NY
Counsel or consultant:
I and J Associates (Ira F. Jersey, Jr., John J. Regan)

Public Interest Computer Ass'n
1025 Connecticut Ave., N.W. Suite 1015, Washington, DC 20036
Telephone: (202) 775-1588
Background: Provides information and education to non-profit use of information technologies. Promotes computer technology use to serve public welfare and democratic institutions.
Represented by:
Robert Schmitt, Exec. Director

Public Interest Video Network
1642 R St., N.W., Washington, DC 20009
Telephone: (202) 797-8997
Background: A non profit media center serving the communications needs of the public interest community and providing nationwide television and radio audiences with greater diversity in programming. Producer of the weekly radio program "New Voices," a service to non-profit organizations.
Represented by:
Arlen Slobodow, Exec. Director

Public Lands Council
1301 Pennsylvania Ave., N.W. Suite 300, Washington, DC 20004
Telephone: (202) 347-5355
Background: A non-profit group that represents livestock operators who hold permits to graze livestock on public lands. Exec. Director is Patty McDonald of the Nat'l Cattlemen's Ass'n.
Represented by:
Betty J. Munis, Staff Assistant

Public Law Education Institute
1601 Connecticut Ave., N.W. Suite 450, Washington, DC 20009
Telephone: (202) 232-1400
Background: Provides information on military law, the draft, selective service and veterans' affairs.

Represented by:
Thomas Alder, President

Public Offender Counselor Ass'n
5999 Stevenson Ave., Alexandria, VA 22304
Telephone: (703) 823-9800
Background: Represented by William Hunter, Lauren Scheib and Richard Yep of the American Ass'n for Counseling and Development.

Public Office Corp.
911 Second St., N.E., Washington, DC 20002
Telephone: (202) 675-4900
Represented by:
Patricia Anderson, President

Public Ownership of Electric Resources Political Action Committee
2301 M St., N.W., Washington, DC 20037
Telephone: (202) 467-2900
Background: Represented by Ruth Gonze of the American Public Power Ass'n.

Public Resource Associates
1815 H St., N.W. Suite 600, Washington, DC 20006
Telephone: (202) 463-7456
Background: Dr. Elvis J. Stahr, Jr., of Cassidy and Associates, serves as V. President.
Represented by:
Thomas S. Barrett, Counsel
Counsel or consultant:
L. Courtland Lee

Public Risk and Insurance Management Ass'n
1117 19th St. North Suite 900, Arlington, VA 22209
Telephone: (703) 528-7701
Represented by:
Bradley Johnson, Exec. Director

Public Securities Ass'n
1000 Vermont Ave., N.W., Suite 800, Washington, DC 20005
Telephone: (202) 898-9390
Represented by:
Betsy Barclay, Director, Legislative Projects
Bonnie Caldwell, Director, Government Relations
Gregory J. Costa, Manager, Political Affairs
Richard B. Geltman, V. President, Inter-Governmental Relats.
Micah S. Green, Sr. V. President, Legislative Affairs
David S. Liebschutz, Manager, External Affairs
Rebecca McAuliffe, Legislative Assistant
Mark P. Moore, Manager, Policy Analysis
Counsel or consultant:
Gold and Liebengood, Inc. (Denise A. Bode)
Squire, Sanders and Dempsey

Public Securities Ass'n Political Action Committee
1000 Vermont Ave., N.W., Suite 800, Washington, DC 20005
Telephone: (202) 898-9390
Background: Contact is Gregory J. Costa of the Association.

Public Service Co. of Indiana
1800 K St., N.W., Suite 1018, Washington, DC 20006
Telephone: (202) 887-0497
Represented by:
John L. Stowell, Director, Federal Affairs
Gregory A. Troxell, Director, Regulatory & Environ. Affairs
Counsel or consultant:
Bruder, Gentile & Marcoux (George F. Bruder)
Powell, Goldstein, Frazer and Murphy (Roger J. Marzulla)
Skadden, Arps, Slate, Meagher and Flom (Mike Naeve)

Public Service Co. of New Hampshire
Manchester, NH
Counsel or consultant:
Bruder, Gentile & Marcoux (George F. Bruder)
Shaw, Pittman, Potts and Trowbridge (Gerald Charnoff)

Public Service Co. of New Mexico
Albuquerque, NM

Counsel or consultant:
Baker, Worthington, Crossley, Stansberry & Woolf (W. Lee Rawls)
Marcus G. Faust
The Eddie Mahe Company
Morgan, Lewis and Bockius

Public Service Co. of North Carolina
Gastonia, NC
Counsel or consultant:
Wright and Talisman

Public Service Co. of Oklahoma
Tulsa, OK
Counsel or consultant:
Donelan, Cleary, Wood and Maser, P.C.

Public Service Electric and Gas Co.
Newark, NJ
Counsel or consultant:
Conner and Wetterhahn, P.C. (Troy B. Conner, Jr., Mark J. Wetterhahn)
Reid & Priest

Public Service Political Action Committee
8330 Old Courthouse Rd. Suite 600, Vienna, VA 22182
Telephone: (703) 790-0700
Background: The political action arm of the Public Service Research Council. Chairman is David Y. Denholm of the Council.
Represented by:
Roman Rice, Treasurer

Public Service Research Council
1761 Business Center Drive Suite 230, Reston, VA 22090
Telephone: (703) 438-3966
Background: A citizens' lobby concerned with union-oriented issues. Opposes unionism and collective bargaining in public employment.
Represented by:
David Y. Denholm, President
Counsel or consultant:
Resources Development, Inc. (Roger H. Zion)

Public Service Research Foundation
1761 Business Center Drive Suite 230, Reston, VA 22090
Telephone: (703) 438-3966
Background: An education and research foundation concerned with the issue of public sector labor relations. Represented by David Y. Denholm of the Public Service Research Council.

Public Service Satellite Consortium
600 Maryland Ave., S.W., Suite 220, Washington, DC 20024
Telephone: (202) 863-0890
Background: A consortium of public service, non-profit organizations representing the fields of education; health and medicine; state government; and professional, trade and civic associations. Provides telecommunications consulting advice and information on policy issues bearing on the telecommunications needs of its members.
Represented by:
Louis A. Bransford, President
Suzanne G. Douglas, Director, Information and Research

Public Technology Inc.
1301 Pennsylvania Ave., N.W. Suite 704, Washington, DC 20004
Telephone: (202) 626-2400
Background: Represents the research and development interests of the largest cities in the U.S., plus more than 170 other U.S. and Canadian cities and counties.
Represented by:
Costis Toregas, President

Public Voice for Food and Health Policy
1001 Connecticut Ave., N.W. Suite 522, Washington, DC 20036
Telephone: (202) 659-5930
Background: A non-profit research, education and advocacy organization active in food and health policy, including nutrition, anti-hunger, disease prevention, food safety, agriculture policy, rural poverty and women's health. Advances consumer interest in national food and health policy making.

ORGANIZATIONS REPRESENTED

Represented by:
Ellen Haas, Exec. Director
Elizabeth Hedlund, Director, Government Relations
Eileen Kugler, Director of Communications
Allen Rosenfeld, Director, Agricultural Policy

Pueblo, Colorado, City of
Counsel or consultant:
Kogovsek & Associates, Inc.

Puerto Rico, Commonwealth of
San Juan, PR
Counsel or consultant:
Bishop, Cook, Purcell & Reynolds (Marlow W. Cook)
Campbell, Falk & Selby (Anne Campbell, Steven Selby)
Covington and Burling (Michael G. Michaelson)
Pagan Internat'l Inc.
Mark A. Siegel & Associates

Puerto Rico Department of Health
San Juan, PR
Counsel or consultant:
Laxalt, Washington, Perito & Dubuc (Paul L. Perito)

Puerto Rico Department of Justice
San Juan, PR
Counsel or consultant:
Jefferson Group, The (Jose Ortiz-Daliot)

Puerto Rico Economic Development Administration
New York, NY
Counsel or consultant:
Neill and Co. (George A. Dalley)
Scott Runkle

Puerto Rico Federal Affairs Administration
1100 17th St., N.W. Suite 800, Washington, DC 20036
Telephone: (202) 778-0710
Represented by:
Jose Roberto Martinez, Director
Counsel or consultant:
Arent, Fox, Kintner, Plotkin & Kahn (Michael D. Barnes, John C. Culver)
Black, Manafort, Stone and Kelly Public Affairs Co. (Richard H. Davis, Paul J. Manafort)
Campbell, Falk & Selby (Anne Campbell, Steven Selby)
Cassidy and Associates, Inc. (Gerald S. J. Cassidy, Robert A. Farmer)
Covington and Burling (Richard D. Copaken)
Podesta Associates (John D. Podesta)
Scott Runkle
Mark A. Siegel & Associates (Mark A. Siegel)

Puerto Rico Manufacturers Ass'n
San Juan, PR
Counsel or consultant:
Hopkins and Sutter (Joaquin A. Marquez)

Puerto Rico Marine Management, Inc.
Elizabeth, NJ
Counsel or consultant:
Randolph G. Flood and Associates

Puerto Rico Maritime Shipping Authority
San Juan, PR
Counsel or consultant:
Morgan, Lewis and Bockius (Dennis N. Barnes, Mario F. Escudero)

Puerto Rico, New Progressive Party Of
San Juan, PR
Background: The party favoring statehood for Puerto Rico.
Counsel or consultant:
Brockbank & Associates
Verner, Liipfert, Bernhard, McPherson and Hand, Chartered (Harry C. McPherson, John A. Merrigan)

Puerto Rico, Popular Democratic Party of
San Juan, PR
Background: The party favoring Commonwealth status for Puerto Rico.
Counsel or consultant:
Arent, Fox, Kintner, Plotkin & Kahn (John C. Culver)
Bishop, Cook, Purcell & Reynolds (Marlow W. Cook)
Covington and Burling (Richard D. Copaken)
Mark A. Siegel & Associates

Puerto Rico Ports Authority
San Juan, PR

Counsel or consultant:
Covington and Burling (William H. Allen)
McNair Group Inc. (Denis J. Dwyer)

Puerto Rico, Senate of
San Juan, PR
Counsel or consultant:
Dutko & Associates (Richard L. Seely)

Puerto Rico Telephone Co.
San Juan, PR
Counsel or consultant:
Snavely, King and Associates
Steptoe and Johnson (Matthew J. Zinn)

Puerto Rico, U.S.A. Foundation
1701 Pennsylvania Ave., N.W., Suite 1200, Washington, DC 20006
Telephone: (202) 857-0620
Counsel or consultant:
Groom and Nordberg (Peter E. Holmes, Carl A. Nordberg, Jr.)

Puget Sound Cruiseship Alliance
Seattle, WA
Counsel or consultant:
Bogle and Gates (Terry L. Leitzell, Irene Ringwood)
Robertson, Monagle and Eastaugh

Puget Sound Power and Light Co.
Bellevue, WA
Counsel or consultant:
Bishop, Cook, Purcell & Reynolds (H. Lawrence Fox)

Purchasing Management Ass'n of Washington
1350 New York Ave., N.W. Suite 615, Washington, DC 20005
Telephone: (202) 393-1780
Counsel or consultant:
Resources for Group Management, Inc. (Marianne McDermott)

Purdue Frederick Co., The
Norwalk, CT
Counsel or consultant:
Chadbourne and Parke

Push Literacy Action Now (PLAN Inc.)
1332 G St., S.E., Washington, DC 20003
Telephone: (202) 547-8903
Background: A literacy advocacy group.
Represented by:
Catherine A. Baker, Director, Special Projects

Putnam's Sons, G. P.
New York, NY
Counsel or consultant:
Akin, Gump, Strauss, Hauer and Feld (Andrew G. Berg, David A. Donohoe)

Puyallup Tribe of Indians
Tacoma, WA
Counsel or consultant:
Griffin, Johnson & Associates
Sonosky, Chambers and Sachse

Pyropower Corp.
San Diego, CA
Background: Energy consultants.
Counsel or consultant:
W. J. William Harsh (J. William W. Harsch)
Kelley, Drye and Warren (Michael R. Lemov)

Pyrotechnic Signal Manufacturers Ass'n
1310 19th St., N.W., Washington, DC 20036
Telephone: (202) 466-6555
Background: The above address is that of the firm O'Neill and Athy, P.C. Director of the Association is Thomas C. Williams of the law firm.
Counsel or consultant:
O'Neill and Athy, P.C. (Thomas C. Williams)

Qantas Airways
Sydney, Australia
Counsel or consultant:
Condon and Forsyth (Thomas J. Whalen)

Qatar, Embassy of
600 New Hampshire Ave., N.W. Suite 1180, Washington, DC 20037
Telephone: (202) 338-0111

Counsel or consultant:
Davis Wright Tremaine (Walter H. Evans, III)

QIT, Inc.
Counsel or consultant:
Prather, Seeger, Doolittle and Farmer (Kurt E. Blase)

Quad Pharmaceutical Inc.
Counsel or consultant:
Kleinfeld, Kaplan and Becker (Alan H. Kaplan)

Quaker Oats Co.
Chicago, IL
Counsel or consultant:
Howrey and Simon (John S. Kingdon)
Mayer, Brown and Platt

Quality Control Council of America, Inc.
P.O. Box 42558, Northwest Station, Washington, DC 20015-0458
Telephone: (301) 933-7430
Counsel or consultant:
Specialty Contractors Management, Inc. (Walter M. Kardy)

Quanex Corp.
Houston, TX
Counsel or consultant:
Schagrin Associates (Carol A. Colza, Roger B. Schagrin)
Winburn, VanScoyoc, and Hooper (H. Stewart VanScoyoc, John P. Winburn)

Quebec, Canada, Government of
Counsel or consultant:
Covington and Burling (Harvey M. Applebaum)

Quebecair
Montreal, Quebec
Counsel or consultant:
Winthrop, Stimson, Putnam & Roberts (Robert Reed Gray)

Queen City Home Health Care Co.
Cincinnati, OH
Counsel or consultant:
Winthrop, Stimson, Putnam & Roberts (Ronna A. Freiberg, Ira S. Shapiro)

Questar Corp.
Salt Lake City, UT
Counsel or consultant:
DGM Internat'l Inc. (Gordon S. Jones)
Skadden, Arps, Slate, Meagher and Flom (Robert E. Lighthizer)
Sutherland, Asbill and Brennan

QuesTech, Inc.
7600A Leesburg Pike, Falls Church, VA 22043
Telephone: (703) 760-1000
Represented by:
Vincent L. Salvatori, Exec. V. President, Government Relations
Counsel or consultant:
Ashby and Associates (R. Barry Ashby)

QuesTech Inc. Political Action Committee
7600 A Leesburg Pike, Falls Church, VA 22043
Telephone: (703) 760-1000
Represented by:
J. Baron Baptiste, Treasurer

Quileute Indian Tribe
WA
Counsel or consultant:
SENSE, INC. (Joe Tallakson)

Quinault Indian Nation
WA
Counsel or consultant:
Hobbs, Straus, Dean and Wilder (Charles A. Hobbs)
SENSE, INC. (Joe Tallakson)

Quintana Petroleum Corp.
Houston, TX
Counsel or consultant:
Carl F. Arnold

R. Duffy Wall and Associates Inc. Political Action Committee
1317 F St., N.W., Suite 400, Washington, DC 20004
Telephone: (202) 737-0100

ORGANIZATIONS REPRESENTED

R. Duffy Wall and Associates Inc. Political Action Committee (Cont'd)
Counsel or consultant:
R. Duffy Wall and Associates (R. Duffy Wall)

R. Lacey, Inc.
Longview, TX
Counsel or consultant:
Akin, Gump, Strauss, Hauer and Feld (Joel Jankowsky)

Radian Corp.
Austin, TX
Counsel or consultant:
Bob Lawrence & Assoc. (Bob Lawrence)

Radio Officers' Union
100 Indiana Ave., N.W. Suite 311, Washington, DC 20001
Telephone: (202) 737-5109
Background: The Radio Officers Union is affiliated with the Nat'l Marine Engineers Beneficial Ass'n.
Represented by:
Joseph M. Penot, Dir., Wash. Office, Legis. & Res. Affrs.

Radio Technical Commission for Aeronautics
One McPherson Sq. 1425 K St., N.W. Suite 500, Washington, DC 20005
Telephone: (202) 682-0266
Represented by:
David S. Watrous, Exec. Director

Radio Technical Commission for Maritime Services
655 15th St., N.W., Suite 300, Washington, DC 20005
Telephone: (202) 639-4006
Represented by:
William T. Adams, President

Radio-Television News Directors Ass'n
1717 K St., N.W. Suite 615, Washington, DC 20006
Telephone: (202) 659-6510
Represented by:
David Bartlett, President
Robert Vaughn, V. Pres. of Membership and Conferences
Counsel or consultant:
Reed Smith Shaw & McClay (J. Laurent Scharff)

Radix Group Internat'l Inc.
Los Angeles, CA
Counsel or consultant:
Mudge Rose Guthrie Alexander and Ferdon (Richard H. Abbey)

Radon Industry PAC
1 D St. S.E., Washington, DC 20002
Telephone: (202) 543-3859
Represented by:
Jeffrey M. Koopersmith, Treasurer

RailPort
Philadelphia, PA
Counsel or consultant:
Montgomery, McCracken, Walker & Rhoads (David F. Norcross)

Railstar Control Technology, Inc.
Merrimack, NH
Counsel or consultant:
McNair Group Inc. (Denis J. Dwyer)

Railway Labor Executives' Ass'n
400 First St., N.W. Suite 804, Washington, DC 20001
Telephone: (202) 737-1541
Background: Chairman is Richard I. Kilroy (see Transportation, Communications Internat'l Union.
Represented by:
James J. Kennedy, Exec. Secretary-Treasurer

Counsel or consultant:
Alper and Mann
Highsaw, Mahoney & Clarke (William G. Mahoney)
J. P. Trainor

Railway Labor Executives' Ass'n Political League
400 First St., N.W. Room 804, Washington, DC 20001
Telephone: (202) 737-1541
Background: The political action arm of the Railway Labor Executives' Ass'n. Represented by Richard I. Kilroy of the Transportation, Communications Internat'l Union.

Railway Progress Institute
700 North Fairfax St., Alexandria, VA 22314

Telephone: (703) 836-2332
Background: The national trade association of the railway equipment and supply industry.
Represented by:
Helen H. Edge, V. President, Government Affairs
Robert A. Matthews, President
Thomas D. Simpson, V. President

Railway Systems Design
Wilmington, DE
Counsel or consultant:
Allan W. Markham

Rainbow Lobby
1660 L St., N.W. Suite 204, Washington, DC 20036
Telephone: (202) 457-0700
Background: An independent citizen's lobby on progressive issues, both domestic and international, including the advancement of democracy and voting rights. Not associated with the Nat'l Rainbow Coalition of the Rev. Jesse Jackson.
Represented by:
Todd P. Bentsen, Legislative Aide
Deborah Green, Administrative Director
Francine Miller, Legislative Assistant
Nancy Ross, Exec. Director
Donna Waks, Legislative Aide
Counsel or consultant:
Abukari

Rainbow Navigations, Inc.
Red Bank, NJ
Counsel or consultant:
Mudge Rose Guthrie Alexander and Ferdon (Richard H. Abbey)

Ralston Purina Co.
2000 L St., N.W., Suite 801, Washington, DC 20036
Telephone: (202) 223-5302
Represented by:
Claude D. Alexander, Director, Government Affairs
Anne Marie Wiedemer, Executive Assistant
Counsel or consultant:
Morgan, Lewis and Bockius (John R. Quarles, Jr.)

Ramirez & Co., T.
San Juan, PR
Counsel or consultant:
Gregory Co., The (Neal Gregory)

Ramsey County, Minnesota
St. Paul, MN
Counsel or consultant:
Craig Associates (Patricia Johnson Craig)

Ranco, Inc.
Columbus, OH
Counsel or consultant:
Ginsburg, Feldman and Bress (David Ginsburg)

RAND Corp.
2100 M St., N.W., 8th Floor, Washington, DC 20037
Telephone: (202) 296-5000
Background: The Washington Office of a private, non-profit institution based in Santa Monica, CA. Engages in research and analysis on national security and public welfare issues.
Represented by:
Peter Reuter, Co-Director, Drug Policy Research Center
Charles R. Roll, Director, Washington Office

Randolph-Sheppard Vendors of America
1010 Vermont Ave., N.W. Suite 1100, Washington, DC 20005
Telephone: (202) 393-3666
Background: Represented by Roberta Douglas of the American Council of the Blind.

Ranieri-Wilson
New York, NY
Counsel or consultant:
Thacher, Proffitt and Wood (Hu A. Benton, Joseph M. Kolar, Louis H. Nevins)

Rasch Elektronik
Rodermark, Germany
Counsel or consultant:
Tendler, Goldberg & Biggins, Chtd. (Paul M. Tendler)

Rayburn County Electric Cooperative
Kaufman, TX

Counsel or consultant:
Verner, Liipfert, Bernhard, McPherson and Hand, Chartered (Harry C. McPherson, Clinton A. Vince)

Raytheon Co.
1215 Jefferson Davis Hwy., Suite 1500, Arlington, VA 22202
Telephone: (703) 486-5400
Represented by:
Gerard A. Smith, V. President, Washington Operations

Reader's Digest Ass'n
1730 Rhode Island Ave., N.W. Suite 406, Washington, DC 20036
Telephone: (202) 223-9520
Represented by:
William Schulz, Managing Editor

Reading and Bates Corp.
Tulsa, OK
Counsel or consultant:
Groom and Nordberg (Carl A. Nordberg, Jr.)

Reading is Fundamental, Inc.
600 Maryland Ave., S.W. Suite 500, Washington, DC 20560
Telephone: (202) 287-3220
Represented by:
Ruth P. Graves, President

Reading Railway System
Philadelphia, PA
Counsel or consultant:
Morgan, Lewis and Bockius

Rebuild America
201 Massachusetts Ave., N.E., Suite C-6, Washington, DC 20002
Telephone: (202) 547-1212
Represented by:
Fred Branfman, Exec. Director

Recontec
Los Angeles, CA
Counsel or consultant:
Robert N. Pyle & Associates

Recording Arts Political Action Committee
1020 19th St., N.W., Suite 200, Washington, DC 20036
Telephone: (202) 775-0101
Background: The political action arm of the Recording Industry Ass'n of America. Represented by Hilary Rosen of the Association.

Recording for the Blind, Inc.
Princeton, NJ
Counsel or consultant:
MARC Associates, Inc. (Robert R. Humphreys)

Recording Industry Ass'n of America
1020 19th St., N.W., Suite 200, Washington, DC 20036
Telephone: (202) 775-0101
Background: Founded in 1952, RIAA represents 90% of all legitimate recordings produced and sold in the U.S. Seeks legislative and regulatory action needed to maintain a healthy industry.
Represented by:
Jason S. Berman, President
Tanya Blackwood, Assistant Director, Public Relations
Michael W. Cover, Dir., Cong. Relations/Asst. to Pres.
Stephen J. D'Onofrio, Dep. General Counsel/Anti-Piracy Opertns
Neal Edelson, Associate General Counsel
Ken Giel, Dep. Dir., Anti-Piracy Investigative Opn
Patricia A. Heimers, V. President, Public Relations
David Leibowitz, Sr. V. President and General Counsel
Anne D. Neal, Deputy General Counsel
Hilary B. Rosen, V. President, Government Relations
Counsel or consultant:
APCO Associates (Neal M. Cohen)
Arnold & Porter (James F. Fitzpatrick)
Williams and Jensen, P.C. (J. Steven Hart)

Recreation Vehicle Dealers Ass'n of North America
3251 Old Lee Hwy. Suite 500, Fairfax, VA 22030
Telephone: (703) 591-7130
Represented by:
Jay Landers, Director, Government Affairs
Robert Strawn, Exec. V. President

The listings in this directory are available as *Mailing Labels*. See last page.

Recreation Vehicle Industry Ass'n
1896 Preston White Drive P.O. Box 2999, Reston, VA 22090
Telephone: (703) 620-6003
Background: The national trade association for manufacturers of recreation vehicles and van conversions, industry suppliers, and service organizations.
Represented by:
Edward F. Conway, Jr., Assistant General Counsel
Dianne Farrell, V. President, Government Affairs
Yvonne Hiott, Manager, Public Relations
David J. Humphreys, President and CEO
Rick Keir, Director, Communications
Gary M. LaBella, V. President, Public Relations
Jerome Loftus, General Counsel
Karen A. Mason, Media Relations Manager
Susan Moriak, Asst. Director, Government Affairs
Christine E. Morrison, Director, Public Relations

Recreation Vehicle Rental Ass'n
3251 Old Lee Hwy. Suite 500, Fairfax, VA 22030
Telephone: (703) 591-7130
Background: Represented by Robert Strawn, Exec. Vice President of the Recreation Vehicle Dealers Ass'n of North America.

Red Tart Cherries
Lansing, MI
Counsel or consultant:
Highley & Associates (Vern F. Highley)

Redmond Industries
Dallas, TX
Counsel or consultant:
Johnson & Gibbs, P.C. (Evan Miller, Steven J. Sacher)

Redondo Beach, California, City of
Counsel or consultant:
The Ferguson Co. (William Ferguson, Jr., Patricia Jordan, Thane Young)

Redwood City, California, Port of
Redwood City, CA
Counsel or consultant:
Lindsay, Hart, Neil & Weigler (Peter Friedmann)

Reebok Internat'l Ltd.
Avon, MA
Counsel or consultant:
Lindsay, Hart, Neil & Weigler (Peter Friedmann)

Reeve Aleutian Airways
Anchorage, AK
Counsel or consultant:
Robertson, Monagle and Eastaugh (Brad Gilman)

Refractory Composites, Inc.
Whittier, CA
Counsel or consultant:
Ashby and Associates (R. Barry Ashby)

Refractory Metals Ass'n
Princeton, NJ
Counsel or consultant:
Robert N. Pyle & Associates

Regan Group Insurance Marketing, The
Novato, CA
Counsel or consultant:
Ginn, Edington, Moore and Wade

Regional Airline Ass'n
1101 Connecticut Ave., N.W. Suite 700, Washington, DC 20036
Telephone: (202) 857-1170
Background: Formerly known as the Commuter Airline Association of America.
Counsel or consultant:
Smith, Bucklin and Associates (Duane H. Ekedahl, Deborah Ladomirak)

Regional Airlines Ass'n Political Action Committee
1101 Connecticut Ave., N.W. Suite 700, Washington, DC 20036
Telephone: (202) 857-1170
Counsel or consultant:
Smith, Bucklin and Associates (Duane H. Ekedahl)

Regional Airport Authority of Louisville
Louisville, KY

Counsel or consultant:
Sparkman and Cole, Inc. (Timothy R. Cole)

Regional Railroads of America
Washington, DC
Counsel or consultant:
RBC Associates, Inc. (Keith O. Hartwell)

Regional Transportation District
Counsel or consultant:
Kogovsek & Associates, Inc.

Registry of Interpreters for the Deaf
8719 Colesville Rd., Suite 310, Silver Spring, MD 20910
Telephone: (301) 608-0050
Represented by:
Don Roose, Exec. Director

Regular Common Carrier Conference
2200 Mill Road Suite 350, Alexandria, VA 22314
Telephone: (703) 838-1967
Background: An affiliate of the American Trucking Ass'ns, Inc. Represents the interests of general freight motor common carriers.
Represented by:
Russell Capelle, Director of Research and Statistics
Shawn F. Dwyer, Director of Public Relations
James C. Harkins, Exec. Director
Kevin Michael Williams, General Counsel

Regulatory Affairs Professionals Soc.
1101 Connecticut Ave., N.W., Suite 700, Washington, DC 20036
Telephone: (202) 857-1148
Counsel or consultant:
Smith, Bucklin and Associates (Carter E. Keithley)

Reinsurance Ass'n of America
1819 L St., N.W., Suite 700, Washington, DC 20036
Telephone: (202) 293-3335
Represented by:
Jack H. Blaine, Executive V. President
Daniel J. Conway, Sr. V. President, General Counsel
Dana D. Duden, Legislative Assistant
Sandra L. LaFevre, Assistant V. President
Andre Maisonpierre, President
James M. Shamberger, Senior Vice President
Counsel or consultant:
Patton, Boggs and Blow (John Jonas)

Religious Coalition for Abortion Rights
100 Maryland Ave., N.E., Washington, DC 20002
Telephone: (202) 543-7032
Background: An organization of national religious bodies which, on the basis of faith and moral principle and in keeping with constitutional rights, works to safeguard religious and reproductive freedom.
Represented by:
Pamela Haughton-Denniston, Director, Legislative Program
Patricia Tyson, Exec. Director

Remodelers Nat'l Funding Corp.
Austin, TX
Counsel or consultant:
Evans Group, Ltd., The (Thomas B. Evans, Jr.)

Renal Physician Ass'n
1101 Vermont Ave., N.W. Suite 500, Washington, DC 20005
Telephone: (202) 898-1562
Counsel or consultant:
Dyer, Ellis, Joseph & Mills (Thomas L. Mills)

Renal Physicians of Texas
Dallas, TX
Counsel or consultant:
Baker and Hostetler (Frederick H. Graefe)

Renault USA, Inc.
1111 19th St., N.W. Suite 1000, Washington, DC 20036
Telephone: (202) 331-9345
Represented by:
Francois Louis, Director, Governmental Affairs

Renew America Project
1400 16th St., N.W. Suite 710, Washington, DC 20036
Telephone: (202) 232-2252

Represented by:
Tina C. Hobson, Exec. Director
Rick Piltz, Associate Exec. Director
Counsel or consultant:
Gallagher-Widmeyer Group Inc., The (Mary Jane Gallagher)

Renewable Fuels Ass'n
201 Massachusetts Ave., N.E. Suite C-4, Washington, DC 20002
Telephone: (202) 543-3802
Represented by:
Eric Vaughn, President
Counsel or consultant:
Edward D. Heffernan
Sills & Brodsky, P.C. (Alvin J. Geske)

Renewable Natural Resources Foundation
5430 Grosvenor Lane, Bethesda, MD 20814
Telephone: (301) 493-9101
Background: A consortium of 16 professional, scientific and educational societies concerned about conserving and replenishing renewable natural resources.
Represented by:
Robert D. Day, Exec. Director

Reno Sparks Indian Colony
Reno, NV
Counsel or consultant:
Lachelli, Waller and Associates (Vincent P. Lachelli)

Rent A Center
Wichita, KS
Counsel or consultant:
Stateside Associates

Reporters Committee for Freedom of the Press
1735 I St., N.W., Suite 504, Washington, DC 20006
Telephone: (202) 466-6312
Background: Formed in 1970 as a national organization to obtain legal assistance and other support for members of the news media profession and in defense of the principles of freedom of the press.
Represented by:
Jane E. Kirtley, Exec. Director

Republic Group, The
5801 Lee Hwy., Arlington, VA 22207
Telephone: (703) 533-8555
Background: An international marketing firm representing domestic and manufacturers of high tech systems.
Represented by:
Margarita T. Castellon, Director of Government Relations

Republic Health Corp.
Dallas, TX
Counsel or consultant:
Johnson & Gibbs, P.C. (David G. Glickman)

Republic Nat'l Bank of New York
New York, NY
Counsel or consultant:
Rogers and Wells (Eugene T. Rossides)
Silverstein and Mullens (William A. Kirk, Jr.)

Republican Governors Ass'n
310 First St., S.E., Washington, DC 20003
Telephone: (202) 863-8587
Represented by:
Michele M. Davis, Exec. Director

Republican Majority Fund
503 Capitol Court, N.E., Suite 100, Washington, DC 20002
Telephone: (202) 547-6200
Background: A political action committee founded in 1980 by Senator Howard Baker for the purpose of electing Republicans to the Congress. Sen. Richard Lugar (R-IN) serves as Chairman.
Represented by:
Chip Andreae, Exec. Director
Donna F. Peters, Treasurer, Administrator

Republican Nat'l Committee
310 First St., S.E., Washington, DC 20003
Telephone: (202) 863-8500

ORGANIZATIONS REPRESENTED

Republican Nat'l Committee (Cont'd)
Represented by:
  Margaret Alexander, Finance Director
  Lee Atwater, Chairman
  Jeanie Austin, Co-Chair
  B. Jay Cooper, Director of Communications
  Norman B. Cummings, Director of Political Division
  Thelma Duggin, Director, Political Outreach
  Kathleen Evers, Chief of Staff to the Co-Chair
  Benjamin L. Ginsberg, General Counsel
  Leslie Goodman, Press Secretary
  John J. Long, Director, Legislative Task Force
  Mary Matalin, Chief of Staff

Republican Nat'l Hispanic Assembly of the U.S.
  440 First St., N.W. Suite 400, Washington, DC 20001
  Telephone: (202) 662-1355
  Background: Supported by the Republican Nat'l Committee, the Assembly works to get Hispanic Americans more involved in the American political process and to enlist their support for the GOP.
  Represented by:
  Armando L. Mena, Exec. Director

Research Corporation Technologies, Inc.
  Tucson, AZ
  Counsel or consultant:
  Parry and Romani Associates Inc. (Romano Romani)

Research and Development Laboratories
  Los Angeles, CA
  Counsel or consultant:
  The William Chasey Organization (William C. Chasey, Ph.D.)

Research Soc. on Alcoholism
  Austin, TX
  Counsel or consultant:
  MARC Associates, Inc. (Daniel C. Maldonado)

Reserve Bank of Australia
  Melbourne, Australia
  Counsel or consultant:
  Finnegan, Henderson, Farabow, Garrett and Dunner (Kenneth E. Payne)

Reserve Officers Ass'n of the U.S.
  1 Constitution Ave., N.E., Washington, DC 20002
  Telephone: (202) 479-2200
  Represented by:
  Col. Herbert M. Hart, USMC (Ret), Director, Public Affairs
  Maj. Gen. Evan Hultman, AUS (Ret), Exec. Director
  Lt. Col. James C. Rodenberg, USAF (Ret), Legislative Counsel
  Rear Adm. Bennett S. Sparks, USCGR, Deputy Exec. Director

Resilient Floor Covering Institute
  966 Hungerford Drive Suite 12-B, Rockville, MD 20850
  Telephone: (301) 340-8580
  Background: Contact is Walter D. Anderson of the Contractors Pump Bureau.

RESNA
  1101 Connecticut Ave., N.W., Suite 700, Washington, DC 20036
  Telephone: (202) 857-1199
  Background: Formerly the Ass'n for the Advancement of Rehabilitation Technology.
  Counsel or consultant:
  Smith, Bucklin and Associates (Patricia I. Horner)

Resource Conservation and Recovery Act Mine Waste Group
  c/o Holland & Hart, Suite 310 1001 Pennsylvania Ave., N.W., Washington, DC 20004
  Telephone: (202) 638-5500
  Counsel or consultant:
  Holland and Hart (Steven G. Barringer)

Resource Deployment, Inc.
  Fort Worth, TX
  Background: A financial services holding company.
  Counsel or consultant:
  Zuckert, Scoutt and Rasenberger (Walter D. Vinyard, Jr.)

Resources for the Future
  1616 P St., N.W., Washington, DC 20036
  Telephone: (202) 328-5000

Background: A non-profit organization established in 1952 to do independent research and educational work in natural resources and environmental quality.
Represented by:
  Douglas R. Bohi, Dir., Energy & Natural Resources Div.
  Robert W. Fri, President
  Raymond J. Kopp, Dir., Quality of the Environment Div.
  Debra Montanino, Director, Institutional Relations
  Paul R. Portney, V. President
  George E. Rossmiller, Dir., Nat'l Ctr. for Food & Agric. Pol.
  K. Storck, Public Affairs

Resources Trucking Inc.
  North Bergen, NJ
  Counsel or consultant:
  Hill, Betts and Nash (Brien E. Kehoe)

Response Dynamics Inc.
  2070 Chain Bridge Road, Vienna, VA 22180
  Telephone: (703) 442-7595
  Counsel or consultant:
  The William Chasey Organization (Virginia Chasey)

Responsible Citizen's Political League
  3 Research Place, Rockville, MD 20850
  Telephone: (301) 948-4910
  Background: A political action committee sponsored by the Brotherhood of Railway, Airline and Steamship Clerks, Freight Handlers, Express and Station Employes.
  Represented by:
  Donald A. Bobo, Treasurer

Restaurant Ass'n of Metropolitan Washington PAC
  Potomac, MD
  Counsel or consultant:
  Wunder, Ryan, Cannon & Thelen (Paul E. Sullivan)

RESULTS
  236 Massachusetts Ave., N.E. Suite 110, Washington, DC 20002
  Telephone: (202) 543-9340
  Background: Internat'l citizens lobby with over 150 groups in seven countries working to create the political will to end the worst aspects of absolute poverty by the year 2000.
  Represented by:
  Alex Counts, Legislative Director
  Sam Harris, Exec. Director

Retail Bakers of America
  Presidential Bldg. 6525 Belcrest Rd., Suite 250, Hyattsville, MD 20782
  Telephone: (301) 277-0990
  Represented by:
  Richard C. Gohla, Exec. V. President
  Patricia Young, Editor
  Counsel or consultant:
  William A. Quinlan
  Webster, Chamberlain and Bean (Gerard Paul Panaro)

Retail Industry Trade Action Coalition
  1616 H St., N.W., Suite 602, Washington, DC 20006
  Telephone: (202) 783-0922
  Background: A group of U.S. importers opposed to import quotas.
  Counsel or consultant:
  Bonner & Associates
  Internat'l Business and Economic Research Corp.
  Patton, Boggs and Blow (Thomas Hale Boggs, Jr., Frank R. Samolis)

Retail Political Action Committee
  1616 H St., N.W., Washington, DC 20006
  Telephone: (202) 783-7971
  Background: Represents legislative and political interests of American Retail Federation. Secretary-Treasurer of the Committee is Joseph P. O'Neill of the American Retail Federation.

Retail Tax Committee
  2550 M St., N.W., Suite 800, Washington, DC
  Telephone: (202) 457-6000
  Background: A group of retail organizations seeking amendment of the Internal Revenue Code to allow investment tax credit to retail structures and increasing allowance of depreciation on buildings and equipment.
  Counsel or consultant:
  Patton, Boggs and Blow (Thomas Hale Boggs, Jr.)

Retail, Wholesale and Department Store Workers Union
  New York, NY
  Counsel or consultant:
  The Kamber Group (Richard A. Weiss)

Retired Officers Ass'n, The (TROA)
  201 N. Washington St., Alexandria, VA 22314
  Telephone: (703) 549-2311
  Represented by:
  Col. Paul W. Arcari, USAF (Ret), Director, Legislative Affairs
  Col. James Barnes, USA (Ret.), Director, Marketing & Membership Devlmnt
  Col. Charles D. Cooper, USAF (Ret), Director, Communications
  Christopher J. Giaimo, Deputy Director, Legislative Affairs
  William R. Hart, Deputy Director, Legislative Affairs
  V. Admiral Thomas J. Kilcline, USN (Ret.), President
  Capt. Henry S. Palau, USN (Ret.), Secretary and General Counsel
  Capt. Donald Repass, USN (Ret), Public Relations Officer

Revere Copper and Brass Co.
  New York, NY
  Counsel or consultant:
  Kilpatrick & Cody (Joseph W. Dorn)

Review and Herald Publishing Co.
  Hagerstown, MD
  Background: A publisher of religious materials. Associated with the Seventh-day Adventist Church.
  Counsel or consultant:
  Johns and Carson

Revlon Group
  New York, NY
  Counsel or consultant:
  Akin, Gump, Strauss, Hauer and Feld (Andrew G. Berg, James P. Denvir, III, David A. Donohoe, Louise E. Teitz)
  Black, Manafort, Stone and Kelly Public Affairs Co. (Nicholas A. Panuzio)

Rexnord, Inc.
  Brookfield, WI
  Counsel or consultant:
  Leighton and Regnery

Reynolds Metals Co.
  1620 Eye St., N.W., Washington, DC 20006
  Telephone: (202) 833-3760
  Represented by:
  Lee H. Califf, Manager, Government Relations
  Stevenson T. Walker, Director, Government Relations

Reynolds Tobacco Co., R. J.
  1455 Pennsylvania Ave., N.W., Suite 525, Washington, DC 20004
  Telephone: (202) 626-7200
  Background: A subsidiary of RJR Nabisco, Inc. Represented in Washington by Burleigh C. W. Leonard, V. President, Federal Government Affairs. (See RJR Nabisco Washington, Inc.)
  Counsel or consultant:
  Collier, Shannon & Scott (Judy Oldham)
  Ragan and Mason (William F. Ragan)

Rhode Island, State of
  Providence, RI
  Counsel or consultant:
  Dickstein, Shapiro and Morin (Andrew P. Miller, Bernard Nash)

Rhone-Poulenc Ag Co.
  Triangle Park, NC
  Counsel or consultant:
  Jellinek, Schwartz, Connolly & Freshman, Inc. (Steven D. Jellinek)
  Neill and Co. (Denis M. Neill, Albert C. Printz, Jr.)

Rhone-Poulenc Inc.
  Metropolitan Square, Suite 225 655 15th St., N.W., Washington, DC 20005
  Telephone: (202) 628-0500

ORGANIZATIONS REPRESENTED

Represented by:
Joseph J. Martyak, Director, Corporate Affairs
William P. Mengebier, Assistant Director, Government Relations
Jean R. Toohey, Manager, Government Relations
Counsel or consultant:
Baker and Botts (B. Donovan Picard)

Rice Growers Ass'n of California
Sacramento, CA
Counsel or consultant:
Robinson, Lake, Lerer & Montgomery (James H. Lake)
Vickers & Vickers (Eugene B. Vickers)

Rice Millers' Ass'n
1235 Jefferson Davis Hwy. Suite 302, Arlington, VA 22202-3270
Telephone: (703) 920-1281
Represented by:
David R. Graves, President
Counsel or consultant:
Patton, Boggs and Blow (Bart S. Fisher)

Ricebelt Warehouses
El Campo, TX
Counsel or consultant:
Meyers & Associates (Larry D. Meyers)

Riceland Foods
Stuttgart, AR
Counsel or consultant:
Jack L. Williams

Rich Internat'l Airways
Miami, FL
Counsel or consultant:
Boros and Garofalo (Gary B. Garofalo)

Richardson Lawrie Associates
London, England
Counsel or consultant:
William L. Hoffman

Richardson Savings and Loan Ass'n
Richardson, TX
Counsel or consultant:
Elias, Matz, Tiernan and Herrick

Richmond, California, City of
Counsel or consultant:
PPED, Inc. (Richard S. Kochan)

Richmond, Fredericksburg and Potomac Railroad
Richmond, VA
Counsel or consultant:
McGuire, Woods, Battle and Boothe

Richmond Power and Light Co.
Richmond, IN
Counsel or consultant:
Spiegel and McDiarmid (Frances E. Francis)

Richmond Transfer and Storage Co.
Richmond, CA
Counsel or consultant:
Denning and Wohlstetter (Alan F. Wohlstetter)

Ricoh Corp.
West Caldwell, NJ
Counsel or consultant:
Dorsey & Whitney

Ricoh Electronics, Inc.
Tustin, CA
Counsel or consultant:
Fleishman-Hillard, Inc

Ridgeview Institute
Smyrna, GA
Counsel or consultant:
Burson-Marsteller (Carolyn Tieger)

Ridgeway Mining Co.
Counsel or consultant:
Prather, Seeger, Doolittle and Farmer (Kurt E. Blase)

Riedel Environmental Services
Portland, OR
Counsel or consultant:
Ball, Janik and Novack (James A. Beall)

Right to Work Political Action Committee
8001 Braddock Road, Springfield, VA 22160
Telephone: (703) 321-9820
Background: Contact is Reed E. Larson (see Nat'l Right to Work Committee).

Ringling Brothers/Barnum & Bailey
New York, NY
Counsel or consultant:
Capitol Associates, Inc.

Rio Grande Valley Sugar Cane Growers Cooperative
Santa Rosa, TX
Background: Michael L. Morton, of the Florida Sugar Cane League, serves as Washington Representative.

Rio Grande Water Conservation District
Alamosa, CO
Counsel or consultant:
Kogovsek & Associates, Inc.

Ripon Soc.
6 Library Court, S.E., Washington, DC 20003
Telephone: (202) 546-1292
Background: A progressive Republican research and policy organization founded in 1962.
Represented by:
William P. McKenzie, Exec. Director
Counsel or consultant:
Kessler and Associates

RIV-SKF Industrie S.p.A.
Torino, Italy
Counsel or consultant:
White & Case (John W. Barnum)

River Bank America
New Rochelle, NY
Counsel or consultant:
James J. Butera, Chartered
Thacher, Proffitt and Wood (Louis H. Nevins)

Riverside, California, City of
Counsel or consultant:
Nat'l Center for Municipal Development (Mark S. Israel)

Riverside, California, County of
440 First St., N.W. Suite 501, Washington, DC 20001
Telephone: (202) 737-7523
Background: Represented by Roger F. Honberger (see San Diego County listing).

RJR Nabisco, Inc.
Parsippany, NJ
Counsel or consultant:
Lee, Toomey & Kent

RJR Nabisco Washington, Inc.
1455 Pennsylvania Ave., N.W., Suite 525, Washington, DC 20004
Telephone: (202) 626-7200
Background: The Washington office of RJR Nabisco Inc. serves also as Federal Government Affairs office for subsidiaries Del Monte-USA, Nabisco Brands, Inc., RJR Archer, Inc. R. J. Reynolds Tobacco USA, and R. J. Reynolds Tobacco Internat'l.
Represented by:
Alan C. Caldwell, Director, Federal Government Affairs
LeAnn R. Hensche, Sr. Assoc., Federal Government Relations
Marsha Lefkovits, Sr. Associate Federal Gov't Affairs
Burleigh C. W. Leonard, V. President, Federal Gov't Affrs.
M. G. Oglesby, Jr., Senior V. President, Government Affairs
Tommy J. Payne, Director, Federal Gov't Affairs
Counsel or consultant:
Akin, Gump, Strauss, Hauer and Feld
Vern Clark & Associates (Vernon Clark)
Gallagher-Widmeyer Group Inc., The (Scott D. Widmeyer)
Jones, Day, Reavis and Pogue (Robert F. McDermott)
Keefe Co., The (William A. Signer)
Lipsen Whitten & Diamond
Ragan and Mason

RKO General, Inc.
New York, NY
Counsel or consultant:
Wilmer, Cutler and Pickering (J. Roger Wollenberg)

Rmax, Inc.
Dallas, TX
Counsel or consultant:
Dutko & Associates (L. L. Hank Hankla)

Road Information Program, The (TRIP)
1200 18th St., N.W. Suite 314, Washington, DC 20036
Telephone: (202) 466-6706
Background: A private, non-profit highway transportation research organization.
Represented by:
Will Wilkins, Executive Director
Counsel or consultant:
Ketchum Public Relations (Paige Eversol, Penny Hill, Martha Hudak, Ronald R. Mueller, Gregory M. Shaw)

Roadway Express, Inc.
1901 North Ft. Myer Drive, Suite 204, Arlington, VA 22209
Telephone: (703) 528-0233
Represented by:
Timothy P. Lynch, V. President, Government Affairs
Elizabeth A. Murphy, Manager, State Government Affairs

Roanoke Companies, The
Schaumburg, IL
Counsel or consultant:
Mudge Rose Guthrie Alexander and Ferdon (Richard H. Abbey)

Rochester Community Savings Bank
Rochester, NY
Counsel or consultant:
James J. Butera, Chartered
Thacher, Proffitt and Wood (Louis H. Nevins)

Rochester Institute of Technology
Rochester, NY
Counsel or consultant:
Cassidy and Associates, Inc. (James P. Fabiani, Vincent M. Versage)

Rochester Tax Council
Rochester, NY
Counsel or consultant:
Ivins, Phillips and Barker (H. Stewart Dunn, Jr., Philip D. Morrison)

Rockefeller Foundation
New York, NY
Counsel or consultant:
Foreman & Heidepriem (Carol Tucker Foreman, Nikki Heidepriem)

Rockport Fine Arts Council
Rockport, MA
Counsel or consultant:
Palumbo & Cerrell, Inc. (Paul A. Skrabut, Jr.)

Rockwell Internat'l
1745 Jefferson Davis Hwy. Suite 1200, Arlington, VA 22202
Telephone: (703) 553-6600
Represented by:
William Robert Andrews, Director, Congressional Relations
Charles W. Cruit, Senior Procurement Policy Representative
John B. Fallon, Sr. V. President, Internat'l
Alison B. Fortier, Manager, Legislative Programs
R. Mark Fowler, Manager, Legislative Programs
Raymond Garcia, Director, Legislative Affairs
James H. Garrett, Jr., V.P., Electronics Gov't Affairs & Mktg
John A. Gonzalez, Manager, Legislative Programs
Clayton M. Jones, V. Pres., Aerospace Gov't Affairs & Mktg
Joseph T. Mayer, Manager, Legislative Programs
James A. McDivitt, Sr. V. President, Government Operations
George W. Pritts, Jr., Senior Legislative Affairs Specialist
Linda C. Sadler, Dir,Industry/Gov't Rltns-Rockwell Commns
Carl E. Watt, Jr., Manager, Legislative Programs

Rocky Co., The
Seattle, WA
Counsel or consultant:
Bracy Williams & Co. (James C. Benfield, Kenneth S. Birnbaum, Terrence L. Bracy, Thomas J. Hennessey, Jr., Kenneth M. Stram, Susan J. Williams)

The listings in this directory are available as *Mailing Labels*. See last page.

ORGANIZATIONS REPRESENTED

Rocky Mountain Oil and Gas Ass'n
Denver, CO
Counsel or consultant:
Direct Impact Co., The (John Brady, Tom Herrity)

Rodale Press, Inc.
Emmaus, PA
Counsel or consultant:
McMahon and Associates (Joseph E. McMahon, Sandra A. Schlicker)

Rogers and Rogers Investments
TX
Counsel or consultant:
Bill Newbold & Assoc. (Bill Newbold)

Rohm and Haas Co.
1667 K St., N.W., Suite 210, Washington, DC 20006
Telephone: (202) 872-0660
Represented by:
Kenneth E. Davis, Director, Government Relations
Geoffrey B. Hurwitz, Director, State Government Relations
Robin L. Williams, Associate Director, Government Relations
Counsel or consultant:
Bishop, Cook, Purcell & Reynolds (James K. Jackson)
Hill and Knowlton Public Affairs Worldwide (John Urbanchuk)
Wunder, Ryan, Cannon & Thelen (W. Stephen Cannon)

Rohr Industries, Inc.
Chula Vista, CA
Counsel or consultant:
McCutchen, Doyle, Brown & Enersen (David Andrews, Philip T. Cummings)

Rollins Environmental Services, Inc.
Wilmington, DE
Counsel or consultant:
Evans Group, Ltd., The (Thomas B. Evans, Jr.)

Rolls-Royce, Inc.
1001 Pennsylvania Ave., N.W., Suite 490, Washington, DC 20004
Telephone: (202) 737-1010
Background: Markets gas turbines on behalf of its parent, Rolls-Royce p.l.c., based in England.
Represented by:
Barry J. New, V. President, Government Programs
Counsel or consultant:
Hyman Fine & Associates Ltd.
Lipsen Whitten & Diamond
Silverstein and Mullens (Leonard L. Silverstein)

Romania, Embassy of the Socialist Republic of
1607 23rd St., N.W., Washington, DC 20008
Telephone: (202) 232-4747
Counsel or consultant:
van Kloberg and Associates (Edward J. van Kloberg, III)

Rongelap Atoll Local Government
Majuro, Marshall Islands
Counsel or consultant:
David M. Weiman

Roses, Inc.
Haslett, MI
Counsel or consultant:
Stewart and Stewart (Eugene L. Stewart)

Rouse Company, The
10275 Little Patuxent Pkwy., Columbia, MD 21044
Telephone: (301) 992-6468
Represented by:
John J. Szymanski, CPA, V.Pres., Dir., Federal Legislat. Affrs.
Counsel or consultant:
Baker and Hostetler (Kenneth J. Kies)
Davidson Colling Group, Inc., The (James H. Davidson)
Driskell and Associates, Paul
Miller & Chevalier, Chartered (Phillip L. Mann, John S. Nolan)

Rowley-Scher Reprographics, Inc.
Beltsville, MD
Counsel or consultant:
Robert N. Pyle & Associates

Royal Air Maroc
Casablanca, Morocco
Counsel or consultant:
Shaw, Pittman, Potts and Trowbridge (Dean D. Aulick)

Royal Bank of Canada
Montreal, Canada
Counsel or consultant:
Prather, Seeger, Doolittle and Farmer (Thomas L. Farmer)

Royal Caribbean Cruise Line
Miami, FL
Counsel or consultant:
Alcalde & Rousselot (Hector Alcalde)

Royal Danish Embassy
3200 Whitehaven St., N.W., Washington, DC 20008
Telephone: (202) 234-4300
Counsel or consultant:
Hill and Knowlton Public Affairs Worldwide (Mary C. Foerster)

Royal Dutch Shell Group
Amsterdam, Netherlands
Counsel or consultant:
Howrey and Simon (Keith E. Pugh, Jr.)

Royal Jordanian Airline, The
New York, NY
Counsel or consultant:
Robert N. Meiser, P.C.

Royal Nepalese Embassy
2131 Leroy Place, N.W., Washington, DC 20008
Telephone: (202) 667-4550
Counsel or consultant:
van Kloberg and Associates (Lance T. Ventry)

Royal Ordnance, Inc.
1101 Wilson Blvd., Suite 1200, Alexandria, VA 22209
Telephone: (703) 516-2731
Represented by:
Peter Williams, President
Counsel or consultant:
Robison Internat'l, Inc.

Royal Trustco Ltd.
Toronto, Ontario, Canada
Counsel or consultant:
Jones, Day, Reavis and Pogue (Randall E. Davis)
Patton, Boggs and Blow (James B. Christian, Jr.)

RRD & B Good Government Committee
1575 I St., N.W., Suite 1025, Washington, DC 20005
Telephone: (202) 289-8660
Background: The political action committee for the law firm of Rivkin, Radler, Dunne and Bayh.
Counsel or consultant:
Rivkin, Radler, Dunne and Bayh (Thomas A. Connaughton)

RREEF Funds, The
San Francisco, CA
Counsel or consultant:
Morrison & Foerster (Tony M. Edwards)

Ruan Leasing Co.
Des Moines, IA
Counsel or consultant:
Chadbourne and Parke

Rubber Manufacturers Ass'n
1400 K St., N.W., Washington, DC 20005
Telephone: (202) 682-4800
Represented by:
Thomas E. Cole, President
Daniel A. Duffy, Government Relations Associate
Edward J. McCarthy, V. President, Industrial Products
Peter Pantuso, Director, Legislative Affairs
John R. Serumgard, V. President, Tire Division
Frank E. Timmons, Deputy Director, Tire Division
George A. White, Secretary
Counsel or consultant:
Hopkins and Sutter (John W. Pettit)

Rubber Manufacturers Ass'n Political Action Committee
1400 K St., N.W., Washington, DC 20005
Telephone: (202) 682-4800
Background: Officers responsible include Thomas E. Cole, Peter Pantuso, and John R. Serumgard, all of the Rubber Manufacturers Ass'n.

Ruff Political Action Committee
501 Capitol Court, N.E. Suite 100, Washington, DC 20002
Telephone: (202) 546-0023
Background: A conservative grassroots political action committee.
Represented by:
Terry L. Bechtold, Assistant Director
Tammy J. Lyles, President

Rural Coalition
2001 S St., N.W., Suite 500, Washington, DC 20009
Telephone: (202) 483-1500
Represented by:
Judith D. Coats, Director

Russ Berrie Corp.
New York, NY
Counsel or consultant:
Camp, Barsh, Bates and Tate (Ronald L. Platt)

Rust Engineering
Birmingham, AL
Counsel or consultant:
Shaw, Pittman, Potts and Trowbridge (William Mike House)

Rutgers, The State University of New Jersey
New Brunswick, NJ
Counsel or consultant:
Rogers and Wells (William Morris)

Ryder System, Inc.
1275 K St., N.W., 10th Floor, Washington, DC 20005
Telephone: (202) 783-1229
Represented by:
Bob Clark, Director, Federal Affairs
Beverley Walker, Director, Federal Affairs
Counsel or consultant:
Baker, Worthington, Crossley, Stansberry & Woolf (III J. E. Murdock)
Hill and Knowlton Public Affairs Worldwide (Gary Hymel)

Ryland Acceptance Advisers, Inc.
Florham Park, NJ
Counsel or consultant:
Dechert Price & Rhoads (Sander M. Bieber)

S&A Restaurants Corp.
Dallas, TX
Counsel or consultant:
Richard B. Berman and Co.,Inc. (Richard B. Berman)

S & F Warehouses, Inc.
Brooklyn, NY
Background: A foreign trade zone operator.
Counsel or consultant:
Smith Dawson & Andrews, Inc. (Gregory B. Andrews, James P. Smith)

S.R.C. Services, Inc.
Columbia, SC
Counsel or consultant:
Paul Suplizio Associates (Paul E. Suplizio)

Saab-Scania of America
Orange, CT
Counsel or consultant:
Winthrop, Stimson, Putnam & Roberts (John E. Gillick, Robert Reed Gray)

SAB Engineering and Construction
Media, PA
Counsel or consultant:
Peyser Associates, Inc.

Sabey Corp.
Seattle, WA
Counsel or consultant:
Denny Miller Associates

Sacramento, California, City of
Counsel or consultant:
Preston Gates Ellis & Rouvelas Meeds (Allen Erenbaum, Craig J. Gehring)

Sacramento Municipal Utility District
Sacramento, CA
Counsel or consultant:
APCO Associates (Deborah R. Sliz)
Spiegel and McDiarmid (Frances E. Francis, Peter K. Matt)

ORGANIZATIONS REPRESENTED

SAE Electric
Milan, Italy
Counsel or consultant:
Sharretts, Paley, Carter and Blauvelt (Alfred R. McCauley)

Safe Buildings Alliance
655 15th St., N.W., Suite 1200, Washington, DC 20005
Telephone: (202) 879-5120
Background: An organization of companies that formerly manufactured asbestos-containing building materials.
Represented by:
John C. Biechman, V. President
John Frederick Welch, President
Counsel or consultant:
Burson-Marsteller (Carolyn Tieger)
Kirkland and Ellis (L. Mark Wine)

Safe Energy Communication Council
1717 Massachusetts Ave., N.W. Suite LL215, Washington, DC 20036
Telephone: (202) 483-8491
Background: A coalition of national public interest, media, environmental and safe energy groups which responds to the public relations campaign of the nuclear power industry, and promotes safe, and renewable energy sources.
Represented by:
Scott Denman, Director
Mary O'Driscoll, Nat'l Press Coordinator

Safeguard America's Family Enterprises
2550 M St., N.W. Suite 450, Washington, DC 20037
Telephone: (202) 457-5671
Counsel or consultant:
Andrews' Associates, Inc. (Mark Andrews, Jacqueline Balk-Tusa)

Safeguard Industries
King Of Prussia, PA
Counsel or consultant:
Morgan, Lewis and Bockius

Safetran Systems Corp.
Louisville, KY
Counsel or consultant:
Arthur E. Cameron

Safety-Kleen Corp.
Elgin, IL
Counsel or consultant:
Morgan, Lewis and Bockius (Eric V. Schaeffer, Arline M. Sheehan)

Safety Soc., The
1900 Association Drive, Reston, VA 22091
Telephone: (703) 476-3440
Background: Formerly known as the American School and Community Safety Ass'n. Contact is Raymond A. Ciszek (see Ass'n for Research, Administration, Professional Councils and Societies).

Saga Communications, Inc.
Grosse Pointe, MI
Counsel or consultant:
Kaye, Scholer, Fierman, Hays and Handler (Jason Shrinsky)

Saga Corp.
Menlo Park, CA
Counsel or consultant:
Power & Coleman (Thomas W. Power)

Sage Communications Corp.
Hartford, CT
Counsel or consultant:
Kaye, Scholer, Fierman, Hays and Handler (Jason Shrinsky)

Saginaw Chippewa Tribe of Michigan
Mount Pleasant, MI
Counsel or consultant:
Karl A. Funke and Associates (Karl A. Funke)

Sahlen and Associates, Inc.
Deerfield Beach, FL
Counsel or consultant:
Kelly and Associates, Inc. (John A. Kelly)

Sahlman Seafoods
Tampa, FL

Counsel or consultant:
Bogle and Gates (Terry L. Leitzell)

Salem Medical Laboratory
Salem, MA
Counsel or consultant:
Arent, Fox, Kintner, Plotkin & Kahn (Alan E. Reider)

Salomon Brothers Inc.
1455 Pennsylvania Ave., N.W. Suite 350, Washington, DC 20005
Telephone: (202) 879-4100
Represented by:
Michael P. Andrews, Director
Stephen E. Bell, Managing Director
Counsel or consultant:
Dow, Lohnes and Albertson (Stuart A. Sheldon)
Gold and Liebengood, Inc. (Martin B. Gold)

Salt Institute
700 North Fairfax St. Suite 600, Alexandria, VA 22314
Telephone: (703) 549-4648
Represented by:
Bruce M. Bertram, Technical Director
Richard L. Hanneman, President
Louis V. Priebe, Director, Public Policy

Salt River Project
214 Massachusetts Ave., N.E. Suite 310, Washington, DC 20002
Telephone: (202) 546-8940
Background: The Project provides water to the owners and occupants of lands within the Salt River reclamation district and produces electricity for use within the region.
Represented by:
Julie Evans, Office Manager/Administrative Asst.
Peter M. Hayes, Manager, Federal Affairs

Salvation Army
1025 Vermont Ave., N.W., Washington, DC 20005
Telephone: (202) 639-8414
Represented by:
Walter C. French, Col., Director, Nat'l Public Affairs
Dean B. Seiler, Exec. Director, World Service Office

Salzgitter AG
Salzgitter, West Germany
Counsel or consultant:
Prather, Seeger, Doolittle and Farmer (Thomas L. Farmer)

SAMA Group of Ass'ns
225 Reinekers Lane Suite 625, Washington, DC 22314
Telephone: (703) 836-1360
Represented by:
Michael J. Duff, V. President, Public Affairs
Cynthia Esher, President
William Strackbein, Exec. Director, Lab Products Ass'n
Counsel or consultant:
Mayer, Brown and Platt (Charles S. Levy)

Samaritan Health Services
Phoenix, AZ
Counsel or consultant:
Squire, Sanders and Dempsey (Michael Scott)

Sambo Copper Co., Ltd.
Tokyo, Japan
Counsel or consultant:
Sharretts, Paley, Carter and Blauvelt (Beatrice A. Brickell)

Sampo Corp.
Taipei, Taiwan
Counsel or consultant:
Willkie Farr and Gallagher (Christopher A. Dunn)

Samsonite Corp.
Denver, CO
Counsel or consultant:
Baker and McKenzie (William D. Outman, II)

Samsung Electronics Co., Ltd.
Seoul, Korea
Counsel or consultant:
Arnold & Porter (Sukhan Kim)
Murphy and Demory, Ltd.
Reid & Priest

San Bernardino, California, City of

Counsel or consultant:
Simon & Co., Inc. (Leonard S. Simon)

San Bernardino County, California
Counsel or consultant:
Craig Associates (Patricia Johnson Craig)

San Carlos Apache Tribe
San Carlos, AZ
Counsel or consultant:
William Byler Associates

San Diego, California, City of
Counsel or consultant:
Arent, Fox, Kintner, Plotkin & Kahn (John C. Culver, Joseph E. Sandler, Burton V. Wides)
Barrett, Montgomery & Murphy (John H. Montgomery)

San Diego, California, County of
440 First St., N.W. Suite 501, Washington, DC 20001
Telephone: (202) 737-7523
Represented by:
Roger F. Honberger, Washington Representative

San Diego Gas and Electric Co.
316 Pennsylvania Ave., S.E., Suite 301, Washington, DC 20003
Telephone: (202) 546-7676
Represented by:
Mel Hall-Crawford, Manager, Federal Governmental Affairs
Patricia L. Harmening, Governmental Affairs Representative
Counsel or consultant:
Richard W. Bliss
Edwin T. C. Ing

San Francisco Bar Pilots Ass'n
San Francisco, CA
Counsel or consultant:
Jim Wise Associates (James W. Wise)

San Francisco, California, City of
Counsel or consultant:
Manatos & Manatos, Inc. (Andrew E. Manatos, Kimberley A. Matthews)
Smith Dawson & Andrews, Inc. (Thomas C. Dawson)

San Francisco, California, Port of
Counsel or consultant:
Flanagan Group, Inc. (Daniel V. Flanagan, Jr.)

San Francisco Chronicle
San Francisco, CA
Counsel or consultant:
Fletcher, Heald and Hildreth

San Francisco Public Utilities Commission
San Francisco, CA
Counsel or consultant:
Smith Dawson & Andrews, Inc. (Thomas C. Dawson, James P. Smith)

San Juan, Puerto Rico, City of
San Juan, Puerto Rico
Counsel or consultant:
Jefferson Group, The (Jose Ortiz-Daliot)

San Leandro, California, City of
Counsel or consultant:
Simon & Co., Inc. (Leonard S. Simon)

San Lorenzo Guaynabo, Puerto Rico, City of
Counsel or consultant:
PPED, Inc. (Richard S. Kochan)

San Mateo, California, County of
Redwood City, CA
Counsel or consultant:
Government Relations, Inc. (Thomas J. Bulger)

San Miguel Corp.
Manila, Phillipines
Counsel or consultant:
Leslie J. Schmidt Assoc., Inc. (Leslie J. Schmidt)

San Tomo Group
Stockton, CA
Counsel or consultant:
Olsson, Frank and Weeda, P.C. (John Bode)

Sandoz Corp.
1615 L St., N.W., Suite 320, Washington, DC 20036

ORGANIZATIONS REPRESENTED

Sandoz Corp. (Cont'd)
Telephone: (202) 223-6262
Represented by:
  Mike Ailsworth, V. President, Government Relations
  Tracy Haller, Manager, Legislative Affairs
Counsel or consultant:
  Barnes, Richardson and Colburn (James H. Lundquist)
  Kessler and Associates

SANE/FREEZE
1819 H St., N.W., Suite 1000, Washington, DC 20006
Telephone: (202) 862-9740
Background: A national membership organization working
to develop public support for policies that will lead to-
ward peace, including nuclear disarmament, reduced mili-
tary spending and a non-interventionist foreign policy.
Represented by:
  Nick Carter, Exec. Director
  William Sloane Coffin, President
  Mark Harrison, Lobbyist
  Ira Shorr, Program Coordinator

SANE/FREEZEPAC
1819 H St., N.W. Suite 1000, Washington, DC 20006
Telephone: (202) 862-9740
Background: The political action committee of SANE/
FREEZE, registered in 1982 with the Federal Election
Commission.
Represented by:
  Lyle Wirg, Treasurer

Sansui Electronics Corp.
Lyndhurst, NJ
Counsel or consultant:
  Patton, Boggs and Blow

Santa Ana, California, City of
Counsel or consultant:
  The Ferguson Co. (William Ferguson, Jr., Patricia Jordan,
  Thane Young)

Santa Ana River Flood Protection Agency
Santa Ana, CA
Counsel or consultant:
  James F. McConnell

Santa Ana Watershed Project Authority
Riverside, CA
Counsel or consultant:
  Will & Muys, P.C. (Robert P. Will)

**Santa Barbara County Air Pollution Control Dis-
trict**
Santa Barbara, CA
Counsel or consultant:
  Leon G. Billings, Inc. (Leon G. Billings)

Santa Clara, California, City of
Background: Duncan, Weinberg, Miller & Pembroke repre-
sents the municipal electric utility.
Counsel or consultant:
  Duncan, Weinberg, Miller & Pembroke, P.C. (Wallace L.
  Duncan, James D. Pembroke)

Santa Clara Indian Pueblo
Espanola, NM
Counsel or consultant:
  Forrest Gerard & Associates (Forrest J. Gerard)

Santa Cruz, California, Port of
Santa Cruz, CA
Counsel or consultant:
  E. Del Smith, Inc. (E. Del Smith)

Santa Cruz Properties, Inc.
Cathedral City, CA
Counsel or consultant:
  The Ferguson Co. (William Ferguson, Jr., Patricia Jordan,
  Thane Young)

Santa Fe Pacific Pipelines, Inc.
Los Angeles, CA
Counsel or consultant:
  Ray Paabo

Santa Monica, California, City of
Santa Monica, CA
Counsel or consultant:
  E. Del Smith, Inc. (E. Del Smith)

Sanwa Bank Ltd.
Osaka, Japan

Counsel or consultant:
  Civic Service, Inc.
  Hill and Knowlton Public Affairs Worldwide (Gary Hy-
  mel)

Sanyo Electronics
Little Ferry, NJ
Counsel or consultant:
  Patton, Boggs and Blow

Sara Lee Corp.
Chicago, IL
Counsel or consultant:
  Akin, Gump, Strauss, Hauer and Feld (Joel Jankowsky)
  Mayer, Brown and Platt (Jerry L. Oppenheimer)
  Skadden, Arps, Slate, Meagher and Flom (Robert E.
  Lighthizer)

**Satellite Broadcasting and Communications
Ass'n**
300 N. Washington St. Suite 600, Alexandria, VA 22314
Telephone: (703) 549-6990
Background: Trade association of manufacturers, dealers
and distributors of satellite equipment, together with own-
ers, manufacturers, and operators of satellite receiving sta-
tions.
Represented by:
  Mark C. Ellison, V. Pres., Gov't Affairs & Gen. Counsel
  Charles C. Hewitt, President
Counsel or consultant:
  Dutko & Associates (Emily Young)

Satellite Syndicated Systems, Inc.
Tulsa, OK
Counsel or consultant:
  Pepper and Corazzini (Robert F. Corazzini)

Saudi Arabia, Royal Embassy of
601 New Hampshire Ave., N.W., Washington, DC 20036
Telephone: (202) 342-3800
Counsel or consultant:
  The Hannaford Co., Inc.
  Institutional Development Associates (John A. Lucas, Jr.)

Saudi Basic Industries Corp.
Riyadh, Saudi Arabia
Counsel or consultant:
  Burson-Marsteller
  Dutton and Dutton, P.C. (Frederick G. Dutton)
  Miller & Chevalier, Chartered (Catherine Curtiss)

Saudi Refining, Inc.
Houston, TX
Counsel or consultant:
  Burson-Marsteller

Saul Real Estate Investment Trust, B. F.
8401 Connecticut Ave., Chevy Chase, MD 20815
Telephone: (301) 986-6282
Represented by:
  Jonathan C. Swindle, V. President, Operations and Secre-
  tary
Counsel or consultant:
  Shaw, Pittman, Potts and Trowbridge (George M. Rogers,
  Jr.)

Sault Ste. Marie Tribe of Chippewa Indians
Sault Ste. Marie, MI
Counsel or consultant:
  Forrest Gerard & Associates (Forrest J. Gerard)

Save Chanute Committee
Champaign, IL
Counsel or consultant:
  Patton, Boggs and Blow (James B. Christian, Jr.)

Save Our Schools
655 15th St., N.W., Suite 310, Washington, DC 20005
Telephone: (202) 639-4419
Background: A grassroots education lobby.
Represented by:
  Fay Alexander, Exec. Director

Save Our Security
1201 16th St., N.W., Suite 222, Washington, DC 20036
Telephone: (202) 822-7848
Background: Supports legislation preserving all aspects of
Social Security.
Represented by:
  Arthur S. Flemming, Co-Chair
  Roberta Havel, Director

Save the Children
2803 M St., N.W., Washington, DC 20007
Telephone: (202) 342-8096
Background: A U.S.-based, private, non-profit, non-sectarian international organization committed to helping children through the process of community development. Position of Director vacant at time of publication.

Savema S.p.A.
Pietrasanta, Italy
Counsel or consultant:
  Dow, Lohnes and Albertson (William Silverman)

Savings Bank of the Finger Lakes
Geneva, NY
Counsel or consultant:
  James J. Butera, Chartered

Savings Banks Ass'n of Massachusetts
Boston, MA
Counsel or consultant:
  Thacher, Proffitt and Wood (Jeremiah S. Buckley)

Savings Banks Ass'n of New York
New York, NY
Counsel or consultant:
  James J. Butera, Chartered

Savings and Loan League of Colorado
Denver, CO
Counsel or consultant:
  McKenna, Conner and Cuneo

Scale Manufacturers Ass'n
932 Hungerford Drive, Suite 36, Rockville, MD 20850
Telephone: (301) 738-2448
Counsel or consultant:
  Lloyd and Associates, Inc. (Raymond J. Lloyd)

Scandinavian Airlines System (SAS)
New York, NY
Counsel or consultant:
  Global Aviation Associates, Ltd. (Jon F. Ash)
  Winthrop, Stimson, Putnam & Roberts (Robert Reed
  Gray)

Scenic America
216 7th St., S.E., Washington, DC 20003
Telephone: (202) 546-1100
Background: Through national and state legislation seeks
controls over highway billboards and other signs and pro-
vides technical assistance to local governments interested
in enacting landscape protection legislation.
Represented by:
  Hal Hiemstra, Policy Director
  Edward T. McMahon, Exec. Director
  Joan Moody, Communications Director

**Scheduled Airlines Traffic Offices, Inc. (Sato-
Travel)**
1005 North Glebe Road,, Arlington, VA 22210
Telephone: (703) 358-1450
Background: A full service travel company that serves mili-
tary and government customers under contract or memo-
randa of agreement.
Represented by:
  Meric L. Legnini, V. Pres, Government & Industry Rela-
  tions

Schering Internat'l
Kenilworth, NJ
Counsel or consultant:
  Weil, Gotshal & Manges (Nancy L. Buc, David B. Hird,
  Laura L. Krakovec)

Schering-Plough Corp.
1850 K St., N.W. Suite 1195, Washington, DC 20006
Telephone: (202) 463-7372
Represented by:
  Diane D. Darneille, Staff V. President, Legislative Affairs
  Dennis Jackman, Director, Legislative Affairs
Counsel or consultant:
  Baker, Worthington, Crossley, Stansberry & Woolf (W.
  Lee Rawls)
  Lee, Toomey & Kent
  Parry and Romani Associates Inc. (Romano Romani)
  Targeted Communications Corp.

Schick Division (Warner-Lambert Co.)
Milford, CT

The listings in this directory are available as *Mailing Labels*. See last page.

ORGANIZATIONS REPRESENTED

Counsel or consultant:
Stovall & Spradlin

Schnitzer Investment Inc.
Houston, TX
Counsel or consultant:
Brand and Lowell, P.C. (Stanley M. Brand)

Schochet Associates
Boston, MA
Counsel or consultant:
Brownstein Zeidman and Schomer (Sheldon L. Schreiberg)

Schutz American School
Wilmington, DE
Counsel or consultant:
Cassidy and Associates, Inc. (William M. Cloherty, Elliott M. Fiedler)

Schwan's Sales Enterprises
Marshall, MN
Counsel or consultant:
Olsson, Frank and Weeda, P.C. (John Bode)

SCI Technology, Inc.
1215 Jefferson Davis Hwy. Suite 307, Arlington, VA 22202
Telephone: (703) 486-0011
Represented by:
Harley Garrett, Manager, Northeast Region

SCIA - Smart Card Industry Ass'n
2026C Opitz Blvd., Woodbridge, VA 22191
Telephone: (703) 490-3300
Represented by:
Dr. Paul Oyer, President

Science Applications, Inc.
La Jolla, CA
Counsel or consultant:
Dressendorfer-Laird, Inc. (David M. Laird)

Science and Engineering Committee for a Secure World
Box 76220, Washington, DC 20013
Telephone: (202) 547-5580
Background: An organization of scientists and engineers with a membership of about 100 which supports continuing research on the Strategic Defense Initiative. Seeks to counter the efforts of groups like the Union of Concerned Scientists. Based in New York and chaired by Dr. Fred Seitz, President-Emeritus of Rockefeller University and former Chairman of both the National Academy of Science and the American Physical Society. Exec. Secretary (in Washington) is John D. Kwapisz of the Center for Peace and Freedom.

Science Industries (S.A.R.L.)
Paris, France
Counsel or consultant:
Swann, Stephen L., Law Offices of

Scientific-Atlanta, Inc.
2011 Crystal Drive, Suite 308, Arlington, VA 22202
Telephone: (703) 486-0701
Represented by:
Bill Loughrey, Director of Government Affairs
Counsel or consultant:
Kilpatrick & Cody (C. Randall Nuckolls, Frederick H. von Unwerth)

Scientists Center for Animal Welfare
4805 St. Elmo Ave., Bethesda, MD 20814
Telephone: (301) 654-6390
Background: A non-profit organization of scientists and others concerned with the well-being of research animals.
Represented by:
Lee Krulisch, Exec. Director
F. Barbara Orlans, Ph.D., Research Fellow

Scotch Whiskey Ass'n
Edinburgh, Scotland
Counsel or consultant:
Morgan, Lewis and Bockius (Michael S. Kelly, E. Carl Uehlein, Jr.)

Scott Paper Co.
1726 M St., N.W., Suite 901, Washington, DC 20036
Telephone: (202) 331-0730

Represented by:
James A. Morrill, Staff V. Pres., Federal Gov't Affairs
Betty-Grace Terpstra, Washington Corporate Affairs Rep.
Counsel or consultant:
Winburn, VanScoyoc, and Hooper (H. Stewart Van-Scoyoc)

Scott Paper Co. Political Action Committee
1726 M St., N.W., Suite 901, Washington, DC 20036
Telephone: (202) 331-0730
Background: Administrator is Betty-Grace Terpstra of Scott Paper Co.

Scott and Sons, O. M.
Marysville, OH
Counsel or consultant:
Jefferson Group, The (David T. Crow, Jack O. Nutter)

Scottish Equitable Life Assurance Society
Edinburgh, Scotland
Counsel or consultant:
Hill and Knowlton Public Affairs Worldwide (Dr. Ira P. Kaminow)

Scott's Liquid Gold
Denver, CO
Counsel or consultant:
Holland and Hart (Lauren E. Brown, J. Peter Luedtke)

Screen Printing Ass'n Internat'l
10015 Main St., Fairfax, VA 22031-3489
Telephone: (703) 385-1335
Represented by:
John M. Crawford, Jr., President
Bruce Joffe, Director of Communications
Marci Kinter, Director, Government Affairs
Tim McSweeney, Director of Technical Services

Scripps League Newspaper, Inc.
Charlottesville, VA
Counsel or consultant:
Wilmer, Cutler and Pickering (Robert P. Stranahan, Jr.)

Sea Containers America Inc.
1440 New York Ave., N.W., Suite 430, Washington, DC 20005
Telephone: (202) 638-4140
Represented by:
Richard A. Lidinsky, Jr., V. President, Governmental Affairs

Sea Hawk Seafoods, Inc.
Valdez, AK
Counsel or consultant:
Dickstein, Shapiro and Morin (John C. Dill)

Sea-Land Good Government Fund
1331 Pennsylvania Ave., N.W. Suite 560, Washington, DC 20004
Telephone: (202) 783-1117
Background: Represented by Peter J. Finnerty, Donald L. O'Hare and Rebecca J. Berg of Sea-Land Service, Inc.

Sea-Land Service, Inc.
1331 Pennsylvania Ave., N.W. Suite 560 National Place, Washington, DC 20004
Telephone: (202) 783-1117
Represented by:
Rebecca Jane Berg, Director, Federal Public Affairs
Peter J. Finnerty, V. President, Public Affairs
Donald L. O'Hare, Director, Public Affairs
Counsel or consultant:
Kaplan, Russin and Vecchi
Laxalt, Washington, Perito & Dubuc
Ragan and Mason (William F. Ragan)
Robertson, Monagle and Eastaugh

Sea Turtle Rescue Fund
1725 DeSales St., N.W. Suite 500, Washington, DC 20036
Telephone: (202) 429-5609
Background: A project of the Center for Marine Conservation.
Represented by:
Mary Adele Donnelly, Director

Seaboard Corp.
Shawnee Mission, KS
Counsel or consultant:
E. A. Jaenke & Associates (Richard J. Cannon)

Seaboard System Railroad Political Action Committee
1331 Pennsylvania Ave., N.W. Suite 560, Washington, DC 20004
Telephone: (202) 783-8124
Background: Sponsored by CSX Transportation.
Represented by:
Betty Ruth Jackson, Treasurer

Seafarers Internat'l Union of North America
5201 Auth Way, Camp Springs, MD 20746
Telephone: (301) 899-0675
Represented by:
Elizabeth C. DeMato, Legislative Representative
Nick Marrone, Director, Dept. of Cong. and Gov't Rtns.
Mike Neuman, Washington Representative
Frank Pecquex, Legislative Director

Seafarers Political Activity Donation (SPAD)
5201 Auth Way, Camp Springs, MD 20746
Telephone: (301) 899-0675
Background: Contact is Nicholas J. Marrone of the Seafarers Internat'l Union.

Seaford, Delaware, City of
Background: Duncan, Weinberg, Miller & Pembroke represents the electric utility department of Seaford.
Counsel or consultant:
Duncan, Weinberg, Miller & Pembroke, P.C. (Janice L. Lower, Frederick L. Miller, Jr.)

Seagram & Sons, Inc., Joseph E.
1455 Pennsylvania Ave., N.W., Suite 600, Washington, DC 20004
Telephone: (202) 638-3090
Represented by:
Richard J. Connor, Jr., Director, Federal Affairs
Stephen Koplan, V. President, Governmental Affairs
Kirstin Thompson, Manager, Public Policy & Gov't Affairs
Counsel or consultant:
Dewey, Ballantine, Bushby, Palmer and Wood (John J. Salmon)
Kessler and Associates (Richard S. Kessler)
McNair Law Firm, P.A. (Michael S. Gelacek)
O'Connor & Hannan (Thomas R. Jolly, Patrick E. O'Donnell)
Rivkin, Radler, Dunne and Bayh (Birch Bayh, Jr.)
Michael L. Tiner & Associates (Michael L. Tiner)

SeaHarvest, Inc.
Cape May, NJ
Counsel or consultant:
Preston Gates Ellis & Rouvelas Meeds (John L. Bloom, William N. Myhre)

Seal Rescue Fund
1725 De Sales St., N.W., Suite 500, Washington, DC 20036
Telephone: (202) 429-5609
Background: A project of the Center for Marine Conservation. Represented by Roger E. McManus of the Center.

Sealaska Corp.
Seattle, WA
Counsel or consultant:
Birch, Horton, Bittner and Cherot (Joseph M. Chomski)
Edward D. Heffernan
Charlie McBride Assoc., Inc. (Charlie McBride)

Seaplane Pilots Ass'n
421 Aviation Way, Frederick, MD 21701
Telephone: (301) 695-2083
Background: Affiliate of Aircraft Owners and Pilots Ass'n.
Represented by:
Robert Richardson, Exec. Director

Search for Common Ground
2005 Massachusetts Ave., N.W., Lower Level, Washington, DC 20036
Telephone: (202) 265-4300
Background: An organization seeking new approaches to defense and foreign policy issues with the fundamental objective of preserving world peace.
Represented by:
John Marks, Exec. Director

Search Group, Inc.
Sacramento, CA
Background: A state criminal justice organization.

ORGANIZATIONS REPRESENTED

Search Group, Inc. (Cont'd)
Counsel or consultant:
Kirkpatrick & Lockhart (Robert R. Belair)

Searle Co., G. D.
Skokie, IL
Counsel or consultant:
Sheehan Associates, Inc. (Gary W. Maloney, John Thomas Sheehan)
Timmons and Co., Inc.

Sears, Roebuck and Co.
633 Pennsylvania Ave., N.W., Washington, DC 20004
Telephone: (202) 737-4900
Represented by:
Randolf H. Aires, Vice President
Brenda Girton, Legislative Counsel
Counsel or consultant:
Morgan, Lewis and Bockius (Stanton P. Sender)

Seatrain Tankers Corp.
Fort Lee, NJ
Counsel or consultant:
Preston Gates Ellis & Rouvelas Meeds (Jonathan Blank, Emanuel L. Rouvelas)

Seattle Metro
Seattle, WA
Counsel or consultant:
Peyser Associates, Inc.

Seattle Organizing Committee, 1990 Goodwill Games
Seattle, WA
Counsel or consultant:
Preston Gates Ellis & Rouvelas Meeds (Lloyd Meeds)
Sagamore Associates, Inc. (David U. Gogol)

Seattle, Washington, Port of
Counsel or consultant:
Preston Gates Ellis & Rouvelas Meeds (Emanuel L. Rouvelas)

Seaview Property Owners Ass'n, Inc.
New York, NY
Background: A non-profit membership corporation.
Counsel or consultant:
Richard Curry and Associates (Richard C. Curry)

Secondary Lead Smelters Ass'n
1701 Pennsylvania Ave., N.W. Suite 200, Washington, DC 20006
Telephone: (202) 662-2700
Background: Above address is that of the DC law firm Andrews & Kurth. Ass'n Nat'l headquarters is in Atlanta, Georgia.
Counsel or consultant:
Andrews and Kurth (Robert N. Steinwurtzel)

Section 482 Study Group
c/o Miller & Chevalier 655 15th St., N.W., Washington, DC 20005
Telephone: (202) 626-5800
Counsel or consultant:
Miller & Chevalier, Chartered (John S. Nolan)

Section 8 Coalition
Glenview, IL
Counsel or consultant:
Wunder, Ryan, Cannon & Thelen (W. Stephen Cannon)

Section 8 Housing Group
Portland, OR
Background: A coalition of 23 housing developers in Oregon, Washington and Idaho seeking Federal Government reimbursement for low-income housing rents.
Counsel or consultant:
Ball, Janik and Novack (Michelle E. Giguere)

SecuraPAC
1155 21st St., N.W., Suite 850, Washington, DC 20036
Telephone: (202) 728-4920
Background: The political action committee of The Secura Group. Treasurer/Contact is Mary Clare Fitzgerald of that firm.
Counsel or consultant:
Secura Group, The (Mary Clare Fitzgerald)

Securities Industry Ass'n
1850 M St., N.W., Suite 550, Washington, DC 20036
Telephone: (202) 296-9410

Represented by:
Donald J. Crawford, Sr. V. Pres. and Dir. of Gov't Rel.
Marc E. Lackritz, Exec. V. President
William L. Larsen, Ass't V. Pres. and Dir., Reg. Relations
Edward I. O'Brien, President
John T. O'Rourke, V. President and Legislative Counsel
Jonathan R. Paret, V. President and Legislative Counsel
Stephan K. Small, V. Pres. and Dir. of Cong. Rel.
Counsel or consultant:
Campbell-Raupe, Inc. (Jeanne M. Campbell)
Mintz, Levin, Cohn, Ferris, Glovsky and Popeo, P.C. (Francis X. Meaney)
O'Connor & Hannan (Thomas H. Quinn)
Reed Smith Shaw & McClay (William A. Geoghegan)
Royer, Mehle & Babyak (Gregory R. Babyak, Robert Stewart Royer)
Sullivan and Cromwell
R. Duffy Wall and Associates (R. Duffy Wall)

Securities Industry Ass'n Political Action Committee
1850 M St., N.W., Suite 550, Washington, DC 20036
Telephone: (202) 296-9410
Background: Represented by Donald J. Crawford of the Securities Industry Ass'n.

Security Companies Organized for Legislative Action
1023 15th St., N.W. 7th Fl., Washington, DC 20005
Telephone: (202) 289-1780
Counsel or consultant:
Rowland & Sellery (Lawrence E. Sabbath)

Security First Group
Los Angeles, CA
Counsel or consultant:
Manatt, Phelps, Rothenberg & Phillips (Robert J. Kabel)

Security, Inc.
Bethesda, MD
Counsel or consultant:
Keefe Co., The (Robert J. Keefe)

Security Life Insurance Co. of Denver
Denver, CO
Counsel or consultant:
Dickstein, Shapiro and Morin (James R. Jones)
Paul, Hastings, Janofsky and Walker (Judith Richards Hope, Deborah F. Winston)
Fred B. Rooney
Scribner, Hall and Thompson (E. Victor Willetts, Jr.)

Security Pacific Bank of Alaska
Anchorage, AK
Counsel or consultant:
Birch, Horton, Bittner and Cherot (Joseph M. Chomski)

Security Pacific Nat'l Bank
1701 K St., N.W., Suite 503, Washington, DC 20006
Telephone: (202) 293-8440
Represented by:
Alfred M. Pollard, Senior V. Pres., Federal Gov't Relations
Counsel or consultant:
Cleary, Gottlieb, Steen and Hamilton (J. Eugene Marans)
O'Melveny and Myers (William T. Coleman, Jr.)
Ragan and Mason
Wilkinson, Barker, Knauer and Quinn (Paul S. Quinn)

Security Pacific Nat'l Leasing
Los Angeles, CA
Counsel or consultant:
Ragan and Mason

Security Pacific Trade Finance
New York, NY
Counsel or consultant:
Douglas Bloomfield Assoc. (Douglas M. Bloomfield)

Security Systems Internat'l Corp., Geneva
1140 Connecticut Ave., N.W. Suite 503, Washington, DC 20036
Telephone: (202) 296-3840
Counsel or consultant:
Ashby and Associates (R. Barry Ashby)

Security Trust Co.
730 15th St., N.W., Washington, DC 20005
Counsel or consultant:
Dow, Lohnes and Albertson (David F. Bantleon)

Sefri Construction Internat'l
Paris, France
Counsel or consultant:
Dow, Lohnes and Albertson (Philip C. Thompson)

Seiko Epson Corp.
Nagono-Ken, Japan
Counsel or consultant:
Saunders and Company (Pete Salavantis, Steven R. Saunders)

Seilbulite Internat'l, Inc.
Rancho Dominguez, CA
Background: A subsidiary of Seibu Polymer Chemical Co. Ltd. of Japan.
Counsel or consultant:
Hill and Knowlton Public Affairs Worldwide (Phil Armstrong)

Selenia Industria Elettronica, S.p.A.
1101 15th St., N.W., Suite 610, Washington, DC 20005
Telephone: (202) 223-5504
Represented by:
Enzo Mazzaglia, U.S. Representative

Self Help for Hard of Hearing People
7800 Wisconsin Ave., Bethesda, MD 20814
Telephone: (301) 657-2248
Background: A volunteer, international organization of hard of hearing people, their relatives and friends.
Represented by:
Howard E. Stone, Sr., Exec. Director
Counsel or consultant:
Duncan and Associates

Self-Insurance Institute of America, Inc.
Santa Ana, CA
Counsel or consultant:
Vedder, Price, Kaufman, Kammholz and Day (George J. Pantos)

SEMATECH
1825 Eye St., N.W. Suite 400, Washington, DC 20006
Telephone: (202) 429-2021
Represented by:
Mark Nelson, Director, Government Relations
Kathy Weaver, Government Relations Specialist
Counsel or consultant:
Dewey, Ballantine, Bushby, Palmer and Wood (Clark McFadden)
Loeffler Group, The
McCamish, Martin, Brown & Loeffler (Tom Loeffler)

Semiconductor Industry Ass'n
San Jose, CA
Counsel or consultant:
Dewey, Ballantine, Bushby, Palmer and Wood (R. Michael Gadbaw, Thomas R. Howell, John J. Salmon, Michael H. Stein, Alan W. Wolff)
Richard H. Stern

Seminole Tribe of Florida
Hollywood, FL
Counsel or consultant:
Hobbs, Straus, Dean and Wilder (Jerry C. Straus)
Keefe Co., The (William A. Roberts, Jonathon A. Slade)

Seneca Nation
Salamanca, NY
Counsel or consultant:
Sonosky, Chambers and Sachse

Seneca Resources, Inc.
Houston, TX
Counsel or consultant:
Van Ness, Feldman & Curtis (Robert G. Szabo)

Senior Executives Ass'n
Box 7610, Ben Franklin Station, Washington, DC 20044
Telephone: (202) 535-4328
Background: Works to advance professionalism of federal government executive-level employees and to advocate their interests.
Represented by:
Virginia Blodgett, Director, Communications
Carol A. Bonosaro, President
Counsel or consultant:
Neill, Mullenholz and Shaw (G. Jerry Shaw, Jr.)

Sentencing Project, The
918 F St., N.W. Suite 501, Washington, DC 20004

The listings in this directory are available as *Mailing Labels.* See last page.

ORGANIZATIONS REPRESENTED

Telephone: (202) 628-0871
Background: An organization established to improve the quality of legal representation at sentencing, to promote greater use of alternatives to incarceration and to increase the public's understanding of the sentencing process.
Represented by:
Marc Mauer, Assistant Director
Malcolm C. Young, Exec. Director

Sequoia Forest Industries
Dinuba, CA
Counsel or consultant:
F. H. Hutchison and Co. (Fred H. Hutchison)

Seragen Inc.
Hopkinton, MA
Counsel or consultant:
Cassidy and Associates, Inc. (Gerald S. J. Cassidy)

Serono Laboratories, Inc.
Norwell, MA
Counsel or consultant:
Fox, Bennett and Turner (Alan R. Bennett)

Service Corporation Internat'l
Houston, TX
Counsel or consultant:
Wallace & Edwards (Donald L. Wallace, Jr.)

Service Employees Internat'l Union
1313 L St., N.W., Washington, DC 20005
Telephone: (202) 898-3200
Background: Formerly (1968) Building Service Employees Internat'l Union.
Represented by:
Nancy Bennett, Asst. Dir., Political Action Program
Amy Chapman, Field Director
Peggy Connerton, Director, Public Policy
Richard W. Cordtz, Secretary-Treasurer
Nancy A. Donaldson, Assistant Director, Legislation
Edgar 'Ned' H. McCulloch, III, Legislative Representative
Geri D. Palast, Director, Politics & Legislation Dept.
Kathleen M. Skrabut, Legislative Representative
John J. Sweeney, Internat'l President
Counsel or consultant:
Challenge America, Inc. (Richard S. Sloan)
Spiegel and McDiarmid
U.S. Strategies Corp. (K. Michael Matthews)

Service Employees Internat'l Union COPE Political Action Committee
1313 L St., N.W., Washington, DC 20005
Telephone: (202) 898-3200
Background: Represented by Geri D. Palast of the Service Employees Internat'l Union.

Service Engineering Co.
San Francisco, CA
Counsel or consultant:
Snyder Ball Kriser and Associates, Inc. (Lou Kriser)

Service Master, Limited Partnership
Downers Grove, IL
Counsel or consultant:
Kirkland and Ellis

Service Station Dealers of America
499 S. Capitol St., S.E. Suite 407, Washington, DC 20003
Telephone: (202) 479-0196
Represented by:
Jim Daskal, Counsel
David Epstein, Government Affairs Specialist
Joseph L. Koach, Exec. Director
Amy Littlefield, Director, Government Affairs

Service Station Dealers of America Political Action Committee
499 S. Capitol St., S.W., Washington, DC 20003
Telephone: (202) 479-0196
Background: Joseph Koach of the Service Station Dealers of America is responsible for the Political Action Committee.

Services Group, The
1815 N. Lynn St. Suite 200, Arlington, VA 22209
Telephone: (702) 528-7486
Background: Encourages free trade zone and privatization development.

Represented by:
Mark Frazier, Chairman
Kishore Rao, President & CEO

Seton Hall School of Law
Newark, NJ
Counsel or consultant:
CR Associates (Domenic R. Ruscio)

SGS Government Programs, Inc.
New York, NY
Counsel or consultant:
Shea and Gardner

SGS North America, Inc.
Hoboken, NJ
Background: An international inspection service; affiliated with Societe Generale de Surveillance.
Counsel or consultant:
Shea and Gardner

Shakespeare Theater at the Folger, The
31 East Capitol St., S.E., Washington, DC 20003
Telephone: (202) 547-3230
Counsel or consultant:
Chernikoff and Co. (Larry Chernikoff)

Shaklee Corp.
San Francisco, CA
Counsel or consultant:
Hill and Knowlton Public Affairs Worldwide (Robert Keith Gray, Gary Hymel, Roger Lindberg, Frank Mankiewicz)

Shared Medical Systems
Malvern, PA
Counsel or consultant:
Wunder, Ryan, Cannon & Thelen (Bernard J. Wunder)

Sharon Steel Co.
Sharon, PA
Counsel or consultant:
Willkie Farr and Gallagher (Ellen A. Hennessy)

Sharp Electronics Corp.
Mahwah, NJ
Counsel or consultant:
Patton, Boggs and Blow

Sharp S.A. Equipamentos Eletronicos
Sao Paulo, Brazil
Counsel or consultant:
L. A. Motley and Co. (Langhorne A. Motley)

Shaw Food Services Co., Inc.
Fayetteville, NC
Counsel or consultant:
Swift Consulting Co., Ltd., The (Ivan, Red Swift)

Shearson Lehman Hutton
1627 I St., N.W., Suite 1100, Washington, DC 20006
Telephone: (202) 452-4700
Represented by:
Susan C. Simon, V. President
Counsel or consultant:
Lord Day & Lord, Barrett Smith (Mahlon Frankhauser)
Mayer, Brown and Platt (Jerry L. Oppenheimer)
Rogers and Wells (William Morris)
Willkie Farr and Gallagher (Matthew R. Schneider)
Wilmer, Cutler and Pickering (William J. Wilkins)

Sheet Metal and Air Conditioning Contractors' Nat'l Ass'n
8224 Old Courthouse Rd., Vienna, VA 22182
Telephone: (703) 790-9890
Background: Also maintains an office on Capitol Hill.
Represented by:
Gretchen Y. Ayres, Staff Asst., Government Affairs
Dennis Bradshaw, Director, Member Services
Phillips T. Kimball, Jr., Director, Labor Relations Designate
Stanley E. Kolbe, Jr., Director of Governmental Affairs
Rosalind Price Raymond, Dir., Public Relations & Communications
J. Robert Roach, Exec. Director, Operations
Thomas J. Soles, Jr., Director, Insurance and Safety
John Sroka, Exec. V. President
Dana S. Thompson, Asst. for Legislative/Political Affairs

Sheet Metal and Air Conditioning Contractors' Nat'l Ass'n Political Action Committee (SMAC-PAC)
305 4th St., N.E., Washington, DC 20002
Telephone: (202) 547-8202
Background: Contacts are Dana Thompson and Gretchen Ayres of the Sheet Metal and Air Conditioning Contractors' Nat'l Ass'n. Stanley E. Kolbe, Jr., of the Ass'n serves as PAC Treasurer.

Sheet Metal Workers' Internat'l Ass'n
1750 New York Ave., N.W. Sixth Floor, Washington, DC 20006
Telephone: (202) 783-5880
Represented by:
Don Buchanan, Director, Railroad Workers
Edward J. Carlough, General President
Lawrence J. Cassidy, General Secretary-Treasurer
William Gonnelly, Internat'l Representative
James Rock, Exec. Assistant to the General President
Ralph E. Willham, Director of Governmental Affairs
Counsel or consultant:
The Kamber Group (Harry Huge)

Sheet Metal Workers' Internat'l Ass'n Political Action League
1750 New York Ave., N.W. Sixth Floor, Washington, DC 20006
Telephone: (202) 783-5880
Background: A political action committee. Responsible contact is Ralph E. Willham. (See Sheet Metal Workers' Internat'l Ass'n.)

Shell Chemical Co.
Houston, TX
Counsel or consultant:
Burson-Marsteller (Sheila Raviv)

Shell Oil Co.
1025 Connecticut Ave., N.W., Suite 200, Washington, DC 20036
Telephone: (202) 466-1405
Represented by:
Rebecca T. Barbour, Government Affairs Representative
Albert D. Bowers, V. President, Government Affairs
Paul Crowley, Tax Representative
Philip C. Holladay, Jr., Washington Rep., House and Senate
Mary Jane Klocke, Government Affairs Representative
William L. Lafield, Jr., Manager, State Government Relations-East
James E. Rich, Jr., Washington Representative
Walter Sczudlo, Washington Representative
L. H. Wells, Senior Staff Representative
Counsel or consultant:
Bonner & Associates
Camp, Barsh, Bates and Tate (John C. Camp)
Howrey and Simon (Alan M. Grimaldi)

Shenzhen Municipality Industrial Development Corp.
Shenzhen, China
Counsel or consultant:
Lachelli, Waller and Associates (Vincent P. Lachelli)

Shepherd Oil Co.
Jennings, LA
Counsel or consultant:
William Bode and Associates (William Bode)

Shipbuilders Council of America
1110 Vermont Ave., N.W. Suite 1250, Washington, DC 20005
Telephone: (202) 775-9060
Represented by:
Cynthia L. Brown, V. President, Legislative Affairs
Beverly C. Kendall, Secretary and Tresurer
W. Patrick Morris, V. President and General Counsel
Silas O. Nunn, V. President, Programs
John J. Stocker, President
Richard W. Thorpe, V. President, Export Activities
Counsel or consultant:
Collier, Shannon & Scott

Shirley Contracting Corp.
Manassas, VA
Counsel or consultant:
Sadur, Pelland & Rubinstein (Joel S. Rubinstein, Marvin P. Sadur)

ORGANIZATIONS REPRESENTED

Shoup Corp., R. F.
Bryn Mawr, PA
Counsel or consultant:
  Kuykendall Co. (Dan H. Kuykendall)

Showa Line, Ltd.
New York, NY
Counsel or consultant:
  Hoppel, Mayer and Coleman (Neal M. Mayer)

ShowBiz Pizza Time
Irving, TX
Counsel or consultant:
  Richard B. Berman and Co.,Inc. (Richard B. Berman)

Shriner-Midland Co.
6432 Quincy Place, Falls Church, VA 22042
Telephone: (703) 795-4356
Represented by:
  Leslie Michaelson, Manager, Ass'n Research & Economics
  Robert D. Shriner, Managing Partner

Shubert Organization Inc.
New York, NY
Counsel or consultant:
  Murray, Scheer & Montgomery (D. Michael Murray)

Shurberg Broadcasting of Hartford Inc.
Hartford, CT
Counsel or consultant:
  Bechtel and Cole (Harry F. Cole)

Si.A.C./Italy
Catania, Italy
Counsel or consultant:
  Jefferson Group, The (Jose Ortiz-Daliot, John Upston)

SICPA Industries of America, Inc.
New York, NY
Counsel or consultant:
  KCI Inc. (Bette B. Anderson)

Siderbras
Sao Paulo, Brazil
Counsel or consultant:
  Internat'l Advisory Services Group Ltd. (Charles H. Blum, Jeffrey W. Carr)
  Willkie Farr and Gallagher (William H. Barringer)

Sidermex Internat'l, Inc.
San Antonio, TX
Counsel or consultant:
  Manchester Trade, Inc. (Stephen L. Lande)
  Mudge Rose Guthrie Alexander and Ferdon (N. David Palmeter)

Siderurgica Lazaro Cardenas, S.A.
Mexico City, Mexico
Counsel or consultant:
  Mudge Rose Guthrie Alexander and Ferdon (N. David Palmeter)

Siemens Capital Corp.
1455 Pennsylvania Ave., N.W. Suite 300, Washington, DC 20004
Telephone: (202) 347-0444
Represented by:
  James F. Conway, Jr., Manager, Government Affairs
  Elaine P. Dedekian, Government Affairs Liaison
  Jeremiah L. Murphy, V. Pres., Public Policy & Gov't Affairs
Counsel or consultant:
  Mintz, Levin, Cohn, Ferris, Glovsky and Popeo, P.C.

Siemens Corp.
Munich, West Germany
Counsel or consultant:
  Collier, Shannon & Scott (Paul D. Cullen, Michael D. Sherman)
  Howrey and Simon
  TransAtlantic Futures, Inc. (Stephan-Gotz Richter, W. Alan Zuschlag)

Siemens Energy and Automation, Inc.
Atlanta, GA
Counsel or consultant:
  Kilpatrick & Cody (C. Randall Nuckolls)

Siemens Medical Systems, Inc.
Iselin, NJ

Counsel or consultant:
  Dixon Arnett Associates (Dixon Arnett)
  Kaye, Scholer, Fierman, Hays and Handler (Christopher R. Brewster)

Sierra Club
408 C St., N.E., Washington, DC 20002
Telephone: (202) 547-1141
Background: A national non-profit public interest organization that promotes conservation of the natural environment by influencing public policy decisions. Works to restore the quality of natural environments and maintain the integrity of ecosystems.
Represented by:
  Daniel F. Becker, Wash. Dir., Global Warming & Energy Prog
  Jim Blomquist, Washington Dir., Public Lands Program
  George Coling, Great Lakes Washington Specialist
  A. Blakeman Early, Wash. Dir., Pollution & Toxics Program
  Leslie England, Conservation Assistant
  Shira A. Flax, Toxics Specialist
  Cathleen A. Fogel, Associate Washington Representative
  David McLane Gardiner, Legislative Director
  Pamela Goddard, Conservation Assistant
  Melanie Griffin, Associate Washington Representative
  Heide Halik, Conservation Assistant
  Kathryn Hohmann, Associate Washington Representative
  Betsy Loyless, Assistant Political Director
  Michael Matz, Washington Dir., Public Lands Program
  Michael McCloskey, Chairman
  Debbie Sease, Washington Dir., Public Lands Program
  Nancy Wallace, Washington Director, Population Program
  Daniel Weiss, Wash. Dir., Pollution & Toxics Program
  Larry Williams, Washington Dir., Internat'l Program
  Reid Wilson, Political Director

Sierra Club Legal Defense Fund
1531 P St., N.W. Suite 200, Washington, DC 20005
Telephone: (202) 667-4500
Background:
Represented by:
  Robert Dreher, Staff Attorney & Co-Director
  Howard I. Fox, Staff Attorney & Co-Director
  Sandra Goldberg, Law Associate
  Elizabeth Ulmer, Asssociate Director, Development
  Ronald Wilson, Of Counsel

Sierra Pacific Industries
Redding, CA
Counsel or consultant:
  Ray Paabo

Sierra Pacific Resources
Reno, NV
Counsel or consultant:
  Bishop, Cook, Purcell & Reynolds (H. Lawrence Fox)
  Marcus G. Faust
  Goldberg, Fieldman and Letham
  Graham and James (Thomas F. Railsback)
  Morgan, Lewis and Bockius
  Reid & Priest

Sierra Press
Reno, NV
Counsel or consultant:
  Lachelli, Waller and Associates (John D. Waller)

Signal Landmark
Irvine, CA
Counsel or consultant:
  E. Del Smith, Inc. (E. Del Smith)
  Will & Muys, P.C. (Robert P. Will)

Signal Produce Co.
El Centro, CA
Counsel or consultant:
  Highley & Associates (Vern F. Highley)

Signet Banking Corp.
Richmond, VA
Background: Formerly Bank of Virginia Co.
Counsel or consultant:
  Lee, Toomey & Kent
  McGuire, Woods, Battle and Boothe

Silent Partner
Grenta, LA

Counsel or consultant:
  Lachelli, Waller and Associates (John D. Waller)

Siletz Tribal Council
Siletz, OR
Counsel or consultant:
  Forrest Gerard & Associates (Forrest J. Gerard)

Silver Group, Inc.
San Francisco, CA
Counsel or consultant:
  Covington and Burling (Eugene I. Lambert)

Silver Institute
1026 16th St., N.W. Suite 101, Washington, DC 20036
Telephone: (202) 783-0500
Counsel or consultant:
  Klein & Saks, Inc. (Michael J. Brown, John H. Lutley)

Silver Reed America
Los Angeles, CA
Counsel or consultant:
  Willkie Farr and Gallagher (Christopher A. Dunn)

Silver Users Ass'n
1730 M St., N.W., Suite 911, Washington, DC 20036
Telephone: (202) 785-3050
Background: Founded in 1947, the Silver Users Ass'n represents the interests of companies that make, sell or distribute products of which silver forms an essential part and exists to keep its members informed on all developments affecting the use and availability of this metal.
Represented by:
  Walter L. Frankland, Jr., Exec. Vice President

Sima-Peru
Lima, Peru
Counsel or consultant:
  Prather, Seeger, Doolittle and Farmer (Edwin H. Seeger)

Simon for President '86
322 Massachusetts Ave., N.E., Washington, DC 20002
Telephone: (202) 546-4204
Counsel or consultant:
  Cynthia Friedman Assoc. Inc. (Cynthia Friedman)

Simon for Senate '90
322 Massachusetts Ave., N.E., Washington, DC 20002
Telephone: (202) 546-5681
Counsel or consultant:
  Cynthia Friedman Assoc. Inc. (Keith F. Abbott, Eileen Filler)

Simon Wiesenthal Center/Museum of Tolerance
Los Angeles, CA
Counsel or consultant:
  Wexler, Reynolds, Fuller, Harrison and Schule, Inc. (Nancy Clark Reynolds)

Simpson Investment Co.
Seattle, WA
Counsel or consultant:
  Preston Gates Ellis & Rouvelas Meeds (Richard L. Barnes)

Simpson Paper Co.
Seattle, WA
Counsel or consultant:
  Jefferson Group, The (Randal Schumacher)

Singapore, Embassy of
1824 R St., N.W., Washington, DC 20009
Telephone: (202) 667-7555
Counsel or consultant:
  Marshall, Tenzer, Greenblatt, Fallon and Kaplan (Sylvan M. Marshall)
  StMaxens and Co. (Thomas F. StMaxens, II)
  White & Case

Singapore Trade Development Board
Singapore
Counsel or consultant:
  C & M Internat'l L.P. (Doral S. Cooper)
  Willkie Farr and Gallagher (Walter J. Spak)

Site Evaluators & Consultants
151 Spring St., Suite 300, Herndon, VA 22070
Telephone: (703) 481-3980
Counsel or consultant:
  H. John Elliott

ORGANIZATIONS REPRESENTED

Sithe Energies USA
New York, NY
Counsel or consultant:
Olwine, Connelly, Chase, O'Donnell and Weyher (W. Harrison Wellford)

Six Flags, Inc.
Los Angeles, CA
Counsel or consultant:
Pierson, Semmes, and Finley (William T. Finley, Jr.)

Skadden Arps Political Action Committee
1440 New York Ave., N.W., Washington, DC 20005
Telephone: (202) 371-7000
Background: Represented by Lynn R. Coleman of the firm.

SKF USA, Inc.
King of Prussia, PA
Counsel or consultant:
Ervin Technical Associates, Inc. (ETA) (James L. Ervin)
Howrey and Simon (Paul Plaia, Jr.)

Skyline Corp.
Elkhart, IN
Background: Manufacturer of mobile homes and recreational vehicles.
Counsel or consultant:
Morgan, Lewis and Bockius

Skywest Aviation, Inc.
St. George, UT
Counsel or consultant:
Bowen & Atkin

Small Business Council of America
4800 Hampden Lane, 7th Floor, Bethesda, MD 20814
Telephone: (301) 656-7603
Represented by:
Paula A. Calimafde, President
Counsel or consultant:
Zuckert, Scoutt and Rasenberger (J. Michael Keeling)

Small Business Legislative Council
1025 Vermont Ave., N.W. Suite 1201, Washington, DC
Telephone: (202) 639-8500
Background: Formed January 1977 as a legislative action affiliate of the Nat'l Small Business Ass'n. Became independent of the Nat'l Small Business Ass'n in 1985. Membership includes 103 trade and professional groups. President is John S. Satagaj, an attorney. Address given is that of the law firm of London and Satagaj.
Counsel or consultant:
London and Satagaj, Attorneys-at-Law (John S. Satagaj)

Smith Barney, Harris Upham and Co.
New York, NY
Counsel or consultant:
Gibson, Dunn and Crutcher
Mayer, Brown and Platt (Jerry L. Oppenheimer)

Smith Corona Corp.
New Canaan, CT
Counsel or consultant:
Dyer, Ellis, Joseph & Mills (Howard A. Vine)
Stewart and Stewart

Smith Industries
1225 Jefferson Davis Hwy., Suite 402, Arlington, VA 22202
Telephone: (703) 920-7640
Background: Supervisors marketing to U.S. military customers through six regional officers.
Represented by:
Douglas Aylward, Director, Systems Development
Richard L. Hellwege, Director, Business Development
Jim Murray, Regional Manager
Paul Seymour, Export Coordination Manager
John J. Todd, V. President

Smith & Wesson
Springfield, MA
Counsel or consultant:
Neill and Co. (John E. Bircher, III, Denis M. Neill)

SmithKline Animal Health Products
West Chester, PA
Background: A division of SmithKline Beckman Corp.

Counsel or consultant:
Hill and Knowlton Public Affairs Worldwide (Barbara Hyde)
Kleinfeld, Kaplan and Becker (Robert H. Becker, Kinsey S. Reagan)
McMillan and Farrell Associates (C. W. McMillan)

SmithKline Beecham
1020 19th St., N.W., Suite 420, Washington, DC 20036
Telephone: (202) 452-8490
Represented by:
Robert A. Holland, Director, Federal Affairs
David M. Jenkins, V. President, Federal Gov't Affairs
Counsel or consultant:
Covington and Burling (Stanley L. Temko)
O'Connor & Hannan (Timothy M. Haake)

Smithsonian Institution
1000 Jefferson Drive, S.W., Washington, DC 20560
Telephone: (202) 357-2962
Represented by:
Margaret C. Gaynor, Director, Office of Cong. Liaison

Smokeless Tobacco Council
2550 M St., N.W., Suite 300, Washington, DC 20037
Telephone: (202) 452-1252
Represented by:
Robert J. Dotchin, V. President, Industry & Federal Relats.
Michael J. Kerrigan, President
Richard W. Kirchhoff, Director, State Relations
Vincent P. Lonergan, Director, State Relations
Counsel or consultant:
Bonner & Associates
Patton, Boggs and Blow (Thomas Hale Boggs, Jr., James B. Christian, Jr., Ray O'Hara)

Smokeless Tobacco Council Political Action Committee
1925 K St., N.W., Suite 504, Washington, DC 20006
Telephone: (202) 452-1252
Background: Represented by Michael J. Kerrigan of the Smokeless Tobacco Council.

SNA Canada Inc.
Canada
Background: A subsidiary of a French defense contractor.
Counsel or consultant:
Hill and Knowlton Public Affairs Worldwide (Robert V. Schneider)

Snack Food Ass'n
1711 King St., Suite One, Alexandria, VA 22314
Telephone: (703) 836-4500
Represented by:
Stephen E. Eure, Director, Government Relations
Al Rickard, Director, Communications

Snack PAC
1711 King St., Suite One, Alexandria, VA 22314
Telephone: (703) 836-4500
Background: The political action committee for the Snack Food Ass'n. Contact is Stephen E. Eure of the Ass'n.

Snake River Farmers Ass'n
Rupert, ID
Counsel or consultant:
Holt, Miller & Associates (Harris N. Miller)

Snappy Car Rental
Mayfield Heights, OH
Counsel or consultant:
Winthrop, Stimson, Putnam & Roberts (Michael W. Dolan, Ronna A. Freiberg, Peter F. Gold)

Snow Aviation Internat'l
Columbus, OH
Counsel or consultant:
Vorys, Sater, Seymour and Pease (Stephen H. Brown)

Soc. for American Archaeology
808 17th St., N.W., Suite 200, Washington, DC 20006
Telephone: (202) 223-9774
Background: Legislative interests include Interior Dept. appropriations, historic and cultural resources management and protection, the National Science Foundation, land management agencies liaison, public outreach, curators and grassroots networking with state archaeologists.
Jerome A. Miller, of the Bostrom Corp., serves as Executive Director.

Counsel or consultant:
Bostrom Corp. (Jerome A. Miller, CAE)

Soc. for Animal Protective Legislation
Box 3719, Georgetown Station, Washington, DC 20007
Telephone: (202) 337-2334
Background: Interested in furthering legislation favoring humane treatment of wildlife and animals in general.
Represented by:
John Gleiber, Exec. Secretary

Soc. for Application of Free Energy
1315 Apple Ave., Silver Spring, MD 20910
Telephone: (301) 587-8686
Background: Seeks to develop and promote free energy sources like solar, geophysical and geothermal energy. President is Dr. Carl Schleicher of the Foundation for Blood Irradiation.

Soc. for Computer Simulation
La Jolla, CA
Background: A Washington contact is John Clement of the American Federation of Information Processing Societies.

Soc. for Coptic Archaeology
2800 Wisconsin Ave., N.W. Suite 702, Washington, DC 20007
Telephone: (202) 363-3480
Represented by:
Dr. Leslie S.B. MacCoull, U.S. Rep. and Sr. Research Scholar

Soc. for Health and Human Values
6728 Old McLean Village Drive, McLean, VA 22101
Telephone: (703) 556-9222
Counsel or consultant:
Degnon Associates, Inc. (George K. Degnon, Carol Ann Kiner)

Soc. for Human Resources Management
606 N. Washington St., Alexandria, VA 22314
Telephone: (703) 548-3440
Background: The world's largest organization dedicated to excellence in human resource management. Includes more than 44,000 individuals working for a cross-section of employers, from smaller family operations to large, multi-national corporations.
Represented by:
Catherine D. Bower, V.P., Communications & Public Relations
Deanna Hodge, Manager, Congressional Affairs
Patricia Digh Howard, Manager, International Relations
Susan R. Meisinger, V. President, Government Affairs
Ronald C. Pilenzo, President
Kurt Rumsfeld, Legislative Representative
Counsel or consultant:
Kelley, Drye and Warren (Lawrence Z. Lorber)

Soc. for Imaging Science and Technology
7003 Kilworth Lane, Springfield, VA 22151
Telephone: (703) 642-9090
Represented by:
Calva Lotridge, Exec. Director

Soc. for Industrial and Applied Mathematics
Philadelphia, PA
Background: A Washington contact is John Clement of the American Federation of Information Processing Societies.

Soc. for Information Display
Playa del Rey, CA
Background: A Washington contact is John Clement of the American Federation of Information Processing Societies.

Soc. for Marketing Professional Services
99 Canal Center Plaza Suite 320, Alexandria, VA 22314
Telephone: (703) 549-6117
Represented by:
Terry L. Peters, Exec. Director

Soc. for Neuroscience
11 Dupont Circle, N.W., Suite 500, Washington, DC 20036
Telephone: (202) 462-6688
Background: An interdisciplinary organization to enhance information exchange. The membership of 13,000 includes clinicians, research scientists and students.
Represented by:
Nancy Beang, Exec. Director

Soc. for Occupational and Environmental Health
P.O. Box 42360, Washington, DC 20015-0360

ORGANIZATIONS REPRESENTED

Soc. for Occupational and Environmental Health (Cont'd)
Telephone: (202) 797-8666
Background: Serves as a forum for the presentation of scientific data and the exchange of information among occupational and environmental health professionals in government, industry, labor, and academia with the risk of reducing the risks of occupational and environmental hazards. President is Dr. Ellen Silbergeld of the Environmental Defense Fund.

Soc. for Risk Analysis
8000 Westpark Drive Suite 130, McLean, VA 22102
Telephone: (703) 790-1745
Counsel or consultant:
Society and Association Services Corp. (Richard J. Burk, Jr.)

Soc. for Technical Communication
901 North Stuart St., Arlington, VA 22203
Telephone: (703) 522-4114
Represented by:
Peter R. Herbst, Assistant Exec. Director
William C. Stolgitis, Exec. Director and Counsel

Soc. for the Advancement of Ambulatory Care Political Action Committee
1330 New Hampshire Ave., N.W. Suite 122, Washington, DC 20036
Telephone: (202) 659-8008
Background: The Society exists to foster support for outpatient ambulatory clinics that provide quality primary health care to low income and uninsured people. Represented by Vincent A. Keane of the Nat'l Ass'n of Community Health Centers.

Soc. of American Florists
1601 Duke St., Alexandria, VA 22314
Telephone: (703) 836-8700
Represented by:
Stephen Daigler, Director, Information Services
Linda D. Flaherty, Sr. Legislative Representative
Drew Gruenburg, V. President, Government Relations
Peter Moran, Sr. V. President, Consumer Relations
Betty O. Sapp, Exec. V. President
Michele Werner, Legislative Assistant

Soc. of American Florists Political Action Committee
1601 Duke St., Alexandria, VA 22314
Telephone: (703) 836-8400
Represented by:
Lee Wilhide, Treasurer

Soc. of American Foresters
5400 Grosvenor Lane, Bethesda, MD 20814
Telephone: (301) 897-8720
Represented by:
William H. Banzhaf, Exec. V. President
Kenneth Beam, Deputy Exec. V. President
H. William Rockwell, Jr., Director, Resource Policy
Paula Tarnapol, Director, Public Affairs
Sarah Zollman, Public Affairs Assistant

Soc. of American Military Engineers
P.O. Box 21289, Alexandria, VA 22320
Telephone: (703) 549-3800
Represented by:
Brig. Gen. Walter O. Bachus, USA (Ret.), Exec. Director

Soc. of American Travel Writers
1155 Connecticut Ave., N.W. Suite 500, Washington, DC 20036
Telephone: (202) 429-6639
Represented by:
Ken Fischer, Administrative Coordinator

Soc. of American Value Engineers
Nat'l Press Bldg., Room 1199, Washington, DC 20045
Telephone: (202) 347-8998
Represented by:
Hal Tufty, Nat'l Director of Federal Liaison

Soc. of American Wood Preservers, Inc.
7297 Lee Hwy., Unit P, Falls Church, VA 22042
Telephone: (703) 237-0900
Background: Represents the home wood preserving industry in regulatory and legislative affairs with emphasis on environmental issues, and product market development activities.

Represented by:
George K. Eliades, CAE, President and Chief Exec. Officer
Counsel or consultant:
Webster, Chamberlain and Bean

Soc. of American Wood Preservers Political Action Committee
7297 Lee Hwy., Unit P, Falls Church, VA 22042
Telephone: (703) 237-0900
Background: Treasurer and contact is George K. Eliades, President and CEO of the Society.

Soc. of Cardiovascular and Interventional Radiology
1891 Preston White Dr., Reston, VA 22091
Telephone: (703) 648-8980
Counsel or consultant:
Baker and Hostetler (Frederick H. Graefe)
Fulbright & Jaworski (Irwin Cohen)

Soc. of Consumer Affairs Professionals in Business
4900 Leesburg Pike Suite 400, Alexandria, VA 22302
Telephone: (703) 998-7371
Represented by:
Lou Garcia, Exec. Director

Soc. of Critical Care Medicine
Fullerton, CA
Counsel or consultant:
Reed Smith Shaw & McClay (Stephan E. Lawton)

Soc. of Eye Surgeons
c/o Internat'l Eye Foundation 7801 Norfolk Ave., Bethesda, MD 20814
Telephone: (301) 986-1830
Represented by:
Sonya Shields, Assistant to the President

Soc. of Glass and Ceramic Decorators
1730 M St., N.W. Suite 505, Washington, DC 20036
Telephone: (202) 728-4132
Counsel or consultant:
Grove, Jaskiewicz, Gilliam and Cobert (James A. Calderwood)

Soc. of Independent Gasoline Marketers of America
1730 K St., N.W., Suite 907, Washington, DC 20006
Telephone: (202) 429-9333
Represented by:
Kenneth A. Doyle, Exec. V. President
Shari Pogach, Director of Member Services
Counsel or consultant:
Collier, Shannon & Scott (R. Timothy Columbus, Jeffrey L. Leiter, William W. Scott)

Soc. of Independent Gasoline Marketers Political Action Committee
1730 K St., N.W., Suite 907, Washington, DC 20006
Telephone: (202) 429-9333
Background: Represented by Kenneth A. Doyle of the sponsoring organization.
Counsel or consultant:
Collier, Shannon & Scott (R. Timothy Columbus)

Soc. of Industrial and Office Realtors
777 14th St., N.W. Suite 400, Washington, DC 20005-3271
Telephone: (202) 383-1150
Background: Affiliated with the Nat'l Ass'n of Realtors.
Represented by:
Nancy B. Bryant, Exec. V. President
Lottie Gatewood, Public Relations & Marketing Director
Sarah Kenney, Manager, Public Relations and Marketing

Soc. of Medical Consultants to the Armed Forces
4301 Jones Bridge Road, Bethesda, MD 20814
Telephone: (301) 295-3106
Represented by:
Dr. John W. Bullard, Staff Asst. to the President

Soc. of Nat'l Ass'n Publications
3299 K St., N.W., 7th Floor, Washington, DC 20007
Telephone: (202) 965-7510
Counsel or consultant:
Ass'n Management Group (Robert J. Dolibois)

Soc. of Park and Recreation Educators
3101 Park Center Drive, Alexandria, VA 22302
Telephone: (703) 820-4940
Background: A branch of the Nat'l Recreation and Park Ass'n.
Represented by:
Dr. Don Henkel, Staff Liaison

Soc. of Professional Benefit Administrators
2033 M St., N.W., Suite 605, Washington, DC 20036
Telephone: (202) 223-6413
Counsel or consultant:
Hunt Management Systems (Frederick D. Hunt, Jr., Anne C. Lennan, Elizabeth Ysla)

Soc. of Professors of Child Psychiatry
3615 Wisconsin Ave., N.W., Washington, DC 20016
Telephone: (202) 966-7300
Represented by:
John Schowalter, President

Soc. of Real Estate Appraisers
600 New Hampshire Ave., N.W. Suite 1111, Washington, DC 20037
Telephone: (202) 298-8497
Background: Main offices are in Chicago.
Represented by:
Lisa M. DeFusco, Legislative Assistant
Donald E. Kelly, VP & Director of Washington Operations
Counsel or consultant:
Laxalt, Washington, Perito & Dubuc (Marc J. Scheineson)

Soc. of Soft Drink Technologists
P.O. Box 259, Brentwood, MD 20722
Telephone: (301) 277-0018
Represented by:
Henry E. Korab, Exec. Director

Soc. of the Plastics Industry
1275 K St., N.W., Suite 400, Washington, DC 20005
Telephone: (202) 371-5200
Represented by:
Ronald G. Bruner, V. President, Communications
Lewis R. Freeman, Jr., V. President, Government Affairs
Maureen Healey, Ass't Director, Federal Gov't Affairs
Bonnie Limbach, External Communications Manager
Joseph M. Pattok, Director, State Government Affairs
Phil Stapleton, Director, Issue Analysis
Larry L. Thomas, President
Hugh Patrick Toner, Director, Tech. and Regulatory Affairs
Counsel or consultant:
Keller and Heckman

Soc. of Toxicology
1133 15th St., N.W.,, Washington, DC 20005
Telephone: (202) 293-5935
Counsel or consultant:
Internat'l Management Group, Inc. (Joan Walsh Cassedy)

Soc. of Vascular Technology
1101 Connecticut Ave., N.W., Suite 700, Washington, DC 20036
Telephone: (202) 857-1149
Background: Patricia I. Horner, of Smith, Bucklin and Associates, serves as Exec. Director.
Counsel or consultant:
Baker and Hostetler (Rebecca L. Jackson)
Smith, Bucklin and Associates (Patricia I. Horner)

Social Democratic and Labor Party of Northern Ireland (SDLP)
Belfast, N. Ireland
Background: Concerned with fundraising in the U.S. for the SDLP.
Counsel or consultant:
Epstein Becker and Green (William G. Kopit)

Social Security Protection Bureau
510 King St., Suite 515, Alexandria, VA 22314
Telephone: (202) 293-8600
Background: Contact is Michael G. Kushnick of Rose, Schimdt, Hasley, and DiSalle.
Counsel or consultant:
Rose, Schmidt, Hasley & DiSalle (Michael G. Kushnick)

Sociedad de Industrias "Comite Textil"
Lima, Peru

The listings in this directory are available as *Mailing Labels*. See last page.

ORGANIZATIONS REPRESENTED

Counsel or consultant:
Prather, Seeger, Doolittle and Farmer (Edwin H. Seeger, Gary M. Welsh)

Societa Cavi Pirelli S.p.A.
Milan, Italy
Counsel or consultant:
Cassidy and Associates, Inc. (James P. Fabiani, C. Frank Godfrey, Jr., Vincent M. Versage)

Societe Chabert Duval, Ltd.
Elkton, MD
Counsel or consultant:
Balsamo & Associates, Chartered (Richard W. Balsamo)

Societe Financiere d'Entreposage et de Commerce International de l'Alcool
Stamford, CT
Counsel or consultant:
Mudge Rose Guthrie Alexander and Ferdon (Richard H. Abbey)

Societe Generale de Surveillance
Geneva, Switzerland
Background: An international inspection service, particularly in import-export trade.
Counsel or consultant:
Shea and Gardner

Societe Nationale des Poudres et Explosifs
Paris, France
Counsel or consultant:
DGA Internat'l
Dorsey & Whitney

Societe Nationale d'Etude et Construction de Moteurs d'Avaition (SNECMA)
Paris, France
Counsel or consultant:
DGA Internat'l (Sandra K. Meredith)

SOFICIA
Stamford, CT
Counsel or consultant:
Dow, Lohnes and Albertson (Arthur H. Silverman)

Sofreavia
Paris, France
Counsel or consultant:
DGA Internat'l (Sandra K. Meredith)

Soft Drink Political Action Committee
1101 16th St., N.W., Washington, DC 20036
Telephone: (202) 463-6732
Background: The political action committee of the Nat'l Soft Drink Ass'n.
Represented by:
Mark N. Hammond, Treasurer

Software Publishers Ass'n
1101 Connecticut Ave., N.W. Suite 901, Washington, DC 20036
Telephone: (202) 452-1600
Background: The trade association for publishers of microcomputer software and related products.
Represented by:
Mary Jane Saunders, General Counsel
Kenneth A. Wasch, Exec. Director
Counsel or consultant:
Swidler & Berlin, Chartered (Bruce A. Lehman)

Software Publishers Ass'n PAC
1101 Connecticut Ave., N.W. Suite 901, Washington, DC 20036
Telephone: (202) 452-1600
Background: Supports candidates that support legislation regarding the creation and enforcement of copyright laws and other issues related to micro computer software publishers. Represented by Kenneth Wasch of the Ass'n.

Software Rental Coalition
Counsel or consultant:
Timothy X. Moore and Co. (Timothy X. Moore)

Sojourners
P.O. Box 29272, Washington, DC 20017
Telephone: (202) 636-3637
Background: An ecumenical Christian community which seeks to promote the biblical vision of economic justice and peace. Involved in advocacy work for the poor and in opposition to the nuclear arms race and current U.S. military policy.

Represented by:
Jim Wallis, Editor

Solano Water Authority
Vacaville, CA
Counsel or consultant:
Wilkinson, Barker, Knauer and Quinn (Paul S. Quinn)

Solar Energy Industries Ass'n
777 N. Capitol St., N.W. 8th Fl., Washington, DC 20001
Telephone: (703) 524-6100
Represented by:
Scott Sklar, Exec. Director

Solarex Corp.
1335 Piccard Drive, Rockville, MD 20850
Telephone: (301) 948-0202
Represented by:
William J. Simms, Manager, Strategic Business Development

Solargistics Corp.
Northbrook, IL
Counsel or consultant:
Tendler, Goldberg & Biggins, Chtd. (Paul M. Tendler)

Solid Waste Agency of Northern Cook County
IL
Counsel or consultant:
Mayer, Brown and Platt

Solidarity
Gdansk, Poland
Counsel or consultant:
John Adams Associates (A. John Adams)

Solvay et Cie
Brussels, Belgium
Counsel or consultant:
Sullivan and Cromwell

Somalia, Government of
Mogadishu, Somalia
Counsel or consultant:
Black, Manafort, Stone and Kelly Public Affairs Co. (Nicholas A. Panuzio)

Somerville, Massachusetts, City of
Counsel or consultant:
Preston Gates Ellis & Rouvelas Meeds (Allen Erenbaum, Craig J. Gehring)

Sonat Inc.
1100 15th St., N.W. Suite 700, Washington, DC 20005
Telephone: (202) 775-0840
Represented by:
Charles L. Roff, Attorney
Luther J. Strange, III, Director, Federal Government Affairs
Counsel or consultant:
Baker and Botts (James A. Baker, IV)
Skadden, Arps, Slate, Meagher and Flom (Mike Naeve)

Songwriters Guild, The
New York, NY
Counsel or consultant:
Jonathan W. Cuneo Law Offices (James J. Schweitzer)
Liz Robbins Associates (Michael J. Lucas, Liz Robbins)

Sonicraft, Inc.
6303 Little River Turnpike Suite 320, Alexandria, VA 22312
Telephone: (703) 642-0371
Represented by:
Bertrand F. Jones, Special Assistant to the President

Sony Corp.
Tokyo, Japan
Counsel or consultant:
Arent, Fox, Kintner, Plotkin & Kahn
Debevoise and Plimpton (Robert R. Bruce, Jeffrey P. Cunard)
Wilmer, Cutler and Pickering

Sony Corp. of America
New York, NY
Counsel or consultant:
Patton, Boggs and Blow
Wunder, Ryan, Cannon & Thelen (Dennis C. Thelen)

Soo Line Railroad, Inc.
Minneapolis, MN

Counsel or consultant:
Neill, Mullenholz and Shaw (John J. Mullenholz)

Sorptive Minerals Institute
1440 New York Ave., N.W., Suite 300, Washington, DC 20005
Telephone: (202) 638-1200
Counsel or consultant:
E. Bruce Harrison Co. (Steven B. Hellem)

Sotheby's Holdings, Inc.
New York, NY
Counsel or consultant:
Jack Ferguson Associates (Jack Ferguson)
McNair Group Inc. (Elizabeth L. Taylor)
Steptoe and Johnson (Blake D. Rubin)

Source One Management, Inc.
1155 15th St., N.W., Suite 1108, Washington, DC 20005
Telephone: (202) 429-1944
Represented by:
Ernest E. Garcia, V. President, Eastern Operations

South Africa, Chamber of Mines of
Johannesburg, South Africa
Counsel or consultant:
Paul H. DeLaney Law Offices (Paul H. DeLaney, Jr.)
Freedman, Levy, Kroll and Simonds (John H. Chettle)
Riley and Fox (Stephen Riley)

South Africa, Embassy of
3051 Massachusetts Ave., N.W., Washington, DC 20008
Telephone: (202) 232-4400
Counsel or consultant:
Philip J. Hare
Pearson & Pipkin, Inc. (Ronald W. Pearson, Robert R. Pipkin, Jr.)
John P. Sears Law Offices (Robert Kelley, John P. Sears)
United Internat'l Consultants (Joan B. Baldwin)

South Africa Foundation
1225 19th St., N.W. Suite 700, Washington, DC 20036
Telephone: (202) 223-5486
Background: Seeks to keep open international channels of communication and to encourage the process of peaceful change in South Africa.
Represented by:
Michael R. Christie, Director for North America
Sylvia Gon, Assistant Director
John Nixon Montgomery, Deputy Director

South Africa, Government of
Pretoria, South Africa
Counsel or consultant:
Riley and Fox
United Internat'l Consultants

South African Sugar Ass'n
Durban, South Africa
Counsel or consultant:
Galland, Kharasch, Morse and Garfinkle (Marc C. Ginsberg)

South Bend, Indiana, City of
Counsel or consultant:
Sagamore Associates, Inc. (David U. Gogol)

South Carolina Economic Development Board
Columbia, SC
Counsel or consultant:
Black, Manafort, Stone and Kelly Public Affairs Co. (Nicholas A. Panuzio)

South Carolina Electric and Gas Co.
Columbia, SC
Counsel or consultant:
Donelan, Cleary, Wood and Maser, P.C.

South Carolina Research Authority
Columbia, SC
Counsel or consultant:
McNair Law Firm, P.A. (John L. Napier)

South Carolina State College
Orangeburg, SC
Counsel or consultant:
McNair Group Inc. (Elizabeth L. Taylor)

South Carolina, State of
444 N. Capitol St., N.W. Suite 234, Washington, DC 20001
Telephone: (202) 624-7784

The listings in this directory are available as *Mailing Labels*. See last page.

679

ORGANIZATIONS REPRESENTED

South Carolina, State of (Cont'd)
Represented by:
Nikki McNamee, Dir., Washington Office of the Governor

South Carolina State Port Authority
Charleston, SC
Counsel or consultant:
Schmeltzer, Aptaker and Sheppard (J. Thomas Esslinger, Edward J. Sheppard, IV)

South Central Air
Kenai, AK
Counsel or consultant:
Steptoe and Johnson

South Central Bell
Birmingham, AL
Counsel or consultant:
Shaw, Pittman, Potts and Trowbridge (William Mike House)

South Coast Air Quality Management District
El Monte, CA
Counsel or consultant:
Leon G. Billings, Inc. (Leon G. Billings)

South Dade Land Corp.
Florida City, FL
Counsel or consultant:
McLeod & Pires (Harold W. Furman, II)

South Dakota Department of Transportation
Pierre, SD
Counsel or consultant:
Preston Gates Ellis & Rouvelas Meeds (John A. DeVierno)

South Hadley, Massachusetts, Town of
Counsel or consultant:
Spiegel and McDiarmid (Ben Finkelstein, Nancy R. Page)

South Louisiana Port Commission
La Place, LA
Counsel or consultant:
Global USA, Inc. (William H. Morris, Jr.)

South Salt Lake, Utah, City of
Counsel or consultant:
The Ferguson Co. (William Ferguson, Jr., Patricia Jordan, Thane Young)

South Seas Charter Service
Marathon, FL
Counsel or consultant:
Roberts & Co. (Richard R. Roberts)

Southdown
Houston, TX
Counsel or consultant:
Bracewell and Patterson (Gene E. Godley)
Kilpatrick & Cody (Joseph W. Dorn, C. Randall Nuckolls)

Southeast Alaska Regional Health Corp. (SEARHC)
Juneau, AK
Counsel or consultant:
Preston Gates Ellis & Rouvelas Meeds (Susan B. Geiger, Lloyd Meeds)

Southeast Alaska Seiners Ass'n
Ketchikan, AK
Counsel or consultant:
C. Deming Cowles, IV

Southeast Banking Corp.
Miami, FL
Counsel or consultant:
Wilmer, Cutler and Pickering (Michael S. Helfer)

Southeastern Lumber Manufacturers Ass'n
Forest Park, GA
Counsel or consultant:
Neece, Cator and Associates (G. Thomas Cator)

Southeastern Pennsylvania Transit Authority
Philadelphia, PA
Counsel or consultant:
Peyser Associates, Inc.

Southeastern Power Resource Committee
Atlanta, GA

Counsel or consultant:
Verner, Liipfert, Bernhard, McPherson and Hand, Chartered (Clinton A. Vince)

Southern Baptist Press Ass'n
Jefferson City, MO
Counsel or consultant:
Liz Robbins Associates (Michael J. Lucas, Liz Robbins)

Southern Bell Telephone and Telegraph Co.
Atlanta, GA
Counsel or consultant:
Wyman, Bautzer, Christensen, Kuchel and Silbert

Southern California Ass'n of Governments
Los Angeles, CA
Counsel or consultant:
McCutchen, Doyle, Brown & Enersen (Philip T. Cummings)

Southern California Edison Co.
1001 Pennsylvania Ave., N.W. Suite 450N, Washington, DC 20004
Telephone: (202) 393-3075
Represented by:
Terrance M. Adlhock, Counsel
Charles E. Cooke, Washington Representative
Thomas J. Dennis, V. President, Washington Region
Barbara J. Santos, Government Relations Assistant
Counsel or consultant:
Akin, Gump, Strauss, Hauer and Feld (Joel Jankowsky)
Baker, Worthington, Crossley, Stansberry & Woolf (W. Lee Rawls)
Groom and Nordberg (Robert B. Harding)
Hunton and Williams
Charlie McBride Assoc, Inc. (Charlie McBride)
Nossaman, Guthner, Knox and Elliott (Murray Zweben)
O'Melveny and Myers (Warren Christopher)
Reid & Priest
Van Ness, Feldman & Curtis (Ben Yamagata)

Southern California Gas Co.
1150 Connecticut Ave., N.W., Suite 717, Washington, DC 20036
Telephone: (202) 822-3700
Represented by:
David W. Freer, Manager, Federal Governmental Affairs
Edward L. Irwin, Manager, Federal Regulatory Affairs
Rufus W. McKinney, V. President, National Public Affairs
Trudy Y. Settles, Governmental Affairs Assistant

Southern California Rapid Transit District
Los Angeles, CA
Counsel or consultant:
Dixon Arnett Associates (Dixon Arnett)
Palumbo & Cerrell, Inc. (Benjamin L. Palumbo)

Southern Cemetery Ass'n
1101 Connecticut Ave., N.W., Suite 700, Washington, DC 20036
Telephone: (202) 857-1198
Counsel or consultant:
Smith, Bucklin and Associates (Harry G., Skip McComas)

Southern Company Services, Inc.
1130 Connecticut Ave., N.W., Suite 830, Washington, DC 20036
Telephone: (202) 775-0944
Represented by:
David P. Burford, Legislative Affairs Coordinator
J. Robert Minter, Coordinator, Governmental Affairs
Charles P. Saunders, Manager, Industry Structure Issues
Counsel or consultant:
Dunaway & Cross (Mac S. Dunaway)
C. V. & R. V. Mauldin (Robert V. Mauldin)
Shaw, Pittman, Potts and Trowbridge (William Mike House)
W. Robert Woodall

Southern Company, The
1130 Connecticut Ave., N.W., Suite 830, Washington, DC 20036
Telephone: (202) 775-0944
Represented by:
E. John Neumann, Director, Governmental Affairs
John G. Richardson, V. President, Governmental Affairs

Southern Governors Ass'n
444 North Capitol St., N.W., Suite 240, Washington, DC 20001

Telephone: (202) 624-5897
Represented by:
Candis Brown Penn, Exec. Director
Counsel or consultant:
Gallagher-Widmeyer Group Inc., The (Mary Jane Gallagher)

Southern Iron and Steel Works
Kuala Lumpur, Malaysia
Counsel or consultant:
Willkie Farr and Gallagher (Walter J. Spak)

Southern Jersey Airways
Atlantic City, NJ
Counsel or consultant:
V. Michael Straus, P.C.

Southern Maryland Electric Cooperative, Inc.
Hughesville, MD
Counsel or consultant:
Duncan, Weinberg, Miller & Pembroke, P.C. (Jeffrey C. Genzer, Robert Weinberg)

Southern Pacific Transportation Co.
816 Connecticut Ave., N.W. Suite 800, Washington, DC 20006
Telephone: (202) 393-0100
Represented by:
Wiley N. Jones, V. President, Governmental Relations
Alexander H. Jordan, Asst. V. Pres., Governmental Affairs
Counsel or consultant:
Williams and Jensen, P.C. (John J. McMackin, Jr.)

Southern Technical Services
Suite 610 Three Metro Center, Bethesda, MD 20814
Telephone: (301) 652-2500
Background: Performs management consulting, contracting engineering services, and corporate application services for the nuclear utility industry, services companies, and government facilities and operations.
Represented by:
William A. Cross, President
Thomas E. Hicks, Senior Consultant
Barry W. Smith, V. President
Robert E. Sweeney, Senior Consultant

Southern Transportation League, Inc.
3426 North Washington Blvd., Box 1240, Arlington, VA 22210
Telephone: (703) 525-4050
Background: An organization of about 150 corporations, universities and government entities such as state port authorities representing shipper interests before the courts, the Interstate Commerce Commission and other agencies. Exec. Director is William P. Jackson, Jr. of the law firm of Jackson and Jessup, P.C.
Counsel or consultant:
Jackson and Jessup, P.C. (William P. Jackson, Jr.)

Southern Ute Indian Tribe
Ignacio, CO
Counsel or consultant:
Kogovsek & Associates, Inc.

SouthernNet, Inc.
Atlanta, GA
Counsel or consultant:
Hogan and Hartson (John S. Stanton)

Southfield, Michigan, City of
Counsel or consultant:
Preston Gates Ellis & Rouvelas Meeds (Craig J. Gehring)

Southland Corp., The
5300 Shawnee Road, Alexandria, VA 22312
Telephone: (703) 642-0711
Counsel or consultant:
Camp, Barsh, Bates and Tate (Ronald L. Platt)
Holland and Hart (William F. Demarest, Jr.)

Southwest Airlines
Dallas, TX
Counsel or consultant:
Williams and Jensen, P.C. (John J. McMackin, Jr.)

Southwest Center for Study of Hospital and Health Care Systems
Houston, TX
Counsel or consultant:
Bill Newbold & Assoc. (Bill Newbold)

ORGANIZATIONS REPRESENTED

Southwest Gas Corp.
Las Vegas, NV
Counsel or consultant:
Laxalt, Washington, Perito & Dubuc (Marc J. Scheineson)

Southwest Realty, Inc.
Dallas, TX
Counsel or consultant:
Chambers Associates Incorporated (Mary S. Lyman, James N. Smith)

Southwest Virginia and Carolinas Peanut Growers
Counsel or consultant:
Meyers & Associates (Larry D. Meyers)

Southwestern Bell Corp.
1667 K St., N.W., Suite 1000, Washington, DC 20006
Telephone: (202) 293-8550
Represented by:
M. Camille Bares, Director, Federal Relations
David Fine, Exec. Director, Federal Relations
R. Brent Regan, V. President, Federal Relations
Karen S. Rogers, Director, Federal Regulatory Affairs
William H. Shute, Director, Federal Relations
Kent M. Wells, Exec. Director, Federal Relations
Horace Wilkins, Jr., V. President, Gov't & Industry Affairs
Counsel or consultant:
Bayless & Boland, Inc. (James L. Bayless, Jr., Michael J. P. Boland)
Paul, Hastings, Janofsky and Walker (Ralph B. Everett)
Williams and Jensen, P.C. (William T. Brack)

Southwestern Bell Telephone Co.
1667 K St., N.W. Suite 1000, Washington, DC 20006
Telephone: (202) 293-8550
Represented by:
Allan Northcutt, Exec. Director, Corporate Communications
Counsel or consultant:
Wyman, Bautzer, Christensen, Kuchel and Silbert

Southwestern Electric Power Co.
Shreveport, LA
Counsel or consultant:
Donelan, Cleary, Wood and Maser, P.C. (John M. Cleary)

Southwestern Power Resource Ass'n
Tulsa, OK
Counsel or consultant:
Verner, Liipfert, Bernhard, McPherson and Hand, Chartered (Clinton A. Vince)

Southwestern Public Service Co.
Amarillo, TX
Counsel or consultant:
Wright and Talisman

Southwestern Water Conservation District
Durango, CO
Counsel or consultant:
Kogovsek & Associates, Inc.

Southwire Co.
Carrollton, GA
Counsel or consultant:
McKenna, Conner and Cuneo (Michael K. Tomenga)
Rose, Schmidt, Hasley & DiSalle
Wigman and Cohen (Victor M. Wigman)

Sovcomflot
Moscow, USSR
Counsel or consultant:
Mudge Rose Guthrie Alexander and Ferdon (Julia Christine Bliss, David P. Houlihan)

Soy Protein Council
1255 23rd St., N.W., Washington, DC 20037
Telephone: (202) 467-6610
Counsel or consultant:
Hauck and Associates (Sheldon J. Hauck, Dinah D. McElfresh)

Space Industries, Inc.
Webster, TX
Counsel or consultant:
James D. Calaway
Garvey, Schubert & Barer (Alan A. Butchman)

Space Services Inc.
600 Water St., S.W., Suite 207, Washington, DC 20024
Telephone: (202) 646-1025
Background: Provides launch services for both orbital and sub-orbital missions, including payload integration and regulatory support. Pioneers in obtaining regulatory approvals and legislation for commercial launches.
Represented by:
Charles M. Chafer, V. President for Government Affairs
Julia M. Sardan, Washington Assistant
Richard W. Scott, Jr., Washington Representative
Counsel or consultant:
Bayless & Boland, Inc. (James L. Bayless, Jr., Michael J. P. Boland)

Spacecause
922 Pennsylvania Ave., S.E., Washington, DC 20003
Telephone: (202) 543-1900
Background: Grassroots supporters of pro-space legislation focued on the creation of a spacefaring civilization.
Represented by:
David Brandt, Administrator

Spain, Government of
Madrid, Spain
Counsel or consultant:
Patton, Boggs and Blow (David E. Dunn, III)

Spalding-Evenflo
Tampa, FL
Counsel or consultant:
Kilpatrick & Cody (C. Randall Nuckolls)

Spanish Broadcasting System, Inc.
New York, NY
Counsel or consultant:
Kaye, Scholer, Fierman, Hays and Handler (Jason Shrinsky)

Spantax, S.A.
Madrid, Spain
Background: A Spanish charter air carrier.
Counsel or consultant:
Boros and Garofalo (Gary B. Garofalo)

Spar Industries
Weston, Ontario
Background: Involved in space station programs.
Counsel or consultant:
Fierce and Associates

Sparks, Nevada, City of
Counsel or consultant:
Nat'l Center for Municipal Development (Thomas N. Duffy)

SPD Technologies
Philadelphia, PA
Counsel or consultant:
Reid & Priest (Stephan M. Minikes)

Special Committee for Workplace Product Liability Reform
c/o Barnes and Thornburg 1815 H St., N.W., Suite 800, Washington, DC 20006
Telephone: (202) 955-4500
Background: Formed in the spring of 1977 by a group of manufacturers' associations to work for reform of the product liability laws as they affect machinery and equipment used in the workplace. Address above is that of Barnes & Thornburg, a DC law firm.
Counsel or consultant:
Barnes and Thornburg (Randolph J. Stayin)

Special Industrial Radio Service Ass'n
1110 North Glebe Road Suite 500, Arlington, VA 22201
Telephone: (703) 528-5115
Represented by:
Mark E. Crosby, President and Managing Director
Counsel or consultant:
Keller and Heckman

Special Libraries Ass'n
1700 18th St., N.W., Washington, DC 20009
Telephone: (202) 234-4700
Represented by:
Richard D. Battaglia, Associate Exec. Director
David R. Bender, Exec. Director
Sandy I. Morton, Director, Gov't Relations
Mary Erb Zimmermann, Director, Communications

Special Olympics Internat'l, Inc.
1350 New York Ave., N.W., Suite 500, Washington, DC 20005
Telephone: (202) 628-3630
Represented by:
Eunice Kennedy Shriver, Chairman of the Board
Jule Sugarman, Exec. Director

Speciality Seafoods
New York, NY
Counsel or consultant:
Patton, Boggs and Blow (James B. Christian, Jr.)

Specialty Advertising Ass'n, Internat'l
Irving, TX
Counsel or consultant:
Keller and Heckman

Specialty Coffee Ass'n of America
1101 14th St., N.W., Suite 1100, Washington, DC 20005
Telephone: (202) 371-1347
Counsel or consultant:
Internat'l Management Group, Inc. (Joan Walsh Cassedy)

Specialty Steel Industry of the United States
1055 Thomas Jefferson St., N.W., Suite 308, Washington, DC 20007
Telephone: (202) 342-8400
Counsel or consultant:
Collier, Shannon & Scott (David A. Hartquist, Thomas F. Shannon)

Specialty Vehicle Institute of America
Costa Mesa, CA
Background: The trade association of all-terain vehicle manufacturers and distributors.
Counsel or consultant:
Manatos & Manatos, Inc. (Andrew E. Manatos)
Fred B. Rooney

Spectacor Management Group
Philadelphia, PA
Counsel or consultant:
Fleishman-Hillard, Inc (W. Douglas Campbell, Paul Johnson, John Overstreet)

Spectrascan Imaging Services
Windsor, CT
Counsel or consultant:
Liz Robbins Associates (Sharon Edwards, Michael J. Lucas)

Spectrum Emergency Care
St. Louis, MO
Counsel or consultant:
Morrison Associates (James W. Morrison, Jr.)

Speech Communication Ass'n
Bldg. E., 5105 Backlick Road, Annandale, VA 22003
Telephone: (703) 750-0533
Represented by:
Dr. James L. Gaudino, Exec. Director

Spiegel Inc.
Oak Brook, IL
Counsel or consultant:
Flack Inc. (Susan Garber Flack)

Spill-Net, Inc.
655 15th St., N.W., Suite 310, Washington, DC 20005
Telephone: (202) 828-1977
Counsel or consultant:
Washington Policy Advocates (Jeffrey C. Smith)

Spillis Candela & Partners, Inc.
Coral Gables, FL
Counsel or consultant:
Keefe Co., The (William A. Roberts)

Spina Bifida Ass'n of America
1700 Rockville Pike, Suite 540, Rockville, MD 20852
Telephone: (301) 770-7222
Background: Executive Director is Catherine B. Hartnett of Hartnett & Associates.
Counsel or consultant:
Hartnett & Associates (Catherine B. Hartnett)

Spokane Region Economic Development (Momentum 90)
Spokane, WA
Counsel or consultant:
Denny Miller Associates

The listings in this directory are available as *Mailing Labels*. See last page.

ORGANIZATIONS REPRESENTED

Spokane, Washington, City of
Counsel or consultant:
Nat'l Center for Municipal Development (Robert E. Gordon)
Preston Gates Ellis & Rouvelas Meeds (Allen Erenbaum, Craig J. Gehring)

Sporicidin Co., The
Rockville, MD
Counsel or consultant:
Dow, Lohnes and Albertson (Arthur H. Silverman)

Sport Fishing Institute
1010 Massachusetts Ave., N.W., Suite 100, Washington, DC 20001
Telephone: (202) 898-0770
Represented by:
Norville S. Prosser, V. President
Gilbert C. Radonski, President

Sporting Goods Manufacturers Ass'n
1625 K St., N.W., Suite 900, Washington, DC 20006
Telephone: (202) 775-1762
Represented by:
Jan Kinney, Director, Washington Operations

Spot Image Corp.
1897 Preston White Drive, Reston, VA 22091-4326
Telephone: (703) 620-2200
Background: Engaged in processing and distributing satellite imagery. A subsidiary of SPOT IMAGE, S.A.
Represented by:
Pierre Bescond, President
David S. Julyan, Exec. V. President
Clark A. Nelson, Director, Corp. Communications

Spring Garden College
Philadelphia, PA
Counsel or consultant:
Cassidy and Associates, Inc. (Thomas M. Gannon)

Springfield, Illinois, City of
Counsel or consultant:
Nat'l Center for Municipal Development (Carolyn Chaney)

Springfield, Missouri, City Utilities of
Springfield, MO
Counsel or consultant:
APCO Associates (Deborah R. Sliz)

Springs Industries, Inc.
Fort Mill, SC
Counsel or consultant:
Hudson, Creyke, Koehler and Tacke
Stockmeyer & Co. (Steven F. Stockmeyer)
Sutherland, Asbill and Brennan

Sprint International
12490 Sunrise Valley Drive, Reston, VA 22096
Telephone: (703) 689-6000
Represented by:
Stuart Chiron, Senior Attorney
Wanda Glanzman, Regulatory Manager
Elizabeth O'Beirne, Director, Public Affairs
Jeanne Schaaf, Director, Legislative Affairs
Philip M. Walker, V. President, Internat'l Affairs

Squaxin Island Indian Tribe
WA
Counsel or consultant:
SENSE, INC. (Joe Tallakson)

Squibb and Sons, Inc., E. R.
Princeton, NJ
Background: A subsidiary of Squibb Corp.
Counsel or consultant:
Kleinfeld, Kaplan and Becker (Robert H. Becker, Kinsey S. Reagan, Peter O. Safir)
Miller & Steuart (Judith M. Greenberg, Marshall V. Miller, George C. Steuart)

SRI International
1611 North Kent St., Arlington, VA 22209
Telephone: (703) 524-2053
Background: A diverse not-for-profit organization which provides research and consulting in such areas as engineering, physical and social sciences, management, economics and international policy.
Represented by:
Paul A. Laudicina, V. President

Sri Lanka, Government of
Colombo, Sri Lanka
Counsel or consultant:
White & Case

St. Ambrose University
Davenport, IA
Counsel or consultant:
Jefferson Group, The (John Coy)

St. George, Alaska, City of
Counsel or consultant:
Birch, Horton, Bittner and Cherot (Joseph M. Chomski)

St. George Tanaq Corp.
Anchorage, AK
Counsel or consultant:
Birch, Horton, Bittner and Cherot (Joseph M. Chomski)

St. George's University School of Medicine
511 Capitol Court, N.E. Suite 300, Washington, DC 20002
Telephone: (202) 544-7499
Counsel or consultant:
Health and Medicine Counsel of Washington (Dale P. Dirks)

St. Joseph Hospital and Health Center
Lorain, OH
Counsel or consultant:
Baker and Hostetler (Frederick H. Graefe)

St. Joseph's University
Philadelphia, PA
Counsel or consultant:
Cassidy and Associates, Inc. (Charles F. Dougherty, Vincent M. Versage)

St. Lawrence Seaway Pilots Ass'n
Massena, NY
Counsel or consultant:
Kurrus and Kirchner (Paul G. Kirchner)

St. Louis, Missouri, City of
Counsel or consultant:
Miller and Holbrooke

St. Norberts College
DePere, WI
Counsel or consultant:
Cassidy and Associates, Inc. (Elliott M. Fiedler)

St. Paul Fire and Marine Insurance Co.
St. Paul, MN
Counsel or consultant:
Baker and Hostetler (Kenneth J. Kies)

St. Paul, Minnesota, City of
St. Paul, MN
Counsel or consultant:
Robins, Kaplan, Miller & Ciresi

ST Systems Corp. (STX)
1577 Spring Hill Road, Suite 500, Vienna, VA 22180
Telephone: (703) 827-6601
Counsel or consultant:
The William Chasey Organization (William C. Chasey, Ph.D.)
Dow, Lohnes and Albertson (Ralph W. Hardy, Jr.)

St. Vincent Hospital and Medical Center
Portland, OR
Counsel or consultant:
Ryan-McGinn (Brent McCaleb)

Staley Manufacturing Co., A. E.
Decatur, IL
Represented by:
Bradley Myers, Legislative Ass't
Counsel or consultant:
Akin, Gump, Strauss, Hauer and Feld (Joel Jankowsky)
Robinson, Lake, Lerer & Montgomery (Carolyn Cheney)

Stamats Film and Video
Cedar Rapids, IA
Background: Designers and producers of interactive media.
Counsel or consultant:
Richard Curry and Associates (Richard C. Curry)

Standard Commerical Tobacco Co.
Wilson, NC

Willkie Farr and Gallagher (Christopher A. Dunn, Matthew R. Schneider)

Standard Federal Savings Bank
481 North Frederick Ave., Gaithersburg, MD
Telephone: (301) 840-8700
Counsel or consultant:
Andrews' Associates, Inc. (Mark Andrews)
Laxalt, Washington, Perito & Dubuc
Patton, Boggs and Blow (James B. Christian, Jr.)
Tammen Group, The (Ronald L. Tammen)
Thacher, Proffitt and Wood (Virginia W. Brown, Louis H. Nevins)

Standard Pacific Corp.
Costa Mesa, CA
Counsel or consultant:
Liz Robbins Associates (Alvin S. Brown, Liz Robbins)

Standing Rock Sioux Tribe
Fort Yates, ND
Counsel or consultant:
Sonosky, Chambers and Sachse

Stanley Bostitch Inc.
East Greenwich, RI
Counsel or consultant:
Collier, Shannon & Scott (David A. Hartquist, Thomas F. Shannon)

STANT, Inc.
Connersville, IN
Counsel or consultant:
Arent, Fox, Kintner, Plotkin & Kahn (Alan R. Malasky)

Star Tribune Co,
Minneapolis, MN
Counsel or consultant:
Van Dyk Associates, Inc. (Jim Dickenson, Ted Van Dyk)

Starrett Housing Corp.
New York, NY
Counsel or consultant:
Powell, Goldstein, Frazer and Murphy (Lawrence B. Simons)

Startron Industries, Inc.
Providence, RI
Counsel or consultant:
St. Germain, Rodio & Ursillo, Ltd. (Fernand J. St. Germain)

State Ass'n of County Retirement Systems
Santa Rosa, CA
Counsel or consultant:
Jones, Day, Reavis and Pogue (Frieda K. Wallison)

State Compliance Systems
1733 Taylor St., N.W., Washington, DC 20011
Telephone: (202) 882-9030
Counsel or consultant:
Wunder, Ryan, Cannon & Thelen (Paul E. Sullivan)

State Farm Insurance Cos.
Bloomington, IL
Counsel or consultant:
APCO Associates (Barry J. Schumacher)
Arnold & Porter (John M. Quinn)
Bonner & Associates
I. S. Weissbrodt

State Governmental Affairs Council
1255 23rd St., N.W., Suite 850, Washington, DC 20037
Telephone: (202) 728-0500
Background: Has liaison with organizations of state officials such as The National Conference of State Legislatures. The Council is a coalition of business companies and associations seeking to improve the governmental process at the state level while promoting better understanding between private industry and state governments. Membership consists of 110 multi-national corporations and several national trade associations.
Counsel or consultant:
Hauck and Associates (Dinah D. McElfresh, Carole M. Rogin)

State Higher Education Executive Officers
Denver, CO

The listings in this directory are available as _Mailing Labels_. See last page.

ORGANIZATIONS REPRESENTED

Counsel or consultant:
  Chambers Associates Incorporated (Letitia Chambers, Jamie P. Merisotis)

State Medicaid Directors Ass'n
  810 First St., N.E., Suite 500, Washington, DC 20002
  Telephone: (202) 682-0100
  Represented by:
  Jan Horvath, Policy Associate

State Policy Research, Inc.
  7706 Lookout Court, Alexandria, VA 22306
  Telephone: (703) 765-8389
  Represented by:
  Denise S. Hovey, Managing Editor
  Harold A. Hovey, President

State and Territorial Air Pollution Program Administrators
  444 North Capitol St., N.W. Suite 306, Washington, DC 20001
  Telephone: (202) 624-7864
  Represented by:
  S. William Becker, Exec. Director

Statoil North America, Inc.
  New York, NY
  Counsel or consultant:
  Washington Policy & Analysis (Scott L. Campbell, William F. Martin)

Stebbins-Ambler Air Transport
  Anchorage, AK
  Counsel or consultant:
  Birch, Horton, Bittner and Cherot (Joseph M. Chomski)

Steel Founders' Soc. of America
  Des Plaines, OH
  Background: Represented by Walter M. Kiplinger, Jr. of the Cast Metals Ass'n.

Steel Manufacturers Ass'n
  815 Connecticut Ave., N.W. Suite 304, Washington, DC 20006
  Telephone: (202) 331-7027
  Represented by:
  James E. Collins, President
  Counsel or consultant:
  Collier, Shannon & Scott
  Wiley, Rein & Fielding

Steel Service Center Institute
  1919 Pennsylvania Ave., N.W. Suite 400, Washington, DC 20006
  Telephone: (202) 785-3642
  Represented by:
  Elizabeth B. Cady, Government Affairs Director
  Counsel or consultant:
  Internat'l Advisory Services Group Ltd. (Charles H. Blum, Jeffrey W. Carr)

Steel Tank Institute
  Northbrook, IL
  Counsel or consultant:
  Kent & O'Connor, Incorp. (Patrick C. O'Connor)

Stelco, Inc.
  Toronto, Ontario
  Counsel or consultant:
  Dow, Lohnes and Albertson (William Silverman)
  Willkie Farr and Gallagher (Christopher A. Dunn)

Stepan Chemical Co.
  Northfield, IL
  Counsel or consultant:
  Evans & Associates, P.C.

Sterling & Associates, Donald T.
  Beverly Hills, CA
  Counsel or consultant:
  Manatt, Phelps, Rothenberg & Phillips (Robert J. Kabel, Charles T. Manatt)

Sterling Chemical Co.
  Houston, TX
  Counsel or consultant:
  Bracewell and Patterson (Gene E. Godley)

Sterling Drug Inc.
  1776 Eye St., N.W. Suite 1060, Washington, DC 20006
  Telephone: (202) 857-3450

Represented by:
  Laura M. Mudryk, Legislative Ass't, Government Affairs
  Kathleen M. Whyte, V. President, Government Affairs
  John H. Wood, V. President, Public Affairs

Sterling Group, Inc., The
  Houston, TX
  Counsel or consultant:
  Vinson and Elkins (James C. Gould)

Stevens Institute of Technology
  Hoboken, NJ
  Counsel or consultant:
  Mark A. Siegel & Associates

Stevenson & Associates
  Cleveland, OH
  Counsel or consultant:
  E. G. Newton & Assoc. (Elisabeth G. Newton)

Stimson Lumber Co.
  Portland, OR
  Counsel or consultant:
  Ragan and Mason (William F. Ragan)

Stock Information Group
  1455 Pennsylvania Ave., N.W., Suite 1200, Washington, DC 20004
  Telephone: (202) 347-2230
  Background: A coalition of stock insurance companies. The address given is that of the law firm of Davis & Harman.
  Counsel or consultant:
  Davis & Harman (William B. Harman, Jr.)
  Graham and James (Eileen Shannon Carlson, Thomas F. Railsback)
  Robert E. Juliano Associates

Stockholders of America
  1625 Eye St., N.W. Suite 724A, Washington, DC 20006
  Telephone: (202) 783-3430
  Represented by:
  Margaret Cox Sullivan, President

Stockton, California, Port of
  Counsel or consultant:
  Baker and McKenzie (Nicholas F. Coward)

Stone and Webster Engineering Corp.
  1201 Connecticut Ave., N.W. Suite 850, Washington, DC 20036-2605
  Telephone: (202) 466-7415
  Background: A subsidiary of Stone and Webster, Inc.
  Represented by:
  Daniel J. Donoghue, Manager
  Counsel or consultant:
  Campbell-Raupe, Inc. (Jeanne M. Campbell)
  McMahon and Associates
  Preston Gates Ellis & Rouvelas Meeds (Tim L. Peckinpaugh)

STRATCO, Inc.
  Kansas City, MO
  Counsel or consultant:
  Madison Group/Earle Palmer Brown, The (Richard Rosenzweig)
  Public Affairs Group, Inc. (Robert S. Boege, Edie Fraser)

Stratcor
  Danbury, CT
  Counsel or consultant:
  Robert N. Pyle & Associates (Robert N. Pyle)

Strategic Leadership, Inc.
  Washington, DC
  Counsel or consultant:
  Public Affairs Group, Inc. (Robert S. Boege, Edie Fraser)

Stratton and Associates
  Denver, CO
  Background: Washington Liaison is Douglas A. Durante of McMahon and Associates.

Stride Rite Corp., The
  Boston, MA
  Counsel or consultant:
  Powell, Goldstein, Frazer and Murphy (Stuart E. Eizenstat)

STS Corp.
  Orlando, FL
  Counsel or consultant:
  LeBoeuf, Lamb, Leiby, and MacRae (John K. Meagher)

Student Loan Funding Corp. of Ohio
  Cincinnati, OH
  Counsel or consultant:
  Clohan & Dean (John E. Dean)

Student Loan Marketing Ass'n
  1050 Thomas Jefferson St., N.W., Washington, DC 20007
  Telephone: (202) 333-8000
  Represented by:
  Anne Carlucci, Manager, Product Development
  Marianne M. Keler, V. President and Assoc. General Counsel
  Albert L. Lord, Exec. V. President and Chief Fin. Off.
  Counsel or consultant:
  Williams and Jensen, P.C. (Winfield P. Crigler)

Student Nat'l Medical Ass'n
  1012 10th St., N.W., Washington, DC 20001
  Telephone: (202) 371-1616
  Represented by:
  Roslyn D. Roberts, Exec. Director
  Counsel or consultant:
  Webster and Fredrickson (Wendell W. Webster)

Student Press Law Center
  1735 Eye St., N.W. Suite 504, Washington, DC 20006
  Telephone: (202) 466-5242
  Background: Provides legal assistance to student publications threatened with censorship.
  Represented by:
  Mark Goodman, Exec. Director

Sturgis, Michigan, Municipality of
  Background: Duncan, Weinberg, Miller & Pembroke represents the electric utility department of Sturgis.
  Counsel or consultant:
  Duncan, Weinberg, Miller & Pembroke, P.C. (Janice L. Lower, James D. Pembroke)

Subaru-Isuzu Automotive Inc.
  Lafayette, IN
  Counsel or consultant:
  Willkie Farr and Gallagher

Subaru of America
  1700 K St., N.W., Suite 1007, Washington, DC 20006
  Telephone: (202) 296-4994
  Represented by:
  Alfred Gloddeck, Manager, Regulatory Affairs

Substance Abuse Management, Inc.
  Milwaukee, WI
  Counsel or consultant:
  Baker and Hostetler (Frederick H. Graefe)

Suburban Maryland Building Industry Ass'n
  Executive Terrace 1400 Mercantile Lane, Landover, MD 20785
  Telephone: (301) 925-9490
  Represented by:
  Daniel Todd Bradfield, Dir, Political Affrs/Sr Legislative Rep
  F. Hammer Campbell, Dir., Gov't. Affrs., Sr. Legis. Rep.
  Bruce Houdesheldt, Assoc. Dir., Gov't. Affrs.
  Counsel or consultant:
  Susan J. Matlick, CAE

Sucocitrico Cutrale
  Rio de Janeiro, Brazil
  Counsel or consultant:
  Willkie Farr and Gallagher (William H. Barringer, Christopher A. Dunn)

Suffolk County, New York
  Riverhead, NY
  Counsel or consultant:
  Evergreen Associates, Ltd. (Robert M. Brooks, Robert Frank, Leigh Pate)

Sugar Ass'n, Inc.
  1101 15th St., N.W., Suite 600, Washington, DC 20005
  Telephone: (202) 785-1122
  Represented by:
  Dr. Charles W. Baker, V. President, Scientific Affairs
  Delta Barbour, V. President/Treasurer
  Sylvia Rowe, V. President, Public Relations
  Sarah Setton, V. President, Public Affairs
  Charles D. Shamel, President and Chief Executive Officer
  Counsel or consultant:
  Daniel J. Edelman, Inc. (Mary Christ-Erwin, Jean Rainey)

ORGANIZATIONS REPRESENTED

Sulphur Institute
1725 K St., N.W., Washington, DC 20006
Telephone: (202) 331-9660
Represented by:
Harold L. Fike, President

Sumitomo Bank Ltd.
Tokyo, Japan
Counsel or consultant:
Shaw, Pittman, Potts and Trowbridge

Sumitomo Corp.
Tokyo, Japan
Counsel or consultant:
Stafford, Burke and Hecker (Kelly H. Burke, Guy L. Hecker, Thomas P. Stafford)

Sumitomo Corp. of America
1747 Pennsylvania Ave., N.W. Suite 703, Washington, DC 20006
Telephone: (202) 785-9210
Represented by:
Takashi Emura, General Manager
Counsel or consultant:
Robert N. Meiser, P.C.

Sumitronics Inc.
Santa Clara, CA
Counsel or consultant:
Robert N. Meiser, P.C.

Summer Island, Inc.
St. Augustine, FL
Counsel or consultant:
O'Connor & Hannan (George J. Mannina, Jr.)

Summit, Ltd.
Omaha, NE
Counsel or consultant:
Kutak Rock & Campbell (Nancy L. Granese)

Sun Co.
555 13th St., N.W., Suite 1010 East, Washington, DC 20004
Telephone: (202) 628-1010
Represented by:
Shannon P. Guiney, Washington Representative
Mary W. Haught, Consultant
Albert B. Knoll, Washington Representative
Thomas L. Wylie, V. President, Government Affairs
Counsel or consultant:
McGuire, Woods, Battle and Boothe (Robert H. Lamb)

Sun Diamond Growers of California
Pleasanton, CA
Counsel or consultant:
Robinson, Lake, Lerer & Montgomery (James H. Lake)

Sun Life Assurance Co. of Canada (U.S. Division)
Wellesley Hills, MA
Counsel or consultant:
Covington and Burling (Michael R. Levy, Eugene A. Ludwig)

Sun Microsystems
San Francisco, CA
Counsel or consultant:
Nossaman, Guthner, Knox and Elliott (Murray Zweben)

Sun Moon Star Group
Taipei, Taiwan
Counsel or consultant:
Willkie Farr and Gallagher (Christopher A. Dunn)

Sun Pipe Line Co.
Counsel or consultant:
Howrey and Simon (A. Duncan Whitaker)

Sun Refining and Marketing Co.
Philadelphia, PA
Counsel or consultant:
Howrey and Simon (Keith E. Pugh, Jr.)

Sunbelt Corp.
Baltimore, MD
Background: Owned by a combination of Indian, Swiss and British companies.
Counsel or consultant:
Powell, Goldstein, Frazer and Murphy

SunCoast Airlines, Inc.
Fort Lauderdale, FL
Counsel or consultant:
Allan W. Markham

Sundstrand Corp.
1000 Wilson Blvd., Suite 2400, Arlington, VA 22209
Telephone: (703) 276-1626
Represented by:
Albert Barbero, Regional Manager
Alan L. Chvotkin, Senior Corporate Attorney
John L. Hills, Corp. Director, Congressional Relations
Counsel or consultant:
Barnes, Richardson and Colburn (Matthew T. McGrath)

Sunflower Electric Cooperative, Inc.
Hays, KS
Counsel or consultant:
Groom and Nordberg (Robert B. Harding, William G. Schiffbauer)

Sunmar Shipping, Inc.
Washington, DC
Counsel or consultant:
Preston Gates Ellis & Rouvelas Meeds (John L. Bloom, William N. Myhre)

Sunrider Internat'l
Torrance, CA
Counsel or consultant:
Richard Richards Law Offices

Sunshine Makers, Inc.
Huntingtn Harbor, CA
Counsel or consultant:
The William Chasey Organization (Virginia Chasey)

Sunshine Mining Co.
Dallas, TX
Counsel or consultant:
Denny Miller Associates

SuperComputers, Inc.
Redmond, WA
Counsel or consultant:
Evergreen Associates, Ltd. (Robert M. Brooks)

Superconducting Core Technologies
Denver, CO
Counsel or consultant:
James J. Magner & Assoc. Inc. (James J. Magner)

Superior Farms
Bakersfield, CA
Counsel or consultant:
Fierce and Associates

Superior Nat'l Insurance Group
Woodland Hills, CA
Counsel or consultant:
Edward H. Forgotson

Supermarket Development Corp.
San Francisco, CA
Counsel or consultant:
Latham and Watkins (Joseph A. DeFrancis)

Superpharm Corp.
Bay Shore, NY
Counsel or consultant:
King and Spalding (Eugene M. Pfeifer)
Wilmer, Cutler and Pickering (Daniel Marcus)

Supima Ass'n of America
Phoenix, AZ
Counsel or consultant:
McAden Associates, Ltd. (H. Wesley McAden)

Suppliers of Advanced Composite Materials Ass'n (SACMA)
1600 Wilson Blvd., Suite 1008, Arlington, VA 22209
Telephone: (703) 841-1556
Background: A non-profit trade association representing the advanced composite materials industry before public, governmental and quasi-governmental bodies. Members include materials suppliers, parts manufacturers, consultants and academia.
Represented by:
Gigi A. Healy, Director of Public Affairs
Joseph C. Jackson, Exec. Director

Support Center
1410 Q St., N.W., Washington, DC 20009
Telephone: (202) 462-2000
Background: Provides management and accounting assistance to nonprofit organizations.
Represented by:
Jonathan Cook, Exec. Director

Support Systems Associates, Inc.
Hauppauge, NY
Counsel or consultant:
Coffey, McGovern and Noel, Ltd. (James H. Falk)

Suquamish Indian Tribe
WA
Counsel or consultant:
SENSE, INC. (Joe Tallakson)

Surface Freight Corp.
Darien, CT
Counsel or consultant:
Galland, Kharasch, Morse and Garfinkle (Edward D. Greenberg)

Surinam Airways
Surinam
Counsel or consultant:
Bowen & Atkin (Harry A. Bowen)

Suriname, Government of
Paramaribo, Suriname
Counsel or consultant:
van Kloberg and Associates (Edward J. van Kloberg, III)
White & Case

Survival Technology, Inc.
8101 Glenbrook Rd., Bethesda, MD 20814
Telephone: (301) 656-5600
Counsel or consultant:
Arnold & Porter

Suzuki Motors Co., Ltd.
Tokyo, Japan
Counsel or consultant:
Pettit & Martin (Harry W. Cladouhos)

Sverdrup Corp.
1500 Wilson Blvd., Arlington, VA 22209
Telephone: (703) 525-1600
Represented by:
William J. Birkhofer, V. President, Director of Gov't Affairs
Carol Borowy, General Manager

Swaziland Sugar Ass'n
Swaziland
Counsel or consultant:
Murray, Scheer & Montgomery (D. Michael Murray)

Swedish Steelproducers' Ass'n (Jernkontoret)
Stockholm, Sweden
Background: Uddeholms is a subsidiary.
Counsel or consultant:
Winthrop, Stimson, Putnam & Roberts (Raymond S. Calamaro, Louis H. Kurrelmeyer, Christopher R. Wall)

Sweetener Users Ass'n
2100 Pennsylvania Ave., N.W. Suite 695, Washington, DC 20037
Telephone: (202) 872-8676
Represented by:
Thomas A. Hammer, President
Counsel or consultant:
McAuliffe, Kelly, Raffaelli & Siemens (James M. Copeland, Jr.)

Swidler & Berlin Political Action Committee
3000 K St., N.W., Suite 300, Washington, DC 20007
Telephone: (202) 944-4300
Counsel or consultant:
Swidler & Berlin, Chartered

Swiss Bankers Ass'n
Basel, Switzerland
Counsel or consultant:
Royer, Mehle & Babyak (Robert Stewart Royer)

Swissair
Zurich, Switzerland
Counsel or consultant:
Steptoe and Johnson (William Karas, Laurence Short)

The listings in this directory are available as *Mailing Labels*. See last page.

ORGANIZATIONS REPRESENTED

Syntex (USA) Inc.
1133 15th St., N.W., Suite 210, Washington, DC 20005
Telephone: (202) 429-2225
Represented by:
Richard Farrell, V. President, Government Affairs
Spencer K. Hathaway, State Government Affairs Manager
Counsel or consultant:
Hill and Knowlton Public Affairs Worldwide

Syntex Laboratories
1133 15th St., N.W., Suite 210, Washington, DC 20005
Telephone: (202) 244-8160
Counsel or consultant:
Bonner & Associates

Synthetic Organic Chemical Manufacturers Ass'n
1330 Connecticut Ave., N.W. Suite 300, Washington, DC 20036
Telephone: (202) 659-0060
Represented by:
Susan A. Kernus, Manager , Government Affairs
Ronald A. Lang, President
Mary James Legatski, Manager, Government Affairs
Gordon Wood, Sr. V. President, Government Relations

Syracuse University
Syracuse, NY
Counsel or consultant:
John G. Campbell, Inc. (John G. Campbell)

Syro Steel Co.
Girard, OH
Counsel or consultant:
Arthur E. Cameron

Syscon Corp. Political Action Committee
1000 Thomas Jefferson St., N.W., Washington, DC 20007
Telephone: (202) 342-4000
Represented by:
Maurice Cove, Treasurer

Systech Environmental Corp.
Xenia, OH
Counsel or consultant:
Parry and Romani Associates Inc.

Systems Technology & Applied Research Corp.
Two Skyline Place, 5203 Leesburg Pike, Suite 1201, Falls Church, VA 22041
Telephone: (703) 931-7773
Represented by:
Frank P. Smith, President

Syva Co.
Palo Alto, CA
Counsel or consultant:
Fleishman-Hillard, Inc (Paul Johnson)

T. A. Associates
Boston, MA
Counsel or consultant:
Latham and Watkins (Eric L. Bernthal)

T and J Electronics
Rocky Point, NY
Counsel or consultant:
I and J Associates (Ira F. Jersey, Jr., John J. Regan)

T. M. Community College
Reno, NV
Counsel or consultant:
State & Local Resources (Bruce D. Henderson, Patrick M. Murphy)

T.M.P. Inc.
3617 N. John Marshall Drive, Arlington, VA 22207
Telephone: (703) 534-1440
Background: Publishes Political Activity Calendar.
Counsel or consultant:
Sheehan Associates, Inc. (Denise L. Sheehan)

TACA Internat'l Airlines
San Salvador, El Salvador
Counsel or consultant:
Bowen & Atkin (Harry A. Bowen)
Neill, Mullenholz and Shaw

Tacoma Boatbuilding Co.
New York, NY
Counsel or consultant:
Jack Ferguson Associates

Tacoma, Port of
Tacoma, WA
Counsel or consultant:
Denny Miller Associates

Tacoma, Washington, City of
Counsel or consultant:
Simon & Co., Inc. (Leonard S. Simon)

Taiwan Ass'n of Machinery Industries
Taipei, Taiwan
Counsel or consultant:
Tucker & Associates (William Tucker)

Taiwan Power Co.
Taipei, Taiwan
Counsel or consultant:
Shaw, Pittman, Potts and Trowbridge (R. Timothy Hanlon)

Taiwan Textile Federation
Taipei, Taiwan
Counsel or consultant:
Ablondi and Foster, P.C. (Italo H. Ablondi)
Saunders and Company (Kim Brown)

Taiwan Transportation Vehicle Manufacturing Ass'n
Taipei, Taiwan
Counsel or consultant:
Howrey and Simon (Herbert C. Shelley)

Tak Communications, Inc.
1577 Spring Hill Road, Vienna, VA 22182
Telephone: (703) 827-6601
Counsel or consultant:
Dow, Lohnes and Albertson (Ralph W. Hardy, Jr.)

Tampa Electric Co.
Tampa, FL
Counsel or consultant:
Alcalde & Rousselot
Donelan, Cleary, Wood and Maser, P.C.
Gallagher, Boland, Meiburger and Brosnan (Peter C. Lesch)
Hunton and Williams

Tampa, Florida, City of
Counsel or consultant:
Keefe Co., The (Clarence L. James, Jr., William A. Roberts)

Tampa Port Authority
Tampa, FL
Counsel or consultant:
Alcalde & Rousselot
Schmeltzer, Aptaker and Sheppard (Edward J. Sheppard, IV)

Tanadgusix Corp.
St. Paul Island, AK
Counsel or consultant:
Birch, Horton, Bittner and Cherot (Joseph M. Chomski)

Tandem Computers Inc.
Cupertino, CA
Background: Washington representation is handled by J. Phillip Halstead, Manager of Government Relations, 10435 North Tantau Ave., LOC 200-17, Cupertino, CA 95014-0709; Tel: (408) 865-4662.

Tandy Corp.
Fort Worth, TX
Counsel or consultant:
Hopkins and Sutter (John W. Pettit, Malcolm R. Pfunder)
Sharretts, Paley, Carter and Blauvelt (Peter Jay Baskin)

Tanner Resources Corp.
Oklahoma City, OK
Counsel or consultant:
Stovall & Spradlin

Targeted Jobs Tax Credit Coalition
5152 Woodmire Lane, Alexandria, VA 22311
Telephone: (703) 931-0103
Background: An ad hoc coalition formed to represent the interests of employers and workers in supporting legislation which utilizes tax incentives to increase employment and training in the private sector.
Counsel or consultant:
Paul Suplizio Associates (Timothy Bobbitt, Jeanne Miller, Paul E. Suplizio)

Task Force Against Nuclear Pollution
Box 1817, Washington, DC 20013
Telephone: (301) 474-8311
Background: Alternative telephone number: (301) 864-3854.
Represented by:
Franklin Gage, Director

Tasty Kake, Inc.
Philadelphia, PA
Counsel or consultant:
Robert N. Pyle & Associates

Tatung Co.
Taipei, Taiwan
Counsel or consultant:
Willkie Farr and Gallagher (Christopher A. Dunn)

Tax Analysts
6830 North Fairfax Drive, Arlington, VA 22213
Telephone: (703) 532-1850
Background: Founded in 1970 as Tax Analysts and Advocates.
Represented by:
Thomas F. Field, Exec. Director

Tax Executives Institute
1001 Pennsylvania Ave., N.W., Suite 320, Washington, DC 20004-2505
Telephone: (202) 638-5601
Background: A professional association of about 4,500 tax executives from the 2,000 largest corporations in North America.
Represented by:
Mary L. Fahey, Assistant Tax Counsel
Thomas P. Kerester, Exec. Director
Timothy J. McCormally, Tax Counsel

Tax Foundation, Inc.
470 L'Enfant Plaza S.W., East Bldg., Suite 7112, Washington, DC 20024
Telephone: (202) 863-5454
Background: A non-profit research and education organization concerned with national, state and local fiscal policies and activities. President is Wayne S. Gable of Citizens for a Sound Economy.
Represented by:
Paul G. Merski, Director of Fiscal Affairs

Tax Reform Action Coalition
1725 K St., N.W., Suite 710, Washington, DC 20006
Telephone: (202) 872-0885
Background: Major corporate and trade association coalition supporting tax reform. Still active with the purpose of protecting rate cuts in Tax Reform Act of 1986. Run out of the office of the Nat'l Ass'n of Wholesaler-Distributors which acts as Exec. Secretariat to the Coalition.

TCOM Systems, Inc.
20001 L St., N.W., Washington, DC 20036
Telephone: (202) 775-0095
Counsel or consultant:
Barksdale Ballard & Co. (D. Michael Ballard)

TDCC: The Electronic Data Interchange Ass'n
225 Reinekers Lane, Alexandria, VA 22314-2822
Telephone: (703) 838-8042
Counsel or consultant:
Tendler, Goldberg & Biggins, Chtd. (James M. Goldberg)

TDK U.S.A. Corp.
Port Washington, NY
Counsel or consultant:
Graham and James (Jeffrey L. Snyder)
Patton, Boggs and Blow

TDS Healthcare Systems Corp.
Rockville, MD
Counsel or consultant:
Capitol Associates, Inc. (Debra M. Hardy-Havens, Terry Lierman, Gordon P. MacDougall)

TEAC Corp. of America
Montebello, CA
Counsel or consultant:
Patton, Boggs and Blow

Teachers Insurance and Annuity Ass'n
New York, NY
Background: Manages nationwide pension system for institutions of higher education.

ORGANIZATIONS REPRESENTED

Teachers Insurance and Annuity Ass'n (Cont'd)
Counsel or consultant:
Dewey, Ballantine, Bushby, Palmer and Wood (Lawrence F. O'Brien, III)
Rogers and Wells (Eugene T. Rossides)

Teamsters for a Democratic Union
2000 P St., N.W. Suite 612, Washington, DC 20036
Telephone: (202) 785-3707
Represented by:
Christine Allamanno, General Counsel

Teamwork America
1050 Connecticut Ave., N.W. Suite 900, Washington, DC 20036
Telephone: (202) 955-8500
Counsel or consultant:
Gibson, Dunn and Crutcher (Peter L. Baumbusch)

Technology Student Ass'n
1914 Association Drive, Reston, VA 22091
Telephone: (703) 860-9000
Represented by:
Rosanne T. White, Exec. Director

Technology Transfer
Bangkok, Thailand
Counsel or consultant:
TCI Washington Group (Merrill Williams)

TECO Transport & Trade Corp.
Tampa, FL
Counsel or consultant:
Anderson, Hibey, Nauheim and Blair (Robert A. Blair)
Global USA, Inc. (William H. Morris, Jr.)

TeknaMed Corp.
Columbus, MS
Counsel or consultant:
McClure and Trotter

TEKNIKA Electronics Corp.
Fairfield, NJ
Counsel or consultant:
Patton, Boggs and Blow

Tektronix, Inc.
1700 N. Moore St., Suite 1620, Arlington, VA 22209
Telephone: (703) 522-4500
Represented by:
Roger Majak, Manager, Federal Government Affairs

Telecommunications for the Deaf
814 Thayer Ave., Silver Spring, MD 20910
Telephone: (301) 589-3786
Background: A non-profit organization supporting technology in the field of visual communication for the deaf and hearing-impaired.
Represented by:
Alfred Sonnenstrahl, Exec. Director

TeleCommunications, Inc.
Denver, CO
Counsel or consultant:
Jones, Day, Reavis and Pogue
Mayer, Brown and Platt (Jerry L. Oppenheimer)
Preston Gates Ellis & Rouvelas Meeds (Bruce J. Heiman, Lloyd Meeds, Drew D. Pettus)

Telecommunications Industry Ass'n
1722 Eye St., N.W., Suite 440, Washington, DC 20006
Telephone: (202) 457-4912
Represented by:
Peter H. Bennett, V. President
J. Hal Berge, V. President
Allen R. Frischkorn, Jr., President
Eric J. Schimmel, V. President
Paul Vishny, Legal Counsel
Patrick H. Williams, Director, Government Relations
Counsel or consultant:
Willkie Farr and Gallagher (Philip L. Verveer)

Telecommunications Research and Action Center
Box 12038, Washington, DC 20005
Telephone: (202) 462-2520
Background: A non-profit tax-exempt organization devoted to promoting the interests of consumers in the electronic media. TRAC is the oldest and largest media reform organization in the United States. TRAC staff and volunteers monitor legislative and regulatory matters of potential importance to consumers, enter legal and legislative appear-

ances on behalf of the consumer position on important public policy issues, and publiish extensive educational materials.
Represented by:
David Wagenhauser, Exec. Director

Teledyne Brown Engineering
Huntsville, AL
Counsel or consultant:
DGA Internat'l (David L. Mahan)

Teledyne Industries Inc.
1501 Wilson Blvd., Suite 900, Arlington, VA 22209
Telephone: (703) 522-2550
Represented by:
Michael W. Deegan, Director, Government Relations
Willard Mitchell, V. President
Counsel or consultant:
Howrey and Simon (Harvey G. Sherzer)

Telephone and Data Systems, Inc.
Chicago, IL
Counsel or consultant:
Koteen and Naftalin (Margot Smiley Humphrey, Alan Y. Naftalin)
Taft, Stettinius and Hollister (Virginia E. Hopkins, Robert Taft, Jr.)
Taggart and Associates, Inc. (William A. Taggart)

Telephone Education Committee Organization
2626 Pennsylvania Ave., N.W., Washington, DC 20037
Telephone: (202) 298-2300
Background: Represents the legislative and political interests of the Nat'l Telephone Cooperative Ass'n. Washington contact is Charlotte Marks of the Association.

Telephone Pioneers of America
930 H St., N.W., 9th Floor, Washington, DC 20001
Telephone: (202) 392-2889
Represented by:
Janet Sullivan, Administrator, Washington Office

Telephonics, CSD
Farmingdale, NY
Counsel or consultant:
Parry and Romani Associates Inc. (Romano Romani)

Telequest, Inc.
Burbank, CA
Counsel or consultant:
Paul, Hastings, Janofsky and Walker (G. Hamilton Loeb)

Television Operators Caucus, Inc.
901 31st St., N.W., Washington, DC 20007
Telephone: (202) 944-5109
Counsel or consultant:
Hill and Knowlton Public Affairs Worldwide (Mary Jo Manning)

Telocator
2000 M St., N.W., Suite 230, Washington, DC 20036
Telephone: (202) 467-4770
Background: Formerly Nat'l Ass'n of Radiotelephone Systems. Members are paging carriers, cellular service providers and manufacturers of mobile radio equipment.
Represented by:
William J. Hotes, President
Maryann Kilduff, Director of Government Relations
Thomas Stroup, V. President/General Counsel
Michael Vernetti, V. President, Public Relations
Counsel or consultant:
Hill and Knowlton Public Affairs Worldwide (Mary Jo Manning)
Wiley, Rein & Fielding (R. Michael Senkowski)

Telocator Political Action Committee
2000 M St., N.W., Suite 230, Washington, DC 20036
Telephone: (202) 467-4770
Background: A political action committee sponsored by Telocator. Represented by Maryann Kilduff of Telocator.

Temple University
Philadelphia, PA
Counsel or consultant:
Burson-Marsteller (Rebecca L. Halkias)

TempNet
1001 Connecticut Ave., N.W., Suite 800, Washington, DC 20036
Telephone: (202) 452-1520

Counsel or consultant:
William S. Bergman Associates (Valerie H. Bergman)

TENAX Corp.
Jessup, MD
Counsel or consultant:
Mudge Rose Guthrie Alexander and Ferdon (David P. Houlihan, Jeffrey S. Neeley)

Tenneco Inc.
490 L'Enfant Plaza East, S.W. Suite 2202, S.W., Washington, DC 20024
Telephone: (202) 554-2850
Represented by:
Alex J. DeBoissiere, Washington Representative
Robert H. Miller, V. President
James L. Thorne, Director, Government Relations
John Thomas White, III, Washington Representative

Tennessee Valley Authority
412 First St., S.E., Suite 300, Washington, DC 20444
Telephone: (202) 479-4412
Represented by:
Christopher Eckl, Assistant Washington Representative
Willard Phillips, Bill Jr., Washington Representative
Mary Ann Simpson, Assistant Washington Representative

Tennessee Valley Public Power Ass'n
Chattanooga, TN
Counsel or consultant:
APCO Associates (Deborah R. Sliz)
Radin & Associates, Inc. (Alex Radin)

Terio Internat'l
7925 Fairfax Road, Alexandria, VA 22308
Telephone: (703) 768-1331
Counsel or consultant:
J. Arthur Weber & Associates (Joseph A. Weber)

Territorial Savings and Loan Ass'n
Honolulu, HI
Counsel or consultant:
Ragan and Mason (William F. Ragan)

Tesoro Petroleum Corp.
1800 K St., N.W. Suite 530, Washington, DC 20006
Telephone: (202) 775-8840
Represented by:
Jo-Ann Herrick, Washington Representative
Perry W. Woofter, Sr. V. President, Government Relations

Tetrapak Inc.
Shelton, CT
Counsel or consultant:
Nixon, Hargrave, Devans and Doyle

Texaco, Inc.
White Plains, NY
Counsel or consultant:
Lee, Toomey & Kent

Texaco U.S.A.
1050 17th St., N.W., Suite 500, Washington, DC 20036
Telephone: (202) 331-1427
Represented by:
John O. Ambler, Federal Government Affrs. Representative
William O. Bresnick, Senior Federal Environmental Affairs Rep
Max Goldman, Sr. Federal Gov't Affairs Representative
James N. Groninger, Federal Gov't Affairs Representative
David G. Koenig, Tax Attorney
Michael V. Kostiw, Sr. Federal Gov't Affairs Representative
James C. Pruitt, V. President, Washington Office
Counsel or consultant:
Bishop, Cook, Purcell & Reynolds (Marlow W. Cook)
Camp, Barsh, Bates and Tate (Harry E. Barsh, Jr.)
Kaye, Scholer, Fierman, Hays and Handler (Christopher R. Brewster)
Lee, Toomey & Kent
Williams and Jensen, P.C. (J. D. Williams)

Texas A & M College of Medicine
College Station, TX
Counsel or consultant:
Ryan-McGinn (Daniel McGinn)

Texas A & M University Research Foundation
College Station, TX

ORGANIZATIONS REPRESENTED

Counsel or consultant:
Meyers & Associates (Larry D. Meyers, Shelley Wilson)

Texas Air Corp.
901 15th St., N.W. Suite 500, Washington, DC 20005
Telephone: (202) 289-6060
Represented by:
David G. Mishkin, Staff V. Pres., Regul. & Internat'l Aff.
Clark H. Onstad, V. President
Rebecca G. Range, Staff V. President, Government Affairs
Elliott M. Seiden, V. President, Assoc. General Counsel
Counsel or consultant:
Akin, Gump, Strauss, Hauer and Feld (John J. Gallagher)
Marshall S. Filler, P.C.
Williams and Jensen, P.C. (J. Steven Hart)

Texas Ass'n of Steel Importers
Houston, TX
Counsel or consultant:
Dorsey & Whitney

Texas Cattle Feeders Ass'n
Amarillo, TX
Counsel or consultant:
McMillan and Farrell Associates (C. W. McMillan)

Texas Cities Legislative Coalition (TCLC)
1620 Eye St., N.W., Suite 300, Washington, DC 20006
Telephone: (202) 429-0160
Counsel or consultant:
Nat'l Center for Municipal Development (Barbara T. McCall)

Texas Civil Justice League
Austin, TX
Counsel or consultant:
Bonner & Associates

Texas Clinical Laboratories
Dallas, TX
Counsel or consultant:
Hecht, Spencer & Associates (William H. Hecht)

Texas Cotton Marketing
Lubbock, TX
Counsel or consultant:
Meyers & Associates (Larry D. Meyers)

Texas Education Agency
Austin, TX
Counsel or consultant:
Akin, Gump, Strauss, Hauer and Feld (Joel Jankowsky)

Texas Electric Service Co.
Fort Worth, TX
Counsel or consultant:
Reid & Priest

Texas Gas Transmission Corp.
555 13th St., N.W. Suite 430 West, Washington, DC 20004
Telephone: (202) 393-8577
Represented by:
Ray H. Lancaster, V. Pres., Federal Governmental Affairs
Counsel or consultant:
Andrews and Kurth (Robert Perdue)
Fulbright & Jaworski (John F. Harrington)
Keller and Heckman

Texas Instruments
1455 Pennsylvania Ave., N.W., Suite 230, Washington, DC 20004
Telephone: (202) 628-3133
Represented by:
John K. Boidock, Mgr., Government Relations (Corporate)
George J. Donovan, V.P., Dir., Wash. Opns. (Def Syst & El)
William B. Driggers, Legislative Liaison (Def. Syst. & Elec.)
Gary Howell, V.P., Cong. Liais. (Def. Sys. & Elect.)
Toni D. White, Legislative Liaison (Def. Syst. & Elec.)
Elizabeth L. Wright, Manager, Llegislative Affairs
Counsel or consultant:
Miller & Chevalier, Chartered (John S. Nolan)

Texas Instruments, Industrial Automation
Hunt Valley, MD

Counsel or consultant:
McNair Group Inc. (Kathy E. Gallegos, Dennis R. Rankin)

Texas Internat'l Education Consortium
Austin, TX
Counsel or consultant:
Meyers & Associates (Rick Meyers)

Texas Nat'l Research Laboratory Commission
Austin, TX
Counsel or consultant:
Akin, Gump, Strauss, Hauer and Feld

Texas Power and Light Co.
Dallas, TX
Counsel or consultant:
Reid & Priest

Texas Ranchers Labor Ass'n
San Angelo, TX
Counsel or consultant:
Holt, Miller & Associates (Harris N. Miller)

Texas Shrimp Ass'n
1110 Vermont Ave., N.W., Suite 1160, Washington, DC 20005
Telephone: (202) 293-5513
Counsel or consultant:
KLV Associates (Kristin L. Vehrs)

Texas, State of, Office of State-Federal Relations
600 Maryland Ave., S.W., Suite 255, Washington, DC 20024
Telephone: (202) 488-3927
Represented by:
Randall H. Erben, Deputy Director

Texas Utilities
Dallas, TX
Counsel or consultant:
Newman & Holtzinger, P.C. (G. Edgar)
O'Neill and Athy, P.C. (Andrew Athy, Jr.)

Texasgulf Inc.
Stamford, CT
Counsel or consultant:
Dale Miller

Texstor
Grand Prairie, TX
Counsel or consultant:
DGM Internat'l Inc. (Donald E. Ellison)

Textile Fibers and By-Products Ass'n (TFBA)
Charlotte, NC
Counsel or consultant:
Fulbright & Jaworski (Carl W. Vogt)

Textile Machinery Good Government Committee
7297 Lee Highway, Suite N, Falls Church, VA 22042
Telephone: (703) 533-9251
Background: Sponsored by the American Textile Machinery Ass'n.
Counsel or consultant:
Ass'n and Society Management Internat'l Inc. (Clay D. Tyeryar)

Textile Museum
2320 S St., N.W., Washington, DC 20008
Telephone: (202) 667-0441
Counsel or consultant:
Chernikoff and Co. (Larry Chernikoff)

Textile Rental Services Ass'n of America
Miami Beach, FL
Counsel or consultant:
Loomis, Owen, Fellman and Howe (Steven John Fellman)

Textron Inc.
1090 Vermont Ave., N.W., Suite 1100, Washington, DC 20005
Telephone: (202) 289-5800

Represented by:
Roy C. Buckner, Director, Congressional Relations
Mary L. Howell, V. President, Government Affairs
John J. Killeen, Director, Legislative Affairs
Eugene Kozicharow, Director, Public Affairs (Washington)
Richard F. Smith, Director, Government Affairs
Gordon M. Thomas, Director, Government Affairs
Steven A. Wein, Manager, Legislative Affairs
Counsel or consultant:
Cambridge Internat'l, Inc. (Justus P. White)

Textron Marine Systems
1090 Vermont Ave., N.W., Suite 1100, Washington, DC 20005
Telephone: (202) 289-5800
Background: A division of Textron, Inc.
Represented by:
Michael J. Hallahan, Director, ACV Marketing
Gordon L. Thorpe, Exec. Director, Washington Office

TGI Friday's
Addison, TX
Counsel or consultant:
Richard B. Berman and Co.,Inc. (Richard B. Berman)

Thailand, Board of Investment of the Government of
Bangkok, Thailand
Counsel or consultant:
Arthur D. Little, Inc.

Thailand, Department of Foreign Trade of
Bangkok, Thailand
Counsel or consultant:
StMaxens and Co. (Thomas F. StMaxens, II)

Thailand, Embassy of
2300 Kalorama Road, N.W., Washington, DC 20008
Telephone: (202) 483-7200
Counsel or consultant:
Mark C. Bisnow
Dorsey & Whitney
Internat'l Trade and Development Agency
Marshall, Tenzer, Greenblatt, Fallon and Kaplan (Sylvan M. Marshall)
White & Case

Thailand, Office of the Prime Minister
Bangkok, Thailand
Counsel or consultant:
Commerce Consultants Internat'l Ltd. (David M. Hatcher, Richard Richards)

The Limited, Inc.
Columbus, OH
Counsel or consultant:
Ivins, Phillips and Barker (Michael F. Solomon)
Keene, Shirley & Associates, Inc. (Darrel Choat, David A. Keene, Craigan P. Shirley)

The University Hospital
Boston, MA
Counsel or consultant:
Cassidy and Associates, Inc. (Carol F. Casey)

The University Museum (University of Pennsylvania)
Philadelphia, PA
Counsel or consultant:
Chernikoff and Co. (Larry Chernikoff)

Thiele Kaolin Co.
Sandersville, GA
Counsel or consultant:
Sutherland, Asbill and Brennan (Gordon O. Pehrson, Jr.)

Third Class Mail Ass'n
1333 F St., N.W., Suite 710, Washington, DC 20004-1108
Telephone: (202) 347-0055
Represented by:
Douglas Berger, Director, Public Affairs
Gene A. Del Polito, Exec. Director
Counsel or consultant:
Cohn and Marks (Ian D. Volner)

Third Class Mail Ass'n Political Action Committee
1333 F St., N.W., Suite 710, Washington, DC 20004-1108
Telephone: (202) 347-0055

The listings in this directory are available as *Mailing Labels.* See last page.

687

ORGANIZATIONS REPRESENTED

Third Class Mail Ass'n Political Action Committee (Cont'd)
Represented by:
Burton Stuttman, Treasurer

Third World Prosthetic Foundation
1015 33rd St., N.W., Washington, DC 20007
Telephone: (202) 333-6435
Counsel or consultant:
The William Chasey Organization (William C. Chasey, Ph.D.)

Thomas Jefferson Equal Tax Soc.
1469 Spring Vale Ave., McLean, VA 22101
Telephone: (703) 356-5800
Represented by:
Michael Tecton, President

Thomas Jefferson University
Philadelphia, PA
Counsel or consultant:
Cassidy and Associates, Inc. (C. Frank Godfrey, Jr.)

Thompson Development Co., Kathryn G.
Irvine, CA
Counsel or consultant:
The Eddie Mahe Company

Thompson Medical Co., Inc.
New York, NY
Counsel or consultant:
Morris J. Amitay, P.C.
Nixon, Hargrave, Devans and Doyle (Stephen Kurzman)

Thomson Consumer Electronics, Inc.
1200 19th St., N.W., Suite 601, Washington, DC 20036
Telephone: (202) 872-0670
Background: A manufacturer and distributor of consumer electronics products, sold under GE and RCA trademarks.
Represented by:
Dr. D. Joseph Donahue, Sr. V. Pres., Tech. & Business Devel'pt.
Wray C. Hiser, Senior Counsel, Government Relations
Counsel or consultant:
Hill and Knowlton Public Affairs Worldwide (Mary Jo Manning, Marci Williams)

Thomson-CSF Inc.
2231 Crystal Drive, Suite 814, Arlington, VA 22202
Telephone: (703) 486-0780
Counsel or consultant:
Burson-Marsteller
Gold and Liebengood, Inc. (Howard S. Liebengood)

Thomson Group
Bagneux Cedex, France
Counsel or consultant:
Burson-Marsteller

Thousand Springs Generating Co.
Reno, NV
Counsel or consultant:
Bishop, Cook, Purcell & Reynolds

Three Afiliated Tribes of Fort Berthold Reservation
New Town, ND
Counsel or consultant:
Hobbs, Straus, Dean and Wilder (Charles A. Hobbs)

Thrifty Rent-A-Car System, Inc.
Tulsa, OK
Counsel or consultant:
Winthrop, Stimson, Putnam & Roberts (Michael W. Dolan, Ronna A. Freiberg, Peter F. Gold)

Thyssen Inc.
New York, NY
Background: Representation of this major West German steel and metal working enterprise by Sharretts, Paley, Carter and Blauvelt includes Thyssen Stahl, Thyssen Edelstahl and Thyssen Uniformtechnik.
Counsel or consultant:
Sharretts, Paley, Carter and Blauvelt (Beatrice A. Brickell, Alfred R. McCauley)

Tibet, Government of (in Exile)
Dharmsala, India
Counsel or consultant:
Wilmer, Cutler and Pickering (William T. Lake)

Tidewater Health Care
Virginia Beach, VA
Counsel or consultant:
Jefferson Group, The (Frederick J. Hannett, David Serwer)

Tiffany & Co.
New York, NY
Counsel or consultant:
Crowell and Moring (Harold J. Heltzer)

Tile Contractors Ass'n of America
112 North Alfred St., Alexandria, VA 22314
Telephone: (703) 836-5995
Background: Exec. Director is Wilhelmina T. Loomis (see Nat'l Ass'n of Decorative Architectural Finishes).

Tile Council of America
Princeton, NJ
Counsel or consultant:
Howrey and Simon (John F. Bruce)

Tillamook Bay, Oregon, Port of
Tillamook, OR
Counsel or consultant:
Ball, Janik and Novack (James A. Beall, Michelle E. Giguere)

Time Warner Inc.
1050 Connecticut Ave., N.W. Suite 850, Washington, DC 20036
Telephone: (202) 861-4000
Represented by:
Timothy A. Boggs, V. President, Public Affairs
Brian Conboy, V. President, Government Affairs
Michael H. Hammer, Dir., Communications Policy Development
Carol A. Melton, Washington Counsel
Arthur B. Sackler, Director, Publishing Policy Development
Counsel or consultant:
Duberstein Group, Inc., The (John Angus, III)
Willkie Farr and Gallagher (Sue D. Blumenfeld, Matthew R. Schneider, Philip L. Verveer)

Times Mirror Co.
1875 Eye St., N.W., Suite 1110, Washington, DC 20006
Telephone: (202) 293-3126
Represented by:
Patrick H. Butler, V. President, Washington
Jacquelyn L. Jackson, Director
Counsel or consultant:
Gold and Liebengood, Inc. (Martin B. Gold)

Timex Corp.
Waterbury, CT
Counsel or consultant:
Hogan and Hartson (Samuel R. Berger)
Howrey and Simon (Stuart H. Harris, Ralph J. Savarese)
StMaxens and Co. (Thomas F. StMaxens, II)

Timken Co.
Canton, OH
Counsel or consultant:
Stewart and Stewart (Eugene L. Stewart)

Tire Industry Safety Council
National Press Bldg. Suite 844, Washington, DC 20045
Telephone: (202) 783-1022
Represented by:
Edward Lewis, Director

Tissue Culture Ass'n
19110 Montgomery Village Ave., Suite 300, Gaithersburg, MD 20879
Telephone: (301) 869-2900
Represented by:
William G. Momberger, CAE, Exec. Director

Titanium Metals Corp. (TIMET)
Pittsburgh, PA
Counsel or consultant:
Pillsbury, Madison and Sutro (Donald E. deKieffer)

Title Industry Political Action Committee
1828 L St., N.W. Suite 705, Washington, DC 20036
Telephone: (202) 296-3671
Background: Represents the legislative and political interests of the American Land Title Ass'n. Robin K. Santagelo of the American Land Title Ass'n serves as contact.

Toa Nenryo Kogyo Kabushiki Kaisha
Tokyo, Japan
Counsel or consultant:
First Associates Inc. (Floyd I. Roberson)

Tobacco Associates
1725 K St., N.W. Suite 512, Washington, DC 20006
Telephone: (202) 828-9144
Represented by:
Kirk Wayne, President

Tobacco Industry Labor Management Committee
P.O. Box 65311, Washington, DC 20005
Telephone: (202) 659-3005
Counsel or consultant:
Wunder, Ryan, Cannon & Thelen (Michael A. Forscey)

Tobacco Institute
1875 Eye St., N.W., Suite 800, Washington, DC 20006
Telephone: (202) 457-4800
Represented by:
Samuel D. Chilcote, Jr., President
C. Hoke Leggett, Director, Agricultural Relations
Robert J. Lewis, Senior V. President, Federal Relations
Kurt Malmgren, Senior V. President, State Activities
Walker Merryman, V. President
George R. Minshew, Northern Sector V. President
Brennan D. Moran, Director, Media Relations
Bonnie Parker, Legislative Representative
Charles H. Powers, Senior V. President, Public Affairs
Margaret A. Rita, Issue Analyst
Ralph Vinovich, V. President, Legislative Affairs
Richard H. White, V. Pres., Legis. Affrs., Federal Relats.
Counsel or consultant:
Bishop, Cook, Purcell & Reynolds
Black, Manafort, Stone and Kelly Public Affairs Co.
Covington and Burling
Griffin, Johnson & Associates
Hill and Knowlton Public Affairs Worldwide (Tamara Cox, Elaine D. Crispen)
Laxalt, Washington, Perito & Dubuc (James M. Christian, Sr.)
Madison Group/Earle Palmer Brown, The (Peggy L. Martin)
Paul, Hastings, Janofsky and Walker
Powell, Adams & Rinehart
Sparber and Associates (Peter G. Sparber)
Webster and Sheffield (L. Andrew Zausner)

Tobacco Institute Political Action Committee
1875 Eye St., N.W. Suite 800, Washington, DC 20006
Telephone: (202) 457-4800
Represented by:
Phyllis M. McGovern, Treasurer

Toborg Associates, Inc.
Landover, MD
Counsel or consultant:
Resources Development, Inc. (Roger H. Zion)

Todd Shipyards Corp. Political Action Committee
2341 Jefferson Davis Hwy., Arlington, VA 22202
Telephone: (703) 418-0133
Represented by:
Stuart S. Adamson, Chairman
E. David Foreman, Director, Government Affairs

Togo, Government of
Lome, Togo
Counsel or consultant:
David Apter and Associates (Marc L. Apter)

Tohoku Electric Power Co.
Sendai Miyagi, Japan
Counsel or consultant:
Washington Policy & Analysis (Scott L. Campbell, William F. Martin)

Tohono O'odham Nation
Sells, AZ
Background: An Indian tribal government.
Counsel or consultant:
William Byler Associates (William Byler)

Tokyo Electric Co., Ltd.
Tokyo, Japan
Counsel or consultant:
Kelley, Drye and Warren (Edward M. Lebow)

ORGANIZATIONS REPRESENTED

Tokyo Electric Power Co.
1901 L St., N.W., Suite 720, Washington, DC 20036
Telephone: (202) 457-0790
Represented by:
Kiichi Suganuma, Manager
Komonsuke Sugiura, Director and General Manager

Tokyo Juki Industrial Co., Ltd.
Tokyo, Japan
Counsel or consultant:
Dorsey & Whitney

Toledo Edison Co.
Toledo, OH
Counsel or consultant:
Shaw, Pittman, Potts and Trowbridge (Gerald Charnoff)

Toledo Zoological Gardens
Toledo, OH
Counsel or consultant:
Vorys, Sater, Seymour and Pease (Randal C. Teague)

Tomen Corp.
Tokyo, Japan
Counsel or consultant:
Sedam and Shearer (Patrick J. McMahon, Glenn J. Sedam, Jr.)

Tooling and Machining Industry Political Action Committee
Box 44162, Fort Washington, MD 20744
Telephone: (301) 248-6200
Background: The political action committee of the Nat'l Tooling and Machining Ass'n. Staff Executive of the Committee is John Cox, Manager of Government Affairs for the Association.
Represented by:
Marjorie V. Carson, Assistant Treasurer

Tootsie Roll Industries
Chicago, IL
Counsel or consultant:
Sidley and Austin (Judith Bello)

Torchmark Corp.
Birmingham, AL
Counsel or consultant:
R. Duffy Wall and Associates (Michael Stern, R. Duffy Wall)

Torrington Co.
Torrington, CT
Counsel or consultant:
Dyer, Ellis, Joseph & Mills (Howard A. Vine)
Stewart and Stewart (Terrence P. Stewart)

Tosco Corp.
Los Angeles, CA
Counsel or consultant:
Legislative Strategies Inc. (Raymond F. Bragg, Jr.)
Nat'l Counsel Associates (Hilma Lou Ivey)

Toshiba America, Inc.
New York, NY
Counsel or consultant:
Mudge Rose Guthrie Alexander and Ferdon (Jeffrey S. Neeley, N. David Palmeter)
Patton, Boggs and Blow
The Whalen Company, Inc. (Richard J. Whalen)

Toshiba Corp.
Tokyo, Japan
Counsel or consultant:
Dickstein, Shapiro and Morin (Leonard Garment, James R. Jones, G. Joseph Minetti)
Mudge Rose Guthrie Alexander and Ferdon (Richard H. Abbey, Julia Christine Bliss, David P. Houlihan, Jeffrey S. Neeley, David A. Vaughan)

Total American Cooperation
2000 Pennsylvania Ave., N.W., Suite 7150, Washington, DC 20006
Telephone: (202) 822-8365
Represented by:
Philip P. Saint-Andrew, President

Total Health Plan
Denville, NJ
Counsel or consultant:
Jefferson Group, The (David Serwer)

Total Petroleum, Inc.
Denver, CO
Counsel or consultant:
Dykema Gossett (Howard E. O'Leary, Jr.)

Totem Ocean Trailer Express, Inc.
Seattle, WA
Counsel or consultant:
Garvey, Schubert & Barer (Alan A. Butchman)

Tougaloo College
Tougaloo, MS
Counsel or consultant:
Cassidy and Associates, Inc. (Gerald S. J. Cassidy, Robert A. Farmer)

Tourist Cablevision Corp.
Rio de Janeiro, Brazil
Counsel or consultant:
Warren W. Koffler

Tousand Spring Generating Co.
Reno, NV
Counsel or consultant:
Bishop, Cook, Purcell & Reynolds (H. Lawrence Fox)

Tower Air, Inc.
New York, NY
Counsel or consultant:
Hewes, Morella, Gelband and Lamberton, P.C. (Stephen L. Gelband)

Towerbank
Miami, FL
Counsel or consultant:
John G. Campbell, Inc.

Towers Financial Corp.
New York, NY
Counsel or consultant:
Evans Group, Ltd., The (Thomas B. Evans, Jr.)

Towers, Perrin, Forster & Crosby
Philadelphia, PA
Counsel or consultant:
Lee, Toomey & Kent

Towing and Recovery Ass'n of America
Winter Park, FL
Counsel or consultant:
Alvin M. Guttman

Toxicology Forum
1575 Eye St., N.W., Suite 800, Washington, DC 20005
Telephone: (202) 659-0030
Represented by:
Charlene D. Anderson, Administrator
Counsel or consultant:
McKenna, Conner and Cuneo

Toyota Motor Corp.
Toyota City, Japan
Counsel or consultant:
Arent, Fox, Kintner, Plotkin & Kahn (John D. Hushon, Burton V. Wides)
Dorsey & Whitney
Hill and Knowlton Public Affairs Worldwide (Andrew G. Durant)
TKC Internat'l, Inc.

Toyota Motor Corporate Services U.S.A.
New York, NY
Counsel or consultant:
Schnader, Harrison, Segal and Lewis (Richard A. Penna)

Toyota Motor Sales, U.S.A.
1850 M St., N.W., Suite 600, Washington, DC 20036
Telephone: (202) 775-1700

Represented by:
Charles E. Ing, Legislative Affairs Manager
Earl C. Quist, State Government Affairs Manager
C. Douglas Smith, Corporate Manager, Gov't & Indus. Rtns.
Robert J. Wade, National Industry Affairs Manager
Counsel or consultant:
Hogan and Hartson (Samuel R. Berger, Clifford S. Gibbons, Gerald E. Gilbert)
Kendall and Associates (William T. Kendall)
Mike Masaoka Associates (Mike M. Masaoka, Patti A. Tilson, T. Albert Yamada)
Miller & Chevalier, Chartered (John S. Nolan)
The Whalen Company, Inc. (David W. Secrest, Richard J. Whalen)

Trackpower Transmissions, Ltd.
Coventry, England
Counsel or consultant:
Lonington, Inc. (Alan G. Gray)

Trade Relations Council of the U.S.
808 17th St., N.W. Fifth Fl., Washington, DC 20006
Telephone: (202) 785-4194
Background: A non-profit research organization established as the American Tariff League in 1885. Collects statistics on trade and industry as they affect foreign economic policy.
Counsel or consultant:
Stewart and Stewart

Tradewinds Airways Ltd.
London, England
Counsel or consultant:
Lord Day & Lord, Barrett Smith (Joanne W. Young)

Traditional Industries
Agoura Hills, CA
Counsel or consultant:
Hecht, Spencer & Associates (William H. Hecht)

Trafalgar Capital Associates, Inc.
Boston, MA
Counsel or consultant:
Coan & Lyons (Carl A. S. Coan, Jr.)

Trailer Hitch Manufacturers Ass'n
1050 Connecticut Ave., N.W., Washington, DC 20036
Telephone: (202) 857-6087
Background: The above address is that of the law firm Arent, Fox, Kintner, Plotkin and Kahn.
Counsel or consultant:
Arent, Fox, Kintner, Plotkin & Kahn (Lawrence F. Henneberger)

Trailer Train Co.
Chicago, IL
Counsel or consultant:
Williams and Jensen, P.C. (John J. McMackin, Jr.)
Wunder, Ryan, Cannon & Thelen (W. Stephen Cannon)

Training Media Distributors Ass'n
Santa Monica, CA
Counsel or consultant:
Wexler, Reynolds, Fuller, Harrison and Schule, Inc. (Joseph W. Waz, Jr.)

Trammell Crow, Inc.
Dallas, TX
Counsel or consultant:
King and Spalding (William S. McKee)
Vinson and Elkins (James C. Gould)

Trans Air Link, Inc.
Miami Springs, FL
Counsel or consultant:
Bowen & Atkin (Harry A. Bowen)

Trans-Alaska Pipeline Liability Fund
Los Angeles, CA
Counsel or consultant:
Wilmer, Cutler and Pickering (Sally Katzen)

Trans Ocean Leasing Corp.
New York, NY
Counsel or consultant:
Wilmer, Cutler and Pickering (Ronald J. Greene)

Trans Ocean Ltd.
San Bruno, CA

The listings in this directory are available as *Mailing Labels*. See last page.

ORGANIZATIONS REPRESENTED

Trans Ocean Ltd. (Cont'd)
Counsel or consultant:
Patton, Boggs and Blow (James B. Christian, Jr.)

Trans-Pacific Freight Conference of Japan/Korea
Tokyo, Japan
Counsel or consultant:
Warren and Associates

Trans World Airlines
808 17th St., N.W., Suite 520, Washington, DC 20006
Telephone: (202) 457-4750
Represented by:
R. Daniel Devlin, Director, Legislative Affairs
John M. Moloney, Manager, Internat'l Government Relations
Stephen J. Slade, V. President, Government Affairs
Counsel or consultant:
Black, Manafort, Stone and Kelly Public Affairs Co.

TransAfrica
545 Eighth St., S.E. Suite 200, Washington, DC 20003
Telephone: (202) 547-2550
Background: Founded in 1977 as the first Black foreign policy lobby in this country. Seeks to inform and organize popular opinion in support of a more progressive U.S. foreign policy toward the nations of Africa and the Caribbean and toward peoples of African descent throughout the world.
Represented by:
Ibrahim Gassama, Legislative Assistant
Randall Robinson, Exec. Director
Counsel or consultant:
Gallagher-Widmeyer Group Inc., The (Mary Jane Gallagher)

Transamerica Airlines
Oakland, CA
Background: Represented by Edward J. Driscoll of the Nat'l Air Carrier Ass'n.
Counsel or consultant:
Burwell, Hansen, Peters and Houston (Walter D. Hansen)

Transamerica Corp.
San Francisco, CA
Counsel or consultant:
McAuliffe, Kelly, Raffaelli & Siemens (James M. Copeland, Jr.)
Scribner, Hall and Thompson

Transamerica Leasing, Inc.
White Plains, NY
Counsel or consultant:
Patton, Boggs and Blow (James B. Christian, Jr.)

Transamerica Occidental Life Insurance Co.
Los Angeles, CA
Background: A subsidiary of Transamerica Corp.
Counsel or consultant:
Braun & Company
Lautzenheiser and Associates (Barbara J. Lautzenheiser)

Transatlantic Security Council
2323 Virginia Ave., N.W., Washington, DC 20037
Telephone: (202) 338-2539
Background: The Council focuses on Western Europe, the United States, and Latin America and analyses and promotes security and economic development among these regions.
Represented by:
William S. Diedrich, President
Viola Drath, Chairman of the Board

Transbrasil
Rio de Janeiro, Brazil
Counsel or consultant:
Lord Day & Lord, Barrett Smith (Joanne W. Young)

TransCanada PipeLines
1701 Pennsylvania Ave., N.W. Suite 1110, Washington, DC 20006
Telephone: (202) 785-5270
Represented by:
Leonard B. Levine, Director, U.S. Government Affairs

Transco Energy Co.
555 13th St., N.W., Suite 430 West, Washington, DC 20004
Telephone: (202) 628-3060

Represented by:
Elizabeth Fritschle, Government Affairs Specialist
Judy Locke, Manager, Regulatory Relations
Curtis E. Whalen, V. President, Governmental Affairs
Counsel or consultant:
Andrews and Kurth (Robert G. Hardy)
Nancy Whorton George & Associates, P.C. (Nancy Whorton George)

Transconex, Inc.
Miami, FL
Counsel or consultant:
Denning and Wohlstetter

Transcontinental Development Corp.
Santa Barbara, CA
Counsel or consultant:
Century Public Affairs (Philip A. Bangert, Richard L. Sinnott)

Transkei, Government of
Umtata, Transkei
Counsel or consultant:
Pagonis and Donnelly Group (Thomas R. Donnelly, Jr., William B. Robertson)

Transmission Agency of Northern California
Sacramento, CA
Counsel or consultant:
Duncan, Weinberg, Miller & Pembroke, P.C. (Wallace L. Duncan, James D. Pembroke, Edward Weinberg)
Will & Muys, P.C.

Transnational Development Consortium
2745 29th St., N.W., Suite 216, Washington, DC 20008
Telephone: (202) 462-8314
Background: Advise both public and private sectors regarding opportunities for foreign direct investment and sources of financing. Develop and implement investing and marketing strategies. Manage economic and development opportunities for industries in domestic and internat'l markets.
Represented by:
Lane F. Miller, Principal, Internat'l Inv./Venture Cap'l

Transport Workers Union of America, AFL-CIO
New York, NY
Counsel or consultant:
O'Donnell, Schwartz & Anderson (Arthur M. Luby)

Transportation, Communications Internat'l Union
815 16th St., N.W. Suite 511, Washington, DC 20036
Telephone: (202) 783-3660
Represented by:
Roger W. Barr, Jr., State Legislative Director-Kansas
Michael M. Cunniff, State Legislative Director-Missouri
John Doerrer, State Legislative Director-Illinois
John P. Dowd, State Legislative Director-Massachusetts
C. Ray Duggan, Regional Legislative Director
Thomas J. Dwyer, State Legislative Director-Minnesota
Gary M. Faley, State Legislative Director-Michigan
George Falltrick, State Legislative Director-California
Brian Kilbry, State Legis. Director-Washington State
Richard I. Kilroy, Internat'l President
Robert Mariani, Regional Legislative Director
Edward McDonald, Regional Legislative Director
Jack F. Otero, Internat'l V. Pres. and Polit. Dir.
Tony Padilla, Ass't to the Nat'l Legislative Director
Kenneth O. Richardson, Nat'l Legislative Director
Counsel or consultant:
The Kamber Group (Donovan McClure)

Transportation Corridor Agencies
Costa Mesa, CA
Counsel or consultant:
James F. McConnell

Transportation Institute
5201 Auth Way, Camp Springs, MD 20746
Telephone: (301) 423-3335
Background: A private non-profit organization dedicated to research and education on a broad range of transportation issues, particularly maritime: oil tankers, foreign and domestic shipping trades, barges and tugboat operations on the Great Lakes and inland waterways.

Represented by:
Herbert Brand, Chairman of the Board
Lawrence H. Evans, Director, Domestic Marine Affairs
James L. Henry, President
Gerard C. Snow, Director of Federal Affairs
Counsel or consultant:
Preston Gates Ellis & Rouvelas Meeds (Jonathan Blank, Emanuel L. Rouvelas)

Transportation Lawyers Ass'n
Topeka, KS
Counsel or consultant:
Kent & O'Connor, Incorp. (Patrick C. O'Connor)

Transportation Reform Alliance
c/o Valis Associates, 1747 Pennsylvania Ave., N.W. #1201, Washington, DC 20036
Telephone: (202) 833-5055
Background: A coalition of rail, air, bus, maritime and surface transportation companies and associations, plus shippers and public interest groups, advocating transportation deregulation, competitiveness and safety. Members include Air Transport Ass'n, Ass'n of American Railroads, American Bus Ass'n, Citizens for a Sound Economy, Nat'l-American Wholesale Grocers' Ass'n, Transportation Brokers Conference of America, Sears Roebuck & Co., Scott Paper Co., American President Lines, Sea-Land Service, Burlington Northern, Norfolk Southern, Greyhound Lines Inc and Nat'l Ass'n of Wholesaler-Distributors.
Counsel or consultant:
Valis Associates (Cheryl E. Hillen, Wayne H. Valis)

Transportation Research Board (of Nat'l Research Council)
2101 Constitution Ave., N.W., Washington, DC 20418
Telephone: (202) 334-2933
Represented by:
Thomas B. Deen, Exec. Director

Transportation Research Forum
1600 Wilson Blvd., Suite 905, Arlington, VA 22209
Telephone: (703) 525-1191
Background: A national organization of professionals in the transportation field, founded in 1960.
Counsel or consultant:
Zuckert, Scoutt and Rasenberger (Rachel B. Trinder)

Transportes Aereos Mercantiles Panamericanos
Miami, FL
Counsel or consultant:
Winthrop, Stimson, Putnam & Roberts (Robert Reed Gray)

Transportes Aeros Nacionales (TAN)
Tegucigalpa, Honduras
Counsel or consultant:
Squire, Sanders and Dempsey (Robert D. Papkin)

Trapp Family Lodge
Stowe, VT
Counsel or consultant:
Dow, Lohnes and Albertson (William B. Ingersoll)

Travel Industry Ass'n of America
1133 21st St., N.W.,, Washington, DC 20036
Telephone: (202) 293-1433
Represented by:
Thomas Berrigan, Director of Communications
Edward R. Book, President

Travel Industry Ass'n of America Political Action Committee
1133 21st St., N.W., Washington, DC 20036
Telephone: (202) 293-1433
Background: Represented by Edward R. Book of the Association.

Travel and Tourism Government Affairs Council
Two Lafayette Center 1133 21st St., N.W., Washington, DC 20036
Telephone: (202) 293-5407
Background: To monitor legislation in the interest of the U.S. Travel and Tourism industry.
Represented by:
Aubrey C. King, Exec. Director
Patrice North-Rudin, Ass't Exec. Director

Travelers Insurance Co.
Hartford, CT
Counsel or consultant:
Baker and Hostetler (Kenneth J. Kies)

ORGANIZATIONS REPRESENTED

Travelers, The
901 15th St., N.W. Suite 520, Washington, DC 20005
Telephone: (202) 789-1380
Represented by:
Roger N. Levy, V. President, Federal Gov't Affairs
Carole T. Roberts, 2nd V. President, Federal Gov't Affairs
Counsel or consultant:
Verner, Liipfert, Bernhard, McPherson and Hand, Chartered (John A. Merrigan, Douglas M. Steenland)
Vinson and Elkins (Ky P. Ewing, Jr.)
I. S. Weissbrodt

Tread Corp.
Roanoke, VA
Counsel or consultant:
Cassidy and Associates, Inc. (William M. Cloherty)

Trenton, New Jersey, City of
Counsel or consultant:
Nat'l Center for Municipal Development (Richard C. Johnson)

Trenton Sales, Inc.
Houston, TX
Counsel or consultant:
Weinberg & Green (Walter G. Talarek)

Tri-City Industrial Development Council
Kennewick, WA
Counsel or consultant:
Charlie McBride Assoc, Inc. (Charlie McBride)
Denny Miller Associates
Preston Gates Ellis & Rouvelas Meeds (Tim L. Peckinpaugh)

Tri-County Metropolitan Transportation District of Oregon
Portland, OR
Counsel or consultant:
Schwabe, Williamson and Wyatt (Frederick P. Hitz)

Tri-Valley Growers of California
San Francisco, CA
Counsel or consultant:
Robinson, Lake, Lerer & Montgomery (James H. Lake)

Triad Development Corp.
Knoxville, TN
Counsel or consultant:
Cashdollar-Jones & Co. (Robert Cashdollar)

Trial Lawyers for Public Justice
2000 P St., N.W., Suite 611, Washington, DC 20036
Telephone: (202) 463-8600
Background: A public interest law firm which brings major damage lawsuits against corporations and the government over health, safety, environmental and other public policy issues.
Represented by:
Arthur Bryant, Exec. Director
Priscilla Budeiri, Staff Attorney
Joy Pritts, Environmental Enforcement Attorney

Triangle Industries
New York, NY
Counsel or consultant:
Nat'l Strategies Inc.

Tribune Broadcasting Co.
1111 19th St., N.W., Suite 1000, Washington, DC 20036
Telephone: (202) 775-7750
Represented by:
Shaun M. Sheehan, V. President, Washington Office
Counsel or consultant:
Dewey, Ballantine, Bushby, Palmer and Wood (John J. Salmon)

TRIDEC/Westinghouse
Counsel or consultant:
Murphy and Demory, Ltd. (Admiral Daniel J. Murphy, USN (Ret.))

Trident Trading Corp.
1911 North Fort Myer Drive, Arlington, VA 22209
Telephone: (703) 528-2002
Counsel or consultant:
The William Chasey Organization (Virginia Chasey)

Trinity Marine Group
Gulfport, MS

Counsel or consultant:
Forster & Associates (Johann R. Forster)

Trinova Corp.
Maumee, OH
Counsel or consultant:
Bettie McCarthy and Assoc. (Bettie S. McCarthy)

Triton Container Co.
San Francisco, CA
Counsel or consultant:
Patton, Boggs and Blow (James B. Christian, Jr.)

Trophy Dealers and Manufacturers Ass'n
Fresno, CA
Counsel or consultant:
Fehrenbacher, Sale, Quinn, and Deese (C. Michael Deese)

Tropical Shipping and Construction Co.
Rivera Beach, FL
Counsel or consultant:
Hoppel, Mayer and Coleman (Paul D. Coleman, Neal M. Mayer)

Tropicana Energy Co.
Irving, TX
Counsel or consultant:
Silverstein and Mullens (William A. Kirk, Jr.)

Tropicana Products Inc.
Bradenton, FL
Counsel or consultant:
Collier, Shannon & Scott (Robin H. Gilbert, Paul C. Rosenthal)

Trout Unlimited
501 Church St., N.E., Vienna, VA 22180
Telephone: (703) 281-1100
Represented by:
Robert L. Herbst, Exec. Director
Pamela McClelland, Resource Director

Truck Mixer Manufacturers Bureau
900 Spring St., Silver Spring, MD 20910
Telephone: (301) 587-1400
Background: Represented by Raymond F. Wisniewski of the Concrete Plant Manufacturers Bureau.

Truck PAC
430 First St., S.E., Washington, DC 20003
Telephone: (202) 544-6245
Background: The political action committee supported by the American Trucking Ass'ns. Gerald J. McKiernan of the American Trucking Ass'ns is contact for the committee.

Truck Renting and Leasing Ass'n
2011 Eye St., N.W., Fifth Floor, Washington, DC 20006
Telephone: (202) 775-4859
Counsel or consultant:
Bregman, Abell & Kay (Stanley I. Bregman)
Newell-Payne Companies, Inc. (Leigh Anne Preston)

Truck Trailer Manufacturers Ass'n
1020 Princess St., Alexandria, VA 22314
Telephone: (703) 549-3010
Represented by:
Richard P. Bowling, President

Trucking Management, Inc.
2233 Wisconsin Ave., N.W. Suite 412, Washington, DC 20007
Telephone: (202) 965-7660
Background: The main collective bargaining arm of the trucking industry.
Represented by:
Arthur H. Bunte, Jr., President

True Oil Co.
Casper, WY
Counsel or consultant:
Groom and Nordberg (Julie M. Rabinowitz)

Trujillo Alto, Puerto Rico, City of
Counsel or consultant:
Jefferson Group, The (Jose Ortiz-Daliot)

Trump Organization, The
New York, NY

Counsel or consultant:
Black, Manafort, Stone and Kelly Public Affairs Co. (Nicholas A. Panuzio)

Trunkline LNG Co.
Houston, TX
Counsel or consultant:
Dyer, Ellis, Joseph & Mills

Trust for Public Land
312 Massachusetts Ave., N.E., Washington, DC 20002
Telephone: (202) 543-7552
Background: Headquartered in San Francisco, California.
Represented by:
Madeline Fishel, Ass't Director of Federal Projects

TRW Inc.
1000 Wilson Blvd., Arlington, VA 22209
Telephone: (703) 276-5000
Represented by:
David J. Anderson, Manager, Federal Relations
John R. Carter, Jr., V. Pres., Space & Defense, Wash. Office
John J. Castellani, V. President, Government Relations
Pat Choate, V. President, Policy Analysis
Brenda J. Gore, Manager, Congressional Relations
Shirley I. Hales, Manager, Constituent Relations
Ernest W. LaBelle, Director, State & Constituent Relations
Laramie F. McNamara, Director, Federal Relations
Kathleen G. Ott, Manager, Government Relations Research
Henry J. Steenstra, Jr., Manager, Congressional Relations
Peter F. Warker, Director, International Affairs
Counsel or consultant:
Verner, Liipfert, Bernhard, McPherson and Hand, Chartered (Lloyd N. Hand)

TU Services
1825 K St., N.W., Suite 303, Washington, DC 20006
Telephone: (202) 822-9745
Represented by:
Don Womack, V. President

Tubos de Acero de Mexico, S.A.
Mexico City, Mexico
Counsel or consultant:
Manchester Trade, Inc. (Stephen L. Lande)
Paul, Hastings, Janofsky and Walker (G. Hamilton Loeb)

Tucson, Arizona, City of
Counsel or consultant:
Bracy Williams & Co. (Terrence L. Bracy, Thomas J. Hennessey, Jr., Susan J. Williams)
Winston and Strawn (Richard Meltzer)

Tufts University
Medford, MA
Counsel or consultant:
Cassidy and Associates, Inc. (Carol F. Casey, Gerald S. J. Cassidy, C. Frank Godfrey, Jr.)

Tulalip Tribes
Marysville, WA
Background: An Indian tribal government.
Counsel or consultant:
Forrest Gerard & Associates (Forrest J. Gerard)

Tuna Canners Ass'n of the Philippines
Manila, Philippines
Counsel or consultant:
Harris & Ellsworth

Tuna Research Foundation
1101 17th St., N.W., Suite 609, Washington, DC 20036
Telephone: (202) 857-0610
Represented by:
Thomas Randi, V. President

Tunisia, Embassy of
1515 Massachusetts Ave., N.W., Washington, DC 20008
Telephone: (202) 862-1850
Counsel or consultant:
Bannerman and Associates, Inc. (M. Graeme Bannerman, Roxanne Perugino)
Marshall, Tenzer, Greenblatt, Fallon and Kaplan (Sylvan M. Marshall)
White & Case

Tuolumne River Expeditions, Inc.
Oakland, CA

ORGANIZATIONS REPRESENTED

Tuolumne River Expeditions, Inc. (Cont'd)
Counsel or consultant:
  Scootch Pankonin

Tupper Lake, New York, Municipality of
Counsel or consultant:
  Duncan, Weinberg, Miller & Pembroke, P.C. (Wallace L. Duncan, Jeffrey C. Genzer)

Turbomeca Engine Corp.
Grand Prairie, TX
Counsel or consultant:
  RBC Associates, Inc. (Keith O. Hartwell)

Turkey, Central Bank of
Ankara, Turkey
Counsel or consultant:
  White & Case

Turkey, Embassy of
1606 23rd St., N.W., Washington, DC 20008
Telephone: (202) 387-3200
Counsel or consultant:
  Hill and Knowlton Public Affairs Worldwide (Gary Hymel, Donald F. Massey, Charles R. Pucie, Jr.)
  Internat'l Advisers, Inc. (Lydia A. Borland, Douglas J. Feith, Engin Holmstrom, Michael J. McNamara)

Turkey, Government of
Ankara, Turkey
Counsel or consultant:
  Hill and Knowlton Public Affairs Worldwide (Robert Keith Gray, Gary Hymel, Frank Mankiewicz, Donald F. Massey, Charles R. Pucie, Jr.)
  McAuliffe, Kelly, Raffaelli & Siemens (John D. Raffaelli)
  White & Case (Carolyn B. Lamm, John J. McAvoy)

Turkish-American Political Action Committee
7921 Woodruff Court, Suite 200, Springfield, VA 22151
Telephone: (703) 321-6175
Represented by:
  Asil Gezen, President

Turkish Republic of Northern Cyprus
1667 K St., N.W., Suite 690, Washington, DC 20006
Telephone: (202) 887-6198
Represented by:
  Dr. Bulent Aliriza, Representative

Turner Broadcasting System, Inc.
111 Massachusetts Ave., N.W. Third Floor, Washington, DC 20001
Telephone: (202) 898-7670
Represented by:
  Peggy K. Binzel, Director, Government Affairs
  Bertram W. Carp, V. President, Government Affairs
  Lisa Dallos, Director, Public Relations
Counsel or consultant:
  Ginn, Edington, Moore and Wade
  Goldberg & Spector
  Mintz, Levin, Cohn, Ferris, Glovsky and Popeo, P.C.
  Williams and Jensen, P.C. (J. Steven Hart)

Turner Corp., The
New York, NY
Counsel or consultant:
  Rogers and Wells (William Morris)

Tuscaloosa Steel Corp.
Tuscaloosa, AL
Counsel or consultant:
  Bond Donatelli Inc. (Frank Donatelli)

Tuteur Associates, Inc.
Houston, TX
Counsel or consultant:
  Jack McDonald Co. (Jack McDonald, Myron G. Sandifer, III)

Twentieth Century Fox
Los Angeles, CA
Counsel or consultant:
  Cassidy and Associates, Inc. (Thomas M. Gannon)

Typeface Design Coalition
Wilmington, MA
Counsel or consultant:
  Timothy X. Moore and Co. (Timothy X. Moore)
  Swidler & Berlin, Chartered

Typographers Internat'l Ass'n
2262 Hall Place, N.W. Suite 101, Washington, DC 20007

Telephone: (202) 965-3400
Background: An internat'l trade association of over 500 commercial typographers.
Represented by:
  Charles W. Mulliken, Exec. Director

Tyson Foods, Inc.
Springdale, AR
Counsel or consultant:
  Cashdollar-Jones & Co. (Robert Cashdollar)
  Jack L. Williams

T2 Medical
Background: Provides intravenous devices for home use.
Counsel or consultant:
  Dyer, Ellis, Joseph & Mills

U.S. Apparel Industry Council
Miami, FL
Counsel or consultant:
  Sandler, Travis & Rosenberg. P.A. (Thomas G. Travis)

U.S. Banknote Corp.
New York, NY
Counsel or consultant:
  KCI Inc. (Bette B. Anderson)

U.S. Canola Ass'n
1150 Connecticut Ave., N.W. Suite 507, Washington, DC 20036
Telephone: (202) 331-4331
Counsel or consultant:
  Wallace & Edwards (Donald L. Wallace, Jr.)

U.S. Central, Inc.
Allentown, PA
Counsel or consultant:
  Birch, Horton, Bittner and Cherot (Joseph M. Chomski)

U.S.-China Business Council
1818 N St., N.W., Suite 500, Washington, DC 20036
Telephone: (202) 429-0340
Background: Established in May, 1973. A private not-for-profit organization of 250 member companies established, with the encouragement of the U.S. and Chinese governments, to assist American companies in doing business with China.
Represented by:
  David L. Denny, Director, Research
  Kathleen Jyron, Manager, Business Information Center
  Roger W. Sullivan, President

U.S. Committee for UNICEF
110 Maryland Ave., N.E. Suite 304, Washington, DC 20002
Telephone: (202) 547-7946
Represented by:
  Alejandro J. Palacios, Director, Congressional Relations

U.S. Council for Energy Awareness
1776 Eye St., N. W. Suite 400, Washington, DC 20006
Telephone: (202) 293-0770
Background: A non-profit educational organization established in 1982, supported by investor-owned public utilities, manufacturers, labor unions and financial institutions, concentrating on the support of nuclear power as an energy source.
Represented by:
  Harold B. Finger, President and Chief Exec. Officer
  Carl A. Goldstein, V. President, Public and Media Relations
  Bill Harris, Senior V. President

U.S. Ecology
Louisville, KY
Counsel or consultant:
  Conner and Wetterhahn, P.C. (Robert M. Rader, Mark J. Wetterhahn)

U.S. English
818 Connecticut Ave., N.W. Suite 200, Washington, DC 20006
Telephone: (202) 833-0100
Background: A nonprofit organization promoting a Constitutional amendment to establish English as the official language of the United States. Established in 1983.

Represented by:
  Kathryn Bricker, Exec. Director
  Hydi Miller, Senior Legislative Associate
  Yale Newman, Director, Public Affairs
  Michael Rolnick, Legislative Associate
  Stephen C. Shaffer, Director, Government Relations
  Cameron Whitman, Field Director
Counsel or consultant:
  Holt, Miller & Associates (Harris N. Miller)

U.S. Escrow
Downey, CA
Counsel or consultant:
  E. Del Smith, Inc. (E. Del Smith)

U.S. Express, Inc.
Ft. Lauderdale, FL
Counsel or consultant:
  Allan W. Markham

U.S. Federation of Small Businesses, Inc.
Albany, NY
Counsel or consultant:
  Ottosen and Associates (Karl J. Ottosen, Carla L. Saunders)

U.S. Federation of Small Businesses PAC
208 G St., N.E., Washington, DC 20002
Telephone: (202) 547-0555
Counsel or consultant:
  Ottosen and Associates (Carla L. Saunders)

U.S. Feed Grains Council
1400 K St., N.W., Suite 1200, Washington, DC 20005
Telephone: (202) 789-0789
Background: A private, non-profit organization that develops and expands markets for U.S. produced feed garins and co-products through a network of 12 international offices.
Represented by:
  Darwin E. Stolte, President

U.S. Healthcare, Inc.
Paramus, NJ
Counsel or consultant:
  Cassidy and Associates, Inc. (C. Frank Godfrey, Jr.)

U.S. Hispanic Chamber of Commerce
111 Massachusetts Ave., N.W., Suite 200, Washington, DC 20001
Telephone: (202) 789-2717
Represented by:
  Veronica Gouabault, Eastern Regional Manager

U.S. Home Corp.
Houston, TX
Counsel or consultant:
  Dow, Lohnes and Albertson (William B. Ingersoll)

U.S. JVC Corp.
Elmwood Park, NY
Counsel or consultant:
  Patton, Boggs and Blow

U.S. Public Interest Research Group
215 Pennsylvania Ave., S.E., Washington, DC 20003
Telephone: (202) 546-9707
Background: The national lobbying office for state Public Interest Research Groups - non-profit, non-partisan consumer and environmental advocacy organizations. Funded by citizen contributions.
Represented by:
  Maria Brousse, Assistant Field Director
  David Hamilton, Field Director
  Carolyn Hartmann, Staff Attorney
  Richard Hind, Environmental Program Director
  Gene Karpinski, Exec. Director
  Bill Magavern, Staff Attorney
  Edmund Mierzwinski, Consumer Lobbyist
  Zoe Schneider, Environmental Lobbyist
  Lucinda Sikes, Staff Attorney

U.S. Rice Producers' Legislative Group
Houston, TX
Counsel or consultant:
  Bishop, Cook, Purcell & Reynolds (Robert M. Bor)

U.S. Surgical Corp.
Norwalk, CT
Counsel or consultant:
  Olsson, Frank and Weeda, P.C. (John Bode)

The listings in this directory are available as *Mailing Labels*. See last page.

ORGANIZATIONS REPRESENTED

U.S. Trademark Ass'n
New York, NY
Counsel or consultant:
  Marlowe and Co.

U.S. Trust Co.
New York, NY
Counsel or consultant:
  Dow, Lohnes and Albertson (David F. Bantleon, Joseph F. Kelly, Jr.)

U.S. Wheat Associates, Inc.
1620 Eye St., N.W., Suite 801, Washington, DC 20006
Telephone: (202) 463-0999
Background: The foreign market development organization of the U.S. wheat industry. Headquartered in Washington, with 14 overseas offices in Asia, Africa, Europe and Central and South America. Also has West Coast Office in Portland, OR.
Represented by:
  Winston L. Wilson, President

U-T Offshore System
Houston, TX
Counsel or consultant:
  Gallagher, Boland, Meiburger and Brosnan

UBA, Inc.
Suite 603, 600 Maryland Ave., S.W., Washington, DC 20024
Telephone: (202) 484-3344
Background: Works on behalf of employers to control the costs of unemployment and workers' compensation programs. Seeks to limit federal government involvement in such programs, preferring state systems as a means of ensuring reasonable benefits at less cost.
Represented by:
  J. Eldred Hill, Jr., President
  Charles B. Little, Exec. Assistant

UI Companies
10 Fourth St., S.E., Washington, DC 20003
Telephone: (202) 544-4522
Represented by:
  Richard H. Bornemann, V. President, Gov'tl Afrs. & Corp. Comm.
Counsel or consultant:
  Akin, Gump, Strauss, Hauer and Feld
  Charlie McBride Assoc, Inc. (Charlie McBride)

Ukrainian Nat'l Ass'n
400 First St., N.W. Suite 710, Washington, DC 20001
Telephone: (202) 347-8629
Background: Over 70,000 members in the USA and Canada.
Represented by:
  Eugene M. Iwanciw, Director, Washington Office
  John A. Kun, Assistant Director, Washington Office

ULLILPAC - Ullilco Inc. Political Action Committee
111 Massachusetts Ave., N.W., Washington, DC 20001
Telephone: (202) 682-6689
Represented by:
  William L. Cross, Treasurer

Ultrasystems Development Corp.
12500 Fair Lakes Circle, Fairfax, VA 22033
Telephone: (703) 968-9317
Counsel or consultant:
  U.S. Strategies Corp. (K. Michael Matthews)

UNC Incorporated
175 Admiral Cochrane Drive, Annapolis, MD 21401-7333
Telephone: (301) 266-7333
Represented by:
  Marc R. Jartman, V. Pres., Gov't Affairs and Marketing
Counsel or consultant:
  Verner, Liipfert, Bernhard, McPherson and Hand, Chartered (Berl Bernhard, John A. Merrigan)

Undersea and Hyperbaric Medical Soc.
9650 Rockville Pike, Bethesda, MD 20814
Telephone: (301) 571-1818
Represented by:
  Dr. Leon J. Greenbaum, Exec. Director

Undersea Tours Inc.
Marina del Rey, CA
Counsel or consultant:
  Lachelli, Waller and Associates

Underwriters Laboratories Inc.
818 18th St., N.W., Washington, DC 20006
Telephone: (202) 296-7840
Represented by:
  Joe Bhatia, V. President, Governmental Affairs

Uniao Nacional Para Independencia Total de Angola (UNITA)
One Thomas Circle, N.W., Washington, DC 20005
Telephone: (202) 775-0958
Background: The Angolan insurgent movement headed by Jonas Savimbi.
Counsel or consultant:
  Black, Manafort, Stone and Kelly Public Affairs Co. (Paul J. Manafort)
  TKC Internat'l, Inc.

Uniden Corp. of America
Indianapolis, IN
Counsel or consultant:
  Baker and Hostetler

Unilever United States, Inc.
816 Connecticut Ave., N.W. 7th Floor, Washington, DC 20006
Telephone: (202) 393-2839
Represented by:
  A. Allan Noe, Director, Washington Affairs
Counsel or consultant:
  APCO Associates (Margery Kraus)

Unimar Internat'l
Seattle, WA
Counsel or consultant:
  Aylward & Finchem

Union Camp Corp.
2021 L St., N.W., Suite 320, Washington, DC 20036-4909
Telephone: (202) 785-0320
Represented by:
  John C. Whitaker, V. President, Public Affairs

Union Carbide Corp.
1100 15th St., N.W., Suite 1200, Washington, DC 20005
Telephone: (202) 872-8555
Represented by:
  Thomas D. Finnigan, Assistant Director of Federal Affairs
  Jeremiah J. Kenney, Jr., Director of Federal Affairs
  Peter Molinaro, Washington Representative

Union de Empresas y Entidades Siderugicas
Madrid, Spain
Counsel or consultant:
  George V. Egge, Jr.

Union Electric Co.
St. Louis, MO
Counsel or consultant:
  McCarthy, Sweeney and Harkaway, P.C.
  Reid & Priest
  Shaw, Pittman, Potts and Trowbridge (Thomas A. Baxter, Gerald Charnoff)

Union Industrial de Argentina
Buenos Aires, Argentine
Counsel or consultant:
  TKC Internat'l, Inc.

Union Labor Life Insurance Co.
111 Massachusetts Ave., N.W., Washington, DC 20001
Telephone: (202) 682-0900
Represented by:
  Joseph Carabillo, Counsel
  Doyle Niemann, Director

Union Mechling Corp.
Pittsburgh, PA
Counsel or consultant:
  Morgan, Lewis and Bockius

Union of American Hebrew Congregations
2027 Massachusetts Ave., N.W., Washington, DC 20036
Telephone: (202) 387-2800
Represented by:
  Rabbi David Saperstein, Director, Religious Action Center
  Rabbi Richard Sternberger, Director, Mid-Atlantic Council

Union of Concerned Scientists
1616 P St., N.W., Suite 310, Washington, DC 20036
Telephone: (202) 332-0900
Background: Promotes arms control, strategic arms limitation talks, balanced energy policies and reduced reliance on nuclear power.
Represented by:
  Deborah Gordon, Energy Analyst
  Kevin T. Knobloch, Legis. Dir., Arms Control & Nat'l Secur.
  Alden Meyer, Director, Climate Change & Energy Prgm.
  Sean Meyer, Coordinator, Arms Cntrl & Nat'l Security
  Bob Pollard, Nuclear Safety Engineer
  Christine Riddiough, Field Coordntr, Climate Chng/Energy Prgm

Union of Councils for Soviet Jews
1819 H St., N.W., Suite 230, Washington, DC 20006
Telephone: (202) 775-9770
Counsel or consultant:
  Powell, Goldstein, Frazer and Murphy (Stuart E. Eizenstat)

Union Pacific Corp.
555 13th St., N.W., Suite 450 West Columbia Square, Washington, DC 20004
Telephone: (202) 662-0100
Represented by:
  Charles Hollister Cantus, Legislative Ass't
  Jeffrey A. Fritzlen, Director of Washington Affairs-Resources
  Kip Hawley, V. President, External Relations
  Mark S. Knouse, Dir., Washington Affairs - Environment
  Mary E. McAuliffe, Dir., Wash. Affairs - Transportat. & Tax
  Julie Brink Straus, Dir., Washington Affairs - Political

Union Pacific Fund for Effective Government
555 13th St., N.W. Suite 450 West Columbia Square, Washington, DC 20004
Telephone: (202) 662-0100
Background: Also represented by Julie Brink Straus, Director, Political Affairs of the Union Pacific Corp.
Represented by:
  Marianne Farnsworth, Administrator

Union Pacific Resources Co.
Ft. Worth, TX
Counsel or consultant:
  Camp, Barsh, Bates and Tate (Harry E. Barsh, Jr.)
  Kogovsek & Associates, Inc.

Union Tank Car Co.
Chicago, IL
Counsel or consultant:
  Gilbert A. Robinson, Inc. (Gilbert A. Robinson)

Union Texas Petroleum
Houston, TX
Counsel or consultant:
  Groom and Nordberg (Robert B. Harding, Carl A. Nordberg, Jr.)

Uniroyal Chemical Co., Inc.
Middlebury, CT
Counsel or consultant:
  Howrey and Simon (John DeQ. Briggs, III)
  Internat'l Business-Government Counsellors, Inc. (James B. Clawson)

Unisys Corp.
2001 L St., N.W., Suite 1000, Washington, DC 20036
Telephone: (202) 293-7720
Background: Provides advanced computer based information systems, networks and services to domestic and international commercial and government markets.
Represented by:
  John E. Arnold, Jay, Dir., Gov't Affrs - Defense Systems
  John S. Autry, V. President, Government Relations
  Richard H. Bierly, V. Pres., Gov't Affrs & Internat'l Trade
  Donna Siss Gleason, Director, Government Affairs
  Elisabeth Hanlin, Dir., Gov't Affairs - State and Federal
  John P. McNicholas, Dir, Gov't Affairs, Gov't Systems Divsn
  Richard J. Murphy, Dir., Legis. Affrs. - Public Sector Syst
Counsel or consultant:
  Robert B. Carleson & Assoc.
  Wilmer, Cutler and Pickering (William J. Wilkins)

ORGANIZATIONS REPRESENTED

Unisys Employees Political Action Committee
2001 L St., N.W., Suite 1000, Washington, DC 20036
Telephone: (202) 293-7720
Background: Contact is John S. Autry, Secretary-Treasurer, of Unisys Corp.

Unitarian Universalist Ass'n of Congregations
100 Maryland Ave., N.E. Box #68, Washington, DC 20002
Telephone: (202) 547-0254
Represented by:
Robert Z. Alpern, Director, Washington Office

United Airlines
1707 L St., N.W., Suite 300, Washington, DC 20036
Telephone: (703) 892-7410
Represented by:
George J. Aste, V. Pres., Gov't and Internat'l Affairs
John M. Philp, Regional Director, Public Affairs
Robert E. Williams, Director, Legislative Affairs
Counsel or consultant:
Kilpatrick & Cody (Elliott H. Levitas, C. Randall Nuckolls)
Manatt, Phelps, Rothenberg & Phillips (Robert J. Kabel)

United Airlines - EXOCT
Chicago, IL
Counsel or consultant:
Lee, Toomey & Kent

United Ass'n of Journeymen & Apprentices of the Plumbing & Pipe Fitting Industry of the US & Canada
901 Massachusetts Ave., N.W., Washington, DC 20001
Telephone: (202) 628-5823
Represented by:
Joe A. Adam, Director, Dept. of Safety and Health
Marvin J. Boede, General President
Michael A. Collins, Legislative Representative
Joseph Cribben, Research and Legislation
Charles J. Habig, Secretary-Treasurer
M. Eddie Moore, Assistant General President

United Ass'n of Steamfitters, Local 476
Cranston, RI
Counsel or consultant:
St. Germain, Rodio & Ursillo, Ltd. (Fernand J. St. Germain)

United Automobile, Aerospace and Agricultural Implement Workers of America (UAW)
1757 N St., N.W., Washington, DC 20036
Telephone: (202) 828-8500
Represented by:
Steve Beckman, International Economist
Alan V. Reuther, Associate General Counsel
Don Stillman, Dir. of Gov't and Internat'l Affairs
Richard D. Warden, Legislative Director
Counsel or consultant:
Gallagher-Widmeyer Group Inc., The (Scott D. Widmeyer)

United Brands Co.
1331 Pennsylvania Ave., N.W. Suite 1100, Washington, DC 20004
Telephone: (202) 879-2410
Represented by:
Robert F. Corrigan, Washington Representative
Counsel or consultant:
Cadwalader, Wickersham & Taft (Donald C. Alexander)

United Brotherhood of Carpenters and Joiners of America
101 Constitution Ave., N.W., Washington, DC 20001
Telephone: (202) 546-6206
Represented by:
Ed Durkin, Coordinator of Special Projects
Joseph L. Durst, Dir., Occupational Safety and Health
Robin Gerber, Assoc. Dir., Political & Legis. Affairs
Allynn Howe, Legislative Representative
Kathy L. Krieger, General Counsel
Sigurd Lucassen, General President
Wayne Pierce, Dir. of Legis. and Gen. Treas.
R. Denny Scott, Collective Bargaining Specialist

United Bus Owners of America
1300 L St., N.W. Suite 1050, Washington, DC 20005
Telephone: (202) 484-5623
Background: A trade association established in 1971 representing over 2,000 bus companies in the United States.

Counsel or consultant:
Wayne Smith Co., Inc. (Wayne J. Smith)

United Cable Television
Denver, CO
Counsel or consultant:
Griffin, Johnson & Associates

United California Savings Bank
Anaheim, CA
Counsel or consultant:
Dave Evans Associates (David W. Evans)

United Cerebral Palsy Ass'ns
1522 K St., N.W., Suite 1112, Washington, DC 20005
Telephone: (202) 842-1266
Background: Seeks to improve the quality of life for persons with cerebral palsy and related disabilities and their families.
Represented by:
Allen I. Bergman, Deputy Director, Governmental Activities
Christopher Button, Senior Policy Assoc., Gov't'l Activities
Michael Morris, Director, Governmental Activities Office
Robert Williams, Policy Assoc., Governmental Activities

United Church of Christ Office for Church in Society
110 Maryland Ave., N.E. Suite 504, Washington, DC 20002
Telephone: (202) 543-1517
Represented by:
Rev. Jay Lintner, Director

United Cities Gas Co.
Brentwood, TN
Counsel or consultant:
Crowell and Moring (Harold J. Heltzer)

United Coconut Ass'n of the Philippines
Manila, Philippines
Counsel or consultant:
Reichler Appelbaum and Wippman (Judith C. Appelbaum)

United Companies Life Insurance Co.
Baton Rouge, LA
Counsel or consultant:
Theodore L. Jones

United Company, The
Bristol, VA
Counsel or consultant:
R. Duffy Wall and Associates (R. Duffy Wall)

United Egg Ass'n
Decatur, GA
Background: Trade association of manufacturers of egg products (liquid, dry and frozen) for use in further processed products.
Counsel or consultant:
McLeod & Pires (Michael R. McLeod, Christine Nelson)

United Egg Producers
2501 M St., N.W., Suite 400, Washington, DC 20037
Telephone: (202) 861-1234
Background: The largest federation of regional cooperatives in the egg industry. Headquartered in Decatur, Georgia.
Counsel or consultant:
McLeod & Pires (Michael R. McLeod, Christine Nelson)

United Electrical, Radio and Machine Workers of America
1411 K St., N.W., Suite 1005, Washington, DC 20005
Telephone: (202) 737-3072
Represented by:
Lance Compa, Washington Counsel
Robert Kingsley, Political Director

United Financial Group
Houston, TX
Counsel or consultant:
Wunder, Ryan, Cannon & Thelen (Bernard J. Wunder)

United Fishermen of Alaska
Juneau, AK
Counsel or consultant:
C. Deming Cowles, IV

United Food and Commercial Workers Internat'l Union
1775 K St., N.W., Washington, DC 20006
Telephone: (202) 223-3111
Represented by:
Willie L. Baker, Jr., Director, Public Affairs
Deborah Berkowitz, Director, Safety and Health
David F. Claxton, Director, Political Affairs
Douglas Couttee, Internat'l V. President, Civil Rights
Segundo Mercado-Llorens, Director, Government Affairs
Janice E. Pieper, Ass't Director, Gov't Affairs
Pat Scarcelli, Int'l V. President, Dir. Women's Affairs
William H. Wynn, Internat'l President
Counsel or consultant:
Foreman & Heidepriem (Carol Tucker Foreman)
The Kamber Group (Jeffrey M. Sandman)
Michael L. Tiner & Associates (Michael L. Tiner)

United Foods, Inc.
Bells, TN
Counsel or consultant:
Cashdollar-Jones & Co. (Robert Cashdollar, Ed Jones)

United Fresh Fruit and Vegetable Ass'n
722 North Washington St., Alexandria, VA 22030
Telephone: (703) 836-3410
Represented by:
Jodean R. Bens, Special Asst., Gov't Relations
Claudia Fuquay, Director, Congressional Relations
John M. McClung, V. President, Government Relations
Counsel or consultant:
Holland and Knight (Dickson R. Loos)

United Fresh Fruit and Vegetable Ass'n Political Action Committee (UNIPAC)
722 North Washington St., Alexandria, VA 22314
Telephone: (703) 836-3410
Background: Treasurer and contact is John McClung of the United Fresh Fruit and Vegetable Ass'n.

United Gerer Institutions
Brooklyn, NY
Counsel or consultant:
Bruce Ray & Company (Bruce A. Ray)

United HealthCare Corp.
Minneapolis, MN
Counsel or consultant:
Stanton & Associates (James V. Stanton)

United Hellenic American Congress
Chicago, IL
Counsel or consultant:
Manatos & Manatos, Inc. (Andrew E. Manatos, Kimberley A. Matthews)

United Hospital Fund of New York
New York, NY
Counsel or consultant:
FMR Group Inc., The (Joseph M. Rees)

United Jewish Appeal Federation of Greater Washington
6101 Montrose Rd., Rockville, MD 20852
Telephone: (301) 230-7200
Represented by:
Ted B. Farber, Exec. V. President
Lisa Moore, Director, Government Division
Nancy Raskin, Director, Professions Division

United Kingdom Defence Export Services Organization
London, England
Background: Affiliated with the British Embassy.
Counsel or consultant:
Leva, Hawes, Mason and Martin (Marx Leva, Robert Martin)

United Kingdom Express
Great Britain
Counsel or consultant:
Denning and Wohlstetter (Joseph F. Mullins, Jr.)

United Kingdom, Ministry of Defence of the
London, England
Counsel or consultant:
Lipsen Whitten & Diamond

United Kingdom of Great Britain and Northern Ireland, Government of the
London, England

The listings in this directory are available as *Mailing Labels*. See last page.

Counsel or consultant:
Morgan, Lewis and Bockius (Michael S. Kelly)

United Methodist Church Board of Church and Society
100 Maryland Ave., N.E. Suite 300, Washington, DC 20002
Telephone: (202) 488-5600
Represented by:
Thom White Wolf Fassett, General Secretary

United Methodist Church Board of Global Ministries, Women's Div.
100 Maryland Ave., N.E., Room 501, Washington, DC 20002
Telephone: (202) 488-5660
Represented by:
Joyce V. Hamlin, Exec. Secretary for Public Policy
Mary Kercherval Short, Secretary for Women's Concerns

United Mine Workers of America
900 15th St., N.W., Washington, DC 20005
Telephone: (202) 842-7280
Represented by:
Michael W. Buckner, Research Director
Michael Dinnerstein, Staff Attorney
Marc P. Gabor, Nat'l Legislative Representative
Mary Lu Jordan, Attorney
William H. Samuel, Legislative Director
Robert Stropp, Jr., General Counsel
Richard L. Trumka, President
Counsel or consultant:
Yablonski, Both & Edelman (Daniel B. Edelman)

United Nations Ass'n of the U.S.A.
1010 Vermont Ave., N.W., Suite 904, Washington, DC 20005
Telephone: (202) 347-5004
Represented by:
Steven A. Dimoff, Director, Washington Office

United Nations Conference on Trade and Development
Geneva, Switzerland
Counsel or consultant:
C & M Internat'l L.P. (Doral S. Cooper)

United Negro College Fund
1025 Vermont Ave., N.W. Suite 810, Washington, DC 20005
Telephone: (202) 785-8623
Represented by:
Denele Leon, Area Development Director
Michelle D. Stent, V. President of Government Affairs
Counsel or consultant:
Clohan & Dean (William A. Blakey)

United Network of Organ Sharing
Richmond, VA
Counsel or consultant:
Fleishman-Hillard, Inc (W. Douglas Campbell, Paul Johnson, Elizabeth C. McLean)

United Palestinian Appeal
2100 M St., N.W., Suite 409, Washington, DC 20037
Telephone: (202) 659-5007
Background: A non-political, tax-exempt charity dedicated to helping alleviate the suffering of the Palestinian people though health services, education, community development and child sponsorship.
Represented by:
Tariq Abu-Jaber, Exec. Director

United Paperworkers Internat'l Union
815 16th St., N.W. Suite 701, Washington, DC 20006
Telephone: (202) 783-5238
Represented by:
George O'Bea, Jr., Vice President

United Paperworkers Internat'l Union Political Education Program
815 16th St., N.W. Suite 701, Washington, DC 20006
Telephone: (202) 783-5238
Background: George O'Bea, Jr., Vice President of the Union, serves as contact.

United Parcel Service
316 Pennsylvania Ave., S.E. Suite 304, Washington, DC 20003
Telephone: (202) 675-4220

Represented by:
Siro DeGasperis, V. President
Rayne G. Poussard, Manager, Public Affairs
James A. Rogers, V. President
Douglas T. Smalls, V. President
Arnold F. Wellman, Manager, Public Affairs
Counsel or consultant:
Bonner & Associates
Daniel J. Edelman, Inc. (Leslie Dach)
Wiley, Rein & Fielding (Paul C. Smith)

United Press Internat'l
1400 Eye St., N.W., Washington, DC 20005
Telephone: (202) 898-8000
Represented by:
Milton F. Capps, Senior V. President, Corporate Affairs
Counsel or consultant:
John Adams Associates (Gene P. Mater)

United Refining Co.
Warren, PA
Counsel or consultant:
Manatos & Manatos, Inc. (Andrew E. Manatos, Kimberley A. Matthews)

United Savings of America
Chicago, IL
Counsel or consultant:
Foley & Lardner (James N. Bierman)

United Savings of Texas, FSB
Houston, TX
Counsel or consultant:
Vinson and Elkins (Cathy A. Lewis)

United Shareholders Ass'n
1667 K St., N.W., Suite 770, Washington, DC 20006
Telephone: (202) 393-4600
Background: An advocacy organization formed by Mesa Ltd. Partnership's T. Boone Pickens to represent the interests of individual shareholders against corporate 'management'.
Represented by:
Ralph V. Withworth, Director
Counsel or consultant:
The Laxalt Corp. (Michelle D. Laxalt)

United Shipowners of America
1627 K St., N.W., Suite 1200, Washington, DC 20006
Telephone: (202) 466-5388
Background: Established in 1978 by eight U.S. liner companies, previous members of the Liner Council of the American Institute of Merchant Shipping, to promote a U.S. Merchant Marine owned, operated, built and manned by U.S. citizens.
Represented by:
Mark D. Aspinwall, Government Affairs Representative
Albert E. May, Exec. Vice President
William P. Verdon, President

United Ski Industries Ass'n
8377-B Greensboro Drive, McLean, VA 22102
Telephone: (703) 556-9020
Represented by:
David Ingemie, President

United South and Eastern Tribes
Nashville, TN
Counsel or consultant:
Karl A. Funke and Associates (Karl A. Funke)

United Spanish War Veterans
Box 1915, Washington, DC 20013
Telephone: (202) 347-1898
Represented by:
Beulah M. Cope, Adjutant General

United Sport Fishermen
One Thomas Circle, Washington, DC 20005
Telephone: (202) 293-3600
Counsel or consultant:
Bogle and Gates (Robert G. Hayes)

United States Army Warrant Officers Ass'n
Box 2040, Reston, VA 22090
Telephone: (703) 620-3986
Represented by:
Don Hess, Exec. V. President
David P. Welsh, President

United States Ass'n of Importers of Textile and Apparel(USITA)
New York, NY
Counsel or consultant:
Mudge Rose Guthrie Alexander and Ferdon (Martin J. Lewin)

United States Beet Sugar Ass'n
1156 15th St., N.W., Washington, DC 20005
Telephone: (202) 296-4820
Represented by:
David C. Carter, President
James W. Johnson, Jr., Director, Public Affairs
Van R. Olsen, V. President
Counsel or consultant:
Ablondi and Foster, P.C. (F. David Foster)
Howrey and Simon (John F. Bruce)

United States Beet Sugar Ass'n Political Action Committee
1156 15th St., N.W., Washington, DC 20005
Telephone: (202) 296-4820
Background: Represented by Van R. Olsen of the Ass'n.

United States Borax and Chemical Corp.
Los Angeles, CA
Counsel or consultant:
Jack Ferguson Associates

United States Business and Industrial Council
220 Nat'l Press Building, Washington, DC 20045
Telephone: (202) 662-8744
Background: Consists of 1500 conservative business leaders. Priority issues are economic security, a national interest trade policy, deficit reduction through non-defense spending restraint, reform and opposition to many labor union legislative initiatives.
Represented by:
John P. Cregan, V. President
Anthony Harrigan, President
Kirk McAlexander, Exec. V. President

United States Cane Sugar Refiners' Ass'n
1001 Connecticut Ave., N.W., Suite 735, Washington, DC 20036
Telephone: (202) 331-1458
Represented by:
Nicholas Kominus, President
Helen P. Lowenstein, V. President
Counsel or consultant:
Ginn, Edington, Moore and Wade

United States Catholic Conference
3200 4th St., N.E., Washington, DC 20017
Telephone: (202) 541-3000
Represented by:
G. Patrick Canan, Assistant Director, Gov't Liaison
John Carr, Sec'y, Social Development & World Peace
Mark E. Chopko, General Counsel
Richard Daw, Director, Dept. of Communications
Rev. Msgr. Nicholas DiMarzio, Exec. Dir., Migration & Refugee Svcs.
Rev. Kenneth J. Doyle, Director, Office of Media Affairs
Richard E. Duffy, Rep. for Fed. Assistance, Dept. of Educ.
Mark Gallagher, Assistant Director, Gov't Liaison
Deidre Halloran, Associate General Counsel
Rev. J. Bryan Hehir, Consultant
Michael Hill, Assistant Director, Gov't Liaison
Rev. Robert N. Lynch, General Secretary
Frank Monahan, Director of Government Liaison
Counsel or consultant:
Hughes Hubbard and Reed

United States Catholic Conference/Secretariat for Hispanic Affairs
3211 Fourth St., N.E., Washington, DC 20017
Telephone: (202) 541-3150
Background: Established 1948 to represent the interests of Catholic Hispanics.
Represented by:
Pablo Sedillo, Jr., Exec. Director

United States Coast Guard Chief Petty Officers Ass'n
5520 G Hempstead Way, Springfield, VA 22151
Telephone: (703) 941-0395
Represented by:
C. R. Castor, Nat'l Exec. Secretary

ORGANIZATIONS REPRESENTED

United States Committee for Refugees
1025 Vermont Ave., N.W. Suite 920, Washington, DC 20005
Telephone: (202) 347-3507
Background: A public information and advocacy program of the American Council for Nationalities Service. Established in 1958; encourages the American public to participate actively in efforts to assist the world's refugees.
Represented by:
Court Robinson, Policy Analyst
Roger Winter, Director

United States Conference of City Human Services Officials
1620 Eye St., N.W., Suite 400, Washington, DC 20006
Telephone: (202) 293-7330
Background:
Represented by:
Lilia M. Reyes, Assistant Exec. Director
Laura DeKoven Waxman, Deputy Exec. Director

United States Conference of Local Health Officers
1620 Eye St., N.W., Washington, DC 20006
Telephone: (202) 293-7330
Background: Affiliated with the United States Conference of Mayors. Exec. Director is J. Thomas Cochran of the United States Conference of Mayors.
Represented by:
Richard D. Johnson, Deputy Exec. Director

United States Conference of Mayors
1620 Eye St., N.W., Washington, DC 20006
Telephone: (202) 293-7330
Background: A non-partisan nat'l organization of city governments established in 1933 as a nat'l forum through which the country's larger cities express their concerns and work to meet the needs of urban America. Members are mayors of cities with populations over 30,000.
Represented by:
Michael W. Brown, Director of Public Affairs
J. Thomas Cochran, Exec. Director
Richard Johnson, Assistant Exec. Director
Eugene Lowe, Assistant Exec. Director
Lance R. Simmens, Assistant Exec. Director, Legislation
Counsel or consultant:
Peyser Associates, Inc.

United States Council for Internat'l Business
1015 15th St., N.W. Suite 1200, Washington, DC 20005
Telephone: (202) 371-1316
Background: Established in 1945 and based in New York City, the Council represents the interests and expresses the positions of U.S. business on a broad range of international trade, finance and investment related issues. Advocates advantages of private enterprise and a free market economy. Members are corporations, associations and law and consulting firms interested in international trade. Represents U.S. business in Washington; and, as the organization that consults with the major intergovernmental bodies influencing international business, in the Business and Industry Advisory Committee to the OECD, in the ILO as the U.S. member of the International Organization of Employers, and as a member of the International Chamber of Commerce, it consults with various U.N. agencies.
Represented by:
Joseph G. Gavin, III, Associate Washington Representative
Robert J. Morris, Senior V. President, Washington

United States Cruises, Inc.
Seattle, WA
Counsel or consultant:
Preston Gates Ellis & Rouvelas Meeds (John L. Bloom, William N. Myhre)

United States Defense Committee
3238 Wynford Drive, Fairfax, VA 22031
Telephone: (703) 914-2010
Represented by:
Mrs. Libby Merrick, Secretary to the President
M. Louise Tate, Secretary-Treasurer
Henry L. Walther, President

United States Energy Ass'n
1620 Eye St., N.W., Suite 615, Washington, DC 20006
Telephone: (202) 331-0415
Background: Seeks to develop and promote sound, objective policy positions on energy issues, drawing on the views of all sectors of the energy community and presenting findings and conclusions to the federal government, the media and the public.
Represented by:
Barry K. Worthington, Exec. Director

United States Hang Gliding Ass'n
1763 R St., N.W., Washington, DC 20009
Telephone: (202) 265-8720
Background: Represented by Everett W. Langworthy of the Nat'l Aeronautic Ass'n of the U.S.A.

United States Holocaust Memorial Council
2000 L St., N.W., Suite 588, Washington, DC 20036
Telephone: (202) 653-9220
Represented by:
Sara Bloomfield, Exec. Director

United States Industrial Fabrics Institute
2000 L St., N.W., Suite 200, Washington, DC 20036-4907
Telephone: (202) 861-0981
Background: Exec. Director is Marcia Thomson of the Industrial Fabrics Ass'n Internat'l.
Counsel or consultant:
Fehrenbacher, Sale, Quinn, and Deese (C. Michael Deese)
Kaye, Scholer, Fierman, Hays and Handler (Christopher R. Brewster)

United States Institute for Peace
1550 M St., N.W. Suite 700, Washington, DC 20005-1708
Telephone: (202) 457-1700
Background: An independent, nonprofit, nonpartisan, noninterventionalist national institution established by the U.S. Congress to develop and disseminate knowledge about the peaceful resolution of international conflict.
Represented by:
Samuel W. Lewis, President
John Norton Moore, Chairman of the Board of Directors
John Richardson, Counselor
Milan Svec, Fellow

United States League of Savings Institutions
1709 New York Ave., N.W., Suite 801, Washington, DC 20006
Telephone: (202) 637-8900
Background: Represents savings and loan associations, commercial banks, savings banks, and thrift holding companies.
Represented by:
James W. Christian, Sr. V. President & Chief Economist
James H. Cousins, Sr. V. President, Legislative Affairs
J. Noel Fahey, V. President & Assoc. Dir. of Research
Philip Gasteyer, Exec. V. Pres./General Counsel
Gary G. Gilbert, Director, Banking Agency Liaison
James Grohl, Sr. VP, Spec Ass't to the Pres, Commun.
Renie Yoshida Grohl, Sr. V. Pres., Group Exec. Regul. Affairs
Dennis J. Jacobe, Sr. V. Pres. & Director, Research Econ.
Randall H. McFarlane, Sr VP & Dep Gen Counsel, Leg & Reg Afrs.
Coleman C. O'Brien, Sr. V. President, Legislative Counsel
J. Denis O'Toole, Exec. V. President, Government Affairs
Brian P. Smith, Exec. V. President, Dep., Chicago Optns.
Michael G. Troop, Sr. V. President & Legislative Rep.
Frederick L. Webber, President & CEO
Counsel or consultant:
Silverstein and Mullens (James C. Corman)

United States League of Savings Institutions Savings Assns Political Elections Committee
1709 New York Ave., N.W., Suite 801, Washington, DC 20006
Telephone: (202) 637-8900
Represented by:
Paul Prior, Treasurer

United States-Mexico Chamber of Commerce
1900 L St., N.W., Suite 612, Washington, DC 20036
Telephone: (202) 296-5198
Represented by:
Brian Marshall, Director, U.S. Membership & Publishing
Gerard J. Van Heuven, Exec. V. President

United States Nat'l Committee for Pacific Economic Cooperation
1755 Massachusetts Ave., N.W., Suite 420, Washington, DC 20036
Telephone: (202) 745-7444
Background: Established in 1984 by Secretary of State George Shultz. Comprised of more than 70 senior U.S. business, government and education leaders who advise the government on U.S.-Pacific Basin economic issues.
Represented by:
Mark Borthwick, Exec. Director
Clifford Ragonese, Assistant Exec. Director

United States Navy Memorial Foundation
1425 North Quincy St., Arlington, VA 22209
Telephone: (703) 524-0830
Counsel or consultant:
Fleishman-Hillard, Inc

United States-New Zealand Council, The
1250 24th St., N.W. Suite 875, Washington, DC 20037
Telephone: (202) 466-0535
Counsel or consultant:
Potomac Partners (Stanley F. Turesky)

United States Olympic Committee
Colorado Springs, CO
Counsel or consultant:
Kogovsek & Associates, Inc.

United States Pan Asian American Chamber of Commerce
1625 K St., N.W., Suite 380, Washington, DC 20006
Telephone: (202) 638-1764
Background: A national organization to assist Americans of Asian descent in business, professional and public life through establishment of networks to disseminate information, provide training and advice and present the views of Asian Americans on issues of importance to them.
Represented by:
Susan Au Allen, President
Fernando Galaviz, V. President, Government Liaison
William 'Mo' Marumoto, Exec. V. President

United States Parachute Ass'n
1440 Duke St., Alexandria, VA 22314
Telephone: (703) 836-3495
Represented by:
Michael Johnston, Director of Safety & Training
William H. Ottley, Exec. Director

United States Pharmacopeial Convention
12601 Twinbrook Parkway, Rockville, MD 20852
Telephone: (301) 881-0666
Represented by:
Jerome Halperin, Exec. Director
Counsel or consultant:
William J. Skinner

United States Student Ass'n
1012 14th St., N.W., Suite 207, Washington, DC 20005
Telephone: (202) 347-8772
Background: The largest student membership organization in the country. Priority concerns include: creation of a quality, universally accessible system of higher education, protection of civil and constitutional rights and the development of statewide coalitions and local student organizations.
Represented by:
Julius A. Davis, V. President
Janet Lieberman, Legislative Director
Julianne Marley, President

United States Suzuki Motor Corp.
Brea, CA
Counsel or consultant:
Pettit & Martin (Harry W. Cladouhos)
Thompson and Co. (Robert J. Thompson)

United States Telephone Ass'n
900 19th St., N.W., Suite 800, Washington, DC 20006-2102
Telephone: (202) 835-3100

The listings in this directory are available as *Mailing Labels.* See last page.

ORGANIZATIONS REPRESENTED

Represented by:
Lindon Boozer, Manager, Government Relations
David B. Cohen, Dir., Small Company and REA Affairs
R. T. Gregg, Director, Government Relations
Kit Hawkins, Director, Government Relations
Gerard L. Lederer, Exec. Director, Government Relations
Martin T. McCue, V. President & General Counsel
John Sodolski, President
Ward H. White, V. Pres., Government and Public Affairs
Henry Wieland, Jr., Exec. Director for Special Events
Counsel or consultant:
Ginsburg, Feldman and Bress (Rodney Joyce)
Murphy and Demory, Ltd. (Margot F. Bester, Willard L. Demory)
Ragan and Mason (William F. Ragan)
Williams and Jensen, P.C. (William T. Brack)
Wunder, Ryan, Cannon & Thelen (Patrick C. Koch, Bernard J. Wunder)

United States Telephone Ass'n Political Action Committee
900 19th St., N.W., Suite 800, Washington, DC 20006-2102
Telephone: (202) 835-3100
Background: Represents the legislative, regulatory and political interests of the United States Telephone Ass'n. Represented by Lindon Boozer of the Ass'n.

United States Trademark Ass'n
6 East 45th St., New York, NY 10017
Telephone: (212) 986-5880
Represented by:
Michele Grasso, Government Relations Manager
Counsel or consultant:
Swidler & Berlin, Chartered (Bruce A. Lehman)

United States Tuna Foundation
1101 17th St., N.W. Suite 609, Washington, DC 20036
Telephone: (202) 857-0610
Background: The trade association of the U.S. tuna fishing industry.
Represented by:
David Burney, General Counsel/ Exec. Director
Counsel or consultant:
O'Connor & Hannan (George J. Mannina, Jr.)

United States Tuna Industry Political Action Committee
1101 17th St., N.W., Suite 609, Washington, DC 20036
Telephone: (202) 857-0610
Background: Jack C. Bowland, of the U.S. Tuna Foundation, serves as the treasurer. Operates out of the Foundation's San Diego, CA office.

United States Windpower, Inc.
San Francisco, CA
Counsel or consultant:
Edwin T. C. Ing

United Steelworkers of America
815 16th St., N.W. Suite 706, Washington, DC 20006
Telephone: (202) 638-6929
Represented by:
Kenneth S. Kovack, Assistant Director, Legislative Dept.
John J. Sheehan, Legislative Director
Counsel or consultant:
Bredhoff and Kaiser (Elliot Bredhoff, George H. Cohen, Michael H. Gottesman)
Collier, Shannon & Scott (David A. Hartquist, Laurence J. Lasoff)
Nordlinger Associates

United Technologies Carrier
Syracuse, NY
Counsel or consultant:
Squire, Sanders and Dempsey (Edward A. Geltman)

United Technologies Corp.
1825 Eye St., N.W. Suite 700, Washington, DC 20006
Telephone: (202) 785-7400

Represented by:
Ronald A. Chiodo, Director, Legislative Liaison
Jonathan W. Fleming, Director, Government Liaison
Ellen L. Frost, Director, International Affairs
Edgar Mullins, Director, Gov't Relations (Sikorsky Div)
William F. Paul, Sr. V. President, Washington Office
Counsel or consultant:
Crowell and Moring (Brian C. Elmer, W. Stanfield Johnson)
Dickinson, Wright, Moon, Van Dusen and Freeman (Lucien N. Nedzi)
Hyman Fine & Associates Ltd.

United Technologies Corp. Political Action Committee
1825 Eye St., N.W. Suite 700, Washington, DC 20006
Telephone: (202) 785-7446
Background: Contact is Ronald Chiodo of the United Technologies Corp.

United Telecommunications
1875 Eye St., N.W., Suite 1250, Washington, DC 20006
Telephone: (202) 659-4600
Background: A holding company that controls 22 telephone companies comprising the United Telephone System, the nation's third largest non-Bell telephone system. Other United Telecom companies distribute telecommunications equipment, provide cellular mobile telephone and paging services. The company controls 50% of the stock of US Sprint and Telenet which provide computer network services and long distance communications services over a national digital- switched fiber optic network.
Represented by:
William J. Barloon, Manager, Federal Government Relations
Carolyn C. Hill, Washington Counsel
Jay C. Keithley, V. President, Law & External Affairs
Counsel or consultant:
Crowell and Moring (James J. Regan)
Pillsbury, Madison and Sutro (Kevin R. Sullivan)
Wiley, Rein & Fielding (Philip V. Permut)

United Television, Inc.
Los Angeles, CA
Counsel or consultant:
Clarence J. Brown & Co. (Robert B. Giese)

United Transportation Union
400 First St., N.W., Suite 704, Washington, DC 20001
Telephone: (202) 783-3939
Represented by:
James M. Brunkenhoefer, Nat'l Legislative Director
E. R. Plourd, Legislative Representative
Counsel or consultant:
Alper and Mann

United Union of Roofers, Waterproofers and Allied Workers
1125 17th St., N.W., Washington, DC 20036
Telephone: (202) 638-3228
Represented by:
Earl J. Kruse, Internat'l President

United Van Lines, Inc.
Fenton, MO
Counsel or consultant:
Grove, Jaskiewicz, Gilliam and Cobert (James A. Calderwood)

United Video Inc.
Tulsa, OK
Counsel or consultant:
Cole, Raywid, and Braverman (Robert L. James)
Evergreen Associates, Ltd. (Gerald Weaver)
Hopkins and Sutter (William D. Phillips)

United Way of America
701 N. Fairfax St., Alexandria, VA 22314-2045
Telephone: (703) 836-7100
Background: National headquarters for about 2,300 autonomous, non-profit local organizations dedicated to fund-raising for community-supported services.

Represented by:
William Aramony, President
Pat Barrett, Director, State & Local Gov't Relations
Robert Canavan, V. President, Public Affairs
Lisle C. Carter, Jr., General Counsel
Jack Moskowitz, V. President, Government Relations
Sunshine Overkamp, V. President, Communications
Cynthia Woodside, Associate, Federal Gov't Relations
Counsel or consultant:
Olwine, Connelly, Chase, O'Donnell and Weyher (W. Harrison Wellford)
R. Duffy Wall and Associates (Michael Stern)

Universal Foods Corp.
Milwaukee, WI
Counsel or consultant:
Williams and Jensen, P.C. (George D. Baker)

Universal Frutrading Cooperative Ltd.
Durban, South Africa
Counsel or consultant:
Paul H. DeLaney Law Offices (Paul H. DeLaney, Jr.)
Freedman, Levy, Kroll and Simonds (John H. Chettle)

Universal Medical Center
Dallas, TX
Background: A part of the University of Texas Health Science Center.
Counsel or consultant:
Cassidy and Associates, Inc. (Gerald S. J. Cassidy, C. Frank Godfrey, Jr., Dr. Otis A. Singletary, Jr.)

Universal Shipping
1911 N. Fort Myer Drive Suite 703, Arlington, VA 22209
Telephone: (703) 298-6100
Counsel or consultant:
van Kloberg and Associates (Edward J. van Kloberg, III)

Universidad Autonoma de Guadalajara
Guadalajara, Mexico
Counsel or consultant:
Kelly and Associates, Inc. (John A. Kelly)

Universities Associated for Research and Education in Pathology
9650 Rockville Pike, Bethesda, MD 20814
Telephone: (301) 571-1880
Background: Francis A. Pitlick of the American Ass'n of Pathologists serves as Exec. Officer.

University City Science Center
Philadelphia, PA
Counsel or consultant:
Bob Lawrence & Assoc. (Bob Lawrence)

University Hospital of Cleveland
Cleveland, OH
Counsel or consultant:
Cassidy and Associates, Inc. (Roy C. Meyers, George A. Ramonas)

University of Alabama System
Tuscaloosa, AL
Counsel or consultant:
Winburn, VanScoyoc, and Hooper (H. Stewart VanScoyoc)

University of Alaska - Fairbanks
Fairbanks, AK
Counsel or consultant:
Charlie McBride Assoc, Inc. (Charlie McBride)

University of Arizona
Tucson, AZ
Counsel or consultant:
Patton, Boggs and Blow (John Moag, Jr.)

University of Bridgeport
Bridgeport, CT
Counsel or consultant:
Cassidy and Associates, Inc. (George A. Ramonas)

University of California
1523 New Hampshire Ave., N.W., Washington, DC 20036
Telephone: (202) 785-2666
Represented by:
Maureen Budeiti, Senior Government Relations Analyst
Ed Furtek, Asst. Dir., Fed. Governmental Relations
Paul E. Sweet, Dir., Federal Governmental Relations

University of California Medical Centers
Berkeley, CA

The listings in this directory are available as *Mailing Labels.* See last page.

697

ORGANIZATIONS REPRESENTED

University of California Medical Centers (Cont'd)
Counsel or consultant:
Dixon Arnett Associates (Dixon Arnett)

University of Colorado, Office of the President
Boulder, CO
Counsel or consultant:
Cutler and Stanfield (Jeffrey L. Stanfield)

University of Delaware
Newark, DE
Counsel or consultant:
McNair Group Inc.

University of Georgia
Athens, GA
Counsel or consultant:
Kilpatrick & Cody (C. Randall Nuckolls)

University of Kentucky Foundation
Lexington, KY
Counsel or consultant:
Cassidy and Associates, Inc. (C. Frank Godfrey, Jr., George A. Ramonas)

University of Miami
Coral Gables, FL
Counsel or consultant:
Keefe Co., The (William A. Roberts)

University of Michigan
Ann Arbor, MI
Counsel or consultant:
Winburn, VanScoyoc, and Hooper (John P. Winburn)

University of Michigan Medical Center
Ann Arbor, MI
Counsel or consultant:
APCO Associates (Nancy R. Barbour)

University of Nebraska
Lincoln, NE
Counsel or consultant:
Cassidy and Associates, Inc. (James P. Fabiani, Donald P. Smith)

University of Nebraska Foundation
Lincoln, NE
Counsel or consultant:
Cassidy and Associates, Inc. (James P. Fabiani, Donald P. Smith)

University of Nevada - Las Vegas
Las Vegas, NV
Counsel or consultant:
Charlie McBride Assoc, Inc. (Charlie McBride)

University of Nevada/Reno
Reno, NV
Counsel or consultant:
McAuliffe, Kelly, Raffaelli & Siemens (Edward E. Allison)

University of New Mexico
Albuquerque, NM
Counsel or consultant:
DeHart and Darr Associates, Inc. (Anne Darr, Edward H. DeHart)

University of North Carolina
Chapel Hill, NC
Counsel or consultant:
Peabody Fitzpatrick Communications (Joyce Fitzpatrick)

University of North Dakota
Grand Forks, ND
Counsel or consultant:
Garland Associates (Sara G. Garland)

University of Oklahoma
1 Dupont Circle, N.W. Suite 340, Washington, DC 20036
Telephone: (202) 223-9147
Represented by:
Mickki Whitt, Program Coordinator

University of Pennsylvania
Philadelphia, PA
Counsel or consultant:
Cassidy and Associates, Inc. (Carol F. Casey, Gerald S. J. Cassidy, C. Frank Godfrey, Jr.)

University of Scranton
Scranton, PA

Counsel or consultant:
Cassidy and Associates, Inc. (Larry F. Ayres, James P. Fabiani)

University of South Carolina
Columbia, SC
Counsel or consultant:
Lane and Mittendorf

University of Southern California
512 10th St., N.W., Washington, DC 20004
Telephone: (202) 638-4949
Represented by:
Ralph C. Bledsoe, Director, Washington Public Affairs Ctr.

University of Southern Mississippi
Hattiesburg, MS
Counsel or consultant:
Cassidy and Associates, Inc. (C. Frank Godfrey, Jr.)

University of the Arts
Cleveland, OH
Counsel or consultant:
Cassidy and Associates, Inc. (Carol F. Casey, Charles F. Dougherty, Thomas M. Gannon, C. Frank Godfrey, Jr.)

University of Utah
Salt Lake City, UT
Counsel or consultant:
Cassidy and Associates, Inc. (George A. Ramonas)

University of Vermont
Burlington, VT
Counsel or consultant:
Cassidy and Associates, Inc. (Carol F. Casey, Gerald S. J. Cassidy)

University of Washington
Seattle, WA
Counsel or consultant:
Denny Miller Associates
Preston Gates Ellis & Rouvelas Meeds (Susan B. Geiger, Lloyd Meeds)

UNOCAL Corp.
1050 Connecticut Ave., N.W., Suite 760, Washington, DC 20036
Telephone: (202) 659-7600
Represented by:
Joseph L. Colaneri, Washington Representative
Thomas F. Hairston, V. President, Washington Office
Barbara J. Haugh, Manager, Federal Affairs
J. William Ichord, Director, Federal Affairs
Francie Phelps, Washington Representative
Counsel or consultant:
Cleary, Gottlieb, Steen and Hamilton (Henry J. Plog, Jr.)
Gibson, Dunn and Crutcher
Wilmer, Cutler and Pickering (Paul J. Mode, Jr.)

UNUM Corp.
Portland, ME
Counsel or consultant:
Hill and Knowlton Public Affairs Worldwide (Larry I. Good)

UNUM Life Insurance Co.
1919 Pennsylvania Ave., N.W. Suite 300, Washington, DC 20006
Telephone: (202) 775-9585
Represented by:
Kenneth R. Adams, Second V. President, Federal Relations

Upjohn Co.
1455 F St., N.W., Suite 450, Washington, DC 20005
Telephone: (202) 393-6040

Represented by:
Edward F. Greissing, Jr., V. President, Government Affairs
Lee A. Pendergast, Government Affairs Manager
Counsel or consultant:
Akin, Gump, Strauss, Hauer and Feld
Covington and Burling (Herbert Dym, Eugene I. Lambert, Stanley L. Temko)
Ginsburg, Feldman and Bress (E. William Henry, Peter M. Kirby)
Hill and Knowlton Public Affairs Worldwide (Dale Lawson)
Kessler and Associates
Lee, Toomey & Kent
Manning, Selvage & Lee/Washington
Parry and Romani Associates Inc.

Upland Industries
Omaha, NE
Background: A subsidiary of Union Pacific Corp. Represented by Kip Hawley of the parent company.

Upper Peninsula Power Co.
Houghton, MI
Counsel or consultant:
Reid & Priest

Upper Yampa Water Conservancy District
Steamboat Spgs., CO
Counsel or consultant:
Kogovsek & Associates, Inc.

Uranium Producers of America
Washington, DC
Counsel or consultant:
Covington and Burling
Van Ness, Feldman & Curtis (Grenville Garside)

Urban Institute, The
2100 M St., N.W., Washington, DC 20037
Telephone: (202) 833-7200
Background: A non-governmental, non-profit policy research and educational organization to study social and economic problems confronting the nation. Cooperates with federal agencies, states, cities and the private sector.
Represented by:
Lee Bawden, Director, Human Resouces Policy Center
Frank D. Bean, Director, Population Studies Center
Susan Brown, Director, Public Affairs
William Gorham, President
Stephen B. Hitchner, Jr., Senior V. President
John Holahan, Director, Health Policy Center
Thomas Kingsley, Dir., Public Finance & Housing Center
E. Blaine Liner, Director, State Policy Center
Richard Michiel, Dir., Income & Benefits Policy Center
Rudolph G. Penner, Senior Fellow
George Peterson, Senior Fellow
Isabel V. Sawhill, Director, Domestic Priorities Program
John Shannon, Senior Fellow
C. Eugene Steuerle, Senior Fellow
Raymond Struyk, Director, Internat'l Activities Center

Urban Land Institute
1090 Vermont Ave., N.W. Suite 300, Washington, DC 20005
Telephone: (202) 289-8500
Background: An independent, non-profit research and education organization which focuses its activities on making the most of America's urban lands on wise, efficient and productive urban growth. Promotes member involvement, research and publications, education and community service.
Represented by:
J. Thomas Black, Staff V. Pres. for Research & Education
Fran Cady, Staff V. President for Finance
Cheryl Cummins, Staff V. President, Programs
David E. Stahl, Exec. V. President
Rick Ventura, Exec. V. President
Counsel or consultant:
Linda Parke Gallagher & Assoc. (Linda Parke Gallagher)

US-Asia Institute
232 East Capitol St., N.E., Washington, DC 20003
Telephone: (202) 544-3181
Background: The US-Asia Institute, established in 1979, is a national nonprofit, nonpartisan organization which focuses on strengthening economic cooperation, communication, and cultural exchange between the United States and countries of Asia. The headquarters are located in Washington with members including Asians, Americans of Asian descent, and those with an interest in Asia from

ORGANIZATIONS REPRESENTED

the business, community, academic, governmental, and quasi-governmental sectors.
Represented by:
Mary Sue Bissell, Exec. Director
Joji Konoshima, President and Trustee

US Sprint Communications Co.
1850 M St., N.W., Suite 1100, Washington, DC 20036
Telephone: (202) 857-1030
Represented by:
MaryBeth Banks, Director, Federal Regulatory Affairs
Susan Buck, V. President, Government Affairs
Michael Fingerhut, General Regional Attorney-Federal
Leon M. Kestenbaum, V. President, Regulatory Affairs
Counsel or consultant:
Bond Donatelli Inc.
Kilpatrick & Cody (C. Randall Nuckolls)

US Tall Ship Foundation
1629 K St., N.W. Suite 401, Washington, DC 20006
Telephone: (202) 293-1322
Counsel or consultant:
Ken Schlossberg Assoc. (William C. Smith)

US WEST, Inc.
1020 19th St., N.W., Suite 700, Washington, DC 20036
Telephone: (202) 429-3100
Background: A telecommunications holding company that is the parent for Mountain States Bell, Northwestern Bell, and Pacific Northwestern Bell as well as several unregulated subsidiaries.
Represented by:
Ellen Burton, Director, Federal Relations
Sheri Jackson, Manager, Federal Affairs
Kim M. Oboz, Assistant V. Pres., Federal Relations
Dana Rasmussen, Assistant V. Pres. & Attorney
David Rubashkin, Director, Federal Relations
Kevin Smith, Director, Federal Relations
H. Laird Walker, V. President, Federal Relations
Counsel or consultant:
Baker and Botts (B. Donovan Picard)
Paul, Hastings, Janofsky and Walker (Ralph B. Everett)

USA Rugby - East
4001 Ronson Drive, Alexandria, VA 22310
Telephone: (703) 960-6123
Background: President is Robert K. Boyd of Washington Gas Light Co.

USA Telecommunications
6267 Franconia Road, Alexandria, VA 22310
Telephone: (703) 971-6700
Counsel or consultant:
Collins & Associates (Sunny Taylor)

USAA
San Antonio, TX
Background: Formerly known as United Services Automobile Ass'n.
Counsel or consultant:
Steponkus and Associates (William P. Steponkus)
Williams and Jensen, P.C. (Ann Costello)

USAA Federal Savings Bank
San Antonio, TX
Counsel or consultant:
Jones, Day, Reavis and Pogue (C. Thomas Long)

USAir Group Inc.
Crystal Park 4 2345 Crystal Dr., Arlington, VA 22227
Telephone: (703) 418-5111
Represented by:
Patricia Goldman, Sr. V. Pres., Corporate Communications
Juliette Heintze, V. President, Investor Relations
J. Ronald Reeves, V. President, Government Affairs
Counsel or consultant:
Patton, Boggs and Blow (Stephen Lachter)

USAir Political Action Committee
2345 Crystal Dr., Crystal Park Four, 8th Floor, Arlington, VA 22227
Telephone: (703) 418-5119
Background: Supported by USAir. Chairman is J. Ronald Reeves of USAir.

USF&G
Baltimore, MD

Counsel or consultant:
Hill and Knowlton Public Affairs Worldwide (John Urbanchuk)
Miller & Chevalier, Chartered (Anne E. Moran)
Van Dyk Associates, Inc. (Ted Van Dyk)
Winburn, VanScoyoc, and Hooper (H. Stewart VanScoyoc)

USG Corporation
655 15th St., N.W, Suite 300, Washington, DC 20005
Telephone: (202) 639-4057
Represented by:
John S. Bush, Jr., V. President, Governmental Affairs
Counsel or consultant:
Morgan, Lewis and Bockius (Eric V. Schaeffer)

Usinor-Sacilor, S.A.
Paris, France
Counsel or consultant:
Donovan Leisure Rogovin Huge & Schiller (William E. Colby)

USIR - The Internat'l Soc. of SIR Users
808 17th St., N.W., Suite 200, Washington, DC 20006
Telephone: (202) 223-9669
Background: Exec. Director is Ramon A. Estrada of Bostrom Corp.
Counsel or consultant:
Bostrom Corp. (Ramon A. Estrada)

USO World
601 Indiana Ave., N.W., Washington, DC 20004
Telephone: (202) 783-8121
Represented by:
Amy Adler, Manager, Publications & Information
Charles T. Hagel, President
Kevin McCarthy, Dir., Communications/Entertainment/Mktg.

USS Constitution Museum
Boston, MA
Counsel or consultant:
Hale and Dorr (Jay P. Urwitz)

USSI, Inc.
Wilmington, DE
Counsel or consultant:
U.S. Strategies Corp. (K. Michael Matthews)

UST Public Affairs, Inc.
1825 Eye St., N.W., Suite 400, Washington, DC 20006
Telephone: (202) 429-2010
Background: Also serves as federal government relations office for subsidiaries, United States Tobaco Co., Internat'l Wine & Spirits Ltd., and UST Enterprises Inc.
Represented by:
John P. McKinney, Representative, Federal Government Affrs
Jake Seher, V. President, Federal Government Affairs
Counsel or consultant:
Alvarado Group, The (Susan Alvarado)
Sheehan Associates, Inc. (John Thomas Sheehan)

USX Corp.
818 Connecticut Ave., N.W., Washington, DC 20006
Telephone: (202) 331-1340
Represented by:
Quinn R. Fisher, Legislative Analyst
Paula D. Freer, Manager, Governmental Affairs
Marilyn A. Harris, Gen Mgr-Govt'l Afrs, Steel & Diversified
Earl W. Mallick, V. President, Public Affairs
John G. Shortridge, Manager, Governmental Affairs
Terrence D. Straub, General Manager - Govt'l Affairs, Energy
Douglas E. Thierwechter, Manager, Governmental Affairs
Patricia M. Wilson, Manager, Governmental Affairs
Counsel or consultant:
George H. Denison
O'Neill and Athy, P.C. (Andrew Athy, Jr.)

USX Corporation PAC
818 Connecticut Ave., N.W., Washington, DC 20006
Telephone: (202) 857-0300
Background: Political Action Committee of the USX Corp. and represented by Marilyn A. Harris of the sponsoring organization.

Utah League of Cities and Towns
Salt Lake City, UT

Counsel or consultant:
Chambers Associates Incorporated (William L. Stringer)

Utah Power and Light Co.
Salt Lake City, UT
Counsel or consultant:
Leighton and Sherline (Lee S. Sherline)
The Eddie Mahe Company

Utah, State of
444 N. Capitol St., N.W., Suite 204, Washington, DC 20001
Telephone: (202) 624-7704
Represented by:
Debbie Turner, Director, Washington Office
Counsel or consultant:
Cassidy and Associates, Inc.
Dickstein, Shapiro and Morin (Andrew P. Miller, Bernard Nash)

Ute Mountain Ute Indian Tribe
Towaoc, CO
Counsel or consultant:
Kogovsek & Associates, Inc.

Utility Air Regulatory Group
2000 Pennsylvania Ave., N.W., Suite 9000, Washington, DC 20006
Telephone: (202) 955-1500
Background: An ad hoc group of 87 utility companies, the Edison Electric Institute and the Nat'l Rural Electric Cooperative Ass'n formed to represent the utility industry's views on regulations concerning air quality standards.
Counsel or consultant:
Hunton and Williams (Henry V. Nickel)

Utility Decommissioning Tax Group
c/o Reid & Preist 1111 19th St., N.W., Washington, DC 20036
Telephone: (202) 828-0100
Counsel or consultant:
Reid & Priest (Raymond F. Dacek, Patricia M. Healy)

Utility Nuclear Waste Transportation Program
1111 19th St., N.W., Suite 600, Washington, DC 20036
Telephone: (202) 778-6511
Background: Private and public electric utilities involved in operation, construction and planning of nuclear power reactors with a special interest in radioactive waste disposal and transportation.
Represented by:
Brian P. Farrell, Program Manager
James E. Flaherty, Program Manager
Christopher J. Henkel, Program Manager
Steven P. Kraft, Director
Counsel or consultant:
Energy Resources Internat'l (Michael H. Schwartz)
Newman & Holtzinger, P.C. (Michael A. Bauser)
Shaw, Pittman, Potts and Trowbridge (Jay E. Silberg)

Utility Workers of America Political Contributions Committee
815 16th St., N.W., Washington, DC 20006
Telephone: (202) 347-8105
Background: The political action committee of the Utility Workers Union of America. Represented by Marshall M. Hicks of the Utility Workers Union.

Utility Workers Union of America
815 16th St., N.W. Suite 605, Washington, DC 20006
Telephone: (202) 347-8105
Represented by:
Marshall M. Hicks, Secretary-Treasurer
James Joy, Jr., President

Vacation Ownership Council of ARRDA
1220 L St., N.W., Fifth Floor, Washington, DC 20005
Telephone: (202) 371-6700
Background: Represents developers offering resort timeshares, i.e. purchase or right to use of units of time at resort condominiums/hotels.
Represented by:
Stephany A. Madsen, V. President, State Government Relations

Vail Valley Associates
Vail, CO
Counsel or consultant:
Liz Robbins Associates (Sharon Edwards)

ORGANIZATIONS REPRESENTED

Valero Energy Corp.
San Antonio, TX
Counsel or consultant:
Bracewell and Patterson (Gene E. Godley)

Valhi, Inc.
Dallas, TX
Counsel or consultant:
Kirkland and Ellis
Ottosen and Associates (Karl J. Ottosen)

Valio Finnish Co-Operative Dairies Ass'n
Helsinki, Finland
Counsel or consultant:
Max N. Berry Law Offices (Max N. Berry)

Valley Children's Hospital
Fresno, CA
Counsel or consultant:
Cassidy and Associates, Inc. (C. Frank Godfrey, Jr.)
McAuliffe, Kelly, Raffaelli & Siemens (Frederick W. Hatfield)

Valmont Industries, Inc.
Valley, NE
Counsel or consultant:
Bob Lawrence & Assoc. (Bob Lawrence)

Value Foundation
Nat'l Press Bldg., Room 1199, Washington, DC 20045
Telephone: (202) 347-7007
Background: A non-profit, private foundation dedicated to the advancement of planning, research and education in value engineering, value management, life cycle costing, design-to-cost and other related cost-containment techniques. President is Hal Tufty of the Soc. of American Value Engineers.

Valve Manufacturers Ass'n of America
1050 17th St., N.W., Washington, DC 20036
Telephone: (202) 331-8105
Represented by:
Malcolm E. O'Hagan, President
Counsel or consultant:
Collier, Shannon & Scott (David A. Hartquist)

Van Eck Funds
New York, NY
Counsel or consultant:
Robert N. Pyle & Associates

Van Ness, Feldman & Curtis Political Action Committee
1050 Thomas Jefferson St., NW Seventh Floor, Washington, DC 20007
Telephone: (202) 298-1800
Counsel or consultant:
Van Ness, Feldman & Curtis (Robert G. Szabo)

Varian Associates Inc.
2101 Wilson Blvd., Suite 832, Arlington, VA 22201
Telephone: (703) 522-8002
Represented by:
Robert A. Lee, Director, Government Liaison
David G. Shultz, Manager, Federal Governmental Affairs
Counsel or consultant:
Miller & Chevalier, Chartered (Alan R. Yuspeh)

Varig Brazilian Airlines
Miami, FL
Counsel or consultant:
Holland and Knight
Winthrop, Stimson, Putnam & Roberts (Robert Reed Gray)

VASP Airlines
San Paolo, Brazil
Counsel or consultant:
Squire, Sanders and Dempsey (Robert D. Papkin, Edward W. Sauer)

Vaupel Artistry
Henryetta, OK
Counsel or consultant:
Cindy Williams Associates (Lucinda L. Williams)

Veda Inc. Employees Political Action Committee
11 Canal Center Plaza Suite 300, Alexandria, VA 22314
Telephone: (703) 684-8005
Represented by:
Carl R. Varblow, Treasurer, Veda PAC

Velsicol Chemical Corp.
Rosemont, IL
Counsel or consultant:
T. G. Brown & Associates

Venezuela, Government of
Caracas, Venezuela
Counsel or consultant:
Kaplan, Russin and Vecchi
Squier & Eskew Communications, Inc. (Thomas Ochs, Robert Squier)

Venice, Florida, City of
Venice, FL
Counsel or consultant:
Marlowe and Co. (Howard Marlowe)

Ventura, California, County of
440 First St., N.W. Suite 501, Washington, DC 20001
Telephone: (202) 737-7523
Background: Represented by Roger F. Honberger (see San Diego County listing).

Vermont Department of Public Service
Montpelier, VT
Counsel or consultant:
McCarthy, Sweeney and Harkaway, P.C. (Harvey L. Reiter)

Vern Clark & Associates, Inc. PAC
1730 M St., N.W. Suite 911, Washington, DC 20036
Telephone: (202) 737-1123
Counsel or consultant:
Vern Clark & Associates (Michael A. Thompson)

Verner, Liipfert, Bernhard, McPherson and Hand Political Action Committee
901 15th St., N.W. Suite 700, Washington, DC 20005
Telephone: (202) 371-6000
Counsel or consultant:
Verner, Liipfert, Bernhard, McPherson and Hand, Chartered (John A. Merrigan)

Vero Beach Oceanfront Investors Limited Partnership
Greenville, SC
Counsel or consultant:
Manatt, Phelps, Rothenberg & Phillips (Robert T. Herbolsheimer)

Versar, Inc.
Springfield, VA
Counsel or consultant:
Hill and Knowlton Public Affairs Worldwide (Charles Francis)

Vertical Flight Foundation
217 N. Washington St., Alexandria, VA 22314
Telephone: (703) 684-6777
Background: Represented by John F. Zugschwert, Exec. Director of the American Helicopter Soc.

Very Special Arts
1331 Pennsylvania Ave., N.W. Suite 1205, Washington, DC 20004
Telephone: (202) 662-8899
Represented by:
Eileen Cuskaden, Director, Program Operations
Eugene Maillard, Chief Executive Officer

Vestal Laboratories
St. Louis, MO
Background: A division of Chemed Corp.
Counsel or consultant:
Keller and Heckman (John B. Dubeck)

Veterans Education Project
Box 42130, Washington, DC 20015
Telephone: (202) 547-8387
Background: Assists veterans in applying for benefits and appealing denials by Department of Veterans Affairs through printed materials.
Represented by:
Keith D. Snyder, Coordinator

Veterans of Foreign Wars of the U.S.
200 Maryland Ave., N.E., Washington, DC 20002
Telephone: (202) 543-2239

Represented by:
Frederico Juarbe, Jr., Director, Nat'l Veterans Service
James N. Magill, Director, Nat'l Legislative Service
Larry W. Rivers, Exec. Director
William G. Smith, Director, Public Affairs
Kenneth A. Steadman, Director, Nat'l Security & For. Affairs

Veterans of World War I of the U.S.A.
941 North Capitol St., N.E. Suite 1201-C, Washington, DC 20002
Telephone: (202) 275-1388
Background: Organized to unite in fraternal, civic, and social comradeship those who served honorably during World War One.
Represented by:
Gilmer T. Carter, National Commander
Muriel Sue Parkhurst, Exec. Director
Don R. Pears, Legislative Director

VFW-Political Action Committee, Inc.
200 Maryland Ave., N.E. Suite 506, Washington, DC 20002
Telephone: (202) 544-5868
Background: The political action committee sponsored by the Veterans of Foreign Wars of the U.S.
Represented by:
James R. Currio, Director

Viacom Internat'l, Inc.
New York, NY
Counsel or consultant:
Lee, Toomey & Kent
O'Neill and Athy, P.C. (Andrew Athy, Jr.)

VIASA
Caracas, Venezuela
Counsel or consultant:
Squire, Sanders and Dempsey (Robert D. Papkin, Edward W. Sauer)

VICAM
Somerville, MA
Counsel or consultant:
Olsson, Frank and Weeda, P.C. (John Bode)

Vickers Shipbuilding and Engineering, Ltd.
London, England
Counsel or consultant:
Lipsen Whitten & Diamond

Video and Film Distributors Council, The
3150 Spring St., Fairfax, VA 22031-2399
Telephone: (703) 273-7200
Background: Consists of 12 associations which have united to solve their common problems with the U.S. Postal Service and U.S. Parcel Service. Represented by Kenton Pattie of the Internat'l Communications Industries Ass'n (ICIA).

Video Software Dealers Ass'n
Cherry Hill, NJ
Counsel or consultant:
Arent, Fox, Kintner, Plotkin & Kahn (Burton V. Wides)

Videotex Industry Ass'n
8403 Colesville Road Suite 865, Silver Spring, MD 20910
Telephone: (301) 495-4955
Background: An organization of 100 member firms which promotes the use of videotex and teletext. Videotex refers to easy-to-use, interactive electronic services that are transmitted via telephone or cable to television sets connected to a terminal or personal computers in homes or offices.
Represented by:
Robert L. Smith, Jr., Exec. Director

Vietnam Veterans of America, Inc.
2001 S St., N.W., Washington, DC 20009
Telephone: (202) 332-2700
Background: A national service organization with over 480 chapters and 42,000 members. Focuses on issues related to the Vietnam experience and Vietnam veterans.
Represented by:
Paul S. Egan, Director of Legislative Affairs
Mary R. Stout, President

Vietnam Veterans Of America Legal Services Program
c/o Nat'l Veterans Legal Svc. 2001 S St., N.W., Suite 610, Washington, DC 20016

The listings in this directory are available as *Mailing Labels*. See last page.

ORGANIZATIONS REPRESENTED

Telephone: (202) 265-8305
Background: Represents veterans in a variety of legal cases. Particular emphasis is on the problems of Vietnam-era veterans, reform of Veterans Administration procedures and the problems of veterans with less than honorable discharges.
Represented by:
David Addlestone, Director
Barton Stichman, Director

Viktor Lenac Shipyard
Rijeka, Yugoslavia
Counsel or consultant:
Dyer, Ellis, Joseph & Mills

Vinnell Corp.
10530 Rosehaven St., Suite 600, Fairfax, VA 22030
Telephone: (703) 385-4544
Represented by:
Kevin M. O'Melia, Assistant V. President/Corp. Secretary

VINTA Mineral and Financial, Inc.
Alexandria, VA
Counsel or consultant:
Wunder, Ryan, Cannon & Thelen (Paul E. Sullivan)

Viobin Corp.
Monticello, IL
Counsel or consultant:
McGuire, Woods, Battle and Boothe (Larry D. Sharp)

VIP Hotel Representatives, Inc.
Hollywood, FL
Counsel or consultant:
Warren W. Koffler

Virgin Island Nat'l Bank
St. Thomas, VI
Counsel or consultant:
Warren W. Koffler

Virgin Island Rum Industries
Frederiksted, St. Croix, VI
Counsel or consultant:
Fried, Frank, Harris, Shriver & Jacobson (Jay R. Kraemer)

Virgin Islands, Government of the
Charlotte Amalie, VI
Counsel or consultant:
Bishop, Cook, Purcell & Reynolds (Peter N. Hiebert)

Virgin Islands, Office of the Governor
900 17th St., N.W., Suite 500, Washington, DC 20006
Telephone: (202) 293-3707
Represented by:
Dr. Carlyle Corbin, Washington Representative

Virgin Islands, University of the
Charlotte Amalie, VI
Counsel or consultant:
Lisboa Associates, Inc. (Elizabeth Lisboa-Farrow, Eileen F. Michaels, Eileen O'Keefe)

Virginia Beach Federal Savings Bank
Richmond, VA
Counsel or consultant:
Dow, Lohnes and Albertson (Reuben B. Robertson)

Virginia, Governor of
444 N. Capitol St., N.W. Suite 246, Washington, DC 20001
Telephone: (202) 783-1769
Represented by:
Glenn K. Davidson, Director, Virginia Liaison Office

Virginia Independent Network Political Action Committee
422 First St., S.E., Suite 210, Washington, DC 20003
Telephone: (202) 544-6675
Counsel or consultant:
Randolph G. Flood and Associates (Randolph G. Flood)

Virginia Letter on Public Business
McLean, VA
Counsel or consultant:
Randolph G. Flood and Associates (Randolph G. Flood)

Virginia Polytechnical Institute and State University
Blacksburg, VA

Counsel or consultant:
McNair Group Inc. (Elizabeth L. Taylor)

Virginia Power Co.
Richmond, VA
Counsel or consultant:
Flanagan Group, Inc. (Daniel V. Flanagan, Jr.)
Hunton and Williams
McCarthy, Sweeney and Harkaway, P.C.

Virginia Wineries Ass'n
Barboursville, VA
Counsel or consultant:
Barksdale Ballard & Co. (D. Michael Ballard)

VISA U.S.A., Inc.
San Mateo, CA
Counsel or consultant:
Morrison & Foerster (L. Richard Fischer, Robert M. Kurucza)
O'Connor & Hannan

Vision Council of America
1800 North Kent St. Suite 1210, Arlington, VA 22209
Telephone: (703) 243-1508
Represented by:
Susan S. Allen, Chief Staff Executive
William J. Wilson, Director, Public Relations

Visiting Nurses Ass'n of America
Denver, CO
Counsel or consultant:
Leighton and Regnery (Alfred S. Regnery)

Vista Chemical Co.
Houston, TX
Counsel or consultant:
Kent & O'Connor, Incorp. (J. H. Kent)

Visually Impaired Data Processors Internat'l
1010 Vermont Ave., N.W. Suite 1100, Washington, DC 20005
Telephone: (202) 393-3666
Background: Represented by Roberta Douglas of the American Council of the Blind.

Visually Impaired Piano Tuners Internat'l
1010 Vermont Ave., N.W., Suite 1100, Washington, DC 20005
Telephone: (202) 393-3666
Background: Represented by Roberta Douglas of the American Council of the Blind.

Visually Impaired Secretarial/Transcribers Ass'n
1010 Vermont Ave., N.W. Suite 1100, Washington, DC 20005
Telephone: (202) 393-3666
Background: Represented by Roberta Douglas of the American Council of the Blind.

Visually Impaired Veterans of America
1010 Vermont Ave., N.W. Suite 1100, Washington, DC 20005
Telephone: (202) 393-3666
Background: Represented by Roberta Douglas of the American Council of the Blind.

Vitarine Pharmaceuticals Inc.
Counsel or consultant:
Kleinfeld, Kaplan and Becker (Alan H. Kaplan)

Vitro, S.A.
Garza Garcia, Mexico
Counsel or consultant:
Vinson and Elkins (John E. Chapoton, Theodore W. Kassinger)

VNA, Inc.
5151 Wisconsin Ave., N.W. Suite 400, Washington, DC 20016
Telephone: (202) 686-2862
Background: The nonprofit parent corporation of the Visiting Nurse Ass'n.
Represented by:
Paul Riger, Exec. Director

Vocational Industrial Clubs of America
Box 3000, Leesburg, VA 22075
Telephone: (703) 777-8810

Represented by:
Stephen Denby, Exec. Director
Thomas W. Holdsworth, Director, Communications & Public Affrs.
Counsel or consultant:
Webster, Chamberlain and Bean (Arthur L. Herold)

Voice of the Electorate (Office and Professional Employees Internat'l Union)
815 16th St., N.W., Suite 606, Washington, DC 20006
Telephone: (202) 393-4464
Background: The political action committee of the Office and Professional Employees Internat'l Union. Represented by Gilles Beauregard of the Office and Professional Employees Internat'l Union.

Volkswagen of America, Inc.
490 L'Enfant Plaza, S.W., Suite 7204, Washington, DC 20024
Telephone: (202) 484-6096
Represented by:
Philip A. Hutchinson, Jr., V.P., Public Aff., Gen. Counsel & Sec'y
Joseph W. Kennebeck, Government Affairs Manager

Voluntary Contributors for Better Government
1620 Eye St., N.W. Suite 700, Washington, DC 20006
Telephone: (202) 785-3666
Background: Supported by Internat'l Paper Co. Treasurer and contact is Arthur W. Brownell, Washington Representative of the company.

Voluntary Hospitals of America, Inc.
1150 Connecticut Ave., N.W. Suite 800, Washington, DC 20036
Telephone: (202) 822-9750
Represented by:
Daniel P. Bourque, Corporate Senior V. President
Kathleen L. Hartley, Exec. Assistant
Counsel or consultant:
Epstein Becker and Green

Voluntary Hospitals of America PAC
1150 Connecticut Ave., N.W. Suite 800, Washington, DC 20036
Telephone: (202) 822-9750
Background: Represented by Daniel P. Bourque of Voluntary Hospitals of America.

Volunteer-The Nat'l Center
1111 North 19th St. Suite 500, Arlington, VA 22209
Telephone: (703) 276-0542
Background: Formed in 1979. The only national voluntary organization with the sole mission of stimulating and strengthening volunteer citizen involvement in addressing human, social and environmental problems.
Represented by:
Frank Bailey, Exec. Director
Richard C. Mock, V. President, Public Information

Volunteer Trustees of Not-for-Profit Hospitals
1625 Eye St., N.W., Suite 810, Washington, DC 20006
Telephone: (202) 659-0338
Represented by:
Linda B. Miller, President

Volunteers in Overseas Cooperative Assistance
50 F St., N.W., Suite 1075, Washington, DC 20001
Telephone: (202) 626-8750
Background: A private, nonprofit organization formed in 1970 to provide short-term technical help through volunteer businessmen and women to cooperatives, agricultural producer ass'ns, and government agencies in developing countries at their request. Core funding from U.S. Cooperatives and the Agency for International Development.
Represented by:
Don Cohen, President

Volvo North America
New York, NY
Counsel or consultant:
Gibson, Dunn and Crutcher

Vons Co.
El Monte, CA
Counsel or consultant:
Latham and Watkins (Joseph A. DeFrancis)

Vote America Foundation
1200 19th St., N.W., Suite 6030, Washington, DC 20036
Telephone: (202) 659-4595

The listings in this directory are available as *Mailing Labels*. See last page.

ORGANIZATIONS REPRESENTED

Vote America Foundation (Cont'd)
Background: Originally formed in 1983 as Americans for Responsible Government, the Vote America Foundation was created to help turn the trend away from voter apathy. It is the goal of Vote America to encourage the political involvement of all Americans specifically youth and traveling Americans.
Represented by:
Linda A. Leinbach, V. President

Voters for Choice
2000 P St., N.W., Suite 515, Washington, DC 20036
Telephone: (202) 822-6640
Background: An organization to provide financial and technical support to political candidates who favor a woman's right to have a safe and legal abortion. Registered as a political action committee with the Federal Election Commission.
Represented by:
Julie Burton, Exec. Director
Kristina Kiehl, President
Deborah Landeau, Chair

VSI Corp.
Pasedena, CA
Counsel or consultant:
Howrey and Simon (Terrence C. Sheehy)

Vulcan Materials Co.
Birmingham, AL
Counsel or consultant:
Mayer, Brown and Platt (John C. Berghoff, Jr.)
McGuire, Woods, Battle and Boothe
Shaw, Pittman, Potts and Trowbridge (William Mike House)

Wachovia Corp.
Winston Salem, NC
Counsel or consultant:
Lee, Toomey & Kent

WAGM-TV
Presque Isle, ME
Counsel or consultant:
Koteen and Naftalin

Wagner and Brown
Midland, TX
Counsel or consultant:
Van Ness, Feldman & Curtis (Howard J. Feldman)

Walbro Corp.
Cass City, MI
Counsel or consultant:
Dunaway & Cross (Mac S. Dunaway)

Wald Manufacturing Co.
Maysville, KY
Counsel or consultant:
Taft, Stettinius and Hollister (Virginia E. Hopkins)

Walk-Haydel & Associates Inc.
New Orleans, LA
Background: An architectural engineering firm.
Counsel or consultant:
James E. Guirard, Jr.

Walker Field Airport Authority
Counsel or consultant:
Kogovsek & Associates, Inc.

Wall and Ceiling Political Action Committee
1600 Cameron St., Alexandria, VA 22314
Telephone: (703) 684-2924
Background: The Political Action Committee of the Ass'n of the Wall and Ceiling Industries. Treasurer is Joe M. Baker, Jr.
Represented by:
Leslie Szejk, Director

Wall Street Journal
New York, NY
Counsel or consultant:
Snavely, King and Associates

Wallcovering Manufacturers Ass'n
Lyndhurst, NJ
Counsel or consultant:
Howrey and Simon (David C. Murchison)

Walter Corp., Jim
Tampa, FL

Counsel or consultant:
Alcalde & Rousselot
Shaw, Pittman, Potts and Trowbridge (William Mike House)

Wang Laboratories Inc.
Lowell, MA
Counsel or consultant:
Abt Associates Inc.
Baker and McKenzie

WANX-TV
Atlanta, GA
Counsel or consultant:
Fisher, Wayland, Cooper and Leader

WAPA-TV
San Juan, PR
Counsel or consultant:
Fletcher, Heald and Hildreth

WAPT-TV
Jackson, MS
Counsel or consultant:
Cohn and Marks

Warburg Pincus & Co., E. M.
New York, NY
Counsel or consultant:
Liz Robbins Associates (Alvin S. Brown, Liz Robbins)
Vinson and Elkins (Christine L. Vaughn)

Wardair Canada, Ltd.
Edmonton, Alberta
Counsel or consultant:
Burwell, Hansen, Peters and Houston (Walter D. Hansen)

Warner-Lambert Co.
1667 K St., N.W., Suite 1270, Washington, DC 20006
Telephone: (202) 862-3840
Background: A multinational health care and consumer products firm.
Represented by:
W. Bradford Gary, V. President, Government Relations
Catherine L. Walker, Manager, Government Affairs
Counsel or consultant:
Akin, Gump, Strauss, Hauer and Feld (Edward S. Knight)
Baker, Worthington, Crossley, Stansberry & Woolf (W. Lee Rawls)
Michael Hugo & Associates (F. Michael Hugo)
O'Connor & Hannan (Timothy M. Haake, Patrick E. O'Donnell)
Parry and Romani Associates Inc. (Romano Romani)
StMaxens and Co. (Thomas F. StMaxens, II)
Stovall & Spradlin

Washington Agriculture GATT Coalition
Olympia, WA
Counsel or consultant:
Bogle and Gates (Irene Ringwood)

Washington Airports Task Force
P.O. Box 17349, Washington Dulles Internat'l Airport, Washington, DC 20041
Telephone: (703) 661-8040
Represented by:
Elizabeth George, Dir, Public Infor. & Public Relations
Leo J. Schefer, President
Counsel or consultant:
Hewes, Morella, Gelband and Lamberton, P.C. (Stephen L. Gelband)

Washington Area Bankers Ass'n
1750 New York Ave., N.W., Suite 240, Washington, DC 20006
Telephone: (202) 783-4555
Represented by:
Maurice Cullinane, Exec. V. President
Counsel or consultant:
Arnold & Porter (John D. Hawke, Jr.)
Covington and Burling (Stuart C. Stock)

Washington Area Bankers Ass'n PAC
1750 New York Ave., N.W., Suite 240, Washington, DC 20006
Telephone: (202) 783-4555
Background: The political action committee of the Washington Area Bankers Ass'n. Represented by Maurice Cullinane of the parent organization.

Washington Area Council of Engineering Laboratories
8811 Colesville Rd. Suite G106, Silver Spring, MD 20910
Telephone: (301) 588-6047
Counsel or consultant:
Bachner Communications, Inc. (John P. Bachner)

Washington Area Lawyers for the Arts
2025 Eye St., N.W. Suite 1114, Washington, DC 20006
Telephone: (202) 861-0055
Background: Provides free legal assistance and business information to low income artists and arts groups. Also provides education programs on arts and business related subjects.
Represented by:
Ruth P. Cogen, Exec. Director
Patricia Pelizzari, Administrative Coordinator

Washington Area State Relations Group
311 First St., N.W. Suite 500, Washington, DC 20001
Telephone: (202) 626-5752
Background: An informal group of trade association and corporate executives concerned with state government relations.

Washington Ass'n Research Foundation
1426 21st St., N.W., Suite 200, Washington, DC 20036
Telephone: (202) 429-9370
Background: Exec. Director is Stephen W. Carey of the Greater Washington Soc. of Ass'n Executives.
Counsel or consultant:
Loomis, Owen, Fellman and Howe (James E. Anderson)

Washington Ballet, The
3515 Wisconsin Ave., N.W., Washington, DC 20016
Telephone: (202) 362-3606
Counsel or consultant:
Chernikoff and Co. (Larry Chernikoff)

Washington Bancorporation
619 14th St., N.W., Washington, DC 20005-2007
Telephone: (202) 537-2000
Counsel or consultant:
Dow, Lohnes and Albertson (Kathleen W. Collins)

Washington Bancorporation Political Action Committee
619 14th St., N.W., Washington, DC 20005
Telephone: (202) 537-2000
Background: Represented by Patricia N. Mathews of The Nat'l Bank of Washington.

Washington Business Group on Health
229 1/2 Pennsylvania Ave., S.E., Washington, DC 20003
Telephone: (202) 547-6644
Background: A membership organization of employers with a common interest in national health insurance and related legislation. Founded in 1974 at the suggestion of the Business Roundtable's Health Legislation Task Force.
Represented by:
Cathy Ellen Certner, Director, Public Policy
Carol A. Cronin, V. President
Elise A. Gemeinhardt, Public Policy Associate
Willis B. Goldbeck, President

Washington Center for Public Policy Research
1776 K St., N.W., Suite 900, Washington, DC 20006
Telephone: (202) 429-7360
Represented by:
Henry Geller, Director

Washington Citizens for World Trade
Seattle, WA
Counsel or consultant:
Garvey, Schubert & Barer (Alan A. Butchman)

Washington Convention and Visitors Ass'n
1212 New York Ave., N.W., Sixth Floor, Washington, DC 20005
Telephone: (202) 789-7000
Represented by:
Daniel E. Mobley, Exec. V. President

Washington Council of Agencies
1001 Connecticut Ave., N.W. Sute 925, Washington, DC 20036
Telephone: (202) 457-0540
Background: A coalition of non-profit organizations.
Represented by:
Betsy Johnson, Exec. Director

The listings in this directory are available as *Mailing Labels*. See last page.

ORGANIZATIONS REPRESENTED

Washington Council of Lawyers
1200 New Hampshire Ave., N.W. Suite 700, Washington, DC 20036
Telephone: (202) 659-5964
Background: An organization of attorneys devoted to providing legal services to those to whom legal representation may otherwise be unavailable and to involvement in issues of significance to the legal profession and the community.
Represented by:
Timothy Lindon, President

Washington Court Hotel
525 New Jersey Ave., N.W., Washington, DC 20001
Telephone: (202) 628-2100
Counsel or consultant:
The Kamber Group (Katherine Kinsella)

Washington, DC, City of
Counsel or consultant:
Laxalt, Washington, Perito & Dubuc (James M. Christian, Sr.)

Washington Ethical Soc.
7750 16th St., N.W., Washington, DC 20012
Telephone: (202) 882-6650
Background: A humanistic, educational and religious community seeking to improve the quality of life through the cultivation of ethical character and a more ethical society. Member of the American Ethical Union. The Society supports projects for peace, human rights, ecology and the abolition of hunger.
Represented by:
Donald Montagna, Senior Leader

Washington Gas Light Co.
1100 H St., N.W., Washington, DC 20080
Telephone: (202) 624-6091
Represented by:
Robert K. Boyd, Special Assistant
Richard L. Fisher, Dir., Federal Regulations & Gas Planning
John M. Raymond, Director of Communications
Counsel or consultant:
Prudence H. Parks, Esq.

Washington Independent Writers
220 Woodward Building 733 15th St., N.W., Washington, DC 20005
Telephone: (202) 347-4973
Background: A membership organization for freelance writers.
Represented by:
Isolde Chapin, Exec. Director
Counsel or consultant:
Goldfarb, Kaufman & O'Toole (Ronald L. Goldfarb)

Washington Institute for Near East Policy
50 F St., N.W., Suite 8800, Washington, DC 20001
Telephone: (202) 783-0226
Represented by:
John Hannah, Deputy Director of Research
Martin Indyk, Exec. Director
Barry Rubin, Senior Research Fellow
David Segal, Senior Research Analyst
Barbi Weinberg, President

Washington Institute for Values in Public Policy
1015 18th St., N.W. Suite, Washington, DC 20036
Telephone: (202) 293-7440
Represented by:
Neil Albert Salonen, Director

Washington Insurance Bureau
Counsel or consultant:
Potomac Partners

Washington Lawyers' Committee for Civil Rights Under Law
1400 Eye St., N.W., Suite 450, Washington, DC 20005
Telephone: (202) 682-5900
Represented by:
Roderic V. O. Boggs, Exec. Director
Joseph M. Sellers, Dir., EEO/Intake & Litigation Project

Washington Legal Clinic for the Homeless
1800 Massachusetts Ave., N.W., Washington, DC 20036
Telephone: (202) 872-1494
Represented by:
Susanne Sinclair-Smith, Director

Washington Legal Foundation
1705 N St., N.W., Washington, DC 20036
Telephone: (202) 857-0240
Background: A pro-business 'public interest law' organization established in 1976 as a counterweight to liberal influence of consumer and similar "public interest" groups. Board of Directors includes Congressman Jack Kemp of New York and Senators Orrin Hatch of Utah and Barry Goldwater of Arizona. 1987 budget $2.2 million. Has also established an extensive weekly publishing effort on legal policy matters through its Legal Studies Division.
Represented by:
Paul D. Kamenar, Exec. Legal Director
Constance C. Larcher, Exec. Director
Daniel J. Popeo, Chairman
Richard A. Samp, Chief Counsel
John C. Scully, Counsel
Alan Slobodin, President, Legal Studies Division

Washington Metropolitan Area Corporate Counsel Ass'n
c/o C. G. Appleby, Booz, Allen & Hamilton, 4330 East-West Hwy, Bethesda, MD 20814
Telephone: (301) 951-2222
Background: Officers are C. G. Appleby of Booz, Allen & Hamilton, Inc., President; Kathleen O. Argiropolous of Airlines Reporting Corp., Vice President; Stephen E. Smith of Martin Marietta Data Systems, Treasurer; and Peter H. Johnson of Entre Computer Centers, Secretary.

Washington Metropolitan Area Transit Authority
600 5th St., N.W., Washington, DC 20001
Telephone: (202) 962-1000
Represented by:
Deborah Swartz Lipman, Director, Government Relations
Beverly R. Silverberg, Director of Public Affairs
Counsel or consultant:
Gartrell & Alexander (Koteles Alexander)
Gold and Liebengood, Inc. (Charles L. Merin)

Washington Mutual Savings Bank
Seattle, WA
Counsel or consultant:
Gibson, Dunn and Crutcher (C. F. Muckenfuss, III)

Washington Natural Gas Co.
Seattle, WA
Counsel or consultant:
Gallagher, Boland, Meiburger and Brosnan (Thomas F. Brosnan)

Washington Office on Africa
110 Maryland Ave., N.E. Suite 112, Washington, DC 20002
Telephone: (202) 546-7961
Background: Established in 1972 to monitor U.S. policy on southern Africa with the purpose of ending minority rule. Sponsored by 22 church agencies and national trade unions.
Represented by:
J. Wilson Asheeke, Legislative Director
Aubrey McCutcheon, III, Exec. Director

Washington Office on Latin America
110 Maryland Ave., N.E. Suite 404, Washington, DC 20002
Telephone: (202) 544-8045
Background: Since 1974, the Washington Office on Latin America (WOLA) has monitored developments in Central and South America and the formulation and implementation of the United States' Latin American policies. WOLA provides information and analysis to Congress, the media, human rights organizations, government agencies, network organizations, nongovernmental and religious groups and academics.
Represented by:
Alexander Wilde, Exec. Director
Carolynn Winters-Hazelton, Deputy Director

Washington Opera, The
Kennedy Center for the Performing Arts, Washington, DC 20566
Telephone: (202) 822-4700
Counsel or consultant:
Chernikoff and Co. (Larry Chernikoff)

Washington Peace Center
2111 Florida Ave., N.W., Washington, DC 20008
Telephone: (202) 234-2000

Background: Founded in 1963 to serve as a clearing house and research center for peace issues. An independent, nonprofit organization manned by volunteers which seeks to stop the arms race and foster peaceful relations among nations.
Represented by:
Lisa Fithian, Coordinator

Washington Performing Arts Soc., The
1029 Vermont Ave., N.W., Washington, DC 20005
Telephone: (202) 393-3600
Counsel or consultant:
Chernikoff and Co. (Larry Chernikoff)

Washington Political Action Committee
444 North Capitol St., N.W. Suite 712, Washington, DC 20001
Telephone: (202) 347-6613
Background: Treasurer/Administrator is Morris J. Amitay.
Counsel or consultant:
Morris J. Amitay, P.C.

Washington Post Co.
1150 15th St., N.W., Washington, DC 20071
Telephone: (202) 334-6642
Represented by:
Guyon D. Knight, V. President, Communications
Counsel or consultant:
Hogan and Hartson
Morgan, Lewis and Bockius
Williams and Connolly (Kevin Baine, David E. Kendall)
Wilmer, Cutler and Pickering

Washington Psychiatric Soc.
1400 K St., N.W. Suite 202, Washington, DC 20005
Telephone: (202) 682-6270
Represented by:
Alvin Golub, Executive Director
Counsel or consultant:
Leach, McGreevy, Eliassen & Leach (Daniel E. Leach)

Washington Psychiatric Soc. Political Action Committee
1400 K St., N.W. Suite 202, Washington, DC 20005
Telephone: (202) 682-6270
Represented by:
Lawrence Y. Kline, M.D., Treasurer

Washington Public Gaming Ass'n
Mountlake Terr., WA
Counsel or consultant:
Denny Miller Associates (Denny Miller)

Washington Public Power Supply System (WPPSS)
Richland, WA
Counsel or consultant:
Bishop, Cook, Purcell & Reynolds (Marlow W. Cook)
Radin & Associates, Inc. (Alex Radin)

Washington Public Utility Districts Ass'n
Seattle, WA
Counsel or consultant:
Radin & Associates, Inc. (Alex Radin)

Washington Raspberry Commission
Olympia, WA
Counsel or consultant:
Kilpatrick & Cody (Joseph W. Dorn)

Washington Real Estate Investment Trust
4936 Fairmont Ave., Bethesda, MD 20814
Telephone: (301) 652-4300
Represented by:
B. Franklin Kahn, President

Washington Researchers
2612 P St., N.W., Washington, DC 20007
Telephone: (202) 333-3499
Represented by:
Leila Kight, President

Washington State Commissioner of Public Lands
Olympia, WA
Counsel or consultant:
Elinor Schwartz

Washington State Democratic Party
Seattle, WA
Counsel or consultant:
Evergreen Associates, Ltd. (Robert M. Brooks)

The listings in this directory are available as *Mailing Labels*. See last page.

ORGANIZATIONS REPRESENTED

Washington State Impact Aid Ass'n
Omak, WA
Counsel or consultant:
Evergreen Associates, Ltd. (Robert M. Brooks)

Washington, State of
Olympia, WA
Counsel or consultant:
Sutherland, Asbill and Brennan (Wright H. Andrews, Jr.)

Washington, State of, Department of Transportation
Olympia, WA
Counsel or consultant:
Denny Miller Associates

Washington Times Corp., The
3600 New York Ave., N.E., Washington, DC 20002
Telephone: (202) 636-3000
Background: A daily newspaper which also publishes the weekly magazine, INSIGHT.
Represented by:
Linda Clark, Public Relations Manager
Counsel or consultant:
Coalitions, Inc. (Roy Jones)

Washington Water Power Co.
Spokane, WA
Counsel or consultant:
Leighton and Sherline (Lee S. Sherline)
Reid & Priest

Waste Conversion Systems, Inc.
Englewood, CO
Counsel or consultant:
Dutko & Associates (L. L. Hank Hankla)

Waste Management, Inc.
1155 Connecticut Ave., N.W., Suite 800, Washington, DC 20036
Telephone: (202) 467-4480
Represented by:
James T. Banks, Director, Government Affairs
Sue M. Briggum, Director, Government Affairs
William Y. Brown, Director, Government Affairs
Kevin J. Igli, Regulatory Affairs Manager
Charles McDermott, Government Affairs Director
James D. Range, Staff V. President, Government Affairs
Jane Seigler, Government Affairs Counsel
Edmund J. Skernolis, Regulatory Affairs Manager
Counsel or consultant:
FMR Group Inc., The
Patton, Boggs and Blow (Katharine R. Boyce)

WATE-TV
Knoxville, TN
Counsel or consultant:
Fletcher, Heald and Hildreth

Water Pollution Control Federation
601 Wythe Street, Alexandria, VA 22314
Telephone: (703) 684-2400
Background: A non-profit, technical organization whose objective is to advance knowledge of all aspects of water pollution control.
Represented by:
Quincalee Brown, Exec. Director
Alan R. Shark, CAE, Assoc. Exec. Dir., Mktg./Communications
John A. Thorner, Director, Gov't Affairs & Gen. Counsel

Water Quality Ass'n
1001 Connecticut Ave., N.W., Suite 407, Washington, DC 20036
Telephone: (202) 452-7855
Represented by:
Patrick M. Theisen, Director of Government Affairs
Counsel or consultant:
Keck, Mahin and Cate

Water Resources Congress
3800 N. Fairfax Drive Suite 7, Arlington, VA 22203
Telephone: (703) 525-4881
Background: A federation of river basin associations; state, municipal and other government agencies; and engineering and other companies concerned with land and water use, conservation and control.
Represented by:
Raymond G. Leonard, President

Water Ski Industry Ass'n
1625 K St., N.W.,, Washington, DC 20006
Telephone: (202) 775-1762
Background: Represented by Jan Kinney of the Sporting Goods Manufacturers Ass'n.

Water Transport Ass'n
New York, NY
Counsel or consultant:
Alper and Mann

Water and Wastewater Equipment Manufacturers Ass'n
Box 17402 Dulles Internat'l Airport, Washington, DC 20041
Telephone: (703) 661-8011
Represented by:
Dawn C. Kristof, President

Water and Wastewater Equipment Manufacturers Ass'n Political Action Committee
Box 17402 Dulles Internat'l Airport, Washington, DC 20041
Telephone: (703) 661-8011
Background: Responsible contact is Dawn Kristof (see Water and Wastewater Equipment Manufacturers Ass'n).

Waterbed Manufacturers Ass'n
Los Angeles, CA
Counsel or consultant:
Fehrenbacher, Sale, Quinn, and Deese (C. Michael Deese)

Waterman Steamship Co.
1000 16th St., N.W. Suite 802, Washington, DC 20036
Telephone: (202) 659-3804
Represented by:
J. Robert Leyh, Sr. V. President, Government Relations
Counsel or consultant:
Hill, Betts and Nash (Brien E. Kehoe)

Watkins Associated Industries, Inc.
Atlanta, GA
Counsel or consultant:
Ginn, Edington, Moore and Wade

Watkins Glen, New York, Municipality of
Counsel or consultant:
Duncan, Weinberg, Miller & Pembroke, P.C. (Wallace L. Duncan, Jeffrey C. Genzer)

Waukegan, Illinois, City of
Counsel or consultant:
Nat'l Center for Municipal Development (Mark S. Israel)

Wayne County, Michigan
Detroit, MI
Counsel or consultant:
Andrews' Associates, Inc. (Mark Andrews)
Patton, Boggs and Blow (James B. Christian, Jr.)

WBAY-TV
Green Bay, WI
Counsel or consultant:
Fletcher, Heald and Hildreth

WBBH-TV
Fort Myers, FL
Counsel or consultant:
Cohn and Marks

WBBS-TV
Chicago, IL
Counsel or consultant:
Fisher, Wayland, Cooper and Leader

WBEN-TV
Buffalo, NY
Counsel or consultant:
Fletcher, Heald and Hildreth

WBFF
Baltimore, MD
Counsel or consultant:
Fisher, Wayland, Cooper and Leader

WBKO
Bowling Green, KY
Counsel or consultant:
Crowell and Moring

WBLN
Bloomington, IL
Counsel or consultant:
Reddy, Begley and Martin

WBNA
Louisville, KY
Counsel or consultant:
Pepper and Corazzini

WBNS-TV
Columbus, OH
Counsel or consultant:
Crowell and Moring

WBRA-TV
Roanoke, VA
Counsel or consultant:
Cohn and Marks

WBRC
Birmingham, AL
Counsel or consultant:
Koteen and Naftalin

WBRZ
Baton Rouge, LA
Counsel or consultant:
Cohn and Marks

WCBB-TV
Augusta-Lewiston, ME
Counsel or consultant:
Tierney & Swift (John L. Tierney)

WCBD-TV
Charleston, SC
Counsel or consultant:
Cohn and Marks

WCCL
New Orleans, LA
Counsel or consultant:
Fletcher, Heald and Hildreth

WCCT-TV
Columbia, SC
Counsel or consultant:
Fisher, Wayland, Cooper and Leader

WCET-TV
Cincinnati, OH
Counsel or consultant:
Cohn and Marks

WCFC-TV
Chicago, IL
Counsel or consultant:
Fisher, Wayland, Cooper and Leader

WCIU-TV
Chicago, IL
Counsel or consultant:
Cohn and Marks

WCKT
Miami, FL
Counsel or consultant:
Koteen and Naftalin

WCLF
Clearwater, FL
Counsel or consultant:
Gammon and Grange

WCLQ-TV
Cleveland, OH
Counsel or consultant:
Crowell and Moring

WCVX
Vineyard Haven, MA
Counsel or consultant:
Arter & Hadden

WDAF-TV
Signal Hill, MO
Counsel or consultant:
Koteen and Naftalin

WDAY-TV
Fargo, ND

ORGANIZATIONS REPRESENTED

Counsel or consultant:
Marmet and McCombs, P.C.

WDAZ-TV
Fargo, ND
Counsel or consultant:
Marmet and McCombs, P.C.

WDBB
Tuscaloosa, AL
Counsel or consultant:
Mullin, Rhyne, Emmons and Topel, P.C.

WDHN
Dothan, AL
Counsel or consultant:
Fletcher, Heald and Hildreth

WDHN-TV
Valdosta, GA
Counsel or consultant:
Fletcher, Heald and Hildreth

WDRB-TV
Louisville, KY
Counsel or consultant:
Marmet and McCombs, P.C.

WEAL-TV
Lancaster, PA
Counsel or consultant:
Marmet and McCombs, P.C.

WEAU-TV
Eau Claire, WI
Counsel or consultant:
Pepper and Corazzini

Web Water Development Ass'n
Aberdeen, SD
Counsel or consultant:
Duncan, Weinberg, Miller & Pembroke, P.C. (Richmond F. Allan, Edward Weinberg)

WEI Enterprises Corp.
Miami, FL
Counsel or consultant:
Morgan, Lewis and Bockius (Sheldon S. Cohen)

Weirton Steel Corp.
Weirton, WV
Counsel or consultant:
Schagrin Associates

WEIU-TV
Charleston, IL
Counsel or consultant:
Cohn and Marks

Weizman Institute of Science
New York, NY
Counsel or consultant:
Powell, Goldstein, Frazer and Murphy (Stuart E. Eizenstat)

WEJC
Lexington, NC
Counsel or consultant:
Gammon and Grange

Welch's Foods, Inc.
Concord, MA
Counsel or consultant:
Robert N. Pyle & Associates (Robert N. Pyle)

Wells Fargo Armored Service Corp.
San Francisco, CA
Counsel or consultant:
McGuiness and Williams (Jeffrey C. McGuiness)

Wendell Investments Ltd.
London England
Counsel or consultant:
Fort and Schlefer (Leonard Egan)
Wilmer, Cutler and Pickering (John H. Pickering)

Wendy's Internat'l, Inc.
Dublin, OH
Counsel or consultant:
Vorys, Sater, Seymour and Pease (Randal C. Teague)

WENY-TV
Elmira, NY

Counsel or consultant:
Cordon and Kelly

Wertheim Co.
New York, NY
Counsel or consultant:
Akin, Gump, Strauss, Hauer and Feld

Wespar Financial Services
Counsel or consultant:
Gibson, Dunn and Crutcher (Robert A. McConnell)

West African Millers Ass'n
1025 Thomas Jefferson St. N.W., Suite 303 W, Washington, DC 20007
Telephone: (202) 342-0007
Represented by:
Simon Pinniger, V. Presidnet

West Bend Co.
West Bend, WI
Background: A part of Dart Industries.
Counsel or consultant:
Barnes, Richardson and Colburn

West German Ceramic Exporters Ass'n
West Germany
Counsel or consultant:
Barnes, Richardson and Colburn

West German Iron and Steel Federation
West Germany
Counsel or consultant:
Coudert Brothers (Milo C. Coerper)

West India Line
New Canaan, CT
Counsel or consultant:
Denning and Wohlstetter (Joseph F. Mullins, Jr.)

West Indies Rum and Spirits Producers' Ass'n
Bridgetown, Barbados
Counsel or consultant:
Dewey, Ballantine, Bushby, Palmer and Wood (John J. Salmon)

West Mexico Vegetable Distributors Ass'n
Nogales, AZ
Counsel or consultant:
Mike Masaoka Associates (T. Albert Yamada)

West Ohio Gas Co.
Lima, OH
Background: A subsidiary of the Consolidated Natural Gas Co. Represented by Charles R. Brown of the parent company.

West Point Pepperell
West Point, GA
Counsel or consultant:
King and Spalding (Abbott B. Lipsky, Jr.)

West Publishing Co.
St. Paul, MN
Counsel or consultant:
Opperman, Heins & Pasquin

West Virginia Bankers Ass'n
Charleston, WV
Counsel or consultant:
Ryan-McGinn (Daniel McGinn)

West Virginia Hospital Ass'n
Charleston, WV
Counsel or consultant:
Ryan-McGinn (Daniel McGinn)

West Virginia Railroad Maintenance Authority
Charleston, WV
Counsel or consultant:
Anderson and Pendleton, C.A. (Francis G. McKenna)

West Virginia, State of
Charleston, WV
Counsel or consultant:
Dickstein, Shapiro and Morin (Andrew P. Miller, Bernard Nash)

West Virginia University
Morgantown, WV

Counsel or consultant:
John G. Campbell, Inc.
Cassidy and Associates, Inc. (Donald P. Smith, Dr. Elvis J. Stahr, Jr.)

Westcoast Transmission Co.
Vancouver, British Columbia
Counsel or consultant:
McHenry and Staffier, P.C. (John R. Staffier)

Western Ass'n of Children's Hospitals
San Diego, CA
Counsel or consultant:
McDermott, Will and Emery

Western Bank
Los Angeles, CA
Counsel or consultant:
Manatt, Phelps, Rothenberg & Phillips (Robert J. Kabel)

Western Carolina Telephone Co.
Merrifield, VA
Counsel or consultant:
Hunton and Williams

Western Coal Traffic League
1224 17th St., N.W., Washington, DC 20036
Telephone: (202) 659-1445
Background: An association of western coal shippers. The address given is that of the law firm of Slover and Loftus.
Counsel or consultant:
Slover and Loftus (C. Michael Loftus, Ira E. McKeever)

Western Coal Traffic League Political Action Committee
1224 17th St., N.W., Washington, DC 20036
Telephone: (202) 659-1445
Background: Howard Pyle of the Houston Lighting and Power Co. serves as Treasurer.
Counsel or consultant:
Slover and Loftus

Western Electrochemical Co.
Henderson, NV
Counsel or consultant:
O'Connor & Hannan (Mary Scott Guest)

Western/English Retailers of America
2011 Eye St., N.W. Suite 600, Washington, DC 20006
Telephone: (202) 347-1932
Background: Represented by Douglas W. Wiegand, Executive Director of the Menswear Retailers of America.

Western Financial Savings Bank
Orange, CA
Counsel or consultant:
Steptoe and Johnson (John T. Collins)

Western Forest Industries Ass'n
Portland, OR
Counsel or consultant:
Jack Ferguson Associates (Jack Ferguson)
Joseph S. Miller
Scootch Pankonin

Western Fuels Ass'n
1625 M St., N.W. Magruder Bldg., Washington, DC 20036-3264
Telephone: (202) 463-6580
Background: A non-profit corporation, formed by a group of rural electric power cooperatives and municipal electric utilities located principally in the western states, to obtain fuel at the lowest possible prices.
Represented by:
Ned Leonard, Manager Communications/Gov't Affairs
Fredrick D. Palmer, General Manager & CEO
Counsel or consultant:
Doherty, Rumble, and Butler (Peter S. Glaser)
Duncan, Weinberg, Miller & Pembroke, P.C. (Frederick L. Miller, Jr., Edward Weinberg)

Western Governors' Ass'n
444 North Capitol St., Suite 526, Washington, DC 20001
Telephone: (202) 624-5402
Background: Consists of governors of 18 western states, Guam, the Northern Mariana Islands and American Samoa. Based in Denver, Colorado.
Represented by:
R. Philip Shimer, Washington Representative

The listings in this directory are available as *Mailing Labels*. See last page.

ORGANIZATIONS REPRESENTED

Western Land Exchange Co.
Denver, CO
Counsel or consultant:
 Kogovsek & Associates, Inc.

Western Range Ass'n
Fair Oaks, CA
Counsel or consultant:
 Holt, Miller & Associates (Harris N. Miller)

Western River Guides Ass'n
Denver, CO
Counsel or consultant:
 Scootch Pankonin

Western Southern
Cincinnati, OH
Counsel or consultant:
 The Hoving Group (John H. F. Hoving)

Western States Land Commissioners Ass'n
Counsel or consultant:
 Elinor Schwartz

Western States Meat Ass'n
Oakland, CA
Counsel or consultant:
 Olsson, Frank and Weeda, P.C. (John Bode)

Western States Petroleum Ass'n
Glendale, CA
Counsel or consultant:
 Braun & Company

Western States Steel Producers Coalition
Counsel or consultant:
 Laxalt, Washington, Perito & Dubuc

Western Townships Utilities Authority
Plymouth, MI
Counsel or consultant:
 Cassidy and Associates, Inc. (Robert K. Dawson, Donald P. Smith)

Western Transportation Co.
Portland, OR
Counsel or consultant:
 LaRoe, Winn, Moerman & Donovan (Paul M. Donovan, Gerald L. Richman)

Western Union Corp.
Upper Saddle Riv, NJ
Counsel or consultant:
 Collier, Shannon & Scott
 Mudge Rose Guthrie Alexander and Ferdon (David A. Vaughan)
 Wiley, Rein & Fielding

Westinghouse Airship
Baltimore, MD
Counsel or consultant:
 Wunder, Ryan, Cannon & Thelen (John J. McGovern, Jr.)

Westinghouse Broadcasting Co., Inc.
1025 Connecticut Ave., N.W., Washington, DC 20036
Telephone: (202) 429-0196
Represented by:
 Gerald E. Udwin, V. President
Counsel or consultant:
 Wilkes, Artis, Hedrick and Lane, Chartered (John D. Lane)

Westinghouse Community Development Group
Coral Springs, FL
Counsel or consultant:
 Dow, Lohnes and Albertson (Robert M. Chasnow)

Westinghouse Electric Corp.
1801 K St., N.W., Suite 800, Washington, DC 20006
Telephone: (202) 835-2300
Represented by:
 J. Paris Fisher, Director, Gov't Relations - Defense
 Janet Hall, Director, International Affairs
 John F. Hay, Assoc. Dir., Gov't Relations - Defense
 Joseph P. Kigin, Director, Government/Public Affairs
 William A. MacLaurin, Manager, Washington Public Relations
 Frank S. Marriott, Director, Public Programs
 John K. Rayburn, V. President, Government Programs
 David C. Shoaf, Director, Advanced Programs
 William M. Spodak, Director, Government Relations
 F. Leo Wright, V. President, Government Affairs
Counsel or consultant:
 Andrews' Associates, Inc. (Mark Andrews, Jacqueline Balk-Tusa)
 John McE. Atkisson, P.C.
 George H. Denison
 Groom and Nordberg (Robert B. Harding, Carl A. Nordberg, Jr.)
 Lipsen Whitten & Diamond
 Charlie McBride Assoc., Inc. (Charlie McBride)
 McMahon and Associates
 Newmyer Associates, Inc.
 O'Connor & Hannan
 J. Arthur Weber & Associates (Joseph A. Weber)
 Willkie Farr and Gallagher (Matthew R. Schneider)
 Winthrop, Stimson, Putnam & Roberts (G. Lawrence Atkins)
 Wunder, Ryan, Cannon & Thelen (John J. McGovern, Jr.)

Westinghouse Environmental Services
1801 K St., N.W., Washington, DC 20006
Telephone: (202) 835-2347
Counsel or consultant:
 McNair Group Inc. (Kathy E. Gallegos, Dennis R. Rankin)

Westinghouse Hanford Co.
Richland, WA
Background: A subsidiary of Westinghouse Electric Corp; prime contractor at Hanford Reservation.
Counsel or consultant:
 Preston Gates Ellis & Rouvelas Meeds (Tim L. Peckinpaugh)

Westinghouse Transportation Division
West Mifflin, PA
Counsel or consultant:
 Keefe Co., The (Clarence L. James, Jr., William A. Roberts)
 Vierra Associates, Inc. (Dennis C. Vierra)

Westland Oil Development Corp.
Montgomery, TX
Counsel or consultant:
 Taft, Stettinius and Hollister (Robert Taft, Jr.)

Westvaco Corp.
New York, NY
Counsel or consultant:
 Hunton and Williams
 Lee, Toomey & Kent

Westwood One, Inc.
Los Angeles, CA
Background: Distributor of radio programming, owner of the Mutual Broadcasting System.
Counsel or consultant:
 Arter & Hadden (Bruce Goodman)
 Kaye, Scholer, Fierman, Hays and Handler (Christopher R. Brewster, Jason Shrinsky)

WETA
Box 2626, Washington, DC 20013
Telephone: (202) 998-2600
Counsel or consultant:
 Holman Communications (Diana L. Holman)

WEVU
Naples, FL
Counsel or consultant:
 Cordon and Kelly

Wexler, Reynolds, Fuller, Harrison and Schule Political Action Committee
1317 F St., N.W. Suite 700, Washington, DC 20004
Telephone: (202) 638-2121
Counsel or consultant:
 Wexler, Reynolds, Fuller, Harrison and Schule, Inc.

Weyerhaeuser Co.
2001 L St., N.W., Suite 304, Washington, DC 20036
Telephone: (202) 293-7222
Represented by:
 Creigh H. Agnew, Government Affairs Manager
 Frederick S. Benson, III, V. President, National Affairs

WFBN
Joliet, IL
Counsel or consultant:
 Reddy, Begley and Martin

WFCB-TV
Miami, FL
Counsel or consultant:
 Fisher, Wayland, Cooper and Leader

WFFT
Baton Rouge, LA
Counsel or consultant:
 Fletcher, Heald and Hildreth

WFME
West Milford, NJ
Counsel or consultant:
 Fletcher, Heald and Hildreth

WFMJ-TV
Youngstown, OH
Counsel or consultant:
 Fisher, Wayland, Cooper and Leader

WFMZ-TV
Allentown, PA
Counsel or consultant:
 Arter & Hadden

WFRV-TV
Green Bay, WI
Counsel or consultant:
 Koteen and Naftalin

WGAL-TV
Lancaster, PA
Counsel or consultant:
 Marmet and McCombs, P.C.

WGBA
Green Bay, WI
Counsel or consultant:
 Arter & Hadden

WGBU-TV
Bowling Green, OH
Counsel or consultant:
 Cohn and Marks

WGGS-TV
Greenville, SC
Counsel or consultant:
 Fisher, Wayland, Cooper and Leader

WGHP-TV
Greensboro, NC
Counsel or consultant:
 Koteen and Naftalin

WGR-TV
Buffalo, NY
Counsel or consultant:
 Koteen and Naftalin

WGTQ
Sault St. Marie, MI
Counsel or consultant:
 Koteen and Naftalin

WGTU
Traverse City, MD
Counsel or consultant:
 Koteen and Naftalin

WGVC-TV
Allendale, MI
Counsel or consultant:
 Cohn and Marks

WGVK-TV
Kalamazoo, MI
Counsel or consultant:
 Cohn and Marks

The listings in this directory are available as *Mailing Labels*. See last page.

ORGANIZATIONS REPRESENTED

WHA-TV
Madison, WI
Counsel or consultant:
Cohn and Marks

WHAE-TV
Atlanta, GA
Counsel or consultant:
Fisher, Wayland, Cooper and Leader

Wheat Export Trade Education Committee
415 2nd St., N.E., Suite 300, Washington, DC 20002
Telephone: (202) 547-2004
Represented by:
Karen Fegley, Director

Wheatland Tube Co.
Wheatland, PA
Counsel or consultant:
Schagrin Associates (Carol A. Colza, Roger B. Schagrin)

Wheelabrator Corp., The
Peachtree City, GA
Counsel or consultant:
Fleishman-Hillard, Inc

Wheelabrator Technologies‡ Inc.
Danvers, MA
Counsel or consultant:
Concord Associates, Inc.
Wunder, Ryan, Cannon & Thelen (Thomas M. Ryan)

Wheeling Hospital
Wheeling, WV
Counsel or consultant:
Ryan-McGinn (Daniel McGinn)

Wheeling Jesuit College
Wheeling, WV
Counsel or consultant:
Ryan-McGinn (C. Michael Fulton)

Wheeling-Pittsburgh Steel Co.
Wheeling, WV
Counsel or consultant:
Gibson, Dunn and Crutcher

Wheels, Inc.
Des Plaines, IL
Counsel or consultant:
French & Company (Mark M. Ellison, Verrick O. French)

White Consolidated Industries
1317 F St., N.W. Suite 510, Washington, DC 20004
Telephone: (202) 638-7878
Represented by:
Linda W. Greiner, Manager, Government Relations
Frederick H. Hallett, V. Pres., Industry & Gov't Relations
Counsel or consultant:
Squire, Sanders and Dempsey (Jeffrey O. Cerar, Edward J. Hawkins, Robert D. Papkin)

White Earth Tribal Council
White Earth, MN
Background: An Indian tribal government.
Counsel or consultant:
Forrest Gerard & Associates (Forrest J. Gerard)

White Mountain Apache Tribe
White Rive, AZ
Counsel or consultant:
McAuliffe, Kelly, Raffaelli & Siemens (Lynnette R. Jacquez)

Whitman Corp.
1667 K St., N.W., Suite 605, Washington, DC 20006
Telephone: (202) 293-6410
Background: A consumer goods and services company with four major operating companies: Pet, Inc.; Pepsi Cola General Bottlers; Midas Internat'l; and Hussman Corp.
Represented by:
Gary A. Lee, Corporate V. President, Gov't Affairs

Whitman Distributing Co.
Mathis, TX
Counsel or consultant:
Hogan and Hartson (Clifford S. Gibbons, George T. Miller, Jr. Chester Taylor)

Whittle Communications
Knoxville, TN

Counsel or consultant:
Gallagher-Widmeyer Group Inc., The (Scott D. Widmeyer)

WHNT-TV
Huntsville, AL
Counsel or consultant:
Koteen and Naftalin

Wholesale Florists and Florist Suppliers of America
5313 Lee Highway, Arlington, VA 22207
Telephone: (703) 241-1100
Represented by:
Archie J. Clapp, Exec. V. President

Wholesale Nursery Growers of America
1250 Eye St., N.W., Suite 500, Washington, DC 20005
Telephone: (202) 789-2900
Background: Exec. V. President is Lawrence E. Scovotto of the American Ass'n of Nurserymen.

Wholesaler-Distributor Political Action Committee
1725 K St., N.W. Suite 710, Washington, DC 20006
Telephone: (202) 872-0885
Background: The political action committee of the Nat'l Ass'n of Wholesaler-Distributors. Alan Kranowitz serves as Exec. Director.

WHTN
Murfreesboro, TN
Counsel or consultant:
Reddy, Begley and Martin

Wickes Companies, Inc.
Santa Monica, CA
Counsel or consultant:
Dewey, Ballantine, Bushby, Palmer and Wood (John J. Salmon)

Wickes Manufacturing Co.
Southfield, MI
Counsel or consultant:
Preston Gates Ellis & Rouvelas Meeds (Richard L. Barnes, Craig J. Gehring)

Wider Opportunities for Women
1325 G St., N.W. Lower Level, Washington, DC 20005
Telephone: (202) 638-3143
Background: A private nonprofit organization that works to ensure economic independence and equality of opportunity for women. Works at the local, state and national levels to: increase public awareness of women's employment and economic needs; design, test and share innovative program and policy approaches to meeting women's employment needs; and expand women's employment options and earnings potential.
Represented by:
Deborah Arrindell, Director of Public Policy
Cynthia E. Marano, Exec. Director
Sally Steenland, Director of Media Programs

WIEC
Ponce, PR
Counsel or consultant:
Fletcher, Heald and Hildreth

Wien Air Alaska
Anchorage, AK
Counsel or consultant:
Seamon, Wasko and Ozment (Theodore I. Seamon)

Wilderness Soc.
1400 Eye St., N.W., 10th Floor, Washington, DC 20005
Telephone: (202) 842-3400
Background: A national, non-profit citizens' organization with a membership of about 350,000 that works to save endangered wildlands and ensure wise management of natural resources.

Represented by:
Sydney J. Butler, V. President, Conservation
Peter Coppelman, V. President
Brien F. Culhane, Assistant Director, Nat'l Parks Program
Pam Eaton, Refuge Program Assistant
Peter Emerson, V. Pres, Rsrch, Planning & Economics
Barry Flamm, Chief Forester
George T. Frampton, Jr., President
Michael A. Francis, Counsel, National Forest Issues
Craig Gehrke, Director, Intermountain Region
Mary Hanley, V. President, Public Affairs
Donald Hellmann, Associate Counselor
Gaylord Nelson, Counselor
Rindy O'Brien, Director, Governmental Affairs
Bill Reffalt, Director, Wildlife Refuge Program
Richard E. Rice, Resource Economist
Karin Sheldon, Senior Counsel
Jim St. Pierre, Maine Woods Project Director
Ronald Tipton, Deputy, Field Operations
Jay Watson, Forest Issues Specialist
Steven C. Whitney, Director, Nat'l Parks Program
Rebecca Wodder, V. President, Membership & Development

Wildlife Legislative Fund of America
1000 Connecticut Ave., N.W., Suite 1202, Washington, DC 20036
Telephone: (202) 466-4407
Represented by:
Ronald J. Somerville, Director, National Affairs
Counsel or consultant:
Birch, Horton, Bittner and Cherot (William P. Horn)

Wildlife Management Institute
1101 14th St., N.W., Suite 725, Washington, DC 20005
Telephone: (202) 371-1808
Background: Programs of the Institute have been in existence under various names since 1911. Incorporated in New York in 1946. Purpose is to advance sound management of natural resources, especially wildlife.
Represented by:
Laurence R. Jahn, President
Lonnie L. Williamson, Vice President

Williams & Co., A. L.
Duluth, GA
Counsel or consultant:
Fierce and Associates (Donald L. Fierce)
O'Brien and Associates, David (David D. O'Brien)

Williams Companies, The
1120 20th St., N.W. Suite S 700, Washington, DC 20036
Telephone: (202) 833-8994
Background: Subsidiaries also represented include Williams Gas Marketing Co., Williams Pipe Line Co., Williams Natural Gas Co., Northwest Pipe Line Co., Williams Telecommunications Co. and Northwest Alaskan Pipeline Co.
Represented by:
Deborah Ball Lynch, Director, Regulatory Affairs
Counsel or consultant:
Jack Ferguson Associates
Keck, Mahin and Cate (Rebecca Schaffer)
Wright and Talisman

Williams and Jensen P.C. Political Action Committee
1101 Connecticut Ave., N.W. Suite 500, Washington, DC 20036
Telephone: (202) 659-8201
Background: A political action committee organized and sponsored by the Washington law firm of Williams and Jensen. Provides financial support to Congressional candidates on nationwide basis.
Counsel or consultant:
Williams and Jensen, P.C.

Wilmington Savings Fund Soc.
Wilmington, DE
Counsel or consultant:
James J. Butera, Chartered
Dow, Lohnes and Albertson (Jeffrey B. Stern)

Wilmorite, Inc.
Rochester, NY
Counsel or consultant:
F. Nordy Hoffmann & Assoc. (F. Nordy Hoffmann)

ORGANIZATIONS REPRESENTED

WILX-TV
Lansing, MI
Counsel or consultant:
Koteen and Naftalin

Windham Community Memorial Hospital
Willimantic, CT
Counsel or consultant:
Jones, Day, Reavis and Pogue (Randall E. Davis)

Wine Institute
1575 Eye St., N.W., Suite 325, Washington, DC 20005
Telephone: (202) 408-0870
Represented by:
Lorraine Gafney, Director
Counsel or consultant:
McAuliffe, Kelly, Raffaelli & Siemens (Frederick W. Hatfield)

Wine and Spirits Wholesalers of America
1023 15th St., N.W., 4th Floor, Washington, DC 20005
Telephone: (202) 371-9792
Represented by:
Joseph C. Gegg, Senior V. President
Douglas W. Metz, Exec. V. President
Alexandra Walsh, Dir., Communications and Education
Harry G. Wiles, II, V. Pres., Federal Government Relations
Counsel or consultant:
Rogers and Wells (William Morris)

Wine and Spirits Wholesalers of America Political Action Committee
1023 15th St., N.W., 4th Floor, Washington, DC 20005
Telephone: (202) 371-9792
Background: Responsible contact is Douglas W. Metz. (See Wine and Spirits Wholesalers of America.)

Wings Holdings Inc.
Los Angeles, CA
Counsel or consultant:
Verner, Liipfert, Bernhard, McPherson and Hand, Chartered (Berl Bernhard)

Wire Industry Suppliers Ass'n
7297 Lee Highway, Suite N, Falls Church, VA 22042
Telephone: (703) 533-9530
Counsel or consultant:
Ass'n and Society Management Internat'l Inc. (Clay D. Tyeryar)

Wire Reinforcement Institute
1760 Reston Pkwy., Reston, VA 22090
Telephone: (703) 709-9207
Represented by:
Milton R. Sees, President
Counsel or consultant:
Loomis, Owen, Fellman and Howe (James E. Anderson)

Wire Rope Technical Board
P.O. Box 849, Stevensville, MD 21666
Telephone: (301) 643-4161
Counsel or consultant:
J. D. Ferry Associates (John D. Ferry)

Wireless Cable Ass'n, Inc.
Des Moines, IA
Represented by:
Robert L. Schmidt, President
Counsel or consultant:
Fox, Bennett and Turner (Nicholas W. Allard)

Wisconsin Distributor Group
Background: A group of seven Wisconsin utility companies.
Counsel or consultant:
Baker and Botts (Bruce F. Kiely)

Wisconsin Electric Power Co.
Milwaukee, WI
Counsel or consultant:
Bruder, Gentile & Marcoux (George F. Bruder)
Keller and Heckman
McCarthy, Sweeney and Harkaway, P.C.
Shaw, Pittman, Potts and Trowbridge (Gerald Charnoff)

Wisconsin Natural Gas Co.
Milwaukee, WI
Counsel or consultant:
Baker and Botts

Wisconsin Power and Light Co.
Madison, WI
Counsel or consultant:
Baker and Botts
McCarthy, Sweeney and Harkaway, P.C.
Shaw, Pittman, Potts and Trowbridge

Wisconsin Public Service Corp.
Green Bay, WI
Counsel or consultant:
McCarthy, Sweeney and Harkaway, P.C.
Shaw, Pittman, Potts and Trowbridge

Wisconsin, State of
444 N. Capitol St., N.W. Suite 345, Washington, DC 20001
Telephone: (202) 624-5870
Represented by:
David Beightol, Director, Washington Office

Wistar Institute, The
Philadelphia, PA
Counsel or consultant:
Capitol Associates, Inc. (Marguerite Donoghue, Terry Lierman)
Hill and Knowlton Public Affairs Worldwide (Henry W. Hubbard, Sr.)

Witness for Peace
P.O. Box 33273, Washington, DC 20033
Telephone: (202) 797-1169
Represented by:
Dennis Marker, Co-director

WIVB-TV
Buffalo, NY
Counsel or consultant:
Cordon and Kelly

WIXT
Syracuse, NY
Counsel or consultant:
Rubin, Winston and Diercks

WJBF
Augusta, GA
Counsel or consultant:
Fletcher, Heald and Hildreth

WJET-TV
Erie, PA
Counsel or consultant:
Reddy, Begley and Martin

WJKS-TV
Jacksonville, FL
Counsel or consultant:
Cohn and Marks

WJMN-TV
Escanaba, MI
Counsel or consultant:
Koteen and Naftalin

WJPR
Lynchburg, VA
Counsel or consultant:
Arter & Hadden

WJSU-TV
Anniston, AL
Counsel or consultant:
Cohn and Marks

WJTC
Pensacola, FL
Counsel or consultant:
Arter & Hadden

WJZY
Belmet, NC
Counsel or consultant:
Fletcher, Heald and Hildreth

WKPT-TV
Kingsport, TN
Counsel or consultant:
Cordon and Kelly

WKRC-TV
Cincinnati, OH

Counsel or consultant:
Koteen and Naftalin

WLEX-TV
Lexington, KY
Counsel or consultant:
Fletcher, Heald and Hildreth

WLIG-TV
Riverhead, NY
Counsel or consultant:
Gammon and Grange

WLJC-TV
Beattyville, KY
Counsel or consultant:
Reddy, Begley and Martin

WLKY-TV
Louisville, KY
Counsel or consultant:
Marmet and McCombs, P.C.

WLNE-TV
New Bedford, MA
Counsel or consultant:
Marmet and McCombs, P.C.

WLOX-TV
Biloxi, MS
Counsel or consultant:
Fletcher, Heald and Hildreth

WLUC-TV
Marquette, MI
Counsel or consultant:
Pepper and Corazzini

WLYJ
Clarksburg, WV
Counsel or consultant:
Gammon and Grange

WMDT
Salisbury, MD
Counsel or consultant:
Cohn and Marks

WMF of America
Farmingdale, NY
Background: A subsidiary of the West German firm of Wuerttembergische Metalwarenfabrik AG.
Counsel or consultant:
Barnes, Richardson and Colburn

WMGM-TV
Swainton, NJ
Background: Formerly WAAT of Wildwood, NJ.
Counsel or consultant:
Cordon and Kelly

WMSY-TV
Marion, VA
Counsel or consultant:
Cohn and Marks

WMW Machinery, Inc.
Blauvelt, NY
Counsel or consultant:
Jack McDonald Co. (Jack McDonald, Myron G. Sandifer, III)

WNDS
Derry, NH
Counsel or consultant:
Reddy, Begley and Martin

WNEP-TV
Scranton, PA
Counsel or consultant:
Koteen and Naftalin

WNET/Channel 13
New York, NY
Counsel or consultant:
Targeted Communications Corp.

WNFT
Jacksonville, FL
Counsel or consultant:
Gammon and Grange

The listings in this directory are available as *Mailing Labels*. See last page.

ORGANIZATIONS REPRESENTED

WNHT
Concord, NH
Counsel or consultant:
Sutherland, Asbill and Brennan

WNNE-TV
Hanover, NH
Counsel or consultant:
Steptoe and Johnson

WOAY-TV
Oak Hill, WV
Counsel or consultant:
Fletcher, Heald and Hildreth

WOI-TV
Ames, IA
Counsel or consultant:
Cohn and Marks

WOKR
Rochester, NY
Counsel or consultant:
Pepper and Corazzini

Wolf Creek Nuclear Operating Corp.
Burlington, KS
Counsel or consultant:
Shaw, Pittman, Potts and Trowbridge (Jay E. Silberg)

Woman's Nat'l Democratic Club
1526 New Hampshire Ave., N.W., Washington, DC 20036
Telephone: (202) 232-7363
Represented by:
Patricia Desoto, General Manager

Women for Meaningful Summits
1301 20th St., N.W. Suite 702, Washington, DC 20036
Telephone: (202) 296-2665
Background: Chair of the Board is Sharon Parker of the Girls Clubs of America.

Women in Communications
2101 Wilson Blvd., Suite 417, Arlington, VA 22201
Telephone: (703) 528-4200
Represented by:
Susan Lowell Butler, Exec. V. President
Louise Ott, Public Affairs Director
Linda Russman, Director, Communications
Leslie Sansom, Media Relations

Women in Community Service
1900 North Beauregard St., Suite 14, Alexandria, VA 22311
Telephone: (703) 671-0500
Background: A coalition of the Nat'l Council of Catholic Women, the Nat'l Council of Jewish Women, the Nat'l Council of Negro Women, the American G.I. Forum Women, and Church Women United.
Represented by:
Ruth C. Herman, Exec. Director

Women in Government Relations
1325 Massachusetts Ave., N.W., Suite 510, Washington, DC 20005
Telephone: (202) 637-6100
Background: An organization of about 500 women with government relations/public affairs responsibilities in corporations, associations, law firms, government agencies and public interest groups. President is Sandy Cook of Electronic Data Systems.
Counsel or consultant:
Degnon Associates, Inc. (Marge Degnon)

Women Judges Fund for Justice
1900 L St., N.W., 300, Washington, DC 20036
Telephone: (202) 331-7343
Represented by:
Marilyn Nejelski, Exec. Director

Women Strike for Peace
105 2nd St., N.E., Washington, DC 20002
Telephone: (202) 543-2660
Background: A women's movement established in 1961 concerned with nuclear disarmament, radiation dangers, and United States intervention in Third World countries.
Represented by:
Edith Villastrigo, Nat'l Legislative Coordinator

Women vs. Smoking
1730 Rhode Island Ave., N.W. Suite 600, Washington, DC 20036
Telephone: (202) 659-8475
Background: Affiliated with The Advocacy Institute.
Represented by:
Michele Bloch, Director

Women's Action for Nuclear Disarmament
305 7th St., S.E., Suite 204, Washington, DC 20003
Telephone: (202) 543-8505
Represented by:
Suzanne S. Kerr, Legislative Director

Women's Campaign Fund
1601 Connecticut Ave., N.W. Suite 800, Washington, DC 20005
Telephone: (202) 234-3700
Background: Identifies and provides financial and technical support to women candidates for public office.
Represented by:
Maura Brueger, Political Director
Jane Danowitz, Exec. Director

Women's College Coalition
1101 17th St., N.W., Suite 1001, Washington, DC 20036
Telephone: (202) 466-5430
Background: A public relations effort on behalf of single sex institutions.
Counsel or consultant:
Hager Sharp Inc. (Marcia Sharp)

Women's Economic Justice Center
c/o NCPA, 2000 Florida Ave., N.W. 4th Floor, Washington, DC 20009
Telephone: (202) 387-6030
Background: Formed in 1987 by the Nat'l Center for Policy Alternatives to mobilize lobbying support to improver women's economic status. Contact is Linda Tarr-Whelan of the Nat'l Center.

Women's Legal Defense Fund
2000 P St., N.W., Suite 400, Washington, DC 20036
Telephone: (202) 887-0364
Background: Secures and advances the legal rights of women at the state and federal levels.
Represented by:
Diane Dodson, Deputy Director, Family Programs
Donna R. Lenhoff, Director, Legal Policy and Programs
Judith L. Lichtman, President
Virginia Sassaman, Communications Manager
Meshall Thomas, Manager, Emerg. Domestic Rels. Project
Judith Winston, Deputy Director, Public Policy
Claudia A. Withers, Deputy Director, Employment Programs
Counsel or consultant:
Bass & Howes (Joanne Howes)

Women's Research and Education Institute
1700 18th St., N.W., Suite 400, Washington, DC 20009
Telephone: (202) 328-7070
Background: Conducts research on women's economic issues. Publishes papers on issues relevant to current legislation. Administers Congressional Fellowship Program on Women and Public Policy.
Represented by:
Alison C. Dineen, Director of Fellowship Program
Betty Dooley, Exec. Director

Women's Sports Foundation
New York, NY
Counsel or consultant:
Holman Communications (Diana L. Holman)

Women's Task Force - LCCR
Nat'l Women's Political Caucus 1275 Eye St., N.W., Suite 750, Washington, DC 20005
Telephone: (202) 898-1100
Background: Represented by Patricia Blau Reuss of the Nat'l Women's Political Caucus.

Won Door Corp.
Salt Lake City, UT
Counsel or consultant:
Parry and Romani Associates Inc. (Romano Romani)

Wood Heating Alliance
1101 Connecticut Ave., N.W. Suite 700, Washington, DC 20036
Telephone: (202) 857-1181

Counsel or consultant:
Perkins Coie (Guy R. Martin)
Smith, Bucklin and Associates (Carter E. Keithley)

Wood Machinery Manufacturers of America
Philadelphia, PA
Counsel or consultant:
London and Satagaj, Attorneys-at-Law (Sheldon I. London, John S. Satagaj)

Woods Research Associates
Columbia, SC
Counsel or consultant:
Woods and Associates (Irvin M. Woods)

Woodward and Lothrop
1025 F St., N.W., Washington, DC 20013
Telephone: (202) 347-5300
Represented by:
Judith Pickering, General Counsel-Secretary

Woodward and Lothrop Federal Political Action Committee
2800 Eisenhower Ave, Alexandria, VA 22314
Telephone: (703) 329-5457
Represented by:
Eric Schweizer, Treasurer

WordPerfect
Orem, UT
Counsel or consultant:
Swidler & Berlin, Chartered (Bruce A. Lehman)

Work Glove Manufacturers Ass'n
1200 17th St., N.W. Suite 400, Washington, DC 20036
Telephone: (202) 296-9200
Counsel or consultant:
Economic Consulting Services Inc. (Deborah Swartz)
Hill Group, Inc. (Joseph A. Cook)

Working Group Coalition, The
c/o Stateside Assoc., 2300 Clarendon Blvd, Suite 407, Arlington, VA 22201
Telephone: (703) 525-7466
Background: A coalition which includes such major corporations as General Electric, RJR Nabisco and Kraft General Foods. Exec. Director is Constance Campanella of Stateside Associates.
Counsel or consultant:
Stateside Associates (Constance Campanella)

World Airways
Herndon, VA
Counsel or consultant:
Camp, Barsh, Bates and Tate (Ronald L. Platt)
McAuliffe, Kelly, Raffaelli & Siemens (Lynnette R. Jacquez)
McNair Group Inc. (Denis J. Dwyer)

World Chiropractic Alliance
Chandler, AZ
Counsel or consultant:
Parry and Romani Associates Inc.

World Council on Free Zones
1815 N. Lynn St. Suite 200, Arlington, VA 22209
Telephone: (703) 528-7444
Counsel or consultant:
Vorys, Sater, Seymour and Pease (Randal C. Teague)

World Federalist Ass'n
418 Seventh St., S.E., Washington, DC 20003
Telephone: (202) 546-3950
Background: A globally oriented organization which asserts that peace can best be achieved through the enforcement of world law.
Represented by:
Anthony Allen, Youth and Communications Director
Olga Gechas, Development Director
Walter F. Hoffmann, Exec. Director
Edward Rawson, Administrative Director

World Federation for Mental Health
1021 Prince St., Alexandria, VA 22314
Telephone: (703) 684-7722
Represented by:
Dr. Eugene B. Brody, Secretary General
Richard C. Hunter, Deputy Secretary General

World Federation for the Protection of Animals
London, England

The listings in this directory are available as *Mailing Labels*. See last page.

ORGANIZATIONS REPRESENTED

World Federation for the Protection of Animals (Cont'd)
Counsel or consultant:
Murdaugh Stuart Madden

World Federation of Public Health Ass'ns
c/o Amer. Public Health Ass'n 1015 15th St., N.W., Washington, DC 20005
Telephone: (202) 789-5600
Represented by:
Catherine Savino, Exec. Secretary

World Freedom Foundation
111 South Columbus St., Alexandria, VA 22314
Telephone: (703) 683-7746
Counsel or consultant:
Keene, Shirley & Associates, Inc. (David A. Keene, Craigan P. Shirley)

World Future Soc.
4916 St. Elmo Ave., Bethesda, MD 20814
Telephone: (301) 656-8274
Represented by:
Edward S. Cornish, President
Frank Snowden Hopkins, V. President
Graham T. T. Molitor, V. President and Secretary

World Government of World Citizens
1012 14th St., N.W. Suite 1101, Washington, DC 20005
Telephone: (202) 638-2662
Background: An international movement founded in 1954 to implement worldwide legal observance of human rights. Represented by Garry Davis, World Coordinator of World Service Authority.

World Hunger Education Service
3018 Fourth St., N.E., Washington, DC 20017
Telephone: (202) 269-1075
Background: Promotes food policy development and justice issues.
Represented by:
Patricia L. Kutzner, Exec. Director

World Mercy Fund
121 S. Saint Asaph St., Alexandria, VA 22314
Telephone: (703) 548-4646
Represented by:
Patrick Leonard, President
Gary D. Thorud, Exec. V. President

World Peace Through Law Center
1000 Connecticut Ave., N.W. Suite 800, Washington, DC 20036
Telephone: (202) 466-5428
Background: A non-profit organization established under the auspices of the American Bar Ass'n in 1963. Seeks peaceful international relations under a rule of law. Holds biennial international conference/and publishes the newsletter, The World Jurist.
Represented by:
Margaretha M. Henneberry, Exec. V. President
Charles S. Rhyne, President

World Peacemakers
2025 Massachusetts Ave., N.W., Washington, DC 20036
Telephone: (202) 265-7582
Background: Seeks an end to the arms race through church renewal.
Represented by:
Bill Price, Director

World Population Soc.
1333 H St., N.W., Suite 760, Washington, DC 20005
Telephone: (202) 898-1303
Represented by:
Frank Oram, Exec. Director

World Relief
220 Eye St., N.E. Suite 200, Washington, DC 20002
Telephone: (202) 544-4447
Background: A subsidiary of the Nat'l Ass'n of Evangelicals headquartered in Wheaton, IL.
Represented by:
Don Bjork, Associate Exec. Director

World Resources Institute
1709 New York Ave., N.W., Washington, DC 20006
Telephone: (202) 638-6300
Background: An independent research and policy institute founded in 1982 to help governments, environmental and development organizations, and private business address the fundamental question of how can societies meet basic needs and nuture economic growth without undermining the natural resource base and environmental integrity.
Represented by:
Roger Dower, Dir, Climate Energy & Pollution Program
Mohamed T. El-Ashry, V. Pres., Research and Policy Affairs
Shirley K. Geer, Press Relations
Jessica Tuchman Mathews, V. President
James J. McKenzie, Senior Associate
Rafe Pomerance, Senior Associate
Robert Repetto, Director, Economic Research Program
S. Bruce Smart, Senior Counselor
James Gustave Speth, President
Donna Wise, Director, Policy Affairs

World Service Authority
1012 14th St., N.W. Suite 1101, Washington, DC 20005
Telephone: (202) 638-2662
Background: The administrative arm of the World Government of World Citizens.
Represented by:
Garry Davis, World Coordinator

World Trade Center Boston
Boston, MA
Counsel or consultant:
Cassidy and Associates, Inc. (William M. Cloherty)

World Wildlife Fund
1250 24th St., N.W., Washington, DC 20037
Telephone: (202) 293-4800
Background: TRAFFIC stands for Trade Records Analysis of Flora and Fauna in Commerce, part of an international network of offices monitoring international trade in wild animals and plants. TRAFFIC is the trade monitoring program of World Wildlife Fund.
Represented by:
Ginette Hemley, Director, TRAFFIC

World Wildlife Fund/The Conservation Foundation
1250 24th St., N.W., Washington, DC 20037
Telephone: (202) 293-4800
Background: In October 1985, World Wildlife Fund-U.S. and The Conservation Foundation formally affiliated. They remain two legally distinct nonprofit organizations though they are served jointly by communications, development, and finance and administration offices. The Conservation Foundation is a national nonprofit research and education organization established in 1948 to promote wise use of the earth's resources. Part of a network of 23 WWF nat'l organizations coordinated by an international secretariat in Gland, Switzerland, the World Wildlife Fund is the world's leading organization working to maintain the biological resources of the earth.
Represented by:
Kathryn S. Fuller, President
Paige MacDonald, Exec. V. President
Julia A. Moore, V. President, Communications
Jan W. Stout, V. President, Development
Russell E. Train, Chairman of the Board
Douglas Wheeler, Executive V. President/Conservation F'dn

WorldCorp
13873 Park Center Road Suite 490, Herndon, VA 22071
Telephone: (703) 834-9200
Represented by:
A. Scott Andrews, V. President, Treasurer
Counsel or consultant:
Hill and Knowlton Public Affairs Worldwide (Charles Francis)

World's Poultry Science Ass'n, U.S.A. Branch
USDA-APHIS, VS, Room 771, Fed. Bldg., 6505 Belcrest Rd., Hyattsville, MD 20782
Telephone: (301) 436-7768
Represented by:
Dr. Irvin L. Peterson, Secretary-Treasurer

Worldwatch Institute
1776 Massachusetts Ave., N.W., Washington, DC 20036
Telephone: (202) 452-1999
Background: A research body established in 1974 to alert the public and policymakers to the emerging problems of long term management and protection of human and natural resources in a interdependent world. Annual Publication is STATE OF THE WORLD, an assessment of global environmental isssues and emerging trends. Also publishes a bi-monthly magazine WORLD WATCH and other papers.
Represented by:
Lester R. Brown, President
Christopher Flavin, V. President

Worldways Canada, Ltd.
Toronto, Ontario
Counsel or consultant:
Lord Day & Lord, Barrett Smith (Joanne W. Young)

WOST-TV
Block Island, RI
Counsel or consultant:
Cohn and Marks

WOUB-TV
Athens, OH
Counsel or consultant:
Cohn and Marks

WOUC-TV
Cambridge, OH
Counsel or consultant:
Cohn and Marks

WOWT
Omaha, NE
Counsel or consultant:
Fletcher, Heald and Hildreth

WPCB-TV
Pittsburgh, PA
Counsel or consultant:
Gammon and Grange

WPEC
West Palm Beach, FL
Counsel or consultant:
Cohn and Marks

WPTT-TV
Pittsburgh, PA
Counsel or consultant:
Fisher, Wayland, Cooper and Leader

WPXT
Portland, ME
Counsel or consultant:
Hopkins and Sutter (John P. Bankson, Jr.)

WQAD-TV
Moline, IL
Counsel or consultant:
Koteen and Naftalin

WQTV-TV
Boston, MA
Counsel or consultant:
Cohn and Marks

WRAL-TV
Raleigh, NC
Counsel or consultant:
Fletcher, Heald and Hildreth

WRCB-TV
Chattanooga, TN
Counsel or consultant:
Cohn and Marks

WREG-TV
Memphis, TN
Counsel or consultant:
Koteen and Naftalin

Wright Schuchart, Inc.
Seattle, WA
Counsel or consultant:
Bogle and Gates (Terry L. Leitzell)

Writing Instruments Manufacturers Ass'n
c/o Holland & Knight 888 17th St., N.W., #900, Washington, DC 20006
Telephone: (202) 955-5550
Counsel or consultant:
Holland and Knight (David H. Baker)

WRTV
Indianapolis, IN
Counsel or consultant:
Koteen and Naftalin

WRWR-TV
San Juan, PR

ORGANIZATIONS REPRESENTED

Counsel or consultant:
Fletcher, Heald and Hildreth

WSBN-TV
Morton, VA
Counsel or consultant:
Cohn and Marks

WSEE-TV
Erie, PA
Counsel or consultant:
Cohn and Marks

WSFP-TV
Fort Myers, FL
Counsel or consultant:
Cohn and Marks

WSIL-TV
Harrisburg, IL
Counsel or consultant:
Pepper and Corazzini

WSIU-TV
Carbondale, IL
Counsel or consultant:
Cohn and Marks

WSJU
San Juan, PR
Counsel or consultant:
Marmet and McCombs, P.C.

WSKP-TV
Syracuse, NY
Counsel or consultant:
Fletcher, Heald and Hildreth

WSNS-TV
Chicago, IL
Counsel or consultant:
Cohn and Marks

WSVI-TV
St. Croix, VI
Counsel or consultant:
Marmet and McCombs, P.C.

WSVN
Miami, FL
Counsel or consultant:
Koteen and Naftalin

WSYT
Syracuse, NY
Counsel or consultant:
Sutherland, Asbill and Brennan

WTAF-TV
Philadelphia, PA
Counsel or consultant:
Koteen and Naftalin

WTEV
New Bedford, MA
Counsel or consultant:
Marmet and McCombs, P.C.

WTGI-TV
Wilmington, DE
Counsel or consultant:
Gammon and Grange

WTHR
Indianapolis, IN
Counsel or consultant:
Crowell and Moring

WTJC
Springfield, OH
Counsel or consultant:
Miller and Fields

WTKR-TV
Norfolk, VA
Counsel or consultant:
Hopkins and Sutter (Neal M. Goldberg)

WTLW
Lima, OH
Counsel or consultant:
Fisher, Wayland, Cooper and Leader

WTOG
Tampa-St. Pete, FL
Counsel or consultant:
Fletcher, Heald and Hildreth

WTRA
Mayaguez, PR
Counsel or consultant:
Fletcher, Heald and Hildreth

WTSP-TV
St. Petersburg, FL
Counsel or consultant:
Koteen and Naftalin

WTTE
Columbus, OH
Counsel or consultant:
Fisher, Wayland, Cooper and Leader

WTVN-TV
Columbus, OH
Counsel or consultant:
Koteen and Naftalin

WTWS
New London, CT
Counsel or consultant:
Reddy, Begley and Martin

WTZH
Tupelo, MS
Counsel or consultant:
Reddy, Begley and Martin

WUCM-TV
Universal City, MI
Counsel or consultant:
Cohn and Marks

WUCX-TV
Bad Axe, MI
Counsel or consultant:
Cohn and Marks

WUSF-TV
Tampa, FL
Counsel or consultant:
Cohn and Marks

WVGA
Valdosta, GA
Counsel or consultant:
Fletcher, Heald and Hildreth

WVII-TV
Bangor, ME
Counsel or consultant:
Mullin, Rhyne, Emmons and Topel, P.C.

WVIR-TV
Charlottesville, VA
Counsel or consultant:
Cohn and Marks

WVSB-TV
West Point, MS
Counsel or consultant:
Cohn and Marks

WVUT-TV
Vincennes, IN
Counsel or consultant:
Fletcher, Heald and Hildreth

WWL-TV
New Orleans, LA
Counsel or consultant:
Marmet and McCombs, P.C.

WXEX-TV
Petersburg, VA
Counsel or consultant:
Fletcher, Heald and Hildreth

WXFL
Tampa, FL
Counsel or consultant:
Cohn and Marks

WXNE-TV
Boston, MA

Counsel or consultant:
Fisher, Wayland, Cooper and Leader

WYAH
Portsmouth, VA
Counsel or consultant:
Fisher, Wayland, Cooper and Leader

Wyatt Communications
1050 17th St., N.W., Suite 1000, Washington, DC 20036
Telephone: (202) 466-3571
Counsel or consultant:
The Kamber Group (Dennis Walston)

Wyeth-Ayerst Internat'l, Inc.
Radnor, PA
Counsel or consultant:
Hill and Knowlton Public Affairs Worldwide (Ken Rabin)

Wyman-Gordon Co.
Worcester, MA
Counsel or consultant:
Collier, Shannon & Scott (Robin H. Gilbert, David A. Hartquist, Michael R. Kershow)

WZZM-TV
Grand Rapids, MI
Counsel or consultant:
Cohn and Marks

Xerox Corp.
490 L'Enfant Plaza East, S.W., Suite 4200, Washington, DC 20024
Telephone: (202) 646-8285
Represented by:
Rita F. Allen, Team Xerox PAC Administrator
Susan Stuebing Anderson, Manager, Government Affairs
Reginald L. Brown, Jr., Mgr, Policy/Gov't Afrs, Integ. Systm Org
Kenneth H. Klein, Counsel, Government Affairs
Martin G. Reiser, Consultant, Government Affairs
Robert H. Scheerschmidt, V. President, Government Affairs
Counsel or consultant:
Dewey, Ballantine, Bushby, Palmer and Wood (John J. Salmon)
Internat'l Business-Government Counsellors, Inc. (Janet Hunter)

XTRA Corp.
Boston, MA
Counsel or consultant:
Patton, Boggs and Blow (James B. Christian, Jr.)

Yale Materials Handling Corp.
Flemington, NJ
Counsel or consultant:
Thompson, Hine and Flory (Rafael A. Madan, Mark Roy Sandstrom)

Yamaha Corp. of America
Buena Park, CA
Counsel or consultant:
Willkie Farr and Gallagher (William H. Barringer)

Yamaha Electronics Corp., U.S.A.
Buena Park, CA
Counsel or consultant:
Patton, Boggs and Blow

Yamaha Motor Corp. U.S.A.
Cypress, CA
Counsel or consultant:
Miller & Chevalier, Chartered (John S. Nolan)
Willkie Farr and Gallagher (William H. Barringer, Matthew R. Schneider)
Wilmer, Cutler and Pickering (Robert C. Cassidy, Jr.)

Yamaichi Internat'l
Tokyo, Japan
Counsel or consultant:
Brownrigg and Muldoon

Yamazaki Machinery Works, Ltd.
Nia-Gun, Japan
Counsel or consultant:
Finnegan, Henderson, Farabow, Garrett and Dunner (Brian G. Brunsvold)

Yankee Atomic Electric Co.
905 Sixth St., S.W., Washington, DC 20024
Telephone: (202) 488-3789

The listings in this directory are available as *Mailing Labels*. See last page.

ORGANIZATIONS REPRESENTED

Yankee Atomic Electric Co. (Cont'd)
Represented by:
James J. Flanagan, V. President
John Kyte, Sr. Legislative Representative

Yavapai Telephone Exchange
Prescott, AZ
Counsel or consultant:
Dutko & Associates (Daniel A. Dutko, Steve Perry)

Yellow Freight System
908 King St., Suite 300, Alexandria, VA 22314
Telephone: (703) 836-9406
Represented by:
Stephen P. Murphy, Sr. V. President and Secretary

Yellow Pages Publishers Ass'n
Troy, MI
Counsel or consultant:
Davidson Colling Group, Inc., The (James H. Davidson)

Yemen Arab Republic, Government of
Sana, Yemen
Counsel or consultant:
Hill and Knowlton Public Affairs Worldwide (Charles R. Pucie, Jr.)

YMCA of Metropolitan Washington
1625 Massachusetts Ave., N.W., Suite 700, Washington, DC 20036
Telephone: (202) 797-4497
Represented by:
Patricia L. Diener, Director of Communications
Counsel or consultant:
Manning, Selvage & Lee/Washington

YMCA of the USA
1701 K St., N.W., Suite 903, Washington, DC 20006
Telephone: (202) 835-9043
Represented by:
Robert A. Boisture, Director, Washington Office
Counsel or consultant:
Olwine, Connelly, Chase, O'Donnell and Weyher (W. Harrison Wellford)

York Internat'l Corp.
8301-B Patuxent Range, Jessup, MD 20794-9620
Telephone: (301) 953-0520
Represented by:
J. W. Chandler, V. President (MM&G Division)

Young Americans for Freedom
380 Maple Ave. West Suite 303, Vienna, VA 22180
Telephone: (703) 938-3305
Background: Founded in 1960, a political organization for young conservatives.
Represented by:
George Lodick, Exec. Director
Jeffrey Wright, National Chairman

Young America's Foundation
11800 Sunrise Valley Drive, Reston, VA 22090
Telephone: (703) 620-5270
Represented by:
Ron Robinson, President

Young Astronaut Council
1211 Connecticut Ave., N.W. Suite 800, Washington, DC 20036
Telephone: (202) 682-1984
Background: Mission is to encourage student interest and skills in math, science, and related fields.
Represented by:
Cecelia Blalock, Director, Public Relations
Counsel or consultant:
Westermann and Hendricks, Inc. (Diane Hendricks, Edith E. Westermann)

Young Democrats of America
430 South Capitol St., S.E., Washington, DC 20003
Telephone: (202) 863-8000
Background: Promotes the Democratic Party among young people. Affiliated with the Democratic Nat'l Committee. Position of Political Director vacant at publication date.

Young Republican Nat'l Federation
310 First St., S.E., Washington, DC 20003
Telephone: (202) 662-1340
Background: Promotes the Republican Party among young people. Affiliated with the Republican Nat'l Committee.

Represented by:
Terry T. Campo, Chairman
Robin Sprague, Exec. Director

Youngstown Mines Corp.
McMurray, PA
Background: A subsidiary of Lykes Corp.
Counsel or consultant:
Smith, Heenan and Althen (Michael T. Heenan)

Youth For Understanding Internat'l Exchange
3501 Newark St., N.W., Washington, DC 20016
Telephone: (202) 895-1125
Represented by:
William A. Porter, V. President, Public Affairs & Devel't.
William M. Woessner, President

Youth in Philanthropy
P.O. Box 500 20th Floor, Tower 1, Washington, DC 20044
Telephone: (202) 276-3444
Represented by:
Larry Stinchcomb, Director
Counsel or consultant:
Public Affairs Group, Inc. (Edie Fraser)

Youths for Democratic Action
1511 K St., N.W., Suite 941, Washington, DC 20005
Telephone: (202) 638-6447
Background: The youth-oriented political action arm of Americans for Democratic Action. Main undertakings include the Summer Campaign Internship Program, a year-long or semester internship program, and college campus chapter formation.
Represented by:
Ward Morrow, National Chair

Yukon Pacific Inc.
Anchorage, AK
Counsel or consultant:
Birch, Horton, Bittner and Cherot (Ronald G. Birch, William P. Horn)
Laxalt, Washington, Perito & Dubuc
Charlie McBride Assoc, Inc. (Charlie McBride)

Yusen Air and Sea Service (USA) Inc.
New York, NY
Counsel or consultant:
Brownrigg and Muldoon (Charles P. Muldoon)

Zaire, Bank of
Kinshasa, Zaire
Counsel or consultant:
White & Case

Zaire, Government of the Republic of
Kinshasa, Zaire
Counsel or consultant:
Black, Manafort, Stone and Kelly Public Affairs Co.
van Kloberg and Associates (Edward J. van Kloberg, III)
Weaver & Associates, Robert A. (Joseph M. Perta, Patrick J. Tyrrell, Robert A. Weaver, Jr.)

Zambelli Internationale
New Castle, PA
Counsel or consultant:
Evergreen Associates, Ltd. (Gerald Weaver)

Zapata Corp.
Houston, TX
Counsel or consultant:
Theodore L. Jones

Zapata Gulf Marine Service Corp.
Houston, TX
Counsel or consultant:
Theodore L. Jones

Zayre Corp.
Framingham, MA
Counsel or consultant:
Kilpatrick & Cody (Mark D. Wincek)

Zenith Electronics Corp.
Glenview, IL
Counsel or consultant:
Frederick L. Ikenson, P.C. (Frederick L. Ikenson)

Zero Population Growth, Inc.
1400 16th St., N.W., Suite 320, Washington, DC 20036
Telephone: (202) 332-2200
Background: Works to achieve a sustainable balance of population, resources, and the environment in the U.S. and worldwide. President is Timothy B. Lovain, of Denny

Miller Associates.
Represented by:
Karl Gawell, Director, Government Relations
Pamela Lichtman, Legislative Assistant
Dianne Sherman, Director of Communications
Susan Weber, Exec. Director

Zinc Corp. of America
Monaca, PA
Counsel or consultant:
Jefferson Group, The

Zink and Co., John
Tulsa, OK
Background: A manufacturer of Thermal Disposal Pollution Control Systems.
Counsel or consultant:
Akin, Gump, Strauss, Hauer and Feld (Joel Jankowsky)

Zionist Organization of America
11710 Hunters Lane, Rockville, MD 20852-2367
Telephone: (301) 468-3900
Represented by:
Rabbi Stuart Weinblatt, Admin. Dir., Louis D. Brandeis District

Zitel Corp.
Milpitas, CA
Counsel or consultant:
Ashby and Associates (R. Barry Ashby)

Zurich-American Insurance
Schaumberg, IL
Counsel or consultant:
Collier, Shannon & Scott (Pamela Allen)

1993 World University Games
Buffalo, NY
Counsel or consultant:
Sagamore Associates, Inc. (David U. Gogol, Michael B. Kraft)

20th Century Fox
Los Angeles, CA
Counsel or consultant:
Cassidy and Associates, Inc. (Gerald S. J. Cassidy, Pete W. Glavas)

21st Century Space Foundation
1146 19th St., N.W., Washington, DC 20036
Telephone: (202) 728-9500
Counsel or consultant:
Gilbert A. Robinson, Inc. (Gilbert A. Robinson)

47th Street Photo
New York, NY
Background: A retailer of camera, audio and video equipment and other machinery.
Counsel or consultant:
Miller, Cassidy, Larroca and Lewin (Jamie S. Gorelick, Nathan Lewin)

70001 Training & Employment Institute
501 School St., S.W. Suite 600, Washington, DC 20024
Telephone: (202) 484-0103
Background: A national youth employment, education and training organization.
Represented by:
Lawrence C. Brown, Jr., President
Francis J. Harkins, Chairman
Owen Peagler, V. President, Communications
Counsel or consultant:
McKevitt Group, The

The listings in this directory are available as *Mailing Labels*. See last page.

WASHINGTON
REPRESENTATIVES
1990

FEDERAL EXECUTIVE BRANCH
LEGISLATIVE AFFAIRS PERSONNEL

Listed on the following pages are the persons responsible for legislative and congressional relations within the White House and the major departments and agencies of the Federal Government. The Executive Branch offices in which these people work are listed under three groupings — The Executive Office of the President, the Cabinet and sub-Cabinet Departments, and the independent Administrative Agencies. Many of the people listed are, in effect, lobbyists for the Administration in its dealings with Congress. Their inclusion is intended to give the researcher a more complete record of the advocacy community of Washington.

THE EXECUTIVE OFFICE OF THE PRESIDENT

EXECUTIVE OFFICE OF THE PRESIDENT - The White House
1600 Pennsylvania Ave., N.W., Washington, DC 20500
Telephone: (202) 456-2230
Represented by:
Frederick D. McClure, Asst to the President for Legis Affrs
Robert J. Portman, Dep Asst to the Pres, Legis Affrs
Becky Anderson, Admin Asst, Legis Affrs
Karen Goff, Exec Asst, Legis Affrs
Bo Bryant, Staff Asst, Legis Affrs
E. Boyd Hollingsworth, Jr., Dep Asst to Pres, Legis Affrs (Senate)
Nell Payne, Spec Asst to Pres, Legis Affrs (Senate)
David P. Sloane, Spec Asst to Pres, Legis Affrs (Senate)
Brian K. Waidmann, Spec Asst to Pres, Legis Affrs (Senate)
Holly Steger, Princ Staff Asst, Legis Affrs (Senate)
Sue Auther, Staff Asst, Legis Affrs (Senate)
Susan Moore, Staff Asst, Legis Affrs (Senate)
Nicholas E. Calio, Dep Asst to Pres, Legis Affrs (House)
Gary J. Andres, Spec Asst to Pres, Legis Affrs (House)
Jack Howard, Spec Asst to Pres, Legis Affrs (House)
Frances M. Norris, Spec Asst to Pres, Legis Affrs (House)
Rebecca Nelson, Princial Staff Asst, Legis Affrs (House)
Mary Gabriel Harpring, Staff Asst, Legis Affrs (House)
Sonya Pleasant, Staff Asst, Legis Affrs (House)
Henry Plaster, Dir, Cong Correspondence
Patricia Cox, Cong Correspondent
Susan McCormack, Cong Correspondent

EXECUTIVE OFFICE OF THE PRESIDENT - Central Intelligence Agency
Washington, DC 20505
Telephone: (703) 482-6121
Represented by:
E. Norbert Garrett, Dir, Cong Affrs

EXECUTIVE OFFICE OF THE PRESIDENT - Nat'l Security Council
1600 Pennsylvania Ave., N.W., Washington, DC 20500
Telephone: (202) 395-3055
Represented by:
Virginia A. Lampley, Spec Asst to Pres & Sr Dir, Legis Affrs
E. Bret Coulson, Dir, Legis Affrs

EXECUTIVE OFFICE OF THE PRESIDENT - Office of Management and Budget
Old Executive Office Bldg., Washington, DC 20500
Telephone: (202) 395-4790
Represented by:
Thomas A. Scully, Assoc Dir, Legis Affrs
Shawn M. Smeallie, Spec Asst, Legis Affrs (Senate)
Jeff Pierson, Spec Asst, Legis Affrs (House)
Terryle Olsen, Confidential Asst, Legis Affrs
Charles Kieffer, Spec Asst, Legis Affrs
Patrick Kenary, Spec Asst, Legis Affrs
David Taylor, Legis Asst
James C. Murr, Asst Dir, Legis Reference
James J. Jukes, Chief, Econ Sci & Gen Govt Br, Legis Ref
Ronald K. Peterson, Chief, Res, Def & Int'l Br, Legis Ref
Julia E. Yuille, Legis Information Center

EXECUTIVE OFFICE OF THE PRESIDENT - US Trade Representative
600 17th St., N.W., Washington, DC 20506
Telephone: (202) 395-6951
Represented by:
Mary Tinsley, Asst Trade Rep, Cong Affrs

FEDERAL EXECUTIVE BRANCH
LEGISLATIVE AFFAIRS PERSONNEL

FEDERAL DEPARTMENTS

DEPARTMENT OF AGRICULTURE
14th and Independence Ave., S.W., Washington, DC 20205
Telephone: (202) 447-7097
Represented by:
Franklin E. Bailey, Asst Secy, Cong Rels
Gary K. Madson, Dep Asst Secy, Cong Rels
Bradley Meyers, Confidential Asst, Cong Rels
Mary Helen Askins, Confidential Asst, Cong Rels
Cindy Ayers, Confidential Asst, Cong Rels
Jim Cahill, Confidental Asst, Cong Relations
Christine Gunderson, Confidential Asst, Cong Rels
Rod Hastie, Confidential Asst, Cong Rels
Paul McAndrew, Confidential Asst, Cong Rels
Mark Scanlan, Confidential Asst, Cong Rels
Wanda Worsham, Confidential Asst, Cong Rels
Lew Walter, Special Asst, Cong Rels

DEPARTMENT OF AGRICULTURE - Agricultural Marketing Staff
14th and Independence Ave. S.W., Room 3510 South Bldg., Washington, DC 20250
Telephone: (202) 447-3203
Represented by:
Sandra Hogan, Legis Liaison Office

DEPARTMENT OF AGRICULTURE - Agricultural Research Service
12th and Independence Ave. S.W., Washington, DC 20250
Telephone: (202) 447-7141
Represented by:
Loretta A. Owens, Chief, Legis Staff

DEPARTMENT OF AGRICULTURE - Animal and Plant Health Inspection Service
14th and Independence Ave. S.W., Room 1147 South Bldg., Washington, DC 20250
Telephone: (202) 447-2511
Represented by:
John Duncan, Dir, Legis & Public Affrs
Steve Poore, Dep Dir, Legis & Public Affrs
Paula Henstrudge, Legis Specialist
Marilyn Kay Peterson, Legis Asst, Legis & Public Affrs

DEPARTMENT OF AGRICULTURE - Farmers Home Administration
14th and Independence Ave. S.W., Washington, DC 20250
Telephone: (202) 447-6903
Represented by:
Joseph E. O'Neill, Dir, Legis Affrs & Publ Info Staff (Act)

DEPARTMENT OF AGRICULTURE - Federal Crop Insurance Corp.
14th and Independence Ave. S.W., Washington, DC 20250
Telephone: (202) 447-3287
Represented by:
Michael Forgash, Info and Govt'l Affrs Div.

DEPARTMENT OF AGRICULTURE - Food and Nutrition Service
3101 Park Center Drive, Alexandria, VA 22302
Telephone: (703) 756-3039
Represented by:
Christy Schmidt, Dir, Off of Analysis & Eval (Act)
Frank Ippolito, Govt'l Affrs Staff

DEPARTMENT OF AGRICULTURE - Food Safety and Inspection Service
14th and Independence Ave. S.W., Washington, DC 20250
Telephone: (202) 447-7943
Represented by:
David B. Schmidt, Dir, Info & Legis Affrs Staff
Denise Clarke, Dep Dir, Info & Legis Affrs Staff
Elizabeth Laugharn, Dep Dir, Legis Affrs

DEPARTMENT OF AGRICULTURE - Foreign Agricultural Service
14th and Independence Ave. S.W., Washington, DC 20250
Telephone: (202) 447-6829
Represented by:
David Hovermale, Dir, Legis Affrs

DEPARTMENT OF AGRICULTURE - Forest Service
12th and Independence Ave. S.W., Washington, DC 20250
Telephone: (202) 447-6663
Represented by:
Jeff M. Sirmon, Dep Chief, Prog & Legis
Mark A. Reimers, Assoc Dep Chief, Prog and Legis
Roger W. Leonard, Legis Affrs Staff

DEPARTMENT OF AGRICULTURE - Rural Electrification Administration
14th and Independence Ave. S.W., Washington, DC 20250
Telephone: (202) 382-1255

Represented by:
Daniel Cummings, Dir, Legis Affrs & Public Information
Ruth Ann Hockett, Dep Dir, Legis Affrs & Public Info

DEPARTMENT OF AGRICULTURE - Soil Conservation Service
12th and Independence Ave. S.W., Washington, DC 20250
Telephone: (202) 447-2771
Represented by:
Dorothy V. Bradbury, Cong and Public Liaison
Jeffrey Vonk, Legis Asst

DEPARTMENT OF AIR FORCE
The Pentagon, Washington, DC 20330
Telephone: (202) 697-8153
Represented by:
Maj. Gen. Burton R. Moore, Dir, Legis Liaison
Brig. Gen. Brett M. Dula, Dep Dir, Legis Liaison
Col. Tom Allison, Cong Inquiry, Legis Liaison
Col. Jack Overstreet, Weapons Syst Liaison, Cong Liaison
Col. Jerry Woods, House Liaison, Legis Liaison
Col. Gene Ronsick, House Liaison, Legis Liaison
Lt. Col. James Tap, Senate Liaison, Legis Liaison
Lt. Col. Robert Topel, Air Opns Officer, Legis Liaison
Capt. Chris Kenyon, Exec Officer, Legis Liaison
Fred Bumgarner, Legis Res Officer, Legis Liaison

DEPARTMENT OF ARMY
The Pentagon, Washington, DC 20310-0101
Telephone: (202) 697-6767
Represented by:
Maj. Gen. Charles E. Dominy, Chief, Legis Liaison
Brig. Gen. Leonard D. Miller, Dep Chief, Legis Liaison
Lt. Col. William B. Loper, Exec Officer, Legis Liaison (Act)
Col. John McNulty, Cong Inquiry, Legis Liaison
Col. Wendell Black, House Liaison, Legis Liaison
Col. Edward W. Shaw, Senate Liaison, Legis Liaison
Col. John C. Cruden, Investigations & Legislation, Legis Lias
Cordis Colburn, Programs Div, Legis Liaison
Morgan Rees, Policy Plng & Legis Affrs Dep, Civil Wks
Lt. Col. Donald Steele, Cong Affrs Coord, Res Devel & Acq (SARD)

DEPARTMENT OF ARMY - Chief of Engineers
20 Massachusetts Ave., N.W., Washington, DC 20314
Telephone: (202) 272-0030
Represented by:
Ronald C. Allen, Asst Chief Couns, Legis & General Law
William Birney, Chief, Legis Svcs Office, Real Estate

DEPARTMENT OF COMMERCE
14th and Constitution Ave. S.W., Washington, DC 20230
Telephone: (202) 377-5485
Represented by:
William D. Fritts, Jr., Asst Secy, Legis & Intergovt'l Affrs
Patricia Knight, Dep Asst Secy, Legis & Intergovt'l Affrs
Donald Bramer, Confidential Asst to the Asst Secy
Martha McGreevy, Admin Officer, Cong Liaison Asst
Robert Reynolds, Cong Liaison Specialist
Michael Gale, Dep Dir, Legis Affrs
Jim McKenna, Special Asst to the Asst Secy
Cappie Alverson, Cong Liaison Specialist
Rob Carter, Cong Liaison Specialist
Jim Winger, Cong Liaison Officer
Bill Price, Cong Liaison Officer
John Ostronic, Cong Liaison Asst
Hague Ollison, Cong Liaison Asst
Gretchen Craft, Cong Liaison Asst

DEPARTMENT OF COMMERCE - Bureau of the Census
Federal Center, Suitland, MD 20233
Telephone: (301) 763-2446
Represented by:
A. Mark Neuman, Dir, Office of Cong Affrs

DEPARTMENT OF COMMERCE - Economic Development Administration
14th and Constitution Ave. N.W., Washington, DC 20230
Telephone: (202) 377-5314
Represented by:
Mary Dewhirst, Dir, Cong Relations

DEPARTMENT OF COMMERCE - Inspector General
15th and Constitution Ave. N.W., Washington, DC 20230
Telephone: (202)-377-4661
Represented by:
Marilyn Depew, Cong Liaison Officer

The listings in this directory are available as *Mailing Labels*. See last page.

FEDERAL EXECUTIVE BRANCH
LEGISLATIVE AFFAIRS PERSONNEL

DEPARTMENT OF COMMERCE - Internat'l Trade Administration
14th and Constitution Ave. N.W., Washington, DC 20230
Telephone: (202) 377-3015
Represented by:
Paul L. Powell, Dir, Office of Cong Affrs

DEPARTMENT OF COMMERCE - Minority Business Development Agency
14th and Constitution Ave. N.W., Washington, DC 20230
Telephone: (202) 377-5641
Represented by:
Nancy Campaigne, Director, Cong Affrs Div

DEPARTMENT OF COMMERCE - Nat'l Institute of Standards and Technology
A-1111 Adm. Bldg., Gaithersburg, MD 20899
Telephone: (301) 975-3080
Represented by:
Esther C. Cassidy, Director, Cong & Legis Affrs

DEPARTMENT OF COMMERCE - Nat'l Marine Fisheries Service
1335 East-West Hwy., Silver Spring, MD 20917
Telephone: (301) 427-2263
Represented by:
John H. Dunnigan, Cong Affrs Officer
Susan Weaver, Cong Affrs Officer

DEPARTMENT OF COMMERCE - Nat'l Oceanic and Atmospheric Administration
14th and Constitution Ave. N.W., Washington, DC 20230
Telephone: (202) 377-4981
Represented by:
Lori Gribbin, Legis Affrs Office
Marilee Bright, Chief, Legis Affrs

DEPARTMENT OF COMMERCE - Nat'l Telecommunications and Information Administration
14th and Constitution Ave. N.W., Washington, DC 20230
Telephone: (202) 377-1551
Represented by:
Nancy H. Mason, Dir., Cong Affrs and Public Programs

DEPARTMENT OF COMMERCE - Nat'l Weather Service
1325 East-West Hwy., Silver Spring, MD 20910
Telephone: (301) 427-7448
Represented by:
John Milholland, General Counsel

DEPARTMENT OF COMMERCE - Office of Policy Analysis
14th and Constitution Ave. N.W., Room 4876, Washington, DC 20230
Telephone: (202) 377-1985
Represented by:
Robert Grant, Dep Dir, Regul/Legis Analysis

DEPARTMENT OF COMMERCE - Patent and Trademark Office
c/o Asst Secy and Commissioner of Patents and Trademarks, Washington, DC 20231
Telephone: (703) 557-3065
Represented by:
Michael K. Kirk, Asst Commissioner for External Affairs
Janie Cooksey, Cong Liaison
Patricia Callahan, Dir of Cong Affrs

DEPARTMENT OF DEFENSE
The Pentagon, Washington, DC 20301
Telephone: (202) 697-6210
Represented by:
David Gribbin, Asst Secy, Legis Affrs
Brig. Gen. Buster C. Glosson, Dep Asst Secy, Plans & Opns, Legis Affrs
Tom Carter, Dep Asst Secy, Senate Affrs, Legis Affrs
Patty Howe, Dep Asst Secy, House Affrs, Legis Affrs
Col. John Richardson, Senate Affrs Dir, Legis Affrs
Lt. Col. Terry Nyhous, House Affrs Dir, Legis Affrs
Phillip J. Bond, Exec Asst, Legis, Affrs
Michelle P. McIntyre, Confidential Asst, Legis Affrs
Andrew Goldman, Spec Asst, Foreign Affrs, Legis Affrs
Col. Joseph Maguire, Acquisitions Policy, Legis Affrs
James Steen, Spec Asst, Foreign Affrs, Legis Affrs
Lt. Col. Michael Powell, Manpower, Health & Reserve, Legis Affrs
Susan A. Lockard, Research & Admin Dir., Legis Affrs
Capt. Sandy Clarke, Weapons Syst & Current Opns, Legis Affrs
Lt. Col. Thomas Harvey, SDI, Legis Affrs
Lt. Cdr. Robert Meissner, Intel & Spec Opns, Legis Affrs

DEPARTMENT OF DEFENSE - Comptroller's Office
The Pentagon, Washington, DC 20301
Telephone: (202) 697-1101
Represented by:
C. W. Dennis, Spec Asst for Legis Affrs

DEPARTMENT OF DEFENSE - Defense Logistics Agency
Cameron Station, Alexandria, VA 22314-6100
Telephone: (202) 274-6133
Represented by:
Gerald C. Flessate, Cong Affrs

DEPARTMENT OF DEFENSE - Defense Security Assistance Agency
The Pentagon, Washington, DC 20301-2800
Telephone: (202) 697-9201
Represented by:
Bettie-Julia Certain, Senate Liaison

DEPARTMENT OF DEFENSE - Joint Chiefs of Staff
The Pentagon, Washington, DC 20301
Telephone: (202) 697-1137
Represented by:
Col. Fred K. Green, Legal & Legis Counsel to Chairman, JCS
Lt. Col. Eric Kunz, Legis Asst to the Chairman, JCS
Susan Ezzell, Cong Afrs Specialist

DEPARTMENT OF DEFENSE - Military Manpower and Personnel Policy, Office of Asst Secy (Force Mgmt)
The Pentagon, Washington, DC 20301
Telephone: (202) 697-3387
Represented by:
Col. Ted Borek, JAGC, USA, Dir, Legis and Legal Policy
Lt. Col. Richard Ketler, USMC, Dep Dir, Legis and Legal Policy

DEPARTMENT OF EDUCATION
400 Maryland Ave., S.W., Washington, DC 20202
Telephone: (202) 732-5020
Represented by:
Nancy Mohr Kennedy, Asst Secy, Legislation
Bill Hansen, Dep Asst Secy, Legislation
Jack Kristy, Asst Gen Counsel, Legis Counsel

DEPARTMENT OF ENERGY
1000 Independence Ave. S.W., Washington, DC 20585
Telephone: (202) 586-5450
Represented by:
Jacqueline Knox Brown, Asst Secy, Cong and Intergovt'l Affrs
Joseph Karpinski, Princ Dep Asst Secy, Cong & Intergovt'l
Wolfgang C. Retke, Assoc Dep Asst Secy, Cong & Intergovt'l
James B. Tapper, Dep Asst Secy, Senate Liaison
Gary D. Knight, Dep Asst Secy, House Liaison
Beverly E. Gaines, Cong Svcs Coordinator
Leo Arnaiz, Cong Hearings Coordinator
Mark C. Schroeder, Dep Gen Couns, Envir, Conserv & Legis
Robert G. Rabben, Asst Gen Couns, Legis

DEPARTMENT OF ENERGY - Federal Energy Regulatory Commission
825 North Capitol St., Washington, DC 20426
Telephone: (202) 357-8004
Represented by:
Kathleene B. Card, Dir, External Affrs
Cristena Bach, Director, Cong Afrs & State Liaison Div

DEPARTMENT OF HEALTH AND HUMAN SERVICES
200 Independence Ave. S.W., Washington, DC 20201
Telephone: (202) 245-7627
Represented by:
Steven Kelmar, Asst Secy, Legislation (Act)
Wendy Strong, Dep Asst Secy, Cong Liaison
Frances White, Assoc Gen Couns, Legislation Div
Selma Floyd, Legis Reference Unit
Sondra Wallace, Attorney, Legislation Div
Susan Burnett, Attorney, Legislation Div
Paul Speigel, Attorney, Legislation Div

DEPARTMENT OF HEALTH AND HUMAN SERVICES - Alcohol Drug Abuse and Mental Health Administration
5600 Fishers Lane Room 12C-26, Rockville, MD 20857
Telephone: (301) 443-4640
Represented by:
Mary C. Knipmeyer, Ph.D., Dir, Div of Legis & Policy Implementat'n

DEPARTMENT OF HEALTH AND HUMAN SERVICES - Food and Drug Administration
5600 Fishers Lane, Rockville, MD 20857
Telephone: (301) 443-3793
Represented by:
Hugh C. Cannon, Assoc Commissioner, Legis Affrs
Phillip Stiller, Dep Assoc Commissioner, Legis Affrs
Dennis Strickland, Legislation & Spec Projects, Legis Affrs
Wayne Mara, Oversight & Investig Staff, Legis Affrs

The listings in this directory are available as *Mailing Labels*. See last page.

FEDERAL EXECUTIVE BRANCH
LEGISLATIVE AFFAIRS PERSONNEL

DEPARTMENT OF HEALTH AND HUMAN SERVICES - Health Care Financing Administration
200 Independence Ave., S.W., Washington, DC 20201
Telephone: (202) 426-3960
Represented by:
Nancy Dapper, Dir, Legislation & Policy Office (Act)

DEPARTMENT OF HEALTH AND HUMAN SERVICES - Health Resources and Services Administration
5600 Fishers Lane, Rockville, MD 20857
Telephone: (301) 443-2460
Represented by:
Ronald Carlson, Assoc Admin, Plng, Eval & Legislation
Lyman Van Nostrand, Dep Assoc Admin, Plng, Eval & Legislat
Lawrence M. Sauer, Legis Div, Plng, Eval & Legislation

DEPARTMENT OF HEALTH AND HUMAN SERVICES - Human Development Services
200 Independence Ave. S.W., Washington, DC 20201
Telephone: (202) 245-7027
Represented by:
Linda G. Eischeid, Dir, Policy, Plng and Legislation
Janet S. Hartnett, Dep Dir, Polcy, Plng and Legislation
William Riley, Policy and Legislation Div
Lois Harris, Admin Ofcr, Policy, Plng & Legislation

DEPARTMENT OF HEALTH AND HUMAN SERVICES - Nat'l Institutes of Health
Bldg. 1, 9000 Rockville Pike, Bethesda, MD 20892
Telephone: (301) 496-3152
Represented by:
Dr. Jay Moskowitz, Assoc Dir for Science Policy & Legislat
Dr. Frank J. Sullivan, Dir., Div of Legis Analysis

DEPARTMENT OF HOUSING AND URBAN DEVELOPMENT
451 Seventh St., S.W., Washington, DC 20410
Telephone: (202) 755-5005
Represented by:
Timothy L. Coyle, Asst Secy, Legislation & Cong Relations
Ivan Ransopher, Dep Asst Secy, Legislation
James L. Bynum, Dep Asst Secy, Cong Relations
Wanda Murrell, Admin Officer, Legis & Cong Rels
Anthony Mitchell, Legis Officer, Legis & Cong Rels
Christopher Lord, Legis Officer, Legis & Cong Rels
Bemis Smith, Legis Officer, Legis & Cong Rels
Kym Couture, Legis Officer, Legis & Cong Rels
Cheryl Weber, Exec Asst, Legis & Cong Rels
Martha Orwig, Sr Asst, Cong Rels, Legis & Cong Rels
J. Bradford Coors, Asst, Cong Rels, Legis & Cong Rels
Michael McSherry, Asst, Cong Rels, Legis & Cong Rels
Sharron Lipscomb, Asst, Cong Rels, Legis & Cong Rels
Susan Hedrick, Asst, Cong Rels, Legis & Cong Rels
Laura Ruse, Asst, Cong Rels, Legis & Cong Rels
Jeffrey Rands, Asst, Cong Rels, Legis & Cong Rels
G. Bryan Slater, Asst, Cong Rels, Legis & Cong Rels
Edward Murphy, Legis and Regul Office, General Counsel
James F. Lischer, Asst Gen Counsel, Legislation
Grady Norris, Asst Gen Counsel, Regulations

DEPARTMENT OF INTERIOR
18th and C Sts., N.W., Washington, DC 20240
Telephone: (202) 343-7693
Represented by:
James Spagnole, Dir, Cong and Legis Affrs
Pamela E. Somers, Legis Counsel
Stofford Canfield, Dep Dir, Senate Liaison
Lydia Hofer, Dir, House Liaison
Nancy F. Harrison, Admin Officer, Cong and Legis Affrs

DEPARTMENT OF INTERIOR - Bureau of Land Management
18th and C Sts., N.W. Room 5558, Washington, DC 20240
Telephone: (202) 343-5101
Represented by:
Jay R. Sullivan, Chief, Div of Cong Affrs
Eleanor Schwartz, Legislation and Regulatory Mgmt.

DEPARTMENT OF INTERIOR - Bureau of Mines
2401 E St., N.W., Washington, DC 20241
Telephone: (202) 634-1282
Represented by:
Cletus R. Uhlenhopp, Cong Liaison Officer

DEPARTMENT OF INTERIOR - Fish and Wildlife Service
18th and C Sts., N.W., Washington, DC 20240
Telephone: (202) 343-2500

Represented by:
Joseph S. Marler, Asst Dir, External Affrs
Owen Ambur, Legis Services Chief

DEPARTMENT OF INTERIOR - Indian Affairs
18th and C Sts., N.W. Room 4641, Washington, DC 20240
Telephone: (202) 343-5706
Represented by:
Daniel N. Lewis, Dir, Cong & Legis Affrs Staff
Marge L. Wilkins, Legis Specialist

DEPARTMENT OF INTERIOR - Nat'l Park Service
18th and C Sts., N.W., Washington, DC 20240
Telephone: (202) 343-5883
Represented by:
George K. Rasley, Jr., Asst Dir for Legis and Cong Affrs
James Michael Lamb, Dep Asst Dir and Chief, Office of Legis

DEPARTMENT OF INTERIOR - Surface Mining
1951 Constitution Ave. N.W., Washington, DC 20240
Telephone: (202) 343-2165
Represented by:
Nancy Smith, Cong Liaison

DEPARTMENT OF INTERIOR - Territorial and Internat'l Affairs
18th and C Sts., N.W., Washington, DC 20240
Telephone: (202) 343-3003
Represented by:
Larry Morgan, Dir, Legis and Public Affrs

DEPARTMENT OF INTERIOR - U.S. Geological Survey
12201 Sunrise Valley Drive MS 112, Reston, VA 22092
Telephone: (703) 648-4455
Represented by:
Talmadge Reed, Cong Liaison Officer

DEPARTMENT OF JUSTICE
10th and Constitution Ave., Washington, DC 20530
Telephone: (202) 633-3752
Represented by:
Bruce C. Navarro, Acting Asst Attorney General
Thomas T. Reinhardt, Dir., Cong Relations

DEPARTMENT OF JUSTICE - Antitrust Division
10th and Constitution Ave. N.W., Washington, DC 20530
Telephone: (202) 633-2497
Represented by:
John C. Filippini, Chief, Legis Unit, Legal Policy Sect

DEPARTMENT OF JUSTICE - Bureau of Prisons
320 First St., N.W., Washington, DC 20534
Telephone: (202) 724-3198
Represented by:
John Pendleton, Exec Asst, Cong Liaison

DEPARTMENT OF JUSTICE - Criminal Division
10th and Constitution Ave. N.W., Washington, DC 20530
Telephone: (202) 633-3202
Represented by:
Roger Pauley, Dir, Office of Legislation

DEPARTMENT OF JUSTICE - Drug Enforcement Administration
700 Army-Navy Drive, Arlington, VA 22202
Telephone: (703) 307-7363
Represented by:
William F. Alden, Cong and Public Affrs Office

DEPARTMENT OF JUSTICE - Immigration and Naturalization Service
425 I St., N.W., Washington, DC 20536
Telephone: (202) 633-5231
Represented by:
Bonnie Derwinski, Director, Cong and Public Affairs

DEPARTMENT OF JUSTICE - Office of Justice Programs
633 Indiana Ave., N.W., Washington, DC 20531
Telephone: (202) 724-7694
Represented by:
Patricia Howard, Cong and Public Affairs Director
Velva Walter, Cong and Public Affrs Deputy Director

DEPARTMENT OF JUSTICE - Tax Division
555 4th St., N.W., Washington, DC 20001
Telephone: (202) 724-6419
Represented by:
Stephen J. Csontos, Sr Legis Couns, Office of Legis & Policy

DEPARTMENT OF JUSTICE - United States Marshals Service
600 Army-Navy Drive, Arlington, VA 22202

The listings in this directory are available as *Mailing Labels.* See last page.

FEDERAL EXECUTIVE BRANCH
LEGISLATIVE AFFAIRS PERSONNEL

Telephone: (202) 307-9065
Represented by:
Stephen T. Boyle, Cong and Public Affrs

DEPARTMENT OF LABOR
200 Constitution Ave., N.W., Washington, DC 20210
Telephone: (202) 523-6141
Represented by:
Kathleen Harrington, Asst Secy, Cong & Intergov'l Affrs
Amparo Bouchey, Dep Asst Secy, Cong & Intergovt'l Affrs
Rebecca Morris, Assoc Asst Secy, Cong Affrs
James Conrad, Assoc Asst Secy, Intergovt'l Affrs
John Bauer, Legis Officer, Cong & Intergovt'l Affrs
Christopher Bowlin, Legis Officer, Cong & Intergovt'l Affrs
Jon Breyfogle, Legis Officer, Cong & Intergovt'l Affrs
Sally Browning, Liaison Officer, Cong & Intergov'l Affrs
Dana Clark, Legis Officer, Cong & Intergovt'l Affrs
Marcel Dubois, Legis Officer, Cong & Intergovt'l Affrs
Susan Eckerly, Legis Officer, Cong & Intergovt'l Affrs
Lori Gremel, Legis Officer, Cong & Intergovt'l Affrs
Susan Ironfield, Liaison Officer, Cong & Intergov'l Affrs
William Killmer, Legis Officer, Cong & Intergovt'l Affrs
Michael Lawrence, Legis Officer, Cong & Intergovt'l Affrs
Robin Miller, Legis Officer, Cong & Intergovt'l Affrs
Peter Roff, Liaison Officer, Cong & Intergov'l Affrs
Virginia Thomas, Legis Officer, Cong & Intergovt'l Affrs
Molly Walsh, Liaison Officer, Cong & Intergov'l Affrs

DEPARTMENT OF LABOR - Employment and Training Administration
200 Constitution Ave., N.W., Washington, DC 20210
Telephone: (202) 535-0664
Represented by:
Lloyd Feldman, Dir, Planning, Policy and Legislation

DEPARTMENT OF LABOR - Mine Safety and Health Administration
4015 Wilson Blvd., Arlington, VA 22203
Telephone: (703) 235-1392
Represented by:
Sylvia Milanese, Cong and Legis Affrs (Act)

DEPARTMENT OF LABOR - Pension and Welfare Benefits Administration
200 Constitution Ave., N.W., Washington, DC 20210
Telephone: (202) 523-7933
Represented by:
Jerry Lindrew, Asst Dir of Policy & Legis Analysis

DEPARTMENT OF NAVY
The Pentagon, Washington, DC 20350-1300
Telephone: (202) 697-7146
Represented by:
Rear Adm. William J. Flanagan, Chief, Legis Affrs
Capt. Ronald F. Testa, Principal Dep Chief, Legis Affrs
Cdr.. Don Nash, House Liaison, Legis Affrs
Capt. Bud Orr, Senate Liaison, Legis Affrs
Capt. Ted Hack, Navy Program, Legis Affrs
Capt. Roger Pitkin, Legislation, Legis Affrs
Cdr. Steve Clawson, Public Affrs, Legis Affairs
Cdr. Rich O'Hanlon, Exec Asst, Legis Affrs

DEPARTMENT OF NAVY - Chief of Naval Operations Office
The Pentagon, Washington, DC 20350-2000
Telephone: (202) 695-3480
Represented by:
Cdr. Ronald Swanson, Legal and Legis Matters

DEPARTMENT OF NAVY - United States Marine Corps
Navy Annex, Arlington Ridge Road, Washington, DC 20380-0001
Telephone: (202) 694-1686
Represented by:
Brig. Gen. P. D. Williams, Legis Asst

DEPARTMENT OF STATE
2201 C St., N.W., Washington, DC 20520
Telephone: (202) 647-4204
Represented by:
Janet G. Mullins, Asst Secy, Legis Affrs
Peter Madigan, Sr Dep Asst Secy, Legis Affrs
Lorne W. Craner, Dep Asst Secy, Legis Affrs
Richard Mueller, Dep Asst Secy, Legis Affrs
Steven K. Berry, Dep Asst Secy, Legis Affairs
Catherine Thibodeau, Cong. Correspondence
Kathleen Moody, Cong Liaison (African Affrs)
Barry F. Gidley, Cong & Public Affrs (Int'l Org Affrs)
Robert Mantel, Sr Adv., Cong & Public Affrs (Polit-Mil)

DEPARTMENT OF TRANSPORTATION
400 Seventh St., S.W., Washington, DC 20590
Telephone: (202) 366-4573
Represented by:
Galen Reser, Asst Secy, Govt'l Affrs
Steven Gaddy, Dep Asst Secy, Govt'l Affrs
Nancy Bruce, Dir, Cong Affrs Office
Thomas Herlihy, Asst Gen Counsel, Legislation

DEPARTMENT OF TRANSPORTATION - Federal Aviation Administration
800 Independence Ave., S.W., Washington, DC 20591
Telephone: (202) 267-3277
Represented by:
Brenda Yager, Asst Admin, Govt and Industry Affrs
Dennis Parobek, Cong Affrs
Albert B. Randall, Asst Chief Counsel, Legislation

DEPARTMENT OF TRANSPORTATION - Federal Highway Administration
400 Seventh St., S.W., Washington, DC 20590
Telephone: (202) 366-0761
Represented by:
Frank L. Calhoun, Asst Chief Counsel, Legis and Regul
Madeline Bloom, Legis and Strategic Plng Div.

DEPARTMENT OF TRANSPORTATION - Maritime Administration
400 Seventh St., S.W., Washington, DC 20590
Telephone: (202) 366-5724
Represented by:
Leonard L. Sutter, Chief, Div of Legis, Off of Gen Counsel

DEPARTMENT OF TRANSPORTATION - Nat'l Highway Traffic Safety Administration
400 Seventh St., S.W., Washington, DC 20590
Telephone: (202) 366-5265
Represented by:
John Womack, Legis Section

DEPARTMENT OF TRANSPORTATION - United States Coast Guard
400 Seventh St., S.W., Washington, DC 20590
Telephone: (202) 366-4280
Represented by:
Capt. Thomas Schaeffer, Chief, Cong and Govt'l Affrs
Capt. Kevin Barry, Legislation Div, Office of Chief Counsel

DEPARTMENT OF TRANSPORTATION - Urban Mass Transportation Administration
400 Seventh St., S.W., Washington, DC 20590
Telephone: (202) 366-4011
Represented by:
Daniel Duff, Asst Chief Counsel, Off of Chief Counsel

DEPARTMENT OF TREASURY
15th and Pennsylvania Ave. N.W., Washington, DC 20220
Telephone: (202) 566-2037
Represented by:
Bryce L. Harlow, Asst Secy, Legis Affrs
Mary C. Sophos, Dep Asst Secy, Legis Affrs (House)
Caroline Haynes, Dep Asst Secy, Legis Affrs (Senate)
Anna Holmquist Davis, Dir, Legis Affrs
Gale Peterson, Dep Dir, Legis Affrs
William MacKay, Legis Mgr - Enforcement
J. Timothy O'Neil, Legis Mgr
Lisa Stoltenberg, Legis Mgr
John Vogt, Legis Mgr - Tax
Gwen Pascale, Confidential Asst, Legis Affrs
Ora Starks, Cong Inquiries Analyst
Richard S. Carro, Assoc Gen Counsel, Legis, Litig & Regul
Robert Wootton, Tax Legis Counsel (Act)
Allan L. Martin, Asst Chief Couns, Tariff, Trade & Legis

DEPARTMENT OF TREASURY - Bureau of Alcohol, Tobacco and Firearms
1200 Pennsylvania Ave., N.W., Washington, DC 20226
Telephone: (202) 566-7376
Represented by:
James O. Pasco, Asst Dir, Cong and Media Affrs

DEPARTMENT OF TREASURY - Comptroller of the Currency
490 L'Enfant Plaza East, S.W., Washington, DC 20219
Telephone: (202) 447-1820
Represented by:
Frank Maguire, Sr Dep Compt, Legis and Public Affrs
Carolyn McFarlane, Cong Liaison
Raija Bettauer, Dir, Legis & Regul Analysis Div
Ford Barrett, Asst Dir (Regs), Legis & Regul Anal Div
Brenda Curry, Asst Dir (Legis), Legis & Regul Anal Div

The listings in this directory are available as *Mailing Labels*. See last page.

FEDERAL EXECUTIVE BRANCH
LEGISLATIVE AFFAIRS PERSONNEL

DEPARTMENT OF TREASURY - Internal Revenue Service

1111 Constitution Ave., N.W., Washington, DC 20224

Telephone: (202) 566-4071

Represented by:

Gayle Morin, Asst to the Commissioner (Legis Liaison)

DEPARTMENT OF TREASURY - Thrift Supervision Office

1700 G St., N.W., Washington, DC 20552

Telephone: (202) 906-6804

Represented by:

Robert J. Holland, Dep Dir, Cong Relations

Karen Solomon, Regul & Legis Div, Office of Chief Couns

DEPARTMENT OF TREASURY - United States Customs Service

1301 Constitution Ave., N.W., Washington, DC 20229

Telephone: (202) 566-9102

Represented by:

Charles R. Parkinson, Cong and Public Affrs

William Lawrence, Office of Cong Affrs

DEPARTMENT OF VETERANS AFFAIRS

810 Vermont Ave., N.W., Washington, DC 20420

Telephone: (202) 233-2817

Represented by:

Edward T. Timperlake, Asst Secy for Cong and Public Affrs

Alonzo M. Poteet, Dep Asst Secy, Cong Affrs

Dennis M. Duffy, Director, Cong Relations

ADMINISTRATIVE AGENCIES

ACTION

1100 Vermont Ave., N.W., Washington, DC 20525

Telephone: (202) 634-9772

Represented by:

Nora Manning, Asst Dir, Legis Affrs (Act)

Nancy Denholm, Spec Asst, Legis Affrs

AGENCY FOR INTERNAT'L DEVELOPMENT

320 21st St., N.W., Washington, DC 20523

Telephone: (202) 663-1449

Represented by:

R. Ray Randlett, Asst Admin, Legis Affrs

Tyler S. Posey, Dep Asst Admin, Legis Affrs

Joe Fredericks, Bur for Africa, Food for Peace

Kate Latta, Bur for Sci & Tech, Bur for Priv Enter

David Liner, Bur for Latin America & the Caribbean

Dorothy Rayburn, Bur for Asia and the Near East

Marianne O'Sullivan, Apprpriations and Budget Committees

Barbara Bennett, Cong Notifications

Bette Cook, Senate For Relats Cttee, Off For Disast

Janet McConnell, Cong Inquiries

Elouise Hood, Cong Correspondence

Robert M. Lester, Asst Gen Counsel, Legis & Policy, OGC

CONSUMER PRODUCT SAFETY COMMISSION

5401 Westbard Ave., Bethesda, MD 20816

Telephone: (301) 492-5515

Represented by:

Edward D. Harrill, Dir, Office of Cong Relations

ENVIRONMENTAL PROTECTION AGENCY

401 M St., S.W., Washington, DC 20460

Telephone: (202) 382-5200

Represented by:

Patrick H. Quinn, Assoc Admin, Cong and Legis Affrs

Deborah Storey, Dep Assoc Admin, Cong and Legis Affrs

Dona DeLeon, Dir, Cong Liaison Div (Act)

Susan Mulvaney, Info Officer, Cong Liaison Div

Judy Rohrer, Cong Liaison Div

Diann Frantz, Cong Liaison Div

Susan Bullard, Cong Liaison Div

Pat Gaskins, Cong Liaison Div

Delia Scott, Cong Liaison Div

R. Todd Koeze, Cong Liaison Div

Leslie Goss, Cong Liaison Div

Diane Hicks, Cong Liaison Div

M. Todd Foley, Cong Liaison Div

Cliff McCreedy, Cong Liaison Div

Jean Durant, Cong Liaison Div

Barbara Brooks, Cong Liaison Div

C. Marshall Cain, Dep Gen Counsel, Litig, Legis & Reg Opns

EQUAL EMPLOYMENT OPPORTUNITY COMMISSION

1801 L St., N.W., Washington, DC 20507

Telephone: (202) 663-4900

Represented by:

Deborah J. Graham, Commo and Legis Affrs

Marcia V. Sayer, Staff Dir/Legis Affrs

FARM CREDIT ADMINISTRATION

1501 Farm Credit Drive, McLean, VA 22102

Telephone: (703) 883-4056

Represented by:

Ronald H. Erickson, Jr., Cong and Public Affrs Officer

FEDERAL COMMUNICATIONS COMMISSION

1919 M St., N.W., Washington, DC 20554

Telephone: (202) 632-6405

Represented by:

Linda Solheim, Dir, Legis Affrs

Stephen Klitzman, Assoc Dir, Legis Affrs

Carolyn Tatum Roddy, Attorney Advisor, Legis Affrs

Dicksie J. Cribb, Cong Liaison Specialist

Ellen M. Rafferty, Cong Liaison Specialist

O. Lou Sizemore, Cong Liaison Specialist

Diana Atkinson, Secy, Legis Affairs

FEDERAL ELECTION COMMISSION

999 E St., N.W., Washington, DC 20463

Telephone: (202) 376-5136

Represented by:

Tina VanBrakle, Congressional Affrs Officer

FEDERAL RESERVE SYSTEM

20th and C Sts., N.W., Washington, DC 20551

Telephone: (202) 452-3456

Represented by:

Donald J. Winn, Asst to the Board

Win Hambley, Cong Liaison

Diane Werneke, Cong Liaison

FEDERAL TRADE COMMISSION

6th and Pennsylvania Ave. N.W., Washington, DC 20580

Telephone: (202) 326-2195

Represented by:

William B. Prendergast, Dir, Cong Relations

Dorian Hall, Dep Dir, Cong Relations (Act)

GENERAL SERVICES ADMINISTRATION

18th and F Sts., N.W., Washington, DC 20405

Telephone: (202) 566-0563

Represented by:

Michael J. DeLoose, Assoc Admin, Cong Affrs

Judith F. Bassett, Dep Assoc Admin, Cong Affrs

J. Christopher Brady, Legis Director, Cong Affrs

INTERSTATE COMMERCE COMMISSION

12th and Constitution Ave. N.W., Washington, DC 20423

Telephone: (202) 275-7231

Represented by:

Jule R. Herbert, Jr., Dir, Govt and Public Affrs Office (Act)

Jeanne Kowolski, Assoc Dir, Govt Affrs

M. Joy Carabisi, Assoc Dir, Govt Affrs

Carolyn I. Johnson, Legis Aide

Andrea Richards, Govt Affrs Asst

Mildred Toman, Admin Asst, Govt and Public Affrs

Patricia A. Hahn, Assoc General Counsel, Legislation

The listings in this directory are available as *Mailing Labels*. See last page.

FEDERAL EXECUTIVE BRANCH
LEGISLATIVE AFFAIRS PERSONNEL

MERIT SYSTEMS PROTECTION BOARD
1120 Vermont Ave., N.W., Washington, DC 20419
Telephone: (202) 653-7162
Represented by:
Mary L. Jennings, Legis Counsel

NAT'L AERONAUTICS AND SPACE ADMINISTRATION
400 Maryland Ave., S.W., Washington, DC 20546
Telephone: (202) 453-1055
Represented by:
Martin P. Kress, Asst Admin, Legis Affrs
Lynn W. Heninger, Asst Admin, Cong Relations (Act)
Everett Southwick, Dep Asst Admin, Cong Relations
Mary D. Kerwin, Dir, Cong Liaison
Michael A. Maguire, Legislation Dir
Lawrence E. Medway, Dir, Cong Inquiries
John J. Madison, Legis Affrs Specialist
Julia Meredith, Legis Affrs Specialist
Helen Rothman, Legis Affrs Specialist
Barbara F. Cherry, Legis Affrs Specialist
Vincent Sansevero, Legis Affrs Specialist

NAT'L CREDIT UNION ADMINISTRATION
1776 G St., N.W., Washington, DC 20456
Telephone: (202) 682-9650
Represented by:
Robert Loftus, Public and Cong Affrs

NAT'L ENDOWMENT FOR THE ARTS
1100 Pennsylvania Ave., N.W. Room 524, Washington, DC 20506
Telephone: (202) 682-5434
Represented by:
Rose DiNapoli, Dir, Cong Liaison

NAT'L ENDOWMENT FOR THE HUMANITIES
1100 Pennsylvania Ave., N.W., Washington, DC 20506
Telephone: (202) 786-0328
Represented by:
Rex O. Arney, Cong Liaison

NAT'L SCIENCE FOUNDATION
1800 G St., N.W., Washington, DC 20550
Telephone: (202) 357-9838
Represented by:
Dr. Raymond Bye, Dir, Legis and Public Affrs
Dr. Allen Shinn, Dep Dir, Legis and Public Affrs

NAT'L TRANSPORTATION SAFETY BOARD
800 Independence Ave., S.W., Washington, DC 20594
Telephone: (202) 382-6757
Represented by:
Brenda Meister, Congressional & Intergovt'l Relations

NUCLEAR REGULATORY COMMISSION
11555 Rockville Pike, Rockville, MD 20852
Telephone: (301) 492-1780
Represented by:
Harold Denton, Dir, Govt'l and Public Affairs Office
Dennis K. Rathbun, Dir, Cong Affairs

OFFICE OF PERSONNEL MANAGEMENT
1900 E St., N.W., Washington, DC 20415
Telephone: (202) 632-6514
Represented by:
Mark Valente, III, Dir, Cong Relations
Mark W. Rodgers, Dep Dir, Office of Cong Relations
Charlene Luskey, Sr Cong Relations Officer
Ronald A. Brooks, Chief, Cong Liaison
James Woodruff, Legis Analysis, Office of General Couns

OVERSEAS PRIVATE INVESTMENT CORP.
1615 M St., N.W., Washington, DC 20527
Telephone: (202) 457-7038
Represented by:
James R. Offutt, Sr Counsel, Admin and Legislation
Richard C. Horanberg, Dir, Legis Affrs

SECURITIES AND EXCHANGE COMMISSION
450 5th St., N.W., Washington, DC 20549
Telephone: (202) 272-2500
Represented by:
Nina Gross, Dir, Legis Affrs
Peter Kiernan, Legis Counsel
Rusty Dillman, Legis Analyst

SELECTIVE SERVICE SYSTEM
1023 31st St., N.W., Washington, DC 20435

Telephone: (202) 724-0413
Represented by:
John S. Rivers, Asst Dir, Cong and Intergovt'l Affrs

SMALL BUSINESS ADMINISTRATION
1441 L St., N.W. Room 1028, Washington, DC 20416
Telephone: (202) 653-7581
Represented by:
Michael P. Forbes, Asst Admin, Cong and Legis Affrs

UNITED STATES INFORMATION AGENCY
301 4th St., S.W., Washington, DC 20547
Telephone: (202) 485-8828
Represented by:
Martha Johnston, Dir, Office of Cong Liaison
Caroline Isacco, Cong Liaison Officer
Jon Beard, Cong Liaison Officer

UNITED STATES INTERNAT'L TRADE COMMISSION
500 E St., S.W., Washington, DC 20436
Telephone: (202) 252-1151
Represented by:
Jane C. Baird, Dir, Cong Liaison

WASHINGTON REPRESENTATIVES
1990

SELECTED SUBJECTS INDEX

Selected clients or employers of the representatives listed in this book have been cross-referenced in this index by significant or timely legislative, manufacturing or professional interest.

If one wishes to know, for example, what companies or associations are likely to be active in discussion of policies or legislation affecting the sugar industry in this country and abroad, a glance at the subject heading SUGAR will show the relevant groups with representation in Washington.

ABORTION see WOMEN

ACCOUNTING
American Bankruptcy Institute
American Institute of Certified Public Accountants
American Soc. of Military Comptrollers
Andersen and Co., Arthur
Ass'n of Government Accountants
Ass'n of Practicing CPAs
Coopers and Lybrand Political Action Committee
Deloitte & Touche Washington Services Group
Ernst & Young
Financial Accounting Foundation
Financial Accounting Standards Board
Government Finance Officers Ass'n
Governmental Standards Accounting Board
KPMG Peat Marwick
Nat'l Accounting and Finance Council
Nat'l Ass'n of Black Accountants
Nat'l Soc. of Accountants for Cooperatives
Nat'l Soc. of Public Accountants
Peat Marwick
Price Waterhouse

ADVERTISING INDUSTRY
Advo-Systems, Inc.
American Advertising Federation
American Advertising Federation Political Action Committee
American Ass'n of Advertising Agencies
American Council of Highway Advertisers

Ass'n of Nat'l Advertisers
Campbell-Mithun
Clarke & Co.
Direct Marketing Ass'n
Freedom to Advertise Coalition
Internat'l Newspaper Advertising and Marketing Executives
Mail Advertising Service Ass'n Internat'l
Naegle Outdoor Advertising
Nat'l Advertising Co.
Nat'l Ass'n of Exposition Managers
Nat'l Electric Sign Ass'n
Outdoor Advertising Ass'n of America
PR Service Co., Ltd.
Response Dynamics Inc.
Sears, Roebuck and Co.
Specialty Advertising Ass'n, Internat'l

AEROSPACE
Advanced Management & Technologies
Aerojet
Aeronautical Radio, Inc.
Aerospace Education Foundation
Aerospace Industries Ass'n of America
Aerospace Industries Ass'n of Canada
Air Force Ass'n
Air-Log Ltd.
Allied-Signal Inc.
American Astronautical Soc.
American Defense Preparedness Ass'n
Americans for the High Frontier

Atlantic Research Corp.
Ball Corp.
Bell Aerospace Textron
Boeing Co.
Bromon Aircraft Corp.
Challenger Center for Space Science Education
Citizens Against Research Bans
Communications Satellite Corp. (COMSAT)
Contract Services Ass'n of America
DynCorp
Earth Observation Satellite Co.
Earth Satellite Corp.
European Space Agency
Fairchild Political Action Committee
Fairchild Space & Defense Corp.
Ferranti Defense and Space Group
Ford Aerospace Corp.
Goodrich Co., BF
Grumman Aerospace Corp.
Harris Government Systems
Hercules Aerospace Co. (Aerospace Products Group)
Institute for Security and Cooperation in Outer Space
Institute of Navigation
Italian Aerospace Industries (USA), Inc.
ITT Corp.
Kaman Corp.
Lockheed Missiles and Space Co.
Loral/Fairchild Systems
LTV Aircraft Products Group
LTV Corp.
LTV Corp. Active Citizenship Campaign

SELECTED SUBJECTS INDEX

SELECTED SUBJECTS INDEX

SELECTED SUBJECTS INDEX

SELECTED SUBJECTS INDEX

SELECTED SUBJECTS INDEX

CANNERS see FOOD INDUSTRY

CASTING see METAL WORKING

CATTLE see LIVESTOCK

CEMENT see BUILDERS and BUILDING MATERIAL

CHEMICALS and CHEMICAL INDUSTRY

The listings in this directory are available as *Mailing Labels*. See last page.

SELECTED SUBJECTS INDEX

SELECTED SUBJECTS INDEX

Allen-Bradley Corp.
Allnet Communications Services Inc. Good Government
  Fund
American Chamber of Commerce Executives
  Communications Council
American Federation of Information Processing Societies
American Home Satellite Ass'n
American Radio Relay League
Ameritech (American Information Technologies)
Argo Communications Corp.
Armed Forces Communications and Electronics Ass'n
  Headquarters
Asia Pacific Space and Communications
Associated Information Managers
AT&T
AT&T Technologies, Inc.
Atlantic Research Corp.
Bay Area Teleport
BDM Internat'l, Inc.
Bell Atlantic
Bell Communications Research, Inc.
BellSouth Corp.
BHC, Inc.
Bolt, Beranek and Newman
British Telecom plc
Business Computing Internat'l
Cable and Wireless North America
Capital Cities/ABC Inc.
Cellular Telecommunications Industry Ass'n
Centel Corp.
China, Directorate General of Telecommunications,
  Ministry of Communications of Republic of
Chris-Craft Industries Inc.
Cincinnati Electronics Inc.
Citizens Communications Center
Cleartel Communication
Committee of Corporate Telecommunications Users
Communication Industries Ass'n of Japan
Communications Internat'l Inc.
Communications Satellite Corp. (COMSAT)
Communications Workers of America
Competitive Telecommunications Ass'n (COMPTEL)
Competitive Telecommunications Ass'n Political Action
  Committee (COMPTELPAC)
Computer and Business Equipment Manufacturers Ass'n
Computer and Communications Industry Ass'n
Computer and Communications Industry Ass'n Political
  Action Committee
Computer Sciences Corp. (Systems Group)
Contel Corp.
Cook Inlet Communications
Darome, Inc.
DataCom Systems Corp.
Datapoint Corp.
DSC Communications Corp.
Edgell Communications
Electronic Data Systems Corp.
Electronic Industries Ass'n
Electronic Mail Ass'n
Fairchild Space & Defense Corp.
First Carolina Communications
General Cellular Corp.
General Instrument Corp.
General Instrument Corp. Political Action Committee
Graphic Communications Internat'l Union
Graphic Communications Internat'l Union Political
  Contributions Committee
GTE Corp.
GTE Government Systems
Guan Haur Industries Ltd.
Harmon Industries, Inc.
Harris Corp.
Hewlett-Packard Co.
Home Recording Rights Coalition
Honeywell, Inc.
Independent Data Communications Manufacturers Ass'n
Information Industry Ass'n
Internat'l Ass'n of Independent Producers
Internat'l Communications Ass'n
Internat'l Microwave Systems Corp. (IMSCO)
Internat'l Telecharge, Inc.
Internat'l Telecommunications Satellite Organization
  (INTELSAT)
Internat'l Teleconferencing Ass'n
INTERSECT Corp.
ITT Corp.
Lin Broadcasting Corp.
LiTel Telecommunications Corp.

Macrovision
Magnavox Government and Industrial Electronics Co.
Marconi Communications Inc.
Massachusetts Corp. for Educational Telecommunications
MCI Communications Corp.
MCI Telecommunications Political Action Committee
Mead Data Central, Inc.
Media Access Project
Media General, Inc.
Michigan Bell Telephone Co.
Micronesian Telecommunications Corp.
Millicom Inc.
Motorola, Inc.
Nat'l Ass'n of Business and Educational Radio Political
  Action Committee
Nat'l Ass'n of County Information Officials
Nat'l Ass'n of Telecommunications Dealers
Nat'l Exchange Carriers Ass'n
Nat'l Telecommunications Network
Nat'l Telephone Cooperative Ass'n
NCR Corporation
NEC America
New York Telephone Co.
North American Telecommunications Ass'n
OPT IN AMERICA
Organization for the Protection and Advancement of
  Small Telephone Cos.
Pacific Telecom, Inc.
Pan American Satellite Corp.
Phase Two Industries
Physical Optics Corp.
Pirelli Cable Corp.
Pony Express Courier Corp.
Power and Communications Contractors Ass'n
Public Service Satellite Consortium
Radio Technical Commission for Maritime Services
Railstar Control Technology, Inc.
Recording Industry Ass'n of America
Ricoh Corp.
Satellite Broadcasting and Communications Ass'n
SCI Technology, Inc.
Scientific-Atlanta, Inc.
Soc. for Technical Communication
Stamats Film and Video
Sun Moon Star Group
Tektronix, Inc.
TèleCommunications, Inc.
Telecommunications Industry Ass'n
Telecommunications Research and Action Center
Telephone and Data Systems, Inc.
Telephone Education Committee Organization
Telocator
TRW Inc.
Turner Broadcasting System, Inc.
U.S. Central, Inc.
United States Telephone Ass'n
United Technologies Corp.
United Telecommunications
United Television, Inc.
USA Telecommunications
Videotex Industry Ass'n
Western Tele-Communications, Inc.
Western Union Corp.
Westinghouse Broadcasting Co., Inc.
Williams Companies, The
Wireless Cable Ass'n, Inc.
Women in Communications
Yavapai Telephone Exchange
Zitel Corp.

CONSERVATION

America the Beautiful Fund
American Ass'n of Zoological Parks and Aquariums
American Institute for Conservation of Historic and
  Artistic Works
American Institute of Biological Sciences
American Rivers
American Soc. of Heating, Refrigerating and Air
  Conditioning Engineers
Barrier Beach Preservation Ass'n
Center for Marine Conservation
Central Arizona Water Conservation District
Coalition for Acid Rain Equity (CARE)
Coastal Soc.
Coastal States Organization
Committee for Humane Legislation
Congress Watch
Conservation Foundation

Consumer Energy Council of America Research
  Foundation
Council on Ocean Law
Defenders of Wildlife
Environmental Action Foundation
Environmental Defense Fund
Environmental Federation of America
Friends of the Earth
Grand Canyon Trust
Internat'l Ass'n of Fish and Wildlife Agencies
Izaak Walton League of America
Kellogg Co., M. W.
League of Conservation Voters
Marine Mammal Protection Fund
Nat'l Alliance for Animal Legislation
Nat'l Ass'n of Conservation Districts
Nat'l Ass'n of Plumbing-Heating-Cooling Contractors
Nat'l Endowment for Soil and Water Conservation
Nat'l Inholders Ass'n
Nat'l Park Foundation
Nat'l Parks and Conservation Ass'n
Nat'l Trust for Historic Preservation
Nat'l Water Resources Ass'n
Nat'l Wetlands Technical Council
Nat'l Wildlife Federation
Natural Resources Defense Council
Nature Conservancy, The
People for the Ethical Treatment of Animals (PETA)
Platte River Whooping Crane Trust
Preservation Action
Public Citizen's Critical Mass Energy Project
Renew America Project
Renewable Natural Resources Foundation
Sea Turtle Rescue Fund
Sierra Club
Sierra Club Legal Defense Fund
Soc. for Animal Protective Legislation
Sport Fishing Institute
Washington State Commissioner of Public Lands
Water Resources Congress
Wilderness Soc.
Wildlife Legislative Fund of America
Wildlife Management Institute
World Federation for the Protection of Animals
World Resources Institute
World Wildlife Fund
World Wildlife Fund/The Conservation Foundation
Worldwatch Institute

CONSTRUCTION see BUILDERS and BUILDING MATERIALS
CONSULTING

Advanced Energy Technology, Inc.
American Ass'n of Healthcare Consultants
American Ass'n of Political Consultants
American Concrete Pipe Ass'n
American Consulting Engineers Council
American Soc. of Agricultural Consultants
American Soc. of Agricultural Consultants Internat'l
  Political Action Committee
Ass'n Management Corp.
Atlantic Research Corp.
Belmont Development
Brown Bridgman & Co Retiree Health Care Group
Burson-Marsteller Political Action Committee
Campbell-Mithun
CANAMCO (The Canadian-American Company)
Capital Hill Group, Inc., The
Coastal Reports, Inc.
Columbia Institute
Compass Internat'l Inc.
Consulting Engineers Council of Metropolitan
  Washington
CRSS Constructors, Inc.
DeLeuw, Cather and Co.
Deleuw/Greeley/Hyman
Federal Employees Ass'n
Foster Wheeler Internat'l Corp.
Fredrickson Associates, Inc., D. S.
Glick & Glick
Good Relations
Grey, Clark, Shih and Associates, Ltd.
Halliburton Co.
Hill and Knowlton Inc. Political Action Committee
Irrigation Ass'n
Linton, Mields Reisler and Cottone Political Action
  Committee
Metcor Inc.

SELECTED SUBJECTS INDEX

Mitsubishi Research Institute
Nat'l Academy of Public Administration
Nat'l Ass'n of Career Development Consultants
Nat'l Ass'n of Legal Search Consultants
Nat'l Ass'n of Tax Consultants
Nat'l Center for Ass'n Resources
NATJ and NATE
New Directions for Policy
New Directions Group, Inc.
Power Technology Inc.
Price Waterhouse
Professional Engineers in Private Practice
Professional Services Council
Public Affairs Internat'l
Pyropower Corp.
Stratton and Associates
STS Corp.

CONSUMERS

ACORN (Ass'n of Community Organizations for Reform Now)
Ass'n of Flight Attendants
Automotive Consumer Action Program
Aviation Consumer Action Project
Bankcard Holders of America
Buyers Up
Center for Study of Responsive Law
Congress Watch
Consumer Energy Council of America Research Foundation
Consumer Federation of America
Consumer Federation of America Political Action Fund
Consumers Union of the United States
Consumers United for Rail Equity
Continental Ass'n of Funeral and Memorial Societies
Council of Better Business Bureaus
Electricity Consumers Resource Council
Nat'l Ass'n of Consumer Agency Administrators
Nat'l Ass'n of Housing Cooperatives
Nat'l Consumer Law Center
Nat'l Consumers League
Nat'l Resource Center for Consumers of Legal Services
Nat'l Women's Health Network
Public Citizen
Public Citizen Litigation Group
Public Voice for Food and Health Policy
Special Committee for Workplace Product Liability Reform
Telecommunications Research and Action Center
Trial Lawyers for Public Justice
U.S. Public Interest Research Group
Unilever United States, Inc.

CONTRACTORS

ABC-PAC
Air Conditioning Contractors of America
American Public Works Ass'n
American Subcontractors Ass'n
Associated Builders and Contractors
Associated General Contractors of America
Associated General Contractors Political Action Committee
Associated Landscape Contractors of America
Associated Specialty Contractors
Ass'n of Bituminous Contractors
Ass'n of the Wall and Ceiling Industries-Internat'l
Bedford Group
Brown & Root, Inc.
Building Service Contractors Ass'n, Internat'l
Coalition for Government Procurement
Coalition for Prompt Pay
Contract Services Ass'n of America
Dillingham Corp.
DynCorp
Internat'l Ass'n of Drilling Contractors
Internat'l Masonry Institute
Japan Federation of Construction Contractors
Kellogg Co., M. W.
Land Improvement Contractors of America
ManTech Internat'l
Marine Contractors Alliance
Mechanical Contractors Ass'n of America
Mechanical Contractors Ass'n of America/PAC
Merit Shop Foundation
Nat'l Asphalt Pavement Ass'n
Nat'l Ass'n of Dredging Contractors
Nat'l Ass'n of Minority Contractors
Nat'l Ass'n of Miscellaneous, Ornamental and Architectural Products Contractors

Nat'l Ass'n of Plumbing-Heating-Cooling Contractors
Nat'l Ass'n of Reinforcing Steel Contractors
Nat'l Ass'n of the Remodeling Industry
Nat'l Constructors Ass'n
Nat'l Contract Management Ass'n
Nat'l Council of Small Federal Contractors
Nat'l Electrical Contractors Ass'n
Nat'l Insulation Contractors Ass'n
Nat'l Utility Contractors Ass'n
Nat'l Utility Contractors Ass'n Legislative and Action Committee
Northwest Marine Iron Works
Ohbayashi Corp.
Painting and Decorating Contractors of America
Power and Communications Contractors Ass'n
Tile Contractors Ass'n of America
Turner Corp., The
Wall and Ceiling Political Action Committee

COOPERATIVES

Allegheny Electric Cooperative, Inc.
American Institute of Cooperation
Arkansas Electric Cooperative Corp.
Basin Electric Power Cooperative
Cajun Rural Electric Power Cooperative, Inc.
CARE
Central Montana Electric Power Cooperative, Inc.
Central Virginia Electric Cooperative, Inc.
Clean Sound
Continental Ass'n of Funeral and Memorial Societies
Cooperative League of the USA Political Action Committee (Nat'l Coop Business PAC)
Craig-Botetourt Electric Cooperative
Credit Union Nat'l Ass'n
Mid-West Electric Consumers Ass'n
Montana Electric Power Cooperatives Ass'n
Nat'l Ass'n of Housing Cooperatives
Nat'l Cooperative Bank
Nat'l Council of Farmer Cooperatives
Nat'l Farmers Union
Nat'l Rural Electric Cooperative Ass'n
Nat'l Soc. of Accountants for Cooperatives
Nat'l Telephone Cooperative Ass'n
Ocean Spray Cranberries
Rayburn County Electric Cooperative
Southern Maryland Electric Cooperative, Inc.
Sunflower Electric Cooperative, Inc.
Universal Frutrading Cooperative Ltd.
Western Fuels Ass'n

COPPER

Anaconda Minerals Co.
ASARCO Incorporated
Copper and Brass Fabricators Council
Cyprus Minerals Corp.
Inspiration Consolidated Copper Co.
Magma Copper Corp.
Marmon Group
McKechnie Brothers (South Africa) Ltd.
Phelps Dodge Corp.
Revere Copper and Brass Co.
Sambo Copper Co., Ltd.

COPYRIGHTS and PATENTS

American Ass'n of Small Research Companies
American Intellectual Property Law Ass'n
American Soc. of Composers, Authors and Publishers
Ass'n of American Publishers
Coalition to Preserve the Integrity of American Trademarks
Committee for America's Copyright Community
Copyright Justice Coalition
Educators' Ad Hoc Committee on Copyright Law
Horticultural Research Institute
Industry Coalition on Technology Transfer
Information Industry Ass'n
Intellectual Property Owners, Inc.
Nat'l Ass'n of Plant Patent Owners
Nat'l Club Ass'n
Nat'l Patent Council
Patlex Corp.

COTTON

American Cotton Growers
American Cotton Shippers Ass'n
Committee for the Advancement of Cotton
Committee Organized for the Trading of Cotton (COTCO)
Cotton Cooperatives
Cotton Council Internat'l

Cotton Warehouse Ass'n of America
Cotton Warehouse Government Relations Committee
Cottongrowers Warehouse Ass'n
Nat'l Cotton Council of America
Nat'l Cottonseed Products Ass'n
Supima Ass'n of America
Texas Cotton Marketing

CREDIT

Ahmanson & Co., H. F.
American Bankruptcy Institute
American Express Co.
American Financial Services Ass'n
Associated Credit Bureaus, Inc.
Bank Card Servicers Ass'n
Bank of America NT & SA
Bankcard Holders of America
Beneficial Corp.
Beneficial Management Corp. of America
Columbia Farm Credit District
Consumer Bankers Ass'n
Council of South Texas Economic Progress
Credit Union Nat'l Ass'n
CSC Credit Services, Inc.
Defense Credit Union Council
Dun & Bradstreet
Equifax Inc.
Farm Credit Council
Federal Home Loan Bank of Boston
Federal Home Loan Bank of Chicago
Federal Home Loan Bank of Cincinnati
Federal Home Loan Bank of Dallas
Federal Home Loan Bank of New York
Federal Home Loan Bank of Pittsburgh
Federal Home Loan Bank of San Francisco
Great Western Financial Corp.
Household Internat'l
Household Internat'l Political Action Committee
Houston Agricultural Credit Corp.
Joseph and Feiss Inc.
MasterCard Internat'l. Inc.
Nat'l Ass'n of Credit Management
Nat'l Ass'n of Federal Credit Unions
Nat'l Ass'n of State Credit Union Supervisors
Nat'l Bank for Cooperatives
Nat'l Check Cashers Ass'n
Nat'l Institute for State Credit Union Examination
VISA U.S.A., Inc.

CRIME

American Correctional Ass'n
Assassination Archive and Research Center
Center for Dispute Settlement
Citizens for a Drug Free America
Conference of Chief Justices
Criminal Justice Statistics Ass'n
Federal Criminal Investigators Ass'n
Internat'l Anti-Counterfeiting Coalition
Internat'l Ass'n of Chiefs of Police
Internat'l Brotherhood of Police Officers
Internat'l Narcotic Enforcement Officers Ass'n
INTERSECT Corp.
Justice Fellowship
Nat'l Ass'n of Criminal Justice Planners
Nat'l Ass'n of Regional Councils
Nat'l Center for Missing and Exploited Children
Nat'l Center for State Courts
Nat'l Center on Institutions and Alternatives
Nat'l Crime Prevention Council
Nat'l Criminal Justice Ass'n
Nat'l District Attorneys Ass'n
Nat'l Institute of Corrections
Nat'l Organization for Victim Assistance
Nat'l Sheriffs' Ass'n
Prison Fellowship Ministries
Prison Industries Reform Council
Public Offender Counselor Ass'n
Search Group, Inc.
Sentencing Project, The

DAIRY INDUSTRY

American Butter Institute
American Dairy Products Institute
Borden Internat'l
Centre National Interprofessionel de L'Economie Laitiere (French Dairy Ass'n)
Cheese Importers Ass'n of America
Dairy and Food Industries Supply Ass'n
Dairy Industry Committee

SELECTED SUBJECTS INDEX

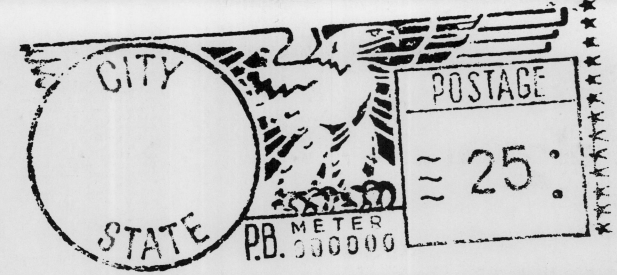

Do you have A PRODUCT ... A SERVICE ... A MESSAGE
to bring to the attention of the 12,000 influential individuals in this book?

Reach them through use of these
accurate, regularly updated
WASHINGTON REPRESENTATIVES

MAILING LIST LABELS OR CARDS

1. All 12,000 Washington Representatives (including employees, law and public affairs consulting firms and individual attorneys and account executives). *Available only as single ZIP listing. No Subject breakdowns.*

2. The Washington offices of the several thousand Organizations Represented (including companies, associations, labor unions, issue groups and professional societies. *Available as a full list or broken down by subject areas of interest* — e.g., Petroleum Industry, Education, Minorities, Banking, Foreign Relations, etc.

CHESHIRE LABELS ... PRESSURE SENSITIVE LABELS ... 3 × 5 CARDS

- -

WASHINGTON REPRESENTATIVE MAILING LIST

☐ Please send me your list of *all* 12,000 *Washington Representatives* (Not available by subject)

☐ Pressure Sensitive Labels $495.00

☐ Cheshire Labels $450.00

☐ 3 × 5 Cards $495.00

☐ Please send me information on counts and prices for labels _____ or cards _____ on Washington offices of *Organizations Represented* in the following subject categories _____ , _____ , _____ .

☐ Check enclosed.

☐ Please bill me.

NOTE: Check of money order must accompany all initial orders!
DC Tax (6%)

Name _____

Title _____

Organization _____

Street _____

City _____ State _____ Zip _____

Date _____

Signature _____

COLUMBIA BOOKS, INC., *Publishers*
1212 New York Ave., N.W., Suite 330
Washington, D.C. 20005

AFFIX
STAMP
HERE

SELECTED SUBJECTS INDEX

Consumer Energy Council of America Research
  Foundation
Corporation for Enterprise Development
Council of Industrial Development Bond Issuers
Council of the Americas
Council on Hemispheric Affairs
Development Group for Alternative Policies
Economic Policy Institute
Enid Joint Industrial Foundation
Government Finance Officers Ass'n
Hawaii State Department of Business and Economic
  Development
Heritage Foundation
Illinois Diversatech Corp.
Institute for Internat'l Economics
Institute for Local Self-Reliance
Institute for Research on the Economics of Taxation
  (IRET)
Interfaith Action for Economic Justice
Internat'l Center for Research on Women
Internat'l Economic Policy Ass'n
Korea Economic Institute of America
Momentum '88
Nat'l Ass'n of Development Organizations
Nat'l Ass'n of Small Business Investment Companies
Nat'l Center for Appropriate Technology
Nat'l Center for Urban Ethnic Affairs
Nat'l Chamber Foundation
Nat'l Community Action Foundation
Nat'l Congress for Community Economic Development
Nat'l Council for Urban Economic Development
Nat'l Economists Club
Nat'l Planning Ass'n
Nat'l Trust for Historic Preservation
Nat'l Urban Coalition
Nat'l Women's Economic Alliance
Nomura Research Institute (America), Inc.
Oregon Economic Development Dept., Ports Division
Oregon, State of, Department of Economic Development,
  Ports Division
Philadelphia Industrial Development Corp.
Puerto Rico Economic Development Administration
Rebuild America
Richardson Lawrie Associates
Spokane Region Economic Development (Momentum 90)
Transnational Development Consortium
Tri-City Industrial Development Council
United States Nat'l Committee for Pacific Economic
  Cooperation
World Council on Free Zones
World Hunger Education Service
World Relief
Worldwatch Institute

EDUCATION

Academy for Educational Development
Academy for State and Local Government
Advisory Council on Historic Preservation
Advocacy Institute, The
Aerospace Education Foundation
Alexander Graham Bell Ass'n for the Deaf
Alliance for Cannabis Therapeutics
Alternative Schools Network
American Alliance for Health, Physical Education,
  Recreation and Dance
American Anthropological Ass'n
American Ass'n for Adult and Continuing Education
American Ass'n for Clinical Chemistry
American Ass'n for Higher Education
American Ass'n for Study of the United States in World
  Affairs
American Ass'n of Colleges of Nursing
American Ass'n of Colleges of Osteopathic Medicine
American Ass'n of Colleges of Pharmacy
American Ass'n of Colleges of Podiatric Medicine
American Ass'n of Collegiate Registrars and Admissions
  Officers
American Ass'n of Community and Junior Colleges
American Ass'n of Immunologists
American Ass'n of Museums
American Ass'n of Petroleum Geologists
American Ass'n of Physics Teachers
American Ass'n of Retired Persons
American Ass'n of School Administrators
American Ass'n of State Colleges and Universities
American Ass'n of University Affiliated Programs
American Ass'n of University Professors
American Ass'n of University Women

American Astronomical Soc.
American Chiropractic Registry of Radiologic
  Technologists
American College Health Ass'n
American College Personnel Ass'n
American Conference of Academic Deans
American Council for Capital Formation
American Council for Drug Education
American Council of Young Political Leaders
American Council on Education
American Defense Foundation
American Driver and Traffic Safety Education Ass'n
American Educational Research Ass'n
American Federation of Teachers
American Forestry Ass'n
American Historical Ass'n
American Institute for Foreign Study
American Institute of Biological Sciences
American Institute of Chemists Foundation
American Labor Education Center
American Legislative Exchange Council
American Medical Student Ass'n
American Occupational Therapy Ass'n
American Podiatric Medical Students Ass'n
American Public Policy Institute
American Rehabilitation Counseling Ass'n
American School Counselors Ass'n
American School Food Service Ass'n
American Soc. for Engineering Education
American Soc. for Pharmacology and Experimental
  Therapeutics
American Soc. for Psychoprophylaxis in Obstetrics
  (ASPO/Lamaze)
American Soc. for Training and Development
American Sociological Ass'n
American Speech-Language-Hearing Ass'n
American University of Beirut
American University, The
American Vocational Ass'n
Americans United for Separation of Church and State
Americans United Research Foundation
Anchorage School District
Arizona State University
ASPIRA Ass'n, Inc.
Associated Universities
Ass'n for Childhood Education Internat'l
Ass'n for Community Based Education
Ass'n for Computing Machinery
Ass'n for Counselor Education and Supervision
Ass'n for Education & Rehabilitation of the Blind &
  Visually Impaired
Ass'n for Educational Communications and Technology
Ass'n for Hospital Medical Education
Ass'n for Humanistic Education and Development
Ass'n for Multicultural Counseling and Development
Ass'n for Persons with Severe Handicaps
Ass'n for Research, Administration, Professional Councils
  and Societies
Ass'n for Supervision and Curriculum Development
Ass'n for the Advancement of Health Education
Ass'n for the Behavioral Sciences and Medical Education
Ass'n of Academic Health Centers
Ass'n of American Colleges
Ass'n of American Geographers
Ass'n of American Law Schools
Ass'n of American Medical Colleges
Ass'n of American Publishers
Ass'n of American Universities
Ass'n of American Veterinary Medical Colleges
Ass'n of Big Eight Universities
Ass'n of Collegiate Schools of Architecture
Ass'n of Community College Trustees
Ass'n of Farmworker Opportunity Programs
Ass'n of Governing Boards of Universities and Colleges
Ass'n of Independent Colleges and Schools
Ass'n of Independent Colleges and Schools Political
  Action Committee
Ass'n of Jesuit Colleges and Universities
Ass'n of Military Colleges and Schools of the U.S.
Ass'n of Minority Health Professions Schools
Ass'n of Navajo Community Controlled School Boards
Ass'n of Physical Plant Administrators of Universities and
  Colleges
Ass'n of Professors of Medicine
Ass'n of School Business Officials Internat'l
Ass'n of Schools and Agencies for the Handicapped
Ass'n of Schools and Colleges of Optometry
Ass'n of Schools of Public Health

Ass'n of Systematics Collections
Ass'n of Teacher Educators
Ass'n of Theological Schools in the United States and
  Canada, The
Ass'n of University Programs in Health Administration
Ass'n of Urban Universities
Atlantic Council of the United States
Auburn University
Aurora University
Autism Soc. of America
Bank St. College
Barry University
Bayonne Board of Education
Beirut University College
Boston College
Boston Museum of Science
Boston University
Bowman Gray School of Medicine of Wake Forest
  University
Brandeis University
Broadcast Education Ass'n
Brookings Institution
Business-Higher Education Forum
California Department of Education
California Institute of Technology
CareerCom Corp.
Carnegie Council on Adolescent Development
Catholic University of America
Cato Institute
Center for Democracy
Center for Health Policy Studies
Center for Immigration Studies
Center for Internat'l Business and Trade
Center for Judicial Studies
Center for Law and Education
Center for Marine Conservation
Center for Nat'l Policy
Center for Nat'l Security Studies
Center for Sickle Cell Disease
Center for Studies in Health Policy
Center for the Study of the Presidency
Challenger Center for Space Science Education
Christian College Coalition
Citizens for Educational Freedom
City University
Clark Atlanta University
Classroom Publishers Ass'n
Clemson University
Clover Park School District
Coalition of Boston Teaching Hospitals
Coalition of EPSCoR States
Coalition of Higher Education Assistance Organizations
College Construction Loan Insurance Ass'n
College Republican Nat'l Committee
College and University Personnel Ass'n
Colorado State University
Columbia University
Committee For Education Funding
Common Fund, The
Concerned Educators Against Forced Unionism
Concord College
Conference of Educational Administrators Serving the
  Deaf
Congressional Black Caucus Foundation
Congressional Institute for the Future
Consortium of State Maritime Schools
Consortium of Universities of the Washington
  Metropolitan Area
Convention II, Inc.
Council for Advancement and Support of Education
Council for American Private Education
Council for Basic Education
Council for Educational Development and Research
Council for Exceptional Children
Council for the Internat'l Exchange of Scholars
Council of Chief State School Officers
Council of Graduate Schools
Council of Independent Colleges
Council of Rehabilitation Specialists
Council of State Administrators of Vocational
  Rehabilitation
Council of the Great City Schools
Council on Continuing Education Unit
Council on Education of the Deaf
Council on Governmental Relations
Council on Hemispheric Affairs
Council on Hotel, Restaurant & Institutional Education
Council on Legal Education Opportunity

SELECTED SUBJECTS INDEX

The listings in this directory are available as *Mailing Labels*. See last page.

SELECTED SUBJECTS INDEX

University of Miami
University of Michigan
University of Michigan Medical Center
University of Nebraska
University of Nebraska Foundation
University of Nevada - Las Vegas
University of Nevada/Reno
University of New Mexico
University of North Carolina
University of Oklahoma
University of Pennsylvania
University of Scranton
University of South Carolina
University of Southern California
University of Southern Mississippi
University of the Arts
University of Utah
University of Vermont
University of Washington
Very Special Arts
Virgin Islands, University of the
Virginia Polytechnical Institute and State University
Vocational Industrial Clubs of America
Washington State Impact Aid Ass'n
Weizman Institute of Science
West Virginia University
Wheeling Jesuit College
Women's College Coalition
Women's Research and Education Institute
Worldwatch Institute
Young America's Foundation

ELECTRICITY and ELECTRONICS

AB Electronics Group Ltd.
Action Committee for Rural Electrification
Ad Hoc Committee for a Competitive Electric Supply System (ACCESS)
Aiwa America, Inc.
Akzo America, Inc.
Alabama Power Co.
Allen-Bradley Corp.
American Electric Power Service Corp.
American Electronics Ass'n
American Electronics Laboratories
AOC Internat'l, Inc.
Arkansas Electric Cooperative Corp.
Armed Forces Communications and Electronics Ass'n Headquarters
Associated Electric Cooperative
Ass'n of Old Crows
Atlantic Research Corp.
AVW Electronics Systems, Inc.
Babcock and Wilcox Co.
Baltimore Gas and Electric Co.
Brother Internat'l, Inc.
Canai Inc.
Car Audio Specialists Ass'n
Carlon Electrical Sciences, Inc.
Central Nebraska Public Power and Irrigation District
Cherokee Nation Industries, Inc.
Chubu Electric Power Co.
Cleveland Electric Illuminating Co.
Colorado River Commission of Nevada
Contract Services Ass'n of America
Council of Defense and Space Industry Ass'ns
Daewoo Electronics Co.
Detroit Edison Co.
Dominion Resources, Inc.
Duquesne Light Co.
E-Systems, Inc.
Eaton Corp.
Edison Electric Institute
EG&G, Inc.
Electric Power Research Institute
Electricity Consumers Resource Council
Electronic Data Processing Auditors Ass'n
Electronic Industries Ass'n
Electronic Industries Ass'n of Japan
Electronic Industries Ass'n of Korea
Elmont AG
Emerson Electric Co.
Empire District Electric Co.
Energy Research Corp.
Fairchild Space & Defense Corp.
Fischbach and Moore
Frontec Logistics Corp.
Fujitsu America, Inc.
Fujitsu Ltd.

G. W. Electronics
General Electric Co.
General Instrument Corp.
General Instrument Corp. Political Action Committee
GNB, Inc.
Go-Video
GTE Corp.
GTE Products Corp.
Harmon-Motive
Harris Corp.
Harris RF Communications
Hewlett-Packard Co.
Hitachi America Ltd.
Hitachi Ltd.
Hitachi Sales Corp. of America
Honeywell, Inc.
Houston Lighting & Power Co.
Hydro-Quebec
Indiana Electric Ass'n
Institute of Electrical and Electronics Engineers, Inc.
Intel Corporation
Internat'l Brotherhood of Electrical Workers
Internat'l Electronics Manufacturers and Consumers of America
Internat'l Microwave Power Institute
Internat'l Union of Electronic, Electrical, Salaried, Machine, and Furniture Workers, AFL-CIO
Iowa Electric Light and Power Co.
Israel Electric Corp., Ltd.
ITT Corp.
Japan Machine Tool Builders Ass'n
Joint Electron Device Engineering Council (JEDEC)
Kenwood U.S.A. Corp.
Kollmorgen Corp.
Kollsman
Kyocera Corp.
Lockheed, Sanders Inc.
LTV Aircraft Products Group
LTV Corp.
Magnavox Government and Industrial Electronics Co.
Matsushita Electric Corp. of America
Matsushita Electronic Corp.
Maxell Corp. of America
Melpar Division Political Action Committee
Micron Technology, Inc.
Mid-West Electric Consumers Ass'n
Mitsubishi Electric Corp.
Mitsubishi Electric Sales America
Mitsubishi Electronics America, Inc.
Motorola, Inc.
MRJ, Inc.
N.V. Philips Gloeilampenfabrieken
Nat'l Ass'n of Video Distributors
Nat'l Computer Systems
Nat'l Electric Sign Ass'n
Nat'l Electrical Contractors Ass'n
Nat'l Electrical Manufacturers Ass'n
Nat'l Hydropower Ass'n
Nat'l Hydropower Ass'n Political Action Committee
Nat'l Lighting Bureau
Nat'l Rural Electric Cooperative Ass'n
Nat'l Semiconductor Corp.
Natural Gas Alliance for Generative Electricity
Nebraska Public Power District
New England Electric System
Nippon Electric Co., Ltd.
North American Philips Corp.
North Carolina Power Co.
Northwest Public Power Ass'n
Orion Electric Co., Ltd.
OTL, Inc.
Pacific Gas and Electric Co.
Pacific Telecom, Inc.
PacifiCorp
Physical Optics Corp.
Plessey Electronic Systems Corp.
Plessey Electronic Systems, Inc.
PolyPhaser Corp.
Power and Communications Contractors Ass'n
Power Electronics
Radio Technical Commission for Aeronautics
Radio Technical Commission for Maritime Services
Rasch Elektronik
Rayburn County Electric Cooperative
Raytheon Co.
Recording Industry Ass'n of America
Ricoh Electronics, Inc.
Rockwell Internat'l

Salt River Project
Sampo Corp.
Samsung Electronics Co., Ltd.
SCI Technology, Inc.
Security Systems Internat'l Corp., Geneva
Selenia Industria Elettronica, S.p.A.
SEMATECH
Semiconductor Industry Ass'n
Sharp Electronics Corp.
Sharp S.A. Equipamentos Eletronicos
Siemens Capital Corp.
Siemens Corp.
Sony Corp.
Sony Corp. of America
Southern Company, The
Southern Maryland Electric Cooperative, Inc.
SPD Technologies
T and J Electronics
Tampa Electric Co.
Tektronix, Inc.
Tennessee Valley Authority
Texas Instruments
Textron Inc.
Thomson Consumer Electronics, Inc.
Tokyo Electric Co., Ltd.
Tokyo Electric Power Co.
Toledo Edison Co.
Toshiba America, Inc.
Toshiba Corp.
TRW Inc.
U.S. JVC Corp.
Varian Associates Inc.
Washington Public Utility Districts Ass'n
Westinghouse Electric Corp.
White Consolidated Industries
Zenith Electronics Corp.

ENERGY

Acurex Corp.
Ad Hoc Committee for Small Hydro Power
Advanced Energy Technology, Inc.
Advanced Transit Ass'n
Air Products and Chemicals, Inc.
Alliance for Acid Rain Control
Alliance to Save Energy
American Ass'n of Blacks in Energy
American Boiler Manufacturers Ass'n
American Consulting Engineers Council
American Council for an Energy-Efficient Economy
American Electric Power Service Corp.
American Institute of Biological Sciences
American Methanol Institute
American Nuclear Energy Council
American Ref-Fuel Co.
American Soc. of Heating, Refrigerating and Air Conditioning Engineers
American Standard Inc.
American Wind Energy Ass'n
Americans for Energy Independence
ANG Coal Gasification Co.
Asea Brown Boveri, Inc.
Atlantic Council of the United States
Babcock and Wilcox Co.
Battelle Memorial Institute
Bonneville Pacific Corp.
Burlington Resources, Inc.
Cabot Corp.
Cabot Oil & Gas
California Energy Co.
Catalyst Energy Corp.
Center for Clean Air Policy
Citizen/Labor Energy Coalition Project
Citizens Against Research Bans
Citizens Utilities Co.
Clean Coal Technology Coalition
Coalition for American Energy Security
Coalition for Reliable Energy
Coalition to Oppose Energy Taxes
Coastal States Organization
Cogeneration and Independent Power Coalition of America
Committee of Hydroelectric Dam Owners
Congress Watch
Consolidated Natural Gas Co.
Consumer Energy Council of America Research Foundation
Council of Energy Resource Tribes
Council of Industrial Boiler Owners

SELECTED SUBJECTS INDEX

SELECTED SUBJECTS INDEX

SELECTED SUBJECTS INDEX

Internat'l Hydrolized Protein Council
Junex Enterprises
Kellogg Co.
Kier English Confectionery, Josephine
Kraft General Foods, Inc.
Land O'Lakes, Inc.
Leprino Foods, Inc.
Lever Brothers Co.
Loma Linda Foods
Long Co. Bakery Cooperative, The W. E.
M&M/Mars, Inc.
Marine Management, Inc.
Marlin Group, The
Marriott Corp.
Mary Jane Bakeries
Maui Land and Pineapple Co., Inc.
McDonald's Corp.
McKesson Corp.
Mead Johnson and Co.
Meat Industry Suppliers Ass'n
Millers' Nat'l Federation
Mushroom Council
Mutual Interest Transactions
Nat'l-American Wholesale Grocers' Ass'n
Nat'l Ass'n for the Specialty Food Trade
Nat'l Ass'n of Food Equipment Manufacturers
Nat'l Ass'n of Margarine Manufacturers
Nat'l Broiler Council
Nat'l Candy Wholesalers Ass'n
Nat'l Cheese Institute
Nat'l Club Ass'n
Nat'l Confectioners Ass'n
Nat'l Confectioners Ass'n Political Action Committee
Nat'l Cottonseed Products Ass'n
Nat'l Food Brokers Ass'n
Nat'l Food Processors Ass'n
Nat'l Food Processors Ass'n Political Action Committee
Nat'l Frozen Food Ass'n
Nat'l Grape Growers Cooperative
Nat'l Grocers Ass'n
Nat'l Honey Board
Nat'l Institute of Oilseed Products
Nat'l Kraut Packers Ass'n, Inc.
Nat'l Pasta Ass'n
Nat'l Peanut Council
Nat'l Pork Board
Nat'l Pork Producers Council
Nat'l Potato Council
Nat'l Watermelon Ass'n
Nelbro Packing Co.
Nestle Enterprises, Inc.
Nestle, S.A.
Norseland Foods
NutraSweet Co.
Ocean Spray Cranberries
Omstead Foods Ltd.
Organic Food Alliance
Peanut Butter and Nut Processors Ass'n
Peanut Butter and Nut Processors Ass'n Political Action Committee
Perdue Farms Inc.
Pet Food Institute
Philip Morris Management Corp.
Pickle Packers Internat'l, Inc.
Pillsbury Co.
Pizza Hut, Inc.
Plantation Foods
Popcorn Institute
Power Packaging Inc.
Processed Apples Institute
Procter and Gamble Mfg. Co.
Promodes
Ralston Purina Co.
Ramirez & Co., T.
Red Tart Cherries
Retail Bakers of America
Riceland Foods
RJR Nabisco Washington, Inc.
S&A Restaurants Corp.
Sahlman Seafoods
Salt Institute
San Miguel Corp.
San Tomo Group
Sara Lee Corp.
Schwan's Sales Enterprises
Sea Hawk Seafoods, Inc.
Shaw Food Services Co., Inc.
ShowBiz Pizza Time

Signal Produce Co.
Snack Food Ass'n
Snack PAC
Southwest Virginia and Carolinas Peanut Growers
Soy Protein Council
Speciality Seafoods
Staley Manufacturing Co., A. E.
Summit, Ltd.
Sweetener Users Ass'n
Tasty Kake, Inc.
TGI Friday's
Tootsie Roll Industries
Tyson Foods, Inc.
U.S. Canola Ass'n
Unilever United States, Inc.
United Brands Co.
United Coconut Ass'n of the Philippines
United Egg Ass'n
United Food and Commercial Workers Internat'l Union
United Foods, Inc.
United Fresh Fruit and Vegetable Ass'n
United Fresh Fruit and Vegetable Ass'n Political Action Committee (UNIPAC)
Universal Foods Corp.
Valhi, Inc.
Welch's Foods, Inc.
Wendy's Internat'l, Inc.
West Mexico Vegetable Distributors Ass'n
Western States Meat Ass'n
Whitman Corp.

FOREIGN RELATIONS

African American Institute
American-Arab Affairs Council
American Ass'n for Study of the United States in World Affairs
American Committee on U.S.-Soviet Relations
American Council for Free Asia
American Council of Young Political Leaders
American Defense Foundation
American Enterprise Institute for Public Policy Research
American Foreign Service Ass'n
American Freedom Coalition
American Hellenic Institute
American Institute for Foreign Study
American Israel Public Affairs Committee
American Jewish Committee
American Jewish Congress
American Security Council
American Security Council Foundation
Americans for Democratic Action
Americas Society
Amnesty Internat'l U.S.A.
Anti-Defamation League of B'nai B'rith
Armenian Assembly of America
Armenian Nat'l Committee of America
Arms Control Ass'n
Arms Control and Foreign Policy Caucus
Asia Foundation, The
Asia Society, The
Ass'n for Internat'l Investment
Ass'n on Third World Affairs
Ass'n to Unite the Democracies
Atlantic Council of the United States
Brookings Institution
Business Executives for Nat'l Security
Campaign for United Nations Reform
CANAMCO (The Canadian-American Company)
Caribbean/Central American Action
Center for Democracy
Center for Foreign Journalists
Center for Foreign Policy Options
Center for Immigration Studies
Center for Internat'l Policy
Center for Internat'l Private Enterprise
Center for Nat'l Security Studies
Center for Peace and Freedom
Center for Privatization
Center for Security Policy
Center for Strategic and Internat'l Studies
Christic Institute
Citizens Network for Foreign Affairs
Committee for a Free Afghanistan
Committee for Nat'l Security
Committee for Production Sharing
Committee on the Present Danger
Conservative Republican Committee

Coordinating Committee of the Hungarian Organizations of North America
Coordination Council for North American Affairs
Council for a Livable World
Council for Inter-American Security
Council for Internat'l Development
Council for the Defense of Freedom
Council of the Americas
Council on Foreign Relations
Council on Hemispheric Affairs
Democratic Unionist Party of Northern Ireland
Diplomatic and Consular Officers, Retired (Dacor)
Egypt, Embassy of
Ethics and Public Policy Center
Federation for American Immigration Reform (FAIR)
Foreign Policy Ass'n
Friends Committee on Nat'l Legislation
Friends of Free China
Gibraltar Information Bureau
Guam Commission on Self-Determination
Henry L. Stimson Center
Heritage Foundation
Hudson Institute
Human Rights Watch
Immigration Reform Law Institute
IMPACT
Indo-U.S. Political Action Committee
Indochina Resource Action Center
Institute for Security and Cooperation in Outer Space
Institute for Soviet-American Relations
Institute on Religion and Democracy
Inter-American Dialogue
Internat'l Center for Development Policy
Internat'l Economic Policy Ass'n
Internat'l Security Council
Internat'l Telecommunications Satellite Organization (INTELSAT)
Irish Nat'l Caucus
Israel, Government of
Japan, Embassy of
Jewish Nat'l Fund
Joint Baltic American Nat'l Committee
Member Committee of the U.S., World Energy Conference
Middle East Institute
Nat'l Ass'n for Foreign Student Affairs
Nat'l Ass'n of Arab Americans
Nat'l Center for Public Policy Research
Nat'l Conference on Soviet Jewry
Nat'l Electrical Manufacturers Ass'n
Nat'l Peace Institute Foundation
Nat'l Republican Institute for Internat'l Affairs
Nat'l Strategy Information Center
Network in Solidarity with the People of Guatemala
New American View
Organization for American-Soviet ExchangeS (OASES-DC)
Palestinian Congress of North America
Physicians for Social Responsibility
Project Orbis
Qatar, Embassy of
Rainbow Lobby
Royal Nepalese Embassy
SANE/FREEZE
Science and Engineering Committee for a Secure World
Search for Common Ground
Social Democratic and Labor Party of Northern Ireland (SDLP)
South Africa Foundation
Third World Prosthetic Foundation
TransAfrica
Transatlantic Security Council
Transnational Development Consortium
U.S. Committee for UNICEF
Union of Councils for Soviet Jews
United Nations Ass'n of the U.S.A.
United States Business and Industrial Council
United States Committee for Refugees
United States Defense Committee
United States Nat'l Committee for Pacific Economic Cooperation
US-Asia Institute
Venezuela, Government of
Washington Institute for Near East Policy
Washington Office on Africa
Washington Office on Latin America
Washington Peace Center
Witness for Peace

The listings in this directory are available as *Mailing Labels*. See last page.

SELECTED SUBJECTS INDEX

The listings in this directory are available as *Mailing Labels*. See last page.

SELECTED SUBJECTS INDEX

SELECTED SUBJECTS INDEX

SELECTED SUBJECTS INDEX

GRAIN

GRAPHIC ARTS see PRINTING

GROCERS see FOOD INDUSTRY

GUNS see FIREARMS

HANDICAPPED

HARBORS see PORTS

HEALTH CARE

SELECTED SUBJECTS INDEX

SELECTED SUBJECTS INDEX

The listings in this directory are available as *Mailing Labels*. See last page.

SELECTED SUBJECTS INDEX

SELECTED SUBJECTS INDEX

SELECTED SUBJECTS INDEX

SELECTED SUBJECTS INDEX

SELECTED SUBJECTS INDEX

Nat'l Consortium for Child Mental Health Services
Nat'l Council of Community Mental Health Centers
Nat'l Institute on Mental Health
Nat'l Mental Health Ass'n
Nat'l Rehabilitation Information Center
Nat'l Women's Health Network
Phobia Soc. of America
Phoenix House
Psychemedics Corp.
Psychiatric Institutes of America
Soc. of Professors of Child Psychiatry
Washington Business Group on Health
Washington Psychiatric Soc.
Watkins Glen, New York, Municipality of
World Federation for Mental Health

MERCHANDISING/RETAILING

Alcoma Packing Co.
Associated Merchandising Corp.
BATUS, Inc.
Belk Stores Services, Inc.
Bureau of Wholesale Sales Representatives
Carson, Pirie, Scott & Co.
Direct Selling Ass'n
Hechinger Co.
Hecht's
Hook-SupeRx, Inc.
Household Merchandising
Internat'l Council of Shopping Centers
Internat'l Franchise Ass'n
Internat'l Mass Retail Ass'n
K mart Corp.
May Department Stores Co.
MayCenters, Inc.
Michigan Retailers Ass'n
Michigan Trade Exchange
Montgomery Ward & Co., Inc.
Nat'l AgriChemical Retailers Ass'n
Nat'l Ass'n of Chain Drug Stores
Nat'l Ass'n of College Stores
Nat'l Automatic Merchandising Ass'n
Nat'l Field Selling Ass'n
Nat'l Independent Automobile Dealers Ass'n
Nat'l Retail Merchants Ass'n Political Action Committee
Nike, Inc.
Penney Co., J. C.
Randolph-Sheppard Vendors of America
Retail Industry Trade Action Coalition
Sears, Roebuck and Co.
Service Station Dealers of America
Supermarket Development Corp.
Woodward and Lothrop
Zayre Corp.
47th Street Photo

METAL WORKING INDUSTRY

Alliance of Metalworking Industries
American Boiler Manufacturers Ass'n
American Cast Metals Ass'n
American Cutlery Manufacturers Ass'n
American Machine Tool Distributors Political Action
  Committee
American Pipe Fittings Ass'n
Ampco-Pittsburgh Co.
Armco Inc.
Ashland Oil, Inc.
Babcock and Wilcox Co.
Cast Iron Pipefittings Committee
Closure Manufacturers Ass'n
Cookware Manufacturers Ass'n
Copperweld Corp.
Davis Walker Corp.
Eaton Corp.
Elkem Metals Co.
Far East Machinery Co. Ltd.
Farberware
Grinnell Corp.
Harsco Corp.
Internat'l Metals Reclamation Co.
Iron Castings Soc.
Korea Metal Industry Cooperative
La Metalli Industriale S.p.A.
Latin American Manufacturers Ass'n
Leggett & Platt
LTV Tubular
Marmon Group
Maverick Tube Corp.
McKechnie Brothers (South Africa) Ltd.
Municipal Castings Fair Trade Council

Nat'l Ass'n of Metal Finishers Political Action
  Committee
Nat'l Certified Pipe Welding Bureau
Nat'l Foundry Ass'n
Nat'l Tooling and Machining Ass'n
Nat'l Welding Supply Ass'n
Nippon Benkan Kogyo Co., Ltd.
NMTBA - The Ass'n for Manufacturing Technology
Non Ferrous Founders' Soc.
Pechiney Corp.
Quanex Corp.
SAE Electric
Silver Users Ass'n
SKF USA, Inc.
Southwire Co.
Stanley Bostitch Inc.
Steel Founders' Soc. of America
Thyssen Inc.
Valve Manufacturers Ass'n of America
Wheatland Tube Co.
White Consolidated Industries
WMF of America
Wyman-Gordon Co.

METALS

Aluminum Co. of America
AM&S/BHAS
Amalgamated Metal Corp. PLC
American Cast Metals Ass'n
American Iron and Steel Institute
American Mining Congress
Anaconda Minerals Co.
Armco Inc.
ASARCO Incorporated
Asturiana de Zinc, S.A.
Ball Corp.
Cabot Corp.
Camara Argentina de la Alumino y Metales Afines
Chase Brass and Copper
China Nat'l Metals and Minerals Import and Export
  Corp.
Chromalloy Gas Turbine Corp.
Cogema, Inc.
Commercial Metals Co.
Dow Chemical
Federation of Materials Societies
Gold Institute
Hamilton Copper and Steel Corp.
Hussey Copper Ltd.
INCO U.S.
Independent Zinc Alloyers Ass'n, Inc.
Industry Council for Tangible Assets
Inspiration Consolidated Copper Co.
Internat'l Lead Zinc Research Organization
Internat'l Magnesium Ass'n
Lead Industries Ass'n
Metal Market and Exchange Co. Ltd.
Metalor USA Refining Corp.
Miller Co.
Minpeco, S.A.
Mocatta Metals Corp.
Non Ferrous Founders' Soc.
Non-Ferrous Metals Producers Committee
Revere Copper and Brass Co.
Reynolds Metals Co.
Sambo Copper Co., Ltd.
Silver Institute
Silver Users Ass'n
Stratcor
Titanium Metals Corp. (TIMET)
Zinc Corp. of America

MILITARY

Adjutants General Ass'n of the United States
Air Force Ass'n
Air Force Sergeants Ass'n
American Defense Foundation
American Defense Preparedness Ass'n
American Legion
American Soc. of Military Comptrollers
American Veterans Committee
American Veterans of World War II, Korea and Vietnam
  (AMVETS)
American War Mothers
Armed Forces Communications and Electronics Ass'n
  Headquarters
Armed Forces Marketing Council
Armed Forces Relief and Benefit Ass'n
Army & Air Force Mutual Aid Ass'n

Associated Enterprises, Inc.
Ass'n of Military Colleges and Schools of the U.S.
Ass'n of Military Surgeons of the U.S.
Ass'n of Old Crows
Ass'n of the United States Army
Bath Iron Works Corp.
Blinded Veterans Ass'n
Bolova System and Instrument Division
Catholic War Veterans of the U.S.A.
Chile, Army Procurement Mission
Contract Services Ass'n of America
Disabled American Veterans
Eberhard Manufacturing
Ex-Partners of Servicemen/Women for Equality
Ferranti Defense and Space Group
Fleet Reserve Ass'n
GKN Defense, Plc.
Internat'l Military Club Executives Ass'n
Israel Military Industries
Israel, Ministry of Defense
Judge Advocates Ass'n
Magnavox Government and Industrial Electronics Co.
ManTech Internat'l
Marine Corps Reserve Officers Ass'n
McDonnell Douglas Systems Integration
Military Boot Manufacturers Ass'n
Military Chaplains Ass'n of the U.S.
Military Educator and Counselor Ass'n
Military Order of the Purple Heart of the U.S.A.
Military Order of the World Wars
Nat'l Ass'n for Uniformed Services Political Action
  Committee
Nat'l Ass'n of Military Widows
Nat'l Guard Ass'n of the U.S.
Nat'l Interreligious Service Board for Conscientious
  Objectors
Nat'l Military Intelligence Ass'n
Nat'l Service Secretariat
Nat'l Strategy Information Center
Naval Reserve Ass'n
Navy League of the United States
No Greater Love
Non Commissioned Officers Ass'n of the U.S.A.
Olin Corp.
Paralyzed Veterans of America
Portsmouth-Kittery Armed Services Committee, Inc.
Reserve Officers Ass'n of the U.S.
Retired Officers Ass'n, The (TROA)
Save Chanute Committee
Science and Engineering Committee for a Secure World
Silent Partner
Soc. of American Military Engineers
Soc. of Medical Consultants to the Armed Forces
Societe Nationale d'Etude et Construction de Moteurs
  d'Avaition (SNECMA)
Toshiba America, Inc.
UNC Incorporated
United Kingdom Defence Export Services Organization
United Spanish War Veterans
United States Army Warrant Officers Ass'n
United States Coast Guard Chief Petty Officers Ass'n
United Technologies Corp.
Veterans Education Project
Veterans of Foreign Wars of the U.S.
Veterans of World War I of the U.S.A.
VFW-Political Action Committee, Inc.
Vietnam Veterans of America, Inc.
Vietnam Veterans Of America Legal Services Program

MILK see DAIRY INDUSTRY

MINERALS

Alpha 21 Corp.
American Institute of Professional Geologists
American Iron and Steel Institute
American Mining Congress
Amselco Minerals, Inc.
Anaconda Minerals Co.
Antimony Products of America
ASARCO Incorporated
Asbestos Information Ass'n/North America
Cabot Corp.
Doe Run Co.
Federation of Materials Societies
Ferroalloys Ass'n
Gypsum Ass'n
Internat'l Minerals and Chemical Corp.
Mineralogical Soc. of America
Minerals Marketing Corp. of Zimbabwe

The listings in this directory are available as *Mailing Labels*. See last page.

SELECTED SUBJECTS INDEX

SELECTED SUBJECTS INDEX

White Earth Tribal Council
White Mountain Apache Tribe
Zionist Organization of America

MOTELS see HOTELS

MOTION PICTURES

American Film Marketing Ass'n
Blockbuster Entertainment Corp.
Columbia Pictures Entertainment, Inc.
Disney Productions, Walt
Internat'l Ass'n of Independent Producers
MCA Inc.
MGM/UA Communications Co.
Motion Picture Ass'n of America
Nat'l Ass'n of Theatre Owners
Paramount Communications, Inc.
20th Century Fox

MOTOR VEHICLES see AUTOMOTIVE INDUSTRY

NATURAL RESOURCES

American Farmland Trust
American Geophysical Union
American Institute of Biological Sciences
American Rivers
Burlington Resources, Inc.
Coastal States Organization
Defenders of Wildlife
Earth Satellite Corp.
Environmental Action Foundation
Environmental Power Corp.
Federation of Materials Societies
Grand Canyon Trust
Illinois Department of Energy and Natural Resources
Internat'l Ass'n of Fish and Wildlife Agencies
Internat'l Economic Policy Ass'n
Izaak Walton League of America
Kenai Natives Ass'n, Inc.
Kootznoowoo, Inc.
Lake Andes-Wagner Water Systems, Inc.
Landscape Architecture Foundation
Liaison Committee of Cooperating Oil and Gas Ass'ns
Nat'l Ass'n of Flood and Stormwater Management Agencies
Nat'l Inholders Ass'n
Nat'l Ocean Industries Ass'n
Nat'l Ocean Industries Ass'n Political Action Committee
Nat'l Parks and Conservation Ass'n
Nat'l Propane Gas Ass'n
Nat'l Wildlife Federation
Natural Gas Vehicle Coalition
Natural Resources Defense Council
Noranda, Inc.
North Carolina Department of Natural Resources
Ormat Energy Systems
Population Institute
R. Lacey, Inc.
Renewable Natural Resources Foundation
Resources for the Future
Soc. for American Archaeology
Tosco Corp.
Transco Energy Co.
Transnational Development Consortium
Wagner and Brown
Western States Land Commissioners Ass'n
Wilderness Soc.
World Resources Institute
World Wildlife Fund/The Conservation Foundation
Worldwatch Institute

NAVAL see also MILITARY

American Defense Preparedness Ass'n
American Soc. of Naval Engineers
Bath Iron Works Corp. Political Action Committee
Conservative Republican Committee
Fleet Reserve Ass'n
Institute of Navigation
Navy League of the United States
Shipbuilders Council of America
Textron Inc.
Toshiba America, Inc.
United States Navy Memorial Foundation

NEWSPAPERS see PRESS

NUCLEAR ENERGY

American Board of Health Physics
American College of Nuclear Physicians
American Nuclear Energy Council
American Nuclear Insurers
Americans for Nuclear Energy

Americans for the Supercollider
Atomic Energy of Canada Ltd.
Babcock and Wilcox Co.
Citizens Against Research Bans
Coalition for Reliable Energy
Cogema, Inc.
Congress Watch
Consumer Energy Council of America Research Foundation
Dairyland Power Cooperative
Edison Electric Institute
EG&G, Inc.
Energy Fuels Nuclear, Inc.
Environmental Action Foundation
FlightSafety Internat'l
Fusion Power Associates
GE Nuclear Energy
General Atomics
GPU Service Corp.
Hanford-Tridec
Health and Energy Institute
Health Physics Soc.
Heart of America Northwest
Indiana Michigan Power Co.
Kerr-McGee Corp.
KMS Industries, Inc.
Lawyers Alliance for Nuclear Arms Control
Long Island Ass'n
Louisiana Energy Services
Missouri Public Service Commission
Mutual Atomic Energy Liability Underwriters
Nat'l Council on Radiation Protection and Measurement
Natural Resources Defense Council
Nuclear Control Institute
Nuclear Information and Resource Service
Oak Ridge Nat'l Laboratory
Pacific Nuclear Systems
Physicians for Social Responsibility
Public Citizen's Critical Mass Energy Project
Research and Development Laboratories
Safe Energy Communication Council
Smith Industries
Stevenson & Associates
Superconducting Core Technologies
Task Force Against Nuclear Pollution
UI Companies
Utility Nuclear Waste Transportation Program
Westinghouse Electric Corp.
Westinghouse Hanford Co.
Wolf Creek Nuclear Operating Corp.

NURSING

American Academy of Nurse Practitioners
American Ass'n of Colleges of Nursing
American Ass'n of Nurse Anesthetists
American College of Nurse-Midwives
American College of Obstetricians and Gynecologists
American Licensed Practical Nurses Ass'n
American Nurses' Ass'n
American Nurses' Ass'n Political Action Committee (ANA-PAC)
Center for Studies in Health Policy
District of Columbia League for Nursing
Federation of Nurses and Health Professionals/AFT
Nat'l Ass'n of Pediatric Nurse Associates and Practitioners
Nat'l Ass'n of Physician Nurses
New MediCo Associates, Inc.
Nurses Ass'n of the American College of Obstetricians and Gynecologists
Nursing Economics
Palomar/Pomerado Hospital District
Pennsylvania Ass'n of Nurse Anesthetists
United States Pharmacopeial Convention
VNA, Inc.

NUTRITION

American Dietetic Ass'n
American Institute of Biological Sciences
American Institute of Nutrition
American Soc. for Clinical Nutrition
American Soc. for Parenteral and Enteral Nutrition
Center for Science in the Public Interest
Center on Budget and Policy Priorities
Child Nutrition Forum
Community Nutrition Institute
Council for Responsible Nutrition
Dietary Managers Ass'n
Food Research and Action Center

Health Insurance Ass'n of America
Herbalife Internat'l
IMPACT
Internat'l Life Sciences Institute Nutrition Foundation
Nat'l Anti-Hunger Coalition
Public Voice for Food and Health Policy
RESULTS
Sandoz Corp.
Soy Protein Council
World Hunger Education Service

PAPER INDUSTRY

Abitibi-Price, Inc.
Adhesives Manufacturers Ass'n
American Paper Institute
American Paper Machinery Ass'n
American Pulpwood Ass'n
Ass'n of Independent Corrugated Converters
BATUS, Inc.
Beckett Packaging, Ltd.
Bowater, Inc.
Champion Internat'l Corp.
Climax Paper Converters Ltd.
Envelope Manufacturers Ass'n
Federal Paper Board Co.
Flexible Packaging Ass'n
Foodservice & Packaging Institute, Inc.
Fort Howard Corp.
Garden State Paper Co.
Great Northern Nekoosa Corp.
Internat'l Paper Co.
James River Corp.
Kimberly-Clark Corp.
Longview Fibre Co.
Mead Corp.
Nat'l Business Forms Ass'n
Paper Industry of Maine
Paperboard Packaging Council
Papeteries Bollore, S.A.
Scott Paper Co.
Scott Paper Co. Political Action Committee
Simpson Investment Co.
Simpson Paper Co.
TRW Inc.
Union Camp Corp.
United Paperworkers Internat'l Union
Wallcovering Manufacturers Ass'n

PATENTS see COPYRIGHTS and PATENTS

PESTICIDES

American Council on Science and Health
American Cyanamid Co.
American Cyanamid Co. (Agricultural Division)
Ass'n of Official Analytical Chemists
Chemical Producers and Distributors Ass'n
Chemical Specialties Manufacturers Ass'n
Dow Chemical
Entomological Soc. of America
Internat'l Sanitary Supply Ass'n
Nat'l AgriChemical Retailers Ass'n
Nat'l Agricultural Aviation Ass'n
Nat'l Agricultural Chemicals Ass'n
Nat'l Pest Control Ass'n
Rhone-Poulenc Ag Co.
Soc. of American Wood Preservers, Inc.

PETROLEUM INDUSTRY

Advance Petroleum, Inc.
Alaska Pacific Refining, Inc.
Alberta Petroleum Marketing Commission
Amerada Hess Corp.
American Ass'n of Petroleum Geologists
American Independent Refiners Ass'n
American Institute of Professional Geologists
American Petroleum Institute
Amoco Corp.
Anadarko Petroleum Corp.
Arabian American Oil Co.
ARCO
ARCO Oil & Gas Co.
Armco Inc.
Ashland Exploration, Inc.
Ashland Oil, Inc.
Ass'n of Oil Pipe Lines
Atlantic Richfield Company (ARCO) Transportation Co.
Baroid Corp.
Beard Oil Co.
BP America Inc.
British Petroleum Oil Marketers Ass'n

SELECTED SUBJECTS INDEX

The listings in this directory are available as *Mailing Labels*. See last page.

SELECTED SUBJECTS INDEX

SELECTED SUBJECTS INDEX

The listings in this directory are available as *Mailing Labels*. See last page.

SELECTED SUBJECTS INDEX

Young Americans for Freedom
Young Democrats of America

POLLUTION and WASTE

Acurex Corp.
Alliance for Acid Rain Control
Alliance for Responsible CFC Policy
American Board of Health Physics
American College of Nuclear Physicians
American Consulting Engineers Council
American Council on the Environment
American Industrial Health Council
American Institute of Biological Sciences
Asbestos Claims Facility
Ass'n for the Safe Handling of Medical Waste
Ass'n of Local Air Pollution Control Officials
Ass'n of Metropolitan Sewerage Agencies
Ass'n of State and Interstate Water Pollution Control
    Administrators
Ass'n of State and Territorial Solid Waste Management
    Officials
Berg-Revoir Corp.
Better Working Environments, Inc.
Brambles USA, Inc.
Browning-Ferris Industries (D.C.), Inc.
California Co-Compost Systems
Center for Clean Air Policy
Chambers Development Co., Inc.
Chemical Specialties Manufacturers Ass'n
Chemical Waste Management, Inc.
CH2M HILL
Citizens Clearinghouse for Hazardous Wastes
Citizens for Sensible Control of Acid Rain
Clean Air Act Project
Clean Air Working Group
Clean Coal Technology Coalition
Clean Sites, Inc.
Clean Sound
Clean Water Action Project
Coastal Coalition
Committee for Environmentally Effective Packaging
Defenders of Wildlife
Detachable Container Ass'n
Ecological and Toxicological Ass'n of the Dyestuffs
    Manufacturing Industry
Ecology & Environment, Inc.
Ecomarine, Inc.
Ensco Fund for Safer Waste Treatment
Environmental Action Foundation
Environmental Air Control Inc.
Environmental Defense Fund
Environmental Design Corp.
Environmental Federation of America
Environmental Industry Council
Friends of the Earth
General Atomics
Government Refuse Collection and Disposal Ass'n
Hazardous Waste Treatment Council
Hazardous Waste Treatment Council Political Action
    Committee
Health and Energy Institute
Health Physics Soc.
In-Situ, Inc.
Infinite Research, Inc.
Institute for Local Self-Reliance
Institute of Scrap Recycling Industries, Inc.
Instrumentation Testing Ass'n
Internat'l Metals Reclamation Co.
Internat'l Sanitary Supply Ass'n
Irrigation Ass'n
Joy Technologies Inc.
Marine Shale Processors, Inc.
Nat'l Clean Air Coalition
Nat'l Coalition Against the Misuse of Pesticides
Nat'l Network to Prevent Birth Defects
Nat'l Organization to Insure a Sound-Controlled
    Environment-N.O.I.S.E.
Nat'l Solid Wastes Management Ass'n
Nat'l Solid Wastes Management Ass'n Political Action
    Committee
Nat'l Water Alliance
Nat'l Wildlife Federation
Natural Resources Defense Council
Orange County Sanitation Districts
Planning Research Corp.
Renewable Natural Resources Foundation
Rohr Industries, Inc.
Safety-Kleen Corp.

Santa Barbara County Air Pollution Control District
Seattle Metro
Solid Waste Agency of Northern Cook County
South Coast Air Quality Management District
Spill-Net, Inc.
State and Territorial Air Pollution Program
    Administrators
Systech Environmental Corp.
Task Force Against Nuclear Pollution
Texstor
Trans-Alaska Pipeline Liability Fund
Utility Air Regulatory Group
Utility Nuclear Waste Transportation Program
Waste Conversion Systems, Inc.
Waste Management, Inc.
Water Pollution Control Federation
Water and Wastewater Equipment Manufacturers Ass'n
Wheelabrator Corp., The
Zink and Co., John

POPULATION

Alan Guttmacher Institute, The
Catholics for a Free Choice
Center for Population Options
Centre for Development and Population Activity
Federation for American Immigration Reform (FAIR)
Global Tomorrow Coalition
Immigration Reform Law Institute
Nat'l Family Planning and Reproductive Health Ass'n
Planned Parenthood Federation of America
Population Ass'n of America
Population Crisis Committee
Population Institute
Population Reference Bureau
Population Resource Center
World Population Soc.
World Resources Institute
Worldwatch Institute
Zero Population Growth, Inc.

PORTS

Alabama State Docks Department
American Ass'n of Port Authorities
American Ass'n of State Highway and Transportation
    Officials
Associated General Contractors of America
Bremer Lagerhaus-Gesellschaft
Canaveral Port Authority
Coastal States Organization
Corpus Christi, Nueces County, Port Authority of
Lake Charles Harbor and Terminal District
Long Beach, California, Port of
LOOP, Inc.
Massachusetts Port Authority
Metro-Dade County
Nat'l Waterways Conference, Inc.
Niagara Frontier Transportation Authority
Norfolk Port and Industrial Authority
North Atlantic Ports Ass'n
Oakland, California, Port of
Oregon, State of, Department of Economic Development,
    Ports Division
PAI, Inc.
Philadelphia Port Corp.
Port Authority of New York and New Jersey
Portland, Oregon, Port of
Ports of Philadelphia Maritime Exchange
RailPort
Redwood City, California, Port of
Sacramento, California, City of
San Francisco, California, Port of
Santa Cruz, California, Port of
Seattle, Washington, Port of
South Carolina State Port Authority
South Louisiana Port Commission
Stockton, California, Port of
Tampa Port Authority
Transportation Institute

POST OFFICE

Alliance of Nonprofit Mailers
American Postal Workers Union
Committee on Letter Carriers' Political Education
Committee on Political Action of the American Postal
    Workers Union, AFL-CIO
Direct Marketing Ass'n
Direct Selling Ass'n Political Action Committee
ElectroCom Automation, Inc.
Mail Advertising Service Ass'n Internat'l

Nat'l Alliance for Political Action
Nat'l Alliance of Postal and Federal Employees
Nat'l Ass'n of Letter Carriers of the United States of
    America
Nat'l Ass'n of Postal Supervisors
Nat'l Ass'n of Postmasters of the U.S.
Nat'l League of Postmasters of the U.S.
Nat'l Postal Mail Handlers Union 'Mail Handlers PAC'
Nat'l Rural Letter Carriers' Ass'n
Nat'l Rural Letter Carriers' Ass'n Political Action
    Committee
Nat'l Star Route Mail Contractors Ass'n
Nat'l Star Route Mail Contractors Political Action
    Committee
Parcel Shippers Ass'n
Pitney-Bowes, Inc.
TCOM Systems, Inc.
Third Class Mail Ass'n
United Parcel Service
Video and Film Distributors Council, The

POULTRY

American Meat Institute
Animal Health Institute
Animal Industry Foundation
ConAgra, Inc.
Nat'l Broiler Council
Nat'l Broiler Council Political Action Committee
Nat'l Turkey Federation
Nat'l Turkey Federation Political Action Committee
United Egg Producers
World's Poultry Science Ass'n, U.S.A. Branch

PRESS

Accuracy in Media
American Newspaper Publishers Ass'n
American Press Institute
American Soc. of Newspaper Editors
Association Trends
Center for Foreign Journalists
Center for Investigative Reporting
Center for Media and Public Affairs
Council on Hemispheric Affairs
Dow Jones & Co., Inc.
Gannett Co., Inc.
Industrial Heating Magazine
Information Industry Ass'n
Internat'l Circulation Managers Ass'n
Internat'l Newspaper Advertising and Marketing
    Executives
Internat'l Newspaper Promotion Ass'n
Japan Times Corp.
Knight-Ridder Newspapers
Korean Overseas Information Service
Lockwood Trade Journal
Media General, Inc.
Media Institute
Nat'l Ass'n of Hispanic Journalists
Nat'l Catholic News Service
Nat'l Newspaper Ass'n
Nat'l Newspaper Publishers Ass'n
Nat'l Press Foundation
New American View
Newspaper Guild, The
PressNet Systems, Inc.
Reader's Digest Ass'n
Reporters Committee for Freedom of the Press
San Francisco Chronicle
Scripps League Newspaper, Inc.
Soc. of Nat'l Ass'n Publications
Star Tribune Co,
Student Press Law Center
Times Mirror Co.
United Press Internat'l
Wall Street Journal
Washington Independent Writers
Washington Post Co.
Washington Researchers
Women in Communications

PRINTING

Ass'n of Reproduction Materials Manufacturers
Columbia Typographical Union - CWA
Donnelley & Sons, R. R.
Financial Stationers Ass'n
Graphic Communications Ass'n
Graphic Communications Internat'l Union
Gravure Research Institute
Gravure Technical Ass'n

The listings in this directory are available as *Mailing Labels*. See last page.

SELECTED SUBJECTS INDEX

Greenwood Press
Information Industry Ass'n
Internat'l Business Forms Industries
Internat'l Electronic Facsimile Users Ass'n
Jeppesen Sanderson, Inc.
Kelly Press, Inc.
Master Printers of America
Meredith Corp.
Nat'l Ass'n of Lithographic Plate Manufacturers
Nat'l Ass'n of Printers and Lithographers
Nat'l Business Forms Ass'n
Nat'l Composition and Prepress Ass'n
Nat'l Computer Graphics Ass'n
Nat'l Printing Equipment and Supply Ass'n
Planeta North America, Inc.
Printing Industries of America
Printing Industries of America Political Action
   Committee (Print PAC)
Public Image Printing
Screen Printing Ass'n Internat'l
Sierra Press
Typographers Internat'l Ass'n
U.S. Banknote Corp.

PUBLIC HEALTH

Action on Smoking and Health
Alan Guttmacher Institute, The
Alexander Graham Bell Ass'n for the Deaf
American Ass'n of Blood Banks
American Cancer Soc. (Public Affairs Office)
American College of Obstetricians and Gynecologists
American Council on Science and Health
American Federation of Home Health Agencies
American Heart Ass'n
American Industrial Health Council
American Lung Ass'n/American Thoracic Soc.
American Medical Ass'n
American Nurses' Ass'n
American Physical Therapy Ass'n
American Public Health Ass'n
American Soc. for Psychoprophylaxis in Obstetrics
   (ASPO/Lamaze)
American Soc. of Cataract and Refractive Surgery
American Social Health Ass'n
Associated Church Press/Evangelical Press Ass'n
Ass'n for the Advancement of Health Education
Ass'n of Schools of Public Health
Ass'n of State and Territorial Health Officials
Ass'n of University Programs in Health Administration
Better Hearing Institute
Center for Studies in Health Policy
Coalition of Religious Press Ass'ns
Commissioned Officers Ass'n of the U.S. Public Health
   Service
Committee for Nat'l Health Insurance
Cooley's Anemia Foundation
Cystic Fibrosis Foundation
Employee Benefit Research Institute
Entomological Soc. of America
Federation of Behavioral, Psychological and Cognitive
   Sciences
Group Health Ass'n of America
Health and Energy Institute
Health Insurance Ass'n of America
Health Security Action Council
Human Rights Campaign Fund
Inova Health Systems
Institute for Professional Health Services Administrators
Internat'l Service Agencies
Nat'l Ass'n of Community Health Centers
Nat'l Ass'n of County Health Officials
Nat'l Ass'n of Plumbing-Heating-Cooling Contractors
Nat'l Ass'n of Regional Councils
Nat'l Ass'n of State Mental Retardation Program
   Directors
Nat'l Coalition of Hispanic Health and Human Services
Nat'l Council on Alcoholism and Drug Dependence
Nat'l Council on Radiation Protection and Measurement
Nat'l Health Policy Forum
Nat'l Hemophilia Foundation
Nat'l Hospice Organization
Nat'l Organization Against Invisible Disease Spread
Nat'l Pest Control Ass'n
Nat'l School Health Education Coalition
Palomar/Pomerado Hospital District
Public Health Foundation
Public Voice for Food and Health Policy
Southeast Alaska Regional Health Corp. (SEARHC)

Third World Prosthetic Foundation
World Federation of Public Health Ass'ns

PUBLISHING

Advance Publications, Inc.
American Book Publishers Political Action Committee
American Geophysical Union
American Newspaper Publishers Ass'n
Ass'n of American Publishers
Ass'n of American Publishers Political Action Committee
Bureau of Nat'l Affairs, Inc., The
Career Communications
CB Representatives
Classroom Publishers Ass'n
Cox-Matthews
Dow Jones & Co., Inc.
Dun & Bradstreet
Elsevier U.S. Holdings, Inc.
Engel Publications
Financial World Partners
Graphic Communications Ass'n
Greenwood Press
Greeting Card Ass'n
Greeting Card Creative Network
Harcourt Brace Jovanovich, Inc.
Hong Kong Press Publishers
Houghton Mifflin Co.
Industrial Heating Magazine
Information Industry Ass'n
Internat'l Circulation Managers Ass'n
Internat'l Data Corp.
Internat'l Law Institute
Japan Times Corp.
Lawyers Co-operative Publishing Co.
MacMillan Publishing Co.
Magazine Publishers of America
Magazine Publishers of American Political Action
   Committee
McGraw-Hill, Inc.
Media General, Inc.
Meredith Corp.
Nat'l Geographic Soc.
Nat'l Music Publishers' Ass'n
Nat'l Newspaper Ass'n
Nat'l Newspaper Publishers Ass'n
News America
Newsletter Ass'n, The
Newspaper Guild, The
Nursing Economics
Pacific Press Publishing Ass'n
Paramount Communications, Inc.
Prentice Hall Information Services
Putnam's Sons, G. P.
Queen City Home Health Care Co.
Reader's Digest Ass'n
Review and Herald Publishing Co.
Scripps League Newspaper, Inc.
Southern Baptist Press Ass'n
Star Tribune Co,
T.M.P. Inc.
Time Warner Inc.
Times Mirror Co.
Training Media Distributors Ass'n
Washington Independent Writers
Washington Researchers
Washington Times Corp., The
West Publishing Co.
Whittle Communications
Yellow Pages Publishers Ass'n

RADIO-TV

Accuracy in Media
Adams Communications Corp.
Ameri-Cable Internat'l, Inc.
American Community TV Ass'n
American Council of the Blind Radio Amateurs
American Radio Relay League
American Women in Radio and Television
Ass'n of Independent Television Stations
Ass'n of Independent Television Stations Political Action
   Committee
Ass'n of Maximum Service Telecasters, Inc.
Barnstable Broadcasting
Blockbuster Entertainment Corp.
Board for Internat'l Broadcasting
Broadcast Education Ass'n
Cable Television Administration and Marketing Soc.
Cable Television Ass'n of Maryland, Delaware and the
   District of Columbia

Cablevision System Development Co.
Capital Cities/ABC Inc.
CBS, Inc.
CBS Records Group
Centel Corp.
Center for Media and Public Affairs
Communications Satellite Corp. (COMSAT)
Community Antenna Television Ass'n
Cook Inlet Communications
Corporation for Public Broadcasting
Detroit Educational TV Foundation
Electronic Industries Ass'n of Japan
Fidelity Television, Inc.
Fox Broadcasting Inc.
Gillett Group Management, Inc.
Go-Video
Golden West Broadcasters
Great American Broadcasting Co.
H & D Communications Group
Holt Communications Corp.
Home Box Office
Information Industry Ass'n
Intermedia Partners
Internat'l Ass'n of Independent Producers
KABY-TV
KADN
KADN-TV
KAIL
KAIT-TV
KAKE-TV
KARK
KATC
KATU
Katz Communications, Inc.
KAUT
KBCP
KBMT
KBMY
KBTX-TV
KCBA
KCEN-TV
KCIK
KCMY
KCNA-TV
KCOS-TV
KCPQ
KCRA-TV
KCSM-TV
KCTZ-TV
KCWC-TV
KCWT
KDLH-TV
KDOC-TV
KDRV
KDSM-TV
KDUH-TV
KEDT-TV
KENI-TV
KERO-TV
KETA-TV
KEVU
Keymarket Communications, Inc.
KFAR-TV
KFBB-TV
KFDX-TV
KFNB
KFNE
KFNR
KFSM-TV
KFTL
KFTY
KGET
KGMC
KGTV
KGW-TV
KHAW-TV
KHNL-TV
KHON-TV
KHSD-TV
KIEM-TV
KIFI
KIHS-TV
KIII
KING-TV
KIRO-TV
KISU-TV
KITN
KIVA-TV

SELECTED SUBJECTS INDEX

The listings in this directory are available as *Mailing Labels*. See last page.

SELECTED SUBJECTS INDEX

WTHR
WTJC
WTKR-TV
WTLW
WTOG
WTRA
WTSP-TV
WTTE
WTVN-TV
WTWS
WTZH
WUCM-TV
WUCX-TV
WUSF-TV
WVII-TV
WVIR-TV
WVUT-TV
WWL-TV
WXEX-TV
WXNE-TV
WYAH
WZZM-TV
Zenith Electronics Corp.
20th Century Fox
810409XO

RAILROADS

American Ass'n of Private Railroad Car Owners, Inc.
American Ass'n of State Highway and Transportation
    Officials
American Railway Car Institute
American Railway Engineering Ass'n
American Short Line Railroad Ass'n
American Standard Inc.
AMTRAK (Nat'l Rail Passenger Corp.)
Ass'n of American Railroads
Atchison, Topeka and Santa Fe Railway Co., The
Bangor and Aroostook Railroad
Brotherhood of Locomotive Engineers
Brotherhood of Maintenance of Way Employees
Brotherhood of Railroad Signalmen
Brotherhood of Railway Carmen of the U.S. and Canada
Burlington Northern Railroad
Canadian Pacific
Chicago and Northwestern Transportation Co.
Committee of American Axle Producers
Consolidated Rail Corp. (CONRAIL)
Consumers United for Rail Equity
CSX Corp.
Dakota, Minnesota & Eastern
Delaware Otsego System
Denver and Rio Grande Western Railroad Co.
Erie Lackawanna Railway Co.
Florida East Coast Railway Co.
Florida High Speed Rail Commission
General Railway Signal Co.
Genesee and Wyoming Corp.
Grand Trunk Corp.
Green Bay and Western Railroad Co.
High Speed Rail Ass'n
Institute of Transportation Engineers
Kansas City Southern Industries
Long Island Rail Road Co.
Nat'l Ass'n of Railroad Passengers
Nat'l Ass'n of Retired and Veteran Railway Employees,
    Inc.
Nat'l Railway Labor Conference
Norfolk Southern Corp.
Pinsly Railroad Co.
Railway Labor Executives' Ass'n
Railway Progress Institute
Railway Systems Design
Reading Railway System
Regional Railroads of America
Responsible Citizen's Political League
Richmond, Fredericksburg and Potomac Railroad
Sea-Land Service, Inc.
Soo Line Railroad, Inc.
Southern Pacific Transportation Co.
Trailer Train Co.
Transportation, Communications Internat'l Union
Union Tank Car Co.
West Virginia Railroad Maintenance Authority

REAL ESTATE

Affordable Housing Preservation Center
Alliance for America's Homeowners
American Institute of Real Estate Appraisers
American Land Title Ass'n

American Real Estate Group
American Resort and Residential Development Ass'n
American Soc. of Appraisers
Amerind Risk Management Corp.
Anden Group, The
Apartment and Office Building Ass'n of Metropolitan
    Washington
Ass'n of Foreign Investors in U.S. Real Estate
Bedford Stuyvesant Restoration Corp.
Benguela Inc.
Building Owners and Managers Ass'n Internat'l
Building Owners and Managers Ass'n Political Action
    Committee
Cabot, Cabot & Forbes Realty Advisors
California Desert Coalition
Carr Company, The Oliver
Centerra Group, The
Centex Corp.
Century 21 Political Action Committee
Century 21 Real Estate Corp.
Chase Enterprises
Citicorp Mortgage Finance, Inc.
College of Property Management, The
Community Ass'ns Institute
Connecticut Ass'n of REALTORS
Cook Inlet Region Inc.
Cooper Communities
Cooperative Housing Foundation
Council for Rural Housing and Development
Council of American Building Officials
Council of Large Public Housing Authorities
Countrywide Credit Industries
Cushman & Wakefield, Inc.
Dean Witter Realty
Diversified Realty Corp. and Financial Group
Escrow Institute of California
Fairfield Communities, Inc.
Federal Home Loan Mortgage Corp.
Federal Nat'l Mortgage Ass'n
Fire Island Ass'n, Inc.
Flo-Sun Land Corp.
Florida Commercial Developers Ass'n
Friendswood Development Corp.
FRISA
Gerald D. Hines Interests
Harsch Investment Corp.
Housing Authority Risk Retention Group
Huskey Realty
Integrated Resources, Inc.
Internat'l Council of Shopping Centers
J & B Management Co.
Kaiser Aluminum and Chemical Corp.
Lehndorff & Babson Real Estate Counsel
Louisiana Land and Exploration Co.
Lusk Company, The
Majestic Realty Co.
Mall Properties, Inc.
Manufactured Housing Institute
Maui Land and Pineapple Co., Inc.
Meredith Corp.
Mid-Atlantic Council of Shopping Center Managers
Mobil Land Development Co.
Mortgage Bankers Ass'n of America
Mortgage Insurance Companies of America
Nat'l American Indian Housing Council
Nat'l Apartment Ass'n
Nat'l Ass'n of Housing Cooperatives
Nat'l Ass'n of Independent Fee Appraisers
Nat'l Ass'n of Industrial and Office Parks
Nat'l Ass'n of Real Estate Brokers
Nat'l Ass'n of Real Estate Investment Trusts
Nat'l Ass'n of REALTORS
Nat'l Center for Housing Management
Nat'l Corp. for Housing Partnerships
Nat'l Council of State Housing Agencies
Nat'l Housing Partnership
Nat'l Inholders Ass'n
Nat'l Leased Housing Ass'n
Nat'l Manufactured Housing Finance Ass'n
Nat'l Multi Housing Council
Nat'l Multi Housing Council Political Action Committee
Nat'l Realty Committee
Nat'l Rural Housing Coalition
Nat'l Second Mortgage Ass'n
Nat'l Soc. for Real Estate Finance
Nationwide Auction Co.
New York City Housing Development Corp.
New York Medical Care Facilities Finance Agency

New York State Housing Finance Agency
O'Connell Management Co.
Palmer Associates, G. H.
Panhandle Eastern Corp.
PHH-Homequity
Philip Morris Cos., Inc.
Property Management Ass'n of America
Property Management Ass'n of Metropolitan Washington
Public Housing Authorities Directors Ass'n
Rouse Company, The
RREEF Funds, The
Saul Real Estate Investment Trust, B. F.
Seaview Property Owners Ass'n, Inc.
Section 8 Housing Group
Site Evaluators & Consultants
Soc. of Industrial and Office Realtors
Soc. of Real Estate Appraisers
Southern Pacific Transportation Co.
Southwest Realty, Inc.
Starrett Housing Corp.
Suburban Maryland Building Industry Ass'n
Thompson Development Co., Kathryn G.
Title Industry Political Action Committee
Trafalgar Capital Associates, Inc.
Trammell Crow, Inc.
Triad Development Corp.
Upland Industries
Vacation Ownership Council of ARRDA
Vero Beach Oceanfront Investors Limited Partnership
Washington Real Estate Investment Trust
Watkins Associated Industries, Inc.
Westinghouse Community Development Group

RECREATION see SPORTS and RECREATION

RELIGION

Adventist Development and Relief Agency Internat'l
Adventist Health System/United States
African Methodist Episcopal Church
American Ass'n of Pastoral Counselors
American Friends Service Committee
American Jewish Congress
Americans United for Separation of Church and State
Americans United Research Foundation
Anti-Defamation League of B'nai B'rith
Archdiocese of Washington
Associated Church Press/Evangelical Press Ass'n
Ass'n for Public Justice
Ass'n for Religious and Value Issues in Counseling
Ass'n of Theological Schools in the United States and
    Canada, The
Baptist Joint Committee on Public Affairs
Baptist World Alliance
B'nai B'rith Internat'l
B'nai B'rith Women
Bread for the World
CASA (Church Alliance of South Africa)
Catholic Health Ass'n of the United States
Catholic Indian Missions, Bureau of
Catholic War Veterans of the U.S.A.
Catholics for a Free Choice
Christian Action Council
Church of the Brethren
Church Women United
Church World Service/Lutheran World Relief
Churches' Center for Theology and Public Policy
Coalition for Religious Freedom
Coalition of Religious Press Ass'ns
Committee for Pro-Life Activities
Conference of Major Superiors of Men of the U.S.A.
Episcopal Church, Washington Office of the
Ethics and Public Policy Center
First Church of Christ-Scientist
Free Congress Political Action Committee
Friends Committee on Nat'l Legislation
Holy Childhood Ass'n
IMPACT
Institute on Religion and Democracy
Interfaith Action for Economic Justice
Interfaith Forum on Religion, Art and Architecture
Internat'l Religious Liberty Ass'n
Jesuit Social Ministries
Larry Jones Ministries
Lutheran Office for Governmental Affairs/Evangelical
    Lutheran Church in America
Lutheran Resources Commission
Lutheran Social Services Community Justice Ministries
Mennonite Central Committee, Peace Section
Military Chaplains Ass'n of the U.S.

The listings in this directory are available as *Mailing Labels*. See last page.

SELECTED SUBJECTS INDEX

The listings in this directory are available as *Mailing Labels*. See last page.

SELECTED SUBJECTS INDEX

SELECTED SUBJECTS INDEX

The listings in this directory are available as *Mailing Labels*. See last page.

SELECTED SUBJECTS INDEX

The listings in this directory are available as *Mailing Labels*. See last page.

SELECTED SUBJECTS INDEX

SELECTED SUBJECTS INDEX

Church Women United
Coalition for Women's Appointments
Coalition of Labor Union Women
Committee for Pro-Life Activities
Concerned Women for America
Daughters of the American Revolution
Eagle Forum
Federally Employed Women, Inc.
Federation of Organizations for Professional Women
General Federation of Women's Clubs
Girl Scouts of the U.S.A.
Internat'l Center for Research on Women
League of Women Voters of the United States
Mexican American Women's Nat'l Ass'n
Mothers Against Drunk Driving (MADD)
Nat'l Abortion Federation
Nat'l Abortion Rights Action League
Nat'l Abortion Rights Action League Political Action
    Committee
Nat'l Ass'n for Girls and Women in Sport
Nat'l Ass'n for Professional Saleswomen
Nat'l Ass'n for Women Deans, Administrators, and
    Counselors
Nat'l Ass'n of Black Women Attorneys
Nat'l Ass'n of Commissions for Women
Nat'l Ass'n of Military Widows
Nat'l Ass'n of Negro Business & Professional Women's
    Clubs, Inc.
Nat'l Beauty Culturists' League
Nat'l Black Women's Political Leadership Caucus
Nat'l Coalition Against Domestic Violence
Nat'l Commission on Working Women
Nat'l Committee for Adoption
Nat'l Committee on Pay Equity
Nat'l Council of Career Women
Nat'l Council of Catholic Women
Nat'l Council of Jewish Women
Nat'l Council of Negro Women
Nat'l Council of Women of the U.S.
Nat'l Family Planning and Reproductive Health Ass'n
Nat'l Federation of Business and Professional Women's
    Clubs
Nat'l Federation of Democratic Women
Nat'l Federation of Republican Women
Nat'l Order of Women Legislators
Nat'l Organization for Women
Nat'l Organization for Women Political Action
    Committee (NOW Equality PAC)
Nat'l Pro-Family Coalition
Nat'l Right to Life Committee
Nat'l Right to Life Political Action Committee
Nat'l Woman's Party
Nat'l Women's Economic Alliance
Nat'l Women's Health Network
Nat'l Women's Law Center
Nat'l Women's Political Caucus
Nat'l Women's Political Caucus Campaign Support
    Committee
Nat'l Women's Political Caucus Victory Fund
Older Women's League
Organization of Chinese American Women
Overseas Education Fund Internat'l
Pension Rights Center
Planned Parenthood Federation of America
Pro-Choice Fund
Public Voice for Food and Health Policy
Religious Coalition for Abortion Rights
United Methodist Church Board of Global Ministries,
    Women's Div.
Voters for Choice
Wider Opportunities for Women
Women for Meaningful Summits
Women in Communications
Women in Community Service
Women in Government Relations
Women Judges Fund for Justice
Women Strike for Peace
Women vs. Smoking
Women's Action for Nuclear Disarmament
Women's Campaign Fund
Women's College Coalition
Women's Economic Justice Center
Women's Legal Defense Fund
Women's Research and Education Institute
Women's Task Force - LCCR
Youths for Democratic Action

WOOD see FORESTRY and FOREST PRODUCTS

WOOL
American Sheep Industry Ass'n
American Sheep Industry Ass'n RAMSPAC
Anodyne, Inc.
Australian Wool Corp.

YOUTH see CHILDREN and YOUTH

The listings in this directory are available as *Mailing Labels*. See last page.

WASHINGTON REPRESENTATIVES
1990

FOREIGN INTERESTS INDEX

Governments, businesses and other organizations of foreign countries which, in addition to their diplomatic missions, retain representation in Washington are listed in this index, together with the individuals and firms providing this service. The index also lists American organizations located in the foreign country under which they appear or principally concerned with some aspect of U. S. relations with that country. (Examples of the latter are the National Council for United States—China Trade and the American Japanese Trade Committee. Their presence in this index in no way implies that they represent the interests of the foreign country under which they are listed.) More information on the representatives may be found in the first two sections of the book.

AFGHANISTAN
Committee for a Free Afghanistan
    Henry Kriegel, Executive Director

ANGOLA
Angola, Government of the People's Republic of
    Fenton Communications, Inc. (David Fenton)
    Laxalt, Washington, Perito & Dubuc (Robert B. Washington, Jr.)
Free Angola Information Service
    Griffin Communications (Frances Griffin)
    Kenneth Barry Schochet, P.C.
Uniao Nacional Para Independencia Total de Angola (UNITA)
    Black, Manafort, Stone and Kelly Public Affairs Co. (Paul J. Manafort)
    TKC Internat'l, Inc.

ARGENTINA
Acindar Industria Argentina de Aceros
    Baker and McKenzie (Thomas P. Ondeck)
Aerolineas Argentinas
    Squire, Sanders and Dempsey (Robert D. Papkin)
Argentina, Government of
    Sharretts, Paley, Carter and Blauvelt (Beatrice A. Brickell)
Camara Argentina de la Alumino y Metales Afines
    Baker and McKenzie (Thomas P. Ondeck, B. Thomas Peele, III)

Camara de la Industria Curtidora Argentina
    Mudge Rose Guthrie Alexander and Ferdon (David P. Houlihan, Julie C. Mendoza)
Camera de la Industria Aceitara de la Republica
    Mudge Rose Guthrie Alexander and Ferdon
Dalmine Siderica
    Mudge Rose Guthrie Alexander and Ferdon (David P. Houlihan, Julie C. Mendoza)
Propulsora Siderugica S.A.I.C.
    Mudge Rose Guthrie Alexander and Ferdon (David P. Houlihan, Julie C. Mendoza)
Tourist Cablevision Corp.
    Warren W. Koffler
Union Industrial de Argentina
    TKC Internat'l, Inc.

AUSTRALIA
AM&S/BHAS
    Sharretts, Paley, Carter and Blauvelt (Alfred R. McCauley)
Ansett Transport Industries
    Squire, Sanders and Dempsey (Robert D. Papkin, Edward W. Sauer)
Australia, Commonwealth of
    Coudert Brothers (Sherman E. Katz)
    Gregory Co., The (Neal Gregory)
    Powell, Adams & Rinehart
Australia, Department of Industry, Technology and Resources of
    Burson-Marsteller

Australia, Embassy of
    Gregory Co., The (Neal Gregory)
Australian Barley Board
    Keene, Shirley & Associates, Inc. (Darrel Choat, David A. Keene, Craigan P. Shirley)
Australian Meat and Livestock Corp.
    Clifford & Warnke
Australian Wool Corp.
    Barnes, Richardson and Colburn (Rufus E. Jarman, Jr.)
Broken Hill Proprietary Co., Ltd.
    O'Melveny and Myers
Colonial Sugar Refineries, Ltd.
    Bishop, Cook, Purcell & Reynolds (Graham B. Purcell, Jr.)
    Cleary, Gottlieb, Steen and Hamilton
Glaxo Australia Pty, Ltd.
    Maupin Taylor Ellis & Adams, P.C. (Scott A. Wilson)
Karlander Kangaroo Lines
    Denning and Wohlstetter (Alan F. Wohlstetter)
Nat'l Farmers' Federation of Australia
    Keene, Shirley & Associates, Inc. (David A. Keene, Craigan P. Shirley)
Qantas Airways
    Condon and Forsyth (Thomas J. Whalen)
Reserve Bank of Australia
    Finnegan, Henderson, Farabow, Garrett and Dunner (Kenneth E. Payne)

FOREIGN INTERESTS INDEX

The listings in this directory are available as *Mailing Labels*. See last page.

FOREIGN INTERESTS INDEX

Costa Rica Shirt Manufacturers
  Internat'l Development Systems
Costa Rican Foreign Trade Committee
  Patton, Boggs and Blow (Frank R. Samolis)
Fundacion de Defensa del Comercio Exterior
  Patton, Boggs and Blow (Frank R. Samolis)
Liga Agricola Industrial de la Cana de Azucar (LAICA)
  Rogers and Wells (Eugene T. Rossides)
Lineas Aereas Costarricicenes (Lasca Airlines)
  Squire, Sanders and Dempsey (Robert D. Papkin, Edward W. Sauer)
Olympic Fibers
  Patton, Boggs and Blow (James B. Christian, Jr.)

CUBA
Cuban-American Committee
  Alicia Torres, Exec. Director
Cuban Patriotic Council
  MacKenzie McCheyne, Inc. (Ana Colomar O'Brien)
Empresa Consolidada Cubana de Aviacion
  Zuckert, Scoutt and Rasenberger (James L. Devall)

CYPRUS
American Hellenic Institute
  Linda Avraamides, Office Manager
  Shaw, Pittman, Potts and Trowbridge (William Mike House)
Cyprus, Government of the Republic of
  Evans Group, Ltd., The
Pancyprian Ass'n of America
  Manatos & Manatos, Inc. (Andrew E. Manatos, Dyck Van Koevering)
Turkish Republic of Northern Cyprus
  Dr. Bulent Aliriza, Representative

CZECHOSLOVAKIA
Czechoslovakia, Chamber of Commerce and Industry of
  Bryan, Cave, McPheeters and McRoberts (J. Michael Cooper)

DENMARK
American Importers Meat Products Group
  Max N. Berry Law Offices (Max N. Berry)
Maersk Inc.
  Mark R. Johnson, General Mgr.-Governmental Affairs
  Lars T. Nyberg, V. President
  Kristi Roos, Government Affairs Representative
Nordisk USA
  Laxalt, Washington, Perito & Dubuc (Michael F. Cole)
Royal Danish Embassy
  Hill and Knowlton Public Affairs Worldwide (Mary C. Foerster)
Scandinavian Airlines System (SAS)
  Global Aviation Associates, Ltd. (Jon F. Ash)
  Winthrop, Stimson, Putnam & Roberts (Robert Reed Gray)

DOMINICAN REPUBLIC
Dominican Republic Internat'l Sugar Policy Coordinating Commission
  McClure and Trotter
Dominican Sugar Institute
  McClure and Trotter
Dominicana Airlines
  Herbert A. Rosenthal

ECUADOR
Aerolineas Nacionales del Ecuador
  Steptoe and Johnson (Richard P. Taylor)
Aeroservicios Ecuatorianos, C.A.
  Lord Day & Lord, Barrett Smith (Joanne W. Young)
Maritima Transligra
  Schmeltzer, Aptaker and Sheppard (Deana Francis Dudley, Suzanne Langford Sanford)

EGYPT
Egypt, Embassy of
  Bannerman and Associates, Inc.
  Brownrigg and Muldoon
  Patton, Boggs and Blow
Egypt, Government of
  Bannerman and Associates, Inc. (M. Graeme Bannerman)

EL SALVADOR
Asociacion Nacional de la Empresa Privada de El Salvador
  O'Connor & Hannan (Joseph H. Blatchford, Patrick E. O'Donnell)

El Salvador Freedom Foundation
  MacKenzie McCheyne, Inc. (I. R. MacKenzie, Ana Colomar O'Brien)
El Salvador, Government of
  O'Connor & Hannan (Joseph H. Blatchford)
  TACA Internat'l Airlines
  Bowen & Atkin (Harry A. Bowen)
  Neill, Mullenholz and Shaw

ETHIOPIA
Eritrean People's Liberation Front
  Hagos Ghebrehiwep, Exec. Director

EUROPE/EUROPEAN COMMUNITY
Airbus Industrie
  Beveridge & Diamond, P.C. (Alexander W. Sierck)
Airbus Industrie of North America
  Alan Boyd, Chairman
Christian Democrat Internat'l
  DC Internat'l, Inc. (Andres R. Hernandez)
Council of European and Japanese Nat'l Shipowners' Ass'ns
  Kirlin, Campbell and Keating (Russell T. Weil)
  Peter G. Sandlund, Washington Representative
Eurofer
  JCLD Consultancy (John C. L. Donaldson)
European Communities, Commission of the
  Kroloff Marshall and Associates (George M. Kroloff)
  TransAtlantic Futures, Inc. (W. Alan Zuschlag)
  Andreas A. M. van Agt, Head of Delegation
European Union of Christian Democrats/European People'sParty
  DC Internat'l, Inc. (Andres R. Hernandez)
Federation of European Bearing Manufacturers Ass'ns
  Mudge Rose Guthrie Alexander and Ferdon (N. David Palmeter)

FIJI
Air Pacific Ltd.
  Condon and Forsyth (Thomas J. Whalen)

FINLAND
Finland, Embassy of
  Marshall, Tenzer, Greenblatt, Fallon and Kaplan (Sylvan M. Marshall)
Outokumpu Oy
  Arent, Fox, Kintner, Plotkin & Kahn (Jerome P. Akman, Stephen L. Gibson, Lewis E. Leibowitz)
Valio Finnish Co-Operative Dairies Ass'n
  Max N. Berry Law Offices (Max N. Berry)

FRANCE
Air France
  V. Michael Straus, P.C.
Air Guadeloupe
  V. Michael Straus, P.C.
Alcatel
  Verner, Liipfert, Bernhard, McPherson and Hand, Chartered (Lloyd N. Hand)
Association Professionnelle de l'Acier Moule de France
  Ross and Hardies (James A. Stenger)
Axa Midi Assurances
  Washington Communications Group/Ruder Finn (James W. Harff)
Bureau National Interprofessionel du Cognac
  Hill and Knowlton Public Affairs Worldwide (Charles R. Pucie, Jr.)
Caisse des Depots et Consignations
  Hill and Knowlton Public Affairs Worldwide (Dr. Ira P. Kaminow)
Casino
  Hill and Knowlton Public Affairs Worldwide (Dr. Ira P. Kaminow)
Centre National Interprofessionel de L'Economie Laitiere (French Dairy Ass'n)
  Max N. Berry Law Offices (Max N. Berry)
Chambre Syndicale des Producteurs d'Aciers Fins et Speciaux
  Covington and Burling (Harvey M. Applebaum)
Compagnie d'Affretement et de Transport USA
  Denning and Wohlstetter (Joseph F. Mullins, Jr.)
Compagnie Financiere de Paris et des Pays Bas
  Rogers and Wells (Anthony F. Essaye, Eugene T. Rossides)
Creusot Loire Steel Products Co.
  Mudge Rose Guthrie Alexander and Ferdon
Federation of Wine and Spirits Exporters of France
  Max N. Berry Law Offices (Max N. Berry)
France, Government of
  Powell, Adams & Rinehart

French-American Chamber of Commerce in the U.S.
  Shaw, Pittman, Potts and Trowbridge
Institut de la Vie
  Laxalt, Washington, Perito & Dubuc (Carroll E. Dubuc)
Manhurin, S.A.
  Shaw, Pittman, Potts and Trowbridge (Steuart L. Pittman)
Matra Aerospace, Inc.
  Gilbert Croze, President & CEO
  Verner, Liipfert, Bernhard, McPherson and Hand, Chartered
Papeteries Bollore, S.A.
  Barnes, Richardson and Colburn
Perrier Group
  Arent, Fox, Kintner, Plotkin & Kahn
Promodes
  Hill and Knowlton Public Affairs Worldwide (Dr. Ira P. Kaminow)
Rhone-Poulenc Ag Co.
  Jellinek, Schwartz, Connolly & Freshman, Inc. (Steven D. Jellinek)
  Neill and Co. (Denis M. Neill, Albert C. Printz, Jr.)
Rhone-Poulenc Inc.
  Baker and Botts (B. Donovan Picard)
  Joseph J. Martyak, Director, Corporate Affairs
  William P. Mengebier, Assistant Director, Government Relations
  Jean R. Toohey, Manager, Government Relations
Science Industries (S.A.R.L.)
  Swann, Stephen L., Law Offices of
Sefri Construction Internat'l
  Dow, Lohnes and Albertson (Philip C. Thompson)
SNA Canada Inc.
  Hill and Knowlton Public Affairs Worldwide (Robert V. Schneider)
Societe Nationale des Poudres et Explosifs
  DGA Internat'l
  Dorsey & Whitney
Sofreavia
  DGA Internat'l (Sandra K. Meredith)
Thomson-CSF Inc.
  Burson-Marsteller
  Gold and Liebengood, Inc. (Howard S. Liebengood)
Total American Cooperation
  Philip P. Saint-Andrew, President
Usinor-Sacilor, S.A.
  Donovan Leisure Rogovin Huge & Schiller (William E. Colby)

GABON
Gabon, Republic of
  White & Case

GERMAN DEMOCRATIC REPUBLIC
German Democratic Republic, Embassy of the
  Marshall, Tenzer, Greenblatt, Fallon and Kaplan (Sylvan M. Marshall)

GERMANY
ADIG-Investment GmbH
  Hill and Knowlton Public Affairs Worldwide (Dr. Ira P. Kaminow)
AEG Aktiengesellschaft
  Ballard, Spahr, Andrews and Ingersoll (Frederic L. Ballard, Jr.)
Akademie Fur Fuhrunskrafte der Deutschen Bundespost
  Porter/Novelli
  Wilkinson, Barker, Knauer and Quinn
American Chamber of Commerce in Germany
  Squire, Sanders and Dempsey (Ritchie T. Thomas)
Amexco
  Ballard, Spahr, Andrews and Ingersoll (Frederic L. Ballard, Jr.)
Baden-Wuerttemberg, State of, Development Corp.
  Hill and Knowlton Public Affairs Worldwide (Mary C. Foerster)
BMW of North America
  Dorsey & Whitney
  Wiley, Rein & Fielding (Mimi Weyforth Dawson)
Bowe Maschinenfabrik GmbH
  Barnes, Richardson and Colburn (Rufus E. Jarman, Jr.)
Bremer Lagerhaus-Gesellschaft
  Prather, Seeger, Doolittle and Farmer (Thomas L. Farmer, Carl B. Nelson, Jr., Edwin H. Seeger)
Bruker Meerestechnik GmbH
  Forster & Associates (Johann R. Forster)

FOREIGN INTERESTS INDEX

Bundesverband der Deutschen Industrie
  Baker and Botts (John P. Babb, Paul Freedenberg, B. Donovan Picard, John B. Veach, III)
  Representative for German Industry and Trade (Dr. Lothar Griessbach, Hartmut Schneider, John Heath Vaughan, Jr,, Bernhard M. Welschke)
Bundesvereinigung der Deutschen Ernahrangsindustrie
  Coudert Brothers (Robert A. Lipstein)
Daimler-Berry A.G.
  Hogan and Hartson
Deutsche Bank AG
  TransAtlantic Futures, Inc. (Stephan-Gotz Richter, W. Alan Zuschlag)
Deutscher Industrie und Handelstag
  Representative for German Industry and Trade (Dr. Lothar Griessbach, Hartmut Schneider, John Heath Vaughan, Jr,, Bernhard M. Welschke)
Dresdnerbank
  Hill and Knowlton Public Affairs Worldwide (Dr. Ira P. Kaminow)
Edelstahlwerke Buderus AG
  Coudert Brothers (Milo C. Coerper)
Electro- & Electronik Appartebau Gesellschaft mbH
  Leva, Hawes, Mason and Martin (Lowell D. Turnbull)
Flachglas A.G.
  Mudge Rose Guthrie Alexander and Ferdon (David P. Houlihan)
Friendship in Freedom Ass'n
  Bergner, Boyette & Bockorny, Inc. (Jeffrey T. Bergner)
German Flatware Manufacturers Ass'n
  Coudert Brothers (Milo C. Coerper)
German Nat'l Tourist Office
  Hill and Knowlton Public Affairs Worldwide (Mary C. Foerster)
German Specialty Steel Ass'n
  Coudert Brothers (Milo C. Coerper)
Germany, Ministry of Posts and Communications of the Federal Republic of
  Wilkinson, Barker, Knauer and Quinn
Gesamtverband der Deutschen Versicherungswirtschaft e.V.
  Wunder, Ryan, Cannon & Thelen (Kenneth S. Levine)
Hallssen & Lyon
  Ballard, Spahr, Andrews and Ingersoll (Frederic L. Ballard, Jr.)
Hannover, City of
  P. W. Anderson & Partners (Philip W. Anderson)
Hapag-Lloyd AG
  Dow, Lohnes and Albertson (Stanley O. Sher)
  Warren and Associates (George A. Quadrino, Charles F. Warren)
Heckler & Koch
  Arent, Fox, Kintner, Plotkin & Kahn (Samuel Efron)
  Marvin Wagner, Legal Counsel
Internat'l Council of Containerships Operators
  Preston Gates Ellis & Rouvelas Meeds (Emanuel L. Rouvelas)
Jauch & Hubener, O.H.G.
  George K. Bernstein Law Off. (George K. Bernstein, Robert B. Shapiro)
Krupp Internat'l
  Coudert Brothers (Milo C. Coerper)
Kuehne and Nagel, Inc.
  Robert N. Meiser, P.C.
LITEF GmbH
  Forster & Associates (Johann R. Forster)
Lufthansa German Airlines
  Powell, Adams & Rinehart
  Wilmer, Cutler and Pickering (James S. Campbell, Robert C. Cassidy, Jr., Dieter G. F. Lange, Carol F. Lee)
Mercedes-Benz of North America, Inc.
  Barnes, Richardson and Colburn (Edgar Thomas Honey)
  Cadwalader, Wickersham & Taft (J. Roger Mentz)
  Hogan and Hartson (Clifford S. Gibbons)
  Mudge Rose Guthrie Alexander and Ferdon (David A. Vaughan)
  O'Connor & Hannan (Patrick E. O'Donnell)
MIP Instandsetzungsbetriebe GmbH
  Ervin Technical Associates, Inc. (ETA) (James L. Ervin)
  Morgan, Lewis and Bockius

North Rhine Westphalia, Government of
  Prather, Seeger, Doolittle and Farmer (Thomas L. Farmer)
Preussag AG
  Jones, Day, Reavis and Pogue (Randall E. Davis, Charles McC. Mathias)
Rasch Elektronik
  Tendler, Goldberg & Biggins, Chtd. (Paul M. Tendler)
Salzgitter AG
  Prather, Seeger, Doolittle and Farmer (Thomas L. Farmer)
Siemens Corp.
  Collier, Shannon & Scott (Paul D. Cullen, Michael D. Sherman)
  Howrey and Simon
  TransAtlantic Futures, Inc. (Stephan-Gotz Richter, W. Alan Zuschlag)
Thyssen Inc.
  Sharretts, Paley, Carter and Blauvelt (Beatrice A. Brickell, Alfred R. McCauley)
West German Ceramic Exporters Ass'n
  Barnes, Richardson and Colburn
West German Iron and Steel Federation
  Coudert Brothers (Milo C. Coerper)

GREAT BRITAIN

AB Electronics Group Ltd.
  Lonington, Inc. (Alan G. Gray)
Accountant's Liability Assurance Co., Ltd.
  Mayer, Brown and Platt (Jerry L. Oppenheimer)
Ace Frosty Shipping Co., Ltd.
  Dyer, Ellis, Joseph & Mills (Thomas M. Dyer, James B. Ellis, II, Michael Joseph, Thomas L. Mills, Howard A. Vine)
Airship Industries, Ltd.
  Ginsburg, Feldman and Bress (David Ginsburg, Robert W. Hawkins)
  Wunder, Ryan, Cannon & Thelen (John J. McGovern, Jr.)
Alexander Laing & Cruickshank
  Hill and Knowlton Public Affairs Worldwide (Dr. Ira P. Kaminow)
Amalgamated Metal Corp. PLC
  Chadbourne and Parke (Cornelius Golden, Jr.)
Apex Ltd.
  Arnold & Porter (Paul S. Berger)
Associated Electric and Gas Insurance Services, Ltd.
  Davis & Harman (Thomas A. Davis, Gail B. Wilkins)
Ass'n of British Insurers
  Lord Day & Lord, Barrett Smith (Brenda Viehe-Naess)
Attorneys' Liability Assurance Soc.
  Mayer, Brown and Platt (Jerry L. Oppenheimer)
Barclays Bank PLC
  Marlene Nicholson, Director, Government Relations
  Sidley and Austin (Margery Waxman)
Bowman Webber Ltd.
  Ross and Hardies (James A. Stenger)
British Aerospace, Inc.
  George Dahlman, Manager, Press Office
  Hyman Fine & Associates Ltd.
  Michael Jolley, V. President, Public Affairs
  Richard Richards Law Offices
British Airports Authority (BAA plc)
  Gold and Liebengood, Inc. (David W. Bushong, Howard S. Liebengood, John F. Scruggs)
British Airtours Ltd.
  Condon and Forsyth (Thomas J. Whalen)
British Ass'n of Investment Trust Companies
  Alcalde & Rousselot (Hector Alcalde)
British Consortium, The
  O'Connor & Hannan (Timothy M. Haake)
British Embassy
  Leva, Hawes, Mason and Martin (Lowell D. Turnbull)
British Independent Steel Producers Ass'n
  Beveridge & Diamond, P.C. (Alexander W. Sierck)
British Steel Corp.
  Steptoe and Johnson (Charlene Barshefsky, Richard O. Cunningham)
British Tourist Authority
  Powell, Adams & Rinehart
Burnett & Hallamshire Holdings, PLC
  Chadbourne and Parke
Christie's Internat'l
  Jack Ferguson Associates (Jack Ferguson)
  Steptoe and Johnson (Blake D. Rubin)

Colebrand Ltd.
  Lipsen Whitten & Diamond
  Shaw, Pittman, Potts and Trowbridge (James H. Burnley, IV)
Cristal Services, Inc.
  Marye T. Miller
F&C Management Ltd.
  Hill and Knowlton Public Affairs Worldwide (Dr. Ira P. Kaminow)
Friends' Provident Life Office
  Hill and Knowlton Public Affairs Worldwide (Dr. Ira P. Kaminow)
Good Relations
  TKC Internat'l, Inc.
Grain and Feed Trade Ass'n, The
  Arnold & Porter (Brooksley E. Born, John M. Quinn, Daniel Waldman)
Grand Metropolitan PLC
  Akin, Gump, Strauss, Hauer and Feld
  Fort and Schlefer (Leonard Egan)
  O'Connor & Hannan
  Wilmer, Cutler and Pickering (John H. Pickering)
Guinness PLC
  Kelley, Drye and Warren
Heron Internat'l, Ltd.
  Jones, Day, Reavis and Pogue (C. Thomas Long)
Hoylake Investments Ltd.
  Akin, Gump, Strauss, Hauer and Feld (Joel Jankowsky)
  Skadden, Arps, Slate, Meagher and Flom (Robert E. Lighthizer)
Internat'l Commodities Clearing House, Ltd.
  Arnold & Porter (Brooksley E. Born, John M. Quinn, Daniel Waldman)
Internat'l Futures Exchange (Bermuda) Ltd.
  Royer, Mehle & Babyak (Robert Stewart Royer)
Internat'l Petroleum Exchange of London
  Arnold & Porter (Brooksley E. Born)
Intex Holdings (Bermuda) Ltd.
  Royer, Mehle & Babyak (Robert Stewart Royer)
Johnson Matthey PLC
  Rose Communications (Robert R. Rose)
Lees Co, J B & S
  L. A. Motley and Co. (Langhorne A. Motley)
London Commodity Exchange Co., Ltd.
  Arnold & Porter (Brooksley E. Born, John M. Quinn, Daniel Waldman)
London Futures and Options Exchange
  APCO Associates
London Internat'l Financial Futures Exchange
  Arnold & Porter
London Metal Exchange, Ltd.
  Mayer, Brown and Platt
Metal Market and Exchange Co. Ltd.
  Arnold & Porter
Morgan Grenfell and Co., Ltd.
  Jones, Day, Reavis and Pogue (James A. Wilderotter)
  O'Connor & Hannan (Thomas H. Quinn)
  Wilson, Elser, Moskowitz, Edelman & Dicker (Robert B. Wallace)
Phillips & Drew
  Hill and Knowlton Public Affairs Worldwide (Dr. Ira P. Kaminow)
Plessey Co. PLC, The
  Akin, Gump, Strauss, Hauer and Feld
Plessey Electronic Systems, Inc.
  Bryan Barrett, V. President- Marconi Underwater Systems
Reebok Internat'l Ltd.
  Lindsay, Hart, Neil & Weigler (Peter Friedmann)
Richardson Lawrie Associates
  William L. Hoffman
Scotch Whiskey Ass'n
  Morgan, Lewis and Bockius (Michael S. Kelly, E. Carl Uehlein, Jr.)
Scottish Equitable Life Assurance Society
  Hill and Knowlton Public Affairs Worldwide (Dr. Ira P. Kaminow)
Sotheby's Holdings, Inc.
  Jack Ferguson Associates (Jack Ferguson)
  McNair Group Inc. (Elizabeth L. Taylor)
  Steptoe and Johnson (Blake D. Rubin)
Sunbelt Corp.
  Powell, Goldstein, Frazer and Murphy
Tradewinds Airways Ltd.
  Lord Day & Lord, Barrett Smith (Joanne W. Young)

The listings in this directory are available as *Mailing Labels*. See last page.

FOREIGN INTERESTS INDEX

FOREIGN INTERESTS INDEX

Italian Aerospace Industries (USA), Inc.
  M. L. Boswell, Chairman
  Stefano P. Ruocco, President
  Riccardo Sarti, Manager, Business Development
La Metalli Industriale S.p.A.
  Cleary, Gottlieb, Steen and Hamilton (Richard deC. Hinds, Daniel B. Silver)
Mirabella
  Wunder, Ryan, Cannon & Thelen (John J. McGovern, Jr.)
OEL/Norfin S.p.A.
  Dow, Lohnes and Albertson (William Silverman)
Order of Sons of Italy in America
  Palumbo & Cerrell, Inc. (Jeffrey D. Doranz, Benjamin L. Palumbo, Paul A. Skrabut, Jr.)
SAE Electric
  Sharretts, Paley, Carter and Blauvelt (Alfred R. McCauley)
Savema S.p.A.
  Dow, Lohnes and Albertson (William Silverman)
Selenia Industria Elettronica, S.p.A.
  Enzo Mazzaglia, U.S. Representative
Si.A.C./Italy
  Jefferson Group, The (Jose Ortiz-Daliot, John Upston)
Societa Cavi Pirelli S.p.A.
  Cassidy and Associates, Inc. (James P. Fabiani, C. Frank Godfrey, Jr., Vincent M. Versage)

IVORY COAST

Air Afrique
  Zuckert, Scoutt and Rasenberger (William H. Callaway, Jr.)
Ivory Coast, Government of
  Neill and Co. (George A. Dalley, Denis M. Neill)

JAMAICA

Air Jamaica
  Galland, Kharasch, Morse and Garfinkle (Morris R. Garfinkle, Susan B. Jollie, Mark S. Kahan)
Jamaica, Government of
  CounterTerrorism Consultants L.P. (L. Carter McCormick, Jr., Gerald S. Walker)
  Fenton Communications, Inc. (David Fenton, Leila McDowell-Head)
  Holland and Knight
  Neill and Co. (George A. Dalley, Denis M. Neill)
Jamaica Nat'l Export Corp.
  Holland and Knight (David H. Baker)
People's National Party
  Curtis A. Ward
Petrojam Ltd.
  William Bode and Associates (William Bode)
  Collier, Shannon & Scott (R. Timothy Columbus)

JAPAN

AIDA Engineering Ltd.
  Arent, Fox, Kintner, Plotkin & Kahn (Stephen L. Gibson)
All Nippon Airways Co.
  Global USA, Inc. (John M. Nugent, Jr.)
  Zuckert, Scoutt and Rasenberger (James L. Devall)
American Koyo Corp.
  Powell, Goldstein, Frazer and Murphy (Peter Suchman)
American Suzuki Motor Corp.
  Dorsey & Whitney
Asahi Chemical Industry Co.
  Barnes, Richardson and Colburn (James S. O'Kelly)
Bank of Tokyo Trust Co.
  Epstein Becker and Green
Brother Internat'l, Inc.
  Tanaka, Ritger and Middleton (Patrick F. O'Leary, H. William Tanaka)
California Steel Industries Inc.
  Arent, Fox, Kintner, Plotkin & Kahn (Michael D. Barnes)
  Squire, Sanders and Dempsey (Robert H. Huey)
  Peter Teeley & Associates
Canai Inc.
  Dorsey & Whitney
Central Union of Agricultural Cooperatives (ZENCHU)
  Arter & Hadden (Georgia H. Burke, William K. Dabaghi)
Chubu Electric Power Co.
  Tatsuo Yagi, Chief Representative
Chugai Pharmaceutical Co., Ltd.
  Hill and Knowlton Public Affairs Worldwide (Ken Rabin)

Communication Industries Ass'n of Japan
  Anderson, Hibey, Nauheim and Blair (Stanton D. Anderson)
  Mintz, Levin, Cohn, Ferris, Glovsky and Popeo, P.C. (Charles D. Ferris)
Council of European and Japanese Nat'l Shipowners' Ass'ns
  Kirlin, Campbell and Keating (Russell T. Weil)
  Peter G. Sandlund, Washington Representative
Daicel Chemical Industries, Ltd.
  Mudge Rose Guthrie Alexander and Ferdon (N. David Palmeter)
Electric Power Development Co., Ltd.
  Tadahisa Miyasaka, Chief Representative
Electronic Industries Ass'n of Japan
  Anderson, Hibey, Nauheim and Blair (Stanton D. Anderson)
  Hill and Knowlton Public Affairs Worldwide (Mary C. Foerster)
  McDermott, Will and Emery (Robert S. Schwartz)
  Mudge Rose Guthrie Alexander and Ferdon (William N. Walker)
  Reese Communications Companies
  Saunders and Company (Pete Salavantis)
  Tanaka, Ritger and Middleton (B. Jenkins Middleton, H. William Tanaka)
Export-Import Bank of Japan
  Dechert Price & Rhoads (Allan S. Mostoff)
Fanuc, Ltd.
  Global USA, Inc. (Dr. Bohdan Denysyk)
Fasteners Institute of Japan
  Tanaka, Ritger and Middleton
Federation of Japan Tuna Fisheries Cooperative Ass'ns
  Anderson and Pendleton, C.A. (Francis G. McKenna)
Flat Glass Ass'n of Japan
  Tanaka, Ritger and Middleton (Patrick F. O'Leary, H. William Tanaka)
Fuji Heavy Industries Ltd.
  Piper Pacific Internat'l (Margaret Parker, W. Stephen Piper, Sara Winslow)
  Willkie Farr and Gallagher (William H. Barringer)
Fuji Photo Film U.S.A.
  Daniel J. Edelman, Inc. (Leslie Dach)
  Patton, Boggs and Blow
  Skadden, Arps, Slate, Meagher and Flom (Thomas R. Graham, William E. Perry)
Fujitsu Ltd.
  Akin, Gump, Strauss, Hauer and Feld (Warren E. Connelly, Richard Rivers)
  Morrison & Foerster (Jonathan Band, Philip D. Bartz, Ronald G. Carr, Tamar R. Schwartz)
  Kuniaki Nozoe, General Manager
  David Olive, Deputy General Manager
Fujitsu Microelectronics, Inc.
  Ball, Janik and Novack (James A. Beall)
Futaba Corp.
  Mudge Rose Guthrie Alexander and Ferdon (Donald B. Cameron, Jr., David P. Houlihan)
Guam-Uranao Development Co., Ltd.
  Gerard F. Schiappa
Hitachi America Ltd.
  McDermott, Will and Emery (Robert S. Schwartz, Carl W. Schwarz)
  Jack McDonald Co. (Jack McDonald, Myron G. Sandifer, III)
  Powell, Goldstein, Frazer and Murphy
Hitachi Ltd.
  Global USA, Inc. (John M. Nugent, Jr.)
  Mitsuhiko Harada, Representative
  Hill and Knowlton Public Affairs Worldwide (Stephen H. Meeter)
  McDermott, Will and Emery (Robert S. Schwartz, Carl W. Schwarz)
  Powell, Goldstein, Frazer and Murphy (Stuart E. Eizenstat)
  TKC Internat'l, Inc.
  Masayuki Yamada, Senior Representative
Hitachi Research Institute
  Hill and Knowlton Public Affairs Worldwide (Andrew G. Durant)
Hitachi Zosen Corp.
  Graham and James (Brian E. McGill, Yoshihiro Saito)

Honda North America, Inc.
  Scott A. Gerke, Government Relations Assistant
  Toni Harrington, Manager, Government and Industry Rtns.
  Shogo Iizuka, Senior V. President
  Barbara Nocera, Asst. Manager, Government Relations
Industrial Bank of Japan, Ltd.
  Wilbur F. Monroe Associates (Wilbur F. Monroe)
Internat'l Public Relations Co.
  Civic Service, Inc. (Roy Pfautch)
  Keefe Co., The (Robert J. Keefe, Terry M. O'Connell)
  Saunders and Company (Eric Edmondson, Steven R. Saunders)
  TKC Internat'l, Inc.
Internat'l Telecom Japan
  Debevoise and Plimpton (Robert R. Bruce, Jeffrey P. Cunard)
Ishikawajima-Harima Heavy Industries Co.
  Arent, Fox, Kintner, Plotkin & Kahn
Japan Aluminum Federation
  Mudge Rose Guthrie Alexander and Ferdon (William N. Walker)
Japan Auto Parts Industry Ass'n
  Robinson, Lake, Lerer & Montgomery (James H. Lake)
Japan Automobile Manufacturers Ass'n
  William C. Duncan, Deputy General Director
  Akihiko Miyoshi, General Director, Washington Office
  John P. Sears Law Offices (John P. Sears)
  Allen Walker, Manager, Public Affairs
Japan Automobile Tire Manufacturers Ass'n
  Tanaka, Ritger and Middleton (James Davenport, B. Jenkins Middleton, Michele N. Tanaka)
Japan Bearing Industrial Ass'n
  Tanaka, Ritger and Middleton (James Davenport, H. William Tanaka)
Japan Chemical Fibers Ass'n
  Internat'l Business and Economic Research Corp.
Japan Economic Institute of America
  Gretchen Green, Government Relations Analyst
  Lerch and Co., Inc. (Donald G. Lerch, Jr.)
  Barbara Warner, Sr. Political Economist
Japan Electronic Industry Development Ass'n
  Graham and James
Japan, Embassy of
  Davis Wright Tremaine (Walter H. Evans, III)
  Dechert Price & Rhoads (Allan S. Mostoff)
  Paul H. DeLaney Law Offices (Paul H. DeLaney, Jr.)
  Hogan and Hartson
  Mike Masaoka Associates
  Milbank, Tweed, Hadley & McCloy
  Saunders and Company (Eric Edmondson, Steven R. Saunders)
  Tanaka, Ritger and Middleton (H. William Tanaka)
  Washington Resources and Strategy, Inc. (William R. Sweeney, Jr.)
Japan Export Metal Flatware Industry Ass'n
  Tanaka, Ritger and Middleton (James Davenport, H. William Tanaka)
Japan External Trade Organization (JETRO)
  Mike Masaoka Associates
Japan Federation of Construction Contractors
  Global USA, Inc. (Dr. Bohdan Denysyk)
Japan Fisheries Ass'n
  Frank, Richard A., Law Offices of
  Garvey, Schubert & Barer
  Ginsburg, Feldman and Bress (David Ginsburg)
Japan General Merchandise Exporters Ass'n
  Tanaka, Ritger and Middleton (James Davenport, H. William Tanaka)
Japan, Government of
  Lerch and Co., Inc. (Donald G. Lerch, Jr.)
  Wilbur F. Monroe Associates (Wilbur F. Monroe)
  Tanaka, Ritger and Middleton (H. William Tanaka)
Japan Iron and Steel Exporters Ass'n
  Steptoe and Johnson
  Willkie Farr and Gallagher (William H. Barringer)
Japan/Korea-Atlantic and Gulf Freight Conference
  Warren and Associates
Japan Lumber Importers Ass'n
  Internat'l Business and Economic Research Corp.
  Mudge Rose Guthrie Alexander and Ferdon (Julia Christine Bliss, David P. Houlihan)

The listings in this directory are available as *Mailing Labels*. See last page.

FOREIGN INTERESTS INDEX

Japan Machine Tool Builders Ass'n
    Anderson, Hibey, Nauheim and Blair (Stanton D.
        Anderson)
Japan Machinery Exporters Ass'n
    Anderson, Hibey, Nauheim and Blair (Stanton D.
        Anderson)
    Willkie Farr and Gallagher (William H. Barringer)
Japan Metal Forming Machine Builders Ass'n
    Anderson, Hibey, Nauheim and Blair (Stanton D.
        Anderson)
Japan, Ministry of Foreign Affairs of
    The Eddie Mahe Company
Japan Pottery Exporters Ass'n
    Tanaka, Ritger and Middleton (H. William Tanaka)
Japan Productivity Center
    Daisaku Harada, Director, U.S. Office
Japan/Puerto Rico and Virgin Islands Freight Conference
    Warren and Associates (Charles F. Warren)
Japan Soc. of Industrial Machinery Manufacturers
    Paul A. London Assoc., Inc. (Paul A. London)
Japan Steel Works, Ltd.
    Marks Murase and White (Matthew J. Marks,
        Frederic B. Rose)
    Popham, Haik, Schnobrich & Kaufman, Ltd. (William
        E. Casselman, II)
Japan Tobacco, Inc.
    Seichi Assako, Chief Representative, Washington
        Office
    Daniel J. Edelman, Inc. (Stephen K. Cook)
    Hoppel, Mayer and Coleman (Neal M. Mayer)
Japan Trade Center
    Hill and Knowlton Public Affairs Worldwide
        (Andrew G. Durant)
    Tanaka, Ritger and Middleton (James Davenport, B.
        Jenkins Middleton, H. William Tanaka)
    TKC Internat'l, Inc.
Japan Tuna Fisheries Cooperative
    Anderson and Pendleton, C.A. (Francis G.
        McKenna)
Japan Woolen and Linen Textiles Exporters Ass'n
    Internat'l Business and Economic Research Corp.
Japanese Aero Engines Corp.
    Global USA, Inc. (Dr. Bohdan Denysyk)
Japanese Aircraft Development Corp.
    Global USA, Inc. (Dr. Bohdan Denysyk)
"K" Line Air Service (U.S.A.), Inc.
    Robert N. Meiser, P.C.
Kawasaki Kisen Kaisha, Ltd.
    O'Connor & Hannan (George J. Mannina, Jr.)
    Warren and Associates (Charles F. Warren)
Kawasaki Motors Corp., USA
    Paul, Hastings, Janofsky and Walker (Mark L.
        Gerchick)
    Fred B. Rooney
Kintetsu World Express (U.S.A.) Inc.
    Robert N. Meiser, P.C.
Kobe Steel Co.
    Willkie Farr and Gallagher (Christopher A. Dunn)
Koito Manufacturing Co.
    Paul, Hastings, Janofsky and Walker (Richard M.
        Fairbanks, III, G. Hamilton Loeb)
Komatsu Ltd.
    Global USA, Inc. (William H. Morris, Jr.)
    Graham and James (Lawrence R. Walders)
    Shearman and Sterling (Robert Herzstein, Thomas B.
        Wilner)
Konishoruku Photo Industry U.S.A.
    Ginsburg, Feldman and Bress
Koyo Seiko
    Powell, Goldstein, Frazer and Murphy (Peter
        Suchman)
Kyocera Corp.
    Global USA, Inc. (William H. Morris, Jr.)
Marubeni America Inc.
    Hill and Knowlton Public Affairs Worldwide
    Takeo Tanaka, Sr. V. President
Matsushita Electric Corp. of America
    Mary Alexander, Manager, Government Affairs
    Cole, Corette & Abrutyn (Robert T. Cole)
    M. McAllister, Government Affairs Coordinator
    Masayuki Nakao, Senior Representative
    Hall Northcott, Director, Government and Public
        Affairs
    Patton, Boggs and Blow
    Mark J. Sharp, Manager, Government Affairs
    Strategic Resources Corp.

Matsushita Electronic Corp.
    Weil, Gotshal & Manges (Jeffrey P. Bialos, A. Paul
        Victor)
Minebea Co.
    Tanaka, Ritger and Middleton (Michele N. Tanaka)
Mitsubishi Corp.
    Barnes, Richardson and Colburn (Edgar Thomas
        Honey)
    Charls E. Walker Associates
    Weil, Gotshal & Manges (Jeffrey P. Bialos, A. Paul
        Victor)
Mitsubishi Electric Corp.
    Baker and McKenzie (Thomas P. Ondeck, William
        D. Outman, II)
    Robinson, Lake, Lerer & Montgomery (James H.
        Lake)
    Saunders and Company (Eric Edmondson, Steven R.
        Saunders)
Mitsubishi Internat'l Corp.
    Michael Call, Manager
    Gordon Epstein, Manager
    Masato Nagase, Manager
    Lawrence Paul, Assistant Manager
    Motoatsu Sakurai, Deputy General Manager
    Saunders and Company (Kim Brown, Steven R.
        Saunders)
    Kazuko White, Assistant Manager
Mitsubishi Trust and Banking Corp.
    Civic Service, Inc. (Roy Pfautch)
Mitsui and Co.
    Barnes, Richardson and Colburn (James S. O'Kelly)
    Marks Murase and White (Matthew J. Marks)
    Steptoe and Johnson (Charlene Barshefsky, Richard
        O. Cunningham, Susan G. Esserman)
Mitsui and Co. (U.S.A.), Inc.
    William C. Bell, Research Associate
    Kent Bossart, Export License Supervisor
    Lawrence Bruser, Deputy General Manager
    Jacalyn Douglas, Research Assistant
    Takatsugu Ohi, General Manager
Mitsui O.S.K. Lines, Ltd.
    Warren and Associates (George A. Quadrino, Charles
        F. Warren)
Murata Machinery, Ltd.
    Global USA, Inc. (Dr. Bohdan Denysyk)
Nakajima All Co.
    Patton, Boggs and Blow (Thomas Hale Boggs, Jr.)
NEC Corp.
    Coudert Brothers (Mark D. Herlach)
    Manatt, Phelps, Rothenberg & Phillips (J. Michael
        Farrell, Charles T. Manatt)
    Paul, Weiss, Rifkind, Wharton and Garrison (Terence
        J. Fortune, Robert E. Montgomery, Jr.)
New Energy and Industrial Technology Development
  Organization
    Toshiaki Yamamoto, Chief Representative
NHK (Japanese Broadcasting Corp.)
    Anderson, Hibey, Nauheim and Blair (Stanton D.
        Anderson)
Nippon Benkan Kogyo Co., Ltd.
    Graham and James (Yoshihiro Saito)
Nippon Cargo Airlines
    Shun-Ichi Fujimura, Chief Representative
    Williams and Jensen, P.C. (John J. McMackin, Jr.)
    Zuckert, Scoutt and Rasenberger (James L. Devall)
Nippon Electric Co., Ltd.
    Coudert Brothers (Milo C. Coerper)
Nippon Kokan K.K.
    Willkie Farr and Gallagher (William H. Barringer)
Nippon Steel Corp.
    Steptoe and Johnson (W. George Grandison, Daniel
        J. Plaine)
Nippon Synthetic Chemical Industry Co.
    Mudge Rose Guthrie Alexander and Ferdon (N.
        David Palmeter)
Nippon Telephone and Telegraph Corp.
    Civic Service, Inc. (Roy Pfautch)
    TKC Internat'l, Inc.
Nippon Yusen Kaisha (NYK) Line
    Warren and Associates (George A. Quadrino, Charles
        F. Warren)
Nissan Aerospace Division
    Charles Louis Fishman, P.C. (Charles Louis Fishman)
Nissan Industrial Equipment Co.
    Arnold & Porter (Patrick F. J. Macrory)

Nissan Motor Co., Ltd.
    Arnold & Porter (Patrick F. J. Macrory)
    Charles Louis Fishman, P.C. (Charles Louis Fishman)
    Manchester Associates, Ltd. (John V. Moller)
    Piper Pacific Internat'l (Margaret Parker, W. Stephen
        Piper, Sara Winslow)
Nissan Motor Corp. in U.S.A.
    Franklin J. Crawford, Director, Government and
        Public Affairs
    Dorsey & Whitney
    Paul D. Ryan, Manager, Government and Public
        Affairs
    Yutaka Suzuki, Vice President, External Relations
    James A. Young, Manager, Industry & Economic
        Affairs
Nissho-Iwai American Corp.
    Donovan Leisure Rogovin Huge & Schiller (William
        E. Colby)
    Dorsey & Whitney
    Yasuo Wataru, Sr. V. President, General Manager
Nomura Research Institute (America), Inc.
    Wilbur F. Monroe Associates (Wilbur F. Monroe)
    Kota Washio, General Manager, Washington Office
NTT America
    Paul Muroyama & Assoc. (Paul Muroyama)
Ohbayashi Corp.
    Graham and James
    Saunders and Company (Eric Edmondson, Steven R.
        Saunders)
Onoda Cement Co., Ltd.
    Tanaka, Ritger and Middleton (Patrick F. O'Leary,
        H. William Tanaka)
PR Service Co., Ltd.
    Civic Service, Inc. (Roy Pfautch)
Ricoh Electronics, Inc.
    Fleishman-Hillard, Inc
Sambo Copper Co., Ltd.
    Sharretts, Paley, Carter and Blauvelt (Beatrice A.
        Brickell)
Sanwa Bank Ltd.
    Civic Service, Inc.
    Hill and Knowlton Public Affairs Worldwide (Gary
        Hymel)
Seiko Epson Corp.
    Saunders and Company (Pete Salavantis, Steven R.
        Saunders)
Seilbulite Internat'l, Inc.
    Hill and Knowlton Public Affairs Worldwide (Phil
        Armstrong)
Sharp Electronics Corp.
    Patton, Boggs and Blow
Showa Line, Ltd.
    Hoppel, Mayer and Coleman (Neal M. Mayer)
Sony Corp.
    Arent, Fox, Kintner, Plotkin & Kahn
    Debevoise and Plimpton (Robert R. Bruce, Jeffrey P.
        Cunard)
    Wilmer, Cutler and Pickering
Subaru-Isuzu Automotive Inc.
    Willkie Farr and Gallagher
Subaru of America
    Alfred Gloddeck, Manager, Regulatory Affairs
Sumitomo Bank Ltd.
    Shaw, Pittman, Potts and Trowbridge
Sumitomo Corp.
    Stafford, Burke and Hecker (Kelly B. Burke, Guy L.
        Hecker, Thomas P. Stafford)
Sumitomo Corp. of America
    Takashi Emura, General Manager
    Robert N. Meiser, P.C.
Sumitronics Inc.
    Robert N. Meiser, P.C.
Suzuki Motors Co., Ltd.
    Pettit & Martin (Harry W. Cladouhos)
Toa Nenryo Kogyo Kabushiki Kaisha
    First Associates Inc. (Floyd I. Roberson)
Tohoku Electric Power Co.
    Washington Policy & Analysis (Scott L. Campbell,
        William F. Martin)
Tokyo Electric Co., Ltd.
    Kelley, Drye and Warren (Edward M. Lebow)
Tokyo Electric Power Co.
    Kiichi Suganuma, Manager
    Komonsuke Sugiura, Director and General Manager
Tokyo Juki Industrial Co., Ltd.
    Dorsey & Whitney

The listings in this directory are available as *Mailing Labels*. See last page.

FOREIGN INTERESTS INDEX

The listings in this directory are available as *Mailing Labels*. See last page.

FOREIGN INTERESTS INDEX

FRISA
Weatherly & Co. (Jin-Hyun Weatherly)
Grupo Industrial Alfa, S.A.
Sills & Brodsky, P.C. (Alvin J. Geske)
HYLSA
Manchester Trade, Inc. (Stephen L. Lande)
Mexico, Government of
Milbank, Tweed, Hadley & McCloy
Mark E. Moran
Morgan, Lewis and Bockius
Shawn, Berger, and Mann
Mexico, Ministry of Commerce
Fleishman-Hillard, Inc
Mexico, Ministry of Finance and Public Credit
Cleary, Gottlieb, Steen and Hamilton (Douglas E. Kliever)
Sidermex Internat'l, Inc.
Manchester Trade, Inc. (Stephen L. Lande)
Mudge Rose Guthrie Alexander and Ferdon (N. David Palmeter)
Siderurgica Lazaro Cardenas, S.A.
Mudge Rose Guthrie Alexander and Ferdon (N. David Palmeter)
Tubos de Acero de Mexico, S.A.
Manchester Trade, Inc. (Stephen L. Lande)
Paul, Hastings, Janofsky and Walker (G. Hamilton Loeb)
Universidad Autonoma de Guadalajara
Kelly and Associates, Inc. (John A. Kelly)
Vitro, S.A.
Vinson and Elkins (John E. Chapoton, Theodore W. Kassinger)
West Mexico Vegetable Distributors Ass'n
Mike Masaoka Associates (T. Albert Yamada)

MONGOLIA
Mongolia People's Republic, Embassy of
Marshall, Tenzer, Greenblatt, Fallon and Kaplan (Sylvan M. Marshall)
van Kloberg and Associates (Edward J. van Kloberg, III)

MOROCCO
Morocco, Kingdom of
Ginsburg, Feldman and Bress (David Ginsburg, Lee R. Marks)
Neill and Co. (John E. Bircher, III, Denis M. Neill)
Stovall & Spradlin
White & Case
Royal Air Maroc
Shaw, Pittman, Potts and Trowbridge (Dean D. Aulick)

MOZAMBIQUE
Mozambique, Government of
Bruce P. Cameron
Mozambique Research Center
Thomas W. Schaaf, Jr., Exec. Director

NAMIBIA
Foundation for Democracy in Namibia
Commonwealth Consulting Corp. (Christopher M. Lehman)

NEPAL
Nepal, Embassy of
Marshall, Tenzer, Greenblatt, Fallon and Kaplan (Sylvan M. Marshall)
Royal Nepalese Embassy
van Kloberg and Associates (Lance T. Ventry)

NETHERLANDS
American Importers Meat Products Group
Max N. Berry Law Offices (Max N. Berry)
Compagnie Financiere de Paris et des Pays Bas
Rogers and Wells (Anthony F. Essaye, Eugene T. Rossides)
Fokker Aircraft U.S.A., Inc.
Robert M. Hawk, Dir., Public Relations & Advertising
Stuart Matthews, President & Chief Exec. Officer
Fokker B.V.
Ehrlich-Manes and Associates (Sherwin B. Stein)
Hoogovens Group BV
Powell, Goldstein, Frazer and Murphy (Peter Suchman)
Martinair Holland
Zuckert, Scoutt and Rasenberger (Frank J. Costello, Rachel B. Trinder)
N.V. Philips Gloeilampenfabrieken
Sullivan and Cromwell (Margaret K. Pfeiffer)

North American Philips Corp.
Randall B. Moorhead, Director, Government Affairs
Thomas B. Patton, V. President, Government Relations
Wunder, Ryan, Cannon & Thelen (W. Stephen Cannon)
Royal Dutch Shell Group
Howrey and Simon (Keith E. Pugh, Jr.)

NETHERLANDS ANTILLES
Air Aruba
Zuckert, Scoutt and Rasenberger (Frank J. Costello)
Anzonia Hotel Corp., N.A.
Rogers Internat'l, Inc. (Joe O. Rogers)
Aruba, Government of
Arnold & Porter (Claire Reade)
Internat'l Public Strategies, Inc. (C. Grayson Fowler)
Keefe Co., The (Clarence L. James, Jr., Robert J. Keefe, Terry M. O'Connell)
TKC Internat'l, Inc.
Central Bureau for Fruit and Vegetable Auctions in Holland
Hill and Knowlton Public Affairs Worldwide
Curacao Internat'l Trust Co.
Anderson, Hibey, Nauheim and Blair (Stephen A. Nauheim)
Institute of Financial and Fiscal Studies of Curacao
Anderson, Hibey, Nauheim and Blair (Stanton D. Anderson, Stephen A. Nauheim)
Netherlands Antilles, Government of
Alcalde & Rousselot (Hector Alcalde)
Cole, Corette & Abrutyn (Robert T. Cole, Steven A. Musher)
Surinam Airways
Bowen & Atkin (Harry A. Bowen)

NEW ZEALAND
New Zealand, Embassy of
Van Dyk Associates, Inc. (Ted Van Dyk)

NICARAGUA
Committee for Free Elections and Democracy in Nicaragua
Burgum & Grimm, Ltd. (Thomas L. Burgum, Rodman D. Grimm, Cynthia Lebrun-Yaffe)
Carmen Group, The (Willie W. Bledsoe, David M. Carmen, Carol Boyd Hallett, George C. Whatley)
Committee for Human Rights for the People of Nicaragua
Carlos Anzoategui, Exec. Director
Nicaragua, Government of
Reichler Appelbaum and Wippman (Judith C. Appelbaum, Paul S. Reichler, David Wippman)
Nicaraguan Resistance- U.S.A.
Ernesto Palazio, Washington Representative
Ann E. W. Stone and Associates (Michael Weintraub)

NIGERIA
Benguela Inc.
Stovall & Spradlin
Nigeria Airways
Winthrop, Stimson, Putnam & Roberts (Robert Reed Gray)
Nigeria, Embassy of
Land, Lemle & Arnold (Millard W. Arnold, J. Stuart Lemle)
van Kloberg and Associates (Edward J. van Kloberg, III)
Nigeria, Government of
Black, Manafort, Stone and Kelly Public Affairs Co.
Evans Group, Ltd., The (L. A., Skip Bafalis, Thomas B. Evans, Jr.)
Prather, Seeger, Doolittle and Farmer (Thomas L. Farmer)

NORWAY
Crystal Globe Ltd.
Bogle and Gates
Internat'l Ass'n of Independent Tanker Owners
Dyer, Ellis, Joseph & Mills
Graham and James (Richard K. Bank, Stuart S. Dye)
Hill, Betts and Nash
Norske Fiskeoppdretternes Salgslag (FO)
Mudge Rose Guthrie Alexander and Ferdon (Jeffrey S. Neeley, N. David Palmeter)
Norway, Government of
Burson-Marsteller
Norwegian Caribbean Lines
Alcalde & Rousselot (Hector Alcalde)

Norwegian Dairies Ass'n
Mudge Rose Guthrie Alexander and Ferdon (N. David Palmeter)
Norwegian Fisheries Ass'n
Bogle and Gates (Terry L. Leitzell)
Scandinavian Airlines System (SAS)
Global Aviation Associates, Ltd. (Jon F. Ash)
Winthrop, Stimson, Putnam & Roberts (Robert Reed Gray)
Statoil North America, Inc.
Washington Policy & Analysis (Scott L. Campbell, William F. Martin)

OMAN
Oman, Embassy of the Sultanate of
Patton, Boggs and Blow (David E. Dunn, III)

PAKISTAN
Pakistan, Government of
Internat'l Public Strategies, Inc.
Pakistan Internat'l Airlines
Zuckert, Scoutt and Rasenberger (James L. Devall)

PALAU
Palau, Government of
Powell, Goldstein, Frazer and Murphy (Michael H. Chanin)

PANAMA
Panama, Government of
Arnold & Porter (Douglas Dworkin, William D. Rogers)

PARAGUAY
Lineas Aereas Paraguayes (LAP)
Boros and Garofalo (Gary B. Garofalo)

PERU
Comite Textil de la Sociedad Nacional
Prather, Seeger, Doolittle and Farmer
Empresa de Transporte Aereo del Peru
Prather, Seeger, Doolittle and Farmer (Edwin H. Seeger)
Flores Esmeralda, S.R.L.
Prather, Seeger, Doolittle and Farmer (Edwin H. Seeger, Gary M. Welsh)
Minpeco, S.A.
Porter/Novelli
Peru, Government of
White & Case
Sima-Peru
Prather, Seeger, Doolittle and Farmer (Edwin H. Seeger)
Sociedad de Industrias "Comite Textil"
Prather, Seeger, Doolittle and Farmer (Edwin H. Seeger, Gary M. Welsh)

PHILIPPINES
Continental Manufacturing Corp.
World Trade Link
Imasco
Lachelli, Waller and Associates (Sam Ballenger)
Orient Airlines Ass'n
Galland, Kharasch, Morse and Garfinkle (Morris R. Garfinkle, Susan B. Jollie)
Philippines, Government of the
Bannerman and Associates, Inc. (M. Graeme Bannerman, Curtis Silvers)
Fidelity Pacific Group (Jack L. Copeland)
Reichler Appelbaum and Wippman
San Miguel Corp.
Leslie J. Schmidt Assoc., Inc. (Leslie J. Schmidt)
Tuna Canners Ass'n of the Philippines
Harris & Ellsworth
United Coconut Ass'n of the Philippines
Reichler Appelbaum and Wippman (Judith C. Appelbaum)

POLAND
American Importers Meat Products Group
Max N. Berry Law Offices (Max N. Berry)
Finryan Internat'l Ltd.
Wealth Management Corp. (Paul W. Mousseau)
Poland, Ministry of Finance of
Arnold & Porter (Jeffrey A. Burt)
Hogan and Hartson (Joseph C. Bell, Samuel R. Berger)
Polish-American Congress
Myra Lenard, Exec. Director
Polskie Linie Lotnicze
Winthrop, Stimson, Putnam & Roberts (Robert Reed Gray)

FOREIGN INTERESTS INDEX

FOREIGN INTERESTS INDEX

Turkey, Government of
    Hill and Knowlton Public Affairs Worldwide (Robert
      Keith Gray, Gary Hymel, Frank Mankiewicz,
      Donald F. Massey, Charles R. Pucie, Jr.)
    McAuliffe, Kelly, Raffaelli & Siemens (John D.
      Raffaelli)
    White & Case (Carolyn B. Lamm, John J. McAvoy)

U.S.S.R.
Institute for Soviet-American Relations
    Harriett Crosby, President
    Nancy A. Graham, Senior Associate
    Eliza K. Klose, Exec. Director
Internat'l Security Council
    Mark P. Barry, Media Liaison
    Dr. Joseph Churba, President
    Steven A.F. Trevino, Senior Associate for Statgy
      Affairs
Nat'l Conference on Soviet Jewry
    Barbara Gaffin, Congressional Liaison
    Mark B. Levin, Assoc. Exec. Director, Washington
      Office
    Robin Saipe, Community Relations Coordinator
Organization for American-Soviet ExchangeS (OASES-
DC)
    Elizabeth Gardiner, EPA/Environment Project
      Manager
    Eleanor Gorman, EPA Project Assistant
    Dr. C. Grant Pendill, Jr., Exec. Director
    Leslie Sherman, Public Relations Coordinator
    Kathy Woelfer, NAS, USIA Interpreting Coordinator
Sovcomflot
    Mudge Rose Guthrie Alexander and Ferdon (Julia
      Christine Bliss, David P. Houlihan)
Summit, Ltd.
    Kutak Rock & Campbell (Nancy L. Granese)
Union of Councils for Soviet Jews
    Powell, Goldstein, Frazer and Murphy (Stuart E.
      Eizenstat)

VENEZUELA
Aero B
    Bowen & Atkin (Harry A. Bowen)
C.V.G. Sideurgica del Orinoco Ca. (SIDOR)
    Mudge Rose Guthrie Alexander and Ferdon (David
      P. Houlihan, William N. Walker)
Christian Democrat Organization of the Americas
    DC Internat'l, Inc. (Andres R. Hernandez)
Petroleos de Venezuela, S.A.
    Cleary, Gottlieb, Steen and Hamilton
    Collier, Shannon & Scott (Paul D. Cullen, William
      W. Scott, Thomas F. Shannon)
    Hill and Knowlton Public Affairs Worldwide (Lauri
      J. Fitz-Pegado)
Venezuela, Government of
    Kaplan, Russin and Vecchi
    Squier & Eskew Communications, Inc. (Thomas
      Ochs, Robert Squier)
VIASA
    Squire, Sanders and Dempsey (Robert D. Papkin,
      Edward W. Sauer)

YEMEN
Yemen Arab Republic, Government of
    Hill and Knowlton Public Affairs Worldwide (Charles
      R. Pucie, Jr.)

YUGOSLAVIA
Viktor Lenac Shipyard
    Dyer, Ellis, Joseph & Mills

ZAIRE
Zaire, Bank of
    White & Case
Zaire, Government of the Republic of
    Black, Manafort, Stone and Kelly Public Affairs Co.
    van Kloberg and Associates (Edward J. van Kloberg,
      III)
    Weaver & Associates, Robert A. (Joseph M. Perta,
      Patrick J. Tyrrell, Robert A. Weaver, Jr.)

ZIMBABWE
Minerals Marketing Corp. of Zimbabwe
    Patton, Boggs and Blow (Frank R. Samolis)

The listings in this directory are available as *Mailing Labels.* See last page.